GUIDE TO
VENTURE CAPITAL
&
PRIVATE EQUITY FIRMS

DOMESTIC & INTERNATIONAL
WITH SEPARATE CANADIAN SECTION

2021 GUIDE TO VENTURE CAPITAL & PRIVATE EQUITY FIRMS

DOMESTIC & INTERNATIONAL
WITH SEPARATE CANADIAN SECTION

GREY HOUSE PUBLISHING

PRESIDENT: Richard Gottlieb
PUBLISHER: Leslie Mackenzie
EDITORIAL DIRECTOR: Laura Mars
PRODUCTION MANAGER: Kristen Hayes
MARKETING DIRECTOR: Jessica Moody
EDITORIAL ASSISTANTS: Krystal Dos Santos; Olivia Parsonson

Grey House Publishing, Inc.
4919 Route 22
Amenia, NY 12501
518.789.8700 • Fax 845.373.6390
www.greyhouse.com
books@greyhouse.com

While every effort has been made to ensure the reliability of the information presented in this publication, Grey House Publishing neither guarantees the accuracy of the data contained herein nor assumes any responsibility for errors, omissions or discrepancies. Grey House accepts no payment for listing; inclusions in the publication of any organization, agency, institution, publication, service or individual does not imply endorsement of the editors or publisher.

Errors brought to the attention of the publisher and verified to the satisfaction of the publisher will be corrected in future editions.

Except by express prior written permission of the Copyright Proprietor, no part of this work may be copied by any means of publication or communication now known or developed hereafter, including but not limited to use in any directory or compilation or other print publication, in any information storage and retrieval system, in any other electronic device, or in any visual or audio-visual device or product.

This publication is an original and creative work, copyrighted by Grey House Publishing, Inc. and is fully protected by all applicable copyright laws, as well as by laws covering misappropriation, trade secrets and unfair competition.

Grey House has added value to the underlying factual material through one or more of the following efforts: unique and original selection; expression; arrangement; coordination; and classification.

Grey House Publishing, Inc. will defend its rights in this publication.
Copyright © 2021 Grey House Publishing, Inc.

All rights reserved
First edition published 1996
Twenty-fifth edition published 2021
Printed in Canada

Publisher's Cataloging-In-Publication Data
(Prepared by The Donohue Group, Inc.)

Names: Grey House Publishing, Inc., publisher.
Title: Guide to venture capital & private equity firms : domestic & international with separate Canadian section.
Other Titles: Guide to venture capital and private equity firms
Description: Amenia, NY : Grey House Publishing, 2021- | Includes indexes.
Subjects: LCSH: Venture capital—Directories. | Venture capital—United States—Directories. | Private equity—Directories. | Private equity—United States—Directories.
Classification: LCC HG4751 .G85 | DDC 332/.04154—dc23

ISBN: 978-1-64265-813-2

Table of Contents

Introduction vii
User Guide & Key ix
KPMG Private Enterprise—Venture Pulse, Q4 2020,
    Global Analysis of Venture Funding xi
PwC | CB Insights MoneyTree™ Report Q4 2020 xv

DESCRIPTIVE LISTINGS

Domestic Firms 3
Canadian Firms 707
International Firms 779
National & State Associations 1001

INDEXES

College & University Index 1011
Executive Index 1077
Geographic Index 1105
Industry Preference Index 1137
Portfolio Companies Index 1245

Introduction

This twenty-fifth edition of the *Guide to Venture Capital & Private Equity Firms, Domestic & International* is a comprehensive database of more than 3,000 of the most active venture capital and private equity firms operating today, domestically and internationally. All company profiles include current contact information and specific industry data for a detailed picture of the firm and its investment parameters. Profiles include headquarters, other locations and branches, industry group preferences, average investment, portfolio companies, investment criteria and detailed lists of key executives.

As with previous editions, this 2021 edition includes a User Guide, followed by two industry reports that offer insight into the current state of this dynamic industry segment: *KPMG Enterprises—Venture Pulse Q4 2020, Global Analysis of Venture Funding;* and *PwC/CB Insights Money Tree™ Report Q4 2020*. Highlights include:

- VC investment in the U.S. reaches record annual high;

- Trends to watch for in the U.S. include: fintech, delivery and logistics, automotive, health and biotech, and cybersecurity;

- COVID-19 is driving disruption across U.S healthcare sector;

- M&A activity remains strong and IPO activity in the U.S. continues to surge.

The firm profiles in this edition present a most current, comprehensive picture of this dynamic industry. Hundreds of domestic and international firms have been updated, with a particular focus on firms based in Canada. More than 3,100 pieces of data have been updated, with a focus on key executives and company branches. In addition to the significant update effort put forth for this edition, we have added 103 completely new venture capital firms, and 489 new data points throughout the body of the work.

All domestic, Canadian and international profiles include, in addition to contact information, a mission statement, industry group preferences, portfolio companies, geographic preferences, average and minimum investments, and investment criteria. Each firm's partners are listed with extensive background information, such as education (degree and school), professional background (previous positions and companies) and directorships held. The specificity of both the firm and its partners add to the value of each firm's profile. Information for firms headquartered overseas include name, phone, fax, email and website.

Guide to Venture Capital & Private Equity Firms is organized into four major sections, Domestic Firms, Canadian Firms, Domestic Associations, and International Firms, each arranged alphabetically by company name. These sections are followed by five valuable indexes:

- **College/University Index** offers an alphabetical list of more than 1,000 educational institutions worldwide—and the venture capital executives who attended them. Each listing includes the reference number of the affiliated VC firm of the executive listed.

- **Executive Index** is an alphabetical list by last name of more than 9,000 key partners and the listing number of their affiliated firm.

- **Geographic Index** organizes all firms by state for domestic listings and by country for international listings.

- **Industry Preference Index** alphabetically lists more than 900 industry segments and the names of the firms that invest in them.

- **Portfolio Companies Index** alphabetically lists the more than 49,500 companies that received venture capital from a listed firm, and is referenced to that listing.

For even easier access to information, *Guide to Venture Capital & Private Equity Firms* is available in our online database platform, http://gold.greyhouse.com. Subscribers will have immediate access to all domestic and international venture capital and private equity firms to:

- Find firms that are specifically interested in their industry group. From agrifood to web infrastructure, this online database can be sorted into over 900 industry group categories.

- Search for firms that match the investment level they need. From $250,000 to $50 million, you'll be able to generate a list to match your requirements, within specific geographic areas.

- Find which venture capital firms have funded specific companies. Simply key in a company to generate a list of firms who funded them.

This online database platform offers a number of ways to search and sort data—Firm Name, Geographic Location, Geographic Preferences, Portfolio Companies, Industry Group Preferences, Average Investment, Fund Size, Investment Criteria, Managing Partners and much more. Visit www.greyhouse.com for a free search of this database and subscription details.

Praise for previous edition:

> "...valuable reference...excellent indexes...recommended for business collections in large public, academic and business libraries..."
> —*CHOICE*

> "...excellent resource for public libraries supporting a business sector..."
> —*ARBA*

> "...extremely user-friendly..."
> —*Library Journal*

> "...only directory to list and index portfolio companies...a useful volume..."
> —*Journal of Business & Finance Librarianship*

The 2021 edition of *Guide to Venture Capital & Private Equity Firms* is our strongest to date, and offers a valuable resource for those needing to research the investment community. Users are encouraged to bring new, unlisted, or changed firms to our attention.

User Guide

Descriptive listings in the *Guide to Venture Capital & Private Equity Firms* are organized into Domestic and International sections, with each arranged alphabetically by company name. The listings are supplemented by five indexes: College & University Index, Executive Index, Geographic Index, Industry Preference Index, and Portfolio Company Index. The record number, shown top left, rather than the page number, is how the listings are referenced.

Shown below is a fictitious listing illustrating the kind of information that is or might be included in an entry. Each numbered item is described on the following page.

1234 1- **GALIVANT VENTURE CAPITAL**
2- 14 State Boulevard
Suite 185
Millerton, NY 12546

3- 060-555-4131

4- 060-555-4132

800-945-7411

5- info@gvaztx.com

6- www.gvaztx.com

7- **Mission Statement:** To identify, support and counsel companies with strong management and proven growth in the communications industry.

8- **Geographic Preference:** Eastern United States

9- **Fund Size:** $20 million

10- **Founded:** 1982

11- **Average Investment:** $1.5 million

12- **Minimum Investment:** $500,000

13- **Investment Criteria:** Seed, Startup, First-Stage, Second-Stage, Mezzanine, LBO, MBO

14- **Industry Group Preference:** Communications, Data Communications, Telecommunications, Internet Services, Television, Radio

15- **Portfolio Companies:** HamStark Inc., Placid Internet, DuBois Inc., Berkshire Radio Co., Shir-Fire.com, Trail Communications, Holyoke Internet Services

16- **Other Locations:**
96 Club Road
Suite 1982
Milwaukee, WI 53212

17- **Key Executives:**
Gabriele O'Laughlin PhD, Managing Director
019-931-6966
Fax: 019-931-4967
e-mail: glord@gvaztx.com
Education: BA, Mount Holyoke College; MBA, PHD, Finance, Texas A&M University
Background: CFO, Whitehouse Inc., IntelliCon Technologies
Directorship: OverDrive Tech, BrynSore Group

User Key

1- **Company Name:** Formal name of the company.

2- **Address:** Location or permanent mailing address of the company.

3- **Phone Number:** The listed phone number is usually for the main office, but may also be for sales, marketing, or public relations as provided by the company.

4- **Fax Number:** This is listed when provided by the company.

5- **E-Mail:** This is listed when provided, and is usually the main office e-mail.

6- **Web Site:** Listed when provided by the company, and is also referred to as a URL address.

7- **Mission Statement:** This information is either provided directly by the company, or abridged from data on the company web site or in company literature.

8- **Geographic Preference:** This lists the geographic location the firm prefers to invest in.

9- **Fund Size:** This is the total amount of money a firm has to invest. International firms often calculate dollar amounts in their own currency.

10- **Founded:** The year in which the firm was established or founded. If the organization has changed its name, the founding date is usually for the earliest name under which it is known.

11- **Average Investment:** The average amount the firm generally invests in a company.

12- **Minimum Investment:** The smallest possible amount the firm would consider investing.

13- **Investment Criteria:** This indicates at what stage the firm is willing to invest in, i.e., Seed, Startup, First-Stage, Second-Stage, Mezzanine, LBO, MBO, etc.

14- **Industry Group Preference:** This indicates what industry the firm is most likely to invest in. Note that most of this information does not follow standard industry language; the Industry Group Preference Index is designed to help the reader summarize information, and should be reviewed carefully.

15- **Portfolio Companies:** This is a listing of the companies that the firm has invested in to date.

16- **Other Locations:** Divisions or subsidiaries of the main company. Also included may be the key executives of that location.

17- **Key Executives:** Names, titles, phone numbers, fax numbers and personal e-mail addresses of key executives—including Presidents, Partners, and Managing Directors. This section can also include educational data, including degree and school, and professional data, including previous positions and companies, backgrounds, as well as a list of directorships held.

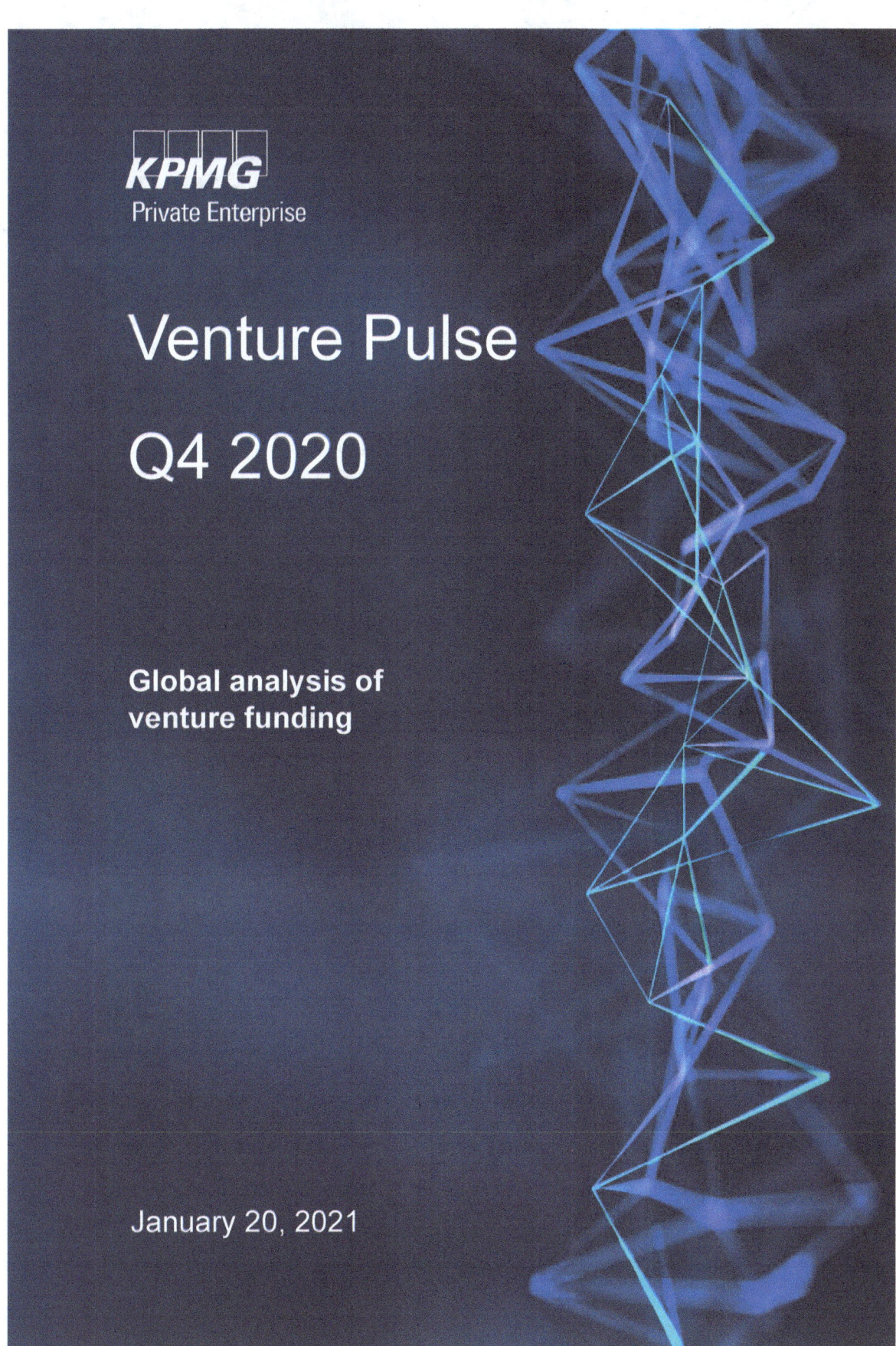

VC investment in the US reaches new annual record high

VC investment in the US stayed robust in Q4'20, helping drive total annual VC investment to a new record high of $156.2 billion in 2020, compared to $138 billion last year. While the US faced a number of uncertainties during the quarter, including the presidential election in November, a seemingly endless supply of cash on the sidelines and an ample exit market helped to keep confidence in the VC market relatively robust through the end of the year.

During Q4'20, VC investment in the US remained focused on key sectors relevant in the current pandemic environment, including fintech, health and biotech, and transportation. These sectors accounted for many of the quarter's largest funding rounds, including Resilience ($725 million), Robinhood ($668 million), Chime ($533 million), Nuro ($500 million), Tempus Labs ($450 million), and Hippo Insurance ($350 million).

Large VC funds grow more attractive, while smaller funds struggle
Fundraising activity in the US reached a near-record high in 2020. In Q4'20, in particular, Andreessen Horowitz announced two mega funds totalling $4.5 billion[6]. Over the course of the year, large US VC funds attracted the lion's share of capital, while some smaller funds had difficulties with capitalization. This trend towards larger funds has been building for a couple of years, although it accelerated in recent quarters as investors increased their focus on metrics like cash-flow, unit economics, and the long-term sustainability of target companies. With a lot of capital sitting on the sidelines, large institutional investors and pension funds moved to put their capital into safe and knowledgeable hands – which predominantly meant larger VC firms with proven fund managers offering a consistent track record for delivering high returns over the lifespan of their funds.

COVID-19 driving disruption across US healthcare sector
The health and biotech sector continued to be a hot priority for US-based VC and corporate investors in Q4'20, with interest stretching well beyond COVID-19 specific activities. Over the last few quarters, the pandemic highlighted significant gaps in the healthcare ecosystem in the US ripe for disruption, which has led to an uptick in investor interest in a wide-range of health and biotech areas, including remote diagnostics, medical imaging solutions, fitness, and wellness. The wellness industry in particular saw significant growth throughout 2020 as consumers became more concerned about their health — a trend expected to continue well into 2021.

IPO activity in the US continues to surge
Following a strong quarter in Q3'20, IPO activity in the US continued to surge in Q4'20, despite the uncertainty related to the US presidential election. December saw a number of highly successful unicorn IPOs, including vacation rental marketplace Airbnb, delivery company DoorDash, and AI-driven enterprise SaaS company C3.ai. Airbnb raised $3.5 billion in its IPO, with shares rising 112 percent on the first day of trading, propelling the company's valuation

[6] https://www.finsmes.com/2020/11/andreessen-horowitz-closes-two-funds-totalling-4-5-billion.html

#Q4VC

VC investment in the US reaches new annual record high, cont'd.

over $100 billion[7]. DoorDash raised $3.3 billion, with shares climbing 85 percent on the first day, giving it a market cap of $44 billion[8]. C3.ai, meanwhile, raised $651 million, with shares spiking over 170 percent on the first day of trading, giving it a market cap of $10 billion[9].

The ongoing march of unicorn exits in the US propelled the exit value of VC backed companies in the US to a record $290 billion in 2020 — well above the previous record of $257 billion seen in 2019.

No slowdown in M&A activity
M&A exit activity remained strong in the US during Q4'20, led by the announcement of the $27.7 billion acquisition of enterprise communications company Slack by Salesforce[10]. The acquisition follows less than two years after Slack's IPO via a direct listing[11].

The strong M&A activity in the US is likely due to a number of competing factors, including acquirers looking for deals from companies hit hard by the pandemic and others acting quickly to acquire companies in growing sectors before they became too expensive. Corporates also continued to make acquisitions during the quarter — primarily targeted at companies able to help them accelerate their digital efforts in order to not be left behind by more nimble and responsive competitors.

Trends to watch for in the US
VC investment in the US is expected to remain strong heading into Q1'21, in addition to M&A and traditional IPO activity. The use of SPACs for IPOs is also expected to continue into Q1'21, although the time horizon of SPACs — which (typically) require target companies to be acquired within a two-year period — could lead to some suboptimal choices over time given the number of SPACs currently in the market looking for targets.

Investment in the fintech, delivery and logistics, automotive, and health and biotech sectors is expected to remain strong well into 2021, while investments related to cybersecurity are expected to heat up given the expectation that digital channels and offerings will remain important to consumers in a post-pandemic world.

The change in administration in the US will also be critical to watch heading into 2021 as it will likely drive a shift in key government priorities and policies over time, which could affect key sectors of VC investment. One area well positioned to see an increase in activity is cleantech — such as cloud-based software solutions and energy storage and battery technologies.

[7] https://www.forbes.com/sites/jonathanponciano/2020/12/10/airbnb-ipo-shares-valuation-billion-more-than-marriott-hilton-hyatt/?sh=6abb42cb20ef
[8] https://investorplace.com/2020/12/why-post-ipo-pullback-doordash-stock-will-likely-continue/
[9] https://www.businessinsider.in/stock-market/news/software-firm-c3-ai-skyrockets-174-after-651-million-ipo/articleshow/79652222.cms
[10] https://www.nytimes.com/2020/12/01/technology/salesforce-slack-deal.html
[11] https://venturebeat.com/2019/06/20/slack-ipo-starts-trading-at-38-50-for-23-billion-valuation/

Source: Venture Pulse, Q4'20, Global Analysis of Venture Funding, KPMG Private Enterprise. *As of 12/31/20.
Data provided by PitchBook, 1/20/21. Reprinted with permission, February 2021.

#Q4VC

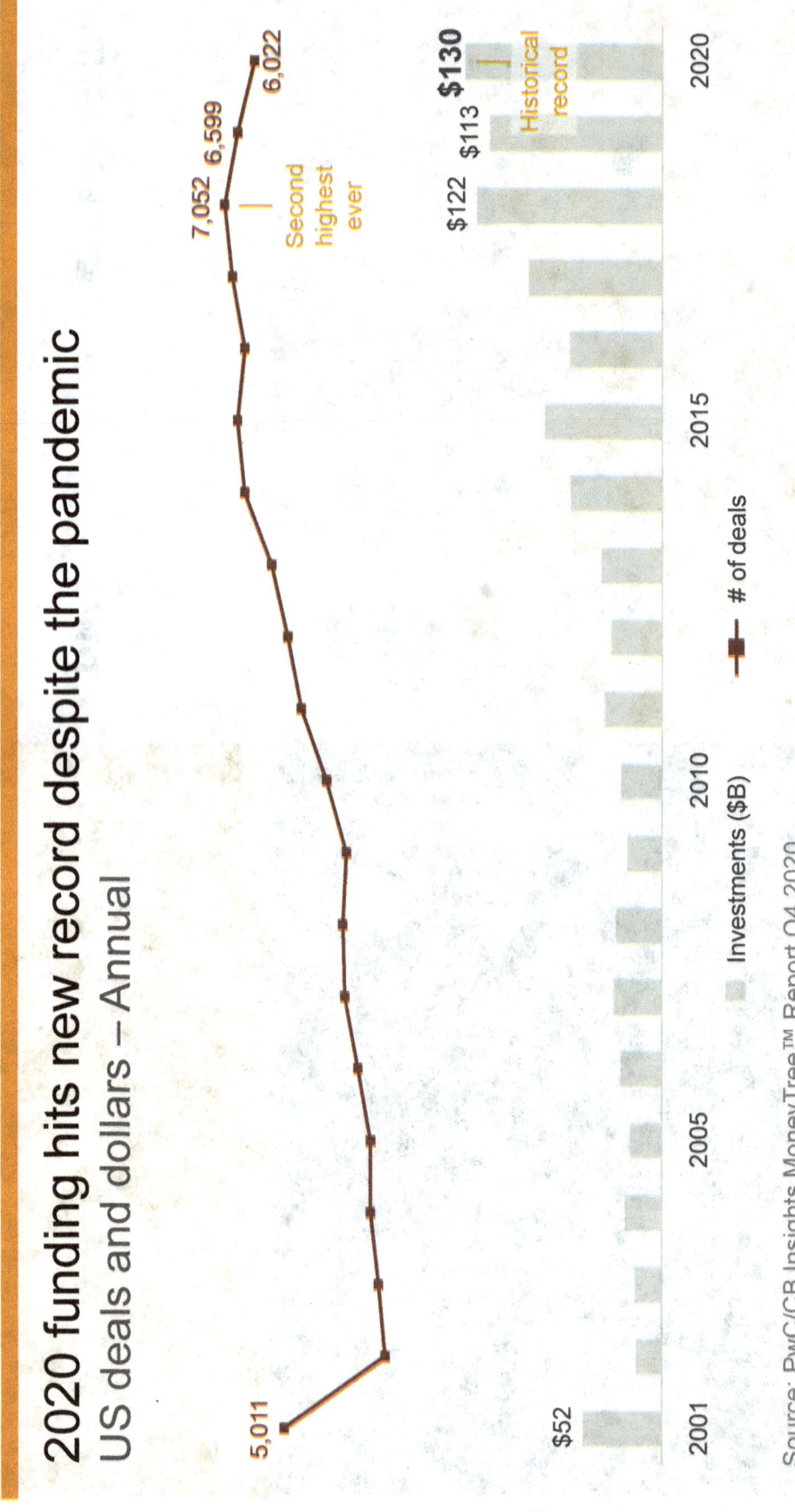

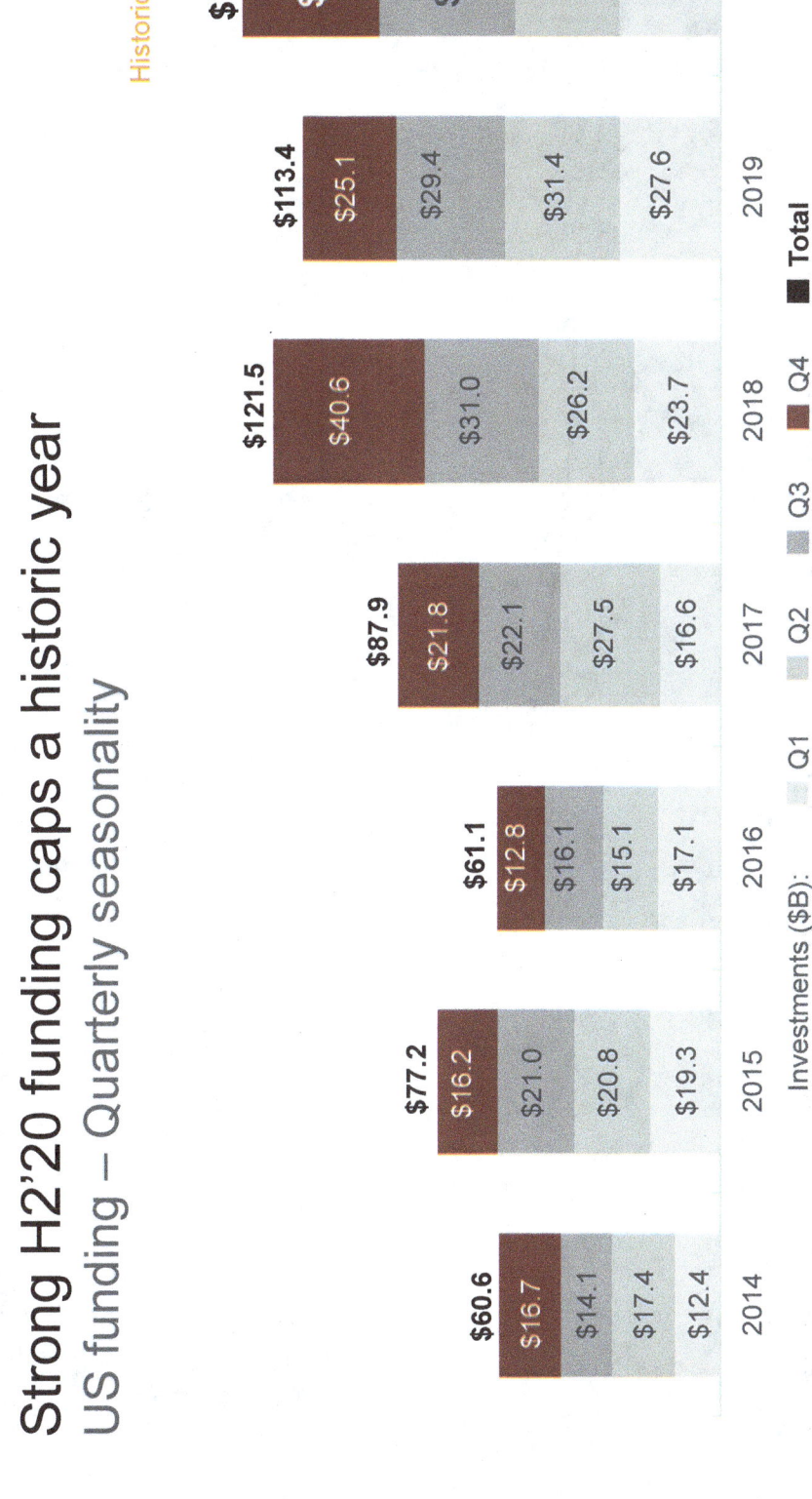

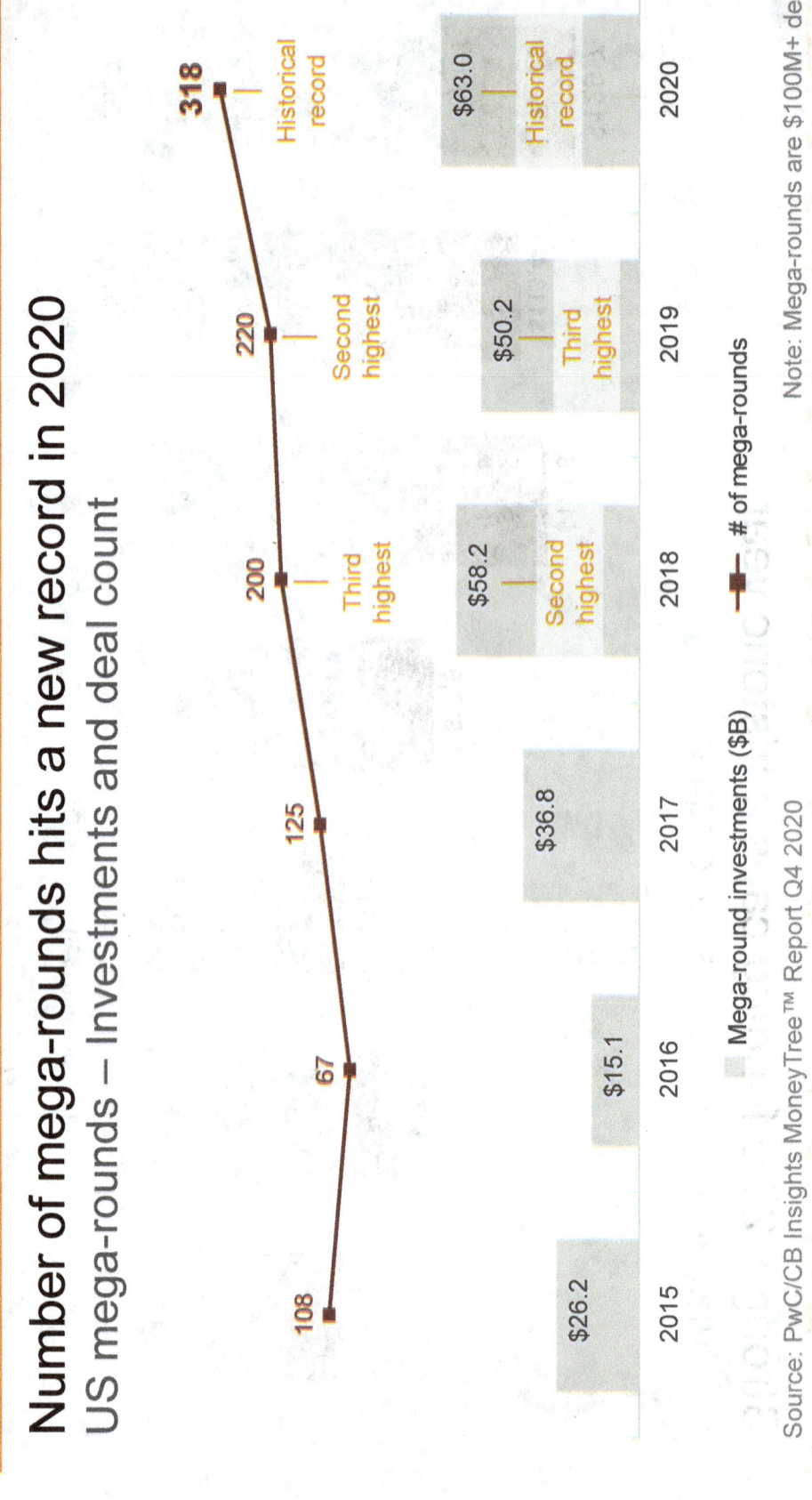

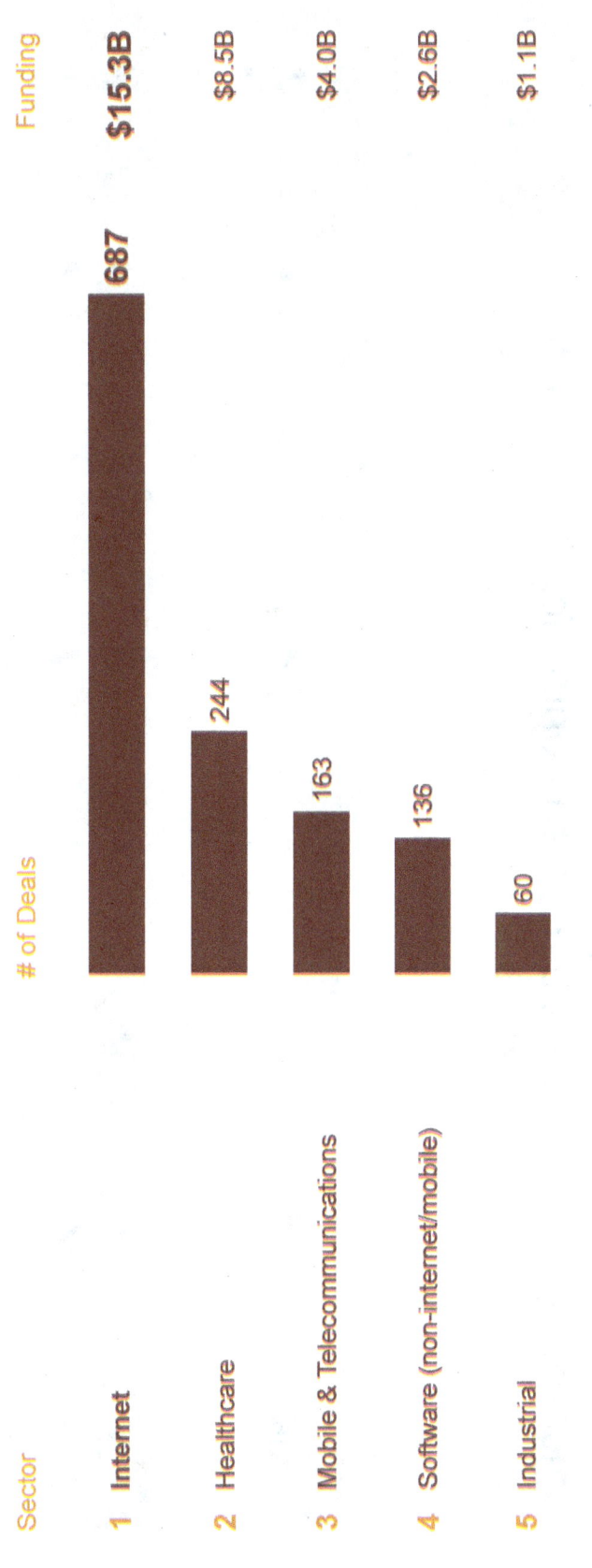

MoneyTree™ Report Q4 2020

The total US unicorn population continues to climb
Unicorns – Total US-based unicorn population

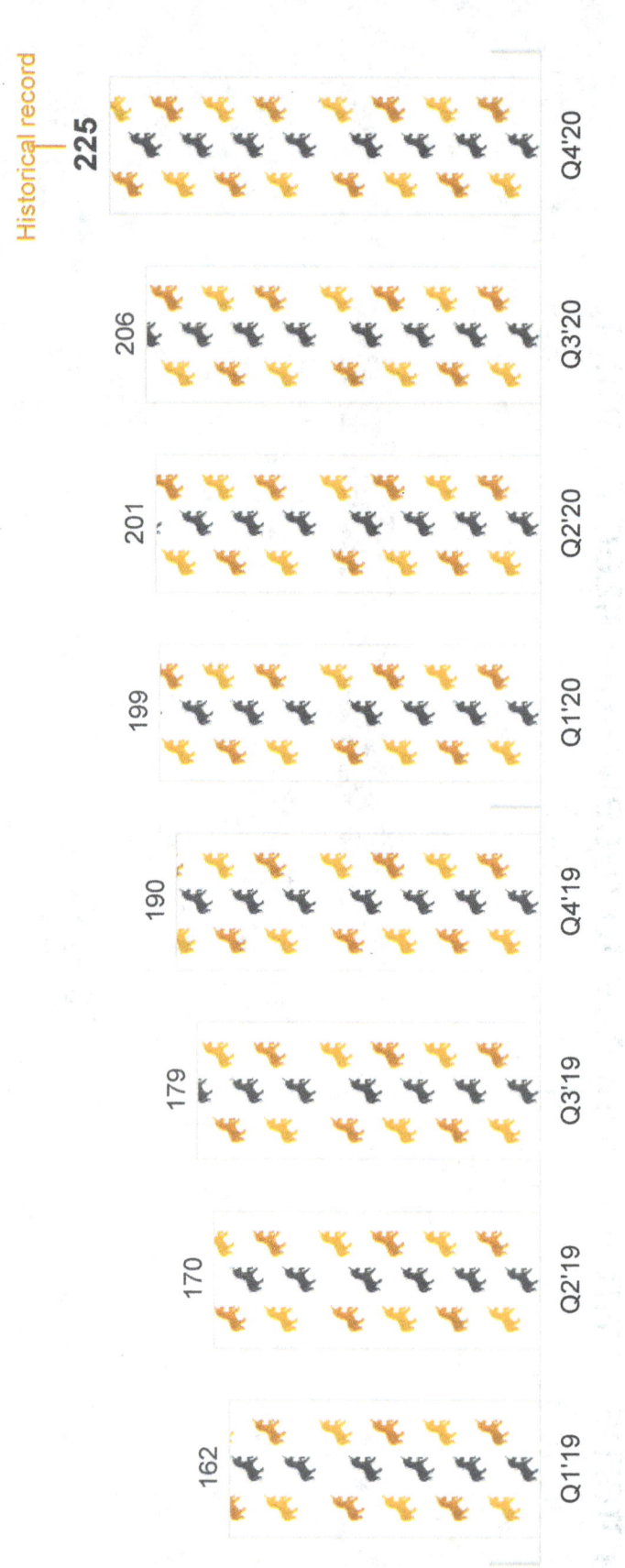

Note: Unicorns are startups valued at $1B or more

Source: PwC/CB Insights MoneyTree™ Report Q4 2020

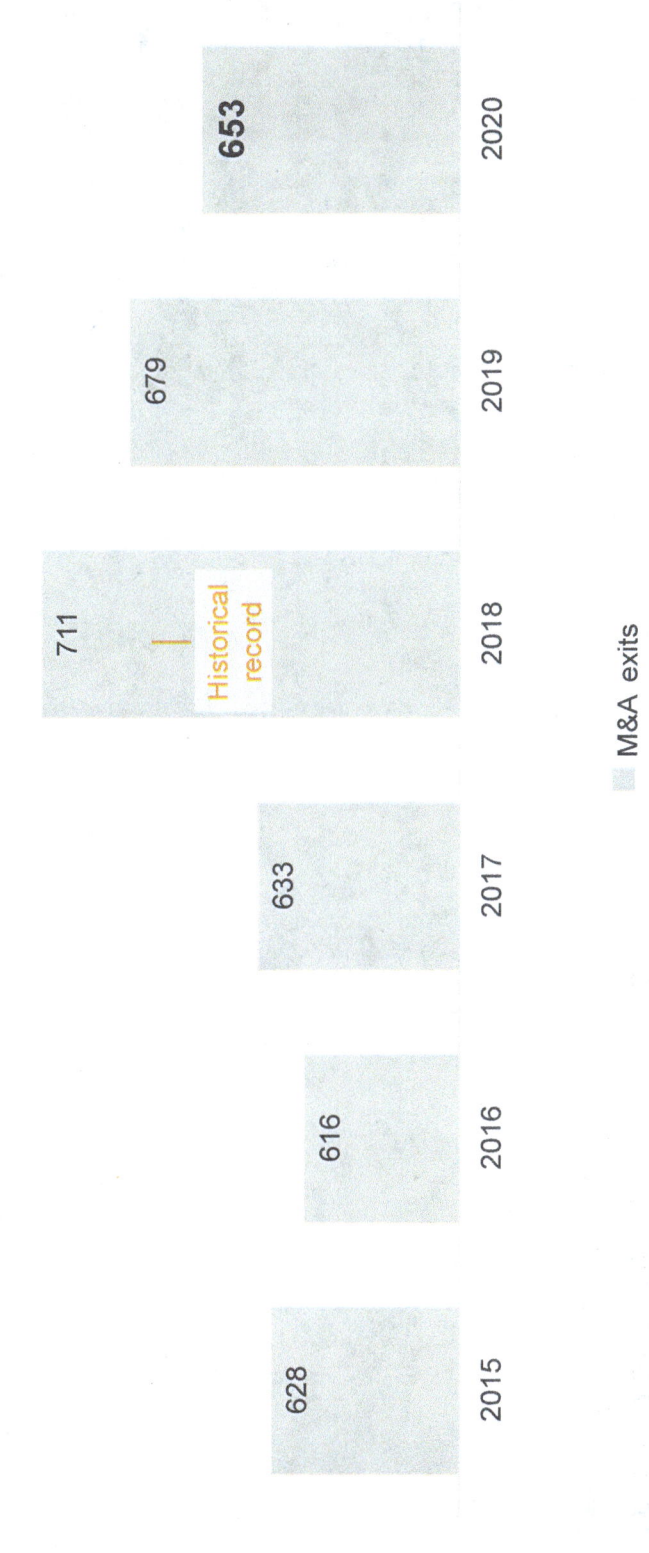

IPO activity jumps in 2020
US IPOs – Annual

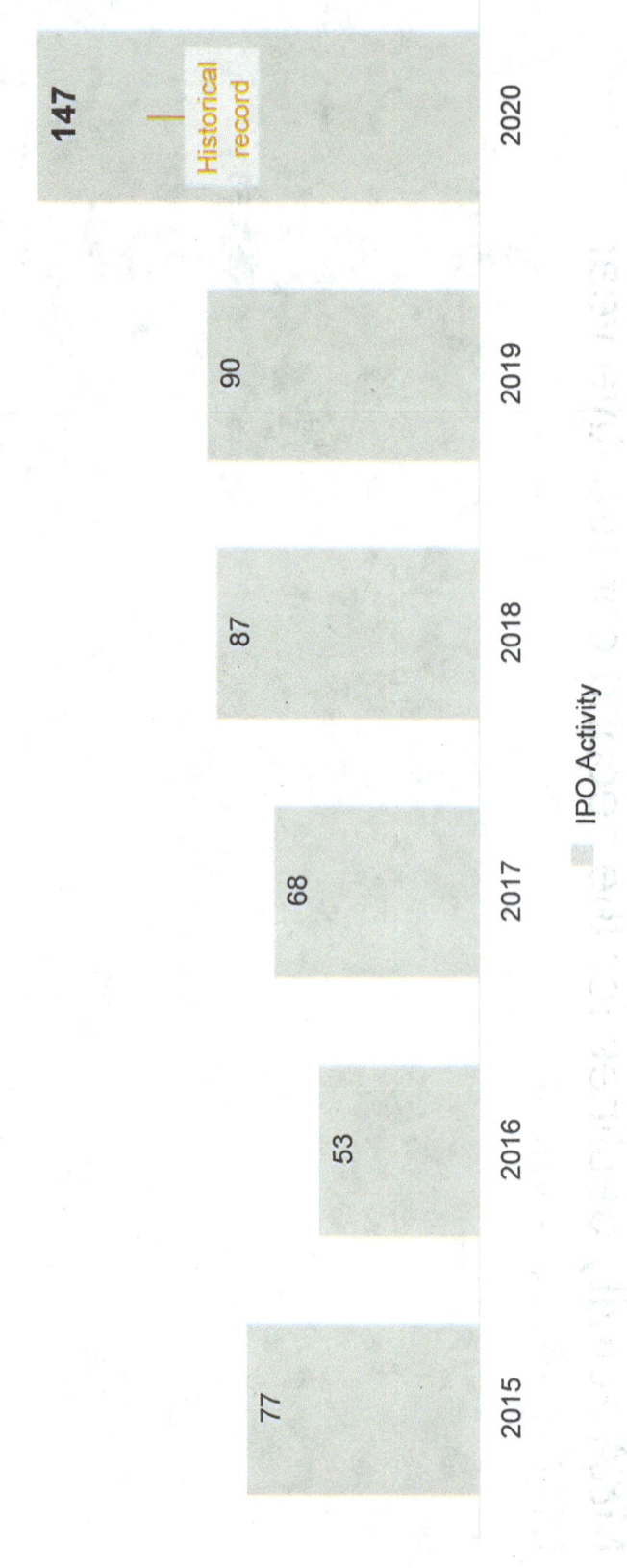

Source: PwC/CB Insights MoneyTree™ Report Q4 2020

Majority of Metros see an increase in deal activity in Q4'20
Top 10 Metros by deal activity

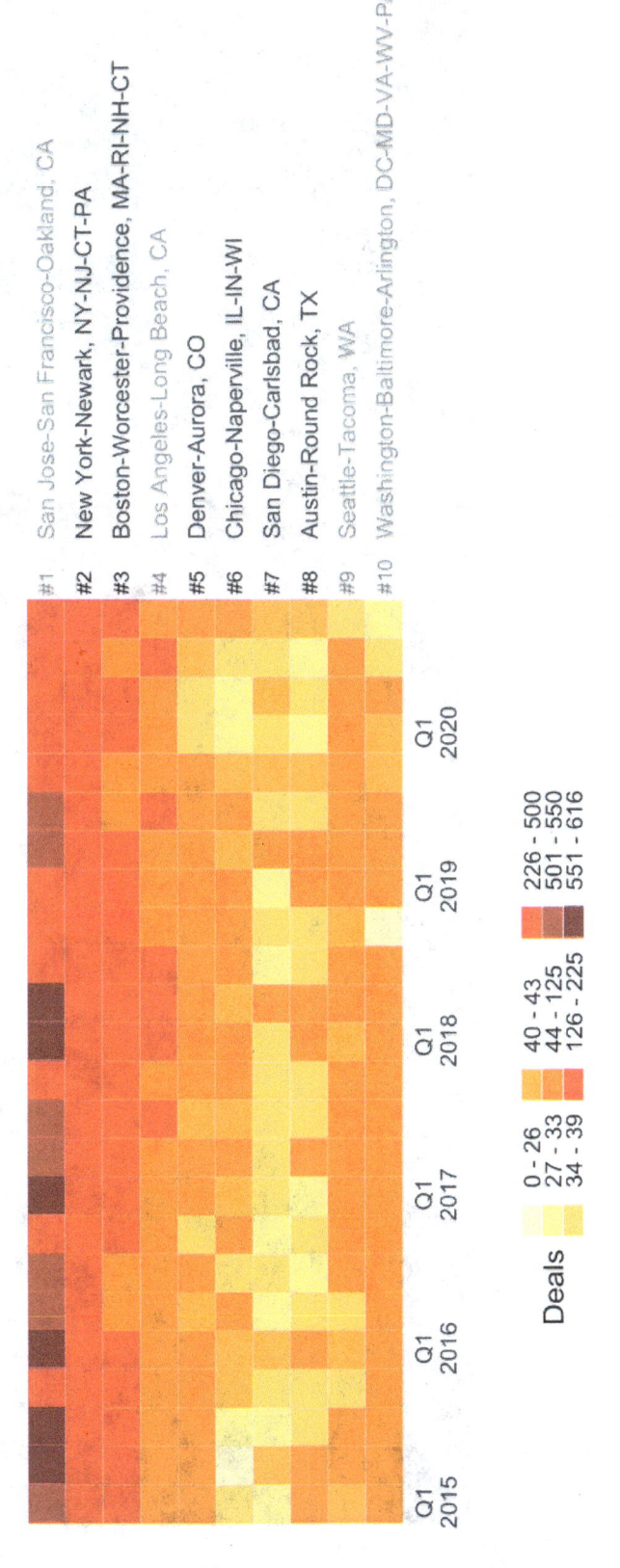

Source: PwC/CB Insights MoneyTree™ Report Q4 2020

Together, startups in the top 3 states raised 74% of US funding

Source: PwC/CB Insights MoneyTree™ Report Q4 2020

Guide to Venture Capital & Private Equity Firms

Four emerging areas dominate deal activity among the top 20

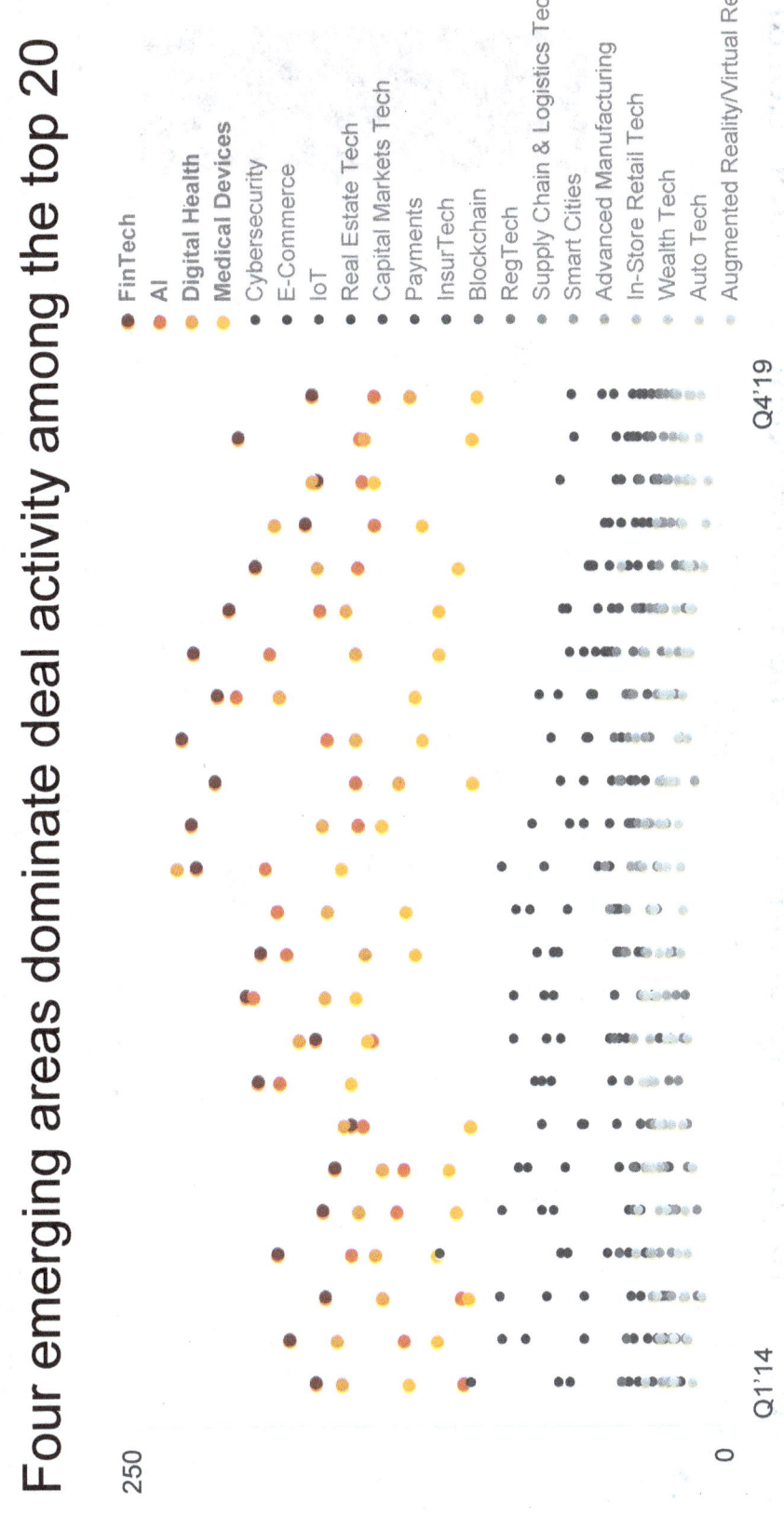

Source: PwC/CB Insights MoneyTree™ Report Q4 2020

Investor fundraising continues to rise, exceeding a trillion dollars
US startup investors – Annual aggregate funds raised

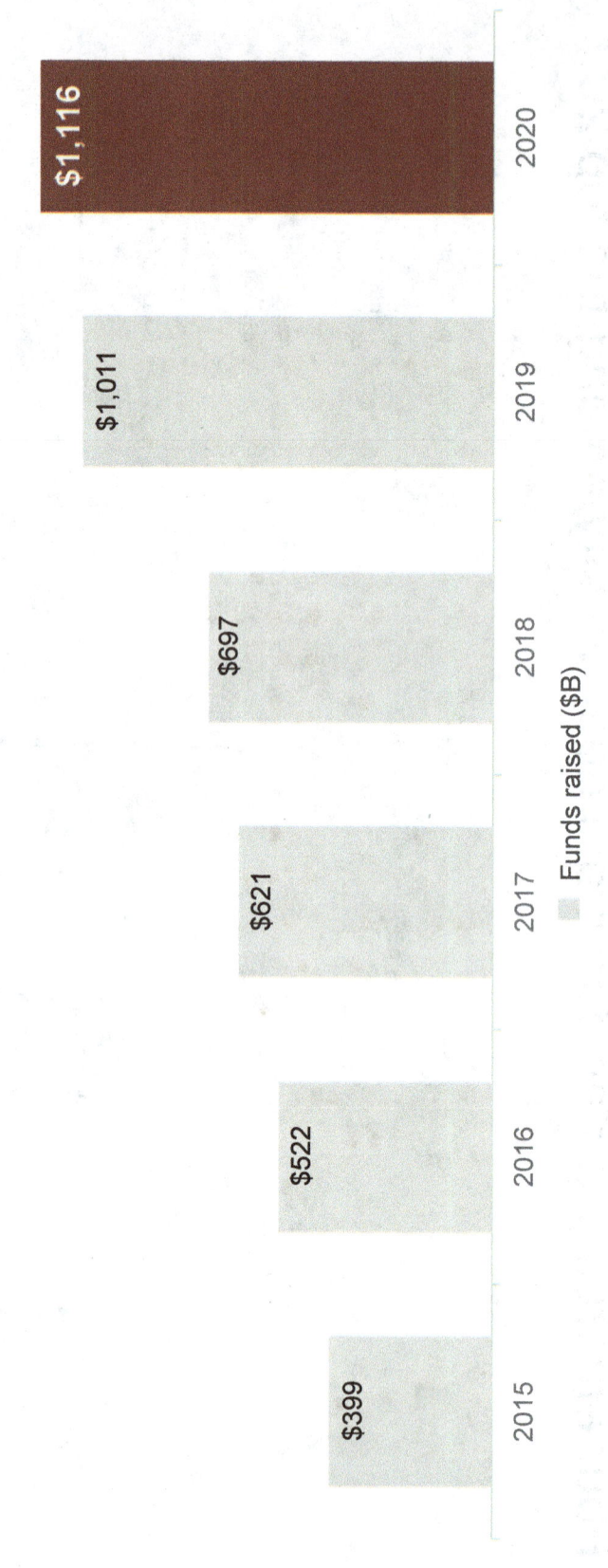

Source: PwC/CB Insights MoneyTree™ Report Q4 2020

Global regional comparison – 2020

- 6,042 / $87.1B Asia
- 3,599 / $33.4B Europe
- 6,454 / $132.9B North America
- 16,773 Deals / $259.4B invested globally

Source: PwC/CB Insights MoneyTree™ Report Q4 2020

© PwC. Not for further distribution without the prior written permission of PwC. PwC refers to the US member firm or one of its subsidiaries or affiliates, and may sometimes refer to the PwC network. Each member firm is a separate legal entity. Please see www.pwc.com/structure for further details.

Domestic Firms

Venture Capital & Private Equity Firms / Domestic Firms

1 (@)VENTURES
1601 Trapelo Road
Suite 170
Waltham, MA 02451

Phone: 978-658-8980 **Fax:** 978-658-8981
e-mail: info@ventures.com

Mission Statement: @Ventures invests in early stage, high value companies in the clean technology sector. The firm seeks to provide valuable resources and establish committed partnerships with portfolio companies in order to bring innovative clean technology products to market.

Geographic Preference: North America
Fund Size: $280 million
Founded: 1995
Average Investment: $5 million
Investment Criteria: Early-Stage, Mid-Stage Technology
Industry Group Preference: Internet Technology, Enterprise Services, Software, Clean Energy, Information Technology, Technology, Security, Enabling Technology, Alternative Energy, Clean Technology
Portfolio Companies: 212 Resources, Cobalt Biofuels, Powerit Holdings, Propel Biofuels, Object Video

Key Executives:
  Peter H Mills, Managing Director
  Education: BS, Communications, Ithaca College; MBA, Marketing, Graduate School of Business, Columbia University
  Background: CEO, United States Display Consortium; Chief Administrative Officer, SEMATECH; Co-Founder/COO, Softrend Inc.; Senior Vice President, BPI
  Directorships: 212 Resources, Cobalt Biofuels, Powerit Solutions, Propel Biofuels

2 .406 VENTURES
470 Atlantic Avenue
12th Floor
Boston, MA 02210

Phone: 617-406-3300
e-mail: contact@406ventures.com
web: www.406ventures.com

Mission Statement: To provide capital, leadership and operational expertise for early stage companies in the technology industry.

Geographic Preference: New England
Fund Size: $1 billion
Founded: 2005
Investment Criteria: Early-Stage
Industry Group Preference: Technology, Digital Media & Marketing, Energy Technology, Fintech, Healthcare Information Technology, Information Services, Internet, Next Generation Software, Open Source, Real-Time Data, Web Infrastructure, Technology-Enabled Services, Cybersecurity, Data & Cloud
Portfolio Companies: Abacas Insights, AbleTo, Axial Healthcare, Bend, Better Life Partners, Business Intelligence Advisors, CHAOSSEARCH, Compass, Corvus, CPX Security, Edgewise Networks, Gamalon, GreatHorn, HYPR, Indico, Iora Health, Kaltura, Laudio, MineralTree, Nomad Health, Onapsis, Randori, Redox, Reltio, Simon Data, Terbium Labs, Threat Stack, Trilio, Virtudent, WelbeHealth, Wellist

Key Executives:
  Maria Cirino, Co-Founder/Managing Partner
  e-mail: mcirino@406ventures.com
  Education: BA, English Literature, Mount Holyoke College
  Background: SVP, VeriSign; CEO, Guardent; SVP, Sales & Marketing, Razorfish
  Directorships: Attend.com, AuthAir, Bit9, Kaltura, Mineral Tree, Onapsis, Pwnie Express, Threat Stack, Vaultive, Veracode

  Liam Donohue, Co-Founder/Managing Partner
  e-mail: ldonohue@406ventures.com
  Education: BS, Chemistry, Georgetown University; MBA, Tuck School of Business, Dartmouth College
  Background: Principal, Foster Management; Co-Founder, Arcadia Partners; CEO, Business Intelligence Advisors; Booz-Allen & Hamilton
  Directorships: Abilto, Axial Healthcare, Bedrock Data, Business Intelligence Advisors, Connotate, Copatient, Healthsense, Indico, Iora Health, Redox, Reltio, WoodPellets.com

  Graham Brooks, Partner
  e-mail: gbrooks@406ventures.com
  Education: BSE, Computer Science, Princeton University; MBA, Tuck School of Business, Dartmouth College
  Background: Business Development Manager, Bose Corporation; Co-Founder, Accentus

  Greg Dracon, Partner
  e-mail: gdracon@406ventures.com
  Education: BS, Electrical Engineering, Pennsylvania State University; MBA, Entrepreneurial Management & Finance, Wharton School
  Background: VP, Core Capital Partners

  Payal Agrawal Divakaran, Partner
  e-mail: payal@406ventures.com
  Education: BS, Electrical Engineering, MIT; MBA, Harvard Business School
  Background: Co-Founder, SpotRocket; Corporate Development, Eventbrite; Associate, Spectrum Equity; J.P. Morgan

3 10X VENTURE PARTNERS
848 Elm Street
Suite 200
Manchester, NH 03104

Phone: 603-838-3828
e-mail: 10xventurepartners@gmail.com
web: www.10xvp.com

Mission Statement: 10X Venture Partners is a seed stage (and beyond) investment group.

Geographic Preference: New England
Average Investment: $50,000 - $500,000
Investment Criteria: Seed-Stage, Revenue between $5 to $10 Million
Industry Group Preference: Mobile, Internet, Wireless, Security, Social Media, SaaS, Cloud Computing, Green Technology
Portfolio Companies: Adored, Akumina, Applied BioMath, Blade, Coach Up, Eversound, Liquidware Labs, MyVBO, Nanocomp Technologies Inc., NBD Nano, Spiro, Splitwise, Uconnect, WOO Sports, XL Hybrids

Key Executives:
  Jason Syversen, Managing Partner
  Background: Founder, Siege Technology; Program Manager DARPA

  Matt Pierson, Partner
  e-mail: mpierson@10xvp.com
  Education: BBA, University of Rhode Island
  Background: Co-Founder, DTC Communications; Managing Director, Dunn Rush & Co.

4 11.2 CAPITAL
818 Mission Street
Suite 200
San Francisco, CA 94103

web: www.112capital.com

Mission Statement: 11.2 Capital invests in tech-based businesses focused on technologies such as AI, cyber security, robotics, new space, and date-driven healthcare.

Founded: 2013
Industry Group Preference: Artificial Intelligence, Cyber Security, Robotics, Space, Data Analytics, Healthcare

Venture Capital & Private Equity Firms / Domestic Firms

Portfolio Companies: Aeva, Anyscale, Auransa, Avaamo, ByteGain, Caption Health, Covariant AI, Cruise Automation, CryptoNumerics, Deep Genomics, Forter, Genturi, Ginkgo Bioworks, Hinge Health, Kindred, Loop Genomics, Lucira Health, Mantle, Mason, Molecular Assemblies, Notable Labs, Orbital Sidekick, Outlier, Passage AI, Placenote, Savioke, Synthace, TigerGraph, Totem Labs, White Ops

Key Executives:
Shelley Zhuang, Founder/Managing Partner
Education: BS, University of Missouri; PhD, University of California, Berkeley
Background: Principal, Draper Fisher Jurvetson; EVP of Business Development, Ecoplast Technologies
Directorships: Passage AI
Yizhen Dong, Principal
Education: BS, Vanderbilt University; MBA, Booth School of Business
Background: Management Consultant, ZS Associates
Jonathan Mo, Senior Associate
Education: Columbia University; The London School of Economics
Background: Associate, TandemLaunch Ventures

5 1315 CAPITAL
2929 Walnut Street
Suite 1240
Philadelphia, PA 19104

Phone: 215-662-1315
web: www.1315capital.com

Mission Statement: 1315 Capital provides expansion and growth to commercial-stage healthcare services, medical technology and specialty therapeutics companies.

Fund Size: $500 million
Founded: 2014
Investment Criteria: Targets $10 to $30 million investments in commercial healthcare that have the potential to grow to $50 to $150 million of revenue

Key Executives:
Adele Oliva, Founding Partner
Education: BSc, St. Joseph's University; MBA, Cornell University
Background: Quaker Partners; Co-Head, US Healthcare, Apax Partners
Michael Koby, Founding Partner
Education: BSc, Cornell University; MBA, The Wharton School
Background: Managing Director, Palm Ventures; Investor, Galen Partners; Analyst, Dillon, Read & Co.

6 180 DEGREE CAPITAL
7 North Willow Street
Suite 4B
Montclair, NJ 07042

Phone: 973-746-4500 Fax: 212-582-9563
e-mail: ir@180degreecapital.com
web: www.180degreecapital.com

Mission Statement: An active investor committed to working side-by-side with the management of its portfolio companies to surmount the many challenges they confront. Formerly known as Harris & Harris Group.

Founded: 1983
Investment Criteria: Early stage, IPO, Acquisition, Tiny Technology
Industry Group Preference: Nanotechnology, Microelectronics
Portfolio Companies: ABS Materials, Adesto Technologies, Accelerator, AgBiome, D-Wave Systems, EchoPixel, Genome Profiling LLC, HALE.Life, HZO, Lodo Therapeutics, Mersana, Nanosys, NGX Bio, ORIG3N, Petra Pharma, Phylagen, ProSep, Synacor, TARA, TheStreet Inc., Xenio

Key Executives:
Kevin M. Rendino, Chairman/CEO
Background: Chairman/CEO, RGJ Capital
Directorships: Rentech Inc.
Daniel B. Wolfe, Ph.D, President/Chief Financial & Compliance Officer
Education: PhD, Chemistry, Harvard University; BA, Chemistry, Rice University
Background: Consultant, Nanosys; CW Group; Bioscale; Co-Founder/President, Scientific Venture Assessments

7 1843 CAPITAL
52 Mason St.
Greenwich, CT 06830

e-mail: info@1843capital.com
web: www.1843capital.com

Mission Statement: 1843 Capital is an early stage, technology venture firm advocating for gender equity to generate superior returns.

Investment Criteria: Early-Stage
Industry Group Preference: Technology, Consumer, Technology-Enabled Services
Portfolio Companies: Agrilyst, Beauty Counter, Finn AI, Glassbreakers, Iotas, Marstone, Modumetal, Rapt, Seedling, Shareablee, Silvernest, TA, Triple Canopy

Key Executives:
Tracy Chadwell, Founding Partner
Education: JD, Loyola University of Chicago
Background: Baker Capital
Alison Andrews Reyes, General Partner
Education: AB, Dartmouth College
Background: COO/Co-Founder, Dezignable.com; CEO/Co-Founder, Vigilant

8 1ST COURSE CAPITAL
541 Jefferson Avenue
Suite 100
Redwood City, CA 94063

web: www.1cc.vc

Mission Statement: 1CC is an early stage venture capital firm investing in entrepreneurs and businesses looking to change how produce is grown, produced and distributed.

Key Executives:
Peter Herz, General Partner
Education: BS, ECE, Carnegie Mellon University
Renske Lynde, General Partner
Education: BA, Boston University; MPP, University of California, Berkeley

9 42 VENTURES
6510 Millrock Dr.
#430
Salt Lake City, UT 84121

Phone: 801-893-2442
e-mail: info@42ventures.com
web: www.42ventures.com

Mission Statement: Partnering with entrepreneurs to grow software-driven businesses that deliver innovative products and services to highly defined markets.

Founded: 2006
Average Investment: $250,000 - $1.5 million
Investment Criteria: Early-Stage
Industry Group Preference: Software, SaaS, Mobile, Cloud Computing, Big Data
Portfolio Companies: Distribion, Fast, Ideal Response, Inside Real Estate, Insurance Technologies, Luminoso, Marketingfx, New Media Gateway, Sharp Analytics, Simpleview, Swipeclock Workforce Management, Verticalnerve, Works Software, TouchPath

Venture Capital & Private Equity Firms / Domestic Firms

Key Executives:
Ned Stringham, Managing Director
801-550-5024
Education: BS, Philosophy & Political Science, University of Utah; MBA, Harvard Business School
Background: Co-Founder, SBI Group; Co-Founder, Impact Group; McKinsey & Company
Bob Howe, Executive Advisory Board
Education: BBA, Southern Methodist University; MBA, Harvard Business School
Background: Managing Partner, Highnote Ventures; Chairman, Montgomery Goodwin Investments; CEO/Chairman, Scient; Senior Vice President, Booz Allen Hamilton
Tim Storer, Executive Advisory Board
214-868-8484
Education: BSc, Engineering and Mathematics, Vanderbilt University; MBA, Southern Methodist University
Background: CEO, Distribion Inc.; Chairman, Vertical Nerve; Chairman, Marketingfx
Blue VanDyke, Partner
Education: MS, International Management, Thunderbird
Background: Co-Founder, Pride-Media Group; COO, Proxicom; Daimler-Benz; Ernst & Young
Troy Wardrop, Operating Principal - Technology
Education: BS, Computer Science, University of Utah
Background: Co-Founder, White Label Marketing
Doug Folsom, Chief Financial Officer
801-703-1625
Education: BSc, University of Utah; CPA

10 4490 VENTURES
111 North Fairchild Street
Suite 240
Madison, WI 53703

Phone: 608-501-0000
e-mail: info@4490ventures.com
web: 4490ventures.com

Mission Statement: 4490 Ventures rings capital, company-building experience and a network of resources to help entrepreneurs build their next great tech company.

Geographic Preference: Outside Silicon Valley
Founded: 2014
Average Investment: $6-10 Million
Investment Criteria: 4490 Ventures looks to invest early in a Company's lifecycle. They focus on Tech Company Start-Ups.

Key Executives:
Greg Robinson, Managing Director
Education: BSc, Arizona State University; MBA, Dartmouth College
Background: Managing Director, Penninsula Ventures; Co-Founder, Cogent Technologies
Dan Malven, Managing Director
Education: BSc, Purdue University; MBA, Northwestern University, Kellogg School of Management
Background: Principal, Flatiron Partners

11 500 STARTUPS
814 Mission Street
6th Floor
San Francisco, CA 94013

web: 500.co

Mission Statement: Based in Silicon Valley, 500 Startups has invested in more than 1,600 companies in 60 countries.

Geographic Preference: Global
Fund Size: $300 million
Founded: 2010
Average Investment: $150,000
Investment Criteria: Seed, Series A
Industry Group Preference: Consumer Commercial, Family Tech and Education, Design, SMB Productivity & Cloud Services, International/Emerging Markets, Food Tech & Digital Healthcare, Mobile & Tablet, Payments & Financial Services, Online Video, Bitcoin, Ad Tech, Components & IoT
Portfolio Companies: Cleanify, ClickMechanic, ContaAzul, Grab, LE TOTE, Mayvenn, RealtyShares, Saucey, STOREMAVEN, Talkdesk, ToutApp, Twilio

Key Executives:
Christine Tsai, Chief Executive Officer
e-mail: christine@500.co
Education: University of California, Berkeley
Background: Google, YouTube

12 5AM VENTURES
501 Second Street
Suite 350
San Fransisco, CA 94107

Phone: 415-933-8569
web: www.5amventures.com

Mission Statement: 5AM Ventures is focused on expanding early stage biotechnology and life science companies.

Fund Size: $350 million
Founded: 2002
Average Investment: $25 million
Minimum Investment: $4 million
Investment Criteria: Seed, Early Stage, Startups
Industry Group Preference: Life Sciences, Biotechnology, Biopharmaceutical, Drug Delivery Technology, Healthcare
Portfolio Companies: Achaogen, Akouos, Alexza, Ambrx, Aprea, Arvinas, Audentes, Bellerophon, Biodesy, Bird Rock Bio, Cabaletta Bio, Calibrium, Cellular Research, Ceterix, Chrono, Cidara, CinCor, Cleave, Crinetics, DVS Sciences, Entrada, Envoy, Epirus, Escient Pharmaceuticals, Expansion Therapeutics, Flexion, Homology Medicines, Ideaya Biosciences, Ikaria, Ilypsa, Impel Neuropharma, Incline Therapeutics, KalaBios, Kinestral, Magnetic Insight, Marcadia Biotech, Miikana, Millendo, Neurogastrx, NodThera, Nohla Therapeutics, Nouscom, Novira, Novome, Panomics, Pear Therapeutics, Pearl, Portal, Precision NanoSystems, Pulmatrix, Purigen, Rallybio, RareCyte, Relypsa, Scientist.com, scPharmaceuticals, Semprus, Synosia, TMRW, VBI Vaccines, Viveve, Vor Biopharma, Wildcat Discovery Technology

Other Locations:
200 Clarendon Street
45th Floor
Boston, MA 02116
Phone: 857-305-1825

Key Executives:
John D Diekman PhD, Founding Partner
Education: BA, Chemistry, Princeton University; PhD, Chemistry, Stanford University
Background: Founder/Managing Director, Bay City Capital; Chairman/CEO, Affymetrix; Chairman/Managing Director, Affymax
Directorships: Ambrx, Igenica, Wildcat, Chemdex, Envoy, Ingenuity, LJL BioSystems, Marcadia
Andrew J Schwab, Founding Partner
Education: BS, Genetics & Ethics, Davidson College
Background: Principal, Bay City Capital; VP, Business Development, Digital Gene Technologies; VP, Montgomery Securities
Directorships: Bellerophon, Biodesy, Cleave, DVS, Flexion, Ikaria, Ilypsa, Miikana, Pear Therapeutics, Precision NanoSystems, RuiYi, Synosia, Viveve
Scott M Rocklage PhD, Founding Partner
Education: BS, Chemistry, University of California, Berkeley; PhD, Chemistry, MIT
Background: Chairman/CEO, Cubist Pharmaceuticals; President/CEO, Nycomed; Salutar; Catalytica
Directorships: Achaogen, Cidara, Epirus, Kinestral, Novira, Pulmatrix, Rennovia
Kush M Parmar, MD, PhD, Managing Partner
Education: AB, Molecular Biology, Princeton University;

Venture Capital & Private Equity Firms / Domestic Firms

PhD, Experimental Pathology, Harvard University; MD, Harvard Medical School
Background: VP, Strategy & Corporate Development, Novira
Directorships: Arvinas, Audentes, Novira, scPharmaceuticals
Rebecca Lucia, CFA, Chief Financial Officer/Chief Operating Officer
Education: MBA, JL Kellogg School Of Management; Chartered Financial Analyst; Canadian Chartered Accountant
Background: CFO, Prospect Venture Partners; CFO Asset Management Ventures
Paul A Stone JD, Chief Operating Officer/General Counsel
Education: University of Wisconsin
Background: SVP/General Counsel, Ethos Pharmaceuticals; SVP/General Counsel, Ilypsa; VP, Chief Patent Counsel, Symyx; Patent Attorney, Senniger, Powers, Leavitt & Roedel
Directorships: Save the Bay
Mason Freeman MD, Venture Partner
Education: BA, Harvard College; MD, University of California, San Francisco
Background: Chief, Lipid Metabolism Unit/Director, Translational Medicine, Massachusetts General Hospital
Directorships: Envoy
Richard J Ulevitch PhD, Venture Partner Emeritus
Education: AB, Washington & Jefferson College; PhD, Biochemistry, University of Pennsylvania
Background: Professor & Chairman, Department of Immunology, The Scripps Resarch Institute
James W Young PhD, Venture Partner Emeritus
Education: BS, Chemistry, Fordham University; PhD, Organic Chemistry, Cornell University
Background: CEO, Sunesis; SVP, ALZA Corporation; President, Pharmaceuticals Division, Affymax, N.V.; SVP/General Manager, Pharmaceuticals Division, Sepracor; VP, Research, Zoecon/Sandoz Crop Protection Corporation
Directorships: Chrono Therapeutics

---

13 645 VENTURES

e-mail: ideas@645ventures.com
web: 645ventures.com

Mission Statement: A tech-based venture capital firm interested in early-stage startups.
Founded: 2013
Investment Criteria: Early-Stage
Industry Group Preference: Technology, Artificial Intelligence, Retail, Consumer, Design, Entertainment, Industry, Health & Wellness, Infrastructure, Security
Portfolio Companies: AaDya, Abacus, Alice, Andrena, AptDeco, Beauty Bakerie, Bespoke Post, Betterview, Eden Health, Fat Llama, FiscalNote, Hire An Esquire, Iterable, League Apps, Negotiatus, Ovetime, Panther, Resident, Rifiniti, Rosie, Source3, Squire, Thinknum, Voodoo Manufacturing

Key Executives:
Nnamdi Okike, Co-Founder/Managing Partner
Education: BA, Harvard University; JD, Harvard Law School; MBA, Harvard Business School
Background: Principal, Insight Venture Partners; Business Development Officer, Verne Global
Aaron Holiday, Co-Founder/Managing Partner
Education: BS, Morehouse College; MBA, Cornell University
Background: Software Engineer, Goldman Sachs; Business Analyst, GFI Group; Associate, DFJ Gotham Ventures; Managing Entrepreneurial Officer, Cornell Tech

---

14 747 CAPITAL
880 Third Avenue
17th Floor
New York, NY 10022

Phone: 212-747-7474
e-mail: info@747capital.com
web: www.747capital.com

Mission Statement: Through the funding of funds and managed accounts, 747 Capital focuses exclusively on the smaller end of the private equity market in North America.
Geographic Preference: United States, Canada
Fund Size: $550 million
Founded: 2001
Minimum Investment: $50 million
Investment Criteria: Later-Stage
Industry Group Preference: Private Equity
Portfolio Companies: Crossplane Capital, Guardian Capital Partners, Hamilton Robinson Captial Partners, Periscope Equity, Tilia, Transom Capital Group

Key Executives:
Gijs FJ Van Thiel, Managing Partner
Education: BA, Webster University; MBA, Thunderbird School of Global Management, Arizona State University
Background: Founder/General Partner, Triad Media Ventures; Director, Financial Services, Icon International; Assistant Area Director, Netherlands Foreign Investment Agency
Marc der Kinderen, Managing Partner
Education: BBA, European University, Belgium; MBA, Nijenrode School of Business
Background: Executive VP, Greenfield Capital Partners; Noro Group of Companies; HomeBanc
Directorships: CapCorp Investments
Joshua Sobeck, Partner
Education: BA, Molecular Biology & Biochemistry, Middlebury College; MBA, Finance, Columbia Business School
Background: Product Marketing Manager, Citadon
James Yang, Vice President
Education: BAA, Finance, University Of Texas at Austin
Background: University Of Texas Investment Management Company
Greg Stupore, Associate
Education: BA, Accounting, Boston College; CPA
Background: Senior Auditor, Deloitte & Touche

---

15 A-GRADE INVESTMENTS
Los Angeles, CA

web: www.agradeinvestments.com

Geographic Preference: United States
Founded: 2011
Investment Criteria: Seed, Early Stage, Debt
Industry Group Preference: Consumer Internet, Technology
Portfolio Companies: Airtable, Amen, Getaround, GoButler, IfOnly, Kopari Beauty, Pair, ResearchGate, Sonic Notify, Tinychat, Willing

Key Executives:
Guy Oseary, Founder
Background: Principal, Untitled Entertainment; Executive Producer, NBC's Last Call
Ron Burkle, Founder
Background: Managing Partner, The Yucaipa Companies; Director, Yahoo; Director, Yucaipa Equity Partners, L.P.; Director, Occidental Petroleum Corp.; Director, KB Home Corporation
Ashton Kutcher, Founder
Background: General Partner, Sound Ventures; Co-Founder, Thorn: Digital Defenders of Children
Chris Hollod, Managing Partner
Education: BA, Economics, Finance, and Philosophy, Vanderbilt University
Background: Founding Partner, Inevitable Ventures

Venture Capital & Private Equity Firms / Domestic Firms

16 AM VENTURES
65 Union Avenue
Suite 500
Memphis, TN 38103

Phone: 901-523-2000
web: www.archermalmo.com

Mission Statement: AM Ventures seeks to invest in early-stage companies by providing expertise and execution.

Geographic Preference: United States
Founded: 2010
Investment Criteria: Early-Stage
Industry Group Preference: Consumer Internet, Software
Portfolio Companies: Capital Farm Credit, Delaware North, Implus, Juice Plus, Massage Heights, Nations Hearing, Palm Beach Tan, Reynolds American, Smile Doctors Braces, Stoller, Valent, Zoetis

Key Executives:
Russ Williams, Principal, Chief Executive Officer
Education: MBA, Darden School Of Business, University of Virginia; BSc, Chemical Engineering, Christian Brothers University
Background: Chemical Engineer, DuPont
Directorships: Kraft Food Ingredients
Gary Backaus, Principal, Chief Creative & Strategic Officer
Education: BFA, Advertising Design, Memphis College of Art
Wally Rose, SVP/Executive Creative Director
Education: University of Memphis
Background: Executive Creative Director, Sullivan Branding

17 AAVIN PRIVATE EQUITY
1245 First Avenue Southeast
Cedar Rapids, IA 52402

Phone: 319-247-1072
web: www.aavin.com

Mission Statement: Generates outstanding investment results by partnering with strong management groups to build companies into profitable acquisition candidates.

Geographic Preference: Mid-America Region
Fund Size: $87 million
Founded: 1999
Average Investment: $5 - $10 million
Minimum Investment: $5 million
Investment Criteria: Late Stage, Expansion Stage, High-Growth Opportunities, MBO, Recapitalization
Industry Group Preference: Medical Devices, Healthcare, Information Technology, Manufacturing, Distribution, Industrial Products, Retail, Consumer & Leisure, Software, Services
Portfolio Companies: American Industrial Machine, Brown Industries, CPI Luxury Group, Dream Giveaway, ECS Learning Systems, FedEx Ground, Graham Waste, Green Diamond Sand Products, Greenleaf Book Group, Happy Joe's, HH Ventures, Montana Silversmiths, Roanwell Corporation, Standard Precast, Transfer Tool Products, Verrex, Weeks Service Company

Key Executives:
James Thorp, Managing Partner
319-200-4354
e-mail: jthorp@aavin.com
Education: BS, Business Administration, Oklahoma State University; MBA, Finance, Wharton School, University of Pennsylvania
Background: Principal, Allsop Venture Partners; Berthel Fisher & Company
Eric Hender, Senior Partner
319-200-4846
e-mail: ehender@aavin.com
Education: Colorado College; Banking Institute, University of Wisconsin; Securities Institute, Wharton School, University of Pennsylvania
Background: Co-Founder/Managing Member, Marshall Venture Capital, LC; SCI Financial Group; President, Securities Corporation of Iowa
Directorships: Destinations Unlimited, Inter-Med
David Schroder, Senior Partner
319-247-1072
e-mail: dschroder@aavin.com
Education: BSFS, International Business, Georgetown University; MBA, University Of Wisconsin
Background: MorAmerica Capital Coproration, InvestAmerica
Directorships: NASBIC, Midwest RASBIC
Paul Rhines, Senior Partner
319-363-8971
e-mail: prhines@aavin.com
Education: BA, Accounting, University of Northern Iowa
Background: Founding General Partner, Allsop Venture Partners; Co-Founder/Managing Member/Executive VP, Marshall Venture Capital, LC; Regional VP, MorAmerica Capital Corporation
Directorships: GreatAmerica Financial Services, Stamats Communications Company, Schebler Company
Thies O Kolln, Partner
319-200-4355
Education: BA, Dartmouth College; JD, University of Chicago
Background: Boston Consulting Group; Orbitz; Kirkland & Ellis; Law Clerk, US Court of Appeals
Kevin Mullane, Partner
816-807-3817
e-mail: kmullane@aavin
Education: BSBA, MBA, Rockhurst Jesuit University
Background: MorAmerica Capital; Co-Founder, Invest America
Directorships: NASBIC, Midwest RASBIC

18 ABBOTT CAPITAL MANAGEMENT LLC
1290 Avenue of the Americas
New York, NY 10104

Phone: 212-757-2700
web: www.abbottcapital.com

Mission Statement: Abbott Capital Management, LLC is an investment management firm focused on building and managing private equity funds worldwide. Abbott Capital provides a number of solutions for institutional investors, and selects funds across venture capital, growth equity, buyouts, special situations and secondaries.

Geographic Preference: Worldwide
Founded: 1986

Key Executives:
Jonathan D Roth, Managing Director/President
Education: AB, Economics, Cornell University; MBA, The Fuqua School of Business, Duke University
Background: Associate, Elmrock Partners; Financial Analyst, Amoco Corporation; Corporate Lending Officer, Chemical Bank
Mary T Hornby, Managing Director/General Counsel
Education: BA, Boston College; JD, Boston College Law School
Background: Counsel, Private Equity Group, Testa Hurwitz & Thibeault LLP
Timothy W Maloney, Managing Director
Education: BS, Accounting, DePaul University; MBA, Finance, New York University; CPA
Background: Frye-Louis Capital Management; General American Transportation Corporation; Hewitt Associates
Lauren M Massey, Managing Director/Finance & Administration
Education: BS, Accounting, State University of New York at Binghamton; MBA, Finance & Marketing, New York University; CPA
Background: Audit Manager, Financial Services Division, Ernst & Young

Venture Capital & Private Equity Firms / Domestic Firms

Paolo Parziale, Managing Director/Chief Financial Officer
Education: BS, Accounting, St. John's University; MBA, Finance, New York University
Background: Audit Senior, Ernst & Young
Meredith L Rerisi, Managing Director
Education: BS, Applied Economics & Business Management, Cornell University; MBA, Duke University
Background: Equity Analyst, American High Growth Equities Corporation
Matthew M Smith, Managing Director
Education: AB, History, MBA, Finance, Georgetown University
Background: Federal Reserve Bank of New York; First Trust Washington; Bank of America
Kathryn J Stokel, Managing Director/Chief Operating Officer
Education: BS, Mathematics, University of Michigan; MBA, Finance, Wharton School, University of Pennsylvania; CFA
Background: Portfolio Manager, General Motors Investment Management Corporation
Charles H van Horne, Senior Advisor
Education: BA, Sociology, University of Pennsylvania
Background: AIG Capital Partners; Creditanstalt International Advisors; Bankers Trust; UBS Securities

19 ABELL FOUNDATION VENTURES
111 South Calvert Street
Suite 2300
Baltimore, MD 21202-6174

Phone: 410-547-1300 Fax: 410-539-6579
e-mail: abell@abell.org
web: www.abell.org

Mission Statement: The Abell Foundation is dedicated to supporting innovative initiatives that will enhance the quality of life in Maryland.
Geographic Preference: Baltimore, Nearby
Fund Size: $25 million
Founded: 1953
Average Investment: $150,000 - $500,000
Investment Criteria: Companies that create jobs in Baltimore and seek to challenge various social and environmental issues
Industry Group Preference: Telecommunications, Internet Technology, Software, Healthcare, Biotechnology, Medical Devices, Energy
Portfolio Companies: AMRM, Awarables, BioMarker Strategies, Breethe, Common Curriculum, CoolTech, CyberSpa, Dipole Materials, eNeura Therapeutics, Factory Four, Gemstone Biotherapeutics, Gliknik, GrayBug, Harpoon Medical, Lawrenceville Plasma Physics, Life Sprout, Longeviti, MF Fire, Network for Good, Next Step Robotics, NAWEC, Noxilizer, Oasis Marinas, OTEC International, PAICE, Perceptive Navigation, Personal Genome Diagnostics, Pixelligent, Propel Baltimore Fund, ReGelTec, Sisu Global Health, Sonavex, Sonify Biosciences, Sunrise, ThermoChem Recovery International, Vasoptic Medical, Vixiar Medical
Key Executives:
Robert C Embry Jr, President
Education: Williams College; Harvard Law School
Background: President, Board of School Commissioners, Baltimore City; Assistant Secretary, US Department of Housing and Urban Development
Directorships: Maryland State Board Of Education
Eileen O'Rourke, Chief Financial Officer
Education: Loyola College; CPA; Registered Securities Broker; Certified Financial and Operations Principal
Background: KPMG, VP, Legg Mason Inc
Directorships: eNeura, Pixelligent, Ceratech

20 ABERDARE VENTURES
235 Montgomery Street
Suite 1230
San Francisco, CA 94104

Phone: 415-392-7442 Fax: 415-392-4264
web: www.aberdare.com

Mission Statement: Experienced venture investors and operators of healthcare technology companies.
Geographic Preference: San Francisco area
Fund Size: $400 million
Founded: 1999
Average Investment: $1 - $15 million
Minimum Investment: $1 million
Investment Criteria: Early Stage
Industry Group Preference: Healthcare, Biopharmaceuticals, Medical Devices, Therapeutics
Portfolio Companies: Castlight, Clovis Oncology, ElationEMR, Gravie, Gritstone Oncology, Indigo Agriculture, Kaleido Biosciences, Kezar Life Sciences, MC10, Piper Bioscience, Vir
Key Executives:
Paul Klingenstein, Founder/Managing Partner
e-mail: pklingenstein@aberdare.com
Education: AB, Harvard College; MBA, Stanford Graduate School of Business
Background: Advisor, Rockefeller Foundation; Accel Partners; Warburg Pincus
Directorships: Aviron, Isis Pharmaceuticals, Glycomed, Neurex, Xomed Surgica Products
Sigrid Van Bladel, PhD, Venture Partner
e-mail: svanbladel@aberdare.com
Education: MA, Chemistry/Biology, University Of Ghent; PhD, Molecular Biology, University Of Ghent; MBA, Stanford Graduate School Of Business
Background: Partner, New Enterprise Associates
Directorships: Myogen, Kai Pharma, Novacept, SurgRx, Xcel Pharmaceuticals, Appriva Medical, Spiration Inc.
Mohit Kaushal MD, Partner
e-mail: mkaushal@aberdare.com
Education: MBA, Stanford University; MD, Imperial College London
Background: Director, Connected Health, Federal Communications Commission; Investment Professional, Polaris Venture Partners; Merrill Lynch; World Health Organization
Directorships: goBalto, RxAnte
Jake Odden, Partner/Chief Operating Officer
e-mail: jodden@aberdare.com
Education: AB, Bowdoin College; MBA, Tuck School of Business, Dartmouth College
Background: Walt Disney Company; Goldman Sachs; Vanguard Group
Directorships: Posit Science
Sigrid Van Bladel, Venture Partner
e-mail: svanbladel@aberdare.com
Education: PhD, Molecular Biology, Ghent University; MBA, Stanford Graduate School of Business
Background: Partner, New Enterprise Associates; Management Consultant, McKinsey and Company
Directorships: Aviir, Conatus, Kai Pharmaceuticals

21 ABRY PARTNERS
888 Boylston Street
Suite 1600
Boston, MA 02199

Phone: 617-859-2959
e-mail: information@abry.com
web: www.abry.com

Mission Statement: ABRY Partners is a private equity investment firm focused on media, communications, business and information services companies based in North America. ABRY provides operational expertise, investment experience, capital and industry insight. The firm partners with superior

Venture Capital & Private Equity Firms / Domestic Firms

management teams with the goal of helping to build stronger companies.
Fund Size: $1.7 billion
Founded: 1989
Average Investment: $25 million - $150 million
Minimum Investment: $10 million
Investment Criteria: Buyouts, Expansion Capital, Backing Platform Acquisitions, Mezzanine, Roll-ups/Consolidations, Recapitalization for partial liquidity
Industry Group Preference: Media, Communications, Business Products & Services, Education, Entertainment, Healthcare Services, Information Services, Digital Media & Marketing
Portfolio Companies: Accela, Access Information Management, Acrisure, AddSecure, AdSwerve, Aduro, Aegis Sciences Corporation, Aftermath, AFS Technologies Inc., Airband, Alliantgroup, American CyberSystems, Anju Software, ArchivesOne, Atlantic Broadband, Avalon Cable, Basefarm, B&H Education, Billing Services Group, Brash Entertainment, Broadcast Electronics, BSO, BTG, CafeMedia, CapRock Holdings, Casamba, Cast & Crew, Charleston Newspaper, CIBT, Citadel Communications, CitiXsys, Claranet, Commerce Connect Media, Commonwealth Business Media, Confie Seguros, Confirma Software, Conoisseur Communications, Consolitated Theatres, Consumer Media Network, Country Road Communications, CyrusOne, DataMentors, Datapipe, DF King World Wide, Direct Travel, Dolan Media Company, Donuts, Dr. Dental, Edgile, EduK Group, Emerging Markets Communications, Executive Health Resources, F+W Media, FanFare Media Works, FastMed Urgent Care, Finest City Broadcasting LLC, FLS Transportation, Franklin Energy, Frontline Performance Group, Gateway EDI, Gould & Lamb, Grande Communications, Hanley Wood, HealthPort, HealthSCOPE Benefits, HealthTrans, Hilb Group, Hispanic Yellow Pages, Home Town Cable, Hosted Solutions, Houghton Mifflin Harcourt, IMG, InfiLaw System, Integra, iTradeNetwork Inc., JAB Broadband, Kidz Bop, Kore Wireless Group, Legendary Pictures, Lighthouse Autism Center, Link Mobility, Masergy, Maya Cinemas, Media Rights Capital, Millennium Trust, Music Reports Inc., Muzak, North American Dental Group, Nuspire,

Key Executives:
Royce G. Yudkoff, Co-Founder
Education: Dartmouth College; Harvard Business School
Background: Partner, Bain & Company; Founder, Information Partners
Andrew Banks, Co-Founder
Education: Harvard Law School; Oxford University; University of Florida
Background: Partner, Bain & Co; TELCO Board, National Association of Broadcasters
Peggy Koenig, Chair
Education: Cornell University; MBA, Wharton School
Background: Partner/Board Member, Sillerman Communications Management Corporation
Jay Grossman, Managing Partner/Co-CEO
Education: Dickinson College; MBA, Harvard Business School
Background: Managing Director/Co-Head, Media and Entertainment Group, Prudential Securities; Corporate Finance, Kidder, Peabody & Company
C.J. Brucato, Managing Partner/Co-CEO
Education: Princeton University
Background: Media and Entertainment Group, Prudential Securities Inc.
John Hunt, Managing Partner
Education: University of Massachusetts Amherst
Background: General Partner, Boston Ventures Management
Brent Stone, Partner
Education: Cornell University
Background: Credit Suisse First Boston; Donaldson, Lufkin & Jenrette; Chase Securities

Robert MacInnis, Partner
Education: Merrimack College; MBA, Boston University; CPA
Background: CFO, Weather Services Corporation; Senior Manager, Mergers & Acquisition Group, PricewaterhouseCoopers
Anders Bjork, Partner
Education: BS, University of Denver; MSF, Daniels College of Business; MBA, Wharton School
Background: Fir Tree Partners; Guggenheim Partners; VSS; Former Professional Hockey Plaer in the American Hockey League, Represented the Swedish National team
Brian St. Jean, Partner
Education: University of Rhode Island; CPA
Background: Manager, Mergers & Acquisition Group, PricewaterhouseCoopers
John Connor, Partner
Education: Columbia University; MBA, Graduate School of Business, University of Chicago; CFA
Background: SVP, Hartford Investment Management Company
Michael Ashton, Partner
Education: BA, MBA, University of Rhode Island
Background: Senior Credit Analyst, Eaton Vance Management; Fortis Investments; Hartford Investment Management
Matt Lapides, Partner
Education: Colby College
Background: Senior Analyst, John Hancock Financial Services Inc.; VP, Finance, Diveo Broadband Networks; Chase Securities Inc.
Nicolas Massard, Partner
Education: HEC Paris
Background: Spectrum Equity Investors; Continuum Group; Morgan Stanley; Lehman Brothers
Directorships: Airband, JAB
T.J. Rose, Partner
Education: MBA, Harvard Business School
Background: Engagement Manager, McKinsey & Company; Associate, Goldman Sachs Capital Partners
Nicholas Scola, Partner
Education: Tufts University
Background: HIG Capital; Capital Resource Partners; Broadview International
Tomer Yosef-Or, Partner
Education: Rutgers Business School, Rutgers University
Background: Financial Instiution Group, Bear Stearns; Securitization Transaction Group, Deloitte & Touche
Tyler Wick, Partner
Education: Amherst College
Background: Ticonderoga Capital; Advest
Azra Kanji, Partner
Education: Duke University
Background: Communications, Media & Entertainment Group, Goldman Sachs
Debbie Johnson, Chief Financial Officer
Education: Boston University; CPA
Background: Senior Accountant, Audit Division, PricewaterhouseCoopers

---

22 **ABS CAPITAL PARTNERS**
400 East Pratt Street
Suite 910
Baltimore, MD 21202-3127

Phone: 410-246-5600
e-mail: abscapital@abscapital.com
web: www.abscapital.com

Mission Statement: To create significant, market-leading companies. Investment strategy focuses on companies in the healthcare, technology, business services, media and communications sectors.

Geographic Preference: United States
Fund Size: $500 million
Founded: 1990

Venture Capital & Private Equity Firms / Domestic Firms

Average Investment: $10 - $40 million
Investment Criteria: Later-Stage Growth, Expansion, Recapitalizations
Industry Group Preference: Business Products & Services, Information Technology, Communications, Healthcare, Media, Education
Portfolio Companies: Accurate Group Holdings, Alarm.com, Aldera, Bambeco, Bask, Bravo Wellness, ConnectYourCare, Defy Media, EXOS, FactorTrust, IgnitionOne, INTTRA, Invision, ISO Group, iZotope, Liquid Environmental Solutions, Modular Space Corporation, Pathology, PaySpan, Paystream, Power Reviews, Purch, Redzone Robotics, Scale Computing, Teachscape, Whitney International University System, Zoom Media Group

Other Locations:
3 Harbor Drive
Suite 108
Sausalito, CA 94965
Phone: 415-262-8100

Key Executives:
Donald B. Hebb, Jr., Chairman/Founding Partner
Education: Kenyon College; Harvard Law School; Harvard Business School
Background: President/CEO, Alex. Brown & Sons
Directorships: INTTRA, ISO Group, Modular Space Corporation, Zoom Media Group
Phil Clough, Managing General Partner
Education: United States Military Academy; Darden School of Business, University of Virginia
Background: CEO, SITEL Corporation; Investment Banking Group, Alex. Brown & Sons; Captain, United States Army
Directorships: Accurate Group Holdings, FactorTrust, Liquid Environmental Solutions, Liquidity Services, Teachscape, Whitney International University, System
John Stobo, Managing General Partner
Education: University of California, San Diego; Johnson Graduate School of Management, Cornell University
Background: Health Care Investment Banking Group, Alex. Brown & Sons
Directorships: Aldera, Bravo Wellness, EXOS, Pathology
Mike Avon, General Partner
Education: University of Virginia; University of Virgina School of Law
Background: Venture Capitalist, Millennial Media; Principal, Columbia Capital; Executive Chairman, ICX Media
Kimberly Kyle, General Partner
Education: Bloomsburg University; University of Baltimore
Ralph Terkowitz, General Partner
Education: Cornell University; University of California, Berkeley
Background: CIO/CTO, Washington Post Company; Founder/CEO, WashingtonPost.Newsweek Interactive
Directorships: Alarm.com, IgnitionOne, PowerReviews, Purch
Tim Weglicki, Founding Partner
Education: Johns Hopkins University; Wharton School
Background: Founder/Head, Capital Markets Group, Alex. Brown & Sons
Directorships: American Public Foundation, ConnectYourCare, PaySpan
Cal Wheaton, General Partner
Education: Colby College; Wharton School
Background: VP, Deutsche Bank, Alex. Brown & Sons; Kidder, Peabody & Co.
Directorships: Accurate Group Holdings, Bambeco, ConnectYourCare, PaySpan, PayStream
Paul Mariani, General Partner
Education: Stanford University
Background: Technology Investment Banking Division, Robertson Stephens; SoundView Technology Group
Directorships: Liquid Environmental Solutions, PowerReviews, Purch, Teachscape

James Stevenson, Chief Financial Officer
Education: University of North Carolina
Background: EVP/CFO, SITEL Corporation; Alex. Brown & Sons; KPMG

23 ABS VENTURES
950 Winter Street
Suite 2600
Waltham, MA 02451

e-mail: abs@absventures.com
web: www.absventures.com

Mission Statement: ABS Ventures is a venture capital firm that invests in mid-stage technology companies. Utilizing primary and secondary direct investing strategies, ABS Ventures works with management teams to help with the growth of portfolio companies.

Geographic Preference: United States
Fund Size: $320 million
Founded: 1983
Average Investment: $5 - $15 million
Minimum Investment: $5 million
Investment Criteria: Bridge, First Stage, Mezzanine, Second Stage, Mid-Stage
Industry Group Preference: Software, Communications, Healthcare, Technology-Enabled Services, Information Technology, Medical Technology
Portfolio Companies: Active Network, Adeptra, Alphablox, Certona Corp., Clearforest, Clicksquared Inc., Cognio, CVRx, End2End, Evalve Inc., Everbridge, Eyeonics, Farechase, Formation Systems, FoxHollow Technology, Gomez Inc., Highroads, Hotbar.com, I-Logix, Ilumin, Intact Medical Corps., Intralinks, Inxight Software, IQ Financial Systems, Lumend, Nuera, Overtone, Paratek, Powerdsine, Qualys, Rib-X Pharmaceuticals, RiskMetrics, Synchronoss, Telogy, Theravance, Trema, Trivascular, Vesta GMS, Wimba, Workbrain

Key Executives:
Bill Burgess, Managing Partner
Education: BA, Dartmouth College; MBA, Harvard Business School
Background: Managing Director/Global Head/Vice Chairman, Deutsche Bank Venture Partners; Head of Technology Investment Banking, Alex. Brown & Sons
Directorships: Certona, ClickSquared, Highroads
Bruns Grayson, Managing Partner
Education: Harvard College; Univ. of Oxford; University of Virginia School of Law
Background: Adler & Company; Associate, McKinsey & Company; Manager, Venture Funds, Alex. Brown & Sons
Directorships: Active Network, Intact Medical, Rib-X Pharmaceuticals, Wimba
Susan Adams, Chief Financial Officer
Education: BS, Pennsylvania State University

24 ABSTRACT VENTURES
South Park
San Francisco, CA 94133

web: abstractvc.com

Mission Statement: A broad partnership of investors that funds the earliest stages of business formation.

Geographic Preference: California
Founded: 2016
Investment Criteria: Pre-Seed, Seed, Series A
Industry Group Preference: Insurance, Finance, Robotics, Healthcare, Software
Portfolio Companies: Ripple, Osaro, Neighborly, Brave Software, Starsky Robotics, Arrivo, Squadrun, Grabango, Contraline, Ccobox, Clara, Simple Health, ID By DNA, Simbi, RBC Signals, Drip, Catalia Health, Poncho, Polychain Capital, Cruncher, Clarity Money, Lunar, Petal, Prodigy, Hippo

Venture Capital & Private Equity Firms / Domestic Firms

Key Executives:
Ramtin Naimi, Founder/General Partner
Background: Founder/Senior Advisor, AutoHub; Partners, Flight Ventures; Core Innovation Capital
Directorships: AppOnboard, Arrivo, AutoHub, Bestow, Brave, BuildUp, Catalia Health, Ccobox, Clara, Clarity Money, Contraline, CUR, DeepCurrent Technologies, Dolo (Tea Time Labs), Drip, Hippo

25 ACACIA CAPITAL
101 S Ellsworth Avenue
Suite 300
San Mateo, CA 94401

Phone: 650-372-6400 Fax: 650-378-8977
web: www.acacia-capital.com

Mission Statement: A private investment banking firm which provides M&A and corporate finance advisory services to middle market businesses in support of client growth, refinance, and sale efforts.

Geographic Preference: United States
Fund Size: $100 million
Founded: 1999
Minimum Investment: $20 million
Investment Criteria: Existing Apartment Communities, 100+ Unites, Value Add & Core Opportunity
Industry Group Preference: Real Estate
Other Locations:
2398 E Camelback Road
Suite 200
Phoenix, AZ 85016
Phone: 602-253-5563 **Fax:** 602-253-0859

Key Executives:
Robert E. Larson, Founder/Co-CEO
Education: BA, MBA, Stanford University
Background: Morgan Stanley & Co.
Robert G. Leupold, Co-CEO
Education: BA, University of California, San Diego
Background: Asset Sales Group, Union Bank

26 ACADIA WOODS PARTNERS
New York, NY

Mission Statement: A New York based investment partnership with particular interest in early stage technology companies.

Investment Criteria: Early Stage
Industry Group Preference: Technology, Biotechnology
Portfolio Companies: Burlywood, Dispersol Technologies, Luminoso, SyncHR, VidMob
Key Executives:
Jeff Samberg, Managing Director
Education: BA, Economics, Princeton University; MBA, Stanford University Graduate School of Business
Background: Vice President of Corporate Strategy, PeopleSoft Inc.; Vice President of Business Development, Wily Technology; Entrepreneur in Residence, Greylock Partners

27 ACARIO INNOVATION
535 Middlefield Road
Menlo Park, CA 94025

web: www.acarioinnovation.com

Mission Statement: Acario Innovation was established by Tokyo Gas and is headquartered in Silicon Valley They aim to bring sustainable energy solutions, collaboratinf with top labs and incubators to support their entrepreneurs and partners.

Key Executives:
Patrick Sagisi, Managing Partner
650-283-7026
e-mail: patrick@acarioinnovation.com

28 ACCEL
500 University Avenue
Palo Alto, CA 94301

Phone: (650) 614-4800
web: www.accel.com

Mission Statement: A venture capital firm dedicated to helping outstanding entrepreneurs build category-defining technology companies.

Geographic Preference: U.S., Europe, India, Israel
Fund Size: $3 billion
Founded: 1983
Minimum Investment: $500K
Investment Criteria: Early-Stage, Growth Stage
Industry Group Preference: Consumer, Infrastructure, Media, Mobile, SaaS, Security
Portfolio Companies: 2Wire, 3LM, 99 Designs, Acalvio, Acko, Acopia, Actuate, Admob, AdRoll, Agile Networks, Agile Software, Agrostar, Airgo Networks, Airwatch, Alfresco, Algolia, Alphabox, Amino, Amitree, Amobee Media Systems, Anchor, ANSR, Aorato, Arcot, Arista, Arrowpoint, Ascend.io, Atlassian Software, Avici Systems, Avito, Away, Axio Biosolutions, BaubleBar, BBN Technologies, Bettercloud, Birch Box, Bird, Bizongo, BlaBlaCar, Blackbuck, Blameless, Blue Jeans Network, Bluestone, Bonobos, BookMyShow, Bounce, Braintree, Brightcove, Brightmail, Browserstack, Calastone, Callsign Inc, Campaignmonitor, Can Capital, Capricoast, Cardspring, Carestack, Carto, Carwow, Catawiki, Celions, Centrify, Chargebee, Check24, CheckR, Clevertap, Cloudera, Code42 Software, Cogoport, Cohesity, Complex Media, Comscore, Consure Medical, Corelight, Cormetrics, Cornershop, Couchbase, Coverfox, Crowdanalytix, CrowdStrike, Crownit, Curefit, Curejoy, Dashdash, Despegar, DocuSign, Dropbox, Dropcam, Educreations, Elo7, Ensatus, Etsy, Fiverr, Flaregames, Flipkart, ForeScout, ForgeRock, Forus Health, GameForge, GoCardless, Hailo, High Gear Media, HolidayIQ, HootSuite, HotelTonight, Hotelogix, HouseTrip, Invoca, Iron Planet, Joyus, Jut, KDS International, Kirusa, Knewton, Krux, KupiVIP, LearnVest, Legendary, LetsVenture, LightSpeed, Lookout, Lot18, Lynda.com, Lyst, Medio Systems, MemSQL, MetraTech, Mind Candy, Mind Lab, MindTickle, Mitra Biotech, MobStac, Model N, MyFitnessPal, Myntra, MySmartPrice, Nextbit, Nimble Storage,

Other Locations:
2 Jack London Alley
San Francisco, CA 94107
Phone: 415-293-1100

1 New Burlington Place
6th Floor
London W1S 2HR
United Kingdom
Phone: 44 0 20 7170 1000

886/A Confident Electra
17th E. Main Road
6th Block, Koramangala
Bengaluru 560095
India
Phone: 91 80 4353 9800

Key Executives:
Andrew Braccia, Partner
Education: BS, Business Administration, University of Arizona
Background: Yahoo!
Directorships: 99designs, Anchor, Braintree, Cloudera, Cornershop, Etsy, Gametime, HotelTonight, Lynda.com, MyFitnessPal, PagerDuty, Prezi, Slack, Squarespace, UserTesting, Vox Media, Xero
Miles Clements, Partner
Education: University of Virginia; Harvard Business School
Background: lynda.com

Venture Capital & Private Equity Firms / Domestic Firms

Directorships: Atlassian, Bird, DJI, HudI, Lynda.com, MessageBird, Podium, SeatGeek, UiPath
Sameer Gandhi, Partner
Education: MSEE, BSEE, MIT; MBA, Stanford Graduate School of Business
Background: Partner, Sequoia Capital; Principal, Broadview
Directorships: Bonobos, CrowdStrike, DJI, Dropbox, Dropcam, Flipkart, Freshworks, Grovo, Jet, Plex Systems, Raise, Rylo, Spotify, Venmo, Yapstone
Amit Kumar, Partner
Education: University of California, Berkeley
Background: CardSpring; Twitter
Directorships: Amino, Cornershop, Deserve, Plays.tv, Skip, Smash.gg, Usertesting, Visor
Daniel Levine, Partner
Education: Yale University
Background: Dropbox; Chartio; TechCrunch
Directorships: Bird, Checkr, Heptio, MessageBird, Mux, Rylo, Scale, Sentry, Trifacta
Ping Li, Partner
Education: AB, Harvard University; MBA Stanford Graduate School of Business
Background: Senior Product Line Manager, Juniper Networks; Singapore Telecom; Goldman Sachs Asia
Directorships: Blue Jeans Network, Cloudera, Code42 Software, Demisto, Heptio, Lookout, Plays.tv, Split Software, Sysdig, Tenable Network Security, Trifacta
John Locke, Partner
Education: Woodrow Wilson School; Princeton University
Background: Senior Associate, Housitonic Partners
Directorships: Braintree, CrowdStrike, GoFundMe, Invoice2Go, Lightspeed, OzForex, Pond5, QMC, SeatGeek, Tenable Network Security, The Zebra, Venmo, WorldRemit, WyzAnt
Steve Loughlin, Partner
Education: Stanford University
Background: SalesforceIQ;
Directorships: Ascend.io, Ironclad, Split Software
Arun Mathew, Partner
Education: University of Pennsylvania; Stanford University
Background: Squarespace
Directorships: Avici Systems
Vas Natarajan, Partner
Education: University of Pennsylvania
Directorships: Blameless, DeepMap, Frame.io, InVision, Ironclad, Propeller Aero, Segment, Skydio, Spoke, Tune
Nate Niparko, Partner
Education: Dartmouth; Stanford Graduate School of Business
Background: Amazon Web Service; Invoice2Go
Directorships: Algolia, BrowserStack, CrowdStrike, Ethos, G2 Crowd, HootSuite, PagerDuty, RiskRecon, Tenable Network Security
Ryan Sweeney, Partner
Education: BBA, University of Notre Dame; MBA, Harvard Business School
Background: Summit Partners; North Bridge
Directorships: AirWatch, Atlassian, Braintree, BrowserStack, GOAT, HootSuite, Invoice2Go, Lightspeed, Narvar, Ozforex, PagerDuty, Qualtrics, Simility, Squarespace, Venmo, VSCO, Xero
Rich Wong, Partner
Education: BS, Materials Science & Engineering, MIT; MBA, MIT Sloane School of Management
Background: Senior Vice President, Openwave; Chief Marketing Officer, Covad Communications; Brand Manager, Proctor & Gamble; Brand Manager, McKinsey
Directorships: Atlassian, Checkr, Instabug, Osmo, Qwilt, ServiceChannel, Tune, UniPath

29 ACCEL-KKR LLC
2500 Sand Hill Road
Suite 300
Menlo Park, CA 94025
Phone: 650-289-2460 Fax: 650-289-2461
web: www.accel-kkr.com

Mission Statement: Accel-KKR seeks investment opportunities in lower middle market technology companies, primarily in the software and technology-enabled services industries, with strong growth potential.
Fund Size: $1.3 billion
Founded: 2000
Average Investment: $10 - $100 million
Minimum Investment: $10 million
Investment Criteria: Middle Market, Mid-Market Buyouts, Acquisitions, Recapitalizations, Going-Private Transactions
Industry Group Preference: Technology, Software, Hardware, Internet Technology, Enterprise Services, Infrastructure, IT Enabled Services, Data Storage, Storage Networking, Internet, Information Technology
Portfolio Companies: Abrigo, Agilence Inc., Cendyn, Cielo, ClickDimensions, Continuity, Datapipe, Delta Data Software, Duett AS, Efreightsolutions, Enverus, Envizi, Energy Services Group, ESO, FastSpring, FM:Systems, Green Mountain Technology, HighWire, Humanforce, InSight Mobile Data, IntegriChain, ISolved HCM, Insurance Technologies Corporation, Jaggaer, KCS, Kimble, Lemontech, Ministry Brands, OrthoFi, Patientco, Paymentus, Pegasus, Peppermint Technology, PointRight, PrismHR, Reapit, Safeguard Global, Salsa Labs, Sandata Technologies, Seequent, ShowingTime, Siigo, Smart Communications, SugarCRM, TEAM Software, TELCOR, ToolsGroup, TrueCommerce, US eDirect, Vistex, Vitu, Vobile

Other Locations:
3284 Northside Parkway Northwest
Suite 475
Atlanta, GA 30327
Phone: 678-809-5989 Fax: 678-905-6809

25 Green Street
London W1K 7AX
United Kingdom
Phone: 44-02077696736

Key Executives:
Tom Barnds, Managing Director
Education: AB, Princeton University; MBA, Stanford Graduate School of Business
Background: Managing Director, Nassau Capital; Business Development Manager, McGaw; Investment Banking Division, Alex. Brown & Sons
Directorships: Abila, Datapipe, EPiServer, Highjump, Kerridge Commercial Systems, Motor Vehicle Software Corporation, North Plains, Transzap
Rob Palumbo, Managing Director
Education: AB, Princeton University
Background: Co-Head, Software Investment Banking, Thomas Weisel Partners; Deutsche Bank; Information Technology Banking, Stephens, Inc.; Mergers & Acquisitions Analyst, Alex. Brown & Sons
Directorships: Cielo, EA Holdings, Infinisource, North Plains, On Center Software, Paymentus
Jason Klein, Managing Director
Education: BS, Finance & Accounting, Pennsylvania State University; MBA, Finance & Strategic Management, Wharton School
Background: Investment Banker, Goldman Sachs; PricewaterhouseCoopers; Financial Advisory Services, Cooper & Lybrand; Arthur Andersen
Directorships: EA Holdings, EPiServer, Highjump, Infinisource, Kerridge Commercial Systems, Motor Vehicle Software Corporation, Paymentus
Greg Williams, Managing Director
Education: AB, History, Harvard College; MBA, Darden School of Business, University of Virginia

Venture Capital & Private Equity Firms / Domestic Firms

Background: Managing Director, CapitalSoruce; Sturm Group; Mergers & Acquisitions Investment Banking, JP Morgan; Bond Corporation; Analyst, Fleet Financial Group
Directorships: Cielo, Clavis Insight, EPiServer, One.com, PageUp People, PrismHR
Patrick Fallon, Managing Director/COO/CCO
Education: AB, Economics, Harvard College; MBA, Amos Tuck School of Business Adminstration, Dartmouth College; CPA
Background: Partner & COO, Gryphon Investors; Investment Banker, Donaldson, Lufkin & Jenrette; Investment Banker, Credit Suisse; KPMG
Directorships: Banker's Toolbox, HighWire Press
Dean Jacobson, Managing Director
Education: AB, Harvard University; MBA, Stanford Graduate School of Business
Background: VP, Summit Partners; Director, Corporate Development, Vonage; Associate Director, 3i; Robertson Stephens
Directorships: Abila, Cielo, EPiServer, Infinisource, North Plains, Oildex
Park Durrett, Managing Director
Education: BS, Cornell University; MBA, Kellogg School of Management, Northwestern University
Background: Principal, The CapStreet Group; Associate, Technology Crossover Ventures; Associate, 3i Group; Robertson Stephens
Directorships: Abila, EA Holdings, HighWire Press, On Center Software
Ben Bisconti, Senior Advisor
Education: AB, Economics, Harvard College; MBA, Anderson School of Management, University of California, Los Angeles
Background: Managing Director, Technology Group, Credit Suisse First Boston; Managing Director, Technology Group, Robertson Stephens
Directorships: HighWire Press

---

30 ACCELEPRISE
San Francisco, CA

web: acceleprise.vc

Mission Statement: Acceleprise focuses investments in SaaS accelerators.
Geographic Preference: US
Fund Size: $70 Million
Founded: 2012
Industry Group Preference: SaaS, Software, Technology
Portfolio Companies: Agreemint, Drishyam AI, ENVision Mobile, GroLens, PassRight, Piio, Sparkir, StoriiCare, TestRigor AI
Key Executives:
  Michael Cardamone, Managing Director/General Partner
  Education: BS, Syracuse University; MBA, Columbia Business School
  Background: Managing Partner, United States Federation of Small Business; VP of Partnerships, AcademixDirect Inc.; Venture Partner, SaaStr; Advisor, Mya Systems
  Whitney Sales, General Partner
  Education: BA, University of California, San Diego
  Background: Inside Sales Manager, Meltwater Group; Director of Sales, SpringAhead; Director of Midwest Sales, Demandbase; VP of Sales, People Data Labs; Creator, The Sales Method
  Nina Stepanov, Principal/Director of Partnerships
  Education: BBA, Northeastern University
  Background: Associate Marketing Manager, Inbound.org; Head of Marketing, ViewPoint Cloud; Associate, Techstars

31 ACCELERATOR LIFE SCIENCE PARTNERS
2815 Eastlake Avenue East
Suite 300
Seattle, WA 98102
  Phone: 206-957-7300 **Fax:** 206-957-7399
  e-mail: info@acceleratorlsp.com
  web: www.acceleratorlsp.com

Mission Statement: Accelerator Corporation, founded in 2003, finances and manages companies in the biotechnology sector. The company has established and built a proprietary array of sources, as well as a key set of start-up resources. Accelerator aims to utilize these resources to help build emerging biotechnology companies and ensure their long-term success.
Fund Size: $305 million
Founded: 2003
Investment Criteria: Startup, Early Stage
Industry Group Preference: Biotechnology, Life Sciences, Healthcare
Portfolio Companies: ApoGen Biotechnologies, Lodo Therapeutics, Magnolia NeuroSciences, Petra Pharma, Proniras, Rodeo Therapeutics
Other Locations:
  430 East 29th Street
  Suite 840
  New York, NY 10016
  Phone: 646-282-5990 **Fax:** 646-828-5989

  10996 Torreyana Road
  Suite 270
  San Diego, CA 92121
  Phone: 206-957-7300 **Fax:** 206-957-7399
Key Executives:
  Thong Q Le, Chief Executive Officer
  Education: BA, Harvard University; Templeton College, Univ. of Oxford
  Background: Managing Director, WRF Capital; President/CEO, MiniMeals Inc.; Consultant, Capital Management Consulting; Raymond James & Associates; Singer & Xenos Investment Management Company; Capital Management Group LLC
  Directorships: Evergreen Venture Capital Association, Washington Biotechnology & Biomedical Association, Washington Global Health Fund
  Ian A.W. Howes, Chief Financial Officer
  Education: BS, Accounting and Finance, University Of Warwick; MBA, Kenan-Flagler Business School at the University Of North Carolina
  Background: CFO, Heart Metabolics; CFO, Scioderm; CFO, Akebia Therapeutics; CFO, Senior VP, Coporate Development Of Serenex
  Kendall Mohler, PhD, Chief Development Officer
  Education: BS, University of Kansas; PhD, Immunology, University of Texas Health Science Center
  Background: Senior Vice President, Chief Science Officer, Juno Therapeutics; Co-Founder, Trubion Pharmaceuticals; Vice President, Biological Sciences Of Imunex Corporation
  Court R. Turner, J.D., Chief Business Officer
  Education: BS, Psychology, San Diego State University; JD, San Diego School Of Law
  Background: Operating Partner, ALSP; Venture Partner, Avalon Ventures; Executive Manager, Kalypsys; Director Of Business Development, Aurora Biosciences
  Directorships: Synthorx, Cellular Approaches, RQx Pharmaceuticals
  Alice Chen, PhD, Vice President
  Education: BS, Chemical Engineering, University of California, Berkeley; PhD, Chemical Engineering, Stanford University
  Background: Director Of Technologies, Quell Pharmaceuticals

Venture Capital & Private Equity Firms / Domestic Firms

Directorships: Evergreen Fund Advisory Committee, Fred Hutch Cancer Research Center, Life Science Washington

32 ACCELERATOR VENTURES
2020 Union Street
San Francisco, CA 94123

e-mail: info@acceleratorventures.com
web: www.acceleratorventures.com

Mission Statement: Accelerator Ventures is a San Francisco-based venture capital firm that invests in early stage technology companies. Accelerator Ventures brings to entrepreneurs its strong understanding of technology, capital, and venture markets. We actively help companies with financing strategy, business development, customer introductions and management team development. Our goal is to invest at the earliest stages of a company's fund raising efforts and to leverage our domain expertise in order to help companies get on the path toward profitability. We leverage our network of angel investors, early stage funds and venture capital firms in order to meet the funding needs of our portfolio companies.

Investment Criteria: Early Stage, Seed, Start-Up
Industry Group Preference: Technology
Portfolio Companies: Appboy, Data Pop, Cloudmark, Cornerstone On Demand, Double Dutch, FairLoan, FlashSoft, Freeform, Gigwalk, Grouply, Hivemapper, Indextank, Influitive, Insikt, iSocket, Lively, Locomobi, Longtail Video, Mytime, Nutanix, Oyster.com, Playnomics, Rinse, Rockbot, SALIDO, Siftery, SixUp, Smartling, Snapdocs, SocialWire, Sproutling, StudySoup, Talkable, Tapulous, Trigo, Trovix, Web Methods, Zappos.com, Zimbio, Zynga

Key Executives:
Alexander Lloyd, Managing Director
Education: BA, International Relations, University Of Pennsylvania; MBA, Entrepreneurial Management, The Wharton School
Background: Venture Partner, Rustic Canyon Partners; Business Development Manager, Microsoft; Product Manager, SGI; Marketing, Activision; Marketing, Apple Computer; Financial Analyst, Goldman Sachs
Directorships: SideLuck
Ben T. Smith, IV, Venture Partner
Education: BS, Mechanical Engineering, University Of California, Davis; MBA, Tepper School of Business
Background: President, Reply Media; Co-Founder & CEO, MerchantCircle; SVP Corporate Development, Bortlan; Co-Founder, Spoke
Directorships: Spoke, Giu Mobile
Tom Cervantez, Venture Partner
Education: BA, Business Administration, Loyola Marymount University; JD/MBA, Harvard
Background: Founder, Business Counsel Law Group LLP.
John Paul Milciunas, Entrepreneur In-Residence
Education: Georgia Institute of Technology
Background: Strategic Partnerships and Business Developmnet, Yahoo!; Product Strategy Consultant, Checkfree; CEO, SPI Dynamics; Business Strategy Consultant, Scient
Linda Jacobson, VR/AR Venture Partner
Education: BS, Journalism, Boston University College of Communication

33 ACCENT CAPITAL PARTNERS LLC
One Embarcadero Center
Suite 1540
San Francisco, CA 94111

Phone: 415-981-7238
web: www.accentcapitalpartners.com

Mission Statement: Accent Capital Partners is a private equity advisory firm based in San Francisco. The firm focuses on growing middle market companies and offers advice on a number of issues, including sources of growth capital and capital structure.

Geographic Preference: United States, California

Founded: 2002
Key Executives:
Milton K Reeder, Managing Partner
Education: BBA, University of Michigan
Background: President & COO, Meridian Industrial Trust; CPA, Deloitte Touche

34 ACCESS BRIDGE-GAP VENTURES
Cambridge, MA 02142

web: www.accessindustries.com

Mission Statement: Access BridgeGap Ventures is a life sciences venture investment initiative to fund early-stage companies in the therapeutics space. Leveraging its team's experience in startup creation, technology commercialization and venture investing, Access BridgeGap will fund early-stage startups and also create de-novo spinoffs around potential high-impact technologies, many of which are still in academic labs. Funding activities will focus on scientists, entrepreneurs, and companies that are developing novel and clinically relevant therapeutic approaches and platforms that can become must-have solutions for patients, physicians, and payers.

Fund Size: $75 million
Founded: 1986
Investment Criteria: Early-Stage
Industry Group Preference: Natural Resources & Chemicals, Media & Telecommunications, Real Estate
Portfolio Companies: 20 East End, Access Technology Ventures, Al Film, Amedia, Clal Industries Ltd., EP Energy, Faena Group, First Access Entertainment, Grand-Hotel du Cap-Ferrat, Grand Peaks, Ice Group, LyondellBesell, MBS Media Campus, One & Only Ocean Club, Perform, R.G.E. Group Ltd., Sunset Tower Hotel, UC RUSAL, Warner Music Group

Key Executives:
Len Blavatnik, Founder/Chairman
Education: MA, Computer Science, Columbia University; MBA, Harvard Business School

35 ACCESS CAPITAL
405 Park Avenue
New York, NY 10022

Phone: 212-644-9300 Fax: 212-644-5488
Toll-Free: 800-421-0034
e-mail: contactus@accesscapital.com
web: www.accesscapital.com

Mission Statement: Access Capital provide immediate capital to small and middle market companies, closely working with law firms and accounting firms.

Geographic Preference: United States
Founded: 1986
Investment Criteria: Early-Stage, Second-Stage
Industry Group Preference: Consumer Services, Distribution, Industrial Equipment, Medical & Health Related, Staffing, IT Consulting, Printing, Software, Transportation
Portfolio Companies: Avatar Alliance, Diagnostek, Inc., ETC, Inc., Inmark Services, Inc., National Tele-Communications (NTC), INC 500 Companies

Key Executives:
Angela Santi, Co-President
Education: BS, St. John's University
Paul Mehring, Co-President
Education: BS, Finance, Villanova University

36 ACCESS VENTURE PARTNERS LLC
8787 Turnpike Drive
Suite 260
Westminster, CO 80031

web: www.accessvp.com

Mission Statement: Access Venture Partners is an early stage venture capital fund. Together over the past 14 years, the partners at Access Venture Partners have invested in over fifty early stage companies and have served as founders and early executives of numerous companies. Through this experience Access Ventures Partners has built an understanding of how to navigate the challenges associated with building successful companies and drive them to success.

Geographic Preference: Mid Continent
Founded: 1999
Average Investment: $2 million
Minimum Investment: $250,000
Investment Criteria: Seed, Early Stage
Industry Group Preference: Computer Hardware & Software, Internet Technology, Telecommunications, Infrastructure, Semiconductors, E-Commerce & Manufacturing, Technology, Clean Technology, SaaS, Data & Analytics, New Media, Digital Media & Marketing, Cloud Computing, Consumer Internet, Data Security
Portfolio Companies: Alces Technology, AlchemyAPI, Accel Graphics, Alert Logic, Ascent 360, Bionumerik, Brightware, CCBN, Channel Technology, Cloud Elemts, Commercial Tribe, Convey, Craftsy, CVA, Dizzion, eSionic, Enterprise Link, ETI, Firehole Composites, Handel Information Technologies Inc., Hotrail, Innova, Inspirato, Kapost, Listen MD, LogRhythm, Nexgen Storage, Pawngo, Osteobiologics, Quickarrow, Rebit, Red Canary, RoundPegg, ShapeShift, Shotzr, Skydex, Slamdata, Spotright, Tap Influence, Tenscorcomm, Thought Equity, Trividia, Taskeasy, Tendril, TopFan, TrackVia

Key Executives:
  Kirk Holland, Managing Director
  Education: BS, Electrical Engineering, University of Washington; MBA, Stanford University
  Background: General Partner, Vista Ventures; Procter & Gamble; Jupiter Media
  Directorships: RoundPegg, NexGen, Sympoz
  Frank Mendicino III, Co-Founder/Managing Director
  Education: BA, Political Science, University of California, Berkeley
  Background: Analyst, Woodside Fund II; Senior Associate, Woodside Fund III
  Directorships: LogRhythm, TrackVia, Thought Equity, Giveo, Inspirato
  Brian D Wallace, Managing Director
  Education: BS, Business Finance, University of Arizona
  Background: Corporate Securities Attorney, Fairfield and Woods PC
  Directorships: PitchEngine, Pawngo, Rebit, Firehole Composites, Alces, Spotright
  Frank Mendicino II, Venture Partner
  Education: BS, Business Administration, Law Degree, University of Wyoming
  Background: General Partner, Woodside Funds; Wyoming Attorney General; Board Director, University of Wyoming; Western Research Institute
  Directorships: Skydex, TensorComm

37 ACCOLADE PARTNERS
2001 M Street North West
Suite 801
Washington, DC 20036

Phone: 202-775-5595
e-mail: info@accoladepartners.com
web: www.accoladepartners.com

Mission Statement: Accolade Partners' mission is to generate superior returns through a diversified portfolio of venture capital and growth equity investments focused on technology and healthcare.

Geographic Preference: United States
Investment Criteria: Early-Stage
Industry Group Preference: Technology, Healthcare
Portfolio Companies: Accel, Accel KKR, Andreessen Horowitz, Amplify Partners, Anthos, August Capital, Bolt, Clarus Ventures, Harrison Metal, IA Ventures, Ignition, JMI Equity, Leerink Transformation Partners, Level Equity, Mucker Capital, North Bridge Growth Equity, Notation Caption, OrbiMed Healthcare Fund Management, Pivot North Capital, Shore Capital Partners, Sverica, Radian Capital, Thoma Bravo, Water Street, Acquia, Avant Credit, Compuware, Hightail, Sun Basket, Tiger Text, Alloy, Centerpoint, Election, FFC, General Catalyst, Golden Gate, HLM, Impact, Sevin Rosen, Skyline, Sternhill, TCV, Telegraph Hill, Telesoft, Trident, Walden

Key Executives:
  Joelle Kayden, Managing Member
  Education: BA, Smith College; MBA, Stanford Graduate School of Business
  Background: CFO, ABS Ventures, Alex Brown & Sons
  Atul Rustgi, Partner
  Education: BBA, University of Michigan; MBA, Harvard Business School
  Background: Senior Management, McKinsey & Company; Robin Hood Foundation
  Andrew Salenbier, Partner/Chief Operating Officer
  Education: BA, University of Virginia; MBA, Georgetown University
  Background: Georgetown Endowment; Cambridge Associates

38 ACCOMPLICE
56 Wareham Street
3rd Floor
Boston, MA 02118

Phone: 617-588-2600
e-mail: hello@accomplice.co
web: www.accomplice.co

Mission Statement: Accomplice, formerly the technology side of Atlas Venture, is a venture capital firm that focuses on early stage technology investments.

Fund Size: $200 million
Founded: 2015
Investment Criteria: Early Stage
Industry Group Preference: Technology
Portfolio Companies: AngelList, Button, Captricity, Carbon Black, Clypd, Currency Cloud, DataRobot, DataXu, DraftKings, Earnest, Hopper, InsightSquared, Integral Ad Science, Joist, Keas, Kinvey, Lagoa, Maiden Lane Ventures, Mojo Motors, Moo, Nutonian, OwnerIQ, OYO Sportstoys, Patreon, PillPack, Plastiq, Quirky, Recorded Future, Reddo Mobility, SimpleReach, Skillz, Sqrrl, Threat Stack, Valore, Veracode

Key Executives:
  Jeff Fagnan, Founding Partner
  Education: BS, Management & Mathematics, University of Alaska; MBA, Finance & Operations, University of Rochester
  Background: Partner, Seed Capital Partners; Booz Allen & Hamilton; Nortel Networks
  Directorships: Bit9, InsightSquared, Objective Logistics, Snapguide, Whoop, Keas
  Ryan Moore, Founding Partner
  Education: AB, Princeton University
  Background: General Partner, GrandBanks Capital; SOFTBANK Venture Capital
  Directorships: Gocella, Plastiq, SimpleTuition, Flashnotes, Clypd, Moo
  Frank Castellucci, Partner/General Counsel
  Education: BA, Economics/History, Bowdoin College; JD, Boston College Law School
  Background: Associate, Testa Hurwitz & Thibeault LLP
  Sam Clemens, Partner
  Education: BS, Applied Math, Yale University; MBA, Harvard Business School

Venture Capital & Private Equity Firms / Domestic Firms

Background: Co-Founder/Chief Product Officer, InsightSquared; VP of Product, HubSpot
Ash Egan, Partner
Education: AB, American Politics, Princeton University
Background: Founding Principal, ConsenSys; Associate, Converge VC
Travis Macinnes, Partner/Chief Financial Officer
Education: BA, Accounting, Michigan State University; MBA, Boston University; CPA
Background: VP of Finance, Berkshire Partners; Godel Capital; Godel Capital; Alta Equity Partners; BV Investment Partners; PricewaterhouseCoopers
TJ Mahony, Partner
Education: BA, Economics, Macalester College
Background: Founder, FlipKey

39 ACCRETIVE LLC
660 Madison Avenue
12th Floor
Suite 1215
New York, NY 10065

Phone: 646-282-3131 Fax: 646-282-3138
e-mail: info@accretivellc.com
web: www.accretivellc.com

Mission Statement: Accretive is a private equity firm focused on working with talented people to build world-class companies that deliver meaningful and unique value to their customers.
Geographic Preference: United States, Western Europe
Fund Size: $200 million
Founded: 1999
Investment Criteria: Startups
Industry Group Preference: Healthcare, Education
Portfolio Companies: Accolade, Accretive Commerce, Accretive Health, Accumen, AlphaStaff, Arise, Equitant, Everspring, Exult, Fandango, Insureon, Quantum Health, Xchanging
Key Executives:
  J Michael Cline, Founding Partner
  Education: BS, Cornell University; MBA, Harvard Business School
  Background: General Partner, General Atlantic Partners; Co-Founder, Exult; Xchanging; Fandango; Accolade; Associate, McKinsey & Company
  Directorships: Panthera, National Fish and Wildlife Foundation
  Edgar Bronfman Jr, Managing Partner
  Background: Chairman/CEO, Warner Music Group; Chairman/CEO, Lexa Partners LLC; Executive Vice Chairman, Vivendi Universal; President/CEO, The Seagram Company Ltd.
  Directorships: Arise, Accolade, Accumen, Everspring, AlphaStaff
  Anne-Marie Shelley, General Councel/Chief Compliance Officer
  Education: BA, Yale University; JD, Villavona University School of Law
  Background: Corporate Attorney, Chadbourne & Park, LLP; Associate, Fried, Frank, Harris, Shiriver & Jacobson
  Tony Shum, Chief Financial Officer
  Education: BA, Pace University; CPA
  Background: Manager, Audit & Advisory Services, KPMG LLP
  Mimi Wolfe Strouse, Senior Advisor
  Education: BA, History & African Studies, Trinity College; University of Cape Town
  Background: Managing Director & Partner, Warburg Pincus; Principal, General Atlantic Partners; Financial Analyst, Credit Suisse First Boston
  Directorships: Everspring
  Ben West, Advisor
  Education: BBA, University of Oklahoma
  Background: Consultant, Boston Consulting Group; Sevin Rosen Funds; RiskMetrics Group

40 ACCUITIVE MEDICAL VENTURES LLC
295 Premiere Parkway
Suite 100
Atlanta, GA 30097

Phone: 678-812-1101
e-mail: charlie@amvpartners.com
web: www.amvpartners.com

Mission Statement: Accuitive Medical Ventures LLC invests in and helps develop early stage and expansion stage medical device and technology companies.
Geographic Preference: United States
Fund Size: $230 million
Founded: 2003
Average Investment: $5 million
Minimum Investment: $1 million
Investment Criteria: Early Stage, Expansion Stage
Industry Group Preference: Health Related, Medical Technology, Information Technology, Medical Devices
Portfolio Companies: AcuFocus, AqueSys, AxoGen, CardioFocus, Inogen, Intuity Medical, LipoSonix, MyoScience, Neuronetics, Nevro, Respicardia, Sadra Medical, Sebacia, Softscope, Torax Medical, WaveTec Vision
Other Locations:
  5542 First Coast Highway
  Suite 301
  Fernandina Beach, FL 32034
  Phone: 904-261-9690
Key Executives:
  Thomas D Weldon, Chairman/Managing Director
  Education: BS, Industrial Engineering, Purdue University; MBA, Indiana University
  Background: The Innovation Factory; Chairman/CEO, Novoste Corporation; Chairman, LipoSonix; Arthur Young & Company; Key Pharmaceuticals
  Directorships: MyoScience, Respicardia, Sebacia
  Charles E Larsen, Managing Director
  Education: BS, Mechanical Engineering, New Jersey Institute of Technology
  Background: Co-Founder/Vice Chairman, The Innovation Factory; Co-Founder, Novoste Corporation; Cordis Corporation; Key Pharmaceuticals; Parke-Davis/Warner Lambert
  Directorships: Acufocus, CardioFocus, Inogen, Intuity
  Gordon T Wyatt, Chief Financial Officer
  Education: BS, Accounting & Finance, Lehigh University
  Background: SVP, Finance, WebMD Corporation; General Electric Company
  Cory S Anderson, Principal
  Education: BS, MS, Biomedical Engineering, Tulane University; MBA, Emory University
  Background: Program Manager, The Innovation Factory; Product Manager, Novoste Corporation
  Directorships: AqueSys
  Anthony V Lando, Partner
  Education: BS, Physics, Manhattan College; Georgia Institute of Technology; University of California
  Background: COO, BTG PLC; Senior Marketing & Product Development, Philips Medical Systems; Stone & Webster Engineering

41 ACERO CAPITAL
2440 Sand Hill Road
Suite 101
Menlo Park, CA 94025

Phone: 650-233-7100 Fax: 650-233-7112
web: www.acerovc.com

Mission Statement: Acero Capital is a venture capital firm that invests in technology enabled services, including enterprise mobility, IT infrastructure, enterprise cloud applications and data analytics. Acero actively pursues companies with resourceful management teams, capital-efficient business mod-

16

Venture Capital & Private Equity Firms / Domestic Firms

els, and innovative approaches to large and established markets.
Fund Size: $150 million
Industry Group Preference: Information Technology, Clean Technology, Energy, Technology-Enabled Services
Portfolio Companies: Argyle Data, Banyan Energy, Bitzer Mobile, Contrast Security, HyperGrid, Livehive, QuantPower, Swrve
Key Executives:
  Rami Elkhatib, General Partner
  e-mail: rami@acerovc.com
  Education: BS, Computer & Electrical Engineering, Purdue University; MBA, Massachusetts Institute of Technology
  Background: General Partner, Southeast Technology Funds; Co-Founder, Datacme Software; Oneworld Software Solutions; UBS Warburg
  Directorships: Argyle Data, Banyan Energy, Contrast Security, Gridstore, LiveHive, Swrve Mobile
  Elena Winefeld, Vice President
  e-mail: jayme@acerovc.com
  Education: BA, Economics and Management, Technion Israel Institute Of Technology
  Background: Fund Controller, Financial Analysis Manager, Nokia Growth Parners
  Elisa del Gaudio, Principal
  e-mail: elisa@acerovc.com
  Education: BA, Human Biology, Stanford University
  Background: Deutsche Bank
  Charles Ho, Venture Partner
  e-mail: charles@acerovc.com
  Education: BS, Chemical Engineering, University of Texas; MBA, Columbia University
  Background: Standard Bank; COO/Director, Lithcon Group; Lehman Brothers; UBS Warburg; Deloitte Consulting

42 ACI CAPITAL
299 Park Avenue
34th Floor
New York, NY 10171

Phone: 212-634-3333 Fax: 212-634-3330
web: www.acicapital.com

Mission Statement: ACI Capital invests in middle-market companies across a variety of industries. The firm partners with exceptional management teams to help build valuable companies.

Geographic Preference: United States
Fund Size: $335 million
Founded: 1986
Average Investment: $20 - $50 million
Minimum Investment: $10 million
Investment Criteria: Middle Market, Lower-Middle Market
Industry Group Preference: Consumer Products, Manufacturing, Transportation, Infrastructure, Alternative Energy, Business Products & Services, Financial Services, Logistics, Media, Healthcare
Portfolio Companies: Accent Energy, Cornhusker Energy, Excel Polymers, Healthy Directions, Hollywood Tans, Sundance, United Logistics
Key Executives:
  Kevin S Penn, Managing Director
  e-mail: kspenn@acicapital.com
  Education: BS, Economics, Wharton School, University of Pennsylvania; MBA, Harvard Business School
  Background: EVP/Chief Investment Officer, First Spring Corporation; Principal, Adler & Shaykin; Founding Member, Leveraged Buyout Group, Morgan Stanley
  Directorships: Accent Energy, Cornhusker Energy, Excel Polymers, Healthy Directions, SEMX, Sundance Catalog, Hollywood Tans, Mt. Sinai Hospital Department of Medicine

  Matthew Bronfman, Managing Director
  e-mail: mbronfman@acicapital.com
  Education: BA, Williams College; MBA, Harvard Business School
  Background: Chairman/CEO, Candle Acquisitions Company; Chairman/CEO, Sterling Cellular Holdings, LP; Goldman Sachs; Cadillac Fairview Corporation Limited
  Directorships: Bronfman Fisher Real Estate Holdings, Earnest Partners, Palace Candles Inc.
  Mitchell Quain, Managing Director
  e-mail: mquain@acicapital.com
  Education: University of Pennsylvania; Harvard Business School
  Background: Schroder Wertheim; Industrial Manufacturing Group, Wall Street; President, Machinery Analysts Group
  Directorships: Hardinge Inc., Titan International, Magnetek Inc.
  Mira Muhtadie, Vice President
  e-mail: mmuhtadie@acicapital.com
  Education: BA, Economics, University of Pennsylvania; MBA, Wharton School, University of Pennsylvania
  Background: Senior Associate, KPS Special Situations; Associate, Lightyear Capital; Analyst, Credit Suisse First Boston
  Directorships: Hollywood Tans
  Chad Ellis, Associate
  e-mail: cellis@acicapital.com
  Education: BA, Economics, University of Virginia
  Background: Analyst, Mergers & Acquisitions Group, Rothschild Group

43 ACKERLEY PARTNERS LLC
1301 Second Avenue
Suite 1936
Seattle, WA 98101

Phone: 206-624-2888
e-mail: info@ackerley.com
web: ackerleypartners.com

Mission Statement: Ackerley Partners invests primarily in media and entertainment entities, including but not limited to: media content and programming, internet based media, digital broadcast and broadband, media metric/delivery technology and wireless marketing services.

Founded: 2002
Industry Group Preference: Media, Communications, Entertainment, New Media
Portfolio Companies: Cequint, CSTV, Elevation Partners, FastChannel, FlexPlay, Hidden City, Howcast, Jott, Judy's Book, Labrador Mobile, LicenseStream, Mobliss, Nascar Members Club, Plum, Screenlife, SpotTaxi.com, Twelvefold
Key Executives:
  Christopher Ackerley, Co-Founder
  Background: President, The Ackerley Group; Capital Markets Group, Bank of America
  Ted Ackerley, Co-Founder
  Background: Vice President, Ackerley Ventures
  Directorships: LicenseStream, Hidden City Entertainment, Nascar Members Club
  Kim Ackerley Cleworth, Co-Founder
  Background: President, The Ginger & Barry Ackerley Foundation

44 ACKRELL CAPITAL
38 Keyes Avenue
South Lobby
Suite 200
San Francisco, CA 94129

Phone: 415-995-2000 Fax: 415-995-2002
e-mail: info@ackrell.com
web: www.ackrell.com

17

Venture Capital & Private Equity Firms / Domestic Firms

Mission Statement: A private investment bank interested in the following industries: Ag tech, cannabis, consumer goods, digital media, energy/alternative energy, entertainment, healthcare, real estate, semiconductors, software, and sports.
Founded: 2003
Investment Criteria: Middle-market
Industry Group Preference: Cannabis, Software, Technology, Healthcare, Consumer Goods, Digital Media, Entertainment, Sports, Semiconductors, Energy, Real Estate
Portfolio Companies: Vuber, Défoncé, PROHBTD, Purch, Street Light Data, Blinkx, BranchOut, Urbansitter, EnergyHub

Key Executives:
  Mike Ackrell, Founder/Managing Partner
  Education: BS, Economics, Wharton School, University of Pennsylvania
  Background: Sr. Managing Director, ABN AMRO's US Technology Investment Banking Group; WR Hambrecht+Co.; SVP of Technology Investment Banking, Donaldson Lufkin & Jenrette; DLJ
  Iian Bunimovitz, Partner
  Education: BA, Psychology, Bar Iian University; Business Admin., Baruch College
  Background: CEO/Founder, Mama's LLC; CEO, Private Media Group
  Bryan Castillo, Managing Director
  Education: BS, Economics, Pennsylvania State University
  Background: Kema Partners

45 ACME CAPITAL
800 Market Street
8th Floor
San Francisco, CA 94102

Phone: 415-805-8500
e-mail: info@acme.vc
web: acme.vc

Mission Statement: ACME invests in companies that leverage technology and data to pursue massive opportunities that have the potential to reshape industies - or create completely new ones; companies led by founders who dream big and execute smartly. ACME invests in founders buulding disruptive models that can capitalize on current platforms, as well as founders building breakthrough technologies that will enable emerging platforms.
Geographic Preference: US, Europe
Fund Size: $181 million
Founded: 2018
Average Investment: $3-8 million
Investment Criteria: Series A & B
Industry Group Preference: Hardware, Infrastructure, Automation, Business Model Innovation
Portfolio Companies: Airbnb, Beyond Games, Brandless, Cue, Curology, Cymmetria, Didi, Doctor On Demand, Fair, Hired, Ipsy, Light Field Lab, Opengov, Owl, PillPack, Quip, Rent the Runway, Replika, Robinhood, Slack, Stance, Stealth Space Company, Uber, Virgin Hyperloop One, Wag, Zendrive

Key Executives:
  Scott Stanford, Co-Founder/Partner
  Education: AB, Harvard College; MBA, Harvard Business School
  Background: Goldman Sachs; General Atlantic Partners
  Kirby Bartlett, Chief Operating/Compliance Officer
  Education: BA, University of California, Berkeley; MBA, University of San Francisco
  Background: Bay City Capital; Burrill & Craves

46 ACON INVESTMENTS
1133 Connecticut Avenue Northwest
Suite 700
Washington, DC 20036

Phone: 202-454-1100 Fax: 202-454-1101
e-mail: contact@aconinvestments.com
web: www.aconinvestments.com

Mission Statement: ACON Investments is a private equity firm that targets middle-market companies based in the United States and Latin America.
Geographic Preference: United States, Latin America
Fund Size: $750 million
Founded: 1996
Average Investment: $20 - $150 million
Investment Criteria: Middle Market
Industry Group Preference: Energy, Financial Services, Healthcare Services, Industrial, Media, Telecommunications, Retail, Consumer & Leisure, Consumer
Portfolio Companies: Amfora Packaging, APR Energy, BetterWare de Mexico, BSM, Cabo Telecom, Cool Gear International, Credivalores, Fiesta Mart, Funko, Grupo Sala, Hidrotenecias, IDX, Igloo Products, Injured Workers Pharmacy, Milagro Exploration, ProEnergy Holdings, Refac Optical Group, Saga Resource Partners, Sequitur Energy Resources, Suzo-Happ Group, Vetra Energia, Videomar Rede Nordeste SA, Waldo's, White Oak Resources

Other Locations:
  4640 Admiralty Way
  Suite 500
  Los Angeles, CA 90292
  Phone: 310-788-5713 Fax: 310-277-7582

  Carrera 7 No. 83-29
  Oficina 604
  Edificio la Cabrera
  Bogota
  Colombia
  Phone: 57 1 616 1684

  Bosque de Alisos 47-A, Piso 2
  Bosques de las Lomas
  Cuajimalpa
  Mexico D.F. 05120
  Mexico
  Phone: 52 55 2167 0999

  Rua Bandeira Paulista 726
  Cj 191
  Sao Paulo SP 04532-002
  Brazil
  Phone: 55 11 3017-7666

Key Executives:
  Bernard Aronson, Founder/Managing Partner
  e-mail: baronson@aconinvestments.com
  Education: BA, Humanities, University of Chicago
  Background: International Advisor, Goldman Sachs; US Assistant Secretary of State for Inter-American Affairs
  Directorships: Sequitur Energy Resources, ACON Franchise Holdings, The Nature Conservancy
  Kenneth Brotman, Founder/Managing Partner
  e-mail: kbrotman@aconinvestments.com
  Education: BSe, Wharton School, University of Pennsylvania; MBA, Harvard Business School
  Background: Partner, Veritas Capital; Associate, Bain Capital; Principal, Wasserstein Perella Management Partners
  Directorships: Credifinanciera, Fiesta Mart, Funko, Grupo Sala, IDX, Igloo Products, ProEnergy, Refac/US Vision, Suzo-Happ, NetUno
  Jonathan Ginns, Founder/Managing Partner
  e-mail: jginns@aconinvestments.com
  Education: BA, History, Brandeis University; MBA, Harvard Business School
  Background: Senior Investment Officer, GEF Funds; Management Consultant, Booz Allen Hamilton
  Directorships: Sequitur Energy Resources

Venture Capital & Private Equity Firms / Domestic Firms

Jorge Dickens, Managing Partner
Education: Harvard Business School
Background: Darby Overseas Investments
Directorships: Grupo Vizion; Hidrotenencias

47 ACORN CAMPUS VENTURES
3235 Kifer Road
Suite 150
Canta Clara, CA 95051

Phone: 408-598-4239
web: www.acorncampus.com

Mission Statement: The Acorn Campus Ventures approach is anchored by innovative methods, differentiated competitive strategies, and key corporate alliances. With access to a vast network of professional and personal connections throughout the Pacific Rim region, Acorn Campus Ventures principals bring expertise, diversity of experience, and exceptional insight to the process of developing a new business.

Fund Size: $100 million
Founded: 2000
Average Investment: $5 million
Investment Criteria: Seed, Startup, First Stage
Industry Group Preference: Communications Equipment, Telecommunications, Networking, Wireless Technologies, Internet, Life Sciences, Semiconductors
Portfolio Companies: Agate Logic, Inc., Atoptech, Inc., Autekbio, Inc., Aviva Communications, Inc., Boly Media Communications, Inc., Crown Bioscience, Inc., Eureka Therapeutics, Nano Photonics, Inc., NStreams Technologies, Inc., Optovue Corporation, Rasilient Systems, Inc., Siargo, Inc., Toplogis, Inc., Waterstone Pharmaceuticals

Key Executives:
Wu-Fu Chen, Chairman
Education: BSEE, National Taiwan University; MSEE, University of Florida; Doctoral program, Computer Science, University of California, Berkeley
Background: Founder/VP Engineering, Cascade Communications;VP, Cisco Systems; Chairman/CEO, Ardent Communications; Arris Networks
Hsing Kung, Managing Partner
Education: BSEE, National Cheng Kung University; PhD EE, University of California at Berkeley; MBA, Santa Clara University
Background: President/CEO, Pine Photonics; Senior VP, Opnext Inc.; Chairman, Luxnet Cororation; Co-Founder/VP, SDL, Inc.; Chairman, Monte Jade
David Tsang, Managing Member/Co-Founder
Education: MSEE, Santa Clara University; honorary PhD, International Technical Universitry
Background: Founder/Chairman, Oak Technology; Founder, Data Technology Corporation; Founder, Xebec
T Chester Wang, Managing Partner
Education: Tsinghua University, Taiwan; PhD Physics, University of Oregon
Background: Founder, Pacific Rim Electronics; Co-Founder, CMC; Developer, Silicon Valley Science Park; Developer, first Chinese-American shopping/community center, Pacific Rim Plaza; College Professor of Computer Science

48 ACORN GROWTH COMPANIES
621 N. Robinson
Suite 550
Oklahoma City, OK 73102

Phone: 405-737-2676
web: www.acorngrowthcompanies.com

Mission Statement: Acorn Growth Companies is a private equity firm dedicated to creating value and assisting with the growth of companies. The firm exclusively invests in the aerospace and defense industries.

Fund Size: $100 million
Investment Criteria: Early Stage, Middle Market, Growth Capital
Industry Group Preference: Aerospace, Defense and Government
Portfolio Companies: Aerospares 2000, AGC AeroComposites, APSE, Berry Aviation, Black Sage, CIS, DIMO Corp., North Coast Composites, Paul Fabs, Raisbeck, Robbins-Gioia, SinglePoint, Tods Aerospace, TSS Solutions, Unitech Composites and Structures

Other Locations:
1015 15th Street NW
Suite 350
Washington, DC 20005

Unit 35
Barratt Way
Industrial Estate
Harrow HA3 5TJ
United Kingdom
Phone: +44 (0)20-8863-8578

Key Executives:
Jeff Davis, Founding Partner
Education: BS, Marketing, Walton College of Business, University of Arkansas; Institute for Organization Management, Southern Methodist University
Background: President, Oklahoma Venture Forum; Founder, Oklahoma Aerospace Alliance
Rick Nagel, Managing Partner
Education: BS, Environmental Science, University of Oklahoma College of Engineering
Background: Platinum Equity; President, DCA
Directorships: State Chamber of Oklahoma
Jeff Morton, Senior Partner
Education: BA, Finance, Baldwin-Wallace College
Background: Senior Manager, Ernst & Young; Deloitte & Touche; CFO, Eateries
Robert Hinaman, Senior Partner
Education: BA, Economics, Lafayette College
Background: Managing Director, Mergers & Acquisitions, Chase Manhattan Bank; Chemical Bank; JP Morgan Chase; Partner, Jefferies Quarterdeck
Directorships: Maden Consulting, Gryphon Emerging Markets, Hunstworth plc
Laura Siegal, Executive Vice President
Education: BA, Economics, University Of California, San Diego; CPA
Background: CFO, NEO Tech; Vice President, Corporate Controller, Kratos Defense & Security Solutions
Directorships: Iteris, Board Of Governors and Supply Chain Executive Committee of Aerospace Industries Association
Gregory Bloom, Chief Operations Officer
Education: BA Economics and Business, University of California, LA; MBA, UCLA Anderson School of Management; Certificate in Defense Technology, Georgia Institute of Technology
Background: President, Seal Science; President/CEO, MSM Industries; Operating General Manager/Financial Executive, KB Home; Founder/CEO, SAFC
Craig Woodruff, Vice President, Finance/Chief Compliance Officer
Education: BS Political Science And Philosophy, Oklahoma State University; MBA, Oklahoma City Univeristy's Meinders School of Business
Background: Finance Director, Chesapeake Energy
Directorships: OKC Metropolitan Library Trust
Matthew Ritchie, Managing Director
Education: BA Public Policy Analysis, University of North Carolina; MBA, McDonough School of Business at Georgetown University
Background: Senior Manager, Northrop Grumman; The Cohen Group; Renaissance Strategic Advisors
Directorships: Young Professionals Committe of USO Metropolitan Washington-Baltimore

Venture Capital & Private Equity Firms / Domestic Firms

49 ACREW CAPITAL
471 Emerson Street
Palo Alto, CA 94301

e-mail: info@acrewcapital.com
web: acrewcapital.com

Mission Statement: Acrew Capital is interested in long-term partnerships with its portfolio companies within the tech industry.

Founded: 2019
Investment Criteria: Early Stage
Industry Group Preference: Artificial Intelligence, Technology, Healthcare, Retail, Consumer
Portfolio Companies: Amino, Aqua, Augtera Networks, BaubleBar Inc., Cato Networks, Chime Banking, CipherTrace, Coinbase, Crew, Deserve Cards, Divvy, Eden Health, Evident, Exabeam, Finix, ForeScout, Future Family, Gusto, Hotel Tonight, Indegy, Integris Software, Klar, The Muse, Pie Insurance, Solv, Stem, Tara AI, The RealReal, Troops, TruStar Technology, Worklete

Other Locations:
3004 16th Street
San Francisco, CA 94103

Key Executives:
Lauren Kolodny, Founding Partner
Background: Partner, Aspect Ventures; Product Marketing, Google
Mark Kraynak, Founding Partner
Background: Investor, Aspect Ventures; General Manager, Imperva Enterprise Business; Product Marketing, Check Point Software Technologies Ltd.; Marketing, CacheFlow; Consutlant, Ernst & Young's Center for Technology Enablement
Theresia Gouw, Founding Partner
Background: Co-Founder/Partner, Aspect Ventures; Managing General Partner, Accel; VP of Business Development & Sales, Release Software; Product Manager, Silicon Graphics
Vishal Lugani, Founding Partner
Education: AB, Economics, Harvard University
Background: Aspect Ventures; Greycroft Partners; Bain & Company
Asad Khaliq, Founding Principal
Education: Stanford University
Background: Investor, Aspect Ventures; PricewaterhouseCooper
Directorships: NextGen Partners

50 ACT ONE VENTURES
662 N Sepulveda
Suite 300
Los Angeles, CA 95066

e-mail: info@actoneventures.com
web: www.actoneventures.com

Mission Statement: Act One Ventures is a venture capital firm investing in software companies. 70% of Act One's portfolio companies were founded by women or minorities.

Founded: 2016
Investment Criteria: Seed
Industry Group Preference: Software, Technology
Portfolio Companies: Aiva Health, AuditBoard, Battery Streak, BLAZE, Bloomlife, Blutag, Branch, Camera IQ, Dray Alliance, Finix Payments, Glitzi, Naked Biome, Narrativ, Ordermark, Polycera, PRZM, QLess, SilverSheet, Social Native, Storyblaster, Tapcart, Veryfi, Wizely Finance, WiZR

Key Executives:
Michael Silton, Managing Director
Background: Executive Director, UCLA Venture Capital Fund; Founder/CEO, Rainmaker Systems; Co-Founder/CEO, UniDirect Systems Inc.
Alejandro Guerrero, Principal
Education: BA, University of California, Los Angeles
Background: Associate, UCLA Venture Capital Fund; Founder/CEO, UniqApp; Co-Founder, Life Entertainment Network

51 ACTA CAPITAL
Washington, DC 20005

e-mail: info@actawireless.com
web: angel.co/company/acta-wireless

Mission Statement: Acta Capital incubates and invests in early stage companies that share their vision for wireless technology to improve the way people live, work, and play.

Founded: 2003
Investment Criteria: Early Stage
Industry Group Preference: Wireless Technologies
Portfolio Companies: Active Mind Technology, Bandsintown, CardStar, FounderFuel, Gimbal, Hook Mobile, Imagine K12, Launchbox Digital, Millenial Media, Moonlighting, Numerai, OZ Communications, Payzer, PopUp, Real Ventures, Snaplytics, Sweet Relish, Task Force X Capital Management, WaveMetrix

Key Executives:
Alan MacIntosh, Managing Partner
Education: BSc, Offshore Engineering, Heriot-Watt University; MBA, INSEAD
Background: Co-Founder, GSM Capital; Schlumberger; Microcell
Directorships: WaveMetrix, Millennial Media, Cellfish Media
Mark McDowell, Executive Chairman
Education: BSEE, MSEE, MIT
Background: Founding Managment Team: Invertix, Telecorp PCS
Directorships: LaunchBox Digital, mphoria

52 ACTIVATE VENTURE PARTNERS
509 Madison Avenue
Suite 1006
New York, NY 10022

Phone: 212-223-7400
web: www.activatevp.com

Mission Statement: Formerly known as Milestone Venture Partners, Activate Venture Partners is a traditional venture capital partnership focusing on early stage, enterprising information technology companies in the New York metropolitan area. The fund targets companies that possess the nucleus of an exceptional management team, a compelling business model, a large market opportunity.

Geographic Preference: Primarily New York, New Jersey, Connecticut, Northeast, Mid-Atlantic
Fund Size: $70 million
Founded: 1999
Average Investment: $1 million
Minimum Investment: $250,000
Investment Criteria: Early
Industry Group Preference: Technology-Enabled Businesses
Portfolio Companies: Access Health, AnyTime Access, AppBus, BA Insight, Benefix, BTG, Canvs, CareGain, CEMA, ClickPay, Cloudnexa, Cosential, Cureatr, Diameter Health, Digital Pharmacist, eHealth Technologies, Elastomeric Technologies, Expert Plan, FSA Store, GQ Life Sciences, Grovo, Halfpenny Technologies, Healthify, High QA, ID Entropy, Innovative Solutions & Support, Integri Chain, IQE, Iris Plans, Katabat, Knovel, M5, Mapmy Fitness, Medidata, Medpage Today, Medtrex, MicroE Systems, Micro Interventional Devices, National Packaging Systems, Natural Insight, Octagon, Othot, Premise, Racemi, Ravisent Technologies, Rights Flow, Sequoia, Shyft Analytics, Skill Survey, Smartanalyst, Surefire Local, Tabula Rasa Healthcare, Turtle Beach, Ultracision, Visual Networks, Vitals

Venture Capital & Private Equity Firms / Domestic Firms

Other Locations:
116 Research Dr.
Bethlehem, PA 18015
Phone: 610-849-1990
Key Executives:
Glen R Bressner, Managing Partner
Education: BSBA, Boston University; MBA, Babson College
Background: NEPA Venture Funds; Originate Growth Fund I
Todd T Pietri, Managing Partner
Education: Duke University; MBA, Georgia State University
Background: VP, Legacy Services Corporation
Edwin A Goodman, Investment Partner
Education: BA, Yale University; MS, Columbia University
Background: Patricof & Company; Hambros Bank

53 ACTUA
555 East Lancaster Avenue
Suite 640
Radnor, PA 19087
Phone: 610-727-6900 **Fax:** 610-727-6901
e-mail: ir@actua.com
web: www.actua.com

Mission Statement: A venture capital firm that aquires and builds cloud companies. Formerly known as Internet Capital Group.
Geographic Preference: Worldwide
Founded: 1996
Industry Group Preference: Business to Business, E-Commerce & Manufacturing, SaaS, Marketing, Internet
Key Executives:
Walter W. Buckley III, Co-Founder/CEO
e-mail: buck@actua.com
Education: BA, Political Science, University of North Carolina
Background: Vice President, Safeguard Scientifics; President/Co-Founder, Centralized Management Systems; Commercial Loan Officer, CoreStates
Directorships: Internet Capital Group; ICG Commerce; Verticalnet; OneCoast Networks
John Loftus, Managing Director
e-mail: john@actua.com
Education: BEE, MSEE, MSCS, Villanova University; MSOD, University of Pennsylvania
Background: Founder, Swinford Group; Managing Director, Safeguard Scientifics; Co-Founder, Gestalt LLC; Senior Vice President, Breakaway Solutions
Directorships: GovDelivery
Vincent P. Menichelli, Managing Director
e-mail: vince@actua.com
Education: Lehigh University; MBA, Finance, Bloomsburg University; BS, Accounting
Background: Senior Manager, Arthur Andersen; Coopers & Lybrand LLP
Directorships: Freeboarders, GovDelivery, Metastorm, SeaPass, StarCite
Suzanne Niemeyer, Managing Director/General Counsel/Secretary
e-mail: suzanne@actua.com
Education: BA, Duke University; JD, Georgetown University Law Center
Background: Dechert LLP
Directorships: Investor Force
Kirk Morgan, Chief Financial Officer
e-mail: kirk@actua.com
Education: BS, Accounting, Pennsylvania State University; CPA
Background: Audit Manager, PriceWaterhouseCoopers LLP

Karen Greene, Managing Director/Investor Relations/Marketing Communications
e-mail: karen@actua.com
Education: BA, University of Rochester; MBA, Finance & Marketing, Temple University School of Business
Background: Investor Relations, Safeguard; Investor Relations, CIGNA
Scott Powers, Managing Director/Assistant General Counsel
e-mail: scott@actua.com
Education: BS, Fordham University; JD, James E Beasley School of Law, Temple University
Background: Dechert LLP

54 ACUITY VENTURES LLC
1960 The Alameda
Suite 200
San Jose, CA 95126-1493
Phone: 408-210-8394
web: www.acuityventures.com

Mission Statement: Based in Silicon Valley, Acuity Ventures offers investment capital and operational expertise to emerging growth companies. The fund provides capital through convertible preferred debit, direct equity investments and other investment participations.
Geographic Preference: United States
Founded: 2004
Investment Criteria: Early Stage, Emerging Growth Companies
Industry Group Preference: Internet, Software
Portfolio Companies: FlashFoto, GCommerce, Protocol Driven Healthcare Inc.
Other Locations:
600 Hansen Way
Palo Alto, CA 94304-1043
Phone: 650-843-8766 **Fax:** 650-843-8768
Key Executives:
Eric Hardgrave, Co-Founder
Education: BA, Economics, Stanford University
Background: Co-Founder, Sand Hill Capital
Larry Hootnick, Managing Partner
Education: BS Industrial Management, MIT; MBA, University of Maryland
Background: SVP Finance/Administration, Intel Corporation; President/CEO, Maxtor Corporation; Consilium Corporation

55 ACUMEN
40 Worth Street
Suite 303
New York, NY 10013
Phone: 212-566-8821 **Fax:** 212-566-8817
web: www.acumen.org

Mission Statement: Acumen is dedicated to creating a world beyond poverty by investing in social enterprises in East Africa, India and Pakistan, with particular focus on the agriculture, education, healthcare and energy industries.
Geographic Preference: India, East Africa, Pakistan
Fund Size: $60 million
Founded: 2001
Average Investment: $250,000 - $3 million
Investment Criteria: Early Stage, Mid-Stage
Industry Group Preference: Healthcare, Energy, Agriculture, Water, Housing, Education
Portfolio Companies: Aarusha Homes, Aga Khan Rural Support Program, Ansaar Management Company, Asian Health Alliance, Avani Bio Energy, Azahar Coffee, Basix Krishi, Biolite, Broadreach, Burn Manufacturing, Cacao De Colombia, Circ Medtech, Consejosano, D.Light, Devergy, Drishtee, Earnup, Edubridge, Esoko, Ethiochicken, Everytable, Farmers Hope, First Access, Frontier Markets, Gigante Central Wet-Mill, Global Easy Water Products,

Venture Capital & Private Equity Firms / Domestic Firms

Green Energy Biofuels, Greenway Grameen, Guardian, Gulu Agricultural Development Company, Healthify, Husk Power Systems, Ignis Careers, Jawabu Microhealth, Juhudi Kilimo, Kashf School Sarmaya, Labournet, Learners Guild, Lifespring, Listo, Micro Drip, Myvyllage, Nasra Public School, National Rural Support Program, Nizam Energy, Orb Energy, Our Family Clinic, Pagatech, Peg, Pharmagen Healthcare Ltd., PVRI, Shayog, Sanergy, Seed Education Corp., Sewa Grih Rin, Siembraviva, Solarnow, Sproxil, SRE Solutions, Uncommon Cacao, Under The Mango Tree, Vikalp, Viridis, Virtual City, Wasi Organics, Waterhealth International, Wellpass, Western Seed, Workamerica, Ziqitza Health Care Ltd.

Other Locations:
203 Dheeraj Plaza
Hill Road, Bandra West
Mumbai 400 050
India
Phone: 91 (22) 6740-1500 **Fax:** 91 (22) 6740-1550

3rd Floor, ABC Towers
Waiyaki Way, Westlands
Nairobi
Kenya

1st Commerical Lane
Shahbaz Commercial Area
Phase VI
Karachi
Pakistan
Phone: 92 (21) 3584-6430-2 **Fax:** 92 (21) 3584-6490

Somerset House, New Wing
Strand
London WC2R 1LA
United Kingdom
Phone: 44-20-3701-7382

Carrera 7 No. 84A-29
Oficina 502
Bogota
Colombia

Key Executives:
Jacqueline Novogratz, Founder/Chief Executive Officer
Education: BA, Economics/International Relations, University of Virginia; MBA, Stanford University
Background: Chase Manhattan Bank, World Bank, UNICEF, Rockefeller Foundation
Directorships: Sonen Capital
Sasha Dichter, Chief Innovation Officer
e-mail: sdichter@acumenfund.org
Education: BA, Harvard College; MPA, International Development, Harvard Kennedy School, Harvard University; MBA, Harvard Business School
Background: Global Manager, Corporate Citizenship, GE Money
Andrew Tarazid-Tarawali, Portfolio Manager
Education: MBA, IE Business School; BSc, Business Admin., Ashesi University
Background: Senior Investment Professional, Injaro Investments
Carlyle Singer, President
Education: BA, History, Harvard College; MBA, Stanford University
Background: President/CEO, Katun Corp.; Senior President of Operations, IKON Office Solutions

56 ADAMS CAPITAL MANAGEMENT
500 Blackburn Avenue
Sewickley, PA 15143
Phone: 412-749-9454 **Fax:** 412-749-9459
web: www.acm.com

Mission Statement: ACM deploys its discontinuity driven investment strategy to identify and invest in companies that have value propositions driven by economics and product roadmaps that have the potential to define and dominate product categories.

Geographic Preference: United States
Fund Size: $815 million
Founded: 1994
Investment Criteria: Startup, Series A, Early-Stage
Industry Group Preference: Information Technology, Telecommunications, Semiconductors, Network Infrastructure & Security, Technology
Portfolio Companies: Airnet Communications, AutoESL Design Technologies, Bluestone Software, CoManage, Context Media, CoreTek, Cytyc, DATAllegro, Dell, Dynamics, Factory Logic, First Insight, Flashline, InSoft, Innovative Solutions & Support, Intrinsity, Landslide Technologies, LibreDigital, Luminescent Technologies, Mirage Network, NetSolve, ON Technology, Optellios, Qspeed Semiconductor, ReturnCentral, Revenue Technologies, RoadRunner Recycling Inc., SmartOps, SnapRetail, The Efficiency Network Inc., Touchdown Technologies, Uplogix, VBrick Systems

Key Executives:
Joel P. Adams, General Partner
412-749-9456
e-mail: jpa@acm.com
Education: MS, Industrial Administration, Carnegie Mellon University; BS, Nuclear Engineering, State University of New York at Buffalo
Background: VP/General Partner, Fostin Capital Corporation; Nuclear Test Engineer, General Dynamics
Directorships: Additech, First Insight, Intrinsity, Precision Therapeutics, SmartOps, TimeSys, Tiversa
Jennifer E. Parulo, Chief Financial Officer
Education: BS, Accounting, Grove City College; CPA
Background: Ernst & Young

57 ADAMS STREET PARTNERS, LLC
One North Wacker Drive
Suite 2700
Chicago, IL 60606-2823
Phone: 312-553-7890 **Fax:** 312-553-7891
web: www.adamsstreetpartners.com

Mission Statement: Private markets investment manager to institutional clients around the world.

Geographic Preference: United States, Western Europe, Israel, Asia
Fund Size: $27 billion
Founded: 1972
Average Investment: $5-$20 million
Minimum Investment: $5 million
Investment Criteria: First Stage, Second Stage
Industry Group Preference: Business to Business, Computer Hardware & Software, Healthcare, Technology, Life Sciences, Medical Devices, Biopharmaceuticals, Consumer Internet, Business Products & Services, Clean Technology, Communications, Components & IoT, SaaS, Fintech
Portfolio Companies: Actelis Networks, Adams Harris, Adesto, Alien Technology, American Wholesale, Amonix, Ancestry.com, APT, ArrowEye Solutions, AtHoc, Atlantis Computing, AVG Technologies, AWAS, Barracuda Networks, BrightRoll, CareCloud, cbanc Network, Cbeyond, Convio, CoreLab Partners, Couchbase, Criteo, Cybera, Damballa, Dolex, Enfora, FiftyOne, Glam Media, Global MailExpress, GlobeImmune, gWallet, INC Research, Integral Development, JasperSoft, Jazz Pharmaceuticals, KPG Ventures, Light Sciences Oncology, Luminous Medical, MachineryLink, Mintigo, Mpex, Neuraltus Pharmaceuticals, NewPath Ventures, NXP Semiconductor, OncoMed Pharmaceuticals, Paylocity, Peerless Networks, PneumRx, Proteus Biomedical, Q2ebanking, Retail Me Not, Revascular Therapeutics, Rimini Street, Sabre Holdings, ServiceMax, Shermans Travel, Shred-it, SnagAJob.com, Solaria, SPS Commerce, Tavve Software, T3Media, TriReme Medical,

Venture Capital & Private Equity Firms / Domestic Firms

Univision, USGI Medical, Visible World, Vocaltec, WhiteFence, YouSendIt, Ziggo

Adams Street Partners (Beijing) Co., Ltd.
77 Jianguo Road
Chaoyang District
Beijing 100025
China
Phone: 86 10 8587 2312 **Fax:** 86 10 8587 0110

745 Atlantic Avenue
8th Floor
Boston, MA 02111
Phone: 312-553-8475 **Fax:** 312-553-8499

Adams Street Partners UK LLP
4th Floor
London W1K 5JN
United Kingdom
Phone: 44 20 7659 7700 **Fax:** 44 20 7659 7701

Adams Street Partners, Inc.
Suite 300
Menlo Park, CA 94025
Phone: 650-331-4860 **Fax:** 650-331-4861

Adams Street (Europe) GmbH
Munich 80539
Germany
Phone: 49 89 2620 7285

Adams Street Partners, Inc.
20th Floor
New York, NY 10020
Phone: 646-647-1000 **Fax:** 646-647-1001

Adams Street Partners, LLC (Korea Branch)
17th Floor
Gangnam-gu
Seoul 06235
Republic of Korea

Adams Street Partners Singapore Pte. Ltd.
#14-02 Raffles City Tower 179101
Singapore
Phone: 65 6303 8730 **Fax:** 65 6303 8740

Adams Street Partners Japan G.K.
Otemachi 1-chome, Chiyoda-ku
Tokyo 100-0004
Japan
Phone: 081 3 6206 3545 **Fax:** 081 3 6206 3547

Key Executives:
T. Bondurant French, Executive Chairman
e-mail: bfrench@adamsstreetpartners.com
Education: Northwestern University
Background: Brinson Partners; Connecticut General Insurance Company
Jeffrey Diehl, Managing Partner & Head of Investments
Education: Cornell University; Harvard University
Background: Brinson Partners; The Parthenon Group
Jim Walker, Partner & Chief Operating Officer
Education: Catholic University of America; MIT
Background: Credit Suisse Private Bank Americas; Morgan Stanley Global Wealth Management; Merrill Lynch
Quintin Kevin, Partner & Chief Financial Officer
Education: University of Illinois; University of Chicago
Background: KPMG
Kelly Meldrum, CFA, Partner & Head of Primary Investments
Education: Bentley College
Background: William and Flora Hewlett Foundation; Morgan Stanley
Jeff Akers, Partner & Head of Secondary Investments
Education: Indiana University; Northwestern University
Background: L.E.K. Consulting; William Blair & Company

58 ADOBE VENTURES LP
345 Park Avenue
San Jose, CA 95110-2704
Phone: 408-536-6000 **Fax:** 408-537-6000
e-mail: newventure@adobe.com
web: www.adobe.com/ventures.html

Mission Statement: The strength and experience of Adobe, partnered with the endorsement and investing experience of Granite Ventures, makes the Adobe Ventures funding model unique, and allows the entrepreneur access to additional resources within one program.

Fund Size: $100 million
Founded: 1982
Average Investment: $3-$5 million
Investment Criteria: Early Stage
Industry Group Preference: Infrastructure, Enterprise Services, Networking, Digital Media & Marketing, Media, Internet Technology, Communications, Publishing
Portfolio Companies: Acrodea, Arcot, AvantGo, BidClerk, Cell Co., Convio, DecisionView, Digimarc, Digital Fountain, DigitalThink, Demandbase, EFI, FiveAcross, Gigya, imeem, Indiagames, Kontiki, Netscape, Objectivity, Oversight Systems, PSS Systems, PlayJam, Scrybe, Sendmail, Siebel System, Skysoft, Shutterfly, Tumbleweed Communications, TuVox, Vignette, Virage, Virtual Ubiquity, 56.com

Key Executives:
John Leckrone, Managing Director
e-mail: jleckron@adobe.com
Education: MBA, Stephen M. Ross School of Business, University of Michigan
Background: Group Product Manager, Adobe; Business Development Manager, Netscape; Management Development Program, Ford Motor Compan

59 ADVANCED TECHNOLOGY VENTURES
500 Boylston Street
Suite 1380
Boston, MA 02116
e-mail: investorrelations@atvcapital.com
web: www.atvcapital.com

Mission Statement: A bio-coastal venture capital firm that takes an active role in their investments, offering a collaborative experience in regards to executive recruitment, market selection, business development, etc.

Geographic Preference: United States
Fund Size: $1.6 billion
Founded: 1979
Average Investment: $10 million
Minimum Investment: $250,000
Industry Group Preference: Information Technology, Healthcare, Clean Technology
Portfolio Companies: Accord Networks, Acme Packet, Actel, AppIQ, Application Networks, Adrian, Cepheid, Credence, CYTYC, DataSage, E-Security, Epigram, Healthshare Technology, Helixis, Hypnion, Microvention, Omneon Video Networks, Plexxikon, Proteolix, Qumu, RFMD, Redline Networks, Striva, Teradata, Tran Switch, Tripwire, Upshot.com, Verastem, Webline, [X+1], Zaperio Technologies, Aquion Energy, Accelero Pharma, Actifio, Alfalight, Alta Rock Energy, Altura Medical, Calithera Biosciences, Catabsis, Cedexis, Cenzic, Channel Advisor, Coskata, EndoGastric Solutions, Evergage, Five Prime, Gi Dynamics, Great Point Energy, Great Point Ventures, Gynesonics, Holaira, Host Analytics, Hydra Biosciences, Modria, Nominum, Oasys Water, Poly Remedy, Portola, Powervision, QuickPay, Rive Technology, Second Genome, Silicor Materials, Thinking Phone Networks, Therasos Therapeutics, Trans1, Valeritas, Wild Tangent, Cool Sculpting

23

Venture Capital & Private Equity Firms / Domestic Firms

Other Locations:
2884 Sand Hill Road
Suite 121
Menlo Park, CA 94025

Key Executives:
Steven Baloff, General Partner
e-mail: sbaloff@atvcapital.com
Education: MBA, Stanford Graduate School of Business; BA, Harvard College
Background: CEO and Founder, Worldview Systems; Co-developer, Travelocity; Executive, Covalent Systems; Strategist, Booz Allen & Hamilton; Founder, Twin Lakes Ventures
Directorships: Covalent Systems

Mike Carusi, General Partner
e-mail: mcarusi@atvcapital.com
Education: MBA, Amos Tuck School of Business Administration Dartmouth College; BS, Lehigh University
Background: Director of Business Development, Inhale Therapeutic Systems; Principal, The Wilkerson Group
Directorships: Acceleron Pharma; Emphasys Medical; EndoGastric Solutions; GI Dynamics; MicroVention; Plexxikon; TranS1; Xtent

Jean George, General Partner
e-mail: jgeorge@atvcapital.com
Education: MBA, Simmons College Graduate School of Management; BS, University of Maine
Background: Various Operational Positions, Genzyme Corporation; Life Sciences Lead Investor, BancBoston Ventures
Directorships: Critical Therapeutics; Five Prime Therapeutics; Hydra Biosciences; Hypnion; Juniper Medical; Proteolix

Bob Hower, General Partner
e-mail: bhower@atvcapital.com
Education: BA, Cum Laude, Harvard College; MBA, Amos Tuck School, Dartmouth College
Background: VP Sales, LHS Group; Sales/Marketing, Lotus Development; Sales/Marketing, General Mills; Director, BancNoston Ventures; Commercial Real Estate, Cabot, Cabot & Forbes
Directorships: Acme Packet; AppIQ; Application Networks; ChannelAdvisor; e-Security

Bill Wiberg, General Partner
e-mail: bwiberg@atvcapital.com
Education: BS, Cornell University; MS, Stanford University; MBA, Columbia University
Background: Telecommunications, Lucent Technologies; President, Lucent's Cellular & PCS Wireless Networks; General Partner, Bowman Capital; General Partner, Orange Ventures; Board of Directors/ Executive Committee, Cellular Telecommunications and Internet Association
Directorships: CombineNet; Great Point Energy; HVVi

Edward Frank PhD, Technology Partner
Education: BS, MS, Electrical Engineering, Stanford University; PhD, Computer Science, Carnegie Mellon University
Background: Co-Founder & EVP, Epigram; VP, R&D, Broadcom Corporation
Directorships: Onstor, Wavesat

Stephen Shapiro, Venture Partner
Education: BS, MIT; MS, Biomedical Engineering & Medical Physics, University of California, Berkeley
Background: Managing Director, The Wilkerson Group
Directorships: Aperio, ONI Corp., Pacific Diagnostic Labs

60 ADVANCIT CAPITAL
846 University Avenue
Norwood, MA 02062

e-mail: info@advancitcap.com
web: www.advancitcapital.com

Mission Statement: Advancit Capital is an early stage investment firm focused on media, entertainment and technology companies. The firm seeks the opportunity to form long-term partnerships with talented, focused and driven entrepreneurs. With its strategic and industry expertise, Advancit Capital provides value-added resources at the critical growth stages of companies.

Founded: 2011
Investment Criteria: Early-Stage
Industry Group Preference: Media, Entertainment, Technology
Portfolio Companies: 8I, MiTú, Maker Studios, HeadSpace, Unikrn, MasterClass, The Business of Fashion, Directr, Epoxy, Reserve, Brickwork, Molio, FitStar, Qualia, Lua, Draft, Wedgies, Victorious, Moat, NewsCred, Panna, MobCrush, Baobab, The Noun Project, Percolate, Skift, Speakaboos, Hyper, Amper, French Girls, Vistar Media, Mic Network, Push.io, BlitzESports, Msg.ai, Silver, Niche, CrowdTangle, SocialRank, Splash, The Outline, Thrive Global, Clique Media Group, Pop, Distractify, Women.com, Crypt TV, Block Six Analytics, REDEF, Base79, AllDefDigital, STRIVR, The Athletic, Mux, All Def Digital, Indigenous Media, Mux, JanusVR, Outpost Games, Woven Orthopedics

Other Locations:
99 University Place
3rd Floor
New York, NY 10003

Key Executives:
Jason Ostheimer, Co-Founder/Partner
Education: BS, Economics, Wharton School, University of Pennsylvania
Background: National Amusements Inc., Blackstone Group

Shari Redstone, Co-Founder/Managing Partner
Education: BS, Tufts University; JD, MA, Boston University
Background: President, National Amusements
Directorships: Vice Chair, Viacom Inc.; Vice Chair, Board of CBS Corp.; Co-Chair MovieTickets.com; Board of Directors & Executive Committee, National Theatre Owners Association

Jonathan Miller, Senior Advisor
Education: BA, Harvard College
Background: CEO/Chairman/Chief Digital Officer, Digital Media Group for News Corp.; CEO, AOL; CEO/President, USA Information and Services; VP, Programming, NBA Entertainment
Directorships: Nickelodeon International

61 ADVANTAGE CAPITAL PARTNERS
156 W 56th Street
Suite 801
New York, NY 10019

Phone: 646-685-8755
web: www.advantagecap.com

Mission Statement: Provides capital and value added services to well-managed companies with superior growth potential.

Geographic Preference: North, Southeast, Midwest
Fund Size: $700 million
Founded: 1992
Average Investment: $10 million
Minimum Investment: $1 million
Investment Criteria: Seed, Startup, Early Stage, Mezzanine, Special Situations
Industry Group Preference: Business Products & Services, Clean Technology, Communications, Energy, Financial Services, Information Technology, Life Sciences, Manufacturing
Portfolio Companies: 3DR Laboratories, Av Smoot, Able Planet, AgencyQ, AGIS, ARCMail Technology, Barton Nelson, BinOptics, Bizzuka, Butler's Pantry, Cardax

Venture Capital & Private Equity Firms / Domestic Firms

Pharmaceuticals, CheckPoint Pumps & Systems, City Carting & Recycling, CodeRed, Computime, Contego Services Group, Crown Plastics, Digium|Asterik, Distech Systems, Elevate Digital, EmergingMed, Enersciences, Esperance Pharmaceuticals, FireRock, FleetCor, Game Equipment, Glori Energy, Greenleaf Biofuels, GridPoint, Group360 Worldwide, Hawaii Biotech, HRI, iCardiac Technologies, Illinois Neurospine Institute, ILMO Products, INDEECO, Inside Higher Ed, Jahabow, Lawrence Group, Lift for Life Academy, MannaPro, MarqueMedicos, Mason Manufacturing, Merill Industries, Mezmeriz, MicroGreen, Mid America Brick, Monarch Machine Tool, New England Linen Supply, NovaTract, Novelos, Owensboro Grain, Pasteuria Bioscience, Quality Wood Products, RepEquity, Rucker's, Selltis, Skyline Innovations, Soft Switching Technologies, Stout Industries, Summit Broadband, Sunburst Farms, Synacor, T&K Machine, TAS Environmental Services LP, TurboSquid, Veran Medical Technologies, Virent Energy, Willert Home Products, Worley Company, XIOLINK, Zadspace, Inc., Voxitas, Waste Remedies, Willert Home Products, Worley Catastrophe Response, Xiolink, Zadspace

Other Locations:
3 Lebanon Street
Hanover, NH 03755
Phone: 603-676-7160

909 Poydras Street
Suite 2230
New Orleans, LA 70112
Phone: 504-522-4850

7733 Forsyth Boulevard
Suite 1400
St. Louis, MO 63105
Phone: 314-725-0800

1028 33rd Street Northwest
Suite 200
Washington, DC 20007
Phone: 202-337-1661

900 South Capital of Texas Highway
Las Cimas Building 4
Suite 480
Austin, TX 78746
Phone: 512-380-1168

c/o Venture Investors
869 Lakeshore Boulevard
Incline Village, NV 89451
Phone: 775-298-1338

174 West Comstocl Avenue
Suite 209
Winter Park, FL 32789
Phone: 407-454-6184

207 East Side Square
Suite 200
Huntsville, AL 35801
Phone: 256-883-8711

6923 Silverado Trail
Napa, CA 94558
Phone: 707-944-2310

318 W Adams
16th Floor
Chicago, IL 60606
Phone: 312-767-2019

208 West Georgetown Street
Crystal Springs, MS 39059
Phone: 601-954-6636

c/o Ironwood Capital
45 Nod Road
Avon, CT 06001-3819
Phone: 860-409-2100

Key Executives:
Steven Stull, President
Education: BS, Finance/Economics & MBA, Washington University
Background: Investment Director, General American Life Insurance Company
Maurice Doyle, Managing Director
Education: BBA, University of Notre Dame; JD, Chicago-Kent College of Law
Background: Senior VP, UBS Securities; VP, Credit Suisse First Boston; VP, Winthrop Securities
Michael Johnson, Managing Director/COO
Education: Stanford School of Law; AB, Harvard College
Background: Jones, Walker, Waechter, Potevent, Carrere & Denegre
Damon Rawie, Managing Director
Education: BA, Wesleyan University; MBA, University of Chicago Graduate School of Business
Background: China International Capital Corporation; JP Morgan Securities
Louis Dubuque, Managing Director
Education: MBA, Washington University; Washington and Lee University
Background: US Bank
Scott Murphy, Managing Director/CIO
e-mail: smurphy@advantagecap.com
Education: AB, Harvard University; CFA
Background: United States Congress, New York
Thomas Keaveney, Advisor
Education: Fordham University
Background: Investment Banker, Credit Suisse First Boston
Jonathan Goldstein, Managing Director
Education: BA, Yale University; Washington University School of Law
Background: SVP, McCormack Baron Salazar; Founder, Taproot Ventures
Charles Booker, Principal
Education: BA, Vanderbilt University; JD, Tulane School of Law
Background: Lawyer, Mayer Brown Platt; Lawyer, McGlinchey Stafford
Jeremy Degenhart, Principal
Education: BSBA, Finance, Economics & Accounting, Washington University, St. Louis
Background: Analyst, Wydown Capital
Directorships: Veran Medical Technologies, Quick Study Radiology, Waste Remedies, Carbolytic Materials Company, Sunflower Food & Spice
Jeffrey Craver, Principal
e-mail: jcraver@advantagecap.com
Education: Duke University; JD, University of Richmond; LLM, Taxation, Washington University, St. Louis
Background: Tax Counsel, Missouri Chamber of Commerce & Industry
W. Anthony Toups, Principal
e-mail: ttoups@advantagecap.com
Education: Louisiana State University; JD, Paul M Herbert Law Center, Louisiana State University
Background: Partner, Adams & Reese

---

62 ADVENT INTERNATIONAL CORPORATION
Prudential Tower
800 Boylston Street
Boston, MA 02199-8069

Phone: 617-951-9400
web: www.adventinternational.com

Mission Statement: Global private equity firm with $32 billion in investments.

Geographic Preference: Worldwide
Founded: 1984
Average Investment: $5 million
Investment Criteria: Buyouts, Growth Equity Investment
Industry Group Preference: Business & Financial Services, Healthcare, Industrial, Retail, Consumer & Leisure, Technology, Media & Telecommunications

Venture Capital & Private Equity Firms / Domestic Firms

Portfolio Companies: ABC Supply, AccentCare, Addiko Bank, Aimbridge Hospitality, BioDuro, Canvia, CCC Information Services Inc., Circet Groupe, Clearent/FieldEdge, Definitive Healthcare, Easynvest, First Watch, Laird Limited, Prisma Medios de Pagos S.A., Quala, QuEST Global Services, Roehm, Transcend Therapeutics, TransUnion, Zentiva

Other Locations:
12 East 49th Street
45th Floor
New York, NY 10017
Phone: 212-813-8300

8-10 rue Lamennais
Paris 75008
France
Phone: 33 0 1 55 37 29 00

Westhafenplatz 1
Frankfurt am Main 60327
Germany
Phone: 49 0 69 955 2700

Serrano, n§ 57 - 2§
Madrid 28006
Spain
Phone: 34 91 745 48 60

160 Victoria Street
London SW1E 5LB
United Kingdom
Phone: 44 0 20 7333 0800

Av. Brig. Faria Lima 3311, 9§ andar
Sao Paulo 04538-133
Brazil
Phone: 55 11 3014 6800

Edificio Omega
Campos Eliseos 345 - 14th Floor
Col. Polanco
Mexico City 11560
Mexico
Phone: 52 55 5281 0303

Avenida Calle 82 #10-33
Oficina 702
Bogota 110221
Colombia
Phone: 57 1 254 4747

HKRI Centre One
Units 3904-3905
288 Shimen Road (No. 1)
Shanghai 200041
China
Phone: 86 21 6032 0788

Unit 1702, 17th Floor
One India Bulls Centre, Tower 2, Wing A
841, Senapati Bapat Marg
Mumbai 400 013
India
Phone: 91 (22) 4057 3000

Suite 5707, 57th Floor
Two International Finance Centre, 8 Finance Street
Central
Hong Kong
China
Phone: 852 2278 3788

Key Executives:
Peter Brooke, Chairman Emeritus
Education: Harvard University, Harvard Business School
Background: Managing Partner, TA Associates
Chris Egan, Managing Partner
Education: Dartmouth College
Background: Financial Sponsors Group, UBS Warburg
Directorships: Ansira Holdings; CCC Information Services Inc.; Clearent/FieldEdge; Definitive Healthcare; P2 Energy, Prisma Medios de Pagos S.A.; BondDesk; RedPrairie; TransUnion
John Maldonado, Managing Partner
Education: Dartmouth College; Harvard Business School
Background: Bain Capital; Parthenon Capital
Directorships: AccentCare; ATI Physical Therapy Holdings LLC; Definitive Healthcare; Health Care Private Equity Association; Syneos Health Inc.; American Radiology Services; Genoa Healthcare
David McKenna, Managing Partner
Education: Dartmouth College
Background: Bain Capital; Monitor Group
Directorships: BOS Solutions; Culligan International Group; NCS Multistage; Serta Simmons Bedding; ABC Supply; Aspen Technology; Boart Longyear; Bradco Supply; Keystone Automotive Operations
David Mussafer, Managing Partner
Education: Tulane University; Wharton School; University of Pennsylvania
Background: Chemical Bank; Adler & Shaykin
Directorships: First Watch; Lululemon Athletica; Serta Simmons; American Radiology Services; Charlotte Russe; Dufry; Five Below; Hudson Group; Kirkland's; Making Memories; Party City; Vantiv
Chris Pike, Managing Partner
Education: Amherst College
Background: Coopers & Lybrand
Directorships: ATI Physical Therapy Holdings; CCC Information Services Inc.; Cotiviti; Genoa Healthcare; Americus Dental; Aspen Technology; BondDesk; GFI Group; Managed Healthcare Associates
Eileen Sivolella, Managing Director & Chief Financial Officer
Education: University of Delaware
Background: CFO, Bain Capital; Partner, Deloitte
Bryan Taylor, Managing Partner
Education: Stanford University; Stanford Graduate School of Business
Background: Co-Head, Technology Group, TPG Capital; Founder & Managing Director, Symphony Technology Group; Manager, Bain & Company
Directorships: Tanium; McAfee; CCC Information Services; Celerity; Decision Insight Information Group; Ellucian; Eze Software; Greensky; IQVIA; Intergraph; Sutherland Global Services
Fred Wakeman, Managing Partner
Education: University of California at Berkley; Georgetown University School of Business
Background: GE Capital
Directorships: IDEMIA; Unit4; DFS Furniture; Fat Face; HMV; ILVA; KMD Holding; Poundland; Radio 538; Venere
James Westra, Managing Partner & Chief Legal Officer
Education: Harvard College; Boston University
Background: Weil, Gotshal & Manges LLP

63 **ADVENT-MORRO EQUITY PARTNERS**
Banco Popular Building
Suite 903
206 Tetuan Street, Old San Juan
San Juan, PR 00902

Phone: 787-725-5285 **Fax:** 787-721-1735
web: www.adventmorro.com

Mission Statement: Advent-Morro Equity Partners is Puerto Rico's leading private equity investment firm with more than $120 million in equity capital under management. It has invested in over 50 companies, most of which are based or have operations in Puerto Rico. From 1997 to 2010, Advent-Morro was affiliated with Boston-based Advent International Corporation.

Geographic Preference: Puerto Rico, United States
Fund Size: $120 million
Founded: 1997
Average Investment: $2.5 - 10 million

Minimum Investment: $2.5 million
Investment Criteria: Later-Stage, Expansion Financing, MBO, Corporate Divestitures, Turnarounds, Re-Capitalizations, Industry Consolidations
Industry Group Preference: Diversified
Portfolio Companies: Abaco PR, AquaVentures Holdings LLC, Centennial Communications, Charlotte Russe Holdings Inc., Codigo Entertainment LLC, Datek Online, Dollar Express, FFI Holdings Inc., Hotel El Convento, ICPR Junior College, Infinity Laser Centers, Infopaginas Inc., Integration Technologies, International Meal Company Holdings SA, Islanet Communications, LendingPoint, Medical Card Systems, Next Level Learning Inc., Packers Provision, Pahteon Inc., Puerto Rico ASC Holdings Co. Inc., QMC Media, Quench USA Inc., QWS Holdings LLC, Trexel, Venture Steel, Vigilant Shipping Holding, Windstream

Key Executives:
Cyril L. Meduna, Managing Partner/President
Education: BS, Mechanical Engineering, Rensselaer Polytechnic Institute; MBA, George Washington University
Background: President, Meduna & Co.; Regional Manager, Ehrlich Bober International
Omar Mejias, Director
Education: BS, Finance, Loyola University; MF, Tulane University
Background: Senior Associate, BMO Capital Markets; Equity Research Associate, Bb&T Capital Markets

64 AEA INVESTORS
666 Fifth Avenue
36th Floor
New York, NY 10103

Phone: 212-644-5900 **Fax:** 212-888-1459
web: www.aeainvestors.com

Mission Statement: AEA's investment activities are primarily focused on the three market sectors in which AEA has developed considerable expertise: value added industrials, specialty chemicals and consumer products.
Geographic Preference: United States, Western Europe
Fund Size: $400 Million
Founded: 1968
Average Investment: $10 Million
Minimum Investment: $1 Million
Investment Criteria: Consolidations, Acquisitions, LBO, MBO, Recapitalization, Special Situations, Mezzanine
Industry Group Preference: Chemicals, Consumer Products, Business to Business, Manufacturing, Distribution
Portfolio Companies: Aramsco Holdings Inc., BOA Group, Brand Networks, Colony Hardware, CPG International, Dayton Parts LLC, Dematic, The Evans Network of Companies, Garden Ridge, Hospitalists Management Group LLC, Industrial Accoustics Company, Lone Star, NEW Global Talent, Phillips Pet Food & Supplies, PLZ Holding Corporation, PPC Industries Inc., Pregis Corporation, Reladyne Inc., SBP Holdings LP, Sextant Education Corporation, Shoes For Crews, Sparrows Group, Suhyang Networks, Swanson Industries Inc., Troxell Communication Inc.

Other Locations:
281 Tresser Boulevard
12th Floor
Stamford, CT 06901
Phone: 203-564-2660 **Fax:** 203-564-2661

78 Brook Street
London W1K 5EF
England
Phone: 44 (20) 7659-7800 **Fax:** 44 (20) 7491-2155

Widenmayerstr 3
Munich 80538
Germany
Phone: 49 (89) 244-173-0 **Fax:** 49 (89) 244-173-860

Suite 2903, 29F
Kerry Center, Tower 2
1539 Nanjing Road West
Jingan District 200040
Shanghai
Phone: 86-21-2308-7888 **Fax:** 86-21-2308-7880

Key Executives:
John Garcia, Executive Chairman
Education: SS, University of Kent, Canterbury England
Background: KFedit Suisse First Boston: Global Head Chemicals Group, European Investment Banking Management Committee, Head European Acquisitions, Leveraged Finance, Financial Sponsors Group, Head European Natural Resources Group; Managing Director, Schroder Wertheim; Atlantic Richfield
Directorships: Icetex Corp
John Cozzi, Partner/Co-Head of Small Business Funds
Education: BA, Union College; MBA, Wharton School
Background: Managing Director, Arena Capital Partners; Managing Director, Leveraged Finance Group of Credit Suisse First Boston; Smith Barney; Harris Upham & Company; NYNEX Corp
Joseph Carrabino, Jr., Partner/Executive Chairman
Education: AB Economics, Harvard College
Background: Co-Head Mezzanine Debt Group, Whitney & Co; Leveraged Finance/Financial Sponsor Coverage, Credit Suisse First Boston
Shivanandan A. Dalvie, Consultant
Education: MBA, Stanford University Graduate School of Business; BS, Yale University
Background: Credit Suisse First Boston
Directorships: Compresison Polymers, Telephia
Brian Hoesterey, Chief Executive Officer
Education: MBA, Harvard University; BBA, Accounting, Texas Christian University
Background: BT Capital Partners; Bankers Trust; Morgan Stanley; McKinsey & Co.
Thomas Pryma, Partner
Education: Georgetown University
Background: Merrill Lynch
Directorships: Pro Mach, TricoBraun, Eviqua Water Technologies
Martin Eltrich III, Partner
Education: BS, Economics, Wharton School, University of Pennsylvania
Background: Greenhill & Co.
Directorships: Acosta, Burt's Bees. Cogen Healthcare, Henry Company, Li & Fung Distribution, Shoes for Crews, Tampico Beverage
Alan Wilkinson, Partner/Co-Head of Small Business Funds
Education: MBA, Columbia University; BS, Mathematics, King's College
Background: Peter J Solomon Company; Lehman Brothers; Principal Investment Group
Scott Zoellner, Partner/Head of Private Debt
Education: BA, Economics and Political Science, Trinity College; MBA, NYU Stern School of Business
Background: Principal, Allied Capital; Director, Callidus Capital Corp; Consultant, Carlyle Group; Credit Suisse First Boston; Leveraged Finance Group
Thomas Groves, Partner
Education: AB, Economics, Bowdoin College
Background: Credit Suisse First Boston
J. Louis Sharpe, Partner
Education: BA, Economics, Yale University
Background: Investment Banking Division, Morgan Stanley
Steven DeCillis II, Partner/Chief Financial Officer
Education: BS, Accounting, Villanova University; MBA, Columbia University; CPA
Background: CFO, Ripplewood Holdings LLC;

Venture Capital & Private Equity Firms / Domestic Firms

Assurance & Business Advisory Services, PricewaterhouseCoopers LLP
Nannette McNally, Partner
Education: BS, Business Administration, University of North Carolina, Chapel Hill
Background: Investment Banking, Credit Suisse First Boston
Barbara Burns, Partner/General Counsel/Chief Compliance Officer
Education: BA, Economics and International Relations, and JD, University of Pennsylvania
Background: Morgan Stanley Real Estate
Baron Carlson, Partner
Education: BA, Government, Dartmouth College
Background: Arena Capital Partners
James Ho, Partner
Education: BA, Economics and Mathematical Methods in the Social Sciences, Northwestern University
Background: Bain & Co.

65 AEP CAPITAL LLC
366 Madison Avenue
8th Floor
New York, NY 10017

Phone: 212-641-5100 Fax: 212-641-5125
web: www.aepcapital.com

Mission Statement: An affiliate of Alpine Capital, principally involved in media, entertainment, communications and financial services.

Geographic Preference: North America
Founded: 1995
Average Investment: $10 - $75 million
Investment Criteria: Early Stage, Consolidations, Leveraged Buyout, Management Buyout, Recapitalization, Second Stage, Special Situations
Industry Group Preference: Advertising, Broadcasting, Consumer Services, Internet Technology, Publishing, Telecommunications, Communications, Information Technology, Media, Entertainment, Business Products & Services
Portfolio Companies: Creme de la Creme, Uplifting Entertainment, Bonded Holdings LLC
Key Executives:
  Richard Goldstein, Senior Managing Director
  Education: Summa Cum Laude, Phi Beta Kappa, Queens College; Magna Cum Laude, Harvard Law School
  Background: Partner, Paul, Weiss, Rifkind, Wharton & Garrison
  Directorships: Alpine Capital Bank, American Community Newspapers, Creme de la Creme
  Bruce Greenwald, Senior Managing Director
  Education: BS, Business Economics & MBA, University of Rochester
  Background: Arthur Young & Company
  Directorships: American Community Newspapers, Creme de la Creme, Destina Theaters

66 AEROEQUITY
2500 N Military Trail
Suite 470
Boca Raton, FL 33431

Phone: 561-372-7820 Fax: 561-392-6908
e-mail: investorrelations@aeroequity.com
web: www.aeroequity.com

Mission Statement: To distinguish themselves from other private equity firms by bringing a unique set of capabilities, relationships and experiences to their portfolio companies in a way seldom seen in the middle market. In addition to providing substantial financial, human and intellectual capital to our platform investments, AE provides portfolio companies and management teams with unmatched access to critical decision makers within key OEMs and operators worldwide.

Founded: 1998
Industry Group Preference: Aerospace, Defense and Government
Portfolio Companies: AC&A, Belcan, BHI Energy, CDIm FMI, Global Jet Capital, Kellstrom Aerospace, Moeller Aerospace
Key Executives:
  David H. Rowe, Co-Founder/Managing Partner
  Education: BS, Tulane University
  Background: EVP, Gulfstream Financial Services Corp.
  Directorships: TurboCombustor Technology, Kellstrom Industries, AeroSat Corp
  Thomas K Churbuck, Operating Partner
  Education: John F Kennedy Special Warfare Center, Department of Defense Systems Management College
  Background: Founder, Power Systems Manufacturing; Founder, Tropic Aviation
  Michael Greene, Managing Partner
  Education: BA, College of the Holy Cross; MBA, Harvard Business School
  Background: Founding Partner, UBS Capital LLC
  Thomas E. Brew Jr., Special Advisor
  Education: BS, LLB, Boston University
  Background: COO, Power Systems Manufacturing; CEO, Laclede Steel
  Wayne P. Garrett, General Partner
  Education: BS, MBA, Boston College
  Background: CFO, Power Systems Manufacturing; CFO, Cambridge SoundWorks

67 AEROSTAR CAPITAL LLC
590 Sandhill Crane Road
PO Box 1270
Wilson, WY 83014-1270

Phone: 888-280-5566 Fax: 888-280-5566
web: www.aerostarcapital.com

Mission Statement: Private equity for aerospace, defense and telecom companies.

Geographic Preference: United States, Europe
Founded: 1997
Investment Criteria: Bridge, Consolidations, Leveraged Buyout, Management Buyout, Mezzanine, Middle Market, Recapitalization, Special Situations
Industry Group Preference: Aerospace, Defense and Government, Communications, Equipment, Telecommunications
Portfolio Companies: Firth Rixon, Ltd., Forged Metals, Inc., WESCO Aircraft, Inc.
Key Executives:
  Robert Paulson, Founder/CEO
  e-mail: bob4aerostar@gmail.com
  Education: BA in Economics, University of California at Santa Barbara; MBA, Harvard
  Background: Army Officer/Analyst, Assistant Secretary of Defense for Systems Analysis; Consultant, McKinsey & Company
  Directorships: Director, Ducommum; Nationwide Health Properties; Forgings International LP; Advisor, McKinsey & Company

68 AFFINITY CAPITAL MANAGEMENT
901 Marquette Avenue
Suite 2820
Minneapolis, MN 55402

Phone: 612-252-9900

Mission Statement: Affinity Capital Management works with innovative and visionary companies and entrepreneurs to create groundbreaking improvements in health care.

Geographic Preference: Upper Midwest US
Fund Size: $80 million

Venture Capital & Private Equity Firms / Domestic Firms

Founded: 1993
Average Investment: $5 million
Investment Criteria: Seed, Start-up, Early Stage, Mid Stage
Industry Group Preference: Healthcare, Medical Devices, Health Related
Portfolio Companies: Data Sciences International, LifeSync Corporation, National Dentex Corporation, Proteus Digital Health, Respicardia, Spineology, Uptake Medical, ValenTx
Key Executives:
   Edson W. Spencer Jr., Founder/Chairman
   e-mail: espencerjr@affinitycapital.net
   Education: BA, Williams College; MBA, Columbia University
   Background: Principal/Co-Founder, Peterson-Spencer-Fansler Company; Senior Officer, Dyco Petroleum
   B. Kristine Johnson, President
   e-mail: bkjohnson@affinitycapital.net
   Education: BA, St. Olaf College
   Background: Senior VP/CAO, Medtronic; Various Executive Positions, Cargill
   Robin Dowdle, Chief Financial Officer
   e-mail: rdowdle@affinitycapital.net
   Education: BS, University of Minnesota
   Background: Analyst/Operations Manager, USTrust;

69 AGILITY CAPITAL LLC
10 E Figueroa Street
Suite 204
Santa Barbara, CA 93101

Phone: 805-568-0425
e-mail: info@agilitycap.com
web: www.agilitycap.com

Mission Statement: A private venture debt fund focused on providing senior debt solutions to venture capital-backed private companies and Small Cap public companies.
Geographic Preference: Western USA
Founded: 2000
Average Investment: $750,000
Minimum Investment: $250,000
Investment Criteria: Mezzanine Financing, Primary Bridge Loans, Lines of Credit, Factoring Lines of Credit, Non-Formula Lines of Credit, Restructuring Debt
Portfolio Companies: Alpha Innotech, Aurionpro, Inc., BlackFog, Blue Sky Research, Bravanta, Cake Marketing, CKL Design Automation, Computer Motion, Cyber Rain, DAX Solutions, DPS Inc., EdgeWave Software, Inc., Emmaus Life Science Inc., Everyone Counts, FastSoft, Flowplay, Fragmob, Fugoo, GCommerce, Gigoptix, GrabGreen, Haht Commerce, Harbinger, Home Chef, iBahn, INgrooves, iPass, Innovative Micro Technologies, Kana, Kanam Lifescript, Lucid, Lunera, MobileStorm, MiaSolé, MicroTech Systems Inc., Monet Software, Moving iMage Technologies, Nimble Commerce, NuvoSun, Oomba, Pathfire, PepperBall Technologies, Permlight, Petnet, Phizzle, Phoenix Energy Technologies, Predixion, Primaxx, Qubera Solutions, THE RESET, SimplyShe, StemCyte, Storactive, Inc., Superconductor Technologies, Inc., Supply Edge, Inc., Strasbaugh, Synapse Design, Tacit, Talenthouse, Triple Ring Technologies, TrueVision Systems Inc., Uniquify, Valant, Vantos, Vimana, Visto, Wordlock, Zhone
Key Executives:
   Jeff Carmody, Managing Director
   e-mail: jeff@agilitycap.com
   Education: University of California, Santa Barbara
   Background: Sand Hill Capital; Tech Coast Angels
   Daniel Corry, Managing Director
   e-mail: daniel@agilitycap.com
   Education: University of California, Santa Barbara
   Background: Co-Founder, Sand Hill Capital; Silicon Valley Bank; Bank of the West

70 AGMAN PARTNERS
12910 Pierce Street
Suite 210
Omaha, NE 68144

Phone: 402-882-0112
e-mail: ir@agmanpartners.com
web: www.agmanpartners.com

Mission Statement: Agman Partners is a multi-strategy investment fund attracted to areas of market inefficiency and fundamental value. Agnostic to industry and geography, the fund has flexibility to invest directly and through partnerships across asset classes and stages of development. Agman Partners emphasizes a long-term perspective to its investment approach.
Founded: 2005
Industry Group Preference: All Sectors Considered
Portfolio Companies: Accomplice, Agman Capital, Ampler, AngelList, Aparium Hotel Group, Atlas Venture, Brook Furniture Rental, Carbon Black, City Place, DataXu, DraftKings, FreshBooks, Malliouhana Resort, Metonic Real Estate Solutions, Nelson Cash, Omaha National, OMNE Partners, RA Capital, RedBird Capital Partners, Seldin Company, Senator Investment Group, Skillz, Stromedix, The Chicago Athletic Association, The Iron Horse Hotel, Tuscany Apartments, Universal Services, Veracode, Virtus, West Glen Town Center
Other Locations:
   10 East Ohio Street
   2nd Floor
   Chicago, IL 60611
Key Executives:
   Scott Silverman, Co-Founder/CEO
   Education: Dartmouth College, University of Oxford
   Background: Principal, Atlas Venture; Consultant, The Boston Consulting Group
   Jeff Silverman, Co-Founder
   Education: BS, Management, MIT
   Background: Vice-Chairman, National Securites Studies, Israel

71 AGRIBUSINESS MANAGEMENT COMPANY
One Burlington Place
1004 Farnam Street
Omaha, NE 68102

Phone: 402-444-1630 **Fax:** 402-930-3066
Toll-Free: 800-283-2357
web: burlingtoncapital.com

Mission Statement: The Burlington International Agribusiness Management Company is a global private equity fund focused on agribusiness and ancillary businesses.
Geographic Preference: Former Soviet Union, Eastern European
Fund Size: $100 million
Founded: 1995
Average Investment: $5 - 25 million
Minimum Investment: $5 million
Investment Criteria: Startup, First Stage, Consolidations, Privatizations
Industry Group Preference: Food Services, Food & Beverage, Distribution, Renewable Resources, Agriculture
Portfolio Companies: Rasko, FoodMaster, Bagrationi, Chicken Kingdom, Acodec, KLP, Polygraph, Saint Springs
Key Executives:
   Michael Yanney, Chairman Emeritus
   Education: Graduate, University of Nebraska; University of Wisconsin
   Background: Management, Valmont; EVP/Treasurer, Omaha National Bank; Omaha National Coarporation
   Directorships: Burlington Northern Santa Fe Corporation; Level 3 Communications

Venture Capital & Private Equity Firms / Domestic Firms

Brad Muse, Vice President of Finance
Education: BSc, Accounting, Indiana State University
Background: Financial Planning and Analysis; ConAgra Foods; Coopers & Lybrand LLP
Lisa Y. Roskens, Chief Executive Officer
Education: Stanford Law School
Background: Twin Compass, LLC; Business Development, Inacom Corporation; Finance Director, US Senate Campaign of Senator Chuck Hagel
Directorships: Cantera Partners, LLC
George Krauss, Managing Director
Education: JD, MA, Business Admin., University of Nebraska
Background: Partner, Kutak Rock
Directorships: Chairman, MFA Mortgage Investment Inc.; Core Bank; Omaha State Bank; Gateway Inc.; West Corp.; First Apartment Investors Inc.; InfoGROUP Inc.

72 AHOY CAPITAL
530 Lytton Avenue
2nd Floor
Palo Alto, CA 94301

web: www.ahoycap.com

Mission Statement: Ahoy Capital is focused on investing in both early-stage venture capital and start-up companies. They seek opportunities in the application of disruptive technologies and ideas that will have profound effects on the ways in which people live and work.

Founded: 2018

Key Executives:
Chris Douvos, Founder/Managing Director
Education: BA, Yale College; MBA, Yale School of Management
Background: Venture Investment Associates; Consultant, Monitor Company
Cliff Gilman, Managing Director
Education: AB, Duke University; MBA, Dartmouth College
Background: Prime Buchholz & Associates; Associate VP/Founding Member, Merrill Lynch Private Equity Partners LP

73 AIRBUS VENTURES
Menlo Park, CA

Mission Statement: Airbus Ventures invests in early and growth-stage companies, acting as lead investors for new and fast-accelerating technologies that will reshape aerospace.

Key Executives:
Thomas D'Halluin, Managing Partner
Education: MS, McGill University
Background: COO, Airbus Ventures; Chief of Staff, Airbus Vetures

74 AISLING CAPITAL
888 Seventh Avenue
12th Floor
New York, NY 10106

Phone: 212-651-6380 **Fax:** 212-651-6379
web: www.aislingcapital.com

Mission Statement: Aisling Capital is a leading investment firm that advises investment funds that invest in products, technologies and global businesses that advance health.

Average Investment: $20 - $50 million
Industry Group Preference: Healthcare, Life Sciences, Therapeutics, Biotechnology
Portfolio Companies: Aclaris Therapeutics, Adams Respiratory Therapeutics, Adma Biologics Inc., Advion, Agile Therapeutics, Aimune Therapeutics, Ajax Health, Allos Therapeutics, Admbit, Aragon Pharmaceuticals, Archimica, Arcus Biosciences, Armgo Pharma Inc., Ascendis Pharma, Aton Pharma, Audentes, Auxilum, Avanza Laboratories, Axcan Pharma, Barried Therapeutics Inc., Bioenvision, BioHaven Pharmaceuticals, Bridgebio, Cardiokine Biopharma, Catalent, Cempra, Chimerix, Cidara Therapeutics, Clovis Oncology, CollaGenex Pharmaceuticals, Colorescience, Cynapsus, Cytos, Dermira, Durata, Earlens, Esperion Therapeutics, F2G, Globalblood Therapeutics, GTx, Imbruvica, Infinity, Intercept, Intersent Ent., Lensar, Lombard Medical, Loxo Oncology, Map Pharmaceuticals, MEI Pharma, Menlo Therpeutics, Miramarlabs, Myogen, Next Wave, Novazyme Pharmaceuticals, Obseva, Oculex Pharmaceuticals, Paratek, Pernix Therapeutics, Pharmaron, Planet Biopharmaceuticals Inc., Powervision, Precision Dermatology, Prolacta Bioscience, Promentis Pharmaceuticals Inc., Proragonist Therapeutics, Quintiles, Roka Bioscience, Seragon Pharmaceuticals, SIrion Therapeutics, SkinMedica, Sorrento, Spirox, Sunesis, Synergy, Syros, T2Biosystems, Topaz, TransEnterix, Tria, Verona Pharma, Versartis, ViewRay, Vivus, Zavante, Zeltiq

Key Executives:
Dennis Purcell, Founder
Education: BS, Accounting, University of Delaware; MBA, Harvard University
Background: Managing Director, Life Sciences Investment Banking Group, Chase H&Q
Directorships: Dynova Laboratories, Xanodyne Pharmaceuticals
Steven A. Elms, Managing Partner
Education: BA, Human Biology, Stanford University; MBA, Kellogg Graduate School of Management
Background: Principal, Life Sciences Investment Banking Group, Hambrecht & Quist; Donaldson Lufkin & Jenrette
Directorships: ADMA Biologics, Advion BioSciences, Ambit Biosciences Corporation, CeNeRx, BioPharma, LensAR, Next Wave Pharmaceuticals, Pernix Therapeutics, Scerene Healthcare
Andrew Schiff, MD, Managing Partner
Education: BS, Neuroscience, Brown University; MD, Cornell University Medical College; MBA, Columbia University
Background: Internal Medicine, New York Presbyterian Hospital
Directorships: ARMGO Pharma, Dynova Laboratories, Planet Technologies, SkinMedica, TransEnterix, Zeltiq Aestetics
Robert J. Wenzel, Chief Financial Officer
Education: BBA, Accounting, Baruch College
Background: Controller, Aisling Capital; Vice President, Lazard Alternative Investments; Eisner & Lubin LLP
JH Bilenker, MD, Operating Partner
Education: BA, English, Princeton; MD, John Hopkins School of Medicine
Background: President/CEO, Loxo Oncology; Medical Officer, Office of Oncology Drug Products, US Foods and Drug Administration
Directorships: Loxo Oncology; LENSAR; Roka Biosciences; T2 Biosystems; ViewRay; Aragon Pharmaceuticals
Eric Aguitar, MD, Partner
Education: MD, Harvard Medical School; Cornell University
Background: Partner, Thomas, Mcnerney and Partners; CEO, Genovo Inc.
Directorships: HealthCare Ventures
Aftab R. Kherani, MD, Operating Partner
Education: BS, Biology, AB, Economics, MD, Duke University
Background: Engagement Manager, McKinsey & Company
Stacey D. Seltzer, Partner
Education: BS, MS, Yale University; MBA, The Wharton School
Background: Business Development, Schering-Plough
Directorships: Miramar Labs, Precision Dermatology

Venture Capital & Private Equity Firms / Domestic Firms

75 AKERS CAPITAL LLC
8436 Marina Vista
Fair Oaks, CA 95628

Phone: 916-966-2236
web: akerscapital.com

Mission Statement: The firm invests in underserved markets in California and the Northwestern US in technology based investment capital in IT, medical devices, and biotechnology.

Geographic Preference: California, Northwest
Founded: 1999
Average Investment: $3 million
Minimum Investment: $1 million
Investment Criteria: First Stage, Second Stage
Industry Group Preference: Computer Hardware & Software, Wireless Technologies, Electronic Components, Internet Technology, Chemicals, Telecommunications, Networking
Portfolio Companies: Telemetric Corporation, CustomerLink Systems Inc., IP Infusion, Inc.

Key Executives:
Roger Akers, Managing Partner
Education: CPA; MA, Business Admin
Background: Prodata Inc.
Directorships: Golden State Capital Network; Emerging Technology Institute; University of California Connect

76 ALACRITY VENTURES
Berkeley, CA 94707

Phone: 510-649-4030
e-mail: alacrity@alacrityventures.com
web: www.alacritymanagement.com

Mission Statement: Alacrity Ventures is an angel capital investment firm. Its main purpose is to fund and guide start-up companies through initial stages of development, offering seed financing and mentorship. Alacrity is primarily oriented toward working with Internet and technological companies with new and innovative ideas. Alacrity's goal is to identify people with a passion to create ground-breaking high-tech firms and to help them achieve success in building those businesses.

Investment Criteria: Seed-Stage, Startup
Industry Group Preference: Internet, High Technology

Key Executives:
Christopher Allen, Founder
Background: Chief Technology Officer, Certicom Corp; Founder, Concensus Development; Founder, Associated Computer Consultants

77 ALANTRA
75 State Street
Suite 1210
Boston, MA 02109

Phone: 617-482-6200
web: www.alantra.com

Mission Statement: To provide M&A services to mid-market family-ownded companies, mid-cap corporate and private equity investors.

Geographic Preference: Worldwide
Fund Size: $1 billion
Founded: 1975
Minimum Investment: $250,000
Investment Criteria: First stage, Second stage, Mezzanine, Corporate Acquisition, Divestiture, Capital Raising Services
Industry Group Preference: Aerospace, Defense and Government, Automotive, Business Products & Services, Consumer Products, Retail, Consumer & Leisure, Retailing, Food & Beverage, Healthcare, Material Handling, Logistics
Portfolio Companies: Adval Tech, Akta US LLC, Arneg SPA, Bruce Foods Corporation, C-4 Analytics, Centrax, conditorei Coppenrath & Wiese GmbH & Co., CHT Group, Crane & Co., Dearborn Mid-West Conveyor Company, Educational Holdings LLC, Equita GmbH & Co. Holdings, Flavor Infusion LLC, Fleetwood, FORTE Industrial Equipment Systems, Fortress, Freudenberg, Greencore Group Plc, Group Uriach, GSI Group Inc., HitecVision AS, HypothenkenZentrum AG, JacquelineBs Gourmet Cookies, Kaydon Corp., KRG Capital Partners, Landshire Inc., Leggett & Platt Incorporated, Lycored, Lydall Inc., Novozymes AS, Nutragenesis, PAS International Holdings, Pietro Rosa TBM, ProTec, Prudential Capital Group, RFE Investment Partners, Rogers Corporation, RTS Holdings Inc., Seabrook International, Smith Co., Superior Controls, TeraDiode, Trescal

Other Locations:
6 Rue Lamennais
Paris 75008
France
Phone: 33 (0) 1-70-91-35-70

6 Mount Street Upper
Grand Canal Dock
Dublin 2 D02 VF44
Ireland
Phone: 353-1-662-0175

77 Queen Victoria Street
2nd Floor
London EC4V 4AY
United Kingdom
Phone: 44 (0)20-7246-0500

Taunusanlage 15
Frankfurt 60325
Germany
Phone: 49 (0)69-977-886-0

Unit 2608, United Plaza
No. 1468 Nanjing West Road
Shanghai 200040
China
Phone: 86-21-68818870

Calle de José Ortega Y Gasset, 29
Madrid 28006
Spain
Phone: 34-91-745-84-84

Stockerstrasse 47
Zurich 8002
Switzerland
Phone: 41-44-552-50-50

Via Borgonuovo 16
Milan 20121
Italy
Phone: 39-02-6367-1601

Paseo de la Reforma 115
Lomas de Chapultepec
Mexico City
Mexico
Phone: 525580007209

Museumplein 11
Amsterdam 1071DJ
Netherlands
Phone: 31-20-305-11-30

Albertgasse 35
Vienna 1080
Austria
Phone: 43 717 28 990

Vasta Tradgardsgatan 15
Stockholm 111 53
Sweden
Phone: 46-705-086-725

Akadimias 35
Athens 106 72
Greece
Phone: 30-210-33-87-140

Rua Duque de Palmela 25
6th Floor

31

Venture Capital & Private Equity Firms / Domestic Firms

Lisbon 1250-097
Portugal
Phone: 351-211522282

Coronel Diaz 2857
Buenos Aires
Argentina
Phone: 54 (11)5218-0030
Key Executives:
  R. Wade Aust, Managing Partner
Education: BA, Finance & Mathematics, Salve Regina University; CFA
  Joseph J. Downing Jr., Managing Partner
Education: BA, Business Management/Finance, Boston University; MBA, University of Aalborg
  Paul A. Colone, Managing Partner
Education: BA, Economics, Boston College; MSc, International Securities Investment, University of Reading

78 ALBION INVESTORS LLC
501 Madison Avenue
Suite 701
New York, NY 10022
    Phone: 212-277-7520
    e-mail: cgonzalez@albioninvestors.com
    web: www.albioninvestors.com

Mission Statement: Seeks to provide mezzanine and private equity capital to attractive middle market companies to facilitate events such as leveraged acquisitions, refinancing/recapitalizations or growth capital requirements.
Geographic Preference: Northeastern, Mid-Atlantic & Southeastern United States
Fund Size: $170 million
Founded: 1996
Average Investment: $15 million
Minimum Investment: $2 million
Investment Criteria: Differentiated Products/Services, Solid Customer Base, Located in the Continental United States, Consistent Operating & Financial Performance
Industry Group Preference: Business Products & Services, Value-Added Distribution, Specialty Manufacturing, Consumer Products
Portfolio Companies: ARTONE Manufacturing, Addison McKee, Rimrock, S.I. Jacobson
Key Executives:
  Mark Arnold, Managing Partner
  212-277-7527
  e-mail: marnold@albioninvestors.com
Education: London University; Fellow, Institute of Actuaries
Background: Partner/COO, BEA Associates; Co-Founder, Albion Asset Advisors
Directorships: Rimrock Corporation; North American Propane, Inc.
  Alastair Tedford, Managing Partner
  212-277-7525
  e-mail: atedford@albioninvestors.com
Education: MBA, INSEAD; MA Law, University College
Background: Co-Founder, Albion Asset Advisors; Co-Head Emerging Market, Goldman Sachs
Directorships: Salomon Brothers
  Charles Gonzalez, Managing Director
  212-277-7537
  e-mail: cgonzalez@albioninvestors.com
Education: BS Finance/Economics, University of Illinois; MBA, University of Chicago
Background: Management, Continental Bank; Management, Bank of America; Managing Director, Banc of America Securities
Directorships: Associated Packaging Technologies; Wood Resources; AddisonMckee; ShelterLogic
  Basil Livanos, Managing Director
  212-277-7524
  e-mail: blivanos@albioninvestors.com
Education: BS Banking/Finance/International Business, MBA Finance, New York University
Background: Management, ACFG; Investments, Equitable
  Christine Vogt, Vice President
  212-277-7521
  e-mail: cvogt@albioninvestors.com
Education: BS, Finance, Villanova University
Background: The Blackstone Group, LP
  Edina Leiher, VP of Operations/Chief Compliance Officer
Education: BS/MPA, Policy Analysis, Marxe School of Public and International Affairs, Bernard M Baruch College

79 ALBUM VC
3451 N Trimpuh Boulevard
Suite 200
Lehi, UT 84043
    e-mail: hello@album.vc
    web: album.vc

Mission Statement: Formerly known as Peak Ventures, the firm focuses on investing in and growing innovative seed-stage companies in Utah and the West Coast through two funds, with a third in progress.
Geographic Preference: Utah, West Coast
Fund Size: $75 million
Founded: 2019
Investment Criteria: Seed Stage
Industry Group Preference: Technology, E-Commerce & Manufacturing, Mobile, Retail, Consumer & Leisure, SaaS, Real Estate Technology, Video Gaming
Portfolio Companies: Andela, BallerTV, Beynd, Bluestar.com, Cake, ClearVoice, ClientSuccess, Consensus, Converus, Degreed, Divvy, EquitySim, Filevine, GrassWire, Homie, Jolt, Lendio, Liingo Eyewear, MarketWare, Mighty, Molio, Mosyle, MX, Nav, Neighbor, ObservePoint, Omadi, Owlet, Pet IQ, PierianDx, Pillow, Podium, Prenda, Pronto, Qwick, Route, SalesRabbit, SaltStack, Spiff, Strala, Studio, TaxBit, Teem, Weave, Wooly, Zipbooks
Key Executives:
  Sid Krommenhoek, Partner
Education: BS, Brigham Young University; University of Utah
Background: Managing Partner, Peak Ventures; Co-Founder, Zinch; Adjunct Professor of Entrepreneurship, Brigham Young University; Advisor, Braid Workshop; Partner, HKK Marketing; Director, Sales, Dealstreet; Founder, Soft Spot
Directorships: Podium, BallerTV, Jolt, Cake, ClientSuccess, EquitySim, SalesRabbit, Marketware, CampusLogic, Consensus,
  John Mayfield, Partner
Education: BS, MBA, Brigham Young University
Background: Partner, Peak Ventures; Sales, Instructure; Marketing, Qualtrics; Senior Associate, Duff & Phelps; Associate, Peterson Ventures; Operations, Innovasis
Directorships: Filevine, Route, Qwick, Neighbor, ZipBooks, Wooly, Consensus, ClearVoice,
  Diogo Myrrha, Partner
Education: BEcon, Brigham Young University
Background: Principal, Peak Ventures; Vice President, Stoneway Capital; Co-Founder, Finance, Operations, Luvaire; Special Projects, Braven
Directorships: Huckabuy, Beynd, TaxBit, Spiff, BlueStar Inspections, Mosyle, SalesRabbit,

80 ALERION PARTNERS
23 Old Kings Highway South
Darien, CT 06820
    Phone: 203-202-9900
    e-mail: info@alerionpartners.com
    web: www.alerionpartners.com

Venture Capital & Private Equity Firms / Domestic Firms

Mission Statement: Alerion's investment professional team offers financial and operating expertise to help accelerate the development of companies.
Founded: 2004
Average Investment: $3 - $10 million
Industry Group Preference: Consumer Products, Business Products & Services, Marketing, Media
Portfolio Companies: DeliverCareRx, EnviroScent, HydroMassage, InStadium, True Citrus
Key Executives:
  Bruce F Failing, Managing Partner
  e-mail: failing@alerionpartners.com
  Education: BA, Tufts University; MBA, Harvard Business School
  Background: Productivity Solutions Inc.; Actmedia; Lamaze Publishing Company; Newborn Channel; Tone Brothers; Spice Company; ERS International
  Directorships: EnviroScent, InStadium, HydroMassage, DeliverCareRx
  Michael B Persky, Managing Partner
  e-mail: persky@alerionpartners.com
  Education: BA, Economics and Organizational Behavior and Management, Brown University; MBA, Stanford Graduate School of Business
  Background: President & COO, Productivity Solutions; President & COO, ERS International; VP, Marketing, Executone Information Systems; VMX
  Directorships: EnviroScent, True Citrus, InStadium, HydroMassage, DeliverCareRx
  Robert Cioffi, Venture Partner
  e-mail: cioffi@alerionpartners.com
  Education: BA, Political Science & Economics, University of Vermont; MBA, Fuqua School of Business, Duke University
  Background: Senior VP, GE Equity; Evaluation Associates Capital Markets; Chase Manhattan; Staff, US Senator James M Jeffords
  Virginia Cargill, Venture Partner
  e-mail: cargill@alerionpartners.com
  Education: BA, Wellesley College; MBA, Kellogg School of Management, Northwestern University
  Background: President & CEO, CBS Outernet; Co-Founder, Caring Today; President, Lamaze Publishing; Actmedia; General Mills; Procter & Gamble
  Sayles Braga, Partner
  e-mail: braga@alerionpartners.com
  Education: BA, Economics, Harvard University
  Background: CEO, ABD3; Restructuring Group, Lazard
  Directorships: EnviroScent, True Citrus, InStadium, DeliverCareRx
  Nissa Bartalsky, Manager
  e-mail: bartalsky@alerionpartners.com
  Education: BA, Neuroscience, Mount Holyoke College; MBA, School of Business, University of Connecticut
  Rick Ruffolo, Venture Partner
  e-mail: rruffolo@enviroscent.com
  Education: BS, Business Administration, University Of Dayton; MBA From Olin School of Business at Washington University, St. Louis
  Background: CEO, Enviroscent; SC Johnson; Bath & Body Works; Yankee Candle; Crabtree & Evelyn

81 ALEUTIAN CAPITAL PARTNERS
100 Wall Street
Suite 900
New York, NY 10005

Phone: 212-652-4000 Fax: 212-652-4030
e-mail: info@aleutiancapital.com
web: www.aleutiancapital.com

Mission Statement: Aleutian Capital Partners is a private equity investment group that invests in and acquires privately-owned companies in North America and internationally.
Geographic Preference: North America
Industry Group Preference: Manufacturing, Distribution, Business Products & Services, Medical Devices, Aerospace, Defense and Government, Security, Consumer Products, Information Technology, Logistics, Transportation
Portfolio Companies: Rev H20, Global Sugar Art, Amtech Corporation
  Daniel Pfeffer, Managing Director
  Education: BA, University of Colorado, Boulder; MBA, University of Colorado, Denver
  Background: President/cEO, Lighting By Gregory; Senior Manager, Linkshare Corporation

82 ALEXANDER HUTTON
Raineier Towerue
Suite 3405
1301 Fifth Avenue
Seattle, WA 98101

Phone: 206-341-9800
e-mail: info@alexanderhutton.com
web: alexanderhutton.com

Mission Statement: Focuses on investments in technology companies in the areas of IT, Internet, telecommunications, medical services and healthcare infrastructure, particularly in business-to-business Internet space. Actively seeking new projects.
Geographic Preference: Northwest
Founded: 1999
Investment Criteria: All Stages, Seed, First Stage, Second Stage
Industry Group Preference: Business to Business, Communications Equipment, Computer Hardware & Software, Transportation, Electronic Components, Healthcare, Internet Technology, Manufacturing, Telecommunications, Networking, Online Content
Portfolio Companies: Madrona Solutions Group, Rite In The Rain, Damar Aerosystems, Olympic Physical Therapy
Key Executives:
  Scott Hardman, Managing Director
  Education: MBA, University of Washington
  Kent Johnson, Managing Director
  Education: BA, University of Washington; MBA, Seattle University

83 ALIGNED PARTNERS
2882 Sand Hill Rd.
Suite 100
Menlo Park, CA 94025

e-mail: info@alignedvc.com
web: www.alignedvc.com

Mission Statement: Aligned Partners believes in aligning the interests of founders and investors to generate high returns and sustainable growth.
Investment Criteria: Early-Stage, Series A
Industry Group Preference: Information Technology
Key Executives:
  Jodi Sherman Jahic, Managing Partner
  Education: Pomona College; MBA, Kellogg School of Management
  Background: Voyager Capital; SCG
  Susan Mason, Managing Partner
  Education: BS, University of Colorado; MBA, University of California, LA
  Background: ONSET Ventures

Venture Capital & Private Equity Firms / Domestic Firms

84 ALLEGIS CYBER CAPITAL
200 Page Mill Road
Suite 100
Palo Alto, CA 94306

e-mail: businessplans@allegiscyber.com
web: www.allegiscyber.com

Mission Statement: Invests in early-stage startup companies developing enabling technology and infrastructure which serve emerging information technology markets. Allegis Cyber Capital is currently seeking new investments with the following criteria: visionary founders and winning managers, compelling products and technologies, ROI potential and realistic exit strategies.

Geographic Preference: West Coast, North America, Western Europe
Fund Size: $500 million
Founded: 1996
Average Investment: $3 - $5 million
Minimum Investment: $50,000
Investment Criteria: Seed, Early-Stage, Startup
Industry Group Preference: Enabling Technology, Infrastructure, Enterprise Services, Software, Broadband, Service Industries, Wireless Technologies, Internet Technology
Portfolio Companies: Area 1, Bracket Computing, Callsign, CyberGRX, Dragos Inc., E8 Security, eFileCabinet, Ironport, Lucidworks, Moki, Platfora, RedOwl Analytics, Shape Security, Signifyd, Solera Networks, Symplified, Synack, vArmour, SafeGuard Cyber, Source Defence, Prevailion

Other Locations:
8110 Maple Lawn Boulevard
Suite 200
Fulton, MD 20759

Key Executives:
Robert R. Ackerman, Jr., Founder/Managing Director
e-mail: ackerman@allegiscapital.com
Education: BS Computer Science, University of California
Background: Manager, Ackerman Group; CEO, UniSoft Corporation; Founder/Chairman, InfoGear Technology Corporation
Directorships: IronPort Systems, RFco
Spencer Tall, Managing Director
Education: BS Political Science/Japanese, Brigham Young University
Background: Co-Founder/General Partner, APV Technology Partners; Strategic Advsior: Motorola, Sony, Fujitsu, Samsung, Canon, TDK, Dacom; US Sales Operations, Marubeni Corporation; Sales Manager, GRE America
Directorships: IMVU; Allegiance; Solera Networks; Symplified
Peter Bodine, Managing Director
Education: MBA, University of Utah; BS, Brigham Young University
Background: Co-Founder, APV Technology Partners; Asia Pacific Ventures
Directorships: AdventureLink; Axcient; iBAHN; iPass
Steve Simonian, Chief Financial/Compliance Officer
Education: BA, Business Economics, University of California, Santa Barbara
Background: CFO, August Capital; CFO, Gabriel Venture Partners; CFO, Meritech Capital Partners

85 ALLIANCE OF ANGELS
719 Second Avenue
Suite 1403
Seattle, WA 98104

e-mail: aoa@allianceofangels.com
web: www.allianceofangels.com

Mission Statement: The Alliance of Angels is one of the largest and most active angel groups in the Pacific Northwest.
Geographic Preference: Pacific Northwest
Founded: 1997
Industry Group Preference: Clean Technology, Information Technology, Life Sciences, Consumer Products, Consumer Services
Portfolio Companies: 1000 Museums, Accium Biosciences, ADAPX, Airbiquity, Amnis, Ansyr, AppAttach, Apptentive, Array Health, Athleon, Balance, Banshee Bungee, Battlefly, Bidadoo Auctions, Blade, Buddy, BuddyTV, Cadence Biomedical, Cardiometrics, Celilo Group Media, Centri Technology, Chelsey Henry, Claim-Maps, Clairsonic, ClarityHealth, Cleverset, Clover, Conenza, Cordance, CourtLink, Crowd Compass, CultureMob, Daptiv, DashWire, Deep Domain, Delve Networks, Dendreon, Dentigenix, DigitalScirocco, DocuSign, Dry Soda Co., Earth Class Mail, Elemental, EnRoute, Entomo, Escapia.com, Esately, Estorian, Every Move, FluxDrive, Food.ee, Full Circle, GenPrime, GeoPage, Geospiza, Giftspot, Globesherpa, Healionics, HomeGrocer.com, iclick, Illumingen, ImageX, Impel Neuropharma, Infomove, Insitu, InSpa, Intelsoft Technologies, Intelligent ION, Julep, Lagotek, Limeade, LiquidPlanner, Livebid.com, Lumencor, Madfiber, MagicWheels, Mailchannels, Marketfish, Marketsync, Mercent, Meteor, Metron Systems, MicroGreen Polymers, Mirador Biomedical, MobiSante, Mobliss, Modumetal, Moprise, Movaya, Mporai, Neah, Nfluence, Novinium, Nuun, Onehub, OraHealth, Others Online, Overcast Media, PakSense, Pathable, PeopleMatter, Perlego, Pharmitas, Photobucket, Pier Systems, POW, PowerTech, Prepared Response, Protelus, Revel Body, Sash, ScaleOut Software, Scayl, Seattle Sensor Systems, Shelfari, Shiftboard, Signature Destinations, Skycast, Snapin, SnapNames, StressWave, Sunstream Boat Lifts, TalentSpring, Tatango, Teachtown,

Key Executives:
Yi-Jian Ngo, Managing Director
Education: MBA, Johnson Graduate School of Management, Cornell University
Background: Founding Team Member, AT&T Corporate Venture Fund; Sierra Ventures

86 ALLOS VENTURES
6340 Westfield Boulevard
Indianapolis, IN 46220

Phone: 317-275-6800
web: www.allosventures.com

Mission Statement: Allos Ventures invests in early-stage companies, executing a hands-on approach with their clients.
Geographic Preference: Indiana, Michigan, Ohio
Founded: 2010
Investment Criteria: Early-Stage
Industry Group Preference: Software, Technology-Enabled Business, Specialty Healthcare, Medical Devices, Diagnostics, Advanced Manufacturing
Portfolio Companies: 7signal, Alung, Aprimo, Assure X Health, BidPal, Blue Pillar, Bolstra, Change Dynamix, Cordata, Dattus, Emplify, Enosix, Foxtrot Code, Fuzic, Healthcare Asset Network, Lessonly, Life Share Technologies, Lumavate, Octiv, Peach Works, Scale Computing, Vendor Registry, WebLink International

Other Locations:
2724 Erie Avenue
Suite 200
Cincinnati, OH 45280
Phone: 513-723-2309

Key Executives:
Dan Aquilano, Managing Director
317-275-6802
Education: BS, Arizona University; MBA, Harvard University
Background: Boston Consulting Group; Fox Group; Gazelle TechVentures

John McIlwraith, Managing Director
513-723-2311
Education: BA, Hillsdale College; JD, Case Western Reserve University
Background: Corporate Lawyer, Jones Day; Quantum Health Resources; Blue Chip Venture Company; Gazelle TechVentures

87 ALLOY VENTURES
1415 Hamilton Avenue
Palo Alto, CA 94301

web: www.alloyventures.com

Mission Statement: Seeks matches between emerging technologies with emerging market opportunities and looks for companies with the potential to achieve a large market capitalization and address a large and growing market. Each year Alloy invests in a small number of entrepreneurial ideas and young companies and strive to achieve long-term relationships.

Geographic Preference: Western United States
Fund Size: $370 million
Founded: 1977
Average Investment: $1 - $5 million
Minimum Investment: $50,000
Investment Criteria: Seed, Early-Stage, Later-Stage
Industry Group Preference: Information Technology, Life Sciences, Bioinformatics, Health Related, Energy, Clean Technology
Portfolio Companies: Aegea Medical, Agari, AnaptysBio, Apptera, Cambrios, CoAlign Innovations, Cortina, Ensenda, Genomatica, The GigaOM Network, Gradient, Hightail, KaloBios, KFx Medical, Labcyte Inc., Mavenir Systems, Molecular Imprints, Novasys Medical, NuGEN Technologies, Optimedica, Pacific Biosciences, RainDance Technologies, Restoration Robotics, Scifiniti, Siluria Technologies, SynergEyes, Teradici, Xactly

Key Executives:

Ammar H. Hanafi, General Partner
e-mail: ahanafi@alloyventures.com
Education: BS Applied/Engineering Physics, Cornell University; MBA, Stanford University
Background: VP New Business Ventures, Cisco Systems; PanAmSat Corporation; Morgan Stanley; Donaldson Lufkin & Jenrette
Directorships: YouSENDit, Retrevo, Mavenir Systems, Cortina Systems, GigaOM, Infineta Systems, Apptera

Michael Hunkapiller, General Partner
e-mail: mwhunk@alloyventures.com
Education: BS, Oklahoma Baptist University; PhD, California Institute of Technology
Background: President/General Manager, Applied Biosystems; Founder, Celera Genomics; Sr VP, Applera Corporation; Senior Research Fellow Biology, California Institute of Technology; Author of more than 100 scientific publications; Patentholder
Directorships: Pacific Biosciences, NuGEN, Verinata Health, RainDance Technologies

Doug Kelly MD, General Partner
e-mail: doug@alloyventures.com
Education: BA, Biochemistry/Molecular Biology, University of California, San Diego; MD, Albert Einstein College of Medicine; MBA, Stanford University
Background: Ligand Pharmaceuticals; Independent Consultant
Directorships: Aegea, Barrx, CoAlign Innovations, Crux Biomedical, Novasys, Restoration Robotics

Daniel I. Rubin, General Partner
e-mail: dan@alloyventures.com
Education: BA Physics, Pomona College
Background: Co-Founder, Artisan Components; Director Product Marketing/Managing Director, Ultratech Stepper
Directorships: CiraNova, Ensenda, Molecular Imprints, Gradient, Teradici, Integrated PhotoVoltaics

John F. Shoch, General Partner
e-mail: shoch@alloyventures.com
Education: BA Political Science, MS, PhD Computer Science, Stanford University
Background: President, Xerox Office Systems Division; CEO, Xerox; Founding Investor, Conductus and Remedy
Directorships: Knowledge Networks, Nitronex, ViVOtech, Xangati

Craig C. Taylor, General Partner
650-687-5000
Fax: 650-687-5010
e-mail: craig@alloyventures.com
Education: BS, MS Physics, Brown University; MBA, Stanford University
Background: Office of Technology Licensing, Stanford University
Directorships: ForteBio, Labcyte, Optimedica, Zyomyx, KFx Medical

Tony Di Bona, General Partner/CFO
e-mail: tony@alloyventures.com
Education: BS, Psychology & Biology, Rice University; MD, University of Texas Health Science Center
Background: Founder, Affymax NV; Founder, FluMist

David W. Pidwell, Venture Partner
e-mail: pidwell@alloyventures.com
Education: MS, Computer System Engineering, Ohio State University; 3 years on PhD in Engineering Economic Systems, Stanford University
Background: Founder/President/CEO, Rasna Corporation; ROLM
Directorships: Rainfinity, iPrint Systems, Informatica

J. Leighton Read, MD, Venture Partner
e-mail: leighton@alloyventures.com
Education: BS, Psychology & Biology, Rice University; MD, University of Texas Health Science Center
Background: Co-Founder, Affymax NV; Founder/Chairman/CEO, Aviron; Partner, Interhealth Limited; Peter Bent Brigham Hospital
Directorships: Avidia Research Institute

88 ALLSTATE INVESTMENTS LLC
3075 Sanders Road
Suite G5D
Northbrook, IL 60062

web: www.allstateinvestments.com

Mission Statement: Allstate Investment is a private equity, real estate, and mezzanine funds firm.

Geographic Preference: United States
Fund Size: $200 million
Founded: 2000
Average Investment: $50 million
Minimum Investment: $10 million
Investment Criteria: Mezzanine, Consolidations, Acquisition, LBO, MBO, Recapitalization, Privatizations
Industry Group Preference: Broadcasting, Cable, Radio, Communications Equipment, Diversified, Education, Electronic Components, Financial Services, Industrial Equipment, Manufacturing, Chemicals, Publishing, Wholesale, Advertising, Distribution

Other Locations:
444 W Lake Street
45th Floor
Chicago, IL 60606

36 Broadway
London SW1H 0BH
United Kingdom

Key Executives:

Peter Keehn, Managing Director, Private Equity
e-mail: pkeehn@allstate.com
Education: AB, Brown University; MBA, Northwestern University
Background: Pricinpal, Waud Capital Partners

Venture Capital & Private Equity Firms / Domestic Firms

Directorships: Northwestern Investment Management Company
John Dugenske, President, Investments & Financial Products
Education: BA, MA, Mechanical Engineering, MBA, University of Illinois
Background: UBS Asset Management; Neuberger Berman; Deutsche Asset Management; Portfolio Manager, NISA Investment Advisors
Russ Mayerfeld, Senior Managing Director, Alternative Investments
Education: BA, University of Illinois; MBA, Harvard University
Background: UBS LLC; Dean Witter Reynolds Inc.
Scott McConnell, Chief Information Officer
Education: BS, Business Admin., Miami University; MBA, University of Chicago Booth School of Business
Background: Technology & Operations, Alltstate; Accenture

89 ALMAZ CAPITAL
3274 Alpine Road
Portola Valley, CA 94028

Phone: 650-644-4530
e-mail: press@almazcapital.com
web: www.almazcapital.com

Mission Statement: Almaz Capital Partners is one of the leading venture capital firms serving entrepreneurs and companies with ties to Russia and the Commonwealth of Independent States (CIS).
Geographic Preference: United States, Russia
Fund Size: $170 million
Founded: 2008
Industry Group Preference: Technology, Digital Media & Marketing, Communications, Internet, Data Storage, Enterprise Software, E-Commerce & Manufacturing
Portfolio Companies: 2can, Acronis, Acumatica, Alawar Entertainment, AlterGeo, AppScotch, CarPrice, Cinarra Systems, Content Analytics, Dabbl, Fasten, FinalPrice, Flirtic, GoodData, GridGain, Hover, If You Can, Jelastic, MakeTime, Mobalytics, NFWare, Nival, nScaled, Odin, Parallels, Petcube, PIQ, Plesk, Qik, Sensity, StarWind Software, Vyatta, Yandex
Key Executives:
  Alexander Galitsky, Co-Founder/Managing Partner
  Education: PhD, Computer Science, Defense Research Institute, Moscow Institute of Physics
  Background: Russian Technologies, Soviet Space Agency and Defense Industry
  Charles E. Ryan, General Partner
  Education: Harvard College
  Background: Chairman, UFG Asset Management; Senior Advisor, Deutsche Bank AG; Associate/Principal Banker, European Bank for Reconstruction and Development; Co-Founder, United Financial Group; Chief Country Officer/CEO, Deutsche Bank Group
  Pavel Bogdanov, General Partner
  Education: BS, Moscow Institute of Physics; MBA, INSEAD; PhD, Stanford University
  Background: Partner, Russian Technologies; Systems Design Engineer, KLA-Tencor
  Directorships: Investment Director, Sistema Telecom
  Geoffrey Baehr, General Partner
  Education: BA, Biochemistry & Natural Sciences, Fordham University
  Background: General Partner, US Venture Partners; Chief Network Officer, Sun Microsystems

90 ALPHA CAPITAL PARTNERS
Chicago, IL 60601

Phone: 312-322-9800
e-mail: info@alphacapital.com
web: www.alphacapital.com

Mission Statement: Actively seeking investments. Provides equity financing for promising growth businesses and for buyouts or recapitalizations of established companies; targets promising young companies with a commercially developed product needing financing primarily for marketing and business expansion.
Geographic Preference: Midwest United States
Fund Size: $90 million
Founded: 1984
Average Investment: $2 - 15 million
Minimum Investment: $500,000
Investment Criteria: Middle-market companies with current run rate revenues of at least $5 million; Buyouts, Recapitalizations, Acquisitions, Expansion, Late-Stage, Growth Stage
Industry Group Preference: Manufacturing, Industrial Distribution, Consumer Products, Consumer Services, Financial Services, Communications, Information Technology, Health Related
Portfolio Companies: America's PowerSports, Emerald BioAgricultre Corp., Factory Connection, NM Group Global LLC
Key Executives:
  Andrew H Kalnow, President
  e-mail: ahkalnow@alphacapital.com
  Education: BA, Lawrence University; MBA, Babson College
  Background: VP, First National Bank of Chicago; VP, First Chicago; CEO, National Machinery LLC; CEO, NM Group Global LLC

91 ALPHA VENTURE PARTNERS
1 Penn Plaza
Suite 3905
New York, NY 10119

Phone: 212-967-3332
web: alphavp.com

Mission Statement: Alpha Venture Partners is a growth-stage fund investing in the tech industry.
Geographic Preference: US
Average Investment: $20 million - $50 million
Minimum Investment: $500,000
Investment Criteria: Growth Stage, Series C, Revenue of $20 million
Industry Group Preference: Software, SaaS, Information Technology, E-Commerce, Mobile
Portfolio Companies: Careem, Cloud Technology Partners, Coupang, Doctor on Demand, Getaround, GoPuff, Lime, LiveIntent, Localytics, Rover, Socure, SportHero, Vroom, Wish.com
Key Executives:
  Steve Brotman, Founder/Managing Partner
  Education: BA, Duke University; JD/MBA, Washington University
  Background: Strategic Advisor, Pritzker Group Venture Capital; Co-Founder/Managing Director, Greenhill SAVP
  Brian Smiga, Co-Founding Partner
  Education: BA, Swarthmore College; MA, Trinity College, Dublin
  Background: Advisor, Priztker Group Venture Capital; Founder/CEO, Preclick; CEO, 3Path; SVP of Marketing, 1ClickCharge

92 ALPINE INVESTORS
One California Street
Suite 2900
San Francisco, CA 94111

Phone: 415-392-9100
web: www.alpineinvestors.com

Mission Statement: Alpine Investors believes in working with and learning from their portfolio companies.
Geographic Preference: United States, Canada

Venture Capital & Private Equity Firms / Domestic Firms

Fund Size: $1.4 Billion
Founded: 2001
Average Investment: $15 million
Minimum Investment: $10 million
Investment Criteria: Acquisition, LBO, MBO, Recapitalization, Special Situations, Minority Investments, EBITDA of $1-40 million, Enterprise Value of $5-400 million
Industry Group Preference: Software, Retail, Consumer & Leisure, Business Services
Portfolio Companies: AuthorityLabs, America's Thrift Stores, Apex Service Partners, ASG, Bill4Time, CarHop, Cleo, Comlinkdata, Cyfe, EcoInteractive, e-Courier Software, Evergreen Services Group, Exym, Foothold Technology, GatherUp, Grade Us, HealthComp Holdings, ImageQuix, Ingenio, Kaleidacare, Light Wave Dental Management, MidAmerica Administrative & Retirement Solutions LLC, Midwest Vision Partners, Minute Menu Systems, Photolynx, PracticePanther, Record 360, ReputationLoop, Reputology, Riverside Insights, Transcendent, Vendstar, Vionic, WebEquity, Windsor Fine Jewelers, YDesign Group, YouCaring

Key Executives:
  Graham Weaver, Partner
  e-mail: gweaver@alpine-investors.com
  Education: BS, Engineering, Princeton University; MBA, Stanford Business School
  Background: Vice President, Oak Hill Capital Management
  Will Adams, Partner
  e-mail: wadams@alpine-investors.com
  Education: BA, Colgate University; MBA, Kellogg Graduate School of Management
  Background: Marketing, Clorox Company; CEO, Great Falls Marketing
  Billy Maguy, Partner
  e-mail: bmaguy@alpine-investors.com
  Education: BS, MS, Industrial Engineering, Stanford University; MBA, Stanford Graduate School of Business
  Background: Director, Business Development, Telephia
  Dan Sanner, Partner
  e-mail: dsanner@alpine-investors.com
  Education: BA, Economics, Dartmouth College
  Background: Partner, Flowerdale Group
  Directorships: YLighting
  Mark Strauch, Partner
  Education: BSc, Lehigh Univ.; MBA, Kellogg School of Management
  Background: Business Engine
  Matt Moore, Partner
  Education: BS, Environmental Studies/Geography, University of California, Santa Barbara
  Background: OpenDNS; Symantec; FireEye; SolidFire; Google; Virident

93 ALSOP LOUIE PARTNERS
943 Howard Street
San Francisco, CA 94103

Phone: 415-625-8752
web: www.alsop-louie.com

Mission Statement: Early-stage technology VC firm in San Francisco.

Founded: 2006
Investment Criteria: Early-Stage
Industry Group Preference: Information Technology
Portfolio Companies: Aerospike, Baton System, Device Authority, Digilens, drop, Gfycat, Hover, Intelyt, Jetlore, Karmic Labs, Keyssa, Looking Glass, Mixed Dimensions, Motive Medical Intelligence, New Matter, Niantic, Phase Four, Phizzle, Remedy, Sapho, The Cipher Brief, Ursa Major Tech, Wickr
  Gilman Louie, Partner
  Background: Founder & CEO, In-Q-Tel; Chief Creative Officer, Hasbro Interactive

Stewart Alsop, Partner
Background: General Partner, New Enterprise Associates; Editor in Chief, InfoWorld; Executive Editor, Inc. Magazine
Nancy Lee, CFO & Partner
Background: Walden International
Jim Whims, Partner
Background: Partner, Techfund Capital; Co-Founder, Worlds of Wonder
Directorships: Smith & Tinker
Joe Addiego, Partner
Background: Investment Partner, In-Q-Tel; EVP, Marketing & Sales, Talarian; Hewlett-Packard; AT&T
Bill Crowell, Partner
Background: Deputy Director, National Security Agency; CEO, Cylink
Directorships: Safenet Holdings, Fixmo, Airpatrol, DRS Technologies, Six3 Systems
Mark Fields, Partner
Education: BA, Rutgers Univ.; MBA, Pepperdine Univ.
Background: CME Ventures
Directorships: Advisory Council, Brennan School of Business; Lauren's Hope

94 ALTA PARTNERS
One Embarcadero Center
Suite 3700
San Francisco, CA 94111

Phone: 415-362-4022
e-mail: alta@altapartners.com
web: www.altapartners.com

Mission Statement: Healthcare venture capital firm with offices in San Francisco and Denver.

Fund Size: $2 Billion
Founded: 1996
Average Investment: $5-$12 million
Investment Criteria: Early-Stage, Later-Stage
Industry Group Preference: Technology, Life Sciences, Biotechnology, Biopharmaceuticals, Medical, Information Technology
Portfolio Companies: Ablynx, Adolor Corporation, Aerie Pharmaceuticals, Allakos, Angiosyn, Aspire Health, Astex Pharmaceuticals, ATS Medical, Augmedix, Avid, Bioventus, Calistoga Pharma, Cartiva, Cerenis Therapeutics, Chimerix, Clovis Oncology, Connetics Corporation, Cotherix, Cutera, Cytokinetics, DeCODE Genetics, Difinity Health, Dispatch Health, Encoded Genomics, Esperion Therapeutics, Esprit Pharma, ESP Pharma, Flamel Technologies FoldRx, Intarcia Therapeutics, InterMune, Immune Design, itriage, Kiadis Pharma, Kite Phrama, Kosan Biosciences, LJL Biosystems, MacroGenics Inc., Mako Surgical Corp., Maestro Health, NovaCardia, Oceana Therapeutics, Paladina Health, PatientKeeper, Plexxikon, PneumRx, Prolacta Bioscience, Proxima Therapeutics, U3 Pharama, US Acute Care Solutions, Sarcode Bioscience, Sienna Biopharmaceuticals, Sutro Biopharma, Tivity Health

Other Locations:
  250 Fillmore Street
  Suite 225
  Denver, CO 80206
  Phone: 415-362-4022

Key Executives:
  Dan Janney, Managing Director
  Education: MBA, Anderson School, University of California, Los Angeles; BA History, Georgetown University
  Background: Senior Investment Banker, Montgomery Securities; Leveraged Buyout/Private Equity Group, Bankers Trust Company
  Directorships: Rebecca & John Moores Cancer Center; Corgentech; Dynavax Technologies
  Bob More, Managing Director
  Education: BA, Middlebury College; MBA, Darden

Venture Capital & Private Equity Firms / Domestic Firms

School of Business
Background: Bill and Melinda Gates Foundation
Directorships: One Revolution; Foundation for Innovative New Diagnostics
Pete Hudson, Managing Director
Education: BA, Colorado College; MD, University of Colorado
Background: Aetna
Directorships: U.S. Acute Care Solutions; Maestro Health
Larry Randall, Chief Financial Officer
Education: BS, Accounting, Santa Clara University
Background: The Gap, Inc., Intel Corporation

95 ALTAIR VENTURES
18416 Chelmsford
Cupertino, CA 95014

Phone: 408-218-1920 Fax: 309-214-3195
web: www.altairventures.com

Mission Statement: An entry-level high-technology investment and consulting firm whose approach is to help with financial investments, human capital, and strategic consulting.

Founded: 2001
Minimum Investment: $250,000
Investment Criteria: Seed, Startup, Early-Stage
Industry Group Preference: Semiconductors, Consumer Products, Biometrics, Infrastructure, Networking, Security, Electronic Technology, Internet Technology
Portfolio Companies: Applied Wave Research, Path Scale, Syabas, Zenasis

Key Executives:
  Sajid A. Sohail, General Partner
  925-413-9286
  Fax: 925-396-6032
  Education: MS, Electrical Engineering, University of Illinois
  Background: Founder/CEO, Dazzle Multimedia; Executive VP/General Manager, SCM Corporation; Director Engineering, C-Cube Microsystems; Tera Microsystems; Engineering/Design, Digital Equipment Corporation
  Naeem Zafar, General Partner
  408-218-1920
  Fax: 309-214-3195
  e-mail: naeem@altairventures.com
  Education: BSEE, Brown University; MSEE, University of Minnesota
  Background: President/CEO, Silicon Design Systems; President/CEO, Veridicom; VP Technology Strategy/VP Worldwide Marketing, Quickturn Design Systems ; VLSI Design Engineer/Research Scientist, Honeywell Research Labs; Lecturer

96 ALTAMONT CAPITAL PARTNERS
400 Hamilton Avenue
Suite 230
Palo Alto, CA 94301

Phone: 650-264-7750
e-mail: acp-info@altamontcapital.com
web: www.altamontcapital.com

Mission Statement: Private equity firm investing in middle market businesses, often ones in transition.

Fund Size: $2.5 Billion
Founded: 2010
Industry Group Preference: Business Products & Services, Financial Services, Industrial Services, Healthcare, Retail, Restaurants & Franchising, Consumer Products & Services
Portfolio Companies: Accelerant Holdings, Access Insurance, Alamo Drafthouse Cinema, Amplity Health, The Bayou Companies, Billabong, Byrider, Brixton, Cascade Windows, Che Behavioral Health Services, Celestite, Colorado Boxed Beef Company, Cotton Patch Cafe, Dakine, Embark General, Douglas Products, Excel Fitness, Fox Head, Hybrid Apparel, Intuitive Health, The Juice Plus Company, Kuvare, Maxi Canada, McLarens, Marvin Manufacturing, Meta Financial Group, ModernHealth, Omniplex, Renegade Brands, Robert Allen Duralee Group, Sequel Youth & Family Services, Tacala, Tall Tree Foods, Wunderlich
  Jesse Rogers, Managing Director
  Education: BA, Stanford University; MBA, Harvard Business School
  Background: Co-Founder/Co-Principal Managing Director, Golden Gate Capital; Bain & Company
  Directorships: Beringer Wine Estates, CCCS, Cydcor/2020, Employer's Direct Insurance
  Randall Eason, Managing Director
  Education: BA, Economics, MA, Sociology, Stanford University
  Background: Principal, Golden Gate Capital; Consultant, Bain & Company
  Keoni Schwartz, Managing Director
  Education: BA, History, Princeton University
  Background: Principal, Golden Gate Capital; Consultant, Bain & Company
  Casey Lynch, Managing Director
  Education: BA, Public Policy, Stanford University; MS, Management, Stanford Graduate School of Business
  Background: Partner, SFW Capital Partners; Partner, Parthenon Capital
  Steve Brownlie, Senior Director
  Education: BSE, Electrical Engineering, Princeton University
  Background: Vice President, Lazard Alternative Investments; Senior Associate, Golden Gate Capital
  Kristin Johnson, Managing Director
  Education: BA, Pomona College; MBA, Stanford Grad. School of Business
  Background: Morgan Stanley
  Carol Pereira, Chief Financial Officer
  Education: MBA, Stanford Grad. School of Business
  Background: Opus Capital Group

97 ALTARIS CAPITAL PARTNERS
10 East 53rd Street
31st Floor
New York, NY 10022

Phone: 212-931-0250
e-mail: info@altariscap.com
web: altariscap.com

Mission Statement: Altaris Capital Partners, LLC is an investment firm focused exclusively on the healthcare industry.

Fund Size: $2.3 Billion
Average Investment: $15-50 million
Industry Group Preference: Healthcare, Pharmaceuticals, Medical Devices, Healthcare Services, Healthcare Information Technology
Portfolio Companies: Acclara, Alterna LLC, AGS Health, Analogic, bk Medical, Brim, Chemical Computing Group, CI Medical Technologies, Clearwater, CMP Pharma, Creganna, CSafe Global, Endocare, Gaffey Healthcare, G&H Orthodontics, HealthTronics, HealthTronics IT Solutions, HSS, Healthcare Waste Solutions, Intralign, JDS Pharmaceuticals, Minnetronix, M2S, Oasis Outsourcing, OsoBio, Paragon Medical, Paramit, Penlon, Precyse, Quantum Health, Senior Helpers, Sparta Systems, SpecialtyCare, Tivity Health, Trean Corporation, US Health Works
  George E. Aitken-Davies, Managing Director
  212-931-0230
  e-mail: george.aitken-davies@altariscapital.com
  Education: MS, Molecular & Cellular Biochemistry, University of Oxford
  Background: Merrill Lynch Private Equity
  Daniel G. Tully, Managing Director
  212-931-0234
  e-mail: daniel.tully@altariscap.com
  Education: BS, Economics, University of Pennsylvania

Wharton Undergraduate Program
Background: Merrill Lynch Private Equity
David G. Ellison, Managing Director
212-931-0241
e-mail: david.ellison@altariscap.com
Education: Washington & Lee University
Background: Investment Banking Group, Lehman Brothers
James D. O'Brien, Managing Director
Education: BA, History, Princeton University
Background: Merrill Lynch

98 ALTIRA GROUP LLC
1675 Broadway
Suite 2400
Denver, CO 80202

Phone: 303-592-5500 **Fax:** 303-592-5519
e-mail: info@altiragroup.com
web: www.altiragroup.com

Mission Statement: Oil and gas investor.

Geographic Preference: North America
Founded: 1996
Average Investment: $5 million
Minimum Investment: $1 - $3 million
Investment Criteria: Seed, Early-Stage, Growth
Industry Group Preference: Energy, Oil & Gas, Information Technology, Power Technologies, Distribution, Renewable Energy, Electric Power, Technology-Enabled Services
Portfolio Companies: Seeq, Agile Upstream, FlexGen Power Systems, Infrastructure Networks

Dirk McDermott, Managing Partner
e-mail: dmcdermott@altiragroup.com
Education: MS Geophysics, MBA, Stanford University
Background: Geophysicist, Louisiana Land & Exploration Company; Co-Founder, Aspect Management; Brigham Oil & Gas; Energy Arrow; SouthTech Exploration; General Atlantic Resources
Directorships: Hyperion Evolutionary Genomics; DHI Services; Amended Silicates; MicroSeiomic; Beyond Compliance

Sean Ebert, Partner
Education: BS, Civil Engineering, MBA, University of Texas
Background: Principal, Booz Allen; CEO, Foresight Weather
Directorships: TransZap, Austin Geomodeling

J.P. Bauman, Principal
Education: BA, MBA, Univ. of Chicago
Background: Perseus LLC
Directorships: Seeq, Agile Upstream, FlexGen Power Systems

99 ALTITUDE INVESTMENT MANAGEMENT, LLC
205 East 42nd Street
20th Floor
New York, NY 10017

Phone: 212-381-9680
e-mail: info@altitudein.com
web: altitudein.com

Mission Statement: Invests in early-stage to growth companies in the cannabis industry.

Geographic Preference: US, Canada, Europe
Founded: 2016
Industry Group Preference: Cannabis
Portfolio Companies: BDS Analytics, C4 Distro, Canndescent, Enlighten, Flowhub, Front Range Biosciences, Grassroots, Grassroots Herbology, Grassroots Greenhouse, Green Flower, Liberty Cannabis, PathogenDx, Privateer Holdings, Segra, Springbig, Sunderstorm, The Green Organic Dutchman, Würk

Key Executives:
John Brecker, Partner
Education: BS, Political Science, American University; JD, St. John's University School of Law
Background: VP, High Yield Department, The Bear Stearns Companies Inc.; Principal & Co-Founder, Longacre Fund Management; Founding Partner, Drivetrain Advisors

Michael Goldberg, Partner
Education: The London School of Economics and Political Science (LSE); BSM, Finance, A.B. Freeman School of Business, Tulane University; MBA, Finance & International Business, Columbia Business School
Background: Managing Director, Longacre Fund Management LLC; Owner/Portfolio Manager, Sonar Asset Management Group, Inc.; Managing Director, Banc of America Securities, LLC; Chase Securities, Inc.

Roderick Stephan, Partner
Education: BS, Biochemistry, University of Notre Dame; MA, Finance, Kellogg School of Management, Northwestern University
Background: Sr. Analyst, First Chicago Capital Corp.; Sr. Analyst, Bank of Montreal; Sr. Analyst, Citadel Investment Group LLC; Principal/Portfolio Manager/CEO, Longacre Fund Management (UK); Portfolio Manager, Cantibury Capital LLC

Jon Trauben, Partner
Education: BA, Political Science, Rutgers University; MSc, Real Estate, New York University
Background: Ernst & Young; VP, APC Realty Advisors; Managing Director, Credit Suisse; Managing Director, Cantor Fitzgerald; Managing Director, Barclays Capital; Sr. Managing Director, Hunt Mortgage Group; Principal, JAC Investments

100 ALTOS VENTURES
2882 Sand Hill Road
Suite 100
Menlo Park, CA 94025

e-mail: info@altos.vc
web: www.altos.vc

Mission Statement: Altos Ventures invests in growing North America and South Korea-based companies in the Internet, software and mobile sectors.

Geographic Preference: North America, South Korea
Fund Size: $300 million
Founded: 1996
Average Investment: $1 - $5 million
Investment Criteria: Early Stage, Growth Stage
Industry Group Preference: Technology, Mobile, Software, Internet
Portfolio Companies: Adop, Allocadia, April, Beat, Bench, Bluehole Studio, Book Jam, Bridea, Brightedge, Coupang, Demandbase, Digitalpath.net, Funizen, HireMojo, Hyperconnect, I-Um, Jobplanet, Joya, LendIt, Lohika, Memebox, My Real Trip, NetBase, One Up, Origin Games, Outbound Engine, PandaDoc, Pandora.TV, Piqora, Quizlet, Retrica, Roblox, Spicus, TrilibisMobile, TVU Networks, Upsight, Vesta, Viva Republica, Vonvon, WhiteHat Security, Xignite, Zigzag

Other Locations:
4th Floor
96-1 Cheongdam-dong
Gangnam-gu
Seoul 135-517
Korea

Key Executives:
Han Kim, Managing Director
Education: BS, United States Military Academy; MBA, Stanford University
Background: Booz Allen & Hamilton; Procter & Gamble; Captain, US Army Corps of Engineers

Venture Capital & Private Equity Firms / Domestic Firms

Anthony Lee, Managing Director
Education: BA, Politics & Economics, Princeton University; MBA, Stanford University
Background: Evolve Software; Strategy Consultant, McKinsey & Company; Chairman, TechSoup Global
Hodong Nam, Managing Director
Education: BS, Engineering, Harvey Mudd College; MBA, Stanford University
Background: Trinity Ventures; Bain & Company; Silicon Graphics; Octel Communications

101 ALTPOINT CAPITAL
600 Steamboat Road
Greenwich, CT 06830

Phone: 212-487-1100
e-mail: info@altpointcapital.com
web: altpointcapital.com

Mission Statement: Venture partner to growing companies in fintech, communications, cryptocurrencies and data-driven marketplaces.

Founded: 2009
Average Investment: $100K - $20MM
Minimum Investment: $100K
Industry Group Preference: Fintech, Communications, Data-driven marketplaces, Blockchain/cryptocurrencies
Portfolio Companies: Aces, Acorn, Brief, ByteGrid, Dreamlines, Edisun Microgrids, Enwoven, Factual, Ford Models, Honk, Just, lyft, Newbook, Redbooth, Saucey, Status, TLL, Vetter, VYTL, Zowdow

Key Executives:
Gerald T. Banks, Founder & Managing Partner
Education: Columbia Univ.; London Business School
Background: Merrill Lynch
Andrew Grapkowski, Managing Director & Partner
Education: Princeton; Univ. of Virginia
Directorships: ByteGrid Holdings; ANARAQ; Vazata

102 ALTRIA VENTURES
Richmond, VA

Mission Statement: Altria Group created Altria Ventures Inc. to invest in technology areas of interest to our core businesses. Our approach to investing is not limited to funding and may include the provision of other assistance, such as technical expertise.

Geographic Preference: Worldwide
Average Investment: $250,000 - $3 million
Investment Criteria: Growth Stage
Industry Group Preference: Safety, Biotechnology, Packaging, Clean Energy, Water, Sustainability, Recycling

103 ALTURA VENTURES LLC
9600 Blue Larkspur Lane
Suite 201
Monterey, CA 93940

Phone: 831-595-7501 Fax: 831-855-0206
e-mail: contactus@altura.com
web: www.altura.com

Mission Statement: Altura Ventures is an evangelist for the entrepreneurial approach to business. Altura believes that both the world's economy and everyone's quality of life will be best served when more motivated individuals (or small teams) tinkering in their garages and taking long brain-storming lunches away from their 9 to 5 jobs decide to take the plunge and start a company.

Founded: 2006
Portfolio Companies: CrossLoop, Living Gluten Free, UserBliss, JobCoin, KallOut

Key Executives:
Lee Lorenzen, President/CEO
e-mail: leel@altura.com
Education: BS, Computer Science, SMU
Background: Founder, SHOP.COM; Founder, Ventura Software; Xerox
Thomas E Mallett, Managing Director
e-mail: tomm@altura.com
Education: University of California, Davis
Background: Buck & Mallett

104 ALTUS CAPITAL PARTNERS
10 Westport Road
Suite C204
Wilton, CT 06897

Phone: 203-429-2000 Fax: 203-429-2010
web: www.altuscapitalpartners.com

Mission Statement: Focus on small and middle market domestic manufacturing companies.

Geographic Preference: Northeast, Mid-Atlantic, Southeast, Midwest, Rocky Mountains
Fund Size: $79.3 million
Founded: 2003
Average Investment: $12 million
Minimum Investment: $3 million
Investment Criteria: LBO, MBO, Recapitalization
Industry Group Preference: Military, Water Purification, Infrastructure, Building Materials & Services
Portfolio Companies: MGC Diagnostics, Max Environmental, Nichols Portland, GED Integrated Solutions, iimak, Thomson Plastics

Other Locations:
250 Parkway Drive
Suite 120
Lincolnshire, IL 60069
Phone: 847-229-0770 Fax: 847-229-9266

Key Executives:
Russell J. Greenberg, Founder & Managing Partner
e-mail: rgreenberg@altuscapitalpartners.com
Education: Graduate Economics with honors, Claremont McKenna College; MBA, Amos Tuck School, Dartmouth
Background: Head Investment Banking, Chatfield Dean and Company; Managing Director, Brean Murray, Foster Securities; Head Mergers/Acquisitions, Daiwa Securities America; Prudential Bache
Directorships: Duramax; Thomson Acquisition
Gregory L. Greenberg, Founder & Senior Partner
e-mail: ggreenberg@altuscapitalpartners.com
Education: Graduate Business Administration, Denver University
Background: SVP, JMB Realty Corporation
Heidi M. Goldstein, Partner
e-mail: hgoldstein@altuscapitalpartners.com
Education: Univ. of Connecticut
Background: GE Antares Capital
Directorships: Intl. Imaging Materials; Max Environmental Technologies; MGC Diagnostics; Nichols Portland
Thomas R. Groh, Partner, Business Development
e-mail: tgroh@altuscapitalpartners.com
Education: MBA, Booth School of Business
Background: KPMG
Peter Polimino, Partner, Chief Financial Officer and CCO
e-mail: ppolimino@altuscapitalpartners.com
Education: Iona College
Background: Fox Sports Net
Directorships: Nichols Portland; Thomson Plastics

Other Locations:
823 Congress Avenue
Suite 205

Venture Capital & Private Equity Firms / Domestic Firms

Austin, TX 78701
Phone: 512-532-2800

106 AMD VENTURES
2485 Augustine Drive
Santa Clara, CA 94054

Phone: 408-749-4000
e-mail: amd.ventures@amd.com
web: www.amd.com

Mission Statement: Through AMD Ventures, AMD's investment program, AMD invests in strategic software and application ecosystem companies that serve large and growing markets.
Industry Group Preference: Software, Data Storage, Analytics, Security, Multimedia, Virtual Reality & Augmented Reality, Machine Learning
Portfolio Companies: BlueStacks, InContext Solutions, Matterport, Nitero, Personify, Raptr, Tango
Key Executives:
   Harry Wolin, Managing Director
   Background: SVP/General Counsel, AMD
   Shantnu Sharma, Managing Director
   Education: MIT
   Background: VP, Corporate Strategy/Business Development, AMD; Consultant, McKinsey & Co.

107 AME CLOUD VENTURES
Palo Alto, CA

e-mail: pr@amecloudventures.com
web: www.amecloudventures.com

Mission Statement: AME Cloud Ventures invests in seed to later stage companies that are involved in developing technology and data.
Investment Criteria: Seed to Later Stage
Industry Group Preference: Technology, Data & Analytics
Portfolio Companies: Accion, Amitree, Arterys, Astranis, AtScale, Atomwise, Berkeley Lights, Blast, BirdEye, Bitpay, Blast Motion, BlockCypher, Blockstream, Bowers & Wilkins, Boxed, Cala Health, Canvas Technology, Capella Space, Catalog, Citrine Informatics, Civil Maps, Clover Health, Cofactor Genomics, Coda, Cohere Technologies, Color Genomics, CrowdAI, Deepscale, DiDi, Docker, Edge Intelligence, Eero, Elementum, Embark, Enfore, Enso Relief, Everlance, Evernote, FiscalNote, Game Closure, Gusto, Holberton School, HyperScience, Illumio, Import.io, Impossible Foods, Inscopix, Interana, Inui Health, Joby, Just Inc., Katerra, Kindred.ai, Layer, Lighthouse, Litbit, Luminist, Lyft, Mammoth Biosciences, Matterport, Megabots, Minio, ModBot, Neurotrack, nStack, Openbucks, Osaro, PepperData, Planet Labs, PlotWatt, Primer, Qadium, QuantiFind, Radius, Recursion Pharma, Rigetti Computing, Ripple Labs, Sapho, Savioke, ShoCard, Siftery, Slack, Talech, Tekion, Tempo Auto, The Grid, TigerGraph, Tile, Transcriptic, Twist Bioscience, uBiome, VIDA, Vectra, Vicarious, Vicarious Surgical, Vium, Viz.AI, Voicera, Wevr, Wattpad, Whole Biome, Wish, Xapo, Zendrive, Zoom, Zume Pizza, Zymergen
Key Executives:
   Nick Adams, Managing Director
   Education: MEng, Imperial College
   Background: Cloud Valley
   Directorships: Zoom, Zume, Zymergen, Eero, Planet, Cruise
   Jeff Chung, Managing Director
   Education: BS, University of California, Berkeley; MBA, Harvard Business School
   Background: Silver Lake
   Directorships: Savioke, Nervana Systems, Freenome, Elementum, Synthego, Rigetti Quantum Computing

108 AMERICA FIRST INVESTMENT ADVISORS
Regency One Building
10050 Regency Circle
Suite 515
Omaha, NE 68114

Phone: 402-991-3388
web: www.am1st.com

Mission Statement: An employee-owned international investment management organization committed to successfully developing unique business opportunities for institutional, private and public fund investors, making investments in agribusiness and food processing companies in the former Soviet Union, and fully investing in companied located in Russia, Kazakhstan, Ukraine, Moldova and Georgia.
Geographic Preference: Former Soviet Union
Fund Size: $270 million
Founded: 1994
Average Investment: $8 million
Minimum Investment: $5 million
Investment Criteria: Agribusiness/Food processing companies that will benefit from capital and management expertise
Industry Group Preference: Agribusiness, Packaging, Food & Beverage
Key Executives:
   Eric M. Ball, Chief Executive Officer/Chief Compliance Officer
   Education: BS, Finance, University of Nebraska, Lincoln; CFA
   Background: VP/Portfolio Manager, Financial Institutions Investment Management; Investment Advisor, Wallace R. Weitz & Company; VP/Manager, FirsTier Westchester Capital Management; Securities Analyst, Kirkpatrick, Pettis, Smith & Polian
   Barry Dunaway, Managing Director
   Education: BS, Economics, University of Nebraska, Omaha
   Background: Portfolio Manager, KPM Investment Management; Securities Analyst, Wallace R Weitz & Company
   David Guthrie, Vice President
   Education: BS, MBA, University of Nebraska, Lincoln
   Background: Vice President, Senior Private Banker, Wells Fargo Private Bank

109 AMERICAN INDUSTRIAL PARTNERS
450 Lexington Avenue
40th Floor
New York, NY 10017

web: www.americanindustrial.com

Mission Statement: A private equity firm that is dedicated to buying and improving manufacturing and industrial service companies based in North America.
Geographic Preference: United States, Canada, Mexico
Fund Size: $1.8 billion
Founded: 1989
Average Investment: $10 - $50 million
Minimum Investment: $10 million
Investment Criteria: MBO, Recapitalizations, Corporate Divestitures, Growth Capital investments to fund acquisitions or internal growth
Industry Group Preference: Manufacturing, Industrial Services
Portfolio Companies: ACPI, AHF Products, AIP Aerospace, Brock, Canam, The Carlstar Group, CQMS Razer, GE Current, Entrans International, Form Technologies, Gerber Technology, Manroland Goss, Molycop, Optimas, Rand Logistics, REV, Shape Technologies, Verico Technology, Vertex Aerospace, Brooks Instrument, Bucyrus, Consoltex, Great Lakes Carbon, Ichor Systems, JHT Holdings, Manac, Mark Andy, Mecs, Micro-Poise Measurement Systems,

41

Venture Capital & Private Equity Firms / Domestic Firms

Northwest Hardwoods, Port Arthur Steam Energy, Stolle Machinery Company, Williams Controls

Key Executives:

John Becker, Senior Managing Partner
Education: BS, Business, Oregon State University
Background: Founder, Newport Shrimp Company; COO, Clearwater Fine Foods, USA; Chairman, Newport Pacific Corporation

Kim Marvin, Senior Managing Partner
Education: BS, Ocean Engineering, Massachusetts Institute of Technology; MBA, Harvard Business School
Background: M&A, Goldman, Sachs & Co; COO, American Original Corporation

Dino Cusumano CFA, Senior Managing Partner
Education: BBA, University of Notre Dame; CFA
Background: Investment Banking, JP Morgan & Co. Inc.; Wedbush Morgan Securities

Paul Bamatter CA, Partner
Education: Accounting and Finance, Bishop's University
Background: CFO & COO, Consoltex Holdings Inc.; Senior Manager, Price Waterhouse; Royal Bank of Canada; Alcan Aluminum Limited

Eric Baroyan, Partner
Education: BS, Business Administration, University of Southern California
Background: Associate, Capital Z Financial Services Partners; Investment Banking Division, Salomon Smith Barney

Ben DeRosa, Partner
Education: BS, Engineering, University of Pennsylvania; MBA, Stanford Graduate School of Business
Background: Managing Director, Liberty Partners; Principal, Donaldson, Lufkin & Jenrette/CSFB Private Equity; Associate, The Harlan Company; Senior Consultant, Coopers & Lybrand

Ryan Hodgson, Partner
Education: BS, Economics, Wharton School, University of Pennsylvania; MBA, Harvard Business School
Background: M&A, The Blackstone Group

Derek Leck, Partner
Education: BS, Mechanical Engineering, Massachusetts Institute of Technology; MBA, Finance & Statistics, University of Chicago Graduate School of Business
Background: Emerging Markets Product Manager, Caterpillar Inc.; VP, Corporate Planning, Fuji Heavy Industries (Subaru); General Motors

Jorge Amador, Partner
Education: BS, Industrial Engineering, University of Costa Rica; MS, Management & Engineering, MIT; MS, Manufacturing Systems Engineering, University of Texas
Background: Manager of Professional Services & Product Development, Factory DNA Inc.; Senior Consultant, Factory Logic Inc.; Project Manager, Applied Materials Inc.; Quality Manager, Central American Division of Unisys Corporation

Stephen Bordes, Partner/CFO
Education: BSM, Management & Accounting, Tulane University; MBA, International Finance, Columbia Business School; CPA
Background: CFO, Castle Harlan; CFO, CHAMP Equity; CFO, CIM Group; Partner, Transaction Services Group, Deloitte

110 AMERICAN SECURITIES LLC
299 Park Avenue
34th Floor
New York, NY 10171

Phone: 212-476-8000
e-mail: cjander@american-securities.com
web: www.american-securities.com

Mission Statement: Private investment firm that makes equity investments into profitable companies in partnership with management teams.

Geographic Preference: Worldwide

Fund Size: $3 billion
Founded: 1947
Average Investment: $20 million
Minimum Investment: $5 million
Industry Group Preference: Consumer Products, Restaurants, Industrial, Aerospace, Defense and Government, Packaging, Agriculture, Environment, Paper, Power, Specialty Chemicals, Media
Portfolio Companies: Air Methods, American Axle & Manufacturing, Aspen Dental, Blount International, Blue Bird, Chromaflo Technologies, Emerald Performance Materials, Fairmount Santrol, Frontier Spinning Mills, Global Tel*Link, Henry Company, Learning Care Group, Milk Specialties Global, Mortgage Contracting Services, MW Industries, North American Partners in Anesthesia, SeaStar Solutions, Ulterra Drilling Technologies, Unifrax, United Distribution Group

Other Locations:
288 South Shaanxi Road, Two ICC
Suite 2808-2810
Shanghai 200031
China
Phone: 86 (21) 5419-1100

Key Executives:

Michael Fisch, Managing Director/CEO
212-476-8051
Education: BA, Dartmouth College; MBA, Stanford University
Background: Consultant, Bain & Company; Mergers & Acquisitions, Goldman Sachs

David Horing, Managing Director
212-476-8059
e-mail: dhoring@american-securities.com
Education: BS, Economics, Wharton School, University of Pennsylvania; BSc, Engineering, University of Pennsylvania; MBA, Harvard Business School
Background: Dyson-Kissner-Moran Corporation; Solomon Brothers; Boston Consulting Group

Kevin Penn, Managing Director
212-476-8020
e-mail: kpenn@american-securities.com
Education: BS, Economics, Wharton School; MBA, Harvard Business School
Background: Founder, ACI Capital; EVP & CIO, First Spring Corporation
Directorships: Healthy Directions, Presido

Will Manuel, Managing Director
212-476-8030
e-mail: wmanuel@american-securities.com
Education: BA, Government, Connecticut College
Background: Principal, Spectrum Equity Investors; Spire Capital Partners; CEA Capital Advisors; M&A, Chase Securities
Directorships: Senior Managing Director, Centerbridge Partners

Helen Chiang, Managing Director
212-476-8012
e-mail: hchiang@american-securities.com
Education: BA, Economics & International Studies, Yale University; MBA, Stanford Grad. School of Business
Background: VP, Morgan Stanley Capital Partners; Warburg Pincus; Weston Presidio
Directorships: Learning Care Group; Milk Specialties Global; United Planet Fitness

Loren Easton, Managing Director
212-476-8029
e-mail: leaston@american-securities.com
Education: BA, University of Pennsylvania; MBA, Wharton School
Background: Vice President, ACI Capital; Analyst, Lazard Freres
Directorships: Healthy Directions, NEP Broadcasting, Unifrax

Venture Capital & Private Equity Firms / Domestic Firms

111 AMERIMARK CAPITAL CORPORATION
320 Decker Drive
Suite 100
Irving, TX 75062
Phone: 214-638-7878
e-mail: admin@amcapital.com
web: www.amcapital.com

Mission Statement: Provides solutions to business owners who need additional capital for growth or personal liquidity. Seeking investment opportunities in a variety of industries. Established companies are preferred with a record of profitability and an opportunity for growth.
Fund Size: $50 million
Founded: 1988
Average Investment: $1 million
Minimum Investment: $500,000
Investment Criteria: Second-Stage, Mezzanine, LBO. Companies ranging in size from $5 - $300 million in annual sales.
Industry Group Preference: Communications, Consumer Services, Distribution, Industrial Equipment, Manufacturing, Service Industries
Portfolio Companies: Protel, Inc., City Mortgage Corporation, MSI Acquisition, Inc., Village Square Cabinet Supply, TTH Holdings, Superior Chaircraft Corporation, Texas B&B, Inc., Chartwell Healthcare, Inc., E.E. Stringer Funeral Homes, Lewis Electric Supply, Inc., Stohlquist Waterware, Inc., Fitting Valve and Control Corporation, Algas Industries, Inc., Commercial Financial Services, Full Vision, Inc., Service Strategies Interntional, Inc., Electronics, Inc.
Key Executives:
   Charles R Martin, Managing Principal/CEO
   e-mail: martin@amcapital.com
   Education: BS Industrial Engineering, Auburn University; MBA, Southerm Methodist University; graduate studies in Marketing, Syracuse University
   Background: VP/Principal, Capital Alliance Corporation; President, building supply distributor; VP Sales/Marketing, major home products manufacturer; Colonel, US Army Reserve
   Directorships: Martin Industries, Amsouth Bank

112 AMGEN VENTURES
One Amgen Center Drive
Thousand Oaks, CA 91320-1799
Phone: 805-447-1000
e-mail: investor.relations@amgen.com
web: www.amgen.com

Mission Statement: Corporate venture capital fund designed to provide emerging biotechnology firms with resources to develop pioneering discoveries focused on human therapeutics. It can offer early stage companies access to Amgen's extensive capabilities while providing Amgen insight into external research paving the way for future collaborations.
Geographic Preference: North America, Asia, Europe
Fund Size: $100 million
Founded: 2004
Average Investment: $2-3 million
Minimum Investment: $1 million
Investment Criteria: Early-Stage, Equity, Venture Fund Investment
Industry Group Preference: Biotechnology, Therapeutics, Life Sciences, Pharmaceuticals
Portfolio Companies: Adheron Therapeutics, Ardelyx, Atara Bio, Avidia, Calistoga, Epizyme, Imago BioSciences, MiRagen, NexImmune, Ra pharma, Surface Oncology, Sutro Biopharma, TeraLogic Pharmaceuticals, Ziarco
Key Executives:
   Janis Naeve, PhD, Managing Director
   e-mail: amgenventures@amgen.com
   Education: BS, Microbiology, Caltech, Pomona; PhD, Pathology, University of Southern California
   Background: Director, Business Development, X-Ceptor Therapeutics; Aurora Biosciences

113 AMHERST FUND
401 East Stadium
Ann Arbor, MI 48104
Phone: 734-662-2102
e-mail: info@amherstfund.com
web: www.amherstfund.com

Mission Statement: To generate sound returns for portfolio companies. Amherst Fund makes venture capital investments (with focus on early stage companies) and private equity investments (with focus on later stage companies) across a broad range of industries.
Geographic Preference: Midwest
Fund Size: $30 million
Founded: 1998
Investment Criteria: Early Stage, Later Stage
Industry Group Preference: Manufacturing, Medical Devices, Advanced Materials, Mobile, Restaurants, Food & Beverage, Drug Development
Portfolio Companies: AdAdapted, BD Accuri, Fusion Coolant Systems, Michigan Ladder, Saline Lectronics Inc., SkySpecs
Key Executives:
   Matt Turner, President/Chief Executive Officer
   Education: BA, Economics, University of Michigan; MA, University of Monaco, Monte Carlo; Webster University, Vienna
   Background: Professional Racecar Driver, Porsche Cars GB
   Directorships: Saline Lectronics, Espresso Royale, FlockTAG, Fusion Coolant
   Amherst Turner, Founder/Fund Advisor
   Education: BA, University of Michigan
   Background: Co-Founder, GT Products
   Directorships: Saline Lectronics

114 AMICUS CAPITAL
1045 Sansome Street
Suite 306
San Francisco, CA 94111
Phone: 415-646-0120
e-mail: ideas@amicuscapital.com
web: www.amicuscapital.com

Mission Statement: Amicus Capital is a seed stage information technology investment fund, investing in entrepreneurs who are developing innovative information technology solutions to problems that affect large numbers of businesses or consumers.
Founded: 1998
Investment Criteria: Seed-Stage
Industry Group Preference: Information Technology
Portfolio Companies: ATMA Software, Adventa, Attributor, Automatic, BrightFunnel, Business Signatures, BuyersEdge, Closely, Corrigo, Food Genius, Greenling, GrubHub, IronPort, Kefta, Marin Software, Moseo, Octopus.com, Odeo, Oneforty, RethinkDB, Snocap, Soundflavor, Spotlife, Three Rings, TravelPotst.com, Visible Markets, Vividence, Vizu Corp., VoxPop Network Corp., W&W Communications, WiredPlanet
Key Executives:
   Bob Zipp, Co-Founder/Managing Director
   Education: Duke University; Texas A&M University

115 AMIDZAD PARTNERS
370 Convention Way
Redwiid City, CA 94063
Phone: 650-216-2384
e-mail: marc@amidzad.com
web: www.amidzad.com

43

Venture Capital & Private Equity Firms / Domestic Firms

Mission Statement: Amidzad is a seed and early-stage investment firm focused on investing in emerging growth companies on the West Coast. They have over 50 years of combined entrepreneurial experience in building profitable, global enterprises from the ground up and over 25 years of combined investing experience in successful information technology and life science companies.
Geographic Preference: West Coast
Investment Criteria: Seed-Stage, Early-Stage
Industry Group Preference: Information Technology, Life Sciences
Portfolio Companies: Aquantia, Bix, Causes, Clear Spring, Clixtr, Course Hero, Danger, Dropbox, Ellie Mae, Equator, Extreme DA, Freewebs, Infoaxe, InMage, Integen, Jaxtr, LendingClub, LiteScape, Milo, Mywaves, Nextbio, OpTrip, ParAllele, Picoboo, Powerset, Preview System, Paypal, Quantenna, Sabio Labs, ScanScout, SGN, Sendori, SignmaQuest, Sonitus Medical, Songbird, SoundHound, Tau-Metrix, Techdirt, TokBox, VentureBeat, Zephyr, Zetta.net, Zoosk,
   Rahim Amidi, Founding General Partner
   e-mail: rahim@amidzad.com
   Background: Co-Founder, Amidi Group
   Saeed Amidi, Founding General Partner
   e-mail: saeed@amidizad.com
   Background: Co-Founder, Amidi Group

116 AMITI VENTURES
1603 Orrington Ave.
Suite 600
Evanston, IL 60201

e-mail: info@amitiventures.com
web: www.amiticapital.com

Mission Statement: Amiti Ventures is a venture capital firm based in Chicago and Tel Aviv that invests alongside leading Israeli venture capital firms in late stage Israeli high tech companies. We help fund Israeli entrepreneurs and partner with them to build great global companies.
Geographic Preference: Israel
Investment Criteria: Early Stage
Industry Group Preference: Mobile Technology, IT Infrastructure, Cloud Computing, Digital Media Delivery, Information Technology
Portfolio Companies: Amimon, Autotalks, Cycognito, Corephotonics, Innoviz, Flash Networks, Nextsilicon, Sckipio, Siklu, Valens Semiconductor, Vayyar
Key Executives:
   Ben Rabinowitz, Managing Partner & Founder
   Education: MBA, Georgetown University
   Background: General Manager, Vice President, AudioCodes
   Directorships: Valens Semiconductor
   Shimrit Samuel, Venture Partner
   Education: LLB, MBA, LLM, Tel Aviv University
   Background: Board Member, Corephotonics Ltd.; Board Member, Cycognito; Teaching Professional, Tel Aviv University
   Vered Digmy, Investor Relations
   Education: BA, English Literature, Tel Aviv University
   Background: Director of Investor Relations, Giza Venture Captial; Investor Relations Manager, Grove Venture Capital
   Yafit Schwartz, Vice President, Finance
   Education: BS, Accounting, Tel Aviv University
   Background: Vice President, Finance, Perion; ERP Finance and Business Leader, Ceragon Networks

117 AMKEY VENTURES
44370 Old Warm Springs Boulevard
Fremont, CA 94538

Phone: 510-668-1816 Fax: 510-668-1017
e-mail: info@amkeyvc.com
web: www.amkeyvc.com

Mission Statement: Amkey Ventures is a California-based VC firm, whose mission is to identify investment opportunities by focusing on cutting-edge biomedical technologies.
Founded: 2001
Industry Group Preference: Biotechnology, Pharmaceuticals, Medical Devices
Portfolio Companies: Cardiva Medical, Inc., Renal Solutions, Inc., MedWaves Incorporated, U-Systems, Inc., Biokey, Inc., VM Discovery, Inc., GenePharm, Inc., Epitomics, Inc., Multispan, Inc. StemCyte, Inc.
Key Executives:
   Woody Sing-Wood Yeh, Managing Director/Founder
   Education: BS, Agricultural Chemistry, National Taiwan University; PhD, Food Science, University of Chicago, Champaign-Urbana
   Background: CEO/Founder, Bioken Laboratories; CEO/Founder, BestLife; CEO/Founder, Soyeh Natural; Research Scientist, INTSOY
   George J Lee, Managing Director/Founder
   Education: BS, Agricultural Chemistry, National Taiwan University; PhD, Chemistry, SUNY Buffalo
   Background: Co-Founder, Pharmout Labs

118 AMPERSAND CAPITAL PARTNERS
55 William Street
Suite 240
Wellesley, MA 02481

Phone: 781-239-0700
e-mail: info@ampersandcapital.com
web: ampersandcapital.com

Mission Statement: A middle market private equity firm focused on investments in two core sectors: Healthcare and Industrial.
Geographic Preference: United States, Canada
Fund Size: $1 Billion
Founded: 1988
Average Investment: $10-30 Million
Investment Criteria: Middle Market Growth Opportunities
Industry Group Preference: Biotechnology, Communications Equipment, Computer Hardware & Software, Electronic Components, Health Related, Medical, Information Technology, Industrial Equipment, Manufacturing, Chemicals, Medical Devices, Pharmaceuticals, Healthcare
Portfolio Companies: Accuratus Lab Services, Aclara, Agilux Labs, Alexis Biochemicals, Assay Designs, Avista Pharma, Bako, BioClinica, Bioventus, Brammer Bio, ChanTest, Confluent, CoreLab, Corpus Medical, CRI Worldwide, CutisPharma, Detector Technology, Dynex Technologies, Elite One Source, ETE Medical, Genewiz, Genoptix, Gyros Protein, Innovative Food Processors, LakePharma, Magellan, MedVenture, Invitrogen, Ortho Organizers, Panacos, Roadrunner Pharmacy, Sanova Dermatology, Signature Genomic, Stereotaxis, Talecris, TREK Diagnostic, TriPath Imaging, Viracor-IBT
Other Locations:
   Gustav Mahlerplein 2
   Amsterdam 1082 MA
   Netherlands
   Phone: 31-207997391
Key Executives:
   Richard A. Charpie, Founder & Managing Partner
   Education: MS, Physics, PhD, Economics, Finance, MIT
   Directorships: CoreLab Partners, NDC, RAND Worldwide
   Herbert H. Hooper, Managing Partner
   Education: BS Chemical Engineering, University of California; PhD, Chemical Engineering, University of California, Berkeley
   Background: Chief Tech Officer/Executive VP, ACLARA BioSciences (Nasdaq: ACLA); Product/Business Development Manager, Air Products and Chemicals

Directorships: ATS Labs, Biomedical Structures, CoreLab Partners, Magellan Biosciences, ViraCor-IBT Laboratories
Stuart A. Auerbach, Advisory Partner
Education: BS Chemical Engineering, Columbia University; MBA, Harvard Business School
Background: Consulting, Bain; Manufacturing/Engineering, Lever Brothers; CFO ADFlex Solutions during the design implementation of its turnaround; Director, ADFlex, Smartflex
Directorships: Agilux Laboratories, MedVenture, Modified Polymer Components
Jared J. Bartok, Advisory Partner
Education: BA, Economics & Computer Science, Middlebury College
Background: Senior Associate, Wellspring Capital Management; JPMorgan Chase & Co.
Directorships: Biomedical Structures, MedVenture, Modified Polymer Components, NDC, ViraCor-IBT Laboratories
David J. Parker, Partner
Education: BA, Government & Economics, Dartmouth; MBA, Wharton
Background: Consultant, Bain; Consultant, Mercer; Bank of Boston
Directorships: Blue Sky BioServices, Modified Polymer Components
David Q. Anderson, Partner
Education: BSc, Universty of Aberdeen; PhD, University of Sheffield; MBA, Olin Graduat School of Business, Babson College
Background: Director, Healthcare Group, Covington Associates; Consultant, Boston Healthcare Associates
Directorships: ATS Labs
Thomas de Jager, Vice President, Business Development
Education: BA, Economics, University of Pretoria; MBA, Pace University
Background: Founder, Savannah Acquisitions; Aleutian Capital Partners

119 AMPLIFIER VENTURE PARTNERS
1614 Brookside Road
McLean, VA 22101

Phone: 703-635-2655 **Fax:** 703-782-0222
web: www.amplifierventures.com

Mission Statement: Amplifier Ventures primary investment focus is emerging technology businesses located in the DC Region, a geographic region stretching from Maryland through Washington DC, and into Virginia. Amplifier Ventures' investment strategy is to capitalize on federal spending on technology research and development and consumption and invest in a balanced portfolio of entrepreneurial technology companies positioned to benefit from proximity to the federal government.

Geographic Preference: Maryland, Northern Virginia
Founded: 2004
Investment Criteria: Seed-Stage
Industry Group Preference: Software, New Media, Enterprise Software, Communication Technology, Materials Technology, Security, Clean Technology
Portfolio Companies: ArcheMedX, CardStar, College Factual, E-Chromic Technologies, Hook Mobile, Spyor Safe Mobile Security, Zenoss
Key Executives:
    Jonathan Aberman, Founder/Managing Director
    Education: BA, Political Science & Economics, George Washington University; MSc, International Economics, London School of Economics; MA, Downing College; LLM, New York University School of Law
    Background: Partner, Fenwick & West; Fish and Richardson; Pillsbury Winthrop; Investment Banking, Daiwa Securities; Donadlson Lufkin & Jenrette; Goldman Sachs International

120 AMPLIFY
Venice, CA

web: amplify.la

Mission Statement: Amplify is a venture capital fund focused on technology, entertainment, and media in Los Angeles, California.

Geographic Preference: US
Investment Criteria: Seed, Early Stage
Industry Group Preference: Artificial Intelligence, SaaS, Software, Consumer, Commerce, Automation, Health & Wellness, Virtual Reality, Blockchain, e-Commerce
Portfolio Companies: Advekit, Alpha Draft, Alto, Battlefy, Bitium, Brighten, The Bouqs Company, Card, CarPay, Cheese, Clutter, Countertop Foods, DSTLD, Estify, Fama, FanBread, The Flex Company, FloQast, Gem, Goodfair, HelloTech, Honeybee Health, HyperVR, Iconery, Lantern, Ledge, Lensabl, Little Labs, Look.io, Mapsense, Manufactured, Markett, MedRepublic, Mover.io, Pete Health, ProGuides, Ready Set Food, Repost, SafeRide, Sensay, Ship Mate, Skylar Body, SmartLane, StackCommerce, Stop Breathe & Think, String AI, Tapcart, Thankful AI, The Kive Company, Trace, Trials AI, Vetted Petcare, Volley, WeeCare, Winc

Key Executives:
    Paul Bricault, Managing Partner
    Background: Venture Partner, Greycroft; EVP, William Morris; Founder, Mailroom Fund
    Oded Noy, Managing Partner
    Background: Co-Founder/CTO, TrueCare; CTO, Zefr; Founder/CTO, TargetClose; Founder/Chair, LA CTO Forum
    Eric Pakravan, Vice President
    Education: University of Southern California
    Background: Founder, LavaLab
    Amanda Schutzbank, Vice President
    Education: BS, Wharton School
    Background: Primary Venture Partners; Karma Mobility; Techstars; Merrill Lynch

121 ANALYTICS VENTURES
6450 Lusk Boulevard
Suite E208
San Diego, CA 92121

Phone: 619-866-4400
web: www.analytics-ventures.com

Mission Statement: Analytics Ventures is the premier early-stage venture capital firm for digital analytics startups in San Diego. They offer world-class entrepreneur experience to founders seeking initial capital. They help entrepreneurs with proven operation and go-to-market experience and bring a broad network of top industry professionals to help ensure their clients' success.

Geographic Preference: San Diego Area
Fund Size: $124 million
Investment Criteria: Early-Stage
Industry Group Preference: Artificial Intelligence, Machine Learning, Technology, Applications, Software, Medicine
Portfolio Companies: AdTheos, AV Lab, Cure Match, Cute Metrix, Kazuhm, Tinoro
Key Executives:
    Blaise Barrelet, Managing Director
    Background: Founder, WebSideStory

122 ANDERSON PACIFIC CORPORATION
Chicago, IL 60611

e-mail: kda@andersonpacific.com
web: www.andersonpacific.com

Mission Statement: Anderson Pacific Corporation leads investor groups in partnerships with strong management teams

Venture Capital & Private Equity Firms / Domestic Firms

who acquire companies in various industries, predominantly in telecommunications, media and distribution.
Geographic Preference: Midwest
Founded: 1978
Average Investment: $5 million
Minimum Investment: $1 million
Investment Criteria: Early, Expansion, Turnaround, Buy-Out
Industry Group Preference: Telecommunications, Communications, Cable, Carriers, Cellular Service & Products, Internet Technology, Satellite Communications, Media
Portfolio Companies: Cityfront Partners LLC, ColoHub LLC, Cypress Cellular LP, Digital Capital Partners LLC, FBL Group LLC, iVelozity LLC, Neutral Path Communications LLC

Key Executives:
Kenneth D. Anderson, Chief Executive Officer
312-951-8500
e-mail: kda@andersonpacific.com
Education: University of Iowa
Background: Combined Cable Corporation

123 ANDLINGER & COMPANY INC
520 White Plains Road
Suite 500
Tarrytown, NY 10591

Phone: 914-332-4900
e-mail: info@andlinger.com
web: www.andlinger.com

Mission Statement: Andlinger & Company look to acquire independent or family-owned companies and corporate divisions or subsidiaries and to grow them into stronger, profitable leaders in their industry.
Geographic Preference: United States, Canada, Western Europe, Eastern Europe
Fund Size: $100 million
Founded: 1976
Average Investment: $25 million
Minimum Investment: $1 million
Investment Criteria: Acquisition, LBO, MBO, Recapitalization, Special Situations, Privatizations
Industry Group Preference: Clean Technology, Biotechnology, Communications Equipment, Computer Hardware & Software, Aerospace, Defense and Government, Diversified, Electronic Components, Energy, Environmental Protection, Industrial Equipment, Manufacturing, Chemicals, Medical Devices, Pharmaceuticals, Telecommunications
Portfolio Companies: Alltec Global, CyberAlert, Clesse, CPI. Crown Van Gelder, ETI, Eska, Global Graphics, Magnum Materials, Seitz, Solvis, Spoolex, Suspa, Steward Advanced Materials, VP360

Other Locations:
Sieveringer Strasse 36/9
Vienna 1190
Austria
Phone: 43-1-328-7145

Avenue Louise 326
Box 12
Brussels 1050
Belgium
Phone: 32-2-647-80-70

660 Beachland Boulevard
Suite 202
Vero Beach, FL 32963
Phone: 772-234-4998

Key Executives:
Merrick Andlinger, President
e-mail: mgandlinger@andlinger.net
Education: AB, Princeton University; MBA, Stanford Grad. School of Business
Background: Associate, Kroll Associates; VP Corporate Finance, Salomon Brothers; Managing Director, Smith Barney; President/CEO/Director, Pure Energy Corporation
Charles E. Ball, Managing Director, FL
Education: MBA, Suffolk University
Background: Managing Director, Bank of Boston Ltd., London
George Doomany, Managing Director, NY
Education: BA, Mathematics and Music, University of Rochester; MBA, Columbia University
Background: Finance and Accounting, Price Waterhouse & Co., New York; Managing Director, Bankers Trust Company; Managing Director, BT Capital Partners; Senior Managing Director, Mandarin Partners, LLC; Acting Chief Financial Officer, United States Manufacturing Co.
Stephen A. Magida, Managing Director, NY
Education: BS, Economics, Wharton School; University of Pennsylvania Columbia Law School, LLB
Background: Assistant Professor of Business Law, Virginia Polytechnic Institute; Assistant Professor of Business Law, The Wharton School University of Pennsylvania; Partner, Olwine, Connelly, Chase, O'Donnell & Weyher; Partner, Dechert Price & Rhoads
Ivar W. Mitchell, Managing Director, FL
Education: BS, University of Bridgeport; LLB, Columbia Law School; LLM, School of Law, New York University
Background: VP Taxes, ITT Levitt & Sons, Inc.; VP/Secretary, The Allen Group, Inc.; VP/CFO, Yusen Management Corp.

124 ANDREESSEN HOROWITZ
2865 Sand Hill Road
Suite 101
Menlo Park, CA 94025

e-mail: businessplans@a16z.com
web: a16z.com

Mission Statement: Aims to invest in seed to late-stage companies in the area of technology.
Fund Size: $7.1 Billion
Founded: 2009
Minimum Investment: $50,000
Investment Criteria: Start-Ups, Technology, Late-Stage
Industry Group Preference: Information Technology, Consumer Services, Enterprise Software
Portfolio Companies: Accolade, Actifio, AIQ, Affirm, Airbnb, Airware, Allset, Alluxio, Alt School, Ampersand, Anki, Apeel Science, Applied Intuition, Apptio, Asana, Asimov, Astranis, Atrium, Axoni, Barefoot Networks, Basis, Bebop, Benchling, Big, Bioage, Bitcoin, Blockspring, Boku, Bonfire, Box, Branch, Bromium, BuzzFeed, Cadre, Caffeine, Camp4, Capriza, Cardiogram, Cazena, Celo, Chia, Ciitizen, CipherCloud, Clear Story Data, CodeCombat, Coinbase, Comma, Compound, Cross River, Cumulus, CYNGN, CryptoKitties, Databricks, DEEPMAP, Descript, DFINITY, Dialpad, DigitalOcean, Dispatch, Dollar Shave Club, Doxel, Drishti, DWOLLA, dYdX, Earn.com, Earnin, Envoy, Ethereum, Everlaw, Facebook, Factual, Fanatics, Filecoin, Forward Networks, Foursquare, Freenome, Fusion.io, Genius, Gigster, GitHub, Glow, Gobble, GoodData, Granular, Groupon, Harbor, Hatch Loyalty, Health IQ, Honor, Human API, HVMN, iCracked, IFTTT, Illumio, Imgur, Imply, Improbable, Insitro, Instabase, Instacart, Instagram, Instart, Journera, Julep, Jungla, Keep, Keybase, Kong, Lime, Lookout, LTSE, Lyft, Lyrebird, Lytro, Magic Leap, Magnet, Maker, Maxta, Mayvenn, Medisas, Medium, Mesosphere, Meteor, Mixpanel, NationBuilder, Netlify, Micira, Oculus VR, OfferUp, Okta, Omada, Onshape, OpenBazaar, Opengov, OpenInvest, Optimizely, Orchid, Overtime, Pagerduty, Patientping, PeerStreet, Pindrop, Pinterest, Point, Polychain Capital, Product Hunt, Propel, Proven., Q Bio, Rabbit, RapidAPI, Rappi, Reflektive, Rigetti, Samsara, Shapeways, Shield AI, Shift,

Venture Capital & Private Equity Firms / Domestic Firms

Key Executives:
Marc Andreessen, Co-Founder & General Partner
Education: BS, Computer Science, University of Illinois at Urbana-Champaign
Background: Netscape; Loudcloud
Directorships: Anki; Bracket Computing; Dialpad; Honor; Lytro; Mori; OpenGov; Samsara; Facebook; Hewlett-Packard Enterprise
Ben Horowitz, Co-Founder & General Partner
Education: BA, Computer Science, Columbia University; MS, Computer Science, UCLA
Background: Lotus Development Corporation; Netscape; AOL; Opsware; Hewlett-Packard
Directorships: Caffeine, Capriza, Databricks, Foursquare, Genius, Lyft, Magnet Systems, Medium, NationBuilder, Okta, SignalFx, Sisu, Tanium, TripActions, United Masters, Usermind, CODE2040
Connie Chan, General Partner
Education: BA, Economics, MS, Management Science & Engineering, Stanford University
Background: HP; Private Equity Investor, Elevation Partners
Jeff Jordan, Managing Partner
Education: BA, Political Science & Psychology, Amherst College; MBA, Stanford University Graduate School of Business
Background: Senior VP/General Manager, eBay; President, PayPal; Chairman/CEO, OpenTable; Chief Financial Officer, Hollywood Entertainment; President, Reel.com; Senior VP of Finance, The Disney Stores
Directorships: Accolade, Airbnb, Hatch, Instacart, Lime, Lookout, OfferUp, Pinterest, Walter & Company, Wonderschool

125 ANGEL STREET CAPITAL
402 Angell Street
Providence, RI 02906

Phone: 401-854-1850
e-mail: rmaccini@angelstreetcapital.com
web: angelstreetcapital.wordpress.com

Mission Statement: Angel Street Capital assists companies in the early stages of their life cycle, providing both consulting services and capital. Principals have a long track record of successfully investing in digital media and related industries, and generating impressive returns.

Founded: 2010
Average Investment: $50,000 - $250,000
Investment Criteria: Early-Stage
Industry Group Preference: Digital Media & Marketing
Portfolio Companies: FlexReceipts, Closely

Key Executives:
Joseph V. Gallagher, Managing Director
401-841-9484
e-mail: jgallagher@angelstreetcapital.com
Education: BA, English & Classics, Georgetown University
Background: CEO, Aritaur Communications
Robert J. Maccini, Managing Director
401-854-1850
e-mail: rmaccini@angelstreetcapital.com
Education: BA, Economics, College of the Holy Cross; MBA, Finance, Babson College
Background: Founder/CEO, Ando Media
Stephan C. Sloan, Director
401-854-1850
e-mail: ssloan@angelstreetcapital.com
Education: Salve Regina University

126 ANGELENO GROUP
2029 Century Park East
Suite 2980
Los Angeles, CA 90067

Phone: 310-552-2790 Fax: 310-552-2727
e-mail: info@angelenogroup.com
web: www.angelenogroup.com

Mission Statement: Angeleno Group specializes in providing growth capital to next generation companies in the clean energy and natural resources sectors. Angeleno Group invests in a wide range of deal types and primarily seeks opportunities in the United States, Asia and Australia. Since its founding in 2001, AG has grown into one of the largest energy growth equity investment firms.

Geographic Preference: United States, Asia, Australia
Fund Size: $200 million
Founded: 2001
Average Investment: $5 - $25 million
Industry Group Preference: Energy, Alternative Energy, Clean Transportation, Emissions Control, Energy Efficiency, Power Infrastructure, Renewable Energy, Solar Energy, Waste & Recycling, Advanced Materials, Logistics
Portfolio Companies: ArzonSolar, Click Energy, Critigen, Crius Energy, eCullet, EdeniQ, Eka Systems, GT Advanced Technologies, INRIX, Kinematics, Konarka Technologies, Metriv, mPrest New Forests, newterra, ParkMe, Patriot Environmental Services, PowerGenix Systems, Renew Financial, Scodix, Soraa, Stem, Sunlink Corporation, Telogis, TPI Composites, Verdiem Corporation, Verengo Solar, Xicato, ZincFive

Key Executives:
Yaniv Tepper, Managing Partner/Co-Founder
Education: BS, Mechanical Engineering, University of California, Berkeley; MS, Civil & Environmental Engineering, MS, Management, Massachusetts Institute of Technology
Background: Aetna/ING Investment Management; Engineering R&D, Bechtel
Daniel Weiss, Managing Partner/Co-Founder
Education: BA, University of California, Berkeley; MA, Stanford University; JD, Stanford Law School
Background: Attorney, O'Melveny & Myers
Jeanne Li, Senior Analyst
Education: BA, Financial Economics, Columbia University; General Securites Representative
Background: Analyst, BNP Paribas; Analyst, Bank of America
William Miller, Chief Operating Officer
Education: BS, Accounting, California State University; CPA
Background: CFO, MuniMac Management Group; CFO, Themis Asset Strategies; COO, Transamerica Investment Management; CFO, Kanye Anderson; VP, Accounting & CCO, Pilgrim Group
Paula Robins, Chief Financial Officer
Education: Stanford University; MBA, Anderson Graduate School of Management, University of California, Los Angeles
Background: CFO, Smart Technology Ventures; Price Waterhouse; Treasury Department, Long Beach Bank; Tenet Healthcare
Danny Jaffe, Principal
Education: BS, Business Administration, Haas School of Business, University of California, Berkeley
Background: Analyst, Leviticus Partners; Financial Analyst, Bay City Capital
Anil Tammineedi, Principal
Education: BE, Electrical Engineering, PSG College of Technology; MS, Electrical Engineering, Iowa State University; MBA, Anderson Graduate School of Management, UCLA
Background: Product Management, Broadcom; Applied Ventures; Clearstone Venture Partners

Venture Capital & Private Equity Firms / Domestic Firms

Michelle Kincanon, Vice President, Finance and Sustainability
Education: BS, Management Science, University of California, San Diego; MBA, University of California, Irvine
Background: Controller, Mayfield Fund; Bingham McCutchen
David Nguyen, Associate
Education: BS, Business Administration, Haas School of Business, University of California, Berkeley
Background: Analyst, Goldman, Sachs & Co.

127 ANGELO, GORDON & CO.
245 Park Avenue
New York, NY 10167
Phone: 212-692-2000 Fax: 212-867-9328
Toll-Free: 800-805-0024
e-mail: information@angelogordon.com
web: www.angelogordon.com

Mission Statement: Angelo, Gordon & Co. seek to generate absolute returns with low volatility by exploiting inefficiencies in selected markets and capitalizing on situations that qualify for alternative investments.

Fund Size: $10 million
Founded: 1988
Average Investment: $30 million
Minimum Investment: $10 million
Investment Criteria: Control Buyouts, Minority Investments, Management Buyouts, Private Company Recapitalizations, Corporate Lift-outs
Industry Group Preference: Financial Services, Retailing, Consumer Products, Healthcare, Business Products & Services
Portfolio Companies: Aveta, National Home Healthcare Corp., AG Semi, KEE Action Sports, Benihana, Firebirds Restaurants, Steve Nash Fitness Clubs, Crunch, Kings Foodmart, ClearBalance, Hamilton State Bank, Oak Street Funding

Other Locations:
2000 Avenue of the Stars
Suite 1020
Los Angeles, CA 90067
Phone: 310-777-5440 Fax: 310-246-0796

111 South Wacker Drive
36th Floor
Chicago, IL 60606
Phone: 312-763-5100

Angelo, Gordon Europe LLP
23 Savile Row
London W1S 2ET
United Kingdom
Phone: 44-207-758-5300 Fax: 44-207-207-758-5420

Angelo, Gordon Netherlands B.V.
Prinsengracht 919
Amsterdam 1017 KD
Netherlands
Phone: 31-020-262-0660 Fax: 31-020-262-0664

Angelo, Gordon Europe LLP
Milan, Galleria Vittorio Emanuele
Via Mengoni 4
Milan 20121
Italy
Phone: 39 02 3031 5120

Angelo, Gordon Asia Limited
Suite 1604, One Exchange Square
Central
Hong Kong
Phone: 852-3416-7300 Fax: 852-3416-7500

Angelo, Gordon Asia Limited
9F, A Tower, The-K Twin Towers
50 Jongno 1-Gil, Jongno-Gu
Seoul 03142
Korea
Phone: 822-721-5200 Fax: 822-721-5225

Angelo, Gordon International LLC
Roppongi Hills Mori Tower, 17th Floor
6-10-1, Roppongi, Minato-ku
Tokyo 106-6117
Japan
Phone: 81-3-5474-5610 Fax: 81-3-5474-5620

Key Executives:
Michael L. Gordon, Chief Executive Officer/Co-Chief Investment Officer
Education: BA, Colby College; JD, Boston Univ. School of Law
Background: Research Analyst, L.F. Rothschild
Directorships: Director, Research, L.F. Rothschild
Josh Baumgarten, Co-Chief Investment Officer
Education: BS, Economics, Wharton School, University of Pennsylvania
Background: Portfolio Manager, AG Super Fund; Portfolio Manager, Blackrock; Investment Banker, Jefferies
Directorships: Senior Managing Director, Blackstone
Kirk Whickman, President
Education: BA, Dartmouth College; JD, MBA, Brigham Young University
Background: General Cousel, Morgan Stanley's Global Wealth Management; Senior Vice President/General Counsel, Aetna Financial Services & Aetna Inc.
Adam Schwartz, Co-Chief Investment Officer
Education: BA, University of Pennsylvania
Background: M&A. Vornado Realty Trust

128 ANGELPAD
New York, NY
web: www.angelpad.org

Mission Statement: An intensive mentorship program to help startups build better products, raise the funding they need to succeed and ultimately grow more successful businesses

Fund Size: $200 million
Founded: 2010
Average Investment: $11 million
Minimum Investment: $ 120,000
Investment Criteria: Startups,
Industry Group Preference: Marketing, API, Data, B2C, Advertising, Mobile, Healthcare, AI
Portfolio Companies: AgentDesks, Allay, Alltrails, Astronomer, Beamery, Buffer, Coverhound, Drone Deploy, Fieldwire, Hive, HumanAPI, Iterable, Kinnek, Loftsmart, Paintzen, Periscope Data, Pipedrive, Postmates, Rolepoint, Sensor Tower, Simplifeye, Tray.io, Truly Wireless, Upcounsel, Vungle, Wove, Zum

Key Executives:
Carine Magescas, Co-Founder
Education: M, Economics, Monetary International Relations, Unversité Paris Daupine; DESS (Post-Masters Degree), Logistics, Marketing and Merchandising, Université Paris Dauphine
Background: Founder, illico design; Moreover Technologies; Semio Corporation; Informatica
Thomas Korte, Co-Founder
Education: University of Mannheim; MBA, Freie Universität Berlin; Stanford Graduate School of Business
Background: Google

129 ANGELS' FORUM LLC
2665 Marine Way
Suite 1150
Mountain View, CA 94043
Phone: 650-857-0700
web: www.angelsforum.com

Mission Statement: The Angels' Forum consists of a group of experienced investors who invest their own wealth in

emerging companies. TAF reviews approximately 20 deals per week and makes 5-15 new investments per year.
Geographic Preference: Silicon Valley, Bay Area-based companies
Fund Size: $18 million
Founded: 1997
Average Investment: $1 - $3 million
Minimum Investment: $100,000
Investment Criteria: Seed, Startups, Early-Stage
Industry Group Preference: Consumer Products, Enterprise Services, Industrial Products, Internet Technology, Medical Devices, Networking, Software, E-Commerce & Manufacturing, Clean Technology
Portfolio Companies: Aravo Solutions, Bell Biosystems, Bouxtie, Cargo Chief, Chimera Bioengineering, DecisionNext, The Detection Group, Ensighten, FE3 Medical, Glue Networks, Intrapace, Kiana Analytics, Kinestral, Laughing Glass Cocktails, Mission Bio, OneMob, PanTerra Networks, RenovoRx, Revfluence, Sonos, Talent Sky, Taulia, Theron Pharmaceuticals, Tiatros, TranscribeMe, Vida, Vidlet
Key Executives:
  Carol Sands Langensand, Managing Member/Founder
  Education: BA, Political Marketing, University of Iowa
  Background: Product Marketing Manager, Motorola; Marketing Officer, First Bank Systems; Director, Marketing, Arthur Young; Director, Marketing, Coopers & Lybrand Consulting; Founder & Owner, Sands MarketingPlus
  Directorships: Silicon Valley Association of Startup Entrepreneurs
  Leif Langensand, Chief Financial Officer
  Education: BS, Forest Products, University of California, Berkeley
  Background: Charles Schwab; Price Waterhouse; First Nationwide Bank; Decision Dynamics

130 ANNEX VENTURES
3031 Tisch Way
Suite 505
Jan Jose, CA 95128

web: www.annexventures.com

Mission Statement: Annex Ventures supports early-stage funding for entrepreneurs in the hi-tech, bio-tech and medical device markets.
Founded: 2005
Average Investment: $2 million
Minimum Investment: $100,000
Investment Criteria: Early-Stage
Industry Group Preference: High Technology, Biotechnology, Medical Devices
Portfolio Companies: Listo!, Lucid, Air Media, Im In, iWin.com, Alta Analog Inc., Blue 7 Communications, Jeda Technologies, iSeek, Loadstar Sensors, Nethra, Shimon Systems, PingPad
Key Executives:
  Ven N. Reddy, General Partner
  Education: BS, Information Systems & Electrical Engineering, San Jose State University
  Background: Intel Corporation, Alliance Semiconductor
  Mark E. Pearson, General Partner
  Education: BS, University of San Francisco
  Background: Founder, Catalyst Real Estate Group

131 ANTARES CAPITAL CORPORATION
PO Box 330309
Miami, FL 33233-0309

Phone: 305-894-2888 Fax: 305-894-3227
e-mail: jkislak@antarescapital.com
web: www.antarescapital.com

Mission Statement: A private venture capital firm investing equity capital in expansion stage companies and management buyout opportunities for firms headquartered in the Southeast and Texas.
Geographic Preference: Southeast, Texas
Fund Size: $2.4 billion
Founded: 1993
Average Investment: $500,000-$5 million
Minimum Investment: $250,000
Investment Criteria: Developmental, Expansion Stage
Portfolio Companies: AEMT, Inc., Alphatronix, Inc., AnyRiver, BancWest Bancorp, Inc., Bankrate, Inc., BML Pharmaceuticals, Inc., BRPH Architects-Engineers, Inc., Cellit, Inc., Clear-to-Send Electronics, Inc., Crystal Dynamics, Inc., Dispatch Management Services, DTx, Inc., Flood Data Services, Inc., ISO Group, JRL Systems, Inc., Masada Security, Inc., Micro Networks/Andersen Laboratories, National Product Services, Inc., Neotonus, Inc., Nueva Cocina Foods, Inc., Outback Steakhouse, Inc., Sano Corporation, SportsLine.com, Inc., StadiaNet Sports, Inc., Summit Financial Services Group, Triage Management Services
Other Locations:
  PO Box 410730
  Melbourne, FL 32941
  Phone: 321-777-4884 Fax: 321-777-5884
Key Executives:
  Randall E. Poliner, Founder/General Partner
  e-mail: rpoliner@antarescapital.com
  Education: BSEE, Georgia Institute of Technology; MSEE, Carnegie-Mellon; MBA, Harvard Business School
  Background: Founder/COO, Macrodyne; President/CEO, Flood Data Services; VP Operations, Scientific Systems Services
  Jonathan I. Kislak, General Partner
  305-894-2888
  Fax: 305-894-3227
  e-mail: jkislak@antarescapital.com
  Education: BA Economics, Harvard College
  Background: Founder, Kislak Capital; Deputy Under Secretary, Small Community/Rural Development, US Department of Agriculture

132 ANTHEM VENTURE PARTNERS
225 Arizona Avenue
Suite 200
Santa Monica, CA 90401

Phone: 310-899-6225 Fax: 310-899-6234
e-mail: info@anthemvp.com
web: www.anthemvp.com

Mission Statement: Anthem Venture Partners seek to provide early-stage investments and operational guidance to distinctive entrepreneurs.
Geographic Preference: United States, Southern California
Fund Size: $100 million
Founded: 2001
Average Investment: $1 - 5 million
Minimum Investment: $1 million
Investment Criteria: Startup, Early Stage, First Stage, Second Stage, MBO
Industry Group Preference: Biotechnology, Communications Equipment, Telecommunications, Computer Hardware & Software, Diversified, Education, Electronic Components, Health Related, Medical, Information Technology, Online Content, Networking, Pharmaceuticals, Internet, New Media
Portfolio Companies: Affinity Networks, Android, Audyssey, Axiom Microdevices, Big Frame, Blurb, Card.com, Cognet, Corus Pharma, Cynvenio Biosystems, DemandMedia, Designers House, Dot Wireless, Entropic Communications, FileTrek, Glossi, Interset, Janrain User Management Platform, Layer, The Lucky Group, Matic, Meez, Madefire, Nevenvision, NewHound, Nextest System Corporation, Ocata Therapeutics, Panna, Planet A.T.E., Plixi, Pricelock, Prism Skylabs, RFmagic, Scopely, Siperian,

Venture Capital & Private Equity Firms / Domestic Firms

SpinMedia, Solarflare, StackIQ, Surfair, Troika Networks, TrueCar, Video Amp, Viewdle, Vuvox, WaveStream

Key Executives:
William Woodward, Founder/Managing Director
Education: BS Business Administration, University of Southern California
Samit Varma, Partner
Education: BS, Mechanical Engineering, United States Naval Academy; MBA, Marshall School of Business, University of Southern California
Background: Audyssey Labs; United States Navy
Claudia L. Llanos, Partner/Chief Financial Officer
Education: BA, California State University at Northridge
Background: Ernst & Young, LlP

---

133 ANZU PARTNERS
44 Manning Road
2nd Floor
Billerica, MA 01821

Phone: 202-742-5870
e-mail: info@anzupartners.com
web: anzupartners.com

Mission Statement: Anzu Partners is an investment firm focusing on breakthrough life science technology companies.

Fund Size: $350 Million

Other Locations:
2223 Avenida De La Playa
Suite 204
La Jolla, CA 92037

12610 Race Track Road
Suite 250
Tampa, FL 33626

1399 New York Avenue NW
Suite 601
Washington, DC 20005

Key Executives:
Whitney Haring-Smith, Managing Partner
Education: Yale University; PhD, Oxford University
Background: Principal, Boston Consulting Group; Co-Founder, College Abacus
David Michael, Managing Partner
Education: BA, Harvard University; MBA, Stanford Business School
Background: Senior Partner, Boston Consulting Group
David Seldin, Managing Partner
Education: BS, University of Pennsylvania; MBA, University of Chicago
Background: President, Jacksonville Jaguars NFL Franchise; President, Catalyst Inc.
Directorships: Nice-Pak Products Inc.

---

134 AOL VENTURES
770 Broadway
4th, 5th, 6th & 9th Floors
New York, NY 10003-9562

e-mail: ventures@corp.aol.com
web: www.oath.com

Mission Statement: AOL Ventures is the venture capital arm of AOL, focused on early stage investing in technology-centric consumer Internet companies.

Geographic Preference: United States, Israel, India
Founded: 2010
Average Investment: $50,000 - $3 million
Investment Criteria: Seed-Stage, Series A, Early-Stage
Industry Group Preference: Consumer Internet

Other Locations:
13031 West Jefferson Boulevard
Building 900
Los Angeles, CA 90094

Key Executives:
Tim Armstrong, Chief Executive Officer
Education: BS, Economics/Sociology, Connecticut College
Background: Director, Integrated Sales & Marketing, Starwave; President, Operations/SVP, Google; The Walt Disney Company
Tim Lemmon, Chief Operating Officer
Education: University of Cambridge; Wharton School, University of Pennsylvania
Background: Vice President, American Express Business Travel

---

135 APAX PARTNERS
601 Lexington Avenue
53rd Floor
New York, NY 10022

Phone: 212-753-6300
web: www.apax.com

Mission Statement: Apax Partners has raised and advised 31 funds. The partnership was a venture investing pioneer in Europe and the U.S.

Geographic Preference: United States, Europe, Asia
Fund Size: $7 billion
Founded: 1969
Average Investment: $20 million
Minimum Investment: $3.5 million
Investment Criteria: All stages
Industry Group Preference: Technology & Telecommunications, Services, Healthcare, Consumer
Portfolio Companies: ADCO Group, Advantage Sales & Marketing, Answers Corporation, AssuredPartners, Attenti, Authority Brands, Auto Trader Group, Boats Group, Candela, Cengage Learning, Cole Haan, Duck Creek Technologies, ECi Software Solutions, Fractal Analytics, FULLBEAUTY Brands, GamaLife, General Healthcare Group Limited, Genius Sports, Global-e, Go Global Travel, Healthium MedTech, Huayue Education, Ideal Protein, Idealista, Inmarsat, Karl Lagerfeld, Kepro, Lexitas, Manappuram Finance Limited, Max, MetaMetrics, Moda Operandi, Neuraxpharm, Paycor Inc., Psagot, Quality Distribution, Ramet Trom, S.R. Accord, Safetykleen, Schulz Catering, Shriram City Union Finance, Signavio, Solita, Sophos, SoYoung, Takko, Ten10, ThoughtWorks, TIVIT, Tommy Hilfiger, Tosca Services, Trade Me, TRADER, Unilabs, Vyaire Medical, Wizeline, Zap Group, Zensar Technologies

Other Locations:
33 Jermyn Street
London SW1Y 6DN
United Kingdom
Phone: 44 20 7872 6300 Fax: 44 20 7666 3441

Apax Partners Betelingungsberatung GmbH
Theatinerstr. 3
Munich 80333
Germany
Phone: 49 89 99 89 09 0 Fax: 49 89 99 89 09 33

Apax Partners (Israel) Ltd.
Museum Tower
4 Berkowitz Street
Tel Aviv 64238
Israel
Phone: 972 3 777 4400 Fax: 972 3 777 4411

Apax Partners Hong Kong Ltd.
16/F Nexxus Building
41 Connaught Road Central
Hong Kong

China
Phone: 852 2200 5813 **Fax:** 852 2200 5820

Apax Partners India Advisers Private Limited
Peninsula Corporate Park, Ganpatrao Kadam Marg
Lower Parel (West)
Mumbai 400 013
India
Phone: 91 22 4050 8400 **Fax:** 91 22 4050 8444

65th Floor, Shanghai World Financial Center
100 Century Avenue
Shanghai 200120
China
Phone: 86 21 5198 5600

Key Executives:
Mitch Truwit, Partner & Co-CEO
Education: Vassar College; Harvard Business School
Background: Orbitz Worldwide; priceline.com
Directorships: AssuredPartners, Inc.; Answers Corporation; Bankrate; Dominion Marine Media; Quality Distribution Inc.
Andrew Sillitoe, Partner & Co-CEO
Education: University of Oxford; INSEAD
Background: LEK
Directorships: Inmarsat; Intelsat; King; TDC; TIVIT; Unilabs
Simon Cresswell, Partner & General Counsel
Education: University of Melbourne; Edith Cowan University
Background: Goldman Sachs; Davis Polk & Wardwell; Mallesons
Ralf Gruss, Partner & Chief Operating Officer
Education: Technical University (Karlsruhe); University of Massachusetts; London School of Economics
Background: Arthur D. Little International Inc.
Directorships: LR Health; Beauty Systems GmbH

136 APERTURE VENTURE PARTNERS
645 Madison Avenue
20th Floor
New York, NY 10022
Phone: 212-758-7325 **Fax:** 212-319-8779
e-mail: info@aperturevp.com
web: www.aperturevp.com

Mission Statement: A venture capital group committed to working with exceptional entrepreneurs to tackle significant problems and create major new opportunities.
Geographic Preference: Northeast, West Coast
Founded: 1974
Average Investment: $1-4 million
Minimum Investment: $1 million
Investment Criteria: Second Stage or later, Healthcare Information Technology, Medical Devices, Healthcare, Biopharmaceuticals, Biotechnology
Portfolio Companies: Avedro, Aclaris Therapeutics, BioHaven Pharmaceuticals, Cameron Health, Cardiocore, Cardiomems, Cardiac Dimensions, Ceptaris Therapeutics, Ception Therapeutics, Channel Medsystems, College Pharmaceuticals, Concerro, Conor Medsystems, Endotronix, Entrigue Surgical, Interlace Medical, Inspire, Lyric Pharmaceuticals, Mako Surgical Corp., Neuros Medical, Therox, Tonomy, Trevi Therapeutics, Spirox, T2 Biosystems, Transmolecular, VenusConcept, Xlumena

Key Executives:
Paul E. Tierney Jr., General Partner
e-mail: paul@aperturevp.com
Education: BA, University of Notre Dame; MBA, Harvard Business School
Background: Co-Founder, Coniston Partners; Founder, Coniston Global Partners; Corporate Value Partners; Darwin Capital Partners
Directorships: Altea Therapeutics, TechnoServe
Thomas P. Cooper, MD, General Partner
e-mail: tom@aperturevp.com

Education: BA, DePauw University; MD, Indiana University
Background: Co-Founder, Spectrum Emergency Care; Co-Founder, Correctional Medical Services; Vericare; Mobilex USA
Directorships: Hanger Orthopedic, Kindred Healthcare
Eric H. Sillman, General Partner
e-mail: eric@aperturevp.com
Education: BA, Brown University; MBA, Harvard Business School
Background: UBS Warburg; Parthenon Group; TechnoServe
Directorships: TechnoServe

137 APEX VENTURE PARTNERS
225 West Washington Street
Suite 1500
Chicago, IL 60606
Phone: 312-857-2800 **Fax:** 312-857-1800
e-mail: apex@apexvc.com

Mission Statement: Apex Venture Partner's philosophy is to build significant value in their portfolio companies in close partnership with their management teams.
Geographic Preference: North America
Fund Size: $140 million
Founded: 1987
Average Investment: $10 million
Minimum Investment: $500,000
Investment Criteria: Seed to Growth Stage
Industry Group Preference: Consumer Services, Environment Products & Services, Information Technology, Software, Retailing, Telecommunications, Enterprise Services, Infrastructure, Applications Software & Services, Clean Technology, Business Products & Services
Portfolio Companies: Advanced Equities Financial Corp., Ali Solutions, Analyte Media, Appolicious, Bloom Energy, Combinenet, Current Analysis, Digitalwork, Dirtt Environmental Solutions, Enkata Technologies, Envestnet, Ifbyphone, Illumitex, IQS Inc., Sittercity, Solfocus, Suniva, Target Data, Timelines, Trunk Club

138 APHELION CAPITAL
100 Tiburon Boulevard
Suite 215
Mill Valley, CA 94941
Phone: 415-944-8123
e-mail: venture@aphelioncap.com
web: www.aphelioncapital.net

Mission Statement: Aphelion Capital is a venture capital firm focused on supporting the growth of innovative medical technology with an emphasis on fast to market, low capital intense products that reduce the cost of delivering quality healthcare.

Founded: 2005
Investment Criteria: Seed-Stage to Later-Stage
Industry Group Preference: Healthcare, Wellness
Portfolio Companies: ClearLab, ClearFlow, Cymedica Orthopedics, CytoPherx, Explorer Surgical, iHear, Mercator MedSystems, Neuroptics, Niveus Medical, Palo Alto Health Sciences, Providence Medical Technology, Siesta Medical, Vynca, Aurora SFC Systems, Catheter Connections, Corium, Insound Medical, Insulet Corp., OrthoScan, Surgicount Medical, Surgiquest, Tria Beauty, Vasonova

Key Executives:
Ned Scheetz, Managing Partner
Education: Colby College, Duke University Fuqua School of Business, Univ. of Oxford
Background: Partner, Piper Jaffray Ventures; Janus Capital
John Kim, MD, Principal
Education: Harvard University, Duke University School

Venture Capital & Private Equity Firms / Domestic Firms

of Medicine, Fuqua School of Business
Background: Bear Stearns & Co.

139 APJOHN GROUP LLC
350 E Michigan Ave
Suite 500
Kalamazoo, MI 49007

Phone: 269-349-8999 **Fax:** 269-349-8993
web: www.apjohngroup.com

Mission Statement: Apjohn Group invests in early-stage life science opportunities, with a special focus on biopharmaceuticals.
Geographic Preference: Midwest
Investment Criteria: Early-Stage
Industry Group Preference: Biopharmaceuticals, Healthcare, Pharmaceuticals, Medical, Information Technology, Medical Devices
Portfolio Companies: Afmedica, Sierra Oncology, Armune BioScience, MuciMed, Tetra Discovery Partners
Key Executives:

   Donald R. Parfet, Managing Director
   e-mail: drparfet@ameritech.net
   Education: BA Economics, University of Arizona; MBA Finance, University of Michigan
   Background: SVP, Pharmacia; Trustee, WE Upjohn Institute for Employment Research; Trustee/Chairman, Bronson Healthcare Group; Chairman, Kalamazoo College
   Directorships: Biocore International AB
   Jack R. Luderer, MD, Founding Partner
   Education: Masters Chemistry, Northwestern University
   Background: ssociate VP Research, Western Michigan University; VP US Medical Affairs, Pharmacia; Board Certified in both Internal Medicine and Clinical Pharmacology
   Peter R. Seaver, Founding Partner
   Education: BA Biology, Bowdoin College
   Background: President Healthcare Group, Kaleidoscope Television; Executive Director, Pharmacia and Upjohn; First Lieutenant, US Army Medical Service Corps
   Directorships: University of Arizona Pharmacy School; National Association of Chain Drug Stores; Barr Laboratories; Nelson Information Systems; Fellows of the Harvard School of Dental
   Joseph T. Sobota, MD, Founding Partner
   e-mail: jts100@sbcglobal.net
   Education: AB Chemistry, Drew University; MD, Georgetown University; Post MD residency, Tulane University
   Background: CEO, Rubicon Genomics; President/COO, Biopure; EVP/COO, Chugai-Upjohn; Board Certifed in Anatomic and Clinical Pathology; Visiting Professor of Pathology, Dartmouth Medical School; Adjunct Professor of Medicine, Northwestern University School of Medicine
   Eli L. Thomssen, Associate Director
   Education: BS Animal Science, University of Nebraska; MBA, Western Michigan University
   Background: Senior Consultant, Brakke Consulting; VP Business Development/Strategic Planning, Pharmacia Animal Health
   Ronald J. Shebuski, PhD, General Partner
   Education: BS, Microbiology, University of Wisconsin; PhD, Pharmacology, University of Minnesota Medical School
   Background: Pharmacia & Upjohn; VP, Afmedica, Inc.; Senior Scientist, Merck Research Laboratories; Smith Kline & French
   Charles M. Hall, PhD, General Partner
   Education: University of the South in Sewanee, TN; PhD, Organic Chemistry, University of Minnesota
   Phillip C. Carra, General Partner
   e-mail: pccarra@sbcglobal.net
   Background: VP, Public Affairs, Pfizer

M. Holly Folk, General Partner
Background: CFO, Afmedica; Peat Marwick & Mitchell

140 APOLLO GLOBAL MANAGEMENT
9 West 57th Street
43rd Floor
New York, NY 10019

Phone: 212-515-3200
web: www.apollo.com

Mission Statement: Apollo Global Management invests in private equity, credit and real estate. Dedicated to creating value, Apollo Global Management raises, manages and provides capital for investors and industry leading businesses.
Geographic Preference: North America, Europe, Asia
Fund Size: $17.5 billion
Founded: 1990
Average Investment: $200 million
Minimum Investment: $20 million
Investment Criteria: Traditional Buyouts, Distressed Buyouts, Debt Investments, Corporate Partner Buyouts
Industry Group Preference: Chemicals, Commodities, Consumer Products, Retail, Consumer & Leisure, Distribution, Transportation, Financial Services, Business Products & Services, Manufacturing, Industrial, Media, Packaging, Satellite Communications, Wireless, Leisure
Portfolio Companies: Berry Plastics, Caesars Entertainment, Claire's, Countrywide plc, CEVA Logistics, Hexion Specialty Chemicals, Jacuzzi Brands, LyondellBasell Industries, McGraw-Hill Education, Momentive Performance Materials, Novitex Enterprise Solutions, Realogy, Rexnord, Vantium Management, Verso Paper

Other Locations:
3 Bryant Park
New York, NY 10036
Phone: 212-515-3200

2000 Avenue of the Stars
Suite 510N
Los Angeles, CA 90067
Phone: 310-843-1900

1 Manhattanville Road
Suite 201
Purchase, NY 10577
Phone: 914-694-8000

7255 Woodmont Avenue
Bethesda, MD 20814
Phone: 240-630-2700

700 Louisiana Street
Suite 2710
Houston, TX 77002
Phone: 832-708-2000

Apollo Management International LLP
25 St. George Street
London W1S 1FS
United Kingdom
Phone: 44-2070165000

Apollo Management Advisors GmbH
mainBuilding
Taunusanlage 16
Frankfurt 60325
Germany
Phone: 49-69789887000

Le Dome, 3rd Floor
2-8, Avenue Charles de Gaulle
Luxembourg L-1653
Luxembourg
Phone: 352-20881300

Apollo Management Asia Pacific Limited
The Hong Kong Club Building
Suites 1301-1303, 3A Chater Road
Central

Venture Capital & Private Equity Firms / Domestic Firms

Hong Kong
Phone: 852-35886300

Apollo Management Singapore Pte. Ltd.
61 Robinson Road
Level 11, Suite 1, Robinson Centre 68893
Singapore
Phone: 65-63725440

AGM India Advisors Pte. Ltd.
The Grand Hyatt Complex
Suite F-11, Maharashtra
Mumbai 400 055
India
Phone: 91-2239571400

Key Executives:
Leon Black, Founder/Chairman/CEO
Education: AB, Philosophy & History, Dartmouth College; MBA, Harvard Business School
Background: Founder, Lion Advisors; Co-Founder, Apollo Real Estate Advisors; Managing Director, Drexel Burnham Lambert
Directorships: Apollo Global Management LLC, The New York City Partnership, The Museum of Modern Art, FasterCures, Port Authority Task Force
Joshua Harris, Co-Founder/Senior Managing Director
Education: BS, Economics, Wharton School, University of Pennsylvania; MBA, Harvard Business School
Background: M&A Group, Drexel Burnham Lambert
Directorships: Berry Plastics Group, LyondellBasell Industries, CEVA Group plc, Momentive Performance Materials, EP Energy and Constellium
Marc Rowan, Co-Founder/Senior Managing Director
Education: BS, MBA, Finance, Wharton School
Background: M&A Group, Drexel Burnham Lambert
Directorships: Athene Holding, Caesars Entertainment Corp., Caesars Acquisition Corp.
Sanjay Patel, Senior Partner/Chairman International
Education: Eton College; Harvard College, Harvard University; MBA, Stanford Graduate School of Business
Background: Goldman Sachs; PIA
Directorships: Brit Insurance, Countrywide Holdings, Aurum Holdings
Scott Kleinman, Co-President
Education: BA, University of Pennsylvania; BS, Wharton School
Background: Investment Banking, Smith Barney
Directorships: Lyondell Basell Industries, Taminco Global Chemicals, Verso Paper, Realogy, Momentive Performance Materials
James Zelter, Co-President/CIO
Education: BS, Economics, Duke University
Background: CIO, Citigroup Alternative Investments; Trader, Goldman Sachs
Directorships: DUMAC

141 APPIAN EDUCATION VENTURES
e-mail: info@appianeducation.com
web: appianeducation.com

Mission Statement: A firm that invests in and operates high-growth, high-impact educational ventures. At the core of AppianBs vision is the idea that well-targeted, socially-conscious private investment in education can have a profound impact on the future.

Geographic Preference: Latin America
Founded: 2012
Industry Group Preference: Education, Vocational Training, Educational Technologies, Publishing

Key Executives:
Luis E Garcia Garcia de Brigard, Founder/Managing Partner
Education: LLB, Universidad Javeriana; MEd, Harvard University; MBA, MIT
Background: CEO, Americas, Inspired Education; Deputy Minister of Education, Government of Colombia
Directorships: Global Education Innovation Initiative; Varkey Foundation; SOS Children's Villages
Juan Uribe, Partner
Alejandro Maldonado, Partner

142 APPIAN VENTURES
4810 Prospect Street
Littleton, CO 80123
Phone: 303-830-2450
web: www.appianvc.com

Mission Statement: Appian's practice is to connect with entrepreneurs by treating them respectfully and their ideas thoughtfully. The firm's whole company investment method sharpens a company's business focus and connects industry resources to help accelerate success.

Geographic Preference: Western United States
Fund Size: $80 million
Founded: 2002
Average Investment: $5 million
Minimum Investment: $3 million
Investment Criteria: Seed, Startup, First Stage, Second Stage, Bridge
Industry Group Preference: Computer Hardware & Software
Portfolio Companies: AdPay, Auctionpay, Cadre, Carefx, Collective Intellect, ETI, IP Commerce, Lefthand Networks, mPay Gateway, OneRiot, OpenLogic, Oxlo, Ping Identity, Roving Planet, SkyeTek, Tendril, Thought Equity Motion, Univa, Valen Technologies

Key Executives:
Stacey McKittrick, Managing Director/Chief Financial Officer
e-mail: stacey@appianvc.com
Education: BA, College of William & Mary
Background: VP Operations, Centennial Ventures; Corporate Finance, Kirkland and Ellis; Hirschler, Fleischer; Founder/President, Timberlike-BEC Inc.
Don Parsons, Managing Director
Education: BS Electrical Engineering, Northwestern University; MBA, University of Michigan
Background: General Partner, Centennial Ventures; Associate Engineer, IBM's Personal Computer Division; Chairman/President, Colorado Venture Capital Association
Directorships: Roving Planet; Oxlo Systems; Univa; National Association for Corporate Directors; Valen Technologies; Collective Intellect
Mark Soane, Managing Director
Education: Graduated with highest distinction in History, Dartmouth College; MBA, Stanford Business School
Background: Managing Partner, Quest Capital Partnership; Senior Operating, Multum Information Services; Trade; Personics Corporation; Investment Associate, Bessemer Venture Partners; Current Chairman, Colorda Venture Capital Association
Directorships: Cadre Technologies, AdPay; OpenLogic; Carefx; Voyant Technologies; Datria Systems; Pixxures; Active Education

143 APPLE TREE PARTNERS
230 Park Avenue
Suite 2800
New York, NY 10169
Phone: 212-468-5800
e-mail: info@appletreepartners.com
web: www.appletreepartners.com

Mission Statement: Apple Tree Investments is a venture capital firm that invests in the healthcare, pharmaceuticals and biotechnology sectors. Apple Tree Investments is dedicated to providing capital and working with its portfolio company entrepreneurs to establish necessary corporate infrastructure.

Fund Size: $1.5 billion

53

Venture Capital & Private Equity Firms / Domestic Firms

Founded: 1999
Investment Criteria: All Stages
Industry Group Preference: Biotechnology, Genomics, Chemicals, Drug Development, Life Sciences, Pharmaceuticals, Healthcare
Portfolio Companies: Akero Therapeutics, Braeburn, Chinook Therapeutics, Corvidia Therapeutics, Elstar Therapeutics, Gala Therapeutics, Limelight Bio, Stoke Therapeutics, Stoke Therapeutics, Syntimmune, Tusker Therapeutics, VytronUS

Other Locations:
245 Main Street
12th Floor
Cambridge, MA 02142

The Stanley Building
7 Pancras Square
Kings Cross
London N1C 4AG
United Kingdom

Key Executives:
Seth L. Harrison, M.D., Founder/Managing Partner
Education: AB, Princeton University; MD, MBA, Columbia University
Background: General Partner, Oak Investment Partners; Venture Partner, Sevin Rosen Funds
Directorships: International Partnership for Microbicides, ASOthera Pharmaceuticals, Cure Forward, Syntimmune, Braeburn Pharmaceuticals, Tokai Pharmaceuticals
Anna Batarina, Partner
Education: MA, Global Affairs, Yale University; MA, Clinical Psychology, Lomonosov Moscow State University; CFA
Background: SVP/Head of Capital Markets & Investor Relations, Uralkali; Associate, A1/Alfa Eco; Senior Consultant, Financial & International Tax Services, Ernst & Young
Andy Bayliffe, Venture Partner
Education: PhD, Molecular Biology, Leeds University
Background: GlaxoSmithKline
Michael Ehlers, Venture Partner/Chief Scientific Officer
Education: BS, Chemistry, Caltech; MD & PhD, Johns Hopkins University School of Medicine
Background: EVP of R&D, Biogen; Group SVP, BioTherapeutics; Chief Scientific Officer, Pfizer; George Barth Geller Professor & Investigator of the Howard Hughes Medical Institute, Duke University Medical Center
Paul Eisenberg, Venture Partner
Education: MD, New York Medical College
Background: Professor of Medicine, Washington University; Director of the Cardiac Intensive Care Unit, Barnes-Jewish Hospital; Cardiovascular Discovery; Translational Medicine; Amgen
Phil Johnson, Venture Partner
Education: University of North Carolina; Fellowship at Vanderbilt University
Background: National Institutes of Health in Bethesda, MD; Nationwide Children's Hospital in Columbia, OH; Chief Scientific Officer & EVP, Children's Hospital of Philadelphia; Professor, University of Pennsylvania Perelman School of Medicine; Chief Scientific Officer, Limelight Bio Inc.
Spiros Liras, Venture Partner
Education: PhD, Organic Chemistry, Iowa State University
Background: Biogen; Pfizer; Adjunct Professor, Dept. of Pharmaceutical Chemistry, University of California

144 APPLIED MATERIALS VENTURES
3050 Bowers Avenue
PO Box 58039
Santa Clara, CA 95054-3299

Phone: 408-727-5555
web: www.appliedventures.com

Mission Statement: Applied Ventures is the venture capital fund of Applied Materials, Inc. Applied Ventures invests in early-stage technology companies that promise to deliver high growth and exceptional returns. They seek to invest in companies that provide technologies that advance or complement Applied Materials' core business and stimulate the growth of applications for semiconductors, displays, solar PV, and related products and services.
Geographic Preference: United States, Israel
Fund Size: $50 million
Founded: 2001
Average Investment: $500,000 - $3 million
Minimum Investment: $500,000
Investment Criteria: Seed, Startup, First Stage, Second Stage
Industry Group Preference: Communications Equipment, Computer Hardware & Software, Semiconductors
Portfolio Companies: ActaCell, Adesto Technologies, Advanced Inquiry Systems, BT Imaging, ClearEdge Power, Devicescape, Enki Technology, Enphase Energy, Fat Spaniel Technologies, Glimmerglass, Grandis, Halation Photonics, Illumitex, Infinera, Infinite Power Solutions, Innolume, Kotak, Liquavista, Lumiode, Menara Networks, MTPV Power Corp., Nanomix, Nanosys Inc., Norsk Titanium, Oncoscope, Passport Systems Inc., Plextronics, Sage Electrochromics Inc., Semprius, Solaicx, SolidEnergy, SuNAM Co., SunEdison, Takumi Technology, Tera-Barrier Films, Tessolve, Twist Bioscience

Key Executives:
Omkaram Nalamasu, Ph.D., Senior Vice President/Chief Technology Officer
Education: PhD, University of British Columbia
Background: Professor, Rensselaer Polutechnic Institute; AT&T Bell Laboratories; Agere Systems Inc.
Directorships: Nanofabrication Research Laboratory, Bell Laboratories; MEMS; Waveguides Research

145 ARAGON VENTURES
1455 Adams Court
Menlo Park, CA 94025

Phone: 650-566-8000

Mission Statement: Aragon Ventures provides investment capital to high technology enterprises at early stages of their development from startup companies through and including expansion financing.
Investment Criteria: Early-Stage
Industry Group Preference: High Technology
Portfolio Companies: ScienceBased Health

Key Executives:
David Brewer, Managing Partner
Education: Business Degree, University of California, Berkeley; Law Degree, University of San Francisco
Background: Explore Technologies, eFax.Com, Monogram Software, Telebit, Packet Technologies
Directorships: HereUare, Notify Technology Corp, Cuica Technologies, FirstStone Incubators, PriaVision
Michael Ballard, Manager
Education: BFA, University of Utah
Background: President & CEO, eLingo; President & CEO, Telebit Corporation

146 ARAVAIPA VENTURES
Boulder, CO

e-mail: info@aravaipaventures.com
web: www.aravaipaventures.com

Mission Statement: Aravaipa Venture Fund LLC is the only fund investing exclusively in Impact Technology, low-capital-intensive, early-stage companies in Colorado.
Geographic Preference: Colorado
Founded: 2008
Investment Criteria: Early-Stage

Venture Capital & Private Equity Firms / Domestic Firms

Industry Group Preference: Technology, Renewable Energy, Energy Efficiency, Clean Technology
Portfolio Companies: aWhere, Bolder Industries, Clear Comfort, Lightning Systems, Raven Window, Silver Bullet, Steelhead Composite, Sundolier, Vision Chemical Systems
Key Executives:
  Robert Fenwick-Smith, Founder/Senior Managing Director
  Education: BA, Economics, HEC Lausanne; MBA, Harvard Business School
  Background: Co-Founder/CEO, Robannic
  Directorships: AXIT AG
  Timothy Reeser, Managing Director
  Education: BS, Mechanical Engineering, Colorado State University
  Background: Co-Founder, Engineering Computer Consultants; Partner, 3t Systems

147 ARBOR INVESTMENTS
676 North Michigan Avenue
Suite 3400
Chicago, IL 60611

Phone: 312-981-3770
e-mail: arborinvestments@arborpic.com
web: www.arborpic.com

Mission Statement: Arbor Investments is a private equity firm focused on middle market companies in the food and beverage sector.
Geographic Preference: North America
Fund Size: $400 million
Founded: 1999
Investment Criteria: Middle Market
Industry Group Preference: Food & Beverage
Portfolio Companies: Best Maid Cookie Co., Columbus Manufacturing, Concord Foods, DPI Specialty Foods, Fieldbrook Foods Corporation, Hudson Baking Company, Keyes Packaging Group, Mister Cookie Face, New French Bakery, PBF Pita Bread Factory, Rice Garden, Trojan Lithograph Corporation
Other Locations:
  410 Park Avenue
  Suite 1620
  New York, NY 10022
Key Executives:
  Gregory J. Purcell, Chief Executive Officer
  Education: BS, Marquette University; MBA, University of Chicago
  Background: Senior VP, M&A, Reyes Holdings; American National Bank of Chicago
  Directorships: Keyes Packaging, Trojan Lithograph Corporation, New French Bakery, Midland Packaging & Display, Chicago Public Library Foundation
  Joseph P. Campolo, President
  Education: BS, Villanova University; MBA, University of Pittsburgh
  Background: VP, M&A, Reyes Holdings; American National Bank of Chicago
  Directorships: Fieldbrook Foods Corporation
  Timothy G. Fallon, Senior Operating Partner
  Education: BS, St. Joseph's University; MBA, Fox School of Business, Temple University
  Background: CEO, Columbus Foods; Operating Partner, Krave Jerky; Senior Exectuvie Positions at various companies, including: Procter & Gamble; Cadbury Schweppes; Pepsi; Vermont Pure; Annie's Homegrown; Kettle Foods
  Ryan R. McKenzie, Chief Administrative Officer
  Education: BA, University of Chicago; MM, Finance & Accounting, Northwestern University
  Background: COO, Automatic Ice; Icemakers LLC; CIO & Head, Corporate Finance, American National Bank of Chicago; President & COO, Pullman Bank
  Directorships: Rice Garden, Columbus Manufacturing, New French Bakery, Gold Standard Baking

148 ARBOR VENTURES
web: www.arborventures.com

Mission Statement: Arbor Ventures is a pioneer venture capital firm focused on technology investments in Hong Kong, Japan, Singapors and ASEAN.
Geographic Preference: Hong Kong, Japan, Singapore, ASEAN
Industry Group Preference: Technology
Portfolio Companies: Abra, Akulaku, A-Saas, BlockApps, Beam, Bob, C1X, Demyst Data, Ever Compliant, Forter, Fundbox, GlobaliD, Karmic, Lufax/Lu.com, NS8, Paidy, Planck Re, TrueAccord, Quancheng, Quottly, Skyline, Silot, Trumid, 2C2P
Key Executives:
  Melissa Guzy, Co-Founder & Managing Partner
  Education: Wellesley College; Master's degree in Finance, University of Florida
  Background: Managing Director and Head of VantagePoint Asia
  Directorships: InvestLab, Denyst.data
  Wei Hopeman, Co-Founder & Managing Partner
  Education: BA, International Relations, Pomona College; MBA, Stanford University Graduate School of Business
  Background: Managing Director, Head of Asia, Citi Ventures
  Directorships: Silot Pte Ltd.; GlobaliD; Akulaku; Karmic; Abra
  Ari Fine, Senior Analyst
  Education: Cornell University
  Evelyn Sun, Senior Analyst
  Education: BA, Economic Statistics, Xi'an Jiaotong University; MA, Management and Financial Engineering, Peking University & the National University of Singapore

149 ARBORETUM VENTURES
303 Detroit Street
Suite 301
Market Place Building
Ann Arbor, MI 48104

Phone: 734-998-3688
e-mail: info@arboretumvc.com
web: www.arboretumvc.com

Mission Statement: A private equity firm targeting investments in early stage life sciences companies.
Geographic Preference: United States
Fund Size: $220 million
Founded: 2002
Average Investment: $5 - 7 million
Investment Criteria: Seed, Startup, First Stage, Second Stage
Industry Group Preference: Biotechnology, Healthcare, Medical & Health Related, Information Technology, Medical Devices, Pharmaceuticals, Life Sciences, Healthcare Services
Portfolio Companies: Adavium Medical, Advance ICU Care, ArborMetrix, Aira, Cardio Dimensions, ConertoHealth, Delphinus Medical Technologies, Ebb Tehrapeutics, KFx Medical, Lucina Health, MyHealthDirect, NeuMoDx Molecular, nVision, NxThera, Pear Therapeutics, Rethink, SI-BONE, Strata Oncology, Swift Biosciences, Wellfount
Other Locations:
  11000 Cedar Avenue
  Cleveland, OH 44106
  Phone: 216-658-3989 **Fax:** 216-658-3998
Key Executives:
  Jan Garfinkle, Founder/Managing Director
  e-mail: jgarfinkle@arboretumvc.com
  Education: BS, University of California, Berkeley; MBA, University of Pennsylvania
  Background: Management, Advanced Cardiovascular

55

Systems; Devices for Vascular Intervention; President, Strategic Marketing Consultants; Manufacturing Engineer, Proctor and Gamble; President, Michigan Venture Capital Association
Directorships: HandyLab; Thermocure; Uptake Medical; NeoGuide
Timothy Petersen, Founder/Managing Partner
e-mail: tpetersen@arboretumvc.com
Education: BA, Williams College; MS, University of Wisconsin; MBA, University of Michigan
Background: Interium President, Thermocure; Managing Director, Zell Lurie Institute; Wolverine Venture Fund; Senior Management, Industrial Economics
Directorships: Asterand; HealthMedia; KFx Medical; Thermocure
Paul McCreadie, Partner/Chief Operating Officer
Education: BS, MS, Mechancial Engineering, University of Michigan; MBA, Ross School of Business
Background: Ford Motor Company
Directorships: Frankel Commercilization Fund
Marcy Marshall, Chief Financial Officer
Education: BA, Economics, University of Michigan; MBA, Ross School of Business, University of Michigan
Background: Davenport Univesity; ITt Consumer Financial Corporation; 3M Corporation; May Department Stores Company
Tom Shehab, Managing Partner
Education: BS, Biology, Bowling Green State University; MD, Wayne State University, MA, Medical Management, Carnegie Mellon University
Background: Chief of Staff, St. Joseph Mercy Hospital, Ann Arbor; Chief of Medicine for Integrated Health Associates
Dan Kidle, Partner
Education: BBA, MBA, Ross School of Business, University of Michigan
Background: Analyst, Arboretum Ventures; Financial Analyst, Eli Lilly & Company

150 ARC ANGEL FUND
885 3rd Avenue
20th Floor
New York, NY 10022

e-mail: info@arcangelfund.com
web: www.arcangelfund.com

Mission Statement: ARC Angel Fund invests in seed and early-stage companies with high growth potential. ARC's primary focus is in software, digital media, internet services and other technology.
Geographic Preference: Northeast, Mid-Adlantic
Average Investment: $50,000 - $250,000
Investment Criteria: Seed-Stage, Early-Stage, Revenues of under $5 million
Industry Group Preference: Software, Information Technology, Internet, Technology-Enabled Services, Business Products & Services, Digital Media & Marketing, Mobile, Healthcare Information Technology
Portfolio Companies: Kanvas, Uptown Network, Human Demand, Nulabel, Statsocial, Offermobi, Prognos, Careerminds, Upnext, Sidecare, Yeildmo, BeneStream, Cirrusdata, Bow & Drape, Movie Pass, Partpic, Radius8, Crowded, Cuebiq, Lynq, Ollie
Key Executives:
Edward Reitler, Founding Partner
Education: Harvard Law School
Background: Senior Partner, Reitler Kailas & Rosebnlatt
Directorships: Business Financial Services
David Freschman, Founding Partner
Education: BS, Accounting, University of Delaware; MBA, Loyola College of Maryland
Background: Managing Principal, Innovation Capital Advisors

Michael Kelley, Founding Partner
Education: BA, History, University of Delaware
Background: Founder/Principal, Formation Capital
Joe Rubin, Founding Partner
Education: BS, Communications, Hofstra University
Background: Director/Co-Founder, FundingPost.com

151 ARCADIAN FUND
9663 Santa Monica Blvd.
Unit 1038
Beverly Hills, CA 90210

Phone: 424-279-8188
e-mail: info@arcadianfund.com
web: arcadianfund.com

Mission Statement: Invests in ancillary cannabis companies.
Founded: 2018
Investment Criteria: Late Stage
Industry Group Preference: Cannabis
Portfolio Companies: Baker Technologies, BDS Analytics, Flow Hub, High Times, Kush Bottles, Meadow, Quanta, Treez, Würk
Key Executives:
Matthew J. Nordgren, Founder/Chief Executive Officer
Education: BA, Government/Business; Business Foundations Certifications, Red McCombs School of Business, University of Texas at Austin; MBA, University of Dallas
Background: CEO, Inspired Builders; Executive Director, Nordco Inc. Energy; Founder, Leadership Foundation; Executive/COO, St. Augustine Holdings; Managing Director, Camden Capital Partners; CEO, Nordco Consulting
Directorships: International Tower Group; Ballybunion Caplain Growth Fund
Krishnan Varier, Principal
Education: BA, Economics, University of Texas at Austin; MBA, Kenan-Flager Business School, University of North Carolina at Chapel Hill
Background: Associate, Morgan Keegan & Co.; Associate, Merrill Lynch; Sr. Investment Analyst, Health Care REIT; Health Care Investment Banking, Cowen & Co.; Principal Varier Venture Consulting
Lisa Riedmiller, Chief Financial Officer
Education: BA, California State University at San Jose
Background: OSCCO Ventures
Stacy Huynh, Director of Operations
Education: BA, Economics, San Francisco State University;
Background: Data Analyst, San Francisco's Hospitality House

152 ARCAPITA INC
1180 Peachtree Street NE
Suite 2280
Atlanta, GA 30309

Phone: 404-920-9000
web: www.arcapita.com

Mission Statement: Invests in established companies throughout the world, targeting growth-oriented private equity acquisitions with a total transaction value between $50 and $500 million.
Geographic Preference: North America, Europe, Russia, Middle East, India, China
Founded: 2005
Average Investment: $50 - $200 million
Industry Group Preference: Healthcare, Information Technology, Industrial Technology, Energy, Business Products & Services, Healthcare, Consumer Products
Portfolio Companies: Veolia, Arcapita Ventures I Limited, Meridian Surgical Partners, Saadiyat, Ascendas India Trust, Dubai Investment Park, MorningStar, The Arbor Company, Layetana Real Estate, Arcapita International Luxury

Residential Developement I, Bainbridge, Bahrain Bay, Ampad, Arpatia India Growth Capital I, B.R. Lee Industries Inc., Bijoux Terner, Caribore Coffee, Church Street Health Management, Church's Chicken, Cirrus, Compagnie Européenne de Prestations Logistique, Computer Generation Inc., Cypress Communications, Falcon Gas Storage, DVT Corp., Freightliner, Loehmann's Medifax EDI, Pods, J. Jill, Profine, Roxar, Smart Document Solutions, South Staffordshire Place, Southland Log Homes, Varel International, Tensar, TLC Health Network, Transportation Safety Technologies Inc., Viridian, Watermark Inc, Al Rajhi Capital, Zephyr Investments Limited, Yakima, Mapletree, Gicram Groupe, Point Park Properties, Shurgard Self-Storage, CapitaLand, Arcapita Qatar Real Estate Investment I, Sunrise, Arcapita US Residential Development II, Arcapita US Residential Developmental III, Prescott Group, Archstone Smith, ProLogis, Riffa Views, Victory Heights, NAS, ARC UAE Logistics II

Other Locations:
Arcapita Investment Management B.S.C.
P.O. Box 1357
Manama
Bahrain
Phone: 973-17-218333

Arcapita Investment Advisors UK Limited
The Shard
32 London Bridge Street
London SE1 9SG
United Kingdom
Phone: 44-20-7824-5600

Arcapita Investment Management Singapore Pte.
24 Raffles Place
#16-03 Clifford Centre
Singapore 048621
Singapore
Phone: 65-6513-0395

Key Executives:
Atif Abdulmalik, Chief Executive Officer
Education: BBA, Saint Edward's University. Texas
Background: Investcorp
Hisham Al Raee, Deputy Chief Executive Officer
Education: MBA, University of Hull, UK; CSD, Business Admin., University of Behrain
Background: Senior Director, Business Development, Reuters Middle East; Finance, Citibank N.A.
Martin Tan, Chief Investment Officer
Education: BA, MBA, Washington State University
Background: CEO, CapitaLand Commericial & Integrated Development
Arthur Rogers, Managing Director/General Counsel
Education: BA, History, Hamilton College; JD, Emory University School of Law
Background: Managing Director, Falconvest; General Counsel, Gatehouse Bank; Director, Arcapita Bank; Corporate Attorney, Gibson, Dunn & Crutcher; Corporate Attorney, Testa, Hurwitz & Thibeault

153 ARCH VENTURE PARTNERS
8755 W Higgins Road
Suite 1025
Chicago, IL 60631

Phone: 773-380-6600 **Fax:** 773-380-6606
web: www.archventure.com

Mission Statement: One of the largest technology venture firms in the U.S.
Geographic Preference: Global
Fund Size: $2 billion
Founded: 1986
Average Investment: $5 million
Minimum Investment: $500,000
Investment Criteria: Seed- and Early-Stage
Industry Group Preference: Semiconductors, Advanced Materials, Clean Technology, Optics & Photonics, Electronic Components, Network Infrastructure & Security, High Performance Computing, Wireless, Pharmaceuticals, Genomics & Bioinformatics, Medical Devices, Diagnostic & Drug Discovery Platforms, Nano- and Microtechnologies
Portfolio Companies: Achaogen, Acylin Therapeutics, Adolor, Agios Pharmaceuticals, Allozyne, Alnylam Pharmaceuticals, Array BioPharma, Aviron, Bind Biosciences, Bluebird Bio, Caliper Life Sciences, Chiasma, Ensemble Therapeutics, Fate Therapeutics, Genvec, Groove Biopharma, Hua Medicine, Idun Pharmaceuticals, Ikaria, Illumina, ISB Accelerator, Kythera Biopharmaceuticals, Lycera, Neurogesx, Nura, Omeros, Oncofactor, Permeon Biologics, Phaserx, Pulmatrix, Receptos, Sorbent Therapeutics, Syros, Theraclone Sciences, Trubion Pharma, VBI Vaccines, VentiRx, VLST, Xcyte Therapies, Xenoport, Xori, deCODE Genetics, Fast Track Systems, Genomica, Medvantix, Nexcura, Ekos, R2 Technology, AgBiome, Cambrios Technology, NanoSys, Sapphire Energy, Twist Bioscience, Adesto Technologies, Artificial Muscle, CoolEdge Lighting, Crystal-IS, Eichrom Technologies, Innovalight, Nanophase Technologies, 908 Devices, Ahura Scientific, Alfalight, Alis, Isco International, Impinj, Intelligent Reasoning Systems, Kotura, Kilimanjaro Energy, Microoptical Devices, Nioptics, Nitronex, Xtera Communications, Semprius, Siluria Technologies, Caliper Life Sciences, Pixelexx Systems, Quanterix, Everyday Learning, Teach.com, Classmates Online, CelebrateExpress.com, Apropos Technology, Ciespace, Netbot, New Era of Networks, Univa UD

Other Locations:
188 E Blaine Street
Suite 125
Seattle, WA 98102
Phone: 206-806-8478

5001 Plaza on the Lake Blvd
Suite 103
Austin, TX 78746
Phone: 512-795-5830 **Fax:** 512-795-5849

1700 Owens Street
Suite 535
San Francisco, CA 94158
Phone: 415-565-7103

Key Executives:
Clinton W. Bybee, Co-Founder & Managing Director
Education: MBA, University of Chicago; BS Engineering, Texas A&M University
Background: Associate, ARCH Development Corporation; Manager, Technology Venture Fund, Illinois Department of Commerce & Community Affairs; Production and Operations Engineer, Amoco Corporation
Directorships: Nanosys, Cambrios, AmberWave Systems, Aveso Displays, ePolicy Solutions
Keith L. Crandell, Co-Founder & Managing Director
Education: MBA, University of Chicago; MS Chemistry, University of Texas; BS Chemistry, Math, St. Lawrence University
Background: Senior Manager, ARCH Development Corporation; President, Eichrom Industries; Marketing, Hercules
Directorships: AlfaLight, Apropos, CelebrateExpress, ALIS, Crystal-IS
Robert T. Nelsen, Co-Founder & Managing Director
Education: MBA, University of Chicago; BS Biology, Economics, University of Puget Sound
Background: Senior Manager, ARCH Development Corporation
Directorships: Fred Hutchison Cancer Research Institute, Adolor Corporation, Accelerator, Xcyte Therapies, NeurogesX, Ikaria, Optobionics
Steven Gillis, Managing Director
Education: BA, Williams College; PhD, Dartmouth College
Background: Immunologist; pioneer in the field of

Venture Capital & Private Equity Firms / Domestic Firms

cytokines; Founder/Director, Corixa Corp; Founder/Director, Immunex Corp; 300 publications
Kristina Burow, Managing Director
Education: BS, Chemistry, University of California, Berkeley; MA, Chemistry, Columbia University; MBA, University of Chicago
Background: Novartis BioVenture Fund; Business Development, Genomis Institute of The Novartis Research Foundation; Co-Founder, Sapphire Energy
Directorships: Sapphire Energy; Ensemble Discovery; Archaeogen; Kythera Biopharmaceuticals; Celula; Accelerator
Paul Thurk, Managing Director
Education: BS, Economics, The Wharton School; MBA, University of Texas at Austin
Background: Director of Operations, NABS; SSM Ventures
Mark McDonnell, Managing Director, CFO & CAO
Education: BS, Marquette University; CPA
Background: CFO, Marquette Venture Partners

154 ARCHTOP VENTURES
Four International Drive
Suite 330
Rye Brook, NY 10570

e-mail: helloarchtop@archtopventures.com
web: www.archtopventures.com

Mission Statement: Archtop Ventures is focused on making investments in emerging growth and middle market companies in media, entertainment and new technology, positioning them for rapid growth and market leadership.

Average Investment: $20 - $75 million
Investment Criteria: Early-Stage
Industry Group Preference: Media, Entertainment, New Technology, Mobile, Social Media, Gaming, E-Commerce & Manufacturing, Publishing, Travel & Leisure, Health & Wellness, Advertising, Big Data, Education, Enterprise Software

Key Executives:
Jeff Demond, Chairman/CEO
Education: Business School Graduate, University of Alabama; CPA
Background: President & CEO, BCI Broadband; President & CEO, Bresnan Communications; Senior Manager, KPMG
Paul Gruenberg, Partner
Background: Founder, Video News International; Founder, Videovation; Founder, Plum Holdings; Rockefeller & Co.; Morgens Waterfall & Vintiadis
John Young, Partner
Background: Tribal DDB Worldwide, Moden Media/Poppe Tyson, Full Contact

155 ARCHYTAS VENTURES
1880 Century Park East
Suite 250
Los Angeles, CA 90067

Toll-Free: 866-822-2662
e-mail: info@archytasventures.com
web: archytasventures.com

Mission Statement: An investment holding firm offering flexible capital to emerging companies in the cannabis industry.

Founded: 2016
Investment Criteria: Early-Stage
Industry Group Preference: Cannabis
Portfolio Companies: Xtraction Services, Halo Labs, Grow Now

Key Executives:
David Kivitz, Co-Founder/Partner
Education: BBA, Finance, George Washington University
Background: Real Estate Analyst, CapitalSource; Fund Investment Analyst, Hamilton Lane; Co-Founder/Managing Principal, Alta Verde Group
Directorships: Xtraction Services
Tim Rotolo, Co-Founder/CIO
Education: BA, History, Tufts University
Background: Financial Analyst, Merrill Lynch; Analyst/VP, Sandalwood Securities; Founder/Managing Partner, Lloyd Harbor Capital Management
Directorships: Xtraction Services
Antony Radbod, Co-Founder/CSO
Background: Marketing Director, Georgetown Private Cliente; VP of Product Development, NuParadigm; Partner, StandAlone Consulting; Director of Marketing NearU Search; Director of Marketing, Creative Asylum; Advisor, Alta Verde Group; Founder/CEO, Pollen Partners; CMO, Xtraction Services
Directorships: Xtraction Services
Brooke Hayes, Partner/COO
Education: BS, Economics; MBA, Wharton School, University of Pennsylvania
Background: Associate, The Stratum Group; Associate, JPMorgan Chase H&Q; Partner, Milestone Partners; Private Equity Consultant, Meadowbrook Capital Advisors; CFO, Xtraction Services
Directorships: Agust Spark; Occasion Brands

156 ARCLIGHT CAPITAL PARTNERS
200 Clarendon Street
55th Floor
Boston, MA 02116

Phone: 617-531-6300 Fax: 617-867-4698
e-mail: info@arclightcapital.com
web: www.arclight.com

Mission Statement: Private equity firm focused on energy infrastructure investments.

Fund Size: $3.33 billion
Founded: 2001
Industry Group Preference: Power Technologies, Energy, Oil & Gas
Portfolio Companies: ACE Cogeneration, AL Gulf Coast Terminals, AL Shore, Anglo Suisse Offshore Partners, Arkoma Pipeline Partners, Atlantic Power Holdings, Bayonne Energy Center, Big Sandy Equipment Company, Black Point Petroleum, Black Bear Power, Blue Ridge Asphalt, Bridger Energy Funding, Bronco Midstream Holdings, Caithness Energy, Cardinal Power Funding, Charger Oil & Gas, Cherokee Partners, Colusa Power Development, CPV Wind Ventures, Crawfish Cogen, DG Power, Element Petroleum, Epsilon Power Holdings, Escalade Energy, Forst Point Power, G3 Global Energy, Galleon Oil & Gas, Grant Peaking Power, Great Point Power, Hurrikan Power, Juno Energy, Key Energy, KGen Power, Leeward Renewable Energy, Liberty Bell Power, Lightyear Holdings, Lincoln Peaking Power, Magellan Power Holdings, Matagorda Island Gas Ops, Mesquite Power, Michigan Power, Midland Cogeneration Venture, Mountaineer Gas Holdings, Navy Power, NET Midstream, North Sea Infrastructure Holdings, North Sea Midstream Partners, Petrotank, Pomifer Power Funding, ReNu Power, RepconStrickland, Republic Midstream, Ridgeline Midstream Holdings, Rockport Georgetown Partners, Scrubgrass, Southeast PowerGen, Southern Pines, Stamford Bridge Power, Terra-Gen Power, Waterside

Other Locations:
41, avenue de la Gare
Luxembourg L-1611
Luxembourg

Key Executives:
Daniel R. Revers, Managing Partner & Founder
Education: BA Economics, Lafayette College; MBA, Amos Tuck School of Business Administration, Dartmouth College
Background: Managing Director Corporate Finance, John Hancock; Wheelabrator Technologies

Venture Capital & Private Equity Firms / Domestic Firms

Kevin M. Crosby, Partner
Education: BS, Finance, University of Maine
Background: Associate, Corporate Finance Group, John Hancock

Mark A. Tarini, Partner & Head, Portfolio Management
Education: BS, Accounting, Boston College
Background: CFO, EP Power Finance; CFO, Energy Investors Funds Group; Vice President, Finance, Legeis Resources; Manager, Utility & Real Estate, Arthur Anderson & Company

Carter A. Ward, Partner
Education: BS, Operations Research & Industrial Engineering, Cornell University
Background: VP, McManus & Miles

John F. Erhard, Partner
Education: BA, Arts in Economics, Princeton University; JD, Harvard Law School
Background: Associate, Blue Chip Venture Company

Timothy M. Evans, Partner
Education: BA, Dartmouth College; MBA, Harvard Business School
Background: Associate, Allegheny Energy Supply; Global Power & Energy Group, Merrill Lynch

Theodore D. Burke, Partner & General Counsel
Education: BA, Economics, University of Vermont; JD, Georgetown University
Background: Chief Executive & Global Managing Partner, Freshfields Bruckhaus Deringer LLP; Partner, Milbank Tweed Hadley & McCloy

Lucius H. Taylor, Principal
Education: BA, Geology, Colorado College; MS, Hydrogeology, University of Nevada; MBA, Wharton School, University of Pennsylvania
Background: Vice President, Energy & Natural Resources, FBR Capital Markets; Geologist, CH2M HILL

Evan M. Schwartz, Principal
Education: Harvard University; Sloan School of Management
Background: DC Energy

157 ARCUS VENTURES
One Grant Central Place
60 East 42nd Street
Suite 1610
New York, NY 10165

Phone: 212-785-2236 Fax: 212-785-2237
e-mail: info@arcusventures.com
web: www.arcusventures.com

Mission Statement: Arcus Ventures (AV) consists of a team of professionals with experience in clinical and academic medicine, drug development, hospital management, healthcare industry consulting and private equity. AV is dedicated to investing in oncology focused companies with innovative biopharmaceuticals and or new drug delivery platforms in development, device companies with products that have pre-marketing approval, and service companies with positive revenue.

Industry Group Preference: Biopharmaceuticals, Healthcare, Drug Delivery

Portfolio Companies: Clear Vascular Inc., Marco Genics, Mi Bioresearch, Tracon Pharma, T2Biosystems, Epic Sciences, Exosome Diagnostics, Xtuit Pharmaceuticals, Cleave Biosciences, Genta, Oncoscope, Palyon Medical, Vascular Pathways

Key Executives:

James B. Dougherty, MD, Co-Founder/General Partner
e-mail: jd@arcusventures.com
Education: BS, Biology, Georgetown University; MD, Pennsylvania State University, Hershey School of Medicine
Background: Venture Partner, Cross Atlantic Partneres; Deputy Physician-in-Chief, Clinical Affairs, Memorial Sloan-Kettering Cancer Center

Steven L. Soignet, MD, General Partner
e-mail: ss@arcusventures.com
Education: BS, University of New Orleans; MD, Louisiana State University
Background: Co-Founder, The Arcus Group; Venture Partner, Cross Atlantic Partners; Faculty, Developmental Chemotherapy Service, Memorial Sloan-Kettering Cancer Center; Department of Medicine, Cornell University Medical Center

158 ARES CAPITAL CORPORATION
2000 Avenue of the Stars
12th Floor
Los Angeles, CA 90067

Phone: 310-201-4200 Fax: 310-432-8632
web: www.arescapitalcorp.com

Mission Statement: Business development company serving private middle-market companies across diverse industries.

Fund Size: $12.3 billion

Investment Criteria: Revolver, first lien, second lien, stretch senior, unitranche, subordinated debt, private/public high yield, non-control equity

Industry Group Preference: All Sectors Considered

Portfolio Companies: 10th Street LLC, 1A Smart Start LLC, 42 North Dental LLC, Absolute Dental Management, ACAS Equity Holdings Corporation, ACAS Real Estate Holdings Corporation, Accomodations Plus Technologies, Acessa Health Inc., ADF Restaurant Group, Alteon Health LLC, Batanga Inc., Birch Permian LLC, Blue Wolf Capital Fund II, BluePay Processing Inc., Borchers Americas Inc., BRG Sports Inc., BW Landco LLC, Cadence Aerospace LLC, Care Hospice Inc., ChargePoint Inc., Chariot Acquisition LLC, Cority Software Inc., Cozzini Bros., CPV Maryland Holding Company II, Creation Holdings Inc., Directworks Inc., Dorner Holding Corp., Doxim Inc., Dynatrace Inc., First Insight Inc., Flow Control Solutions Inc., Foundation Risk Partners Corp., Liason Acquisition LLC, Masergy Holdings Inc., MB Aerospace Holdings II Corp., MB2 Dental Solutions LLC, McKenzie Creative Brands, Microstar Logistics, Moxie Patriot LLC, Nationwide Marketing Group LLC, NECCO Realty Investments, Nodality Inc., Nordco Inc., Southeast, nThrive Inc., Production Resource Group LLC, ProVation Medical Inc., Puerto Rico Waste Investment LLC, Pyramid Management Advisors, Pyramid Investors LLC, QC Supply LLC, QF Holdings, R2 Acquisition Corp., Radius Aerospace Inc., Raptor Technologies LLC, RecoveryDirect Acquisition, Reddy Ice Inc., Regent Education Inc., Respicardia Inc., Riverview Power LLC, RMP Group Inc., Synergy HomeCare Franchising LLC, Sundance Energy Inc., Teligent Inc., TimeClock Plus Inc., West Dermatology LLC

Key Executives:

Michael Arougheti, Director, Co-Founder, CEO & President
Education: Yale University
Background: Royal Bank of Canada; Indosuez Capital; Kidder, Peabody & Co.

159 ARES MANAGEMENT LLC
2000 Avenue of the Stars
Los Angeles, CA 90067

Phone: 310-201-4100
e-mail: IRARES@aresmgmt.com
web: www.aresmgmt.com

Mission Statement: Specializes in managing assets in both the private equity and leveraged finance markets.

Geographic Preference: United States
Fund Size: $4 million
Founded: 1997
Investment Criteria: LBO, Special Situations, Distressed Debt

Venture Capital & Private Equity Firms / Domestic Firms

Industry Group Preference: Business Products & Services, Consumer Products, Manufacturing, Aerospace, Defense and Government, Energy, Healthcare
Portfolio Companies: 99 Cents Only Stores, Air Lease Corporation, AmeriQual Group LLC, Aspen Dental Management, Inc., CHG Healthcare Services, City Ventures LLC, CPG International Inc., EXCO Resources, Inc., Floor & Decor Outlets of America, Insight Global, Jacuzzi Brands Corp., Marietta Corporation, National Bedding Company LLC, Neiman Marcus Group LTD Inc., Nortek, Inc., OB Hospitalist Group, Inc., Oro Negro, Plasco Energy Group, Inc., Sandridge Energy, Inc., Simmons Bedding Company, Smart & Final Stores LLC, Sotera Defense Solutions, Stram Global Services, Inc., True Oil Company LLC, Unified Physician Management LLC

Other Locations:
245 Park Avenue
44th Floor
New York, NY 10167

3344 Peachtree Road NE
Suite 1950
Atlanta, GA 30326
Phone: 678-538-1900

71 S Wacker Drive
Suite 3500
Chicago, IL 60606

591 Redwood Highway
Suite 3100
Mill Valley, CA 94941
Phone: 415-380-0520

2 Bethesda Metro Center
Mezzanine Level
Suite 250
Bethesda, MD 20814
Phone: 301-951-6122

10 New Burlington Street
6th Floor
London W1S 3BE
United Kingdom
Phone: 44 (0) 20-7434-6400

25 Rue Blazac
Paris F-75008
France
Phone: 33 (0) 17039-4150

Taunusanlage 18
Frankfurt 60325
Germany
Phone: 49 (0)69-97086-3400

Strandvagen 7A
4th Floor
Stockholm 114 56
Sweden
Phone: 46 (0) 8-450-39-69

14-16 Avenue Pasteur
Luxembourg L-2310
Luxembourg

1601 West Nan Jing Road
Unit 3701
Park Place Office Building
Shanghai 200040
China

Office 44 Gate, Building Level 15
Dubai International Financial Centre
P.O. Box 121208 UAE
Dubai
Phone: 971-4-401-9115

MLC Centre, Level 56
19-29 Martin Place
Sydney NSW 2000
Australia
Phone: 612-9238-2200

Bennett Rosenthal, Founding Partner
Education: MBA, BS, Econmics, Wharton School, University of Pennsylvania
Background: Senior Advisor, Ares Capital Markets; Managing Director, Global Leveraged Finance Group; Senior Member, Merrill Lynch Leveraged Transaction Commitment Committee
Directorships: Douglas Dynamics; MF Acquisition Corporation; Marietta Corporation; National Bedding Company

David Kaplan, Founding Partner
Education: BBA, Finance, University of Michigan School of Business Administration
Background: Shelter Capital Partners, LLC; Apollo Management LP; Investment Banking, Donaldson, Lufkin & Jenrette Securities Corp

Anthony Ressler, Co-Founder/Executive Chairman
Education: BSFS, Georgetown University; MBA, Columbia Business School
Background: Senior Advisor, Ares Capital Markets Group; Co-Founder, Apollo Management; SVP, Drexel Burham Lambert; Founding Member, Painted Turtle's Camp
Directorships: Allied Waste Industries; Samsonite Corporation

160 ARETE CORPORATION
Arete Corporation
PO Box 1299
Center Harbor, NH 03226

Phone: 603-253-9797 **Fax:** 603-253-9799
e-mail: aretecorp@roadrunner.com
web: www.arete-microgen.com

Mission Statement: The Arete Corporation is a venture fund focused on alternative energy technologies.

Founded: 1983

Key Executives:
Robert Shaw, Jr., President
Education: BEP, MS, Cornell University; MPA, American University; PhD, Stanford University
Background: Managing Member, SC Green Tech Ventures; SVP, Booz, Allen & Hamilton Energy Division; Bell Laboratories

161 ARGENTUM GROUP
60 Madison Avenue
Suite 701
New York, NY 10010

Phone: 212-949-6262 **Fax:** 212-949-8294
e-mail: tag@argentumgroup.com
web: www.argentumgroup.com

Mission Statement: A private equity firm that provides expansion capital to rapidly growing small and mid-sized businesses with market leading potential. Argentum emphasizes the concept of partnership investing.

Geographic Preference: United States
Fund Size: $215 million
Founded: 1988
Average Investment: $3-10 million
Minimum Investment: $3 million
Investment Criteria: Later-Stage, Expansion Capital, Growth, MBO, Platform Acquisition Strategies, Recapitalizations
Industry Group Preference: Software Services, Outsourcing & Efficiency, Manufacturing, Technology, Healthcare
Portfolio Companies: Afs Technologies, Applieddata.net, Buyerquest, Chromeriver, CrossMedia Services, Cyclone Commerce, etouches, Expert Plan, Fleet Worth Solutions, Flightdocs, Hanweck, Image Cafe, Margin Point, Mediant Communications, Micro Focus, Netboa, NuOrder, Orion

Venture Capital & Private Equity Firms / Domestic Firms

Labs, Paciolan, Parallaz Capital Partners LLC, Resonate, Structured Web, TCI, Trustwave, Tut Systems, VPNet, Wimba, Yello, Ytel

Key Executives:
  Walter Barandiaran, Managing Partner
  e-mail: walter@argentumgroup.com
  Education: BBA, Baruch College (CUNY); attended New York University School of Business
  Background: Senior VP, Steinberg & Lyman
  Directorships: HorizonWimba, AFS Technologies, Conner Industries, LifeStar, M3 Technologies, Medsite.com, Metalico, StructuredWeb
  Daniel Raynor, Managing Partner
  e-mail: draynor@argentumgroup.com
  Education: BS Economics, Wharton School, University of Pennsylvania
  Background: Senior VP, Steinberg & Lyman
  Directorships: Applied Data Systems, Community Education Centers, NuCo2, Paciolan, ReSearch Pharmaceutical Services, Transforce, ExpertPlan, FutureHealth, Bio-Kinetic Clinical Applications
  Steve Berman, Partner/CFO
  e-mail: sdberman@argentumgroup.com
  Education: BS, Accounting, Temple University; MA, Taxation, Villanova University
  Background: Assistant Controller/Tax Manager, Caxton Corporation; Tax Supervisor, Laventhol & Horwath; Certified Public Accountant
  Directorships: Bio-Kinetic Clinical Applications
  Chris Leong, Partner/Head of Business Development
  e-mail: cleong@argentumgroup.com
  Education: Wharton School
  Background: VP, Sirit Inc.; Analyst, Lehman Brothers Merchant Banking Partners
  Federica Norreri, Fund Administrator
  e-mail: fregec@argentumgroup.com

162 ARGO GLOBAL CAPITAL
401 Edgewater Place
Suite 120
Wakefield, MA 01880
Phone: 781-213-9344 **Fax:** 781-213-9345
e-mail: info@argoglobal.com
web: www.argoglobal.com

Mission Statement: Venture capital firm focused on global investments in wireless communications companies.

Fund Size: $300 million
Founded: 1997
Average Investment: $4-$7 million
Investment Criteria: Initial Funding, Later-Stage, Startup, Through Buyout, Special Emphasis, Financings
Industry Group Preference: Wireless Technologies, Internet Technology, Communications
Portfolio Companies: 12snap AG, Amperion Cayman, ArgNor Wireless Ventures BV, Birdstep Technology ASA, Bytemobile Inc., Cambridge Positioning Systems, Ltd., Casero, Inc., Chinatron Group Holdings, Ltd., Digital Bridges, Ltd., Digital Route, Eftia OSS Solutions, Inc., Empower Interactive Group, Ltd., General Wireless, Handmark, Inc., Hotsip AB, inCode Telecom Group, Inc., IPeria, Inc., Kabira Technologies, Inc., LGC Wireless, Inc., Neural Technologies Ltd., Nuera Communications, Inc., OnMobile Systems, Inc., PhyFlex Networks, Inc., Q-go.com B.V., RV Technology, Ltd., SenseStream Ltd., SurfKitchen, Sylantro Systems Corporation, uReach Technologies, Inc., Vallent Corporation, VoluBill, Webraska Mobile Technologies SA, World Wide Packets

Other Locations:
  40-44 Bonham Strand
  28th Floor, EIB Center
  Sheung Wan
  Hong Kong
  Phone: 852-22952209 **Fax:** 852-22953111

  1250 Rene-Levesque Blvd West
  38th Floor
  Montreal, QC H3B 4W8
  Canada
  Phone: 514-397-8444 **Fax:** 514-397-8445

Key Executives:
  H H Haight, President/CEO
  781-592-5250 x18
  e-mail: hhaight@argoglobal.com
  Education: BS, University of California, Berkeley; MBA, Harvard Business School
  Background: Founder/Managing Director, Advent International Corporation
  Directorships: OnMobile, Neural Technologies Ltd., ArgNor, OnMobile Systems Global, Ltd., uReach, Surfkitchen, Nostix
  Charles Sirois, Senior Partner
  781-592-5250 x20
  Education: Bachelors, Finance, Universite de Sherbrooke; Masters, Finance, Universite Laval; Honorary Doctorates, Universite du Quebec a Montreal, University of Ottawa, Concordia University, Laval University
  Background: National Pagette; National Mobile Radio Communications Inc.; BCE Mobile Communications Inc.; Chairman/CEO, Teleglobe
  Directorships: Chairman, Telesystem International Wireless; Microcell Telecommunications; Canadian Imperial Bank of Commerce; Chairman/CEO, Enablis Entrepreneurial Network
  Amy Ssuto, Financial Controller
  Education: BA, Commerce, Concordia University
  Background: Chief Accountant, Ipex, Inc.

163 ARGONAUT VENTURES
180 Harbor Drive
Suite 101
Sausalito, CA 94965
Phone: 415-332-0707
web: www.argonautventures.com

Mission Statement: Argonaut Ventures provides funding, strategic consulting, and technical expertise to early-stage companies to build, manager on monetize new businesses. With 15 years of direct experience in building online businesses from the ground up, our goal is to create a portfolio of successful companies and share in the success of our clients.

Founded: 1995
Investment Criteria: Early-Stage
Industry Group Preference: Internet
Portfolio Companies: Malaria.com, MedNews, Heal.com, PhysiciansNet.com

Key Executives:
  Matthew Naythons MD, Partner
  Education: BS, Muhlenberg College; MS, Hahnemann University
  Background: Founder, Epicenter Communications; PlanetRx; Co-Founder, EpiCom Media
  Peter Goggin, Partner
  Background: Vice President, NetHealth; Director of Project Management; PlanetRx; ISL Consulting

164 ARGOSY CAPITAL
950 West Valley Road
Suite 2900
Wayne, PA 19087
Phone: 610-971-9685 **Fax:** 610-964-9524
web: www.argosycapital.com

Mission Statement: Argosy Capital invests entrepreneurial capital in basic businesses in the lower middle market, focus-

61

Venture Capital & Private Equity Firms / Domestic Firms

ing primarily on business services and manufacturing companies based in the United States.
Geographic Preference: Eastern, Midwestern United States
Fund Size: $600 million
Founded: 1990
Average Investment: $5 - $15 million
Minimum Investment: $3 million
Investment Criteria: Later Stage Expansion, Buyout, Recapitalization, Acquisitions, Growth Equity, revenues in the range of $15 - $100 million
Industry Group Preference: Manufacturing, Business to Business, Franchising, Distribution, Aviation Services, B2B Services, Engineered Materials, Industrial Electronics, Industrial Services
Portfolio Companies: AbelConn, American Huts, American Leather, Atlantic Diagnostic Laboratories, Capewell Aerial Systems, Casual Living and Trigon Plastics, CBT Technologies, Combined Public Communications, Component Sourcing International, CRS Reprocessing Services, Dan-Loc, ECS Environmental Solutions, Enefco International, Fairway Architectural Railing Solutions, Flow Dry Technology, GenServe, Great Western Leasing & Sale, Groome, HB&G Building Products, Joliet Holdings, KMCO, Library Systems & Services, Linkage, Linx Technologies, MFM, Nationwide Industries, Olympia Chimney Supply, Oneida Molded Plastics, Panhandle Oilfield, Paragon Energy Solution, Ranger Aerospace, Ranger AirShop, Reed City Tool, Revive Personal Products, Rita's, Roll Rite, SinterFire, SirsiDynix, Sound Lounge, Southerland, Vanguard Modular, Walpole

Key Executives:
  Kirk B Griswold, Founding Partner
  e-mail: kirk@argosycapital.com
  Education: BS, Physics, University of Virginia; MBA, Wharton School, University of Pennsylvania
  Background: Manager & Consultant, Mercer Management Consulting; Manager & Avionics Engineer, Integrated Logistics Support Division, Westinghouse Electric Corporation
  Directorships: Managing Director, Odyssey Capital Group LP
  John Paul Kirwin III, Founding Partner/CEO
  e-mail: john@argosycapital.com
  Education: BA, Dickinson College; JD, George Washington University
  Background: Partner, McCausland, Keen & Buckman
  Sarah G Roth, COO/CFO
  e-mail: sroth@argosycapital.com
  Education: BA, Political Science, William College; MBA, Kellogg School of Management at Northwestern University
  Background: Partner, The Riverside Company; Merrill Lynch Ventures
  Jason M Cunningham, Vice President, Business Development
  e-mail: jcunningham@argosyprivateequity.com
  Education: BS, Economics West Chester University
  Background: Vice President, Ardenton Capital; Managing Director, Baker Tilly Captical; Senior Associate, Fleet M&A Advisors
  Paul M Grassinger, Vice President, Finance and Accounting
  e-mail: paul@argosycapital.com
  Education: BS, Business Administration, Rowan University; CPA
  Background: CFO, cOO, Vice President, Corporate Controller, Ernst & Young
  Steven J Morgenthal, Managing Director
  e-mail: steven@argosycapital.com
  Education: BS, Pace University; MS, Stevens Institute of Technology
  Background: Venture Partner, SCP Private Equity Partners; COO, Unified Systems Solutioins
  Melanie C Lyren, CCO/Vice President, Investor Reporting
  e-mail: melanie@argosycapital.com
  Education: BS, Economics, Wharton School, University Of Pennsylvania; CPA
  Background: Senior Accountant, Enterprise Group Of Arthur Andersen
  Lane W Wiggers, Managing Director
  e-mail: lane@argosycapital.com
  Education: Clemson University; MBA, Smith School of Business, University of Maryland
  Background: Founder, Cordam Group; Partner, CS Capital Partners; Wachova Securities/Wells Fargo; Rockwell International

165 ARISTOS VENTURES
8300 Douglas Avenue
Suite 800
Dallas, TX 75225

Phone: 214-306-9554
e-mail: plans@aristosventures.com
web: www.aristosventures.com

Mission Statement: Aristos Ventures is a venture capital firm focusing on efficient technology companies primarily in Texas that need early capital in order to create their product.
Geographic Preference: Texas
Fund Size: $35 Million
Average Investment: $200,000 - $1,000,000
Investment Criteria: Aristos invests in companies that already have a product or service and need up to $1 million to get to profitability

Key Executives:
  Felipe Mendoza, Managing Director
  Education: BS, Texas Tech University; MBA, Southern Methodist University
  Background: Engineer, Cisco Systems; CFO/Associate, Silver Creek Ventures; Co-Founder, TAC Portfolio Advisors

166 ARLINGTON CAPITAL PARTNERS
5425 Wisconsin Avenue
Suite 200
Chevy Chase, MD 20815

Phone: 202-337-7500 Fax: 202-337-7525
e-mail: requestinfo@arlingtoncap.com
web: www.arlingtoncap.com

Mission Statement: A middle market private equity firm focused on buyouts and recapitalizations in targeted growth industries in partnership with management. The firm leverages a combination of private equity and operating experience.
Geographic Preference: United States, Canada, Europe
Fund Size: $452 Million
Founded: 1999
Average Investment: $20-$75 Million
Minimum Investment: $20 Million
Investment Criteria: LBO, Recapitalization
Industry Group Preference: Business to Business, Aerospace, Defense and Government, Healthcare Services, Information Technology, Media, Education, Healthcare, Manufacturing, Outsourcing & Efficiency, Business Products & Services
Portfolio Companies: Ad Venture Interactive, Apogen Technologies, AHM, Avalign Technologies, Cambridge Major Laboratories, Chandler/May, Cadence Aerospace, Compusearch, Consolidated Precision Products Corp., Endeavor Robots, Grand River Aseptic Manufacturing, MB Aerospace, Micron Technologies, Micropact, Molecular, NLX, Novetta, Ontario Systems, Polaris Alpha, Quantum Spatial, Secor, Signal Tree Solutions, Textech Industries, TSI, United Flexible, Virgo, Xebec, Zemax

Key Executives:
  Peter M. Manos, Managing Partner
  Education: MBA, Harvard Business School; BA, Stanford University

Venture Capital & Private Equity Firms / Domestic Firms

Background: VP, Carlyle Group; Managing Partner, Capitol Partners; Fayez Sarofim & Co; Investment Banker, Donaldson Lufkin & Jenrette; Peers & Co; Founder/Manager, iFINANCE
Directorships: SECOR
Matthew L. Altman, Managing Partner
Education: BA, Economics, Duke University; MBA, Stanford Grad. School of Business
Background: Stonington Partners; Packard BioScience Corp.; Obagi Medical Products
Directorships: Advanced Health Media, Avalign Technologies, Endeavor Robotics. Grand River Aseptic Manufacturing, Molecular Products, Ontario Systems, Tex Tech Industries, United Flexible
Michael H. Lustbader, Managing Partner
Education: AB, Harvard College
Background: Lazard Freres & Co
Directorships: MicroPact, Polaris Alpha, Quantum Spatial, Zemax, Xebec
David C. Wodlinger, Partner
Education: AB, Economics, Georgetown University
Background: Deutsch Bank
Directorships: Polaris Alpha, Quantum Spatial, Xebec
C. Malcolm Little, Partner
Education: BS, University of Virginia; MBA, Harvard Business School
Background: Vice President, Avista Capital Partners; Associate, Oak Hill Capital Partners; Bear, Stearns & Co.
Directorships: Digital River; New Vision Group; Cherry Creek Radio
A. Bilal Noor, Vice President
Education: BS, Commerce, University of Virginia; MBA, Harvard Business School
Background: H.I.G. Capital; Leveraged Finance Group, Bank of American Merrill Lynch
Directorships: Cadence Aerospace, United Flexible, Zemax
Erica S. Son, Vice President
Education: BS, Finance/Accounting, Wharton School, University of Pennsylvania; MBA, Harvard Business School
Background: Associate, Thomas H. Lee Partners; Analyst, The Blackstone Group
Directorships: Tex Tech Industries
Benjamin J. Ramundo, Vice President
Education: BS, Finance, Georgetown University
Background: Jefferies' Aerospace, Defense, and Government Services
Directorships: Xebec

167 ARMY VENTURE CAPITAL INITIATIVE
Mission Statement: The Army Venture Capital Initiative is a strategic private equity investor. They invest in companies that support all branches of the US army in defense and commercial markets. They invest at all stages of the investment lifecycle.
Average Investment: $500,000-$2,000,000

168 ARROWHEAD INVESTMENT MANAGEMENT
33 Benedict Place
1st Floor
Greenwich, CT 06830

Phone: 203-485-0700 **Fax:** 203-295-3771
web: www.arrowheadmgt.com

Mission Statement: Formerly Arrowhead Mezzanine, Arrowhead Investment Management provides mezzanine capital to middle-market companies. Arrowhead provides capital in the form of subordinated debt, preferred stock and non-control common equity.
Fund Size: $479 million
Founded: 1996
Average Investment: $10 - 100 million

Investment Criteria: Acquisitions, Buyouts, Recapitalizations, Growth Capital
Industry Group Preference: Consumer Products, Industrial Manufacturing, Value-Added Distribution, Business Products & Services, Value-Added Distribution, Healthcare, Chemicals, Packaging
Portfolio Companies: Bare Escentuals, Berkshire, C.H.I. Overhead Doors, CPI, CMS, Driven Brands, Edwin Watts Golf, Express Oil Change and Service Center, Hoffmaster Group, ILP, Implus, Kurt Versen, Meineke, Multi Packaging Solutions, MW Industries, Otis Spunkmeyer, Polaris, PQ Corp., Quest, Ranpak Corp., Reef, Rough Country Suspension Systems, The Sheridan Group, SPI Polyols, Sram, Tempur World, Tidi Products, United Pet Group Inc.
Other Locations:
10877 Wilshire Boulevard
21st Floor
Los Angeles, CA 90024
Phone: 301-551-0101
Key Executives:
Elliott Jones, Chief Investment Officer
e-mail: ejones@arrowheadmgt.com
Education: Colgate University; MBA, Columbia University
Background: Subordinated Debt Group, The Chase Manhattan Bank; Gleacher NatWest; Lieutenant, US Navy
Mary Gay, Managing Director
e-mail: mgay@arrowheadmgt.com
Education: BS, University of Richmond
Background: Leveraged Finance Group, Gleacher NatWest; Consultant, Ernst & Young
Craig Pisani, Managing Director
e-mail: cpisani@arrowheadmgt.com
Education: BA, Lafayette College; MBA, New York University
Background: Leveraged Finance Group, Gleacher NatWest; Prudential Investment Corporation
Jennifer Cerminaro, Chief Financial Officer
e-mail: jcerminaro@arrowheadmgt.com
Education: BS, Accounting, William Paterson University
Background: Senior Associate, Goldman Sachs

169 ARROWPATH VENTURE PARTNERS
4477 Adams Drive
Houston, TX 77002

Phone: 979-475-2200
web: www.arrowpathvc.com

Mission Statement: Arrowpath Ventures seek companies in the storage, security, networking, infrastructure and other data center-related markets.

Geographic Preference: United States
Fund Size: $325 million
Founded: 1997
Average Investment: $3 - 10 million
Minimum Investment: $200,000
Investment Criteria: Seed, First Stage, Second Stage
Industry Group Preference: Computer Hardware & Software, Internet Technology, Telecommunications, Networking
Teresa McDaniel, Chief Financial Officer
Education: BS, Business Administration, Finance, San Jose State University
Background: KPMG Peet Marwick LLP; Apple Computer

170 ARSENAL CAPITAL PARTNERS
100 Park Avenue
31st Floor
New York, NY 10017

Phone: 212-771-1717
e-mail: info@arsenalcapital.com
web: www.arsenalcapital.com

Venture Capital & Private Equity Firms / Domestic Firms

Mission Statement: A private equity firm that invests in middle market manufacturing, healthcare and business service companies. In particular, Arsenal invests where it believes it can add value by providing capital and resources to support management-led initiatives that accelerate growth, upgrade key business processes, and improve productivity.
Geographic Preference: United States
Fund Size: $3 billion
Founded: 2000
Average Investment: $300 million
Minimum Investment: $50 million
Investment Criteria: Buyouts, Recapitalizations, Growth Equity Investments
Industry Group Preference: Business to Business, Healthcare, Manufacturing, Retailing, Financial Services
Portfolio Companies: Accella, BIOIVT, Breen & Carolina Color, Certara, Charter Brokerage, Chromaflo Technologies, Cyalume, DG3, Elite Comfort Solutions, Flowchem, Genovique Specialties, IDQ, IGM Specialties, IMDS, Inhance Technologies, Kel-Tech, Novolyte Technologies, Polymer Solutions Group, Priority Solutions, Renaissance Mark, Royal Adhesives & Sealants, Scientific Protein Laboratories, Sermatech International, Solvaira Specialties, Sources Refrigeration & HVAC Inc., Spartech, TallyGenicom, TractManager, Vertellus Specialties, WCG
Key Executives:
  William Farrell, Firm Advisor
  212-771-1717
  e-mail: bfarrell@arsenalcapital.com
  Education: BEE, Manhattan College; MBA, Wharton School, University of Pennsylvania
  Background: President, Farrell Marsh & Co.; Managing Director, Salomon Brothers
  Joelle Marquis, Senior Partner
  e-mail: jmarquis@arsenalcapital.com
  Education: BS, Business Admin., Western New England College; MS, Organizational Development, American International College; University of Michigan's Executive Leadership Certificates
  Background: Chief Operating Officer, Baltimore Technologies; Senior Operating, National Grange Mutual Insurance; Senior Operating, Big Y Foods
  Directorships: Renaissance Mark Holdings, TallyGenicom Holdings
  Stephen McClean, Senior Partner
  e-mail: smclean@arsenalcapital.com
  Education: BS, Economics, MBA, Wharton School, University of Pennsylvania
  Background: Managing Director, Courtagen Capital Group LLC; Founding Partner, Merrill Lynch Capital Partners Inc.
  Directorships: BioIVT, TractManager Holdings, WIRB Copernicus Group, Certara
  John Televantos, Senior Partner
  e-mail: jtelevantos@arsenalcapital.com
  Education: BS, Chemical Engineering, University of London; PhD, Chemical Engineering, University of London
  Background: President, Hercules Inc.; President/Founder, Helios Chemical Co.; CEO, Foamex International; Vice President, Lyondell Chemical Co.; Vice President, Arco Chemical Co.; Director, R&D, Union Carbide Corp.
  Timothy Zappala, Senior Partner
  e-mail: tzappala@arsenalcapital.com
  Education: BS, Chemical Engineering, Univerisity of New Hampshire; MBA, University of Houston
  Background: President/CEO, Vertellus Specialties Inc.; Executive Vice President, Borden Chemical Inc.; The Dow Chemical Company; W.R. Grace & Co.
  Terrence Mullen, Co-Managing Partner & Co-CIO
  e-mail: tmullen@arsenalcapital.com
  Education: BBA, University of Notre Dame; MBA, Harvard Business School
  Background: Morgan Stanley & Co.; Principal, Thomas H Lee Partners
  Directorships: DG3 Holdings Inc.; KGS Holdings LP; Source Refridgeration & HVAC Inc.; IDQ Holdings Inc.; Renaissance Mark Holdings Corp.; Sermatech International Holdings Corp.
  Jeffrey Kovach, Co-Managing Partner & Co-CIO
  e-mail: jkovach@arsenalcapital.com
  Education: Dartmouth College; Tuck School of Business
  Background: Thomas H Lee Partners; Leveraged Finance, Merrill Lynch
  Directorships: Elit Comfort Solutions Inc.; Frontstream Payments Inc.; Breckenridge IS Inc.; Novolyte Technologies Corp.; Tempo Financial Corporation; DG3 Holdings Inc.; FirstAgain LLC

171 ARSENAL VENTURE PARTNERS
750 South Orlando Avenue
Suite 200
Winter Park, FL 32789

Phone: 407-838-1439
web: arsenalgrowth.com

Mission Statement: Arsenal Venture Partners invests in early-stage companies that target extremely large commercial markets, but can also leverage the defense industrial complex in a manner that is beneficial to both the company and the defense community. This focus enables AVP to source and identify high-quality opportunities, reduce the risk of each investment, and minimize the capital required to reach the market. This is accomplished by (1) activating defense resources to source opportunities or provide due diligence assessments, (2) obtaining synergistic funding for research, development and productization, or (3) attracting development partners, field trials or customers far in advance of the commercial market.
Geographic Preference: United States
Investment Criteria: Early-Stage
Portfolio Companies: Filter Easy, Blue Talon, Health Integrated, Thrive Market, Onapsis, Sharecare, Peach Works, Caremerge, Process Map, Highwinds, Protectwise, Le Tote, BoxC, CounterTack, UltraCell, Trust Digital, A123 Systems, Power Precise Solutions Inc., Varsity News Network, Root3, PowerGenix, Petra Systems, Byte Foods, The NanoSteal Company, MyUS.com, REG, InVisage, TravelTab, CrossFiber, 37.5, Blue Pillar, Sirrus, Arctic, MashNetworks
Other Locations:
  385 Homer Avenue
  Palo Alto, CA 94301
  Phone: 650-838-9200

  6701 Carnegie Avenue
  Suite 100
  Cleveland, OH 44103
  Phone: 216-456-2678

  303 Detroit Street
  Suite 100
  Ann Arbor, MI 48104
  Phone: 734-436-1496
Key Executives:
  Jason Rottenberg, General Partner
  e-mail: jason@arsenalvp.com
  Education: BS, Georgetown University; MBA, Harvard Business School
  Background: Founder, Muse Ventures; IT Angel; Manager, Arthur Andersen
  Directorships: PowerPrecise Solutions, Trust Digital, OnPoint Technologies, SpectrumBridge, PowerGenix, Ultracell, InVisage, Nanosteel, Teranex
  Christopher Fountas, General Partner
  Education: BS, Finance, Ohio State University; JD, University of Miami
  Background: Partner, Baker & Hostetler
  Directorships: PetraSolar, Atraverda, Akermin, Cocona, OnPoint Technologies, Z-Power, The Nanosteel Company
  John Trbovich, General Partner
  Education: School of Engineering, Columbia University;

Venture Capital & Private Equity Firms / Domestic Firms

Harvard Business School
Background: Co-Founder/Principal, E*OFFERING; Senior Technology Banker, Robertson Stephens & Co.; Metzler Corp.
Directorships: A123 Systems, Nanosolar, Iosil Energy, SuperProtonics
Denny Behm, Strategic Advisor
e-mail: denny@arsenalvp.com
Background: Lockheed Martin Western Development Labs, McDonnell Douglas, US Navy
Jennifer Dunham, Partner
e-mail: jennifer@milcomvp.com
Education: BSBA, SUNY College of Technology; MBA, Rollins College
Henry Huey, Strategic Advisor
Education: PhD, Electrical Engineering, University of Southern California
Background: Director, Systems Engineering, Alidian Networks; Lockheed Martin Western Development Labs, TRW Electronic Systems Group, Hughes Aircraft Ground Systems, IBM Federal Systems

172 ARTHUR P GOULD & COMPANY
Scarsdale, NY 10583

Phone: 914-729-9116
e-mail: andrew@gouldco.com
web: www.gouldco.com

Mission Statement: To help clients conceptualize, identify, execute and finance acquisitions of new businesses, and license manufacture and distribution of new products worldwide.
Geographic Preference: Worldwide
Founded: 1967
Investment Criteria: Seed, Research and Development, Startup, Early Stage, First-Stage, Second-Stage, Mezzanine, LBO
Industry Group Preference: Technology, Seafood, Consumer Services, Distribution, Electronic Components, Medical & Health Related, Energy, Natural Resources, Genetic Engineering, Industrial Equipment
Key Executives:
  Arthur P. Gould, Chairman
  e-mail: arthur@gouldco.com
  Education: BA, New York University
  Background: Founder/President, Golden Shield Corp; Founder/General Manager, Bulova Radio Company; Manufacturer, transistor radios marketed worldwide
  Andrew G Gould, President
  e-mail: andrew@gouldco.com
  Education: BA, Yale University; MA, Finance/Economics, New York University
  Robert Frankel, Special Limited Partner/Senior Technology Analyst
  e-mail: rfrankel@gouldco.com
  Education: BS Electrical Engineering, State University of New York, Buffalo; PhD, Physiology, Buffalo Medical School State University of New York
  Background: R&D Management
  Harris Landgarten, Special Limited Partner
  Education: BS, Mathematics, Queens College of the City of New York
  Background: Co-Founder/Principal, SamsungCCTV; Co-Founder/President, Techland Systems; expert with Linux and embedded control systems
  Frank Simon, Operating Partner
  e-mail: fsimon@gouldco.com
  Education: BA, English Literature, University of Colorado
  Background: Founder, Rain Forest Aquaculture Products; Co-Founder, Great Eastern Mussel Farms, Inc.
  J. Russell Chapman, Operating Partner
  e-mail: rchapman@gouldco.com
  Education: BA, Earlham College; MBA, Harvard Business School

Background: Managing Director, Atlantic Capital; CEO, Ecce Panis

173 ARTHUR VENTURES
210 Broadway North
Suite 301
Fargo, ND 58102

Phone: 701-232-3521 Fax: 701-232-3530
web: www.arthurventures.com

Mission Statement: Arthur Ventures began believes in the power of the growth cycle and the positive effect that well-managed businesses can have in society. Businesses that Arthur Ventures works with help solve crucial problems for customers while providing an opportunity for founders and team-members to create and impact powerful change in society.
Geographic Preference: Upper Midwest
Founded: 2008
Average Investment: $500,000 - $2 million
Investment Criteria: Early-Stage
Industry Group Preference: Information Technology, Enterprise Software, Web Applications & Services, Healthcare, Agriculture, Energy
Portfolio Companies: 250OK, Agronomic Technology, Ambassador, Avalara, Clariondoor, Cybrary, DataCamp, Datica, Everything Benefits, Flipgrid, Infusion Soft, Intelligent InSites, Invinsec, Ionic, Lead Pages, Linus Academy, Loyalty Builders, New Ocean Health Solutions, Preventice Solutions, Protenus, Rhiza, Stream, Talk Route, Terminus, Tiny Pulse, Total Expert, When I Work, Zipnosis
Other Locations:
  IDS Center
  80 South 8th Street
  Suite 3760
  Minneapolis, MN 55402
Key Executives:
  Doug Burgum, Founding Partner
  Education: North Dakota State University, Stanford Graduate School of Business
  Background: McKinsey & Co.; Founder, Great Plains Software; SVP, Microsoft Corporation
  Directorships: Atlassian, Intelligent InSites
  James Burgum, Co-Founder/Managing Partner
  Education: BSBA, North Dakota State University
  Background: President, Advenio Partners; Founding Team Member, North Dakota Trade Office
  Dave O'Hara, Venture Partner
  Education: BS, Economics, MBA, University of South Dakota
  Background: COO, Microsoft Advertising
  Lauris Molbert, Venture Partner
  Education: BSBA, JD, University of North Dakota
  Background: CEO, TMI Hospitality; EVP/COO, Otter Tail Corporation
  Patrick Meenan, Partner
  Education: BS, Business, Miami University
  Background: Corporate Development Group, Microsoft

174 ARTIMAN VENTURES
1731 Embarcadero Road
Suite 212
Palo Alto, CA 94303

Phone: 650-845-2020
e-mail: info@artiman.com
web: www.artiman.com

Mission Statement: Artiman typically supplies the first institutional capital, often at the concept phase. Artiman works are active partners with entrepreneurs, helping with all aspects of strategy, market definition, and execution.
Geographic Preference: United States
Fund Size: $1 billion
Founded: 2001

Venture Capital & Private Equity Firms / Domestic Firms

Average Investment: $2 - $6 million
Minimum Investment: $2 million
Investment Criteria: Seed, Startup, First Stage, Second Stage
Industry Group Preference: Business to Business, Communications Equipment, Computer Hardware & Software
Portfolio Companies: Aditazz, AppleBoard, Boxbot, Capella Space Inc., CellMax Life, Cellworks, Click Diagnostics, CORE Diagnostics, Crossbar, MedECUBE Healthcare, Niron Magnetics, OncoStem Diagnostics, Pavilion Data, Prysm, Silniva Inc., TeraPore, Tonbo Imaging, Virsec Systems Inc., Yanta Financial Technologies, zSpace Inc.

Other Locations:
Artiman Capital India Pvt. Ltd.
Brigade Hulkul Centre, Ground Floor
No. 82, Lavelle Road, Near Bangalore Club
Bangalore 560 001
India
Phone: 91 (80) 6176 9400 **Fax:** 91 (80) 6176 9401

Key Executives:
Amit Shah, Founding Partner
e-mail: amit@artimancapital.com
Education: BSEE, MS University Baroda; University of California, Irvine
Background: General Partner, Anthelion; VP New Markets/Technology, Cisco Systems Business Development; Founded/CEO, PipeLinks; Founded, Zietnet; Taught coarses and seminars, University of California, Berkeley; InterOp
Directorships: Auryn; Sierra Design Automation; NetDevices; InvenSense; SiOptical; Zyme

Tom Dennedy, Partner
e-mail: tom@artiman.com
Education: BS, Electrical Engineering, US Air Force Academy; MS, Electrical Engineering, MIT; JD, Stanford Law School
Background: Managing Director, Telesoft Partners, Inc.; Attorney, Brobeck Phleger & Harrison, LLP; Captain, US Air Force; Project Officer, Milstar Communication Satellite Joint Program Office

Yatin Mundkur, Partner
e-mail: yatin@artiman.com
Education: BSEE, MSU of Baroda, India, MSEE, University of Texas at Austin
Background: Managing Director, TeleSoft Partners; President, Equator Technologies; Vice President, Conextant; Chief Architect, Sun Microsystems; Ross Technology; Cypress Semiconductor

Ramesh Radhakrishnan, Partner
Education: BE, Indian Institute of Technology; ME, Systems Engineering, University of Virginia
Background: VP, Engineering, FireEye; Airgo Networks

Akhil Saklecha, Partner
Education: BS/MD, Northwestern Ohio Universities College of Medicine; MBA, University of Tennessee
Background: Medical Director; President/CEO, Canton Aultman Emergency Physicals

Ajit Singh, Partner
Education: BS, Electrical Engineering, Banaras Hindu University; PhD, Computer Science, Columbia University; MS, Computer Engineering, Syracuse University
Background: President/CEO, BioImagene
Directorships: Aditazz, CardioDx, Oncostem

Tim Wilson, Partner
Education: BS, Physics, Bowdoin College; MBA, Fuqua School of Business
Background: General Partner, Paratech International; CMO, Digital Island

175 ARTIS VENTURES
809 Montgomery St.
San Francisco, CA 94133

Phone: 415-344-6200
e-mail: contact@artisventures.com
web: www.av.co

Mission Statement: Artis Ventures focuses on elegant solutions that are solving the world's greatest challenges, in turn creating tomorrow's extraordinary companies.
Industry Group Preference: Semiconductors, Advanced Energy, Energy, New Media, Internet, Healthcare, Telecommunications, Networking, Cloud Computing, Data Storage
Portfolio Companies: Aruba Networks, Chefsfeed, Cohesity, Eko, Excision Biotherapeutics, ID by DNA, Locus Biosciences, Modern Meadow, Nimble Storage, Quid, Stemcentrx, Tae Life Sciences, Versa Networks, YouTube, Zenrex

Key Executives:
Stuart Peterson, Founding Partner
e-mail: stuart@artisventures.com
Education: BA, Economics, UCLA; MBA, Analytic Finance, University of Chicago Graduate School of Business
Background: Managing Director, The Cypress Funds; Vice President & Co-Portfolio Manager, Portfolio Advisory Services

Michael Harden, Founding Partner
e-mail: mike@artisventures.com
Education: BA, East Asian Studies, Washington & Lee University; MS, Finance, Olin Graduate School of Business, Babson College
Background: Analyst, CSFB Technology Group
Directorships: Chefs Feed, Practice Fusion

Robert Riemer, Chief Operating Officer
Education: BS, Accounting, Bradley University; JD, DePaul University College of Law
Background: Controller, Blum Capital Partners; CFO & COO, Fort Point Capital Management

176 ASCENSION HEALTH VENTURES LLC
101 South Hanley Road
Suite 200
Clayton, MO 63105

e-mail: info@ascensionventures.org
web: www.ascensionventures.org

Mission Statement: Provides strategic funding to companies that offer healthcare-related products, services or technologies that represent potential service breakthroughs for Ascension Health's hospitals and health facilities.
Geographic Preference: United States
Fund Size: $800 million
Founded: 2001
Average Investment: $5 million
Minimum Investment: $2 million
Investment Criteria: Expansion- to Late-Stage
Industry Group Preference: Medical & Health Related, Information Technology, Medical Devices, Healthcare, Healthcare Information Technology
Portfolio Companies: Accretive Health, Advanced Practice Strategies, Aethon, Apama Medical, Augmenix, BardyDx, Body Media, Bio Imagene, Cheetah Medical, CHF Solutions, Cofactor Genomics, Comprehensive Pharmacyservices, Confluent Surgical, CSA Medical, EBR Systems, Ekos, Emageon, GetWellNetwork, Haven Behavioral Healthcare, Impulse Monitoring Inc., Ingenious Med, Instylla, IMO, Interventional Spine, ISTO Technologies, Ivantis. MedWentive, Millennium Pharmacy System Inc., MindFrame Inc., NaviHealth, NeuroLutions, NeuroStar, Novasys Medical, OB Hospitalist Group, Ocular Therapeutix, Omnicell, OptiScan, PathoGenetix, Phreesia, Quantros, Radianse, Reputation.com, SeQual, Servicys, Solstas Lab Partners, Sonoma, Stereotaxis, Steril Med, Syapse,

Venture Capital & Private Equity Firms / Domestic Firms

TomoTherapy, TriMedx, Vascular Pathways, Visit Pay, Vivify Health, Voalte, Zipnosis, Zonare

Key Executives:
Tara Butler, MD, Managing Director
Education: MBA, Wharton School; MD, University of Pennsylvania School of Medicine
Background: Honeywell; Laboratory Assistant, University of Pennsylvania School of Medicine
Matthew Hermann, Senior Managing Director
e-mail: mhermann@ascensionhealth.org
Education: BS, Engineering, Tufts University; MBA, Finance, NYU Stern School of Business
Background: VP, Atlantic Medical Management; Financial Management, Nutrition 21; Regeneron Pharmaceuticals; JP Morgan Chase and Company; PricewaterhouseCoopers
Victor Kats, Managing Director
Education: University of North Carolina, Chapel Hill; MBA, Wharton School
Background: Allscripts-Misys; Vice President, Lehman Brothers Holdings
John Kuelper, Managing Director
Education: BA, Washington University; JD, Pritzker School of Law, Northwestern University; MBA, Kellogg School of Management
Background: Founder/President, Qualia Holdings LLC
Ryan Schuler, Managing Director
Education: BS, Accounting, Christian Brothers University; MBA, Washington University
Background: Investment Banking, AG Edwards & Sons; Associate, PricewaterhouseCoopers
Jamie Wehrung, Senior Director, Finance & Administration
Education: BA, Accountancy, Southern Illinois University, Carbondale
Background: Accountant, Catholic Healthcare Systems; Deloitte & Touche LLP

177 ASCENT BIOMEDICAL VENTURES
142 West 57th Street
Suite 4A
New York, NY 10019

Phone: 212-303-1680 Fax: 212-752-3633
e-mail: info@abvlp.com
web: www.abvlp.com

Mission Statement: Ascent Biomedical Ventures (ABV) is a venture capital firm investing in seed and early-stage biomedical technology companies developing medical devices, biopharmaceuticals, healthcare services, and information technology. ABV's principals and advisors work closely with entrepreneurs to manage the risks associated with deploying capital in startup companies.

Investment Criteria: Seed-Stage, Early-Stage
Industry Group Preference: Medical Devices, Biopharmaceuticals, Healthcare Services, Healthcare Information Technology
Portfolio Companies: Arstasis, Ary Therapeutics, Azevan Pharmaceuticals, Biomerix, Cara Therapeutics, Cross Trees Medical, Curaseal, Guided Delivery Systems, InnerPulse, Metronome, Ouroboros Medical, SpinalKinetics, SpineView, Synecor, TargAnox, Vivasure Medical, Xlumena

Key Executives:
Steve Hochberg, Managing Partner
Education: BS, University of Michigan; MBA, Harvard Business School
Background: Co-Founder: Biometrix Corporation, Eminent Research, Clinsights, Med-E-Systems, Physicians' Online
Directorships: Biometrix Corporation, Synecor, Crosstrees Medical, Ouroboros, SpineView, Solar Capital, Solar Senior Capital
Geoffrey W. Smith, Managing Partner
Education: BA, Williams College; JD, University of Pennsylvania Law School
Directorships: Azevan Pharmaceuticals, Anterios, BackBeat Medical, Biometrix, Caliber Therapeutics, TargAnox, Vivasure Medical
Avi Kometz, MD, Partner
Education: MD, University of the Witwatersrand Medical School
Background: Healthcare Practice, McKinsey & Co.
Lawrence S. Atinsky, Partner/General Counsel
Education: BA, University of Wisconsin; JD, New York University School of Law
Background: ABV; M&A Attorney, Skadden Arps Slate Meagher & Flom
Jeffrey M. Sauerhoff, Partner/Chief Financial Officer
Education: BS, Accountancy, CW Post Campus, Long Island University
Background: CFO, Erisco
Jon Edelson, MD, Venture Partner
Education: BA, Yale University; MD, University of Chicago Pritzker School of Medicine
Background: Co-Founder/CEO, Aureon Laboratories

178 ASCENT VENTURE PARTNERS
255 State Street
5th Floor
Boston, MA 02109

Phone: 617-720-9400
web: www.ascentvp.com

Mission Statement: Ascent is dedicated to financing and supporting innovative entrepreneurs striving to build emerging market leaders. Ascent is committed to backing companies with innovative and courageous ideas about how technology can transform business.

Geographic Preference: East Coast
Fund Size: $400 million
Founded: 1985
Average Investment: $2 - 5 million
Minimum Investment: $2 million
Investment Criteria: Early Stage, Investment Growth
Industry Group Preference: Technology, Networking, Communications, Information Technology, Enterprise Services, Software, SaaS
Portfolio Companies: BryterCX, Cloud Bees, CPX Security, Connected2fiber, Empow Networks, Exchange Solutions, Gr8 People, Invaluable, Knoa, Nova Scientific, Promo Boxx, Rapidminer, Revulytics, Sidecar, Splash, Startapp, Synovia Solutions, Timetrade, Vee24

Key Executives:
Geoffrey S. Oblak, General Partner
e-mail: goblak@ascentvp.com
Education: BA Economics, Hamilton College; MBA, Boston University; Certified Public Accountant with a CFA Charter
Background: Investment Analyst, Norwest Venture Partners; Audit/Business Advisory, Arthur Andersen LLP
Directorships: Auction Holdings, ClickFox, Exchange Solutions, Fidelis Security, Forefield, VI Labs, WebLayers, Guardium, Network Intelligence
Brian J. Girvan, General Partner
Education: BBA, Accounting, Manhattan College
Background: COO/CFO, Argo Global Capital; Various Positions, Fidelity Investments; Senior VP/CFO/Treasurer, Affiliated Managers Group; Senior VP/CFO, PIMCO Advisors
Directorships: BlueSocket, Knoa Software, Placemark Investments, Pyxis Mobile, TimeTrade
Christopher W. Lynch, Special General Partner
e-mail: clynch@ascentvp.com
Education: BS, Political Science, Colgate University; MBA, Harvard Business School
Background: TA Associates, Investment Officer/VP, Massachusetts Capital Corporation; President, MCC Corp.
Directorships: Everyday Wireless, Innoveer, The Corporate Marketplace, ZoomInfo

67

Venture Capital & Private Equity Firms / Domestic Firms

Christopher W. Dick, General Partner
Education: BS, Agricultural Economics, Cornell University; MBA, Babson College
Background: President, Venture Capital & Corporate Finance Subsidiaries, UST Corp
Directorships: BEZ Systems, Nova Holdings, Nova Scientific, Terascala, Whaleback Systems
Matt Fates, General Partner
Education: Double Major in Computer Science and Economics, Yale University; MBA, Tuck School of Business at Dartmouth College
Background: Business Development, Gold Wire Technology; Management, Norwest Venture Partners; Technology Investment Banking, Alex Brown & Sons
Directorships: The Corporate Marketplace, HubCast, StrikeIron, Terascala
Luke Burns, General Partner
Education: AB, Chemistry & Physics, Havard University; MBA, MIT Sloan School of Management
Background: Management Consultant, Bain & Company; Co-Founder & CEO, Emercis Corporation

179 ASHBY POINT CAPITAL
1240 Ashby Court
Arnold, MD 21012

Phone: 410-544-6250 Fax: 410-544-3264
web: ashbypointcapital.com

Mission Statement: Ashby Point Capital is a private equity firm investing in the payment services and financial services industries.

Average Investment: $100K - $5MM
Minimum Investment: 100K
Investment Criteria: All Stages
Industry Group Preference: Payment Services, Financial Services
Portfolio Companies: PayKii, Card.com, HalCash North America, SVM Cards, Trade Harbor, Shanghai Harvest Network Technology, InstaMed

Key Executives:
William J. Westervelt, Jr., Partner
e-mail: bill@ashbypoint.com
Education: BA, Economics, McDaniel College; MBA, University of Baltimore
Background: Co-Founder, First Annapolis Consulting
James D. Leroux, Partner
e-mail: jim@ashbypoint.com
Education: BA, Economics, Tufts University; JD, Boston College Law School
Background: First Annapolis Consulting

180 ASPECT VENTURES
471 Emerson Street
Palo Alto, CA 94301

e-mail: info@aspectventures.com
web: www.aspectventures.com

Mission Statement: Aspect Ventures was launched with the goal of working with entrepreneurs in the emerging mobile industry. The firm invests in Seed and Series A companies that focus on the creation of multi-platform, multi-device technologies, with particular emphasis on the mobile, consumer Internet, healthcare IT, SaaS and enterprise software sectors.

Fund Size: $150 million
Founded: 2014
Average Investment: $500,000 - $2 million
Investment Criteria: Seed-Stage, Series A, Early-Stage
Industry Group Preference: Mobile, Consumer Internet, Enterprise Software, SaaS, Healthcare Information Technology
Portfolio Companies: Amino, Aqua, Astro, Athena Health, Balenda, Baublebar, Cato Networks, Chime, Cipher Trace, Crew, Deserve, Dfinity, Edgy Bees, Exabeam, Flurry, FollowAnalytics, ForeScout, Future Family, Grokker, Gusto, Hotel Tonight, Imperva, Indegy, Integris Software, Kosmix, Learn Vest, Mapper, Nano String Technologies, OHM Connect, People Support, PredictHQ, Qordoba, ShieldX, Solv, Stem, TalkIQ, Tari, The Muse, TheRealReal, Troops, Trulia, Tru Star Technology, UrbanSitter, Vida

Key Executives:
Theresia Gouw, Co-Founder/Managing Partner
Education: ScB, Engineering, Brown University; MBA, Stanford University
Background: Partner, Accel; VP, Business Development & Sales, Release Software; Bain & Company; Product Manager, Silicon Graphics
Jennifer Fonstad, Co-Founder
Education: Georgetown University; MBA, Harvard Business School
Background: Managing Director, Draper Fisher Jurvetson; Goto.com; Co-Founder, Broadway Angels; Bain & Company
Directorships: Flurry, iCix, Intematic, Nantero
Lauren Kolodny, Principal
Education: BA, Brown University; MBA, Stanford University Graduate School of Business
Background: Product Marketing, Google; Cowboy Ventures; Clinton Foundation
Kamil Saeid, Associate
Education: Stanford University
Background: Associate Consultant, Bain & Company

181 ASSET MANAGEMENT VENTURES
2595 E Bayshore Road
Suite 240
Palo Alto, CA 94303

Phone: 650-621-8808
e-mail: plans@assetman.com
web: www.assetman.com

Mission Statement: Emphasizes involvement in seed or start-up companies in the information technology and life sciences sectors; often facilitates company formation, to take advantage of opportunities in markets and technologies.

Geographic Preference: Western, Northeastern Regions
Fund Size: $500 million
Founded: 1965
Average Investment: $4 million
Minimum Investment: $1 million
Investment Criteria: Seed, Early-Stage
Industry Group Preference: Telecommunications, Computer Hardware & Software, Environment Products & Services, Networking, Applications Software & Services, Information Technology, Database Services, Tools, Semiconductors, Nanotechnology, Energy, Healthcare
Portfolio Companies: Aegis, Amgen, Applied Biosystems, Applied Micro, Arterys, Audentes, Benefitter, Biogen Idec, BiPar Sciences, CardioDX, Cadiogen Sciences, Chmerix Inc., Coherent, CT Therapeutics, Evidation, Esperion Therapeutics, Freenome, Health, Icon, Huiseoul, InCarda Therapeutics Inc., Immune Cellular, Indi Molecular, KeepSafe, Kii, Lark, Liquid M, Maverix Biomics, Provade VMS, Mozio, Nuance, Ooma Pharmacyclics, Profusa, Properly, PMC, Proteus Digital Health, SenseOmics, Rally Point, Rapidscan, Reify, Stratavia, SignaVine, Skybox Imaging, Tandem Computers, Thunder, Twist Bioscience, Uni Key, Virtio, View Point Therapeutics, Welkin Health, WellDoc, Womply, 1 Doc Way, 3T Biosciences

Key Executives:
Skip Fleshman, Partner
Education: BS, Mechanical Engineering, University of California, Davis; MS, Management, Sloan Fellow, Stanford Grad. School of Business
Background: Fighter Pilot, United States Air Force; Founder/Executive, BGI
Lou Lange, MD, PhD, Partner
Education: BA, University of Rochester; MD, PhD,

Venture Capital & Private Equity Firms / Domestic Firms

Biological Chemisty, Harvard University
Background: Founder, CV Therapeutics; Chief of Cardiology/Professor of Medicine, Jewish Hospital
Richard Simoni, Partner
Education: PhD, Electrical Engineering, Stanford University; BA/MA, Stanford University; and Rice University
Background: Co-Founded Talkway Communications

182 ASTELLAS VENTURE MANAGEMENT
2882 Sand Hill Road
Suite 121
Menlo Park, CA 94025

web: www.astellasventure.com

Mission Statement: Astellas Venture Management LLC (AVM) is the corporate venture capital organization dedicated to helping Astellas Pharma Inc. to achieve its strategic goals. The venture capital activity of AVM can be traced back to the year 1999. Through its strategic investments in private early-stage companies, the funds aim to forge relationships with Astellas Pharma which may lead to larger collaborations in the future. AVM is able to provide portfolio companies with invaluable advice and assistance.

Founded: 1999
Investment Criteria: Early-Stage
Industry Group Preference: Therapeutics, Pharmaceuticals, Biotechnology
Portfolio Companies: Bicycle Therapeutics, Cleave Biosciences, Crescendo Biologics, DecImmune Therapeutics, eFFECTOR Therapeutics, Innocrin Pharmaceuticals, Oncorus Inc., PhaseBio Pharmaceuticals Inc., Raze Therapeutics Inc., Tacurion Pharma Inc., Tizona Therapeutics, Twentyeight-Seven, Viamet Pharmaceuticals

Key Executives:
Shunichiro Matsumoto, PhD, President
Education: MBA, McGill University; PhD, Medicine, University oF Tsukuba; MS, Agriculture, Kyoto University
Background: VP, Innovation Management, Astellas Pharma Inc.; Investment Director, AVM
Kazunori Maruyama, PhD, Executive Investment Director
Education: PhD, Agricultural Chemistry, University of Tokyo
Background: Director, Business Development, Astellas Pharma Inc.; Research Scientist, Yamanouchi
Ryosuke Munakata, PhD, Investment Director
Background: Associate Director, Innovation Management, Astellas Pharma Inc.

183 ATA VENTURES
4300 El Camino Real
Suite 205
Los Altos, CA 94022

Phone: 650-594-0189
e-mail: contact@ataventures.com
web: www.ataventures.com

Mission Statement: ATA Ventures offers seed and early-stage growth capital along with decades of proven operating experience to assist startups in their pursuit of building companies of tremendous value.

Fund Size: $400 million
Founded: 2003
Investment Criteria: Seed, Startup, First Stage
Industry Group Preference: Information Technology, Wireless Technologies, Consumer Internet, Enterprise Software
Portfolio Companies: Accelops, Argyle Data, Billeo, Cinova, Clustrix, FastScale, Givit, HarvestMark, Jobvite, Jolata, Lavante, Medagate, Milyoni, SalesPortal, Siaras, Sikka, Theranos, Trilibis Mobile, YottaMark, ZooskottaMark, Zoosk, Actelis, Adesto Technologies, Altierre, EdgeWave, NE Photonics, PureWave Networks, Revera, Shocking Technologies

Key Executives:
Michio Fujimura, Director Emeritus
e-mail: mfujimura@ataventures.com
Education: Bachelor Law, Chuo University
Background: Owned/Operated, Vanguard Systems Consulting; Founded, Aisys Corporation; Product Marketing, David Systems
Directorships: Aisys Corporation; IT-Farm Corporation; Vadem
Hatch Graham, Managing Director
e-mail: hgraham@ataventures.com
Education: BS Engineering, Idaho State University
Background: Co-Founded, Wave7; Optics in Georgia; Resonext; CEO, Zoran Corporation; Executive Officer, World Access; TCSI Corporation; Stanford Telecom
Directorships: College of Engineering Advisory Committee
Pete Thomas, Managing Director
e-mail: pthomas@ataventures.com
Education: BSEE magna cum laude, Utah State University; MS Computer Science, University of Santa Clara
Background: General Partner, Institutional Venture Partners; OEM Engineering Manager, Intel Corporation; Engineering, Fairchild Communications; Sylvania EDL
Michael Hodges, Managing Director
e-mail: mhodges@ataventures.com
Education: BSEE, MSEE, UC Berkeley
Background: Spectra-Physics
Nancy McCroskey, Chief Financial Officer
e-mail: nmccroskey@ataventures.com
Education: University of California, Berkeley; MBA, College of Notre Dame
Background: Redpoint Ventures
John Loiacono, Venture Partner/Market Strategist
e-mail: jloiacono@ataventures.com
Background: CMO, Sun Microsystems; SVP/General Manager, Adobe's Systems' Digital Media & Creative Solutions

184 ATEL CAPITAL GROUP
The Transamerica Pyramid
600 Montgomery Street
9th Floor
San Francisco, CA 94111

Phone: 415-989-8800 Fax: 415-989-3796
web: www.atel.com

Mission Statement: ATEL provides secured financing to emerging growth companies.

Founded: 1977
Portfolio Companies: Adenosine Therapeutics LLC, Adesto Technologies, ALBA Therapeutics, Altierre, AlveolUs, Amyris, Arbinet, Arsenal, ARYX Therapeutics, Asempra, Aspen Aerogels, Audience Science, Axial BioTech, AxoGen, Bloom Energy, Boingo Wireless, Cambrios, CedarPoint Communications, Chelsio Communications, Complete Genomics, Convio, CryoCor, Cymbet Corporation, Danger Inc, Deeya Energy Inc, DeliveryAgent, Doppelganger, Dorado, ecoATM, EcoLogic, EdeniQ, Enerkem Technologies, Enevate, Enphase Energy, Five9, Forma Therapeutics, GangaGen, Good, InfiniRoute Networks, Innovalight, InSite One, IntelePeer, Ioxus, Iperian, Kabam, Kaminario, Linden Lab, Lightship Telecom, Locus, LS9, Metabolon, Miasole, Microfabrica, Millennium Pharmacy Systems, MotoSport, ON24, NanoGram Corporation, NexPlanar, OpenPages, OpSource, Primet, QSr, Raydiance, Recyclebank, RenalSolutions, Reply.com, RewewData, Rubicon Technology, SilverPOP, Sixtron Advanced Materials, Sling Media, Solaria, SolFocus, Sorra, StarCite, Step Labs, Technorati, TelePacific Communications, Xlumena, Zeevo

69

Venture Capital & Private Equity Firms / Domestic Firms

Key Executives:
Steven Rea, President
e-mail: srea@atel.com
Education: BS, Finance, San Diego State University; EMBA, Business, Saint Mary's College of California
Background: Vice President, Imperial Bank; Vice President, LINC Capital Partner

186 ATHENAEUM FUND
3100 East Foothills Blvd
2nd Floor
Pasadena, CA 91101

Phone: 626-584-0913 Fax: 626-584-0953
web: www.athenaeumfund.com

Mission Statement: A venture capital limited partnership that provides seed funding to emerging technology companies based in Southern California. The Athenaeum Fund is committed to offering funding, management, and marketing skills to early stage companies in order to generate capital gains and help with the advancement of company products.

Geographic Preference: United States, Southwest, California, Northwest
Fund Size: $6 million
Founded: 1999
Average Investment: $250,000
Minimum Investment: $50,000
Investment Criteria: Seed, First Stage
Industry Group Preference: Biotechnology, Communications Equipment, Computer Hardware & Software, Chemicals, Pharmaceuticals, Telecommunications, Networking, Materials Technology
Portfolio Companies: Eidogen, Inc.

Key Executives:
Dr Philippe H Adam, Founder/General Partner
Education: Polytechnic University, Brooklyn; MS, PhD, Aeronautics, California Institute of Technology; MBA, Wharton School, University of Pennsylvania
Background: Jet Propulsion Lab, Caltech/NASA; AlliedSignal/Honeywell; Houlihan Lokey; Avery Dennison; Beckman Coulter
Dr John Baldeschwieler, Founder/General Partner
Education: BS, Chemical Engineering, Cornell University; PhD, Physical Chemistry, University of California, Berkeley
Background: US Army; Teaching & Research, Harvard University; Professor, Chemistry, Stanford University; Deputy Director, Office of Science & Technology, White House; Professor, Chemistry, California Institute of Technology; Founder, Vestar; Founder & Director, Combion
Directorships: NeXstar
Malcolm Cloyd, Founder/General Partner
Background: Manager, Mergers & Acquisitions, Geosource Inc.; International Technology Corp.

187 ATHENIAN VENTURE PARTNERS
340 West State Street
Suite 137B
Athens, OH 45701

Phone: 614-360-1155 Fax: 740-593-9311
e-mail: info@athenianvp.com
web: www.athenianvp.com

Mission Statement: A venture capital firm that specializes in early stage information technology, digital health and healthcare investments.

Geographic Preference: United States
Fund Size: $100-$150 million
Founded: 1997
Average Investment: $1 - $5 million
Minimum Investment: $1 million
Investment Criteria: Early through Later Stage

Industry Group Preference: Information Technology, Life Sciences, Communications, Internet Technology
Portfolio Companies: Advanced Digital Internet Corp., Aerpio Therapeutics, Akebia Therapeutics, Alloptic, Analect Instruments, Archemix Corp., Asset Management Outsourcing, Baxano, Candera, Chaparral Network Storage, Comet Solutions, Cyber-Rain, DiAthegen, Manta Media, Integrated Energy Services, Intellispace, LigoCyte Pharmaceuticals, Micromet, PacketMotion, Pain Therapeutics, Phobos Corporation, Sendio, Servion Global Solutions, StorageApps, Verus Pharmaceuticals, Windy Hill Medical

Other Locations:
2400 Eat Commercial Boulevard
Suite 410
Ft. Lauderdale, FL 33308
Phone: 954-289-3000

Key Executives:
Daniel H. Kosoy, MD, Partner, Healthcare
614-360-1589
e-mail: kosoy@athenianvp.com
Education: BA, Philosophy/Biosciences, Yale University; MD, McGill University
Background: Management Consultant, Generics Group
Directorships: Windy Hill Medical; Akebia Therapeutics; LigoCyte Pharmaceuticals; Archemix; Verus Pharmaceuticals; CancerVax
David R. Scholl, Partner, Healthcare (Part-Time)
e-mail: scholl@athenianvp.com
Education: BS, Biology, Indiana University; PhD Microbiology, Ohio University
Background: President/CEO/Director of Research/VP of Research, Diagnostic Hybrids; Post-Doctoral Fellow, Roche Institute for Molecular Biology
Directorships: Pain Therapeutics; CancerVax; Ohio Governor's Technology Action Board; Trustee, BioOhio; The Ohio Business Development Corporation (OBDC); Ohio University ESP Advisory Council
Francois Helou, Senior Partner, Information Technology
e-mail: helou@athenianvp.com
Education: MS, Electrical Engineering, Federal Institute of Technology; MBA, INSEAD
Background: Strategic Consultant, Cambridge Positioning Systems; Logica; Operations, Brown Boveri; Compugraphic; Fujitsu-ICL
Directorships: Manta Media; Sendio; Chaparral Network Storage; StorageApps; Alloptic; Advanced Digital Internet Corp

188 ATHYRIUM CAPITAL MANAGEMENT
530 Fifth Avenue
25th Floor
New York, NY 10036

Phone: 212-402-6925
e-mail: info@athyrium.com
web: www.athyrium.com

Mission Statement: Athyrium invests in a wide range of financial instruments including royalties, structured credit, and equities as well as select special situations.

Founded: 2008
Average Investment: $25 - $75 million
Industry Group Preference: Healthcare, Biotechnology, Pharmaceuticals, Medical Devices, Diagnostics, Healthcare Services
Portfolio Companies: BioFire Diagnostics, Horizon Pharma, Ikaria, InnoPharma, Ironwood Pharmaceuticals, Lannett Company, MedPro Safety Products, Pernix Therapeutics Holdings, Progenity, Retrophin, Synarc-Biocore Holdings, SynCardia Systems, Tecomet, Tria Beauty, Universal Biosensors, Verenium, VIVUS, Zealand Pharma A/S

Key Executives:
Jeffrey A. Ferrell, Managing Partner
Education: AB, Biochemical Sciences, Harvard College

Venture Capital & Private Equity Firms / Domestic Firms

Background: Lehman Brothers; Principal, Schroder Ventures Life Sciences
Directorships: Lpath, Progenity
Laurent D. Hermouet, Partner
Education: BS, Economics, MS, Banking & Finance, University of Paris-Dauphine; CFA
Background: Vice President, Senior Credit Analyst, Tribeca Global Managment; Goldman Sachs
Jeremy D. Lack, Partner
Education: School of Industrial & Labor Relations, Cornell University; Doctorate, Biochemistry, University of Oxford
Background: Managing Director, Cortec Group; Principal, New Leaf Ventures; Associate, Oxford Bioscience Partners
Uttam Jain, Partner
Education: B.Tech, Chemical Engineering, Indian Institute of Technology; MS, Cheminical Engineering Practice, MIT; MBA, Healthcare Management, Wharton School at the University of Pennsylvania;
Background: Director, Thomas H. Lee Partners; Consultant, Boston Consulting Group
Hondo Sen, Partner
Education: A.B., Economics, Dartmouth College
Background: Sr. Associate, Littlejohn & Co.; Financial Analyst, J.P. Morgan Securities

189 ATLANTA VENTURES

Phone: 404-590-4660
web: www.atlantaventures.com

Mission Statement: Focused on serving entrepreneurs in earlier stages. Offers a unique community in partnership with the Atlanta Tech Village. Their platform is designed for entrepreneurs looking to launch at the ground floor of their business.
Average Investment: $250K - $1 million
Investment Criteria: Annual Recurring Revenue of less than $1 Million; Target for Current Capital Raise of less than $1 Million; Unaffiliated
Industry Group Preference: Technology, Sustainable Energy
Portfolio Companies: Actively Learn, Atlanta Tech Village, Calendly, Copient Health, Dragon Army, Gimme, GreenPrint, Greenzie, Hannon Hill, Intown Golf Club, LeaseQuery, Musical Overture, Sales Force Pardot, Rigor, SalesLoft, Sequr, SingleOps, Teamworks, Terminus

Key Executives:
David Cummings, Partner
Education: BS, Duke University
Background: Managing Director, Shotput Ventures; Founder/CEO, Pardot LLC; Founder/Chairman, Hannon Hill; Co-Founder, Rigor; SalesLoft; Dragon Army; Terminus Software
AT Gimble, Partner
Education: BS, Georgia Institute of Technology; MBA, Harvard Business School
Background: Manager, Bain & Company; Sr Director, LexisNexis Risk Solutions; Advisor, Atlanta Tech Village
Jon Birdsong, Partner
Education: University of Georgia
Background: Marketing Manager, OpenStudy; Head of Growth, SalesLoft; VP, AA-ISP; CEO, WideAngle
Karen Houghton, Venture Partner
Education: BS, Berry College; MA, Richmont Graduate University
Background: Retreats Director, YMCA; Consultant/Conselor, Hope Counseling Center/Family Conseling Associates; Business Consultant, Golden Coaching and Consulting; Founder/Director, Land of a Thousand Hills Coffee Co.; Marketing Manager, Pardot; VP, Atlanta Tech Villages
David Lightburn, Venture Partner
Education: BBA, Rhodes College
Background: Founder/CEO, Clickspace;

Founder/Owner/Advisor, Village Realty - Atlanta; Co-Founder/President, Atlanta Tech Village

190 ATLANTIC CAPITAL GROUP
1 Olympic Place
Suite 1220
Towson, MD 21204

Phone: 410-602-6020
e-mail: info@atcapgroup.com
web: www.atcapgroup.com

Mission Statement: Atlantic Capital Group is a real estate and private equity investment firm.
Geographic Preference: United States
Industry Group Preference: Real Estate, Diversified
Portfolio Companies: Residence Inn by Marriott, Oil Purification Systems, 200-208 Sixth St. Jersey City NJ, Carchex, F.T. Silfies, Mariner Village, Lumiere Hotel, Noble Logistic Services, GigaTrust, Epic at Cub Run, Miami Green, 60 Erie St. Jersey City NJ, Castlefield, Ziggs.com, Honest Tea, Biometric Access Co.

Key Executives:
Steven B. Fader, Founder and Chairman
Education: BA, Western Maryland College; JD, University of Baltimore School of Law
Background: CEO, Atlantic Automotive Corp.
James M. Bannantine, Managing Partner
Education: Distinguished Graduate, West Point; MBA, Wharton School
Background: Founder, Acumen Capital; Dorsal Networks
Peter M. Rubin, Founder and Partner
Education: BA, Political Science, Duke University; JD, University of Baltimore Law School
Background: Litigator, Transactional Attorney
Directorships: Carchex, Affordable Hearing Networks
Howard Kra, Partner
Education: Political Science, Business Administration, University of Maryland
Background: Wealth Advisor, Lehman Brothers; SVP, Morgan Stanley; Streamline.com
Directorships: Carchex
Bruce Taub, Partner
Education: BA, University of Maryland; JD, California Western School of Law; LLM, Taxation, Georgetown University Law School
Background: Head of Acquisitions, Storage USA

191 ATLAS VENTURE
400 Technology Square
10t Floor
Cambridge, MA 02139

Phone: 857-201-2700
web: www.atlasventure.com

Mission Statement: Atlas Venture invests in the earliest stages of technology and life science innovation.
Geographic Preference: United States, Europe
Fund Size: $283 million
Founded: 1986
Average Investment: $500,000 - $5 million
Minimum Investment: $500,000
Investment Criteria: Seed, Startup, Early-Stage
Industry Group Preference: Information Technology, Life Sciences, Communications
Portfolio Companies: Acetelion, Adnexus Therapeutics, Alnylam Pharmaceuticals, Annovation Biopharma, ArQule, Arrow Therapeutics, Arteaus Therapeutics, Avila Therapeutics, Avrobio, Bicycle Therapeutics, Cadent Therapeutics, CoStim Pharmaceuticals, Crucell, deCODE Genetics, Delinia, Disarm Therapeutics, Egalet Corp., Exelis, F-Star Alpha Limited, Gemini Therapeutics, Harbour Antibodies, Horizon Pharma, IFM Therapeutics, Infacare, Intellia Therapeutics, JenaValve, Kymera Therapeutics, Kyn Therapeutics, Lysosomal Therapeutics Inc., Magenta

Venture Capital & Private Equity Firms / Domestic Firms

Therapeutics, Micromet, MiRagen Therapeutics, Momenta Pharmaceuticals, MorphoSys, Navitor Pharmaceuticals, Nimbus Therapeutics, Novexel, Numerate, Obsidian Therapeutics, Padlock Therapeutics, Replimune, Robin Therapeutics, Spero Therapeutics, Stromedix, Surface Oncology, Synlogic, Translate Bio, U3 Pharma, Unum Therapeutics, Vitae Pharma, Zafgen

Key Executives:

Bruce Booth, Partner
Education: BS, Biochemistry, Pennsylvania State University; PhD, Molecular Medicine, University of Oxford
Background: Principal, Caxton Health Holdings LLC, Associate Principal, McKinsey & Company
Directorships: Zafgen; Lysosomal Therapeutics; Magenta Therapeutics; Unum Therapeutics

Peter Barrett, Partner, Legacy Funds
e-mail: pbarrett@atlasventure.com
Education: BS, Chemisty, Lowell Technological Institute; PhD, Analytical Chemistry, Northeastern University; Harvard Business School Management Development Program
Background: Co-Founder/Executive VP/Chief Business Officer, Celera Genomics; VP Corporate Planning/Business Development, Perkin-Elmer Corporation
Directorships: Alnylam Pharmaceuticals, Archemix Corporation, Aureon Biosciences, Momenta Pharmaceuticals

Kevin Bitterman, PhD, Partner
Education: BA, Rutgers University; PhD, Harvard Medical School
Background: Co-Founder, Genocea Biosciences; CEO, Editas Medicine; Partner, Polaris Partners
Directorships: InSeal Medical; Kala Pharmaceuticals; Neuronetics; Taris Biomedical

Jason Rhodes, Partner
Education: BA, Yale University; MBA, Wharton School
Background: Founder/CEO, Disarm Therapeutics; Founder/CEO, Torus Therapeutics; President, Epizyme; Business Development, Alnylam; Founder, Fidelity Biosciences

Michael Gladstone, Principal
Education: AB, Biochemical Sciences, Harvard College
Background: Consultant, L.E.K. Consulting; Fellow, Eutropics; Viral Pathogenesis

David Grayzel, MD, Partner
Education: BA, Stanford University; MD, Harvard Medical School
Background: Infinity Pharmaceutical; Director, Coporate Development, Dyax Corp.; Curriculum Director, Stanford University Medical Center
Directorships: Acera

Jean-Francois Formela, MD, Partner
Education: MD, Paris University of Medicine; MBA, Columbia University
Background: Senior Director, Medical Marketing and Scientific Affairs, Schering-Plough; Practiced Emergency Medicine, Necker University Hospital in Paris; Involved in formation of companies such as ArQule; MorphoSys; Exelixis; deCODE Genetics; Nuvelo; Structural GenomiX; CellZome; Archemix; Aureon Biosciences

192 ATRIUM CAPITAL
3000 Sand Hill Road
Building 2
Suite 130
Menlo Park, CA 94025

Phone: 650-233-7878 Fax: 650-233-6944
web: www.atriumcapital.com

Mission Statement: Atrium has been co-managing strategic venture funds on an outsourced basis for Global 1000 corporations for 25 years.

Founded: 1991

Average Investment: $5 million
Minimum Investment: $1 million
Investment Criteria: Seed, Startup, First Stage, Second Stage
Industry Group Preference: Software, Natural Resources, Internet Technology, Chemicals, Publishing, Wireless Technologies, Energy, Materials Technology, Advertising
Portfolio Companies: Acal Energy, Adforce, Canto, Ciespace, ClassOwl, ClearGuage, CPC, Dataware Technologies, DigitalPersona, Fastsoft, FieldCentrix, Incentive Logic, InfoUSA, IPT, Landmark, Mapquest.com, Marketlive, Mediatel, MetaTV, ModViz, Multex.com, MyOffers, MyTango, NewsEdge, NxtGen Emission Controls, Pixim, RedEenvelope, ShowEvidence, Spectra, ThinkCERCA, Tumbleweed Communications, Virent, Vocabulary.com, Xeikon

Key Executives:

Russell Pyne, Founder & Managing Partner
e-mail: rpyne@atriumcapital.com
Education: AB, Princeton University; JD, MBA, Stanford University
Background: General Partner, Sprout Group

Bart Faber, Partner
Education: BA, Arizona State University; MBA, New York University
Background: CEO, Document Sciences Corporation

George Petracek, Partner
e-mail: gpetracek@atriumcapital.com
Education: MS Cybernetics, CVUT Institute of Technology; MBA, Stanford University
Background: Venture Investments, Hewlett-Packard; Investment Banker, UBS; Morgan Stanley; Computer Programmer, 3M

Jon Rattner, Chief Operating Officer
Education: BA, Economics & Business Administration, Vanderbilt University; JD, Columbia University School of Law
Background: General Counsel, SummerHill Homes; Partner, Gray Cary Ware & Freidenrich

Bob Shaw, Advisor
Education: BEP, MS, Cornell University; MPA, American University; PhD, Applied Physics, Stanford University
Background: President, Arete Corporation; Senior Vice President, Energy Division, Booz Allen & Hamilton; Bell Laboratories; Cavendish Laboratory
Directorships: Distributed Energy Systems Corporation, H2Gen Innovations

Chris Heivly, Advisor & Venture Partner
Education: BS, West Chester University; MA, University of South Carolina
Background: Executive Vice President, Ultimus Software; Chairman, Angular Systems; President, Rand McNally; Andersen Consulting; Founder, MapQuest
Directorships: Alphagraphics, MediaTel, Hands-On-Technology

Jim Hornthal, Venture Partner
Education: AB Economics, Princeton University; MBA, Harvard Business School
Background: Vice Chairman, Travelooty; Chairman/Founder, Preview Travel; General Partner, Oak Grove Ventures; Consultant, The Boston Consulting Group; Co-Founder, Healthcentral.Com
Directorships: University of California, Berkeley; Wingspring Companies

193 AUA PRIVATE EQUITY PARTNERS
666 Fifth Ave
27th Floor
New York, NY 10103

Phone: 212-231-8600 Fax: 212-231-8601
e-mail: info@auaequity.com
web: auaequity.com

Mission Statement: AUA Private Equity Partners focuses on lower-middle market businesses that target the growing U.S.

Hispanic population, or that take ethnic brands to the mainstream.
Geographic Preference: United States
Fund Size: $275MM
Industry Group Preference: Consumer Products, Consumer Services, Media, Business Products & Services
Portfolio Companies: Associated Foods, Cirque Dreams, Desi, Elegant Desserts, Gourmet Culinary Partners, Gourmet Foods, Gourmet Kitchen, Joey's Fine Foods, Kabobs, Love & Quiches, Indulge Desserts, Noga Dairy, Raymundos, Tijuana Flats, Trufood, Van-Lang Foods, Vistar Entertainment, Water Lilies

Key Executives:
Andy Unanue, Managing Partner
e-mail: andy.unanue@auallc.com
Education: BA, University of Miami; MBA, Thunderbird
Background: COO, Goya Foods
Directorships: KABR Real Estate Partners, Opt-Intelligence, TruFoods, eSchoolData
Steven Flyer, Partner
e-mail: steven.flyer@auaequity.com
Education: BA, Columbia University; JD, Cornell Law School
Background: Managing Director, Trimaran Capital Partners; CIBC World Markets
David Benyaminy, Partner
e-mail: david.benyaminy@auaequity.com
Education: BA, MBA, Hofstra University
Background: Investment Professional, CNPE Management; Executive Director, Trimaran Capital Partners
Kyce Chihi, Managing Director
e-mail: kyce.chihi@auaequity.com
Education: BS, Economics, Wharton School
Background: Investment Professional, CNPE Management
John Moore, Chief Financial/Compliance Officer
e-mail: john.moore@auaequity.com
Education: BA, Davidson College; MBA, University of Rochester
Background: ALPS Fund Services

194 AUDAX GROUP
101 Huntington Avenue
25th Floor
Boston, MA 02199

Phone: 617-859-1500
web: www.audaxgroup.com

Mission Statement: Audax Group is a premier investor in middle market companies. Audax manages over $5.0 billion of capital through its private equity, mezzanine debt, and senior secured debt funds. Audax focuses on building companies with leading market positions and superior management teams. Its mission is to partner with management to build long term value in its companies. Audux handles a variety of transactions, including leveraged buyouts and recapitalizations, corporate divestitures spin-offs and roll-outs.

Geographic Preference: United States
Fund Size: $5 billion
Founded: 1999
Investment Criteria: Small Cap, Lower-Middle Market
Industry Group Preference: Building Materials & Services, Business Products & Services, Distribution, Direct Marketing, Energy, Niche Manufacturing, Technology, Media, Consumer Products, Environment Products & Services, Education, Food & Beverage, Waste & Recycling, Water
Portfolio Companies: A & A Manufacturing Company, AAMP of America, A-D Technologies, Advanced Dermatology & Cosmetic Surgery, Affordable Interior Systems, API Heat Transfer, Arnold Magnetic Technologies, Artisan Entertainment, Astrodyne Corporation, ATG Rehab, Bridgeport Tank Trucks, Chart Industries, CIBT Global, Cinelease, Coast Crane, Colormatrix, Correct Care Solutions, Cozzini Bros, Denver Biomedical, Distribution International, Dynisco, Elgin Equipment Group, Elgin Fastener Group, Endurance International Group, Fibersense Technology, Flexstar Technology, Great Expressions Dental Centers, Help/Systems, Herald Media Holdings, In The Swim, Injured Workers Pharmacy, Koda Distribution Group, Kurt Versen, Laborie Medical Technologies, Lewis-Goetz and Company, Macgregor, Nash_Elmo, Neptune-Benson, Nivel Holdings, Northern Digital, Overton's, Phillips & Temro Industries, Phoenix Children's Academy, Quest Specialty Chemicals, Ready Mixed Concrete, Reed Group, Silent Preferred Partners, Silver State Materials, Thermon Industries, Trimark Usa, United Recovery Systems, Utex Industries, Winchester Electronics

Other Locations:
320 Park Avenue
19th Floor
New York, NY 10022
Phone: 212-703-2700

101 California Street
Suite 4750
San Francisco, CA 94111
Phone: 650-252-0600

Key Executives:
Geoffrey Rehnert, Co-Founder & Co-CEO
e-mail: grehnert@audaxgroup.com
Education: JD, Stanford Law School; AB, Duke University
Background: Managing Director, Bain Capital; Bain & Company; JP Morgan & Company
Marc Wolpow, Co-Founder & Co-CEO
e-mail: mwolpow@audaxgroup.com
Education: JD, Harvard Law School; MBA, Harvard Business School; BS, Wharton School, University of Pennsylvania
Background: Managing Director, Bain Capital; Founder, Sankaty Advisors; Drexel Burnham Lambert; Donaldson Lufkin & Jenrette
Richard Joseph, Managing Director & Chief Operating Officer
e-mail: rjoseph@Audaxgroup.com
Education: Boston College School of Management
Background: CFO, Streamline.com; CFO, Software Emancipation Technology; CFO, Planet Direct Corp.; CFO, ESSENSE Systems Inc.; Senior Manager, Ernst & Young
Daniel Weintraub, Managing Director, Chief Legal Officer & CAO
e-mail: dweintraub@audaxgroup.com
Education: Dartmouth College; Boston College Law School
Background: Ropes & Gray; Law Clerk to the Honorable Mark L. Wolf, United States District Judge for the District of Massachusetts

195 AUGMENT VENTURES
206 South 4th Avenue
Ann Arbor, MI 48104

e-mail: info@augmentventures.com
web: www.augmentventures.com

Mission Statement: To invest in innovative technology-based companies that can make an impact on quality of life and business efficiency around the world.

Fund Size: $20 million
Founded: 2010
Investment Criteria: Startups, Early-Stage
Industry Group Preference: Software, Cloud Computing, SaaS, Big Data, Analytics & Analytical Instruments, Energy
Portfolio Companies: Aperia Technologies, Cloud Agronomics, Crowdz, Fluid Screen, Flume, GeoTix, Iteros, LARQ, Llamasoft, Lumenetix, Mercatus, RayVio, Revolights, Slive

Venture Capital & Private Equity Firms / Domestic Firms

Key Executives:
Sonali Vijayavargiya, Founder/Managing Director
Education: BS, Statistics, Fergusson College; MBA, Symbiosis Institute of Business Management
Background: Founder, Augment Capital LLC; Industrial Development Bank of India; PricewaterhouseCoopers; Edelweiss Capital
Directorships: RayVio
David Armstrong, Partner/Chief Financial Officer
Education: BBA, Accounting, University of Michigan-Dearborn; MS, Taxation, Walsh College
Background: Partner, Edwards Ellis Armstrong & Company; Principal & CFO, Pinnacle Investment Advisors LLC; Treasurer, Riverside Arts Center

196 AUGURY CAPITAL PARTNERS
8025 Forsyth Blvd
2nd Floor
St. Louis, MO 63105

Phone: 314-448-1316 Fax: 314-335-7637
web: www.augurycapital.com

Mission Statement: Mid- and later-stage investors in the life sciences and financial services industries.
Investment Criteria: Mid-Stage, Later-Stage
Industry Group Preference: Life Sciences, Financial Services, Information Technology, Medical Devices, Biopharmaceuticals
Portfolio Companies: Force10 Networks, Clearent, Circle Medical, Texcel Medical, Paranet, PEX Card
Key Executives:
David W. Truetzel
Education: MBA, Wharton School
Background: Founder/General Partner, Hela Capital Partners; CFO, Paymentech
Directorships: Clearent
Robert B. Wetzel
Education: MBA, Carnegie Mellon Tepper School of Business
Background: Founder, Alchemy Advisors
Directorships: Circle Medical, Texcel Medical

197 AUGUST CAPITAL
893A Folsom Street
San Francisco, CA 94107

Phone: 650-234-9900 Fax: 650-234-9910
web: www.augustcap.com

Mission Statement: Believes in the creative power of successful information technology entrepreneurs to envision sizable market opportunities, construct lasting technologies, and build enduring companies; prefers to act as a company's lead investor, moving swiftly on closing deals, helping management evaluate and complete their next financing stages, and providing counsel on how to create the most effective board of director teams.
Geographic Preference: Northwest, Southwest, Rocky Mountains, West Coast
Fund Size: $2 billion
Founded: 1995
Average Investment: $5 - $20 million
Minimum Investment: $2 million
Investment Criteria: Startup, Early-Stage, First Round, Special situations
Industry Group Preference: Communications, Computer Related, Distribution, Electronic Components, Information Technology, Business Products & Services
Portfolio Companies: Aardvark, Actional Corporation, Adara Media, Adchemy, Alibre, Alta Devices, Atheros Communications, Be, Bill.Com, Blippy, BroadLogic, Bubbli, Cobalt Networks, Compaq Computer, Crystal Decisions, Cygnus Solutions, Devicescape Software, DITTO, Done Right!, Dotnetnuke, Ebates, Encentuate, Enuvis, Evite, Flingo, Frame Technology, Genoa, Gigwalk, Grand Junction Networks, Gravity, Guru, Inrix, Intuit, Iridigm Display Corp, Jaxtr, Listen, Livemocha, LiveOps, Luminate, Luxtera, Magnum Semiconductor, Mainstreet Networks, Mavenir Systems, Memolane, Metrofi, Microdisplay Corporation, Microsoft, Mimosa Systems, MMC Networks, Neopath Networks, Netcell, Netopia, Netpulse, Nomis Solutions, Notiva, Ohai, Openlane, Packettrap, Paradise Electronics, Paycycle, Paynearme, Postini, Printpaks, Pubmatic, Pulsecore Semiconductor, Quantum, Radlan Computer Communications, Reconnex, Relayrides, Reputation.Com, Retailnext, Rocket Lawyer, SAY Media, Scintera, Seagate Technology, Sequence Design, Shopping.Com, Silicon Architects, Silicon Image, Six Apart, Skypilot, Snagajob, Splunk Technology, Stratus Computer, Stumbleupon, Summit Microelectronics, Sun Microsystems, SuVolta, Swoopo, Sybase, Symantec, Technorati, Tegile Systems, Telocity, Threatmetrix, Tickle, Topica, Trumba, Tumbleweed Communications, Tzero Technologies, Ubicom, Unity Semiconductor, Valicert, Virsto Software, Visio, WePay, Xilinx, Xirrus, Zulily

Key Executives:
David Hornik, General Partner
Education: Computer Music, Stanford University; MPhil, Criminology, Cambridge University; JD, Harvard Law School
Background: Corporate Attorney, Venture Law Group; Cravath Swaine & Moore; Perkins Coie LLP
Directorships: Nomis Solutions; Notiva; PayCycle; Six Apart; Splunk Technology; Actional Corporation
John Johnston, Founding Partner
Education: AB, English, Princeton University; MBA, Harvard University
Background: General Partner, Technology Venture Investors; Hambrecht & Quist Venture Partners; Inter-Asia Management Company Ltd; Past Director, Western Association of Venture Capitalists
David Marquardt, Founding Partner
Education: BSME, Columbia University; MBA, Stanford University; MSEE, Stanford University
Background: Co-Founder, Technology Venture Investors; Institutional Venture Associates; Design Engineer/Development Manager, Diablo Systems; President, Western Association of Venture Capitalists; Director, National Venture Capital Association; President, Western Assn of Venture Capitalists
Howard Hartenbaum, General Partner
e-mail: howard@augustcap.com
Education: BS, Mechanical Engineering, MIT
Background: General Partner, Draper Richards LP; Hughes Electronics; Honda Motor Company; Teledyne Relays
Directorships: Livemocha, Pizazza, Soopo
Eric Carlborg, General Partner
e-mail: eric@augustcap.com
Education: BA, Economics, University of Illinois; MBA, University of Chicago
Background: Partner, Continental Investors; Investment Banking, Merrill Lynch & Co.
Directorships: Blue Nile, CarHop, Dydacomp, PubMatic, SnagAJob, Zulily
Tripp Jones, General Partner
e-mail: tripp@augustcap.com
Education: BA, Psychology, Princeton University
Background: Spectrum Equity Investors, JMP Securities
Directorships: Adara Media
Vivek Mehra, Partner Emeritus
Education: BS, Electronics, Punjab University; MS, Computer Engineering, Iowa State University
Background: VP/General Manager, Cobalt Business Unit, Sun Microsystems; Co-Founder, Cobalt Networks; Apple; SGI; Digital Equipment
Directorships: NeoPath Networks; Encentuate

Venture Capital & Private Equity Firms / Domestic Firms

198 AUGUSTUS VENTURES
1302 Colwell Ln.
Conshohocken, PA 19428

Mission Statement: Augustus Ventures is a leading venture capital advisory and consulting firm helping early-stage companies. We believe that building a business requires full-time attention of the management team. We help entrepreneurs stay focused on growing the business and assist them with the fundraising process and secure funding in the minimal time.

Investment Criteria: Early-Stage
Portfolio Companies: Legend3D, Legend Films, RiffTrax

Key Executives:
  Utkarsh Kanal, Founder
  Education: BS, Engineering, Regional Engineering College; MS, Mechanical Engineering, Oregon State University; MBA, University of Iowa
  Background: Blueprint Ventures, MCI Ventures

199 AURORA CAPITAL GROUP
10877 Wilshire Boulevard
21st Floor
Los Angeles, CA 90024

Phone: 310-551-0101
e-mail: info@auroracap.com
web: www.auroracap.com

Mission Statement: Using a discipline approach to selecting industries and cultivating high level contacts with senior executives, Aurora focuses on proactive and direct origination efforts.

Geographic Preference: United States, Canada
Fund Size: $2 billion
Founded: 1991
Average Investment: $200 million
Minimum Investment: $150 million
Investment Criteria: Middle Market, Consolidations, Acquisition, LBO, MBO, Recapitalization
Industry Group Preference: Aerospace, Defense and Government, Logistics, Energy, Healthcare, Industrial, Software, Technology-Enabled Services, Manufacturing, Distribution, Transportation
Portfolio Companies: ADCO Global, Aftermarket Technology, Ames Taping Tools, Anthony, Astor Corporation, Autocam, Coast Gas Industries, Cold Chain Technologies, Douglas Dynamics, DuBois Chemicals, FleetPride, Impaxx, Industrial Container Services, Inhance Technologies, Joerns, K&F Industries, Market Track, Mitchell, National Technical Systems, Newport Media, NuCO2, Pace Analytical, Petroleum Service Corporation, Porex Corporation, Randall-Reilly, RBC Bearings, Restaurant Technologies, SRP Companies, United Plastics Group, VLS Recovery Services, Western Nonwovens, Zywave

Key Executives:
  John Mapes, Partner
  Education: BA, University of California, LA; MBA, Harvard Business School
  Background: Corporate Finance Group, Salomon Brothers
  Directorships: National Technical Systems; Restaurant Technologies; The UCLA Foundation
  Josh Klinefelter, Partner
  Education: BA, Tulane University; MBA, Harvard Business School
  Background: Bear Stearns
  Directorships: Randall-Reilly; Zywave
  Matthew Laycock, Partner
  Education: BS, University of North Carolina; MBA, Harvard Business School
  Background: Castle Harlan; JP Morgan
  Directorships: Petroleum Service Corporation; VLS Recovery Services
  Mark Rosenbaum, Partner
  Education: BS, Wharton School, University of Pennsylvania; MBA, Anderson School of Management, University of California, LA
  Background: Summit Partners; Montgomery Securities
  Directorships: Restaurant Technologies; SRP Companies
  Robert Fraser, Partner
  Education: BA, Stanford University; MBA, Harvard Business School
  Background: Senior Associate, BC Partners
  Directorships: Randall-Reilly; SRP Companies; Zywave
  Randy Moser, Partner
  Education: BA, Claremont McKenna College; MBA, Wharton School
  Background: Senior Associate, Bertram Capital Management; Investment Banker, Merrill Lynch
  Directorships: Cold Chain Technologies; Inhance Technologies; National Technical Systems; Pace Analytical
  Andrew Wilson, Partner
  Education: BS, Princeton University; MBA, Harvard Business School
  Background: Bank of America
  Directorships: Petroleum Service Corporation; VLS Recovery Services
  Michael Marino, Partner, Investor Relations
  Education: BA, Boston College; MBA, Harvard Business School
  Background: Banking Division at Goldman Sachs
  Directorships: Inhance Technologies; National Technical Systems; Pace Analytical
  Bob West, Chief Financial Officer
  Education: BA, Miami University
  Background: CFO, Northgate Capital; CFO, BGC Partners; CFO, Thomas Weisel Partners Group

201 AUSTIN CAPITAL PARTNERS LP
30799 Pinetree Road
#424
Perpper Pike, OH 44124

Phone: 216-574-2284 Fax: 216-574-4850
web: www.austincapitalpartners.com

Mission Statement: A private equity fund focusing on smaller private companies that are transitioning ownership to acquire growth capital or achieve liquidity. Austin Capital's objective is to partner with superior management teams to build a portfolio of profitable companies with competitive advantages.

Geographic Preference: Midwest, North Central United States
Founded: 2002
Average Investment: $5 - $20 million
Minimum Investment: $750,000
Investment Criteria: Acquisition, LBO, MBO, Recapitalization
Industry Group Preference: Industrial Equipment, Manufacturing, Chemicals, Medical Devices, Materials Technology, Wholesale Distribution
Portfolio Companies: Leather Resources of America Inc., Vanner Inc., Westny Building Products Company

Key Executives:
  Darrell W Austin, Principal
  Education: BA, Ohio Wesleyan University; MBA, Carroll School of Mangement, Boston College
  Background: Vice President, Leveraged Capital Group; Vice President, Citicorp Investment Bank
  Directorships: Westny Building Products Company, Vanner Inc., Omega Sea LLC, Leather Resources of America Inc.
  Sam Hartwell, Principal
  Education: BA, Yale University; MBA, Harvard University
  Background: CEO, Southern Mill Creek Products; Founding Partner, Newmarket Partners; Sealy Inc.; McKinsey & Co.; Booz, Allen & Hamilton Inc.
  Directorships: Vanner Inc.
  William E Conway, General Partner
  Education: BS, Yale University; Executive Program,

75

Venture Capital & Private Equity Firms / Domestic Firms

University of California, Berkeley
Background: Executive Vice President, Pickands Mather & Co; Executive Vice President, Diamond Shamrock Corporation; Group Vice President, Capital Goods, Midland-Ross Corporation
Directorships: Fairmount Santrol Inc.

202 AUSTIN VENTURES
100 Congress Avenue
Suite 1600
Austin, TX 78701-2746
web: www.austinventures.com

Mission Statement: Austin Ventures is a venture capital firm invests in early stage and middle market companies, and form partnerships with their portfolio companies.
Geographic Preference: Texas
Fund Size: $3.9 billion
Founded: 1979
Average Investment: $20 million
Minimum Investment: $100,000
Investment Criteria: Seed-Stage, Growth Opportunities
Industry Group Preference: Business Products & Services, Enterprise Services, Computer Hardware & Software, Hardware, Applications Software & Services, Internet Technology, Semiconductors, Electronic Components, Financial Services, New Media, Internet
Portfolio Companies: 724 Solutions, Acorn Systems, Active Network, Active Power, Adometry, Agere, Alchemy Semiconducter, All Star Directories, AlterPoint, Ambiq Micro, AnswerSoft, Asset International, Augmentix, Bazaarvoice, Beecher Carlson, Benchmarq, BenefitMall, BetweenMarkets, Black Sand Technologies, Bloomfire, Boca, Boundless Network, BreakingPoint Systems, BroadJump, BuildForge, Careline, Caringo, Celarix, Century Payments, Civitas Learning, ClearCommerce, ClearCube, ColdWatt, Complex Media, CompUSA, Conformative, Convio, Copan Systems, Credant Technologies, Credence Systems, CreditCards.com, CrimeReports, Crossroads Systems, CrunchFund, Crystal Semiconductor, Cygnal, D2 Audio, Dachis Group, Datical, Dazel, Delta Rigging & Tools, Donuts, Draker, Edgecase, Egenera, Emerus Hospital Partners LLC, Entact, Entorian Technologies, ESO Solutions, Explorys Inc., Exterprise, FiveRuns, Flash Valet, Floodgate, Food On The Table, Gazzang, Graduation Alliance, Grande Communications, Hire.com, HomeAway, Human Code, Idera, Ignite Technologies, iMark, Innography, Innovative Silicon, Intelliquest, ITinvolve, Jigsaw Data Corp., KD1, LDR Medical, LEAP Auto Loans, LifeSize Communications, Lincoln Clean Energy, Lion Street, Listen.com, Lombardi Software, Magnablend, Map My Fitness, Mass Relevance, Mavenir Systems, McData, Metasolv, MIQ Logistics, Mission Critical, Mobestream Media, MojoPages, Monitronics International, Motive, MyDocket, Naviant, Navini Networks, NetBotz, NetEffect, NetStream, New Hope Bariatric

Key Executives:
Chris Pacitti, General Partner
Education: BA, Economics, Johns Hopkins University
Background: Vice President, TL Ventures; Co-Founder/COO, Elsewhere Partners
Directorships: Microsoft Venture Capital Advisory Group; Entrepreneurs Foundation of Central Texas
John Thornton, General Partner
e-mail: johnt@ausven.com
Education: MBA, Stanford Graduate School of Business; BA, Trinity University
Background: McKinsey & Company
Joe Aragona, General Partner
Education: AB, Harvard University; MBA, Harvard Business School
Background: Bank of Boston
Directorships: National Venture Capital Association; Livestrong Foundation
Ken DeAngelis, General Partner
Education: BA, Harvard Uiversity; MBA, Wharton School, University of Pennsylvania
Background: Bank of Boston

203 AUSTRALIS CAPITAL
376 East Warm Springs Road
Suite 190
Las Vegas, NV 89119
Toll-Free: 800-898-0648
e-mail: ir@ausacap.com
web: www.ausacap.com

Mission Statement: Invests in the cannabis industry.
Geographic Preference: US, Canada
Founded: 2018
Investment Criteria: Early-Stage
Industry Group Preference: Cannabis
Portfolio Companies: Aurora Cannabis, Body and Mind, Quality Green, ShowGrow, Wagner Dimas Inc.

Key Executives:
Scott Dowty, Director/CEO
Education: National Sales Manager/Director, CIBC; SVP/General Manager, First Data Corp.; EVP Sales/CMO, Everi Holdings Inc.; Founder/Chairman, Passport Technology Inc.
Mike Carlotti, EVP/CFO
Education: BS, Finance, Boston College; MBA, Anderson School of Management, University of California, LA
Background: Investment Banking Analyst, Smith Barney; VP of M&A, Donaldson Lufkin & Jenrette; Partner, Palmyra Capital Advisors, SVP, Wachovia; VP of Treasury & Investor Relations, Bally Technologies; VP/Treasurer, Scientific Games; SVP/Treasure, MGM Resorts International
Daniel Norr, SVP/General Counsel
Education: JD, Chicago-Kent College of Law, Illinois Institute of Technology; MBA, Northern Illinois University
Cleve Tzung, SVP, Mergers & Acquisitions
Education: BS, Economics, University of Pennsylvania; Anderson School of Management, University of California, LA
Background: Strategist, PepsiCo; Product Manager, Airtouch; Associate, Deutsche Bank; VP, Berenson & Co.; Analyst, Lakeway Capital; Portfolio Manager, Ivory Capital; Head of Global Corp. Development/M&A, Mattel; Founder/CSO, Kidify
Casey Jones, Director, Business Development
Education: BS, Criminal Justice, Virginia Commonwealth University

204 AUTO TECH VENTURES
525 Middlefield Rd.
Menlo Park, CA 94025
e-mail: qg@autotechvc.com
web: www.autotechvc.com

Mission Statement: Auto Tech Ventures is a global independent transportation technology venture capital firm.
Founded: 2014
Investment Criteria: Early-Stage
Industry Group Preference: Transportation, Technology, Semiconductors, Energy Storage, Recycling
Portfolio Companies: Cogniac, Deepscale, Frontier Car Group, HDVI, Indie Semiconductor, Lyft, Metawave, Outdoorsy, Rollick, ShipHawk, Sport Hero, Volta, Work Truck Solutions, Xnor.Ai

Key Executives:
Quin Garcia, Managing Director
Education: BS, Applied Economics & Management, Cornell University; MSc, Management Science & Automotive Engineering, Stanford University
Background: Business Analyst, Management Consulting Strategic Management Solutinos; Founding Employee, Global Automotive AlliancesBetter Place; Advisor,

Controlled Power Technologies
Directorships: Peloton Technology, Lyft
Alexei Andreev, Managing Director
Education: BS, Ph.D., Theoretical Physics, Moscow Institute of Steel and Alloys; MBA, Stanford Business School
Background: Managing Director, Harris & Harris Group
Maurice Gunderson, Managing Director
Education: BA, Mechanical Engineering, Oregon State; MS, Mechanical Engineering & Thermodynamics, Oregon State; MBA, Stanford University
Background: Control Systems Engineer, CH2M Hill; Systems Engineer, Garrett AiResearch; Director of Advanced Technologies, BOC; Founder & Managing Director, Nth Power; Co-Founder & Senior Advisor, Runway Capital Partners
Directorships: Gentherm, Contour Energy Systems, Scion-Sprays, Clean Air Power, Capstone Turbine
Daniel Hoffer, Managing Director
Education: BA, Philosophy, Harvard College; MBA, Columbia Business School
Background: Partner, Tandem Capital; Senior Director, Concur; Co-Founder and CEO, CouchSurfing; Entrepreneur-In-Residence, Benchmark Capital

205 AUTOTECH VENTURES
525 Middlefield Rd.
Menlo Park, CA 94025

e-mail: info@autotechvc.com
web: autotechvc.com

Mission Statement: The firm aims to generate financial returns by helping passionate entrepreneurs to deploy revolutionary transportation technologies and business models.
Geographic Preference: Worldwide
Minimum Investment: $1 - 5 million
Investment Criteria: Early & Growth-Stage Startups
Industry Group Preference: Transportation, Ground Transportation
Portfolio Companies: Lyft, Realine, Outdoorsy, Volta, Deepscale, Work Truck Solutions, Spot Hero, Metawave, Rollick, Cogniac, Frontier Car Group
Key Executives:
Alexei Andreev, Managing Director
Education: MBA, Stanford University; PhD In Solid State Physics, Moscow Steel and Alloys Institute; MA, Liberal Sciences, Dartmouth College
Background: Managing Director, Harris & Harris Group; Draper Fisher Jurvetson.
Directorships: D-Wave Systems, Adesto Technologies, NeoPhotonics, Molecular Imprints
Quin Garcia, Managing Director
Education: BS, Applied Economics and Management, Cornell University; MS, Management Science and Automotive Engineering, Stanford University
Background: Co-Founder, Better Place; Management Consultant, Strategic Management Solutions; Stanford University's Dynamic Design Lab
Directorships: D-Wave Systems, Adesto Technologies, NeoPhotonics, Molecular Imprints
Maurice Gunderson, Managing Director
Education: BA, MS, Thermodynamics & Mechanical Engineering, Oregon State University; MBA, Stanford University
Background: Senior Partner, CMEA Ventures; Co-Founder, Nth Power
Directorships: Gentherm, Clean Air Power, Capstone Turbine, Pentadyne, NuScale Power, NeoPhotonics, Visyx

206 AVALON VENTURES
1134 Kline Street
La Jolla, CA 92037

Phone: 858-348-2180 **Fax:** 858-348-2183
e-mail: info@avalon-ventures.com
web: www.avalon-ventures.com

Mission Statement: Avalon Ventures is an early stage venture capital fund focused on information technology and life sciences. Avalon partners are passionate about backing talented entrepreneurs seeking to build market-leading companies.
Geographic Preference: United States, California
Fund Size: $200 million
Founded: 1983
Average Investment: $6 million
Minimum Investment: $250,000
Investment Criteria: Seed-Stage, Early-Stage
Industry Group Preference: Biotechnology, Communications Equipment, Computer Hardware & Software, Pharmaceuticals, Telecommunications, Networking, Wireless Technologies, Life Sciences, Information Technology
Portfolio Companies: Acceleron Pharma, AeroFS, Afraxis, Ambit Biosciences, Anaptys Biosciences, Ansa Software, Aratana Therapeutics, Ariad, Arista, MD, Attena Neurosciences, Aurora Biosciences Corp., Avelas Biosciences, Aware Point, Backupify, WeChi, BookBub, Byliner, Calliper, Cambrios, Cardeas Pharma, Carolus Therapeutics, Chart.io, Cheezburger, Cloudant, Cloudkick, Coi Pharmaceuticals, Conjur, E Band Communications, Edge Makers, FASTech Integration, Figure 8 Wireless, GenPharm, Good, Idun, Impath, Indix, Inogen, Insight, Juliet Marine Systems Inc., Kaltura, Kinvey, Korrelated, Loop It, Memrise, Metra Biosystems, MPI, Mogi, Ningans, NeoRx, Network Switching Systems, Neurocrine, Node, Onyx, Orion, Ortiva Wireless, Otonomy, Panmira, Pharmacopeia, Pictela, Pingup, Pronoun, Proximal Data, Quippi International Gift Card Center, Redbooth, RethinkDB, River Medical, RQX Pharmaceuticals, Score Stream, Selectable Media, Sequana, Shelby.tv, Sidecar, Simulmedia, Skycatch, Smyte, Software Transformation Inc., Sova Pharmaceuticals, Spectra Biomedical Inc., StackIQ, Standingcloud, TechStars, Synaptics, Syndax, Synthorx, Talarian, Talla, Tapad, TheHappyCloud, Twinstrata, Uwanna?, Vertex, Vocera, Zacharon Pharmaceuticals, Zynga
Other Locations:
1770 Massachusetts Avenue
Suite 708
Cambridge, MA 02140
Phone: 617-299-2237
Key Executives:
Kevin J. Kinsella, Managing Director
e-mail: kkinsella@avalon-ventures.com
Education: BS, Management, MIT
Background: Solar Turbines International
Directorships: Amira, Anaptys, InCode
Steve Tomlin, Managing Director
e-mail: stomlin@avalon-ventures.com
Education: BA, American Studies, Yale University; MBA, Harvard Graduate School of Business
Background: Co-Founder, President & CEO, PersonaLogic; VP & General Manager, QVC Interactive; Director, New Business Development, Walt Disney Computer Software
Directorships: chumby industries, E-Band Communications Corporation
Jay Lichter, PhD, Managing Director
e-mail: jlichter@avalon-ventures.com
Education: BS/PhD, University of Illinois
Background: Co-Founder, Sequana Therapeutics
Rich Levandov, Managing Director
e-mail: rich@avalon-ventures.com
Education: BS, Binghamton University

Venture Capital & Private Equity Firms / Domestic Firms

Background: Co-Founder, Masthead Venture Partners; Affiliate Partner, Softbank Technology Ventures
Brady Bohrmann, Managing Director
e-mail: brady@avalon-ventures.com
Education: BS, Finance, Babson College
Background: General Partner, Masthead; President & COO, Watson Technologies
Directorships: Ad Summos, Afraxis, Backupify, Carolus, Cloudant, Cloudkick, Nabbr, Pictela, Twinstrata, Simulmedia
Tighe Reardon, Chief Financial Officer
Education: BS, Accounting, MS, Taxation, San Diego State University; CPA
Background: SVP, Tax & Treasury, DJO Global Inc.; Arthur Andersen LLP

207 AVANSIS VENTURES
Clifton, VA

web: www.avansis.com

Mission Statement: Avansis Ventures is a Mid-Atlantic, early-stage technology value fund that helps talented people build pioneering technology companies. As fellow entrepreneurs, the Avansis principals understand the difficulties of raising venture capital and the challenges of starting a new company.
Geographic Preference: Baltimore, Washington DC
Founded: 2000
Average Investment: $500,000-$1 million
Minimum Investment: $500,000
Investment Criteria: Early-Stage, Seed Stage
Industry Group Preference: Wireless Technologies, Software, Telecommunications, New Media, Enterprise Software, Internet Technology

Key Executives:
Laura L. Lukaczyk, Founder/Managing General Partner
Education: MBA, University of Virginia Darden School; BS, Chemical Engineering, University of Wisconsin-Madison
Background: Consultant, New Enterprise Associates, Founding CFO, Denwa Communications; Director of Sales, International Communications Corporation; Multifinance Holding Corporation
Brownell Chalstrom, Venture Partner
Education: MIT; University of California Berkeley
Background: General Manager, Lotus Notes; VP, BBN

208 AVENUE CAPITAL GROUP
11 West 42nd Street
9th Floor
New York, NY 10036

Phone: 212-850-7500
e-mail: investorrelations@avenuecapital.com
web: www.avenuecapital.com

Mission Statement: Headquartered in New York with offices in Europe and Asia, Avenue Capital specializes in distressed debt.
Geographic Preference: United States, Canada, Europe, Asia
Fund Size: $10.6 billion
Founded: 1995
Investment Criteria: Mezzanine, Bankruptcy, Recapitalization, Special Situations, Distressed Debt
Industry Group Preference: Diversified, Energy, Healthcare, Industrial Equipment, Manufacturing, Chemicals, Real Estate, Construction, Retailing, Telecommunications, Materials Technology, Transportation, Natural Resources

Key Executives:
Marc Lasry, Chairman, Co-Founder & CEO
Education: Clark University; New York Law School
Background: Amroc Investments; Clerk for the Honorable Edward Ryan, former Chief Bankruptcy Judge of the Southern District of New York.
Directorships: Bankruptcy and Corporate Reorganization Dept. at Cowen & Company; Private Debt Dept. at Smith Vasiliou Management Company
Sonia Gardner, President, Managing Partner, Co-Founder
Education: Clark University; Cardozo School of Law
Background: Co-Founder, Amroc Investments
Directorships: Mount Sinai Medical Center; Client Advisory Board of Citi Private Bank
Jane Castle, Senior Portfolio Manager
Education: Yale University; Stanford University
Background: Managing Director & Head of U.S. Distressed Research, Lehman Brothers Inc.; High Grade Analyst, Citigroup Inc.
Shawn Foley, Senior Portfolio Manager
Education: University of Notre Dame
Background: Merrill Lynch; Baker Nye Greenblatt
Matthew Kimble, Senior Portfolio Manager
Education: University of Illinois; NYU Stern School of Business
Background: Bellport Capital Advisors LLC; Gordian Group LP; International Business Machines Corporation
Randal Klein, Senior Portfolio Manager
Education: University of Virginia; Wharton School, University of Pennsylvania
Background: SVP, Lehman Brothers; Aerospace Engineer, The Boeing Company
Craig Hart, Portfolio Manager
Education: Colorado College; Yale School of Management; Yale School of Forestry & Environmental Studies
Background: EVP & CFE, U.S. Power Generating Company; Managing Consultant, PA Consulting Group

209 AVISTA CAPITAL PARTNERS
65 East 55th Street
18th Floor
New York, NY 10022

Phone: 212-593-6900
e-mail: info@avistacap.com
web: avistacap.com

Mission Statement: Specializes in private equity investments in growth oriented energy, healthcare and media companies.
Geographic Preference: United States
Fund Size: $6 Billion
Founded: 2005
Industry Group Preference: Healthcare, Energy, Media, Communications, Consumer Products, Consumer Services, Industrial Services
Portfolio Companies: Accellent, Acino, AngioDynamics, BioReliance, Braeburn, Charles River, ConvaTec, Fisher Scientific, Focus Diagnostics, INC Research, Inform Diagnostics, IVAC, KCI, Lantheus Medical Imaging, MedServe, National Spine & Pain Centers, Nycomed, Optinose, Osmotica Pharmaceutical, Oxford Health Plans, Prometheus Therapeutics & Diagnostics, Shoppers Drug Mart, Strategic Partners, Trimb Healthcare, United BioSource, VWR Intl, Warner Chilcott, Zest Dental

Key Executives:
Thompson Dean, Managing Partner & Co-CEO
Education: BA, University of Virginia; MBA, Harvard Business School
Background: DLJ Merchant Banking Partners
Directorships: ConvaTec, IWCO, Nycomed, VWR
David Burgstahler, Managing Partner & Co-CEO
Education: BS, Aerospace Engineering, University of Kansas; MBA, Harvard Business School
Background: Partner, DLJ Merchant Banking Partners
Directorships: BioReliance, Cidron, Lantheus Medical Imaging, Navilyst Medical, Visant, Warner Chilcott, WideOpenWest
Sriram Venkataraman, Partner
Education: MS, Electrical Engineering, University of Illinois; MBA, Wharton School
Background: Vice President, Credit Suisses; GE Medical

Systems
Directorships: AngioDynamics, Lantheus Medical Imaging, OptiNose
Robert Girardi, Partner
Education: BS, Univ. of North Carolina; MBA, Wharton School
Background: Quadrangle Group
Directorships: ACP Mountain Holdings, Telular Corp., United BioSource

210 AWEIDA VENTURE PARTNERS
500 Discovery Parkway
Suite 300
Superior, CO 80027

Phone: 303-664-9520 Fax: 303-664-9530
e-mail: info@aweida.com
web: www.aweida.com

Mission Statement: Aweida Ventures invests in companies in data storage, software, and the life sciences, from seed through mezzanine rounds, encompassing the lifespan of a company. Industry specific skills are made available to partners with the intent of maximizing return for portfolio companies.

Fund Size: $100 million
Founded: 1988
Investment Criteria: Seed-Stage through Mezzanine
Industry Group Preference: Data Storage, Software, Life Sciences
Portfolio Companies: Atrato, Inc., Benchmark Storage Innovations, Channel Intelligence, Chaparral Network Storage, EStarCom, Illumitex, Info Trust, Permacharge Corp, RxKinetix, Storage Genetics, TerraXML, Turnleaf, Vertos Medical

Key Executives:
  Jesse Aweida, General Partner
  Background: Chairman & President, Storage Technology Corporation
  Dan Aweida, General Partner
  Education: BS, Business, University of Northern Colorado; MBA, Finance, Regis University
  Background: President, Aweida Properties

211 AXIA CAPITAL
84 State Street
Suite 320
Boston, MA 02109

Phone: 617-830-1117 Fax: 978-375-6784
e-mail: phunter@axia-partners.com
web: www.axia-partners.com

Mission Statement: Axia Capital is a private equity investment and advisory firm.

Investment Criteria: All Stages
Industry Group Preference: Automation, Robotics, Enterprise Software, Sensors, Instrumentation, Industrial Equipment
Portfolio Companies: Fiberoptic Components, Hydroid, Innovative Pressure Technologies, Network Vision, Segue Manufacturing Services

Key Executives:
  Peter A. Hunter, Managing Director
  e-mail: phunter@axia-partners.com
  Education: BS, Accounting, Suffolk University
  Background: CEO, Innovative Microplate; CEO, Inspectron Corporation
  James A. Pelusi, Managing Director
  e-mail: jpelusi@axia-partners.com
  Education: BS, Operations Research, Columbia University; MBA, Harvard Business School
  Background: SVP & General Manager, Factory Software Division, Brooks Automation

212 AXIOM VENTURE PARTNERS
185 Asylum Street
Suite 17
Hartford, CT 06103

Phone: 860-548-7799

Mission Statement: Serves investors, employees, and portfolio companies in a manner that generates superior returns for investors, fosters a challenging and collegial environment for employees, and engenders the respect of portfolio companies; provides capital and strategic assistance to rapidly growing high technology companies.

Geographic Preference: United States
Fund Size: $200 million
Founded: 1994
Average Investment: $5 million
Minimum Investment: $1 million
Investment Criteria: Early-Stage, Late-Stage
Industry Group Preference: High Technology, Communications, Software, Infrastructure, Information Technology, Biotechnology
Portfolio Companies: Aironet, Airwide Solutions, Alphion, Carrier Access Corporation, CiDRA, CenterPost, CipherOptics, LightSurf, Motia, Nufern, Sabre Communications, Tangoe, WellDog, WiDeFi, YDI Wireless, Albridge Solutions, DataTrak International, Shopping.com, Eprise Corporation, Evoke Software Corp., I-Film, Proximities, Inc., MetaStorm, Inc., MXLogic, Inc., Open Solutions, Inc., SilverStorm Technologies, Inc., SPS Commerce, Inc., Anika Therapeutics, Inc., Advancis Pharmaceutical Corp., Anesiva, Asprevea Pharmaceuticals, AVANT Immunotherapeutics, Inc., BioArray Solutions, Ltd., BioMimetic, Inc., Cellomics, Inc. Corixa Corp., Cyber-Care, Inc., Diversa Corp., Dynavax Corp., Exelixis Pharmaceuticals, Nextec Applications, Inc., PuriLens, Primera Biosystems, Rib-X Pharmaceuticals, Sagres Discovery, Small Bone Innovations

Key Executives:
  Alan Mendelson, Co-Founder/General Partner
  Background: Aetna Life & Casualty; Founding Investor/CEO, SyStemix; Founder, Thermoscan; President/CEO, Aetna, Jacobs & Ramo
  Directorships: ZipLink, Battery Ventures, Syncom II, Investment Committee of Connecticut Innovations
  Samuel McKay, Co-Founder/General Partner
  Background: Manager, CIGNA Insurance Company; Manager, Connecticut Seed Ventures; Manager, Ventech Partners; Founder/CEO, Targetech
  Directorships: Anika Therapeutics, Open Solutions, Aironet Wireless Communications, Sabre Communications

213 AZALEA CAPITAL
One Liberty Square
55 Beattie Place
Suite 1500
Greenville, SC 29601

Phone: 864-235-0201 Fax: 864-235-1155
web: www.azaleacapital.com

Mission Statement: A private equity firm that invests in lower middle-market firms in the Southeast region of the United States. Azalea specializes in management buyouts, business recapitalizations, and growth plans.

Geographic Preference: Southeast
Fund Size: $83 million
Founded: 1995
Average Investment: $1 - $10 million
Investment Criteria: Lower Middle-Market, Buyouts, Recapitalizations, Family-Owned
Industry Group Preference: Manufacturing, Distribution, Business Products & Services, Consumer Products, Healthcare, Energy, Aerospace, Defense and Government, Family-Owned

Venture Capital & Private Equity Firms / Domestic Firms

Portfolio Companies: ACL Airshop, Ark Naturals, InTech Aerospace, Jones Naturals, Modus, Muffin Mam, Power Services Group

Key Executives:

Pat Duncan, Managing Partner
Education: BA, MA, Economics, Clemson University
Background: CFO & Director, Kent Manufacturing Company; First Union National Bank; Senior VP & Group Manager, Corporate Banking Group
Directorships: Power Services Group, Orbital Tool Technologies, Star Packaging

R Patrick Weston CFA, Managing Partner
e-mail: patrick@azaleacapital.com
Education: BS, Business Administration, University of South Carolina; MBA, Fiqua School of Business, Duke University
Background: VP, Transamerica Mezzanine Financing; Liberty Capital Advisors; Merrill Lynch
Directorships: MODUS, KLMK Group, Sunbelt Chemicals, ETAK Systems

Marshall Cole, Chief Financial Officer/Managing Partner
Education: BS, Business Administration, Middle Tennessee State University; CPA
Background: CFO, National Electrical Carbon Corp.; CEO, Wright Metals
Directorships: MODUS, KLMK, Star Packaging

Meredith Pflug, Chief Compliance Officer/Controller
Education: BS, Accounting, Bob Jones University
Background: Senior Associate, KPMG

Ben Wallace, Partner
Education: BA, Davidson College; MBA, Vanderbilt University
Background: Product Manager & Business Analyst, ScanSource
Directorships: Power Services Group, Orbital Tool Technologies

214 AZCA
525 Middlefield Road
Suite 120
Menlo Park, CA 94025

Phone: 650-324-9100
e-mail: twilson@azcainc.com
web: www.azcainc.com/en

Mission Statement: AZCA Venture Partners is a corporate venture capital firm that assists corporations in developing new business. AZCA focuses on North American and Asian companies in IT, clean technology and life science industries.

Geographic Preference: North America, Asia
Founded: 1985
Industry Group Preference: Information Technology, Medical Devices, Diagnostics, Chemicals, Biotechnology, Life Sciences, Healthcare, Solar Energy, Telecommunication, Pharmaceuticals, Waste Water Treatment, Recycling Systems
Portfolio Companies: 360ip, Actel, ALCOM, Ballard, BigFix, Brookstone, Business Computer News, Ebara, Evergreen Solar, Exchange Resources, Fry's Electronics, Fulcrum Technologies, Gehl, Haas School of Business, iFire, Kaiser Permanente, KPMG, LecTec, Logitech, Marathon Products, Maxager, Micro Vision, Mitsubishi, Motorola, Nanogen, Nektar, Nikkiso, Nippon Steel, Oki, Panasonic, PARC, Quantum, Ricoh, Savvion, Shell, Shoshin, Sierra Ventures, Sony, SunPower, Sybase, Therma-Wave, Union Bank of California, Yamaha, Zaxel

Other Locations:
One Broadway
14th Floor
Cambridge, MA 02142
Phone: 650-73-71929

Ark Hills Executive Tower
Suite 601
1-15-5 Asaka, Minato-ku
Tokyo 107-0052
Japan
Phone: +81 (0)50-3567-9100

Key Executives:

Masazumi Ishii, Managing Director
e-mail: mishii@azcainc.com
Education: BE, Mathematical Engineering & Instrumentation Physics, University of Tokyo; MS, Computer Science, Stanford University
Background: Managing Director, Noventi; Senior Management Consultant, McKinsey & Company; Technical/Management, IBM, Japan
Directorships: Japan Society of Northern California, Japanese Chamber of Commerce

Wayne Doiguchi, Managing Director
e-mail: wdoiguchi@azcainc.com
Education: BA, Univesity of California, LA; MBA Santa Clara University
Background: Bank of Toyon; Union Bank of California; Park Plaza Investment Company; Strata Ventures
Directorships: Pan Pacific Bank

Leo Kim PhD, Managing Director
e-mail: lkim@azcavp.com
Education: BS, California State University; PhD, University of Kansas
Background: Founder & Managing Director, POSCO BioVentures; EVP, Research & CTO, Mycogen Corporation; Research Director, Shell Oil Company

215 AZURE CAPITAL PARTNERS
505 Sansome Street
Suite 1575
San Francisco, CA 94111

web: www.azurecap.com

Mission Statement: Investor in early-stage technology companies.

Geographic Preference: United States, Canada
Fund Size: $750 million
Founded: 2000
Average Investment: $25 million
Minimum Investment: $1 million
Investment Criteria: Post-Seed, Series A
Industry Group Preference: Advertising, Applications Software & Services, Broadband, Cloud Computing, Digital Media & Marketing, Education, Networking, Financial Services, Gaming, Healthcare Information Technology, Mobile, Open Source, E-Commerce & Manufacturing, SaaS, Security
Portfolio Companies: BillMeLater, Broadlight, Calix, Cyan, Luminate, Native, NeoNova, phanfare, PSS Systems, Rooftop Media, Slide Rocket, Tripit, Top Tier Software, Vapps, VMWare, World Wide Packets, Zend

Other Locations:
713 Santa Cruz Avenue
Suite 5
Menlo Park, CA 94025

2100 - 150 9th Avenue SW
Calgary, AB T2N 1Z6
Canada

Paul Ferris, General Partner
Education: BA, Computer Science/English Literature, Amherst College
Background: Investment Banking, Credit Suisse First Boston; Morgan Stanley
Directorships: Calix, Personeta

Mike Kwatinetz, General Partner
Education: MA, PhD, University of California, Berkeley; MBA Accounting, New York University
Background: Global Head of Equity, Credit Suisse First Boston
Directorships: Education.com, I4 Commerce, Jacent, Knowledge Adventure, Medsphere OQO, ROME Corporation

Paul Weinstein, General Partner
Education: BS, Babson College
Background: Credit Suisse First Boston
Directorships: InterModal Data, K2 Software, Virtual Instruments, Switchfly, Unitas Global
Andrea Drager, Principal
Education: BComm, McGill University

216 B CAPITAL GROUP
1240 Rosecrans Avenue
Manhattan Beach, CA 90266

Phone: 310-698-1270
e-mail: info@bcapgroup.com
web: www.bcapgroup.com

Mission Statement: B Capital Group invests in B2B startups across four technology-enabled ategories: Enterprise technology and Consumer enablement, Healthcare Tech and Bio IT, Industrial and Transportation, and Fintech and Insurtech

Average Investment: $10 to 50 Million
Investment Criteria: Transformative Technology Start-Ups; Early Expansion Stage; Prepared for Rapid Growth and Acceleration

Other Locations:
2 Embarcadero Center
Suite 2400
San Francisco, CA 94111
Phone: 415-732-8052

10 Hudson Yards
New York, NY 10001

50 Raffles Place 048623
Singapore
Phone: 65 6429-2418

Key Executives:
Howard Morgan, Co-Founder and Chair
Raj Ganguly, Co-Founder and Managing Partner
Eduardo Saverin, Co-Founder and Managing Partner

217 BABSON CAPITAL MANAGEMENT LLC
New York, NY

Mission Statement: Babson Capital Management LLC is an investment management firm that specializes in a variety of asset classes, including structured credit, private debt and high yield loans.

Geographic Preference: Worldwide
Fund Size: $182 billion
Founded: 1940

218 BACKSTAGE CAPITAL
Los Angeles, CA

web: backstagecapital.com

Mission Statement: Invests in seed and startup ventures whose founders identify as a woman, person of color, and/or LGBTQ+.

Geographic Preference: United States
Fund Size: $36 Million
Average Investment: $1,000,000
Investment Criteria: Seed, Startup, Women, People of Color, LGBTQ+
Industry Group Preference: All Sectors Considered
Portfolio Companies: Airfordable, Aquaai, Astral AR, Avisare, Bandwagon, BeVisible, Blendoor, CapWay, CareAcademy, Carrot, CEEK VR, Civic Eagle, CurlMix, Dibs, Drop, Filament, Flat Out of Heels, GoGrab, HabitAware, Haute Hijab, Healthy Roots, Hostfully, Houghton NYC, Ilerasoft, Jewelbots, Kairos, Laughly, Localeur, Mahmee, Mars Reel, NailSnaps, nedl, Nicolette, Nomiku, Novoron Bioscience, O.school, OmniSpeech, On Second Thought, Partake Foods, Pilotly, Please Assist Me, PopCom, Quarrio, Radial, Radiant RFID, Revry, Seeds, Seed&Spark, ShearShare, Siempo, Solstice Energy Solutions, Sunhouse, SUPA, Swivel Beauty, TextEngine, The Difference, The Door, The Mentor Method, Thesis Couture, Thurst, Tinsel, TresseNoire, Uncharted Power, Wedspire, Wildfang, Win-Win, Workfrom, XO, Zyrobotics

Key Executives:
Arlan Hamilton, Founder/Managing Partner
Background: Tour Manager, Atlantic Records
Christie Pitts, General Partner
Education: BA, San Jose State University; MBA, University of Phoenix
Background: Venture Development Manager, Verizon Ventures
Lisa Atia, Chief Revenue Officer
Education: MA, Entrepreneurship & Strategy, Pepperdine University
Background: Brand Strategist, Blavity

219 BAIDU VENTURES
463 Bryant Street
San Francisco, CA 94107

e-mail: hi@bv.ai
web: bv.ai/en/

Mission Statement: Baidu Ventures seeks to invest in the AI sector, from algorithms and sensors to computing paradigms and storage systems.

Geographic Preference: US, China
Investment Criteria: Seed, Series A & B
Industry Group Preference: Artificial Intelligence, Data Analysis
Portfolio Companies: 8i, Airmap, Alces, AMP Robotics, Catalog DNA, CiDi, Cytovale, Covariant, Engine Bio, Falcon Computing, Flow ++, Lightelligence, Magnetic Insight, MORE Health, OpenSpace, Pointcloud, RBC Signals, Ripcord, AutomationHero, Sensoro, Subtle Medical, Vesper Technologies, YI Tunnel, ZingFront, YunDing, Loock, Yunhan Financial Technology

Other Locations:
China World Tower A, Suite 1601
#1 Jianguomenwai Dajie
Chaoyang District
Beijing 100020
China

Key Executives:
Wei Liu, Chief Executive Officer
Education: BS, University of Electronic Science and Technology of China; MS, Cambridge University
Background: General Partner, Legend Star; Chairman, Comet Labs
Saman Farid, Partner
Education: BS, Control Systems Engineering, Cooper Union; MBA, MIT
Background: Founder, Comet Labs; Honeywell; Verizon; Deloitte Consulting; Microsoft

220 BAIN CAPITAL PRIVATE EQUITY
John Hancock Tower
200 Clarendon Street
Boston, MA 02116

Phone: 617-516-2000 Fax: 617-516-2010
e-mail: privateequity@baincapital.com
web: www.baincapitalprivateequity.com

Mission Statement: Bain Capital Private Equity partners with management teams to help build and grow great companies.

Geographic Preference: Worldwide
Fund Size: $65 billion
Founded: 1984
Minimum Investment: $20 million
Investment Criteria: Seed, Late Growth, Buyout
Industry Group Preference: Consumer, Retail & Dining, Financial Services, Healthcare, Industrial, Technology, Media & Telecommunications, Energy

Venture Capital & Private Equity Firms / Domestic Firms

Portfolio Companies: Accellent, Air Medical Group Holdings, AMC Entertainment, Applied Systems, ASIMCO, Bellsystem24, Bloomin' Brands, Bombardier Recreational Products, Brakes Group, Bravida, Brenntaq, Bright Horizons, Broder Brothers Co., Burlington Coat Factory, Casda Biomaterials, Cerved, China Fire & Security Group, Clear Channel Communications, Consolidated Container Company, Contec, CRC Health Group, Cumulus Media, D&M Holdings, Denon & Marantz, Dollarama, Domino's Pizza Japan, Dunkin Brands, Edcon, Epoch, FCI, FleetCor, GA Pack, GOME Electrical Appliances, Guitar Center, Gymboree China, Gymboree Corporation, HCA, HD Supply, Hero Investments, Himadri, Ideal Standard, IMCD, International Market Centers, JinSheng International, Jupiter Shop Channel, Keystone Automotive Operations, Lilliput Kidswear, MEI Group, Michaels, MYOB, Novacap, NXP, Physio Control, QSI Restaurant Partners, Quintiles, Securitas Direct, Sensata Technologies, Sinomedia Holding Limited, SkillSoft, Skylark, Square Trade, Startronics, Styron, Sunac, SunGard, SunTelephone, Suzhou HiPro Polymers, TeamSystem, The Weather Channel, Toys 'R Us, Unisource, Uniview, Village Ventures, Warner Chilcott, Warner Music Group, WorldPay

Other Locations:
535 Madison Avenue
29th Floor
New York, NY 10022
Phone: 212-326-9420 **Fax:** 212-421-2225

Devonshire House
Mayfair Place
London W1J 8AJ
United Kingdom
Phone: 44 20 7514 5252 **Fax:** 44 20 7514 5250

Maximilianstrasse 11
Munich 80539
Germany
Phone: 49-89244410700 **Fax:** 49-89244410731

One Pacific Place
Suite 2501, Level 25
88 Queensway, Admiralty
Hong Kong
China
Phone: 852-36566800 **Fax:** 852-36566801

2nd Floor, Free Press House
Nariman Point
Mumbai 400 021
India
Phone: 91-2267528000 **Fax:** 91-2267528010

Room 3669, 36/F Two IFC
8 Century Boulevard
Shanghai 200120
China
Phone: 86-2160626120 **Fax:** 86-2160626121

Level 19, Suite 1903, Deutsche Bank Place
126 Phillip Street
Sydney NSW 2000
Australia
Phone: 61 2 9093 5500

1-1-1 Marunouchi
Chiyoda-ku
Tokyo 100-0005
Japan
Phone: 81-362127070 **Fax:** 81-362127071

Key Executives:
Stephen Pagliuca, Co-Chairman
Education: BA, Duke University; MBA, Harvard Business School
Background: VP, Bain & Company; Peat Marwick Mitchell & Company
Josh Bekenstein, Co-Chairman
Education: BA, Yale University; MBA, Harvard Business School
Background: Bain & Company
Blair Hendrix, Managing Director
Education: BA, Brown University
Background: EVP & COO, DigiTrace Care Services; Corporate Decisions
Ian Loring, Managing Director
Education: BA, Trinity College; MBA, Harvard Business School
Background: VP, Berkshire Partners; Corporate Finance, Drexel Burnham Lambert
Phil Loughlin, Managing Director
Education: AB, Dartmouth College; MBA, Harvard Business School
Background: Consultant, Bain & Company; Eagle Snacks; Norton Company
Robert Ehrhart, Managing Director
Education: BSBA, University of Missouri, Columbia
Background: Managing Director, Head of the Americas, Private Equity Group, Goldman Sachs & Co.
John Kilgallon, Managing Director
Education: BSE, Princeton University; MBA, Amos Tuck School of Business
Background: Leveraged Finance, Citadel
Luca Bassi, Managing Director
Education: Bocconi University; Columbia Business School
Background: Goldman Sachs
Nancy Lotane, Managing Director/Chief HR Officer
Education: BA, Tufts University; MBA, Amos Tuck School of Business
Background: Mercer Management Consulting
Amit Chandra, Managing Director
Education: Boston College
Background: DSP Merrill Lynch
Patrick Sullivan, Managing Director
Education: BS, ME, Rensselaer Polytechnic Institute; MBA, Columbia Business School
Background: Goldman Sachs Asset Management
Cécile Belaman, Managing Director
Education: Cornell University; London City University
Background: Morgan Stanley
Drew Chen, Managing Director
Education: Harvard Business School
Background: China Investment Corporation
John Connaughton, Co-Managing Partner
Education: BS, University of Virginia; MBA, Harvard Business School
Background: Consultant, Bain & Company
Ryan Cotton, Managing Director
Education: Princeton University; Stanford Grad. School of Business
Background: Bain & Company
Stuart Gent, Managing Director
Education: Bristol University
Background: Avis UK
Chris Gordon, Managing Director
Education: AB, Economics, Harvard College; MBA, Harvard Business School
Background: Consultant, Bain & Company
Steven Barnes, Managing Director
Education: BS, Syracuse University
Background: CEO, Dade Behring; President, Executone Business Systems; President, Holson Burnes Group; Senior Management, PriceWaterhouseCoopers
David Gross-Loh, Managing Director
Education: BS, Wharton School; MBA, Harvard Business School
Background: Consultant, Bain & Company

221 BAIN CAPITAL VENTURES
200 Clarendon Street
Boston, MA 02116

Phone: 617-516-2000
web: www.baincapitalventures.com

Venture Capital & Private Equity Firms / Domestic Firms

Mission Statement: Venture capital arm of Bain Capital.
Fund Size: $2 billion
Founded: 1984
Minimum Investment: $1 million
Investment Criteria: All Stages
Industry Group Preference: Infrastructure Software, SaaS & Data Services, Marketing Technology, Fintech, Healthcare
Portfolio Companies: 1-800-Dentist, Ability Network, Accelecare Wound Centers, Ameritox, AppNeta, Appriss, Aria Systems, Billtrust, Blip.TV, Bloomreach, Bluestem Brands, Booker Software, Boston Heart Diagnostics, BTI Systems, Captora, Celerion, CQuotient, Digital Compliance, Dynamics, Enservio, Evertrue, Experticity, GainSight, Garantia Data, Hazelcast, Hook Logic, InfoScout, INRIX, LiaZon, Linkable Networks, MedeAnalytics, Media Radar, MyEdu, National Cardiovascular Partners, Nomis Solutions, Novus, Nubisio, ObserveIt, Optimizely, Oyster.com, Persado, PGOA Media, Precision Therapeutics, Quanterix, Rapid7, Rave Mobile Safety, Regulatory Datacorp, Rent The Runway, ScaleBase, Scorebig, SevOne, Skyhook Wireless, Square Trade, Stack Driver, Symphony Commerce, Synapdx, Targetspot, Tellapart, Tennis Channel, The Receivables Exchange, Thefind, Travelclick, VMTurbo, Vonage, ZeroTurnaround, US Lec Corp., Vauto, Vmlogix, VMturbo, Vonage, Webputty, Wharton Economics, Work 'n Gear

Other Locations:
632 Broadway
New York, NY 10012
Phone: 212-822-2900

524 Hamilton Avenue
2nd Floor
Palo Alto, CA 94301

301 Howard Street
Suite 2200
San Francisco, CA 94105

Key Executives:
Ajay Agarwal, Partner
Education: BSEE, Stanford University; MBA, Harvard Business School
Background: Senior Executive, Trilogy Software; Consultant, McKinsey & Company; Patentholder
Directorships: AdReady, BloomReach, INRIX, Kiva Systems, m-Qube, Memento, Oyster.com, Rave Mobile Safety, Skyhook Wireless, Thumbplay, VMLogix
Scott Friend, Partner
e-mail: sfriend@baincapital.com
Education: BA, Electrical Engineering & Economics, Brown University; MBA, Harvard Business School
Background: Chairman, VP, Marketing, Oracle Retail; President & Co-Founder, ProfitLogic
Directorships: CQuotient, MagazineRadar, Norris Solutions, ProfitLogic, Rent The Runway, TheFind, TokBox
Matt Harris, Partner
e-mail: mharris@baincapitalventures.com
Education: Williams College
Background: Co-Founder, Village Ventures; Private Equity Group, Bain Capital
Mike Krupka, Partner
Education: BA, Chemistry, Dartmouth College
Background: Managing Director, Bain Private Equity Group; Principal, Information Partners
Directorships: Bluestem Brands, DataSynapse, Enservio, Invoke Solutions, iPay Technologies, Lala, Liberty Dialysis, MAXM Systems, MyEdu, The Learning Company, The Princeton Review
Enrique Salem, Partner
Education: BA, Computer Science, Dartmouth College
Background: CEO, Symantec; President & CEO, Brightmail
Directorships: DocuSign; FireEye; Atlassian; ForeScout
Sarah Smith, Partner
Education: BA, Music Education, University of Wisconsin-Madison; MBA, Stanford University
Background: VP of Advertising Sales/Operations & VP of HR/Recruiting, Quora; Director of Online Operations, Facebook
Yumin Choi, Partner
Education: BS, Entrepreneurship & Finance, Babson College
Directorships: AbleTo; Centivo; Datica; Iodine Software; Vetsource; ABILITY; MPulse Mobile; Oceans Healthcare; Payspan; Spinal Kinetics; Vets First Choice
John Connolly, Senior Advisor
e-mail: jconnolly@baincapital.com
Education: BA, St. Norbert College; Executive Education Program, INSEAD
Background: President, CEO & Chairman, M|C Communications; President & CEO, Institutional Shareholder Services
Directorships: EDGAR Online, Memento
Salil Deshpande, Senior Advisor
e-mail: salil@baincapital.com
Education: BS, Cornell University; MS, Stanford University
Background: Co-Founder/CEO, The Middleware Company
Ben Nye, Senior Advisor
e-mail: bnye@baincapital.com
Education: Harvard College, Harvard Business School
Background: SVP, Veritas Software; COO & CFO, Precise Software Solutions
Directorships: Apparent Networks, AppAssure Software, Archer Technologies, dynaTrace software, Network Intelligence, Rapid7, SolarWinds, VMTurbo

---

222 BAIRD CAPITAL PARTNERS
777 E Wisconsin Avenue
Milwaukee, WI 53233

Toll-Free: 800-792-2473
web: www.bairdcapital.com

Mission Statement: Seeks to provide financial advice and service to clients, helping them achieve their wealth management, investment banking and asset management goals.

Geographic Preference: United States, Europe, Asia
Fund Size: $512 million
Founded: 1919
Average Investment: $25 - $150 million
Minimum Investment: $5 million
Investment Criteria: Later Stage Growth, Change of Control, LBO
Industry Group Preference: Business to Business, Internet Technology, Telecommunications, Healthcare, Industrial Services, E-Commerce & Manufacturing, Life Sciences
Portfolio Companies: Accume Partners, American Auto Auction Group, AiCure, Alpha Source Inc., Amphora Medical, Apervita, Appcast, Arroweye, Autobooks, ADG, Bfinance, Car King, Ice Protection, Clear Water, Coal Fire, Datica, Eckler's, Elucent Medical, Emids, FullContact, Gabbro, Genome DX Biosciences, ChemDry, Hireology, Housecall Pro, Indi, Kason, Kedu Healthcare, Kindstar Global, Bioresearch, Montage, Muyingzhijia.com, Myelin Health, Neochord, NeuMoDx Molecular, New Vitality, Nigel Wright, NowSecire, ParkWhiz, Prescient Healthcare Group, R2I, Radius Global Growth Experts, RQI, SGX Sensortech, Signal, Sittercity.com, SloanLED, Snagajob, Startwire, Strata Oncology, Synap, Talent Academy, The SR Group, Veniti, Vitalyst, WordStream, Workforce Insight, Zaloni, Zurex Pharma Inc.

Venture Capital & Private Equity Firms / Domestic Firms

Other Locations:
227 West Monroe Street
Chicago, IL 60606

15 Finsbury Circus
London EC2M 7EB
United Kingdom

50 California Street
Suite 450
San Francisco 94111

Key Executives:
Paul Purcell, Chairman
Education: University of Notre Dame; MBA, Booth School of Business
Background: Managing Director, Kidder, Peabody & Co.
Directorships: RiverFront Investment Group LLC; Securities Industry and Financial Markets Association
C. Andrew Brickman, Partner
312-609-4702
Education: BA, Middlebury College
Background: M&a, Drexel Burnham Lambert; Private Equitym Wesray Capital; Heller Equity Capital
Directorships: Kason Corp., SloanLED, New Vitality, Harris Research Inc.
Martin Beck, Partner
49-172-852-71-24
Education: Business Administration, Catholic University of Eichstaett, Germany
Background: Senior Advisory Board, ZT Management Holding GmbH; CEO, MEC Holding GmbH
Gordon G. Pan, President
312-609-5498
Education: BA, Economics and Asian Studies, Colgate University; MBA, Kellogg School of Management, Northwestern University
Background: Principal, One Equity Partners; Marquette Venture Partners; Founder, The Pangaea Group; Associate, Berkshire Partners

223 BAKER CAPITAL
575 Madison Avenue
8th Floor
New York, NY 10022

Phone: 212-848-2000 **Fax:** 212-646-0660
web: www.bakercapital.com

Mission Statement: A private equity fund that invests in digital communications at all stages.
Geographic Preference: Europe, North America
Fund Size: $1.5 billion
Founded: 1995
Average Investment: $30 million
Minimum Investment: $5 million
Investment Criteria: Early Stage, Later Stage
Industry Group Preference: Communications Equipment, Services, Applications Software & Services
Portfolio Companies: Adaptix, Akamai, Broadview Networks, Canal+, Cherry Road Technologies, Connected, CoreValue Software, Dotster, EM4, Immedia Semiconductor, Interxion, IQNavigator, Medianet, NTent, Offermatica, ParStream, PlusTV, QSC AG, SandVideo, Sequoia Software, Teem Photonics, Totality, Voltaire, Wine.com

Key Executives:
John Baker, Founding Partner
Education: Harvard College; Harvard Business School
Background: Patricof & Company Ventures
Directorships: Cherry Road Technologies, QSC AG
Henry G. Baker, Founding Partner
Education: BS/MS Electrical Engineering, PhD Computer Science, Massachusetts Institute of Technology
Background: Consultant, Privately
Directorships: Permabit, Sand Video
Joseph Saviano, CFO & COO
Education: BS, Finance, Lehigh University; MBA, Fordham University
Background: VP, Harvest Partners

224 BALLAST POINT VENTURES
401 E Jackson Street
Suite 2300
Tampa, FL 33602

Phone: 813-906-8500 **Fax:** 813-906-8514
e-mail: info@ballastpointventures.com
web: ballastpointventures.com

Mission Statement: Growth equity investors in companies in Florida, the Southeast and Texas.
Geographic Preference: Southeast, Texas
Fund Size: $164 Million
Founded: 2002
Average Investment: $6 Million
Minimum Investment: $4 Million
Investment Criteria: Late-stage expansion
Industry Group Preference: Healthcare, Software, Technology-Enabled Services, Communications, Consumer Products & Services
Portfolio Companies: Avoxi, Advanced Processing and Imaging, Blue Medical, Cbeyond Inc., Florida Bank, FSV Payment Systems, GHN Online, HotSchedules, InComm, Iconixx, Instawares, Innocutis, Intelligent Retinal Imaging Systems, KBI Biopharma, Knology, KSep Systems, Lifestyle Family Fitness, Matrix Medical Network, MeYou Health, MolecularMD, Optical Experts Manufacturing, PDQ South Texas, PDSHeart, PowerChord, PowerDMS, Prepaid Technologies, QOL Medical, SkuVault, SleepMed, Symphonic Distribution, TicketBiscuit, TissueTech, Theragen, Tower Cloud, Vazata, Wave7 Optics, YPrime, The Zebra

Key Executives:
Drew Graham, Partner
e-mail: dgraham@ballastpointventures.com
Education: BBA, Harvard Business School
Background: South Atlantic Venture Funds; Morgan Stanley & Co.
Paul Johan, Partner
Education: BA, Emory University; MBA, Darden School of Business
Background: Raymond James & Associates
Directorships: Prepaid Technologies, Instawares Holding Company, Vazata, InsuranceZebra
Matt Rice, Partner
Education: BComm, University of Virginia; MBA, Harvard Business School
Background: Raymond James
Directorships: MolecularMD, TissueTech, Y-Prime, MeYou Health, Theragen, Iconixx
Robert Faber, Partner
Education: BA, Princeton University; MBA, Tuck School of Business
Background: Wachovia Capital Partners

225 BALMORAL FUNDS
11150 Santa Monica Boulevard
Suite 825
Los Angeles, CA 90025

Phone: 310-473-3065 **Fax:** 310-479-1740
e-mail: thaynes@balmoralfunds.com
web: balmoralfunds.com

Mission Statement: Balmoral Funds LLC is a Los Angeles-based private equity firm which invests in recapitalization, special situations, and acquisitions of small and middle-market companies.
Geographic Preference: United States, Canada
Fund Size: $200 Million
Founded: 2005
Average Investment: $5-20 Million
Investment Criteria: Recapitalizations, Special Situations

Industry Group Preference: Manufacturing, Business Products & Services, Consumer Products, Retail, Consumer & Leisure, Value-Added Distribution
Portfolio Companies: Aero Interiors Company, Bennington Marine, Concurrent Manufacturing, Dispatch Transportation, Enesco LLC, GlobalOptions, IGPS Logistics LLC, Interstate Soutwest, KP Aviation, Mooyah, Silver Aero, tara Technologies, Things Remembered, VESTA Modular
Key Executives:
  Jonathan Victor, Senior Managing Director
  e-mail: jvictor@balmoralfunds.com
  Education: AB, Economics, Princeton University; MBA, Stanford University; MA, Oxford University; JD, Stanford University
  Background: Senior Advisor, Chanin Capital Partners; President/CEO, eBility Inc.; SVP of Finance, The Irvine Company' VP, Kaufman & Broad Inc.
  Directorships: Bennington Marine; Dispatch Transportation; Concurrent Holdings; iGPS Holdings, Enesco Holdings, AgileX; Silver Aero; Mooyah
  Skip Victor, Managing Director
  e-mail: svictor@balmoralfunds.com
  Robin Nourmand, Managing Director
  e-mail: rnourmand@balmoralfunds.com
  Education: BA/JD, University of California, Los Angeles; MBA, Anderson School of Management
  Background: Sidley Austin LLP; Canyon Partners; Analysis Group Inc.
  Directorships: Bennington Marine; Dispatch Transportation; Things Remembered; iGPS Logistics; KP Aviation; LifePort
  Travis Haynes, Managing Director
  e-mail: thaynes@balmoralfunds.com
  Education: BA, University of California, Los Angeles
  Background: VP, Platinum Equity
  Directorships: Enesco LLC
  David Shainberg, Principal
  e-mail: dshainberg@balmoralfunds.com
  Education: BA, New York University
  Background: Brookfield Asset Management; JP Morgan
  Luke Mau, Chief Financial Officer
  e-mail: lmau@balmoralfunds.com
  Education: BS, Finance & Accounting, University of Utah; MBA, ESADE, Spain
  Background: JP Morgan; Citco Fund Services

226 BAND OF ANGELS LLC
750 Battery Street
7th Floor
San Francisco, CA 94111
Phone: 650-695-0400
e-mail: bandhq@bandangels.com
web: www.bandangels.com

Mission Statement: The Band of Angels is a seed funding organization based in Silicon Valley. The Band of Angels consists of over 150 high-tech executives dedicated to investing their money into startup companies.

Geographic Preference: California
Fund Size: $50 million
Founded: 1994
Average Investment: $300,000 - $1.5 million
Minimum Investment: $200,000
Investment Criteria: Seed, Startup, First Stage
Industry Group Preference: Semiconductors, Life Sciences, Biotechnology, Networking, Telecommunications, Software, Internet, Web Applications & Services
Portfolio Companies: Arovia, Basepaws, Car IQ, Cartogram, Cello Lighting, CNote, CoLabs, Combinati, Crater, Deep Blue Medical Advances, eyecandylab, Gravyty, HitCheck, Hupnos, HyperKey, IrisVision, IrriGreen, Kango, Mechanodontics, MisFit, Muzit, mxHero, Nwave Technologies, OneDome, OnScale, PlayFull, Purissima, RAM Medical Innovations, Raydiant Oximetry, Resonado, Rune Labs, Shyft, Snapwire, Strategikon Pharma, TrueData, U-Nest, Valfix, Visgenx, Your Fare
Other Locations:
Key Executives:
  Ian Sobieski, PhD, Chairman
  Education: BA, Philosophy, BS, Aerospace Engineering, Virginia Polytechnic Institute; MS, PhD, Aeronautics & Astronautics, Stanford University
  Background: Evite.com; Enact Health Management; Kaman Aerospace
  Directorships: Angel Capital Association, Venture Capital Network
  Ed Canty, Chief Financial Officer
  Background: General Partner, CFO, BayCom Partners; CFO, Teknowledge
  Sonja Markova, MBA, Executive Director
  Education: BS, Management, University Of St. Cyril and Methodius; MBA, Finance, California State University
  Background: Vice President, Point Reyes Managment; Keiretsu Forum; Advisor, Camp BizSmart
  Nicola Corzine, Partner/Deal Manager
  Background: Founder & Executive Director, Financing Partners; Credit Suisse First Boston; Fundraising Forum

227 BANNEKER PARTNERS
600 Montgomery St
24th Floor
San Francisco, CA 94111
e-mail: khufford@bannekerpartners.com
web: www.bannekerpartners.com

Mission Statement: Banneker Partners is a private equity firm focused on investing in software/SaaS, Internet and business services companies.

Industry Group Preference: SaaS, Software, Internet, Business Products & Services
Portfolio Companies: Ancestry.com, Genesys, IQMS, Magento, Pepperjam
Key Executives:
  Stephen Davis, Partner
  Education: Carleton College; JD, MBA, Columbia University
  Background: Co-Founder, Vista Equity Partners
  Matthew McDonald, Partner
  Education: BS, California Poly; MS, Santa Clara Univ.
  Background: Square, Inc.; CVC Capital Partners
  Adrian van Schie, Partner
  Education: LLB, BComm, Univ. of Otago; Univ. of Chicago
  Kyle Hufford, Vice President
  Education: BS, W.P. Carey School of Business
  Background: Serent Capital Partners

228 BARODA VENTURES
245 South Beverly Drive
Beverly Hills, CA 90212
web: www.barodaventures.com

Mission Statement: Baroda Ventures is a Los Angeles based venture capital firm who work side-by-side with scrappy entrepreneurs who are passionate about building lasting businesses.

Geographic Preference: Los Angeles
Founded: 1998
Investment Criteria: Seed-Stage, Series A
Industry Group Preference: Consumer Internet, E-Commerce & Manufacturing, Mobile, SaaS, Digital Media & Marketing
Portfolio Companies: Amplify, Blade, Bridg, Crexi, DSTLD Premium Denim Co., Embrace.io, Gem, HelloTech, Healthvana, ID90 Travel, Koh Founders, Launchpad LA, Local ID, Overnight, Pathmatics, Policy Genius, Retention Science, Revolution Credit, Science, Steelhouse, Surf Air,

Venture Capital & Private Equity Firms / Domestic Firms

Thayer Ventures, Travo, Trebeca, Unglue, Chromatik, DogVacay, Gradient X, Lettuce, OVGuide, Shift

Key Executives:
David Bohnett, Founder
Education: BBA, University of Southern California; MBA, Finance, University of Michigan
Background: Founder, Geocities
Peter Lee, Managing Partner
Education: BS, MS, Engineering Product Development, MIT; MBA, Harvard Business School
Background: Investor, Clearstone Ventures; Investor, Prism Ventures; VP Operations & Product Development, Goldpocket; Manager, McKinsey

229 BASE VENTURES
Berkeley, CA

e-mail: hello@base.ventures
web: base.ventures

Mission Statement: Invests in seed-stage technology companies in various sectors including cannabis, health & wellness, information technology, real estate, and consumer goods.

Founded: 2012
Investment Criteria: Seed, Early-Stage
Industry Group Preference: Cannabis, Health & Wellness, Technology, Data Technology, Food & Beverage, Consumer Goods, Entertainment
Portfolio Companies: Olly, Luma, Dirty Lemon, Rapchat, inDinero, Style Seat, Netki, Genies, Cleanify, Ink, Armory, Rinse, PlanGlid, Mayvenn, Virool, 6 Sence, Travel Joy, Baker Technologies, Pigeonly, World View, Angellist, Pando Daily, Modest, Balanced, Buffer, Rolltech, Naja, CultureIQ, BlackJet, SwapBox, Thinair, Revip, Glambot, Parade, GrowX

Key Executives:
Erik Moore, Founder/Managing Director
Education: AB, Dartmouth College; MA, International Relations; MBA, Wharton School, University of Pennsylvania
Background: VP, Gen Re; Director, Merill Lynch
Directorships: Surf Air; Pigeon.ly; Wildfang.com
Kirby Harris, Partner
Education: BA, Morehouse College; MBA, California State University Hayward
Background: VP/Consultant, Impact Capital Management; Principal, Monte Cresta Capital
Lisa Parks, Operations Partner
Education: BA, Political Science/Government, University of California, Berkeley
Background: Sr. Development Officer, Right to Play; Operations Partners, Three Bridges Venture
Directorships: PACE
Tami Flores, Director of Operations
Education: BA, English, University of California, Berkeley
Background: Production Associate, Clockdrive Productions; Finance Manager, Claremont Creek Ventures; Team Lead for Quality Control Operations, Googles; Technology Preferred Banker, First Republic Bank

230 BASECAMP VENTURES
1 Executive Drive
Suite 8
Moorestown, NJ 08057

Phone: 856-813-1100
e-mail: mel@basecampventures.com
web: www.basecampventures.com

Mission Statement: To invest in new technology companies with great potential and to offer support to management teams. BaseCamp's objective is to lead its portfolio companies to success.

Geographic Preference: Mid-Atlantic
Fund Size: $10 million
Founded: 2000
Average Investment: $250,000
Investment Criteria: Seed, Startup, First Stage, Mezzanine
Industry Group Preference: Technology, Internet Technology, Internet Infrastructure, Cloud Computing
Portfolio Companies: Coredial, IonField Systems

Key Executives:
Mel Baiada, Managing Partner
Education: BSEE, Computers, MA, Communications, Drexel University
Background: Founder, Bluestone
Directorships: Drexel University, New Jersey Technology Council, Bayada Home Health Care

231 BASELINE VENTURES
web: www.baselinev.com

Mission Statement: To help founders build and grow their early stage companies into change affecting enterprises.

Geographic Preference: United States
Founded: 2006
Investment Criteria: Seed-Stage
Industry Group Preference: Consumer Internet, Digital Media & Marketing
Portfolio Companies: Aardvark, Adara, Afresh, Alt School, Apiary, Appuri, Avocado, Backplane, Blekko, Bloc, BlueFox, BookFresh, Boombotix, Cake Financial, CarePort, CircleCI, Citrus Lane, Cluster, Copper, CoTweet, Crashlytics, Crayon, Datalot, Digit, Dishcraft Robotics, DocVerse, Dusty Robotics, ExactTarget, Expensify, Figure, Finxera, Flowtown, Freck, Formspring, Giftly, Gild, GoInstant, Good Eggs, Heartwork, Heroku, Homebase, Hunch, Indextank, Instagram, Instructables, Iron.io, J. Hilburn, LaunchKit, Librato, Liftoff, LoanSnap, Lucid, MachineZone, Mango Health, Metaresolver, MixerLabs, mLab, nWay, Okanjoya, OMGPop, OwnLocal, PacketZoom, Pagerduty, Pantheon, Parakey, Path, Peel, Pickwick & Weller, Piqora, Pocket, Projector, Pronoun, Reverb, Revere, Rivet & Sway, ROI DNA, Rupture, ScanScout, Seesaw, Sendori, Sendwithus, Shape, Smartbiz, Smyte., SoFi, Soma, Spruce, StackMob, Stax, Stitch Fix, StumbleUpon, Sun Basket, TaskRabbit, TastemakerX, TellApart, Threadflip, TINYpulse, Trazzler, TrialPay, TRUSTe, Twitter, Uservoice, Versly, Weebly, Xobni, Yardbarker

Key Executives:
Steve Anderson, Founder
Education: University of Washington, Stanford Graduate School of Business
Background: eBay, Microsoft, Kleiner Perkins, Starbucks, Digital Equipment Corporation

232 BASIS SET VENTURES
San Francisco, CA

web: www.basisset.ventures

Mission Statement: Mission is to invest in early stage startups in the area of artifical intelligence.

Fund Size: $140 Million
Investment Criteria: Seed/Series A Startups, Artificial Intelligence
Industry Group Preference: Artificial Intelligence
Portfolio Companies: Clara Labs, FarmWise, Falkonry, Foresight AI, Lime, Oasis Labs, Rasa, Rylo, Turing Video, Verge Genomics, Workstream

Key Executives:
Dr. Lan Xeuzhao, Founding/Managing Partner
Education: MA, Statistics, PhD, University of Michigan
Background: McKinsey; Dropbox
Andrew Kim, Operations Manager
Background: Meeno Babies; Project Gina

Venture Capital & Private Equity Firms / Domestic Firms

233 BATTELLE VENTURES
181 Rice Terrace Drive
Columbia, SC 29229

Phone: 843-535-2336

Mission Statement: The fund will principally, but not exclusively, focus on seed, startup, and first stage investments that will commercialize the technologies that emerge from Battelle and the laboratories that Battelle manages or co-manages for the US Department of Energy.
Geographic Preference: United States
Fund Size: $220 million
Founded: 2003
Investment Criteria: Seed, Startup, Early, First Stage
Industry Group Preference: Technology, Health Related, Life Sciences, Energy, Environment, Security
Portfolio Companies: 360ip Pte. Ltd., Aldis, BioNano Genomics, BioVigilant, Hepregen, Hi-G-Tek, Micro Interventional Devices, Proterro, Rajant, RemoteReality, SafeView, SmartSynch

234 BATTERSON VENTURE CAPITAL LLC
web: www.battersonvc.com

Mission Statement: Batterson Venture Capital provides venture capital to promising new or growing businesses. The firm's goal is to offer capital, operational expertise and strategic partnership to emerging entrepreneurs.
Geographic Preference: United States
Fund Size: $30 million
Founded: 1995
Average Investment: $100,000 - $12 million
Minimum Investment: $25,000
Investment Criteria: Seed, Startup, First-Stage, Second-Stage
Industry Group Preference: Biotechnology, Communications, Computer Related, High Technology, Materials Technology, Medical & Health Related
Portfolio Companies: Cleversafe, NextGen Solar LLC, ThirdStream BioScience
Key Executives:
Len Batterson, Chairman/CEO
Education: BA, JD, Washington University, St. Louis; MBA, Harvard Business School
Background: Managing General Partner, Batterson, Johnson & Wang; Director, Allstate Insurance Company; Control Video Corporation; Principal, Leonard Batterson Associates
Directorships: Illinois Coalition
James Vaughan, Managing Principal
Education: San Francisco State University
Background: CEO, JE Vaughan Financial Services; Founder & Manager, William Blair Select
Annie Piotrowski, Vice President, Administration
Education: BS, Legal Administration, Loyola University
Background: Executive Assistant, Stein & Company; Environmental Paralegal, American National Can Company

235 BATTERY VENTURES
1 Marina Park Drive
Suite 1100
Boston, MA 02210

Phone: 617-948-3600 **Fax:** 617-948-3601
web: www.battery.com

Mission Statement: Focuses on investing in technology companies at all stages of growth, leveraging expertise and capital to actively guide companies to category dominance.
Geographic Preference: United States, Canada, Israel, India, China, Europe
Fund Size: $6.8 billion
Founded: 1983
Average Investment: $35 million
Minimum Investment: $5 million
Investment Criteria: Seed, Startup, Later Stage
Industry Group Preference: Communications, Infrastructure, Software, Technology, Media, Networking, Telecommunications, Online Content, Semiconductors, Digital Media & Marketing, Financial Services, Clean Technology, Industrial Technology
Portfolio Companies: 2nd Address, 6sense, AED-SICAD, Affirm, Agari, Alogent, Amplitude, Audio Precision, AuditBoard, BigPanda, Black Diamond IT Services, BloomReach, Blue Jeans Network, Boost Media, BounceX, BPSC, Braze, BrightEdge, Brookhaven Instruments, Catchpoint Systems, Champions Oncology, Chef, Cheq, ClearCare, Clip Industie, Clubessential, Clubhouse, ClubReady, Cohesity, Coinbase, Colibra, Concurrent Real-Time, Contrast Security, Cortera, Coupa, CrediFi, Cross River Bank, CrunchTime!, Cumulus Networks, Curve Dental, Dantec Dynamics, Data Physics, Databricks, Dataiku, Delphix, DGSI, Duetto, Dynament, EDR, Elastifile, Entelo, Enviance, Excelero, Expel, Fastly, FirstFuel, Forterro, Fungible, Gainsight, GetYourGuide, GoEuro, GuardiCore, Habana Labs, HotelTonight, Influxdata, Interana, InVision, Istra Research, J. Hilburn, James Heal, Jask, Jeeves, JFrog, JOOR, KeyMe, Kodiak Robotics, Lansmont, Latitude Geographics, LDetek, Leadspace, Learnosity, LiveIntent, Local Bushel, Lotame, Machinify, Mecmesin, Michell Instruments, Minute Media, N26, Narrative Science, Narvar, NDT Systems, Newforma, Niantic Inc., Nitro Software, Nova Instruments, Nova Metrix, NTRON, Nutanix, NVT Group, Optimizely, Outlyer, PageUp, Pendo, Performance IQ, Physical Property Testing, Plixer, PowerInbox, Precidian Investments, PrestoSports, Primerevenue, Process Sensing Technologies, Qognify, Quantum Machines, Quinyx, Reflektion, RelayFoods.com, RickIQ, Robotiq, Roctest, Rotronic, Scodix, SensorNet, Sensu, Serena & Lily,

Other Locations:
2882 Sand Hill Road
Suite 280
Menlo Park, CA 94025
Phone: 650-372-3939 **Fax:** 650-372-3930

6 Hahoshlim Street
6th Floor
Herzliya 46724
Israel
Phone: 972 (9) 972-4300 **Fax:** 972 (9) 950-9484

260 Townsend Street
7th Floor
San Francisco, CA 94107
Phone: 415-426-5900 **Fax:** 415-426-5901

1 Duchess Street
Ground Floor
Suite 2
London W1W 6AN
United Kingdom
Phone: 44 (0)20-7299-1480 **Fax:** 44 (0)20-3689-7163

215 Park Avenue South
Floor 12
New York, NY 10003
Phone: 212-466-6340 **Fax:** 212-466-6341

Key Executives:
Dharmesh Thakker, General Partner
Education: BS, Electrical Engineering, University of Texas; MBA, Wharton School, University of Pennsylvania
Background: Managing Director, Intel Capital; Advanced Technology Ventures; Keynote Systems; InterNetwork; Peakstone; Manhattan Associates
Directorships: Agari, Collibra, Contrast Security, Databricks, Expel, Fungible, InfluxDatam JFrog, Machinify, Narvar, Reflektion, Sensu, StreamSets, UpKeep, Woven
Dave Tabors, Senior Advisor
Education: Dartmouth College

Venture Capital & Private Equity Firms / Domestic Firms

Background: Financial Consulting, Cambridge Associates
Directorships: CrunchTime!, Enviance, Forterro,
Scott Tobin, General Partner
Education: BA, International Relations, Islamic and Middle Eastern Studies, Brandeis University
Background: Investment Banking, First Albany Corporation; Director Corporate Development, Future Vision
Roger Lee, General Partner
Education: BA, Political Science, Yale University
Background: Co-Founder, Corio; Manager Internet Products, Edify Corporation; Co-Founder/President, NetMarket
Directorships: 6Sense, Blue Jeans Network, BrightEdge, Coinbase, Entelo, Gainsight, HotelTonight, Joya Communications, Live Intent, Lotame, Narrative Science, Narvar, Niantic Inc., etc.
Neeraj Agrawal, General Partner
Education: BS, Computer Science, Cornell University; MBA, Harvard Business School
Background: Product Manager, Real Networks; Management Consultant, Booz-Allen; Operative Executive, SkyTV
Michael Brown, General Partner
Education: BS, Finance & International Business, Georgetown University
Background: High Technology Group, Goldman, Sachs & Co; Financial Anaylst, Goldman's Financial Institutions Group
Jesse Feldman, General Partner
Education: BA, Science in Society, Wesleyan University; MBA, Harvard Business School
Background: Ionian Management; GE Commercial Finance
Directorships: Healthvision, HighJump Software, Industrial Safey Technology, Nova Analytic, Nova Technologies, Rogue Wave Software
Brian Leiber, Partner
Education: BA, Political Science, Wittenberg University
Background: Senior Associate, The Bowdoin Group; SCO, Inc.; Allegis Group
Itzik Parnafes, General Partner, Israel
Education: BSc, Computer Science & Mathematics, Technion Institute of Technology
Background: Co-Founder, Kagoor Networks; R&D, Class Data Systems
Directorships: 90min, Cheq, Elastifule, GoEuro, Insert, Kodiak Robotics, Quantum Machines, Sisense, Zeitgold
Alex Benik, Partner
Education: BA, Government, Wesleyan University
Background: Analyst, The Yankee Group
Directorships: Cask, Catchpoint, Cumulus Networks, Fungible, GuardiCore, Interana, Nutanix, Plixer, Stratoscale, Thundra, Vivid Cortex
Chelsea Stoner, General Partner
Education: BS, Chemical Engineering, Northwestern University; MBA, University of Chicago
Background: Associate, Key Principal Partners; Manager, Accenture; Principal, Battery Ventures; Merrill Lynch; Classified Ventures

236 BAXTER VENTURES
One Baxter Parkway
Deerfield, IL 60015-4625

e-mail: ventures@baxter.com
web: www.baxter.com

Mission Statement: Baxter Ventures identifies companies with promising, early-stage technologies, products and/or therapies, and provides them with the capital and expertise needed to drive successful innovation. Baxter Ventures was created by Baxter International Inc., which has an 80-year legacy of healthcare innovation and saving and sustaining lives worldwide.
Founded: 2011
Investment Criteria: Early-Stage
Industry Group Preference: Healthcare, Pharmaceuticals

237 BAY CITY CAPITAL LLC
750 Battery Street
Suite 400
San Francisco, CA 94111

Phone: 415-676-3830 Fax: 415-837-0503
web: www.baycitycapital.com

Mission Statement: To provide investment capital and strategic and transaction advisory review to publicly traded and privately held companies.
Geographic Preference: United States
Fund Size: $1.3 billion
Founded: 1997
Average Investment: $5 - $10 million
Minimum Investment: $100,000
Investment Criteria: All Stages
Industry Group Preference: Life Sciences, Pharmaceuticals, Biomedical, Diagnostics, Nutrition, Agribusiness, Biopharmaceuticals, Medical Devices
Portfolio Companies: Accriva Diagnostics, Aciex Therapeutics, Amerifit Nutrition, Antriabio, AquaBounty Technologies, Aragon Surgical, Ascendancy Healthcare, BioRen, BioSeek, Cadence Pharmaceuticals, Calupso Medical, Chemdex, Civitas Therapeutics, Conatus Pharmaceuticals, Cydan, CymaBay Therapeutics, Dermira, EnteroMedics, Eos, Epizyme, Epoch Biosciences, Epocrates, Fabric Genomics, GenturaDx, Gritstone Oncology, Hyperion Therapeutics, Idev, Imara, Ingenuity Systems, Intarcia Therapeutics, Interleukin Genetics, Ion Torrent, Itamar Medical, Iterum Therapeutics, Kezar Life Sciences, Lexicon, LJL BioSystems, Madrigal Pharmaceuticals, MAP Pharmaceuticals Inc., Maxia Pharmaceuticals Inc., Medarex, Menlo Therapeutics, Merus, Neorx, Nevro, Next Wave Pharmaceuticals, NuPathes, OcuLex, OmegaTech, Panomics, Pathway Diagnostics, Pharm Akea Therapeutics, Pharmanex, Pharmion, Presidio Pharmaceuticals Inc., Protez Pharmaceuticals, PTC Therapeutics, Radiant Medical, Reliant Pharmaceuticals Inc., Reset Therapeutics, Sembiosys, Senomyx. Sunesis, Symyx, SynGen, Syntonix, Syrrx, Tetraphase, Tria, Twist Bioscience, Vivaldi Biosciences, VNUS Medical Technologies Inc., Vtesse, Xeris Pharmaceuticals

Other Locations:
Baarerstrasse 14
Zug 6300
Switzerland
Phone: 415-835-9341

Key Executives:
Fred Craves, PhD, Founder/Managing Director
Education: PhD Pharmacology/Toxicology, University of California San Francisco; BS Biology, Georgetown University
Background: Executive VP, Shering Beruin Inc; CEO and President, Berlex Buiosciences; Founding Chairman and CEO, Codon; Co-Founder of Creative BioMolecules/NeoRx
Directorships: Incyte Genomics, Medarex, Bioseek, Galileo Laboratories, Reliant Pharmaceuticals
Carl Goldfischer, MD, Managing Director
Education: MD, Albert Einstein College; BA, Sarah Lawrence College
Background: CFO, ImClone Systems; Research Analyst, Reliance Insurance Company
Directorships: Diametrics Medical, Avera Pharmaceuticals, Etex, Metabolex, NeoRx, Oculex Pharmaceuticals, PTC Therapeutics, Syntonix Pharmaceuticals
Lionel Carnot, Managing Director
Education: MS, Molecular Biology, University of Geneva; MBA, INSEAD
Background: KFitzker Organization; Principal, Oracle

Venture Capital & Private Equity Firms / Domestic Firms

Partners; Product Manager for Prozac, Eli Lilly; Sales/Marketing, Booz Allen & Hamilton; Accenture Strategic Services
Directorships: Mervus BV
Dayton Misfeldt, Managing Director
Education: BA Economics, University of California, San Diego
Background: KFce President, Roth Capital Partners; Project Manager, LifeScience Economics
Directorships: Aciex, Sunesis Pharmaceuticals
Manuel Lopez-Figueroa, Managing Director
Education: MS, Molecular & Cell Biology, University of La Laguna; PhD, Medicine & Surgery, University of Las Palmas
Background: Scientific Liason, Pritzker Neuropsychiatric Disorders Research Consortium
Mervyn Turner, PhD, Advisor
Background: Chief Strategy Officer, Merck & Co.

---

238 BAY PARTNERS
2180 Sand Hill Road
Suite 345
Menlo Park, CA 94025

web: www.baypartners.com

Mission Statement: Bay Partners aim to build high value companies that provide exceptional returns to both the investors and entrepreneurs. Bay Partners works to create a strong alignment between the interests of the investors and those of the entrepreneur.
Geographic Preference: United States
Fund Size: $1 Billion
Founded: 1976
Average Investment: $7 - $10 million
Minimum Investment: $3 million
Investment Criteria: Seed and early-stage companies with validated concepts facing execution risk.
Industry Group Preference: Wireless Technologies, Semiconductors, Enterprise Software, SaaS, Equipment, Components & IoT, Consumer Services, Hardware, Energy Services
Portfolio Companies: AMEC, Apigee, BoardVantage, Code Green Networks, Covestor, DropCam, Engine Yard, Enphase Energy, Envia Systems, Eventful, Grand Junction, Interact Public Safety Systems, Lending Club, Mimoni, MuleSoft, OncoMed, RS LiveMedia, Sonatype, Xactly, FinancialContent, Vaxart, Yapta, Junglee Games, Brocade Communications, Buddy Media, Cornerstone, Digital Island, Dynatrace, Eloqua, Excelan, Exodus Communications, G2One, Geoworks, Guidewire Software, Informatica, Like.com, Macromedia, Maxtor, NCM Services, Protocol Systems, Red Brick Systems, Shiva, SonicWALL, SpringSource, Tealeaf, WebLogic, Zenprise

Key Executives:
Stu Phillips, General Partner
e-mail: stu@baypartners.com
Education: BS, Electronics, University of Wales
Background: Founder, Ridgelift Ventures; General Partner, US Venture Partners; Cisco Systems
Neal Dempsey, General Partner
e-mail: neal@baypartners.com
Education: MBA, University of Washington
Background: CEO, Quibix Graphics Systems; CEO, Envision Technology; Senior Management, Sentec/Harris

---

239 BAYSIDE CAPITAL
1450 Brickell Avenue
31st Floor
Miami, FL 33131

Phone: 305-379-8686 Fax: 305-379-3655
e-mail: bayside@bayside.com
web: www.bayside.com

Mission Statement: Bayside Capital is an investment firm that provides debt and equity capital to middle market companies.
Geographic Preference: United States, Canada
Fund Size: $7 billion
Average Investment: $10 - $100 million
Investment Criteria: Recapitalizations, Debtor in Possession Financing
Industry Group Preference: Diversified
Other Locations:
500 Boylston Office
20th Floor
Boston, MA 02116
Phone: 617-425-5650 Fax: 617-262-1505

600 Fifth Avenue
22nd Floor
New York, NY 10020
Phone: 212-314-1000 Fax: 212-506-0559

H.I.G. European Capital Partners LLP
2nd Floor
London W1K 4QB
United Kingdom
Phone: 44 0 207 318 5700 Fax: 44 0 207 318 5749

H.I.G. European Capital Partners GmbH
Hamburg 20354
Germany
Phone: 49 40 41 33 06 100 Fax: 49 40 33 06 200

H.I.G. European Capital Partners Spain, S.L.U.
4th Floor
Madrid 28014
Spain
Phone: 34 91 737 50 50 Fax: 34 91 737 50 49

Ih.I.G. European Capital Partners Italy S.r.l.
Milan 20121
Italy
Phone: 39 02 45 37 5200 Fax: 39 02 45 37 5250

H.I.G. European Capital Partners SAS
5th Floor
Paris 75008
France
Phone: 33 0 1 53 57 50 60 Fax: 33 0 1 53 57 50 89

Sensu Serpen, Managing Director
Education: METU University
Background: Barclays Capital; Bank of America; Credit du Nord

Key Executives:
John Bolduc, Executive Managing Director
Education: BS, Computer Science, Lehigh University; MBA, University of Virginia
Background: Bain & Company; Chemed Corporation
Jackson Craig, Managing Director
Education: BS, Business Administration, University of Vermont
Background: DDJ Capital Management; Morgan Stanley
Sean Britain, Managing Director
Education: BS, Business Administration, Wake Forest University
Background: Principal, Apax Partners; Saunders Karp & Megrue; First Union Securities
Duncan Priston, Managing Director
Education: Bristol University
Background: Strategic Value Partners; Houlihan Lokey; Morgan Stanley
Roman Krislav, Managing Director
Education: BSE, Wharton School, BAS, School of Engineering and Applied Sciences, University of Pennsylvania; MBA, Columbia Business School
Background: VP, Mercantile Capital Partners; Goldman Sachs
Adam Schimel, Managing Director
Education: BS, Electrical Engineering & Economics, Duke University; MBA, Kellogg School of Management,

Venture Capital & Private Equity Firms / Domestic Firms

Northwestern University
Background: Associate, Lindsay Goldberg; Goldman Sachs
Steven Schwartz, Managing Director
Education: Boston University School of Management; NYU Stern School of Business
Background: Partner, Torchlight Investors; JP Morgan
Andrew Scotland, Managing Director
Education: Oxford University
Background: Special Situations Group, RBS; Equity Research, ABN AMRO; Citigroup; Credit Suisse

240 BBH CAPITAL PARTNERS
140 Broadway
New York, NY 10005-1101

Phone: 212-483-1818
web: www.bbh.com

Mission Statement: Provides highly customized, one-stop junior capital solutions to lower middle market companies.
Geographic Preference: United States
Fund Size: $2 billion
Founded: 1989
Average Investment: $20 to $50 million
Minimum Investment: $20 million
Investment Criteria: Leveraged Buyouts, Growth Initiatives, Recapitalizations, Balance Sheet Refinancings, Ownership Transactions, Generational Transfers, Buy & Build Strategies, Acquisitions
Industry Group Preference: Business Products & Services, Distribution, Healthcare, Niche Manufacturing, Communications, Consumer Products, Consumer Services
Portfolio Companies: Americam Physician Partners, Best Doctors, EdgeConneX, Haven Behavioral Healthcare, Heniff Transporation Systems, KabaFusion Holdings, Microban International, PrimeRevenue, Utility Pipeline, Vyve Broadband

Other Locations:
Brown Brothers Harriman Business Services Co.
Unit 2002-04, 20/F, Tower 2, China World Trade Center
No. 1 Jianguomenwai Avenue, Chaoyang District
Beijing 100004
China
Phone: 86-10-5783-2300

Brown Brothers Harriman Trust Company, N.A.
50 Post Office Square
Boston, MA 02110-1548
Phone: 617-772-1818

Brown Brothers Harriman Trust Company, N.A.
227 West Trade Street
Suite 2100
Charlotte, NC 28202-1675
Phone: 704-370-0500

Brown Brothers Harriman Trust Company, N.A.
150 South Wacker Drive
Suite 3250
Chicago, IL 60606
Phone: 312-781-7111

6801 South Tuscon Way
Suite 100
Centennial, CO 80112
Phone: 303-566-6600

Fund Administration Services Limited
Trustee Services Limited
30 Herbert Street
Dublin 2
Ireland
Phone: 353-1-603-6200

Brown Brothers Harriman Trust Company Limited
18 Forum Lane
Camana Bay
Grand Cayman KY1-1106
Cayman Islands
Phone: 354-945-2719

Brown Brothers Harriman Limited
13/F Man Yee Building
68 Des Voeux Road Central
Hong Kong
China

185 Hudson Street
Suite 1150
Jersey City, NJ 07311-4003
Phone: 201-418-5600

Brown Brothers Harriman Sp. z o.o.
Orange Office Park
ul. Klimeckiego 1
Krakow 30-705
Poland
Phone: 48-12-340-6000

Brown Brothers Harriman Investor Services Ltd
Park House
16-18 Finsbury Circus
London EC2M 7EB
United Kingdom
Phone: 44-207-588-6166

Brown Brothers Harriman S.C.A.
80, Route D'Esch
Luxembourg L-1470
Luxembourg
Phone: 352-47-4066-1

3100 West End Avenue
Suite 450
Nashville, TN 37203
Phone: 615-279-8880

BBH Trust Company of Delaware, N.A.
1 Logan Square
14th Floor
Philadelphia, PA 19103-6908
Phone: 215-864-1818

Toranomon Kotohira Tower 15F
1-2-8- Toranomon
Minato-Ku
Tokyo 105-0001
Japan
Phone: 81-3-6361-6500

BBH Trust Company of Delaware, N.A.
Delle Donne Corporate Center
1013 Centre Rd, Suite 101
Wilmington, DE 19805
Phone: 302-552-4040

Brown Brothers Harriman Services AG
Talstresse 83
Zurich 8001
Switzerland
Phone: 41-44-227-1818

Key Executives:
Jeffrey A. Schoenfeld, Partner/Institutional Business Development & Relationship Mgmt
Education: BA, Economics, University of California, Berkeley; MBA, Wharton School
Daniel J. Greifenkamp, Managing Director/Head of Funds/CEO of BBH Investments
Education: BBA, Carroll University; MBA, University of Chicago
Background: Director of Business Development, Abbey Capital; Partner, Artisan Partners LP
Jean-Pierre Paquin, Co-Manager/Partner/Investment Management
212-493-8413
e-mail: jp.paquin@bbh.com
Education: Colgate University; MBA, Wharton School
Directorships: Tower Ventures, KabaFusion Holdings, Vyve Broadband

Venture Capital & Private Equity Firms / Domestic Firms

Anita K. Kerr, Managing Director/COO
Education: BA, Spanish, New York University
Background: Managing Director & Global Head of Regulatory Reform, Goldman Sachs Asset Management
Vincent D'Angelo, SVP/Head of Risk & Governance
Education: BS, Economics, Saint Michael's College; MBA, Lubin School of Business, Pace University
Background: Global Head of Operational Risk, AIG; Morgan Stanley; Goldman Sachs

241 BCM TECHNOLOGIES
2 Greenway Plaza
Suite 910
Houston, TX 77046

Phone: 713-795-0105 Fax: 713-795-4602

Mission Statement: An early stage venture capital firm formed by Baylor College of Medicine with a 20-year investment history in the Houston area.
Geographic Preference: Southwest
Fund Size: $20 million
Founded: 1983
Average Investment: $1 million
Minimum Investment: $500,000
Investment Criteria: Seed, Early Stage
Industry Group Preference: Biotechnology, Information Technology, Medical Devices, Life Sciences
Portfolio Companies: Diversigen, HGHI, Kardia Therapeutics, Kryptiq Corporation, Molecular Logix, Opexa Therapeutics, Progression Therapeutics, Relievant MedSystems, StepStoneMed, Synced Care

Key Executives:
Caroline Popper MD MPH, President
Education: MPH, Johns Hopkins University; MD, University of the Witwatersrand
Background: Becton Dickinson; Founding General Manager, BDGene; CBO, MDS Proteomics
Cynthia S Sheridan
Education: BBA, Economics, University of Memphis; MBA, Finance & Strategic Planning, University of Texas at Austin
Background: Division VP, GE Capital Consulting; CEO, IBT Technologies; Associate Professor, St. Edward's University
Stephanie Kreml MD
Education: BS, Electrical Engineering, University of Texas at Austin; MD, Baylor College of Medicine
Background: Product Engineer, Texas Instruments; Motorola Semiconductor; Medical Advisor, Televero Health

242 BEDFORD FUNDING
10 New King Street
Suite 104
White Plains, NY 10604

Phone: 914-287-4880
e-mail: info@bedfordfunding.com
web: www.bedfordfunding.com

Mission Statement: Bedford Funding is a private equity firm focused on software and IT services in the human capital management and healthcare IT sectors.
Geographic Preference: Worldwide
Founded: 2006
Industry Group Preference: IT Services, Healthcare IT
Portfolio Companies: MDLive, Voalte, KZO Innovations, Socialtext, Strategia, Aquire, Peopleclick, Authoria

Key Executives:
Charles S. Jones, Managing Partner and Founder
Background: President & CEO, Geac Computer Corporation
Larry Kaplan, Managing Director and Chief Financial Officer
Education: BS, Mathematics, SUNY Stony Brook; MBA, Carnegie Mellon University
Background: SVP, Geac; CFO, Healthology; Shandwick International
Jonathan D. Salon, Managing Director and General Counsel
Education: BA, Colgate University; JD, Boston University School of Law
Background: VP & General Counsel, Unica Corporation

243 BEE PARTNERS
50 Osgood Place
Suite 220A
San Francisco, CA 94133

e-mail: hello@beepartners.vc
web: www.beepartners.vc

Mission Statement: Bee Partners, a genesis-stage venture firm, pollinates visionary entrepreneurs with financial, human and social capital. The firm actively supports teams with customer development, marketing strategy, financing strategy and more.
Geographic Preference: United States
Founded: 2008
Average Investment: $200,000 - $400,000
Industry Group Preference: Business to Business
Portfolio Companies: TubeMogul, Indiegogo, Tradesy, Skycatch, Embroker, Magoosh, Parsec, LeadGenius, OrderGroove, Zipongo, BuildingConnected, StatMuse, Node.io, Vacatia, RBC Signals, Neighborly, Xola, AxleHire, SnapTravel, Identify3D, LocalWise, Voltaiq, Florence Healthcare, Capio, Iris Automation, VentureScanner, Airbanq, Sideqik, tbh, Zeus, Breezy, Preact, Modify Watches, Columbia Green, Pudget, FiveRun, Earbits, Bear Naked, Evol Foods, Phonio, Enliken, Pencil, Enthuse, Illumobile

Key Executives:
Michael Berolzheimer, Founder/Managing Partner
Education: BS, Economics & Computer Science, Vanderbilt University
Background: DLJ/Credit Suisse, Harvest Partners

244 BEECKEN PETTY O'KEEFE & COMPANY
131 S Dearborn Street
Suite 2800
Chicago, IL 60603

Phone: 312-435-0300 Fax: 312-435-0371
e-mail: partners@bpoc.com
web: www.bpoc.com

Mission Statement: Beecken Petty O'Keefe & Company (BPOC) is a private equity firm based in Chicago. The firm focuses exclusively on middle-market companies in the healthcare industry.
Geographic Preference: United States
Fund Size: Fund III: $400 million; Fund IV: $500 million
Founded: 1996
Average Investment: $7 million
Minimum Investment: $1.5 million
Investment Criteria: Middle-Market Buyout Transactions, Recapitalizations, Growth Platforms
Industry Group Preference: Healthcare, Medical Devices, Medical & Health Related
Portfolio Companies: Absolute Dental, ClareMedica Health Partners, Cranial Technologies, D4C Dental Brands, EMSI, Health-E Commerce, himagine Solutions, Maxor, Medicus Healthcare Solutions, MPE, Spectrum Professional Services, Zenith American Solutions

Key Executives:
David Beecken, Founder
Education: University of the South; MBA, Finance, University of Chicago; MS, Economics, London School of Economics
Background: Investment Banker, First National Bank of Chicago; Managing Director, Smith Barney
Directorships: AbilityOne, Corizon, D4C Dental Brands

Venture Capital & Private Equity Firms / Domestic Firms

Holdings, DentalCare Partners, Heartland Information Systems, ISG Holdings, Paragon Medical, Sirona Dental Systems
Kenneth O'Keefe, Founder
Education: BA, Economics, Northwestern University; MBA, Finance, University of Chicago
Background: Managing Director, First National Bank Chicago; Corporate Finance, Smith Barney
Directorships: Corizon, Himagine Solutions, Jazz Pharmaceuticals, Origin Healthcare Solutions, PerfectServe, Same Day Surgery, Team Health
Gregory Moerschel, Managing Partner
Education: BA, Economics, Northwestern University; MBA, Finance & Health Services Administration, Kellogg Graduate School of Management
Background: VP/Sr Healthcare Analyst, ABN AMRO; Healthcare Investment Banking Group, The First National Bank of Chicago
Directorships: EMSI, Genezen Healthcare, Genoa Healthcare, Hospital Physician Partners, The Hygenic Corporation, Maxor, Medical Solutions, NetRegulus, NeuroSource, Preferred Homecare
David J Cooney, Managing Director
Education: BS, History, University of Illinois; MPP, International Finance, Georgetown University
Background: Corporate Finance, Smith Barney; Analyst, Overseas Private Investment Corporation
Directorships: ISG Holdings, Paragon Medical, Reichert, The MED Group
John Kneen, Partner, CFO/COO
Education: College of Wooster; MBA, Accounting & Finance, Kellogg Graduate School of Management
Background: Acquisitions & Corporate Development, Evergreen Healthcare; CFO, Alterra Healthcare; Healthcare Financial Consulting, Coopers & Lybrand
William Petty Jr, Founder
Education: BS, Business, University of Illinois
Background: Co-Founder, Omega Capital Ltd.; Evergreen Healthcare; Forum Group; Alterra Healthcare
Directorships: Sunrise Assisted Living, Omega Healthcare Investors, Forum Group, Axentis, Complient, DentalCare Partners, Genezen Healthcare, Take Care Health Systems
Thomas A Schlesinger, Managing Director
Education: BA, Economics, Rutgers University; MBA, Finance, University of Chicago
Background: Healthcare Investment Banker, ABN AMRO
Directorships: AbilityOne Corporation, DentalCare Partners Inc., Heartland Information Services, PerfectServe Inc., Scrip Holdings Corporation
Timothy D Sheehan, Managing Director
Education: BA, University of Virginia
Background: Director, Madison Dearborn Partners; Investment Banking Group, Solomon Brothers
Directorships: Hospital Physicians Partners, Path Lab Holdings, Sirona Dental Systems, Team Health Holdings, VWR International
Peter N Magas, Managing Director
Education: BS, Miami University (Ohio); MBA, Kellogg Graduate School of Management, Northwestern University
Background: Director, Healthcare Finance Group, CapitalSource Finance; GE Healthcare; Heller Healthcare Finance
Directorships: Hospital Physician Partners, Paragon Medical, Medical Solutions
Grant A Patrick, Managing Director
Education: BBA, Finance & Management, Emory University; MBA, Finance & Economics, University of Chicago Graduate School of Business
Background: Associate, BlueStar Ventures; Investment Banking, ABN AMRO
Directorships: Himagine Solutions, Origin Healthcare Solutions, Sunrise Assisted Living
M Troy Phillips, Managing Director
Education: BS, Finance & Computer Applications, University of Notre Dame; MBA, Harvard Business School; CFA
Background: Vice President, Edgewater Growth Capital Partners; Triple Tree Capital; Associate, Frontenac Company
Directorships: Corizon, EMSI, Genoa Healthcare, Maxor, Preferred Homecare, RSA Medical
Julian L Carr, Operating Partner
Education: BS, Economics, University of Tulsa; MBA, Indiana University
Background: Chairman & CEO, Valitas Health Services; Executive VP, Aramark Corporation
Directorships: Corizon, DentalCare Partners, Himagine Solutions, Living Centers of America, The MED Group, Medcor Holdings, Sanford-Brown, TIDI Products, VHA
Scott R Kabbes, Operating Partner
Background: Founder & CEO, EagleSoft; President, Professionals' Software Company
Directorships: Heartland Dental Care, Preferred Homecare, Scrip Product Corporation, TIDI Products

245 BEHRMAN CAPITAL
126 East 56th Street
27th Floor
New York, NY 10022
Phone: 212-980-6500 Fax: 212-980-7024
web: www.behrmancap.com

Mission Statement: Private equity investment firm invests in middle-market buyouts of growth companies.

Fund Size: $3 billion
Founded: 1991
Average Investment: $25 - $100 million
Minimum Investment: $2 million
Investment Criteria: All Stages, Management Buyouts, LBO, Recapitalizations
Industry Group Preference: Defense & Aerospace, Healthcare Services, Specialty Manufacturing & Distribution
Portfolio Companies: Ark Holding Company, Athena Diagnostics, Atherotech Diagnostics, Brooks Equipment Company, Condor Systems, Corfin Industries LLC, Emmes Corporation, Esoterix Inc., Executive Greetings Inc., Hunter Defence Technologies, ILC Dover, KSARIA, Nimbus CD International Inc., Peacock Engineering Company, Pelican Products, Plastics Industries Inc., Selig Sealing Products, Tandem Health Care, Tresys Technology, Waterline Renewal Technologies, WIL Research Laboratories

Other Locations:
One Letterman Drive
Suite D4900
Building D, The Presidio
San Francisco, CA 94129
Phone: 415-434-7300 Fax: 415-434-4004

Key Executives:
Grant Behrman, Managing Partner
Education: MBA Marketing/General Management, Wharton School; University of Witwatersrand
Background: Fouding Member, Morgan Stanley Venture Capital Group; Consultant, Boston Consulting Group
Directorships: Esoterix, The Management Network Group, Brooks Equipment
William Matthes, Managing Partner
Education: MBA, Harvard Business School; AB Economics, Stanford University
Background: COO, Holsted Marketing; General Partner, Brentwood Associates; Analyst, Morgan Stanley
Directorships: The Management Network Group, Tandem Health Care, The Kinetics Group, ILC Industries
Simon Lonergan, Managing Partner
Education: BA, University of Cambridge; MBA, Harvard Business School
Background: Partner & Senior Managing Director, The Blackstone Group

Venture Capital & Private Equity Firms / Domestic Firms

Directorships: Selig Sealing Products, Data Device Corppration
Mark Visser, Partner
Education: BS, Engineering, Physics, Rensselaer Polytechnic Institute
Background: Investment Banking Group, Merrill Lynch
Directorships: Ark Holding Company, Peacock Engineering Company
Jeffrey Wu, Partner
Education: BS, Economics, Wharton School; BS, Electrical Engineering, University of Pennsylvania
Background: Financial Analyst, Merrill Lynch Technology Investment Banking Group

246 BEN FRANKLIN TECHNOLOGY PARTNERS
4801 S Broad Street
Suite 200
Building 100 Innovation Center
Philadelphia, PA 19112
Phone: 215-972-6700 Fax: 215-972-5588
e-mail: info@sep.benfranklin.org
web: www.sep.benfranklin.org

Mission Statement: Ben Franklin Technology Partners of Southeastern Pennsylvania provides technology entrepreneurs and established businesses with the capital, knowledge and networks they need to compete in the global marketplace.
Geographic Preference: Southeastern Pennsylvania
Founded: 1982
Average Investment: $200,000
Minimum Investment: $50,000
Investment Criteria: Seed, Early Stage, Growth Capital
Industry Group Preference: Technology
Portfolio Companies: Monetate, Health Market Science, Boomi, Brad's Raw Foods, Morphotek, Neat
Key Executives:
 RoseAnn B. Rosenthal, CEO Emeritus
 e-mail: roseann@sep.benfranklin.org
 Education: BA, Temple University; Honorary PhD, Humane Letters, Philadelphia University
 Background: Executive Director, Philadelphia Industrial Development Corp; Associate Director, Landing Corp; Executive Director, Children's Village
 Directorships: Digital Delaware
 Scott Nissenbaum, President/CEO
 e-mail: scott@sep.benfranklin.org
 Education: BS, Pennsylvania State University; MBA, Saint Joe's University
 Anthony P. Green, PhD, Vice President, Science & Technology
 215-972-6700
 e-mail: anthony@sep.benfranklin.org
 Education: BSc, Immunology, Brown University; PhD, Microbiology & Immunology, Temple University School of Medicine

247 BENAROYA COMPANIES
3600 136th Place SE
Suite 250
Bellevue, WA 98006
Phone: 425-440-6700 Fax: 425-440-6730
e-mail: larryb@benaroya.com

Mission Statement: Invest in high growth opportunities with strong management and developed technology.
Geographic Preference: Pacific North
Founded: 1995
Average Investment: $4 million
Minimum Investment: $500,000
Investment Criteria: Equity, Equity-Bridge Financings in Post Seed Stage Growth
Industry Group Preference: Telecommunications, Infrastructure, Manufacturing, Consumer Services, Data Communications
Portfolio Companies: Audiosocket, Avalara, Avail-TVN, Calico Energy Services, Capital Stream, Coinstar, CommQuest, DNA Response, Open Interface, Peapod, Prepared Response, Swype, Starbucks, Sparkbuy, Tegic
Key Executives:
 Larry Benaroya, Manager
 425-440-6704
 e-mail: larryb@benaroya.com
 Education: University of Pennsylvania

248 BENCHMARK
140 New Montgomery Street
San Francisco, CA 94105
web: www.benchmark.com

Mission Statement: Venture capital firm behind a number of successful startups. Noted for its compensation structure in which partners share profits equally.
Founded: 1995
Investment Criteria: Early-Stage
Industry Group Preference: Mobile, Cloud Computing, Social Media
Portfolio Companies: 1stdibs, Amplitude, Asana, Confluent, Couchsurfing, Docker, Dropbox, eBay, elastic, Glassdoor, Good Eggs, Grubhub, HackerOne, Hortonworks, Instagram, Lithium Technologies, Minted, New Relic, One Medical, OpenTable, Optimizely, Potbelly, Proofpoint, ResearchGate, Sailthru, Silver Peak, Snapchat, Software Integrity, Tinder, Twitter, Uber, Upwork, WeWork, Wix.com, Zendesk, ZipCar, Zuora
Other Locations:
 2965 Woodside Road
 Woodside, CA 94062
Key Executives:
 Peter Fenton, General Partner
 Education: BA, Philosophy, MBA, Stanford University
 Background: Managing Partner, Accel Partners
 Directorships: Buoyant, Docker, Cockroach Labs, Elasticsearch, Hortonworks, Minted, New Relic, Optimizely, Revinate, TimescaleDB, Yelp, Zuora
 Matt Cohler, General Partner
 Education: BA, Yale Universty
 Background: VP & Special Advisor, Facebook; VP & General Manager, LinkedIn; Consultant, McKinsey & Company
 Directorships: Tinder, Duo Security, Edmodo, 1stdibs, Domo, ResearchGate, Quora, Asana, Instagram
 Mitch Lasky, General Partner
 Education: Harvard College; University of Virginia
 Background: Irell & Manella; Walt Disney Company; Serum Entertainment Software; Activision; JAMDAT
 Directorships: Snapchat; Riot Games; Hammer & Chisel; Outpost Games; thatgamecompany; PlayFab; Manticore Games; Cyngn
 Eric Vishria, General Partner
 Education: Stanford University
 Background: Rockmelt; Yahoo
 Directorships: Benchling, Blue Hexagon, Contentful, Cerebras Systems, Bugsnag, Amplitude Analytics, Confluent

249 BENHAMOU GLOBAL VENTURES
540 Cowper Street
Suite 200
Palo Alto, CA 94301
Phone: 650-324-3680 Fax: 650-473-1347
web: www.benhamouglobalventures.com

Mission Statement: Early-stage venture capital firm focused on enterprise information technology with a particular empha-

Venture Capital & Private Equity Firms / Domestic Firms

sis on mobility, cloud architectures and technologies, and cyber security.
Geographic Preference: Silicon Valley
Investment Criteria: Early-Stage
Industry Group Preference: Cloud Infrastructure, Business Software, SaaS, Networking, Communications, Enterprise Mobility, Cyber Security
Portfolio Companies: 4IQ, 3com, 6d, Atricia, Ayehu, Bayshore, Blue Cedar, Carfit, Connected Signals, Contextream, Cyberinc, Dasient, DialOnce, Drishti, EcoPlant, Finjan, Flytrex, GoNetworks, Grid Dynamics, Identity Mind, IntelliVision, Kaptivo, Load Dynamix, Macrometa, MyTopia, NGD Systems, OneMob, Onymos, Palm, Platform.sh, Profitect, Qubell, Ripples, Scalefast, Secret Double Octopus, Spikes Security, SwanLabs, Tagnos, Tilera, Totango, Virtual Instruments, Voltaire, Webscale, Zentri

Key Executives:
   Eric Benhamou, Founder/General Partner
   e-mail: eric@benhamouglobalventures.com
   Education: MS, Stanford University School of Engineering
   Background: CEO, 3Com
   Directorships: Swan Labs, Dasient, Voltaire, Finjan, Contextream, Load Dynamix, Grid Dynamics, Ayehu, Totango, Secret Double Octopus, 6d
   Anik Bose, General Partner
   e-mail: anik@benhamouglobalventures.com
   Education: BA, Economics, University of Delhi; MBA, Boston College
   Background: H3C; Partner, Deloitte Management Consulting
   Directorships: Cyberinc, WebScale, Blue Cedar Networks
   Eric Buatois, General Partner
   e-mail: buatois@benhamouglobalventures.com
   Education: MSc, Computer Science, Ecole Nationale Suprieure des Telecommunications; INSEAD
   Background: General Partner, Sofinnova Ventures; Texas Instruments, Hewlett-Packard, Ericsson

250 BERGGRUEN HOLDINGS
304 S Broadway
Suite 550
Los Angeles, CA 90013

Phone: 213-430-2350
e-mail: pipeline@berggruenholdings.com
web: www.berggruenholdings.com

Mission Statement: Investment arm of the Nicholas Berggruen Charitable Trust.
Geographic Preference: Worldwide
Fund Size: $2 billion
Industry Group Preference: Real Estate, Alternative Energy, Financial Services
Portfolio Companies: Berggruen Car Rentals, Bonded Kayit Sistemleri AS, Equipwell, Gemini Equipment & Rents, Global Supply Chain Finance, International Education Corporation, NBP Capital LLC, Oreko Metal Mining, Transport Labor Holding Company, UEI Global

Key Executives:
   Nicolas Berggruen, Chief Executive Officer
   Education: BS, Finance, New York University
   Background: Jacobson & Co.
   Koonal Gandhi, Chief Investment Officer
   Justin Topilow, Chief Financial Officer
   Education: BA, Yale Univ.; MBA, NYU Stern School of Business
   Samuel Czarny, Managing Director, Germany
   e-mail: sc@berggruenholdings.com
   Background: Hamburgische Immobilien Handlung GmbH
   Mehmet Kosematoglu, Managing Director, Turkey
   e-mail: mk@berggruenholdings.com
   Education: BSc, Cornell University; MA, Public Administration, Harvard University
   Background: CEO, AIG Blue Voyage Advisors
   Kabir Kewalramani, Managing Director, India
   e-mail: kk@berggruenholdings.com
   Background: CEO, RDC Concrete India; Crosby Capital Partners; JP Morgan Partners

251 BERINGEA
32330 W 12 Mile Road
Farmington Hills, MI 48334

Phone: 248-489-9000
e-mail: info@beringea.com
web: www.beringea.com

Mission Statement: Beringea is a private equity firm that invests in and nurtures companies across a wide range of growth industries, including life sciences, healthcare, Internet technology, manufacturing, clean technology and media. Beringea, which has offices in Detroit and London, offers capital, experience and expertise to entrepreneurs and utilizes these resources to create value for portfolio companies.
Geographic Preference: United States
Fund Size: $65 million
Founded: 1988
Average Investment: $2 - $10 million
Minimum Investment: $1 million
Investment Criteria: Expansion, Small Buyout, Later Stage
Industry Group Preference: Healthcare, Manufacturing, Media, Food Services, Retailing, Entertainment, Clean Technology, Information Technology
Portfolio Companies: Arrive, Avid Ratings, Blis, Brideside, Complion, D30, Delphinus, DIME, dscout, Fiber By-Products, Floyd, Freeosk, Gas Station TV, Hygenica, InContext Solutions, Intervention Insights, InTouch Health, Popular Pays, Sharecare, UICO, Xanitos

Other Locations:
   39 Earlham Street
   Covent Garden
   London WC2H 9LT
   United Kingdom
   Phone: 44-02078457820

   WeWork
   1 St Peter's Square
   Manchester M2 3DE
   United Kingdom
   Phone: 44-01615048500

Key Executives:
   Charlie Rothstein, Founder/Senior Managing Director
   Education: BBA, MBA, University of Michigan
   Background: VP, Corporate Finance, JW Korth; European Gateway Acquisition Corp.
   Directorships: Mophie, Detroit Institute of Music Education, Sakti3
   Malcolm Moss, Founding Partner
   Education: BA, MBA, Business Studies, Kingston Buiness School, Kingston University
   Background: Planning Head, Baxter International/Uniroyal; Sr Strategist, Lloyds/TSB Group
   Directorships: ProVen VCT, Income VCT
   Michael Gross, Managing Director
   Education: BA, Finance, Michigan State University; CFA
   Background: VP, Investment Banking, P&M Corporate Finance; Stout Risius Ross
   Directorships: Molecular Imaging, D3O, Delphinus Medical Technologies, InTouch Health, Intervention Insights, Xanitos, Freeosk, Rethink, Fiber By-Products
   Harry Thomas, Principal
   Education: MA, History, University of St Andrews
   William Blake III, Vice President
   Education: BA, Finance, Stephen M. Ross School of Business, University Of Michigan
   Background: P&M Corporate Finance
   Directorships: Brideside, Complion, Avid Ratings, Fiber By-Products
   Stuart Veale, Managing Partner
   Background: Senior Director, Lloyds Development

Venture Capital & Private Equity Firms / Domestic Firms

Capital; 3i plc
Directorships: Contact Engine, DeepCrawl, Exonar, Firefly Learning, InSkin Media, ResponseTap

252 BERKELEY VC INTERNATIONAL LLC
PO Box 591748
San Francisco, CA 94159-1748

Phone: 415-249-0450
e-mail: info@berkeleyvc.com
web: www.berkeleyvc.com

Mission Statement: Berkeley VC International LLC is a venture capital firm that makes private placement investments into growing technology companies. The firm's investments typically serve as development capital for later-stage companies which are close to conducting alpha testing on their launch products.

Fund Size: $1 billion
Founded: 1977
Average Investment: $5 million - $50 million
Minimum Investment: $1 million
Investment Criteria: Second-stage, Late Stage
Industry Group Preference: Communications, Computer Related, Consumer Services, Distribution, Electronic Components, Industrial Equipment, Medical & Health Related
Portfolio Companies: Agility Communications Inc., Alacritech Inc., BeamReach Networks, BRECIS Communications Corporation, Catena Networks, Ceon Corporation, Fastchip Inc., KnowledgeNet Inc., LightChip Inc., LongBoard Inc., Mahi Networks Inc., Telera Inc., Triscend Corporation, Westwave Communications Inc., Xtera Communications
Key Executives:
Arthur Trueger, Founder/Chairman
Education: AB, MA, JD, University of California

253 BERKELEY VENTURES
727 Allston Way
Suite C
Berkeley, CA 94710

web: www.berkeleyventures.com

Mission Statement: Berkeley Ventures is an accelerator which helps serious entrepreneurs bring their innovations to the world. The firm is focused on helping startups in sectors including, but not limited to, internet, software, mobile, clean energy, and gaming. The firm offers access to mentors and advisors, introductions to investors, incubator space, connections to local talent/resources, and a year round program to help these companies grow.

Geographic Preference: California
Founded: 2009
Investment Criteria: All Stages
Industry Group Preference: Internet, Software, Mobile, Clean Energy, Gaming
Portfolio Companies: Blaze Mobile, BuySquare, CodeEval, FI Info Net, Power2Switch, Proxpur Labs, Virtual Labs, WAPIS
Key Executives:
Chris Doner, Founder/Executive Director
Background: Founder & CEO, Access Softek
Barak Berkowitz, Advisor
Background: Chairman/CEO, Six Apart; Apple; Logitech; Infoseek; Co-Founder, Omnisky
Jeff Braun, Advisor
Background: Founder & CEO, Maxis; SVP, North American Studios, Electronic Arts
Dean Frost, Advisor
Education: BA, University of California, Berkeley; MBA, Harvard Business School
Background: CEO, StockPower; Founder, Frost Capital Partners

Jonathan Morgan, Advisor
Background: Founder/Managing Partner, Rostrevor Partners; CEO, FirstVirtual Communications; Managing Director, Prudential Volpe Technology; Managing Director/Head of Investment Banking Operations, Sutro & Co.; M&A, Montgomery Securities
Rick Moss, Advisor
Education: Trinity College; MBA, Amos Tuck School, Dartmouth College
Background: Sun Microsystems; Oracle; Computer Sciences Corp.; Investment Banker, Salomon Brothers
Anthony Patek, Advisor
Education: BS, Philosophy & Biochemistry, University of Michigan; MS, Chemistry, Stanford University; JD, Boalt School of Law
Background: Cooley Godward
Joel Serface, Advisor
Education: BS, Chemical & Environmental Engineering, University of Texas, Austin; MBA, MIT Sloan School of Management
Background: Entrepreneur in Residence, Kleiner Perkins

254 BERKSHIRE PARTNERS LLC
200 Clarendon Street
35th Floor
Boston, MA 02116

Phone: 617-227-0050 **Fax:** 617-227-6105
web: www.berkshirepartners.com

Mission Statement: Private equity firm that strives to partner with management teams to increase the value of their businesses.

Geographic Preference: United States, Canada, Western Europe, Australia
Fund Size: $16 billion
Founded: 1986
Average Investment: $50 - $250 million
Minimum Investment: $20 million
Investment Criteria: LBO, Recapitalizations, Minority Investments, Privatizations Industry consolidations
Industry Group Preference: Consumer Products, Retailing, Business Products & Services, Transportation, Energy, Manufacturing, Communications
Portfolio Companies: Accela, Access, Advanced Drainage Systems, Affordable Care, Asurion, Consolidated Precision Products Corp., Curriculum Associations, Implus, Kendra Scott, Masergy, Parts Town, Portillo's, Precision Medicine Group, Protellindo, SRS Distribution, Teraco Data Environments, TransDigm, U.S. Anesthesia Partners, Vapor IO, Vi-Jon
Key Executives:
Samantha A. Adams, Managing Director
Education: AB, Harvard College; MBA, Harvard Business School
Background: SVP, Enterprise Brand Straegy, Bank of America; Hill Holliday Advertising; Discovery Health Channel; Bain & Co.
Michael C. Ascione, Managing Director
Education: BS, Boston College; MBA Harvard Business School
Background: Golman Sachs
Directorships: Advance Drainage Systems; Consolidated Precision Products Corp.; TransDigm
David C. Bordeau, Managing Director
Education: AB, Princeton University; MBA, Harvard Business School
Background: Ripplewood Holdings; Gleacher Partners
Directorships: Implus; SRS Distribution
Kenneth S. Bring, Managing Director & Chief Financial Officer
Education: BS, Duke University; M.Acc., University of North Carolina
Background: PrincewaterhouseCoopers
Kevin T. Callaghan, Managing Director
Education: BSE, Princeton University; MBA, Stanford

Venture Capital & Private Equity Firms / Domestic Firms

Grad. School of Business
Background: Lehman Brothers
Directorships: Implus; Kendra Scott; Parts Town
Blake L. Gottesman, Managing Director
Education: MBA, Harvard Business School
Background: Deputy Chief of Staff at the White House; Special Assistant and Personal Aide to former U.S. President George W. Bush
Directorships: Consolidated Precision Products Corp.; Portillo's; Protelindo; Curriculum Associates; Vi-Jon
Christopher J. Hadley, Managing Director
Education: BS, University of Wisconsin; MBA, Wharton School, University of Pennsylvania
Background: Bain & Co.; Trustee, Dana-Farber Cancer Institute
Lawrence S. Hamelsky, Managing Director
Education: AB, Duke University; MBA, Harvard Business School
Background: Boston Consulting Group; Financial Analyst, Bowles, Hollowell, Conner & Co.
Directorships: Parts Town; Teraco Data Environment
Sharlyn C. Heslam, Managing Director & General Counsel
Education: BA, Cornell University; JD, Harvard Law School
Background: Weil, Gotshal & Manges LLP
Directorships: Vi-Jon
Beth Hoffman, Managing Director
Education: BA, Macalester College; MBA, Kellogg School of Management, Northwestern University
Background: Sprout Group; Morgan Stanley
Directorships: Masergy; Protelindo; Vapor IO
Matthew A. Janchar, Managing Director
Education: BBA, University of Notre Dame
Background: Oak Hill Advisors; Goldman Sachs
Ross M. Jones, Managing Director
Education: BA, Dartmouth College; MBA, Stanford Grad. School of Business
Background: Bain & Co.
Directorships: Access; Advanced Drainage Systems; Asurion
Thomas Y. Kuo, Managing Director
Education: AB, Harvard College; MBA, Stanford Grad. School of Business
Background: General Atlantic; Goldman Sachs
Directorships: Accela; Masergy; TransDigm
Joshua A. Lutzker, Managing Director
Education: AB, Duke University; MBA, Harvard Business School
Background: Bain & Co.
Directorships: Portillo's; SRS Distribution
Greg J. Pappas, Managing Director
Education: BS, Lehigh University; MBA, Harvard Business School
Background: Senior Partner, The Parthenon Group; M&A Advisor, Deloitte
Directorships: Accela; U.S. Anesthesia Partners; Implus; SRS Distribution
Marni F. Payne, Managing Director
Education: BA, Dartmouth College; MBA, Harvard Business School
Background: McKinsey & Co.
Directorships: Kendra Scott
Raleigh A. Shoemaker, Jr., Managing Director
Education: AB, Duke University; MBA, Harvard Business School
Background: Sterling Capital Management; Audax Group; Bain & Co.; Bowels, Hollowellm Conner & Co.
Robert J. Small, Managing Director
Education: BA, Yale University; MBA, Harvard Business School
Background: Bain & Co.
Directorships: TransDigm; Active Aero Group; AmSafe; Citizens of Humanity; Cypress; Electro-Motive Diesel; Gordon Brothers; Hexcel; Party City; Skillsoft; Tranz Rail; WordWave
Samuel W. Spirn, Managing Director
Education: AB, Harvard College; MBA, Harvard Business School
Background: Summit Partners
Directorships: U.S. Anesthesia Partners; Parts Town; Farm Boy; Grocery Outlet; Mattress Firm; Tower Development Corporation
Edward J. Whelan, Managing Director
Education: BA, Dartmouth College; MBA, Harvard Business School
Background: Sterling Auto Boduy Centers; Bain & Co.
Directorships: Accela; Access; Curriculum Associations; AmSafe; Mattress Firm; Melissa & Doug; Party City; Skillsoft
Tim Heston, Partner
Education: BS, Finance, Boston College; MBA, HAAS School of Business
Background: Calera Capital; JP Morgan; Carl Marks & Co.
Directorships: Anord Mardix Group; Perennials and Sutherland

256 BERTELSMANN DIGITAL MEDIA INVESTMENTS
1745 Broadway
20th Floor
New York, NY 10019

e-mail: info@bdmifund.com
web: www.bdmifund.com

Mission Statement: Drawing upon the vast resources of Bertelsmann SE & Co. KGaA, BDMI is a strategic investor that brings a wealth of experience and opportunities to emerging companies. BDMI provides not only capital, but also a worldwide network of diverse businesses. The firm's goal is to partner with companies that can benefit from their innovative spirit and media leadership across the globe. BDMI is a wholly owned subsidiary of Bertelsmann SE & Co. KGaA.

Geographic Preference: Europe, North America, Israel
Fund Size: $180 million
Founded: 2006
Average Investment: $1 - $5 million
Minimum Investment: $500,000
Investment Criteria: Series A & B
Industry Group Preference: Digital Media & Marketing, Virtual Reality & Augmented Reality, Pub Tech, E-Commerce, Gaming, AD Tech
Portfolio Companies: 89, Adspert, Art19, The Athletic, Audible, Boostr, Fatherly, FloSports, Frank & Oak, Inked, Jukin Media, Marfeel, Nativo, Omaze, Pathmatics, Semasio, Skimlinks, Whisbi, Wibbitz, Wondery, ZergNet

Key Executives:
Urs Cete, Managing Partner
Education: Finance Degree, HHL Leipzig Graduate School of Management; MBA, Tulane University
Background: Chief of Staff, Bertelsmann
Keith Titan, Partner
Education: BA, English, University of Michigan; EdM, Harvard University; MBA, Rutgers University
Background: Random House Ventures; Simon & Schuster; Penguin Group; J. Walter Thompson
Directorships: Trion Worlds, Art19
Sim Blaustein, Partner
Education: MBA, MIT Sloan School of Management
Background: High Line Venture Partners; Gabriel Ventures

Venture Capital & Private Equity Firms / Domestic Firms

257 BERTRAM CAPITAL
950 Tower Lane
Suite 1000
Foster City, CA 94404
Phone: 650-358-5000 Fax: 650-358-5001
web: www.bertramcapital.com

Mission Statement: Private equity firm in Northern California targets lower middle market companies.
Fund Size: $1.3 billion
Average Investment: $25-100 million
Investment Criteria: MBO, Liquidity Events
Industry Group Preference: Business Products & Services, Consumer Products, Consumer Services, Industrial, Healthcare, Technology
Portfolio Companies: Anord Mardix, Bearcom, Best Version Media, Clarus Glassboards, CreativeDrive, ECS Tuning, Flow Control Group, Maxcress, PaulaBs Choice, Perennials and Sutherland LLC, Registrar Corp., Rowmark, Solo Stove, Spectrio, Spireon, Trademark Global, TydenBrooks, Author Solutions, Datavail, Extrusion Dies Industries, One Distribution, Power Distribution
Key Executives:
 Jeff Drazan, Managing Partner
 e-mail: jeff@bertramcapital.com
 Education: New York University; MBA, Stern School of Business
 Background: Co-Founder/Managing Director, Sierra Ventures
 Directorships: Spireon, One Distribution, Sanare, Webex, Paula's Choice
 Tom Beerle, Partner
 Education: University of California, Berkeley; HAAS School of Business
 Background: Opus Capital; Carl Zeiss Vision; Deloitte Consulting; Deloitte Audit
 Directorships: ECS Tuning; Registrar; Trademark Global
 Ryan Craig, Partner
 e-mail: rcraig@bertramcapital.com
 Education: BA, Stanford University; MBA, Stanford Graduate School of Business
 Background: Health Net
 David Hellier, Partner
 e-mail: dhellier@bertramcapital.com
 Education: BS, Business Administration, MA, Economics, University of Florida
 Background: President & CEO, The Gemesis Corporation; Iomega
 Jared Ruger, Partner
 e-mail: jruger@bertramcapital.com
 Education: BA, Princeton University; MBA, Stanford Graduate School of Business
 Background: Oak Hill Capital Management; Investment Banking Group, DLJ
 Brian Wheeler, Partner, Head of Bertram Labs
 e-mail: bwheeler@bertramcapital.com
 Education: BA, Chemistry, Pomona College
 Kevin Yamashita, Partner
 e-mail: kyamashita@bertramcapital.com
 Education: BS, UCLA
 Background: Calera Capital, Salomon Smith Barney

258 BERWIND CORPORATION
2929 Walnut Street
Suite 900
Philadelphia, PA 19104
Phone: 215-563-2800 Fax: 215-575-2314
e-mail: information@berwind.com
web: www.berwind.com

Mission Statement: Berwind Corporation is a family-owned investment management company that provides financial and operational support to manufacturing and service businesses.
Founded: 1886
Investment Criteria: Acquisitions
Portfolio Companies: Caplugs, Colorcon, CRC Industries Inc., Ecco Safety Group, Maxcess, Oliver Products, Tasi Group
Key Executives:
 Charles Lewis, Vice President
 e-mail: clewis@berwind.com
 Education: BS, Electrical Engineering, MBA, Business, Drexel University
 Background: VP, Corporate Development, Exelon

259 BERWIND PRIVATE EQUITY
200 Ayer Rd
Harvard, MA 01451
Phone: 978-391-1244 Fax: 978-391-1255
e-mail: info@berwindprivateequity.com
web: www.berwindprivateequity.com

Mission Statement: Berwind Private Equity is a multi-generational company that identifies investment opportunities for the Berwind family.
Portfolio Companies: Boston Color Graphics, Coolerado, Free Flow Power, MacDougalls' Cape Code Marine Service, PRE Resources, Southwest Nanotechnologies, Tantaline, ThermImage, MacuLogix

260 BESSEMER VENTURE PARTNERS
1865 Palmer Avenue
Suite 104
Larchmont, NY 10538
Phone: 914-833-5300 Fax: 914-833-5499
e-mail: businessplans@bvp.com
web: www.bvp.com

Mission Statement: Invests in and helps build innovative, high-growth companies. Primary focus is investing in companies in the start-up or development phases. Plays an active role in partnering with entrepreneurs to build companies that dominate their sectors. Interested in working with exceptional people and experienced management teams who have a strong business model, growing market, defensible technology and industry leadership position.
Geographic Preference: United States, Israel, India, Brazil, Europe, Emerging Markets
Fund Size: $300 million
Founded: 1970
Average Investment: $4 - $10 million
Minimum Investment: $1 million
Investment Criteria: Seed, First-stage, Second-stage, Mezzanine, Late stage, MBI, MBO, LBO, Expansion
Industry Group Preference: Cloud Computing, Consumer, Cyber Security, Developer Platforms, Financial Services, Healthcare, Industry Software, Infrastructure, Marketplaces, Mobile, Space Technology
Portfolio Companies: 2U, 42 Floors, Abacus, Acceleron Pharma, AccuVein, ACTIV Financial Systems, Adap.Tv, ART, Affymax, Allena Pharmaceuticals, Allscripts, Alnara Pharmaceuticals, Altair Semiconductor, Altiga, American Federal Bank, American Superconductor, Anant Raj, Apperian, Applied Solar Technologies, Aptis, Arris Pharmaceutical, Avalanche Technology, AVEO Pharmaceuticals, Avnera, Axis Network Technology, Babycenter, Berkeley Design Automation, Betterment, BigBasket, BillGuard, Bizo, Bladelogic, Blue Nile, Box, Bright Horizons, Broadsoft, Businessland, BuyerZone, C-Port, Car Wash Partners, Castle Networks, Celcore, CellAccess, Celtel, Cerulean Pharma, ChinaEdu, Chrysalis, Ciena, Circadian, Clearslide, Community First, Compumotor, Convertro, Cornerstone OnDemand, Counterpane Internet Security, CPower, Criteo, CrowdFlower, Cyota, Dashlane, Diapers.com, Dick's Sporting Goods, DocuSign, DSP Group, Eagle, Echelon, eEye Digital Security, EKOS, Element14, Eloqua, Endeca, Enforta, Enzytech, Epic Therapeutics, Epix, eToys.com, Fiverr, Flarion, Flex Pharma, Flycast, FourPhase Systems, Fractyl, Ganesh Housing, Gartner, Gerson Lehrman

Venture Capital & Private Equity Firms / Domestic Firms

Group, GetInsured.com, Glint, GMIS, Goal.com, Gracenote, GTS, Habana Labs, Harman International, Health Essentials, HFFC, Horizon Cellular Group, HotJobs.com, Hunch, IAG Research, Icot, IL&FS, Immulogic, Impact HQ, Ibpil, IEX, Individual.com, Insight Squared, Intacct, Intego, Intersil, Intucell, Involver, IPC, Iris, Fort James, K2, Kilkenny, Keynote, Kiran Energy, KnowMe,

Other Locations:
196 Broadway
2nd Floor
Cambridge, MA 02139
Phone: 617-588-1700 **Fax:** 617-588-1701

285 Madison Avenue
Suite 1401
New York, NY 10017
Phone: 212-653-1900

889 Winslow Street
Suite 500
Redwood City, CA 94062
Phone: 650-853-7000

539 Bryant Street
Suite 301
San Francisco, CA 94107
Phone: 415-800-8982

40 Vittal Mallya Road
3rd Floor
Bangalore 560 001
India
Phone: 91-80-3082-9000 **Fax:** 91-80-3082-9001

Key Executives:
Ed Colloton, Partner
Education: BA, Cornell University; JD, Harvard Law School
Background: COO, JP Morgan Capital; Mergers/Acquisitions Lawyer, Davis Polk & Wardwell; Officer, US Navy
Kent Bennett, Partner
Education: University of Virginia; Harvard Business School
Background: Bain & Co.
Charles Birnbaum, Partner
Education: BA, Northwestern University; MA, University of Pennsylvania; MBA, The Wharton School
Background: Foursquare
Directorships: 2U, August Home, Betterment, Bread Finance, BrightBytes, Eave, Fabric, Kroll Bond Ratings, Main Street Hub, Quantopian, Spruce, United Capital, Yodle, Zopa
David Cowan, Partner
Education: MBA, AB, Computer Science/Mathematics, Harvard University
Background: Co-Founder/Chairman/CFO, VeriSign
Directorships: Rocket Lab, Spire, GetInsured, Smule, Endgame, Claroty, Tile, Iris Automation, Auth0, Zapier
Byron Deeter, Partner
Education: Honors degree Political Economy, University of California, Berkeley
Background: Executive, IBM; Founding President/CEO, Trigo Technologies; TA Associates; McKinsey & Company
Brian Feinstein, Partner
Education: Harvard University
Background: Opera New Media; Blackstone
Alex Ferrara, Partner
Education: University of Pennsylvania; Columbia Business School
Background: Salomon Brothers; Goldman Sachs
Adam Fisher, Partner
Education: BSFS, International Economics, Georgetown University School of Foreign Service
Background: General Partner, Jerusalem Venture Partners
Directorships: Cloudinary, CTERA, Dynamic Yield,

Fiverr, Habana Labs, HiBob, MyHeritage, Oryx, Prospera, ScyllaDB, Stratoscale, SiSense, Vayyer, Wandera, YotPo
Bob Goodman, Partner
Education: BA, Brown University; MBA, Columbia University
Background: Founder & CEO, Celcore; Founder & Celcore, Boatphone
Directorships: Affirmed Networks, Anaqua, Blue Apron, Capsule8, Disco, Fuze, Light, MealPal, Qwilt, Sedona Systems, Sisense, Smashfly, Vayyar
Vishal Gupta, Managing Director, BVP India
Education: BA, Commerce, GS College; MBA, Indian Institute of Management
Background: Senior Manager, Reliance Group
Directorships: Anunta Technologies, Applied Solar Technologies, Bigbasket, Home First Finance, Hungama, Innoviti, LivSpace, MediAssist, NephroPlus, Perifos, Pharmeasy, Swiggy, Urbanclap
Felda Hardymon, Partner
Education: BS, Rose Polytechnic; MA and PhD, Duke University; MBA, Harvard
Background: Investor, Ungermann-Bass, Stratus Computer and Western Digital; Taught and served as Director Systems/Research, Duke University
Amit Karp, Partner
Education: BS, Technion; MBA, MIT Sloan School of Management
Background: Senior Associate, McKinsey & Company; Product Leader, Mercado
Directorships: Dynamic Yield, HiBob, Oryx Vision, otonomo, Prospera, ScyllaDB
Stephen Kraus, Partner
Education: BA, Yale University; MBA, Harvard Business School
Background: Director, Ironwood Equity Fund
Directorships: Alcresta, Bright Health, Collective Medical Technologies, Docent Health, Health Essentials, Groups, Qventus, Welltok
Rob Stavis, Partner
Education: Engineering School of University of Pennsylvania; Wharton School
Background: Co-Head, Global Arbitrage Trading, Salomon Smith Barney
Directorships: 2U, Betterment, BrightBytes, Knewton, Gerson Lehrman Group, Main Street Hubs, United Capital Financial Partners, Yodle
Ethan Kurzweil, Partner
Education: Stanford University; Harvard Business School
Background: Dow Jones & Co.
Jeremy Levine, Partner
Education: Duke University
Background: McKinsey & Co.; AEA Investors; Dash

261 BEVERAGE MARKETING CORPORATION
143 Canton Road
2nd Floor
Wintersville, OH 43953
Phone: 212-688-7640 **Fax:** 740-314-8639
e-mail: advisors@beveragemarketing.com
web: www.beveragemarketing.com

Mission Statement: BMC Advisors provides advisory services to middle-market beverage companies around the world. BMC Advisors specializes in a number of areas, including equity funding and asset sales and acquisitions.
Geographic Preference: United States, Latin America, Europe, Asia
Founded: 1972
Investment Criteria: Middle Market
Industry Group Preference: Beverages
Key Executives:
Michael C Bellas, Chairman/Chief Executive Officer
Education: Yale University; JD, University of Michigan; MBA, Columbia University
Background: Co-Founder, The Beverage Forum; Staff

Venture Capital & Private Equity Firms / Domestic Firms

Consultant & Project Manager, Cresap McCormick & Paget

262 BEZOS EXPEDITIONS
e-mail: info@bezosexpeditions.com
web: www.bezosexpeditions.com

Mission Statement: Manages Jeff Bezos' personal venture capital investments.

Investment Criteria: Seed, Early Stage, Late Stage
Industry Group Preference: Biotechnology, Clean Technology, Business Products & Services, Computers & Peripherals, Consumer Products, Education, Electronics, Financial Services, Food & Beverage, Gaming, Healthcare Services, Industrial, Internet/Web Services, IT Services, Lifestyle & Recreation
Portfolio Companies: 37 Signals, Airbnb, Aviary, Basecamp, Blue Origin, Business Insider, Chacha, Convoy, Denali Therapeutics, Domo, Doxo, D-Wave, Everfi, Fundbox, General Assembly, General Fusion, Glassybaby, Grail, Juno Therapeutics, Linden Lab, Makerbot, Mark43, MFG.com, Nextdoor, Plenty, Pioneer Square Labs, Qliance, Remitly, Rescale, Rethink Robotics, Sapphire Energy, Sonder, Stack Overflow, Twitter, Uber, Vicarious, Workday, ZocDoc

263 BIA DIGITAL PARTNERS LP
14150 Parkeast Circle
Suite 110
Chantilly, VA 20151

Phone: 703-227-9600
e-mail: contactdp@bia.com
web: www.biadigitalpartners.com

Mission Statement: A private equity firm providing flexible, cost-effective junior capital to growing middle market companies in the media, telecommunications, entertainment, and information services sectors.

Fund Size: $283 Million
Average Investment: $5-15 Million
Minimum Investment: $3-6 Million
Investment Criteria: Mezzanine
Industry Group Preference: Media, Telecommunications, Entertainment, Information Services, Business Products & Services, Education
Portfolio Companies: Ariston Global, Cash Cycle Solutions, Cooking.com, DigitalBridge Communications, Eli Research, EyeWonder, Global Telecom & Technology, Hibernia Atlantic, Hoffman Media, Manifest Digital, Market Tech Media Corporation, The Motley Food, Total Attorneys, Trio Video, United Metro Media, Vantage Media, Willamette Broadband

Key Executives:
Thomas J. Buono, Principal
e-mail: tbuono@bia.com
Education: BS, Applied Mathematics, Clarkson University; MBA, Tuck School of Business, Darmouth College
Background: BIA Financial Network; BIA Consulting; BIA Research; BIA Capital Corp.
Gregg E. Johnson, Managing Principal
e-mail: gjohnson@bia.com
Education: BS, Commerce, University of Virginia; MBA, University of Rochester
Background: Division Manager of Communications Lending, American Security Bank; Chase Lincoln First Bank
Charles A. Wiebe, Principal
e-mail: cwiebe@bia.com
Education: BA, Comparative Literature and History, Cornell University
Background: VP, Mellon Bank; VP, American Security Bank
Scott E. Chappell, Principal
e-mail: schappell@bia.com
Education: BS, Business Administration, University of Georgia; MBA, Fuqua School of Business, Duke University
Background: Media and Telecommunications Corporate Financial Team, Thomas Weisel Partners; Investment Banker, First Union Securities
Damien A. Dovi, Vice President
Education: BS, Ithaca College
Background: Danc of America Securities
Directorships: Cooking.com; Total Attorneys; Cross MediaWorks; Eyewonder; Hibernia Atlantic; Manifest Digital; The Motley Fool
Lloyd R. Sams, Managing Principal
e-mail: lsams@bia.com
Education: BS, Business Administration, Washington and Lee University; MBA, University of North Carolina
Background: First Union; First Chicago

264 BILTMORE VENTURES
1825 West Knudsen
Unit B-100
Phoenix, AZ 85027

Phone: 480-510-5550
web: www.biltmoreventures.com

Mission Statement: Biltmore Ventures works with talented entrepreneurs to build great companies. The firm invests during the early development stage with the following business goals: create rapid growth through access to capital, expertise, and relationships; build long-term sustainable value; provide substantial returns to entrepreneurs, employees and investors, most often through subsequent merger or acquisition; and lead investment rounds involving other firms, funds, or partners.

Average Investment: $10 million
Investment Criteria: Early-Stage
Industry Group Preference: Internet
Portfolio Companies: My Job Chart, GolfNow, Lifelock, American Legal Fund, Investar, Insymphony, Airpower Insurance, Mytrade, Adaptive Blue

Key Executives:
Adam Bruss, Managing Partner
Education: Art Center College of Design
Background: Founder/President, GD MAC

265 BINARY CAPITAL
1550 Bryant Street
Suite 700
San Francisco, CA 94103

e-mail: info@binarycap.com

Fund Size: $300 million
Founded: 2014
Investment Criteria: Early-Stage
Portfolio Companies: Twitter, Instagram, Snapchat

266 BIOADVANCE
3711 Market Street
8th Floor
Philadelphia, PA 19104

Phone: 610-230-0544
web: www.bioadvance.com

Mission Statement: Investing in emerging life sciences technologies with the most promising commercialization prospects.

Geographic Preference: Southeastern Pennsylvania
Fund Size: $20 million
Founded: 2002
Investment Criteria: Pre-Seed, Seed-Stage
Industry Group Preference: Therapeutics, Medical Devices, Research Tools, Diagnostics, Health IT
Portfolio Companies: Allevi, Bainbridge Health, BioDetego, CarePartners Plus, Cohero Health, Cytovas, Eagle Vision Pharmaceuticals, Enzium, GenPro Profiling, Group K Diagnostics, Halo Labs, Hsiri Therapeutics, Imiplex,

Venture Capital & Private Equity Firms / Domestic Firms

Immunome, InfraScan, Innovative Supply Solutions, Intezyne, iView Therapeutics, Jenrin Discovery, Keriton, Mebias Discovery, Melior Discovery, Midway Pharmaceuticals, Olive Devices, Oncora Medical, The One Health Company, Opsidio, Ossianix, Palvella Therapeutics, PeriRx, Phoenix S&T, Pillo, QR Pharma, Relmada RiboNova, Ride Health, TalexMedical, TowerView Health, Treventis Corp., VenatoRx, WellSheet, WellTrackOne

Key Executives:
Barbara Schilberg, Managing Director and CEO
Education: JD, University of Virginia
Background: Incara Pharmaceuticals; VP/General Counsel, Locus Discovery, Inc.; Morgan, Lewis & Brockius
Shahram Hejazi, Partner
Education: PhD, Engineering, Stanford University
Background: President, Kodak Life Science Division; CEO, Zargis Medical Corporation
Gregory Harriman, Venture Partner
e-mail: gharriman@bioadvance.com
Education: University of California, Berkeley; MD, University of California, San Diego
Background: Founder, Main Line Ventures; Member, Robin Hood Ventures
Rick Jones, Partner
Education: BA, MD, MBA, Univ. of Pennsylvania
Background: Anchor Therapeutics

267 BIOGENERATOR
20 South Sarah St
St. Louis, MO 63108

Phone: 314-615-6355
e-mail: info@biogenerator.org
web: biogenerator.org

Mission Statement: BioGenerator's mission is to support bioscience in St. Louis.

Geographic Preference: St. Louis Region
Founded: 2003
Average Investment: Pre-Seed: $10K - $50K; Seed: $50K - $250K
Minimum Investment: $10,000
Investment Criteria: Seed-Stage, Early-Stage
Industry Group Preference: Therapeutics, Agriculture, Research Tools, Healthcare Services, Healthcare IT, Animal Health, Nutrition, Diagnostics, Research Services, Medical Devices
Portfolio Companies: Accuronix, Adarza, RNAgri, Arch Innotek, Arvegenix, Atomation, BacterioScan, Benson Hill Biosystems, Canopy Biosciences, Cardialen, Cofactor Genomics, Daya CNS, Edison Agrosciences, Electrochaea, Elira Therapeutics, EPharmix, Euclises, Galera Therapeutics, GeneriCo, Graematter, Immuno Photonics, Indalo Therapeutics, Katalyst Surgical, Kogent Surgical, Kypha, Medaware Solutions, MediBeacon, MedSocket, Mobius Therapeutics, Nanopore Diagnostics, NeuroLutions, Nitrogenics, Plastomics, PM Diagnostics, Pulse Therapeutics, S4 Agtech, Sentiar, Tioma Therapeutics, Unleash Immuno Oncolytics, YourBevCo

Key Executives:
Eric Gulve PhD, President
Education: BA, Chemistry, Occidental College; PhD, Physiology, Harvard University
Background: Cardiovascular Research, Pfizer; Associate Director, Cardiovascular & Metabolic Diseases, Pharmacia Corporation
Dan Broderick, Vice President
Education: BS, Biology, Iowa State University
Background: Prolog Ventures, Mason Wells Biomedical Fund
Edward Hamati, Director
Education: BS, Cellular Biology, University of California, Davis; MBA, California State University
Background: The Chi Rho Group, The Broadband Group

Charlie Bolten, Vice President
Education: University of Missouri, St. Louis
Background: Principal Scientist & Project Leader, Pfizer Exploratory Immunobiology
Directorships: Vasculox

268 BIOMATICS CAPITAL
719 2nd Avenue
Suite 1402
Seattle, WA 98104

e-mail: info@biomaticscapital.com
web: www.biomaticscapital.com

Mission Statement: A for-profit venture firm investing in companies that focus on healthcare technology.

Geographic Preference: United States
Fund Size: $200 Million
Founded: 2016
Minimum Investment: $5-10 Million
Investment Criteria: Series A
Industry Group Preference: Healthcare Technology
Portfolio Companies: AiCure, Aledade, BlackThorn Therapeutics, BlueTalon, Compass Therapeutics, Cytrellis, Denali Therapeutics, eGenesis Bio, Encodia, GRAIL, Omniome, Twist Bioscience, Verana Health

Key Executives:
Dr. Boris Nikolic, Managing Director
Education: MD, University of Zagreb School of Medicine; PhD, Transplantation Immunology, Harvard Medical School
Background: Assistant Professor of Medicine, Massachusetts General Hospital/Harvard Medical School; Chief Advisor For Science And Technology, Bill Gates
Julie Sunderland, Managing Director
Education: BA, Harvard University; MBA, Wharton Business School; MA, Johns Hopkins School of Advanced International Studies
Background: Bill & Melinda Gates Foundation
Liz Birch, Investment Associate
Education: BA, Keble College; DPhil, University of Oxford
Background: Consultant in Life Sciences, L.E.K. Consulting
Yeon Cramer, Business Operations Manager
Background: bgC3; Research Assistant, Farallon Capital

269 BIOSTAR VENTURES
560 W Mitchell Street
Suite 500
Petoskey, MI 49770

Phone: 231-487-9186 Fax: 231-487-9183
e-mail: info@biostarventures.com
web: www.biostarventures.com

Mission Statement: BioStar Ventures invests in companies their key focus of cardiovascular, orthopedic and neuroscience areas.

Fund Size: $68.8 million
Founded: 2005
Average Investment: $2 - $6 million
Investment Criteria: Seed-Stage, Early-Stage
Industry Group Preference: Medical Devices, Medical Technology
Portfolio Companies: Ablative Solutions, Inc., Angioslide, Aria CV Inc., Autonomix Medical Inc., Avantis Medical Systems, CathWorks Ltd., Cibiem Inc., Conventus Orthopaedics Inc., Corindus Vascular Robotics Inc., Foldax Inc., Kona Medical Inc., MiCardia Corp., NewPace Ltd., OmniGuide Inc., Ortho-Space Ltd., SynergEyes Inc., TransMedic, Trice Medical Inc., TriVentures II Fund; V-Wave Ltd., VytronUS Inc., AorTx Inc., Atritech Inc., Bioabsorable Therapeutics Inc., Broncus Technologies, CD Diagnostics Inc., CV Ingenuity Corp., Devax Inc., Doman Surgical Inc., Ellipse Technologies Inc., Embrella Cardiovascular Inc.,

100

Hotspir Technologies Inc., Interventional Spine Inc., Nellix Endovascular Inc., Onset Medical Corp., ReVascular Therapeutics Inc., Reverse Medical Corp., Setagon Inc.

Key Executives:
Louis Cannon, MD, Founder/Senior Managing Director
Background: President, Cardiac & Vascular Research Center of Northern Michigan
Directorships: Medtronic, Abbott, Boston Scientific, HotSpur, CardioVascular Ingenuity, TransLuminal Therapeutics, Nellix
Renee Masi, Managing Director
Education: BA, Stanford University; MBA, Wharton School
Background: Partner, Windward Ventures; Advisor, Ventures Medical
Directorships: SynergEyes, Axis Surgical, CardiacMD, Embrella Cardiovascular
Steven L. Almany, MD, Managing Director
Background: Director of Cardiac Cath Lab, William Beaumont Hospital; Partner, Michigan Heart Group
Paul A. Scott, Managing Director/Chief Financial Officer
Education: BA, Ithaca College; MBA, Loyola University of Chicago
Background: CFO/Administrative Partner, Windward Ventures; President/CEO, VSI Enterprises Inc.
Directorships: AdvancedMD
William H. Kucheman, Director
Education: BS, Virgina Polytechnic Institute; MBA, Virginia State University
Background: Senior Advisor, Global Health Exchange; CEO, Boston Scientific

270 BIOVENTURES INVESTORS
70 Walnut Street
Suite 302
Wellesley, MA 02481

Phone: 617-252-3443 **Fax:** 617-621-7993
e-mail: info@bioventuresinvestors.com
web: www.bioventuresinvestors.com

Mission Statement: BioVentures invests in companies commercializing breakthrough life science and healthcare technology with clear application, a strong proprietary position and a well-understood development pathway. Seeks opportunities with a defined 'entrepreneurial advantage' that will enable a new venture to prevail in an extremely competitive environment.

Geographic Preference: Eastern Massachusetts
Fund Size: $133 million
Average Investment: $3 - $7 million
Investment Criteria: Life-Science Technology
Industry Group Preference: Life Sciences, Healthcare, Human Therapeutics, Medical Devices, Diagnostics, Healthcare Information Technology
Portfolio Companies: Cardiosolutions, CoNextions, Deep Vein Medical Inc., Endotronix, HydroCision, Locemia, POC Medical Systems Inc., Orachiotek, Verax BioMedical

Key Executives:
Peter Feinstein, Co-Founder/Venture Partner
Education: BA, English Literature, New York University
Background: Feinstein Kean Healthcare; Co-Founder, Massachusetts Biotechnology Council; Financial Journalist, University Film Study Center, MIT
Directorships: BioValve Technologies, Inc., HospitalCare Online, Inc.
Walter Gilbert, PhD, Venture Partner
Education: AB, Chemistry & Physics, Harvard College; MA, Physics, Harvard University; PhD, Mathematics, Cambridge University
Background: Co-Founder, Biogen; Co-Founder, Myriad Genetics; Co-Founder, Paratek Pharmaceuticals; Co-Founder, Memory Pharmaceuticals; Co-Founder, Pintex Pharmaceuticals; Director, Transkaryotic Therapies

Marc Goldberg, Co-Founder/Managing Partner
Education: AB, Harvard College; MBA, Harvard Business School; JD, Harvard Law School
Background: President/CEO, Massachusetts Biotechnology Research Institute; Safer, Inc.; Manager of Business Development, Genetics Institute, Inc.; Co-Founder, Massachusetts Biotechnology Council
Jeffrey Barnes, Managing Director
Education: BS, Physiology & Biophysics, MS, Biomedical Engineering, Duke University; MS, Management, Stanford University
Background: Managing Partner, Oxford Bioscience Partners

271 BIP CAPITAL
Piedmont Center
3575 Piedmont Road
Building 15, 7th Floor, Suite 730
Atlanta, GA 30305

Phone: 404-495-5230 **Fax:** 404-495-5239
Toll-Free: 866-435-8877
web: bip-capital.com

Mission Statement: Atlanta-based investors in the Southeastern U.S.

Geographic Preference: Southeastern U.S.
Average Investment: $2-5 million
Investment Criteria: Growth Capital, Add On Acquisition, Partial Shareholder Liquidity
Industry Group Preference: Technology, SaaS, Business Products & Services, Franchising, Healthcare, Specialty Finance
Portfolio Companies: AchieveIt, Aspirion, Crescerance, Huddle, Ingenious Med, Inked, Ipreo, M Level, PlayOn! Sports, QASymphony, ReachHealth, Tin Drum Asian Kitchen, Tropical Smoothie Cafe

Key Executives:
Mark Buffington, Co-Founder and CEO
e-mail: mbuffington@bipfund.com
Education: Georgia Institute of Technology; MBA, Tulane University
Background: Founder, Buckhead Investment Partners; Peachtree Financial Management, Phoenix Capital
Scott Pressly, Co-Founder and Managing Director
e-mail: spressly@bipfund.com
Education: BS, Chemical Engineering, University of Florida; MBA, Harvard Business School
Background: Partner, Roark Capital Group; US Franchise Systems
Paul Iaffaldano, Managing Director

272 BIRCHMERE VENTURES
2000 Smallman Street
Suite 201
Pittsburgh, PA 15222

web: www.birchmerevc.com

Mission Statement: Focus on early-stage, IP-differentiated companies creating Engineering Driven Innovation. Specialize in being the first institutional investor in cleantech, medical and technology start-ups.

Geographic Preference: Mid-Atlantic Region
Fund Size: $250 million
Founded: 1996
Minimum Investment: $500,000
Investment Criteria: Start-Up, Early Stage
Industry Group Preference: Technology, Drug Development, Clean Technology, Medical Devices, Advanced Materials, Mobile, SaaS, Semiconductors, Social Media
Portfolio Companies: Admiral, BloomBoard, ContainerShip, Crystal, Cvent, Eargo, Earshot, Encentivenergy, Estimote, FreeMarkets, Gem, GradeSlam, Healthie, Idelic, Identified Technologies, Ikos, Jazz, Joany, Legal Sifter, Mapper, Modsy, Mom Trusted, Mona, Mosss, Neolinear, Nowait, One Kloud,

Venture Capital & Private Equity Firms / Domestic Firms

Peloton, Presence Learning, Senic, Sleeperbot, Spidr Tech, SubCenter.io, Ten Marks, Treatspace, Umano, Yaypay, The Zebra

Other Locations:
701 Minnesota Street
Unit 113
San Francisco, CA 94107

Key Executives:
Sean Sebastian, Partner
e-mail: sean@birchmerevc.com
Education: BS, Mechanical Engineering, Worcester Polytechnic Institute; MBA, Rensselaer Polytechnic Institute
Background: Assistant VP, Corporate Finance Group, PNC Bank; Founder/CEO, The Telford Group; International Systems Services; General Electric Information Services; American Management Systems; US Air Force; President, Pittsburgh Venture Capital Association
Directorships: CyOptics, Precision Therapeutics
Ned J Renzi, Partner
e-mail: ned@birchmerevc.com
Education: BS, Electrical Engineering, Pennsylvania State University; MBA, Katz Graduate School of Business at the University of Pittsburgh; MA, Engineering Management, George Washington University
Background: Manager, Information Transfer Technology, Concurrent Technologies Corporation; Sr Manager, US Department of Defense Special Projects Group
Directorships: Cvent, Plextronics, Solexant
Sean Ammirati, Partner
e-mail: sean@birchmerelabs.com
Education: BS, Computer Information Systems, Grove City College
Background: Partner, Birchmere Labs; Adjunct Professor of Entrepreneurship, Carnegie Mellon University's Tepper School

273 BIRD DOG EQUITY PARTNERS
221 South Phillips Avenue
#202
Sioux Falls, SD 57104
Phone: 605-310-2923 **Fax:** 605-357-5303

Mission Statement: As a private equity firm, we invest in companies with big dreams. We look for entrepreneurs throughout the Midwest with strong cash flow, experienced management, and an eye for growth. Formerly known as Nordic Venture Partners.

Geographic Preference: Midwest United States

Key Executives:
Chad Hatch, Managing Partner
Background: CFO, Destination Golf Ventures; Managing Partner, Sweet Deals; SVP, Strategic Capital, POET
Paul Schock, Managing Partner
Background: Founding Partner, Bluestem Capital Company; Chairman, Destination Golf Ventures

274 BISON CAPITAL ASSET MANAGEMENT LLC
233 Wilshire Boulevard
Suite 425
Santa Monica, CA 90401
Phone: 310-260-6573
web: www.bisoncapital.com

Mission Statement: A private equity firm which makes non-control investments in fundamentally strong middle-market companies, to finance their growth, balance sheet restructuring and/or recapitalization.

Average Investment: $10 million
Investment Criteria: Middle Market Companies with Revenues of $20 to $500 Million

Industry Group Preference: Business Services, Healthcare, Technology, Distribution, Logistics
Portfolio Companies: Advantmed, BC2Environmental Corp., Big Rock Sports LLC, Cartasite, Clinical Research Laboratories LLC, CutisCare, CVE Technology Group Inc., Ease Entertainment Services, EmpirecLS Worldwide Chauffeured Services, Fuel Systems Solutions Inc., Fyfe Group LLC, General Finance Corp., Global Benefits Group Inc., Helinet Aviation Services LLC, Indi Semiconductor, KeyTech Limited, Lime Energy Co., Metagenics Inc., Midwestern BioAg, Miva, MVConnect, Overland, Pacific & Cutler, Performance Team Freight Systems Inc., Royal Wolf Australia, Sentinel Offender Services LLC, Solarsilicon Recycling Services LLC, The Center for Wound Healing, Twin Med LLC, United Therapies Holding LLC

Other Locations:
780 Third Avenue
30th Floor
New York, NY 10017
Phone: 646-792-2080

Key Executives:
Douglas B. Trussler, Partner
310-260-6582
e-mail: dtrussler@bisoncapital.com
Education: MBA, Richard Ivey School of Business, University of Western Ontario
Background: Principal, Windward Capital Partners
Directorships: GTS Holdings, Inc., Performance Team Freight Systems, Inc.; Royal Wolf Australia, Ltd., Royal Wolf Trading New Zealand Limited, BC2 Environmental Corp, Big Rock Sports LLC
Yee-Ping Chu, Partner
310-260-6574
e-mail: pchu@bisoncapital.com
Education: BS, Economics, Wharton School, University of Pennsylvania
Background: VP, Lehman Brothers; Credit Suisse First Boston; Trust Company; Senior Analyst, TCW's International Private Equity; Public Accountant, Price Waterhouse
Directorships: Metagenics, Inc; Bc2 Environmental Corp; Performance Team Freight Systems, Inc
Lou Caballero, Partner
310-260-6573
e-mail: lcaballero@bisoncapital.com
Education: BA, Economics and Business, Westmont College; MBA, UCLA Anderson School of Management
Background: Senior Associate, Roth Capital Partners; Financial Analyst, Catellus Development Corporation
Directorships: BC2 Environmental Corp.
Peter Macdonald, Partner
646-792-2080
e-mail: pmacdonald@bisoncapital.com
Education: BS, Business Administration, University of Southern California; MBA, Wharton School, University of Pennsylvania
Background: Managing Director, BlackRock Kelso Corporation; Partner, Windward Capital Partners
Directorships: GTS Holdings, Inc.
Kurt Pilecki, Vice President
310-260-6578
e-mail: kpilecki@bisoncapital.com
Education: BS, Commerce with Concentrations in Finance & Accounting, University of Virginia
Background: Senior Analyst, CIBC World Markets / Oppenheimer & Co.; Associate, Bison Capital

275 BLACK DIAMOND VENTURES
450 North Brand Boulevard
Suite 600
Glendale, CA 91203
Phone: 818-245-6250 **Fax:** 818-245-6255
e-mail: info@bdventures.com
web: bdventures.com

Mission Statement: Black Diamond Ventures provides individual investors the opportunity to invest alongside institutional investors and first-tier venture capital firms in technology-leading companies.

Founded: 1998
Average Investment: $2 - $10 million
Industry Group Preference: Technology, Telecommunications, Biotechnology, Medical Devices, Semiconductors, Mobile Apps, Clean Technology
Portfolio Companies: Altwork, Berkeley Lights, Capella, Consumer Brands, Engage3, LiquidSpace, Mumo, NEI Treatment Systems, Obalon, Tela Innovations, Theranos

Other Locations:
  475 Alberto Way
  Los Gatos, CA 95032
  Phone: 408-558-6300 **Fax:** 408-884-8840

  19 Vista Tramonto
  Newport Coast, CA 92657
  Phone: 949-644-4288 **Fax:** 949-644-4628

Key Executives:
  Christopher Lucas, Managing Director
  e-mail: chris@bdventures.com
  Education: BS, Mechanical Engineering, UCLA; MBA, University of Southern California
  Background: Global One Distribution & Merchandising, Peripheral Systems
  Rob Ukropina, Managing Partner
  e-mail: rob@bdventures.com
  Education: University of Southern California, Marshall School of Business
  Background: Founder, Overnight Express
  Directorships: Allyance Communications, Arenda Capital Management, C2 Reprographics, United Document Storage
  Ana Quintana, Principal
  e-mail: ana@bdventures.com
  Education: BA, English Literature, California State University, Los Angeles
  Background: Senior Editor, Goto.com; Corporate Finance, ING Barings

276 BLACKFORD CAPITAL LLC
190 Monroe Ave. NW
Suite 600
Grand Rapids, MI 49503
  Phone: 616-233-3161 **Fax:** 616-828-5042
  e-mail: info@blackfordcapital.com
  web: www.blackfordcapital.com

Mission Statement: Acquires, manages, and builds middle-market manufacturing companies; provides attractive exit options for owners and operators of small to medium-sized privately held manufacturing enterprises, an provides divestiture opportunities for division of corporate parent companies that no longer reflect the company's strategic focus.

Geographic Preference: Midwest Region, Mid-Atlantic Region, New England
Founded: 2000
Average Investment: $50 million
Minimum Investment: $10 million
Investment Criteria: Small to medium-sized privately held manufacturing enterprises; Divestitures
Industry Group Preference: Distribution, Business Products & Services, Low-Tech Manufacturing
Portfolio Companies: Bond Street, Burgaflex, Custom Profile, Davalor, Dickinson, Ellison Bakery, Grand Equipment, Grand Power Systems, Hall Research, Industrial Piping, Key Health, McClarin Plastics, Mopec, Online Tech Stores, Quality Aluminium Products, Snowhite, Staging Concepts, Rhinotek Heavy Duty Computer Products

Other Locations:
  150 West Second Street
  Suite 400
  Royal Oak, MI 48067

Key Executives:
  Martin Stein, Founder & Managing Director
  e-mail: mstein@blackfordcapital.com
  Education: BA, University of Chicago; MBA, Harvard Business School
  Background: Consultant, Mercer Management Consulting; Consultant, Council for Excellence in Government
  Jeffrey Johnson, Managing Director
  Education: MBA, Harvard Business School; BA, Claremont McKenna College
  Background: Managing Director, Gilbert Global Equity Partners; Director, Alternative Investments, Russell Investments
  Directorships: Mopec, Quality Aluminium Products, Ellison Bakery
  Carmen Evola, Managing Director
  Education: BS, Electrical Engineering, University of Toledo
  Background: President & CEO, Vari-Form Group (formerly Crowne Group)
  Directorships: Grand Power Systems, Burgaflex, Grand Equipment, Davalor Mold

277 BLACKSTONE PRIVATE EQUITY GROUP
345 Park Avenue
New York, NY 10154
  Phone: 212-583-5000 **Fax:** 212-583-5749
  web: www.blackstone.com

Mission Statement: Blackstone Private Equity Group's approach to investing is guided by a set of proven principles: accountability, excellence, integrity, teamwork and entrepreneurship. The firm is committed to establishing corporate partnerships, focusing on opportunities in under-appreciated industries, and actively managing its portfolio companies.

Geographic Preference: North America, Western Europe, Latin America
Fund Size: $18 billion
Founded: 1987
Average Investment: $100 - $400 million
Minimum Investment: $100 million
Investment Criteria: Leveraged Buyouts, Middle Market, Growth Capital
Industry Group Preference: Business Products & Services, Consumer Products, Retail, Consumer & Leisure, Energy, Financial Services, Healthcare, Pharmaceuticals, Industrial, Media, Telecommunications, Travel & Leisure, Technology
Portfolio Companies: Allcargo, Bayview Financial, Bujagali Hydropower Project, Center Parcs, Cheniere, Crestwood Midstream Partners, Crocs, DJO, Emdeon, Gateway Rail Freight, Gokaldas Exports Limited, Intelenet, Jack Wolfskin, Leica, LLOG, Merlin Entertainments, Michaels Stores, MTAR, PBV Partners, Performance Food, Pinnacle Foods, Seaworld Parks and Entertainment, Steifel Laboratories, Summit Materials, Vivint

Other Locations:
  100 Wilshire Boulevard
  Suite 200
  Santa Monica, CA 90401
  Phone: 310-310-6949 **Fax:** 310-310-6998

  40 Berkeley Square
  London W1J 5AL
  United Kingdom
  Phone: 44-2074514000 **Fax:** 44-2074514001

  Two International Finance Centre
  Suite 901
  8 Finance Street
  Central

Venture Capital & Private Equity Firms / Domestic Firms

Hong Kong
Phone: 852-36568600 **Fax:** 852-26568601

Winland International Finance Center
Unit F817-18, No. 7, Financial Street
Xicheng District
Beijing 100140
China
Phone: 86-1066497300 **Fax:** 86-1066497301

Abu Dhabi Global Market Square
Al Sila Tower, 24th Floor
PO Box 128666
Abu Dhabi
United Arab Emirates
Phone: 971-26948617

Tuborg Boulevard 12
2900 Hellerup
3rd Floor
Copenhagen
Denmark
Phone: 45-36944057

Express Towers
Nariman Point
Mumbai 400 021
India
Phone: 91-2267528500 **Fax:** 91-2267528531

278 Boulevard Saint-Germain
Paris 75007
France
Phone: 33-0170982330 **Fax:** 33-0170982331

16th Floor, Tower 8
7 Jongro 5-gil
Jongro-gu
Seoul 03157
Korea
Phone: 82-262267110 **Fax:** 82-262267010

Unit 3901-3903, 39th Floor
HKRI Centre One HKRI
Taikoo Hei, 288 Shumen Yi Road
Shanghai 200041
China
Phone: 86-2161698188 **Fax:** 82-2161698189

Marina Bay Financial Centre Tower 2
Suite 13-01/02
10 Marina Blvd. 018983
Singapore
Phone: 65-68507500 **Fax:** 65-68507501

Gateway One
MacQuarie Place
Suite 3901
Sydney NSW 2000
Australia
Phone: 61-280167200 **Fax:** 61-280167201

Midtown Tower, 22nd Floor
9-7-1 Akasaka
Minato-ku
Tokyo 107-6222
Japan
Phone: 81-0345778400 **Fax:** 81-0345778401

101 California Street
Suite 3200
San Francisco, CA 94111
Phone: 212-583-5000

Key Executives:
Stephen A. Schwarzman, Chairman, Co-Founder & CEO
Education: BA, Yale University; MBA, Harvard Business School
Directorships: The Asia Society, New York-Presbyterian Hospital
Jonathan Gray, President & Chief Operating Officer
Education: BA, University of Pennsylvania; BS, Wharton School
Background: Chairman, Hilton Worldwide
Directorships: Harlem Village Academies
Joseph Baratta, Global Head, Private Equity
Education: Georgetown University
Background: Tinicum; McCown De Leeuw & Company; M&A, Morgan Stanley
Directorships: Seaworld Parks and Entertainment, Penn Engineering
Michael Chae, Senior Managing Director & Chief Financial Officer
Education: AB, Harvard College; MPhil, Cambridge University; JD, Yale Law School
Background: The Carlyle Group LP; Dillon, Read & Co.
Prakash A. Melwani, Senior Managing Director/Chief Investment Officer
Education: Cambridge University; MBA, Harvard Business School
Background: Founding Partner, Vestar Capital Partners; The First Boston Corporation; NM Rothschild & Sons
Directorships: Crocs, Kosmos Energy, Performance Food Group, RGIS Inventory Specialists
David I. Foley, Senior Managing Director/CEO, Blackstone Energy Partners
Education: BA, MA, Economics, Northwestern University; MBA, Harvard Business School
Background: AEA Investors; Monitor Company
David Calhoun, Senior Managing Director
Education: Virginia Polytechnic Institute
Background: Vice Chairman, The General Electric Company; President & CEO, GE Infrastructure
Directorships: The Boeing Company, Caterpillar
Angelo Acconcia, Senior Managing Director
Education: Queen's University
Background: Morgan Stanley; Canadian Imperial Bank of Commerce
Directorships: Alta Energy, GeoSouthern Energy, Hunter Oil & Gas, LLOG Exploration, Osum Oil Sands, Royal Resources
Lionel Assant, Senior Managing Director
Education: Ecole Polytechnique
Background: M&A, Asset Management & Private Equity, Goldman Sachs
Directorships: Tangerine, Intertrust, Alliance Automotive Group
Gautam Banerjee, Senior Managing Director
Education: BS, LLD, University of Warwick
Background: Executive Chairman, PricewaterhouseCoopers Singapore
Directorships: Singapore Airlines, Piramal Enterprises, The Indian Hotels Company, GIC Private Limited
Martin Brand, Senior Managing Director
Education: BA, MA, Mathematics & Computation, Univ. of Oxford; MBA, Harvard Business School
Background: Goldman Sachs; McKinsey & Company
James Carnegie, Senior Managing Director
Education: BComm, University of Melbourne; MBA, Harvard University
Background: Partner, Archer Capital; Director, MacQuarie Direct Investment Group
Jeffrey Iverson, Managing Director & Chief Compliance Officer
Education: BA, University of Colorado; JD, University of California
Background: General Counsel, Blackstone; General Counsel & CCO, Pulse Capital Partners; CCO, RiverRock Europen Capital Partners; Executive Director, Lehman Brothers; Associate, Cooley Godward
Directorships: Harlem Grown
Thomas Iannarone, Managing Director & COO, Liquid Credit Strategy Unit
Education: BA, Siena College; JD, Villanova University
Background: Morrison & Foerster; Bingham McCutchen
Edward Huang, Senior Managing Director
Education: BA, Yale University; MBA, Harvard Business School

Venture Capital & Private Equity Firms / Domestic Firms

Background: Managing Director & Partner, Morgan Stanley; Merrill Lynch
Directorships: Pactera Technology International
Joan Solotar, Senior Managing Director & Head of Private Wealth Solutions
Education: BS, State University of New York; MBA, New York University
Background: Head of Equity Research, Bank of America Securities; Services Analyst, Credit Suisse; Services Analyst, Donald Lufkin & Jenrette
Directorships: First Eagle Investment Management
Julia Kahr, Senior Managing Director
Education: BA, Classical Civilization, Yale University; MBA, Harvard Business School
Background: Project Leader, Boston Consulting Group
Directorships: DJ Orthopedics, Summit Materials
Robert McMullan, Senior Managing Director
Education: BS, History, Vanderbilt University; MBA, Wharton School, University of Pennsylvania
Background: Co-Head, Financial Sponsors Group, FBR Capital Markets; DLJ/CSFB
Seth Meisel, Senior Managing Director
Education: BA, Economics, Princeton University; MBA, Harvard Business School
Background: Partner, Bain Capital; Mercer Management Consulting
Dwight Scott, Senior Managing Director & President of GSO
Education: University of North Carolina; McCombs School of Business, University of Texas
Background: EVP & CFO, El Paso Corporation; Managing Director, Donald Lufkin & Jenrette
Directorships: FourPoint Energy; GEP Haynesville
Stephen Can, Senior Managing Director & Co-Head of Strategic Partners
Education: MS, Krannert Business School, Purdue University
Background: IBM Pension Funds; IBM Corporation
Neil P. Simpkins, Senior Managing Director
Education: University of Oxford; MBA, Harvard Business School
Background: Principal, Bain Capital; Consultant, Bain & Company
Directorships: Gates Corporation, Apria Healthcare Group, Summit Materials, Emdeon
Michael Sotirhos, Senior Managing Director
Education: BA, JD, Georgetown University
Background: Partner, Atlantic Pacific Capital; Merrill Lynch
Peter Wallace, Senior Managing Director
Education: Harvard College
Directorships: Allied Barton Security Services, GCA Services, Michaels Stores, Outerstuff, SeaWorld Parks & Entertainment, Service King, Vivint, The Weather Channel Companies

278 BLADE VENTURES
27762 Antonio Parkway
Suite L1-426
Mission Viejo, CA 92694

Phone: 949-298-4595 Fax: 949-554-0181
e-mail: admin@bladeventures.com
web: www.bladeventures.com

Mission Statement: Blade Ventures' focus is on companies that drive the adoption of leading edge information, media, sensor and related systems technologies. Through select partners the firm also invests in life science opportunities such as medical devices, diagnostics, and operations-enhancing information technology. Blade Ventures' portfolio companies are capable of playing a disruptive role in emerging, high growth markets, and they are led by management teams that have a long term commitment to the success of their company.

Geographic Preference: United States
Average Investment: $250,000 - 1.5 million

Industry Group Preference: Media, Life Sciences, Medical Devices, Diagnostics
Portfolio Companies: 5iSciences, Apollo Enterprise Solutions, Clear Access, Good Technology, Infinera, LaserCure Sciences, Metric Stream, Motricity, Neilsoft, Vigilistics

Key Executives:
  Craig Gunther, Managing Director
  Education: BS, Engineering, UCLA; MS, Electrical Engineering, University of Southern California; JD, Loyola Law School
  Background: President, Blade Capital Management
  Directorships: ClearAccess, 5iScience, Lasercure, Vigilistics
  Brian Flucht, Principal
  Education: Northwestern University; MBA, University of Southern California
  Background: Senior Analyst, Shepherd Ventures
  Rajeev Varshneya, Venture Partner
  Education: BSc, Electronics & Telecommunications Engineering, New Delhi, India; ME, Electronics, Eindhoven, The Netherlands
  Directorships: Metric Stream, Vigilistics

279 BLAST FUNDING
900 Diamond Circle
Naples, FL 34119

Phone: 877-580-5754
e-mail: brian@blastfunding.com
web: www.blastfunding.com

Mission Statement: A private direct lender investing in various industries.

Fund Size: $500M
Minimum Investment: $200k
Investment Criteria: $3M Annual Revenue, Startups
Industry Group Preference: Cannabis, Oil & Gas, Aerospace Defense, Energy, Transportation, Gaming, Consumer Goods, Security, Technology, Software, HOA Financing

280 BLAZER VENTURES

e-mail: info@blazerventures.com
web: www.blazerventures.com

Mission Statement: Blazer Ventures is an early-stage investment firm primarily interested in consumer services.

Investment Criteria: Early-Stage
Industry Group Preference: Consumer Services, Business Products & Services
Portfolio Companies: Clothia, ClassPass, Combatant Gentlemen, Fondu, Keychain Logistics, Lovely, PlanGrid, Priceonomics, SpotOn, True & Co.

Key Executives:
  Michael Wolf, Managing Partner
  Education: Columbia University; Wharton School, University of Pennsylvania
  Background: ClassPass

281 BLEU CAPITAL
110 E 25th Street
New York, NY 10010

web: www.bleucap.com

Mission Statement: Bleu Capital is a venture capital firm investing in supply chain optimization, data intelligence, AI voice intelligence, nd sustainable consumption.

Key Executives:
  Jean Pierre Chesse, Founder

Venture Capital & Private Equity Firms / Domestic Firms

282 BLH VENTURE PARTNERS
75 5th Street NW
Suite 311
Atlanta, GA 30308

Phone: 404-941-8780
web: www.blhventures.com

Mission Statement: BLH Venture Partners invests in bright entrepreneurs tackling innovative opportunities and support them in any way possible. BLH understands entrepreneurs and the phases start-ups and young companies traverse on their path to success. BLH insights stem from hands-on experience operating companies and having faced many of the same challenges current and prospective partners face as well.

Investment Criteria: Early-Stage
Industry Group Preference: Technology-Enabled Services, Enterprise Software, Consumer Internet, E-Commerce & Manufacturing
Portfolio Companies: 3Birds, BetterCloud, Call Rail, Chrono.gg, Cypress.io, Evident, Forbes Travel Guide, Gro, Haste, KontrollFreek, Ionic Security, Mashburn, Salesfusion, Shinesty, StrataCloud, TripLingo, UserIQ, Vidyo, Acumen, Digital Assent, KidsLink, nCrowd, Overdog, SaveUp, Vocalocity

Key Executives:
  Billy L. Harbert, Partner
  Education: Auburn University; MBA, Goizueta Business School, Emory University
  Background: President & CEO, BL Harbert International
  Ashish H. Mistry, Partner
  Education: Emory University
  Background: Co-Founder, Virtex Networks; RCMS Group

283 BLOCKCHAIN CAPITAL
440 Pacific Avenue
San Francisco, CA 94133

Phone: 415-677-5340
e-mail: contact@blockchaincapital.com
web: blockchain.capital

Mission Statement: Blockchain Capital is a leading venture firm in blockchain technology.

Fund Size: $500 Million

Key Executives:
  W Brad Stephens, Co-Founder and Managing Partner
  Education: BA, Duke University
  Background: Managing Partner, Stephens Investment Management LLC; Senior Analyst, CSFB Techonology Group; Research Analyst, Furman Selz
  P Bart Stephens, Co-Founder and Managing Partner
  Education: BA, Princeton University
  Background: Co-Founder/Head, Business Development, Oncology.com; EVP, Ivanhoe Capital Corporation; Managing Partner, Stephens Investment Management

284 BLOOMBERG BETA
140 New Montgomery Street
22nd Floor
San Francisco, CA 94105

web: github.com/bloomberg-beta

Mission Statement: Venture firm backed by Bloomberg L.P.

Fund Size: $150 million
Investment Criteria: Early-Stage
Industry Group Preference: Data Services, Content, Media Distribution, Technology Platforms, Networks and Communities, Human-Computer Interaction, New Organizational Models

Other Locations:
  731 Lexington Ave.
  New York, NY 10022

  James Cham, Partner
  Education: Harvard College; Massachusetts Institute of Technology - Sloan School of Management
  Background: Principal, Trinity Ventures; Vice President, Bessemer Venture Partners; Consultant, Boston Consulting Group; Principal, Zefer; Senior Consultant, Accenture
  Karin Klein, Founding Partner
  Education: BA, University of Pennsylvania; BS/MBA, Wharton School
  Background: VP, Softbank; Head of New Initiatives, Bloomberg
  Directorships: Paramount Group; Regency Centers; Harvey Mudd College
  Roy Bahat, Head
  Education: Harvard University; University of Oxford; UC Berkeley
  Background: President, IGN Entertainment; Vice President, News Corporation; Director of International Strategy, NYC2012; Senior Policy Director at Office of the Mayor, New York City; Associate, McKinsey & Co.
  Shivon Zilis, Partner
  Education: Yale University
  Background: Chief Adventurer, Bloomberg Ventures; Senior Strategy Consultant, IBM; Strategy Consultant, IBM; Thought Leadership Analyst, IBM Institute for Business Value

285 BLU VENTURE INVESTORS
1577 Spring Hill Road
Suite 405
Vienna, VA 22182

web: www.bluventureinvestors.com

Mission Statement: Blu Venture Investors is a venture capital investment company that supports early stage entrepreneurs in the Mid-Atlantic Region. The firm's investors are experienced, successful operating executives with experience in a broad range of industries and business models. Each team member has successfully launched new companies, products or services.

Geographic Preference: Maryland, Virginia, Washington Dc, North Carolina
Average Investment: $250,000 - $1 million
Minimum Investment: $250,000
Investment Criteria: Early-Stage
Industry Group Preference: Technology, Business to Business, Software
Portfolio Companies: 3C Logic, Atomicorp, Avizia, Axon AI, Bandura Systems, Blue Triangle Technologies, Bright Greens, CyberSponse, Cybrary, Dark Cubed, Emu Solutions, Fischer Block, Graphus, GroupSense, Huntress Labs, ID.me, Immuta, Interfolio, Latista, Technologies, Link Labs, LKC Technologies, N5 Sensors, NewConnect, NS8, PacketSled, Pathsensors, PFP Cybersecurities, Pixspan, SenseWare, Sensics, Shevirah, SocialToaster, Solid Carbon Products, StreamLink Software, ThreatQuotient, Trip Tribe, Unveillance, Urgant, Vagabond Vending, VanGogh Imaging, Virgil Security

Key Executives:
  J.S. Gamble, Co-Founder
  Education: BS, McIntire School of Commerce; MBA, Wharton School, University of Pennsylvania
  Background: CEO, Smart Imaging Systems; McKinsey & Company
  Jim Hunt, Co-Founder
  Education: BBA, University of Notre Dame
  Background: Founder, BDS; System Integration Practice, Price Waterhouse
  Bob Proctor, Co-Founder
  Education: BS, MS, PhD, Applied Physics, Cornell University
  Background: CEO, FlexEl; Co-Founder, Wiser Together

Venture Capital & Private Equity Firms / Domestic Firms

286 BLUE BRIGHT VENTURES
713 Greenwood Road
Chapel Hill, NC 27514-5924
Phone: 919-971-1377
e-mail: lee@bluebrightventures.com
web: bluebright.com

Mission Statement: Blue Bright Ventures invests in early-stage technology companies in the Southeast with a focus on the Raleigh-Durham area.
Geographic Preference: Southeast United States
Founded: 2009
Investment Criteria: Early-Stage
Industry Group Preference: Technology
Portfolio Companies: Adroit Digital, Aims, Bandsintown, Fabl, MarketBrief, Ocean Watch, Shoeboxed.com, Science Inc., Spring Metrics, Sweet Relish, Tethis, Windsor Circle, Womply, Wylan Energy, Zana

Key Executives:
Lee Buck, Founder
Education: BS, Systems Engineering, University of Virgina
Background: Partner, LaunchBox Digital; Co-Founder, Near-Time

287 BLUE CHIP VENTURE COMPANY
1308 Race Street
Suite 200
Cincinnati, OH 45202
Phone: 513-723-2300
web: bcvc.com

Mission Statement: Helps entrepreneur partners build lasting enterprises, providing capital and business-building assistance to entrepreneurs seeking to build growth companies. Blue Chip provides 'last financing round' or 'pre-exit' capital for early stage investors and venture-backed companies.
Geographic Preference: United States, Canada
Fund Size: $600 million
Founded: 1990
Average Investment: $1 - $4 million
Minimum Investment: $1 million
Investment Criteria: Later Stage
Industry Group Preference: Information Technology, Enterprise Services, Media, Communications, Healthcare, Marketing, Internet, Healthcare Services
Portfolio Companies: Adelphic, Aprecia Pharmaceuticals, Bidtellect, Blue Chip Surgery Centers Partners, Endocyte, Genesis Media, Kinetic Social, Linkable, PCIX, Rocketfuel, Scale Computing, ShareThis, UberMedia, Verance, Vestmark, Wild Things, XOS Digital

Key Executives:
Jack Wyant, Co-Founder/Managing Director
e-mail: jack@bcvc.com
Education: BA, Denison University; JD, Salmon P Chase College of Law
Background: Brand Management; Proctor & Gamble Company; Taft Broadcasting Company
Directorships: Blue Chip Broadcasting, Evergreen Assurance, Health Care Solutions, IntelliSeek/PlanetFeedback, Regent Communications, USinternetworking
Richard Kiley, Advisor/Venture Partner
e-mail: rlkiley@yahoo.com
Education: BS, Rensselaer Polytechnic Institute
Background: Procter & Gamble; CincyTech USA
Mark Wright, Venture Partner
e-mail: mark@bcvc.com
Education: BA, Northwestern University; MBA, Vanderbilt University
Background: Founder, Inforum; Founder, @plan
Directorships: Atomic Dog Publishing, InternetWire, Space Holdings

Christopher McCleary, Managing Director
Education: BA, University of Kentucky
Background: Founder/CEO, Evergreen Assurance; Co-Founder/Chairman/CEO, USinternetworking; Founded, USi; Chairman/CEO, DIGEX; Recipient, Ernst & Young Entrepreneur of the Year Award for software services

288 BLUE HERON CAPITAL
8730 Stony Point Parkway
Suite 280
Richmond, VA 23235
Phone: 804-212-3400 Fax: 804-212-3401
e-mail: info@blueheroncap.com
web: www.blueheroncap.com

Mission Statement: Invests in venture capital and management buyout opportunities in a broad range of industries. Blue Heron Capital's flexible and opportunistic investment philosophy allows them to creatively evaluate and structure investments to meet the individual needs of each situation.
Geographic Preference: Mid-Atlantic Region
Founded: 2006
Average Investment: $3 - $7 million
Minimum Investment: $3 million
Investment Criteria: Early-Stage, Growth Capital, Acquisitions, Direct Investments, Secondary Loans, Revenues between $5 to $25 million
Industry Group Preference: Healthcare, Tech-Enabled Business Services, Technology, Business Services
Portfolio Companies: Apogee IT Services, Avizia, Presence Learning, STARC Systems, Tricast, Verisma, Cartes Networks, CSA Medical, innRoad, Local Voice, WiserTogether

Key Executives:
Tom Benedetti, Co-Founder/Managing Partner
Education: BS, Government, College of William & Mary; MBA, Georgetown University
Background: Co-Founder, Benedetti & Farris
Andrew Tichenor, Co-Founder/Managing Partner
Education: BS, Accounting, University of Richmond; MBA, Georgetown University
Background: CPA, McGladrey & Pullen
Sam Sezak, Partner
Education: BS, Cornell University School of Hospitality Management; MBA, Georgetown University
Background: Co-Founder & Managing Partner, Breo International
Mike Marcantonio, Principal
Education: BS, Finance & Accounting, James Madison University; MBA, Duke University
Background: Harris Williams & Co.

289 BLUE OLIVE PARTNERS
web: www.linkedin.com/company/blue-olive-partners-llc

Mission Statement: Blue Olive Partners is a team of business operating executives devoted to identifying early-stage companies with tremendous growth potential. Blue Olive adheres to a comprehensive due diligence process prior to making equity investments. Blue Olive only invests in opportunities with a management team that embraces the Partners' hands-on involvement in the company's management, operations, finance and marketing strategies.

Founded: 2008
Investment Criteria: Preferred Equity

Key Executives:
Ben Sheridan, Partner
Education: BA, Duke University; MBA, Harvard University
Background: General Manager, Progressive Insurance
Larry Porcellato, Partner
Education: BComm, University of Toronto
Background: CEO, ICI Paints

107

Venture Capital & Private Equity Firms / Domestic Firms

George L. Buzzy, Partner
Education: BS, Business Administration, Lawrence University; CPA
Background: CEO, Novagard Solutions
Ed Weinfurtner, Partner
Education: BA, Harvard University
Background: EVP, Pella Window & Door Company

290 BLUE POINT CAPITAL PARTNERS
127 Public Square
Suite 5100
Cleveland, OH 44114-1312
Phone: 216-535-4700 **Fax:** 216-535-4701
web: www.bluepointcapital.com

Mission Statement: Blue Point Capital Partners is a private equity firm that invests in lower middle-market companies. Blue Point uses a range of operating resources to provide strategic support to its portfolio businesses.

Geographic Preference: United States, China
Fund Size: $1.5 billion
Founded: 1990
Average Investment: $10 - $50 million
Minimum Investment: $10 million
Investment Criteria: LBO, MBO, Middle Market, Recapitalizations
Industry Group Preference: Manufacturing, Distribution, Business Products & Services, Aerospace, Apparel & Footwear, Chemicals, E-Commerce, Environmental Services, Healthcare, Industrial Products, Transportation, Safety, Testing & Inspection
Portfolio Companies: Area Wide Protective, Consolidated Precision Products, Country Pure Foods, Fire & Life Safety America, FM Sylvan, Gesco Group of Companies, Italian Rose Gourmet Products, Kendall Vegetation Services, Mattco Forge, Next Level Apparel, Premier Needle Arts, Russell Hendrix, SASE Company, Spector & Co., TAS Environmental Services, Vetta, VRC Holdings

Other Locations:
601 Union Street
Suite 3022
Seattle, WA 98101
Phone: 206-332-9200 **Fax:** 206-332-9209

201 S Tryon Street
Suite 850
Charlotte, NC 28202
Phone: 704-347-1111 **Fax:** 704-347-1107

Suite 4604B
Wheelock Square
1717 Nan Jing W Road
Shanghai 200040
China
Phone: 86-2150474700

Key Executives:
Colleen Greenrod, CFO/CCO
216-353-4711
e-mail: cgreenrod@bluepointcapital.com
Education: BSBA, Accounting, Ohio State University; CPA
Background: J.P. Morgan; Citadel Investment; Arthur Andersen
Dennis Wu, Managing Director
86-2150474708
e-mail: dwu@bluepointcapital.com
Education: BE, Material Science, Shanghai University; MBA China Europe International Business School
Background: Purchasing Director Asia Pacific, Delphi Packard Electric Systems; Shanghai Printronics Circuit Board Co.
Directorships: Premier Needle Arts and Vetta
Charles Gedge, Operatinos Vice President
e-mail: cgedge@bluepointcapital.com
Education: BS, Finance, Fordham University
Background: VP, One Equity Partners; Bank of J.P. Morgan
John LeMay, Partner
Education: BS, Economics & Finance, Miami University; MBA, Kellogg Graduate School of Management, Northwestern University
Background: Manager, Boston Consulting Group; Mergers & Acquisitions, Salomon Brothers
Directorships: Hilco Vision
Juli Marley, Partner
Education: BS, State University of New York, Oswego; CPA
Background: Mergers & Acquisitions, Ernst & Young
Directorships: The Lion Brewery, OrthoLite, Smith-Cooper International
Mark Morris, Partner
Education: BS, Finance, Miami University
Background: Structured Capital Markets & Investment Banking, KeyCorp
Directorships: Russell Food, Selmet
Sean Ward, Partner
Education: BS, Economics, Allegheny College; MBA, John Carroll University
Background: Investment Banking & Credit Administration, KeyCorp
Directorships: Alco Manufacturing, AWP, Handi Quilter, LineStar Services, Shnier-Gesco, Trademark Global
Jim Marra, Director, Business Development
216-535-4703
e-mail: jmarra@bluepointcapital.com
Education: BS, Psychology, Pennsylvania State University; MBA, University of Pittsburgh
Background: Leveraged Capital, Investment Banking & Venture Capital Groups, Citicorp
Brian Castleberry, Principal
Education: BA, Economics & Mathematics, Washington and Lee University
Background: VP, Red Ventures; HOPE International; Harris Williams & Co.
Jonathan Pressnell, Principal
Education: BSBA, Accounting, University of Pittsburgh; MS, Accountancy, University of Notre Dame; MBA, Tuck School of Business, Dartmouth College
Background: Principal, Greenbriar Equity Group; Analyst, M&A, KeyBanc Capital Markets; Auditor, Ernst & Young

291 BLUE SAGE CAPITAL
2700 Via Fortuna
Suite 300
Austin, TX 78746
Phone: 512-536-1900 **Fax:** 512-236-9215
web: www.bluesage.com

Mission Statement: Blue Sage Capital is a private equity firm based in Austin, Texas. The firm invests across a wide range of sectors and specializes in growth financings, recapitalizations and buyouts of smaller middle-market businesses.

Geographic Preference: Texas, Southwest
Fund Size: $300 million
Founded: 2003
Average Investment: $20 - $40 million
Minimum Investment: $5 million
Investment Criteria: Small Middle-Market, Recapitalizations, Buyouts
Industry Group Preference: Industrial Equipment, Distribution, Service Industries, Healthcare, Manufacturing, Energy, Media
Portfolio Companies: All-State, Americo Manufacturing, BACOM, Frontier Waste Solutions, Ligchine International, Magnum System, Timber Automation

Key Executives:
Peter Huff, Founder/Managing Member
Education: Southern Methodist University; MBA, Stanford Graduate School of Business

Venture Capital & Private Equity Firms / Domestic Firms

Background: Partner, Austin Ventures; Managing Member, JH Whitney; McKinsey and Company
Directorships: Cobalt Environmental Solutions, Primus Sterilizer
Jim McBride, Founder/Managing Member
Education: BBA, Finance, MBA, University of Texas at Austin
Background: Senior Executive, The LBJ Holding Company
Directorships: C&M Conveyor, Marine Accessories, Baxley-LogPro, Cobalt Environmental Solutions
Jonathan Pearce, Partner
Education: BBA, MPA, Accounting, University of Texas; CPA
Background: Senior Associate, Avista Capital Partners; Analyst, Global Energy Group, Credit Suisse; Analyst, JP Morgan Chase
Eric Weiner, Partner
Education: BBA, Finance, BA, Government, University of Texas; MBA, Stanford Graduate School of Business
Background: Associate, Berkshire Partners; Senior Associate Consultant, Bain & Company
Jonathan Kaskow, Vice President
Education: BA, Economics, Stanford University; MBA, University of Texas
Background: SunTx

292 BLUE SKY CAPITAL
3525 Del Mar Heights Rd
PO Box 862
San Diego, CA 92130

Phone: 877-424-7479 **Fax:** 877-424-7480
e-mail: info@blueskycapital.com
web: www.blueskycapital.com

Mission Statement: A private equity company that buys and sells distressed real estate.

Geographic Preference: Southern California
Founded: 2005
Industry Group Preference: Real Estate

293 BLUE TREE ALLIED ANGELS
PO Box 1323
Wexford, PA 15090

Phone: 724-475-4538 **Fax:** 888-550-3093
e-mail: info@bluetreecapital.com
web: www.bluetreealliedangels.com

Mission Statement: BlueTree Allied Angels is a network of private equity investors that invests in early stage companies. The organization seeks to leverage the experience and expertise of its members to mitigate investment risk and increase the probability of investment success.

Geographic Preference: Western Pennsylvania, Eastern Ohio, Northern West Virginia
Founded: 2003
Average Investment: $200,000 - $3 million
Investment Criteria: Early Stage, Exit Potential
Portfolio Companies: 101, 4moms, Aeronics, ALung Technologies, Angler Labs, ApartmentJet, Aspinity, Augement Therapy, Aurochs Brewing, Austin Coctails, Baebies, Bergen Medical Products, Bioptigen, BIOSAFE, BlastPoint, BoardBookit, C360, Carmell Therapeutics, ChromaTan, coeo, Cognition Therapeutics, Columbia Northwest, Complexa, Inc., Cryothermic Systems, CytoAgents, Edge Case Research, Figure8 Surgical, FlyCast, Holganix, INRange Management Systems, Iteros, JoyLux, Kold-Draft, LegalSifter, Lia Diagnostics, Lyndy Biosciences, Malcovery Security, Medrobotics, medSage, Neuros Medical, PECA Labs, Peptilogics, Physcient, Inc., PICKUP, PittMoss, RedPath Integrated Pathology, Rinovum, Shoefitr, StageMark, TalkShoe, Voci Technologies, Westmoreland Advanced Materials, Wombat Security, Wright Therapy Products, Zive, Zone2

Key Executives:
Catherine Mott, Founder
Education: BS, Education; Masters of Education; MBA, Finance
Sreekar Gadde, Executive Director
Education: BS, Cognitive Science, BS, MSc, Electrical and Computer Engineering, Carnegie Mellon Unveristy; JD, George Washington University Law School; MBA, Tepper School of Business, Carnegie Mellon University
Background: Ropes and Gray; Dynamics, Inc.; Intel

294 BLUEFISH VENTURES
San Francisco, CA

Phone: 415-614-1161

Mission Statement: Bluefish Ventures is a venture capital firm that invests in seed and early-stage Internet and technology companies. Bluefish targets markets with significant growth potential and specifically companies involved in, but not limited to, Internet infrastructure, enterprise software, wireless applications and power technology. Key criteria when making an investment decision include the strength of the company's management team, the potential size of the company's target market and the competitive advantages the company has versus other industry participants.

Investment Criteria: Seed-Stage, Early-Stage
Industry Group Preference: Internet, Technology, Internet Infrastructure, Enterprise Software, Wireless Applications, Power Technologies
Portfolio Companies: LiveVox, Powercell, Tangerine Technologies, Varro Technologies, Vivaro, vVault

Key Executives:
Alex Millar, Partner
e-mail: alex@bluefishventures.com
Education: School of Engineering & Applied Sciences, MBA, Wharton School, University of Pennsylvania
Background: Investment Banking Division, Donaldson Lufkin & Jenrette
Directorships: Epana Networks, LiveVox
David Istock, Partner
e-mail: distock@bluefishventures.com
Education: Wharton School, University of Pennsylvania
Background: Director/Head of Technology M&A, Cowen & Company; Executive Director, M&A, USB Investment Bank; VP, M&A, PaineWebber Inc.

295 BLUEPOINTE VENTURES
999 Baker Way
Suite 150
San Mateo, CA 94404

Phone: 650-293-4545
e-mail: info@bluepointeventures.com
web: www.bluepointeventures.com

Mission Statement: Seeks to invest in game-changing companies within the tech industry, including innovations in AI, Virtual Reality, and Big Data.

Founded: 2014
Investment Criteria: Early Stage
Industry Group Preference: Artificial Intelligence, Virtual Reality, Big Data, Cloud Data
Portfolio Companies: AngelPad, Avaamo, AdRise, Arkin, Boomtrain, Bullpen Capital, ClassPass, Compound, Cota Capital, Estate Assist, Fanduel, The Hive, Lemonade, Next Force Technology, Paintzen, Periscope Data, PipeDrive, Pogoseat, Postmates, Streamlined Ventures, Tadem Capital, Tekion Cloud, UpCounsel, Wanderu, Zodius

Key Executives:
Sandeep Sardana, Co-Founder/Managing Director
Education: BS, Rutgers University; MBA, Columbia Business School

109

Venture Capital & Private Equity Firms / Domestic Firms

296 BLUERUN VENTURES
545 Middlefield Road
Suite 250
Menlo Park, CA 94025

Phone: 650-462-7250
e-mail: ventures@brv.com
web: www.brv.com

Mission Statement: BlueRun operates globally as a single, ROI driven fund that invests in early stage mobile and information technology companies.

Founded: 1998
Average Investment: $1-6 million
Investment Criteria: Early-Stage
Industry Group Preference: Mobile Communications Devices, Information Technology, Internet, Media, Enterprise Software, Semiconductors, Components & IoT, Social Media, Digital Media & Marketing
Portfolio Companies: Airobotics, Apricot Forest, Availink, App Central, Banjo, BlueCart, BetterCompany, Changba, Chunyu, Channel Breeze, Coupa, Enpocket, FreedomPay, Foodspotting, Ganji, HumanAPI, Kitman Labs, Kabbage, Location Labs, Meilishuo, Nom, PPTV, PayPal, Radius, SoundWall, Topsy, uMake, Verve, VisionScape, Varolii, Waze, ZeeMee, 140 Proof

Other Locations:
BlueRun Investment Consulting (Shanghai) Co.
Room 2361, 23/F, 5 Corperate Avenue
150 Hubin Road
Shanghai 200021
China
Phone: 86-21-8013-5016

BlueRun Investment Consulting (Shanghai) Co.
Suite 1308, Office Tower 1, China Central Place
No. 81 Jianguo Road, Chaoyang District
Beijing 100025
China
Phone: 86-10-5969-5680 **Fax:** 86-10-5969-5681

BRV Korea Advisors Co. Ltd.
4th Floor
Eonju-ro 168gil 6, Gangnam-gu
Seoul 06020
Korea
Phone: 82-2-2088-3900 **Fax:** 82-2-2088-3901

Key Executives:
John Malloy, Co-Founder/General Partner
Education: BA, Boston College; JD, George Mason School of Law
Background: Nokia; MCI; Co-Founder, Go Communications
Jonathan Ebinger, General Partner
Education: BS, Finance, Virginia Polytechnic Institute; MBA, Darden Grad. School of Business, University of Virginia
Background: VP Marketing, Qwest Communications; Bell Atlantic Internet Solutions; MCI Communications; Founder, Simply Savings
Directorships: ASIP; Enpocket; LightningCast; Qovia; SunRocket
Cheryl Cheng, General Partner
Education: BA, Stanford University; MBA, Kellogg School of Management, Northwestern University
Background: Clorox; The Sharper Image
Kwan Yoon, General Partner
Education: BA, Economics, MS, Management Science & Engineering, Stanford University
Jui Tan, General Partner
Education: BS, Electrical & Electronics Engineering, Nanyang Technological University; MBA, International Institute of Management Development
Background: Director Global Service Development, Singapore Telecom; Engineering Management, IBM

Jeff Tannenbaum, Venture Partner
Background: Founder, PhotoCrank; Co-Founder, DreamFront;

297 BLUESTEM CAPITAL COMPANY
101 S Phillips Avenue
Suite 501
Sioux Falls, SD 57104

Phone: 605-331-0091
e-mail: info@bluestemcapital.com
web: www.bluestemcapital.com

Mission Statement: Provides investors and portfolio companies with service and returns by creating an environment that fosters professional investing and stewardship of capital in accordance with proven strategies and beliefs.

Geographic Preference: Midwest United States
Fund Size: $66 million
Founded: 1989
Average Investment: $500,000 - $3 million
Minimum Investment: $500,000
Investment Criteria: Early Stage, Mid-to-Late Stage Companies
Industry Group Preference: Business Products & Services, Information Services, Agriculture, Retail, Consumer & Leisure, Healthcare, Real Estate, Energy, Manufacturing
Portfolio Companies: ACTV8me, Ambient Clinical Analytics, Clarify Medical, Conventus Orthopaedics, CRA Continental Realty Advisors, Dakotaland Manufacturing, EDCO, Equinox, eyeBrain Medical, ianTECH, Intelliflux, LENTECHS, MembranePRO, NoteSwift, Pivitol Health Solutions, POET, PolyCera Membranes, Regency Midwest, sight4all, SpringCM, Surface Pharmaceuticals, SYNQ3, Tear Film Innovations, TearClear, The Community Company, The Pairie Club, TherOptix, Virtual Incision, VIRUN

Key Executives:
Steve Kirby, Founding Partner
Education: BS, Political Science, Arizona State University; JD, University of South Dakota School of Law
Background: Western Surety Company; Lieutenant Governor, State of South Dakota
Tyler J Stowater, Partner/Vice President
Education: BS, Agriculture Economics, MS, Economics, South Dakota State University
Background: Budget Analyst, State Economist & Deputy Commissioner, Bureau of Finance & Management, State of South Dakota; Assistant Vice President, Citibank
Sandy Horst, Partner/CFO
Education: BS, Accounting, University of South Dakota
Background: Senior Manager, Tax Department, McGladrey & Pullen
Nikole Mulder, Partner/Vice President
Education: BS, Business Administration, Master of Professional Accountancy, University of South Dakota
Background: CPA, Eide Baily LLP

298 BLUETREE VENTURE FUND
PO Box 1323
Wexford, PA 15090

Phone: 724-475-4538
e-mail: info@bluetreeventurefund.com
web: www.bluetreeventurefund.com

Mission Statement: A venture capital firm based in Pittsburgh, the BlueTree Venture Fund invests in early stage companies across a variety of technology-based sectors.

Geographic Preference: Mid-Adlantic Region
Fund Size: $10 million
Investment Criteria: Early Stage
Industry Group Preference: Technology, Medical Technology, Information Technology, Software
Portfolio Companies: ALung Technologies, ApartmentJet, C360, ChromaTan, Encentiv Energy, Gemmus Pharma,

Venture Capital & Private Equity Firms / Domestic Firms

HealthTell, Niche.com, Physcient, Rinovum Women's Health, SLED Mobile, Thread

Key Executives:
Catherine Mott, Managing Partner
Education: MBA, Finance
Background: Chairman, Angel Capital Education Foundation; Founder, Synergetic Sales Performance Group; Founder, Indigo Capital Development
David Motley, Managing Partner
Education: BS, Mechanical Engineering, University of Pittsburgh; MBA, Harvard Business School
Background: VP & General Manager, Covidien Inc. Surgical Devices; Respironics
Directorships: First National Bank, Optimal Strategix Group, Gemmus Pharma, ALung
Roger Byford, Managing Partner
Education: MA, Electrical Engineering, University of Cambridge
Background: President, Vocollect Healthcare Systems
Jon Pastor, Venture Partner
Education: BA, Chemistry & Economics, Case Western Reserve University; MBA, Harvard Business School
Background: Engagement Manager, McKinsey & Company; President & Co-Founder, Rent Jungle; President & CTO, The Rainmaker Group

299 BLUFF POINT ASSOCIATES
274 Riverside Avenue
Westport, CT 06880

Phone: 203-557-9450
web: www.bluffpt.com

Mission Statement: Bluff Point Associates is a private equity firm based in Westport, Connecticut. Bluff Point actively invests in information services companies supporting the banking, trust, securities, retirement and wealth management sectors of the financial services industry, as well as the healthcare information services sector.

Investment Criteria: Growth Companies
Industry Group Preference: Fintech, Healthcare Technology
Portfolio Companies: fi360, FPS Group, HealthSavings Administrators, Innovest, PEX Card, TSA Consulting Group

Key Executives:
Thomas E. McInerney, CEO
Education: St. John's University
Background: General Partner, Welsh Carson Anderson & Stowe; Co-Founder/President, Dama Telecommunications
Paula G. McInerney, President
Education: BA, Manhattanville University; MBA, Stern School of Business
Background: COO, Oppenheimer Funds; Managing Director, Bankers Trust Company
Neil Q. Gabriele, Managing Director
Education: BA, Political Science, University of Richmond; MBA, Vanderbilt University
Background: Optech Systems
John L. McInerney, Managing Director
Education: BA, JD, St. John's University
Background: Cullen & Dykman; Counsel, New York City Police Department
John P. Gilliam, Managing Director
Education: BBA, Ohio University
Background: SVP, Finance, The BISYS Group
Kevin P. Fahey, Managing Director
Education: BBA, Accounting, Saint Bonaventure University
Background: SVP/CFO, Healthland
Jamie J. DeRubertis, Managing Director
Background: Matrix Settlement & Clearance Services

300 BLUM CAPITAL PARTNERS
909 Montgomery Street
San Francisco, CA 94133

Phone: 415-434-1111 Fax: 415-434-3130
web: www.blumcapital.com

Mission Statement: Blum Capital has established a record of generating superior risk-adjusted returns for its institutional and high net worth partners by adhering to a highly focused, distinctive investment strategy.

Fund Size: $3 Billion
Founded: 1975
Average Investment: $10 million
Portfolio Companies: Aimia Inc., American Reprographics Inc., Axipointe Inc., Athlon Holdings, The Bisys Group, BankThai, Ceridian Corp, Convergys Corp., CareFusion, CIMB Group Holding, CoreLogic, Career Education, Current Media, CBRE Group, Copart Inc., Dianon Systems Inc., Electronics for Imaging, Echostar Corp., Fairmont Hotels, Fair, Isaac & Company, First Health Group Corp., First American Financial, Glenrose Instruments, Haemonetics Corp., ITT Educational Services, JDA Software, John H. Harland Company, Janus Capital Group, Kinetic Concepts Inc., Korea First Bank, Laboratory Corp. of America, Lincoln Educational Services, Magellan Health Services Inc., MoneyGram International, Montpelier Re Holdings, Nu Skin Enterprises, NutriSystem Inc., National Data Corp., NCR Corp., Novell Inc., Nova Corp., Paxar Corp., Pegasus Solutions, PRGX Global, Pediatrix Medical Group Inc., Payless ShoeSource, Playtex Products Inc., Rovi Inc., Skillsoft PLC, Suntron Corp., Synopsys Inc., Ross Stores, Renal Care Group, Scott Technologies Inc., TCF Financial Corp., Thomson, Tiffany & Co., Timberland Corp., Western Wireless Corp., Tokeheim Corp., Waddell Reed Financial Inc., Washington Mutual, Williams Sonoma, Websense, Xtralis Group, Zebra Technologies

Key Executives:
Richard C. Blum, Chairman
Education: BA, MBA, University of California, Berkeley
Background: Co-Founder, Newbridge Capital
Directorships: PAG
Murray McCabe, Managing Partner
Education: BA, University of Texas
Background: JPMorgan
Directorships: Columbia Property Trust Inc; RREEF Property Trust Inc.; Sunstone Hotel Investors Inc.
Peter Westley, Partner
Education: BA, Dartmouth College; MBA, Stanford University
Background: Managing Director, Salomon Smith Barney; Partner, ThinkEquity Partner; Partner, North Point Advisors; Canyon Partners
Directorships: Avid Technology Inc.; Payless ShoeSource
T.C. Ostrander, Vice President
Education: BA, Stanford University
Background: United States Senator Advisor

301 BLUMBERG CAPITAL
501 Folsom St
Suite 400
San Francisco, CA 94105

Phone: 415-905-5000 Fax: 415-357-5027
e-mail: info@blumbergcapital.com
web: www.blumbergcapital.com

Mission Statement: Early-stage venture capital firm.

Fund Size: $40 million
Founded: 1991
Average Investment: $3 million
Minimum Investment: $500,000
Investment Criteria: Seed, Early Stage
Industry Group Preference: Networking, Enterprise Services, Wireless Technologies, Security, Technology, Infrastructure, Information Technology, Software, Digital

Venture Capital & Private Equity Firms / Domestic Firms

Media & Marketing, Social Media, Mobile, Consumer Internet, SaaS
Portfolio Companies: Addepar, Any.do, Appboy, BrainRush, Carwoo, CaseStack, Chirpme, Cook Taste Eat, CoverHound, Credorax, Cyvera, Damballa, Dealsquare, Dekko, DoubleVerify, Elevator, Ellie, ePet World, Fanzila, FEEX, HootSuite, Isocket, Kreditech, Lenddo, LiteScape, mAdvertise, Mentad, Merchant Atlas, Mishor, Moment.Me, Mom Trusted, Mygola, Nutanix, Paid Piper, Parse.ly, Paymill, Revionics, Sonar, The One Page Company, Trulioo, Upfront Digital Media, Urbanara, VideoGenia, Wummel Kiste, Yap.tv, Zanbato, ZipZap

Other Locations:
39 Montefiore St
Tel Aviv 6520108
Israel
Phone: 972-3-7573107

Key Executives:
David J. Blumberg, Founder and Managing Partner
Education: AB, Government, Harvard College; MBA, Stanford Graduate School of Business
Background: Investment Manager, Claridge Investments; Investment Manager, Adler & Co; Investment Manager, Apax Partners; Investment Manager, T Rowe Price Associates
Directorships: CaseStack; Siperian; IP Infusion; Seclarity; Insightix; Board Member, Jewish Community Federation of San Francisco; Member, Pacific Council on International Policy
Bruce K. Taragin, Managing Director
Education: BA, Finance/Communications, Yeshiva University; MBA, JD, Fordham University
Background: Senior Management, Charles River Computers; Manager, Hambrecht & Quist; Manager, Mayer Brown & Platt; Manager, Bankers Trust Company
Directorships: CaseStack; Go Networks; Insightix; LiteScape; PureSight; Vista Research

302 BMW I VENTURES
2606 Bayshore Parkway
Mountain View, CA 94043

web: www.bmwiventures.com

Mission Statement: Seeks start-ups with the potential to create a lasting impact in the area of mobility services, primarily through cooperation with the BMW i brand. Additionally, these start-ups should have a strong focus on improving personal mobility in urban areas - automotive or otherwise. Whether it be intermodal travel, smart parking, recommendations, communication or other avenues, these services should deliver innovative and intelligent benefits to today's growing urban population.

Founded: 2011
Industry Group Preference: E-Mobility, Autonomous Driving, Digital Cars, Artificial Intelligence, Clean Energy
Portfolio Companies: Bus.com, Carbon, Caroobi, Charge Master, Charge Point, Desktop Metal, DSP Concepts, Embark, Fair, Gan Systems, Just Park, Life360, Moovit, Nauto, Proterra, Rever, RideCell, Shift, Skurt, Stratim, Strivr, Scoop, Xometry, ZenDrive

Key Executives:
Uwe Higgen, Managing Director
Background: Project Manager, BMW Group; Strategic Council, NAUTO
Directorships: Gan Systems Inc.
Ulrich Quay, Managing Director
Zach Barasz, Partner
Education: Stanford Graduate School of Business
Background: Kleiner Perkins Caufield & Byers
Michael Christoph Hammer, Chief Financial Officer

303 BNY MELLON CAPITAL MARKETS
240 Greenwich Street
New York, NY 10286

Phone: 212-495-1784
web: www.bnymellon.com

Mission Statement: BNY Mellon Capital Markets is dedicated to providing flexible and responsive financing solutions to private equity firms and middle market companies that seek junior capital solutions to finance growth, acquisitions or recapitalizations.

Geographic Preference: United States
Founded: 1991
Minimum Investment: $500,000
Investment Criteria: Prefer $3 - $20mm of subordinated debt or $2 - $10mm of private equity. Annual sales in excess of $25mm and operating cash flow of at least $3mm.

Key Executives:
Thomas P (Todd) Gibbons, Chief Executive Officer
Education: BS, Wake Forest University; MBA, Pace University
Background: CEO, Clearing, Market & Client Management; CFO, BNY Mellon; CFO, Bank of New York; Assistant Treasurer, Handy & Harman
Bridget E Engle, Chief Operating Officer/Chief Technology Officer
Background: Executive/CIO, Bank of America; Managing Director, Depository Trust & Clearing Corporation; CIO, Lehman Brothers

304 BOLDCAP VENTURES LLC
750 Lexington Avenue
6th Floor
New York, NY 10022

Phone: 212-730-5498 **Fax:** 917-591-0880

Mission Statement: Boldcap Ventures LLC invests in early to mid-stage companies and focuses primarily on the healthcare and technology industries.

Average Investment: $5 - $15 million
Investment Criteria: Early-Stage, Mid-Stage
Industry Group Preference: Healthcare, Technology
Portfolio Companies: AgraQuest, Aquea Scientific, Cylex, Go Fish, The NewsMarket, Pivot Solutions, Proto Software, Precision Therapeutics

Key Executives:
Amy Rosen Wildstein, Fund Manager
Background: Blackstone Group; Principal, Solera Capital; Morgan Stanley

305 BOLDSTART VENTURES
30 East 23rd Street
5th Floor
New York, NY 10010

web: www.boldstart.vc

Mission Statement: BoldStart Ventures is interested in IT infrastructure and software development.

Founded: 2010
Industry Group Preference: Information Technology, Data Analytics, Software, SaaS, Cyber Security, Virtual Reality, Artificial Intelligence, Mobility
Portfolio Companies: AskWonder, Auxon, BigID, Blaze Software, BlockDaemon, Catalytic, Clay, Coherent Path, Dark, Divide, Dropout Labs, Emissary, FortressIQ, Front, GoInstant, GoToMeeting, Greenplum, Handshake, HYPR, IOpipe, Init.ai, Jyve, Klipfolio, Kustomer, LivePerson, Manifold, MState, Pinpoint, Preact, Rapportive, Replicated, Robin, Security Scorecard, Sling, Smallstep, Snyk, SocialRank, Superhuman Labs, Rebel Mail, ThinkNear, Truly, Wallaroo Labs, WEVR, WorkRails, Yhat, Yipit Data

Key Executives:
Ed Sim, Founder/General Partner
Education: AB, Harvard University

Venture Capital & Private Equity Firms / Domestic Firms

Background: Co-Founder, MState; Managing Director, Dawntreader Ventures; Investment Analyst, JP Morgan; Sr. Investment Analyst, Equitable Real Estate
Charlotte Chapanoff, General Manager
Education: BA, Long Island University
Background: Assistant Account Manager, Under Armour
Eliot Durbin, General Partner
Education: BA, Georgetown University
Background: Assistant VP, Permal Asset Management; Managing Director/Co-Founder, Penny Black Holdings LLC; Co-Founder, MState
Jeff Leventhal, Partner
Education: Binghamton University School of Management
Background: Founder/CEO/Chairman, OnForce; Founder, Spinback Inc.; Founder/CEO, Work Market; Co-Founder/CEO, WorkRails

306 BONFIRE VENTURES
725 Arizona Ave.
Suite 400
Santa Monica, CA 90401

web: www.bonfirevc.com

Mission Statement: Bonfire Ventures invests in companies that are designing software solutions that change the way business is conducted.
Investment Criteria: Early-Stage
Industry Group Preference: Business to Business, Software
Portfolio Companies: Adstage, Bitium, BlueCasa, Boulevard, Branch, Burstly, Cadforce, Campus Explorer, ChowNow, Clearwire, Clique, Comparably, Connexity, ConversionLogic, Credit Key, DataPop, Disqo, Divshot, Earnest, EdgeCast, Elephant Drive, Emailage, Embrace.io, EvConnect, Fama, FieldTest, Fuel 50, FutureVault, Gradient, Haawk, HiQ, HG Data, Honk, Inspire, InVia Robotics, Invoca, InvolveSoft, JazzHR, Kaleo, Keen IO, Kittyhawk, Launchpad LA, Lettuce, LiftIgniter, Local Market Launch, MessageLabs, Mobcrush, MomentFeed, mPulse, Niantic, Nord Sense, OpenDrives, OpenPath, Orbitera, Packet Island, Particle, Pathmatics, Pingg, PingThings, Pledgeling, Postie, Prevoty, Prompt.ly, Qordoba, Quietly, Rainforest, Raken, Ranker, Reaction Commerce, Remote.it, Rentlytics, RESC, Respondly, Rockbot, Saferide, Scopely, Sense360, Shift, Shippabo, Sideqik, Silversheet, SimpleLegal, SteelHouse, TallyGo!, TaxJar, theTradeDesk, ThinkIQ, Tradesy, Tray, Trinity Mobile Networks, Tuition.io, Vintra, Windfall, Yello Mobile, Zingle

Other Locations:
803 Chapala St.
Santa Barbara, CA 93101

Key Executives:
Jim Andelman, Co-Founder/Managing Director
Education: BS, Economics, Wharton School; MBA, Tuck School of Business
Background: Managing Partner, Rincon Venture Partners; Broadview Capital Partners
Directorships: Campus Explorer, Conversion Logic, Keen IO, Qordoba, Rentlytics, Rainforst QA, Rockbot, SteelHouse, Tradesy
Mark Mullen, Co-Founder/Managing Director
Education: BSBA, University of Denver; MBA, Thunderbird School of Global Management
Background: Managing Partner, Double M Partners; Managing Partner, Mull Capital
Directorships: Fama, Trinity Mobile Networks, Altice USA

307 BOOST VC
55 East Third Avenue
San Mateo, CA 94401

e-mail: info@boost.vc
web: www.boost.vc

Mission Statement: Boost VC invests in innovative technology with a speciality in virtual realities and blockchain.
Geographic Preference: International
Founded: 2012
Average Investment: up to $50,000
Investment Criteria: Ownership of 7%
Industry Group Preference: Virtual Reality & Augmented Reality, Robotics, Space Technology, AI, Technology
Portfolio Companies: Mindshow, Kite & Lightingm, 89, Boom, Realities.io, TheWaveVR, SculptiVR, Fearless, JanusVR, Unimersiv, Vizor, Spaces, Casino VR Poker, VArchive, Aemass, Lingoland, BinaryVR, Beloola, Kokowa, Construct, Primitive, Jig Space, Twindom, Quark VR, Ease, Pixel Ripped, Jump, Ralph, Surreal, Bouncy, Imgnation, Virt, Orb, Spacesys, One Caring Team, Metaphysics VR, 3D-SensIR, Collect, Uraniom, Samo, Karobi, Beast, Dimension IO, Flipside, Galatea, Microtrip, Virtual Speech, Vrart, Xploadr, Wyre, Etherscan, Coinbase, Veem, Blockcypher, Ripio, T3, Abra, Aragon, Sfox, Unocoin, Polychain Capital, IPFS, Yours, Hijro, JoyStream, BitRefill, Filecoin, Volabit, Stampery, Coinut, Shake, BlinkTrade, Lawnmower, Hashrabbit, Leet, Coinprism, Celery, Bitquick, Simply Vital Health, The Sun Exchange, Pop Chest, Coinage, Atlas, Coin Jar, Factury, Loanbase, Mego, Coinhako, Blossom, Ownershipp, Rainvow, Rehive, Ubby, BitWall, Bitproof.io, Gliph, Surebits, Follow The Coin, Volt Markets, CleverCoin, Favor, Octane AI, 7 Shifts, & Ava, Blockscore, DeepGram, Pillow, Cobalt, Eagaveev, Mirror, Rebel Coast Winery, Swiftly, Trending, Kubos, CommitChange, Volley, Gravity, Feastly, Gun, GlycoProx, Listenloop, AuditFile.com, & Sunsama, Strengthportal, Eva, Unaptent, Globevestor, + GNEO, Appfuel, Perch, Checkbook, Swell Rewards, Seeds, Down, Scalpr, Ziibra, WorkingOn, Roam, AirBoard, Kriya, Launcher, LeadFlip, NearGroup, SenseiHub, Teamwork.ai, TensorFlight, Waylo

Key Executives:
Adam Draper, Founder/Managing Director
Education: University of California, LA
Background: Founder, Xpert Financial
Brayton Williams, Founder/Partner
Background: Morgan Stanley; Boost Bitcoin Fund, Xpert Financial; Northrop Grumman, Taylor Frigon Capital Management; Advisor at, Miffiel, 7 Shifts, Etherscan.io, Aragon, MyEtherWallet
Maddie Callander, Director of Operations
Education: BA, Art History & Spanish, Denison University
Background: Private Aviation Department, Yellowstone Club; Event Coordination, Van Wyck & Van Wyck

308 BOREALIS VENTURES
10 Allen Street
Hanover, NH 03755

Phone: 603-643-1500
e-mail: team@borealisventures.com
web: www.borealisventures.com

Mission Statement: Borealis Ventures is a seed and early-stage venture capital firm uniquely focused on investing in companies in Northern New England and throughout the Dartmouth College network.
Average Investment: $2.5 million
Minimum Investment: $100,000
Investment Criteria: Seed, Early-Stage
Industry Group Preference: Applications Software & Services, Internet, Mobile Media, Technology
Portfolio Companies: Adimab, At Last Software, Avedro, Avitide, Blockable, Builtr Labs, Compass Therapeutics, CoUrbanize, Dandelion Energy, Dyn, Envista, Fieldlens, Foodbuzz, Flurry, Flux, GlyciFi, Handmark, Honest Buildings, Icovia, M2S, Makeover Solutions, Measurabl, Newforma, OmniEarth, Scribe Software, SketchFab, Smartvid.io, Spaceclaim, Tinkercad, Vets First Choice, VICO Software, Wingu

Venture Capital & Private Equity Firms / Domestic Firms

Other Locations:
31 St. James Avenue
6th Floor
Boston, MA 02116
Key Executives:
   Jesse Devitte, Managing Director/Co-Founder
   e-mail: jdevitte@borealisventures.com
   Background: Softdesk; Autodesk; Handmark
   Directorships: Envista, Handmark, Newforma, Vico
   Phil Ferneau, Managing Director/Co-Founder
   e-mail: phil@borealisventures.com
   Education: BA, Dartmouth College; JD, University of Virginia School of Law; MBA, Tuck School of Business, Dartmouth College
   Background: Executive Director, Center for Private Equity & Entrepreneurship, Tuck School of Business, Dartmouth College
   Matt Rightmire, Managing Director
   e-mail: matt@borealisventures.com
   Education: MBA, Tuck School of Business at Dartmouth College; BS, Industrial Engineering, Stanford University
   Background: COO, Efficient Frontier; Yahoo

309 BOSTON CAPITAL
One Boston Place
Boston, MA 02108

Phone: 617-624-8900
e-mail: bcinfo@bostoncapital.com
web: www.bostoncapital.com

Mission Statement: Boston Capital is the nation's leading provider of equity investments in multifamily real estate funds.

Geographic Preference: Nationwide
Fund Size: $250 million
Founded: 1974
Investment Criteria: Class A Apartments, Tax Credit Funds
Industry Group Preference: Real Estate, Property Development
Key Executives:
   Jack Manning, President/Chief Executive Officer
   617-624-8501
   e-mail: jmanning@bostoncapital.com
   Education: Boston College
   Background: President's Export Council; President's Advisory Committee on the Arts
   Directorships: Chairman, Distinguised Visitors Program; Liberty Mutual Group
   Jeffrey H. Goldstein, Executive Vice President/Chief Operating Officer
   617-624-8640
   e-mail: jgoldstein@bostoncapital.com
   Education: BA, University of Colorado; MBA, Northeastern University
   Background: Manager of Finance, A.J. Lane & Co.; Manager, Homeowner Financial Services
   Kevin P. Costello, Executive Vice President/Director, Institutional Investing
   617-624-8550
   e-mail: kcostello@bostoncapital.com
   Education: Stonehill College; MBA, Finance, Rutgers Graduate School of Business Administration
   Directorships: FamilyAid Boston

310 BOSTON CAPITAL VENTURES
Boston, MA 02109

e-mail: info@bcv.com
web: www.bcv.com

Mission Statement: Boston Capital Ventures is a private venture capital firm which invests in early-stage companies in the information technology and telecommunications services industries.

Geographic Preference: United States, Europe, Asia, Latin America
Fund Size: $150 million
Founded: 1982
Average Investment: $1 - $10 million
Minimum Investment: $1 million
Investment Criteria: Start-Up, Niche, Regional, Multinational, Fortune 100
Industry Group Preference: Technology, Software, Telecommunications, Enterprise Software, Infrastructure, Retailing, Transportation, Business to Business, Marketing
Portfolio Companies: Availant, Centric Software, Exa Corporation, FareChase, HubX, iBreva, ImpactXoft, Khimetrics, RealManage, Reflexion Network Solutions, Signiant, Thor Technologies, Veridiem, Wandrian, Yokel
Key Executives:
   Johan von der Goltz, General Partner
   e-mail: jgoltz@bcv.com
   Education: Massachusettes Institute of Technology, Harvard Business School
   Background: Otto Wolff AG; Trinkhaus Bank; Compania Argo Comercial SA; Cerveceria del Sur SA
   Directorships: International Cornerstone Group, Fast Channel Networks, Conservative Tourism
   Jack Shields, General Partner
   e-mail: jshields@bcv.com
   Education: Sorcester Polytechnic Institute's School of Industrial Management; Harvard Business School PMD; Honorary Doctorate of Engineering, WPI
   Background: KFgital Equipment Corporation; President/CEOComputervision
   Directorships: Iirector, Centric Software; Director, Exa; Director, ImpactXoft
   Alex von der Goltz, Partner
   e-mail: agoltz@bcv.com
   Education: Brown University, MIT Sloan School of Management
   Background: International Music Division, Bertelsmann Entertainment; Management Consultant, Roland Berger; Professional Services/Technical Sales, Oracle Corporation & Techgnosis
   Directorships: Centric Software; Reflexion Network Solutions; Signiant; Thor Technologies

311 BOSTON GLOBAL VENTURES, LLC
One Broadway
14th Floor
Cambridge, MA 02142

Mission Statement: Boston Global Ventures is a Boston based venture capital firm supporting early-stage high-impact technology companies.

Investment Criteria: Early Stage
Industry Group Preference: Technology

312 BOSTON MILLENNIA PARTNERS
30 Rowes Wharf
Suite 400
Boston, MA 02110

Phone: 617-428-5150 Fax: 617-428-5160
web: www.bostonmillenniapartners.com

Mission Statement: Boston Millennia Partners is a private equity and venture capital firm active nationwide.

Geographic Preference: United States, Canada
Fund Size: $700 million
Founded: 1984
Average Investment: $10 - $15 million
Minimum Investment: $3 million
Investment Criteria: Early Stage, Later Stage, Expansion
Industry Group Preference: Healthcare, Business Services, Information Technology

Portfolio Companies: Arthrosurface, Athenix, CardioMEMS, Coapt Systems, Collegium, CombinatoRx, eMed Technologies, EpiGenesis Pharmaceuticals, EPIX Pharmaceuticals, Galt Associates, GlycoFi, Histogenics Corporation, ILEX, MedAptus, MedAptus, Medical Management of New England, MedSpan, Novalar, Parexel, PHT, Proteome, Sapphire Therapeutics, Tektagen

Key Executives:
Dana Callow, Managing General Partner
e-mail: dana@bmpvc.com
Education: MBA, Amos Tuck School, dartmouth college; tufts university
Background: General Partner, Co-Founder, Boston Capital Ventures; Sr Consultant, Braxton Associates
Directorships: Bright Horizons, Collegium, HotJobs, ILEX Oncology, Infotrieve, iVillage, Knowledge Impact, MedAptus, Medical Management of New England, PAREXEL International, PHT, Tektagen
Rob Sherman, Operating Partner
e-mail: robs@bmpvc.com
Education: MBA, Harvard Business School; Amherst College
Background: Boston Capital Ventures; General Partner, Hambro International Venture Fund
Directorships: Concentrix, MedSpan, Neoworld, NuVox Communications, TechSmart, UNIsite, V-Span
Marty Hernon, General Partner
e-mail: marty@bmpvc.com
Education: BA Economics, Boston College; MA Economics, University of Maryland; JD, Georgetown University
Background: President, Boston Capital Ventures; Asst General Counsel, Lifetime Corporation; Of Counsel Business Department, Warner & Stackpole/Kirkpartrick & Lockhart
Directorships: Dawntreader Funds, VIA Net.Works, WebCT, YankeeTek
Bruce Tiedemann, Partner/CFO
e-mail: bruce@bmpvc.com
Education: Graduate, Bentley College
Background: Founder, Tiedemann & Company; CFO/Controller, serveral startup venture funded companies; Certified Public Accountant

313 BOSTON SEED CAPITAL
37 Walnut Street
Suite 110
Wellesley, MA 02347

e-mail: info@bostonseed.com
web: www.bostonseed.com

Mission Statement: Boston Seed Capital provides seed state funding for internet-enabled businesses. The firm's approach is to identify and help extraordinary talent to create great new companies, and to contribute to the culture of invention, leadership and learning in Boston. Boston Seed's team is made up of operators who have founded companies, grown companies, raised capital, acquired companies, taken companies public, and exited companies.
Geographic Preference: United States
Founded: 2010
Industry Group Preference: Internet, Consumer Internet, Business to Business, SaaS
Portfolio Companies: Alignable, Altiscale, Blaze.io, Bostlnno, Careport Health, Clypd, Codeship, Contactually, Directr, Draft Kings, Evertrue, FamilyID.com, FlyWire, Gamersensei, GrapeviceLogic.com, Horse Network, Humanize, Indico.co, Jebbit, Kindara, Kinvey, Mylestoned, NBD Nano, OfferLogic, Openbay, Promoboxx, UberSense, RunKeeper, Shareaholic, Smackhigh, Sold.

Key Executives:
Nicole M. Stata, Founder/Managing Director
e-mail: nstata@bostonseed.com

Background: Founder, Deploy Solutions; Restrac; Lotus Development Corporation
Peter Blacklow, Senior Partner
e-mail: pblacklow@bostonseed.com
Education: Harvard University
Background: President, Worldwinner; EVP, Digital, GSN; SVP, Marketing, Monster
Directorships: eSkill.com, WGBH
Dave Balter, Venture Partner
e-mail: davebalter@gmail.com
Background: CEO, BzzAgent; Co-Founder, Word of Mouth Marketing Association
Directorships: Promoboxx, Relay Rides, eLaCarte, ProctorCam, HelpScout

314 BOSTON UNIVERSITY - TECHNOLOGY DEVELOPMENT
One Silber Way
8th Floor
Boston, MA 02215

web: www.bu.edu/researchsupport/project-lifecycle/bring-to-market

Mission Statement: Provides venture capital to early-stage companies. The Fund focuses on companies within the Information Technology and Life Sciences industries.
Geographic Preference: Northeast United States
Fund Size: $30 million
Founded: 1975
Average Investment: $500,000 to $1.5 million
Minimum Investment: $250,000
Investment Criteria: Early Stage
Industry Group Preference: Information Technology, Life Sciences
Portfolio Companies: Arradial, Artel Video, Boston Medical Technologies, C-Port Corporation, CardioFocus, Cellicon, Centagenetix, Cetaccean Networks, Commonwealth Network Technologies, Concord Communications, Continental Cablevision, Coriolis Networks, Crossbeam Systems, Cynosure, CytoLogix Corporation, Emperative, Evrest Broadband Networks, FASTech Integration, HPR, Holographix, InfoLibria, Invisable Hand Networks, Maple Tree Networks, MicroCHIPS, MicroE Systems, Nitro med, Nitronex, OutStart, Pharmadyne, Predictive Networks, Quanhtum Bridge Communications, Quarry Technologies, QuitNet, Sandburst Corporation, Scion, Seragen, SilverBack Technologies, StarGen, Synchrologic, Vibrant Technologies, Viewlogic Systems, Wave Systems

315 BOULDER VENTURES LTD
1941 Pearl Street
Suite 300
Boulder, CO 80302

Phone: 303-444-6950
e-mail: james@boulderventures.com
web: www.boulderventures.com

Mission Statement: Identifies exceptional entrepreneurs building market-leading technology companies and provides funding, contacts and experience needed to succeed in today's highly competitive environment.
Geographic Preference: Mid-Atlantic, Colorado, California
Fund Size: $300 million
Founded: 1995
Average Investment: $5-$10 million
Minimum Investment: $2-$4 million
Investment Criteria: Early-Stage
Industry Group Preference: Information Technology, Internet Technology, Retailing, Life Sciences, Biotechnology, Health Related, Nutrition, Food & Beverage, Data Storage, Communications
Portfolio Companies: ARCA Biopharma, Array BioPharma, Barofold, BiOptix, Bluesocket, BroadHop, Cadre

115

Venture Capital & Private Equity Firms / Domestic Firms

Technologies, CenterStone Technologies, ClaraBridge, Cogent Communications, Compatible Systems, Datavail, Dharmacon, Entelos, Entevo Corp., Era, Estorian, Everest Software, Exactis.com, Federated Media Publishing, Finali Corporation, Genomica, Hiberna Corporation, iLumin Software, Interland, kSaria Corporation, LeftHand Networks, Lijit Networks, Market Force Information, Metron Aviation, Millennium Pharmacy Systems, MiRagen Therapeutics, ProStor Systems, Rally Software, SafeRent, TidalTV, Videology, Wall Street On Demand, XIFIN, Zenoss

Other Locations:
5425 Wisconsin Avenue
Suite 704
Chevy Chase, MD 20815
Phone: 301-913-0213

Key Executives:
Kyle Lefkoff, General Partner
e-mail: kyle@boulderventures.com
Education: BA, Vassar College; MBA, University of Chicago
Directorships: Metabolite Laboratories, Trust Company of America, Symetix, Vexcel Corporation, ArrayBioPharma, LeftHand Networks, Dharmacon
Peter Roshko, General Partner
e-mail: peter@boulderventures.com
Education: MBA, Harvard Graduate School; BS, Industrial Engineering, Stanford University
Background: General Partner, Mohr, Davidow Ventures
Directorships: Trust Company of America, Finali, Xifin, BitBlitz, f4 Technologies
Jonathan Perl, General Partner
e-mail: jonathan@boulderventures.com
Education: BA, Tufts University; MBA, Tuck School of Business, Dartmouth College
Background: Kauffman Fellows

316 BOUNDS EQUITY PARTNERS
600 Central Avenue
Suite 230
Highland Park, IL 60035

Phone: 847-266-6300
e-mail: mab@boundsequity.com
web: www.boundsequity.com

Mission Statement: A private equity investment firm that invests in well-managed, entrepreneurial businesses.
Geographic Preference: United States, Canada
Fund Size: $100 million
Founded: 1998
Minimum Investment: $1 million
Investment Criteria: Companies With Minimum EBITDA of $1.5 Million
Industry Group Preference: Building Materials & Services, Business Products & Services, Distribution, Manufacturing, Healthcare Services
Portfolio Companies: Beacon Promotions, Clad-Rex, CrossCom, EastPoint Sports, Hollinee, L&S Mechanical, Norcraft Companies, Sportcraft, Thermo-Tech Windows

Key Executives:
Mark Bounds, Managing Director
e-mail: mab@boundsequity.com
Education: BA, Marketing, University of Iowa; MBA, University of Chicago
Background: Managing Director, Goense Bounds & Partners; Director, Allstate Private Equity; VP, Corporate Development, GAF Corporation; Co-Founder/Principal, Heller Equity Capital Corporation
Stuart Skinner, Chief Financial Officer
Education: BS, Accounting, Northeastern Illinois University
Background: Controller, Goense Bounds & Partners; Controller, Allstate Private Equity
Andy Reed, Operating Advisor
Education: BA, History, Principia College; MBA, Indiana University
Background: CEO, Shurline; CEO, US Builder Services, Goense Bounds; USBS

317 BOWERY CAPITAL
37 West 20th St.
New York, NY 10011

web: www.bowerycap.com

Mission Statement: We are a thesis-driven early-stage investor backing exceptional founders modernizing business through technology. From marketing and sales to analytics and infrastructure, our startups are changing the way business is done. We work hard on behalf of our founders and believe in a model of concentrated value-add with a central focus: building the base of flagship customers that startups need to achieve outsized early growth. We move fast, never waste an entrepreneur's time, always strive to be more resourceful than most, and focus our day-to-day on being the best possible partner to each and every founder we back, If you are a seed-stage entrepreneur and this is for you, let's talk.
Founded: 2010
Investment Criteria: Early-Stage
Industry Group Preference: Business Products & Services
Portfolio Companies: ActionIQ, Block Six Analytics, Carnival Mobile, ChannelEyes, Codeacademy, CredSimple, Drawbridge Networks, Electric AI, Elliot, Expedi, Fero Labs, Inpher, Leapfin, Metricly, Moat, Moment Snap, mParticle, msg.ai, Oncue, Oomnitza, Outlaw, Premise, Sailthru, Selfie Networks, StreetCred, SupplyShift, SwiftShift, TrackMaven, Transfix, VNDLY, Voxy, Wizeline, Zeus

Key Executives:
Mike Brown Jr., Founder & Managing Partner
Education: Columbia University
Background: Co-Founder, AOL Ventures; Virgin Group; Morgan Stanley
Nic Poulos, Partner
Education: AB, History, Princeton University
Background: Associate, AOL Ventures; Manager, Advertising.com; Technology Investment Banking Analyst, GCA Savvian Advisors

318 BOXGROUP
New York, NY

e-mail: hello@boxgroup.com
web: boxgroup.com

Mission Statement: Early stage investment fund in New York among the most active micro venture capital firms.
Geographic Preference: New York, Silicon Valley, Los Angeles
Average Investment: $50-250K
Investment Criteria: Pre-Seed, Seed
Industry Group Preference: Marketplaces, E-Commerce & Manufacturing, SaaS, Fintech
Portfolio Companies: 64x Bio, Aether Bio, Agora, Airtable, Amino, Amplitude, Apply, Arcadia, Artemys, Artsy, Astranis, Atom Computing, Baobab, Balsa, Binti, Blink Health, Boxed, Braavo, Brat TV, Bravo Sierra, The Browser Company of New york, By Humankind, Candidate Labs, Canopy Servicing, Capchase, Casetext, Celevity, Classpass, Clay, Cleancut, Codecov, Collective Retreats, Colu Technologies, CommandDot, Cricket Health, Crowd AI, Customer.io, Dataminr, David Energy, Dooly, Embrace.io, EnterMedicare, FairShake, Flexport, Giant Swarm, Goodcover, Good Dog, Harry's, Karuna Health, Kula Bio, Lotus Flare, Mantra Bio, memphis Meats, Modern Fertility, Modern Animal, Muze, Omni Labs, One Chronos, One Tap Away, OpenSpace, PaperSpace, Pickle Robot Co., Timebyping, PlanetScale, Prime Discovery, RankScience, Reverie Labs, Rockets Of Awesome, Scoot Science, Skillshare, Something Navy, Standard Bots, Terminal49, TrueAccord, Verto Education, Warby Parker, WayUp, WeRecover, Yoni Circle, OpenZeppelin, Zestful, Zipline, Zira.ai

Key Executives:
David Tisch, Co-Founder & Managing Director
Education: University of Pennsylvania; New York University
Background: Vornado Realty Trust; LightsOver
Adam Rothenberg, Co-Founder & Partner
Education: University of Pennsylvania
Background: Zimmer Lucas Partners; TechStars

---

319 BP ALTERNATIVE ENERGY VENTURES
501 Westlake Park Boulevard
Houston, TX 77079

Phone: 281-366-2000
e-mail: bpventures@bp.com
web: www.bp.com

Mission Statement: Invests in growth stage companies offering low carbon and secure energy solutions. Alternative Energy Ventures seeks to identify new technologies and business opportunities with the potential of making sound financial returns in the clean energy sector.

Fund Size: $150 million
Founded: 2006
Average Investment: $10 - $30 million
Investment Criteria: Early-Stage, Growth Stage
Industry Group Preference: Energy, Wind Power, Clean Technology, Alternative Energy, Renewable Energy, Carbon Management
Portfolio Companies: Advanced BioCatalytics, Beyond Limits, BiSN, Biosynthetic Technologies, Bright Source, Carbonfire, Chromatin, Drover, EOS, Fotech, Fulcrum, Helie Power, Lightning Hybrids, Modumetal, Peloton, Repair Pal, RocketRoute, Saltworks, Solidia Technologies, Synthetic Genomics, SMG, Tricoya, Verdezyne, Victor, Xact, Zubie

Key Executives:
David Hayes, Chief Investment Officer/Managing Director
Education: BA, Sheffield Hallam University
Directorships: Chromatin, Lightning Systems, Xpansiv Data Systems, Mendal Biotechnology

---

320 BR VENTURE FUND
Johnson Graduate School of Management
Cornell University
106 Sage Avenue
Ithaca, NY 14853

Phone: 607-255-9395
e-mail: contact@brventurefund.com
web: www.brventurefund.com

Mission Statement: Early-stage venture capital fund operated by MBA students at Cornell University's Johnson Graduate School of Management.

Geographic Preference: Northeast United States
Average Investment: $50,000-$250,000
Investment Criteria: Seed-Stage
Portfolio Companies: Adenios, Appinions, e2e Materials, GNS Healthcare, Medical Care Corporation, NovaSterilis, Venga

---

321 BRADFORD EQUITIES MANAGEMENT LLC
360 Hamilton Avenue
7th Floor
White Plains, NY 10601

Phone: 914-922-7171 **Fax:** 914-922-7172
web: bradfordequities.com

Mission Statement: Investor in middle-market companies.
Geographic Preference: United States
Fund Size: $200 million
Founded: 1974
Average Investment: $15 - $75 million
Minimum Investment: $5 million
Investment Criteria: Middle-Market
Industry Group Preference: Distribution, Industrial Equipment, Retailing, Technology, Manufacturing
Portfolio Companies: Connecticut Color, Electron Beam Technologies, Metals Technology Corp., Sunbelt Modular, United Brass Works

Key Executives:
Robert J. Simon, Senior Managing Director
212-218-6917
Fax: 212-218-6901
Education: MBA, New York University Graduate School of Business Administration; BS in Finance, University of Minnesota School of Management
Background: Securities Analyst, Kidder, Peabody & Company; Acquisition Finance, Bancorp
Directorships: CR Gibson Company, Pamarco Technologies, Portugese Baking Company LP, VSC Corporation, Trimark USA, Wolverine Brass, Overseas Callander Fund Limited
David W. Jaffin, Senior Advisor
Education: BA, History, Harvard College; MBA, Finance/Accounting, New York University
Background: HoloPak Technologies Inc.; Poliwogg Holdings; B2B SFO; XShares Advisors LLC; Arthur Andersen & Co.
Neil J. Taylor, Principal/Chief Financial Officer
Education: BA, City of London University England; Graduate Enterprise Program, Cranfield School of Management England
Background: Senior Accountant, Dreyfus Corporation

---

322 BRAEMAR ENERGY VENTURES
350 Madison Avenue
New York, NY 10017

Phone: 212-697-0900
web: www.braemarenergy.com

Mission Statement: Braemar's mission is to partner with the most promising innovators to help unlock the enormous potential that exists in creating profitable solutions to the issues shaping the future of energy.

Founded: 2002
Average Investment: $1-10 million
Investment Criteria: Venture-Stage, Expansion-Stage, Early-Stage, Later-Stage
Industry Group Preference: Energy
Portfolio Companies: EnerNOC, BrightVolt, PowerGenix, Verenium, CoalTek, Utility, Stion, Afina, Fractal Systems, Cerion, CirisEnergy, Luminus, Climos, Enerkem, Laser Light Engines, Nuventix, Ioxus, Solazyme, Proterro, Opxbio, Fulham, Gridnet, Convey, General Fusion, Powervation, ViridityEnergy, LumEnergi, Amc10, Sirrus, Nexsteppe, Utilidata, Albeo, Sefaira, Chargepoint, Engine Efficiency, Aledia, Storiant, Flywheel, Next Step Living, Voxel8, Skyonic, Renew Financial, Getaround

Key Executives:
Neil S. Suslak, Managing Director
Education: BA, University of Rochester; MBA, Columbia Business School
Background: SG Warburg; Swiss Bank Corporation
Directorships: Venture Investors Association of New York; North American Advisory Board of The Cleantech Oganization
William D. Lese, Managing Director
Education: BA, Physics, MS, Energy Science; New York University
Dennis R. Costello, Partner
Education: BA, Economics, SUNY Fredonia; MA, Economics, Ohio State University; MS, Business, MIT
Background: Partner, Advent International; Managing Director, Rock Maple Ventures; General Partner, Zero Stage Capital; Executive Director, Colorado Advanced Technology Institute; Project Manager, Midwest Research Institute

Venture Capital & Private Equity Firms / Domestic Firms

Directorships: Nuventix, Climos, Fulham, Luminus, Laser Light Engines
Jiong Ma, Venture Partner
Education: PhD, Electrical Engineering, University of Colorado; MS, Electrical Engineering, Worcester Polytechnic Institute
Background: Lucent Technologies; Bell Labs

323 BRAIN TRUST ACCELERATOR FUND
800 Airport Boulevard
Suite 508
Burlingame, CA 94010

Phone: 650-375-0200 **Fax:** 650-375-0230
e-mail: john.reher@braintrustvc.com
web: www.braintrustvc.com

Mission Statement: Unique features of the fund include the focus and experience in brain related diseases, potential deal flow from philanthropies, operational as well as venture capital experience, and a focus on social as well as economic considerations.
Investment Criteria: Early-Stage
Industry Group Preference: Healthcare, Life Sciences, Therapeutics
Portfolio Companies: Anmestix, BrainScope Company, Chase Pharmaceuticals, NeuroFluidics, Satoris

Key Executives:
John M. Reher, Partner
Education: BS, Mathematics & Business Economics, Illinois Benedictine University; MS, Management, Northwestern University
Background: Co-Founder/General Partner, Medicus Venture Partners

324 BRAINSTORM VENTURES
4 Embarcadero Center
Suite 1400
San Francisco, CA 94111

e-mail: team@brainstorm.vc
web: brainstorm.vc

Mission Statement: BrainStorm Ventures was founded with a mission to fund emerging technology companies and actively assist them in their development.
Geographic Preference: Silicon Valley & San Francisco Bay Area
Founded: 1999
Investment Criteria: Seed-Stage, Early-Stage
Industry Group Preference: Enabling Technology, Enterprise Software, Broadband, E-Commerce & Manufacturing
Portfolio Companies: Adspace Networks, Aravo Solutions, Bid4assets, Cerego, Friend2friend, Kio Networks, Krush, Lightt, Lively, Me.com, OpenTable, Treatful, Uniscape, Vacatia, Yattos, Zappos.com

Key Executives:
Ariel Jaduszliwer, Managing Director
Education: BS, University of California Berkeley; MS, Georgia Institute of Technology; MBA, Wharton School
Background: Consultant, The Bridgespan Group; VP, Pacific Community Ventures; Fellow & Mentor, Kauffman Fellows
Directorships: ICU Eyewear Inc.; Bentek Corporation; New Leaf Paper; Freshology Inc.; Adina for Life
Eduardo Rallo, Co-Founder, Managing Director
Education: BA, Economics, University of California, San Diego; MBA, Harvard University
Background: Co-Founder, World Wrapps; Director of Special Projects, Cifra

325 BRAND FOUNDRY VENTURES
109 Nassau Street
New York, NY 10038

web: brandfoundryvc.com

Mission Statement: Brand Foundry Ventures is focused on consumer-based projects.
Industry Group Preference: Consumer, Retail
Portfolio Companies: Allbirds, Barnraiser, Birchbox, Bonobos, Brilliant Bicycles, Burrow, Clove, CoEdition, Cotopaxi, Crown Affair, Eden Health, Floravere, Floyd, Goby, Good Stock, Harry's, Haus, Henry The Dentist, Jinx, Judy, Keen Home, Kids On 45th, Kite, Kiwi Co., Koio, Leap, Lola, MixLab, Mosaic, NAJA, Nineteenth Amendment, Peachy, Peloton, Prefix, RMDY, Rockets of Awesome, Scratch Kitchen, Small Door, Smilo, Starface, Stay Tuned, The Still, The Wing, The Wonder, Warby Parker, Weller, Trace, Yumi

Other Locations:
119 Nueces Street
Austin, TX 78701

Key Executives:
Andrew Mitchell, Founder/General Partner
Education: BA, Lafayette College
Background: Co-Founder, Aspen Industries; Angel Investor
Wesley Gottesman, Principal
Education: BA, University of Virginia; MBA, Red McCombs School of Business, University of Texas
Background: Head of Product, PHLUR; Head of Product, Buzz Points Inc.; Special Projects Associate, The Idea Village
David Bell, Venture Partner
Education: BComm, University of Auckland; MA, University of Pennsylvania; MS, Stanford University; PhD, Stanford Grad. School of Business
Background: Co-Founder, Idea Farm Ventures; Associate Professor, Wharton School; Visiting Associate Professor, MIT Sloan School of Management
John Yang, Venture Partner
Education: BBA, Stephen M. Ross School of Business, University of Michigan; MBA, Wharton School
Background: Head of Strategy, Global Footwear, Nike; Director of Product Strategy & Marketing, Magic Leap; Director of Corporate Strategy & Development, NBCUniversal Media; Director of Customer Analytics, Comcast

326 BRANDON CAPITAL GROUP
459 Hamilton Avenue
Suite 205
Palo Alto, CA 94301

e-mail: info@mrcf.com.au
web: www.brandoncapital.com.au

Mission Statement: Seeks to invest in smaller middle-market business in the Northeastern US that have a defensible market position opportunity for growth, either internally or through acquisition.
Geographic Preference: Northeastern United States
Average Investment: $3 million
Minimum Investment: $1 million
Investment Criteria: Smaller Middle Market
Industry Group Preference: Manufacturing, Services, Distribution

Key Executives:
Leighton Read, Venture Partner
Education: BS, Rice University; MD, University of Texas Health Science Center
Background: Managing Director, Alloy Ventures; Managing Director/President, Pharma Division, Affymax NV; Chairman/CEO, Aviron

Venture Capital & Private Equity Firms / Domestic Firms

327 BRANFORD CASTLE
150 East 58th Street
37th Floor
New York, NY 10155

Phone: 202-317-2004 Fax: 212-317-2053
web: branfordcastle.com

Mission Statement: Branford Castle is a long-term investor in small- to medium-sized private companies.
Geographic Preference: North America
Fund Size: $200 million
Founded: 1986
Average Investment: $10 million equity
Minimum Investment: $1 million
Investment Criteria: Small to Medium Companies, Expansion
Industry Group Preference: Industrial, Oil and Gas, Marine, Chemicals, Consumer, Aerospace and Defence, Restaurants, Transportation and Infrastructure, Distribution, Media & Telecommunications, Energy, Healthcare Services, Business Services
Portfolio Companies: ABC Industries, Canada Metal Pacific, Drew Foam Companies Inc., EarthLite, Morton's The Steakhouse, PulseVet, Titan, TooJay's Restaurant & Deli, Vitrek, Washington Chain & Supply

Key Executives:
John S. Castle, President/CEO
212-317-2020
e-mail: jsc@branfordcastle.com
Background: Current Chariman/CEO, Castle Harlan, Former President/CEO, Donaldson, Lufkin & Jenrette
David Castle, Managing Partner
Education: Skidmore College; Cornell Law School
Background: Santa Fe Steakhouse; GE Capital
Eric R. Korsten, Senior Managing Director
212-317-2219
e-mail: ekorsten@branfordcastle.com
Education: BA, University of Pennsylvania; MBA, NYU Stern School of Business
Background: VP, Jefferies & Co.; Senior Analyst, Dunbar Capital Management
Directorships: ABC Industries; Pulse Veterinary Technologies; TooJay's Restaurant & Deli; Surface Preparation Technologies
Laurence Lederer, Senior Managing Director
212-317-2037
e-mail: lbl@branfordcastle.com
Education: BA, Carleton College; MBA, Harvard Business School
Background: Founder, Rubicon Associates; Principal, ACG Capital; Associate, Morgan Stanley & Co.; Associate, Castle Harlan
Directorships: Earthlite Massage Tables; Vitrek; Drew Foam

328 BRAZOS PRIVATE EQUITY PARTNERS
100 Crescent Court
Suite 1777
Dallas, TX 75201

Phone: 214-301-4201 Fax: 214-853-5090
web: www.brazosinv.com

Mission Statement: Specializes in leveraged acquisitions and recapitalizations of middle market companies that offer the potential for substantial capital appreciation.
Geographic Preference: Southwestern U.S., Texas
Fund Size: $1.4 billion
Founded: 1999
Average Investment: $25 - $100 million
Minimum Investment: $10 - $25 million
Investment Criteria: Buyouts, Recapitalizations, CEO-Backed Buy-and-Builds, Corporate Divestitures/Divisional Spin-Offs, Public-To-Privates
Industry Group Preference: Manufacturing, Consumer Products, Services, Healthcare, Media, Telecommunications, Business Products & Services, Financial Services, Distribution
Portfolio Companies: BlackHawk Industrial, Cheddar's Restaurants, Comark Building Systems, Eberly Design Inc., Ennis-Flint, European Wax Center, Fuel Systems, Healthcare Solutions, Impact Confections, Lone Star Overnight, Morton Industrial Group, National Surgical Care, ORS Nasco, Rennhack Marketing Services, Repulic Insurance, Sadler's Smokehouse, Shelter Distribution, Southern Tide, Strategic Equipment and Supply, TriNorthern Security Distribution, Vision Source, Walls Industries, Windebow Inc.

Key Executives:
Randall S. Fojtasek, Co-Founder and Co-CEO
214-756-6511
Fax: 214-756-6505
e-mail: rfojtasek@brazosinv.com
Education: Associate Arts Degree, Franklin College Switzerland; BBA & MBA, Cox School of Business at Southern Methodist University
Background: CEO, Atrium Companies; Board, Rennhack Marketing Services
Directorships: Cox School of Business at Southern Methodist University; Distinguished Alumni Award; Investment Committee at St Marks School of Texas; Young Presidents' Organization
Jeff S. Fronterhouse, Co-Founder and Co-CEO
214-756-6501
e-mail: jfronterhouse@brazosinv.com
Education: BBA Honors, University of Texas; MBA, Harvard Business School
Background: Principal, Hicks Muse; Specialist Merger/Acquisitions, The First Boston Corporation
Directorships: Baylor Healthcare System Foundation; The Rise School of Dallas; The Mike Modano Foundation; Dallas Citizens Council; Young Presidents' Organization
Patrick K. McGee, Co-Founder and Partner
214-756-6544
Fax: 214-756-6505
e-mail: pmcgee@brazosinv.com
Education: BS Engineering Science/Economics/Business Administration, Vanderbilt University
Background: Principal, Hicks Muse; VP Investment Banking Division, Merrill Lynch & Co; Board, Rennhack Marketing Services
Directorships: Young Presidents' Organization
Glenn W. Askew, Managing Director
214-756-6524
e-mail: gaskew@brazosinv.com
Education: BBA High Honors, University of Texas; MBA, University of Chicago
Background: VP Investment Banking Division, Goldman Sachs & Co
Lucas T. Cutler, Managing Director
Education: BBA, University of Texas
Background: Leveraged Finance Group, Banc of America Securities; Analyst, Corporate Finance Group, BancAmerica Robertson Stephens
Directorships: Golden County Foods, Impact Confections
Jason D. Sutherland, Managing Director
Education: BA, Harvard College; MBA, Harvard Business School
Background: Vice President, Specialty Lending Group, Goldman Sachs & Co.; Associate, Banc of America Securities; Investment Banking, James & Associates
Douglas L. Kennealey, Managing Director
Education: BA, Boston College; MBA, Harvard Business School
Background: Principal, Silver Lake Partners; Senior Associate, Summit Partners
Gayla W. Hightower, Fund Controller
Education: BBA, Accounting, University of Houston

Venture Capital & Private Equity Firms / Domestic Firms

329 BREAKAWAY VENTURES
399 Boylston Street
5th Floor
Boston, MA 02116

Phone: 617-399-0635
web: www.breakawayventures.com

Mission Statement: Breakaway is a unique combination of strategic consultancy, creative agency and venture capital firm. Actively investing in early to growth stage businesses and trusted partners to established brands looking for agents of change.

Average Investment: $3 - $8 million
Investment Criteria: Early-Stage, Growth-Stage, Revenues greater than $2 million
Industry Group Preference: Consumer Products, E-Commerce & Manufacturing, Retail, Consumer & Leisure, Apparel, Accessories, Footwear, Entertainment, Sports
Portfolio Companies: Spartan Race, EverybodyFights, Oath, Rue Lala, Yasso, Mission, Sweetgreen, M.Gemi, Drizly, CoachUp, Idea Point, True Fit, Nic+Zoe, Draft, Convergent Dental

Key Executives:
  Dennis Baldwin, Founder/Managing Partner
  617-399-0635
  e-mail: dbaldwin@breakaway.com
  Education: Union College; MS, Industrial Relations, Cornell University
  Background: Chief Marketing Officer, Reebok International; Management Consultant, Ernst & Young
  John Burns, Managing Director
  617-399-0637
  e-mail: jburns@breakaway.com
  Education: Boston College; MBA, Babson College
  Directorships: Spartan Race, Oath Pizza, EverybodyFights
  Chaz Bertrand, Managing Director
  617-399-0635
  e-mail: cbertrand@breakaway.com
  Education: BS, Economics, US Naval Academy; MBA, Harvard Business School
  Background: CEO, RHG LLC; Investment Banker, Adams Harkness; Investment Banker, Roberston Stephens

330 BREAKWATER INVESTMENTS
1999 Avenue of the Stars
Suite 3430
Los Angeles, CA 90067

Phone: 424-777-4000 Fax: 424-777-4001
e-mail: info@breakwatermgmt.com
web: www.breakwatermgmt.com

Mission Statement: Breakwater Investment Management is a private investment firm that specializes in direct investments in small to lower middle market businesses ranging in annual sales of $10 million to $150 million. The firm serves as general partner of Breakwater Structured Growth Opportunities Fund, LP, a $100 million open-ended private investment partnership. The Fund's investment objective is to generate both current income and capital appreciation through secured debt investments, primarily in growth-oriented companies across a variety of industries.

Fund Size: $100 million
Founded: 2008
Average Investment: $2 - $20 million
Investment Criteria: Lower Middle Market: Growth Capital, Recapitalizations, Acquisitions, Bridge Financing, Liquidity-Based
Industry Group Preference: Healthcare, Medical Devices, Consumer Products, Retailing, Information Technology, Telecommunications, Business Products & Services, Financial Services, Energy, Alternative Energy, Manufacturing
Portfolio Companies: Alpha Media, Argo Tea, Bear Down Brands, Bleach Group, BMM Compliance, Consensus Orthopedics, Global Restoration Holdings, Hamilton Captive Management, Loot Crate, Open Road Entertainment, Planet Blue, Smarty Pants Vitamins, Split Rail Fence & Supply Co., The Madera Group, Veggie Grill

Key Executives:
  Saif Mansour, Managing Partner
  424-777-4010
  Fax: 424-777-4001
  e-mail: smansour@breakwatermgmt.com
  Education: BS, International Relations, Brown University
  Background: Vice President, Sunset Holdings; Strategy Consultant, Office of the President, Union Bank of California
  Eric Beckman, Managing Partner
  424-777-4024
  Fax: 424-777-4001
  e-mail: ebeckman@breakwatermgmt.com
  Education: BA, Cornell University; JD, Yale Law School
  Background: Senior Investment Professional, Ares Management; Golman Sachs

331 BREAKWATER MANAGEMENT
1999 Avenue of the Stars
Suite 3430
Los Angeles, CA 90067

Phone: 424-777-4000
e-mail: info@breakwatermgmt.com
web: www.breakwatermgmt.com

Mission Statement: Invests in various industries with a focus on companies within the lower-middle market size. Areas of interest include media & entertainment, retail, consumer products, health & wellness and cannabis.

Geographic Preference: US, Canada
Fund Size: 75M
Founded: 2008
Average Investment: 10-75M
Minimum Investment: 10M
Investment Criteria: Lower Middle Market
Industry Group Preference: Food & Beverage, Entertainment, Radio, Media, Health & Wellness, Consumer Products, Cannabis, Apparel
Portfolio Companies: Alpha Media, Argo Tea Inc., Bear Down Brands, Bleach Group Inc., BMM Compliance, Consensus Orthopedics, Hamilton Captive Management, Global Restoration Holdings, Loot Crate Inc., Open Road Entertainment, Planet Blue, SmartyPants Inc., U.S. Fence Solutions, Tocaya Organica, Toca Madera, Casa Madera, The Veggie Grill Inc., Isatori Inc, Optimus EMR Inc., Training Partners USA Limited, Yurbuds, Zealot Networks Inc.

Key Executives:
  Eric Beckman, Managing Partner
  424-777-4024
  Fax: 424-777-4001
  e-mail: ebeckman@breakwatermgmt.com
  Education: BA, Political Theory/Economics, Cornell University; JD, Yale Law School; Jawaharlal Nehru University
  Background: Associate, Investment Banking Division, Goldman Sachs; Sr. Partner, Ares Management; Investor/Advisor, Carmelina Capital Management
  Directorships: The Posse Foundation
  Saif Mansour, Managing Partner
  424-777-4010
  Fax: 424-777-4001
  e-mail: smansour@breakwatermgmt.com
  Education: BA, International Relations, Brown University
  Background: Strategy Counsultant to the Office of the President at Union Bank of California
  Darrick Geant, Management Director
  424-777-4020
  Fax: 424-777-4001
  e-mail: dgeant@breakwatermgmt.com
  Education: BA, Ivey Business School, Western University
  Background: Analyst, Donaldson Lufkin & Jenrette; VP,

Credit Suisse; Managing Director, Goldman Sachs
Directorships: Barclays Investment Bank
Joe Kaczorowski, Managing Director/CFO
424-777-4025
Fax: 424-777-4001
e-mail: joek@breakwatermgmt.com
Education: BS, Accounting/Business Management, St. John's University
Background: EVP/CFO, The Cannell Studios; EVP/CFO/President, House of Blues Entertainment; President, Grosvenor Park Media; Principal, Oakridge Partners
Directorships: Napster; Roxio
Walter Chung, Director
424-777-4017
Fax: 424-777-4001
e-mail: wchung@breakwatermgmt.com
Education: BA, Business Economics/Accounting, University of California, LA
Background: Associate, FTI Consulting Inc.; Associate, Libra Securities
Directorships: THL Credit
Tammy Funasaki, Head of Investor Relations
424-777-4028
Fax: 424-777-4001
e-mail: tfunasaki@breakwatermgmt.com
Education: BA, International Business, University of Southern California; Pre-MBA, Anderson School of Management; MBA, NYU Stern School of Business
Background: Marketing/Strategy Associate, Lexus; Private Wealth Advisor, Goldman Sachs; VP, Evolution Financial Group

332 BREGAL ENERGY
277 Park Avenue
29th Floor
New York, NY 10172

Phone: 212-704-3000 **Fax:** 212-704-3001
web: bregalenergy.com

Mission Statement: Bregal Energy, formerly known as Good Energies Capital is a private equity firm focused on the energy sector in North America, investing in companies in the growth stage of development.
Geographic Preference: North America
Founded: 2002
Average Investment: Up to $100 million
Industry Group Preference: Energy, Renewable Energy, Energy Services, Transmission, Midstream
Portfolio Companies: Atlantic Wind Connection, Champlin Wind, Fortune Greek Gas Gathering and Processing, IMG Midstream, Inflection Energy, SolarReserve
Key Executives:
  Raluca Florea, Senior Associate
  Education: BS, Interational Business, Academy of Economic Studies; MBA, Harvard Business School
  Background: McKinsey & Company; Procter & Gamble
  Sylvester Burley, Senior Associate
  Education: BA, Economics & Mathematics, Harvard University
  Background: Basalt Infrastructure Partners; Riverstone Holdings; JP Morgan

333 BREGAL SAGEMOUNT
277 Park Avenue
29th Floor
New York, NY 10172

Phone: 212-704-5370
e-mail: info@bregalsagemount.com
web: sagemount.com

Mission Statement: Bregal Sagemount is focused on investing in and acquiring high-growth companies.
Fund Size: $1.7 billion
Average Investment: $15-$75 million
Investment Criteria: Growth Stage
Industry Group Preference: Software, Enterprise Software, SaaS, Technology-Enabled Software, Business Products & Services, Cloud Computing, Internet, Healthcare, Healthcare Information Technology, Financial Services, Consumer Services, Direct Marketing, Education
Portfolio Companies: Accela, Adreima, Advanced Solutions, Align, Bite Squad, Buyers Edge Platform, CallTower, Connectria, Critical Start, DiscoverOrg, Discovery Data, Enprecis, Fluent Home, GPS Insight, Information Builders, Interface Security Systems, Irth Solutions, Keg Logistics, Key Health, LabVantage, Lux Research, MicroEdge, MOBI Wireless, Network Merchants, Open Lending, Options Technology, Procurement Advisors, Purchasing Power, RDX, Recondo Technology, Single Digits, STEELE Compliance Solutions, SurePrep, TradeGlobal, Trapp Technology, Truckstop.com, TrustArc, Vital Insights, Yapstone, ZeOmega
Key Executives:
  Cene Yoon, Managing Partner
  212-704-5375
  e-mail: gene.yoon@bregalsagemount.com
  Education: BS, Economics, MBA, Wharton School
  Background: Head of Private Equity, Goldman Sachs & Co.
  Daniel Kim, Partner
  212-704-5379
  e-mail: daniel.kim@bregalsagemount.com
  Education: BS, Biological Sciences, BA, Music, Stanford University; MBA, Harvard Business School
  Background: Vice President, Goldman Sachs Americas Special Situations Group; Senior Associate, JMI Equity
  Phil Yates, Partner
  212-704-5377
  e-mail: phil.yates@bregalsagemount.com
  Education: BS, Business Administration, University of North Carolina, Chapel Hill
  Background: Great Hill Partners; Associate, Carousel Capital
  Clayton Main, Partner, Head of Credit
  212-704-5372
  e-mail: clayton.main@sagemount.com
  Education: BBA, Southern Methodist Univ.
  Background: Goldman Sachs
  Curt Witte, Partner, Head of Sagemount Growth Factors
  212-704-5390
  e-mail: curt.witte@sagemount.com
  Background: Symphony Technology Group
  Adam Fuller, Partner
  Education: BA, Economics, Stanford University
  Background: Goldman Sachs; Arbord Advisors
  Blair Greenberg, Partner
  Education: BBA, Kelley School of Business; MBA, Kellogg School of Management
  Background: VP, Technology Crossover Ventures; UBS Investment Bank
  Michael Kosty, Partner
  212-704-5380
  e-mail: michael.kosty@sagemount.com
  Education: BSBA, Georgetown University
  Background: Goldman Sachs
  Pavan Tripathi, Partner
  212-704-5383
  e-mail: pavan.tripathi@safemount.com
  Education: BEng, Electrical Engineering & Economics, University of California, LA; MBA, Stanford Grad. School of Business
  Background: Goldman Sachs

Venture Capital & Private Equity Firms / Domestic Firms

334 BRENTWOOD ASSOCIATES
11150 Santa Monica Blvd.
Suite 1200
Los Angeles, CA 90025

Phone: 310-477-6611 Fax: 310-317-7200
e-mail: info@brentwood.com
web: www.brentwood.com

Mission Statement: Brentwood Associates is a leading consumer-focused private equity investment firm based in Los Angeles.
Geographic Preference: Midwest
Fund Size: $2.4 billion
Founded: 1972
Average Investment: $20 - $150 million
Minimum Investment: $1 million
Investment Criteria: Middle Market, Consumer Related Businesses
Industry Group Preference: Business to Business, Consumer Products, Consumer Services, Direct Marketing, Distribution, Education, Health Related, Marketing
Portfolio Companies: Allen Edmonds, Ariat, Array, Aspen Marketing Group, Bell Sports, Blaze Pizza, Boston Proper, Cardinal Business Media Inc., Chamilia, Chicken Salad Chick, Classroom Connect, ClassWallet, Credential Solutions, Excelligence Learning Corp., Exhale, Filson, FleetPride Inc., HIMS, J.Mclaughlin, Jefferson Dental Care, KFC, Marshall Retail Group, MD Now, Oriental Trading, Orange Theory Fitness, Pacific Catch, Pacific Island Restaurants Inc., Paper Source, Saxx, Soft Surroundings, Spectrum Athletic Clubs, Three Sixty Sourcing, Veggie Grill, Wiland, Z Gallerie, Zumiez

Key Executives:
   William Barnum, Partner
   Education: Stanford University; Stanford Law School; Stanford Graduate School of Business
   Background: Investment Banking Division, Morgan Stanley & Comapny
   Directorships: Filson Holdings; Oriental Trading Company; ThreeSixty Asia; Exhale Enterprises; FleetPride Corporation; Zumiez; Quicksilver; Stanford University; St Matthews Parish School
   Roger Goddu, Partner
   Education: Adrian College; University of Toledo; Completed, Executive Development Program, Harvard Business School
   Background: Independent Director, Array Marketing Group; Chairman/CEO, Montgomery Ward; President, Toys R Us; Senior Management Positions, Target; RH Macy & Co; Federated Department Stores
   Steven Moore, Partner
   Education: BA, Mechanical Engineering, University of Michigan
   Background: Merger/Acquisitions/Corporate Finance, Donaldson, Lufkin & Jenrette; Deloitte & Touche Consulting Group
   Directorships: Filson Holdings; ThreeSixty Asia; Zumiez
   Eric Reiter, Partner
   Education: Dual Degree, in Finance/Operation/Information Management, magna cum laude, Wharton School University of Pennsylvania
   Background: Merchant Banking Division, Donaldson, Lufkin & Jenrette
   Directorships: Array Marketing; Oriental Trading Company; Monarch Designs
   Rahul Aggarwal, Partner
   Education: BS, Finance/International Relations, magna cum laude, University of Pennsylvania Wharton School of Business; BA International Relations, College of Arts and Sciences
   Background: Financing, Donaldson, Lufkin & Jenrette
   Directorships: Pacific Island Restaurants; Spectrum Clubs; Exhale Enterprises; FleetPride Corporation

335 BRERA CAPITAL PARTNERS
244 Fifth Avenue
Suite 2345
New York, NY 10001

web: www.brera.com

Mission Statement: Global private equity investment firm.
Geographic Preference: United States, Asia, Japan, Southern Europe, Italy
Fund Size: $680 million
Founded: 1997
Average Investment: $150 million
Investment Criteria: Management Buyouts, Recapitalizations, Restructurings
Industry Group Preference: Telecommunications, Healthcare, Financial Services, Outsourcing & Efficiency
Portfolio Companies: 2-10 Home Buyers Warranty, GAB Robins, Italtel, Western Industries

336 BREYER CAPITAL
2500 Sand Hill Road
Suite 300
Menlo Park, CA 94025

Phone: 650-681-3069 Fax: 650-433-4243
e-mail: info@breyercapital.com
web: breyercapital.com

Mission Statement: Breyer Capital is a global private equity and venture capital investor.
Geographic Preference: United States, China, India
Founded: 2006
Industry Group Preference: Social Media, Artificial Intelligence, Entertainment, Digital Health, Data Analytics, Fintech
Portfolio Companies: Facebook, Legendary, Kensho, IDG Capital Partners, Etsy, Circle, Marvel, C3 IoT

Key Executives:
   Jim Breyer, Founder and CEO
   Education: BS, Stanford University; MBA, Harvard University
   Background: Partner, Accel; President, Accel Management Company; Management Consultant, McKinsey & Company

337 BRIDGE INVESTMENT FUND
Cleveland, OH

web: www.bridgefundllc.com

Mission Statement: Bridge Investment Fund is a venture capital fund focused on investing in Israeli medical device companies with strong synergies with the leading health care institutions and industries in Cleveland. Bridge is specifically focused on companies that have completed their initial clinical trials and are looking to the US market for further clinical validation and to establish a US sales marketing organization. Bridge's team brings excellent access to Israeli companies, deep regional networks and hands-on support to help their portfolio companies successfully enter the US market.
Geographic Preference: Israel
Average Investment: $250,000 - $1 million
Minimum Investment: $250,000
Industry Group Preference: Medical Devices
Portfolio Companies: EarlySense, IceCure Medical, Navotek, Medic Vision

Other Locations:
   Tenram Investments
   11 Tuval Street
   Ramat Gan 52522
   Israel

Key Executives:
   Avshalom Horan, Managing Partner
   Education: PhD, Engineering-Economic Systems, Stanford University
   Background: Colonel, Israeli Defense Forces, Israeli

Venture Capital & Private Equity Firms / Domestic Firms

Military Intelligence; VP, Bank Leumi Investment Group
Directorships: Simbionix
Michael Goldberg, Managing Partner
Education: BA, Woodrow Wilson School of Public and International Affairs, Princeton University; MA, International Relations, Johns Hopkins University
Background: Director, International Business Development, America Online

338 BRIDGE STREET CAPITAL
171 Monroe Avenue NW
Suite 410
Grand Rapids, MI 49503

Phone: 616-732-1050 Fax: 616-732-1055
web: www.bridgestreetcapital.com

Mission Statement: Bridge Street Capital Partners works with entrepreneurial companies throughout the Midwest and Great Lakes region and invests in a variety of industries, including healthcare, business services, manufacturing and consumer products. The firm provides the capital, operational expertise and practical experience necessary to meet the needs of portfolio companies.

Geographic Preference: Midwest & Great Lakes Region
Fund Size: $30 million
Average Investment: $2.5 - $7.5 million
Investment Criteria: Middle-Market Firms
Industry Group Preference: Industrial Manufacturing, Distribution, Logistics, Consumer Products, Healthcare, Business Products & Services
Portfolio Companies: Affy Tapple, Callpod, Jacob Ash, Performance Fabrics, Superior Fibers, V.I.O., Callpod, Zorch

Other Locations:
52 Village Place
Hinsdale, IL 60521
Phone: 630-323-9222 Fax: 630-323-9224

Key Executives:
Bill Kaczynski, Managing Director
Education: BS, Accounting, University of Illinois at Urbana-Champaign; MBA, Kellogg School of Management, Northwestern University
Background: Managing Director, Trivest Partners; Heller Financial; Fidelcor Business Credit; Price Waterhouse
John Meilner, Managing Director
Education: BS, Accounting, Drake University; Kellogg School of Management
Background: Managing Director, Investment Banking Group, McDonald Investments; Partner, Deloitte & Touche

339 BRIDGESCALE PARTNERS
Menlo Park, CA

Phone: 650-854-6100
web: www.bridgescale.com

Mission Statement: Bridgescale invests in technology companies that require equity to accelerate growth.

Geographic Preference: United States, Canada
Industry Group Preference: Information Technology, Consumer Internet, Digital Media & Marketing, Communications, Infrastructure, Business Products & Services, Mobile Technology
Portfolio Companies: Axonify, BlueCat Networks, Dayforce, Jasper Wireless, J. Hilburn, Plum Organics, Proofpoint, Rypple, Shutterfly, Xactly, Neonova, BitGo, IMVU, Vision Critical, Chronometriq

340 BRIGHTPATH CAPITAL PARTNERS
One Kaiser Plaza
Suite 650
Oakland, CA 94612

Phone: 510-488-4140
e-mail: info@bcplp.com
web: www.brightpathcapitalpartners.com

Mission Statement: Brightpath Capital Partners invests in talented management teams and high-growth businesses, creating jobs, wealth and sustainable environments in communities. BCP provides innovative investment solutions rooted in in-depth research and a disciplined investment process.

Geographic Preference: California, Western United States
Founded: 2010
Average Investment: $1-5 million
Investment Criteria: Late-Stage
Industry Group Preference: Clean Energy, Business Products & Services, Education, Food & Beverage, Manufacturing, Health & Wellness
Portfolio Companies: Blu Homes, Ecologic Brands, Sungevity

Key Executives:
Robert R. Davenport III, Managing Partner
510-488-4140
e-mail: rob@bcplp.com
Education: AB, MBA, Harvard University
Background: Chairman, Up Communication Services; President & CEO, Covad International
Directorships: MCI, Sungevity, One Pacific Coast Ank, FSB
Jonathan Mi, Principal
510-488-4143
e-mail: jonathan@bcplp.com
Education: BA, University of California, Berkeley
Background: Associate, Gryphon Investors

341 BRIGHTSTONE VENTURE CAPITAL
510 First Avenue North
Suite 200
Minneapolis, MN 55403

web: www.brightstonevc.com

Mission Statement: Brightstone Venture Capital Fund has a long history of helping build successful companies in the early-growth stage.

Fund Size: $100 million
Founded: 1985
Average Investment: $250,000 - $10 million
Minimum Investment: $250,000
Investment Criteria: Early Growth-Stage
Industry Group Preference: Technology, Digital Media & Marketing, Mobile, Virtual Reality, Cloud Computing, Data Storage, Enterprise Software, Consumer Internet, Energy, Life Sciences, Medical Devices, Healthcare Information Technology, Biotechnology, Clean Technology
Portfolio Companies: HomeSpotter, Bnocular, Celcuity, Fortus Medical Inc., Miromatrix, Flipgrid, TruBrain, Bite, Gravie, VR Chat, Real Vision, Stemonix, Atavium, Wasabi

Key Executives:
David Dalvey, Partner
e-mail: david@brightstonevc.com
Directorships: Homespotter, Definity Health, App Tec Laboratories, Navarre Corp, chf Solutions, Agiliti, Nature Vision, Celcuity, Bite Squad
Patrick O'Shaughnessy, Partner
e-mail: patrick@brightstonevc.com
Seth Degroot, Partner
e-mail: seth@brightstonevc.com

342 BRILLIANT VENTURES
520 Broadway
Suite 200
Santa Monica, CA 90401

web: www.brilliant.ventures

Mission Statement: Brilliant Ventures invests capital, experience, and a powerful network to build companies that are leveraging technology and data to accelerate growth and to shape the future of media, marketing, and commerce.

Industry Group Preference: Media, Marketing, Commerce, Technology, Data

123

Venture Capital & Private Equity Firms / Domestic Firms

Portfolio Companies: Beam Impact, CameraIQ, Cherrypick, Cognitiv, Happy Returns, Harper Wilde, Haute Hijab, Parachute, Postie, Relovv, RevCascade, Tamara Mellon, The Riveter, Skylar Body, Vela

Key Executives:
  Kara Weber, Founder, Partner
  Education: Williams College
  Directorships: Happy Returns, CameraIQ, Cognitiv, RevCascade
  Lizzie Francis, Founder, Partner
  Education: BA, Cornell University
  Directorships: Parachute Home, Tamara Mellon, Vow to be Chic

343 BROADHAVEN CAPITAL PARTNERS
521 Fifth Avenue
New York, NY 10175

Phone: 212-418-1240
e-mail: info@broadhaven.com
web: broadhaven.com

Mission Statement: Broadhaven Capital Partners is an independent investment bank and growth equity investor serving the financial technology sector.

Fund Size: $100 million
Founded: 2009
Average Investment: $5 - $15 million
Investment Criteria: Early-Stage, Growth Equity, Buyout
Industry Group Preference: Financial Services, Technology
Portfolio Companies: Binary Event Network, Mantara, UNX

Other Locations:
150 North Riverside Plaza
Chicago, IL 60606
Phone: 312-621-9800

2 Embarcadero Center
San Francisco, CA 94111
Phone: 415-295-4447

Key Executives:
  Gerard von Dohlen, Co-Founder/Partner
  Education: BS, Industrial Engineering, Columbia University; MBA, Columbia Business School
  Background: Managing Director, Investment Banking, Goldman Sachs; UBS Investment Bank; Credit Suisse First Boston
  Greg Phillips, Co-Founder/Partner
  Education: BA, Economics, University of Chicago
  Background: M&A Group, UBS Investment Bank; Wasserstein Perella & Co.
  James T. Denton, Partner
  Education: BA, Economics & Languages, Rutgers College; MBA, Columbia Business School
  Background: Co-Head, Financial Institutions Group, Rothschild
  Michael Deleray, Partner
  Education: BA, History, University of California, Berkeley
  Background: Founder, Bendigo; President, US Equity Services, Computershare
  Todd G. Owens, Partner
  Education: Williams College
  Background: Fifth Street Finance Corp.
  John H. Simpson, Partner
  Education: Williams College; Harvard Law School
  Background: Wasserstein Perella & Co.
  Directorships: Lurie Children's Hospital
  Christopher Spofford, Partner
  Education: Amherst College
  Background: Goldman Sachs
  Kurt von Holzhausen, Partner
  Education: Tufts University
  Background: Goldman Sachs

  Joseph J. Zabik, Partner
  Education: Kent State University
  Background: Sterne Agee
  Esther Tian, Managing Director
  Education: AB, Economics, Harvard University
  Background: Davidson Kempner Capital Management, SAC Capital

344 BROADHORN CAPITAL
West Des Moines, IA

e-mail: info@broadhorn.com
web: www.broadhorn.com

Mission Statement: Broadhorn Capital is a venture development firm specializing in early and seed stage technology companies. Business services include: business plan advisment, board and management development, technology strategy and architecture, proof of concept, sales and marketing development and private placement services.

Investment Criteria: Seed-Stage, Early-Stage
Industry Group Preference: Technology
Portfolio Companies: AmericasOne, Appcore, ARC Center, Broadhorn Farm, Computility, Family Arc, GForce Group, Growth Ventures Group, Micoy, MinistryHub.com, MobileSmith, Palisade

Key Executives:
  Brian Donaghy, Partner
  e-mail: brian.donaghy@broadhorn.com
  Background: Founder/CEO, Appcore; Partner/CTO, Growth Ventures Group

345 BROADMARK CAPITAL
1800 One Union Square
600 University Street
Seattle, WA 98101

Phone: 206-623-1200 Fax: 206-623-2213
web: www.broadmark.com

Mission Statement: Merchant bank that provides financing and management services and direct investment to help emerging companies grow and create shareholder value.

Founded: 1987
Average Investment: $5 - $75 million
Minimum Investment: $5 million
Investment Criteria: Early-Stage, First-Stage, Mid-Stage, Second-Stage, Mezzanine, LBO, Emerging Growth, Middle Market, Mergers & Acquisitions
Industry Group Preference: Information Technology, Life Sciences, Healthcare, Communications
Portfolio Companies: Pyatt, Vesiflo, NewsCrafted, FedTax

Key Executives:
  Joseph L. Schocken, President
  e-mail: jls@broadmark.com
  Education: Graduate, honors, University of Washington; MBA, Harvard University
  Background: Partner, New York Stock Exchange; Member, National Advisory Board of the Democratic National Committee
  Adam J. Fountain, Managing Director
  e-mail: afountain@broadmark.com
  Education: BA, International Relations, Stanford University
  Background: Associate, L.E.K. Consulting

347 BROADVIEW VENTURES
265 Franklin Street
Suite 1902
Boston, MA 02110

Phone: 617-459-4686
e-mail: ccolecchi@broadviewventures.org
web: www.broadviewventures.org

Mission Statement: Broadview's mission is to accelerate the development of promising technology in cardiovascular and

Venture Capital & Private Equity Firms / Domestic Firms

neurovascular disease through targeted investments in and support of early stage ventures.
Geographic Preference: United States, Europe
Founded: 2008
Average Investment: $1 - 1.5 million
Investment Criteria: Early-Stage
Industry Group Preference: Healthcare, Life Sciences, Therapeutics, Medical Devices, Diagnostics
Portfolio Companies: 480 Biomedical, Acesion, Adient Medical, Aeromics, Aggamin, Allosteros, Apama, Aria CV, BioKier, Capricor, Cardero, CardiAQ Valve, CardiaLen, CellAegis, DecImmune, EP Sciences, FineHeart, GI Windows, Gila Therapeutic, InfoBionic, Intravascular Imaging Inc., Ischemia Care, Herantis, Mellitus, MiRagen, Nido Surgical, NuPulse, Provasculon, Pulmokine, Remedy, Vascular Graft Solutions, Vectorious, VentriNova, Zumbro Discover, ZZ Biotech

Key Executives:
Christopher Colecchi, Managing Director
Education: BA, Holy Cross College; MPH, University of Massachusetts School of Public Health
Background: Vice President, Research Ventures & Licensing, Partners Healthcare; Director, Clinical Trials & Industrial Relations, Massachusetts General Hospital

---

348 BROCKWAY MORAN & PARTNERS
225 NE Mizner Boulevard
Suite 700
Boca Raton, FL 33432

Phone: 561-750-2000 **Fax:** 561-750-2001
e-mail: info@brockwaymoran.com
web: www.brockwaymoran.com

Mission Statement: Brockway Moran & Partners is a private equity firm with an unusual combination of financial resources, strategic expertise & operational know-how brought together to support management teams in maximizing opportunities for growth-oriented, middle-market companies.
Fund Size: $1.3 billion
Founded: 1998
Investment Criteria: $50-$300 Million in Value
Industry Group Preference: Consumer Products, Industrial Products, Services
Portfolio Companies: MD Now, Pennant Foods Corp., Turning Technologies, The Winebow Group

Key Executives:
Peter C Brockway, Managing Partner
e-mail: pbrockway@brockwaymoran.com
Education: BBA, Stetson University; MBA, Harvard Business School
Background: Senior Advisor, Blue Sea Capital;
Directorships: Crisis Prevention Institute Inc., MD Now Medical Centers Inc., The Winebow Group, Turning Technologies, MW Industries Inc., Woodstream Corp., Gold's Gym, Norwesco, ElectroStar
Michael E Moran, Managing Partner
e-mail: mmoran@brockwaymoran.com
Education: BS, Drake University; MBA, DePaul University
Background: Founder, Moran Capital Partners
Directorships: Pennant Foods Corp., Crisis Prevention Institute Inc., The Winebow Group, Turning Technologies, MD Now Medical Centers Inc., ElectroStar Inc.
Peter W Klein, Partner/General Counsel
e-mail: pklein@brockwaymoran.com
Education: BA, Albion College; JD, Cleveland-Marshall College of Law; LLM, Taxation, New York University
H Randall Litten, Partner
e-mail: rlitten@brockwaymoran.com
Education: BS, Ohio University; MBA, University of Toledo
Background: General Manager, Owens-Illinois
Directorships: Celesete Industries Corp.; Norweso Inc.;

Cosmetic Essense Inc.; Woodstream Corp.; MW Industries Inc; Penda Corp.
Ari M. Zur, Partner
e-mail: azur@brockwaymoran.com
Education: BS, Economics, Wharton School; BA, University of Pennsylvania; MBA, Kellogg School of Management, Northwestern University
Background: Associate, Cambridge Capital Partners; Investment Analyst, Frontenac Company; Financial Analyst, Bear, Stearns & Co.

---

349 BROOK VENTURE FUND
301 Edgewater Place
Suite 425
Wakefield, MA 01880

Phone: 781-295-4000 **Fax:** 781-295-4007
e-mail: rspencer@brookventure.com
web: www.brookventure.com

Mission Statement: To invest capital in high-growth, expansion-stage companies, within a focused set of industries, with the objective of realizing venture level returns for us, our investors, and for the other shareholders and managers of each portfolio company.
Geographic Preference: Northeastern, Mid-Atlantic States
Fund Size: $100 million
Founded: 1998
Average Investment: $2-15 million
Minimum Investment: $1 million
Investment Criteria: Expansion Stage
Industry Group Preference: Medical Devices, Information Technology, Chemicals, Optical Technology, Biotechnology, Publishing, Electronic Technology, Healthcare Information Technology
Portfolio Companies: Affordable Interior Systems, AHP Billing, Allegience Software, Anodyne, Apogee IT Services, Arigo G360, Atlas Water, BabyEarth, Certica, Cole Information, Coronis Health, D2 Hawkeye, Farm Market iD, HistoRX, IMN, Interwoven, itrac LLC, Laser Projection Technologies, LearnWell, Medicus IT, Mobile Medical International Corporation, OnBoard Security, Orbis Technologies Inc., PointCare, Relevate, Reveal, Robbinskertsten Direct, Security Innovation, SilverRail, Software Unlimited, Spectral Dimensions, Texerity, Union Biometrica, Universal Software, V12 Data, Verge Health

Key Executives:
Frederic H. Morris, Partner
e-mail: morris@brookventure.com
Education: Economics, Yale University; MBA Finance, Harvard Business School
Background: Lieutenant, Navy's Reserve Officer Training; CFO Assistant, First National City Bank
Walter Beinecke, Partner
e-mail: wbeinecke@brookventure.com
Education: University of California
Background: President, RewardsNow; President/Co-Managing Partner, Affinity Marketing Group; CEO, S&H Partners; Founder/Executive VP, S&H Greenpoints; President/CEO, Biological Technologies International; Co-Founder/Managing Partner, MHB Partners; Founder/President/CEO, Silvan
Edward C. Williams, III, Partner
e-mail: ewilliams@brookventure.com
Education: University of Massachusetts; BS, Harvard University
Background: Private Equity, Winthrop Financial Associates; Equity Sales, Morgan Stanley; Investment Banking, Bank of Boston
Brennan Mulcahey, Partner
e-mail: bmulcahey@brookventure.com
Education: BA, University of Rochester; MBA, Simon School of Business
Directorships: Medicine-On-Time
Kyle Stanbro, Partner
e-mail: kstanbro@brookventure.com

125

Venture Capital & Private Equity Firms / Domestic Firms

Education: BS, St. John Fisher College; MBA, Simon School of Business
Background: Travelers; Kodak

350 BROOKE PRIVATE EQUITY ASSOCIATES
20 Custom House St
Suite 610
Boston, MA 02110

Phone: 617-227-3160 Fax: 617-227-4128
e-mail: info@brookepea.com
web: www.brookepea.com

Mission Statement: A private equity firm with a a diversified focus.

Founded: 2002
Industry Group Preference: Consumer, Retail, Healthcare, Industrial
Key Executives:
  Peter Brooke, Co-Founder
  Education: Harvard College, Harvard Business School
  Background: Founder, TA Associates; Co-Founder, Sofinnova SA
  John Brooke, Managing Director
  Education: Harvard College, Harvard Business School
  Background: Advent International, The Tucker Anthony Private Equity Group
  Christopher Austen, Managing Director
  Education: Duke University, Fuqua School of Business
  Background: Partner, Southeast Interactive Technology Funds; BBDO, Foote Cone & Belding

351 BROOKLYN BRIDGE VENTURES
55-C 9th Street
Brooklyn, NY 11215

e-mail: charlie@brooklynbridge.vc
web: www.brooklynbridge.vc

Mission Statement: Brooklyn Bridge Ventures is a seed-stage investor. Brooklyn Bridge Ventures seeks to connect community leaders together, support new events, and encourage the creation of a thriving ecosystem.

Geographic Preference: New York City
Fund Size: $23 million
Average Investment: $500,000
Investment Criteria: Seed-Stage
Industry Group Preference: Technology
Portfolio Companies: Bravely, Wethos, Petal, Bazaar, Waggle, The Wing, Amper Music, Bizly, Radius, Talla, Agrilyst, C And Co., Seed, Ample Hills Creamery, Clubhouse, Homer, Drip, Wheelhouse, Hungry Root, Tinker Garten, Even Financial, Bezar, Plum Print, Vixxenn, LogCheck, ProofPilot, BioDigital, GoTenna, Ringly, Canary, Orchard, Makr, SocialSign.in, Tinybop, Floored, Windowfarms, Editorially, Superhuman, Versa
Key Executives:
  Charlie O'Donnell, Founder
  e-mail: charlie@brooklynbridge.vc
  Background: Union Square Ventures, First Round Capital, General Motors Asset Management Private Equity Group

352 BROOKS HOUGHTON & COMPANY
1 Stamford Plaza
9th Floor
Stamford, NY 06901

Phone: 212-753-1991 Fax: 212-753-7730
web: www.brookshoughton.com

Mission Statement: Brooks, Houghton & Company provides investment banking services and direct investments to emerging growth companies as well as middle market companies. The firm has experience in a number of industries, including healthcare, media and entertainment.

Geographic Preference: United States
Founded: 1989
Average Investment: $15 million
Minimum Investment: $2 million
Investment Criteria: Middle Market, Public and Private Companies, Debt and Equity Private Placements, Mergers & Acquisitions, Growth and Expansion, Recapitalizations, Refinancings
Industry Group Preference: All Sectors Considered
Portfolio Companies: Competitive Technology, Happy Hour Creative, Mad Catz Interactive, Hennessy Capital Solutions
Key Executives:
  Kevin Centofanti, President
  e-mail: kcentofanti@brookshoughton.com
  Education: BS, Pharmacy & Business, State University of New York at Buffalo; MBA, Finance & International Business, Columbia University; CFA
  Background: Partner, The Nassau Group; Managing Director, WR Hambrecht & Co.; Daiwa Securities America
  Anthony Moretti, Senior Managing Director/Head of Investment Banking
  212-329-1667
  e-mail: amoretti@brookshoughton.com
  Education: BA, Business Economics, Brown University
  Background: Director, BMO Capital Markets; Vice President, RBC Capital Markets
  Domenico Pecorini, Senior Managing Director
  e-mail: dpecorini@brookshoughton.com
  Background: COO, Fondazione Parco Biomedico San Raffaele of Rome; Executive Director, Stilbon SA; President/CEO, Inveni Engineering
  Directorships: Intensivecare SpA; Chairman, Life Episteme Group
  David M Maher, Executive Director
  212-329-1661
  e-mail: maher@brookshoughton.com
  Education: BA, Dartmouth College; MBA, Darden School of Business, University of Virginia
  Background: Equity Capital Market Group member, Deutsche Bank Securities; Derivatives Trader, JP morgan Chase

353 BROOKSIDE EQUITY PARTNERS LLC
One Stamford Forum
201 Tresser Blvd
Suite 320
Stamford, CT 06901

Phone: 203-595-4520
e-mail: info@brooksideequity.com
web: www.brooksideequity.com

Mission Statement: Brookside Equity Partners, a part of The Brookside Group, focuses on private equity investments. The firm seeks to assist companies in creating long-term value.

Geographic Preference: United States
Founded: 1977
Average Investment: $3 - $8 million
Minimum Investment: $3 million
Investment Criteria: Leveraged Buyouts, Mezzanine, Growth Capital
Industry Group Preference: Food & Beverage, Plastics, Environment, Manufacturing, Distribution, Industrial, Financial Services, Specialty Chemicals
Portfolio Companies: Guardian Compliance, Hillsdale Furniture, Margaritaville Holdings, Meta Financial Group, New Energy, NSi, Operator of Full Service Restaurants, Performance Health & Wellness, SelectQuote, Superior Automotive, Tellermate Holdings, US Century Bank, Valterra Products
Key Executives:
  Donald L Hawks III, Managing Director/President
  Education: Georgetown University; MBA, Wharton School, University of Pennsylvania
  Background: Strategy Consultant, Monitor Group

Venture Capital & Private Equity Firms / Domestic Firms

Raymond F Weldon, Managing Director
Education: La Salle University; Villanova University
Background: PricewaterhouseCoopers
Richard T Dell'Aquila, Managing Director
Education: BA, Economics, Hamilton College
Background: Managing Director, Parallel Investment Partners; Principal, Southfield Capital Advisors; Research Analyst, Sasco Capital

354 BRUCKMANN, ROSSER, SHERRILL & COMPANY
126 East 56th Street
29th Floor
New York, NY 10022

Phone: 212-521-3700 Fax: 212-521-3799
e-mail: info@brs.com
web: www.brs.com

Mission Statement: Private equity investment firm specializes in buyouts and recapitalization.

Fund Size: $1.2 billion
Founded: 1995
Investment Criteria: Management Buy-Outs, Recapitalizations of high quality, Middle Market Companies
Industry Group Preference: Consumer Services, Commercial Services, Healthcare, Consumer Products, Industrial Services, Industrial Equipment, Restaurants, Retailing
Portfolio Companies: 2nd Ave LLC, Airxcel Holdings Inc., Alliance Laundry Systems LLC, AmerisourceBergen Corporation, Anvil Holdings, Au Bon Pain Inc., B&C Foods Inc., Bally Engineering, Bravo Brio Restaurant Group Inc., California Pizza Kitchen Inc., Canada Pooch Ltd., Cort, Daisy Manufacturing Co., Davco Restaurants LLC, Del Monte Foods, Doane Pet Care Enterprises Inc., DTLR Inc., EOS Fitness Holdings LLC, Eurofresh Inc., Evolv Sports & Designs, Farm Fresh, Fox Photo, Galey & Lord, Gamo Outdoor SL, Gilbarco Veeder-Root, Golden Corral, H&E Equipment Services Inc., Hancor Inc., Healthplus Corporation, Heritage-Crystal Clean Inc., Inmotion Entertainment Group, J&L Specialty Steel, Logan's Roadhouse, Marshall Retail Group, McCormick & Schmick's Seafood Restaurants Inc., Milk Specialties Co., Morse Shoe Inc., MWI Veterinary Supply Inc., New Archery Products Corp., Not Your Average Joe's Inc., Organika Health Products, Penhall International Inc., Polyfibron Technologies Inc., Rax Restaurants Inc., Real Mex Restaurants Inc., Reliance Electric, Restaurant Associates Corporation, Royal Robbins Inc., Ruth's Hospitality Group, Reroyal Holdings LP, Simpson Performance Products, Steak & Ale Restaurant, Sheridan Group Inc., Things Remembered Inc., Totes Isotoner Corporation, Town Sports International Inc., Triumph Group Inc., Unwired Group Limited, Wilson Farms Inc., Zatarain's

Key Executives:
Bruce C. Bruckmann, Managing Partner & Founder
Education: AB, Harvard College; JD, Harvard Law School
Background: CVC Associate, Patterson, Belknap, Webb & Tyler
Directorships: Mohawk Industries, Town Sports International, Anvil Knitwear, MWI Veterinary Supply, HealthEssentials, Penhall International, Copelands' Enterprises, H&e Equipment Services
Stephen C. Sherrill, Managing Partner & Founder
Education: BA, Yale University; JD, Columbia Law School
Background: CVC, Paul, Weiss, Rifkind, Wharton & Garrison
Directorships: Galey & Lord, Doane Pet Care Enterprises, B&G Foods, HealthPlus Corporation, MWI Veterinary Supply, HealthEssentials, Alliance Laundry Systems, Eurofresh, Remington Arms
Thomas J. Baldwin, Managing Partner
Education: BBA, Siena College; MBA, Harvard Business School
Background: VP/Managing Director, INVUS Group; Boston Consulting Group
Directorships: B&G Foods, Eurofresh, The Sheridan Group
Rashad Rahman, Managing Director
Education: Economics, Wharton School, University of Pennsylvania
Background: DB Capital Partners; Investment Banking, Credit Suisse First Boston
Directorships: Seroyal Holdings
Tory Rooney, Managing Director
Education: BA, Goizueta Business School
Background: Wachovia Capital Markets
Directorships: Royal Robbins
Duwain Robinson, Managing Director & CFO
Education: CPA
Background: Manager, Asset Management Practice, PricewaterhouseCoopers
Oren Yerushalmi, Vice President
Education: Emory University
Background: Wells Fargo Securities
Directorships: Gamo Outdoor; Royal Robbins

355 BRUML CAPITAL CORPORATION
1801 East Ninth Street
Ohio Savings Plaza
Suite 1620
Cleveland, OH 44114

Phone: 216-771-6660 Fax: 216-771-6673
e-mail: info@brumlcapital.com
web: www.brumlcapital.com

Mission Statement: Independent investment banking firm in Cleveland.

Geographic Preference: Great Lakes
Fund Size: $15 million
Founded: 1986
Average Investment: $5 - $50 million
Minimum Investment: $1 million
Investment Criteria: Middle Market Companies, Management Buyouts, Acquisitions, Recapitalizations
Industry Group Preference: Manufacturing, Wholesale, Metals, Publishing, Chemicals, Retailing, Business to Business, Technology, Industrial Equipment, Distribution

Key Executives:
Robert W. Bruml, President
e-mail: bob@brumlcapital.com
Education: BA Economics, University of Rochester; MBA, Wharton School
Background: KPMG Peat Marwick
Andrew S. Gelfand, Senior Vice President
e-mail: andy@brumlcapital.com
Education: BA Mathematics, Colgate University; MBA, Columbia University Graduate School of Business
Background: Investment Banking Officer, KeyCorp
James R. Deitzer, Asst. Vice President
e-mail: jim@brumlcapital.com
Education: BS, Univ. of Pittsburgh; MA, Columbia Univ.
Background: FTN Equity Capital Markets; RBC Capital Markets

356 BRYANT PARK VENTURES
web: bryantparkventures.com

Mission Statement: Bryant Park Ventures is a private investment fund and advisory services business.

Investment Criteria: Early-Stage
Industry Group Preference: Technology, Homeland Security, Law Enforcement, Healthcare

Key Executives:
Michael G. Levine, Chairman & CEO
e-mail: mgl@bryantparkventures.com
Education: BS, SUNY Buffalo; MBA, Wharton School

Venture Capital & Private Equity Firms / Domestic Firms

Background: President, Xact Technology; CFO, Maler Technologies

357 BRYNWOOD PARTNERS
8 Sound Shore Drive
Suite 265
Greenwich, CT 06830
Phone: 203-622-1790 Fax: 203-622-0559
e-mail: info@brynwoodpartners.com
web: www.brynwoodpartners.com

Mission Statement: Lower middle market buyout fund.
Fund Size: $725 million
Founded: 1984
Average Investment: Up to $80 million
Investment Criteria: Middle Market
Industry Group Preference: Manufacturing, Food & Beverage, Consumer Products, Business Products & Services
Portfolio Companies: Back To Nature, Balance Bar, Carolina Beverage Group LLP, DeMet's Candy Company, Harvest Hill Beverage Company, High Ridge Brands, Hometown Food Company, J.B. Williams Company, Joseph's Frozen Foods, Kretschmer, Lightlife Foods, Lincoln Snacks, Pearson's, Richelieu Foods Inc., Stella D'Oro

Key Executives:
Hendrik J. Hartong III, Chairman/CEO
e-mail: hhartong@brynwoodpartners.com
Education: BA, History, Lafayette College; MBA, Harvard Business School
Background: President/CEO, Lincoln Snacks Company; VP Marketing, Activision; Sales/Marketing: Baskin Robbins USA, Nestle USA
Hendrik J. Hartong, Jr., Founder Partner Emeritus
e-mail: huppsv@brynwoodpartners.com
Education: BA, Economics, University of Cincinnati; MBA, Harvard Business School
Background: President/CEO, Pittston Company; President/CEO, The Brink's Company; Group VP, North American Philips Corporation; Chairman/President/CEO, Simplex Wire & Cable Company; Consultant, McKinsey & Co
Ian B. MacTaggart, President/COO/CFO
e-mail: imactaggart@brynwoodpartners.com
Education: BBA, Boston College; MBA, Fuqua School of Business, Duke University
Background: M&A/Corporate Finance, Merrill Lynch & Co
David A. Eagle, Managing Director
Education: BS, Commerce, University of Virginia; MBA, Wharton School
Background: Emigrant Capital, GC Andersen Partners, Stifel Nicolaus
Vipul B. Soni, Managing Director
Education: BS, Economics, University of Wisconsin-Madison; MBA, University of Chicago, Booth School of Business
Background: Procter & Gamble

358 BULLPEN CAPITAL
215 2nd Street
3rd Floor
San Francisco, CA 94105
web: www.bullpencap.com

Mission Statement: Bullpen Capital is an early-stage venture fund which makes follow-on investments in start-ups funded by super-angels. Bullpen's market focus is on the social-mobile web sector (both enterprise and direct to consumer).
Fund Size: $85 million
Founded: 2010
Investment Criteria: Early-Stage
Industry Group Preference: Consumer Internet, Social Media, Enterprise Software

Portfolio Companies: About.me, Airmap, Aggregated Knowledge, Ayasdi, Bentobox, Betable, Beyond Pricing, Braze, Carbon, Chartio, Circulate, Citus Data, Classy, Cleanify, Confident Cannabis, CoverHound, Derby Jackpot, +Desk.com, Doubledutch, Drive Motors, Fanduel, Filament, FlashSoft, GameFlip, Grassroots Unwired, Grove Collaborative, Herb, HomeLight, Illumeo, Ipsy, Jump Ramp, Life360, LiveIntent, Lumoid, Mango Health, Marketo, Millennial Media, Namely, Navistone, Jackpocket, Paintzen, PayNearMe, Ranker, Reniac, Saucey, Sourceeasy, Splitwise, Spot Hero, Suiteness, Tanium, TubeMogul, Twenty20, Udemy, Urban Airship, Verbling, Wag, WedPics, Xumii, Zynga

Key Executives:
Paul Martino, General Partner
Education: BS, Mathematics, Lehigh University; MA, Computer Science, Princeton University
Background: Founder, Ahpah Software; Founder, Tribe; Founder, Aggregated Knowledge
Duncan Davidson, General Partner
Education: BS, Physics/Mathematics, Brown University; JD, Michigan Law School
Background: Founder, Covad Communications; Founder, Sky Pilot Networks; SVP, Business Development, InterTrust; Managing Director, VantagePoint Venture Partners
Directorships: Drive Motors, Filament, Hologram, Illumeo, SpaceIQ
Richard Melmon, Emeritus Partner
Education: BA, Physics, University of California, Berkeley; MBA, Stanford University
Background: Co-Founder, Electronic Arts; Co-Founder, Melmon Tawa & Partners; Co-Founder, Objective Software; Co-Founder, NetService Ventures Group
James Conlon, Partner
Education: BA, Bucknell University; JD, Washington College of Law, American University
Background: Co-Founder, Venture Scanner

359 BUNKER HILL CAPITAL
16 Laurel Avenue
Suite 10
Wellesley Hills, MA 02481
Phone: 617-720-4030 Fax: 617-720-4037
web: www.bunkerhillcapital.com

Mission Statement: Bunker Hill Capital is a private equity firm with a singular focus on lower middle-market companies in four industry sectors: industrial products, business services, consumer products and specialty retail. Bunker Hill Capital invests in companies with exceptional management teams and the potential for significant growth.
Fund Size: $200 million
Average Investment: $30 - $50 million
Industry Group Preference: Industrial Products, Business Products & Services, Specialty Retail, Consumer Products
Portfolio Companies: Dyno Holdings, Hubbardton Forge, Medicinal Genomics, Taos
Other Locations:
12625 High Bluff Drive
Suite 320
San Diego, CA 92130
Phone: 858-793-4560 Fax: 858-793-4562

Key Executives:
Mark DeBlois, Co-Founder/Managing Partner
617-720-4035
Education: BA, Boston College
Background: Managing Director, BancBoston Capital; Bank of Boston
Directorships: ASPEQ Heating Group, Dyno Holdings, Hubbardton Forge, ImportLA, Rizing, Specialty Brands Holdings, Taos Mountain
Robert Clark Jr, Co-Founder/Managing Partner
617-720-4032

Venture Capital & Private Equity Firms / Domestic Firms

Education: BA, Harvard College
Background: Managing Director, BancBoston Capital; Bank of Boston
Directorships: ASPEQ Heating Group, California Family Fitness, Dyno Holdings, Hubbardton Forge, ImportLA, Rizing, Specialty Brands Holdings, Taos Mountain
Brian Kinsman, Co-Founder/Managing Partner
Education: BA, Yale University; MS, New York University
Background: Senior Managing Director, Pacific Corporate Group; Principal, Charterhouse Group International; Founding Partner, Milley & Company; Dyson-Kissner-Moran Corporation
Directorships: California Family Fitness, ImportLA
Jason Hurd, Co-Founder/Managing Partner
617-720-4034
Education: BA, Harvard College
Background: Director, BancBoston Capital
Directorships: Hubbardton Forge, Rizing, Specialty Brands Holdings
David L Gold, Partner
617-720-4033
e-mail: david.gold@bunkerhillcapital.com
Education: BA, Hobart College; MBA, Harvard Business School
Background: Procter & Gamble; Gerber; Aramark; CEO, Source4Teachers; Operating Partner, The Riverside Company
Directorships: ASPEQ Heating Group, Dyno Holdings
Robert Dreier, Principal/Director of Business Development
617-398-5517
e-mail: rob.dreier@bunkerhillcapital.com
Education: BS, University of Arizona; MBA, Kellogg School of Management, Northwestern University
Background: Managing Director & Co-Head, Financial Sponsors Group, BB&T Capital Markets; Vice President, M&A, RBC Capital Markets; Tucker Anthony
Jared B Paquette, Principal
617-398-5513
e-mail: jared.paquette@bunkerhillcapital.com
Education: AB, Bowdoin College; MBA, University of Chicago Booth School of Business
Background: Senior Associate, Nautic Partners; Associate, Weston Presidio; Associate, M&A, RBC Capital Markets; Tucker Anthony
Directorships: ASPEQ Heating Group, Dyno Holdings
Nathaniel P Bacon, Vice President
617-398-5518
e-mail: nat.bacon@bunkerhillcapital.com
Education: BA, Bucknell University
Background: Analyst, Morgan Stanley
Austin Wright, Vice President
617-398-5514
e-mail: austin.wright@bunkerhillcapital.com
Education: BBA, Stephen M. Ross School of Business, University of Michigan
Background: Analyst, Deutsche Bank
Anthony Giannobile, Associate
617-398-5524
e-mail: anthony.giannobile@bunkerhillcapital.com
Education: BS, Carroll School of Management, Boston College
Background: Analyst, Technology Services Group, Raymond James & Associates

360 BUSINESS CONSORTIUM FUND
39 West 37th Street
7th Floor
New York, NY 10018

Phone: 212-243-7360 Fax: 212-243-7647
web: www.bcfcapital.com

Mission Statement: A source of capital for certified minority-owned firms having difficulty obtaining financing from conventional sources on reasonable terms.
Geographic Preference: United States
Founded: 1994
Industry Group Preference: Diversified
Key Executives:
  Serafin Mariel, President & COO
  Background: New York National Bank, National Minority Supplier Development Council
  Ruben Rodriguez, Sr. Vice President and Chief Lending Officer
  Education: BA, Economics, Lehman College
  Background: Relationship Manager, Seedco Financial Services
  Thomas C. Fitzgerald, Advisor
  Education: BA, Economics, Western Kentucky State University
  Background: Vice President & Treasurer, Hershey Foods Corporation

361 BV INVESTMENT PARTNERS
125 High Street
17th Floor
Boston, MA 02110

Phone: 617-350-1500 Fax: 617-350-1509
e-mail: info@bvlp.com
web: www.bvlp.com

Mission Statement: Investment firm focused on the intersection of business and big data.
Geographic Preference: North America
Fund Size: $2.6 billion
Founded: 1983
Minimum Investment: $20 million
Investment Criteria: Middle Market Buyouts, Recapitalizations, Growth Equity, Industry Roll-Ups
Industry Group Preference: Business Services, Information Technology
Portfolio Companies: Albridge Solutions, Apps Associates, Butterfield Fulcrum Group, C-4 Analytics, CAMP Systems International, CF Stinson, CivicPlus, Consero Global, Decision Resources Inc., DTIQ, ECRM Holdings, EDCO, Edtech Holdings, Franco Signor, Geologic Systems LTD., Harron Communications LP, INetU Holdings, Intelliteach, Marshall & Swift Holdings, Medley Global Advisors, PetroSkills, Precision Nutrition, REAN Cloud, Reimagine Holdings Group, Right Networks, Risk International, RKD Group, SJI Holdings, SSI Holdings, TriCore Solutions, Vista III Media Holdings, Veracross LLC, WIRB Group Holdings
Key Executives:
  Vikrant Raina, Managing Partner
  Education: BS, Computer Science, Yale University; MBA, Harvard Graduate School of Business
  Background: Executive Director, Communications, Media & Technology Group, Goldman Sachs (Asia); Project Leader, The Boston Consulting Group
  Justin Harrison, Managing Director
  Education: BA, Economics, Middlebury College
  Background: Analyst & Associate, Chase Securities
  Matt Kinsey, Managing Director
  Education: BS, Finance, Ithaca College; MBA, Columbia Business School
  Background: Analyst & Associate, Chase Securities
  Jerry Hobbs, Operating Partner
  Education: New York University, American Institute of Banking
  Background: Chairman/CEO, VNU

Venture Capital & Private Equity Firms / Domestic Firms

362 BVM CAPITAL
820 Garrett Drive
Bossier City, LA 71111

Phone: 318-746-8430
web: www.bvmcap.com

Mission Statement: BVM Capital LLC is a Southeast-based venture capital firm that invests opportunistically. We provide equity capital to early and expansion stage companies with proprietary technology platforms or unique products addressing large markets.
Geographic Preference: Southeast United States
Founded: 2000
Portfolio Companies: Arcmail Technology, Cadforce, Cellfor, Embera Neurotherapeutics, Esperance Pharmaceuticals, LifeSync Corporation, NuPotential, SteriFx, Body Evolution, Jenrin Discovery, Calosyn Pharma, Chow Town, Fitness Interactive Experience
Key Executives:
  Ross P. Barrett, Managing Partner
  Background: Co-Founder, VC Experts; Capitol Hill, Legislative Aide to Senior US Senator, J Bennett Johnston

363 C&G CAPITAL PARTNERS
302 Merchants Walk
Suite 250
Tuscaloosa, AL 35406

web: www.candgcapitalpartners.com

Mission Statement: Christian values-oriented investment company in Tuscaloosa, Alabama.
Geographic Preference: Southeastern U.S.
Average Investment: $500,000 - $3 million
Investment Criteria: Early-Growth to Mature Stage
Industry Group Preference: Diversified
Key Executives:
  John Gaffney, Principal
  e-mail: jgaffney@candgcapitalpartners.com
  Education: Vanderbilt University
  Background: Management Committee Member, Commercial Banking Group Head, AmSouth Bank
  Mike Chambers, Principal
  e-mail: mchambers@candgcapitalpartners.com
  Education: University of Texas
  Background: Co-Founder/CEO/Chairman, River Gas Corporation

364 C3 CAPITAL PARTNERS LP
1511 Baltimore Avenue
Suite 500
Kansas City, MO 64108

Phone: 816-756-2225
web: www.c3cap.com

Mission Statement: To back successful and strong management teams and businesses with a vision for growth.
Geographic Preference: United States, Midwest, South
Fund Size: $500 million
Founded: 1994
Average Investment: $2 - $15 million
Minimum Investment: $2 million
Investment Criteria: Mezzanine, Later Stage, Strategic Acquisitions, Ownership Transitions, Recapitalizations
Industry Group Preference: Chemicals, Plastics, Energy, Business to Business, Distribution, Manufacturing
Portfolio Companies: A5, Air Waves, BP Express, Custom Steel Processing, Dynamatic, Equivalent Data, Flojos, GradLeaders, Green Compass, Grun Style, Hobbs Rental Corporation, iOR Partners, Lev, Market Fresh Produce, Monster XP, National Power, Nemaha Environmental, New World Natural Brands, Professional Environmental Engineers, Reynolds Plymer, Scrap Partners, SG360, Southern Spine Institute, SPOKE Custom Products, Steak 44, Stouse, SuccessEd, Sweet Additions, Transnational Foods, Warne, Wise Connect
Other Locations:
  15169 North Scottsdale Road
  Suite 320
  Scottsdale, AZ 85254
  Phone: 480-389-6955 Fax: 816-756-5552
Key Executives:
  Andy Butler, Director
  816-360-1808
  e-mail: abutler@c3cap.com
  Education: BS, Business, MAcc, University Of Missouri
  Background: KPMG; BKD
  Jared Poland, Managing Director
  816-360-1827
  e-mail: jpoland@c3cap.com
  Education: BS, Accounting, Rockhurst University
  Background: Senior Securities Analyst, Kansa City Life Insurance; Deloitte & Touche
  Robert Smith, Partner
  816-360-1805
  e-mail: rsmith@c3cap.com
  Education: BS, Engineering, University of Kansas; MBA, University of Chicago
  Background: President, Koch Producer Services; EVP, Koch Oil; Koch Energy
  Patrick Healy, Partner
  816-360-1804
  e-mail: phealy@c3cap.com
  Education: BS, Accounting, University of Kansas
  Background: Senior Tax Partner, Mayer Hoffman McCann
  A Baron Cass III, Partner
  214-292-2000
  e-mail: bcass@c3cap.com
  Education: BBA, Finance, Southern Methodist University; MBA, Wharton School, University of Pennsylvania
  Background: Goldman Sachs & Company; Bear Stearns & Company
  Steven Swartzman, Partner
  816-360-1806
  e-mail: sswartzman@c3cap.com
  Education: AB, Harvard College; MBA, Columbia Business School
  Background: President, Small Business Investment Alliance; KC Venture Group; VP, Citibank
  D Patrick Curran, Partner
  816-360-1802
  e-mail: pcurran@c3cap.com
  Education: BA, Economics, Stanford University; MBA, Kellogg School of Management, Northwestern University
  Background: CEO, Cook Composites & Polymers; CEO, Cook Paint
  Directorships: Applebee's International, Gold Banc, Lockton Companies, Unitog, Sealright, JPS Packaging, American Safety Razor

365 CAI CAPITAL PARTNERS
300 Cadman Plaza W
One Pierrepont Plaza
12th Floor
New York, NY 11201

web: caifunds.com

Mission Statement: Founded in 1989, CAI is a private equity firm specializing in buyouts, restructurings, acquisitions, recapitalizations and other corporate growth initiatives. CAI offers financial expertise and access to capital, and aims to establish partnerships with capable management teams in order to ensure superior returns for investors.
Geographic Preference: Canada, United States
Founded: 1989
Average Investment: $20 - $75 million
Minimum Investment: $20 million

Investment Criteria: Lower Middle Market
Industry Group Preference: Consumer Products, Consumer Services, Business Products & Services, Infrastructure, Manufacturing, Aerospace, Defense and Government, Energy, Healthcare, Financial Services
Portfolio Companies: CustomAir, Javelin, Montigo, Sympli, CSAT Solutions, Feeney Brothers Utility Services
Other Locations:
510 Burrard Street
Suite 1000
Vancouver, BC V6C 3A8
Canada
Phone: 604-637-3411 **Fax:** 604-694-2524
Key Executives:
Peter Restler, Senior Advisor
212-319-3056
e-mail: prestler@caifunds.com
Education: BS, Wharton School, University of Pennsylvania
Background: Advisor, Island Natural Gas; Senior Vice President, Canada, Lehman Brothers; Vice President/Director, Wood Gundy
Directorships: Plastube, The Corix Group, Livingston International
Tracey McVicar, Managing Partner
e-mail: tmcvicar@caifunds.com
Education: BComm, Sauder School of Business, University of British Columbia; CFA Chartholder
Background: RBC Dominion Securities; Raymond James Ltd.; Goepel Shields & Partners
Directorships: Feeney Brothers Excavation, GeoStabilization International, White House Design, Tervita Corporation, Teck Resources
Curtis Johansson, Partner
604-694-2527
e-mail: cjohansson@caifunds.com
Education: BComm, Haskayne School of Business, University of Calgary
Background: RBC Capital Markets
Directorships: GeoStabilization International
Ashton Herriott, Director
604-637-1288
e-mail: aherriott@caifunds.com
Education: BComm, Finance, University of British Columbia; CFA
Background: Investment Banking Analyst, CIBC World Markets
Directorships: GeoStabilization International, Tervita Corporation, White House Design
Sherri Pittman, Managing Director

---

367 CALCEF CLEAN ENERGY FUND
5 Third Street
Suite 900
San Francisco, CA 94103

e-mail: info@calcef.org
web: calcef.org

Mission Statement: The Fund deploys deep industry networks and experience to support capital-efficient companies focusing on renewable energy, energy efficiency, energy storage and related products and services.
Fund Size: $24 million
Average Investment: $600,000
Investment Criteria: Seed-Stage, Early-Stage
Industry Group Preference: Clean Technology, Energy, Renewable Energy, Energy Efficiency
Key Executives:
Danny Kennedy, Managing Director
Christina Borsum, Chief Financial Officer

---

368 CALERA CAPITAL
580 California Street
Suite 2200
San Francisco, CA 94104

Phone: 415-632-5200
web: www.caleracapital.com

Mission Statement: Calera Capital invests in middle-market companies with proven management teams, sound business franchises and substantial unrealized potential. They accept public or private companies, family-controlled enterprises and corporate divestitures in virtually any sector.
Fund Size: $2.8 billion
Founded: 1991
Average Investment: $50 - $250 million
Investment Criteria: Leveraged Recapitalizations, Restructurings, Growth Investments, Corporate Spin-Offs, Take-Private Transactions
Industry Group Preference: Financial Services, Business Products & Services, Food Products & Services, Consumer Products, Healthcare, Building Materials & Services, Industrial Manufacturing
Portfolio Companies: Arnott, Bay State Physical Therapy, Carnegie Fabrics, Coldwell Banker, Crown Pacific, Direct General, Evans, First Republic Bank, Grandpoint, ImageFIRST, IPS Corporation, Ironshore, Juno Lighting, Kerr Group, Kinetic Concepts, LoopNet, Petro Shopping Centers, Transaction Services, RFIB, Rock-It Cargo, Sleepy's, Software Architects, Specialty Brands, SterlingBackcheck, Tapco International, United Dental Partners, United Site Services
Other Locations:
800 Boylston Street
Suite 1460
Boston, MA 02199
Phone: 617-578-0790
Key Executives:
Jim Farrell, Managing Partner
Education: AB, Princeton University; MBA, Harvard Business School
Background: Independent Investor; Associate, ESL Partners
Directorships: Modular Space Corporation, LoopNet, Rock-It Cargo
Mark N. Williamson, Managing Partner
Education: BA, Univ. of Oxford; MBA, Harvard Business School
Background: Managing Director, Harvard Private Capital Group; Associate, ESL Partners
Directorships: Direct General Corporation, IPS Corporation, Ironshore Corporation
Kevin Baker, Managing Director & General Counsel
Education: BA, Economics & Accounting, Claremont McKenna College; JD, Harvard Law School
Background: Partner, O'Melveny & Myers; Arthur Andersen & Co
Paul Walsh, Senior Managing Director
Education: BS, Engineering, Tufts University; MBA, Boston University
Background: Chairman & CEO, eFunds Corporation; CEO, Wright Express; CEO, BancOne Diversified Services; SVP, Norwest Capital Managment; CEO, Diners Club Germany
Ethan Thurow, Managing Director
Education: AB, Harvard University; MBA, Harvard Business School
Background: Associate, Audax Group; The Parthenon Group
Directorships: IPS Corporation
Brian Fearnow, Managing Director
Education: BS, Industrial Engineering, Stanford University; MBA, Stanford Graduate School of Business
Background: Investment Banking Group, Morgan Stanley; Franklin Templeton

Venture Capital & Private Equity Firms / Domestic Firms

James Halow, Managing Director
Education: BA, Stanford University
Background: Technology Investment Banking Group, Salomon Smith Barney
Directorships: Ironshore Corporation, Rock-It Cargo

369 CALGARY ENTERPRISES
Four Park Avenue
Suite 12G
New York, NY 10016

Phone: 212-683-0119 Fax: 212-683-3119
e-mail: insalaco@calgaryenterprises.com
web: www.calgaryenterprises.com

Mission Statement: Calgary Enterprises provides management consulting and advisory services to early stage and emerging middle market companies across a variety of industry sectors.

Geographic Preference: United States, Canada
Founded: 1988
Investment Criteria: Emerging, Early Stage, Growth, Middle Market, Management Buyouts, Acquisitions, Restructurings, Turnarounds
Industry Group Preference: All Sectors Considered
Key Executives:
  Steven Insalaco, President
  e-mail: insalaco@calgaryenterprises.com
  Education: BA, Social Science & Economics, St. John's University; MBA, Finance Management, Long Island University
  Background: Bank of America; Chemical Bank; Manufacturers Hanover Trust Corporation; Wood Gundy Corp; Merrill Lynch

370 CALIBRATE VENTURES
130 W Union Street
Pasedena, CA 91103

web: www.calibratevc.com

Mission Statement: Calibrate Ventures invests in early-revenue automation and AI technology companies.

Investment Criteria: Less than $5 million revenue; Recurring revenue business models and ambition to scale beyond $100 Million in sales
Key Executives:
  Kevin Dunlap, Co-Founder and General Partner
  Jason Schoettler, Co-Founder and General Partner

371 CALIFORNIA TECHNOLOGY VENTURES
670 N Rosemead Boulevard
Suite 201
Pasadena, CA 91107

e-mail: info@ctventures.com
web: www.ctventures.com

Mission Statement: California Technology Ventures (CTV) is a venture capital fund that makes direct investments in technology and life science companies. CTV has built a strong reputation for its entrepreneurial approach to investing and working with companies. CTV believes in guiding entrepreneurs through the strategic, operational, and management decisions critical to a company's success.

Average Investment: $250,000 - $2 million
Minimum Investment: $250,000
Investment Criteria: Seed-Stage/Startup, Early-Stage, First & Second Round, Later-Stage
Industry Group Preference: Life Sciences, Biopharmaceuticals, Medical Devices, Information Technology, Communications, Telecommunications, Electronics, Semiconductors, Software Systems, Multimedia, Internet
Portfolio Companies: Ablexis, Agile Materials & Technologies Inc., Akiva Inc., AngioScore, Aurora SFC Systems, Avita Biomedical, Blade Games World Inc., Ceregene Inc., China Genetics Holdings, Clear Flow Inc., Education.com, Dolphinsearch Inc., GoingOn Networks Inc., FanXChange, Health Hero Network, Gamevice, Insert Therapeutics, InSound Medical, MariaDB, MingPlan.com, Moss Software, Oerthalign Inc., Orthoscan Inc., Photothera Inc., Surgrx Inc., Spine Wave Inc., SupplyEdge Inc., SurgiQuest Inc., Vasonova Inc., Thinglefin, Travelmuse Inc., Turbine Inc., Vivant Medical Inc.

Key Executives:
  Alex Suh, Managing Director/Founder
  e-mail: asuh@ctventures.com
  Education: BSBA, Management, University of Denver's School of Business
  Background: Jacobs Capital Group, LLC; JJ Jacobs Enterprises
  William A. Hanna, Managing Director
  e-mail: william@jacobscapitalgroup.com
  Education: MBA, Harvard University; BComm, McGill University
  Background: Jacobs Capital Group, LLC; Founding President/Director, Cedars Bank; Senior VP, Credit of Bank Audi USA; VP, Corporate Finance Department, Smith Barney & Company
  Andrea Devita, Director of Finance
  e-mail: andrea@ctventures.com
  Background: Controller, Main Line Equipment; Controller, CTL Environmental Services

372 CALLAIS CAPITAL MANAGEMENT
401 Focus Street
Thibodaux, LA 70301

Phone: 985-492-2323
web: callaiscapital.com

Mission Statement: Callais Capital leverages generations of entrepreneurship to pursue regional startup investment opportunities.

Geographic Preference: Louisiana and Regional
Key Executives:
  Harold Callais II, Managing Partner/Chief Investment Officer
  985-272-1324
  Education: BS, Nicholls University
  Corey Callais, Managing Partner/Chair
  985-492-2323
  e-mail: corey.callais@callaiscapital.com
  Education: BS, Nicholls State University
  Background: CEO, KLEB/KZZQ; CEO, Callais Cablevision; CEO Solid Waste Disposal Inc.
  Nicholas Callais, Managing Partner/CFO and Chief Compliance Officer
  985-492-2323
  e-mail: nicholas.callais@callaiscapital.com
  Education: BA, MBA, Tulane University
  Background: VP, Terrebonne Parish Republican Party; Credit Analyst, United Community Bank

373 CALTIUS EQUITY PARTNERS
11766 Wilshire Blvd
Suite 850
Los Angeles, CA 90025

Phone: 310-996-9585
e-mail: info@caltius.com
web: www.caltius.com

Mission Statement: Makes equity investments in small and medium sized businesses throughout the United States.

Geographic Preference: United States
Founded: 1999
Average Investment: $10 - $30 million
Minimum Investment: $5 million
Investment Criteria: Late-Stage, Growth Capital, Leveraged Recapitalizations, Corporate Divestitures, Acquisitions, Buyouts

Industry Group Preference: Consumer Products, Consumer Services, Business Products & Services, IT & Managed Services, Industrial Services

Portfolio Companies: ACIS, Arrowhead Brass Products, CampGroup, Consolidated Fire Protection, CRC Health, DavexLabs, Diversified Human Resources, Electra Bicycle Company, Health Payment Systems, Impact Fire Services, La Dove, MC Sign Company, MCC Control Systems, MC Sign, Nicoat, Northwest Coatings, OrthoClassic, Polytex Environmental Inks, Scientech, SeniorBridge, SM&A, Starpoint Health, Talent Systems, Vision Holdings

Key Executives:

Jim Upchurch, President/CEO
e-mail: jupchurch@caltius.com
Education: BS, Accounting, Northern Arizona University
Background: President, Bancorp Libra; Libra Investments; Portfolio Manager, Columbia Savings & Loan Association; KPMG
Directorships: CampGroup, DavexLabs, Kiss My Face, OrthoClassic, SM&A, Starpoint Health

Garrick Ahn, Managing Director
e-mail: gahn@caltius.com
Education: BS, MS, Electrical & Computer Engineering, Johns Hopkins University; MBA, Harvard Business School
Background: Associate, Bastion Capital Corporation; Associate, McKinsey & Company; Financial Analyst, Morgan Stanley & Company
Directorships: Electra Bicycle Company, Health Payment Systems, Kiss My Face, Ortho Classic, Scientech

Jeffrey Holdsberg, Managing Director
Education: BS, Business, Eastern Illinois University
Background: CEO/President, Northwest Coatings; Advisor, Charlesbank Capital Partners; President, Alper Ink Group; Arthur Andersen
Directorships: Diversified Human Resources, Health Payment Systems, National Industrial Coatings, The Institute of Audio Research

Michael Morgan, Managing Director
e-mail: mmorgan@caltius.com
Education: BA, Economics, University of Pennsylvania; MBA, Anderson School of Management, University of California, Los Angeles
Background: Salomon Smith Barney; Kline Hawkes & Co.; Continental Illinois Venture Corporation
Directorships: Starpoint Health, MCC Control Systems, Diversified Human Resources, Kiss My Face

Justin Benshoof, Principal
e-mail: jbenshoof@caltius.com
Education: BA, Economics, Beloit College; MBA, University of Minnesota
Background: Analyst, Norwest Equity Partners
Directorships: Diversified Human Resources, Health Payment Systems, Impact Facility Services, MCC Control Systems, MC Sign

Greg Brackett, Chief Financial Officer
e-mail: gbrackett@caltius.com
Education: BA, Business Economics, University of California, Los Angeles
Background: Senior Accountant, Investment Management Services Assurance Group, KPMG

---

374 CALTIUS STRUCTURED CAPITAL
11766 Wilshire Blvd
Suite 850
Los Angeles, CA 90025

Phone: 310-996-9585
e-mail: info@caltius.com
web: www.caltius.com

Mission Statement: Makes investments in businesses with diverse customer bases, experienced management teams and strong market positions throughout the United States.

Geographic Preference: United States
Founded: 1999

Average Investment: $7 - $50 million
Minimum Investment: $7 million
Investment Criteria: Late-Stage, Growth Capital, Leveraged Recapitalizations, Acquisitions, Buyouts, Acquisition Financing, Management Buyouts, Refinancing, Shareholder Liquidity

Industry Group Preference: Consumer Products, Consumer Services, Business Products & Services, Healthcare, Specialty Manufacturing, Specialty Staffing, Tech Services

Portfolio Companies: Adrenaline, American Consolidated Media, Aspen Education Group, BrightHeart, Building Systems Design, Bulk Handling Systems, CampGroup, Closet world, CRC Health, Dickinson Frozen Foods, Diversified Human Resources, Divisions Maintenance Group, ETT, EXOS, ForeFront Education, Fullerton, GLM, Griplock Systems, Harris Research, HealthPlan, Healthy Pet, Hill Country Holdings, Homegrown Natural Foods, HSS, Imagenet, Insight Global, Integrated Healthcare Strategies, Intellectual Technology, J-B Weld, KCAEP, Kids Care Dental, Lucky Strike, Mercer Advisors, Meridian Surgical Partners, Monitor Group, MCRA, Nu Visions Manufacturing, Pacific Crest, Parking Company America, Pearl Meyer & Partners, PlanMember Financial, Plassein Packaging, Pritikin, QCI Marine Offshore, Quantic Industries, Radiant Logistics, Radiant Research, Scientech, Select Rehabilitation, SM&A, Soff-Cut, Spinnaker Support, Tri-Star Electronics, True Home Value, U.S. Pole Company, UHY Advisors, Unitech Aerospace, Universal Services Of America, Vantage Mobility International, Walker Edison, Wyle Laboratories, Zenith Adminstators

Key Executives:

Jim Upchurch, President/CEO
e-mail: jupchurch@caltius.com
Education: BS, Accounting, Northern Arizona University
Background: President, Bancorp Libra; Libra Investments; Portfolio Manager, Columbia Savings & Loan Association; KPMG
Directorships: CampGroup, DavexLabs, Kiss My Face, OrthoClassic, SM&A, Starpoint Health

Michael Kane, Managing Director
e-mail: mkane@caltius.com
Education: BA, Economics, MBA, Accounting, Rice University
Background: Building and Construction Capital Partners; General Electric Capital Corporation; Metropolitan Life Insurance
Directorships: Bulk Handling Systems, Fullerton Engineering, Perl Meyer & Partners, SM&A, Unitech Aerospace

Greg Howorth, Managing Director
e-mail: ghoworth@caltius.com
Education: BS, University of Southern California
Background: Senior Credit Officer, FINOVA Capital; Heller Financial
Directorships: Adrenaline, GLM Energy Services, Imagenet, J-B Weld

Alisa Frederick, Managing Director
e-mail: afrederick@caltius.com
Education: BA, Wellesley College
Background: Senior Vice President, Portfolio Manager, Fleet Capital Corporation; Chemical Bank
Directorships: MCRA, Pearl Meyer & Partners, SM&A, Spinnaker Support

Gavin Bates, Managing Director
e-mail: gbates@caltius.com
Education: BA, University of Nottingham; MBA, Haas School of Business at the University of California
Background: Director, CapitalSource; Compass Partners and Permira; HSBC Investment Bank
Directorships: Adrenaline, GLM Energy Services, J-B Weld, SM&A

Rick Shuart, Managing Director
e-mail: rshuart@caltius.com
Education: BA, Columbia University; MBA, UCLA Anderson School of Management

Venture Capital & Private Equity Firms / Domestic Firms

Background: Financial Analyst, Dillon, Read & Company; Donaldson, Lufkin & Jenrette
Directorships: Bulk Handling Systems, Fullerton, Imagenet, Select Rehabilitation, Unitech Aerospace
Don Jamieson, Vice President
e-mail: djamieson@caltius.com
Education: BA, Economics, Harvard University
Background: Financial Analyst, Salomon Smith Barney
Directorships: Adrenaline, Fullerton, GLM Energy Services, Imagenet, J-B Weld, MCRA, Pearl Meyer & Partners, Spinnaker Support
Alan Chen, Vice President
e-mail: achen@caltius.com
Education: BS, Finance and Business Economics, University of Southern California; MBA, Columbia Business School
Background: Associate, Endeavour Capital; Banking Analyst, Piper Jaffray & Co.

375 CALUMET VENTURE FUND
1245 E Washington Avenue
Suite 210
Madison, WI 53703
Phone: 308-310-3242 Fax: 888-310-3989

Mission Statement: Calumet Venture Fund was formed to invest in the next generation of high-growth technology companies in the Midwest.
Geographic Preference: Midwest United States
Founded: 2008
Investment Criteria: Early-Stage
Industry Group Preference: SaaS, Business Products & Services, Education, Healthcare, E-Commerce & Manufacturing, Mobile Technology, Wireless, Software, Networks, Bioinformatics
Portfolio Companies: CraftArtEdu, Craft Media Network, Montage Talent, OptiMine

Key Executives:
Judy M. Owen, General Partner
Education: BSEE, University of Wisconsin, Madison
Background: Silicon Graphics, Chips & Technologies, Teknekron Communication Systems; CEO/Co-Founder, Wireless Access
Directorships: Picazo Communication, SigmaQuest
Toni F. Sikes, General Partner
Education: BS, Mathematics, University of Alabama; MS, Market Research, University of Wisconsin, Madison
Background: Investment Banking, Gruppo Levey & Co.

376 CALVERT INVESTMENT MANAGEMENT
1825 Connecticut Ave. NW
Suite 400
Washington, DC 20009-5727
Phone: 301-951-4800 Fax: 301-657-1982
Toll-Free: 800-368-2748
web: www.calvert.com

Mission Statement: Invests in high-risk, socially and environmentally responsible enterprises. Calvert is part of a larger financial services family, The AmeritasAcacia Companies.
Geographic Preference: United States
Fund Size: $9 billion
Founded: 1976
Average Investment: $100,000-$700,000
Minimum Investment: $1,000
Investment Criteria: Early-to-expansion stage; generally not a seed or start-up investor
Industry Group Preference: Environment, Education, Energy, Health Related
Portfolio Companies: Cylex, H2Gen Innovations

Key Executives:
John Streur, President & Chief Executive Officer
Education: BS, Agriculture & Life Sciences, University of Wisconsin
Background: President & CEO, Managers Investment Group LLC
Anthony Eames, Vice President, Director of Responsible Investment Strategy
Education: BA, Wittenberg University
Background: Vice President, Eaton Vance Management; Sr. Vice President and National Sales Manager, Calvert Investment Management.
Hope Brown, Vice President, Chief Compliance Officer
Education: BA, English, University of Maryland
Background: Vice President & Chief Compliance Officer, Wilmington Funds; Assistant Vice President, Risk Management & Compliance Lead Manager, T. Rowe Price Associates
Stu Dalheim, Vice President, Shareholder Advocacy
Education: BA, Philosophy, Wesleyan University
Jessica Milano, Vice President, Director of ESG Research
Education: BSc, Government, London School of Economics; MA, Applied Economics, Johns Hopkins University
Background: Deputy Assistant Secretary, U.S. Treasury Department; Compass Lexecon; Promontory Interfinancial Network

377 CAMBER CREEK
5410 Edson Lane
Suite 220
Rockville, MD 20852
Phone: 240-621-3177
web: www.cambercreek.com

Mission Statement: Camber Creek is a venture capital firm providing strategic value and capital to operating technology companies focused on the real estate market. The investment team at Camber Creek has investing, operating, and technology experience and expertise across a range of real estate businesses, including construction, property management, development, and leasing.
Geographic Preference: United States
Investment Criteria: Seed-Stage, Early-Stage
Industry Group Preference: Real Estate, Software
Portfolio Companies: 42 Floors, Canvas, ClearEdge, Optii Solutions, Parkifi, Vedero Software, SalesWarp, Compstak, Fundrise, Motista, Latch, VTS, Revmetrix, BuildingEngines, Rachio, 3C Logic, Task Easy, Mobideo, Red IQ, Notion, Turbo Appeal, Latista, Bowery

Other Locations:
450 West 17th Street
Suite 1222
New York, NY 10011

Key Executives:
Jeffrey Berman, General Partner
Directorships: LoftSmart, SalesWarp, AquaSeca
Casey Berman, Managing Director
Education: University of Michigan
Background: NextGen Venture Partners; Founder, DATG Security Company; Advisor, Pervazive

378 CAMBRIA GROUP
Commonwealth Hall at Old Parkland
3899 Maple Avenue
Suite 150
Dallas, TX 75219
Phone: 469-513-2200 Fax: 469-513-2201
web: www.cambriagroup.com

Mission Statement: The Cambria Group is a private equity firm which invests in small and mid-sized businesses. The group targets control positions in stable, historically profitable entities with operating profits in excess of $1 million annually. the group does not invest in startups or turnarounds.
Geographic Preference: United States
Founded: 1996

Venture Capital & Private Equity Firms / Domestic Firms

Average Investment: $5 million
Minimum Investment: $500,000
Investment Criteria: Leveraged Buyouts, Management Buyouts, Recapitalizations, Industry Consolidations, Growth Equity, Transfers, Restructurings, Strategic Acquisitions
Industry Group Preference: Business Products & Services, Transportation, Consumer Products, Consumer Services, Manufacturing, Industrial Products, Retail, Consumer & Leisure, Education
Portfolio Companies: 8 Enterprises, Advanced Network Solutions, Allen Edmonds, Allrecipes.com, Ames Taping Tools, Ancient Mosaic Studios, Apartment Data Services, Bacrac Supply Company, Behavioral Health Group, Blue Dog Bakery, Boca Executive Beauty, Business Networking International, CalNet Technology Group, Care2.com, Classroom Connect, Cobblestone Golf Group, ConvenientMD, Crossbow Technology, Dakota Arms, Data Fusion Technologies, Dolce Hotels & Resorts, DSA/Phototech, DuBois Chemicals, Excelligence, Eyewitness Surveillance, FastSpring, Filson, FleetPride, Flexstar Technology, Funko, Gizmo Beverages, Globys, Gogotech, Griswold Home Care, Gwynnie Bee, Identified, iLight Technologies, iNet Interactive, InSight Eye Care, ISC Water Solutions, Ivize, KPI Consulting, Krueger-Gilbert Health Physics, Leader Technologies, Leocorpio, Liftoff Mobile, LM Foods, Lund Van Dyke, MarketTrack, Marshall Retail Group, Midwest Supplies, Mitchell, National Technical Systems, National Video Monitoring Corporation, NuCO2, O'Brien Veterinary Management, OOHA Wilkins, Ooyala, Opengov.com, Oriental Trading Company, Paragon Products, PEAK Broadcasting, Penn Warranty Corporation, Pet Loss Center, Planet DDS, Polaroid, Restaurant Technology, River Point Farms, Rock Ridge Stone, Rod and Tubing Services, Roman Decorating Products, Root Metrics, Scottish-American Insurance, Shoreline Solutions, SkyPipeline, Social Sentinel, Soft Surroundings, Sonoma Creamery, Sundance, Teaching Company, US Labs, Vector Disease Control, Veri

Key Executives:
  Paul L Davies III, Founder/Managing Principal
  469-513-220 ext.870
  e-mail: davies@cambriagroup.com
  Education: BS, Industrial Engineering, Stanford University; MBA, Stanford Graduate School of Business
  Background: Principal, Brentwood Associates; The Fremont Group; Operating & Financing, Bechtel Group; Foreign Operations, Chevron Corporation
  Directorships: Hoover Institution, National Trustee of the Boys & Girls Clubs of America
  René Lajous, Principal
  469-513-200 ext. 878
  e-mail: lajous@cambriagroup.com
  Education: BAS, Industrial Engineering, University of Toronto; MBA, Wharton School, University of Pennsylvania
  Background: Consultant, Boston Consulting Group; Logistics & Operations, Procter & Gamble; Pillsbury
  Natalie D Cryer, Vice President
  469-513-220 ext. 861
  e-mail: cryer@cambriagroup.com
  Education: BS, Stanford University; MBA, Stanford Graduate School of Business
  Background: Senior Analyst, Accenture; Salt Creek Capital
  Natalie L Davies, Senior Associate
  e-mail: nld@cambriagroup.com
  Education: BS, Management Science & Engineering, Stanford University
  Background: Senior Analyst, Business & Systems Integration, Accenture

379 CAMBRIDGE ASSOCIATES
125 High Street
Boston, MA 02110
Phone: 617-457-7500
e-mail: contactca@cambridgeassociates.com
web: www.cambridgeassociates.com

Mission Statement: To deliver outperformance with a portfolio that is right for each entrepreneur.

Industry Group Preference: Diversified

Key Executives:
  David Druley, Chief Executive Officer
  Education: BBA/MBA, University of Texas
  Background: Founder, Druley Investment Management

380 CAMBRIDGE CAPITAL
525 S Flagler Drive
Suite 200
West Palm Beach, FL 33401
Phone: 561-932-1600 **Fax:** 561-655-6232
web: www.cambridgecapital.com

Mission Statement: Cambridge Capital provides private equity and supply chain knowledge to growth companies in the applied supply chain sector. The firm utilizes its resources and operational expertise to create value for portfolio companies. Cambridge Capital is an investment partner of BG Strategic Advisors.

Fund Size: $81 million
Founded: 2009
Average Investment: $10 - $50 million
Investment Criteria: Growth Capital, Leveraged Buyouts, Recapitalizations, Build Up Strategies
Industry Group Preference: Manufacturing, Packaging, Distribution, Recycling, Logistics, Supply Chain Technology, Transportation
Portfolio Companies: American Capital, DHL, Geologistics, Kuehne Nagel, Meritex, New Breed Logistics, Odyssey Logistics & Technology, Old Dominion Freight Line, Supervalu, Tibco, Translink, USCO Logistics

Key Executives:
  Benjamin Gordon, Managing Partner
  e-mail: ben@cambridgecapitcal.com
  Education: BA, Yale College, Yale University; MBA, Harvard Business School
  Background: Founder, 3Plex; Mercer Management Consulting; AMI
  Directorships: Palm Beach United Way, Palm Beach Federation, Pal Beach Youn Presidents' Organization
  Bill Conley, Operating Partner
  Education: BS, Aeronautics, St. Louis University
  Background: CEO, Sky-Trax; President, ATC Technologies Corporation; Vice President/General Manager, FedEx
  Herb Shear, Operating Partner
  Education: Southern Illinois University
  Background: CEO, GENCO Supply Chain Solutions
  Dave Stubbs, Operating Partner
  e-mail: dave@cambridgecapital.com
  Education: BA, Economics, Haverford College; MBA, Finance, Wharton School, University of Pennsylvania
  Background: Senior Vice President/General Manager, Kuehne + Nagel; Vice President, Supply Chain, Champion International
  Rimas Kapeskas, Partner
  e-mail: rimas@cambridgecapitcal.com
  Education: BS, University of Connecticut; MBA, Goizueta Business School, Emory University; Stanford Business School
  Background: VP Of Strategy, Managing Director, UPS
  Directorships: National Venture Capital Association, Junior Achievement of Georgia
  Shai Greenwald, Director Of Business Development
  e-mail: shai@cambridgecapital.com

Venture Capital & Private Equity Firms / Domestic Firms

Education: MBA, Boston University
Background: FleetBoston Financial; EMC; Heidrick and Struggles
Matt Smalley, Vice President
e-mail: matt@cambridgecaptical.com
Education: Bachelor's, Leonard N. Stern School of Business, New York University
Background: Macquarie Capital; Insight Venture Partners

381 CAMBRIDGE CAPITAL CORPORATION
200 Madison Avenue
Convent Station, NJ 07960
Phone: 973-401-1414 Fax: 973-401-1417
e-mail: kjm@camcapcorp.com
web: www.camcapcorp.com

Mission Statement: Financial services including venture capital, capital sourcing, market planning, and consultation.
Geographic Preference: Middle Atlantic States
Founded: 1992
Average Investment: $2.5 million
Minimum Investment: $500,000
Investment Criteria: Early Stage, Well Capitalized, Institutional Investors, Affluent Individuals
Industry Group Preference: Assisted Living, Graphic Arts, Healthcare, Biotechnology, Manufacturing, Distribution, Computer Hardware & Software, Manufacturing, Financial Services, Banking

Key Executives:
Kenneth J Mathews, Managing Director
e-mail: kjm@camcapcorp.com
Education: BS, Economics, St. Peter's College
Background: Executive VP, First Fidelity Bancorporation

382 CAMBRIDGE VENTURES LP
4181 E 96th Street
Suite 200
Indianapolis, IN 46240
Phone: 317-843-9704 Fax: 317-844-9815
web: www.cambridgecapitalmgmt.com

Mission Statement: Invests in growth companies within a 200 mile radius of Indianapolis.
Geographic Preference: Mid-West
Fund Size: $20 million
Founded: 1991
Average Investment: $750,000
Minimum Investment: $100,000
Investment Criteria: Second-Stage, Mezzanine, LBO, Expansion, Acquisition
Industry Group Preference: Diversified

Key Executives:
Jean Wojtowicz, President
317-843-9704 ext. 126
e-mail: jwojtowicz@cambridgecapitalmgmt.com
Charles Kennedy, Portfolio Manager
317-843-9704 ext. 124
e-mail: ckennedy@cambridgecapitalmgmt.com

383 CAMDEN PARTNERS HOLDINGS LLC
500 East Pratt Street
Suite 1200
Baltimore, MD 21202
Phone: 410-878-6800 Fax: 410-878-6850
e-mail: info@camdenpartners.com
web: www.camdenpartners.com

Mission Statement: Capitalizes on the disconnect between business fundamentals and valuation in small and micro-cap markets.
Founded: 1995
Average Investment: $10 million
Minimum Investment: $3 million
Investment Criteria: Equity, Preferred Equity, Equity-Linked Debt Securities acquired directly from issuer in negotiated private placement
Industry Group Preference: Business Products & Services, Healthcare, Education, Financial Services
Portfolio Companies: Blisplay, Bluefin, Clavert Education Services LLC, CMC, eNeura, EGHC, Implantable Provider Group, InGo, Metabolon, Network For Good, New Horizons, Orpheris, OutMathc, Paragon Bioservices, Patient Safe Solutions, Pinnacle Automotive Hospitally, Planet Payment, PreScience Labs, Proposal Software.com, Ranir, Santa Rosa Consulting, Sisu Global Health, Tracx, Triumpth Higher Education Group, Viventium

Key Executives:
David L. Warnock, Founder/Partner
410-878-6810
e-mail: ssprigg@CamdenPartners.com
Education: BA, University of Delaware; MS, University of Wisconsin
Background: President/Consultant, T Rowe Price Strategic Partners; Co-Manager, T Rowe Price New Horizons Fund; Welch and Forbes
Directorships: Concorde Career Colleges, Environmental Safeguards, Touchstone Applied Science Associates, Blue Rhino Corporation, Nobel Learning Communities
Donald W. Hughes, Strategic Advisor
e-mail: ssprigg@camdenpartners.com
Education: BA, Lycoming College; MSF, Loyola University; CPA
Background: Executive VP/CFO, Broventure Company; Arthur Andersen LLP; CFO, Capstone Pharmacy Services
Directorships: Occupational Health + Rehabilitation, Touchstone Applied Science Associates, AqilQuest
Meghan M. McGee, Partner
e-mail: cbeal@camdenpartners.com
Education: BS, Family Studies, University of Maryland; MBA, Robert H. Smith School of Business, University of Maryland
Richelle P. Parham, Strategic Advisor
e-mail: richelle@camdenpartners.com
Education: BS, Business Admin. & Design Arts, Drexel University
Background: Visa Inc.; Digitas Inc.; Citibank; VP Chief Marketing Officer, eBay
Jason R. Tagler, Partner
e-mail: cbeal@camdenpartners.com
Education: BS, Applied Economics, MBA, Cornell University
Background: Alliant Partners
Directorships: Ranir, IncentOne

384 CAMP ONE VENTURES
101 California St.
Suite 2710
San Francisco, CA 94111
Phone: 415-856-7248 Fax: 415-856-7348
web: www.camponeventures.com

Mission Statement: Camp One Ventures seeks to combine the expertise, insights and relationships that the team possesses from their years of advising early stage companies with the core team's investment experience. The synergies among the team create unparalleled access into the realm of early stage technology investments, and bring to investors a unique opportunity to participate in exciting growth companies that would otherwise be reserved for Sand Hill Road insiders. Camp One Ventures will leverage the local team's client base, founder referral network, and proximity to Stanford and Silicon Valley to identify early stage companies. We want to keep a hands-on relationship with the company and help build out the team, as well as make introductions.

Geographic Preference: San Francisco, Silicon Valley
Investment Criteria: Early Stage
Industry Group Preference: Technology, Social Media, Mobility, Fintech, Cloud Computing, SaaS

Portfolio Companies: Aarki, Apple Pie Capital, Augmate, Balance, Booking Pal, Boomtown, CommerceSync, Credit Sesame, DoubleBeam, Earnin, Earn Up, Even, Fanbank, Fenway Summer, Float, Goodworld, InDinero, Karmic Labs, MetaBrite, Mobius, Momentum, One Inc., Otelic, Pulse.io, Rhiza, Ripple, Simple Disability Insurance, Stellar, Terabit Radios, Wade & Wendy, Xola, Zooz

Other Locations:
2501 20th Place South
Suite 275
Birmingham, AL 35223
Phone: 205-202-1083 **Fax:** 205-639-5678

Key Executives:
Robert Claassen
650-714-0538
e-mail: rob@camponeventures.com
Thomas P. Brown
415-856-7248
Fax: 415-856-7348
e-mail: tom@camponeventures.com
Madding King III
205-202-1083
Fax: 205-639-5678
e-mail: madding@camponeventures.com
J. Rainer Twiford
205-202-1083
Fax: 205-639-5678
e-mail: rainer@camponeventures.com

---

385 CAMP VENTURES
1216 Woodview Terrace
Los Altos, CA 94024-7046

Phone: 650-949-0804 **Fax:** 650-618-1719
e-mail: justin@campventures.com
web: www.campventures.com

Mission Statement: To engage with great companies in their earliest stage of development.

Founded: 1997
Average Investment: $500,000 - $1.5 million
Minimum Investment: $500,000
Investment Criteria: Seed-Stage
Industry Group Preference: Mobile Apps, Technology, Computer Software, Communications, Data, Semiconductors
Portfolio Companies: Abertis, AllTrails, Altera, Broadcom, Cepheid, deCarta, Dell, Qualcomm, GainSpan, GeoVector, LifeLock, Picaboo, Quantance, Riverbed, Seagate, Sierra Wireless, SiTime, Skype, SpreadTrum, YesVideo

Key Executives:
Justin Camp, Founder & Managing General Partner
e-mail: justin@campventures.com
Education: BA, Economics & Political Science, UCLA; JD, University of Pennsylvania Law School
Background: Corporate Attorney, Cravath Swaine & Moore; Author, Venture Capital Due Dilligenc
Jerome Camp, Founder & General Partner
Education: BS, Mechanical Engineering, University of Arkansas; BS, Electrical Engineering, University of Maryland; MS, Mechanical Engineering, Purdue University; PhD, Electrical Engineering, University of Arizona
Background: Founder, ComTier; Consultant, Lockheed-Martin
Kevin Negus, General Partner
e-mail: kevin@campventures.com
Education: BASc, MASc, Mechanical Engineering, University of Waterloo
Background: CTO, Proxim Corporation; VC Investments, Atheros Communications

386 CANAAN PARTNERS
2765 Sand Hill Road
Menlo Park, CA 94025

Phone: 650-854-8092
e-mail: hello@canaan.com
web: www.canaan.com

Mission Statement: Helps companies successfully grow over time by taking an active role in their development; investment capabilities range from $4 million to $20 million. The firm can invest in any stage of development from early through expansion stage; it has investments in over 100 companies, and has created a number of public companies.

Geographic Preference: United States, Israel
Fund Size: $2.0 billion
Founded: 1987
Average Investment: $4 - $20 million
Minimum Investment: $2 million
Investment Criteria: Seed- and Early-Stage
Industry Group Preference: Technology, Healthcare
Portfolio Companies: Abryx, AdNear, AdverCar, Aldea Pharmaceuticals, Artspace, Arvinas, Axial Exchange, Beckon, Bharat Matrimony, Blurb, Borro, Butterfly, Call My Name, Cardlytics, CarTrade, Chimerix, Inc., Civitas Therapeutics, CompStak, Cortina, Cuyana, CytomX Therapeutics, Data Sciences International, Dermira, Dicom Grid, Durata Therapeutics, ee4, Ebates, Echopass, Efficient Finance, EndoGastric Solutions, EnStorage, Envisia, Equitas, Gemvara, Groundwork, Happiest Minds, IndiaProperty.com, Instacart, ItBit, iYogi, Joor, Kabam, Koolbit, Labrys Biologics, Lancope, LendingClub, Liquidia Technologies, LiveU, Loyalty Rewardz, Marinus Pharmaceuticals, mCarbon, Metacloud, Minimally Invasive Devices, Inc., N-trig, Naaptol, Novira Therapeutics, On24, OneFineStay, OpenSky, Orchard, Prime Sense, Relievant, Revision Optics, Sample6, Semnur, ShopKeepPOS, SilverRail, Skybox Imaging, Soasta, Spine Wave, Stayful, Switchfly, Talena, The RealReal, Theraclone Sciences, Tobira Therapeutics, Transcend Medical, Tremor Video, UnitedLex, UrbanSitter, VaxInnate, Verance, Victorious, ViewBix, Vivox, Wibidata, Xirrus, Zoosk

Other Locations:
285 Riverside Avenue
Suite 250
Westport, CT 06880
Phone: 203-855-0400

821 Broadway
3rd Floor
Entrance at 51 East 12th
New York, NY
Phone: 646-374-4949

27 South Park
Suite 201
San Francisco, CA 94107
Phone: 415-405-4655

Key Executives:
John Balen, Partner
e-mail: jbalen@canaan.com
Education: MBA, BS, Electrical Engineering, Cornell University
Background: Managing Director, Horsley Bridge Partners; Sales Application Engineer, Codentoll Technology Corporation; Fiber Communications Start-Up/Engineer, Digital Equipment Corporation
Directorships: Blurb; Cardlytics; eStamp; ID Analytics; SilverRail; SOASTA; Switchfly; UberSitter
Guy M. Russo, General Partner & COO
e-mail: grusso@canaan.com
Education: BS, Accounting, University of Connecticut; CPA & MBA, University of Connecticut
Background: Senior Accountant, Entrepreneurial Services Group of Ernst & Young
Deepak Kamra, General Partner
e-mail: dkamra@canaan.com

Venture Capital & Private Equity Firms / Domestic Firms

Education: BC, Carleton University; MBA, Harvard Business School
Background: Marketing, Aspect Communications; General Manager, TRW Datacomm International; ROLM Corporation
Directorships: Acme Packet; Capella Space; DoubleClick; Kickplay; Kustomer; Match.com; Matrimony; Node; ON24; Spark Networks; SuccessFactors; Turo; World View; Zoosk
Eric Young, Partner & Co-Founder
e-mail: eyoung@canaan.com
Education: BS, Mechanical Engineering, Cornell University; MBA, Finance, Northwestern University
Background: Senior VP, GE Venture Capital; Marketing, GE
Directorships: Capstone Turbine Corporation; Diffusion Software; Ebates; Lancope; Xirrus; Snyk
Brent Ahrens, General Partner
e-mail: bahrens@canaan.com
Education: BS & MS Mechanical Engineering, University of Dayton; MBA, Tuck School of Business at Dartmouth College
Background: General Surgical Innovations; Ethicon Endo-Surgery; IAp Research
Directorships: Abyrx; Calixa Therapeutics; Cerexa; Data Sciences International; DexCom; EndoGastric Solutions; Grey Wolf Therapeutics; Patios Therapeutics; Unchained Labs
Maha Ibrahim, General Partner
e-mail: mibrahim@canaan.com
Education: BA Economics; MA Organizational Behavior, Stanford University; PhD Economics, MIT
Background: Numerous Roles; Qwest Communications; Management Consultant, Boston Consulting Group & Price Waterhouse
Directorships: Agile Stacks; Cuyana; Forte; Gen.G; Kabam; Komprise; ManiMe; The RealReal; Twenty20; Unifi
Brendan Dickinson, General Partner
e-mail: bdickinson@canaan.com
Education: BA, Political Science, Bowdoin College; MS, Computer Science, Brown University; MBA, NYU Stern School of Business
Background: Senior Quantitative Analyst, Lehman Brothers; Barclays Capital
Directorships: Embroker; Even Financial; Hugo; Journey Meditation; Ladder; Paxos; Quantum Circuits Inc.
Stephen Bloch, General Partner
e-mail: sbloch@canaan.com
Education: MA, History and Science, Harvard University; AB, History, Dartmouth College
Background: CEO, Radiology Management Sciences; Medical Director Omnisonics Medical Technologies
Directorships: Ambra Health; Amicus Therapeutics; Envisia; Genome Medical; Liquidia Technologies; Marinus Pharmaceuticals; Onkos Surgical; Truveris
Daniel Ciporin, General Partner
e-mail: dciporin@canaan.com
Education: AB, Princeton University's Woodrow Wilson School of Public & International Affairs; MBA, Yale University
Background: Chairman, Shopping.com; Chairman, Internet Lab
Directorships: Bellhops; Bond; Bumped; CircleUp; Homeis; JOOR; LendingClub; Ollie; Orchard; Peer39; ShopKeep; Velocity
Wende Hutton, General Partner
e-mail: whutton@canaan.com
Education: AB, Human Biology, Stanford University; MBA, Harvard Business School
Background: Mayfield Fund; Spring Ridge Ventures
Directorships: Alsius Corp; Apieron, Antiva Biosciences; BiPar Sciences Inc.; Calibra Medical; Chimerix; Dermira; Glooko; Hyalex Orthopaedics; OncoResponse; Theraclone Sciences

Tim Shannon, General Partner
e-mail: tshannon@canaan.com
Education: BA, Chemistry, Amherst College; MD, University of Connecticut
Background: President, CuraGen; Bayer's Pharmaceutical Business Group
Directorships: Arvinas; CytomX; IDEAYA Biosciences; NextCure; Rallybio; Vivace Therapeutics
Byron Ling, General Partner
e-mail: bling@canaan.com
Education: BS, Economics, Case Western Reserve University; MBA, Wharton School
Background: Investor, Primary Venture Partners; Operator, Gilt Groupe;
Directorships: Bravo Sierra; Kin Euphorics; Papa; Ro; Uniform Teeth

387 CANAL PARTNERS
7114 E Stetson Dr
Suite 360
Scottsdale, AZ 85251

Phone: 480-264-0238
e-mail: info@canalpartners.com
web: canalpartners.com

Mission Statement: Canal Partners is a venture capital firm that provides professional investor services and capital to B2B software and internet technology companies.

Average Investment: $1 - $3 million
Industry Group Preference: Software, Internet Technology, SaaS
Portfolio Companies: PetDesk, Allbound, CallRail, Edaris Health, Iris PR Software, LightPost Digital, Firepoint, MobileLogix, Picmonic

Key Executives:
Todd Belfer, Managing Partner
Education: BS, Finance & Real Estate, University of Arizona
Background: Co-Founder, Employee Solutions; Co-Founder, MD Labs
Jim Armstrong, Managing Partner
Background: CEO, JDA Software
Directorships: JDA Software Group

388 CANNA ANGELS LLC
San Francisco, CA

Phone: 415-722-4849
e-mail: inquiries@cannaangelsllc.com
web: cannaangelsllc.com

Mission Statement: An angel investment firm focused on the cannabis industry. Areas of focus include genetics, plan & bio-science, real estate, data analytics, agriculture technology, business consulting & compliance, cultivation, and lab research.

Founded: 2016
Investment Criteria: Seed
Industry Group Preference: Cannabis, Agriculture, Business Consulting, Biotech, Research

Key Executives:
Sherri Haskell, Founder/CEO
Education: Washington University; Webster University
Background: Sr. Partner/Marketing & Business Development, Bridgeway Capital; Investor Relations Specialist, National Financial Consultants; Investor Relations Dir., ZAP!; Praxis Capital; SVP of Marketing, Drever Capital Management; Marketing Communications, Granite Peak Partners; Principal, Capital Dynamics

389 CANNABIS CAPITAL
1 World Trade Centre
Long Beach, CA 90831

Toll-Free: 888-680-5548
web: www.cannabiscapitalinc.com

Venture Capital & Private Equity Firms / Domestic Firms

Mission Statement: An investment consulting and private equity firm focused on the cannabis industry.
Founded: 2013
Investment Criteria: Early-Stage
Industry Group Preference: Cannabis

390 CANNABIS CAPITAL GROWTH
1099 Main Avenue
Suite 215A
Durango, CO 81301

Phone: 970-403-4686
web: cannabiscapitalgrowth.com

Mission Statement: Managed by McMillan Capital Management, Cannabis Capital Growth focuses on investments within the cannabis industry.
Founded: 2007
Average Investment: $250,000
Minimum Investment: $5,000
Industry Group Preference: Cannabis
Portfolio Companies: Origin House, Aurora Cannabis, Green Thumb Industries, CannTrust Holdings, Aphria, Green Organic Dutchman, Acreage Holdings, Charlotte's Web Holdings, GW Pharmaceuticals, Ianthus, Kuschco Holdings, Emblem Corp.
Key Executives:
  Jaime McMillan, Founder, Managing Advisor
  Education: BA, Political Science, North Carolina State University; JD, Trinity Law School
  Background: Private Client Financial Advisor, Charles Schwab; Founder/Managing Advisor, McMillan Capital Management

391 CANNABIS STRATEGIC VENTURES
Beverly Hills, CA

web: cannabisstrategic.com

Mission Statement: To strive for evolution in the cannabis industry through people, products, and processes, as well as providing access to safe and high-performing cannabis products.
Geographic Preference: California and Canada
Founded: 2003
Investment Criteria: Leaders who are passionate about improving the cannabis industry.
Industry Group Preference: Cannabis
Portfolio Companies: Asher House Wellness, Budhire, Fitamins, Halo Filters, Lyxr, Pure Organix
Key Executives:
  Simon Yu, CEO
  Education: University of Southern California
  Arlene Guzman, Vice President of Communications & Operations
  Background: VantagePoint Capital Partners

392 CANOPY BOULDER
1002 Walnut Street
Boulder, CO 80302

Phone: 303-586-4745
e-mail: info@canopyboulder.com

Mission Statement: Dedicated to investing in and educating entrepreneurs in the cannabis industry.
Founded: 2014
Investment Criteria: Seed
Industry Group Preference: Cannabis, Data Analysis, Technology
Portfolio Companies: BDS Analytics, Leaf, PotGuide.com, Grownetics, Hemp Business Journal, Front Range Biosciences, Würk, The Beak Beyond, Andia, Sana Packaging, WeGrow, Estrohaze, Redfield Proctor, Adistry, Firesale, KNXit, GreenScreens, Miele Events, 420 Klean, BDTNDR, Vapor Slide, Cannabis Big Data, The Herbalista Set, Deepgreen, Treatment X, Canna Zoning, Who Is Happy, Grass-Pass, iDro, Virtugro, Spare, Croptimize Inc., Stashbox, Snapp Digital, Solutions Vending International, PenSimple, TwoCubes Inc., Serene Green, Elevate Accessories, MyStrain, Hello People Ops, Paragon, Dispensarly, Bloom Automation, Gram, Icatus RT, BudTender, DCN Media Inc., Event Hi, Apothecarry, Lodestone Data Technologies, Yobi, Cannactrl, MJ Hybrid Solutions, Ripe Metrics, Traffic Roots, VertiCann, Mycocann, Collectif, Urban Labs, Ganjaboxes, Ananas, Gupta Daniel, Acro Vape, Leaf Cart, Healthy Headie Lifestyle, Campfire, Blujays Brand, Trellis Research Group, Pot Scientist, Glasshouse, Tradiv, Highest Reward
Key Executives:
  Patrick Rea, Co-Founder/Chief Executive Officer
  Education: BA, Geology; BA, Organizational Behavior & Management, Brown University
  Background: Financial Analyst, Health Business Partners; Director of Research, Nutrition Business Journal; Director of eMedia, New Hope Natural Media/Penton Media; Market Leader, Penton; Managing Director, Health Business Partners; Executive Editor, The ArcView Group
  Directorships: GreenBroz, Pure Prescriptions, Co-Chair, The NBJ Summit
  Micah Tapman, Managing Director
  Education: MBA, George Washing University School of Business
  Background: Managing Partner, Aerstone; Founder/CEO, CBMT Creative; Founder/CEO, The Tapman Group; Advisor, FlapJacked; Advisor, Front Range Biosciences; Managing Director, Canopy Ventures
  Directorships: BDS Analytics, PotGuide.com, Tradiv
  Celia Daly, Marketing Manager
  Education: BS, Economics/International Relations, American University; MBA, Colorado State University
  Background: Research Associate, Geo Strategy Partners; Market Process Coordinator, Alexander Proudfoot; Co-Founder, Chaka Fibers; Market Strategy Design Consultant, Factor(E) Ventures; Freelance Counsultant; Marketing Coordinator, Surna Inc.
  Bob Goodman, Managing Director
  Education: BS, Engineering, United States Military Academy at West Point; MBA, St. Edward's University
  Background: CEO, Kentron Technologies; President/CEO, Phiar Corp.; President/CEO, Qs Semiconductor Corp.; Executive-in-Residence, Infield Capital; President/CEO, BASiC 3C; Founder/President/CEO, OpiSafe; Counsulting CEO, Blackbox AI
  Directorships: Partner/Board Member, Blackbox Foundation

393 CANROCK VENTURES
720 Northern Boulevard
Brookville, NY 11548

Phone: 516-828-2673

Mission Statement: Canrock Ventures is an early-stage technology venture capital fund focused on turning good technology ideas into great technology businesses.
Fund Size: $400 million
Average Investment: $500,000 - $1.5 million
Minimum Investment: $500,000
Investment Criteria: Early-Stage
Industry Group Preference: Technology, Software
Portfolio Companies: Crowdster, General Sentiment, ThriveMetrics, Sentiment Alpha, SEO Pledge

394 CANTOR VENTURES
499 Park Avenue
New York, NY 10022

web: www.cantorventures.com

Mission Statement: Cantor Ventures is the venture capital and enterprise development arm of Cantor Fitzgerald, which has over 65 years of expertise in providing capital raising and

139

Venture Capital & Private Equity Firms / Domestic Firms

advisory services to growth oriented companies. Cantor Ventures invests in companies with business models focused on the development of innovative, technology-focused products, services and marketplaces. As an active partner, Cantor Ventures has guided and accelerated growth for numerous e-commerce businesses.

Founded: 2011
Investment Criteria: Early-Stage
Portfolio Companies: Delivery.com, Ritani, Topline Game Labs, AdFin

395 CANTOS VENTURES
San Francisco, CA

web: www.cantos.vc

Mission Statement: Cantos Ventures is an early-stage venture capital fund that invests in the newest technologies influencing industries like real estate, healthcare, and finance.

Founded: 2016
Average Investment: $25,000-$50,000
Investment Criteria: Pre-Seed, Seed-Stage
Industry Group Preference: Real Estate, Healtcare, Logistics, Parenting, Accessbility, Finance
Portfolio Companies: Alice, Advano, Aizon, Anagram, Arable, Astranis, Atom, Catalog, Chameleon, Circularis, Clara, Clover Tx, Concha, Curie Co., Debut Bio, Dhrama, Dusty, Earth AI, Eridan, Ethic, Helium, Humane, Knowde, Legit, Lively, Maxwell, Mission Barns, Opus 12, Phenomic, Pow Bio, Prellis, Public, Qwil, Shipamax, Skyryse, Solugen, Space Tango, Standard Cyborg, Super-Medium, Symbio, Vence, Visolis, X Genomes

Key Executives:
  Ian Rountree, Founder/Managing Partner
  Education: Vanderbilt University
  Background: Invisible Technologies, Inc.

396 CANVAS VENTURES
3200 Alpine Road
Portola Valley, CA 94028

Phone: 650-388-7600 Fax: 650-388-7601
e-mail: press@canvas.vc
web: www.canvas.vc

Mission Statement: Silicon Valley firm focused on early-stage investments in fintech, marketplaces and digital health.

Geographic Preference: Silicon Valley
Founded: 2013
Average Investment: $5 - $15 million
Investment Criteria: Early-Stage
Industry Group Preference: Fintech, Digital Health, Marketplaces, New Enterprise
Portfolio Companies: CrowdFlower, Eden, Everwise, Folloze, FutureAdvisor, HealthLoop, Totango, Transfix, Vida, Viewics, Zola

Key Executives:
  Gary Little, General Partner
  e-mail: glittle@canvas.vc
  Education: Harvard University; UCLA
  Background: Morganthaler Ventures; Apple Computer; Sun Microsystems
  Rebecca Lynn, General Partner
  e-mail: rebecca@canvas.vc
  Education: University of Missouri; University of California, Berkeley
  Background: Procter & Gamble; NextCard; Morgenthaler Ventures
  Paul Hsiao, General Partner
  e-mail: paul@canvas.vc
  Education: MIT, Harvard Business School
  Background: Mazu Networks
  Mike Ghaffary, General Partner
  e-mail: mike@canvas.vc
  Background: General Partner, Social Capital; CEO, Eat24;

VP of Business & Corporate Development, Yelp; Director of Business Development, TrialPay; Co-Founder, Stitcher; Co-Founder, BarMax; Associate, Summit Partners

397 CANYON CREEK CAPITAL
Santa Monica, CA 90404

e-mail: buck.jordan@canyoncreekcapital.com
web: www.canyoncreekcapital.com

Mission Statement: Canyon Creek Capital strives to build game changing companies, investing in the "Bridge to A" stage of early development.

Geographic Preference: West Coast
Founded: 2010
Investment Criteria: Mature Seed, Series A
Industry Group Preference: Technology, Consumer Services, Media
Portfolio Companies: ChowNow, Jukin Media, Winc, HoneyBook, HelloTechm Gyft, ShipHawk, Amplify, Bridg, Relativity, Bringhub, Misco Robotics Kitchen Assistant, Vertical Mass, Figs, Blue Bottle Coffee Co., Pixalate, Harri, Social Annex, Study Soup, Verbling, Meadow, TrueChoice, Iconery, Wedgies, Native Tap, Lawn Guru, Final, Vydia, Matic, Tonx, Anymeeting, StrikeAd, ShopSavvy, Afinity, Pongolo

Key Executives:
  Buck Jordan, Partner
  e-mail: buck.jordan@canyoncreekcapital.com
  Education: MBA, Anderson School of Management, University of California, LA

398 CAPITAL E
1054 31st Street NW
Suite 314
Washington, DC 20007

web: www.cap-e.com

Mission Statement: Capital-E invests in and works with leading corporations, cities, and technology firms to accelerate the transition to zero net carbon green buildings and cities.

Industry Group Preference: Renewable Energy, Green Building
Portfolio Companies: Bloom Energy, Skyline Innovations, Sunnovations, Calstar Products, BuildingIQ, MyEnergy, Green Wizard, Bright Frams, Better Workplace, Sage, GSI, Playa Viva, Scream Point, Sustainability Roundtable

Key Executives:
  Greg Kats, President
  e-mail: gkats@cap-e.com
  Education: BA, University of North Carolina; MBA, Stanford University; MPA, Princeton University
  Background: Managing Director, Good Energies

399 CAPITAL FOR BUSINESS, INC
11 South Meramec
Suite 1330
St. Louis, MO 63105

Phone: 314-746-7427 Fax: 314-746-8739
e-mail: info@cfb.com
web: cfb.com

Mission Statement: Capital For Business is a private investment firm that targets middle market companies with a potential for significant growth. The firm provides industry, operational and financial expertise to assist management teams with the growth of their businesses.

Geographic Preference: Central United States
Fund Size: $150 million
Founded: 1959
Average Investment: $3 - $5 million
Minimum Investment: $500,000
Investment Criteria: LBO, MBO, Recapitalizations, Corporate Divestitures, Growth Financings

Industry Group Preference: Plastics, Communications, Distribution, Electronic Components, Manufacturing, Industrial Equipment, Specialty Chemicals, Aerospace, Defense and Government, Education, Energy, Food & Beverage, Medical Devices, Diagnostics
Portfolio Companies: Arrow Material Handling Products, Bennett Tool & Die Company, Buse Industries, Central States Bus Sales, Custom Marketing, Domaille Engineering, Hi-Grade Welding & Manufacturing, Kieffer & Co., Lanair Holdings, Legacy Technologies, McNally Industries, Perennial Energy, Polymer Technology, Presence From Innovation, Preston-Eastin, Sun Graphics, Vanguard Graphics International, Waples Manufacturing, Wayne Trademark Printing & Packaging, Whitworth Tool, Winco Mfg, Wisconsin Coil Spring
Key Executives:
Stephen Broun, Managing Partner
e-mail: steve.broun@capitalforbusiness.com
Education: BBA, St. Louis University; MBA, Olin Business School, Washington University
Background: Investment Analyst, AG Edwards; Senior Associate, Missouri Venture Partners
Directorships: Kansas Venture Capital, Missouri Venture Forum
Bill Witzofsky, Senior Vice President
e-mail: bill.witzofsky@capitalforbusiness.com
Education: BBA, Accounting, University of Missouri St. Louis
Background: Landmark Commercial Corporation; Norwest Business Credit; Boatmen's Bank of St. Louis; Deutsche Financial Services; Corporate Accountant, Save-A-Lot Foods
Brett A Parr, Vice President
Education: BS, Business Administration, University of Kansas; MBA, Olin School of Business, Washington University
Background: Banking Officer & Assistant VP, US Bank
Chris Redmond, Senior Vice President
e-mail: chris.redmond@cfb.com
Education: BBA, University of Notre Dame; MBA, Kellogg School of Management
Background: A.G. Edwards & Sons; Morgan Stanley & Co.; COO, Argent Capital Management
Matt Leinauer, Assistant Vice President
e-mail: matt.leinauer@cfb.com
Education: BS, Finance, DePaul University
Background: Analyst, JP Morgan Chase; Peabody Energy

400 CAPITAL MIDWEST FUND
10556 North Port Washington Road
Suite 201
Mequon, WI 53092

Phone: 414-453-4488 Fax: 414-453-4831
e-mail: seinhorn@capitalmidwest.com
web: www.capitalmidwest.com

Mission Statement: Capital Midwest Fund is a venture capital firm that invests primarily in areas where the Midwest spends most of its research dollars: life science and information technology. The fund concentrates on investments where companies have excellent management and technology, are performing an important function, and will address significant markets. The firm looks for management teams with successful previous experience; markets that are established and growing; defensible IP positions; and sustainable competitive advantages.
Geographic Preference: Midwest United States
Founded: 2010
Industry Group Preference: Life Sciences, Information Technology, Manufacturing, Business to Business, Healthcare Technology
Portfolio Companies: Adello Biologics, Always In Touch, Centron, CytoPherx, EpiCare, Gemphire Therapeutics, HarQen, Intellihot, LiquidCool Solutions, NanoStatics, NuCurrent, Ocularis Pharma, OPS Solutions, PegEx, Physician Software Systems, PreEmptive Meds, PrevaCept Infection Control, Rapid Diagnostek, ScholarCentric, Sierra Oncology
Key Executives:
Stephen Einhorn, Principal
Education: BA, Chemistry, Cornell University; MS, Chemical Engineering, Brooklyn Polytechnic Institute
Background: Founder, Einhorn Associates
Daniel Einhorn, Principal
Education: BS, Cornell University; MBA, Cox School, Southern Methodist University

401 CAPITAL PARTNERS
301 Merritt 7
Norwalk, CT 06851

Phone: 203-625-0770 Fax: 203-625-0423
e-mail: info@capitalpartners.com
web: www.capitalpartners.com

Mission Statement: Private equity investment firm that invests in and supports small and mid-sized companies.
Geographic Preference: North America
Founded: 1982
Industry Group Preference: Manufacturing, Distribution, Business to Business, Franchising, Education, Food & Beverage, Aftermarket Products
Portfolio Companies: American Leather, CMI Limited, M&Q Packaging Corp., Parkway Products, Premier Performance Products, Roll Rite
Key Executives:
Brian Fitzgerald, Founder & Chairman
Education: BA, History, Princeton University; MBA, Harvard Graduate School of Business
Background: Industrial Capital Group, General Electric Co., The Vencap Group
Mark Allsteadt, Managing Partner
e-mail: mallsteadt@capitalpartners.com
Education: BA, Bucknell University; MBA, Stanford Graduate School of Business
Background: Partner, Saugatuck Capital Company; SVP, Operations, Eye Care Centers of America
Robert Tucker, Managing Partner
e-mail: rtucker@capitalpartners.com
Education: BA, Physics & Economics, Middlebury College; MBA, Finance & Management, Columbia University Graduate School of Business
Background: Partner, Saugatuck Capital Company; Partner, Rutledge Capital
John Willert, Principal
Education: BA, Gettysburg College; MBA, Finance & Accounting, Ohio State University
Background: Principal, Family Capital Growth Partners; VP, de Visscher & Co.
Thorsten Suder, Principal
Education: BA, Economics, Manhattanville College; MBA, Cornell University
Background: Vice President, Hartford Investment Management Company
James Sidwa, Principal, CFO & COO
Education: BS, University of Connecticut; CPA
Background: Transaction Services Group, PricewaterhouseCoopers
Edwin Tan, Managing Director
Education: BSE, MSE, University of Pennsylvania; MBA, Booth School of Business
Background: Prospect Capital Corporation
Mark Langer, Principal
Education: BSBA, Management, Bucknell University; MBA, Columbia University Graduate School of Business
Background: The Compass Group

Venture Capital & Private Equity Firms / Domestic Firms

402 CAPITAL RESOURCE PARTNERS
83 Walnut Street
Unit 10
Wellesley, MA 02481

Phone: 617-478-9600 Fax: 617-478-9605
e-mail: asilverman@crp.com
web: www.crp.com

Mission Statement: CRP invests in proven businesses, often in niche markets.
Geographic Preference: North America
Fund Size: $1 billion
Founded: 1987
Average Investment: $30 million
Minimum Investment: $5 million
Investment Criteria: Later Stage, Mezzanine, LBO, MBO, Special Situations, Management Quality, Security of Principal
Industry Group Preference: Business Services, Consumer Products & Services, Healthcare Services, Products & Technology, Proprietary Industrial Products & Services, Software & Information Services
Portfolio Companies: AllianceCare, Altra, Ardence, Aspen Dental Management, Athletes' Performance, Buckeye Nutrition, Commercialware, Context Integration, Coyne Textile Services, DynamicImaging, Ecollege, Enfield Logistics, ePartners, Epredix Campus Tele Video, Fantasy Entertainment, Fludrive, Gamma Medica-Ideas, Ganeden Biotech, Infotrieve, JDR Recovery Corporation, K2 Industrial Services, Kirkland's, Lamont Digital System, Lionbridge, L'Occitane, Lois Law Library, Loyaltyworks, MedMark Services, Monitronics, Odyssey Health Care, Paysys, Polar Beverages, PreVisor, Pro Group, Prometheus Laboratories, Revenue Cycle Solutions, The Richardson Group, RogersCasey, Rowland Coffee Roasters, Sam Seltzer's Steakhouse, SemperCare, Softbrands, Solis Women's Health, Specialty Filaments, Spirit Brands, Summit Global Partners, Supportkids.com, The Art of Shaving, Thrifty Lavanderia, Todd Combustion, Trintel, TVR Communications, United Country Real Estate, VMW Paducahbiltwpt, Women's Diagnostic of Texas, World Power Technologies

Key Executives:
  Robert C. Ammerman, Managing Partner
  e-mail: rammerman@crp.com
  Education: BA, History/BS, Mathematics, Carnegie Mellon University; MS, Industrial Administration, Graduate School of Industrial Administration at Carnegie Mellon University
  Background: General Partner, Advanced Technology Ventures II; VP, BT Capital; VP/Section Manager, Portfolio Investment Management Group, Bankers Trust Company
  Andrew A. Silverman, Partner
  617-478-9615
  e-mail: asilverman@crp.com
  Education: BA, Economics, Tufts University
  Background: Consultant, Aitman Vilandrie & Co.; Senior Associate, Investor Group Services; Equity Division Sales Trader, Optiver Derivatives Trading

403 CAPITAL SOUTHWEST CORPORATION
5400 Lyndon B Johnson Freeway
Lincoln Center Tower 1
Suite 1300
Dallas, TX 75240

Phone: 214-238-5700 Fax: 214-238-5701
e-mail: request@capitalsouthwest.com
web: www.capitalsouthwest.com

Mission Statement: Capital Southwest is a public company making long-term investments.
Geographic Preference: United States
Fund Size: $628 million
Founded: 1961
Investment Criteria: Small and Medium Sized Businesses, MBO, Recapitalizations, Industry Consolidations, Early-Stage Financings, Expansion Financings
Industry Group Preference: Aerospace, Defense and Government, Energy, Specialty Chemicals, Industrial Technology
Portfolio Companies: AAC Holdings Inc., Ace Gathering Holdings LLC, Adams Publishing Group, AG Kings Holdings Inc., Alliance Sports Group, Amware Fulfillment LLC, American Nuts, Apollo MedFlight, Binswanger Glass, California Pizza Kitchen Inc., Capital Pawn, Chandler Signs, Clickbooth, Blaschak Coal Corp., Danforth Advisors LLC, Delphi Behavioral Health Group, Digital Media Agency, Digital River, Driven Inc., Dunn Paper Inc., Dynamic Communicaties, Environmental Pest Service, Envocore, Fast Sandwich LLC, GrammaTech Inc., IEnergizer Limited, LGM Pharma, OrthoBethesda, Precision Spine Care, Premier Global Services Inc., Relevant Rental Solutions, Research Now Group Inc., RJO Holdings Corp., Scrip Companies, STATinMed, Tax Advisors Group Inc., Trinity3 Technology, Vertex Business Services, Vistar Media Inc., Zenfolio Inc.

Key Executives:
  Bowen S. Diehl, President/CEO
  e-mail: bdiehl@capitalsouthwest.com
  Education: Vanderbilt University; University of Texas
  Background: American Capital
  Michael S. Sarner, Chief Financial Officer
  e-mail: msarner@capitalsouthwest.com
  Education: James Madison University; George Washington University
  Background: American Capital
  Douglas M. Kelley, Managing Director
  e-mail: dkelley@capitalsouthwest.com
  Education: University of Texas
  Background: American Capital
  Joshua S. Weinstein, Managing Director
  214-884-3835
  e-mail: jweinstein@capitalsouthwest.com
  Education: Columbia University; University of Southern California
  Background: H.I.G. WhiteHorse

404 CAPITAL Z PARTNERS
142 West 57th Street
4th Floor
New York, NY 10019

Phone: 212-965-2400 Fax: 212-965-2301
e-mail: czpproposals@capitalz.com
web: www.capitalz.com

Mission Statement: Capital Z Partners identifies and selects financial services companies with the promise for growth. Through capital investments and ongoing support, Capital Z helps these companies to realize their full potential.
Geographic Preference: United States, Europe
Fund Size: $2.8 billion
Founded: 1990
Average Investment: $25 - $75 million
Industry Group Preference: Financial Services
Portfolio Companies: Aaccredited Home Lenders, Anchor BanCorp Wisconsin Inc., Argo Group, British Marine Holdings Ltd., Brookdale Senior Living Inc., Catlin Group Limited, Centrue Financial Corporation, Endurance Specialty Holdings Ltd., Hamilton Insurance Group Ltd., Jelf Group Plc., Kemper Corporation, Lancashire Holdings Limited, Minova Insurance Holdings Ltd., MountainView Capital, NACOLAH Holding Corporation, National Re Corporation, Opportunity Bancshares Inc., Pearl Capital, Permanent General Company Inc., Portfolio Group, Prestige Insurance Holdings Limited, Provident Companies Inc., SBJ Group Limited, Tarquin Plc., Transport Holdings Inc., Unionamerica Insurance Company Limited, Universal American Financial Corporation, UP&UP Inc., Health Extras Inc., USI Holdings Corporation

Venture Capital & Private Equity Firms / Domestic Firms

Key Executives:
Bradley E. Cooper, Partner
e-mail: brad.cooper@capitalz.com
Education: BBA, University of Michigan
Background: Financial Institutions Group, Salomon Brothers
Robert A. Spass, Partner
e-mail: bob.spass@capitalz.com
Education: BA, Business, State University of New York, Buffalo
Background: Director, Investment Banking Division, Salomon Brothers; Senior Manager, Peat Marwick Main & Co
Directorships: Lancashire Holdings
Jonathan D. Kelly, Partner
e-mail: jonathan.kelly@capitalz.com
Education: BS, Economics, Wharton School, University of Pennsylvania; BS, Electrical Engineering, School of Engineering & Applied Science
Background: Senior Vice President, Donaldson Lufkin & Jenrette
Trevor W. Pieri, Principal
e-mail: trevor.pieri@capitalz.com
Education: BA, Economics, Hobart College
Background: Investment Banker, Citadel & Citigroup
Roland V. Bernardon, Chief Financial Officer
e-mail: roland.bernardon@capitalz.com
Education: BBA & MBA, Accounting, Pace University
Background: Audit Director, Deloitte & Touche LLP

405 CAPITALA
4201 Congress Street
Suite 360
Charlotte, NC 28209

web: www.capitalagroup.com

Mission Statement: To provide private equity and mezzanine capital to lower middle-market companies.

Geographic Preference: Southern United States
Fund Size: $700 Million
Founded: 1998
Average Investment: $5-$25 million
Minimum Investment: $5 million
Investment Criteria: Lower Middle-Market
Industry Group Preference: Business Products & Services, Consumer Products, Energy, Healthcare
Portfolio Companies: Advantage Medical Electronics, Aerial Access Equipment, American Clinical Solutions, American Exteriors, AmeriMark, B&W Quality Growers, BigMouth, BlueStem Brands, BTM Company, Burgaflex Holdings, Burke America Parts Group, CableOrganizer, California Pizza Kitchen, Caregiver Services, Cedar Electronics, CIS Secure Computing, City Gear, Corporate Visions, CSM Bakery Solutions, Currency Capital, Eastport Holdings, Flavors Holdings, Fresh Dining Concepts, GA Communications, Hale and Hearty Soups, Immersive Media Tactical Solutions, Installs Inc., J&J Produce, Kelle's Transport Service, Long John Silver's, Micro Precision, MMI Holdings, myAgway, Nth Degree, On-Site Fuel Service, Portrait Innovations, Print Direction, Regent Education, Security Solutions of America, CarePoint Health, Sierra Hamilton, Staging Concepts, Stride Tool, Sur La Table, Taylor Precision Products, Tubular Textile, US Well Services, Velum Global Credit Mgmt., Vintage Stock, Vology, Western Windows Systems, Xirgo Technologies

Other Locations:
500 E Broward Blvd
Suite 1710
Fort Lauderdale, FL 33301
Phone: 954-848-2860

1450 Raleigh Rd
Suite 100
Chapel Hill, NC 27517
Phone: 704-376-5502 **Fax:** 704-376-5877

75 14th Street NW
Suite 2700
Atlanta, GA 30309
Phone: 678-666-3699 **Fax:** 678-999-8118

Key Executives:
Joseph B. Alala III, Chairman/CEO
Education: AB, Economics, Princeton University; MBA, Wake Forest University
Background: Director, Centura Bank; Principal, Halcyon Investments
M. Hunt Broyhill, Partner
e-mail: hbroyhill@capitalsouthpartners.com
Education: BA, Wake Forest University
Background: CEO, Broyhill Asset Management, LLC; President, Broyhill Investments
Jack McGlinn, Senior Managing Director
e-mail: jmcglinn@capitalsouthpartners.com
Education: BA, Accounting, University of Notre Dame
Background: President, Triangle Biomedical Sciences, Inc.; Senior Accountant, Price Waterhouse LLP
Michael S. Marr, Director of Portfolio Monitoring
704-936-4923
e-mail: mmarr@capitalsouthpartners.com
Education: BSBA, University of North Carolina; JD, Campbell University; Master of Laws in Taxation, Emory University
Background: Partner, Business Law Advisors
Christopher B. Norton, Director of Underwriting
e-mail: cnorton@capitalsouthpartners.com
Education: MBA, University of Virginia
Background: VP, Business Development, Waveguide Solutions; Associate, Bowles Hollowell Conner; First Union Securities; Summer Associate, Merrill Lynch-Mergers & Acquisitions; Senior Analyst, First Union Capital Markets

406 CAPITOL PARTNERS
7475 Wisconsin Avenue
Suite 750
Bethesda, MD 20814

Phone: 301-364-9020 **Fax:** 301-364-9022
e-mail: info@capitolpartners.com
web: www.capitolpartners.com

Mission Statement: Capitol Partners aims to achieve exceptional medium-term capital gains through investments in large, high growth industries, as well as partnerships with strong management teams.

Geographic Preference: Mid-Atlantic
Average Investment: $25 - $50 million
Investment Criteria: Recapitalizations, Management-Led Buyouts, Mergers and Acquisitions, Capital Investments
Industry Group Preference: Information Technology, Healthcare, Internet Technology, Infrastructure, Telecommunications, Energy
Portfolio Companies: Able Home Health, Advantage Home Health, Alliance Care, Amedisys Resource Management Division, Baylor Home Care, Baylor Home Infusion Therapy, Calvert Healthcare Partners, CareSouth Health System, Community Home Health, CS Indemnity, eCareOne.com, Family Care, Florida Pallative Homecare, Hand-In-Hand Home Health Care, HC360, Health at Home, Home Care of St. Francis, Integrity Services, Middle Tennessee Home Health Services, Paramount Healthcare, Rutherford Polk McDowell Home Health, Tenet Home Care, Total Home Health Care, US CareNet

Key Executives:
TJ Jubeir, Founder/Managing Partner
Education: BA, Quantitative Economics, MS, Engineering-Economic Systems, Stanford University; MBA, Harvard Business School
Background: Founder/Managing Partner, New Horizons

143

Venture Capital & Private Equity Firms / Domestic Firms

Venture Capital; Investment Officer, International Finance Corporation; Strategy Consultant, Bain & Company; Strategy Consultant, Booz-Allen & Hamilton; Advisor, Office of the Saudi Arabian Minister of Petroleum and Mineral Resources
Directorships: CareSouth Health System, CarePartners@Home, CS Indemnity
Julie Jubeir, Senior Vice President
Education: BA, Economics & Environmental Studies, Bowdoin College; MBA, Marketing & Strategic Management, Kellogg Graduate School of Management, Northwestern University
Background: Management Consultant, Booz Allen & Hamilton Inc.; Marketing Consultant, Nestle USA Inc.
Alex Radcliffe, Associate
Education: BS, Systems Engineering & Financial Economics, University of Virginia; MBA, George Washington University School of Business
Background: Investment Director, The Legacy Foundation

407 CAPX PARTNERS
155 North Wacker Drive
Suite 1760
Chicago, IL 60606

web: www.capxpartners.com

Mission Statement: CapX Partners strives to be the premier capital provider to private equity and venture capital backed companies. The company invests in and supports small and medium sized growth stage businesses.
Geographic Preference: United States
Fund Size: $225 million
Founded: 1999
Average Investment: $7 million
Minimum Investment: $500,000
Investment Criteria: Private Equity & Venture Capital Backed Firms, High Growth, Turnaround, Rebuilding Companies, Recapitalization
Industry Group Preference: Consumer Products, Energy, Healthcare, Manufacturing, Technology
Portfolio Companies: Acumentrics Holding Corporation, All Around Roustabout, Aquion Energy, Arandell Corporation, Arro Corporation, Digital Ocean, Gro-Well Brands, Karmaloop, Lake County Press, Rupari Food Services, TGI Systems Corporation

Other Locations:
4370 La Jolla Village Drive
Suite 400
San Diego, CA 92122

1460 Broadway
New York, NY 10036

33 Arch Street
15th Floor
Boston, MA 02110

Key Executives:
Jeffry S. Pfeffer, Managing Partner
Education: BA, Economics, Brandeis University; MBA, Finance, Kellstadt Graduate School of Business, DePaul University
Background: VP/Regional Manager, Bac One Leasing Corporation; American National Bank & Trust Company of Chicago
James N. Hallene, Founding Partner
Education: BA, University of Illinois; MBA, Kellogg Graduate School of Management, Northwestern University
Background: Founder, Capital Concepts Holdings; Co-Founder, MaxMiles Inc.; American National Bank
Directorships: KeHE Distributors, HallStar Company, VSA Partners
Barrett D. Carlson, Partner
Education: University of Illinois
Background: Partner, Capital Concepts Holdings; Founder/Managing Partner, Nine Iron LLC; Co-Founder,

Waterstone Consulting; Andersen Consulting
Directorships: VSA Partners, Illinois Venture Capital Association
Eric D. Starr, Partner
Education: Brandeis University; New York University Stern School of Business
Background: Risk Committee, Forest Investment Management; Owner, Starr Capital Management; Co-Founder, Aventine Investment Management; Refco; Union Bank of Switzerland

408 CARBON VENTURES
261 Madison Avenue
New York, NY 10016

e-mail: invest@carbonventures.com
web: www.carbonventures.com

Mission Statement: Carbon Ventures invests in technology serving a variety of industries, including education, agriculture, waste management, and transportation.
Founded: 2017
Average Investment: $500,000
Investment Criteria: Seed, Series A, Company Value of $5 million
Industry Group Preference: Technology, Education, Energy, Agriculture, Waste Management, Transportation, Manufacturing, Robotics, Artificial Intelligence, Machine Learning, Language Processing
Portfolio Companies: Andium, Fortify, Idelic, Mobius, Novel Effect, Sayspring, Smarter Sorting, Summit Sync, Transit Screen, Wasteplace

Key Executives:
Jason Cahill, Founder/Managing Partner
Education: MBA, Carnegie Mellon University
Background: Founder, Traansmission; Engineer, CSRA; Adjunct Professor, Columbia University; Veteran, Special Forces
Katherine Zamsky, Managing Partner
Education: MBA, Columbia University
Background: Fund Manager, Merrill Lynch; FinTech Builder, Bank of America
Gary Ragusa, Venture Partner
Education: MBA, Columbia University
Background: Consultant, PricewaterhouseCoopers; Head of Business Development, Outbrain; Co-Founder, StudioXchange; Co-Founder, Lustr Fasion App
Directorships: Savings United

409 CARDINAL EQUITY PARTNERS
8801 River Crossing Boulevard
Suite 320
Indianapolis, IN 46240

Phone: 317-663-0205 Fax: 317-663-0215
web: www.cardinalep.com

Mission Statement: To buy, build and operate a small number of middle-market businesses for long-term value creation.
Geographic Preference: Eastern United States
Founded: 1993
Minimum Investment: $250,000
Investment Criteria: Management Buyouts, Recapitalizations, Lower to Middle-Market
Industry Group Preference: Light Manufacturing, Distribution, Service Industries, Pharmaceuticals, Consumer Products, Industrial Equipment, Recreational Vehicles, Horticulture, Publishing, Healthcare, Financial Services, Home Improvement, Water Treatment
Portfolio Companies: Aqua Systems, Contour Industries, Eagle Battery, Guardian Pharmacy, MotionTech Automation, Poly-Wood, Wild Sports

Key Executives:
John F Ackerman, Co-Founder/Managing Director
e-mail: jackerman@cardinalep.com
Education: University of Michigan; Kellogg School of

Management, Northwestern University
Background: Quaker Oats Company; National Bank of Detroit
Directorships: Eskenazi Health Foundation, Avondale Meadows Academy Charter School, Teach For America
James L Smeltzer, Managing Director
e-mail: jsmeltzer@cardinalep.com
Education: BS, Accounting, Ball State University
Background: CFO, Cardinal Communications; Senior Tax Advisor, KPMG Peat Marwick
Directorships: Contour Industries, Corporate Imaging Concepts, Essco, Guardian Pharmacy, New Aqua, Oak Security Group, Williams Sound
Peter Munson, Managing Director
e-mail: pmunson@cardinalep.com
Education: BA, Economics, DePauw University
Background: Senior Vice President, JPMorgan Chase
Directorships: Contour Industries, Motion Tech Automation, OrthoPediatrics, Williams Sound
Michael L Smith, Senior Advisor
Education: DePauw University
Background: EVP & CFO, Anthem; Chairman, President & CEO, Mayflower Group; Arthur Andersen & Co.
Directorships: HHGregg, Envision Healthcare Holdings, Vectren Corporation, Carestream Health Services, USI, Hulman & Company, Go Health
Darell E Zink Jr, Senior Advisor
Education: BA, Vanderbilt University; MBA, University of Hawaii; JD, Indiana University
Background: Duke Realty Corporation; Partner, Bose McKinney & Evans; Captain, United States Air Force

410 CARDINAL PARTNERS
230 Nassau Street
Princeton, NJ 08542

Phone: 609-924-6452 Fax: 609-683-0174
e-mail: info@cardinalpartners.com
web: www.cardinalpartners.com

Mission Statement: Venture capital partnership focused exclusively on healthcare.

Fund Size: $400 million
Founded: 1996
Average Investment: $6-12 Million
Investment Criteria: Early Stage
Industry Group Preference: Healthcare, Life Sciences, Medical Devices, Service Industries, Healthcare Information Technology, Biopharmaceuticals
Portfolio Companies: Abide Therapeutics, Alnylam Pharmaceuticals, aTyr Pharma, Cubist Pharmaceuticals, Momenta Pharmaceuticals, Rib-X Pharmaceuticals, Sirtris Pharmaceuticals, Verastem

Key Executives:
John Clarke, General Partner
e-mail: johnclarke@cardinalpartners.com
Education: AB, Harvard University; MBA, Wharton School
Background: General Partner, DSV; interim CEO, Alkermes/Arris/DNX Corporation/Cubist Pharmaceuticals; General Electric Company
Directorships: Alnylam, Molecular Mining, Momenta Pharmaceuticals, Rib-X, TechRx, Visicu, Jackson Laboratory
Thomas McKinley, General Partner
Education: BS, Harvard University; MS, Accounting, New York University; MBA, Stanford Graduate School of Business
Background: Co-Founder & Co-Managing Partner, Paratech International
John Park, Partner/CFO
e-mail: johnpark@cardinalpartners.com
Education: BS, Villanova University; MBA, University of Michigan
Background: CFO, DSV Partners; Financial Analyst/Corporate Tax Manager, Day & Zimmermann

Directorships: Biotechnology and Life Sciences Advisory Committee for Ben Franklin Technology, Life Sciences Greenhouse of Central PA

411 CARDINAL VENTURE CAPITAL
325 Sharon Park Drive
Suite 107
Menlo Park, CA 94025-6805

Mission Statement: Cardinal Venture Capital is dedicated to investing in early-stage software companies in four specific focus areas: Digital Media, Financial Technology, Mobility and Software-as-a-Service. Cardinal takes a hands-on approach to partnering with their companies, dedicating significant time and resources into creating a successful company.

Founded: 2008
Investment Criteria: Early-Stage
Industry Group Preference: Software, Technology, Digital Media & Marketing, Financial Services, Mobility, SaaS
Portfolio Companies: Adaptive Insights, Chipcon, deCarta, DeliveryAgent, DIVX, GuardianEdge, ipinfusion, LiveCapital, PlayPhone, SuccessFactors, Wireless Security Corp., Zilliant

Key Executives:
Derek Blazensky, General Partner
e-mail: derek@cardinalvc.com
Education: BA, Fairfield University; BS, Engineering & Computer Science, University of Connecticut
Background: Adobe Ventures
Directorships: GuardianEdge Technologies, Nimblefish Technologies, deCarta
Christian Borcher, General Partner
e-mail: christian@cardinalvc.com
Education: Bachelor of Laws, Copenhagen University; MBA, Stanford Business School

412 CARE CAPITAL
Avon by the Sea, NJ 07717

Phone: 609-683-8300 Fax: 609-683-5787
e-mail: info@carecapital.com
web: www.carecapital.com

Mission Statement: Care Capital invests in companies developing pharmaceutical assets.

Geographic Preference: United States, Europe
Fund Size: $500 million
Founded: 2001
Average Investment: $5-20 million
Investment Criteria: Late Stage
Industry Group Preference: Life Sciences, Pharmaceuticals, Biotechnology
Portfolio Companies: Agile Therapeutics, NormOxys, Resolvyx Pharmaceuticals, Sentinella Pharmaceuticals, Vaxart

Key Executives:
Jan Leschly, Partner
Education: BBA, Copenhagen School of Economics and Business Administration; MS Pharmacy, Copenhagen College of Pharmacy
Background: Chief Executive, SmithKline Beecham; President/COO, Squibb Corpoartion; Novo Nordisk
Directorships: American Express, Viacom, Maersk Group, DaimlerChrysler, International Tennis Hall of Fame
Argeris Karabelas, Partner
Education: PhD Pharmacokinetics, Massachusetts College of Pharmacy
Background: Head Healthcare/CEO Worldwide Pharmaceuticals, Novartis AG; Executive VP, SmithKline Beecham; Founder/Chairman, Novartis Bio Venture Fund
Directorships: Massachusetts General Hospital, Visiting Committee for Health Sciences and Technology at MIT, SykePharma, Human Genome Sciences, Nitromed, Anadys

Venture Capital & Private Equity Firms / Domestic Firms

David Ramsay, Partner
Education: AB, Mathematics, Princeton University; MBA, Stanford Grad. School of Business
Background: Managing Director, Rhone Group; Rhone Capital; Director, Primus International; Straightline Communications; Terphane; Nation One Mortgage; Investment Committee, Morgan Stanley Capital Partners

413 CARLYLE GROUP
1001 Pennsylvania Avenue Northwest
Washington, DC 20004-2505
Phone: 202-729-5626 **Fax:** 202-347-1818
web: www.carlyle.com

Mission Statement: Originates, structures and acts as lead equity investor in management-led buyouts, strategic minority equity investments, equity private placements, consolidations and buildups and growth capital financings.

Geographic Preference: United States, Asia, Africa, Europe, South America

Founded: 1987

Investment Criteria: Buyouts, Privatizations, Strategic Minority Investments

Industry Group Preference: Aerospace, Defense and Government, Telecommunications, Automotive, Transportation, Consumer Products, Retail, Consumer & Leisure, Energy, Power, Financial Services, Healthcare, Industrial, Infrastructure, Technology, Business Products & Services

Portfolio Companies: 4Gas Holding BV, 7 Days Group Holdings, Accudyne Industries, Acosta, AcuFocus, Addison Lee Group, ADT CAPS Co., Al Nabil Food Industries, Alamar Foods, Alamosa Solar Generating Project, Alliance Boots plc, Allsec Technologies, Altice S.A., Apex Parks Group, Arabela Holding, ArtGo Holdings, ARUHI Corporation, Asia Satellite Telecom Holdings, Atlas Aerospace LLC, ATMU, Authentix, Avalon Advisors, AvanStrate, Axalta Coating Systems, AxieTech International Holdings, B&B Hotels, Bahcesehir Schools, Bank Of N.T. Butterfield & Son, Black Sea Oil & Gas SRL, Blyth, Bonotel, Booz Allen Hamilton, Bottle Rock Power, Brand Group Holdings, Brintons Carpets, BTI Studios, C.H.I. Overhead Doors, CalPeak Power, Cap Vert Finance SA, Carroll Cuisine, Catapult Learning, CDM MAX LLC, China Agritech, China Fishery Group, China Recycling Energy Group, Coalfire Systems, Coastal Carolina Clean Power LLC, Coates Hire, Cobalt International Energy, Cogentrix Power Management, Collingwood Ethanol, Combined Systems, CommScope, CommunityOne Bancorp, Companeo, Concord Medical Service Co., ConvaTec, Crystal Orange Hotel Holdings, Custom Sensors & Technologies, CVC Brasil Operadora e Agencia de Viagens S.A., CxS Corporation, Cyient, Dealogic, Dee Development Engineers, Diamond Bank, Discover Exploration, Document Technologies, Duff & Phelps, Dynamic Industries, Dynamic Precision Group, Eastern Broadcasting Company, ECi Software Solutions, Edelweiss Financial Services, Edgewood Partners Holdings, Ensus, Est

Other Locations:
Jachthavenweg 118
Amsterdam 1081
Netherlands
Phone: 31-205407575 **Fax:** 31-205407500

Pau Casals, 13
Barcelona 8021
Spain
Phone: 34-932000906 **Fax:** 34-932093510

China World Tower
No. 1 Jianguomenwai Avenue
Chaoyang District
Beijing 100004
China
Phone: 86-1057067000 **Fax:** 86-1057067003

201 North Illinois Street
Suite 1530
Indianapolis, IN 46204

One Vanderbilt Avenue
Suite 3400
New York, NY 10017
Phone: 212-813-4900 **Fax:** 212-813-4901

Dubai International Financial Centre
Gate Village, Building 5, Office 206
PO Box 506564
Dubai
United Arab Emirates
Phone: 971-44275600 **Fax:** 971-44275610

2 Pacific Place
88 Queensway
Hong Kong
China
Phone: 852-28787000 **Fax:** 852-28787007

Connaught House
1 Burlington Road
Floor 5
Dublin 4
Ireland
Phone: 353-16319738

15/F, One Pacific Place
J1. Jnd. Sudirman No. 52-53
Jakarta 12190
Indonesia

1 st. James's Market
London SW1Y 4AH
United Kingdom
Phone: 44-2078941200 **Fax:** 44-2078941600

C Las Begonias 415
Torre Begonias, 16th Floor
San Isidro
Lima
Peru
Phone: 51-12066830

11100 Santa Monica Blvd
Los Angeles, CA 90025
Phone: 310-575-1700 **Fax:** 310-575-1740

2 Avenue Charles de Gaulle L-1653
Luxembourg
Phone: 35-226102747 **Fax:** 35-226862110

2710 Sand Hill Road
1st Floor
Menlo Park, CA 94025

Piazza Cavour 2
Milan 20121
Italy
Phone: 39-026200461 **Fax:** 39-0229013559

Quadrant A, The IL&FS Financial Centre
Bandra-Kurla Complex
Bandra East
Mumbai 400 051
India
Phone: 91-2266470800 **Fax:** 91-2266470803

Promenadeplatz 8
Munich D-80333
Germany
Phone: 49-892444600 **Fax:** 49-89244460460

299 Park Avenue
35th Floor
New York, NY 10171
Phone: 212-332-6240 **Fax:** 212-332-6241

112, avenue Kleber
Paris 75116

Venture Capital & Private Equity Firms / Domestic Firms

France
Phone: 33-153703520 **Fax:** 33-153703530

Av. Brigadeiro Faria Lima 3900
Sao Palo Sp 04538-132
Brazil
Phone: 55-1135687700 **Fax:** 55-1135687750

15F, Centropolis Tower A
26, Ujeongguk-Ro
Jongno-gu
Seoul 03161
Korea
Phone: 822-20048400 **Fax:** 822-20048440

Unit 4001, 40th Floor, Tower 2
Jing An Kerry Centre
1539 Nanjing Road West
Shanghai 200040
China
Phone: 86-2161033200 **Fax:** 86-2161033210

1 Temasek Avenue
Millenia Tower 039192
Singapore
Phone: 65-62129600 **Fax:** 65-62129620

Level 33
The Chifley Tower, 2 Chifley Square
Sydney NSW 2000
Australia
Phone: 61-292703500 **Fax:** 61-292703520

Shin-Marunouchi Building
1-5-1 Marunouchi Chiyoda-ku
Tokyo 100-6535
Japan
Phone: 81-352084350 **Fax:** 81-352084351

Key Executives:
  William E Conway Jr, Founder/Co-Executive Chairman
  Education: Dartmouth College; University of Chicago Graduate School of Business
  Background: CFO, MCI Communications; The First National Bank of Chicago
  Daniel A D'Aniello, Founder/Chairman Emeritus
  Education: Syracuse University; Harvard Business School
  Background: VP, Finance & Development, Marriott Corporation; Financial Officer, PepsiCo Inc.; Trans World Airlines
  Directorships: AlpInvest
  David M Rubenstein, Founder/Co-Executive Chairman
  Education: Duke University; University of Chicago Law School
  Background: Paul, Weiss, Rifkind, Wharton & Garrison; Shaw, Pittman, Potts & Trowbridge; Chief Counsel, Subcommittee on Constitutional Amendments, US Senate Judiciary Committee
  Directorships: Lincoln Center for the Performing Arts, Memorial Sloan-Kettering Cancer Center, Johns Hopkins Medicine, Institute for Advanced Study
  Glenn A Youngkin, President/Chief Operating Officer
  Education: BS, Mechanical Engineering, BA, Managerial Studies, Rice University; MBA, Harvard Business School
  Background: Management Consultant, McKinsey & Company
  Directorships: Ri-Happy Brinquedos S.A., Rice Management Company
  Curtis L Buser, Chief Financial Officer
  Education: Georgetown University
  Background: Ernst & Young LLP; Arthur Andersen
  Jeffrey W Ferguson, General Counsel
  Education: University of Virginia
  Background: Associate, Latham & Watkins; Vinson & Elkins
  Kewsong Lee, Chief Executive Officer
  Education: AB, Harvard College; MBA, Harvard Business School
  Background: Deputy Chief Investment Officer, Corporate Private Equity; Partner, Warburg Pincus
  Brooke B Coburn, Managing Director/Partner
  Education: BA, Princeton University
  Background: Salomon Brothers
  Directorships: ECi Software Solutions, PrimeSport, Coalfire, Catapult Learning, Worldstrides
  Christopher Finn, Chief Operating Officer
  Education: Harvard College
  Background: Former Managing Director, Global Head of Operations, Carlyle

414 CAROLINA FINANCIAL GROUP
100 Elks Club Road
Brevard, NC 28712
Phone: 828-393-5401
e-mail: info@carofin.com
web: www.carofin.com

Mission Statement: An investment banking firm that specializes in raising debt and equity capital for privately-held middle market growth companies.

Founded: 1995

Key Executives:
  Bruce Roberts, President/CEO
  e-mail: bruceroberts@carofin.com
  Education: BSE, Civil Engineering, Duke University
  Background: Founder, Rehabilitation Support Services; Director, Investment Banking, Credit Suisse First Boston; Corporate Finance Specialist, Bank of America
  Directorships: Accelerate Appalachia, North Carolina Aquarium
  Craig Gilmore, Chief Operating Officer
  e-mail: cgilmore@carofin.com
  Education: BS, Bentley College
  Background: Survey Center Manager & Database Specialist, REDA International Inc.
  Bruce Smith, VP, Investor Development
  e-mail: bsmith@carofin.com
  Education: BA, American History, Princeton University
  Background: Morgan Stanley; Merrill Lynch

415 CAROUSEL CAPITAL
201 N Tryon Street
Suite 2450
Charlotte, NC 28202
Phone: 704-372-2040
web: www.carouselcapital.com

Mission Statement: Carousel Capital is a private equity firm that invests in companies based in the Southeastern United States. The firm partners with management teams to build leading companies in the business services, consumer services and healthcare services sectors.

Geographic Preference: Southeastern United States
Fund Size: $265 million
Founded: 1996
Investment Criteria: Leveraged Buyouts, Recapitalizations
Industry Group Preference: Business Products & Services, Consumer Products, Consumer Services, Healthcare Services
Portfolio Companies: AG Data, Apex Analytix, Axium Healthcare Pharmacy, Brasseler USA, Caldwell & Gregory, Copac, Crescent, Crown Column, Driven Brands, Express Oil Change & Service Center, Hepaco, Jameson, Joe Hudson's Collision Center, Med Data, Meineke Car Care Center, Mergent, Nestor Sales, Pegasus TransTech, Southeastern Automotive Aftermarket Service Holdings, Simpson Performance Products, Sona

Key Executives:
  Charles S. Grigg, Managing Partner
  e-mail: cgrigg@carouselcapital.com
  Education: BA, Economics, Yale University; MBA, Wharton School
  Background: Orion Partners; Smith Barney
  Directorships: Apex Analytix, Caldwell & Gregory, Mergent, Brasseler USA, Nestor Sales, HEPACO

Venture Capital & Private Equity Firms / Domestic Firms

Peter L. Clark, Jr., Partner
Education: BA, Economics, Davidson College
Background: Harris Williams & Co.
Directorships: Palmetto Infusion; Huseby; Consolidated Claims Group; Expedited Travel; Apex Analytix
Jason C. Schmidly, Managing Partner
e-mail: jschmidly@carouselcapital.com
Education: BBA, Finance & Organizational Behavior, Southern Methodist University
Background: M&A, Gregory & Hoenemeyer Inc.; M&A, Morgan Stanley
Directorships: Southeastern Automotive Aftermarket Service Holdings, Joe Hudson's Collision Center, Pegasus TransTech
Nelson Schwab III, Senior Advisor
e-mail: nschwab@carouselcapital.com
Education: BA, English, University of North Carolina at Chapel Hill; MBA, Wharton School, University of Pennsylvania
Background: Chairman & CEO, Paramount Parks; Chairman & CEO, Kings Entertainment Company; EVP, Attractions Group, Taft Broadcasting Company
Directorships: Herschend Family Entertainment, Messer Corporation

416 CARRICK CAPITAL PARTNERS
One California Street
Suite 1900
San Francisco, CA 94111

Phone: 415-432-4100
web: carrickcapitalpartners.com

Industry Group Preference: SaaS, Business Process Outsourcing, Transaction Processing
Portfolio Companies: Accolade, Axiom Law, Bay Dynamics, Complia Health, Everspring, Infinia ML, Infrascale, InstaMed, LaunchPoint, MavenLink, Perfect Sense, Saama, Seven Lakes Technologies

Key Executives:
Jim Madden, Co-Founder and Managing Director
Education: BBA, Finance, Southern Methodist University
Background: Founder/Chairman/CEO, Exult; Special Advisor, General Atlantic
Marc McMorris, Co-Founder and Managing Director
Education: BS, Economics, University of Pennsylvania; MBA, Wharton School
Background: Managing Director, General Atlantic; Vice President, Goldman Sachs
Alex Mason, Managing Director
Education: BS, Economics, University of Washington; Harvard Business School
Background: Vice President, Accel-KKR
Steve Unterberger, Managing Director, Operations
Directorships: Bay Dynamics, Infrascale, LaunchPoint, Mavenlink, Seven Lakes Technologies
Mike Salvino, Managing Director
Paul Zolfaghari, Managing Director, Operations
Mitchell Slodowitz, Managing Director & CFO

417 CASA VERDE CAPITAL
12530 Beatrice Street
Los Angeles, CA 90066

web: www.casaverdecapital.com

Mission Statement: Invests in companies focused on the ancillary cannabis industry, including health & wellness, financial services, technology, media, compliance, and laboratory technology.

Founded: 2015
Industry Group Preference: Cannabis
Portfolio Companies: Metrc, Dutchie, Oxford Cannabinoid Technologies, Green Tank Technologies, Weconnect, Vangst Talent Network, Green Bits, Cannalysis, Trellis, Leeflink, Eaze, Merry Jane

Key Executives:
Karan Wadhera, Managing Partner
Education: BA, Finance, Babson College
Background: Indian Equities, Goldman Sachs; VP of Equities, IIFL Capital; Head of India Sales Trading, Nomura Securities; Managing Director, Cashmere Asia; Advisor, MissMalini Publishing; Partner, Thursday Capital; Strategic Advisor, Stampede Management
Yoni Meyer, Partner
Education: BA, Economics, Tufts University
Background: Analyst, Herbert J. Sims & Co.; VP, Citigroup; Partner, TVP NYC

418 CASABONA VENTURES
2 Keil Avenue
Suite 244
Kinnelon, NJ 07405

e-mail: info@casabonaventures.com
web: www.casabonaventures.com

Mission Statement: Casabona Ventures provides management services, strategic planning, and early stage/Angel investment capital to technology driven start-up companies, with an emphasis on the Northeast region. By partnering with dynamic executive teams, the firm works to commercialize innovative, industry-impacting technologies, driving them from the laboratory to the marketplace.

Geographic Preference: Northeast United States
Investment Criteria: Early-Stage
Industry Group Preference: Technology, Renewable Energy, Environment, Communications, Electronics, Medical Technology, Information Technology
Portfolio Companies: AlgometR, NeuroFlow, Tech Launch, UBuildNet, Adaptive, Bluum, Fusar Technologies, Mobile Xoom, Mobile Arq, Outdoor Exchange, Retail Shopping Systems, Shielf Tech, Weldobot, BeautyStat.com, Inbox, Electro-Radiation Inc., StearClear, Nickle Bus, Powerhouse Dy Dynamics, Go-Now, SpeechTrans, Inc., Ray Sat, Skyworks Interactive, Fortress Technologies, Nuskool, MM Guardian, Untethered Labs

Key Executives:
Mario Casabona, Founder/Managing Director
Background: Founder/CEO, Electro-Radiation

419 CASDIN CAPITAL
1350 Avenue of the Americas
Suite 2600
New York, NY 10019

Phone: 212-897-5430
e-mail: info@casdincapital.com
web: www.casdincapital.com

Mission Statement: Casdin Capital, LLC is an investment firm focused on the life sciences and healthcare industry.

Industry Group Preference: Life Sciences, Healthcare
Key Executives:
Eli Casdin, Founder/Chief Investment Officer
Education: BS, Columbia University; MBA, Columbia Business School
Background: VP, Alliance Bernstein; Bear Stearns; Cooper Hill Partners
Brian Shim, Chief Financial Officer
Suzanne Angell, Director of Therapeutic Research
Education: BA, Yale University; MA, Johns Hopkins University
Background: COO/CFO, Jungell Inc.; Managing Director/Advisor, Alpine ESD; Research Analyst, Cooper Hill Partners

Venture Capital & Private Equity Firms / Domestic Firms

420 CASE TECHNOLOGY VENTURES Case Western Reserve University
10900 Euclid Avenue
Cleveland, OH 44106-7219

Phone: 216-368-2000
e-mail: techventures@cwru.edu
web: case.edu

Mission Statement: CWRU Technology Ventures (CTV) is Case Western Reserve University's pre-seed technology validation fund. CTV focuses on creating and supporting new companies for the Northeast Ohio region by providing capital to early stage companies based on intellectual property developed at CWRU and its affiliate institutions.

Geographic Preference: Northeast Ohio
Founded: 2002
Average Investment: $50,000 - $250,000
Investment Criteria: Seed-Stage, Early-Stage
Industry Group Preference: Life Sciences, Physical Sciences, Information Technology
Portfolio Companies: Neuros Medical Inc., CardioInsight Technologies Inc., Interventional Imaging Inc., Arteriocyte Inc., Synapse Biomedical Inc., Great Lakes Pharmaceuticals, Intwine Connect

---

421 CASTANEA PARTNERS
Three Executive Park Drive
Suite 304
Newton, MA 02462

Phone: 617-630-2400 Fax: 617-630-2424
e-mail: info@castaneapartners.com
web: www.castaneapartners.com

Mission Statement: Castanea is a middle-market consumer-focused private equity firm.

Geographic Preference: US, Canada
Fund Size: $600 million
Founded: 2001
Average Investment: $15-150 million
Investment Criteria: MBOs, Consolidations, Growth Equity, Acquisition Equity Capital Raises, Corporate Carve-Outs
Industry Group Preference: Publishing, Education, Training, Consumer Products, Specialty Retail, Marketing
Portfolio Companies: 4moms, Brew Dr. Kombucha, The Bruery, Drybar, Essentia, Jeni's, Mackenzie-Childs, Simms Fishing Products, Thymes, West Coast Fitness, Yasso

Key Executives:
  Steven T. Berg, Managing Partner
  617-630-2416
  e-mail: sberg@castaneapartners.com
  Education: MBA, The Wharton School of Business; BS, Engineering, magna cum laude, University of Michgian
  Background: Founder, Bain Outreach, Bain & Company
  Brian J. Knez, Managing Partner
  617-630-2401
  e-mail: bknez@castaneapartners.com
  Education: JD, cum laude, Boston College Law School; BS, Phi Beta Kappa, University of Arizona
  Background: Vice Chairman/Board of Directors, The Neiman Marcus Group Inc.; CEO, Harcourt General; General Cinema Beverages; Associate, Choate, Hall and Stewart
  Robert A. Smith, Managing Partner
  617-630-2410
  e-mail: rsmith@castaneapartners.com
  Education: AB, Harvard College; MBA, Harvard University
  Background: Vice Chairman/Board of Director, The Neiman Marcus Group Inc.; CEO, Harcourt General; President, General Cinema Corporation; Associate, Bain & Company
  Directorships: Children's Hospital, Facing History & Ourselves, Pan-Mass Challenge, Jumpstart, Harvard Committee on University Resources

---

422 CASTILE VENTURES
396 Washington Street
Suite 188
Wellesley, MA 02481-6209

Phone: 781-890-0060 Fax: 781-890-0065
web: www.castileventures.com

Mission Statement: Castile Ventures invests in entrepreneurs and visionaries pioneering disruptive innovations that will define tomorrow's technology markets.

Fund Size: $200 million
Founded: 1998
Average Investment: $1-10 million
Investment Criteria: Early Stage
Industry Group Preference: Communications, Enterprise Applications, Infrastructure, Software, Wireless Technologies, Internet Technology
Portfolio Companies: Agilance, Agito Networks, Ahura Scientific, ASPEED Software, Aurora Networks, BNI Video, Brix Networks, ByAllAccounts, ChosenSecurity, Connotate, Funambol, GeoTrust, HealthGuru, NanoMedical Diagnostics, Neah Power Systems, NetDevices, Network Intelligence, Optiant, Quantiva, RetailExchange's, Sandbridge Technologies, SilverStorm Technologies, Sonus, Stargus, Trapeze Networks, VGo Communications, Whaleback Managed Services

Key Executives:
  Nina Saberi, Founder & Managing General Partner
  Education: BS Electrical Engineering, University of Rhode Island
  Background: General Partner, OneLiberty Ventures; President/CEO Netlink; General Manager, Amnet; Manager, Data General; Sr Hardware/Software Engineering, BBN/Avanti Communications
  Directorships: Agilance, Ahura Scientific, Aurora Networks, ChosenSecurity, North End, RatePoint
  Roger Walton, General Partner
  Education: MA Mathermatics, Univ. of Oxford
  Background: Advisor to start-up and established businesses; Sr. Marketing Executive, NetLink; Carrier Marketing; Cabletron; Sr. Executive, Motorola; Sr. Executive, Octocom Systems
  Directorships: North End, Sandbridge Technologies, Whaleback Systems
  Skip Besthoff, General Partner
  Education: BA Economics, Hamilton College; MBA, Cornell University
  Background: Principal, Rho Ventures; Manager, Anderson Consulting
  Directorships: Enquisite, Health Guru
  Jason King, Partner/Chief Financial Officer
  Education: BS, Accounting, Bryant Univ.; CPA
  Background: Manager, Summit Partners; Senior Associate, Deloitte & Touche

---

423 CASTLE HARLAN
150 East 58th Street
New York, NY 10155

Phone: 212-644-8600 Fax: 212-207-8042
e-mail: info@castleharlan.com
web: www.castleharlan.com

Mission Statement: Invests in companies with the potential to grow and accrue successful returns with the help of capital and management expertise.

Fund Size: $900 million
Founded: 1987
Average Investment: $30 - $200 million
Minimum Investment: $5 million
Investment Criteria: Established
Industry Group Preference: Consumer Products, Consumer Services, Energy, Manufacturing, Distribution
Portfolio Companies: Baker & Taylor, Caribbean Restaurants, Gold Star Foods, Shelf Drilling, Tensar Corporation

Venture Capital & Private Equity Firms / Domestic Firms

Key Executives:
  John K. Castle, Chairman/CEO
  Education: Massachusetts Institute of Technology; MBA, Harvard Business School
  Background: Chairman/CEO, Branford Castle; President/CEO, Donaldson, Lufkin & Jenrette
  Directorships: Baker & Taylor, Equitable Life Assurance Society
  Leonard M. Harlan, Chairman, Castle Harlan Executive Committee
  Education: BS, Mechanical Engineering, Cornell University; MBA, Harvard Business School
  Background: Chairman/CEO, Harlan Company; VP/Stockholder, Donaldson, Lufkin & Jenrette
  Directorships: IDQ Holdings, The America for Bulgaria Foundation, Harvard Business School Club
  Marcel Fournier, Senior Managing Director
  Education: MBA, University of Chicago; Ecole Speciale des Travaux Publics; Paris-Sorbonne University
  Background: Managing Director, Investment Banking, Lepercq, de Neuflize & Co.; Assistant Director, US Office of the Agency of the French Prime Minister
  David B. Pittaway, Senior Managing Director
  e-mail: dpittaway@castleharlan.com
  Education: BA, University of Kansas; MBA, JD, Harvard University
  Background: VP, Strategic Planning, Lufkin & Jenrette; Management Consultant, Strategic Planning, Bain & Company; Attorney, Morgan, Lewis & Bockius
  Directorships: Gold Star Foods, Caribbean Restaurants
  Eric Schwartz, Vice President
  Education: BSE, Biomedical & Electrical Engineering, Duke University; MBA, Stanford Graduate School of Business
  Background: Citigroup
  Directorships: Baker & Taylor, Caribbean Restaurants, Shelf Drilling
  Sylvia F. Rosen, Vice President/Controller
  Education: BA, Accounting, Queens College; MBA, Taxation, St. John's University
  Background: Corporate Accounting Manager, Tishman Realty & Construction; Senior Auditor, Ernst & Young

424 CASTLELAKE
90 S Seventh Street
4600 Wells Fargo Center
Minneapolis, MN 55402

web: www.castlelake.com

Mission Statement: Castlelake strives to unlock value and generate risk-adjusted returns.

Founded: 2005

Other Locations:
  510 Madison Avenue
  24th Floor
  New York, NY 10022

  100 Crescent Court
  Suite 825
  Dallas, TX 75201

  15 Sackville Street
  London W1S 3DJ
  United Kingdom

  5 Rue De Strasbourg
  Luxembourg L-2561
  Luxembourg

Key Executives:
  Dax Atkinson, Managing Director

425 CATALYST GROUP
1375 Enclave Parkway
Houston, TX 77077

e-mail: inquiries@tcgfunds.com
web: www.tcgfunds.com

Mission Statement: The Catalyst Group provides middle-market business owners access to capital and operational expertise, with the objective of achieving growth and exceptional returns for its partners.

Geographic Preference: United States, Southwest
Founded: 1990
Average Investment: $2 - $20 million
Minimum Investment: $1 million
Investment Criteria: Acquisitions, Buyouts, Expansion, Recapitalization, Middle-Market
Industry Group Preference: Manufacturing, Distribution, Services, Consumer Products, Media, Telecommunications, Energy
Portfolio Companies: Allocation Specialists, Auberge Resorts Collection, Axio, CellerateRX, Rochal Industries, Superior Plant Rentals, Triad Life Sciences, Trillian Surgical, YPS Anesthesia Services

Other Locations:
  7500rialto Boulevard
  Building II
  Suite 220
  Austin, TX 78735

Key Executives:
  Ron Nixon, Founder/Managing Member
  713-580-5231
  e-mail: rnixon@tcgfunds.com
  Education: BS, Mechanical Engineering, University of Texas
  Background: TGC; LHC Group
  Directorships: LHC Group, Ascent Automotive Group
  David McWhorter, Principal
  713-580-5254
  e-mail: dmcwhorter@tcgfunds.com
  Education: BS, Mechanical Engineering, University of Texas; MBA, Texas A&M University
  Background: VP & General Manager, Control Business Unit, Cameron International; Director, Engineering, Texas Oil Tools
  Brad Gurasich, Vice President/Principal
  512-320-8600
  e-mail: bgurasich@tcgfunds.com
  Education: BBA, Finance, University of Notre Dame; MBA, University of Texas, Austin; CFA
  Background: CFO/Investment Analyst, Goshawk Global Investments; Senior Finance Manager, Alta Colleges; Investment Banking Analyst, Credit Suisse First Boston
  Directorships: Rochal Industries
  Robert Norris, Principal
  Education: BA, Economics, MBA, University of Texas, Austin
  Background: VP, Corporate Development & Strategy, Civeo Corporation; VP, Corporate Development, Oil States

426 CATALYST HEALTH VENTURES
50 Braintree Hill Office Park
Suite 301
Braintree, MA 02184

Phone: 781-228-5228
e-mail: info@catalysthealthventures.com
web: www.catalysthealthventures.com

Mission Statement: Catalyst Health Ventures is an early-stage venture capital firm targeting technology solutions applied within the health care and life science industries. At the core of this strategy is a committed, hands-on approach to working with management and syndicate partners to build successful companies. This investment process leverages both intellectual and financial capital to originate deals, cultivate opportunities, and realize the full potential of emerging ventures in the health care and life science marketplace.

Geographic Preference: Northeast United States
Founded: 1998
Investment Criteria: Early-Stage

Venture Capital & Private Equity Firms / Domestic Firms

Industry Group Preference: Healthcare, Life Sciences, Medical Devices, Diagnostics
Portfolio Companies: Allegro Diagnostics, Aria CV, Augmenix, Biocius Life Sciences, Bio Trove, Cruzar Medical, Endo Via, G1 Dynamics, Hansen Medical, Kaleidoscope Medical, Lantos Technologies, Maxwell Health, Nova Zyme Pharmaceuticals, nVision, Pavilion Medical Innovations, Saphena Medical, Sera Prognostics, Seven Oaks Biosystems, Vortex Medical

Key Executives:
   Joshua S. Phillips, Managing Partner
   e-mail: jphillips@catalysthealthventures.com
   Education: BE, Electrical Engineering, Vanderbilt University; MBA, Harvard Business School
   Background: Manager, Lucas Group
   Kevin M. McCafferty, Founder/Special Partner
   e-mail: kmccafferty@catalysthealthventures.com
   Education: BA, Harvard College; MBA, University of Chicago
   Background: First Chicago Venture Capital, Madison Dearborn Partners
   Robert A. Vigoda, Founder/Special Partner
   e-mail: rvigoad@catalysthealthventures.com
   Education: BA, University of Rochester; JD, University of Miami
   Background: Partner, Rubin & Rudman LLP
   Darshana Zaveri, Partner
   e-mail: dzaveri@catalysthealthventures.com
   Education: BS, Biochemistry, Bombay University; MS, Cell & Molecular Biology, Boston University; MPA, Harvard University
   Background: Genome Therapeutics Corporation
   Directorships: Lantos

427 CATALYST INVESTORS
711 Fifth Avenue
Suite 600
New York, NY 10022

Phone: 212-863-4848 Fax: 212-319-5771
e-mail: businessplans@catalyst.com
web: catalyst.com

Mission Statement: Catalyst Investors invests in technology-enabled businesses.
Geographic Preference: North America
Average Investment: $10 - $40 million
Investment Criteria: All Stages, Growth Buyouts, Expansion Capital, Roll-Ups
Industry Group Preference: Cloud Computing, Internet, SaaS, E-Commerce & Manufacturing, Internet-Enabled Hardware, Digital Media & Marketing, Healthcare Information Technology, Education, Business Products & Services, Consumer Services, Wireless, Mobile
Portfolio Companies: BrightFarms, ChowNow, Clinicient, Conductor, Datavail, Envoy, Fusion Risk Management, Insite Wireless Group, Jobvite, MediaMath, PresenceLearning, Reputation Institute, Videology, Weave, WeddingWire, Xplornet

Key Executives:
   Brian Rich, Managing Partner & Co-Founder
   e-mail: brian@catalystinvestors.com
   Education: BS, Industrial Engineering, SUNY Buffalo; MBA, Columbia University
   Background: Founder, TD Capital
   Ryan McNally, Partner & Co-Founder
   e-mail: ryan@catalystinvestors.com
   Education: AB, Harvard College
   Background: Vice President, Daniels & Associates; Bear Stearns & Co.
   Chris Shipman, Partner & Co-Founder
   e-mail: chris@catalystinvestors.com
   Education: BA, MA, Boston University; MBA, Anderson School of Management, UCLA
   Background: Vice President, TD Capital
   Todd Clapp, Partner
   e-mail: todd@catalystinvestors.com
   Education: BA, McGill University; MBA, Columbia University
   Background: Lightyear Capital
   Tyler Newton, Partner
   e-mail: tyler@catalystinvestors.com
   Education: BA, Middlebury College; CFA
   Background: Vice President, TD Capital
   Gene Wolfson, Partner, Investor Relations & Business Development
   e-mail: gene@catalystinvestors.com
   Education: BS, Marketing & Management, Montclair State University; MBA, Finance, Pace University
   Background: Managing Director, Citigroup

428 CATAMOUNT VENTURES LP
400 Pacific Avenue
3rd Floor
San Francisco, CA 94133

Phone: 415-277-0300
e-mail: info@catamountventures.com
web: www.catamountventures.com

Mission Statement: Catamount Ventures is a venture capital firm investing in mission-driven companies, bringing with them connecttions and coaching to help grow leaders with a strong mission at their core.
Fund Size: $200 million
Founded: 2000
Investment Criteria: Early-Stage
Industry Group Preference: Information Technology, Environment, Consumer Internet, Enterprise Applications
Portfolio Companies: Amourvert, Banyan Water, Carezone, EdSurge, eSilicon, GridNet, Linden Lab, LuxResearch, MasteryConnect, ModuMetal, Numi Organic Tea, Plum Organics, Presence Learning, Quri, Revolution Foods, Seventh Generation, Ten Marks, Upworthy

Other Locations:
   3000 Sand Hill Road
   1-100
   Menlo Park, CA 94025

Key Executives:
   Jed Smith, Partner
   Education: BA, Middlebury College; MBA, Harvard Business School
   Background: Founder, drugstore.com; Co-Founder, Cybersmith; VP, Sales, Tribe Computer Works; Oracle Corporation
   Directorships: Linden Lab, Numi Organic Tea, Banyan Water, Plum Organics, Revolution Foods
   Mark Silverman, Partner
   Education: JD, University of California, Los Angeles; BA, History, University of California, Berkeley
   Background: President/CEO, Bocada; VP, Business Development, drugstore.com; Partner, Venture Law Group
   Tory Patterson, Partner
   Education: BA, Economics, Williams College; MBA, Stanford Graduate School of Business
   Background: Investment Banking, GCA Sawian, Wells Fargo Securities
   Directorships: MasteryConnect, Presence Learning, Ecologic Brands
   Kate Chhabra, CFO/Partner
   Education: BA, George Washington University
   Background: Human Resources/Operations, ATEL Capital; Human Resources, CriticalArc Technologies Inc.

429 CATAPULT VENTURES
Los Altos, CA

e-mail: admin@catapultventures.vc
web: catapultventures.vc

Venture Capital & Private Equity Firms / Domestic Firms

Mission Statement: A tech-based venture capital firm seeking to work with entrepreneurs with an interdisciplinary perspective.
Founded: 2018
Investment Criteria: Seed
Industry Group Preference: Artificial Intelligence, Automation, Robots, Industrial Manufacturing, Aerospace, Construction, Smart Buildings, Consumer Electronics, Healthcare
Portfolio Companies: Advanced Farm Technologies, Anello Photonics, Aulera Autentication, Elroy Air, Engine ML, FlightWave Aero, Left Hand Robotics, Resonado, SpinLaunch, Starsky Robotics, Xnor.ai
Key Executives:
  Darren Liccardo, Co-Founder/Managing Director
  Education: BS/MS, Electrical Engineering & Computer Science, University of California, Berkeley
  Background: Crossbow Technology Inc.; BMW Group; Tesla Motors; DJI
  Rouz Jazayeri, Co-Founder/Managing Director
  Education: BS/MS, Electrical Engineering, Purdue University
  Background: Account Manager, Intel Corporation; Partner/Head of Business Development, Kleiner Perkins Caufield & Buyers

430 CATO BIOVENTURES
4364 South Alston Avenue
Durham, NC 27713
Phone: 919-361-2286 Fax: 919-361-2290
e-mail: cbvinfo@cato.com
web: www.catobioventures.com

Mission Statement: Cato BioVentures is the venture capital affiliate of Cato Research. Cato BioVentures primarily invests in biotechnology and pharmaceutical companies, and focuses on the successful development and commercialization of products.
Geographic Preference: United States, Canada
Founded: 1990
Investment Criteria: Early Stage, Mid Stage, Late Stage, Mezzanine
Industry Group Preference: Life Sciences, Biotechnology, Pharmaceuticals
Portfolio Companies: Avicin Therapeutics Ltd., Cancer Advances Inc., Hemodynamic Therapeutics Inc.
Other Locations:
  1100 Winter Street
  Bay Colony Corporate Center
  Waltham, MA 02451-1427
  Phone: 781-890-4477 Fax: 781-890-8118

  9605 Medical Center Drive
  Suite 390
  Rockville, MD 20850
  Phone: 301-309-8242 Fax: 301-308-8470

  6480 Weathers Place
  San Diego, CA 92121
  Phone: 858-452-7271 Fax: 919-361-2290

  9900 Cavendish Blvd
  Suite 400
  Saint-Laurent, QC H4M 2V2
  Canada
  Phone: 514-856-2286 Fax: 514-856-0100

Key Executives:
  Allen Cato MD PhD, Co-Founder/Principal
  Education: MD; PhD
  Directorships: Advanced Pain Remedies, Cancer Advances, Hemodynamic Therapeutics, Nutritional Restart Pharmaceuticals
  Lynda Sutton, Co-Founder/Principal
  Education: BS
  Directorships: Advanced Pain Remedies, Cancer Advances, Hemodynamic Therapeutics, Nutritional Restart Pharmaceuticals
  Daniel Pharand, Principal
  Education: CPA, CA
  Background: CFO, Pharmacia Canada; Pharmacia KK; Innovatech Grand Montreal
  Jo Cato, Vice President
  Education: BS, Pharmacy, University of North Carolina at Chapel Hill; PhD, Biopharmaceutics, University of North Carolina at Chapel Hill
  Background: Pharmacokineticist, Abbott Laboratories; Pharmacokineticist, Ligand Pharmaceuticals
  Directorships: Cato Research
  Daniel Pharand, Principal
  Education: BCom, Concordia University
  Background: CFO, Pharmacia Canada; CFO, Pharmacia KK; Portfolio Manager, Innovatech Grand Montreal

431 CAVA CAPITAL
132 B Water Street
Norwalk, CT 06854
Phone: 203-210-7477
e-mail: info@cavacapital.com
web: www.cavacapital.com

Mission Statement: Cava Capital is an innovative, early-growth stage investor, actively supporting talented entrepreneurs as they build their companies through various stages of expansion. Cava Capital's team members are experts in scaling revenue growth and are focused on enlisting the resources and connections to do so.
Founded: 2008
Average Investment: $1 - $5 million
Investment Criteria: Early Growth Stage
Industry Group Preference: Marketing, Mobile, Technology, Information Services, E-Commerce & Manufacturing, Social Media, Digital Media, Healthy Active Lifestyle
Portfolio Companies: Confirm.io, Drizly, Dstillery, Etouches, Freeletics, Gwynnie Bee., MVMNT, NeueHouse, Ocean's Halo, PageScience
Key Executives:
  Geoff Schneider, Founder/Managing Partner
  Education: BS, Business & Economics, Lehigh University; MBA, George Washington University
  Background: Iconoculture, Gartner Groupscient, PointCast
  Bob Geiman, Managing Partner
  Education: BA, Dartmouth College; MBA, Harvard Business School
  Background: Founder/President/CEO, EveryScreen Media; General Partner, Polaris Venture Partners; Envoy Networks
  Kevin Lynch, CFO & Fund Administrator
  Education: BS, Fordham University; CPA
  Background: AlpInvest Partners; Wall Street Technology Partners; Annex Capital; Equinox Capital; PJSC-JOSS Real Estate Partners; Atlantic Medical Capital; Kleinwort Benson Holdings; Credit Suisse First Boston; KPMG

432 CAYUGA VENTURE FUND
15 Thornwood Drive
Ithaca, NY 14850
Phone: 607-266-9266 Fax: 607-266-9267
e-mail: info@cayugaventures.com
web: cayugaventures.com

Mission Statement: Cayuga Venture Fund is a venture capital firm working to create and establish a thriving community of leading edge, high tech start-up companies in Ithaca and upstate New York by providing the necessary capital and other resources they need to grow and prosper.
Geographic Preference: New York
Founded: 1994

Investment Criteria: Seed to Growth Stage
Industry Group Preference: All Sectors
Portfolio Companies: Advion BioSciences, Adapt-N, Allworx, BinOptics, Calient Technologies, Cheribundi, e2E Materials, Ecovation, EkoStinger, GiveGab, Incomeda3D, Instinctiv, Intrinsiq Materials, Ioxus, iTellio, Kionix, Mezmeriz, Outmatch, Pathlight, Pom-Co, Primet, Rheonix, Silicon Video Inc., SocialFlow, SoundCloud, True Gault, VenueBook

Key Executives:
Zachary Shulman, Managing Partner
Education: BS, Industrial & Labor Relations, JD, Cornell University
Background: Corporate Law, Ropes & Gray
Phil Proujansky, Managing Partner
Education: BS, Engineering Physics, Cornell University
Background: Founder, IAD
Jennifer Tegan, Partner/VP Finance & Administration
Education: BA, MS, Geology, Smith College; MBA, Cornell University
Background: Consultant, Gemini Ernst & Young; Business Manager, EMF Corporation
Cliff Lardin, Venture Partner
Education: BA, English, MBA, Cornell University
Background: CEO, Cyan Data Systems; Founder, VP Systems, MiniGram

433 CCMP CAPITAL
277 Park Avenue
27th Floor
New York, NY 10172

Phone: 212-600-9600
web: www.ccmpcapital.com

Mission Statement: Private equity firm focused on buyouts and growth equity investments.

Geographic Preference: North America, Europe
Fund Size: $12 Billion
Founded: 1984
Average Investment: $100-500 million
Investment Criteria: Buyouts, Growth Equity
Industry Group Preference: Consumer Products, Industrial, Healthcare
Portfolio Companies: Aramark, BGIS, Cabela's, CareMore Health, Chaparral Energy, Chromalox, Crosstown Traders Inc., Eating Recovery Center, Edwards Group, Founder Sport Group, Francesca's Collection, Generac Power Systems, Infogroup, Hayward, The Hillman Group, Jamieson Wellness, Jetro Cash & Carry, LHP Hospital Group, Medpace, Milacron, Newark Energy, Ollie's Bargain Outlet, PQ Corporation, Pure Gym, Shoes for Crews, Truck Hero, Volotea

Other Locations:
24 Waterway Avenue
Suite 750
The Woodlands, TX 77380
Phone: 281-363-2013

Almack House
28 King Street
London SW1Y 6XA
United Kingdom
Phone: 44 20 7389 9100

Key Executives:
Greg Brenneman, Executive Chairman
Education: BA, Accounting/Finance, Washburn University; MBA, Harvard Business School
Background: Chairman & CEO, Burger King Corporation; President & CEO, PwC Consulting
Timothy Walsh, President & CEO
Education: BS, Trinity College; MBA, University of Chicago Graduate School of Business
Background: The Chase Manhattan Corporation
Directorships: Generac Power Systems, MetoKote

Christopher Behrens, Managing Director
Education: BA, University of California, Berkeley; MA, Columbia University
Background: Vice President, Merchant Banking Group, The Chase Manhattan Corporation
Directorships: Chaparral Energy, Newark E&P Holdings, Noble Environmental Power
Ryan Anderson, Managing Director
Education: BSE, Wharton School, University of Pennsylvania
Background: M&A Group, JP Morgan
Directorships: Eating Recovery Center; Founder Sport Group
Mark McFadden, Managing Director
Education: BA & BBA, College of William and Mary
Background: CSFB; Bowles Hollowell Conner
Directorships: Hayward; PQ Corporation; BGIS
Kevin O'Brien, Managing Director
Education: BA, University of Notre Dame; MBA, Wharton School
Background: High Yield Capital Markets, Chase Securities; Chemical Securities
Directorships: Infogroup, LHP Hospital Group, Medpace, National Surgical Care, Octagon Credit Investors
Joseph Scharfenberger, Managing Director
Education: BA, University of Vermont
Background: Bear Stearns Merchant Banking; Toronto Dominion Securities
Directorships: Founder Sport Group; The Hillman Group; Shoes for Crews; Truck Hero
Kristin Steen, Managing Director
Education: BS, McIntire School of Commerce, University of Virginia
Background: Lone Star Funds; HBK Capital Management
Directorships: Shoes for Crews; The Hillman Group
Richard Zannino, Managing Director
Education: BS, Finance & Economics, Bentley College; MBA, Finance, Pace University
Background: CEO, Dow Jones & Company; EVP, Liz Claiborne; EVP/CFO, General Signal
Directorships: Francesca's Collections, Infogroup, IAC, Estee Lauder

434 CCP EQUITY PARTNERS
100 Pearl Street
14th Floor
Hartford, CT 06103

Phone: 860-249-7104 Fax: 860-249-7001
web: www.ccpequitypartners.com

Mission Statement: CCP Equity Partners is a private equity firm focused on financing innovative companies with exceptional growth potential, placing particular emphasis on the financial services and healthcare services sectors. CCP combines operating expertise, industry experience and the talents of proven executives to help build profitable companies.

Fund Size: $150 million
Founded: 1985
Average Investment: $5 - $20 million
Minimum Investment: $5 million
Investment Criteria: Growth Equity, Middle-Market, Later Stage
Industry Group Preference: Financial Services, Insurance, Healthcare, Business to Business
Portfolio Companies: Evolution Markets, GlobalView, Kinloch Holdings, Mezz Cap, MMV Financial, Prism Education Group, Vantage Oncology

Key Executives:
Michael E. Aspinwall, Managing Partner
203-904-3832
e-mail: maspinwall@ccpequitypartners.com
Education: BS, Worcester Polytechnic Institute; MBA, University of Chicago Graduate School of Business
Background: Managing Partner, Bear Stearns Health Innoventures; Senior VP, GE Equity; Chase Manhattan

Venture Capital & Private Equity Firms / Domestic Firms

Bank; Pitney Bowes; FMC Corporation
Directorships: Vantage Oncology
Steven F. Piaker, Managing Partner
860-233-8959
e-mail: spiaker@ccpequitypartners.com
Education: BA Economics, University of Rochester; MBA, Duke University; CFA
Background: Senior VP, Conseco; VP, Financial Institutions Group, GE Capital; Chase Manhattan
Directorships: Mezz Cap, MMV Financial
David W. Young, Managing Partner
860-415-0834
e-mail: dyoung@ccpequitypartners.com
Education: BA, Rutgers University
Background: Chief Investment Officer, Progressive Corporation; Brown Brothers Harriman & Company; Salomon Brothers
Directorships: Evolution Markets, GlobalView
Diane M. Daych, Partner
203-314-5580
e-mail: ddaych@ccpequitypartners.com
Education: BA, Economics, Lehigh University; MBA, Tuck School of Business, Dartmouth College
Background: GE Capital; Signal Capital; President, Connecticut Venture Group
Directorships: Prism Education Group

Key Executives:
Hai Yang, Director
Background: Founder/CEO, Beijing SEL System; Chief Representative, Vantone Investment Group

436 CEDAR FUND
1050 Winter Street
Suite 2700
Waltham, MA 02451

Fax: 781-895-9099
Toll-Free: 800-844-3469
e-mail: info@cedarfund.com
web: www.cedarfund.com

Mission Statement: A venture capital firm investing in early stage, Israel-related high technology companies.
Geographic Preference: Israel
Fund Size: $225 million
Investment Criteria: Pre-Seed, Early Stage, First Round
Industry Group Preference: Telecommunications, Networking, Enterprise Services, Infrastructure, Internet Technology, Communications, Enterprise Software, Wireless Technologies, SaaS, Clean Technology
Portfolio Companies: 365Scores.com, Amimon, Appilog, BigBand Networks, ClickFox, CloudLock, Datorama, e-Glue, Guardium, HIRO, Iamba, Intigua, IPlight, iSonar, Kenesto, Netotiate, NewACT, Nolio, Octalica, Onaro, Orsus, PeerApp, Pentalum, Pixie, Personali, Primary Data, Red-C, StartApp, WebCollage, WiNetworks, Wochit

Key Executives:
Amnon Shoham, Co-Founder
Background: Managing Partner, Star Ventures Israel; Board of Directors, Accord Networks, BreezeCOM, Fourth Dimension Software, Fundtech, Jacada, NICEcom, Paradigm Geophysical, ViraNet; Attorney, Skadden, Arps, Slate, Meagher & Flom
Directorships: Intigua, ClickFox, PeersApp, Jsonar, Appilog, CloudLock, Guardium, Orsus, Onaro
Gal Israely, Co-Founder
Background: Managing Director, High Tech Investment Banking Group, Bear Stearns
Directorships: Wochit, StartApp, Pixie, Pentalum, Amimon, BigBand Networks, Celtro, NewAct, Octalica, WiNetworks, Red-C
Motti Vaknin, Partner
Background: CEO, BelnSync; CEO & Co-Founder, WebLayers; CEO, Bridges for Islands; VP, Sales & Marketing, Shiron Satellite Communications

Directorships: 365Scores, Datorama, Primary Data, Personali, Curiyo
Hila Leibovitz, Inhouse Counsel
Education: LLB, LLM, Bar Ilan University
Background: Herzog Fox & Neeman
Shlomi Shiloni Shem Tov, VP of Finance
Education: BA, Economics/Business, Bar Ilan University; MBA, Tel Aviv University; CPA
Background: Financial Controller/Analyst, Fortissimo Capital; Senior Auditor, EY

437 CEDAR VENTURES LLC
2870 Peachtree Road
Suite 450
Atlanta, GA 30305

Phone: 404-239-8416 **Fax:** 404-239-8417
web: www.cedarventures.com

Mission Statement: Cedar Ventures is an investment banking and financial advisory services firm that specializes in raising debt and equity capital for a variety of companies.
Geographic Preference: Louisiana, Texas, Alabama, Gulf Coast, North & South Carolina
Industry Group Preference: Medical Devices, Consumer Products, Food & Beverage, Energy, Technology, Life Sciences, Healthcare Information Technology

Key Executives:
Karen Kassouf, Founder/Managing Member
e-mail: kassouf@cedarventures.com
Education: BA, Economics & Political Science, Bucknell University; JD, Villanova University School of Law
Background: Cedar Equities, Western Indemnity Insurance Company; Healthcare Investment Banking Unit, Chemical Banking Corporation; Texas Commerce Bank

438 CEI VENTURES
30 Federal Street
Suite 100
Brunswick, ME 04011

Phone: 207-504-5900
Toll-Free: 877-340-2649
e-mail: info@ceimaine.org
web: www.ceiventures.com

Mission Statement: To create jobs and ownership opportunities for people with low income, to create socially beneficial products and services, and to promote progressive management practices while striving toward a competitive rate of return.
Geographic Preference: Northeast
Fund Size: $25.54 million
Founded: 1994
Average Investment: $750,000
Minimum Investment: $500,000
Investment Criteria: Job creation, socially responsible, good management, practical exit plan
Industry Group Preference: Industrial Services, Energy, Biotechnology, Financial Services, Consumer Products, Information Technology, Software, Healthcare, Business to Business, Networking, Media, Entertainment
Portfolio Companies: A&B Electronics, Avia Boisystems, Beacon Analytical Systems, BlueTarp Financial, BroadcastAmerica.com, Bush Equities dba Cuddledown, Certify Inc., Chemogen, Chomp, CitySoft, Clickshare Service, Coast of Maine Organic Products, Cormier Textile Products, CV Finer Foods, Definition6, eCopy, Ektron Inc., EnvisionNet Computer Services, Foreside Company, FreeBorders, Genicon Inc., HCI Systems, HomeBistro Foods, Hyperlite Mountain Gear, Innov-X Systems, Intellicare America, Juno Rising, Look's Gourmet Food, Maine Craft Distilling, Maine Trailer, Metrobility Optical Systems, Mingle Analytics, Native Energy, Navigator Publishing, NBT Solutions, New England 800 dba Taction, New England Audio Resource, NextMark, Ogee Inc., PenBay Solutions,

Pika Energy Inc., RecruiterNet, RedZone Wireless, Research Enhanced Design + Development Inc., Rustic Crust, SciAps Inc., SmartPak Equine, Soleras, Stillwater Scientific Instruments, Sun & Earth, The Gelato Fiasco, Tilson Technology Management, Wentworth Technology Inc.

Key Executives:
Betsy Biemann, Chief Executive Director
e-mail: betsy.biemann@ceimaine.org
Education: BA, Harvard University; MPA, Princeton University
Background: President, Maine Technology Institute; Associate Director, The Rockefeller Foundation
Keith Bisson, President
e-mail: keith.bisson@ceimaine.org
Education: BA, McGill University; MA, Yale School of Forestry & Environmental Studies

439 CELERITY PARTNERS
12121 Wilshire Boulevard
Suite 512
Los Angeles, CA 90025

Phone: 310-268-1710
web: www.celeritypartners.com

Mission Statement: Manages private equity and is dedicated to building businesses in partnership with management to achieve preeminence in their respective markets.

Geographic Preference: United States
Fund Size: $200 million
Founded: 1995
Minimum Investment: $1 million
Investment Criteria: Growth Equity, De-Leveraging Investments, MBO, Corporate Divestitures, Recapitalizations
Industry Group Preference: Manufacturing, Security, Outsourcing & Efficiency, Database Services, Niche Manufacturing, Marketing, Information Technology, Aerospace, Defense and Government, Military, Consumer Products, Life Sciences, Healthcare
Portfolio Companies: 360 PT Management, ABC Industries, ABC Laboratories, Advanced Accessory Systems, All Aboard America!, Ascension Insurance, Dynamic Details, estudy Site, Meridien Research, National Research Institute, OnCore Manufacturing Services, O Premium Waters, Ortho Organizers, PC Helps, Peer 1, Pinnacle Treatment Centers, Project Leadership Associates, Rincon Industries, SMTC Corporation, Streamline Circuits, SynteractHCR, Total Care RX, Tru Fit Athletic Clubs, Verari Systems, Vince & Associates Clinical Research, Well-Foam, Western Jet Aviation

Other Locations:
3000 Sand Hill Rd
Building 3
Suite 100
Menlo Park, CA 94025
Phone: 650-646-3624

Key Executives:
Mark Benham, Managing Director
e-mail: mbenham@celeritypartners.com
Education: BA English, University of California, Berkeley; MA, MBA, University of Chicago both with honors
Background: Senior Investment Officer, Citicorp Venture Capital; Principal, Merchant Banking Group, Crocker/Montague
Directorships: SMTC Corporation, several private companies
Matt Kraus, Managing Director
e-mail: mkraus@celeritypartners.com
Education: BA Political Science, Bucknell University
Background: Founder/Managing Director, Harvey & Company; Analyst, W.E. Myers & Company
Directorships: AdB Industries; The New Release

440 CENTANA GROWTH PARTNERS
855 El Camino Real
Building 4, Suite 240
Palo Alto, CA 94301

web: www.centanagrowth.com

Mission Statement: Centana invests in rapidly growing companies in order to sustain or accelerate growth.

Founded: 2015

Other Locations:
1412 Broadway
Suite 1504
New York, NY 10018

Key Executives:
Steven Swain, Co-Founder/Partner
212-256-8452
e-mail: sswain@centanagrowth.com
Education: BA, Clark University; JD, Villanova University; MBA, George Washington University
Background: President, Global X Management; COO, Lyster Watson & Co.
Ben Cukier, Co-Founder/Partner
212-256-8451
e-mail: bcukier@centanagrowth.com
Education: BA, University of Pennsylvania; MBA, Stanford University
Background: Partner, FTV Capital; Consultant, McKinsey & Co.

441 CENTENNIAL VENTURES
10901 West Toller Drive
Suite 206
Littleton, CO 80127

Phone: 303-405-7500 Fax: 303-405-7575

Mission Statement: Centennial Ventures is a venture capital firm investing in network, software and technology companies with the potential to be market leaders.

Fund Size: $341 million
Founded: 1982
Average Investment: $4 - $10 million
Minimum Investment: $500,000
Investment Criteria: Early Stage, Later-Stage
Industry Group Preference: Global Industries, Media, Broadband, Infrastructure, Software, Internet Technology
Portfolio Companies: Accellos, Alereon, Extenet, FDN Communications, Grande, Hoak Media Corporation, InnerWireless, MarketForce Information, Masergy, Panasas, Siterra, Slackers, TriStar, Zayo

Key Executives:
Duncan Butler, Managing Director
Education: BBA, MBA, University of Texas; Doctor of Jurisprudence, University of Texas School of Law
Background: Principal, Prime New Ventures; VP, Corporate Development, Prime Cable
Steve Halstedt, Managing Director
Education: BS, Management Engineering, Worcester Polytechnic Institute; MBA, Tuck School of Business, Dartmouth College
Background: EVP/Director, Daniels & Associates; US Army; US Army Engineer School; Dartmouth College
Directorships: National Venture Capital Association
David Hull, Managing Director
Education: BS, Chemical Engineering, MBA, University of Texas, Austin
Background: Managing General Partner, Criterion Venture Partners, TransAmerica; SVP, Finance/Treasure/Director, General Leisure Corporation
Rand Lewis, Managing Director
Education: BS, Electrical & Computer Engineering, Brigham Young University; MS, Computer Science, University of Colorado; MBA, Kellogg School of Management, Northwestern University

Venture Capital & Private Equity Firms / Domestic Firms

Background: Management Consultant, McKinsey & Company; Software Engineer, US WEST
Neel Sarkar, Managing Director
Education: BS, Electrical Engineering, Massachusetts Institute of Technology; MBA, Kellogg School of Management, Northwestern University
Background: Director, Strategy & Business Development, Dell; Management Consultant, McKinsey & Company; Operations Manager, GE & Excelon
Jeffrey Schutz, Managing Director
Education: BA, Economics, Middlebury College; MBA, Colgate Darden Graduate School of Business Administration, University of Virginia
Background: VP/Director, PNC Venture Capital Group
Directorships: Small Business Administration

442 CENTERBRIDGE PARTNERS
375 Park Avenue
New York, NY 10152

Phone: 212-672-5000
web: www.centerbridge.com

Mission Statement: A private equity firm focusing on leveraged buyouts and distressed securities.
Fund Size: $5.5 billion
Founded: 2005
Investment Criteria: Leveraged Buyouts
Portfolio Companies: Aktua, American Renal, Banca FarmaFactoring, Bank United, Carefree, Dana, Extended Stay America, Great Wolf Lodge, Green Tree, GSI, Hearland, HydroChem, IPC, Kenan Advantage Group Inc., KIK Custom Products, Ligado Networks, Santander Consumer USA, Satmex, Senvion, Superior Vision

Key Executives:
Jeffrey Aronson, Co-Founder and Managing Partner
Education: BA, Johns Hopkins University; JD, New York University School of Law
Background: Partner, Angelo, Gordon & Co.; Senior Corporate Counsel, L.F. Rothschild & Co.; Securities Attorney, Stroock & Stroock & Lavan

443 CENTERFIELD CAPITAL PARTNERS
3000 Market Tower
10 W Market Street
Indianapolis, IN 46204

Phone: 317-237-2323 Fax: 317-237-2325
web: www.centerfieldcapital.com

Mission Statement: Provides growth and expansion capital to privately held companies in the Midwest.
Geographic Preference: Midwest
Fund Size: $150 million
Founded: 1985
Average Investment: $2 - $15 million
Minimum Investment: $2 million
Investment Criteria: Most interested in companies with annual revenues between $15 and $75 million and at a stage where they have a positive cash flow and proven products and customers.
Industry Group Preference: Healthcare, Business to Business, Information Technology, Telecommunications, Financial Services, Manufacturing, Distribution, Consumer Products, Specialty Chemicals, Food & Beverage, Education, Healthcare Services
Portfolio Companies: A&D Environmental Services, Advanced Physical Therapy, Aero Systems Engineering, Aerostar Global Logistics, Alpha Imaging, Automated Systems Design, Backyard Products, Banner Service Corp., Battery Solutions, Beacon Communications, Bell Automotive Products, Bil-Jax, California Medical Evaluators, Cargo Airport Services, CE Rental, Coast Composites, D.S. Brown, DCL Medical Laboratories, Dedicated Transport, Digital Medica Services, Direct Marketing Solutions, Diversified Graphics, eGix, Evrihoulder Products, First Source, Fresh Food Concepts, Gabriel Performance Products, Heartland Steel Products, Hunter's Specialties, IF&P Foods, Imaginetics, Indo-European Foods, Matilda Jane Clothing, MicroMass, Midland Container, Millennium Custom Foods, Pipp Mobile Storage Solutions, PowerWay, PRISM Plastics, Rice's Honey, RIO Brands, Roehm Marine, Rose America Corp., SCT, Shred All, Silbond Corp., Standard Locknut, Swiff-Train Co., TCI, Thermafiber, Transolutions, Venture Technology Groups, Wild Sports, Woodmarc, Y-T Holdco

Key Executives:
Scott Lutzke, Founding Partner
e-mail: scott@centerfieldcapital.com
Education: Physcics, Purdue University; MBA, Finance, Indiana University
Background: First VP/Manager, Indiana Public Banking; 11 Years Experience in Private Equity; 20 Years in Corporate Banking
Directorships: Venture Club of Indiana
Farraz Abassi, Senior Partner
e-mail: faraz@centerfieldcapital.com
Education: MBA Finance, Indiana University; BS Chemical Engineering, University of Texas
Background: Senior Product Engineer, Praxair; Sales Engineering, Rodel; Vice President, Young Professionals, 10 Years Experience in Private Equity
Mark Hollis, Partner
e-mail: mark@centerfieldcapital.com
Education: BBA, University of Southern Indiana; MBA, Kelley School of Business, Indiana University
Background: Vice President, National City Bank
Michael Miller, Partner
e-mail: michael@centerfieldcapital.com
Education: BBA, Economics, Hanover College; MBA, Fuqua School of Business, Duke University
Background: Eli Lilly & Company, Hatteras Venture Partners
Jill Margetts, Partner
e-mail: jill@centerfieldcapital.com
Education: MBA, Kelley School of Business, Indiana University; BS, Chemical Engineering, MIT
Background: Business Analyst, Midwest Independent Transmission System Operator; Process Engineer, ETEX Corporation

444 CENTERPOINT VENTURE PARTNERS
Two Galleria Tower
13455 Noel Road
16th Floor
Dallas, TX 75240

Phone: 972-702-1101 Fax: 972-702-1103
web: www.cpventures.com

Mission Statement: Leverages expertise and resources to help entrepreneurs in building productive management teams, implementing business models and developing strategic technologies that can revolutionize major market areas; constantly scans the horizon for inspired entrepreneurs with innovative business concepts to help them build successful ventures.
Geographic Preference: Texas, Southwest United States
Fund Size: $450 million
Founded: 1996
Average Investment: $5 - $15 million
Minimum Investment: $5 million
Investment Criteria: Early, Expansion, Seed
Industry Group Preference: Communications, Software Services, Semiconductors, Industrial Services, Infrastructure
Portfolio Companies: Active Power, Applied Science Fiction, Covaro Networks, D2Audio, Neoworld, NetBotz, Silicon Labs, Voyence

Other Locations:
One Bridgepoint
6300 Birdge Point Parkway
Building 1, Suite 500

Venture Capital & Private Equity Firms / Domestic Firms

Austin, TX 78730
Phone: 512-795-5800 **Fax:** 512-795-5849
Key Executives:
Bob Paluck, Managing Director
Education: BS, Electrical Engineering, University of Illinois
Background: Co-Founder/Chairman/CEO, Convex Computer Corporation; VP Product Development/Marketing, Mostek
Cam McMartin, Managing Director/Chief Financial Officer
Education: MBA, University of Michigan; BA, Trinity University
Background: Senior VP Operations, Dazel Corporation; Senior Vice President/CFO, DataCard Corporation; CFO, Convex Computer Corporation
Terry Rock, Managing Director
Education: BS, Mechanical Engineering, South Dakota School of Mines & Technology
Background: President, Convex; Operating Management, Texas Instruments; Co-Founded, STARTech Technology Incubator; Managing General Partner, STARTech Seed Fund

445 CENTRAL TEXAS ANGEL NETWORK
PO Box 5435
Austin, TX 78763-5435

Phone: 512-518-6054
e-mail: director@ctan.com
web: ctan.com

Mission Statement: The Central Texas Angel Network is a Texas-based angel organization dedicated to providing strong investment opportunities for angel investors as well as financial and educational resources for early stage growth businesses and entrepreneurs.

Geographic Preference: Central Texas
Founded: 2006
Investment Criteria: Startups, Early Stage
Industry Group Preference: Consumer Products, Consumer Services, Food & Beverage, Healthcare, Industrial, Internet, Mobile, Telecommunications, Software
Portfolio Companies: AccuWater, AdBm Technologies, Admittance Technologies, Agile Planet, Alzeca Biosciences, Apptive, Atonometrics, Autowraptec, Beauty Box 5, Better Voicemail, Bing Outdoor Media, Boomerang's, Bouldin Creek Distillery, Boxer, Cache IQ, CelAccess, City Bebe, ClearBlade, CSID, Curb, Cutting Edge Gamer, Daily Juice, DealerHQ, Deep Eddy, DiFusion Technologies, DisplayPoints, Dulce Vida, Edioma, EDHC, Enlyton, ENTvantage Diagnostics, ESO Solutions, FantasySalesTeam, Firefly LED Lighting, FlowBelow, Friends & Allies Brewing, Frontier Bank of Texas, Global Material Exchange, Goodybag, Greenling, GreenWorld Restoration, GRIDbot, Guidepath Medical, Guns & Oil Brewing, HeatGenie, HUVRData, Hyperwear, Infinite, JamHub, Job Cannon, Karmaback.com, KENGURU, KIMBIA, Localeur, Loku, MacuCLEAR, Mahana, ManagerComplete, Meals to Live, Meshify, MicroTransponder, Mixbook, MommyMixer, NanoMedical Systems, NanoRacks, Netsurion, NeuroChaos Solutions, Nexersys iPower Trainer, NuHabitat, NurturMe, Nuve, OneSpot, Order Corner, Ordoro, Ortho Kinematics, ParLevel, Perception Software, Phunware, Pioneer Bank, Quarri, Querium, Recursion, Rhythm Superfoods, Salient Pharmaceuticals, Savara, Senscient, Smart Picture Solution, SmarteSoft, SonarMed, Sports Tradex, StreamVine, Structured Polymers, Student Loan Genius, Suvola, TalentGuard, TEKVOX, Televero, TextureMedia, The Corner Vet, The Good Promise, Traitwise, Traumatec, Upspring Baby, Verb, VolunteerSpot, Wenzel, Wisegate, Wonder, Xeris, Zilker Brewing

Key Executives:
Victoria Dominguez-Edington, Program Director
Education: BA, Southwestern University; MA, University of Texas

446 CENTRE LANE PARTNERS
One Grand Central Place
60 East 42nd Street
Suite 1250
New York, NY 10165

Phone: 646-843-0710
e-mail: info@centrelanepartners.com
web: centrelanepartners.com

Mission Statement: Centre Lane is a private investment firm focused on making equity and debt, control and non-control, investments in North American middle market companies.

Geographic Preference: North America
Average Investment: $5 - $250 million
Minimum Investment: $5 million
Industry Group Preference: Diversified
Portfolio Companies: Alternative Biomedical Solutions, Clickbooth, Crown Brands, Infobase, Jobe's, Luminex Home Decor & Fragrance, MDC Vacuum Products, The Merit Group, Oracle Packaging, Saladworks, Sure Fit Home Decor, Vexos, WIS Intl., Zenfolio Inc.

Key Executives:
Quinn Morgan, Managing Director
Education: London School of Economics
Background: D.B. Zwirn & Co.
Kenneth Lau, Managing Director
Education: MIT
Background: D.B. Zwirn & Co.
Luke Gosselin, Managing Director
Education: Syracuse Univ.; Fordham Univ.
Background: Fort Hill Investment Partners
Mayank Singh, Managing Director
Education: Colgate Univ.; Stern School
Background: Monomoy Capital Partners

447 CENTRE PARTNERS MANAGEMENT LLC
601 Lexington Avenue
55th Floor
New York, NY 10022-4611

Phone: 212-332-5800 **Fax:** 212-758-1830
e-mail: info@centrepartners.com
web: www.centrepartners.com

Mission Statement: Private equity firm specializing in middle market businesses in the consumer and healthcare markets.

Geographic Preference: North America
Fund Size: $850 million
Founded: 1986
Average Investment: $20 - $60 million
Minimum Investment: $20 million
Investment Criteria: Buyouts, Spin-Outs, Growth Investments, Leveraged Build-Ups, Going Private Transactions
Industry Group Preference: Consumer Products, Industrial Products, Financial Services, Healthcare, Media, Retailing, Food & Beverage, Business Products & Services
Portfolio Companies: American Seafoods LP, Autoland Inc., Bellisio Food LLC, Bradford Health Services, Bravo Sports, Bumble Bee Foods LP, Catlin Westgen Group, Centre Pacific Holdings LLC, Covenant Care, Dan Howard Industries, Distant Lands Trading Co., Filament Brands Inc., Firearms Training Systems Inc., Garden Fresh Holdings, Gray Energy Services, Golding Farms Foods Inc., Guy & O'Neill Inc., Group Dekko Holdings Inc., Hyco International Inc., Jeepers! Inc., K2 Pure Solutions LP, Kaz Inc., Kinburn Corp, Laundry Mart Inc., MacNeill Pride Group, Manor House Retirement Centers Inc., Maverick Media LLC, Monte Nido Holdings LLC, Muzak Limited Partnership, Nationwide Credit Inc.,

157

Venture Capital & Private Equity Firms / Domestic Firms

Nearly Natural Inc., Nexus Gas Parttners, One World Fitness PFF, Orion ICG, Patient Education Media Inc., Q2 Publishing Inc., Quickie Manufacturing Corp, Rembrandt Photo Services, Rocky Mountain Financial Corporation, Ross Aviation, Salton Inc., Scientific Games Holdings Corp, Seaview Petroleum Co. LP, Sphere Drake Holdings Limited, Stonewall Kitchen LLC, Sun Orchard Inc., The Johnny Rockets Group, The Learning Company Inc., The Golden Financial Group Inc., United New Mexico Financial Corporation, United Retail Grop Inc., Uno Restaurant Holdings Corp, Vinters International Inc., Vision Innovation Partners, Wind River Environmental LLC, Wisconsin Cheese Group Holding LLC

Other Locations:
11726 San Vicente Blvd
Suite 450
Los Angeles, CA 90049
Phone: 310-207-9170 **Fax:** 310-207-9180

Key Executives:
Bruce Pollack, Managing Partner
e-mail: bruce.pollack@centrepartners.com
Education: Brandeis University
Background: TSG Holdings; RSG Partners; Becker; Merrill Lynch Capital Markets
Directorships: Salton, Bravo Sports, BumbleBee Seafoods, Maverick Media, Johnny Rockets Group, KIK Corporation Holdings, OSF, The Tiffen Company, Centre Palisades Ventures

David Jaffe, Managing Partner
e-mail: david.jaffe@centrepartners.com
Education: AB, Harvard University; MBA, Wharton School
Background: Managing Director, Merchant Banking Partners; DLJ Securities Corporation
Directorships: Catlin Westgen Group, Kaz, International Imaging Materials, Hyco International, Autoland, Target Media Partners

Jeffrey Bartoli, Partner
e-mail: jeffrey.bartoli@centrepartners.com
Education: BS, Georgetown University
Background: M&A, Smith Barney
Directorships: Environmental Logistics Services, K2 Pure Solutions, Maverick Media, Ross Aviation, US Retirement Partners

Michael Schnabel, Partner
e-mail: michael.schnabel@centrepartners.com
Education: BS, Duke University
Background: Director of Finance, OmniSky Corporation; Donaldson Lufkin & Jenrette Securities Corp.
Directorships: Centre Environmental Partners, Covenant Care, DSI Holding Company, Uno Restaurant Holdings

William Tomai, COO & CFO
e-mail: bill.tomai@centrepartners.com
Education: MBA, Wharton School; Vanderbuilt University
Background: Donaldson, Lufkin & Jenrette; Bank of New York; AspenTree Capital

448 CENTRIPETAL CAPITAL PARTNERS
Six Landmark Square
3rd Floor
Stamford, CT 06901

Phone: 203-326-7600
e-mail: info@centricap.com
web: www.centricap.com

Mission Statement: Centripetal Capital Partners, LLC. is an innovative venture capital firm with a distinctive investing and membership structure that provides greater flexibility and opportunity for limited partners than a traditional fund. We have an opportunistic growth capital investment approach, and seek investments in revenue generating companies with proprietary advantages, proven business models, and relevantly experienced management teams.

Founded: 2004
Average Investment: $2 - $7 million
Investment Criteria: Early-Stage, Growth Stage
Portfolio Companies: APJeT, Choice Pet, Cytogel, Dashbid, Earth Animal, IMCS Group, Meelo, Zing

Key Executives:
Steven Chrust, Senior Partner & Managing Director
Education: BA, Baruch College
Background: Founder, SGC Advisory Services; Sanford C Bernstein & Co.

Stephen Rossetter, Partner
Education: BA, Hartwick College; MBA, Pace University
Background: CFO/Partner, L&L Capital Advisors

Jeff Brodlieb, Partner
Education: BA, Brown University; MBA, Harvard Business School
Background: VP, Strategic Transactions, GE Capital

449 CENTURY PARK CAPITAL PARTNERS
2101 Rosencrans Avenue
Suite 4275
El Segundo, CA 90245

Phone: 310-867-2210 **Fax:** 310-867-2212
web: www.centuryparkcapital.com

Mission Statement: A private equity firm that partners with owners/managers to build successful companies.

Geographic Preference: North America
Average Investment: $10 - $40 million
Investment Criteria: Companies with a revenue of $20-100 million, historical and projected growth, manageable cyclicality, and diversified customer base
Industry Group Preference: Chemicals, Medical Products & Services, Business Services, Engineered Products, Consumer Products
Portfolio Companies: The Mochi Ice Cream Company, Better Life Technology LLC, Covercraft Industries LLC, ICM Products Inc., Cirtec Medical LLC, Hi-Tech Rubber Inc., Dickinson Frozen Foods Inc., Becker Underwood Inc., Eckler's Enterprises Inc., Kidsline Inc., Lynx Grills Inc., Specialty Manufacturing Inc., ROM Corp., Moss Inc., Packaging Plus LLC, Ryan's Express Transportation Services Inc., Aqua-Flo LLC

Other Locations:
750 Menlo Avenue
Suite 200
Menlo Park, CA 94025
Phone: 650-324-1956 **Fax:** 650-325-7757

Key Executives:
Martin A. Sarafa, Managing Partner
e-mail: msarafa@cpclp.com
Education: BS, Economics & Computer Science, University of Michigan; MBA, Wharton School, University of Pennsylvania
Background: Managing Director, Houlihan Lokey Howard & Zulkin
Directorships: Ryan's Express Transportation Services, Lynx Grills, Moss, Speciality Manufacturing Group, Cirtec Medical Systems, ICM Products

Charles W. Roellig, Managing Partner
e-mail: croellig@cpclp.com
Education: BA, Economics, Stanford University; MBA, Anderson Graduate School of Management, University of California, LA
Background: Principal, BT Capital Partners
Directorships: ROM Corporation, Lynx Grills, Eckler's Enterprises

Guy Zaczepinski, Managing Partner
e-mail: gzaczepinski@cpclp.com
Education: BS, Wharton School, University of Pennsylvania, MBA, Harvard Business School
Background: ACI Capital, DCMI

Venture Capital & Private Equity Firms / Domestic Firms

Directorships: Eckler's Enterprixes, Moss, Lynx Grills, ICM Products
Adam Zacuto, Vice President
e-mail: azacuto@cpclp.com
Education: BS, Finance, University of Southern California
Background: Analyst, Wells Fargo Securities

450 CEO VENTURES
600 Northpark Building
1200 Abernathy Road
17th Floor
Atlanta, GA 30328

Phone: 770-998-9999
e-mail: info@ceoventures.com
web: www.ceoventures.com

Mission Statement: CEO Ventures manages an angel fund that focuses on Software as a Service (Saas) seed stage companies and startups. CEO Ventures seeks to help entrepreneurs with the development and growth of new technology companies.

Investment Criteria: Seed-Stage, Startups
Industry Group Preference: Business to Business, Technology, SaaS
Portfolio Companies: CriticalFit, FindMatic, GoPresent, TeamEx

Other Locations:
Market Acceleration Center
Atlantic Station
201 17th Street, 12th Floor
Atlanta, GA 30363

228 Hamilton Avenue
3rd Floor
Palo Alto, CA 94301

Key Executives:
Michael Price, General Partner
e-mail: mprice@ceoventures.com
Education: Ohio State University, University of Akron
Background: IBM/Deibold

451 CERBERUS CAPITAL MANAGEMENT
875 Third Avenue
New York, NY 10022

Phone: 212-891-2100
e-mail: info@cerberuscapital.com
web: www.cerberuscapital.com

Mission Statement: Cerberus specializes in providing both financial resources and operational expertise to help transform undervalued companies into industry leaders for long-term success and value creation. Cerberus has numerous branches acorss the US, Europe and Asia.

Geographic Preference: United States, Europe, Asia
Fund Size: $20 billion
Founded: 1994
Industry Group Preference: Aerospace, Defense and Government, Transportation, Apparel, Automotive, Building Materials & Services, Commercial Services, Consumer Products, Financial Services, Healthcare, Manufacturing, Distribution, Paper, Real Estate, Technology

Other Locations:
10 South Riverside Plaza
Suite 875
Chicago, IL 60606
Phone: 312-474-7846

11812 San Vincente Blvd
Suite 300
Los Angeles, CA 90049
Phone: 310-826-9200

580 California Street
16th Floor
San Francisco, CA 94104
Phone: 415-568-2109

Key Executives:
John W. Snow, Chairman
Education: University of Toledo, George Washington University Law School, MS, Johns Hopkins University; PhD, Economics, University of Virginia
Background: United States Secretary of the Treasury
Stephen A. Feinberg, Co-Founder & CEO
Education: Princeton University
Background: Gruntal & Co.
Frank W. Bruno, Co-CEO & Senior Managing Director
Education: Cornell University; MBA, Wharton School, University of Pennsylvania
William L. Richter, Co-Founder
Education: Harvard College; MBA, Harvard Business School
Background: President, Richter Investment Corp.

452 CERES VENTURE FUND
1750 Harding Road
Northfield, IL 60093

e-mail: contact@ceresventurefund.com
web: www.ceresventurefund.com

Mission Statement: Ceres Venture Fund is an established Chicago-based venture capital fund dedicated to funding high growth companies located in the Midwest in their early stages of growth. As growth-oriented investors, the fund seeks to partner with entrepreneurs of proven ability and provide them with the resources needed to achieve extraordinary success.

Geographic Preference: Midwest United States
Industry Group Preference: Healthcare, Information Technology, Business Products & Services
Portfolio Companies: Brill Street + Company, Coverity, Eved, INRange Systems, SynCardia Systems, SynTherix, TrafficCast International, Vormetric, Zorch International

Key Executives:
Sona Wang, Managing Partner
Education: BS, Industrial Engineering, Stanford University; MBA, Kellogg School of Management
Background: Investment Manager, Allstate Insurance; Co-Founder, Batterson Johnson & Wang; Co-Founder, Inroads Capital Partners
Donna Williamson, Managing Director
Education: ScB, Applied Mathematics, Brown University; Graduate Degree, MIT Sloan School of Business
Background: Managing Director, ABN Amro; Founding Officer & SVP, Caremark International
Laura Pearl, Managing Director
Education: BS, Accountancy, University of Illinois, Urbana-Champaign; MBA, University of Chicago
Background: Ernst & Young; Partner, Frontenac

453 CERRACAP VENTURES
650 Town Center Drive
Suite 1870
Costa Mesa, CA 92626

Phone: 949-309-8598
e-mail: info@cerracap.com
web: www.cerracap.com

Mission Statement: Cerracap Ventures is focused on investing globally in early stage B2B companies. Their sectors include healthcare, enterprise AI and cybersecurity.

Key Executives:
Saurabh Suri, Managing Partner
Education: MS, University of Reading

454 CERVIN VENTURES
705 Forest Avenue
Palo Alto, CA 94301

e-mail: info@cervinventures.com
web: www.cervinventures.com

159

Venture Capital & Private Equity Firms / Domestic Firms

Mission Statement: The Cervin Ventures team consists of entrepreneurs who have a deep understanding of what it takes to start, build and grow a business. The firm brings an extensive network of technology, venture capital, and business professionals to advise and help early stage companies through their life cycle. The partners work closely with their portfolio companies to help them realize their full potential.
Investment Criteria: Early-Stage
Industry Group Preference: Software, Business to Business
Portfolio Companies: Ampool, ArmorText, Bedrock Analytics, BetterCompany, Bright Pattern, Claritics, EdCast, Folloze, Involver, Software, Nexient, Reveel, PayStand, Punchh, QuanticMind, SnapLogic, Soha Systems, Spotzot, Tynker, Zephyr, Zycada Networks
Key Executives:
   Preetish Nijhawan, Managing Director
   Education: BSEE, Birla Institute of Technology & Science; MS, Computer Engineering, University of Southern California; MBA, MIT Sloan School of Management
   Background: CFO, Neon Enterprise Software; McKinsey & Company
   Neeraj Gupta, Managing Director
   Education: BSEE, Punjab University; MSEE, University of Alabama
   Background: Patni; Founder, Cymbal Corporation

455 CHARLES RIVER VENTURES
855 Boylston Street
10th Floor
Boston, MA 02116
Phone: 781-768-6000 **Fax:** 781-768-6100
web: www.crv.com

Mission Statement: To contribute to the creation of significant new enterprises by working in constructive partnership with driven, talented entrepreneurs. To invest in early-stage, high potential companies with the objective of building rigorous, high-growth businesses, which produce substantial capital gains.
Geographic Preference: Northeast United States
Fund Size: $1.5 billion
Founded: 1970
Average Investment: $10-$25 million
Minimum Investment: $25,000
Investment Criteria: Early Stage, Series A
Industry Group Preference: Communications, Software, Information Technology, E-Commerce & Manufacturing, Consumer Internet, Infrastructure, SaaS, Cloud Computing
Portfolio Companies: 24M, Affirmed, Ark, Aveksa, Capriza, CarrierIQ, Cloudshare, Crossbeam Systems, Crushpath, DailyBreak, DataGravity, EnterpriseDB, Fiksu, Geni, Glyde, GrabCad, Greatcall, HubSpot, iControl Networks, Intellectual Ventures, InVisage, LearnBoost, Live Gamer, Magnetic, Maxthon, Millennial Media, Nantero, Neologin, Optaros, Progresso Financiero, Public Mobile, Qubole, Rethink Robotics, Rive Technology, RPX, Samplify, Scribd, SessionM, Simplivity, Sincerely, SpiderCloud Wireless, TalenBin, TerraPower, Tonian, ToyTalk, Twitter, Udacity, Vanu, Verenium, Viki, Wangyou.com, Wave Accounting, Xamarin, Yammer, Zendesk, CoTap, Dropbox, Gupshup, Pebble, Refresh, TopHatter, Usermind
Other Locations:
   300 Hamilton Avenue
   3rd Floor
   Palo Alto, CA 94301
   Phone: 650-687-5600 **Fax:** 650-687-5699

   855 Boylston Street
   10th Floor
   Boston, MA 02116
   Phone: 781-768-6000 **Fax:** 781-768-6100
Key Executives:
   Izhar Armony, Partner
   e-mail: izhar@crv.com
   Education: MBA, Wharton School of Business, University of Pennsylvania; MA, Cognitive Psychology, University of Tel Aviv; MA, International Studies, University of Pennsylvania
   Background: Enterprise Software, General Atlantic Partners; Software Designer, Director, Buisiness Development, Onyx Interactive; Officer, Israeli Army
   Jon Auerbach, Partner
   781-768-6000
   Education: BA, University of Pennsylvania
   Background: General Partner, Highland Capital Partners; Technology Reporter & Editor, The Wall Street Journal
   Saar Gur, Partner
   Education: BS, Biochemistry, University of Wisconsin, Madison; MBA, Stanford University
   Background: Co-Founder, Brightroll; Co-Founder, Carebadges.com; VP, Customer Acquisition, Adteractive; Founder, FounderDating
   Bruce Sachs, Partner
   Education: Master in Electrical Engineering, Cornell University; MBA, Northeastern University
   Background: AT&t Bell Laboratories; Memotec/Infinet; Xylogics; Bay Networks;
   Devdutt Yellurkar, Partner
   Education: BS, Fergusson College, India
   Background: Venture Partner, Rho Ventures; Co-Founder & CEO, Yantra Corporation; Senior Vice President, Infosys Technologies
   George Zachary, Partner
   Education: BS, MIT Sloan School of Management
   Background: General Partner, Mohr Davidow Ventures; Development, Nintendo/Silicon Graphics; Marketing Manager, VPL Research; CATS Software
   Max Gazor, Partner
   e-mail: max@crv.com
   Education: BS, EECS, UC Berkeley; MS, EECS, MIT, MBA, Harvard Business School
   Background: Corporate Development, Cisco
   Chris Baldwin, Partner Emeritus
   Education: AB, Electrical Engineering, Brown University; MS, Optical Physics, University of Rochester
   Background: VP Marketing, Argon Networks; Cascade Communications; Chipcom Corporation; Digital Equipment Corporation
   Directorships: Acopia Networks, EqualLogic, Nauticus Networks, Picolight, Revivio and Storigen Systems
   Richard Burnes, Partner Emeritus
   e-mail: rick@crv.com
   Education: MBA, Boston University; BA, Harvard University
   Background: Co-Founder, Charles River Ventures; Chairman of the Board, The Middlesex School
   Directorships: Concord Communications, Passport Corporation, SpeechWorks, Boston Science Museum, Sea Education Association
   Ted Dintersmith, Partner Emeritus
   e-mail: ted@crv.com
   Education: PhD, Stanford University; BA, William and Mary College
   Background: General Manager, Digital Signal Processing Division, Analog Devices; Congressional Staff Assistant

456 CHARLESBANK CAPITAL PARTNERS
200 Clarendon Street
54th Floor
Boston, MA 02116
Phone: 617-619-5400
web: www.charlesbank.com

Venture Capital & Private Equity Firms / Domestic Firms

Mission Statement: Charlesbank Capital Partners is a private equity firm committed to providing flexible capital and valuable collaboration to middle-market companies across a variety of sectors. The firm seeks to build companies with exceptional growth prospects.
Fund Size: $1.75 billion
Founded: 1991
Average Investment: $50 - $150 million
Investment Criteria: Growth Through Acquisition, Leveraged Acquisition, Middle Market, Small & Mid-Capitalization Public Companies, Later Stage
Industry Group Preference: Consumer Products, Distribution, Energy, Financial Services, Food & Beverage, Healthcare, Manufacturing, Media, Communications, Education
Portfolio Companies: American Residential Services, American Tire Distributors, Animal Health International, Aurora Organic Dairy, Bankruptcy Management Solutions, Blacksmith Brands, Blueknight Energy Partners, Catlin, Cedar Creek, CIFC, Citadel Plastics, CSI Leasing, DEI Holdings, Del Taco, Doit International, Ensono, Fullbeauty Brands, Galls, Gray Wolf Industrial, HDT Global, Hearthside Food Solutions, Helpsystems, Montpelier RE, Myeyedr., National Surgical Hospitals, Neo Tech, Park Place, Papa Murphy's, Peacock Foods, Plaskolite, Polyconcept, The Princeton Review, QC Supply, Regency Gas Services, RGL Reservoir Management, Rockport, Shoppers Drug Mart, Sightpath Medical, Six Degrees, Southcross Energy, StoneCastle, Tecomet, Technisource, Trojan Battery, United Road Services, Universal Technical Institute, Varsity Brands, Vestcom, Vision Group Holdings, Wolfpak Software, WorldStrides, Zayo Group, Zenith Products Corp.

Other Locations:
70 East 55th Street
20th Floor
New York, NY 10022
Phone: 212-903-1880

Key Executives:
Kim G. Davis, Managing Director/Co-Chairman
Education: BA, MBA, Harvard University
Background: Managing Director, Harvard Private Capital Group; General Partner, Kohlberg & Co.; Partner, Weiss, Peck & Greer
Directorships: Cedar Creek, HDT Global, Horn Industrial Services, Southcross Energy, Varsity Brands
Michael R. Eisenson, Managing Director/Co-Chairman
Education: BA, Economics, Williams College; MBA, JD, Yale University
Background: President, Harvard Private Capital Group; Managing Director, Harvard Management Company; Boston Consulting Group
Directorships: Blueknight Energy, DEI Holdings, Penske Auto Group, StoneCastle Partners, United Road Services
Michael Choe, Managing Director/CEO
Education: BA, Biology, Harvard University
Background: Harvard Private Capital Group; McKinsey & Company
Directorships: Acxiom ITO, DEI Holdings, Horn Industrial Services, Six Degrees, United Road Services, Zayo
Samuel Bartlett, Managing Director
Education: BA, History, Amherst College
Background: Bain & Company
Directorships: American Residential Services, HDT Global, Horn Industrial Services
J. Ryan Carroll, Managing Director
Education: BA, Economics, Harvard University
Background: LEK Consulting
Directorships: Acxiom ITO, DEI Holdings, Peacock Engineering, Six Degrees, Trojan Battery
Andrew S. Janower, Managing Director
Education: BS, Economics, Wharton School, University of Pennsylvania; MBA, Harvard University; CPA
Background: Harvard Private Capital Group; Research Associate, Harvard Business School; Consultant, Bain & Company
Directorships: American Residential Services, FULLBEAUTY Brands, WorldStrides, Varsity Brands
Joshua A. Klevens, Managing Director
Education: BA, Woodrow Wilson School of Public Policy & International Affairs, Princeton University; MBA, Stanford University
Background: Bain Capital; Business Analyst, McKinsey & Company
Directorships: FULLBEAUTY Brands, HDT Global
Brandon C. White, Managing Director
Education: BA, Economics, Brigham Young University
Background: Harvard Private Capital Group; Business Analyst, McKinsey & Company
Directorships: Sightpath Medical, StoneCastle Partners, Trojan Battery, Varsity Brands, Vision Group Holdings
Mark Rosen, Advisory Director
Education: BA, Amherst College; JD, Yale University
Background: Managing Director, Harvard Private Capital Group; Principal, The Conifer Group; President, Morningside/North America Limited; Senior Partner, Hale and Dorr
Tim R. Palmer, Co-Founder & Senior Advisor
Education: BA, Purdue University; JD, University of Virginia; MBA, University of Chicago
Background: Managing Director, Harvard Private Capital Group; The Field Corporation; Sidley & Austin
Michael G. Thonis, Co-Founder & Senior Advisor
Education: BS, Geology, Syracuse University; MS, Geology, MIT; MBA, Harvard Business School
Background: Director of Research/Portfolio Management, Harvard Management Company; Managing Director, Harvard Private Capital Group

457 CHART VENTURE PARTNERS
555 Fifth Avenue
19th Floor
New York, NY 10017

Phone: 212-350-8200
web: www.chartventure.com

Mission Statement: Chart Venture Partners invests in security related technologies with government and commercial applications. The firm invests in highly differentiated opportunities with large markets where value can be added through their industry experience, network of relationships and technology insight.
Fund Size: $100 million
Founded: 1994
Industry Group Preference: Homeland Security, Security, Aerospace, Defense and Government
Portfolio Companies: CoolIT, DisperSol, Flyby Media, GeoiQ, IntegriCo Composites, Nextreme Thermal Solutions, Ogmento, PacStar, PureEnergy Solutions, RemoteReality, Twisted Pair Solutions, WiSpry

Key Executives:
Christopher D. Brady, Founding Managing Partner
Education: BA, Middlebury College; MBA, Columbia University Graduate School of Business
Background: Lehman Brothers; Dillon Read
Chris Brady, Jr., Managing Partner
Education: BA, Yale University
Background: InSitech; Flyby Media
Directorships: CoolIT Systems, IntegriCo Composites, Flyby Media, Pacific Star Communications, RemoteReality

458 CHARTER LIFE SCIENCES
325 East Middlefield Road
Mountain View, CA 94043

Phone: 650-318-5411 **Fax:** 650-318-3425
web: www.clsvc.com

161

Venture Capital & Private Equity Firms / Domestic Firms

Mission Statement: Early-stage life sciences investor.
Fund Size: $300 million
Founded: 1982
Average Investment: $500,000-$5 million
Minimum Investment: $100,000
Investment Criteria: Early stage
Industry Group Preference: Life Sciences
Portfolio Companies: Amaranth Medical, MEI Pharma, CoMentis, EnteroMedics, Great Lakes Pharmaceuticals, Health Fidelity, Inviragen, Kereos, KFx Medical, Minimally Invasive Devices, Mirabilis Medica, Revascular Therapeutics, Visioneering Technologies, Xlumena
Other Locations:
   3130 Highland Avenue
   Suite 3A
   Cincinnati, OH 45219
   Phone: 513-475-6626
Key Executives:
   A. Barr Dolan, Managing Partner
   Education: BA, Chemistry, MS, Engineering, Cornell University; MBA, Stanford University; MA, Applied Science, Harvard University
   Background: Arthur Andersen; CM Capital Corporation
   Directorships: Heska Corporation, Integrated Biosystems, Metabolex, ShieldIP, UMD
   Donald C. Harrison, Managing Partner
   Education: BA, Birmingham Southern College; MD, University of Alabama School of Medicine; Honorary Doctor of Law Degree, Birmingham Southern College
   Background: Senior VP/Provost Health Affairs, University of Cincinnati Medical Center; Chief of Department of Cardiology, Stanford University School of Medicine; Chief of Cardiology, Stanford University Hospital; Co-Director, Falk Cardiovascualr Research Center; President, AHA
   Directorships: Co-Founder, EP Technologies; Co-Founder, Vesta; Founder, BIO/START; Kendle International; SciMed
   Nelson Teng, Managing Partner
   Education: Graduate of Postgraduate Program at the Stanford University Graduate School of Business; MD, University of Miami; PhD Biophysics, University of California Berkeley
   Background: Chief Gynecologic Oncology, Stanford University School of Medicine; Research Scientist, MIT; President, Western Association Gynecoscualr Oncology; Chairman, National Comprehensive Cancer Network

459 CHATTANOOGA RENAISSANCE FUND
201 W. Main Street
Suite 205
Chattanooga, TN 37408

e-mail: info@chattanoogarenaissancefund.com
web: chattanoogarenaissancefund.com

Mission Statement: To invest in seed and early-stage campnaies that display great habits and solid growth potential.
Geographic Preference: Chattanooga, Knoxville, Nashville, North Atlanta
Founded: 2010
Industry Group Preference: Diversified
Portfolio Companies: Collider, Vendor Registry, Branch Technology, Felt, TN Stillhouse, Aegle Gear, GreenPrint, Alumnify, Everly, BattleBin, Ambition Solutions, Blue Light, Rapid RMS, DataFlyte, XOEye Technologies, ReadyCart, PriceWaiter, Interntional Coffee Group, Iron Gaming, The Convenience Network, RecruitTalk, RentStuff, Tensor Surgical, Inova Payroll, Glenveigh Medical, RootsRated, Variable, Quickcue, Advanced Catheter Therapies, AudiencePoint, SupplyHog
Key Executives:
   Miller Welborn, General Partner
   Education: BA, Political Science & Government, University of Alabama
   Background: Chairman, Cornerstone Community Bank; Chairman, SmartFinancial; President, Welborn Transport, Boyd Bros. Transportation; Co-Founder, Lamp Post Group; Chairman, Big Oak Ranch
   Directorships: Federal Reserve Board of Atlanta

460 CHAZEN CAPITAL PARTNERS
150 East 58th Street
27th Floor
New York, NY 10155

Phone: 212-888-7800 Fax: 212-888-4580
e-mail: info@chazen.com
web: www.chazen.com

Mission Statement: Established in 1997, Chazen Capital Partners offers support and equity capital to economy businesses across a variety of sectors.
Founded: 1997
Industry Group Preference: Consumer Products, Consumer Services, Technology, Software
Portfolio Companies: 7thOnline, Black Book Magazine, eChalk.com, Kalisaya, LivePerson, Naked, Nerve, Nina McLemore, Return Path, Verterra
Key Executives:
   Jerome A Chazen, Founder/Chairman
   Education: University of Wisconsin; MBA, Columbia Business School
   Background: Chairman, Liz Claiborne Inc.
   Directorships: Taubman Centers Inc.
   David F Chazen, Managing Director
   Education: BS, Wharton School, University of Pennsylvania; MBA, Columbia Business School
   Background: President, The Good Stuff Company; Principal, JLB Capital Partners; Manager, Strategic Government Partners; Goldman Sachs
   Directorships: Jazz Aspen
   Sid Banon, Managing Director
   Education: BS, Accounting, State University of New York at Albany
   Background: Co-Founder, The Good Stuff Company; Co-Founder, Win Stuff; Sony Corporation of America; Gulf & Western; Citicorp

461 CHB CAPITAL PARTNERS
299 Milwaukee Street
Suite 450
Denver, CO 80206

Phone: 303-571-0100 Fax: 303-571-0114
web: www.chbcapital.com

Mission Statement: Provide closely held and family-owned businesses with the equity capital and expertise for smooth ownership transition and sustained growth.
Geographic Preference: United States
Fund Size: $75 million
Founded: 1995
Average Investment: $5 - $15 million
Minimum Investment: $5 million
Investment Criteria: Leveraged Recapitalizations, Management-Led Buyouts, Growth Equity Investments
Industry Group Preference: Niche Manufacturing, Distribution
Portfolio Companies: Blu Dot, CanGen, Logic PD, Sorrento Networks, Alternative Technology Inc., Brandbase Holdings Inc., Champion Technologies Inc., HiRel Systems LLC, MACTEC, Newline Products Inc., Shoe Corp. of America, Spyder Active Sports, Trussway Holdings Inc., USA Capital Holdings Inc., Valent Aerostructures
Key Executives:
   John W. Flanigan, Managing Partner
   e-mail: jwflanigan@chbcapital.com
   Education: BA, English & Economics, Amherst College; MBA, Harvad Business School
   Background: Bain & Company; Cannon Associates

Venture Capital & Private Equity Firms / Domestic Firms

Thomas L. Kelly II, Managing Partner
e-mail: tlkelly@chbcapital.com
Education: BA, Economics, BS, Administrative Sciences, Yale University; MBA, Harvard Business School
Background: Bass Brothers; Richard Rainwater
David J. Anderson, Chief Financial Officer
e-mail: djanderson@chbcapital.com
Education: BA, Accounting, University of Wisconsin
Background: Independent Consultant; Financial Management, Capital Associates and Systems Marketing; Management Consultant, Ernst Whinney; Internal Auditing/Systems Development, Los Alamos National Laboratory; CPA

462 CHEROKEE & WALKER
6440 South Wasatch Blvd
Suite 200
Salt Lake City, UT 84121

Phone: 801-278-7800 **Fax:** 801-278-7818
web: cherokeeandwalker.com

Portfolio Companies: Green Light Auto Solutions, TopNoggin, Rimrock Construction, Red Bridge Capital, inthinc, Gold's Gym, Rockworth Companies, Vital Signs Staffing, Visible Equity, Campus Book Rentals, Financial Guard, Fortius Financial, Cornerstone Concrete, SYMBII, Wentworth Senior Living Services, Cottonwood Capital

Key Executives:
  Shane R. Peery, Partner
  e-mail: shane@cherokeeandwalker.com
  Education: BS, MS, Accounting, Brigham Young University
  Background: Ernst & Young
  Paul K. Erickson, Partner
  e-mail: paul@cherokeeandwalker.com
  Education: BS, Accounting, Brigham Young University
  Background: SunGard, IBM
  J. Blair Jenkins, Partner
  e-mail: blair@cherokeeandwalker.com
  Education: BS, University of Utah; MS, Real Estate Development, Columbia University
  Brent Wilson, Partner
  e-mail: brent@cherokeeandwalker.com
  Background: Progressive Finance LLC

463 CHEROKEE INVESTMENT PARTNERS
310 South West Street
Suite 200
Raleigh, NC 27603

Phone: 919-743-2500 **Fax:** 919-743-2501
web: www.cherokeefund.com

Mission Statement: To acquire environmentally impaired assets and protect sellers from the associated risks and liabilities. Cherokee invests through both private equity and venture capital.
Geographic Preference: North America, Europe
Fund Size: $2 billion
Founded: 1984
Average Investment: $130 million
Minimum Investment: $10 million
Investment Criteria: Primary and Secondary Markets
Industry Group Preference: Industrial Services, Manufacturing, Research & Development, Property Management, Real Estate, Commercial Services
Key Executives:
  Bret Batchelder, Managing Director
  e-mail: bbatchelder@cherokeefund.com
  Education: BA, Morehead Scholar, University of North Carolina; MBA, JL Kellogg Graduate School of Management, Northwestern University; CPA; CFA; NC Real Estate License
  Background: VP Mergers/Acquisitions, First Union

Securities; Associate, Goldman, Sachs & Company; Portfolio Manager, Bank South N.A.
Tom Darden, Founder & CEO
919-743-2500
e-mail: tdarden@cherokeefund.com
Education: BA, Morehead Scholar, MRP, University of North Carolina; JD, Yale Law School
Background: Cherokee Sanford Group; Consultant, Bain & Company; Research Triangle Transit Authority; NC Board of Transportation
Directorships: Woodberry Forest School; Shaw University; University of North Carolina Environmental Department; REIT, Winston Hotels; Research Triangle Institute
John Mazzarino, Founder & Managing Principal
e-mail: jmazzarino@cherokeefund.com
Education: BA, Phi Beta Kappa, Colgate University; MS, Sloan School of Management, MIT
Background: Cherokee Sanford Group; President, Hackney Holdings; Carolina Ceramics; Manager, Bain & Company; Peat, Marwick, Mitchell & Company
Directorships: Center for Sustainable Enterprise, Kenan-Flagler School of Business; Oak Ranch Children's Home; Hometown America
Steven Hartanto, Senior Associate
Education: BA, Economics & Chinese Studies, Occidental College
Elizabeth Merritt, Managing Director
Education: BA, Economics & English, University of North Carolina, Chapel Hill
Background: Associate, Leveraged Finance Group, Goldman, Sachs & Co

464 CHERRY TREE COMPANIES
301 Carlson Parkway
Suite 103
Minnetonka, MN 55305

Phone: 952-893-9012
e-mail: info@cherrytree.com
web: www.cherrytree.com

Mission Statement: Cherry Tree provides investment banking services to middle market businesses and raises capital for growth companies through private placements.
Founded: 1980
Investment Criteria: Middle Market, Recapitalizations, Acquisitions, Growth Capital
Key Executives:
  Tony Christianson, Managing General Partner
  e-mail: tchristianson@cherrytree.com
  Education: BS, St. John's University; MBA, Harvard Business School
  Background: VP, Norwest Venture Capital; Consultant, Arthur Andersen
  Directorships: AmeriPride Services, Arctic Cat, Capella Education Company, Computer Petroleum Corporation, The Dolan Company, J3 Learning, Titan Machinery
  Gordon Stofer, Managing General Partner
  e-mail: gstofer@cherrytree.com
  Education: BS, Industrial Engineering, Cornell University; MBA, Harvard Business School
  Background: VP, Norwest Venture Capital; Marketing Manager, Honeywell; Westinghouse; Maine National Bank
  Directorships: VEE Corporation, Bright Start, Buffets, DataMyte Corporation, FilmTec, Harmony Brook, Insignia Systems, MakeMusic, National Information Systems
  Chuck Gorman, Senior Executive Director
  e-mail: cgorman@cherrytree.com
  Education: BA, Business, University of St. Thomas
  Background: President & CEO, Kobixx Systems; President, KnowledgeSoft; President & CEO, J3 Learning; Executive Vice President, Wilson Learning

Venture Capital & Private Equity Firms / Domestic Firms

Chad Johnson, Managing Director
e-mail: cjohnson@cherrytree.com
Education: BA, MBA, University of Minnesota
Background: VP, The M&A Group; General Manager, Ultralingua; Manager, Business Development, PLATO Learning; Venture Capital Analyst, Sherpa Partners
Dave Latzke, Managing Director
e-mail: dlatzke@cherrytree.com
Education: BA, Accounting, University of Northern Iowa
Background: SVP & CFO, SoftBrands; EVP & CFO, Fourth Shift Corporation; Manager, Arthur Andersen & Co.
Elmer Baldwin, Senior Executive Director
e-mail: ebaldwin@cherrytree.com
Education: BBA, Finance, Loyola Marymount University
Background: President & CEO, Internet Broadcasting Systems; SVP, Fujitsu Consulting; President & CEO, BORN Information Services; President & CEO, Nuvolution
Directorships: Lifesprk, EA Sween Company, FileControl International
Jane Bortnem, Chief Financial Officer
e-mail: jbortnem@cherrytree.com
Education: BS, Accounting, Minnesota State University
Background: Consultant & Audit Manager, Boulay Heutmaker Zibell & Company; Accountant, Pepin Heights
Mik Gusenius, Director
e-mail: mgusenius@cherrytree.com
Education: BA, Economics & Scandinavian Studies, Gustavus Adolphus College; MBA, Carlson School of Management, University of Minnesota
Background: Analyst, Bayview Capital Group; Managing Director, Carlson Fixed-Income Fund; Assistant Director, The Gustavus Fund, Gustavus Adolphus College
Mike Buttry, Senior Executive Director
e-mail: mbuttry@cherrytree.com
Education: BS, Creighton University
Background: VP of Public Affairs and Strategy, Capella Education Company; Entrepreneur-In-Residence, Whiteboard Advisors; Managing Director, Chlopak Leonard & Schecter
Directorships: Capella University; Angel Foundation; Shank Institute for Innovation in Education

465 **CHESTNUT HILL PARTNERS**
520 Madison Avenue
3rd Floor
New York, NY 10022

Phone: 212-687-3123 **Fax:** 212-972-2921
e-mail: info@chestnuthillpartners.com
web: www.chestnuthillpartners.com

Mission Statement: Chestnut Hill Partners is an investment banking boutique specializing in merger and acquisition originations for private equity investors.

Portfolio Companies: ERC Wiping Products Inc., Ecoscape Solutions, Caring People, Krauss Craft, Spill Magic Inc., Construction Labor Contractors, Sprayglo, Superior Contract Cleaners, Natural Balance Pet Foods Inc., Greg C. Rigamer & Associates, Contessa Premium Foods Inc., Berry Family Nurseries, DCS Sanitation Management, Uno Restaurant Holdings Corp., Granny's Kitchen Ltd., Crompco Corp., American Furniture Manufacturing, Compression Polymers Group, Andrews International Inc., Polar Plastics Ltd., Beckett Corp., Saisha Tehnology, Action Labs Inc., Contract Services Limited, ADS Technologies Inc., Advance Technology Services, Hickery Farms, Roscoe Manufacturing, AD-Tech Plastic Systems, K.G. Box Inc., Spacetec IMC Corp., Remco Maintenance Corp., Hooven Heat Treating, Michigan Induction Inc., Meer Corp., Buckner Equipment Rental, Chemseco, Merlin 200,000 Mile, American Stencil, Brentax Inc., Four Star Lighting Co., American Products Co., Compressor Controls Corp., Chamberlain Gard

Key Executives:
Paul L. Schaye, Managing Director
Education: BA, PhD, Business, University of Massachusetts
Background: Consultant, A.T. Kearney and Booz Allen & Hamilton
Jeff Davidson, Managing Director
Education: University of Delaware
Background: Managed Accounts Advisor, SEI; Co-Founder, Cathedral Partners; Director, Head of Americas, Palico
David Rowley, Managing Director
Education: University of Delaware
Background: Co-Founder & Partner, Cathedral Partners; Vice President, SRS Capital
Daniel Terpak, Director
Education: BS, Villanova University

466 **CHEVRON TECHNOLOGY VENTURES**
1500 Lousiana
39th Floor
Houston, TX 77002

e-mail: techventures@chevron.com
web: www.chevron.com/technology/technology-ventures

Mission Statement: Identifies new technologies and business opportunities that can create value for Chevron. Then, using disciplined venture capital practices, Chevron invests in those opportunities that promise clear competitive advantages and superior financial returns.

Fund Size: $250 million
Founded: 1999
Investment Criteria: Early Stage, Mid Stage
Industry Group Preference: Technology, Energy, Power Technologies, Information Technology, Biotechnology, Networking, Oil & Gas, Alternative Energy, Advanced Materials, Communications, Networking
Portfolio Companies: Acumentrics, Amphora, Apprion, Arisdyne, BlueArc, BrightSource Energy, Codexis, Cubility, DeepFlex, DynaPump, Ember Resources, Five Star Technologies, Frictionless Commerce, Foro Energy, Inficomm, Ironport Systems, Konarka Technologies, MetaCarta, Microfabrica, MicroSeismic, Moblize, Network International, Nimbus, OsComp Systems, Oxane, PanGeo Subsea, Panzura, PathScale, Production Science, Radiance Technologies, Reality Mobile, Sample6 Technologies, SchemaLogic, Silixa, Soane Energy, SpectraSensors, Spotfire, Southwest Windpower, Stingray Digital, Sub-One Technology, Tacit Technologies, Teros, TradeCapture, Tubel Technologies, Xenogen, Zi-Lift

Key Executives:
Richard Pardoe, Venture Executive
Education: BS, Chemical Engineering, University of California, Davis
Background: Process Engineer, Chevron; Principal, Chevron Technology Ventures

467 **CHEYENNE CAPITAL**
1430 Wynkoop Street
Suite 200
Denver, CO 80202

Phone: 303-454-5453
e-mail: contact@cheyennefund.com
web: www.cheyennefund.com

Mission Statement: Private equity firm in Denver, Colorado.

Geographic Preference: United States
Investment Criteria: LBO, Recapitalizations, Expansion or Growth Equity
Industry Group Preference: Manufacturing, Financial Services, Business Products & Services, Consumer Products, Consumer Services, Media, Energy

Venture Capital & Private Equity Firms / Domestic Firms

Key Executives:
John Fitzgerald, Managing Director & Co-Founder
Education: BS, SUNY Oneonta; JD, New England School of Law
Background: Partner, Kirkland & Ellis
Brian Knitt, Managing Director
Education: BS, Mathematics, Colorado State University; MS, Systems Management, University of Southern California; MBA, UCLA Anderson School of Management
Background: Meritage Funds; Officer, U.S. Air Force
Mike West, Chief Financial Officer
Education: BS, Accounting, MBA, University of Denver; CPA
Background: Arthur Andersen LLP
Phil Parrott, Co-Founder
Education: BA, Colorado State University; JD, University of Colorado
Background: Chief Deputy District Attorney, Denver District Attorney's Office; Partner, Kirkland & Ellis

468 CHICAGO GROWTH PARTNERS
Attn: Parker Gale Suite 2.02
222 Merchandise Mart
12th Floor
Chicago, IL 60654
Phone: 312-698-6300 Fax: 312-201-0703
e-mail: info@cgp.com
web: www.cgp.com

Mission Statement: Helps companies achieve their goals by providing expansion and buyout capital, to create success for companies, their managers and investors.
Average Investment: $5 - $25 million
Investment Criteria: Middle-Market, Expansion Capital, Buyout Capital
Industry Group Preference: Education, Business Products & Services, Consumer Services, Healthcare, Healthcare Services, Industrial Services, Technology-Enabled Services, Industrial Technology
Portfolio Companies: 2Checkout, AC Lordi, Advanced Pain Management, Airpax, AnaJet, Benetech, Caprion Proteomics, CLP Resources, Compete, Comtempo Ceramic Tile, CryoCor, Daisytek International, DJ Pharma, eInstruction, Encore Paper, EndoGastric Solutions, FineLine Technologies, Footprint Retail Services, Genoptix, HouseValues, Jonathan Engineered Services, Lanx, Marathon Data Systems, Morton Grove Pharmaceuticals, NuVasive, Paramount Services, PharmaResearch, Point Biomedical, PRIMIS Marketing Group, Royall & Company, SchoolMessenger, Scribe America, Specialized Education Services, TargeGen, Teaching Strategies, The Tie Bar, U.S. Education Corporation, World 50, Workwave, Zogenix

Key Executives:
David G Chandler, Managing Partner
e-mail: dchandler@cgp.com
Education: BA, Princeton University; MBA, Amos Tuck School, Dartmouth
Background: Managing Director, William Blair Capital Partners; Investment Banking, Morgan Stanley
Robert P Healy, Managing Partner
e-mail: rhealy@cgp.com
Education: United States Military Academy, West Point; MBA, Harvard Business School
Background: Managing Director, William Blair Capital Partners; General Partner, ClearLight Partners; Principal, William E Simon & Sons
Directorships: ABC Window Company, Advanced Pain Management, Aimnet Solutions, Apripax Corporation, AnaJet, Benetech, Contempo Ceramic Tile, eInstruction Corp., Footprint Retail Services
Arda M Minocherhomjee, Managing Partner
e-mail: arda@cgp.com
Education: MS, Pharmacology, University of Toronto; PhD, MBA, University of British Columbia
Background: Managing Director, William Blair Captial Partners; Senior Healthcare Analyst, William Blair & Company
Directorships: Advanced Pain Management, DJ Pharma, EndoGastric Solutions, Genoptix, Lanx, Morton Grove Pharmaceuticals, NuVasive, PharmaResearch Corporation, Proteon, TargeGen, Zogenix
Devin Mathews, Managing Partner
e-mail: dmathews@cgp.com
Education: BA, State University of New York, Binghamton; MBA, Tuck School of Business, Dartmouth
Background: Baird Venture Partners, Great Hill Partners, William Blair Capital Partners
Directorships: World 50, Vigo Remittance Corporation, Fellon-Mccord & Associates, Arroweye Solutions, LatinVest, TrueAdvantage, Encover, Payroll Associates
Robert D Blank, Partner
e-mail: rblank@cgp.com
Education: BA, Economics, Miami University; MBA, Kellogg School of Management, Northwestern University
Background: Managing Director, William Blair Capital Partnes; Partner, Private Market Group, Brinson Partners; Investment Manager, Wind Point Partners
Directorships: AC Lordi Financial Services, Alternative Resources Corporation, Contractors Labor Pool, Cypress Medical Products, DJ Pharma, Jefferson-Wells, PRIMIS Marketing Group
Timothy M Murray, Partner
e-mail: tmurray@cgp.com
Education: BA, Duke University; MBA, University of Chicago
Background: Managing Director, William Blair Capital Partners
Directorships: Airpax Holdings, CES, Compete, Daisytek Corp., Engineered Materials Corp., Extended Care Info. Network, Paramount Services, Sanford Corp., TimePlus Payroll, Towne Holdings
James F Milbery, Operating Partner
e-mail: jmilbery@cgp.com
Education: BS, Management, Babson College
Background: Director, Competitive Intelligence, Oracle Corporation; Compuware; Computer Associates; Elevon; Digital Equipment Corporation
Jeff Farrero, Principal
e-mail: jfarrero@cgp.com
Education: BS, University of Illinois; MBA, Kellogg School of Management, Northwestern University
Background: Associate, Credit Suisse First Boston
Directorships: Airpax, AnaJet, Benetech, eInstruction, FineLine Technologies, Footprint Retail Services, Royall & Company, Specialized Education Services, Teaching Strategies
Kristina Heinze, Principal
e-mail: kheinze@cgp.com
Education: BS, Finance, University of Illinois
Background: Analsyt, Credit Suisse First Boston
Directorships: 2Checkout, Paramount Services, Contempo Ceramic Tile, Specialized Education Services, The Plastics Group, Union Corrugating
Sean Barrette, Principal
e-mail: sbarrette@cgp.com
Education: BS, SUNY Binghamton; MBA, Booth School of Business
Background: Associate & Analyst, Credit Suisse; Staff Accountant, Ernst & Young
Directorships: Advanced Pain Management, Caprion Proteomics
Ryan Milligan, Principal
e-mail: rmilligan@cgp.com
Education: BS, Management, Boston College; MBA, Kellogg School of Management
Background: Investment Banking, Analyst, Robert W Baird
Directorships: 2Checkout, Jonathan Engineered

Venture Capital & Private Equity Firms / Domestic Firms

Solutions, Marathon Data Systems, SchoolMessenger, World50

469 CHICAGO PACIFIC FOUNDERS
980 North Michigan Ave.
Suite 1998
Chicago, IL 60611

Phone: 312-273-4750
e-mail: info@cpfounders.com
web: www.cpfounders.com

Mission Statement: Chicago Pacific Founders manages private funds with an exclusive interest in healthcare services. Chicago Pacific Founders is actively seeking to partner with companies that are dedicated to providing high quality healthcare services to patients, providers, and payers.
Industry Group Preference: Healthcare
Portfolio Companies: CPF Living Communities; Florida Elite Medical Group; It's Never 2 Late; Marquee Dental Partners; P3 Health Partners; Pinnacle Dermatology; Recovery Ways, Sage, SightMD
Other Locations:
135 Main St.
Suite 1350
San Francisco, CA 94111
Phone: 415-539-0630
Key Executives:
Mary Tolan, Founder/Managing Partner
Education: BBA, Loyola University; MBA, University of Chicago
Background: Founder, Accretive Health; Group Chief Executive, Accenture
Vance Vanier, Founder/Managing Partner
Education: MD, Johns Hopkins School of Medicine; MBA, Stanford University
Background: President, Verinata Health; CEO, Navigenics; Partner, Mohr Davidow Ventures

470 CHICAGO VENTURE PARTNERS LP
303 E Wacker Drive
Suite 1040
Chicago, IL 60601

Phone: 312-297-7000 Fax: 312-819-9701
web: www.chicagoventure.com

Mission Statement: Chicago Venture Partners helps entrepreneurs build successful technology companies. The firm seeks companies that have the potential to achieve leading positions in their industry. In addition to providing capital, Chicago Venture Partners works with its portfolio companies to provide advice on competitive positioning, establish strategic alliances, recruit key management and forge other key relationships.
Geographic Preference: United States
Fund Size: $45 million
Founded: 1998
Average Investment: $500,000 - $10 million
Investment Criteria: Emerging, Growth Stage, Small Cap
Industry Group Preference: Internet Technology, E-Commerce & Manufacturing, Software, Information Technology, Telecommunications, Consumer Products, Applications Software & Services, Networking, Equipment, Computer Related, Media, Energy
Portfolio Companies: Emergent Trading, Miller Fabrication, Pulse Systems, Typenex Medical,
Key Executives:
John Fife, Managing Partner
Education: BS, Statistics & Computer Science, Brigham Young University; MBA, Harvard Business School
Background: President, CEO & Chairman, Utah Resources International; Assistant VP, Continental Illinois Venture Corporation; Consultant, Oracle Corporation
Directorships: Edwards Trucking, Typenex Medical, Pulse Systems

Colin Robinson, Senior Associate
Education: BS, Management, Brigham Young University
Background: Consultant, Accenture
Tina Saxton, Project Manager
Education: University of Denver
Background: Assistant VP, Private Equity Fund Services, JPMorgan Chase; KPMG
Christopher R Stalcup, Associate
Education: BA, Finance & Economics, University of Illinois at Urbana-Champaign; CFA
Background: VP, Northern Trust Hedge Fund Services; Associate, Omnium

471 CHICAGO VENTURES
222 West Merchandise Mart Plaza
Suite 1212
Chicago, IL 60654

e-mail: info@chicagoventures.com
web: chicagoventures.com

Mission Statement: Chicago Ventures invests in well-managed seed-stage technology companies in Chicago and the Greater Midwest that have demonstrated a value proposition in a given market for their product or services.
Geographic Preference: Midwest
Founded: 2011
Average Investment: $750K - $1 million
Investment Criteria: Seed
Industry Group Preference: Analytics & Analytical Instruments, Business to Business, Sales & Marketing SaaS, Payments & Financial Services, Healthcare Information Technology, Marketplace/On-Demand Services, Loyalty
Portfolio Companies: Donde, Rocketmiles, Spring, Catalyze.io, MdotLabs, BloomNation, TempoDB, FindIt, Zipments, Blitsy, Pangea, Picturelife, Betterfly, Cartavi, Shiftgig, Kapow Events, UpCity, SimpleRelevance, Retrofit, HealthFinch, Food Genius, Power2Switch
Key Executives:
Rob Chesney, Partner
Education: BA, McGill University; MBA, Kellogg School of Management, Northwestern University
Background: Associate, Lehman Brothers; VP of Buyer Experience & Verticals, eBay; COO, Trunk Club
Directorships: CoPilot; Cameo; LandscapeHub; TaskRabbit
Stuart Larkins, Partner
Education: BS, Southern Methodist University
Background: Branch Manager, Penske Logistics; Founder/Managing Director, Twin Capital;
Directorships: Ureeka; Forager; Veryable; Sunbit; Meritize; Project44; PerformLine Inc.; G2 Crowd; itemMaster; Shedd Aquarium; Spring Marketplace; Shiftgig; Trunk Club; Netconcepts

472 CHINAROCK CAPITAL MANAGEMENT VENTURES
475 Sansome St.
Suite 730
San Francisco, CA 94111

Phone: 415-578-5700
e-mail: vc@crcm.com
web: www.crcmvc.com

Mission Statement: Invests in startup companies in the areas of artificial intelligence, machine learning, augmented reality, virtual reality, emerging media, financial technology, blockchain, and smart cities. Has additional offices in Palo Alto, CA, and in China.
Geographic Preference: Global
Fund Size: $158 Million
Founded: 2006
Investment Criteria: Early Stage, Startup, Tech

Venture Capital & Private Equity Firms / Domestic Firms

Industry Group Preference: Artificial Intelligence, Machine Learning, Emerging Media, Financial Technology, Blockchain, Smart Cities
Portfolio Companies: Agentiq, Airy:3D, Arraiy, Baobab Studios, Cargo, Chariot, Civil Maps, Deep Motion, Drone Racing League, Fan AI, Felix & Paul, Gamer Sensei, Ming Yi Zhu Dao, Musical.ly, Orbeus, Ripple, Roam, Senyi, Sonavex, Vreal, Youku
Key Executives:
Chun Ding, Managing Partner
Education: BA, Economics, Middlebury College; MBA, Harvard Business School
Background: Farallon Capital Management; The Goldman Sachs Group, Inc.
Toby Zhang, Partner
Education: BA, MA, University of Michigan; MBA, The Wharton School, University of Pennsylvania
Background: Tradeversity Inc.; NBC Universal; Microsoft; Edison Partners
Matt Lee, Partner
Education: BE, MA, University of New South Wales; MBA, New York University; MBA, London Business School
Background: MacQuarie Group; Capco; authentiQ; Pobble; Pereg Ventures
Jessica Ngo, Partner/CFO
Education: BA, Economics, University of California, Berkeley
Background: Primarius Capital

473 CHINAVEST
P.O. Box 170985
San Francisco, CA 94147

e-mail: info@chinavest.com.cn
web: www.chinavest.com

Mission Statement: To provide long-term investment capital and management expertise to growing companies doing business in or with the economies of Greater China: China, Hong Kong and Taiwan.
Geographic Preference: Greater China
Founded: 1981
Average Investment: $5 million
Minimum Investment: $3 million
Investment Criteria: Early-Stage, Expansion Stage, Acquisitions, Buyouts
Industry Group Preference: Logistics, Healthcare, Media, Manufacturing, Telecommunications, Information Technology, Consumer Services
Portfolio Companies: AGI, Arima Communications, AsiaInfo, Brinks Home Security, Chubb, Clearwater, Coca-Cola, Danone, Domino's Pizza, evian, First Quality, Fosun, Heineken, Heinz, HNA Group, Hodo, Honeywell, IBM, ITW, John Deere, Kellogg Company, McDonald's, PrimeCredit Limited, Rockwekll Automation, Santa Fe Relocation, Suning.com, TGI Fridays, Valeo, Wendy's, XCMG

Other Locations:
19-27 Wyndham Street
Room 1103
Wilson House
Central
Hong Kong
Phone: 852-28101638 Fax: 852-28683788

Beijing China Resources Building
5th Floor, No. 8 Jian Guo Men Bei Avenue
Suite 508B
Beijing 100005
China
Phone: 8610-85191535 Fax: 8610-85191530

2801 Huaihai International Plaza
1045 Huaihai Middle Road
Xuhui Distric
Shanghai 200031
China
Phone: 8621-63232255 Fax: 8621-63293951
Key Executives:
Robert A Theleen, Chairman/CEO
Education: BA, Duquesne University; MBA, Thunderbird School of Global Management
Directorships: Beijing Enterprises
Jenny Hsui, President
Education: University of Singapore
André Dallaire, Senior Managing Director & COO
Education: BS, Business Adminstration and Management, Université Laval
Background: CEO, Chubb; Senior Vice President, Asia Pacific; AIG;
Kenneth Petrilla, Managing Director
Education: BA, Business Administration and Management, Bowling Green State University; MA, Golden Gate University
Background: U.S. Representative, American Chamber of Commerce in Shanghai; Executive Director, California-China Office of Trade and Investment; Executive Vice President, Wells Fargo
Steve Nelson, Vice President
e-mail: snelson@chinavest.com.cn
Education: BS, Business, Chapman University
Background: Halter Financial Services; Sterne Agee; The Seidler Companies

474 CHL MEDICAL PARTNERS
1055 Washington Boulevard
6th Floor
Stamford, CT 06901

Phone: 203-324-7700 Fax: 203-324-3636
web: www.chlmedical.com

Mission Statement: Create opportunities for entrepreneurs who have the skills necessary to build leading companies. We invest at the seed, start-up phases of companies, frequently as the lead investor. As portfolio companies grow, we continue our active support at the board level and through follow-on financings.
Geographic Preference: United States
Fund Size: $250 million
Founded: 1990
Average Investment: $4 million
Minimum Investment: $250,000
Investment Criteria: Startup, Early Stage
Industry Group Preference: Biotechnology, Pharmaceuticals, Genomics, Healthcare, Drug Development, Diagnostics, Medical Devices, Health Related, Instrumentation
Portfolio Companies: Ambra Health, Care Management Technologies, Inc., CareWell Urgent Care, Comprehensive Clinical Development, DICOM Grid, Ella Health, Fidelis Seniorcare, MedMark Services, Millenium Pharmacy Systems
Key Executives:
Jeffrey J Collinson, Partner
e-mail: jcollinson@chlmedical.com
Education: Degree in Economics, Yale University; MBA Harvard Business School
Background: Baxter International, Inc.
Timothy F Howe, Partner
203-324-7700 x223
e-mail: thowe@chlmedical.com
Education: BA, MBA, Columbia University
Background: Schroder Ventures, Collinson Howe Venture Partners, Biotechnology Investment Group
Gregory M Weinhoff MD, Partner
e-mail: gweinhoff@chlmedical.com
Education: Harvard College, Harvard Medical School, Harvard Business School
Background: Whitney & Company, Fidelity Select

Venture Capital & Private Equity Firms / Domestic Firms

Biotechnology, Healthcare Corporate Finance Group at Morgan Stanley & Company
Myles D Greenberg, Partner
e-mail: mgreenberg@chlmedical.com
Education: BAS, University of Pennsylvania, MD, Yale University, MBA, Harvard Business School
Background: A.M. Pappas & Associates, Assistant Professor At University Of North Carolina School Of Medicine, Assistant Clincial Director, Beth Israel Deaconess Medical Center
Directorships: CareWell Urgent Care Centers

475 CHRYSALIS VENTURES
101 S Fifth Street
Suite 1650
Louisville, KY 40202-3122
Phone: 502-583-7644
e-mail: info@chrysalisventures.com
web: www.chrysalisventures.com

Mission Statement: Chrysalis Ventures is a leading source of equity capital for young, growing companies in Mid-America. Chrysalis invests primarily in early-and growth-stage Healthcare and Technology companies.

Geographic Preference: Midwest, South
Fund Size: $400 million
Founded: 1993
Average Investment: $3 - $5 million
Minimum Investment: $2 million
Investment Criteria: Early-Stage, Expansion-Stage
Industry Group Preference: Healthcare, Technology
Portfolio Companies: AfterBOT, Connecture, Edj Analytics, Foundation Radiology Group, GoNoodle, Health Information Designs, Intervention Insights, ITC Compounding Pharmacy, Lucina Health, MeQuilibrium, MyHealthDIRECT, Regent Education, StraighterLine, Xlerant

Key Executives:
David Jones, Jr., Chairman/Managing Director
Education: BA, Yale University; JD, Yale University Law School
Background: Chairman, Humana, Inc.; US Department of State Legal Adviser; Commercial Banker, Bank of Boston
Wright Steenrod, Partner
Education: BA, Princeton University
Background: Ygnition; Genscape; Appriss; VP, Business Development, Darwin Networks; SunTrust Bank; US Marine Corps
Directorships: bCatalyst, Inc., Cybera Inc., Information Outfitters
Charlie Crawford, Vice President
Education: BA, Williams College
Background: Innova Memphis

476 CI CAPITAL PARTNERS
500 Park Avenue
8th Floor
New York, NY 10022
Phone: 212-752-1850 Fax: 212-832-9450
e-mail: info@cicapllc.com
web: www.cicapllc.com

Mission Statement: CI Capital Partners, formerly Caxton-Iseman Capital, is a leading private equity investment firm specializing in leveraged buyouts of middle market companies located primarily in North America.

Geographic Preference: North America
Founded: 1993
Average Investment: $50 - 100 million
Investment Criteria: Leveraged Buyouts
Industry Group Preference: Consumer Services, Business Products & Services, Distribution, Aerospace, Defense and Government, Light Manufacturing
Portfolio Companies: AlliedPRA, Epiphany Dermatology, Galls, Hero Digital, Impact Group, Maroon Group, Pivot Physical Therapy, Ply Gem Industries, SavATree, Simplified Logistics, Summit Companies, Tech Air

Key Executives:
Frederick J Iseman, Chairman & Chief Executive Officer
Education: BA, English Literature, Yale University
Background: Chairman, Anteon International Corporation; Hambro International Equity Partners
Directorships: Conney Safety Products, KIK Custom Products, CoVant Technologies, American Residential Services, Ply Gem Industries
Jordan S. Bernstein, General Counsel
Education: BA, History, University of Pennsylvania; JD, Havard Law School
Background: General Counsel, AGM Partners; Associate General Counsel, Wasserstein Perello & Co.; M&A, Paul, Weiss, Rifkind, Wharton & Garrison
Timothy T. Hall, Managing Director
Education: BS, Lehigh University; MBA, Columbia Business School
Background: Vice President, Frontline Capital; Assistant Vice President, GE Equity
Directorships: KIK Custom Products, Prodigy Health Group, Ply Gem Industries
Joost F. Thesseling, Managing Director
Education: BA, Economics, MBA, Erasmus University School of Economics, Rotterdam
Background: Director, Transplace; Director, Valley National Gases

477 CIC PARTNERS
3879 Maple Ave.
Suite 400
Dallas, TX 75219
Phone: 214-871-6812 Fax: 214-880-4491
e-mail: info@cicpartners.com
web: www.cicpartners.com

Mission Statement: As a mid-market private equity firm, Dallas-based CIC Partners has invested in more than 40 companies with revenues of $10 million to $1 billion in industries including energy exploration, food, healthcare services, restaurants and retail.

Average Investment: $5 - $100 million
Investment Criteria: Growth Capital, Recapitalizations, Buyouts
Industry Group Preference: Energy, Food & Beverage, Healthcare Services, Restaurants, Retail, Consumer & Leisure
Portfolio Companies: Activa Resources, Castex Energy, CIC Minerals, Continental Structural Plastics, Cornerstone Automation Systems, CraftMark Bakery, Dale Gas Partners, DynaGrid Construction Group, East Hampton Sandwich Co., Granite City Food & Brewery, L&L Foods, Magnolia Petroleum Co., OmniSYS, Pogo Resources, Red Mango, River Point Farms, RMX Resources, Schuepbach Energy, Select Product Group, Taco Mac, Tiff's Treats, Willie's Grill & Icehouse

Key Executives:
Fouad Bashour, Founding Partner
214-871-6825
Education: BA, Duke University
Background: The Boston Consulting Group
Directorships: Granite City Food & Brewery, Schuepbach Energy, Willie's Grill & Icehouse
Marshall Payne, Founding Partner
214-871-6807
Education: BS, Stanford University; MBA, Harvard Business School
Background: Cardinal Investment Company
Directorships: Activa Resources, CraftMark Bakery, Pogo Resources, RMX Resources, Schuepbach Energy
Michael Rawlings, Founding Partner
214-871-6864
Education: BA, Boston College

Venture Capital & Private Equity Firms / Domestic Firms

Background: President, Pizza Hut; CEO, DDB Needham Dallas Group; CEO, Legends Hospitality Management
Directorships: Willie's Grill & Icehouse

478 CID CAPITAL
10201 N. Illinois St.
Suite 200
Indianapolis, IN 46290
Phone: 317-818-5030 Fax: 317-644-2914
web: www.cidcap.com

Mission Statement: CID Capital's Private Equity Group makes majority investments in lower-middle-market companies with a strong history of consistent performance. Our focus is on companies that have the potential to grow significantly but have been constrained by lack of capital, operating systems, or management experience. CID provides the resources and capital to overcome these critical constraints.

Geographic Preference: United States
Fund Size: $75 million
Founded: 1981
Average Investment: $2-$10 million
Investment Criteria: Control Buyouts, Recapitalizations
Industry Group Preference: Consumer Products, Industrial, Distribution, Food & Beverage, Security, Medical & Health Related, Manufacturing, Medical Devices, Healthcare Services, Education, Value-Added Distribution
Portfolio Companies: ABC Industries, BigMouth, Chef'n, Classic Accessories, Fit & Fresh, Grandview Gallery, Matilda Jane, ProSource, Strahman Valves, Team Drive-Away

Key Executives:
John C Aplin, Managing Director
317-708-4852
e-mail: john@cidcap.com
Education: BA, Drake University; MBA, PhD, University of Iowa
Background: President/CEO, Fuller Brush Company; Consultant, Marathon Oil Company; Eli Lilly and Company; Borg-Warner; Faculty Member, Graduate School of Business, Indiana University; Chairperson, Master of Business Administration Program, Indiana University
Steve A Cobb, Managing Director
317-708-4853
e-mail: steve@cidcap.com
Education: BA, Economics, DePauw; MBA, Harvard Business School
Background: Director and Founding Member, Indiana Chapter of Association for Corporate Growth; Finance Manager, Proctor & Gamble; Business Valuation Group; Deloitte & Touche
Eric J Bruun, Managing Director
317-708-4857
e-mail: eric@cidcap.com
Education: BS, MBA, Purdue University
Background: Conseco Companies
Scot E Swenberg, Managing Director
317-708-4856
e-mail: scot@cidcap.com
Education: BEE, Purdue University; MCS, Arizona State University; MBA, University of Chicago
Background: Software Engineer/Financial Analyst, Bull Worldwide Information Systems; Irwin Financial Corporation

479 CINCYTECH
1311 Vine St.
Suite 300
Cincinnati, OH 45202-3559
Phone: 513-263-2720 Fax: 513-381-5093
e-mail: contactus@cincytech.com
web: www.cincytechusa.com

Mission Statement: CincyTech is a public-private seed-stage investor whose mission is to strengthen the regional economy by driving talent and capital into scalable, investable technology companies in Southwest Ohio.

Geographic Preference: Southwest Ohio
Fund Size: $10.4 million
Investment Criteria: Seed-Stage, Startup
Industry Group Preference: Enterprise Software, Technology-Enabled Services, Marketing, Digital Media & Marketing, Biosciences, Healthcare Information Technology
Portfolio Companies: Abre. Action Streamer, Aerpio Therapeutics, Aha!ogy, Airway Therapeutics, Akebia Therapeutics, AssureRx, Astronomer, Batterii, Blue Ash Therapeutics, Clarigent Health, ConnXus, Cordata, Data Inventions, Data Role, Eccrine Systems, Enable Injections, Family Tech, Genetesis, Ilesfay, Include Fitness, Invirsa, Jersey Watch, Lisnr, Losant, Myonexus, Nano Detection Technology, Navistone, Ready Set Surgical, Road Trippers, Sirrus, Stack, Standard Bariatrics, StoreLynkm StreamSpot, Talmetrix, Think Vine, Workflex Solutions, Xact Medical, ZipScene

Key Executives:
Mike Venerable, Chief Executive Officer
513-263-2727
e-mail: mvenerable@cincytechusa.com
Education: University of Dayton
Background: Co-Founder/CEO, Talus; Co-Author, Data Warehouse Design Solutions; Managing Director, Scius Capital
Doug Groh, Director
Education: University of Notre Dame
Background: Director of Sales & Marketing, Verifi; Investor and VP of Sales & Marketing, RS Solutions; Investor and VP of Sales & Marketing, Ohmart/VEGA Corp.
John M. Rice, Director of Life Sciences
Education: BS, MS, PhD, Microbiology & Virology, Ohio State University
Background: Co-Founder & Managing Partner, Triathalon Medical Ventures; Managing Director, Senmed Medical Ventures; Research & Business Development, Battelle Memorial Institute

480 CINTRIFUSE
1311 Vine Street
Cincinnati, OH 45202
Phone: 513-246-2700
e-mail: info@cintrifuse.com
web: www.cintrifuse.com

Mission Statement: Cintrifuse is a community of talented people. We connect, we teach, we learn. We strive to foster inspiration. We support our city, and the people within it.

Founded: 2012
Investment Criteria: Startup
Industry Group Preference: Technology

Key Executives:
Pete Blackshaw, Chief Executive Officer
Education: BA, Politics, University of California; MBA, Harvard Business School
Background: Global Head of Digital Marketing & Social Media, Nestle; EVP, Digital Strategic Services, Nielsen Online

481 CIRCLE PEAK CAPITAL
New York, NY 10019
Phone: 917-992-6400 Fax: 646-349-2743
web: circlepeakcapital.com

Mission Statement: Circle Peak Capital invests in private companies based in the United States, focusing primarily on businesses with established or emerging brands that also demonstrate high growth potential.

Geographic Preference: United States
Founded: 2002
Average Investment: $10 - 100 million

169

Venture Capital & Private Equity Firms / Domestic Firms

Investment Criteria: Management Buyouts, Recapitalizations, Acquisition Platforms
Industry Group Preference: Consumer Products, Financial Services
Portfolio Companies: Hill & Valley, Luxury Optical Holdings, Rocket Dog, Shari's Management Corporation
Key Executives:
   R Adam Smith, Founder/CEO
   Education: BA, International Relations & Economics, Boston University; MBA, Columbia University
   Background: Financial Sponsors Group, Lehman Brothers; Caxton-Iseman Capital; Castle Harlan; Columbus Advisors
   Directorships: Rocket Dog Holdings, Fischbein, WealthTrust, Luxury Optical Holdings, Shari's Mangement Corp, Hill & Valley, Stride Capital

482 CIRCLEUP
San Francisco, CA 94108

e-mail: partners@circleup.com
web: circleup.com

Mission Statement: CircleUp focuses on the small American businesses in the early-stage of development.
Fund Size: $125 million
Founded: 2017
Industry Group Preference: Consumer Products
Portfolio Companies: Kettle & Fire, Nut Pods, Rhythm Superfoods, Smarty Pants, Winky Lux
Key Executives:
   Ryan Caldbeck, Co-Founder/Chief Executive Officer
   Rory Eakin, Co-Founder
   Education: Princeton University
   Background: Humanity United, The Boston Consulting Group

483 CISCO INVESTMENTS
300 East Tasman Drive
San Jose, CA 95134

web: www.ciscoinvestments.com

Mission Statement: The venture capital arm of Cisco Systems, Cisco Investments invests in innovative technology companies around the world, focussing on big data and analytics, internet of things, data centre, SaaS, security, semiconductor, and more.
Geographic Preference: United States, Canada, Europe, China, India, Israel
Fund Size: $220 million
Founded: 1993
Investment Criteria: Start-Ups, Early Stage, Late Stage, Pre-IPO
Industry Group Preference: Information Technology, Big Data & Analytics, IoT, Data Centre, SaaS, Infrastructure, Security, Semiconductor, Connected Mobility
Portfolio Companies: 3TS Capital Partners, 6WIND, Aavishkaar, Actility, AIMotive, Alchemist Accelerator, Algebra Ventures, Almaz Capital, Altiostar Networks, Ambiq Micro, AnDAPT, Apptio, Aravo, Archetype Ventures Fund, Ascendify, Aspect Ventures, Avi Networks, Ayla Networks, BehavioSec, Belly, Blackbird Ventures, BNI Video, Bolt, Bull City Venture Partners, CafeX Communications, Capnamic Ventures, Celeno, Cinarra, City Cloud International, CloudCherry, CloudFX, CNEX Labs, Cohda Wireless, Cohesity, Corvil, Covacsis, CRCM Ventures, CTERA, DataRobot, Deskera, Dremio, Dynamic Signal, Elastifile, eSilicon, Evolution Equity, Evrythng, Exabeam, Exent, Flashpoint, FuturePlay, Gainsight, Georgian Partners, Global Talent Track, Gobi Partners, Gong, Grid Net, GuardiCore, Helpshift, HyTrust, IDG Ventures India, Idinvest Partners, ILFS Technologies, illusive networks, Ineda Systems, Innovid, Inspur-Cisco Networking Technology, Intersec, Invitalia Ventures, Involvio, ItsOn, Kaszek Ventures, Kespry, KeyTone Cloud, Kii, Kumu Networks, Kustomer, Kyligence, LiveAction, Mapr, McRock Capital iNFund, Mist Systems, MobStac, Monashees, Moogsoft, Moxtra, mozaiq operations, N3N, Nantero, Near Pte Ltd, Netronome, Nexpa, Nimbus, Notion Capital, OMERS Ventures Fund II, One Mobikwik Systems Private Ltd., Ozon, Panaseer, Paris Saclay Fund, Partech, Paxata, Phunware, Pixvana, Plexo Capital, Prospera, PubNub, Puppet, Quantcast, Qwilt, Qyuki, Real Image, Redpoint eventures, RiverMeadow, SecurView, Sensity Systems, Servion,

Other Locations:
126 Post Street
5th Floor
San Francisco, CA 94108

101 Collins Street
Levels 11, 14
Melbourne
Victoria 3000
Australia

Great Eagle Centre
23 Harbour Road
Wan Chai
Hong Kong
China

Dawning Centre West Tower
No. 500 Hongbaeshi Road
Changning District
Shanghai 201103
China

10 Finsbury Square
London, England EC2A 1AF
United Kingdom

Brigade South Parade
No. 10 Mahatma Gandhi Road
Bangalore, Karnataka 560001
India

Rothschild Boulevard 3
Tel Aviv-Yafo
Tel Aviv 6688106
Israel

UE BizHub East
8 Changi Business Park Avenue 1
Singapore 486018
Asia

Key Executives:
   Rob Salvagno, Head, Corporate Development/Cisco Investments
   Education: BA, Economics, Stanford University
   Janey Hoe, Vice President
   Education: BS, University of California, Berkeley; MS, Massachusetts Institute of Technology
   Background: Management Consultant, McKinsey & Company; MIT LCS Laboratory; AT&T Laboratories; HP Laboratories
   Derek Idemoto, Vice President
   Education: BS, Finance & Marketing, University of California, Berkeley; MBA, Anderson School of Management, UCLA
   Background: Managing Director, ITOCHU Technology; VP, Corporate Development, Overture Services
   Phil Kirk, Senior Director
   Education: MBA, Wharton School, University of Pennsylvania; AB, Economics, University of Chicago
   Background: Microsoft Corporate Strategy Team; Associate, DTEC Venture Capital

484 CIT GROUP
One CIT Drive
Livingston, NJ 07039

Toll-Free: 866-542-4847
web: www.cit.com

Venture Capital & Private Equity Firms / Domestic Firms

Mission Statement: Financing solutions for small and middle market businesses and the transportation sector.
Geographic Preference: United States, Canada, Worldwide
Fund Size: $28 billion
Founded: 1908
Average Investment: $3.5 million
Minimum Investment: $1 million
Industry Group Preference: Aerospace, Defense and Government, Business Aircraft, Commercial & Industrial, Commercial Air, Communications, Consumer Goods, Energy, Entertainment, Healthcare, Maritime, Office Imaging & Technology, Rail, Restaurants, Retail, Consumer & Leisure
Other Locations:
11 West 42nd Street
New York, NY 10036
Key Executives:
Ellen R. Alemany, Chairwoman and CEO
Education: Fordham University
Background: Royal Bank of Scotland
David Harnisch, President, CIT Commercial Finance
Education: BA, Boston College; MBA, New York University
Background: Santander Bank; Citizens Financial Group; RBS Citizens

485 CITARETX INVESTMENT PARTNERS
1120 NASA Parkway
Suite 600
Houston, TX 77058

Phone: 281-984-7331 Fax: 281-984-7374
e-mail: jsheldon@citaretx.com
web: www.citaretx.com

Mission Statement: CitareTx Investment Partners is a venture development, investment, and start-up management company concentrated on promising new medical devices, technology, and business opportunities throughout the State of Texas and beyond.
Geographic Preference: Texas
Founded: 2008
Average Investment: $500,000 - $7 million
Investment Criteria: Seed-Stage and Series A
Industry Group Preference: Medical Devices
Portfolio Companies: EMIT Corporation, Houston Medical Robotics Inc., Coagulex Inc.
Key Executives:
Jeffrey Sheldon, General Partner
Education: BS, Aerospace Engineering, University of Minnesota; MBA, University of Houston, Clear Lake
Background: Founder, iDev Technologies; Nittany Polymedics

486 CITI VENTURES
260 Homer Avenue
Suite 101
Palo Alto, CA 94301

Phone: 650-798-8140
e-mail: citiventures@citi.com
web: www.citi.com/ventures

Mission Statement: Citi Ventures is Citi's global corporate venturing arm, chartered to collaborate with internal and external partners to conceive, partner, launch, and scale new ventures that have the potential to disrupt and transform the financial services industry, drive client success, and generate new value for Citi.
Geographic Preference: Worldwide
Founded: 2010
Industry Group Preference: Marketing, Security, Financial Services, Enterprise IT, Commerce, Data Analytics, Machine Learning
Portfolio Companies: Appboy, Ayasdi, Betterment, BlueVine, C2FO, Chain, Chef, Claritymoney, Cylance, Datameer, DB Networks, DocuSign, Dyadic, FastPay, Feedzai, HomeLight, Illusive Networks, Jet, Joist, Kinetica, Linkable Networks, LiveNinja, M-DAQ, Optimizely, Pepperdata Networks, Persado, Pindrop Security, Plaid, Platfora, SilverTrail Systems, Shopkick, Square, Tanium, Tealium, Trade It

Other Locations:
Citi Canary Wharf Office
33 Canada Square
10th Floor
London E14 5LB
United Kingdom

1 Court Square
18th Floor
Long Island City, NY 11101

1 Market Street
Steuart Tower
Suite 1550
San Francisco, CA 94105

Key Executives:
Vanessa Colella, Chief Innovation Officer
Education: MA, Columbia University; MA, MIT; PhD, MIT Media Lab
Background: Entrepreneur in Residence, US Ventures Partners; Head of NA Marketing/SVP of Insights, Yahoo; Partner, McKinsey & Co.
Emily Turner, Director/Head of Strategic Growth Initiatives
Education: BA, Sociology, Dartmouth College; MBA, Columbia Business School
Background: Management Consultant, McKinsey & Co.; Merrill Lynch; ABN Amro; UBS
Ramneek Gupta, Managing Director
Education: B-Tech, Mechanical Engineering, Indian Institute of Technology; MS, Mechanical Engineering, Stanford University
Background: Partner, Battery Ventures
Maja Lapcevic, Director/Co-Head of Strategic Growth Initiatives
Education: BA, Economics/Internation Affairs, Georgetown University
Background: Founder, SML Strategic Media
Arvind Purushotham, Managing Director
Education: B-Tech, Electrical Engineering, Indian Institute of Technology; MSEE, Case Western Reserve University; MBA, Harvard Business School
Background: Managing Director, Menlo Ventures

487 CITY HILL VENTURES
4653 Carmel Mountain Road
Suite 501
San Diego, CA 92130

web: www.cityhillventures.com

Mission Statement: City Hill Ventures is a healthcare focused investment firm whose mission is to restore human health through innovation, by building or helping other health care entrepreneurs build great companies that collectively have a transformative impact on patients, the healthcare industry, and society.
Founded: 2010
Industry Group Preference: Healthcare
Portfolio Companies: Bonti Inc., Eclipse Therapeutics Inc., Flex Pharma Inc., Independa Inc., Ignyta Inc., Inhibrx LLC, Medenovo LLC, Patara Pharma LLC
Key Executives:
Jonathan E. Lim, MD, Founder/Managing Partner
Education: BS, MS, Stanford University; MD, McGill University; MPH, Harvard College
Background: President, Halozyme Therapeutics
Directorships: Eclipse Therapeutics
Karen Gilmore, Controller
Education: BS, CalTech, Pomona; CPA

171

Venture Capital & Private Equity Firms / Domestic Firms

Background: CFO/VP, Finance, HRE Performance Wheels; CFO/Controller, QLogic Corp.; PacifiCare; FutureKids; Madge Networks; Auditor, PricewaterhouseCoopers
Zachary Hornby, Operating Partner
Education: BS, MS, Biology, Stanford University; MBA, Harvard Business School
Background: Vice President, Corporate Development, Ignyta; Halozyme Therapeutics; LEK Consulting

488 CITY LIGHT CAPITAL
335 Madison Ave
16th Floor
New York, NY 10017

Phone: 212-403-9514
e-mail: info@citylightcap.com
web: www.citylightcap.com

Mission Statement: We look for the most dynamic and experienced entrepreneurs passionate about leveraging the power of technology and markets to create substantial economic, social and environmental value.
Geographic Preference: United States
Founded: 2004
Investment Criteria: Early-Stage
Industry Group Preference: Security, Environment, Education, Information Services, Energy
Portfolio Companies: 2U, Arcadia Power, Envoy, Glacier Bay Technology, HeroX, iBeat, Identilock, Kinetic, Koru, Loris.ai, Legends of Learning, LiveSafe, Meritize, OhmConnect, Omnidian, Open Energy Efficiency, Practice, RapidSOS, Ready Responders, SafeTraces, Senet, ShotSpotter, SkyRyse, Square Roots, Straighterline, SVAcademy, Tinkergarten, Topcoder, Trilogy Education Services, Xage
Key Executives:
  Josh Cohen, Managing Partner
  Education: Angell Scholar, University of Michigan
  Background: SV Group; Director, Business Development, Mobility Electronics
  Directorships: 2U, HeroX, Straighterline, Practice, OhmConnect, Koru, Trilogy
  Tom Groos, Partner
  Education: Cornell University; MBA, Columbia Business School
  Background: President, Viking Group
  Directorships: Minimax-Viking
  Bill Lyons, Environmental Expert
  Education: BS, Operations Analysis, United States Naval Academy
  Background: President, Climate Solutions Group, AES; Co-Founder, Seneca Creek Energy
  Greg Gunn, Education Expert
  Education: BS, University of Chicago; MS, MBA, MIT
  Background: Founder, Wireless Generation; Product Manager, InterDimensions
  Directorships: StraighterLine

489 CIVC PARTNERS
191 N Wacker Drive
Suite 1100
Chicago, IL 60606

Phone: 312-873-7300 Fax: 312-873-7301
e-mail: civc_partners@civc.com
web: www.civc.com

Mission Statement: To develop partnerships with exceptional business leaders and management teams.
Geographic Preference: United States, Canada
Fund Size: $650 million
Founded: 1970
Average Investment: $15 to $85 million
Minimum Investment: $15 million
Investment Criteria: Middle Market, Growth Capital, Acquisition Capital, Management Buyouts, Leveraged Acquisitions, Recapitalizations, Shareholder Liquidity Events
Industry Group Preference: Communications, Consumer Services, Business Products & Services, Financial Services, Media, Industrial Services, Education, Insurance, Telecommunications
Portfolio Companies: Computer Aided Technology, KPA, LendCare, Magna Legal Services, Magnate Worldwide, Right Pointe, Specialized Elevator Services, StoneRidge Insurance Brokers
Key Executives:
  Chris Perry, Partner
  e-mail: cperry@civc.com
  Education: MBA, Pepperdine University; BS, Accountancy, University of Illinois; CPA
  Background: Continental Bank's Mezzanine Investments & Structured Finance Groups; VP Corporate Finance, Northern Trust Company; Public Accounting, Coopers & Lybrand
  Directorships: Brickman Group Ltd., RAM Reinsurance Company, TransWestern Publishing, Wastequip, LA Fitness International, Kellermeyer Building Services
  Chris Geneser, Partner & CFO
  e-mail: cgeneser@civc.com
  Education: BBA, Accounting, University of Notre Dame; CPA
  Background: Senior Manager, Ernst & Young; Managing of Financial Planning, US Robotics Inc.
  John Compall, Partner
  e-mail: jcompall@civc.com
  Education: BS, Computer Science, University of Illinois; MBA, University of Chicago
  Background: Ameritech Corporation; McKinsey & Company
  Scott Schwartz, Partner
  e-mail: sschwartz@civc.com
  Education: BS, Economics, MBA, Wharton School, University of Pennsylvania
  Background: VP, American Industrial Partners; Engagement Manager, McKinsey & Company
  Marc McManus, Partner
  e-mail: mmcmanus@civc.com
  Education: BS, Economics & Computer Science, Vanderbilt University; MBA, Harvard Business School
  Background: Director, HSBC North America; Strategy Consultant, Accenture; Associate, Lehman Brothers
  J.D. Wright, Partner
  e-mail: jwright@civc.com
  Education: BA, Economics, Vanderbilt University
  Background: Investment Banking Analyst, Harris Williams & Co.
  Alex Lieberman, Vice President
  e-mail: alieberman@civc.com
  Education: BBA, Finance/Accounting, Kellogg School of Management
  Background: Senior Associate, RoundTable Healthcare Partners; Analyst, Deutsche Bank
  Andrew Roche, Vice President
  e-mail: aroche@civc.com
  Education: BEng, Chemical Engineering/Mathematics, Vanderbilt University
  Background: Raymond James
  Directorships: CATI
  Brian James, Vice President
  e-mail: bjames@civc.com
  Education: BBA, Finance, University of Notre Dame; MBA, Kellogg School of Management, Northwestern University
  Background: Vice President, H.I.G. Capital; Associate, CIVC; Analyst, JPMorgan

490 CJV CAPITAL

web: www.cjvcapital.com

Mission Statement: Invests in companies within the cannabis industry that focus on consumer products and agro-breeding solutions for research and medical use.
Founded: 2016
Investment Criteria: Seed, Early-Stage
Industry Group Preference: Cannabis
Portfolio Companies: Corsica Innovations Inc.

491 CLAREMONT CREEK VENTURES
300 Frank H. Ogawa Plaza
Suite 350
Oakland, CA 94612

Phone: 510-740-5001
web: www.claremontcreek.com

Mission Statement: A venture capital firm investing in early stage information technology companies. Claremont maintains an expertise in the IT sector, with an interest in energy efficiency, sensor based systems, and securities markets.
Geographic Preference: California
Fund Size: $130 million
Average Investment: $500,000 - $3 million
Investment Criteria: Early Stage
Industry Group Preference: Information Technology, Healthcare, Energy Efficiency, Security, Mobility
Portfolio Companies: Alphabet Energy Inc., Alter G, Assurerx Health, Billeo, Blue Pillar, CellScope, Clean Power Finance Inc., Comfy, Cureus, DNAnexus, EcoATM, EcoFactor, Element Energy, Energy Cache, Fluxion Biosciences, Genalyte, GeneWEAVE Inc., GigaGen, Lefora, Natera, Numedii Inc., Project Frog, PropertyBridge, Renewable Funding, RidePal, Root3, Sentilla, ShotSpotter, SmartZip Analytics, Yerdle, ZipLine Medical

Key Executives:
  Nat Goldhaber, Managing Director
  Education: MA, Education, University of California, Berkeley
  Background: CEO, Cybergold; Founder, Centram Systems West; Founding CEO, Kaleida Labs; Vice President, Sun Microsystems
  Randy Hawks, Managing Director
  Education: BSEE, University of Arkansas; Stanford University Exective Management Program
  Background: General Partner, Novus Ventures; Venture Partner, Horizon Ventures
  Harsh Patel, Director
  Education: BS, Engineering, University of Illinois; MBA, Stanford Grad. School of Business
  Background: General Partner, PRE Ventures; In-Q-Tel; President, Bina Technologies; Co-Founder, Orbit Commerce; R&D, Accenture
  Ted Driscoll, PhD, Venture Partner
  Education: BA, University of Pennsylvania; MA, Computer Graphics & Remote Sensing, Harvard University; PhD, Digital Imaging, Stanford University
  Background: Founder, Be Here Technologies; Division President, Diasonics; Vice President, Engineering, Identix
  Brad Webb, PhD, Venture Partner
  Education: PhD, Biochemistry & Molecular Biology, University of California, Santa Barbara
  Background: Founder, Vision Biology; R&D, 3M Company
  Paul Straub, Director
  Education: BS, Commerce, University of Virginia McIntire School of Commerce; MBA, Duke University Fuqua School of Business
  Background: Product Management, VERITAS Sofware; Consultant, Red Hat Software
  Directorships: TargetCast Networks, Adura Technologies
  Gianna Conci Orozco, Finance Manager
  Education: BS, Economics, Santa Clara University
  Background: Virgin Green Fund; Sierra Ventures; Silver Lake Partners

492 CLARION CAPITAL PARTNERS LLC
527 Madison Avenue
10th Floor
New York, NY 10022

Phone: 212-821-0111 Fax: 212-371-7597
web: www.clarion-capital.com

Mission Statement: A private equity firm which seeks to make primarily control private equity investments in a diversified portfolio of middle-market companies.
Fund Size: $50 million
Founded: 1999
Average Investment: $15-50 million
Investment Criteria: Leverage Buyouts, Growth Equity, Recapitalizations, Revenue greater than $7.5 million
Industry Group Preference: Business Products & Services, Healthcare Services, Specialty Finance, Consumer Products, Specialty Retail, Media & Entertainment
Portfolio Companies: All-Clad Holdings Inc., AML RightSource, Ametros Financial Corp., Cascade Entertainment Group, Cross, Cross Mediaworks, Crowe Paradis Servicing Corp., Encore Capital Group Inc., Great Northwest Insurance Co., Hartmann, HROI, IMAX Corp., Lenox, Madison Logic, Moravia, Reliant Healthcare Professionals, Strategic Outsourcing Inc., SQAD, The Oceanaire Inc.

Key Executives:
  Marc A Utay, Managing Partner
  e-mail: mutay@clarion-capital.com
  Education: BS, Wharton School, University of Pennsyvlania
  Background: Managing Director, Wasserstein Perella & Company; Managing Director, BT Securities; Managing Partner, Kent Capital Partners; Partner, Drexel Burnham Labert Inc.; Financial Associate, Beverage Division, General Foods Corporation
  Eric D Kogan, Partner
  e-mail: ekogan@clarion-capital.com
  Education: MBA, University of Chicago; BA, BSE, Wharton School, University of Pennsylvania
  Background: Triarc Companies, Inc.; Associate, Mergers/Acquisitions, Farley Inc.; Analyst, Oppenheimer Inc.
  Jonathan M Haas, Managing Director
  e-mail: jhaas@clarion-capital.com
  Education: MBA, Northwestern University Kellogg School of Management; BA, Dartmouth College
  Background: Investment Banking Division, Credit Suisse First Boston; Associate, Industrials Group; Associate, A.T. Kearney Inc.
  David B Ragins, Managing Director
  e-mail: dragins@clarion-capital.com
  Education: MBA, Wharton School, University of Pennsylvania; BS, Finance, Babson College
  Background: Seaport Capital Partners; Merrill Lynch & Co.; NationasBanc Capital Markets, Inc.
  Doug K. Mellinger, Managing Director/Head of Marketing
  e-mail: dmellinger@clarion-capital.com
  Education: Entrepreneurship, Syracuse University
  Background: Managing Director, Palm Ventures; Founder, Foundation Source; Founder, Young Entrepreneurs Organization
  Matthew S. Feldman, Managing Director
  e-mail: mfeldman@clarion-capital.com
  Education: BBA, University of Michigan
  Background: Investment Banking Division, Bear Stearns & Co; Principal, Clarion Capital
  Brandon M. Katz, Principal
  e-mail: bkatz@clarion-capital.com
  Education: BS, Business Admin., Boston University
  Background: PioneerPath Capital; Investment Banking Division, Bear, Stearns & Co.
  Edward W Martin, Principal
  e-mail: emartin@clarion-capital.com

Venture Capital & Private Equity Firms / Domestic Firms

Education: BS, Systems Engineering, University of Pennsylvania; MBA, Columbia Business School
Background: Investment Banking, Merrill Lynch & Co.

493 CLARITAS CAPITAL
30 Burton Hills Blvd
Suite 100
Nashville, TN 37215

Phone: 615-690-7179
web: www.claritascapital.com

Mission Statement: Our overall approach is to be partners with our entrepreneurs, to provide value to them, to assist in their growth and success, and to drive the investment return targets we have for each investment through those efforts. These returns are achieved by sourcing, underwriting, post-investment portfolio management, network building, assessing market trends, and a combination of other operational tasks and processes we currently have and are continually enhancing. As a firm, we focus on sourcing the highest quality investment opportunities, and following our investment providing those companies and management teams with value creation services from building out management teams, accessing new customers, and assisting with acquisitions.

Founded: 2002
Investment Criteria: Early-Stage, Growth Equity
Industry Group Preference: Healthcare, Technology, Real Estate
Portfolio Companies: A Head For Profits, Apcela, Blue Chip Partners Surgery Centers, BuyHappy, Continuum, Counsel On Call, Cybera, Dobie Media, Employment Staffinf, Empyrean, Entrada, Expensable, Forbes Travel Guide, Genomind, Hospital Corporation of America, HCCA International, HCTec Partners, Innovatel, I-Payment, LearnVest, Nsight, Oasis Marinas, Pace, Pear, Rubicon, ShareCare, Snag A Slip, StudioNow, Tristar License Group, Tristar 600, TwelveStone Health Partners

Key Executives:
  John H Chadwick, Partner
  615-665-8250
  e-mail: jhchadwick@claritascapital.com
  Education: BA, University of Virginia; MBA, Wharton School
  Background: Principal, Richland Ventures
  Directorships: Empyrean Benefit Solutions, Forbes Travel Guide, Genomind, Sharecare, StudioNow, TwelveStone Health Partners
  Theresa Sexton, Partner
  615-690-7182
  e-mail: tsexton@claritascapital.com
  Education: BBA, Belmont University; MBA, MACC, Belmont University Massey Graduate School of Business
  Background: Director, Investor Services, CAO, Massey Burch Capital Corp.
  Directorships: Apcela, Forbes Travel, Genomind, nSight for Travel, Oasis Holdings, TwelveStone Health Partners
  Bob Fisher, Partner
  615-665-8419
  e-mail: bfisher@claritascapital.com
  Background: Founder/CEO, Jet Finance Group; Partner, Massey Burch Capital Corp.
  Don McLemore, Partner
  615-665-8419
  e-mail: dmclemore@claritascapital.com
  Background: Partner, Massey Burch Capital Corp.
  Directorships: StudioNow, nSight, A Head for Profits, Apcela, Dobie Media, HCTec

494 CLARITY PARTNERS
100 North Crescent Drive
Beverly Hills, CA 90210

web: www.claritypartners.net

Mission Statement: Private equity firm focused on investment in communications, media and related services. More recently, Clarity Partners has broadened their interest to include energy and natural resources.
Geographic Preference: United States, China
Fund Size: $1 billion
Founded: 2000
Average Investment: $15 to $100 million
Minimum Investment: $15 million
Investment Criteria: Growth Equity, Leveraged Buyouts, Divisional Divestitures, Recapitalizations
Industry Group Preference: Broadband, Wireless Technologies, Business Products & Services, Communications, Media, Information Technology
Portfolio Companies: BASE Entertainment, Buytime Media, CaseStack, Crescent Entertainment, Comstellar, Critical Media, ImpreMedia, International Silver, IP Wireless, Liberation Entertainment, MetroPCS, Modern Luxury, Naylor, OpenReach, Opnext, Oxygen Media, PrimeCo, Skye Mineral Partners, TPx, Vaca Energy, Vue Entertainment, Westec Interactive, Woosh Wireless

Key Executives:
  Dr. David Lee, Co-Founder/Managing General Partner
  Education: McGill University; PhD, California Institute of Technology
  Background: Arthur Andersen & Company; Comsat; TRW Information Systems Group; Pacific Capital Group; Global Crossing
  Directorships: Opnext, Impremedia, University of Southern California Keck School of Medicine
  Barry Porter, Co-Founder/Managing General Partner
  Education: BS, Wharton School; JD, MBA, University of California, Berkeley
  Background: Wyman, Bautzer, Rothman, Kuchel & Silbert; Bear, Stearns & Company, Pacific Capital Group, Global Crossing
  Directorships: PrimeCo Personal Communications, Vue Entertainment, eMind, MetroPCS, Board of Public Counsel
  Stephen P. Rader, Co-Founder/Managing General Partner
  Education: BS, University of Southern California School of Business; JD, University of Southern California School of Law
  Background: Rader, Reinfrank & Company; Chartwell Partners; Bear, Stearns & Company; CPA
  Directorships: Vue Entertainment, Impremedia, TelePacific Communications, eMind, Oxygen Media
  Joshua L. Gutfreund, General Partner
  Education: BA, Columbia University; MBA, New York University Business School
  Background: Rader, Reinfrank & Company; Chartwell Partners; EM Warburg, Pincus & Company
  Directorships: Oxygen Media, eMind, xSides Corporation
  Clinton W. Walker, General Partner
  Education: BBA, Pacific Union College; CPA
  Background: VP, Global Crossing; VP, Pacific Capital Group; Price Waterhouse
  Directorships: Woosh Wireless
  W. Jack Kessler Jr., General Partner/CFO
  Education: MBA, JD, University of Southern California Graduate Schools of Business and Law; Business Administration; Theology, Ambassador College; CPA; California State Bar
  Background: CFO, Rader, Reinfrank & Company; Executive Director, Alschuler Grossman & Pines; Rader and Kessler; CFO, Lamborghini of North America
  Mark Swaine, Managing Director
  Education: BA, Economics, Emory University; JD, Pepperdine University School of Law; California State Bar
  Background: The Wonderful Company
  Andrea Caoile, Controller
  Education: BS, Business Admin., University oF California, Riverside; CPA

Background: Senior Accountant, Clarity Partners; Senior Accountant, Maryanov Madsen Gorden & Campbell

495 CLARUS VENTURES
101 Main Street
Suite 1210
Cambridge, MA 02142

Phone: 617-949-2200 **Fax:** 617-949-2201
web: www.clarusfunds.com

Mission Statement: Clarus Ventures is a dedicated life sciences venture capital firm founded by a team of accomplished investment and operating professionals. The investment team has extensive and broad backgrounds in research and development, commercialization, business development and operations management, which have enabled Clarus to establish a long history of success in creating value across multiple disciplines within the healthcare-investing universe.

Fund Size: $2.6 billion
Founded: 2005
Industry Group Preference: Life Sciences, Biopharmaceuticals, Medical Technology, Healthcare
Portfolio Companies: Achillion Pharmaceuticals, Aerie, Annexon Biosciences, Avanir, Avillion, Avrobio, Catabsis, Cleave Biosciences, Comentis, Delenex Therapeutics, eDev, Entasis Therapeutics, ESBATech, ESSA, FerroKin Biosciences, Flowonix, Forty Seven, Globus Medical, Greybug Vision, Gristone, Heptares Therapeutics, Imago Biosciences, Imbruvica, Intercept Pharmaceuticals, Link Medicine, Lumos Pharma, Lycera, NanoString Technologics, Neomend, Neothetics, Nuvelution, Ophthotech, Oxford Immunotec, Pearl, Restoration Robotics, Sarcode Bioscience, SFI, Sientra, Taligen Therapeutics, TetraLogic Pharmaceuticals, TYRX, VBI, Virdante, Zogenix

Other Locations:
601 Gateway Boulevard
Suite 1270
South San Francisco, CA 94080
Phone: 650-238-5000

Key Executives:
Nicholas Galakatos, PhD, Managing Director
e-mail: ngalakatos@clarusventures.com
Education: PhD, Organic Chemistry, MIT; Post-Doctoral Studies, Harvard Medical School
Background: General Partner, MPM Capital; VP, New Business, Millennium Pharmaceuticals; Head of Molecular Biology Research, Novartis; Venrock Associates
Directorships: Entasis Therapeutics, Nanostring, Nuvelution Pharma Inc., Praxis Precision Medicine
Dennis Henner, PhD, Chief Scientific Advisor
Education: PhD, Department of Microbiology, University of Virginia
Background: General Partner, MPM Capital; SVP, Research, Genentech
Directorships: Cleave, Forty Seven Inc., Imago, SFJ Pharmaceuticals
Robert W. Liptak, Managing Director
Education: MBA, Columbia University; CPA
Background: Partner, Geometry Group; VP, Finance, Global Asset Management
Directorships: Avillion Cayman Corp., SFJ Cayman Corp., Globus Medical Inc.
Nicholas J. Simon, Managing Director
Education: BS, Microbiology, University of Maryland; MBA, Loyola College
Background: VP, Business Development, Genentech; General Partner, MPM Capital
Directorships: Gritstone Oncology, Lycera, Nuvelution Pharma Inc., Sientra
Kurt C. Wheeler, Managing Director
e-mail: kwheeler@clarusventures.com
Education: BA, Brigham Young University; MBA, Northwestern University
Background: Founder & CEO, InControl; Principal, Mayfield Fund; General Partner, MPM Capital
Directorships: Avillion, Globus Medical Inc., Flowonix
Emmett Cunningham Jr., Managing Director
e-mail: ecunningham@clarusventures.com
Education: MD, MPH, Epidemiology & Statistics, Johns Hopkins University; PhD, Neuroscience, University of California, San Diego
Background: SVP, Medical Strategy, Eyetech Pharmaceuticals
Scott Requadt, Venture Partner
e-mail: srequadt@clarusventures.com
Education: Bcom, McGill University; JD, University of Toronto; MBA, Harvard Business School
Background: Director, TransForm Pharmaceuticals
Directorships: AvroBio, Edev, VBI Vaccines, ESSA Pharma, Tridendimidine Finance Company
William Young, Venture Partner
e-mail: wyoung@clarusventures.com
Education: BS, Chemical Engineering, Purdue University; MBA, Indiana University
Background: CEO, Monogram Biosciences; COO, Genentech; Eli Lilly and Company
Directorships: Vertex, Theravance

496 CLAYTON ASSOCIATES
5314 Maryland Way
Suite 100
Brentwood, TN 37027

Phone: 615-320-3070
web: www.claytonassociates.com

Mission Statement: Clayton Associates is an investment firm that is passionate about building businesses. We make seed, angel, and venture stage investments in helathcare and technology companies.

Founded: 1996
Investment Criteria: Seed Stage, Angel, Venture Stage
Industry Group Preference: Healthcare, Technology
Portfolio Companies: Catavolt, ChartWise Medical Systems, Clinical Ink, Haven Behavioral, KeraFAST, LogoGarden, MediQuire, Pathfinder Health Innovations, One Medical Passport, StudioNow

Key Executives:
Stuart McWhorter, Founder and President
Education: Masters in Health Administration, The University of Alabama-Birmingham; BS, Management, Clemson University
Background: CEO and Chairman, Medical Reimbursements of America; Vice President, Managed Care and Acquisitions, OrthoLink Physicians Corporation
Directorships: FirstBank of Tennessee, LaunchTN, Tennessee Business Roundtable, Belmont Unviersity
R. Clayton McWhorter, Founder and Chairman Emeritus
Education: BS, Pharmacy, Samford University
Background: Founder, Chairman and CEO, HealthTrust; Chairman, Hospital Corporation of America
John R. Burch, Managing Partner
Background: Co-Founder, MyOfficeProducts; Exec. Vice-President, Motorent
Directorships: Entrada, LogoGarden, KeraFAST, ProviderTrust, ChartWise, Armor Concepts, Thalerus Group, Gemino Healthcare Finance, Pathfinder Therapeutics, PharmMD
Matthew King, Managing Partner
Background: Vice President, Third National Bank; CEO, Radar Business Systems; Regional Vice President, U.S. Office Products; CEO, MyOfficeProducts
Directorships: NuScript Rx, edo Interactive, Entrada, onFocus Healthcare, Silvercare Solutions, LogoGarden, KeraFAST, ProCharging, HCCA International

Venture Capital & Private Equity Firms / Domestic Firms

497 CLEAN ENERGY VENTURE GROUP
Brookline, MA

Phone: 877-531-9017
web: cevg.com

Mission Statement: Clean Energy Venture Group is an investment group that provides seed capital and management expertise to early stage clean energy companies. The group is comprised of seasoned operating executives with strong capabilities in the energy and environmental sectors. The fund's primary focus is New England, but will occasionally consider investments located in other areas.

Geographic Preference: New England
Founded: 2005
Investment Criteria: Seed-Stage
Industry Group Preference: Clean Technology, Energy
Portfolio Companies: 7AC Technologies, Acumentrics, Autonomous Marine Systems Inc., Bevi, CIMCON Lighting, Energetic Insurance, EnergySage, eQuilibrium, FINsix Corp., MTPV, Multisensor Scientific, MyEnergyn, NG Advantage LLC, Pika Energy, Powerhouse Dynamics, PurposeEnergy, Quidnet Energy, REsurety, Solantro Semiconductor Corp., Ultracell, VCharge, Voltserver, WeSpire, Zagster

Key Executives:
David S. Miller, Founder/Executive Managing Director
Education: BS, MS, Computer Science & Engineering, MIT
Background: Founder, Quantum Telecom Solutions; Lucent
Directorships: Azima DLI, Next Step Living, MyEnergy, Cambrian Innovation

498 CLEAN PACIFIC VENTURES
425 California Street
Suite 2400
San Francisco, CA 94104

Mission Statement: Clean Pacific Ventures is a venture capital fund that invests in promising early stage clean technology companies. Clean Pacific focuses primarily on clean technologies related to energy, water, agriculture and materials.

Average Investment: $2 to $4 million
Investment Criteria: Early-Stage
Industry Group Preference: Clean Technology, Energy, Water, Agriculture, Energy Storage, Energy Efficiency, Advanced Materials, Renewable Energy
Portfolio Companies: American Efficient, Aquacue, Clean Power Finance, HydroNovation, LumiGrow, Marrone Bio Innovations, SunLink, Wireless Glue

Key Executives:
Sean Schickedanz, General Partner
Education: BA, English, Brigham Young University; JD, MBA, Duke University
Background: Managing Partner, Sunflower Capital Partners; Managing Director, Montgomery Securities; Investment Banking, Merrill Lynch
Directorships: The Renewables Exchange Inc.
Dave Herron, General Partner
Education: BA, English, University of California, Berkeley; MBA, University of Michigan
Background: Vice President, Robertson Stephen's Energy Technology Investment Banking; Senior Vice President, Van Kasper & Co
Directorships: SunLink; Wireless Glue Networks; The Renewables Exchange Inc.

499 CLEANPATH VENTURES
448 Pennsylvania Avenue
San Francisco, CA 94107

Phone: 415-244-6787
e-mail: info@cleanpath.com
web: www.cleanpath.com

Mission Statement: CleanPath is a premier solar project investment firm with deep development and engineering roots. CleanPath invests in, develops, builds and delivers high quality renewable energy assets to external long-term owners, or to their own portfolio. CleanPath was formed by pioneers of the U.S. clean energy industry, with deep industry and capital markets experience, execution capability and exceptional relationships. The fund's solutions provide significant capital resources coupled with proven project finance, development, engineering, and asset construction and management capabilities.

Fund Size: $300 million
Founded: 2001
Industry Group Preference: Renewable Energy
Key Executives:
Matt Cheney, Chief Executive Officer
Education: BS, American University; MS, Johns Hopkins University School of Advanced International Studies
Background: CEO, Fotowatio Renewable Ventures; MMA Renewable Energy

500 CLEARLAKE CAPITAL
233 Wilshire Boulevard
Suite 800
Santa Monica, CA 90401

Phone: 310-400-8800
e-mail: info@clearlakecapital.com
web: www.clearlakecapital.com

Mission Statement: A leading investment firm focused on private equity and special situations transactions.

Geographic Preference: United States
Fund Size: $3.5 billion
Founded: 2006
Investment Criteria: Buyouts, Acquisitions, Carve-Outs, Growth Capital, Platform Investments, Special Situations
Industry Group Preference: Business Products & Services, Consumer Products, Consumer Services, Energy, Industrial Services, Technology, Communications, Aerospace, Defense and Government, Healthcare, Media
Portfolio Companies: 3alioty Technica, American Construction Source, AmQuip, Appriss, Ashley Stewart, Bluefly, Buy.com, Calero, Chef's Cut Real Jerky, CompuDyne Corporation, ConvergeOne, Diligent, Dude Solutions, Eagleview, From the Ground Up, Futuris, Gravity Oilfield Services Inc., International Textile Group, Inventus, Ivanti, Jacuzzi, Janus, JetSmarter, Knight Oil Tools, Lytx, MetricStream, Mformation, MYCOM OSI, NetDocuments, OnShift, OWYN, Perforce Software, Platinum Energy Solutions, Pomeroy, PrimeSport, Provation, Purple Communications, Sage Automotive Interiors, Sensible Problems, Smart Sand, Solutionary, Sunbelt Supply, Symplr, Team Technologies Inc., Syncsort, Thinsters, Unifrax, Vision Solutions, Wheel Pros

Key Executives:
Martin Arzac, Managing Director
Education: AB, Economics, Stanford University; MBA, Stanford Grad. School of Business
Background: Analyst, Donaldson Lufkin & Jenrette; Director/Associate Director, UBS Investment Bank; Managing Director, Deutsche Bank

501 CLEARLIGHT PARTNERS
100 Bayview Circle
Suite 5000
Newport Beach, CA 92660

Phone: 949-725-6610 Fax: 949-725-6611
web: www.clearlightpartners.com

Mission Statement: ClearLight Partners is a private equity firm that invests in profitable middle-market companies across a variety of sectors, including education, healthcare, business services, consumer products and services, and specialty manufacturing. ClearLight Partners offers financial and

176

operating expertise, and seeks to establish partnerships with management teams to help with the growth of companies.

Geographic Preference: United States, Canada
Fund Size: $300 million
Founded: 2000
Average Investment: $10 - $50 million
Investment Criteria: Middle-Market, Growth Capital
Industry Group Preference: Manufacturing, Distribution, Business Products & Services, Education, Healthcare Services, Financial Services, Consumer Products, Consumer Services
Portfolio Companies: Austin Fitness Group, Handel's Ice Cream, Katzkin Leather Interiors Inc., Moore Landscapes, Paul Fredrick, United Tactical Systems, Walker Advertising

Key Executives:
Michael S Kaye, Founder/Managing Partner
952-725-6628
e-mail: msk@clearlightpartners.com
Education: BA, Stanford University; JD, Harvard Law School
Background: President & CEO, Westec Security Group; Corporate Law, Gibson, Dunn and Crutcher
Joshua Mack, Partner
949-725-6625
e-mail: jmack@clearlightpartners.com
Education: BS, Finance, Pepperdine University
Andrew Brennan, Partner
949-725-6642
e-mail: ajb@clearlightpartners.com
Education: BA, Economics, Williams College
Background: EVP & COO, ValleyCrest Companies; Senior Associate, ClearLight; McKinsey & Company

---

502 CLEARSTONE VENTURE PARTNERS
1351 4th Street
4th Floor
Santa Monica, CA 90401

web: www.clearstone.com

Mission Statement: Clearstone embraces a longtime and active role in the business community as an incubator and financier of early-stage startups.

Geographic Preference: Southern California
Fund Size: $650 million
Founded: 1997
Investment Criteria: Early Stage
Industry Group Preference: Computer Related, Internet, Infrastructure, E-Commerce & Manufacturing, Social Media, Mobile
Portfolio Companies: AOptix, Apture, BillDesk, Clearfly Communications, Comet Systems, Composite Systems, Cooking.com, DiVitas, Games2Win.com, Geodelic Systems, Good Technology, HealthAllies, Idealab, Integrien, Intersperse, Kazeon, Leisurelink, Meru Networks, Mimosa Systems, MP3.com, Nokeena, Novariant, Overture Services, PayPal, PeopleSupport, Phasebridge, Presto, Rubicon Project, Six Degrees Games, Soonr, Spock, SupplyFrame, ThisNext, United Online, UserTesting, Vast

Other Locations:
720 University Avenue
Suite 200
Palo Alto, CA 94301
Phone: 650-234-0400 Fax: 650-234-0401

Key Executives:
Bill Elkus, Founder & Managing Director
Education: BS, Mathematics, MS, Management, MIT; JD, Harvard Law School
Background: Boston Consulting Group; President, Nathan Todd & Company
Directorships: United Online, Overture, PayPal.com, Chronicle Publishing Company, Presto Services, Cooking.com, WeddingChannel.com
Jim Armstrong, Managing Director
Education: BA, Economics, University of California, Los Angeles; MBA, McCombs School, University of Texas at Austin
Background: Austin Ventures
Directorships: SupplyFrame, Internet Brands, Vast, Six Degrees Games, LeisureLink, Inegrien, Composite
William Quigley, Managing Director
Education: BS, Accounting, University of Southern California; MBA, Harvard Business School; CPA
Background: Mid-Atlantic Venture Funds; The Walt Disney Company; Senior Consultant, Arthur Andersen Financial Services Group
Directorships: AOptix, SoonR, Meru Networks, Novariant, Communicado, Spock Networks, Spock.com
Anil Patel, Venture Partner
Education: AB, Economics & Philosophy, Stanford University; MBA, Columbia Business School; JD, Columbia University School of Law
Background: Azure Capital Partners; Bessemer Venture Partners; Attorney, Wilson Sonsini Goodrich & Rosati; Software Developer, Information Management Consultants
Dana Moraly, Chief Financial Officer
Education: BA, Economics, UCLA; MBA, Anderson School of Management, University of California, LA
Background: Trust Company of the West; Senior Manager, Coopers & Lybrand; Senior Auditor, Deloitte & Touche
Vish Mishra, Venture Director
Education: BS, Electrical Engineering, Institute of Technology at Benares Hindu University; MS, Electrical Engineering, North Dakota State University; MBA, University of Minnesota
Background: Founder, Telera; Co-Founder, Excelan; VP, Operations, Excelan; VP, Novell; EVP, iPlanet; CEO, Info-Objects; CEO, Mindworks; CEO, InteliMatch; CEO, Ace Software
Directorships: Abeama, Cofix, Onjibe, PostMedia Group, Quantros, Ramp Networks, SloMedia, Verano, Xalted IP Networks
Prabakar Sundarrajan, Venture Advisor
Education: MS, Computer Science, University of Massachusetts, Amherst
Background: CTO, EVP Strategic Planning & Corporate Development, NetScaler, Inc.; Senior Vice President of Technology, Exodus Communications
David Stern, Venture Partner
Education: Cornell University; San Diego School of Law
Background: President, M Networks
Directorships: Apture, Geodelic Systems, The Rubicon Project, SoonR
Rajan Mehra, Venture Partner
Education: Sydenham College, Mumbai; MBA, Darden School, University of Virginia
Background: Country Manager, eBay India; eBay Asia Pacific Leadership Team; Baazee.com

---

503 CLEARVIEW CAPITAL
1010 Washington Blvd.
11th Floor
Stamford, CT 06901

Phone: 203-698-2777 Fax: 203-698-9194
e-mail: info@clearviewcap.com
web: www.clearviewcap.com

Mission Statement: A private investment firm specializing in the acquisition and recapitalization of North American companies with operating profit of $4 - $20 million. The firm's principals have a long track record of completing transactions and of working collaboratively with management to create and realize value.

Geographic Preference: North America
Investment Criteria: Recapitalizations
Industry Group Preference: Manufacturing, Specialized Services, Branded Goods

Venture Capital & Private Equity Firms / Domestic Firms

Portfolio Companies: Advanced Medical Personnel Services, Apothecare, Community Medicla Services, Controlled Products, Elevation Labs, Mudlick Mail, Nielsen-Kellerman, Wilson, Novik, Pediatric Health Choice, Pyramid Healthcare

Other Locations:
12100 Wilshire Blvd.
Suite 800
Los Angeles, CA 90025
Phone: 310-806-9555 **Fax:** 310-806-9556

Key Executives:
James G Andersen, Founder/Managing Partner
203-698-2777
Fax: 203-698-9194
e-mail: janderson@clearviewcap.com
Education: BSE, Civil Engineering, Princeton University; MBA, Wharton School
Background: Managing Director, Capital Partners; Management Consultant, Mars & Company
Calvin A Neider, Founder/Managing Partner
203-698-2777
Fax: 203-698-9194
e-mail: cneider@clearviewcap.com
Education: BA, Business Administration, SUNY Oneonta; MBA, University of Connecticut
Background: Managing Director, Capital Partners; SVP, LaSalle Business Credit
William F Case Jr, Partner
e-mail: wcase@clearviewcap.com
Education: BA, Union College; MBA, Wharton School
Background: Huntington Holdings
Paul Caliento, Partner
203-698-2777
Fax: 203-698-9194
e-mail: pcaliento@clearviewcap.com
Education: BA, Accounting & Marketing, University of Rhode Island
Background: Flackman Goodman & Potter
Lawrence R Simon, Partner
310-806-9555
Fax: 310-806-9556
e-mail: lsimon@clearviewcap.com
Education: Wharton School; MBA, Columbia Business School
Background: Principal, Triton Pacific Capital Partners
Anthony J Veith, Partner
203-698-2777
Fax: 203-698-9194
e-mail: aveith@clearviewcap.com
Education: BS, Finance, University of Arizona; MBA, City University of New York
Background: Senior Vice President, LaSalle Business Credit
Mathias Rumilly, Partner
203-698-2777
Fax: 203-698-9194
e-mail: mrummily@clearviewcap.com
Education: BS, Finance, University of Connecticut
Matthew Blevins, Partner
203-698-2777
Fax: 203-698-9194
e-mail: mblevins@clearviewcap.com
Education: BS, Business Administration, Accounting & Finance, Cental Michigan University
Background: Senior Consultant, Deloitte & Touche USA

504 CLEARWATER CAPITAL PARTNERS
15 River Rd.
Suite 15B
Wilton, CT 06897

Phone: 212-201-8544
e-mail: information@clearwatercp.com
web: www.clearwatercapitalpartners.com

Mission Statement: Clearwater Capital Partners provides investors with access to a full spectrum of special-situation investments in public and private debt or equity of local, Asia-region issuers. In doing so, Clearwater also assists owners and management, particularly of the region's often capital-constrained small-to-medium-sized enterprises (SMEs), to create financial and operating restructurings that will allow their companies to succeed. In addition, by facilitating these successful restructurings, the firm has become a valuable and trusted resource to the region's banks, brokers and other business intermediaries.

Geographic Preference: Asia, United States
Founded: 2001
Investment Criteria: Restructurings, Turn-Arounds
Other Locations:
Suite 3205
No. 9 Queen's Road
Central
Hong Kong
Phone: 852-3713-4800

Key Executives:
Robert Petty, Co-Founder/Managing Partner
Education: BA, Political Science, Brown University
Background: Amroc Investments, Peregrine Fixed Income, Lehman Brothers Holdings
Amit Gupta, Co-Founder/Partner
Education: B.Eng, Electronics & Communications, Indian Institute of Technology; Post Graduate Diploma, Management, Indian Institute of Management
Background: Goldman Sachs Asia, Peregrine Fixed Income, ICICI

505 CLOQUET CAPITAL PARTNERS
285 Hawks Hill Rd.
New Cannan, CT 06840

Phone: 203-286-6818
e-mail: contact@cloquetcapital.com
web: www.cloquetcapital.com

Mission Statement: Cloquet Capital Partners is a private equity firm that, along with its operating partners and affiliates, manages in excess of $50 million of available or invested capital. Its mission is to acquire and build a portfolio of exceptional businesses in niche markets. Cloquet invests in venture-stage communication software companies, management buyouts, growth equity investments and special situations. Cloquet seeks to enter into close operating partnerships with the managers of its portfolio companies, with Cloquet's resources providing support to help them achieve their strategic objectives and growth. Cloquet invests its own private capital, not that of third parties, with an investment approach based on trust, integrity and honesty.

Fund Size: $50 million
Founded: 2002
Investment Criteria: Management Buyouts, Growth Equity Investments, Special Situations
Industry Group Preference: Communications, Software
Portfolio Companies: Aeris, BitMinutes, FarmLogix, InSight Management, Micromatic, Qv21 Technologies, Side by Side, Tespo

Key Executives:
Burton McGillivray, Partner
Education: AB, Economics, Harvard College; MBA, Harvard Business School
Background: Continental Illinois Venture Corp., Carlisle Enterprises, First Chicago Equity Capital
Directorships: FarmLogix, Qv21 Technologies, Micromatic, Insight Management Group
Jim Zucco, Partner
Education: BA, Western Maryland College; MBA, Loyola College
Background: SVP, MCI Corp.; VP & General Manager, Business Communications Group; VP & General Manager, Lucent Technologies; CEO, Shiva Corp.

Venture Capital & Private Equity Firms / Domestic Firms

Krishnamurty Kambhampati, Partner
Education: MS, Computer Science, Cornell University; MS, Mathematics, Indian Institute of Technology
Background: Founder & CEO, monitor-io; Co-Founder, uReach Technologies

506 CLYDESDALE VENTURES
201 Spear Street
Suite 1150
San Francisco, CA 94105

Phone: 415-391-4085 **Fax:** 415-243-3000
web: www.clydesdaleventures.com

Mission Statement: Clydesdale Ventures is a seed and early-stage venture investment firm who partner with and invest in passionate entrepreneurs with big ideas for capital efficient and highly scalable businesses.

Average Investment: $25,000 - $1.5 million
Investment Criteria: Seed-Stage, Early-Stage
Industry Group Preference: Consumer Products, Food & Beverage, Consumer Internet, Enterprise Technology, SaaS, Financial Services, Leisure, Health & Wellness, Restaurants
Portfolio Companies: HealthFusion, Inc., Bishop Rock Software, LLC, RemoteMDx, Inc., New Momentum LLC, UBmatrix LLC, Cleantech America, Inc., California Bank of Commerce, Chime Entertainment LLC, Mixonic, Inc., Airtreks, Inc., Java Detour, Inc., Duncan Media Group, Dream Dinners, Novint Technologies, Inc., Organic Style, Inc., NowMedia, Pangea World Corporation, QOOP, Inc., Hooja, Inc., The Concery Network, Inc., PayEase, Inc

Key Executives:
Paul Klapper, Partner
Background: PFK Acquisition Company, Creative World Travel; Chairman, A&W Restaurants
Brad Klapper, Partner
Background: Siebel Systems, Freepoint Telecom
Directorships: Bishop Rock Software, NowMedia Corp., The Concert Network Inc.

507 CM EQUITY PARTNERS
900 Third Avenue
33rd Floor
New York, NY 10022

Phone: 212-909-8400 **Fax:** 212-829-0553
e-mail: dcolon@cmequity.com
web: www.cmequity.com

Mission Statement: Specializes in investing in government contract service businesses. Since 1995, CMEP has purchased multiple platform companies that primarily serve the US federal government. CMEP is affiliated with Carl Marks & Co., LP.

Geographic Preference: United States
Fund Size: $200 million
Founded: 1995
Average Investment: $5 - 40 million
Minimum Investment: $500,000
Investment Criteria: Middle Market
Industry Group Preference: Federal Services, Aerospace, Defense
Portfolio Companies: A-TEK, Bogart Associates, Citizant, GracoRoberts, JANUS Research Group Inc., The Level Playing Field Corporation, Preferred System Solutions, Systems Planning and Analysis

Other Locations:
1430 K Street NW
12th Floor
Washington, DC 20005

Key Executives:
Joel R. Jacks, Co-Founder, Managing Partner
Education: BComm, University of Cape Town; MBA, Wharton School; Chartered Accountant
Background: Founding Manager, Carl Marks Consulting Group; Private Consultant; CFO/CEO, USSCO; Director Financial Planning, Penn Central Corporation; Deloitte Haskins & Sells
Directorships: Echo Bridge Entertainment, ICF International, Falcon Communications, RGS Associates, Laguna Ventures, Preferred Systems Solutions, ATS Corporation
Peter M. Schulte, Co-Founder, Managing Partner
Education: BA, Harvard College; MPPM, Yale School of Management
Background: Arnhold & S Bleichroeder; VP, Salomon Brothers; IBM
Directorships: ICF International, ATS Corporation, Falcon Communications, Xebec Global Corporation, RGS Associates, Laguna Ventures, Preferred Systems Solutions
Jeffrey Mark, Partner
Education: BBA, Isenberg School of Management, University of Massachusetts
Background: Director, Risk Arbitrage Group, Royal Bank of Canada; Managing Director, Bear Stearns & Co.
Wesley H.R. Gaus, Managing Partner
Education: BS, Economics, Wharton School; BS, Systems Engineering, University of Pennsylvania
Background: ING Baring Furman Selz
Directorships: Martin Designs
Daniel Colon, Jr., Partner
212-909-8445
Fax: 212-371-7254
e-mail: dcolon@cmequity.com
Education: BA, University of Miami; MBA, Zicklin School of Business, Baruch College
Background: Carl Marks & Co

508 CNF INVESTMENTS Clark Enterprises, Inc.
7500 Old Georgetown Road
15th Floor
Bethesda, MD 20814-6195

Phone: 301-657-7100 **Fax:** 301-657-7263
e-mail: info@clarkenterprises.com
web: www.clarkenterprises.com

Mission Statement: CNF focuses on early and growth stage companies, but will consider investments in later stages and selective public investments as well. CNF looks to partner with other venture capital and private equity firms and is an active investor providing strategic advice to its management teams.

Fund Size: $225 million
Founded: 1972
Investment Criteria: Early-Stage, Growth-Stage
Industry Group Preference: Life Sciences, Oil & Gas, Technology, Telecommunications, Alternative Energy
Portfolio Companies: American Honors, Blitsy, Brown Advisory, Calvert Education Serices, Carbon 38, Ceros, Circle Back, Eagle Oil & Gas Co., Echo 360, Enven Energy Corporation, EU Networks, Gigya, Hubub, In Go Money, Kareo, Media Math, MonoSol RX PharmFilm Technology, Neotract, NUO Therapeutics, Placecast, Print Syndicate, Regent Education, Shared Spectrum Company, Sonatype, Surf Watch, Svelte Medical Systems, Sweet Green, TerraGo, Trov, Up Skill, Vascular Therapies, Verax Biomedical, View Lift

Key Executives:
Robert J Flanagan, President
Education: BBA, Georgetown University; MS, Taxation, American University School of Business
Directorships: Brown Advisory, Eagle Oil & Gas, Svelte Medical Systems, Vascular Therapies
Joe Del Guercio, SVP & Managing Director
Education: BS, Boston College; MBA, Harvard Business School
Background: Director, LPL Financial Services; Robertson Stephens; Goldman Sachs
Directorships: American Honors College, Placecast, Terrago Technologies, Verax Biomedical

Venture Capital & Private Equity Firms / Domestic Firms

James J Brinkman, SVP & Chief Financial Officer
Education: BA, Accounting, University of Delaware
Background: SVP, Financial Operations, Allied Capital

509 COATUE MANAGEMENT
9 West 57th Street
25th Floor
New York, NY 10019
web: www.coatue.com

Mission Statement: Hedge fund investor focused on the technology sector in both public and private equity markets.

Fund Size: $700 million
Founded: 1999
Investment Criteria: Early Stage
Industry Group Preference: Artificial Intelligence, Technology, Information Technology, Software, Applications
Portfolio Companies: Anaplan, Box, Careem, HONKON, Jet, Lending Club, Lyft, Meituan-Dianping, SnapChat, Uber

Other Locations:
2885 Sand Hill Road
2nd Floor
Menlo Park, CA 94025

21 South Park Street
2nd Floor
San Francisco, CA 94107

2 International Finance Centre
F8 Finance Street 6701
Hong Kong

Key Executives:
Philippe Laffont, Founder
Education: MS, Computer Science, MIT
Kris Fredrickson, Managing Partner
Education: BS, Universith of Southern California; JD, University of California, LA; MBA, Harvard Business School
Background: VP, Goldman Sachs; SVP of Operations & Strategy, Munchery; Principal, Benchmark; Co-Founder, Curology
Andy Chen, Partner
Education: BS/MS, Mechanical Engineering, University of California, San Diego
Background: Mechanical Engineer, Los Alamos National Laboratory; Mechanical Engineer, Sensor Metrix; Manager, Engineer Recruiting, Riviera Partners; Analyst, Central Intelligence Agency; Partner, Kleiner Perkins
Directorships: Challenge Success

510 COHEN PRIVATE VENTURES
Stamford, CT

Mission Statement: Invests long term capital in direct private investments in the areas of direct private equity, venture and growth equity financing, concentrated public markets positions, and real estate.

Geographic Preference: United States
Founded: 2010
Investment Criteria: Direct Private Equity, Growth Equity & Venture Capital, Structured Securities, Specialized Credit Investments, Real Estate
Industry Group Preference: Private Equity, Real Estate
Portfolio Companies: Autonomous Partners

Key Executives:
Andrew B. Cohen, Co-Founder/Chief Investment Officer
Education: BA, University of Pennsylvania; MBA, Wharton School, University of Pennsylvania
Background: Dune Capital Management LP; Morgan Stanley; Point 72
Directorships: The New York Mets Baseball Club; Laureate Education Inc.; Republic First Bancorp Inc.; Advisory Board of Metro Bank PLC

511 COLLABORATIVE FUND
web: www.collaborativefund.com

Mission Statement: Collaborative Fund uses capital to merge projects that are motivated by both self interest and by broader interest. The company looks to invest in successful businesses that are making the world a better place in the broader categories of cities, fincances, consumer products, and children's needs.

Fund Size: $300 million
Founded: 2010
Industry Group Preference: Transportation, Technology, Banking, Sustainable Products, Children, Healthcare, Pharmaceuticals
Portfolio Companies: Beyond Meat, Blue Bottle Coffee, Dandelion Energy, Impossible, Kickstarter, LTSE, Lyft, Outdoor Voices, Quora, Reddit, SOCAR, sweetgreen, Tala, The Farmer's Dog, Upstart

Key Executives:
Craig Shapiro, Founder/Managing Partner
Background: Investment Committee, Goldhirsh Foundation
Sophie Bakalar, Venture Partner
Education: BS, Math, Public Health, Tufts University
Background: III Captical Management; President & Co-Founder, di8it charts; Co-Founder, fable
Tehinder Gill, Principal
Education: BS, Evolutionary Biology, Harvard University
Background: Insight Venture Partners; Social Capital LP; Delivery Hero; Altman Vilandrie & Company

512 COLOMA VENTURES
10795 West Twain Avenue
Suite 100
Las Vegas, NV 89135

Mission Statement: Coloma Ventures is a venture capital group with a focus on Internet based start-ups, representing a consortium of accredited investors including many of Las Vegas' most influential and preeminent business luminaries. Coloma seeks to invest in talented entrepreneurial teams and provide founders and developers access to capital for vetted and viable Internet start-ups in web, software, mobile, digital media, social, and gaming sectors.

Geographic Preference: Las Vegas
Founded: 2010
Investment Criteria: Early-Stage
Industry Group Preference: Internet, Software, Mobile, Digital Media & Marketing, Social Media, Gaming
Portfolio Companies: Break-Up Alert, Design Genie, Kemistry, Las Vegas Film Festival, Momentous, Progressive REI, Promise Pictures, Salon Share, Thought Division, Zip The Strip

Key Executives:
Monty Lapica, Founder/Managing Partner
Education: Loyola Marymount University
Background: Founder, Recognition Networks
Directorships: Thought Division
Thomas Bell, Partner
Education: University of Nevada, Las Vegas
Background: Founder, Salon Share; Founder, Rakeless Room; Founder, KemistryHair.com
Joey Paulos, Partner
Background: Manager, Hotel Administration, MGM Grand Hotel & Casino; Financial Analyst/Hotel Operations Manager, New York, New York Hotel & Casino

513 COLORADO MILE HIGH FUND
e-mail: comilehighfund@gcmlp.com

Mission Statement: The Colorado Mile High Fund is a $50 million co-investment program designed to invest in a diversified, high-quality portfolio of companies with a nexus to Colorado. Investments will generally be in the form of co-investments alongside financial sponsors, with ultimately 12 to

15 investments targeted for the portfolio. With established industries, strong growth opportunities, a dedicated research community, and an active private equity market, the state is ripe for investment. The fund is managed by GCM Grosvenor.

Geographic Preference: Colorado
Fund Size: $50 million
Investment Criteria: Mezzanine, Buyout, Growth Capital, Infrastructure/Energy
Industry Group Preference: Business Products & Services, Clean Technology, Renewable Resources, Information Technology, Communications, Aerospace, Defense and Government, Aerospace, Defense and Government, Manufacturing, Infrastructure, Energy

---

514 COLT VENTURES
2101 Cedar Springs Road
Suite 1230
Dallas, TX 75201

Phone: 214-397-0176
web: www.coltventures.com

Mission Statement: Colt Ventures is a privately-held opportunistic investment firm primarily focused on the following investment activities: Private Equity, Venture Capital, Proprietary Trading, Oil and Gas, Hedge Funds and Real Estate. Colt engages in a broad range of investment activities and has the flexibility to invest in a wide variety of asset classes.

Industry Group Preference: Oil & Gas, Infrastructure, Biotechnology, Financial Services, Technology
Portfolio Companies: Rocket Pharma, Bonti, La Jolla Pharmaceutical, Ignyta, Intrexon, NeoStem, Maple, Colt WTX Resources, Colt CTX Resources, Acapella, Alamito Minerals, Colt Mineral Interests, The Realtime Group, VizSense, High Brow Cat, Waggoner Ranch, Euroseas, Waste Corporation of America, Barilla Draw, Colt Unconventional Resources, Credo West, Smith Pipe, Anterios, CardioSpectra, Halozyme Therapeutics, Highlands Bank, Paetec International, ServiceNow Inc., Eloqua, Trulogica, Motive, OpsTechnology, Oscar Mike Games, Craft International

Key Executives:
  Darren Blanton, Founder/Managing Director
  Background: Perry E. Espin; Able Investments
  J.D. McCulloch, Managing Director
  Education: BS, Mechanical Engineering; MBA, University of Texas, Austin; CFA
  Background: VP, Investments, TRT Holdings; Industrial/Consumer Investment Banking Group, JPMorgan

---

515 COLUMBIA CAPITAL
204 South Union Street
Alexandria, VA 22314

Phone: 703-519-2000
e-mail: info@colcap.com
web: colcap.com

Mission Statement: Columbia Capital is a premier venture capital franchise in wireless, broadband, media, and enterprise information technology investing. Since its formation, Columbia Capital has taken a sector-focused approach to investing, and has funded over 130 global companies. This sector focus enables the fund to regularly identify disruptive emerging companies and to recognize and build value throughout a company's lifecycle - from early-stage investments, to large growth stage financings and any singular situations.

Fund Size: $441 million
Founded: 1989
Average Investment: $15 - $40 million
Minimum Investment: $1 million
Investment Criteria: Early Stage, Late Stage
Industry Group Preference: Communications, Communication Technology, Information Technology, Enterprise Technology, Software, Wireless, Broadband, Media, Cyber Security, Internet Infrastructure

Portfolio Companies: 2nd Watch, Access Sports Media, Altamira, BillingPlatform, Canara, Cologix, Contino, Daz 3D, Devas Multimedia, Endgame, euNetworks, Fuse, Landways, Lemongrass, Local Media, Mandalay Sports Media, Mobile Posse, NewSignature, Nextnav, Omnispace, OPAQ Networks, Open Media, RockYou, Slacker Radio, SoundHouse LLC, SummitIG, TerraPact, Verato, VuBiquity

Other Locations:
  Reservoir Place
  1601 Trapelo Road
  Suite 154
  Waltham, MA 02451
  Phone: 781-290-2240

Key Executives:
  Jim Fleming, Partner
  Education: BA, Stanford University
  Background: President, Prime Cellular; Price Waterhouse
  Directorships: Nuvox Communications, Tennis Channel, WCS Wireless
  Arun Gupta, Venture Partner
  Education: BS, Electrical Engineering, MS, Engineering Economics, Stanford University; MBA, Harvard Business School
  Background: Carlyle Venture Partners; Arthur D Little
  Directorships: Approva, Avail Media, Brickstream, Devas Multimedia, Envysion, FreeWebs, Gizmoz, InnerWireless, Intelliworks, Millenial Media, Netuitive
  Patrick Hendy, Partner
  Education: BA, Economics, Vanderbilt University
  Background: Financial Analyst, Global Telecommunications and Media Investment Banking Group of J.P. Morgan; Financial Analyst, Debt Capital Markets Group
  Jennifer Krusius, Venture Partner
  Education: BS, Applied Economics & Management, Cornell University; MBA, Harvard Business School
  Background: General Manager, Uber Technologies; Investor, IFC Asset Management Company; Investor, Emerging Capital Partners; Investment Banker, Credit Suisse Group
  John Leibovitz, Venture Partner
  Education: BA, University of Pennsylvania; M.Phil, Cambridge University; JD, Yale Law School
  Background: Deputy Chief, Wireless Bureau/Special Advisor, Spectrum Policy, FCC; McKinsey & Co.
  Evan DeCorte, Principal
  Education: BS, Economics/Political Science, George Washington University
  Background: Head of Marketing, Roshan TDCA; Analyst, JPMorgan Chase
  Directorships: Landways, TerraPact
  Jeff Patterson, Venture Partner
  Education: BA, Bowdoin College; MBA, Kellogg School of Management
  Background: First National Bank of Boston; European Cable & Telephony, London
  Directorships: Rapid Communications, Si TV
  John Siegel, Partner
  Education: BA, Princeton University; MBA, Harvard Bsuiness School
  Background: Morgan Stanley Private Equity Group; Fidelity Ventures; Alex Brown & Sons
  Directorships: mindSHIFT Technologies, FDN Communications, Netifice Communications, ICG Communications, Integrated Solutions
  Jason Booma, Partner
  Education: BS, Computer Engineering, Northwestern University; MBA, Kellogg School of Management
  Background: Centennial Ventures
  Directorships: Cloud Sherpas, Envysion
  Monish Kundra, Partner
  Education: BS, Wharton School; BS, Chemical Engineering, University of Pennsylvania
  Background: Senior VP, Corporate Development, Mobile

Venture Capital & Private Equity Firms / Domestic Firms

Satellite Ventures
Directorships: NexNav, Local Media Partners

516 COLUMBUS NOVA
900 Third Avenue
New York, NY 10022

Phone: 212-418-9600
e-mail: info@columbusnova.com
web: www.columbusnova.com

Mission Statement: Columbus Nova is a multi-strategy investment firm managing over $15.0 billion of assets through its own funds and affiliated portfolio companies. CN has a broad investment mandate which allows investments across all levels of the capital structure from senior secured debt to equity. CN takes a value-oriented, long-term view to investing and seeks consistent returns with an emphasis on capital preservation.

Fund Size: $15 billion
Founded: 2000
Investment Criteria: Senior Structured Debt, Equity
Key Executives:
 Andrew Intrater, Chief Executive Officer
 Education: BS, Chemical Engineering, Rutgers University
 Background: Founder, ATI; President & COO, Oryx Technology Corp
 Directorships: Renova Management
 Jason Epstein, Managing Partner
 Education: BA, Tufts University
 Background: Co-Founder, elink Communications

517 COLUMN GROUP
1700 Owens Street
Suite 500
San Francisco, CA 94158

Phone: 415-865-2050 Fax: 415-255-2048
e-mail: info@thecolumngroup.com
web: www.thecolumngroup.com

Mission Statement: The Column Group is a venture capital firm that provides capital and operational support to life sciences and biotechnology companies. The Column Group focuses on early stage drug discovery companies and is dedicated to the development of breakthrough therapies.

Fund Size: $176 million
Average Investment: $15 - $30 million
Investment Criteria: Seed, Early Stage
Industry Group Preference: Biotechnology, Pharmaceuticals, Life Sciences
Portfolio Companies: Carmot Therapeutics, Constellation Pharmaceuticals, eFFECTOR Therapeutics, FLX Bio, Gritstone Oncology, Igenica Biotherapeutics, Immune Design, Kallyope, Neurona Therapeutics, NGM Biopharmaceuticals, Nurix, Oric Pharmaceuticals, Peloton Therapeutics
Key Executives:
 Peter Svennilson, Founder/Managing Partner
 Background: Founder & Managing Partner, Three Crowns Capital; Associate Managing Director, Nomura Securities
 Directorships: Immune Design, NGM Biopharmaceuticals, ORIC Pharmaceuticals, Gritstone Oncology
 David V. Goeddel PhD, PhD, Managing Partner
 Education: BA, Chemistry, University of California, San Diego; PhD, Biochemistry, University of Colorado
 Background: Co-Founder, Tularik; Senior Scientific Vice President, Amgen
 Directorships: Constellation Pharmaceuticals, FLX Bio, Igenica Biotherapeutics, NGM Biopharmaceuticals, Nurix, Peloton Therapeutics
 Tim Kutzkey, PhD, Managing Partner
 Education: Stanford University; PhD, University of California, Berkeley
 Background: Scientist, KAI Pharmaceuticals
 Directorships: Carmot Therapeutics, Nurix, Peloton Therapeutics
 Larry Lasky, PhD, Partner
 Education: BA, PhD, University of California, Los Angeles
 Background: Founding Scientist, Genetics Institute; Scientist, Genentech; General Partner, Latterell Venture Partners; Partner, USVP
 Directorships: Carmot Therapeutics, eFFECTOR Pharmaceuticals
 JJ Kang, PhD, Partner
 Education: Harvard University; PhD, California Institute of Technology
 Background: FibroGen
 Directorships: Escient Pharmaceuticals; Tenaya Therapeutics
 Leon Chen, PhD, Partner
 Education: BA, Biochemistry, University of California, Berkeley; PhD, Molecular Pharmacology, Stanford School of Business; MBA, Stanford Grad. School of Business
 Background: Founder, KAI Pharmaceuticals; Venture Partner, OrbiMed; Partner, Skyline Ventures
 Directorships: E-Scape Bio; TranscripTx; Adicet

518 COMCAST VENTURES
One Kearny Building
23 Geary Street
10th Floor
San Francisco, CA 94108

web: www.comcastventures.com

Mission Statement: To turn startups into profitable businesses through innovation and business resources.

Geographic Preference: United States, Europe, Israel
Fund Size: $600 million
Founded: 1999
Investment Criteria: Seed-Late Stage; dedicated management team with clearly defined target market combined with strategic opportunities
Industry Group Preference: Media, Broadband, E-Commerce & Manufacturing, Data Communications, Communications, Applications Software & Services, Networking, Infrastructure, Advertising, Consumer Products, Enterprise Software
Portfolio Companies: Accolade, Atscale, Automat, Autonomic, Away, Axial, B8ta, Baobab, Baublebar, Bay Dynamics, Bento, Benu Networks, BigID, Birchbox, BitSight, Blink, Blockdaemon, Brightside, Bunker, Cheddar, Cloud Passage, College Ave Student Loans, Color, Comparably, Creative Live, Cross Mediaworks, CTI Towers, Cut, Data Plus Math, Datastax, Docu Sign, Dray Now, Earny, Eden, Edge Connex, Enigma, Fan Duel, Felix & Paul Studios, Flipboard, Fortress, Grokker, Heleo, Hippo, Hired, Hollar, Houseparty, Houzz, Instacart, Integrate, Interactions, Italic, Jornaya, K Health, KeyMe, KiwiCo, KodaCloud, Lendio, Life House, Lyft, Lytics, Madison Reed, MealPal, Meta, Modsy, Nextdoor, NextVR, Ninth Decimal, OfferUp, Osaro, Pony.ai, PrecisionHawk, Quantifind, Ramp, Retina AI, SevenR Rooms, SheKnows, Shine, Slack, SnagFilms, Spaces, Stella Service, SundaySky, Taboola, Talix, Tastemade, The Athletic, Trion, TuneIn, UberMedia, Uptycs, Videology, Vox Media, Windsor Circle, YouNow, Zenefits, Zola, ZoomData

Other Locations:
 480 Cowper Street
 Suite 200
 Palo Alto, CA 94301

 One Comcast Center
 55th Floor

182

Venture Capital & Private Equity Firms / Domestic Firms

1701 John F. Kennedy Boulevard
Philadelphia, PA 19103-2838

588 Broadway
Suite 202
New York, NY 10012

11111 Santa Monica Boulevard
Suite 950
Los Angeles, CA 90025

Key Executives:
Amy Banse, Managing Directory/Head of Funds
Education: BA, Harvard University; JD, Temple University Law School
Background: Attorney, Comcast; Founder, Comcast Interactive Media
Andrew Cleland, Managing Director
Education: Economics, Edinburgh University; MBA, INSEAD
Background: Managing Director, Time Warner Investments; Booz Allen & Hamilton; COO, TrustTheDJ
Gil Beyda, Managing Director
Education: BS, Computer Science, MBA, California State University, Northridge
Background: Managing Partner, Genacast Ventures; CTO, TACODA; Founder, Real Media; Founder, Mind Games for Apple II
Dinesh Moorjani, Managing Director
Education: BS, Chemical Engineering, Northwestern University; MBA, Harvard Business School
Background: Founder/CEO, Hatch Labs; Co-Founder, Tinder; LP & Advisor, Warburg Pincus; InterActiveCorp; Samsung Electronics; Co-Founder, Saffronart; AD Little; Mainspring; Goldman Sachs
Directorships: American Express, Assurant
David Zilberman, Managing Director
Education: BS, Finance, Binghamton University
Background: Business Development Manager, Flarion Technologies; Associate, Lehman Brothers

519 COMET LABS
703 Market Street
19th Floor
San Francisco, CA 94103

e-mail: hi@cometlabs.io
web: cometlabs.io

Mission Statement: Comet Labs is a venture capital firm and startup platform with an exclusive focus on AI and robotics technology.
Founded: 2015
Industry Group Preference: Artificial Intelligence, Robotics, Deep Technology, Industry Applications, Machine Learning
Portfolio Companies: 3scan, Abundant Robotics, Airmap, Akin, Alces Technology, AMP Robotics, Arch, Cobalt, Creator, Deep Vision, Doc AI, DotDashPay, Esperanto Technologies, Grabango, IAM Robotics, InsightRX, Iron Ox, Lightform, Maidbot, Matternet, Oculii, OtoSense, Percolata, Plutoshift, Point One Navigation, PRENAV, RBC Signals, Ripcord, Roost, SalesHero, Shaper, Simbe, SunTouch, Transcend Robotics, WiBotics

Key Executives:
Mingyao Wang, Chairman
Education: IMBA, Tsinghua University
Background: Manager, Dacheng Fund Management Co.; SVP, Zeo2IPO Group; Partner, Ninesail Capital; Executive Director, Legend Holdings
Lucas Wang, Managing Partner
Education: BA, Finance, National Taiwan University; MBA, National Sun Yat-Sen University
Background: Market Manager, Microelectronics Technology Inc.; Partner, WI Harper Group; Execution Partner/Founder, TMI Holding Corp.; CEO/Found, HWTrek; US Operations Partner, Legend Star;

520 COMMONS CAPITAL
320 Washington Street
4th Floor
Brookline, MA 02445

Phone: 617-739-3500 **Fax:** 617-739-3550
web: www.commonscapital.com

Mission Statement: Invests in early stage businesses whose products and services address significant social and environmental issues in the areas of healthcare, environment, energy and education.
Investment Criteria: Early-Stage
Industry Group Preference: Healthcare, Energy, Environment, Education
Portfolio Companies: Apex Learning, Claros Diagnostics, CodeRyte, Combinent BioMedical Systems, CTP Hydrogen, H2Gen Innovations, HistoRx, Medical Metrix Solutions, Niman Ranch, OutStart, Passport Systems, Pelamis Wave Power, Protonex, Solstice Capital, Sun & Earth, Teladoc

Key Executives:
William Osborn, Investment Manager
e-mail: wosborn@commonscapital.com
Education: BA, Princeton University; JD, George Washington University Law School
Background: Partner, Arete Corporation; Principal, Venture Investment Management Company, LLC; Management Consultant, Arthur D Little
Directorships: Evergreen Solar, World Power Technologies, Evolutionary Technologies, Surgical Sealants, Fingerlakes Aquaculture, Conservation Services Group

521 COMMONWEALTH CAPITAL VENTURES LP
400 West Cummings Park
Suite 1725-134
Woburn, MA 01801

Phone: 781-890-5554
web: www.commonwealthvc.com

Mission Statement: Commonwealth Capital Ventures' experienced team works closely with entrepreneurial management teams to help them build outstanding growth companies and deliver superior returns to investors.
Geographic Preference: Northeast United States
Fund Size: $580 million
Founded: 1995
Average Investment: $2-6 million
Minimum Investment: $1 million
Investment Criteria: Early Stage, Venture Growth Stage
Industry Group Preference: Software Services, Internet Technology, Communication Technology, Instrumentation, Internet, Digital Media & Marketing, Communications, Wireless
Portfolio Companies: Aberdeen Group, Acacia, Accurev, Akibia, Altiga Networks, American Internet Corp, Antenna Software, Auction Holdings, BBN Technologies, BitSight, Brooks24x7, BuyerZone, ByAllAccounts, Carbon Design Systems, CardScan, Centra Software, Cerulean Technology, CloudSwitch, Compete, Constant Contact, Crossbeam Systems, Direct Hit Technologies, e-Dialog, Echo Nest, Envoy Networks, Expressor Software, Extraprise, HubCast, i-Logix, Inframetrics, Innoveer Solutions, JAZD Markets, MacGregor Group, NBX Corp., Net2Net Corp., NeuroMetrix, Nova Analytics Corp., OneRiot, Oneshape Inc., Ounce Labs, Pactolus Communications, Qiave Technologies, Qvidian, RAMP, Reval, Sand 9, Seahorse Bioscience, SeniorLink, SoundBite Communications, Tally Systems, TIM Group, Vela Systems, Verivo, Visible Assets, Wavesmith Networks, Zinio Systems, Zoom Information

Key Executives:
Michael T. Fitzgerald, General Partner/Founder
Education: Amherst College; Harvard Business School
Background: General Partner, Palmer Partners

183

Venture Capital & Private Equity Firms / Domestic Firms

Jeffrey M. Hurst, General Partner/Founder
Education: MBA, Tulane University; BA History & Economics, Duke University
Background: GE Capital's Corporate Finance Group; Cox Partners; Bamkers Trust Company
Stephen McCormack, General Partner/Founder
Education: MBA, University of Michigan; Graduate, Psychology, Dartmouth College
Background: 3i Corporation, Merrill Lynch Venture Capital, Massachusetts Technology Development Corporation, Bank of New York, Interactive Data Corporation
Justin J. Perreault, General Partner
Education: MBA, Harvard Business School; BS Mechanical Engineering, Rensselaer Polytechnic Institute
Background: CEO, Object Deisgn; Harvard Management Company; McKinsey & Company
Elliot M. Katzman, General Partner
Education: BSBA, Salem State College
Background: General Partner, Kodiak Venture Partners; Founder, Myteam.com
Directorships: CloudSwitch, OneRiot, My Perfect Gig, Vela Systems, The Echo Nest

522 COMPASS GROUP
135 Eest 57th Street
30th Floor
New York, NY 10022

Phone: 212-355-7630 Fax: 212-355-2015
web: cgcompass.com

Mission Statement: A registered investment adviser servicing institutional and private clients specializing in Latin American investments. Compass Group aims to provide consistently better returns than competitors and the highest level of service and the best range of products to serve their clients' investment needs.

Geographic Preference: Latin America
Founded: 1995

Other Locations:
Carlos Pellegrini 1023
14th Floor
Buenos Aires
Argentina
Phone: 54-11 4878 8000 Fax: 54-11 4878 8008

Av. Rosario Norte 555
Piso 14
Las Condes
Santiago 1001
Chile
Phone: 562-364-4660

Av. La Paz 1049
Piso 3
Miraflores
Lima
Peru
Phone: 511-611-5350 Fax: 511-611-5351

Paseo de los Tamarindos No. 90
Torre 1
Piso 21
Mexico DF 05120
Mexico
Phone: 5255-5010-2150 Fax: 5255-5570-9583

Carrera 7 No. 113-43
Suite 1508
Bogota
Columbia
Phone: 57-1748-6096 Fax: 57-1214-3101

Key Executives:
Manuel Jose Balbontin, Founder & Managing Partner
Education: BS, Catholic University; MBA, Harvard University
Background: Managing Director, Banco Santander; Citibank/Citicorp
Jorge Aguilo, Partner/CEO
Education: Civil Engineering, Catholic University, Chile; MBA, Instituto de Empresa Business School, Madrid

523 COMPASS GROUP MANAGEMENT LLC
301 Riverside Avenue
2nd Floor
Westport, CT 06880

Phone: 203-221-1703 Fax: 203-221-8253
web: www.compassequity.com

Mission Statement: Private investing in small to middle market companies for growth, ownership change and recapitalization.

Geographic Preference: United States, Canada
Fund Size: $300 million
Founded: 1998
Average Investment: $15-150 million
Minimum Investment: $4 million
Investment Criteria: Middle-Market, Acquisitions, MBO
Industry Group Preference: Manufacturing, Distribution, Services, Retailing, Diversified
Portfolio Companies: 55.1 Tactical, Advanced Circuits, Aeroglide Corporation, American Furniture Manufacturing, Arnold Magnetic Technologies, Camelbak, Clean Earth, Ergobaby, Foam Fabrications, Fox Racing Shox, Halo Branded Solutions, Liberty Safe, Manitoba Harvest, Silvue, Staffmark, Sterno Group, Tridien Medical, Velocity Outdoor Corporation

Other Locations:
2010 Main Street
Suite 1220
Irvine, CA 92614
Phone: 949-333-5033 Fax: 949-333-5043

Key Executives:
Ryan J. Faulkingham, Executive Vice President/CFO
Education: Lehigh University; Fordham University
Background: Merrill Lynch; WebMD Corp.; Arthur Andersen
Elias J. Sabo, Partner/CFO
Education: Rensselaer Polytechnic Institute
Background: Investment Banker, CIBC Oppenheimer; President/Chief Investment Officer, Boundary Partners; Acquisition Department, Colony Capital
Directorships: TransMarine Navigation, Venturi Partners, KBell Holdings, CBS Personnel Holdings
Patrick A. Maciariello, Partner/COO
Education: BBA, University of Notre Dame; MBA, Columbia University
Background: Management Consultant, Bain & Company; Deutsche Banc Alex. Brown

524 COMPASS TECHNOLOGY PARTNERS LP
1155 Broadway Street
Suite 210
Redwood City, CA 94063

Phone: 650-366-7595
e-mail: darscott@compasstechpartners.com
web: www.compasstechpartners.com

Mission Statement: Focused on investments in emerging companies with innovative products or services addressing high-growth markets.

Geographic Preference: San Francisco
Fund Size: $10 million
Founded: 1988
Average Investment: $500,000
Minimum Investment: $500,000
Investment Criteria: Seed/First Round
Industry Group Preference: Information Technology, Communications, Medical Devices, Computer Related, Silicon-Related Technologies

Venture Capital & Private Equity Firms / Domestic Firms

Portfolio Companies: Atherotech, Oculex Pharmaceuticals, Radio Therapeutics Corporation, NanoNexus, Photodigm, SoftBook Press, Dragnet Solutions, Torrex Equipment Corporation, Boxer Cross, DataCycles, Metara, Ripfire, Yield Dynamics, Tesla Motors, Toolwire, Percutaneous Systems, Sentinel Vision, Applied MicroStructures

Key Executives:
David G. Arscott, General Partner
e-mail: darscott@compasstechpartners.com
Education: BA, College of Wooster; MBA, University of Michigan
Background: Citicorp Venture Capital; Arscott, Norton & Associates
Directorships: Lam Research, Toolwire, Star Vox
Martha P.E. Arscott, General Partner/CFO
e-mail: marscott@compasstechpartners.com
Education: BA Economics, Hollins College; MBA, Darden School, University of Virginia
Background: Crocker National Bank

525 COMPOUND
156 Fifth Ave.
Suite 600
New York, NY 10010

Phone: 646-794-1330
e-mail: info@compound.vc
web: www.compound.vc

Mission Statement: Compound, formerly Metamorphic Ventures, is a New York City based venture capital fund that invests in start-up and early stage technology businesses focused on the digital media and digital commerce sectors. Compound believes that vast new waves of innovation and business opportunity are on their way leveraging the build out of the fixed and mobile broadband internet network. In fact, many are already here. Compound funds those early stage businesses in the digital media and digital commerce sectors. While it may appear that these are two distinct sectors, it is our view that they are in fact in the process of converging and that Compound is one of a few venture firms with the expertise in both domains.

Investment Criteria: Early-Stage
Industry Group Preference: Technology, Digital Media & Marketing, E-Commerce & Manufacturing
Portfolio Companies: Agrilyst, Allset, Alreverie, Ample, Away, BetterView, Boost Biomes, Blockstack, Braze, Buzz Points, Casa, Catalyst, Chango, Clear Genetics, Compound, Computable, Counselytics, CrowdAI, CryptoKitties, Deepgram, Digital Genius, Easecentral, Fetch Back, Finova Financial, Gem, Genies, Indiegogo, Indio, Kadena, Lenddo, Livepeer, Lotus Flare, Lune, Mass Relevance, Mattereum, Mode, Modsy, Movable Ink, Nearbuy, Nectar, Noteworth, Nucypher, Ono, Orch1d, Osaro, Payjoy, Pluot, Rayv, Rebag, Remote.it, Sayspring, Sense360, Songza, Stamped, Stanza, StowAway, Symphony Commerce, Switch, Talkspace, Tap Commerce, Tapad, Thinknear, Thrive Market, Tia, Transactis, Trusted, TV Time, Upcounsel, Vitae, Wanderu, Wayve, Xperiel, Zipdrug, Zodiac

Key Executives:
David Hirsch, Managing Director
Education: BA, University of Maryland
Background: Google; Co-Founder, Google Vertical Markets Group; Snowball; AdSmart
Marc Michel, Managing Director
Education: BA, Emory University; MBA, Wharton School
Background: Group Head, TD Capital; Managing Partner, EOS Partners; Co-Founder, Precyse Solutions
Michael Dempsey, Partner
Education: BA, New York University
Background: Rothenberg Ventures; CB Insights; Crane Partners
Joshua Nussbaum, Partner
Education: BS, New York University

Background: Business Development, JustDecide; Digital Marketing, Bayard Advertising

526 COMSPACE
web: www.comspacedev.com

Mission Statement: Offers interim executive management, advisory, and early stage private equity investment to firms in the aerospace/defense, wireless telecom, and information technology fields.

Geographic Preference: Worldwide
Founded: 1997
Average Investment: $500,000
Minimum Investment: $50,000
Investment Criteria: Early Stage
Industry Group Preference: Aerospace, Defense and Government, Information Technology, Telecommunications, Wireless Technologies
Portfolio Companies: CEL Polska, eLink Communications, Fiberight, Give More Media, Global Radio, Knight-Hub Computing, Peracon, Technikom Polska, Tracer Net, Tucana Technologies, Wall Street Sports

Key Executives:
Michael W. Miller, President/Managing Director
Education: MBA Finance, University of Chicago; Aeronautical/Astronautical Engineering/Electrical Engineering, University of Illinois
Background: Fourtune 500; CEO, TracerNet; Arc Second; Sr Executive, Rockwell International/Orbital Science/Center for Innovative Technology
Thien-Ly Ngo, Managing Director
Education: BS, Electrical Engineering, General Motors Institute; MA, Telecommunications, George Mason University

527 COMSTOCK CAPITAL PARTNERS LLC
9430 Readcrest Drive
Beverly Hills, CA 90210

Phone: 310-278-6444 Fax: 310-861-5010
e-mail: info@comstockpartners.com
web: www.comstockpartners.com

Mission Statement: A private capital firm that provides growth and buy-out capital, from senior debt to equity, and actively works with management to transform public and private companies from good to great. With extensive operating experience, they have created over $12 billion of value across a range of companies focused on consumer-facing and customer relationship business. The firm will consider deals across the nation, but focuses on the West Coast.

Geographic Preference: West Coast
Founded: 1992
Average Investment: $10 million - $500 million
Investment Criteria: Middle-market, minimum of $5 million EBIT, $50 million to $750 million in revenue
Industry Group Preference: Financial Services, Media, Entertainment, Distribution, Consumer Products, Outsourcing & Efficiency

Key Executives:
Jeffrey L Balash, Partner
Education: Summa cum laude, Princeton University; Baker Scholar, Harvard Business School; Cum laude, Harvard Law School
Background: Managing Director, Lehman Brothers; Managing Director, Drexel Burnham; Co-Founder, Anthem Partners; Co-Founder, JL Furnishings; CFO/Chief Strategic Officer, Telephony@Work; Director Export Operations, Avon Products; CEO, Louis Dreyfus & Cie

Venture Capital & Private Equity Firms / Domestic Firms

528 COMVEST PARTNERS
525 Okeechobee Blvd
Suite 1050
West Palm Beach, FL 33401

Phone: 561-727-2000
web: www.comvest.com

Mission Statement: Comvest Partners provides equity capital to middle-market companies based in the United States.
Geographic Preference: United States
Fund Size: $893 million
Founded: 2000
Average Investment: $25 - $100 million
Investment Criteria: Divestitures, Management Buyouts, Restructurings, Industry Consolidations, Public-to-Private Transactions, Turnaround
Industry Group Preference: Software, Information Technology, Transportation, Healthcare, Industrial Manufacturing, Consumer Products, Fintech, Financial Services, Education
Portfolio Companies: AxisPoint Health, BEL USA, Cartera Commerce, Convey Health Solutions, D&S Community Services, EVCI Career Colleges, GroundLink, Haggen, Innovative Health Products, Old Time Pottery, Priority Holdings, Red Hawk Fire & Security, Robbins Brothers, Sunteck, US Pipe

Other Locations:
181 West Madison Street
Suite 3815
Chicago, IL 60602
Phone: 312-637-8455

Key Executives:
Michael Falk, CEO & Managing Partner
Education: BA, Economics, Queens College
Background: Founder & CEO, Commonwealth Associates
Roger Marrero, Managing Partner
Education: BA, BBA, University of Texas at Austin; MBA, Harvard Business School
Background: Principal, ABRY Partners; Apax Partners; Hicks, Muse, Tate & Furst; Goldman Sachs
Tom Clark, Partner
Education: BA, International Relations, Johns Hopkins University; MBA, Harvard Business School
Background: Principal, Retail & Consumer, Apax Partners; Principal, Private Equity, Bain Capital; Analyst, M&A Group, Goldman Sachs
Lee Bryan, Partner
Education: BA, Georgia Institute of Technology; MBA, Harvard Business School
Background: Director, Private Equity Group, Harbert Management Corporation; Bain & Company; Procter & Gamble; Delta Airlines
Marshall Griffin, Principal
Education: BS, Finance, Boston College; MBA, Duke University
Background: Senior Associate, Crossbow Ventures; Analyst, TD Capital

529 CONCENTRIC EQUITY PARTNERS
Financial Investments Corporation
50 East Washington Street
Suite 400
Chicago, IL 60602

Phone: 312-494-4513
web: www.ficcep.com

Mission Statement: Concentric Equity Partners provides financial and operating expertise to profitable growth companies. The firm seeks opportunities in the service industry, including business, consumer, financial, and technology-enabled services.
Fund Size: $650 million
Average Investment: $10 - $30 million
Investment Criteria: Management Buyouts, Leveraged Buyouts, Growth Equity Investments, Majority & Minority Investment Structures
Industry Group Preference: Business Products & Services, Consumer Services, Financial Services, Healthcare Services, Technology-Enabled Services
Portfolio Companies: Airway Services, Aperture, Catastrophe Solutions International, Chicago Deferred Exchange Company, Coastal Waste & Recycling, Cole Taylor Bank, Colonial Claims, Consulting Solutions, Ellison Bakery, Energy Distribution Partners, Environmental Pest Services, Lario Oil & Gas Company, Liberty Oilfield Services, Marathon Data Systems, Market Express, MB Financial Bank, Mortgage Contracting Services, Microsystems, Mountain Waste & Recycling, Nine Four Ventures, NSC Technologies, Online Tech Stores, Puttman Infrastructure, SaaS Capital, Southpaw Live, Stay Alfred, Tricoci University, UsAmeriBank, Vision, World Energy Partners

Key Executives:
Ken Hooten, Partner
Education: BS, University of Illinois; MBA, Kellogg School of Management
Background: Founder, ServiceMaster Ventures; President & Founder, ServiceMaster Home Services Center
Jennifer Steans, Partner
Education: BA, Davidson College; MBA, Kellogg School of Management, Northwestern University
Background: Consultant, Deloitte & Touche; Treasurer, Prime Graphics; Founder, Financial Investments Corporation
Directorships: Chicago Deferred Exchange Corp., Prime Graphics
Frank Reppenhagen, Partner
Education: BS, Industrial Engineering, University at Buffalo; MBA, University of Chicago Booth School of Business
Ian Ross, Partner
Education: BA, Finance, Michigan State University; MBA, University of Chicago Booth School of Business
Background: Edgewater Funds; Lincoln International; GE Capital Corporation
David Gervase, Chief Financial Officer
Education: BS, Accounting, University of Illinois; CPA
Background: Director of Finance, Arena Football League

530 CONNECTICUT INNOVATIONS
470 James Street
Suite 8
New Haven, CT 06513

Phone: 860-258-7858 Fax: 860-563-5851
e-mail: info@ctinnovations.com
web: www.ctinnovations.com

Mission Statement: State of Connecticut's leading investor in high technology, making risk capital investments in high tech companies throughout the state. They offer a wide range of support from research assistance to financing for product development and marketing.
Geographic Preference: Connecticut
Founded: 1989
Average Investment: $1 million
Minimum Investment: $500,000
Investment Criteria: Seed, Start-up, First Stage, Second Stage. Applicants must be located in Connecticut, have a management team in place, provide a business plan and demonstrate sustainable competitive advantage.
Industry Group Preference: Advanced Marine Applications, Aerospace, Defense and Government, Energy, Photonics, Advanced Materials, Biotechnology, Information Technology, Renewable Energy, Applications Software & Services, Environment Products & Services, High Technology, Clean Technology, Medical Devices
Portfolio Companies: Achillion, Affomix Corp., Alexion, ATMI, Axiomx, Biohaven, Bioplexus, Bristol Technology, Cara Therapeutics, Cardium, CGI, Curagen, Cyberian

Venture Capital & Private Equity Firms / Domestic Firms

Outpost, Cyvek, Cyvera, DEOS, Digital Graphics, Discover Video, EDR, Genaissance Pharmaceuticals, Hadapt, Idevices, Imstem Biotechnology, International Telecommunication Data Systems, Ipsogen Cancer Profiler, Job Direct, Keisense, Lexibridge, Lifecodes, Linksoft, Memry, Meta Server, Netkey, Neuvis, Nufern, NXT-ID, Online Tech, Open Solutions, Paragon, PCC Technology, Perosphere Inc., Photonics Applications, PolyVision, Post-N-Track, Preferred Systems, Premise, Proton, Silversky, Standing Stone

Key Executives:
Peter Longo, Senior Managing Director, Investments
860-258-7858
e-mail: peter.longo@ctinnovations.com
Education: BBA, University of Connecticut; MBA, University of Hartford; CPA; CFA
Background: Senior Accountant, Ernst & Young
Kevin Crowley, Managing Director, Investments
860-258-7858
e-mail: kevin.crowley@ctinnovations.com
Education: MBA, Quinnipiac University
Background: Director, Office of BioScience, Connecticut Department of Economic & Community Development
Directorships: frevvo, Oil Purification Systems, RemoTV, Retail Optimization
Pauline Murphy, Senior Managing Director, Investments
e-mail: pauline.murphy@ctinnovations.com
Education: BS Accounting, University of Connecticut; CPA
Background: Controller, early stage software development company; Ernst & Young
Matthew McCooe, Chief Executive Officer, Connecticut Innovations
Education: BA, Boston College; MBA, Columbia University
Background: Chart Venture Partners; Director, Columbia University Science and Technology Ventures; Co-Founder, Eureka Networks; Fortune 500; Becton Dickinson; MCI
Philip Siuta, COO/CFO
Education: BS, Accounting, Villanova University
Background: Project Manager, Jackson Laboratory; Project Manager, Connecticut Ecosystem
David Wurzer, Executive Vice President/Chief Investment Officer
e-mail: david.wurzer@ctinnovations.com
Education: BBA, Accountancy, University of Notre Dame
Background: Executive Vice President, CuraGen Corporation; Senior Vice President, Value Health
Daniel Wagner, Managing Director, Investments
e-mail: daniel.wagner@ctinnovations.com
Education: BS, Biology, University of Dayton; MBA, MS, Health Sciences, Quinnipiac University
Background: CuraGen Corporation
Directorships: Innovatient Solutions, RemoteReality Corp., FMP Products

531 CONSOR CAPITAL
Sausalito, CA

web: www.consorcapital.com

Mission Statement: Consor Capital LLC was formed by Josh and Jay Huffard to manage venture capital investments. Consor Capital focuses on early-stage companies serving consumers and small businesses. We seek to partner with companies run by strong leaders, focused on rapidly changing markets and leveraging technology as a key aspect of their business model.

Investment Criteria: Early-Stage
Portfolio Companies: Coveroo, NewCross Technologies, vSocial, Wallop
Key Executives:
Jay Huffard, Manager
Education: BA, Yale University; MBA, Stanford Graduate School of Business
Background: Managing Director, Huffard & Co.; Managing Director & Principal, Prima Managment Corp.

532 CONSTELLATION TECHNOLOGY VENTURES
web: technologyventures.constellation.com

Mission Statement: The mission of Constellation Technology Ventures is to drive innovation through Exelon by investing in venture stage energy technology companies that can provide new solutions to Exelon and its customers.

Fund Size: $650 million
Founded: 1998
Average Investment: $15 million
Minimum Investment: $5 million
Investment Criteria: Early to mid-stage companies with emerging digital networks
Industry Group Preference: Digital Media & Marketing, Communications, Enterprise Services, Media, Information Technology
Portfolio Companies: Bidgely, C3 Energy, ChargePoint, Cool Planet Energy Systems, DemandQ, LevelTen Energy, Measurabl, Ouster, Owl Analytics, PosiGen, PrecisionHawk, Proterra, Qnovo, Sparkfund, Stem, V-Grid Energy Systems, XL Hybrids

Key Executives:
Scott Dupcak, Managing Director
e-mail: scott.dupcak@constellation.com
Education: BS, Accounting, Fairfield University; MBA, Robert H. Smith School of Business, University of Maryland
Background: Strategic Systems/Business Operations, Exelon Corp.
Curtis Schickner, Principal, Investments
e-mail: curtis.schickner@constellation.com
Education: BA, Economics, University of Maryland
Background: Exelon Generation Finance
Megan Sparks, Director, Commercialization
e-mail: megan.sparks@constellation.com
Education: BS, Finance/Logistics, University of Maryland College Park; MA, Applied Economics, Johns Hopkins University
Background: Constellation Retail & Wholesale
Shounok Sinha, Principal, Investments
e-mail: Shounok.Sinha@constellation.com
Education: BS, Instrumentation Engineering, BMS College Of Engineering, India; MBA, University of Maryland

533 CONTOUR VENTURE PARTNERS
475 Park Avenue South
6th Floor
New York, NY 10016

Phone: 212-644-5482
e-mail: businessplan@contourventures.com
web: www.contourventures.com

Mission Statement: Contour Venture Partners is a venture capital firm based in New York. The firm invests in early stage companies that provide technology solutions to established sectors, including financial services, business services, software, and digital media. Contour Venture Partners seeks to help entrepreneurs and management teams to build companies that will transform their industries.

Geographic Preference: Northeast United States
Average Investment: $250,000 - $1.5 million
Investment Criteria: Seed-Stage, Early-Stage
Industry Group Preference: Financial Services, Digital Media & Marketing, Internet, Business Products & Services, Software, Technology, Information Technology
Portfolio Companies: Bench, BounceExchange, Clothes Horse, Contently, Datadog, Dstillery, EachScape, Edgecase, Ellevest, Estimize, EveryScreen Media, FieldLens, FinTech Innovation Lab, LeagueApps, Movable Ink, Octane Lending,

187

Venture Capital & Private Equity Firms / Domestic Firms

Oggifinogi, OnDeck, OwnEnergy, Pathgather, Pendo, Punchbowl Software, Qwiki, Routehappy, Scratch Music Group, ShopKeep, Simpli.fi, Source3, SwapDrive, Ticketfly, TiqIQ, True Office, Ufora, Voxy, YellowJacket, Yhat, YouBeauty, Zipmark

Key Executives:
Bob Greene, Managing Partner
Education: BS, Wharton School, University of Pennsylvania; MBA, MIT Sloan School of Management
Background: Managing Partner, Flatiron Partners; General Partner, Chase Capital Partners; Chemical Venture Partners
Directorships: New York Venture Capital Association
Matt Gorin, Managing Partner
Education: BA, Economics & American Studies, Brandeis University; MBA, Harvard Business School
Background: Promotory Financial Group; Strategic Planning & Corporate Development Group, Red Hat; Morgan Stanley; PricewaterhouseCoopers; Founder, StreetWise Partners

534 CONVERGE VENTURE PARTNERS
101 Main Street
Cambridge, MA 02142

web: converge.vc

Mission Statement: Converge Venture Partners provides capital to early stage technology companies in the software, cloud, mobile, digital media, Internet and SaaS sectors.
Geographic Preference: Boston, New England, New York City
Fund Size: $27 million
Founded: 1998
Average Investment: $100,000 - $1 million
Investment Criteria: Seed, Early Stage, Early Series A
Industry Group Preference: Information Technology, Software, Internet, Digital Media & Marketing, Mobile, SaaS, Cloud Computing
Portfolio Companies: Apperian, Coherent Path, Curoverse, Disruptor Beam, DocTracker, HapYak, HNW, Influitive, InsightSquared, InStream, Linkable Networks, N-of-One, Offerpop, ownCloud, OwnerIQ, ParElastic, Powerhouse Dynamics, Practically Green, Prime Student Loan, Promoboxx, Scratch Wireless, Skyhook Wireless, TimeTrade, TripleShot, TrueLens, Xconomy, YieldBot, wymsee

Key Executives:
Maia Heymann, Senior Managing Director
e-mail: maia@convergevp.com
Education: BA, Wellesley College
Background: Managing Director, Shott Capital Management; BancBoston Ventures; Bank of Boston
Nilanana Bhowmik, Founder/General Partner
Education: BEng, Computer Science, Indian Institute of Technology; MS, Computer Science, University of South Carolina; MBA, INSEAD
Background: Managing Director, Longworth Venture Partners

535 CONVERSION CAPITAL
902 Broadway
Suite 1611
New York, NY 10010

e-mail: info@conversioncapital.com
web: www.conversioncapital.com

Mission Statement: Provides financial services venture capital.
Investment Criteria: Early Stage, Growth Stage
Industry Group Preference: Financial Services, Technology
Portfolio Companies: Blend, Booster, Dataminr, Fauna, Figure, FiscalNote, Frame.ai, Immuta, Improbable, LearnVest, Orchard, Osper, Paribus, Perpetua, Planetary Resources, Predata, Redowl, Sperical Defence

Key Executives:
Christian Lawless, Founder & Managing Partner
Education: BA, Economics, Wesleyan University
Background: Managing Director, Capital Markets, Lehman Brothers
Directorships: Booster Fuels, Immuta, Improbable, Blend Labs, Dataminr, WillCall, Paribus, Orchard Platform, LearnVest, Redowl Analytics

536 CORAL GROUP
Phone: 612-335-8682
web: www.coralgrp.com

Mission Statement: Coral Group has partnered with entrepreneurs and management teams to bring a new approach to solving problems and transforming companies. The group uses three strategies in parallel to achieve this goal. Those strategic values are venture capital, holistic solutions and transformations.
Fund Size: $300 million
Founded: 1990
Average Investment: $2 million - $12 million
Minimum Investment: $100,000
Investment Criteria: Enterprises that exploit major industry trends, focus on substantial markets, grow through execution or effort as opposed to being research or equipment intensive and develop a global scope
Industry Group Preference: Communications, Information Technology, Media, Software, Healthcare, Life Sciences, Medical
Portfolio Companies: Advanced Fibre, AeroScout, Alfy, Baystone Software, BroadRiver Communications, Calix, Call Connect, Cerus, Computer Aided Services, Damark International, Delivery Agent, Digital Generation Systems, E/O Networks, ebix.com, Elity Systems, Entone, Exanet, FaxSav, Firetide, FlexLight Networks, Fon, Force10 Networks, Freeborders, Gearworks, Gift Certificate Center, GoDigital Networks, GoToCall.com, Iconoculture, Infinera, InfoGin, Integral Access, Macromedia, Magnet Communications, Movius, Myocor, NewCity Communications, NextNet Wireless, Optical Solutions, Picolight, Prodea, Racotek, Red Bend Software, RichFX, Systems & Networks, Teltech Resource Network, Tricord Systems, Veracicom, Vertical Communications, Vicarious, Vizrt, Zoran

Key Executives:
Yuval Almog, Chairman
e-mail: yuval.almog@coralgrp.com
Education: BA, BS, University of Alabama; Massachusetts Institute of Technology
Background: Co-Founder, Zoran Corporation; Raychem Corporation; Systems Officer/Fighter Pilot, Israeli Air Force
Mark Headrick, Managing Director/General Counsel
e-mail: mark@coralgrp.com
Education: BA, Economics, Lake Forest College; JD, William Mitchell College of Law
Robert Goldberg, Managing Director
e-mail: robert@coralgrp.com
Education: BS, Engineering & Applied Science, Columbia University
Background: SVP, Busines Operations & Corporate Development, Zynga; Managing Director, Idealab
Eyal Shaked, Managing Director
e-mail: eyal@coralgrp.com
Education: BA, Electrical Engineering, Technion Institute of Technology; MSc, Electrical Engineering & Computer Science, Tel Aviv University
Background: COO, Playtika; EVP & General Manager, Network Solutions Division, ECI Telecom
Miki Granski, Managing Director
e-mail: miki@coralgrp.com
Education: BSc, MSc, Electrical Engineering & Computer Science, Technion Institute of Technology; MBA, Kellogg

Venture Capital & Private Equity Firms / Domestic Firms

School of Management, Northwestern University
Background: Zoran; NeoMagic; LSI Logic
Linda Watchmaker, Managing Director/Chief Financial Officer
e-mail: lindawatchmaker@coralgrp.com
Education: BBA, MBA, Finance & Marketing, University of Wisconsin, Madison; CPA
Background: Consulting Manager, Ernst & Young; Financial Analyst & Manager, Kimberly-Clark Corporation

537 CORDOVA VENTURES
4080 McGinnis Ferry Road
Suite 1201
Alpharetta, GA 30005
Phone: 678-942-0300 Fax: 678-942-0301

Mission Statement: Experienced venture capital company managing a range of venture funds that provide both capital and value-added resources for growing companies.

Geographic Preference: Southeast
Fund Size: $130 million
Founded: 1989
Average Investment: $1 - $5 million
Minimum Investment: $250,000
Investment Criteria: Privately held, Seed, Start-Up, Early Stage, Later Stage
Industry Group Preference: Information Technology, Industrial Equipment, Real Estate, Life Sciences, Biotechnology, Communications, Healthcare, Financial Services, Telecommunications
Portfolio Companies: EcoSMART Technologies, Nexidia

Key Executives:
Gerald F Schmidt, Co-Founder/Managing Partner
e-mail: js@cordovaventures.com
Education: BS, North Dakota State University; University of Minnesota
Background: Jostens; Manderson & Associates
Directorships: National Executive Committee for the Council of Growing Companies
Charles E Adair, Partner
e-mail: ea@cordovaventures.com
Education: Vanderbilt University; BS, Accounting, University of Alabama; Advanced Management Program, Harvard Business School
Background: Accountant, Haskins & Sells; Controller, Durr-Fillauer Medical
Directorships: Tech Data Corporation, Performance Food Group Company, Torchmark Corporation, PSS World Medical, Sterling Bank, Jenkins Brick Company, UAB Health System
Paul R DiBella, Partner
e-mail: pd@cordovaventures.com
Education: State University of New York at Albany; University of Miami School of Law
Background: Founder, Industrial Technology Ventures
Directorships: ASPEX, Ecovation, Axonn, Five Star Technologies, SkyBitz, EcoSmart Technologies, DemandPoint Systems
Frank X Dalton, Partner
e-mail: fxd@cordovaventures.com
Education: BS, Accounting, University of South Carolina; UGA Board of Directors College; KPMG Audit Committee Institute
Background: Partner, BDO Seidman; Ernst & Ernst
Directorships: Technology Executives Roundtable, Atlanta Venture Forum, Moore School of Business, Xpanxion
L Edward Wilson PE, Partner
e-mail: lewdux@aol.com
Education: BCE, Tennessee Technological University
Background: President, L Edward Wilson & Associates; Founder, EDGe Group; CEO, OSCO Environmental Management; Sirrom Capital Corporation
Directorships: Tennessee Tech

538 CORE CAPITAL PARTNERS
1717 K Street NW
Suite 920
Washington, DC 20006
Phone: 202-589-0090 Fax: 202-589-0091
e-mail: info@core-capital.com
web: www.core-capital.com

Mission Statement: Backed by sophisticated and experienced institutional and individual investors who are often actively involved in investment work. Each year thousands of potential transactions are reviewed. They have access to an extensive network of investors, bankers, service providers and entrepreneurs.

Geographic Preference: East Coast
Fund Size: $350 million
Founded: 1999
Average Investment: $6 million
Minimum Investment: $2 million
Investment Criteria: Early-Stage, Small to Mid-Sized Growth companies with disruptive technologies
Industry Group Preference: Communications, Information Technology, Internet Technology, Microelectronics, Nanotechnology, Networking, Optical Technology, Semiconductors, Enabling Technology, Infrastructure, Digital Media & Marketing, Technology-Enabled Services
Portfolio Companies: Aptology, BridgeWave Communications, buySAFE, DivvyCloud, Foresight, FreedomPay, Fugue, Genband, Infinite Power Solutions, Inlet Technologies, InPhonic, IXI, JackBe, KnowledgeTree, Load Dynamix, MedVentive, Mobile System7, NewEdge, OLO, Pendo.io, Radius Networks, Rally Software, Revulytics, Rollstream, Roundbox, RulesPower, Silver Storm Technologies, Soft Module, Solstice Software, Source Fire, Staq, Stardog, SwapDrive, Triumfant, Trust Digital, Twisted Pair, Univa, Update Logic, Valen Analytics, Vizbee, Vocal Data, ZeroFOX

Key Executives:
William Dunbar, Managing Director
e-mail: wdunbar@core-capital.com
Education: MBA, Harvard University; BA, Davidson College
Background: CEO/Founder, Pebble Hill Capital; Portfolio Manager, Allied Capital; President, Allied Capital Corporation II; LBO Lending, Chase Manhattan Bank; Technology Operations, NationsBank; Venture America
Directorships: Young Presidents Organization; Venture Philanthropy Partners; Meyer Foundation; Madeira School
Mark Levine, Managing Director
e-mail: mlevine@core-capital.com
Education: MBA Finance, George Washington University
Background: GCI Venture Partners; GEO-CENTERS; Subcommittee Staff Director, Small Business Committee, US House of Representatives
Directorships: ZeroFOX, Staq, Medventive, BuySAFE, New Edge, Revulytics, Valen, Univa, UpdateLogic, FreedomPay, Roundbox, InPhonic, Vizbee, VocalData
Randy Klueger, Chief Financial Officer
e-mail: rklueger@core-capital.com
Education: BS, Business Administration, George Washington University
Background: President, Klueger & Associates LLC; CFO, Global Material Technologies; President & CFO, Millennium Laser Eye Centers

539 CORIOLIS VENTURES
160 Mercer Street
3rd Floor
New York, NY 10012
web: coriolisventures.com

Mission Statement: Coriolis Ventures is a New York based early stage Venture and incubation fund specializing in new media and infrastructure technology related to Internet advertising. Coriolis provides its portfolio companies with both

189

Venture Capital & Private Equity Firms / Domestic Firms

capital (and in many cases) incubation assistance to help nascent early stage companies accelerate their growth and development. Coriolis Ventures is associated with Coriolis Labs, a New York based marketing information research laboratory.

Investment Criteria: Early-stage
Industry Group Preference: Infrastructure Technology, Internet Advertising, New Media
Portfolio Companies: AppNexus, Crisp Media, Devpost, Dstillery, Every Screen Media, Integral Ad Science, Magnetic, NeueHouse, Triton Web Properties

Key Executives:
Joshua Abram, Founding Partner
Directorships: TMRW Life Sciences, Dstillery, Integral Ad Science, NeueHouse
Alan Murray, Founding Partner
Directorships: Dstillery, Integral Ad Science, NeueHouse

540 CORNERSTONE CAPITAL HOLDINGS
315 S Beverly Drive
Suite 320
Los Angeles, CA 90212
Phone: 310-499-5670 Fax: 312-275-7855
web: www.cstonecapital.com

Mission Statement: Cornerstone Capital Holdings is a private equity firm that invests in companies in the lower end of the middle market, with particular emphasis in aerospace, space, defense and industrial services sectors.

Geographic Preference: United States
Founded: 2000
Investment Criteria: Middle Market, Buyouts, Recapitalizations
Industry Group Preference: Industrial Services, Machinery, Manufacturing, Aerospace, Space, Defense
Portfolio Companies: AeroGen-TEK, Essner Manufacturing, N2 Imaging Systems, NuSpace, Powers Equipment Company, RSA Engineered Products, UST-Aldetec Group, Walbar Engine Components

Other Locations:
650 Sentry Parkway
Suite One
Blue Bell, PA 19422
Phone: 215-628-4486 Fax: 215-647-7473

Key Executives:
Jonathan H Alt, Founder/Principal
e-mail: jalt@cstonecapital.com
Education: BA, Finance, College of Commerce and Business Administration, University of Illinois
Background: BGL Capital Partners; Associate, Banque Paribas
Andrew M Bushell, Founder/Principal
e-mail: abushell@cstonecapital.com
Education: BA, Economics, Cornell University; JD, Rutgers Law School; MBA, Kellogg School of Management; CPA
Background: BGL Capital Partners; President, Sentry Fire Protection Systems
Lili Zhou, Chief Financial Officer
e-mail: lzhou@cstonecapital.com
Education: BSBA, Accounting, Northeastern University, China; CPA
Background: CFO, RSA Engineered Products; Corporate Finance Executive, Klune Industries
Tim Martin, Executive Advisor/Board Member
e-mail: tmartin@cstonecapital.com
Education: BA, Business Administration
Background: Chief Commercial Officer, President, Doncasters; VP Supply Chain and Strategic Initiatives, UTC Aerospace Systems

541 CORNERSTONE EQUITY INVESTORS LLC
281 Tresser Blvd
12th Floor
Stamford, CT 06901
Phone: 212-753-0901 Fax: 212-826-6798

Mission Statement: Strives to generate attractive investment returns by providing equity capital to growth companies and management buyouts and recapitalizations. Key strategies employed by the firm to achieve this goal include lead investor roles, active participation, and industry specialization. Seeks to invest in businesses that have validated their business concept and are shipping products or providing services, are staffed with experienced management team, and are either profitable or forecast profitability in the near future.

Fund Size: $1.2 billion
Founded: 1996
Average Investment: $100 million
Minimum Investment: $10 million
Investment Criteria: Later-Stage, Leveraged Buyouts, Middle Market
Industry Group Preference: Business to Business, Healthcare, Manufacturing
Portfolio Companies: ArrayComm, Auspex, Card Establishment Services, Centurion Wireless Technologies, Comdata, Commodites Corp., Conner, Continental Medical, CrossLand Mortgage Corp., Dell, Equitrac, GeoTrace, Health Management Associates, IMS, Inflow, Interim, Keystone, Linear Technology, Lionbridge, Neptco, Novatel Wireless, Optum, PerSe, PictureTel, Specialty Healthcare Services, Spectrum Healthcare Services, StoroMedia, TeamHealth, TrueTemper Sports, Vestcom, VIPS

542 CORNERSTONE HOLDINGS
385 Interlocken Crescent
Suite 250
Broomfield, CO 80021
Phone: 303-410-2510
e-mail: info@bvcv.com
web: www.bvcv.com

Mission Statement: Cornerstone Holdings is a private equity and real estate development company. Privately owned, the company focuses on opportunistic investments in profitable middle market companies via direct investments. Cornerstone partners with strong management teams to actively add value and grow businesses. The team at Cornerstone has substantial private company investment experience which spans from startup ventures to traditional leverage buyouts to distressed turnarounds. The real estate development division acquires land in resort markets and takes it through the development process.

Geographic Preference: United States
Average Investment: $4-$15 million
Investment Criteria: Recapitalizations, LBO, MBO, Growth Capital
Portfolio Companies: Apex Towers, B Media, Flat Iron Energy Partners, Gracon, Horizon Organic, Magna Energy Services, PetroCloud, Trispan

Other Locations:
1746 Union St.
San Francisco, CA 94123

Key Executives:
Tom McCloskey, Chairman/CEO
Education: BA, University of Notre Dame; MBA, Wharton School
Background: Chairman, Horizon Organic Holdings; Palmer Communications
Directorships: Magna Energy Services, Petro Cloud, B Media
Neville Vere Nicoll, President
Education: European Business School, Paris
Background: President & CEO, Kryptonics; CEO, Magna Energy Services

Venture Capital & Private Equity Firms / Domestic Firms

Clark Lipscomb, President, Real Estate
e-mail: clipscomb@cstoneholdings.com
Education: BBA, University of Texas, Austin
John Ord, Chief Financial Officer
e-mail: jord@cstoneholdings.com
Education: BS, Economics & Business Administration, Colorado State University; MoTM, University of Denver; CPA
Background: Co-Founder/CFO, BV-Cornerstone Ventures; CFO, Kryptonics; VP, Finance, Rustco Products
Ryan Williams, Principal
e-mail: rwilliams@cstoneholdings.com
Education: BS, Business Administration, Colorado State University; MS, Finance, University of Colorado, Denver; CFA
Background: Senior Consultant, Corporate Finance Group, FTI Consulting

543 CORNERSTONE VENTURE PARTNERS
120 East 23rd Street
New York, NY 10010

Phone: 646-942-0019
e-mail: contact@cornerstonevp.com
web: cornerstonevp.com

Mission Statement: Cornerstone Venture Partners is a tech-based fund interested in the Business-to-Business sector.
Geographic Preference: US, Israel
Average Investment: $1.5 million
Industry Group Preference: IoT, Big Data, FinTech, Cloud
Portfolio Companies: Axonize, DBSH, Dealhub, DeskForce, OptimalQ, Sixdof Space, Texel, User 1st, Youtiligent
Key Executives:
Michael Ozechov, Partner
Education: BS, University of Michigan
Background: Emerging Ventures Limited; Pall Mall Capital; EXP Federal; Jerusalem Venture Partners
Hanan Brand, Partner
Education: BA, Hebrew University; MBA, Israel Institute of Technology
Background: Jerusalem Venture Partners; Ofer Brothers Group; Made in Jerusalem

544 CORRELATION VENTURES
9255 Towne Centre Drive
Suite 350
San Diego, CA 92121

Phone: 858-412-8500
e-mail: dec@correlationvc.com
web: www.correlationvc.com

Mission Statement: Correlation Ventures is a new breed of venture capital firm, leveraging world-class analytics to offer entrepreneurs and other venture capitalists a dramatically better option when they are seeking additional capital to complete a financing round.
Geographic Preference: United States
Fund Size: $165 million
Investment Criteria: All Stages
Industry Group Preference: Life Sciences, Clean Technology, Information Technology, Consumer Services, Business Products & Services, Fintech, Healthcare, Enterprise Software
Portfolio Companies: 10% Happier, Able Lending, Admittedly, AirPR, AirXpanders, AlienVault, Alloy, Ando, Ankasa, Annexon Biosciences, Appthority, Apsalar, Arista MD, Betterworks, Bloomz, BlueVine Capital, Brandcast, Bravely, Care Well Urgent Care, Casper, Cloud Passage, Codefights, Contactually, Cotopaxi, Crossbar, Crowdpac, Descartes Labs, Distil Networks, Dizzion, Dolls Kill, Dropoff, Earnest, Earnup, Employee Channel, Empyr, Enlibrium, Entelo, FlexPharma, Fluid, Framehawk, FreeRange Games, Galera Therapeutics, Getaround, Gethuman, Goby, Good Eggs, Grokker, Gynesonics, Hello Tech, iBeat, Imperfect Produce, InstaEDU, Intervene, IOpipe, Ioxus, Karmic, Knock, Kwik, Labdoor, LeanData, Lemonaid Health, Lever, Litbit, Lytro, Madefire, Manticore Games, Mirna Therapeutics, Mirror, MNectar, Nexlas, NumberFire, Ollie, Optimizely, Overtime, Pepo, Personal Capital, Pley, Inbox, Powervision, Prattle, Project Cohort, Prose, Reelgood, RQX Pharmaceuticals, Scale Arc, Scribble Live, SEE Forge, ShoCard, SigniFAI, Source3, Spirox, Splice Machine, Sun Basket, Sundar, SynthoRX, Talent Sonar, TBH, Trefoil Therapeutics, Trumaker & Co., Upstart, Urjanet, VigLink, Virsto Software, Wonderschool, Yumi, Zebit

Other Locations:
650 California Street
7th Floor
San Francisco, CA 94108
Phone: 415-890-5425

79 Madison Avenue
7th Floor
New York, NY 10016
Phone: 917-297-6295

Key Executives:
David Coats, Managing Director
858-412-8500 x115
e-mail: dec@correlationvc.com
Education: BS, Biology, Princeton University; MBA, Harvard Business School
Background: Managing Director, Hamilton BioVentures; Venture Partner, Windamere Venture Partners; President, Forge Medical Ventures; Founder, Spine Wave
Trevor Kienzle, Managing Director
650-843-3210 x10
e-mail: trevor.kienzle@correlationvc.com
Education: BA, University of Virginia; MBA, Harvard Business School
Background: Managing Director, Newbury Ventures; Vice President, GE Equity; Management Consultant, Deloitte & Touche
Grace Chui-Miller, Chief Financial Officer
858-412-8500 x123
e-mail: gcm@correlationvc.com
Education: BA, Quantitative Economics & Decision Sciences, University of California, San Diego; MBA, Anderson School, University of California, LA
Background: Audit Manager, KPMG; Chief Financial Officer, DCM
Anu Pathria, Partner, Analytics
858-412-8500 x117
e-mail: akp@correlationvc.com
Education: BS, Mathematics & Computer Science, University of Waterloo; MS, Computer Science, PhD, Operations Research, University of California, Berkeley
Background: HNC Software
Moiz Saifee, Principal, Analytics
858-412-8500 x127
e-mail: mas@correlationvc.com
Education: BS, Computer Science, IIT Kharagpur
Background: Info Edge

545 CORSA VENTURES
103 E 5th Street
Suite 208
Austin, TX 78701

web: www.corsaventures.com

Mission Statement: The Corsa philosophy is to actively help build businesses and not just monitor investments. The Fund's Managing Partners are patient investors with a long term view and are actively involved across all functional areas including financial strategy, talent acquisition, technology and product roadmap planning, sales and marketing, business development and company operations.
Geographic Preference: Texas, Southwest
Investment Criteria: Early-Stage

Venture Capital & Private Equity Firms / Domestic Firms

Industry Group Preference: Information Technology, Cloud Computing, Big Data, Mobile, Social Media
Portfolio Companies: Ad Mass, Bold Metrics, Clear Blade, Convey, Eye Q, Favor, Good Shepherd Entertainment, Gravitant, Help Social, Ideal Spot, Key Concierge, Local Libations, Optimizely, Real Savvy, Revival, Social Matterz, Tasting Room, Toopher, Violin Memory, Yellow Bird Sauce

Key Executives:
  Brian Grigsby, Managing Partner
  e-mail: brian@corsaventures.com
  Education: BS, Mechanical Engineering & Physics, MS, Optical Electronics, University of Oklahoma
  Background: Founder/General Partner, Raven Venture Partners & Venio Capital Partners
  Directorships: Open Lending, Perception Software
  Alex Gruzen, Partner
  e-mail: alex@corsaventures.com
  Education: BS, MS, Aeronautical & Astronautical Engineering, MIT; MBA, Harvard Business School
  Background: Senior Vice President, Dell; Hewlett Packard
  Directorships: Gravitant, Toopher
  Kevin Green, Partner
  Education: LLM, London School of Economics; JD, Baylor Law School; BA, Southern Methodist University
  Background: U.S. Department of State; Patton Boggs

546 CORTEC GROUP
140 East 45th Street
43rd Floor
New York, NY 10017

Phone: 212-370-5600
e-mail: info@cortecgroup.com
web: www.cortecgroup.com

Mission Statement: Cortec Group is a private equity investment firm which uses the extensive operating experience of our principals to help management teams grow companies and meaningfully add value to their businesses.
Geographic Preference: United States
Fund Size: $2.6 billion
Founded: 2000
Average Investment: $25 million
Minimum Investment: $10 million
Investment Criteria: Equity Investments
Industry Group Preference: Manufacturing, Business to Business, Distribution
Portfolio Companies: 101 Mobility, Aspen Medical Products, Barcodes Inc., Center for Vein Restoration, Chauvet, Community Veterinary Partners, EVP EyeCare, Groome Transportation, Harmar, Rotating Machinery Services Inc., Urnex, Viradis, Weiman, Window Nation, Yeti

Key Executives:
  R. Scott Schafler, Managing Partner
  Education: BA, Johns Hopkins University; MBA, Harvard Graduate School of Business Administration
  Background: VP Operations/Director, Condec Corporation; Founder/Chairman, UC Industries; Director, Fidelity Bank; Director, Unimation; Chock-ful-o-Nuts
  Directorships: Sequa Corporation
  David L. Schnadig, Managing Partner
  212-370-5600
  Fax: 212-682-4195
  e-mail: dschnadig@cortecgroup.com
  Education: BS, Economics, Trinity College; MM, Kellogg School of Management, Northwestern University
  Background: Assistant Chairman, SunAmerica; Investment Banker, Lehman Brothers; Management Consultant, Cresap, McCormick & Paget
  Jeffrey A. Lipsitz, Managing Partner
  e-mail: jlipsitz@cortecgroup.com
  Education: BA, Union College; MBA, Columbia University Graduate School of Business
  Background: VP Corporate Development, PLY GEM Industries

  Michael E. Najjar, Managing Partner
  e-mail: mnajjar@cortecgroup.com
  Education: BA, Cornell University; MBA, Wharton School, University of Pennsylvania
  Background: Managing Director, Cornerstone Equity Investors; Investment Banker, Donaldson Lufkin & Jenrette
  Eugene P. Nesbeda, Senior Managing Partner
  Education: BS, Columbia University School of Engineering; MBA, Harvard Graduate School of Business Administration
  Background: Managing Director, CITIC Capital Partners; Corporate Officer, General Electric
  Jonathan A. Stein, Partner
  e-mail: jstein@cortecgroup.com
  Education: BA, Harvard College
  Background: Principal, Three Cities Research
  Jeffrey R. Shannon, Partner
  e-mail: jshannon@cortecgroup.com
  Education: US Naval Academy, BS, Ocean Engineering, Texas A&M University; MS, Civil Engineering, University of Illinois
  Background: Analyst, Saloman Smith Barney
  James W. Tucker, Managing Director
  e-mail: btucker@cortecgroup.com
  Education: BBA, Accounting, College of William & Mary; MBA, Columbia Business School
  Background: Analyst, M&A Group, Wachovia Capital Markets

547 COSTANOA VENTURE CAPITAL
160 Forest Ave.
Palo Alto, CA 94301

Phone: 650-388-9310
e-mail: info@costanoavc.com
web: www.costanoavc.com

Mission Statement: Costanoa Venture Capital is an early stage investor in cloud-based services leveraging data and analytics to solve real problems for businesses and consumers. We aren't afraid of sectors before they are high profile and don't shy away from hard work. We've been there before and enjoy the journey. Our insight, network and business development skills can help change the trajectory of a company's business. We understand the challenges of leading young companies. We provide hands-on guidance while allowing entrepreneurs and CEOs the room to operate, improve and ultimately succeed.

Investment Criteria: Early Stage
Industry Group Preference: Cloud-Based IT Services
Portfolio Companies: 3scale, 6sense, Acme Technologies, Alation, Amplify.ai, AppOrbit, Apptimize, Aquabyte, Auterion, Bugcrowd, Datalogix, Demandbase, Directly, Elevate Security, Fauna, Focal Systems, GameChanger, Grovo, Guardian Analytics, Inflection, Intacct, Isocket, Kahuna, Kenna Security, Kepler, Krypton, Landit, Leap, Lex Machina, Lively, NovoED, Parallel Domain, PayNearMe, PepperData, Propeller, Quizlet, Rayfay, Return Path, Roadster, Skedulo, Springboard, Stitch Labs, Upcounsel, VictorOps

Other Locations:
  251 Rhode Island St.
  Suite 107
  San Francisco, CA 94103

Key Executives:
  Greg Sands, Founder & Managing Partner
  Education: BA, Harvard; MBA, Stanford Graduate School of Business
  Background: Sutter Hill Ventures; Netscape Communications; Cisco; Corporate Decision, Inc (now Mercer Consulting)
  Directorships: Alation, Directly, Focal Systems, Guardian Analytics, Inflection, Kepler Communications, Return Path, Roadster, Stitch Labs, VictorOps

192

Venture Capital & Private Equity Firms / Domestic Firms

Neill Occhiogross, Partner
Education: BS, Computer Science, Duke University; MBA, Wharton School
Background: Investor Growth Capital; Highland Capital Partners; InnaPhase
Directorships: Acme Technologies, Apptimize, Bugcrowd, Kenna Security
Mark Selcow, Partner
Education: BA, English, Brown University; MBA, Stanford Graduate School of Business
Background: President, BabyCenter; President, Merced Systems
Directorships: Lively, Quizlet, Skedulo, Springboard

548 COSTELLA KIRSCH
3500 Alameda de las Pulgas
Suite 150
Menlo Park, CA 94025

Phone: 650-462-1890
e-mail: info@costellakirsch.com
web: www.costellakirsch.com

Mission Statement: Costella Kirsch is a venture lending firm that offers capital support to emerging technology companies.

Founded: 1986
Investment Criteria: Start-Up, Emerging
Industry Group Preference: Technology
Portfolio Companies: Accolo, AdBrite, AdvancePath, Aeris Communications, Athersys, Boombotix, BridgeLux, Centerbeam, Coyuchi, Discera, Doctor Evidence, Domain Surgical, Echo, Enkata, ID Watchdog, InfraScale, Invivodata, Kontera, Mantara, Maxwell Health, OnPharma, PaySimple, Remedy Interactive, RiseSmart, Silver Tail Systems, SnapLogic, Solaria, SpectraSensors, SpeedInfo, Toktumi, Twelvefold Media, U-Systems, Vast, Verimatrix, Zep Solar, Zolo Technologies, Zoosk

Key Executives:
  Richard Ginn, Managing Director/Chief Financial Officer
  650-462-1890
  e-mail: rich@costellakirsch.com
  Education: Stanford University; MBA, Anderson School, University of California, Los Angeles
  Background: Program Manager, Philips Electronics
  Bill Kirsch, Managing Director
  650-462-5790
  e-mail: bill@costellakirsch.com
  Education: BS, Accounting & Economics, Lehigh University; MBA, Anderson School, University of California, Los Angeles
  Background: Rolm Credit Corporation; GATX Capital Corporation
  Beth Kelsey, Portfolio Manager
  650-462-5792
  e-mail: beth@costellakirsch.com
  Background: Senior Administrator, Borland Software; Harmony Foods; Plantronics; Sprint Communications

549 COTTONWOOD TECHNOLOGY FUND
422 Old Santa Fe Trail
Santa Fe, NM 87501

Phone: 505-412-8537
e-mail: info@cottonwood.vc
web: www.cottonwoodtechnologyfund.com

Mission Statement: Cottonwood Technology Fund offers venture services and capital to seed-stage technology companies with significant commercial potential.

Geographic Preference: Paso del Norte Region from Los Alamos, NM to El Paso, TX
Investment Criteria: Seed-Stage, Early-Stage
Industry Group Preference: Technology, Biosciences, New Energy, Nanotechnology, Information Technology, Clean Technology, Aerospace, Defense and Government
Portfolio Companies: Clear Flight Solutions, Eurekite, Exagen Diagnostics, FibeRio Technology Corporation, Respira Therapeutics, Skorpios Technologies, xF Technologies

Other Locations:
  Hengelosestraat 541
  Enschede 7521 AG
  Netherlands

Key Executives:
  Dave Blivin, Managing Director
  505-412-8537
  e-mail: dave@cottonwoodtechnologyfund.com
  Education: MBA, Fuqua School of Business, Duke University
  Background: Managing Director, Southeast Interactive
  Alain le Loux, General Partner
  Education: University of Twente
  Background: Getronics PinkRoccade; CEO, Virobuster Technologies

550 COUNCIL CAPITAL
30 Burton Hills Blvd.
Suite 576
Nashville, TN 37215

Phone: 615-255-3707 Fax: 615-255-3709
e-mail: pfulner@councilcapital.com
web: www.councilcapital.com

Mission Statement: Founded in 2000, Council Capital has approximately $150 million of capital under management and is actively investing out of its second fund, which was raised in 2008. The success of the initial fund, which is ranked in the top quartile in its vintage year by Private Equity Intelligence, is a credit to the deep expertise and extensive capabilities the partners and CEO Council members possess as healthcare investors and operators.

Fund Size: $150 million
Founded: 2000
Investment Criteria: Growth-Stage, Early Growth-Stage
Industry Group Preference: Healthcare, Healthcare Services, Healthcare Information Technology
Portfolio Companies: Adva-Net, Benefit Informatics, Caregiver Inc., CNNH NeuroHealth, Emids Experience Partnership, EndoChoice, EspriGas, EVault, EWC, Ingenious Med, Lancope, Medseek, NotifyMD, REACH Health, Senior Whole Health, Triad Behavioral Health

Key Executives:
  Dennis C Bottorff, Co-Founder/Managing General Partner
  615-255-3707 x326
  e-mail: dbottorff@councilcapital.com
  Education: BE, Electrical Engineering, Vanderbilt University; MBA, Northwestern University
  Background: President/Chairman, Commerce Union; Vice Chairman/COO, Sovran Bank; President/COO, C&S Sovran; President/CEO, First American National Bank
  Directorships: NuScriptRX, CapStar Bank, Ingram Industries
  Katie H Gambill, Co-Founder/Managing General Partner
  615-255-3707 x314
  e-mail: kgambill@councilcapital.com
  Education: BA, Economics, Vanderbilt University; CFA
  Background: President, Equitable Securities; President, SunTrust Equitable Securities
  Directorships: Reach Health
  Grant A Jackson, Managing General Partner
  e-mail: gjackson@councilcapital.com
  Education: Florida State University; MBA, Kellogg Graduate School of Management
  Background: Accenture, Compaq
  Directorships: eMids, EspriGas, Experience Wellness Centers
  Eric Keen, General Partner
  e-mail: ekeen@councilcapital.com

193

Venture Capital & Private Equity Firms / Domestic Firms

Education: BA, Finance and Political Science, University of Illinois
Background: DW Healthcare Partners; Riverside Company; Northwest Equity Partners; Credit Suisse First Boston; Marakon Associates
Directorships: AdvaNet, Caregiver, Triad Learning Systems

551 COURT SQUARE VENTURES
455 Second Street Southeast
Suite 401
Charlottesville, VA 22902

Phone: 434-817-3300

Mission Statement: A venture capital firm that invests in early-stage communications, information technology, and media companies, with a particular interest in points of convergence between these industries.

Geographic Preference: United States
Fund Size: $118 million
Founded: 1945
Investment Criteria: Early Stage
Industry Group Preference: Communications, Information Technology, Media
Portfolio Companies: Automated Insights, Bug Labs, Continuum, Echo 360, Great Call, Mobile Posse, Seakeeper, Verance

Key Executives:
James B Murray Jr, General Partner
Education: BA, University of Virginia; JD, Marshall-Wythe School of Law, College of William and Mary
Background: Founding Partner, Columbia Capital
Directorships: Imagine Communications, GreatCall, Seakeeper, Continuum 700, Technology Crossover Ventures Internet Advisory Committee
Randy Castleman, General Partner
Education: BA, Princeton University; MBA, Darden School of Business, University of Virginia
Background: Founder/Manager, Media & Technology Strategy Group, ASCAP; RheoGene; Egg Pictures; Interscope Communications; Ogilvy & Mather; BellSouth
Directorships: Automated Insights, Bug Labs, TRAFFIQ, SNOCAP, Labrador Mobile, Grand Central, Optinel Systems
Chris Holden, General Partner
Education: Davidson College
Background: Senior Executive, Rupert Murdoch's News Corporation; CEO, Kesmai Corporation; Vice President, News Technology Group; HarperCollins Publishers
Directorships: Emerging Media Group, Grab Networks, Echo360, Mobile Posse
Douglas Burns, Principal/Chief Financial Officer
Education: BS, Accounting & Business Administration, Washington & Lee University; MBA, Darden School of Business, University of Virginia
Background: Senior Auditor, Arthur Andersen's Enterprise Group
Directorships: GreatCall, Imagine Communications, Seakeeper, Continuum 700

552 COWBOY VENTURES
Palo Alto, CA

e-mail: hello@cowboy.vc
web: www.cowboy.vc

Mission Statement: Cowboy Ventures is a seed-stage focused fund. We seek to back exceptional founders who are building products that 're-imagine' work and personal life in large and growing markets - we call it 'Life 2.0'.

Geographic Preference: United States
Founded: 2012
Investment Criteria: Seed-Stage
Industry Group Preference: Technology
Portfolio Companies: Abstract, Accompany, After School, Area 1, August, Aura, Aviso, Branch, Brandless, Brava, Brickwork, Brit+Co., Chime, Crunchvase, DocSend, Dollar Shave Club, Fullcast.io, Gixo, Guild, Guildery, HeartWork, Homebase, Hooked, Joyride, LendingHome, Librato, LightStep, LumaTax, Manifest, Massdrop, Memebox, Mighty Networks, Mutiny, NuOrder, nWay, Pantry, Philz Coffee, Polar, Product Hunt, Rise, Seneca Systems, Soma, Spruce, StyleSeat, Tally, Tenor, Textio, True, Vic.ai, Vorstella

Key Executives:
Aileen Lee, Founder & Partner
Education: MIT, Harvard Business School
Background: Partner, Kleiner Perkins Caufield & Byers; Founding CEO, RMG Networks
Ted Wang, Partner
Education: AB, History & Latin, Duke University; JD, University of Virginia
Background: Partner, Fenwick & West
Samantha Kaminsky, Partner
Education: Harvard Business School; Middlebury College
Background: Operator, Eventbrite; Investor, J.P. Morgan; Co-Founder, vcgc

553 CRAWLEY VENTURES
600 S Cherry Street
Suite 1125
Denver, CO 80246

Phone: 303-592-1135
e-mail: info@crawleyventures.com
web: www.crawleyventures.com

Mission Statement: Crawley Ventures is the Denver-based private equity subsidiary of Crawley Petroleum Corporation. Crawley Ventures pursues investment opportunities in early stage companies with the potential for growth. The firm invests in a number of industries, including software, manufacturing, financial services, and wireless technologies.

Average Investment: $250,000 - $1.5 million
Investment Criteria: Seed-Stage, Early-Stage, Expansion-Stage
Industry Group Preference: Optics, Financial Services, Software, Manufacturing, Wireless Technologies
Portfolio Companies: CCELP Holding, CenterStone Technologies, Cequint, CertiPath, Collective Intellect, CSP Holdings, DNA Response, Energy Financial and Physical, Enertia Software, First Western Financial, Jetta Corp, NHW Holding, Perlego, REALD, Skydex Technologies, Taaz, TerraLUX, UsingMiles Inc., VarVee

Key Executives:
Jason Garner, President
Education: BEng & MS, Petroleum Engineering, West Virginia University
Background: VP/COO, HighMount Exploration & Production
S Kim Hatfield, Chief Executive Officer
Education: BS, Petroleum Engineering, MS, Petroleum Finance, University of Oklahoma
Directorships: Crawley Petroleum, Enertia Software, CSP Holdings, Oklahoma Independent Producers Association
Martha Tracey, Vice President
Education: Williams College; MBA, Yale University
Directorships: Crawley Petroleum, CenterStone Technologies, First Western Financial, Collective Intellect, Opera Colorado

554 CREDIT SUISSE PRIVATE EQUITY Credit Suisse Group
11 Madison Avenue
New York, NY 10010

Phone: 212-325-5527
web: www.credit-suisse.com

Mission Statement: Comprised of investment funds that focus on domestic and international leverage buyouts, struc-

Venture Capital & Private Equity Firms / Domestic Firms

tured equity investments, mezzanine investments, real estate investments, venture capital and growth investments, and investments in other private equity funds.
Geographic Preference: Worldwide
Fund Size: $3 billion
Founded: 1856
Minimum Investment: $20 million
Investment Criteria: Leverage buyouts, Mezzanine, Private/Structured Equity
Industry Group Preference: Real Estate
Other Locations:
Credit Suisse First Boston
One Cabot Square
London E14 4QJ
United Kingdom
Phone: 011-44-20-7888-8888

Kalandergasse 4
Zurich 8070
Switzerland
Phone: 41 (0)800-88-88-74
Key Executives:
Tidjane Thiam, Chief Executive Officer
Education: MBA, INSEAD
Background: CFO/Group Chief Executive, Prudential Plc; Chief Executive, Aviva; Partner, McKinsey & Co.; Chairman, National Bureau for Technical Studies & Development
Helman Sitohang, CEO, Asia Pacific
Education: BS, Engineering, Bandung Institute of Technology
Background: Derivatives Group, Bankers Trust
Lara J. Warner, Chief Risk Officer
Education: BS, Pennsylvania State University
Background: Equity Research Analyst, Lehman Brothers; Director of Investor Relations/CFO, AT&T
Romeo Cerutti, General Counsel
Education: MA, JD, University of Fribourg; MA, Law, University of California, LA
Background: Attorney, Latham & Watkins; Attorney, Homburger Rechtsanwälte, Zurich; Partner, Lombard Odier Darier Hentsch & Cie
Lydie Hudson, Chief Compliance Officer
Education: BA, International Politics & Economics, Middlebury College; MBA, Harvard Business School
Background: Lehman Brothers; Boston Consulting Group; Various Management Positions at Credit Suisse
David Mathers, Chief Financial Officer
Education: BA, MA, Natural Sciences, University of Cambridge
Background: Global Head of Equity Research, HSBC
James B. Walker, Chief Operating Officer
Education: BS, Mathematics, University of Glasgow; Postgraduate Diploma Finance, University of Stirling
Background: Morgan Stanley; Merrill Lynch; Barclays Capital; Various Management Positions at Credit Suisse

555 CRESCENDO VENTURES
405 El Camino Real
Suite 126
Menlo Park, CA 94025
Phone: 650-470-1200 **Fax:** 650-470-1201
e-mail: investorservices@crescendoventures.com
web: www.crescendoventures.com

Mission Statement: Focuses exclusively on early-stage investments in the communications and enterprise infrastructure sectors.

Fund Size: $400 million
Founded: 1993
Investment Criteria: Early-Stage
Industry Group Preference: Communications, Enterprise Software, Infrastructure, Software, Components & IoT

Portfolio Companies: Airband Communications Holdings, Algety Telecom, Arteris, BDNA, Broadsoft, CREDANT Technologies, Compellent Technologies, CoreOptics, Cybrant, Cygent, Dash Navigation, Dust Networks, Ejasent, Ensemble Communications, Entera, Envivio, Fultec Semiconductor, Jasper @ Cisco, Metaplace, Morphics Technology, Netcentrex, Pure Digital Technologies, Quorum Systems, RHK. Salient Surgical Technologies, ShoZu, Sistina Software, StoneFly Inc., Transitive, Tropic Networks, WhereNet
Key Executives:
David Spreng, Managing General Partner
Education: BS, Accounting, University of Minnesota
Background: President, IAI Ventures; Mutual Fund Manager, Investment Advisers; Investment Banker, Salomon Brothers; Investment Banker, Dain Bosworth
Directorships: Ciena, CoSine, Digital Island, Lightspeed, Novalux, OneSecure, Oplink, Tut Systems
John Borchers, General Partner
Education: BS, University of Richmond; MBA, Harvard Business School
Directorships: BDNA Corporation; Credant Technologies; Dust Networks; SealedMedia; Worksoft Inc; Transitive Corporation
Wayne Cantwell, General Partner
Education: BSEE, DeVry Institute of Technology
Background: President/CEO, inSilicon Corporation; Worldwide Field Operations, Phoenix Technologies; Sales/Engineering, Intel Corporation; NEC Corporation
Peter Van Cuylenburg, General Partner
Education: Electrical Engineering diploma, Bristol Polytechnic
Background: SealedMedia; Transitive; President, Quantum Corporation/S DSS Group; Executive VP, Xerox Corp; President, NeXT Computer; CEO, Mercury Communications; Marketing/General Manager, Texas Instruments
Directorships: SealedMedia; Transitive Corp; QAD Inc; Elixent Ltd

556 CRESCENT CAPITAL GROUP LP
11100 Santa Monica Blvd
Suite 2000
Los Angeles, CA 90025
Phone: 310-235-5900
web: www.crescentcap.com

Mission Statement: A source of capital for private equity-backed companies in the United States. Crescent Capital Group invests in mezzanine debt and offers private capital to middle market companies in Europe.

Geographic Preference: United States, Europe
Fund Size: $3.4 billion
Founded: 1991
Average Investment: $50 - $150 million
Minimum Investment: $15 million
Investment Criteria: Mezzanine, Buyouts, Acquisitions, Recapitalizations, Refinancings
Industry Group Preference: All markets Considered
Portfolio Companies: Connect-Air International, The Copernicus Group IRB, Double E Company, Fairchild Industrial Products Company, Insource Contract Services, Lazer Spot, Mallet & Company, MooreCo, National Display Systems LLC, The Outsource Group, Precision Manufacturing Group LLC, Solidscape, Thorne Research Inc. & Diversified Natural Products, Tital Fitness LLC, Utrecht Art Supplies, Wearwell, Winchester Electronics
Other Locations:
10 Hudson Yards
41st Floor
New York, NY 10001
Phone: 212-364-0200

100 Federal Street
31st Floor

195

Venture Capital & Private Equity Firms / Domestic Firms

Boston, MA 02110
Phone: 617-854-1500
Key Executives:
Jean-Marc Chapus, Managing Partner
e-mail: jm.chapus@crescentcap.com
Education: AB, MBA, Harvard University
Background: Group Managing Director, TCW; Managing Director, Cresent Capital Corporation; Drexel Bumham Lamert
Mark Attanasio, Managing Partner
e-mail: mark.attanasio@crescentcap.com
Education: AB, Brown University; JD, Columbia University School of Law
Background: Group Managing Director, TCW; Co-Chief Executive Officer, Crescent Capital Corporation; Drexel Burnham Lambert; Attorney, Debevoise & Plimpton
Christopher G. Wright, Managing Director
e-mail: chris.wright@crescentcap.com
Education: BA, Michigan State University; MBA, Harvard Business School
Background: Managing Director, TCW; General Electric Company; GE Industrial Systems

557 CRESCO CAPITAL PARTNERS
8214 Westchester Drive
Dallas, TX 75225

web: www.crescocapitalpartners.com
Mission Statement: Invests in the cannabis industry.
Founded: 2014
Industry Group Preference: Cannabis
Portfolio Companies: FLRish, Alternative Solutions, Acres Cultivation & Cannabis, Libertas, Grow Healthy, Aurora Flower Co., Ebbu, Koan Agroscience, Vanguard Scientific, Pot Pots, Sakti, Faces Human Capital Management, High Street Capital Partners, National CC, Green Thumb Industries, Gesundheit Foods, Casimir Partners, Planted Supply Co., Harvest Cannabis Co.
Key Executives:
Matt Hawkins, Managing Partner
Education: University of Texas at Austin
Background: Principal, San Jacinto Partners; Managing Principal, Adjacent Capital Advisors
Todd Boren, Managing Partner
Education: University of Miami
Background: President/COO, International Assets Advisory; Partner, Arizona Rattlers; Team President/Managing Member, Tampa Bay Storm; President/CEO, Pinnacle Financial Group; VP, Bernstein Global Wealth Management; Partner, Orlando Predators Football Team; Managing Partner, MacArthur Capital
Andrew Sturner, Managing Partner
Education: BS, Washington University; JD, Bankruptcy, Brooklyn Law School
Background: Co-Founder/Director, Miami Angels; Co-Founder, Boatsetter; Founder, Orange Island Ventures; Manager, MacArthur Capital; Founder/Chairman, Aqua Marine Partners
Directorships: Snap-A-Slip; Boatyard; Oasis Marinas
Dov Szapiro, Managing Partner
Education: The Wharton School, University of Pennsylvania
Background: Co-Founder/CEO, AFS Acceptance; Director of Business Development, GovWorks Inc.
Matthew Bryant, Vice President
Education: BS, Finance/Accounting, University of Texas at Austin
Background: Hunt Realty Investments; Advisor, JPMorgan; Co-Founder/CFO, Drive Casa

558 CRESSEY & COMPANY LP
155 N Wacker Drive
Suite 4500
Chicago, IL 60606

Phone: 312-945-5700 **Fax:** 312-945-5701
web: www.cresseyco.com
Mission Statement: Cressey & Company invests in high-potential companies in the US healthcare market. The firm seeks to provide its capital and expertise to accelerate the growth of its portfolio companies and help build leading healthcare businesses.
Geographic Preference: United States
Fund Size: $615 million
Founded: 2008
Average Investment: $10 - $100 million
Investment Criteria: Middle Market, Later Stage, Growth Equity
Industry Group Preference: Healthcare, Healthcare Services, Information Technology
Portfolio Companies: Concentra, Dental Services Group, Haven Behavioral Healthcare, InnerChange, QualDerm Partners, RestorixHealth, Spine Wave, Unitek Information Systems, US Renal Care, VetCor, Wound Care Specialists
Other Locations:
2525 West End Avenue
Suite 1250
Nashville, TN 37203
Phone: 615-369-8400 **Fax:** 615-369-8444
Key Executives:
Bryan Cressey, Partner
312-945-5710
Education: BS, Economics, University of Washington; MBA, Harvard Business School; JD, Harvard Law School
Background: Co-Founder, Golder, Thoma, Cressey, Rauner; First Chicago Equity Group
Merrick Axel, Partner
312-945-5717
Education: BA, Economics & Political Science, Duke University; MBA, Harvard Business School
Background: Harvest Partners; JW Childs Associates; Morgan Stanley
Directorships: Academy for Urban School Leadership
Paul Diaz, Partner
Education: BS, Finance/Accounting, Kogod School of Business, American University; JD, Georgetown University Law Center
Background: President/CFO, Kindred Healthcare Inc.
Directorships: DaVita; PharMerica Corporation
Peter Ehrich, Partner
312-945-5724
Education: BS, Economics, Wharton School, University of Pennsylvania; MBA, Stanford University Graduate School of Business
Background: Principal, Black Diamond Capital Partners; Associate, Aurora Capital Partners
Sen. William H. Frist, MD, Partner
615-369-8400
Education: BA, Princeton University; MD, Harvard Medical School
Background: United States Senator, State of Tennessee; Majority Leader, United States Senate; Founder, Vanderbilt Multi-Organ Transplant Center
Directorships: Robert Wood Johnson Foundation, Kaiser Family Foundation
Bary Bailey, Operating Partner
312-945-5737
Education: BS, Finance, California State University, Long Beach
Background: CFO, AMN Healthcare Services Inc.; PacifiCare Health Systems Inc.; Premier Inc.; Tenet Healthcare; American Medical Holdings Inc.; Arthur Andersen & Co.

Venture Capital & Private Equity Firms / Domestic Firms

559 CRESTVIEW PARTNERS
590 Madison Avenue
36th Floor
New York, NY 10022

Phone: 212-906-0700
e-mail: information@crestview.com
web: www.crestview.com

Mission Statement: Crestview Partners is a private equity firm seeking opportunities with healthcare, media, energy, industrials and financial services companies.

Geographic Preference: United States
Fund Size: $3 billion
Founded: 2004
Average Investment: $100 - $250 million
Industry Group Preference: Financial Services, Media, Healthcare, Energy, Industrial
Portfolio Companies: Accuride Corporation, Arxis Capital Group, ATC Drivetrain, Camping World Holdings, Capital Bank Financial, Charter Communications, Concours Mold, Congruex Holdings, CP Energy, Cumulus Media, DARAG Group, DS Services, Elo Touch Solutions, Endurance Lift Holdings, FBR & Co., Fidelis Insurance Holdings Limited, H2Oil Energy, Hornblower Holdings, ICM Partners, Industrial Media, Insight Communications, Interoute Communications, JR Automation, Key Safety Systems, Lancashire Holdings, Martin Currie, Munder Capital Management, NEP Group, NYDJ Apparel, OneLink Communications, Oxbow Carbon, PartnerRe, Protect My Car, Samson Resources, Select Energy Services, Silver Creek Oil & Gas, Silver Creek Permian, Stackpole International, Symbion, US Well Services, ValueOptions, Venerable Holdings, Victory Capital, W Energy Partners, WOW!

Key Executives:
  Tom Murphy, Co-Founder & Partner
  Education: AB, Princeton University; MBA, Harvard Business School
  Background: Head, Financial Sponsors Group, Goldman Sachs
  Directorships: JR Automation
  Barry Volpert, Co-Founder & CEO
  Education: AB, Amherst College; MBA, Harvard Business School; JD, Harvard Law School
  Background: Partner, Goldman Sachs
  Directorships: Key Safety Systems, Oxbow Carbon
  Bob Hurst, Vice Chairman
  Education: AB, Clark University; MBA, Wharton School, University of Pennsylvania
  Background: Vice Chairman, Goldman Sachs
  Directorships: Oxbow Carbon, VF Corporation
  Jeff Marcus, Vice Chairman
  Education: BA, Economics, University of California, Berkeley
  Background: President & CEO, AMFM; Founder & CEO, Marcus Cable; CEO, WestMarc Communications
  Directorships: Camping World/Good Sam Enterprises, NEP Group
  Brian Cassidy, Partner
  Education: AB, Physics, Harvard College; MBA, Stanford Graduate School of Business
  Background: Boston Ventures; Investment Banking Analyst, Alex Brown & Sons
  Directorships: Camping World/Good Sam Enterprises, NEP Group, Cumulus Media, Interoute Communications, WOW!
  Quentin Chu, Partner
  Education: AB, Classics, Harvard College; MBA, Harvard Business School
  Background: Associate, The Carlyle Group; Analyst, Healthcare Investment Banking, Goldman Sachs
  Directorships: Arxis Capital Group, Breakthrough New York
  Bob Delaney, Partner
  Education: AB, Hamilton College; MS, Accounting, New York University Stern School of Business; MBA, Harvard Business School
  Background: Goldman Sachs
  Directorships: Samson Resources, Select Energy Services, Silver Creek Oil & Gas, Synergy Energy, CP Energy
  Rich DeMartini, Partner
  Education: BA, San Diego State University
  Background: President, Asset Management Group, Bank of America; Morgan Stanley
  Directorships: Capital Bank Financial, Arxis Capital Group, Fidelis Insurance Holdings, Victory Capital Management
  Adam Klein, Partner
  Education: AB, Harvard College; MBA, Harvard Business School
  Background: Analyst, Centennial Ventures; Analyst, Compass Partners; Financial Analyst, Donaldson Lufkin & Jenrette
  Directorships: Select Energy Services, Silver Creek Oil & Gas, Synergy Energy, CP Energy
  Alex Rose, Partner
  Education: AB, Government, Harvard College; MBA, Wharton School, University of Pennsylvania
  Background: Business Development Associate, General Electric Company; Investment Banking Analyst, Goldman Sachs
  Directorships: JR Automation, Key Safety Systems

560 CROSS CREEK ADVISORS
505 Wakara Way
Suite 215
Salt Lake City, UT 84108

Phone: 801-214-0010 Fax: 801-214-0020
e-mail: info@crosscreekadvisors.com
web: www.crosscreekadvisors.com

Mission Statement: Cross Creek Capital seeks to invest in late-stage private companies with significant return potential. Our late-stage venture investments mean shorter time to liquidity and lower risk relative to early stage venture investments.

Investment Criteria: Late Stage
Industry Group Preference: Internet, IT Services, Life Sciences
Portfolio Companies: Accolade, Alta Devices, Anaplan, Angie's List, AppDynamics, Assurex Health, BlueArc Corporation, Bounce Exchange, Bravo Health, Braze, Bright Health, Cardica, Care.com, CENX, Coupang, Cryocor, Data Science International, Dataminr, Datastax, Docker, DocuSign, Drillinginfo, e2Open, Earnest, ExactTarget, Extreme Reach, Fluidigm, ForeScout, FrameMax, Genvault, Gigya, Gusto, Hubspot, Icertis, IntegenX, Integral Ad Science, IronPlanet, Kollective, Legalzoom, Lifelock, Looker, Mavenir, MedManage, mFormation, Miramar Labs, MyHeritage, Netuitive, Neurogesx, Neutral Tandem, newScale, NxStage Medical, Ocera Therapeutics, OpGen, Ophthonix, OREXIGEN Therapeutics, ORQIS Medical, PCH International, Pendo.io, Pindrop, Pluralsight, Poshmark, RealtyShares, Responsys, Rocket Fuel, Rover, Rules Based Medicine, Scopely, ServiceMax, Shiftgig Silver Spring Networks, Simplus, Slice, Solera Networks, Sourcefire, Sumo Logic, Tegile, Telogis, Tethys Bioscience, TherOx, Thumbplay, Ticketfly, True Fit, TubeMogul, Vapotherm, Veracode

Key Executives:
  Karey Barker, CFA, Founding Managing Director
  Background: Portfolio Manager, Wasatch Small Cap Ultra Growth
  Peter Jarman, MBA, Managing Director
  Education: MBA, Northwestern Kellogg Graduate School of Management
  Background: Senior Investment Manager, Fort Washington Capital Partners Group; Ancestry.com; Campus Pipeline; Icon Health and Fitness

Venture Capital & Private Equity Firms / Domestic Firms

Tyler Christianson, MBA, Managing Director
Background: President, American Investment Financial
Barbara Reininger, Director, Finance & Operations
Background: Operations Manager, Duty Free Americas; Assistant Vice President, Moody's; Product Manager, InterSearch; Founder, BainbridgeBusinessWomen.com; Founder, MyKidsCookies.com

561 CROSSCUT VENTURES
373 Rose Avenue
Venice, CA 90291

web: www.crosscutventures.com

Mission Statement: Seeking dedicated entrepreneurs who have the foresight and personal fortitude to take their ideas and make them happen in a big way.
Geographic Preference: Southern California
Founded: 2008
Portfolio Companies: Arsenic, Blitz, Boom, Boon & Gable, Branch Messenger, CandyClub, Comparably, ConversionLogic, DataScience, FanBank, FieldDay, Foray, GumGum, Hijro, HelloTech, Iconery, Immortals, Inspire, Jyve, Ledger, LittleLabs, Measurabl, MobCrush, Narvar, Omaze, Overnight, ProspectWise, Purple Squirrel, Reaction Commerce, Science, StreamLabs, StyleSaint, Super Evil Megacorp, TechStyle, The Black Tux, Trace, Unmute, Verve Mobile, WeDo, Winc, Zingle

Key Executives:
Rick Smith, Co-Founder/Managing Director
Education: BS, Finance, University of Illinois; JD, Harvard Law School
Background: Founder, SunAmerica Ventures; Partner, Palomar Ventures
Directorships: DocStoc, Zadspace, Postcard on the Run, Pulpo Media, GraphEffect
Brian Garrett, Co-Founder/Operating Partner
Education: BS, Industrial Engineering, MBA, Stanford University
Background: Partner, Palomar Ventures
Directorships: StyleSaint, GraphEffect, GumGum, Verve Wireless, MyGlam, Lettuce Apps
Brett Brewer, Co-Founder/Operating Partner
Education: BA, Business/Economics, University of California, Los Angeles
Background: Co-Founder, Intermix Media; President & Chairman, Adknowledge.com; CEO, Sensa
Directorships: Sensa, Eventup
Adam Goldenberg, Venture Advisor
Background: Founder, Gamer's Alliance; COO, Intermix Media; Founder, Intelligen Beauty
Clinton Foy, Managing Director
Education: BA, University of Notre Dame; JD, University of Washington School of Law; MA, Stanford University
Background: COO, Square Enix; Attorney, Heller Ehrman Venture Law Group

562 CROSSHILL FINANCIAL GROUP
201 North Union Street
Suite 300
Alexandria, VA 22314

Phone: 703-717-6420 Fax: 703-518-6122
e-mail: info@crosshill.com
web: www.crosshill.com

Mission Statement: CrossHill Financial Group provides private equity funding, bridge financing and advisory services to companies.
Investment Criteria: Growth Financing, Acquisitions, Restructurings, Crisis Management
Key Executives:
Stephen X Graham, Principal
Education: Georgetown University; MBA, University of Chicago
Background: Principal, Kidder Peabody & Co.; Merrill Lynch & Co.; Ernst & Young; Founder, Prestwick Companies; Founder, ACell Inc.

563 CROSSLINK CAPITAL
2 Embarcadero Center
Suite 2200
San Francisco, CA 94111

Phone: 415-617-1800
web: www.crosslinkcapital.com

Mission Statement: Seeks to identify sectors of the economy where the rate of business change is greatest and investment opportunities are most profound; focuses efforts exclusively on the sectors that the firm believes offer outstanding opportunity in order to identify companies, add value, and help them achieve greater success.
Fund Size: $800 million
Founded: 1999
Average Investment: $7-15 million
Minimum Investment: $250,000
Investment Criteria: Any stage from seed to pre-IPO to PIPES
Industry Group Preference: Alternative Energy, Data & Analytics, Cloud Infrastructure, Consumer Internet, Software, Digital Health, Digital Marketing, Fintech, IP Services, Lighting, Semis/Coretech, Wireless Systems
Portfolio Companies: 365 Data Centers, 500friends, Adept, Alpha, UX, AmberPoint, Ancestry.com, Armory, Autofi, Ayla, BetterUp, Bigfinite, Bityota, Bizo, Bleacher Report, BlueArc, Bonfire, Brightfunnel, Brightwheel, Broderbound, Building Connected, Carbonite, Case Text, Casper, Cendura, Centerrun, Chart.io, Chime, Cirrus Logic, Comparably, Comprehend, Coupa, Cypress Semiconductor, Datastax, Descartes Labs, Devonway, Digital Cognition Technologies, Eargo, Educents, Enigma, Enview, Equinix, Espresa, Fairclaims, Fatherly, Filament, Flurry, Force10, Fountain, Global Analytics, Good, Great Jones, Haven, Hired, Homelight, Hotel Booking Solutions, Huckleberry, Hungry Root, ICurrent, IMlogic, Infinicon, Inpher, Insight Engines, Intematix, Inverse, Jack Erwin, Kinetic, Kinnek, Koan, Like.com, Livescribe, Madefire, Magma, Marble Security, Marin Software, Marketdial, Marketworks, Mavrx, Mirador Financial, Molekule, Nav, Newscale, Nodesource, Nucore, NWP Services, Omniture, On Display, Op Source, Pandora, Personal Capital, Phil, Phonespots, Pica, Postmates, Power To Fly, Prenav, Primer, Prosper, Protect Wise, Radiumone, Rainforst QA, Rebag, Red Swoosh, Reltio, Rentlytics, Revera, Richrelence, SABA, Schoolmint, Science Exchange, Seamicro, Servicemax, Set Media, Silicon Blue, Silk Road, Sionyx, Sonia, Stratalight, Surgient, Swift Shift, Synapsense, Take Lessons, TIVO, True & Co., Truspan, Validity, Verodin, Vertrue, Virage Logic, Visual.Ly, Vitalstream, Vitesse, Vungle, Weave, Werecover, Xilinx, Xsigo, Yipes,

Other Locations:
2925 Woodside Road
Woodside, CA 94062
Phone: 415-617-1800

Key Executives:
Michael Stark, Co-Founder/Portfolio Manager
e-mail: mjs@crosslinkcapital.com
Education: BS, Engineering, Northwestern University; MBA, University of Michigan
Background: Director Research/Equity Analyst, Robertson Stephens; Intel Corporation
Directorships: Espresa, Apttus
Samantha Wang, Partner
Education: BA, Economics, Stanford University
Background: Vice President, Marketing, T2Media; Director, Legalzoom; Vice President, eCommerce, Marc Ecko Enterprises; Vice Presient, Marketing, Home Décor Products; 3i; Deutsche Bank
McLain Southworth, Venture Partner
Education: BSBA, Georgetown University; MBA, Stanford Graduate School of Business

Background: Currenex; State Street; SV Angel; Apparent; CircleUp
David Silverman, Partner
e-mail: dsilverman@crosslinkcapital.com
Education: BA, Dartmouth College; JD, Stanford University
Background: Partner, 3i Ventures; Senior Officer, Robertson Stephens; Senior Officer, Piper Jaffray
Directorships: BuildingConnected, Vungle, Weave, Casper, Enigma, AutoFi, BetterUp, BrightFunnel, Reltio
Eric Chin, Partner
Education: BA, Dartmouth College; MBA, Harvard Business School
Background: Partner, Artiman Ventures; Partner, Bay Partners; IBM; MILCOM
Directorships: Datastax, Hired, Postmates, Casper, Protectwise, TakeLessons, Vungle, Comparably, Descartes Labs, Nodesource, Flo, Molekule, Verodin, Enigma, JackErwin, Yotascale, Reltio
Jim Feuille, Partner
e-mail: jmpf@crosslinkcapital.com
Education: BA, Chemistry, Dartmouth College; JD, MBA, Stanford University
Background: Global Head Technology Investment Banking, UBS Warburg; COO, Volpe Brown Whelan & Company; Robertson Stephens
Directorships: Pandora, Coupa, Personal Capital, Reltio, Global Analytics, Zebit, Chime, Parkifi, Devon Way, Zoosk, SilkRoad
Omar El-Ayat, Partner
Education: BS, Management Science & Engineering, Stanford University
Background: Piper Jaffray; Iroquois Capital
Directorships: Casper, Enigma, Hired, Potmates, Phil, Building Connected, Descartes Labs, HungryRoot, BigFinite, GreatJones, Kinetic, WeRecover
Matt Bigge, Partner
Education: BSFS, Georgetown University; MBA, Harvard Business School
Background: Venture Partner, Paladin Capital; Co-Founder/CEO, Strategic Social Holdings; Co-Founder/President, MILCOM Technologies; U.S. Army
Directorships: Protectwise, Verodin, Descartes Labs, Nodesources, Enview, Inpher

564 CRUNCHFUND
410 Townsend Street
San Francisco, CA 94107

e-mail: partners@crunchfund.com
web: www.crunchfund.com

Mission Statement: Crunchfund invests in and works with information technology companies at any stage, but is primarily focused on seed and early stage investments.
Fund Size: $20 million
Founded: 2011
Investment Criteria: Seed Stage, Early Stage
Industry Group Preference: Technology
Portfolio Companies: Knowhere, Manticore Games, Marble, nTopology, Nylas, One Concern, Overclock Labs, Prodigy, Truework, Wonolo
Key Executives:
  Michael Arrington, General Partner
  Education: Claremont McKenna College, Stanford Law School
  Background: Founder/Board of Directors, Edgeio, Co-Founder of Achex, Founder of TechCrunch
  Patrick Gallagher, General Partner
  Education: BA, Economics & Literature, Claremont McKenna College
  Background: Partner, VantagePoint Capital Partners; Board of Directors, Core Security Technologies/Constant Contact/TouchTunes Interactive Networks/Grocery Shopping Network, Air2Web, YouMail, Board Observer, IntelePeer

565 CRYSTAL RIDGE PARTNERS
111 Dunnell Road
Suite 102
Maplewood, NJ 07040

Phone: 973-275-1100 Fax: 973-275-1120
e-mail: don@crystalridgepartners.com
web: www.crystalridgepartners.com

Mission Statement: Crystal Ridge Partners is a New Jersey based private equity firm with $70 million of committed capital that invests in smaller middle-market companies in partnership with management. CRP focuses primarily on the manufacturing, distribution, consumer products, and business services sectors. CRP invests in management buyouts, recapitalizations and growth equity transactions, it and has the flexibility to take control of minority positions.
Geographic Preference: United States, Northeast, Southeast, Mid-Atlantic, North Central Regio
Fund Size: $70 million
Founded: 2004
Average Investment: $3 - $10 million
Minimum Investment: $3 million
Investment Criteria: $10 to $50 million in sales, Management Buyouts, Recapitalizations, Growth Equity Transactions, Middle-Market Companies
Industry Group Preference: Manufacturing, Distribution, Consumer Products, Business to Business, Healthcare
Portfolio Companies: A.R.E. Accessories, Bronco Manufacturing
Key Executives:
  Jack Baron, Managing Principal
  e-mail: jack@crystalridgepartners.com
  Education: BS, Lehigh University; MBA, Fordham University
  Background: Partner, JP Morgan Partners
  Directorships: Executive in Residence, MBA Program, Lehigh University
  Don Hofmann, Managing Principal
  e-mail: don@crystalridgepartners.com
  Education: BA, Hofstra University; MBA, Harvard Business School
  Background: Senior Partner, JP Morgan Partners; Founder, MH Equity, Manufacturers Hanover Trust Company
  Mark G Solow, Senior Advisor
  Background: Co-Founder, GarMark Partners; Senior Executive Vice President/Global Head, Investment & Corporate Banking, Chemical Banking Corporation; Manufacturers Hanover Trust Co.
  Andrew Tananbaum, Senior Advisor
  Education: BA, University of Michigan; JD, Fordham University Law School
  Background: President & CEO, Capital Factors; President & CEO, Century Business Credit Corporation

566 CSA PARTNERS
333 N Plankinton Ave.
Suite 205
Milwaukee, WI 53203

web: www.csapartners.com

Mission Statement: CSA Partners, LLC is a venture fund investing in early stage, high growth, companies in the Midwest, with particular focus in Wisconsin. We partner with entrepreneurs to help them build and grow great innovative companies in our community.
Geographic Preference: Midwest
Investment Criteria: Early-Stage
Industry Group Preference: Software, Business Products & Services

Venture Capital & Private Equity Firms / Domestic Firms

Portfolio Companies: Bright Cellars, Carson Life, Dattus, Docalytics, Ease, EatStreet, Eventup, Gener8tor, Music Dealers, Openhomes, Prettylitter, Review Trackers, Scanalytics, Spiritshop, Understory, Yachtlife

Key Executives:
Chris Abele, Managing Director
Steve Mech, Managing Director
Education: BA, Lawrence University; Certificate in Real Estate, University of Wisconsin-Madison

567 CUE BALL GROUP
1 Faneuil Hall Square
7th Floor
Boston, MA 02109

Phone: 617-542-0100 Fax: 617-542-0033
e-mail: ping@cueball.com
web: www.cueball.com

Mission Statement: Cue Ball Group is a venture capital firm focused on companies in the consumer services, enterprise Internet and digital media sectors. The firm helps to build businesses by pursuing innovative ideas and creating close partnerships with management teams. Cue Ball Group is committed to adding value to its portfolio companies.

Founded: 2008
Average Investment: Startup: $500K - $1.5MM; Scaleup: $2 - $5MM
Investment Criteria: Start-Up, Scale-Up
Industry Group Preference: Digital Media & Marketing, Business Products & Services, Specialty Consumer Brands
Portfolio Companies: Argent, Athena Club, Banyan Water, Bread, Cambridge Blockchain, Centrl, ChatGrid, CMG, Codeverse, Ditto, Dubset, Eave, Epic Burger, Funding Gates, Futuredontics, Halo Neuroscience, Haute Hijab, Helpr, Ianacare, Ideeli, Inventables, Jopwell, JW Player, Kapost, Knovel, Landt, Leaders, Lex Machina, Livefyre, Miniluxe, Pex, PlanetTran, ProofPilot, Redline Trading Solutions, Rentlytics, Roti, ScrollMotion, Shade Up, SmartZip Analytics Inc., Sopris Health, StyleSight, TB12, Tea Drops, TeachBoost, True Botanicals, Virgin Pulse, Wahed Invest, Wait What, Wynd, Yapp

Key Executives:
Richard J Harrington, Chairman Emeritus
Education: BS, Honorary Doctorate of Laws, University of Rhode Island
Background: President & CEO, Thomson Reuters Corporation
Directorships: Xerox Corporation, Aetna, MiniLuxe, PlanetTran, Knovel, StyleSight
Tony Tjan, Managing Partner
Education: AB, Harvard College; MBA, Harvard Business School
Background: Senior Partner, The Parthenon Group; Chief Strategic Counselor, Thomson Reuters; Founder & CEO, ZEFER
Directorships: Cyberplex, Knovel, Shape Up, Epic Burger, MiniLuxe
John Hamel, Partner
Education: AB, Harvard College
Background: Director, Business Intelligence, Answerthink; Technology Advisor, ZEFER
Directorships: MiniLuxe, Epic Burger, PlanetTran, Shape Up
Mats Lederhausen, Operating Partner
Education: Business Administration, Bromma Gymnasium; MS, Stockholm School of Economics
Background: Managing Director, McDonald's Ventures; The Boston Consulting Group
Ali Rahimtula, Partner
Education: BA, Memorial University; MBA, Harvard Business School
Background: Principal, Aquiline Capital Partners; VP, Financial Institutions Group, Goldman Sachs

568 CULTIVATE CAPITAL
17 West 76th Street
Suite 2D
New York, NY 10023

Toll-Free: 800-420-0634
e-mail: hello@cultivatecapital.com
web: www.cultivatecapital.com

Mission Statement: Offers capital loans, startup funding, bridge & inventory loans, real estate financing, and cannabis equipment financing.

Geographic Preference: US, Canada
Founded: 2018
Industry Group Preference: Cannabis, Finance

569 CULTIVATION CAPITAL
911 Washington Avenue
Suite 801
St. Louis, MO 63101

Phone: 314-216-2051
web: www.cultivationcapital.com

Mission Statement: Cultivation Capital is an early-stage venture capital firm managed by experienced entrepreneurs seeking to partner with the next generation of great founders. All portfolio companies get the benefit of Cultivation Capital's General Partners and Entrepreneurs in Residence. These business-savvy entrepreneurs have built successful companies and thrive at getting great start-ups through the challenging early stages of business development.

Geographic Preference: Missouri
Average Investment: $250,000 - $1.5 million
Minimum Investment: $250,000
Investment Criteria: Post-Seed/Pre-Series A
Industry Group Preference: Technology, Life Sciences
Portfolio Companies: Aisle411, Host Analytics, Gainsight, Gremlin Social, Hatchbuck, Label Insight, Lockerdome, Salesvue, TopOPPS, TrackBill, Tunespeak, WealthAccess, Adarza BioSystems, Arvegenix, Benson Hill Biosystems, BlueStrata EHR, Cardialen, Euclises Pharmaceuticals Inc., Galera Therapeutics, Immuno Photonics, Mobius Therapeutics, Molecular Sensing, Pulse Therapeutics, Sequoia Vaccines, Tioma Therapeutics, Veniti, Emplify, CloudBeds, DealCloud, Sfara, FinLocker, Assembly, S4, SafeTrek, Yurbuds, Upside, Cheddar, NarrativeDx, Rentalutions

Other Locations:
CIC@CET
4041 Forest Park Avenue
Suite 116
St. Louis, MO 63108
Phone: 314-216-2051

1100 Corporate Square Drive
Suite 184
St. Louis, MO 63132

Key Executives:
Brian Matthews, Co-Founder/Managing Partner
Education: BS, Mechanical Engineering, Missouri University of Science & Technology
Background: Mentor, Capital Innovators; Founder, River City Internet Group
Peter Esparrago, Co-Founder/General Partner
Education: BS, Chemical Engineering, University of Missouri; MBA, Finance, Rockhurst University
Background: Managing Partner, Growspar; CEO, IntraISP; President, Cigital; President, Mycroft; COO, Ariel Research; Partner, Accenture
Jim McKelvey, Co-Founder/General Partner
Education: Washington University, St. Louis
Background: Co-Founder, Square; Co-Founder, Mira Digital Publishing
Rick Holton Jr., Co-Founder/General Partner
Education: BS, Engineering & Economics, Vanderbilt University School of Engineering; MBA, Olin Business

School
Background: Founding Partner, Holton Capital Group; Co-Founder, Classic Car Studio
Directorships: Anchor Packaging
Cliff Holekamp, Co-Founder/General Partner
Education: BA, Washington & Lee University; MBA, Washington University, St. Louis
Background: Founder, Foot Healers, Back Experts & Pacheco Capital
Directorships: LockerDome, Yurbuds, SoMoLend, Schoology, The Danube Fund, City Academy
Kyle Welborn, Co-Founder/Partner
Education: Political Science, Loyola University Chicago
Background: Founder, FinServe Tech Angels; Chicagoland Entrepreneurial Center; Analyst, I2A Fund

570 CULTIVIAN SANDBOX VENTURES
1000 West Fulton Market
Suite 213
Chicago, IL 60607

e-mail: contactus@cultiviansbx.com
web: www.cultiviansbx.com

Mission Statement: Cultivian Sandbox Ventures is a venture capital firm focused on cultivating the next generation of leading food and agriculture technology companies. The firm is a partnership between Cultivian Ventures and Sandbox Industries.
Geographic Preference: North America
Fund Size: $115 million
Average Investment: $5 - $15 million
Investment Criteria: Seed through Late Stage
Industry Group Preference: Food & Beverage, Agriculture, Water, Animal Health, Environment, Food Safety, Sustainability, Technology
Portfolio Companies: AbCelex Technologies, Advanced Adnimal Diagnostics, Agrivida, Allylix, AquaSpy, Aratana Therapeutics, Conservis, Corvium, Descartes Labs, Divergence, EnEvolv, Full Harvest, Geltor, Harvest Automation, HarvestPort, Novihum Technologies, Novogy, Nuritas, Phylagen, Proterro, Rivertop Renewables, Sound Agriculture, Vestaron, Virgin Plants
Key Executives:
Ron Meeusen, PhD, Managing Director
Education: PhD, Plant Cell Biology, University of California, Berkeley
Background: Global Leader of Biotechnology, Dow AgroSciences; Founder, Immuneworks
Directorships: AbCelex, Agrivida, Asilomar Bio, EnEvolv, Proterro, Rivertop Renewables, Vestaron, Virgin Plants
Andy Ziolkowski, Managing Director
Education: BS, Engineering, University of Pennsylvania; MBA, Wharton School
Background: Managing Director, SAE Ventures; Forest Street Capital; Director, Venture Capital, Credit Suisse First Boston
Directorships: AquaSpy, Descartes Labs, EOSi, Harvest Automation, Novihum Technologies, Sample6
Bob Shapiro, Managing Director
Education: AB, Harvard College; JD, Columbia University School of Law
Background: Chairman & CEO, Monsanto Agriculture Group; CEO, The NutraSweet Company; VP & General Counsel, GD Searle & Co.
Directorships: Chromatin, Elevance Renewable Sciences, Intrexon Corporation, Conservis Corp., Advanced Animal Diagnostics
Nick Rosa, Managing Director
Education: BS, Political Science, Northern Illinois University; MBA, DePaul University
Background: CEO, NutraSweet Company; Senior Executive, Monsanto

571 CUSTER CAPITAL
14 Sout High Street
New Albany, OH 43054

Phone: 614-855-9980

Mission Statement: Established to make investments in a diversified portfolio of growth and expansion companies.
Geographic Preference: Midwest United States
Fund Size: $5 million
Founded: 1985
Average Investment: $200,000
Minimum Investment: $50,000
Investment Criteria: Debt Expansion, Spinoffs, Management Buyouts, Recapitalizations, Leveraged Acquisitions
Industry Group Preference: Healthcare, Manufacturing, Distribution, Business Products & Services, Technology
Key Executives:
William M. Custer, President/CEO
Education: BS, Corporate Finance, University of Southern California, NASD Series 7 and Series 63 License
Donald O'Shea, Managing Director
Education: MBA, Vrunel University; DMS, University of the West of England; BSc, University of London
Background: Managing Director, Leather Agencies; President/CEO, Minit Canada; Founder, BDF Group Ltd.

572 CUTLASS CAPITAL LLC
229 Marlborough Street
Boston, MA 02116

web: www.cutlasscapital.com

Mission Statement: Cutlass Capital is a private venture capital firm that exclusively pursues opportunities in the healthcare industry, with particular emphasis on the specialty healthcare services and medical device sectors. Cutlass Capital's objective is to provide its expertise to create value for its portfolio companies and to help cultivate the next generation of leading healthcare businesses.
Fund Size: $57 million
Founded: 2001
Industry Group Preference: Healthcare, Healthcare Services, Medical Devices
Portfolio Companies: Alere Medical Inc., Apneon Inc., Byram Holdings Inc., CardioKinetix Inc., Evalve Inc., GI Dynamics Inc., Hemsphere Inc., IntelliCare america Inc., Titan Health Corporation, TranS1 Inc., Xoft Inc.
Other Locations:
1750 Montgomery Street
San Francisco, CA 94111
Key Executives:
Jonathan W Osgood CFA, Co-Founder/Managing Member
617-867-0820
e-mail: jonosgood@cutlasscapital.com
Education: BA, Dartmouth College; MBA, Amos Tuck School of Business Administration, Dartmouth College
Background: Research Analyst, Deutsche Banc Alex Brown; Global Head, Health Care Research
Directorships: CardioKinetix, GI Dynamics, Hemsphere, TranS1, Xoft
E David Hetz, Co-Founder/Managing Member
415-806-4611
e-mail: hetz@cutlasscapital.com
Education: BA, Claremont McKenna College; MBA, Harvard Business School
Background: Investment Banker, Robertson Stephens & Co
Directorships: Titan Health Corporation, Xoft
Raymond Larkin, Venture Partner
e-mail: raylarkin@cutlasscapital.com
Education: BS, La Salle University
Background: CEO, Eunoe; CEO, Nellcor Puritan Bennett;

Venture Capital & Private Equity Firms / Domestic Firms

National Sales Manager, Bentley Laboratories; Captain, United States Marine Corps.
Stephen B Solomon MD, Venture Partner
410-303-6901
e-mail: ssolomon@cutlasscapital.com
Education: AB, Biochemistry & Molecular Biology, Harvard College; MD, Yale School of Medicine
Background: Faculty Member, Johns Hopkins School of Medicine

573 CVF CAPITAL PARTNERS
1590 Drew Avenue
Suite 110
Davis, CA 95618

Phone: 530-757-7004 Fax: 530-757-1316
e-mail: info@cvfcapitalpartners.com
web: cvfcapitalpartners.com

Mission Statement: CVF Capital Partners grew out of California's Central Valley to become a lower middle market investor in the Western U.S. with special knowledge of the Hispanic market.
Geographic Preference: Western U.S.
Founded: 2005
Average Investment: $2 - $5 million
Investment Criteria: Later-Stage, Expansion, Strategic Acquisitions, Ownership Transitions, Recapitalizations
Industry Group Preference: Business Services, Distribution and Logistics, Manufacturing, Healthcare, Telecommunications
Portfolio Companies: Utility Telecom, ComAv, Pioneer Recycling, LightRiver Technologies, Signature Coast

Key Executives:
José Blanco, Managing Partner
Education: Saint Michael's College; MS, Economics, University of Utah; MBA, Claremont Graduate University; PhD, Economics, Utah State University
Background: Regional Vice President, CIO, AIG Investment Corporation
Edward McNulty, Managing Partner
Education: BA, Colgate University; MIA, Finance, Columbia University
Background: Founding Partner, ACI Capital America Fund
Brad Triebsch, Managing Partner
Education: Saint Mary's College
Background: Westhoff Cone & Holmstedt

574 CXO FUND
3031 Tisch Way
Suite 704
San Jose, CA 95128

web: thecxofund.com

Mission Statement: To create long-term value by helping entrepreneurs build companies and provide attractive returns to our investors. CXO is a venture capital firm that works hands on with management to build innovative companies.
Geographic Preference: California
Investment Criteria: Early Stage, Seed/Pre-Series A
Industry Group Preference: Fintech, Health Care, Technology, Deep Tech, Software, Internet, Food Technology
Portfolio Companies: Avocado Systems, Breinify, Censia, Coddle, Cogni, CogX, Modjoul, TruU, Uniphore, Zapata

Key Executives:
Gary Gauba, Founder/Managing Director
Education: BEng, Gujarat University; MS, Chemical Engineering, West Virginia University
Background: CEO/Founder, Softline; Systech Integrators; Cognilytics Inc.; TruU; Sr Partner, KPMG; President, ACS Systech Integrators; President, CenturyLink

575 CYPRESS GROUP
437 Madison Avenue
33rd Floor
New York, NY 10022

Phone: 212-705-0150 Fax: 212-705-0199
web: www.cypressgp.com

Mission Statement: Invests equity capital in privately negotiated transactions and builds value for investors. Investments are made in promising established companies, which are then helped to grow dynamically and profit as their plans are realized.
Fund Size: $2.5 billion
Founded: 1989
Minimum Investment: $500,000
Industry Group Preference: Manufacturing, Consumer Products, Media
Portfolio Companies: Affinia Group Inc., American Marketing Industries Holdings Inc., Anglian Group Plc., Atlanta Cable Systems, Brand Connections LLC, Catlin, Cinemark USA Inc., ClubCorp Inc., Communications & Power Industries Inc., Cooper-Standard Automotive Inc., Dank Business Systems Plc., Evergreen Media Corporation, Financial Guaranty Insurance Company, Illinois Central Corporation, Infinity Broadcasting Corporation, K&F Industries Inc., Lear Corporation, Loral Aerospace Holdings Inc., McBride Plc., MedPointe Inc., Meow Mix Company, Montpelier Re Holdings Ltd., Parisian Inc., Republic National Cabinet Corporation, RP Scherer Corporation, Scottish Re Group Limited, Stone Canyon Entertainment Corporation, WESCO International Inc., Williams Scotsman Inc.

Key Executives:
James A. Stern, Chairman/CEO
e-mail: jstern@cypressgp.com
Education: BS, Tufts University; MBA, Harvard Business School
Background: Head Merchant Banking, Lehman Brothers
Directorships: Lear Corporation; AMTROL; Affinia Group; MedPointe; WESCO International

576 CYPRESS GROWTH CAPITAL
3899 Maple Ave.
Suite 100
Dallas, TX 75219

Phone: 214-304-7645
e-mail: inquiries@cypressgrowthcapital.com
web: www.cypressgrowthcapital.com

Mission Statement: An alternative to traditional debt and equity instruments, royalty financing offers entrepreneurs access to significant capital while preserving ownership and control. As one of the first and largest royalty financing firms in the United States, Cypress Growth Capital is actively investing in technology-enabled business services companies in the Southwest.
Geographic Preference: Southwest
Average Investment: $1 - $8 million
Investment Criteria: Growth Capital
Industry Group Preference: Technology-Enabled Services, SaaS, Software, Business Products & Services

Key Executives:
Ed Mello, Co-Founder/Managing Director
Education: University of Notre Dame
Background: COO/Managing Partner, Computer Sciences Corporation Consulting Group; Co-Founder, Cypress Point Partners; President, Global Sales & Operations, nGenera; EDS
Barton Goodwin, Co-Founder/Managing Partner
Education: Economics & Managerial Studies, Rice University
Background: Co-Founder, Cypress Point Partners; Information Technology, Accenture

Venture Capital & Private Equity Firms / Domestic Firms

Vik Thapar, Venture Partner
Education: BS, University of Texas, Dallas; MBA, Southern Methodist University
Background: Director, Texas Regional Center for Innovation & Commercialization
Directorships: TeXchange, TiE Dallas

577 CYPRIUM PARTNERS
200 Public Square
Suite 2020
Cleveland, OH 44114

Phone: 216-453-4500
web: www.cyprium.com

Mission Statement: A private investment firm that provides mezzanine and equity capital to profitable, middle-market companies. Cyprium strives to be a value-added investor that supports the growth, acquisition, refinancing or liquidity needs of private company owners and their management teams.

Geographic Preference: United States, Canada
Founded: 1998
Average Investment: $10 - $60 million
Investment Criteria: Mezzanine, Equity
Industry Group Preference: Manufacturing, Distribution
Portfolio Companies: ACT Lighting Inc., Backyard Products LLC, Bensussen Deutsch & Associates, Hobbico Inc., Irvin Automotive Products Inc., MC Assembly, M-D Building Products, MGS Mfg. Group Inc., Paper Machinery Corp., Phantom Fireworks, Weaber Inc.

Other Locations:
461 Fifth Avenue
26th Floor
New York, NY 10017
Phone: 616-571-1620

77 West Wacker Drive
Suite 4500
Chicago, IL 60601
Phone: 312-283-8800

Key Executives:
John Sinnerberg, Partner
Education: BA Economics, Bucknell University; MBA, Wharton School, University of Pennsylvania
Background: CEO & Managing Partner, Key Principal Partners; Co-Founder, Key Mezzanine Capital Fund; Founder, Regis Capital Partners; Investment Banking, Barclays Group
Cindy Babbit, Managing Partner
Education: BS Biology, University of Miami; MBA, Case Western Reserve University
Background: Partner, Key Principal Partners; Investment Banking, Carleton, McCreary, Holmes and Company; Laboratory Technical, Siebert Powder Coatings; Statistician, University Hospitals of Cleveland
Drew Molinari, Principal
Education: BBA, Finance, Kent State University; MBA, Booth School of Business, University oF Chicago
Background: Associate, Corporate Development, Agilysys Inc.; Analyst, Croft & Bender; Analyst, Brown, Gibbons Lang & Co.
Daniel Kessler, Partner
Education: BS, Accounting, Indiana University; MBA, University of Chicago; CPA
Background: Key Principal Partners; GlobalStreams
Beth Haas, Partner
Education: BA, Government, Dartmouth College; MBA, Wharton School, University of Pennsylvania
Background: Key Principal Partners; KeyBanc Capital Markets

578 CapitalG

web: capitalg.com

Mission Statement: Formerly known as Google Capital, CapitalG is a growth equity fund that invests in companies that harness long-term technology trends to drive market disruption. Our connection to Google is our key asset.

Geographic Preference: Global
Industry Group Preference: Technology
Portfolio Companies: Airbnb, Applied, Aye, Care.com, Car Dekho, Cloudflare, Commonfloor.com, Convoy, Credit Karma, Crowd Strike, Cuemath, Duolingo, Fanduel, Freshworks, Glassdoor, Gusto, Inno Light, Lending Club, Looker, Lyft, Mapr, MultiPlan, Oscar, Practo, Renaissance, Robinhood, Snap, Stripe, Survery Monkey, Ten-X, Thumbtack, UiPath, Zscaler

Key Executives:
Gene Frantz, Partner
Education: BS, University of California, Berkeley; MBA, Stanford Graduate School of Business
Background: Partner, TPG Capital
David Lawee, Partner
Education: McGill University; University of Western Ontario; MBA, University of Chicago
Background: VP, Corporate Development, Google; VP, Marketing, Google; Founder, Mosaic Venture Partners
Laela Sturdy, Partner
Education: AB, Harvard College; MSc, Trinity College Dublin; MBA, Stanford Graduate School of Business
Background: Director, Sales & Business Operations, Google; Consultant, Bain & Company

579 D.E. SHAW & CO. LP The D.E. Shaw Group
1166 Avenue of the Americas
9th Floor
New York, NY 10036

Phone: 212-478-0000 Fax: 212-478-0100
e-mail: inquiries@deshaw.com
web: www.deshaw.com

Mission Statement: The D.E. Shaw Group is a global investment firm that invests in a wide array of companies in both public and private markets across the world.

Geographic Preference: Worldwide
Fund Size: $39 billion
Founded: 1988
Investment Criteria: Early-Stage, Later-Stage
Industry Group Preference: All markets considered

Other Locations:
180 Linden Street
2nd Floor
Wellesley, MA 02482

7300 College Boulevard
Suite 620
Overland Park, KS 66210
Phone: 212-478-0050 **Fax:** 212-478-0060

821 Alexander Road
Suite 202
Princeton, NJ 08540

2735 Sand Hill Road
Suite 105
Menlo Park, CA 94025
Phone: 650-526-4300 **Fax:** 650-526-4301

3 Bermudiana Road
Third Floor
Hamilton HM 08
Bermuda
Phone: 441-278-4850 **Fax:** 441-278-4860

D.E. Shaw & Co. London LLP
55 Baker Street
Seventh Floor
London W1U 8EW

Venture Capital & Private Equity Firms / Domestic Firms

United Kingdom
Phone: 44-2074094300 Fax: 44-2074094350

D.E. Shaw & Co. Asia Pacific Limited
19th Floor, York House
The Landmark, 15 Queens Road
Central
Hong Kong
Phone: 852-35212500 Fax: 852-35212600

D.E. Shaw Investment Management Co., Ltd.
Level 35, Unit 3506, International Finance Center Tower 2
8 Century Avenue, Pudong
Shanghai 200120
China

D.E. Shaw India Private Limited
Plot No. 573, B & C, No. 1
Jubilee Hills
Hyderabad, Telangana 500 096
India
Phone: 91-4066390000 Fax: 91-4040164284

Key Executives:
David E. Shaw, Founder
Education: PhD, Stanford University
Background: Chief Scientist, D.E. Shaw Research LLC; Senior Research Fellow, Center for Computational Biology & Bioinformatics, Columbia University; Adjunct Professor, Biochemistry & Molecular Biophysics, Columbia Medical School

580 DACE VENTURES
405 Waltham Street
Suite 140
Lexington, MA 02421
Phone: 781-250-0600 Fax: 781-250-0611
e-mail: info@daceventures.com
web: www.daceventures.com

Mission Statement: Dace Ventures actively invests in innovative businesses in the Internet industry, with particular focus on the mobile services, digital media and consumer marketing sectors. The firm seeks to work with passionate entrepreneurs and innovative companies with advantages in high-potential markets.

Fund Size: $70 million
Average Investment: $250,000 - $3 million
Investment Criteria: Early-Stage
Industry Group Preference: Digital Media & Marketing, Consumer Marketing, Mobile Services, Marketing
Portfolio Companies: Apptient, Cartera Commerce, Cityvoter, EveryScape, Healthguru, Howcast, Ticket Evolution, YieldMo

Key Executives:
Dave Andonian, Managing Partner
e-mail: dave@daceventures.com
Education: BA, Business, University of Massachusetts, Amherst
Background: Entrepreneur-in-Residence, Flagship Ventures; Chairman & CEO, Affinnova; President & COO, CMGI; PictureTel; IBM
Directorships: CityVoter, EveryScape, Ticket Evolution
Jon Chait, General Partner
e-mail: jon@daceventures.com
Background: Principal, Pod Holding; Managing Director, Garage Technology Ventures; CEO & Founder, Reality Bytes
Directorships: Cartera Commerce, Marlin Mobile
Doug Chertok, Venture Partner
Background: Founder, Vast Ventures; Founder, StreetEasy
Directorships: Daylife, StreetEasy, Hashable

581 DAG VENTURES
251 Lytton Avenue
Suite 200
Palo Alto, CA 94301
Phone: 650-543-8180 Fax: 650-328-2921
e-mail: info@dagventures.com
web: www.dagventures.com

Mission Statement: DAG Ventures is a venture capital partnership that helps promising entrepreneurs to build leading companies across a range of technology sectors.

Fund Size: $500 million
Investment Criteria: Early Stage, Mid-Stage
Industry Group Preference: Information Technology, Energy, Life Sciences, Software
Portfolio Companies: 3VR, Adamas Pharmaceuticals, Admob, Aerohive Networks, Aggregate Knowledge, Agrivida, Alta Devices, Altor Networks, Ambarella, Amyris Biotechnologies, Aoptix Technologies, Atara Biotherapeutics, Avnera, Avvo, Axiom Global, Birst, BitTorrent, Bloom Energy, Boku, CardioDx, Chegg, Clarizen, ClearStory Data, Cleartrip, Clickatell, Cloudera, D2S, DisplayLink, Engine Yard, Eventbrite, FireEye, Fortify Software, Funny or Die, Gigya, Glam Media, Glassdoor, GrubHub, Harvest Power, High Gear Media, Inspirato, Jasper Wireless, Kovio, LearnVest, Lithium Technologies, LiveOps, Loopt, Marin Software, Mcube, NEOS, New Relic, Newport Media, Nextdoor, Ninjan Solutions, One Medical Group, OpenDNS, OpenX Software, Oportun, Origami Logic, Pacific Biosciences of California, Pentaho, Picarro, Pinger, Proofpoint, Quantenna Communications, Raptr, RightScale, Ring Central, Seeking Alpha, Silver Peak Systems, SilverSpring Networks, Solexel, StrongView Systems, SunRun, Taulia, TrialPay, True Ultimate Standards Everywhere, Upwork, uShip, Vectra Networks, Visible Measures, Wealthfront, Wetpaint, WeWork, Wixpress, Xoom, Yelp, YuMe, Zlango, Zuora, Zynga

Key Executives:
John Caddedu, Managing Director
Education: BA, Harvard College; MBA, Stanford Graduate School of Business
Background: Managing Director, Amsterdam Pacific; Octel Communications; Tandem Computers; JP Morgan
Young Chung, Managing Director
Education: BA, Harvard College; MBA, Harvard Business School
Background: Investment Banking Analyst, Goldman Sachs; Entrisphere
Tom Goodrich, Managing Director
Education: AB, Dartmouth College; MBA, Stanford Graduate School of Business
Background: Principal, Bechtel Investments; Co-Founder & Vice President, Dimensional Corporate Finance
Nick Pianim, Managing Director
Education: BSc, Electrical Engineering, Tufts University; MBA, Stanford Graduate School of Business
Background: Vice President, Corporate Development, Juniper Networks; CEO, iAsiaWorks
Greg Williams, Managing Director
Education: BSc, McGill University
Background: Portfolio Manager, Teachers' Private Capital; Summerhill Ventures
Joseph Zanone, Chief Financial Officer
Education: BS, Pennsylvania State University; MBA, Santa Clara University; CPA
Background: Finance Director, Siemens Venture Capital; Audit Manager, PricewaterhouseCoopers

582 DALLAS VENTURE PARTNERS
2801 Woodside St.
Dallas, TX 75204
e-mail: info@dallasventurepartners.com
web: www.dallasventurepartners.com

Mission Statement: Our mission at Dallas Venture Partners is to become the financial partner of choice for technology entrepreneurs seeking to build a world-class business. At DVP, we believe in creating and sustaining long term relationships within our own local venture community as well as within the larger venture industry. That means, if we think we can help you, we will - even if we are not able to invest in your business. It also means that if we choose to invest in your company, you can expect us to use every resource at our disposal to ensure that you will succeed.

Geographic Preference: Texas, Midwest
Investment Criteria: Early-Stage
Industry Group Preference: Software, Clean Technology, Networking, Mobile Apps, Gaming, Web Applications & Services
Portfolio Companies: AgSolver, Averify, Data Vision Resources, Device Fidelity, Eyelation, Parrable, PHYND, SmartyPig, Yvolver, Zest Health
Key Executives:
  Michael Coppola, Managing Partner
  Education: BBA, Southern Methodist University
  Background: President, Coppola Enterprises; Co-Founder, DataVision; Co-Founder, Businessolver.com; Co-Founder, Workcomp.net
  Directorships: Datavision, Businessolver, Social Money
  Jim Duda, Managing Partner
  Education: BA, Northwestern University; MBA, Fuqua School
  Background: Executive Vice President, Genus Holdings

583 DANEVEST TECH FUND ADVISORS
8215 Greenway Blvd.
Suite 560
Midleton, WI 53562

Phone: 608-830-2990

Mission Statement: DaneVest Tech Fund Advisors, LLC invests in privately held, early stage growth businesses with special technology and other advantages in the information technology, life science and consumer goods/service industries.

Geographic Preference: Midwest
Investment Criteria: Early-Stage
Industry Group Preference: Technology, Information Technology, Life Sciences, Consumer Products, Consumer Services
Portfolio Companies: Alice.com, Compact Particle Acceleration Corporation, Eso-Technologies, Sologear, Stemia Biomarker Discovery, TrafficCast China, TrafficCast International
Key Executives:
  Terrence R Wall, General Partner
  Education: Graaskamp Real Estate Program, University of Wisconsin-Madison
  Background: Founder, President & General Partner, T. Wall Properties Master Limited Partnership
  Joseph P Hildebrandt, General Partner
  Background: CEO/Manager, H Venture Management; Managing Director, Penomenelle Angels Fund I; Partner Emeritus, Foley & Lardner LLP
  Leon R Wilkosz, President
  Education: Univeristy of Wisonson, Madison
  Background: President/Owner, Resource Consulting LLC

584 DARBY OVERSEAS INVESTMENTS LTD
1133 Connecticut Avenue Northwest
Suite 400
Washington, DC 20036

Phone: 202-872-0500 **Fax:** 202-872-1816
web: www.darbyoverseas.com

Mission Statement: Darby Overseas Investments, Ltd. is the private equity arm of Franklin Templeton Investments. Experienced in the field of infrastructure, Darby pursues investments in sectors such as energy, transportation, waste management, water treatment and telecommunications, and specifically targets markets in Asia, Central and Eastern Europe and Latin America.

Geographic Preference: Latin America, Asian, Central Europe, Eastern Europe
Fund Size: $250 million
Founded: 1994
Average Investment: $10 - $15 million
Investment Criteria: Late Stage Venture Capital, Minority, Shared Control Stakes, Acquisitions, Mezzanine, Restructuring, Buyouts, Growth Capital, Middle-Market, Consolidation
Industry Group Preference: Financial Services, Energy, Consumer Products, Telecommunications, Information Technology, Healthcare, Industrial
Portfolio Companies: Amalgamated Bean Coffee Trading Company, ART Group, AUPU Group Holding Company, Bioerix SRL, Bhoruka Power, Brightex Industries, Bugukgangbyung Co., Career Point Infosystems, Daechun Greenwater, Daesan Energy, Datapoint, Electrosteel Steels, Empresa Generadora de Electricidad Haina, Energy Network, Enzen Global Solutions, ERG Services, Escorts Construction Equipment, Gangwon Wind Power, GKC Projects, Golden Harvest, Gramex 2000, Gyeonggi Expressway, Heemang Dream Haksa Co., Hisarlar, Hyosung Wind Power Holdings, Injae Tongil Village Co., Intertug, Junggwan Library Operation Co., Kerrera Company, Kimaya Fashions, Koza Gida, Leadcorp, Machang Bridge, Myungsung Environment, Nara-Sarang Co., Newgen Knowledge Works, OCI Solar, OCENSA, OCENSA Transportation Rights, Orion Holding, Paju Yangju Tongil Village Co., PECH, PSM Investments, Seoul Beltway Corporation, SFO Technologies, Shayne International Holdings, Storent Holding, Sun-Jin Boramae Co., Symbiotec Pharmalab, Tabacarcen, Top Image, Ver Se Innovation, Vital Renewable Energy Company, Walnut Investment Holding, Water Oasis Group, Yeongcheon Daegu Tongil Madang Co., Yuchai

Other Locations:
  Fiduciary Trust International of the South
  2 Alhambra Plaza
  Penthouse 1
  Coral Gables, FL 33134
  Phone: 305-372-1260 **Fax:** 305-982-1593

  Franklin Templeton Investments Svcs Mexico
  Darby Private Equity, Paseo de la Reforma No. 342, piso 8
  Col. Juárez
  Delegación Cuauhtémoc 06600
  Mexico
  Phone: 52-5550020696 **Fax:** 52-5526232643

  Darby Colpatria Capital SAS
  Cra. 7 80-49
  Suite 201
  Bogota
  Colombia
  Phone: 57-13131188

  Franklin Templeton Investimentos Ltda
  Avenida Brigadeiro Faria Lima
  331 - 5o andar
  Sao Paulo SP 04538-133
  Brazil
  Phone: 55-1132060080 **Fax:** 55-1130713775

  Darby Asia Investors Limited
  17th Floor Charter House
  8 Connaught Road
  Central
  Hong Kong
  Phone: 852-29109200 **Fax:** 852-25219815

  Darby-Hana Infrastructure Fund Management Co.
  10th Floor, CCMM Building
  12 Youido-Dong, Youngdungpo-Gu
  Seoul 150-968

Venture Capital & Private Equity Firms / Domestic Firms

Korea
Phone: 822-37740605 Fax: 822-37740667

Darby Asia Investors Private Limited
Indiabulls Finance Center, Tower 2, 13th Floor
Senapati Bapat Marg, Elphinstone (W)
Mumbai 400013
India
Phone: 91-02267519100 Fax: 91-02266391277

Franklin Templeton Austria GmbH
Dr. Karl Lueger-Ring 10
Vienna A-1010
Austria
Phone: 43-1532265500 Fax: 43-1532265550

Franklin Templeton Slovakia cro
Aupark Tower
Einsteinova 24
Bratislava 851 0
Slovakia
Phone: 421-232113720 Fax: 421-232113730

Franklin Templeton Magyarország Kft
Granit Tower, Sixth Floor
Szabadsag ter 7
Budapest 1054
Hungary
Phone: 36-13543700 Fax: 36-13543710

Darby Overseas Investments
Buyukdere Caddesi No. 191
Apa Giz Plaza Kat 12
Levent / Istanbul 34330
Turkey
Phone: 90-2123679204 Fax: 90-2123679202

Franklin Templeton Investments Poland sp
Z.O.O., Rondo 1, 29th Floor
Rondo ONZ 1
Warsaw 00-124
Poland
Phone: 48-223371380 Fax: 48-223371373

Key Executives:
Richard H. Frank, President/CEO
Education: BS, Mechanical Engineering, South Dakota School of Mines and Technology; MS, Sloan School of Management, Massachusetts Institute of Technology
Background: World Bank; CFO, International Finance Corporation

585 DATA COLLECTIVE
500 2nd Street
Suite 200
San Francisco, CA 94107

e-mail: press@dcvc.com
web: www.dcvc.com

Mission Statement: Data Collective invests in entrepreneurs building Big Data companies. Big Data companies capture, store, secure, transmit, transform, and analyze data for economic advantage, either with huge volumes (terabytes to exabytes), or at tremendous speed (microseconds to seconds), or both. Big Data companies can come to market solving hard infrastructure problems, taking leadership in vertical B2B markets, or as truly data-driven consumer products. The common thread is that the founding team has the experience and discipline to solve data problems at novel scale, speed, or level of insight, and ideally all three.

Investment Criteria: Seed, Series A, Growth
Industry Group Preference: Data Storage, Cloud Computing, Internet, Software
Portfolio Companies: Amiato, Apcera, Appurify, Authy, BackOps, BitDeli, CardSpring, Carsabi, CircleCI, CitusData, Cloudability, Continuity, Cube, Elasticsearch, Feedzai, Firebase, FlipTop, FloType, FreshPlum, GetGOing, HeavyBit Industries, Ink, Kaggle, Keen IO, LevdUp, MatterMark, Memsql, Meteor, MindSumo, MixRank, Moleculo, MongoHQ, Morta Security, Parse, ParStream, Piston Cloud Computing, Planet Labs, Platfora, Priceonomics, PrimaTable, Prism Skylabs, Qumulo, Ranker, Rescale, RolePoint, Sentinel, ShopLogic, Signifyd, Simpler, SinoLending, SolidStage, Space Monkey, Srch2, Swiftype, Teambox, Tempo, Trifacta, TrustedInsight, Virool, Vurb, Weotta, Womply, ZenPayroll

Other Locations:
270 University Avenue
Palo Alto, CA 94301

Key Executives:
Zachary Bogue, Co-Managing Partner
Education: BS, Environmental Science, Harvard University; JD, Georgetown Law School
Background: Co-Founder, Founders Den; Co-Founder, Montara Capital Partners; Associate, Wilson Sonsini Goodrich & Rosati; Law Partner, Virtual Law Partners
Matt Ocko, Co-Managing Partner
Education: Physics, Yale University
James Hardiman, Partner
Education: University of California, Berkeley; University of Chicago
Background: ZS Associates; Blackstone Group

586 DATA POINT CAPITAL
One Marina Park Drive
10th Floor
Boston, MA 02210

Phone: 617-874-5152
e-mail: info@datapointcapital.com
web: www.datapointcapital.com

Mission Statement: Data Point Capital focuses on companies that can be leveraged and scaled on the Internet and touch the consumer. Categories of interest include mobile, gaming, social networks, payments, comparison shopping, e-commerce and emerging technologies. The fund is stage-agnostic, allowing for investments in all business stages or controlling interest deals and is made up of business executives and internet leaders who have created tremendous value through building a number of very successful companies.

Founded: 2012
Investment Criteria: All Stages
Industry Group Preference: Mobile, Gaming, Social Media, E-Commerce & Manufacturing, Internet
Portfolio Companies: Aperio, Blitsy, Clypd, CouchUp, Jebbit, Luxury Garage Sale, Paintzen, Print Syndicate, Smart Lunches, Vee24, Yieldify, YourMechanic

Key Executives:
Scott Savitz, Founder/Managing Partner
Education: BA, English, University of Colorado
Background: CEO, Shoebuy.com
Directorships: Olejo Stores, On The Spot Systems, Bluestem Brands
Mike Majors, Managing Partner
Education: BSE, Machine Learning/Robotics, Cambridge University
Background: Managing Partner, Siemens Venture Capital; CFO, Visible World; CFO, Indeed; Brand Equity Ventures
Mary Shannon, Principal of Finance
Education: MBA, Boston College
Background: Director, Planning & Analysis, Zefer; Director, Special Projects, Libery Mutual Group; Analyst, Burr Egan Deleage & Co.

587 DAUPHIN CAPITAL PARTNERS
108 Forest Avenue
Locust Valley, NY 11560

Phone: 516-759-3339 Fax: 516-759-3322
web: www.dauphincapital.com

Mission Statement: Dauphin Capital Partners is a venture capital firm that focuses primarily on the medical and healthcare industries.

Geographic Preference: Eastern Half of United States

Venture Capital & Private Equity Firms / Domestic Firms

Fund Size: $30 million
Founded: 1998
Average Investment: $2 - $3 million
Minimum Investment: $2 million
Investment Criteria: Early Stage
Industry Group Preference: Healthcare, Healthcare Services
Portfolio Companies: Supplemental Health Care Services

Key Executives:
  James B Hoover, Founder/Managing Member
  e-mail: jhoover@dauphincapital.com
  Education: BS, Elizabethtown College; MBA, Finance, Indiana University
  Background: General Partner, Welsh, Carson, Anderson & Stowe; General Partner, Robertson, Stephens & Company; VP, Investment Management Group, Citibank NA
  Directorships: Quovadx, US Physical Therapy

588 DAVENPORT RESOURCES LLC
7 Seir Hill Road
Unit 21
Norwalk, CT 06850

Phone: 203-276-1600
e-mail: hebingham@davenportresources.com
web: www.davenportresources.com

Mission Statement: Direct investments and fund sponsorship for high growth in valuation.

Geographic Preference: United States, Europe
Fund Size: $2.5 million to $100 million
Founded: 1995
Minimum Investment: $50,000
Investment Criteria: Seed, Start-up, Early Rounds, Buy-Ins
Industry Group Preference: Clean Technology, Infrastructure, Renewable Energy, Technology, Energy
Portfolio Companies: Halite Energy Group, Castion Corp., CyGene Inc., Mensch & Natur AG, Mycotech Corp., Room Temperature Superconductors Inc. (ROOTS), Interative Retail Management Inc., Demegen Inc, I/SCRIBES Corp.

Key Executives:
  Hiram A. Bingham, Managing Director
  Education: BA, Yale, Columbia LLB
  Background: President, Caithness Energy, Associate, Shearman & Sterling
  Douglas S. Perry, Managing Director
  Education: Law Degree, Emory University & Georgetown University; MBA, Duke University
  Background: President, Constellation Holdings; Special Counsel/Attorney, SEC's Divisions of Corporation Finance and Enforcement

589 DAVID N DEUTSCH & COMPANY LLC
Westchester Financial Center
50 Main Street
10th Floor
New York, NY 10606

Phone: 212-980-7800
e-mail: office@dndco.com
web: www.dndco.com

Mission Statement: David N. Deutsch & Company is an investment banking firm and independent advisor based in New York. The firm provides financial services to closely-held private and public companies, including advisory services and merger, acquisition, divestiture and financing transactions.

Geographic Preference: US, Canada, Mexico, Western Europe, Israel, Asia, Pacific Rim
Founded: 1993
Industry Group Preference: Business to Business, Communications, Computer Related, Retailing, Real Estate, Consumer Services, Diversified, Financial Services, Food & Beverage, Industrial Equipment, Manufacturing, Chemicals, Publishing, Construction, Technology

Key Executives:
  David N Deutsch, Founder/President
  212-980-7800 x1
  e-mail: dndeutsch@dndco.com
  Education: AB, Economics, Middlebury College; MBA, Columbia University
  Background: Managing Partner, The Presidents Council; Managing Director, Congress Financial; VP, Bear Stearns & Company; Lehman Brothers

590 DAVID SHEN VENTURES
e-mail: info@davidshenventures.com
web: www.davidshenventures.com

Mission Statement: David Shen Ventures focuses mainly on early-stage Internet and Internet-related businesses. The goal is to quickly bring a product to market in an inexpensive way, employ innovation to differentiate from competitors and delight consumers, and test its viability live in the marketplace. Once a product's viability has been validated, David Shen Ventures helps its businesses strategize on growth to the future.

Investment Criteria: Early-Stage
Industry Group Preference: Internet
Portfolio Companies: 5mina, Aerin Medical, Betaworks, Bit.ly, BombFell, Dekko, ElaCarte, Evoz, Ideeli, Knack, Liquor.Com, Micello, Miso Music, Nutrivise, Outspark, Proven, Quincy, Supplyhog, Tie Society, Tripping, User Voices

Key Executives:
  David Shen, President
  Education: BS, Computer Engineering, Renssalaer Polytechnic Insitute; MS, Computer Science, Stanford University
  Background: Vice President, User Experience & Design, Yahoo!; Product Designer, Frog Design

591 DAVIS, TUTTLE VENTURE PARTNERS LP
110 West 7th Street
Suite 1000
Tulsa, OK 74103-3703

Phone: 918-584-7272 **Fax:** 918-582-3404
web: www.davistuttle.com

Mission Statement: Davis, Tuttle Venture Partners is a private investment partnership dedicated to providing long-term development capital and operating expertise to emerging companies.

Fund Size: $100 million
Average Investment: $5 million - $20 million
Minimum Investment: $500,000
Investment Criteria: Seed, Early Stage, Acquisitions, Expansion, LBO, Mezzanine
Industry Group Preference: Corporate Services, Financial Services, Asset Management
Portfolio Companies: AmPro Mortgage Corporation, EnLink Geoenergy Services, Hydrade, Outlast, Nationwide Graphics, Web Tpa

Other Locations:
8 Greenway Plaza
Suite 1320
Houston, TX 77046
Phone: 713-993-0440 **Fax:** 713-621-2297

Key Executives:
  Barry M Davis, Managing General Partner
  Education: BBA, Finance, University of Oklahoma
  Background: Alliance Business Investment Company; Davis Venture Partners; Board Chairman, NASBIC; Director, NVCA; Founder, Venture Capital Institute; Chairman, Oklahoma Innovation Institute
  Philip A Tuttle, General Partner
  Education: BS, Rice University; MBA, Northwestern University; CPA

207

Venture Capital & Private Equity Firms / Domestic Firms

Background: Allied Bancshares Capital; Davis Venture Partners; Founder, Houston Venture Capital Association
W Michael Partain, Partner
Education: BS, Business Management, BS, Accounting, Oklahoma Christian University; CPA
Background: Deloitte, Haskins and Sells; Price Waterhouse; Gerrity Oil and Gas Corp.; Capital Management Company
H Lee Frost, Chief Financial Officer
Education: BS, Accounting, Northwestern Oklahoma State University; CPA
Background: Arthur Young & Company; Williams Companies; Mabee Petroleum Corporation; Capital Management Company

592 DAWNTREADER VENTURES
P.O. Box 571
Southport, CT 06890
Phone: 203-659-0346 Fax: 203-842-4098

Mission Statement: An early-stage venture capital firm collaborating with entrepreneurs to build the next generation of software, internet and digital media companies.

Fund Size: $270 million
Founded: 1998
Investment Criteria: Early-Stage
Industry Group Preference: Software, Internet, Digital Media & Marketing, Infrastructure, Technology-Enabled Services
Portfolio Companies: Answers.com, Colloquis, DeepNines Technologies, FlashBase, Gizmo5, GoToMyPC, Greenplum, HNW, Intersan, iPrint.com, Liverperson, Moreover, MortgageIT, NetForensics, Peer39, Perfect Commerce, ProactiveNet, Tutor.com, Visible World, Xora

593 DAY ONE VENTURES
e-mail: pitch@dayoneventures.co
web: dayoneventures.co

Mission Statement: Technology investor and marketing and communications partner.

Founded: 2018
Average Investment: $100K - $1 million
Investment Criteria: Early-Stage, Startups
Industry Group Preference: AI, Virtual Reality & Augmented Reality, Quantum, Fintech, Education, Healthcare, Self-Driving Cars
Portfolio Companies: DigitalGenius, Piper Inc., Domuso, lvl5, Feastly, Home61, Monscierge, Truebill, Unity Influence

Key Executives:
Masha Drokova, Founding Partner
Background: Houzz, HotelTonight, Gett, Toptal
Directorships: Oceanic
Natalie Issa, Head of Communications
Background: D-Wave Systems, Drive.ai, EchoPixel, Woopra

594 DAYLIGHT PARTNERS
e-mail: info@daylightpartners.com
web: www.daylightpartners.com

Mission Statement: Daylight Partners is a unique venture capital firm which seeks out entrepreneurs who value our operational experience and functional expertise as much as our capital commitment to their venture. Eleven former executives with expertise in marketing, operations, manufacturing, finance, information technology, technological innovation, accounting, real estate, oil and gas, as well as overall corporate management, are driven to have Daylight Partners take an active role in helping mid-stage companies turbo-charge their growth initiatives. While having made investments nationally, Daylight Partners has a particular affinity for Texas-based companies.

Geographic Preference: Texas
Minimum Investment: $250,000 - $750,000
Investment Criteria: Mid-Stage
Industry Group Preference: Technology
Portfolio Companies: CS Identity, DadLabs, Digby, DIYSEO, Edioma, Energetic Solutions, Fantrail, FGA Media, KLD Energy, FISOC, Pawngo, PlanetHS, SmarteSoft, Uplogix, YMAX

Key Executives:
William J. Amelio, Partner
Education: BS, Chemical Engineering, Lehigh University; Honorary Doctorate in Engineering, Lehigh University; MS, Management, Stanford Graduate School of Business
Background: President and CEO, Lenovo Group Limited; Senior Vice President, Asia-Pacific and Japan, Dell Inc; Executive Vice President and COO, NCR Corp's Retail and Financial Group; President and CEO, Honeywell International Inc's Transportation and Power-Systems Division; Senior Management Positions, IBM
Gil Burciaga, Partner
Education: BS, Engineering, Texas A&M University
Background: Senior Vice President, DYNEGY; President, NGC Energy Resources; Senior Vice President, Natural Gas Supply/Trading; Co-Founder, Asset Risk Management
Scott C. Helbing, Partner
Background: President, Scott Helbing Inc; Senior Officer and Executive Vice President, AT&T; Dell; YUM; Reebok; Whittle Communications
Dick Hunter, Partner
Education: Mechanical Engineering, Georgia Institute of Technology
Background: Vice President, Dell Americas Operations, Dell; General Electric; Texas Instruments; Ericcson
Directorships: Massachusetts Institute of Technology China Leaders for Manufacturing Governing Board
Terry Klein, Partner
Background: Vice President of the Advanced Systems Group, Dell;
Rod MacDonald, Partner
Education: BA, University of Missouri, St. Louis
Background: Vice President of Finance, Dell Inc; CFO, iChat/Acuity; CFO, GaSonics; CFO, GRiD; Emerson Electric; Monsanto
Rocky Mountain, Partner
Education: University of Texas at Austin; State University of New York, Albany
Background: Vice President and General Manager of Dell's US Consumer Business; Vice President and General Manager of Dell's Americas Transactional Group; Principle, The Galt Group
Directorships: FGA Media, Frontier Renewal
Scott O'Hare, Partner
Education: BA, Political Science, Stanford University; MS, Geophysics, Stanford University; MBA, Tuck School at Dartmouth College
Background: Vice President and General Manager of Dell's Software and Peripheral Group; Management Consultant, McKinsey and Company; Exploration Geophysicist, Chevron
Ro Parra, Partner
Background: SVP and General Manager, Dell Americas; Vice President and General Manager, Federal Division, GRiD; Radio Shack
Susan Sheskey, Partner
Education: Miami University
Background: Senior Vice President and Chief Information Officer, Dell; Ameritech; Ohio Bell
Directorships: StoredIQ, Digby
Elias "Lee" Urbina, Partner
Education: BBA, Accounting, University of Texas at Austin
Background: Co-Founder and CFO, US Infrastructure

Venture Capital & Private Equity Firms / Domestic Firms

595 DBL PARTNERS
One Montgomery Street
Suite 2375
San Francisco, CA 94104

Phone: 415-568-2901 Fax: 415-956-2561
web: www.dblpartners.vc

Mission Statement: DBL Partners employs a 'Double Bottom Line' investment strategy, which entails investing in businesses that can generate superior returns and working with portfolio companies to help enact positive social, environmental and economic change. DBL focuses on companies in the clean technology, information technology, healthcare and sustainable products and services sectors.

Geographic Preference: Western United States
Fund Size: $400 million
Founded: 2015
Industry Group Preference: Clean Technology, Healthcare Services, Information Technology, Sustainability
Portfolio Companies: Advanced Microgrid Solutions, Akros, Bentek, BrightSource Energy, Ecologic Brands, EcoScraps, eLoan, eMeter, Farmers Business Network, Five Prime Therapeutics, If You Can, Imergy, InSpa, Kaiam, Kateeva, Labcyte, Livescribe, Maiyet, Mapbox, The Muse, NEXTracker, Off Grid Electric, Ogin Energy, OPX Biotechnologies, Pandora, Peninsula Pharmaceuticals, Planet Labs, PowerGenix, PowerLight Corporation, Primus Power, RallyPoint, The RealReal, Revolution Foods, Ruby Ribbon, Siva Power, SolarCity, Solexel, SpaceX, Tesla, UrbanSitter, View Dynamic Glass, Wholeshare, XDx, Yerdle

Key Executives:

Nancy Pfund, Managing Partner
e-mail: nancy@dblpartners.vc
Education: BA, MA, Anthropology, Stanford University; MBA, Yale School of Management
Background: Managing Director, JPMorgan; Intel Corporation; Stanford University; State of California; Sierra Club
Directorships: SolarCity, Brightsource Energy, Primus Power, Farmers Business Network

Ira Ehrenpreis, Managing Partner
e-mail: ira@dblpartners.com
Education: BA, University of California, Los Angeles; JD, Stanford Law School; MBA, Stanford Grad. School of Business
Background: President, Western Association of Venture Capitalists; Chairman, VCNetwork; Founder/Chairman, World Energy Innovation Forum

Cynthia Ringo, Senior Partner
e-mail: cynthia@dblpartners.vc
Education: BS, Legal Systems, Georgia State University; JD, Emory University School of Law
Background: Managing Director, VantagePoint Venture Partners; CEO, Coppercom; SVP, Corporate Development, Madge Networks; VP, Marketing, Red Brick Systems

Mark Perutz, Partner
e-mail: mark@dblpartners.vc
Education: BS, MS, Mechanical Engineering, MIT; MBA, Sloan School of Management, MIT
Background: Investment Professional, JPMorgan; Equity Research Analyst, Robertson Stephens
Directorships: Revolution Foods, RallyPoint

Lisa Hagerman, Director, Programs
e-mail: lisa@dblpartners.vc
Education: BA, Bucknell University; MA, Political Science, University of North Carolina at Chapel Hill
Background: Director, More for Mission, Harvard Kennedy School; VP, Economic Innovation International

Carol Wong, Chief Administrative Officer
e-mail: carol@dblpartners.vc
Education: BS, Business Administration, California Polytechnic State University
Background: Fund Manager, Bay Area Equity Fund, JPMorgan

596 DCM
2420 Sand Hill Road
Suite 200
Menlo Park, CA 94025

Phone: 650-233-1400 Fax: 650-854-9159
web: www.dcm.com

Mission Statement: To build high-impact, global technology companies that maximize the success of our entrepreneurs.

Founded: 1996
Investment Criteria: Seed Stage, Early Stage, Mid Stage
Industry Group Preference: Mobile, Consumer Internet, Software & Services
Portfolio Companies: 1Mainsteam, 2Wire, 51job, 51Talk, 58.com, 99Bill.com, @Motion, About.com, Adspace Networks, Adways, AHAlife, AllAbout, Amalfi Semiconductor, Analogix, Appia, Apsalar, Arrayent, Arroyo, Auto Radio, Baike.com, Basis, Bill.com, BitAuto, BitTorrent, Bridgelux, Caring.com, Celsys, Cenx, Clearwire, Cmune, Coffee Meets Bagel, Cognitive Networks, Coradiant, Cortina, Crowdtilt, Dangdang.com, Digital Media Professionals, DXY.com, eDreams, Embark, Enovix, Etouch, Exablox, Fivestars, FocusEdu.cn, Force10, Fortinet, Foundry Networks, FreedomPop, Freee, Green Box, HaoDF.com, Happy Elements, Hi Corp., HireRight, Huodongxing, IMS, Internap, IPivot, Jaspersoft, Jawbone, Japan Communications, Kabu.com, Kakao, Kanbox, Keep Holdings, KNTV, LASO, Learn Zillion, Life360, Loki Studios, Lumi, Mbaobao.com, Mobix, MediaShare, Miox, MobilePeak Systems, Mobileum, Neopath Networks, Neutral Tandem, Nok Nok Labs, nQuire Software, NxEdge, OneChip Photonics, Oriental Standard, Pandora.TV, Papaya, PayCycle, PayPerks, Pedestal Networks, PGP, Pharmaron, PlayFirst, Playstudios, Pokelabo, Pose, RayVio, RealScout, Recourse Technologies, Renren, Revel Systems, Rockyou, SandForce, SavingStar, Scigineer, Ivxinevotech, SigFig, Sigmatel, Sihe Wood, Slice, Sling Media, SMIC, SoFi, Starflyer, SwanLabs, Tab, TransLattice, Trion, Trusper, Tuniu.com, UCloud, UStream, VanceInfo, Vendavo, ViMicro, Vindicia, Vip.com, Wandoujia, Wanxue, WePow, Whistle, Xishiwang, Yesmywine.com, Yongche.com, Youxinpai, Zenverge

Other Locations:
No. 1 East Chang An Avenue
Tower W2, Unit 1, Level 10
Oriental Plaza
Beijing 100738
China
Phone: 011-8610-6511-1700 Fax: 011-8610-6511-1799

The ARGYLE Aoyama 15F
2-14-4 Kita-Aoyama, Minato-Ku
Tokyo 107-0061
Japan
Phone: 011-81-3-4520-2310 Fax: 011-81-3-4520-2311

Key Executives:

David Chao, Co-Founder & General Partner
e-mail: dchao@dcm.com
Education: B.A. Brown University; MBA Stanford University
Background: Co-Founder/CTO, Japan Communications; Management Consultant, McKinsey & Company; Apple Computer; Account Executive, Recruit
Directorships: 51job, 99Bill, All About Japan, Careem, Eaze, eDreams, Fortinet, Kabu.com, Musical.ly, Resource Technologies, Sling Media, SMIC, SoFi, StarFlyer, UCloud

Dixon Doll, Co-Founder & Partner Emeritus
Education: B.S. Electrical Engineering, Kansas State University; M.S./PhD Electrical Engineering, University of Michigan
Background: IBM Systems Research Institute
Directorships: @Motion, About.com, Clearwire, Coradiant, Force10 Networks, Foundry Networks, IMS, Internap, IPivot, Neutral Tandem, nQuire, Vimicro

209

Venture Capital & Private Equity Firms / Domestic Firms

Osuke Honda, General Partner
e-mail: ohonda@dcm.com
Education: BA, MA, Law, Hitotsubashi University; MBA, Keio University Grad. School of Business Administration; Wharton School, University of Pennsylvania
Background: Principal, Globis Capital Partners; Mitsubishi Corporation; Machinery Group
Directorships: atama plus, Blind, CADDi, Coffee Meets Bagel, Coubic, DMP, every.tv, Folio, Fond, Freee, Happy Elements, Kakao, LASO, Loki Studios, Pandora.TV, PECO, PicsArt, RealScout
Jason Krikorian, General Partner
e-mail: jkrikorian@dcm.com
Education: BA, Psychology, University of CA, Berkeley; JD, MBA, University of Virginia
Background: Co-Founder, Sling Media; Partner, id8 Group
Directorships: 1 Mainstream, ART19, Basis, Brigit, Caavo, Cognitive Networks, Emprove, FiveStars, FloSports, fubo TV, Galore, Jackpocket, Kespry, Life360, Matterport, Mendel Health

597 DDJ CAPITAL MANAGEMENT
130 Turner Street
Building 3
Suite 600
Waltham, MA 02453
Phone: 781-283-8500 Fax: 781-419-9180
e-mail: inforequest@ddjcap.com
web: www.ddjcap.com

Mission Statement: DDJ Capital Management is an investment management firm focused on generating outstanding investment returns for its client base.

Founded: 1996
Minimum Investment: $5 million
Investment Criteria: High Yield Bonds, Bank Loans, Contol Distressed, Non-Control Distressed, Special Situations

Key Executives:
David J Breazzano, President/Chief Investment Officer
Education: BA, Union College; MBA, Johnson School, Cornell University
Background: VP & Portfolio Manager, High Income Group, Fidelity Investments; VP & Portfolio Manager, T Rowe Price Associates; VP & High Yield Analyst, First Investors Asset Management
Directorships: Bush Industries, Key Energy Services, Wornick Holding Company
Benjamin Santonelli, Portfolio Manager
Education: BA, Amherst University
John W Sherman, Portfolio Manager
Education: BBA, University of Notre Dame
Background: Associate, Healthcare Group, Thoma Cressey Equity Partners; Analyst, Global Healthcare Group, Citigroup
Michael S Weissenburger, Head of Origination
Education: BA, University of Connecticut; MBA, Northeastern University
Background: Director, Direct Loan Origination, Wells Fargo Capital Finance; Sonus Networks; Cognos; Converge

598 DE NOVO VENTURES
PO Box 2160
Saratoga, CA 95070
web: www.denovovc.com

Mission Statement: To provide financial capital to assist entrepreneurs in building leading healthcare companies.

Geographic Preference: California
Fund Size: $650 million
Founded: 2000
Average Investment: $8 - $15 million
Minimum Investment: $8 million

Investment Criteria: All Stages
Industry Group Preference: Medical & Health Related, Life Sciences, Technology, Healthcare, Medical Devices
Portfolio Companies: Asante Solutions, Astute Medical, Avedro, Axogen, Benvenue, BioParadox, C2 Therapeutics, Hansen Medical, MyoScience, OncoMed Pharmaceuticals, ProMed, Pulmonx, Simpirica, Spinal Kinetics, Spinal Modulation, Spiracur, Synergeyes, TearScience, TRIA Beauty, WaveTec Vision

Key Executives:
Frederick J Dotzler, Managing Director
e-mail: fred@denovovc.com
Education: BS, Iowa State University; University of Louvain, Belgium; MBA, University of Chicago
Background: Managing General Partner, Medicus Venture Partners; General Partner, Crosspoint Venture Partners; Searle; Merrimack; Millipore; IBM
Directorships: Bayhill Therapeutics, Microvention, Point Biomedical, Senorx, Talima
Richard M. Ferrari, Managing Director
e-mail: rich@denovovc.com
Education: BS, Ashland University; MBA, University of South Florida
Background: CEO, Cardiovascular Imaging Systems; CardioThoracic Systems; Co-Founder, CTS; Co-Founder, Medical Technology Group; EVP & GM, ADAC Laboratories; Founder, Saratoga Ventures
Directorships: Bacchus Vascular, Sinus Rhythm Technologies
Joe Mandato, Managing Director
e-mail: joe@denovovc.com
Education: BS, Nasson College; MA, Long Island University; Advanced Executive Program, Northwestern University; Doctorate, Management, Case Western Reserve University
Background: Chairman, Confer Software; President & CEO, Origin Medsystems; Co-Founder & CEO, Gynecare; Entrepreneur-in-Residence, Mayfield Fund; CEO, Ioptex Research; Captain, US Army Medical Service Corps
Directorships: Axogen, Endogastric Solutions, Facet Solutions, Hansen Medical, InSound Medical, M2 Medical, Tear Science, WaveTec Vision Systems

599 DECIENS CAPITAL
267 Dorland St.
San Francisco, CA 94105
e-mail: partners@deciens.com
web: www.deciens.com

Mission Statement: Deciens Capital is a venture capital firm that focuses on making angel and seed investments. We invest time and money in founders who are seeking to reduce inefficiencies in large industries with demonstrable disruptive information technology or to create disruptive offerings in de novo industries. We are particularly interested in online-to-offline offerings, marketplaces, financial technology, and civic and education tech.

Investment Criteria: Angel Investments, Seed Investments
Industry Group Preference: Online To Offline Offerings, Marketplaces, Fintech, Civic Technology, Education, Financial Services
Portfolio Companies: 7 Cups of Tea, EarnUp, Funding University, TenderTree, Fuze Network, Keychain Logistics, Simple Legal, Sponsorhub, Subledger, True Link Financial, Wevorce, Work Hands

Key Executives:
Daniel Kimerling, Co-Founder & General Partner
Education: BA, MA, University of Chicago
Background: Policy Analyst, Hudson Institute and Center for Strategic and International Studies; COO, Giftly

Venture Capital & Private Equity Firms / Domestic Firms

600 DEEP FORK CAPITAL
580 Howard Street
Suite 404
San Francisco, CA 94105

web: www.deepforkcapital.com

Mission Statement: Deep Fork Capital (DFC) is a venture capital firm focused on consumer innovations through online, software, mobile or other advances. Whether a company is pre-product, pre-revenue or growth-focused, we look for inspired, creative teams with great ideas.

Investment Criteria: All Stages
Industry Group Preference: Consumer Internet, Digital Media & Marketing, E-Commerce & Manufacturing
Portfolio Companies: Algorithmia, Amplify, Artivest, Battlefy, Bkstg, Bowery, Boxed Wholesale, Canopy, Dash, Dataminr, Delectable, Digital Artists, Ease Central, Educents, Genius, MaestroIQ, Oodle, Paracosm, Playdeck, Radpad, Rebelmail, Robin, Songza, Transfix, Trulia, Vsporto, Wevr, Zebra

Key Executives:
Tim Komada, Co-Founder/Managing Director
e-mail: tim@deepforkcapital.com
Education: BS, BA, The Citadel; JD, MPP, William & Marry; MBA, Wharton School
Background: Co-Founder, Vintrust
Directorships: Songza, Spling, Playdek, Cloudy, weplay, Digital Artists Entertainment

601 DEERFIELD MANAGEMENT
345 Park Avenue S
New York, NY 10010

Phone: 212-551-1600 Fax: 212-599-3075
web: deerfield.com

Mission Statement: Deerfield Management is an investment firm dedicated to advancing healthcare for the sake of curing disease, improving the quality of life and reducing the cost of healthcare.

Fund Size: $13 billion
Founded: 1994

Other Locations:
K Wah Center 3906
Middle Huaihai Road 1010
Shanghai 200031
China
Phone: 86 21-6079-3988

602 DEFTA PARTNERS
111 Pine Street
Suite 1410
San Francisco, CA 94111

Phone: 415-433-2262
e-mail: information@deftapartners.com
web: www.deftapartners.com

Mission Statement: DEFTA Partners pursues opportunities in core technology sectors, with a focus on innovative healthcare and information technology businesses. A global venture capital firm, DEFTA Partners has invested in companies based in the United States, United Kingdom, Bangladesh, Japan and Israel.

Geographic Preference: Worldwide
Fund Size: $50 million
Founded: 1985
Average Investment: $500,000 - $3 million
Investment Criteria: Seed, Early Stage, Expansion
Industry Group Preference: Communications, Electronic Components, Information Technology, Medical, Medical Devices, Optical Technology, Software, Technology, Healthcare Information Technology
Portfolio Companies: 1World Online, Allocade, BracNet, Cloudfiling, Fortinet, Oplus, Oren Semiconductor, Orig3n, Tmsuk

Key Executives:
George Hara, Group Chairman/CEO
Education: LLB, Keio University; MS, Stanford University
Background: Partner, Accel Partners
Directorships: Pixera, Actuate Co. Ltd, Chemtrix
Masa Isono, Principal
Education: BA, Waseda University; MA, Economics, MBA, Boston University
Background: Director, Joint Venture Company, Hong Kong; The Security Analysts Association of Japan

603 DELL VENTURES
e-mail: DTCapital@dell.com
web: www.delltechnologies.com

Mission Statement: Dell Technologies Capital is the venture capital arm of Dell Inc. The fund invests in early-stage companies with a focus in areas such as software storage, security, machine learning, big data and analytics, cloud, and other internet ventures.

Founded: 2012
Average Investment: $2 - $5 million
Investment Criteria: Early-Stage
Industry Group Preference: Data Storage, Networking, Cloud Computing, Mobility, Software, Machine Learning, Security, Data Analytics
Portfolio Companies: Agari, Appdome, Aria, Barefoot Networks, Big Switch Networks, Binaris, Bluedata, Cloud66, CloudEndure, CNEXLabs, Cylance, Datometry, DocuSign, Druva, Edico Genome, Elatifile, FogHorn, Graphcore, GuardiCore, Iguazio, Jask, JFrog, Lastline, Minio, Mirantis, Moogsoft, Nantero, Nasuni, Netskope, Nexenta, OpsMx, Otonomo, Packet, Primary Data, Quali, Redislabs, Rich Relevance, Risk Lens, Risk Recon, Striim, Twistlock, ZingBox, Zscaler

Key Executives:
Scott Darling, President
Education: BS, Economics/Computer Science, University of California, Santa Cruz; MBA, Stanford Grad. School of Business
Background: President, EMC Corporate Developement and Ventures; General Partner, Frazier Technology Ventures; VP/Managing Director, Intel Capital; Product Marketing, Apple Computer
Raman Khanna, Managing Director
Education: Electrical/Electronics Engineering, Delhi College of Engineering; MS, Computer Science, Virginia Tech; MBA, Golden Gate University
Background: CIO, Stanford University IT; Co-Founder, Diamondhead Ventures; Managing Director, ONSET Ventures
Daniel Docter, Managing Director
Education: BS, Electrical Engineering, University of Minnesota; PhD, University of Bradford
Background: Director, Intel Capital; Advisor, Merrill Lynch; AT&T Bell Labs; Hughes Research Labs

604 DELPHI VENTURES
3000 Sand Hill Road
Menlo Park, CA 94025

Phone: 650-854-9650
web: www.delphiventures.com

Mission Statement: Focused in early-stage healthcare investing, including medical devices and diagnostics, biotechnology, and healthcare services companies.

Fund Size: $1.1 billion
Founded: 1988
Average Investment: $500,000 - $12 million
Investment Criteria: Seed, Start-Up, Early Stage, First-Stage, Second-Stage
Industry Group Preference: Biotechnology, Medical & Health Related, Medical Devices, Healthcare Services

Venture Capital & Private Equity Firms / Domestic Firms

Portfolio Companies: Aegea Medical, Alder Biopharmaceuticals, Calithera Biosciences, Cardeas Pharma, EBR Systems Inc., Ivantis, Karyopharm Therapeutics, Labcyte Inc., Onco Med Pharmaceuticals, Relypsa Inc., Senseonics, Sequent Medical, SynergEyes, Tandem Diabetes Care, Trivascular

Key Executives:
James J. Bochnowski, Partner Emeritis
Education: MBA, Harvard University; BS Massachusetts Institue of Technology
Background: President, Shugart Associates; General Partner, Donaldson Lufkin & Jenrette's; Sprout Capital Group
David Douglass, Partner Emeritis
Education: MBA, MA, Stanford University; BA Amherst College
Background: Matrix Partners; Paladin Software Corporation; Collagen Corporation; McKinsey & Company
Matthew T. Potter, Parner/CFO
Education: BS, California Polytechnic State University
Background: Controller, Bluecurve Inc.; Public Accountant, Arthur Andersen
Deepa Pakianathan, PhD, Managing Partner
Education: BS, MS, University of Bombay; MS, PhD, Wake Forest University
Background: VP, Healthcare Group, JPMorgan; Biotechnology Research Analyst, Genesis Merchant Group
Doug Roeder, Managing Partner
Education: AB, Dartmouth College
Background: Associate, Healthcare Investments Group, Alex.Brown; Consultant, Putnam Associates

605 DENALI VENTURE PARTNERS
web: www.denalivp.com

Mission Statement: A partnership that invests capability and capital in entrepreneurial ventures, in order to build sustainable, high performance environments where people love what they do.

Founded: 1999
Investment Criteria: Early-Stage
Industry Group Preference: Cloud Computing, Data Infrastructure, Analytics, Enterprise Services, Consumer Products, Retail, Consumer & Leisure
Portfolio Companies: Aconex, FanPlayr, Heffron Consulting, Redbubble

Key Executives:
Richard Cawsey, Founder/Executive Chairman
Education: Australian National University
Background: St. George Bank; NatWest Financial Products; ANZ Banking Group; Managing Director, Morgan Stanley

606 DESCO CAPITAL
7795 Walton Parkway
Suite 175
New Albany, OH 43054

e-mail: info@descocapital.com
web: www.descocapital.com

Mission Statement: The investment arm of Desco Corporation, Desco Capital is a privately held company that focuses on working closely with management in the developing growth of businesses. Desco offers capital and management expertise with the objective of creating long-term value for its portfolio companies.

Fund Size: $75 million
Founded: 1992
Average Investment: $1 - $5 million
Minimum Investment: $500,000
Investment Criteria: Growth Businesses, Underperforming Businesses, Controlling or Minority Equity Positions
Industry Group Preference: Industrial Products, Manufacturing, Distribution, Building Materials & Services, Energy Products, Rubber, Plastics, Process Controls, Consumer Products
Portfolio Companies: ARPAC, Blackeagle Energy Services, Crown Group, Marsh Bellofram Corporation, MDT Software, Medical Indicators, Mueller Electric Company, Republic Doors & Frames, Tek-Air Systems

Key Executives:
Arnold B Siemer, Chief Executive Officer
Education: BA, Banking & Finance, John Carroll University; Foreign Trade, American Graduate School; JD, Cleveland Marshall College of Law
Background: Sprayon Products Inc.; Air-O-Matic Power Steering
Paul D Kestler, Operating Director
972-869-9099
e-mail: pkestler@descocapital.com
Education: BS, Marketing, Arizona State University
Background: Senior Manager, Marsh Instrument-Juarez; Thermo-Couple Products; Tek-Air; Medical Indicators
Roger D Bailey, Director/Chief Financial Officer
614-888-8855 x101
e-mail: rbailey@descocapital.com
Education: BBA, Business Management, Texas Christian University; MBA, Marketing & Finance, Indiana University; MS, Chemical Engineering, Carnegie Mellon University Graduate School
Background: PPG Industries; Treasurer & Chief Financial Officer, Asten Group

607 DETROIT VENTURE PARTNERS
1555 Broadway Street
3rd Floor
Detroit, MI 48226

web: www.detroitventurepartners.com

Mission Statement: To help rebuild the Detroit area by assisting entrepreneurs in growing meaningful businesses in the digital media, marketing technology, social media, e-commerce, software, and sports and entertainment sectors.

Geographic Preference: Detroit, Michigan
Fund Size: $28 million
Founded: 2010
Investment Criteria: Seed-Stage, Early-Stage
Industry Group Preference: E-Commerce & Manufacturing, Digital Media & Marketing, Social Media, Internet, Software, Sports, Entertainment, Marketing Technology
Portfolio Companies: 100 Thieves, Airspace Link, Are You A Human, Autobooks, Benzinga, Bloomscape, Branch, Breadless, Cargo, Dering Hall, detroit Labs, Digital Onboarding, Dwolla, Ethos, FarmLogs, Finicity, floyd, Genius, Grand Circus, Guardhat, Homie, Instore, IRule, Crossover, LevelEleven, MagicBus, Marxent, May Mobility, Opsmatic, PriorAuthNow, Quickly, Reach Influence, Rockbot, Sift, Skillo, Stylecaster, StockX, Sweet, Velos, Vroom, Waymark WSC Sports

Key Executives:
Dan Gilbert, Founding Partner
Background: Founder & Chairman, Quicken Loans
Jake Cohen, Partner
Education: BA, MBA, JD, University of Michigan
Background: Co-Founder, eatBlue.com; Ugrub.com; Ubars.com
Gabe Karp, Operating Partner
Education: University of Michigan; Wayne State University
Background: Executive Team, ePrize
Jared Stasik, Partner
Education: BBA, Ross School of Business, University of Michigan; MBA, University of California, Berkeley
Background: Consultant, ZS Associates

Venture Capital & Private Equity Firms / Domestic Firms

608 DFJ GOTHAM VENTURES
44 South Broadway
Suite 100
White Plains, NY 10601

Phone: 212-279-3980
web: www.gothamvc.com

Mission Statement: DFJ Gotham is a generalist information technology investor, meaning that the firm will invest in all sub-sectors of the IT space. These sub-sectors include, but are not limited to: digital media, e-commerce, financial technology, mobile and network infrastructure.

Geographic Preference: East Coast
Average Investment: $100,000 - $500,000
Investment Criteria: Seed Stage, Series A Round
Industry Group Preference: Information Technology, Digital Media & Marketing, E-Commerce & Manufacturing, Fintech, Mobile, Infrastructure
Portfolio Companies: ADstruc, Altruik, DailyWorth, Drop.io, Gen.Video, Ingenio, JIBE, Lendkey, Local Response, Magnolia Broadband, Massive, Medialets, Mimeo.com, Nano Opto, Pantero, Panvideo, Philo, Pickie, Pivot, Pulse Point, Q Link Technologies, Quantiva, Sailthru, Seamless Receipts, Searchandise Commerce, Single Platform, Stella Service, Techstar, Totsy, Verterra, Vivo Tech, Widetronix, XO Soft, Yipit

Key Executives:
  Ross Goldstein, Co-Founder & Managing Director
  Education: BS, Applied Mathematics-Economics, Brown University; MBA, Stanford University Graduate School of Business
  Background: EVP & CFO, Interactive Imaginzations; Morgan Stanley
  Directorships: Mimeo.com, Lumeta, ContextWeb, Searchandise Commerce, Drop.io, Medialets, Altruik
  Daniel Schultz, Co-Founder & Managing Director
  Education: BA, Economics, Columbia University
  Background: Senior Banker, Lehman Brothers
  Directorships: Pivot Solutions, Magnolia Broadband

609 DFJ VENTURE CAPITAL
2882 Sand Hill Road
Suite 150
Menlo Park, CA 94025

Phone: 650-233-9000
e-mail: plans@dfj.com
web: www.dfj.com

Mission Statement: To support entrepreneurs who want to change the world. We focus on companies specializing in consumer and enterprise IT, commerce, cloud, enterprise, big data, and bold new technologies.

Investment Criteria: Early Stage, Growth Stage
Industry Group Preference: Technology, Software
Portfolio Companies: AngelList, Athena Health, Azuqua, Baidu, Balena, BetterUp, Box, BrightSource, Chartbeat, Chef Code Can, CircleCI, Diamanti, Doximity, DWave, Edeniq, Elation Health, Enernoc, Epocrates, FeedBurner, Flurry, Forward Networks, Front, Genomatica, Good Technology, Helix, Highlight, Hotmail, Human Longevity Inc., Insight Squared, Intematix, Kaiima, iYogi, Launch Darkly, Lendkey, Livongo, Location Labs, Loftium, Lumity, Memphis Meats, Mindshow, Mobile 365, Mythic, Nervana, Newsle, Ooda Health, Path, Periscope Data, Ping Identity, Planet Labs, Polaris Wireless, Pro.com, Raydiance, Redfin, Remity, Retrofit, Rich Relevance, Seamicro, Selligy, ShareThis, Shift, Skype, SolarCity, SpaceX, Spiral Genetics, SugarCRM, SugarSync, Swell, Synthetic Genomics, Talk Desk, Tango, Tesla Motors, Tremor Video, Twilio, Verge Genomics, Vineti, Wellframe, Xtime, Yammer, Yellowbrick, Yodle, Z2Live, Zillabyte, Zoox, Zymergen

Key Executives:
  John Fisher, Managing Director
  Education: Harvard College; Harvard Business School
  Background: ABS Ventures; Alex, Brown & Sons; Bank of America
  Directorships: Katerra, Pulsepoint, Renovate America
  Timothy Draper, Managing Director
  Education: BS Electrical Engineering, Stanford University; MBA Harvard Business School
  Josh Stein, Partner
  Education: BA Dartmouth College; MBA Stanford University
  Background: Vice President, Telephia; Co-Founder/Director/Chief Strategy Officer, ViaFone; Product Management, Microsoft/NetObjects
  Directorships: Box, Chartbeat, LaunchDarkly, LendKey, Loftium, Lumity, Periscope, Talkdesk
  Randy Glein, Partner - DJF Growth
  Education: BSEE University of Florida; MSEE University of Southern California; MBA Anderson School of Management
  Background: CFO, FeedBurner; DIRECTV; Screenz; Tribune Ventures; GM Hughes Electronics; Martin Marietta

610 DFW CAPITAL PARTNERS
300 Frank W. Burr Boulevard
Glenpointe Centre East
7th Floor
Teaneck, NJ 07666

Phone: 201-836-6000 Fax: 201-836-5666
web: www.dfwcapital.com

Mission Statement: DFW Capital Partners is a private equity investment firm that focuses on lower middle-market companies. DFW works with entrepreneurs and management teams and provides them with the support necessary for significant growth.

Geographic Preference: United States
Fund Size: $162 million
Founded: 1983
Average Investment: $5 - $20 million
Minimum Investment: $5 million
Investment Criteria: High-Growth, Lower Middle-Market Companies
Industry Group Preference: Business to Business, Industrial Services, Healthcare Services
Portfolio Companies: Children's Dental Health Associates, Envocore, Insight2Profit, Lotus Clinical Research, Regulatory and Quality Solutions, ReSource Pro, Restoration + Recovery, Saol Therapeutics, Sebela Pharmaceuticals, Sev1Tech, Theraplay, VertexOne

Other Locations:
4445 Willard Avenue
11th Floor
Chevy Chase, MD
Phone: 202-827-0722 Fax: 202-204-0724

Key Executives:
  Donald F. DeMuth, Founder
  Education: BA, BSEE, Rutgers University; MBA, Harvard University
  Background: Systems Engineer, IBM; Investment Banker, Kidder, Peabody & Co.
  Directorships: Tech Pharmacy Services, Garden State Dental, Copernicus Group, SoftWriters, Meta, Nurses 24/7
  Keith W. Pennell, Managing Partner
  Education: BA, Economics & Art History, Middlebury College
  Background: Dean Witter; First Atlantic
  Directorships: Versatech, Venio, Copernicus Group, SoftWriters
  Brett L. Prager, Partner
  Education: BA, Wharton School; BAS, Moore School of Engineering, University of Pennsylvania; MBA, Columbia Business School
  Background: Founder & Partner, Theo Capital Partners;

Venture Capital & Private Equity Firms / Domestic Firms

JP Morgan
Directorships: Venio, Garden State Dental
Douglas H. Gilbert, Partner
Education: BA, Political Economy, Williams College; MBA, Harvard University
Background: Managing Director, MCG Capital Corporation; Partner, Winston Partners; Thayer Capital Partners
Brian C. Tilley, Partner
Education: BS, Finance, Ohio University; MBA, Kellogg School of Management, Northwestern University
Background: Founder & Managing Member, Wenzi Capital Partners; United HealthGroup
Directorships: Garden State Dental

611 DIAMOND STATE VENTURES LP
200 River Market Avenue
Suite 400
Little Rock, AR 72201

Phone: 501-374-9247 Fax: 501-374-9425
Toll-Free: 800-216-7234
web: new.diamondstateventures.com

Mission Statement: Diamond State Ventures invests in growing companies and established industry leaders. The firm seeks to work with experienced management teams across a range of industry segments.

Geographic Preference: South, Southeast, Midwest
Fund Size: $100 million
Founded: 1999
Average Investment: $3 - $7 million
Investment Criteria: Growth Expansion, Buyouts, Acquisitions, Recapitalizations, Lower Middle-Market, Established Companies
Industry Group Preference: Manufacturing, Business Products & Services, Consumer Products, Consumer Services, Healthcare Services
Portfolio Companies: Evergreen Holdings, Integrated Aerospace Manufacturing, Jahabow, Mob Scene, NewKota Energy Group, Rio Ranch Markets, Sure Shot Drilling, Transfer Tool Products, Waples Manufacturing, Whitworth Tool

Key Executives:
Joe T. Hays, Co-Founder/Managing Director
e-mail: jhays@dsvlp.com
Education: University of Arkansas; MBA, Wharton School, University of Pennsylvania
Background: President, Southern Regional Association of Small Business Investment Companies
Directorships: UAMS Biotechnology Center
Larry B. Carter, Managing Director
e-mail: lcarter@dsvlp.com
Education: BS, Business Administration, University of Arkansas
Background: Investment Banking, PaineWebber; Equity Syndications, First Chicago Corp.; Deal Originations, Bank of America
Tyler A. Bozynski, Vice President
e-mail: tbozynski@dsvlp.com
Education: BS, Business Administration, University of Arkansas
Background: Associate, Diamond State Ventures; Stephens Inc.

612 DIAMOND TECHVENTURES
350 Oakmead Pkwy
Suite 200
Sunnyvale, CA 94085

web: www.diamondtechventures.com

Mission Statement: Diamond TechVentures is a venture capital firm focused on investing in technology companies based in China.

Geographic Preference: China

Investment Criteria: Start-Ups, Early-Stage
Industry Group Preference: Technology, Wireless
Portfolio Companies: Broadsoft, ClearAccess IP, IWatt, LGC Wireless, Packet Island, percolata, STEPLabs

Key Executives:
Henry Wong, Managing Partner
Education: BSc, Finance, University of Utah; MBA, Telecom Management, Golden Gate University
Background: Venture Partner, Crystal Ventures; Founder, Chairman & CEO, SS8 Networks; President, CNet Technology
Dr. Robert P Lee, Senior Venture Partner
Education: BA, University of California Berkeley; MS/PhD, University of California Los Angeles
Background: CEO, Accela; Achievo; Insignia; Inxight Software; EVP, Symantec
Directorships: chairman, AAMA (Asia America Multi-Technology Association)

613 DIAMONDHEAD VENTURES
1350 Bayshore Highway
Suite 920
Bulringame, CA 94010

Phone: 650-687-7550 Fax: 650-529-0777
web: www.dhven.com

Mission Statement: Invests in early stage technology companies. Affiliated with Diamondhead Ecosystem, a pool of venture capital advisors.

Geographic Preference: California, Bay Area
Fund Size: $140 million
Founded: 2000
Average Investment: $1 - $5 million, total of $8 - $10 million
Investment Criteria: Primarily Seed, Start-Up, Early Stage, First Stage, Limited Second Stage
Industry Group Preference: Internet Technology, Business to Business, IT Infrastructure
Portfolio Companies: Cavium Networks, Danger, Entercept Security Technologies, Orative, Passmark Security, Reactivity, Serus, Truviso, UPEK

Key Executives:
David Lane, Founding Managing Director
Education: MBA, Harvard University; BSEE, University of Southern California
Background: Hughes Aircraft; IBM; Harvard Management Company

614 DIFFERENTIAL VENTURES
40 Exchange Place
Suite 1110
New York, NY 10005

Phone: 212-300-2879
e-mail: info@differential.vc
web: www.differential.vc

Mission Statement: Differential Ventures focuses on early stage capital, looking to invest in companies that have advantages in data or machine intelligence. They especially look for Enterprise Tech, FinTech and Cybersecurity.

Investment Criteria: Pre-Seed or Seed stage ($250,000-$1 million); B2B or a Unique advantage in Data/Machine Intelligence

Key Executives:
David Magerman, Co-Founder/Managing Partner
Education: BA, BS, University of Pennsylvania; PhD, Stanford University
Background: Renaissance Technologies
Nick Adams, Co-Founder/Managing Partner
Education: BA, Brandeis University; MBA, Northeastern University
Background: Venture Partner, Supernode; Senior Sales Manager, Opower

Venture Capital & Private Equity Firms / Domestic Firms

Mitchell Kleinhandler, Managing Partner
Background: Venture Partner, Scout Ventures; Entrepreneur
Key Executives:
Yuri Milner, CEO/Founding Partner
Education: Moscow State University; MBA, Wharton School of Business
Background: Lebedex Physical Institute

616 DIMELING SCHREIBER & PARK
1629 Locust Street
Philadelphia, PA 19103

Phone: 215-546-8585 Fax: 215-546-5398
web: www.dsppartners.com

Mission Statement: An investment partnership that offers capital and strategic support to middle market companies. The firm pursues opportunities with superior management teams and specializes in leveraged acquisitions, management buyouts and assisting in generational ownership changes.

Fund Size: $1 billion
Founded: 1982
Average Investment: $5 - $30 million
Minimum Investment: $5 million
Investment Criteria: Middle Market, Acquisitions, Recapitalizations, LBO
Industry Group Preference: Manufacturing, Services
Portfolio Companies: Boston Ship Repair, Martin Color-Fi, Orchids Paper Products Company, Piper Aircraft, Rocky Mountain Helicopters, Wiser Oil Company
Key Executives:
Richard R Schreiber, Principal
e-mail: rschreiber@dsppartners.com
Education: BS, Wharton School, University of Pennsylvania
Background: Strouse, Greenberg & Company; Coldwell Banker
Steven G Park, Principal
e-mail: spark@dsppartners.com
Education: BS, Pennsylvania State University
Background: VP, Strouse, Greenberg & Company; Senior VP, Reading Company
Peter D. Schreiber, Principal
e-mail: pschreiber@dsppartners.com
Education: BS, Finance, Pennsylvania State University
Background: Corporate Banking Representative, Fidelity Bank

617 DISRUPTOR CAPITAL
315A Cameron St.
Alexandria, VA 22314

Phone: 703-659-1100
e-mail: info@disruptor.com

Mission Statement: Disruptor Capital is a Virginia-based seed and angel capital investment company focused on funding and growing disruptive technologies, ideas and entrepreneurs.

Investment Criteria: Seed, Angel Capital
Industry Group Preference: Technology
Portfolio Companies: Data Analytics Media, Echelon Insights, IJReview, Imge, Ledbury, Liftbump, Media Group of America, Pascal Metrics, Potomac Research Group
Key Executives:
Pete Snyder, CEO
Background: Founder & CEO, New Media Strategies; President of Emerging Markets Group, Meredith Xcelerated Marketing, Meredith Corporation

618 DIVERGENT VENTURES
1652 20th Avenue
Seattle, WA 98122

e-mail: ober@divergent.com
web: www.divergentvc.com

Mission Statement: An early-stage venture capital investment firm headquartered in Seattle Washington. The Managing Directors are Kevin Ober and Rob Shurtleff, both highly experienced and successful early-stage investors. The firm invests in early-stage companies, with an emphasis on big data, mobile data, virtualization/cloud and storage.

Geographic Preference: Northwest, West Coast United States
Investment Criteria: First Round
Industry Group Preference: Data Storage, Cloud Computing
Portfolio Companies: SpaceCurve, TempoDB, Shippable, Proximal Data, Piston Enterprise OpenStack, Iron.MQ
Key Executives:
Kevin Ober, Managing Director
e-mail: ober@divergent.com
Education: BS, Business Administration, St. John's University; MBA, Santa Clara University
Background: Vulcan Ventures, Conner Peripherals
Rob Shurtleff, Managing Director
e-mail: shurtleff@divergent.com
Education: BA, Computer Science, University of California, Berkeley
Background: Founder, Sightline Partners
Directorships: Flashsoft, Piston, Asta Networks
Todd Warren, Managing Partner
e-mail: warren@divergent.com
Education: BA, Northwestern University
Background: Corporate Vice President, Microsoft; Adjunct Professor, Northwestern University

619 DN PARTNERS LLC
180 N LaSalle Street
Suite 3001
Chicago, IL 60601

Phone: 312-332-7960
web: www.dnpartnersllc.com

Mission Statement: DN Partners is a Chicago-based private equity firm that invests in lower middle-market companies. The firm generally focuses on businesses based in the Midwestern region of the United States and specializes in recapitalizations, management buyouts, buy and build strategies, and corporate spin-offs.

Geographic Preference: Midwest United States
Founded: 1995
Average Investment: $3 - $15 million
Investment Criteria: Lower Middle Market, Strong Market Position, Growth Potential, High Revenues $20 to $100 Million
Industry Group Preference: Distribution, Manufacturing, Services
Portfolio Companies: Central Can Company, Country Pure Foods, Crysteel Manufacturing, FCL Graphics, M&M Pump & Supply, Primary Packaging, PrimeCo Wireless Communications
Key Executives:
John E Dancewicz, Managing Partner/Founder
Education: BA, Economics, Yale University; MBA, Finance, Harvard Business School
Background: Senior Managing Director, Bear Stearns; Manager, Midwest Corporate Finance; US Investment Banking Department, Continental Illinois National Bank
Directorships: Central Can Company, Country Pure Foods, FCL Graphics
Maurey J Bell, Managing Partner
Education: BA, Economics, Northwestern University
Background: M&A Group, EVEREN Securities;

Venture Capital & Private Equity Firms / Domestic Firms

Managing Director, Midwest Corporate Finance Department, Bear, Stearns & Co.
Directorships: FCL Graphics
Christopher J Blum, Chief Financial Officer
Education: BBA, Finance & Accounting, University of Notre Dame
Background: CFO & Director of Corporate Development, Clayton Holdings; Principal, Diamond Management and Technology Consultants; CFO, MindBuilder Group
Directorships: M&M Pump & Supply, Chinada Holdings

620 DOCOMO INNOVATIONS
3301 Hillview Avenue
Palo Alto, CA 94304

web: www.docomoinnovations.com

Mission Statement: A corporate venture arm of NTT DOCOMO of Japan. DOCOMO invests in companies introducing leading-edge mobile services based on innovative technologies.

Fund Size: $100 million
Founded: 2005
Industry Group Preference: Telecommunications, Communications, Wireless Technologies
Portfolio Companies: Elemtnal, Coinbase, Netpulse, Centrify, Nanosys, Beceem, GCT, Kyte, GestureTek, Daz3D, WiSpry, Verient, InvenSense, Arteris, Forté Media, Quantance, Tensilica, Evernote, Swyper, Tune Wiki, SkyCross, Couchbase, Cooliris, Fab, Anfacto, Cyphort

Key Executives:
Neil Sadraranganey, Managing Director
Education: BEng, University of Waterloo; MBA, Stanford University
Background: Former VP of Business Development; General Partner, Bay Partners; Investor

621 DOMAIN ASSOCIATES LLC
202 Carnegie Center
Suite 104
Princeton, NJ 08540

Phone: 609-683-5656 **Fax:** 609-683-9789
web: www.domainvc.com

Mission Statement: Manages venture capital and provides early-stage financing and support to technology-based companies in the life sciences industry, with primary focus on the pharmaceuticals, diagnostics and medical devices sectors. Domain Associates offers experience in technology asssessment, operations, finance, and strategic planning, and pursues opportunities with high growth potential businesses with superior management teams and outstanding breakthrough technologies.

Fund Size: $500 million
Founded: 1985
Average Investment: $1 - $20 million
Minimum Investment: $500,000 (except seed financing)
Investment Criteria: Seed, First-Stage, Second-Stage
Industry Group Preference: Biopharmaceuticals, Life Sciences, Medical Devices, Instrumentation, Diagnostics, Advanced Materials, Healthcare Information Technology, Information Technology, Pharmaceuticals
Portfolio Companies: Achaogen, Achillion Pharmaceuticals, Adynxx, Afferent Pharmaceuticals, Aldeyra Therapeutics, Alimera Sciences, Applied Proteomics, Ascenta Therapeutics, Astute Medical, Atara Biotherapeutics, aTyr Pharma, Benvenue Medical, BioNano Genomics, Cantex Pharmaceuticals, Carticept Medical, Cartiva, Celator Pharmaceuticals, Celtaxsys, Clovis Oncology, CoDa Therapeutics, Colorescience, CoLucid Pharmaceuticals, Cotera, Dicerna Pharmaceuticals, Domain Elite Holdings, DRI Holdings Limited, Eddingpharm International Holdings Limited, Epic Sciences, Esperion Therapeutics, Evoke Pharma, Five Prime Therapeutics, Fractyl Laboratories, GI Dynamics, Glaukos Corporation, IntegenX, Kona Medical, Marinus Pharmaceuticals, Medico (Hong Kong) Limited, Milestone Pharmaceuticals, Miramar Labs, Neothetics, NeuroPace, Novadigm Therapeutics, Obalon Therapeutics, Ocera Therapeutics, Oraya Therapeutics, Orexigen Therapeutics, Otonomy, REVA Medical, ReVision Optics, RightCare Solutions, ROX Medical, Sebacia, Sequent Medical, Sera Prognostics, Smart Medical Systems, Syndax Pharmaceuticals, Tandem Diabetes Care, Tragara Pharmaceuticals, VentiRx, Veracyte, Xagenic, Zyga Technology

Other Locations:
12481 High Bluff Drive
Suite 150
San Diego, CA 92130
Phone: 858-480-2400 **Fax:** 858-480-2401

Key Executives:
Jim Blair, PhD, Partner
Education: BSE, Princeton University; MSE, PhD, Electrical Engineering, University of Pennsylvania
Background: Managing Director, Rothschild Inc.; FS Smithers & Co.; White, Weld & Co.; Engineering Manager, RCA Corporation
Directorships: Prostate Cancer Foundation, Sanford-Burnham Medical Research Institute
Brian Dovey, Partner
Education: BA, Mathematics, Colgate University; MBA, Harvard Business School
Background: President, Rorer Group; President, Survival Technology; Howmedica; Howmet Corporation; New York Telephone
Directorships: Orexigen Therapeutics, REVA Medical, Center for Venture Education, La Jolla Playhouse
Brian K. Halak, PhD, Partner
Education: BSE, Bioengineering, University of Pennsylvania; PhD, Immunology, Thomas Jefferson University
Background: Associate, Advanced Technology Ventures; Consultant, Wilkerson Group
Directorships: Alimera Sciences, BioNano Genomics, Carticept Medical, Dicerna Pharmaceuticals, Kona Medical, Oraya Therapeutics
Kim Kamdar, PhD, Partner
Education: BA, Northwestern University; PhD, Biochemistry & Genetics, Emory University
Background: Kauffman Fellow, MPM Capital; Research Director, Novartis; Founder, Aryzun Pharmaceuticals
Directorships: Epic Sciences, Neothetics, Obalon Therapeutics, ROX Medical, Sera Prognostics, Syndax Pharmaceuticals, Tragara Pharmaceuticals, CONNECT Foundation, Hastings Center
Dennis Podlesak, Advisory Partner
Education: BA, Western Illinois University; MBA, Pepperdine University; Wharton School
Background: Senior VP & Head, North American Business Unit, Novartis AG; VP & Head, CEC Division, Allergan; SmithKline Beecham
Directorships: Adynxx, Syndax Pharmaceuticals, Tobira Therapeutics, RightCare Solutions, DRI Holdings
Kathleen Schoemaker, Partner/Chief Financial Officer
Education: BA, Wheaton College; MA, Middlebury College; MBA, New York University
Background: Auditor & Tax Specialist, KPMG
Jesse Treu, PhD, Partner Emeritus
Education: BS, Rensselaer Polytechnic Institute; MA, PhD, Princeton University
Background: VP, Wilkerson Group; CW Ventures; President & CEO, Microsonics; Technicon Instruments Corporation
Directorships: Afferent Pharmaceuticals, Aldeyra Pharmaceuticals, CoLucid Pharmaceuticals, RightCare Solutions, Sebacia, Tandem Diabetes Care, Veracyte, Xagenic
Nicole Vitullo, Partner
Education: BA, Mathematics, MBA, Finance, University of Rochester

Venture Capital & Private Equity Firms / Domestic Firms

Background: Senior VP, Rothschild Asset Management; Director, Corporate Communications & Investor Relations, Cephalon; Eastman Kodak
Directorships: Achillion Pharmaceuticals, Celator Pharmaceuticals, Celtaxsys, Esperion Therapeutics, Marinus Pharmaceuticals, VentiRx Pharmaceuticals
Eckard Weber, MD, Advisory Partner
Education: BS, Kolping College, Germany; MD, University of Ulm Medical School, Germany; Stanford University Medical School
Background: Professor of Pharmacology, University of California, Irvine
Directorships: Ocera Therapeutics, Orexigen Therapeutics, Adynxx, Tobira Therapeutics

622 DORM ROOM FUND

e-mail: info@dormroomfund.com
web: www.dormroomfund.com

Mission Statement: A student-run venture firm that invests in student-run companies.
Average Investment: $15,000 - $20,000
Portfolio Companies: 101, 3DFortify, A&B American Style, Acculis, Acention Digital, AdsNative, Aegis AI, Airbud, Airmada, Analytical Space, Athelas, AutismSees, Ava, Bevi, BevSpot, BioCollection, Blockstack, Blueprint Income, Boom Fantasy, Booya Fitness, BottleRocket, BrainSpec, Brooklinen, Bruzd Foods, Bungalow, C. Light Technologies, Capella, Cathbuddy, Clara, Cognitive Toybox, Colibri, CommonCents, Concierge Stat, Cookin, Cresilon, Curative Orthopaedics, Dagne Dover, Dash, Databetes, DegreeChamp, DribbleUp, Droice Labs, EagerPanda, Eat Makhana, EmCasa, Farther Farms, FeastFox, Finfox, FireHUD, Firefly, FiscalNote, Five, Five to Nine, Flare Technologies, Floating Point Group, Flourish, Flowtune, Forest Device, Forge, FreeWill, Gainful, Gauge Insights, Geneoscopy, Greo, Grove Labs, Harper Wilde, Harvest Labs, HealthWiz, Healthie, Homesuite, Humon, Hydrant, Immudicon, Infinite Uptime, InnaMed, Intelligent Flying Machines, Inventory Connections, Keriton, KitSplit, Laws of Motion, LeapYear Technologies, LearnLux, LightUp, LogRocket, Lovepop, MaestroQA, Markit Medical, Mati, Miramix, MoveButter, NERv, NEU, NeuroMesh, NextWave Hire, Nimble, Noken, OliLux Biosciences, Oncora Medical, Onfleet, PageVamp, PandaPay, Parable Health, Parsegon, Pavlov, Pison Technology, Pixorize, Plan, Plasticity, Players' Lounge, Podium, Polymorph, ProducePay, Project Applecart, Pundit, Py, Quithelp, Radiator Labs, RapidSOS, Reach Labs, Resonado, Reveal Media, RocketBolt, Rorus, Scholly, SheFly, ShieldAI, Solisite, Solstice

Key Executives:
Molly Fowler, CEO
Education: BA, Political Science, Yale University
Chauncey Hamilton, COO
Education: BA, History, Trinity College, Hartford
Background: Partner Operations Manager, First Round Capital; WIRED

623 DOT EDU VENTURES
514 Bryant Street
Suite 110
Palo Alto, CA 94301

e-mail: contact@doteduventures.com
web: www.doteduventures.com

Mission Statement: The firm provides seed funding along with strong technical and strategic support for early stage technology businesses.
Founded: 2000
Average Investment: $10,000 - $250,000
Investment Criteria: Seed-Stage
Industry Group Preference: Enterprise Software, Database Services, Data & Analytics, Communications Software, Wireless Communications
Portfolio Companies: 23 and Me, Accel Growth Fund, Accel IX Strategic Partners, Acromedia Inc., Adchemy, AH Parallel Fund III-Q, Andreessen Horowitz Fund II-A, Aster Data, Audiencescience Inc., August Capital Management V, Baynote, Belwater Capital Fund, Braigo Labs, ByteMobile, Coast Access, Concept 10 Inc., Composite Software, Criteria Investment Partners LLC, CSP II Destressed Opportunities Trust, Digmine, DilMil, Eatime Inc., FlexLogics, Fin Robotics, Fireweed Fund, Fraudwall/Anchor Intelligence, Funny or Die (Sabse Technologies Inc.), Gigya, GReply, Greylock XII Limted, Gridants Inc., Gwynnie Bee, Hive II, Inventus Capital Management, Ixoraa Media Inc., Jaxtr, Kawi Safi Ventures, Kluttr, Korra, Loomia, Mashery, Mayfield Associates Fund, MC Pelican Fund LP, Mechanical Zoo, Medio Systems, Menlo Entrepreneurs Fund X, Meraki Networks Inc., Meru Networks, Metamachinix, Mimosa Systems, Mixer Labs Inc., ML-CSP II Trust, Nanonet, NextForce, Nokeena Networks, Northgate Capital LLC, NthOrbit, PeerNova, Pinterest, Plusmo, ReckOne Inc., Renkoo, Revenue Science, RocketFuel, Rupture, Scintera Networks, Score Data, Seligman Spectrum Focus Fund, Sequoia Tech Partners, Simplyhired Inc., Snaptell, Stumbleupon Inc., Sunflower New Co., Supyo, SV Angel III, Tapulous/GoGoApps, Teapot Inc., Technology IQ US LLC, Teracent Corp., Threads, TiE LaunchPad, Tizor, TokBok Inc., Genie, Urban Engines, UTV LLC, Vdopia, Wifidabba, WowkKast, Xambala, Xinlab, Zazzle.com

Key Executives:
Asha Jadeja, Founder
Education: Stanford University
Background: CEO, iScale, Inc.

624 DOUBLE M PARTNERS
725 Arizona Ave.
Suite 400
Santa Monica, CA 90401

web: www.doublempartners.com

Mission Statement: Double M Partners is a $7.2MM early stage venture fund based in Los Angeles and formed in August 2012. The Fund invests in Internet, Media and Communications companies who primarily are either business to business infrastructure, software, management platform and/or technology focused companies. The Fund is managed by Mark Mullen who has more than 20 years of investing and investment banking experience across the IMC sector. The Fund's current portfolio is comprised of 21 companies primarily in Southern California, but also including companies in San Francisco, Oregon and Canada. The Fund is supported by a premier group of investors, as well as fund advisors who are all successful entrepreneurs, investors, and business leaders.

Geographic Preference: Southern California, Oregon, Canada
Fund Size: $7.2 million
Founded: 2012
Investment Criteria: Early Stage
Industry Group Preference: Internet, Media, Communications
Portfolio Companies: Adomic, AdStage, Bitium, ChowNow, Clique Media, EV Connect, Gradient, HiQ, Idealists, Kaleo Software, Lettuce, MediaPass, MindClick, MomentFeed, Mover, Postcard on the Run, Prevoty, Quiet.ly, Retention Science, Scopely, Seismic Games, Sense360, Shift, Solfo, The Trade Desk, Tradesy

Key Executives:
Mark Mullen, Managing Partner
Education: BA, University of Denver; International MBA, Thunderbird School of Global Management; University of Michigan
Background: Senior Advisor, McCafferty & Co; Managing Director, International M&A, RBC Capital Markets; Senior Partner, Daniels & Associates; Senior Advisor to Los Angeles Mayor Antonio Villaraigosa;

Venture Capital & Private Equity Firms / Domestic Firms

Chief Operating Officer, Office of Economic and Business Policy, City of Los Angeles

625 DOUBLEROCK VENTURE CAPITAL
1 Sansome Street
Suite 3500
San Francisco, CA 94104

Phone: 415-910-0943
e-mail: admin@doublerock.com
web: www.doublerock.com

Mission Statement: DoubleRock invests primarily in early and growth stage technology companies.

Founded: 2012
Average Investment: Early: $2-5 million; Growth: $10-15 million
Investment Criteria: Early-Stage, Growth-Stage
Industry Group Preference: Consumer Internet, Cloud Computing, Mobile, Wireless, Software, Consumer Services
Portfolio Companies: Addvocate, Aromyx, Buzzstarter, Circa, Instawork, Jawbone, Oomnitza, Optim.al, Peer, Real5D, Silk Labs, SolveBio, Switch.co, TrustedInsight, Vurb, Wealthminder

Key Executives:
Suraj Rajwani, Co-Founder/Managing Partner
e-mail: suraj@doublerock.com
Background: Managing Director, Global Entrepreneurs Network Organization
Nick Dani, General Partner

626 DRAPER ATHENA
55 East Third Avenue
San Matea, CA 94401

e-mail: info@draperathena.com
web: www.dfjathena.com

Mission Statement: Uses a team-oriented approach, making available the complete mix of talents and resources of all partners and affiliates to the investment companies; maintains interest in building companies for the long-term and in helping the companies fulfill their complete vision.

Geographic Preference: Worldwide, West Coast
Fund Size: $100 million
Founded: 1997
Average Investment: $1 - $3 million
Minimum Investment: $500,000
Investment Criteria: Seed, Early-Stage
Industry Group Preference: Big Data, Software, Semiconductors, Robotics, Clean Technology, Security, Fintech, Machine Learning
Portfolio Companies: CallGate, Coinplug, Idea, Minigate, MXD3D, Nexia Device, OG Planet, Ramsway (JSC), Relay2, Creative Deign Systems, Demandtec, Imparto Software, Impli, Pivot, Khancera, Mobeam, Persist Technologies, Profitlogic, Vivd Semiconductor, Zantaz

Other Locations:
7th Floor
#712 Seocho-gu Heolleung-no 7
Seoul 137-749
South Korea
Phone: 82 (2)554-3131 Fax: 82 (2)553-2201

Key Executives:
Tim Draper, Chairman, USA
e-mail: tim@dfj.com
Education: BS, Electrical Engineering, Stanford University; MBA, Harvard Business School
Background: Founding Partner, Draper Fisher Jurvetson; DFJ Global Network
Perry Ha, Managing Director
e-mail: perry@draperathena.com
Education: BS, MS, MIT; MBA, Harvard Business School
Background: Product Development/Technology Management, Gemini Consulting; Amicon
Directorships: FirstIP, Impli, ProfitLogic, Zantaz.com

Henry Chung, Managing Director, Korea
e-mail: henry@draperathena.com
Education: BA, English Literature, MBA, Seoul National University
Background: Arthur D Little; SK Group
Directorships: CEO, eCommunity
Steven Tang, Managing Director, Hong Kong
e-mail: steven@draperathenagp.com
Education: BS, Electiral Engineering, Nottingham University; MBA, Bradford University
Background: National Semiconductor, Honeywell, Coolsand Semiconductor, RDA Microelectronics, Mills & Partners; Warburg Pincus
Charles Rim, Venture Partner
e-mail: chasrim@gmail.com
Education: BA, University of Pennsylvania; JD, Emory University
Background: Corporate Development, Google; Director, Yahoo! Korea; Investment Banking, Credit Agricole

627 DRAPER RICHARDS KAPLAN FOUNDATION
1600 El Camino Real
Suite 155
Menlo Park, CA 94025

Phone: 650-319-7808 Fax: 650-323-4060
web: www.drkfoundation.org

Mission Statement: Draper Richards is a venture capital firm dedicated to helping entrepreneurs and early-stage technology-based companies achieve maximum growth. The firm provides its portfolio companies support in the areas of raising capital and strategy development.

Geographic Preference: United States
Fund Size: $35 million
Founded: 1996
Average Investment: $1 million
Minimum Investment: $75,000 - $250,000
Investment Criteria: Early, Expansion, Seed
Industry Group Preference: Communications, Software, Internet Technology, Electronic Components, Information Technology, Telecommunications
Portfolio Companies: Axiom Legal, Blue Vector Systems, Brilliant Telecommunications, EoPlex Technologies, Flurry, Kyte, Lohika, LucidPort Technologies, Nusym Technologies, ObjectVideo, Ooma, Polaris Wireless, Prolacta Bioscience, Tsumobi, Ultriva

Key Executives:
William H Draper III, Co-Chair
e-mail: bill@draperrichards.com
Education: BA, Yale University; MBA, Harvard Graduate School of Business
Background: Founder, Sutter Hill Ventures; President & Chairman, Export-Import Bank of the US; Head, United Nations Development Program
Robin Richards Donohoe, Co-Chair
e-mail: robin@draperrichards.com
Education: Stanford Graduate School of Business; University of North Carolina
Background: Managing Director, Seaboard Management Corporation

628 DRAPER TRIANGLE VENTURES
2 Gateway Center
Suite 2000
Pittsburgh, PA 15222

Phone: 412-288-9800 Fax: 412-288-9799
web: www.drapertriangle.com

Mission Statement: Draper Triangle Ventures is a venture capital firm that partners with high-technology companies based in Pennsylvania and the Midwest.

Geographic Preference: Pennsylvania, Ohio, Midwest
Fund Size: $68 million

Venture Capital & Private Equity Firms / Domestic Firms

Founded: 1999
Average Investment: $250,000 - $2 million
Investment Criteria: Seed-Stage, Early-Stage
Industry Group Preference: Technology
Portfolio Companies: Acrobatiq, Aethon, Amplifinity, Bjond, Commuter Advertising, Directworks, OnShift, Pixel Velocity, RE2, Rhiza, ThinkVine, Thread
Other Locations:
21 East State Street
Suite 2200
Columbus, OH 43215
Phone: 614-450-2888

303 Detroit Street
Suite 100
Ann Arbor, MI 48104
Phone: 734-215-7577
Key Executives:
Jay Katarincic, Founder/Managing Director
e-mail: jay@dtvc.com
Education: BA, Economics, College of the Holy Cross; JD/MSIA, University of Pittsburgh School of Law & Carnegie Mellon University Graduate School of Industrial Administration
Background: Associate, M&A Group, Skadden Arps Slate Meagher & Flom
Directorships: Amplifinity, DirectWorks, Thread, Acrobatiq, Pittsburgh Technology Council, 3RiversConnect
Mike Stubler, Founder/Managing Director
e-mail: mike@dtvc.com
Education: BBA, University of Notre Dame
Background: Co-Founder & VP, Finance, IndustryNet; VP & CFO, International Cybernetics Corp.; Touche Ross & Company
Directorships: Unitask, OnShift, Aethon, Rhiza, Ohio Venture Association, Innovation Works
Tom Jones, Managing Director
e-mail: tom@dtvc.com
Education: BS, College of Wooster
Background: VP, Marketing, IndustryNet; VP, Marketing, Exonic Systems
Directorships: Commuter Advertising, Thinkvine, RE2, Directworks, Bjond, Pittsburgh DataWorks
Jonathan Murray, Venture Partner
e-mail: jonathan@dtvc.com
Background: Spectra Laboratories; President, Volk Optical; Co-Founder, Early Stage Partners
Zach Malone, Principal
e-mail: zach@dtvc.com
Education: BS, Finance, Virginia Polytechnic Institute
Background: Analyst, UPMC; Gateway Financial
Directorships: Pittsburgh Venture Capital Association Emerging Leaders

629 DRESNER COMPANIES
10 S LaSalle Street
Suite 2170
Chicago, IL 60603

Phone: 312-726-3600 **Fax:** 312-726-7448
web: www.dresnerpartners.com

Mission Statement: Dresner Partners is an investment bank focusing on middle market companies in a variety of industries, including technology, business services, consumer products, healthcare and industrials. The firm specializes in mergers and acquisition advisory, private institutional financing and finance restructuring.
Geographic Preference: Worldwide
Founded: 1991
Investment Criteria: Corporate Divestitures, Acquisitions, Management Buyouts
Industry Group Preference: Communications, Computer Related, Consumer Products, Distribution, Electronic Components, Industrial Equipment, Medical & Health Related, Technology
Other Locations:
200 Park Avenue
Suite 1700
New York, NY 10166
Phone: 212-203-8449

401 E Las Olas Boulevard
Suite 1400
Fort Lauderdale, FL 33301
Phone: 954-951-0272
Key Executives:
Steven M Dresner, President
312-780-7206
e-mail: sdresner@dresnerco.com
Education: BS, Economics, Wharton School, University of Pennsylvania; MBA, Finance, University of Chicago
Background: First Chicago Corporation; Arthur Andersen; Heller Financial; GE Capital Corporation
Kevin W McMurchy, Senior Managing Director, Financial Institutions
212-444-8029
Education: AB, Harvard University; MBA, Wharton School, University of Pennsylvania
Background: Merrill Lynch Capital Markets; Deutsche Morgan Grenfell, Keefe, Bruyette & Woods; Houlihan Lokey
Omar Diaz, Managing Director, Industrials
312-780-7221
Education: BS, Mechanical Engineering, Cornell University; MBA, Finance, Kelley School of Business, Indiana University
Background: Managing Director, Allegiance Capital; SVP, Industrial Group, Houlihan Lokey; VP, Acquest Advisors; Associate, M&A Group, JP Morgan; Bank of America; Deloitte & Touche
W Robert Friedman Jr, Managing Director, Healthcare
212-390-0503
Education: BA, MBA, Wharton School, University of Pennsylvania
Background: Managing Director, Deutsche Morgan Grenfell; Managing Director, Prudential Bache Capital Funding; General Partner, Montgomery Securities; LF Rothschild Unterberg Towbin
Directorships: MaxiCare Health Plans, Health Plan of California
Brian Graves, Managing Director
312-780-7237
Education: BS, Industrial Engineering, Purdue University; MBA, Finance, University of Chicago Graduate School of Business
Background: Ernst & Young; Credit Suisse; Mesirow Financial; Motorola
Michelle Moreno, Managing Director
312-780-7207
Education: BA, Economics & French, University of Illinois at Urbana-Champaign; MBA, California State University, Fullerton
Background: First Analysis; CIBC World Markets
Directorships: Chicago Finance Exchange
Stephen P Mullin, Director, Marketing & Business Development
312-780-7213
Education: BS, Finance, Drake University
Background: Dun & Bradstreet Information Services; American National Bank
Paul E Hoffman, Director
312-780-7229
Education: BA, Economics, University of Chicago
Background: Bank of America Securities

Venture Capital & Private Equity Firms / Domestic Firms

630 DRIVE CAPITAL
629 North High Steet
Columbus, OH 43215

e-mail: info@drivecapital.com
web: www.drivecapital.com

Mission Statement: Drive Capital invests in innovative technology, healthcare, and consumer companies in the Midwest. Actively seeking innovative entrepreneurs addressing big market opportunities. Drive Capital partners with entrepreneurs that have audacious goals and strive to build large sustainable companies.

Geographic Preference: Midwest
Industry Group Preference: Technology, Technology-Enabled Services, Healthcare, Consumer Services, Consumer Products
Portfolio Companies: Aver Inc., Beam, Channel IQ, Civis Analytics, Clinc, Comply 365, CrossCHX, Duolingo, FarmLogs, Hologram, Immuta, Kapow, LeadPages, Muve, Nowait, Roadtrippers, Root, TriggrHealth, Trove, Udacity, When I Work

Key Executives:
Mark D. Kvamme, Co-Founder
Education: University of California, Berkeley
Background: Partner, Sequoia Capital; Chief Investment Officer/President, JobsOhio
Chris Olsen, Co-Founder
Background: Partner, Sequoia Capital; Technology Crossover Ventures

631 DUBILIER & COMPANY
Stamford, CT 06902

web: www.dubilier.com

Mission Statement: A private investment firm focused on buying and building companies in partnership with management.

Investment Criteria: Middle Market
Industry Group Preference: Consumer Products, Media, Publishing, Information Technology, E-Commerce & Manufacturing, Marketing
Portfolio Companies: Acrow Bridge, Amplified Technology Holdings, Bluegrass Dairy And Food Inc., Bulletin Intelligence, Cleareon Fiber Networks, Cavario, DC Safety, FourQ, MDT, ODC Nimbus, Old london, Ooska News, Phoenix, Rio SEO, Systech International, Zim's Crack Creme

Key Executives:
Michael M Cone, Director
Education: BA, Princeton University; PhD, Organic Chemistry, Yale University
Background: Partner, Crossway Ventures; Chemical Research, DuPont Company; Venture Manager, Somos
Dana Donovan, Director
Education: BA, Duke University; MBA, Amos Tuck School, Dartmouth College
Background: President, Clarion Capital; Managing Director, John Hancock Financial
Michael J Dubilier, Managing Partner
Education: Connecticut College; MBA, Garvin School of International Management; New York University Graduate School of Business Administration
Background: Partner, Clayton Dubilier & Ric; Drexel Burnham Lambert
Directorships: Phoenix Packaging Company, Magnetic Data Technologies, HEM Pharmaceuticals, APS, Old London Foods
Peter D Goodson, Director
Education: Stanford University; Harvard Business School
Background: Partner, CD&R; Managing Director, Kidder Peabody & Co

632 DUBIN CLARK & COMPANY
323 Newbury Street
Boston, MA 02115

Phone: 203-629-2030 **Fax:** 203-547-7444
web: www.dubinclark.com

Mission Statement: Dubin Clark & Company seeks to partner with management teams and help build businesses by providing capital and assisting with the development of new strategies.

Geographic Preference: North America
Founded: 1984
Investment Criteria: Platform company sales of $10-$100+ million and adjusted EBITDA of $2-$20 million (smaller for add-ons); businesses in transition; strong growth trajectory
Industry Group Preference: Construction, Building Materials & Services, Transportation, Manufacturing, Infrastructure, Aerospace, Defense and Government, Healthcare Services, Energy
Portfolio Companies: Action Target, Johnny on the Spot, Merex Group, Peterson Party Center, Reel Power International, Restoration Parts Unlimited, Sentient Medical Systems, SGA Production Services, USSC

Other Locations:
1030 2nd Street S
Suite 301
Jacksonville Beach, FL 32250
Phone: 203-629-2030 **Fax:** 203-547-7444

Key Executives:
Thomas J Caracciolo, Managing Partner
203-629-2030 x225
e-mail: caracciolo@dubinclark.com
Education: BS, Northeastern University; MBA, Harvard Business School
Background: Partner, TCW Capital; Corporate Finance Group, GE Capital
Directorships: Driven Performance Brands, Action Target, Reel Power International, Sentient Medical Systems, Merex Group
Brent L Paris, Managing Partner
203-629-2030 x228
e-mail: paris@dubinclark.com
Education: BS, Accounting, Indiana University School of Business; MBA, Finance & Entrepreneurship, University of Chicago Graduate School of Business
Background: Associate, Latek Capital Corp.; Analyst, Waveland Capital Management; Brinson Partners
Directorships: Driven Performance Brands, Restoration Parts Unlimited, Peterson Party Center, Association for Corporate Growth
Michael P Hompesch, Partner
203-629-2030 x223
e-mail: hompesch@dubinclark.com
Education: BS, Business Administration, American University; MBA, Finance, Wharton Graduate School of Business; CFA
Background: General Electric Financial Management Program, Commercial Finance
Directorships: Action Target, Reel Power International, Merex Group, Johnny on the Spot
Frank J Pados Jr, Senior Advisor
203-629-2030 x229
e-mail: pados@dubinclark.com
Education: BA, Economics, Boston College; MBA, Finance, University of Pennsylvania
Background: EVP & Head, Private Equity, Desai Capital Management; Managing Director & Co-Founding Partner, TCW Capital
Directorships: Sentient Medical Systems, Reel Power International, Merex Group, Johnny on the Spot

Venture Capital & Private Equity Firms / Domestic Firms

633 DUCHOSSOIS CAPITAL MANAGEMENT
444 W Lake Street
Suite 2000
Chicago, IL 60606

Phone: 312-586-2080
e-mail: info@dcmllc.com
web: www.dcmllc.com

Mission Statement: Duchossois Capital Management is a privately held investment company that seeks to create long term value by providing capital and operational expertise.
Geographic Preference: Midwest United States
Average Investment: $2 - $7 million
Investment Criteria: Growth Stage, Later Stage
Industry Group Preference: Networking, Semiconductors, Software, Technology, Information Technology, Communications
Portfolio Companies: Critical Signal Technologies, Echo Active Learning, GetWellNetwork, Infoblox, Milestone AV Technologies

Key Executives:
   Michael E Flannery, Chief Executive Officer
   Education: BS, Finance, University of Illinois; Indiana University School of Law
   Background: CEO, Trinity Rail Group; Vice Chairman, Thrall Car; Corporate Counsel, Cummins Engine Company
   Directorships: The Chamberlain Group, Milestone AV Technologies
   Eric A Reeves, Managing Director/Head, Private Capital Investments
   Education: BA, University of Michigan; JD, Ohio State University
   Background: EVP & General Counsel, The Chamberlain Group; Partner, Corporate Department, McDermott Will & Emery
   Directorships: Seaway Bank and Trust Company, Milestone AV Technologies
   Lauren K Bugay, Managing Director
   Education: BBA, University of Notre Dame; MBA, Booth School of Business, University of Chicago; CFA
   Background: Director of Business Development, The Duchossois Group; Corporate Finance, William Blair & Company
   Jason B Moskowitz, Managing Director
   Education: BBA, University of Notre Dame; MBA, Finance, Kellogg School of Management, Northwestern University
   Background: VP, Merit Capital Partners; Associate, Pfingsten Partners
   Michelle A Waldusky, Manager, Investment Operations
   Education: BS, Accounting, University of Illinois; CPA
   Background: Deloitte & Touche

634 DUFF ACKERMAN & GOODRICH
251 Lytton Avenue
Suite 200
Palo Alto, CA 94301

Phone: 650-543-8180 Fax: 415-788-7311

Mission Statement: To achieve superior returns through investments in private companies in the communications industries.
Geographic Preference: United States
Fund Size: $1.8 billion
Founded: 1991
Average Investment: $5 - $10 million
Minimum Investment: $3 million
Investment Criteria: Stage Independent, Industry Specific
Industry Group Preference: Communications, Infrastructure, Media, Manufacturing
Portfolio Companies: 3VR, Adamas, Admob, Aerohive Networks, Aggregate Knowledge, Agrivida, Alta, Altor, Ambarella, Amyris, Arresto Biosciences, Atara Bio, Avi Networks, Avnera, Avvo, Axiom, Birst, Bloomenergy, BlueLane, Boku, Brighter, CardioDX, Chegg, Clarizen, ClearStory, Cleatrip, Clearwell, Clickatell, Cloudera, Convertro, D2S, DisplayLink, Engine Yard, Eventbrite, FireEye, Fortify Software, Funny or Die, Gigya, Glassdoor.com, Grouper, GrubHub.com, Harvest, HighGear Media, Huddle, Inspirato, Jasper Wireless, Kovio, LearnVest, Lithium, LiveOps, Loopt, Marin Software, Matrix Memory, MCube, Meraki, Metaweb, Mind.com, Mu Dynamics, Neos Geosolutions, New Relic, Newport Media, Nextdoor, NimbleRX, Oakley Networks, One Medical Group, Open DNS, OpenX, Oportun, OptiMedica, Origami Logic, Pacific Biosciences, Pentaho, Picarro, Pinger, Pixtronix, Plaxo, Plays TV, Polyvore, Proofpoint, Quantenna Communications, Right Scale, Ring Central, RMI Corp. Seeking Alpha, Silver Peak, Silver Spring Networks, Spring Source, Stoke, StrongView, Runrun, Taulia, Terracotta, Tokbox, Trialpay TRUSTe, Upwork, uShip, Vectra, Vudu, Wealthfront, Wet Point, WeWork, Wix, Xoom, Xsigo Systems, Yelp, YuMe, Zimbra, Zlango, Zuora, Zynga

635 DUNDEE VENTURE CAPITAL
3717 Harney Street
2nd Floor
Omaha, NE 68131

web: www.dundeeventurecapital.com

Mission Statement: Dundee Venture Capital is a venture capital firm that invests in early stage technology companies with high growth potential.
Fund Size: $20 million
Founded: 2010
Average Investment: $50,000 - $750,000
Investment Criteria: Startups, Early Stage
Industry Group Preference: E-Commerce & Manufacturing, SaaS, Consumer Networks, Technology
Portfolio Companies: ABODO, ABPathFinder, AgLocal, Briefcase, Built In Chicago, BuluBox, Business Exchange, Cosmic Cart, DivvyHQ, DonorPath, HuntForce, Inventables, Leap.It, Lockr, MindMixer, Phone2Action, RoundPegg, Techstars Ventures, TripleSeat, Viirt, Vine Street Ventures, Wide Open Spaces

Key Executives:
   Mark Hasebroock, Founder
   Education: BS, Business Administration, University of Nebraska-Lincoln; MBA, Finance, Creighton University
   Background: Co-Owner, Tranquility Bay Resort; Co-Founder, Hayneedle; COO, GiftCertificates.com
   Beth Engel, Advisor
   Education: BS, Biochemistry, University of Notre Dame; MBA, Georgetown University
   Background: Hayneedle; Co-Founder, Interface: The Web School; Straight Shot

636 DUNRATH CAPITAL
641 Courtland Circle
Western Springs, IL 60558

Phone: 312-546-4700
web: www.dunrath.com

Mission Statement: Dunrath Capital is a private equity and strategic advisory firm that invests in early and growth stage infrastructure surety companies.
Geographic Preference: United States
Fund Size: $100 million
Investment Criteria: Early-Stage, Growth-Stage
Industry Group Preference: Infrastructure, Aerospace, Defense and Government, Security
Portfolio Companies: Critical Signal Technologies, Exadigm, Keri Systems, Quantum Secure, RedSky Technologies

Key Executives:
   John I Abernethy, Founder/Managing Director
   312-546-4782
   Fax: 866-255-7299

221

Venture Capital & Private Equity Firms / Domestic Firms

e-mail: john@dunrath.com
Education: BS, Accounting, Northern Illinois University
Background: CFO, Revere Group; CFO, APAC Customer Services; EVP & CFO, Commerce Clearing House; Audit Partner, Deloitte & Touche
Stephen S Beitler, Founder/Managing Director
847-847-4414
Fax: 847-432-4420
e-mail: steve@dunrath.com
Education: School of International Service, American University; University of Chicago; Defense Intelligence College
Background: Managing Director, Trident Capital; Sears Roebuck & Co.; Helene Curtis
Richard P Earley, Founder/Managing Director
630-871-8940
e-mail: rich@dunrath.com
Education: BA, University of Notre Dame; MBA, Benedictine University
Background: CEO & Chairman, Arxan Technologies; Arxan Defense Systems; President, Synergy Software Inc.

637 DUPONT CAPITAL
1 Righter Parkway
Suite 3200
Wilmington, DE 19803

Phone: 302-477-6000
e-mail: kimberly.a.fetterman@usa.dupont.com
web: www.dupontcapital.com

Mission Statement: DCM offers a diversified private equity program that was designed with the objective of providing superior, risk-adjusted, long-term private equity returns for investors. Fundamentally, the Private Markets Group (PMG) are value investors and believe the inherent inefficiency of the private market provides opportunities to acquire assets at prices below their intrinsic values. The PMG has diligently applied value investment principles to the private equity market since 1989.

Fund Size: $3.7 billion
Founded: 1989
Investment Criteria: Buyouts, Co-Investments, Mezzanine, Special Situations

Key Executives:
  Lode J Devlaminck, Managing Director, Equities
  Education: MA, Applied Economics, University of Antwerp
  Background: CIO, Global Equities, Hermes North America; Portfolio Manager, Global Equities and Sector Specialist, Fortis Investments; Global Sector Manager, Fimagest
  Krzysztof A. Kowal, CFA, Managing Director, Fixed Income Investments
  Education: MS, Physics, Jagiellonian University; PhD, Materials Science and Engineering, University of Pennsylvania
  Antonis Mistras, CFA, Managing Director, Alternative Investments
  Education: BS, Forestry, Aristotellian University; MS, Wood Science and Technology, University of California, Berkeley; MBA, University of California, Berkeley
  Background: Manager of Production, BARRA
  Timothy R Sweeney, Managing Director, Business Development and Client Service
  Education: BS, United States Military Academy; MBA, Amos Tuck School of Business Administration, Dartmouth College
  Background: Managing Director, Morgan Stanley; Principal, Vanguard Group; Partner, Trammell Crow Company
  Daryl B Brown, Director/Portfolio Manager
  Education: BS, Mathematics, University of Texas; MBA, University of Delaware; CFA
  Background: Associate Actuary, DuPont

638 DUTCHESS CAPITAL
50 Commonwealth Avenue
Suite 2
Boston, MA 02116

Phone: 617-301-4701
e-mail: dleighton@dutchesscapital.com
web: www.dutchesscapital.com

Mission Statement: Invests in several types of industries, including technology, ecommerce, and consumer products.

Geographic Preference: 7S, Canada, UK, Europe, Australia, Asia, Latin America
Founded: 1996
Average Investment: Up to $25M
Investment Criteria: Seed, Early-Stage, Late-Stage
Industry Group Preference: Technology, Ecommerce, Consumer Goods, Cannabis
Portfolio Companies: American Cannabis Company, Baobab Resources, Big Night Entertainment Group, CampusTap, Continental Coal Ltd., Dixie Elixirs, Foria, Independent Bank, Kandy Pens, Mannatech, Mass Roots, Nanigans, ProPhase Labs, Range Resources Ltd., Safety Quick Light, SMTP

Other Locations:
  1110 Route 55
  Suite 206
  LaGrangeville, NY 12540
  Phone: 845-575-6770 x202

  New Broad Street House
  35 New Broad Street
  London EC2M 1NH
  United Kingdom

  Room 11A1, Block A, Han Wei Plaza
  7 Guang Hua Road
  Chaoyang District
  Beijing 100004
  China

  Rua Itapeva, 378 - 120 Andar
  Sao Paulo, SP 01332-000
  Brasil

Key Executives:
  Douglas H. Leighton, Founder/Managing Partner
  e-mail: dleighton@dutchesscapital.com
  Education: BS, Economics, University of Hartford
  Michael A. Novielli, Founder/Managing Partner
  845-575-6770 ext. 202
  e-mail: mnovielli@dutchesscapital.com
  Education: BS, Business, University of South Florida
  Theodore J. Smith, Managing Director/COO
  617-301-4702
  e-mail: tsmith@dutchesscapital.com
  Education: BS, Finance, Boston College
  Jessica Geran, Head of Corporate Finance
  617-301-4703
  e-mail: jgeran@dutchesscapital.com
  Education: BA, Economics, University of Colorado
  Background: Financial Representative, Northwestern Mutual

639 DW HEALTHCARE PARTNERS
1413 Center Drive
Suite 220
Park City, UT 84098

Phone: 435-645-4050
web: www.dwhp.com

Mission Statement: DW Healthcare Partners invests exclusively in healthcare businesses across North America.

Geographic Preference: North America
Fund Size: $265 million
Founded: 2002
Average Investment: $15 - $40 million
Minimum Investment: $5 million

222

Investment Criteria: Middle-Market, Growth Capital, Management Buyouts
Industry Group Preference: Healthcare
Portfolio Companies: ABC Home Medical Supply, Arteriocyte Medical Systems, Med-Pharmex, Reliant Rehabilitation, Reliant Renal Care, Z-Medica
Other Locations:
  1 Toronto Street
  Suite 401
  Toronto, ON M5C 2V6
  Canada
  Phone: 416-583-2420
Key Executives:
  Andrew Carragher, Founder/Managing Director
  416-583-2421
  e-mail: acarragher@dwhp.com
  Education: BS, University of Western Ontario; MBA, Harvard Business School
  Background: VP, Business Development, Ventro Corporation; Total Renal Care; Divisional Manager, Weston Foods; Bain & Company
  Directorships: Genesis Technology Partners, Verathon, Tandem Labs, Reliant Renal Care, Reliant Rehabilitation, Pentec Health, Career Step, Z-Medica Corporation, Health & Safety Institute
  Jay Benear, Founder/Managing Director
  435-645-4052
  e-mail: jay@dwhp.com
  Education: BA, Psychology, Rice University; MD, Oklahoma University
  Background: President, Cancer Care Associates
  Directorships: Arteriocyte Medical Systems, BGS Pharmacy Partners, Emphusion, Genesis Technology Partners, Global Physics Solutions, Hill Top Research, The Radlinx Group
  Doug Schillinger, Managing Director
  435-645-4056
  e-mail: doug@dwhp.com
  Education: BS, Cornell University; MBA, Harvard Business School
  Background: Bain & Company; Manager, Accenture Consulting
  Directorships: Tandem Labs, Pentec Health, Hill Top Research, Global Physics Solutions, ClinOps, BGS Pharmacy, Arteriocyte Medical
  Lance Ruud, Managing Director/Chief Financial Officer
  435-645-4054
  e-mail: lance@dwhp.com
  Education: BS, Accounting, University of Utah
  Background: Senior VP & CFO, HTD Corporation; CFO & Director, TransAmerican Waste Industries; CFO, Republic Waste Industries
  Directorships: Arteriocyte Medical Systems, Z-Medica Corporation

640 DYNAMO VC
800 Market Street
Suite 200
Chattanooga, TN 37402

e-mail: hello@dynamo.vc
web: www.dynamo.vc

Mission Statement: A venture capital fund investing in technology businesses that have the potential to transform commerce and trade.

Founded: 2016
Industry Group Preference: Commerce and Trade, Clean Technology, Energy, Software, Robotics, Entertainment, Travel, Network Infrastructure & Security, Data & Analytics
Portfolio Companies: Steam Logistics, Starksky Robotics, Skupos, Slope, Skydrop, Armada.ai, Numadic, Sennder, Zeelo, Autit, Wise, SynapseMX, Locatible, Shipamax, Work Hound, Stord, Sirenum
Key Executives:
  Barry Large, Founder/Managing Director
  Background: Founder, Lamp Post Group; Advisor, Bellhops; Advisor, FanJam
  Ted Alling, Founder/Managing Director
  Education: Samford University
  Background: Founder/CEO, Access America Transport; Advisor, Skupos; Advisor, PriceWaiter; Advisor, Tripr; Advisor, Breeze; Advisor, Bellhops; Founder, Lamp Post Group
  Directorships: Skupos
  Allan Davis, Founder/Managing Director
  Background: Founder, Lamp Post Group; Access America Transport; Advisor, Bellhops; Advisor, FanJam
  Directorships: Bellhops
  Santosh Sankar, Founder/Managing Director
  Education: BS, Finance, Pennsylvania State University
  Background: Citigroup; Wells Fargo Securities

641 E.VENTURES
600 Montgomery Street
43rd Floor
San Francisco, CA 94111

Phone: 415-869-5200 **Fax:** 415-869-5201
e-mail: info@eventures.vc
web: www.eventures.vc

Mission Statement: Focuses on emerging opportunities in new media, information technology and communications. With a team in each of our five regions, we have access to teams, markets, and investors in all the important places. And because we work together closely, we can offer significant synergies and benefits for entrepreneurs. These include global insights, recognition of emerging trends, and a strategic advantage for startups with global goals. In essence, we can bring you global virtually overnight.

Geographic Preference: United States, Europe
Investment Criteria: Early Stage, Growth Stage
Industry Group Preference: Media, Information Technology, Communications
Portfolio Companies: 36Kr, 9flats.com, Acorns, Add, Angie's List, Amplify, App Annie, Appfolio, Aptoide, Asana Rebel, Asap54, Axios, Azimo, BackOps, BankFacil, BetaWorks, BetterCloud, Bird, Blinkist, Bluekai, Braavo, Bright Health, Candid Co., CarPrice, Class Box, Clicksign, Clique Media Group, Code Fights, Copa90, Cornerjob, Cortex, Coya, Daily Secret, Del.Icio.Us, Delta Method, Deposit Solutions, Eucalyptus, Everything but the House, Experteer.dE, Exporo, FanTV, FarFetch, Flux, Fotolog, Freee, Friendsurance, Futrli, GamersFirst, Global Savings Group, GoPuff, GoToMeeting, Goyoo, Graylog, Groupon, Gympass, Hashgo, Hi-Media, Honeycomb.io, HouseCall, Huckleberry, Icertis, JMTY, Jow, JW Player, Karma, Kauf.da, LastLine, Layer, Made, Maker Studios, Medicinia, Memed, Merchantry, Mightybell, Minuto Seguros, Minutrade, MoyoGame, Munchery, Muse & Co., Nativo, Natural Cycles, nCircle, Nibo, Nginx, Nomnomnom, Online Tours, Order With Me, Ozon.ru, PasseiDireto, PayKey, Peanut Labs, Pink.oi, Plain Vanilla, Plated, PlayHaven, PSafe, Pulse, Recurly, Reelio, Rekoo, Resultados Digitais, Saatchi Art, Sapato, Savoteur, Scopely, Segment, Semrush, Shipt, Shopping.com, Shutl, Smartfrog, Soldsie, Sonim Technologies, Sonos, SpotHero, Stackshare, Staffbase, Streamlabs, Strikingly, StyleSaint, Tandem, Teamo.ru, TechTemple, Test.ai, The Real Real, The Young Turks, The Family, ThisClicks, Thrive Market, Trippy, TVSmiles, Upsight, Verse, ViajaNet, Vicampo, Waptx, WealthNavi, When I Work, Wine In Black, Wonderschool, YuMe
Other Locations:
  Hohe Bleichen 21
  Hamburg 20354

Venture Capital & Private Equity Firms / Domestic Firms

Germany
Phone: 49-4082225550 **Fax:** 49-408222555999
Friedrichstr. 206
Berlin 10969
Germany
Phone: 49-30467249770
Rua Joaquim Floriano, 1120 A, cj. 92
Itaim Bibi
Sao Paulo SP 04534-004
Brazil
Phone: 55-1140636061
Taikouen Bld.3F, 1-3-8
Shibakoen Minato-ku
Tokyo 105-0011
Japan
Phone: 81-9014672730
Tianhai Business Building B
Suite 107
Dongsi Bei St, Dongcheng District
Beijing
China

Key Executives:
Mathias Schilling, Co-Founder/Managing Partner
Education: Masters Finance, University of St. Gallen
Background: Consultant, Bertelsmann AG; Bertelsmann's Book Group, New York; Roland Berger & Partner
Thomas Gieselmann, Co-Founder/General Partner
Education: BA Economics/Business Administration, Rhodes College
Background: Chief Technology Officer, AOL Europe
Directorships: NGINX, Playhaven, Pulse News, Gamersfirst
Andreas Haug, Co-Founder/General Partner, Hamburg
Background: Co-Founder, InfoMedia Group, Co-Founder, Diligenz Management Consulting; Bertelsmann AG
Christin Leybold, Co-Founder/Managing Partner, Hamburg & Berlin
Education: Masters Degree, Electrical Engineering, University of Illinois at Urbana
Background: Detecon International; Daimler Chrysler Research
Akio Tanaka, Partner, Tokyo & Beijing
Education: MS, University of British Columbia
Background: Head of Venture Investment Program, Adobe
Anderson Thees, Partner, Sao Paulo
Education: BS, Computer Engineering, University of Campinas; MBA, Yale School of Management
Background: CEO, Apontador; Investment Principal, Naspers/MIH
Charles Yim, Venture Partner
Education: BA, Philosophy, Carleton College
Background: Head of Mobile Application Partnerships, Google; AdMob

642 EARLY STAGE PARTNERS
1801 East Ninth Street
Suite 1700
Cleveland, OH 44114
Phone: 216-781-4600
web: www.esplp.com

Mission Statement: Early Stage Partners is a venture capital firm dedicated to investing in Midwest-based early stage companies across a range of technology sectors.
Geographic Preference: Ohio, Michigan, Midwest
Fund Size: $55 million
Founded: 2001
Investment Criteria: Early Stage
Industry Group Preference: Information Technology, Clean Technology, Manufacturing, Healthcare, Industrial Technology
Portfolio Companies: Amplifinity, Arisdyne, AxioMed Spine, Ayalogic, Blue Spark Technologies, Cardiox, Cleveland Medical Polymers, CytoPherx, EcoSmart, Gensyn Technologies, Great Lakes Pharmaceuticals, HealthSpot, HistoSonics, Intelligent Clearing Network, Imalux, Juventas Therapeutics, LineStream, MAR Systems, NineSigma, OnShift, OPTEM, Reverse Medical Corp., Simbionix, SironRX, TOA Technologies, UniTask

Key Executives:
Jim Petras, Managing Director
Education: BA, Oberlin College; MA, MBA, University of Michigan
Background: President & Managing Director, Capital One Partners; Founder, Wolfensohn Ventures; Citicorp
Directorships: Blue Spark, EcoSmart, Simbionix, Arisdyne, OPTEM, Linestream, ICN
Jonathan Murray, Co-Founder
Education: BA, Biology & English Literature, George Washington University; MBA, University of Michigan
Background: President, Incubation Services; President, Volk Optical; Spectra Laboratories
Directorships: TOA Technologies, OnShift, ICN, Imalux, Ayalogic, Unitask, Amplifinity
Charlie MacMillan, Chief Financial Officer
Education: Ohio Wesleyan University
Background: CFO, Capital One Partners; VP, Administration, Manco; Manager, Entrepreneurial Services Group, Ernst & Young

643 EARTHRISE CAPITAL
80 Broad Street
5th Floor
New York, NY 10004
Phone: 212-757-1007
web: www.earthrisecapital.com

Mission Statement: Earthrise Capital Fund is a venture fund investing in emerging technologies for energy, power and water, primarily in North America. Areas of interest include lower-carbon energy sources; energy and materials efficiency improvement, cost-effective energy storage; and environmental technologies and services. The Earthrise team has decades of collective experience in energy and environmental technology investing.
Geographic Preference: North America
Investment Criteria: Early-Stage, Later-Stage
Industry Group Preference: Energy, Water, Energy Efficiency, Energy Storage, Environment, Renewable Energy, Clean Energy, Green Technology
Portfolio Companies: Axion Power International, CoolChip Technologies, Forest2Market, NanoMas Technologies, Powerhouse Dynamics, TSO Logic Inc.

Key Executives:
Ann Partlow, Co-Founder/General Partner
e-mail: apartlow@earthrisecapital.com
Background: Portfolio Manager, Rockefeller & Co
James LoGerfo, Co-Founder/General Partner
e-mail: jlogerfo@earthrisecapital.com
Education: BA, International Studies, University of Washington; PhD, Political Science, Columbia University; CFA
Background: Energy Technology Energy Research, Bank of America; General Motors Pension Fund; BOVARO Partners; Vortex Energy

644 EASTON CAPITAL INVESTMENT GROUP
767 Third Avenue
7th Floor
New York, NY 10017
Phone: 212-702-0950 **Fax:** 212-702-0952
web: www.eastoncapital.com

Mission Statement: Easton Capital Investment Group is a venture capital firm focusing on the healthcare and life sciences sectors. The firm invests in companies with capital effi-

Venture Capital & Private Equity Firms / Domestic Firms

cient business models and seeks to generate superior returns while minimizing risks.
Geographic Preference: Eastern Seaboard, United States
Fund Size: $20 - $100 million
Founded: 1999
Average Investment: $10 - $20 million
Minimum Investment: $500,000
Investment Criteria: Early Stage, Mid-Stage, Late Stage, Growth Capital, PIPEs
Industry Group Preference: Life Sciences, Healthcare, Healthcare Services, Diagnostics, Medical Devices, Therapeutics, Healthcare Information Technology
Portfolio Companies: Bluebird Bio, Cardiomems, Claret Medical, Comprehend, Conor Medsystems, ElectroCore, EM Kinetics, Expanding Orthopedics, Kitcheck, Medikly, PerceptiMed, Precise Light Surgical, Promedior, Resolve Therapeutics, Shimojani, SOLX, TigerText, Trellis Bioscience, WellTrackOne, Wildflower, Within3
Key Executives:
  John H Friedman, Founding Partner/Managing Partner
  e-mail: friedman@eastoncapital.com
  Education: BA, Yale College, Yale University; JD, Yale Law School
  Background: Founder & Managing General Partner, Security Pacific Capital Investors; Manging Director & Partner, EM Warburg Pincus & Company
  Directorships: Promedior, Trellis Bioscience, MedCPU, PerceptiMed, TigerText, Within3, Precise Light
  Francisco Garcia, Managing Director
  e-mail: garcia@eastoncapital.com
  Education: AB, Harvard College, Harvard University; JD, Harvard Law School
  Background: Head, Corporate Finance, Cramer Rosenthal McGlynn; Neptune Management Company; VP, Corporate Finance, Kidder Peabody & Company; Attorney, Sullivan & Cromwell
  Directorships: Archibald, Autonet, Gentis, TransMolecular
  Charles B Hughes III, Managing Director/General Counsel
  e-mail: hughes@eastoncapital.com
  Education: AB, Princeton University; LLM, New York University School of Law; JD, University of Virginia School of Law
  Background: Partner, Torys LLP
  Kresimir Letinic MD PhD, Managing Director
  e-mail: kletinic@eastoncapital.com
  Education: MBA, PhD, Neuroscience, Yale University; MD, University of Zagreb
  Background: Fletcher Spaght Ventures; The Channel Group; Lesanne Life Sciences
  Directorships: Medikly, Wildflower Health
  Richard Lipkin, Managing Director
  e-mail: rlipkin@eastoncapital.com
  Education: Princeton University; MBA, Columbia University
  Background: Partner, Commerce Health Ventures; Laird & Co.; Goldman Sachs; Executive Director, Strang Cancer Prevention Center
  Ting-Pau Oei, Executive Partner
  e-mail: toei@eastoncapital.com
  Education: BA, Union College; MBA, Columbia University Graduate School of Business
  Background: Johnson & Johnson; Ortho Pharmaceutical International; Abbott Laboratories; Merck

645 EASTVEN VENTURE PARTNERS
17 Old Kings Highway South
Suite 140
Darien, CT 06820

Mission Statement: Seeks investments in companies with exceptional management teams, that have unique and proprietary technology, and that seek to capitalize on sizeable market opportunities.
Geographic Preference: North America
Fund Size: $50 million
Founded: 2001
Investment Criteria: Primary Focus Early Stage, Will Except All Stages Including Spin-Outs
Industry Group Preference: Software, Technology, Infrastructure, Communications, Semiconductors, Networking, Information Technology, Enabling Technology
Portfolio Companies: ByteMobile, Kirusa, Photobucket, RadioFrame Networks, Atrua, ReefEdge, Vallent
Key Executives:
  Mark Maybell, Founder/Partner
  Education: MBA, Taxation and Accounting, Indiana University; AB, Finance, University of Illinois
  Background: Merrill Lynch, Bear, Stearns and Company
  Directorships: WatchMark Corporation, RadioFrame Networks
  Mark McAndrews, Partner
  Education: BA, Economics, Yale University; MA, Accounting and Finance, New York University
  Background: Merrill Lynch
  Directorships: Bytemobile Corporation
  Jeff Low, Partner
  Education: Business Management degree, Harvard University; BA, MA, comparative literature, University of California, Unibersity of Massachusetts
  Background: Ericsson's Data Networking Division
  Directorships: I-Controls

646 EASTWARD CAPITAL PARTNERS
432 Cherry Street
West Newton, MA 02465
Phone: 617-969-6700 Fax: 617-969-7900
e-mail: contacts@eastwardcp.com
web: www.eastwardcp.com

Mission Statement: To work with venture capital firms to provide venture debt and equity financing to their portfolio companies.
Fund Size: $300 million
Founded: 1994
Industry Group Preference: Information Technology, Communications, Alternative Energy, Clean Technology, Healthcare
Portfolio Companies: Aurion Pro Solutions, Best Doctors, Blue Cod Technologies, Booker Software, Brickstream, Clearent, Conductor, Digital Ocean, Dormeo, eChalk, Ecosense Lighting, Edgewater Networks, Everbridge, FirstBest Systems, Gilt, Hillcrest, Host Analytics, Invaluable, Lifescript, Linkwell Health, Management Health Solutions, Menara, MinuteKey, Mutual Mobile, myThings, Neat, NetBio, The New Orleans Exchange, Next Step Living, Nomis Solutions, NutraClick, Persado, Plated, PlumChoice, Qualtre, Quantenna, Resilient Systems, Rocksbox, ScaleMP, Simplicity, SnagaJob, Solarflare Communications, Tabula Rasa, Tracx, Trade Desk, TraderTools, Travora, Triad Semiconductor, UStream, Vanu, View, Wealth Engine, Xactly, Xiotech, xMatters, Xtalic, Zest Finance
Key Executives:
  Dennis P Cameron, Founding Partner
  e-mail: dennis@eastwardcp.com
  Education: BS, Marketing & Finance, Northeastern University
  Background: Founder, CommVest; John Hancock Leasing; CIT; MeesPierson
  Edward I Dresner, Investment Partner
  e-mail: edward@eastwardcp.com
  Education: BA, Economics, Hamilton College
  Background: Managing Director, MeesPierson; Credit Analyst, Chemical Bank
  Nick Bologna, Investment Partner
  e-mail: nick@eastwardcp.com

Venture Capital & Private Equity Firms / Domestic Firms

Education: BS, Finance, University of Connecticut
Background: Applied Telecommunications Technologies; VP, Marketing, Stratus Computer; VP, Sales, Marketing & Service, Sequoia Systems; Senior Advisor, Needham & Company; IBM
Tim O'Loughlin, Investment Partner
e-mail: tim@eastwardcp.com
Education: BA, Economics, Boston College
Background: Vencore Capital; Silicon Valley Bank
Chris Bodnar, Investment Partner
e-mail: chris@eastwardcp.com
Education: Boston University; MBA, Cornell University
Background: Advisor, Metabolix; Bear Stearns; Great Hill Partners; Ladenburg Thalmann

647 ECHELON VENTURES
300 Fifth Ave.
3rd Floor
Waltham, MA 02451
Phone: 781-419-9850 Fax: 781-419-9851

Mission Statement: Seeks investments in companies with a proprietary enabling technology in IT, communications, and life sciences.

Geographic Preference: New England
Fund Size: $1-5 million
Investment Criteria: Early Stage
Industry Group Preference: Software, Hardware, Communications, Drug Discovery, Medical Devices, Semiconductor Manufacturing, Alternative Power
Portfolio Companies: BioTrove, LumeRx, Inc., Avedro, Inc., SiteScape, Inc.

Key Executives:
Alfred S Woodworth Jr, Managing Director
Education: AB, Harvard College; MBA, Amos Tuck School at Dartmouth
Background: State Street Bank; Director, Strategic Development, Commercial Banking Group
A Leigh Fulmer, Director Investor Relations
Education: cum laude, Finance, Boston University
Background: Manager, Investor Relations, Brodeur Worldwide

648 ECLIPSE VENTURES
514 High Street
Suite 4
Palo Alto, CA 94301
Phone: 650-720-4667
e-mail: admin@eclipse.vc
web: eclipse.vc

Mission Statement: Eclipse Ventures partners with companies who wish to transform and redefine industries.

Founded: 2015
Investment Criteria: Early Stage
Industry Group Preference: Artificial Intelligence, Automotive, Semiconductor, Manufacturing, Networking, Communications
Portfolio Companies: 6 River Systems, Angury, AxleHire, Bright Machines, BrightInsights, Cerebras Systems, Cheetah, ClearMetal, Clearpath Robotics, Common Networks, Flex Logix Technologies, InsidePacket, Impossible Aerospace, Instrumental, Invicta Medical, June Life, Kindred, Kinema Systems, Light, Lucira Health, Owlet Baby Care, Oxide, Reliable Robotics, Skyryse, Spell, Swift Navigation, SwipeSense, Symbio Robotics, Tenstorrent, Third Wave Automation, Tortuga Logic, Veev, VulcanForms, Wayve

Key Executives:
Lior Susan, Founding Partner
e-mail: lior@eclipse.vc
Background: Advisor, Intucell; Founder, Flextronics; General Partner, Formation 8; Co-Founder, Farm2050; Co-Founder, Bright Machines; Angel Investor

Pierre Lamond, Partner
e-mail: pierre@eclipse.vc
Education: MS, Physics, University of Toulouse, France
Background: Co-Founder/CTO/GM, National Semiconductor; General Partner, Sequoia Capital; General Partner, Khosla Ventures; Senior Advisor, Formation 8
Greg Reichow, Partner
e-mail: greg.reichow@eclipse.vc
Education: BS, Mechanical & Industrial Engineering, University of Minnesota
Background: Cypress Semiconductor; SVP of Operations, SunPower; VP of Operations/Production, Tesla Motors
Seth Winterroth, Partner
e-mail: seth@eclipse.vc
Directorships: Invicta Medical; Third Wave Automation; Wayve
Adam Bryant, Partner
e-mail: adam@eclipse.vc
Education: BS, Mechanical Engineering, Worcester Polytechnic Institute; MS, Mechanical Engineering, Northeastern University; MBA, Harvard Business School
Background: Lead Design Engineer, GE Aviation; Director of Product Control, Tesla Motors, Director of Customer Programs, Proterra Inc.
Justin Butler, Partner
e-mail: justin@eclipse.vc
Education: BS, Chemical Engineering, University of California, Santa Barbara; MBA, MIT Sloan School of Management
Background: Process Engineer, DuPont; Director of Business Development, Synthetic Genomics; VP of Commercial Development, Misfit Wearables
Directorships: Lucira Health; Tenstorrent Inc.; Common Networks; Tortuga Logic Inc.; Dragonfly Group; Spell; BrightInsight
Greg Lyon, Operating Partner/CFO
e-mail: greg@eclipse.vc
Education: BS, Accounting, Sonoma State University
Background: Manager, Financial Services, PricewaterCooper; Financial Manager, Sequoia Capital; Controller, Formation 8

649 ECOAST ANGEL NETWORK
Portsmouth, NH
e-mail: ecoastangels@gmail.com
web: www.ecoastangels.com

Mission Statement: The eCoast Angel Network was formed in July 2000 by a group of like-minded investors from the Portsmouth NH area. Our members come from diverse backgrounds but have a unified purpose: to support economic development, principally in the Coast region, to foster entrepreneurial spirit and to identify investment opportunities.

Geographic Preference: New Hampshire Coastal Region
Average Investment: $250,000 - $2 million
Investment Criteria: Early-Stage
Industry Group Preference: Technology, E-Commerce & Manufacturing, Healthcare, Industrial Products
Portfolio Companies: Aras, AtlasWatersystems, Bortech, CitySquares, Content Raven, Environments@Work LLC, Groove Mobile, IAM Registry, In Addition, FastAsset, Parcxmart, Punchbowl, SemiNex, SingleToken Security, SmartPackets, SourceIQ, StatSocial, Thebizmo, V-Kernel, Vaward Communications, ZipRealty

650 ECOSYSTEM VENTURES
P.O. Box 3347
Saratoga, CA 95070
Phone: 408-426-8040 Fax: 408-867-1441
e-mail: info@ecosystemventures.com
web: www.ecosystemventures.com

Mission Statement: A venture capital investment and strategic consulting firm that is dedicated to building sustainable companies around significant technologies and innovative business ideas. We focus primarily, but not exclusively on companies that are based in Europe or have strong European ties.

Investment Criteria: Startup/Seed, Early Stage
Industry Group Preference: Clean Technology, Industrial, Technology, Energy
Portfolio Companies: AngelList, Appstores Inc., Attolight AG, Autonet Mobile, Bartab, Checkbook, Cleanify, cloudGuide SA, Collanos AG, Dekko, Draft, Facebook, Gladiator Entertainment, GolfNet, Graphic.ly, Illumenix, I Need MD, Investiere.ch, Lagotek, LESS, MamaMancini's, Microventures LLC, MixRank Inc., Mobile Mantra Inc., MothersClick, MXD3D Inc., Nanotion AG, NexTier Networks, NoiseToys, Oasis Media Corporation, OpenPeak, Philz Coffee, PlaySpanTM, Pooch, PowerInbox, Pure Swiss Water AG, Rainforest, rVita, SchooLa Inc., SDK Biotechnologies, shopobot Inc., Simplibuy, SpaceX, Spectralus Corporation, Squirro AG, StarStreet Inc., Storefront Inc., SVOX AG, TimeSight Systems, Twitter, VEENOME Inc., visual.ly, VoiceBase, Zikon, Zubio

Other Locations:
60 Weingartenstrasse
Zurich 8708 Mannedorf
Switzerland
Phone: +41 (44) 586-7108 **Fax:** +41 (44) 790-2187

Key Executives:
Alexander Fries, General Partner
Education: BA Finance/MBA Telecommunications, University of San Francisco; Swiss Banking Diploma, UBS
Background: Telecommunications Analyst, Credit Suisse; Executive Vice President of Sales & Marketing, Advance Visual Communications; Senior Market Manager, Lucent Technologies Wireless Broadband Division

651 EDELSON TECHNOLOGY PARTNERS
180 Summit Avenue
Suite 205
Montvale, NJ 07645
Phone: 201-930-9898 **Fax:** 201-930-8899
web: www.edelsontech.com

Mission Statement: Edelson Technology Partners is a venture capital firm focused on providing support to multinational technology corporations in the areas of venture capital, consulting, and mergers and acquisitions.

Geographic Preference: Mostly United States, Europe, Asia, Canada
Fund Size: $150 million
Founded: 1984
Average Investment: $1 - $3 million
Investment Criteria: Seed, Startups, First-Stage, Second-Stage, Later Stage, Mezzanine
Industry Group Preference: Technology, Telecommunications, Life Sciences, Software, Environment, Consumer, Internet
Portfolio Companies: EXA, GIGA, Lifelines Technology, Lithium Technology, Portable Energy Products, Satcom, Savoy Entertainment Group, Vehicular Technologies, xSides

Key Executives:
Harry Edelson, Founder/Managing Director
e-mail: harry@edelsontech.com
Education: BS, Physics, Brooklyn College; MBA, Management, New York University
Background: Computer Engineer, Unisys; Transmission Engineer, AT&T; CEO, Special Purpose Acquisition Company; Founder & President, China Investment Group

652 EDF VENTURES
425 North Main Street
Ann Arbor, MI 48104-1147
Phone: 734-663-3213 **Fax:** 734-663-7358

Mission Statement: EDF Ventures invests in growing companies that are early in their development, with a focus on untapped markets.

Geographic Preference: Midwest
Fund Size: $170 million
Founded: 1987
Average Investment: $1.5 - $5 million
Minimum Investment: $500,000
Investment Criteria: Early-Stage
Industry Group Preference: Healthcare, Information Technology
Portfolio Companies: AlfaLight, Alure, Arbor Networks, Arxan, BioSet, Cerensis Therapeutics, DirectFlow Medical, Eleme Medical, GenVec, Greenplum, HandyLab, HealthCareSolutions, IntelePeer, IntraLase, Lycera, Pixelworks, QuadraSpec, Sircon, Sonoma Orthopedic Products, TransCorp, ValenTx, Vontoo, Xtera, Zyray Wireless

Key Executives:
Mary Lincoln Campbell, Founder/Managing Director
Education: BA, English, MBA, University of Michigan; MA, Special Education, Fairfield University
Directorships: IntelePeer, ValenTx
Mike DeVries, Managing Director
Education: BA, Calvin College; MBA, Grand Valley State University
Background: President & CEO, A-Med Systems; Medtronic; DLP
Directorships: CardioMetrix, Direct Flow Medical
Linda Fingerle, Chief Financial Officer/Principal
Education: Michigan State University; MBA, Ross School of Business, University of Michigan; CPA
Background: Group Operating President, MascoTech; Senior Audit Manager, Arthur Andersen & Co.

653 EDGEWATER CAPITAL PARTNERS
5005 Rockside Road
Suite 840
Independence, OH 44131
Phone: 216-292-3838
e-mail: info@edgewatercapital.com
web: www.edgewatercapital.com

Mission Statement: Private equity investment firm focused on investing in lower middle market specialty performance material companies.

Geographic Preference: North America
Fund Size: $85 million
Founded: 1980
Average Investment: $10 - $50 million
Minimum Investment: $2 million
Investment Criteria: Corporate Divestitures, Family Businesses, Management Buyouts
Industry Group Preference: Technology, Chemicals, Distribution, Manufacturing, Pharmaceuticals
Portfolio Companies: Callery, ChemQuest chemicals, DanChem, Far Chemical Inc., FMI, Gabriel Performance Products, H&S, Haematologic Technologies, Lycus Ltd., Naprotek, Particle Dynamics, PChem, PolyAd Services, Preferred Rubber, Pure Wafer, Royal Adhesives & Sealands, Syrgis Performance Initiators, Tractech Inc., Tritec Performance Solutions, Turbonetics

Key Executives:
Christopher Childres, Founder/Managing Partner
Education: BA, English & American Literature, Northwestern University; JD, Fordham University School of Law
Background: Attorney, M&A Department, Winthrop, Stimson, Putnam & Roberts
Directorships: Lycus Chemical, Hahn Elastomer, Royal Adhesives and Sealants
Ryan Meany, Managing Partner
Education: BS, Business Administration, Miami University; MBA, Case Western Reserve University
Background: Investment Analyst, NatCity Investments

Venture Capital & Private Equity Firms / Domestic Firms

Richard Schwarz, Partner
Education: BS, Chemical Engineering, Ohio State University; MBA, Case Western Reserve University
Background: Founder, Sycamore Partners LLC; Director & President, Laurel Industries; Management Consultant, AT Kearney
Directorships: Syrgis

Brian Leonard, Chief Financial Officer/Chief Compliance Officer
Education: BS, Accounting, Miami University
Background: Director, Transaction Advisory Services, Grant Thornton LLP; VP, Finance, Workflow.com
Directorships: Cleveland Chapter of the Association for Corporate Growth

654 EDGEWATER FUNDS
900 North Michigan Avenue
Suite 1800
Chicago, IL 60611

Phone: 312-649-5666
web: www.edgewaterfunds.com

Mission Statement: Based in Chicago, The Edgewater Funds is a private equity firm focused on providing lower middle market companies with resources to help drive their growth.

Fund Size: $1.4 billion
Minimum Investment: $10 - $20 million
Investment Criteria: Lower Middle Market, Buyouts, Growth Equity
Industry Group Preference: Business to Business, Information Technology, Software, Consumer Services, Service Industries, Services, Biotechnology
Portfolio Companies: Accutest Laboratories, American Piping Products, AMF, Apex Parks Group, Avante Health Solutions, BarrirerSafe Solutions International, Beverage House, Bolder Healthcare Solutions, Brilliance Financial Technology, Confluent Health, Dantom Systems Inc., DataBank, DBS Communications Inc., Deflecto, Dental Services Group, ETX, Extended Care Information Network, ExteNet Systems, Family Home Health Services, FishNet Security, Genesis Financial Solutions, G&H Orthodontics, Harrington Holdings Inc., Helicon Re, Horseburgh & Scott Co., Industrial Service Solutions, ITSolutions, Med America Recycling, Teddy Bear Portraits, NetCentrics, Nielsen-Kellerman, Orizon, PGI International, PowerQuest, Priority Express, Private Bancorp Inc., Rensa Filtration, Salter Labs, Sechrist Industries Inc., Sensor Solutions Holdings, Skyware Global, Testing Services Holdings, Southern Petroleum Laboratories Inc., State National Companies, Steel & OBbrien Manufacturing, TAL International, Technical Solutions Holdings Inc., Trausch Industries, Triwater Holdings, Unitech Aerospace, Vertical Bridge, Westar Aerospace & Defense Group, Would Care Solutions Inc., WRSCompass

Key Executives:

James Gordon, Founder/Managing Partner
e-mail: jim@edgewaterfunds.com
Education: BA, Northwestern University
Background: President, Gordon Foods; Gordon's Wholesale

Gregory Jones, Partner
e-mail: greg@edgewaterfunds.com
Education: BS, Miami University; MBA, Kellogg Graduate School of Management, Northwestern University
Background: President & COO, Reliable Corporation; Senior VP, APAC Teleservices; Chairman & CEO, uBid.com

David Tolmie, Partner
e-mail: dave@edgewaterfunds.com
Education: BA, University of Virginia; MBA, Harvard Business School
Background: CEO & President, Yesmail; Senior VP, Operations, Bally Total Fitness; Consultant, McKinsey & Company; Product Manager, General Mills
Directorships: Field Museum of Natural History, Opportunity International, Illinois Venture Capital Association, Chicagoland Entrepreneurial Center

Scott Brown, Partner
e-mail: scottbedgewaterfunds.com
Education: BA, Economics, Colgate University; MBA, Booth School of Business
Background: Baird Capital Partners; JP Morgan

Jeffrey Frient, Partner
e-mail: jeff@edgewaterfunds.com
Education: BS, US Air Force Academy; MBA, Harvard Business School
Background: Partner, William Blair & Company; F-16 Pilot, US Air Force

Brian Peiser, Partner
e-mail: brianp@edgewaterfunds.com
Education: BS, Electrical Engineering, Cornell University; MBA, University of Michigan Business School; CFA
Background: Senior Associate, Deloitte & Touche Corporate Finance; Senior Analyst, Lehman Brothers

Gerald Saltarelli, Partner
e-mail: gerald@edgewaterfunds.com
Education: BA, Bucknell University; MBA, University of Michigan Business School
Background: Director, Conway MacKenzie & Dunleavy; Associate, One Equity Partners; Analyst, M&A Group, William Blair & Company

Stephen Natali, Partner
e-mail: stephen@edgewaterfunds.com
Education: BA, Economics, Northwestern University
Background: Associate, Investment Banking Division, JP Morgan Securities

Scott Meadow, Associate Partner
e-mail: scott.meadow@chicagobooth.edu
Education: AB, Harvard College; MBA, Harvard Business School
Background: Clinical Professor of Entrepreneurship, University of Chicago; General Partner, The Sprout Group

655 EDISON PARTNERS
281 Witherspoon Street
Princeton, NJ 08540

Phone: 609-896-1900
web: www.edisonpartners.com

Mission Statement: Edison Partners provides financing and guidance to growth companies. They are a leading investor focused on information technology companies located in the Mid-Atlantic region of the United States.

Geographic Preference: Boston to DC Corridor
Fund Size: $550 million
Founded: 1986
Average Investment: $6 - 10 million
Minimum Investment: $5 - 8 million
Investment Criteria: Venture Capital, Expansion, Acquisition, Consolidation, Secondary Stock, MBO, Corporate Spinout, Recapitalization
Industry Group Preference: Information Technology, Software, Communications, Internet Technology, Electronic Technology, Financial Services, Pharmaceuticals, Fintech, Healthcare Information Technology, Marketing, E-Commerce & Manufacturing, Enterprise Applications
Portfolio Companies: Act!, All Traffic Solutions, Andera, Archive Systems, Arkadium, Axent, Axial, Best!, BFS Capital, Bill Trust, Blue Cod Technologies, Bricata, Cadient Group, CambridgeSoft, Check Point HR, Clearpool, ClearPoint, Clinverse, ComplySci, Dendrite, DPM, Diagnosis One, Edge Trade, Esentire, EVO, Fiberlink, Fishbowl, FolioDynamix, Gain Capital, GAN Integrity, Giant Realm, Health Market Science, High Branch Software, IContracts, Itemmaster, IQ Media, Incurrent, Jornaya, Kemp Technologies, Kds, Liberty Tax Service, Lincor, Logfire, LookBookHQ, M5, Magnetic, Mathsoft, MDY, MoneyLion, Motionsoft, Neat, Netprospex, NFR Security, Notable

Venture Capital & Private Equity Firms / Domestic Firms

Solutions, Octagon Research Soltuions Inc., Operative, Options City, PHX, Pixability, Plum Choice, Portico, Predata, Presidium, Princeton Financial Systems, Realmatch, Receptiv, Red Vision, Rewards Now, Salsa, Scivantage, Sentori, Signet Accel, Smartanalyst, Softgate Systems, Solovis, Sonicbids, Tangoe, Tartec, Telarix, Terminus, TetraData, Tracx, TraderTools, TrialScope, TripleLift, Truecommerce, Uptivity, Verilogue, VFA, VirtualEdge, Virutal Health, Visual Networks, Vocus, VoxMobile, Wyng, Zagster, Zelis

Key Executives:
Ryan Ziegler, General Partner
609-873-9225
e-mail: ryan@edisonpartners.com
Education: BS, Business Administration, BA, Biology, Bucknell University
Background: Associates Program, SEI
Directorships: Jornaya, Magnetic, Receptiv, Offerpop, Tracx, Terminus, TripleLift
Chris Sugden, Managing Partner
e-mail: csugden@edisonpartners.com
Education: BA, Accounting, Michigan State University
Background: EVP, Princeton eCom; Supervisor, PricewaterhouseCoopers
Tom Vander Schaaff, General Partner
e-mail: tvanderschaaff@edisonpartners.com
Education: BEng., Engineering/Management Systems, Princeton University
Background: Senior Associate, MMC Capital; Associate, CIBC Capital Partners; Financial Analyst, CIB Oppenheimer's Technology Investment Banking Group
Michael Kopelman, General Partner
e-mail: mkopelman@edisonpartners.com
Education: BA, Economics, University of Pennsylvania; MBA, Wharton School
Background: Investment Banker, Credit Suisse First Boston; Founder, E*OFFERING; Co-President, Wharton Private Equity Partners
Lenard Marcus, General Partner
e-mail: lmarcus@edisonpartners.com
Education: BA, Industrial Engineering, Stanford University; MBA, Columbia Business School
Background: Financial Analyst, IBM Global Services; Manager, Princeton eCom; Investment Banker, Wachovia Securities
Kelly Ford Buckley, General Partner
e-mail: kford@edisonpartners.com
Education: BA, Michigan State University
Background: SundaySky; LivePerson; Lotus; Groove Network

656 EGL HOLDINGS
3017 Bolling Way NE
No 18 Buckhead
Atlanta, GA 30305

Phone: 404-949-8300
e-mail: salmassaro@eglholdings.com
web: www.eglholdings.com

Mission Statement: Venture capital and corporate finance advisory services to companies in a wide variety of industries and geographical markets.

Geographic Preference: Southwestern United States
Fund Size: $70 million
Founded: 1988
Average Investment: $100,000 - $500,000
Investment Criteria: Mergers & Acquisitions, Divestiture, Expansion, Later Stage
Industry Group Preference: Medical Devices, Enterprise Software, Communications, Information Technology, Healthcare, Technology
Portfolio Companies: Echo11, Intellinet, MET-TEST, The Pedowitz Group, Purple Cows, SimCraft, SpeedTracs

Key Executives:
Richard V Lawry, Co-Founder/Chairman/Managing Partner
404-949-8306
e-mail: rlawry@eglholdings.com
Background: Co-Founder & President, British American Business Group; Divisional Accountant, BICC plc; Glynwed International; Atlanta Arrangements
Directorships: Airo Wireless, Alliance Theater
David O Ellis, Managing Partner
404-949-8310
e-mail: doellis@eglholdings.com
Education: BS, Chemistry, PhD, Biophysics, St. Andrews University; Senior Executive Program, MIT
Background: COO & CEO, BH Blackwell; CFO, Software Sciences International; Oxford Instruments plc
Salvatore A Massaro, Managing Director
404-949-8303
e-mail: samassaro@eglholdings.com
Education: BS, Business Administration, Georgetown University; MBA, Harvard University
Background: Prudential-Bache Venture Capital; Telesphere International; Price Waterhouse
Charles Elliott, Senior Vice President
704-300-8650
e-mail: celliott@eglholdings.com
Education: MBA, University of North Carolina, Charlotte
Tom McDermott, Managing Director
e-mail: tmcdermott@eglholdings.com
Education: MBA, University of North Carolina at Chapel Hill

657 ELEMENT PARTNERS
565 E Swedesford Road
Suite 207
Wayne, PA 19087

Phone: 610-964-8004 Fax: 610-964-8005
e-mail: patti@elementpartners.com
web: www.elementpartners.com

Mission Statement: Element Partners is a private equity firm focused on growth equity investments in companies that offer innovative products and services to the industrial, energy and environment industries.

Fund Size: $800 million
Founded: 1995
Average Investment: $10 - $50 million
Investment Criteria: Greater than $20 million in revenue, enterprise values between $20 to $200 million, Acquisitions, MBO, LBO, Corporate Divestitures, Industry Consolidations, Minority Investments
Industry Group Preference: Energy, Clean Technology, Manufacturing, Water, Environmental Controls, Chemicals, Advanced Materials
Portfolio Companies: 212 Resources, Agility Fuel Systems, Amp Electrical Distribution Services, AquaVenture Holdings, Detechtion Technologies, Ecore, Energex, Hayward Gordon, LumaSense Technologies, Petra Systems, Quench USA, Seven Seas Water, Soleras Advanced Coatings, TAS Energy, TPI Composites

Key Executives:
David Lincoln, Founder & General Partner
e-mail: david@elementpartners.com
Education: BA, Geology, Colgate University; MS, Energy Management & Policy, University of Pennsylvania
Background: Co-Founder & Managing Director, EnerTech Capital Partners; President & CEO, Deven Resources; Partners, CMS Companies; UGI Corporation
Directorships: 212 Resources, Amp, Detechtion, Electro-Petroleum, Environmental Drilling Solutions, Petra Solar, Wasatch Wind
Michael DeRosa, General Partner
e-mail: mderosa@elementpartners.com
Education: BS, Electrical Engineering, Georgia Tech; MBA, Wharton School, University of Pennsylvania

Venture Capital & Private Equity Firms / Domestic Firms

Background: Partner, Industrial Technology Fund, Cordova Ventures; Principal, EnerTech Capital Partners; Senior Associate, Safeguard International Fund
Directorships: Agility Fuel Systems, AMP Electrical Distribution Services, Detechtion Technologies, Ecore International, TPI Composites, TAS Energy
Michael Bevan, General Partner
e-mail: michael@elementpartners.com
Education: BA, English, Denison University; MBA, Wharton School
Background: Partner, Advent International; Principal, EnerTech Capital Partners; SEI Investments

658 ELEVATE VENTURES
50 East 91st Street
Suite 213
Indianapolis, IN 46240

Phone: 317-975-1901
web: www.elevateventures.com

Mission Statement: Elevate Ventures nurtures and develops emerging and existing high-potential businesses into high-performing, Indiana-based companies.
Geographic Preference: Indiana
Founded: 2011
Industry Group Preference: Life Sciences, Information Technology, Advanced Manufacturing
Portfolio Companies: 3BG Supply Co., Apl Next Ed, AgenDx Biosciences, AIT Bioscience, Animated Dynamics Inc., Apexian Pharmaceuticals, App Press, AquaSpy, Atlas 3D, Baby Plus, Blue Pillar, Bolstra, Clear Object, Clear Scholar, Compendium, Confuence Pharmaceuticals, Costello, Curvo, Diagnotes, Emerging Threats, Fast BioMedical, FNEX, Go Electric, Hc1.com, Healthcare Anywhere, Immune Works, Inscope, Jada Beauty, Kinney Group, Lumavate, Market Wagon, MyCoi, Oak Financial, Owl Manor Veterinary, PactSafe, PartTec, PayK12, PDS Biotechnology, Edwin, PolicyStat, Prosolia, RedPost, Salesvue, Sharpen, Sigstr, Smarter HQ, Smartfile, Solstice Medical, SonarMed, Spensa, Springbuk, SproutBox, SteadyServ Technologies, Stray Light, Sword Diagnostics, Targamite, The Bee Corp, Theratome Bio, Trek10, Ultra Angkle, Upper Hand Managed Sports, Vennli, Verve Health, VoCare, Wellfount, Wolfe Diversified, Wolfpack, Wordsentry, Xtreme Alternative Defense Systems, Zio

Key Executives:
Chris LaMothe, Chief Executive Officer
Education: Kelley School of Business, University of Indiana
Ting Gootee, Chief Investments Officer
Education: BA, Beijing University; MA, Purdue University; MBA, Finance, Indiana University
Background: Deputy Director, 21 Fund
Ken Miller, Chief Operating Officer
Background: Partner, DeveloperTown; IT Operations, MISCO

659 ELEVATION PARTNERS
352 Sharon Park Drive
Suite 522
Menlo Park, CA 94025

Phone: 650-687-6700 Fax: 650-687-6710
e-mail: info@elevation.com
web: www.elevation.com

Mission Statement: A leading private equity firm focused on large-scale investments in media, entertainment and technology businesses.
Industry Group Preference: Media, Entertainment, Digital Media & Marketing, Software
Portfolio Companies: BioWare/Pandemic Studios, Facebook, Forbes, MarketShare, Move, Palm, Yelp

Key Executives:
Fred Anderson, Managing Director & Co-Founder
Education: BA, Whittier College; MBA, University of California, LA
Background: Executive Vice President, Apple Computer
Directorships: Apple, Crystal Decisions, 3COM
Roger McNamee, Managing Director & Co-Founder
Education: BA, Yale College; MBA, Amos Tuck School of Business Administration, Dartmouth College
Background: Co-Founder, Silver Lake Partners; Co-Founder, Integral Capital Partners
Bret Pearlman, Managing Director & Co-Founder
Education: BS, Economics, Wharton School, University of Pennsylvania; BS, Engineering, Moore School of Electrical Engineering
Background: Analyst, Blackstone Group
Directorships: BioWare/Pandemic Studios, SDI Media, Forbes Media
Avie Tevanian, Managing Director
Education: BA, Mathematics, University of Rochester; MS & PhD, Computer Science, Carnegie Mellon University
Background: Senior Executive Team, Apple, Inc.; Vice President, Software Engineering, NeXT Computer
Directorships: Dolby Laboratories, Tellme Networks
Adam Hopkins, Managing Director & Founding Member
Education: AB, Economics, Princeton University; MBA, Stanford University Graduate School of Business
Background: Associate, Silver Lake Partners; Morgan Stanley Capital Partners

660 ELM STREET VENTURES
33 Whitney Avenue
New Haven, CT 06510

Phone: 203-401-4201
e-mail: venture@elmvc.com
web: www.elmvc.com

Mission Statement: Elm Street Ventures offers experience and venture capital to seed and early stage businesses and is dedicated to helping entrepreneurs, scientists and engineers build significant technology and life sciences companies.
Fund Size: $22 million
Average Investment: $100,000 - $2.5 million
Minimum Investment: $100,000
Investment Criteria: Seed-Stage, Early-Stage
Industry Group Preference: Life Sciences, Diagnostics, Medical Devices, Therapeutics, Healthcare Information Technology, Healthcare Services
Portfolio Companies: Accelerated Orthopedic Technologies, Affomix Corporation, Ancera Corporation, Arvinas Corporation, AxioMx, BioRelix, Desmos, Iconic Therapeutics, Kolltan Pharmaceuticals, Occam Sciences, P2 Science, Retail Optimization, Samara Innovations, ScrollMotion, ShareGrove

Key Executives:
Rob Bettigole, Managing Partner
Education: BS, Engineering & Applied Science, Yale University; MPPM, Yale School of Management
Background: Partner, Rothschild Inc.; Partner, Investor AB; Founder, Surety Technologies
Directorships: AxioMx, Samara Innovations, Affomix Corporation, Metagenomix
Chris McLeod, Managing Partner
Education: BS, Yale University; MS, Sloan School of Management, MIT
Background: CEO, AxioMx; President/CEO, 454 Life Sciences; EVP, CuraGen; CEO, Havas Interative
Brian Dixon, Venture Partner
Education: BS, University of Michigan; PhD, Organic Chemistry, MIT
Background: VP, Bayer HealthCare; Presient/CEO, BioRelix Inc.
Rick Stahl, Venture Partner
Education: BS, Physics, Emory University; MD,

Vanderbilt University; MBA, University of New Haven
Background: Limited Partner, Sachem Ventures; Senior Associate Dean for Strategic Relationships, Frank H. Netter MD School of Medicine, Quinnipiac University; VP, Yale New Haven Health System

661 ELYSIUM VENTURE CAPITAL
440 N Wolfe Road
Sunnyvale, CA 94085

Phone: 408-524-1600
e-mail: contact@elysium.vc
web: ely.vc

Mission Statement: Elysium's experienced team offers guidance in Business Development, International Markets, Deal Structuring, Strategy, Recruiting, and Product Marketing.
Geographic Preference: US, Europe, China
Investment Criteria: Early Stage, Growth Stage
Industry Group Preference: Consumer Tech, Blockchain, Fintech, Artificial Intelligence
Portfolio Companies: Acquired.io, Alpaca, Anchorage, Capture.io, Flo, Knack, LoóNa, Node, Prisma, Telegram
Key Executives:
   Peter Xu, Managing Partner
   Background: Head of Alternative Investments, Galaxy Group
   Nikolai Roeshkin, Managing Partner
   Eric Ly, Venture Partner
   Background: Co-Founder/CTO, LinkedIn
   William O'Brien, Venture Partner

662 EMBARK HEALTHCARE
web: www.embarkhc.com

Mission Statement: Embark Healthcare invests in repurposing drugs. The company works with pharmaceutical companies in the later stage of their business to license and increase the potential benefit of both investors and patients in need.
Founded: 2001
Average Investment: $250,000 - $1 million
Investment Criteria: Later Stage
Industry Group Preference: Healthcare, Pharmaceutical
Portfolio Companies: Learmont Pharmaceuticals, Martin Pharmaceuticals, Remedy Pharmaceuticals, Woolsey Pharmaceuticals
Key Executives:
   David M Geliebter, Managing Partner
   e-mail: david@embarkhc.com
   Background: Founder, Carson Group; Founding Principal/President, Evolution Capital; Founder, Harvard Capital
   Directorships: Chairman/CEO, Critical Diagnostics; Executive Chairman, Remedy Pharmaceuticals
   Sven M Jacobson, Partner
   e-mail: sven@embarkhc.com
   Education: BSc, Electrical Engineering, MBA, Business Administration & Management, University of the Witwatersrand
   Background: Vice President, Leisureplanet; Board Member, Rennies Travel and Financial Services Group
   Directorships: Critical Diagnostics, Remedy Pharmaceuticals

663 EMBARK VENTURES
610 Santa Monica Boulevard
Suite 226
Santa Monica, CA 90401

web: www.embark.com

Mission Statement: Embark Ventures invests in "deep tech" companies, within sectors such as life sciences, material science, robotics, automation, semiconductors, software computing and manufacturing.
Founded: 2017
Investment Criteria: Pre-Seed, Seed
Industry Group Preference: Security, Life Science, Manufacturing, Robotics, Material Science, Semiconductors
Portfolio Companies: Avro Life Sciences, CellFE, InVia Robotics, Jiko, K2 Cyber Security, Kebotix, Kula Bio, SafeAI, SeqOnce, Syntiant, Truvian Health, Via Separations
Key Executives:
   Yipeng Zhao, Managing Partner
   Education: BS, Michigan State University; MS, University of California, San Diego
   Background: Managing Partner, ArcheMatrix Investment Group
   Directorships: ZMXY Global Investment Inc.
   Peter Lee, Managing Partner
   Education: BS/MS, MIT; MBA, Harvard Business School
   Background: Product Manager/Senior Engineer, Virtual Ink; Junior Engagement Manager, McKinsey & Company; Managing Director, Fortis Partners; Associate, Clearstone Venture Partners; Investor, Prism Venture; Managing Partner, Baroda Ventures

664 EMERALD OCEAN CAPITAL
1300 Dove Street
Suite 210
Newport Beach, CA 92660

Phone: 949-468-7474

Mission Statement: Invests in companies focused on technology, life sciences and media within the cannabis industry.
Founded: 2013
Industry Group Preference: Cannabis, Life Sciences, Technology
Key Executives:
   Doug Francis, Managing Partner
   Education: BS, George L. Argyros School of Business Economics, Chapman University
   Background: Co-Founder/COO, Canna-Centers; CEO, Weedmaps
   Justin Hartfield, Managing Partner
   Education: BS, Computer & Information Sciences, University of California Irvine; MBA, Paul Merage School of Business
   Background: CEO/Chairman, Weedmaps; SearchCore
   Jerry Lotter, Managing Partner
   Education: BA, International Relations; BS, International Business, Marshall School of Business, University of Southern California
   Background: Co-Founder/Managing Member, Bonfire.com; COO, SearchCore

665 EMERGENCE CAPITAL PARTNERS
160 Bovet Road
Suite 300
San Mateo, CA 94402

Phone: 650-573-3100
e-mail: hello@emcap.com
web: www.emcap.com

Mission Statement: Venture capital firm focused on investing in early and growth-stage enterprise technology companies.
Geographic Preference: United States
Fund Size: $335 million
Founded: 2003
Average Investment: $1 - $10 million
Investment Criteria: Early-Stage, Growth-Stage
Industry Group Preference: Technology-Enabled Services, SaaS, Consumer Services, Digital Media & Marketing, Social Media, Information Services, Cloud Computing
Portfolio Companies: Augmedix, Bill.com, Box, Civitas Learning, Cotap, Crunchbase, Digital Air Strike, Donuts,

Venture Capital & Private Equity Firms / Domestic Firms

Doximity, Drivewyze, DroneDeploy, EchoSign, Eversight, Gusto, Handshake, High Alpha, Hightail, InsideView, Insightly, Intacct, Janrain, Lithium, Lotame, Medeanalytics, Navera, Quasar Ventures, Replicon, Restorando, Salesforce.com, SalesLoft, ServiceMax, SteelBrick, SuccessFactors, Textio, Top Hat, TouchCommerce, Veeva Systems, VigLink, Welltok, Xad, Xapo, Yammer, Zoom

Key Executives:
   Jason Green, Founder/General Partner
   e-mail: jgreen@emcap.com
   Education: BA, Economics, Dartmouth College; MBA, Harvard University
   Background: General Partner, US Venture Partners; Bain & Company; Carson, Anderson & Stowe
   Directorships: CoTap, Lotame, Replicon, ServiceMax, SteelBrick, SalesLoft, xAd
   Gordon Ritter, General Partner
   e-mail: gritter@emcap.com
   Education: BA, Economics, Princeton University
   Background: Co-Founder & CEO, Software As Service; Co-Founder & President, Whistle; Co-Founder, Tribe Communications; VP, Capital Markets, Credit Suisse First Boston
   Directorships: Ketera Technologies, MarketingGenius
   Brian Jacobs, General Partner
   e-mail: bjacobs@emcap.com
   Education: BS, MS, Mechanical Engineering, Massachusetts Institute of Technology; MBA, Stanford University
   Background: General Partner, St. Paul Venture Capital; Security Pacific Venture Capital; Raychem Corporation
   Directorships: Visage Mobile, Krugle, Intacct, DVDPlay
   Kevin Spain, General Partner
   e-mail: kspain@emcap.com
   Education: BBA, University of Texas, Austin; MBA, Wharton School, University of Pennsylvania
   Background: Corporate Development, Microsoft; Electronic Arts; Co-Founder & CEO, atMadison.com
   Santi Subotovsky, Partner
   e-mail: ssubotovsky@emcap.com
   Education: BS, Economics, St. Andrew's University, Argentina; MBA, Harvard Business School
   Background: Advisor, Aqua Capital Partners; Associate, Storm Ventures; Founder, AXG Tecnonexo
   Everett Cox, Venture Partner
   e-mail: ecox@emcap.com
   Education: BS, MS, Stanford University; MBA, University of Southern California
   Background: General Partner, St. Paul Venture Capital; Senior VP, Security Pacific Capital
   Joe Floyd, General Partner
   e-mail: jfloyd@emcap.com
   Education: BA, Economics, BS, Business Administration, University of California, Berkeley; MBA, Wharton School, University of Pennsylvania
   Background: Senior Associate, Technology Group, American Capital

666 EMERGENT MEDICAL PARTNERS
1735 North First Street
Suite 290
San Jose, CA 95112

Phone: 650-851-0091 Fax: 650-851-0095
e-mail: eassist@empllp.com
web: www.emvllp.com

Mission Statement: A life sciences investment firm experienced in the medical field, Emergent Medical Partners focuses on early stage healthcare and medical devices companies.

Fund Size: $37 million
Investment Criteria: Early-Stage
Industry Group Preference: Life Sciences, Medical Devices, Healthcare, Medicine

Portfolio Companies: Biomimedica, Cianna Medical, Crux Biomedical, CyberHeart, CytoPherx, Figure 8, Focal Therapeutics, HeartFlow, Hemosphere, ImaCor, Incline Therapeutics, InSite Medical Technologies, Intuity Medical, Nanostim, Niveus Medical, Novare, NovaSom, OncoHealth, Orlucent, Relievant Medsystems, Reverse Medical, Satiety, Sonoma Orthopedic Products, SP Surgical, Stimwave Technologies, TransCorp Spine, Venous Health Systems

Key Executives:
   Thomas J Fogarty MD, Managing Director
   e-mail: info@emvllp.com
   Education: Xavier University; MD, University of Cincinnati
   Background: Clinical Professor of Surgery, Stanford University; President, Medical Staff, Stanford University Medical Center; Director, Cardiovascular Surgery, Sequoia Medical Center; Founder & General Partner, Three Arch Partners
   Kirt Kirtland, Managing Director
   e-mail: jkirtland@empllp.com
   Education: BS, Biology, Stanford University; MBA, Stanford University School of Business
   Bob Brownell, Managing Director
   e-mail: rbrownell@emvllp.com
   Education: BA, University of California, Berkeley; JD, UCLA Law School
   Background: Partner, MedVenture Associates; VP & General Counsel, TheraSense

667 EMIGRANT CAPITAL
6 East 43rd Street
8th Floor
New York, NY 10017

Phone: 917-262-5245
web: www.emigrantcapital.com

Mission Statement: The private equity division of Emigrant Bank, Emigrant Capital provides financial, operational and strategic experience and resources to middle-market companies.

Geographic Preference: United States
Fund Size: $150 million
Founded: 1999
Average Investment: $5 - $20 million
Minimum Investment: $2 million
Investment Criteria: Middle Market, Growth Equity, Recapitalizations, Turnarounds, Buyouts
Industry Group Preference: Branded Goods, Chemicals, Distribution, Financial Services, Healthcare, Manufacturing, Business to Business, Technology, Education, Consumer Products, Consumer Services, Plastics
Portfolio Companies: AC Label, Cascade Drilling LP, CSA Service Solutions, East West Manufacturing, Fire Door Solutions, Intechra, M Cubed

Key Executives:
   William Staudt, Partner
   e-mail: staudtw@emigrant.com
   Education: BA, Economics, Yale University; JD, University of Michigan Law School
   Background: Founding Managing Partner, Environmental Capital Partners; Managing Partner, Hamilton Capital Partners; President & CEO, Sirit
   Robert Nardelli, Partner
   e-mail: nardellir@emigrant.com
   Education: Western Illinois University; MBA, University of Louisville
   Background: Senior Advisor & CEO, Cerberus Operations & Advisory Company; Chairman, President & CEO, The Home Depot; CEO, GE Transportation Systems; GE Power Systems
   Directorships: Pep Boys, Wounded Warrior Project, BWXT Technologies
   Christopher Staudt, Partner
   e-mail: staudtc@emigrant.com

Venture Capital & Private Equity Firms / Domestic Firms

Education: BA, Physics, Pomona College; MBA, Harvard Business School
Background: Co-Founder & Principal, Environmental Capital Partners; CIBC World Markets
Rafael Romero, Principal
e-mail: romeror@emigrant.com
Education: BA, Business Administration, Augustana College; MBA, Harvard Business School
Background: Invesment Professional, Prospect Capital Management; Analyst, Rockwood Equity Partners

668 EMIL CAPITAL PARTNERS
67 Mason Street
Greenwich, CT 06830

Phone: 203-900-1301
web: www.emilcapitalpartners.com

Mission Statement: Emil Capital is an entrepreneurial, private investment company based in Greenwich, Connecticut, and managed by the fifth generation of one of the world's most successful and venerable family business concerns. We select a small number of investments each year enabling us to complement strong, dedicated management teams with our skills, experience and relationships.

Geographic Preference: United States, Canada, Europe
Industry Group Preference: Consumer Products, Distribution, E-Commerce & Manufacturing
Portfolio Companies: 2|Beans, Aloha, American Giant, Amour Vert, Balance Water, Base Culture, Bare Snacks, Bright Farms, Chef's Plate, Cheribundi, Consumer Physics, Data Council, Goodbelly, Green & Tonic, Kidfresh, Kin Community, Klarna, Milk & Honey, NibMor, Ollie, Pasta Chips, Peach, Persona, Sipp, TCHO, Uber, United by Blue, VariBlend Dual Dispensing Systems, Volition Beauty, Whistle Sports, Wish, YouDinner, Zeel

Key Executives:
Christian W.E. Haub, Co-Founder & President
Education: University of Economics & Business Administration, Vienna
Background: Co-CEO, Tengelmann Group; Chairman/President/CEO, The Great Atlantic & Pacific Tea Company; Investment Banking, Dillon Read
Andreas Guldin, Founding Partner & Chief Executive Officer
Education: MS, Psychology, MBA, PhD
Background: EVP/Co-CFO, Tengelmann Group; CSC Index; PA Consulting

669 EMINENT CAPITAL PARTNERS
245 Park Avenue
39th Floor
New York, NY 10167

Phone: 212-372-8950 Fax: 212-419-9499
web: www.eminentcp.com

Mission Statement: Eminent Capital Partners is a private equity investment firm providing operating expertise to ensure the growth of companies.

Geographic Preference: United States
Fund Size: $100 million
Founded: 1999
Average Investment: $5 - $25 million
Minimum Investment: $5 million
Investment Criteria: Revenues of $10 to $100 million, operating margins of at least 10%
Industry Group Preference: Consumer Products, Light Manufacturing, Distribution, Imports/Exports, Business Products & Services, Industrial Products, Luxury Goods
Portfolio Companies: Bi Coastal Media, Card Personalization Solutions, CP Media LLC, Echolab, Jill-e Designs LLC

Key Executives:
Edward Anchel, Partner
Education: Pennsylvania State University
Background: Founder, President & CEO, Sparkomatic Corporation; Altec Lansing
Directorships: Three Springs Bottling Company
Chuck Parente, Partner
Education: King's College; CPA
Background: Haskins & Sells; Founder & CEO, Parente Randolph PC; President & CEO, C-Tec Corporation
Directorships: Bertels Can Co., Circle Bolt & Nut Co., WP Carey & Co., Community Bank Systems
Hagai Barlev, Venture Partner/Board Member
Education: BA, Economics, Hebrew University of Jerusalem; MBA, Kellogg School of Management
Background: Corporate Finance, Deloitte Consulting; Co-Founder, Addwise

670 EMP GLOBAL
1901 Pennsylvania Avenue NW
Suite 300
Washington, DC 20006

Mission Statement: A worldwide private equity firm with the resources and expertise to source, evaluate and manage private investments globally in both developed and developing markets and across many industrial and commercial sectors.

Geographic Preference: Latin America, Africa, Central and Eastern Europe
Founded: 1994
Investment Criteria: Strategic Partner, Local Partner, minimum rate of return criteria, must be infrastructure project
Industry Group Preference: Telecommunications, Water, Power Technologies, Natural Resources, Infrastructure, Transportation, Agriculture, Retailing

Key Executives:
Donald C. Roth, Managing Partner
Education: BA, Politics, Princeton University; MBA, International Finance, University of Chicago; MSc, The London School of Economics in International Monteary Economics
Background: VP/Treasurer, World Bank

671 ENCAP FLATROCK MIDSTREAM
1826 North Loop 1604 West
Suite 200
San Antonio, TX 78248

Phone: 210-494-6777 Fax: 210-494-6762
e-mail: info@efmidstream.com
web: www.efmidstream.com

Mission Statement: Focuses on providing growth capital to proven midstream management teams in North America.

Geographic Preference: North America
Fund Size: $3 billion
Founded: 2008
Average Investment: $25 - $100 million
Investment Criteria: Growth Stage
Industry Group Preference: Energy, Natural Gas, Oil & Gas, Energy Infrastructure
Portfolio Companies: Aspen Midstream, Caiman Energy II, Candor Midstream, Cardinal Midstream III, Clear Creek Midstream, Cogent Midstream, Edgwater Midstream, Evolution Midstream, Greenfield Midstream, Ironwood Midstream Energy Partners II, Lotus Midstream, Moda Midstream, Nuevo Midstream Dos, Rangeland Energy III, Stakeholder Midstream, Tall Oak Midstream

Other Locations:
3856 South Boulevard
Suite 210
Edmond, OK 73013
Phone: 405-341-9993 Fax: 405-341-9973

1100 Louisiana Street
Suite 5025

233

Venture Capital & Private Equity Firms / Domestic Firms

Houston, TX 77002
Phone: 281-829-4901 **Fax:** 281-829-4902
Key Executives:
William D. Waldrip, Founder/Managing Partner
Education: BS, Civil Engineering, Louisiana Tech University; Executive Management Program, Indiana University Graduate School of Business
Background: COO, Lewis Energy Group; VP, Delhi Gas Pipeline
Dennis F. Jaggi, Founder/Managing Partner
Education: BS, Mechanical Engineering, Missouri University of Science & Technology
Background: VP & COO, Enogex; VP & Regional Manager, Delhi Pipeline Corporation
William R. Lemmons, Jr., Founder/Managing Partner
Education: BS, Petroleum Engineering, Texas A&M University; MBA, Mays Graduate School of Business, Texas A&M University
Background: VP, Enron Corporation; Texas Oil & Gas Corporation

672 ENCAP INVESTMENTS LP
1100 Louisiana Street
Suite 4900
Houston, TX 77002
Phone: 713-659-6100 **Fax:** 713-659-6130
web: www.encapinvestments.com
Mission Statement: Provider of private equity to independent oil and gas companies.
Geographic Preference: United States
Fund Size: $6.5 billion
Founded: 1988
Industry Group Preference: Oil & Gas
Portfolio Companies: Advance Energy Partners, American Resource Development, Bold Energy III, Brigadier Oil & Gas, Broad Oak Energy II, Cinco Oil & Gas, Common Resources III, Cornerstone Natural Resources, Council Oak Resources, Dorado E&P, Eclipse Resources, ER Energy Group, EV Energy Partners, Excalibur Resources, Felix Energy, FireWheel Energy, Forge Energy, Fossil Creek Resources, Fuse Energy, Grenadier Energy Partners II, Halcon Resouces, Laramie Energy, Limestone II Holding Company, Lone Star Land & Energy II, Manti Exploration, Marlin Resources, Modern Resources, Oak Valley Resources, OGX Holding II, Paloma Partners IV, PayRock Energy, PennEnergy Resources, Phillips Energy Partners III, Piedra Resources III, Plantation Petroleum Holdings V, Protege Energy III, QStar, Sabalo Energy, Scala Energy, Sierra Oil & Gas, Silver Oak Energy, Silverback Exploration, Southland Royalty Company, Staghorn Petroleum, Talon Oil & Gas II, Tracker Resources Development III, Travis Peak Resources, Unconventional Resources, Venado Oil & Gas

Other Locations:
3811 Turtle Creek Blvd
Suite 2100
Dallas, TX 75219
Phone: 214-599-0800 **Fax:** 214-599-0200

Key Executives:
David B. Miller, Founder & Managing Partner
Education: BBA, MBA, Southern Methodist University
Background: President, PMC Reserve Acquisition Company; Co-CEO, MAZE Exploration; Republic National Bank of Dallas
Gary R. Petersen, Founder & Managing Partner
Education: BBA, MBA, Texas Tech University
Background: SVP, Corporate Finance, Energy Banking Group, Republic Bank; EVP, Nicklos Oil & Gas Company; US Army
D. Martin Phillips, Founder & Managing Partner
Education: BS, MBA, Louisiana State University
Background: SVP, Energy Banking Group, NationsBank; Republic Bank

Robert L. Zorich, Founder & Managing Partner
Education: BA, Economics, University of California, Santa Barbara; MS, International Management, American Graduate School of International Management
Background: SVP, Trust Company of the West; Co-Founder & Co-CEO, MAZE Exploration
Jason M. DeLorenzo, Managing Partner
Education: BBA, University of Texas
Background: Corporate Finance, ING Barings; Assocate, Energy Group, Wells Fargo Bank
E. Murphy Markham IV, Managing Partner
Education: BBA, Texas Tech University; MBA, University of Houston
Background: Managing Director & Group Head, Oil & Gas Finance, JP Morgan; Republic Bank; Bank of America
Directorships: Independemt Petroleum Association of America
Douglas E. Swanson Jr., Managing Partner
Education: BA & MBA, University of Texas
Background: Frost National Bank; Amegy Bank
Directorships: Houston Producers' Forum

673 ENDEAVOUR CAPITAL
920 Southwest 9th Avenue
Suite 2300
Portland, OR 97205
Phone: 503-223-2721
web: www.endeavourcapital.com
Mission Statement: Partners with companies based in the Western United States region.
Geographic Preference: Western United States
Fund Size: $675 million
Founded: 1991
Average Investment: $25 - $100 million
Minimum Investment: $5 million
Investment Criteria: Growth Equity, Industry Consolidation, Management Acquisitions, Recapitalizations, Ownership Transfers
Industry Group Preference: Business Products & Services, Manufacturing, Food & Beverage, Consumer Products, Transportation, Logistics, Education
Portfolio Companies: The Aladdin Group, Alpha Media, Arizona Nutritional Supplements, Bristol Farms, DTC Logistics, ESCO Corporation, Genesis Financial Solutions, GlobalWide Media, Grant Victor, Johnny Was, K2 Insurance Services, Metropolitan Market, New Seasons Market, Nor-Cal Products, Port Logistics Group, ProKarma, Providien Medical, Tall Oak Learning, USNR, Vigor Industrial, Zoom+

Other Locations:
1001 Fourth Avenue
Suite 4301
Seattle, WA 98154
Phone: 206-621-7060

444 S Flower Street
Suite 4300
Los Angeles, CA 90071
Phone: 213-891-0115

1860 Blake Street
Suite 200
Denver, CO 80202
Phone: 303-355-3553

Key Executives:
Stephen E. Babson, Managing Director
e-mail: seb@endeavourcapital.com
Education: BA, Stanford University; JD, Stanford Law School; MBA, Stanford Graduate School of Business
Background: Chairman, Stoel Rives LLP; Member, Stanford University Committee for Undergraduate Education
Directorships: ESCO Corporation, Zoom+, USNR, New Seasons Market, Bristol Farms, Vigor Industrial, Genesis

Venture Capital & Private Equity Firms / Domestic Firms

Financial Solutions, Johnny Was, Columbia Sportswear Company
Rocky Dixon, Managing Director
e-mail: jwd@endeavourcapital.com
Education: BS, University of Oregon
Background: West Coast Director, Earl Kinship Capital Corporation; Marketing & Sales Management, Stanley Tools; Co-Founder, Support Technologies
Directorships: Bi-Mart Corporation, El Aero Services, Adventure Funds, Beef Northwest
Mark Dorman, Managing Director
e-mail: dmd@endeavourcapital.com
Education: BS, Lewis & Clark College; MBA, Harvard Business School
Background: Partner, Green Manning & Bunch; Boettcher & Company; Morgan Stanley; President, Lake Oswego Schools Foundation
Directorships: Alpha Media, Arizona Nutritional Supplements, Grant Victor, Providien Medical, Nor-Cal Products
John Von Schlegell, Managing Director
e-mail: jevs@endeavourcapital.com
Education: BA, MBA, Stanford University
Background: Golder, Thoma, Cressey & Rauser Partner; Undersecretary, Health and Human Services, Massachusetts; Caterpillar Tractor
Directorships: K2 Insurance Services, GlobalWide Media, The Aladdin Group, ProKarma, Port Logistics Group, DTC Logistics, National Fish and Wildlife Foundation, Nature Conservancy
Chad Heath, Managing Director
e-mail: cnh@endeavourcapital.com
Education: BS, Business Administration, Georgetown University
Background: Charterhouse Group International; Merrill Lynch
Directorships: GlobalWide Media, Tall Oak Learning, Johnny Was
Leland Jones, Managing Director
e-mail: lmj@endeavourcapital.com
Education: BA, University of California, Davis; MBA, Stanford Graduate School of Business
Background: Coopers & Lybrand
Directorships: Bristol Farms, K2 Insurance Services, DTC Logistics, The Aladdin Group, Genesis Financial Solutions, Port Logistics Group
Aaron Richmond, Managing Director
e-mail: asr@endeavourcapital.com
Education: AB, Harvard College; MBA, Stanford Graduate School of Business
Background: Consultant, McKinsey & Company
Directorships: USNR, Vigor Industrial, Nor-Cal Products, ProKarma
Dietz Fry, Managing Director
e-mail: jdf@endeavourcapital.com
Education: University of Colorado Boulder
Background: Green Manning & Bunch
Directorships: Grant Victor, Providien Medical, Tall Oak Learning
Bradaigh Wagner, Managing Director
e-mail: bow@endeavourcapital.com
Education: AB, Princeton University; MBA, Wharton School, University of Pennsylvania
Background: Fenway Partners; The Beacon Group
Directorships: Arizona Nutritional Supplements, New Seasons Market
Derek Eve, Principal
e-mail: dae@endeavourcapital.com
Education: BABA, University of Washington; MBA, Columbia Business School
Background: Associate, Diamond Castle; Analyst, Financial Sponsors Group, Credit Suisse
Directorships: The Aladdin Group, Arizona Nutritional Supplements, USNR, Vigor Industrial

674 ENERGIA VENTURES
346 Queen Street
Fredericton, NB E3B 1B2
Canada

Phone: 506-261-0871
e-mail: unbenergiaventures@gmail.com

Mission Statement: Energia Ventures provides funding, mentoring and programming to take enertrepreneurs in the energy, smart grid, artificial intelligence, cleantech, and cybersecurity sectors to the next stage.

Joe Allen, Managing Director
Education: BBA, University of New Brunswick
Background: Director, Investments, New Brunswick Innovation Foundation; Chief Financial Officer, HJ Crabbe & Sons Ltd.

675 ENERGY CAPITAL PARTNERS
51 John F. Kennedy Parkway
Suite 200
Short Hills, NJ 07078

Phone: 973-671-6100 **Fax:** 973-671-6101
e-mail: info@ecpartners.com
web: www.ecpartners.com

Mission Statement: Energy Capital Partners is a private equity firm focused on investing in North America's energy infrastructure.

Geographic Preference: North America
Founded: 2005
Industry Group Preference: Power Generation, Midstream Oil & Gas, Electric Transmission, Energy Equipment & Services, Environmental Infrastructure, Other Energy Related Assets
Portfolio Companies: ADA Carbon Solutions, Brayton Point Power, Broad River Power, Calpine Corporation, Cardinal Gas Storage Partners, CE2 Carbon Capital, Chieftain Sand and Proppant, CIG Logistics, CM Energy, Cormetech, Dynegy, Empire Generating, EnergySolutions, EquiPower Resources Corp., FirstLight Power Enterprises, Furie Operating Alaska, Gopher Resource, NCSG Crane & Heavy Haul, NESCO, Next Wave Energy, NextLight Renewable Power, Odessa Power Holdings, PLH Group, ProPetro Services, Ramaco Resources, Red Oak Power, Rimrock Midstream, Sendero Midstream Partners, Southcross, Summit Midstream Partners, Sungevity, Sunnova, SunZia Southwest Transmission Project, Targa Resources, Terra-Gen, Triton Power Partners, US Development Group, Wheelabrator Technologies

Other Locations:
12680 High Bluff Drive
Suite 400
San Diego, CA 92130
Phone: 858-703-4400 **Fax:** 858-703-4401

One World Trade Center
Suite 48D
New York City, NY 10006
Phone: 212-266-2900 **Fax:** 212-266-2901

1000 Louisiana Street
52nd Floor
Houston, TX 77002
Phone: 713-496-3100 **Fax:** 713-496-3101

450 East Las Olas Blvd.
Suite 1400
Fort Lauderdale, FL 33301

Key Executives:
Doug Kimmelman, Senior Partner
Education: BA, Economics, Stanford University; MBA, Wharton School
Background: General Partner, Goldman Sachs
Directorships: Calpine Corporation, NESCO, Summit Midstream Partners, Sunnova, US Development Group

Venture Capital & Private Equity Firms / Domestic Firms

Pete Labbat, Managing Partner
Education: BA, Economics, Georgetown University; MBA, Wharton School
Background: Managing Director, Goldman Sachs
Directorships: NCSG Crane & Heavy Haul, Next Wave Energy, Sundero Midstream Partners, Summit Midstream Partners, Triton Power Partners

Tom Lane, Vice Chairman
Education: BA, Economics, Wheaton College; MBA, University of Chicago
Background: Managing Director, Goldman Sachs
Directorships: Sendero Midstream Partners, Summit Midstream Partners, US Development Group

Tyler Reeder, Managing Partner
Education: BA, Economics, Colgate University
Background: Vice President of Power and Fuel Markets, Texas Genco; Director for Energy Markets and Finance Manager, Orion Power Holdings; Goldman Sachs
Directorships: Calpine Corporation, EnergySolutions, Gopher Resource, Ramaco Resources, Terra-Gen, Wheelabrator Technologies

Andrew Singer, Partner & General Counsel
Education: BS, Electrical Engineering, Cornell University; JD, Harvard University
Background: Partner, Latham & Watkins LLP
Directorships: Calpine Corporation; Cormetech Inc.; Terra-Gen LLC; Furie Operating Alaska LLC

Schuyler Coppedge, Partner
Education: BA, Middlebury College; MBA, Wharton School
Background: Energy Investment Banking Division, JP Morgan
Directorships: CIG Logistics; Cormetech; Terra-Gen LLC; U.S. Development Group

Rahman D'Argenio, Partner
Education: BA, Mathematics and Economics, University of Pennsylvania
Background: First Reserve Corporation; Deutsche Bank Securities; Sempra Energy Trading
Directorships: CM Energy; NESCO; PLH Group; Sunnova; Triton Power Partners

Scott Rogan, Partner
Education: BBA and MPA, University of Texas at Austin; MBA, University of Chicago
Background: Managing Director and Co-Head of Barclay's Houston office
Directorships: Next Wave Energy; Sendero Midstream Partners; Summit Midstream Partners

Trent Kososki, Partner
Education: BS, Electrical Engineering, Duke University
Background: Financial Sponsors Investment Banking Group, Credit Suisse First Boston
Directorships: Furie Operating Alaska; Ramaco Resources

Kevin Clayton, Partner
Education: BA, Government, Lehigh University; MBA, St. Joseph's University
Background: Marketing and Client Relations, Oaktree Capital Management
Directorships: Aquicore

Matt DeNichilo, Partner
Education: BSE, Operations Research and Financial Engineering, Princeton University
Background: Energy Investment Banking Group, JP Morgan
Directorships: Sunnova; Terra-Gen

Murray Karp, CPA, Partner, CFO, COO
Education: BS, Accounting, Rutgers University School of Business
Background: CFO, AEA Investors LLC; Controller, Accordia; Assistant Controller, Caxton Corporation

676 ENERTECH CAPITAL
One Tower Bridge
100 Front Street
Suite 1225
West Conshohocken, PA 19428

Phone: 416-515-2759
e-mail: mmiles@enertechcapital.com
web: www.enertechcapital.com

Mission Statement: EnerTech Capital, a pioneer in energy and clean energy, is a firm focused on funding energy ventures and micro-infrastructure projects that address the global opportunity for cleaner, cheaper and more efficient energy usage.

Geographic Preference: North America
Fund Size: $500 million
Founded: 1996
Average Investment: $5 - $6 million
Minimum Investment: $1 million
Investment Criteria: Early to Mid Stage; Energy Tech
Industry Group Preference: Digital Networks, Clean Energy, Technology, Transportation, Waste & Resources, Solar Energy, Automation, Cyber Security, AI
Portfolio Companies: Blue Pillar, Enbala, Encycle, GeoDigital, N-Dimension, NanoSteel, Power Survey, Sofdesk, Tangent Energy Solutions, Vertex Downhole, Western Oilfield Equipment Ltd.

Other Locations:
333 7th Avenue SW
Suite 970
Calgary, AB T2P 2Z1
Canada

5 Place Ville Marie
Suite 1400
Montreal, QC H3B 2G2
Canada
Phone: 514-864-5500

1235 Bay Street
Suite 801
Toronto, ON M5R 3K4
Canada

2000 PGA Boulevard
Suite 4440
Palm Beach Gardens, FL 33408

755 Sansome Street
Suite 450
San Francisco, CA 94111

Key Executives:
Scott Ungerer, Founder/Managing Director
e-mail: sungerer@enertechcapital.com
Education: BS, Mechanical Engineering, Princeton University
Background: President/COO, Atlantic Energy Enterprises
Directorships: Enbala Power Networks, GeoDigital, NanoSteel, N-Dimension Solutions, Tangent Energy Solutions

Wally Hunter, Managing Director
e-mail: whunter@enertechcapital.com
Education: BA, University of Western Ontario
Background: Managing Director, RBC Capital Partners
Directorships: FilterBoxx, HPC Energy Services, N-Dimension Solutions, Western Oilfield Equipment Ltd.

Dean Sciorillo, Managing Director
e-mail: dsciorillo@enertechcapital.com
Education: BS, Finance, LaSalle University; MBA, Fox School of Business, Temple University
Background: Exelon Corporation; Business Planning Manager, Enterprise

Jarett Carson, Managing Director
e-mail: jcarson@enertechcapital.com
Education: BSc, Chemical Engineering, Louisiana Tech University; MBA, A.B. Freeman School, Tulane University

Venture Capital & Private Equity Firms / Domestic Firms

Background: Sound Energy Partners; Director, Energy Technology Research, Royal Bank of Canada.
Dean Sciorillo, Director
e-mail: dsciorillo@enertechcapital.com
Education: BS, Finance, La Salle University; MBA, Fox School, Temple University
Background: Exelon Corporation
Directorships: EnergySavvy
Anne-Marie Bourgeois, Vice President
e-mail: ambourgeois@enertechcapital.com
Education: BS, Geology, BA, Management, BA, Political Science, University of Ottawa; MA, International Management, University of Quebec
Background: Regional Director, Partnerships, Sustainable Technology Canada; Business Development Specialist, International Services for Sustainable Development
Eric Schmadtke, Vice President, Investments
e-mail: eschmadtke@enertechcapital.com
Education: BBA, Finance, Bishop's University; MBA, University of Ottawa; MBA, Haskayne School of Business, University of Calgary
Background: Director, Business Development, Suncor Energy

677 ENGAGE VENTURES
75 5th Street NW
Suite 2100
Atlanta, GA 30308

e-mail: info@engage.vc
web: engage.vc

Mission Statement: An independent venture fund collaborating with entrepreneurs emerging in the tech industry.

Founded: 2017
Average Investment: $500,000 - $25 million
Minimum Investment: $500,000
Investment Criteria: Early Stage
Industry Group Preference: Diversified

Key Executives:
Blake Patton, Managing Partner
Education: BS, Georgia Tech College
Background: Managing Partner, Tech Square Ventures; General Manager, Advanced Technology Development Center; President/COO, Interactive Advisory Software; Associate, SEI Corporation
Daley Ervin, Managing Director
Education: BS, Arizona State University
Background: VP of Business Development & Strategy, Nucleus; GM/Head of North American Operations for Students.com
Thiago Olson, Managing Director
Education: BEE, Vanderbilt University
Background: Venture Partner, Tech Square Ventures; CEO, Stratos Technologies
Scott Lopano, Principal
Education: Wharton School
Background: Associate, Tech Square Ventures; Associate Director/Lead Coverage Officer, Insurance Debt Capital Markets Group
Joelle Fox, Operating Partner/CFO
Education: BS, Accounting, University of Tennessee
Background: CFO/Operating Partner, Tech Square Ventures; Velocity Medical Solutions; Varian Medical Systems; iXL Inc.; PricewaterhouseCoopers

678 ENHANCED CAPITAL
601 Lexington Avenue
Suite 1401
New York, NY 10022

Phone: 212-207-3385 **Fax:** 212-207-9031
web: www.enhancedcapital.com

Mission Statement: Enhanced Capital is a small business investment firm focused on established lower middle market companies. We invest in growing businesses often overlooked by traditional sources of capital due to location or size.

Average Investment: $500,000 - $3 million
Investment Criteria: Lower Middle Market
Industry Group Preference: Renewable Energy, Real Estate Rehabilitation, Affordable Housing
Portfolio Companies: Accelerated Orthopedic Technologies, Advanced Network Solutions, Affinity Lab, Alereon, American Log Handlers, Aquasana, Autotether, BroadStar Energy, CK Mechanical Plumbing & Heating, CloudX, CMD Bioscience, Community Cars, Dreyfus-Corney, Elm City Food Cooperative, Emme E2MS, Energy Source Partners, EnteGreat, Envirelation, FSI, Fire Rock, Fireside Glamping, Floop, FlowTech Feuling, Greenleaf Biofuels, GreyWall Software, Hadapt, Heliovolt, Invinia, Innovatient Solutions, Knoa Software, Lapolla Industries, Knoa Software, Lapolla Industries, Local Yokel Media, MedAdherence, Motion Computing, New Haven Pharmaceuticals, NovaTract Surgical, NuScriptRX, Optimal IMX, Optiwind, Oxford Performance Materials, PART Point, Payment America Systems, Peak Builders, Pinkgirls, Precipio Diagnostics, Queralt, RepEquity, SciApps, Session Title Services, Shareholder InSite, Sierra Industries, Solar Change, Southern Theaters, Sustainable Real Estate, Taurus, Teton Gravity Research, Townsend, Two Roads Brewing Company, Vacuum Technologies Corporation, Vault, WC Leasing, WRJ Design Associates, WhiteGlove Health, Wyoming Authentic Products, YouRenew.com

Other Locations:
201 St. Charles Ave.
Suite 3400
New Orleans, LA 70170
Phone: 504-569-7900

Key Executives:
Michael A.G. Korengold, President/CEO
e-mail: mkorengold@enhancedcapital.com
Education: Vassar College, University of Minnesota Law School
Background: Lawyer
Paul S. Kasper, Managing Director, New York City
e-mail: pkasper@enhancedcapital.com
Education: BS, Accounting, MS, Business Adminstration, Penn State University; MBA, Stanford Graduate School of Business
Background: Principal, American Securities Capital Partners; Hicks Muse Tate & Furst; Merrill Lynch
Shane McCarthy, CPA, Managing Partner/CFO, New Orleans
e-mail: smccarthy@enhancedcapital.com
Education: BS, MS, Accounting, University of Southern Mississippi
Background: Audit Manager, Ernst & Young

679 ENIAC VENTURES
San Francisco, CA

web: eniac.vc

Mission Statement: Seed-stage firm named after the world's first computer, developed at the University of Pennsylvania.

Founded: 1996
Investment Criteria: Seed
Industry Group Preference: Mobile, Financial Services
Portfolio Companies: 1upHealth, Airbnb, Alloy, Anchor, AutoFi, B8ta, Basket Savings, BioBeats, Bleximo, Boxed, Breezy, Brightwheel, Briq, Cameo, Chatgrid, CMRA, DemandSage, Dubsmash, Eden, Elevate, Embrace, Esports One, Fitocracy, Fleksy, Fondu, FortressIQ, Fritz AI, Fuzz Pet Health, Ginger, Grouparoo, Hinge, Imagine, IMRSV, Instinctive, Iovation, Iron Ox, isee, Jobr, Jump Ramp Games, Kanvas Labs, KitchenMate, LaunchKey, Lawmatics, Legit, LevelOps, Localytics, Luxe, MaestroQA, Medallia, MedCrypt, Meta Resolver, Mighty Meeting, Mio, MirrorMe, mParticle, N3twork, Neumob, Nextpeer, Onswipe, Owlet, Passbase, Pienso, ProdPerfect, Qualia, Quilt, Raken, Ready

237

Venture Capital & Private Equity Firms / Domestic Firms

Robotics, Recharge, Sea Machines, Shaper, Shine, ShowMe, Simperium, Snips, SoundCloud, Spansive, Statsbot, SugarCRM, Superpeer, TalentShare, Tap to Learn, TapCommerce, Tempo AI, Vence, Virgin Hyperloop One, Vistar Media, Visual Vocal, Vungle, Workflow, Xwing, Zero

Key Executives:
Hadley Harris, Founding General Partner
Education: University of Pennsylvania; Wharton School
Background: Vlingo; Thumb
Nihal Mehta, Founding General Partner
Education: University of Pennsylvania
Background: LocalResponse
Vic Singh, Founding General Partner
Education: University of Pennsylvania; Columbia Business School
Background: RRE Ventures; NearVerse; Tracks; Kanvas
Tim Young, Founding General Partner
Education: University of Pennsylvania
Background: WebYes; Bridge; Quoteship

680 ENLIGHTENMENT CAPITAL
4445 Willard Avenue
Suite 1120
Chevy Chase, MD 20815

e-mail: info@enlightenment-cap.com
web: www.enlightenment-cap.com

Mission Statement: Enlightenment Capital is a private investment firm that provides flexible capital solutions to businesses in the Aerospace, Defense & Government sector.
Investment Criteria: Senior Debt, Mezzanine Debt, Minority Equity
Industry Group Preference: Aerospace, Defense and Government, Security, Government
Portfolio Companies: 1901 Group, Aurora Flight Sciences, Byte Cubed, Cadmus, CyberCore Technologies, The Diplomat Group, Emagine IT, EverWatch, Gleason Research Associates, MicroPact, North American Rescue, Opera Solutions, Phase One Consulting Group, PIXIA, REI, SolAero Technologies, Telos Corporation, Vanguard Space Technologies, Vistronix

Key Executives:
Devin Talbott, Co-Founder/Managing Partner
Education: BA, Law & Spanish, Amherst College; JD, MBA, Georgetown University
Background: Vice President, D.E. Shaw; TCG Financial Partners; M&A Group, Lazard
Pierre Chao, Co-Founder/Operating Partner
Education: Dual Degrees, MIT; CFA
Background: Co-Founder, Renaissance Strategic Advisors; Institutional Investor, Smith Barney; Morgan Stanley Dean Witter; Credit Suisse First Boston

681 ENTER VENTURES
350 Cambridge Avenue
Suite 225
Palo Alto, CA 94306

Phone: 650-323-5088 Fax: 650-323-5084
e-mail: info@enterventures.com
web: www.enterventures.com

Mission Statement: A business accelerator that works closely with early stage high-growth emerging technology companies towards the successful launch of and execution of their business models by providing guidance and support.
Geographic Preference: Worldwide
Fund Size: $100 million
Investment Criteria: Seed, Early Stage
Industry Group Preference: Financial Services, Ancillary Services, Management, Business to Business, Corporate Services

Other Locations:
601 California Street
Suite 2000
San Francisco, CA 94108
Phone: 415-505-5003
19-31 Pitt Street
Level 6
Sydney NSW 2000
Australia

Key Executives:
Rob Allan, Co-Founder/CEO/General Partner
e-mail: rob.allan@enterventures.com
Education: MBA, LLM, BSC
Background: Managing General Partner/CEO, PoleStar Business Development; Partner, The Anvil Group; Management Consultant, McKinsey & Company; Consultant, Egon Zehnder International
Directorships: VCMentors; Avelin Capital
Diana Saca, Co-Founder/COO
415-505-5003
e-mail: diana.saca@enterventures.com
Education: Political Science and Administration of Justice degrees; JD, Santa Clara University School of Law; Certification, Hong Kong International & Comparative Law Institute
Background: Partner, Hagan, Saca & Hagan Law Corporation; Outside General Counsel; Associate Editor, Santa Clara Law Review
John Chaisson, Co-Founder/Partner
e-mail: john.chaisson@enterventures.com
Education: Law degree, Stanford University
Background: Vice President Business/Corporate Development, DataMain; President, Interbiznet Group; General Counsel, several Bay Area technology companies; Vice President Business Development, Resumix; Wilson, Sonsini, Goodrich & Rosati
Bill Kelsall, Co-Founder/Partner
(0419) 811-988
e-mail: bill.kelsall@enterventures.com
Education: MBA, Cranfield School; Curtin University, Australia
Background: Strategy Practice, Arthur Andersen Melbourne; Strategy Consultant, McKinsey & Company/Mckinsey Global Innovation; Founder/CEO, Fresh Cosmetics; Physical Therapist (opened eight successful practices)

682 ENTREPIA VENTURES
101 Eisenhower Parkway
Suite 300
Roseland, NJ 07068

Phone: 973-467-0880
e-mail: info@entrepia.com
web: www.entrepia.com

Mission Statement: Entrepia Ventures manages venture capital funds that invest in private technology companies in the United States and Canada. The company further funds the business development initiatives of these companies in Asian markets.
Geographic Preference: United States, Japan, Canada
Founded: 1999
Investment Criteria: Early-Stage, Expansion-Stage, Private Companies, Japanese Startups, Japanese Seed Businesses
Industry Group Preference: Technology, Information Technology, Multimedia, Mobility, Web Applications & Services, Next Generation Computing, IT Infrastructure
Portfolio Companies: Achronix Semiconductor Corp., Bluestreak Technology Inc., Business Search Technologies Corp., FreeLinc, MagSil Corp., Vantrix

Other Locations:
1200 McGill College Avenue
Suite 1100
Montreal, QC H3B 4G7

Venture Capital & Private Equity Firms / Domestic Firms

Canada
Phone: 866-305-9610 Fax: 866-305-9610
2-5-7, Hirakawacho
Chiyada-ku
Tokyo 102-0093
Japan
Key Executives:
  Amit Srivastava, Managing Partner
  Education: BSc, Electrical Engineering, Indian Institute of Technology; MSc, Electrical Engineering, Rensselaer Polytechnic Institute; MBA, Wharton School, University of Pennsylvania
  Background: JP Morgan Chase; Mercer Management Consulting
  Directorships: Achronix, Bluestreak, Freelinc, Vantrix

683 ENTREPRENEUR PARTNERS
123 South Broad Street
Suite 1843
Philadelphia, PA 19109

Phone: 267-322-7000
e-mail: info@epfunds.com
web: www.epfunds.com

Mission Statement: Entrepreneur Partners brings operating insight to the assessment and ownership of direct marketing companies in the middle-market.
Geographic Preference: United States
Average Investment: $3 to $10 million
Minimum Investment: $3 million
Investment Criteria: Company Revenue of $10 to $150 million
Industry Group Preference: Business to Business, Direct Marketing, Retailing, Compliance/Traning/Certification, Publishers
Portfolio Companies: AmeriFile, Competitor Group, Future Publishing, Intelsat, Medical Arts Press, NEP Broadcasting, Northern Brewer, Peachtree Business Products
Key Executives:
  Salem Shuchman, Managing Partner
  e-mail: sshuchman@epfunds.com
  Background: Senior Partner, Apax Partners; Principal, Odyssey Partners
  Bruce Newman, Partner
  e-mail: bnewman@epfunds.com
  Background: Operating Partner, Graham Partners; President, Franklin Mint Company; President, Paramount Citrus
  Lori Lombardo, Principal
  Education: BA, Bates College; MS, University of Pennsylvania
  Background: AVP, Lending Services & Operations, Merrill Lynch

684 ENTREPRENEURS ROUNDTABLE ACCELERATOR
415 Madison Avenue
4th Floor
New York, NY 10017

e-mail: pr@eranyc.com
web: www.eranyc.com

Mission Statement: Helps startup companies acclerate their visibility, access, and credibility with customers, mentors and investors.
Average Investment: $100,000
Investment Criteria: Seed Stage, Early Stage, Middle Stage
Industry Group Preference: Media, Business to Business, B2B, Business to Consumer, B2C, Marketing, Real Estate, Logistics, Fintech, E-Commerce
Portfolio Companies: ArtistOnGo, Coinapoly, FieldCLIX, Hailify, Hazel, Mouth Off Health, Nayya, Parento, RillaVoice, Salusion, Spotter, Top Corp, Undock

Key Executives:
  Murat Aktihanoglu, Managing Director
  Education: BSc, Electrics and Electronics, MSc, Computer Science, Bilkent University in Turkey
  Background: Founder, Centrl; Founder, Entrepreneurs Roundtable; Co-Author, Location-Aware Applications; AT&T; Sony; Panasonic; Logitech; Pioneer
  Directorships: Belgian American Chamber Of Commerce, MIT Enterprise Forum
  Jonathan Axelrod, Managing Director
  Education: AB, Social Studies, Harvard University
  Background: Co-Founder, Co-CEo, MusicGremlin; Co-Founder, President, Music123
  Directorships: Beth Israel Medical Center

685 EONCAPITAL

Phone: 303-850-9300
e-mail: inquiry@eoncapital.com
web: www.eoncapital.com

Mission Statement: Our experience working with and in start-up businesses, prompted us to establish our own private venture funds. eonCapital Venture Fund I and II invest in seed and early-stage Software as a Service (SaaS) and mobile application businesses. Like the creative entrepreneur, we saw a problem and desired a solution. Our goal is to help fill the funding gap for entrepreneurs of seed and early-stage companies. As entrepreneurs, we understood what it takes to build a company from the ground up and the challenges presented from concept through development and into the growth phase.
Investment Criteria: Start-Up, Seed-Stage, Early-Stage
Industry Group Preference: SaaS, Mobile Apps
Portfolio Companies: AllAboardToys, BirdBox, Circa, Closely, CollectiveIP, CrowdTwist, DailyBurn, eonMedia, FlexTrip, FlixMaster, Forkly, FullContact, GameChanger, GoChime, GoSpotCheck, Go Toast, Highlighter, LgDb, MadKast, Nextly, MobileStorm, Mocapay, Mocavo, Nimble, ReTel Technologies, Remitly, Roximity, Rubicon Project, Socialthing, Sycara, TeamSnap, TechStars, Vanilla, VerbalizeIt, Vizify
Key Executives:
  Dave Carlson, Managing Director
  Education: BA, Communications, Bethany College; MS, International Business Management, Thunderbird School of Global Management
  Background: Founder, Go Toast; Founder, eonMedia
  Directorships: MobileStorm

686 EOS PARTNERS LP
437 Madison Avenue
14th Floor
New York, NY 10022

Phone: 212-832-5800 Fax: 212-832-5815
web: www.eospartners.com

Mission Statement: To work with stellar management teams and provide strategic and financial expertise and knowledge in order to grow businesses into industry leading companies.
Geographic Preference: National
Fund Size: $1.5 billion
Founded: 1994
Average Investment: $20 - $100 million
Minimum Investment: $1 million
Investment Criteria: Lower Middle Market, Growth Equity, Recapitalizations, Buyouts, Acquisitions, Shareholder Liquidity, Corporate Divestitures
Industry Group Preference: Consumer Products, Consumer Services, Energy, Healthcare Services, Business to Business, Transportation, Logistics, Media
Portfolio Companies: Addus Healthcare, Arbonne, BeavEx, Country Fresh, CRS Proppants, KeyImpact Sales & Systems, MC2, Mercury Media, ProEnergy Services, RCG Global Services, Residential Mortgage Services, ShelterPoint Life, Summit Business Media, True Science

239

Venture Capital & Private Equity Firms / Domestic Firms

Key Executives:
  Steven M. Friedman, Founding Partner
  e-mail: sfriedman@eospartners.com
  Education: AB, MBA, University of Chicago; JD, Brooklyn Law School
  Background: VP, Citibank, NA; General Partner, Odyssey Partners
  Brian D. Young, Founding Partner
  e-mail: byoung@eospartners.com
  Education: AB, Harvard University
  Background: General Partner, Odyssey Partners; Managing Director, First Boston Corporation
  Mark L. First, Parnter
  e-mail: mfirst@eospartners.com
  Education: BS, Wharton School; MBA, Harvard Business School
  Background: Morgan Stanley
  Brendan M. Moore, Managing Director
  e-mail: bmoore@eospartners.com
  Education: AB, Dartmouth College; BEng, Thayer School of Engineering, Dartmouth College
  Background: Harbourton Enterprises; First Dominion Capital; Schroder & Co.
  Adam S. Gruber, Principal
  e-mail: agruber@eospartners.com
  Education: BBA, University of Wisconsin, Madison
  Background: Windward Capital Partners; Cred Suisse First Boston
  John Lee, Principal
  Education: BBA, Finance, Terry School of Business, University of Georgia
  Background: Associate Principal, Kamylon Capital
  Matthew Young, Associate
  e-mail: myoung@eospartners.com
  Education: BA, Franklin & Marshall College
  Background: Analyst, Kayne Anderson Mezzanine Partners
  Beth L. Bernstein, Chief Financial/Compliance Officer
  e-mail: bbernstein@eospartners.com
  Education: BS, Fairleigh Dickenson University; CPA
  Background: Senior Accountant, Coopers & Lybrand

---

687 EPIC PARTNERS
116 W 23rd Street
5th Floor
New York, NY 10011

web: www.epicpartnersllc.com

Mission Statement: A merchant banking firm focused exclusively on investing in the education and training sector.

Geographic Preference: United States, Canada
Founded: 2000
Investment Criteria: Minimum $2 Million in EBITDA; Company Revenue of $10 to $150 million; Experienced Management Teams
Industry Group Preference: Training, Education, Healthcare Services, Business Services
Portfolio Companies: EDUSS, Oasis Children's Services, Provant, St. Matthew's University, University of Sint Eustatius School of Medicine

Key Executives:
  Robert Puopolo, Partner
  646-375-2123
  e-mail: rtpuopolo@epicpartnersllc.com
  Education: AB Economics, Harvard University; MBA, Harvard Business School
  Background: Partner, Leeds Equity Partners; Oppenheimer & Co; Bear Stearns & Co; Kidder, Peabody & Co
  Directorships: Helma Institute; Oasis Children Services

---

688 EPIC VENTURES
15 West South Temple
Suite 500
Salt Lake City, UT 84101

Phone: 801-524-8939
e-mail: info@epicvc.com
web: www.epicvc.com

Mission Statement: To invest in companies positioned to become leaders in the technology industry.

Geographic Preference: Mountain & Western States
Fund Size: $60 million
Investment Criteria: Early-Stage
Industry Group Preference: High Technology, Clean Technology, Communications, Consumer Services, Business Products & Services, Enterprise Software, Internet Technology, Life Sciences
Portfolio Companies: Adaptive Computing, Alliance Health, Canopy, Clinkle, Cloud Lending, The Clymb, Dotgo, eSionic, Everspin, Exagen Diagnostics, Health Catalyst, HG Data, HyTrust, Insidesales.com, Instructure, Iovation, Janrain, Joyent, Knod, Lavu, Le Tote, Medsphere, Moki, NetDocuments, Nuvi, Primary Data, Q Therapeutics, Signal, SolutionReach, SpinGo

Key Executives:
  Nick Efstratis, Managing Director
  Education: BS, Entrepreneurship, Brigham Young University; MBA, Marriott School, Brigham Young University
  Background: Business Development Group, Excite; Founder, Management Team, NetDocuments; Founder, Ranchlife Adventures
  Kent Madsen, Managing Director
  Education: BS, Mechanical Engineering & Applied Mechanics, MA, International Studies, University of Pennsylvania; MSE, University of Michigan; MBA, Wharton School
  Background: Managing Director, Wasatch Venture Fund; Advanced Technology Group, Ford Motor Company
  Directorships: Pivot Solutions, Q Therapeutics, Zettacore, Everspin, S5 Wireless
  Ryan Hemingway, Managing Director
  Education: BS, Psychology, MSS, Economics, Utah State University; MBA, University of Oxford
  Background: Zions Bank Capital Markets Group; Nevada State Bank
  Katie Szczepaniak Rice, Venture Associate
  Education: BS, Engineering, Massachusetts Institute of Technology; MBA, University of Chicago
  Background: Strategic Market Analyst, Cabot Corporation; Consultant, Kline & Co.
  Directorships: Lavu, DOTGO, Figaro

---

689 EPIDAREX CAPITAL
7910 Woodmont Avenue
Suite 1210
Bethesda, MD 20814

Phone: 301-298-5455 Fax: 301-357-8517
e-mail: info@epidarex.com
web: www.epidarex.com

Mission Statement: Epidarex Capital is a venture capital fund that invests in early-stage, high-growth life science companies in the Unites Stages and United Kingdom. Their focus is on providing start-up and growth equity capital to young companies currently developing commercial applications of novel research.

Geographic Preference: United States, United Kingdom
Investment Criteria: Early-Stage
Industry Group Preference: Life Sciences
Portfolio Companies: AdoRx Therapeutics, Apellis Pharmaceuticals, Caldan Therapeutics, Clyde Biosciences, Confluences Life Sciences, Edinburgh Molecular Imaging, Enterprise Therapeutics, Eternygen, IGEM Therapeutics,

Harpoon Medical, Mironid, NodThera, SIRAKOSS, Topas Therapeutics

Other Locations:
4F Le Gratte-Ciel Building 3
5-22-3 Shimbashi, Minatoku
Tokyo 105-0004
Japan
Phone: 81-3-6459-0258

137a George St.
Edinburgh EH2 4JY
United Kingdom
Phone: 44-131-243-3700

Key Executives:
A. Sinclair Dunlop, Managing Partner
Education: MA, International Relations, Syracuse University; MA, Political Economy, Glasgow University; MBA, Columbia Business School
Background: MASA Life Science Ventures
Directorships: Apellis Pharmaceuticals; Clyde Biosciences; EM Imaging; Mironid; Sirakoss
Kyparissia Sirinakis, CPA, Managing Partner
Education: Boston College School of Management
Background: Founder & Managing Director, WomenAngels.net; MLSV
Directorships: Confluence Life Science; Harpoon Medical; Nodthera; Sirakoss

690 EPLANET CAPITAL
99 Almaden Blvd
Suite 600
San Jose, CA 95113

Phone: 408-236-6500
e-mail: siliconvalley@eplanetcapital.com
web: www.eplanetcapital.com

Mission Statement: ePlanet Capital seeks to partner with management teams and offer the contacts, resources, and expertise necessary to help portfolio companies achieve growth and success.

Geographic Preference: United States, Asia, Europe
Founded: 1999
Investment Criteria: Growth Capital, Expansion Stage
Industry Group Preference: Internet, E-Commerce & Manufacturing, Semiconductors, Electronics, Wireless, Telecommunications, Healthcare, Medical Technology, Green Energy, Energy Efficiency, Gaming
Portfolio Companies: Baidu, End2End, Focus Media, Friendi, High Power Lithium, HiSoft Technology International, iKang, Moreens, Naseeb Networks, Newgen, OrderDynamics, Palringo, Silicon Mitus, Skype, Tribe Mobile, Virgin Mobile

Other Locations:
71-75 Uxbridge Road
Ealing W5 5SL
United Kingdom
Phone: 44-20-3859-0140

ePlanet Ventures Investment Group (HK) Ltd.
RM152515F China World Tower A No 1
Jianguomenwai Avenue, Chaoyang District
Beijing 100004
China
Phone: 86-10-5737-2520

Key Executives:
Asad Jamal, Founder/Chairman/Managing Partner
Education: BSc, London School of Economics
Background: Peregrine Investment Holdings
Dennis Atkinson, Managing Partner, London
Education: BS, Physics, Exeter University; MBA, Harvard Business School
Background: Principal, Softbank Europe Ventures; Global Product Manager, Reuters Business Information
Jerry Ilhuyn Cho, Managing Partner, Beijing
Education: BEng, Dongguk University, Seoul; MS, Electrical Engineering, University of Southern California
Background: Samsung Electronics
Amira Atallah, Chief Financial Officer
Education: BA, Economics, University of California, Davis; CPA
Background: Deloitte Tax LLP; Arthur Andersen
Hemant Khatwani, Vice President, Bangalore
Education: BMS College of Engineering; MBA, Indian Institute of Management
Background: AMP Capital Investors; Project Finance & Principal Investments, Infrastructure Development Finance Company

691 EQUINOX CAPITAL
41 W Putnam Avenue
Greenwich, CT 06830

Phone: 203-622-1605 **Fax:** 203-622-4684
web: www.equinox-capital.com

Mission Statement: Equinox Capital makes equity investments in small- to medium-sized companies facing constraints and provides the corporate environment necessary to help build emerging market leaders.

Founded: 1996
Investment Criteria: Owner Recapitalizations, Add-On Acquisitions, Growth Capital, Management Buyouts, Turnarounds
Industry Group Preference: Healthcare, Communications
Portfolio Companies: Care Management Technologies, Comprehensive NeuroScience, Cushcraft Corporation, Medical University of the Americas, Saba University, St. Matthew's University

Key Executives:
Steven C Rodger, Founder
Education: BA, University of Virginia; MBA, Harvard Business School
Background: Principal, Bessemer Securities; Mergers & Acquisitions, Bear Stearns & Co.; Donaldson Lufkin & Jenrette
Gregory S Czuba, Managing Director
Education: BS, MS, Electrical Engineering & Computer Science, Massachusetts Institute of Technology
Background: CEO, Cushcraft Corporation; VP, Celient Corporation; President, Remec Wireless; Senior Director, Hughes Network Systems
Donald J Donahue Jr, Managing Director
Education: BA, Georgetown University; MBA, NYC Stern School of Business
Background: President, 1st Worldwide Financial Partners; Managing Director, Banc One Capital Markets
Patrick J Donnellan, Managing Director
Education: BS, Bates College; MBA, Carnegie Mellon University
Background: Principal, Booz Allen Hamilton

692 EQUITEK CAPITAL
3659 Green Road
Suite 101
Beachwood, OH 44122

Phone: 216-360-0151 **Fax:** 216-373-9399
web: www.equitekcapital.com

Mission Statement: Equitek Capital is a venture capital firm that focuses on growth-stage deals. The firm invests in companies in the technology sector.

Investment Criteria: Growth Stage
Industry Group Preference: Technology
Portfolio Companies: Alien Technology, Chorum Technologies, DFT Microsystems, Eclipse Aviation, Embedded Planet, Flarion Technologies, Fsona Communications, Quicksilver Technology, Viztec

Key Executives:
Ken Ehrhart, Founding Managing Director
Education: BA, University of California, Berkeley

Venture Capital & Private Equity Firms / Domestic Firms

Background: Director of Research, Gilder Technology Report
Greg Somer, Founding Managing Director
Education: BSEE, MIT; MSEE, Stanford University
Background: Manager, New Products Planning Group, Cypress Semiconductor; Foreign Exchange Derivative Specialist, J.P. Morgan; BNP
Paul Grim, Founding Managing Director
Education: BSME, MIT; MBA, MIT Sloan School of Management
Background: Strategy Managing Consultant, Telecoms and Media Group, Gemini Consulting; Coopers & Lybrand France; IT Specialist, IBM France/CGI
John Gannon, Founding Managing Director
Education: BSAE, Pennsylvania State University; MBA, University of Chicago
Background: Orbit Specialist, General Electric Astro-Space Division; Risk Manager, Merrill Lynch; Barclays Capital

693 EQUITY SOUTH
2855 Marconi Drive
Suite 370
Alpharetta, GA 30005

Phone: 678-612-9876
e-mail: dld@equity-south.com
web: www.equity-south.com

Mission Statement: Pursues acquisitions or substantial equity investments in businesses with revenues from $10 million to $50 million and who have growth potential from internal efforts or through acquisitions.

Geographic Preference: Northeast, Southeast, Southwest
Fund Size: $42 million
Founded: 1987
Average Investment: $3 million - $5 million
Minimum Investment: $1 million
Investment Criteria: Mezzanine, LBO, Recapitalizations, Controlblock Purchases
Industry Group Preference: Services, Software, Manufacturing, Distribution
Portfolio Companies: American Screen Art, Carstar, F.B. Leopold Company, Loyaltyworks, Octane5 International LLC, PaySys International Inc., PolyVision Inc., Saunders Inc., Sherman & Reilly Inc., Sports & Recreation Inc., VCG Inc., VisAer Inc.

Key Executives:
Douglas Diamond, Managing Director
Education: BS, Commerce, University of Virginia
Background: CPA, Arthur Anderson and Co.; Director, Grubb and Williams, Ltd.; CEO, Octane5 International
Directorships: VisAER, Carstar, American Screen Art, LoyaltyWorks Inc.
Michael Dunn, Managing Director
Education: Liberal Arts, Pierce College
Background: Chairman, Octane5 International; CEO, PolyVision Corp.; CEO, Alliance International Group;

694 EQUUS TOTAL RETURN
700 Louisiana Street
48th Floor
Houston, TX 77002

Fax: 212-671-1534
Toll-Free: 888-323-4533
e-mail: info@equuscap.com
web: www.equuscap.com

Mission Statement: Focuses on the potential for long-term capital gains or a combination of capital gains with some level of current income.

Geographic Preference: United States
Fund Size: $70 million
Founded: 1983
Average Investment: $15 million
Minimum Investment: $1 million
Investment Criteria: Recapitalizations, Acquisitions
Industry Group Preference: Consumer Products, Distribution, Industrial Equipment, Medical & Health Related
Portfolio Companies: 5th Element Tracking, Biogenic Reagents, Equus Energy, Equus Media Development Company, MVC Capital, PalletOne Inc.

Other Locations:
2800 Park Place
666 Burrard Street
Vancouver, BC V6C 2Z7
Canada

Key Executives:
Robert Knauss, Chairman
Background: CEO, Baltic International USA; Chairman, Philip Services Corp.; Dean/Professor, University of Houston Law School; Dean, Vanderbilt Law School
John A. Hardy, Chief Executive Officer
Background: Chairman/CEO, Versatile Systems; Professor, University of British Columbia
Kenneth I. Denos, Director/Secretary/Chief Compliance Officer
Background: Chairman/CEO/President, London Pacific & Partners Inc.; CEO, MCC Global NV
Directorships: Start Scientific Inc.
Henry W. Hankinson, Director
Background: Co-Founder/Managing Partner, Global Business Associates; Senior Regional Executive, Haliburton/Brown & Root
L'Sheryl D Hudson, Senior Vice President, CFO & CCO
Bertrand Des Pallieres, Director
Background: Global Head of Structured Credit, JP Morgan
Directorships: Orco Property Group, SPQR Capital Holdings, Cadogan Petroleum, Attali Investment Partners, Versatile Systems, Euromax Capital Grlobal Finance
Richard F. Bergner, Director
Background: Attorney
Fraser Atkinson, Director
Background: Chairman, Green Power Motor Company Inc.; CFO, Versatile Systems Inc.; Partner, KPMG

695 ESCALATE CAPITAL PARTNERS
6300 Bridgepoint Parkway
Building 1
Suite 480
Austin, TX 78701

Phone: 512-651-2100
web: www.escalatecapital.com

Mission Statement: A mezzanine firm that invests in later stage companies experiencing growth. Escalate Capital focuses on the technology industry, particularly the tech-enabled services, healthcare and Internet sectors.

Investment Criteria: Mezzanine, Growth Capital, Permanent Working Capital, Acqusitin Financing, Recapitalizations, Later Stage
Industry Group Preference: Software, Mobile, Wireless, Technology-Enabled Services, Healthcare, Medical Devices
Portfolio Companies: Accolade, Adaptly, Allconnect, Arcadia, Arteriocyte, BlackDuck, Certona, ControlScan, Donuts, Dstillery, eFolder, Entrada, FireApps, Fishbowl, Glowpoint, HealthX, HotChalk, J.Hilburn, Kareo, LiveIntent, MarketForce, MoPro, Motionsoft, Needle, OneCommand, OwnerIQ, PaySimple, Peerless Network, Phreesia, Revionics, Signiant, SportVision, Viverae, WorkFront

Key Executives:
Tony Schell, Managing Director
Education: BBA, MBA, University of Texas
Background: Managing Director, Comerica Bank; Imperial Bank; The Sabre Group; Coopers & Lybrand; MBank Dallas; First Gibraltar Bank
Ross Cockrell, Managing Director
Education: BA, Harvard University; MBA, University of

242

Venture Capital & Private Equity Firms / Domestic Firms

Texas
Background: General Partner, Austin Ventures; Lomas Financial
Simon James, Chief Financial Officer
Education: BBA, University of Washington
Background: Chief Administrative Officer, Technology & Life Sciences Division, Comerica; VP, Semiconductor Industry, Silicon Valley Bank
Larry Bradshaw, Principal
Education: BS, Duke University; MBA, University of Texas
Background: Associate, Healthcare Corporate Finance Group, JP Morgan; Research Analyst, Joel Mogy Investment Counsel
Chris Julich, Principal
Education: BA, Wake Forest University
Background: Senior Market Manager, RBC Centura Bank; VP, Technology & Life Sciences Group, Comerica Bank; Associate, Capital Investment Partners

696 ESCHELON ENERGY PARTNERS
712 Main Street
Suite 2200
Houston, TX 77002-3290
Phone: 713-546-2621 Fax: 713-546-2620
e-mail: tsg@eschelonadvisors.com
web: www.eschelonadvisors.com

Mission Statement: Eschelon Energy Advisors provides private equity capital to companies in the energy sector with the objective of giving its partners the chance to become involved in the growth of the North American energy industry.

Geographic Preference: North America
Average Investment: $5 million
Minimum Investment: $500,000
Investment Criteria: Management, Business Plan, Co-Investors, Valuation
Industry Group Preference: Energy, Oil & Gas
Portfolio Companies: Itron, Strand Energy
Key Executives:
  Tom Glanville, Managing Partner
  Education: BS, Economics, University of Virginia; MS, Mineral Economics, Colorado School of Mines
  Background: Reliant; Enron Corp.; Bankers Trust Company
  Directorships: Itron, Chroma Exploration & Production, Strand Energy

697 ESSEX WOODLANDS HEALTH VENTURES LLC
21 Waterway Avenue
Suite 225
The Woodlands, TX 77380
Phone: 281-364-1555 Fax: 281-364-9755
e-mail: houston@ewhealthcare.com
web: www.ewhealthcare.com

Mission Statement: Essex Woodlans Healthcare Ventures make growth equity investments in proven healthcare companies. The fund seeks opportunities with rapidly growing revenues and earnings, low to no risk of capital loss, and that are well positioned for a predictable exit.

Geographic Preference: United States, Europe, China, Latin America
Fund Size: $2.5 billion
Founded: 1985
Average Investment: $20 - $80 million
Minimum Investment: $20 million
Investment Criteria: Seed-Stage, Early Stage, Growth Stage, Private Equity, Later Stage PIPE
Industry Group Preference: Pharmaceuticals, Medical Devices, Healthcare, Life Sciences, Biotechnology, Medical Technology, Healthcare Services, Information Technology
Portfolio Companies: AxoGen, Biotoscana, Bioventus, BreatheAmerica Inc., Breg, Cognate Biosciences, Cota, Encore Dermatology, Endologix, EUSA Pharma, EyePoint Pharmaceuticals Inc., Healthgrades, Metabolon, Prolacta Bioscience, Suneva Medical, TissueTech, Venus Concept, Xenex Disinfection Services Inc., Yantai Beacon
Other Locations:
280 Park Avenue
27th Floor East
New York, NY 10017
Phone: 646-429-1251 Fax: 212-922-0551

335 Bryant Street
3rd Floor
Palo Alto, CA 94301
Phone: 650-543-1555 Fax: 650-327-9755

Berkeley Square House
Berkeley Square
London W1J 6BR
United Kingdom
Phone: 44 (0)20 7529-2500 Fax: 44 (0)20 7529-2501

Key Executives:
  Martin Sutter, Managing Director
  e-mail: houston@ewhealthcare.com
  Education: BS, Louisiana State University; MBA, University of Houston
  Background: President, Woodlands Venture Capital Co.; various operations, marketing and finance positions in the health care industry
  Directorships: Aronex Pharmaceuticals, Cell Therapeutics, EluSys, eNos, Sontra, NotifyMD, Zonagen, Rinat Neuroscience, Confluent Surgical
  Immanuel Thangarai, Managing Director
  e-mail: paloalto@ewhealthcare.com
  Education: BA & MBA, University of Chicago
  Background: ARCH Venture Partners
  Directorships: iKnowMed Systems, Sound ID, CBR Systems
  Jeff Himawan, PhD, Managing Director
  e-mail: paloalto@ewhealthcare.com
  Education: BS, MIT; PhD, Harvard University
  Background: Co-Founder, Seed-One Ventures
  Petri Vainno, MD, PhD, Managing Director
  e-mail: london@ewhealthcare.com
  Education: MD, PhD Biochemistry with highest academic honors, Helsinki University of Technology; MBA, Stanford University
  Background: General Partner, Sierra Ventures
  Directorships: Chroma Theupeutics, Molecular Partners, Elisa Pharma, Prism
  Ron Eastman, Managing Director
  e-mail: paloalto@ewhealthcare.com
  Education: BA, Williams College; MBA, Columbia University
  Background: American Cyanamid Company; Pfizer
  Directorships: OMT, Cerium, RaduSys, Cell Biosciences
  Guido Neels, Operating Partner
  e-mail: paloalto@ewhealthcare.com
  Education: MBA, Stanford University; Business Degree, Engineering, University of Leuven, Belgium
  Background: COO, Guidant
  Directorships: LeMaitre Vascular, WMR Biomedical, EndGenitor Technologies, Radiant Medical
  Steve Wiggins, Operating Partner
  e-mail: newyork@ewhealthcare.com
  Education: BA, Macalester College; MBA, Harvard University
  Background: Founder, Oxford Health Plans
  Directorships: Millennium Pharmacy Systems
  Goran Ando, MD, Senior Advisor
  44-20-7529-2500
  e-mail: london@ewhealthcare.com
  Education: BA, Uppsala University; MD, Linkoeping University
  Background: Medical Director, Pfizer; VP, Medical &

Venture Capital & Private Equity Firms / Domestic Firms

Scientific Affairs, Bristo-Myers
Directorships: Chroma Therapeutics, EUSA Pharma, Molecular Partners, Symphogen
George W. Carmany III, Senior Advisor
281-264-1555
e-mail: houston@ewhealthcare.com
Education: BA, Amherst College
Background: Bankers Trust, American Express
Scott Barry, Managing Director
e-mail: newyork@ewhealthcare.com
Education: BA, Wesleyan University; MBA, New York University
Background: Novartis Pharma AG
Directorships: Victory Pharma, Orthovita, United Orthotic Group, Ziopharm Oncology
Evis Hursever, Partner
e-mail: london@ewhealthcare.com
Education: BA, Macalester College; PhD, University of Pennsylvania
Background: LEK Consulting, Merrill Lynch

698 EUREKA GROWTH CAPITAL
1717 Arch Street
34th Floor
Philadelphia, PA 19103

Phone: 267-238-4200 **Fax:** 267-363-3109
web: www.eurekaequity.com

Mission Statement: Makes private capital investments in lower middle market growth companies.

Geographic Preference: Mid-Atlantic, Eastern United States
Fund Size: $175 million
Founded: 1999
Average Investment: $8 - $15 million
Minimum Investment: $4 million
Investment Criteria: Acquisitions, Corporate Divestitures, Minority-Interest Growth Equity
Industry Group Preference: Healthcare Services, Manufacturing, Business Products & Services, Consumer Products, Consumer Services
Portfolio Companies: CCA Floors & Interiors, Everite Machine Products, Jansy Packaging, NetBoss Technologies, Project Leadership Associates, Toxicology Holdings, UTC Retail, West Academic Publishing

Key Executives:
Christopher G Hanssens, Managing Partner
267-238-4218
e-mail: chanssens@eurekagrowth.com
Education: BS, Accounting, Villanova University; MBA, Wharton School, University of Pennsylvania
Background: VP, Murray, Devine & Co.; Management Consultant, Accenture
Directorships: CCA Floors & Interiors, Project Leadership Associates, West Academic Publishing
Jonathan Y Chou, Partner
267-238-4203
e-mail: jchou@eurekagrowth.com
Education: BA, Economics, Columbia University; MBA, Wharton School, University of Pennsylvania
Background: Engagement Manager, LEK Consulting; Associate, Value Asset Management; Financial Analyst, Alex. Brown
Directorships: Everite Machine Products, Project Leadership Associates
Christian T Miller, Partner
267-238-4204
e-mail: cmiller@eurekagrowth.com
Education: AB, Economics, Princeton University; MBA, Wharton School, University of Pennsylvania
Background: Consultant, LEK Consulting; Investment Banking Associate, Berwind Financial Group; Accenture
Directorships: CCA Floors & Interiors, Jansy Packaging, NetBoss Technologies, Toxicology Holdings, UTC Retail, West Academic Publishing

699 EVERCORE CAPITAL PARTNERS
55 East 52nd Street
New York, NY 10055

Phone: 212-857-3100 **Fax:** 212-857-3101
web: www.evercore.com

Mission Statement: Evercore is an advisory and investment banking firm offering advisory and management services on corporate transactions and institutional asset, wealth, and private equity funds management.

Founded: 1996
Average Investment: $10 - $90 million
Investment Criteria: LBO, MBO, Early Stage, Mergers & Acquisitions, Divestitures
Industry Group Preference: Communications, Storage, Enterprise Services, Technology, Internet Technology, Data Services, Software

Other Locations:
666 Fifth Avenue
11th Floor
New York, NY 10103
Phone: 212-446-5600

One International Place
Boston, MA 02110
Phone: 617-449-3502

One North Wacker Drive
Suite 4010
Chicago, IL 60606
Phone: 312-619-4260

2 Houston Center at 909 Fannin
Suite 1750
Houston, TX 77010
Phone: 713-403-2440 **Fax:** 713-403-2444

515 South Figueroa Street
Suite 1000
Los Angeles, CA 90071
Phone: 213-443-2620 **Fax:** 313-443-2630

11111 Santa Monica Blvd
Suite 1480
Los Angeles, CA 90025
Phone: 310-473-0362

2494 Sand Hill Road
Suite 200
Menlo Park, CA 94025
Phone: 650-561-0100 **Fax:** 650-561-0101

150 South Fifth Street
Suite 1330
Minneapolis, MN 55402
Phone: 612-656-2820 **Fax:** 612-656-2830

Three Embarcadero Center
Suite 1450
San Francisco, CA 94111
Phone: 415-989-8900 **Fax:** 415-989-8929

425 California Street
Suite 1500
San Francisco, CA 94104
Phone: 415-288-3000

5359 Highway North
Suite 103
St Charles, MO 63304
Phone: 636-447-7422

4030 Boy Scout Blvd
Suite 475
Tampa, FL 33607
Phone: 813-313-1190 **Fax:** 813-434-2462

1000 Winter Street
Suite 4400
Waltham, MA 02451
Phone: 781-370-4700 **Fax:** 781-370-4747

1130 Connecticut Avenue Northwest
Suite 625

Venture Capital & Private Equity Firms / Domestic Firms

Washington, DC 20036
Phone: 202-530-5626

15 Stanhope Gate
London W1K 1LN
United Kingdom
Phone: 44-2076536000 **Fax:** 44-2076536001

50 St Mary Axe
4th Floor
London EC3A 8FR
United Kingdom
Phone: 44-2078473500

7 Queens Gardens
Aberdeen AB15 4YD
United Kingdom
Phone: 44-1224619214 **Fax:** 44-1224218510

Torre Virreyes
Pedregal 24, Piso 15
Col Molino del Rey, Miguel Hidalgo
Mexico City, Distrito Federal 11040
Mexico
Phone: 52-5552494300 **Fax:** 52-5552494317

Batalion de San Patricio 111, Piso 29
Torre Comercial America
Col. Valle Oriente
San Pedro Garza Garcia 66269
Mexico
Phone: 52-8181335550 **Fax:** 52-8181335526

Two Exchange Square
Suite 1405-1407
Central
Hong Kong
Phone: 852-39832600 **Fax:** 852-28690319

12 Marina Blvd
33-01 Marina Bay Financial Centre
Tower 3 018982
Singapore
Phone: 65-62907000 **Fax:** 65-62907001

Av Brigadeiro Faria Lima 3311
10th Floor
Sao Paulo 04538-133
Brazil
Phone: 55-1130146868 **Fax:** 55-1130146869

Av Borges de Medeiros
633 Sala 206
Rio de Janeiro 22430 042
Brazil
Phone: 55-2132059180 **Fax:** 55-2132059181

181 Bay Street
Suite 3630
Toronto, ON M5J 2T3
Canada
Phone: 416-304-8100 **Fax:** 416-352-5897

Paseo de la Castellana 36-38
Pl 10
Madrid 28046
Spain
Phone: 34-911190584

Ulmenstr 37-39
Frankfurt am Main 60325
Germany
Phone: 49-697079990 **Fax:** 49-6970799910

Key Executives:
Ralph Schlosstein, Co-Chair/Co-CEO
Education: BA, Economics, Denison University; MPP, University of Pittsburgh
Background: CEO, HighView Investment Group; Co-Founder & President, BlackRock; Managing Director, Investment Banking, Lehman Brothers
Directorships: Pulte Corporation
John Weinberg, Co-Chair/Co-CEO
Education: BA, Princeton University; MBA, Harvard Business School
Background: Vice Chair, Goldman Sachs; Co-Head, Global Investment Banking
Roger Altman, Founder/Senior Chair
Education: AB, Georgetown University; MBA, University of Chicago
Background: General Partner, Lehman Brothers; Vice Chair, The Blackstone Group
Robert Walsh, Senior Managing Director/Chief Financial Officer
Education: BS, Villanova University
Background: Senior Partner, Deloitte & Touche LLP
Directorships: New York Cares, IFA Insurance Company

700 EVEREST GROUP
PO Box 27395
Omaha, NE 68127

Phone: 402-548-5600
web: www.everestusa.net

Mission Statement: Everest Group focuses specificlaly on Service-based businesses such as marketing, financial and business outsourcing services.

Key Executives:
Vinod Gupta, Managing General Partner
Education: MBA, University of Nebraska
Background: Founder, Business Research Services; Founder, American Business Lists

701 EVERGREEN ADVISORS
9256 Bendix Road
Suite 300
Columbia, MD 21045

Phone: 410-997-6000
e-mail: info@evergreenadvisorsllc.com
web: www.evergreenadvisorsllc.com

Mission Statement: Provides investment banking services to emerging growth businesses and middle market companies throughout the Mid-Atlantic region.

Geographic Preference: Mid-Atlantic
Founded: 2001
Investment Criteria: Emerging Growth, Corporate Finance, Exit Strategies, Middle Market, Mezzanine, Debt Financing, Divestitures
Industry Group Preference: Consumer Services, Financial Services, Database Services, Marketing, Business to Business, Information Technology, Healthcare Services, Medical Devices, Internet, Digital Media & Marketing

Other Locations:
2010 Corporate Ridge
Suite 320
McLean, VA 22102
Phone: 571-406-5230

Key Executives:
Rick Kohr, Founding Member/Chief Executive Officer
Education: BA, Accounting, MBA, Finance & Marketing, Loyola University
Background: Managing Member, Chesapeake Emerging Opportunities Club
Directorships: LifeJourney, Pathsensors, Economic Alliance of Greater Baltimore, Howard County Economic Development Authority, Healthcare Interactive, BWTech
Joseph Statter, Managing Director
Education: BS, Accounting, University of Maryland
Background: CFO, CTB Group; CFO, Capitol Acquisition Corp.; Managing Director, Friedman Billings & Ramsey & Co.; Senior Manager, Arthur Andersen
Directorships: iCore Networks
Greg Huff, Partner
Education: Harvard College; JD, University of Maryland School of Law
Background: Director, M&A, CoreStates Securities Corp.;

245

Venture Capital & Private Equity Firms / Domestic Firms

VP, Corporate Finance Department, Mercantile-Safe Deposit & Trust Company

702 EVOLVE CAPITAL
P.O. Box 181569
Dallas, TX 75218

Phone: 214-220-4800
e-mail: jeff@evolvecapital.com
web: www.evolvecapital.com

Mission Statement: A private equity firm focused exclusively on leveraged capitalizations of entrepreneurial businesses.

Founded: 2005
Investment Criteria: $2 to $5 million EBITDA
Industry Group Preference: Healthcare, Industrial Services, Life Sciences
Portfolio Companies: Aspire Home Care, Biologos, Controlled Contamination Services, Doctor's Choice Home Care, Indigo Biosystems, Power Design Services

Key Executives:

Jeff Baker, Partner
e-mail: jeff@evolvecapital.com
Education: BA, Government, JD, University of Texas, Austin
Background: Attorney, Locke Lord Billell & Liddell; DLA Piper

Mike Crothers, Founder
e-mail: mike@evolvecapital.com
Education: BA, International Relations, University of Virginia
Background: Founder, Transition Capital Partners; Best Associates

Heidi Hargrove, Partner
e-mail: heidi@evolvecapital.com
Education: Texas A&M University, Commerce
Background: General Accounting, Transition Capital Partners; Accounting, Renshaw Davis & Ferguson

Matt Becker, Partner
e-mail: matt@evolvecapital.com
Education: BS, Physics, University of North Carolina; Siemens AG Executive Business Leadership Program
Background: CEO, Data Division, Volex Plc.; CEO, KVT Koenig; Operations, Siemens VDO

Ryan Shulz, Partner
e-mail: ryan@evolvecapital.com
Education: BBA, Master of Professional Accounting, McCombs School of Business, University of Texas, Austin
Background: CFO, Glass & Associates

703 EXCEL VENTURE MANAGEMENT
200 Clarendon Street
17th Floor
Boston, MA 02116

Phone: 617-450-9800 Fax: 617-450-9749
web: www.excelvm.com

Mission Statement: Excel Venture Management builds companies that are devoted to developing innovative and transformative life science technologies.

Fund Size: $125 million
Average Investment: $1 - $5 million
Investment Criteria: Early- to Late-Stage
Industry Group Preference: Life Sciences, Healthcare, Information Technology, Diagnostics, Medical Devices, Agriculture, Energy
Portfolio Companies: Activate Networks, Aileron Therapeutics, Aventura, Ayogo, Biocius Life Sciences, BioTrove, Catch, ClearDATA, Cleveland HeartLab, Gemphire Therapeutics, IlluminOss, InfoBionic, Lantos Technologies, MedVentive, Molecular Templates, NanoMR, Neosensory, N-of-One, Oculus Health, Openwater, Orionis Biosciences, Qstream, Saladax, ShapeUp, Synthetic Genomics, Tetraphase Pharmaceuticals, Virgin Pulse, WellDoc, Zipongo

Key Executives:

Rick Blume, Managing Director
Education: University of the Pacific; MBA, Stanford University
Background: Genentech; Co-Founder, CB Health Ventures
Directorships: Saladax Biomedical, Cytyc, EdenTec, Lantos Technologies, AbT, Zonare

Juan Enriquez, Managing Director
Education: BA, Harvard University; MBA, Harvard Business School
Background: Founding Director, Life Sciences Project, Harvard Business School; Founder, Biotechonomy Ventures
Directorships: Cabot Corporation, Genetics Advisory Council of Harvard Medical School, Visiting Committee of Harvard's David Rockefeller Center

Steve Gullans PhD, Managing Director
Education: BS, Union College; PhD, Duke University
Background: Co-Founder, RxGen; Senior Executive, US Genomics; CellActPharma GmbH; Senior Advisor, CB Health Ventures
Directorships: Molecular Templates, Cleveland HeartLab

Caleb Winder, Managing Director
Education: BA, Biology, Colby College; MBA, Babson College
Background: Principal, Biotechonomy; Synthetic Genomics; BioTrove; Biocius; Xcellerex
Directorships: Aileron, Aventura, Ayogo, ClearData, InfoBionic, Molecular Templates, ShapeUp, Saladax Biomedical, MedVentive

Gaye Bok, Venture Partner
Education: BA, Harvard College; MBA, Finance & International Management, MIT Sloan School of Management
Background: Microbia; Senior Director, Business Development, Synthetic Genomics; Business Development Manager, Cabot Corporation
Directorships: QStream

Chris Seitz, Venture Fellow
Education: BA, Williams College
Background: Consultant, Health Advances; Partner, Dorm Room Fund; ZocDoc

Kathryn Taylor, Associate
Education: BA, Quantitative Economics & International Relations, Tufts University
Background: Project Manager, New Product Development, The Advisory Board Company; Consultant, Putnam Associates

704 EXCELL PARTNERS, INC.
343 State St.
Rochester, NY 14650

Phone: 585-458-7333
e-mail: info@excellny.com
web: www.excellny.com

Mission Statement: Excell is a VC fund that invests in Seed and Early Stage high-tech startups in New York State focused on Upstate NY. Excell has the dual mission of generating returns through its funds' that rank in the top-quartile of its benchmarks, and supporting regional economic development by providing entrepreneurs with hands-on support as well as investment capital.

Geographic Preference: Finger Lakes Region of Upstate New York
Founded: 2005
Industry Group Preference: High Technology
Portfolio Companies: Adarza, Advantage Home Telehealth, American Fuel Cell, Augmate, Cerebral Assessment Systems, Cerion Energy, Conamix, CypherWorX, Diffinity Genomics, Diligence Labs, Efferent Labs, EkoStinger, First Crush, Full Circle Feed, GiveGab, Glauconix, Graphenix Development,

Venture Capital & Private Equity Firms / Domestic Firms

GRYT, IMSWorkX, Kinvolved, Koning, Mezmeriz, MicrOrganic Tech., Molecuar Glasses, OSM Environmental, PharmAdva, Rialto, SanaBit, Sensor Films, Splyce, StrongArm Tech., TenCar, Tetragenetics, Traverse Biosciences, Viggi Corp., VitaScan, WexEnergy

Key Executives:
Theresa B Mazzullo, Chief Executive Officer
Rami Katz, Chief Operating Officer

705 EXIUM PARTNERS
144 Village Landing
#276
Fairport, NY 14450

Phone: 888-983-9486
e-mail: info@exiumpartners.com
web: www.exiumpartners.com

Mission Statement: We invest in healthy businesses with strong growth potential. In doing so, we bring liquidity to owners looking to sell majority ownership to a partner that will respect what they've built, care for their employees, and continue to grow the business in the future.

Geographic Preference: Upstate New York, Southeast, Midwest
Investment Criteria: Change of Control, Recapitalization, Corporate Spin-Outs, Public-to-Private

Key Executives:
Jeff Valentine, Co-Founder/Partner
Education: Materials Science & Engineering, Cornell University
Background: CEO, Callfinity
Josh Bouk, Partner
Education: BS, Computer Science and Mathematics, State University of New York, College at Brockport
Background: VP, Sales and Marketing, Expense Management Division, Cass Information Systems; Veramark Technologies; COO, Connected Energy Corp.

706 EXPANSION CAPITAL PARTNERS
58 Andrews Drive
Darien, CT 06820

Phone: 203-202-2109
e-mail: info@expansioncapital.com

Mission Statement: To partner with entrepreneurs to grow clean technology companies that become respected industry leaders. We invest in companies that offer improvements in resource efficiency and productivity, while creating more economic value with less energy and materials, or less waste and toxicity.

Founded: 2002
Average Investment: $2 - $7 million
Investment Criteria: Growth Stage; Revenues of $5-30 Million
Industry Group Preference: Clean Technology, Energy, Water, Manufacturing, Advanced Materials, Transportation
Portfolio Companies: Agile Systems, Biorem, CPower, Dirtt, ElementLabs, Orion, Powerit Solutions, Sensortran, TigerOptics

Key Executives:
Bernardo H. Llovera, General Partner
e-mail: bernardo@expansioncapital.com
Education: BA, Engineering Sciences, Dartmouth College; Diploma Accounting & Finance, London School of Economics; MBA, Kellogg Graduate School of Business Administration, Northwestern University
Background: Senior Vice President, GE Equity; Senior Manager, Sara Lee Corporation
Directorships: Biorem, Powerit Holdings, Tiger Optics
Diana Propper de Callejon, General Partner
e-mail: diana@expansioncapital.com
Education: BA, Duke University; MBA, Harvard Business School
Background: Founder & Managing Director, EA Capital
Directorships: Echoing Green
John A. (Tony) Mayer, Board Memeber/Advisor
Education: BA, Princeton University; MBA, Harvard Business School
Background: Managing Director/CEO, JP Morgan

707 EXPANSION VENTURE CAPITAL
250 West 57th Street
RM 1301
New York, NY 10107

Phone: 212-265-1220 Fax: 516-882-5307
e-mail: info@expansionvc.com
web: www.expansionvc.com

Mission Statement: Expansion VC is an angel/VC firm that provides capital investments to early-stage companies focused on the Internet, e-commerce, education, biotechnology, and energy markets.

Founded: 2011
Investment Criteria: Early-Stage
Industry Group Preference: Internet, E-Commerce & Manufacturing, Education, Biotechnology, Energy
Portfolio Companies: Able, Agentero, Alchemy 43, Allbirds, AngelList, Apptopia, Ark, Astro, Aurora Labs, Bear Flag Robotics, Beyond Games, Bizly, Boatbound, Boomtown!, Booster, Bowery, Bulletin, Caarbon, Capsalus, Carrot Fertility, Chalkable, Compstak, Crius Energy, Dataminr, Decartes Labs, Emergent One, Engrade, Enigma, eShares, Esquire Bank, FanAI, Firebase, Fitmob, Fitocracy, HelloTech, Honk, Instamotor, InVenture, Latch, LegitParents, Lemonade, Life360, LoftSmart, Lola, Lunar, Maker's Row, May Mobility, Maz, Mino Monsters, Naadam, NewHound, Nexar, OrderUp, Outbox, Paintzen, Peek, Periscope, Pillow, PopExpert, Postmates, Pricing Engine, Recharge, Red Tricycle, Redcap, RelayRides, Rinse, See Me, Shuddle, Skurt, Slide, Socratic Labs, Sols, Stream, Student Loan Hero, Super, Tender Tree, TheFutureFM, The RealReal, Transfix, Turo, Unbound Concepts, Verificient Technologies, Via, VidIQ, Viridian, Viridis, Vive, YieldStreet, ZenDrive

Key Executives:
Joseph Melohn, Founder/CEO
Background: Owner, Platinum Brokerage Group LLC
Ryan Melohn, Co-Founder/COO
Education: BS, Business Management
Background: President, Expansion Group

708 EXPERIMENT FUND
67 Mt. Auburn St.
Cambridge, MA 02138

Phone: 650-204-1636
e-mail: start@xfund.com
web: xfund.com

Mission Statement: The Experiment Fund, anchored in Cambridge, invests in world-changing startups. We catalyze bold ideas and build transformative companies. XFund offers experimenters seed capital, expert guidance, and unparalleled access to America's top-tier universities and venture capital firms.

Geographic Preference: East Coast
Investment Criteria: Seed-Stage
Industry Group Preference: Information Technology, Healthcare, Energy, Technology
Portfolio Companies: 23andMe, Curebase, Fort Awesome, Guideline, Halo Neuro, Kensho, Kiite, Landit, Nebula Genomics, NewtonX, Parts Market, Philo, Ravel, Rest Devices, Service, Synapse, Tonic.ai, Zumper

Other Locations:
390 Lytton Ave.
Palo Alto, CA 94301

Key Executives:
Patrick Chung, Partner
e-mail: patrick@xfund.com

Venture Capital & Private Equity Firms / Domestic Firms

Education: JD, Harvard Law School; MBA, Harvard Business School; MS, Oxford University; AB, Harvard College
Background: Co-Head, NEA Seed
Directorships: 23andMe; Philo; Ravel Law
Brandon Farwell, Partner
e-mail: brandon@xfund.com
Education: BA, Economics and International Relations, Stanford University; MBA, Harvard Business School
Background: Investment Professional, DFJ; Rothenberg Ventures

709 EcoR1 CAPITAL
409 Illinois St.
San Francisco, CA 94158

Phone: 415-754-3517
e-mail: info@ecor1cap.com
web: ecor1.wpengine.com

Mission Statement: EcoR1 Capital invests in companies that seek to move medical research and biotechnology forward to advance an improve drug development.

Industry Group Preference: Biotechnology, Drug Development, Therapeutics
Portfolio Companies: Aldila Therapeutics, Accent Therapeutics, Anagin, Arcus Biosciences, Atara Bio, Atreca, aTyr Pharma, Avidity NanoMedicines, Clementia, Codiak, Collegium Pharmaceutical, Denali Therapeutics, Editas Medicine, FlexPharma, GossamerBio, Intellia Therapeutics, Kezar Life Sciences, Kindred Bio, Kura Oncology, Magenta Therapeutics, Metacrine, Morphic Therapeutic, Nabriva Therapeutics, Naurex, OmniOx, Oric Pharmaceuticals, Pellepharm, Prevail Therapeutics, Relay Therapeutics, Rubius Therapeutics, Sage Therapeutics, Scholar Rock, Syndax, Unity Biotechnology

Key Executives:
Oleg Nodelman, Founder/Managing Director
Education: BS, Georgetown University
Background: Portfolio Manager, BVF Partners; Mercer Management Consulting
Scott Platshon, Principal
Education: BS, Stanford University
Background: Aquilo Partners
Caroline Stout, Principal
Education: BA, Georgetown University
Background: Investment Banking Analyst, Credit Suisse

710 F-PRIME CAPITAL PARTNERS
1 Main Street
13th Floor
Cambridge, MA 02142

Phone: 617-231-2400
e-mail: info@fprimecapital.com
web: www.fprimecapital.com

Mission Statement: F-Prime Capital Partners combines two former venture funds, Fidelity Biosciences and Devonshire Investors. A global venture capital firm, F-Prime Capital invests in healthcare and technology companies in all stages of development.

Geographic Preference: Global
Investment Criteria: All Stages
Industry Group Preference: Biopharmaceuticals, Medical Technology, Therapeutics, Medical Devices, Healthcare Information Technology, Enterprise Software, Fintech
Portfolio Companies: AcaciaPharma, Aclaris Therapeutics, Adagene, Adaptimmune, Amphora Medical, AppsFlyer, Avidity Nanomedicines, Bang Er Medical, Better Life Medical, BioConnect Systems, BioRegen, Caribou Biosciences, Codeship, Cygnus Hospitals, Cytoville, Denali Therapeutics, Dimension Therapeutics, Eris Exchange, EVEN Financial, Eyebright Medical, Flywire, Forum Pharmaceuticals, Good Data, Gu Sheng Tang, HQ Medical Technology, Hua Medicine, Ikano Therapeutics, Innovent Biologics, Iora Health, Ivenix, Kensho Technologies, Kyruus, Laurus Labs, Madaket Health, MDDF, Medwell, Mersana Therapeutics, Neo4j, Novaerus, Orient Speech Therapy, OwnCloud, PatientPing, Ping Identity, Precision Biosciences, Procured Health, Prosper, Proteostasis, Pulmocide, Quartet Health, ReadMe, Receivables Exchange, Recurly, ReGenX Biosciences, Semma Therapeutics, Stride Health, Surface Oncology, Symbiomix, TraceLink, TradeBlock, Tradier, Trivitron Healthcare, Unum Therapeutics, US HealthVest

Other Locations:
33 Foley Street
London W1W 7TL
United Kingdom

Key Executives:
Stephen Knight MD, President/Managing Partner
Education: BS, Biology, Columbia University; MD, Yale University School of Medicine; MBA, Yale School of Organization & Management
Background: Researcher, AT&T Bell Laboratories; Consultant, Arthur D. Little; President & COO, EPIX Pharmaceuticals
Directorships: Innovent Biologics, Proteostasis Therapeutics, Iora Health, Pulmocide, Semma Therapeutics, Denali Therapeutics
Robert Weisskoff PhD, Partner
Education: AB, Physics, Harvard University; MBA, Columbia University; PhD, Physics, Massachusetts Institute of Technology
Background: Associate Professor, Radiology, Harvard Medical School; Faculty, Harvard-MIT Health Sciences Technology Program; Associate Director, MGH-NMR Center, Massachusetts General Hospital
Directorships: Bioconnect Systems, Caribou Biosciences, FORUM Pharmaceuticals, Laurus Labs, Surface Oncology, Trivitron Healthcare, ViewRay
David Jegen, Managing Partner
e-mail: david@fprimecapital.com
Education: Indiana University; Harvard Law School
Background: Senior Executive, Cisco Systems; JP Morgan & Company; The Boston Consulting Group
John Raguin, Venture Partner
Education: BS, Electrical Engineering, Cornell University; MBA, New York University Stern School of Business
Background: Co-Founder & CEO, Guidewire Software; VP, Sourcing Solutions Group, Ariba; MRO Software; Work Technology Corporation

711 FA TECHNOLOGY VENTURES
1000 Winter Street
Waltham, MA 02451

Phone: 781-786-8780
web: www.fatechventures.com

Mission Statement: FA Technology Ventures seeks opportunities with innovative businesses founded on the development of breakthrough technologies. The firm places particular emphasis on early and expansion stage companies in the technology and enterprise software sectors.

Geographic Preference: Northeast NY
Fund Size: $125 million
Founded: 2000
Average Investment: $3 - $8 million
Minimum Investment: $3 million
Investment Criteria: Early Stage, Expansion Stage, Growth Capital
Industry Group Preference: Technology, Energy Technology, Enterprise Software, Robotics
Portfolio Companies: Auterra, CreditSights, Knoa Software, OnePIN

Key Executives:
Gregory Hulecki, Founder/General Partner
Education: BSEE, Kettering University; MBA, Harvard Business School

Background: Founder & Managing Director, Seacoast Capital; Principal, Capital Growth Partners
Directorships: Auterra
Kenneth Mabbs, Founder/General Partner
Education: BA, Denison University; MBA, Wharton School, University of Pennsylvania; PhD, Harvard University
Background: Director, Investment & Merchant Banking, Gleacher and Company; Bear Stearns and Company
Directorships: Knoa Software, OnePIN

712 FAIRHAVEN CAPITAL
1 Hampshire Street
Suite 3
Cambridge, MA 02139

Phone: 617-452-0800 **Fax:** 617-452-0801
e-mail: info@fairhavencapital.com
web: www.fairhavencapital.com

Mission Statement: Fairhaven Capital invests in and helps to build early stage technology companies that are positioned for growth.
Fund Size: $250 million
Founded: 2001
Investment Criteria: Early-Stage
Industry Group Preference: Technology, Consumer Products, Digital Media & Marketing, Financial Services, Materials Technology, Security, Mobile, SaaS, Data Storage, Semiconductors, Network Infrastructure, Advertising
Portfolio Companies: Celtra, Cloakware, Cocona, Contour Semiconductor, CounterTack, CrowdTwist, Cylance, Digital Guardian, Drizly, EqualLogic, Exoprise Systems, HelloSoft, Icera, InnoPad, Ionic Materials, iPhrase, Jibo, NanoSteel, Prelert, Pwnie Express, Ramp, Resilient, ShopWell, SiGe Semiconductor, SocialFlow, Softricity, Statisfy, Third Screen Media, TrackVia, Trust Digital, VeloBit, YottaMark

Key Executives:
Paul Ciriello, Partner
Education: BA, Political Science, State University of New York at Buffalo; MPA, Northeastern University
Background: Founder, TD Capital Ventures; President, Fidelity Interactive, Fidelity Investments
Directorships: Cloakware, Fortisphere, iPhrase, SiGe Semiconductor, Softricity, Spring Partners, Surge Trading, Third Screen Media
Jim Goldinger, Partner
Education: BS, MS, Electrical Engineering, Massachusetts Institute of Technology; MBA, MIT Sloan School of Management
Background: Co-Founder, TD Capital Ventures; Chief Technical Architect, Adero
Directorships: Cocona, Contour Semiconductor, HelloSoft, InnoPad, Lilliputian Systems, NanoSteel, SiRiFIC Wireless
Rick Grinnell, Partner
Education: BS, MS, Electrical Engineering, Massachusetts Institute of Technology; MBA, Harvard Business School
Background: Co-Founder, TD Capital Ventures; Marketing, Content Bridge Division, Adero; ClearOne Communications
Directorships: Brabeion, Bridgeport Networks, Dataupia, Everypoint, EqualLogic
Rudina Seseri, Partner
Education: BA, Economics & International Relations, Wellesley College; MBA, Harvard Business School
Background: Senior Manager, Corporate Development, Microsoft Corporation; Investment Banking, Technology Group, Credit Suisse
Directorships: Fashion Playtes
Wan Li Zhu, Partner
Education: Massachusetts Institute of Technology; MBA, Harvard Business School
Background: Global Product Manager, Microsoft Dynamics CRM; General Manager, Online Sales & Operations in Asia Pacific, Google; Technology Investment Banking, Morgan Stanley

713 FAIRMONT CAPITAL
18340 Yorba Linda Blvd
Suite 107
Yorba Linda, CA 92286

Phone: 714-524-4770
web: www.fairmontcapital.com

Mission Statement: Fairmont Capital is a private equity firm that invests in middle-market businesses in the consumer-related sector.
Fund Size: $300 million
Founded: 1986
Average Investment: $10 - $20 million
Minimum Investment: $1 million
Investment Criteria: Leveraged Acquisitions, MBO, LBO, Private Restructurings, Recapitalization
Industry Group Preference: Manufacturing, Retailing, Restaurants, Distribution, Services
Portfolio Companies: Expressions Furniture, Garden Fresh Restaurant, Insurance Auto Auctions, Krause's Sofa Factory, Shari's Management Corporation, Stampede Meat, VICORP Restaurants, White Pine Company

Key Executives:
Michael W Gibbons, President
Education: BA, Harvard University; MBA, Stanford University
Background: Co-Founder & EVP, Equivest Partners; VP, Crocker Bank; Senior Associate, ICF International; Consultant, Booz Allen Hamilton
Mark J Gill, Managing Director
Education: BA, Economics, University of California, Davis; MBA, Finance, Golden Gate University
Background: VP Controller, John Breuner Company; Weinstocks

714 FAIRVIEW CAPITAL PARTNERS
75 Isham Road
Suite 200
West Hartford, CT 06107

Phone: 860-674-8066
e-mail: info@fairviewcapital.com
web: www.fairviewcapital.com

Mission Statement: Fairview Capital Partners is a venture capital and private equity investment management firm that offers fund of funds as well as investment strategies and services to investors.
Geographic Preference: United States
Fund Size: $3.7 billion
Founded: 1994
Investment Criteria: Growth Equity, Buyouts, Expansion
Industry Group Preference: All markets considered
Other Locations:
156 2nd Street
San Francisco, CA 94105
Phone: 860-470-0353
Key Executives:
JoAnn H. Price, Co-Founder/Managing Partner
e-mail: jprice@fairviewcapital.com
Education: Howard University
Background: President, National Association of Investment Companies
Directorships: YMCA of Greater Hartford
Laurence C. Morse PhD, Co-Founder/Managing Partner
e-mail: lcmorse@fairviewcapital.com
Education: Howard University; MA, PhD, Princeton University
Background: TSG Ventures; Equico Capital Corporation; UNC Ventures
Directorships: Webster Financial Corporation, Institute of International Education

Venture Capital & Private Equity Firms / Domestic Firms

Kola Olofinboba, Managing Partner
e-mail: kolofinboba@fairviewcapital.com
Education: University of Ibadan, Nigeria; MBA, Financial Management, Massachusetts Institute of Technology Sloan School of Management
Background: Engagement Manager, McKinsey & Company; Assistant Professor, University of Connecticut Health Center
Directorships: National Association of Investment Companies, Connecticut Children's Medical Center
Matthew Schaefer, Partner
e-mail: maschaefer@fairviewcapital.com
Education: BA, College of the Holy Cross; CPA
Background: VP & Treasurer, Bigler Investment Management Company; Senior Manager, M&A, Arthur Andersen
Directorships: UConn Ventures
Alan Mattamana, Partner
e-mail: alanm@fairviewcapital.com
Education: BSE, Chemical Engineering, Princeton University; MBA, Harvard Business School
Background: Principal, Polaris Venture Partners; Strategy Consultant, McKinsey & Co.
Directorships: West Hartford YMCA
Howard A. Halligan, Senior Advisor
Education: BA, Williams College; MBA, Columbia Business School
Background: President & CIO, Bigler Investment Management Company; President, CIGNA Investment Management Company
Directorships: Alternative Asset Investment Committee, Williams College Endowment Fund; Finance Committee, Francine Clark Art Institute
Edwin Shirley, Senior Advisor
e-mail: eshirley@fairviewcapital.com
Education: BA, Hampton University; MPA, Woodrow Wilson School of Public and International Affairs, Princeton University
Background: Equitable Capital Management Corporation
Directorships: Milestone Growth Fund, The Amistad Center for Art & Culture, Bushnell Performing Arts Center, Hartford Symphony Orchestra

715 FALCON FUND
100 N Barranca Street
Suite 920
West Covina, CA 91791

Phone: 626-966-6235 **Fax:** 626-966-0193

Mission Statement: We invest both in companies we alone have conceived, and in companies based on concepts that are brought to us by their founders. We do not invest in ideas, but in people who are willing to commit five or more years of their lives to making a company, and who have good knowledge of the markets they intend to serve. We can and do invest in ventures without complete management teams, and with very rudimentary business plans.

Geographic Preference: Southern California
Fund Size: $30 million
Founded: 1982
Investment Criteria: Seed, Very Early Stage
Industry Group Preference: Telecommunications, Software, Aerospace, Defense and Government
Portfolio Companies: Constellation Services International, IQinvision, NanoRacks, Napo Pharmaceuticals, Pascal's Pocket Corporation; Social Fabric Corporation, Touchdown Technologies, Vivature

716 FALCON INVESTMENTS
21 Custom House Street
10th Floor
Boston, MA 02110

Phone: 617-412-2700
web: www.falconinvestments.com

Mission Statement: Falcon Investments is a private equity firm that invests in subordinated debt and equity capital in leading middle market companies.

Fund Size: $1 billion
Founded: 2000
Average Investment: $10 - $75 million
Investment Criteria: Acquisition Financings, Recapitalizations, MBO, LBO, Growth Capital Financings, Liquidity, Structured Finance
Portfolio Companies: Accurate Metal Fabrications, Allion Healthcare, American Institute of Technology, AMPAC Packaging, Anton Capital Entertainment SCA, Bellisio Foods, BrightStar, Capital Sports Holdings, Capitain D's, Connect America Holdings, Dearborn Mid-West Conveyor Company, Digital Domain, EcoATM, Education One D/B/A Penn Foster, Gas Station TV, Ignition Group, Jason Incorporated, Jobson Healthcare Information, Kendrick Electric, Lapmaster International, LVI Services, MSX International, Northcentral University, One On One, Protect America, Purchasing Power, RFS Goldings, RoadSafe Traffic Systems, Rook Media, Saveology, Shari's Restaurants, Triad Retail Media, Village Roadshow Entertainment Group, WealthTrust, WL Plastics

Key Executives:
Sandeep D Alva, Managing Partner
617-412-2701
Education: BComm, Bombay University; MBA, Cornell University
Background: President, Hancock Mezzanine Investments; Joseph Littlejohn & Levy
William J Kennedy Jr, Managing Partner
617-412-2702
Education: BS, Business Management, Susquehanna University; CFA
Background: John Hancock Life Insurance Company
John S Schnabel, Managing Partner
212-300-0206
Education: BS, Chemistry, Adelphi University; MBA, Operations Research, Hofstra University
Background: Partner, Canterbury Capital Partners
Matthew J Hurley, Partner/CFO
617-412-2703
Education: BS, Business Administration, Bryant University
Background: John Hancock Financial Services
Eric Y Rogoff, Partner
212-300-0207
Education: BBA, University of Michigan School of Business
Background: Executive Director, Leveraged Finance, CIBC World Markets Corp.
Sven K. Grasshoff, Partner
617-412-2712
Education: BS, Business Administration, University of Colorado; MBA, Johnson School at Cornell University
Background: Corporate Development Group, Fischer Scientific International; Latona Associates; Citigroup Global Markets

717 FALCONHEAD CAPITAL
75 Rockefeller Plaza
Suite 1600B
New York, NY 10019

Phone: 212-634-3304
e-mail: info@falconheadcapital.com
web: www.falconheadcapital.com

Mission Statement: Falconhead Capital is a private equity firm that invests in companies in the consumer services, media, sports, lifestyle and food and beverage sectors. Falconhead Capital seeks to establish partnerships with stellar management teams and to create long-term value for its portfolio companies.

Fund Size: $500 million

Venture Capital & Private Equity Firms / Domestic Firms

Founded: 1998
Average Investment: $10 - $100 million
Minimum Investment: $5 million
Investment Criteria: MBO, LBO, Expansion, Middle Market
Industry Group Preference: Leisure, Sports, Media, Entertainment, Wellness, Food & Beverage, Consumer Services
Portfolio Companies: GPSI Holdings, Javo Beverage Company, Multi-Flow Industries, Rita's Water Ice Franchise Company
Key Executives:
  David Moross, Founder/Chairman/CEO
  Education: BA, Economics, University of Texas at Austin
  Background: Vice Chairman, Whitehall Financial Group; Chairman, Insco; President, Kalvin-Miller International
  Directorships: ESPN Classic Sports Europe, Maritime Telecommunications Network, National Power Sport Auctions, NYDJ Apparel Company, ESCORT Holdings
  David Gubbay, General Partner
  Background: Chairman & CEO, Whitehall Insurance Holdings, Whitehall Financial Group; Chairman, NHP Holdings; Head, Operations, Norwegian Cruise Lines; Digital Seas International; Conseco; Fellow, Institute of Chartered Accountants, England
  Directorships: EXL Service, Whitehall Financial Group
  Robert J Fioretti, Managing Director
  Education: BSc, MBA, Wharton School, University of Pennsylvania
  Background: Managing Director, Mistral Equity Partners; Trimaran Capital Partners; CIBC World Markets Corp.
  Directorships: Worldlynx Wireless, Worldwise, Abe's Market

718 FCA VENTURE PARTNERS
110 Winners Circle
Suite 100
Brentwood, TN 37027
Phone: 615-326-4848 **Fax:** 615-963-3847
web: www.fcavp.com

Mission Statement: FCA Venture Partners believes that by focusing on healthcare services and healthcare technology as well as information technologies opportunities, particularly in early and growth stage companies in the Southeastern region of the United States, it can take advantage of excellent investment opportunities. With its location in Nashville, Tennessee, as well as FCA Venture Partners deep involvement in the growth of the Nashville healthcare community, the Fund is poised to take advantage of the multiple opportunities provided by the current disruptions in the economy and efforts by the healthcare industry to reduce costs and become more efficient in this changing marketplace.
Geographic Preference: Southeast United States
Fund Size: $75 million
Founded: 1996
Average Investment: $2 million
Minimum Investment: $500,000
Investment Criteria: Start-Up, First Round, Second Round
Industry Group Preference: Healthcare, Information Technology, Wireless Technologies, Technology
Portfolio Companies: Catavolt, Clinical Ink, ChartWise Medical Systems, Entrada Health, Health iPass, IdentalSoft, KeraFAST, LogoGarden, Lumere, MediQuire, MRA Medical Reimbursements of America, One Medical Passport, Pathfinder Health Innovations, ProviderTrust, Remedly, Silvercare Solutions, Spiras Health, StudioNow, Vericred, Vivante Health
Key Executives:
  Matthew A King, Managing Partner
  Background: VP, Third National Bank; Chairman, President, and CEO, Radar Business Systems; Founder, MyOfficeProducts, Inc.
  Directorships: Clinical Inc.; KeraFAST; MediQuire; StudioNow; Vericred
  John Burch, Partner
  Background: Clayton Associates; Co-Founder, MyOfficeProducts
  Directorships: Armor Concepts; ChartWise; Lumere; One Medical Passport; Pathfinder Health Innovations; ProviderTrust; Thalerus Group
  Nancy S Allen, Partner & Chief Financial Officer
  Background: Partner, Heathcott & Mullaly & Hill

719 FCF PARTNERS LP
250 West Coventry Court
Suite 201
Milwaukee, WI 53217
Phone: 414-213-7091
web: www.fcffunds.com

Mission Statement: Wisconsin based private equity fund, established as an SBIC and investing in established companies located in the upper Midwest.
Geographic Preference: Upper Midwest
Fund Size: $62 million
Founded: 1999
Average Investment: $2 - $15 million
Minimum Investment: $2 million
Investment Criteria: Management Buyout, Corporate Spinout, Leveraged Buyout, Growth Investment
Industry Group Preference: Manufacturing, Distribution, Food Services, Food & Beverage, Medical Devices, Specialty Chemicals, Paper, Capital Equipment, Niche Manufacturing, Financial Services, Outsourcing & Efficiency, Packaging
Portfolio Companies: Alkar-RapidPak, CERAC, Kolpin Outdoors, Kolpin Powersports, Oshkosh Floor Designs, Riverside Engineering, Riverside Products, Rondele Specialty Foods, Sani-Matic, Seattle Systems, Sivyer Steel Corporation, Thiel Cheese & Ingredients, Waukesha Kramer
Key Executives:
  Gus Taylor, Senior Managing Director
  414-807-4204
  e-mail: taylor@facilitatorfunds.com
  Education: Middlebury College; Stanford Business School
  Background: Operations, Firststar Bank; Partner, Lubar & Company
  Scott D. Roeper, Managing Director
  414-881-2760
  e-mail: roeper@facilitatorfunds.com
  Education: Lawrence University
  Background: Prudential Capital; Firstar Bank; Harris Bank
  Paul J. Raab, Managing Director
  414-807-4178
  e-mail: raab@facilitatorfunds.com
  Education: Marquette University; University of Chicago; CFA
  Background: Firstar Bank
  G. Woodrow Adkins, Managing Director
  414-861-0168
  Education: University of Maryland
  Background: President, ConAgra's Deli Company; Armour Food Service; Wis-Pak Foods; Swift & Co.; Turnaround Capital Partners; New Glarus Foods Inc.; Acme Machell Rubber Products Company

720 FELICIS VENTURES
530 Lytton Avenue
Suite 305
Palo Alto, CA 94301
web: www.felicis.com

Mission Statement: Felicis Ventures targets innovative companies in five principal areas of focus: mobile, e-commerce,

Venture Capital & Private Equity Firms / Domestic Firms

enterprise, education and health. Felicis Ventures strives to provide quality support to its portfolio companies.
Geographic Preference: United States, International
Fund Size: $270 Million
Average Investment: $100,000 - $1,000,000
Investment Criteria: All Stages
Industry Group Preference: Consumer Internet, Mobile, SaaS, E-Commerce & Manufacturing, Education, Enterprise Applications, Financial Services, Gaming, Healthcare, Media
Portfolio Companies: aira.io, Alma, Aloha, Any.do, Ascend.io, Astranis, AvidBots, Azumio, Bioage Labs, bitpay, Bluecore, Breezy, Bright, Canva, CarDash, Chloe & Isabel, Civitas Learning, Class Dojo, Clear Labs, Cleo, Codesignal, Creative Live, Credit Karma, CrunchBase, Culture Amp, Cymmetria, Cyphy Works, Dedrone, Dialpad, Diffbot, dinda, DNAnexus, Dots, Drivetime, Earnin, EduK, Elevate, Emailage, ERPLY, Everalbum, Factual Beta, Figure Eight, First Opinion, Flexport, Fluxx, FundersClub, Gamalon, Gigster, Ginkgo Bioworks, Gobble, Granular, Greenhouse.io, Grove, Guideline, Guild, Happiest Baby, Hearsay Systems, Hippo, HireArt, HyperScience, Juniper Square, Kahuna, KISSmetrics, KiwiCo, Komodohealth, LeanData, Lighthouse, Matterport, Metromile, MightyHive, Mobile Action, Muse, Octave, Okera, Opendoor, Optimizely, PeerStreet, PetaSense, Philo, Piazza, Pindrop, Plaid, Planet., plotwatt, Practicefusion, Predict Spring, Recursion Pharmaceuticals, Rich Relevance, Rigetti, Roadmunk, Sano Intelligence, Sapho, Savioke, Scaled Inference, Scopely, Simplifeye, Smartling, SoundHound Inc., Spoke, Spring, Survios, Swift Navigation, Thirdlove, Top Hat, Trackvia, TripleByte, Troops, TrueAccord, Tynker, Vicarious, Warby Parker, Wild Earth, Wish, Zaarly, Zefr, Zipline
Key Executives:
Aydin Senkut, Founder/Managing Director
Education: BS, Business Administration, Boston University; MBA, Marketing, Wharton School; MA, International Studies, School of Arts, University of Pennsylvania
Background: Senior Manager, Google; Product Manager, MineSet, SGI
Sundeep Peechu, Managing Director
Education: BS, Computer Science, Indian Institute of Technology, Madras; MS, Computer Science, University of Illinois, Urbana-Champaign; MBA, Stanford Graduate School of Business
Background: Product Manager, Intel; NEA; Simbol Mining
Victoria Treyger, Managing Director
Education: Business/International Studies, University of Washington; MBA, Harvard Business School
Background: Chief Revenue Officer, Kabbage; Amazon; American Express; Travelocity; RingCentral
Directorships: Hippo Analytics; Deluxe Holdings
Wesley Chan, Managing Director
Education: BS/MS, Computer Science, Electrical Engineering, Massachusetts Institute of Technology
Background: General Partner, Google Ventures; Founder, Google Analytics & Google Voice, Google; HP Labs; Microsoft

721 FENOX VENTURE CAPITAL
2680 North First Street
Suite 250
San Jose, CA 95134

Phone: 408-645-5532
e-mail: contact@fenoxvc.com
web: www.fenoxvc.com

Mission Statement: Fenox Venture Capital is a Silicon Valley-based venture capital firm founded by an exceptional team of seasoned entrepreneurs and proven international business leaders. Fenox VC works with emerging technology companies worldwide and specializes in assisting entrepreneurs in North America achieve global expansion in Asian and European markets. Fenox VC seeks to work with world-class management and technical teams that are targeting disruptive opportunities in the consumer internet, retail, and software sectors.
Geographic Preference: North America, Asia, Middle East, Europe
Founded: 2011
Industry Group Preference: Consumer Internet, Retailing, Software
Portfolio Companies: Jibo, Genius, Affectiva, Meta, Afero, Color Genomics, Blockstream, X.ai, ShareThis, MindMeld, Terra Motors, Money Forward, TechninAsia, Metaps, Ossia, Lark, Scanadu, Evolable Asia, Gobble, Bluesmart, Zuu, Edyn, Jetlore, Sense.ly, Block Cypher, QVentus, Osaro, Sano, FiNC, Ahlijasa, Darmiyan, Sidecar, Medikly, True Vault, Kii, Money Design, Bop.fm, Dream Link Entertainment, I and C-Cruise.Co, NextCaller, Memebox, Pomelo, 500V, Moshimo, AloDoketer, Bride Story, Circa, HijUp, Third Love, IMoney, Regalii, MNectar, 99.co, Socialize, Rigetti, Roximity, Deepgram, 3Sourcing, Priyo.com, Talenta, Nova, Jurnal, Mailtime, Optilly, Wevorce, AirHelp, Panda Whale, GTar, BellaBeat, Women.com, Schematic Labs, Code Combat, Joyful Frog Digital Incubator, Belazee, Geniee, Crossfader, Xwork, KlikDaily, Jojonomic, Ajker Deal, Moka, 4doctor, Exvivo, Local, Multiply Labs, TeleCTG, Pesanlab, Bulletin, PopLegal, Sinovia Technologies, Paprika, Millibatt, Digicon Technologies, Monstar Lab, BagDoom.com
Key Executives:
Bill Reichert, Partner
Education: BA, Harvard College; MBA, Stanford University
Background: Chief Evangelist, Startup World Cup; Managing Director, Garage Technology Ventures; McKinsey & Co.; Brown Brothers Harriman & Co.; World Bank
Anis Uzzaman, General Partner
Education: BEng, Tokyo Institute of Technology; MS, Engineering, Oklahoma State University; PhD, Computer Engineering, Tokyo Metropolitan University
Background: Business Development, IBM
Brent Traidman, Advisor
Education: BA, Psychology & Economics, University of Michigan
Directorships: Edyn
Chris Abshire, Venture Partner
Education: BS, Petroleum Engineering, University of Kansas
Background: Evangelist, Startup World Cup

722 FENWAY PARTNERS
1251 Avenue of the Americas
17th Floor
New York, NY 10020

Phone: 212-698-9400 Fax: 212-581-1205
e-mail: info@fenwaypartners.com
web: www.fenwaypartners.com

Mission Statement: Based in New York, Fenway Partners is a middle-market private equity firm that focuses primarily on the consumer products and transportation, logistics, and distribution sectors. Fenway Partners works with management teams to help build valuable companies.
Fund Size: $2.1 billion
Founded: 1994
Average Investment: $50 - $75 million
Minimum Investment: $25 million
Investment Criteria: LBO, Middle Market of $100 - $600 million
Industry Group Preference: Consumer Products, Transportation, Logistics, Distribution
Portfolio Companies: 1-800 Contacts, American Achievement, Aurora Foods, Blue Capital, BRG Sports, Coach America, DCI Holdings, Delimex, Fastfrate, Elogex, Greatwide Logistics, Harry Winston, Iron Age, M2, MW Windows, North American Archery, Panther Expedited,

Venture Capital & Private Equity Firms / Domestic Firms

Preferred Freezer Services, Quality Farm & Country, RoadLink, Refrigerated Holdings, Simmons, SunTek, Sleep Country, Targus, Transport Industries, Valley-Dynamo, VB&P

Key Executives:
  Peter Lamm, Co-Founder/Managing Director
  e-mail: plamm@fenwaypartners.com
  Education: BA, English Literature, Boston University; MBA, Columbia University
  Background: Managing Director, Butler Capital Corporation; Co-Founder, Photoquick of America
  Directorships: Easton-Bell Sports, Fastfrate, Preferred Freezer
  Gregg Smart, Managing Director
  e-mail: gsmart@fenwaypartners.com
  Education: BA, Davidson College; MBA, Wharton School, University of Pennsylvania
  Background: Managing Director, Merrill Lynch & Company; First Union National Bank
  Directorships: American Achievement, SunTek, Preferred Freezer, RoadLink Workforce Solutions
  Walter Wiacek, Vice President/Chief Financial/Compliance Officer
  e-mail: wwiacek@fenwaypartners.com
  Education: BS, Business Administration, Bryant College
  Background: CFO, Jupiter Partners
  Chris Stevenson, Vice President
  e-mail: cstevenson@fenwaypartners.com
  Education: BS, Accounting & Business Administration, Washington and Lee University
  Background: Analyst, BB&T Capital Markets

---

723 FERRER FREEMAN & COMPANY LLC
10 Glenville Street
Greenwich, CT 06831
  Phone: 203-532-8011 Fax: 203-532-8016

Mission Statement: Invests exclusively in healthcare and healthcare related companies. Ferrer Freeman & Company aims to build leading healthcare businesses by helping to drive the growth of its portfolio companies.

Fund Size: $900 million
Founded: 1995
Average Investment: $10 - $40 million
Investment Criteria: Mezzanine, LBO, MBO, Later Stage
Industry Group Preference: Medical & Health Related, Healthcare
Portfolio Companies: AeroCare Holdings, AgaMatrix, Ancillary Advantage, Arcadia Healthcare Solutions, Ardent Health Services, Biotix, IC Axon, K2M, Medical Depot, Reliant Renal Care

---

724 FF VENTURE CAPITAL
989 Avenue of the Americas
3rd Floor
New York, NY 10018

Mission Statement: FF Venture Capital is one of the oldest early-stage venture capital firms in New York, with over 160 investments in over 50 companies. FFVC's strategy is to be the institutional-quality investor in the Seed/Series A space by identifying and helping to build startups that can be the low cost, disruptive player in their industry. FFVC has a dozen employees and extensive resources dedicated to portfolio acceleration, including strategy consulting, an experienced mentor network, recruiting assistance, pre-negotiated discounts with preferred service providers, an executive portfolio community, and in-house accounting.

Geographic Preference: United States, Canada, Isreal
Founded: 2008
Average Investment: $500,000 - $750,000
Minimum Investment: $500,000
Investment Criteria: Early-Stage, Series A
Industry Group Preference: Internet, Software
Portfolio Companies: 500px, Addepar, Alarts.com, Alpha Vertex, Appy Couple, Authorea, The Better Software Company, Bitesnap, Bloomz, Bowtie, Cambrian Intelligence, CardFlight, Cielo24, Clarity Money, Contently, Conerstone, CyberX, Dashbot, Deem, Distil Networks, Doc Authority, .tv, Drop, Earnest, Elicit, Estify, Founder Suite, Four Mine, GameSalad, GlucoVista, Gooten, GreatHorn, Hello Vera, Hijro, HowAboutWe.com, Identified, Indiegogo, InfoChimp, Ionic, Jazz, Klout, Klustera, Lithium, Livefyre, Mainframe, Movable Ink, Mount Cleverest, Muse, OfferIQ, Omaze, Omek, OpenCare, Owlet, Parse.ly, Parents.com, Pear, Pebblepost, Phone.com, Plated, Playdek, Qualia, Quigo, Rescale, Rhino, Rinse, SecondMind, SignUp.com, Skip, Skycatch, Socure, Software.com, Stae, Sure, Surfair, Tackk, Theatermania, ThinkNear, Top Flight Technologies, Track.com, Transactis, UniKey, Voxy, Wade & Wendy, Whisk, Wonder, YieldMo

Key Executives:
  John Frankel, Founder/Partner
  Education: BA, New College, Oxford
  Background: Goldman, Sachs & Co.
  Directorships: 500px, Apparel Media Group, Alerts.com, BlueDomains, Centzy, ClearPath, Immigration, Infochimps, Interaxon, Media Gobbler, Klout, Patents.com, Parse.ly, Phone.Com, Quigo, Voxy
  Alex Katz, Managing Partner
  Education: BSBA, Drexel University; JD, Temple University School of Law
  Background: Mesirov Gelman; Founding Partner, Katz & Miele, LLP; CEO, Fastener Distribution & Marketing Company
  David Teten, Venture Partner
  Education: BA, Yale University; MBA, Harvard Business School
  Background: Founder & Chairman, Navon Partners; CEO, Vertical Key; Bear Stearns

---

725 FGA PARTNERS
99 Wall Street
Suite 1770
New York, NY 10005
  Phone: 646-397-0588
  e-mail: info@fgapartners.com
  web: www.fgapartners.com

Mission Statement: A private equity firm that has a focus on disruptive software and technology in the areas of Artificial Intelligence, Machine Learning, Augmented Reality, Virtual Reality, Smart Technology and Advanced Blockchain Technology. Looks to invest and build with partners that are looking to change the world in some way for the better. During Mid 2021 an accelerator program initiative will commence in which FGA will partner with various small companies globally to spark rapid growth and innovation in a number of industries.

Geographic Preference: United States, Europe
Fund Size: $1 Billion
Founded: 1998
Average Investment: $100K to $50 million
Minimum Investment: $500K
Investment Criteria: Startups & Turnaround situations in Tech
Industry Group Preference: Technology, Blockchain, Business to Business, Real Estate, Enterprise Software, Cybersecurity
Portfolio Companies: Megahoot LLC, Spartan MTech

Key Executives:
  Louis Velazquez, Managing Partner
  Background: CS First Boston; Smith Barney; Morgan Stanley; Bear Stearns; Lehman Brothers; Paine Webber
  Directorships: Chariman, Spartan Modular Technologies; CEO, Megahoot.

253

Venture Capital & Private Equity Firms / Domestic Firms

Jenner Bendele, EVP of Acquisitions
Background: Clark Thomas & Winters; Assoc. Dir. of Development, University of Texas
Kenneth J. Kulaga, Executive Vice President
Education: MBA, Seton Hall University
Background: Consulting CFO/CAO for Start Ups; VP of Finance/Chief of Staff, CFO Global Foundries; Finance Director, ABM Industries; CFO, Consumer Electronics Division, Sirius Satellite Radio

726 FIELDSTONE PRIVATE CAPITAL GROUP
120 West 45th Street
Suite 1400
New York, NY 10036

Phone: 212-626-1400
web: www.fpcg.com

Mission Statement: Fieldstone Private Capital Group is an investment banking firm providing advisory services on leveraged buyouts, mergers and acquisitions, and private capital raises. Fieldstone specializes in global energy and infrastructure finance.

Geographic Preference: United States
Founded: 1990
Investment Criteria: Mergers & Acquisitions, Restructurings, Debt Financings, Equity, Divestitures, Leveraged Buyouts
Industry Group Preference: Natural Resources, Financial Services, Telecommunications, Transportation, Infrastructure, Energy

Other Locations:
11 Bolton Street
London W1J 8BB
United Kingdom
Phone: 44-2078081500

Kronenstr 3
Berlin 10117
Germany
Phone: 49-302123370 Fax: 49-3021233720

2nd Floor, Katherine and West
114 West Street, Sandown
PO Box 781589
Sandton 2146
South Africa
Phone: 27-117752000 Fax: 27-117752009

4B, Suryodaya, 1-10-60/3
Begumpet
Hyderabad, A.P. 500 016
India
Phone: 91-4066331960 Fax: 91-4066331965

Unit E-2-1
Plaza Damas
60 Jalan Sri Hartamas
Kuala Lumpur 50480
Malaysia
Phone: 6-0362017111 Fax: 6-0362019299

Key Executives:
Andrew Smith-Maxwell, Chairman
Jason Harlan, Chief Executive Officer

727 FIFTH WALL
13160 Mindanao Way
Suite 100B
Marina Del Rey, CA 90292

e-mail: lpinquiry@fifthwall.com
web: fifthwall.com

Mission Statement: Fifth Wall is a venture capital firm that takes an advisory-based approach when partnering with companies.

Founded: 2016

Industry Group Preference: Artificial Intelligence, Information Technology, Software, Applications, Building Sciences, Real Estate, Consumer, Retail
Portfolio Companies: Appear Here, Aquicore, Aurora Solar, b8ta, Blend, Blueprint Power, BUILT Robotics, Built Technologies, ClassPass, Clutter, Cobalt Robotics, Cobli, Convene, Cotopaxi, Eden, Enertiv, Foxtrot, Harbor, Heyday, Hippo, Honest Networks, Hydra Studios, Industrious, Interior Define, Lime, Loft, Loggi, Lyric, Madison Reed, Notarize, Opendoor, PollyEx, Shipwell, States Title, Taft, UNTICKit, Urbint, VTS, WiredScore

Key Executives:
Andriy Mykhaylovskyy, Managing Partner
Education: BS, Princeton University; MBA, Stanford Grad. School of Business
Background: Principal, Evergreen Coast Capital; VP, The Gores Group; CFO, Identified; Investment Banker, Morgan Stanley; Associate, Francisco Partners
Brad Greiwe, Managing Partner
Education: BA, Economics, Harvard University
Background: Co-Founder, Invitation Homes; Investment Banker, UBS; Tishman Speyer; Starwood Capital
Brendan Wallace, Managing Partner
Education: BA, Political Science & Economics, Princeton University; MBA, Stanford Grad. School of Business
Background: Co-Founder, Identified; Co-Founder, Cabify; Goldman Sachs

728 FIKA VENTURES
1950 Sawtelle Blvd.
Suite 183
Los Angeles, CA 90025

web: www.fika.vc

Mission Statement: Fika Ventures is a boutique seed fund that invests in founders engaged in problem solving through the use of data, artificial intelligence, and automation.

Geographic Preference: Los Angeles, Bay Area, Seattle, New York
Investment Criteria: Seed-Stage
Industry Group Preference: Data, Artificial Intelligence, Technology, Automation
Portfolio Companies: Atticus, Bowery, Chatdesk, FairClaims, Fullcast.io, Noyo, Openpath, Papaya, PathSpot, Policy Genius, Pull Request, Sierra Labs, Specright, Tolemi, Visor, WeeCare

Key Executives:
Eva Ho, General Partner
Education: BA, Harvard University; MBA, Cornell University
Background: General Partner, Susa Ventures; Google; YouTube
TX Zhuo, General Partner
Education: BA, Wesleyan University; MBA, Stanford University
Background: McKinsey & Co.; Co-Founder, Karlin Ventures

729 FINAVENTURES
541 Jefferson Avenue
Suite 100
Redwood City, CA 94063

Phone: 650-799-7725
e-mail: contact@finaventures.com
web: www.finaventures.com

Mission Statement: Finaventures focuses on early-stage to mid-stage growth equity technology companies. The firm seeks businesses with stellar management teams and a clear value proposition to its targeted market segment.

Geographic Preference: United States, Europe
Fund Size: Fund I: $20 million; Fund II: $80 million; Fund III: $120 million
Founded: 1999

Average Investment: $5 million
Minimum Investment: $3 million
Investment Criteria: Early-Stage, Mid-Stage, Growth Equity
Industry Group Preference: Software, Applications Software & Services, Mobile, Fintech, Components & IoT, Virtual Reality & Augmented Reality, Semiconductors
Portfolio Companies: Chartboost, DocuSign, Entropic Communications, General Photonics, Global Communications, Jawbone, Jumio, Kabam, Koinify, OEwaves, RockYou, Semiconductors

Other Locations:
20715 N. Pima Rd.
Scottsdale, AZ 85255

Key Executives:
Rachid Sefrioui, Managing Director
Education: BS, Operations Research & Management Science, Case Western Reserve University
Background: Managing Director, Credit Agricole Indosuez (Wafabank/Wafatrust); Managing Director, Bowco Investment Management
Sam Lee, Senior Advisor
Education: BS, Electrophysics, National Chiao Tong University; MS, PhD, Electrical Engineering, Ohio State University
Background: President, Raytheon Semiconductor Division; AMCC; Motorola; NCR
David Espitallier, Principal
Education: Reims Management School, France
Background: Manager, Transaction Services, KPMG; Founder, DealFlowFinder

---

730 FIRELAKE CAPITAL
350 Rhode Island St.
Suite 228
San Francisco, CA 94301-1648

Phone: 650-321-0880 **Fax:** 650-321-0882
e-mail: fkittler@firelakecapital.com

Mission Statement: While other firms look to invest in the tried-and-true, we seek out the disruptive. The ideas everyone else writes off as outrageous or impossible. The ones most venture capitalists would consider weird. We take the so-called wild and crazy ideas and develop them into intelligent, scalable solutions. We are early-stage investors with a long-term investment horizon. We aim to solve our world's most pressing problems through transformational, rather than incremental, change. That's why we invest in areas where we believe new technologies or even an early-stage idea can significantly change the economics of current markets: areas like energy, water, material sciences, and global supply chains.
Investment Criteria: Early-Stage
Industry Group Preference: Energy, Water, Materials Technology, Global Supply Chains
Portfolio Companies: Airware, Array Power, BluWrap, C2F, EnerG2, EOS Climate, HydroPoint Data Systems, Kurion, Liquidia Technologies, Nano-Tex, NovaTorque, Plextronics, QBotix, Ruckus Wireless, Scifiniti, Simbol Materials, Siva Power, Solicore, Sungevity, ZeaChem, ZT3 Technologies

Key Executives:
Fred Kittler, Managing Director
e-mail: fkittler@firelakecapital.com
Education: BA, Architecture, Princeton University; MA, Economics, Columbia University
Background: Co-President, Velocity Capital Management; JP Morgan Investment Management
Directorships: Kurion

---

731 FIRESTARTER FUND
e-mail: proposals@firestarterfund.com
web: www.firestarterfund.com

Mission Statement: We are not a traditional venture fund - we are 42 successful entrepreneurs who have come together to help fund the next generation of leading companies.
Geographic Preference: United States, Illinois, Midwest
Fund Size: $5.7 million
Minimum Investment: $25,000
Investment Criteria: Any Stage
Industry Group Preference: Digital Media & Marketing, SaaS, E-Commerce & Manufacturing
Portfolio Companies: Retrofit, Kapow Events, Hireology, GiveForward, ShiftGig, UpCity, Pangea, Blitsy, Cartavi, Mighty Nest, Food Genius

Key Executives:
Shradha Aharwal, Member
Background: Current: Co-Founder & Chief Strategy Officer, ContextMedia
Stopher Bartol, Member
Background: Current: Founder & CEO of Legacy.Com
Alex Campbell, Member
Background: Current: Co-Founder of Vibes Media
Cary Chessick, Member
Background: Current: Founder & CEO of Restaurant.com
Jamie Crouthamel, Member
Background: Current: Founder of Old Town Capital; Past: Founder & CEO of Performics
Brandon Cruz, Member
Background: Current: Co-Founder & President of Norvax
George Deeb, Member
Background: Current: Managing Director, Red Rocket Venture Partners; Past: Founder & Former CEO iExplore and Former CEO of Media Recall
Steve Farsht, Member
Background: Current: COO of Tap.me; Past: Partner of Norwest Equity Partners
Michael Fassnacht, Member
Background: President of DraftFCB Chicago; Founder & CEO of Loyalty Matrix
Gian Fulgoni, Member
Background: Current: Executive Chairman and Co-Founder of comScore; President and CEO of Information Resources

---

732 FIRST ANALYSIS
One South Wacker Drive
Suite 3900
Chicago, IL 60606

Phone: 312-258-1400
web: www.firstanalysis.com

Mission Statement: First Analysis is a private growth equity investor that focuses on emerging growth companies in the healthcare, technology, software, clean technology and chemicals sectors. The firm seeks to help established businesses grow into market leaders. First Analysis also provides equity research and investment banking services.
Geographic Preference: United States
Fund Size: $700 million
Founded: 1981
Average Investment: $3 - $10 million
Minimum Investment: $1 million
Investment Criteria: Emerging, Growth Equity, Expansion
Industry Group Preference: Healthcare, Information Technology, Clean Technology, Broadband, Infrastructure, Medical Devices, Clinical Research, Pharmaceuticals, Behavioral Management, Diagnostics, Network Infrastructure & Security, Wireless, Outsourcing & Efficiency, Chemicals, Energy
Portfolio Companies: ANI Pharmaceuticals, BuyerQuest, Checkpoint Surgical, Chrome River, Courtagen, CSA Medical, DataSphere Technologies, Freeosk, GAPbuster Worldwide, Gyrodata, ITS Compliance, Learning.com, Mediant, QPS Pharmaceutical Services LLC, Scale Computing, Sonoma Orthopedic, SquareTwo Financial, UniversityNow, VisiQuate, Yello

Venture Capital & Private Equity Firms / Domestic Firms

Key Executives:
Matthew Nicklin, Managing Director
Education: BS, Biology, Lehigh University; MBA, University of Chicago
Background: William Blair & Co.
Michael Siemplenski, Managing Director Emeritus
Education: BA, Policial Science, Northern Illinois University; MBA, Marketing/Information Systems, University of Illinois
Background: Burroughs; ITT Courier; Sanders Associates
Richard Conklin, Managing Director, Investment Banking
Education: BA, Economics, University of Notre Dame; MBA, Finance, Wharton School
Background: Managing Director, Robert W. Baird & Co.; Principal, William Blair & Co.; Managing Director of Investment Management, ProLogis; SVP/Head of Equity Capital Markets, Jones Lang LaSalle
Tracy Marshbanks, Managing Director
Education: BS, Chemical Engineering, Colorado State University; PhD, Chemical Engineering, Purdue University; MBA, University of Chicago
Background: Amoco Corp.
Eric Terhorst, Vice President
Education: BS, Chemistry/Environmental Engineering, California Polytechnic State University; MS, Industrial Administration, Purdue University; MS, Chemical Engineering, Stanford University
Background: Former Management Consultant

733 FIRST ATLANTIC CAPITAL LTD.
477 Madison Avenue
Suite 330
New York, NY 10022

Phone: 212-207-0300 Fax: 212-207-8842
web: www.firstatlanticcapital.com

Mission Statement: Investment firm that targets middle market companies.
Geographic Preference: United States
Fund Size: $500 million
Founded: 1989
Average Investment: $75 - $300 million
Minimum Investment: $5 million
Investment Criteria: LBO, MBO, Add-on-Acquisitions
Industry Group Preference: Consumer Products, Food & Beverage, Plastics, Aerospace, Defense and Government
Portfolio Companies: C-P Flexible Packaging, Resource Label Group, Sprint Industrial Holdings, TestEquity
Key Executives:
Roberto Buaron, Chairman/CEO
e-mail: rbuaron@first-atlantic.com
Education: Politechnco of Milan; MBA, INSEAD; MBA, Harvard Graduate School of Business
Background: Senior Partner, Overseas Partners; General Partner, First Century Partnership; Partner, McKinsey & Company
Thomas A Berglund, Managing Director
e-mail: tberglund@first-atlantic.com
Education: BS, Lehigh University; MS, Purdue University; MBA, Wharton School, University of Pennsylvania
Background: Partner, Jupiter Partners; Principal, Invus Group; Manager, Boston Consulting Group; Researcher, Bell Laboratories
Emilio S Pedroni, Managing Director
e-mail: epedroni@first-atlantic.com
Education: Bocconi University, Italy
Background: Engagement Manager, Corporate Finance & Strategy, McKinsey & Company; Executive Director, CIBC World Markets

734 FIRST CAPITAL GROUP
750 East Mulberry
Suite 305
P.O. Box 15616
San Antonio, TX 78212

Phone: 210-736-4233 Fax: 210-736-5449
e-mail: jpblanchard@firstcapitalgroup.com
web: www.firstcapitalgroup.com

Mission Statement: To realize an exemplary return on a diversified portfolio of well-managed companies having the potential to achieve exceptional growth in earnings and value.
Geographic Preference: Southwest Texas
Fund Size: $150 million
Founded: 1984
Average Investment: $5 - $10 million
Minimum Investment: $5 million
Investment Criteria: Growth Capital Investments in Well-Managed Expansion Stage and Mature Growth Stage Companies and other Special Situation Investments, Revenues of $20 Million
Industry Group Preference: Communications, Information Technology, Medical Products, Life Sciences, Manufacturing, Distribution
Portfolio Companies: Bluestreak Media, CCI Telecom, Extreme Communications, Hicks Broadcasting Partners, Lifestyle Media, Pr0Net, TransCom, Data Race, Digital Motorworks, Injury Sciences, FairPay Solutions, Mimix Broadband, Pavilion Technologies, SecureLogix, Wellogix, Biomedical Development Corporation, BioNumerik Pharmaceuticals, Chase Medical, Phi, BOXX Technologies, DL Industries, IntelliPack, Meyer Industries, Microwave Networks, Protective Packaging Corporation, Pulsetech Products Corporation, Shockwatch, Baseball Express, Media Recovery, Sav-On, WorldPass

Other Locations:
12400 Coit Road
Suite 910
Dallas, TX 75251
Phone: 214-382-1916 Fax: 214-382-1915

Key Executives:
Jeffery P. Blanchard, Founder/Managing Member
e-mail: jpblanchard@firstcapitalgroup.com
Education: BBA, MBA, University of Texas
Background: Founder, First Capital Group; First Dallas Capital Corporation, Rust Capital LTD, Victoria Capital Corporation, First Capital Group of Texas; COO, CFO, TESCORP, Inc., CEO, Baseball Express, Inc.
Directorships: Baseball Express; Boxx Technologies; Data Race; EZ Talk Communications;Media Recovery; Rewind Holdings, Specialty Bags, Injury Science
James A. O'Donnell, Managing Member
214-382-1916
e-mail: jaodonnell@firstcapitalgroup.com
Education: BA, Rhodes College; MBA Wharton School, University of Pennsylvania; CFA
Background: Carvey, Green & Wahlen; O'Donnell & Masur LP; Sherry Lane Partners LP; First Republic Venture Group; InterFirst Venture Corporation; First Dallas Capital Corporation; The Equitable Life Assurance Society
Paul S. Williams, Principal
e-mail: pswilliams@firstcapitalgroup.com
Education: BS, Accounting, Liberty University; CFA
Background: Senior Analyst/Director, USAA Federal Savings Bank; USAA Investment Management Company; Sr Auditor, KPMG;

735 FIRST CAPITAL VENTURE
50 South Steele Street
Suite 500
Denver, CO 80209

Phone: 303-955-4394
web: www.firstcapitalventures.com

256

Venture Capital & Private Equity Firms / Domestic Firms

Mission Statement: Invests in various innovative technology companies serving emerging industries. Their Viridis Fund focuses on cannabis.
Founded: 2005
Investment Criteria: Early-Stage, Production-Ready, Serves a Niche Market, Foreseeable exit in 24 to 36 months.
Industry Group Preference: Technology, Cannabis, Healthcare, eSports, Biotech
Portfolio Companies: BuildingDNA, CereScan, Coda Signature, DigyScores, Esports Entertainment Group, Kaonetics Technologies, KromaTiD

Key Executives:
  Gary Graham, Executive Managing Director
  Education: BS, Business Management, Meyers College
  Background: President, First Capital Investments Inc.
  Scott Morris, CPA, Chief Financial Officer
  Education: BS, Accounting, University of Colorado; MBA, Finance/Accounting, Regis University
  Background: Controller, Bay4 Capital/Convergent Capital; CFO, Fortress Investment Group
  Paul Spieker, VP, Operations
  Education: BS-EE, Electircal Engineering, Iowa State University; MIT Sloan School of Management
  Background: VP, Voltelcon; VP of Network Services, Webb Interactive Services; SVP of Network Operations, Webb Interative; President, Spieker Consulting

737 FIRST FLIGHT VENTURE CENTER
2 Davis Drive
P.O. Box 13169
Research Triangle Park, NC 27709-3169

Phone: 919-990-8558
web: www.ffvcnc.org

Mission Statement: The corporate mission of the First Flight Venture Center is to increase the number of successful technology-based small companies originating in or relocating to the Research Triangle Park region.
Geographic Preference: North Carolina
Fund Size: $140 million
Founded: 1991
Average Investment: $500,000
Minimum Investment: $50,000
Investment Criteria: Seed, Startup
Industry Group Preference: Information Technology, Life Sciences, Technology
Portfolio Companies: MAA Laboratories Inc., Iprobelabs Inc., Zenomics, InnoVision Imagine Laboratory, Microgrid Labs, Jericho Sciences, Techverse Inc., Hi Fidelity Genetics, Clairvoyant Networks, Ascent Bio-Nano Technologies, Learning Machines, CleanVolt Energy, Cell Microsystems, Indexus Biomedical, SonoVol, Gift Boogle, Clinical Sensors, ViraTree, 21st Century Creations, ElectroChemical Systems Inc., Excelerate Health Ventures, Verinetics, SciKon Innovation, Sirga Advanced BioPharma, Vindrauga Holdings; Inanovate, NIRvana Sciences Inc., Dignify Therapeutics, Trio Labs Inc., Camras Vision, Network Development Group

Key Executives:
  Andrew Schwab, President
  Education: BS, Electrical Engineering, Duke University; MS, PhD, Electrical Engineering, University of Virginia
  Background: COO, Panacea Biomatx; Director/Secretary, RTP Capital Associates
  Joe Spratt, Financial Specialist
  e-mail: jspratt@nctda.org
  Education: BA, Accounting/Finance, West Virginia State University; MBA, Marshall University

738 FIRST GREEN PARTNERS
221 East Myrtle Street
Stillwater, MN 55082

Phone: 952-288-2760

Mission Statement: To invest in innovative early stage companies that intersect agriculture and technology.
Founded: 2011
Investment Criteria: Startups, Early Stage
Industry Group Preference: Agricultural Technologies
Portfolio Companies: Digital H2O, Monolith Materials, Rivertop Renewables, Trelys

Key Executives:
  Doug Cameron, Managing Director
  Education: BS, Biomedical Engineering, Duke University; PhD, Biochemical Engineering, Massachusetts Institute of Technology
  Background: Chief Scientist & Research Director, Cargill; Investor & Advisor, Cargill Ventures; Khosla Ventures; Piper Jaffray; Professor, University of Wisconsin-Madison
  Directorships: Trelys, Renmatix, Sirrus Chemistry
  Thomas Erickson, Managing Director
  Education: BA, Mathematics, St. Olaf College; MBA, Kellogg School of Management, Northwestern University; CFA
  Background: Co-Founder & General Partner, BlueStream Ventures; Managing Director, Dain Rauscher Wessels
  Directorships: Monolith Materials, Rivertop Renewables, Trelys
  Constance Paiement, Chief Financial Officer/General Counsel
  Education: BA, Accounting, University of St. Thomas; JD, University of Minnesota; CPA
  Background: CFO & General Counsel, BlueStream Ventures; Co-Founder, Paiement Law Office; Gray Plant Mooty; Coopers & Lybrand
  Matthew Strongin
  Education: BA, Carleton College
  Background: Piper Jaffray; Co-Founder, MS Consulting; Co-Founder, WaterQuant
  Directorships: International Education Center

739 FIRST NEW ENGLAND CAPITAL LP
998 Farmington Avenue
Suite 216
West Hartford, CT 06107

Phone: 860-293-3334 **Fax:** 860-293-3338

Mission Statement: First New England Capital specializes in providing debt and equity financing to small and medium sized later stage companies in the United States. FNEC assists portfolio companies with capital raising, strategic planning, financing decisions, and personnel recruiting.
Geographic Preference: Northeast, Southeast
Fund Size: $50 million
Founded: 1988
Average Investment: $2 - $5 million
Minimum Investment: $1 million
Investment Criteria: Later Stage, Equity Capital, Mezzanine
Industry Group Preference: Aerospace, Defense and Government, Healthcare, Business Products & Services, Consumer Services, Manufacturing, Distribution, Technology
Portfolio Companies: Awareness Technologies, Cecilware, Ranger International Services Group, VaultLogix

Other Locations:
  285 Riverside Avenue
  Suite 200
  Westport, CT 06880

Key Executives:
  Richard C Klaffky, Co-Founder/Managing Principal
  860-293-3333
  e-mail: rklaffky@fnec.com
  Education: Brown University; MBA, Columbia University Graduate School of Business
  Background: VP & Manager, Intermediate Term Lending Division, Barclays Business Credit; Securities Analyst, Travelers Corporation
  Directorships: National Association of Small Business Investment Companies

Venture Capital & Private Equity Firms / Domestic Firms

John L Ritter, Co-Founder
860-293-3333
e-mail: jritter@fnec.com
Education: BA, Macalester College; MA, Religion, Yale University; JD, University of Connecticut School of Law
Background: Attorney, Blume & Elbaum; General Counsel, Independent Energy Corporation; Legislator, Connecticut State House of Representatives
Directorships: West Hartford Town Council
Seth W Alvord, Partner
203-341-9257
e-mail: salvord@fnec.com
Education: BA, Connecticut College; MBA, Cornell University
Background: Founder & Managing Partner, Balance Point Capital Partners; VP, Investment Banking Division, CRT Capital Group LLC; Morgan Stanley

740 FIRST RESERVE
290 Harbor Drive
Stamford, CT 06902

Phone: 203-661-6601 **Fax:** 203-661-6729
web: www.firstreserve.com

Mission Statement: First Reserve Corporation is a private equity firm focused exclusively on investment opportunities in the energy industry.

Geographic Preference: United States, Canada
Fund Size: $3.4 billion
Founded: 1981
Average Investment: $200 million
Minimum Investment: $50 million
Investment Criteria: Add-On Acquisitions, Buyouts, Growth Capital
Industry Group Preference: Industrial Equipment, Energy, Oil & Gas, Alternative Energy, Renewable Energy
Portfolio Companies: 9Ren Group, Abengoa, AF Global Corporation, American Energy Permian Basin, Amromco Energy, Ascent Resources, Barra Energia, Century Midstream, CHC Helicopter Corporation, Cobalt International Energy, Connect Resource Services, Deep Gulf Energy, Diamond S, Dixie Electric, DOF Subsea, Energy Credit Partners, FR Midstream Holdings, Hoover Group, KrisEnergy Holdings, Midstates Petroleum, Mountaineer Keystone, NewWoods Petroleum, PrimeLine Utility Services, Sabine Oil & Gas, Templar Energy, TNT Crane & Rigging, TPC Group

Other Locations:
600 Travis
Suite 6000
Houston, TX 77002
Phone: 713-227-7890 **Fax:** 713-224-0771

First Reserve Intl. Ltd.
25 Victoria Street
7th Floor
London SW1H 0EX
United Kingdom
Phone: 44 20 7930 2120 **Fax:** 44 20 7930 2130

Key Executives:
William E. Macaulay, Chairman
Education: BBA, City College of New York; MBA, Wharton School
Background: Co-Founder, Meridien Capital Company; Director, Corporate Finance, Oppenheimer & Company; Founder, Peppermill Oil Company
Gary D. Reaves, Managing Director
Education: BBA, University of Texas
Background: Analyst, UBS Investment Bank; Analyst, Howard Frazier Barker Elliott Inc.
Alex T. Krueger, President/CEO
Education: BS, Chemical Engineering, BS, Finance & Statistics, Wharton School
Background: Energy Group, Donaldson Lufkin & Jenrette
Brooks Shugharts, Managing Director
Education: BBA, University of Texas

Background: Credit Suisse; Lazard Freres; Donaldson Lufkin & Jenrette
Will Honeybourne, Managing Director
Education: BSc, Oil Technology, Imperial College, London
Background: Senior Vice President, Western Atlas International; President & CEO, Computalog; Baker Hughes
Directorships: CNOOC
Jeffrey K. Quake, Managing Director
Education: BA, Economics, Williams College; MBA, Harvard Business School
Background: JP Morgan; Lehman Brothers
Claudi Santiago, Managing Director
Education: Universidad Autonoma de Barcelona; INSEAD; Georgetown University
Background: President & CEO, GE Oil & Gas, General Electric
Alan G. Schwartz, Managing Director
Education: BS, University of New Hampshire; JD, Fordham University School of Law
Background: Partner, Simpson Thacher & Bartlett
Joshua R. Weiner, Managing Director
Education: BA, Bowdoin College
Background: Associate, Warburg Pincus LLC; Associate, Morgan Stanley
Neil A. Wizel, Managing Director
Education: BA, Emery University
Background: Greenbriar Equity Group; Financial Analyst, Credit Suisse

741 FIRST ROUND CAPITAL
151 10th Street
San Francisco, CA 94103

web: www.firstround.com

Mission Statement: Collectively, First Round partners have more than 100 years of experience working with founding teams.

Geographic Preference: San Francisco, New York, Los Angeles
Average Investment: $500-750K
Investment Criteria: Seed
Industry Group Preference: Enterprise, Consumer, Hardware, Fintech, Healthcare
Portfolio Companies: 33across, 64-x, 9GAG, Abl, Abra, Abstract, Against Gravity, Agari, Alma, Aloha, AltSchool, Amino, AppNexus, Area 1, Aster Data Systems, Atrium, Augury, Aviso, Axial, Bazaarvoice, Beautiful AI, Binti, Birchbox, Blue Apron, Boom.tV, Boulder, Bowery, Boxed, Bright, Caredox, Caspida, Castle, Civitas Learning, Clare, Clearbit, Clover Health, Collective Retreats, Confide, Continuity Control, Court Buddy, Cricket Health, Crossbeam, CrowdJustice, Curalate, Discourse, Dishcraft Robotics, DNAnexus, DoubleVerify, Drift, Dynasty, EAT Club, Eero, Engagio, Evie, Flatiron Health, Flexport, Flurry, Forward, Fundera, FundersClub, Gauntlet, Gem, Gigya, Gnip, Goat, Good Uncle, Gregor Diagnostics, Grokker, GroupMe, Grove, GumGum, Gumroad, Haven, Health IQ, HotelTonight, Human DX, Influitive, Inspirato, Instrumental, Intrinsic, June, Karuna Health, Keeps, Kentik, Kindred, KiwiCo, Knewton, Koru, Legion, LendingHome, Liftopia, LiveIntent, Lob, Looker, Lygos, Mango Health, Mashery, Massdrop, MemSQL, Metric Insights, Metromile, Mighty Networks, Mint, Mirror, Moat, Mobcrush, Modern Fertility, Monetate, Nimble Pharmacy, Nomad Health, North, Notable Labs, Notion, Nova Credit, Numerai, On Deck Capital, OpenX, Ossium Health, Outlier, Pantheon, Parsable, PatientPing, Perceptive Automata, Percolate, PerformLine, Ping, Pique Tea, Planet Labs, Poppin, Promise, PullString, RaiseMe, Rare Bits, RebelMouse, Refinery29, Relay Network, Remind, Righthook, Ring, Roblox, Rover, Sano, SavingStar, Shipwell,

Other Locations:
37 E 28th St.
Suite 900
New York, NY 10016

2400 Market Street
Suite 237
Philadelphia, PA 19103

Key Executives:
Phin Barnes, Partner
Education: BA, Economics & Sociology, Haverford College; MBA, Wharton School, University of Pennsylvania
Background: Founder, ResponDesign; Creative Director, Footwear, AND1 Basketball
Chris Fralic, Partner
Education: BS, Finance, Villanova University; MBA, St. Joseph's University
Background: VP, Business Development, del.icio.us; Ad Sales & Business Development, eBay; VP, Business Development, Nextron; Director, Business Development, America Online
Rob Hayes, Partner
Education: BA, University of California, Berkeley; MBA, Columbia University
Background: Venture Investor, Omidyar Network; Palm
Josh Kopelman, Partner
Education: BS, Entrepreneurial Management & Marketing, Wharton School, University of Pennsylvania
Background: Co-Founder, Infonautics Corporation; Founder, Half.com; Founder, TurnTide
Bill Trenchard, Partner
Education: BA, Science & Technology Studies, Cornell University
Background: LiveOps; Founder, Jump Networks; Founder Partner, Founder Collective
Directorships: Readyforce, LiveOps, Looker, Samasource
Hayley Barna, Partner
Education: Harvard Business School
Background: Bain & Company; Birchbox
Brett Berson, Partner
Education: New York University

742 FIRST STEP FUND
600 Reniassance Center
Suite 1710
Detroit, MI 48243-1802

Phone: 313-259-6368 Fax: 313-259-6393
e-mail: info@investdetroit.vc
web: www.investdetroit.com/managed-funds/first-step-fund

Mission Statement: The First Step Fund is an early stage investment fund in partnership with the Invest Detroit Foundation, TechTown, Bizdom, Ann Arbor SPARK and Automation Alley serving emerging and newly-formed high growth, businesses in Southeast Michigan.

Geographic Preference: Southeast Michigan
Average Investment: $10,000 - $50,000
Investment Criteria: Early-Stage
Industry Group Preference: High Technology, Clean Technology, Life Sciences, Advanced Manufacturing, Consumer Products
Portfolio Companies: Accio Energy, Air Movement Systems, Algal Scientific, Are You A Human, Bandals, Clean Emission Fluids, Coliant Corporation, Current Motor Company, Delphinus, ERT Systems, FamilyMint, Fusion Coolant, GradeCheck, Heart Graffiti, IC Data Com, InfoReady Corporation, Ix Innovations, Launch Learning, Local Orbit, Myine Elecronics, NextCat, OWN POS, Reveal Design Automation, Wedit, UniTask, Apolife, SideCar, Estrakon, ArdentCause, Relume, Envy Modular Systems, Epsilon, Denovo Sciences, Larky, New Eagle, Molecular Imaging Research, Llamasoft, Stik.com, Ann Williams Group, FarmLogs

Key Executives:
David Blaszkiewicz, President
Background: President, Detroit Investment Fund

743 FIRSTMARK CAPITAL
100 Fifth Avenue
New York, NY 10011

Phone: 212-792-2200 Fax: 212-391-5700
e-mail: info@firstmarkcap.com
web: www.firstmarkcap.com

Mission Statement: Committed to investing in leading technology innovators who share our passion for making an impact by building exceptional, world-changing businesses.

Founded: 2008
Investment Criteria: All Stages
Industry Group Preference: Fintech, Gaming, Entertainment, Communications, Healthcare, Hardware, Mobile, Applications Software & Services, Infrastructure, Data & Analytics, Commerce, Education
Portfolio Companies: ActionIQ, Aereo, Airbnb, AppFirst, Aveksa, BioDigital, Blispay, Bluecore, Body & Labs, Bonusly, Boomi, Brooklinen, Cockroach Labs, Conductor, Dashlane, Data Iku, Digital Currency Group, Disconnect, Dovetail, Draft Kings, Eagle Eye Analytics, Emergent Payments, Engagio, Fame and Partners, Frame.ai, Frame.io, Gravie, Greenphire, Guru, HealthPlanOne, Helium, HopSkipDrive, HowGood, Hubble, HyperScience, IMImobile, Insikt, Invision, Jirafe, Kinsa, Knewton, Lolly Wolly Doodle, Lot18, Lumosity, MarketFactory, Medico, Methodology, Mission U, NewsCred, Omaze, OpenGamma, Optimus Ride, Payoff, Phosphorus, Pinterest, Playnomics, Proletariat, Public Stuff, Recombine, Riot Games, Robin, Roli, Schoology, Secondmarket, Selfmade, Sence360, Shopify, Sketchfab, Spadac, Sproutling, Starry, Straighterline, Symphony Commerce, Tapad, TestFire, Tommy John, TraceLink, Tubular, Upgrade, Upwork, Virgin Mega, Welcome, X., Zipments

Key Executives:
Matt Turck, Managing Director
Education: LLM, Yale Law School
Background: Managing Director, Bloomberg Ventures; Co-Founder, TripleHop Technologies
Catherine Ulrich, Managing Director
Education: AB, Engineering, Harvard College
Background: Chief Product Officer, Shutterstock; Chief Product Officer, Weight Watchers
Beth Ferreira, Managing Director
Education: BA, University of Pennsylvania; MBA, Wharton School
Background: Managing Partner, WME Ventures; COO, Fab; Flatiron Partners; BCG; UBS
Rick Heitzmann, Managing Director
Education: BS, Georgetown University; MBA, Harvard Business School
Background: Partner, Pequot Ventures; Founding Member, First Advantage; Nationsbanc Montgomery Securities; Booz Allen Hamilton; Houlihan Lokey Howard & Zukin
Amish Jani, Managing Director
Education: BS, MBA, Wharton School, University of Pennsylvania
Background: Partner, Pequot Ventures
Greg Raiten, General Counsel
Education: BS, Computer Science, John Hopkins University; JD, New York University School of Law
Background: General Counsel, 500 Startups; Corporate Attorney, Gunderson Dettmer; Securities Attorney, Latham & Watkins

Venture Capital & Private Equity Firms / Domestic Firms

744 FISHER LYNCH CAPITAL
2929 Campus Drive
Suite 420
San Mateo, CA 94403
Phone: 650-287-2700 Fax: 650-287-2701
web: www.fisherlynch.com

Mission Statement: Fisher Lynch Capital is a boutique investment firm that focuses exclusively on private equity sectors around the world. FLC offers investors private equity solutions in the form of co-investments, fund-of-funds, and customized investment strategies.

Geographic Preference: Worldwide
Fund Size: $2 billion
Founded: 2003
Average Investment: $10 - $100 million
Investment Criteria: Buyouts, Growth Equity, Distressed, Mezzanine
Portfolio Companies: ADT Security, Aernnova, Allegro, Atlice, Coty Inc., CPA Global, Edward Don & Company, Endeavor, Finastra, Flexential, Biotoscana, HD Vest Financial Services, IQVIA, Ista International GmbH, Lifetime Fitness, McAfee, MultiPlan, NXP Semiconductors, Performance Food Group, Picard, Quest, SonicWall, Securus Technologies, Solera Holdings Inc., Vivint Smart Home, Woodstream, Zayo, Ziggo

Other Locations:
200 Clarendon Street
25th Floor
Boston, MA 02116
Phone: 617-406-3120 Fax: 617-406-3121

12 Hay Hill
Mayfair
London W1J 8NR
United Kingdom
Phone: 44-2071180603

Key Executives:
Marshall Bartlett, Managing Director
e-mail: marshall@fisherlynch.com
Education: BA, History, Yale University; MBA, Tuck School of Business, Dartmouth College
Background: Partner, Parthenon Capital; The Parthenon Group; Saugatuck Capital; Brown Brothers Harriman & Co.
Brett Fisher, Founder/Managing Director
e-mail: brett@fisherlynch.com
Education: BA, Economics & Mathematics, Yale University; MBA, Stanford Graduate School of Business
Background: SVP, GIC Special Investments; Director, Corporate Development, AirTouch Communications; VP, Genstar Investment Corporation; Marakon Associates
Leon Kuan, Managing Director
e-mail: leon@fisherlynch.com
Education: BS, Engineering & Business, Jerome Fisher Program in Management & Technology, MBA, Wharton School, University of Pennsylvania
Background: SVP, GIC Special Investments
Anthony Limberis, Senior Advisor
e-mail: anthony@fisherlynch.com
Education: ScB, Applied Mathematics & Economics, Brown University; MBA, Stanford Graduate School of Business
Background: Porfolio Manager, The Andrew W. Mellon Foundation; Senior Analyst, Lucent Asset Management; Consultant, Cambridge Associates
Linda Lynch, Founder/Senior Advisor
e-mail: linda@fisherlynch.com
Education: BA, English, Yale University; MBA, Stanford Graduate School of Business
Background: VP & Director, Private Equity, Lucent Asset Management; Managing Director, Cambridge Associates
Marcus Wood, Managing Director, London
e-mail: marcus@fisherlynch.com
Education: BSc, Mathematics, University of London
Background: Partner, Cinven; Intermediate Capital Group plc; PricewaterhouseCoopers
Georganne Perkins, Senior Advisor
e-mail: georganne@fisherlynch.com
Education: BA, Fine Arts, University of California, Irvine
Background: Director, Private Equity, Stanford Management Company

745 FIVE ELMS CAPITAL
4801 Main St.
Suite 700
Kansas City, MO 64112
Phone: 913-953-8960
e-mail: ws@fiveelms.com
web: www.fiveelms.com

Mission Statement: Five Elms Capital is a global growth equity firm that invests in fast-growing B2B software businesses that users love. Five Elms provides capital and resources to help companies accelerate growth and further cement their role as industry leaders. Since firm inception in 2007, Five Elms has focused exclusively on software investing, building an unmatched network and deep domain expertise. Today with $700+ million AUM and a global team of over 50 investment professionals, Five Elms has invested in more than 40 software platforms globally.

Fund Size: $557 million
Founded: 2007
Average Investment: $5 -$50 million
Investment Criteria: Expansion Stage
Industry Group Preference: Business Products & Services, Consumer Services, Information Technology, Internet, Financial Services, SaaS, Advertising, Outsourcing & Efficiency, E-Commerce & Manufacturing
Portfolio Companies: ActiveProspect, Apptegy, Crelate Talent, Dark Owl, DeepCrawl, Field Agent, Go React, Hubb, LaborChart, MemberClicks, Outfit, Panopta, Passageways, PlayVox, Powwr, ProxyClick, Reachdesk, RFP360, Saylent, Sherpa, SimpliField, SingleOps, Skynamo, Smart Warehousing, Spring Venture Group, Userlane

Key Executives:
Fred Coulson, Founder/Managing Partner
e-mail: fred@fiveelms.com
Education: BS, Business Administration, University of Kansas
Background: TH Lee Putnam Ventures; Investment Banking, Morgan Stanley
Thomas Kershisnik, Partner
Joe Onofrio, Partner
Ryan Mandl, Partner
Stephanie Schneider, Partner
Austin Gideon, Partner

746 FIVE POINTS CAPITAL
101 N Cherry Street
Suite 700
Winston-Salem, NC 27101
Phone: 336-733-0350
e-mail: bkulman@fivepointscapital.com
web: www.fivepointscapital.com

Mission Statement: Makes control investments in privately-held companies in the lower-middle market.

Geographic Preference: United States
Fund Size: $230 million
Founded: 1998
Minimum Investment: $10 million
Investment Criteria: Buyouts, Acquisitions, Growth Capital, Recapitalizations
Industry Group Preference: Business & Commercial Services, Healthcare Services, Industrial Services, Value-Added Distribution, Niche Manufacturing
Portfolio Companies: Aaron Industries, Advanced Disposal Services, Alzheimers Research & Treatment Center,

Venture Capital & Private Equity Firms / Domestic Firms

BrandFX, CareerStep, Cavalier Telephone, Cline Driving Solutions, ECP/CH Industries, Fire & Life Safety America, Five Star Foods, GrammaTech, Flint Trading Inc., Glassock Company, JML Optical Industries, Jones & Frank, Outsolve, PHC, Quick Med Claims, Safety Infrastructure Solutions, Smith-Cooper International, Specialty Applicances, Synoptek, The Lion Brewery, Thompson Industrial Services, TransGo, Triangle Ice, Unishippers Global Logistics, Universal Solutions International, Village Tavern, Women's Marketing, Young Innovations

Key Executives:
  David G Townsend, Managing Partner
  336-733-0355
  e-mail: dtownsend@fivepointscapital.com
  Education: BA, History, University of North Carolina, Chapel Hill; MBA, Finance & Accounting, University of North Carolina, Chapel Hill
  Background: Investment Banking, Stephens Inc.; Ernst & Young
  Directorships: BrandFX Holdings, JML Optical, Thompson Industrial Services
  Martin P. Gilmore, Managing Partner
  336-733-0361
  e-mail: mgilmore@fivepointscapital.com
  Education: BA, Finance, University of South Carolina
  Background: Partner, Ernst & Young Corporate Finance Group; Vice President, Green Capital Investors; Wells Fargo
  Directorships: Fire & Life Safety America, Five Star Food Services, TransGo, U.S. Drinks
  Christopher N. Jones, Managing Partner
  336-733-0360
  e-mail: cjones@fivepointscapital.com
  Education: BS, Mathematics, Davidson College; MBA, Wharton School, University of Pennsylvania
  Background: CFO, Mega Force; Ernst & Young Corporate Finance Group; Kidder Peabody & Company
  Directorships: JML Optical, Quick Med Claims, Thompson Industrial Services
  Thomas H. Westbrook, Managing Partner
  336-733-0359
  e-mail: twestbrook@fivepointscapital.com
  Education: BA, Economics, Wofford College; MBA, Finance, Kenan-Flagler School of Business, University of North Carolina
  Background: Managing Director, Allied Capital Corporation; Associate, North Carolina Enterprise Fund
  Directorships: Linkage, Outsolve, Quick Med Claims
  Jonathan B. Blanco, Partner
  336-733-0358
  e-mail: jblanco@fivepointscapital.com
  Education: BA, Economics, University of North Carolina, Chapel Hill; MBA, Darden School of Business Administration, University of Virginia
  Background: Carousel Capital, Bowles Hollowel Conner & Co., Chase Securities
  S. Whitfield Edwards, Partner
  336-733-0353
  e-mail: wedwards@fivepointscapital.com
  Education: BA, Economics, University of North Carolina, Chapel Hill; MBA, Darden School of Business Administration, University of Virginia
  Background: Gilbarco Veeder-Root; Vice President, Corporate Development, FairPoint Communications; Bowles Hollowel Conner & Co.
  Scott L. Snow, Partner
  336-733-0357
  e-mail: ssnow@fivepointscapital.com
  Education: BS, Business Management, Brigham Young University; MBA, Harvard Business School
  Background: Investment Banking, Wachovia Securities; GE Capital; GE Plastics
  Marshall C. White, Partner
  336-733-0351
  e-mail: mwhite@fivepointscapital.com
  Education: BS, Finance and Accounting, Georgetown University
  Background: American Capital, JP Morgan
  Directorships: Thompson Industrial Services, TransGo
  W. Brent Kulman, Director of Business Development
  e-mail: bkulman@fivepointscapital.com
  Education: BA, English, University of North Carolina, Chapel Hill; MBA, Wharton School, University of Pennsylvania
  Background: Fund Executive, Charlotte Angel Partners; Investment Banking, Raymond James & Associates; Bank of Boston

---

747 **FLAGSHIP PIONEERING**
55 Cambridge Parkway
Suite 800E
Cambridge, MA 02142

Phone: 617-868-1888 Fax: 617-868-1115
web: flagshippioneering.com

Mission Statement: A venture capital firm investing in entrepreneurial scientists and their life sciences companies.
Fund Size: $1 billion
Founded: 2000
Industry Group Preference: Life Sciences, Therapeutics, Healthcare, Technology, Sustainability, Pharmaceuticals
Portfolio Companies: Acceleron Pharma, Accuri, Adnexus, Advanced Electron Beams, Affinnova, Agios, Alinea, Alvine Pharmaceuticals, Anvil, Avedro, Aveo, Avidimer Therapeutics, Axcella, Be Power Tech, BGMedicine, Bind Biosciences, BlackDuck, Cadena Bio, Celera, Celexion, CGI, CiBo, Codiak, Codon Devices, Concert Pharmaceuticals, Denali Therapeutics, Ecosense, Editas Medicine, Eleven Biotherapeutics, Emsemble Therapeutics, Epitome Biosystems, Evelo Biosciences, Everyday Solutions, Foghorn Therapeutics, Genomics Collaborative, Helicos BioSciences Corp., Hypnion, Idexx Laboratories, Inari, Incredible Foods, Indigo, Interactive Supercomputing, Intio, Joule, Kaleido, KSQ, LS9, Mascoma, MedidaMetrics, Midori Health, Moderna, Morphotek Inc., Nanostream, Novomer, Oasys, Permeon Biologies, Pervasis, Quanterix, Receptos, Red Rock Biofuels, Renovis, Resolvyx, Rubio Therapeutics, Seahorse Biosciences, Selecta Biosciences, Selventa, Seres Therapeutics, SeventhSense Biosystems, Sigilon Therapeutics, Syros, T2 Biosystems, Taris, Tarveda, Tetraphase, Torque, Transmedics, Visen, Visterra, Zalicus

Key Executives:
  Noubar Afeyan, Founder/CEO
  Education: PhD, Biochemical Engineering, MIT
  Background: Founder/CEO, PerSeptive Biosystems; SVP/Chief Business Officer, Applera;
  Directorships: Chemgenics Pharmaceuticals; Color Kinetics; Adnexus Therapeutics; Affinnova
  Karen Hodys, Partner, Legal
  Education: BA, Philosophy, University of Michigan; JD, Case Western Reserve University School of Law; MBA, Weatherhead School of Management, Case Western University
  Background: Senior Counsel, Latham & Watkins; Proskauer Rose
  Stephen Berenson, Executive Partner
  Education: BS, Mathematics, MIT
  Background: Investment Banker, JP Morgan
  Directorships: Moderna Therapeutics, CiBO Technologies
  David Berry, General Partner
  Education: PhD, Biological Engineering, MIT; MD, Harvard Medical School, Harvard-MIT Health Sciences and Technology Program
  Background: Co-Founder, Seres Therapeutics; Joule Unlimited; Evelo Biosciences; Eleven Biotherapeutics; LS9; Axcella Health; Indigo Agriculture
  Doug Cole, Managing Partner
  Education: AB, English, Darmouth College; MD, University of Pennsylvania School of Medicine
  Background: Instructor, Harvard Medical School;

Venture Capital & Private Equity Firms / Domestic Firms

Assistant in Neurology, Massachusetts General Hospital; Medical Director, Cytotherapeutics; Program Executive, Vertex Pharmaceuticals Inc; Co-Founder, Ensemble Therapeutics; Permeon Biologics; Moderna Therapeuticsl Syros Pharmaceuticals; Sigilon Therapeutics
Directorships: Denali, Editas, Fogorn, Quanterix, Sigilon, Taris, Torque
Jim Gilbert, Senior Partner
Education: BS, Industrial Engineering, Cornell University; MBA, Harvard Business School
Background: Managing Director, Bain & Co.; VP, Corporate Strategy, Boston Scientific; Senior Advisor, General Atlantic; Senior Operating Executive, Welsh Carson Anderson & Stowe
Directorships: Nestle Health Science, TransMedics, Rubius Therapeutics, Sigilon
Avak Kahvejian, Partner
Education: PhD, McGill University
Background: Founding President/CEO, Cygnal Therapeutics; Co-Founder, Rubius Therapeutics; VP, Business Development, Helicos BioSciences
Ignacio Martinez, General Partner
Education: BS, Economics/Business Admin., Deusto University (Spain); MBA, Instituto de Empresa
Background: Managing Director, Syngenta Ventures; CFO, Progenika Group; Najeti Ventures Fund
Directorships: Indigo Agriculture, Novomer, Agtech Accelerator, CiBO Technologies
Stacie Rader, Partner/Chief People Officer
Education: BS, Business, Babson College
Background: SVP/Executive Operations/Human Resources, BG Medicine; Corporate Director, Applera Corp.; Human Resources, PerSeptive; Interim VP/Human Resources, Celera Genomics
Leda Trivinos, Partner, Intellectual Property
Education: Law Degree, University of California, Berkeley; PhD, Cell & Molecular Biology, Northwestern University Medical School
Background: Chief Patent Counsel, Momenta Pharmaceuticals Inc.; Assistant General Counsel for Intellectual Property, Biogen Idec.; Associate, Fish & Richardson PC
Geoffrey von Maltzahn, Partner
Education: BS, Chemical Engineering, MIT; MS, Bioengineering, University of California, San Diego; PhD, Biomedical Engineering/Medical Physics, MIT
Background: Co-Founder, Sienna Biopharmaceuticals; Chief Innovation Officer/Director, Kaleido Biosciences; Chief Innovation Officer, Indigo Agriculture; VP of Discovery, Axcella
Harry Wilcox, General Partner
Background: CFO/General Partner, Highland Capital Partners; CFO, Charles River Ventures; CFO/SVP, EXACT Sciences; Interim CEO, Thrasos Therapeutics; Interim CEO, Biostratym; President/CEO, Cambridge NeuroScience Inc.; SVP/CFO, Cellcor
Directorships: Seventh Sense Biosystems; Incredible Foods; MidoriUSA; BG Medicine; Be Power Tech

748 FLARE CAPITAL PARTNERS
800 Boylston Street
Suite 2310
Boston, MA 02199

Phone: 617-607-5060
web: www.flarecapital.com

Mission Statement: To provide support, strategic resources and industry insight to innovative healthcare technology companies.
Fund Size: $200 million
Founded: 2001
Investment Criteria: Early-Stage, Growth Equity
Industry Group Preference: Medical Devices, Biopharmaceuticals, Predictive Medicine Technology, Diagnostics, Healthcare Services

Portfolio Companies: CardioMEMS, CardioNet, Clear Data, Direct Flow Medical, Explorys, Functional Neuromodulation, Iora Health, Rise Health, SetPoint Medical, SynapDx, Valence Health, Welltok
Key Executives:
Michael Greeley, General Partner/Co-Founder
Education: BA, Chemistry, Williams College; MBA, Harvard Business School
Background: Founding General Partner, Flybridge Capital Partners; Polaris Venture Partners; SVP & Founding Partner, GCC Investments; Wasserstein Perella & Company; Morgan Stanley; Credit Suisse First Boston
Directorships: BlueTarp Financial, Explorys, Functional Neuromodulation, Iora Health, MicroCHIPS, Nuvesse, PolyRemedy, Predictive Biosciences, Predilytics, T2 Biosystems, TARIS Biomedical
Bill Geary, General Partner/CoFounder
Education: Carroll School of Management, Boston College
Background: Partner, North Bridge Venture Partners; Partner, Hambro International Equity Partners; CFO, MathSoft; CPA, Arthur Andersen & Company
Chris Kryder, Executive Partner
Education: BA, University at Buffalo; MD, Georgetown University; MBA, Massachusetts Institute of Technology
Background: Founder, D2Hawkeye; Co-Founder, Generation Health
Tom Mac Mahon, Executive Partner
Education: BS, Marketing, St. Peter's College; MBA, Fairleigh Dickinson University
Background: Chairman & CEO, LabCorp; CEO, Laboratory Group, America Holdings; SVP, Hoffman-La Roche; President, Roche Diagnostics Group

749 FLETCHER SPAGHT VENTURES
500 Boylston Street
Boston, MA 02116

Phone: 617-247-6700 Fax: 617-247-7757
e-mail: info@fletcherspaght.com
web: www.fletcherspaght.com

Mission Statement: Fletcher Spaght Ventures is a venture capital firm focused on providing expertise and capital to high growth healthcare, life sciences and information technology companies.
Geographic Preference: United States
Fund Size: $100 million
Founded: 1983
Average Investment: $4 - $6 million
Investment Criteria: All Stages
Industry Group Preference: Healthcare, Life Sciences, Biotechnology, Diagnostics, Healthcare Information Technology, Medical Devices
Portfolio Companies: CardioFocus, Cayenne Medical, HistoSonics, Metabolon, Proteus Digital Health, Soleo Communications, Swift Biosciences
Key Executives:
John Fletcher, Managing Partner/Founder
Education: BBA, Marketing, George Washington University; MBA, Southern Illinois University; PhD Candidate, The Wharton School, University of Pennsylvania
Background: CEO, Fletcher Spaght; Senior Manager, The Boston Consulting Group; Captain & Jet Pilot, U.S. Air Force
Directorships: Axcelis, Metabolon
Pearson Spaght, General Partner
Education: BS, Mechanical Engineering, MS, Aeronautical/Astronautical Engineering, MBA, Stanford University
Background: VP, Corporate Strategy & International, Raymark Corporation; Senior Manager, The Boston Consulting Group; Engineer, NASA

Venture Capital & Private Equity Firms / Domestic Firms

Directorships: Soleo Communications, Battery Resourcers
Linda Tufts, General Partner
Education: SB, Electrical Engineering, SB, Humanities & Science, MIT; SM, Finance Management, MIT Sloan School of Management
Background: Internal Consultant, Sony Corporation of America; Manager, Bain & Company; Consultant, Strategic Planning Associates
Directorships: Juventas

750 FLEXPOINT FORD LLC
676 North Michigan Avenue
33rd Floor
Chicago, IL 60611
Phone: 312-327-4520 Fax: 312-327-4525
web: www.flexpointford.com

Mission Statement: Flexpoint Ford is a private equity investment firm focused on providing operational and financial expertise, industry contacts, and development strategies to assist with the building of portfolio companies.

Geographic Preference: United States
Fund Size: $950 million
Founded: 2005
Average Investment: $200 million
Industry Group Preference: Healthcare, Financial Services
Portfolio Companies: AMD Holdings, CFGI, Credibly, GeoVera, Great Ajax, Jefferson Capital International, JetPay, Kastle Therapeutics, KingStar, Pelican AutoFinance, Service Finance Company, Summit Behavioral Healthcare, Top Rx, Vericlaim, WisdomTree Investments

Other Locations:
717 Fifth Avenue
20th Floor
New York, NY 10022
Phone: 646-217-7555 Fax: 646-217-7855

Key Executives:
Christopher J. Ackerman, Managing Director
312-327-4540
e-mail: cackerman@flexpointford.com
Education: BA, Mathematical Economics, Colgate University; MBA, Kellogg School of Management
Background: Executive Director, Investment Banking Division, Morgan Stanley
Perry O. Ballard, Managing Director
312-327-4539
e-mail: pballard@flexpointford.com
Education: BA, Economics, University of Michigan; MBA, Harvard Business School
Background: VP, Healthcare Group, GTCR; Analyst, Credit Suisse First Boston
Steven L. Begleiter, Managing Director
646-217-7572
e-mail: sbegleiter@flexpointford.com
Education: BA, Economics, Haverford College
Background: Director, MarketAxess Holdings; Senior Managing Director, Bear Stearns & Co.
Ethan A. Budin, Managing Director
312-327-4535
e-mail: ebudin@flexpointford.com
Education: AB, Mathematics, Harvard University
Background: Principal, GTCR; Principal, Leeds Group; Associate, The Boston Consulting Group; M&A Analyst, Lazard Freres & Co.
Charles E. Glew, Jr., Managing Director
312-327-4533
e-mail: cglew@flexpointford.com
Education: AB, Harvard University; MBA, Stanford University Graduate School of Business
Background: Principal, GTCR; Summit Partners; Analyst, Corporate Finance Group, Citicorp
Jonathan T. Oka, Managing Director
312-327-4547
e-mail: joka@flexpointford.com

Education: BA, Yale University; MBA, Harvard Business School
Background: Associate, GTCR; McKesson Corporation; M&A Analyst, Lazard Freres & Co.
Donald J. Edwards, Chief Executive Officer
312-327-4530
e-mail: dedwards@flexpointford.com
Education: BS, Finance, University of Illinois, Urbana-Champaign; MBA, Harvard Business School
Background: Principal, GTCR; Lazard Ltd.

751 FLOODGATE FUND
820 Ramona Street
Suite 200
Palo Alto, CA 94301
Phone: 650-204-7990
e-mail: mediarequests@floodgate.com
web: floodgate.com

Mission Statement: Floodgate helps today's most ambitious entrepreneurs develop tomorrow's great business success stories.

Geographic Preference: California, Texas
Founded: 2010
Average Investment: $150,000 - $1 million
Industry Group Preference: Enterprise Software, Business to Business, Consumer Internet, Software, Hardware
Portfolio Companies: 6D.AI, Aceable, Aconite, Adroll, Angellist, Applied Intuition, Atlas Obscura, Ayasdi, Bazaarvoice, Bigcommerce, Bolt Financial, Bot MD, Business Connect China, Camio, Chairman Mom, Cheetah Technology, Chegg, Civitas Learning, Clever, Clover Health, Consecutive Capital, Data.World, Demandforce, Dispatchr, Doubledutch, Egnyte, Enhatch, Finxera, Giftly, Goformz, Greatist, Greo, Handle Financial, Hodinkee, Hopscotch, IFTTT, Illumeo, Inscopix, IRL, Jodel, Joyrun, Kanler, Kapost, Keepsafe, Kindly Care, Labdoor, Liquidspace, LOB, Ligistics Exchange, Loris.AI, Lyft, Maker Media, Mango Health, Mighty Networks, Mixmax, Mobilize, Monetate, Myra Labs, N3twork, Newscred, NGMOCO, Nirvana, OHMConnect, OKTA, Openmind, Origin, OutboundDengine, Outreach, Pantheon, Parallel Wireless, Piccollage, Pingpad, Pley, Praxis, Rafay Systems, Rappi, Recharge, Refinery29, Reputation.Com, Rev Worldwide, Robin Systems, Sano, SBR Health, Sharethrough, Skale Labs, Smule, Snaplogic, Solarwinds, Sonos, Sparefoot, Spiceworks, Starkware, Swivel, Tango Card, Tapatalk, Taskrabbit, Tesorio, TetraScience, TextIQ, Thankx, The Zebra, Thinkful, Touch Of Modern, Townsquared, Try.Com, TTYL, Twitch, Twitter, Unitive, Virtual Instruments, Wanleo, Weebly, Whipclip, Workboard, Xamarin, Yup Technologies, Zeplin, Zeus

Key Executives:
Mike Maples Jr., Managing Partner
Education: BS, Engineering, Stanford University; MBA, Harvard Business School
Background: Co-Founder, Motive; Product Marketing, Tivoli
Directorships: Dasient, Swiftest, ModCloth
Ann Miura-Ko, Partner
Education: BS, Electrical Engineering, Yale University; PhD, Mathematical Modeling of Computer Security, Stanford University
Background: Lecturer, School of Engineering, Stanford University; Charles River Ventures; McKinsey & Company
Iris Choi, Partner
Education: BA, Harvard University; MBA, Wharton School, University of Pennsylvania
Background: M&A, Goldman Sachs
Arjun Chopra, Partner
Education: BS, University of Texas, Austin; MBA, Harvard Business School
Background: CTO, Cambridge Technology Enterprises; Microsoft; Motive; IBCC

263

Venture Capital & Private Equity Firms / Domestic Firms

Ryan Walsh, Partner
Education: BS, Computer Science, MS, Telecommunications, University of Pittsburgh
Background: Product Management, Apple; VP of Products, Beats by Dre

752 FLORIDA CAPITAL PARTNERS
500 N Westshore Blvd
Suite 605
Tampa, FL 33609

Phone: 813-222-8000 Fax: 813-222-8001
e-mail: newdeals@fcpinvestors.com
web: www.fcpinvestors.com

Mission Statement: To help build private, middle-market companies into successful businesses.
Geographic Preference: United States
Fund Size: $350 million
Founded: 1988
Minimum Investment: $3 million
Investment Criteria: Recapitalizations, MBO, MBI, Family Successions, Corporate Divestiture, Industry Consolidation
Industry Group Preference: Consumer Products, Industrial Equipment, Services, Distribution, Manufacturing, Business to Business
Portfolio Companies: Bell'O International, Custom Molded Products, E-Z Shipper Racks, Levin HomeCare, Precision Aviation Group, United States Environmental Services
Key Executives:
Peter B Franz, Partner
e-mail: franz@fcpinvestors.com
Education: BS, Economics, Wharton School, University of Pennsylvania; MBA, JL Kellogg Graduate School of Management, Northwestern University
Background: VP, NationsCredit Commercial Corporation
Felix J Wong, Partner
e-mail: fjw@fcpinvestors.com
Education: BS, Business Administration, Wake Forest University
Background: Corporate Finance, Stephens

753 FLUKE VENTURE PARTNERS
520 Kirkland Way
Suite 300
Kirkland, WA 98033

Phone: 425-896-4322 Fax: 425-827-4683
e-mail: weston@flukeventures.com
web: www.flukeventures.com

Mission Statement: Fluke invests in early-stage companies located in the Pacific Northwest.
Geographic Preference: Pacific Northwest United States
Fund Size: $65 million
Founded: 1982
Average Investment: $2.5 - $4 million
Minimum Investment: $500,000
Investment Criteria: Seed, Startup, First-Stage, Second-Stage, Mezzanine
Industry Group Preference: Technology, Consumer Services, Consumer Products, Healthcare
Portfolio Companies: AcryMed, Aldus, Calidora, Carena, Chatham Technologies, Coinstar, Concordia Coffee Company, Coinstar, Confirma, Creative Multimedia, Dantz Development Corporation, Drug Emporium, Eagle Hardware & Garden, Fios, Genoa Healthcare, Innova, Innovation, Integrex, Interlinq Software, Ioline Corporation, Klir Technologies, Luxar, MedManage Systems, MidStream Technologies, NetMotion Wireless, Pacific Edge Software, Pacific Star Communications, Panlabs International, Payscale, Pet's Choice, Phoseon Technology, RedHook Ale Brewery, Sightward, Starbucks, Sur La Table, Tegic Communications, Vantos, Viathan, Xcyte Therapies

Key Executives:
Denny Weston, Senior Managing Director
e-mail: weston@flukeventures.com
Education: BA, Central Washington University; MBA, University of Washington
Background: Certified Public Accountant; Founder, Evergreen Venture Capital Association
Directorships: PayScale Inc., Pacific Star Communications Inc., Carena Inc., Sur La Table, Confirma, Redhook Brewery
Kevin Gabelein, Managing Director
e-mail: gabelein@flukeventures.com
Education: BA, Business Admin., University of Washington; JD, Souther Methodist Univerity School of Law
Background: Attorney, Corporate Finance Group of Ridedell Williams PS; Certified Public Accountant, PricewaterhouseCoopers LLP
Directorships: Concordia Coffee Company; Phoseon Technology; Vantos Inc.; Genoa Healthcare; MedManage Systems; Fios

754 FLYBRIDGE CAPITAL PARTNERS
31 St. James Ave.
6th Floor
Boston, MA 02116

Phone: 617-307-9292 Fax: 617-307-9293
e-mail: hello@flybridge.com
web: www.flybridge.com

Mission Statement: Our goal is to find talented entrepreneurs and then partner with them to build exceptional and valuable companies. We focus on providing guidance and perspective in a complimentary way to the entrepreneurs we invest in and help them build connections to soar to the next level.
Geographic Preference: United States
Fund Size: $560 million
Founded: 2001
Investment Criteria: Seed-Stage, Early-Stage
Industry Group Preference: Consumer Technology, Energy Technology, Healthcare Information Technology, Information Technology
Portfolio Companies: 33Across, Aiera, Analytical Space, BetterCloud, BitSight, Bloxroute Labs, BlueTarp Financial, Bowery, Bulletin, Chief, Codecademy, Datalogue, DataXu, Eager, Enigma, Feature Labs, Hyr, I4CP, Imperfect, Infracommerce, Jibo, Kebotix, Lorem, Madeira Madeira, Minim, MongoDB, Narrator AI, Nasuni, NS1, Omni, Open English, Parachute, Philo, Pitzi, Plastiq, Precognitive, Proscia, Redox, Remote Year, Restorando, Saving Star, Sentenai, Shine, Skillist, Splice, Tracx, Valimail, Vidsys, Wanderset, Welltok, Wethos, Zest Finance

Other Locations:
27 W 24th St.
New York, NY 10010
Phone: 917-522-0065

Key Executives:
David Aronoff, General Partner
Education: BS, Computer Science, University of Vermont; MS, Computer Engineering, University of Southern California; MBA, Harvard Business School
Background: Grelock Partneres, Chipcom
Directorships: BetterCloud, Bitsight, Minim, NS1, Valimail
Jeffrey Bussgang, General Partner
Education: BA, Computer Science, Harvard University; MBA, Harvard Business School
Background: Co-Founder, Upromise; Executive, Open Market
Directorships: 33Across, Analytical Space, BloXroute, BlueTarp Financial, Bowery Farming, Codecademy, DataXu, Enigma, Open English, Plastiq, Precognitive, Wanderset, ZestFinance

Venture Capital & Private Equity Firms / Domestic Firms

Jesse Middleton, General Partner
Education: Drexel University
Background: WeWork; CEO, Backstory
Directorships: Bulletin, Chief, Hyr, Imperfect Produce, Narrator, Omni, Remote Year, Skillist, Splice, Wethos
Chip Hazard, General Partner
Education: BA, Stanford University; MBA, Harvard Business School
Background: General Partner, Greylock Partners; Company Assitance Limited
Directorships: Datalogue, Feature Labs, Lorem, MongoDB, Nasuni, Parachute Home, Redox, VidSys, Welltok

755 FLYING FISH
Seattle, WA

e-mail: info@flyingfish.vc
web: www.flyingfish.vc

Mission Statement: Mission is to fund startups in the areas of cloud computing, artificial intelligence, speech and natural language, machine learning and internet and technology.
Geographic Preference: United States
Fund Size: $85 Million
Average Investment: $500,000 - $5,000,000
Minimum Investment: $500,000
Investment Criteria: Early Stage Startups, Cloud Computing, AI, Speech & Natural Language, Machine Learning, Info & Tech
Industry Group Preference: Artificial Intelligence, Cloud Computing, Speech and Natural Language, Machine Learning, Information and Technology
Portfolio Companies: Ad Lightning, Element Data, Finn.ai, Gradient, Joe, Message Yes, Streem, Tomorrow, Vivi
Key Executives:
  Geoff Harris, Partner
  Education: BA, Political Science, Brown University
  Background: Microsoft
  Directorships: Board Member, Seattle Angel Board of Directors
  Heather Redman, Partner
  Education: BA, Reed College; JD, Stanford University
  Background: AtomShockwave, Inc.; Getty Images, Inc.; PhotoDisc, Inc.; Indix Corporation; Summit Power Group
  Directorships: Washington Technology Industry Association; Greater Seattle Chamber; Hawthown Club; Global EIR Coalition & Beneficial State Bank
  Frank Chang, Partner
  Education: BA, Computer Science, Princeton University
  Background: Reef Technologies; Amazon; Microsoft

756 FLYWHEEL VENTURES
341 East Alamada Street
Santa Fe, NM 87501-2229

Phone: 505-225-1618 Fax: 505-672-7053
web: www.flywheelventures.com

Mission Statement: Flywheel Ventures invests in seed-stage and early-stage companies with the potential to provide solutions to global challenges in digital services, as well as energy, water and infrastructure technology.
Fund Size: $35 million
Average Investment: $100,000 - $1 million
Investment Criteria: Seed-Stage, Early-Stage
Industry Group Preference: Digital Services, Infrastructure Software, Energy Technology, Water, Software, Clean Technology
Portfolio Companies: AfterCollege, Angaza Design, AppCityLife, Aravo Solutions, Bitsbox, Bytelight, Cinnafilm, Comet Solutions, Digabit, Jana, Jive Software, Lingotek, Lotus Leaf Coatings, MicroProbe, MIOX Corporation, RentPayment, SalmData, ShowEvidence, SkyFuel, Submittable, TempoDB, TheRetailPlanet.com, Tiatros, TrackVia, Tribogenics, TruTouch Technologies

Other Locations:
9204 San Mateo Northeast
Albuquerque, NM 87113
Key Executives:
  Trevor R Loy, General Partner
  e-mail: trevor@flywheelventures.com
  Education: BS, MS, Electrical Engineering, MS, Management Science & Engineering, Stanford University
  Background: Gigabeat; Brooktree; ParkingNet; Teradyne; Intel Corporation
  Directorships: Astria Semiconductor Holdings, TrackVia, Tuscany Design Automation
  David Jargiello, Venture Partner
  e-mail: david@flywheelventures.com
  Education: BA, Case Western Reserve University; MS, Stanford University; JD, University of California, Berkeley
  Background: Co-Founder, Venture Law Group; Heller Ehrman White & McAuliffe; Virtual Law Partners
  Chris Traylor, Venture Partner
  e-mail: chris@flywheelventures.com
  Education: BS/BA, Management, Kansas State University; MBA, University of New Mexico
  Background: CEO, PureColor; Global Director, Commercial & Institutional Markets, MIOX Corporation; Pumping Solutions

757 FOCUS VENTURES
525 University Avenue
Suite 225
Palo Alto, CA 94301

Phone: 650-325-7400 Fax: 650-325-8400

Mission Statement: Seeking companies that have completed initial development of their product or service. These leading technology companies have demonstrated clear market acceptance and are seeking additional capital to expand their sales and marketing efforts or to execute strategic acquisitions.
Fund Size: $830 million
Founded: 1997
Average Investment: $3 - $8 million
Minimum Investment: $500,000
Investment Criteria: Expansion-Stage
Industry Group Preference: Communications, Software, Technology, Semiconductors, Consumer Services, Internet
Portfolio Companies: 3VR, Acta Technology, Active Software, Agile Software, Alteon WebSystems, Aruba Networks, Apigee, Atmosphere Networks, Aventail, Barracuda Networks, Black Duck Software, Brand.net, Broadbase Software, BuzzMedia, Cedar Point Communications, CenterBeam, Centrality Communications, Choridiant Software, ClearCube, Com 21, Commerce One, Copper Mountain, Corio, CoSine Communications, Crossbeam Systems, Cyan Optics, DATAllegro, Delivery Agent, Digital Fuel, Drobo, DSL.Net, Ecast, edocs, Elance, Ensim, Entropic, EqualLogic, Exigen, Extricity Software, Fanfare, Financial Engines, FrontBridge, G-Log, Hara Software, inCode Telecom, Infoblox, Interwoven, Isilon Systems, Kace, Kazeon, LogLigic, MarkMonitor, Marin Software, Mimosa, Miradia, MuDynamics, Netmoshere, NetScaler, Niku, Oblix, Opsware, Orchestria, Outer Bay, PA Semi, Panasas, PCH International, Picarro, Pivot3, Pixelworks, Pure Digital, QuinStreet, Rafter, Ramp Networks, Repeater Technology, Reputation.com, RGB Networks, Ruckus Wireless, SAY Media, Sequence Design, Sepaton, ShoreTel, Silicon Optix, Six Apart, Sojern, Starent Networks, Stoke, Teknovus, Telera, Turn, Verisity, Vina Technologies, Virtusa, WebVisible, Wily Technology

758 FOG CITY CAPITAL
San Francisco, CA 94105

e-mail: deals@fogcitycapital.com
web: www.fogcitycapital.com

265

Venture Capital & Private Equity Firms / Domestic Firms

Mission Statement: A private equity firm that invests in lower middle-market software and business services companies and assists with growing them into leading businesses.
Average Investment: $2 - $10 million
Investment Criteria: Middle Market, Growth Capital Funding, Recapitalizations, Management Buyouts
Industry Group Preference: Business Products & Services, Technology, Media, Marketing, Software
Key Executives:
  Adit Abhyankar
  e-mail: adit@fogcitycapital.com
  Education: BS, Electrical Engineering & Economics, MS, Engineering, Tulane University
  Background: Co-Founder & VP, Gadgetworks; Xigo; BARRA
  Ravi Bhaskaran
  e-mail: ravi@fogcitycapital.com
  Education: BS, Unversity of California, Berkeley; MBA, University of Chicago; London Business School
  Background: Co-Founder & CEO, Pyramid Consulting; Management Consultant, Booz Allen & Hamilton

759 FOGEL INTERNATIONAL
5110 North 32nd Street
Suite 206
Phoenix, AZ 85018
Phone: 602-508-0728 Fax: 602-840-4970
e-mail: lfogel@fogelinternational.com
web: www.fogelinternational.com

Mission Statement: An investment/merchant banking firm dedicated to assisting companies throughout the United States in the fulfillment of their business and personal strategies and goals.
Geographic Preference: United States
Founded: 1969
Average Investment: $75 million
Minimum Investment: $10 million
Investment Criteria: Merger & Acquisition, Private Placements for Mature Companies
Industry Group Preference: All Sectors Considered
Key Executives:
  Lawrence M Fogel, Senior Managing Principal
  e-mail: lfogel@fogelinternational.com
  Background: Account Executive, Walston & Company; HO Peet & Company
  Ahim Kandler, Managing Director, Israeli & European Investments
  Education: Graduate Degree, Business Administration, LMU University, Munich
  Background: Founder & Managing Partner, AHIM Business Development; PricewaterhouseCoopers; Daimler Benz Aerospace
  P Frank Limbaugh, Consultant, Specialty Finance
  Education: MA, Management, Peter Drucker School of Management, Claremont University
  Background: President, Technology Division, Deutsche Financial Services; Division Vice President, Borg Warner Acceptance Corporation
  Bryan J. Toth, Senior Financial Analyst/Consultant
  Education: BBA, University of Toledo; Obtained Series 7 and Series 66 licensing
  Background: Management, Merrill Lynch; Deutsche Financial Services; Security Pacific; Bank One; Pacific Century Bank.

760 FONTINALIS PARTNERS
One Woodward Avenue
Suite 1600
Detroit, MI 48226
e-mail: info@fontinalis.com
web: www.fontinalis.com

Mission Statement: To find innovative companies in the transportation technology sector; bring its resources to bear and help companies grow and expand across markets on a global scale.
Industry Group Preference: Transportation, Communications
Portfolio Companies: Life 360, Masabi, Nano-C, ParkMe, Parkmobile, QuickPay, RelayRides, SQLstream, Streetline, Synovia Solutions, Zagster
Key Executives:
  Ralph Booth, Founder/Managing Partner
  Education: BA, Harvard University
  Background: CEO/Chairman, Booth American Company
  Directorships: Diveo Broadband Networks
  Bill Ford, Founder/Partner
  Education: BA, Princeton University; MS, Management, MIT
  Background: Executive Chairman, Ford Motor Company
  Chris Cheever, Founder/Managing Director
  Education: BA, Harvard University; MBA, Yale School of Management
  Background: Launch Capital; Wealth Management & Business Banking, UBS
  Laura Petterle, Partner/CFO
  Education: BA, University of Michigan
  Background: EVP/CFO, Booth American Company

761 FORERUNNER VENTURES
1161 Mission St.
Suite 300
San Francisco, CA 94103
e-mail: info@forerunnerventures.com
web: forerunnerventures.com

Mission Statement: Forerunner Ventures invests in early-stage ventures by ambitious entrepreneurs who seek to challenge industry norms.
Investment Criteria: Early-Stage
Portfolio Companies: 11 Honoré, Alchemy 43, Away, Birchbox, Birdies, Bloomthat, Bonobos, Brickwork, Chime, Choosy, Cleo, Cotopaxi, Curology, Darby Smart, Dollar Shave Club, Draper James, Faire, Flow, Glossier, Hims, Hollar, Homebase, Hotel Tonight, Inturn, Jet, KiwiCo, Lolli, Lumi, M.Gemi, MoveWith, Nécessaire, Neighborhood Goods, Outdoor Voices, Packagd, Phil, Prose, Reformation, Rep, ReSci, Ritual, Rockets of Awesome, Serena & Lily, ShopShops, Sproutling, Stadium Goods, Stockwell, The Farmer's Dog, The Inside, Warby Parker, Zesty, Zola, Zyper
Key Executives:
  Kirsten Green, Founder/Managing Director
  Education: BA, Business Economics, UCLA; CPA; CFA
  Directorships: Glossier, Outdoor Voices, Ritual, Inturn, Indigo Fair, Dollar Shave Club, Bonobos
  Eurie Kim, Partner
  Education: BS, Business Administrations, UC Berkeley; MBA, Wharton School
  Background: Management Consultant, Bain & Co.; Investor, Castanea Partners
  Directorships: Away, Alchemy 43, Curology, MoveWith, ShopShops, The Farmer's Dog
  Brian O'Malley, Partner
  Education: BS, Economics, Wharton School
  Background: Accel; General Partner, Battery Ventures

762 FORESITE CAPITAL
600 Montgomery St.
Suite 4500
San Francisco, CA 94111
Phone: 415-877-4887
web: www.foresitecapital.com

266

Venture Capital & Private Equity Firms / Domestic Firms

Mission Statement: Foresite Capital invests at all stages in companies across all areas of healthcare including diagnostics, medical devices, therapeutics, and services.
Investment Criteria: All Stages
Industry Group Preference: Healthcare, Diagnostics, Healthcare Services, Medical Devices, Therapeutics
Portfolio Companies: 10x Genomics, Acceleron Pharma, Achaogen, Aclaris Therapeutics, Adaptimmune, Adaptive Biotechnologies, Aerie Pharmaceuticals, Aimmune Therapeutics, Akari Therapeutics, Alder Biopharmaceuticals, Alector, Ambit, Anacor, Arbutus Biopharma, Arcus Biosciences, Ardelyx, Argenx, Ascendis Pharma, Audentes, Auspex, Avanir, Avexis, Bellicum, Biodelivery Sciences, Biohaven Pharmaceuticals, Biotie Therapies, Blueprint Medicines, Bracket, Color, ConnectiveRx, CymaBay Therapeutics, Jenali, Dermira, DNAnexus, Dyax, Editas Medicine, Eidos, Epizyme, FibroGen, Fount Therapeutics, Fulcrum Therapeutics, Generation Bio, Genomics PLC, Global Blood Therapeutics, Grail, Immunomedics, Inscripta, Insitro, Insmed, Intarcia, Intellio Therapeutics, iRhythm, Iventis, Jounce, Juno, Juvenescence, LifeMine, Lipocine, Loxo Oncology, Mindstrong, Momenta, MyoKardia, NanoString, Natera, NeuroDerm, Nexvet, Optinose, OrexiGen, Oric Pharmaceuticals, PacBio, Pact Pharma, Peloton, Protagonist, RegenxBio, Replimune, Rhythm, RxSight, Sage, Sangamo, Scynexis, Solid Biosciences, Solta Medical Tocagen, Tricida, UniQure, Universal American, VenatoRx, Verona Pharma, Vitae Pharmaceuticals, Wave Life Sciences, WaveTec Vision, Zafgen

Other Locations:
1345 Ave. of the Americas
3rd Floor
New York, NY 10105
Phone: 212-804-6303

Key Executives:
Jim Tananbaum, CEO & Managing Director
Education: BS, BSEE, Yale University; MS, MIT; MD, MBA, Harvard University
Background: Co-Founder, GelTex; Co-Founder, Theravance
Dennis D Ryan, CFO & Managing Director
Education: BA, University of California, Berkeley; MBA, University of Santa Clara; CPA
Background: KPMG; Western Properties Trust; Lighthouse Capital Partners; Berkeley Advisors Group
Vikram Bajaj, Managing Director
Education: PhD, MIT
Background: Chief Scientific Officer, GRAIL; Co-Founder, Verily; Associate Professor, Stanford School of Medicine; Advisor, Department of Defense
Matthew Buten, Managing Director
Background: Healthcare Portfolio Manager, Catapult/Millennium Partners; Co-Founder, Sapphire Capital
Dorothy Margolskee, Managing Director
Education: BS, Harvard University; MD, Johns Hopkins Medical School
Background: Managing Director, Prospect Ventures; SVP, Marck Research Labs
Brett Zbar, Managing Director
Education: Yale University; MD, Harvard Medical School
Background: Partner, Aisling Capital

763 FORGEPOINT CAPITAL
400 S El Camino Real
Suite 1050
San Mateo, CA 94402

Phone: 650-289-4455
web: forgepointcap.com

Mission Statement: ForgePoint Capital is a venture investor for early stage cybersecurity companies.
Fund Size: $750 Million
Founded: 2015

Key Executives:
Will Lin, Co-Founder/Managing Director
Education: University of California
Donald Dixon, Co-Founder/Managing Director
Education: BSE, Princeton University; MBA, Stanford University
Background: Co-President, Partech International; Managing Director, Alex, Brown & Sons; VP, Morgan Stanley & Co.
Sean Cunningham, Managing Director
Education: MBA, Gonzaga University
Background: Intel Capital
Alberto Lopez, Managing Director
Background: Apple; Oracle; CEO, enCommerce, Entrust and Thor Technologies

764 FORMATIVE VENTURES
2905 Stender Way
Suite 2
Santa Clara, CA 95054

Phone: 650-245-7088
web: www.formative.com

Mission Statement: Works with early-stage entrepreneurial teams that are seeking a value-added partner for institutional financing.
Founded: 2000
Average Investment: $2 - $5 million
Investment Criteria: Early-Stage
Industry Group Preference: Communications, Wireless, Internet, Semiconductors, Infrastructure
Portfolio Companies: Capella, InboundWriter, InnoCOMM Wireless, IP Infusion, Marketocracy, Mashery, Pyxis Technology, Samplify Systems, Silicon Clocks, Smalltown, SOASTA, Veebeam, Zyray Wireless

Key Executives:
Brian Connors, Managing Director
e-mail: brian@formative.com
Education: BS, Egineering, Northern Arizona University
Background: Institutional Venture Partners; C-Cube; VP, North American Sales, Synopsys
Directorships: IP Infusion, Pyxis Technology, Samplify Systems
Clint Chao, Managing Director
e-mail: clint@formative.com
Education: BS, Electrical Engineering/Computer Science, University of California, Berkeley
Background: VP Marketing, SkyStream; Senior Director Marketing, C-Cube Microsystems; Sales Management, Motorola's Semiconductor Products Sector
Dino Vendetti, Managing Director
e-mail: dino@formative.com
Education: MSEE, MBA, University of Washington; BSEE, San Diego State University
Background: Co-Founder, FoundersPad; General Partner, Bay Partners; Vulcan Ventures

765 FORREST BINKLEY & BROWN
Irvine, CA

Phone: 808-441-5001

Mission Statement: Focuses on investing in middle-market buyouts and providing growth capital to companies that offer potential for a substantial increase in shareholder value and exceptional rates of return to investors.
Geographic Preference: Southern California
Fund Size: $215 million
Founded: 1993
Average Investment: $4 million
Minimum Investment: $2 million
Investment Criteria: First Stage, Second Stage, MBO, Middle Stage, Later Stage
Industry Group Preference: Technology, Communications, Computer Related, Consumer Services, Consumer Products

267

Venture Capital & Private Equity Firms / Domestic Firms

Portfolio Companies: AD PathLabs, AirClic, American Asphalt & Grading, American Lighting Supply, Artifact Entertainment, Ascendent Telecommunications, CallConnect Communications, Comcore Semiconductor, Cooking.com, Crosman Acquisition Corporation, Cytovia, DispenseSource, FieldCentrix, Golden State Vintners, HFSC Holdings, InnoTech, IPNet Solutions, Maxima Corporation, NextCard, OfficeSource, OnPrem Networks Corporation, Pearl Izumi, SpectraSensors, Stamps.com, Tekni-Plex, Teradiant Networks, Trikon Technologies, Tunable Photonics Corporations, UltraLink, Vativ Technologies, Vendavo, Vista Medical Technologies

Other Locations:
265 Santa Helena
Suite 110
Solana Beach, CA 92075
Phone: 858-259-4105 **Fax:** 858-259-4108

Key Executives:
Gregory J Forrest, Co-Founder\Partner
e-mail: greg@fbbvc.com
Education: BS, Chemical Engineering, Arizona State University; MBA, University of Southern California Graduate School of Business
Background: President/CEO, Security Pacific Corporation; Chairman/President, BankAmerica Venture Capital
Nicholas B Binkley, Co-Founder\Partner
e-mail: nick@fbbvc.com
Education: BA, Political Science, Colorado College; MA, International Studies, Johns Hopkins School of Advanced International Studies
Background: Assistant VP, Security Pacific National Bank; Deputy Administrator, Security Pacific Financial Systems; Vice Chairman, Security Pacific Corporation
Jeffrey J. Brown, Co-Founder/Partner
Joseph Galligan, Chief Financial Officer
Education: BA, Accounting, University of Northern Iowa; CPA
Background: Controller, Automotive Safety Components International
Ashish Kaul, Principal
Education: BS, Electronics Engineering, Mangalore University, India; MS, Electrical Engineering, Virginia Tech; MBA, Kellogg School of Management, Northwestern University

---

766 FORT WASHINGTON CAPITAL PARTNERS GROUP
303 Broadway
Suite 1200
Cincinnati, OH 45202
Phone: 513-361-7600 **Fax:** 513-361-7605
Toll-Free: 888-244-8167
web: www.fortwashington.com

Mission Statement: Fort Washington Capital Partners Group is a private equity fund-of-funds manager and serves as the private equity division of Fort Washington Investment Advisors.
Fund Size: $450 million
Average Investment: $250,000 - $2 million
Investment Criteria: Growth Equity, Buyouts, Special Situations, Mezzanine
Industry Group Preference: Diversified

Other Locations:
The Huntington Center
Suite 1670
41 South High Street
Columbus, OH 43215
Phone: 614-222-6500 **Fax:** 614-222-6535

25800 Science Park Drive
Suite 100
Cleveland, OH 44122
Phone: 216-378-2235 **Fax:** 513-357-4010

Key Executives:
Maribeth Rahe, President and CEO
Education: BS, Bowling Green State University; MBA, Thunderbird School of Global Management
Background: JP Morgan; US Trust Company of NY
Stephen A Baker, Managing Director/Co-Head, Private Equity
Education: BA, History, University of Cincinnati; MBA, Finance, New York University Stern School of Business
Background: Principal, Seaport Capital Partners; Providence Journal Company
Robert Maeder, Managing Director/Co-Head, Private Equity
Education: BA, MBA, Northwestern University
Background: LEK Consulting; CIVC Partners; Merrill Lynch & Co.

---

767 FORTRESS INVESTMENT GROUP LLC
1345 Avenue of the Americas
46th Floor
New York, NY 10105
Phone: 212-798-6100
e-mail: grunte@fortress.com
web: www.fortress.com

Mission Statement: Fortress has one of the largest private equity businesses focused on acquiring undervalued assets and companies that can be improved through intensive asset management.
Geographic Preference: International
Fund Size: $36 billion
Founded: 1998
Industry Group Preference: Financial Services, Transportation, Energy, Infrastructure, Healthcare
Portfolio Companies: Air Castle, Brookdale Senior Living, CW Financial Services, Florida East Coast Industries, Florida East Coast Railway, Global Signal, Holiday Retirement, NationStar, New Fortress Energy, OneMain

Other Locations:
3290 Northside Parkwat NW
Suite 350
Atlanta, GA 30327
Phone: 404-264-4779

5221 North O'Connor Boulevard
Suite 700
Irving, TX 75039
Phone: 972-532-4300

GmbH FPM Deutschland GmbH
Fortress Germany Asset Management GmbH
An Der Welle 4
Frankfurt 60322
Germany
Phone: 49-69-2549-6700

Fortress Real Estate (HK) Limited
No. 8 Queen's Road Central
28th Floor
Central, Hong Kong
China
Phone: 852-5803-6500

FCF UK (A) III Limited
7 Clarges Street
London W1J 8AE
United Kingdom
Phone: 44-20-7290-5600

10250 Constellation Boulevard
Suite 1600
Los Angeles, CA 90067
Phone: 310-228-3030

220 Elm Street
Suite 201

New Canaan, CT 06840
Phone: 203-442-2442

Fortress Investment Consulting (Shanghai) Co.
Bldg 5, 858 Huanzhen Road South
Baoshan District
Shanghai 200436
China
Phone: 86-21-5650-8989

Fortress Investment Group (Australia) PTY
Level 19 Getaway
1 McQuarie Place
Sydney NSW 2000
Australia
Phone: 61-2-8239-1900

Fortress Investment Group (Japan) GK
Roppongi Hills Mori Tower 2gF
6-10-1 Roppongi, Minato-Ku
Tokyo 106-6129
Japan
Phone: 81-3-6438-4400

Key Executives:
Wesley R. Edens, Co-Founder/Co-CEO/Principal
Education: BS, Finance, Oregon State University
Background: Managing Director, BlackRock Financial Management Inc.; Partner/Managing Director, Lehman Brothers
Peter L. Briger Jr., Principal/Co-CEO
Education: BA, Princeton University; MBA, Wharton School
Background: Partner, Goldman Sachs
Directorships: Tipping Point, Caliber School
Randal A. Nardone, Co-Founder/Principal
Education: BA, English & Biology, University of Connecticut; JD, Boston University School of Law
Background: Managing Director, UBS; Principal, BlackRock Financial Management; Partner, Thacher Proffitt & Wood

768 **FORTÉ VENTURES**
Atlanta Technology Village
3423 Piedmont Road, NE
Suite 520 (225A)
Atlanta, GA 30303

Phone: 404-480-3090 Fax: 404-855-2840
web: www.forteventures.com

Mission Statement: Forté Ventures launched in January 2012 with a clear mission to deliver exceptional financial returns on a risk-reduced basis to limited partner investors by providing national visibility and privileged access to investment opportunities that are validated by a global network of strategic partners and corporate co-investors. We actively collaborate with a large cadre of corporate strategic partners to identify the most innovative and promising technology companies to invest in throughout North America. We invest across a diversified set of industry sectors including Information Technology, Mobility, Digital Media, Financial Technology and Industrial Technology.

Geographic Preference: North America
Founded: 2012
Minimum Investment: $100,000
Industry Group Preference: Information Technology, Digital Media & Marketing, Mobility, Internet, E-Commerce & Manufacturing, Fintech, Industrial Technology
Portfolio Companies: Adstage, AppBus, Aspen Aerogels, Ecosmart, Fision, Integrate, Liaison, News Distribution Network, RapidSOS, Remedy Informatics, SpringBot Commerce, Stella Service, Stockpile, TaDa Innovations, TidalScale, Urgent.ly, Ushr, Zeuss

Other Locations:
310 De Guigne Dr.
Sunnyvale, CA 94085

Key Executives:
Tom Hawkins, Managing Partner
Education: BA, Duke University; MBA, Kellogg School of Management
Background: Arcapita; Siemens Venture Capital; Cordova Ventures; Radiant Systems
Directorships: AppBus, Urgent.ly, Springbot, RapidSOS, StellaService
Louis Rajczi, Partner
Education: BS, Computer Engineering, University of Michigan; MBA, Southern Methodist University
Background: Siemens Venture Capital; Nortel Networks; TaDa Innovations
Directorships: AdStage, Integrate, IntelliVision, StellaService, Ushr, Urgent.ly
Paul Dibella, Partner
Education: University of Miami School of Law; SUNY Albany
David Nagel, PhD, Partner
Education: Bachelors and Masters, Engineering, UCLA; PhD, Perception and Mathematical Psychology, UCLA
Background: PalmSource; AT&T; Apple Computer; NASA's Ames Research Center
Melanie Martin, Director
Education: BS, Education, University of Georgia
Background: Cordova Ventures

769 **FORWARD VENTURES**
4747 Executive Drive
Suite 700
San Diego, CA 92121

Phone: 858-677-6077
e-mail: info@forwardventures.com
web: www.forwardventures.com

Mission Statement: Seeks both to accelerate the development of innovative and effective treatments for serious diseases and produce significant returns for its investors in three to five years.

Geographic Preference: United States, Europe
Fund Size: $500 million
Founded: 1990
Average Investment: $3 - 5 million
Minimum Investment: $500,000
Investment Criteria: Seed, Startup, First Round, Later Stage;
Industry Group Preference: Pharmaceuticals, Healthcare, Life Sciences, Medical Devices, Biopharmaceuticals
Portfolio Companies: Acorda Therapeutics, Adiana, Affinium Pharmaceuticals, Ambit Biosciences, Applied Molecular Evolution, Ariad, Cabrellis Pharmaceuticals, Collective Therapeutics, Combichem, Conforma Therapeutics, Corixa, Dynavax, Essentialis Therapeutics, Hypnion, LigoCyte Pharmaceuticals, Micromet, Morphotek, Nereus, NovaCardia, Onyx Pharmaceuticals, Predix Pharmaceuticals, Proprius Pharmaceuticals, Sequana, Somatix, Syndax, TargeGen, Tioga Pharmaceuticals, Triangle Pharmaceuticals, Viracta

Key Executives:
Standish Fleming, Founding Managing Partner
Education: BA, Amherst College; MBA, University of California, LA
Background: President, Biotechnology Venture Investors' Group
Directorships: Ambit, Aventa Biosciences Corporation, Coverge Medical, Kemia, MitoKor, Sanarus Medical, Arizeke Pharmaceuticals, Nereus Pharmaceuticals
Stuart Collinson, Partner
Education: MBA, Harvard Business School; PhD, Physical Chemistry, University of Oxford
Background: Chairman, CEO & President, Aurora

Venture Capital & Private Equity Firms / Domestic Firms

Biosciences Corporation; CEO, Andaris Limited; GlaxoWellcome PLC; Baxter International, Consultant, The Boston Consulting Group
Directorships: Affinium Pharmaceuticals, Asteres, Essentialis, Sequel Pharmaceuticals, Tioga Pharmaceuticals, Vertex Pharmaceuticals
Kristen Bailey, Director, Finance & Administration
Education: BA, Business Economics, University of California, Santa Barbara; MBA, San Diego State University
Background: Financial Accountant, Advent Venture Partners

770 FOUNDATION CAPITAL
250 Middlefield Road
Menlo Park, CA 94025

Phone: 650-614-0500
web: www.foundationcapital.com

Mission Statement: To build great companies, organizations that make a difference, not only in the lives of their constituents, but in the impact they have on their markets.
Geographic Preference: West Coast
Fund Size: $80 million
Founded: 1995
Average Investment: $10 million
Minimum Investment: $1 million
Investment Criteria: Early-Stage, Small-Seed
Industry Group Preference: Consumer Services, Internet Technology, Telecommunications, Data Communications, Software, Information Technology, Networking, Semiconductors, Clean Technology, Consumer Products, Data Storage, Cloud Computing
Portfolio Companies: 2nd Address, Acco, AdRoll, Aggregate Knowledge, Aquion Energy, Arthena, AutoGrid, Aux Money, Azure Power, Block Cypher, Board Vantage, Bold Threads, Calix, Cantaloip, Catalytic, Chegg, CliQr, CloudOn, Cohesity, Confer, Control4, Conviva, Converity, CoverWallet, Custora, Cyphort, DogVacey, Ebates, EMeter. Enernoc, Entropix, Envestnet, Everyday Health, Fastback Networks, Financial Engines, Finxera, ForgeRock, For Us All, Free Wheel, Funds India, Genies, Graphcore, Guardian Analytics, Health IQ, HomeBay, Hustle, Immersv, InsideView, Kik, League, LendingClub, LendingHome, Localytics, Luxe, MaestrolQ, MarkMonitor, Mesosphere, MobileIron, Mode, Motif Investing, Moxie, Mya, Netflix, OnDeck, Openspace, Pachyderm, Paribus, Peespace, Peribit, PhantomCyber, Plate Joy, Pocket, Prevedere, Private Core, QuanticMind, Quilt, Rappi, Refresj, Oracle Responsys, Lollicam, Sentient Energy, Shopular, ShoreTel, SilkRoad, Silver Spring Networks, SimplyHired, Skycure, Spotzot, Spring CM, SunRun, Tea Leaf, Triple, Trufa, TubeMogul, Tubi, Uber, Venafi, Visier, Wevorce, Xmos, Yozio, Zero Stack, Zetta.net

Key Executives:
   Bill Elmore, General Partner
   e-mail: belmore@foundationcapital.com
   Education: MBA, Stanford Graduate School of Business; BSEE & MSEE, Purdue University
   Background: President, Visual Engineering; General Partner, Inman & Bowman; Marketing Management, Hewlett-Packard; President, Western Association for Venture Capitalist
   Directorships: Onyx Software, Wind River Systems, Atheros Communications, Markmonitor, Packet Design, TeaLeaf Technology, Vernier Networks, Wherenet, Biz360, Uxcomm, Adexs
   Mike Schuh, General Partner Emeritus
   e-mail: mschuh@foundationcapital.com
   Education: BSEE, University of Maryland
   Background: CFO/Co-Founder/Chairman, Intrinsa Corporation; VP Sales, Clarify; VP Sales, Cadence Design Systems; VP Sales, Computervision
   Directorships: Netflix, Responsys, Barcelona, BoardVantage, CoWare, OnStor, Jasper Design Automation

Ashu Garg, General Partner
e-mail: agarg@foundationcap.com
Education: BA, Indian Institute of Technology, New Dehli; MA, Indian Institute of Management, Bangladore
Background: General Manager, Microsoft On-Line Service; McKinsey & Company
Directorships: Vienova
Paul Holland, General Partner
e-mail: pholland@foundationcapital.com
Education: MBA, University of California, Berkeley; MA, Foreign Affairs, University of Virginia; BS, James Madison University
Background: Senior VP, Kana Communications; Pure Software; SRI International
Directorships: Talking Blocks, manageStar, Ketera, RouteScience, TuVoxo Video Solutions, Silver Spring Networks
Paul Koontz, General Partner Emeritus
e-mail: pkoontz@foundationcapital.com
Education: MA, Engineering Management, Stanford University; BS, Mechanical Engineering, Princeton University
Background: VP Marketing, Netscape Communications; Sr Management, Silicon Graphics; Hewlett-Packard
Directorships: United Online, Financial Engines, Apexon, Oberon Financial Technology, Pacific Edge, Vivecon, CloudShield
Skip Glass, Operating Partner
e-mail: sglass@foundationcapital.com
Education: BS, Sacramento State University; MBA, University of Arizona
Background: Canaan Partners; Sygate; SleepyCat Software; eHealth Insurance; Retention Education
Directorships: Voyence; Groundwork Open Solutions
Joanne Chen, Partner
e-mail: kbasco@foundationcap.com
Education: BS, University of California, Berkeley; MBA, Booth School of Business, University of Chicago
Background: Engineer, Cisco Systems; Jefferies & Company; Probitas Partners; Hyde Park Angels
Charles Moldow, General Partner
e-mail: cmoldow@foundationcapital.com
Education: BS, The Wharton School; MBA, Harvard University
Background: Tellme Networks; @Home Network; Co-Founder, OnTime Guide
Zach Noorani, Partner
e-mail: ecavanaugh@foundationcapital.com
Education: BS, Economics, Stanford University; MBA, Sloan School of Management, MIT
Background: Sherpa Ventures; Capital One Financial; North Hill Ventures
Dave Armstrong, Administrative Partner
e-mail: jslimmer@foundationcapital.com
Education: BS, Finance, Virginia Tech; JD, George Mason University School of Law
Background: Gunderson Dettmer
Steve Vassallo, General Partner
e-mail: svassallo@foundationcapital.com
Education: BS, Mechanical Engineering, Worcester Polytechnic Institute; MS, Mechanical Engineering, Stanford University; MBA, Stanford Graduate School of Business
Background: Ning; Director of Mechanical Engineering, Immersion; Project Leader, IDEO
Warren Weiss, General Partner
e-mail: wweiss@foundationcapital.com
Education: BS, Western Illinois University
Background: President & CEO, Asera; President, Prism Solutions
Directorships: eMeter.com; Guardian Analytics; InterAct; MarkMonitor; nGenera; Purfresh; Quantivo; Rearden

Commerce; SilkRoad Technologies; Silver Spring Networks
Angela Nuttman, Operating Coordinator
e-mail: anuttman@foundationcap.com
Education: Santa Clara University
Background: Director of Operations, Olive Grove Consulting

771 FOUNDER COLLECTIVE
81 Greene Street
2nd Floor
New York, NY 10012

web: www.foundercollective.com

Mission Statement: Founder Collective is a venture capital fund investing in seed-stage companies around the world.

Geographic Preference: San Francisco, New York
Fund Size: $70 million
Investment Criteria: Seed
Industry Group Preference: Advertising Technology, Business to Business, Consumer, E-Commerce & Manufacturing, Health Related, Mobile
Portfolio Companies: BuzzFeed, Coupang, Cruise, Dia & Co., Hotel Tonight, Kuvee, Periscope, PillPack, SeatGeek, theTradeDesk, Uber

Key Executives:
David Frankel, Managing Partner
Education: Harvard Business School; University of the Witwatersrand
Background: Internet Solutions
Eric Paley, Partner
Education: Harvard Business School
Background: Brontes Technologies
Micah Rosenbloom, Partner
Education: Cornell University; Harvard Business School
Background: Brontes Technologies; Handshake; Sample6

772 FOUNDER PARTNERS
San Francisco, CA

web: www.founderpartners.co

Mission Statement: Seeking to partner with and invest in technical founders focused on mobile, internet and software products.

Founded: 2013
Industry Group Preference: Mobile, Internet, IoT, Software, Applications, Technology
Portfolio Companies: AddEvent, Admovate, Check Point Software Technologies LTD., Chairish, Cobalt, Dealix, Meltwater, Mixbook, Pinkoi, Relevad, Roblox, Wheelhouse, Yahoo!

Key Executives:
Brian Flynn, Co-Founder/Partner
e-mail: brian@founderpartners.co
Education: BA, University of Notre Dame; MBA, Harvard Business School
Background: Principal, Robertson Stephens & Co.; Partner, Investment Group of Santa Barbara; Co-Founder, IMsecure; Head of Corporate Development, Macromedia Inc.; Co-Founder, AdMovate Inc.; Co-Founder, Relevad Corporation; Founder, Esplanade Partners; Co-Founder, Braintrust Network
Greg Baszucki, Co-Founder/Partner
e-mail: greg@founderpartners.co
Education: BSEE, University of Minnesota
Background: Co-Founder/Executive, Knowledge Revolution; Co-Founder/President, Dealix; Divisional General Manager, The Cobalt Group; Co-Founder, AdMovate Inc.; Founder/CEO, Wheelhouse Enterprises
Directorships: Roblox; Mixbook; iDentalSoft; Band of Angels
Adam Jackson, Partner
e-mail: adam@founderpartners.co
Education: BS, Vanderbilt University
Background: Co-Founder/CEO, Doctor On Demand; Founder, Dopamine Labs; Co-Founder/Managing Partner, Cambrian Asset Management LLC
Directorships: Cleanshelf
Ted West, Partner
e-mail: ted@founderpartners.co
Education: BA, Princeton University; MBA, Harvard Business School
Background: Partner, Sage Partners LLC; Executive Director, Giving Assistant Inc.; Executive Director, CFO Plans; Strategic Advisor, Fresh Victor; Founding Chair, BOHH Labs; Co-Founder/CEO, Strateq Health Inc.
Directorships: BlueSpace Software; Colarity; RealNames
Dimitri Steinberg, Partner
Education: BA, Princeton University; MBA, Harvard University
Background: Morgan Stanley; Lazard; Merrill Lynch; HSBC
Steve McKay, Partner
e-mail: steve@founderpartners.co
Education: BSEE, University of Notre Dame; MBA, Kellogg School of Management
Background: Associate Partner/Management Consultant, Accenture; CEO, Entone Inc.; Mentor, Founder Institute; President of Global Sales & Business Development, Amino Communications; Founder/CEO, Ignite
Xavier Casanova, Partner
e-mail: xavier@founderpartners.com
Education: MS, Stanford University
Background: Founder, Fireclock; General Manager, Digital River; Founder/CEO, Wambo; Founder/CEO, Liveclicker

773 FOUNDER'S CO-OP
1100 NE Campus Parkway
2nd Floor
Seattle, WA 9810G

web: www.founderscoop.com

Mission Statement: Founders Co-op is a seed-stage investment fund dedicated to working with talented entrepreneurs in the Pacific Northwest region.

Geographic Preference: Pacific Northwest
Investment Criteria: Seed-Stage, Early-Stage
Industry Group Preference: Mobile, Internet
Portfolio Companies: Amperity, Appature, AppFog, Apptentive, Apsalar, Array Health, Auth0, BigDoor, BloomAPI, Boomz, Bluecore, Bonanza, Boundless, Brand AI, C-sATS, Clipboard, Cody, Innervate, Instagift, Jobalign, KITT.ai, Komiko, Level Ten Energy, LiveStories, LendUp, Lighter Capital, Loftium, Meldium, MobileDevHQ, Moment, Onewed, Outreach, Reflect, Remitly, The Riveter, Shelf Engine, Shippable Simply Measured, SkyWard, Smore, Stackery, TalentWorks, Tavour, Thinkfuse, Tindie, Tred, TrueFacet, Tune, Unbounce, Urban Airship, Zappli

Key Executives:
Chris DeVore, General Partner
Education: BA, American Studies, Yale University
Background: Co-Founder, Judy's Book; Vice President, Sapient Corporation; Senior Product Management, McCaw Cellular
Andy Sack, General Partner
Education: Brown University; MBA, Sloan School of Management, MIT
Background: Co-Founder/CEO, Judy's Book; Co-Founder, Kefta; Co-Founder, Abuzz; Co-Founder, Firefly Network
Directorships: Zango, Cooler Planet, Orange Line Media

Venture Capital & Private Equity Firms / Domestic Firms

774 FOUNDERS EQUITY
545 Fifth Avenue
Suite 401
New York, NY 10017

Phone: 212-829-0900 Fax: 212-829-0901
e-mail: info@fequity.com
web: www.fequity.com

Mission Statement: Committed to long-term value creation that generates above average returns.

Geographic Preference: East of the Rockies
Fund Size: $160 million
Founded: 1969
Average Investment: $10 million
Minimum Investment: $3 million
Investment Criteria: Small Buyout, Later Stage, Accelerating Stage, MBO, Recapitalizations, Special Situations/Turnarounds, Corporate Divestitures
Industry Group Preference: Business to Business, Marketing, Outsourcing & Efficiency, Logistics, Healthcare, Environment Products & Services, Security, Consumer Products, Food & Beverage, Food Services, Franchising, Manufacturing, Consumer Services
Portfolio Companies: Advantedge Healthcare Solutions, Core Business Technology Solutions, Glass America, In The Swim Inc., Pay-O-Matic Corporation, Richardson Foods, Stone Source

Key Executives:
  Warren H. Haber, Founding Partner
  212-829-0900 x201
  Fax: 212-829-0901
  e-mail: whaber@fequity.com
  Education: BBA Finance, Baruch College
  Background: Equity Research/Investment Banking, Merrill Lynch; Bear Stearns
  Directorships: CoStar Group; Warnex;
  John L. Teeger, Founding Partner
  Education: BS, University of Witwatersrand; MBA, Columbia University
  Background: VP, Bear Stearns & Company
  Directorships: American LifeCare, Bevglen Medical Systems of Delaware, Ensure Technologies
  John D. White, Founding Partner
  Education: BS, Finance and Accounting, Babson College; MS, Business Admin., Wharton School, University of Pennsylvania
  Background: Executive VP/CFO 3-D Geophysical; Senior VP, Laidlaw Holdings; Paine Webber; Digital Equipment Corporation
  Directorships: ForeAmerica
  J. Ryan Kelly, Partner
  e-mail: rkelly@fequity.com
  Education: BS, Finance & Accounting, Fairfield University
  Background: JH Whitney & Co.; RFE Investment Partners; Arthur Andersen Worldwide

775 FOUNDERS FUND
One Letterman Drive
Building C, Suite 420
San Francisco, CA 94129

e-mail: info@foundersfund.com
web: www.foundersfund.com

Mission Statement: Founders Fund is a venture capital firm that finances companies developing innovative and revolutionary technologies. The firm invests across a wide range of industries and seeks to help build great companies from the ground up.

Fund Size: $625 million
Founded: 2005
Average Investment: $500,000 - $150 million
Investment Criteria: Seed, Early Stage, Later Stage
Industry Group Preference: Aerospace, Defense and Government, Energy, Healthcare, Software, Biotechnology, Internet
Portfolio Companies: Airbnb, AltSchool, Asana, Bolt Threads, Collective Health, Counsyl, Emerald Therapeutics, Facebook, Flexport, Knewton, Lyft, Misfit, Nanotronics Imaging, Oscar, Palantir, Quantcast, Radius, ResearchGate, SpaceX, Spotify, Stemcentrx, Stripe, Wish, ZocDoc

Key Executives:
  Peter Thiel, Partner
  Education: BA, Philosophy, Stanford University; JD, Stanford Law School
  Background: Co-Founder, Chairman & CEO, PayPal; Founder, Clarium Capital Management; Palantir Technologies
  Napoleon Ta, Partner
  Education: BS, University of Colorado; MBA, Stanford University
  Directorships: RigUp; The Athletic; Zenreach
  Brian Singerman, Partner
  Education: BS, Computer Science, Stanford University
  Background: Executive, Google
  Lauren Gross, Partner/Chief Operating Officer
  Education: Stanford University
  Background: Clarium Capital Management; Citigroup Investment Bank
  Keith Rabois, Partner
  Education: BA, Policial Science, Stanford University; JD, Harvard University
  Background: Senior Executive, PayPal; COO, Square
  Directorships: Yelp; Xoom; YouTube; Palantir; Lyft; Airbnb; Eventbrite; Wish; Quora
  Scott Nolan, Partner
  Education: BS, MEng, Mechanical & Aerospace Engineering, Cornell University; MBA, Stanford University
  Background: SpaceX; Bain & Company
  Directorships: CollectiveHealth, Tachyus, Tribogenics
  Neil Ruthven, Chief Financial Officer
  Education: University of Johannesburg
  Background: Controller, VantagePoint Capital Partners; Controller, 3i; Accounting Manager, Merriman Curhan Ford; Audit Manager, Ernst & Young

776 FOUNDRY GROUP
1050 Walnut Street
Suite 210
Boulder, CO 80302

Phone: 303-642-4050 Fax: 303-642-4001
web: www.foundrygroup.com

Mission Statement: Focused on making investments in early-stage information technology, internet and software startups.

Geographic Preference: North America
Fund Size: $225 million
Founded: 2007
Minimum Investment: $250,000 - $500,000
Investment Criteria: Early Stage
Industry Group Preference: Information Technology, Internet, Software
Portfolio Companies: 3D Robotics, About.me, Amper, AppDirect, Authentic8, Avidxchange, Beeswax, Betabrand, Boudless, Brightleaf, Broadly, Chewse, Chorus Fitness, Chowbotics, Chute, Cloudability, Crowdtap, Data Nerds, Distil Networks, Dwolla, Ello, FormLabs, FullContact, GlowForge, Harmonix, Havenly, Hellosign, Help Scout, Integrate, Joany, Jump Cloud, June, Leadpages, littleBits Electronics, Looking Glass, Maketime, Mapbox, Mattermark, Mighty Ai, Misty Robotics, Mlab, Modular Robotics, Moz, Nima, Nix Hydra, Oblong Industries Inc, Occipital, Pantheon, Pi Charging, Pilot, Pioneer Square Labs, Return Path, Roli, Rover.com, Sensu, Sourcepoint, Sovrn, Sphero, StockTwits, Taunt, Team Snap, Tech Stars, The Pros Closet, Tidelift,

TrackR, Two Bit Circus, Urban Airship, VictorOps, VigLink, Wootmath, Work Market, Yesware

Key Executives:
Brad Feld, Managing Director
e-mail: brad@feld.com
Education: BS, MS, MIT
Background: Co-Founder, Mobius Venture Capital
Directorships: Gnip, Oblong, Zynga
Seth Levine, Managing Director
Education: Macalester College
Background: Mobius Venture Capital; FirstWorld Communications; ICG Communications
Ryan McIntyre, Managing Director
e-mail: ryan@foundrygroup.com
Education: BS, Symbolic Systems, Stanford University
Background: Co-Founder, Excite; Oracle Corporation; Software Engineer, Canon Research of America
Jason Mendelson, Managing Director
e-mail: jason@foundrygroup.com
Education: BA, University of Michigan
Background: Managing Director, Mobius Venture Capital; Attorney, Cooley Godward Kronish LLP
Directorships: Accelergy, eCast, Stratify

777 FOUR RIVERS GROUP
156 2nd Street
San Francisco, CA 94105

web: www.fourriversgroup.com

Mission Statement: Four Rivers Group is an expansion stage venture capital firm that invests in high-growth, market leading technology companies globally. The fund provides custom, flexible financing and have no minimum threshold for investment size or ownership percentage.

Founded: 2008
Investment Criteria: Expansion-Stage
Portfolio Companies: Aerohive, Availink, Carbonite, Clutter, Corrigo, FireEye, GameFly, Kahuna, Namely, Numerify, PowerReviews, Return Path, ResearchGate, Sabrix, Satmetrix, ThousandEyes, Vidyo, New Relic. AssureRx Health, Nexenta, Talari Networks, Check, Agilone, Simply Measured, Tintri, Brightspace, Instart Logic, Dtex Systems, Outreach, Everwise, CloudPassage

Key Executives:
Farouk Ladha, Founder/Managing Partner
Education: BA, Economics, Dartmouth College; MBA, Harvard Business School
Background: Managing Director, SVB Capital; Broadview; PricewaterhouseCoopers
Aamir Virani, Strategic Limited Partner
Education: BS, Electrical Engineering; Rice University
Background: Co-Founder/COO/SVP, Product, Dropcam Inc.

778 FOX PAINE & COMPANY LLC
2105 Woodside Road
Suite D
Woodside, CA 94062-1153

Phone: 650-235-2075 Fax: 650-295-4045
e-mail: info@foxpaine.com
web: www.foxpaine.com

Mission Statement: Fox Paine specializes in providing solutions and capital for management buyouts, public-to-private transactions and growth capital investments.
Fund Size: $1.2 billion
Founded: 1996
Average Investment: $50 million
Investment Criteria: Management Buyouts, Public-To-Private Trasactions, Growth Capital
Industry Group Preference: Financial Services, Insurance, Industrial, Consumer Products, Energy, Oil & Gas, Agriculture

Portfolio Companies: ACMI, Alaska Communications Systems, Advanta, Byram Healthcare, Erno Laszlo, Global Indeminity Limited, L'Artisan Parfumeur, Maxxim Medical, Paradigm B.V., Penhaigon's, Seminis, United American Energy Corp., VCST, WJ Communications

Key Executives:
Saul A. Fox, Chief Executive Officer
Education: BS, Temple University; JD, University of Pennsylvania Law School
Background: General Partner, Kohlberg Kravis Roberts & Co.
Directorships: American Cytoscope Manufacturers, American Reinsurance, Canadian General, Global Indemnity, L'Artisan Parfumeur, Motel 6, Paradigm, Penhaligon's, Res-Fuel, Union Texas Petrol

779 FRANCISCO PARTNERS
One Letterman Drive
Building C, Suite 410
San Francisco, CA 94129

Phone: 415-418-2900 Fax: 415-418-2999
e-mail: info@franciscopartners.com
web: www.franciscopartners.com

Mission Statement: Working in close concert with management teams, we seek to reposition, rejuvenate, and grow businesses. With an intense focus on corporate strategy, operational excellence, and financial performance, we leverage our network, resources and experience to help build value for customers, employees, and shareholders.

Industry Group Preference: Software, Business Products & Services, Security, Internet, Healthcare Information Technology, Hardware, Industrial, Communications, Semiconductors, Components & IoT
Portfolio Companies: 2Checkout, Aconex, Aderant, Advanced M, Aesynt, Akqa, Allston Trading, AMI Semiconductor, API Healthcare, Attachmate, Attenti, Availity, Avalon, Barracuda Networks, Betterment, Blue Coat, Blu Jay, Bomgar, ByBox, C MAC Microtechnology, Capsilon, CityIndex, Click, Connecture, Corsair, CoverMyMeds, Crossmatch, Dextrys, Discovery Education, Dynamo, EFJohnson, EFront, eSolutions, ExLibris, Foundation9, Frontrange, GoodRx, Grass Valley, GXS, HealthcareSource, Healthland, Hypercom, Ichor Systems, Iconectiv, K2, Landmark, LegalZoom, Legerity, Lumata, Lynx Medical Systems, Masternaut, Metaswitch, Metrologic, Mincom, Mitel, MyOn, Nextech, NexTraq, NMI, Np Text, Numonyx, OfficeTiger, Operative, Optanix, PayLease, Paymetric, Paysafe, Petcircle.com.au, Plex, Primavera, Prometheus Group, Prosper, QGenda, QuadraMed, Quantros, Quest, R2Net, RedPrairie, Renaissance, Sandvine, Sectigo, ShoreGroup, Smart Modular Technologies, SmartBear, Smart Focus, SonicWall, Source Photonics, Specific Media, The T System, Therapeutic Research Center, Trellis, Ultra Clean Technology, Vendavo, Verifone, WatchGuard, Webtrends, Xcellenet

Other Locations:
207 Sloane Street
Second Floor
London SW1W 9QX
United Kingdom
Phone: 44-020-7907-8600 Fax: 44-0-20-7907-8650

Key Executives:
Dipanjan (DJ) Deb, Founding Partner & CEO
e-mail: deb@franciscopartners.com
Education: BS, Electrical Engineering & Computer Science, UC Berkeley; MBA, Stanford Graduate School of Business
Background: Principal, Texas Pacific Group; Director of Semiconductor Banking, Robertson Stephens & Company; Managment Consultant, McKinsey & Company
Directorships: Bomgar, Cross Match Technologies,

Venture Capital & Private Equity Firms / Domestic Firms

GoodRx, K2, LegalZoom, Plex, Quest, Sectigo, Sonicwall, Verifone
Ben Ball, Founding Partner
e-mail: ball@franciscopartners.com
Education: AB, Harvard College; MBA, Stanford Graduate School of Business
Background: TA Associates, Genstar Capital
Directorships: Cross Match Technologies, MetaSwitch Networks, WatchGuard
Neil Garfinkel, Founding Partner
e-mail: garfinkel@franciscopartners.com
Education: AB, Harvard College; JD, Columbia Law School
Background: Managing Director, Friedman Fleischer & Lowe
Directorships: Quantros
Keith Geeslin, Partner
e-mail: geeslin@franciscopartners.com
Education: BS, Electrical Engineering, Stanford University; MS, Philosophy, Politics & Economics, Univ. of Oxford; MS, Engineering-Economic Systems, Stanford University
Background: Sprout Group
David Golob, Chief Investment Officer
e-mail: golob@franciscopartners.com
Education: AB, Harvard College; MBA, Stanford Graduate School of Business
Background: Managing Director, Tiger Management; General Atlantic Partners; McKinsey & Company
Directorships: Betterment, Bomgar, K2, Optaniz, Prosper, Quest, Sectigo, SmartBear, Sonicwall
Ezra Perlman, Co-President
e-mail: perlman@franciscopartners.com
Education: BA, Applied Mathematics, Harvard University; MBA, Stanford Graduate School of Business
Background: Battery Ventures, Advanta
Directorships: Availity, Avalon Healthcare, Cennecture, eSolutions, HealthcareSource, Landmark, Nextech, QGenda, Quantros, Renaissance
Deep Shah, Co-President
e-mail: shah@franciscopartners.com
Education: MA, Economics, University of Cambridge
Background: Morgan Stanley
Directorships: BluJay Solutions, ByBox, MetaSwitch Networks, Operative, Prometheus Group
Sanford Robertson, Co-Founder/Partner Emeritus
e-mail: robertson@franciscopartners.com
Education: BA, University of Michigan; MBA, University of Michigan
Background: Chairman, Robertson Stephens & Company; Founder, Robertson Coleman Siebel & Weisel

780 FRANKLIN STREET EQUITY PARTNERS
1450 Raleigh Road
Suite 300
Chapel Hill, NC 27517

Phone: 919-489-2600 Fax: 919-489-1666
Toll-Free: 877-489-2600
e-mail: franklin@franklin-street.com
web: www.franklin-street.com

Mission Statement: To provide independent, trusted and personalized advice, complementing in-house expertise with carefully selected external resources.
Geographic Preference: Southeastern United States
Fund Size: $2 billion
Founded: 1990
Minimum Investment: $500,000
Investment Criteria: Companies with rational business model and strong management team
Industry Group Preference: Technology, Business to Business
Key Executives:
Robert C. Eubanks Jr., Founder/Chairman Emeritus
Education: University of North Carolina, Chapel Hill
Background: Co-Founder/President, McMillion Eubanks Capital Management
Directorships: All Kinds of Minds Foundation, Kenan-Flagler Business School Foundation
William B. Thompson, Managing Director
Education: MBA, Darden Graduate School of Business; BS Chemical Engineering, North Carolina State University
Background: President/Co-Founder, Peacock-Thompson Investment Management; Management, Carolina Securities Corporation

781 FRASER MCCOMBS CAPITAL
1035 Pearl Street
Suite 401
Boulder, CO 80302

Phone: 210-382-6822
e-mail: chase@fmcap.com
web: www.fmcap.com

Mission Statement: Fraser McCombs Capital is a venture firm focused on early-stage technology companies within the automotive space. Fraser McCombs is the first and only venture fund that has managed by automotive entrepreneurs and dealers. The team has long standing relationships with Tier 1, 2, and 3 vendors, and connections with leading OEM executives and principals of the largest dealer groups. This allows the fund to provide key introductions for their portfolio companies.
Investment Criteria: Early-Stage
Industry Group Preference: Automotive, Transportation
Portfolio Companies: Autoniq, Confident Financial Solutions, Dataium, Dealer HQ, ESupply Systems, Gazillion, Kapost, Phunware, Relevant Solutions, Roximity, Scout, Showroom Logic, Smart Picture, Smule UParts, Verve, Autopay, Autotalks, Frontier Car Group, Keeps, Optimus Ride
Other Locations:
755 Mulberry Avenue
Suite 600
San Antonio, TX 78212

220 North Green Street
Chicago, IL 60607
Key Executives:
Chase Fraser, Managing Partner
210-382-6822
e-mail: chase@fmcap.com
Education: University of Texas, Austin
Background: Managing Partner, Circle P Capital; Founder, MarketQuiz; Vice President, IFCO Containers
Tony Rimas, Managing Partner
e-mail: tony@fmcap.com
Background: Director of Operations, McCombs Automotive Group

782 FRAZIER HEALTHCARE VENTURES
601 Union Street
Two Union Square
Suite 3200
Seattle, WA 98101

Phone: 206-621-7200
web: www.frazierhealthcare.com

Mission Statement: Makes partnerships with entrepreneurs who benefit from the company's network of technical, industry, academic, research and financial contacts; considers each opportunity on an individual basis, knowing that emerging companies are dynamic by nature, and looks for visionaries in emerging healthcare who have promising concepts.
Geographic Preference: United States
Fund Size: $3.4 billion
Founded: 1991
Average Investment: $2 million
Minimum Investment: $250,000

Venture Capital & Private Equity Firms / Domestic Firms

Investment Criteria: Seed, Series A, Series B, Early-Stage, Growth Equity, Later Stage
Industry Group Preference: Medical Devices, Healthcare, Life Sciences, Biopharmaceuticals
Portfolio Companies: Abode Healthcare, Acerta Pharma, Acheogen, Alcresta Therapeutic, Allena Pharmaceuticals, Alnara Pharmaceuticals, Alpine Immune Sciences, Alteon Health, Amicus, Anaptys Bio, Aptinyx, Array BioPharma, Ascension Orthopedics, Barrx Medical, Bravo Health, Cadence Pharmaceuticals, Calibra Medical, Calibrium, Calistoga, Calixa Therapeutics, Cerexa, CHG Healthcare Services, Chimerix Inc., Cidara Therapeutics, Cirius Therapeutics, Clovis Oncology, Collegium Pharmaceutical, Corixa, Cotherics, CVT Therapeutics, DSI Renal, Elements Behavioral Health, Entasis Therapeutics, FlowCadia Inc., Glaukos, Gritstone Oncology, Ignyta, Imago BioSciences, Incline Therapeutics, Iovance Biotherapeutics, Iterum Therapeutics, Labsco, Leiter's, Marcadia Biotech, Matrix Medical Network, Mavu Pharma, MedPointe, Millendo Therapeutics, Northfield, Oceana Therapeutics, OraPharma Inc., Ohi, Outpost Medicine, PCI Pharma Services, Pentec Health, Portola Pharmaceuticals, Powervision, Precision Dermatology, Priority Solutions, Quatrx, Rempex Pharmaceuticals, Rigel, Semnur Pharmaceuticals, Sierra Oncology, Silvergate Pharmaceuticals Inc., Sojournix, Solis Mammography, South Side, Stromedix, Sutrovax, TCG RX, The Core Institute, Threshold Pharmaceuticals, Tobira Therapeutics, Trident USA Health Services, Trubion Pharmaceuticals, Tularik, United Dermpartners, US Renal Care, VentiRx, ViroPharma, Vivus, XenoPort, Zavante, Zeltic, Zymo Genetics

Other Locations:
70 Willow Road
Suite 200
Menlo Park, CA 94025
Phone: 650-325-5156

Key Executives:

Alan D. Frazier, Founder/Chairman
e-mail: alan@frazierco.com
Education: BA, University of Washington
Background: EVP/CFO, Immunex Corporation; Senior Financial Advisor/CFO, Affymax; Co-Head of Technology Practice, Arthur Young & Company (Ernst & Young)
Directorships: UW Medicine Board, UW Medicine Strategic Initiatives Committee, University of Washington School of Medicine

James N. Topper, MD, PhD, Managing Partner
650-325-5156
e-mail: james@frazierhealthcare.com
Education: BS, University of Michigan; MD, PhD, Stanford University
Background: Director Cardiovascular R&D, Millennium Pharmaceuticals; Director, Millennium San Franciso; VP Biology, COR
Directorships: Amicus Therapeutics; Arete Therapeutics; MacuSight; Zelos Therapeutrics; Point Biomedical; Portola Pharmaceuticals; Harvard-Partners Center for Genetics and Genomics

Patrick Heron, Managing Partner
650-325-5156
e-mail: patrick@frazierco.com
Education: BA, University of North Carolina, Chapel Hill; MBA, Harvard Business School
Background: McKinsey & Company
Directorships: Tobira Therapeutics, Marcadia, Calixa, Cerexa, PreCision Dermatology, MedPointe, Collegium, Imago BioSciences, Iterum Therapeutics, Silvergate Pharmaceuticals, SutroVax

Nathan R. Every, MD, MPH, General Partner, Seattle
e-mail: nathan@frazierhealthcare.com
Education: BA, University of Pennsylvania; MD, Emory University School of Medicine; MPH, University of Washington School of Public Health
Background: Associate Professor of Medicine/Director, Cardiovascular Outcomes Research Center; Management, Merck & Company; Johnson & Johnson
Directorships: Apneon; BaroSense; BARRx; FlowCardia; MacuSight; SyneCor; Interventional Rhythm Management; PowerVision; Xoft Microtube; Alexza Pharmaceuticals; FoviOptics

Daniel Estes, PhD, General Partner
e-mail: dan.estes@frazierhealthcare.com
Education: BS, Electrical Engineering, Stanford University; PhD, Biomedical Engineering, University of Michigan
Background: Management Consultant, McKinsey & Company
Directorships: Semnur Pharmaceuticals, Outpost Medicine, Sierra Oncology, Cirius Therapeutics

Philip Zaorski, Principal
e-mail: philip.zaorski@frazierhealthcare.com
Education: BS, Wharton School, University of Pennsylvania
Background: Analyst, RBC Capital Markets

Kent Berkley, Principal
e-mail: kent.berkley@frazierhealthcare.com
Education: BS, Northwestern University; MBA, Kellogg School of Management, Northwestern University
Background: The Edgewater Funds; Associate, CIVC Partners, Dresner Partners; Lehman Brothers

Nader Naini, Managing Partner, Seattle
e-mail: nader@frazierco.com
Education: MBA, New York University; BA, University of Pennsylvania
Background: Aspen Education Group; Goldman, Sachs & Company; Chairman, CHG Healthcare
Directorships: Elements Behavioral Health, Northfield, Solis Mammography, Alteon Health

Carol Eckert, Director, Investor Relations, Seattle
e-mail: carol.eckert@frazierhealthcare.com
Education: BS, Accounting, University of Idaho
Background: Westin Hotels; Deloitte Touche
Directorships: Immunex Corporation

Elizabeth Park, Vice President, Investor Relations
e-mail: liz.park@frazierhealthcare.com
Education: BA, Mass Communications, University of California, Berkeley
Background: Product Project Manager, Amgen; Associate Project Manager, MacuSight

Brian Morfitt, General Partner, Seattle
206-621-7200
e-mail: brian@frazierhealthcare.com
Education: BS, MS, Management Science & Engineering, Stanford University
Background: Associate, Summit Partners
Directorships: Health Care Private Equity Association

James W. Brush, MD, Partner
Education: BA, Middlebury College; MD, University of Southern California
Background: Boston Consulting Group

Steve Bailey, Chief Financial Officer/Partner
e-mail: steveb@frazierhealthcare.com
Education: BS, Accounting, Central Washington University; MS, Tax, Portland State University
Background: Vice President, Finance, LapLink; Finance & Corporate Development, Elixis Corporations; Data Critical Corporation; Senior Manager, Tax Department, Ernst & Young LLP

Ben Magnano, Managing Partner, Seattle
e-mail: ben@frazierhealthcare.com
Education: BBA, University of Notre Dame; MBA, Tuck School of Business, Dartmouth College
Background: Associate, Morgan Stanley Venture Partners; Arthur Andersen
Directorships: Woodland Park Zoo; Matrix Medical Network, Northfield, TCGRx, United Derm Partners, US Renal Care

Ryan Lucero, Principal
e-mail: ryan.lucero@frazierhealthcare.com

Venture Capital & Private Equity Firms / Domestic Firms

Education: BS, Marriott School of Management, Brigham Young University
Background: JPMorgan Chase & Co.; TARP, US Department of the Treasury; Kohlberg & Co.
Anna H. Chen, PhD, Senior Associate
e-mail: anna.chen@frazierhealthcare.com
Education: AB, Biochemical Sciences, Harvard College; PhD, Systems Biology, Harvard University
Background: L.E.K.; Entrepreneurial Fellow, Flagship Pioneering; Business Mentor, National Science Foundation Innovation Corps program
Jeremy Janson, Senior Associate
e-mail: jeremy.janson@frazierhealthcare.com
Education: BA, Economics, Middlebury College
Background: Robert W. Baird

783 FREEMAN SPOGLI & CO.
11100 Santa Monica Boulevard
Suite 1900
Los Angeles, CA 90025

Phone: 310-444-1822
web: www.freemanspogli.com

Mission Statement: Private equity firm focused on middle market companies in the consumer and distribution sectors.

Fund Size: $13 billion
Founded: 1983
Minimum Investment: $25 million
Investment Criteria: Exclusively middle-market
Industry Group Preference: Retailing, Direct Marketing, Distribution, Restaurants
Portfolio Companies: Arhaus, Batteries Plus Bulbs, Cafe Rio, City Barbeque, CRH Healthcare, El Pollo Loco, FASTSIGNS, Five Star Food Service, Floor & Decor, ISN, MicroStar, Osprey, PF Baseline Fitness, Plantation Products, Regent Holding, Sur La Table

Other Locations:
299 Park Avenue
20th Floor
New York, NY 10171
Phone: 212-758-2555

Key Executives:
Bradford M. Freeman, Co-Chairman
Education: BA, Stanford University; MA Business Administration, Harvard University
Background: Managing Director, Dean Witter Reynolds
Ronald P. Spogli, Co-Chairman
Education: Stanford University; MA Business Administration, Harvard University
Background: Managing Director Investment Banking, Dean Witter Reynolds
John M. Roth, Chief Executive Officer
Education: BA Accounting/MA Business Administration/Finance, Wharton School
Background: VP Mergers/Acquisitions, Kidder Peabody; Management Consultant, McKinsey & Co; Investment Banking, Dean Witter Reynolds
Jon D. Ralph, President & Chief Operating Officer
Education: BA History, Amherst College
Background: Analyst Investment Banking, Morgan Stanley
Brad J. Brutocao, Partner
Education: BS, Economics, University of California, Los Angeles
Background: Analyst, M&A, Morgan Stanley & Co.
Benjamin D. Geiger, Partner
Education: BS, Economics, Cornell University
Background: Analyst, M&A, Merrill Lynch & Co.
Todd W. Halloran, Partner
Education: Economics Graduate, Colby College; MA Business Administration
Background: VP Mergers/Acquisitions, Soldman Sachs & Co; Financial Analyst, Amerian Brands/Manufacturers Hanover

John S. Hwang, Partner
Education: BS, Business Economics, University of California, LA
Background: Analyst, Citigroup Global Markets
Christian B. Johnson, Partner
Education: History, Colgate University
Background: Analyst, Leveraged Finance Group, Wachovia Securities
J. Frederick Simmons, Partner
Education: Bachelor's, Williams College, Masters, New York University
Background: Vice President, Los Angeles Office Of Bankers Trust Company
William M. Wardlaw, Chief Compliance Officer
Education: Bachelor's (Honors), Whittier College
Background: Riordan & McKinzie, Managing Partner

784 FREESTYLE

e-mail: media@freestyle.vc
web: www.freestyle.vc

Mission Statement: Freestyle Capital is a seed stage investor and mentor for Internet software startups. Freestyle's community of veteran entrepreneurs offers real-world experience and business finesse without stuffy investor baggage or hidden agendas.

Fund Size: $216 million
Founded: 2009
Investment Criteria: Seed-Stage
Industry Group Preference: Internet
Portfolio Companies: 9gag, About.me, Adstage, Agentology, Airtable, Alpha Draft, Applie Pie Capital, Aviate, Backtype, BetterUp, Boomtown, BuildingConnected, Byliner, Camiocam, Cardpool, Chartbeat, Chute, Clarity, Clypd, CREXi, CrowdFlower, Easecentral, Embark, French Girls, Giftbit, Golnstant, Gradescope, Heart This, Impermium, Indextank, Joyfride, Juvo, Kite, LaunchKit, Leo, Memoir, Mongolab, Nestio, New Co., Opsmatic, Payable, PicCollage, Range Me, Recurly, Riffsy, Rixty, SimpleGeo, Singly, Snapdocs, SnappyTV, Stitch, Swift Shift, Text Now, Trizic, TrueFacet, Typekit, UXPin, Webshots, Yobongo

Key Executives:
Josh Felser, Founder
Education: Duke University, Fuqua Business School
Background: Co-Founder, FYI Living; Founder, Spinner; Founder, Grouper
Dave Samuel, Founder
Education: MIT
Background: Founder, Thriller Designs; Oracle; Founder, Spinner; Founder, Brondell; Founder, Grouper

785 FRESH VC
San Francisco, CA

web: www.freshvc.com

Mission Statement: A venture capital and angel firm investing in the cannabis industry.

Founded: 2014
Industry Group Preference: Consumer Products, Cannabis, Healthcare, Technology, Hospitality
Portfolio Companies: Aptible, Bannerman, Crunchbutton, Eaze, Eight Sleep, FiscalNote, Gyroscope, Pijon, The Sails Company, Shyp, Unwind Me, Vessel

Key Executives:
Shri Ganeshram, Founder/Managing Partner
Education: BS, Mathematics/Computer Science, Massachusetts Institute of Technology
Background: Founder/CTO, FlightCar; Software Consultant, Credit Suisse; VP of Growth, Analytics & Strategy, Eaze
Brian Sheng, Co-Founder/Managing Partner
Education: Princeton University
Background: Founder, IvyBound; Analyst, Shenzhen Capital Group Co.; Partner, DreamTech Ventures; Foreign

Venture Capital & Private Equity Firms / Domestic Firms

Investment Advisor, URI Investment Fund; General Partner, The Arcview Group
Directorships: Eaze

786 FRESHTRACKS CAPITAL
29 Harbor Road, Suite 200
PO Box 849
Shelburne, VT 05482

Phone: 802-923-1500 **Fax:** 802-923-1506
web: www.freshtrackscap.com

Mission Statement: FreshTracks combines $25 million in venture capital with the strategic resources needed by entrepreneurs to build thriving companies throughout Vermont and beyond. Our Fund Managers have deep backgrounds in business finance and strategy, as well as direct operating experience with numerous growth companies. FreshTracks' resources, capital and networks support innovative businesses through multiple rounds of financing and stages of growth.
Geographic Preference: Vermont, New York, Massachusetts, New Hampshire
Fund Size: $25 million
Industry Group Preference: Technology
Portfolio Companies: Auterra, Bridj, Budnitz Bicycles, Caledonia Spirits, CPS, Draker, DRINKmaple, Ello, Faraday, Horse Network, IrisVR, ISIS, Kohort, Lincoln Peak Partners, Mamava, Morphie, Native Energy, NEHP, Ogee, Patient Engagement Systems, Quirky, Redd, Reilly's Hempvet, Social Sentinal, Solais, SolarOne, SunCommon, THINKmd, Vermont Teddy Bear, Virtual Peaker, Vocate, Wuu
Key Executives:
  Cairn G Cross, Co-Founder/Managing Director
  Education: BS, Montana State University; MBA, New Hampshire College; Stonier Graduate School of Banking
  Background: Owner, Cross Vermont Financial; Assistant General Manager, Green Mountain Capital; Co-Chair, Vermont Investors Forum
  Directorships: Budnitz Bicycles, Faraday, Mamava, NativeEnergy, Vermont Teddy Bear
  Charles F Kireker, Co-Founder/Senior Advisor
  Education: Princeton University; MPP, Harvard University
  Background: Co-Founder, Green Mountain Capital; Co-Founder, North Country Angels
  Directorships: EatingWell Media Group, Vermont Teddy Bear, VEMAS, Autumn Harp
  Timothy C Davis, Managing Director
  Education: University of Vermont; MBA, Harvard Business School
  Background: Management, Advanced Materials Companies
  Directorships: Auterra, Moscow Mills, Solais, SolarOne
  Lee E Bouyea, Managing Director
  Education: Colgate University; MBA, Tuck School of Business
  Background: eBay, Nextel Communications, Ebates
  Directorships: Auterra, Ello, Horse Network, IrisVR, Mamava, Social Sentinal
  T.J. Whalen, Managing Director
  Education: BA, Economics and Education, Dartmouth College
  Background: Chief Strategy Officer & Chief Sustainability Officer, Keurig Green Mountain
  Directorships: Budnitz Bicycles, NativeEnergu, Ogee, Reilly's HempVet, SunCommon

787 FRIEDMAN, FLEISCHER & LOWE LLC
One Maritime Plaza
Suite 2200
San Francisco, CA 94111

Phone: 415-402-2100 **Fax:** 415-402-2111
e-mail: contact@fflpartners.com
web: www.fflpartners.com

Mission Statement: Actively seeking investment opportunities and encourage owners, managers, legal, financial and accounting professionals, and intermediaries to reach out with any questions, investment opportunities or ideas.
Geographic Preference: United States, Canada
Fund Size: $2 billion
Founded: 1997
Average Investment: $50 - $300 million
Minimum Investment: $15 million
Investment Criteria: Middle Market Companies: Ownership Restructuring, Going-Private Transactions, Growth Equity Funding, Recapitalizations, Management Buyouts (Public and Private)
Industry Group Preference: Education, Business to Business, Media, Marketing, Healthcare, Consumer Products, Financial Services
Portfolio Companies: Advanced Career Technologies, American Advisors Group, Bacharach, Banner Bank, BearingPoint, Benevis, CapitalSource, CHI, Church's Chicken, CPI, Curo, DataOnline, Discovery Foods, Enjoy Beer, Eyecare Partners, Eyemart Expreess, GeoVera Holdings Inc., Green Bank, Guardian, Icynene, Interactive Health, Iracore International Inc., JonesTrading, Korn Ferry, Midwest Dental, Milstone AV Technologies Inc., Monpelier RE, ProService Hawaii, Snap Financial Group, SteelPoint, Strategic Investment Group, Summit BHC, Tempur-Pedic, Transtar, Tritech, Well Street Urgent Care, Wilton Re
Key Executives:
  Tully M. Friedman, Managing Partner
  e-mail: tfriedman@fflpartners.com
  Education: AB, Stanford University; JD, Harvard Law School
  Background: Hellman & Friedman; Co-Chairman, American Enterprise Institute; Vice Chairman, Telluride Foundation
  Directorships: George Lucas Museum of Narrative Art
  Spencer Fleischer, Managing Partner
  e-mail: sfleischer@fflpartners.com
  Education: MS, Univ. of Oxford; BA, University of Witwatersrand
  Background: Morgan Stanley
  Directorships: Eyemart Express; Korn Ferry International; Milestone AV Technologies; BearingPoint Inc.; Jones Trading Institutional Services LLC; Transtar Holdings; Wilton Re Holdings Ltd.
  Christopher Masto, Co-Founder/Senior Advisor
  e-mail: cmasto@fflpartners.com
  Education: MBA, Harvard Business School; ScB, Brown University
  Background: Bain & Company; Morgan Stanley & Company
  Directorships: Curo Financial Technologies; Enjoy Beer LLC; TriTech Holdings; Tempur Sealy International
  Rajat Duggal, Partner
  Education: BS, Indiana University; JD, Yale Law School
  Background: Bain Capital; Kirkland & Ellis; Deloitte & Touche
  Directorships: Church's Chicken; Summit Behavioral Healthcare LLC; Benevis LLC; GeoVera Insurance Group; Jones Trading; Transtar Holdings; Guardian Home Care; Discovery Foods
  Aaron Money, Partner
  Education: AB, Economics, Duke University
  Background: Assciate, DB Capital; Investment Banking Analyst, Chase Securities
  Directorships: Guardian Home Care Holdings, Speedy Cash Holdings Corp
  Cas Schneller, Partner
  Education: BBA, Finance & Business Economics, University of Notre Dame; MBA, Harvard Business School
  Background: GTCR Golder Rauner; Analyst, William Blair & Company
  Directorships: JonesTrading Institutional Services

Venture Capital & Private Equity Firms / Domestic Firms

Chris Harris, Partner
Education: BS, Management Science & Engineering, Stanford University; MBA, Stanford Graduate School of Business
Background: Associate, Berkshire Partners; Associate Consultant, Bain & Company
Directorships: EyeMart Express; Eye Care Partners; Summit Behavioral Healthcare; Strategic Investment Group; TriTech Software Systems
David Crussel, Operating Partner
Background: COO, SumTotal Systems; ADAC Laboratories; GE Medical Systems
Greg Long, Partner
Education: BS, Mechanical Engineering, Stanford University
Background: Senior Associate, The Parthenon Group
Directorships: American Advisor Group; CHI Overhead Doors; Big Brothers Big Sisters; Icynene

788 FRIEND SKOLER & COMPANY LLC
160 Pehle Avenue, Suite 303
Saddle Brook, NJ 07663

Phone: 201-712-0075 Fax: 201-712-1525
web: www.friendskoler.com

Mission Statement: Invests in leading middle market companies across a range of industries in partnership with skilled management teams who want to invest in and grow the businesses they operate.
Geographic Preference: United States
Fund Size: $231 million
Founded: 1998
Average Investment: $20 million - $200 million
Minimum Investment: $5 million
Investment Criteria: Minimum EBITDA of $5 million; Strong management; Good growth prospects, Middle Market
Industry Group Preference: Manufacturing, Distribution, Retailing, Services, Consumer Products, Industrial Services, E-Commerce & Manufacturing, Business Products & Services
Portfolio Companies: Hex Performance, Iconic Group, Slon Lofts Group, Banza, Madan Plastics Inc., Petmatrics LLC, Hopkins Manufacturing, Accessories Marketing Inc., Woodstream Corp., United Pet Group Inc., Ballet Jewels, Box, CNC Global, AllHeart, Fashion Cents, Kenlin Pet Supply,

Key Executives:
Alexander A. Friend, Managing Director
201-712-0075
Fax: 201-712-1525
e-mail: alex@friendskoler.com
Education: BA, Harvard University; MBA, Stanford Graduate School of Business
Background: Venture Partners Inc; Merrill Lynch; Mercer Consulting
Directorships: CNC Global Limited, United Pet Group, HAS Holding Corp, Madan Plastics, Kenlin Pet Supply, Woodstream Corporation
Steven F. Skoler, Managing Director
e-mail: steve@friendskoler.com
Education: BA, Harvard; MBA, Stanford
Background: Venture Partners; Morgan Stanley; Braxton Associates
Directorships: CNC Global, NAS Holdings, Madan Plastics, Kenlin Pet Supply, Woodstream
Gregory P. Sullivan, Director, Finance
Education: BBA/MBA, Iona College; Post Grad. Certificate, Accounting, Seton Hall University
Background: Kenlin Pet Supply; APS; Loral Electronics International; MacMillan Publishing/American Brands
Cheryl Moss, Director
e-mail: cmoss@friendskoler.com
Education: BS, Business Admin., McDonough School of Business, Georgetown University
Background: Senior Analyst, Prudential Capital Group

789 FRONTENAC COMPANY
One South Wacker
Suite 2980
Chicago, IL 60606

Phone: 312-368-0044 Fax: 312-368-9520
e-mail: reception@frontenac.com
web: www.frontenac.com

Mission Statement: Frontenac Company provides resources and capital to help portfolio companies achieve long-term growth and success.
Geographic Preference: United States, Europe
Fund Size: $250 million
Founded: 1971
Average Investment: $15 - $50 million
Investment Criteria: Lower Middle Market, Recapitalizations, Buyouts, Growth Capital
Industry Group Preference: Business Products & Services, Technology, Commercial Services, Healthcare, Food & Beverage, Consumer Products
Portfolio Companies: AH Harris, Behavioral Health Group, Diversified Maintenance Systems, e+ CancerCare, GNAP, H-E Parts International, La Tavola Fine Linen Rental, Mercer Foods, Portfolio Group, Salient CRGT, SIGMA, Spice Chain Corporation, Wenner Bread Products, Whitebridge Pet Brands

Key Executives:
Paul D Carbery, Managing Partner
312-759-7315
e-mail: pcarbery@frontenac.com
Education: BA, Yale University; MBA, Stanford University Graduate School of Business
Background: Strategic Planning Associates
Directorships: GNAP, H-E Parts, La Tavola, Portfolio Group
Walter C Florence, Managing Partner
312-629-3152
e-mail: wflorence@frontenac.com
Education: Dartmouth College; MBA, Kellogg School of Management, Northwestern University
Background: Analyst, Bear Stearns & Company
Directorships: Mercer Foods, Salient CRGT, Sigma, Spice Chain Corporation, Wenner Bread Products, Whitebridge Pet Products
Ronald W Kuehl, Managing Director
312-759-7330
e-mail: rkuehl@frontenac.com
Education: University of Notre Dame; MBA, Kellogg School of Management, Northwestern University
Background: Churchill Capital; H.I.G. Capital; Analyst, Morgan Stanley
Directorships: AH Harris, Diversified Maintenance Systems, Portfolio Group, Sigma, Wenner Bread Products
Michael S Langdon, Managing Director
312-759-7348
e-mail: mlangdon@frontenac.com
Education: University of Michigan; MBA, Harvard Business School
Background: Senior Associate, Genstar Capital; Analyst, DLJ Merchant Banking
Directorships: AH Harris, Behavioral Health Group, H-E Parts, Salient CRGT
Elizabeth C Williamson, Managing Director
e-mail: ewilliamson@frontenac.com
Education: Dartmouth College; MBA, Harvard Business School
Background: Associate, Thomas H. Lee Partners; Lehman Brothers; Director, Schlotterbeck & Foss; Director, Spice Chain Corporation
Julie A Bender, Vice President/Chief Financial Officer/Chief Compliance Officer
312-759-7345
e-mail: jbender@frontenac.com
Education: Indiana University; MBA, Kellogg School of Management, Northwestern University

Venture Capital & Private Equity Firms / Domestic Firms

Background: Associate, Heller Financial; NES Rentals; Chicago Corporation; Auditor, Arthur Andersen & Co.
Joseph R Rondinelli, Principal
312-759-7319
e-mail: jrondinelli@frontenac.com
Education: Northwestern University; MBA, University of Chicago Booth School of Business
Background: Analyst, Citigroup Global Markets
Directorships: GNAP, La Tavola, Whitebridge Pet Brands
Neal G Sahney, Principal
312-759-7335
e-mail: nsahney@frontenac.com
Education: University of Michigan; MBA, Wharton School, University of Pennsylvania
Background: Engagement Manager, McKinsey & Company; Senior Analyst, Corporate Strategy & Business Development, The Walt Disney Company
Directorships: AH Harris

---

790 FRONTIER CAPITAL
525 N Tyron St.
Suite 1900
Charlotte, NC 28202

Phone: 704-414-2880 Fax: 704-414-2881
e-mail: info@frontiercapital.com
web: www.frontiercapital.com

Mission Statement: Frontier Capital was founded in 1999 to provide capital and support to high growth business services companies. At the time, many of these companies were being overlooked by both investors and lenders. Many investors felt business services did not have the allure of high-tech venture investments and lenders were more interested in asset intensive, traditional businesses. We recognized an opportunity to help fill this void by focusing our investments on a sector that we believed would benefit from the rise of the service economy and a growing trend toward outsourcing.

Founded: 1999
Industry Group Preference: Business Products & Services
Portfolio Companies: AccessOne, Agreement Express, Aviacode, Dinova, Igloo, InteliSecure, Listen First, MediaPro, MediaRadar, Planet Risk, PowerDMS, Price Spider, Talent Reef, Tango, Vibe HCM, Viverae

Key Executives:
Richard Maclean, Managing Partner
e-mail: richard@frontiercapital.com
Education: College of Charleston; MBA, Darden School of Business
Background: Investment Banking Group, NationsBank; General Partner, Blue Ridge Capital
Directorships: Agreement Express, Anodyne Health, Celergo, Healthx, Peak 10, PMG Research, SecureWorks, VibeHCM, WilsonHCG, Zephyr
Andrew Lindner, Managing Partner
e-mail: andrew@frontiercapital.com
Background: Stephens, Inc., Bank of America, Weiss, Peck & Greer
Directorships: AccessOne, Azaleos, Conclusive Analytics, Daxko, Digital Envoy, Gazelle, Healthiest You, Igloo, Lanyon, Planet Risk, Quickparts, Ryla, Social Solutions, Tango, Teladoc, Vivera
Michael Ramich, Partner
e-mail: michael@frontiercapital.com
Education: Duke University; MBA, Harvard Business School
Background: General Electric
Directorships: Anodyne Health, Aviacode, Celergo, Daxko, Dinova, Healthx, Lanyon, ListenFirst, MediaRader, MultiLing, Netdocuments, PowerDMS, Simpli.fi, Social Solutions, TalentReef, Viverae
Joel Lanik, Partner
e-mail: joel@frontiercapital.com
Education: Duke University; MBA, Darden School of Business
Background: VP, Finance & Strategy, LURHQ

Directorships: Anodyne Health, Azaleos, ConnectSolutions, InteliSecure, LurHQ, Peak10, PMG Research, WilsonhCG, Zephyr
Seth Harward, Partner
Education: BA, University of North Carolina
Background: Research Triangle's Council for Entrepreneurial Development
Directorships: Aviacode, Celergo, Dinova, HealthiestYou, InteliSecure, Lanyon, MediaPro, MultiLing, Netdocument, Simpl.fi, Tango, Wilson HCG, Zephyr
Scott Hoch, Partner
e-mail: scott@frontiercapital.com
Education: Furman University
Background: Edgeview Partners
Directorships: Aviacode, Celergo, Daxko, eVerifile, HealthiestYou, Healthx, InteliSecure, Lanyon, MediaPro, PMG Research, Simpl.fi, Social Solutions, TalentReef, Viverae, Wilson HCG, Zephyr

---

791 FRONTIER VENTURE CAPITAL
100 Wilshire Blvd
4th Floor
Santa Monica, CA 90401

Phone: 424-354-2244
e-mail: info@frontiervc.com
web: www.draperfrontier.com

Mission Statement: Frontier invests in start-up businesses with the potential to make significant changes in the world. Frontier aims to help entrepreneurs to create value and transform their ideas into self-sustaining businesses.

Geographic Preference: Western United States
Fund Size: $55 million
Average Investment: $100,000 - $1 million
Investment Criteria: Startups, Seed Stage
Industry Group Preference: Software, Information Services, Biotechnology, Nanotechnology, Alternative Energy
Portfolio Companies: Appletree.com, BigFrame, BondMart, Boom Studios, Chimeros, D.Light Design, Dragnet Solutions, Dx Biosciences, Game Salad, Graph Effect, HydraDx, Iconix, Instantly, Intematix, JanRain, Lottay, Marval Bioscience, Mogreet, MomentFeed, Netpulse, Neurovigil, NinthDecimal, OnTech, Planitax, Predixion Software, Prolacta Bioscience, Seismic Games, SkyGrid, SmartRG, Super Heat Games, Swink.tv, SynapSense, Synthetic Games, Tethys Bioscience, Tioga Energy, Zadspace

Key Executives:
David Cremin, Founder/Managing Director, Los Angeles
Education: BS, Industrial Engineering, Stanford University
Background: Founding Partner, Zone Ventures; Founder & CEO, Vis-a-Vis Entertainment
Directorships: Instantly, Janrain, MomentFeed, OnTech, UCode
Scott Lenet, Founder/Managing Director, Los Angeles
Education: AB, Comparative Literature, Princeton University; MBA, Entrepreneurial Management, Wharton School, University of Pennsylvania
Background: CEO, SmartFrog.com; Product Marketing, Trilogy Software
Directorships: Boom Studios, NinthDecimal, Seismic Games, Sacramento Philharmonic
Frank Foster, Managing Director, Santa Barbara
Education: BA, Harvard University; MBA, Harvard Business School
Background: Investment Manager, Gideon Hixon Fund; General Partner, Allen & Buckeridge Pty Ltd
Directorships: Dx Biosciences, HydraDx, Marval Biosciences, Predixion Software, Prolacta Bioscience, Swink.tv, Zadspace
Eric Rosenfeld, Venture Partner, Portland
e-mail: eric@frontiervc.com
Education: Stanford University; MBA, Institute for Management Development, Lausanne, Switzerland
Background: Founding Partner, Oregon Angel Fund;

279

Venture Capital & Private Equity Firms / Domestic Firms

Capybara Ventures; Director, Corporate Business Development, Mentor Graphics
Directorships: Catlin Gabel School
Jim Schraith, Venture Partner, Sacramento
Background: Quantum; ShareWave; Compaq; President & COO, AST Research; Co-Founder, QTV Capital
Directorships: Achievo, Semtech, VisualCalc

792 FRONTIER VENTURES
19925 Stevens Creek Boulevard
Suite 100
Cupertino, CA 95014-2358

Phone: 650-250-1224
e-mail: media@frontier.ventures
web: frontier.ventures

Mission Statement: Frontier Ventures is a venture fund investing in early stage technology companies with network effects in the United States and globally.

Geographic Preference: North America, Asia, Europe
Founded: 2012
Industry Group Preference: Virtual Reality & Augmented Reality, Machine Intelligence, Robotics, Drones & 3D, Space Technology, Enterprise & Consumer
Portfolio Companies: 8i, AltspaceVR, Emergent, Fove, Immersv, Jaunt, matterport, Meta, River Studios, Wevr, booshaka, eBrevia, Gridspace, Tissue Analytics, Wade & Wendy, Auro Robotics, Boosted, maidbot, Scanse, Vicarious Surgical, Drone Base, HiveUAV, Kespry, Sols, Vantage Robotics, boom, Planet Labs, SpaceX, Ursa, World View, 1-Page, AngelList, Board Vitals, CarePort, Gusto, Hello Giggles, Luxe, Propeller, Revel Systems, Robinhood

Key Executives:
Dmitry Alimov, Founder/Managing Partner
Education: BS, Samara State Aerospace University; BSBA, University of Missouri; MBA, Harvard Business School
Background: VP, Sputnik Group; First Deputy CEO, TNT Broadcasting Network; COO/Manging Director, Amedia; Managing Partner, RTP Global; Investor

793 FTV CAPITAL
555 California Street
Suite 2850
San Francisco, CA 94104

Phone: 415-229-3000 Fax: 415-229-3005
e-mail: businessplans@ftvcapital.com
web: www.ftvcapital.com

Mission Statement: FTV Capital invests in companies with innovative ideas, established business models and proven management teams that value a collaborative approach to building great companies.

Geographic Preference: United States
Fund Size: $1 billion
Founded: 1998
Average Investment: $10 to $75 million
Minimum Investment: $10 million
Investment Criteria: Any Stage, Middle Stage, Later Stage, Consolidations, Spinouts
Industry Group Preference: Software, Business Products & Services, Financial Services, Technology
Portfolio Companies: Actimize, Apex Fund Services, Aspire Financial Services, Aveksa, BlueGill Technologies, Cardconnect, CashStar, Castle Pines Capital, Catalyst, Cedar Capital, Centro, Clearent, Cloudmark, Company.com, Coremetrics, Covario, Credorax, Daylight Forensic & Advisory, Eloan, eBaoTech, Edgewater Markets, Empyrean, Enfusion, ETF Securities, EXL Service, Finanical Engines, Fleet One, Giga Spaces, Globant, GMI, Health Credit Services, ID.me, Index IQ, Intrepid Learning, Invest Cloud, KVS, LiveIntent, Markets and Markets, MarketShare, MedSynergies, Mu Sigma, NewsCred, Open Span, Perfecto, Powershares by Invesco, Presidio, Reliaquest, Rio Seo, Risk Alyze, Site Hands, Source Code, Predfast, Swan Global Investments, Symbio, True Potentional LLP, Trustwave, Varicent, VelocityShares, Verus, Vindicia, Vpay, WePay, Worldfirst, Xign

Other Locations:
535 Madison Avenue
32nd Floor
New York, NY 10022
Phone: 212-682-4800 Fax: 212-682-4480

Key Executives:
Richard Garman, Managing Partner
Education: BS, Southwest Missouri State University; MBA, Oklahoma State University
Background: President/CEO, Electronic Payment Services
Robert Anderson, Partner
Education: AB, Economics, Princeton University
Background: Merrill Lynch
Brad Bernstein, Managing Partner
Education: BA, Tufts University
Background: Partner, Oak Hill Capital Management; Patricof & Company Ventures; Merrill Lynch
Karen Derr Gilbert, Partner
Education: BA, Economics, University of California, LA; MBA, Johnson Grad. School oF Management, Cornell University
Background: Marketing, Wells Fargo; Merrill Lynch Capital Markets; Shearson Lehman Brothers
Liron Gitig, Partner
Education: BS, Wharton School, University of Pennsylvania; JD, Columbia Law School; MBA, Columbia Business School
Background: Lazard Technology Partners; Giza GE Venture Fund; BRM Capital; Fundtech Corp.; Lehman Brothers
Chris Winship, Partner
Education: BA Government, Dartmouth College
Background: Investment Banker, Salomon Smith Barney's Media & Telecommunications Group; Sales/Marketing, Putnam Investments
Directorships: CapitalStream; Freeborders; MedSynergies; Verus Financial Management
David Haynes, Partner & COO
Education: BS, Mechanical Engineering, MBA, JD, University of California, Berkeley
Background: Executive Vice President & General Counsel, OffRoad; Executive Vice President & General Counsel, Examen; Montgomery Securities
Kyle Griswold, Partner
Education: BA, Economics & Mathematics, Trinity College
Background: Investment Banking Associate, Berkshire Capital Securities

794 FULCRUM EQUITY PARTNERS
Glenridge Highlands One
5555 Glenridge Connector
Suite 930
Atlanta, GA 30342

Phone: 770-551-6300 Fax: 770-551-6330
web: www.fulcrumep.com

Mission Statement: Fulcrum Equity Partners is a private equity firm that provides financing to high growth companies.

Fund Size: $93 million
Average Investment: $1 - $5 million
Investment Criteria: High Growth
Industry Group Preference: Technology, Information Technology, Healthcare
Portfolio Companies: Addiction Campuses of America, ALS Resolvion, Bright Light Systems, Logfire, m2M Strategies, Mobile Health Engagement Strategies, Path-Tec, PhishLabs, Prevalent, Red Bag Solutions, Regenesis Biomedical, Rival Health

Venture Capital & Private Equity Firms / Domestic Firms

Other Locations:
Tampa Bay Innovation Centre
501 First Avenue N
Suite 901
St Petersbourg, FL 33701
Key Executives:
Jeffrey S Muir, Partner
Education: BA, JD, University of Georgia
Background: COO, OnTarget; Executive VP, T2 Medical; VP, Information Systems of America; Managing Director, Corporate Finance, KPMG
Directorships: Red Bag Solutions, Bright Light Systems, Enduracare Acute Care Services, Partners Healthcare Group, Bruder Healthcare, Southern Capital Forum
Thomas L Greer, Partner
Education: BS, Finance, Clemson University; MBA, Wake Forest University
Background: Founder, President & CEO, Regency Healthcare; VP, Healthcare Investment Banking, Robinson Humphrey; Eli Lilly & Company; Director, Corporate Finance, KPMG
Directorships: Enduracare Acute Care Services, Regenesis Biomedical, Five Points Healthcare, Medical Direct Club, Addiction Campuses, Special Olympics Georgia
Frank X Dalton, Partner
Education: BS, Accounting, University of South Carolina
Background: General Partner, Cordova Ventures; CEO, Market Velocity; Chairman & CEO, Axonn; CFO, Caetec Systems; Director, Operations, Microsouth
Directorships: ContactatOnce, Mfg.com, Preparis, Path-Tec, Bruder Healthcare, Xpanxion
James S Douglass, Partner
Education: BBA, Finance & Accounting, Georgia State University
Background: CEO, Vesdia; CEO, Visionary Systems; Executive VP, Corporate Development & CFO, CheckFree Corporation; VP & Corporate Controller, Medaphis Corporation
Directorships: Cartera Commerce, FactorTrust, GetOne Rewards, Thumb-Friendly
Alston Gardner, Founder/Venture Partner
Education: BA, University of North Carolina
Background: CEO, OnTarget; Dun & Bradstreet Computing Services; ADP; Wallace Computer Services
Directorships: Human Rights First, Chatham Capital
Philip Lewis, Partner
Education: BS, Business Administration, Washington University, St. Louis
Background: Investment Banking Analyst, AG Edwards & Sons; Michelson Organization
Directorships: RivalHealth, MFG.com, ALS Resolvion, Venture Atlanta

795 FUNDERS CLUB
237 Kearny Street
Suite 424
San Francisco, CA 94108

Toll-Free: 888-405-9335
e-mail: contact@fundersclub.com
web: www.fundersclub.com

Mission Statement: The Funders Club builds around a unique online marketplace that allows accredited investors to become equity holders in managed venture funds, which then fund pre-screened, private companies.
Investment Criteria: Seed Stage, Startups, Series A Stage
Portfolio Companies: Actiondesk, Anyplace, Arpeggio Biosciences, AXDRAFT, Biorender, Caper, CognitionIP, CoLab, Convictional, Demodesk, Embrace, Envkey, Golinks, Grin, Habit Analytics, HRI, InsideSherpa, Intersect Labs, JetLenses, JITx, Kyte, Leena AI, Negotiatus, Obie, Patch, PopSQL, Precious, Pronto, Qulture.Rocks, Rain Neuromorphics, RevenueCat, Runa HR, Shogun, Substack, The Podcast App, Together, Treble.ai, Vathys, Worklytics, Xgenomes, YoGov, zeroheight

796 FUNG CAPITAL USA
Four Embarcadero Center
Suite 3400
San Francisco, CA 94111

Phone: 415-315-7440
e-mail: contact@fungcap.com
web: www.fungcapitalusa.com

Mission Statement: Core business is to help entrepreneurial companies achieve success by providing equity capital, Asian sourcing expertise, and operational support during their critical growth stage.
Geographic Preference: United States
Fund Size: $100 million
Founded: 1982
Average Investment: $1 - $10 million
Minimum Investment: $5 million
Investment Criteria: Early-Stage; Later Stage Expansion Rounds, Refinancings, MBOs, Turnaround Situations
Industry Group Preference: E-Commerce & Manufacturing, Internet, Enabling Technology, Consumer Products, Retailing
Portfolio Companies: 500friends, BodyFX, Celect, Centric Software, CYRK, Danskin, ecVision, Flow, Galoob, GT Nexus, Hook Logic, The Lodge, Millworks, Narvar, Onestop, Order Groove, Proclivity, Studio Direct, Third Channel, Tulip Retail, Wilke-Rodriguez, Wood Associates
Other Locations:
11812 San Vicente Boulevard
Suite 610
Los Angeles, CA 90049
Phone: 415-315-7440
Key Executives:
Michael Hsieh, President
Education: BA, Harvard College; MBA, Harvard Business School
Background: RH Chappell Company; Merrill Lynch's Corporate Finance Division; Sun Hung Kai Securities (Hong Kong)
John Seung, Partner
Education: BSE, University of Pennsylvania
Background: Chief Information Officer, Li & Fung Group; Co-Founder, Castling; Advanced Technology Group, Andersen Consulting/Accenture
Janie Yu, Partner
e-mail: janie@fungcap.com
Education: MA, Havard University
Background: Burt's Bees; Journalist, BBC & PRI

797 FUNK VENTURES
15332 Antioch Street
Suite 119
Pacific Palisades, CA 90272

web: www.funkventures.com

Mission Statement: Provides business development, resources, expertise and management to companies generally too young to receive venture funding.
Industry Group Preference: Health & Wellness, Medical Devices, Lifestyle & Recreation, Clean Technology
Portfolio Companies: Alter G, Cyber Rain, Encore Fitness, Fuji Food Products, Game Ready, Organic To Go, Own, Prolacta Bioscience, UsedCardboardBoxes.com, Virgin Charter
Key Executives:
Andy J. Funk, President
Background: Founder/CEO, Microdyme; Founder/CEO, Helping.org; Co-Founder, Daily F1
Directorships: Fuji Food Products, UsedCardboardBoxes, Strata Development Group

281

Venture Capital & Private Equity Firms / Domestic Firms

798 FUSE CAPITAL
P.O. Box 1251
Menlo Park, CA 94026-1251

Phone: 650-325-9600
web: www.fusecapital.com

Mission Statement: Invests in early stage communications and infrastructure companies, building them into market leading enterprises.

Geographic Preference: United States, India, China
Fund Size: $1.5 billion
Founded: 1974
Average Investment: $15 million
Minimum Investment: $12 million
Investment Criteria: Seed and Early Stage companies that are creating new markets, developing new technologies and addressing emerging business needs
Industry Group Preference: Communications, Digital Media & Marketing
Portfolio Companies: Vyatta, SpectraLinear, Radar Networks, PacketHop, ONStor, Next New Networks, NetDevices, MonoSphere, KOTURA, Hatteras Networks, Generate, Fultec Semiconductor, CloudShield Technologies, Caymas Systems, BBE, Ambric, Ahura Scientific, 5to1

Key Executives:
 David Britts, Partner
 Education: MBA, Wharton School; BA Economics, University of California, Berkeley
 Background: JP Morgan Partners; Founding Team, Deutsche Morgan Grenfell Technology Group
 Directorships: Celestial
 Mickie Rosen, Investment Partner
 Education: BA, Economics, University of California, San Diego; MBA, Harvard Business School
 Background: Fox Interactive Media; Fandango; McKinsey & Company
 Roland Van der Meer, Partner
 Education: BSE, University of Pennsylvania; BS, Wharton School
 Background: Partner, Partech International; Co-Founder, Communications Ventures; PairGain; ConferTech; Hambrecht & Quist Venture Partners; GTE Labs; Sprint

799 FUSION FUND
550 Lytton Avenue
Palo Alto, CA 94301

e-mail: info@fusionfund.com
web: www.fusionfund.com

Mission Statement: A venture capital fund seeking to partner with entrepreneurs making waves in the tech industries, particularly AI.

Investment Criteria: Seed, Series A, Early Stage
Industry Group Preference: Artificial Intelligence, Healthcare, Network Technology, Industry, Applications, Software
Portfolio Companies: Assembly, Bluefox, Bluespace, Bodo, Catalia Health, Chat Sports, CodeSpark, Constructor.io, Cuseum, DreameGGs, Edge Compute, GrubMarket, Huma.ai, IAMRobotics, Locomation, Loop Genomics, Looptify, Lyft, Macrometa, MissionBio, Mojo Vision, NeuVector, Nucypher, NView, OTO.ai, Paperspace, Paradromics, Plexuss, PopularPays, Proscia, Quantapore, Safehub, Savonix, Scansite 3D, SpaceX, Sonavex, Stratifyd, Strongsalt, Stryde, Subtle Medical, This Is l, TVision Insights, Whoknows

Key Executives:
 Lu Zang, Founder/Managing Partner
 Education: MS, Materials Sciences & Engineering, Stanford University
 Background: World Economic Forum - Young Global Leader
 Homan Yuen, Partner
 Education: BA, University of California, Berkeley;
MS/PhD, Stanford University
 Background: Co-Founder/CTO, Solar Junction
 Carol Mao, Principal
 Education: BS, Peking University; MS, HKUST; MBA, Columbia Business School
 Background: Senior Investment Banking Associate, Deutsche Bank

800 FUTURE VENTURES
San Francisco, CA

e-mail: kate@pluckpr.com
web: future.ventures

Mission Statement: A venture capital firm seeking to invest in trailblazing entrepreneurs focused on the AI industry.

Fund Size: $1 Billion
Investment Criteria: Seed, Early Stage
Industry Group Preference: Artificial Intelligence, Information Technology, Robotics, Blockchain, Sustainable Transportation, Quantum Computing
Portfolio Companies: Atai Life Sciences, The Boring Company, BrdgAI, Cambrian BioPharma, Capital, Commonwealth Fusion Systems, Deep Genomics, Latent AI, Medcorder, Memphis Meats, Mythic, Neuralink, Ockam, Skype, SpaceX, Sutro Biopharma, Synthetic Genomics, Tesla, Tradex Technologies, Zoox

Key Executives:
 Steve Jurvetson, Co-Founder
 Education: BS/MS, Electrical Engineering, Stanford University; MBA, Stanford Grad. School of Business
 Background: R&D Engineer, Hewlett-Packard; Management Consultant, Bain & Company
 Maryanna Saenko, Co-Founder
 Education: BS, BioMedical Engineering/MS, Materials Science & Engineering, Carnegie Mellon University
 Background: Khosla Ventures; Partner, Airbus Ventures; Consultant, Lux Research; Research Engineer, Cabot Corporation

801 FdG ASSOCIATES LP
499 Park Avenue
26th Floor
New York, NY 10022

Phone: 212-940-6260
e-mail: info@fdgassociates.com
web: www.fdgassociates.com

Mission Statement: To maximize the potential of its portfolio companies.

Geographic Preference: United States
Fund Size: $500 million
Founded: 1993
Average Investment: $15 - $50 million
Minimum Investment: $8 million
Investment Criteria: Recapitalizations, Management Buyouts, Growth Investments, Industry Consolidations
Industry Group Preference: Business to Business, Consumer Products, Consumer Services, Distribution, Manufacturing, Retailing, Financial Services, Construction, Transportation, Logistics
Portfolio Companies: Hercules, Infrastructure and Industrial Constructors USA, Limbach Facility Services, Proficio Bank, Seabrook International, USA Bouquet

Key Executives:
 David S. Gellman, Managing Director
 Education: AB, Cornell University; MM, Kellogg School of Management
 Background: Managing Director, AEA Investors; Trump Group
 Directorships: Hercules Tires, Seabrook International, ReTrans

802 G SQUARED
205 North Michigan Avenue
Suite 3770
Chicago, IL 60601

web: gsquared.com

Mission Statement: G Squared is a venture capital firm whose mission is to invest in companies challenging the status quo and shaking up industries. G Squared partners with world-class entrepreneurs tackling big problems by investing in businesses throughout their life cycle as performance is strong-a fundamentally different approach than the classical early-, mid-, or late-stage venture capital firms. Formerly known as Gentry Venture Partners.

Founded: 2006
Industry Group Preference: Cloud Computing, Big Data, Mobility, Social Media, New Age Media
Portfolio Companies: 23andMe, Agrivida, Alibaba Group, Bloom Energy, Coursera, Dropbox, Enjoy, Fair, Instacart, JAMF Software, Kik, Lyft, Palantir, Pinterest, Postmates, Snapchat, Spacex, Spotify, Twitter, Uber

Key Executives:
  Larry L. Aschebrook, Managing Partner
  Education: MBA, Arizona State University
  Background: CEO, Gentry Financial Corporation
  Thomas R. Raterman, Managing Partner
  Education: MS, Management, Kellogg School of Management
  Background: President, Building Street Capital; CFO, LKQ Corporation

803 G-51 CAPITAL LLC
3939 Bee Caves Road
C-100
Austin, TX 78746

Phone: 512-929-5151

Mission Statement: To identify, nurture and grow great people, technology, and business. G51 provides value-added resources to assist companies bridge the numerous support and financing gaps that companies encounter on the road to success.

Geographic Preference: United States
Fund Size: $9 million
Founded: 1996
Average Investment: $500,000
Minimum Investment: $200,000
Investment Criteria: Seed, Start-up, First Stage, Second Stage, Mezzanine
Industry Group Preference: Hardware, Software, Business to Business
Portfolio Companies: E5 Systems Inc., Motion Computing, Pilot Software Inc., Socialware

Key Executives:
  Rudy Garza, Founder/Managing General Partner
  e-mail: rudy@g51.com
  Education: MBA, University of Texas; BBA, Saint Edwards University
  Bill Kennedy, Founding Partner
  Education: BA, History Education, MA, Mathematics & Physics, University of Texas, Austin
  Background: Founder, Beacon Professional Services; Co-Founder, Waveset Technologies
  Directorships: SailPoint; Bomgar

805 GABRIEL VENTURE PARTNERS
999 Baker Way
Suite 400
San Mateo, CA 94404

Phone: 650-551-5000 Fax: 650-551-5001
e-mail: info@gabrielvp.com
web: www.gabrielvp.com

Mission Statement: Gabriel invests in early-stage startups run by passionate entrepreneurs that are taking advantage of changing markets with next-generation technologies and innovative business models.

Geographic Preference: United States
Fund Size: $260 million
Founded: 1999
Average Investment: $3-6 million
Minimum Investment: $500,000
Investment Criteria: Start-Up, Early Stage
Industry Group Preference: Software, Technology, Wireless Technologies, Infrastructure, Mobile, Communications, Consumer Products, Enterprise Applications, Systems & Hardware, Clean Technology
Portfolio Companies: AccessLine, Allsec Technologies, Arula Systems, Aurora Algae, Boston-Power, Chegg, Concord Communications, Connetbeam, CrossMedia Services, Encentuate, Exodus, iForem, IL & FS Investment Limited, IPWireless, Iridigm, Jacked, Kajeet, Level 7 Systems, MakeMyTrip.com, NeoPath Networks, NetScaler, NetG Networks, Persistent Systems, PlaceWare, PlantSense, Provogue, SkyCross, STEP Labs, Tejas Networks, YLX Corp.

Key Executives:
  Scott Chou, Managing Director
  Education: MS, Engineering, Stanford University; MS, Computer Science, Harvard University; BS, Electrical Engineering, California Institute of Technology
  Background: Poqet Computers, ICE, Bellcore, IBM, Onset Ventures
  Rick Bolander, Managing Director/Co-Founder
  Education: MBA, Harvard Business School; BS/MS Electrical Engineering, University of Michigan
  Background: Apex Investment Partners; Founder, Blue Sky Venture; AT&T; Engineer, Chevron Oil
  Directorships: Jacked, iForem, Chegg, Kajeet, Persistent Systems
  Jim Long, Partner
  Education: BS, Electrical Engineering, UC Berkeley; MBA, Harvard University
  Background: Hewlett Packard; Fred Adler Ventures
  Directorships: Aurora BioFuels, Connectbeam, PlanetSense, YLX
  Phil Samper, Co-Founder/Partner Emeritus
  Education: BS, Business Administration, UC Berkeley; BFT, International Management, American Graduate School of International Management; MSM, Management, MIT
  Background: Vice-Chairman/Executive Officer, Eastman Kodak Company; President, Sun Microsystems Computer Corp.; CEO/Chairman, Cray Research;

806 GALEN PARTNERS
680 Washington Blvd
10th Floor
Stamford, CT 06901

Phone: 203-653-6400
e-mail: info@galen.com
web: www.galen.com

Mission Statement: Invests in emerging healthcare companies, with focus on the healthcare information technology, specialty pharmaceuticals, and medical devices sectors. Galen Partners is committed to working collaboratively with entrepreneurs and management teams.

Geographic Preference: United States
Fund Size: $250 million
Founded: 1990
Average Investment: $10 - $30 million
Minimum Investment: $10 million
Investment Criteria: Mid-to-Late Stage, Growth Equity
Industry Group Preference: Healthcare Information Technology, Healthcare, Medical Devices, Pharmaceuticals

Venture Capital & Private Equity Firms / Domestic Firms

Portfolio Companies: Acura Pharmaceuticals Inc., Cambrooke Therapeutics, Cardiva, Consensys Imaging Services, Dakim, Derma Sciences, Integrated Diagnostic Centers, InTouch Health, LifeIMAGE, PeriGen, Quotient Biodiagnostics Holdings, Sharecare, SonaCare Medical, Tactile Systems Technology, Tech Pharmacy Services

Key Executives:

David W Jahns, Managing Partner
203-653-6440
e-mail: djahns@galen.com
Education: BA, Political Science & Economics, Colgate University; MBA, Health Services Management, Kellogg School of Management, Northwestern University
Background: Financial Analyst, Corporate Finance Division, Smith Barney
Directorships: Stamford Health System

Zubeen Shroff, Managing Partner
203-653-6430
e-mail: zshroff@galen.com
Education: BA, Biological Science, Boston University; MBA, Wharton School
Background: Principal, Wilkerson Group; Schering-Plough Pharmaceuticals

Philip Borden, Managing Director
e-mail: pborden@galen.com
Education: BS, Duke University; MBA, Harvard Business School
Background: Healthcare Analyst, Dain Rauscher Wessels; Sr Analyst, Frazier Healthcare Partners; Associate, Oxford Bioscience Partners; General Partner, Riverside Partners

Bruce Wesson, Founding Partner Emeritus/Senior Advisor
203-653-6420
e-mail: bwesson@galen.com
Education: BA, Colgate University; MBA, Columbia University Graduate School of Business
Background: Managing Director, Corporate Finance Division, Smith Barney
Directorships: MedAssets, Derma Sciences, Acura Pharmaceuticals, TPS

L John Wilkerson, Founder/Senior Advisor
203-653-6450
e-mail: wilker@galen.com
Education: Biological Sciences, Utah State University; PhD, Cornell University
Background: Group Product Director, Ortho Diagnostics; VP, Medical Analysis & Research, Smith Barney; Channing, Weinberg & Co.
Directorships: Cardiva, Quotient BioDiagnostics Holdings, TPS

Stacey Bauer, Chief Financial Officer
203-653-6473
e-mail: sbauer@galen.com
Education: BA, Business Administration, University of Massachusetts at Amherst
Background: Controller & CFO, Bedrock Capital Partners; Tax Manager, Financial Services, PriceWaterhouseCoopers

807 GARAGE TECHNOLOGY VENTURES
1059-1069 East Meadow Circle
Palo Alto, CA 94303

Phone: 650-397-1359
e-mail: info@garage.com
web: www.garage.com

Mission Statement: A seed-stage and early-stage venture capital fund looking to invest in entrepreneurial teams with big ideas and a need for seed capital to turn their ideas into great companies.

Geographic Preference: California, West Coast
Fund Size: $10 million
Founded: 1997
Average Investment: $2 million, up to $3 millin
Minimum Investment: $500,000

Investment Criteria: High Technology Startups, Seed Stage, Early Stage
Industry Group Preference: Software, Materials Technology, Technology, Clean Technology
Portfolio Companies: Business Layers, CastStack, CFares, Claria, ClearFuels Technology, ClearAccessIP, ClearFuels Technology, Digital Envoy, Digital Fountain, D.light Design, FilmLoop, FutureTrade, GuruNet Corp., Hoku Scientific, Immunix, iNest, Innovative Robotics, IP3 Networks, Kaboodle, Knightscope, LeftHand Networks, Miasole, The Motley Fool, NetConversions, NovaCentrix, Packet Island, Pandora, People, ai, PhatNoise, Price.com, Psionic, PûreSight Inc., Qumu, Razz, Sapias, SignaCert, Simply Hired, Sixense, STEP Labs, Synacor, Thermo Ceramix, Tripwire, U-Nav Microelectronics, Vigilistics, Virtualis, VISANOW, VOKE, WebOrder, WhiteHat Security, Xora, Yoics

Key Executives:

Guy Kawasaki, Managing Director
e-mail: kawasaki@garage.com
Education: BA, Stanford University; MBA, University of California, Los Angeles
Background: Apple Computer
Directorships: BitPass, FilmLoop, SimplyHired

Bill Reichert, Managing Director
e-mail: reichert@garage.com
Education: BA, Harvard College; MBA, Stanford University
Background: Co-Founder/VP, Academic Systems Corporation; McKinsey & Company; Brown Brothers Harriman & Company
Directorships: CaseStack, IP3 Networks, Miasole, WhiteHat Security, ClearFuels Technology, SimplyHired, D.light Design, ThermoCeramix, VisaNow

Joyce Chung, Managing Director
e-mail: joyce@garage.com
Education: SB, Chemical Engineering, MIT; MBA, Stanford Graduate School of Business
Background: Founding Partner, Cardinal Venture Capital; Adobe Ventures

Henry Wong, Managing Director
e-mail: henry@garage.com
Education: BS, Business, University of Utah; MBA, Telecom Management, Golden Gate University
Background: Founder, Diamond TechVentures; Venture Partner, Crystal Ventures

808 GE CAPITAL
901 Main Avenue
Norwalk, CT 06851

Phone: 203-357-3100 Fax: 203-357-3945
Toll-Free: 800-976-0675
web: www.gecapital.com

Mission Statement: To build a premier global investing business that creates value by leveraging GE Systems.

Geographic Preference: Worldwide
Fund Size: $28 billion
Founded: 1992
Average Investment: $20 million
Minimum Investment: $5 million
Industry Group Preference: Financial Services, Transportation, Logistics, Information Technology, Telecommunications, Healthcare, Insurance, Retailing, Consumer Products, Media, Industrial Equipment, Real Estate, Mining, Aviation, Energy

Other Locations:
622 3rd Avenue
New York, NY 10017-4669
Phone: 212-880-7000

6-12 Clarges Street
London W1J 8DH

United Kingdom
Phone: 44-0-207-302-6310 **Fax:** 44-0-207-302-6810

5th Floor Via G Casati
Milan 20123
Italy
Phone: 39-02-7259-591310 **Fax:** 37-02-7259-5959

GE International
Eliahu House
Tel Aviv 64077
Israel
Phone: 972-3-695-8466 **Fax:** 972-3-696-9436

Level 14
255 George Street
Sydney NSW 2000
Australia
Phone: 61-2-9324-7565 **Fax:** 61-2-9324-7570

16/F Three Exchange Square
Central
Hong Kong
Phone: 852-2100-6871 **Fax:** 852-2100-6733

Kowa 35 Building 2F
14-14- Akasaka 1-chome
Tokyo 107-8453
Japan
Phone: 81-3-3588-6126 **Fax:** 81-3-3588-6159

8/F Blk 4A DLF Corporate Park
DLF Qutub Enclave, Phase III
Mehrauli-Gurgaon Road
Gurgoan 122002
India
Phone: 91-124-6358-030 **Fax:** 91-1246-6356-037

Avenue LN Alem 619
4th Floor
Buenos Aires 1001
Argentina
Phone: 54-11-4317-8755 **Fax:** 54-11-4317-87897

Av Nove de Julho 11
andor
Sao Paulo
Brazil
Phone: 55-11-3067-8369 **Fax:** 55-11-3067-8398

Prolongacion Reforma 490
3rd Floor
Col Santa Fe 01217DF
Mexico
Phone: 525-257-6200 **Fax:** 525-257-6239

Key Executives:
Alec Burger, President & CEO
Education: BEng, Trinity College; MBA, Northeastern University
Background: VP, General Electric Corporation; Bain & Company; Cabot Corporation
Dan Colao, Chief Financial Officer
Education: BS, Boston College
Background: Lehman Brothers

809 GE VENTURES
2882 Sand Hill Rd.
Suite 240
Menlo Park, CA 94025
Phone: 650-233-3900
web: www.ge.com/ventures

Mission Statement: GE Ventures assists entrepreneurs and start-ups by providing access to GE's technical expertise, capital, and network.

Industry Group Preference: Software, Analytics & Analytical Instruments, Advanced Manufacturing, Energy, Healthcare

Portfolio Companies: 1366 Technologies, Acutus Medical, Advanced Microgrid Solutions, Alchemist Accelerator, Ambyint, Apervita, Aras Corp., Arcadia, Arterys, Ascendify, Aver, Avitas Systems, Ayasdi, Balena, BiSN, Carbon, Caremerge, Catalant, China Materialia, Chrono, Clear Path Robotics, Cooledge, Desktop Metal, Drawbridge Health, Element Analytics, Elementum, Enbala, Equalum, Evidation, eVolution Networks, FlexGen Power Systems, FogHorn, Foro Energy, Freightos, Genome Medical, Gravie, Grid Net, Headsense, Health Reveal, Hyperloop One, i3 Equity Partners, Igenu, Iora Health, IoTium, Labcyte, LM, Maana, MedAware, Menlomicro, Mocana, Morphisec, mPrest, Nexar, Nuvolo, Nyshex, Oblong, Omada, Omni-ID, Optomec, Ornim, PingThings, Portworx, Rig Up, Sarcos, Sentient, Sight Machine, Sonnen, Stem, Syapse, Tamr, TTTech, Tendril, The Hive, Thetaray, Trilliant, Up Skill, Veran, Varana Health, View Dynamic Glass, Vineti, Volta, Xage Security, Xometry, Zinc, Zola Electric

Other Locations:
33-41 Farnsworth St.
Boston, MA 02210

Key Executives:
Leslie Bottorff, Managing Director
Education: BS, Biomedical Engineering, Purdue University; MBA, Harvard Business School
Background: General Partner, ONSET Ventures
Lisa Coca, Managing Director
Education: Wharton School; MBA, Stanford Graduate School of Business
Background: GE Capital; Bankers Trust; Deutsche Bank
Alex De Winter, Managing Director
Education: Amherst College; PhD, Stanford University; MBA, University of California, Berkeley
Background: Partner, Mohr Davidow Ventures; Senior Scientist, Pacific Biosciences
Michael Dolbac, Senior Managing Director
Education: BS, MS, Stanford University; MBA, Wharton School
Background: LG Electronics
Daniel Hullah, Managing Director
Education: BS, PhD, University of Oxford; MBA, INSEAD
Background: Director of Ventures, National Grid
Karen Kerr, Executive Managing Director
Education: AB, Bryn Mawr College; PhD, University of Chicago
Background: Managing Director, ARCH Venture Partners
Jonathan Pulitzer, Managing Director
Education: New York University
Ralph Taylor-Smith, Managing Director
Education: BA, MA, MIT; MA, PhD, Princeton University
Background: Cofounfer/General Partner/Managing Director, Battelle Venture Partners; Investment Banker, Goldman Sachs; Investment Banker, JP Morgan
Victor Westerlind, Managing Director
Education: BA, Cornell University; MA, Stanford University; MBA, Harvard Business School
Background: Intel Capital; General Partner, RockPort Capital; InterWest Partners

810 GEFINOR CAPITAL
2700 Westchester Avenue
Suite 303
Purchase, NY 10577
Phone: 212-308-1111 **Fax:** 212-308-1182
web: www.gefinorcapital.com

Mission Statement: Provides the reach, and power of presence of a large organization, with a focused entrepreneurial approach that enables devoted time and resources to companies from their inception.

Geographic Preference: United States
Fund Size: $10 million
Founded: 2002
Average Investment: $2 - 5 million
Investment Criteria: Early-Stage, Mid-Stage, Late-Stage

Venture Capital & Private Equity Firms / Domestic Firms

Industry Group Preference: Financial Services, Telecommunications, Semiconductors, Software, Services, Medical & Health Related, Manufacturing, Consumer Products

Portfolio Companies: Advion Inc., Anokiwave Inc., Beenz, BinOptics, BlueSpace Software Corp., Calient Technologies Inc., Carmichael Training Systems, Genesant Technologies Inc., GridApp Systems Inc., GoNoodle Inc., Kionix Inc., Knoa Software Inc., Metros Corp., Mimix Broadband Inc., ModbiTV Inc., Myriad Development, NetSpend Corp., Nextivity, Patton Surgical Corp., PeerNova Inc., RemitDATA Inc., Rheonix Inc., SciAps Inc., Scuf Gaming LLC, SocialFlow Inc., SiVerio Inc., Silicon Navigator Corp., Unwired Nation, Volaris Advisors, Wimba Inc., XAware Inc., ZeeWaves Systems Inc.

Key Executives:

Mimo Ousseimi, Managing Director
Education: MBA, John E Anderson School of Management, University of California, LA; BA Political Economy, University of California, Berkeley
Background: Merrill Lynch; State Street Research and Management Company
Directorships: Knoa Software

William Beckett, Partner
Education: MBA, Stanford Graduate School of Business
Background: Investment Banking, Merrill Lynch

Robert Porell, Chief Financial Officer
Education: BA, Economics, Harvard College; MS, Accounting, New York University
Background: CFO/CEO, Alexander Doll Company Inc.; Manager, Coopers & Lybrand; CPA

Chris Davis, Principal
Education: BComm, Information Systems, Queen's University; MBA, Financial Engineering, Sloan School of Management, MIT
Background: Systems Analyst, Credit Suisse First Boston; High Yield Origination Group, TD Securities

---

811 GELT VC
Ann Arbor, MI

e-mail: turner@gelt.vc
web: www.gelt.vc

Mission Statement: Gelt Venture Capital has networks in Los Angeles, San Francisco, New York City, and Ann Arbor.

Founded: 2019
Average Investment: $25,000 - $250,000
Minimum Investment: $25,000
Investment Criteria: Pre-Seed, Seed, Series A
Industry Group Preference: Diversified
Portfolio Companies: Alpha Foods, Babyscript, Domuso Inc., FlightWave Aero, Forelinx, Hykso, Jobs For Vets, Lambda, Marble Robot, May Mobility, Natilus Inc., OpenSponsorship, Phase Four, Sixa, Standard Cyborg, Starsky Robotics, Streamloan, SuperPhone

Key Executives:

Turner Novak, General Partner
Education: BBA, Grand Valley State University
Background: Credit Analyst, Mercantile Bank of Michigan; Investment Analyst, Van Andel Institute; Founder, TDN Capital

Keith Wasserman, General Partner
Education: BBA, Marshall School of Business, University of Southern California
Background: Co-Founder, Resident Relief Foundation; Co-Founder, Happy Home Communities; Co-Founder, Domuso Inc.; Co-Founder, Gelt Inc.

Damian Langere, General Partner
Education: University of California, Santa Barbara
Background: Co-Founder, Domuso Inc.

---

812 GEMINI INVESTORS
20 William Street
Suite 250
Wellesley, MA 02481

Phone: 781-237-7001 **Fax:** 781-237-7233
web: www.gemini-investors.com

Mission Statement: Based in Massachusetts, Gemini Investors is a private equity firm that makes investments in lower middle-market companies in a wide range of industries. Gemini Investors targets established companies with significant growth potential.

Geographic Preference: United States
Fund Size: $64 million
Founded: 1993
Average Investment: $3 - $8 million
Investment Criteria: Established companies with at least three years operating history, Lower Middle Market, Growth Capital, Recapitalizations, MBO
Industry Group Preference: Technology, Business to Business, Consumer Services, Manufacturing, Distribution, Consumer Products, Healthcare, Education, Waste & Recycling
Portfolio Companies: 360 PT Management, Action Target, Advanced AV, All Aboard America, American Signcrafters, Bag Balm, Beryllium, Bonded Filter, Brady Enterprises, Center Rock, Conditioned Air, Coventor, Datacom Systems, Disaster Kleenup International, Dorsey Schools, DTT Surveillance, Express Window Films, FabEnCo/BlueWater, Garbanzo Mediterranean Grill, Geronimo Alloys, Hilco Technologies, Jan Pro, Jersey Precast, Just Brakes, KP Corporation, Marinello, Newpro, Phillips Screw Company, Phoenix Aromas and Essential Oils, Pinnacle Treatment Centers, PI Worldwide, Primestream, Quality Powder Coating, Scotia Technology, SGA, SolmeteX, Star Career Academy, TGaS Advisors, TJ Hale, Trois Petits Cochons, Ultracor, Valence Surface Technologies, Vanderveer Plastics, Vision Government Solutions, Wake Research Associates, Well-Foam, Workplace

Key Executives:

James J Goodman, President
e-mail: jgoodman@gemini-investors.com
Education: AB, MBA, JD, Harvard University
Background: Berkshire Partners; Bain & Company

Jeffrey T Newton, Managing Director
e-mail: jnewton@gemini-investors.com
Education: BS, University of Vermont; MBA, Tuck School of Business, Dartmouth College
Background: President, Concord Partners; Senior VP & Treasurer, Lifetime Corporation; VP, Investment Banking, Prudential Securities

David F Millet, Managing Director
e-mail: dmillet@gemini-investors.com
Education: BA, Physical Sciences, Harvard University
Background: President, Chatham Venture Corporation; Group Executive, NEC Corporation; Senior Consultant, Arthur D Little

James T Rich, Managing Director
e-mail: jrich@gemini-investors.com
Education: AB, Dartmouth College
Background: Senior Associate, Citizens Energy; Analyst, JP Morgan

Matthew E Keis, Managing Director
e-mail: mkeis@gemini-investors.com
Education: BS, Boston College
Background: Senior Associate, Arthur Andersen

---

813 GEN Y CAPITAL PARTNERS Young Entrepreneur Council
745 Atlantic Ave.
Boston, MA 02110

Phone: 484-403-0736
e-mail: info@yec.co
web: yec.co

Venture Capital & Private Equity Firms / Domestic Firms

Mission Statement: We invest in early stage companies that will benefit from the leverage provided by a network of many of the world's top young entrepreneurs through our partnership with the YEC (the Young Entrepreneur Council). We work with early stage, consumer facing mobile and internet companies where a network of highly connected young entrepreneurs from around the world can increase the likelihood that they become the leaders in their space.
Average Investment: $250,000 - $500,000
Investment Criteria: Early-Stage
Portfolio Companies: Classic Specs, Levo League, Flow, Virool, Sellercrowd
Key Executives:
  Scott Gerber, Co-Founder/Director of Communications
  Background: Founder, Young Entrepreneurs Council
  Carissa Reiniger, Founding Partner & Fundraising Chair
  Background: Founder, Silver Lining Ltd.

814 GENACAST VENTURES
One Comcast Center
55th Floor
Philadelphia, PA 19103

e-mail: hello@genacast.com
web: www.genacast.com

Mission Statement: A seed fund that invests in technology-centric Internet startups.
Geographic Preference: Northeastern United States, Boston to Washington DC corridor
Average Investment: Up to $1 million
Investment Criteria: Seed or Early-Stage
Industry Group Preference: Technology, Consumer Internet, Digital Media & Marketing, E-Commerce & Manufacturing, Gaming, Mobile, Online Advertising, Software, SaaS, Cybersecurity, Business to Business, B2B
Portfolio Companies: BigID, Blockdaemon, Confetti, Datadog, Demdex, Divide, DoubleVerify, DrayNow, Invited Media, Jornaya, Mortar Data, Overlap, PackLate, Revmetrix, Rocketrip, Staq, Uptycs, YieldMo, ZeroFox
Other Locations:
  588 Broadway Street
  Suite 202
  New York, NY 10012
Key Executives:
  Gil Beyda, Founder/Managing Partner
  Education: BS, Computer Science, MBA, California State University, Northridge
  Background: Founder, Mind Games; Founder, Real Media; CTO, TACODA; Managing Director, Comcast Ventures
  Directorships: Neural Magic, Confetti, goTenna, Zapata Computing, Blockdaemon, DrayNow, BigID, STAQ
  Morgan Polotan, Principal
  Education: BS, Northeastern University
  Background: Bloomberg Beta; Tapad; Charles Koch Institute

815 GENERAL ATLANTIC PARTNERS
Park Avenue Plaza
55 East 52nd Street
33rd Floor
New York, NY 10055

Phone: 212-715-4000 **Fax:** 212-759-5708
web: www.generalatlantic.com

Mission Statement: General Atlantic is a growth equity firm that offers capital and expertise to growth companies worldwide.
Geographic Preference: Globally
Fund Size: $900 million
Founded: 1980
Average Investment: $250 million
Minimum Investment: $25 million
Investment Criteria: Private and Public Companies
Industry Group Preference: Information Technology, Business Products & Services, Consumer Products, Financial Services, Healthcare
Portfolio Companies: Acumen Brands, Adyen, Affinion Group, Aimbridge, Airbnb, Alignment Healthcare, Amherst Pierpont Securities, AppDynamics, Appirio, Asian Genco, Avant, Axel Springer Digital Classifieds, Barteca, Bazaarvoice, Box, BuzzFeed, C&J Energy Services, Citco, CitiusTech, CLEAResult, Decolar.com, EN Engineering, EviCore Healthcare, Exp, Flixbus, FNZ, Garena, Gilt Groupe, House of Anita Dongre, Hyperion Insurance Group, IBS Software Services, Indusind Bank, KCG, Klarna, Markit, Meituan, MeteoGroup, Mu Sigma, National Stock Exchange, Network International, Oak Hill Advisors, OptionsHouse, Ourofino Saude Animal, Pague Menos, Privalia, QTS, Red Ventures, Sanfer, Santander Asset Management, SAS Sistema de Ensino, Saxo Bank, SnapAV, Squarespace, Studio Moderna, Sun Art Retail Group, Sura Asset Management, Tenfu, Too Faced Cosmetics, Tory Burch, TriNet, Uber, Vox Media, Xiabu Xiabu, XP Investimentos, Zhongsheng Group
Other Locations:
  600 Steamboat Road
  Suite 105
  Greenwich, CT 06830
  Phone: 203-629-8600 **Fax:** 203-622-8818

  228 Hamilton Avenue
  Palo Alto, CA 94301
  Phone: 650-251-7800 **Fax:** 650-251-9672

  23 Savile Row
  London W1S 2ET
  United Kingdom
  Phone: 44-2074843200 **Fax:** 44-2074843290

  Luitpoldblock
  Amiraplatz 3
  Munich 80333
  Germany
  Phone: 49-089558932710 **Fax:** 49-089558932730

  5901-5903 & 5912, 59F China World Office Tower B
  1 Jianguomenwai Avenue
  Beijing 100004
  China
  Phone: 86-1059652500 **Fax:** 86-1058669533

  Suite 5704-5706, 57F
  Two IFC
  8 Finance Street
  Central
  Hong Kong
  Phone: 852-36022600 **Fax:** 852-22196600

  Level 19, Birla Aurora
  Dr. Annie Besant Road
  Worli
  Mumbai 400 030
  India
  Phone: 91-2266561400 **Fax:** 91-2266317893

  Av Brigadeiro Faria Lima, 3477
  7th Floor
  Tower A, Itaim Bibi
  Sao Paulo 04538-133
  Brazil
  Phone: 55-1132966100

  Raamplein 1
  Amsterdam 1016 XK
  Netherlands
  Phone: 31-206090301

  Asia Square Tower 1
  8 Marina View, 41-04 018960
  Singapore
  Phone: 65-66616700

  Pedregal No. 24 Piso 4
  Colonia Molino del Rey

Venture Capital & Private Equity Firms / Domestic Firms

Delegacion Miguel Hidalgo
Mexico 11600
Mexico
Phone: 52-5541646500
Key Executives:
Steven Denning, Chairman
Education: BS, Georgia Institute of Technology; MS, Naval Postgraduate School; MBA, Stanford Graduate School of Business
Background: Consultant, McKinsey & Company
Directorships: The Nature Conservancy, Council on Foreign Relations, Next Generation
William E. Ford, Chief Executive Officer
Education: BA, Amherst College; MBA, Stanford Graduate School of Business
Background: Investment Banking, Morgan Stanley & Co
Directorships: Tory Burch, Oak Hill Advisors, Markit
Frank Brown, Managing Director/Chief Risk Officer
Education: BSBA, Bucknell University
Background: Dean, INSEAD; PricewaterhouseCoopers
Directorships: The Home Depot
Thomas Murphy, Advisory Director
Education: BA, Economics, Colgate University; MBA, Stern School of Business, New York University
Background: Senior Accountant, Deloitte & Touche
Gabriel Caillaux, Managing Director, Europe
Education: MBA, Finance, ESCP-EAP European School of Management
Background: Analyst & Associate, Merrill Lynch
Directorships: Santander Asset Management, Axel Springer Digital Classifieds, Citco, Network International, Privalia
Andrew Crawford, Managing Director, United States
Education: BS, Washington and Lee University; MBA, Harvard Business School
Background: Advent International
Directorships: Too Faced Cosmetics, Barteca
Cory Eaves, Operating Partner
Education: BSEE, University of Iowa; MBA, Babson College; Advanced Management Program, Harvard Business School
Background: EVP, CTO & CIO, Misys plc
Directorships: CitiusTech, EviCore, The Marfan Foundation, NetHope
Martin Escobari, Managing Director, Latin America
Education: BS, Harvard College; MBA, Harvard Business School
Background: Managing Director, Advent International; Co-Founder & CFO, Submarino.com; Associate, Boston Consulting Group
Directorships: Ourofino, Pague Menos, Sanfer, Sura Asset Management, XP Investimentos
David Hodgson, Vice Chairman
Education: AB, Mathematics & Social Sciences, Dartmouth College; MBA, Stanford University Graduate School of Business
Background: President, New England Software
Directorships: Alignment Healthcare, Hyperion Insurance Group, Amherst Pierpont Securities, TriNet
Rene Kern, Advisory Directpr
Education: BS, University of California, Berkeley; MBA, Wharton School, MA, School of Arts and Sciences, University of Pennsylvania
Background: VP, Morgan Stanley; Management Consultant, Bain & Company
Directorships: OptionsHouse, KCG
Chris Lanning, Managing Director/General Counsel
Education: BA, History, JD, University of Virginia
Background: Senior Associate, Corporate Finance, Hunton & Williams; Associate, Paul, Weiss, Rifkind, Wharton & Garrison
Directorships: Dice Holdings, Webloyalty
Anton Levy, Managing Director/Global Head of Technology
Education: BS in Commerce, Finance & Computer Science, University of Virginia; MBA, Columbia University
Background: Investment Banker, Morgan Stanley
Directorships: Squarespace, Acumen Brands, Klarna, Red Ventures, Gilt Groupe
Sandeep Naik, Managing Director, India
Education: BTech, Instrumentation Engineering, University of Mumbai; MS, Biomedical Engineering, Medical College of Virginia; MBA, Wharton School, University of Pennsylvania
Background: Partner, Apax; Global Marketing Manager, Medtronic; Consultant, McKinsey & Company; Co-Founder, InfraScan
Joern Nikolay, Managing Director, Munich
Education: WHU Otto Beisheim Graduate School of Management; Institut d'Etudes Politiques
Background: TA Associates; Case Team Leader, Bain & Company; Analyst, Morgan Stanley
Directorships: Axel Springer Digital Classifieds, Klarna, Flixbus
David Rosenstein, Managing Director/General Counsel
Education: BA, University of North Carolina; JD, New York University School of Law
Background: Associate, Paul, Weiss, Rifkind, Wharton & Garrison
Graves Tompkins, Managing Director/Head of Capital Partnering
Education: AB, Princeton University; MBA, Harvard Business School, MPA, Harvard Kennedy School of Government, Harvard University
Background: Merchant Banking Division, Goldman Sachs; McKinsey & Company
Directorships: Oak Hill Advisors
Robbert Vorhoff, Managing Director/Global Head of Healthcare
Education: BS, Commerce, McIntire School of Commerce, University of Virginia
Background: Greenhill Capital Partners; M&A Advisory Group, Greenhill & Co.
Directorships: Alignment Healthcare, EviCore Healthcare, Echoing Green

816 GENERAL CATALYST PARTNERS
20 University Road
4th Floor
Cambridge, MA 02138

Phone: 617-234-7000
e-mail: gcinfo@generalcatalyst.com
web: generalcatalyst.com

Mission Statement: General Catalyst Partners is a venture capital firm that seeks to help entrepreneurs build market leading companies. The firm targets innovative technology businesses that can transform industries. General Catalyst Partners focuses on making early stage and growth equity investments.

Fund Size: $1.4 billion
Founded: 2000
Investment Criteria: Early Stage, Growth Equity
Industry Group Preference: Infrastructure, Applications Software & Services, Industrial Equipment, Software, Clean Energy, Consumer, New Media, Internet, Fintech
Portfolio Companies: 6D.AI, Airbnb, AirMap, All Turtles, Allego, Anaconda, Anduril, Angle, Anomali, Atrium, Audius, B12, BigCommerce, Blade, Bowery, Brainly, Bustle, Cadre, Catalant, Circle, Clarabridge, ClassDojo, ClassPass, ClearSky, CoachUp, Color, Common Networks, Contentful, Contrast Security, Corelight, Corevia Medical, CouchSurfing, Cozy, Curai, Custora, CyPhy, Deliveroo, Digit, Drift, Elysium, Envoy, Espressive, Evolv Technology, Fancy, Feedvisor, Fractyl, Freebird, Fundbox, Giphy, GoodData, Grammarly, Gusto, Highfive, Hive, Hometap, HubHaus, Illumio, Ionic, Julia Computing, Kin Community, Kuvee, Lemonade, Livongo, Lola, Loom, Lose It!, M.Gemi, Major League Hacking, Mark43, Menlo Security, Merlin,

Venture Capital & Private Equity Firms / Domestic Firms

Mindstrong, Monzo, Naturebox, Newstore, Nova, Oceans Healthcare, OM1, Oscar, Outdoor Voices, PathAI, Photoshelter, Preempt, Pumpup, Rebag, Remesh, Riskrecon, Ro, Rockets of Awesome, R Studio, Sabre, Samsara, Shift Technology, SignalFX, Singular, Spring Discovery, Strip, Super Evil Megacorp, Superpedestrian, Swirl, Teamworks, The Honest Company, ThoughtSpot, Tidelift, TrueMotion, Tunein, VerneGlobal, Viajanet, Vroom, Wag!, Warby Parker, WayUp, Yottaa

Other Locations:
434 Broadway
6th Floor
New York, NY 10013
Phone: 212-775-4000

564 University Avenue
Palo Alto, CA 94301
Phone: 650-618-5900

2 South Park Street
Suite 100
San Francisco, CA 94107

Key Executives:
Adam Valkin, Managing Director
Education: AB, Economics, Harvard University
Background: Venture Partner, Accel Partners; Global Head, Digital Media & New Business, Endemol; Partner, Arts Alliance; Co-Founder & Interim CEO, LOVEFiLM; Co-Founder, Propertyfinder; Marketing Manager, Firefly Network; Market Manager, BarnsandNoble.com
Directorships: Brainly, Bustle, ClassPass, Fundbox, Giphy, Super Evil Megacorp, Vroom, WayUp
Bill Fitzgerald, Strategic Advisor
Education: BA, College of the Holy Cross; JD, Suffolk University Law School
Background: Interim CFO, Miami Cruise Holdings; Manager, KPMG; Adjunct Professor, Boston College
Directorships: Private Equity CFO Association
David Orfao, Venture Partner
Education: BS, Business & Accounting, Norwich University
Background: President & CEO, Allaire Corporation; Senior VP, Sales Operations & Marketing, Frame Technology Corporation; Claris Corporation; SQA Corporation
Directorships: Circle Financial, Clearsky, Imprivata, RStudio
Dr. Steve Herrod, Managing Director
Education: BA, University of Texas, Austin; MS, Computer Science, PhD, Stanford University
Background: CTO & SVP, VMware; Transmeta Corporation; SGI
Directorships: Anomaly, Curai, Illumio, Menlo Security, Preempt Security, Contrast Security, SignalFX, Espressive, RiskRecon
Hemant Taneja, Managing Director
e-mail: htaneja@generalcatalyst.com
Education: BS, MS, Electrical Engineering & Computer Science, BS, Biology & Biomedical Engineering, BS, Mathematics, MS, Operations Research, Massachusetts Institute of Technology
Background: Founder, Advanced Energy Economy; Founder & CEO, Isovia; SVP, Operations, JP Mobile; Founder & Co-Chairman, New England Clean Energy Council
Directorships: ARC Energy, ClassDojo, Corvia Medical, CyPhy Works, Digit, FlightCar, Fractyl Laboratories, Fundbox, Gridco Systems, Gusto, Hey, Highfive, JuiceBox Games, Khan Academy
Joel Cutler, Co-Founder & Managing Director
e-mail: jcutler@generalcatalyst.com
Education: Colby College; Boston College Law School
Background: National Leisure Group; Retail Growth ATM Systems
Directorships: Airbnb, Cadre, Chloe + Isabel, Freedbird, Handy, Lemonade, Lola, M.Gemi, Oscar Insurance, Rockets of Awesome, Warby Parker
Larry Bohn, Managing Director
e-mail: lbohn@generalcatalyst.com
Education: BA, English, University of Massachusetts, Amherst; MA, English Linguistics, Clark University
Background: Chairman, President & CEO, NetGenesis; President, PC DOCS; SVP, Marketing & Business Development, Interleaf; Data General
Directorships: B12, Bigcommerce, Clarabridge, Drift, Feedvisor, GoodData, Mark43, Yottaa
David Fialkow, Co-Founder & Managing Director
e-mail: dfialkow@generalcatalyst.com
Education: Film, Colgate University; Boston College
Background: Co-Founder, National Leisure Group; Co-Founder, Alliance Development Group; Retail Growth ATM Systems; Starboard Cruise Services
Directorships: Facing History and Ourselves, Debate Mate, The Pan-Mass Challenge
Niko Bonatsos, Managing Director
e-mail: nbonatsos@generalcatalyst.com
Education: Dipl.-Ing, Electrical Engineering & Computer Science, Natl. Tech. University of Athens; MPhil, Manufacturing Engineering & Management, University of Cambridge; MS, Management Science & Engineering, Stanford University
Background: Yokogawa Electric Corporation
Directorships: 6d.ai, All Turtles, Atrium, Audius, Hive, HubHaus, ClassDojo, Cover, Livongo Health, Wag!

817 GENERAL MOTORS VENTURES
30470 Harley Earl Blvd
Warren, MI 48092

web: www.gmventures.com

Mission Statement: General Motors Ventures LLC, the venture capital arm of General Motors, was established in 2010 to build relationships with innovative businesses and other venture capital firms. GM Ventures invests in growth stage automotive-related technology companies with the objective of making the best technology available to GM's customers.

Geographic Preference: United States
Fund Size: $100 million
Founded: 2010
Investment Criteria: Early Stage, Growth Stage
Industry Group Preference: Automotive, Clean Technology, Transportation, Advanced Materials
Portfolio Companies: Algolux, Empower Energies, Envisics, Geodigital, Nanosteel, Nauto, Powermat, Proterra, Savari, Seaurat Technologies, Solid Energy, Springcoin, Tula, Weizuche, Yoshi

Key Executives:
Matt Tsien, President
Education: BS, Kettering University; MS, Stanford University; MS, MIT
Background: VP of Planning and Program Management, GM China; EVP, SAIC-GM-Wuling; Executive Director of Vehicle Systems; Electrical Engineer, Delco Electronics
Wade Sheffer, Managing Director
Education: BS, Michigan Technology University; MS, Rensselaer Polytechnic Institute
Background: Test Engineer, Milford Proving Ground; Global Commodity Manager for Vehicle Infotainment; Deputy Executive Director, Shanghai General Motors; Executive Director, Chassis Purchasing
Rohit Makharia, Investment Manager
Education: MS, Chemical Engineering, University of Rochester
Background: Tech Specialist & Program Manager, Global Battery Systems, General Motors

Venture Capital & Private Equity Firms / Domestic Firms

818 GENERATION PARTNERS
Two Lafayette Court
Greenwich, CT 06830
Phone: 203-422-8200 Fax: 203-422-8250
web: www.generation.com

Mission Statement: To invest in technology-enabled services businesses that can make a positive impact on society, and to create value for these companies.
Geographic Preference: United States
Fund Size: $350 million
Founded: 1996
Average Investment: $10 - $40 million
Minimum Investment: $6 million
Investment Criteria: Early Stage, Mid-Stage, Late Stage
Industry Group Preference: Business to Business, Media, Information Technology, Outsourcing & Efficiency, Communications, Healthcare Services, Healthcare Information Technology, Business Products & Services
Portfolio Companies: 3seventy, American Cellular Corporation, Captivate Network, Demand Media, DiscoverMusic, Donuts, High End Systems, Hotjobs.com, iCrossing, LVI Services, MedVance Institute, MethodCare, Muzak, New Wave Broadcasting, Office Media Network, Post University, Promatory Communications, ReCept Pharmacy, Rightside, Scientific Games, ShopWiki, Sterling InfoSystems, thePlatform, Virtual Radiologic Corporation, Zirmed

Other Locations:
Los Angeles, CA
Phone: 424-204-9683

Austin, TX 78759
Phone: 203-422-8200

Key Executives:
Mark Jennings, Managing Partner
512-459-7100
e-mail: jennings@generation.com
Education: BS, Mechanical Engineering, University of Texas at Austin; MBA, Harvard Graduate School of Business
Background: General Partner, Centre Partners; Corporate Finance Department, Goldman Sachs & Company
Directorships: Captivate Network, Virtual Radiologic Corporation, inVentiv Health, MedVance Institute, Agility Recovery Solutions, Sterling Infosystems, Post University
John Hawkins, Managing Partner
415-385-9575
e-mail: hawkins@generation.com
Education: BA, English, Harvard College; MBA, Harvard Graduate School of Business
Background: General Partner, Burr, Egan, Deleage & Company; Corporate Finance Department, Alex. Brown & Sons; Woodman, Kirkpatrick & Gilbreath; Salomon Brothers
Directorships: Captivate Network, P-Com, HotJobs, Demand Media, ShopWiki, ZirMed, iCrossing
Andrew Hertzmark, Managing Partner
203-422-8215
e-mail: hertzmark@generation.com
Education: BA, Economics & Political Science, MBA, Wharton School, University of Pennsylvania
Background: Associate, Galen Partners; Analyst, UBS; Analyst, Dillon Read & Co.; Business Development Group, Pfizer; National Economic Council
Directorships: Captivate Network, Post Education, ReCept Pharmacy, ShopWiki, Virtual Radiologic Corporation
Louis Marino, Senior Vice President/Chief Financial Officer
203-422-8212
e-mail: marino@generation.com
Education: BS, Accounting, Boston College; CPA
Background: Senior Associate, PricewaterhouseCoopers
Directorships: Agility Recovery Solutions, Captivate Network, MedVance Institute, Post Education, ReCept Pharmacy, ShopWiki

819 GENSTAR CAPITAL LP
4 Embarcadero Center
Suite 1900
San Francisco, CA 94111-4191
Phone: 415-834-2350 Fax: 415-834-2383
e-mail: ir@gencap.com
web: www.gencap.com

Mission Statement: Seeks opportunities to invest in unique businesses that can benefit from the productive relationship between proactive shareholders and a motivated management team.
Geographic Preference: United States, Canada
Fund Size: $2 billion
Founded: 1988
Average Investment: $15-75 million
Minimum Investment: $15 million
Investment Criteria: Companies with minimum revenues of $50 million, strong management, prospects for long-term growth and profitability, competitive advantages
Industry Group Preference: Life Sciences, Industrial Technology, Healthcare Services, Software, Financial Services
Portfolio Companies: Accruent, Acrisure, AleraGroup, AWL, Altegris, Apex, Ascensus, Association Member Benefits Advisors, Blue Star Sports, Boyd Corp., Blacket, Bullhorn, ConnectiveRx, Infinite Electronics Inc., Innovative Aftermarket Systems, Institutional Shareholder Services, Insurity, Mercer Advisors, Ministry Brands, Palomar Specialty, PDI, Power Products LLC, Pretium Packaging, Sphera, Stratetic Insight, Tekniplex, Telestream

Key Executives:
Jean-Pierre L. Conte, Chairman/Managing Director
415-834-2350
Fax: 415-834-2383
e-mail: jpconte@gencap.com
Education: MBA, Harvard Graduate School of Business; BA Colgate University
Background: NTC Group, Drexel Burnham Lambert, Chase Manhattan Bank
Directorships: BioSource International, PRA International
Ryan Clark, President/Managing Director
Education: AB, Environmental Science & Public Policy, Harvard College; MBA, Harvard Business School
Background: Associate, Hellman & Friedman
Katie Solomon, Managing Director/Talent Management
Education: BA, American Studies, MA, English, Stanford University; MBA, Stanford Grad. School of Business
Background: Vice President, Vector Capital; Executive Research, Russell Reynolds Associates; Marketing, Harvard Business School Career Services; Consultant, Bain & Company
Directorships: Global Investment Banking Recruitment Department, Robertson Stephen
Anthony Salewski, Managing Director
Education: Harvard College; MBA, Harvard Business School
Background: Chief of Staff, Operations, Barclays Global Investors; Associate, Hellman & Friedman
Directorships: MidCap Financial, TravelCLICK, International Aluminum Corporation
Rob Rutledge, Managing Director
Education: BComm, Queen's University; MBA, Stanford University
Background: Associate, Investment Banking, Salomon Smith Barney
Directorships: Woods Equipment Corporation, Confie Seguros, Voice Construction
Eli Weiss, Managing Director
Education: Yale University; MBA, Stanford Graduate School of Business
Background: Associate, Hellman & Friedman LLC;

Venture Capital & Private Equity Firms / Domestic Firms

Greenhill & Co.
Directorships: Evolution1, Insurity, IAS

820 GEODESIC CAPITAL
950 Tower Lane
Suite 1100
Foster City, CA 94404

Phone: 650-781-0400
e-mail: info@geodesiccap.com
web: www.geodesiccap.com

Mission Statement: A venture capital firm investing in technologies. Geodesic Capital is dedicated to maintaining a strong connection between Sillicon Valley and Japan.
Geographic Preference: California, Japan
Founded: 2015
Investment Criteria: Early-Stage
Industry Group Preference: Technology, Applications, Hospitality, Media, Entertainment
Portfolio Companies: Airbnb, Tanium, Looker, Uber, Databricks, Duo, Netskope, Orbital Insight, Invision, Pindrop, Snapchat, Thoughtspot, Instartlogic
Key Executives:
   John Roos, Partner/Co-Founder
   Education: AB, Political Science, Stanford University; JD, Stanford Law School
   Background: Senior Advisor, Centerview Partners; CEO, Wilson, Sonsini, Goodrich & Rosati
   Directorships: Salesforce.com; Sony
   Ashvin Bachireddy, Partner/Co-Founder
   Education: BS, Management Science, University of California, San Diego
   Background: Head of Growth Stage Investing, Andreessen Horowitz; VC Invester, Lightspeed Venture Partners; VC Investor, 3i Group; VC Investor, JMI Equity; Investment Banker, Montgomery & Co.; Investment Banker, Salomon Smith Barney
   Nate Mitchell, Partner
   Education: Dartmouth College
   Background: Vulcan Capital; Index Ventures; Draper Fisher Jurvetson; Summit Partners
   Charlie Friedland, Partner
   Education: BA, Economics, Dartmouth College
   Background: Ipsy; Summit Partners; Morgan Stanley
   Jon Rezneck, Partner/Chief Operating Officer
   Education: MBA, Finance, Wharton School, University of Pennsylvanial; AB, Economics & East Asian Studies, Harvard College
   Background: Investment Banker, Greenhill & Co.; Investment Banker, JP Morgan & Co.
   Directorships: Business Development, Crowley Technologies
   Matt Fuller, Partner
   Education: MA, LBJ School of Public Affairs, University of Texas; Pepperdine University
   Background: National Security Council; Coalition Provisional Authority Administrator L. Paul Bremer's Special Assistant
   Morgan Livermore, Partner
   Education: BA, Government, Dartmouth College
   Background: Investor, Accel; Investment Bank, Vista Point Advisors
   Susie Roos, Partner/Chief Administrative Officer
   Education: AB, Stanford University; JD, University of Southern California
   Background: Co-Founder, The TOMODACHI Initiative
   James Kondo, Senior Advisor
   Education: BA, Keio University; Visiting Student, Brown University; MBA, Harvard Business School; World Fellow, Yale University
   Background: Co-Chairman, Silicon Valley Japan Platform; President, Rebuild Japan Initiative Foundation; Visiting Scientist, MIT Media Lab; VP, Twitter Inc.

821 GEORGIA OAK PARTNERS
The Office Tower at the Four Seasons
75 14th St. NE
Suite 2150
Atlanta, GA 30309

Phone: 404-961-7201
web: www.georgiaoakpartners.com

Mission Statement: Georgia Oak Partners is a highly differentiated investment platform focused on growth private equity investments in the Southeast US. Our model uniquely combines operational and financial expertise throughout the investing process: from deal sourcing, to strategic appraisal, to post-acquisition value creation. We believe our strategic approach and operational philosophy can generate long-term stakeholder value through the spectrum of business lifecycles, from turnaround situations to acquisition growth strategies.
Geographic Preference: Southeast
Average Investment: $5 - $20 million
Investment Criteria: Control Buyouts, Co-Investments, Minority Equity, Debt-for-Equity
Industry Group Preference: Business Products & Services, Transportation, Logistics, Consumer Services, Consumer Products, Restaurants, Manufacturing, Niche Manufacturing, Packaging, Building Materials & Services
Portfolio Companies: Farm Burger, Sailfish Boats, Spectrum Staffing, TeamOne Logistics, Your Pie
Key Executives:
   Michael A. Lonergan, Managing Partner
   Education: BBA, Finance & Management, Terry College of Business, University of Georgia
   Background: Vice President, Strategic Value Partners; Sun European Partners; Houlihan Lokey; Wells Fargo
   Doug Fisher, Partner
   Education: MBA, Emory University Goizueta Business School; MA, Terry College of Business, University of Georgia
   Background: Director of Finance
   David Barr, Director
   e-mail: dbarr@georgiaoakpartners.com
   Background: Chairman, Samuels Jewelers; Price Waterhouse
   Directorships: Your Pie, Del Frisco's Restaurant Group, BrightStar Care, The Spice & Tea Exchange, Capriotti's Sandwich Shops, Bistro Group, PMTD Restaurants

822 GERKEN CAPITAL ASSOCIATES
110 Tiburon Boulevard
Suite 5
Mill Valley, CA 94941

Phone: 415-383-1464 Fax: 415-383-1253
web: www.gerkencapital.com

Mission Statement: Investment firm and alternative asset fund manager specializing in private equity investment products.
Geographic Preference: Europe
Fund Size: $1.5 billion
Founded: 1989
Investment Criteria: LBO, MBO
Industry Group Preference: Data & Analytics, Financial
Portfolio Companies: Datalink, Infinite English, Sapiens Data Science, Zympay
Key Executives:
   Lou Gerken, Founder/Chief Executive Officer
   e-mail: lou@gerkencapital.com
   Education: University of Redlands; American Graduate School; MBA, Southern Methodist University Graduate School of Business
   Background: Managing Director & Group Head, Prudential Securities Technology; Montgomery Securities; Wells Fargo Capital Markets; Founder, TCG International; Senior Research Analyst, GT Capital Management

Venture Capital & Private Equity Firms / Domestic Firms

Anthony J. Moore, Managing Director
e-mail: anthony@gerkencapital.com
Education: MA, Cambridge University; MBA, Finance & Accounting, Kellogg School of Management, Northwestern University
Background: Wells Fargo Institutional Investments; Bankers Trust Company; Ziegler Securities; Northern Trust Company

823 GGV CAPITAL
3000 Sand Hill Road
Building 4
Suite 230
Menlo Park, CA 94025

Phone: 650-475-2150 **Fax:** 650-475-2151
web: www.ggvc.com

Mission Statement: GGV Capital leads venture capital investments across the United States and China.

Geographic Preference: United States, China
Fund Size: $2.6 billion
Founded: 2000
Average Investment: $5 - $25 million
Investment Criteria: All Stages
Industry Group Preference: Software, Internet, Digital Media & Marketing, Gaming, Marketing, Mobile, Cloud Computing
Portfolio Companies: 1More Design, 21Vianet, 7k7k, AAC Technologies, Aero, Affirm, Airbnb, Agora.io, Alibaba, AlientVault, Allume, Appirio, athenahealth, AvidBots, Baobao, BigCommerce, BingoBox, BitSight Technologies, BlackLake Technology, BlueKai, Brightwheel, Bowery Farming, Boxed, Buddy Media, Bustle Digital Group, CashShield, CDG, Chaoli, China Talent Group, Chukong Technologies, Chushou TV, Citrus Lane, Citybox, CityShop, Clobotics, Conviva, Curse, Diandian Yangche, Didi Chuxing, DOMO, Douguo, DraftKings, Drive.ai, EHANG, Electric, Endeca, Evolv, Farmland Keeper, FlightCar, Flipboard, Function of Beauty, Giphy, Giska, Gladly Software, Global Scanner, Glow Concept, Glu Mobile, Grab, GrubMarket, Haitunjia, HaoHaoZhu, HashiCorp, Hello ChuXing, Heptagon/AMS, HotelTonight, Houzz, Ibotta, Immotor, Iris Nova, Isilon, IWJW, Keep, Kingsoft WPS, Kintana, Ku6, Kuaidian, Kujiale, LAIX, Lambda School, Light Chaser, Lively, MediaV, Meicai, Meihua, Meili/Mogu, Misfit, Moka, Musical.ly, Namely, Netli, Netscaler, New Knowledge, Nimble Storage, NIU, Nozomi, NS1, OfferUp, OpenDoor, Pactera, Pandora, P-Cube, Peloton, Percolate, Petkit, Philm, Phoenix Labs, Phononic, PlushCare, Poshmark, Qpass, QuinStreet, Quixey, Qunar, Reebonz, Shiftgig, Shoppo, SinoSun Technology, Slice, SkyStream Networks, Slack, SmartMI, Social Touch, SoundCloud, Square, Structo, SuccessFactors, Synack, Tangdou, The Mighty, ThinCI, Tile, Tujia, Turbine, u51.com, UCWeb, Unravel Data, Vincross, Vocera, Wish, XCharge, Xfire, Xiangwushuo,

Other Locations:
70 South Park St.
San Francisco, CA 94107
Phone: 650-475-2150 **Fax:** 650-475-2151

Unit 1806, Tower West, Genesis Beijing
No. 8 Xinyuan South Road
Chaoyang District
Beijing 100027
China
Phone: 86-1059897988

Unit 3501, Two IFC
8 Century Avenue, Pudong District
Shanghai 200120
China
Phone: 86-2161611720 **Fax:** 86-2154035580

Key Executives:
Jixun Foo, Managing Partner, Shanghai
Education: MSc, National University of Singapore
Background: Director, Draper Fisher Jurvetson ePlanet Ventures; Hewlett Packard
Jenny Lee, Managing Partner, Shanghai
Education: BSc, MS, Engineering, Cornell University; MBA, Kellogg School of Management, Northwestern University
Background: Singapore Technologies Aerospace; Morgan Stanley; JAFCO Asia
Directorships: eHang Technology, Yingying Finance, 51zhangdan, Xiaozhan
Eric Xu, Managing Partner, Shanghai
Education: Shanghai University; Master of Finance, University of Manchester School of Business
Background: Managing Director, SIG Investment Asia; Investment Professional, CITIC Capital; TDF Capital
Directorships: Zhaoyou, Cityshop, BingoBox, Citybox, Xinshang
Jeff Richards, Managing Partner, Silicon Valley
Education: BA, Government, Dartmouth College
Background: VP, Digital Content Services, VeriSign; Founder & CEO, R4 Global Solutions, Founder, QuantumShift
Directorships: Appirio, Boxed, Percolate, Reebonz, Tile
Glenn Solomon, Managing Partner, Silicon Valley
Education: BA, MBA, Stanford University
Background: General Partner, Partech International; Goldman Sachs; SPO Partners
Hans Tung, Managing Partner, Silicon Valley
Education: BS, Industrial Engineering, Stanford University
Background: Qiming Venture Partners; Bessemer Venture Partners; HelloAsia; Asia2B
Directorships: Wish, Xiaohongshu, GrubMarket, Totspot, FlightCar, Curse
Stephen Hyndman, Partner/CFO, Shanghai
Education: BS, Commerce, JD, Santa Clara University
Background: CFO, Prospero Ventures; CFO, ASCII Corporation
Erica Yu, Principal, Beijing
Education: Zhejiang University
Background: Senior Associate, China Renaissance Partners

824 GI PARTNERS
188 The Embarcadero
Suite 700
San Francisco, CA 94105

Phone: 415-688-4800 **Fax:** 415-688-4801
e-mail: info@gipartners.com
web: www.gipartners.com

Mission Statement: GI Partners' private equity and real estate groups work closely with portfolio investments to help them realize their full potential.

Portfolio Companies: Access, AdvoServ, Consilio & Advanced Discovery, California Cryobank Life Sciences, Daxko, Digital Reality, Doxim, Duckhorn, Far Niente, First Republic Bank, Flexential, Kellermeyer Bergensons Services, Ladder Capital, The Linc Group, Logibec, MRI Software, Netsmart, Plum, Softlayer, Telx, Together Work, Viawest, Wave, Waypoint Homes

Key Executives:
Rick Magnuson, Executive Managing Director
Education: BA, Dartmouth College; MBA, Stanford Graduate School of Business
Background: Director of Investment Banking, Merrill Lynch & Co.; Founder of Interactive Software
Directorships: Flexential, Far Niente Wine Estates, CenterPoint Properties Trust
David Smolen, Managing Director, General Counsel, Chief Compliance Oficer
Education: BA, International Relations, MA, Political Science, Stanford University; JD, Stanford Law School
Background: Senior Counsel & Chief Compliance Officer,

Silver Lake; General Counsel, CFO & COO, Fort Mason Capital
Dave Kreter, Managing Director
Education: BA, Economics, Princeton University; MBA, Harvard Business School
Directorships: Logibec, Netsmart Technologies, California Cryobank Life Sciences
David Mace, Managing Director
Education: BA, Economics, Dartmouth College; MBA, Harvard School of Business
Directorships: Flexential, Far Niente Wine Estates
Howard Park, Managing Director
Education: BA, Rice University; MBA, Tuck School of Business, Dartmouth College
Directorships: Logibec, Netsmart Technologies, California Cryobank Life Sciences
Travis Pearson, Managing Director
Education: BA, MA, Duke University; JD, Harvard Law School
Background: Bain & Company
Directorships: Togetherwork, Doxim, Flexential, Logibec, MRI Software, Daxko
John K. Saer Jr., Managing Director
Education: AB, Economics, Dartmouth College; MBA, Stanford Graduate School of Business
Background: CFO, KSL Recreation Corporation
Directorships: CalEast Global Logistics, CenterPoint Properties
Philip Yau, Managing Director
Education: BA, Princeton University; MBA, Northwestern University
Background: UBS Private Funds Group
Hoon Cho, Managing Director
Education: BA, Princeton University; MBA, Harvard Business School
Directorships: Kellermeyer Bergensons Services, Access, Consilio

825 GIC GROUP
4328 Montgomery Ave.
Bethesda, MD 20814

Phone: 301-799-0840
e-mail: info@gicgroup.com
web: www.gicgroup.com

Mission Statement: Provides clients in agrobusiness and biotech with resources to reach their potential.

Investment Criteria: Later Stage, Expansion, Early Stage, Startup/Seed
Industry Group Preference: Biotechnology, Financial Services, Agribusiness
Key Executives:
  Richard Gilmore, President/CEO
  Education: MA, International and Development Economics, Johns Hopkins University; PhD, International Economics/Trade, Graduate Institute of International Studies

826 GIDEON HIXON FUND
2476 Lillie Ave.
Summerland, CA 93067

Phone: 805-962-2277 x11 Fax: 805-565-0929
web: www.gideonhixon.com

Mission Statement: The Gideon Hixon Fund is a venture capital investment fund representing the interests of the extended Hixon family. We take a long-term traditional approach to venture capital investing by supporting passionately committed entrepreneurs with visions of revolutionizing industries and by building strong lasting businesses. Our investment philosophy perpetuates the principals of Gideon Cooley Hixon-principles honored for six generations. The Gideon Hixon Fund believes that investors and entrepreneurs must align to build great companies, which ultimately will make the world a better place.

Geographic Preference: United States
Average Investment: $500,000 - $1.5 million
Investment Criteria: All Stages
Industry Group Preference: Biosciences, Biotechnology
Portfolio Companies: Boom Entertainment, Capella, Edufii, Genbad, Blycos Biotechnologies, Hansen Engine, Boka Sciences, Igrok, Illumitex, Instructure, Prolacta Bioscience, Shotspotter, Percona, Zadspace
Other Locations:
  315 East Commerce Street
  Suite 300
  San Antonio, TX 78205
  Phone: 210-225-3053 Fax: 210-225-5910
Key Executives:
  Frank H Foster, Managing Partner
  Education: BS, Harvard University; MBA, Harvard Business School
  Background: Managing Director, DFJ Frontier; Venture Partner, Southern Cross Venture Partners; General Partner, Allen & Buckeridge
  Directorships: Hixon Properties, Boka Sciences, Edufii, Prolacta Biosciences, Buyology, Predixion Software, Onsert Media
  Dylan Hixon, Managing Partner
  Education: BS, Yale University; MS, Mechanical Engineering, California Institute of Technology
  Background: President, Arden Road Investments; PCI; Reel EFX
  Debra P Geiger, General Partner
  Education: BS, University of Colorado; JD, Santa Barbara College of Law
  Background: Consultant, Santa Barbara District Attorney's Office
  Eric Hixon, General Partner
  Education: BS, , MS, Computer Science, New York University
  Background: Founder, WebCal; Yahoo Mail; Torque Systems
  Bryan Simpson Jr., General Partner
  Education: BS, University of North Carolina; JD, University of Florida
  Background: CEO/Chairman, Medcom Services; Chairman, Hixon Properties Inc.
  Directorships: Compass Bank

827 GILBERT GLOBAL EQUITY PARTNERS
767 Fifth Avenue
15th Floor
New York, NY 10153-0028

Phone: 212-584-6200 Fax: 212-584-6211
web: www.gilbertglobal.com

Mission Statement: Makes private equity and equity-related investments in both public and private companies around the world, seeking attractive opportunities across global markets and industries.

Geographic Preference: United States, Europe, Latin America, Asia-Pacific
Fund Size: $1.2 billion
Founded: 1997
Average Investment: $20 to $150 million
Minimum Investment: $20 million
Investment Criteria: Mezzanine, LBO, MBO
Industry Group Preference: Telecommunications, Infrastructure, Optical Technology, Industrial Services, Consumer Services, Internet Technology, Business to Business, Networking
Portfolio Companies: Amkor Technology, CPM Holdings, Montpelier Re Holdings, Olympus Re Holdings, True Temper

Venture Capital & Private Equity Firms / Domestic Firms

Other Locations:
P.O. Box 984
New Canaan, CT 06840
Phone: 203-966-6022 **Fax:** 203-972-0250

Key Executives:
Steven J. Gilbert, Chairman
e-mail: sgilbert@gilbertglobal.com
Education: Wharton School; Harvard Law School; Harvard Business School
Background: Founder, Soros Capital; Founder, Commonwealth Capital Partners; Founder, Chemical Venture Partners; EF Hutton International; Wertheim & Company; Morgan Stanley & Co.
Richard W. Gaenzle Jr., Partner
e-mail: rgaenzle@gilbertglobal.com
Education: Hartwick College; Fordham Graduate School of Business
Background: Soros Capital; PaineWebber
Jeffrey W. Johnson, Partner
e-mail: jjohnson@gilbertglobal.com
Education: Claremont McKenna College; Harvard Business School
Background: Soros Capital; Frank Russell Company; Goldman, Sachs & Company; Hallmark Cards
Steven Kotler, Partner
e-mail: skotler@gilbertglobal.com
Education: City College of New York
Background: President/CEO, Schroder & Company; Co-Head, Investment and Merchant Banking Activities Worldwide

---

828 GLADSTONE CAPITAL
1521 Westbranch Drive
Suite 100
McLean, VA 22102

Phone: 703-287-5800
e-mail: information@gladstonecompanies.com
web: www.gladstonecompanies.com

Mission Statement: The Gladstone Companies invests in small to middle-market companies based in the United States. The firm provides capital and traditional debt financing to businesses in a broad range of sectors, including industrial products, specialty manufacturing, transportation, specialty chemicals, media and communications, and business, healthcare and energy services.

Geographic Preference: United States
Fund Size: $280 million
Founded: 2001
Average Investment: $5 - $30 million
Minimum Investment: $5 million
Investment Criteria: Second Lien, Subordinated, Mezzanine
Industry Group Preference: Service Industries, Manufacturing, Distribution, Specialty Manufacturing, Media, Communications, Business Products & Services, Government Services, Consumer Products, Healthcare Services, Transportation, Specialty Chemicals, Energy Services
Portfolio Companies: ACME Cryogenics, Ag Trucking, Allison Publications, Alloy Die Casting, BAS Broadcasting, B-Dry, Behrens Manufacturing, Brunswick Bowling Products, B+T Group, Cambridge Sound Management, Circuitronics, Channel Technologies Group, Counsel Press, Country Club Enterprises, Danco Machine, Defiance Stamping Company, Drew Foam Companies, Edge Adhesives Holdings, Flight Trampoline Parks, Francis Drilling Fluids, Frontier Packaging, Galaxy Tool Corporation, GFRC Cladding Systems, GI Plastek, Ginsey Holdings, Head Country, Heartland Communications Group, JackRabbit, J.America, Legend Communications of Wyoming, Lignetics, LogoSportswear, Mathey Dearman, Meridian Rack & Pinion, Mikawaya, Mitchell Rubber Products, NDLI Logistics, Nth Degree, Old World Christmas, Precision, Precision Southeast, Profit Systems, Quench USA, Reliable Biopharmaceutical Corporation, Saunders & Associates, SBS Industries, Schylling, SOG Specialty Knives & Tools, Southern Petroleum Laboratories, Star Seed, Stellar Outdoor Media, StrataTech Education Group, Sunburst Media-Louisiana, Sunshine Media Holdings, Tread Corporation, United Flexible, Vision Government Solutions, WadeCo Specialties, Westland Technologies

Other Locations:
245 Park Avenue
39th Floor
New York, NY 10167
Phone: 203-661-1397

200 South Wacker Drive
Suite 3100
Chicago, IL 60606

17 E Gabilan Street
Salinas, CA 93901
Phone: 831-225-0883

Key Executives:
David Gladstone, Founder/Chairman/CEO
Education: BA, Government & Economics, University of Virginia; MA, American University; MBA, Harvard Business School
Background: Chairman, American Capital Strategies; Chairman & CEO, Allied Capital Corporation; Allied Capital Lending Corporation; Allied Capital Commercial Corporation; Allied Capital Advisors; President, CEO & Director, Business Mortgage Investors
Directorships: Capital Automotive REIT
Terry Brubaker, Vice Chairman/COO
703-287-5820
e-mail: terry.brubaker@gladstonecapital.com
Education: BSE, Aerospace & Mechanical Sciences, Princeton University; MBA, Harvard Business School
Background: Chairman & Founder, Heads Up Systems; VP, Paper Group, American Forest & Paper Association; President, Interstate Resources; President, IRI; James River Corporation; Strategic Planning & Marketing Manager, Boise Cascade; Senior Engagement Manager, McKinsey & Company
David Dullum, Director/President/Executive Managing Director, Private Equity
703-287-5891
e-mail: david.dullum@gladstonecompanies.com
Education: BME, Georgia Institute of Technology; MBA, Stanford Graduate School of Business
Background: Partner, New England Partners; Managing General Partner, Frontenac Company
Laura Gladstone, Managing Director, Gladstone Capital
212-792-4187
e-mail: laura.gladstone@gladstonecompanies.com
Education: BBA, George Washington University
Background: Associate, Equity Research, ING Barings; Assistant Analyst, Salomon Smith Barney
Erika Highland, Managing Director, Gladstone Investment
703-287-5840
e-mail: erika.highland@gladstonecompanies.com
Education: BS, Business Administration, Boston College
Background: Account Executive, Wells Fargo Retail Finance; Financial Analyst, AG Edwards
Kyle Largent, Senior Managing Director, Gladstone Investment
703-287-5880
e-mail: kyle.largent@gladstonecompanies.com
Education: BSBA, University of Tulsa; MBA, Georgetown University
Background: VP, National Capital; Associate Analyst, Research, Friedman Billings Ramsey
Christopher Lee, Managing Director, Gladstone Investment
703-287-5887
e-mail: christopher.lee@gladstonecompanies.com
Education: BA, MBA, Georgetown University
Background: VP, MCG Capital; Consultant, KPMG Consulting

Venture Capital & Private Equity Firms / Domestic Firms

829 GLASSWING VENTURES
275 Newbury St.
Boston, MS 02116

e-mail: info@glasswing.vc
web: glasswing.vc

Mission Statement: Glasswing Ventures in an early stage venture capital firm that invests in artificial intelligence and technology startups.
Geographic Preference: East Coast
Investment Criteria: Early-Stage
Industry Group Preference: Artificial Intelligence, SaaS, Technology, Cybersecurity
Portfolio Companies: Allure Security Technology, Armored Things, Autit, Base Operations, BotChain, ChaosSearch, Devcon Detect, Elsy, Terbium Labs, Zylotech
Key Executives:
  Rudina Seseri, Founder/Managing Partner
  e-mail: rudina@glasswing.vc
  Education: BA, Wellesley College; MBA, Harvard Business School
  Directorships: AUTIT, Celtra, ChaosSearch, CrowdTwist, Inrupt, Plannuh, SocialFlow, Talla, Zylotech
  Rick Grinnell, Founder/Managing Partner
  e-mail: rick@glasswing.vc
  Education: BS, MS, MIT; MBA, Harvard Business School
  Background: Managing Director, Fairhaven Capital
  Directorships: Allure Security, Armored Things, Terbium Labs
  Sarah Fay, Managing Partner
  e-mail: sarah@glasswing.vc
  Education: BA, University of Vermont

830 GLENCOE CAPITAL
444 N Michigan Avenue
Suite 2970
Chicago, IL 60611

Phone: 312-795-6300 Fax: 312-795-6301
web: www.glencap.com

Mission Statement: Targets control investments in lower middle-market companies.
Geographic Preference: United States, Canada
Fund Size: $789 million
Founded: 1993
Minimum Investment: $7 million
Investment Criteria: Lower Middle Market, Lead-Sponsored Acquisitions, Growth Equity
Industry Group Preference: Consumer Products, Industrial Equipment, Food & Beverage, Chemicals, Financial Services, Business to Business, Media
Portfolio Companies: Allegra Direct Communications, Budco, Campbell Grinder Company, Child Development Schools, Dialogue Marketing, Dixie Chemical Company, Fortis Energy Services, NOVO 1, Polyair Inter Pack
Other Locations:
  36700 Woodward Avenue
  Suite 107
  Bloomfield Hills, MI 48304
Key Executives:
  David S. Evans, Chairman/CEO/CIO
  Education: BGS, University of Michigan; MBA, University of Chicago Graduate School of Business
  Background: M&A Specialist, Donaldson, Lufkin & Jenrette; Associate Director, Growth Capital Foundation, University of Michigan
  Paul Smith, Managing Director
  Education: BS, Miami University; MBA, Kellogg School of Management
  Background: W.W. Grainger Inc.; General Electric
  Scott Mygind, Vice President, Finance/IT
  Education: BA, Finance/Economics, University of Illinois
  Background: Director of Financial Planning/Analyst, LKQ Corporation; Orbitz Worldwide; Whitehall Jewelers; Electronic Data Systems
  Nicholas Iovino, CCO/Vice President, Accounting
  Education: BA, Wesleyan University; CPA
  Background: Portfolio Accountant, Aurora Investment Management LLC; Senior Fund Accountant, Woodfield Fund Administration; Financial Services Tax Associate, McGladrey

831 GLENGARY LLC
25200 Chagrin Boulevard
Suite 300
Beachwood, OH 44122

Phone: 216-378-9200
e-mail: shaynes@glengaryllc.com

Mission Statement: Glengary combines an unparalleled network of support services with investment capital. The initial investment in an early-stage company is typically made after its product or service has been validated in the market. The firm then works with its leadership to achieve mutually-defined milestones before participating in follow-on rounds of financing.
Average Investment: $100,000 - $1.5 million
Minimum Investment: $100,000
Investment Criteria: Early-Stage
Industry Group Preference: Healthcare, Information Technology, Applied Technology, Business Products & Services
Portfolio Companies: Cardinal Commerce, Cleveland HeartLab, Connected Living Inc., Guardian Technologies, Germguardian, Juventas Therapeutics, Monarch Teching Technologies Inc., Neuros Medical Inc., On Shift, Predictive Service, Procuri, SupplierInsight, ToolingU
Key Executives:
  Stephen R Haynes, Founder/Chairman/Managing Partner
  Education: BS, Accountancy, Miami University; CPA
  Background: General Partner, Key Equity Capital; Kirtland Capital; Corporate Finance, McDonald & Company Securities
  Directorships: Cleveland HeartLab

832 GLENTHORNE CAPITAL
200 West Lancaster Avenue
Suite 206
Wayne, PA 19087

Phone: 610-688-6313 Fax: 610-688-3410
e-mail: dkollock@glenthornecapital.com
web: www.glenthornecapital.com

Mission Statement: Assists company owners and senior management groups to successfully meet the important strategic challenges of today's changing markets by providing financial advisory and investment banking services.
Geographic Preference: North America, Europe, South America
Founded: 1984
Average Investment: $1 million
Minimum Investment: $250,000
Investment Criteria: Mezzanine, LBO, MBO
Industry Group Preference: Chemicals, Life Sciences, Transportation, Packaging, Financial Services, Manufacturing, Medical
Portfolio Companies: Adco Technologies, Adco Products Inc, American Mirrex, Asplundh Tree Expert Co., Colorcraft Packaging, Crane Company, Heritage Inks International, Houghton International Inc, IMI Express, Inco Limited, Industrial Valley Title, Island Chemical, Lavino Shipping Company, Michael Huber Gmbh, Pecora Corporation, Philadelphia Financial Group, Public Financial Management, Quality Coach Inc., Resco Products Inc., Stixi Ag, Tasty Banking Company, Teleflex Inc., Thatcher Tubes, Valquip Corporation

Venture Capital & Private Equity Firms / Domestic Firms

Key Executives:
David P Kollock, Founder/Managing Director
e-mail: dkollock@glenthornecapital.com
Education: BS, MBA, Wharton School of the University of Pennsylvania
Background: American Mirrex Corporation; JM Huber Company; CoreStates Financial; Towers Perrin Forester; Selby Battersby & Company
Roy C. Carriker, PhD, Director
e-mail: roy@global-advisors.net
Education: BS, MS, PhD, Physics, Washington State University
Background: Vice Chairman, Teleflex Inc.; Founder & Chairman, Global Advisors LLC
Directorships: Indivers BV
Craig N. Johnson, Advisory Director
Education: BS, Engineering, University of Pennsylvania; MBA, Wharton School
Background: President & CEO, Lavino Shipping Company
Directorships: Blair Corporation

833 GLOBAL CATALYST PARTNERS
530 Lytton Ave.
2nd Floor
Palo Alto, CA 94301
Phone: 650-486-2420 **Fax:** 650-560-6218
e-mail: plans@gc-partners.com
web: www.gc-partners.com

Mission Statement: Global Catalyst Partners is an international, multistage, technology-oriented venture capital firm. Our partners have significant operating experience serving in large public companies as well as building entrepreneurial ventures into major public companies.
Geographic Preference: United States, China, Israel, Japan
Investment Criteria: All Stages
Industry Group Preference: Technology
Portfolio Companies: Actelis Networks, Advanced Micro-Fabrication Equipment, Beceem Communications, Greenfield Networks, KargoCard, SoundHound, Newport Media, P-Cube, Teranetics, Velio, Verient

Other Locations:
1-1-1 Minami-Aoyama Minato-Ku
West Wing 7F
Tokyo 107-0062
Japan
Phone: 81-3-6455-5950 **Fax:** 81-3-6455-5950

Key Executives:
Kamran Elahian, Chairman/Co-Founder
Education: BS, Computer Science, BS, Mathematics, MS, Engineering, Computer Graphics, University of Utah
Background: Co-Chair, UNDESA-gAID
Directorships: SoundHound
Koji Osawa, Managing Principal/Co-Founder
Education: BS, Electronics, Keio University; PhD, Engineering, Tohoku University
Background: Mitsubishi Corporation
Directorships: Verient, KargoCard, Advanced Micro-Fabrication Equipment, SoundHound
Vijay C Parikh, Managing Principal
Education: BSEE, Birla Institute of Technology & Science; MBA, University of Michigan
Background: President, StratumOne Communications
Directorships: KargoCard, Verient
Arthur Schneiderman, Principal & Co-Founder
Education: Beloit College; JD, University of Wisconsin Law School
Background: Partner, Wilson Sonsini Goodrich & Rosati

834 GLOBAL ENVIRONMENT FUND
2 Bethesda Center
Suite 440
Bethesda, MD 20814
Phone: 240-482-8900 **Fax:** 301-656-1612
web: gefcapital.com

Mission Statement: To be the premier alternative asset management firm in the domain of energy and environment by delivering favorable risk-adjusted invested returns to our limited partners over multiple vintage years and through varied macroeconomic climates.
Geographic Preference: United States, China, India, Brazil, Turkey, Mexico, South Africa
Founded: 1990
Industry Group Preference: Renewable Energy, Energy Efficiency, Environment Products & Services, Forestry, Food & Agriculture
Portfolio Companies: Afram Plantation Limited, AGV Logistica, America Latina Logistica, athena Controls, Aurora Flight Sciences, Blue Ridge ESOP Associates, Blue Ridge Numerics, Cantaloupe Systems, Cape Pine Investment Holdings, CHAINalytics, ComRent, Concord Enviro, Dentistanbul, Dequingyuan, Derive Systems, Duoyuan, Empresas Verdes Argentina, Essex, Euromedic, Geodex Communications, Global Forest Products, Global Woods, Greenergy, Greenko, Gro-Well Brands, Haverfield, Hijauan Bengkoka, Imvelo Forests, indian Energy Exchange, IClean, IHC, Kalkitech, KEYW, Kilombero Valley, Knight & Carver Wind Group, Luminae, MAEH, Monte Alto Forestall, Mozwood, Neogas, Niko Resources Ltd., Peak Timbers, Pemba Sun and Mozwood, Product Software Development, Ramanas Farms, Red Ambiental, Renew Power, Reva, Rishabh Instruments, Rocklands, Saisudhir, Sanepar, Sensicast, Shakti, Signature Control Systems Inc., SPG Solar, Tecverde, Terszol, Unirac, UPC Renewable, Xymetrex

Other Locations:
WeWork, C20 - G Block
Bandra Kurla Complex
Bandra East
Mumbai 400051
India
Phone: 91-22-4445-1139

Rua Pais de Araujo, 29
14th Floor
Sao Paulo, SP 04531-090
Brazil
Phone: 55-11-3073-0444

Key Executives:
H Jeffrey Leonard, President/Founding Partner/CEO
Education: BA, Harvard University; MS, London School of Economics; PhD, Princeton University
Background: VP, World Wildlife Fund; VP, Conservation Foundation; Chairman, International Pepsi-Cola Bottlers Investments
Directorships: Global Forest Products
John Earhart, Chairman/Founding Partner
Education: BS, California State University; MA, Forestry, Yale School of Forestry and Environmental Studies
Background: Senior Fellow, World Wildlife Fund; Sr Fellow, Conservation Foundation; Associate Director, Peace Corporation
Alexandre Alvim, Managing Director, Sao Paulo
Education: BS, Electrical Engineering, Universidade Estadual de Campinas; MBA, Kellogg School of Management, Northwestern University
Background: Co-Founder/Managing Partner, Greentech Capital
Directorships: Energy & Business Development, Estre Ambiental
Scott MacLeod, Managing Partner
Education: BA, Yale University; MBA, Columbia University Graduate School of Business
Background: Division Manager, Finance Corporation

Venture Capital & Private Equity Firms / Domestic Firms

Stuart Barkoff, Managing Director/COO
Education: AB, Vassar College; JD & MBA, Emory University
Background: Attorney, Arnold & Porter LLP
Sridhar Narayan, Managing Director, GEF Advisors India
Education: Post Graduate Diploma, Management, Indian Institute of Management; Bachelor of Technology, Mechanical Engineering, Indian Institute of Technology
Background: JRE Partners; American International Group; Zurich Asset Management India
Daniel Prawda, Managing Director
Education: BA, Economics & International Relations, Tufts University
Background: ACON Investments; Latin America Corporate Finance Group, JP Morgan
Directorships: Gro-Well Brands Inc.
Anibal Wadih, Managing Director
Education: BS, Electrical Engineering, Universidad Simon Bolivar; MA, Finance, IESA; MBA, NYU Stern School of Business
Background: Managing Director, MacQuarie Capital; M&A, Deutsche Bank
Steve Guffey, Chief Financial Officer
Education: BBA, Accounting, James Madison University; CPA
Background: Assistant Controller, The Carlyle Group
Marta De La Cruz, Executive Services Associate
Education: BA, Marketing, Bernard Baruch College, Zicklin School of Business
Nupur Jalan, Vice President, GEF Advisors India
Education: BS, Computer Applications, University of Bangalore; MBA, Narsee Monjee Institute of Management Studies
Background: GE Capital
Raj Pai, Managing Director
Education: BS, Computer Engineering, University of Bombay; MA, Computer Science, Arizona State University; MBA, University of Chicago
Background: Managing Director, CID Capital
Katie Vasilescu, Chief Compliance Officer
Education: BA, Anthropology, University of Maryland
Background: Office Manager, GEF
Aditya Arora, Principal
Education: BComm, University of Calcutta; MBA, Indian School of Business
Background: Investment Manager, Navis Capital; JM Financial
Lisa Schule, Managing Director
Education: BA, Amherst College; JD, Georgetown University School of Law
Background: Vice President, Perseus LLC; PECO Energy
Derek Beaty, Principal
Education: BS, Accounting, University of Illinois; MBA, Kellogg School of Management, Northwestern University; CPA
Background: CIVC Partners; M&A, BMO Capital; M&A, Arthur Andersen
Nick Morriss, Senior Investment Partner, Managed Accounts
Education: BA, Economics, University of York
Background: Co-Founder & Managing Partner, EMAlternatives; Coopers & Lybrand
Justin Heyman, Principal
Education: BS, Economics, Wharton School, University of Pennsylvania; MBA, Columbia Business School
Background: Senior Associate, Oliver Wyman; Investor Growth Capital
Alipt Sharma, Principal
Education: BA, Economics, Shri Ram College of Commerce, Dehli University; MBA, Indian School of Business
Background: AMP Capital Investors; Ambit Corporate Finance; Arthur Andersen; Ernst & Young

835 GLOBESPAN CAPITAL PARTNERS
One Boston Place
Suite 2810
Boston, MA 02108

Phone: 617-305-2300
web: www.globespancapital.com

Mission Statement: Invests in Internet, mobile, IT infrastructure and SaaS businesses. Globespan Capital Partners is dedicated to establishing partnerships with entrepreneurs and helping companies to realize their potential.

Geographic Preference: Worldwide
Average Investment: $250,000 - $15 million
Investment Criteria: Early-Stage, Middle-Stage, Late-Stage
Industry Group Preference: Information Technology, Internet, Mobile Technology, Clean Technology, Communications, Software, Systems & Peripherals
Portfolio Companies: Analogix, BitSight, Coskata, Credit Sesame, Gild, Kaminario, Linden Lab, MarketLive, Nantero, Nominum, OpenSpan, Overture Networks, Pelican Imaging, Perfecto Mobile, Redfin, Rev, Roku, Silicor Materials, SMS GupShup, Solar Silicon Technology, Sonics, SundaySky, Upwork, VMTurbo, ZeaChem

Other Locations:
300 Hamilton Avenue
Palo Alto, CA 94301

Key Executives:
Andy Goldfarb, Co-Founder/Executive Managing Director
Education: AB, East Asian Studies & Economics, Harvard College; MBA, Harvard Business School
Background: Senior Managing Director, JAFCO Ventures; Founder & Director, TN Ventures; Corporate Development, Kikkoman Corporation
Directorships: Gild, Nominum, Overture Networks, Pelican Imaging, Redfin, Rev, SundaySky
Dave Fachetti, Managing Director
Education: BBA, University of Massachusetts, Amherst; MBA, Boston University, CPA
Background: Principal, JAFCO Ventures; SVP, Sales & Marketing, Family Education Network; SVP, Business Marketing, Trans National Group
Directorships: BitSight, Credit Sesame, Kaminario, Nantero, OpenSpan, Perfecto Mobile
Steve Wood, Chief Financial Officer
Education: BS, University of Vermont; MBA, Carroll School of Management, Boston College

836 GLYNN CAPITAL MANAGEMENT
3000 Sand Hill Road
Building 3, Suite 230
Menlo Park, CA 94025

Phone: 650-854-2215
web: www.glynncapital.com

Mission Statement: An investment management firm that focuses on generating substantial long-term capital gains for a small number of individual high-net-worth clients.

Fund Size: $50 million
Founded: 1970
Average Investment: $500,000
Minimum Investment: $250,000
Investment Criteria: Companies that can grow 20% of revenue and profits annually
Industry Group Preference: Business Products & Services, Medical & Health Related, Electronic Technology, Software, Digital Media & Marketing, Internet
Portfolio Companies: Intel, Electronic Arts, Sun Microsystems, Facebook, Linkedin, Palantir, Pure Storage, Cloudera, Dropbox, Etsy, Oscar, Domo, VS, Nimble Storage, Bonobos, Birchbox, Responsys, Suumologic, DocuSign, Redfin, Radius, OpenDNS, Financial Engines, SalesforceIQ, Xoom, Zappos.com, Okta, Evernote, Dataminr, The Climate

Venture Capital & Private Equity Firms / Domestic Firms

Corporation, Giphy, Bigpanda, Rhumbix, Science37, Kalo, SeatGeek, Couchbase

Key Executives:
John W. Glynn, Founder & Managing Director
Education: BS, University of Notre Dame; JD, University of Virginia; MBA, Stanford University
Background: General Partner, Lamoreaux, Glynn Associates; Special Partner, New Enterprise Associates
Directorships: Molecular Design, The Learning Company
Steven J Rosston, Managing Director
Education: Harvard University; MBA & JD, Stanford University
Background: Product Manager, ROLM
Carl T Anderson, Managing Director
Education: BA, Economics, Princeton University; MBA, Stanford University Graduate School of Business
Background: Partner, Stonebrook Fund Management; AllAdvantage.com
Jacqueline Glynn, Managing Director
Education: Davidson College; MBA, Darden Graduate School of Business, University of Virginia
Background: Analyst, Alex Brown & Sons; Roberton Stephens
Sarah Rogers, Chief Operaring & Compliance Officer
Education: BA, Philosophy, Princeton University; MFA, University of Iowa; MBA, Stanford Graduate School of Business
Background: Lecturer, College of Business, University of Iowa; Director, Hawkinson Institute of Business Finance; Co-Founder, West Lake Partners
Scott Jordon, Managing Director
Education: University of California, Berkeley; MBA, Stanford University Graduate School of Business
Background: Associate, Westbrook Partners; Senior Analyst, Morgan Stanley, Hong Kong
David Glynn, President/Managing Director
Education: University of Notre Dame; MBA, Stanford Graduate School of Business
Background: Eric Gotland Management
Vivian Loh Nahmias, Chief Financial Officer
Education: MBA, Santa Clara University
Background: Consultant, RMC Group
John Fogelsong, Managing Director
Education: BS, Computer Science, Stanford University; MBA, Stanford University Graduate School of Business
Background: Co-Founder & CEO, Wearit; Zazzle.com

837 GOAHEAD VENTURES
Menlo Park, CA

web: www.goaheadvc.com

Mission Statement: GoAhead Ventures strives to work with entrepreneurs in the earliest stages of their company. They enjoy working with students and recent graduates, believing that young entrpreneurs possess a transformative ability when building a company.

Key Executives:
Clancey Stahr, Managing Partner
Education: BS, Stanford University
Background: ZenShin Capital
Phil Brady, Managing Partner
Education: BS, Stanford University
Background: Founder, Copernican Solutions; Andreessen Horowitz
Takeshi Mori, Managing Partner
Education: BS, University of Tokyo; MS, Stanford University
Background: Co-Founder/Managing Director, ZenShin Capital; VP, OnFiber Communications Inc.

838 GOENSE & COMPANY LLC
850 West Adams Street
Chicago, IL 60607

Phone: 312-870-9511
web: www.goense.com

Mission Statement: Goense & Company is an entrepreneurial, Chicago-based private equity firm which seeks to partner with dynamic management teams to make control investments in and help grow smaller middle market businesses & services companies.

Geographic Preference: United States, Canada
Founded: 2008
Average Investment: $5 - $30 million
Investment Criteria: Industry Cosolidations, Family-Owned Business Transactions, Shareholder Liquidity, Leveraged or Mangement Buyouts, Growth Equity
Industry Group Preference: Business Products & Services
Portfolio Companies: Bayview Financial, BKA Restoration, Capital Drywall, Crosscom National, ER Experts, Imagine Technology Group, Kirby Lester Group, Melco Electric, Response Team 1, US Builder Services, Latite Roofing & Sheetmetal Company

Key Executives:
John M. Goense, Partner
312-543-2721
e-mail: jmg@goense.com
Education: MBA, University of Chicago; BS, Accounting/Business Administration, Aquinas College
Background: Managing Partner, Goense Bounds & Partners; Founder/President, Heller Equity Capital Corporation; Managing Director, Allstate Insurance Company; Harris Bank; Co-Founder/Manager, American Paging; Kidder Peabody & Company
Directorships: Indian Head Industries, Imagine Technology Group, Bayview Financial, BSI Holdings
Erik W. Bloom, Partner
312-870-9511
e-mail: ewb@goense.com
Education: BA, Economics/Business Administration, Vanderbilt University; MBA, Wharton School, University of Pennsylvania
Background: Managing Parnter, Goense Bounds & Partners; Allstate Private Equity; Management Consultant, Bain & Company; Continental Illinois Venture Corporation
Directorships: Barjan Products, L&S Plumbing, Norcraft Industries, Sportcraft, USA Media

839 GOLDEN GATE CAPITAL
One Embarcadero Center
39th Floor
San Francisco, CA 94111

Phone: 415-983-2700 Fax: 415-983-2701
web: www.goldengatecap.com

Mission Statement: A leading private equity firm that generates superior returns for our investors through buyout and growth equity investments across a wide variety of industries.

Fund Size: $12 billion
Investment Criteria: Buyouts, Growth Equity
Industry Group Preference: Software, Information Technology, Semiconductors, Electronics, Retailing, Restaurants, Consumer Products, Financial Services, Media, Industrial Services
Portfolio Companies: Aeroflex, Apogee, Appleseed's, Aspect Software, Atrium, Attachmate Group, Blair, B-Line, California Check Cashing Stores, California Pizza Kitchen, Cedarcrestone, Celetronix, Clover, Coldwater Creek, Conexant, Critigen, Crosstown Traders, Cydcor, Data Direct, Devcon, Draper's & Damon's, Eddie Bauer, Employer's Direct Insurance Company, Endurance Specialty Insurance, Ep Minerals, Escalate, Ex Libris, Express, Eye Care Centers Of America, Inc., Gxs, Haband, Hansen, Herbalife, Infor, Interstate, Itronix, J. Jill, Jazz Pharmaceuticals , Lantiq,

Lawson, Lexicon, Macaroni Grill, Massif, Max Media, Micro Focus, National Warranty Corporation, Neways, Next Model Management, Norm Thompson, On The Border, Oncore Manufacturing Services, Orchard Brands, Pacific Sunwear, Payless, Pinnacle Security, Plantcml, Rocket Dog, Sierra Systems, Signstorey, Symon, Teridian Semiconductor, Tollgrade, U.S. Silica, Vistec Semiconductor Systems, Wellco, Zale

Key Executives:
David Dominik, Managing Director
Education: AB, Harvard College; JD, Harvard Law School
Background: Manging Director, Bain Capital; Investment Committee, Brookside
Rishi Chandna, Managing Director
Education: BA, Economics, University of California, Berkeley; MBA, Harvard Business School
Background: Associate Consultant, Bain & Company
Josh Cohen, Managing Director
Education: Wharton School
Background: Vice President, Sun Capital Partners; Audax Private Equity; Morgan Stanley
Robert Kirby, Managing Director
Education: BS, Chemical Engineering, University of New Hampshire
Background: CEO, Atrium; CEO, Vi-Jon; CEO, Accellent
Rob Little, Managing Director/COO
Education: BA, English, University of Notre Dame; MBA, Duke University
Background: Limited Partner, Hellman & Friedman; Vice President, Goldman Sachs; Officer, US Navy
Felix Lo, Managing Director
Education: AB, Public Policy, Brown University
Background: Bain Capital
Steve Oetgen, Managing Director
Education: BS, Accountancy, University of Illinois; JD, Georgetown University Law Center
Background: Senior Partner, Kirkland & Ellis LLP
Josh Olshansky, Managing Director
Education: BA, Economics, University of Pennsylvania; MBA, Harvard Business School
Background: Vice President, RightOrder; Vice President, Ventro Corporation
Jim Rauh, Managing Director
Education: BA, Economics & Mathematical Methods in the Social Sciences, Northwestern University
Background: JLL Partners; Investment Banking, JP Morgan
Dave Thomas, Managing Director
Education: BBA, Finance, University of Notre Dame
Background: Senior Associate Consultant, Bain & Company

840 GOLDEN PINE VENTURES
201 West Main Street
Suite 300
Durham, NC 27701

Phone: 919-473-9296
e-mail: information@goldenpineventures.com
web: www.goldenpineventures.com

Mission Statement: Golden Pine Ventures is a venture capital firm that targets companies in the biotechnology and biomedical fields. The firm identifies companies developing revolutionary technologies and helps to create value for these businesses.

Geographic Preference: North Carolina, Southeast United States
Founded: 2004
Industry Group Preference: Life Sciences, Biotechnology, Biomedical
Portfolio Companies: Arcato Laboratories, Kylin Therapeutics, Pique Therapeutics

Key Executives:
Christopher S Meldrum, Managing Director
Education: BA, Chemistry, University of Utah; MBA, Carlson School of Management, University of Minnesota
Background: Director, Corporate Alliances, Paradigm Genetics; Licensing Associate, Purdue University
John E Hamer PhD, Director
Education: PhD, Microbiology, University of California, Davis
Background: Burrill & Company; CSO & CEO, Paradigm Genetics; Professor, Biological Sciences, Purdue University
James A Severson PhD, Director
Education: BS, Zoology, PhD, Physiology, Iowa State University
Background: VP, Global Networks for Veratect Corporation; President, Cornell Research Foundation; Amersham Corporation; President, Association of University Technology Managers

841 GOLDEN SEEDS
FDR Station
Box 642
New York, NY 10150

Phone: 888-629-6774
e-mail: info@goldenseeds.com
web: www.goldenseeds.com

Mission Statement: Golden Seeds is an investment group dedicated to supporting women entrepreneurs. Golden Seeds consists of an angel investing network as well as venture funds that focus on early stage growth companies.

Geographic Preference: United States
Founded: 2005
Average Investment: $250,000 - $2 million
Investment Criteria: Early Stage
Industry Group Preference: Consumer Products, E-Commerce & Manufacturing, Financial Services, Life Sciences, Social Media, Technology
Portfolio Companies: AboutOne, Amplyx Pharmaceuticals, Avaxia Biologics, Bergen Medical Products, Bespoke Global, Cabinet M, Chromis Fiberoptics, Cisse Cocoa, Cognition Therapeutics, Consensus Point, Crimson Hexagon, Dancing Deer Baking, Day One Response, Dry Soda, DxUpClose, Eachwin Capital, EpiEP, Gracious Eloise, Groupize, Gummicube, HarQen, Hatsize, HitFix, Kalion, Lark, Little Passports, Little Pim, Lovesac, Microenergy Credits, ModuMetal, NovaTract Surgical, nVision Medical, Open Road Media, OtoNexus, Paradigm4, Playrific, Plum Perfect, Poshly, ProSeeder, Rapt Media, RenovoRx, RuMe, Saladax, Shareablee, Source4Style, Sweetriot, Sylvatex, Tempo Automation, The Alberleen Group, TowerCare Technologies, United Catalyst, Wisegate, Work Truck Solutions, Zenflow

Key Executives:
Ao Ann Corkran, Managing Partner
Education: BS, Mathematics, New York University
Background: Global Head, Cash & Short Duration, Credit Suisse; Consulting Actuary, Econometric Modeling Area, Buck Consultants
Directorships: Crimson Hexagon
Loretta McCarthy, Managing Partner
Education: BA, University of Arizona; MBA, University of Colorado
Background: Executive VP & CMO, Oppenheimer Funds; VP, Marketing, American Express
Peggy Wallace, Managing Partner
Education: BA, George Washington University
Background: JP Morgan Chase

Venture Capital & Private Equity Firms / Domestic Firms

842 GOLDMAN SACHS INVESTMENT PARTNERS
200 West Street
New York, NY 10282

Phone: 212-902-1000
web: www.gsipventures.com

Mission Statement: Goldman Sachs targets late stage and growth equity companies with a focus on consumer and business technologies.
Geographic Preference: United States
Fund Size: $4 billion
Investment Criteria: Late Stage, Growth Equity
Industry Group Preference: Consumer, Business, Technology
Portfolio Companies: Baozen, Boqii, BOSS, Cadre, Care/of, CompareAsia, Compass, Doctor on Demand, FabHotels, Facebook, Fluid, foodpanda, GoEuro, Hubba, M-Service, Meican, Networks Insights, NextNav, Outcome Health, Pinterest, Plaid, Ring, ResearchGate, Shift, SMS Assist, Spotify, Tarena, thredUp, Uber, Zola

843 GOLDNER, HAWN, JOHNSON & MORRISON
3700 Wells Fargo Center
90 S 7th Street
Minneapolis, MN 55402-4128

Phone: 612-338-5912
e-mail: reporting@ghjm.com
web: www.ghjm.com

Mission Statement: Investment philosophy is based on flexibility, patience, and the desire to deliver those resources that will make each portfolio company successful.
Geographic Preference: Mid-West
Fund Size: $200 million
Founded: 1989
Minimum Investment: $25 million
Investment Criteria: Middle-market companies that have sound performance records, high growth potential and distinct market advantages
Industry Group Preference: Business Products & Services, Consumer Services, Industrial Products, Distribution, Consumer Products, Food & Beverage, Manufacturing, Transportation, Niche Manufacturing
Portfolio Companies: Allen Edmonds Shoe Corp., American Engineered Components, American Lock, Animart LLC, Applied Adhesives, Bankers Systems, Byerly's, Cameron's Coffee & Distribution Co., Claire-Sprayway, Control Devices LLC, Crescent Sleep Products, CTM Group Inc., Deltak, Hartzell Manufacturing, Havco Wood Products, Houlihan's Restaurants Inc., Imperial Plastics Inc., Jacobson Machine Works, Knutson Mortgage, Lancaster Laboratories, Mark VII Equipment, Michael Foods, Mid-America Entertainment, Mid Valley Industries LLC, North America Central School Bus LLC, Petermann Bus Co., Quest Events LLC, Samuel Lawrence Furniture Co., Specialty Commodities Inc., Stellar Materials LLC, Stouse LLC, Transport Corp. of America Inc., Union Metal, Universal Turbine Parts LLC, VICORP Restaurants, Vitality Foodservice, Western Reserve Products, Westlake Hardware Inc., Wilson Leather, Woodcrafts Industries

Key Executives:
Van Zandt Hawn, Managing Director/Advisor
612-347-0154
e-mail: hawn@ghjm.com
Education: Williams College; University of Virginia Law School
Background: Managing Director, Piper Jaffray; Corporate Lawyer, Davis Polk & Wardwell
Directorships: Regis Corporation; Claire-Sprayway, Union Metal Corporation, Mark VII Equipment, Lancaster Laboratories

John L. Morrison, Co-Founder/Managing Director
612-347-0159
e-mail: morrison@ghjm.com
Education: Yale University; Harvard Business School
Background: Executive VP, Pillsbury; VP, Kidder, Peabody & Company
Directorships: Andersen Corporation, Hormel Corporation, Claire-Sprayway, American Engineered Components

Timothy D. Johnson, Managing Director
612-347-0161
e-mail: johnson@ghjm.com
Education: Denison University; Kellogg School of Management, Northwestern University
Background: Group VP, First Bank System; Corporate Finance, JP Morgan
Directorships: American Engineered Components, Woodstuff Manufacturing

Chad M. Cornell, Managing Director
612-347-1070
e-mail: cornell@ghjm.com
Education: Marquette University; University of Pennsylvania Law School; CPA; CFA
Background: Corporate Development Group, Medtronic Inc.; Corporate Lawyer, Sidley Austin

Jason T. Brass, Managing Director
612-347-0172
Education: University of St. Thomas, University of Notre Dame Mendozza College of Business
Background: Norwest Equity Partners; Arthur Andersen
Directorships: Specialty Commodities, Westlake Hardware

Joseph H Heinen, Managing Partner
612-347-0171
e-mail: heinen@ghjm.com
Education: Knox College
Background: Corporate Development Group, Arthur Andersen
Directorships: Transport America, Remmele Engineering

844 GOLUB CAPITAL
666 Fifth Avenue
18th Floor
New York, NY 10103

Phone: 212-750-6060 Fax: 212-750-3756
web: www.golubcapital.com

Mission Statement: Invests in both privately and publicly held businesses, opportunistically selecting industries and geographic locations in which to invest; provides subordinated debt and equity capital to middle-market companies.
Geographic Preference: United States
Fund Size: $20 billion
Founded: 1994
Average Investment: $40 million
Minimum Investment: $10 million
Investment Criteria: Revenues in excess of $20 million, EBITDA margins greater than 10%, experienced management team, proprietary market positions, products with strong growth potential
Industry Group Preference: Consumer Products, Consumer Services, Manufacturing, Distribution, Media, Retailing, Healthcare, Food Services, Aerospace, Defense and Government, Healthcare Services, Restaurants

Other Locations:
4 Embarcadero
Suite 1400
San Francisco, CA 94111
Phone: 415-766-3549

150 South Wacker Drive
5th Floor

Chicago, IL 60606
Phone: 312-205-5050 **Fax:** 312-205-5050

139 Harbour Place
Suite 340
Davidson, NC 28036
Phone: 980-231-5657

Key Executives:
Lawrence E. Golub, Founder & Chief Executive Director
e-mail: lgolub@golubcapital.com
Education: AB, Economics, Harvard University; MBA, Harvard Business School; JD, Harvard Law School
Background: Editor, Harvard Law Review; Managing Director, Bankers Trust Company; Managing Director, Wasserstein Perella & Co; Officer, Allen & Company; Chairman, Mosholu Preservation Corporation; Treasurer, White House Fellows Foundation; President, Harvard JD-MBA Alumni Association
David B. Golub, President
e-mail: dgolub@golubcapital.com
Education: AB, Government, Harvard College; MPhil, International Relations, Univ. of Oxford; MBA, Stanford Graduate School of Business
Background: Managing Director, Centre Partners Management LLC
Gregory W. Cashman, Senior Managing Director
e-mail: gcashman@golubcapital.com
Education: BS, Commerce, University of Virginia; MBA, Darden School of Business
Background: Manager Business Development, Bristol-Myers Squibb Consumer Products Division; Sr. Accountant, Arthur Andersen & Company
Andrew H. Steuerman, Head of Middle Market & Late Stage Lending
e-mail: asteuerman@golubcapital.com
Education: BBA, Finance, Pace University; MBA, Finance, St. John's University
Background: Managing Director, Albion Alliance; Vice President, Bankers Trust Alex Brown
Gregory A. Robbins, Managing Director/Co-Head of Investor Partners Group
Education: BS, Economics, Wharton School, University of Pennsylvania
Background: Officer, Golub Capital BDC Inc.; VP, Merchant Banking Group, Indosuez Capital; Associate, Saw Mill Capital
Alissa Grad, Managing Director/Co-Head of Investor Partners Group
Education: BS, American Labor History, Cornell University
Background: Head of Marketing & Investory Relations, Jemmco Capital
Directorships: Marketing & Investor Relations, D.B. Zwirn & Co.; Business Development, TAG Associates
Christina D. Jamieson, Managing Director
Education: BBA, Accounting & MBA, Finance, University of Michigan
Background: Portfolio Manager, Senior Loan Group, Morgan Stanley Investment Management; SVP & Senior Credit Officer, First National Bank of Chicago
Directorships: Loan Syndications and Trading Association
Pierre-Olivier Lamoureux, CFO, GC Advisors LLC
Education: BBA, Accounting, HEC; MBA, Finance, NYU Stern School of Business; CPA; CFA
Background: VP, Merchant Banking Group, National Bank of Canada; Associate, Putnam Lovell NBF Securities; Associate, Arthur Andersen
Joshua M. Levinson, Co-General Counsel/Chief Compliance Officer
Education: BS, Political Science, Vanderbilt University; JD, Georgetown University Law Center
Background: Counsel, Magnetar Capital; Associate, King & Spalding; Corporate Associate, Wilson Sonsini Goodrich & Rosati; Associate Editor, Georgetown Law Journal

845 GOTHAM GREEN PARTNERS
489 5th Avenue
Suite 29A
New York, NY 10017
e-mail: info@gothamgreenpartners.com
web: gothamgreenpartners.com

Mission Statement: Invests in companies serving the cannabis industry.

Industry Group Preference: Cannabis
Portfolio Companies: The High Note, Flow Kana, Grow Generation, iAnthus

Key Executives:
Jason Adler, Managing Partner
Background: CEO, Saiers Capital; Managing Partner, Alphabet Ventures
Directorships: Cronos Group
Devin Quarles, Operating Partner
Education: BS, Integrative Biology; MS, Plant Biology, University of Illinois at Urbana-Champaign
Background: Cultivator/IPM Specialist, PureGreens; Operations Manager, MJardin
Michael Henderson-Cohen, Principal
Education: BA, Economics, Colby College; MBA, Columbia Business School
Background: Analyst/Associate, Bear Stearns; VP, JPMorgan; Analyst, Andalusian Capital Partners; Principal, 838 Partners
Daniel Finkelstein, Principal
Education: BSM, A.B. Freeman School of Business, Tulane University
Background: Founder/Owner/Manager, Storyville Spirits Co.; Founder/Owner/Manager, HenryScott Ventures; Sales Consultant, Pacific Solar; Consultant, FTRE; Owner/Principal, Timber Ridge Stable
Directorships: CID Stables

846 GRAHAM PARTNERS
3811 West Chester Pike
Building 2
Suite 200
Newtown Square, PA 19073
Phone: 610-408-0500 **Fax:** 610-408-0600
web: www.grahampartners.net

Mission Statement: Seeking to invest in privately held middle market industrial companies.

Geographic Preference: United States, Canada, Western Europe
Fund Size: $1.5 billion
Founded: 1988
Average Investment: $50 million
Minimum Investment: $10 million
Investment Criteria: Domestic industrial businesses with revenues between $20-$250 million
Industry Group Preference: Plastics, Business Products & Services, Manufacturing, Industrial Equipment, Building Materials & Services, Transportation, Packaging
Portfolio Companies: Abrisa Technologies, Acme Cryogenics, Anaheim, Asahi Tec/Trimas, The Atlas Group, B+B SmartWorx, Berry, BrightPet Nutrition Group, Chelsea, Comar, Creative Mines, Desser Tire, Dynojet, EasyPak, Eberle, Eldorado Stone, Exteria, HB&G Building Products Inc., HemaSource, Henry, ICG Commerce, Infiltrator Systems, Line-X, The Masonry Group, Mercer Foods, Mitten, NDS, OptConnect, Schneller, SP Industries, Strata, Supreme Corq, Tidel, Transaxle, Universal Pure, Western Industries

Key Executives:
Steven C. Graham, Chief Executive Officer
Education: BA, Philosophy/English, Williams College; MBA, Amos Tuck School of Business, Dartmouth College
Background: Senior Group VP, Graham Packaging Company; Investment Banking Division, Goldman, Sachs

& Company; Acquisition Officer, RAF Group
Directorships: Western Industries, National Diversified Sales, Eldorado Stone, HB&G Building Products, Nailite International, ICG Commerce
Bill McKee Jr., Chief Operating Officer
e-mail: bmckee@grahampartners.net
Education: BS, Economics, Wharton School, University of Pennsylvania
Background: Investment Banking Division, Bear Stearns
Directorships: National Diversified Sales, HB&G Building Products, Eldorado Stone
Christopher Lawler, Managing Principal
e-mail: clawler@grahampartners.net
Education: BS, Business Administration, University of Richmond; MBA, Wharton School, University of Pennsylvania
Background: Vice President, Financial Sponsors Gropu, NationsBanc Montgomery Securities; Vice President, NationsBank's Corporate Finance Group
Directorships: Dynojet, Schneller, Supreme Corq, Western Industries
Christina Morin, Managing Principal/Investor Relations
e-mail: cmorin@grahampartners.net
Education: BA, Economics, University of Virginia; MBA, Wharton School, University of Pennsylvania
Background: Investment Banking, Goldman Sachs & Co.; Borders, Inc.
Directorships: Abrisa, Eldorado, HB&g
Robert Newbold, Managing Principal
e-mail: rnewbold@grahampartners.net
Education: BA, Business Administration, MA, Accounting, University of Texas; MBA, Wharton School, University of Pennsylvania
Background: Private Equity Group, Investcorp; Goldman Sachs & Co.
Directorships: B&B, Dynojet, Eldorado, HB&G, Infiltrator, National Diversified Sales, StormTech, TransAxle
Adam Piatkowski, Managing Principal
e-mail: apiatkowski@grahampartners.net
Education: BA, Economics, Williams College; CFA
Background: Equity Analyst, Monitor Asset Management; Mangement Consultant, Monitor Group
Directorships: Schneller
Andrew Snyder, Managing Principal
e-mail: asnyder@grahampartners.net
Education: BA, Political Science, Amherst College; MBA, Wharton School, University of Pennsylvania
Background: Concert Capital Partners; Adams Harkness Inc.
Directorships: Abrisa, B&B, TransAxle
Joshua Wilson, Managing Principal
e-mail: jwilson@grahampartners.net
Education: BA, Finance, James Madison University
Background: Global Investment Banking Division, Chase Securities
Directorships: Dynojet, Exteria Building Products, HB&G, Infiltrator, Line-X, Supreme Corq, TransAxle
Joseph Heinmiller, Managing Principal
e-mail: jheinmiller@grahampartners.com
Education: BS, Accountancy, Villanova University
Background: Investment Banking Analyst, Banc of America Securities
Directorships: Exteria Building Products, Infiltrator
William Timmerman III, Managing Principal
e-mail: wtimmerman@grahampartners.net
Education: BA, Economics, Vanderbilt University
Background: Director, M&A Group, UBS Securities

847 GRAND CENTRAL HOLDINGS
475 Park Avenue South
4th Floor
New York, NY 10016

Phone: 212-625-9710
web: www.grandcentralholdings.com

Mission Statement: Invests in technology-related businesses, with a fund consisting of ten holdings in the healthcare information, financial service technology and transportation industries.
Geographic Preference: Northeast
Founded: 1999
Average Investment: $1-$3 million
Minimum Investment: $250,000
Industry Group Preference: Healthcare Information Technology, Financial Services, Transportation
Portfolio Companies: Castle Connolly, Ez-Ways.Com, Free Decision, Japan Internet Ventures, MedEViewing, Online Benefits, Peanutpress.Com, Performance Logic

Key Executives:
Gregory C. Belmont, Managing Partner
Education: MIT; Harvard University
Background: Arthur D Little; Mercer Management Consulting; The Wilkerson Group

848 GRANDBANKS CAPITAL
75 Second Avenue
Suite 360
Needham, MA 02494

Phone: 781-997-4300 Fax: 781-997-4301
e-mail: info@grandbankscapital.com
web: www.grandbankscapital.com

Mission Statement: To offer operating expertise and industry experience, build successful companies, and secure long-term capital gains. GrandBanks Capital seeks opportunities with early stage companies in the software, security, mobile media, financial technology, wireless technology and Internet technology sectors. The firm primarily invests in businesses based in the eastern region of the United States.
Geographic Preference: East Coast
Fund Size: $125 million
Founded: 2000
Average Investment: $1 - $5 million
Minimum Investment: $1 million
Investment Criteria: Early Stage
Industry Group Preference: Infrastructure, Software Services, Security, Media, Financial Services, Wireless Technologies, Internet Technology, Storage, Software, Mobile Media, Wireless Services, Fintech
Portfolio Companies: Achievers, Celtra Technologies, Clearfit, Coherent Path, Defense Mobile, Dispatch, EachScape, Knowledge Vision, SilverRail Technologies, TIM Group

Key Executives:
Charles R Lax, Co-Founder/Managing General Partner
Education: BS, Boston University
Background: Founding General Partner, SOFTBANK Venture Capital; VP, SOFTBANK Holdings; Venture Partner, VIMAC Ventures; Co-Founder, Flatiron Partners; Phoenix Technologies
Directorships: Defense Mobile, GlassHouse Technologies, KnowledgeVision, SilverRail Technologies, TIM Group
Tim Wright, General Partner
Education: BS, City University, London
Background: CEO, International Operations, Geac Computer Corporation; Senior VP, CTO & CIO, Terra Lycos SA; Senior VP & CIO, The Learning Company
Directorships: Celtra, Achievers, EachScape, Nexage, Coherent Path, Bison, TechStars Boston, ClearFit
Jeffrey P Parker, Venture Partner
Education: Bachelor & Master of Engineering, MBA, Cornell University
Background: Founder, Technical Data Corporation; Founder, First Call Corporation; Chairman & CEO, Thomson Financial; Co-Founder, 38 Newbury Ventures; Co-Founder, Chairman & CEO, CCBN.com
Directorships: KnowledgeVision, First Coverage

Venture Capital & Private Equity Firms / Domestic Firms

JJ Healy, Venture Partner
Education: BS, Chemistry, Saint Anselm College; MBA, International Finance, American Graduate School of International Management
Background: VP, Corporate Development, Yahoo!; Principal, Von Gehr International; VP, Credit Suisse First Boston; EMC Corporation

849 GRANITE BRIDGE PARTNERS
420 Lexington Avenue
Suite 920
New York, NY 10170
Phone: 646-599-9900
e-mail: info@granitebridge.com

Mission Statement: Private equity firm that seeks to invest in and build successful middle-market companies.

Founded: 1991
Average Investment: $10-$30 million
Minimum Investment: $8 million
Investment Criteria: Expansion, Consolidation, Recapitalizations
Industry Group Preference: Services, Consumer Products, Manufacturing
Portfolio Companies: All Island Media, American Higher Educaion Development, Best Lighting Products, Century Fire Protection, Custom Wood Products, Freedom Scientific, Integrated Cable Assembly Holdings, MariTEL, Microdynamics Group, Mitchell Gold + Bob Williams, Phelps Industries, Smiles Services, Teraco

Key Executives:
Peter Petrillo, Managing Partner
Education: MBA, New York University; BS, Accounting, State University of New York Albany
Background: Partner, Claymore Partners, Vice President, Lambert Brussels Capital Corporation; CPA
Michael D Goodman, Partner
Education: MBA, New York University; BS, Economics, Cornell University
Background: Principal, Equinox Investment Partners, Vice President, Chase Manhattan Bank
Ryan Wierck, Partner
Education: MBA, Columbia Business School; BS Economics, Wharton School, University of Pennsylvania
Background: Oppenheimer & Co - M&A and Corporate Finance Departments
Jeffrey P Gerson, Partner
Education: BA, History, University of Pennsylvania; MBA, MIT Sloan School of Management
Background: Associate, Lane, Berry & Co.; Associate, Rhone Capital LLC; Analyst, Salomon Smith Barney

850 GRANITE EQUITY PARTNERS
122 12th Avenue North
Suite 201
St. Cloud, MN 56303
Phone: 320-251-1800 Fax: 320-251-1804
e-mail: rick@graniteequity.com
web: www.graniteequity.com

Mission Statement: Private equity firm seeking co-ownership for portfolio companies in industrial companies focused on energy and manufacturing.

Geographic Preference: Minnesota, Wisconsin, Iowa, North Dakota, South Dakota
Founded: 2002
Investment Criteria: Companies with at least $5 million of revenue, Buyouts, Recapitalizations, Business Expansions and managers who have proven track records
Industry Group Preference: Manufacturing, Service Industries, Media, Distribution, Agriculture, Communications
Portfolio Companies: Aeration Industries, All Flex, Altimate Medical, Dezurik, GeoComm, Geotek, Massman Automation, Microbiologics, Vector

Other Locations:
Calhoun Beach Club
2925 Dean Parkway
Suite 300
Minneapolis, MN 55416
Phone: 612-925-8350 Fax: 612-925-8320

Key Executives:
Richard Bauerly, Managing Partner/CEO
e-mail: rick@graniteequity.com
Education: MA, Business Administration, Harvard Business School; MA, Public Administration, Harvard University; BA, Economics, Saint John's University
Background: Founder, Venture Allies; Bauerly Brothers Incorporated; Deloitte & Touche Consulting Group
Directorships: DeZurik Water Controls; UniqueScreen Media; Anderson Entrepreneurial Center; CentraCare Health System
Patrick Edeburn, Partner
Education: MA, Business Administration, Harvard Business School; BA, Carleton College
Background: Medtronic; Deloitte & Touche Consulting Group
Directorships: Vinylite Windows; Heartland Communications; Anderson Entrepreneurial Center
Arthur Monaghan, Senior Advisor
e-mail: art@graniteequity.com
Education: BA, University of Notre Dame
Background: Principal, Norwest Equity Partners; Arthur Andersen's Management Consulting Group
Directorships: Heartland Communications; UniqueScreen Media; Vinylite Windows

851 GRANITE HILL CAPITAL PARTNERS, LLC
750 Battery St.
Suite 400
San Francisco, CA 94111
Phone: 415-903-1457
web: www.granitehill.net

Mission Statement: Granite Hill India Opportunities Fund is a venture and growth equity fund focused on India-related as well as selected High Tech investment opportunities. The fund is distinguished by the deep operating experience, investment track record, and the strong business network of the Partners. The three investment professionals have over 40 years of total investment and operating experience in Silicon Valley and India. India's economic growth, along with the wide range of private business which need to scale to meet robust demand, provides a unique opportunity for investment returns. In particular, we believe Financial Services, High Tech, Sustainability and Education are among the most promising verticals.

Geographic Preference: India, United States,
Industry Group Preference: Technology, Financial Services, Retail, Consumer & Leisure, Sustainability, Life Sciences
Portfolio Companies: Airspace, Aptus, Arceo Analytics, Attero Recycling, The Beer Café, CL Educate, Craxel, Efflux Systems, Imubit, Manappura, NAFA, nCrypted Cloud, Netcitadel, Orange Retail Finance India, Palantir, Seed Infotech, SentinelOne, Tamr, Treatful

Key Executives:
Shailesh Mehta, General Partner
e-mail: shailesh@granitehill.net
Education: BS, Mechanical Engineering, IIT-Bombay; PhD, Operations Research, Case Western Reserve
Background: Chairman and CEO, Providian Financial; Executive VP, AmeriTrust (now KeyCorp); Operating General Partner, WestBridge Capital
Sameet Mehta, Managing General Partner
e-mail: sameet@granitehill.net
Education: BS, Electrical Engineering, Princeton; MBA, Stanford University
Background: Cisco; Lehman Brothers

303

Venture Capital & Private Equity Firms / Domestic Firms

Kamil Hassan, General Partner
e-mail: kamil@granitehill.net
Education: MS, Engineering, MIT; PhD, Engineering, UC Berkeley
Directorships: America India Foundation

852 GRANITE VENTURES
300 Montgomery Street
Suite 638
San Francisco, CA 94104

Phone: 415-591-7700 Fax: 415-591-7720
web: www.granitevc.com

Mission Statement: Partners with promising and successful entrepreneurs to create businesses that have a competitive edge and achieve category leadership.

Geographic Preference: United States
Fund Size: $1 billion
Founded: 1998
Average Investment: $500,000 - $4 million
Investment Criteria: Seed, Series A & B, Early-Stage
Industry Group Preference: Technology, Application Software
Portfolio Companies: Agilence, Airbnb, AirPair, Anaplan, Aspen Avionics, Blockcypher, Fastback Networks, HireVue, Hobo Labs, HyTrust, Kindly, Kity, Lucidworks, Marqeta, Mojo Networks, Motiv, SellPoints, Smule, Survios, Telltale Games, Workboard, Arcot Systems, Auditude, AvantGo, Bidclerk, Bunchball, Cardiff Software, Connected, Convio, Digimarc, DigitalThink, Direct Medical Knowledge, Empowered Careers, Entropic Communications, Episodic, Five Across, Fractal Design, Fulcrum Microsystems, GigaNet, InfoGear Technology, Internap, Kontiki, Liquent, LSSi Data, Managing Editor, Mixamo, Navini Networks, NetBoost, Nexabit Networks, Oversight Systems, Ozmo, Percello, Plumtree, PSS Systems, Purisma, Quantance, Salon.com, Sense, Shutterly, Siebel Systems, Sierra Wireless, Skytide, SnapTrack, Speakeasy, StepUp Commerce, Symplified, Trovix, Tumbleweed Communications, Vignette, Virage

Key Executives:
Chris McKay, Managing Director
e-mail: cmckay@granitevc.com
Education: BA, University of Virginia
Background: Hambrecht & Quist
Directorships: HireVue, Lucidworks, Marqeta, Arcot Systems, Purisma, Sendmail, Symplified
Standish O'Grady, Managing Director
e-mail: sogrady@granitevc.com
Education: BSE, Chemical Engineering, Princeton University; MBA, Dartmouth College Tuck School of Business Administration
Background: Hambrecht & Quist
Directorships: Anaplan, Telltale Games, HyTrust, SellPoint
Jackie Berterretche, Managing Director/CFO
e-mail: jackieb@granitevc.com
Education: BS, Accounting, University of San Francisco; CPA
Background: CFO, Hambrecht & Quist Venture Capital; Audit Manager, Ernst & Young

853 GRANTHAM CAPITAL
5335 Wisconsin Ave. NW
Suite 400
Washington, DC 20015

Phone: 202-495-5939
web: www.granthamllc.com

Mission Statement: Grantham Capital makes select investments in US-based small businesses where we can provide significant value.

Geographic Preference: United States
Investment Criteria: Small Businesses
Industry Group Preference: Healthcare Services, Medical Devices, Infrastructure, Logistics, Business Services, Distribution, Transportation, Light Manufacturing
Portfolio Companies: Capstone Logistics, EDI, Energy Source, Fisk, Image Ware Systems, Intra Links, Iridian Technologies, NDS, Pharma Logic, Quantum Medical Imaging, Raleigh, Superior Recreational Products, Tegra Medical, Wave

Key Executives:
William Ford, Managing Partner
e-mail: bford@granthamllc.com
Education: BS, St. Lawrence University; MBA, Tuck School of Business, Dartmouth College
Background: SVP & Managing Director, MCG Capital; Managing Director, Perseus LLC; VP, Butler Capital Corp.; Price Waterhouse; General Electric
Michael Van Vleck, Managing Partner
202-247-0673
e-mail: mvanvleck@granthamllc.com
Education: BS, University of New Hampshire; MA, University of Pennsylvania; MBA, Wharton School
Background: Co-Founder & President, GeoGlobal Energy; Founder, Integra Partners

854 GRAPHENE VENTURES
530 Lytton Avenue
2nd Floor
Palo Alto, CA 94301

web: www.graphenevc.com

Mission Statement: Graphene bring strength, tranparency, and flexibility to their projects. They propel tech startups towards growth and maximize their returns.

Key Executives:
Nabil Borhanu, President and Managing Member
Education: MBA
Background: Guest Speaker; Entrepreneur

855 GRAY GHOST VENTURES
2200 Century Parkway
Suite 100
Atlanta, GA 30345

Phone: 678-365-4700 Fax: 678-365-4752
e-mail: info@grayghostventures.com
web: www.grayghostventures.com

Mission Statement: Gray Ghost Ventures is dedicated to investing in early-stage businesses who seek to serve low-income communities in developing nations.

Geographic Preference: India, South Asia, Sub-Saharan Africa
Fund Size: $100 million
Founded: 2005
Average Investment: $5 million
Investment Criteria: Start-Ups, Early-Stage
Industry Group Preference: Microfinance, Clean Technology, Information Technology
Portfolio Companies: Babajob, Beam, bKash, CellBazaar, d.light, Emergence BioEnergy, iSend, mDhil, M-Kopa, Movirtu, ParaLife, PharmaSecure, Range Networks, RentBureau, SourceTrace Systems, United Villages

Other Locations:
8/16, Seethammal Extension
2nd Cross Street
Chennai 600 018
India

Key Executives:
Arun Gore, President/Chief Executive Officer
Education: BSc, Sciences, BS, Accounting, MBA, Finance
Background: CFO, T-Mobile USA
Ashwini Sahasrabudhe, Chief Financial Officer
Education: BComm, University of Mumbai; CPA; CA

Venture Capital & Private Equity Firms / Domestic Firms

Background: Larsen & Toubro; Western Union; Marico Industries; Mattel & Ashok Piramal Group
Brian Cayce, Vice President, Investments
Education: BA, University of Georgia; MBA, Finance, Georgia State University
Background: Benevolink; Deputy Director, CARE International; Consultant, KPMG
Brenda Bracken, Treasurer
Education: Virginia Commonwealth University
Background: Controller, Robert Pattillo Properties; AP DW Industrial Portfolio; American Resurgens Management Corporation; Fleitz Construction Company; Weyman & Kruse; Graphic Ads
Bahniman Hazarika, Director of Investments
Education: BComm, Accounting, Shriram College of Commerce, University of Delhi; MBA, Finance and Accounting, Emory University
Background: Viscogliosi Brothers; Navigation Capital Partners; Ernst & Young

856 GRAYHAWK CAPITAL
4250 N Drinkwater Blvd
Suite 300
Scottsdale, AZ 85251

Phone: 602-956-8700
web: www.grayhawkcapital.us

Mission Statement: Invests in early stage and growth stage companies based in the southwestern region of the United States. Grayhawk Capital seeks companies with outstanding management teams and innovative product offerings in quickly growing technology markets.

Geographic Preference: Southwestern United States
Fund Size: $70 million
Founded: 2000
Average Investment: $1 - $15 million
Minimum Investment: $1 million
Investment Criteria: Early Stage, Growth Stage
Industry Group Preference: Financial Services, Consumer Products, Software, Internet Technology, Telecommunications, Healthcare Information Technology, Semiconductors, Business to Business, Cloud Computing, Mobile, Security
Portfolio Companies: Account Now, Alianza, AppsFreedom, Apptentive, BlueCedar, BroadHop, Camstar, CareFx, CellzDirect, Coinstar, Communispace, Efficient Networks, Environmental Support Solutions, eVisit, Folloze, Golfnow, Horizon Organic Dairy, Health Outcomes Sciences, Innovasic, Intesource, Itax Group, Lucid Software, MarketTools, MX Logic, Myriad Genetics, New Century Financial Corporation, P-Com, Plastc, PowerQuest, Profitect, Quality Care Solutions, Response Analytics Inc., Ribbit, Ryver, Siverion, Small Box Energy, SOCi, StackIQ, SyncHR, Totango

Key Executives:
  Sherman I Chu, Co-Founder/Managing Partner
  Education: BS, Marketing, University of Arizona; MBA, Texas A&M University
  Background: Partner, Cornerstone Equity Partners; Assistant VP, Banc One Capital Partners
  Directorships: AccountNow, Intesource, TM International
  Brian N Burns, Co-Founder/Managing Partner
  Education: BS, Accounting, Arizona State University; CPA
  Background: VP, SunVen Capital; Anderson & Wells; VP & CFO, Pinnacle West Capital Corp.; Senior Manager, Audit Division, Arthur Andersen & Co.
  Directorships: AppsFreedom, Innovasic, TM International
  Brian S Smith, Managing Partner
  Education: BS, Brigham Young University; MBA, Kelley School of Business, Indiana University
  Background: Managing Director, Peninsula Ventures; Dominion Ventures; Emerging Business Services Consultant, Deloitte Haskins & Sells
  Directorships: Contatta, Integrated Photovoltaics, Intesource, Response Analytics

857 GREAT HILL PARTNERS LLC
200 Clarendon Street
29th Floor
Boston, MA 02116

Phone: 617-790-9400 **Fax:** 617-790-9401

Mission Statement: Great Hill Partners is a private equity firm that invests in growing middle market businesses in the software, media, communications, financial technology, business services, consumer services and healthcare industries.

Fund Size: $1.1 billion
Founded: 1998
Average Investment: $25 - $150 million
Investment Criteria: All investment stages beyond early stage, Acquisitions, Recapitalizations, Consolidations, Growth Equity
Industry Group Preference: Business to Business, Consumer Services, Fintech, Healthcare, Information Technology, Media, Communications, Software
Portfolio Companies: AffiniPay, BlueSnap, Bombas, CliqStudios, Custom Ink, Evolve IP, Examity, G/O Media, Ikon Science, Intapp, Mineral Tree, NMI, Pareto Health, PartsSource, Paytronix Systems Inc., Quantum Health, Reflexis, Reward Gateway, RxBenefits, The RealReal, TodayTix, Vanco, Vatica Health, YogaWorks

Key Executives:
  Christopher S. Gaffney, Managing Partner
  617-790-9420
  e-mail: cgaffney@greathillpartners.com
  Education: BS, Economics & Accounting, Boston College
  Background: Associate, Principal & General Partner, M/C Partners; Commercial Lending Officer, First National Bank of Boston
  Directorships: IntApp, Recruiting.com
  John G. Hayes, Senior Advisor
  617-790-9418
  e-mail: hayes@greathillpartners.com
  Education: BA, Economics, Williams College; MBA, Harvard Business School
  Background: Senior Associate, M/C Partners; Loan Officer, Bank of Boston
  Directorships: Ascenty, Symmetry Holdings
  Michael A. Kumin, Managing Partner
  e-mail: mkumin@greathillpartners.com
  Education: BA, Woodrow Wilson School of Public & International Affairs, Princeton University
  Background: Co-Founder & Executive VP, Creative Planet Incorporated; Associate, Apollo Advisors; Analyst, Goldman Sachs
  Directorships: Momondo Group, YogaWorks, The Shade Store, Legacy.com, Wayfair, SheKnows Media, Educaedu, Recruiting.com
  Mark D. Taber, Managing Partner
  617-790-9448
  e-mail: taber@greathillpartners.com
  Education: BA, Public Policy Studies, Duke University; JL Kellogg Graduate School of Management
  Background: Boston Consulting Group; Westlake Capital Group
  Directorships: RxBenefits, Qualifacts, DealerRater
  Matthew T. Vettel, Managing Partner
  617-790-9432
  e-mail: mvettel@greathillpartners.com
  Education: BS, Industrial Engineering & Management, North Dakota State University; MBA, Harvard Business School
  Background: Associate, GTCR Golder Rauner; Senior Associate, Accenture; Founding Member, PureSpeech
  Directorships: AffiniPay, Chrome River Technologies, Network Merchants, PlanSource, Reward Gateway, Vanco Payment Solutions, BlueSnap

Venture Capital & Private Equity Firms / Domestic Firms

Christopher M. Busby, Partner
e-mail: busby@greathillpartners.com
Education: BA, Political Science & History, University of North Carolina at Chapel Hill; MBA, Harvard Business School
Background: Analyst, JP Morgan; Associate, GCC Investments
Directorships: Reward Gateway, PlanSource, Vanco Payment Solutions, BlueSnap

858 GREAT OAKS VENTURE CAPITAL
660 Madison Avenue
Suite 1600
New York, NY 10065

Phone: 212-821-1800
e-mail: info@greatoaksvc.com
web: www.greatoaksvc.com

Mission Statement: Great Oaks Venture Capital is a seed-stage investment firm committed to identifying, financing and developing early-stage growth businesses led by promising entrepreneurs.

Average Investment: $50,000 - $500,000
Investment Criteria: Seed-Stage, Early-Stage
Industry Group Preference: E-Commerce & Manufacturing, Consumer Products, Advertising, Education, SaaS, Cloud Computing, Mobile, Social Media, Gaming
Portfolio Companies: 1 Doc Way, 33 Across, 500friends, Able Health, Acorns, Adcade, Affinity, Akido, Allbirds, Aloha, AptDeco, Arbor, Atomic, AugMedix, Away, Beaconhome, Bellhops, Despoke Post, Bluecrew, Blueshift, Boatsetter, Bolt, Bomfell, Bonobos, Breakthrough, Brewster, Built Robotics, Call9, Cameo, Canopy, Captain401, CardFlight, Cardpool, Chartio, Choozle, Circulate, Classkick, Cleanify, ClearGraph, Collective Health, Conduit, Conselytics, Counsyl, Course Hero, CoVenture, Cover, Crimson Hexagon, Directr, Discover.ly, Down, Dramafever, Drunc, Eat Club, Eat Street, Eaze, Eero, EquipmentShare, Expii, Fatherly, Fathom, Fetch, Flatiron, FlightCar, Future Advisor, Genies, GrubMarket, Health AP, Helix Sleep, Herb, Hinge, Hired, Homer, Houzz, HowGood, Huckleberry, Hullabalu, Hungry Root, Ibotta, Icon, ImageBrief, Interior Define, Interviewed, Invite Media, Joor, Jumpcut, Kickback, Kinnek, Kip, Knock, Knotch, Knowsy, Le Souk, Levo League, Locket, Lofty, Loom, Loverly, Love With Food, Mettermark, Maven, MemSQL, MightyBell, Minibar, Mino Games, ModCloth, Mojilala, Momentum Machines, Mortar, Move Loot, Notable Labs, Nylas, Okcupid, Olapic, Oportun, OrderAhead, Parcel, Pay Off, Peek, Permutation, Petal, Picasso Labs, PicnicHealth, Plastiq, Plated, Pluto, PocketGems, Popular Pays, Porter Road, Priori Legal, Propeller, Pure Wow, ReadMe, RecoverX, Replenish, Rep The Squad, RigUp, Rinse, Rise, Rise Art, Rock Health, Roostock, Roomi, Rumble, Sapho, Schoology, Scoutible, Seed Invest, Shift, SkyVu, SmithRx

Key Executives:

Andy Boszhardt, Founder/Managing Partner
Education: BS, Accounting, MBA, University of Wisconsin-Madison
Background: Managing Director & Portfolio Manager, Neuberger Berman; Goldman Sachs

Ben Lin, Venture Partner
Education: BS, Economics, Wharton School, University of Pennsylvania
Background: Global Investment Research, Goldman Sachs & Co.

John Philosophos, Partner, Business Development
Education: BS, Finance & Marketing, University of Wisconsin-Madison
Background: Co-Founder, Managing Partner, Wellspring Capital Advisors

Celine Kwok, Chief Financial Officer
Education: BA, Economics, Columbia University
Background: Analyst, Morgan Stanley

859 GREAT POINT PARTNERS
165 Mason Street
Third Floor
Greenwich, CT 06830

Phone: 203-971-3300 Fax: 203-971-3320
web: www.gppfunds.com

Mission Statement: The principals of Great Point Partners have a long history of helping executives build successful healthcare companies.

Geographic Preference: United States
Fund Size: $156 million
Founded: 2003
Average Investment: $7 million - $25 million
Minimum Investment: $7 million
Investment Criteria: Recapitalizations, Growth Capital, Acquisitions, Management Buyouts, Corporate Spin-Offs
Industry Group Preference: Healthcare, Life Sciences, Healthcare Services, Healthcare Information Technology, Medical Devices, Pharmaceuticals
Portfolio Companies: American Surgical Professionals, Aris Teleradiology, Autism Learning Partners, Biotronic NeuroNetwork, Caprion Proteomics, Citra Health Solutions, Clinical Supplies Management, Connecture, Corrona, Cytovance Biologics, Equian, Mediatech Inc., Pro PT, Softbox Systems, United Claim Solutions, VitaLink Research

Key Executives:

Jeffrey R. Jay, MD, Managing Director
e-mail: jjay@gppfunds.com
Education: BA, MD, Boston University; MBA, Harvard Business School
Background: JH Whitney & Co., Canaan Partners, Salomon Brothers

David E. Kroin, Managing Director
e-mail: dkroin@gppfunds.com
Education: BS, University of Michigan
Background: JH Whitney & Co.; Merrill Lynch & Co.

Adam B. Dolder, Managing Director
e-mail: adolder@gppfunds.com
Education: BS, Wake Forest University; MBA, Harvard Business School
Background: JP Morgan Partners; JP Morgan Securities

Joseph Pesce, Managing Director/Operating Partner
e-mail: jpesce@gppfunds.com
Education: AB, Boston College; MBA, Wharton School, University of Pennsylvania
Background: Thomas H Lee Partners, Renaissance Worldwide, Concentra Managed Care

Noah F. Rhodes III, Managing Director
e-mail: nrhodes@gppfunds.com
Education: BS, Washington & Lee University
Background: Wachovia Securities, Forest Hill Capital

Rohan Saikia, Manaing Director
e-mail: rsaikia@gppfunds.com
Education: BA, Columbia University
Background: Cowen & Company

860 GREEN LION PARTNERS
2209 Larimer Street
Denver, CO 80205

e-mail: contact@greenlionpartners.com
web: www.greenlionpartners.com

Mission Statement: Invests in various consumer product companies within the cannabis industry. Green Lion is dedicated to elevating the public perception of cannabis through responsible and respectable business practices and partnerships.

Founded: 2015
Investment Criteria: Early-Stage
Industry Group Preference: Cannabis
Portfolio Companies: LeafList, Natural Order Supply, Dip Devices, America Isreal Cannabis Association, Two Bridges Design

Venture Capital & Private Equity Firms / Domestic Firms

Key Executives:
Jeffrey M. Zucker, President
Education: BS, Business Admin./Management, Questrom School of Business, Boston University
Background: Co-Founder, Raining Combos; Director of Business Development, The InterTech Group; President/Co-Founder, Leaflist; President, America Isreal Cannabis Association; President, Devices; Co-Founder, Big Smits Entertainment; President, Two Bridges Design; Founder/President/CEOm, Saltshaker Holdings
Directorships: Marijuana Policy Project
Mike Bologna, Chief Executive Officer
Education: BS, Marketing/Operations, School of Management, Boston University
Background: Supply Chain Buyer, General Dynamics C4 Systems; Subcontracts Manager, UTC Aerospace Systems; Trade & Logistics Consultant, Edgewater Fullscope

861 GREEN TOWER CAPITAL
20595 Arrow Creek Drive
Leesburg, VA 20175

Mission Statement: A hedge fund investing in companies serving the cannabis industry.

Founded: 2017
Industry Group Preference: Cannabis, Big Data, Info Technology, Machine Learning
Key Executives:
Ryan Gehringer, Chief Executive Officer
Background: CEO, Ripplechrome; Co-Founder, FindaFixr
Dan Chiriaev, Managing Director
Education: BA, Economics/Applied Math; Undergraduate Certificate in Conflict Management, Pepperdine University
Background: Chief Marketing Officer, CoArt; Co-Founder/CEO, Aarde.io

862 GREENBRIAR EQUITY GROUP LLC
555 Theodore Fremd Avenue
Suite A-201
Rye, NY 10580

Phone: 914-925-9600
e-mail: info@greenbriarequity.com
web: www.greenbriarequity.com

Mission Statement: Private equity firm focused exclusively on making investments in the global transportation industry, an area to which it brings distinct expertise and substantial resources.

Fund Size: $1.1 billion
Founded: 1999
Average Investment: $75 to $150 million
Minimum Investment: $50 million
Investment Criteria: LBO, Recapitalization, Growth Capital, Joint Ventures
Industry Group Preference: Global Industries, Transportation, Aerospace, Defense and Government, Logistics, Distribution
Portfolio Companies: Active Aero Group Holdings Inc., AerGen Leasing, Align Aerospace Holdings Inc., American Tire Distributors Inc., AmSafe Partners Inc., Ardmore Shipholding Ltd., Argo-Tech Corporation, Arotech, BDP International, DART Aerospace, EDAC Technologies, Electrical Source Holdings, Electro-Motive Diesel Inc., Frauscher Sensor Technology, GB Auto Service Inc., GENCO Distribution System Inc., Grakon International Inc., Hexcel Corporation, LaserShip, Lazer Spot Inc., Morgan Auto Group, Muth Mirror Systems, Nordco Holdings LLC, PetroChoice Holdings Inc., Ryan Herco Flow Solutions, SEKO Logistics, Stag-Parkway Inc., Spireon Inc., STS Aviation Group, Tinnerman Palnut Engineered Products Inc., Transplace Holdings, Western Peterbilt Inc., Whitcraft Group, World Freight Company International

Key Executives:
Gerald Greenwald, Chair
Education: BA, Princeton University; MA, Wayne State University
Background: Chairman/CEO, UAL Corporation; Vice Chairman/CFO, Chrysler Corporation
Reginald L. Jones III, Co-Founder/Managing Partner
Education: BA, Williams College; MBA, Harvard Business School
Background: Investment Banker, Goldman Sachs
John Daileader, Managing Director
Education: BS, Management, Renssalaer Polytechnic Institute; MBA, Stern School of Business, New York University
Background: Principal, JP Morgan Partners; Chemical Bank; Manufacturers Hanover Trust Company; National Westminster Bank
Jill C. Raker, Managing Director
Education: BS, Boston College Carroll School of Management; MBA, Harvard Business School
Background: Principal, Compass Partners International; Associate, The Blackstone Group
Noah Roy, Managing Director
Education: BS, Georgetown University
Background: Managing Director, Goldman Sachs & Co.; Rothschild Inc.
Niall McComiskey, Managing Director
Education: BA, Economics, Yale University
Background: M&A Group, Deutsche Bank AG
Michael Weiss, Managing Director
Education: BA, Duke University
Background: Financial Sponsor & Leveraged Finance Group, Merrill Lynch & Co.

863 GREENHAVEN PARTNERS
9 W Broad Street
Suite 430
Stamford, CT 06902

Phone: 203-930-2702
web: www.greenhavenpartners.com

Mission Statement: Greenhaven Partners invests in and builds emerging businesses focused on developing information products and software.

Investment Criteria: Startups, Acquisitions
Industry Group Preference: Media, Publishing, Software
Portfolio Companies: Affirmify, Bongarde Holdings, Chief Executive Group, Dashboard Director, Institute of Finance & Management, Kennedy Information, LA 411, Pyramid Research, RecruitingTrends, Vizeum

Key Executives:
Wayne Cooper, Managing Partner
Education: BA, Stanford University; MBA, Harvard Business School
Background: CEO, Kennedy Information; Chairman & CEO, Visium; Consultant, Bain & Company; Monitor Company
Directorships: Bongarde Media, Chief Executive Group, Institute of Finance & Management
Marshall Cooper, Managing Partner
Education: BA, History & Political Science, University of Michigan; MBA, Tuck School of Business, Dartmouth College
Background: M&A, K-III Communications; The New York Times Company; Editor, Daily White House News Summary; President, Kennedy Information
Directorships: Bongarde, Chief Executive Group, Institute of Finance & Management, AIPAC
Giles Goodhead, Partner
Education: Cambridge University; MBA, Stanford University
Background: Stategy Consultant, Monitor Company; CEO, LA411/Media Publishing International
Directorships: Bongarde, Pyramid Research, TGI

Venture Capital & Private Equity Firms / Domestic Firms

864 GREENHILL SAVP
300 Park Avenue
New York, NY 10022
Phone: 212-389-1600 Fax: 212-389-1805
e-mail: rfg@greenhill.com
web: www.greenhill.com

Mission Statement: Specializes in small, worthy companies, providing them with money and high-quality advice and when the companies are ready, bringing them to the attention of later-stage funds for additional funding. Provides a vehicle for angel investors, founders and entrepreneurs, as well as top-tier investment banks and VCs, institutional investors and other limited partners to participate in a diversified pool of top-line, early-stage Internet investments.
Geographic Preference: Greater Tri-State Area
Fund Size: $102 million
Founded: 2006
Average Investment: $1 - $8 million
Investment Criteria: Early-Stage
Industry Group Preference: Software, Information Technology, Internet Technology, Telecommunications
Other Locations:
Landsdowne House
57 Berkeley Square
London W1J 6ER
United Kingdom
Phone: +44 20 7198 7400 Fax: +44 20 7198 7500

Neue Mainzer Strasse 52
Frankfurt am Main D-60311
Germany
Phone: +49 69 272 272 00 Fax: +49 69 272 272 33

Av. Brigadeiro Faria Lima, 2277
19th Floor
Sao Paulo, SP 01452-000
Brazil
Phone: +55 11 2039 0600

Gustav Adolfs torg 16
Stockholm SE-111 52
Sweden
Phone: +46 (8) 402 1370

Level 43, Governor Phillip Tower
1 Farrer Place
Sydney NSW 2000
Australia
Phone: +61 2 9299 1410 Fax: +61 2 9229 1490

79 Wellington Street West
Suite 3403
P.O. Box 333
Toronto, ON M5K 1K7
Canada
Phone: +1 416 601 2560 Fax: +1 416 214 4886

155 North Wacker Drive
Suite 4550
Chicago, IL 60606
Phone: 312-846-5000 Fax: 312-846-5001

1301 McKinney Street
Suite 2850
Houston, TX 77010
Phone: 713-739-2000 Fax: 713-739-2001

Suite 1201 York House, The Landmark
15 Queen's Road Central
Hong Kong S.A.R.
China
Phone: 852-3896-6400 Fax: 852-3896-6401

Level 30
101 Collins Street
Melbourne VIC 3000
Australia
Phone: +61 3 9935 6800 Fax: +61 3 9935 6850

600 Montgomery Street
33rd Floor
San Francisco, CA 94111
Phone: 415-216-4150 Fax: 415-216-4140

Marunouchi Building
2-4-1, Marunouchi
Chiyoga-ku
Toyko 100-6333
Japan
Phone: +81 3 4520 5100 Fax: +81 3 4520 5101

Key Executives:
Robert F. Greenhill, Founder/Chairman
212-389-1500
Fax: 212-389-1700
e-mail: rfg@greenhill.com
Background: Chairman/CEO, Smith Barney Inc.; Chairman/President, Morgan Stanley Group
Directorships: Travelers Corp.
Scott L. Bok, Chief Executive Officer
212-389-1520
Fax: 212-389-1720
e-mail: sbok@greenhill.com
Background: M&A, Wachtell, Lipton, Rosen & Katz
Directorships: M&A, Morgan Stanley & Co.
Kevin Costantino, President/Co-Head of US M&A
212-389-1528
Fax: 212-389-1728
e-mail: kevin.costantino@greenhill.com
Education: BBA, University of Michigan; JD, University of Michigan Law School
Background: Wachtell, Lipton, Rosen & Katz
Harold J. Rodriguez Jr., Managing Director/COO/CFO
212-389-1516
Fax: 212-389-1716
e-mail: hrodriguez@greenhill.com
Background: VP, Finance/Controller, Silgan Holdings; Ernst & Young

865 GREENHILLS VENTURES, LLC
The Chrysler Landmark Building
405 Lexington Avenue
26th Floor
New York, NY 10174
Phone: 917-368-8390
web: www.greenhillsventures.com

Investment Criteria: Early-Stage
Industry Group Preference: Healthcare Technology, Medical Devices, Mobile Software, Wireless Software, Cloud Software
Portfolio Companies: ACE*COMM, Acta Vascular Systems, Cyberis Group, Digital Angel, Extra Space Storage, Facet Pricing, Global Wireless Unified Messaging, I/OMagic Corporation, Infocrossing, Medarex, Netease.com, Nfocus Neuromedical, Photronics, Sigouria Groupe, Sysview Technology, True Share Vault, Viisage Technology, Vital Images, Wasabi Life
Other Locations:
The Hemsley Building
230 Park Ave.
10th Floor
New York, NY 10169

Key Executives:
Emanuel Martinez, General Managing Director
Education: M.B.A. Finance, B.A. Accouting, St. John's University
Background: Managing Director for Mergers & Acquisition, Citibank; Vice President of Finance, American Express Corporation
Patrick Tan, Managing Director
Education: B.A. Mathematics & Computer Science, SUNY Buffalo
Background: CIO Azerty Inc.

Venture Capital & Private Equity Firms / Domestic Firms

866 GREENHOUSE VENTURES
2401 Walnut Street
Suite 102
Philadelphia, PA 19103

e-mail: info@greenhouse.ventures
web: greenhouse.ventures

Founded: 2014
Average Investment: $2-5M
Minimum Investment: $250K
Investment Criteria: Seed, Startup
Industry Group Preference: Cannabis

Key Executives:
Kevin Provost, Co-Founder/CEO
Education: BA, Business Management, La Salle University
Background: Franchise Manager, College Pro; Founder, Crowdcampuses; Founder/CEO, CoFund360 LLC
Tyler Dautrich, Co-Founder/Operations Manager
Education: BBA, West Chester University of Pennsylvania; BBA, Fox School of Business, Temple University
Background: Community Manager, coPhilly; Director of Business Development, MoreBetter Ltd.

867 GREENSPRING ASSOCIATES
100 Painters Mill Road
Suite 700
Owings Mills, MD 21117

Phone: 410-363-2725 **Fax:** 410-363-9075
e-mail: info@gspring.com
web: www.greenspringassociates.com

Mission Statement: Greenspring Associates is a global venture investment firm that offers investment expertise and a number of investment solutions, including fund-of-funds, direct investment funds and secondary funds. The firm was founded in 2000 and has clients in North America, Europe, Asia and Australia. Greenspring Associates invests primarily in the healthcare and technology-enabled sectors.

Geographic Preference: United States, China, India, Israel, Europe
Fund Size: $430 million
Founded: 2000
Average Investment: $15 million
Minimum Investment: $5 million
Investment Criteria: Seed, Early-Stage, Growth Equity VC Funds, Late-Stage & Growth Equity Co-Investments
Industry Group Preference: Technology, Life Sciences, Technology-Enabled Services, Information Technology, Communications, Healthcare
Portfolio Companies: Chewy.com, CloudFlare, Cologix, Cyara, Demandbase, Entellus Medical, Everything But The House, Exinda, FanDuel, G5, Gigya, IL&FS Transportation, Intarcia Therapeutics, Intrinsic Therapeutics, JW Player, Kareo, Lithium Technologies, MapR Technologies, Namely, NeoTract, Nutanix, Ocera Therapeutics, Packaging Coordinators, PhotoBox, SolidFire, Sonos, Spredfest, TeamViewer, Teladoc, Ticket Monster, TriVascular, Turn, WalkMe, Woowa Brothers, WorkFront, Zayo Group

Other Locations:
228 Hamilton Avenue
3rd Floor
Palo Alto, CA 94301
Phone: 650-798-5392 **Fax:** 650-798-5001

Key Executives:
Ashton Newhall, Co-Founder/Managing General Partner
e-mail: ashton@gspring.com
Education: Elon College
Background: T. Rowe Price Associates
Directorships: National Venture Capital Association, Domain Associates, Pelion Venture Partners, QuestMark Partners

Jim Lim, Managing General Partner
e-mail: jlim@gspring.com
Education: Washington University; MBA, Finance, Indiana University
Background: Director, Commonfund Capital; Pfizer
Directorships: Bullpen Capital, Columbia Capital, Foundry Group, High Alpha Ventures, Lightspeed China, Meritech Capital Partners, Cloud Sherpas, Kareo
John Avirett, General Partner
e-mail: john@gspring.com
Education: BA, Political Science, Johns Hopkins University
Background: Associate, Zurich Financial Services
Directorships: Workfront, Volition Capital, Shasta Ventures
Deric Emry, Venture Partner
e-mail: deric@gspring.com
Background: General Partner, ABS Capital Partners; Deutsche Bank Alex Brown
Eric Thompson, Chief Operating Officer
e-mail: ethompson@gspring.com
Education: BBA, Accounting, MBA, Finance, Sellinger School of Business & Management, Loyola University
Background: Manager, Assurance & Business Advisory Services Practice, PricewaterhouseCoopers
Nathan Campbell, Partner
Education: BComm, Australian National University; MA, Applied Finance & Invetsment, Financial Services Institute of Australasia
Background: Associate Director, Macquarie Capital; Deutsche Bank AG
Directorships: Agile Energy, Atlantic Wind Connection, Nexamp

869 GREIF & COMPANY
633 West Fifth Street
65th Floor
Los Angeles, CA 90071-2005

Phone: 213-346-9250 **Fax:** 213-346-9260
e-mail: owl@greifco.com
web: www.greifco.com

Mission Statement: Provides financial advisory services and execution to meet the specialized corporate finance needs of middle market growth companies.

Geographic Preference: United States, Canada, Latin America
Fund Size: $100 million
Founded: 1992
Average Investment: $1-$5 million
Minimum Investment: $1 million
Investment Criteria: Second-stage, Mezzanine, LBO, Control-block purchases
Industry Group Preference: Food and Beverage, Healthcare, Technology, Financial Services, Manufacturing, Media, Retailing, Aerospace and Defence, Consumer Products, Entertainment, Real Estate
Portfolio Companies: ABM Industris Inc., Advent International, Aerosol Servives Holdings Corp., Aerosol Services Company Inc., Outsourcing Services Group, Air Lease Corp., Allen Foods Inc., Allied Waste, American Apparel, AGS, AMF, Aquaria Inc., ASA Events, Back9 Network, Bebe, Blue Ribbon Baking Inc., Boone, Bossa Nova, Bristol Farms, Lazy Acres Merket, BF Acquisitions Company LLC, Buenavision Cable TV, Bumble Bee Seafoods, Uni Group Inc., Caesars Entertainment, California Manufacturing Enterprises, Center For Discover & Adolescent Change, Chromium Graphics Inc., City Center, Cole Real Estate Investments, Commericial Advance, Compel, Continental North Penn Technology, Contour Aerospace, Costco Wholesale, Century 21. CRL, Dacor, DTN, Del Amo Diagnostic Center, Dogswell, Dynamic Medical Systems Inc., E.B. Bradey Co., Evergreen, Express Energy Services, EZ Lube, Fantastic, First American Title Company of Marin, Fontainebleau, Ford Wholesale Co. Inc.,

309

Venture Capital & Private Equity Firms / Domestic Firms

Fred Sands, Fresh Express, Gaiam, Gary's Tux Shops, Gold Star Foods, Empire CLS, Hilton Worldwide, Inland American Real Estate Trust Inc., Interior Specialists Inc., Ixia, Kidsline, Kidsmart, Label-Aire, Landry's, Leisure Concepts, Levlad Inc., Lindora, LoopNet, Luciz, Lucky Brand, Malibu Grand Prix, Malone Mortgage Co., Marshall & Swift, Meico Crown Entertainment, MGM Resorts, MSA, Modnique, Mollie Stone's Markets, Morherhood Maternity, Mrs. Gooch's, Nordstrom, Orange Plastics, Rose Hills, Skechers, UnitedHealth Group, WestwoodOne, Wynn Resorts

Key Executives:
Lloyd Greif, President/CEO
e-mail: greif@greifco.com
Education: BA, Economics, University of California, Los Angeles; MBA, Entrepreneurship, University of Southern California; JD, Loyola Law School
Background: Investment Banker, Sutro & Company; Management Consultant, Touche, Ross & Company
David S. Felman, Managing Director
213-346-9225
e-mail: felman@greifco.com
Education: BA, Economics & Political Science, Stanford University; MBA, Finance & Entrepreneurship, University of California, Los Angeles
Background: Co-Founder, Cardinal Advisors; M&A, Moelis & Co.; Investment Banker, Morgan Stanley; UBS; Stanford Management Company; White House Concil of Economic Advisers; Goldman Sachs
Kevin T. Dugan, Director
213-346-9257
e-mail: dugan@greifco.com
Education: BS, University of Miami; MBA, Marshall School of Business, University of California
Background: General Management, Enterprise Holdings Inc.
Brad Money, Vice President
213-346-9268
e-mail: money@greifco.com
Education: BS, Finance & Economics, David Eccles School of Business, University of Utah
Background: Financial Analyst, RSM EquiCo; Financial Analyst, Ameriprise Financial
Brian R. Nelson, Vice President
213-346-9267
e-mail: nelson@greifco.com
Education: BA, Business Economics, Brown University; MBA, Anderson School of Management, University of California, Los Angeles
Background: Vice President, Guggenheim Securities; Investment Banker, Citigroup Global Markets; Investment Banker, Focalpoint Partners; Trading Assistant, JP Morgan; Bear Stearns

870 GREY SKY VENTURE PARTNERS
10400 Northeast 4th St.
Suite 700
Bellevue, WA 98004

e-mail: info@gsvp.com
web: gsvp.com

Mission Statement: Grey Sky Venture Partners makes early-stage investments in healthcare and medical technology companies with the aim of improving clinical outcomes, enhancing quality of life, and reducing system costs.
Investment Criteria: Early-Stage
Industry Group Preference: Healthcare, Medical Technology
Portfolio Companies: Biolinq, Care Wave, Immunovalent Therapeutics, MatriSys Bioscience, Modulated Imaging, Nodexus, Persephone Biome, Quantum Diamon Technologies, Sonavex, Soundstim Therapeutics, WestFace Medical, Winterlight

Other Locations:
2710 Sand Hill Rd.
Menlo Park, CA 94025
Key Executives:
Michael Banks, Founder/Partner
Education: BA, MA, Stanford University; MBA, Anderson School
Background: Intel Capital; Steamboat Ventures; Palisades Ventures; DE Shaw Ventures; Windy Hill Capital
Todd McIntyre, Founder/Partner
Education: BA, Hendrix College; MBA, Stanford University
Background: Invention Science Fund; Microvision; Lumera Corp.
Paul Wu, Partner
Education: MBA, MIT Sloan School; PhD, Northwestern University
Background: Invention Science Fund; KLA-Tencor

871 GREYCROFT PARTNERS
292 Madison Avenue
New York, NY 10017

Phone: 212-756-3508 **Fax:** 212-832-0117
web: greycroft.com

Mission Statement: Greycroft Partners is a venture capital partnership, formed to invest in promising digital media companies.
Geographic Preference: New York, Los Angeles
Fund Size: $800 million
Founded: 2009
Average Investment: $2 million
Minimum Investment: $100K
Investment Criteria: Seed, Series A
Industry Group Preference: Digital Media & Marketing, Advertising, Marketing, SaaS, E-Commerce & Manufacturing, Mobility, Infrastructure, Gaming
Portfolio Companies: 33across, 9flats.com, 9gag, Ad.ly, AppAnnie, BalconyTV, Bauble Bar, BetterCloud, Boxed, Buzz Points, Ceros, Collective, Combatant Gentlemen, CrowdComputing Systems, Daily Secret, Elicit, Epoxy, ETouches, ExtremeReach, Fanhattan, Fight My Monster, Floored, Fortumo, FriendBuy, Game Salad, Glam Media, Hashgo, HealthPlanOne, Highlight, HIP Digital, HipSwap, Joyent, JWPlayer, GamersFirt, Kaleo, Klout, Knozen, Koding, Layer, Livefyre, Local Response, Maker, Media Armor, Merchantry, MightyBell, Moonfrye, Nativo, Netsertive, NewsCred, Nifty Thrifty, NimbleTV, Nomi, NuOrder, OpenBucks, ParentMedia, PeopleLinx, Phg, Plain Vanilla, Playdek, PrecisionDemand, ProdThink, Radiate Media, Resonate, Scopely, Skimlinks, SteelHouse, Sulia, TagMan, The Dodo, The RealReal, ThisClicks, Trunk Club, Trustev, uSamp, Viddy, Vitals, Who What Wear, WideOrbit, WochIt

Other Locations:
1375 East 6th Street
Suite 1
Los Angeles, CA 90021
Phone: 213-896-7126 **Fax:** 213-402-2859
Key Executives:
Alan Patricof, Co-Founder/Chairman Emeritus
Background: Founder, Patricof & Co. Ventures
Dana Settle, Co-Founder/Partner
Education: BA, Finance & International Studies, University of Washignton; MBA, Harvard Business School
Background: Business Development, Truveo; Investment Banking, Lehman Brothers; International Business Development, McCaw Cellular Communications
Directorships: Fanhattan, Gamersfirst, GameSalad, Joyent, Lucid Commerce, Maker Studios, Pulse, Sometrics, TrunkClub, uSamp, WideOrbit
Ian Sigalow, Co-Founder/Partner
Education: BS, Economics, MIT; MBA, Columbia

University Graduate School of Business
Background: Founder, StrongData Corporation; Boston Millenia Partners
Directorships: Buddy Media, Buzzd, Collective, CrowdFusion, Extreme Reach, Oggifinogi, Tynt, Vizu

872 GREYLOCK PARTNERS
2550 Sand Hill Road
Suite 200
Menlo Park, CA 94025

Phone: 650-493-5525 **Fax:** 650-493-5575
web: www.greylock.com

Mission Statement: Greylock Partners supports entrepreneurs who are building software companies that define new markets.

Investment Criteria: All Stages
Industry Group Preference: Software
Portfolio Companies: AI Fund, Airbnb, Angle Technologies, Apollo Fusion, Apptio, Aurora, Avi Networks, Awake Security, Blend, BountyJobs, Caavo, Caffeine, Cato Networks, Censys, Cleo, Coda, Coinbase, Convoy, CreativeLive, Crew, Delphix, Demisto, Discord, Docker, Domo, Entrepreneur First, Figma, Gixo, Gladly, GoFundMe, Grand Rounds, HealthHiway, Houseparty, Innovium, Instabase, Lightbend, Lyra Health, Mammoth Media, Matrixx Software, Medium, Nauto, Nextdoor, Notable Health, Nuro, Obsidian Security, Operator, Oportun, PullString, Rhumbix, Ribbon, richrelevance, Ritual, Roblox, Rockset, Rubrik, Silver Peak Systems, Solv, Sonder, Spoke, Sumologic, TechProcess Solutions, Trifacta, Trove, Upserve, Wealthfront, WildTangent, Wrapp, Xapo

Other Locations:
1600 District Avenue
Suite 104
Burlington, MA 01803

457 Bryant Street
San Francisco, CA 94107

Key Executives:
Reid Hoffman, Partner
Education: Bachelor's Stanford University; Master's Univ. of Oxford
Background: Co-Founder, LinkedIn; Executive Vice President, PayPal
Directorships: Airbnb, Apollo Fusion, Aurora, Coda, Convor, Entrepreneur First, Gixo, Nauto, Xapo
Jerry Chen, Partner
e-mail: jerry.chen@greylock.com
Education: BS, Industrial Engineering, Stanford University; MBA, Harvard Business School
Background: VP, Cloud and Application Services, VMware
Directorships: Blend, Cato Networks, Cloudera, Docker, Gladly, Isntabase, Notable Health, Rhumbix, Rockset, Spoke
Sarah Guo, Partner
e-mail: sguo@greylock.com
Education: Wharton School; University of Pennsylvania
Background: Casa Systems; Goldman Sachs
Directorships: AI Fund, Awake Security, Clea, Demisto, Obsidian Security
Josh McFarland, Partner
e-mail: jmcfarland@greylock.com
Education: BA, Economics, Stanford University
Background: VP of Product, Twitter; Product Manager, Google
Directorships: Coinbase, Ribbon
David Sze, Partner
e-mail: dsze@greylock.com
Education: BA Yale University; MBA Stanford University
Background: SVP Product Strategy, Exite; Product Marketing & Development, Electronic Arts/Crystal Dynamics; Management Consultant, Marakon Associates/Boston Consulting Group
Directorships: Caavo, Medium, Nextdoor, PullString, Roblox
Asheem Chandna, Partner
e-mail: achandna@greylock.com
Education: B.S./M.S. Electrical and Computer Engineering, Case Western Reserve University
Background: Vice President of Business Development, Check Point Software; Vice President of Marketing, CoroNet Systems; Strategic Marketing, SynOptics/Bay; AT&T Bell
Directorships: Avi Netowrks, Awake Security, Censys, Delphix, Innovium, Obsidian Security, Palo Alto Networks, Rubrik

873 GRIDIRON CAPITAL
220 Elm Street
New Canaan, CT 06840

Phone: 203-972-1100 **Fax:** 203-801-0602
web: www.gridironcapital.com

Mission Statement: A private equity firm focused on creating value by acquiring and building middle-market manufacturing, service and specialty consumer companies.

Geographic Preference: United States, Canada
Investment Criteria: Contol Equity Investments, $8-50 Million in EBITDA
Industry Group Preference: Manufacturing, Services, Specialty Consumer Products
Portfolio Companies: Consel On Call, Dent Wizard, Electronic Systems Protection, Engage2Excel, Essential Cabinetry Group, H.M. Dunn AeroSystems Inc., McKenzie Sports Products, Motion Recruitment Partners, PAS Technologies, Performance Health, Ramsey Industries, Rough Country, Schutt Sports, Tokyo Joe's, Travel Nurse Across America

Key Executives:
Thomas A. Burger Jr., Managing Partner & Co-Founder
e-mail: tburger@gridironcapital.com
Education: Mechanical Engineering Degree, Duke University; MBA, Wharton School, University of Pennsylvania
Background: Managing Director, RFE Investment Partners; Managing Director, Butler Capital Corporation
Eugene P. Conese Jr., Managing Partner & Co-Founder
e-mail: gconese@gridironcapital.com
Education: BA, Economics, Denison University
Background: President, Greenwich Air Services; President, Haskon Corporation
Directorships: Audit Committee
Kevin M. Jackson, Senior Managing Partner
e-mail: kjackson@gridironcapital.com
Education: BA, Economics & Latin American Studies, Oberlin College; MBA, Columbia Business Schoool
Background: Senior Associate, CCMP Capital; Analyst, Credit Suisse
Kallie Hapgood, Managing Director
e-mail: khapgood@gridironcapital.com
Education: BA, Dartmouth College
Background: Principal, NovaFund Advisors; Vice President, Knight Capital Partner; State Street Global Advisors; Merrill Lynch
Joseph A. Saldutti Jr., Managing Director
e-mail: jsaldutti@gridironcapital.com
Education: MBA, Harvard Business School
Background: President, TDA Capital Partners; Engineer, General Electric
Geoffrey D. Spillane, Managing Director
e-mail: gspillane@gridironcapital.com
Education: BA, Economics, Boston College
Background: Principal, Brookside International Inc; Creditanstalt Corporate Finance; Fleet Financial Group
Owen G. Tharrington, Managing Director
e-mail: otharrington@gridironcapital.com
Education: BS, Accounting, Fairfield University; MBA, Columbia Business School

Venture Capital & Private Equity Firms / Domestic Firms

Background: Vice President, Saugatuck Capital Company; KPMG LLP
Christopher M. King, Vice President
e-mail: cking@gridironcapital.com
Education: BSBA, Finance & International Business, Georgetown University; Wharton School, University of Pennsylvania
Background: Analyst, Lehman Brothers; M&A, Barclays Capital
Douglas J. Rosenstein, Vice President
e-mail: drosenstein@gridironcapital.com
Education: BS, Business, Indiana University; MBA, Booth School of Business, University of Chicago
Background: Analyst, Merrill Lynch
Sean M. Kelley, Principal/Director of Business Development
e-mail: skelley@gridironcapital.com
Education: BA, Economics, Wake Forest University; MBA, Darden School of Business, University of Virginia
Background: Vice President, Investment Banking Division, BB&T Capital Markets; Associate, Equity Research Division, Credit Suisse; Analyst, Investment Banking Division, Deutsche Bank

874 GRISHIN ROBOTICS
New York, NY

e-mail: info@grishinrobotics.com
web: www.grishinrobotics.com

Mission Statement: Grishin Robotics is a global investment company that is dedicated to supporting personal robotics around the world. Grishin Robotics is focused on raising the profile of the robotics industry and helping robotics entrepreneurs advance their products and ideas.

Fund Size: $100 million
Founded: 2012
Industry Group Preference: Robotics, Internet
Portfolio Companies: Bolt, Double Robotics, Eero, Embodied, Gobee.Bike, littleBits Electronics, OBike, Occipital, Petnet, Planetary Resources, Ring, Sphero, Spin, Spire, Starship, Swivi, Ring, Robots Lab, Wonder

Key Executives:
Dmitry Grishin, Founder
Education: Faculty of Robotics & Complex Automation, Moscow State Technical University
Background: CEO, Mail.Ru

875 GROSVENOR FUNDS
888 17th Street NW
Suite 214
Washington, DC 20006

Phone: 202-861-5650 **Fax:** 202-861-5653

Mission Statement: Strives to invest in small businesses that stimulate the economic development and create new jobs in local communities.

Geographic Preference: Washington DC
Fund Size: $90 million
Founded: 1994
Average Investment: $1.5 million
Minimum Investment: $1 million
Investment Criteria: Early, Expansion
Industry Group Preference: Healthcare, Information Technology, Wireless Technologies

Key Executives:
Bruce B. Dunnan, Managing Partner
Education: Washington & Lee University; University of North Carolina School of Business
Background: President, Dunnan Securities Advisors; Alex Brown & Sons; Dean Witter Reynolds; First National Bank Atlanta
Douglas M. Dunnan, Managing Partner
Education: Cornell University, Harvard Law School, University of Chicago School of Business

Background: Attorney, Kirkland & Ellis; Investment Banking, Salomon Brothers; Founder, Grosvenor Fund
C. Bowdoin Train, Managing Partner
Education: Trinity College; JD, Georgetown University
Background: Counsel, Clean Air Capital Markets; Corporate Finance Law, Shaw Pittman Potts & Trowbridge; Environmental Protection Agency-George Bush Administration
Directorships: SnappCloud, Three Stage Media, iMove Inc., Inside Higher Ed
Oak Strawbridge, Partner
Education: George Washington University
Background: New Product Development Gropu, Concert Communications; Marketing Consultant, IGOR Communications
Directorships: DoublePOSITIVE, Appfluent, Generic Medical Devices, Inside Higher Ed, Omeros

876 GROTECH VENTURES
3033 Wilson Boulevard
Suite 200
Arlington, VA 22201

Phone: 703-637-9555
web: www.grotech.com

Mission Statement: Private equity investment firm investing in both emerging technology and traditional industry companies.

Geographic Preference: United States
Fund Size: $1 billion
Founded: 1984
Average Investment: $500,000 - $5 million
Minimum Investment: $500,000
Investment Criteria: All Stages, Recapitalization, Management Buy-Outs, Early, Emerging and Later Stages
Industry Group Preference: Enterprise Services, Business to Business, Communications, Healthcare, Consumer Products, Technology, Software, Infrastructure, Information Technology, Internet, Digital Media & Marketing
Portfolio Companies: Advertising.com, Adwerx, Airside, Anypresence, Atavium, Aztek Networks, Booker, Broadsoft, BuySafe, CDNow, Ceroc, Ceterus, Churnzero, CircleBack, Clarabridge, Closely, Cloud Elements, Collective Intellect, Commericial Tribe, Contactually, DB Networks, Digex, Direct Scale, Dizzion, Fieldglass, Fluid, Fusient Media Ventures, GutCheck, Healthcare Interactive, HealthScribe, HellaWaller, Hillcrest Labs, HiveLive, iBiquity, ICX Media, Intellinote, Invincea, Livingsocial, Login Analytics, LogRhythm, MedAssets, Medecision, Micro Prose, My Alerts, Nexgen Storage, Omnilink, OpenQ, Optoro, Overture, ParkiFi, Parsely, Passport, Payzer, Promoboxx, Rebit, RedPoint, RollStream, Secure, Social Radar, Spotright, Stardog Union, Synchrologic, TapInfluence, Taskeasy, Tethr, Royalty Exchange, ThreatConnect, TwoSix Labs, UrbanBound, Urbanstems, Urjanet, USI, Verity, WebScal, WhiteOps, Wiser Together, Yet Analytics, Zenoss

Other Locations:
230 Schilling Circle
Suite 362
Hunt Valley, MD 21031
Phone: 703-637-9555

1685 South Colorado Boulevard
Unit S-251
Denver, CO 80222
Phone: 720-399-4952

Key Executives:
Frank A. Adams, Founder/Chaiman
703-637-9555
e-mail: fadams@grotech.com
Education: BS/JD, University of Baltimore; Management Programs in Finance & Information Technology, Stanford University; Harvard University
Background: Co-Founder, Mid-Atlantic Venture Association

Venture Capital & Private Equity Firms / Domestic Firms

Directorships: DIGEX; Global Software; Healthscribe; iBiquity Digital Radio; Interspec; Lloyds Foods; MasterPower; SimonDelivers.com; Thunderbird Technologies; USinternetworking
Chuck Cullen, General Partner/CFO/COO
703-637-9555
e-mail: ccullen@grotech.com
Education: BBA, Accounting, Loyola University; JD, University of Notre Dame Law School; MBA, Kellogg School of Management
Background: CFO/CAO, Avatech Solutions; AT Kearney
Directorships: buySAFE, Pelican Life Sciences, OpenQ, Sagittarius Brands
Steve Fredrick, General Partner
703-462-1343
e-mail: sfredrick@grotech.com
Education: BS, MS, Electrical Engineering, Virginia Tech
Background: General Partner, Novak Biddle Venture Partners; Research & Develpment, IBM
Directorships: LogiXML, Omnilink Systems, RollStream, Secure Command, TRAFFIQ
Don Rainey, General Partner
703-462-1348
e-mail: drainey@grotech.com
Education: BBA, James Madison University; MS, Bioscience Management, George Mason University
Background: Emerging Technology Consultant, US Department of Defense, DeVenCI Program; President, Attitude Network; IBM
Directorships: ARPU, Clarabridge, LivingSocial, Zenoss
Joseph Zell, Venture Partner
703-399-4952
e-mail: jzell@grotech.com
Education: BS, Marketing, Southwest Missouri State University
Background: US West Communications; CEO, Convergent Communications; Management, WilTel, LDXNet, United Technologies Communications, MCI Communications, Xerox
Lawson DeVries, Managing General Partner
703-637-9555
e-mail: ldevries@grotech.com
Education: BA, English Literature, Harvard University
Background: Associate, Institutional Equity Sales, The Buckingham Research Group

877 GROUND UP VENTURES
web: www.groundup.vc

Mission Statement: A seed and early stage venture capital firm investing in innovative companies from the group up.
Geographic Preference: US, Israel
Founded: 2017
Average Investment: $250,000 - $500,000
Minimum Investment: $250,000
Investment Criteria: Pre-Seed, Seed
Industry Group Preference: Artificial Intelligence, Automation, Consumer, Data Management, Finance, Retail, Cyber Insurance, Software
Portfolio Companies: build Ops, Catch, Dandelion, Frank., Jones, MeetElise, Neighborhood Goods, Paladin Cyber, Shapeshift, Wardrobe
Key Executives:
 David Stark, Founding Partner
 e-mail: david@groundup.vc
 Education: BS, University of Pennsylvania
 Background: Analyst, The Blackstone Group; General Partner, OurCrowd
 Cory Moelis, Founding Partner
 e-mail: cory@groundup.vc
 Education: MBA, Wharton School
 Background: Analyst, Moelis & Company; Research & Analytics Manager, AEG; Product Manager, Derby Games
 Jordan Odinsky, Investor, Head of Platform
 e-mail: jordan@groundup.vc
 Education: BS, Queens College
 Background: Business Development Manager, OurCrowd; Co-Chair, VC Platform Global Community; Global Mentor, WeWork Labs; Angel Investor

878 GROVE GROUP MANAGEMENT
New York, NY
Phone: 212-671-1951
e-mail: contact@grovegroupmanagement.com
web: grovegroupmanagement.com

Mission Statement: Grove's team is compiled of finance, markting, and operational experts with vast knowledge of the cannabis industry.
Geographic Preference: US, Canada
Founded: 2018
Industry Group Preference: Cannabis
Key Executives:
 Kevin Shin, Co-Founder/CEO
 Education: University of Michigan
 Background: Financial Consultant, AXA; Founder, Craving; Founder, Paedea Inc.; Limited Partner/Senior Advisor, NewOak Capital; Co-Founder, iFood Korea
 James Frischling, President
 Education: BA, Government, Wesleyan University; MBA, Finance, Columbia Business School
 Background: VP, UBS Securities; Managing Director/Head of US Structured Credit, Fortis Securities; Partner/Finance Director, Branded Restaurants; Principal, MuniRisk; Co-Founder/Strategic Advisor, NewOak Capital; Principal, Oak Branch Advisors; Co-Founder/Principal, Branded Strategic Hospitality
 Directorships: Oak Branch Advisors
 Tiki Barber, Co-Founder/Chief Business Development Officer
 Education: BComm, Management Information Systems, University of Virginia
 Background: Running Back, New York Football Giants; Co-Founder, Thuzio; Co-Host, Tiki & Tierney Show
 Directorships: Chairman, Thuzio
 Chris Chung, Chief Investment Officer
 Education: BA, Economics, Northwestern University; University of Pennsylvania; NYU Stern School of Business
 Background: SVP, RBC Dain Rauscher; SVP/Head of Fixed Income, Janney Montgomery Scott; Founder/CEO, Clubstest.com; SVP, UBS Investment Bank; SVP, Bank of America; President/CEO, AGI LLC; Head of Business Development, The PreTesting Company; President/CEO, Altibase; EVP-Cyber Security Analytics, Antuit
 Bob DeSena, Chief Marketing & Communications Officer
 Education: BS, Quantitative Analysis, Manhattan College; MBA, Saint John's University
 Background: CEO, Engagement Marketing Group; CMO, TouchVision; Director of Relationship Marketing, Masterfoods USA; VP of Digital Media, Time Inc.; Adjunct Professor, NYU Graduate Program of Integrated Marketing' EVP/General Manager, Draft (now FCB)

879 GROVE STREET ADVISORS LLC
2221 Washington Street
Building 1
Suite 201
Newton, MA 02462
Phone: 781-263-6100
web: www.grovestreet.com

Mission Statement: Established with the objective of reengineering the traditional relationships between gatekeeper, fund manager and the major institutional investors in private equity.
Geographic Preference: North America, Western Europe, Isreal, China

Venture Capital & Private Equity Firms / Domestic Firms

Fund Size: $8.5 billion
Founded: 1998
Investment Criteria: Buy-outs, Mezzanine, Growth Equity
Industry Group Preference: Energy, Technology, Cloud Computing, Life Sciences, Healthcare, Agriculture
Portfolio Companies: Bedrock Capital, Flagship Pioneering, Hyperplane, M33 Grwoth, Quantum Energy Partners, Trive Capital

Key Executives:
  Frank Angella, Managing Partner
  Education: BA, Interdisciplinary Studies, University of Virginia; MBA, Harvard Business School
  Background: Co-Founder/VP, Biocode; Analyst, Advent Venture Partners; Associate, Innotage Management
  Catherine Crockett, Co-Founder & Managing Partner
  Education: BA, Business Admin./Government, University of Notre Damn; MPA, Kennedy School of Government, Harvard University
  Background: 14 years of experience designin and building private equity programs
  Christopher Quinn, CPA, Managing Partner & Chief Financial Officer
  Education: BS, Bryant University; MT, Taxation, University of Denver
  Background: CFO, Regiment Capital Advisors; Director of Tax, Bain Capital; Tax Manager, Highfields Capital; Senior Tax Consultant, Deloitte
  Bruce Ou, Managing Partner
  Education: BA, Williams College; MBA, Tuck School of Business, Dartmouth College
  Background: Monitor Group
  Chris Yang, Managing Partner
  Education: BA, Economics, MIT; JD, Harvard Law School; MBA, MIT Sloan School of Management
  Background: Consultant, Integral Inc.; Alliance Consulting Group; HomeGrocer; SchoolStop; Rottentomatoes; Associate, I-Group HotBank/Seed Capital

880 GROWTH FUND PRIVATE EQUITY
14929 Highway 172
Suite 302
P.O. Box 367
Ignacio, CO 81137

Phone: 970-563-5000 Fax: 970-764-6301
web: www.gfprivateequity.com

Mission Statement: The principal mission of GF Private Equity Group, LLC is to invest capital provided to it by the Southern Ute Growth Fund on behalf of the Southern Ute Indian Tribe in a variety of private equity funds and direct investments in companies for three primary reasons: pursue above-average investment returns, contribute to asset diversification of the Southern Ute Growth Fund, and provide long-term economic benefits to the Southern Ute Indian Tribe.

Founded: 2003
Portfolio Companies: Ahura Scientific, Applied Wave Research, Impinj, Kotura, Pixtronix, Redline Communications, Teknovus, Venda

Key Executives:
  James Thompson PhD, President/COO
  Jonathan Abshagen, Portfolio Manager

881 GRYPHON INVESTORS
One Maritime Plaza
Suite 2300
San Francisco, CA 94111

Phone: 415-217-7400 Fax: 415-217-7447
e-mail: info@gryphoninvestors.com
web: www.gryphon-inv.com

Mission Statement: Gryphon actively seeks companies where strong results can be achieved when the right management team is combined with Gryphon's focused industry approach and operational expertise.

Geographic Preference: United States
Fund Size: $900 million
Founded: 1995
Average Investment: $50 - $150 million
Minimum Investment: $25 million
Investment Criteria: Traditional Buyouts, Leveraged Build-Ups, Growth Equity Investments, Revunue of $25 to $250 million
Industry Group Preference: Education, Specialty Retail, Business Products & Services, Healthcare, Manufacturing, Consumer Products, Consumer Services
Portfolio Companies: Accelerated Rehabilitation Centers, Alliedbarton Security, Bright Now! Dental, C.B. Fleet Laboratories, Consolidated Fire Protection, Cora Health Services, Delta Career Education Corp., ECG Management Consultants, Eight O'Clock Coffee, Envision, Flagstone Foods, Hepaco, Intelligrated, Jen Sen Hughes, K&N Engineering Inc., Medfinders, Miller Heiman, MSD Ignition, OB Hospitalist Group, Orchid Underwriters, PHNS, Sheplers, Smile Brands, Synteratchr, TASQ Technology, The Original Cakerie, Trinity Consultants, Trusthouse Services Group, Update Legal, Washing Systems LLC, Wind River Environmental

Key Executives:
  R. David Andrews, CEO/Managing General Partner
  415-217-7410
  e-mail: andrews@gryphoninvestors.com
  Education: BA, Economics, Stanford University; JD, Stanford University; MBA, Stanford University
  Background: Managing Director, Oak Hill Partners; Investor, Adler & Shaykin; Salomon Brothers; Shearson Lehman Brothers
  Directorships: Delta Career Education, Envision, HEPACO, Jen Sen Hughes, Wind River Environmental
  Alex Earls, Partner
  415-217-7405
  e-mail: earls@gryphoninvestors.com
  Education: BA, Government, Harvard College
  Background: Associate, Castle Harlan; Analyst, Princes Gate; Morgan Stanley
  Directorships: DLC, HEPACO, Jen Sen Hughes, Orchid Underwriters, Wind River Environmental
  Kevin Blank, Partner/General Manager, Healthcare
  415-217-7449
  e-mail: blank@gryphoninvestors.com
  Education: BA, Medical Sociology, Boston University; MPH, Health Systems, Boston University School of Medicine
  Background: CEO, FastMed Urgent Care; EVP, Evolution Benefits; President/COO, Benefit Point; nson
  Directorships: OB Hospitalist Group
  Will Lynn, Partner
  415-217-7409
  e-mail: lynn@gryphoninvestors.com
  Education: Case Western Reserve University; Baldwin Wallace College
  Background: President, LaChoy/Rosarita Foods Division, ConAgra; Group Vice President, Clorox Company; Private Equity Consultant, Oak Hill
  Directorships: CORA Health Services, Delta Career Education, Envision, Smile Brands
  Dennis O'Brien, Partner/General Manager, Consumer Products & Services
  415-217-7414
  e-mail: obrien@gryphoninvestors.com
  Education: BS, Marketing, University of Connecticut
  Background: President/COO, ConAgra; Armstrong Industries; Campbell's Soup; Nestle Foods; Procter and Gamble
  Directorships: DLC, The Original Cakerie
  Nick Orum, President
  415-217-7440
  e-mail: orum@gryphoninvestors.com

Education: BA, Quantitative Economics, Stanford University
Background: Principal Investor, Oak Hill Partners; High Yield Finance Group, Merrill Lynch
Directorships: Delta Career Education, CORA Health Services. DLC, ECG Management Consultants, OB Hospitalist Group, Orchid Underwriters, Smile Brands
Dorian Faust, Partner
415-217-7424
e-mail: faust@gryphoninvestors.com
Education: BA, University at Buffalo; MBA, Columbia Business School
Background: Principal, Norwest Equity Partners; Vice President, Thomas Weisel Capital Partners; Associate, JP Morgan Partners
Dell Larcen, Partner
415-217-7441
e-mail: larcen@gryphoninvestors.com
Education: BA, Sociology, Carson Newman College; MS, Psycology/Psychiatric Social Work, University of Tennessee
Background: CEO, Larcen Consulting Group; Founder/CEO, Overlook Center; Founding Member, Mental Health Risk Rention Group; Adjunct Faculty Professor, University of Tennessee
Directorships: ECG Management Consultants, Jen Sen Hughes, Washing Systems LLC
Keith Stimson, Partner
415-217-7430
e-mail: stimson@gryphoninvestors.com
Education: BS, Economics, MBA, Wharton School, University of Pennsylvania
Background: Principal, Saunders Karp & Megrue; Big Flower Press Holdings; Bankers Trust
Directorships: The Original Cakerie; Lawler's Foods

---

882 GRYPHON MANAGEMENT COMPANY
101 Federal Street
Suite 1900
Boston, MA 02108
Phone: 617-619-3800 Fax: 617-619-3801
e-mail: wfa@gryphoninc.com
web: www.gryphoninc.com

Mission Statement: A diversified financial services firm which is actively seeking new investments. Focusing on the capital needs of technology-based companies in New England.
Geographic Preference: United States
Fund Size: $56 million
Founded: 1984
Average Investment: $3 million
Minimum Investment: $1 million
Investment Criteria: Early, Start Up
Industry Group Preference: Energy, Environment Products & Services, Industrial Services, Petrochemicals, Specialty Chemicals, Biotechnology

Key Executives:
   William F Aikman, President/CEO
   Education: Brown University; University of Pennsylvania; Harvard University
   Background: President, Gryphon Management Company, Inc.; President and Chief Executive Officer, Massachusetts Technology Development Corporation
   Directorships: Massachusetts Certified Development Corporation, Geltech, Optex

---

883 GSV VENTURES
171 2nd Street
San Francisco, CA 94105
Phone: 415-757-5634
e-mail: info@gsvaccelerate.com
web: gsvaccelerate.com

Mission Statement: Partners with entrepreneurs in the learning and talent technology sector.
Investment Criteria: Early-Stage
Industry Group Preference: Technology, Education, Human Resources
Portfolio Companies: Amira Learning, Andela, Ansaro, Begin, Campuslogic, ClassDojo, Clever, CLI Studios, Course Hero, Coursera, Create&Learn, Creativelive, Degreed, Educents, Fairygodboss, Glimpse, Goodtime, Gradescope, Handshake, HotChalk, Hustle, Intellispark, Lightneer, Masterclass, Mastery Connect, Mighty, Motimatic, Nearpod, NoRedInk, PeopleGrove, Pluralsight, RaiseMe, Remind, ScholarMe, Stride, Tara, Think Through Math, Toucan, Turnitin, Tynker, Verto Education, Voxy

Key Executives:
   Michael Cohn, Co-Founder and Partner
   Education: MBA, Kellogg School of Management, Northwestern University; BBA, University of Michigan
   Directorships: GSV Advisors
   Michael Moe, Co-Founder and Partner, GSV Asset Management
   Education: BA, University of Minnesota; Chartered Financial Analyst
   Background: Co-Founder, Chair And CEO, ThickEquity Partners; Head of Global Growth Research, Merrill Lynch; Head of Growth Research and Strategy, Montgomery Securities
   Directorships: Coursera, Curious, GSVlabs, Course Hero, Class Dojo, Parchment, SharesPost, StormWind, OZY Media
   Deborah Quazzo, Managing Partner and Co-Founder, ASU GSV Summit
   Education: BA, History, Princeton University; MBA, Harvard University
   Directorships: Aakash Educational Services Ltd., Ascend Learning, Degreed, Educational Testing Service, Intellispark, Mighty, Remind, Turnitin

---

884 GTCR
300 North LaSalle Street
Suite 5600
Chicago, IL 60654
Phone: 312-382-2200
e-mail: info@gtcr.com
web: www.gtcr.com

Mission Statement: GTCR is a private equity firm that seeks to partner with outstanding management leaders; leverage its expertise within the financial technology, healthcare, media, telecommunications, and technology industries; and acquire and build companies with the potential to become market leaders.
Fund Size: $3.85 billion
Founded: 1980
Average Investment: $30 - $250 million
Minimum Investment: $20 million
Investment Criteria: Operating profits $5-$150 million, Mezzanine, Growth Capital, Buyouts, PIPES Financing, Acquisitions
Industry Group Preference: Business to Business, Communications, Distribution, Financial Services, Health Related, Information Technology, Media, Telecommunications
Portfolio Companies: Avention, Callcredit Information Group, CAMP Systems, Cedar Gate Technologies, Cision, Cole-Parmer Instrument Company, Convergex, Correct Care Solutions, Crealta Pharmaceuticals, Fairway Outdoor, Global Traffic Network, IQNavigator, Maravai LifeSciences, Mondee, Opus Global Holdings, Rural Broadband Investments, Rx30, Sterigenics, The Townsend Group, XIFIN, Zayo Group

Key Executives:
   Mark M. Anderson, Managing Director
   312-382-2239

Venture Capital & Private Equity Firms / Domestic Firms

Education: BS, McIntire School of Commerce, University of Virginia; MBA, Harvard Business School
Background: Gracie Capital; Bowles Hollowell Conner & Company
Directorships: CAMP Systems, Cision, Global Traffic Network, IQNavigator, Mondee, Rural Broadband Investments, XIFIN
Craig A. Bondy, Managing Director
312-382-2224
Education: BBA, Finance, MBA, University of Texas
Background: Credit Suisse First Boston
Directorships: Avention, CAMP Systems, Fairway Outdoor, Mondee
Philip A. Canfield, Managing Director
312-382-2234
Education: BBA, University of Texas; MBA, University of Chicago
Background: Corporate Finance Group, Kidder Peabody and Company
Directorships: Avention, Global Traffic Network, IQNavigator, Rural Broadband Investments, Zayo Group
Aaron D. Cohen, Managing Director
312-382-2169
Education: BS, Accountancy, University of Illinois at Urbana-Champaign
Background: Hicks, Muse, Tate & Furst; M&A Group, Salomon Smith Barney
Directorships: Callcredit Information Group, Opus Global/Hiperos
Sean L. Cunningham, Managing Director
312-382-2260
Education: AB, BE, Dartmouth College; MBA, Wharton School
Background: Consultant, The Boston Consulting Group
Directorships: Cedar Gate Technologies, Cole-Parmer, Correct Care Solutions, Maravai LifeSciences, Rx30, Sterigenics
David A. Donnini, Managing Director
312-382-2240
Education: BA, Economics, Yale University; MBA, Stanford University
Background: Associate Consultant, Bain and Company
Directorships: Fairway Outdoor, Sterigenics, AssuredPartners, Classic Media, Coinmach, Gensar, HSM Electronic Protection Services
Constantine S. Mihas, Managing Director
312-382-2204
Education: BS, Finance & Economics, University of Illinois; MBA, Harvard Business School
Background: CEO & Co-Founder, Delray Farms; McKinsey & Company
Directorships: Cedar Gate Technologies, Cole-Parmer, ConvergEx, Crealta Pharmaceuticals, Maravai LifeSciences, Rx30, Sterigenics, XIFIN
Collin E. Roche, Managing Director
312-382-2214
Education: BA, Political Economy, Williams College; MBA, Harvard Business School
Background: Associate, EVEREN Securities; Analyst, Goldman Sachs & Company
Directorships: Callcredit Information Group, ConvergEx, Opus Global/Hiperos, Aligned Asset Managers
Anna May L Trala, Chief Financial Officer/Managing Director
312-382-2215
Education: BS, Accounting, Goldey Beacom College
Background: Partner, Transaction Advisory Services Group, Ernst & Young

885 GUGGENHEIM PARTNERS
330 Madison Avenue
New York, NY 10017

Phone: 212-739-0700
web: www.guggenheimpartners.com

Mission Statement: Guggenheim Partners is a privately held, diversified financial services firm characterized by a deep commitment to creating exceptional value for our clients throughout the world.
Fund Size: $210 billion
Investment Criteria: Early-Stage Venture Capital, Growth Capital, Distressed Venture Capital
Industry Group Preference: Technology, Semiconductors, Communications, Software, Digital Media & Marketing, Wireless

Other Locations:
227 West Monroe Street
Chicago, IL 60606
Phone: 312-827-0100

3414 Peachtree Road, NE
Suite 960
Atlanta, GA 30326
Phone: 404-585-2200

500 Boylston Street
Boston, MA 02116
Phone: 617-859-4600

500 E Morehead St.
Suite 350
Charlotte, NC 28202
Phone: 704-805-1000

3000 Internet Blvd.
Suite 570
Frisco, TX 75034
Phone: 214-872-4000

1301 McKinney
Houston, TX 77010
Phone: 713-300-1330

401 Pennsylvania Parkway
Suite 300
Indianapolis, IN 46280
Phone: 317-574-6201

100 Wilshire Boulevard
Santa Monica, CA 90401
Phone: 310-576-1270

702 King Farm Boulevard
Rockville, MD 20850

50 California St.
San Francisco, CA 94111

231 South Bemiston Avenue
St. Louis, MO 63105
Phone: 314-862-4848

Office 602
Burj Daman Office Tower 6th Floor
Dubai International Financial Centre
Dubai
United Arab Emirates
Phone: +971 (4) 425-0605

South Dock House
Hanover Quay
Dublin 2
Ireland
Phone: +353 1616-8400

5th Floor, The Peak
5 Wilton Road
London SW1V 1AN
United Kingdom
Phone: +44 20 3059 6600

Unit 1, 7th Floor, B-Wing
Prism Towers, Mindspace
Link Road, Malad West
Mumbai 400064
India

Otemachi First Square
West Tower 13F

Venture Capital & Private Equity Firms / Domestic Firms

1-5-1, Otemachi Chiyoda-Ku
Tokyo 100-0004
Japan

Key Executives:
Mark R. Walter, Chief Executive Officer/Co-Founder
Background: Co-Founder, Liberty Hampshire
Thomas J. Irvin, Managing Partner
Alan D. Schwartz, Managing Partner
Background: CEO, The Bear Stearns Companies
B. Scott Minerd, Managing Partner
Background: Managing Director, Morgan Stanley & Credit Suisse
Peter O. Lawson-Johnston II, Managing Partner
Andrew M, Rosenfield, Managing Partner

886 GUIDE MEDICAL VENTURES
2 Oliver Street
Suite 616
Boston, MA 02109

web: www.guidemedicalventures.com

Mission Statement: Guide Medical Ventures was founded in 2011 to develop innovative medical devices that improve patient outcomes and reduce costs. GMV focuses on technology improvements for existing medical procedures and applications. Our team members have proven track records at both large companies and start-ups in the medical device industry, including experience leading companies from formation through acquisition. GMV guides its projects and start-ups from inception through acquisition, creating value for our shareholders and strategic partners in the most capital efficient manner.

Founded: 2011
Investment Criteria: Early-Stage
Industry Group Preference: Medical Devices
Portfolio Companies: CardioSolv Ablation Technologies, CSA Medical, Enspire DBS Therapy, NeuroAccess Technologies, Qr8 Health

Key Executives:
Vince Owens, Founder/Managing General Partner
Education: BS, Mechanical Engineering, Carnegie Mellon University; MBA, Ashland University
Background: Co-Founder/CEO, Intelect Medical
Scott Kokones, Founder/General Partner
Education: BS, Mechanical Engineering, University of Michigan; MBA, Boston University
Background: Co-Founder/SVP, Intelect Medical; Medtronic, Enpath Medical
Keith Carlton, Founder/General Partner
Education: BS, Biomedical Engineering and Engineering Mechanics, Johns Hopkins University; MBA, Boston University
Background: CEO, HUINNO; Director of New Therapy Development, Boston Scientific
Greg Schulte, Partner
Education: BS, Mechanical Engineering, University of Michigan
Background: 525 Medical; Mechanical Engineering, Intelect Medical; EnteroMedical, Enpath Medical; Medtronic

887 GUIDE VENTURES
12509 Bel-Red Road
Suite 201
Bellevue, WA 98005-2535

Fax: 425-688-7980
web: www.guideventures.com

Mission Statement: Actively work with each portfolio firm and their team to create the highest value possible through building a strong company culture, solid financial models, and leading-edge intellectual property.

Geographic Preference: West Coast, Western Canada
Fund Size: $21 million
Founded: 1999
Average Investment: $1.5 million
Minimum Investment: $500,000
Investment Criteria: Seed, Early
Industry Group Preference: Life Sciences, Infrastructure, Wireless Technologies
Portfolio Companies: AdRelevance, BOCADA, nCircle, Sharebuilder, Virtual Relocation

Key Executives:
Russ Aldrich, Managing Director
Education: Long Beach City College
Background: VP/Co-Founder, Simba Technologies; Hal (Fujitsu) Computer Systems; Silicon Graphics; Altos Computer Systems; Covergent Technologies; SoftTech, Xerox Corporation; McDonnell-Douglas Aircraft
Directorships: Flatrock, Netstock
Jim Thornton, Managing Director
Education: MBA, Rutgers University
Background: Newsweek Magazine; VP of Finance & Operations, Aldus Corporation; CEO, Lifespex Corporation
Directorships: Bocada
Dave Kowalick, Senior Associate
Education: Graduate Degree, MIT
Background: Naval Officer, United States Naval Academy; Fund Manager, CKW LLC; Advanced Marine Technology; Tidemark Solutions
Directorships: Detto
Mike Templeman, Managing Director
Education: BS, Zoology, University of Washington; MSE, Seattle University
Background: Graphics & Systems Programmer, Boeing; Co-Founder, Aldus Corporation; Co-Founder, MetaBridge Corporation; Co-Founder, Netpodium
Directorships: nCirle Network Security

888 GULFSTAR GROUP
700 Louisiana Street
Suite 3800
Houston, TX 77002-2731

Phone: 713-300-2020 **Fax:** 713-300-2021
e-mail: info@gulfstargroup.com
web: www.gulfstargroup.com

Mission Statement: Gulfstar provides investment and merchant banking services to a variety of industries, to both public and private middle market companies. Gulfstar is one of the South West's largest and most active investment banking firms serving the middle market, having completed over 225 assignments in over 15 industries.

Founded: 1990
Average Investment: $20 million
Minimum Investment: $5 million
Investment Criteria: Company with revenues between $10-$150 million
Industry Group Preference: Business Products & Services, Technology, Software, Energy, Manufacturing, Wholesale, Health Related, Consumer Products, Security, Consumer Services, Infrastructure, Financial Services, Information Technology, Transportation, Logistics

Key Executives:
Cliff Atherton Jr., Managing Director
713-300-2060
e-mail: catherton@gulfstargroup.com
Education: BA, Rice University; PhD, MBA, University of Texas; CFA
Background: Managing Director, McKenna & Company; President, Emprise Consulting Group; Rice University's Jesse H Jones School of Administration; Adjunct Professor of Finance, University of Houston.
Directorships: Teas Nursery Company Inc
Alan J. Blackburn, Managing Director
713-300-2048
e-mail: ablackburn@gulfstargroup.com

Venture Capital & Private Equity Firms / Domestic Firms

Education: BBA, Accounting & Finance, University of Texas, Austin; MBA, Wharton School, University of Pennsylvania
Background: Managing Director, Growth Capital Partners; Investment Banking Group, Merrill Lynch
Chip Cureton, Advisory Director
713-300-2033
e-mail: ccureton@gulfstargroup.com
Education: AB, History, Stanford University; MBA, Harvard Business School
Background: Cureton & Company; VP, Rotam Mosle; United States Navy
Directorships: Hankey Oil Company, Mobley Environmental Services, Modular Environmental Technologies, Midway Importing
Bryan C. Frederickson, Managing Director
713-300-2030
e-mail: bfrederickson@gulfstargroup.com
Education: BS, Economics, MBA, Finance, Vanderbilt University
Background: Navigant Capital Advisors; Wachovia Securities
Thomas M. Hargrove, Managing Director/Co-Founder
713-300-2050
e-mail: thargrove@gulfstargroup.com
Education: BA, Economics, University of Texas
Background: Senior VP, Rotan Mosle Inc.; First VP, Underwood, Neuhaus & Company; Assisitant VP, Corporate Finance, First City National Bank
Directorships: Entrix, Stellar Event & Presentation Resources, Rimco Production Company
G. Kent Kahle, Managing Director/Co-Founder
713-300-2025
e-mail: kkahle@gulfstargroup.com
Education: MBA, Wharton School, University of Pennsylvania; AB, Brown University
Background: Senior VP, Investment Banking; Director, Rotan Mosle; Manager of Investor Relations, Geosource; Special Assistant to the Secretary of Commerce and Secretary of Interior, Ford Administration.
Directorships: US Legal Support; Total Safety
Stephen A. Lasher, Managing Director
713-300-2010
e-mail: slasher@gulfstargroup.com
Education: BA, Vanderbilt University
Background: Executive Vice President, Rotan Mosle Inc.
Directorships: Weingarten Realty
Colt Leudde, Managing Director
713-300-2015
e-mail: cluedde@gulfstargroup.com
Education: BBA, Finance, University of Texas, Austin
Background: Corporate Banking Group, NationsBank Corporation
Eric Swanson, Managing Director
713-300-2008
e-mail: eswanson@gulfstargroup.com
Education: BA, Biochemistry/Molecular Biology, MS, Evaluative Clinical Sciences, Dartmouth College; MBA, Kellogg School of Management, Northwestern University
Background: Investment Banker, Morgan Stanley; Deutsche; JP Morgan; ExxonMobil Corp.
Pamela L. Reiland, Senior Vice President
713-300-2003
e-mail: preiland@gulfstargroup.com
Education: BA, Spanish, Duke University; MBA & MPA, Rice University
Background: Director of Alumni Engagement, Rice University; Willbros USA; Galveston-Houston Company
Brian J. Lobo, Managing Director
713-300-2047
e-mail: blobo@gulfstargroup.com
Education: BBA, Finance, University of Texas, Austin
Background: Lazard Middle Market; Analyst, Advanced Micro Devices Inc.

Rupert Gerard, Vice President
713-300-2051
e-mail: rgerard@gulfstargroup.com
Education: BA, Government, Georgetown University; MBA, INSEAD
Background: Castleton Commodities International; Taylor Woods Capital
Scott D. Winship, Managing Director
713-300-2011
e-mail: swinship@gulstargroup.com
Education: BA, Poltical Science & Business Communcations, University of California, Davis
Background: Managing Director, 6Pacific Partners; BMO Capital Markets; JPMorgan Chase & Co.; Cowen & Co.
Ben Stanton, Vice President
713-300-2040
e-mail: bstanton@gulfstargroup.com
Education: BA, Business Admin., MS, Finance, Mays Business School, Texas A&M University; CPA
Background: Senior Associate, PricewaterhouseCoopers

---

889 GV
1600 Ampitheatre Parkway
Mountain View, CA 94043

Phone: 650-253-0000
web: www.gv.com

Mission Statement: GV, formerly Google Ventures, provides venture capital funding to innovative new companies across a range of industries, including healthcare, life sciences, consumer Internet, robotics, and artificial intelligence.

Geographic Preference: United States
Fund Size: $2.4 billion
Founded: 2009
Investment Criteria: All Stages
Industry Group Preference: Consumer Internet, Software, Mobile Technology, Robotics, Life Sciences, Healthcare, Artificial Intelligence, Enterprise Software, Transportation, Cybersecurity
Portfolio Companies: 23andMe, 2nd Address, Abacus, About.me, Abundant Robotics, Acalvia, Agent, Airtime, Airwave, Alector, Aledade, Ambition, Amino, Anchor, Andela, AngelList, Anomali, Apptentive, Apptimize, Aspire Health, Basis, Benson Hill Biosystems, BlackThorn Therapeutics, Blavity, Blockchain, Bowery, Brandless, Breather, Bugsnag, Cambly, Cambridge Epigenetix, Carbon, Carmera, Carrick Therapeutics, Celsius Therapeutics, Censys, Checkr, CircleUp, CircuitHub, Clarifai, ClassPass, Clear Labs, ClearStory Data, Clever, Clover Health, Clutter, Cockroach Labs, Cohesity, Collective Health, Compass Therapeutics, Confide, Cool Planet Energy Systems, Copper, Corduro, Cozy, creativeLIVE, Creator, CTRL-Labs, Currencycloud, CyberGRX, DaileyTech, DataFox, Datanyze, Decibel Therapeutics, Delighted, Desktop Metal, Desmos, Dialpad, Digit, Disruptor Beam, DNAnexus, Doctor On Demand, Duo, Easy Post, Egnyte, Emergent, Emissary, English Central, Ethos, Evelo Bioscience, Evox Therapeutics, Farmers Business Network, Fauna, Flexport, Flux, FLX Bio, FogPharma, Freenome, FullStory, Gametime, Genomics Medicine Ireland, Giphy, GitLab, Grail, Gritstone Oncology, Gusto, Happiest Babby, HeadSpin, Helium, HelloSign, High Fidelity, Highfive, HomeLight, HOVER, Hustle, Ideaya Bioscience, Impossible Foods, Incorta, insitro, Intercom, IonQ, Ionic Security, Jaunt, JumpCam, KeepTruckin, Kitched United, Kindred, Kobalt, Lambada School, Le Tote, LedgerX, Lemonade, LendUp, LevelUp, LifeMine Therapeutics, Light, Lime, Lola, LostMyName

Other Locations:
345 Spear Street
San Francisco, CA 94105
Phone: 415-736-0000

355 Main Street
5th Floor

Venture Capital & Private Equity Firms / Domestic Firms

Cambridge, MA 02142
Phone: 617-575-1300

76 Ninth Avenue
4th Floor
New York, NY 10011
Phone: 212-565-0000

146-148 Clerkenwell Road
London EC1R 5DG
United Kingdom

Key Executives:
 David Krane, CEO & Managing Partner
 Education: BA, Journalism, Indiana University, Bloomington
 Background: Director, Global Communications & Public Affairs, Google; Apple Computer; QUALCOMM; Four11
 Blake Byers, General Partner
 Education: BS, Biomedical Engineering & Economics, Duke University; MS, PhD, Bioengineering, Stanford University
 Tyson Clark, General Partner
 Education: BS, Industrial Engineering, Stanford University; MBA, Harvard Business School
 Background: Partner, Andreessen Horowitz; Corporate Development Group, Oracle; Investment Banker, Morgan Stanley; United States Navy
 Karim Faris, General Partner
 Education: BS, Computer Engineering, Brown University; MS, Electrical Engineering, University of Michigan; MBA, Harvard Business School
 Background: Corporate Development, Google; Atlas Venture; Director, New Ventures, Level 3 Communications; Intel; Siemens
 Tom Hulme, General Partner
 Education: BS, Physics, University of Bristol; MBA, Harvard Business School
 Background: Design Director, IDEO Europe; Managing Director, Marcos; Founder, Magnom
 Joe Kraus, Venture Partner
 Education: BA, Stanford University
 Background: Co-Founder, Excite.com; Co-Founder, JotSpot
 Directorships: Electronic Frontier Foundation
 Dave Munichiello, General Partner
 Education: BS, Mathematics & Computer Science, Emory University; MBA, Harvard Business School
 Background: Senior Executive, Kiva Systems; Management Consultant, The Boston Consulting Group; Captain, United States Military
 M.G. Siegler, General Partner
 Education: University of Michigan
 Background: 500ish; Founding Partner, CrunchFund; Writer, TechCrunch; Writer, VentureBeat
 Andy Wheeler, General Partner
 Education: BS, MEng, Electrical Engineering & Computer Science, Massachusetts Institute of Technology
 Background: CTO, Adura; CTO, Tendril Networks; Co-Founder, Ember Corporation; Zipcar; MIT Media Lab
 Krishna Yeshwant, General Partner
 Education: BS, Computer Science, Stanford University; MD, Harvard Medical School; MBA, Harvard Business School
 Background: New Business Development Team, Google
 Directorships: Editas Medicine, Flatiron, One Medical Group
 John Lyman, Partner
 Education: Georgetown University; MA, Public Policy, University of California, Berkeley
 Background: Clinton Global Initiative; Center for American Progress; Google
 Shaun Maguire, Partner
 Education: MA, Stanford University; PhD, Caltech
 Background: Qadium; Escape Dynamics; Defense Advanced Research Projects Agency

890 GVA CAPITAL
906 Broadway
San Francisco, CA 94133

web: gva.capital

Mission Statement: The US investment arm of the Global Venture Alliance funds early-stage companies with a focus on education.

Geographic Preference: North America
Fund Size: $120 million
Founded: 2011
Investment Criteria: Early-Stage, Late-Stage, Secondary Market, Seed
Industry Group Preference: Fintech, Artificial Intelligence, Neural Networks, Big Data, Data Mining, Cloud Technologies
Portfolio Companies: Acquired.io, Cherry Labs, Establishment Labs, Opus12, WISeKey, Storj.iO, Diamond Factory, AstroDigital, Mlvch, Nopassword, People.ai, Qwil, I.AM+, Virool, Luminar, PolyUp, Omniscience, Pixlee, Mubert, SoLoMoTo, COUB, Kiana, Fiscal Note, RoboCV

Other Locations:
 Plug and Play Tech Center
 440 N Wolfe Road
 Sunnyvale, CA 94085
 US

Key Executives:
 Pavel Cherkashin, Managing Partner
 Roman Sobachevskiy, Managing Partner
 Education: MBA, Stephen M. Ross School of Business, University of Michigan
 Daria Gonzalez, Chief Executive Officer
 Education: MBA, Stanford University

891 H KATZ CAPITAL GROUP
Southampton Office Park
928 Jaymor Road
Suite A-100
Southampton, PA 18966-3823

Phone: 215-364-0400 **Fax:** 215-364-5025
web: www.katzgroup.com

Mission Statement: H. Katz Capital Group is a private equity firm seeking to provide funding to companies with experienced management teams, unique products or services, and the ability to generate financial returns.

Investment Criteria: Management Buyouts, Recapitalizations, Early Stage, Expansion Stage, Growth Stage
Industry Group Preference: Consumer Services, Food & Beverage, Media, Healthcare, Financial Services, Franchising, Real Estate

Key Executives:
 Harold Katz, Chairman
 Background: Nutri/System Center; Owner, Philadelphia 76ers
 Directorships: United Valley Bank, Hero Scholarship Fund of Philadelphia, Police Athletic League
 Brian J Siegel, Managing Director
 e-mail: bsiegel@katzgroup.com
 Education: BS, Accounting & Finance, La Salle University; LLM, Taxation, Georgetown University; JD, University of Pennsylvania Law School
 Background: Partner, Duane Morris & Heckscher; Lecturer, Accounting, University of Pennsylvania Wharton School of Finance & Commerce; Attorney Advisor, Arnold Raum, United States Tax Court; Coopers and Lybrand
 David A Katz, Executive Vice President/Secretary
 e-mail: davidkatz@katzgroup.com
 Background: Co-Owner & Founder, Camp Big Pocono; D&S Camps; Sixer's Camp; Owner & President, Innovative Staffing Services; Analyst, Finance Department, Nutri System; Executive Investment

Venture Capital & Private Equity Firms / Domestic Firms

Advisors; VP & Director, Marketing, Philadelphia 76ers Basketball Club

892 H&Q ASIA PACIFIC
228 Hamilton Avenue
3rd Floor
Palo Alto, CA 94301
Phone: 650-838-8025 Fax: 650-618-1699
web: www.hqap.com

Mission Statement: H&Q Asia Pacific is a private equity firm based in Asia.

Geographic Preference: Asia Pacific
Fund Size: $1.8 billion
Founded: 1986
Investment Criteria: Early Stage, Later Stage, Emerging, Buyout, Middle Market, Growth Capital
Industry Group Preference: All Sectors Considered
Portfolio Companies: Access, Acer, Advanced Analog Technology, Advanced Systems Automation, Amperex Technology, Aplix, Array Networks, Atop Holdings, Aztech Systems, Biosensors International, Bluebird, CareNet, Chimei Innolux, Dalipal Pipe Company, Darfon Electronics, D-Link, Esquire, Fabrinet, Falmac, Foxlink, Gonzo, Good Morning Securities, Grace THW Holdings, Groundhog Technologies, Hainan Airline, HANA Micron, Headstrong, Headway Technologies, Hi-mart, Hyunjin Materials and Yonghyun Base Materials, Korea Petrochemical, KSNet, The LeadCorp, Macronix International, MAG Technology, Mando, Megastudy, MTV Japan, Music Semiconductors, Mustek, Nan Ya PCB, Nitgen Technologies, O2Micro, One, Opto Tech, Optovue, Penta Securities Systems, PhiSkin, Primax Electronics, Ralink Technology, RITEK, Roly International Holdings, Semiconductor Manufacturing International, Shandong Winery, SiGen, Siliconware Precision Industries, SinoGen International, Sky Vision, Starbucks Beijing, SVI Public, Taiwan Semiconductor Manufacturing Company, Taiwan Sumida Electronics, Thai Cane Paper Public, TICON Industrial Connection Public, VIBE, Viscovery, Weltrend Semiconductor, Winbond Electronics, Wintek, You Yi Shopping City, Yuchai Engineering

Other Locations:
1650B, 16th Floor
The Hong Kong Club, Building 3A
Chater Road
Central
Hong Kong
Phone: 852-28684800 Fax: 852-28104883

3F Wonseo Building
171 Wonseo-Dong
Jongno-Gu
Seoul 110-280
Korea
Phone: 82-27872288 Fax: 82-237754589

32F-1, International Trade Building
333 Keelung Road
Sec. 1
Taipei 110
Taiwan
Phone: 8862-27209855 Fax: 8862-27222106

Suite 708, 7/FL Citigroup Tower
33 Hua Yuan Shi Qiao Road
Shanghai 200120
China
Phone: 86-2168878080 Fax: 86-2168878011

Key Executives:
Ta-Lin Hsu, Chairman/Founder
Education: BS, Physics, National Taiwan University; MS, Electrophysics, Polytechnic Institute of Brooklyn; PhD, Electrical Engineering, University of California, Berkeley
Background: Research, IBM; General Partner, Hambrecht & Quist
Directorships: ASE, Sinogen International, One

Benson He, Managing Director
Education: BEng, Electrical Engineering, Shanghai Jiao Tong University; CFA
Background: PwC Business Modelling and Valuation; JP Morgan; KPMG Corporate Finance
Mark Hsu, Managing Director
Education: BA, University of California, Los Angeles; JD, Columbia University
Background: Director, Business Development, Sina.com; Attorney, Simpson Thacher & Bartlett
Directorships: AAMA, East West Players, The Churchill Club, Vision New America
William Chung, Managing Director
Education: BS/MS, Agriculture, National Taiwan University
Background: VP, CIDC Consultants Ltd.; Deputy Manager, Industrial Bank of Taiwan Group
Robert Shen, Managing Director
Education: BS, National Cheng Kung University; MS, Marquette University; PhD, Southern Methodist University
Background: Chief Technical Officer & General Manager, Lucent Microelectronics; Founder, Enable Semiconductor; President, 8x8 Inc.; General Manager, VLSI Technology

893 HADDINGTON VENTURES LLC
2603 Augusta
Suite 900
Houston, TX 77057
Phone: 713-532-7992 Fax: 713-532-9922
web: www.hvllc.com

Mission Statement: Providing superior returns to its investors by focusing on the midstream energy sector.

Geographic Preference: United States
Fund Size: $850 million
Founded: 1998
Average Investment: $20 to $50 million
Minimum Investment: $20 million
Industry Group Preference: Energy, Natural Gas, Power Storage, Underground Hydrocarbon Storage, Midstream Growth
Portfolio Companies: Apax CAES, Bear Paw Energy, Bobcat Gas Storage, CAES Development Company, Endicott Biofuels, Eureka Resources, Fairway Energy, Gulf Coast LNG, IACX Energy, Lodi Gas Storage, Magnum NGLS, Magnum Energy, Nations Energy, Proton Energy Systems, Sago Energy, Silicon Energy, Tristream Energy, Zechstein Energy Storage

Key Executives:
J. Chris Jones, Managing Director
Education: BBA, Accounting, University of Texas, Austin
Background: SVP/CFO/COO, Tejas Power Corp.; Secretary/Treasurer/CFO, The Fisk Group Inc.
Directorships: Market Hub Partners, Dayton Power & Light, New Jersey Resources, NIPSCO, Public Service Electric and Gas
John A. Strom, Managing Director
Education: BS, Finance, University of Illinois
Background: Fish Engineering; Union Carbide; Co-Founder/President, TPC
Jim P. Wise, Advisory Board
Education: University of Houston, Bauer College of Business
Background: Managing Director, Haddington Ventures; CEO/Vice Chairman, Integrated Electrical Services; VP, Finance/CFO, Sterling Chemicals; EVP/CFO, Transco Energy Company
M. Scott Jones, Managing Director
Education: BA, Pomona College; JD, University of Texas School of Law
Background: VP/General Counsel, TPC; Dickerson, Carmouch & Jones

James K. Lam, Managing Director
Education: BBA, Finance, University of Houston
Background: Jefferies & Company; Merrill Lynch
Sam H. Pyne, Director
Education: BA, Quantitative Economics, BS, Chemical Engineering, Tufts University; MBA, Rice University
Background: Equity Analyst, Howard Weil; Process Engineer, Lyondell
Directorships: Endicott Biofuels, Eureka, Apex CAES

894 HALIFAX GROUP LLC
1133 Connecticut Avenue NW
Suite 300
Washington, DC 20036

Phone: 202-530-8300
e-mail: inquiry@thehalifaxgroup.com
web: www.thehalifaxgroup.com

Mission Statement: Seeks to create substantial equity value for management teams and its investment partners. Halifax's goal is to form partnerships with proven management teams, bringing not only capital to the middle market but also a wealth of strategic, financial, and operating experience.

Geographic Preference: United States
Fund Size: $1.5 billion
Founded: 1999
Average Investment: $20 million
Minimum Investment: $10 million
Investment Criteria: The last twelve months EBITDA is between $5-$15 million.
Industry Group Preference: Consumer Products, Distribution, Financial Services, Health Related, Information Technology, Manufacturing, Telecommunications, Transportation, Logistics, Consumer Services
Portfolio Companies: Animal Supply Company, Aptiv Solutions, BCI Burke, Caring Brands International, Delphi Behavioral Health Group, Envision Pharma Group, Familia Dental, Golden State Overnight, IASIS Healthcare, InSight Health Services Corp. Inc., K2 Industrial Services, Maverick Healthcare, Meineke Car Care Centers, MTW Corp., North American Video, Nutrition Physiology Company LLC, NPSG, Papa Johns, Pirtek, PolyPipe, The PromptCare Companies, Service Champ, SoilSafe, Taylor Logistics LLC, Universal Hospital Services, U.S. Environmental Services, XLA

Other Locations:
200 Crescent Court
Suite 1030
Dallas, TX 75201
Phone: 214-855-8700

3605 Glenwood Avenue
Suite 490
Raleigh, NC 27612
Phone: 919-786-4420

Key Executives:
David Dupree, Founder/Senior Partner
202-530-8300
e-mail: ddupree@thehalifaxgroup.com
Education: BS, University of North Carolina-Chapel Hill; MBA, Graduate School of Management, Wake Forest University
Background: The Carlyle Group; Montgomery Securities; Alex.Brown & Sons
Directorships: K2 Industrial Services Inc., XLA, Aptiv Solutions, Envision Pharma Group, IASIS Healthcare Corp, InSight Health Services Corp., Meineke Car Care Centers, Soil Safe Inc.
Kenneth M. Doyle, Senior Partner
202-530-8300
e-mail: kdoyle@thehalifaxgroup.com
Education: BS, Boston College; MBA, Duke University
Background: GE Equity; Telecommunications Corporate Finance Group-Merrill Lynch; Chase Manhattan Bank-Media Telecommunications Group; Ernst & Young
Directorships: Famalia Dental, Pirtek Europe, XLA Inc., Caring Brands International, Sinsight Holdings, Maverick Healthcare, Meineke Car Care Centers Inc, North American Video, PJ United
Brent Williams, Senior Partner
214-855-8700
e-mail: bwilliams@thehalifaxgroup.com
Education: BA, University of Texas; MBA, Rice University
Background: Painewebber; Smith Barney; Sumitomo Bank
Directorships: Animal Supply Company, BCI Burke, GSO Delivery, Maverick Healthcare, MTW Corp., PolyPipe Holdings Inc., Taylor Logistics, Universal Hospital Services Inc.
Michael Marshall, Senior Partner/CFO/COO
919-786-4420
e-mail: mmarshall@thehalifaxgroup.com
Education: BA, Accounting, North Carolina State University
Background: KPMG; PricewaterhouseCoopers
Chris Cathcart, Managing Partner
202-530-8300
e-mail: ccathcart@thehalifaxgroup.com
Education: BA, Wake Forest University; MBA, Kellogg School of Management, Northwestern University
Scott Plumridge, Managing Partner
202-530-8300
e-mail: splumridge@thehalifaxgroup.com
Education: BS, Business, Wake Forest University; MBA, Stanford Grad. School of Business
Background: Chartwell Investments; JP Morgan & Co.
Davis Hostetter, Vice President
214-855-8705
e-mail: dhostetter@thehalifaxgroup.com
Education: BS, Economics & Political Science, Duke University; MBA, Wharton School, University of Pennsylvania
Background: Investment Analyst, Hayman Capital; Associate, Diamond Castle Holdings; M&A, Deutsche Bank

895 HALLEY VENTURE PARTNERS
876 Revere Road
Lafayette, CA 94549

Phone: 925-451-3310
web: www.halleyvp.com

Mission Statement: Invests in companies across the various sectors of the cannabis industry.

Founded: 2017
Industry Group Preference: Cannabis, Agriculture, Biosciences, Technology
Portfolio Companies: Front Range Biosciences, SpringBig

Key Executives:
Steve Schuman, Founder/Managing Director
Education: BS, Chemical Engineering, University of Dayton; BS, Ohio State University; MBA, Haas School of Business, University of California, Berkeley
Background: Coordinator/Process Engineer, The Dow Chemical Company; Marketing Manager, Bandwidth9; Sr. Equity Analyst, Prudential Equity Group; Sr. Equity Analyst, New Vernon Associates; Owner/Sr. Equity Analyst, Lafayette Research; Sr. Analyst/PM, Agriculture & Chemicals, Passport Capital

896 HALOGEN VENTURES
e-mail: hello@halogenvc.com

Mission Statement: Halogen Ventures is an early stage venture capital fund focused on female founded consumer technology companies.

Industry Group Preference: Consumer, Technology
Portfolio Companies: Armoire, Barn & Willow, BeautyCon, Block Cypher, Blue Fever, Broadway Roulette, Bulletin, Carbon38, Clover Letter, Dog Parker, Eloquii, Finery, Goodr,

Venture Capital & Private Equity Firms / Domestic Firms

Handwriting.io, HopSkipDrive, Inked Brands, L., Laurel & Wolf Interior Design, Levo League, Molly, Naja, Naya, One Potato, PartySlate, Peek, Preemadonna, Seedling, Senreve, Shipsi, Silvernest, Sugarfina, Tea Drops, Tentrr, The Flex Company, The Relish, The Sill, The Skimm, Tinted, Trust & Will, Vida, Werk

Key Executives:
Jesse Draper, Founding Partner
Education: University of California, LA
Background: Creator/Host, The Valley Girl Show
Directorships: The Skimm, Laurel & Wolf, Carbon38, HopSkipDrive, The Flex Company, Sugarfina

897 HALYARD CAPITAL
140 E 45th Street
Floor 37
New York, NY 10017

Phone: 212-554-2121
e-mail: info@halyard.com
web: www.halyard.com

Mission Statement: Halyard Capital is a middle market private equity firm focused on creating value within the Information and Knowledge economies through thesis-driven investments. The firm invests in technology-enabled Information, Data Analytics, Communications and Business Services companies.

Geographic Preference: North America, Europe
Fund Size: $300 million
Average Investment: $10 - $40 million
Investment Criteria: Growth Equity, Acquisition Capital, Leverage Buyouts, Consolidations, Platform Builds, Turnarounds, Structured Equity, Going-Private Transactions
Industry Group Preference: Information Technology, Marketing, Communications, Business Products & Services, Healthcare, IT Cyber Risk, Data Analytics, Outsourced Solutions
Portfolio Companies: Aberdeen Group, Datamyx, Digital Fortress, Education Dynamics, Engauge, Focal Point Data Risk, Greeley Company, Hanley-Wood, Herld Media, impreMedia, Inflow Group, Inner City Media Corporation, Jun Group, NETGEAR, North Dakota Holdings, NuLink, OneSource Virtual, Pfingsten Publishing, Practice Insight, Presidion Inc., Smith Broadcasting Group, StratEx, Tama Broadcasting, TCP Communications, TI Health, TRANZACT, WMI

Key Executives:
Robert B Nolan Jr, Founding Partner
212-554-2144
e-mail: rnolan@halyard.com
Education: BS, BA, Georgetown University; JD, Fordham University School of Law
Background: CEO, BMO Private Equity Group; Managing Director, CIBC World Markets; Telecommunications Group Head, UBS Securities; Goldman, Sachs & Co.
Directorships: Digital Fortress, Education Dynamics, Jun Group, Practice Insight
Bruce A Eatroff, Managing Partner
212-554-2145
e-mail: beatroff@halyard.com
Education: BA, Lafayette College; MBA, Wharton School
Background: Goldman Sachs; UBS Securities; CIBC World Markets
Directorships: Cyber Risk Management, Education Dynamics, Jun Group, NuLink, OneSource Vital
Jonathan P Barnes, Partner
212-554-2122
e-mail: jbarnes@halyard.com
Education: AB, Harvard University; MBA, Columbia Business School
Background: Morgan Stanley; Consolidated Press Holdings

Directorships: Aberdeen Group, OneSource Virtual, Stratex
Jonathan Grad, Managing Director
212-554-2194
e-mail: skim@halyard.com
Education: BA, Economics & Political Science, Colgate University
Background: Managing Director, Media, Communications & Technology, BMO Capital Markets
Directorships: Digital Fortress, Engauge Marketing, Women's Marketing Inc.
Brendyn T Grimaldi, Principal
212-554-2131
e-mail: bgrimaldi@halyard.com
Education: BS, Finance, Boston College
Background: Analyst, Credit Suisse
Directorships: Aberdeen Group, Stratex, TI Health
Kyle Grace, Associate
212-554-2143
e-mail: kgrace@halyard.com
Education: BA, Economics & Finance, University of Richmond
Background: Investment Banking Analyst, Jefferies & Company

898 HAMILTON BIOVENTURES
990 Highland Drive
Suite 302
Solana Beach, CA 92075

Phone: 858-314-2350
e-mail: info@hamiltonbioventures.com

Mission Statement: A venture capital firm investing in talented entrepreneurs bringing new Life Science technology enterprises to market.

Geographic Preference: United States/West Coast
Fund Size: $100 million
Average Investment: $1-$5 million
Minimum Investment: $1 million
Investment Criteria: Generally early-stage
Industry Group Preference: Life Sciences, Biopharmaceuticals, Therapeutics, Drug Development, Medical Devices, Healthcare
Portfolio Companies: Angstrom Power, CargoTech, Ceregene, Converge Medical, Egea Biosciences, Entropic Communications, Kemia, Mohomine, PhotoThera, Q3DM, Santarus, Transcept Pharmaceuticals, Troika Networks, Voyager Systems

Key Executives:
Robert Ellsworth, Chairman/Founding Partner
Education: BSME, University of Kansas; JD, University of Michigan
Background: General Partner, Lazard Freres & Company; Chairman, Fairchild Space & Defense Corp.; Howmet Corp
Richard Crosby, Managing Director
e-mail: richard@hamiltonbioventures.com
Education: BS, Accounting, University of California, LA
Elliot Parks, Director
e-mail: elliot@hamiltonbioventures.com
Education: PhD, Microbiology & Immunology, University of Washington School of Medicine
Background: Managing Director, Ventana Capital Management; President & CEO, Myelos Neurosciences Corp.; Director, Johnson & Johnson Biotechnology Center; President/cEO, Hawaii Biotech Inc.
Dr. Kerry Dance, Managing Director
e-mail: kerry@hamiltonbioventures.com
Education: PhD Mechanical Engineering, Stanford University
Background: CEO, Advanced Distillation Technology; Maxwell Laboratories; VP Technology, Aerojet General Corporation; President, General Atomics Corporation
Malcolm Finayson, Venture Partner
e-mail: malcolm@hamiltonbioventures.com

Education: BA, Molecular Biology, San Jose State University; PhD, Pharmacology & Toxicology, University of British Columbia
Background: President, Egea Biosciences; President, Invitrogen Corporation
Donald W. Grimm, Director
e-mail: don@hamiltonbioventures.com
Education: BS, Pharmacy, MBA, University of Pittsburgh
Background: President, CEO & Chairman, Hybritech; Founder, Strategic Design

899 HAMILTON ROBINSON CAPITAL PARTNERS
301 Tresser Boulevard
3 Stamford Plaza
Suite 1333
Stamford, CT 06901

Phone: 203-602-0011 Fax: 203-602-2206
e-mail: cld@hrco.com
web: www.hrco.com

Mission Statement: A private equity firm that specializes in serving small to medium size companies seeking equity capital for management buyouts, corporate growth, and recapitalizations for shareholder equity.
Geographic Preference: United States
Founded: 1984
Average Investment: $2-$20 million
Minimum Investment: $2 million
Investment Criteria: LBO, MBO, Recapitalization, Revenue of $25-$200 Million
Industry Group Preference: Industrial Equipment, Outsourcing & Efficiency, Energy, Business to Business, Manufacturing, Distribution, Business Products & Services
Portfolio Companies: Automatan LLC, Custom Engineered Wheels Inc., GrayMatter LLC, Horizon Food Equipment Inc., Sound Seal Inc., Systec Corp., Unifiller Systems Inc., W-Technology Inc.

Key Executives:
Scott I. Oakford, Managing Partner
203-602-0566
e-mail: sio@hrco.com
Education: BS, Economics, Claremont McKenna College
Background: CFO, AGCO; President, Maloney Industries; Goldome Strategic Investments; Chemical Bank
Directorships: W-Technology Holdings, Sound Seal Holdings, Inspire Automation, MEGTEC Holdings
Steve Crihfield, Senior Advisor
203-602-0085
e-mail: osc@hrco.com
Education: BA, Government, Pomona College; MBA, Harvard Business School
Background: General Partner, Saugatuck Capital Company; Merrill Lynch
Directorships: Horizon Bradco, Dexter Magnetic Technologies, Lifestyle Media, The Fitzpatrick Company, Custom Engineered Wheels
Phil Cagnassola, Partner/CFO
203-602-0514
e-mail: pjc@hrco.com
Education: BS, Accounting, Fairfield University
Background: VP, Walker Digital; CFO, PC Flowers and Gifts; Ernst & Young; GE Capital
Directorships: Black Clawson Converting Machinery
Chris Lund, Partner
203-602-0012
e-mail: cel@hrco.com
Education: BA, St. Lawrence University; MBA, Tuck School of Business, Dartmouth College
Background: GE Equity; Chase Manhattan Bank; Chemical Bank
Directorships: Sound Seal Holdings Inc, Inspire Automation, Unifiller Systems, Magnatech International, All Island Media

Stephen B. Connor, Director, Business Development
203-602-3309
e-mail: sbc@hrco.com
Education: BS, Wharton School; University of Pennsylvania; MBA, Columbia Business School; CPA; CFA
Background: SVP, Business Development, GE Capital; Smith Barney Venture Capital Group; Prudential Bache Corporate Finance Group; PricewaterhouseCoopers

900 HAMMOND, KENNEDY, WHITNEY & COMPANY
420 Lexington Avenue
Suite 2633
New York, NY 10170

Phone: 212-867-1010 Fax: 212-867-1312
e-mail: info@hkwinc.com
web: www.hkwinc.com

Mission Statement: Concentrates investments on private and public, small middle market manufacturing companies with low risk of technological obsolescence, providing transaction experience, investing in people and companies with solid fundamentals and creating shareholder value.
Geographic Preference: North America
Fund Size: $255 million
Founded: 1903
Average Investment: $20 - $150 million
Minimum Investment: $5 million
Investment Criteria: MBO, recaps, Revenues of $20 - $200 Million
Industry Group Preference: Manufacturing, Industrial Services, Distribution, Automotive, Medical Devices, Aerospace, Infrastructure, Energy, Cosumer Products
Portfolio Companies: Allied Vision Group Inc., Brant Instore Corp., Gatekeeper Systems Inc., GCR Inc., PANOS Brands LLC, Partners in Leadership Inc., ProAct Services Corp., Protect Plus Air Holdings, Royal Camp Services, Specialized Desanders, Xirgo Technologies

Other Locations:
8888 Keystone Crossing
Suite 600
Indianapolis, IN 46240
Phone: 317-574-6900 Fax: 317-574-7515

Key Executives:
Glenn Scolnik, Senior Advisor
317-705-8814
e-mail: gs@hkwinc.com
Education: BS, Indiana University School of Business, JD, Indiana University School of Law
Background: Partner, Sommer, Barnard, Ackerson Attorneys, Professional Football
Jeffrey G Wood, Senior Partner
207-650-0780
e-mail: jgw@hkwinc.com
Education: BS & MBA, University of Maine
Background: CEO, First Technology PLC; Control Devices Inc.
James O. Futterknecht Jr., Senior Advisor
248-334-9464
Education: BA, University of Texas, Austin
Background: Chairman/CEO/President, Excel Industries Inc.
James C. Snyder, Partner
317-705-8815
e-mail: jcs@hkwinc.com
Education: BA, Wabash College; JD, Indiana University School of Law
Background: Vice President, Browing Investments
Constantine J. Rakkou, Chief Financial & Operations Officer
201-447-1388
e-mail: cjr@hkwinc.com
Education: BA & MBA, Fairleigh Dickinson University

Venture Capital & Private Equity Firms / Domestic Firms

Background: Accounting Managing, Palmeri Fund Administrators Inc.; Putnam Lovell Capital Partners
Ted H. Kramer, President/CEO
317-705-8824
e-mail: tk@hkwinc.com
Education: BS, University of Michigan; MBA, Kelley School of Business, Indiana University
Background: Investment Manager, White River Venture Partners; Arthur Andersen
Luke A. Phenicie, Lead Transaction Partner
317-705-8826
e-mail: lap@hkwinc.com
Education: BS, Indiana University Kelley School of Business; MBA, University of Chicago Graduate School of Business
Background: Financial Analyst, Prospect Partners; M&A, A.G. Edwards & Sons
Caroline L. Young, Partner
317-705-8823
e-mail: cly@hkwinc.com
Education: BA, University of Vermont; JD, University of Virginia School of Law
Background: Wooden & McLaughlin, LLP
John M. Carsello, Partner
317-705-8735
e-mail: jmc@hkwinc.com
Education: BS, Indiana University Kelley School of Business; MBA, Kellogg School of Management, Northwestern University
Background: Analyst, Norwest Equity Partners; Investment Banking, Credit Suisse
Michael A. Foisy, Lead Operations Partner
207-807-8695
e-mail: maf@hkwinc.com
Education: BS, University of Maine; MBA, University of New Hampshire Whittemore School of Business
Background: Business Unit Manager, First Technology Unit, Sensata Technlogy/Bain Capital Partners
Thomas P. Shaw, Vice President
317-663-6492
e-mail: tps@hkwinc.com
Education: BA, Kelley School of Business, Indiana University; MBA, Booth School of Business, University of Chicago
Background: Associate, Wynnchurch Capital; Global Industrials Group, Merrill Lynch
Ralph R. Whitney Jr., Chairman Emeritus/Senior Advisor
212-867-1010
Education: BA & MBA, Rochester University
Christopher M. Eline, Principal
317-705-8827
e-mail: cme@hkwinc.com
Education: BA, Indiana University
Background: Analyst, Sagent Advisors

901 HANCOCK CAPITAL MANAGEMENT
197 Claredon Street
1st Floor
Boston, MA 02116
web: www.hancockcapitalllc.com

Mission Statement: Provides junior capital to support the business objectives of experienced management teams and shareholders.

Fund Size: $4.5 billion
Founded: 1862
Average Investment: $10-50 million
Minimum Investment: $10 million
Investment Criteria: Growth capital, LBO, refinancing, acquisitions
Industry Group Preference: Technology, Construction, Energy, Industrial Services
Portfolio Companies: Compuware, CPG International, DTI, Dynatrace, Exal, Industrial Container Services, Inland, KeyPoint Government Solutions, Nellson Nutraceutical LLC, Old World Industries, Pexco, SolAero Technologies, Sterling, Swanson Industries, Waterjet Holdings, Woodside Homes, Zywave

Other Locations:
1251 Avenue of the Americas
Suite 2300
New York, NY 10020

200 South Wacker Drive
Suite 820
Chicago, IL 60606

Key Executives:
Scott A. McFetridge, Senior Managing Director
e-mail: smcfetridge@jhancock.com
Education: BS, Applied Economics & Management, Cornell University
Background: John Hancock North America Corporate Finance Group
Paul Fishbin, Managing Director
e-mail: pfishbin@jhancock.com
Education: BA, Economics, University of Pennsylvania; MBA, Booth School of Business, University of Chicago
Background: Investment Banker, Citicorp; Dillon Reed; Putnam Lovell
Scott Garfield, Managing Director
e-mail: sgarfield@jhancock.com
Education: BA, Economics, Williams College; MBA, Fuqua School of Business, Duke University
Background: Partner, FinanStar Group; Wachovia Capital Markets Group
Daniel Budde, Senior Managing Director
e-mail: dbudde@jhancock.com
Education: BS, Economics, University of New Hampshire; MBA, Babson College; CFA
Background: Partner, ABRY Partners; Managing Director, John Hancock North Americ Corporate Finance Group

902 HANCOCK PARK ASSOCIATES
10350 Santa Monica Boulevard
Suite 295
Los Angeles, CA 90025
Phone: 310-228-6900 Fax: 310-228-6939
e-mail: info@hpcap.com
web: www.hpcap.com

Mission Statement: A private equity firm with an investment approach distinguished by its strong orientation towards operations. Each of the firm's principals has significant operating experience which allows HPA to seek out investments in businesses where present management needs to be supplemented.

Geographic Preference: California, Western Region
Fund Size: $30 million
Founded: 1986
Average Investment: $10 million
Minimum Investment: $5 million
Investment Criteria: Controlling Investements in Small to Medium-Sized Companies; Revenues of $25 - $200 million
Industry Group Preference: Manufacturing, Retailing, Aerospace
Portfolio Companies: American Home/American Furniture Company, ASC Specialty Vehicle, Advent Aerospace Inc., Barcalounger, Charming Charlie, Crimson Well Services Inc., Priject Time & Cost, The Marktets LLC, Synchronous Aerospace Group

Other Locations:
1980 Post Oak Boulevard
Suite 2150
Houston, TX 77056
Phone: 713-940-8100 Fax: 713-986-8410

Key Executives:
Michael J. Fourticq Sr., Managing Partner
e-mail: mjfourticq@hpcap.com
Education: BA, LLB, Texas University, MBA Harvard

Business School
Background: General Partner, Brentwood Associates
Directorships: Member, State Bar of Texas
Michael J. Fourticq Jr., Partner
Education: BA, Economics, University of Texas, Austin; CPA
Background: Corporate Finance, KPMG
Kevin L. Listen, Partner
e-mail: klisten@hpcap.com
Education: BBA, Finance & Real Estate, Southern Methodist University; MBA, University of California, Los Angeles
Background: The TCW Group Inc.
Kenton S. Van Harten, Partner
e-mail: kvanharten@hpcap.com
Education: BS, Accounting, Brigham Young University; CPA
Background: CEO, Fitness Holdings International; Interim CEO, American Furniture Corp.
Kenneth G. Walter Jr., Partner
e-mail: kwatler@hpcap.com
Education: BA, University of Texas, Austin
Martin Irani, Vice President
e-mail: mirani@hpcap.com
Education: BA, Economics, MBA, Finance, University of Southern California
Ted Fourticq, Principal
e-mail: tfourticq@hpcap.com
Education: BA, Vanderbilt University; JD & MBA, Loyola Marymount University
Directorships: Borga, American Furniture Corp, Project Time & Cost
Michael F. Gooch, Vice President, Finance
e-mail: mgooch@hpcap.com
Education: BS, Business Administration, University of Southern California; CPA

903 HANOVER PARTNERS
425 California Street
Suite 2000
San Francisco, CA 94104

Phone: 415-788-8680
e-mail: aaron@hanoverpartners.com
web: www.hanoverpartners.com

Mission Statement: Change of control acquisitions only. Hanover Partners acquires privately owned middle market companies with a minimum of $2 million of operating cash flow annually.
Geographic Preference: United States, Canada
Founded: 1994
Average Investment: $8 million
Minimum Investment: $5 million
Investment Criteria: LBO, MBO, Middle market companies with earnings of at last #8 million
Industry Group Preference: Service Industries, Manufacturing
Portfolio Companies: Audio Precision, Bri-Mar Manufacturing LLC, Consolidated Equipment Group, Freedom Communication Technologies, Hamer LLC, Handi Quilter, Pyramid Technologies Inc., Rugby Manufacturing Company, Solidscape, Wohler Technologies Inc.

Other Locations:
201 B Avenue
Suite 270
Lake Oswego, OR 97034
Phone: 503-699-6410

Key Executives:
Andrew N. Ford, Co-Founder/Principal
503-699-6410
e-mail: andyf@hanoverpartners.com
Education: BA, Government, Dartmouth College; MBA, Kellogg School, Northwestern University
Background: Chairman, Freedom Communication Technologies; Consolidated Equipment Group; Pyramid Technologies; Solidscape; Bri-Mar Manufacturing; Product & Marketing Manager, Atlast Telecom; Management Consultant, Gemini Consulting
Directorships: Hamer LLC, Wohler Technologies, Handi-Quilter, Rugby Manufacturing
John E. Palmer, Co-Founder/Principal
415-788-8222
e-mail: johnp@hanoverpartners.com
Education: BA, Dartmouth College; MBA, Kellogg School of Business; Northwestern University; CFA
Background: VP, Wells Fargo; Management Consultant, Mercer Management Consulting; Chairman, Wohler Technologies; Hamer LLC
Directorships: Pyramid Technologies, Consolidated Equipment Group, Solidscape Inc., Bri-Mar Manufacturing
Aaron C. Aiken, Principal
415-788-8680
e-mail: aaron@hanoverpartners.com
Education: BA, History & Political Science, Northwestern University
Background: Analyst, Baird Capital Partners; LaSalle Capital Group
Directorships: Freedom Communication Technologies, Wohler Technologies

904 HARBERT MANAGEMENT CORPORATION
2100 Third Avenue North
Suite 600
Birmingham, AL 35203

Phone: 205-987-5500
e-mail: irelations@harbert.net
web: www.harbert.net

Mission Statement: To partner with successful business leaders to build viable, dynamic companies. Harbert invests in a variety of asset classes to build a portfolio with the diversification that can balance risk and return.
Geographic Preference: Mid-Atlantic, Southeastern US
Fund Size: $150 million
Founded: 1995
Average Investment: $3 - $7 million
Minimum Investment: $500,000
Investment Criteria: Early Stage, Experienced Management Teams, Scalable Operating Platforms
Industry Group Preference: Communication Technology, Software, Communications Equipment, Semiconductors, Healthcare, Information Technology, Services, Technology
Portfolio Companies: Agility, Anutra Medical, Axial Exchange, Caresync, Clarabridge, Clinipace Worldwide, Cloud Elements, ControlScan, Envera, Healthcare Interative, Iconixx, Invincea, Jack Be, Kaleo, Ledbury, MapAnything, Mobile Posse, MaxCyte, Netsertive, nContact, NovaMin, Racemi Inc., Sidecar, Snagajob, Social SafeGuard, Springbot, Shipt, UniTrends, Wellcentive, Wiser Together, Yap

Other Locations:
1210 East Cary Street
Suite 400
Richmond, VA 23219
Phone: 804-782-3800

555 Madison Avenue
25th Floor
New York, NY 10022
Phone: 212-521-6970

618 Church Street
Suite 500
Nashville, TN 37219
Phone: 615-301-6400

Brookfield House
5th Floor
44 Davies Street

Venture Capital & Private Equity Firms / Domestic Firms

London W1K 5JA
United Kingdom
Phone: 44 (0) 207 408 4120

3060 Peachtree Road NW
Suite 885
Atlanta, GA 30305
Phone: 404-760-8340

575 Market Street
Suite 2925
San Francisco, CA 94105
Phone: 415-442-8380

Suite 204
2nd Floor
Pinar, 5
Madrid 28006
Spain
Phone: 34-91-745-6859

200 Cresent Court
Suite 440
Dallas, TX 75201
Phone: 214-756-6590

29 rue de Bassano
Paris 75008
France
Phone: 33-17-225-6527

Key Executives:
Raymond J. Harbert, Chairman & Chief Executive Officer
Education: BS, Business, Auburn University
Background: Vice President, Harbert Properties Corp.
Directorships: Birmingham Business Alliance
Charles D. Miller, EVP, Global Head oF Distribution
Education: BS, Civial Engineering, Auburn University; Wharton Executive Program, Financial Management, University of Pennsylvania
Background: Operations, Harbert Corp.
Sonja J. Keeton, EVP, Chief Financial Officer
Education: BA, Accounting, University of South Alabama; CPA
Background: Director, Corporate Taxation & Assistant Controller, Hartbert Corporation; PricewaterhouseCoopers
John W. McCullough, EVP, General Counsel
Education: BA, Economics, Washington and Lee University; JD, Cumberland School of Law, Samford University
Background: Partner, Balch & Bingham LLP
J. Travis Prichett, VP/Senior Managing Director, Global Real Estate Strategies
Education: BS, Biology, Davidson College; MA, Environmental Management, Duke University; MBA, Kenan-Flagler Business School, University of North Carolina

905 HARBINGER VENTURE MANAGEMENT
3 Results Way
Cupertino, CA 95014
Phone: 408-861-3983
e-mail: uscontact@harbingervc.com

Mission Statement: Harbinger's mission is to be a value-added venture investor in the core technologies that will enhance the productivity and experience at the workplace or at home. Leveraging the MiTAC-SYNNEX Group's strong financial backing and web of networks, we strive to create synergy and forge strategic relationships among our investee companies and the Group's affiliated companies at every opportunity. Welcoming challenge, Harbinger will continue to be a forerunner in the technologies that will change the communications and computing networks of tomorrow while generating tangible results and real value for both its investees and investors.

Geographic Preference: North America, Asia
Average Investment: $1 - $5 million

Investment Criteria: Early-Stage to Late-Stage
Industry Group Preference: Communications, Networking, Wireless Technologies, Semiconductors, Internet, Software, Infrastructure, Computer Hardware & Software
Portfolio Companies: A10 Networks, ACTi, Alpha & Omega Semiconductor, Applied Optoelectronics, BroadSound, Cardiva Medical, Centrality Communications, CGCG, Continuous Computing Corp, CP Secure, EpiStar, Envivo, GemTek, HEP Tech, LighTuning, MedSphere International, Plaxo, Tsang Yow, Tyan, VeriSilicon, vvlogger, YeePay

Other Locations:
7th Floor, No. 187
Tiding Blvd, Sec 2
Neihu
Taipei 114
Taiwan
Phone: 886-22657-9368

Key Executives:
C.K. Cheng, General Partner
Education: BS, Physics, Tsing-Hua University; MBA, Chiao-Tung University
Background: Senior Vice President, Product Marketing, SYNNEX
M.R. Lin, Venture Partner
Education: BSEE, National Taiwan University; MBA, National Chiao Tung University
Background: Managing Director, H&Q Taiwan Co.; President, Hantech Venture Capital
Matthew Miau, Chairman
Education: University of California, Berkeley; MBA, Santa Clara University
Background: Chairman, MiTAC-SYNNEX Group
T.C. Chou, President, Harbinger Taiwan
Education: BS, National Taiwan University; MBA, Wharton Business School; PhD, Rutgers University
Background: Special Assistant to Chairman, MiTAC-SYNNEX Group; Director, Corporate Development, Roll International
John Tzeng, Vice President, Harbinger Taiwan
Education: BS, Business Administration, National Taiwan University; MBA, Purdue University
Background: Senior Manager, O'Melvery & Myers; President, CT Tainjn Datian-Rel Estate
Tzyy-Po Wang, Senior Vice President, Harbinger Taiwan
Education: BSEE, MSEE, National Taiwan University
Background: MIC/III
Ronald Han, Vice President, Harbinger Taiwan
Education: BS, Fu-Jen Catholic University, Taiwan; MBA, George Washington University
Background: MITAC-SYNNEX Group; Union Petrochemical Corporation; Westpac Banking Corporation
Ru-Guang Bal, Vice President, Harbinger China
Education: BS, Physics, Beijing Normal University
Background: Senior Investment Manager, RuYing Investment Management Co.
Ronald Han, Vice President, Harbinger Taiwan
Education: BS, Fu-Jen Catholic University; MBA, Finance, George Washington University
Background: MiTAC-SYNNEX Group, Union Petrochemical Corporation

907 HARBOR LIGHT CAPITAL PARTNERS
91 Court St.
Keene, NH 03431
Phone: 603-355-9954 **Fax:** 603-355-1158
e-mail: info@hlcp.com
web: www.hlcp.com

Mission Statement: Harbor Light Capital Partners is a private investment firm seeking to invest in early and growth stage companies located in the Northeast. Our unique approach combines flexible capital and collaborative support to build successful, sustainable operating companies. Harbor

Light's legacy, values, and experience provide the guiding light for superior results.
Geographic Preference: Northeast United States
Average Investment: $1 - $5 million
Investment Criteria: Early-Stage, Growth Stage
Industry Group Preference: Technology, Clean Technology, Healthcare
Portfolio Companies: Alcyone Lifesciences, Carmell Therapeutics, Courtagen Life Sciences, Direct Vet Marketing, Micronotes, Senet
Key Executives:
  Todd Warden, Managing Partner
  Education: BS, Mathematics, University of Vermont; MBa, Boston University
  Background: Vice President, Marketing & Business Development, MARKEM Corporation
  Directorships: Tauck, Senet
  Richard Upton, General Partner
  Education: BA, Economics & English, Amherst College; MBA, Darden School, University of Virginia
  Background: Founder & President, Upton Advisors
  Directorships: Alcyone, Courtagen Life Sciences, Castlewood Surgical, Carmell Therapeutics, Home Diagnostics
  Darby Kopp, General Partner
  Education: BA, Swarthmore College; MBA, Tuck School of Business, Dartmouth College
  Background: Business Development, MARKEM Corporation; Strategy Consultant, Pembroke Consulting
  Directorships: EBSCO Information Services

908 **HARBOUR GROUP**
7701 Forsyth Boulevard
Suite 600
St. Louis, MO 63105
Phone: 314-727-5550
e-mail: bmichel@harbourgroup.com
web: www.harbourgroup.com

Mission Statement: A privately owned operating company with a demonstrated record of success in acquiring and developing market leading companies for long term investment.
Geographic Preference: North America
Fund Size: $400 million
Founded: 1976
Investment Criteria: Companies with revenues between $30-$500 million
Industry Group Preference: Manufacturing, Distribution, Business Products & Services, Digital Media & Marketing, Logistics, Industrial Products
Portfolio Companies: LLP Holding Corporation, Green Creative LLC, Marshall Excelsior Company, Koch & Associates Inc., BASE Engineering Inc., SP Industries Inc., PennTech Machinery Corporation, Phillips & Temro Industries Inc., Wolverine Heaters, ONICON Incorporated, Greyline Instruments Inc., Air Monitor Corporation, Fox Thermal Instruments Inc., Seattle Metrics Inc., Cleaver-Brooks Inc., Holman Boiler Works, Affiliated Power Services, Camus Hydronics Ltd., CPS Products Inc., Uview Ultraviolet Systems Inc., AAB Smart Tools LLC, STAR EnviroTech Inc., Lindsstrom LLC, Bossard Metrics Inc., Titan Fastener Products Inc., Anda Tool and Fastener Ltd., Fleetgistics Enterprises Inc., Top Knobs USA Inc., Hardware Resources, Atlast Homewares Inc., SloanLED, Watchfire, Haydon Enterprises Inc., Kerk Motion Products Inc., Pearlman Industries Inc., Dimensional Tools Inc., Stone Tool Supply Inc., GranQuartz Holdings LLC, Somaca, Granite City Tool Company Inc., Lincoln International Corporation, Alemite LLC, Reelcraft Industries, Lincoln Helios Ltd., Tech Lighting LLC, LBL Lighting Inc., Merit Industries Inc., Rowe International Inc., Games Warehouse Ltd., View Interative, Tap.tv, Rock-Ola, NSM Music Group, Auto Meter Products Inc., STACK Ltd., Dedenbear Products, SIMCO Ltd., ProParts, Eckler Industries, Classic Chevy International, Late Great Chevy, Copperfield Chimney Supply, California Comfort Corp., Hancock's Wholesale Supply, Tubular Textile, Ashby Industries, RFG Enterprises, Marshall & Williams Co.
Key Executives:
  Jeff Fox, Chairman & CEO
  Education: BS, Universith of Southern California; MBA, Washington University
  Directorships: Lincoln Industrial Corp.; JLG OmniQuip Inc.

909 **HARBOURVEST PARTNERS LLC**
One Financial Center
Boston, MA 02111
Phone: 617-348-3707 **Fax:** 617-350-0305
web: www.harbourvest.com

Mission Statement: A global private equity investment firm seeking investments in all types of private equity funds, and also directly in operating companies.
Geographic Preference: United States, Europe, Asia, Australia, South America
Fund Size: $4.4 billion
Founded: 1973
Average Investment: $12 million
Minimum Investment: $5 million
Investment Criteria: Late-Stage, Leveraged buyouts, Recapitalization, Mezzanine, Growth Equity
Industry Group Preference: Software, Hardware, Data Communications, Telecommunications, Financial Services, Asset Management, Technology, Media, Advertising, Consumer Products, Healthcare, Biotechnology
Portfolio Companies: Ability, ACG, Acrisure, Advance Health, Advanced Instruments Inc., Allegro, Alliant, Amri, Appriss, Advidxchange, BenefitMall, Benestra, Capsugel, CareCentrix, Catalina, Clix, Colisee, Consol, Cortefiel, EatonTowers, Exxcelia, Finanzcheck.De, Finjan Vital Security, Five Star Food Service, Flash Networks, Flinn Scientific Inc., GB Foods, Get Back, GCS, Gotha Cosmetics, Harbor Community Bank, Healthgrades, Heritage Foodservice Group, Hub International, Love'em Ingham, Intelex, Ista, Lionbridge Capital, Lucid, MedOptions, Mimeo.com, Ministry Brands, Moeller Aerospace, MultiPlan, Nero, OTG, Outbrain, Peloton, Pinnacle, Planview, Polyconcept, Polynt, Press Ganey, Preston Hollow Capital, Profi, Project Arriendo, Q4, RCN, Re Commmunity Recycling, Risk Strategies Company, Riverbed, Roland, Roompot, Saba, Safe, Salad Signature, Samba Safety, Schenck Process, SeaSwift, Sebia, Secure-24, Securus Technologies, ServOne, Sign-Zone Inc., Sirius Computer Solutions, Solace Systems, Solarwinds, Staples, Super Max, Team Viewer, Third Bridge, ThoughtSpot, Towne Park, Tritech Software Systems, Triton, Tyntec, United Surgical Partners International, Veriato, Vestcom, Videology, Vironclinics Biosciences, Vix, Wave Accounting, Wayfair, Xpressdocs, Zayo
Other Locations:
  Champion Tower
  3 Garden Road
  Suite 1207
  Central
  Hong Kong
  Phone: 852-2525-2214 **Fax:** 852-2525-2241

  3rd Floor
  33 Jermyn Street
  London SW1Y 6DN
  United Kingdom
  Phone: 44 (0)20 7399 9820

  Suite 5608 56/F China World Tower A
  1 Jianguomenwai Avenue
  Chaoyang District
  Beijing 100004

Venture Capital & Private Equity Firms / Domestic Firms

China
Phone: 86 10 5706 8600 **Fax:** 86 10 5706 8601

Marunouchi Building, 34th Floor
2-4-1 Marunouchi
Chiyoda-ku
Tokyo 100-6326
Japan
Phone: 81 3 3284 4320 **Fax:** 81 3 3217 1077

Carrera 7 #113 - 43
Oficina 904
Edificio Samsung
Bogota
Colombia
Phone: 57 1 552 1400

Gran Seoul Tower 1 18th Floor
33 Jongro
Jongno-gu
Seoul 03159
South Korea
Phone: 82 2 6410 8020 **Fax:** 82 2 6937 1012

3 HaNechoshet Street
Building B
Tel Aviv 6971068
Isreal
Phone: 972 3 3720001 **Fax:** 972 3 7618120

Bay Adelaide Centre
333 Bay Street
Suite 2720
Toronto, ON M5H 2R2
Canada
Phone: 647-484-3022 **Fax:** 647-498-1448

Key Executives:
Frederick Maynard, Senior Advisor
617-348-3723
e-mail: fmaynard@harbourvest.com
Education: BA, Wesleyan University; MBA, Amos Tuck School of Busines Administration, Dartmouth College
Background: Loan Officer, Manufacturers Hanover Trust
Directorships: Apax Partners, First Capital-Oklahoma, Genesis Holdings International Management-London
Robert Wadsworth, Senior Advisor
617-348-3715
e-mail: rwadsworth@harbourvest.com
Education: MBA, Harvard University; BS Systems Engineering/Computer Science, University of Virginia
Background: Booz Allen and Hamilton
Directorships: Concord Communications, ePresence, Network Engines, Trintech Group PLC, Switchboard and several international companies
George Anson, Senior Advisor
44 (0)20 7399 9822
e-mail: ganson@harbourvest.com
Education: BA, Finance, University of Iowa
Background: Pantheon Ventures
William Johnston, Senior Advisor
Education: BA, Colgate University; MBA, Syracuse University
Background: Corporate Finance, John Hancock; State Street Bank
Directorships: Boston Communications Group, Masada Security, Transit Communications
Brett Gordon, Managing Director
617-348-3764
e-mail: bgordon@harbourvest.com
Education: MBA, Babson College; BS/BA Management, Boston University
Background: VP, Princeton Review of Boston
John Morris, Managing Director
617-348-3732
e-mail: jmorris@harbourvest.com
Education: BA Economics, Clark University; MBA, Columbia University
Background: Abbott Capital Management; VP Corporate Finance, CIBC; Canadian Imperial Bank of Commerce; Board of Directors, Applied Molecular Evolution
Directorships: Blackstone Communications, Bruckmann Rosser Sherrill & Co II, Concord Israel Ventures II, Cypress Merchant Banking Partners II, Domain Partners II-V, Draper Fisher Jurveston
John Fiato, Principal
617-348-3540
e-mail: jfiato@harbourvest.com
Education: BSBA, Accounting, Minor in Economics, Salem State College
Amanda Outerbridge, Managing Director
617-348-3518
e-mail: aouterbridge@harbourvest.com
Education: BS, Business Administration from Babson College
Background: XL Capital; Bank of Bermuda
Kathleen Bacon, Senior Advisor
44 (0)20 7399 9823
e-mail: kbacon@harbourvest.com
Education: BA, Russian, Dartmouth College; MBA, Tuck School of Business, Dartmouth College
Background: First National Bank of Boston
Gregory Stento, Managing Director
617-348-3588
e-mail: gstento@harbourvest.com
Education: BS, Cornell University; MBA, Harvard Business School
Background: Comdisco Ventures; Bridge Partners; NCR Corporation
Peter Lipson, Managing Director
617-348-3595
e-mail: plipson@harbourvest.com
Education: BA, Economics, Univesity of California San Diego; MS, Information Ssytems, University of Virginia; MBA, Harvard Business School
Background: Financial Analyst, M&A Group, Salomon Brothers
Julie Ocko, Managing Director
617-348-3532
e-mail: jocko@harbourvest.com
Education: BS, Business Administration, University of North Carolina; MBA, Darden School of Business Administration, University of Virginia
Background: AEW Capital Management; Narragansett Capital
Alex Rogers, Managing Director
647-348-3555
e-mail: arogers@harbourvest.com
Education: BA, Economics, Duke University; MBA, Harvard Business School
Background: McKinsey & Company
Michael Taylor, Managing Director
617-348-3721
e-mail: mtaylor@harbourvest.com
Education: BS, United States Naval Academy; MBA, Finance, The Wharton School, University of Pennsylvania
Background: Morgan Stanley; Lieutenant Commander, United States Navy; Naval Aviator
John Toomey Jr., Managing Director
617-348-3525
e-mail: jtoomey@harbourvest.com
Education: BS, Chemistry & Physics, Harvard University; MBA, Harvard Business School
Background: Analyst, Smith Barney
Martha DiMatteo Vorlicek, Senior Advisor
617-348-3709
e-mail: mvorlicek@harbourvest.com
Education: BS, Business Administration, Babson College
Background: Senior Audit Manager, Ernst & Young
Mary Traer CPA, Managing Director & Chief Administrative Officer
617-348-3778
e-mail: mtraer@harbourvest.com
Education: BS, Economics, MS, Accounting, University

Venture Capital & Private Equity Firms / Domestic Firms

of Virginia
Background: Ernst & Young; University of Virginia's Treasurer's Office
Peter Wilson, Managing Director
44-20-7399-9824
e-mail: pwilson@harbourvest.com
Education: BA, McGill University; MBA, Harvard Business School
Background: European Bank for Reconstruction & Development; The Monitor Company
David Atterbury, Managing Director
44-20-7399-9836
e-mail: datterbury@harbourvest.com
Education: BSc, International Management & France, University of Bath
Background: Director of Private Equity, Abbey National Treasury Services; PricewaterhouseCoopers
Julie Eiermann, Managing Director/Chief Data Officer
617-348-3727
e-mail: jeiermann@harbourvest.com
Education: BA, University of New Hampshire
Background: Advent International Corporation
Jeffrey Keay, Managing Director
617-348-3536
e-mail: jkeay@harbourvest.com
Education: BA, Economics & Accounting, College of the Holy Cross
Background: Ernst & Young
Karin Lagerlund, Managing Director/CFO
617-348-3752
e-mail: klagerlund@harbourvest.com
Education: BA, Business Administration, Washington State University
Background: AEW Capital Management; Audit Manager, EY Kenneth Leventhal
Edward W Kane, Senior Advisor
Education: BA, University of Pennsylvania; MBA, Harvard Business School
Background: Co-Founder, HarbourVest Partners; New England Merchants National Bank; Board Member of Xylogics, Al Corp, Mutual Risk Management
Directorships: Advisory Committee Member to: Battery Ventures, Canadover (UK), Transpac Equity Investment, Latin American Enterprise Fund
Tatsuya Kubo, Managing Director
81 3 3284 4321
e-mail: tkubo@harbourvest.com
Education: BA, Economics, Waseda University; MBA, Duke University
Background: Managing Director, Fortress Investment Group Japan; Senior Manager, Norinchukin Bank
Scott Voss, Managing Director
852-2878-5630
e-mail: svoss@harbourvest.com
Education: BS, Marketing, Bryant College; MBA, Babson College
Background: Cannondale Corporation
McComma Grayson III, Principal
e-mail: mgrayson@harbourvest.com
Education: BA, Government, Harvard College; MBA, Harvard Business School
Background: Financial Analyst, Morgan Stanley's Global Energy Group

910 HARREN EQUITY PARTNERS
200 Garrett Street
Suite F
Charlottesville, VA 22902
Phone: 434-245-5800 **Fax:** 434-245-5802
e-mail: info@harrenequity.com
web: www.harrenequity.com

Mission Statement: Harren Equity Partners seeks to create long-term value for companies by forming strong partnerships with stellar management teams and assisting with operational improvement and strategic planning.

Geographic Preference: North America
Fund Size: $275 million
Founded: 2001
Average Investment: $10 million
Minimum Investment: $7 million
Investment Criteria: Lower Middle Market, Management Buyouts, Recapitalizations, Industry Consolidations
Industry Group Preference: Manufacturing, Distribution, Business Products & Services, Consumer Products, Industrial, Healthcare Services, Aerospace, Defense and Government, Restaurants, Energy Services, Transportation
Portfolio Companies: ARKLATEX Energy Services, Circa Corporation of America, Energy Fishing & Rental Services, Marianna Industries, Med-Legal, Persante Health Care, SimplyShe, Spartan Energy Services, Virginia Tile Company
Key Executives:
Thomas A. Carver, Co-Founder & Managing Partner
Education: BS, McIntire School of Commerce, MBA, Darden School of Business, University of Virginia
Background: Partner, HIG Capital; Interim President, Plastic Fabricating Company; Interim President, Virginia Explosives & Drilling Company
Directorships: Professional Directional Holdings, Keystone Air & Drill Supply
Lee J. Monahan, Partner
e-mail: leem@harrenequity.com
Education: BS, Finance, DePaul University; MBA, Harvard Business School
Background: Associate, HIG Capital; Lazard Freres & Co
Directorships: Keystone Air & Drill Supply, Med-Legal, Energy Fishing & Rental Services
C Taylor Cole Jr, Partner
e-mail: tcole@harrenequity.com
Education: University of Virginia; Darden School of Business
Background: Morgan Stanley; Kirkland Investment Corp.; Lehman Brothers; Charterhouse Group
Directorships: MedPro Healthcare Staffing
George McCabe, Partner
e-mail: gmccabe@harrenequity.com
Education: University of Virginia
Background: Freidman Billings Ramsey; Pine Creek Partners
Directorships: Shrimp Basket, Inc.

911 HARRISON METAL
2430 3rd St.
San Francisco, CA 94107
e-mail: info@harrisonmetal.com
web: www.harrisonmetal.com

Mission Statement: Harrison Metal invests in early stage technology companies leg by exceptional founders. We help founders build products that improve the daily lives of users, successfully take those products to market, and create a thriving business. If we do that right, we return many times our investors capital and help perpetuate the work of great institutions.

Founded: 2008
Investment Criteria: Early Stage
Industry Group Preference: Technology
Key Executives:
Michael Dearing, Founder
Education: AB, Economics, Brown University; MBA, Harvard Business School
Background: Senior Vice President & General Merchandise Manager, eBay.com; Bain & Company; Filene's Basement; The Walt Disney Company; Industrial Shoe Warehouse
Andrew Humphries, Head of School
Education: BS, Biology, Duke University; MA, Education, Stanford University

Venture Capital & Private Equity Firms / Domestic Firms

Background: Performer, Second City; Teacher, Francis W. Parker School; Teacher, Chicago Public School

912 HARTFORD VENTURES
690 Asylum Avenue
Hartford, CT 06155

Phone: 860-547-5000
e-mail: hartfordventures@thehartford.com
web: www.thehartford.com

Mission Statement: Hartford Ventures, partners with and invests in people with big ideas to spawn a new generation of possibilities to transform the insurance and wealth management industry.
Geographic Preference: Hartford, CT
Average Investment: $1 - $3 million
Investment Criteria: Early-Stage, Expansion-Stage
Portfolio Companies: DriverSide, Coulomb Technologies, GreenRoad, Insurance.com, Buysafe, Intelleflex, Co3Systems
Key Executives:
　Tom Whiteaker, Managing Director
　e-mail: thomas.whiteaker@thehartford.com
　Education: MBA, International Management, Thunderbird School of Global Management
　Background: Corporate Ventures, Visa

913 HARVARD CAPITAL GROUP
1800 Century Park East
6th Floor
Los Angeles, CA 90067

Phone: 213-290-0048
e-mail: corporate@harvardcapital.com
web: www.harvardcapital.com

Mission Statement: The Harvard Capital Group is an investment bank focused on providing advisory services and capital raising solutions to startups and middle-market private companies.
Average Investment: $1 - $20 million
Investment Criteria: Startups to Mezzanine Financing
Key Executives:
　Ailliam Knoke, President/Managing Director
　e-mail: bill.knoke@harvardcapital.com
　Education: BA, Economics, Stanford University; MBA, Harvard Business School
　Background: Founder, Badjao Foundation; VP, M&A, VI Capital
　Rashid Alvi, Managing Director
　e-mail: rashid.alvi@harvardcapital.com
　Education: Columbia Law School
　Background: Acro Healthcare; Davis Polk & Wardwell; Lehman Brothers; Goldman Sachs
　Louie Ucciferri, Managing Director
　e-mail: louie.ucciferri@harvardcapital.com
　Education: Stanford University
　Background: CCO & Financial Principal, EdgeLine Capital; CEO, Regent Capital Group; VP, Operations, Commonwealth Financial Network

914 HARVEST PARTNERS
280 Park Avenue
26th Floor
New York, NY 10017

Phone: 212-599-6300
e-mail: info@harvestpartners.com
web: www.harvestpartners.com

Mission Statement: To pursue a risk-return approach that will generate stable, consistent and superior returns, as well as ensure the preservation of capital.
Geographic Preference: North America
Fund Size: $1.125 billion
Founded: 1981
Average Investment: $50 - $250 million
Investment Criteria: High free cash flow, revenue driven business model, control investment
Industry Group Preference: Manufacturing, Distribution, Industrial Services, Business Products & Services, Consumer Products, Specialty Retail, Healthcare Services
Portfolio Companies: Advanced Dermatology & Cosmetic Surgery, APC Automotive Technologies, Aquilex Corporation, Associated Materials Inc., Athletico, AxelaCare Holdings Inc., Bartlett Holdings Inc., Communications Supply Corporation, Continuum Energy, Coveright Surfaces Holding GmbH, Cycle Gear Inc., Dental Care Alliance, Driven Brands Inc., DTI Inc., Encanto Restaurants Inc., Epiq, Evenflo Company Inc., EyeCare Services Partners, FCX Performance Inc., Garretson Resolution Group, Green Bancorp Inc., Insight Global Inc., Integrity Marketing Group, Lazer Spot Inc., Natural Products Group Inc., Neighborly, New Flyer Industries Ltd., OnPoint Group, Packers Holdings LLC, PRO Unlimited, Regency Energy Partners LP, Service Express, TruckPro LLC, US Silica Company, Valet Living, VetCor, Yellowstone Landscape
Key Executives:
　Thomas W. Arenz, Partner
　Education: BS, Mechanical Engineering, United States Naval Academy; MBA, Harvard Business School
　Background: Principal, Joseph Littlejohn & Levy; Kidder Peabody; Drexel Burnham Lambert
　Directorships: Truck Pro, Cycle Gear, Coveright
　Michael B. DeFlorio, President
　Education: BS, Economics, Wharton School, University of Pennsylvania; MBA, Harvard Business School
　Background: Partner, JH Whitney & Co.; American Industrial Partners; Donaldson, Lufkin & Jenrette
　Directorships: FCX, Bartlett Holdings, Continuum Energy, Valet Waste
　Stephen Eisenstein, Partner
　Education: BA, Economics, Tufts University; MBA, Wharton School, University of Pennsylvania
　Background: Founding Partner, Paribas Principal Partners; Corporate Finance, Chase Manhattan Bank; Equity Research, Paine Webber Inc.
　Directorships: Packers Holdings, Green Bancorp, Encanto Restaurants
　Ira D. Kleinman, Partner
　Education: BS, Accounting, State University of New York, Binghamton; MBA, St. John's University
　Background: Regional Controller, American International Group; Financial Analyst, Bank of New York; National Benefit Life Insurance Co.
　Directorships: Athletico, Dental Care Alliance, Garretson Resolution Group, Insight Global, VetCor
　Jay Wilkins, Chief Operating Officer
　Education: BS, Vanderbilt University
　Background: Principal, DLJ Merchant Banking Partners; North Castle Partners; Analyst, Leveraged Finance Group, Donaldson, Lufkin & Jenrette
　Directorships: Athletico, Dental Care Alliance, Insight Global, Packers Holdings, VetCor

915 HATTERAS VENTURE PARTNERS
280 S Mangum Street
Suite 350
Durham, NC 27701

Phone: 919-484-0730 Fax: 919-484-0364
web: www.hatterasvp.com

Mission Statement: Hatteras Venture Partners is a venture capital firm that invests in early stage companies based in North Carolina and the Southeastern United States. The firm focuses primarily on human medicine-related sectors, including healthcare informational technology, biopharmaceuticals, diagnostics, and medical devices. Hatteras Venture Partners seeks innovative businesses with the potential to transform

the practice of medicine and is dedicated to creating value for these companies.
Geographic Preference: North Carolina, Southeast United States
Fund Size: $125 million
Founded: 2000
Investment Criteria: Early-Stage
Industry Group Preference: Biopharmaceuticals, Medical Devices, Diagnostics, Life Sciences, Healthcare Information Technology
Portfolio Companies: Artus Labs, Clearside Biomedical, Clinipace Worldwide, Clinverse, Coferon, Contego Medical, Curoverse, Device Innovation Group, Embrella, G1 Therapeutics, GeneCentric, Graybug, Histosonics, Lysosomal Therapeutics, Medfusion, Medikidz, NeuroTronik, Nu Sirt Sciences, Orig3n, Pathfinder Technologies, PhaseBio, Qvella, Sideris Pharmaceuticals, SpineAlign, Spyryx Biosciences, TetraLogic, Viamet, Wildflower Health

Key Executives:
John Crumpler, General Partner
Education: AB, Harvard University
Background: Founder & CEO, E-Comm; XcelleNet
Directorships: Clinipace Worldwide
Robert A Ingram, General Partner
Education: BS, Business Administration, Eastern Illinois University
Background: Chairman & CEO, GlaxoWellcome; VP Chairman, Pharmaceuticals, GlaxoSmithKline
Directorships: Cree, Valeant Pharmaceuticals International, BioCryst Pharmaceuticals
Kenneth B Lee, General Partner
Education: BA, Lenoir-Rhyne College; MBA, University of North Carolina at Chapel Hill
Background: Co-Head, International Life Sciences, Ernst & Young; Genentech
Directorships: Clinverse, Clinipace
Douglas Reed MD, General Partner
Education: BA, Biology, MD, University of Missouri, Kansas City; MBA, Wharton School, University of Pennsylvania
Background: Vector Fund Management; SR One; VP, Business Development, NPS Pharmaceuticals; GelTex Pharmaceuticals
Directorships: Coferon, SpineAlign Medical, TetraLogic Pharmaceuticals
Christy Shaffer PhD, General Partner
Education: PhD, Pharmacology, University of Tennessee
Background: Associate Director, Pulmonary & Critical Care Medicine, Burroughs Wellcome; President & CEO, Inspire Pharmaceuticals
Directorships: G1 Therapeutics, Spyryx, Clearside, KinoDyn, GrayBug
Clay B Thorp, General Partner
Education: BA, Mathematics & Art History, University of North Carolina at Chapel Hill; MPP, Harvard University
Background: Co-Founder, Chairman & CEO, Synthematix; Co-Founder & Head, Corporate Development, Novalon Pharmaceutical Corporation; Co-Founder & President, Xanthon
Directorships: Clearside Biomedical, Curoverse, Lysosomal Therapeutics, Orig3n

916 HAWTHORN EQUITY PARTNERS
200 W Madison
Suite 2100
Chicago, IL 60606

Phone: 312-277-4010
e-mail: investors@hawthornep.com
web: www.hawthornep.com

Mission Statement: Formerly known as Genuity Capital Partners, Hawthorn invests in growth-oriented, knowledge-based middle market companies.

Geographic Preference: North America
Founded: 2005
Average Investment: $10 million - $45 million
Investment Criteria: Middle Market
Industry Group Preference: Specialty Consumer, Business Services, Infrastructure Services, Technology, Media
Portfolio Companies: Front Porch Digital, Green For Life, Ice Mobility, J Brand, Natural Food Holdings, Navantis, NGrain, One Floral Group, Railroad Controls Limited, Rx Label Technology, Solace Systems, Waterworks

Key Executives:
Christopher Payne, CEO & Managing Partner
416-687-5299
e-mail: christopher.payne@hawthornep.com
Education: BComm, Queen's University; MBA, The Wharton School
Background: CIBC; BMO Nesbitt Burns; Merrill Lynch; The Blackstone Group
John Tomes, Senior Partner
847-736-3844
e-mail: tomes@hawthornep.com
Education: BA, Kenyon College; Masters, University of Chicago
Background: Hilco Equity Partners; Wynnchurch Capital; Continental Bank; GE Capital
Eric Ceresnie, Partner
734-276-5632
e-mail: ceresnie@hawthornep.com
Education: BSc, MSc, Industrial & Operations Engineering, University of Michigan
Background: Monomoy Capital Partners; Ernst & Young LLP; Sleep Innovations; A.T. Kearney

917 HCI EQUITY PARTNERS
1730 Pennsylvania Avenue, NW
Suite 525
Washington, DC 20006

Phone: 202-371-0150 Fax: 202-312-5300
e-mail: info@hciequity.com
web: www.hciequity.com

Mission Statement: Deliver superior risk adjusted returns to our limited partners through long duration investments in middle-market businesses based in the United States.

Geographic Preference: United States
Fund Size: $1.5 billion
Founded: 1993
Average Investment: $25 - $100 million
Minimum Investment: $5 million
Investment Criteria: MBO, LBO, Consolidations, Growth
Industry Group Preference: Industrial Equipment, Industrial Services, Aerospace, Defense and Government, Logistics, Automotive, Distribution, Industrial Distribution, Power Generation, Test & Measurement, Transportation
Portfolio Companies: Adept Plastic Finishing, AmerCareRoyal, Amtex, Certified Safety, Commercial Steel Trating Corporation, The Delaney Hardware Company, Dynamic Systems, Express Packaging, Go To Logistics, Group Transportation Services, HVH Transportation, JGB Enterprises, Milan Supply Chain Solutions, Naumann/Hobbs Material Handling, Power & Composite Technologies, Quadel Consulting Corporation, Regent Cabinetry, Roadrunner Transportation Systems, Southern Ag Carriers, Summit Interconnect, TDS, Tribar Manufacturing, TSM Corporation, Wellborn Forest

Other Locations:
IDS Center
80 South 8th Street
Suite 4508
Minneapolis, MN 55402
Phone: 612-332-2335 **Fax:** 612-332-2012

1033 Skokie Boulevard
Suite 260

Venture Capital & Private Equity Firms / Domestic Firms

Northbrook, IL 60062
Phone: 847-291-9259 **Fax:** 847-897-6212
Key Executives:
Daniel Dickinson, Managing Partner & Co-Founder
e-mail: dand@hciequity.com
Education: JD, MBA, University of Chicago, BS, Duke University
Background: Merrill Lynch
Douglas McCormick, Managing Partner & Co-Founder
e-mail: dmccormick@hciequity.com
Education: MBA, Harvard Business School, BS, U.S. Military Academy
Background: Morgan Stanley & Company, Captain, U.S. Army's 25th Infantry
Scott Gibaratz, Managing Director
e-mail: sgibaratz@hciequity.com
Education: MBA, Kellogg School of Management, BA, University of Michigan
Background: Merrill Lyncht
Dan Moorse, Managing Director
e-mail: dmoorse@hciequity.com
Education: BS, Accounting, St. John's University
Background: CFO, Famous Daves
Carl Nelson, Managing Director
e-mail: cnelson@hciequity.com
Education: BS, Accounting, Winona State University
Background: Accounting & Advisory Group, Arther Andersen & Co

918 HEALTH ENTERPRISE PARTNERS
565 Fifth Avenue
26th Floor
New York, NY 10017

Phone: 212-981-6901 **Fax:** 212-981-9378
e-mail: info@hepfund.com
web: www.hepfund.com

Mission Statement: Health Enterprise Partners is a New York based private equity firm that invests in healthcare services and technology businesses.
Fund Size: $134 million
Founded: 2006
Average Investment: $5 - $15 million
Investment Criteria: Later Stage
Industry Group Preference: Healthcare, Biotechnology, Administrative Automation, Behavioral Health, Data Security, Genomics, Patient Safety, Pharma Data, Social Determinants
Portfolio Companies: Access Physicians, AllyAlign Health, AxiaMed, Bardy Diagnostics, Catapult Health, CenterPointe Behavioral Health, ContinuumRx, Evariant, HealthQx, InDemand Interpreting, Intraprise Health, Jet Health, Jvion, Nordic Consulting, Payer Compass, Sapphire Digital, Twistle, Wildflower Health
Key Executives:
Bob Schulz, Managing Partner
Education: BS, MS, Chemical Engineering, Massachusetts Institute of Technology; MBA, Columbia Business School, Columbia University
Background: Managing Member & Co-Founder, CB Health Ventures; President & COO, Harris & Harris Group; Credit Suisse First Boston
Directorships: ContinuumRx, SCIOinspire, AllyAlign Health, Skylight Healthcare Systems
Rick Stowe, Managing Partner
Education: BSEE, Rensselaer Polytechnic Institute; MBA, Harvard Business School
Background: Senior Advisor, CB Health Ventures; Senior Advisor, Capital Counsel; Principal, New Court Securitites Corporation; General Partner, Welsh, Carson, Anderson & Stowe
Directorships: InDemand Interpreting, HMS Holdings Corp., HT-GAF Holdings
Dave Tamburri, Managing Partner
Education: United States Military Academy; MBA, Harvard Business School
Background: VP, Susquehanna Growth Equity; President/COO, Onward Healthcare; EVP, Pinnacor
Directorships: Bardy Diagnostics, Catapult Health, eVariant, Intraprise Health, Jet Health, Paer Compass, Access Physicians
Ezra Mehlman, Managing Partner
Education: BA, Wasthington University, St. Louis; MBA, Columbia Business School
Background: Senior Analyst, Advisory Board Company; Senior Consultant, Booz Allen Hamilton
Directorships: AxialMed, CenterPointe Behavioral Health System, Jvion, Twistle, Wildflower Health
Pete Tedesco, Principal
Education: AB, Princeton University; MBA, Kellogg School of Management, Northwestern University
Background: VP, Olympus Partners; Waud Capital Partners; Becton Dickinson & Co.; UBS Investment Bank
Elizabeth Colonna, Vice President
Education: BA, University of Virginia; MBA, Columbia Business School
Background: Senior Consultant, FTI Consulting; UCLA Health
Directorships: Wildflower Health, AxiaMed, Access Physicians

919 HEALTHCARE VENTURES LLC
47 Thorndike Street
Suite B1-1
Cambridge, MA 02141

Phone: 617-252-4343
e-mail: info@hcven.com
web: www.hcven.com

Mission Statement: Creates, finances and manages high science health care companies with significant growth potential, making investments in early-stage and emerging growth companies.
Geographic Preference: United States
Fund Size: $1.6 billion
Founded: 1985
Average Investment: $10 million
Investment Criteria: Early-Stage, Emerging Growth; Late-Preclinical & Early Clinical-Stage
Industry Group Preference: Biopharmaceuticals, Healthcare, Life Sciences
Portfolio Companies: Anchor Therapeutics, Apellis, Asterand Bioscience, Catalyst Biosciences, Cleveland HeartLab, Colore Science, DecImmune Therapeutics, InfaCare Pharmaceutical, Leap Therapeutics, Mosaic Biosciences, Promedior, Radius, Theraclone Sciences, Trevena, Vaxxas
Key Executives:
James H. Cavanaugh, PhD, Managing Director
Education: PhD, Health Economics, University of Iowa
Background: President, SmithKline & French Laboratories US; President, Allergen International; Deputy Assistant to the President, Domestic Affairs; Deputy Chief of White House Staff; Special Assistant to the Surgeon General; Director, Office of Comprehensive Health Planning; Founding Director, Marine Nat'l Bank
Augustine Lawlor, Managing Director
Education: BA, University of New Hampshire; MM, Yale University
Background: COO, LeukoSite; CFO/VP Corporate Development, Alpha-Beta Technology; CFO/VP Business Development, BioSurface Technology
Directorships: Slater Center
John W. Littlechild, Managing Director
Education: BS, University of Manchester; MBA, Manchester Business School
Background: Founder, Advent International Corporation; Citicorp Venture Capital; Rank Xerox; ICI
Christopher K. Mirabelli, PhD, Managing Director
Education: PhD, Molecular Pharmacology, Baylor

Venture Capital & Private Equity Firms / Domestic Firms

University
Background: Chairman/CEO, LeukoSite; Founder, Isis Pharmaceuticals; Director, Molecular Pharmacology Department, SmithKlein & French
Douglas E. Onsi, Venture Partner
Education: BS, Biology, Cornell University; JD, University of Michigan Law School
Background: Vice President, Campath Product Operations & Oncology Portfolio Management; Vice President, Business Development, Genzyme Corporation; CFO, TolerRx
Harold R. Werner, Co-Founder/Senior Advisor
Education: BS, MS, Princeton University; MBA, Harvard Graduate School
Background: Director New Ventures, Johnson & Johnson Development Corporation; Sr VP, Robert S First

920 HEALTHINVEST EQUITY PARTNERS
2507 Post Road
Southport, CT 06890

Phone: 203-324-7700
web: healthinvestequity.com

Mission Statement: HealthInvest Equity Partners aim to invest in early stage healthcare services companies.

Key Executives:
Timothy Howe, Managing Partner
Education: Columbia College
Background: Co-Founder, CHL Medical Partners; Co-Manager
Wilfred Jaeger, Managing Partner
Education: BS, MD, University of British Columbia; MBA, Stanford University
Background: Co-Founder, Three Arch Partners; General Partner, Schroder Ventures

921 HEALTHQUEST CAPITAL
1301 Shoreway Rd.
Suite 350
Belmont, CA 94002

web: www.healthquestcapital.com

Mission Statement: HealthQuest Capital invests in healthcare innovation companies that are at or approaching the growth stage.
Average Investment: $7-25 million
Investment Criteria: Growth Stage
Industry Group Preference: Medical Devices, Diagnostics, Digital Health, Consumer Medicine, Technology-Enabled Services
Portfolio Companies: Ajax Health. Alcresta Therapeutics, Avedro, Avizia, BioIQ, Bio Theranostics, Castle Biosciences, CleanSlate, HealthChannels, inMediata, Lineagen, Magnolia Medical Technologies, Spirox, Springbuk, Trice Medical, Venus Concept, Vestagen, VirMedica

Key Executives:
Garheng Kong, Managing Partner
Education: BS, Stanford University; MD, PhD, MBA, Duke University
Background: Intersouth Partners; Sofinnova Ventures
Directorships: Ajax, Alcresta, Avedro, Avizia, Castle Biosciences, CleanSlate, Health Channels, Magnolia Medical, Spirox, Trice Medical, Venus, VirMedica
Randy Scott, Partner
Education: BS, Management, Georgia Institute of Technology
Directorships: Vestagen, VirMedica, Springbuk, Magnolia Medical, Avizia, Trice Medical
Todd Creech, Partner
Education: BA, Finance and Accounting, Miami University; MBA, Duke University
Background: CFO, Femasys; CFO, ZS Pharma; CFO, Sarcode; CFO, Sirion Therapeutics; Quintiles

Directorships: BioIQ, HealthChannels, Springbuk, InMediata, Avedro, Venus Concept
David Kabakoff, Partner
Education: BA, Chemistry, Case Western Reserve University; PhD, Yale University
Background: EVP, Dura Pharmaceuticals; CEO, Spiros Development; CEO, Salmedix
Directorships: Lineagen, Castle Biosciences, Biotheranostics

922 HEARST VENTURES
300 West 57th Street
New York, NY 10019

Phone: 212-649-2000
web: www.hearst.com

Mission Statement: Hearst takes minority positions in startups that focus on the intersecting worlds of media and technology.
Founded: 1995
Average Investment: $2 - $10 million
Investment Criteria: Expansion-Stage
Industry Group Preference: Media, Technology
Portfolio Companies: 8i, Acrobatiq, Atzuche, BuzzFeed, Caavo, Drone Racing League, Flash Delivery, HootSuite, Kujiale, LingoChamp, LiveSafe, MobiTV, Otonomo, PowerToFly, RAMP, Relationship Science, Roku, Science, Sharecare, Signal, Spartan Race, Stylus, Swirl, Via, WideOrbit, Wyng, Yoka, Zcool, Zinc, Pandora, XM, Brightcove, E Ink, Sling Media, Local.com, Broadcast.com, Exodus, Netscape, Drugstore.com, Circles, Zip2, I/Pro, Sphere, Medscape, IGG, Nexage, Yieldex

Key Executives:
Steven R. Swartz, President/CEO
Education: Harvard University
Background: President, Hearst Newspapers; President/CEO, SmartMoney; Reporter, The Wall Street Journal

923 HEARTLAND INDUSTRIAL PARTNERS
300 Atlantic Street
7th Floor
Stamford, CT 06901

Phone: 203-327-1200 Fax: 203-327-1201
e-mail: info@heartlandpartners.com
web: www.heartlandpartners.com

Mission Statement: Combines strong financial and operating acumen in order to create a uniquely positioned firm that facilitates growth and significantly increases corporate value.
Founded: 1999
Investment Criteria: Buyouts, Industrial Operations, Debt Financing
Industry Group Preference: Industrial Services, Industrial Equipment
Portfolio Companies: Metaldyne, Springs, Trimas

Key Executives:
Jim McConoughey, Chief Executive Officer
Background: Active Fund Manager, Early Stage Partners; Singapore EDB; Bloomberg LP; Central Illinois Angels; Voice of America; Fox News Channel; NBCUniversal; NPR
Directorships: Zuchem; ViMedicus

924 HELLMAN & FRIEDMAN LLC
415 Mission Street
Suite 5700
San Francisco, CA 94105

Phone: 415-788-5111
e-mail: info@hf.com
web: www.hf.com

Mission Statement: Invests in long-term equity capital to support the strategic and financial objectives of outstanding

333

Venture Capital & Private Equity Firms / Domestic Firms

teams operating businesses with defensible positions in growing markets.
Geographic Preference: United States, Europe
Fund Size: $3.5 billion
Founded: 1984
Average Investment: $300-$1 billion
Minimum Investment: $100 million
Investment Criteria: Leveraged Recapitalization, Acquisition Financing, Buy & Builds, Traditional Buyouts, Financial Restructurings
Industry Group Preference: Business Products & Services, Media, Technology, Marketing, Communications, Information Technology, Financial Services, Healthcare, Software, Internet, Digital Media & Marketing, Industrial Products, Energy, Insurance
Portfolio Companies: Abra, Activamt, Advanstar Communications, Alix Partners, All Funds Bank, Applied, Arch Capital Group Ltd., Artisan Partners, Associated Materials, Axel Springer, Blackbaud, CarProof, Catalina, Change Healthcare, Digitas, Double Click, Edelman Financial Services, Eller Media, Ellucian, Formula 1, Franlin Templeton Investments, Gartmore, Genesys, GTT, GeoVera Insurance, Getty Images, Goodman, Grocery Outlet Bargain Market, GCM Grosvenor, HUB, Intergraph, Internet Brands, Iris, Kronos, LPL Financial, Mitchell, Mondrian Investment Partners Ltd., MultiPlan, Nasdaq, Nielsen, OpenLink, Paris RE, PPD, ProSiebenSat1 Media SE, Renaissance, Scout 24, Sedgwick, Sheridan, Snap Av, SSP, TeamSystem, Texas Genco, Verisure Smart Alarms, Vertafore, Web Reservations International, Wood Mackenzie, Young & Rubicam

Other Locations:
390 Park Avenue
21st Floor
New York, NY 10022
Phone: 212-871-6680

30th Floor, Millbank Tower
21-24 Millbank
London SW1P 4QP
United Kingdom
Phone: 44 (0)20 7839 5111

Key Executives:
Brian Powers, Senior Advisor/Chairman Emeritus
Education: Yale University; University of Virginia School of Law
Background: Partner, James D Wolfensohn; Manager/Chief Executive, Jardine Matheson Group; Managing Director/CEO, Consolidated Press Holdings Limited; Managing Director/CEO, Publishing and Broadcasting Limited
Directorships: Blackbaud
Philip Hammarskjold, Executive Chairman
Education: Princeton University; Harvard Business School
Background: Corporate Advisory Department, Dominguez Barry Samuel Montagu; Merchant Banking Department, Morgan Stanley & Company
Directorships: Digitas, Upromise
Patrick Healy, Chief Executive Officer
Education: Harvard College; Harvard Business School
Background: James D Wolfensohn; Consolidated Press Holdings
Directorships: Digitas; Scout24; Verisure; TeamSystem
Jeffrey Goldstein, Advisor Emeritus
Education: Vassar College; PhD, MPhil, MA, Economics, Yale University; London School of Economics
Background: Under Secretary of the Treasury for Domestic Finance, Counselor ot the Secretary of the Treasury; Manging Director/CFO, World Bank; Co-Chairman, BT Wolfensohn
Directorships: AlixPartners, Grosvenor Capital Management Holdings
Stefan Goetz, Partner
Education: MA, Electrical Engineering, RWTH Aachen & Ecole Centrale Paris; MBA, Kellogg School of Management, Northwestern University
Background: Executive Director, Principal Investments area, Goldman Sachs International; McKinsey & Co.
Judd Sher, Partner/Chief Financial Officer
Education: University of Maine; JD, University of Dayton School of Law; LLM, Taxation, Georgetown University School of Law
Background: Principal, Deloitte Tax LLP
Zita Saurel, Partner
Education: Georgetown University
Background: Investcorp; Leveraged Finance, Lehman Brothers
Directorships: Wood Mackenzie; Web Reservations
Erik Ragatz, Partner
Education: Stanford University; MBA, Stanford Graduate School of Business
Background: Bain Capital; Chairman, SnapAV; Grocery Outlet; ABRA; Associated Materials
Directorships: Sheridan Holdings, LPL Holdings, Goodman Global
Roanne Daniels, Partner
Education: University of Virginia; MBA, Harvard Business School
Background: Operating Partner, Bain Capital; Consultant, McKingsey & Co.; Correspondent/Editor, Reuters
Allen Thorpe, Partner
Education: Stanford University; MBA, Harvard Business School
Background: Vice President, Pacific Equity Partners; Manager, Bain & Company; Chairman, Sheridan Healthcare
Directorships: MultiPlan; Change Healthcare; Edelman Financial; LPL Financial; Artian Partners; Mondrian Investment Partners; Gartmore Investment Management
David Tunnell, Partner
Education: Harvard University; Harvard Business School
Background: Banking Group, Lazard Freres & Company; Chairman, Applied Systems; Kronos; Activant; GeoVera; Vertafore
Directorships: Genesys; HUB; OpenLink; Arch Capital; Blackbaud; Ellucian; Intergraph; Sedgwick; PARIS RE
Blake Kleinman, Partner
Education: Harvard College
Background: M&A Group, Morgan Stanley & Co.
Directorships: Scout24; TeamSystem; Gartmore; Iris; SSP; Wood Mackenzie
Deepak Advani, Partner
Education: Michigan State University; MS, Computer Engineering, Wright State University; MBA, Wharton School, University of Pennsylvania
Background: IBM; Global Chief Marketing Officer, Lenovo
Directorships: Applied Systems; Renaissance Learning; OpenLink
Arrie Park, Partner/Chief Legal Officer
Education: University of California, Los Angeles; JD, Yale Law School
Background: Corporate Law, Wachtell Lipton Rosen & Katz
Trevor Watt, Partner
Education: Princeton University; MBA, Stanford Graduate School of Business
Background: Executive Director, Morgan Stanley

---

925 **HERCULES TECHNOLOGY GROWTH CAPITAL, INC**
400 Hamilton Avenue
Suite 310
Palo Alto, CA 94301

Phone: 650-289-3060
e-mail: info@htgc.com
web: www.htgc.com

Venture Capital & Private Equity Firms / Domestic Firms

Mission Statement: Hercules Capital is a venture lending company with an interest in technology, life science, and sustainable and renewable energy
Geographic Preference: United States, Israel, Canada
Fund Size: $1.6 billion
Founded: 2003
Minimum Investment: $1 million
Industry Group Preference: Technology, Life Sciences, Clean Technology, Renewable Energy
Portfolio Companies: Acceleron Pharma, AcelRx Pharmaceuticals, Achronix Semiconductor, Adiana, Aegerion Pharmaceuticals, Affinity VideoNet, Affinity Express, Agami Systems, Ageia Technologies, Alexza Pharmaceuticals, Althea Technologies, Ancestry.com, Annie's, Anthera Pharmaceuticals, Atrenta, AVEO Pharmaceuticals, BabyUniverse, BARRx, BIND Biosciences, Blurb, Box.Net, Braxton Technologies, BrightSource Energy, Bullhorn, Buzz Media, Calera, Central Desktop, Cha Cha, Chroma Therapeutics, Cittio, ClickFox, Compete, Cornice, Cozi Group, Cradle Technologies, Crux Biomedical, deCODE Genetics, Dicerna Pharmaceuticals, Diomed Holdings, E-Band Communications, EcoMotors, EKOS, Elixir Pharmaceuticals, Enphase Energy, Enpiorion, ENTrique Surgical, EpiCept, Everyday Health, ForeScout Technologies, GameLogic, Glam Media, Gomez, GreatPoint Energy, Guava Technologies, Gynesonics, HedgeStreet, hi5 Networks, HighJump, HighRoads, Horizon Therapeutics, Ikano Communications, InfoLogix, Inotek Pharmaceuticals, IntelePeer, Intelliden, Intelligent Beauty, Interwise, Invoke Solutions, Inxite Software, InXpo, IPA, iWatt, Jab Broadband, Kamada, Kovio, KXEN, Labcyte, LaboPharm, Light Sciences Oncology, Lilliputian Systems, Market Force Information, MaxVision, Memory Pharmaceuticals, Merrimack Pharmaceuticals, Merrion Pharmaceuticals, Nanosolar, Navidea Biopharmaceuticals, NeoNova, Neosil, NeurogesX, NEXX Systems, Novasys Medical, NuGEN Technologies, OATSystems, Occam Networks, Omtrix Biopharmaceuticals, OpSource, Optovia

Other Locations:
31 St. James Avenue
Suite 730
Boston, MA 02116
Phone: 617-314-9973

777 Church Road
Elmhurst, IL 60126
Phone: 847-542-1858

100 Park Avenue
16th Floor
New York, NY 10017
Phone: 650-600-5405

4800 Hampden Ln
Suite 200
Bethesda, MD 20814
Phone: 202-446-1634

20 Church Street
Suite 1780
Hartford, CT 06103
Phone: 617-851-5416

Key Executives:
Michael Hara, Managing Director of Investor Relations/Corp. Communications
650-433-5578
e-mail: mhara@htgc.com
Education: BS, Electronics Engineering, DeVry University
Background: VP of Investor Relations/Business Development, Cortina Systems; SVP of Investor Relations, NVIDIA; Wyse Technology; Radius; Verticom Graphics; Vermont Microsystems; GE Healthcare
Scott Bluestein, Chief Executive/Investment Officer
617-314-9976
e-mail: sbluestein@htgc.com
Education: BBA, Finance, Emory University
Background: Founder/Partner, Century Tree Capital Management; Managing Director, Laurus-Valens Capital Management; Financial Technology Coverage Group, UBS
Steve Kuo, Senior Managing Director/Group Head, Technology
650-289-3065
e-mail: skuo@htgc.com
Education: BS, Hass Business School, University of California, Berkeley
Background: Ligthcross; Principal, Comdisco Ventures
Roy Y. Liu, Managing Director
617-314-9982
e-mail: rliu@htgc.com
Education: BS, Electrical Engineering, MBA, University of Michigan
Background: Vice President, GrandBanks Capital; Founding Principal, VantagePoint Structured Investments; Co-Founder of Imperial Bank's Emerging Growth Industries; R&D, IBM
Melanie Grace, General Counsel/Chief Compliance Officer
212-774-3611
e-mail: mgrace@htcg.com
Education: BA, MA, History, University of California, Riverside; JD, Boston University School of Law
Background: Chief Legal & Compliance Officer/Corporate Secretary, WHV Investments; Chief Counsel, New York Stock Exchange; Associate, Fenwick & West; General Counsel, FINRA
Kristen Kosofsky, Senior Managing Director
617-314-9980
e-mail: kkosofsky@htgc.com
Education: BS, Business, Central Connecticut State University
Background: Managing Director, Horizon Technology Finance; VP, Life Sciences, Comerica Bank; GATX Corporation; Transamerica Technology Finance
April Young, Managing Director
703-245-3184
e-mail: ayoung@htgc.com
Education: BA, MS, Urban & Regional Planning, George Washington University; PhD, Public Policy & Administration, Saint Louis University
Background: Senior Vice President & Managing Director, MMV Financing; Senior Vice President & Managing Director, Comerica Bank; Executive Director, Potomac KnowledgeWay Project; Director, Virginia Department of Economic Development
Raj Seth, Managing Director
857-206-8963
e-mail: rseth@htgc.com
Education: BS, Electrical Engineering, University of Illinois; MS, Cornell University; MBA, Kellogg School of Business
Background: Executive, Bulger Partners; Managing Director, GE Capitals' Sponsor Finance (TMT) Group
Lesya Kulchenko, Managing Director, Portfolio Management
650-289-3062
e-mail: lkulchenko@htgc.com
Education: BS, Computer Engineering, Marquette University
Background: Nourish Capital; Hopewell Ventures; Corporate Credit Monitoring Manager, Raiffeisen Bank Ukraine; Product Management, Rockwell Automation
Janice Borque, Managing Director
617-314-9992
e-mail: jborque@htgc.com
Education: BS, Veterinary Science; MBA, Finance & Accounting, University of New Hampshire
Background: Commons Capital; Oxford Bioscience Partners; Senior Vice President/Group Head, Life Sciences, Comerica Bank; President/CEO, Massachusetts Biotechnology Council

Venture Capital & Private Equity Firms / Domestic Firms

Lake McGuire, Managing Director
517-304-0382
e-mail: lmcguire@htgc.com
Education: BS, Construction Management, Michigan State University; MBA, Finance, University of Michigan
Background: Vice President, Business Development, Comerica Bank
R. Bryan Jadot, Senior Managing Director/Group Head, Life Sciences
617-314-9981
e-mail: bjadot@htgc.com
Education: BA, Economics & Government, California State University, Sacramento
Background: 0ice President, Life Sciences Group, Silicon Valley Bank; Corporate Banking, Banque Nationale de Paris

926 HERITAGE PARTNERS
800 Boylston Street
Suite 1535
Boston, MA 02199

Phone: 617-439-0688 Fax: 617-439-0689
web: www.newheritagecapital.com

Mission Statement: Invests preferred and common stock, on a minority or majority basis, in mature, successful manufacturing, distribution and service companies.
Geographic Preference: United States
Fund Size: $1.4 billion
Founded: 1987
Average Investment: $15 - 40 million
Minimum Investment: $15 million
Investment Criteria: Acquisitions, Equity-Based Recapitalizations, Revenues of $4- 20 million EBITDA
Industry Group Preference: Aerospace, Defense and Government, Business Products & Services, Consumer Products, Distribution, Education, Food & Beverage, Healthcare, Healthcare Services, Industrial Products, Manufacturing, Pet Products, Specialty Chemicals, Test & Measurement
Portfolio Companies: Continental, Covalent Health, Centra Industries, Eptam Plastics, The Execu|Search Group, Flying Colours Corp., OneSource Distributors, Reach Air Medical, Rhythmlink, Welcome Dairy
Key Executives:
Mark Jrolf, Managing Senior Partner
617-428-0108
e-mail: mjrolf@heritagepartnersinc.com
Education: BS, Finance, Babson College; MS, Management, MIT
Background: Equity Partners; McKinsey & Company; Heritage Partners; Bank of Boston
Directorships: Continental; The Execu|Search Group; Eptam Plastics; Covalent Health
Charlie Gifford, Senior Partner
617-428-0104
e-mail: cgifford@newheritagecapital.com
Education: BA, Denison University; MBA, Kellogg School of Management, Northwestern University
Background: Heritage Partners; The New England Revolution; Smith Barney
Nickie Norris, Senior Partner/Chief Operating & Compliance Officer
617-428-3616
e-mail: nnorris@newheritagecapital.com
Education: BS, Business Management, Cornell University
Background: Dolandson Lufkin & Jenrette; Phoenix Private Equity Partners; Heritage Partners
Directorships: Continental; The Execu|Search Group; Eptam Plastics; Covalent Health
Melissa Barry, Partner
617-429-8427
e-mail: mbarry@newheritagecapital.com
Education: BA, University of Virginia
Background: Heritage Partners; Banc of America Securities
Directorships: Continental; Covalent Health
Judson Samuels, Partner
617-428-0106
e-mail: jsamuels@newheritagecapital.com
Education: BA, University of Virgnia; MBA, Wharton School, University of Pennsylvania
Background: HIG Capital; Bain & Company; Heritage Partners
Directorships: The Execu|Search Group; Eptma Plastics
Kyle Veatch, Vice President
e-mail: kveatch@newheritagecapital.com
Education: BA, Economics, Yale University; MBA, Booth School of Business
Background: Raymond James & Company; PSP Capital Partners
Tristan Velez, Vice President, Finance
617-428-0014
e-mail: tvelez@newheritagecapital.com
Education: BS, MBA, University of Windsor, Ontario
Background: Investors Bank & Trust (Alternative Investments Group); Bisys Hedge Fund Servives

927 HEWLETT PACKARD ENTERPRISE
6280 America Center Drive
San Jose, CA 95002

web: www.hpe.com

Mission Statement: Hewlett Packard identifies and invests in leading startup companies. They invest in disruptive innovation in cybersecurity, analytics and infrastructure.
Key Executives:
Anhishek Shukla, Managing Director/Global Head of Investing
Education: MBA, University of California, Berkeley
Background: Managing Director, GE Ventures

928 HIG CAPITAL
1450 Brickell Avenue
31st Floor
Miami, FL 33131

Phone: 305-379-2322 Fax: 305-379-2013
e-mail: info@higcapital.com
web: www.higprivateequity.com

Mission Statement: A leading global private equity firm focused on management buyouts and recapitalizations of leading middle market companies as well as growth equity investments.
Geographic Preference: United States, Europe
Fund Size: $1.75 billion
Founded: 1993
Average Investment: $2 million - $10 million
Minimum Investment: $1 million
Investment Criteria: First Stage, Second Stage, LBO, MBO, Recapitalizations, Growth Equity
Industry Group Preference: Aerospace, Defense and Government, Building Materials & Services, Business Products & Services, Specialty Chemicals, Consumer Products, Distribution, Healthcare, Infrastructure, Manufacturing, Media, Energy, Information Technology, Transportation, Education, Food & Beverage
Portfolio Companies: 37.5, A10 Capital, Accupac, ACG Materials, AERT, Albertville Quality Foods, All American Group, Amerijet International, AMPAC, ARBOC Specialty Vehicles, Arctic Glacier Holdings, ATX Networks, Caraustar Industries, CEL LEP, CFMG, Classmates, Comverge, Constructive Media, Cornerstone Chemical, CPower, Creme Mel, DHISCO, Die Cuts With a View, Eletromidia, Fox River Fiber, Hart InterCivic, HealthSTAR, HelpSystems, Higher Gear Group, Holland Services, Infogix, Innovative Building Systems, Intelius, InterDent, Lexmark, LG Lugar de Gente, Matrixx, Milestone Technologies, Mr. Cat, Net Trans, NextSource, Office Total, Onyx Payments, Pendum, Pro-Pet, Progrexion, Protocol Global Systems, Raymond Express

Venture Capital & Private Equity Firms / Domestic Firms

International, Ready Pac Produce, Redfish Rentals, Rennhack Marketing Services, Rolland, Rotorcraft Leasing Company, Ship Supply, Soleo Health, Southern Quality Meats, Stant Corporation, Surgery Partners, T-Bird Restaurant Group, TestAmerica, TLC Vision, TRAKAmerica, Trinity, Universal Fiber Systems, US MED, Valtris Specialty Chemicals, VIP Petcare

Other Locations:
1380 West Paces Ferry Road
Suite 1290
Atlanta, GA 30327
Phone: 404-504-9333 **Fax:** 404-504-5315

500 Boylston Street
20th Floor
Boston, MA 02116
Phone: 617-262-8455 **Fax:** 617-262-1505

One Sansome Street
37th Floor
San Francisco, CA 94104
Phone: 415-439-5500 **Fax:** 415-439-5525

600 Fifth Avenue
22nd Floor
New York, NY 10020
Phone: 212-506-0500 **Fax:** 212-506-0559

151 N Franklin Street
21st Floor
Chicago, IL 60606
Phone: 312-214-1234 **Fax:** 312-345-5999

200 Crescent Court
Suite 1414
Dallas, TX 75201
Phone: 214-855-2999 **Fax:** 214-855-2998

HIG European Capital Partners LLP
2nd Floor
London W1K 4QB
United Kingdom
Phone: 44-2073185700 **Fax:** 44-2073185749

Key Executives:
Sami Mnaymneh, Founder/Co-CEO
Education: BA, Columbia University; JD, Harvard Law School; MBA, Harvard Business School
Background: Managing Director, The Blackstone Group; VP, Mergers & Acquisitions, Morgan Stanley
Tony Tamer, Founder/Co-CEO
Education: Rutgers University; Stanford University; MBA, Harvard Business School
Background: Partner, Bain & Company; Marketing, Engineering & Manufacturing, Hewlett-Packard; Sprint
Douglas Berman, Executive Managing Director
Education: BA, Economics, University of Virginia; MBA, Wharton School, University of Pennsylvania
Background: Consultant, Bain & Company
Rick Rosen, Co-President
Education: Stanford University; MBA, Harvard Business School
Background: General Electric Company; GE Capital
Brian D. Schwartz, Co-President
Education: BS, University of Pennsylvania; MBA, Harvard Business School
Background: Dillon Read & Co., PepsiCo
Camilo E. Horvilleur, Managing Director
Education: BBA, Finance, Texas A&M University; MBA, Harvard Business School
Background: Associate, Morgan Stanley; Atticus Capital
Directorships: ATX Networks, PMSI, Capstone Logistics, Safe-Guard Products, Service Net, Align Networks
Matthew Hankins, Managing Director
Education: BS, University of Michigan College of Engineering; MBA, Booth School of Business
Background: Sterling Partners; Co-Founder, Metropolitan Capital Bank; JP Morgan; Accenture

Michael Gallagher, Managing Director
Education: BS, Finance & Accounting, Indiana University; MBA, Wharton School
Background: Apax Partners; Qualitest Pharmaceuticals
Elliot Maluth, Managing Director
Education: BBA, University of Washington; MBA, Harvard Business School
Background: Partner, Behrman Capital; Associate, Golder Thoma Cressey Rauner; Manager, Strategic Consulting Group, Price Waterhouse; Sales Manager, Beverage Division, Procter & Gamble
Fernando Marques Oliveira, Managing Director
Education: BBA, Fundacao Getulio Vargas
Background: Partner, General Atlantic; Partner & Head, Illiquid Strategies Group, Icatu
Directorships: Cel Lep Idiomas, Creme Mel Sorvetes, LG Sistemas, Eletromidia, Office Total, Grupo NZN, Casa Franca-Brasil Foundation
William Nolan, Managing Director
Education: BS, Computer Engineering, Villanova University; MBA, Harvard Business School
Background: Bain & Company; Arthur Andersen Business Consulting
Keval Patel, Managing Director
Education: BA, Economics, Wharton School, University of Pennsylvania
Background: Graham Partners; Salomon Smith Barney
Rodrigo Feitosa, Managing Director
Education: MBA, INSEAD
Directorships: Grupo NZN; Selfit Academias; Eletromidia; Grupo Meridional
Marcelo Cecchetto, Managing Director
Education: BA, Economics, Universidade Federal do Rio de Janeiro
Background: Group Icatu
Directorships: Cel-Lep Idiomas; Mr. Cat; LG; Elekeiroz; Tecfil; Office Total
Richard Stokes, Managing Director
Education: Cornell University
Background: M&A Group, Salomon Smith Barney
Tenno Tsai, Managing Director
Education: Williams College; MBA, Harvard Business School
Background: Principal, Warburg Pincus; Associate, AEA Investors; Consultant, McKinsey & Company
Rob Wolfson, Managing Director
Education: Northwestern University; MBA, Harvard Business School
Background: VP, Sales & Business Development, IPWireless; Consultant, LEK Consulting
Jeff Zanarini, Managing Director
Education: BS, BA, Southern Methodist University; MBA, Harvard Business School
Background: Bain & Company, Goldman Sachs

---

929 HIGH ALPHA
830 Massachusetts Avenue
Suite 1500, 4th Floor
Indianapolis, IN 46204

web: highalpha.com

Mission Statement: High Alpha creates and funds B2B SaaS companies.

Key Executives:
Scott Dorsey, Managing Director
Education: BA, Indiana University; MBA, Northwestern University
Background: Co-Founder and CEO, Salesforce

Venture Capital & Private Equity Firms / Domestic Firms

930 HIGH COUNTRY VENTURE
Boulder, CO 80302

Mission Statement: To invest in innovative early stage Colorado-based companies, and to work closely with entrepreneurs to drive growth and create profitable businesses.

Fund Size: $50 million
Founded: 2005
Investment Criteria: Early-Stage
Industry Group Preference: Life Sciences, Biotechnology, Clean Technology, Medical Devices, Technology, Software, Internet
Portfolio Companies: AktiVax, BirdBox, Collective IP, Digabit, Endoshape, Full Contact, Kapost, LogRhythm, Mosaic Biosciences, Nutrinsic, QualVu, Sinopsys, Surefire Medical, TheraTogs, ViroCyt

Key Executives:
  Mark T Lupa PhD, Managing Director
  Education: BSc, Bioengineering, Northwestern University; MPhil, Bioengineering, University of Sussex; PhD, Pharmacology, University of Lund
  Background: Founder, CEO & CFO, Tabernash Brewing Company
  Directorships: LeftHand/Tabernash, Oberon, TheraTogs, Surefire Medical, Endoshape, Mosaic Biosciences

931 HIGH ROAD CAPITAL PARTNERS
1251 Avenue of the Americas
Suite 4102
New York, NY 10020

Phone: 212-554-3265
web: www.highroadcap.com

Mission Statement: To collaborate with management teams to develop growth plans for portfolio companies. High Road Capital Partners is focused primarily on investing in smaller middle market businesses.

Fund Size: $320 million
Founded: 2007
Average Investment: $3 - $25 million
Investment Criteria: Buyouts, Recapitalizations
Industry Group Preference: Manufacturing, Distribution, Media, Healthcare, Services
Portfolio Companies: Accurate Component Sales, Advanced Sleep Medicine Services, BlueSpire, Cali Bamboo, Celco Controls, The Crown Group, General Tools & Instruments, Guidemark Health, PANOS Brands, SMB Machinery Systems, York Wallcoverings

Key Executives:
  Robert J Fitzsimmons, Managing Partner
  e-mail: rfitzsimmons@highroadcap.com
  Education: BS, Accounting, University of Pennsylvania; MBA, Finance, University of Chicago
  Background: Managing Partner, The Riverside Company; Citicorp Venture Capital; Price Waterhouse
  Directorships: Advanced Sleep Medicine Services, BlueSpire, The Crown Group, Guidemark Health, PANOS Brands, SMB Machinery Systems
  William C Connell, Partner
  e-mail: wconnell@highroadcap.com
  Education: BA, English, Boston College; MBA, Harvard Business School
  Background: Vice President, The Riverside Company; Connell Limited Partnership
  Directorships: Advanced Sleep Medicine Services, PANOS Brands, The Crown Group
  Jeffrey M Goodrich, Partner
  e-mail: jgoodrich@highroadcap.com
  Education: BS, Economics, BA, International Relations, University of Pennsylvania; MBA, Finance & Accounting, New York University Stern School of Business
  Background: Vice President, The Riverside Company; Corporate Finance, IBJ Whitehall Bank & Trust Company
  Directorships: Accurate Component Sales, BlueSpire, Celco, Guidemark Health, General Tools & Instruments

  Ben A Schnakenberg, Partner
  e-mail: bschnakenberg@highroadcap.com
  Education: BA, Political Science & English, Valparaiso University; MBA, Wharton School, University of Pennsylvania; CFA
  Background: Senior VP, LaSalle Bank; Madison Capital Funding
  Directorships: Accurate Component Sales, Cali Bamboo, Guidemark Health, SMB Machinery Systems

932 HIGH STREET CAPITAL
150 North Wacker Drive
Suite 2420
Chicago, IL 60606

Phone: 312-423-2650 Fax: 312-267-2861
web: www.highstreetcapital.com

Mission Statement: High Street Capital pursues opportunities with lower middle market businesses and implements strategies to build valuable niche manufacturing, outsourced business services, and distribution and logistics companies.

Geographic Preference: Central United States
Fund Size: $100 million
Founded: 1997
Average Investment: $8 million
Minimum Investment: $4 million
Investment Criteria: Revenues up to $100 million, Management-Led Buyouts, Growth Capital, Recapitalizations
Industry Group Preference: Outsourcing & Efficiency, Niche Manufacturing, Distribution, Logistics, Healthcare Services
Portfolio Companies: Applied Process, Avomeen, Banner Services Corporation, BeneSys, Bock & Clark, Can-Do National Tape, Commodity Blenders, Countryside Hospice, CRFS Services, DataSource, DiversiTech, Koontz-Wagner Electronic, Massey Fair, ORB Packing, ShoreMaster, Suburban Team, Superior Fibers, TLC Companies

Key Executives:
  Joseph R Katcha, Founder/Principal
  312-423-2651
  e-mail: joe@highstreetcapital.com
  Education: University of Wisconsin, Madison; Harvard University Graduate School of Business
  Background: Director, SG Warburg; Partner, Managing Director & COO, KC-CO Investments; Associate, First Atlantic Capital; Associate, M&A, PaineWebber; Peat, Marwick, Mitchell & Co.
  Directorships: BeneSys, Countryside Hospice, DataSource, Bock & Clark, MST Analytics, Koontz-Wagner
  William J Oberholtzer, Principal
  312-423-2652
  e-mail: will@highstreetcapital.com
  Education: Kalamazoo College; MBA, University of Chicago Graduate School of Business
  Background: Alpha Capital; Bank of Nova Scotia; Comerica Bank
  Directorships: Superior Fibers, Massey Fair, DiversitTech, DocuForce
  Kent C Haeger, Principal
  e-mail: kent@highstreetcapital.com
  Education: University of Wisconsin, Madison
  Background: Managing Director, SG Warburg & Company; Founder & Managing Partner, KC-CO
  Directorships: DocuForce, Bock & Clark, MST Analytics, Massey Fair
  Richard McClain, Principal
  312-423-2654
  e-mail: dick@highstreetcapital.com
  Education: BS, Engineering, University of Michigan; MBA, University of Texas
  Background: VP, Global Business Development & Strategy, Tenneco Automotive; TRW
  Directorships: BeneSys, DataSource, Superior Fibers, Koontz-Wagner

Venture Capital & Private Equity Firms / Domestic Firms

933 HIGHBAR PARTNERS
545 Middlefield Road
Suite 175
Menlo Park, CA 94025

e-mail: info@highbarpartners.com
web: www.highbarpartners.com

Mission Statement: HighBAR Partners is an early-stage and structured growth capital firm that helps align Management and Investors to build great companies. HighBAR invests in companies that develop infrastructure software and solutions. HighBAR Partners are hands-on investors and bring significant experience and strategic relationships to every project.

Founded: 1995
Investment Criteria: Early-Stage, Structured Growth Capital
Portfolio Companies: Autotask, Blazent, Clustrix, Janrain, Patientsafe Solutions, Virtual Instruments, Zettaset, Brightmail, Brocade, Cawnetworks, CDS, Dantz, Ingrian, Load Dynamix, Mirapoint, Neopath Networks, Sanlight, Soonr, Tapulous, Tazznet, Vyatta

Key Executives:
Roy Thiele-Sardina, Managing Partner
e-mail: roy@highbarpartners.com
Education: BS, Electrical Engineering & Computer Science, University of Wisconsin, Madison; MBA, Stern School of Business
Background: Managing Director, Steelpoint Capital; EIR, Mayfield Fund; Co-Founder & CEO, Ingrian Networks; Brocade Communications
John Kim, Managing Partner
e-mail: john@highbarpartners.com
Education: BS, Economics, University of Chicago; MBA, Columbia Business School
Background: W Capital Partners; Director of Corporate Development, Zeborg; Director of Investments, ISL Managment
Brian Peters, Managing Director
Education: BSE, Computer Engineering, University of Michigan, MBA, Columbia Business School
Background: Investment Banker, Barclays Capital; Analyst, Rosemounth Capital Management; Software Developer, Nextel Telecomunications
Chris Kitching, Operating Partner
Education: BS, MS, Electrical Engineering, Stanford University; MBA, Harvard Business School
Background: CFO, Sound United; CFO, ClariPhy Communications Inc.; Ethernet

934 HIGHER GROUND LABS
626 W Jackson Boulevard
Suite 600
Chicago, IL 60661

e-mail: info@highergroundlabs.com
web: highergroundlabs.com

Mission Statement: Seeks to discover new techniques for effective campaigning, spark and nurture new collaborations, and strengthen connectivity across progressive tech. Invests in companies building solutions to the most pressing campaign challenges and provides programming and mentorship.

Industry Group Preference: Technology
Portfolio Companies: Avalanche Insights, BallotReady, CallTime, Change Research, Civic Eagle, Civitech, Countable, Deck, FactSquared, Field Day, GroundBase, Grow Progress, Hope, Human Agency, Hustle, Icebreaker, Main Street One, Mobilize, New'Mode, OpenField, Outfox AI, OutreachCircle, Outvote, PredictWise, Qriously, SameSide, Speakeasy Political, Survey 160, Swayable, The tuesday Company, Torch, Victory Guide, Warchest, Wethos

Key Executives:
Shomik Dutta, Partner
Education: BA, Williams College; MBA, Wharton School
Background: Chief Revenue Officer, Romeo Power Technology; Managing Director, Renewable Energy Private Equity
Directorships: Mobilize
Betsy Hoover, Partner
Education: BA, Xavier University
Background: Partner, 270 Strategies; Online Organizing Director, Obama for America; Regional Director, Democratic National Committee
Andrew McLaughlin, Partner
Education: BA, Yale University; JD, Harvard Law School
Background: President/COO, Assembly OSM; Exec Director, Tsai CITY; Head of Various Bits, Medium.com; CEO/Exec Chairman, Digg; CEO, Instapaper; EVP, Tumblr; Exec Director, Civic Commons; Deputy CTO of the United States; Director of Global Public Policy, Google Inc.; VP/Chief Policy Officer, Internet Corp.

935 HIGHLAND CAPITAL PARTNERS
One Broadway
16th Floor
Cambridge, MA 02142

Phone: 617-401-4500
e-mail: info@hcp.com
web: www.hcp.com

Mission Statement: Invests in seed, early and growth stage companies in the communications, consumer, digital media, healthcare and information technology markets.

Fund Size: $1.8 billion
Founded: 1988
Minimum Investment: $500,000
Investment Criteria: Early, Growth, Seed
Industry Group Preference: Communications, Information Technology, Healthcare, Consumer Products, Internet, Digital Media & Marketing
Portfolio Companies: Aloha, Anova Data, Avidyne, BAROnova, Beeswax, BetterLesson, BlueTrap Financial, Bromlum, Cafe Media, Carbon Black, Catlant, Cenx, ClearSky, Datiphy, Disconnect, Enjoy, Exagrid, Fidelis SeniorCare, Freshly, Gigamon, Handy Expert Home Services, Harry's, Iddiction, Infinio, Inxpo, Jaunt, Kascend, Kyruus, Leap Motion, LevelUp, Lovepop, Alwarebytes, Netentsec, Omni, OneSpace, Open Sky, Pharmaca Integrate Pharmacy, Photoboxm QD Vision, Qumulo, Rapidsos, Redbrick Health, Remote Year, Rent The Runway, Rethink Robotics, RethinkDB, Scopely, Session M, Shift, Signifai, Spartoo, Thred Up, Trilogy Education Services, Tuache.com, Tuniu.com, Turbonomic, US Search, vArmour, Violin Memory, Viva, Weeby.co, Wooga, Xometry, Yipit, ZeroFOX

Other Locations:
537 Hamilton Avenue
Palo Alto, CA 94301
Phone: 650-687-3800

5-9 Union Square West
3rd Floor
New York, NY 10003

451 Jackson Street
San Francisco, CA 94111

Key Executives:
Paul Maeder, Chair/Founding Partner
617-401-4500
e-mail: pmaeder@hcp.com
Education: BSE, Princeton University; MS, Stanford University; MBA, Harvard Business School
Background: Director, Avid Technology/CheckFree/Chipcom HighGround Systems/Mainspring/SCH/SQA/Sybase/WebLine Communications; Novacon; Synemed
Directorships: Imprivata, Performix Technologies, Relicore, Village Ventures, VistaPrint
Daniel Nova, Partner
617-401-4500
e-mail: dnova@hcp.com
Education: BS, Computer Science, Boston College; MBA, Harvard Business School

Venture Capital & Private Equity Firms / Domestic Firms

Background: Former Partner, CMG@Ventures; Sr Associate, Summit Partners; Sales, Wang Laboratories
Directorships: CMI Marketing, Coremetrics, GlobalStreams, Gotuit Media, N2 Broadband, Banic Networks, NuGenesis Technologies, Topica, Whole Body
Craig Driscoll, Partner
617-401-4500
Education: BE, Mechanical Engineering, Vanderbilt University
Background: Korn/Kerry International; JacobsRimell; Fidelity Ventures; Beacon Power Corp.; SatCon Technology Corp.
Directorships: Remote Year, Trilogy Education Services, Bullhorn, Quattro
Manish Patel, Partner
650-687-3800
e-mail: mpatel@hcp.com
Education: BA, Economics, BS, Engineering, Stanford University
Background: Advanced Imagery & 3D Mapping Programs at Google
Bob Davis, Partner
617-401-4500
e-mail: bdavis@hcp.com
Education: BS, Northeastern University; MBA, Babson College
Background: CEO, Terra Lycos; Founder, Lycos, Inc.
Directorships: Bullhorn, Genvara, Hangout Industries, NameMedia, OpenSky, Turbine
Corey Mulloy, Partner
650-687-3800
e-mail: cmulloy@hcp.com
Education: BA, Swarthmore College; MBA, Harvard Business School
Background: Corporate Development, ONI; Healthcare Investment, Roberson Stephens & Co; Assistant CEO, Whitman Group
Directorships: AccentCare, Whole Body, Conor Medsystems, NuGenesis Technologies, Radian Medical, US Labs

936 HIGHWAY1
1040 Mariposa Street
San Francisco, CA 94107

e-mail: info@highway1.io
web: www.highway1.io

Mission Statement: Hardware startup accelerator in San Francisco.

Founded: 2013
Average Investment: $50K
Minimum Investment: $50K
Investment Criteria: Seed-Stage
Industry Group Preference: Hardware
Portfolio Companies: Modbot, Navdy, Ringly

Key Executives:
  Brady Forrest, Co-Founder

937 HILCO BRANDS
5 Revere Drive
Suite 206
Northbrook, IL 60062

web: www.hilcobrands.com

Mission Statement: A specialized private equity firm with an exclusive focus on investing in successful and struggling consumer brand companies.

Geographic Preference: United States, Canada
Founded: 2006
Average Investment: $25 - $100 million
Investment Criteria: Acquisitions
Industry Group Preference: Consumer Products, Consumer Services, Retailing
Portfolio Companies: Altec, Clipper Marine, Dealgenius.com, Denby, Halston, Haute Hippie, Hillier's, Le Tigre, LetsBab, MadaLuxe Group, Misco, Portico, Powerbilt, Staples, StreetTrend, The Shoe Box, Tradepoint Atlantic, Under the Canopy, Xcel Brands, Xtra-vision

Other Locations:
  65 Queen Street West
  Thomson Building, Suite 1100
  Toronto, ON M5H 2M5
  Canada
  Phone: 416-361-6336

  80 New Bond Street
  London W1S 1SB
  United Kingdom
  Phone: 44-2073172050

Key Executives:
  Eric Kaup, Managing Director/General Counsel
  e-mail: akaup@hilcoglobal.com
  Education: Yale University; JD, Moritz College of Law, Ohio State University
  Background: Skadden, Arps, Slate, Meagher & Flom
  Edward J Siskin, Executive Vice President
  e-mail: esiskin@hilcoglobal.com
  Education: BA, Economics, State University of New York at Albany; MBA, Finance & International Business, New York University
  Background: Principal, Crystal Financial; President, Back Bay Capital; Managing Director, Bankers Trust; Head of Corporate Development, Red Apple Group; COO, Bank of America Retail Finance Group
  Gary C Epstein, Chief Marketing Officer
  e-mail: gepstein@hilcoglobal.com
  Education: BA, English, Journalism & Political Science, University of Michigan
  Background: CEO, Abundant Ventures; CEO/CMO, ReachMD LLC; CMO, American Medical Association; Euro RSCG Worldwide
  Jeff Branman, Managing Director
  e-mail: jbranman@hilcoglobal.com
  Education: University of California, Santa Cruz; University of California, Berkeley; Carnegie Mellon University
  Background: President, Interactive Technology Partners; Senior Vice President, Corporate Development, Foot Locker; Investment Banker, Financo; VP, Strategic Planning, May Department Stores Company; Strategy Consultant, Boston Consulting Group
  Directorships: Fanatics Inc., Polaroid, Rue La La Inc.

938 HLM VENTURE PARTNERS
116 Huntington Avenue
9th Floor
Boston, MA 02116

Phone: 617-266-0030
web: www.hlmvp.com

Mission Statement: Invests in US-based healthcare technology companies whose products and services provide direct improvements to the organization and distribution of healthcare.

Geographic Preference: United States
Fund Size: $65 million
Founded: 1983
Average Investment: $4 - $10 million
Investment Criteria: Early Stage, Mid-Stage
Industry Group Preference: Healthcare Services, Healthcare Information Technology, Medical Technology, Medical Devices, Diagnostics
Portfolio Companies: AbilTo, ArroHealth, Aventura, Binary Fountain, ClearDATA, Imagine Health, Linkwell Health, Medicalis, mPulse Mobile, Nordic Consulting, OnShift, Payspan, Persivia, Phreesia, Prism Education Group, RedBrick Health, Sanovia Corporation, Spinal Kinetics, Tandem Diabetes Care, Teladoc, Transcend Medical,

Venture Capital & Private Equity Firms / Domestic Firms

Valeritas, Vantage Oncology, Vericare, Vets First Choice, Welltok

Key Executives:
Ed Cahill, Partner
e-mail: ecahill@hlmvp.com
Education: Williams College; Yale University
Background: Founding Partner, Cahill Warnock & Company; Managing Director, Alex. Brown & Sons
Directorships: Binary Fountain, Persivia, Phreesia, Tandem Diabetes
Steve Tolle, Partner
Background: SVP/General Manager, Optum, VP of Product Management, Allscripts; Director of Product Management, Pfizer
Vin Fabiani, Partner
e-mail: vfabiani@hlmvp.com
Education: BS, American University
Background: VP & General Manager, First Data Investor Services
Directorships: ClearDATA Networks, Prism Education
Peter Grua, Partner
e-mail: pgrua@hlmvp.com
Education: AB, Bowdoin College; MBA, Columbia University
Background: Managing Director, Alex. Brown & Sons; Research Analyst, William Blair & Company; Strategy Consultant, Booz Allen Hamilton
Directorships: ArroHealth, Imagine Health, Linkwell, Medicalis, Nordic Consulting, OnShift, The Advisory Board Company
Enrico Picozza, Venture Partner
e-mail: epicozza@hlmvp.com
Education: University of Connecticut
Background: Co-Founder, COO & CTO, HTS Biosystems; PerkinElmer; Applied Biosystems
Directorships: Aventura, Transcend Medical, Vericare
Mike Wong, Chief Financial Officer
Education: BSBA, Accounting & Finance, Boston University; MBA, Finance, Boston College
Background: Financial Analyst, Summit Partners; Senior Auditor, Deloitte

---

939 HMS HAWAII MANAGEMENT
Davies Pacific Center
841 Bishop Street
Suite 860
Honolulu, HI 96813

Phone: 808-545-3755 Fax: 808-531-2611

Mission Statement: Makes venture capital investments in start-up, emerging and established companies with a preference for seed and early-stage Hawaii-based companies and later-stage non-Hawaii-based companies.

Geographic Preference: Hawaii
Founded: 1994
Investment Criteria: Seed-Stage, Early-Stage, Later-Stage with Co-Investors
Industry Group Preference: Telecommunications, Health & Wellness, Biotechnology, Earth Sciences
Portfolio Companies: Firetide, Hawaii Biotech, Hoku Scientific, InterWave, Kona Bay Marine Resources, MobiCom Corporation, Pacific DirectConnect, Pacific Island Resources

Key Executives:
Richard G. Grey, General Partner
Education: BS, MBA, University of California, Los Angeles; JD, University of California, Santa Barbara
Background: Founder, Vidar Corporation; Founder, Transwitch Associates
Directorships: Pacific Island Resources, Kona Bay Marine Resources, Firetide, MedDev Corporation
William K. Richardson, General Partner
Education: University of California, Santa Barbara; Duke University School of Law
Background: Commercial Law & Finance Attorney; Wang Laboratories
Directorships: Pacific DirectConnect, Kona Bay Marine Resources, Hawaii Biotech, HealthScape, Digital Island
John Dean, Special Limited Partner
Education: Holy Cross College; MBA, Finance, Wharton School, University of Pennsylvania
Background: CEO, Silicon Valley Bancshares; CEO, Silicon Valley Bank
Ron Higgins, Special Limited Partners
Background: Founder, CEO, Chairman, Digital Island; CEO, RSHF

---

940 HOLDING CAPITAL GROUP
104 West 40th Street
19th Floor
New York, NY 10018

Phone: 212-486-6670 Fax: 212-486-0843
web: www.holdingcapital.com

Mission Statement: Holding Capital Group specializes in acquisitions and investments across a variety of industries.

Geographic Preference: United States
Founded: 1975
Average Investment: $2 - $150 million
Investment Criteria: Acquisitions, Recapitalizations, Growth Financing, Management Buyouts
Industry Group Preference: Food Services, Financial Services, Apparel, Distribution, Manufacturing, Retail, Consumer & Leisure
Portfolio Companies: Berkeley Contract Packaging, ChicagoLand Commissary, Haskell Jewels, Haskins Electric, HCG Energy, Innerstave, L&S Industries, Malabar Investments, Premise One, Robert Lee Morris, Samara, Southern States, Star-Glo Industries, Value Partners

Other Locations:
5965 Willow Lane
Dallas, TX 75230

1301 Fifth Avenue
Suite 3405
Seattle, WA 98101
Phone: 206-792-1973

Key Executives:
Steven Leischner, President
e-mail: sleischner@holdingcapital.com
Education: BS, Accounting & Business Administration, Wagner College; CPA
Karl D Dillon, Portfolio Advisor
e-mail: kdillon@holdingcapital.com
Education: BA, Whitman College; MBA, Wharton School, University of Pennsylvania
Background: Gilliam Joseph & Littlejohn; HAL Investments; Antfactory
Thomas M Galvin, Portfolio Advisor
e-mail: tgalvin@holdingcapital.com
Education: BS, Business Administration, University of Nebraska; CPA
Background: President & Chairman, HCG Energy Corporation

---

941 HOMEBREW MANAGEMENT
436 Bryant St.
3rd Floor
San Francisco, CA 94107

web: www.homebrew.co

Mission Statement: Our focus is on startups supporting the Bottom Up Economy - helping businesses, developers and individuals drive economic growth and innovation through simpler, cheaper and more direct access to technology, information and customers.

Investment Criteria: Seed
Portfolio Companies: Building Connected, Chime, De-Ice, Finix Payments, Honor, Hummingbird, Intellimize, Joymode,

Venture Capital & Private Equity Firms / Domestic Firms

Layer, Lumi, Q, Outlier, Primary.com, Pulse Data, Ravti, Ride Report, Seriforge, Shield AI, Stockwell, TheSkimm, Tia, Traptic, Upcounsel, Weave, Winnie

Key Executives:
 Hunter Walk, Partner
 e-mail: hunter@homebrew.co
 Education: BA, History, Vassar; MBA, Stanford University
 Background: YouTube; Google; Linden Lab
 Satya Patel, Partner
 e-mail: satya@homebrew.co
 Education: BS in Finance and BS in Psychology from The University of Pennsylvania
 Background: Twitter; Battery Ventures; Google; DoubleClick

942 HONE CAPITAL
530 Lytton Avenue
Suite 305
Palo Alto, CA 94301

Phone: 650-251-4930
e-mail: info@honecap.com
web: honecap.com

Mission Statement: A venture capital fund focused on tech-based startup companies.

Fund Size: $150 million
Founded: 2015
Investment Criteria: Seed, Early Stage
Industry Group Preference: Diversified
Portfolio Companies: Aifi, Airtable, Albert, Alto Pharmacy, Amitree, Ample, Apartment List, AspireIQ, Atrium, BetterView, BIOAGE, Blendid, Blockstack, Bluecore, Bolt, Boom, Boon + Gable, Branch, Brave, BuildingConnected, Carbon Black, Catalia Health, Clara, Clover, Cronofy, Cruise, DataRobot, Dia & Co., Dil Mil, Elroy Air, Embark, Emulate, Flexport, Fysical, Grove Collaborative, Guardant Health, Gusto, Haven, Intellimize, June, Juniper Square, Labelbox, Landis, Ledger Investing, Lever, Mattermost, Medisas, Molekule, Nav, Notion, Nurx, Ouster, PayJoy, Protocol Labs, Rappi, Renoviso, Rentlytics, Zrinse, Rippling, Rocksbox Jewelry, Roofstock, Schoolmint, Shift, SketchDeck, Starsky Robotics, Tenjin, Troops, True Facet, uMake, Vantage Robotics, Vesper, Weave, Wigwag, Wonderschool, Woodtric, Your Mechanic, Zeel

Key Executives:
 Veronica Wu, Managing Partner
 Education: BS, Yale University; MS/PhD, University of California, Berkeley
 Background: Tesla Motors; Apple; Motorola; McKinsey & Company
 Purvi Gandhi, Partner/Chief Financial Officer
 Education: BBA, University of California, Berkeley; CPA
 Background: CFO, H&Q Asia Pacific; CFO, MedVantage; Deloitte; Charles Schwab

943 HOPEN LIFE SCIENCE VENTURES
171 Monroe Avenue NW
Grand Rapids, MI 49503

Phone: 616-325-2110
e-mail: info@hopenls.com
web: www.hopenls.com

Mission Statement: Hopen Life Science Ventures is a venture capital firm that invests in early- to mid-stage companies in the life sciences industry.

Geographic Preference: Midwest United States
Fund Size: $65 million
Founded: 2006
Average Investment: $3 - $5 million
Investment Criteria: Seed-Stage, Early-Stage, Mid-Stage
Industry Group Preference: Life Sciences, Therapeutics, Medical Devices, Diagnostics, Healthcare Information Technology

Portfolio Companies: Alphabeta Therapeutics, BjondHealth, ConcertoHealth, Delphinus Medical Technologies, Great Lakes Pharmaceuticals, Intervention Insights, Metabolic Solutions Development Company, NeoChord, Nymirum, ProNAi Therapeutics, Transcorp Spine

Other Locations:
159 Crocker Park Blvd
Suite 400
Westlake, OH 44145
Phone: 440-385-4225

Key Executives:
 Mark Olesnavage, Managing Director
 Education: BS, Economics & Marketing, MBA, Grand Valley State University
 Background: EVP & General Manager, Perrigo Company
 Directorships: Michigan Venture Capital Association
 Michael Fulton MD, Managing Director
 Education: BA, Northwestern University; MD, Cornell University
 Background: Founder, Director & CEO, Lanx
 Michael Jandernoa, Managing General Partner
 Education: University of Michigan
 Background: Chairman & CEO, Perrigo Company; Co-Founder, Bridge Street Capital Partners; Co-Founder, Grand Angels
 Directorships: Business Leaders for Michigan, Lack Industries, ADAC Corp, Metabolic Solutions Development Company, Grand Valley University Foundation
 Jerry Callahan PhD, Venture Partner
 Education: PhD, Organizational Leadership
 Background: VP, Business Development, Van Andel Research Institute; CIO & VP, Supply Chain, Twinlab/Metabolife

944 HOPEWELL VENTURES
207 East Ohio Street
Suite 248
Chicago, IL 60611

Phone: 312-357-9600
web: www.hopewellventures.com

Mission Statement: Hopewell Ventures partners with strong management teams of high-growth businesses in the Midwest, bringing equity capital, expertise and over a century of experience.

Geographic Preference: Midwest United States
Average Investment: $2 - $7 million
Investment Criteria: Early-Stage, Growth-Stage, Change in Control
Industry Group Preference: Technology, Healthcare, Manufacturing, Medical Devices, Media, Life Sciences, Energy, Information Technology
Portfolio Companies: Pioneer Surgical Technology, INRange Systems, Mersive Technologies, Helios Coatings, SageQuest, Symbios Holdings, National Pasteurized Eggs, VHT, iTRACS Corporation, TLContact, InStadium

Key Executives:
 William P. Sutter Jr., Senior Managing Director
 Education: BS, Economics, Yale University; MBA, Stanford University
 Background: Corporate Finance, Smith Barney; Mesirow Financial
 Directorships: Regent Communications
 Thomas Parkinson, Partner
 Education: BS, Economics, Northwestern University; MBA, Kellogg Graduate School of Management
 Background: General Partner, Adena Ventures; Executive Director, Evanston Business Investment Corporation
 Craig Overmyer, Principal
 Education: Indiana University
 Background: Adena Ventures; Regional VP, Ridgewood Capital; VP, Cooper Investment Partners

945 HORIZON PARTNERS, LTD
3838 Tamiami Trail N
Suite 408
Naples, FL 34103

Phone: 239-261-0020 Fax: 239-261-0225
web: www.horizonpartnersltd.com

Mission Statement: A private investment holding company that acquires companies with significant growth prospects and potential for above-average profitability.

Fund Size: $100 million
Founded: 1990
Average Investment: $6 million
Minimum Investment: $10 million
Investment Criteria: Sales between $10-$100 million, gross margins in excess of 25%, medium size companies, privately held or divisions/subsidiaries of larger corporations
Industry Group Preference: Manufacturing, Distribution, Business to Business, Retailing, Packaging, Food & Beverage, Plastics, Consumer Products, Electronics, Financial Services, Specialty Chemicals
Portfolio Companies: Xymox Technologies, TGR Financial, Inc.

Other Locations:
9099 West Dean Road
Milwaukee, WI 53224
Phone: 414-271-2200 Fax: 414-271-4016

Key Executives:
Robert M. Feerick, Chairman/Founder
e-mail: rfeerick@horizonpartnersltd.com
Education: Phi Beta Kappa, Georgetown University; MBA, University of Chicago
Background: Chairman, The Corporate Development Group; General Partner, Frontenac Company
Directorships: WinterQuest LLC, Xymox Technologies, Lantor International, Climax Portable Machine Tools, Groeb Farms, Karl's Event Rental
William H. Schaar, Chief Financial Officer
239-261-4588
e-mail: wschaar@horizonpartnersltd.com
Education: DePaul University; MBA, University of Chicago
Background: EVP & CFO, Church Pension Group; ARMCO; Brunswick Corporation; Ford Motor Company; Federal Reserve Bank of Chicago

946 HORIZON TECHNOLOGY FINANCE
312 Farmington Avenue
Farmington, CT 06032

Phone: 860-676-8654 Fax: 860-676-8655
e-mail: jerry@horizontechfinance.com
web: www.horizontechfinance.com

Mission Statement: A venture lending, investment and financial services management company that offers creative financing solutions to technology, life science, healthcare information and services, and cleantech companies.

Founded: 2004
Average Investment: $2 - $25 million
Industry Group Preference: Technology, Life Sciences, Healthcare, Clean Technology, Information Technology
Portfolio Companies: Additech, Aquion Energy, Avalanche Technology, Bolt, Bridge2Solutions, ControlScan, CrowdStar, Decisyon, Digital Signal, eAsic, eBureau, Education Elements, Ekahau, MaaS360, Gwynnie Bee, IgnitionOne, Jump Ramp, Kixeye, Le Tote, Lotame, Luxtera, Mblox, Nanocomp, Nanosteel, Netuitive, NMI, NexPlanar, Optaros, Overture, PebblePost, Powerhouse Dynamics, RazorSight, Receptiv, Rocket Lawyer, SavingStar, Shopkeep, Signix, SilkRoad, Simpletuition, Skyword, Social Intelligence, Soraa, Springcm, Streambase, Systech, Brick, VidSys, WebLinc, Xtera, Xtreme Power, Zinion, AccuVein, Anacor, Argos, Celsion Corp., Direct Flow Medical, Inotek, IntegenX, Lantos Technologies, Mederi, Mitralign, N30 Pharma, Nine Point Medical, OraMetrix, Palatin Technologies Inc., Sample6, Strongbridge Biopharma, Sunesis, Supernus, Titan Pharmaceuticals, Tryton Medical, VTV Therapeutics, Xcovery, Accu Metrics, BioScale, Interleukin Genetics, Genepeeks, Healthedge, Medsphere, Precisi Therapeutics, Radisphere, Recondo, Enphase Energy, Lehigh Technologies, Renmatix, Rypos, Semprius, Tigo Energy

Other Locations:
349 Main Street
Suite 203
Pleasanton, CA 94566
Phone: 925-935-2924 Fax: 925-977-9488

1818 Library Street
Suite 500
Reston, VA 20190
Phone: 703-956-3504

Key Executives:
Rob Pomeroy, Chief Executive Officer/Chairman
860-676-8656
e-mail: rob@horizontechfinance.com
Education: BS, MBA, University of California, Berkeley
Background: President, GATX Ventures; EVP, Transamerica Business Credit; General Manager, Transamerica Technology Finance; Crocker Bank
Gerald A. Michaud, President/Director
860-676-8659
e-mail: jerry@horizontechfinance.com
Education: Northeastern University; Rutgers University; University of Phoenix; Harvard Business School
Background: SVP, GATX Ventures; SVP, Transamerica Business Credit; Senior Business Development Executive, Transamerica Technology Finance; President, Venture Leasing & Capital
Chris Mathieu, Senior Vice President, Chief Financial Officer
860-676-8653
e-mail: chris@horizontechfinance.com
Education: BS, Business Administration, New England College; CPA
Background: VP, Life Sciences, GATX Ventures; VP, Life Sciences, Transamerica Business Credit Technology Finance; VP, Finance, Science International
John C. Bombara, Senior Vice President/General Counsel/Chief Compliance Officer
860-676-8657
e-mail: jay@horizontechfinance.com
Education: BA, Colgate University; JD, Cornell Law School
Background: In House Counsel, GATX Ventures; Partner, Pepe & Hazard LLP
Dan Devorsetz, Senior Vice President/Chief Investment Officer
860-674-1208
e-mail: dan@horizontechfinance.com
Education: BS, Cornell University; MBA, Clark University, CFA
Background: vP, General Electrical Capital Corporation; Credit Manager, GATX Ventures; VP, Director of Analysis for Student Loans, Citigroup; Advest, Inc.; Ironwood Capital
Gregory E. Clark, Managing Director
860-676-8651
e-mail: greg@horizontechfinance.com
Education: BA, Columbia University; JD, MBA, University of Connecticut
Background: VP, GATX Ventures; Business Development, Transamerica Technology Finance; Connecticut Innovations; Attorney, Shipman & Goodwin
Kevin J. May, Senior Managing Director
925-935-2924 x100
e-mail: kevin@horizontechfinance.com
Education: BS, Finance, University of Florida
Background: Director, Credit & Portfolio, Oxford Finance

Venture Capital & Private Equity Firms / Domestic Firms

Corporation; VP, Credit & Portfolio Management, GATX Ventures; Finova Capital; Deutsche Financial Services
Mishone B. Donelson, Managing Director
860-674-9949
e-mail: mishone@horizontechfinance.com
Education: BS, Chemical Engineering, MIT; MBA, Kellogg School of Management, Northwestern
Background: Principal, Fairview Capital Partners; Analyst, Ariel Investments
Kevin T. Walsh, Managing Directory
925-935-2924 x101
e-mail: kwalsh@horizontechfinance.com
Education: BS, Business Administration, California State University, Hayward
Background: SVP, Market Manager, Bridge Bank Technology Banking & Capital Finance Division; VP, Relationship Manager, Silicon Valley Bank

947 HORIZON VENTURES LLC
Four Main Street
Suite 20
Los Altos, CA 94022

Phone: 650-917-4100
web: www.horizonvc.com

Mission Statement: A venture capital partnership with exclusive focus on technology-based companies. Offers traditional venture capital strengths to innovative young companies that want to capitalize in the growing information technology market.
Geographic Preference: Northern California
Fund Size: $150 million
Founded: 1999
Average Investment: $2-4 million
Minimum Investment: $1 million
Investment Criteria: Seed, First Round, Second Round, Financing
Industry Group Preference: Software, Wireless Technologies, Technology, Communications, Healthcare Information Technology, Business Products & Services
Portfolio Companies: Chelsio Communications, Identity Engines, Inc., InfiniRoute Networks, Sensys Networks, Venturi Wireless, Applied MicroStructures, Inc., Discera, Inc., iWatt, Inc., LefEngin, Inc., NuCORE Technology, Inc., SpectraLinear, Inc., Theta Microelectronics, Alignment Software, Hipbone, Inc., NativeMinds, Inc., Onstation Corporation, PINC Solutions, Right90, Inc,. Toolwire, Inc., WhiteHat Security, Inc., InterVideo Corp., Knowledge Revolution Inc., SalesLogix, Cholestech Corp., Invivodata, Laser Diagnostics, Neurex Corp., Alien Technology, Photon Dynamics Inc., Silicon Motion Inc., Vertex Networks, AudioTalk Networks, Harmonic Inc., Palm Inc., RapidStream Inc., Sandpiper Networks Inc, SpectraLink Corp.

Key Executives:
Jack Carsten, Managing Director
650-917-4100
e-mail: jack@horizonvc.com
Education: BA, Duke University; MBA, Southern Methodist University
Background: Technology Investments; US Venture Partners; VP, Intel Corporation
John E. Hall, Managing Director
650-917-4100
e-mail: john@horizonvc.com
Education: MBA, BS, San Jose State University; PhD, University of Santa Clara
Background: Newtek Ventures; Intel Corporation
Doug Tsui, Managing Director
650-917-4100
e-mail: doug@horizonvc.com
Education: BSEE, University of California; MBA, Santa Clara University
Background: AudioTalk; VP Marketing, Precept Software; Cisco Systems; 3Com/Bridge Communications; Hewlett-Packard

Art Reidel, Managing Director
650-917-4100
e-mail: art@horizonvc.com
Education: BS, Mathematics, MIT
Background: CEO, Scintera; Chairman/CEO, Pharsight Corp.; President/CEO, Sunrise Test Systems; Venture Partner, Lightspeed Ventures Partners; General Partner, ABS Ventures
Directorships: WhiteHat Security, Eye-Fi, Entelos, Materna Medical

948 HOULIHAN LOKEY
10250 Constellation Boulevard
5th Floor
Los Angeles, CA 90067

Phone: 310-553-8871 **Fax:** 310-553-2173
web: www.hl.com

Mission Statement: An international, advisory-focused investment bank with expertise in mergers and acquisitions, capital markets, financial restructuring, and valuation.
Geographic Preference: United States
Fund Size: $250 million
Founded: 2001
Average Investment: $6 million
Minimum Investment: $1 million
Investment Criteria: Early Stage, Growth Capital, Acquisition
Industry Group Preference: Manufacturing, Retailing, Education, Healthcare, Financial Services

949 HOUSATONIC PARTNERS
800 Boylston Street
Suite 2220
Boston, MA 02199

Phone: 617-399-9200 **Fax:** 617-267-5565
e-mail: wthorndike@housatonicpartners.com
web: www.housatonicpartners.com

Mission Statement: A private equity investment firm that has invested in over 25 companies. Seeking to invest in and build companies in cooperation with experienced and entrepreneurial managers. Housatonic plays an active role in their portfolio companies as board members, working with management to formulate company strategy, develop operating budgets, arrange additional financial rounds, and recruit seasons operating executives.
Geographic Preference: United States
Fund Size: $350 million
Founded: 1994
Average Investment: $5 to $20 million
Minimum Investment: $3 million
Investment Criteria: MBO, Recapitalizations, Consolidations
Industry Group Preference: Business Products & Services, Media, Communications
Portfolio Companies: Access, Accurate, Aegis, Aircraft Fasteners, ArchivesOne, Asurion, Beacon Fire & Safety, BirdDog Solutions, Calo, Carillion, CaseCentral, Classic Party Rentals, Continental Fire & Safety, Diamond Rental, Efficient Forms, FDH, FIMC, First American Records Management, HealthWyse, Healhcare Financial Resources Inc., Hema Source, LeadQual, LeMaitre, MedOptions, Oasis, Oneline Radiology, Onramp, Onsite Health, Pro Service Hawaii, Response Linl, Service Source, Sprout Health Group, WCCT, Wind River, ZicroData

Other Locations:
One Post Street
Suite 2600
San Francisco, CA 94104-5203
Phone: 415-955-9020 **Fax:** 415-955-9053

Key Executives:
Barry D. Reynolds, Managing Director
Education: University of California; Stanford Graduate

School
Background: Principal, Trident Capital; Manager, Bain & Company; Texas Pacific Group
William N. Thorndike, Managing Director
Education: Harvard University; Stanford Graduate School
Background: T Rowe Price Associates; Walker & Co.
Directorships: Carillon Assisted Living; Lincoln Peak Holdings; OASIS Group; QMC International; ZircoData
Joseph M. Niehaus, Managing Director
Education: Dartmouth College; Harvard Business School
Background: Managing Director, Hellman & Friedman; M&A, Morgan Stanley & Co.
Directorships: Accurate Monitoright; Fastener Distribution Holdings; FIMC; ResponseLinkcircle Graphics; 365 Data Centers; HealthWyse; Calo Programs; ZircoData
Michael C. Jackson, Special Limited Partner
Education: Dartmouth College; Johns Hopkins University
Background: Partner/Managing Director, Lehman Brothers
Directorships: LeMaitre Vascular Inc.; South Florida Media Group; Vox Communications
Eliot Wadsworth II, Special Limited Partner
Education: Harvard University; Harvard Business School
Background: CEO, White Flower Farm; Managing Partner, Boston Common Press
James H. Greene III, Vice President
Education: University of Pennsylvania
Background: Milestone Partners; Financial Sponsors Group, Morgan Stanley & Co.
Directorships: Accurate Monitoring; FIMC
Mark G. Hilderbrand, Managing Director
Education: BS, Boston University; MS, Stanford University; MBA, Harvard Business School
Background: General Partner, Onset Ventures; Summit Partners; Fox Paine & Company; Bain & Company
Jill A. Raimondi, Chief Financial Officer
Education: BS, Business Admin., University of California, Berkeley; CPA
Background: Controller, Trident Capital; Manager, Ernst & Young
Amy L. Laforteza, Controller
Education: BS, Business Admin., Univerity of California, Riverside; CPA
Background: Manager, Ernst & Young
Kirsi Fontenot, Tax Director
Education: BS, Business Admin., San Francisco State University; CPA
Background: Senior Manager, Ernst & Young
H. Irving Grousbeck, Special Limited Partner
Education: Amherst College; Harvard Business School
Background: Consulting Professor, Stanford Business School; Lecturer, Harvard University Graduate School of Business Administration; Co-Founder, Continental Cablevision
Directorships: Alta Colleges; Ancora Capital and Management; Asurion Corporation; Beacon Fire & Safety; Carillon Assisted Living; Rent-Wise; Med-Mart; Wind River Environmental
Mark A. McLaughlin, Principal
Education: Stanford Graduate School of Business
Background: Vice President, Technology Crossover Ventures; TA Associate/Consultant, Oliver Wyman; Sageview Capital; Wealthfront
Stephen M. Johnson, Vice President
Education: BS, Wharton School, University of Pennsylvania; MBA, Kellogg School of Management, Northwestern University
Background: M&A, Credit Suissel Citigroup; General Electric; American International Group
Directorships: Onrad Inc.; Sprout Health; Calo Programs; ZircoData
Charlotte D. MacDonald, Fund Administrator/Executive Assistant
Education: Colby-Sawyer College

950 HOUSTON ANGEL NETWORK
410 Pierce Street
PO Box 12
Houston, TX 77002

web: www.houstonangelnetwork.org

Mission Statement: The Houston Angel Network is a Texas-based angel organization focused on providing capital and support to early stage businesses.

Geographic Preference: Texas, United States
Fund Size: $4 million
Founded: 2001
Investment Criteria: Early Stage
Industry Group Preference: Life Sciences, Information Technology, Healthcare Information Technology, Energy Technology
Portfolio Companies: Adient Medical, Assistant Coach, BiologicsMD, Blausen Medical Communications, Bonfire Wings, Boomerang's, Cerebro Tech Medical Systems, Cinegif, CS Identity, Deep Imaging Technologies, End The Lix, Fairway Medical Technologies, Fannin Partners, Greenling, Houston Health Ventures, Kewl, Kimbia, Mercury Fund, Metric Medical Devices, Molecular Match, Monster Mosquito Systems, Nanospectra Biosciences, Nurtur Me, NutshellMail, On It, Ortho Accel, Personal Wine, Rhythm Superfoods, Rock My Run, Salient Pharmaceuticals, See Forge, Senscient, SioTex, SpringCharts, Strike Brewing Company, Surge, Sweet Leaf Iced Teas, Texas Ventures

Key Executives:
Stephanie Campbell, Managing Director
Education: BASc, Spring Hill College; MBA, Jones Graduate School of Business, Rice University
Background: Government Affairs Consultant, Potomac Partners DC; Independent Research Consultant, Texas Medical Center; Director of Recruiting, Security & Investigative Placement Consultants; General Partner, The Artemis Fund
Directorships: Goodfynd
Mark Leigh, President
Education: BS, University of Illinois; MBA, Kellogg School of Management, Northwestern University
Background: Regional Sales Manager, Evonik Degussa; VP of Pigments, Degussa Engineered Carbons; VP of Marketing/VP/Business Director, Evonik; SVP/GM, Orion Engineered Carbons; President, Americas, GSE Environmental

951 HOUSTON HEALTH VENTURES
Houston, TX

web: www.houstonhealthventures.com

Mission Statement: Invests in various companies serving the healthcare industry including innovative information technology, medical supplies, and medicinal cannabis.

Founded: 2013
Average Investment: $30,000
Investment Criteria: Seed, Early-Stage
Industry Group Preference: Healthcare, Technology, Medical Supply, Cannabis, Information Technology
Portfolio Companies: INRFOOD, I'm Sick Mobile, myRoundUp, myLAB Box, The Hippo Kitchen, Alltrope Medical, Legworks, Adient Medical, Luminostics

Key Executives:
David C. Franklin, Co-Founder/Managing Director
Education: BSE, Bio-Medical/Electrical Engineering, Duke University; MBA, Venture Capital, Anderson School of Management
Background: Consultant, Accenture; Manager, DaVita; Director of Venture Capital Programs, UCLA Anderson School of Management; Co-Founder, DCF Ventures; EVP, HigherEducation.com; CEO, BestAgents.com; Co-Founder, Joycare Pediatric Day Health Center
Directorships: Joycare Pediatric Day Health Center; Allotrope Medical

345

Venture Capital & Private Equity Firms / Domestic Firms

Huan Le, Co-Founder/Managing Director
Education: JD, University of Texas School of Law; BA, International Relations/Biology, University of Southern California
Background: Founder/Director/Advisor, Caphin Inc.; Co-Founder/President, Medifr Inc; CAO/General Counsel, DiCentral Corp.

952 HQ CAPITAL
1290 Avenue of the Americas
10th Floor
New York, NY 10104

Phone: 212-863-2300 **Fax:** 212-593-2974
web: hqcapital.com

Mission Statement: HQ Capital is a combination of alternative investment managers Auda, Real Estate Capital Partners and Equita.

Geographic Preference: United States
Fund Size: $6.5 Billion
Founded: 2015
Average Investment: $15 million
Investment Criteria: Partnership Investments, Secondary Investments, Co-Investments, Venture Capital and Buyouts
Industry Group Preference: Real Estate

Key Executives:
Dr. Bernd Turk, Chief Executive Officer
Tim Avery, CFO/COO, US & Asia
Ferdinand von Sydow, Managing Director

953 HT CAPITAL ADVISORS LLC
437 Madison Avenue
Suite 19D
New York, NY 10022-7001

Phone: 212-759-9080
e-mail: info@htcapital.com
web: www.htcapital.com

Mission Statement: HT Capital offers advice to middle market and closely-held companies that is firmly anchored by decades of experience on Wall Street.

Geographic Preference: United States; International
Founded: 1999
Minimum Investment: $100,000
Investment Criteria: Established, emerging middle market companies
Industry Group Preference: Food & Beverage, Healthcare, Pollution, Industrial Equipment, Electronic Technology, Manufacturing, Electrical Distribution
Portfolio Companies: Cellotape, Cidade, Tablewerks Inc., Hillsidecandy, Richardeyres, Justin's

Key Executives:
Eric J. Lomas, President
Education: BS, Business, New York University Graduate School of Administration
Background: Managing Director/Co-Head of Banking, Gruntal & Co; Deloitte & Touche; Non-Executive Chairman, Rexel; Troster, Singer & Co
C.A. Burkhardt, Senior Managing Director
Education: AB, Brown University; MBA, Columbia University Graduate School of Business
Background: Investment Banker, Janney Montgomery Scott; Financial Analyst, Aetna Life and Casualty; Deloitte Touche & Raquos
Florence J. Mauchant, Partner/Managing Director
e-mail: fmauchant@htcapital.com
Education: Graduate Degree, Institut Commercial de Nancy (France); MBA, Indiana University of Pennsylvania
Background: Schroders (UK based merchant bank); Generale Bank; Banque Nationale de Paris
Directorships: NYSSA; FWA
Thomas Girardi, Managing Director
Education: BS, Accounting, Montclair State University;
MBA, Finance, Rutgers Business School
Background: Unilever; Reckitt & Colman
Jean-Damien Perrier, Managing Director
Education: Sup de Co Tours (France)
Background: BNP Paribas Corporate Finance Group
Stephen C. Tardio, Managing Director
e-mail: stardio@htcapital.com
Education: MBA, Corporate Finance, The Fuqua School of Business at Duke University; BS, Computer Science, University of Illinois
Background: Manager of Technology Integration, Andersen Consulting
David S. Slackman, Managing Director
Education: BA/MA, Economics, University of Michigan
Background: President, Commerce Bank; Federal Reserve Bank of New York; The Dime Savings Bank of New York; Atlantic Bank of New York

954 HUDSON VENTURE PARTNERS
545 Fifth Avenue
Suite 401
New York, NY 10017

Phone: 212-644-9797 **Fax:** 212-371-9305
e-mail: info@hudsonptr.com

Mission Statement: To invest in and advise early stage companies with strong management and good market opportunities in the technology industry.

Geographic Preference: Northeastern United States
Fund Size: $170 million
Founded: 1997
Average Investment: $3 million
Minimum Investment: $1 million
Investment Criteria: Early stage, outstanding business and revenue models, revenues of $2-6 million, A product or service with a proprietary technology
Industry Group Preference: Infrastructure, Information Technology, Software, Enterprise Software, Technology, Communications, Financial Services, Marketing, Advertising, Media, Internet
Portfolio Companies: Acorda, Albridge Solutions, Bigfoot Interactive, Bla-Bla.com, Blue Lobster Software, Centor Software, CertifiedMail, Certpoint, ClientSoft, Comet Systems, Constant Contact, DataMotion, Didera, Dynamic Mobile Data Systmes, E-Tran, Elity Systems, GlobalServe, Greenplum, Guardent, Home Director, iClick, InQ, iHello, iTraffic, Integral, IPI Scrittura, Intellibridge, Knoa Corporation, LogMatrix, MarketSoft, MIDAS Vision Systems, Marketing Technology Solution: (MTS), Metapa, NetKey, OpenServices, Pathlight Technology, PeanutPress, Peminic, Pivot Solutions, Poindexter Systems, PowerOne Media, PowerSteering Software, Prescient Systems, QualityHealth, QueryObject Systems, Relegence, Roving, ScanBuy, Scrittura, TechRx, TheSquare, TouchCommerce, UGO Networks, Verge Solutions, VuePoint, Wasabi Systems, WebMethods, [x + 1]

Key Executives:
Kim P. Goh, Senior Managing Director
212-644-9797
e-mail: kgoh@hudsonptr.com
Education: BA, Southamptom College, Long Island University; MA, Columbia University; Harvard University; Carnegie-Mellon University
Background: Merck/Medco; Chemical Banking Company; Capital Market Group; Citibank
Directorships: Center Software, Elity Systems, E-Tran Solutions, Peminic
Jay N. Goldberg, Senior Managing Director
212-644-9797
e-mail: jgoldberg@hudsonptr.com
Education: BA, New York University
Background: Opcenter LLC; Lexstra PLC; Business Systems Corporation; Zeitech; Software Design Associates

Venture Capital & Private Equity Firms / Domestic Firms

Directorships: Bigfoot Interactive, GlobalServe, Metapa, i-Hello, PowerSteering, OpenService
Lawrence Howard MD, Senior Managing Director
212-644-9797
Fax: 212-583-1857
e-mail: lhoward@hudsonptr.com
Education: BS, University of New Hampshire; MD, New York Medical College
Background: President/CEO, Presstek; Consultant, The Villages
Directorships: Intellibridge Vuepoint.com, Intuitive Products International, CertifiedMail
Glen Lewy, Senior Managing Director
212-644-9797
e-mail: glewy@hudsonptr.com
Education: BA, Amherst College; JD, University of Chicago Law School
Background: Wolfensohn & Company; Bankers Trust; Debvoise & Plimpton
Directorships: NetKey, Relegence, Intellibridge, Peminic
Bill Carson, Managing Director
212-644-9797
e-mail: bcarson@hudsonptr.com
Education: Undergraduate Degree, Engineering & Economics, University of Notre Dame; MBA, University of Chicago
Background: Citigroup's Strategic Investment Group; IBM
John P. Truehart, Chief Financial Officer
Education: BS, Accounting, State University College of Arts & Sciences
Background: Controller, Charterhouse Group; Manager, Alliance Capital Management Corporation

955 HUMANA VENTURES
500 West Main Street
Louisville, KY 40202

Phone: 502-580-3906
web: www.humana.com

Mission Statement: Humana Ventures fosters innovation in the delivery of healthcare services and the development and use of healthcare information technology, while pursuing financial returns commensurate with the risks of early stage investing.

Geographic Preference: United States
Founded: 1961
Average Investment: $1-$5 million
Minimum Investment: $1 million
Investment Criteria: Early-Stage
Industry Group Preference: Communications, Computer Related, Consumer Services, Distribution, Natural Resources, Industrial Equipment, Medical & Health Related, Energy, Healthcare, Healthcare Services, Healthcare Information Technology
Portfolio Companies: Abaton.com, AirLogix, Aperture Credentialing, BenefitMall.com, CMG Health, CorSolutions Medical Corporation, Essex WoodlandsFund, Healthcare Recoveries, JSA Healthcare Corporation, Latin Healthcare Fund, Paidos Health Management Services, Paradigm Healthcare Corporation, Physics Ventures, Quality Metric, Raytel Medical, TriZetto Group, US Behavioral Health, Workscape
Key Executives:
  Paul Kusserow, SVP/Chief Strategy Officer/Corporate Development Officer
  Education: Wesleyan University; Master's Degree, Univ. of Oxford
  Background: Managing Director, Private Equity, BC Ziegler & Company; Managing Director & CIO, Ziegler HealthVest Fund
  Charles W Beckman, Vice President
  Education: BBA, University of Texas; MBA, University of Louisville

956 HUMMER WINBLAD VENTURE PARTNERS
50 Francisco Street
Suite 450
San Francisco, CA 94133

Phone: 415-979-9600 Fax: 415-979-9601
web: www.hwvp.com

Mission Statement: A venture capital firm focused exclusively on software. HWVP's goal is to provide the capital, experience, and vision that will help companies become leaders in this software-driven economy.

Geographic Preference: United States
Fund Size: $1 billion
Founded: 1989
Investment Criteria: Early-stage, software companies
Industry Group Preference: Applications Software & Services, Consumer Services, Infrastructure, Software, Business to Business, Retailing, Cloud Computing, SaaS, Internet, Enterprise Software
Portfolio Companies: 6connect, AceMetrix, Alpharank, Amberdata, Aria Systems, AspireIQ, Blissfully, Kiip, NeuVector, NuoDB, OptiMine, Sonatype, Stackery, Symbium, TidalScale, XANT
Key Executives:
  John Hummer, Founding Partner, Seattle
  Education: AB, English, Princeton University; MBA, Stanford Business School
  Ann Winblad, Founding Partner
  Education: BA, Mathematics & Business Administration, College of St. Catherine; MA, Education & International Economics, University of St. Thomas
  Background: Systems Programmer, Federal Reserve Bank; Co-Founder, Open Systems
  Directorships: Ace Metricsx, Krillion, MuleSoft, Star Analytics, Voltate Security
  Ann Winblad, Founding Partner
  Education: BA, Mathematics & Business Administration, St. Catherine University; MA, Education, University of St. Thomas; Honorary Doctorate of Law, University of St. Thomas
  Background: Systems Programmer, Federal Reserve Bank; Co-Founder, Open Systems Inc.; Strategy Consultant for various companies: IBM, Microsoft, Price Waterhouse Cooper
  Directorships: Hyperion; Mulesoft; The Knot; Net Perceptions; Liquid Audio; AceMetrix; OptiMine; Sonatype
  Mitchell Kertzman, Managing Director
  Background: Chairman/CEO, Liberate Technologies; CEO, Sybase; CEO, Powersoft
  Directorships: AspireIQ; NuoDB; Peerlyst; 6connect
  Lars Leckie, Managing Director
  Education: Engineering Physics degree, Queen's University; MS, Engineering, Stanford University; MBA, Stanford Graduate School of Business
  Background: Co-Founder, Auto-Farm
  Directorships: Kiip; InsideSales.com; Innovative Leisure; Aria Systems
  Ingrid Chiavacci, Chief Financial Officer
  Education: BS, Business Admin., University of Colorado, Boulder
  Background: Controller, PlumpJack Management Group; Senior Associate, PricewaterhouseCoopers

957 HUNT INVESTMENT GROUP
1900 North Akard Street
Dallas, TX 75201-2300

Phone: 214-978-8000 Fax: 214-978-8888
e-mail: bjolly@huntinvestment.com
web: www.huntinvestmentgroup.com

Venture Capital & Private Equity Firms / Domestic Firms

Mission Statement: An investment firm seeking to deploy capital with equity and hedge fund managers, private investment fuds and select direct co-investments.
Geographic Preference: United States, Western Europe, Japan
Fund Size: $100 million
Founded: 2014
Average Investment: $1 million - $5 million
Minimum Investment: $1 million
Industry Group Preference: Oil & Gas, Real Estate
Key Executives:
  McCall Cravens, Senior Vice President/Chief Investment Officer
  Education: BA, Economics, BS, Engineering Science, Vanderbilt University; MBA, Harvard Business School
  Background: Managing Director, SMU; Pamlico Capital; Lehman Brothers; Analyst, Wachovia
  Brian Jolly, Vice President
  Education: BBA/MPA, University of Texas, Austin; MBA, Southern Methodist University; CPA
  Background: Controller, Hunt Investment Group; Financial Analyst, Hunt Consolidated; Senior Accountant/Advisor, KPMG LLP

958 HUNTINGTON CAPITAL
3636 Nobel Drive
Suite 401
San Diego, CA 92122
Phone: 858-259-7654 Fax: 858-452-2003
web: www.hcapllc.com

Mission Statement: Huntingon Capital seeks to be the best-of-class mezzanine fund serving the lower middle market in the western United States with a particular emphasis on California. We provide capital and strategic assistance to small business entrepreneurs while making a positive and measurable contribution to the community.
Founded: 2000
Investment Criteria: Mezzanine Debt
Portfolio Companies: Advanced Structural Alloys, Altrec, Autumn Years at Newport Mesa, Autumn Years at Ojai, Arosa+LivHome, Burke Williams, CNCdata, Color Labs Enterprises, Cubex, Diamond Contract Services, Eaton Veterinary Pharmaceutical, Environment Furniture, Geary LSF, gen-E, Michael's Bakery Products LLC, Native Foods Café, ONCampus Media, Paragon Technology, PriMetrica, Inc., Progistics Distribution, Protect Plus Air Holdings, Reischling Press, Residential Design Services, RJE International, RPI, Summit Estates, Turbo International, Vertical Management Systems, Wave Technology Solutions Group
Key Executives:
  Tim Bubnack, Managing Partner
  Background: Managing Director, Silicon Valley Bank, Senior Executive, Comerica Ventures Inc.
  Directorships: Cubex Systems, Reischling Press, LLT Corp.
  Frank Mora, Partner
  Education: B.S. Economics, Wharton School of the University of Pennsylvania, M.B.A. Columbia Business School
  Background: DBI Capital, Vice President, Fixed Income Capital Markets team at Citigroup, Venture Capital Officer, Economic Development Bank for Puerto Rico
  Directorships: Paragon Technology, Baked In The Sun, PriMetrica, Burke Williams, Progistics Distribution

959 HUNTSMAN GAY GLOBAL CAPITAL
1950 University Avenue
Palo Alto, CA 94303
Phone: 650-321-4910 Fax: 650-321-4911
e-mail: ir@hggc.com
web: www.hggc.com

Mission Statement: A private equity fund focusing on leveraged buyout, recapitalizations and growth transactions in the middle-market.
Geographic Preference: North America
Fund Size: $300 million
Average Investment: $25 - $100 million
Investment Criteria: Leveraged Buyouts, Recapitalizations, Growth Equity, Public To Private, Corporate Carve-Outs
Industry Group Preference: Business Services, Consumer Products, Financial Services, Healthcare, Industrial Services, Information, Software
Portfolio Companies: AutoAlert, Davies Group, Dealer-FX, Denodo, etouches, FPX, Gee Holdings, IDERA, Innovative, Integrity, iQor, MyWebGrocer, Nutraceutical, Pearl, Sandbox, Selligent, SSI, Citadel, GIS, Hollander, Hybris, MaMa Rosa's, Power Holdings, Serena, Sunquest, Turner
Key Executives:
  Bob Gay, Executive Director
  Education: AB, University of Utah; PhD, Business Economics, Harvard University
  Background: Mamaning Director, Bain Capital; Executive Vice President, GE Capital; Engagement Manager, McKinsey & Co.
  Greg Benson, Co-Founder/Managing Partner
  e-mail: gbenson@hggc.com
  Education: BS, Business Administration, University of Minnesota
  Background: Bain Capital, General Electric
  Directorships: Medical Edge Healthcare Group, ICON Health & Fitness, Nutraceutical International Corp., American Nutritional Casualty Insurance, American Pad & Paper
  Gary Crittenden, Executive Director
  e-mail: gcrittenden@hggc.com
  Education: BS, Brigham Young University; MBA, Harvard Business School
  Background: CFO, Citigroup; CFO, American Express; CFO, Monsanto; CFO, Sears Roebuck & Company
  Directorships: Chairman, iQor; Pearl Holding Group
  Rich Lawson, Co-Founder/CEO
  Education: BA, Interdisciplinary Studies, Amherst College; MBA, Harvard Business School
  Background: Co-Founder, Sorenson Capital Partners
  Directorships: Wasatch Adaptive Sports
  Steve Young, Co-Founder/Managing Partner
  Education: BS, Finance/Political Science, Brigham Young University; JD, J. Reuben Clark Law School
  Background: Co-Founder, Sorenson Capital; NFL

960 HURON CAPITAL PARTNERS LLC
500 Griswold
Suite 2700
Detroit, MI 48226
Phone: 313-962-5800
e-mail: info@huroncapital.com
web: www.huroncapital.com

Mission Statement: A Midwest based equity investment firm focused on investing in growing, established and profitable companies.
Geographic Preference: United States, Canada
Fund Size: $1.8 billion
Founded: 1999
Average Investment: $20 - $50 million
Minimum Investment: $5 million
Investment Criteria: Corporate spin-offs, family succession transactions, recapitalizations, buy & build strategies, management buyouts
Industry Group Preference: Manufacturing, Consumer Products, Consumer Services, Business Products & Services, Healthcare
Portfolio Companies: Albireo Energy, Aquamar Holdings, Atlantic Beverage Company, B&B Roadway Security Solutions, Direct Connect Lofistix, Drake Automotive,

Venture Capital & Private Equity Firms / Domestic Firms

Hansons, High Street Insurance Partners, InterVisions Systems, IQ Brands, Norwest Pallet Supply, Pacific Shoring, Pueblo Mechanical & Controls, Pure Dental Brands, Ronnoco Beverage Solutions, Sciens Building Solutions, StayOnline, Valentus Specialty Chemicals, WD Diamonds, XLerate Group

Other Locations:
225 Ross Street
4th Floor
Pittsburgh, PA 15219
Phone: 412-201-7040 **Fax:** 412-201-7041

4 King Street West
Suite 1300
Toronto, ON M5H 1B6
Canada
Phone: 416-234-0313 **Fax:** 416-234-1980

Key Executives:
Brian Demkowicz, Co-Founder/Managing Partner
313-962-5801
e-mail: bdemkowicz@huroncapital.com
Education: BS, Accounting, Purdue University; MBA, Kellogg School of Management, Northwestern University
Background: Director, Bulkley Capital; Principal, Waud Capital Partners; VP, Heller Equity Capital Corporation; CPA
Directorships: Albireo Energy LLC, Direct Connect Logitix, High Street Insurance Partners, InterVision
Michael Beauregard, Senior Partner
313-962-5802
e-mail: mbeauregard@huroncapital.com
Education: BA, Economics, University of Michigan; MBA, Joseph M. Katz Graduate School of Business, University of Pittsburgh; JD, School of Law, University of Pittsburgh
Background: Managing Director, Macam Corporation; Principal, Japonica Partners; VP, Strategic Planning, Sunbeam Corporation; VP, Finance & Investments, Duchossois Enterprises
Directorships: IQ Brands, Aquamar Holdings, Valentus Specialty Chemicals, Brunder Polymer
Peter Mogk, Senior Partner
313-962-5803
e-mail: pmogk@huroncapital.com
Education: BS, Economics, Miami University of Ohio; MBA, University of Chicago
Background: Vice President, Treasurer, Penske Corporation; Nesbitt Burns Securites; Bank of montreal; Northern Trust Company
Directorships: InterVision Systems, Good Sportsman Marketing, XLerate Group, Pueblo Mechanical & Control, Direct Connect Logistix
Peter E Mogk, Senior Partner
313-962-5803
e-mail: pmogk@huroncapital.com
Education: BS, Economics, Miami University, Oxford; MBA, University of Chicago
Background: VP/Treasurer, Penske Corporation; Senior Management, Nesbitt Burns Securities Inc.; The Northern Trust Company
Directorships: Agri-Carriers Group, Jensen Hughes, Victoria Fine Foods, XLerate Group
David Reynolds, Senior Partner, CFO & CCO
e-mail: dreynolds@huroncapital.com
Education: BA, Mathematics, Kenyon College; MBA & Master of Professional Accountancy, Georgia State University
Background: CFO, Printegra Corporation; General Manager, Datagraphic
Directorships: Printegra, OneTouchpoint, Maple Leaf Automotive, LeadingResponse
Christopher S Sheeren, Partner, Business Development
313-962-5805
e-mail: csheeren@huroncapital.com
Education: BA, University of Nebraska; MBA, University of Michigan; CPA
Background: Conway MacKenzie Inc.; Audit Manager, PricewaterhouseCoopers
Directorships: Maple Leaf Automotive, Apex Laboratories International, Mosaic Youth Theatre of Detroit
Gretchen B Perkins, Partner, Business Development
313-962-5806
e-mail: gperkins@huroncapital.com
Education: BBA, University of Michigan
Background: Long Point Capital; VP, Business Development, IRN Inc.; Fleet Capital Corporation; GE Capital Corporation
Directorships: Association for Corporate Growth Inc., International Women's Insolvency & Restructuring Confederation
Nicholas H Barker, Partner, Deal Execution
e-mail: nbarker@huroncapital.com
Education: BA, Economics, University of Michigan; MBA, University of Chicago
Background: Corporate Development/Finance Professional, CCC Information Services Inc.; Analyst, Ryan Enterprises Group; Bear Stearns & Co. Inc.
Directorships: Dynamic Dental Partners, Jensen Hughes, Six Month Smiles Inc., Sock & Accessory Brands Global Inc., Spring & Sprout Dental Holdings LLC
James Mahoney, Senior Partners
e-mail: jmahoney@huroncapital.com
Education: BA, Economics & Political Science, Villanova University; MBA, University of Chicago
Background: Conway MacKenzie Inc.; Robert W Baird & Company
Directorships: Sciens Building Solutions, Alireo Energy, XLerate Group, Valentus Specialty Chemicals, Pure Dental Brands, Ronnoco Beverage Solutions

961 HURON RIVER VENTURES
303 Detroit Street
Suite 100
Ann Arbor, MI 48108

web: www.huronrivervc.com

Mission Statement: Huron River Ventures invests in early-stage, Michigan-based, energy technology, Cleanweb, and smart transportation companies offering innovative, cost-effective and higher performing products and solutions to large global problems.

Geographic Preference: United States, Midwest
Average Investment: $1 - $5 million
Investment Criteria: Seed, Series A & B
Industry Group Preference: Energy, Agriculture, Manufacturing, Mobility
Portfolio Companies: Ambiq Micro, ArborMetrix, Cribspot, Deliv, FarmLogs, Opto Atmosphere, PeachWorks, Postmates, Sigh Machine, SkySpecs, Sportsman Tracker, Tachyus, Tackk

Key Executives:
Ryan Waddington, Founding Partner
e-mail: ryan@huronrivervc.com
Education: BS, Aerospace Engineering, University of Michigan; MS, Civil & Environmental Engineering, University of Wisconsin; MBA, Ross School of Business
Background: Ziff Brothers Investments, DTE Energy Corporate Venture Group

962 HYDE PARK VENTURE PARTNERS
415 N LaSalle Street
Suite 502
Chicago, IL 60654

web: hydeparkvp.com

Mission Statement: Hyde Park Venture Partners (HPVP) is an early stage venture capital fund investing in early stage technology companies in the Midwest, with particular focus in Chicago. HPVP draws on its strategic relationship with Hyde Park Angels (HPA) to provide industry and business expertise to its portfolio companies through a network of more

Venture Capital & Private Equity Firms / Domestic Firms

than 90 seasoned business executives, entrepreneurs and service professionals. HPVP's principals, Ira Weiss and Guy Turner, and the HPA network take an active role in mentoring and guiding portfolio companies in product development, business strategy, financing and exit through both formal director roles and informal mentorship relationships.

Geographic Preference: Chicago
Average Investment: $750,000 - $1.5 million
Investment Criteria: Early-Stage
Industry Group Preference: Business to Business, Consumer Marketplace
Portfolio Companies: Ahalogy, FarmLogs, FindIt, FoodGenius, InContext Solutions, Iris Mobile, LevelEleven, NoRedInk, ParkWhiz, Protean, SimpleRelevance, Sqrl, TempoDB, Zaranga

Other Locations:
10401 N Meridian Street
Suite 215
Indianapolis, IN 46290

Key Executives:
Ira Weiss, Partner
Education: MBA, PhD, Booth School of Business
Background: Managing Director, RK Ventures; Accountant, Coopers & Lybrand
Directorships: ReTel Technologies
Guy Turner, Partner/Managing Director, Chicago
Education: BS, Mechanical Engineering, Cornell University; MBA, Booth School of Business
Background: Boston Consulting Group; Mechanical Engineer, Raytheon, General Electric
Directorships: InContext Solutions
Tim Kopp, Partner/Managing Director, Indianapolis
Background: Coca-Cola; Procter & Gamble; Webtrends; ExactTarget
Directorships: Ahalogy, G2Crowd, Level11

963 HYPUR VENTURES
7812 East Acoma Drive
Suite 7
Scottsdale, AZ 85260

Phone: 480-409-4599
web: hypurventures.com

Mission Statement: Invests in various companies within the cannabis industries. Areas of focus include compliance, business intelligence and consumer products.

Founded: 2012
Industry Group Preference: Cannabis, Technology
Portfolio Companies: Blue Line Protection Group, DOPE Magazine, Calyx, Cannasure, Headset, Hypur, Simplifya, Willie's Reserve

964 I-HATCH VENTURES LLC
270 Lafayette Street
Suite 814
New York, NY 10012

Phone: 212-651-1750 Fax: 212-208-4590
e-mail: info@i-hatch.com
web: www.i-hatch.com

Mission Statement: To provide capital and support to early-stage technology companies, with focus on the communications, enabling technology, mobile data services and broadband sectors.

Founded: 1999
Investment Criteria: Early Stage
Industry Group Preference: Communications, Technology, Mobile Data Services, Broadband, Enabling Technology
Portfolio Companies: AtHoc, Datasnap.Io, Equator, M:Metrics, Mobliss, OpenAir, Salsa, SignalSoft, Thumbplay, Vindigo, Widerthan

Key Executives:
Chip Austin, Managing Partner
Education: Duke University; MBA, Harvard Business School
Background: Co-Founder, Interactive Practice, McKinsey & Co.; Morgan Stanley; IBM; President & CEO, Bertelsmann Online; SVP, Sales & Business Development, Prodigy
Brad Farkas, Managing Partner
Education: BA, Harvard College; MBA, Harvard Business School
Background: Founding Partner, Lazard Technology Partners; CFO & Director, Compatible Systems; Founder, Argosy Technology; Director & Principal, pcAnywhere Inc.; Founder, Metropolitan Asset Technology; Co-Founder, Phonetix Inc.; Associate, First Boston

965 IA VENTURES
920 Broadway
15th Floor
New York, NY 10010

web: www.iaventures.com

Mission Statement: Invests in companies that create competitive advantage through data.

Investment Criteria: Early-Stage
Industry Group Preference: Software, Digital Media, Healthcare, Consumer Services
Portfolio Companies: Recorded Future, NewsCred, DataRobot, Kinsa, DigitalOcean, MemSQL, Datadog Inc., Drift, Transcriptic, Vectra AI, PlaceIQ, Simple, Next Big Sound, The Trade Desk Inc.

Key Executives:
Roger Ehrenberg, Founder/Managing Partner
Education: BBA, Finance, Economics & Organizational Psychology, University of Michigan; MBA, Finance, Accounting & Management, Columbia Business School
Background: IA Capital Partners; President & CEO, DB Advisors; Investment Banking & Managing Director, Citibank
Directorships: DataSift, Metamarkets, Recorded Future, The Trade Desk, Twice
Brad Gillespie, Partner
Education: PhD, Electrical Engineering, University of Washington
Background: Technology Advisor, Microsoft; Lockheed-Martin

966 IANTHUS CAPITAL MANAGEMENT
420 Lexington Avenue
Suite 414
New York, NY 10170

Phone: 646-518-9411
e-mail: info@ianthuscapital.com
web: www.ianthuscapital.com

Mission Statement: iAnthus operates and invests in cannabis companies.

Geographic Preference: US
Founded: 2014
Industry Group Preference: Cannabis, Agriculture, Financial Services, Healthcare
Portfolio Companies: Citiva, Grassroots Vermont, The Green Solutions, GrowHealthy, Mayflower Medicinals, Organix, Reynold Greenleaf & Associates

Other Locations:
22 Adelaide Street West
Suite 2740
Toronto, ON M5H 4E3
Canada

Key Executives:
Hadley Ford, Director/CEO
Education: BS, Boston University; MBA, Stanford University Graduate School of Business

Background: VP, Goldman Sachs; CFO, Clearway Technologies; Managing Director, Banc of America Securities; CEO, ProCure Treatment Centers
Randy Maslow, Director/President
Education: AB, Government, Cornell University; JD, Rutgers Law School
Background: SVP, Business Development/General Counsel, XO Communications; Managing Partner, Electric Ventures; SVP/General Counsel, IGE
Julius Kalcevich, Director/CFO
Education: BA, McGill University; MBA, Columbia University
Background: Partner, BG Partners Corp.; Director of Investment Banking, CIBC World Markets
Carlos Perea, Chief Operating Officer
Education: BS, Mechanical Engineering, University of New Mexico; MBA, Stanford University Graduate School of Business
Background: President, Qynergy; Founding Partner, Entrada Ventures; Advisor, Flywheel Ventures; Special Advisor, Verge Fund; Chairman/CEO, MIOX Corp.; President/Director, Nuvita
Directorships: Chairman, YPO New Mexico; InnovateABC; Puralytics
John Henderson, Managing Director/Chief Development Officer
Education: BA, English, Northwestern University; MBA, Tuck School of Business, Dartmouth College
Background: President, George B.H. Macomber Co.; Founding Principal/COO/Development Officer, ProCure Treatment Centers; Founding Partner, Proton International

967 IBM VENTURE CAPITAL GROUP
1 New Orchard Road
Armonk, NY 10504-1722

Phone: 914-499-1900
Toll-Free: 800-426-4968
web: www.ibm.com/innovation/venture-development

Mission Statement: IBM Venture Capital Group's objective is to bring innovation into the venture capital community. Typically, IBM Venture Capital Group does not engage in equity or seed funding, and instead works closely with venture capital firms to discover new technologies and develop business strategies. In 2014, IBM launched the IBM Watson Venture Fund, a venture fund designed to support startups interested in utilizing IBM's own business platform, IBM Watson.

Fund Size: $100 million
Investment Criteria: Startups
Industry Group Preference: Technology, Aerospace and Defense, Automotive, Banking, Education, Electronics, Energy, Healthcare, Insurance, Manufacturing, Metals, Oil & Gas, Retail, Telecommunications & Media, Transportation
Portfolio Companies: BigFix, Claranet, Clearscope, Cloud Temple, Coronado Curragh Pty., CyFir, dan.com, DATEV eG, Deloitte, Elektronabava, Emnotion, Fosen IKT, Geisinger Health System, Veristat

Key Executives:
Angie Grimm, Managing Director
Education: BS, Finance and Marketing, Indiana University, Bloomington; Kelley School of Business, Indiana University
Background: Donaldson, Lufkin & Jenrette
Christoph Auer-Welsbach, Partner
Thomas Whiteaker, Partner
Background: Partner, Propel Venture Partners; Executive Director, BBVA Ventures; Hartford Ventures; Visa Inc.; Omnium Worldwide
Wendy Lung, Director, Corporate Strategy
Education: BBA, Finance & Marketing, University of Washington
Deborah Magid, Director, Software Strategy
Education: University of Pennsylvania; University of Connecticut
Background: Taligent; GE Information Services; AT&T
Savitha Srinivasan, Partner
Education: MS, Computer Science, Pace University

968 ICON VENTURES
505 Hamilton Avenue
Suite 310
Palo Alto, CA 94301

Phone: 650-463-8800
e-mail: info@iconventures.com
web: www.iconventures.com

Mission Statement: An independent venture capital firm investing in emerging technology companies.

Fund Size: $260 million
Founded: 2003
Average Investment: $4 - $8 million
Investment Criteria: Early Stage, Middle Stage
Industry Group Preference: Consumer Internet, Clean Technology, Digital Media & Marketing, Software, Cloud Computing, Communications, Mobile, Security
Portfolio Companies: 41st Parameter, Alation, Aera 1, Aster Data, Attributor, Avnera, Awarepoint, Bill.com, Brion, Calypto, ClairMail, Clicker, Cloud Physics, Cortina, Data Allegro, Delphix, Device Scape, Duetto, Ever, Exabeam, FireEye, Huddle, Infinera, Inkling, Ionic Security, Kixeye, Marketlive, Meebo, Mimosa Systems, Moovweb, Mopub, Ocarina Networks, Oodle, Opcity, Origami Logic, Paloalto, Playstudios, Posterous, PostPath, Proofpoint, Quellan, RedSeal, Reputation.com, Ripcord, Sencha, Si Time, Solidcore, Synack, Teladoc, Thanx, The Muse, True X Media, Trust Arc, Tune, Tunein, Voltage Security, Clip, WGT, Xambala, Yodle, Zephyr Health

Key Executives:
Joe Horowitz, Managing General Partner
e-mail: joe@iconventures.com
Education: BA, Economics, Columbia University; MBA, Wharton School, University of Pennsylvania
Background: US Venture Partners; Exxon Enterprises; Chairman & CEO, Geocast Network Systems
Directorships: Area 1 Security, Devicescape, KIXEYE, Moovweb, PlayStudios, Sencha, Synack, TuneIn, Zephyr Health
Tom Mawhinney, General Partner
e-mail: tom@iconventures.com
Education: BA, Harvard College; MBA, Stanford Graduate School of Business
Background: Canaan Partners; Co-Founder, President & COO, North Systems
Directorships: Area 1 Security, Awarepoint, Bill.com, Huddle, Ionic Security, KIXEYE, MarketLive, Reputation.com, Synack, Teladoc, Yodle, Zephyr Health
Jeb Miller, General Partner
e-mail: jeb@iconventures.com
Education: BA, Economics, Harvard College
Background: The Carlyle Group; Managing Director, Business Development, Scient; Morgan Stanley
Directorships: CloudPhysics, Duetto, Exabeam, Origami Logic, TRUSTe, WGT Sports
Michael Mullany, General Partner
e-mail: michael@iconventures.com
Education: BA, Economics, Harvard College; MBA, Stanford University
Background: CEO, Sencha; VP, Products & Marketing, Engine Yard; PeakStream; Netscape; Loudcloud; VMware
Directorships: Moovweb
Ben Shih, Partner
e-mail: ben@iconventures.com
Education: Massachusetts Institute of Technology; MBA, Stanford Graduate School of Business
Background: Crystal Ventures; Analyst, MDT Advisers; Lotus Development
Peter Yi, Principal
e-mail: peter@iconventures.com

Venture Capital & Private Equity Firms / Domestic Firms

Education: BA, University of California, Berkeley
Background: Worldview Technology Partners

969 ICV PARTNERS
810 7th Avenue
35th Floor
New York, NY 10019

Phone: 212-455-9600 Fax: 212-455-9603
e-mail: emailicv@icvpartners.com
web: www.icvpartners.com

Mission Statement: A private equity firm exclusively investing in companies in the lower end of the middle market, commited to the realities of growing a mid-size business. A certified Minority Business Enterprise (MBE), iCV invests in companies owned by members of ethnic minorities.

Fund Size: $130 million
Average Investment: $5-20 million
Minimum Investment: $5 million
Investment Criteria: Buyouts, recapitalizations, growth equity, corporate Divestitures, family successions and revenues between $25-$250 million
Industry Group Preference: Healthcare, Consumer Products, Processing, Commercial Services, Industrial Equipment, Food & Beverage, Consumer Services, Manufacturing, Business Products & Services
Portfolio Companies: American Alliance Dialysis Holdings, Coverall, LeadingResponse, OneTouchPoint, Physician IMS Control, Safe Security, SG360, SirsiDynix, UTP, AAMP of America, Cargo Airport Services USA, Chung's, Entertainment Cruises, The Hilsinger Company, Innovative, Mallet, Marshall Retail Group, Press A Point, The PFM Group, Stauber Performance Ingredients Inc., Sterling Foods

Other Locations:
1201 West Peachtree
Suite 2800
Atlanta, GA 30309
Phone: 404-682-1401 Fax: 212-504-0842

Key Executives:
Willie E. Woods Jr., President/Managing Director
e-mail: wwoods@icvcapital.com
Education: BA, Accounting, Morehouse College; MBA, Harvard Business School
Background: VP, Deutsche Bank Alex Brown; Levmark Capital; Lehman Brothers; NDB Bank
Lloyd M. Metz, Managing Director
Education: BS, Industrial Engineering, Stanford University; MBA, Harvard Business School
Background: Warburg Pincus; High Yield Capital Markets Group, Morgan Stanley; M&A, JP Morgan
Cory D. Mims, Managing Director
Education: BBA, Howard University; MBA, Harvard Business School
Background: Principal, TSG Capital Group; Salomon Brothers, NY, London
Ira L. Moreland, Managing Director
Education: BS, Accounting, Morehouse College; MBA, University of Chicago
Background: Managing Director, Financial Sponsors Group, SunTrust Robinsin Humphrey; Managing Director, Mid-Cap Investment Banking Group, Banc of America Securities; Citigroup
Directorships: ACG Atlanta
Qian W. Elmore, Principal
Education: BA, Finance, Morehouse College; MBA, Harvard Business School
Background: Principal, Reliant Equity Investors; Senior Associate, Wind Point Partners; Senior Associate, McCown De Leeuw
Zeena Rao, Managing Director
Education: BS, Economics, Wharton School, University of Pennsylvania; MBA, Harvard Business School
Background: Consumer Industrial Group, Lehman Brothers; Investment Banking Division, Deutsche Bank

Sheldon Howell, Principal
Education: BA, Economics & Political Science, Rutgers University; MBA, Ross School of Business, University of Michigan
Background: Churchill Financial, Merrill Lynch, Landenburg Thalmann, American International Group
Jermaine L. Warren, Principal
Education: BS, Business, Hofstra University; MBA, Harvard Business School
Background: Starwood Capital Group, Goldman Sachs

970 ID VENTURES AMERICA LLC
5201 Great America Parkway
Suite 355
Santa Clara, CA 95054

Phone: 408-894-7900 Fax: 408-894-7939
web: www.idsoftcapital.com

Mission Statement: To commit full resources to the building of portfolio companies and the creation of long-term value for these businesses. iD Ventures America, formerly Acer Technology Ventures America, invests primarily in early stage companies in the United States.

Geographic Preference: United States, Canada
Fund Size: $150 million
Founded: 1998
Average Investment: $500,000 - $3 million
Minimum Investment: $500,000
Investment Criteria: Startups, Seed, First Round, Second Round, Early Stage
Industry Group Preference: Communications, Electronic Technology, Information Technology, Semiconductors, Hardware, Software, Computer Related, Internet Technology, Online Content, Energy Efficiency, Medical Devices, Cloud Computing
Portfolio Companies: Applied Biocode, ATS Advanced Telematic Systems, Bandwidth 10, CoAdna Photonics, CounterPoint Health Solutions, Dragonfly, Ginkgo Bioworks, mCube, Neumitra, Optovue, SiFotonics Technologies, Silicon Frontline Technology, Striiv, Voltafield Technology

Key Executives:
Dr Ronald Chwang, Chairman/President
Education: BEng, Electrical Engineering, McGill University; PhD, Electrical Engineering, University of Southern California
Background: President & CEO, Acer America Corporation; Intel; Bell Northern Research
Directorships: mCube, Striiv, Voltafield Technology, CoAdna, iRobot Corporation, AU Optronics Corporation
Ted Lai, Partner/Chief Financial Officer
Education: BS, MA, Accounting, National Cheng Chi University; MBA, Michigan State University
Background: Controller & CFO, Acer America Corporation; Deloitte & Touche
Ed Yang, Partner
Education: BS, Electrical Engineering, National Cheng-Kung University; Philips International Institute; MS, Electrical Engineering, Oregon State University
Background: Hewlett-Packard Company

971 IDEA FUND PARTNERS
1415 W NC Highway 54
Suite 206
Durham, NC 27707

web: www.ideafundpartners.com

Mission Statement: IDEA Fund Partners invests in seed and early stage technology companies in the Southeast and Mid-Atlantic regions of the United States.

Geographic Preference: North Carolina, Southeast & Mid-Atlantic Regions
Founded: 2006
Minimum Investment: $100,000
Investment Criteria: Seed-Stage, Early-Stage

Venture Capital & Private Equity Firms / Domestic Firms

Industry Group Preference: Information Technology, Materials Technology, Medical Devices, Diagnostics, Software
Portfolio Companies: 71lbs, Antenna, Brightdoor, Canopy, CloudTags, Distil Networks, FilterEasy, First, GradSave, Joicaster, NextRay, Pendo, Physcient, Reveal Mobile, Sarda Technologies, WedPics, Windsor Circle

Key Executives:
  Aohn Cambier, Managing Partner
  Education: BA, International Relations, Michigan State University; MBA, University of North Carolina at Chapel Hill
  Background: CFO, NC IDEA; Microelectronics Center of North Carolina
  Directorships: 71lbs, Brightdoor Systems, Sarda Technologies, Royalty Exchange, CloudTags
  Lister Delgado, Managing Partner
  Education: ScB, Electrical Engineering, Brown University; MS, Computer Engineering, University of Texas, Austin; MBA, University of North Carolina at Chapel Hill
  Background: NC IDEA; AT&T Bell Labs; Lucent Technologies
  Directorships: Oncoscope, Windsor Circle, GradSave
  Richard Fox, Venture Partner
  Education: BS, Physics, Massachusetts Institute of Technology
  Background: Founding Partner, Astralis Group
  Directorships: National Association of Seed and Venture Funds

972 IDEALAB
130 West Union Street
Pasadena, CA 91103
Phone: 626-585-6900 **Fax:** 626-535-2701
web: www.idealab.com

Mission Statement: Invests in technology companies in the incubation stage.
Geographic Preference: California
Fund Size: $400 million
Founded: 1996
Industry Group Preference: E-Commerce & Manufacturing, Entertainment, Software, Technology, Clean Technology, Communications, Security, Internet, Digital Media & Marketing
Portfolio Companies: aiPod, Branch, Candy Club, CodeSpark, Cool Energy, Edisun Microgrids, Enplug, eSolar, Factual, Flexa, Gem, HelloTech, Kaleo, Lumin, Mightytext, Migo, Mount Wilson Ventures, New Matter, Open, Papaya, Refer.com, Scoutables, Sellbrite, Simbi, Tag Pop, Teleport Me, Tenor, Tint, Trinity Mobile Networks, UberMedia, UCode, WhiteCoat, WorldHaus, X1, Zowdow

Key Executives:
  Bill Gross, Chairman
  Education: BS, Mechanical Engineering, California Institute of Technology
  Background: Solar Devices; GNP Development
  Marcia Goodstein, President & CEO
  Education: Pomona College
  Background: Enfish Corporation; Gemstar Development Corporation; California Institute of Technology Research facility
  Alex Maleki, Vice President, Business Development
  Education: BA, University of California, Santa Barbra; JD, Southwestern University
  Craig Chrisney, Chief Financial Officer
  Education: BS, California Polytechnic University
  Background: Audit Senior Manager, PricewaterhouseCoopers
  Wes Ferrari, Vice President, Information Technologies
  Education: BS, Biology & Anthropology, Loma Linda University; MBA, Fisher School of International Business, Monterey Institute of International Studies
  Background: Managing Director, IKON Office Solutions

973 IDG CAPITAL
1345 Avenue of Americas
33rd Floor
New York, NY 10105
Phone: 212-337-5200
web: www.idgcapital.com

Mission Statement: An early stage venture capital firm that invests in New Media, E-Commerce and IT companies in the US.
Geographic Preference: United States
Fund Size: $100 million
Founded: 1997
Average Investment: $1 - $5 million
Minimum Investment: $1 million
Investment Criteria: Early-Stage
Industry Group Preference: Infrastructure, Computer Hardware & Software, Enterprise Services, Mobile Communications Devices, Wireless Technologies, E-Commerce & Manufacturing, Healthcare, Information Technology, Internet Technology, New Media
Portfolio Companies: Bilibili, App Annie, Jiguang, Wiseasy, Zapya, Rokid, Tongdun, 5miles, Wecash, Live.Me, CreditEase, Amlogic, Archermind, Iobit, Royole, Pacific Construction, RDA, AsiaTelco Technologies, Anker, Circle, Yixin Group, LongShine, Technology Tarena, Ctrip, Kingdee, Tencent, +360, OriGene, Shenogen Pharma Group, Pai+, Sentieon, Shuangcheng Pharma, China Biologic Products Inc., Funzio G-Bits, Artsy, Sheln, Farfetch, Moncler, Gentle Monster, IGG, Legendary, Apollo Solar, Hyper Strong, Ecovacs Robotics, IDG Energy, HC Semitek, OSRAM, Aikosolar, Xpeng

974 IGNITION PARTNERS
350 106th Avenue NE
1st Floor
Bellevue, WA 98004
Phone: 425-709-0772
e-mail: info@ignitionpartners.com
web: www.ignitionpartners.com

Mission Statement: Ignition invests in emerging and future leaders in communications, internet, software, and services across business and consumer targets.

Investment Criteria: Seed, Series A & B
Industry Group Preference: Machine Learning, Mobile Enterprise, Software, Security, Digital Transformation, Infrastructure, Information Technology
Portfolio Companies: Acalvio, Accompany Beta, Airbiquity, Amplero, Appfog, Apprenda, Aviatrix, Avist, Avvo, Azuqua, Bluedata, BlueStacks, Bromium, Cask, Chef, Cloudmark, Couchbase, DataSphere, Docker, DocuSign, Fire Apps, Glympse, Icertis, KenSci, Korrio, LiveStories, MotifInvesting, Moz, Nymi, Onehub, PaxVax, Previser, Skytap, SnapLogic, Spoken, StreamSets, Talent Sonar, Tempered Networks, Tractable, Trifacta, Verity Solutions, WePay

Other Locations:
108 First Street
Los Altos, CA 94022
Phone: 650-825-6909

Key Executives:
  Cameron Myhrvold, Founding Partner
  e-mail: cam@ignitionpartners.com
  Education: BA, University of California, Berkeley
  Background: Microsoft Corporation; Co-Founder, Dynamical Systems
  Directorships: Azaleos, Cloudmark, Likewise, Seven, Teranode, Zenprise
  Johnathan Roberts, Founding Partner
  e-mail: jonro@ignitionpartners.com

353

Venture Capital & Private Equity Firms / Domestic Firms

Education: BA, History, University of Washington
Background: Microsoft Corporation
Directorships: Docusign, HyperQuality, Spoken Communications, Earth Class Mail
Brad Silverberg, Founding Partner
e-mail: brad@ignitionpartners.com
Education: BS, Computer Science, Brown University; MS, Computer Science, University of Toronto
Background: Senior Vice President, Executive Committee, Microsoft Corporation
Directorships: Avvo, Fotopedia, GlobalScholar, Keas, Seven, SourceLabs, ice.com, Skytap
John Connors, Managing Partner
e-mail: johncon@ignitionpartners.com
Education: BA, Accounting, University of Montana
Background: Microsoft Corporation; PIP Printing; SAFECO Corp; Deloitte, Haskins & Sells
Directorships: Nike, Recruiting.com, FIREapps, AdmitOne, Datasphere, Splunk
Richard Fade, Partner
e-mail: rfade@ignitionpartners.com
Background: Microsoft Corporation
Directorships: Appature, Azaleos, Likewise, InstallFree, One Hub, Talyst, GotVoice
Robert Headley, Administrative Partner
e-mail: rheadley@ignitionpartners.com
Education: MS & BS, Industrial Engineering, Stanford University
Background: Vice President, Finance & Treasurer, Starbucks Corporation; Principal Investment Area & Investment Banking Division, Goldman Sachs
Directorships: Enclarity, Earth Class Mail, FiREapps
Steve Hooper, Founding Partner
e-mail: shooper@ignitionpartners.com
Education: BS, Civil Engineering, Seattle University; MBA, The Wharton School
Background: Chairman & CEO, Netxlink Communications; Co-CEO, Teledesic; CEO, AT&T Wireless
Directorships: Modiv Media, TTMI, SeaMobile, Sparkplub, Airbiquity, AVST, OpenWave, UIEvolution
Michelle Goldberg, Partner
e-mail: michelle@ignitionpartners.com
Education: BA, Columbia University; MA, Harvard University
Background: Consultant, Microsoft's Developer Division; Investment Banking, Ollympic Capital Partners; Management Consultant, A.T. Kearney
Directorships: Visible Technologies, SEOmoz, TrackSimple, Mpire
Adrian Smith, Partner
e-mail: adrian@ignitionpartners.com
Background: Nextlink; AT&T Wireless; McCaw Cellular Communication; British Telecom Research Laboratories
Directorships: SinglePoint, Twisted Pair Solutions, Melodeo, Xeround
Chris Howard, Principal
e-mail: chris@ignitionpartners.com
Education: BS, Psychology, Occidental College; MBA, University of Washington
Background: Advertising & Marketing, Heckler Associates; Pilot + Levy
Directorships: Batch, Hipmunk, Datasphere, Fotopedia, Keas, Parse, SocialEyes

975 ILLINOIS VENTURES
2242 West Harrison Street
Suite 201
Chicago, IL 60612

web: www.illinoisventures.com

Mission Statement: IllinoisVENTURES is a venture capital firm that invests in seed and early-stage companies based on research done in federal laboratories and universities in the Midwest. The firm focuses primarily on businesses in the life sciences, clean technology, physical sciences and information technology sectors.

Geographic Preference: Midwest United States
Founded: 2002
Investment Criteria: Seed-Stage, Early-Stage
Industry Group Preference: Information Technology, Physical Sciences, Life Sciences, Clean Technology
Portfolio Companies: Advanced Diamond Technologies, ANDalyze, Autonomic Materials, Cbana Labs, Chromatin, ClearStream, Cortex Pharmaceuticals, Diagnostic Photonics, EdenPark Illumination, Fluensee, iCYT, Local Offer Network, Mirror.me, Personify, Semprius, ShareThis, SolarBridge Technologies, Solidware Technologies, Tetravitae Bioscience

Other Locations:
60 Hazelwood Drive
Suite 226
Champaign, IL 61820

Key Executives:
Nancy Sullivan, Chief Executive Officer/Senior Managing Director
Education: BBA, Loyola University; MBA, Kellogg School of Management, Masters, Biotechnology, Northwestern University
Background: Director, Office of Technology Management, University of Illinois; Senior Director, Business Development, KeraCure; Director, Northwestern University
Thomas Parkinson, Senior Director
Education: BA, Northwestern University; MBA, Kellogg School of Management

976 ILLUMINATE VENTURES
6114 La Salle Avenue
Unit 323
Oakland, CA 94611

e-mail: contact@illuminate.com
web: www.illuminate.com

Mission Statement: Illuminate Ventures seeks new and innovative business ideas led by committed, talented and diverse teams, particularly those that are inclusive of women entrepreneurs.

Geographic Preference: United States
Investment Criteria: Early-Stage
Industry Group Preference: Internet, SaaS, Information Technology
Portfolio Companies: Allocadia, Bedrock, Brightedge, CafeX Communications, CalmSea, Channeleyes, Coupang, Hoopla, Influitive, Jacobi, Litbit, Nitrio, Opsmatic, Peerlyst, Pex, Red Aril, Sense, Wild Pocketsm Xactly, Yozio, Vivant, DigitalFuel

Key Executives:
Cindy Padnos, Founder/Managing Partner
Education: AB, University of Michigan; MSIA/MBA, Tepper School of Business, Carnegie Mellon University
Background: Director, Outlook Ventures; Founder & CEO, Vivant; President/CEO, Acumen; IDE; Ingres; AT&t
Directorships: BrightEdge, CalmSea, Hoopla, Xactly Corporation
Rebecca Norlander, Venture Partner
Education: BS, Computer Science, Boston University
Background: General Manager, Microsoft
Cliff Higgerson, Strategic Portfolio Advisor
Education: BS, University of Illinois; MBA, University of California, Berkeley
Background: Founding Partner, ComVentures; General Partner, Vanguard Venture Partners; Managing Partner, Hambrecht & Quist
Directorships: Hatteras Networks, Kotura, World of Good, Xtera Communications, Ygnition

Venture Capital & Private Equity Firms / Domestic Firms

977 IMAGINATION CAPITAL
New York, NY

e-mail: info@imaginationvc.com
web: www.imaginationvc.com

Mission Statement: Imagination Capital invests in early stage companies that are aiming to create change in their industry of choice. They focus in the areas of esports, big data, machine learning, and digital media.

Geographic Preference: United States
Founded: 2017
Average Investment: $250,000 - $500,000
Minimum Investment: $250,000
Investment Criteria: Early Stage, U.S. Based
Industry Group Preference: Esports, Big Data, Machine Learning, Digital Media
Portfolio Companies: Boom, Co Star, Epics, Forge, Overtime, Roam, Upcomer, Veritonic

Key Executives:
  Rachel Lam, Co-Founder/Managing Partner
  Education: BS, Industrial Engineering & Operations, University of California Berkeley; MBA, Harvard Business School
  Background: Time Warner Investments Group; Quetzal/Chase Capital Partners; Time Warner Inc.; Credit Suisse First Boston; Morgan Stanley
  Richard D. Parsons, Co-Founder/Partner
  Education: JD, Union University Albany Law School; BA, University of Hawaii
  Background: Citigroup; Time Warner; Dime Bancorp; Patterson Belknap Webb & Tyler

978 IMPLEMENT CAPITAL
17 State Street
40th Floor
New York, NY 10004

Phone: 212-739-0822
e-mail: info@implementcapital.com
web: www.implementcapital.com

Mission Statement: Implement Capital invests in financial technology and services companies focused on the front, middle and back office.

Industry Group Preference: Financial Services, Business Products & Services

Key Executives:
  Jean-Edouard van Praet, Managing Partner
  Education: European Univeristy Brussels
  Background: CFO/Partner/Director, RIMES Technologies; Portfolio Manager, Sofaer Capital; Managing Director, Lawhill Capital

979 IN-Q-TEL
2107 Wilson Boulevard
Suite 1100
Arlington, VA 22201

Phone: 703-248-3000
e-mail: info@iqt.org
web: www.iqt.org

Mission Statement: In-Q-Tel identifies, adapts and delivers innovative technology solutions to support the missions of the Central Intelligence Agency and the broader U.S. intelligence community.

Geographic Preference: United States
Fund Size: $28 million
Founded: 1999
Average Investment: $3 million
Minimum Investment: $1 million
Investment Criteria: Start-Ups, Mezzanine, Emerging and Established companies
Industry Group Preference: Internet Technology, Security, Data Services, Data Communications, Information Technology, Energy, Infrastructure, DNA
Portfolio Companies: 3VR, AdaptivEnergy, Adapx, Advanced Photonix, Alfalight, Arcxis, Asankya, Basis Technology, Bay Microsystems, Biomatrica, Boreal Genomics, CallMiner, Cambrios Technology, Carnegie Speech, Cleversafe, Cloudera, Connectify, Convera, CopperEye, Contour Energy Systems, Decru, Destineer, Digital Reasoning, Digital Solid State Propulsion, Dust Networks, Electro Energy, Elemental Technologies, Ember Corporation, Etherstack, febit, Fetch Technologies, FireEye, Fluidigm, FMS Advanced Systems Group, Gainspan, GATR Technologies, GeoIQ, Geosemble, Genia Photonics, Iatroquest, Idelix Software, Innocentive, iMove, Infinite Power Solutions, Infinate Z, IntegenX, Intelliseek, InView Technology Corporation, Inxight, KZO Innovations, LensVector, Lingotek, Lucid Imagination, MedShape Solutions, Metacarta, Metricstream, MiserWare, MotionDSP, Nanosys, NetBase, Network Chemistry, Nextreme Thermal Solutions, NovoDynamics, Oculis Labs, OpGen, OpenSpan, Palantir Technologies, Paratek Microwave, Pelican Imaging, Perceptive Pixel, Pixim, piXlogic, Platfora, Power Assure, QD Vision, Quantum4D, Quanterix, Qynergy, Recorded Future, RedSeal Systems, ReversingLabs, Seahawk Biosystems Corporation, Semprius, Seventh Sense Biosystems, Skybuilt Power, Signal Innovations Group, SitScape, Silver Tail Systems, Sonitus Medical, SpectraFluidics, SpotterRF, StreamBase Systems, T2 Biosystems, Tendril, Teradici, TerraGo Technologies, Traction Software, Veracode, Visible Technologies, VSee, WiSpry

Other Locations:
  890 Winter Street
  Suite 310
  Waltham, MA 02451
  Phone: 781-529-1100

  800 El Camino Real
  Suite 300
  Menlo Park, CA 94025
  Phone: 650-234-8999

Key Executives:
  Christopher Darby, President & Chief Executive Officer
  Education: University of Western Ontario
  Background: Vice President & General Manager, Intel; President & CEO, Sarvega; Chairman & CEO, @stake; President & CEO, Interpath Communications
  Steve Bowsher, Managing General Partner
  Education: Harvard University; MBA, Stanford University
  Background: General Partner, InterWest Partners; E*TRADE
  Bruce Adams, Legal & General Counsel
  Education: BA, Swarthmore College; JD, Boston University
  Lisbeth Poulos, Chief of Staff
  Education: BA, International Relations, College of William & Mary
  Background: National Security Agency, Central Intelligence Agency; BAE Systems, MicroStrategy
  Lisa Porter, Executive Vice President & IQT Labs
  Education: BS, Nuclear Engineering, MIT; PhD, Applied Physics, Stanford University
  Background: President, Teledyne Scientific & Imaging; Intelligence Advanced Research Projects Activity, ODNI; Associate Administrator, Aeronautics Research Mission Directorate, NASA; Project Manager/Senior Scientist, DARPA
  Matthew Strottman, Chief Operating Officer
  Education: BA, University of Notre Dame; MBA, Georgetown University; CPA
  Background: Technology Investment Banking Group, Friedman Billings Ramsey & Co.; PricewaterhouseCoopers LLP

Venture Capital & Private Equity Firms / Domestic Firms

980 INCUBE VENTURES
2051 Ringwood Avenue
San Jose, CA 95131

Phone: 408-457-3700
e-mail: contact@incubevc.com
web: www.incubevc.com

Mission Statement: InCube Ventures is a life science venture capital firm focused on investing in innovative life sciences companies that can provide solutions to unfulfilled clinical needs.

Founded: 2008
Investment Criteria: Early Stage, Mid-Stage, Late Stage
Industry Group Preference: Life Sciences, Medical Devices, Pharmaceuticals
Portfolio Companies: BodyMedia, Corhythm, Entrack, Fe3 Medical, IntraPace, Neurolink, Nfocus, Python, Rani Therapeutics, Sonoma Orthopedics, Spinal Modulation, WhiteSwell

Key Executives:
   Mir Imran, Chairman/CEO
   Education: BS, Electrical Engineering, MS, Bioengineering, Rutgers University
   Background: Chairman & CEO, InCube Labs LLC
   Directorships: Bodymedia, Corhthym, eGeen, Entrack, Fe2, Intrapace, Modulus, Neurolink, NFocus, Spinal Modulation
   Andrew Farquharson, Managing Director
   Education: University of California, Berkeley; MBA, Harvard University
   Background: Partner, Halo Funds; EVP, Sales, Marketing & Research, Operon Technologies; Genentech
   Wayne Roe, Managing Director
   Background: Founding Officer, Covance Health Economics & Outcomes Services; VP, Economic & Health Policy, Health Industry Manufacturers Association
   Directorships: ISTA Pharmaceuticals, Celera Genomics, Hemaquest, Fe2, Intrapace, Spinal Modulation

981 INCWELL VENTURE CAPITAL
1000 South Old Woodward Avenue
Suite 105
Birmingham, MI 48009

Mission Statement: IncWell Venture Capital is a venture capital firm seeking opportunities with early stage companies in consumer-based and industrial markets.

Geographic Preference: United States, Canada
Founded: 2013
Average Investment: $50,000 - $250,000
Investment Criteria: Startups, Early Stage
Industry Group Preference: Consumer Products, Healthcare, Industrial Technology, Industrial Manufacturing, Software, Enterprise Software, Information Technology, Clean Technology
Portfolio Companies: BeautyTouch, BoostUp, Bridgefy, Bubl, Calendly, Career Now, Clicktivated Video, CoolChip Technologies, CureLauncher, Eve Medical, Everykey, Illumitex, Jewelbots, Kiwi Wearables, KnipBio, LabDoor, Learnmetrics, LocoMobi, Map My Beauty, Meditory, OwnThePlay, OXX, Pavlok, PharmRight Corporation, Plasc Card, Preo, Sentinl, SkySpecs, Stkr.it, Stylekick, Sutro, Theia Interactive, TrackR, Vivid Vision, XOEye Technologies

Key Executives:
   Tom LaSorda, Founder/Managing Partner
   Background: Founder & General Managing Partner, LaSorda Group; Co-Founder, Stage 2 Innovations; CEO, Fisker Automotive; CEO, Chrysler
   Simon Boag, Chief Executive Officer/Managing Partner
   Education: University of Toronto; MS, Management, Stanford University
   Background: CEO, Stage 2 Innovations; Chrysler; Case New Holland; General Motors; CAMI Automotive
   Evonna Karchon, Partner
   Education: BA, Economics &
   Management/Communication Studies, Albion College
   Background: TechArb; Program Manager, Stage 2 Innovations
   John Melstrom, General Partner
   Education: Michigan State University
   Background: Partner, Fenner Melstrom & Dooling
   Wayne Sales, General Partner
   Education: Harvard Business School
   Background: CEO & President, Canadian Tire Corporation; CEO & President, SUPERVALU Inc.
   Directorships: Tim Hortons, Toys R Us, Albertson's, Canadian Tire

982 INCYTE VENTURES
2911 Turtle Creek Boulevard
Suite 300
Dallas, TX 75219

Phone: 214-599-8700
e-mail: mgineris@incytecapital.com
web: www.incytecapital.com

Mission Statement: Incyte employs a focused, partner-intensive approach intended to result in measurable benefits to the invested capital and management well beyond the initial providing of capital.

Geographic Preference: United States, Canada
Founded: 2000
Average Investment: $20 - $150 million
Minimum Investment: $20 million
Investment Criteria: Early-Stage, Revenues between $25 to $200 million
Industry Group Preference: Telecommunications
Portfolio Companies: American Messaging Services, Paging Network of Canada

Key Executives:
   Marc A. Gineris, Founder & Managing General Partner
   e-mail: mgineris@incytecapital.com
   Education: BA, Pomona College; MBA, Harvard Business School
   Background: M&A; Kidder Peabody & Co.
   Directorships: Aileen, New Dimensions in Medicine, eVIN, Madison Telecommunications

983 INDEPENDENCE EQUITY
2100 Sanders Road
Suite 170
Northbrook, IL 60062

Phone: 847-739-0100 Fax: 224-723-5071
web: www.independence-equity.com

Mission Statement: Independence Equity is an early-stage venture capital firm that invests in companies commercializing technologies that improve resource utilization.

Geographic Preference: United States
Founded: 2010
Average Investment: $500,000 - $1 million
Investment Criteria: Early-Stage
Industry Group Preference: Clean Technology, Material Science
Portfolio Companies: Tagnetics, 10x Technology, Autonomic Materials, Intellihot Green Technologies, NanoStatics, EatStreet, Algal Scientific, Nucurrent, Swapbox, Advanced Diamond Technologies

Key Executives:
   Donald Sackman, Managing Partner
   Education: BS, Mechanical Engineering, Stanford University; MBA, University of Chicago
   Background: Principal, Oryx Capital
   Directorships: Mottahedeh & Co., Advanced Diamond Technology, Digital Acoustics, In-Pipe Technology, Tagnetics
   Michael Gruber, Investment Partner
   Education: BA, International Relations & Economics, University of Pennsylvania; MBA, Kellogg School of

Venture Capital & Private Equity Firms / Domestic Firms

Management
Background: Partner/Co-Founder, G4 Capital; Director, Taproot Ventures
Laurence Hayward, Investment Partner
Education: BS, Psychology, MBA, University of Illinois
Background: Founder, VentureLab; Managing Partner, SCIUS Capital Group
Michael McCullough, Administrative Partner
Education: BBA, Accounting, University of Iowa; MBA, Kellogg School of Management
Background: CFO, Oryx Capital

984 INDEPENDENT BANKERS CAPITAL FUND
1700 Pacific Avenue
Suite 3660
Dallas, TX 75201

Phone: 214-722-6200
e-mail: bconrad@ibcfund.com
web: www.ibcfund.com

Mission Statement: A private equity partnership providing equity capital to established lower-middle-market companies primarily in the Southwestern United States.

Geographic Preference: Southwest
Fund Size: $70 million
Founded: 2000
Average Investment: $2 - $5 million
Minimum Investment: $2 million
Investment Criteria: Recapitalizations, late stage, lower middle market companies and companies with revenues between $10-$50 million
Industry Group Preference: Manufacturing, Distribution
Portfolio Companies: Adao Global, Anthony Machine, Aqueos, Azimuth Technology, Berry Aviation Inc., Burrow Global, Casi, Champion, CPS Houston, DSW Homes, Integrated Advantage Group, Lane Supply Inc., PMA PhotoMetals of Arizona Inc., Raisbeck Engineering, AccuSource Solutions, Alsay Inc., Cohn & Gregory, CareCycle Solutions, Ergo Genesis, GranQuartz, Graco Supply & Integrated Services, Granite & Marble Holdings Inc., Jardine's, Painless, The Finial Company

Key Executives:
  Barry B Conrad, Founder/Managing Member
  e-mail: bconrad@ibcfund.com
  Education: AB, Marshall University
  Background: Founder/Managing Partner, Conrad/Collins Merchant Banking Group; Senior VP/Manager of Corporate Finance, Rauscher Pierce Refsnes; CEO, Hart Delta; Partner, Howard, Weil, Labouisse Friedrichs & Company
  Thomas B. Hoyt, Managing Member
  e-mail: thoyt@ibcfund.com
  Education: BA, Economics, University of Virginia; University of Richmond and Virginia Commonwealth University
  Background: President & Investment Manager, Hibernia; Founder, Audubon Capital Fund; Managing Director, Rodman & Renshaw; Regional VP, Prudential Capital Corporation; The First National Bank of Chicago; Crestar Financial Corporation
  Meg Taylor, Managing Memeber/CFO
  e-mail: mtaylor@ibcfund.com
  Education: BBA, Accounting, Texas Tech University
  Background: Controller, Hicks, Muse, Tate & Furst; Assistant Controller, Nickels & Dimes; Assistant Controller, Sunwestern Investment Group; Ernst & Young
  William H. Miltenberger, Managing Member
  e-mail: bmiltenberger@ibcfund.com
  Education: BBA, Loyola University; MBA, Kellogg School of Management
  Background: Portfolio Manager, Highland Capital Management; Venture Capital Officer, Hibernia Capital Corporation

985 INDUSTRIAL GROWTH PARTNERS
101 Mission Street
Suite 1500
San Francisco, CA 94105

Phone: 415-882-4550 Fax: 415-882-4551
web: www.igpequity.com

Mission Statement: A private investment partnership that provides equity capital to private sector, middle-market manufacturing companies, the firm invests equity in a broad range of transactions involving a change of ownership, such as management buyouts, recapitalization, management buy-ins and corporate divestitures. The firm also provides growth capital to privately held companies in the manufacturing sector which require capital in order to expand their businesses.

Geographic Preference: United States
Fund Size: $2.2 billion
Founded: 1997
Average Investment: $10
Minimum Investment: $5 million
Investment Criteria: MBO, Recapitalizations, Growth Financings, Co-Operative, Divesitures, Private Companies/Family Owned and revenues up to $250 million
Industry Group Preference: Manufacturing
Portfolio Companies: Amercable Inc., API Heat Transfer, Associated Chemist Inc., Atlas Material Testing Solutions, Breeze Industrial Products Corp., Cambridge International Inc., Climax Portable Machine Tools, Consolidayed Precision Products Corp., Controls Southeast Inc., Des-Case Corp., Electronic Packaging Products Inc., FMH Aerospace, Global Power Systems, Grakon, Group360 Inc., Ideal-Tridon, Integrated Global Services, Integrated Polymer Solutions, IOTA Engineering, Jonathan Engineered Solutions, Microporous Products, North American Substation Services, O'Brien Corp., Power Protection Products Inc., Q Holding Company, Royal Die and Stamping Co., Seaboard International Inc., SPL, The Felters Group, The TASI Group, Thermal Sensing Products Inc., Weasler Engineering Inc., West American Rubber Company, Xaloy Inc.

Key Executives:
  Michael H. Beaumont, Co-Founder, Partner
  e-mail: mhb@igpequity.com
  Education: MM, Kellogg School of Management; BS, Chemical Engineering, University of Witwatersrand
  Background: Principal, American Industrial Partners; General Electric Capital Corporation; Bank of Montreal
  Directorships: Power Protection Products, Thermal Sensing Products, Breeze Industrial Products, Felters Company, Group360, Weasler Engineering, West America Rubber, Associated Chemists
  Gottfried P. Tittiger, Co-Founder, Partner
  e-mail: gpt@igpequity.com
  Education: BBA Finance, San Francisco State University
  Background: Principal, American Industrial Partners; General Electric Capital Corporation
  Directorships: Associated Chemists, Sweetheart Holdings, Power Protection Products, Thermal Sensing Products, West America Rubber Company, Breeze Industrial Products Corporation
  R. Patrick Forster, Co-Founder, Partner
  e-mail: rpf@igpequity.com
  Education: BA, Stanford University; MA, University of Manchester; International Business, Northwestern University
  Background: Senior Advisor, American Industrial Partners; Senior Management, Litton Industries
  Directorships: Electronic Packaging Products, Breeze Industrial Products Corporation, Group360, Weasler Engineering, West America Rubber Company
  Eric D. Heglie, Managing Director
  e-mail: edh@igpequity.com
  Education: MBA, Wharton School, University of Pennsylvaniva; BA, University of California, LA
  Background: Jeffries & Company; Morgan Stanley Dean Witter

Venture Capital & Private Equity Firms / Domestic Firms

Directorships: Breeze Industrial Products Corporation, Group360
Jeffrey M. Webb, Director
e-mail: jmw@igpequity.com
Education: BA, Economics, Cornell University; MBA, University of Chicago Graduate School of Business
Background: Ridge Capital Partners; Equity Research, William Blair & Company
Directorships: API Heat Transfer, Microporous Products, O'Brien Holding Co., Total Automated Solutions
Daniel L. Delaney, Director
e-mail: dld@igpequity.com
Education: BS, Business Administration, California Polytechnic State University; MBA, Operations & Accounting, University of Chicago Graduate School of Business
Background: Glencoe Capital; Investment Banking, AG Edwards
Directorships: Seaboard Wellhead
Robert M Austin, Vice President
e-mail: rma@igpequity.com
Education: BS, Commerce, University of Virginia; MBA, JL Kellogg School of Management, Northwestern University
Background: Vice President, Lake Capital; The Riverside Company
Matthew P. Antaya, Vice President
e-mail: mpa@igpequity.com
Education: BBA, Finance, College of William & Mary
Background: Analyst, Citigroup
Matthew L. Brennan, Vice President
e-mail: mlb@igpequity.com
Education: BS, Industrial Engineering, Northwestern University; MBA, University of Chicago
Background: Operating Principal, Key Principal Partners

986 INDUSTRY VENTURES
30 Hotaling Place
3rd Floor
San Francisco, CA 94111
Phone: 415-273-4201 **Fax:** 415-483-7177
e-mail: info@industryventures.com
web: www.industryventures.com

Mission Statement: A leading investment firm that capitalizes on inefficiencies in venture capital and technology growth equity.

Fund Size: $3 billion
Founded: 2000
Investment Criteria: Seed, Early-Stage
Industry Group Preference: Technology, Communications, Applications, Venture Capital, Pharmaceuticals
Portfolio Companies: Access Closer, Alert Logic, Alibaba, Alphablox, Ancestry.com, AngioScore, AppDynamics, Arch Venture Partners, Arista Networks, ArrowPath Venture Partners, AskMe, Astex Pharmaceuticals, Atherotech, Azure Capital Partners, Baker Communications, Battery Ventures, BitCentral, Blueprint Ventures, Blumberg Capital, BOLDstart Ventures, Boulder Ventures, Broadsoft, Cambridge Display, CellzDirect, CenterPoint Ventures, Chegg, ChemConnect, Chrysalix Venture Capital, ClairMail, ClariPhy, Coleman Swenson Booth, Columbia Capital, CoreOptics, Credant Technologies, Crescendo Ventures, Dejima Inc., DFJ Venture Capital, Draper Espirit, Easton Capital, eBags, Ellie Mae, Eloqua Corp., Enanta Pharmaceuticals, Endforce, Entrade, Envivio, Epocrates, Extended Systems, Facebook, Focus Ventures, Fortinet, Fougera Pharmaceuticals, Foundation Capital, Foundry Group, Frontier Ventures, FT Partner, FTV Capital, Fuse Capital, Garage Technology Ventures, Generation Capital Partners, GetWellNetwork, Green Dot, Horizon Ventures, Ingenuity Systems, Innovation Capital, Instill, Intarcia Therapeutics, InterXion, Jajah Jasper Technologies, JK&B Capital, JMI Equity, Kiodex Inc., LifeLock, Lightspeed Venture Partners, Maveron Equity Partners, MedeAnalytics, Metastorm, Mobius Venture Capital, Model N Inc., Narus, New Enterprise Associates, Newlight Management, Novak Biddle, Once24 Inc., Opsware, Pure Digital, Redpoint Ventures, Rembrandt Venture Partners, Sevin Rosen Funds, Softbank Capital, SoftTech VC,

Other Locations:
204 South Union Street
Alexandria, VA 22314
Phone: 415-689-9947 **Fax:** 415-483-7177

96 Kensington High Street
2nd Floor
London W8 4SG
United Kingdom
Phone: 44 020-3890-3322 **Fax:** 415-483-7177

Key Executives:
Hans Swildens, Founder/CEO
e-mail: hans@industryventures.com
Education: BA, University of California, Santa Barbara; MBA, Columbia Business School
Background: Co-Founder & President, Microline Software
Justin Burden, Managing Director
e-mail: justin@industryventures.com
Education: BA, University of California, Berkeley; MS, London School of Economics
Background: GE Equity, Wells Fargo
Robert May, Managing Director/Chief Operating & Compliance Officer
e-mail: robert@industryventures.com
Education: BS, Finance, San Jose State Uiversity
Background: Consultant, Standish Management; COO/CFO, Founders Fund; CFO, Thomas Weisel Venture Partners; Controller, Mohr Davidow Ventures; Senior Financial Analyst, Hewleet-Packard; Product Control Analyst, Drexler Technologies
Directorships: Financial Executives Alliance
Jonathan Roosevelt, Managing Director
e-mail: jr@industryventures.com
Education: BA, Harvard College; MBA, Harvard Business School
Background: VP of Sales, SoFi; Analyst, Battery Ventures
Victor Hwang, Managing Director
e-mail: victor@industryventures.com
Education: BA, Stanford University; MBA, Stanford Graduate School of Business
Background: Managing Partner, Agile Capital Partners; CEP, ICG Asia; Goldman Sachs
Directorships: MyPerfectSale.com
Roland Reynolds, Senior Managing Director
e-mail: roland@industryventures.com
Education: Princeton University; MBA, Harvard Business School
Background: Managing Partner, Little Hawk Capital Management; Principal, Columbia Capital
Directorships: Kearny Venture Partners
Ken Wallace III, Managing Director
e-mail: ken@industryventures.com
Education: BA, Economics, Wake Forest University; MBA, Haas School of Business, University of California, Berkeley
Background: Associate Vice President, Bessemer Trust
Directorships: Rincon Venture Partners, SoftTech VC

987 INETWORKS ADVISORS LLC
820 Evergreen Avenue
Suite 202
Pittsburgh, PA 15209
Phone: 412-904-1014
e-mail: info@inetworkspe.com
web: www.inetworkspe.com

Mission Statement: To provide capital, operational expertise, industry insight, and experienced executives to assist entre-

Venture Capital & Private Equity Firms / Domestic Firms

preneurs in accelerating the development of their technology-based product or service.

Founded: 1999
Investment Criteria: Early Stage, Mid-Stage, Late Stage, Restructuring, Leverage Buyouts
Industry Group Preference: Healthcare, Medical Devices, Pharmaceuticals, Diagnostics, Healthcare Information Technology, Healthcare Services, Clean Technology, Energy, Environment, Information Technology, Software, Communications
Portfolio Companies: Cognition Therapeutics Inc., Novian Health, One Logos Education Solutions, PennAlt Organics Inc., Propel IT, Sparkt, Unequal Technologies LLC, Vizsafe, Wenzel Spine

Key Executives:
   Anthony M Lacenere, Senior Managing Director
   412-927-1793
   Fax: 412-294-0492
   e-mail: tlacenere@inetworkspe.com
   Education: BS, Economics & Finance, University of Dayton; MS, Business Economics, Ohio State University
   Background: President, MDX Fund; VP, Financial Affairs & Managing Director, Investments, AMSCO International; Rockwell International; Westinghouse Electric Corporation; Battelle Memorial Institute
   Anthony L Tomasello, Senior Managing Director
   412-927-1790
   Fax: 412-294-0492
   e-mail: ttomasello@inetworkspe.com
   Education: University of Pittsburgh
   Background: Chairman, Novian Health; EVP & CTO, Stericycle
   Directorships: Community Schools
   Michael T Dieschbourg, Senior Vice President of Investments
   Education: BBA, Loyola University
   Background: Head of Responsibility & Stewardship, Hermes Investment Management; Co-Founder/CEO of Global Currents Investment Management LLC

---

988 INFIELD CAPITAL
1002 Walnut Street
Suite 202
Boulder, CO 80302

Phone: 303-449-2921 Fax: 303-449-2936
e-mail: info@infieldcapital.com
web: www.infieldcapital.com

Mission Statement: The Infield Capital model is centered around a unique orientation the firm creates between the Limited Partners and Portfolio Companies in the fund. Infield chose to raise capital from companies that are strategically interested in the transportation industry and can, in turn, create unique opportunities for those companies in which we invest. These opportunities begin with our investment, which is equal parts financial and intellectual capital.

Founded: 2008
Investment Criteria: Early-stage
Industry Group Preference: Clean Technology, Green Technology, Stored Energy, Mobile Energy Transmission, Nontechnology, Alternative Energy, Transportation
Portfolio Companies: Basic 3C, Mission Motors, Pinnacle Engines, Simbol Materials, Solix BioSystems, VanDyne SuperTurbo, Wildcat Discovery Technologies

Key Executives:
   David Moll, Founder/Managing Director
   Education: Baldwin Wallace College, MBA, Northwestern University
   Background: CEO, Webroot Inc.; MTD Products
   Directorships: Pinnacle Engines
   William Perry, Venture Advisor
   Education: Harvard Business School, MIT
   Background: President, Precision Visuals Inc.; Co-Founder, Softbridge Advisors

---

989 INFLECTION POINT VENTURES
Delaware Technology Park
One Innovation Way
Suite 302
Newark, DE 19711

Phone: 302-452-1120
web: www.inflectpoint.com

Mission Statement: Provides venture capital and business support for early stage telecommunications, information technology, and electronic commerce companies with the potential to generate rapid growth in revenue, profitability, and shareholder value. As of 2010, Inflection Point is managing its current portfolio and is not making new investments.

Geographic Preference: Mid-Atlantic, New England
Average Investment: $2 million
Minimum Investment: $500,000
Investment Criteria: Early Stage
Industry Group Preference: Telecommunications, Information Technology, E-Commerce & Manufacturing
Portfolio Companies: Alternative Fuels Group, CareGain, ComBrio, CurrentAnalysis, Epion, ExoGenesis, Fidelis, Histogenics, Infoether, IntraPoint, LongWatch, LPInnovations, Premise, ReturnCentral, Searchandise Commerce, SkillSurvey, SourceFire, Synchris, Triumfant, TrueLemon

Other Locations:
   Delaware Technology Park
   One Innovation Way
   Suite 302
   Newark, DE 19711
   Phone: 302-452-1120 Fax: 302-452-1122

Key Executives:
   Jeff Davison, General Partner
   e-mail: jdavison@inflectpoint.com
   Education: Masters, MIT; Bachelor's, Hampshire College
   Background: Co-Founder, Tritech Partners; Senior Management, Massachusetts Technology Development Corporation
   Mike O'Malley, General Partner
   e-mail: momally@inflectpoint.com
   Education: JD, Suffolk University; MBA, Babson College; Bachelors, Colby College
   Background: MDT Advisers; Massachusetts Technology Development Corporation
   Diane Messick, Chief Financial Officer
   Education: BS, Accounting, University of Delaware
   Background: Student Finance Corporation, Young Conaway Stargatt & Taylor LLP, Solomon & Solomon PC, MBNA America

---

990 INFLEXION PARTNERS
2156 SW 98th Drive
Gainesville, FL 32608

Phone: 352-339-6669
e-mail: dan@inflexionvc.com
web: www.inflexionvc.com

Mission Statement: An early-venture capital fund organized with an emphasis on company building and harnessing regional, national, and international resources of the fund's managers and strategic partners.

Geographic Preference: Florida
Average Investment: $100,000 - $1 million
Investment Criteria: Seed-Stage, Early-Stage
Industry Group Preference: Communications, Software, Life Sciences
Portfolio Companies: CallMiner, Celsia Technologies, DataBanq, IZEA, Persystent Enterprise, Proximities, RedPath, Visible Assets, WiDeFi

Key Executives:
   Jim Boyle, Managing Partner
   Education: HBSc, Chemistry, Lakehead University; MBA, Finance & Accounting, McMaster University

359

Venture Capital & Private Equity Firms / Domestic Firms

Background: Union Carbide Canada Limited; Nortel; Telinvest Management Corporation
Charles Resnick, Managing Partner
Education: AB, MBA, St. Louis University
Background: Danka Business Systems; Tropicana Products; Mellon Bank; PepsiCo; The Procter & Gamble Company; Mimeo, Inc.
Dan Rua, Managing Partner
Education: BS, Computer Engineering, University of Florida; JD, University of North Carolina School of Law; MBA, Kenan-Flagler Business School
Background: Partner, Draper Atlantic; IBM
Michael Barach, Venture Partner
Education: BA, Amherst College; JD, Harvard Law School; MBA, Harvard Business School
Background: General Partner, Village Ventures; Partner, Bessemer Venture Partners; President/CEO, MotherNature.com
Carolyn Ticknor, Venture Partner
Education: BS, Psychology, University of Redlands; MS, Industrial Psychology, San Francisco State University; MBA, Stanford Graduate School of Business
Background: President, Imaging & Printing Business, Hewlett-Packard
Directorships: AT&T Wireless Services, Boise Cascade Corporation

991 INITIALIZED CAPITAL
San Francisco, CA

e-mail: contact@initialized.com
web: initialized.com

Mission Statement: Venture capital firm focused on software startups at seed stage or earlier.
Fund Size: $160 million
Founded: 2012
Investment Criteria: Seed stage or earlier
Industry Group Preference: Software
Portfolio Companies: reddit, patreon, Flexport, Lever, soylent, Triplebyte

Key Executives:
 Garry Tan, Managing Partner
 Education: Stanford University
 Background: Posterous; Palantir
 Alda Leu Dennis, General Partner
 Education: BS, Stanford University; JD, University of California LA
 Background: Associate, Wilson Sonsini Goodrich and Rosati; Associate/General Counsel, Clarium Capital Management; General Counsel, The Founders Fund; COO, Airtime; Founder, Sproutkin Inc.; Managing Partner, 137 Ventures
 Directorships: The Mom Project; Landed; SkySelect; A-Frame Brands
 Brett Gibson, General Partner
 Education: BA, University of California Santa Barbara
 Background: Software Engineer, Grand Central Communications; Developer, Sonific; Co-Founder, Slkinset; Co-Founder, Posterous; Co-Founder, Posthaven
 Jen Wolf, Partner/Chief Operating Officer
 Education: University of Washington
 Background: Director of User Experience, Sapient; Partner, Millimeter Design; VP of Products, Deem Inc.; CEO/Founder, Plumfile Product Consulting; Chief Product Officer, Reserve

992 INITIO GROUP
195 Page Mill Road
Palo Alto, CA 94306

web: www.initiogroupadvisors.com

Mission Statement: An early-stage investment fund that invests in people first. Initio is a 21st century investment and business consulting firm that specializes in emerging and expanding markets focusing on niched forms of real estate and business investment.
Founded: 2010
Investment Criteria: Early-Stage
Industry Group Preference: Real Estate

Key Executives:
 Maria Neal, Chief Executive Officer
 Rahsaan Dean, President
 Education: BA, University of California Berkeley
 Dan Policy, Director, International Finance

993 INLAND TECHSTART FUND
Phone: 561-322-9660

Mission Statement: The Inland TechStart Fund invests seed capital in early stage companies and entrepreneurs with great ideas. The Fund is focused on providing rewarding returns for investors, while building great companies with the next generation of entrepreneurs, and having fun doing it. The Fund invests in technology based companies only.

Geographic Preference: United States, Northwest
Investment Criteria: Early-Stage
Industry Group Preference: Software, Cloud Computing, Internet, E-Commerce & Manufacturing, Mobile, Entertainment, Media, Social Media, Gaming, Energy, Healthcare, Medical Devices, Telecommunications, Clean Technology

Key Executives:
 Scott Broder, Chief Executive Officer
 Education: BS, Computer Science, University of Miami
 Background: CEO, CanAM Internet; CEO, Opalis Software; Citrix Systems
 Steven King Neff, Co-Founder/Senior Manager
 Education: BA, University of Nebraska
 Background: Principal, Revita Institute Northest; Advisor, Signia Capital; Vice President, Marketing, ICM Asset Management

994 INNOSPRING
3401 El Camino Real
Palo Alto, CA 94306

Phone: 408-550-2818
web: www.innospringus.com

Mission Statement: InnoSpring is Silicon Valley's first US-China technology start-up incubator. Its focus is on encouraging startups to expand beyond their home countries to lead huge market opportunities in the US and China. InnoSpring is a joint project between Tsinghua University Science Park (TusPark), Shui On Group (Shui On), Northern Light Venture Capital and Silicon Valley Bank (SVB).

Geographic Preference: United States, China
Fund Size: $405 million
Founded: 2012
Investment Criteria: Seed-Stage, Startup
Industry Group Preference: Consumer Products & Services, Technology, Software
Portfolio Companies: Agentdesks, Akido Labs, Audacy, Cafe X, Celentail.ai, Dine Market, Drive.ai, HackHands, Haitou, Instamotor, Jaunt VR, Jist.tv, Labdoor, Leapmind, Meadow, Meta, Paperspace, Pluralsight, PlushCare, Savioke, Securly, SLIVER.tv, Teaforia, VideoStitch, WiseBanyan

Key Executives:
 Xiao Wang, General Manager, US
 Lara Kwong, Operations & Accounting
 Education: BBA, Accouting, San Jose State University

995 INNOVA MEMPHIS
20 Dudley St.
Suite 620
Memphis, TN 38103

e-mail: info@innovamemphis.com
web: www.innovamemphis.com

Mission Statement: Innova focuses on creating and funding high-growth biotechnology companies, especially in the earliest stages.

Founded: 2007
Investment Criteria: Pre-Seed, Seed, Early-Stage
Industry Group Preference: Biotechnology, Technology, Agriculture, Healthcare, Diagnostics, Medical Devices
Portfolio Companies: Advanced Catheter Therapies, AgriSync, AgSmarts, Ajax Intel, AlwazPro, arGentis, Arkis Biosciences, ArtSquare, BetterWalk, BioNanovations, Bionova, Blood Monitoring Solutions, Cagenix, CareIT, Cast21, Cattlog, Centiba, Cirquest, ClearMedicare, Community Health TV, Compression Kinetics, Coursicle, Cuff-Gard, Dermaflage, Dev/Con Detect, DivorseSecure, EarthSense, EcoSurg, EMBrace Design, EndoInsight, Entac Medical, ExtraOrtho, Fairway Biomed, Feather, FitNexx, FlexSpark, Frontdesk Connect, GlucosAlarm, Growers Holdings, Handminder, Health & Bliss, HelloHome, Hera Health Solutions, HerdDogg, Homey, Innometrix, Inspire Living, IRT, iScreen, iShipdit, Kilimo, L7 Logistics, LawnTap, LendMed, Life Detection Systems, Life Links, LiLoE, Lineus Medical, MedHaul, Mobilizer, Mozak, Nanophthalmics, NCrease, NuscriptRx, Parental Health, Path Ex, Persistence Data Mining, Please Assist Me, Powermet, Preteckt, Pro Hydration Therapy, Prolific Earth Sciences, ProxBox, Quire, Rabbit Tractors, Rantizo, Reemo, Rescue Forensics, Resolute Games, Restore Medical, RistCall, Roundabout Markets, S2 Interactive, SecondKeys, Secure Food Solutions, ServiceBot Software, Shurpa, SILQ, SixFix, Skycision, Soil Nerd, SOMAVAC, SweetBio, SwineTech, Tensor Surgical, Thaddeus Medical Systems, ThroughPut, Tractor Zoom, TradeLanes, TrakLok, Truck Driver Power, Truckish, Urova, Vaxent, View Medical, Vital Metrix, ZoomThru

Key Executives:
   Ken Woody, Partner
   Education: BS, North Carolina State University
   Background: SVP, Global Sales, Smith & Nephew Orthopedics; VP, Sales, DePuy Spine; GE
   Directorships: Cagenix, S2 Interactive, Tensor Surgical, ACT, BioNova Medical
   Jan Bouten, Partner
   Education: MBA, Duke University
   Background: Aurora Funds
   Directorships: Quire, iScreen Vision, Restore Medical, Silicone Art Labs, Compression Kinetics
   Dean Didato, Partner
   Education: BS, Marietta College
   Background: Strategic Accounts Manager, The Vincit Group
   Directorships: Secure Food Solutions

996 INNOVATION ENDEAVORS
1845 El Camino Real
Palo Alto, CA 94306

e-mail: info@innovationendeavors.com
web: www.innovationendeavors.com

Mission Statement: Innovation Endeavors invests in companies of all sizes in the tech industry.

Founded: 2010
Industry Group Preference: Data, Engineering, Technology
Portfolio Companies: Afresh, AlphaSense, Beamr, Blue River Technology, Bolt Threads, Claroty, Citrine Informatics, Clearmetal, Color, Cropx, Datorama, Dewpointx, Dynamic Yield, Eko, Fabric, FarmerBs Fridge, Form Labs, Freenome, Gatik, GRO Biosciences, Hysolate, Illusive, Karius, Keywee, Planet, Plenty, Rebellion, Replica, SkyTran, Slice, SoFI, Team8, Uber, Ukko, Unbound, Vicarious Surgical, Yotpo, Zymergen

Other Locations:
10 E 53rd Street
14th Floor
New York, NY 10022

121 Menachem Begin Street
57th Floor
Tel Aviv
Israel

Key Executives:
   Eric Schmidt, Founding Partner
   Education: BS, Electrical Engineering, Princeton University; MS/PhD, Computer Science, University of California, Berkeley
   Background: Technical Advisor, Alphabet Inc.; CEO, Google; CEO, Novell; CTO, Sun Microsystems Inc.; Researcher, Xerox Palo Alto Research Center; Bell Laboratories; Zilog
   Scott Brady, Partner
   Education: BS, Finance, University of Florida; MS, Stanford Grad. School of Business
   Background: CEO, Slice; Co-Founder/CEO, FibertTower; CTO, Clarus Corporation; CTO, SQLFinancials; Lecturer in Management, Stanford Grad. School of Business
   Sam Smith-Eppsteiner, Partner
   Education: BA, Political Science, Stanford University; MBA, Stanford Grad. School of Business
   Background: Management Consultant, Bain & Company; Product Manager, Kigali Farms (Rwanda)
   Rick Scanlon, Partner
   Education: BA, Middlebury College
   Background: Morgan Stanley; Credit Suisse
   Harpinder Singh, Partner
   Education: MS, Computer Science, Indiana University; MBA, Stanford Grad. School of Business
   Background: Co-Founder/CEO, Slice Technologies; Co-Founder/Head of Product & Marketing, FiberTower; Software Developer, Oracle; Architect, Bull Honeywell
   Dror Berman, Partner
   Education: BS, Computer Science, Ben-Gurion University; MBA, Stanford Grad. School of Business
   Background: Team Leader of R&D, NICE Systems; Part of Special Forces United of Intelligence Corps of the Israeli Defense Force
   Daniel Goldstein, Partner
   Education: BA, Communications, IDC Herzliya
   Background: Head of Business Development, Red Onion Game
   Bridget Storm, Partner/CFO
   Education: BA, Gonzaga University; MA, Washington State University
   Background: CFO, Makena Capital Management

997 INNOVATION PLATFORM CAPITAL
2450 Holcombe Blvd
Houston, TX 77021

web: innovationplatformcapital.com

Industry Group Preference: Healthcare, Education, Infrastructure, Energy, Finance, Manufacturing & Distribution, Technology

Key Executives:
   Gursh Kundan, CEO
   Education: Simon Fraser Univ.
   Background: Invesco
   Ionel V. Nechiti, President
   Background: Platform Management LLC

998 INNOVATION WORKS
Nova Tower 2
Two Allegheny Center
Suite 100
Pittsburgh, PA 15212

Phone: 412-681-1520
web: www.innovationworks.org

Venture Capital & Private Equity Firms / Domestic Firms

Mission Statement: Innovation Works invests in Southwestern Pennsylvania's technology economy.
Geographic Preference: Southwestern Pennsylvania
Founded: 1999
Average Investment: $340,000
Investment Criteria: Seed
Industry Group Preference: Technology, Life Sciences, Medical Devices, Biotechnology, Information Technology, Software, Internet Infrastructure, Advanced Materials, Consumer Electronics, Energy, Enterprise Software, Mobile, Network Infrastructure, Robotics
Portfolio Companies: AardvarQ, Accipiter Systems, Aethon, Agentase, Alertek, AllFacilities Energy Group, ALung Technologies, American Roadprinting, Appalachian Lighting Systems, ATRP Solutions, BIOSAFE, BitArmor Systems, Blue Belt Technologies, Bossa Nova Concepts, BPL Global, Bridge Semiconductor, Bueda, Caliber Infosolutions, Carmell Therapeutics, Carnegie Speech Company, CastGrabber, Celluman, Cepstral, Ciespace Corporation, Circadiance, Civic Science, ClearCount Medical Solutions, Cognition Therapeutics, Cohera Medical, Compliance Assurance Corporation, Concurrent Electronic Design Automation, Crono, Crystaplex Corporation, Deeplocal, Diamyd, Epiphany Solar Water Systems, Etcetera Edutainment, FASTTAC, Fluorous Technologies, Health Monitoring Systems, High Performance Building Systems, HyperActive Technologies, Immunetrics, ImpactGames, Industry Weapon, INTEG Process Group, Intimate Bridge 2 Conception, InvestEdge, KeyBay Pharmaceutical, Knopp Neurosciences, Landslide Technologies, LeftRight Studios, Lightfoot, Medallion Anayltics, medSage Technologies, Memory Medallion, Metis Secure Solutions, Mobile Aspects, MobileFusion, ModCloth, mSpoke, My Payment Network, nanoLambda, NeuroInterventions, NuRelm, Penthera Partners, PeriOptimum, PetsDx Imaging, Pittsburgh Iron Oxides, Plextronics, Powercast Corporation, RedPack Logistics, RedPath Integrated Pathology, RedZone Roboticss, ReGear Life Sciences, SEEGRID Corporation, ShowClix, Slim Ops Studios, SMASH, Songwhale, STARR Life Sciences

Key Executives:
Rich Lunak, President & CEO
Education: Carnegie Mellon University; University of Pittsburgh
Background: McKesson

999 INNOVENTURES CAPITAL PARTNERS
150 South State
Suite 100
Salt Lake City, UT 84111

Phone: 801-243-6674
e-mail: steve@innoventures.com
web: www.innoventurescapitalpartners.com

Mission Statement: A licensed Small Business Investment Company (SBIC) in Salt Lake City, Utah. Innoventures invests in small companies by providing subordinated debt to start-up and growing businesses.
Geographic Preference: Utah, Neighboring States
Fund Size: $9.6 million
Founded: 1983
Average Investment: $50,000 - $250,000
Minimum Investment: $50,000
Investment Criteria: Mezzanine, Start up, Early stage
Industry Group Preference: Information Technology, Manufacturing
Portfolio Companies: BetterBody Foods, Five Star Franchising, Property Solutions

Key Executives:
Steve Grizzell, Managing Director
e-mail: sgrizzell@utfc.biz
Education: MBA, University of Utah; University of Massachusetts; BS, Anthropology, Michigan State

Background: Consultant, World Bank and U.S. Agency for International Development
Robert Lund, General Counsel
Education: JD, Brigham Young University Law School
Background: Utah Technology Finance Corp.
Scott Stenberg, CFO
e-mail: sstenberg@utfc.biz
Education: Master of Professional Accountancy, Weber State University
Background: Internal Auditor, University of Utah

1000 INSIGHT VENTURE PARTNERS
1114 Avenue of the Americas
36th Floor
New York, NY 10036

Phone: 212-230-9200
e-mail: growth@insightpartners.com
web: www.insightpartners.com

Mission Statement: A private equity and venture capital firm that invests in companies in the software-based segments of the information technology industry.
Geographic Preference: United States
Fund Size: $6.3 billion
Founded: 1995
Average Investment: $15 million
Minimum Investment: $5 million
Investment Criteria: Expansion
Industry Group Preference: Infrastructure, Software Services, Applications Software & Services, Consumer Internet, E-Commerce & Manufacturing, Education, Energy, Financial Services, Gaming, Government, Graphics, Healthcare, Marketing, Media, Telecommunications
Portfolio Companies: 1stdibs, 5Nine, 6Waves, Aaptiv, Academic Partnerships, Achieve 3000, Alteryx, AMCS, Anaqua, Appriss, Automattic, Automile, Azuqua, BlaBlaCar, Blinkist, Branding Brand, BrightBytes, BrightEdge, Bullhorn, Bynder, Calm, Campaign Monitor, Caremerge, Cartrawler, CentralReach, CeresImaging, Chargbee, Checkmark, Cherwell, Chrono24, CloudBolt Software, CommunityBrands, Conga, Copado, CoreView, Cylance, DarkTrace, DataCore, Delivery Hero, Despegar.com, Detectify, Devo, Diligent, Divvy, Docker, DocuSign, DrillingInfo, Duco, E2open, Elo7, Ensighten, Episerver, EquipmentShare.co.nz, Everyaction, EzCater, Famous, Fanatics, Fenergo, Film Track, Firemon, Flipboard, Flipp, FloQast, Force, Fourth, Freshly, Gainsight, GoSpotCheck, GraphPad Software, Harver, Hello Fresh, Hinge Health, HomeToGo, Hootsuite, Hotel Urbano, Hustle, Illuminate Education, Ilumno, Indiegogo, Intent Media, Interfolio, Invaluable, iSpot.tv, Jama Software, JFrog, JoyTunes, Kaseya, Kira, Kony, LeanIX, LeanTaaS, Lease Accelerator, Lightricks, LiveAction, Marketing Evolution, Mediaspectrum, Menu Next Door, Mimecast, Ministry Brands, Mirantis, Monday.com, N26, nCino, Nearpod, Nextdoor, NNG, Numetric, Nymbus, OneCommand, OpenEnglish, Optibus, OwnBackup, Parachute Health, Parallels, PicsArt, Pipedrive, Planview, PluralSight, PrecisionLender, Prevalent, Project44, PropertyBrands, Prose, QASymphony, Qualtrics, Quantum Metric, ReceiptBank, Recorded Future, Resolve Systems, Ritual, SalesLoft, Showpad, Sift Science, SimpleNexus,

Key Executives:
Jeff Horing, Managing Director/Co-Founder
Education: BS, MIT; MBA, Wharton School, University of Pennsylvania
Background: Warburg Pincus; Goldman Sachs
Richard Wells, Managing Director
Education: BS, Economics, Wharton School, University of Pennsylvania; MBA, Harvard Business School
Background: Veritas Software; Pacioclan Systems; Associate, Technology Crossover Ventures; Consultant, Mercer Management Consulting
Peter Sobiloff, Managing Director
Background: Datalogix; Ross Systems; Think Systems

Venture Capital & Private Equity Firms / Domestic Firms

Directorships: Achieve3000, DrillingInfo, Duco, Fenergo, Filmtrack, Kony Sultions, NYMBUS, Planview, Mediaspectrum, Workforce Software
Deven Parekh, Managing Director
Education: BS, Wharton School, University of Pennsylvania
Background: Principal, Berenson Minella & Company; The Blackstone Group
Directorships: Bullhorn, DrillingInfo, Turnitin, Ministry Brands, Apriss, Campaign Monitor, Fanatics, Diligent, 1stdibs, Vela, Chrono24, LetGo, Wallapop
Michael Triplett, Managing Director
Education: BA, Economics, Dartmouth College
Background: Investment Professional, Summit Partners; Financial Analyst, Morgan Stanley & Co.; Midland Data Systems
Directorships: N2W, 5nine Software, Acronis, GFI Software, IKANO/Virtacore, Kaseya, Parrallels, SmartBear, ThreatTrack, Unitrends, Veeam
Jeff Lieberman, Managing Director
Education: Systems Engineering & Finance, Pennsylvania's Moore School of Engineering; Wharton School, University of Pennsylvania
Background: Management Consultant, McKinsey & Company
Ryan Hinkle, Managing Director
Education: BS, Engineering, School of Engineering & Applied Science, University of Pennsylvania; BS, Wharton School
Background: Morgan Stanley; PPL Corporation

1001 INSTITUTIONAL VENTURE PARTNERS
3000 Sand Hill Road
Building 2
Suite 250
Menlo Park, CA 94025

Phone: 650-854-0132
e-mail: gbauman@ivp.com
web: www.ivp.com

Mission Statement: One of the premier later-stage venture capital and growth equity firms in the United States. The partnership is focused on later-stage companies, investing in rapidly growing technology and digital media companies.
Geographic Preference: United States, West Coast
Fund Size: $7 billion
Founded: 1980
Average Investment: $25 million
Minimum Investment: $10 million
Investment Criteria: Later-Stage, Expansion, Public
Industry Group Preference: Software, Data Communications, Components & IoT, Technology, Digital Media & Marketing, Internet, Enterprise Software, Information Technology, Mobile, Communications
Portfolio Companies: AddThis, Adroll, Aerohive Networks, Alien Vault, Amplitude, Anomali, App Annie, AppDynamics, Arcsight, Aster Data Systems, Ayasdi, Buddy Media, Business Insider, Business.com, Care.com, Casper, Checkr, Coinbase, Compass, Comscore Networks, Concur Technologies, Cyence, Danger, Datalogix, Dataminr, Domo, DoubleVerify, Dropbox, Dropcam, Fleetmatics, Gaia Interative, General Assembly, Giphy, Github, Glossier, Grammarly, Ground Truth, H5, Hipmunk, HomeAway, Indiegogo, Inspirato, Juniper Networks, Kayak, Klarna, Klout, Legal Zoom, Lifelock, LiveOps, LSI, Marketo, Markmonitor, Masterclass, Mindbody, Mobile 365, Mobileiron, Mulesoft, MYSQL, NerdWallet, Netflix, NGMOCO, Moniture, Ondeck Capital, One Kings Lane, Oportun, Personal Capital, Pindrop, Polycom, Popsugar, Prosper, Pure Storage, Qadium, Qubole, Quigo Technologies, Retail Me Not, Rubrik, Sauce Labs, Seagate Technologies, Shazam, Skytream Networks, Slack, Snapchat, SOFI, Soundcloud, Spiceworks, Steelbrick, Sumo Logic, Supercell, Synchronoss, Tala, Tanium, The Honest Company, The Player's Tribune, Thrive Global, Tivo, Transferwise, Tripwire, Tuniein, Twitter, Twyla, Uproxx, Vessel, Voxer, Walker & Company, Whip Networks, Wikia, Yext, Yodlee, Zefr, Zendesk, Zenefits, Zerto, Zipprecruiter, Zynga
Other Locations:
747 Front Street
Suite 100
San Francisco, CA 94111
Phone: 415-432-4660
Key Executives:
Todd C. Chaffee, Advisory Partner
e-mail: tchaffee@ivp.com
Education: BS, University of Minnesota Carlson Business School; Venture Capital Program, Harvard Business School; Advanced Management College, Stanford Graduate Business School
Background: President, Visa International's Venture Capital Group; Norwest; American Express; TRW Information Systems Group; Grand Expeditions
Norman A. Fogelsong, Advisory Partner
e-mail: nfogelsong@ivp.com
Education: BS, Management Science & Engineering, Stanford University; MBA, Harvard Business School; JD, Harvard Law School
Background: Mayfield Fund; McKinsey & Company; Hewlett-Packard Company; Actively Involved in IVP; Integrated Circuit Works; Platinum Software; Polycom/TelCom
Directorships: Aspect Communications, Concur Technology
Steve Harrick, General Partner
e-mail: sharrick@ivp.com
Education: BA, History, Yale University; MBA, Harvard Business School
Background: Internet Capital Group; Highland Capital Partners; Netscape; Morgan Stanley
Directorships: Teros and several other portfolio companies.
Sandy Miller, General Partner
e-mail: smiller@ivp.com
Education: BA, University of Virginia; MBA & JD, Stanford University
Background: Senior Partner, 3i; Co-Founder, Thomas Weisel Partners; Senior Partner, Montgomery Securities; Managing Director, Merrill Lynch; Donaldson Lufkin & Jenrette; Manager, Bain & Company; Securities Lawyer, Pillsbury Winthrop
Dennis Phelps, General Partner
e-mail: dphelps@ivp.com
Education: BA, Government & Economics, Dartmouth College
Background: Battery Ventures; Internet Capital Group; Hambrecht & Quist
Jules Maltz, General Partner
e-mail: jmaltz@ivp.com
Education: BA, Economics, Yale University; MBA, Stanford University
Background: 3i, Admob

1002 INTEGRA VENTURES
300 E Pine Street
2nd Floor
Seattle, WA 98112

Phone: 206-832-1990 **Fax:** 206-832-1991

Mission Statement: To develop a portfolio of outstanding regional and national biomedical companies chosen within the framework of our partner's extensive biomedical, service and device expertise.
Geographic Preference: West Coast United States
Fund Size: $38 million
Founded: 1998
Average Investment: $2 million
Minimum Investment: $500,000

Venture Capital & Private Equity Firms / Domestic Firms

Investment Criteria: Early Stage, Late Stage and Growth Stage
Industry Group Preference: Life Sciences, Healthcare Services, Drug Development, Medical Devices
Portfolio Companies: Acorda Therapeutics, Amnis, Ampla Pharmaceuticals, Blue Heron, Calypso Medical Technologies, Cara Vita, Cardax, ClearMedical, Corus Pharma, Guava Technologies, Hawaii Biotech, HealthHelp, MediQuest, Napo Pharmaceuticals, National Healing, Novasite Pharmaceuticals, PLx Pharmaceutical, Raven Biotechnologies, Targeted Growth, Tepha, WellPartner

Key Executives:
Joseph Piper JD, Founder/Managing Director
206-229-5001
Fax: 206-329-5105
e-mail: piper@integraventures.net
Education: BA, Arizona State; JD, Seattle University; MBA, University of Colorado
Background: President, Capital Services
Directorships: National Healing, HealthHelp, Physicians Edge, Vara Vita
Hans Lundin, Chief Financial Officer
206-229-3814
Fax: 206-329-5105
e-mail: lundin@integraventures.net
Education: BS, US Coast Guard Academy; MBA, University of Colorado
Background: Chairman, Clear Medical
Directorships: Blue Heron Biotechnologies, ClearMedical
Timothy Thompson Black, Partner/Chief Operating Officer
206-229-3814
Fax: 206-329-5105
e-mail: black@integraventures.net
Education: JD, Seattle University; BA, Colorado College
Background: SunWest International
James Nelson MD, Partner
Education: Harvard University, Harvard Medical School
Background: Professor of Radiology, UW

1003 INTEGRAL CAPITAL PARTNERS
2750 Sand Hill Road
Menlo Park, CA 94025

e-mail: john@icp.com
web: www.icp.com

Mission Statement: Integral Capital Partners operates a family of partnerships that invests in expansion-stage private and growth-stage public companies in the information and life sciences industries.
Founded: 1991
Investment Criteria: Expansion-Stage, Growth-Stage
Industry Group Preference: Information Technology, Life Sciences
Portfolio Companies: Iolon Inc., Zaffire, Visible Path, Vertical Networks, Tropos Networks, TherOx, Stoke, Silicon Energy, Qpass, Peppers & Rogers, Opsware, OpenTable, Octane Software, NewPort Communications, NetClerk, MyPlay, MetaMatrix, Matrix Semiconductor, Lytx Inc., LogMeln, Lockdown Networks, Lantern Communications, Ketera, Jasper, Ingenio, Informative, Health Hero Network, Grockit, Event Zero, Drugstore.com, Concept Shopping, Celarix, CareDx, Calix, Blue Nile, Asera, ArcSight, Aragon Surgical, AlphaBlox

Key Executives:
Pamela Hagenah, Opertations Partner
Education: BS, University of California, Los Angeles; JD, University of California, Los Ageles
Background: Attorney, Brobeck Phleger & Harrison
John Powell, Co-Founder & Managing Director
Education: BA, University of North Carolina, Chapel Hill; MBA, Darden Graduate School of Business Administration, University of Virginia
Background: T. Rowe Price

Brian Stansky, Managing Director
Education: BS, Accounting, Boston College; MS, Finance & Applied Economics; Sloan School of Management, MIT
Background: Director, Johns Hopkins Technology Ventures

1004 INTEL CAPITAL
2200 Mission College Boulevard
Santa Clara, CA 95054-1549

Phone: 408-765-8080
web: www.intelcapital.com

Mission Statement: Venture capital arm of Intel invests in mergers, acquisitions and tech startups.
Geographic Preference: Worldwide
Fund Size: $1.28 billion
Founded: 1991
Average Investment: $50-100 million
Investment Criteria: All Stages
Industry Group Preference: Enterprise, Mobility, Consumer Internet, Digital Media & Marketing, Semiconductors, Big Data, Cloud Infrastructure, Aritificial Intelligence, Autonomous Vehicles, IoT, Security, Software, Sports, Entertainment, Health
Portfolio Companies: 99Cloud, Adaptive Mobile, Ad Hawk Microsystems, Aerial, AEye, Airy3D, Alauda.cn, Alcide, Aledia, Almalence, Trace, AlterGeo, Altia Systems, Amenity Analytics, AnD APT Inc., Appionics Holdings, APPScomm, Arcadia Data, ASML, Avaamo, Avegant, Ayar Labs, Awcloud, Beijing UniSoc Technology Ltd., Betaworks, Big Switch Networks, Bigstream, Bluebank, BlueStacks, Borqs, Bossanova, Braigo Labs, Bright Edge, Brit + Co, Bromium, Cafe Communications, CareCloud, Certisign, Cgtrader, Chargifi, Chipsbank, Cloud Genix, Cloudian, Cloudify, Cognitive Scale, CTACCEL, CubeWorks, CYVision, Data Robot, Delair, Denovo, DSC, Dot Product, Dysonics, Eazytec, Echo Pixel, Eclypsium, Element, eLoupes, Embodied, Empathy, Enovix, Eruditor Group, Espressif, Eye Smart Technology, Alcon Computing, Fibocom Wireless, Fictiv, Fileforce, Fino, Flowplay, Forte Media, Fort Scale, Fortumo, Funders Club, Gamalon, Gengo, GenXcomm, Giga Spaces, Goldbely, Good Way Technologies, Good Data, Grameen Intel Social Business, Grand Chip Microelectronics, Griti, Habana, Happist Minds, Help Shift, Here, Horizon Robotics, Huaqin, Huiying Medical Technology, Hungama.com, HY Trust, Ice Tech, Identec Group, Imanis Data Inc., Immersed, InContext Solutions, Indiamart.com, Inpria, Inrix, Interlude, Intezer, Iotas, Jasper Infotech Pvt Ltd., Joby Aviation, KH Connect, KDS China, Kaltura, KM Labs, Kazan Networks, Keyssa, Kinduct, KiraKira3D, KupiVip.ru, Leapmind, Learnmetrics, LegUp, Lintes, Lisnr, Lumiata, Lyncean, Maana, Mango Telecom,

Key Executives:
Anthony Lin, Vice President/Senior Managing Director
Education: BA, Economics, University of California Berkeley
Background: Banc of America Securities; ASAT; Merrill Lynch; PaineWebber
Directorships: Intel Capital Investment Committee
Dave Flanagan, Vice President/Senior Managing Director
Education: BA, Economics, University of Colorado; MBA, Georgetown University
Background: Van Kasper & Company; Transamerica
Sean Doyle, Managing Director
Education: BA, University of California Berkeley; MBA, UCLA
Background: Laidlaw Equities; Oracle Corporation
Andy Fligel, Senior Managing Director
Education: MBA, Kellogg Graduate School of Management; BS, Commerce, University of Virginia
Background: Robinson-Humphrey
Directorships: ScienceLogic; Maana; Guavus
Dave Johnson, Managing Director
Education: MBA, Cornell University; BA, Vanderbilt

364

Venture Capital & Private Equity Firms / Domestic Firms

University
Background: Procter and Gamble; Chevron Corporation
Mark Rostick, Vice President/Senior Managing Director
Education: JD/MBA, University of South Carolina
Tammi Smorynski, Managing Director
Education: MBA, The Anderson School, UCLA; BA, Accounting/International Management, Georgetown University
Background: J.P. Morgan & Co.
Directorships: Embodied
Tamiko Hutchinson, Vice President/Senior Managing Director
Education: BA, International Relations, University of California; MBA, Finance, Anderson School of Management, UCLA
Background: Solomon Smith Barney
Mark Lydon, Managing Director
Education: BS, Electrical Engineering, California Polytechnic State University
Background: Dialogic Corporation; Engineer, IBM

1005 INTELLECTUAL VENTURES
3150 139th Avenue SE
Building 4
Bellevue, WA 98005

Phone: 425-467-2300
e-mail: info@intven.com
web: www.intellectualventures.com

Mission Statement: Pioneer in the invention capital market with one of the world's largest intellectual property portfolios.

Geographic Preference: Global
Fund Size: $6 billion
Founded: 2000
Industry Group Preference: Invention
Portfolio Companies: Echodyne Corp., Evolv Technologies, Kymeta, TerraPower

Other Locations:
7 Harcourt Street
Dublin 2
Ireland
Phone: 353 0 1 472 0100 **Fax:** 353 1 475 85 82

Intellectual Ventures Lab
14360 SE Eastgate way
Bellevue, WA 98007
Phone: 425-691-3353

19620 Stevens Creek Boulevard
Suite 270
Cupertino, CA 95014
Phone: 650-397-3100

Key Executives:
Nathan Myhrvold, Founder & Chief Executive Officer
Education: UCLA; Princeton University; Cambridge University
Background: Microsoft
Edward Jung, Founder
Background: Deep Thought Group; Microsoft
Peter Detkin, Founder
Education: University of Pennsylvania
Background: Wilson Sonsini
Directorships: Brady Campaign and Center to Prevent Gun Violence

1006 INTERLACE VENTURES
New York, NY 10003

e-mail: hello@interlacevc.com
web: interlaceventures.com

Mission Statement: Interlace Ventures is focused on technology serving the Commerce sector.

Founded: 2019
Average Investment: $200,000 - $600,000
Minimum Investment: $200,000

Industry Group Preference: Consumer, Commerce, Retail, Technology, Artificial Intelligence
Portfolio Companies: Algopix, B8ta, BlueFox.io, Cargo, For Days, French Founders, Goodeed, Hyphen, Oliver, OTO Systems Inc., Presence AI, SelfMade, Senders, Skip

Key Executives:
Vincent Diallo, Managing Partner
Background: Co-Founder, Bleu Capital; CFO, Sinodis; Auditor, Deloitte
Joseph Sartre, Managing Partner
Background: Partner, Bleu Capital; Finance Manager, Evian Asia Pacific; Finance Manager, MinuteBuzz

1007 INTERNATIONAL FINANCE CORPORATION (IFC)
2121 Pennsylvania Avenue NW
NW Washington, DC 20433

Phone: 202-473-1000
e-mail: mannanbrown@ifc.org
web: www.ifc.org

Mission Statement: Promotes sustainable private sector investment in developing countries as a way to reduce poverty and improve people's lives.

Geographic Preference: Worldwide
Fund Size: $2.45 Billion
Founded: 1956
Average Investment: $50.5 Million
Minimum Investment: $1 Million
Industry Group Preference: Agribusiness, Financial Services, Healthcare, Information Technology, Infrastructure, Oil & Gas, Mining, Chemicals, Education, Communications
Portfolio Companies: Arcor Group, Armenia Tomato, Asia Opportunity Fund LP, Baku Coca-Cola Bottlers II, Ciment Blanc d'Algerie, Fushe Kruje Cement, Haripur Power Project, Kabul Serena Hotel, Olam-Africa, LaFarge Surma Cement, Nova Cimangola

Key Executives:
Philippe Le Houérou, Chief Executive Officer
Education: MBA, Columbia University; PhD, Economics, Institut d'Études Politiques de Paris
Background: World Bank; European Bank for Reconstruction and Development;
Stephanie Von Friedeburg, Chief Operating Officer
Education: Undergraduate Degree from the School of Foreign Services, Georgetown University; MA, Lauder Institute, University of Pennsylvania; MBA, Wharton School
Background: World Bank

1008 INTERSOUTH PARTNERS
4711 Hope Valley Road
Suite 4F-632
Durham, NC 27707

Phone: 919-493-6640 **Fax:** 919-493-6649
e-mail: marketing@intersouth.com
web: www.intersouth.com

Mission Statement: One of the most active and experienced early-stage venture funds in the Southeast, having invested in more than 75 private companies over the last twenty years.

Geographic Preference: Southeast United States
Fund Size: $780 million
Founded: 1985
Average Investment: $500,000 to $6 million
Minimum Investment: $500,000
Investment Criteria: Early-Stage to Startup
Industry Group Preference: Life Sciences, Information Technology, Communications, Internet, Digital Media & Marketing, Semiconductors, Software, Biotechnology, Medical Technology, Pharmaceuticals
Portfolio Companies: 480 Biomedical, 6fusion, ABT Molecular Imaging, Accipiter, Accordant Health Systems, Adaptify, Advanced Animal Diagnostics, Advanced

365

Venture Capital & Private Equity Firms / Domestic Firms

Biomarker Technologies, AGTC, Aldagen, Alimera Sciences, Applied Genetic Technologies, Argos Therapeutics, Arsenal Medical, Athenix, Azalea, Biolex Therapeutics, ArtiCure, Bright Hub, Burl Software, Calibra Medical, CallMiner, Cellective Therapeutics, Cempra Pharmaceuticals, Clarabridge, Comstock Systems Corporation, Covelight Systems, CSA Medical, Digital Optics, Encelle, Esanex, Extensibility, HexaTech, Infoglide Software, Innocrin, Insmed Inc., Inspire Pharmaceuticals, Integrated Silicon Systems, InvoiceLink, KAI Pharmaceuticals, Lambda Technologies, LOC-AID, Location Smart, Marathon Group, MaxCyte, Microchips Biotech, nContact, Neolinear, New River Innovation, Nitronex, NovaMin Technology, nTouch Research, OpenSite Technologies, Overture Networks, Paradigm Genetics, PeopleMatter, PharmaNetics, Proteon Therpeutics, Row Sham Bow, SciQuest, Semprius, Sentillion, Serenex, SimplifyMD, SmartPath, Snagajob, Sphinx Pharmaceuticals, SunPharm Corporation, TapRoot Systems, Trancept Systems, TransEnterix, Trinity Convergence, UOL Publishing, Vascular Pharmaceuticals, Viamet Pharmaceuticals, Zenoss, Zenph Sound Innovations, Ziptronix

Key Executives:
Dennis Dougherty, Founding Partner
e-mail: dennis@intersouth.com
Education: BA, Oklahoma City University; Postgraduate, Accounting & Finance, Duke University
Background: Office Managing Partner, Accounting Firm
John Glushik, Partner
e-mail: john@intersouth.com
Education: BS, Mechanical Engineering & Materials Science, Duke University; MS, Aeronautics & Astronautics, MIT; MBA, Kellogg School of Management, Northwestern University
Background: Booz-Allen & Hamilton; General Electric
Richard Kent MD, Partner
e-mail: rick@intersouth.com
Education: University of California, Berkeley; MD, University of California, San Diego
Background: President & CEO, Serenex; CEO, Ardent Pharmaceuticals; Senior Vice President, Global Medical Affairs & Chief Medical Officer, GlaxoSmithKline; GlaxoWellcome; Burroughs Wellcome
Mitch Mumma, Member Manager
e-mail: mm@intersouth.com
Education: AB, Management Science, Duke University
Background: Manager, Touche Ross & Co.

1009 INTERVALE CAPITAL
One Mifflin Place
Suite 400
Office 402
Cambridge, MA 02138

e-mail: info@intervalecapital.com
web: www.intervalecapital.com

Mission Statement: Intervale Capital is a private equity firm that invests in companies in the oilfield service and manfuacturing sectors. Intervale works closely with management teams to help drive the growth of companies.

Geographic Preference: North America, Europe
Fund Size: $1.3 billion
Founded: 2006
Minimum Investment: $5 million
Investment Criteria: Middle-Market, Buyouts, Growth Equity
Industry Group Preference: Oil & Gas, Manufacturing
Portfolio Companies: Aegis Chemical Solutions, Certus Energy Solutions, EnerCorp, Entegra, FlexEnergy, Innovex Downhole Solutions, Milestone Environmental Services, Pro Oilfield Services, Sentry Energy, Soane Energy, Taurex Drill Bits, Tier 1 Energy Solutions, Transform Materials

Other Locations:
1221 McKinney Street
Suite 4100
Houston, TX 77010
Phone: 281-605-3900

Key Executives:
Charles Cherington, Chairman
e-mail: charles@intervalecapital.com
Education: BA, History, Wesleyan University; MBA, University of Chicago
Background: Vice President, Vietnam Fund; Credit Suisse
Patrick Connelly, Partner
e-mail: pconnelly@intervalecapital.com
Education: BS, United States Military Academy; MBA, Harvard Business School; MPA, Harvard Kennedy School
Background: Managing Director, SCF Partners; Forum Energy Technologies
Jason Turowsky, Partner
e-mail: jt@intervalecapital.com
Education: BA, Economics, University of Pennsylvania
Background: Falconhead Capital; UBS Investment Bank
Tuan Tran, Partner
e-mail: tuan@intervalecapital.com
Education: BA, Government, Harvard College, Harvard University
Background: Lehman Brothers
Stephen Cherington, Director
e-mail: stephen@intervalecapital.com
Education: BA, Economics, Wheaton College; MBA, Kent Business School, University of Kent
Background: Section Manager, MFS Investment Management

1010 INTERWEST PARTNERS
2710 Sand Hill Road
Suite 200
Menlo Park, CA 94025

Phone: 650-854-8585 Fax: 650-854-4706
e-mail: info@interwest.com
web: www.interwest.com

Mission Statement: InterWest provides valuable industry, strategic, and corporate development expertise, as well as venture capital, to help young life sciences and IT companies succeed.

Geographic Preference: United States
Fund Size: $650 million
Founded: 1979
Average Investment: $10-15 million
Minimum Investment: $10 million
Investment Criteria: Early-Stage
Industry Group Preference: Information Technology, Healthcare
Portfolio Companies: AGTC, Alt12Apps, Alvine Pharmaceuticals, AMEC, AppMesh, Arcion Therapeutics, Aria, Aryaka, Autonomic Technologies, Badgeville, Biba, Brite Semiconductor, C3 Energy, C9, Carbylan Biosurgery, Cardiac Dimensions, Cebix, Convery Computer, Damballa, Doximity, Drais, Eiger, Empowered, Exalt, Fluidigm, Flurry, GainFitness, Get Satisfaction, Glaukos, Gobiquity Mobile Health, Gojee, Gynesonics, Hangtime, HireArt, iDoneThis, Indi, Invidi, InVisage, Invuity, Joyus, Knotch, Labrys Biologics, Locbox, Lycera, MacroGenics, Marketo, Microfabrica, Mobee, Neuronetics, NeuroPace, NewsCred, NexPlanner, Nuventix, Obalon, Ocera, OnDemand Therapeutics, Optimizely, Pelican Imaging, Pivot, PMW Pharma, PrimeraDx, Quantance, QuatRx, RadioRx, Restoration Robotics, Revision Optics, Sera Prognotics, Splice Machine, Spredfast, Swell, TapJoy, Tesaro, TheRealReal, Transcept, Triposo, USDS, Vendavo, Vidora, Welltok, Xenon, Xirrus

Key Executives:
Flip Gianos, Managing Director, Information Technology
e-mail: flip@interwest.com

Education: BS, Stanford University; MBA, Harvard University
Background: Engineering Manager, IBM
Directorships: Xilinx, T/R Systems
Gil Kliman, Managing Director, Healthcare
e-mail: gkliman@interwest.com
Education: BA, Harvard University; MD, University of Pennsylvania; MBA, Stanford University
Background: LCA Vision; Aris Vision Laser; Norwest VC
Arnie Oronsky, Managing Director, Healthcare
e-mail: aoronsky@interwest.com
Education: BS, New York's University College; PhD, Columbia University's College of Physicians and Surgeons
Background: VP, Drug Discovery, Lederle Lab Division
Directorships: Corixa Corporation, BioTransplant
Khaled Nasr, Partner & COO
Education: BA & MA, Mathematics, Social & Political Sciences, Cambridge University
Background: Alta Partners; President, FlowWise Networks; General Manager, Ipsilon; COO, Advanced Computer Communications
Directorships: Exalt Communications, Gear6, InVisage Technologies, NexPlanar, Xirrus
Stephen Holmes, General Partner Emeritus
Education: BS, Business Administration, Lehigh University; MBA, Harvard Graduate School of Business Administration
Background: Vice President, Finance & Administration, Specialty Brands
Directorships: National Venture Capital Association; International Private Equity & Venture Capital Valuation Guidelines Board
Keval Desai, Partner, Information Technology
Education: BE, Electrical Engineering, University of Mumbai; MS, Computer Science, UC Santa Barbara; MBA, Haas School of Business, UC Berkeley
Background: Director, Product Management, Google; Vice President, Digg
Doug Fisher, Partner, Healthcare
Education: Stanford University; University of Pennsylvania School of Medicine; Wharton School
Background: The Boston Consulting Group; New Leaf Venture Partners
Directorships: Gynesonics; Indi Molecular; Obalon Therapeutics; QuatRx
Drew Harman, Director
Education: Harvard University; INSEAD
Background: TradingDynamics; Ariba
Karen Wilson, Chief Financial Officer
Education: University of California, Berkeley
Background: Frank, Rimerman & Co.

1011 INVENCOR
San Francisco, CA

Phone: 415-531-5003 Fax: 707-257-2196
e-mail: information@invencor.com
web: www.invencor.com

Mission Statement: A seed and early stage equity provider with an investment focus on high growth rate business opportunities in its prime target markets. An active co-investor and leverages investment opportunities in the ever present gap between the angel investors and larger venture funds.

Geographic Preference: Silicon Valley, Southeast
Founded: 1997
Investment Criteria: Seed, Early Stage, Mezzanine
Portfolio Companies: 4Charity.com, AdOn Network, Arcanvs, AssistGuide, Bioreason, Cardax Pharmaceuticals, Hawaii Biotech, HotU, Kona Bay Marine Resources, Lumidigm, MyGeek.com, NAPO Pharmaceuticals, Perimeter Labs, Sandpiper Software

Key Executives:
Debra Guerin Beresini, President
e-mail: debra@invencor.com
Education: Dominican College; Global Biotechnology Program, University of California, Berkeley
Background: AR&D Corp; Ford/US Leasing; Hambrecht & Quist; Technology Funding; Senior VP/Manager National Division, Silicon Valley Bank
Kirk Westbrook, President/Chief Financial Officer
e-mail: kirk@invencor.com
Education: San Jose State University
Background: VP, Silicon Valley Bank
Directorships: Hawaii Venture Capital Association; HiBEAM
Richard Harding, Managing Partner
e-mail: richard@invencor.com
Education: BA, University of Montana; Graduate International Management, American Graduate School; MBA, Golden Gate University
Background: Managing Committee, Silicon Valley Bank; First Interstate Bank; American Express International Banking Corporation
Directorships: Founder, Santa Fe Venture Partners; Concise Logic Systems, Lumidigm, Access Anytime Bancorporation/First Bank of New Mexico

1012 INVENT
1930 Ocean Avenue
Suite 305
Santa Monica, CA 90405

web: www.invent.vc

Mission Statement: Invent VC is the only public company in the US that is focused exclusively on building tech startups. The Invent structure provides stakeholders with access to early-stage venture capital through their curated and actively managed portfolio of technology businesses.

Geographic Preference: United States
Average Investment: up to $250,000
Investment Criteria: Early-Stage, Pre-Seed
Industry Group Preference: Technology
Portfolio Companies: Revenue.Com, Sanguine Biosciences

Key Executives:
Demetrios Mallios, Chief Executive Officer
Alan D. Lewis II, Chief Operating Officer

1013 INVENTUS
400 S El Camino Real
Suite 700
San Mateo, CA 94402

Phone: 650-292-2530 Fax: 650-292-2570
e-mail: jk@inventuscap.com
web: www.inventuscap.com

Mission Statement: We seek to support entrepreneurs, first and foremost. Particularly those building disruptive digital services businesses, often integrating consumer or business software into a technology-enabled service. While products have dominated past waves of technology innovation, the industry is in the midst of a transformation from product to service-led businesses. Our team has a highly relevant entrepreneurial and operating background combined with two decades of success partnering with Silicon Valley and Indian entrepreneurs accessing India's natural advantages in adding value to digital services businesses.

Geographic Preference: United States, India
Founded: 1993
Average Investment: $1 - $10 million
Industry Group Preference: Digital Media & Marketing, SaaS, Consumer Internet, Media, Mobile, Technology-Enabled Services, E-Commerce & Manufacturing, Advertising, Software, Financial Services, Communications, Healthcare, Education, Mobile Apps
Portfolio Companies: Aasaan Jobs, Activity Hero, Assured Risk Cover, Avaz, Cbazaar, Credit Sesame, Dhingana, Disco, eDreams Edusoft, Espresso Logic, Farfaria, Funds India, Genwi, Healthify Me, Insta Health Solutions, IntelliVision,

Venture Capital & Private Equity Firms / Domestic Firms

Knolskape, Motivo, MoveInSync, Next, Peel-Works, Policy Bazaar, Poshmark, Power2sme, Redbus.in, Resilinc, Savaari Car Rentals, Sensy, Sierra Atlantic, Spotzot Mobile Shopping, Sokrati, StatX, Sys Cloud, Tricog, Truebil, Unbxd, Vivu, Vizury

Other Locations:
Inventus Advisory Service
1st Floor, G.R. Primus
69-1, 1st Cross, Domlur (near Post Office)
Bangalore 560 071
India
Phone: 91-80-4125-6747

Key Executives:
Kanwal Rekhi, Managing Director
Education: BSEE, IIT-Bombay; MSEE, Business & Engineering, Michigan Tech
Background: Co-Founder, Excelan; CEO, Ensim; CEO, Cybermedia
Directorships: Assured Risk Cover, Espresso Logic, GenWi, Funds India, Intellivision, Poshmark, Sierra Atlantic, Statx
Manu Rekhi, Managing Director
Education: BS, Boston University; MBA, Columbia Business School & Haas School of Business
Background: VP, Products, NewsCorp Digital Division; Lolapps; Google
Directorships: Credit Sesame, Dhingana, FarFaria, Genwi, Growbot, Spotzot, Vivu, NextForce
John Dougery, Managing Director
Education: BA, University of California, Berkeley; MBA, Haas School of Business
Background: Sun Microsystems, IBM, Mircosoft, Intel
Directorships: Activity Hero, Credit Sesame, Dhingana, Motiva, Reslinc, Sokrati, Spotzot, Syscloud, Vivu
Samir Kumar, Managing Director, India
Education: BSEE, Indian Institute of Technology; MBA, Indian Institute of Management
Background: Wipro, Acer Technology Ventures
Directorships: Cbazaar, Instahleath Solutions, MoveInSync, Savaari, Sokrati, Knolskape
Parag Dhol, Managing Director, India
Education: BSME, Indian Insitute of Technology; MBA, Indian Institute of Management
Background: Associate Director, Intel Capital
Directorships: Avaz. Funds India, Peel Works, Policy Bazaar, Power2sme, redBus, Tricog, Vizury
Rutvik Doshi, Managing Director, India
Education: BTech, Indian Institute of Technology; MBA, INSEAD
Background: Google; CEO, Taggle
Directorships: Aasaanjobs, Avaz, eDreams Education, HealthifyMe, Sensara, Syscloud, Truebil, Unbxd

1014 INVERNESS GRAHAM INVESTMENTS
3811 West Chester Pike
Building 2, Suite 100
Newtown Square, PA 19073

Phone: 610-722-0300 Fax: 610-251-2880
e-mail: myoung@invernessgraham.com
web: www.invernessgraham.com

Mission Statement: Inverness acquires high growth, innovative manufacturing and service companies through partnership with management and well executed building strategies.

Fund Size: $250 million
Founded: 1997
Investment Criteria: Buyouts, Recapitalizations, Divestitures
Industry Group Preference: Manufacturing, Business Products & Services
Portfolio Companies: Advanced Cath, B+B SmartWorx, Danville, DemandPoint, Energy Solutions International, Extrumed, Faxitron, Global ID Group, ICC Nexergy, Infiltrator Systems Inc., MarginPoint, Mesker, Nobles Worldwide, RacoWireless, SkyBitz, DataSource, GPS Trackit, Kalkomey, SmartFlow Technologies, Spirion, Swipeclock Workforce Management

Key Executives:
Kenneth A. Graham, Founder/Chairman
Education: BA, Dartmouth College; MBA, Amos Tuck School of Business
Background: Senior Vice President, Graham Packaging; Co-Founder, Media Stream
Directorships: Energy Solutions, ExtruMed, Faxitron, Infiltrator, ICCNexergy, SmartFlow, SkyBitz
Scott A. Kehoe, Founder/Managing Principal
Education: BA, Dartmouth College; MBA, Kellogg Graduate School of Management, Northwestern University
Background: President & CEO, MediaStream; Advisor, Graham Group Legacy Businesses; Senior Manager, Ernst & Young
Directorships: B&B Electronics, ExtruMed, Faxitron, Bioptics, TechDevice
Michael B. Morrissey, Managing Principal
Education: BA, University of Pennsylvania; MBA, Wharton School
Background: Vice President, Business Development, Audax Group
Directorships: B&B Electronics, Energy Solutions, FaxitronBioptics, Nobles, SmartFlow, TechDevice
Steven F. Wood, Founder/Vice Chairman
Education: BS, Connecticut State University; CFA
Background: Chairman & CEO, Graham Engineering Corporation; Senior Group Vice President & CFO, Graham Companies and Graham Packaging; Senior Manager, Ernst & Young
Directorships: B&B Electronics, DemandPoint, Energy Solutions, ExtruMed, Nexiant, ICCNexergy, TechDevice
Trey Sykes, Managing Principal
Education: BS, University of California, Berkeley; MBA, Wharton School, University of Pennsylvania
Background: GE Equity, Lehman Brothers Venture Partners, Houlihan Lokey Howard & Zukin
Directorships: ElectriTek AVT, Nexergy

1015 INVESCO PRIVATE CAPITAL
Two Peachtree Pointe
1555 Peachtree Street NE
Suite 1800
Atlanta, GA 30309

web: www.invesco.com

Mission Statement: A private equity firm backing industry leading venture, buyout and other private equity firms and investing directly in private venture capital companies.

Geographic Preference: United States, Worldwide
Fund Size: $3 billion
Founded: 1982
Average Investment: $20 million
Minimum Investment: $10 million
Investment Criteria: Early and Expansion Stage
Industry Group Preference: Information Technology, Life Sciences, E-Commerce & Manufacturing, Communications, Infrastructure

Other Locations:
1166 6th Avenue
New York, NY 10036
Phone: 212-278-9000

Key Executives:
Kelvin Liu, Partner/Senior Portfolio Manager
Education: BEng, MS, Management, National University of Singapore; MBA, Finance, Wharton School
Background: Director, North American Operations, TIF Ventures
Evan Jaysane-Darr, Partner
Education: BA, History, Washington & Lee University; MBA, INSEAD

Venture Capital & Private Equity Firms / Domestic Firms

Background: Vice President, Alternative Investments, Atlantic Trust Private Wealth Management

1016 INVESTAMERICA VENTURE GROUP
101 2nd Street SE
Suite 800
Cedar Rapids, IA 52401
Phone: 319-363-8249 **Fax:** 319-363-9683
web: www.investamericaventure.com

Mission Statement: InvestAmerica is a private equity and venture capital management group investing in management buyouts, ownership changes and later-stage growth opportunities. Formerly known as InvestAmerica Investment Advisors.
Geographic Preference: United States
Fund Size: $44 million
Founded: 1985
Average Investment: $1 - $2 million
Minimum Investment: $1 million
Investment Criteria: Management buy-outs, Particular interest in later-stage companies; sales revenues between $10-$50 million
Industry Group Preference: High Technology, Manufacturing, Distribution, Service Industries
Other Locations:
 10000 NE 7th Avenue
 Suite 330H
 Vancouver, WA 98685
 Phone: 360-573-5067 **Fax:** 360-573-7462

 51 Broadway
 Suite 500
 Fargo, ND 58102
 Phone: 701-298-0003 **Fax:** 701-293-7819

 911 Main Street
 Commerce Tower
 Suite 2424
 Kansas City, MO 64105
 Phone: 816-842-0114 **Fax:** 816-471-7339

 801 Nicollet Mall
 Suite 1700W
 P.O. Box 2289
 Minneapolis, MN 55402
 Phone: 651-632-2140

Key Executives:
 David R. Schroder, President
 319-363-8249
 Fax: 319-363-9683
 e-mail: david@investam.com
 Education: BSFS, Georgetown University; MBA, University of Wisconsin
 Background: President, Director, MorAmerica Capital Corporation; VP, Kentucky Highlands Investment Corporation
 Robert A. Comey, Executive Vice President
 319-363-8249
 Fax: 319-363-9683
 e-mail: rcomey@investam.com
 Education: BA, Economics, Brown University; MBA, Fordham University
 Background: Executive VP/Director, MorAmerica Capital Corporation; VP, RIHT Capital Corporation; President, Tower Ventures
 Kevin F. Mullane, Senior Vice President
 816-842-0114
 Fax: 816-471-7339
 e-mail: kmullane@investam.com
 Education: BSBA, MBA, Rockhurst College
 Background: Senior VP, MorAmerica Capital Corporation
 Michael H. Reynoldson, Vice President
 360-573-5067
 Fax: 360-573-7462
 e-mail: jcosgriffe@fedc.com
 Education: MBA, Finance, University of Iowa; BSBA, Washington State University
 Background: Price Waterhouse; Co-Founder, Iowa-Based Fund Company
 John G. Cosgriff, Manager
 701-298-0003
 Education: BS, Business Economics; MS, Economics, North Dakota State University
 Background: US Small Business Administration, Minnesota State Univesity, Moorhead

1017 INVESTCORP
280 Park Avenue
New York, NY 10017
Phone: 212-599-4700 **Fax:** 212-983-7073
e-mail: info@investcorp.com
web: www.investcorp.com

Mission Statement: To select and arrange private equity investments in mid to large size companies with capable managers, prominent positions in their industries, a strong track record and potential growth.
Geographic Preference: North America, Western Europe
Fund Size: $2.1 billion
Founded: 1982
Investment Criteria: Company value of $100 million-$1 billion, mid-size, a good established track record, can operate in almost any industry sector
Industry Group Preference: Diversified
Portfolio Companies: Impero, Ageras, Calligo, AlixPartners, Arrowhead, Agromillora, Corneliani, The Wrench Group, SecureLink, NDT CCS, Nobel Learning Communities, Dainese, Arvento, PRO Unlimited, SPGPrints Group B.V., Totes ISOTONER, Namet, AYTB, Paper Source, Leejam, Theeb, Hydrasun, Georg Jensen, Automak Automotive Company, Orka Group, Esmalglass, Archway Marketing Services, Wazee Digital, Sur La Table, Eviivo, Tiryaki Agro, OpSec, Gulf Cryo, L'Azurde, CEME, Kgb, Magnum Semiconductor, TelePacific, Optiv, Fleetmatics, Kentrox, IPH Group, Tyrrells, Armacell, Mania Technologies, Stratus Technologies, CCC, FleetPride, InnerWireless, Mobileway, GL Education Group, Skrill, Moody International, Avecia, Associated Materials, Aero Products, Aurora Systems, Wells-CTI, Veritext, Sophos, American Tire, CSIdentity, Spectel, N&W, Redington Gulf, Platform Solutions, TDX, Asiakastieto, Welcome Break, Randall-Reilly, Softek, Berlin Packaging, Trema, Icopal, Harborside Healthcare, APCOA, Helly Hensen, Hilding Anders, Aspective, Dialogic, Minimax, Stahl, Saks Inc., Autodistribution, ObjectStar, PortalPlayer, US Unwired, Polyconcept, Utimaco, Gerresheimer, ECI, SourceMedia, CSK Auto, Taqua, MW Manufacturers, ZettaCom, Zeta Interactive, Atrenta, Willtek, Neptune, Jostens, 4th Pass, Acta, Carter's, Leica, Main Street Dairy, Chaumet, Falcon, Ebel, SI Corp., Breguet, Star Market, Simmons, Prime Equipment, Dellwood, Circle K, Gucci, Thorn Lighting, Ny Department Stores, Sports & Recreation, Catherines, Fox Photo,
Other Locations:
 48 Grosvenor Street
 London W1K 3HW
 United Kingdom
 Phone: 44 (0)20 7629 6600 **Fax:** 44 (0)20 7499 0371

 Investcopr House
 P.O. Box 5340
 Manama
 Bahrain
 Phone: 973-17-532-000 **Fax:** 973-17-530-816

 Qatar Financial Centre - Tower 1
 Suite 701
 West Bay Area - P.O. Box 24995
 Doha
 Qatar
 Phone: 974-4496-0381 **Fax:** 974-4435-2750

 Al Faisaliah Tower
 29th Floor

Venture Capital & Private Equity Firms / Domestic Firms

P.O. Box 61992
Riyadh 11575
Saudi Arabia
Phone: 966-11-484-7600 **Fax:** 966-11-273-0771

Level 24-01, CapitaGreen
138 Market Street
Singapore 048946
Phone: 65-69115300

Key Executives:
Mohammed Alardhi, Executive Chairman
Education: BS, Military Science, Royal Air Force UK Staff College; MA, Public Pilicy, John F. Kennedy School of Government, Harvard University
Hazem Ben-Gacem, Co-Chief Executive Officer
Education: BA, Harvard University
Background: Credit Suisse First Boston; Chairman, Corneliani; Chairman, Georg Jensen; Vice-Chair, Dainese
Rishi Kapoor, Co-Chief Executive Officer
Education: BS, Electrial/Computer Engineering, Indian Institute of Technology; MBA, Duke University
Background: CFO, Citigroup
Firas El Amine, Head of Corporate Communications
Education: BA, Communication Arts, Beirut University College; MA, Political Science, Lebanese American University
Background: Corporate Communications Director, Dubai Holdings; Public Relations Director, Alsalam Holding; Public Relations Director, Impact & Echo

1018 INVUS GROUP
750 Lexington Avenue
30th Floor
New York, NY 10022
Phone: 212-371-1717 **Fax:** 212-371-1829
e-mail: nyoffice@invus.com
web: www.invus.com

Mission Statement: Invus looks for transformational opportunities where we can partner with owner-managers to create extraordinary business performance and enjoy the resulting financial rewards. Given this high bar and our small team, we are very selective about the companies with which we get involved. We only make a handful of sizable investments each year.

Geographic Preference: United States, Europe
Investment Criteria: Turnarounds, Growth Capital, Expansion-Stage
Industry Group Preference: Consumer Products, Consumer Services, Food & Beverage, Specialty Retail, Software, Biotechnology, Medical Devices
Portfolio Companies: Avantec Vascular, Blue Buffalo, Bluemercury, The Grow Network, Harry's, Keebler, OdontoPrev, Provalliance-Franck Provost, Weight Watchers

Other Locations:
275 Grove Street
Suite 2-400
Newton, MA 02466
Phone: 617-663-4917

2nd Floor Lansdowne House
57 Berkeley Square
London W1J 6ER
United Kingdom
Phone: 44-20-7493-9133 **Fax:** 44-20-7518-9629

21, Avenue Kléber
Paris 75116
France
Phone: 33-1-56-90-50-00 **Fax:** 33-1-56-90-50-10

22/F, St. George's Building
2 Ice House St.
Central
Hong Kong
Phone: 852-3758-2536 **Fax:** 852-3105-0358

Key Executives:
Raymond Debbane, President/CEO
Education: BS, Agricultural Sciences & Agricultural Engineering, American University of Beirut; MBA, Stanford Graduate School of Business
Background: CEO, Artal Group; Manager, Boston Consulting Group
Christopher Sobecki, Managing Director
Education: BS, Engineering, Purdue University; MBA, Harvard Business School
Background: Engineer, Eastman Kodak Company
Philippe Amouyal, Managing Director
Education: MS, Engineering, DEA, Management, Ecole Centrale de Paris
Background: Vice President & Director, Boston Consulting Group; Research Fellow, Center for Policy Alternatives, MIT
Jonas Fajgenbaum, Managing Director
Education: BS, Wharton School; BA, Economics, University of Pennsylvania
Background: Management Consultant, McKinsey & Company
Aflalo Guimaraes, Managing Director
Education: BA, Economics & Political Science, Yale University; MBA, Wharton School
Background: Manager, Marakon Associates; Federal Reserve
Evren Bilimer, Managing Director
Education: BS, Electrical Engineering & Economics, Yale University
Background: Management Consultant, McKinsey & Company
Benjamin Felt, Managing Director
Education: BA, Economics, Yale University
Background: Management Consultant, The Boston Consulting Group

1019 IRISH ANGELS
Chicago, IL

web: www.irishangels.com

Mission Statement: Founded in September 2012, the new IrishAngels investing group is dedicated to furthering startup growth through early stage investments in which a founder, Board member, or investor is a student, graduate, parent, or faculty member at the University of Notre Dame.

Founded: 2012
Average Investment: under $3 million
Investment Criteria: Notre Dame Affiliation; Seed-Stage, Series A
Industry Group Preference: Internet, Mobile, Healthcare, Social Enterprises, Software, Enterprise Software, Cloud Computing, Manufacturing, Retailing, Business Products & Services
Portfolio Companies: AgenDx, Appcast, Ash & Erie, Baby Scripts, Blue Triangle, Caretaker Medical, CargoSense, Catalyst Orthosience, Chime, Coolfire Solutions, Elevate K-12, Emu Technology, Hatfield & McCoy Whiskey, Kidizen, Genomenon, Groupsense.io, Margin Edge, Micro-LAM, The Mom Project, myCOI, Nurture Life, PageVault, Pattern89, The Renewal Workshop, Rivet Smart Audio, Rivs Digital Interviews, Shot Tracker, Superstar Games, Techstars, Trading View, UpCity, Vagabond, Vapogenix, Vennli, Wolf & Shepherd, Zipfit Denim

Key Executives:
Gale Bowman, Managing Director
Education: BBA, University of Notre Dame; MBA, University of Chicago Booth School of Business
Background: Nielsen; Orbitz.com
Kaitlyn Doyle, Director
Education: BBA, University of Notre Dame; MBA, University of Chicago Booth School of Business

Caroline Yeager, Analyst
Education: BBA, Boston College; MSM, University of Notre Dame

1020 IRON GATE CAPITAL
842 W South Boulder Road
Suite 200
Louisville, CO 80027

Phone: 303-395-1335
e-mail: info@irongatecapital.com
web: www.irongatecapital.com

Mission Statement: Iron Gate Capital is a private equity firm seeking to invest in growth stage companies and assist those businesses in realizing their growth plans.

Founded: 2005
Average Investment: $1 - $5 million
Investment Criteria: Growth Stage
Industry Group Preference: Business to Business, Services, Energy, Healthcare, Real Estate, Retail, Consumer & Leisure
Portfolio Companies: AcuStream, Branded Online, CPX Lone Tree Hotel, Encino Energy, HZO, Kapost, MBH Enterprises, Meritage Energy, Northeastern Ohio Energy Hotel Fund, Smashburger, Syncardia Systems, Techstars

Key Executives:
Doug Fahoury, Founder/Managing Partner
Education: BS, Business Administration, Colorado State University; MBA, California State University, Sacramento
Background: CIO & Principal, Inventure Partners; VP, iBelay; VP, Tango Partners; VP, Consumer Products & Business Development, Exactis.com; Founder & Managing Director, McNatt, Douglas & Co.
Ryan Pollock, Managing Partner
Education: University of Cape Town; Univ. of Oxford; MBA, University of Texas, Austin
Background: Managing Director, Meritage Funds; Investec Asset Management
Directorships: Rocky Mountain Venture Capital Association
Steve McConahey, Co-Founder/Partner
Education: University of Wisconsin; MBA, Harvard Business School
Background: Chairman, SGM Capital; President & COO, EVEREN Securities, EVEREN Capital; President, Kemper Securities
Directorships: Cal Dak International, Great-West Funds, IMA Financial Group, Guaranty BanCorp
Rob Cohen, Co-Founder/Partner
Education: University of Texas, Austin
Background: CEO, IMA Financial Group; Chubb and Son
Directorships: USR, ccintellect

1021 IRONWOOD CAPITAL
45 Nod Road
Suite 2
Avon, CT 06001-3819

Phone: 860-409-2100
web: www.ironwoodcap.com

Mission Statement: Ironwood Capital is a private equity firm based in Connecticut. The firm targets middle market companies and provides growth capital in addition to operational and strategic support.

Fund Size: $300 million
Average Investment: $5 - $20 million
Investment Criteria: Leveraged Buyouts, Growth Financings, Recapitalizations
Industry Group Preference: Business Products & Services, Consumer Products, Education, Environment Products & Services, Healthcare, Manufacturing, Distribution, Aerospace, Defense and Government
Portfolio Companies: Acelero Learning, Action Carting, Advanced Recycling Systems, Capewell Holdings, City Carting Holding, Curtis Bay Energy, Dancing Deer Baking, Diamond Packaging, DocuLynx, Femco Machine, Fiber-Line, FitLinxx, Flow-Dry, Gold Medal Services, Healthtrax, Hobbs Bonded Fibers, Imperial Machining, iPacesetters, Joliet Equipment, Katahdin Industries, The Learning Experience, MedVantx, Morgan Contracting, My Alarm Center, NEBC, New England Linen, Numet Machining, Pharmaceutic Litho & Label Company, Professional Rental Tools, Red River Waste Solutions, RM Techtronics, Roberts Company, Rostra Tool Company, St. George Warehouse, Tidewater Equipment Company, Tulip Molded Plastics

Key Executives:
Marc Reich, Chairman/Chief Executive Officer
860-409-2101
e-mail: reich@ironwoodcap.com
Education: University of California, Los Angeles; MBA, University of Connecticut
Background: Chairman, Greater Bristol Realty Corporation; Investment Banking, Aetna
Carolyn Galiette, President/Chief Investment Officer
860-409-2105
e-mail: galiette@ironwoodcap.com
Education: BA, English, Dartmouth College
Background: Investment Professional, Aetna; Investment Banking, PaineWebber
Roger Roche, Senior Managing Director
860-409-2129
e-mail: roche@ironwoodcap.com
Education: BS, Accounting & Finance, Babson College
Background: SVP & Managing Director, BankBoston; SwingBridge Capital
Directorships: Action Carting, FEMCO Machine, Tulip Corporation, Katahdin Industries, New England Linen Supply, High Hopes Therapeutic Riding
Victor Budnick, Senior Managing Director
860-409-2108
e-mail: budnick@ironwoodcap.com
Education: Yale University; Harvard Law School; Yale School of Management
Background: President & Executive Director, Connecticut Innovations
Jim Barra, Managing Director
860-409-2113
e-mail: barra@ironwoodcap.com
Education: Bryant University; MBA, University of Connecticut
Background: President, Northeast Regional Association of Small Business Investor Alliance
Directorships: Medport, Advanced Concrete, Genesis Solutions, Columbus House
Dickson Suit, Managing Director
860-409-2128
e-mail: suit@ironwoodcap.com
Education: Brown University; MBA, Columbia Business School
Background: Investment Manager, Environmental Opportunities Fund; Pitney Bowes; PricewaterhouseCoopers
Directorships: Action Carting Environmental Services, VLS Recovery Services
Alex Levental, Managing Director
860-409-2109
e-mail: levental@ironwoodcap.com
Education: BA, Economics & Russian Literature, Colby College
Background: VP, Market Development & Strategic Planning, CCA Global Partners; Analyst, Morgan Stanley; Associate, Advent International
Directorships: Merrill Industries

Venture Capital & Private Equity Firms / Domestic Firms

1022 IRVING PLACE CAPITAL
745 Fifth Avenue
New York, NY 10151

Phone: 212-551-4500
e-mail: info@irvingplacecapital.com
web: www.irvingplacecapital.com

Mission Statement: A private equity firm focused on making equity investments in middle-market companies. The firm partners with talented managers, providing them with the resources they need to sustain growth, build world-class companies and unlock value.

Geographic Preference: North America
Fund Size: $2.7 billion
Founded: 1997
Average Investment: $50 - $250 million
Investment Criteria: Growth Capital, Corporate Divestitures, Byouts, Recapitalizations, Build-Ups, Public-To-Private Transactions
Industry Group Preference: Retail, Consumer & Leisure, Consumer Products, Consumer Services, Industrial Products, Packaging
Portfolio Companies: Alpha Packaging, Bendon, Coker Tire, Dynojet, Mold-Rite Plastics, New York & Company, Rag & Bone

Key Executives:
John Howard, Co-Managing Partner
Education: BA, Trinity College; MBA, Yale School of Management
Background: Co-CEO, Vestar Capital Partners; SVP & Partner, Wesray Capital Corporation
Directorships: Bendon, New York & Co., Rag & Bone, Aeropostale, Dots, Integrated Circuit Systems, Multi Packaging Solutions, Nice-Pak Holdings
Phil Carpenter III, Co-Managing Partner
Education: BS, State University of New York, Binghamton
Background: Brockway Moran & Partners; Bear Stearns & Co.
Directorships: Alpha Packaging Holdings, Dynojet Research, Mold-Rite Plastics, Multi Packaging Solutions, Ohio Transmission Corp., Reddy Ice, Chesapeake
Blake Austin, Principal/Strategic Services
Education: BS, Indiana University
Directorships: Alaris Consulting
Kevin Culp, Senior Advisor
Education: BS, Indiana University; MBA, University of Chicago Graduate School of Business; CPA
Background: CFO, Rotorcraft Leasing Company; Partner, Crowe Horwath; Arthur Andersen; KPMG
David Knoch, Partner/Head of Strategic Services
Education: BBA, MBA, Loyola University of Chicago
Background: Senior Managing Director, Chief Administrative Officer, Alaris Consulting
Bob Bode, Principal/Strategic Services
Education: BBA, University of Iowa; MS, Stuart School of Business, Illinois Institute of Technology
Background: Principal, The Keystone Group; Consultant, Alaris Consulting; Consultant, Crowe Chizek
Paul Lehman, Senior Advisor
Education: BA, Vassar College; MBA, Harvard Business School
Background: COBB Tuning; Edge Products; Bear Stearns Merchant Banking
Michael Hyatt, Senior Advisor
Education: BA, Syracuse University; JD, Emory University School of Law
Background: Senior Managing Director, Bear Stearns & Co.
Joe El Chami, Principal
Education: BS, State University of New York, Binghamton; MBA, Wharton School, University of Pennsylvania
Background: Analyst, Merrill Lynch

Tom Robertshaw, Senior Advisor
Education: BS, University of Virginia; MS, University of West Florida
Background: Motion Industries
Devraj Roy, Partner
Education: BA, Yale University; MBA, Columbia Business School
Background: Associate, Parthenon Capital
Directorships: Caribbean Financial Group Holdings, Pet Supplies Plus Holdings, Ohio Transmission Corp.
Keith Zadourian, Partner
Education: AB, Dartmouth College; MBA, Columbia Business School
Background: Associate, Veritas Capital Management
Directorships: Alpha Packaging Holdings, Chesapeake Holdings, Mold-Rite Plastics, Mold-Rite Plastics, Chromalox

1023 J. BURKE CAPITAL PARTNERS
655 Madison Avenue
25th Floor
New York, NY 10065

web: www.jburkecapital.com

Mission Statement: A private equity firm investing in a wide range of small to mid-size companies.

Average Investment: $3 - $30 million
Investment Criteria: Corporate or Large Spin Offs, Leveraged Recapitalizations, Generational Sales, Industry Consolidations, Under-Performing Companies, Special Situations
Industry Group Preference: Education, Financial Services, Business Products & Services, Consumer Services, Manufacturing, Retail, Consumer & Leisure, Environment Products & Services, Healthcare, Food & Beverage
Portfolio Companies: Apique, Command Health, Leading Edge Innovations, VariBlend Dual Dispensing Systems, Verity Wine Partners

Key Executives:
James J. Burke Jr., Founder
Education: BA, Brown University; MBA, Harvard Business School
Background: Senior Partner & Co-Founder, Stonington Partnerse
Directorships: Ann Taylor Stores Corporation, Lincoln Education Services Corporation
Eric Lauerwald, Partner
Education: BS, Mechanical Engineering, Union College; MBA, Columbia Business School
Background: Principal, Arena Capital Partners; Associate Principal, Churchill Equity & Industrial Equity Partners
Christopher Delaney, Portfolio Manager
Education: BA, Economics, Williams College; MBA, Darden School of Business, University of Virginia
Background: Fixed Income & Commodity Trader, Lehman Brothers

1024 JACKSON SQUARE VENTURES
727 Sansome St.
Suite 300
San Francisco, CA 94111

Phone: 415-229-7100
e-mail: info@jsv.com
web: www.jsv.com

Mission Statement: Jackson Square Ventures is a small venture capital firm leading seed And Series A deaks in SaaS and marketplace companies.

Investment Criteria: Seed, Series A
Industry Group Preference: SaaS, Marketplaces, Consumer, Security, Storage, Enterprise
Portfolio Companies: Alien Vault, Alto Pharmacy, Atrium, Bus.com, Centrify, Contently, Cornershop, Crexi, Crownpeak, Demandbase, DigitalFuel, DocuSign, Doxo,

Venture Capital & Private Equity Firms / Domestic Firms

Empyr, EqualLogic, Fortify, Hightail, Intacct, Jackbox Games, Jellyvision, Kace, Kindly Care, Lanetix, Marketlive, Mynd, OfferUp, Omniata, Plume, Rented, Responsys, ScanCafe, Seismic, Sparkcentral, Strava, Talking Blocks, Tapio, ToutApp, Upwork, Vormetric, Waterline Data, Zenput, Zetta

Key Executives:
   Josh Breinlinger, Managing Director
   e-mail: josh@jsv.com
   Education: MIT
   Background: oDesk; Rev; Adroll
   Directorships: Omniata, OfferUp, rented.com, Contently, Kindly Care, Bus.com, Crexi, Atrium
   Greg Gretsch, Managing Director
   e-mail: greg@jsv.com
   Directorships: Upwork, Responsysm Strava, Toutapp, Equallogic, Jellyvision, Jackbox Games, Sugarsync, Doxo, Talking Blocks
   Pete Solvik, Managing Director
   e-mail: pete@jsv.com
   Directorships: Docusign, Centrify, KACE, Seismic, Topio, Lanetix, Mogl, Scancafe

1025 JAGUAR CAPITAL PARTNERS
PO Box 198
Haverford, PA 19041

   Phone: 610-585-0285
   web: www.jaguar-capital.com

Mission Statement: Jaguar Capital Partners is a private equity investment firm dedicated to investing in and building companies based in Europe, Asia and the United States.

Geographic Preference: Europe, Asia, United States
Investment Criteria: Early- to Expansion-Stage
Industry Group Preference: Technology, Media, Telecommunications, Financial Services
Portfolio Companies: Arcadian Networks, China Cablecom, Inveshare, Return on Intelligence, UNIRISX, Vizant Technologies

Key Executives:
   Jonathan Kalman, Managing Partner
   e-mail: jkalman@jaguar-capital.com
   Education: BS, Applied Physics, Cornell University; MBA, Kellogg School of Management, Northwestern University
   Background: Executive Chairman, UNIRISX; Chairman & CEO, Jaguar Acqusition Corporation; Founder & Managing Partner, Katalyst Venture Partners; IBM
   Directorships: Vizant Technologies

1026 JANE VC
Cleveland, OH

   e-mail: hello@janevc.com
   web: www.janevc.com

Mission Statement: Mission is to invest in early-stage female-founded companies accross a variety of industries.

Geographic Preference: United States
Fund Size: $2 Million
Average Investment: $25,000 - $150,000
Minimum Investment: $25,000
Investment Criteria: Early Stage, Female Founded
Industry Group Preference: All Sectors Considered
Portfolio Companies: Akin, Hatch Apps, Kinside, Proformex, Sown To Grow

Key Executives:
   Jennifer Keiser Neundorfer, Founding Partner
   Education: BA, Harvard; MBA, Stanford University
   Background: 21st Century Fox; YouTube
   Maren Thomas Bannon, Founding Partner
   Education: BA, Engineering, Dartmouth; MBA, Stanford University
   Background: CEO/Co-Founder, LittleLane; Genentech

1027 JARVINIAN VENTURES
One International Place
Suite 1400
Boston, MA 02110

   e-mail: info@jarvinian.com
   web: www.jarvinian.com

Mission Statement: Jarvinian focuses exclusively on the wireless sector and seeks to support the development of wireless technologies.

Fund Size: $150 million
Average Investment: $1 - $5 million
Investment Criteria: Early Stage
Industry Group Preference: Wireless

Key Executives:
   John Dooley, Founder/Managing Director
   Background: Director, AWS Spectrum Bidco; Founder, Nanoton; FiberTower Corporation
   Tom Eddy, Managing Director
   Education: BS, University of Virginia; JD, Duquesne University School of Law; MBA, Harvard Business School
   Background: COO & Senior General Partner, Atlas Venture; Managing Director, Robertson Stephens & Company; VP, Technology Investment Banking Group, Morgan Stanley & Co.
   Directorships: First Marblehead Corporation

1028 JAVELIN VENTURE PARTNERS
221 Main Street
Suite 1300
San Francisco, CA 94105

   Phone: 415-471-1300
   web: www.javelinvp.com

Mission Statement: Javelin Venture Partners was founded by former entrepreneurs with a first-hand appreciation of what it takes to develop a company from concept to thriving enterprise.

Geographic Preference: Worldwide
Average Investment: $250,000 - $5 million
Minimum Investment: $250,000
Investment Criteria: Seed, Searies A
Industry Group Preference: Technology, Digital Media & Marketing, Internet, Mobile Communications Devices, Healthcare Information Technology
Portfolio Companies: 3scale, Appvance, Armory, Boost Media, Carbon Health, Clutter, Correlated Magnetics Research, Cyberrinc, Engrade, Estimote, ExecThread, Fair, Famo.us, FEM Inc., Filld, GameCo, ImageVision, Kidpass, KopoKopo, Linqia, Lithium, MasterClass, Netpulse, Nexenta, Niantic Labs, Nuvon, Overstat, Pixalate, Plug.dj, PowerCloud Systems, Prismatic, Rinse, Ritter Pharmaceuticals, Rixty, RxVantage, ScoutLabs, Seismos, Sense Networks, Skytree, Smartasset, Smartzip, Spotsetter, Telerivet, Thanx, The Hunt, Thumbtack, Trumaker, Vacatia, Weddington Way, WellnessFX

Key Executives:
   Noah J. Doyle, Managing Director
   e-mail: ndoyle@javelinvp.com
   Education: BA, Economics, MBA, University of California Berkeley
   Background: Co-Founder, MyPoints.com; Overseas Sales & Marketing, Matsushita's Communications
   Jed Katz, Managing Director
   e-mail: jkatz@javelinvp.com
   Education: BA, Business Economics, UCLA; MBA, Haas School of Business, University of California, Berkeley
   Background: Managing Director, DFJ Gotham Ventures; COO & Founder, Rent Net

Venture Capital & Private Equity Firms / Domestic Firms

1029 JAZZ VENTURE PARTNERS
123 South Park Street
San Francisco, CA 94107

e-mail: info@jazzvp.com
web: jazzvp.com

Mission Statement: Jazz VP seeks breakthroughs in digital technology and neuroscience that influence the human experience. THey focus primarily on augumented reality, AI, immersive gaming and closed-loop human-computer systems.

Key Executives:
  John Harris, Managing Partner
  Education: BS, Stanford University; MBA, Northwestern University
  Background: Founder, Heartstream; Co-Founder, ClearFlow; Co-Founder, MDX Partners; Founder, President and CEO, NeuroVista
  Zack Lynch, Managing Partner
  Education: BS, MA, Univerity of California, Los Angelos
  Background: Founder, Neurotechnology Industry Organization; Author; Founder, Experential Technology and NeuroGaming Conference; Founder and CEO, NeuroInsights
  John Spinale, Managing Partner
  Education: Yale University
  Background: Founder, Bitmo; General Manager, Disney Interactive, Mobile and Social Games Division

1030 JB POINDEXTER & COMPANY
600 Travis Street
Suite 400
Houston, TX 77002

Phone: 713-655-9800 Fax: 713-951-9038
e-mail: info@jbpco.com
web: www.jbpoindexter.com

Mission Statement: JB Poindexter & Co. aquires companies from private owners and require additional financiaing or operating resources to develop and grow.

Geographic Preference: United States
Fund Size: $500 million
Founded: 1988
Minimum Investment: $2 million
Investment Criteria: Later Stage
Industry Group Preference: Transportation, Machinery, Metals, Industrial Equipment
Portfolio Companies: EFP Corp., MIC Group, Morgan Corp., Morgan Olson, Reading Truck Body, Specialty Vehicles Group, Truck Accessories Group

Key Executives:
  John Poindexter, Chairman/CEO
  e-mail: jpoindexter@jbpco.com
  Education: MBA/PhD in Economics and Finance, New York University
  Background: KD/P Equities; Smith Barney Capital Corporation; Salomon Brothers

1031 JC2 VENTURES
P.O. Box 10195
Dept. 12
Palo Alto, CA 94303

Phone: 650 762-5101
web: www.jc2ventures.com

Mission Statement: JC2 invests in and mentors startup companies dealing with digital technologies in the areas of digital communications, security, agricultural technology, internet, and more.

Geographic Preference: United States
Fund Size: $100 Million
Founded: 2018
Investment Criteria: Startup, Technology
Industry Group Preference: Security, Social Media, Agriculture Technologies, Technology, Internet

Portfolio Companies: Aspire Food Group, Balbix, Bloomenergy, Dedrone, IoTium, Lucideus, Opengov, Pindrop, Privoro, Rubrik, Sparkcognition, Sprinklr, Uniphore

Key Executives:
  John Chambers, CEO/Founder
  Education: BA, BSc, JD, West Virginia University; MBA, Finance/Management, Indiana University
  Background: Cisco

1032 JEFFERIES CAPITAL PARTNERS
520 Madison Avenue
Suite 11
New York, NY 10022

Phone: 212-284-1700
web: www.jefferies.com

Mission Statement: Jefferies provides insight, expertise, and execution to investors, companies and government entitites. The firm offers services in investment banking, equities, fixed income and wealth management.

Geographic Preference: North and South America, Europe, Middle East, Asia
Founded: 1967
Average Investment: $10 to $100 million
Minimum Investment: $10 million
Investment Criteria: LBO, MBO, Industry Consolidation, Recapitalization, Growth
Industry Group Preference: Consumer Products, Education, Energy, Financial Services, Healthcare, Manufacturing, Media, Telecommunications, Transportation, Restaurants, Distribution, Logistics

Key Executives:
  Brian P. Friedman, President
  Education: BS, Economics, MS, Accounting, Wharton School, University of Pennsylvania; JD, Columbia University School of Law
  Background: Attorney, Wachtell Lipton Rosen & Katz
  Nicholas Daraviras, Managing Director
  Education: BS & MBA, Wharton School, University of Pennsylvania
  Background: Equity Research Analyst, Oppenheimer & Co.
  James J. Dowling, Managing Director
  Education: BS & MBA, Farleigh Dickinson University
  Background: Senior Securities Research Analyst, Furman Selz LLC
  George R. Hutchinson, Managing Director
  Education: BS, Boston University School of Management
  Background: Senior Managing Director, Jefferies Randall & Dewey; Friedman Billings & Ramsey
  Directorships: Patara Oil & Gas

1033 JEGI CAPITAL The Jordan Edminston Group, Inc.
150 East 52nd Street
18th Floor
New York, NY 10022

Phone: 212-754-0710
e-mail: adamg@jegi.com
web: www.jegi.com

Mission Statement: The leading provider of independent investment banking services for the media, information, marketing services and technology sectors.

Geographic Preference: United States, Europe, Australia
Fund Size: $100 million
Founded: 1987
Average Investment: $1 - 3 million
Minimum Investment: $1 million
Investment Criteria: Early Stage, Late Stage
Industry Group Preference: Publishing, Information Technology, Media, Infrastructure, Marketing, Communications

Other Locations:
One Liberty Square
Boston, MA 02109
Phone: 617-294-6555

90 Long Acre
London WC2E 9RA
United Kingdom
Phone: 44 (0)20 3402 4900

L35, Tower One
International Towers
100 Barangaroo Avenue
Sydney NSW 2000
Australia
Phone: 61 2 8046 6840

Key Executives:
Wilma Jordan, Founder & Chief Executive Officer
e-mail: wilmaj@jegi.com
Education: University of Tennessee
Background: Founder/CEO, The Jordan Edmiston Group; Co-Founder, 13-30 Corporation; COO, Esquire Magazine Group
Directorships: Guideposts; Blyth
Amir Akhavan, Managing Director
Education: BS, Corporate Finance, University of Southern California; MS, University of Virginia
Background: Deloitte Corporate Finance, Deloitte Consulting, Ernst & Young Assurance & Advisory Business
Sam Barthelme, Managing Director
Education: BS & MBA, NY Stern School of Business
Background: AIG; Production Resource Group; Time Warner/CNN
Kathleen Thomas, Managing Director
Education: BA, Architecture, University of North Carolina; MBA, Baruch College
Background: Managing Partner, Drake Star Partners; Marketing, Berkery Noyes; Veronis Suhler Stevenson

1034 JESSELSON CAPITAL CORPORATION
450 Park Avenue
New York, NY 10022-2605

Phone: 212-751-3666

Portfolio Companies: AllCloud, Happy Cloud, Jifiti

Key Executives:
Michael Jesselson, President
Background: Director, American Eagle Outfitters

1035 JETBLUE TECHNOLOGY VENTURES
999 Skyway Road
Suite 350
San Carlos, CA 94070

e-mail: crew@jetblueventures.com
web: www.jetblueventures.com

Mission Statement: JetBlue Technology Ventures focuses investments on aviation technology.

Founded: 2016
Industry Group Preference: Aviation, Technology, Industry
Portfolio Companies: Betterez, Bizly, Claire By 30 Seconds To Fly, Climacell, CoinFlip, Flyr, Gladly, Joby Aviation, Lumo, Miles, Mozio, Node, Redeam, Shape, Slice, Skyhour, Stride, Unicoaero, Volantio

Key Executives:
Bonny Simi, President
Education: BA, Communications; MS, Management; MS, Engineering, Stanford University
Raj Singh, Managing Director, Investments
Education: BS, Imperial College London; MBA, INSEAD, Fontainebleau, France
Background: Mentor, Founder Institute; CEO, Sooqini; General Partner/Co-Founder, Pervasive Technology Ventures; Principal, Investcorp

Amy Burr, Managing Director, Operations & Partnerships
Education: BS, American University; MBA, Moore School of Business, University of Carolina
Background: Founders, Virgin America; Revenue Manager, Continental Airlines

1036 JF SHEA VENTURES
655 Brea Canyon Road
Walnut, CA 91789

Phone: 909-594-9500
web: www.jfshea.com

Geographic Preference: United States
Investment Criteria: Early-Stage
Industry Group Preference: Software, Semiconductors, Biotechnology, Medical Devices

1037 JH WHITNEY & COMPANY
130 Main Street
New Canaan, CT 06840

Phone: 203-716-6100
e-mail: info@whitney.com
web: www.whitney.com

Mission Statement: One of the first US private equity firms. JHW provides private equity capital for small and middle market companies.

Geographic Preference: Untied States
Fund Size: $750 million
Founded: 1946
Average Investment: $50 to $500 million
Minimum Investment: $50 million
Investment Criteria: Buyouts, Turnarounds, Acquisitions, Recapitalizations, Revenues of $50 - $500 Million
Industry Group Preference: Consumer Products, Retailing, Niche Manufacturing, Business Products & Services, Healthcare
Portfolio Companies: 3B Scientific, Accupac, Aarrowcast, Autosplice, Aveanna Healthcare, Cabi, Caris Life Sciences, CJ Foods Inc., CPG International, Confluence Outdoor, Encanto, FNF Construction Inc., Igloo, Precision for Medicine, Pure Fishing, RBC Bearings, Stevens, TIDI Products, United BioSource, US Bioservices, Uncle Julio's, Wellman Plastics

Key Executives:
Paul R. Vigano, Senior Managing Director
Education: BBA, University of Michigan; MBA, Stanford University Graduate School of Business
Background: M&A, Goldman Sachs & Co.
Robert M. Williams Jr., Senior Managing Director
Education: BA, Bucknell University; MBA, Columbia University
Background: Financial Advisory Services Group, CIBC; Partner, Duff & Phelps
Shaneel D. Patel, Senior Associate
Education: BA, Economics, BS, Commerce, University of Virginia
Background: Hamilton Lane
David J. Zatlukal, Chief Financial Officer
Education: BBA, St. Bonaventure University; CPA
Background: PricewaterhouseCoopers
Kevin J. Curley, Advisor/Chief Compliance Officer
Education: BA, College of the Holy Cross; JD, Columbia Law School
Background: Partner, Morgan Lewis & Bockius; Lord Day & Lord Barrett Smith
Daniel J. O'Brien, Avisor
Education: BS, Fordham University; CPA
Background: Partner/National Chairman, Emerging Business Services Practive, PricewaterhouseCoopers

Venture Capital & Private Equity Firms / Domestic Firms

1038 JK&B CAPITAL
Two Prudential Plaza
180 N Stetson Avenue
Suite 4500
Chicago, IL 60601

Phone: 312-946-1200 Fax: 312-946-1103
web: www.jkbcapital.com

Mission Statement: JK&B Capital is a venture capital firm focused in the software, IT and communications markets.

Geographic Preference: United States
Fund Size: $1.1 billion
Founded: 1996
Industry Group Preference: Telecommunications, Software, Internet Technology, Information Technology, Applications, Pharmaceuticals, Infrastructure, Semiconductors
Portfolio Companies: 21st Century Telecom Group, Actiance, AlterPoint, Anchor Intelligence, Andromedia, Aperto Networks, AppStream, Atrica, Baynote, Bluefire Security Technologies, Cambria Security, Cenzic, Chumby Industries, ClearPoint Metrics, ColdSpark, Commerce One, Continuum Photonics, CoreTek, CounterStorm, Cranite Systems, Daleen Technologies, E2open, Entercept Security Technologies, Exodus Communications, EZ Chip Technologies, FaceTime Communications, Instantis, Intacct Corporation, Interwoven, Intrado, iVivity, Jareva Technologies, Kazeon Systems, Lenslet, Liquidware Labs, Nanochip, nCircle Network Security, NextIO, Novarra, Openwave Systems, Paragon Networks International, Polatix, Reactivity, Scalent Systems, Seaway Networks, Selectica, Sequation, Sheer Networks, SiCortex, Silver Stream Software, SnapTell, Synchrologic, TenXc, Trusted Network Technologies, UNIsite, Ubiquity Software Corporation, UNIsite, Vantrix, Verimatrix, Viewfinity, VMIX Media, Vormetric, XOSoft, Zone Labs

Key Executives:
David Kronfeld, Chairman
e-mail: dkronfeld@jkbcapital.com
Education: BSEE, MS Computer Science, Stevens Institute of Technology; MBA, Wharton School
Background: General Partner, Boston Capital Ventures; VP Acquisitions/Venture Investments, Ameritech; Senior Manager, Booz Allen & Hamilton; Systems Analyst, Electronic Data Systems (EDS)
Thomas Neustaetter, Partner, Software
e-mail: tneustaetter@jkbcapital.com
Education: MBA, MS, University of California, Los Angeles; BA Philosophy, University of California, Berkley
Background: Partner, The Chatterjee Group; Founder/President, Bancroft Capital;Chemical Venture Partners-Northeast of Chemical Bank (now JP Morgan); CFO, First Reserve Corporation; Senior Tax Accountant, Price Waterhouse
Directorships: Cambria Security; Intacct Corporation; FaceTime Communications; Instantis; Selectica; XOSoft
Robert Humes, Partner, Communications
Education: BSEE, Purdue University; MSEE, Polytechnic Institute of Brooklyn
Background: VP Engineering/Technology, Ameritech; VP Operations, Michigan Bell; original design team on cellular tellephony, Bell Labs
Directorships: EZchip Technologies
Tasha Seitz, Partner, Software
e-mail: tseitz@jkbcapital.com
Education: MBA, Stanford Graduate School of Business; BA, Wellesley College
Background: IT Analyst, Gartner Group; Founder, Gartner's Multimedia
Directorships: Bluefire Security Technologies; Cambria Security; Novarra; Trusted Network Technologies; Reactivity; Baynote
Ali Shadman, Partner, Communications
Education: BSEE, MSEE, PhD, Oregon State University
Background: President New Media, Ameritech; Boardmember, Americast; VP Corporate Strategy, Ameritech; Director Technology Development, MCI Telecommunications; Technical Staff, INTELSAT
Directorships: Atrica; Ivivity; Lenslet; Seaway Networks; Sheer Networks; TenXc
Albert DaValle Jr., Partner, Communications
Education: BSEE, Purdue University; MA, Management, Kellogg School of Management
Background: VP Engineering/Construction, Ameritech; VP Technology, Belgacom (Belgium); Senior Planner, Sprint
Directorships: Aperto Networks; Nanochip; Continuum Photonics; SiCortex; Purdue University School of Engineering Advisory Board
Marc Sokol, Partner, Software
Background: SVP/GM Global Marketing, Computer Associates International; Co-Founder, Realia; Co-Author, Realia COBOL compiler; Software Developer, NASA Goddard Space Flight Center
Directorships: AppStream; XOsoft; Cenzic; Cranite Systems; ClearPoint Metrics; Vormetric; Scalent Systems; AlterPoint; CounterStorm
Nancy O'Leary, Partner/CFO
Education: BS, Psychology, Bradley University
Background: Founder, Keystone Associates; Controller, Capital Health Venture Partners; Lanac Technology; Director Finance, CORS

1039 JLL PARTNERS
245 Park Avenue
Suite 1601
New York, NY 10167

Phone: 212-286-8600 Fax: 212-286-8626
web: www.jllpartners.com

Mission Statement: To create value for portfolio companies by providing operational and financial expertise. JLL Partners, a private equity firm with headquarters in New York, targets middle market companies in the financial services, business services, healthcare, industrial, education, aerospace and defense sectors.

Fund Size: $624 million
Founded: 1988
Industry Group Preference: Healthcare, Financial Services, Business Products & Services, Industrial, Education, Aerospace, Defense and Government, Building Materials & Services
Portfolio Companies: ACE Cash Express, American Dental Partners, BioClinica, Builders FirstSource, DPx, Education Affiliates, FC Holdings, IASIS Healthcare, JG Wentworth, Loar Group, Medical Card System, Pioneer Sand Company, Point Blank Enterprises, Ross Education

Key Executives:
Alexander R Castaldi, Managing Director
Education: BA, Central Connecticut State University
Background: CFO & CAO, Remington Products; CFO, Uniroyal Chemical; CFO, Kendall International; Controller, Duracell; KPMG Peat Marwick
Paul S. Levy, Managing Director
Education: BA, Lehigh University; JD, University of Pennsylvania Law School
Background: Managing Director, Drexel Burnham Lambert; CEO, Yves Saint Laurent; VP, Administration, Quality Care; Attorney, Stroock & Stroock & Lavan LLP
Frank J. Rodriguez, Managing Director
Education: BS, Wharton School, University of Pennsylvania
Background: Merchant Banker, Donaldson, Lufkin & Jenrette
Directorships: Mosaic Sales Solutions, Education Affiliates, Motor Coach Industries
Daniel Agroskin, Managing Director
Education: BA, Stanford University; MBA, Wharton School, University of Pennsylvania

Venture Capital & Private Equity Firms / Domestic Firms

Background: Associate, JP Morgan Partners; Analyst, M&A Group, Merrill Lynch
Eugene Hahn, Managing Director
Education: BA, Economics, Cornell University; MBA, Wharton School, University of Pennsylvania
Background: Associate, Warburg Pincus; Analyst, M&A Group, Lazard Freres
Kevin T. Hammond, Managing Director
Education: BS, McIntire School of Commerce, University of Virginia
Background: Analyst, Greenhill & Co.

1040 JMH CAPITAL
155 Federal Street
Suite 502
Boston, MA 02110

Phone: 617-910-2602
web: www.jmhcapital.com

Mission Statement: A private equity firm based in Boston, JMH Capital primarily focuses on growth-oriented companies across a variety of sectors, including food products and services, niche manufacturing, distribution, specialty chemicals and medical devices.

Founded: 2003
Investment Criteria: Recapitalizations, Mangement Buyouts, Leveraged Buyouts, Growth Equity
Industry Group Preference: Niche Manufacturing, Specialty Chemicals, Building Materials & Services, Medical Devices, Business Products & Services, Value-Added Distribution, Analytics & Analytical Instruments, Food Services
Portfolio Companies: Alternative Hose LLC, All4, carlisle Wide Plank Floors, Currie Medical Specialties Inc., Endres Processing, kenexa, MedAssets, Morningside Venture Group, Parterre Flooring Systems, Richard Brady & Associates, Service Radio Rentals, The Signature Group, Spheris, Tri-Star Protector

Key Executives:
John Nies, Managing Partner
781-522-1604
e-mail: jnies@jmhcapital.com
Education: BA, Dartmouth College; MBA, Harvard Business School
Background: Managing Director, Operations, Parthenon Capital; Founding Member & Managing Director, The Parthenon Group; Bain & Co.
Directorships: Carlisle Wide Plank Floors, Service Radio Rentals, Currie Medical Specialties, The Signature Group, Parterre Flooring Systems
Scott Steele, Managing Partner
781-522-1603
e-mail: ssteele@jmhcapital.com
Education: BBA, University of Michigan; MBA, New York University Stern School of Business
Background: Principal, Parthenon Capital; Electra Fleming Americas; Senior Associate, Coopers & Lybrand; Associate, Heller Financial
Directorships: Carlisle Wide Plank Floors, Currie Medical Specialties, Service Radio Rentals, The Signature Group, Parterre Flooring Systems
Michael Stanek, Management Partner
716-870-4298
e-mail: mstanek@jmhcapital.com
Education: BS, Accounting, Rochester Institute of Technology; CPA
Background: CEO, Classifieds Plus; CEO, Northern Group Retail; Akron Manufacturing
Directorships: Carlisle Wide Plank Floors, Parterre Flooring Systems
Tate Bevis, Managing Director
781-522-1613
e-mail: tbevis@jmhcapital.com
Education: BS, MS, Accounting, Carroll School of Management, Boston College
Background: Wachovia Securities; Associate, Deloitte
Directorships: The Signature Group, Parterre Flooring Systems

1041 JMI EQUITY FUND LP
100 International Drive
Suite 19100
Baltimore, MD 21202

Phone: 410-951-0200 **Fax:** 410-637-8360
web: www.jmi.com

Mission Statement: Focused on enterprise application and infrastructure software and services - investing in companies with rich intellectual property that automates and optimizes business and information technology processes.

Fund Size: $350 million
Founded: 1992
Average Investment: $6 million
Minimum Investment: $1 million
Investment Criteria: Early, Late Stage
Industry Group Preference: E-Commerce & Manufacturing, Software, Internet, Healthcare Information Technology, Business Products & Services
Portfolio Companies: ACI, Activant, Adaptive Insights, Adknowledge, Airclic, Applied, AppNeta, Appriss, Arena, Aarowhead, Attachmate, Automotive Mastermind, Autotask, Avecto, Axeda, Axonify, Benevity, BigMachines, Bindview, Blackbaud, Businessolver, Capsule, Catapult Learning, Classy, Code42, Compusearch, ConfigureSoft, CoreHr, Courion, Double Click, DoubleVerify, eBenx, Ellucian, Eloqua, Empathica, EMS, Gemcom, Global360, Granicus, Halogen Software, Harmony Information Systems Inc., HealthX, Higher Logic, Innovative, Intelex, Intergraph, Internet Brands, Intradiem, Jackson Hewitt Tax Service, Kronos, Level Access, Lytx, Meta Group, Mision Critical Software, Mitchell, Navicure, Neon, Netpro, Network Intelligence Corp., Nimsoft, Paradigm, PointClickCarem PowerPlan, Pros, Quiave, Quic, RSam, Schoology, Seismic, SMT Kingdom, ServiceBench, ServiceNow, Sirius Decisions, Studer Group, TC3, The Search Agency, Triple Point Technology, Trustwave, Undertone, Unica, Vertafore, Vocalocity, Vocus, WhiteHat Security, WorkFront, X Matters, Yello

Other Locations:
7776 Ivanhoe Avenue
Suite 200
La Jolla, CA 92037
Phone: 858-362-9880 **Fax:** 858-362-9879

Key Executives:
Harry Gruner, Founder & Managing General Partner
410-951-0207
e-mail: hgruner@jmi.com
Education: BA, Yale; MBA, Harvard Business School
Background: Principal, Technology Group, Alex Brown; Marketing, Sigma Design; Investment Banking, Technology Group, Blyth Eastman PaineWebber
Directorships: Appriss, Aptela, Autotask Corp, Catapult Learning, Courion Corp, Halogen Software, Intellitactics, Naivcure
Charles E. Noell, Founder
Education: BA, University of North Carolina; MBA, Harvard Business School
Background: President, John J. Moores; Founder/CEO, BMC Software Inc.; Managing Director, Alex Brown's Technology Group; Associate, American Security Bank; Associate, Pittsburgh National Bank
Directorships: Authentify, Alex Brown Realty Inc., Greystar Real Estate Partners
Paul Barber, Managing General Partner
858-362-9881
e-mail: pbarber@jmi.com
Education: AB, Economics, Stanford University; MBA, Harvard Business School
Background: Manating Director, Alex Brown; Product

377

Venture Capital & Private Equity Firms / Domestic Firms

Marketing, Microsoft; Investment Banker, Merrill Lynch
Directorships: Applied Systems, Healthx, Innovative Interfces, Kronos
Peter Arrowsmith, General Partner
858-362-9882
e-mail: parrowsmith@jmi.com
Education: AB, History/Literature, Harvard University
Background: AEA Investors, Mckinsey & Co.
Directorships: Seismic, The Search Agency, WhiteHat Security, Workfront, xMatters, Yello
Kathy Fields, General Partner/General Counsel
858-362-9884
e-mail: kfields@jmi.com
Education: BS, Business, Indiana University; JD, Stanford Law School
Background: Goodwin Procter LLP; Partner, Testa Hurwitz & Thibeault LLP
David Greenberg, General Partner
410-951-0231
e-mail: dgreenberg@jmi.com
Education: BBA, Finance/Accounting, Goizueta Business School, Emory University
Background: Associate, Cascadia Capital; Analyst, Houlihan Lockey
Directorships: Businessolver, CoreHR, Intelex, Sirius Decisions
Randy Guttman, General Partner & CFO
410-951-0213
e-mail: rguttman@jmi.com
Education: BS, Accounting/Finance, Robert H. Smith School of Business, University of Maryland; CPA
Background: Senior Associate, EY
Brian Hersman, General Partner
858-362-9886
e-mail: bhersman@jmi.com
Education: BA, Economics/Computer Science, MS, Management of Information Systems, Weatherhead School, Case Wetern Reserve University; MBA, Harvard Business School
Background: Senior Associate, Vista Equity Partners; Analyst, McKinsey & Co.
Directorships: Arena, Classy, EMS Software, Innovative Interfaces, Intradiem

Key Executives:
Stacy Feld, Head, Johnson & Johnson Innovation
Education: BA, University of Pennsylvania; JD, Vanderbilt Law School
Background: Former Sr Director of Consumer Scientific Innovation; Partner, Physic Ventures; Business Development, Genentech; Business Development, Third Wave Technologies

1043 JOHNSON & JOHNSON INNOVATION
New Brunswick, NJ 08901

e-mail: jnjinnovation@its.jnj.com
web: jnjinnovation.com

Mission Statement: Johnson & Johnson Innovation, the venture capital arm of Johnson & Johnson, invests in emerging healthcare companies. Johnson & Johnson Development Corporation seeks to generate both financial returns and options for strategic growth for Johnson & Johnson. JJDC targets opportunities with large markets, competitive advantages, and experienced management teams.

Founded: 1973
Investment Criteria: Early-Stage to Advanced Stages
Industry Group Preference: Medical Devices, Diagnostics, Pharmaceuticals, Biotechnology, Consumer Products, Wellness, Prevention
Portfolio Companies: Accelerator Corporation, Asceneuron, Merus, Navitor Pharmaceuticals, NovoCure, Padlock Therapeutics, Protagonist Therapeutics, Vivo Capital

1044 JOHNSTON ASSOCIATES
155 Lambert Drive
Princeton, NJ 08540

Phone: 609-924-2575 **Fax:** 609-924-3135
e-mail: info@jaivc.com
web: www.jaivc.com

Mission Statement: Provides seed capital to emerging companies in the general Princeton, NJ area for healthcare related businesses. Johnston Associates typically invests in one enterprise a year. The firm invests its own private capital and has no pre-set investment horizons, investment limits or size, or return objectives.

Geographic Preference: New Jersey
Founded: 1968
Investment Criteria: Seed, Startup
Industry Group Preference: Biotechnology, Pharmaceuticals, Healthcare, Therapeutics, Drug Development
Portfolio Companies: Cerus Endovascular, Cytogen Corp., Envirogen, Genex, I-STAT, JDS Therapeutics, Myosotis, PharmaStem, Pharmos, Retrotope, Sepracor, Targent, Zywie LLC

Other Locations:
2205 Trakehner Lane
Reno, NV 89521

Key Executives:
Robert Johnston, Founder
Education: BA, Princeton University; MBA, New York University
Background: Investment Banker: FS Smithers & Company, Smith Barney & Company
Directorships: Envirogen Inc., Vela Pharmaceuticals

1045 JORDAN COMPANY
399 Park Avenue
30th Floor
New York, NY 10022

Phone: 212-572-0800 **Fax:** 212-755-5263
web: www.thejordancompany.com

Mission Statement: A private investment firm specializing in the buyout and building up of businesses in partnership with management.

Geographic Preference: United States, Europe
Fund Size: $6 billion
Founded: 1982
Investment Criteria: LBO, MBO, Recaps, Private-to-Public, Restructuring, Consolidation, Strategic Buildup, Growth Capital, Established Middle Market Companies with Revenues between $100 Million to $2 Billion
Industry Group Preference: Aerospace, Defense and Government, Building Materials & Services, Consumer Products, Education, Metals, Energy, Transportation, Financial Services, Insurance, Industrial Products, Packaging, Healthcare, Telecommunications, Automotive
Portfolio Companies: ACR Group, Agility, American Freight, Anchor, Arch, Bojangles', Borchers, Bruin II, Capstone, CFS Brands, Dimora, Gulfstream, Harvey Gulf, Odyssey, Parts Authority, Polymer Additives, Production Resource Group, RFJ Auto, Sabre, Silvus, Simpleview, Syndigo, Vantage, Venari, Vertical Bridge, VT Services, Vyne, Watchfire, Worldwide Clinical Trials, Young Innovations

Other Locations:
One North Wacker Drive
Suite 4140
Chicago, IL 60606
Phone: 312-668-0400 **Fax:** 312-668-0496

Key Executives:
Jay Jordan, Chairman & Founding Partner
Education: BBA, University of Notre Dame; Columbia University Grad. School of Business
Background: Carl Marks & Co.

Venture Capital & Private Equity Firms / Domestic Firms

Directorships: Gulfstream Services, Worldwide Clinical Trials, Young Innovations
Rich Caputo, Managing Principal
Education: BA, Mathematical Economics, Brown University
Background: Analyst, High Yield Department, Prudential-Bache Capital Funding
Directorships: American Fast Freight, American Freight, Borchers, Capstone, Harvey Gulf, Pats Authority, Venari
Dave Butler, Partner
Education: BA, English/Economics, University of Notre Dame; JD, Fordham University School of Law
Directorships: DiversiTech, Watchfire, Worldwide Clinical Trials, Young Innovations
Krisin Custar, Partner
Education: BS, Finance, University of Illinois, Urbana; MBA, University of Chicago Booth School of Business
Background: Director, Investor Relations, First Reserve Corporation; GE Equity; Arthur Andersen
Michael Denvir, Partner
Education: BA, Economics, University of Notre Dame
Directorships: Dimora, Vantage, Worldwide Clinical Trials
Mark Emery, Partner & Co-Head, Operations Management Group
Education: BS, Civil Engineering, Bristol University; MBA, Booth School of Business, University of Chicago
Background: President/CEO, Northstar Aerospace Inc.; President/CEO, Indalez Aluminum Solutions Group; President, Caradon Terrain; President, Hubbard Group; President, Margaux CVC Ltd.; Senior Engagement Manager, McKinsey & Co.
Directorships: Drew Marine, Gulfstream Servives, RFJ Auto, Vantage, VT
Brian Higgins, Partner
Education: BA, Economics, Williams College; CFA
Background: Global Natural Resources Group, Lehman Brothers
Directorships: American Fast Freight, Capstone, Harvey Gulf, Odyssey, Quick
Eion Hu, Partner
Education: AB, Economics, Harvard University; MBA, Harvard Business School
Background: M&A, Salomon Smith Barney
Directorships: RFJ Auto, Vertical Bridge
Joseph Linnen, Partner
Education: BBA, Finance, University of Notre Dame
Directorships: Worldwide Clinical Trials
Lisa Ondrula, Partner & Co-Head, Operations Management Group
Education: BS, Accounting, Miami University
Background: Ernst & Young LLP
Directorships: American Freight; Borchers; Parts Authority; Syndigo
Douglas Zych, Partner
Education: BBA, University of Notre Dame
Background: Mergers/Acquisitions Group, Merrill Lynch & Co

1046 JUMP CAPITAL LLC
600 West Chicago Avenue
Suite 625
Chicago, IL 60654

e-mail: info@jumpcap.com
web: jumpcap.com

Mission Statement: Jump Capital is a venture capital firm based in Chicago. The firm pursues opportunities with scalable technology companies and implements long-term investment strategies.
Average Investment: $2 - $15 million
Investment Criteria: Expansion Stage, Growth Capital, Startups
Industry Group Preference: Enterprise Technology, Healthcare Information Technology, Marketing, Financial Services
Portfolio Companies: 4C, AVIA, Booker, Champion Medical Technologies, Doctor on Demand, HealthExpense, LISNR, MediBeacon, NarrativeScience, NowSecure, Opternative, Pangea, ParkWhiz, Personal Capital, Pixability, Procured Health, ProPharma Group, ShareThis, SIM Partners, Spire, Spring, Swiftpage, True Fit, Tulip Retail, Wholesome Goodness, Zettics, ZipScene
Other Locations:
15 E 26th Street
New York, NY 10010
Key Executives:
Michael McMahon, Managing Partner
Education: BS, Finance, Pennsylvania State University
Background: Co-Founder & Senior Partner, Excelar Group LLC; President, SIRVA; CFO, Rail Services & Card Services, GE Capital
Sach Chitnis, Managing Partner
Education: BS, Chemical Engineering, University of Rochester; MBA, Kellogg School of Management, Northwestern University
Background: Operating Partner, Tarsus Holdings; VP, Consumer Moving & Corporate Development, SIRVA; GE Corporate
Saurabh Sharma, General Partner
Education: Cornell University; MBA, University of Chicago Booth School of Business
Background: Groupon; Lightbank; Barclays Capital; Lehman Brothers; French Institute for Research in Computer Science and Automation; Co-Founder, Benchprep

1047 JUMPSTART INC
6701 Carnegie Avenue
Suite 100
Cleveland, OH 44103

Phone: 216-363-3400 Fax: 216-363-3401
e-mail: askjs@jumpstartinc.org
web: www.jumpstartinc.org

Mission Statement: JumpStart ventures guides Northeast Ohio entrepreneurs with high potential businesses down the path toward wealth creation by providing seed capital, experienced advisors, and a network of vital resources. JumpStart Ventures is the investment arm of JumpStart, Inc., a nationally recognized non-profit transforming the economic impact of entrepreneurial ventures and the ecosystem supporting their growth.

Geographic Preference: Northeastern Ohio
Founded: 2003
Industry Group Preference: Life Sciences, Healthcare, Digital Media, Software
Portfolio Companies: Wiretap, Wisr, StreamLink Software, ExpenseBot, Complion, Markers Workstation, EnosiX, LISNR, 02 RegenTech, Apollo Medical Devices, BioMendics, Vox Mobile, Casentric, BoxCast, eFuneral, Zuga Medical, Movable, Guided Interventions, Sociagram, 7signal, Big River, Amvonet, Intellirod Spine, Milo Biotechnology, Cryothermic Systems, GenomOncology, Enforcer eCoaching, Cureo, Securus Medical Group, Anderson Aerospace, Intelligent Mobile Support, Segmint, SPR Therapeutics, SpearFysh, Caralo Global, MedCity Media, SironRX Therapeutics, CoverMyMeds, Endotronix, Thermalin Diabetes LLC, TheraVasc, Checkpoint Surgical, ABS Materials Inc., Catacel, Myers Motors, Wireless Environment, OnShift, Neuros Medical, IGuiders, Freedom Meditech Inc., Juventas Therapeutics, Inspiron Logistics, CervilLenz, STACK Media, Echogen Power Systems, Great Lakes Pharmaceuticals, AnalizaDX LLC, CardioInsight, MAR Systems, Inspherion, Knotice, Banyan Technology, PreEmptive Solutions, Embrace Pet Insurance, Synapse Biomedical Inc., Ayalogic, Phycal, MesoCoat, Electron

379

Venture Capital & Private Equity Firms / Domestic Firms

Database Company, Amplified Wind Solutions, CFRC Water and Energy Solutions Inc., Design Flux Technologies, Ento Bio, Full Circle Technologies, MET Innovations, Paragon Robotics, Skysun LLC, Body Phyx, Disease Diagnostic Group, iRxReminder, Micro DataStat, Pulmonary Apps, SpireSano, Apply Board, NGageContent, BOLD Guidance, Lauren Loft Social, Enfusen, Flight Deck, Groupmatics, InStore Finance, The Learning Egg LLC, LogiSynn, Projitech,

Key Executives:
  Ray Leach, Chief Executive Officer
  e-mail: ray.leach@jumpstartinc.org
  Education: University of Akron; MIT Sloan School of Managment
  Background: IBM; Founding Member, US Commerce Department's National Advisory Council on Innovation and Entrepreneurship; Chair, National Venture Capital Association
  Cathy Belk, President
  e-mail: cathy.belk@jumpstartinc.org
  Education: BA, Economics, Davidson College; MBA, Duke University
  Background: COO, JumpStart Inc.; Director, Innovations, American Greetings; The Coca-Cola Company; Procter and Gamble; Bank of America

1048 JW ASSET MANAGEMENT
515 Madison Avenue
New York, NY 10022

Phone: 212-446-5362

Mission Statement: Specializes in early-stage investments.
Geographic Preference: US, Canada
Industry Group Preference: Cannabis, Healthcare, Pharmaceuticals
Portfolio Companies: TerrAscend, Vensun Pharmaceuticals, Aralez Pharmaceuticals, Establishment Labs, Vitruvias Therapeutics

Key Executives:
  Jason Wild, President/CIO
  Education: Arnold and Marie Schwartz College of Pharmacy
  Background: Chairman, TerrAscend

1049 JW CHILDS ASSOCIATES
500 Totten Pond Rd.
6th Floor
Waltham, MA 02451

Phone: 617-753-1100 **Fax:** 617-753-1101
e-mail: jwcinfo@jwchilds.com
web: www.jwchilds.com

Mission Statement: Specializing in leveraged buyouts and recapitalizations of middle-market growth companies.
Geographic Preference: North America
Fund Size: $1.75 billion
Founded: 1995
Average Investment: $600 million
Minimum Investment: $150 million
Investment Criteria: Leveraged buyouts and recapitalizations of middle-market growth companies in partnership with company management
Industry Group Preference: Consumer Products, Healthcare, Retailing, Asset Management
Portfolio Companies: Comoto Holdings, EbLens, Honors Holdings, KeyImpact Sales and Systems, Outward Hound, Shoe Sensation, Siromed, Urology Management Associates, Walker Edison

Key Executives:
  John W Childs, Chairman & CEO
  Education: BA, Yale University; MBA, Columbia University
  Background: Senior Managing Director, Thomas H Lee Company; Senior Managing Director, Prudential Insurance Company of America
  Adam L Suttin, Managing Partner
  e-mail: asuttin@jwchilds.com
  Education: BS magna cum laude, University of Pennsylvania; Bachelor Applied Science magna cum laude, Moore School of Engineering
  Background: Associate, Thomas H Lee Company
  Directorships: Comoto Holdings, KeyImpact Sales and Systems, Outward Hound, Shoe Sensation, Siromed, Urology Management Associates, Walker Edison
  David A Fiorentino, Partner
  e-mail: dfiorentino@jwchilds.com
  Education: BA, Amherst College; MBA, Harvard Business School
  Background: Investment Banking, Morgan Stanley
  Directorships: KeyImpact Sales and Systems, Outward Hound, Siromed, Urology Management Associates, Walker Edison
  Jeffrey J Teschke, Partner
  e-mail: jteschke@jwchilds.com
  Education: BA, University of Rochester; MBA, Harvard Business School
  Background: Quad-C Management; Merrill Lynch & Co.
  Directorships: Comoto Holdings, EbLens, Honors Holdings
  William E Watts, Partner
  e-mail: bwatts@jwchilds.com
  Education: BA, State University of New York, Buffalo
  Background: President & CEO, General Nutrition Companies
  Directorships: Comoto Holdings, EbLens, Honors Holdings, Shoe Sensation

1050 K9 VENTURES
Palo Alto, CA

web: www.k9ventures.com

Mission Statement: K9 Ventures is a true 'early stage' venture fund that provides funding and support for concept-stage and seed-stage technology companies. We work with entrepreneurs, sometimes even before a company has been formed, to help evaluate, evolve and fund a company in its nascent stages. K9 Ventures focuses on startups in the San Francisco Bay Area that have a strong entrepreneur/team, an idea that has a clear path to revenue, which can be capital efficient and where we can add value.

Geographic Preference: San Francisco Bay Area
Average Investment: $100,000 - $1 million
Investment Criteria: Early-Stage, Seed-Stage
Industry Group Preference: Technology
Portfolio Companies: Auth0, Baydin, Bugsee, Caarbon, CrowdFlower, Dishero, DNAnexus, eShares, Enuma, Everlaw, Gradescope, HighlightCam, KidAdmit, Lucidchart, Lyft, Lytro, Occipital, Osmo, Tapcanvas, Twilio

Key Executives:
  Manu Kumar, Founder
  Education: BS, Electrical & Computer Engineering, MS, Software Engineering, Carnegie Mellon University; Masters & PhD, Computer Science, Stanford University
  Background: Founder/President/CEO, SneakerLabs; Vice President, Interactive Technologies, E.piphany; Chairman/CEO, iMeet; Lecturer, School of Computer Science, Carnegie Mellon University
  Directorships: Auth0, Gradescope, Lyft, KidAdmit, Osmo, Enuma, eShares, Occipital, Boomerang, LucidChart

Venture Capital & Private Equity Firms / Domestic Firms

1051 KAIROS VENTURES
9440 South Santa Monica Boulevard
Suite 710
Beverly Hills, CA 90210

Phone: 310-271-1866
e-mail: info@kairosventures.com
web: www.kairosventures.com

Mission Statement: Kairos Ventures invests in the world's leading scientific discoveries, working with scientists, engineers, and entrepreneurs to help them transform those discoveries into businesses. Kairos is dedicated to invest in projects that will help improve student debt, cost of rent, childcare, and retirement.

Fund Size: $25 million
Founded: 2008
Average Investment: $150,000-$20 million
Industry Group Preference: Energy, Engineering
Portfolio Companies: 1200 Pharma, 3DBio, Actinobac Biomed, Inc., Amorphology, Applaud Medical, Inc., Auspion, Axial Biotherapeutics, Behavioral Signals, Chimera Bioengineering, Compellon, Dear Health, Delpor, El Pharma, Foldax, GeneSciences, Holoclara, KM Labs, Memiray, MemVerge, Mixcomm, NanoClear Technologies, Neuro-Bio, Provivi, Repairogen, Sienza, Symbiotix Biotherapies, Translent Plasma Systems

Key Executives:
  Jim Demetriades, Founder/Manager Partner
  e-mail: jimd@kairosventures.com
  Education: BSc, Economics & Computer Science, Loyola Marymount University
  Background: PHS; Founder, SeeBeyond; Inspero.net
  Alex Andrianopoulos, Chief R&D Officer
  e-mail: alexa@kairosventures.com
  Education: Electrical Engineering; Computer Engineering; MBA, Finance & Marketing
  Background: Oracle
  Nikos Iatropoulos, Regional Partner, Central US
  e-mail: nikosi@kairosventures.com
  Education: BSc, Computer Science, Columbia University; MBA, MIT Sloan School of Management
  Background: CEO, Lingospot; Senior Vice President of Business Development, Piksel; CEO, Upstream

1052 KAISER PERMANENTE VENTURES
One Kaiser Plaza
22nd Floor
Oakland, CA 94612

web: www.kpventures.com

Mission Statement: Supports Kaiser Permanente's mission and brand by investing in products and services that improve the health status of KP members and communities, enhance access to affordable quality health services, innovate ways for providers to organize and deliver healthcare, improve KP's cost structure, and access markets beyond KP's membership.

Geographic Preference: United States
Fund Size: $20 million
Founded: 1945
Average Investment: $1 million
Minimum Investment: $500,000
Investment Criteria: First Stage, Second Stage, Later Stage, Beta Sites, Strategic Alliance
Industry Group Preference: Medical Devices, Healthcare, Information Technology, Therapeutics, Diagnostics, Healthcare Information Technology, Healthcare Services
Portfolio Companies: BigHealth, CollectiveMedical Technologies, Ginger.io, Health Catalust, Ingenious Med, Kitcheck, MetricStream, Omada, Protenus, Proteus Digital Health, Rock Health, Startip + Health, Talix, Validic, Vidyo, BDNA, Concerro, Mageon, Healthline, NexlWeb, Silverlink

Key Executives:
  Chris Grant, Executive Managing Director
  e-mail: chris.m.grant@kp.org
  Education: BA Business/Finance, University of California Santa Barbara
  Background: Rockwell International
  Directorships: Five portfolio companies.
  Amy Belt Raimundo, Managing Director
  e-mail: amy.b.raimundo@kp.org
  Education: BA, Economics, Yale University; MBA, University of California, Berkeley
  Background: Chief Business Officer, Evidation Health; Vice President, Covident Venturesl Vice President, Advanced Technology Ventures; Management Consultant, APM/CSC Healthcare
  Sam Brasch, Senior Managing Dirrection
  e-mail: sam.e.brasch@kp.org
  Education: BA, Public Policy, Stanford University; MBA, Healthcare Management, Wharton School, University of Pennsylvania
  Background: Executive in Residence & Vice President, Frazier Healthcare Ventures; Global Management, Medtronic

1053 KANSAS VENTURE CAPITAL
40 Corporate Woods
Suite 200
9401 Indian Creek Parkway
Overland Park, KS 66210

Phone: 913-262-7117 Fax: 913-262-3509
e-mail: mparker@kvci.com
web: www.kvci.com

Mission Statement: An SBIC providing equity and mezzanine capital to Mid-Western based companies with talented management in a variety of industries for expansion, buy-out acquisition or recapitalization.

Geographic Preference: Mid-Western United States
Fund Size: $50 million
Founded: 1977
Average Investment: $1 - 3 million
Minimum Investment: $1 million
Investment Criteria: Mezzanine
Industry Group Preference: Diversified
Portfolio Companies: Airworx Construction Equipment & Supply, ALM Positioners, Arrow Material Handling Products, B12 Transportation Group, Bennett Tool & Die Company, The Carlson Company Inc., Carlson Products, Central States Bus Sales, Crain Hot Old Services, C&W Manufacturing and Sales, Cutler Repaving Inc., Delco Corp., Eagle Precision, English Boiler Tube, Full Vision, High Sierra Energy Partners, In2itive Bsuiness Solutions LLC, KCAS, Legacy Technologies Inc., Perennial Energy LLC, Presence From Innovation, Power I.T. LLC, Remtec Inc., Reynolds Polymer Technologies, Superior Boiler Works Inc., Transfer Tool Products, Vanguard Graphics International

Key Executives:
  Marshall D. Parker, President/CEO
  Education: BA, Kansas State University; CPA
  Background: Marketing, Allen Gibbs and Houlik; Management Services, Ernst & Young; Investment Banker, Blunt Ellis & Loewi; Co-Founder, Snelgrove Parker & Co.
  Brian Lueger, Principal
  Education: MS, Accountancy, Kansas State University; CPA
  Background: Senior Manager, Audit Practice, KPMG

1054 KAPOR CAPITAL

e-mail: info@kaporcapital.com
web: www.kaporcapital.com

Mission Statement: Kapor Capital is an investment fund based in Oakland, CA that invests in seed stage information technology companies which aspire to generate economic value and positive social impact. Investment sectors include but are not limited to education, health and consumer finance.

Geographic Preference: United States

381

Venture Capital & Private Equity Firms / Domestic Firms

Investment Criteria: Seed-Stage
Industry Group Preference: Information Technology, Education, Healthcare, Consumer Finance
Portfolio Companies: Accredible, Allovue, Always Hired, AngelList, Applauze, Asana, Atipica, BeneStream, Binti, Birdi, Bitly, Blockboard, BlocPower, Blokable, Bloom Technologies, Bolstr, Breakthrough, Brilliant, Call9, Captricity, Catchafire, Citizen, Citrus Lane, ClasDojo, Classkick, Cleanify, Clever, CodeHS, Codespark, Compaas, Compology, Constant Therapy, Desmos, Dropcam, Earn Up, EdCast, Edovo, Educents, Elation Health, Elevate, emocha Mobile Health, Endaga, Engrade, Enuma, Ethic, Fidelis, Flowtown, Formlabs, FounderDating, Front Row, Fundly, FutureAdvisor, Gengo, Genius Plaza, Get Satisfaction, Ginger.io, Glassbreakers, Gojee, Good Eggs, GroupRaise, Handle Financial, Healthify, HealthLoop, Health Sherpa, High Fidelity, Hingeto, Honor, Hopscotch, Human Dx, Hustle, inDinero, Inkling, Interviewing.io, Joonko, Jopwell, Josephine, Junyo, Kairos, Kiverdi, LeadGenius, Learners Guild, LendStreet, LendUp, Life360, Linden Lab, Livestar, Looksharp, Love With Food, Magoosh, Make School, Maker's Row, Managed By Q, Mercaris, Modria, Motion Math, Muzy, Mytonomy, Newsela, NoRedInk, NovoEd, OKpanda, Omada Health, Optimizely, Orchestra, Peel, Piazza, Pigeonly, Plum Perfect, Posterous, Propeller, Prosky, Proven, Rd Rabbit, Regalii, Revivn, SchoolMint, Schoolzilla, SendHub, Shift Payments, ShiftMessenger, Socialize, Sparked, Student Loan Genius, Style Seek, Sweep, Swing Education, Talent Sonar, Talko, Thrive, Tinybop, True Link, Twilio, Uber, UBiome, Uncharted Power, Velano Vascular, Verificient, Via, Visually,

Key Executives:
 Mitchell Kapor, Partner
 Background: Founder, Lotus Development Corporation; Co-Founder, The Electronic Frontier Foundation; Founding Chair, The Mozilla Foundation; Founding Investor, Linden Lab
 Freada Kapor Klein, Partner
 Background: Director of Organizational Development, Lotus Development Corporation

1055 KARLIN VENTURES
11755 Wilshire Boulevard
Suite 1400
Los Angeles, CA 90025

Phone: 310-806-9700
e-mail: info@karlinvc.com
web: www.karlinvc.com

Mission Statement: Karlin Ventures is an early-stage venture capital fund based in Los Angeles. Karlin Ventures is compiled of value-add partners helping entrepreneurs who take contrarian approaches to create impactful solutions to big, interesting problems. Karlin Ventures is an affiliate of Karlin Asset Management, a private investment firm managing over $1.4 billion of unleveraged equity capital.

Geographic Preference: United States, West Coast
Fund Size: $145 million
Average Investment: $250,000 - $2 million
Minimum Investment: $250,000
Investment Criteria: Early-Stage
Industry Group Preference: Education, Digital Media & Marketing, Healthcare, Financial Services, Consumer Products
Portfolio Companies: Bark, Bitium, Bridg. Brightfunnel, ChowNow, CREXi, DataRPM, Figs, The Grid, HelloTech, Honk, Investedin, Jukin Media, Kaleo, Laurel & Wolf, Markkit, Noun Project, Pathmatics, Percolata, Pixalate, Policy Genius, Preact, Prevoty, Retention Science, Saygent, ShipHawk, Social Annex, TetraScience, True Link, Verge Genomics, Victorious, Yoi, Cirro Secure, Game Mix, Gyft, Kimono, StrikeAd, Tonx, Walla.by

Key Executives:
 TX Zhuo, Managing Partner
 Education: BA, Economics & Mathematics, Wesleyan University; MBA, Stanford Graduate School of Business
 Background: CFO, Lit Motors; Innovation Endeavors; McKinsey & Co.

1056 KB PARTNERS
600 Central Avenue
Suite 325
Highland Park, IL 60035

Phone: 847-681-1270
e-mail: info@kbpartners.com
web: kbpartners.com

Mission Statement: Established for the purpose of pursuing investment opportunities in the golf and sports worlds. The principals of VSP plan to utilize their diverse entrepreneurial, real estate, financial, investment and management experience, along with extensive industry contacts, to pursue those select opportunities that provide the potential for the greatest return.

Founded: 2010
Industry Group Preference: Golf, Sports, Real Estate, Consumer Products
Portfolio Companies: Club Champion, GAGA, Hammerhead Navigation

Key Executives:
 Keith Bank, Founder/Managing Partner
 e-mail: keith@versp.com
 Education: BS, Economics, Wharton School; MBA, Kellogg Graduate School of Management, Northwestern University
 Background: Co-Founder, KB Partners; Principal, Hiffman Shaffer Associates
 Directorships: Kirtas Technologies, SteadyMed, Versatile Sports Partners, Club Champion Golf

1057 KB PARTNERS LLC
600 Central Avenue
Suite 390
Highland Park, IL 60035

Phone: 847-681-1270 Fax: 847-681-1370
e-mail: keith@kbpartners.com
web: www.kbpartners.com

Mission Statement: Provides equity financing for early-stage technology companies in the Midwest. KB's objective is to work with talented entrepreneurs and experienced managers to build market leading organizations.

Geographic Preference: Central US, Midwestern US, Chicago
Fund Size: $95 million
Founded: 1996
Average Investment: $1 - $5 million
Minimum Investment: $1 million
Investment Criteria: Seed, Early-Stage, First Round, Second Round
Industry Group Preference: Infrastructure, Information Technology, Telecommunications, Medical Devices, Semiconductors, Computer Hardware & Software, Industrial Services, Communications, Diagnostics, Engineering, Internet Technology
Portfolio Companies: Accumetrics, Active.com, Cadant, Cobotics, Cognitive Concepts, Corona Optical Systems, Data TV Networks, EthnicGrocer.Com, Exacq Technologies, Firefly Energy, iLink Global, Ischemia Technologies, Kirtas Technologies, LeagueLink, Mezzia, Midi, NetRegulus, Orbit Commerce, Performics, Rubicon Technology, Sarvega, Silver Creek, Verax Biomedical

Key Executives:
 Keith Bank, Co-Founder/CEO
 e-mail: keith@kbpartners.com
 Education: BSE, Wharton School, University of Pennsylvania; MBA, Kellogg School of Management,

Venture Capital & Private Equity Firms / Domestic Firms

Northwestern University
Background: Principal, Hiffman Shaffer Associates; Co-Founder, deep discount drugstore chain; Turnaround, women's apparel manufacturing & sales company; feature film financing for film - Heaven Is A Playground
Directorships: Chairman, Illinois Venture Capital Association; Chairman/Founder, Chicago Select Golf Invitational; NetRegulus; Data TV Networks; Kirtas Technologies
Raja M. Parvez, Venture Partner
e-mail: raja@kbpartners.com
Education: BS, Mechanical Engineering, University of Peshawar; MS, Industrial Engineering/Management Science, New York University
Background: President/CEO, Rubicon Technology Inc.; President, Optigain Inc.; COO, CyOptics Inc.
Directorships: Xerion Advanced Battery Corp., SiNode Systems Inc., Shasta Crystals Inc.

1058 KBL HEALTHCARE VENTURES
52 East 72nd Street
New York, NY 10021

Phone: 212-319-5555 Fax: 212-319-5591
e-mail: admin@kblvc.com
web: www.kblvc.com

Mission Statement: Physician-run venture capital firm dedicated to discovering and developing innovative companies that create real, lasting value within the U.S. healthcare system.

Geographic Preference: United States
Fund Size: $115 million
Founded: 1991
Minimum Investment: $100,000
Investment Criteria: Seed, Startup, First-Stage, Second-Stage, Early-Stage, Emerging Growth
Industry Group Preference: Biopharmaceuticals, Drug Development, Medical Devices, Healthcare Services, Information Technology
Portfolio Companies: Achillion Pharmaceuticals, Candela, CardioFocus, Magellan Health, Neuronetics, PneumRx, Prolong Pharmaceuticals, Summer

Zachary C. Berk, Managing Director
e-mail: zberk@kblhealthcare.com
Education: BS/Doctorate of Optometry, Pacific University
Background: Concord Health Group; Cambridge Heart; KBL Healthcare Acquisition
Directorships: Lumenos. Comprehensive Medical Management, Gynetics

Marlene R. Krauss, Managing Director
e-mail: mkrauss@kblhealthcare.com
Education: MBA, Harvard Business School; MD, Harvard Medical School; BA, Cornell University
Background: KBL Healthcare Acquisition; Concord Health Group; Cambridge Heart; Lumenos;
Directorships: Lumenos, APS Healthcare, Gynetics

1059 KEARNY VENTURE PARTNERS
One Embarcadero Center
Suite 3700
San Francisco, CA 94111

Phone: 415-875-7777
e-mail: info@kearnyvp.com
web: www.kearnyvp.com

Mission Statement: Kearny Venture Partners is a venture capital firm that invests exclusively in emerging drug and healthcare products. The firm seeks to find solutions to unsolved medical problems, and is willing to invest in innovative companies across a wide range of development stages and medical sectors.

Fund Size: $330 million
Average Investment: $10 - $15 million
Minimum Investment: $2 - $8 million
Investment Criteria: Early-Stage to Late-Stage

Industry Group Preference: Healthcare, Medical Devices, Pharmaceuticals
Portfolio Companies: Aerpio Therapeutics, Akebia Therapeutics, Baxano Surgical, Boreal Genomics, CVRx, Keryx, QuatRx Pharmaceuticals, Repros Therapeutics, SpinalMotion, Tandem Diabetes Care, TriVascular, ViewRay

Key Executives:

Caley Castelein MD, Founder/Managing Member
Education: AB, Harvard College; MD, University of California, San Francisco
Background: Founder & Managing Member, KVP Capital
Directorships: Alivecor, Boreal, Newbridge Pharmaceuticals, Neos Therapeutics, ViewRay, WellPartner, Waterstone Pharmaceuticals

Anupam Dalal MD, Managing Director
Education: BA, Economics, University of California, Berkeley; MD, University of California, San Francisco; MBA, Harvard Business School
Background: Flagship Ventures
Directorships: Aerpio Therapeutics, Akebia Therapeutics, Neurotech, NewBridge Pharmaceuticals, Nora Therapeutics

Jim Shapiro, Managing Director
Education: AB, Princeton University; MBA, Stanford University Graduate School of Business
Background: Co-Founder, SpinalMotion; Investment Banking, Alex. Brown; Associate, Goldman Sachs; Financial Analyst, Bank of America
Directorships: Baxano, CVRx, Hansen Medical, SpinalMotion, Tandem Diabetes Care, TranS1, TriVascular

Dick Spalding, Managing Director
Education: AB, Harvard College; JD, Columbia Law School
Background: Vice President & CFO, Portal Software; CFO, Fusion Medical Technologies; Alex. Brown & Sons; Brobeck Phleger & Harrison
Directorships: Align Technology, Kai Pharmaceuticals, SpinalMotion

Andrew Jensen, Chief Financial Officer
Education: BA, Finance & Accounting, University of California, Berkeley; CPA
Background: CFO, Liquid Realty Partners; Senior Controller, Gryphon Investors; Director, Finance, Sanderling Ventures

1060 KEGONSA CAPITAL PARTNERS
5520 Nobel Drive
Suite 150
Fitchburg, WI 53711

Phone: 308-310-4454
web: www.kegonsapartners.com

Mission Statement: Kegonsa Capital Partners pursues a Money for Minnows strategy. The primary goal of Money for Minnows is to be the first investor in new Wisconsin companies. Money for Minnows promotes new company creation by spreading venture capital across diverse industries, technologies and locations throughout Wisconsin.

Geographic Preference: Wisconsin
Founded: 2005
Investment Criteria: Seed-Stage, Early-Stage
Industry Group Preference: Manufacturing, Biotechnology, Pharmaceuticals, Medical Devices, Internet
Portfolio Companies: Jellyfish, Bio Systems, Idle Free, Semba Biosciences, Networked Insights, Stealth, Brazen, NanoMedex

Key Executives:

Ken Johnson, Managing Director
Background: Associate, Paramount Capital

383

Venture Capital & Private Equity Firms / Domestic Firms

1061 KEIRETSU FORUM
29 Orinda Way
Suite 415
San Francisco, CA 94563

e-mail: info@keiretsuforum.com
web: www.keiretsuforum.com

Mission Statement: Global investment community of private equity investors, venture capitalists and corporate/institutional investors with 47 chapters on three continents.

Geographic Preference: North America, Europe, Asia
Founded: 2000
Average Investment: $250,000 - $2 million
Investment Criteria: Early-stage
Industry Group Preference: Clean Technology, Consumer, Financial, Healthcare, Real Estate, Technology
Portfolio Companies: 20/20 GeneSystems, 5i Medical, Abom, Acceleration Systems, Agralogics, AlwaysOn, AMHC Healthcare, AnaBios Corporation, Aqueduct Critical Care, Asius Technologies, AttachedApps, BarTrendr, BlueCamroo, Building Energy, BYNDL, CareCap, Clearpath Robotics, Clinovo, Conceptua Math, Corvida Medical, Direct Lending Investments, Drever Capital Management, Embera Neurotherapeutics, EV Connect, Exergyn, Exponential Entertainment, Fairway America, Fingi, Fireman's Brew, Flight Office, Going Green, Graphene Technologies, HeatGenie, HoneyComb, House of Matriach, IBIS Networks, iHealtHome, Immunomic Therapeutics, Infantium, Iomando, Keonn, Kineta, Kiwi Crate, Lightpoint, Linkstorm, LiquidSpace, LumiThera, LYNK Capital, Minetta Brook, MobiCash, MOGL, Ninja Metrics, Nuritas, NuvoMed, Onics, Orpheus Interactive, OtoNexus Medical Technologies, OtoSense, Overlake Capital, Owlized, Pacific West Land, Perfect Point, PetHub, Precision Image Analysis, Plasticity, Plum, Pyatt/Broadmark Management, Quantion, RABBL, Respect Network, Respiratory Motion, RSportz, Safe-H2O, Savara Pharmaceuticals, Schiller Bikes, Scratch-It, Smart Planet Technologies, SnoBar Cocktails, Swyft, SYNQY, Tectonic Audio Labs, Temp Automation, TesoRx Pharma, Tether Technologies, Textile Based Delivery, ThinkSpider, Tilting Motor Works, TranscribeMe, U Grok It, Veristone Capital, VetDC, Viakoo, Voyager Pacific Capital, Wellesley Pharmaceuticals, Worldwise Education, Woven Orthopedics, YouSolar

Key Executives:
Randy Williams, Founder & CEO
415-493-9875
Education: University of California, Berkeley
Background: Co-founder & director, Diablo Valley Bank; President, Pacific Union Commercial Brokerage; Founder, Lamorinda National Bank; Managing Director, Kennedy-Wilson International

1062 KELSO & COMPANY
320 Park Avenue
24th Floor
New York, NY 10022

Phone: 212-751-3939 Fax: 212-223-2379
web: www.kelso.com

Mission Statement: Kelso & Company is a private equity firm that focuses its efforts and resources on investment opportunities in partnership with highly capable management teams in middle market companies.

Geographic Preference: United States, Canada
Fund Size: $5.1 billion
Founded: 1971
Average Investment: $100-250 million
Minimum Investment: $40 million
Investment Criteria: LBO
Industry Group Preference: Manufacturing, Communications, Retailing, Healthcare, Transportation, Chemicals, Media, Consumer Services
Portfolio Companies: 4Refuel, American Beacon, Audio Visual Services Corporation, Augusta Sportswear, Cronos, Delphin Shipping, EACOM Timber, Eagle Foods, Elara Caring, Ellis Communication Group, Foundation Consumer Healthcare, Global Geophysical Services, Harbor Community Bank, Hunt Marcellus, KdocTV Los Angeles, Logan's Roadhouse, Newport Group, Nivel, Oasis Outsourcing, Physicians Endoscopy, The Poseidon Companies, PowerTeam Services, Premia, Progressive-PMSI, Renfro, Risk Strategies, Sandler O'Neill & Partners, Sentinel Data Centers, Sirius, Southern Carlson, Tallgrass Energy, Tervita, Third Point Re, The Traxys Companies, Truck-Lite, U.S. LBM, Venari Resources, Zenith Energy

Key Executives:
Frank T Nickell, Chairman
212-751-3939
e-mail: fnickell@kelso.com
Education: BS Business Administration/Accounting, University of North Carolina
Background: Public Accountant, A.M. Pullen & Company; Member, American Institute of Certified Public Accountants; Director, The Bear Stearns Companies; BlackRock; Earle M. Jorgensen Company; Member, Board of Visitors of the University of North Carolia; Certified Public Accountant

Philip E Berney, Co-Cheif Executive Officer
e-mail: pberney@kelso.com
Education: BS Business Administration, University of North Carolina where he was a Morehead Scholar
Background: Senior Managing Director/Head High Yield Finance, The First Boston Corporation
Directorships: DEL Laboratories, DS Waters, EACOM Timber, Eagle Foods, PowerTeam Services, Sandler O'Neill & Partners, Venari Resources, Wilton Re

Frank J Loverro, Co-Chief Executive Officer
212-751-3939
e-mail: floverro@kelso.com
Education: BA Economics with distinction, University of Virginia
Background: Associate, Private Equity Investing, Clipper Group; High Yield Finance Group, CS First Boston
Directorships: Ajax Resources, Buckeye GP Holdings, Endo, Helios, Oceana Therapeutics, Physicians Endoscopy, Tallgrass Energy, Zenith Energy

Lynn Alexander, Managing Director
Education: BBA, Finance & Accounting, Texas Tech University; MBA, University of Michigan
Background: Director, Investment Banking, Merrill Lynch & Co.; Associate, Natural Resources Investment Banking, Kidder Peabody & Co.

Thomas R Wall, IV, Managing Director
e-mail: twall@kelso.com
Education: BS Business Administration with special attainments in Commerce, Washington & Lee University
Background: Lending Officer, Corporate Division, Chemical Bank
Directorships: Augusta Sportswear, B-Way, Charter, Nivel, Renfro, Sandler O'Neill & Partners, Sentinel, Transdigm

George E Matelich, Managing Director
e-mail: gmatelich@kelso.com
Education: MBA Finance/Business Policy, Stanford Grad. School of Business; Holds a Certificate in Management Consulting
Background: Mergers & Acquisitions, Corporate Finance, Lehman Brothers Kuhn Loeb; Consultant, Ernst & Whinney; Certified Public Accountant
Directorships: Charter, CVR Energy, EACOM Timber, Hunt Marcellus, Optigas, Venari Resources, WSI Waste Services

Michael B Goldberg, Managing Director
e-mail: mgoldberg@kelso.com
Education: BS Business Administration/Finance with high honors, University of Florida; JD, University of Virginia, member of the Order of the Coif, Law Review
Background: Managing Director/Co-head, Mergers & Acquisitions, The First Boston Corporation; Corporate

384

Venture Capital & Private Equity Firms / Domestic Firms

Law/Partner, Skadden, Arps, Slate, Meagher & Flom; Associate, Cravath, Swaine & Moore; Member, Phoenix House Foundation, Wilson Council of the Woodrow International Center for Scholars
Directorships: Buckeye GP Holdings, Cronos, Delphin Shipping, Eagle Bulk Shipping, Endo, KAR Auction Services, Oceana Therapeutics, Overwatch, Tallgrass Energy

David I Wahrhaftig, Managing Director
e-mail: dwahrhaftig@kelso.com
Education: BA Economics, Western Maryland College; MBA Finance, Wake Forest University; Holds a Certificate in Management Accounting
Background: Associate Director Mergers & Acquisitions/Management Consultant, Arthur Young & Company;
Directorships: Augusta Sportswear, B-Way, DS Waters, Endo, KAR Auction Services, Nivel, Renfro, Transdigm

Frank K Bynum, Jr, Managing Director
e-mail: fbynum@kelso.com
Education: BA History, University of Virginia
Background: Investment Analyst, New York Life Insurance Company
Directorships: Custom Buildings Products, Nivel, PSAV Presentation Services, Sentinel Data Centers, Sirius, Truck-Lite, U.S. LBM

Steve Dutton, Managing Director
Education: BS, Commerce, University of Virginia
Background: Investment Banking, Bear Stearns & Co.
Directorships: American Beacon, Newport Group, Oasis Outsourcing, Premia, PSAV Presentation Services, Risk Strategies, Sandler O'Neill & Partners, Third Point Re, Wilton Re

James J Connors II, Managing Director
e-mail: jconnors@kelso.com
Education: BA, History, College of William & Mary; JD, University of Virginia
Background: Associate, Debevoise & Plimpton
Directorships: Custom Building Products

Matt Edgerton, Managing Director
Education: BA, Economics & History, Duke University
Background: Investment Banking, Deutsche Bank
Directorships: Augusta Sportswear, EACOM Timber, Eagle Foods, Foundation Consumer Healthcare, Southern Carlson, U.S. LBM

Church M Moore, Managing Director
e-mail: cmoore@kelso.com
Education: BA, English, University of Virginia
Background: Associate, Investcorp International
Directorships: 4Refuel, DEL Laboratories, DS Waters, Elara Caring, Foundation Consumer Healthcare, Helios, KAR Auction Services, Physicians Endoscopy, Truck-Lite

Sandy Osborne, Managing Director
e-mail: sosborne@kelso.com
Education: BA, Government, Dartmouth College
Background: Associate, Summit Partners; Associate, Private Equity Group, JP Morgan & Co
Directorships: Ajax Resources, B-Way, Custom Building Products, CVR Energy, PowerTeam Services, Southern Carlson, Tallgrass Energy, U.S. LBM, Zenith Energy

Christopher L Collins, Managing Director
e-mail: ccollins@kelso.com
Education: BA, English, Duke University; MBA, Stanford Graduate School of Business
Background: Analyst, Stonington Partners
Directorships: American Beacon, Augusta Sportswear, Cronos, Eagle Bulk Shipping, Newport Group, Oasis Outsourcing, Premia, PSAV Presentation Services, Risk Strategies, Third Point Re

Alec Hufnagel, Managing Director
Education: BA, Economics, Dartmouth College
Background: Leveraged Finance, Deutsche Bank
Directorships: Sirius Computer Solutions, Zenith Energy

John Kim, Managing Director
Education: AB, Brown University; MBA, Harvard Business School
Background: Partner, Court Square Capital; Ivestor Relations & Marketing, Capital Z Investments; Sr. Fundraiser, J.P. Morgan

Mike Letourneau, Managing Director
Education: BA, Accounting, Michigan State University; CPA
Background: PrimeSource Building Products

Hank Mannix, Managing Director
Education: BS, Math & Economics, College of the Holy Cross
Background: Investment Banking, Credit Suisse First Boston
Directorships: Custom Building Products, Eagle Bulk Shipping, Elara Caring, Helios, Physicians Endoscopy, Poseidon Containers, PowerTeam Services, Sentinel Data Centers, Sirius

Howard Matlin, Managing Director
Education: BA, Political Science, Queens College; MBA, St. John's University
Background: CFO & Principal, Butler Capital Corporation; Deloitte & Touche; Colgate-Palmolive; Riverbank America

1063 KENMONT CAPITAL PARTNERS
401 Louisiana Street
Suite 800
Houston, TX 77002

Phone: 713-223-9922 Fax: 713-223-0930
Toll-Free: 877-337-8499

Mission Statement: Provides creative vehicles to generate attractive returns from opportunities in private equity utilizing disciplined institutional investment processes.

Fund Size: $60 million
Founded: 1998
Average Investment: $5 million
Minimum Investment: $500,000
Investment Criteria: All Stages
Industry Group Preference: Diversified

Key Executives:

Donald R Kendall Jr, Founding Managing Director/CEO
e-mail: dkendall@kenmontcap.com
Education: AB, Hamilton College
Background: Palmetto Partners; Cogen Technologies Capital Company LP; Morgan Stanley; Drexel Burnham; First Boston
Directorships: Cogen Technologies Energy Group, Fremont Partners, Rosecliff, Growth Capital Partners, Murray's Discount Auto Parts, Finalco, MetOx

Laura Dotson, Managing Director
e-mail: ijdotson@kenmontcap.com
Education: BBA, University of Cincinnati
Background: Shells Pension Trust; FBI

John T Harkrider, Managing Director/CFO
e-mail: jkharkrider@kenmontcap.com
Education: BBA, Stephen F Austin State Universtiy
Background: Consolidated Graphics; Hines Interests Limited Partnerhsip; Arthur Andersen, CPA

1064 KENTUCKY HIGHLANDS INVESTMENT CORPORATION
PO Box 1738
362 Old Whitley Road
London, KY 40743-1738

Phone: 606-864-5175 Fax: 606-864-5194
web: www.khic.org

Mission Statement: Locates aspiring entrepreneurs and finances new businesses with capital intended for development; operating in a fiscally conservative manner, makes equity investments, loans, and assists businesses in developing financing packages leveraged by extensive contacts.

Geographic Preference: Southeastern Kentucky

Venture Capital & Private Equity Firms / Domestic Firms

Fund Size: $40 million
Founded: 1968
Average Investment: $2 million
Minimum Investment: $500
Investment Criteria: Startup, Expansion, Buyout, Divestiture
Industry Group Preference: Manufacturing
  Jerry Rickett, President/CEO
  Education: Cumberland College; MS, Eastern Kentucky University
  Background: Chairman, Corbin Planning Commission; Kentucky Tourism Association; Corbin Industrial Commission; Director, Cumberland Valley Area Development District
  Brenda McDaniel, EVP/CFO
  Education: MBA, Eastern Kentucky University; Accounting, Union College; BS, Business Administration/Accounting, Cumberland College
  Background: National Congress for Community Economic Development; Vice Chairman, Rural Local Initiative Support Corporation
  Mark Bolinger, Vice President, Business Lending
  Education: BS, Business Adminisration, Berea College
  Background: Mountain Association for Community Economic Development

1065 KEPHA PARTNERS
303 Wyman Street
Suite 300
Waltham, MA 02451

web: www.kephapartners.com

Mission Statement: Kepha Partners is a venture capital firm that invests in pre-seed, seed, and early stage companies.

Fund Size: $100 million
Investment Criteria: Seed-Stage, Early Stage
Industry Group Preference: Technology
Portfolio Companies: Azuki, Boundless, Goby, Linkable Networks, Mavrck, NorthPage, OwnerIQ, Paradigm4, Shareaholic, Triblio, Volt DB

Key Executives:
  Jo Tango, Founder/Partner
  Education: BA, Yale University; MBA, Harvard Business School
  Background: General Partner, Highland Capital Partners; Bain & Company
  Eric Hjerpe, Partner
  Education: Brown University; MS, Management, Massachusetts Institute of Technology Sloan School of Management
  Background: Partner, AtlasVenture; Siebel Systems; Center for Information Systems Research

1066 KERN WHELAN CAPITAL
One Ferry Building
Suite 255
San Francisco, CA 94111

Phone: 415-685-0628 Fax: 415-675-8794
e-mail: info@kernwhelan.com
web: www.kernwhelan.com

Mission Statement: Kern Whelan Capital manages a diversified investment portfolio stretching from new ventures to established and profitable businesses across many industry sectors. We invest in only a few companies each year, and partner with outstanding management teams for the long term. While we typically are active members of the board of directors for our businesses, we do not seek involvement in their daily operations. Through a long term approach to the liquidity horizon, Kern Whelan investments are not beholden to a single exit strategy, but are instead opportunistic about investor capital return whether through M&A, IPO, recap, dividend, or otherwise.

Portfolio Companies: Arcadia Communications, Cohera Medical, InvestCloud, Quri, TAB Products, UserTesting, Vignette Wine Country Soda

Key Executives:
  Jay Kern, Founder\General Partner
  Education: BA, Princeton University; JD, MBA, University of Chicago
  Background: Managing Director, Reynolds DeWitt & Co.; McKinsey & Company
  J.P. Whelan, General Partner
  Education: BA, MA, Stanford University; JD, University of Chicago Law School
  Background: M&A Group, JPMorgan, Hambrecht & Quist

1067 KERRY CAPITAL ADVISORS
260 Franklin St.
6th Floor
Boston, MA 02110

Phone: 617-717-8521
e-mail: tjanes@kerrycapital.com
web: www.kerrycapital.com

Mission Statement: Kerry Capital Advisors, Inc., is a principal and advisory firm focused on middle market private equity investment opportunities in the North America and Europe. The firm has been founded by Thomas W. Janes who has a successful 25-year private equity and investment banking track record in working with superior management teams to provide creative capital solutions to a wide variety of financing transactions.

Average Investment: $5 - $50 million
Investment Criteria: Leverage Buyouts, Recapitalizations, Growth Financings
Industry Group Preference: Manufacturing, Consumer Products, Business Products & Services, Healthcare, Logistics, Distribution, Energy, Media, Publishing, Technology, Software
Portfolio Companies: Abbey Healthcare Staffing, Alarmguard Holdings, Ascent Pediatrics, Benchmark, Claricom Solutions, Clark, Cutters Wireline Services, D2Hawkeye, DairyMart, Dalbo, EnvironWorks, Generation Health, Jenzabar, NextWave, Paddock Pools Patios & Spas, PHC, Plymouth Opportunity REIT, Precision Components, Revstone, Rule, Vik Brothers Insurance

Key Executives:
  Thomas Janes, Founder/CEO
  e-mail: tjanes@kerrycapital.com
  Education: AB, Harvard College; MBA, Harvard Business School
  Background: Managing Director, Lincolnshire; Co-Founder/Managing Director, Triumph Capital Group

1068 KESTREL ENERGY PARTNERS
520 Broad Hollow Road
Melville, NY 11747

Phone: 631-421-2711 Fax: 631-214-4238

Industry Group Preference: Energy, Oil & Gas
Portfolio Companies: Downeast LNG, Kestrel Heat

Key Executives:
  Paul A Vermylen Jr, President/Managing Director
  e-mail: vermylen@kestrelenergypartners.com

1069 KHOSLA VENTURES
2128 Sand Hill Road
Menlo Park, CA 94025

Phone: 650-376-8500 Fax: 650-926-9590
e-mail: kv@khoslaventures.com
web: www.khoslaventures.com

Venture Capital & Private Equity Firms / Domestic Firms

Mission Statement: Khosla Ventures is a venture capital firm that invests in innovative technology opportunities across a wide range of industries.
Fund Size: $5 billion
Founded: 2004
Investment Criteria: Early & Late-Stage, Seed Fund, Very Early-Stage Experiments
Industry Group Preference: Consumer, Enterprise, Education, Advertising, Financial Services, Semiconductors, Health, Big Data, Agriculture, Sustainable Energy, Robotics, Chemicals, Storage, Transportation, Space
Portfolio Companies: Affirm, Aguamarina, Akash Systems, AliveCor, Alpine Oral Tech, AltaRock Energy, Apton Biosystems Inc., Arevo, Artrendex, At-Bay, Bay Labs Inc., Berkshire Grey, Bidgely, BigSwitch, BioConsortia, BlockStream, Boku, Boosted Boards, Bridge International Academies, Bungalow, Cadre, Caelux Corporation, Calera, Canary Connect Inc., Carrot Inc., Chain, Citus Data, Coda Project Inc., Color Genomics, Consumer Physics, Cylance, Datera, DB Networks, Deep Genomics Inc., Digital Alloys, DoorDash, eGenesis, Eight, Eligo Bioscience, Ellipsis Health, EtaGen, Ethos Lending, Even, Everlane, Faire, Feetz, Forward, Fundbox, Fundera, Genalyte, Ghost, Giant.AI, Ginger.io, GitLab, Go, Grokker, Guardant Health, HeartVista, Helium Systems, Homebase, Imply, Impossible Foods, Inflammatix Inc., Instacart, Judicata, Just Inc., Karius Inc., Katerra Inc., Kiddom, Koding, Kumu Networks, Lookout, Lumiata, MDalgorithms Inc., Medisas, MemSQL, Mesosphere, MetaMind, Mojo Vision, Momentum Machines, NakedPoppy, Natron Energy, Neurotrack, Nimble Pharmacy, NuTek Salt, Okta, Opendoor, Opentrons, Ori, Owl Cameras Inc., PatternEx, PayNearMe, Pellion, Plastiq, Plum, Pymetrics, Q Bio, Quantopian, QuantumScape, Quartzy, Realm, Replika, Roofstock, Rubrik, Scaled Inference, Scipher Medicine, Scribd, Silicium Energy, Siren Care Inc., Soraa, Spyce Inc., Square, Stripe, Tapingo, TerraPower, Theatro, Tile, Toytalk, True Accord, Truework, Tule, Two Pore Guys Inc., Ukko Inc., Upstart Network, Varentec, Velo3D, Vert, Vibrado,

Key Executives:
Vinod Khosla, Founding General Partner
e-mail: ovk@khoslaventures.com
Education: BS, Electrical Engineering, Indian Institute of Technology; MS, Biomedical Engineering, Carnegie Mellon University; MBA, Stanford University Graduate School of Business
Background: Founder, Daisy Systems; Sun Microsystems; General Partner, Kleiner Perkins Caufield and Byers
Samir Kaul, Founding General Partner
e-mail: sk@khoslaventures.com
Education: BS, Biology, University of Michigan; University of Maryland; MBA, Harvard Business School
Background: Flagship Ventures; CEO, Codon Devices; TIGR
David Weiden, Partner
e-mail: dw@khoslaventures.com
Education: BA, Organizational Behavior & Economics, Harvard University; MIT; New York University
Background: Morgan Stanley; Netscape; SVP, Marketing & Business Development, Tellme Networks; McCaw Cellular; AOL
Sven Strohband, Chief Technology Officer
e-mail: sst@khoslaventures.com
Education: BS, Mechanical Engineering, Purdue University; PhD, Mechanics & Computation, Stanford University
Background: CTO, Mohr Davidow Ventures; Project Manager, Electronics Research Lab, Volkswagen
Brian Byun, Venture Partner
e-mail: bb@khoslaventures.com
Education: SB, Electrical Engineering & Computer Science, MIT
Background: Rhapsody Networks; AOL; Netscape; HP; VMware

1070 KICKSTART SEED FUND
2750 East Cottonwood Parkway
Suite 160
Cottonwood Heights, UT 84121
Phone: 801-308-0440
web: www.kickstartseedfund.com

Mission Statement: Kickstart is a seed venture fund dedicated to kickstart companies in the Mountain West by aligning technology creators, industry, entrepreneurs, and capital sources behind the funding and mentoring of seed investments.
Geographic Preference: Mountain West
Fund Size: $8 million
Founded: 2008
Portfolio Companies: Alianza, Artemis, Banyan, Big Squid, Blyncsy, Bookly.co, Brainstorm, Bubble, Catheter Connections, C7 Data Centers, Capshare, Chargeback, Chatbooks, CoNextions, Converus, Cotopaxi, DirectScale, Disco, EcoScraps, Estify, Galileo, Grow, Havenly, Hire Vue, Idaciti, Infusion Soft, In Go, Jack Rabbit, Janiis, Juxta Labs, Lineagen, Lucid Software, Mainframe, Market Dial, Nav, Needle, Nuvi, Omadi Mobile Management, Operational Results, Panoptic Security, Pebble Post, Penblade, PhotoPharmics, Podium, Pop Art, Power Practical, qZZR, Rackware, Radiate Media, Robotic Skies, Room Choice, Ryvers, Sage Bin, Sales Rabbit, Savonix, Self Lender, Simple Citizen, SpinGo, Stance, Studio Design, Suralink, T3S Technologies, Taskeasy, Teal, Teem, Veritract, VidAngel, Vutara, Vutiliti, Wave, ZenPrint, Cheddar Up, Homie, Monarx, Mountain Hub, Nanobox, Reaction, Trilumina, Zerista, GroSocial, eVisit, Wavelet, Fixes 4 Kids, JSK Therapeutics, Campus Founders Fund, ConexED, Blue Matador, Rags, Cake, Vence, Wastewater Compliance Systems, Fuze Network

Key Executives:
Gavin Christensen, Managing Director
Education: BS, Economics, Brigham Young University; MBA, Kellogg School of Management
Background: Principal, vSpring; Vertical Strategy Associate, Google
Directorships: Chargeback Guardian, Fuze Network, Grosocial, Jackrabbit Systems, Juxta Labs, NanoMR, Panoptic Security, Symbiot, Zenprint, Zerista
Dalton Wright, Partner
Education: BA, Finance, University of Utah; MA, International Studies, Lauder Institute; MBA, Wharton School, University of Pennsylvania
Background: Alta Ventures
Directorships: Big Squid, DirectSale
Alex Soffe, Administrative Partner
Education: BS, Accounting, University of Utah
Background: Director of Finance, vSpring/Signal Peak

1071 KIDD & COMPANY
1455 East Putnam Avenue
Old Greenwich, CT 06870
Phone: 203-661-0070 **Fax:** 203-661-1839
e-mail: wkidd@kiddcompany.com
web: www.kiddcompany.com

Mission Statement: A principal investment firm that designs businesses that transform their industry segments combined with the hands-on involvement required to successfully execute those strategies.
Founded: 1976
Minimum Investment: $10 million
Investment Criteria: LBO
Industry Group Preference: Industrial Services, Consumer Products
Portfolio Companies: Chatham Technologies, Colerain RV, Imaginetics, iPacesetters, Logistyx Technologies, Nexcore Technology, Numet

387

Venture Capital & Private Equity Firms / Domestic Firms

Key Executives:
William J Kidd, Founding Partner
e-mail: wkidd@kiddcompany.com
Education: BA, MBA, Cornell University
Gerard A Debiasi, Partner
e-mail: gdebiasi@kiddcompany.com
Education: BA, Economics, Summa Cum Laude, Dartmouth College; MBA, Harvard Business School
Background: Chatham Technologies
Matthew A Cook, Principal
e-mail: mcook@kiddcompany.com
Education: BS, Accounting, BS, Business Administration, Villanova Univeristy; MBA Yale University School of Managemet
Background: MHT Partners; Canaccord Adams; Braemar Energy Ventures; PricewaterhouseCoopers
James G Benedict, Principal
e-mail: jbenedict@kiddcompany.com
Education: BA, Baylor University; PhD, International Economics, Columbia University
Background: Senior Managing Director & Chief Talent Officer, Spencer Trask; Managing Director, Diversified Search Companies
Kenneth J Heuer, Principal
e-mail: kheuer@kiddcompany.com
Education: BS, Civil Engineering, Lehigh University; MBA, New York University Stern School of Business
Background: Managing Director, Spencer Trask; Investment Banker, JPMorgan

1072 KINETIC VENTURES
Two Wisconsin Circle
Suite 660
Chevy Chase, MD 20815

Phone: 301-652-8066
web: www.kineticventures.com

Mission Statement: Seeks partnerships with entrepreneurs dedicated to building the leading companies in high-growth market segments.

Geographic Preference: United States
Fund Size: $100 million
Founded: 1985
Average Investment: $7 million
Minimum Investment: $2 million
Investment Criteria: Early, Growth, Seed, Late-Stages
Industry Group Preference: Internet Technology, Information Technology, Communications, Clean Technology
Portfolio Companies: 9Lenses, AnyPresence, APX, Calix, Cardlytics, Clear Standards, Coraid, Cyan, Genband, HotSchedules, Instant, InterModal Data, ITC Capital Partners, Kwater, Lease Term Solutions, Logic Blox Predixlix, Navistone, PlumSilce, ProctorFree, Schoox, Seasoned Staq, Tower Cloud, Vertical Acuity, Virtual Instruments, Vizbee, Weather Analytics, Zift Solutions

Other Locations:
75 Fifth Street NW
Suite 316
Atlanta, GA 30308-1060
Phone: 404-995-8811

Key Executives:
Jake Tarr Jr., Managing Director
301-652-8066
Education: BA, Roanoke College; MBA, Harvard Business School
Background: Goldman, Sachs and Company; Bank of New York
Directorships: Mycotech
William Heflin, Managing Director
301-652-8066
Education: MS, BS, Mechanical Engineering, University of Illinois; MSM, MIT, Sloan School of Management
Background: Research Investment Advisors, Marcam Corporation, IBM

Nelson Chu, Managing Director
404-995-8811
Education: BS, Electrical Engineering, Virginia Tech; MS, Electrical Engineering, MIT; MBA, Harvard Business School
Background: Management Consultant, McKinsey & Company; Development Manager, Oracle Corporation
Cam Lanier, Senior Director
Background: Founding Investor & Chairman, Powertel; Founding Investor, Mindspring
Directorships: Cardlytics, LeaseTerm Solutions, Tower Cloud, Red Book Connect, LogicBox-Predictix, Chairman, ITC Holdings Company

1073 KINSEY HILLS GROUP
PO Box 999
Menlo Park, CA 94026-0999

e-mail: ekinsey@mac.com

Portfolio Companies: Hotswap, Labmeeting, Mill River Labs, Scribd

Key Executives:
Michael Hills, Co-Founding Partner
Education: BS, Political Science, University of Illinois, Urbana-Champaign
Background: CEO, MJH Capital; SVP Operations, Ariba; Oracle Corporation
Edward Kinsey, Co-Founding Partner
Education: BBA, University of Toledo; CPA
Background: CEO, Co-Founder, Quueue; CEO, Determination Ventures

1074 KIRENAGA
66 Palmer Avenue
Suite 49
Bronxville, NY 10708

Phone: 914-202-6046
web: kirenaga.com

Mission Statement: Kirenaga is a Japenese term used to describe a knife or sword blade. Kirenaga represents the principles they aspire to embody as a company — to stay sharp and find and maintain a distinctive edge in everything they do.

Other Locations:
189 S Orange Avenue
Suite 1400
Orlando, FL 32801

Key Executives:
David Scalzo, Founder/Managing Partner
Education: BS, MBA, Northwestern University
Background: Co-Founder/CFO, AdvisorEngine Inc.; COO, Credit Suisse; Managing Director, Bear Stearns; Director, Operations, Precision Plating Company, Chicago
Terrence Berland, Managing Partner
Education: University of Notre Dame; MBA, Northwestern University
Background: CEO, Violet Defense Group; Officer, US Navy; Instructor, Naval Nuclear Power School

1075 KLEINER PERKINS
2750 Sand Hill Road
Menlo Park, CA 94025

e-mail: plans@kpcb.com
web: www.kpcb.com

Mission Statement: Kleiner Perkins is committed to helping entrepreneurs build sustainable technology businesses. For thirty years they have invested in hundreds of market-defining ventures and are constantly on the lookout for promising ideas that either invents new business categories or radically alters existing ones.

Fund Size: $4.6 billion
Founded: 1972

Venture Capital & Private Equity Firms / Domestic Firms

Industry Group Preference: Biotechnology, Communications, Computer Related, Electronic Components, High Technology, Information Technology, Medical & Health Related, Green Technology, Life Sciences

Portfolio Companies: 3-V Biosciences, Aeye, Affectiva, Airbnb, Airtime, Alkira, Ambiqmicro, Amprius, AngelList, Apporbit, Aquion Energy, Area1, Audius, Ayasdi, Beam, Better, BetterWorks, Beyond Meat, Border X Lab, Breathe, Bulletin, Bump, ClearStory, CloudPhysics, Codecademy, CollectiveMedical, Coursera, Crossbar, Datameer, Datastax, DIY, DJI, DoorDash, Drawbridge, Duolingo, Dust Identity, Egnyte, Endame, Enjoy, Epic Games, EssenceHealthcare, Expansion Therapeutics, Farmers Business Network, Feather, Figma, Fleksy, Flipboard, FLX Bio, Fullstory, GeneralRadar, GoEuro, GraphIQ, Gusto, Handshake, Helix, Hixme, Hollar, Houzz, Incorta, Indiegogo, Inspirato, Instacart, Instartlogic, Intercom, Ionic, IronNet Cybersecurity, Jask, Kapwing, Knack, Kinsa, Labelbox, Leanplum, LegalZoom, Livongo, Looker, Magic Leap, Mango Health, Mason Finance, mCube, Mist, Mobcrush, Motiv, N3twork, Nav, Netlify, Newsela, Nextdoor, Nuna, Nurx, Packagd, Paviliondata, Peloton, Pinger, Pinterest, Plaid, Plastiq, Prisma, Productboard, Progyny, Proxy, Puppet, QuantumScape, Qumulo, Remind, Rentmatix, Rent The Runway, Reputation.com, Ripcord, Robinhood, Segment, SessionM, Shape Security, Shoof Technologies, Slack, Smile Direct Club, SpinLaunch, Stance, SoundCloud, SpotAHome, Spruce, Strip, Synack, Tally, Terminal, The Wing, Tmunity, Toss, Tradesy, Trendyol.com, TrueCaller, Trusona, Tulip, Turo, UiPath, Ujet, UntuckIt, Uber, UpStart, Uship, Weem, Victorious, Viz.ai, voloAgri, Willo, Xendit, Zaarly, Zazzle, Zumper

Other Locations:
Unit 2101, BEA Finance Tower
66 Hua Yuan Shi Qiao Road
Pudong
Shanghai 200120
China

Key Executives:
Brook Byers, Founder/Advisor
e-mail: brookb@kpcb.com
Education: MBA, Stanford University; BA, Electrical Engineering, Georgia Tech
Background: Director, Idec Pharmaceuticals; President/Director, Western Association of Venture Capitalists; Contributing Author
Directorships: University of California, SF Medical Foundation; California Healthcare Institute; New Schools Foundation; Stanford Eye Council; USCF Capital Campaign; Asian Art Museum, SF

Bing Gordon, Advisor
e-mail: bingg@kpcb.com
Education: BA, Yale University; MBA, Stanford University
Background: Chief Creative Officer, Electronic Arts

Beth Seidenberg, Advisor
e-mail: beths@kpcb.com
Education: BS, Barnard College; MD, University of Miami
Directorships: 3-V Biosciences, Breathe Technologies, Expansion Therapeutics, FLX Bio, Hixme, Kinsa, Progyny, Tmunity

Ilya Fushman, Partner
Education: PhD, Applied Physics, MS, Electrical Engineering, Stanford University; BS, Physics, Caltech
Background: General Partner, Index Ventures; Head of Product, Dropbox; Principal, Khosla Ventures; Director Of Technology, Solar Junction
Directorships: DUST Identity, Labelbox, Plastiq, Productboard, Robinhood, UiPath

Mamoon Hamid, Partner
Education: BS, Electrical Engineering, Purdue University; MS, Stanford University; MBA, Harvard Business School
Background: Co-Founder & General Partner, Social Capital; Partnerm US Venture Partners; Xilinx

Directorships: Alkira, Figma, Intercom, Kapwing, Mist Systems, Netlify, Prisma, Slack, Tally, Terminal.io, Viz.ai

Wen Hsieh, Partner
e-mail: wenh@kpcb.com
Education: BS, MS, PhD, Electrical Engineering, Caltech
Background: McKinsey & Company; Founder, OnChip Technologies
Directorships: AEye, Ambiq Micro, Amprius, Crossbar, Desktop Metal, DJI, General Radar, mCube, Motiv, Pavilion Data, Proxy Technologies, Qumulo, Ripcord, Shoof Technologies, SpinLaunch

Ted Schlein, Partner
e-mail: teds@kpcb.com
Education: BA, Economics, University of Pennsylvania
Background: Fortify Software; Symantec; DeVenCI
Directorships: App Orbit, Area 1 Security, Ayasdi, Endgame, FullStory, Incorta, Inspirato, Ionic Security, IronNet Cybersecurity, Jask, Reputation.com, Segment, Shape Security, Synack, ujet

1076 KLINE HILL PARTNERS
325 Greenwich Avenue
3rd Floor
Greenwich, CT 06830

Phone: 203-987-6120
e-mail: info@klinehill.com
web: www.klinehill.com

Mission Statement: Kline Hill focuses on the private equity secondary market with sellers of all types.

Fund Size: $1 Billion
Founded: 2015

Key Executives:
Michael Bego, Founder/Managing Partner
203-340-2463
e-mail: mike.bego@klinehill.com
Education: BS, Cornell University; MBA, Columbia University
Background: Partner, Willowridge Partners; Consultant, McKinsey & Co.

1077 KNIGHTSBRIDGE ADVISERS
122 SW Frank Phillips Boulevard
Bartlesville, OK 74003

Phone: 918-336-0978 Fax: 918-336-0824
web: www.knightsbridgeusa.com

Mission Statement: A registered investment adviser that assists European and North American institutional investors to invest in leading early stage venture capital partnerships and specialist public managers that specialize in 'high delta' type companies.

Fund Size: $1.1 billion
Founded: 1983
Minimum Investment: $2,000,000
Investment Criteria: Early-Stage
Industry Group Preference: Communications, Computer Related, Internet Technology, Medical & Health Related

Other Locations:
125 Cambridge Park Drive
Suite 400B
Cambridge, MA 02140
Phone: 617-354-0042 **Fax:** 617-876-0204

Key Executives:
Joel Rommines, Founder
e-mail: jr@knightsbridgeUSA.com
Education: BS, Economics, Drury College
Background: Consultant, Horsley Bridge & Partners; Executive Director, Orion Bank Limited; Citibank NA

Barbara Piette, Managing Principal
Education: BS, Boston College; MBA, Harvard Business School
Background: General Partner, Charles River Ventures; Partner, Schroder Ventures; President, Blackwood Capital

Venture Capital & Private Equity Firms / Domestic Firms

George Arnold, Managing Principal
Education: Swiss Institute of Technology; MS, Electrical Engineering, Stanford University; MBA, Santa Clara University
Background: Director, Citigroup Private Equity
Matthew Ahern, Managing Principal
Education: BA, Boston University; MBA, FW Olin Graduate School of Business, Babson College
Background: Managing Director, Merrill Lynch; Founder & Director, Capitalyst Ventures; Fleet Bank

1078 KNOX CAPITAL
350 N Orleans Street
Suite 9000n
Chicago, IL 60654

web: knox-cap.com

Mission Statement: Knox capital aims to dispense with traditional private equity and prides themmselves on being more nimble and more flexible. They pinpoint where they see potential growth, then seek out partners who match those criteria.

Key Executives:
Alex Gregor, Founder/Partner
312-402-1425
e-mail: aeg@knox-cap.com
Education: BBA, University of Michigan; MBA, Northwestern University, Kellogg School of Management
Background: VP, Pfingsten Partners
Mike Bryant, Partner
708-837-2632
e-mail: mb@knox-cap.com
Education: BBA, University of St. Francis; MBA, MIT Sloan School of Management
Background: Co-Founder/CEO, nSource; President, Legal Services, Integreon
Peter Pacelli, Principal
847-494-4747
e-mail: pjp@knox-cap.com
Education: BA, Yale University; MBA, University of Chicago
Background: Bank of America; Wind Point Partners; Victory Views; Intelligence Officer, US Navy

1079 KODIAK CAPITAL
260 Newport Center Drive
Newport Beach, CA 92660

Phone: 949-432-6900

Mission Statement: A private equity firm investing in pharmaceutical, cannabis, biotech, and Health & Wellness companies.

Geographic Preference: North America
Founded: 2009
Average Investment: $1 million to $25 million
Minimum Investment: $1 million to $5 million
Investment Criteria: Lower Middle Market; $5-$500 Million in Revenue
Industry Group Preference: Cannabis, Agriculture, Pharmaceuticals, Biotech, Health & Wellness
Portfolio Companies: OWCP Pharmaceutical Research, Affinor Growers, Nutritional High, MyDx, Pazoo, Cür, CannaSys Inc., CannaPharmaRx, UCann, Empire Global, THaT, Rx Safes, Icon Vapor, Soligenix, Uluru, Signal Bay Inc., Upper, Corgreen Technologies, Music Of Your Life

Other Locations:
600 B Street
San Diego, CA 92101

1080 KODIAK VENTURE PARTNERS
PO Box 550225
Waltham, MA 02455

Phone: 781-214-6855 Fax: 978-293-1003
web: www.kodiakvp.com

Mission Statement: Kodiak Venture Partners is a seed and early stage venture capital firm focused on commitment.
Geographic Preference: North America
Fund Size: $681 million
Founded: 1999
Investment Criteria: Seed, Early
Industry Group Preference: Communications, Semiconductors, Software, Information Technology, Wireless, Internet, Digital Media & Marketing, Healthcare Information Technology
Portfolio Companies: Airwide Solutions, ALIS, Allegro Diagnostics, Application Security, AppNexus, Astadia, AuroraNetics, Azimuth Systems, BTI Photonic Systems, ChannelAdvisor Corporation, CXO Systems, Chaoticom, CipherOptics, Cortina Systems, DAFCA, Egenera, Enfora, Extreme Packet Devices, Fluxion Biosciences, GTESS Corporation, GlassHouse Technologies, GreenLight Biosciences, Groove Mobile, High Roads, iAmplify, Ideeli, IE-Engine, IMlogic, Kadient, Legra Systems, Live Gamer, Lumicell, Millennial Net, Mindreef, Motia, Newforma, Potentia Semiconductor, Pragmatech Software, Qvidian, Raza MicroElectronics, RMI Corporation, RulesPower, Sentito Networks, Silicon Dimensions, SIMtone, SpaceClaim Corporation, Symwave, TRA, Taral Networks, TeraConnect, Tiaris, Tropic Networks, uLocate, Vesta Retail Network, Vette, Watchfire, Weather Trends International, WHERE, Wireless China

Key Executives:
Dave Furneaux, Founder/Managing Partner
Education: BA, Colorado College
Background: Furneaux & Company; Chrysalis Symbolic Design; Telecomunications Analyst, Natioal Conference
Directorships: GreenLight Biosciences, Lumicell, Qvidian, Fluxion
Lou Volpe, Managing Partner
Education: BA, Tufts University; MBA, Boston University
Background: ArrowPoint Communications; GeoTel Communications; Parametric Technology
Directorships: Atria, Softdesk
Chip Meakem, Managing Partner
Education: BA, Cornell University; MBA, Columbia University
Background: Draper Fisher Juvetson Gotham; Interactive Imaginations

1081 KOHLBERG & COMPANY LLC
111 Radio Circle
Mount Kisco, NY 10549

Phone: 914-241-7430
web: www.kohlberg.com

Mission Statement: A leading US private equity firm which acquires middle market companies.

Geographic Preference: United States
Fund Size: $3.7 billion
Founded: 1987
Average Investment: $60 million
Minimum Investment: $15 million
Investment Criteria: LBO, MBO, Recaps
Industry Group Preference: Manufacturing, Service Industries, Healthcare Services, Consumer Products, Building Materials & Services, Business Products & Services, Financial Services
Portfolio Companies: AGY Holding Corporation, Alitacare, Aurora Products Group, Bauer Performance Sports Ltd., BioScrip, Inc., Cadence, Chronos Life Group, CIBT, Concrete Technologies Worldwide, e+ Cancer Care, Franklin Energy, Interstate Hotels & Resorts, K2-MDV Holdings, Katy Industries, Inc., Kellermeyer Bergensons Services, MarketCast, Nellson Nutraceutical, Nielsen & Bainbridge, Packaging Dynamics, Inc., Osmose, Phillips-Medisize Corporation, Pittsburgh Glass Works, Risk Strategies Company, Sabre Industries, Inc., Sara Lee Frozen Bakery,

Venture Capital & Private Equity Firms / Domestic Firms

Senneca Holdings, SouthernCare, Inc., Specialty Care, Spinal Elements, Stanadyne Corporation, Standard Parking Corporation, SVP Worldwide, Trico Products, Inc., U.S. Retirement & Benefits Partners, U.S. Risk

Key Executives:
James A Kohlberg, Chairman
Education: BA, Golden Gate University; MBA, New York University
Background: Merrill Lynch; Kohlberg Kravis Roberts & Co.
Directorships: Troon Golf, LLC
Samuel P Frieder, Managing Partner
Education: AB, Harvard College
Background: Security Pacific Business Credit
Gordon H Woodward, Partner, Chief Investment Officer
Education: AB, Harvard College
Background: Financial Analyst, James D Wolfensohn
Directorships: Alita Care, Cadence, CIBT Global, e+CancerCare, Franklin Energy Group, Interstate Hotels & Resorts, K2-MDV Holdings, MarketCast, Nellson Nutraceutical, Osmose Utilitie Service
Shant Mardirossian, Partner & Chief Financial Officer
Education: BBA, MBA, Pace University
Background: McKinsey & Company, Senior Staff Accountant, Paneth Haber & Zimmerman
Directorships: Spinal Elements
Benjamin Mao, Partner
Education: AB, Harvard College
Background: Ewing Management Group, Donaldson Lufkin & Jenrette, Credit Suisse First Boston
Directorships: e+CancerCare, Franklin Energy Group, Osmose Utilities Services, Sabre Industries, Senneca Holdings
Seth H Hollander, Partner
Education: BBA, University of Michigan, Ann Arbor
Background: Financial Analyst, Bear Stearns & Co
Directorships: Interstate Hotels & Resorts, Nellson Nutraceutical, Sara Lee Frozen Bakery, Stanadyne Corporation
Andrew P. Bonanno, Partner
Education: BA, Connecticut College; MBA, Washington University
Background: VP of Business Development, New York Butouts Team, American Capital
Christopher Anderson, Partner
Education: BA, Princeton University
Background: Financial Analyst, Warburg Dillon Read
Directorships: Cadence, K2-MDV Holdings LP, Spinal Elements, U.S. Risk Insurance Group
Evan Wildstein, Partner
Education: BBA, University of Michigan
Background: Financial Analyst, Dean Witter Reyolds
Directorships: Alita Care, e+CancerCare, SpecialtyCare, Stanadyne Corporation, U.S. Retirement & Benefit Partners
Ahmed Wahla, Partner
Education: BA, Northwestern University
Background: Lazard Frères & Co.
Directorships: CIBT Global, Interstate Hotels & Resorts, MarketCast, Nellson Nutraceutical, Sabre Industries

1082 KOHLBERG KRAVIS ROBERTS & COMPANY
9 W 57th Street
Suite 4200
New York, NY 10019

Phone: 212-750-8300
web: www.kkr.com

Mission Statement: KKR is an investment firm that makes equity investments in management buyouts on behalf of itself and its investors.

Geographic Preference: North America, Europe, Asia Pacific

Fund Size: $118 billion
Founded: 1976
Minimum Investment: $15,000,000
Investment Criteria: LBO, MBO
Industry Group Preference: Chemicals, Consumer Products, Energy, Education, Financial Services, Healthcare, Infrastructure, Media, Communications, Retail, Consumer & Leisure, Technology
Portfolio Companies: 58 Daojia, A-Gas, ACCO Material Handling Solutions, Academy Sports + Outdoors, Accelerated Oil Technologies, Acciona Energia Internacional, Acteon, Activate Capital Ltd., AcuFocus, Ajax Health, Ambea AB, AppLovin, Apple Leisure Group, Arago, Arbor Pharmaceuticals, Associated Partners, Australian Venue Co., Avendus Capital, BMC, Bay Club, Beach, Beijing Capital Juda, Bharti Infratel, Blue Sprig Pediatrics, BridgeBio Pharma, BrightView, CHI Overhead Doors, COFCO Meat, Calabrio, Calsonic Kansei, Calvin Capital, Cardenas, Carter Haston JV, Cascade Sensior Living, Castel Portfolio, Cementos Balboa, Channel Control Marchants, Cherwell Software, China Int'l Capital Corp. Ltd., China Outfitters Holdings, Clarify Health Solutions, Clicktale, Coffee Day Resorts, Cognita Schools, Cohera Medical, Coherus BioSciences, Colonial Pipeline Co., Comstock Resources, Copper, Covenant Surgical Partners, The Crosby Group, Cue & Co., Cylance, Darktrace, Deutsche Glasfaser, DoubleDutch, Drawbridge, Exco Resources, Ebb Therapeutics, EchoNous, Eclipse, Embarcadero Maritime, Emerald Media, Engility, Entellus Medical, Envision Healthcare, Epicor, European Locomotive Leasing, FanDuel, First Data Corp., Focus Financial Partners, ForgeRock, Gambol Pet Group, Gardner Denver, Genesis Energy, GetYourGuide, GfK SE, Global Medical Response, Go Daddy, Go-Jek, Golden Data, Goodpack, HeTian Hospital Management, Heartland Dental Care, Hensoldt, Hilding Anders, Hipoges, Hitachi Kokusai Electric, Hyperion, Internet B

Other Locations:
2800 Sand Hill Road
Suite 200
Menlo Park, CA 94025
Phone: 650-233-6560

555 California St.
50th Floor
San Francisco, CA 94104
Phone: 415-315-3620

600 Travis Street
Suite 7200
Houston, TX 77002
Phone: 713-343-5142

201 South Orange Ave.
Suite 720
Orlando, FL 32801
Phone: 713-332-7090

Kohlberg Kravis Roberts & Co. SAS
42 Avenue Montaigne
Paris 75008
France
Phone: 33-153539600

Stirling Square
7 Carlton Gardens
London SW1Y 5AD
United Kingdom
Phone: 44-2078399800

KKR Asia Limited
Level 56, Cheung Kong Center
2 Queen's Road
Central
Hong Kong
Phone: 852-63027300

KKR Japan Limited
11F, Meiji Yasuda Seimei Building
2-1-1 Marunouchi, Chiyoda-ku

Venture Capital & Private Equity Firms / Domestic Firms

Tokyo 100-0005
Japan
Phone: 81-362686000

KKR Investment Consultancy (Beijing) Co Ltd
41/F China World Tower 3
No. 1 Jianguomenwai Street, Chaoyang District
Beijing 100004
China
Phone: 86-1058953800

KKR India Advisors Private Limited
2nd Floor, Piramai Tower, Peninsula Corporate Park
Ganpatrao Kadam Marg, Lower Parel West
Mumbai 400 013
India
Phone: 91-2243551300

KKR MENA Limited
Gate Village 4, Levels 5 & 6
DIFC, PO Box 506804
Dubai
United Arab Emirates
Phone: 971-043781500

KKR Korea LLC
35/F, West Tower, Mirae Asset Center 1 Building
26 Eulji-ro 5-gil, Jung-gu
Seoul 100-210
Korea
Phone: 82-263217700

KKR Australia Pty Limited
Level 42, Gateway Building
1 Macquarie Place
Sydney NSW 2000
Australia
Phone: 91-282985500

Key Executives:
Henry R Kravis, Co-Chair & Co-Chief Executive Officer
Education: MBA, Columbia University
George Roberts, Co-Chair & Co-Chief Executive Officer
Education: JD, University of California Law School; BA, Claremont McKenna College
Background: Bear Sterns & Company

1083 KOHLBERG VENTURES
3000 Alpine Road
Portola Valley, CA 94028
Phone: 650-463-1480 **Fax:** 650-463-1481
e-mail: info@kohlbergventures.com
web: www.kohlbergventures.com

Mission Statement: Kohlberg Ventures invests in early stage digital media, consumer product and clean tech companies. Kohlberg Ventures draws on over twenty years experience of bringing patient capital to compelling business opportunities. Since we're investing our own capital, we're equipped to remain active in all market cycles - to take risks in up markets, and to double-down in tighter times. We provide ongoing support with strategic guidance, supplemental talent and an extensive network of domain experts. We recognize that few ventures grow as originally planned, and we're proud of our record in helping entrepreneurs navigate the tactical shifts necessary to thrive.

Fund Size: $35 million
Investment Criteria: Early-Stage
Industry Group Preference: Digital Media & Marketing, Consumer Products, Clean Technology, Advertising, Distribution, Food & Beverage, Power, Energy Efficiency, Enabling Technology
Portfolio Companies: Alibris, Akadémos, Blue Bottle Coffee Company, Business Insider, ClearEdge Power, Current TV, Lunera Lighting, Open Road Integrated Media, Real Gravity, Scharffen Berger Chocolate Maker, Shakti Battery, Social Chorus, Socialmedian, Vintners' Alliance, Wordlock, XQuest

Key Executives:
James A. Kohlberg, Investment Partner
Background: Chairman, Kohlberg & Company
Directorships: Open Road Integrated Media, SocialChorus, The New York Times
John S. Eastburn Jr., Investment Partner
Background: Partner, Kohlberg & Company; Executive, Crystal Dynamics; Vestron; Columbia Pictures; Scovill Fasteners
Greg Shove, Digital Media Partner
Education: Sloan Fellow, Stanford University Graduate School of Business
Background: Founder/CEO, SocialChorus; Executive, America Online; Co-Founder, 2Market; Apple Computer; Sun Microsystems; Digital Equipment
Bill Youstra, Digital Media Partner
Education: MBA, Stanford University; BA, Film, BS, Computer Science, BA, Marketing, University of Maryland; MA, Education, Stanford University
Background: SVP, Marketing & Business Development, Revel Touch

1084 KPG VENTURES
Berkeley, CA 94705
Phone: 925-234-3557
web: www.kpgventures.com

Mission Statement: KPG Ventures provides funding for seed and early stage companies. The firm focuses primarily on tech-centric businesses.

Investment Criteria: Seed-Stage
Industry Group Preference: Consumer Internet, Technology
Portfolio Companies: Bai Du, BrightRoll, Geomagical, Ludic Labs, MindMeld, Nile Guide, Ribbit, Solariat, Sphere, Sportgenic, Teracent, Wowd

Key Executives:
Vince Vannelli, Founder/Managing Partner
Education: BS, MS, Industrial Engineering, Stanford University
Background: SVP & General Manager, Network Products Division, Inktomi Corporation; SVP & General Manager, United States, Hitachi Data Systems; IBM
Directorships: Expect Labs, Sociable Labs, Lingonautics, National Payment Card Association

1085 KPS CAPITAL PARTNERS
485 Lexington Avenue
31st Floor
New York, NY 10017
Phone: 212-338-5100 **Fax:** 646-307-7100
e-mail: dgray@kpsfund.com
web: www.kpsfund.com

Mission Statement: Focuses on constructive investing in restructurings, turnarounds, and other special situations. KPS invests in companies challenged by the need to effect immediate and significant change.

Geographic Preference: North America, Europe
Founded: 1991
Average Investment: $100 - $500 million
Investment Criteria: Special Situations, Restructurings, Turnarounds; Revenues of $250 Million or higher
Industry Group Preference: Manufacturing, Transportation, Business Products & Services
Portfolio Companies: American & Efird LLC, C&D Technologies, Chassis Breaks International, DexKo Global, Electrical Components International, Expera Specialty Solutions, Heritage Home Group, Interational Equipment Solutions, TaylorMade, Winoa, Anchor Glass Container, United Copper Industries, MCI, WWRD, Waupaca, Global Brass and Copper Inc., North American Breweries, Attends, HHI Holdings LLC, Genesis Worldwide Inc., Blue Ridge Paper Products Inc., Bristol Compressors International Inc., United Road, Cloyes, WRCA, Speedline Technologies,

AmeriCast Technologies, Blue Heron Paper Company, Ashcroft Inc., New Flyer, Curtis Papers Inc.

Other Locations:
Barckhausstr 1
Frankfurt D-60325
Germany
Phone: 49-6913814777 **Fax:** 49-6913814774

Key Executives:
Michael Psaros, Managing Partner
Education: BS, Business Administration, Georgetown University
Background: Investment Banker, Bear Stearns & Co.
Directorships: WWRD Holdings, HHI Group Holdings, Global Brass & Copper, North American Breweries, Motor Coach Industries, United Copper Industries

David Shapiro, Managing Partner
Education: BA, History, University of Michigan; MBA, Finance, University of Chicago Graduate School of Business
Background: Investment Banker, Drexel Burnham Lambert; Dean Witter Reynolds
Directorships: WWRD Holdings, HHI Group Holdings, Global Brass & Copper, North American Breweries, Motor Coach Industries, United Copper Industries

Raquel Palmer, Partner
Education: BS, Political Science, Stanford University
Background: Investment Banker, Kidder Peabody & Co.
Directorships: WWRD Holdings, HHI Group Holdings, Global Brass & Copper, North American Breweries, Motor Coach Industries, United Copper Industries

Jay Bernstein, Partner
Education: BA, Economics, University of Michigan; MBA, Columbia University Graduate School of Business
Background: Investment Banking, Schroders
Directorships: WWRD Holdings, Global Brass & Copper, North American Breweries, Motor Coach Industries, United Copper Industries, International Equipment Solutions

1086 KRG CAPITAL PARTNERS
1800 Larimer Street
Suite 220
Denver, CO 80202

Phone: 303-390-5001 **Fax:** 303-390-5015
web: www.krgcapital.com

Mission Statement: KRG Capital Partners is a middle market private equity group that partners with entrepreneurs and management teams to build industry-leading companies through organic growth and a customer-centric add-on acquisition strategy

Investment Criteria: Early Stage, Later Stage
Industry Group Preference: Business Products & Services, Financial Services, Healthcare, Industrial, Infrastructure, Life Sciences, Media & Entertainment, Retail, Consumer & Leisure, Energy

Portfolio Companies: Accellent, ANSIRA, Aspen Marketing Services, ATI Physical Therapy, Aurora Diagnostics, Avizent, Case Logic, CCS Medical, Celebrity Inc., Cetero Research, CIVCO, Convergint Technologies, Diversified Foodservice Supply, Federal, Fire & Life Safety America, FMI International, The Focus Corporation, Fort Dearborn Company, Global Employment Solutions, HMS Healthcare, Home Solutions, Interior Specialists, Inventus Power, Liberty Dialysis, Marquette Transportation, Modtech, NCTI, OLSON, PAS Technologies, PetroChoice, Scivex, Specialty Finance Company, The Sun Valley Group, Texta America, The Tensar Corporation, TerraMarc Industries, Trafficware, TransCore, Trinity Hospice, Tronair, UniversalPegasus International, Varel International, Vention Medical, White Cap Industries

Key Executives:
Bruce Rogers, Co-Founder/Managing Director
303-390-5018
Education: Law Degree, Duke University; Rome Center for International Law; Bachelor's of Business in Management & Finance, Stetson University
Background: Partner, Hogan & Hartson LLP; Partner, Kirkland & Ellis LLP

Charles Gwirtsman, Co-Founder/Managing Director
303-390-5019
Education: MBA English, Columbia University
Background: Senior Vice President, Fiduciary Capital Management Company; Corporate Vice President, Paine Weber, Inc.; Investment Banker, E.F. Hutton
Directorships: Friends of Yemin Orde

Christopher Lane, Managing Director
303-390-5006
Education: MBA Management/BA Economics, University of California, Irvine
Background: CFO, White Cap

Charles Hamilton, Managing Director
303-390-5031
Education: BS Finance, University of California Berkeley
Background: Managing Director, First Analysis Corporation; Managing Director, Robertson, Stephens & Co,

Bennett Thompson, Managing Director
Education: BA, Economics, Washington and Lee University
Background: Vice President, Heritage Partners; Analyst, Harris Williams & Co.

Colton King, Managing Director
Education: BS, Preprofessional Studies, University of Notre Dame; MBA, Kellogg School of Management
Background: CHS Capital; Analyst, Merrill Lynch

Stewart Fisher, Managing Director
Education: MBA Finance, University of Pennsylvania Wharton School; BS Accounting, Lehigh University
Background: Chief Financial Officer/Executive Vice President of Administration, Accellant; Chief Financial Officer/Vice President GenTek

Ted Nark, Managing Director
Education: BS Business Administration, Washington State University
Background: CEO/Chairman, White Cap Construction Supply; Operating Partner, Leonard Green & Partners; CEO, Corporate Express Australia

1087 KTB VENTURES
1 California St.
Suite 2800
San Francisco, CA 94111

Phone: 650-324-4681

Mission Statement: KTB is recognized as one of the top private equity firms in Korea. With KTB's domestic experience and global investment networks in some of Asia's most important financial centers, KTB aims to become one of Asia's leading private equity firms. KTB focuses on finding undervalued proprietary deals to ensure higher profitability by increasing corporate value.

Geographic Preference: Asia
Industry Group Preference: Information Technology, Digital Media & Marketing, Healthcare
Portfolio Companies: 17 Media, Airespace, Alteon WebSystems, Internet Auction, Babbaco, Beceem, Berkanna Wireless, Big Cafe, Brightstorm, Bitfone, CARsgen Therapeutics, Cell Biologics, Centillium, Chips & Media, China Stem Cell, Cintel, Clobotics, Com2Us, Com21, Coolman Entertainment, Copper Mountain, CrucialTec, Epoch Systems, Focus Media, Fortress Technologies, Gravity, Gushan Environmental, IC Works, IDIS, Il Mare, Inphi Corp., Integrant Technologies, Knowre, Koyj, Lmeca, Lumens, Magnum, MCNex, MCubeWorks, Meebo, Mindray Medical, Moloco, Netro Corporation, Neurotech, NoBroker, Novera Optics, ORIG3N, Palm Commerce, Pantech & Curitel, Park Scientific, Polyfuel, Quickturn Design, Satrec Initiative, Sesil, Seven Media, Sino Forest, SNU Precision, Sonus Networks, Spreadtrum, S&S Tech, Standard Diagnostics,

Venture Capital & Private Equity Firms / Domestic Firms

Stoke, Telcom Semicon, Tera Semiconductor, Terawave, Terayon, Todou, Valicert, VeriSilicon, Wayfarer, Wireless Access, WiseNut, Xueersi, Xylan Corporation

1088 L CATTERTON PARTNERS
599 West Putnam Avenue
Greenwich, CT 06830

Phone: 203-629-4901 Fax: 203-629-4903
e-mail: info@lcatterton.com
web: www.lcatterton.com

Mission Statement: A leading private equity firm with an exclusive focus on providing equity capital to small to middle market consumer companies in North America who are well positioned for attractive growth.

Geographic Preference: United States, Canada
Fund Size: $1 billion
Founded: 1989
Investment Criteria: Acquisitions, MBO, Recapitalizations, Turnarounds, continued growth and development
Industry Group Preference: Food & Beverage, Retailing, Restaurants, Media, Marketing, Consumer Products, Consumer Services
Portfolio Companies: 2XU, 360 Fly, Ainsworth Pet Nutrition, Alasko, Antenna79, Anthony's Coal Fired Pizza, Artsy, Asiaray Media Group, Baccarat, Ba&sh, Bateel, Beanitos, Bliss, Bodytech, Bruxie, Captain Tortue Group, Caredent, CE LA VI, Cellular Line, Chopt, ClearChoice Holdings LLC, CLIO, Cover FX, CorePower Yoga, Crystal Jade, Donup, Dr. Wu, Edible Arrangements, Elemis, Equinox, El Ganso, Espaçolaser, Ferrara Candy Company, Ganni, Genesis Luxury, Gental Monster, Getaway, Giuseppe Zanotti, Gill Mix Green, Hanna Andersson, HelloWorld, Home Chef, Hopdpddy, "I and Love And You", Ideal Image, IL MAKIAGE, Innis & Gunn, Intercos, John Hardy, Jones The Grocer Group, JustFoodForDogs, Kopari, Leslie's, Lily's Kitchen, Marubi, Mendocino Farms, Mizzen+Main, Naya, Noodles & Co., Ole & Steen, One Spa World, O Luxe Holdings Limited, Pain Doctor, PatientPoint, Peloton, Pepe Jeans, PetVet Care Centers, PIADA Italian Street Food, Pinarello, PIRCH, Princess Yachtz International, Primanti Bros., Protein Bar and Kitchen, Punch Bowl Social, Pure Barre, Rapsodia, Rhone, R.M. Williams, Sasseur, Seafolly, Snap Kitchen, SteelSeries, Steiner Education Group, St. Marche Group, StriVectin, Sweaty Betty, Trendy International Group, Tula, Uncle Julio's, VER, Velvet Taco, Vroom, Advanced Bio Development, Xin Hee Co. Limited, YG Entertainment, Zarbee's

Other Locations:
1, Rue Euler
Paris 751008
France
Phone: 33-1-44-95-91-22

1 Kim Seng Promenade
#18-07/12 Great World City 237994
Singapore
Phone: 65-6672-7600

30 Rockefeller Plaza
Suite 5405
New York, NY 10112
Phone: 212-600-2139

40 Avenue Monterey
Luxembourg L 2163
Luxembourg
Phone: 352-28-86-80-40

Key Executives:
J Michael Chu, Global Co-CEO
Education: BA, Psychology and Economics, Bates College
Background: First Pacific Company; Director Finance, Hagemeyer NV; VP/Treasurer, Hibernia Bank; COO, Comtrad; COO, Doyle Graf Raj
Directorships: Committee of 100

Scott A. Dahnke, Global Co-CEO
Education: BS Mechanical Engineering, University of Notre Dame; MBA, Harvard Business School
Background: Managing Director, Deutsche Bank Capital Partners; Managing Director, AEA Investors; CEO, infoUSA; Partner, McKinsey & Company; Merger Department, Goldman, Sachs & Co; General Motors

Julian C. Mack, Senior Advisor
Education: Harvard College; MBA, Stanford University
Background: Managing Director, McKinsey & Company; Mark Controls Corporation

Michael J. Farello, Managing Partner, Growth Fund
Education: BS, Industrial Engineering, Stanford University; MBA, Harvard Business School
Background: Dell, McKinsey & Company

David Heidecorn, Partner/Chief Risk Officer
Education: BA Economics, Lehigh University; MBA Finance, Columbia Business School
Background: CFO, Alarmguard Holdings; Nantucket Holding; Corporate Finance, GE Capital

Andrew C. Taub, Managing Partner, Buyout Fund
Education: BA, University of Michigan; MBA, Columbia Business School
Background: VP, Nantucket Holding; Senior Associate, Coopers & Lybrand

Jonathan H. Owsley, Managing Partner, Growth Fund
Education: BA Political Science, Middlebury College; JD with Honors, Cornell Law School
Background: Senior Principal, Parthenon Group; Corporate Attorney, Hale & Dorr; Assistant Brew Master, Otter Creek Brewing; College Lacrosse Coach

Nikhil Thukral, Managing Partner, Buyout Fund
Education: BS Finance with High Honors, University of Illinois; MBA, University of Chicago
Background: VP, MidOcean Partners; DB Capital Partners; Associate Healthcare Group, JP Morgan & Co

Marc Magliacano, Managing Partners, Buyout Fund
Education: BS, Economics, Wharton School; MBA, Columbia Business School
Background: Principal, North Castle Partners; NMS Capital

Howard Steyn, Partner, Global Opportunities
Education: AB, Social Studies, Harvard College; MBA, Wharton School
Background: Principal, Bain Capital; McKinsey & Company

Marc-David Bismuth, Operating Partner
Education: University Institute of Technology, France; MBA, Financial Management, University of Paris X
Background: President, Danone Naya Waters North America; Food Division Gineral Manager, Carefour Group

1089 LABRADOR VENTURES

Phone: 650-366-6000
e-mail: labrador@labrador.com
web: www.labrador.com

Mission Statement: Labrador Ventures is one of the oldest, premier seed stage funds in Silicone Valley.

Geographic Preference: West Coast
Fund Size: $100 million
Founded: 1989
Average Investment: $2 million
Minimum Investment: $500,000
Investment Criteria: Seed, Startup, First-Stage
Industry Group Preference: Information Technology, Digital Media & Marketing, Software, Communications, Semiconductors
Portfolio Companies: Altierre Corporation, Carsala Inc., Delve Networks, EoPlex Technologies Inc., Infoaxe, Integrated Materials Incorporated, Integrated Photovoltaics, Marrone Bio Innovations, MeeVee Inc., Meteor Solutions, Mi5 Networks, Mixbook, Pandora Media Inc., Phonezoo Communications Inc., PlayPhone Inc., Podaddies Inc., Reveal

Venture Capital & Private Equity Firms / Domestic Firms

Technology Inc., Rocketfuel Inc., Shotspotter Inc., Solaicx, Transperra, Traverse Networks Incorporated, Ultriva Inc., UStream, Wiredbenefits Inc., Yardbarker Inc.

Key Executives:
Larry Kubal, Founder/Partner
Education: Duke University; MBA Stanford Graduate School of Business
Background: Founder, Pandora Media; Booz Allen & Hamilton; McGraw-Hill Publications
Directorships: iPV
Sean Foote, Venture Partner
Education: BS, Electrical Engineering, University of Missouri Rolla, MBA, Darden School of Business
Background: Boston Consulting Group; AT&T Bell Laboratories
Stuart Davidson, Partner
Education: Harvard College, Harvard University; Harvard Business School
Background: Founder/CEO, Combion; President, Alkermes; MCI Communications; Warner Communications
Directorships: iPV, Shotspotter, Ultriva, Ustream

1090 LACUNA GAP CAPITAL
1100 Spruce Street
Suite 202
Boulder, CO 80302

Phone: 303-447-1700 Fax: 303-447-1710

Mission Statement: Lacuna seeks to accelerate the growth of our portfolio companies while mitigating investment risk. We collaboratively invest our unique skill sets and experience in order to help build leading companies of tomorrow and create superior returns for our investing partners.

Average Investment: $500,000 - $3 million
Investment Criteria: Early-Stage
Portfolio Companies: Balihoo, concept3D, IntraOp Medical Corporation, Mocapay, Tribute Direct

Key Executives:
Rawleigh Ralls, Chief Investor
Sanford Keziah, Chief Strategist
JK Hullet, Chief Financial Officer
Background: CEO, @Last Software; CEO, Net Identity

1091 LAKE CAPITAL
875 N Michigan Avenue
Suite 3520
Chicago, IL 60611-2896

Phone: 312-640-7050 Fax: 312-640-7051
e-mail: info@lakecapital.com
web: www.lakecapital.com

Mission Statement: Investing selectively in a limited number of middle-market, service-based companies with the potential for growth.

Geographic Preference: North America, Western Europe
Fund Size: $100 million
Average Investment: $50 - $75 million
Investment Criteria: Buyout, Partnership, Starups
Industry Group Preference: Marketing, Healthcare, Technology, Specialty Servaces, Business Outsourcing, Financial
Portfolio Companies: Driveline Retail, Engine, Viamedia

Key Executives:
Terrence M. Graunke, Co-Founder/Principal
Education: BA/MBA, University of Chicago
Paul G. Yovovich, Co-Founder/Principal
Education: BA, MBA, University of Chicago; CPA
Background: Founder, Director, Lighthouse Global Network; President, Advance Ross Corporation; Centel Corporation
Douglas Rescho, Principal
Education: BS, Finance, University Of Illinois

Background: Citigroup Global Markets; Standard & Poor's
Collin Abert, Principal
Education: BS, Accountancy, University of Illinois
Background: JP Morgan

1092 LANCET CAPITAL
100 Technology Drive
Suite 200
Pittsburgh, PA 15219

Phone: 412-402-9914 Fax: 412-452-9480
web: www.lancetcapital.com

Mission Statement: Investing in exceptional researchers, clinicians and entrepreneurs to commercialize innovative technologies in the biomedical field.

Founded: 1998
Investment Criteria: Early Stage
Industry Group Preference: Biopharmaceuticals, Medical Devices, Bioinformatics, Therapeutics, Diagnostics
Portfolio Companies: Ardais, Dyax, Enanta, Scion Pharmaceuticals, Stemnion, Stentntor, VivoQuest

Key Executives:
William J Golden, Managing Director
617-330-9345
Fax: 617-330-9349
e-mail: wgolden@lancetcapital.com
Education: MBA, Harvard Business School; BS, University of Notre Dame
Background: Management Consultant, Arthur D. Little; Director, Community Technology Fund
George L Sing, Managing Director
212-332-3220
Fax: 212-332-3221
e-mail: sing@lancetcapital.com
Education: MBA, Harvard Business School; BE, Stevens Institute of Technology
Background: Co-Founder/Senior Partner, Advanced Technology Ventures; Merrill Lynch
Directorships: Regeneron

1093 LASALLE CAPITAL GROUP
70 West Madison Street
Suite 5710
Chicago, IL 60602

Phone: 312-236-7041 Fax: 312-236-0720
e-mail: contact@lasallecapital.com
web: www.lasallecapital.com

Mission Statement: To create value for investors by investing in family and entrepreneur-owned businesses in the food and beverage and business services sectors.

Geographic Preference: United States
Fund Size: $210 million
Founded: 1984
Average Investment: $20 million
Minimum Investment: $10 million
Investment Criteria: MBO, Growth, Consolidations, Recaps, LBO
Industry Group Preference: Food & Beverage, Technology, Business Products & Services
Portfolio Companies: Avantech Testing Services, Brown & Joseph, Delorio Foods, Eclipse Advantage, Fresh Origins, Gen3 Marketing, MetaSource, National Gift Card, Processing.com, Westminster Foods

Key Executives:
Rocco J. Martino, Co-Founder/Partner
e-mail: rmartino@lasallecapital.com
Education: BBA, Finance, University of Notre Dame; MBA, Loyola University of Chicago; CPA
Background: Partner, PriceWaterhouseCoopers
Jeffrey M. Walters, Co-Founder/Managing Partner
e-mail: jwalters@lasallecapital.com
Education: BA, Tufts University

395

Venture Capital & Private Equity Firms / Domestic Firms

Background: Partner, Managing Director, BT Securities Corporation; Chicago/Europe Partners L.P.; Vice President, Citicorp Leveraged Capital Group; American National Bank; Trust Company of Chicago
I. Donald Rosuck, Senior Operating Advisor
e-mail: drosuck@lasallecapital.com
Education: BS, City University of New York
Background: President & CEO, Culligan International; President, Home Products Division, Beatrice Company; Controller, W.R. Grace & Company
Walter G. Freedman, Senior Operating Advisor
e-mail: wfreedman@lasallecapital.com
Education: BA, Dartmouth College; MBA, Tuck School of Business Administration, Dartmouth
Background: COO, Wheels, Inc.; Co-Investor & CEO, Yoplait USA; Presient, Fuller Brush Company; IBM
Steven W. Parks, Senior Operating Advisor
e-mail: sparks@lasallecapital.com
Education: Valparaiso University; MBA, Kellogg School of Management, Northwestern University; CPA
Background: President & COO, HAVI Group LP; EVP & COO, Wico Corporation
Nicholas S. Christopher, Partner
e-mail: nchristopher@lasallecapital.com
Education: BA, Albion College; MBA, University of Chicago Booth School of Business
Background: Senior Associate, UIB Capital; CIVC Partners; Goldman Sachs & Co
Kelly A. Cornelis, Partner
e-mail: kcornelis@lasallecapital.com
Education: BBA, University of Notre Dame; MBA, Kellogg School of Management, Northwestern University
Background: Vice President, SB Partners; William Blair & Company

1094 LATTERELL VENTURE PARTNERS
1603 Camino Ramon
Suite 200
San Ramon, CA 94583

Phone: 925-242-2618
web: www.lvpcapital.com

Mission Statement: To help entrepreneurs create important new healthcare companies treating major diseases and medical disorders.
Geographic Preference: United States
Fund Size: $300 million
Founded: 2001
Average Investment: $50,000 to $10 million
Minimum Investment: $50,000
Investment Criteria: Early Stage, Medium Stage, Late Stage, Spinouts
Industry Group Preference: Biotechnology, Pharmaceuticals, Research & Development, Bio Materials, Medical Devices, Diagnostics, Healthcare, Instrumentation
Portfolio Companies: Aptinyx, Calistoga, Cellective Therapeutics, Ensure Medical, Evoke, ForteBio, Inova Labs, IntegenX, Meritage, Naurex, OncoMed, Pathway, PerceptiMed, ProteinSimple, Proteolix, Pulmonx, Revascular Therapeutics, TetraLogic, Transcend, Viracta

Key Executives:
Patrick Latterell, General Partner
e-mail: pat@lvpcapital.com
Education: SB, MIT; MBA, Stanford Business School
Background: General Partner, Venrock Associates; General Partner, Rotschild Ventures
Peter Fitzgerald, General Partner
e-mail: peter@lvpcapital.com
Education: BS, University Of Santa Clara; RA, Stanford University; MS, Renseelaer Polytechnic Institute; MD, PhD, Dartmouth College
Directorships: Interventional Cardiology Research Laboratory, FDA Medical Device Advisory Panel
Jim Woody, General Partner
e-mail: jim@lvpcapital.com
Education: MD, Loma Linda University; Pediatric Immunology, Duke University & Children's Hospital in Boston (Harvard); PhD in Immunology, University of London, England
Background: CEO, OncoMed; President, General Manager, Roche Bioscience; CSO, Senior VP, Centocor; US Navy Transplant Research Program
Directorships: Viracta Therapeutics, ForteBio, ProteinSimple
Steve Salmon, General Partner
e-mail: steve@lvpcapital.com
Education: BS in Chemical Engineering, University of Maine
Background: Engineering Manager, CVIS; VP of R&D, Boston Scientific; Co-Founder, Integrated Vascular Systems; Co-Founder, Ensure Medical
Ken Widder, General Partner
e-mail: ken@lvpcapital.com
Education: MD, Northwestern University; Pathology, Duke University
Background: Founder, CEO, NovaCardia; Founder, Chairman, CEO, Santarus; Chairman, CEO, Converge Medical; Chairman, CEO, Molecular Biosystems
Directorships: Evoke Pharma, Meritage Pharma, Naurex Inc.
Bob Curry, Venture Consultant
e-mail: bob@lvpcapital.com
Education: Bs, Physics, University of Illinois; MS, PhD, Chemistry, Purdue Univesity
Background: Partner, Alliance Technology Ventures; Partner, Sprout Group; President, Merrill Lynch Venture Capital

1095 LAUDER PARTNERS LLC
Phone: 650-323-5700 **Fax:** 650-232-2171
e-mail: gary@lauderpartners.com
web: www.lauderpartners.com

Mission Statement: Lauder Partners is an entity investing in various realms of the technology field. We invest both in companies as well as in funds, both venture and others.
Geographic Preference: United States, Canada
Average Investment: $500,000 - $5 million
Industry Group Preference: Technology, Information Technology, Internet
Portfolio Companies: AirVine Scientific, Beyond Meat, Caavo Inc, Cortene, Didi Chuxing, Elevian, Heal, Hidden Level, Hippo Insurance, Hyperloop Transportation Technologies, Kheiron Medical Technologies, Level, LVL Technologies, NaNotics, OpenGov, Openwater, Polystream, Raftr, Solius, SpinLaunch, Uber, UniKey, Via Transportation, Visu, WaterGuru, XCures

Key Executives:
Gary Lauder, Managing Director
e-mail: gary@lauderpartners.com
Education: BA, International Relations, University of Pennsylvania; BS, Economics, Wharton School; MBA, Stanford Graduate School of Business
Background: Aetna, Jacobs & Ramo Technology Ventures, Wolfensohn Associates
Directorships: ActiveVideo Networks, Promptu, MediaFriends, ShotSportter

1096 LAUNCHBOX DIGITAL
76 Cedar Street
Seattle, WA 98121

Mission Statement: LaunchBox Digital is a seed-stage investment firm helping entrepreneurs maximize their chance of success. It is a place for cutting-edge ideas and cutting-edge talent. New entrepreneurs face lots of obstacles in making their vision a reality, and many great ideas and great talent never get out of the starting gate. LaunchBox Digital brings entrepreneurs the seed capital, advice, practical guidance, and

Venture Capital & Private Equity Firms / Domestic Firms

connections to help new technology and digital media businesses succeed.

Geographic Preference: North Carolina
Investment Criteria: Early-Stage
Industry Group Preference: Technology, New Media
Portfolio Companies: Altec Lansing, AT&T, Banana Boat, Brunton, Cisco, Costco, Ecova, Hewlett-Packard, IKEA, Johnson & Johnson, Kodak Dental Systems, Lilly, Microsoft, Motorola, neea, NetGear, OfficeMax, Pfizer, Plantronics, Playtex, Samsung, Seagate, Staples, Wacom

Key Executives:

John McKinley, Founding Partner
e-mail: john@launchboxdigital.com
Education: Wharton School
Background: CTO and Founder and President of Digital Services for AOL; Founder and CEO, OurParents; Executive Vice President and head of Global Technology and Services, Merrill Lynch; Senior Vice President and Chief Technology and Information Officer, GE Capital; Partner, Ernst & Young

Mark McDowell
e-mail: mark@launchboxdigital.com
Education: BSEE and MSEE Degrees, MIT
Background: Co-Founder and Managing Partner, Acta Wireless; Manager, MLJ; Officer, United States Air Force

Matthew Jacobson
e-mail: matt@launchboxdigital.com
Education: BA, University of Pennsylvania; MBA, Wharton School
Background: AOL; ABN AMRO; WR Hambrecht; Peter J. Solomon Co.; Toronto Dominion Securities

Steve Lerner, Partner
Education: MA and PhD, University of North Carolina at Chapel Hill
Background: Capstrat; FGI; Yankelovich Partners; KBM; Sterling Cellular; Blue Hill Group

Lee Buck, Partner
Education: BS, Systems Engineering, University of Virginia
Background: Blue Bright Ventures; Near-Time; Extensibility, Inc; Software Designs Unlimited; Arthur Andersen

1097 LAUNCHCAPITAL
195 Church Street
Suite 1700
Cambridge, MA 06510

web: www.launchcapital.com

Mission Statement: LaunchCapital addresses the capital needs of companies that are in the earliest stages of funding by providing a needed source of financing to companies that can quickly advance to the next level of development.

Founded: 2008
Investment Criteria: Seed-Stage
Industry Group Preference: Technology, Consumer Products, Healthcare, Mobile, Software, Internet
Portfolio Companies: Abbey Post, Aerin Medical, Affinimark Technologies, AI Exchange, Amasten, amSTATZ, Apparel Media Group, Apperian, Bluetrain Mobile, C8 Sciences, CardioPhotonics, CardStar, Carsala, Case Continuum, Centri, CMD Bioscience, Collaborate.com, Compology, Continuity, Copiun, Crew, CustomMade, Dailey Grommet, Dekko.co, Diffinity Genomics, Digital Pickle, Domino, Double Dutch, Draker, Eat Club, Eight Spokes, EpiEP, Equityzen, EyelCo, Faraday, Fashion Playres, FMP, FormLabs, Freight Farms, Genomera, Ginger.io, TheGreenBridge.com, Hadapt, Helium, Hodo Soy Beanery, Hyperink, IncentiveTargeting, Innovatient, Intelligent Clearing Network, InterVene, inVino, iQuartic, i-Team, JackCards, Just the Right Book, Karmic Labs, LaunchPad, Leapset, LearnLaunch, Lefora, Life36, LiQuifix, Liquor.com, LittleBorrowedDress, Localytics, LOCJ, LP33, Marlin Mobile, Mayvenn, MerchantAtlas, Mobee, MoMeland Technologies, Nanny Caddy, Niveus Medical, NovaTract, Novogy, Nutrivise, OnFarm, OurStage.com, Ovuline, Paper G, Parelastic, Petnet, Physcient, Play Vs., Profounder, Project Decor, Promoboxx, QDrinks, Quincy, RentJuice, ReportGrid, REsurety, RunKeeper, SafePorche, SecretBuilders, Semantifi, SemiProbe, SKYstream, Socialsci, STR, Supply Hog, Sustainable Real Estate Manager, Techstars, Traackr, Transparent Healthcare, Tripping, True Body, Vicix, Viral Gains, Voltage, Xconomy, Young Broadcasters of America, Your Mechanic, Zadspace, Zagster, Zozi, YouRenew.com

Other Locations:
142 Temple Street
Suite 206
New Haven, CT 06510

500 7th Avneue
17th Floor
New York, NY 10018

Key Executives:

Elon S Broms, Managing Director
Education: BA, Economics, George Washington University; MBA, Yale School of Management
Background: Management Consultant, Fidelity Investments; Corporate Finance, Citigroup

Konstantine Drakonakis, Venture Partner
Education: Civil & Environmental Engineering, University of Vermont; MS, Environmental Management, Yale University
Background: Connecticut Innovations

Bill McCullen, Chief Investment Officer
Education: BS, MS, Electrical Engineering, Worcester Polytechnic Institute; MBA, MIT Sloan School of Business
Background: Sell Side Equity Analyst, Susquehanna Financial Group

Dave Shen, Venture Partner
Background: Yahoo!

1098 LAUNCHCYTE
2403 Sidney Street
Suite 270
Pittsburgh, PA 15203

Phone: 412-481-2200 Fax: 412-592-0349
e-mail: patty@launchcyte.com
web: www.launchcyte.com

Mission Statement: To build value by creating, seeding and harvesting life sciences companies. LaunchCyte's experience, network and resources offer the opportunity to develop early stage technologies into market-leading companies.

Founded: 2000
Investment Criteria: Early-Stage
Industry Group Preference: Life Sciences
Portfolio Companies: Celsense, Crystalplex, Immunetrics, Knopp Biosciences LLC, Reaction Biology

Key Executives:

Tom Petzinger, Founder/Chairman/President/CEO
Education: BS, Journalism, Northwestern University
Background: EVP, Business Development, Knopp Neursciences
Directorships: Knopp Biosciences

Babs Carryer, Co-Founder/Director
Education: Masters, Management, Carnegie Mellon University
Background: President & CEO, RemComm; President, Carryer Consulting

Gregory T Hebrank MD, Director
Education: BS, Biomedical Engineering, Vanderbilt University; MD, Tulane University School of Medicine; MBA, Carnegie Mellon Unversity Tepper School of Business
Background: Founder & Director, Knopp Neurosciences
Directorships: Knopp Biosciences

397

Venture Capital & Private Equity Firms / Domestic Firms

Robert Unkovic, Director
Education: BS, Ohio State University
Background: Partner, BPU Investment Management

1099 LAUNCHPAD LA
Los Angeles, CA

web: www.launchpad.la

Mission Statement: Launchpad LA is 'the top startup accelerator in Southern California.' We offer each accepted company $25k - $100k, free office space in the heart of Santa Monica (one block from the beach) for four months, a ton of perks and discounts, and most importantly, access to a massive network of mentors, advisors, and investors.

Geographic Preference: Los Angeles
Founded: 2010
Investment Criteria: Seed-Stage
Industry Group Preference: Technology
Portfolio Companies: Adomic, Advocus, Atlas, AudioMicro, BigFrame, ChowNow, Chromatik, CircleSt, Cojoin, Combatant Gentleman, Connectifier, Cramster.com, DanceOn, Datapop, Divshot, Elephant Drive, Fitzroy, Flipgloss, Focus:Trainr, Gendai Games, Guide, Gumgum, Ibeatyou.com, InheritedHealth, JobSync, Jukin Media, Lettuce, Listn, Mark43, Melon, Milk & Honey, Mobile Roadie, Mogreet, Monospace, MoVoxx, Panna, Paratinova.com, Parachute, Periodical, Pop-Up Pantry, Pose, Preact.io, Prevoty, Prospectwise, Ranker, Shopnation, Sometrics, Survly, Swing by Swing, TechForward, Ticket Mob, Totspot, Tradesy, Triptrotting, TrueVault, Tuition.io, Vessix, Victorious, Vow to be Chic, Weilos, Zefr

Key Executives:
Sam Teller, Co-Founder/Managing Director
Education: BA, Harvard College
Background: Charlie, Google AdWords, Credit Suisse
Nicholas Green, Entrepreneur-in-Residence
Education: BA, Economics, Harvard College
Background: Ivy Insiders, Revolution Prep
Chelsea Kent, Entrepreneur-in-Residence
Background: Founder, Scratch

1100 LAUNCHPAD VENTURE GROUP
Boston, MA

web: www.launchpadventuregroup.com

Mission Statement: Launchpad Venture Group, a Boston-based angel investment group, provides funding and advice to early-stage companies. Launchpad looks for innovative, technology-driven startup companies addressing a significant market opportunity where our investment can make a difference. We introduce entrepreneurs to potential investors through business plan presentations at monthly meetings. Launchpad Venture Group consists of individual angel investor members interested in achieving superior returns by financing privately held companies at an early stage of development.

Average Investment: $250,000 - $1 million
Investment Criteria: Early-Stage
Industry Group Preference: High Technology, Financial Services, Industrial, Life Sciences, Healthcare, Software, Information Technology, Internet, E-Commerce & Manufacturing, Media, Social Media, Mobile, Wireless, Medical Devices, Diagnostics
Portfolio Companies: 3Play Media, 7AC Technology, Building Engines, CabinetM, Cambridge Blockchain, CIMCON, Clean Fiber, Cognoptix, Concentric, Content Raven, Crowdly, Electra Vehicles, EnergySage, EveryScape, ezCater, GeoOrbital, Gravyty, Groupsize, InCrowd, Infobionic, iTeam, Kalion, KnipBio, ListenWise, Localytics, ManufactOn, Medumo, MultiSensor Sci., Mobius Imaging, Netra, Parkloco, Peach, Pepperlane, Pixability, Powerhouse Dynamics, Precision Ventures, Prolific Works, Punchbowl, QStream, Repsly, Siamab, Smart Lunches, SmartVid.io, Testive, Tetragenetics, TimeTrade, TruTouch, WeSpire, WindGap, Woo Sports, Zagster, Ziiproom, Zippity

Key Executives:
Hambleton Lord, Chairman
Education: Computer Science, Brown University
Background: Co-Founder, Advanced Visual Systems
Directorships: Cambridge Trust, EveryScape, Netra, Qstream, Repsly
Christopher Mirabile, Managing Director
Education: BA, Colgate University; JD, Boston College Law School
Background: CFO, IONA Technologies; Corporate Lawyer, Testa Hurwitz & Thiebeault; Managment Consultant, Price Waterhouse

1101 LDV CAPITAL
111 East 14th Street
Suite 102
New York, NY 10003

web: www.ldv.co

Mission Statement: LDV Capital seeks to invest in visual technology businesses, such as virtual reality and digital learning.

Geographic Preference: US, Canada, Europe
Founded: 2012
Average Investment: $300,000 - #500,000
Investment Criteria: Pre-Seed, Seed, Early Stage
Industry Group Preference: Artificial Intelligence, Technology, Consumer, Retail, Robotics, Virtual Reality, Satellite Imaging, Medical Imaging, Security, Photonics, Machine Learning
Portfolio Companies: Camio, Carbon Robotics, Clarifai, Ezra, Fantasmo, Farmeron, Geniachip, Lookmark, Mapillary, Mediachain Labs, Narrative, Newco, Unsplash, Sea Machines, ShopPad, Synthesia, TVision Insights, Uizard, UPSKILL, Voyant Photonics

Key Executives:
Evan Nisselson, Founder/General Partner
Education: University of Vermont
Background: VP of Business Development, Eyetide Media; Founder/CEO, Digital Railroad Inc.; Consultant, Nisselson Co.; Advisor/Mentor, TechPeaks
Abigail Hunter-Syed, Vice President, Operations
Education: BA, University of Rochester; MA, International University, Geneva
Background: Co-Founder, WorldBrain LLC; Economic Researcher, World Trade Organization; Operations, Von Essen Group; Senior Associate, Morgan Stanley

1102 LEAPFROG VENTURES
830 Menlo Avenue
Suite 100
Menlo Park, CA 94025

Phone: 650-926-9900 Fax: 650-233-1301

Mission Statement: Our mission is to help our portfolio companies Leapfrog their competitors and achieve industry-leading levels of competitive and market performance as quickly as possible.

Geographic Preference: Western United States
Founded: 2000
Average Investment: $1 - $3 million
Investment Criteria: Seed Stage
Industry Group Preference: Computer Related, Software, Information Technology, Communications, Wireless, Consumer Technology
Portfolio Companies: Avaak, Ace Metrix, Cloud9 Analytics, Global Analytics, HotLink, IronKey, PureWave, RedSeal, SilverTail, Vast, Zebit

Key Executives:
Peter Sinclair, Director
e-mail: pete@leapfrogventures.com
Education: SB, Engineering, MIT; Stanford Business

School
Background: Hewlett Packard
Andy Fillat, Director
e-mail: andy@leapfrogventures.com
Education: SB, SM, MIT; MBA, Harvard
Background: Advent International Corp.; Fidelity Investments

1103 LEASING TECHNOLOGIES INTERNATIONAL INC.
221 Danbury Road
Wilton, CT 06897

Phone: 203-563-1100 **Fax:** 203-563-1112
web: www.ltileasing.com

Mission Statement: To preserve working capital through innovative equipment financing. We acquire/lease business equipment essentials like security devices, computers and servers, lab/test equipment, communications equipment, manufacturing/production equipment and office automation equipment.

Fund Size: $30 million
Founded: 1983
Average Investment: $500,000
Minimum Investment: $250,000
Investment Criteria: Seed, Startup, First-Stage, Second-Stage, Mezzanine, LBO
Industry Group Preference: Software, Telecommunications, Biotechnology, Health Related, Internet Technology, Hardware, E-Commerce & Manufacturing, Life Sciences, Education
Portfolio Companies: About.com, Akamai Technology, Array BioPharma, Axolotl, BeFree, Inc. (TriVida Corp.), Carr Separations/Kendro Lab Products, Coordinated Care Solutions, Digitrace/Sleepmed Inc., Earthlink Network Inc., General Bandwidth, Healtheon-WebMD, LTX Corporation, Metavante, National Semiconductor, NetZero Inc., Pyxis - Helpmate Robotics, Sonexis, SPSS Inc., Superconductor Technologies Inc., TheStreet.com, TransMeta, Triton Network Systems, Virage Logic

Other Locations:
10 Liberty Square
Boston, MA 02109
Phone: 617-426-4116 **Fax:** 617-482-6475

27068 La Paz Road
Suite 270
Aliso Viejo, CA 92656
Phone: 949-290-4312 **Fax:** 949-215-9761

Key Executives:
Jerry Sprole, President/CEO
203-563-1100 ext 212
e-mail: jsprole@LTILeasing.com
Education: BA, Yale University
Background: Founder, President, CEO, LTI Ventures Leasing Corporation; CFO, Intech Capital Corporation; VP, Bank of Boston
William I MacDonald, Senior Vice President
617-426-4116
e-mail: wmacdonald@LTILeasing.com
Education: BA, Tufts University; Advanced Management Program, Harvard University
Background: Senior VP, Bank of Boston; Thirty-one years managing NYC Lending Corresponding Banking and Banking Services Division
Arnold J Hoegler, Executive VP/Founder/COO
203-563-1100 ext 213
e-mail: ahoegler@ltileasing.com
Education: BA, St. John's University
Background: Seven years as leasing and financial services manager at KPMG Peat Marwick; CPA
George A Parker, Executive VP/CFO/Founder
203-563-1100 ext 214
e-mail: gparker@LTILeasing.com
Education: BS Mathematics, Wake Forest; MBA Finance, University of North Carolina
Background: VP, Finance of DPF Computer Leasing; Second VP, Continental Illinois Bank; Founder, LTI Ventures Leasing
Skip Baum, General Counsel/Secretary
203-563-1100
e-mail: sbaum@ltileasing.com
Education: LL.B, Harvard Law School, Yale University

1104 LEE EQUITY PARTNERS
40 West 57th Street
Suite 1620
New York, NY 10019

Phone: 212-906-4900
e-mail: Leeequitypartners@leeequity.com
web: www.leeequity.com

Mission Statement: To work with strong management teams and invest in companies with high growth potential.

Geographic Preference: United States
Founded: 2006
Average Investment: $50 - $150 million
Investment Criteria: Middle Market, Buyouts, Acquisitions, Growth Capital
Industry Group Preference: Business Products & Services, Healthcare Services, Financial Services, Retail, Consumer & Leisure, Consumer, Distribution, Logistics, Media
Portfolio Companies: Aimbridge Hospitality, Captive Resources, Carlile Bancshares, Cross Mediaworks, Deb Shops, Eating Recovery Center, Interluxe Holdings, Midcap Financial, Papa Murphy's International, PDR Network, Skopos Financial, The Edelman Financial Group, Universal American

Key Executives:
Thomas H Lee, Chairman
Education: AB, Economics, Harvard College
Background: Chairman & CEO, Thomas H Lee Partners; VP, First National Bank of Boston; Analyst, LF Rothschild & Company
Directorships: Aimbridge Hospitality, The Edelman Financial Group, Papa Murphy's International
Mark K Gormley, Partner
Education: BSBA, Finance & Economics, University of Denver; MBA, New York University
Background: Co-Founder & Partner, Capital Z Financial Services Partners; Managing Director, Donaldson Lufkin & Jenrette; Merrill Lynch
Directorships: The Edelman Financial Group, Skopos Financial Group, Captive Resources, Carlile Bancshares, MidCap Financial, PDR Network, Universal American
Benjamin A Hochberg, Partner
Education: AB, Chemistry, Harvard College; MBA, Harvard Business School
Background: Principal, Odyssey Investment Partners; Principal, Bain Capital Partners
Directorships: Aimbridge Hospitality, The Edelman Financial Group, Papa Murphy's International, Skopos Financial Group
Yoo Jin Kim, Partner
Education: AB, Biochemistry, Dartmouth College; MBA, Harvard Business School
Background: Principal, Bain Capital; Consultant, Corporate Decisions Inc.
Directorships: Aimbridge Hospitality, Cross Mediaworks, Eating Recovery Center, Interluxe Holdings, Papa Murphy's International, Paragon Industries
Caitlyn MacDonald, Partner/Head of Investor Relations
Education: BS, Emerson College; MBA, Babson College
Background: Director, First Reserve; Investment Manager, SVG Advisers; Wellington Management
Joseph B Rotberg, Partner/Chief Financial Officer/Chief Compliance Officer
Education: BS, Accounting, School of Professional Accountancy, Long Island University; CPA
Background: CFO, Specialty Consulting, Mercer

Venture Capital & Private Equity Firms / Domestic Firms

Management Consulting; Worldwide Director, Internal Audit, Booz Allen Hamilton; Analyst, Salomon Brothers; Senior Auditor, Coopers & Lybrand
Directorships: Captive Resources, Eating Recovery Center

1105 LEEDS EQUITY PARTNERS
590 Madison Ave.
41st Floor
New York, NY 10022

Phone: 212-835-2000 **Fax:** 212-835-2020
e-mail: info@leedsequity.com
web: www.leedsequity.com

Mission Statement: Leeds Equity partners with successful management teams to invest in established companies with strong track records. Our investment approach is to concentrate on a limited number of high-quality investments, which allows us to devote substantial time and resources to each portfolio company in order to drive the necessary growth that can produce significant capital appreciation.

Industry Group Preference: Education, Training, Information Services, Business Products & Services
Portfolio Companies: Amplifire, BARBRI, Campus Management, CeriFi, Covenant Review, Edcentric, Education Management Corporation, EduK Group, Endeavor Schools, Evanta, Exterro, Fusion, iModules, INTO University Partnerships, Lrn, Knowledge Factor Nobel Learning Communities, Project Management Academy, Prosci, Simplify Compliance

Key Executives:
Jeffrey T Leeds, Co-Founder & Managing Partner
e-mail: jeffrey.leeds@leedsequity.com
Education: BA, History, Yale University; Marshall Scholar, Univ. of Oxford; JD, Harvard Law School
Background: Corporate Finance, Lazard Freres & Co.; Law Clerk, Hon. William J. Brennan Jr, Supreme Court of the United States
Directorships: Amplifire, BARBRI, CeriFi, Endeavor Schools, Exterro, Fusion Education Group, INTO University Partnerships, LRN, Simplify Compliance
Robert A Bernstein, Co-Founder & Managing Partner
e-mail: robert.bernstein@leedsequity.com
Education: BS, Economics, Wharton School
Background: M&A, Lazard Freres & Co.
Directorships: Campus Management, Edcentric, Project Management Academy, Prosci
Jacques V Galante, Partner
e-mail: jacques.galante@leedsequity.com
Education: BS, Finance, University of Illinois Champaign-Urbana
Background: Principal, Buyout Team, The Carlyle Group; Investment Banking, M&A Group, Salomon Smith Barney
Directorships: Amplifire, BARBRI, Campus Management, CeriFi, Edcentric, Exterro, LRN
Peter A Lyons, Partner & Chief Financial Officer
e-mail: peter.lyons@leedsequity.com
Education: BS, Accounting, Saint Michael's College; MBA, Stern School of Business
Background: Senior Manager, Ernst & Young LLP
Scott VanHoy, Partner
e-mail: scott.vanhoy@leedsequity.com
Education: BA, Economics, University of North Carolina; MBA, University of Chicago Graduate School of Business
Background: Vice President, DLJ Merchant Banking Partners; Associate, Quad-C Management; Investment Banking, Banc of America Securities LLC
Directorships: Endeavor Schools, Fusion Education Group, Project Management Academy, Prosci, Simplify Compliance
Eric Gevada, Managing Director
e-mail: eric.geveda@leedsequity.com
Education: BBA, Finance & Economics, University of Notre Dame; MBA, Stanford Graduate School of Business
Background: Senior Associate, Arsenal Capital Partners;

Associate, Lightyear Capital
Directorships: Amplifire, BARBRI, CeriFi, Edcentric
Christopher J Mairs, Managing Director
e-mail: christopher.mairs@leedsequity.com
Education: BSc, Mathematics, University of St. Andrews
Background: Greenhill & Co.
Directorships: Endeavor Schools, INTO University Partnerships, Project Management Academy, Prosci, Simplify Compliance
David C Neverson, Principal
e-mail: david.neverson@leedsequity.com
Education: BA, Business Administration, Morehouse College; MBA, Wharton School
Background: ICV Capital Partners
Directorships: Campus Management, Fusion Education Group
Kevin Malone, Principal
e-mail: kevin.malone@leedsequity.com
Education: BSBA, Finance and International Business, Olin Business School at Washington University
Background: Analyst, Harris Williams & Co.
Directorships: Amplifire, BARBRI, Edcentric, Exterro, LRN

1106 LEGACY VENTURE
180 Lytton Avenue
Palo Alto, CA 94301

Phone: 650-324-5980 **Fax:** 650-324-5982
e-mail: info@legacyventure.com
web: www.legacyventure.com

Mission Statement: Legacy is a unique organization tapping into the financial power of venture capital and combining it with an extensive philanthropic community.

Founded: 1999

Key Executives:
Russell B Hall, Co-Founder & Managing Partner
Education: MBA, Stanford Graduate School; MS, University of California; BS, United States Military
Background: Operator, Merrill Pickard Anderson & Eyre; Sr. Vice President, R. Eliot King & Associates
Kelli Cullinane, Managing Partner & Chief Financial Officer
Education: BA, Economics, MA, Accounting, University of Michigan
Background: HRJ Capital, Ernst & Young
Ben Choi, Managing Partner
Education: BA, Computer Science, Harvard University; MBA, Columbia Business School
Background: Adobe Creative Cloud; Greystripe; Co-Founder, CoffeeTable
Alan Marty, Managing Partner
Education: MBA, Stanford University; Iowa State University
Background: NASA; Hewlett-Packard

1107 LEMHI VENTURES
12800 Whitewater Dr.
Suite 100
Hopkins, MN 55343

Phone: 952-908-9680 **Fax:** 952-908-9780
e-mail: info@lemhiventures.com
web: www.lemhiventures.com

Mission Statement: Lemhi Ventures invests in companies that disrupt and transform the delivery of health care services. We seek entrepreneurs with market-driven new ideas, competitive assets and experienced teams that promise to create and sustain a more imaginative, more efficient, and more responsible health care system.

Industry Group Preference: Healthcare
Portfolio Companies: Bind, Digital Reasoning, PlanSource, PokitDok, Recondo Technology, Sandlot Solutions, Shareable Ink, TransEngen, Inc.

Key Executives:
Tony Miller, Managing Partner
Education: St. Olaf College; MS, University of Illinois; MBA, Cornell University
Background: UnitedHealth, Deloitte Consulting; CEO, Definity Health
Directorships: Bind
Jodi Hubler, Managing Director
Education: MAIR, BBA, Tillie College of Business, University of Iowa
Background: Cargill, Accoa, Definity Health
Directorships: Bind, Digital Reasoning, PokitDok, PlanSource, Recondo Technology

1108 LEO CAPITAL HOLDINGS, LLC
400 Skokie Blvd.
Suite 410
Northbrook, IL 60062

Phone: 847-418-3240 **Fax:** 847-418-3424

Mission Statement: Leo Capital Holdings, LLC is a privately funded venture investor making investments in early and later stage private companies. Our focus is primarily on consumer oriented technology and applications. We like ventures that target very large markets, and consider investment opportunities across the United States. Leo maintains a broad network of contacts, investors, and advisors with whom we work after investing to help build value, and usually make investments that allow for our active involvement.

Geographic Preference: United States
Minimum Investment: $1 million - $3 million
Investment Criteria: Early-stage, Late-stage
Industry Group Preference: Entertainment, Internet, Wireless, Technology, Consumer Technology
Portfolio Companies: EpiWorks, FunMobility, GirlSense, GrubHub, JabberSmack, Mighty Cast, NetNearU, PopStarClub, Shoutlet, Starnet Interactive, Tickr

Key Executives:
Randy O. Rissman, Founder and Managing Director
Education: BBA, The University of Michigan; MBA, The Harvard Business School
Background: Founder and CEO, Tiger Electronics

1109 LEONARD GREEN & PARTNERS LP
11111 Santa Monica Boulevard
Suite 2000
Los Angeles, CA 90025

Phone: 310-954-0444 **Fax:** 310-954-0404
e-mail: investorrelations@leonardgreen.com
web: www.leonardgreen.com

Mission Statement: To partner with management to enhance the value of companies through operational improvements, acquisitions, financial engineering and other strategic initiatives.

Geographic Preference: United States
Fund Size: $5.3 billion
Founded: 1989
Average Investment: $150 million
Minimum Investment: $50 million
Investment Criteria: LBO, MBO. Focus on companies worth more than $100 million. No start-ups, no technology-centric ventures
Industry Group Preference: Consumer Services, Business Products & Services, Consumer Products, Distribution, Financial Services, Healthcare, Media, Retail, Consumer & Leisure
Portfolio Companies: Advantage Sales & Marketing, AerSale Holdings, Animal Health International, Aspen Dental Management, Authentic Brands Group, BJ's Wholesale Club, Caliber Collision, Cascade Bancorp, CCC Information Services, Charter Nex Films, CHG Healthcare Services, Clean Energy Fuels, The Container Store, CPA Global, David's Bridal, Del Taco Holdings, Ellucian, Equinox Fitness, ExamWorks, HITS, IMS Health, InsightGlobal, IQVia, Jcrew Group, Jetro Cash & Carry, Jo-Ann Stores, LifeTime, Lucky Brand, MD VIP, Mister Car Wash Holdings, Motorsport Aftermarket Group, MultiPlan, North American Partners in Anesthesia, Palms Casino Resort, PDC Brands, Petco Animal Supplies, Promach, Prospect Medical Holdings, Puregym, Restorix Health, Savers, Scitor Corporation, The Shade Store, Shake Shack, Signet Jewelers, SoulCycle, The Sports Authority, SRS Distribution, Tank Holdings Corp., The Tire Rack, Topshop/Topman Holdings, Tourneau, Troon, Union Square Hospitality Group, United States Infrastructure Corporation, US Renal Care, Veritext

Key Executives:
John G Danhakl, Managing Partner
e-mail: danhakl@leonardgreen.com
Education: BA Economics, University of California, Berkeley; MBA, Harvard Business School
Background: Managing Director, DLJ; VP Corporate Finance, Drexel
Directorships: Advantage Solutions, Charter NEX, Genani Corp., Insight Global, IQVIA, J.Crew, Life Time Fitness, Mister Car Wash, MultiPlan, Savers, SRS Distribution
Jonathan Sokoloff, Managing Partner
e-mail: sokoloff@leonardgreen.com
Education: BA Political Economy and History, Williams College
Background: Managing Director, Drexel; Principal, Hambrecht & Quist; Woodman, Kirkpatrick & Gilbreath; Merrill Lynch & Co
Directorships: Advantage Solutions, The Container Store, J.Crew, Jetro Cash & Carry, JOANN Stores, Shake Shack, Signet Jewelers, Topshop/Topman, Union Square Hospitality Group
John M Baumer, Senior Partner
e-mail: baumer@leonardgreen.com
Education: BBA, University of Notre Dame; MBA, Wharton School
Background: VP, DLJ; Fidelity Investments; Arthur Andersen
Directorships: Aspen Dental, CHG Healthcare Services, ExamWorks, Prospect Medical, ResotirxHealth, SoulCycle, U.S. Renal Care
Jonathan Seiffer, Senior Partner
e-mail: seiffer@leonardgreen.com
Education: BS, Bachelor of Applied Science, University of Pennsylvania
Background: Corporate Finance, DLJ
Directorships: Aersale, Authentic Brands Group, BJ's Wholesale Club, Caliber Collision Centers, Mister Car Wash, Savers, SRS Distribution, The Tire Rack
Usama Cortas, Partner
Education: BA, Economics & Political Science, Columbia University
Background: M&A, Retail/Consumer Products Group, Morgan Stanley
Directorships: Authentic Brands Group, CPA Global, Ellucian, Tank Holdings
Timothy J Flynn, Partner
Education: BA, Economics & Political Science, Brown University
Background: Director, Investment Banking, Credit Suisse First Boston; DLJ; M&A, Paine Webber Inc.
Directorships: Authentic Brands Group, CPA Global, Ellucian, Tank Holdings
J Kristofer Galashan, Partner
Education: BA, Business Administration, Richard Ivey School of Business, University of Western Ontario
Background: Investment Banking, Credit Suisse First Boston
Directorships: BJ's Wholesale Club, The Container Store, Life Time Fitness, Mister Car Wash, Pure Gym, The Shade Store, Troon Golf, Union Square Hospitality Group
W. Christian McCollum, Partner
Education: BA, Economics and Government, Cornell

Venture Capital & Private Equity Firms / Domestic Firms

University; MBA, Wharton School at University of Pennsylvania
Background: Managing Director, Investcorp; Chemical Securities
Directorships: Charter NEX, Ellucian, ProMach, Veritext
Michael S Solomon, Partner
Education: BA, Economics, Pomona College; CFA
Background: Financial Sponsors Group, Deutsche Banc Alex Brown
Directorships: PDC Brands, Prospect Medical
Alyse Wagner, Partner
Education: BS, Economics, Wharton School
Background: Investment Banking, Credit Suisse First Boston
Directorships: Aersale, Aspen Dental, CHG Healthcare Services, ExamWorks, MDVIP, Prospect Medical, RestorixHealth, U.S. Renal Care
Pete Zippelius, Partner
Education: BS, Finance, Virginia Polytechnic Institute
Background: Managing Director & Co-Head, North American Healthcare Investment Banking, J.P. Morgan
Peter J Nolan, Senior Advisor
e-mail: nolan@leonardgreen.com
Education: BS Agricultural Economics and Finance, Cornell University; MBA, Johnson Graduate School of Management, Cornell University
Background: Managing Director/Co-Head, DLJ Investment Banking; First VP, Drexel; VP, Prudential Securities; Associate, Manufacturers Hanover Trust
Directorships: Activision, Aersale

1110 LERER HIPPEAU VENTURES
100 Crosby St.
Suite 308
New York, NY 10013

Phone: 646-237-4837
e-mail: contact@lererhippeau.com
web: www.lererhippeau.com

Mission Statement: Lerer Hippeau Ventures is a seed stage venture capital fund. We invest in founders in the earliest stages of a startup's life. We respect and seek out entrepreneurs with product vision, consumer insight, focused execution, and unwavering ambition. Lerer Ventures also operates SohoTechLabs, an incubator that builds start-ups from the idea up. When we are lucky enough to meet founders with these qualities, our hope is that they will choose us as a partner. Everyone here starts and runs companies for a living. Lerer Ventures is where we invest in our peers.

Investment Criteria: Seed-Stage
Portfolio Companies: Abra, Adaptly, Airtime, Allbirds, Ample Hills, Augury, AutoFi, Ava, Axial, Axios, Bark Box, BaubleBar, Bench, Betaworks, Bkstg, Blade, Block, Bloglovin', Bowery, Brami, Brat, Brit+Co, BuzzFeed, Camp, Casa, Casper, Chartbeat, Chubbies, Class Dojo, Clique Media Group, Clubhosue, Code Climate, Confide, Conversion Logic, Cotopaxi, Crexi, Crypt, CultureIQ, Dering Hall, Dia & Co., Digital Genius, DocSend, Doctor on Demand, Dragon Innovation, Drift, DRL, Even Financial, Everlane, Everytable, Expa, Fancy Hands, Fatherly, Fitplan, Food 52, FoxTrot, Fresh Nation, Friendsly, Fundera, Furnishare, Genies, Genius, Giphy, Glamsquad, Glossier, Goby, Good Uncle, Green Matters, Group Nine, Grovo, Guideline, Heartbeat, Herb, Heyday, Homer, Hungry Root, IFTTT, Inturn, JanusVR, Jibe, Joor, Jott, June, Keezy. K Health, Klara, Leaf Link, Le Tote, Little Bits, LiveIntent, Lola, Maxwell Health, Metric Insights, Mic, Mirror, Namely, Neighborhood Fuel, Neighborland, NewsCred, Ollie, Opentrons, OrderGroove, Ordway, Oscar, OwnLocal, Paintzen, Palmetto, Pando, Panna, Parsec, Percolate, Plus One Robotics, Poncho, Pop Dust, Power to Fly, Properly, Prose, Quartzy, Realm, Rebel Mouse, Refinery 29, Resy, Revere, Revolution Credit, Rockets of Awesome, Rubica, Sailthru, Science Exchange, Scout Mob, SeatGeek, Seller Crowd, Sfara, Skift, Social Sentinel, Soma, Soylent, Spacious, Spectrum, Splash, Splice, Sportsrocket, Spring, Stitch, Studypool, The Black Tux, The Inside, Thrive Global, Tikl, Tracksmith, Transfix, Tr

Key Executives:
Kenneth Lerer, Managing Partner
Background: Co-Founder, Huffington Post
Directorships: Buzzfeed, Group Nine Media, Blade, Thrive Global
Ben Lerer, Managing Partner
Education: University of Pennsylvania
Directorships: Group Nine Media, Casper, RaisedByUs, Refinery29
Eric Hippeau, Managing Partner
Education: Sorbonne University
Background: CEO, Huffington Post; Managing Partner, Softbank Capital
Directorships: Buzzfeed, Marriott International

1111 LEVINE LEICHTMAN CAPITAL PARTNERS
345 N Maple Drive
Suite 300
Beverly Hills, CA 90210

Phone: 310-275-5335 **Fax:** 310-275-1441
e-mail: main@llcp.com
web: www.llcp.com

Mission Statement: To provide capital to industry leading companies owned and managed by entrepreneurs.

Geographic Preference: United States
Fund Size: $452 million
Founded: 1984
Average Investment: $25 million
Minimum Investment: $10 million
Investment Criteria: Late Stage Venture, Growth/Expansion Capital, Recaps
Industry Group Preference: Aerospace, Defense and Government, Consumer Products, Entertainment, Equipment, Financial Services, Processing, Franchising, Healthcare, Radio, Real Estate, Security, Software, Food & Beverage, Telecommunications
Portfolio Companies: Allied Aerofoam Products, Beef 'O' Brady's, Bertucci's Corporation, Best Lawyers, Brass Smith Innovations, Capsa Healthcare, Caring Brands International, Champion Manufacturing, CJ Fallon, Deter Magnetic Technologies, FASTSIGNS International, FlexRay, Genova Diagnostics, GL Education, Global Franchise Group, Hand & Stone, HomeVestors, Jonathan Engineered Solutions, Law Business Research, Lawn Doctor, Magnolia Bluffs Casino, Mander Portman Woodward Limite, Mckenzie Sports Products, Monte Nido, Nobles Worldwide, Nothing Bundt Cakes, Pacific Handy Cutter, Pacific Wave Systems, Pacific World Corporation, The Poma Companies, Polyform Products Company, Regional Rail, Revenew International, Senior Helpers, SFERRA, Smith System Driver Improvement Institute, Squla, Synyron Maerial Handling, Therapeutic Research Center, Trinity Consultants, Tronair, Inc., Werner Holdings, West Academic, Wetzel's Pretzels, Zorg Domein

Key Executives:
Lauren B Leichtman, CEO/Founding Partner
Education: JD, Southwestern University; LLM, Columbia Law School
Background: Law, Public/Private Sectors; Securities and Exhange Commission
Arthur Levine, President/Founding Partner
Education: MBA, Anderson School of Management; JD, Columbia Law School
Background: Principal, Westwood One
Paul W. Drury, Senior Managing Director
Education: BS, Finances and Accounting, Texas Tech University; MBA, Booth School of Business at University of Chicago
Background: Vice President, The CIT Group; Bank of America

Monica J. Holec, Senior Managing Director
Education: HBA, Richard Ivey School of Business at University of Western Ontario
Background: Partner, Triago; Private Equity Funds, Merrill Lynch; Analyst, Investment Banking, DLJ Securities
Andrew M. Schwartz, Senior Managing Director
Education: BS, Economics, Wharton School; BSE, Computer Science and Engineering, University of Pennsylvania
Background: Vice President, Liberty Partners; Investment Banking Analyst, Jefferies & Company
David Wolmer, Senior Managing Director
Education: BA, University of Michigan; JD, Fordham University School of Law
Background: Associate, Milbank Tweed Hadley & McCloy LLP
John O'Neill, Senior Managing Director
Education: BComm, MA, Accounting, University College Dublin
Background: Partner, Graphite Capital; Hawkpoint Partners; Deloitte

1112 LEXINGTON PARTNERS
660 Madison Avenue
23rd Floor
New York, NY 10065
Phone: 212-754-0411 **Fax:** 212-754-1494
e-mail: info@lexpartners.com
web: www.lexingtonpartners.com

Mission Statement: Lexington Partners is the leading manager of secondary private equity fund investments and co-investments in leveraged equity transactions. Focus to provide liquidity to private equity investors interested in selling limited partnership interests.
Geographic Preference: United States, United Kingdom, Western Europe, Asia-Pacific
Fund Size: $15 billion
Founded: 1994
Minimum Investment: $1,000,000
Investment Criteria: Newly formed buyout, mezzanine, venture capital and international partnerships
Portfolio Companies: CardioKinetix, Emerald Solutions, Forcepoint, Movik Networks, PowerVision, Sovrn, Websense

Other Locations:
111 Huntington Avenue
Suite 2920
Boston, MA 02199
Phone: 617-247-7010 **Fax:** 617-247-7050

3000 Sand Hill Road
Building 1, Suite 220
Menlo Park, CA 94025
Phone: 650-561-9600 **Fax:** 650-561-9696

Lexington Partners UK LLP
50 Berkeley St.
London W1J 8HA
United Kingdom
Phone: 44-20-7399-3940 **Fax:** 44-20-7399-3941

Lexington Partners Asia Limited
15/F York House, The Landmark
15 Queen's Road Central
Central
Hong Kong
Phone: 852-3987-1600 **Fax:** 852-3987-1631

Lexington Partners Chile SpA
3477 Isidora Goyenechea Ave.
17th Floor, Suite 170 B
Las Condes, Santiago
Chile
Phone: 56-2-2487-6700
Key Executives:
Brent Nicklas, Founder & Chairman
212-754-0411
e-mail: brnicklas@lexpartners.com
Education: BA, Amherst College; MBA, Stanford Business School
Background: Founding Partner, Landmark Partners; Vice President, Merrill Lynch Capital Markets
Wilson S Warren, Partner & President
212-754-0411
e-mail: wswarren@lexpartners.com
Education: BA, Economics, Williams College
Background: Associate, Landmark Partners; Analyst, LaSalle Partners
Mark M Andrew, Partner, Boston
617-247-7010
e-mail: mmandrew@lexpartners.com
Education: BS, Management, University of Massachusetts Amherst
Background: Principal, Banc of America Securities
Charles R Grant, Partner, Boston
617-247-7010
e-mail: crgrant@lexpartners.com
Education: BCom, University of New South Whales
Background: Director, BancBoston Capital; Associate Director, BZW's Private Equity Group; Vice President, BankBoston LBO Lending Group
Lee J Tesconi, Partner, Boston
617-247-7010
e-mail: ljtesconi@lexpartners.com
Education: BS, Boston College; MBA, MIT Sloan School of Management
Background: Managing Director, BancBoston Capital; Vice President, BankBoston's LBO Lending Group
Duncan A Chapman, Partner, New York
212-754-0411
e-mail: dachapman@lexpartners.com
Education: BA, Economics, Columbia University
Background: President, Butler Chapman & Co; Senior Vice President, Lehman Brothers
Thomas Giannetti, Partner, New York
212-754-0411
e-mail: tgiannetti@lexpartners.com
Education: BS, Accounting, New York University
Background: Senior Manager, Audit, Ernst & Young
John G Loverro, Partner, New York
212-754-0411
e-mail: jloverro@lexpartners.com
Education: BA, Economics, Fairfield University; MBA, Darden School, University of Virginia
Background: Vice President, Investment Banking, JPMorgan; Portfolio Manager, PIMCO/Oppenheimer Capital; InverMexico
Bart D Osman, Partner, New York
212-754-0411
e-mail: bdosman@lexpartners.com
Education: BA, History, Dartmouth College; MBA, Tuck School of Business, Dartmouth College
Background: Director of Acquisitions & Investments, Reuters America; Analyst, Merrill Lynch
David B Outcalt, Partner, New York
212-754-0411
e-mail: dboutcalt@lexpartners.com
Education: BA, Economics, Williams College; MBA, The Wharton School
Background: Associate, Landmark Partners; Analyst, Bear Stearns
Marshall W Parke, Partner, New York
212-754-0411
e-mail: mwparke@lexpartners.com
Education: BA, George Washington University; MIM, American Graduate School of International Management

Venture Capital & Private Equity Firms / Domestic Firms

Background: Director, Pomona Capital; Hong Kong Bank; Wells Fargo Bank; Chase Manhattan Bank
John G Rudge, Partner, New York
212-754-0411
e-mail: jgrudge@lexpartners.com
Education: BA, American Civilizations, Middlebury College; MBA, Tuck School of Business, Dartmouth
Background: Associate, Investment Banking, Morgan Stanley
Victor L Wu, Partner, New York
212-754-0411
e-mail: vlwu@lexpartners.com
Education: BBA, University of Michigan Busines School; MBA, The Wharton School
Background: Analyst, Investment Banking, Goldman Sachs
Tom Newby, Partner, Menlo Park
650-561-9600
e-mail: tnewby@lexpartners.com
Education: BS, Business Administration, University of North Carolina; MBA, Stanford Graduate School of Business
Background: Managing Director, Montgomery & Co; General Partner, Technology Crossover Ventures
Jennifer W Kheng, Partner, Menlo Park
650-561-9600
e-mail: jwkheng@lexpartners.com
Education: BS, Biological Sciences, MS, Management Science & Engineering, Stanford University
Background: Analyst, Morgan Stanley
James D.C. Pitt, Partner, London
44-20-7399-3940
e-mail: jpitt@lexpartners.com
Education: BSc, Management Science, City University, London; MBA, INSEAD, France
Background: Managing Director, AXA Private Equity; Managing Director, Whitney & Co; Vice President, Morgan Stanley's Leveraged Finance Group
Anthony W. Garton, Partner, London
44-20-7399-3940
e-mail: agarton@lexpartners.com
Education: BA, Hispanic and Latin American Studies, University of Bristol
Background: Principal, Conven; Vice President, Investment Banking, Credit Suisse; Associate Director, UBS Investment Bank
Pal B Ristvedt, Partner, London
44-20-7399-3940
e-mail: pbristvedt@lexpartners.com
Education: BS, Business Administration, University of California Berkeley; MBA, INSEAD, France
Background: Investment Banking, Morgan Stanley
Kirk M. Beaton, Partner, Hong Kong
852-3987-1600
e-mail: kbeaton@lexpartners.com
Education: LLB, University of Strathclyde; Universität Hamburg; Universidad Complutense de Madrid
Background: Analyst, Investment Banking, Morgan Stanley
Timothy Huang, Partner, Hong Kong
852-3987-1600
e-mail: thuang@lexpartners.com
Education: BS, Business Administration, Cornell University; MBA, Booth School of Business at University of Chicago
Background: Executive Director, LGT Capital Partners; Engagement Manager, Investment AB Kinnevik
Jose M. Sosa del Valle, Partner, Santiago
56-2-2487-6700
e-mail: jsosadelvalle@lexpartners.com
Education: MS, Industrial Engineering, Instituto Technológico de Buenos Aires; MBA, Columbia Business School
Background: Associate, Investment Banking, Goldman Sachs

1113 LFE CAPITAL
319 Barry Ave. South
Suite 215
Wayzata, MN 55391

Phone: 612-752-1809 Fax: 612-752-1800
e-mail: laurent@lfecapital.com
web: www.lfecapital.com

Mission Statement: LFE Capital invests in businesses with revenues of $5 to $50 million that need capital to support a plan of rapid growth.

Geographic Preference: Upper Midwest Region
Founded: 1999
Average Investment: $2 - $5 million
Industry Group Preference: Business Products & Services, Healthcare, Medical Devices, Consumer Services, Consumer Products
Portfolio Companies: API Outsourcinv, Avant Healthcare Professionals, The Big Know, Coolibar, eMindful, Fitness on Request, M.A. Gedney, Gentra Systems, Global ID Group, Halo Innovations, Immaculate Baking Co., Inlet Medical, Jackson's Honest, JobDig, Portero, SimonDelivers, Wellbeats

Other Locations:
649 Fifth Ave. South
Suite 226
Naples, FL 34102

Key Executives:
Leslie Frécon, Founder & Managing Partner
Education: BA, Stanford University; MBA, Finance, UCLA
Background: SVP, Corporate Finance, General Mills; Corporate Lending Officer, Bank of America

1114 LIBERTY CAPITAL PARTNERS
Naples, FL

Phone: 203-323-6666
e-mail: info@libertycapitalpartners.com
web: www.libertycapitalpartners.com

Mission Statement: Liberty Capital Partners provides wealth management services, private equity opportunities, and corporate advisory services to its clients.

Founded: 1994
Investment Criteria: Early-Stage, Growth-Stage
Industry Group Preference: Software, Equipment, Financial Services, Food & Beverage
Portfolio Companies: All Seasons Services, Armstrong Franklin, ASP, Asure Software, ConnectEDU, Dynadec, Finale, GCA Services Group, Global Asset Alternatives, Heartlab, Impact, Liberty Tire Recycling, Meyer Materials, Nattagansett Beer, Portfolio Solutions, Remotely, Rentbits, Spada Media, Windward Petroleum

Other Locations:
Stamford, CT
Troy, MI

Key Executives:
James S Gladney, Founder/Managing Partner
e-mail: jgladney@libertycapitalpartners.com
Education: BS, University of Rhode Island
Background: Managing Partner, Park Avenue Equity Partners
Directorships: All Seasons Services, Rentbits, Remotely

1115 LIBERTY CITY VENTURES
East 45th St.
New York, NY 10017

e-mail: info@libertycityventures.com
web: www.libertycityventures.com

Mission Statement: Liberty City Ventures is a seed stage fund headquartered in New York City. We invest in startups that are innovating at the cross-sections of technology, media and commerce. We began operations in the summer of 2012

Venture Capital & Private Equity Firms / Domestic Firms

and are led by experienced technology executives and investors.

Founded: 2012
Investment Criteria: Seed
Industry Group Preference: Technology, Media, Commerce
Portfolio Companies: BitGo, Boost, BRD, Faith Street, Farm Hill, Hullabalu, itBit, LibraTax, Parcel, Parenthoods, Paxos, Pickie, Solid Partners, TripleLift

Key Executives:
  Charles Cascarilla, CFA, Founding Partner
  Education: BBA, Finance, Univesity of Notre Dame
  Background: Co-Founder, Cedar Hill Capital Partners; Portfolio Manager, Claiborne Capital; Analyst, Bank of America Securities; Analyst, Goldman Sachs
  Andrew Chang, Founding Partner
  Education: BS, Operation and Technology Management, Boston College; MBA, New York University
  Background: COO, ConditionOne; Associate, TechStars; Operations, Kantar Video; Consumer Insights and Research Division, 360i
  Dorothy Jean Chang, Founding Partner
  Education: Yale University
  Background: VP, Brew Media Relations; Edelman; Text 100
  Emil Woods, Founding Partner
  Education: BSE, Wharton School
  Background: Portfolio Manager (Current) And Co-Founder, Cedar Hill Capital Partners, LLC; Portfolio Manager, SAC Capital Management; Equities and Asset Management Division, Goldman Sachs

1116 LIBERTY PARTNERS
750 Third Ave.
9th Floor
New York, NY 10017

Phone: 212-541-7676 Fax: 212-649-6076
e-mail: mfram@libertypartners.com

Mission Statement: To generate additional value in middle-market and growth enterprises by partnering with management to merge our capital and intellectual resources with management's operational expertise.

Geographic Preference: North America
Fund Size: $1 billion
Founded: 1992
Average Investment: $20 - $75 million
Minimum Investment: $5 million
Investment Criteria: Buyouts, Recapitalizations, Consolidations, Build-Ups, Growth Equity
Industry Group Preference: Niche Manufacturing, Software, Services, Healthcare, Business Products & Services, Communications, Software Services, Education
Portfolio Companies: Avenues: The World School, Concorde Career Colleges, Edison Learning, Edgenet, Fortress Technologies, Henley-Putnam University, High Tower Software, Padcom, Secure Data in Motion, Step2

Key Executives:
  Peter Bennett, Chairman
  e-mail: pbennett@libertypartners.com
  Education: BS, Lehigh University; MBA, Columbia University
  Background: Manager Private Financing/Managing Director, Merrill Lynch Capital Markets; Senior VP, Merrill Lynch Interfunding; US Army
  G Michael Stakias, President & CEO
  e-mail: mstakias@libertypartners.com
  Education: BA, College of William & Mary; JD, Thomas M Cooley Law School; LLM Corporate Finance, New York University School of Law
  Background: Senior Partner, Blank Rome Comisky & McCauley; Corporate Finance Division, US Securities & Exchange Commission
  Thomas G Greig, Senior Managing Director
  Education: BS Electrical Engineering, Princeton University; MS Electrical Engineering, New York University; MBA, Harvard Business School
  Background: Head Technology Investment Banking, Donaldson Lufkin & Jennette
  Michael S. Levine, Senior Managing Director
  Education: BS Economics, Wharton School of the University of Pennsylvania
  Background: General Partner, Joseph Littlejohn & Levy; Managing Director, Chase Manhatte/Merrill Lynch/Drexel Burnham Lambert/McKinsey & Co
  Michael J Fram, Managing Director
  e-mail: mfram@libertypartners.com
  Education: BS Business Economics, University of California; MBA, New York University; CPA
  Background: Transaction Support Group, Ernst & Young

1117 LIFE SCIENCES GREENHOUSE OF CENTRAL PA
225 Market Street
Suite 500
Harrisburg, PA 17101

Phone: 717-635-2100 Fax: 717-635-2010
web: www.lsgpa.com

Mission Statement: The Life Sciences Greenhouse is a public/private venture whose mission is to commercialize bioscience technologies.

Geographic Preference: Pennsylvania
Investment Criteria: Early-Stage
Industry Group Preference: Life Sciences, Biosciences
Portfolio Companies: Azevan Pharmaceuticals, Chromatan, Immunomic Therapeutics, Indigo Biosciences, INRange Systems, MacuLogix, Micro Inverventional Devices, NanoHorizons, Novasentis, QuantumBio, Ras Therapeautics, Saladax Biomedical

Key Executives:
  Mel Billingsley PhD, President & CEO
  Education: BS, Biophysics & Microbiology, University of Pittsburgh; Doctoral Degree, Pharmacology, George Washington University; Postdoctoral Degree, Neuropharmacology, Yale School of Medicine
  Background: Professor, Pharmacology, Pennsylvania State University Milton S Hershey College of Medicine
  Ronald P Thiboutot PhD, Executive Vice President
  717-635-2102
  Education: BS, MS, PhD, Massachusetts College of Pharmacy
  Background: President, RT Consultants; Plant Director, Wyeth Pharmaceuticals
  Steve Carpenter, Vice President, Venture Operations
  717-635-2131
  Education: BS, Mechanical Engineering, Lehigh University; MBA, Pennsylvania State University
  Background: DuPont, Berg Electronics, FCI USA

1118 LIGHTBANK
600 West Chicago Avenue
Suite 775
Chicago, IL 60654

e-mail: press@lightbank.com
web: www.lightbank.com

Mission Statement: Provides a solid business model, technology that works, top talend and an experienced connected partner.

Investment Criteria: Early-Stage
Industry Group Preference: Social Media, Consumer Internet, Business to Business, Consumer Products
Portfolio Companies: Ark, Babba Co., BeachMint, Beautylish, Belly, BenchPrep, Benzinga, Betterfly, Beyond Games, Bonfaire, Boom, Carlease, Catalytic, Classkick, Clearcover, Cleversense, Coffee Meets Bagel, Contently, Crowdrise, Doubledutch, Dough, Draft Day, Drivin, ElaCarte, Eventup, Expel, Fiverr, Fooda, Frank & Oak,

405

Venture Capital & Private Equity Firms / Domestic Firms

FreeAgent, GameFlip, GetGoing, HDVI, HighGround, Hipster, Hireology, Ionic, Lifecrowd, Lightswitch, Locality, Locu, Markkit, Needle, Neumob, Nubundle, Obaz, Onswipe, Ovia Health, Ovuline, Paladin Cyber, Pawngo, PerBlue, Qwiki, Reverb, Riskmatch, SkyVu, Snapsheet, SnapTravel, Socialkaty, SoCore Energy, Soundsupply, SpotHero, Sprout Social, Tagkast, Take Lessons, Talent Bin, TastyTrade, TastyWorks, Team Liquid, Tempus, Udemy, Uptake, Vettery, Whos Here, Zaarly, Zeel, Zero, Zest Health

Key Executives:
Eric Lefkofsky, Partner & Co-Founder
Education: JD, University of Michigan Law School
Background: Founder & CEO, Tempus; Co-Founder & Chairman, Groupon
Brad Keywell, Partner & Co-Founder
Education: BBA, JD, University of Michigan
Background: Founder, Echo Global Logistics, MediaBank, Groupon
Vic Pascucci III, Managing Partner
Background: USAA; Partner, Munich Re/HSB Ventures
Directorships: Clearcover, Snapshet, Carlease, Sprout Social, Fooda, Paladin Cyber, Hireology, Ionic, Hatch Loyalty, Benchprep, Udemy, NuBundle, Billtrim

1119 LIGHTHOUSE CAPITAL PARTNERS
3555 Alameda de las Pulgas
Suite 200
Menlo Park, CA 94025

Phone: 650-233-1001
e-mail: info@lcpartners.com
web: lcpartners.com

Mission Statement: A private venture capital partnership specializing in providing debt financing to technology based start-up companies which have already received financing commitments from top tier venture capital firms.
Geographic Preference: United States
Fund Size: $650 million
Founded: 1994
Average Investment: $5 million
Minimum Investment: $1 million
Investment Criteria: Startups, Early-Stage, Growth Capital, Equipment Financing
Industry Group Preference: Technology, Life Sciences
Portfolio Companies: Angie's List, ARYx Therapeutics, Azelon Pharmaceuticals, BiPar Sciences, Cogit.com, DiVitas Networks, HDmessaging, if(we), iHear Medical, Kala Pharmaceuticals, Life360, LVL7 Systems, Mimosa Systems, NanoH2O, Rafter, Responsys, Revivio, Santur Corporation, Shansong (FlashEX), Shixianghui, Transera Communications, ZestFinance

Other Locations:
255 Main St.
Kendall Center
Cambridge, MA 02142
Phone: 617-441-9192 **Fax:** 617-354-4374

303 Wyman St.
Suite 300
Waltham, MA 02451
Phone: 617-441-9192

336 Bon Air Center
Suite 527
Greenbrae, CA 94904
Phone: 415-464-5900

Key Executives:
Richard Stubblefield, Co-Founder/Managing Director
415-484-5977
e-mail: rick@lcpartners.com
Education: BS, University of California; MBA, Golden Gate University
Background: Senior VP, Comdisco Ventures
Gwill York, Co-Founder/Managing Director
617-441-9192 ext 601
e-mail: gwill@lcpartners.com
Education: AB, Harvard University; MBA, Harvard Business School
Background: Senior VP, Comdisco Ventures
Cristy Barnes, Managing Director
650-233-1007
Education: BA Psychology, University of California, Los Angeles
Background: Senior Associate, Highland Capital Partners; Internet Research Group, Robertson Stephens
Jeff Griffor, Managing Director
617-441-9192 x 604
e-mail: jeff@lcpartners.com
Education: BS Business Economics/Finance, Ohio University; MBA, Loyola University Chicago
Background: Commercial/Technology Lending Experience, Fleet Boston; Loan/Credit Analysis, CIT Groupo/First Chicago National Bank
Ned Hazen, Mangaging Director
617-441-9192 x 603
e-mail: ned@lcpartners.com
Education: AB Political Science, Brown University; MBA Harvard Business School
Background: Investment Banker, Venture Capitalist, Senior Finance Operations Executive, Avid Technology/Robertson Stephens and Company
Damian Arroyo, Managing Director
Background: Manager, Private Banking, Banc Sabadell Banco Banif and Banco Madrid

1120 LIGHTHOUSE PARTNERS
3801 PGA Boulevard
Suite 500
Palm Beach Gardens, FL 33410

Phone: 561-741-0820 **Fax:** 561-748-9046
web: www.lighthousepartners.com

Mission Statement: Lighthouse Partners provide an alternative to traditional fixed income investments to offer flexibility to companies.
Geographic Preference: North America
Fund Size: $5 billion
Founded: 1996
Industry Group Preference: All Sectors Considers

Other Locations:
71 S Wacker Drive
Suite 1860
Chicago, IL 60606
Phone: 312-592-1820 **Fax:** 312-592-1839

437 Madison Avenue
21st Floor
New York, NY 10022
Phone: 212-588-0342 **Fax:** 212-588-0338

4th Floor
St. Albans House
57/59 Haymarket
London SW1Y 4QX
United Kingdom
Phone: 44-0-203-189-9470

20/F, Central Tower
28 Queen's Road
Central
Hong Kong
Phone: 852-2159-9612 **Fax:** 852-2159-9688

W22F Sjibuya Mark City
1-12-1 Dogenzaka
Shibuya-ku
Tokyo 150-0043
Japan
Phone: 81-0-3-4360-5415 **Fax:** 81-0-3-4360-5301

Key Executives:
Sean McGould, President/Co-Chief Investment Officer
Education: BSc, Accounting, Butler University

Venture Capital & Private Equity Firms / Domestic Firms

Directorships: Outside Trader Investment Program, Trout Trading Management Co.; HFA Holdings Ltd.; Price Waterhouse
Kelly Perkins, Co-Chief Investment Officer
Education: BBA, Accounting, College of William and Mary; CFA
Background: Coopers & Lybrant LLP
Directorships: Accounting, Trout Trading Management Co.
Robert Swan, Chief Operating Officer
Education: BA, Business Economics, University of California
Background: Senior Treasury Consultant, Computer Sciences Corp.; Ernst & Young
Directorships: Accounting, Trout Trading Management Co.
Scott Perkins, Executive Managing Director
Education: BBA, Accounting, College of William and Mary; JD, Washington & Lee University School of Law
Background: Corporate Attorney, Mays & Valentine LLP; Coopers & Lybrand LLP
Jack Swan, Executive Managing Director
Education: BA, English, University of Georgia
Background: Trout Trading Management Co.; Financial Counsultant, Merrill Lynch

---

1121 LIGHTSPEED VENTURE PARTNERS
2200 Sand Hill Road
Menlo Park, CA 94025

Phone: 650-234-8300 **Fax:** 650-234-8333
web: lsvp.com

Mission Statement: To serve as lead investors on early stage consumer and enterprise ventures in the areas of fintech, media, commerce, security, infrastructure, saas, big data, analytics, and more.
Geographic Preference: United States, Israel, China, India
Fund Size: $4 Billion
Founded: 1971
Average Investment: $5 million
Minimum Investment: $2 million
Investment Criteria: Early
Industry Group Preference: Enterprise, Big Data, Analytics, Infrastructure, Security, Social, Consumer, Fintech, E-Commerce & Manufacturing, Media, SaaS
Portfolio Companies: 51VR, 99Bill, Aerohive, Affirm, Affirmed Networks, Airbug, Alooma, Amec, AppDynamics, Aqua Security, Aquantia, Arbor Networks, Arctic Wolf, Athos, Audius, Avamar, Avere Systems, Avi Networksm Barefoot Networks, Basis.io, Beme, Betterup, Binaris, Bitmain, Blend, Blockchain, Bloomreach, Blue Nile Bluevine, Bonobos, Brandable, Brocade, Bromium, BTCC, Building Connected, BYJU's, Calista Technologies, Candis, Celequest, Che101, Cheddar, Ciena, Citadel, Clark, Clever, Cloud Moment, Cloudbees, Coding, Cohere Technologies, Companion, Comprehend, Craftsvilla, Crowdamp, Daily Harvest, Darwinbox, Datastax, Datorama, Datos IO, Datrium, Delphix, Dianping, Docker, DOTC United, Dote, Double Click, Dr.2, Dremio, EastMachinery, Edaijia, Edgespring, Ehealth, Elastifile, Elementum, Ensilo, Epic Games, Epsagon, Evariant, Eve.com, Everstring, Evolv, Exabeam, Extensity, Eyeview, Face U, Faire, FangDD, Fashionara, Fastfox, Fireglass, Fivestars, Flip, Flixster, Forty Seven, Freight Tiger, FreshMenu, Fushion-IO, Gainsight, Galileo Technology, Giphy, Girlboss, Global Peersafe, GMedia, Goop, Grab, Growth Networks, GrubHub, Guardant Health, Handshake, Hanshow, Heptio, HighFive, Hollar, Hongchizhineng, HungryRoot, IEver, IfChange, IHaveU, Illumix, Indian Energy Exchange, Influitive, Informatica, Innolight, Innovaccer, Insightera, IO Turbine, Iplas, Itzcash Card, Karius, Kenandy, Kespry, Kiva Software, Kixeye, KJK, Kodiak Robotics, Kongregate, Kosmix, Ladder, Laiye, Ledgerx, Lele Global, Lian Luo,

Other Locations:
1st Floor, Commercial Annex
Hotel Grand, Nelson Mandela Road
Vasant Kunj II
New Dehli 110070
India
Phone: 91 11 4980 0800

Sarona
4 Zvi Strachilevich Street
Tel Aviv 6473957
Israel
Phone: 972 3 974 6800 **Fax:** 972 3 974 6851

21/F, Suite 2105
Platinum Building, No. 233 Tai Cang Road
Huang Pu District
Shanghai 200020
China
Phone: 86 21 5386-6500 **Fax:** 86 21 5386-6668

Unit 3007, Tower 2
China Central Place, No. 79 Jian Guo Road
Chaoyang District
Beijing 100025
China
Phone: 86 10 5969-5980 **Fax:** 86 10 5969-6690

Key Executives:
Andrew Moley, Operating Partner & CFO
e-mail: andrew@lsvp.com
Education: The Wharton School; Stanford University
Background: eGreetings Network; CMC Industries; Mercer Management Consulting
Arif Janmohamed, Partner
e-mail: arif@lsvp.com
Education: University of Waterloo; The Wharton School
Background: Cisco Systems; WebTV; Andes Network
Barry Eggers, Founding Partner
Education: BA Economics/Business, UCLA; MBA, Stanford University
Background: Weiss, Peck & Greer Venture Partners; Director Business Development, Cisco Systems
Bipul Sinha, Partner
Education: Indian Institute of Technology; The Wharton School
Background: Blumberg Capital; Oracle Corporation; American Megatrends; IBM
Christopher Schaepe, Partner
Education: BS/MS, Massachusetts Institute of Technology; MBA, Stanford Graduate School of Business
Background: Weiss, Peck & Greer Venture Partners; Corporate Finance/Capital Markets, Goldman, Sachs & Company; Software Engineer, IBM
David Gussarsky, Partner
Education: BA, Economics, LLB, Tel Aviv University; MBA, Insead, Fountainebleu, France
Background: Partner, BRM Capital; CEO, Paspar2; Corporate Attorney, Rosensweig & Company; Israeli Defense Forces; Eudentics
Jeremy Liew, Partner
e-mail: jeremy@lsvp.com
Education: BA/BSc, Australian National University; MBA, Stanford University
Background: SVP, Corporate Development, AOL; Chief of Staff, Netscape; CitySearch; Interactive Corp.
John Vrionis, Partner
Education: BA, Harvard University; MS, Computer Science, University of Chicago; MBA, Stanford University
Background: Product Management, Determina; Freedom Financial Network
Peter Nieh, Partner
Education: BS Electrical Engineering, AB Economics, MBA, Stanford University
Background: Weiss, Peck & Greer Venture Partners; Business Development/Product Marketing, General Magic; Acer; Strategy Consultant, Bain & Comapny

407

Venture Capital & Private Equity Firms / Domestic Firms

Ravi Mhatre, Partner
Education: BS Electrical Engineering, BA Economics, MBA, Stanford University
Background: Weiss, Peck & Greer Venture Partners; Bessemer Venture Partners; Market Development, Silicon Graphics; Lehman Brothers; Booz Allen Hamilton; BDIS
Yoni Chiefetz, Partner
e-mail: yoni@lightspeedvp.com
Education: MSc, Applied Mathematics & Computer Science, Weizmann Institue of Science; BSc, Applied Mathematics, Tel-Aviv University
Background: Partner, Star Ventures

1122 LIGHTSTONE VENTURES
2884 Sand Hill Road
Suite 121
Menlo Park, CA 94025
Phone: 650-388-3676 Fax: 650-388-3675
web: www.lightstonevc.com

Mission Statement: Lightstone Ventures, formed by the life science teams of Advanced Technology Ventures and Morgenthaler Ventures, targets early stage life sciences companies with the potential to transform medicine.

Fund Size: $172 million
Founded: 2012
Investment Criteria: Early Stage
Industry Group Preference: Life Sciences, Biotechnology, Medical Devices, Biopharmaceuticals, Therapeutics
Portfolio Companies: Acceleron, Alexo Therapeutics, Calithera, Catabasis, Catalyst Biosciences, Claret Medical, EarLens, Elcelyx, EndoGastric Solutions, FIRE1, Flex Pharma, ForSight VISION4, ForSight VISIONS, Galleon, GlobeImmune, Holaira, Hydra Biosciences, Kona Medical, Miramar Labs, Mosaic Biosciences, Moximed, Nexis Vision, Nimbus Therapeutics, OncoMed, Optiscan, Powervision, Principia, Promedior, Ra Pharma, Relievant Medsystems, Scioderm, Second Genome, SetPoint Medical, Spine Wave, Stemgent, Thrasos Therapeutics, Tragara, Transcend Medical, Twelve, Vapotherm

Other Locations:
500 Boylston Street
Suite 1380
Boston, MA 02116
Phone: 617-933-3770 Fax: 617-933-3769

9 Pembrook Street
Dublin 2
Ireland

OCBC Centre #27-07
65 Chulia Street 049513
Singapore

Key Executives:
Mike Carusi, General Partner
e-mail: mcarusi@lightstonevc.com
Education: BS, Mechanical Engineering, Lehigh University; MBA, Amos Tuck School of Business Administration, Dartmouth College
Background: Director, Business Development, Inhale Therapeutic Systems; Principal, The Wilkerson Group
Directorships: National Venture Capital Association
Chris Christoffersen PhD, Special Partner
e-mail: rchris@lightstonevc.com
Education: BS, Chemistry & Mathematics, Cornell College; PhD, Chemistry, Indiana University
Background: President & CEO, Ribozyme Pharmaceuticals; Senior VP, Research, SmithKline Beecham; VP, Discovery Research, The Upjohn Company; President, Colorado State University
Directorships: GlobeImmune, Catalyst Biosciences, Galleon Pharmaceuticals, Tragara Pharmaceuticals, Stemgent, Elcelyx, Calithera Biosciences
Jean George, General Partner
e-mail: jgeorge@lightstonevc.com
Education: BS, University of Maine; MBA, Simmons College Graduate School of Management
Background: VP, Global Sales & Marketing, Genzyme Corporation; BancBoston Ventures
Hank Plain, General Partner
e-mail: hplain@lightstonevc.com
Education: BS, Finance, University of Missouri
Background: Founder, Ardian; President & CEO, Perclose; Chairman, Embolic Protection; Director, TransVascular
Directorships: EarLens, Claret
Jason Lettmann, General Partner
e-mail: jason@lightstonevc.com
Education: BA, University of Iowa; MBA, Ross School of Business, University of Michigan
Background: VP, Split Rock Partners; Co-Founder, Tarsus Medical; Guidant Corporation; Accenture; Genetic Research Analyst, University of Iowa
Directorships: Alexo Therapeutics, FIRE1, Promedior, Ra Pharmaceuticals, Relievant Medsystems, Second Genome, Spinewave, Vapotherm

1123 LIGHTYEAR CAPITAL
9 West 57th Street
New York, NY 10019
Phone: 212-328-0555 Fax: 212-328-0516
e-mail: proposals@lycap.com
web: www.lycap.com

Mission Statement: Lightyear Capital is a leading private equity firm providing buyout and growth capital to companies across the financial services industry.

Fund Size: $3 billion
Founded: 2000
Investment Criteria: Buyouts, Growth Capital
Industry Group Preference: Financial Services
Portfolio Companies: Advisor Group, Alegus Technologies, Antares Holdings Limited, ARGUS Software, Athilon Group Holdings Corp., Augeo FI, BakerCorp, Cascade Bancorp, Cerity Partners, Cetera Financial Group, Clarion Partners, Collegiate Funding Services, Community & Southern Bank Holdings, Datalot, eCommission, Ed., First Sun Capital, Flagstone Reinsurance Holdings Limited, Goldleaf Financial Solutions, Kepler Equities, NAU Country Insurance Company, Paradigm Management Services, Ridgeworth Investments, Therapy Brands, Ygrene Energy Fund, Wealth Enhancement Group

Key Executives:
Chris C Casciato, Managing Director
Education: BS, Civil Engineering, United States Military Academy; MBA, Harvard Business School
Background: Partner, Goldman Sachs & Co.
Daniel Freyman, Managing Director
Education: BS, Applied Economics and Business Management, Cornell University
Background: Credit Suisse, Alex. Brown
Stewart KP Gross, Managing Director
Education: BA, Government, Harvard University; MBA, Columbia Business School
Background: Warburg Pincus
Thierry F Ho, Managing Director
Education: BA, Economics, Harvard University; MBA, Wharton School; CFA; CMA
Background: PainWebber, JP Morgan & Co., Goldman Sachs & Co.
Michal Petrzela, Managing Director
Education: BS, Accounting and Finance, Syracuse University; MBA, Stanford Graduate School of Business
Background: Barclays, Credit Suisse, Arthur Andersen
Boris Rapoport, Managing Director
Education: BA/BS, International Studies and Economics, University of Pennsylvania
Background: Principal, FTV Capital; Investment Banker, W.R. Hambrecht & Co.
Donald B Marron, Founder/Chairman
Education: City University of New York

Background: Co-Founder, Data Resources Inc.; Chairman & CEO, Paine Webber Group
Mark F Vassallo, Managing Partner
Education: BA, Economics, Harvard University; MBA, Columbia Business School
Background: Managing Director, PaineWebber

1124 LILLY VENTURES
115 West Washington Street
Suite 1680 - South
Indianapolis, IN 46204

Phone: 317-429-0140 **Fax:** 317-75928191
web: www.lillyventures.com

Mission Statement: Lilly Ventures is the venture capital arm of Eli Lilly and Company responsible for life science investing in North America and Europe. Our primary goal is to facilitate the success of companies in our areas of focus through early to expansion stage investments and value-adding resources.

Geographic Preference: North America, Europe
Fund Size: $200 million
Founded: 2001
Investment Criteria: Early - Expansion Stage, Start-Up
Industry Group Preference: Biotechnology, Pharmaceuticals
Portfolio Companies: Aeglea Biotherapeutics, Aileron Therapeutics, Avid Radiopharmaceuticals, Cavion, Cerulean Pharma, CGI Pharmaceuticals, Coherus Biosciences, esanex, Esanex, Forma Therapeutics, GlobeImmune, Hydra Biosciences, InCube Ventures, InnoCentive, Innocrin, Intradigm Corporation, Kymera Therapeutics, Lysomal Therapeutics, Nimbus Discovery, Numerate, Protagonist Therapeutics, Receptos, Surface Oncology, Sutro Biopharma, Symic Biomedical, Viamet Pharmaceuticals

Key Executives:
S Edward Torres, Managing Director
e-mail: ed@lillyventures.com
Education: BA, Creighton University; MBA, University of Michigan Business School
Background: CFO, Lilly Argentina
Directorships: Innocrin Pharmaceuticals, Viamet Pharmaceuticals
Steven E Hall, General Partner
e-mail: steve@lillyventures.com
Education: BS, Chemistry, Central Michigan University; PhD, Organic Chemistry, MIT
Background: Co-Founder & Senior Vice President, R&D, Serenex; Site Director, Sphinx Labs
Directorships: Cavion Pharma, Esanex, FORMA Therapeutics, Hydra Biosciences, Kymera Therapeutics, Lysosomal Therapeutics, Nimbus Therapeutics
Armen B Shanafelt, General Partner
e-mail: armen@lillyventures.com
Education: BS, Chemistry & Physics, Pacific Lutheran University; PhD, Chemistry, University of California, Berkeley
Background: CSO, Biotherpeutic Pipeline, Eli Lilly & Company; DNAS Research Insitute; Director of Research, Roche Diagnostic Corporation; Bayer Corporation
Directorships: Aeglea BioTherapeutics, Aileron Therapeutics, Protagonist Therapeutics, Surface Oncology, Sutro Biopharma, Symic Biomedical

1125 LIME ROCK PARTNERS
Heritage Plaza
Suite 4600
1111 Bagby Street
Houston, TX 77002

Phone: 713-292-9500
web: www.lrpartners.com

Mission Statement: Private equity firm focused on the oil and gas sector.

Fund Size: $7.4 billion
Founded: 1998
Industry Group Preference: Energy, Engineering, Oil & Gas, Mining
Portfolio Companies: AccessESP, Airis Wellsite Services, Archer, Ardyne, Arena Gulf, Augustus Energy Partners II, Axis Energy Services, Basin Properties, Blackjewel, Capstone Natural Resources II, Cor4 Oil, CrownRock, CrownRock Minerals, OilSERV, Prime Rock Resources, Reelwell, Reveal Energy Services, San Jacinto Minerals, SDI Gas, Shelf Drilling, Silixa, Silvertip Completion Services, TGT Oilfield Services, Wayfinder Resources

Key Executives:
Will Franklin, Managing Director
Education: University of Texas, Austin; Harvard Business School
Background: Riverstone Holdings
Directorships: Airis, GEODynamics, OilSERV, Shelf Drilling, Xtreme Drilling
Jonathan Farber, Co-Founder & Managing Director
Education: School of Foreign Service of Georgetown University
Background: Goldman Sachs
Directorships: Augustus Energy Partners II; Cor4 Oil; CrownRock; CrownRock Minerals; San Jacinto Minerals; Arena Exploration; Black Shire Energy; Coronado Resources; Deer Creek Energy
John Reynolds, Co-Founder & Managing Director
Education: BA, Bucknell University
Background: Goldman Sachs
Directorships: Blackjewel; Shelf Drilling; Archer; Eastern Drilling; EnerMech; Hercules Offshore; IPEC; Noble Tesco; Torch Offshore; VEDCO Holdings
Trevor Burgess, Managing Director
Education: Oxford University
Background: Director of Global Business Units & Group Director of Marketing and Technology, Expro; VP of Sales, Baker Hughes
Directorships: Acoustic Zoom; Ardyne; Reelwell; Reveal Energy Services; Silixa; TGT Oilfield Services; Gas2; Senscient; TerraSpark; Geosciences

1126 LIMESTONE VENTURES
98 San Jacinto Blvd.
Suite 320
Austin, TX 78701

Phone: 512-346-7111 **Fax:** 512-346-2111
e-mail: info@limestonevc.com
web: www.limestonevc.com

Mission Statement: To grow innovative high technology companies.

Founded: 1999
Investment Criteria: Seed-Stage, Early-Stage
Industry Group Preference: High Technology
Portfolio Companies: BlueSpace Software, Collider, CTS, Kionix, Metreos Corporation, Mimix Broadband, MobiTV, NetSpend, Sharklet Technologies, SiVerion, Rheonix, Wimba

Key Executives:
Bob Inman, Chairman
Education: BA, University of Texas, Austin
Background: Managing Director, Gefinor Ventures; Managing Director, Inman Ventures
Tom Inman, Managing Director
Education: BS, Electrical Engineering, MBA, University of Texas, Austin
Background: Principal, Gefinor Ventures

Venture Capital & Private Equity Firms / Domestic Firms

1127 LINCOLNSHIRE MANAGEMENT
780 Third Avenue
40th Floor
New York, NY 10017
    Phone: 212-319-3633 **Fax:** 212-755-5457
    e-mail: info@lmi780.com
    web: www.lincolnshiremgmt.com

Mission Statement: A private equity firm focused on acquiring and growing small and middle market companies.
Geographic Preference: Worldwide
Fund Size: $835 million
Founded: 1986
Average Investment: $25 million
Minimum Investment: $3 million
Investment Criteria: LBO, Recaps
Industry Group Preference: Niche Manufacturing, Distribution
Portfolio Companies: The Alaska Club, Allison Marine, Cutters, Dalbo Holdings, Desch Plantpak, Fallon Visual Products, Flight Training Acquisitions, Holley, Latite Holdings, National Pen, Nursery Supplies Inc., PADI, Phoenix Brands, True Temper Sports, Wireline

Other Locations:
 22 West Washington Street
 15th Floor
 Chicago, IL 60602
 Phone: 312-899-9000 **Fax:** 312-899-9009

Key Executives:
 TJ Maloney, Chairman & CEO
 Education: BA, Boston College; JD, Fordham University School of Law
 Background: Managing Director, Lincolnshire; Attorney/Founder, Maloney Mehlman Katz
 Michael J Lyons, President
 e-mail: mlyons@lincolnshiremgmt.com
 Education: BS, BA, Boston University; MBA, Harvard University
 Background: CPA, PriceWaterhouse
 Vineet Pruthi, Senior Managing Director
 e-mail: vpruthi@lincolnshiremgmt.com
 Education: BS, Bombay University; MBA, Rutgers University
 Background: CFO, Credentials Services International
 Thomas R Callahan, Managing Director
 e-mail: tcallahan@lincolnshiremgmt.com
 Education: AB, Harvard University
 Background: Executive Managing Director, Equity Capital Markets HSBC Securities; Treasurer/The China Fund
 George J Henry, Managing Director
 e-mail: ghenry@lincolnshiremgmt.com
 Education: BA, Harvard University; MBA, Darden Graduate School of Business Administration, University of Virginia
 Background: Associate, Bowles Hollowell Conner; GAMA Corporation
 Philip Kim, Managing Director
 Education: AB, Economics, Harvard University
 Background: Associate, Knickerbocker LLC; Analyst, Fortress Investment Group LLC
 James G Binch, Managing Director
 e-mail: jbinch@lincolnshiremgmt.com
 Education: BScE, Princeton University; MBA, Wharton School, University of Pennsylvania
 Background: President & CEO, Memry Corporation; Combustion Engineering; Cresap McCormick & Paget Inc.
 Phil Jakeway, Managing Director
 Education: BA, Georgetown University; MBA, Columbia University
 Background: CEO, American Business Institute; Founder & CEO, The Supporting Cast
 James McLaughlin, Managing Director
 e-mail: jmclaughlin@lincolnshiremgmt.com
 Education: BA, Bucknell University; JD, Cornell Law School
 Background: Partner, Pillsbury Winthrop LLP
 Pieter Kodde, Managing Director
 Education: Amsterdam School of Business
 Background: Rabobank International, ABN AMRO
 John O'Connor, Managing Director
 Education: BA, University College Dublin; Tuck School of Business
 Background: Managing Director, Barclays Bank Ireland; Nat West; KPMG
 Ottavio Serena, Managing Director
 Education: Universita' degli Studi di Roma
 Background: Citicorp Venture Capital; Italian Armed Forces

1128 LINDEN LLC
150 N. Riverside Plaza
Suite 5100
Chicago, IL 60606
    Phone: 312-506-5600 **Fax:** 312-506-5601
    e-mail: info@lindenllc.com
    web: www.lindenllc.com

Mission Statement: Linden is a healthcare and life science private equity firm that builds exceptional value in mature businesses. We specialize in traditional management buyouts of independent companies as well as investments in non-core businesses owned by large corporations.

Founded: 2002
Investment Criteria: Management Buyouts
Industry Group Preference: Healthcare, Life Sciences
Portfolio Companies: Ability One, Advarra, Avalign Technologies, BarrierSafe Solutions International, Behavioural Centers of America, Corpak Medsystems, Drayer Physical Therapy Institute, ERG, Flexan, Focused Health Solutions, Hycor, The Hydrafacial Company, Inovision, Kendro Laboratory, LifeStream, Merical, Northwestern Management Services, Pinnacle Treatment Centers, ProPharma Group, Ranir, SeraCare Life Sciences, Smile Doctors Braces, Strata Dx, SutureExpress, Virtus Pharmaceuticals, Young Innovations, Z-Medica

Key Executives:
 Anthony B Davis, President & Managing Partner
 e-mail: tdavis@lindenllc.com
 Education: BA, Economics, Northwestern University; MBA, University of Chicago Graduate School of Business
 Background: Partner, One Equity Partners; Strategy Consultant, Cresap McCormick & Paget
 Directorships: ProPharma, Smile Doctors, Spear Education, Advarra, Sage Dental, Virtus Pharmaceuticals
 Brian C Miller, Managing Partner
 e-mail: bmiller@lindenllc.com
 Education: BA, Princeton University; MBA, Harvard Business School
 Background: First Chicago Equity Capital, Salomon Brothers
 Directorships: Flexan, HydraFacial, MeriCal, Solara, Z-Medica
 Michael Farah, Partner
 e-mail: mfarah@lindenllc.com
 Education: BA, Finance, Carnegie Mellon University; MBA, Harvard Business School
 Background: VP, Metalmark Capital; Private Equity Associate, Summit Partners
 Michael Watts, Partner
 e-mail: mwatts@lindenllc.com
 Education: BA, Economics and History, Washington & Lee University; MBA, Kellogg School of Management
 Background: Brockway Moran & Partners; Stephens Inc.

1129 LINDSAY GOLDBERG
630 Fifth Avenue
30th Floor
New York, NY 10111

Phone: 212-651-1100 Fax: 212-651-1101
e-mail: contact@lindsaygoldbergllc.com
web: www.lindsaygoldbergllc.com

Mission Statement: Lindsay Goldberg seeks to become long-term partners with family business owners, management teams and experienced CEOs who have as their goal significant long-term growth in their enterprise.

Geographic Preference: Worldwide
Investment Criteria: Growth Equity
Portfolio Companies: Alliant Insurance Services, Ambulatory Services of America, Aptitude Investment Management, Aviv REIT, Bell Nursery Holdings, Bluegrass Materials Company, Brightstar Corp., Continental Energy Systems LLC, Crane & Co., Dealer Tire, ECS Federal, EnergySolutions, First American Payment Systems, Formation Energy, FSB Global Holdings, Intermex Holdings, Keystone Foods Holdings, Klöckner & Co. AG, Maine Beverage Company, MBI Energy Services, Pacific Architects and Engineers, PetroLogistics, Pike Electric Corporation, PL Midstream, PSC Holdings I, RECON Holdings III, Rosetta LLC, Scandza AS, The Brock Group, Vitruvian LC, Wacker Construction Equipment AG, Weener Plastic GmbH, WoodSpring Hotels Holdings

Key Executives:

Alan E Goldberg, CEO & Co-Founder
Education: BA, Philosophy & Economics, New York University; MBA, New York University Graduate School of Business; JD, Yeshiva University
Background: Chairman & CEO, Morgan Stanley Private Equity
Directorships: Aptitude Investment Management, Crown Point International, Odfjell Termials BV, Stelco

Robert D Lindsay, Chairman & Co-Founder
Education: BA, English & American Literature, Harvard College; MBA, Stanford University
Background: Managing General Partner, Bessemer Holdings; Managing Director, Morgan Stanely Private Equity
Directorships: The Bessemer Group

Krishna K Agrawal, Managing Director
Education: BS, Finance and Information Systems, New York University; MBA, Stanford Graduate School of Business
Background: Investment Banking Analyst, Morgan Stanley
Directorships: Odfjell Terminals, Intermodal Holdings, Stelco

Megan Lundy, Managing Director
Education: BA, History, Columbia University
Background: DLJ Investment Partners, Barclays

Michael W Dees, Partner
Education: BA, Economics, Harvard College; MBA, Harvard Business School
Background: M&A, Morgan Stanley
Directorships: Odfjell Terminals BV, Paccor, Schur Flexibles GmbH, VDM Metals, Stelco

J Russell Triedman, Partner
Education: ScB, Applied Mathematics, Brown University; JD, University of Chicago Law School
Background: Principal, Bessemer Holdings; Director, Fox Paine & Company
Directorships: Golden West Packaging Group, BA Solutions, Crown Point International, Crown Paper Group, Second Spring Healthcare Investments

John F Aiello, Partner
Education: BA, Political Science, New York Univerity; JD, Georgetown University
Background: Managing Director, Goldman Sachs; Weil Gotshal & Manges LLP
Directorships: Aptitude Asset Management, Trygg Pharma Group AS

Jeffrey B Bunder, Partner
Education: BA, Emory University; MBA, New York Univerity; CPA
Background: Ernst & Young
Directorships: Stelco

Stephen P DeFalco, Partner
Education: BS, Mechanical Engineering, MIT; MS, Computer Engineering, Syracuse University; MBA, MIT Sloan School of Management
Background: CEO, Crance & Co.; CEO, MDS; CEO, Senseonics; CEO, PathoGenetix; Strategy Consultant, McKinsey & Company;

Eric T Fry, Partner
Education: BA, Economics, Wharton School; MBA, Harvard Business School
Background: Managing Director, Morgan Stanley Private Equity

Brian P Kelley, Partner
Education: BA, Economics, College of the Holy Cross
Background: CEO, Keurig Green Mountain; President, North American Operations, Coca-Cola Company; General Electric; Proctor & Gamble
Directorships: Keurig Green Mountain, Blue Apron, BA Solutions

Christopher M Laitala, Partner
Education: BA, Government, Harvard College; MBA, Harvard Business School
Background: Managing Director, HIG Capital; JH Whitney & Co.; Great Point Partners
Directorships: PT Solutions, Women's Care Holdings, Refresh Mental Health

Jacob J Lew, Partner
Background: United States Senate; Managing Director, Citigroup; Executive VP & COO, New York University
Directorships: Stelco

1130 LINLEY CAPITAL
601 Lexington Avenue
43rd Floor
New York, NY 10022

Phone: 646-863-7200 Fax: 646-863-7201
e-mail: info@linleycapital.com
web: www.linleycapital.com

Mission Statement: Linley Capital is a New York-based private equity firm that invests in mid-sized companies, in the United States, Europe and Latin America, through leveraged buyouts, recapitalizations and growth equity investments. The company invests in a wide variety of industries and sectors that include branded consumer products as well as selected subsectors of industrial and manufacturing businesses. Linley Capital has an investment strategy that is both long-term and conservative and works in close partnership with the management team to develop comprehensive and sustainable operating and growth strategies.

Geographic Preference: United States, Europe, Latin America
Founded: 1993
Investment Criteria: Linley Capital generally invests in companies with a $100 million to $2 billion range in revenue.
Industry Group Preference: Technology, Financial Services, Business Products & Services, Energy, Clean Technology, Industrial, Manufacturing, Aerospace, Defense and Government, Retail, Consumer & Leisure, Consumer

Key Executives:

John R Jonge Poernik, Founder & Managing Partner
Education: MA, Marketing & Communications, University of Amsterdam; MBA, Finance, Wharton School
Background: Partner, Circle Peak Capital; Vice President, Limited Brands

Sebastian C. Widmann, Senior Associatie
Education: BA, Tufts University

Venture Capital & Private Equity Firms / Domestic Firms

Matthew Croft, Senior Associate
Education: BA, Finance, Baruch College

1131 LINN GROVE VENTURES
5012 53rd St. S
Fargo, ND 58104

Phone: 701-356-5655
web: www.linngroveventures.com

Mission Statement: Linn Grove Ventures seeks to identify the best early and mid stage life science companies with outstanding technology that can benefit from our strategic capital and business strategies, while creating growth within the Corridor.

Geographic Preference: Upper Midwest Region
Investment Criteria: Early-Stage, Mid-Stage
Industry Group Preference: Life Sciences, Agriculture
Portfolio Companies: FarmQA, Next Healthcre, Virgin Plants
Key Executives:
Dan Hodgson, Managing Partner
Education: BS, English, Bemidji State University
Directorships: FarmQA, Next Health Care, Virgin Plants
Dennis O'Brien, Managing Partner
Education: BS, Chemical Engineering, Rensselaer Polytechnic Institute; Simon School, University of Rochester; Columbia Business School
Directorships: Next Health Care
Steve Polski, Managing Director
Education: BA, Marketing, University of St. Thomas
Background: Andersen Windows; Cargill; Enerfo USA
Directorships: Living Well Disability Services, Clean Energy Economy Minnesota

1132 LINSALATA CAPITAL PARTNERS
5900 Landerbrook Drive
Suite 280
Mayfield Heights, OH 44124

Phone: 440-684-1400 Fax: 440-684-0984
e-mail: info@linsalatacapital.com
web: www.linsalatacapital.com

Mission Statement: Private equity firm focused on middle market leveraged and management buyouts.

Geographic Preference: United States
Fund Size: $425 million
Founded: 1984
Average Investment: $25 million
Minimum Investment: $10 million
Investment Criteria: LBO, MBO
Industry Group Preference: Building Materials & Services, Plastics, Distribution, Automotive, Business to Business, Direct Marketing, Convergent Technologies
Portfolio Companies: Eatem Foods Co., Glynlyon, Happy Floors, Harden Manufacturing, The Home Decor Companies, Home Helpers, Hospitality Mints, Manhattan Beachwear LLC, NeuroTherm, Paradigm Packaging, Randy's Worldwide Automotive, Signature Systems Group, Spartan Foods of America, Stag-Parkway, Transpac, U-Line, Wellborn Forest Products, Whitcraft Group
Key Executives:
Frank Linsalata, Chairman
e-mail: flinsalata@linsalatacapital.com
Education: BS, Case Western Reserve University; MBA, Harvard Business School
Background: Founder/Edgecliff Investment; Executive VP/COO, Midland-Ross
Directorships: Home Helpers, Randy's Worldwide Automotive
Eric V Bacon, Senior Managing Director
e-mail: ebacon@linsalatacapital.com
Education: Albion College; MBA, Stanford University
Background: Consultant, McKinsey & Company; Allied-Signal
Directorships: Randy's Worldwide Automotive, Signature Systems Group, Manhattan Beachwear Holding Company, Hospitality Mints
Stephen B Perry, Senior Managing Director
e-mail: sperry@linsalatacapital.com
Education: Lake Erie College
Background: Senior VP/CFO, CFA Window Group; Auditor, Touche Ross; Controller, Elektrapak; Director Planning/Analysis, FL Industries; VP Finance, CMS Holding
Directorships: Glynlyon Holding Company, Happy Floors, Wellborn Forest Products

1133 LIQUID CAPITAL GROUP
1420 Spring Hill Rd.
Suite 600
McLean, VA 22102

Phone: 703-626-3757
e-mail: info@liquidcapitalgroup.com
web: www.liquidcapitalgroup.com

Mission Statement: Offers accredited investors and families access to a diversified portfolio of superior emerging information technology companies and top venture capital funds.

Founded: 2000
Investment Criteria: Early-Stage
Industry Group Preference: Information Technology, Digital Security, Mobile Computing, Communications, Digital Rights Management, E-Commerce & Manufacturing, Networking
Portfolio Companies: InterSAN, Lightningcast, MaterialNet, Matrics, MortgageIT.com, netForensics, Object Video, Overture Technologies, Parature, ServiceBench, Visto, WiderThan
Key Executives:
Randolph C Domolky, Managing Director
Education: BA, Economics & Environmental Studies, University of Pennsylvania
Background: Managing Director, GKM Newport; Pricipal, NextStep Partners; Vice President, NEON Communications; General Manager, Carrier Sales Division, Winstar Communications

1134 LITTLEJOHN & COMPANY LLC
8 Sound Shore Drive
Suite 303
Greenwich, CT 06830

Phone: 203-552-3500
e-mail: info@littlejohnllc.com
web: www.littlejohnllc.com

Mission Statement: A private equity firm that makes control equity investments in mid-sized companies that are underperforming their potential or struggling with financial or operational challenges.

Geographic Preference: Canada, Europe, United States
Fund Size: $1.3 billion
Founded: 1996
Average Investment: $75 million
Minimum Investment: $50 million
Investment Criteria: LBO, MBO
Industry Group Preference: Industrial Equipment, Chemicals, Automotive, Food & Beverage, Healthcare, Plastics, Textiles, Distribution, Consumer Products, Processing
Portfolio Companies: Accuride, Alvogen, Angiotech, ASG Technologies, Alphabroder, Ameriqual, Aquilex, Benevis Practice Services, Brown Jordan International, Chemtura, Clean Earth, CoActive Technologies, Contech Engineered Solutions, Cook & Boardman Group, Cornerstone Chemical Company, Cosmetic Essence Innovations, CTI Foods, Cunningham Lindsey, Direct Chassis Link Inc., Dex One, Diamond Innovations, Eliokem Materials & Concepts, Erickson, Evergreen, Express Energy Services, General

Venture Capital & Private Equity Firms / Domestic Firms

Trailers, GSE Environmental, Gulf Coast Shipyard Group, Hanleywood, HDT Global, Hennings Automotive, Horsehead, Hostway, HydroChemPSC, Installed Building Products, Interior Logic Group, Jerr-Dan, Joerns Healthcare, Kenan Advantage Group, Keystone Automotive Operations, Latham International, Luxfer, Motion Recruitment, Nellson, Newgistics, NewCold, Noranda, Northwest Hardwoods, Pameco Corp., Penda Corporation, Perfect Fit, Pernix Therapeutics, PlayPower, Prince, PSC, Sequa, Sitel, Smile Brands Inc., Sotera Defense Solutions, Soundview Maritime LLC, Stallion, Stolle Machinery, Strategic Materials, Sun Source, Synchronous Aerospace Group, Synventive, S&S Industries, Tidel, Total Safety, Tronox, Unitek, Universal Lighting Technologies, Van Houtte Cafe, vRad, Wastequip, WireCo WorldGroup, Weight Watchers, World and Main, Wyle

Key Executives:
Angus C Littlejohn Jr., Chairman
Education: BS Economics, University of Pennsylvania
Background: Joseph, Littlejohn & Levy; Quadrex Securities
Michael I Klein, Chief Executive Officer
Education: MBA, Harvard Business School; BS Accounting, New York University
Background: S&S Industries; Senior Associate, Joseph, Littlejohn & Levy; Sumitomo Corporation
Directorships: Brown Jordan, PlayPower, Cornerstone Chemicals
Edmund J Feeley, Managing Director
Education: MBA, College of William & Mary; BSE, Naval Architecture, University of Michigan
Background: President/COO, Fleer Corporation; Timberland Company; Booz Allen & Hamilton
Directorships: Northwest Hardwoods, Cornerstone Chemicals Corp.
Brian W Michaud, Managing Director
Education: BA, Economics and Spanish, Middlebury College
Background: Analyst, CIBC World Markets
Directorships: Total Safety, HydroChemPSC, Strategic Materials Group
Robert E Davis, Managing Director
Education: BA, Economics, Northwestern University; MBA, JL Kellogg School of Management, Northwestern University
Background: Managing Director, Oaktree Capital Management's Mezzanine Fund; Principal, Halcyon Asset Management; Prudential Insurance Company
Directorships: Alphabroder, Interior Logic Inc.
Michael B Kaplan, Managing Director
Education: BA, Communications, SUNY Albany
Background: Senior Associate, Ripplewood Holdings; Associate Attoney, Cravath Swaine & Moore
Directorships: Hostway, Unitek, Total Safety, HydroChemPSC
Richard E Maybaum, Managing Director
Education: BA, Philosophy & Political Science, University of Rochester; JD, American University
Background: Portolio Manager, Ramius Capital Group; Managing Director, Alpine Associates; Chase Securities
Antonio Miranda, Managing Director
Education: AB, Harvard College; MBA, Stanford Graduate School of Business
Background: Associate, Clayton Dubillier & Rice; JP Morgan & Co
Directorships: Tidel
Steven G Raich, Managing Director
Education: BA, Duke University; MBA, Stern School of Business, New York University
Background: Golub Associates; Ernst & Young LLP
Directorships: Strategic Materials Inc., Stallion Oilfield Services, Interior Logic Inc., Cook & Boardman
David E Simon, Managing Director
Education: BS, Economics, Wharton School; MBA, Wharton School
Background: Fenway Partners; Financial Entrepreneurs Group
Directorships: Alphabroder, PlayPower, Brown Jordan, Benevis, Motion Recruitment Partners, Joerns
Gentry S Klein, Managing Director
Education: BS, Economics, Wharton School
Background: Associate, Rothschild; Credit Analyst, Rock Hill Partners; Analyst, Chanin Capital Partners
Directorships: Total Safety

1135 LIZADA CAPITAL LLC
8259 East Alameda Road
Scottsdale, AZ 85255

web: www.lizadacapital.com

Mission Statement: Invests in the cannabis industry. Areas of interest include research & data, dispensaries & retail, cultivation, lab testing, packaging, equipment, paraphernalia, security, business services, and information management.

Geographic Preference: US, Canada
Fund Size: $5 million
Founded: 1998
Average Investment: $100,000
Minimum Investment: $10,000
Industry Group Preference: Cannabis, Information Technology, Consumer Products
Portfolio Companies: AmeriCann, Aphria, Auntie Dolores, The Arcview Group, Budding Enterprise Fund, BDS, Calyx, CDX, CannLabs, Canopy Boulder, CannaRoyalty Corp., Elixirs, DigiPath Inc., Electrum Partners, Ebbu, FLRish, GW Pharmaceuticals, Growcentia, GrowBLOX Science, GFarmalabs, Green Flower Media, Green Thumb Industries, Harborside Health Center, Healthy Headie Lifestyle, Herban Planet, High Times, Jane West, Lexaria Energy, Las Vegas Cannaplex, Mass Roots, Medicine Man Technologies, MJIC, Mirth Provisions, MedBox, MedMen, NeWAY, New Frontier, Noble Blends, Notis Global, Nutritional High, Peter Tosh, PROHBTD, Quigley's, Steep Hill, Therabis, Sunniva, Temescal Wellness, Treatibles, Tech Holdings, Panther Capital, Vapor Slide

Key Executives:
Steve Trenk, Founder/Managing Member

1136 LLR PARTNERS INC
2929 Arch Street, Cira Center
Philadelphia, PA 19104

Phone: 215-717-2900 Fax: 215-717-2270
web: www.llrpartners.com

Mission Statement: LLR is opportunistic, investing in companies with strong growth potential, proven business models and outstanding management.

Geographic Preference: Mid Atlantic & Eastern United States
Fund Size: $800 billion
Founded: 1999
Average Investment: $15 million
Minimum Investment: $10 million
Investment Criteria: Growth, Acquisition, Buyouts, Recapitalizations
Industry Group Preference: Business Products & Services, Information Technology, Healthcare Services, Financial Services, Retailing, Processing, Consumer Services, Software, Education, Manufacturing
Portfolio Companies: 3SI Security Systems, Agility Recovery, Alsbridge, American Renal Associates, Avenues: The World School, Benefit Express, BluVector, BrightHeart, Brightside Academy, Cedar Capital, Celero Accelerated Commerce, Cigital, Codiscope, CollabNet, ComNet, CompoSecure, Coredial, Crothall Healthcare, CyberShift, Digital Guardian, Edlio, Edmund & Associates, EKR Therapeutics, eLocal, eOriginal, eResearch Technology, excelleRx, Eye Health America, Eyewitness Surveillance, Five Below, Fleet One, Gestalt, Healthcare Finance Group,

Venture Capital & Private Equity Firms / Domestic Firms

Heartland Payment Systems, HighPoint Solutions, Illuminate Education, InfoHighway, InnaPhase, IO Education, IOD, JGWPT Holdings, Kemberton, Key2Act, Learn Behavioural, Logi Analytics, Maxwell Systems, Medbridge, Medical Science & Computing, Medmark, Mercury Security, Midigator, Numotion, Onapsis, Opinion Research Corporation, Orbis Education, Pet 360, Phish Labs, Phreesia, Physicians Immediate Care, Princeton Softech, Professional Capital Services, Prophet 21, Quintiq, Rapid Ratings, Reading Truck Body, Relias Learning, Revitas, Rizing, Schweiger Dermatology Group, SDI Health, SDI Inc., Sicom, Singer Equities, Spark Post, Sterling Trading Tech, Sun Behavioural Health, Taratec, Tribridge, Ultimus Fund Solutions, UltiSat, Vanderbilt, Vector Solutions, Vivere Health, Welocalize, World Aware

Key Executives:
Mitchell L Hollin, Partner
e-mail: mhollin@llrpartners.com
Education: BS, Economics, University of Pennsylvania; MBA, Finance, Wharton School
Background: Co-Founder/Managing Director, Advanta Partners; Patricof & Co Ventures (Apax)
Directorships: Celero Commerce, CompoSecure, Midigator, Professional Capital Services, Sterling Trading Tech, Ultimus Fund Solutions
Seth J Lehr, Partner
e-mail: slehr@llrpartners.com
Education: BS, Economics, University of Pennsylvania; MBA, Finance, Wharton School
Background: Managing Director, Legg Mason; Co-Founding Partner, The Middle Market Group; Investment Banking VP, Lehman Brothers; Investment Banking Analyst, First Boston; Sales, IBM
Directorships: Avenues: The World School, IO Education, Mercury Security, SDI Inc., Vanderbilt
Ira M Lubert, Partner
e-mail: ilubert@llrpartners.com
Education: BS Human Development, Pennsylvania State University
Background: Principal/Founder, Independence Capital Partners; Managing Director/Co-Founder, TL Ventures; Founder, Radnor Venture Partners; Chairman/President, CompuCom Systems; Sales, IBMA
Directorships: Safeguard Scientifics, The Franklin Institute, National Constitution Center
Howard D Ross, Partner
e-mail: hross@llrpartners.com
Education: BA, University of Pennsylvania
Background: Senior Partner, Arthur Andersen LLP; CPA
Directorships: Agility Recovery, Key2Act, Numotion, Rapid Ratings, Rizing
Jack Slye, Partner
e-mail: jslye@llrpartners.com
Education: BS, University of Maryland; MBA, Wharton School
Background: Principal, Sterling Partners; COO & Vice President of Corporate Development, Sylvan Learning
Directorships: Edlio, Illuminate Education, Learn Behavioural, MedBridge, Orbis Education, Sun Behavioural Health
Scott A Perricelli, Partner
e-mail: sperricelli@llrpartners.com
Education: BS, Accounting, Bucknell University; MBA, Finance & Entrepreneurship, JL Kellogg School of Management, Northwestern University
Background: Investment Banker, William Blair & Co
Directorships: BenefitExpress, Eye Health America, Kemberton Healthcare Services, Learn Behavioural, Orbis Education, Phreesia, Physicians Immediate Care, Schweiger Dermatology Group
David J Reuter, Partner
e-mail: dreuter@llrpartners.com
Education: BS, Business & Economics, Lehigh University; CPA
Background: Arthur Andersen

Directorships: CollabNet, CoreDial, Edmunds & Associates, eLocal, eOriginal, SparkPost
David A Stienes, Partner
e-mail: dsteines@llrpartners.com
Education: BBA, Accounting, James Madison University; CPA
Background: Arthur Andersen
Directorships: 3SI Security Systems, Agility Recovery, BluVector, ComNet, Digital Guardian, Eyewitness Surveillance, Onapsis, Vanderbilt Industries, WorldAware

1137 LM CAPITAL SECURITIES
2385 NW Executive Center Drive
Suite 100
Boca Raton, FL 33431

Phone: 561-351-4114
e-mail: info@lmcap.net
web: lmcapitalcorp.com

Mission Statement: Dedicated to providing high quality investment management and investment banking services to private and public entities. Built on the cornerstones of integrity, professionalism and superior performance, LM Capital Securities, is an emerging full service investment firm.

Founded: 1993
Minimum Investment: $1 million
Investment Criteria: Strong Management Team; 5-Year Record of Profitability; Above Average Investment Returns of 20%
Industry Group Preference: Consumer Products, Distribution, Industrial Equipment, Medical & Health Related

Key Executives:
Leslie M Corley, President/CEO
e-mail: LeslieCorley@LMCapitalSecurities.com
Education: BS, University of Illinois; MBA, Harvard Graduate School of Business Administration
Background: Founder, LM Capital; Kelso & Company; Fidelity Investments, Boston; Norton Simon, Inc.

1138 LOCUS VENTURES
Redwood City, CA 94065

web: www.locus.vc

Mission Statement: A tech-based venture capital firm that offers its portfolio companies insights on product design, professional development and team-building.

Geographic Preference: US, Asia
Fund Size: $300 million
Founded: 2016
Industry Group Preference: Artificial Intelligence, Information Technology, Software, Applications
Portfolio Companies: Allure Systems, Blue Bottle Coffee, Branch, Brilliant, CareerTu, Cattle Care, Convictional, Digi-Prex, Doorstead, Framer, Glowing.io, Grabb-It, Grin Scooters, HomeCourt.ai, Interative.ai, LemonBox, Lob, Masterclass, Matternet, Meesho, Miso, Notable Labs, One Medical, Orchid Labs, Oxygen, Panther Labs, Passport, Portside, Precious, Proper, Razorpay, Recko, Simple Habit, Standard Cognition, Uber, Vahan, Very Good Security, VideoSlick

Key Executives:
Eric Kwan, Managing Partner
Education: BS/MS, Carnegie Mellon University; MS, Stanford University
Background: Senior Member of Technical Staff, Oracle; Senior Technical Yahoo, Yahoo!; Software Engineer, Facebook; Founding Engineer, Operator; Advisor, Cozymeal Inc.; Investor, Panther Labs
Tommy Tsai, Managing Partner
Education: BS, Stanford University
Background: Director of Engineering, Loopt; Founding Engineer, Shopkick; Co-Founder, Shopular; Co-Founder, Coefficient

Venture Capital & Private Equity Firms / Domestic Firms

William Chan, Managing Partner
Education: BS/MS, Stanford University
Background: Software Engineer, NeoPath Networks; Tech Lead, Google; Co-Founder, S Loyalty; Co-Founder, Wave Commerce

1139 LOMBARD INVESTMENTS
One Embarcadero Center
Suite 320
San Francisco, CA 94111-3607

Phone: 415-397-5900 **Fax:** 415-397-5820
web: www.lombardinvestments.com

Mission Statement: Lombard provides strategic advice to its portfolio companies, adds further value through introducing innovations and improved business practices and by leveraging its extensive relationships in North America and Asia.

Geographic Preference: North America, Asia
Fund Size: $1 billion
Founded: 1985
Average Investment: $30 million
Minimum Investment: $5 million
Investment Criteria: Acquisition, LBO, MBO, Recapitalization
Industry Group Preference: Business to Business, Education, Financial Services, Industrial Equipment, Manufacturing, Materials Technology, Chemicals, Wholesale, Distribution, Retailing, Media, Entertainment, Healthcare, Energy
Portfolio Companies: Asia Books, Asiasoft, Career Choices, Centara Hotels and Resorts, Central Pattana, Concung, Dakota Minnesota & Eastern Railroad, Easy Buy, Express Food Group, Fu Sheng Industrial, Good Morning Shinhan Securities, Hansol Gyoyook Company, JWD, Kantana Group, Krungthep Land, KSNET, MC Group, Mega Lifesciences, Mermaid Maritime, Mithmitree, Nok Airlines, Overseas Dragon China, Pomelo, Pruska Real Estate, Robinson Department Store, S. Pack & Print, San Shing Fastech Corporation, S&P Syndicate, Silkspan, SNC Former, Somboom Advance Technology, Syn Mun Kong Insurance, The Medical City, TICON Industrial, Trinity Watthana, Viet-UC Group, Workpoint Creative TV

Other Locations:
Room 1107, 11/F
Tower 2, Lippo Center
89 Queensway
Hong Kong
Phone: 852-28787388 **Fax:** 852-28787288

10/F CRC Tower
87/2 Wireless Road
Lumpini, Phathumwan
Bangkok 10330
Thailand
Phone: 662-6853599 **Fax:** 622-6853588

Suite 1358, 13th Floor
M Plaza Saigon
39 Le Duan St., District 1
Ho Chi Minh City
Vietnam
Phone: 848-62883959

Key Executives:
Thomas Smith, Managing Director
e-mail: tsmith@lombardinvestments.com
Education: Graduated Cum Laude From Harvard College
Background: CEO/CFo ACI
Peter Sullivan, Senior Advisor
Education: AB, Princeton University; JD, Yale Law School
Background: Asian Development Bank; Lawyer, Sullivan & Cromwell
Scott Sweet, Managing Director/CFO
e-mail: ssweet@lombardinvestments.com
Education: BS, Cornell University, MBA, University of California, La
Background: Audit Manager, Deloitte & Touche
Pote Videt, Managing Director
e-mail: pote@privateequitythai.com
Education: Graduated Summa Cum Laude, Phi Beta Kappa From Yale University With A B.A. M.B.A., Harvard Business School
Background: Managing Director, Credit Suisse First Boston, Managing Director, Goldman, Sachs
Anita Chik Lin Oi, Director, Hong Kong
e-mail: anita@lombardinvestments.com
Education: Management Accounting, Hong Kong Polytechnic University
Background: Transpac Capital; Amoy Industries International; Shiu Pong Group
Margaret Lee Lai Chu, Director, Hong Kong
e-mail: margaret@lombardinvestments.com
Education: Accounting, Hong Kong Polytechnic University
Background: Asia Regional Manager, Circuit Protection Division, Tyco Electronics
Cindy Rose Quackenbush, Director, San Francisco
e-mail: crose@lombardinvestments.com
Education: BS, University of Maryland, College Park; Graduate Studies, Taxation, American University
Background: Controller, VantagePoint Venture Partners; Ernst & Young
Kim Sichel, Director, San Francisco
e-mail: ksichel@lombardinvestments.com
Education: BS, Bentley College
Background: Vice President, Finance, Crimson Ventures; Controller, RS Investment Management

1140 LONE STAR FUNDS
2711 North Haskell Avenue
Suite 1700
Dallas, TX 75204

Phone: 214-754-8300
e-mail: investorrelations@lonestarfunds.com
web: www.lonestarfunds.com

Mission Statement: Invests globally in secured and corporate unsecured debt instruments, real estate related assets and select corporate opportunities.

Fund Size: $24 billion
Founded: 1995

Other Locations:
888 7th Avenue
11th Floor
New York, NY 10019
Phone: 917-286-3300

1450 Brickell Ave.
Suite 1720
Miami, FL 33131
Phone: 786-482-2100

800 de la Gauchetiere West
South East Portal - Suite 9400
P.O. Box 1458
Montréal, QC H5A 1K6
Canada
Phone: 514-879-6310

Washington Mall
Suite 304
7 Reid Street
Hamilton HM11
Bermuda
Phone: 441-2961754

Marunouchi Kitaguchi Building
12th Floor
1-6-5- Marunouchi, Chiyoda-ku
Tokyo 100-0005

Venture Capital & Private Equity Firms / Domestic Firms

Japan
Phone: 81-352245300
Suite 2003, York House
The Landmark
15 Queen's Road
Central
Hong Kong
Phone: 852-3700-6900
10 Collyer Quay
#05-08, Ocean Financial Centre 049315
Singapore
Phone: 65-6800-9520
Level 23
Governor MacQuarie Tower
1 Farrer Place
Sydney, NSW 2000
Australia
Phone: 61-2-8379-4200
Lone Star Europe Acquisitions Lts.
12 Queen Anne St.
London W1G 9LF
England
Phone: 44-2076166800
Niedenau 61-63
Frankfurt am Main 60325
Germany
Phone: 49-69710422600
5 rue de Castiglione
Paris 75001
France
Phone: 33-1-8565-9020
Paseo de la Castellana 20
4ø Planta izquierda
Madrid 28046
Spain
Phone: 34-917-931-705
Av. Presidente Juscelino Kubitschek, 1909
Torre Norte - 18ø Andar
Conjunto 181-B
Sao Paulo 04543-907
Brazil
Phone: 55-11-3527-8800
Av. Leandro N. Alem 815
6th Floor "B"
Buenos Aires C1001AAD
Argentina
Phone: 54-11-7090-0900

Key Executives:
  John Patrick Grayken, Founder/Chairman/CEO
  Education: MBA, Harvard University
  Directorships: Patriot Equities

1141 LONG POINT CAPITAL
26700 Woodward Avenue
Royal Oak, MI 48067

Phone: 248-591-6000 **Fax:** 248-591-6001
web: www.longpointcapital.com

Mission Statement: Focuses on partnering with successful entrepreneurs of middle market businesses to help them achieve their financial goals.

Geographic Preference: North America
Fund Size: $315 million
Average Investment: $10-20 million
Minimum Investment: $10 million
Investment Criteria: Recaps, MBO, Consolidations
Industry Group Preference: Manufacturing, Distribution, Business Products & Services
Portfolio Companies: Arch Aluminum and Glass, Arrow Tru-Line, Artistic Holdings, Atlantic Plywood, Broadcasting Partners, CentriLogic, CHI Overhead Doors, CHA Consulting, Corsicana Mattress Company, Cumming Group, EuroDesign Cabinets, EYP Architecture & Design, Gradall, Haynes International, Hire Counsel & Mestel, Interlogix, National Print Group, Outdoor Seasons, Precision Products Group, Quaker Fabric, Savage Sports, St. George Logistics, Sunbury Textile Mills, The Saxton Group, Therma-Tru Doors, Torrent Resources, UMA Enterprises, Woolpert

Other Locations:
747 Third Avenue
22nd Floor
New York, NY 10017
Phone: 212-593-1800 **Fax:** 212-593-1888

Key Executives:
  Gerry Boylan, Managing Director
  e-mail: gboylan@longpointcapital.com
  Education: BS, Grand Valley State University
  Background: VP Business Development, Masco Corporation
  Eric Von Stroh, Managing Director
  e-mail: evonstroh@longpointcapital.com
  Education: BA, Economics and Political Science, Colgate University
  Background: CFO, Five Star Food Service; Vice President, SG Capital Partners LLC; Chase Securities
  Ira Starr, Managing Director
  e-mail: istarr@longpointcapital.com
  Education: BSE, Princeton University; MBA, Harvard Business School
  Background: Partner, MLG&A; Investment Banker, Merrill Lynch; Management Consultant, Booz, Allen & Hamilton
  Naimish Patel, Senior Advisor
  e-mail: npatel@longpointcapital.com
  Education: B.B.A., University of Michigan, M.B.A. Kellogg School of Management at Northwestern University

1142 LONG RIVER VENTURES
50 Milk St
Boston, MA 02109

Phone: 617-326-3770
e-mail: tpeake@longriverventures.com
web: www.lrvhealth.com

Mission Statement: Long River Ventures invests in seed and early stage companies in healthcare, IT, and other technology-driven sectors. Formed by a group of experienced entrepreneurs and venture capitalist, Long River is designed and structured to invest smaller amounts of capital with typically initial investments of $500,000 to $1MM. We back exceptional entrepreneurs who are focused on building capital efficient businesses.

Geographic Preference: Northeast: Boston, New York
Fund Size: $50 million
Average Investment: $500,000 - $1 million
Investment Criteria: Seed-Stage, Early-Stage
Industry Group Preference: Healthcare Information Technology, Medical Devices, Diagnostics, Information Technology, Software, Telecommunications, Media, Internet, Clean Technology, Business Products & Services
Portfolio Companies: Convergent Dental, Eggrock, Extreme Reach, Health Guru, Healthrageous, Gate Rocket, GetWellNetwork, LifeIMAGE, M2S, MedVentive, Omedix, Optasite, Pervacio, Phreesia, Profile Systems, Protedyne, Qteros, Reconda International, Retail Optimization, Solais Lighting, Verax BioMedical

Key Executives:
  Tripp Peake, Managing Partner
  e-mail: tpeake@longriverventures.com
  Education: BA, Dartmouth College; MBA, Yale University
  Background: Partner, Kestrel Venture Management; Co-Founder, Mass Ventures; Co-Founder, Science Park Associates
  Directorships: Extreme Reach, Health Guru, Optasite,

Profile Systems, Protedyne, Qteros, Sovereign Hill Software
Will Cowen, Managing Partner
e-mail: wcowen@longriverventures.com
Education: BA, University of Colorado; MBA, MIT
Background: Founder, NaviNet; CEO, Pegasus Medical Technologies
Directorships: Eggrock, GetWellNetwork, Healthrageous, LifeIMAGE, Medical Metrx Systems, MedVenture, Phreesia, Solais, Verax Biomedical
Mike Cataldo, Venture Partner
e-mail: mcataldo@longriverventures.com
Education: BA, Economics, Columbia University
Background: CEO, Convergent Dental; CEO, Cambridge Semantics; Founder, MediVation
John Kole, Venture Partner
e-mail: jkole@longriverventures.com
Education: BA, Princeton University's Woodrow Wilson School of Public & Internaitonal Affairs; JD, University of Michigan Law School
Background: President, Merrimack Capital; Managing Director, Comcast Interactive Capital

1143 LONGITUDE CAPITAL
2740 Sand Hill Rd.
2nd Floor
Menlo Park, CA 94025

Phone: 650-854-5700
web: www.longitudecapital.com

Mission Statement: Longitude Capital is a life sciences venture capital firm specializing in investments in medical devices, biotechnology, pharmaceutical product development, and diagnostics and R&D tools.

Founded: 2006
Average Investment: $10 - $30 million
Industry Group Preference: Life Sciences, Medical Devices, Biotechnology, Pharmaceuticals, Diagnostics
Portfolio Companies: 89bio, Aimmune Therapeutics, Akebia Therapeutics, Alphaeon, Amphora Medical, Aptinyx, Axonics Modulation Technologies, Baronova, California Cryobank, CardioDX, CrownWheel Partners, Curasen Therapeutics, Cydan, Encore Dermatology, Inflazome, Inozyme Pharma, Kala Pharmaceuticals, KaNDy Therapeutics, Molecular Templates, Murj, Nabriva, Nalu Medical, Neurana Pharmaceuticals, Orbus Therapeutics, Poseida Therapeutics, Rapid Micro Biosystems, Renew Inserts, RxSight, Sublimity Therapeutics, Sutrovax, Tricida, Velicept Therapeutics, Venus Concept, Welbe Health

Other Locations:
One Fawcett Place
Greenwich, CT 06830
Phone: 203-769-5200

Key Executives:
Juliet Tammenoms Bakker, Managing Director, Greenwich
e-mail: jbakker@longitudecapital.com
Education: BS, Biological Sciences, Cornell University; MPA, Kennedy School of Government, Harvard University
Background: Managing Director, Pequot Ventures; Director, Strategic Planning, Waste Management Internationa
Directorships: Alphaeon, Axonics Modulation Technologies, Encore Dermatology, Nalu, RxSight, Venus Concept
Patrick Enright, Managing Director, Menlo Park
e-mail: penright@longitudecapital.com
Education: BS, Biological Sciences, Stanford University; MBA, Wharton School
Background: Managing Director, Pequot Ventures; Managing Member, Delta Opportunity Fund; PaineWebber Development Corporation
Directorships: Aimmune, Aptinyx, CardioDx, CuraSen Therapeutics, Jazz Pharmaceuticals, Orbus Therapeutics, SutroVax
Marc-Henri Galletti, Managing Director, Menlo Park
e-mail: mgalletti@longitudecapital.com
Education: AB, Princeton University; MBA, Kellogg School of Management
Background: SVP, Pequot Ventures; Amerindo Investment Advisors; Vector Fund Management
Directorships: Amphora, Medical, Murj
David Hirsch MD, PhD, Managing Director, Greenwich
e-mail: dhirsch@longitudecapital.com
Education: BA, Biology, Johns Hopkins University; MD, Harvard Medical School; PhD, Biology, MIT
Background: VP, Pequot Ventures; Engagement Manager, McKinsey & Company
Directorships: Inflazome, Molecular Templates, Poseida Therapeutics, Rapid Micro Biosystems, Tricida, Velicept
Sandip Agarwala, Managing Director, Greenwich
Education: BSE, Systems Engineering, University of Pennsylvania; MBA, Wharton School
Background: VP, Auven Therapeutics; Consultant, Boston Consulting Group
Directorships: Cydan Development, Inozyme, Aptinyx
Gregory Grunberg, Managing Director, Menlo Park
Education: AB, Amherst College; MD, MBA, Duke University
Background: Principal, Rho Ventures; Engagement Manager, McKinsey & Company
Directorships: 89bio, BaroNova, Kala Pharmaceuticals, WelbeHealth, Sydnexis
Josh Richardson, Managing Director, Greenwich
Education: BS, University of South Florida; MD, University of Virginia
Background: Engagement Manager, McKinsey & Company
Directorships: KaNDy Therapeutics; Neurana Pharmaceuticals; Sublimity Therapeutics

1144 LONGUEVUE CAPITAL LLC
111 Veterans Boulevard
Suite 1020
Metairie, LA 70005

Phone: 504-293-3600 **Fax:** 504-293-3636
web: www.lvcpartners.com

Mission Statement: Our goal is to realize substantial long-term capital gains through investments in a diversified portfolio of companies by leveraging our experience, creativity, capital and network of resources.

Fund Size: $82 million
Founded: 2001
Investment Criteria: Recaps, Distressed, Turnarounds, MBO
Portfolio Companies: Advanced Metering Data Systems, Ardent Services, Arnold Logistics, Ascent Aviation Services Corporation, Azimuth Technology, Blue Dot Energy Services, ECA Medical Instruments, Jackson Offshore Holdings, Pod Pack International, Premier Store Fixtures, Prime Health Services, Professional Rental Tools, Quality Senior Living Partners, St. George Logistics, Zavation Medical Products

Other Locations:
733 Third Ave.
15th Floor
New York, NY 10017
Phone: 646-660-3994 **Fax:** 504-293-3636

136 Herber Ave.
Suite 204
P.O. Box 8000
Park City, UT 84060
Phone: 435-655-3605 **Fax:** 435-655-7676

Key Executives:
Rick S Rees, Co-Founder & Managing Partner
e-mail: rrees@lvcpartners.com
Education: BA & MBA, Tulane University

Venture Capital & Private Equity Firms / Domestic Firms

Background: CFO, Halter Marine Group; CFO, FGI; President, Texas Drydock; Principal, Maritime Capital
John C McNamara II, Co-Founder & Managing Partner
e-mail: jmcnamara@lvcpartners.com
Education: BS, Georgetown University; MBA, Harvard Business School
Background: President & CEO, Stewart Capital; Investment Banking, Drexel Burnham Lambert; Donaldson Lufkin & Jenrette
Charles A Cox, Director
e-mail: ccox@lvcpartners.com
Education: BA, University of Georgia; JD, Cumberland School of Law, Samford University; MBA, Kenan-Flagler School, University of North Carolina
Background: Covey Capital Management; Attorney, Allen Kopet & Associates
Raymond J Jeandron III, Partner
e-mail: rjeandron@lvcpartners.com
Education: BS, Management, Boston College
Background: Investment Banking, Jeffries & Company; Global Hunter Securities
Ryan K Nagim, Partner
e-mail: rnagim@lvcpartners.com
Education: BBA, Finance, Southern Methodist University; MBA, Wharton School
Background: Principal, American Capital; Investment Banking Analyst, J.P. Morgan

1145 LONGWOOD FUND
The Prudential Tower
800 Boylston Street
Suite 1555
Boston, MA 02199

Phone: 617-351-2590
e-mail: info@longwoodfund.com
web: www.longwoodfund.com

Mission Statement: Longwood's mission is to identify technologies and to found companies that will advance new therapeutics that can not only make a difference in the lives of patients worldwide, but also create significant value for investors. This is achieved by leveraging the management team's history of successful healthcare company formation and operational leadership.
Industry Group Preference: Healthcare, Therapeutics, Pharmaceuticals
Portfolio Companies: Alnara Pharmaceuticals, ArcherDX, Axial Biotherapeutics, Bicycle Therapeutics, Calithera Biosciences, Channel Medsystems, Colorescience, Flex Pharma, GRAIL, IlluminOss, KalVista Pharmaceuticals, Millendo Therapeutics, Mitobridge, OvaScience, PTC Therapeutics, Pulmocide, Recros Medica, Renovia, Scan Therapeutics, Sitryx Therapeutics, Twentyeight-Seven, Verastem

Key Executives:
Rich Aldrich, Co-Founder & General Partner
Education: Boston College; MBA, Amos Tuck School
Background: Co-Founder, Sirtis Pharmaceuticals, Concert Pharmaceuticals; Founding Employee, Vertex Pharmaceuticals
Directorships: KalVista Pharmaceuticals, Colorescience, Axial, Renovia, Sitryx Therapeutics
Christoph Westphal, Co-Founder & General Partner
Education: BA, Columbia University; MD, Harvard Medical School; PhD, Genetics, Harvard University
Background: Co-Founder/CEO, Alnlam Pharmaceuticals, Momenta Pharmaceuticals
David H Donabedian, Partner
Education: BA, Chemistry, St. Anselm College; PhD, Polymer Chemistry, University of Massachusetts; MBA, University of North Carolina
Background: VP & Global Head of Ventures, AbbVie; VP Global New Deal Strategy and Development, GlaxoSmithKline; Sr. Manager, Accenture's Strategic Services Consulting Group

Directorships: Alcyone Life Sciences, Axial Biotherapeutics, Millendo Therapeutics

1146 LONGWORTH VENTURE PARTNERS
303 Wyman St.
Suite 300
Waltham, MA 02451

Phone: 781-663-3600 Fax: 781-663-3619
e-mail: info@longworth.com
web: www.longworth.com

Mission Statement: Build leading technology companies in conjunction with top entrepreneurs by leveraging our extensive industry expertise and contacts.
Geographic Preference: United States
Fund Size: $130 million
Average Investment: $2 - $3 milllion
Minimum Investment: $250,000
Investment Criteria: Early and expansion-stage
Industry Group Preference: Enterprise Services, Infrastructure, Business to Business, Applications Software & Services, Internet, Digital Media & Marketing
Portfolio Companies: Applause, Constant Contact, Creative Market, DFA Capital Management, Estimize, Fliptop, Genesis Networks, Grab Media, Hospital IQ, iJet, Innovectra, Kaon, Kitsy Lane, Jibe, Marathon, MCA Solutions, Mobiquity, Moodlerooms, NuoDB, Olapic, OwnerIQ, Parlano, PLUMgrid, Power Inbox, RAIDCore, Rapid Miner, Rivermine, Rize, Scanbuy, Scarpblog, Sermo, Softricity, StraighterLine, Swirl, Symform, Thinking Screen Media, Thor Technologies, TrackVia, Triblio, Tylted, Varolii, VeloBit, Viewfinity, VKernel

Key Executives:
Paul Margolis, Founding Partner
e-mail: p.margolis@longworth.com
Education: BA, Brown University; MBA, Harvard Business School
Background: Founder/Chairman/CEO/President of Marcam Corporation; Co-Founder/ Chairmanlications Group
Directorships: Mobiquity, VeloBit
Jim Savage, Founding Partner
e-mail: j.savage@longworth.com
Education: BA, Harvard University
Background: Founder and General Manager of ZD-Net; CEO of PlanetAll.com; Executive VP, Simon & Schuster/Prentice Hall; Digital Media, Mcgraw-Hill
Directorships: Constant Contact, Triblio, Grab Media, Softricity, Sermo, Moodlerooms, Applause
John Lawrence, Partner & CFO
e-mail: j.lawrence@longworth.com
Education: BA Accounting, Assumpton College
Background: CFO, Quail Piping Products; Assistant VP/M&A/SEC/IR, Asani/America; Auditor, Arthur Andersen
Nilanjana Bhowmik, Partner
e-mail: n.bhowmik@longworth.com
Education: BE Computer Science, Indian Institute of Technology; MS Computer Science, University of South Carolina; MBA, INSEAD
Background: VP Mergers/Acquisitions, Broadview International; Director Professional Services, eXcelon Corporation; Technical/Managament, Object Design
Directorships: Jibe, NuoDB, PLUMgrid, RapidMiner, Swirl, TrackVia

1147 LOVELL MINNICK PARTNERS LLC
2141 Rosencrans Avenue
Suite 5150
The Plaza at Continental Park
El Segundo, CA 90245

Phone: 310-414-6160
web: www.lovellminnick.com

Venture Capital & Private Equity Firms / Domestic Firms

Mission Statement: An independent, management-controlled private equity firm formed to provide buyout capital and growth capital to developing companies in the financial services industry.
Fund Size: $800 million
Founded: 1999
Average Investment: $10-$40 million
Minimum Investment: $5 million
Investment Criteria: Leveraged Buyouts, Recapitalizations, Growth Capital
Industry Group Preference: Financial Services, Business Products & Services
Portfolio Companies: 361 Capital, Alps, AssetMark, Atlantic Asset Management, Attom Data Solutions, Berkeley Capital Management, Center Square Investment Management, Centurion Capital Group, ClariVest Asset Management, Commercial Credit, Currency, Dahlam Rose & Co., Duff & Phelps, Engage, First Allied, Foreside, Global Financial, HD Vest Financial Services, JS Held, Kanaly Trust, Keane, Leerink, Lincoln Investment, LSQ Funding, Matthews Asia, Mercer Advisors, National Auto Care, Plan Member Services, Powell Johnson, Seaside National Bank & Trust, SRS Acquiom, Stein Rose Investment Counsel, Tortoise, Trea Asset Management, TriState Capital, UNX, Worldwide Facilities

Other Locations:
555 E. Lancaster Ave.
Suite 510
Radnor, PA 19087
Phone: 610-995-9660

450 7th Ave.
Suite 909
New York, NY 10123
Phone: 646-971-3230

Key Executives:
Jeffrey D Lovell, Co-Chairman
Education: BS, Business Administration, University of Colorado; University of Southern California
Background: Co-Founder, Putnam Lovell Securities; SEI Investments
James Minnick, Co-Chairman
Education: United States Air Force Academy; BA, Economics, University of Denver
Background: President/CEO, Morgan Grenfell Capital Managment; Executive VP, SEI Investments
Robert M Belke, Managing Partner
Education: BBA, Finance & Accounting, University of Wisconsin; MBA, Finance & Accounting, University of Chicago
Background: Associate, Direct Private Equity Group, TIAA-CREF; Senior Analyst, Wilshire Associates
Directorships: Keane Holdings, JS Held Holdings, Tortoise Investments, Worldwide Facilities
Steven C Pierson, Managing Partner
Education: BS, Finance & Management, Virginia Tech University; MBA, Fuqua School, Duke University
Background: UBS, Credit Suisse, Putnam Lovell Securities
Directorships: Global Financial Credit, National Auto Care, SRS Acquiom, Trea Asset Management
Spencer P Hoffman, Partner
Education: BA, African American Studies, Brown University; MBA, Private Equity, Wharton School, University of Pennsylvania
Background: Principal, Safeguard Scientifics; Associate, Mellon Ventures; Global Investment Banking Group, Merrill Lynch; Manager, Corporate Affairs, MicroStrategy
Directorships: Engage People, Foreside Financial Group, Worldwide Facilities
John D Cochran, Partner
Education: BA, English, University of California, Los Angeles; MS & MBA, Manufacturing Systems Engineering, Stanford University
Background: Principal, SV Investment Partners; Analyst, JW Childs Associates; Financial Analyst, Salomon Brothers
Directorships: Seaside National Bank & Trust, Commercial Credit, LSQ Group Holding, Currency Capital, ATTOM Data Solutions
Brad Armstrong, Partner
Education: BS, Business Administration, Kenan-Flagler Business School, University of North Carolina; MBA, Finance & Accounting, Kellogg School of Management, Northwestern University
Background: Financial Institutions Group, Bank of America Merrill Lynch
Directorships: ATTOM Data Solutions, Commercial Credit, Global Financial Credit, LSQ Group Holding, Tortoise Investments
Jason S Barg, Partner
Education: BS, Accounting, Schreyer Honors College, Pennsylvania State University; MBA, Wharton School
Background: Financial Institutions Group, Goldman Sachs; Senior Associate, Forensics, PricewaterhouseCoopers
Directorships: ATTOM Data Solutions, CenterSquare Investment Management, Foreside Financial Group, JS Held Holdings
Trevor C Rich, Partner
Education: BA, Economics, Brigham Young University; MBA, Wharton School
Background: Corporate Development, Morgan Stanley; Analyst, JP Morgan
Directorships: National Auto Care, Worldwide Facilities

1148 LOVETT MILLER & COMPANY
1700 South MacDill Ave.
Suite 300
Tampa, FL 33629

Phone: 813-222-1477 **Fax:** 813-222-1478
e-mail: info@lovettmiller.com
web: www.lovettmiller.com

Mission Statement: Provides growth capital and shareholder liquidity for rapidly-growing, privately-held companies, with a particular emphasis on technology-enhanced services and healthcare companies.
Geographic Preference: Southeastern United States
Fund Size: $175 million
Founded: 1997
Average Investment: $3 - $10 million
Minimum Investment: $2 million
Investment Criteria: Early-stage, growth capital, growth buyouts.
Industry Group Preference: Communications, Consumer Services, Financial Services, Information Technology, Medical Devices, Technology, Software, Healthcare, SaaS, Healthcare Services, Business Products & Services, Telecommunications, Retailing
Portfolio Companies: 360Commerce, Alphamed, Careanyware, Centennial Healthcare Corporation, Cybex Computer Products Corporation, Docufree Corporation, Employease, Everbank Financial Coporation, Florida Bank Group, Go Software, Healthcare Solutions, Inc., K&G Men's Centers, Inc., Key-Trak, Inc., Kinetic Books Company, Main Bank Corporation, Med3000 Group, Peopleclick, Powertel, Proxima Therapeutics RXStrategies, Sigma International General Medical Apparatus, Southcoast-Boca Associates, Southeast Healthplan, Telovations, Towercom Development, Towercom Enterprises, Towercom Limited, United Dental Care

Other Locations:
One Independent Drive
Suite 1600

419

Venture Capital & Private Equity Firms / Domestic Firms

Jacksonville, FL 32202
Phone: 904-634-0077
Key Executives:
W Scott Miller, Co-Founder & Managing Partner
e-mail: Scott@LovettMiller.com
Education: MBA, Harvard Business School; BA, University of the South
Background: Global Trade Technologies; South Atlantic Venture Partners II; Bowles Hollowell Conner & Company; Morgan Stanley & Company
Directorships: 360 Commerce, Centennial HealthCare, K&G Men's Centers, PeopleClick, United Dental Care, Sigma International, Med 3000, Employease, Proxima Therapeutics
Rad Lovett, Co-Founder
e-mail: Rad@LovettMiller.com
Education: AB, Harvard University
Background: Founder/Chairman/CEO, TowerCom Enterprises/Development/Limited; President, Southcoast Capital; Corporate Finance, Merrill Lynch; Lincoln Property
Directorships: Healthcare Solutions, EverBank Financial, RxStrategies, CareAnyware, DocuFree, TowerCom V

1149 LOWERCASE CAPITAL
San Francisco, CA

web: www.lowercasellc.com

Mission Statement: At Lowercase Capital, we invest in startups, acquire later stage companies and advise businesses and funds of all sizes on strategy and execution.

Geographic Preference: United States
Fund Size: $40 million
Founded: 2007
Investment Criteria: Seed-Stage, Startup, Later-Stage Acquisitions
Portfolio Companies: 9gag, Automattic, Bee Free Honee, Bellhops, Binti, Brightwheel, Bytegain, ChartBeat, Common, Comparably, DigitalGenius, Digital Objects, Docker, Dubsmash, Envoy, Electric Imp, Fanbridge, Flirtey, Gimlet Media, Grove, Handshake, Happy Returns, Hatch Baby, Heavybit, Hodinkee, Joymode, Kickstarter, Liftopia, Little Labs, Lookout, LTSE, Lumi, MakeSpace, Mark43, Medium, Mobcrush, Mux, Noun Project, Nurx, Omnity, Optimizely, Poll Everywhere, Radish, Ranker, RecordSetter, RescueTime, Shape, Slack, Smash.gg, Snowshoe, Stensul, Streak, Stripe, StyleSeat, Synervoz, Tala, TalentWorks, Toymail, Tred, Triller, Uber, Urban Airship, Viro Media, Veggie Grill, VidIQ, VoiceOps, Waggle, Webshots, Wizeline, Women.com
Key Executives:
Chris Sacca, Founder
Education: Georgetown University Law Center
Background: Head of Special Initiatives, Google; Speedera Networks; Attorney, Fenwick & West

1150 LUDLOW VENTURES
Detroit, MI 48226

web: www.ludlowventures.com

Mission Statement: To help entrepreneurs transform startups into industry leading companies.

Geographic Preference: United States
Fund Size: $15 million
Founded: 2010
Investment Criteria: Startups, Seed Stage, Early Stage
Industry Group Preference: Technology, Consumer Products
Portfolio Companies: Alpha Outpost, Ambassador, AngelList, Boxbee, Campaign, Canvs, Circa, Cleanly, Density, Final, Flud, Flywheel, Fundly, Gather, Giftcard Zen, HeadOut, Honey, Hooked, Instore, Kickback, Launchkey, Lob, Luka, Lumi, MinBox, Mirror, Navdy, Nestio, NetPlenish, Notarize, Ordr.In, Paperspace, Point, Product Hunt, Quikly, Rentabilities, Roadtrippers, Roximity, Scentbird, Shots, Snowshoe, SpokenLayer, Sprig, Sqwiggle, Stealth, Stem, Tribe, Try, uBeam, UpTo, Videolicious, Vive, Wag, Wantworthy, WorkLife
Key Executives:
Jonathon Triest, Founder/Managing Partner
Education: BS, University of Michigan
Background: Founder & Managing Partner, Sandwich Fund; Creative Director, Discovery Productions; Founder, Triest Group
Directorships: The Trico Foundation, Venture for America
Brett deMarrais, Partner
Education: University of Michigan
Background: Founder, Wedit; Out of the Blue Entertainment
Blake Robins, Partner
Education: BS, Michigan State University
Background: Campus CEO, Zaarly Inc.; Community Manager, General Assembly

1151 LUX CAPITAL
1600 El Camino Real
Suite 290
Menlo Park, CA 94025

Phone: 650-681-0183 **Fax:** 650-618-0372
e-mail: info@luxcapital.com
web: www.luxcapital.com

Mission Statement: To find outstanding early stage companies and support them as a long-term partner. To build lasting companies while providing superior rates of return to our investors.

Founded: 2000
Minimum Investment: $100,000
Investment Criteria: Seed & Early-Stage
Industry Group Preference: Nanotechnology, Life Sciences, Energy, Technology, Healthcare
Portfolio Companies: 3scan, Aeva, Aira.io, Airmap, Alluvium, AltspaceVR, Applied Intuition, Aptible, Aria Insights, Arraiy, Astranis, Auransa, Auris, Authorea, Blockstack, Bright Machines, Cala Health, Cape Analytics, Cerulean, Citizen, Clarifai, Cloud MedX, Common Networks, Computable, Crystal IS, CTRL-Labs, Deep Sentinel, Desktop Metal, Drone Racing League, Echodyne, Embodied Intelligence, Everspin Technologies, Evolv Technology, Flex Logix, G2X Energy, Geocea Biosciences, Halo Neuroscience, Hangar Technology, Happiest Baby, Hometeam, Kala Pharmaceuticals, Kallyope, Kurion, Kymeta, Kyruus, Latch, LightForm, Looking Glass, Loom Vision, Lux Research, Luxtera, Madaket, Magen Biosciences, Mahana Therapeutics, Matterport, Molecular Imprints, Moment, Mythic, Nanosys, Nervana Systems, New Knowledge, Noon, Novel Effect, Nozomi Networks, Oasis Labs, OpenSpace, Orbital Insight, Pager, Pinscreen, Pivotal Commware, Planet Las, Plethora, Primer, RDMD, Recursion Pharmaceuticals, Rigetti Computing, Ripcord, Saildrone, Scaled Inference, Scatter, Science 37, SentiBiosciences, Shapeways, SiBeam, Silicon Clocks, Siluria Technologies, SOLS Systems, Subspace, Survios, Tempo Automation, Transphorm, Veo Robotics, Visla, Visor, Visterra, Vium, Workit Health, Zipdrug, Zoox

Other Locations:
920 Broadway
11th Floor
New York, NY 10010
Phone: 646-475-4385 **Fax:** 646-349-2960

Key Executives:
Peter Hébert, Co-Founder/Managing Partner
Education: BS Communications, Syracuse University Newhouse School
Background: Lehman Brothers Equity Research; American Express International, London; DMB&B; Sports Illustrated
Directorships: Auris Health, Bright Machines, Cape Analytics, Everyspin Technologies, Flex Logix, G2X

Venture Capital & Private Equity Firms / Domestic Firms

Energy, Halo Neuroscience, Lux Research, Luxtera, Matterport, Pivotal Commware, Ripcord
Robert Paull, Co-Founder/Venture Partner
Education: University of Virginia
Background: CEO, Rob Paull Consulting; CTO, VMDO Architects; Co-Founder, Virtucom; Author
Directorships: Cala Health, Cerulean Pharma, Genocea Biosciences, Kala Pharmaceuticals, Kyruus, Magen, Molecular Imprints, Visterra
Josh Wolfe, Co-Founder/Managing Partner
Education: BS Economics and Finance with Honors, Cornell University
Background: Investment Banker, Salomon Smith Barney; Merrill Lynch; Prudential Securities; AIDS Research, Cell Vision; Journal of Leukocyte Biology; Co-Founder, NanoBusiness Alliance; Author
Directorships: 3Scan, Aira.io, CTRL-Labs, Crystal IS, Echodyne, Kallyope, Kurion, Kymeta, Looking Glass, Lux Research, Nanosys, Shapeways, Silicon Clocks, Siluria Technologies
Adam Kalish, General Partner
e-mail: adam.kalish@luxcapital.com
Education: BS, Economics & Communications, University of Miami; University of Westminster
Background: Director, Everest Capital; Quellos Capital Management; DreamWorks SKG

1152 LYNWOOD CAPITAL PARTNERS
Denver, CO

Phone: 303-885-7166 Fax: 303-573-7810
e-mail: dh@lynwoodcapital.com
web: www.lynwoodcapital.com

Mission Statement: Lynwood Capital is a private equity investment firm based in the Rocky Mountain Region that acquires and invests in businesses with initial values from $5 million to $100 million.
Geographic Preference: United States
Industry Group Preference: Natural Resources, Distribution, Food & Beverage, Business Products & Services, Manufacturing
Portfolio Companies: Avalara, Chieftain Sand and Proppant, Communications Products and Services, Dickinson Frozen Foods, Owl Cybersecurity, Rocket Seals, UPF Services, Work Options Group
Key Executives:
 David Hanson, Partner
 e-mail: dh@lynwoodcapital.com
 Education: BS, Economics & Engineering, Yale University
 Ned Doubleday, Advisor
 Education: BA, East Asian Studies, Yale University; MBA, UCLA

1153 M/C PARTNERS
75 State Street
Suite 2500
Boston, MA 02109

Phone: 617-345-7200 Fax: 617-345-7201
e-mail: mcp@mcpartners.com
web: www.mcpartners.com

Mission Statement: Invests in early stage companies in the emerging segments of the communications industry, as well as telecom-related information technology services.
Geographic Preference: North America, Europe
Fund Size: $550 million
Founded: 1976
Average Investment: $50 million
Minimum Investment: $5 million
Investment Criteria: Early-Stage
Industry Group Preference: Communications, Media, Infrastructure, Technology, Software, Wireless Technologies, Advertising

Portfolio Companies: AccentHealth, Attenda, Baja Broadband, Benestra, Carbon60, Cavalier Telephone, CellularOne, CoreLink Data Centers, CSDVRS, Denovo, Ensono, Everstream, Fusepoint, Involta, GTS, Legendary, Lightower, Melita, MetroPCS, Mobi PCS, Neutral Connect Networks, Nuvox, Omega Wirless, Plum Choice, PR Wireless, Public Mobile, SpeechCycle, Thrive Networks, Triad 700, Zayo Bandwidth
Key Executives:
 James F Wade, Managing Partner
 e-mail: jwade@mcpartners.com
 Education: BBA, University of Notre Dame; MBA, Harvard Business School
 Background: Harris Bank
 Directorships: Involta, Neutral Connect Networks, Thrive Networks
 David D Croll, Managing Partner
 e-mail: dcroll@mcpartners.com
 Education: BS, Cornell University; MBA, Harvard Business School
 Background: TA Associates
 Gillis C Cashman, Managing Partner
 e-mail: gcashman@mcpartners.com
 Education: AB, Economics, Duke University
 Background: Salomon Smith Barney
 Directorships: Carbon60, Denovo, Ensono, Involta, Thrive Networks
 Brian M Clark, Managing Partner
 e-mail: bclark@mcpartners.com
 Education: BBA, Finance & Accounting, University of Michigan
 Background: Salomon Smith Barney
 Directorships: Neutral Connect Networks, PR Wireless
 Edward J Keefe, CFO
 e-mail: ekeefe@mcpartners.com
 Education: BS, Business Administration, University of Maine; MBA, Suffolk University; MS, Taxation, Bentley College
 Background: VP of Finance, Atlas Venture; Instrumentation Laboratory; Tax Consultant, Coopers & Lybrand; Senior Financial Analyst, Raytheon Company
 John W Watkins, Senior Advisor
 e-mail: jwatkins@mcpartners.com
 Education: BA, Economics, Northwestern University; MBA, Amos Tuck School of Business Administration at Dartmouth College
 Background: Co-Founder, Telegraph Hill Communications Partners; J.P. Morgan Capital
 Robert Savignol, Senior Advisor
 e-mail: rsavignol@mcpartners.com
 Education: Finance & Economics, Boston University; MBA, Harvard Business School
 Background: Director of Corporate Development, NTL; Investment Banker, Salomon Brothers
 Directorships: Denovo, Ensono, Everstream

1154 M12
San Francisco, CA

web: m12.vc

Mission Statement: Invests in the areas of artificial intelligence, machine learning, automotive, big data, analysis, business SaaS, cloud infrastictire, emerging trends, productivity, communications, and security.
Geographic Preference: North America, Europe, Israel
Fund Size: $65 Million
Founded: 2016
Investment Criteria: Series A-D
Industry Group Preference: Artificial Intelligence, Machine Learning, Automotive, Big Data, Analysis, Cloud Infrastructure, Productivity, Communications, Security, Emerging Markets, Sectors & Technologies, SaaS
Portfolio Companies: Acerta, Agolo, Airmap, Airobotics, Aqua, Beamery, BlueVine, Bonsai, Cerebri, ClearMotion, CloudLanes, Cloud Simple, CNEX Labs, Code Fresh,

Venture Capital & Private Equity Firms / Domestic Firms

Cognitive Scale, Comfy, Contract Security, Directly, Dynamic Signal, Element, Envisagenics, Figure Eight, Frame, Ground Truth, Hazy, Help Shift, HYAS, i3 Equity Partners, Illusive, Incorta, Inter Ana, Kahoot!, Layer, Livongo, Login Radius, Make.tv, Markforged, Mental Canvas, Netradyne, Onfido, Outreach, PandaDoc, Paxata, Pickit, Pixvana, Prevedere, Rapidsos, Rescale, Snaproute, Synack, Syntiant, Tact.ai, Team8, Trusona, Twentybn, Unbabel, Unravel, Voiceitt, Voicera, Volterra, White Source, Work Board, Zencity, Zipwhip

Key Executives:
 Nagraj Kashyap, Corporate VP/Global Head
 Education: BEng, Computer Science, University of Mysore; MS, Computer Science, University of Texas; MBA, J.L. Kellogg Graduate School of Management, Northwestern University
 Background: Qualcomm Ventures
 Leo de Luna, General Manager/Managing Director
 Education: BBA, University of Texas; MBA, Haass School of Business, University of California Berkeley
 Background: Principal, Split Rock Ventures; Saints Capital; AMD; St. Paul Venture Capital; Lehman Brothers; Singapore Armed Forces
 Rashmi Gopinath, Partner
 Education: BEng, University of Mumbai; MBA, J.L. Kellogg Graduate School of Management, Northwestern University
 Background: Investment Director, Intel Capital; Couchbase; BlueData; GE; Oracle
 Mony Hassid, General Manager/Managing Director
 Education: BSc/MSc, Electrical Engineering, Tel Aviv University; MBA, Tel Aviv University
 Directorships: Managing Director, Qualcomm Ventures; Managing Director, Motorola Ventures
 Samir Kumar, Managing Director
 Education: BSc, Mechanical Engineering, Cornell University
 Background: Qualcomm; Microsoft; Enterprise Mobility; Palm; Samsung
 Lisa Nelson, Managing Director
 Education: BA, Univeristy of Washington
 Background: Microsoft

1155 M25 GROUP
Chicago, IL

web: m25group.com

Mission Statement: Chicago-based, early-stage micro-VC fund investing solely in the Midwest.
Geographic Preference: Midwest
Founded: 2015
Average Investment: $500K to $2 million
Investment Criteria: Early-Stage
Industry Group Preference: Agriculture, E-Commerce & Manufacturing, Education, Fashion, Finance, Food & Beverage, Health, Logistics, Manufacturing, Marketing, Materials, Media, Legal, Social Media, Software
Portfolio Companies: Anglr, Ballot Ready, Block Six Analytics, BoxFox, branch, Chowly Inc., Cladwell, ConceptDrop, dabble, DATTUS, The Eastman Egg Company, EXPLORER, Jetpack Workflow, KnowledgeHound, Luna Lights, PactSafe, PAGEVAULT, PrintWithMe, realync, regroup, REWARDS21, Scanalytics Inc., SPATIAL, Sportsman Tracker

Key Executives:
 Victor Gutwein, Managing Director
 Education: University of Chicago
 Mike Asem, Partner
 Education: Purdue University

1156 MADISON DEARBORN PARTNERS
70 West Madison St.
Suite 4600
Chicago, IL 60602

Phone: 312-895-1000 Fax: 312-895-1001
e-mail: info@mdcp.com
web: www.mdcp.com

Mission Statement: The objective is to invest in companies in partnership with outstanding management teams to achieve significant long term appreciation in equity value. A flexible investment approach, encompassing both management buyouts and structured minority investments, has been a key tenet to MDP's investment philosophy for several decades.

Geographic Preference: United States
Fund Size: $8 billion
Founded: 1992
Average Investment: $100-$600 million
Minimum Investment: $50 million
Investment Criteria: MBO, LBO, Recapitalizations, Growth Capital, Acquisition Financing
Industry Group Preference: Financial Services, Healthcare, Consumer Services, Communications, Energy, Manufacturing, Consumer Products, Telecommunications, Media, Technology-Enabled Services
Portfolio Companies: Aderant Holdings, Alcami, Amynta Group, Ankura, Ardonagh Group, Asurion Corporation, BlueCat Networks, Boise Cascade Company, Bolthouse Farms, Buckeye Cellulose Corporation, B-Way Holding, CapitalSource, Cbeyond, CDW, Centennial Towers, Cinemark, Cornerstone Brands, EVO Payments International, Fieldglass, First Wind Holdings, Fleet Complete, Great Lakes Dredge & Dock Corporation, Ikaria, Intelsat, Intermedia, Kaufman Hall & Associates, LA Fitness International, LGS Innovations, LinQuest Corporation, Liquid Web, Magellan Midstream Partners, MetroPCS, Multi Packaging Solutions, National Mentor Holdings, Navacord, Nextel Partners, NextG Networks, NFP Corporation, Nordic Packaging and Container International, Nuveen Investments, Option Care, Packaging Corporation of America, PayPal, Performance Health, Q9 Networks, QuickPlay Media, RDX, Ruth's Hospitality Group, Ryder TRS, Sage Products, Schrader International, Sirona Dental Systems, SIRVA, Smurfit Kappa, Solis Mammography, Sorenson Communications, Stericycle, Team Health Holdings, The Topps Company, Things Remembered, TransUnion, Tuesday Morning, U.S. Lumber, U.S. Power Generating Company, Univision Communications, Valitas Health Services, VWR International, Wind Telecom S.p.A., XM Satellite Radio Holdings, Yankee Candle

Key Executives:
 John A Canning Jr, Chairman
 Education: AB, Denison University; JD, Duke University
 Background: Executive Vice President, The First National Bank; President, First Chicago Venture Capital
 Directorships: Corning Inc., Milwaukee Brewers Baseball Club
 Paul J Finnegan, Co-CEO
 Education: AB, Harvard College; MBA, Harvard Graduate School of Business Administration
 Background: First Chicago Venture Capital
 Directorships: CDW Corp., AIA Corp., Government Sourcing Solutions
 Samuel M Mencoff, Co-CEO
 Education: AB, Brown; MBA, Harvard
 Background: First Chicago Venture Capital; Industrial National Bank
 Directorships: Packaging Corporation of America, World Business Chicago
 Zaid F Alsikafi, Managing Director
 Education: BS, Wharton School; MBA, Harvard Business School
 Background: Goldman Sachs
 Directorships: Centennial Towers, Intermedia, Liquid Web, RDX, Univision Communications

Venture Capital & Private Equity Firms / Domestic Firms

Elizabeth Q Betten, Managing Director
Education: AB, Brown University; MBA, Stanford University Graduate School of Business
Background: JPMorgan
Directorships: Option Care, Solis Mammography
Karla J Bullard, Managing Director & CFO
Education: BS, CPA, University of Illinois; MBA, University of Chicago
Background: Managing Director & CFO, Deerfield Capital Management; VP, Finance, JP Morgan Chase; Arthur Andersen LLP
Richard H Copans, Managing Director
Education: BA, Duke University; MBA, Northwestern University Kellogg Graduate School of Management
Background: Thomas H Lee Partners, Morgan Stanley & Co.
Directorships: Nordic Packaging and Container International, SIRVA, U.S. Lumber
Vahe A Dombalagian, Managing Director
Education: BS, Georgetown University; MBA, Harvard Graduate School of Business Administration
Background: Texas Pacific Group; Bear Stearns & Co.
Directorships: Amynta Group, Ankura, Ardonagh Group, EVO Payments, Navacord, NFP Corporation
James N Perry, Managing Director
Education: BA, University of Pennsylvania; MBA, University of Chicago
Background: First Chicago Venture Capital
Directorships: Asurion Corporation, Centennial Towers, Intermedia, Liquid Web, The Topps Company, Univision Communications
Timothy P Sullivan, Managing Director
Education: BS, United States Navy; MS, University of Southern California;, MBA, Stanford University Graduate School of Business
Background: First Chicago Venture Capital, United States Navy
Directorships: Alcami, Kaufman Hall & Associates, Option Care, Performance Health, Solis Mammography
Thomas S Souleles, Managing Director
Education: AB, Princeton University; JD, Harvard Law School; MBA, Harvard Graduate School of Business Administration
Background: Wasserstein Perella & Co Inc.
Directorships: Nordic Packaging and Container International, SIRVA, U.S. Lumber
Michael J Dolce, Managing Director & Head of Capital Markets
Education: BS, Babson College
Background: Bank of America Merrill Lynch
Jason Shideler, Managing Director
Education: BS, University of Texas; MBA, Stanford Graduate School of Business
Background: Investment Banking Analyst, Health Care Group, JP Morgan
Directorships: Alcami, Kaufman Hall & Associates, Performance Health
Annie S Terry, Managing Director, General Counsel & Chief Compliance Officer
Education: BS, Accountancy, University of Illinois; JD, Georgetown University Law Center
Background: Associate, Kirkland & Ellis LLP
Douglas C Grissom, Managing Director
Education: BA, Amherst College; MBA, Harvard Graduate School of Business Administration
Background: Bain Capital; McKinsey & Company; Goldman Sachs & Co.
Directorships: BlueCat Networks, Fleet Complete, LGS Innovations, LinQuest Corporation
John E Knutsen, Managing Director
Education: BS, Boston University
Background: Managing Director, Private Fund Group, Credit Suisse; Goldman Sachs & Co.; Donaldson Lufkin & Jenrette

Matthew W Norton, Managing Director
Education: BS, Wharton School; MBA, Wharton School
Background: Merrill Lynch
Directorships: BlueCat Networks, Fleet Complete, Kaufman Hall & Associates, LGS Innovations, LinQuest Corporation, NFP Corporation
Scott G Pasquini, Managing Director
Education: BSE, Princeton University; MBA, Harvard Business School
Background: Associate, GTCR Golder Rauner; M&A Group, Merrill Lynch
Directorships: Centennial Towers, Liquid Web, RDX, The Topps Company
David E Pequet, Managing Director
Education: BS, Indiana University
Background: Private Fund Group, Credit Suisse
Matthew W Raino, Managing Director
Education: BBA, University of Michigan; MBA, Northwestern University Kellogg School of Management
Background: Credit Suisse First Boston
Directorships: Amynta Group, Ankura, Ardonagh Group, EVO Payments, Navacord, NFP Corporation

1157 MADISON PARKER CAPITAL
715 Boylston St.
Boston, MA 02116

Phone: 650-229-8676
e-mail: info@madisonparkercapital.com
web: www.madisonparkercapital.com

Mission Statement: Madison Parker Capital provides liquidity and growth capital to select middle-market enterprises. We provide the value-added capital and resources to help these firms realize their maximum potential. In addition, we seek to provide attractive exit opportunities for owners and operators and divestiture opportunities for divisions of corporate parent companies that no longer reflect the overall strategic focus. Madison Parker Capital endeavors to partner with management and execute seamless transactions.

Average Investment: up to $50 million
Investment Criteria: MBO, Expansion Financings, Recapitalizations
Industry Group Preference: Advanced Materials, Enabling Technology, Business Products & Services, Consumer Products, Retailing, Restaurants, Manufacturing
Portfolio Companies: A123 Systems, Aquis, beRecruited, Boloco, Ceramem, ChargePoint, InnerProduct Partners, IPATH, Klone Lab, Paper House Productions, SonicCloud, Utrecht Art Supplies, Venyu, Village Power Finance

1158 MADRONA VENTURE GROUP
999 Third Avenue
34th Floor
Seattle, WA 98104

Phone: 206-674-3000 **Fax:** 206-674-8703
e-mail: information@madrona.com
web: www.madrona.com

Mission Statement: Madrona's investment approach is to make early-stage investments in promising ventures and build long-term relationships, actively assisting its portfolio companies.

Geographic Preference: Pacific Northwest
Fund Size: $650 million
Founded: 1995
Investment Criteria: Seed, Start-up, Early Stage
Industry Group Preference: Internet Technology, Infrastructure, Technology, Consumer Services, Software Services, Business Products & Services, Wireless Technologies, Consumer Internet, Digital Media & Marketing, Advertising, Networking, Infrastructure
Portfolio Companies: 2nd Watch, Accolade, Algorithmia, Amperity, Animoto, Answer IQ, Atsu, Boomerang Commerce, Booster, Branch, Cape, Chatitive, Crowd Cow, Datacoral, Domicile, Echodyne, Eclypsium, Envisagenics,

Venture Capital & Private Equity Firms / Domestic Firms

Eventbase, Evocalize, ExtraHop, GawkBox, HelloTech, Highspot, Igneous, Indochino, Integris Software, IO Pipe, iSpot.tv, Jama, JinTronix, Jobalign, Lumatax, M87, Mato-Erno.com, Mighty AI, MobileWalla, Moz, Opal, Peach, Pixvana, Player Tokens, Pluto, Pro.com, Pulselabs, Pulumi, Qumulo, Renew, Rigado, Rover.com, Saykara, Seeq, Shippable, Shyft, Skytap, Smartsheet, Snowflake, Spruce Up, Suplari, Terraclear, The Riveter, Tigera, TraceMe, UiPath, Unearth, Wicket Labs, WildTangent, Wonder Workshop, Wrench, Xnor.Ai

Key Executives:

Thomas A Alberg, Co-Founder/Managing Director
e-mail: thomas@madrona.com
Education: Harvard College; Law Degree, Columbia Law School
Background: Partner, Perkins Cole; Cravath, Swain & Moore; President, LIN Broadcasting Corporation; Executive VP, McCaw Cellular Communications
Directorships: Impinj, Amazon.com, ACES Northwest Network, TechNet Northwest, Pacific Science Center, Challenge Seattle

Paul Goodrich, Co-Founder/Managing Director
e-mail: paul@madrona.com
Education: Amherst College; University of Utah Law School
Background: Partner, Perkins Cole Law Firm; Co-Founder, William D. Ruckelshaus Associates; General Partner, Environmental Venture Fund
Directorships: Evenbase, Jintronix

S Somasegar, Managing Director
e-mail: soma@madrona.com
Education: BS, Electronics and Communication Engineering, Anna University; MS, Computer Engineering, Louisiana State University
Background: SVP, Developer Division, Microsoft Corporation
Directorships: AnswerIQ, Branch, Envisagenics, Might Ai, Pixvana, Pulumi, Shyft, Snowflake, Suplari, Tigera, UIPath, Unearth

Matt McIlwain, Managing Director
e-mail: matt@madrona.com
Education: Dartmouth College; MBA, Harvard Business School; MA, Public Policy, Harvard's Kennedy School of Government
Background: Vice President, Genuine Parts Company; Engagement Manager, Mckinsey & Company; CS First Boston
Directorships: 2nd Watch, Accolade, Amperity, Animoto, Booster, ExtraHop, Igneous, Pluto, Qumulo, SkyTap, Smartsheet, Suplari, TraceMe, Xnor.Ai

Scott Jacobson, Managing Director
e-mail: scott@madrona.com
Education: BS, Applied Mathematics & Economics, Northwestern University; MBA, Stanford Graduate School of Business
Background: Senior Product Manager, Amazon.com
Directorships: Boomerang Commerce, Chatitive, Crowd Cow, Evocalize, Indochino, Mighty AI, MobileWalla, Peach, Player Tokens, Pro.com, Rover, Wonder Workshop

Tim Porter, Managing Director
e-mail: tim@madrona.com
Education: BS, Mechanical Engineering, MIT; MBA, Stanford Graduate School of Business
Background: Corporate Development, Microsoft
Directorships: Algorithmia, Echodyne, Eclypsium, HighSpot, Integris, Jama Software, JobAlign, Pixvana, Saykara, Shippable

Len Jordan, Managing Director
e-mail: len@madrona.com
Education: BS, Finance & Economics, Eccles School of Business, University of Utah
Background: General Partner, Frazier Technology Ventures
Directorships: HelloTech, iSpot.tv, M87, Opal, Rigado, Wicket Labs, Wrench

1159 MAIN STREET CAPITAL HOLDINGS LLC
301 Grant Street
14th Floor
Pittsburgh, PA 15219

Phone: 412-904-4020 Fax: 412-904-1794
web: www.mainstcap.com

Mission Statement: A private equity firm that has an outstanding track record of creating value with its entrepreneur partners. Our solid performance has been achieved by carefully selecting unique, well-positioned middle-market companies with superior management teams and then providing the proper incentives and resources required to maximize value.

Geographic Preference: Eastern United States
Average Investment: $3 - $25 million
Industry Group Preference: Manufacturing, Food & Beverage, Homeland Security, Niche Manufacturing, Distribution
Portfolio Companies: AccuSpec Electronics, C&K, Coining of America, Conelec, Harry's Fresh Foods, Hi-Rel Group, I-Deal Optics, Lloyd's Barbeque Company, LTS Scale Company, NABCO Inc., Pinnacle Electronics, Sajar Plastics, Steak-ummm, Stiffel, W&W Dairy, Wisconsin Cheese Group

Key Executives:

Dennis G Prado, Managing Partner
412-904-3561
e-mail: dprado@mainstcap.com
Education: BA, Economics, Bucknell University; MS, Information Systems, MBA, University of Pittsburgh
Background: Fortune Brands; Manager, Price Waterhouse LLP Corporate Finance Group
Directorships: Conelec of Florida, I-Deal Optics, W&W Dairy

W Ryan Davis, Managing Partner
412-224-2734
e-mail: wrdavis@mainstcap.com
Education: BS, Physics, Dickinson College; JD, Dickinson School of Law, Pennsylvania State University
Background: Partner, Morgan Lewis & Bockius LLP
Directorships: I-Deal Optics, W&W Dairy

1160 MAINE ANGELS

e-mail: contactmaineangels@gmail.com
web: www.maineangels.org

Mission Statement: The Maine Angels is a group of accredited investors who provide financial resources and mentorship to early stage companies and entrepreneurs in New England, with particular focus on Maine-based businesses.

Geographic Preference: Maine, New England
Founded: 2003
Average Investment: $10,000 - $710,000
Investment Criteria: Early Stage
Industry Group Preference: Biotechnology, Diagnostics, Therapeutics, Clean Technology, Software, Internet, Consumer Products, Financial Services, Media, IT Services, Nanotechnology, Retail, Consumer & Leisure
Portfolio Companies: Abierto Networks, AboGen, Academic Merit, Avaxia Biologics, Broadcast Pix, CEI Coastal Ventures III, Cerahelix, Cognoptix, Corbus Pharmaceuticals, Digital Life Technologies, ezCater, Gelato Fiasco, Goodlux Technology, HoneyTree Films, Introspective Systems, IW Financial, Jam Hub, LeaseQ, Linkstorm, Maine Wealth Partners, Morpheus Technologies, Nanocomp, NetClarity, Newfield Design, Northern Equity Investments, Ocean Renewable Power Co., Pika Energy, Pixability, Playrific, Regroup, Respiratory Motion, Siamab Therapeutics, Tego, Zylo Media

Key Executives:

Ralph Nodine, Chair
Matt Ware, Vice Chair
Background: Senior Partner, Partners In Performance; Mentor, Top Gun Startup Accelerator Program

Venture Capital & Private Equity Firms / Domestic Firms

1161 MAINE VENTURE FUND
PO Box 63
Newport, ME 04953

Phone: 207-924-3800
e-mail: terri@maineventurefund.com
web: maineventurefund.com

Mission Statement: The Maine Venture Fund is a Maine-based fund that focuses exclusively on investing in promising growth companies. The fund considers Maine based companies in almost all industry sectors, though the return potential of the investment must be high enough to justify the risk taken.

Geographic Preference: Maine
Industry Group Preference: All Sectors Considered
Portfolio Companies: Abierto Networks, Aiko Biotechnology, Bar Harbor Biotechnology, BlueTarp Financial, Bourgeois Guitars, Cerahelix, Certify, Chemogen, Chimani, Coast of Maine, CourseStorm, DreamLocal, Emergent Discovery, Finetune, Fly The Wave, Gelato Fiasco, Genextropy, HarborTechnologies, Hyperlite Mountain Gear, InterSpec, Looks Gourmet Food Company, LulaWed, Maine Craft Distilling, MedRhythms, Mingle Healthcare Solutions, Mobile Price Card, Mousam Valley, NBT Solutions, Newfield Design, Nyle Systems, Ocean Approved, Orono Spectral Solutions, PenBay Solutions, Pika Energy, R.E.D.D., RedZone, Sea Bags, Wentorth Technology

Key Executives:
   John Burns, Managing Director
   e-mail: john@maineventurefund.com
   Education: Undergraduate Degree, University of Maine; MS, Resource Economics, Penn State; MBA, Babson College
   Background: Adjunct Faculty, University of Maine

1162 MANAGEMENT CAPITAL
60 Bay Spring Avenue
Suite B4
Barrington, RI 02806

Phone: 401-246-0050 Fax: 401-246-0051
web: www.mgtcapital.com

Mission Statement: Investment firm providing consulting and capital to small and middle market companies.

Fund Size: $275 million
Founded: 2003
Average Investment: $1 - $10 million
Minimum Investment: $1 million
Investment Criteria: All Stages except Start-Up
Portfolio Companies: BioSensory, FAF Inc., Sencorp, White Systems, Wire Weld USA

Key Executives:
   Ernest D Humphreys, Principal
   e-mail: ernie@mgtcapital.com
   Education: University of Michigan, University of Michigan Law School
   Background: Legal Advisor; Co-Founder, Lincoln Group
   Robert D Manchester, Principal
   e-mail: bob@mgtcapital.com
   Education: Boston University; MBA, Tuck School of Business Administration, Dartmouth College
   Background: Director, Narragansett Capital Corp

1163 MANHATTAN INVESTMENT PARTNERS
200 Park Avenue
Suite 1700
New York, NY 10022

Phone: 646-354-6520 Fax: 646-349-1987
web: www.manhattaninvest.com

Mission Statement: Private investment and merchant firm providing advisory services and investment capital to leading middle market companies, emerging-growth enterprises, and entrepreneurial ventures.

Geographic Preference: East Coast
Fund Size: $5 billion
Founded: 1990
Average Investment: $13 million
Minimum Investment: $5 million
Investment Criteria: Mezzanine, Second Stage, MBO, Common Stock, Convertible Debt, Senior Debt, Growth Financing, Management Buyouts, Platform Build-Ups, Special Situations
Industry Group Preference: Industrial Equipment, Broadcasting, Communications, Computer Related, Electronic Components, Energy, Entertainment, Internet Technology, Medical, Pharmaceuticals, Consumer Products, Real Estate

Key Executives:
   David J Machlica, Managing Partner
   e-mail: dmachlica@manhattaninvest.com
   Education: University of Massachusetts, Pennsylvania State University
   Background: Laventhol and Howath, Dunn Corporation
   Michael E Bogucki, Senior Principal
   Education: BS, Ithaca College; MBA, The Wharton School
   Background: Managing Partner, Paradigm Economics
   Frederick H Hager, Special Partner
   Education: BA, Vassar College; MBA, The Wharton School
   Background: Director, Commercial Travelers Mutual Insurance
   Richard S Melrose, Special Partner
   e-mail: rmelrose@manhattaninvest.com
   Education: BS in Engineering Sciences, Purdue University; MBA, Amos Tuck School, Dartmouth
   Background: Chariman/CEO, Hyco International; Managing Director, Pacoma GmbH; Seitz Manufacturing; General Manager, Gould

1164 MANSA CAPITAL
5444 Westheimer
Suite 1000
Houston, TX 77056

Phone: 713-974-9327
e-mail: info@mansallc.com
web: www.mansallc.info

Mission Statement: Mansa Capital seeks to become key stakeholder in the economic development of Ghana through strategic alliance with established global companies.

Geographic Preference: Ghana, Global
Investment Criteria: Project Development, Mezzanine
Industry Group Preference: All Sectors Considered
Portfolio Companies: HydroDive, Intership, Kavin Engineering, Ocean Installer, Van Dyke Energy Company, Wyndham Garden, Zomay Marine and Logistics

Other Locations:
   307/308 3rd Floor, Emporium Section
   Movenpick Ambassador Hotel
   Independence Ave.
   Accra
   Ghana
   Phone: 233-030-3961305

Key Executives:
   George Y Owusu, Founder/CEO

1165 MANSA EQUITY PARTNERS
500 Boylston Street
5th Floor
Boston, MA 02116

Phone: 617-424-4940 Fax: 617-977-9162

Mission Statement: Mansa Equity Partners is a health care private equity investment firm specializing in high growth

425

Venture Capital & Private Equity Firms / Domestic Firms

companies in the health care services and health care technology sectors. Mansa focuses on companies as they prepare for expansion, acquisition, privatization or IPO. We integrate strong expertise in health care policy, regulation, and reimbursement with vast experience in health care operations, marketing, finance, and medical administration.

Investment Criteria: Early-Stage
Industry Group Preference: Healthcare
Portfolio Companies: Accreon, E4 Health, HealthPrize Technologies, HealthSense, Independent Living Systems, Skipta
Key Executives:
  Ruben J King-Shaw Jr, Managing Partner/CIO
  Education: BS, Industrial & Labor Relations, Cornell University; MS, Health Services Administration, Florida International University; Master of International Business, Center for Industrial Studies, Madrid
  Background: COO & Deputy Administrator, Centers for Medicare & Medicaid Services; Senior Advisor, Secretary of the Treasury
  Directorships: Independent Living Systems
  Jason P Torres, Partner/COO
  Education: BS, Finance & Information Systems, Rensselaer Polytechnic Institute; MBA, Stanford Graduate School of Business
  Background: Deutsche Bank High Yield Group, Salomon Smith Barney Asset Finance Group
  James Renna, Partner

1166 MARANON CAPITAL
303 West Medison St.
Suite 2500
Chicago, IL 60606

Phone: 312-646-1200 Fax: 312-578-0047
e-mail: info@maranoncapital.com
web: www.maranoncapital.com

Mission Statement: Maranon Capital provides senior financing, mezzanine debt and equity co-investments for both private equity-backed as well as entrepreneur-owned middle market transactions. We have the flexibility to structure a one-stop financing solution or provide stand-alone senior or mezzanine debt. Maranon Capital does not take control equity positions, but will consider a minority equity role in conjunction with a financing relationship.

Geographic Preference: North America
Investment Criteria: Middle-Market Businesses
Industry Group Preference: Consumer Products, Business Products & Services, Consumer Services, Healthcare Services, Distribution, Manufacturing
Portfolio Companies: Affinitiv, Aircraft Technical Publishers, All States Ag Parts, Ameda, Ancile Solutions, AquaChem, Aristotle Corporation, Atlantic Beverage Company, BBJ Rentals, Bix Produce, Care Hospice, CHA Consulting, Clearant, Coastal Companies, Counsel On Call, CRS Temporary Housing, Dermatology Group, Digital Room, DirectPath, Drillinginfo, Dunn Paper, edriving, EMPG, Engage2Excell, Enviro Vac, EyeSouth, Fidelity Payment Services, Fisher Unitech, Global Knowledge, Gold Standard Baking, GPRS, Haystack, Health & Safety Institute, Hunt Valve, Idaho Pacific, Infogroup, Innovative Chemical Products, J.S. Held, Jensen Hughes, Keane, Kepro, Kronos, Laces, Lakeview Health, LBP Manufacturing, Lionbridge, Magnate Worldwide, Mercer Advisors, Mid Atlantic Capital, Millennium Trust, Miller Heiman, Milton Industries, Momentum, Monroe Truck Equipment, National Spine & Pain Centers, New Era Technology, Niacet, Northstar Travel, Nuvei, OnePath, PathGroup, Phillips & Temro, PKWare, PowerStop, PRV Metals, Sage Hospice, Simplify Compliance, Smile Doctors, Specialty Sales, Spinrite, Tax Guard, Tender Greens, Top Rx, US Salt, Vision Group, Wedgewood Pharmacy, Women's Care Florida, World 50, Young America

Key Executives:
  Ian Larkin, Co-Founder/Managing Director
  312-646-1202
  e-mail: iml@maranoncapital.com
  Education: BBA, University of Notre Dame
  Background: American Capital Strategies, William Blair Capital Partners, Dean Witter & Company
  Laura Albrecht, Managing Director
  312-646-1214
  e-mail: lka@marnoncapital.com
  Education: BS, Indiana University; MBA, Kellogg Graduate School of Management
  Background: American Capital Strategies, Adams Street Partners
  Rich Jander, Managing Director
  312-646-1216
  e-mail: rtg@maranoncapital.com
  Education: BSBA, Miami University; MBA, Kellogg Graduate School of Management
  Background: CapitalSource, LaSalle Bank, PNC Bank
  Demian Kircher, Managing Director
  312-646-1203
  e-mail: dk@maranoncapital.com
  Education: BBA, University of Michigan; MBA, Kellogg School of Management
  Background: American Capital Strategies, Franklin Street Equity Partners, DocuSystems, Arthur Andersen
  Greg Long, Managing Director
  312-646-1204
  e-mail: gml@maranoncapital.com
  Education: BBA, University of Notre Dame; MBA, Harvard Business School
  Background: American Capital Strategies, LEK Consulting, William Blair Capital Partners, Morgan Stanley Group
  Mike Parilla, Managing Director/Chief Compliance Officer
  312-646-1205
  e-mail: msp@maranoncapital.com
  Education: BS, Finance, University of Illinois, Urbana; MBA, University of Chicago Graduate School of Business; CPA
  Background: Heller Financial, Ernst & Young
  Rommel Garcia, Managing Director
  312-646-1211
  e-mail: rpg@maranoncapital.com
  Education: AB, University of Chicago; MBA, University of Chicago Graduate School of Business
  Background: LaSalle Bank, JP Morgan Chase

1167 MARKPOINT VENTURE PARTNERS
15770 Dallas Pkwy
Suite 800
Dallas, TX 75248

Phone: 972-490-1976 Fax: 972-490-1980
Toll-Free: 888-627-5764

Mission Statement: To provide individual investors an affordable opportunity to participate in the same high quality venture capital investment opportunities that have historically been restricted to only large institutional investors.

Geographic Preference: Southwestern United States
Founded: 1996
Average Investment: $250,000 - $1 million
Portfolio Companies: Airwide Solutions, Aether Partners, Dataside, L.I.T. Surgical, Maystreams, Vizionware, Softricity, Spatial Wireless, SyChip, X-EMI, Xtera Communications
Key Executives:
  Tex Sekhon, Managing Partner
  e-mail: tsekhon@markpt.com
  Education: BBA, University of North Texas
  Background: Co-Founder, Markpoint Company; Founder & Managing Partner, Markpoint Realty Group
  Kirk Fichtner, Managing Director
  e-mail: kfichtner@markpt.com

Venture Capital & Private Equity Firms / Domestic Firms

Education: BBA, Texas Tech University; MBA, Finance & Investments, George Washington University
Background: Dillon Read & Co.; NationsBank; DuPont

1168 MARWIT CAPITAL LLC
100 Bayview Circle
Suite 550
Newport Beach, CA 92660
Phone: 949-861-3636 Fax: 949-861-3637
e-mail: info@marwit.com
web: www.marwit.com

Mission Statement: Marwit is a private investment firm that partners with management teams to build industry leading companies in the lower middle market.
Geographic Preference: Western United States
Fund Size: $184 million
Founded: 1962
Average Investment: $10 - $30 million
Minimum Investment: $10 million
Investment Criteria: MBO, LBO, Recaps, Expansion, Growth Equity
Industry Group Preference: Manufacturing, Distribution, Services, Infrastructure, Healthcare, Retail, Consumer & Leisure, Entertainment, Business Products & Services, Renewable Resources
Portfolio Companies: ARC Machines, Driftwood Dairy Holding, Fire Grill, Granite Seed Company, Promax Nutrition, Solis Women's Health, Western Emulsions
Key Executives:
  Matthew L Witte, Managing Partner
  e-mail: mwitte@marwit.com
  Education: Cornell University
  Background: IndX Software; The Related Companies
  Directorships: Solis Women's Health, Promax Nutrition, ARC Machines, Granite Seed, Fire Grill, STEC, Paciolan, IndX Software, Marina Medical, Infotec, New West Communications
  Chris L Britt, Founding Partner
  e-mail: britt@marwit.com
  Education: BA, Economics, Stanford University; MBA, Finance, Anderson Graduate School of Management at UCLA
  Background: Levine Leichtman Capital Partners; Partner, BCC Capital Partners
  Directorships: Boot Barn, Western Emulsions, Storyteller Theatres, Driftwood Dairy, Fire Grill, Nupla, Signature Theatres, Gregg Gift Co., Columbia Aluminum Products, T and T Industries
  David M Browne, Partner
  e-mail: browne@marwit.com
  Education: MBA, Kellogg School of Management at Northwestern University; BS, Economics, Wharton School of the University of Pennsylvania
  Background: The Compass Group International; Aurora Capital Group; Merrill Lynch & Co.; Dell Ventures
  Directorships: Boot Barn; ARC Machines, Promax Nutrition; Driftwood Dairy

1169 MARYLAND VENTURE FUND
7021 Columbia Gateway Dr.
Suite 200
Columbia, MD 21046
Phone: 410-715-4191
web: www.marylandventurefund.com

Mission Statement: The Maryland Venture Fund (MVF) is a regionally recognized leader in seed and early-stage investing and a national model for state-supported investment programs. With nearly two decades of experience and numerous successful investments, MVF invests in highly innovative technology companies across the full range of industry sectors including software, communications, cybersecurity and life sciences companies in the areas of healthcare IT, medical devices and diagnostics.
Geographic Preference: Maryland
Fund Size: $84 million
Investment Criteria: Seed-Stage, Early-Stage
Industry Group Preference: Technology, Software, Communications, Cyber Security, Life Sciences, Healthcare Information Technology, Medical Devices, Diagnostics
Portfolio Companies: 20/20 GeneSystems, 3C Logic, 410Labs, 6th Treet Inc., A&G Pharmaceutical, Advanced BioNutrition, Akonni Biosystems, Aledade, Apkudo, Ashvattha, Bambecco, BrainScope Company, CoFoundersLab, Cover My Test, Curbio, Cytimune Sciences, Cytomedix, Fidelis Security Systems, Fugue, Geostellar, Gold Lasso, Gray Bug, Groupsite.com, Harpoon Medical, HomeCare.com, iLearning Engines, KoolSpan, LifeSprout, Luminal, Maxtena, Moodlerooms, Naviscan PET Systems, Optoro, Paratek, Pathsenors, Personal Genome Diagnostics, Plasmonix, Pulse 8, Racktop, Reel Genie, Sensics, Sequella, Social Toaster, StayNTouch, Tales2Go, Theranostics Health, TRX Systems, Vorbeck Materials, Weather Analytics, Xometry, Zenoss, ZeroChroma, Zeuss
Key Executives:
  Andy Jones, Managing Director
  Education: BS, MS, Electrical Engineering, Cornell University; MBA, Chicago Booth School of Business
  Background: Chief Investment Officer, Maryland Technology Development Corporation; General Partner, Boulder Ventures

1170 MASCHMEYER GROUP VENTURES
46 South Park Street
San Francisco, CA 94107
web: www.mgv.vc

Mission Statement: MGV is an early stage venture capital firm investing in emerging tech companies.
Average Investment: Up to $500,000
Key Executives:
  Marc Schroder, Managing Partner/Co-Founder
  Background: Investor, Seed + Speed Ventures
  Carsten Marschmeyer, Founding Partner

1171 MASON WELLS
411 E Wisconsin Avenue
Suite 1280
Milwaukee, WI 53202
Phone: 414-727-6400 Fax: 414-727-6410
Toll-Free: 800-313-2277
web: www.masonwells.com

Mission Statement: Creates value for investors by organizing, acquiring and strategically repositioning privately held businesses in partnership with management. Helps entrepreneurial managers build successful private companies by providing investment capital for the purchase of an existing business or the expansion of its operations by internal improvements and/or acquisition.
Geographic Preference: Midwest
Fund Size: $500 million
Founded: 1982
Average Investment: $15 million
Minimum Investment: $5 million
Investment Criteria: Later-Stage, LBO, MBO, Recapitalization
Industry Group Preference: Packaging, Information Technology, Printing, Software, Materials Technology, Business Products & Services
Portfolio Companies: A&R Logistics, AWT Labels & Packaging, Aquion, Buffalo Games, Charter NEX Films, Coating Excellence International, Converting, Creative Forming, Dedicated Computing, EastPoint Sports, Eddy Packing, GAMFG Precision, General American, HyperEdge, InterBay Technologies, King Juice Company, L.B. White

Venture Capital & Private Equity Firms / Domestic Firms

Company, MGS Manufacuring, Mullinix Packages, Nelipak, NGI Holdings, Oilgear Company, Oliver Products, Pacon Corp., Paragon Development Systems, Paris Presents, Premix, Prime Distribution, Qualas Power Services, Structural Concepts, Sturm Foods, Whitehall Specialties

Key Executives:
Tom Smith, Executive Managing Director
414-727-6416
e-mail: tgsmith@masonwells.com
Education: BA, University of Wisconsin, Madison
Background: Marshall & Illsley Corp
Directorships: Aquion, Buffalo Games, Coating Excellence International, Pacon Corporation, Mullinix Packages
Jay Radtke, Senior Managing Director
414-727-6405
e-mail: jradtke@masonwells.com
Education: BA, Vanderbilt University; MBA, Columbia Business School
Background: Cornerstone Equity Investors, Lehman Brothers
Directorships: AWT Labels & Packaging, L.B. White Company, Nelipak Healthcare Packaging, Structural Concepts, Charter NEX Films, Mullinix Packaging, Oliver Products, Pacon Corp.
Greg Myers, Senior Managing Director
414-727-6404
e-mail: gmyers@masonwells.com
Education: MBA, Marquette University; BS, University of Iowa
Background: Marshall & Illsley
Directorships: EastPoint Sports, Eddy Packing, MGS Manufacturing, Nelipak Healthcare Packaging, Whitehall Specialties
Kevin P Kenealey, Senior Managing Director
414-727-6417
e-mail: kkenealey@masonwells.com
Education: BS, University of Minnesota; JD, Northwestern School of Law
Background: Kirland & Ellis
Directorships: A&R Logistics, King Juice Co., NGI Holdings Corp., Paris Presents, Qualus Power Services
Ben Holbrook, Managing Director
414-727-6422
e-mail: bholbrook@masonwells.com
Education: BS, Psychology, Brown University
Background: Research Associate, Janney Montgomery Scott; Corporate Finance Analyst, Thomas Weisel Partners
Directorships: A&R Logistics, Buffalo Games, Eddy Packing, King Juice Co., Paris Presents, Whitehall Specialties
Jim Domach, Chief Financial Officer
414-727-6412
e-mail: jdomach@masonwells.com
Education: BS, Business Administration, St. Norbert College; MBA, Marquette University
Background: Loan Audit Manager, Marshall & Ilsley Corporation Commercial Audit Group
Directorships: Eddy Packing, Dedicated Computing, General American, Premix, Oilgear

---

1172 MASS VENTURES
308 Congress Street
5th Floor
Boston, MA 02210

Phone: 617-723-4920 Fax: 617-723-5983
web: www.mass-ventures.com

Mission Statement: The Massachusetts Technology Development Corporation, a leading edge venture capital firm that addresses the 'capital gap' for start-up and expansion of early stage technology companies operating in the Commonwealth of Massachusetts.

Geographic Preference: Massachusetts
Fund Size: $62 million
Founded: 1978
Average Investment: $250,000
Minimum Investment: $100,000
Investment Criteria: Seed, Startup, First-Stage, Second-Stage
Industry Group Preference: Systems & Software, Industrial, Robotics, Internet, Digital Media & Marketing, Healthcare Information Technology, Clean Technology, Energy, Mobile, Medical Devices, Hardware
Portfolio Companies: Applause, Armored Things, BoardOnTrack, ClearGov, Edaris Health, Fairmarkit, Ginkgo Bioworks, Grapevine, Harvest Automation, HorsePower, Inside Tracker, Jebbit, Life Image, Machine Metrics, OwnerIQ, Raven360, Spiro Technologies, Veritas,

Key Executives:
Walter M (Jerry) Bird, President
617-226-2822
e-mail: jbird@mass-ventures.com
Education: BA, Dartmouth College; MBA Tuck School at Dartmouth
Background: Brook Venture Partners; Nova MedVentures; Claflin Capital Management
Directorships: Forerun, lifeIMAGE, uTest
Jason Allen, Vice President
617-207-5576
e-mail: jallen@mass-ventures.com
Education: BA, Denison University; MA, Theological Studies, Harvard Divinity School; JD, Northeastern University School of Law
Background: Launch Capital; General Manager, Ovia Insights
Charlie Hipwood, Vice President
617-306-4512
e-mail: chipwood@mass-ventures.com
Education: BA, Boston College; MBA, Booth School of Business, University of Chicago
Background: JP Morgan

1173 MASSACHUSETTS CAPITAL RESOURCE COMPANY
420 Boylston Street
5th Floor
Boston, MA 02116

Phone: 617-536-3900
web: www.masscapital.com

Mission Statement: MCRC is a source of risk capital for Massachusetts' business and invests across the entire range of business development financings.

Geographic Preference: Massachusetts
Founded: 1977
Average Investment: $5 million
Minimum Investment: $1 million
Investment Criteria: Second-Stage, Mezzanine, LBO, Growth Capital, Acquisitions, Recapitalizations
Industry Group Preference: Communications, Computer Related, Electronic Components, Instrumentation, Genetic Engineering, Industrial Equipment, Equipment, Internet Technology, Medical & Health Related, Consumer Products, Healthcare, Manufacturing, Software, Technology
Portfolio Companies: Advanced Practice Strategies, Aquent, Aspen Tech, Bainbridge, Baynes Electric Supply, Bigbelly Solar, Curaspan Health Group, Exergen, Harbar, Harmonix Music Systems, Litecontrol, Lytron, Magnemotion, Marshall Tube, Medtouch, Network Allies, Phillips Screw Company, Polar Beverages, Pure Incubation, Quadrant Software, Rypos, Seaman Paper, Tri-Wire, Valet Park, WTE Corporation

Key Executives:
Suzanne L Dwyer, Managing Director
617-536-8251
e-mail: sdwyer@masscapital.com
Education: BS/BA, Bridgewater State College; MBA, Babson Graduate School of Bussiness

Venture Capital & Private Equity Firms / Domestic Firms

Background: State Street Bank & Trust Company; Brown Brothers Harriman & Co
Dan Corcoran, Managing Director
617-536-5323
e-mail: dcorcoran@masscapital.com
Education: BA, Economics, Boston College; MBA, Babson College
Background: Bank of New England; BankBoston; Citizens Financial Group

1174 MASSACHUSETTS GROWTH CAPITAL CORPORATION
529 Main Street
Schrafft Center
Suite 201
Charlestown, MA 02129

Phone: 617-523-6262 Fax: 617-523-7676
web: www.massgcc.com

Mission Statement: To provide financing to small businesses in Massachusetts to which private capital is not readily available with the purpose of creating or preserving jobs and promoting economic development.

Geographic Preference: Massachusetts
Founded: 1975
Average Investment: $300,000
Minimum Investment: $100,000
Investment Criteria: Seed, Startup, First-Stage, Second-Stage, LBO, MBO
Industry Group Preference: Communications, Computer Related, Electronic Components, Instrumentation, Genetic Engineering, Industrial Equipment, Equipment, Internet Technology, Medical & Health Related

Key Executives:
Lawrence D Andrews, President & CEO
617-337-2800
e-mail: landrews@massgcc.com

1175 MASTHEAD VENTURE PARTNERS
301 Newbury St.
Suite 241
Danvers, MA 01923

Phone: 617-621-3000 Fax: 617-621-3055
e-mail: info@mvpartners.com
web: www.mvpartners.com

Mission Statement: Masthead's partners possess successful track records creating long-term value in early-stage companies. We seek market-making ventures with strong teams and powerful intellectual property in high-growth segments.

Investment Criteria: Early Stage
Industry Group Preference: Software, Internet Technology, Communication Technology, IT-Intensive Life Science Applications, Internet Infrastructure
Portfolio Companies: AEP Networks, Bitpipe, Ecount, Centric Software, Chumby, ExpoTV, Genesis Networks, Intercasting Corporation, Liquid Machines, NewsGator Technologies, Nexaweb Technologies, Packet Design, RuleStream Corporation, Scanbuy, Tremor Media, TripConnect

Key Executives:
Braden M (Brady) Bohrmann, General Partner
Education: BS, Finance & Communications, Babson College
Background: COO, Watson Technologies; CFO, Alpha-Beta Technology
Directorships: ExpoTV, inOvate Communications, RuleStream
Daniel K Flatley, General Partner
Education: AB, University of Notre Dame; JD, Georgetown University School of Law
Background: Managing Director, Credit Suisse First Boston And Donaldson
Directorships: AEP Networks, Genesis Networks, Newsgator, Scanbuy, Tacoda Systems, TripConnect, Phillips Plywood, Nuron, Mail.com
Richard W Levandov, General Partner
Education: BS, Binghamton University
Background: Partner, Softbank Technology Ventures
Directorships: Chumby, Liquid Machines, Newsgator, Nexaweb, Tacoda, Tremor
Stephen K Smith, General Partner
Education: First Class Honors Degree, Computer Science, Brighton Polytechnic University; MBA Harvard Business School
Background: Analyst, PaineWebber
Directorships: Maine Technology Institute
Timothy P Agnew, Principal
Education: University of Virginia School of Law; Vassar College
Background: CEO, Finance Authority of Maine
Directorships: CEI Community Ventures, the Great Schools Partnership, the Maine Trust for People with Disabilities, HealthInfoNet, Senator George J. Mitchell Scholarship Reserach Institute
Mary M Shannon, Principal
Education: Holy Cross; MBA, Boston College
Background: Director of Planning & Analysis, Sefer; Liberty Mutual Group

1176 MATCHSTICK VENTURES
Twin Cities, MN

e-mail: hello@matchstickventures.com
web: www.matchstickventures.com

Mission Statement: To support innovation and diverse entrepreneurs in startup communities.

Average Investment: $50,000 - $1,000,000
Investment Criteria: Early-Stage, Seed
Industry Group Preference: Technology
Portfolio Companies: Addstructure, AdHawk, Air Tailor, Ambassador, Blueprint Registry, Branch, Bybe, Ilos, Inspectorio, Itsbyu, Kapta, Kidizen, Kipsu, Kokko, Learn To Live, Local Crate, Localize, Nexosis, Savitude, Scale Factor, Shopturn, Spot Crowd, Sprucebot, Story Xpress, Structural, Upsie

Key Executives:
Ryan Broshar, Founder & Managing Partner
e-mail: ryan@matchstickventures.com
Education: BSB, Entrepreneurship and Marketing, University of Minnesota; MBA, University of Colorado Boulder
Background: Managing Partner, Confluence Energy; Co-Founder, Beta.MN; Managing Partner, Confluence Capital Partners; Managing Director, Techstars
Natty Zola, Managing Partner
e-mail: natty@matchstickventures.com
Education: BA, Finance, University of Maryland - Robert H. Smith School of Business
Background: Managing Director, Techstars; Sr. Director, MapQuest; Co-Founder & CEO, Everlater

1177 MATERIAL IMPACT
131 Dartmouth Street
3rd Floor
Boston, MA 02116

web: materialimpact.com

Mission Statement: Material Impact transforms materials into companies that makes an impact. They focus on quantum leap advancements in technology and material technologies that will impact basic human needs and quality of life.

Fund Size: $200 Million

Key Executives:
Carmichael Roberts, Co-Founder and Managing Partner
Education: BS, PhD, Duke University; MBA, Massachussets Institute of Technology
Background: General Partner, North Bridge Venture

429

Venture Capital & Private Equity Firms / Domestic Firms

Partners; Co-Founder, Diagnostics For All; President and CEO, Arsenal Medical
Adam Sharkawy, Co-Founder and Managing Partner
Education: PhD, Duke University
Background: VP, Research, Ventrica Inc.; VP, Research, Abbott Ventures; SVP, The Medicines Company

1178 MATH VENTURE PARTNERS
Chicago, IL 60654

web: www.mathventurepartners.com

Mission Statement: MATH Venture Partners is a venture capital fund investing in early to growth-stage technology companies. MATH seeks to create partnerships with talented and committed digital entrepreneurs.
Geographic Preference: United States
Fund Size: $28 million
Founded: 2014
Average Investment: $500,000 - $1 million
Investment Criteria: Startups, Seed Stage, Early Stage, Expansion Stage, Growth Stage
Industry Group Preference: Technology
Portfolio Companies: Acorns, All4Staff, Apervita, CardFlight, Digital Golf Technologies, GameWisp, InRentive, MightyNest, Music Audience Exchange, NoRedInk, NowSecure, RedSeal, Roost, SocialSignIn, Spoon University, Telnyx, ThinkCERCA

Key Executives:
  Mark Achler, Managing Director
  Education: BA, History & Economics, Purdue University
  Background: Senior VP, New Business, Strategy & Innovation, Redbox; President, Emmi Solutions; Founding Partner, Kettle Partners; President, Kinesoft Development; CEO & Co-Founder, The Whitewater Group
  Troy Henikoff, Managing Director
  Education: BS, Engineering, Brown University; Northwestern University
  Background: Lecturer, Kellogg School of Management; Managing Director, Techstars; Co-Founder, Excelerate Labs; CEO, OneWed.com; President, Amacal; Co-Founder & CEO, SurePayroll.com; President, Systemetrics

1179 MATLINPATTERSON
70 East 55th St.
9th Floor
New York, NY 10022

Phone: 212-651-9500
web: www.matlinpatterson.com

Mission Statement: A global distressed private equity firm.
Key Executives:
  David J Matlin, Chief Executive Officer
  Education: BA, Wharton School; JD, University of California
  Directorships: Flagstar Bank, Standard Pacific

1180 MATON VENTURE
1601 S De Anza Boulevard
Suite 115
Cupertino, CA 95014

Phone: 408-786-5168 Fax: 408-996-0728
web: www.maton.com

Mission Statement: To help new entrepreneurs by investing in privately owned companies offering promising new technologies.
Geographic Preference: United States, Taiwan, Japan, Germany
Investment Criteria: All Stages
Industry Group Preference: Technology
Portfolio Companies: Advanced Analogic Technologies, Analogic Tech, Apherma Corporation, Bit Bliz, Breveon, Broadband Communications, Crosslayer Networks, eBest, Envivio, Innovative Robotics, Intelligent Epitaxy Technology, Martsoft, Octasoft, OmniVision, Oplink, Ortega Innfosystems, PicoNetics, Primanex Corporation, Storactive, Syscan, Tsunami Visual Technologies, ZYNX Networks

Key Executives:
  Connie Chuang, Co-Founder
  Jesse Chen, Co-Founder
  Background: Co-Founder, President & CEO, BusLogic
  Jaff Linn, Co-Founder
  Background: Vice President, Engineering, BusLogic

1181 MATRIX PARTNERS
101 Main Street
17th Floor
Cambridge, MA 02142

Phone: 617-494-1223 Fax: 617-866-4999
e-mail: info@matrixpartners.com
web: www.matrixpartners.com

Mission Statement: Committed to building long-term relationships with outstanding entrepreneurs and helping them build significant, industry-leading companies.
Geographic Preference: United States, India, China
Founded: 1977
Average Investment: $2 to $10 million
Minimum Investment: $2 million
Investment Criteria: All Stages
Industry Group Preference: Enterprise Software, Communications, Semiconductors, Internet Technology, Wireless Technologies, Consumer Internet, Networking, Clean Technology, Energy
Portfolio Companies: Acacia, Adelphic, Affirmed, Aibang.com, Almond Systems, Ambarella, Anjuke.com, ApartmentList, Aquto, Aylus Networks, BabyTree, Canopy, Canva, Carbon Black, Carbon Design, Care.com, Circle, CloudBees, Conductor, Confer, Crossbeam Systems, Cyphort, Didi Chuxing, Digital Fountain, Digium, Earnin, Ele.me, Emphirix, Enservio, The Flatiron School, Fuze Network, Gilt Groupe, GOAT, GrabCad, HubSpot, Huddle, Hyper9, Inflection, Intent Media, Jetsetter, JustFabulous, Kalido, Klip, Koding, Koudai, Lever, Locality, MarkForged, minuteKEY, Mitro, Momo, Namely, Oculus VR, Ola, OpenSpan, Panzura, Plexx, Polyvore, Poynt, Qihoo, QPID Health, Qualtré, Quora, Quri, Rocksbox, Salsify, Sila, SpiderCloud Wireless, Storiant, Taulia, TechStyle, textPlus, The Echo Nest, TribeHR, UniDesk, VeriVue, VeVeo, VideoIQ, Xiaomi, Xtalic, Zaius, Zendesk, ZestFinance

Other Locations:
  260 Hormer Avenue
  Suite 201
  Palo Alto, CA 94301
  Phone: 650-798-1600 Fax: 650-798-1601

  535 Mission St.
  Suite 2600
  San Francisco, CA 94105
  Phone: 650-798-1600 Fax: 650-798-1601

  Ceejay House #306
  Annie Besant Road
  Worli
  Mumbai 400 018
  India
  Phone: 91-2267680000 Fax: 91-2267680001

  Suite 2601, Taikang Financial Tower, No.38,
  East 3rd Ring Road North
  Chaoyang District
  Beijing 100026
  China
  Phone: 86-1065000088 Fax: 86-1065000066

  Suite 1001, Citigroup Tower
  No. 33, Hua Yuan Shi Qiao Road
  Pudong Garden
  Shanghai 200120

China
Phone: 86-2161210600 **Fax:** 86-2161210660

Room 2807, 28th Floor
AIA Financial Centre
1 Connaught Rd.
Central
Hong Kong
Phone: 852-3960-6592 **Fax:** 852-3669-8008

Key Executives:
Timothy A Barrows, General Partner
617-494-1223
e-mail: tbarrows@matrixpartners.com
Education: Williams College; MBA, Stanford University
Background: Merrill Lynch Capital Markets
Directorships: Affirmed Networks, Carbon Black, Cloud Zero, nference, Qrativ
Paul J Ferri, Co-Founder
e-mail: pjf@matrixpartners.com
Education: MBA, Columbia University; MSEE, Polytechnic University of New York; BSEE, Cornell University
Background: Founder, Hellman Ferri Investment Associates; General Partner, WestVen Management
Directorships: Airvana, Aylus Networks, Empirix, Netezza, VeriVue, Veveo
Stan J Reiss, General Partner
617-494-1223
e-mail: sreiss@matrixpartners.com
Education: BSEE, Cornell University; SMEE, SMOR, Massachusetts Institute of Technology
Background: McKinsey & Company
Directorships: Acacia Communications, LogRocket, RightHand Robotics, Xtalic, Lightmatter
David R Skok, General Partner
781-890-2244
e-mail: dskok@matrixpartners.com
Education: BSc, Computer Science, University of Sussex (England)
Background: SilverStream Software; President/CEO, Watermark Software
Directorships: Apollo GraphQL, CloudBees, Conductor, Digium, Enservio, GrabCAD, Hubspot, Meteor, Namely, OpenSpan, SageCloud, Salsify, Video IQ, Zaius
Andrew W Verhalen, General Partner
650-796-1600
e-mail: averhalen@matrixpartners.com
Education: MBA, MSEE, BSEE, Cornell University
Background: Divisional VP, 3Com Corporation; Intel Corporation
Directorships: Panzura, Sila Nanotechnologies
Antonio Rodriguez, General Partner
e-mail: antonio@matrixpartners.com
Education: AB, Social Studies, Harvard University; MBA, Stanford Graduate School of Business; Graduate Studies, Computer Science, Stanford University
Background: CTO, HP; Founder & CEO, Tabblo; VP, Engineering, MyPublisher; Memora; Abuzz; The Boston Consulting Group
Directorships: Adelphic, Canopy, Care.com, Ctrl Labs, Echo Nest, Intent Media, Koding, MarkForged, Oculus VR, Owl Labs, Sqrrl, TalkTo
Dana Stalder, General Partner
650-798-1600
e-mail: dana@matrixpartners.com
Education: BS, Commerce, Santa Clara University
Background: Senior Vice President, Product Sales, PayPay; Vice President, Internet Marketing, eBay; Founding Executive, Respond.com; Vice President, Finance, Netscape
Directorships: Afterpay, ApartmentList, Bugsnag, Earnin, Gilt Groupe, iRise, Lever, minuteKEY, Polyvore, Poynt, Quin Street, textPlus, Work4Labs, Zendesk, ZestFinance
Hardi Meybaum, General Partner
Education: MS, Production Engineering, Tallinna Tehnikülikool

Background: GrabCAD
Directorships: Smartcat, Starship Technologies, CARMERA
Ilya Sukhar, General Partner
Education: BS, MEng, Computer Science, Cornell University
Background: Ooyala, Etacts, Parse, Facebook
Directorships: Fivetran, Flock Safety, Height, Hustle, Mashgin, Parabola, Slab

1182 MAVERICK VENTURES
1 Letterman Drive
Building D
San Francisco, CA 94129

Phone: 415-343-1900
web: www.maverickventures.com

Mission Statement: Maverick Ventures invests in entrepreneurs across the healthcare and technology sectors.

Founded: 1993

Key Executives:
Lee Ainslie, Founder
Education: BS, University of Virginia; MBA, University of North Carolina
Background: Managing Director, Tiger Management

1183 MAVERON LLC
411 First Avenue South
Suite 600
Seattle, WA 98104

Phone: 206-288-1700
web: www.maveron.com

Mission Statement: A financial and strategic partner to those companies who demonstrate both passion and vision in transforming the consumer experience.

Fund Size: $600 million
Founded: 1997
Industry Group Preference: Consumer Services
Portfolio Companies: Against Gravity, Allbirds, Arivale, August, Axius, Big Box, Boon + Gable, Booster, Bread, Capella Education, CircleUp, Clarity Money, Common, Course Hero, Cover, Cranium, Crowd Cow, Darby Smart, Decide.com, Dia & Co., Direct Buy, Dolls Kill, Dolly, Drugstore.com, Dwellable, Eargo, Earnest, eBay, Elysium, Everlane, Fabric, Fit XR, Flywire, General Assembly, Genies, Good, Groupon, Handle, Happy Returns, Homeroom, HopSkipDrive, iBeat, Illumix, Imperfect Produce, Inkbox, JetClosing, Jott, Jumpcut, Keeps, Kids on 45th, Kinetix Living, KonMari, Koru, Leaftail Labs, Lovevery, Lucy, Madison Reed, Masse, MegaBots, Mode.ai, Modern Fertility, Moment, Naja, Nécessaire, Neighborhood Goods, Newsle, Nextfoods, Nomadic, NovoED, Panna, Peach, Periscope, PetCoach, Pinkberry, Pioneer Square Labs, Pluto, Potbelly, Pro.com, Prose, Quellos, Red Tricycle, SafeTrek, Sana, Scoot, Seatme, Service, Shutterfly, Simbi, Splash, Spyce, Study Edge, Svrf, The Guild, The Wrap, Tile, True Facet, Trupanion, Vacatia, Vhoto, Vicarious, Virtuix Omni, Visor, Wander Beauty, Way Up, Zulily, Zume Pizza

Other Locations:
463 Pacific Avenue
San Francisco, CA 94133
Phone: 415-373-6250 **Fax:** 415-373-6255

Key Executives:
Dan Levitan, Co-Founder/Partner
Education: Horace Mann School, Duke University, Harvard Business School
Background: Managing Director, Schroders
Directorships: Allbirds, Arivale, CircleUp, Peach, Pluto VR, Pro.com, Spyce, The Wrap, Trupanion
Anarghya Vardhana, Partner
e-mail: anarghya@maveron.com
Directorships: Masse, Illumix, Imperfect Produce, Inkbox, Pluto VR, Spyce, The Guild Hotels

Venture Capital & Private Equity Firms / Domestic Firms

David Wu, Partner
e-mail: dave@maveron.com
Directorships: Booster, Darby Smart, Eargo, Illumix, Inkbox, Modern Fertility
Pete McCormick, Partner
e-mail: pmccormick@maveron.com
Education: BA, Economics, University of Washington
Background: Partner, Graham & Dunn Law Firm
Directorships: Madison Reed
Clayton Lewis, Partner
e-mail: clewis@maveron.com
Background: President & COO, HouseValues.com
Directorships: Allconnect, Arivale, Koru, Lively, NextFoods
Jason Stoffer, Partner
e-mail: jstoffer@maveron.com
Education: BA, Economics, University of Michigan; MBA, Wharton School
Background: Senior Director, Career Education Corp.
Directorships: Common, Course Hero, Dolls Kill, Dolly, Everlane, Flywire, General Assembly, Imperfect Produce, Keeps, The Guild Hotels, TrueFacet
Elise Hebb, Partner/COO
e-mail: ehebb@maveron.com
Cat Lee, Partner
e-mail: cat@maveron.com

1184 MAYFIELD FUND
2484 Sand Hill Road
Quadrus Complex, Building 4
Menlo Park, CA 94025

Phone: 650-854-5560 **Fax:** 650-854-5712
e-mail: marketing@mayfield.com
web: www.mayfield.com

Mission Statement: Mayfield has always been about the people - experienced, committed partners; smart, innovative entrepreneurs; loyal, knowledgeable investors -all working together to build sustainable technology companies that solve tough customer problems.

Geographic Preference: United States
Fund Size: $2.7 billion
Founded: 1969
Average Investment: $3 million
Minimum Investment: $500,000
Investment Criteria: Seed, Startup, First-Stage, Second-Stage, Third-Stage, Series A, Growth Stage, Later Stage
Industry Group Preference: Communications, Computer Related, E-Commerce & Manufacturing, Electronic Components, Education, Media, Software, Internet Technology, Biotechnology, Medical & Health Related, Life Sciences, Environment Products & Services, Consumer Services, Energy Technology, Telecommunications
Portfolio Companies: 3DRobotics, AgilOne, Alignable, Alfresco, Appcelerator, Arcadia Data, AudienceScience, Baihe.com, Balbix, BigPanda, Blackarrow, Brighter, C9, Centrify, ClassPass, CloudGenix, CloudPhysics, CloudVelox, Couchbase, Crunchbase, Earny, EasilyDo, Edison, Elatica, Electric Cloud, Fab, fitmob, Fixya, Fungible, Gigya, GroundWork, Grove, HashiCorp, HealthTap, if(we), IndiaProperty.com, InfluxDB, Jawbone, Lantern, LatticePower, Lyft, Mammoth Biosciences, MapR Technologies, Massdrop, Matrimony.com, Mission Bio, Moat, NewsCred, Outreach, OUYA, Portworx, Poshmark, Qunar.com, Qventus, Rancher, Rubicon Project, ServiceMax, ShiftLeft, ShineOn, Skilljar, SmartRecruiters, SMiT, Stockpile, SwiftStack, Tejas Networks, Tonal, Tripp, TrustRadius, Versa Networks, Vexata, Viralheat, Webroot, WideOrbit, WorkSpan, Zipongo

Key Executives:
James Beck, Managing Director & COO
e-mail: jbeck@mayfield.com
Education: BS, Business Administration, University of the Pacific; Executive Program, Haas School of Business
Background: Audit Manager, Aurthur Andersen
Directorships: Anita Borg Institute for Women and Technology
Navin Chaddha, Managing Director
e-mail: nchaddha@mayfield.com
Education: MS, Electrical Engineering, Stanford University
Background: Partner, Gabriel Venture Partners; CTO, VXtreme; Co-Founder, iBeam Broadcasting
Raj Kapoor, Venture Advisor
e-mail: rkapoor@mayfield.com
Education: BS, Robotics Engineering, Carnegie Mellon University; MBA, Harvard Business School
Background: Chief Strategy Officer, Lyft; Co-Founder, Snapfish; Excite@Home; Bell Atlantic
Directorships: Carnegie Mellon Silicon Valley Advisory Council, California Research Center Advisory Board, DoSomething.org Board of Directors
Rajeev Batra, Partner
e-mail: rbarta@mayfield.com
Education: MEng, Electrical Engineering, Cornell University; BSEE Honors, University of Maryland, College Park; MBA, Harvard Business School
Background: Siebel Systems, Scopus Technology, Open Environment Corporation
Nikhil Khattau, Managing Director
Education: BA, University of Mumbai
Background: Founding CEO, SUN F&C
Directorships: Matrimony, Box8, IndiaProperty, Licious, Securens, Sohan Lal Commodity, Talview, TripHobo
Vikram Godse, Managing Partner
Education: BComm, University of Bombay
Background: Founding Member, JM Financial Investment Managers; Infinity Venture Fund
Directorships: Fources, Indiagames.com, Amagi, Centum Learning, Emiza, Genesis Colors, Knowlarity, Leap, LendingKart, Simplilearn, The Beer Cafe

1185 MAYFLY CAPITAL
web: www.mayflycapital.com

Mission Statement: Mayfly Capital LLC invests and partners with entrepreneurs developing innovative, environmentally conscious technologies for the graphic arts and printing industries. Before it emerged as an independent firm in 2009, Mayfly was the internal investment and development arm of a family-owned commercial printing company based in Cleveland, Ohio. Now, as a standalone firm, Mayfly can provide its investments the support and resources needed to achieve their near-term goals while increasing their long-term value by developing operational and financial strategies.

Founded: 2009
Industry Group Preference: Graphic Arts, Printing
Portfolio Companies: Ross PPD Corporation, 121nexus
Key Executives:
Charlie Kim, Managing Partner/Founder
Education: BS, Economics & Finance, Ohio Northern University; MS, Accounting, Boston College
Background: Intervale Capital; Merrill Lynch

1187 MB VENTURE PARTNERS
17 West Pontotoc Ave.
Suite 101
Memphis, TN 38103

Phone: 901-322-0330 **Fax:** 901-322-0339
web: www.mbventures.com

Mission Statement: MB Venture Partners is a Memphis, Tennessee venture capital firm that provides equity capital and strategic direction to life science companies.

Fund Size: $76 million
Founded: 2001
Investment Criteria: Seed-State, Early-Stage, Later-Stage
Industry Group Preference: Life Sciences, Biotechnology, Medical Devices

432

Venture Capital & Private Equity Firms / Domestic Firms

Portfolio Companies: AxioMed Spine, Better Walk, Biomimetic, BioNanovations, BioSet, Blood Monitoring Solutions, Calosyn Pharma, Cayenne Medical, Compression Kinetics, CrossRoads, Cuff-Mate, EcoSurg, Endoinsight, Expanding Orthopedics, Focal Point Pharmaceuticals, GTx, Handminder, Hapten Sciences, Health & Bliss, Hubble Telemedical, Innometrix, iScreen Vision, Jumpstart Foundy, Kereos, KFx Medical, MB Innovations, Mobilizer, Nanopthalmics, Ortho Kinematics, Protein Discovery, Restore Medical Solutions, S2 Interactive, Salient Surgical, Spine Wave, Sweetbio, Tidal Wave Technology, Urova Medical, Veracity Medical Solutions, View Medical, Visioneering Technologies, Zyga

Key Executives:
  Gary Stevenson, Co-Founder/Managing Partner
  Education: University of Missouri; MBA, Kellogg School of Business
  Background: Abbott Laboratories
  Directorships: AxioMed Spine, BioSET, Kereos, KFx Medical, Hapten Sciences, S2 Interactive, Visioneering, Focal Point Pharmaceuticals, iScreen, Restore Medical Solutions, MB Innovations
  Mike Sherman, Partner
  Education: BS, Biomedical Engineering, University of Texas
  Background: Sofamor Danek
  Directorships: Anulex Technologies, Cayenne Medical, Calosyn Pharma, Expanding Orthopedics, Hubble Telemedical, Tidal Wave Technology, Veracity Medical, Urova Medical, Nanopthalmics, Zyga

1188 MBF CAPITAL CORPORATION
12 East 49th Street
28th Floor
New York, NY 10017

Phone: 212-339-2861 Fax: 212-339-2834
web: www.mbfcapital.com

Mission Statement: An investment firm specializing in making private equity investments principally in technology driven, early stage information technology and medical technology companies.

Investment Criteria: Early Stage, Turnarounds, Growth Capital
Industry Group Preference: Information Technology, Medical Devices, Telecommunications, Networking, Software, Semiconductors, Biopharmaceuticals, Healthcare Services, Drug Development
Portfolio Companies: eMotion, ExSar Corporation, Gunther International, IQ Systems, Lamar, Network-1 Software & Technology, Network Specialists, Syntonix Pharmaceuticals, Vela Pharmaceuticals

Key Executives:
  Mark Fisher, President
  Background: Principal, Alex Brown; Senior Vice President/Investments, Lehman Brothers; Vice President, Merrill Lynch Futures
  Directorships: Vela Pharmaceuticals, ExSar Corporation

1189 MCG CAPITAL CORPORATION
1001 19th Street North
10th Floor
Arlington, VA 22209

Phone: 703-247-7500 Fax: 703-247-7505
e-mail: mcg@mcgcapital.com

Mission Statement: A provider of capital and strategic advice to small to mid-size companies, focusing on growth and value creation.

Geographic Preference: United States
Founded: 1990
Investment Criteria: Revenue between $20-$200 million, $3-$25 million in EBITDA, Proven business models, Operating leverage
Industry Group Preference: Communications, Information Technology, Media, Technology, Broadcasting, Plastics, Business Products & Services, Consumer Products, Healthcare, Entertainment, Education
Portfolio Companies: Accurate Group Holdings, Broadview Networks Holdings, C7 Data Centers, Community Investors, GMC Television Broadcasting, IDOC, Industrial Safety Technologies, Intrafusion Holding Corporation, Legacy Cabinets Holdings II, Maverick Healthcare Equity, RadioPharmacy Investors, South Bay Mental Health Center, Surefire Medical, Velocity Technology Solutions

Key Executives:
  B Hagen Saville, President/COO
  e-mail: hsaville@mcgcapital.com
  Background: First Union National Bank, Signet Bank
  E Peter Malekian, Managing Director
  e-mail: pmalekian@mcgcapital.com
  Education: BS, George Mason University; MBA, Cornell University, Johnson School of Management
  Background: Ferris Baker Watts; Financial Analyst, Arthur Andersen; Consultant, Hoffman Morison & Fitzgerald
  Keith Kennedy, CFO/Managing Director
  Background: GE Capital; Earnst & Young LLP

1190 MCG CAPITAL MANAGEMENT
750 Kearns Blvd.
Suite 295
Park City, UT 84060

Phone: 435-214-7127
web: www.mcgcapitalmgt.com

Mission Statement: MCG Capital Management is committed to producing consistent profitability for clients.

Key Executives:
  Michael C Giese, President
  e-mail: mgiese@mcgcapitalmgt.com
  Education: BS, Astronautical Engineering, US Air Force Academy

1191 MCGOVERN CAPITAL
230 West 56th Street
New York, NY 10019

Phone: 212-688-9840
e-mail: katey@mcgoverncapital.com
web: www.mcgoverncapital.com

Mission Statement: Invests in startup companies in various industries, including Health & Wellness, Food & Beverage, medicinal cannabis, air & water purification, eSports, and media.

Investment Criteria: Seed, Early-Stage
Industry Group Preference: Health & Wellness, Skincare, Food & Beverage, eSports, Cannabis, Technology, Media, Communications
Portfolio Companies: Sobe, The Water Initiative, K&A Water, KX Industries, Narragansett Beer, Beverage Innovations, Celsius, Rise Brewing Co., Neostrata, Skinphonic, Regimend MD, Optigenex, Isreal Plant Sciences, PlantEXT, Intiva, Intiva Biopharma, WeedMD, Wellness Centers, Esports, iItoo, Clean Coal Technologies Inc., Perimeter Internetworking, Wealthtracking, Angstrom Publishing, Counsel Press,

Key Executives:
  Kevin M. McGovern, Chairman/CEO
  Education: AB, Cornell University; JD, Saint John's University School of Law
  Background: Chairman/CEO, The Water Initiative

433

Venture Capital & Private Equity Firms / Domestic Firms

1192 MCGOWAN CAPITAL GROUP
101 North Main Avenue
Suite 325
Sioux Falls, SD 57104

Phone: 605-357-5302 Fax: 605-357-5303
e-mail: info@mcgowancapitalgroup.com
web: www.mcgowancapitalgroup.com

Mission Statement: To provide private equity opportunities for investors and to assist with the building of successful enterprises.
Geographic Preference: Midwest
Founded: 2004
Investment Criteria: Early Stage, Mid-Stage
Industry Group Preference: Diversified
Portfolio Companies: Classified Verticals, Dakotaland Autoglass, Grand Prairie Foods, Granite City Food & Brewery, Maverick Air Center, NB Golf Cars, Progressive Acute Care, Sajan, Savigent, South Dakota Innovation Partners, The Prairie Club, ZeaChem

Key Executives:
Gene McGowan Sr, Founder/Chief Executive Officer
Background: Entrepreneur in Residence, Bluestem Capital Company; COO, Individual Investor Services; Piper Jaffray

1193 MCKELLAR & COMPANY
8686 N. Central Ave
Suite 106
Phoenix, AZ 85020

Phone: 602-265-3400

Mission Statement: To help companies with sales of over $5 million to grow through venture capital and with management.
Geographic Preference: United States
Fund Size: $300 million
Founded: 1989
Average Investment: $5 million
Minimum Investment: $500,000
Investment Criteria: Second Stage, Third Stage, Revenue of $5 million or more
Industry Group Preference: Diversified

Key Executives:
Winston P. McKellar, Owner/President
e-mail: winston@mckellarandcompany.com

1194 MEAKEM/BECKER VENTURE CAPITAL
603 Beaver Street
Suite 201
Sewickley, PA 15143

Phone: 412-749-5720 Fax: 412-749-5721
e-mail: info@mbvc.com
web: www.mbvc.com

Mission Statement: To help build leading, next-generation companies of significant value.
Geographic Preference: Eastern & Midwestern United States
Founded: 2005
Investment Criteria: Early-Stage
Industry Group Preference: Life Sciences, Information Technology
Portfolio Companies: Spreecast, Schoology, Shipwire, Cloudmeter, HotPads, Kiva Systems, CollegeProwler.com, Leostream, RapidBuyr, 3form, BeatBox, Tiversa

Key Executives:
David Becker, Co-Founder/Managing Director
e-mail: dbecker@mbvc.com
Education: BS, Chemical & Petroleum Refining Engineering, Colorado School of Mines; MS, Chemical Engineering, West Virginia College of Graduate Studies (Marshall University); MBA, Harvard University
Background: President & Chief Investment Officer, Clearwater Capital Management; COO, FreeMarkets; Dole Fresh Fruit International
Directorships: Hotpads, Shipwire, Leostream, Kiva, Schoology

Mark G Miller, Senior Director
e-mail: mmiller@mbvc.com
Education: BS, Chemical Engineering, MS, Metallurgy, Georgia Tech; MBA, University of Pittsburgh Katz School of Business
Background: Chairman, CEO & President, Solutions Consulting; Accenture

David Koegler, Principal/CFO
e-mail: dkoegler@mbvc.com
Education: BA, Slippery Rock University
Background: VP, Finance & Administration, Meakem Venture Partners; Senior Manager, FreeMarkets

1195 MEDIA VENTURE PARTNERS
255 California Street
Suite 850
San Francisco, CA 94111

Phone: 415-391-4877 Fax: 415-549-0515
web: www.mvpcapital.com

Mission Statement: Media Venture Partners identifies opportunities and makes the vital connections necessary to expedite successful transactions and maximize value for its clients.
Geographic Preference: Worldwide
Founded: 1987
Minimum Investment: Less than $100,000
Investment Criteria: Seed, Startup, First-Stage, Second-Stage, LBO, MBO
Industry Group Preference: Communications, Computer Related, Publishing, Consumer Products, Technology, Wireless Technologies, Infrastructure, Radio, Television, Broadcasting

Other Locations:
420 Nichols Road
Kansas City, MO 64112
Phone: 816-249-1630 Fax: 415-549-0515

3 Allied Drive
Suite 120
Dedham, MA 02026
Phone: 617-345-7316 Fax: 415-549-0515

2033 11th Street
Suite 6
Boulder, CO 80302
Phone: 303-284-3965 Fax: 415-549-0515

Key Executives:
Elliot B Evers, Managing Director & Co-Founder
e-mail: eevers@mediaventurepartners.com
Education: BA, Journalism, University of California, Berkeley; JD, Hastings College of the Law, University of California; Diplome Semestriel, University of Paris

Jason Hill, Managing Director
e-mail: jhill@mediaventurepartners.com
Education: BS, Finance & Economics, Boston College
Background: Associate, Amsterdam Pacifi Securities; Analyst, Investment Banking Division, Goldman Sachs & Co

Brian Pryor, Managing Director
Education: BS, Finance & Economics, Boston College

Gred Widroe, Managing Director
e-mail: gwidroe@mediaventurepartners.com
Education: BS, Agricultural & Managerial Economics, University of California, Davis; MBA, Cornell University
Background: Amsterdam Pacific Securities; COO, Apollo Communications; Product Management, Pacific Bell

R Clayton Funk, Managing Director
e-mail: cfunk@mediaventurepartners.com
Education: BA, Communications, Washburn University
Background: Nations Media Partners

Venture Capital & Private Equity Firms / Domestic Firms

1196 MEDIMMUNE VENTURES
One MedImmune Way
Gaithersburg, MD 20878
Phone: 301-398-0000 Fax: 301-398-8170
e-mail: medimmuneventures@medimmune.com

Mission Statement: To foster innovation and entrepreneurship by investing in healthcare start-up companies. MedImmune Ventures seeks to deliver superior financial returns by investing in private biopharmaceutical, medical technology and healthcare IT companies across therapeutic areas and geographies.

Geographic Preference: Worldwide
Fund Size: $300 million
Founded: 2002
Investment Criteria: Early-Stage to Late-Stage
Industry Group Preference: Healthcare, Biopharmaceuticals, Medical Technology, Healthcare Information Technology, Medical Devices, Diagnostics, Imaging
Portfolio Companies: Adheron Therapeutics, Applied Genetic Technologies, Abmit Biosciences, Catabasis, Cerapedics, Coferon, Corridor Pharmaceuticals, Elusys Therapeutics, G1 Therapeutics, Hydra Biosciences, Inotek Pharmaceuticals, NeuProtect, NKT Therapeutics, VaxInnate, VentiRx Pharmaceuticals, Xencor

Other Locations:
121 Oyster Point Blvd.
South San Francisco, CA 94080

Sir Aaron Klug Building
Granta Park
Cambridge CB21 6GH
UK

Key Executives:
Ron Laufer MD, Senior Managing Director
Education: BSci, MD, MPH, Hebrew University; MBA, Harvard Business School
Background: Co-Founder, Lilly Ventures; Managing Director, Visium Asset Management
Isai Peimer, Managing Director
Education: BS, Chemistry, Emory University; MBA, Tuck School of Business, Dartmouth
Background: Visium Asset Management; Investment Banking, JP Morgan; Specialty Pharmaceuticals Analyst, Alliance Bernstein; Scientist, Merck

1197 MEDIPHASE VENTURE PARTNERS
2150 Washington St.
Suite 200
Newton, MA 02462
Phone: 617-332-3408 Fax: 617-332-8463
e-mail: administration@mediphasefunds.com

Mission Statement: A venture capital firm focusing on health care/life sciences companies. We seek rapidly growing companies with outstanding market opportunities.

Investment Criteria: Early Stage
Industry Group Preference: Healthcare, Life Sciences, Biopharmaceuticals
Portfolio Companies: Concert Pharmaceuticals, DiscoveRx, PatientKeeper, Relypsa, STARTech, Supplemental Health Care, Tetraphase Pharmaceuticals, Wellpartner

Key Executives:
Lawrence G Miller, MD, Founding Partner
Education: Harvard College, Cambridge University, Harvard Medical School
Background: Senior Vice President, Hambrecht & Quist Capital Management; Exectutive Vice President & Director, Internal Operations, Avicenna Systems Corp; Vice President, HPR; Physician & Pharmacologist, Faculty Member, Department of Pharmacology & Experimental Therapeutics, Tufts University School of Medicine

Paul A Howard, Founding Partner
Education: AB, Bowdoin College; MS, University of Massachusetts, Amherst; SM, Sloan School of Management, MIT
Background: Senior Vice President, Hambrecht & Quist Capital Management; Senior Technical Sales Executive, Miles Biotechnology Division, Bayer AG
W Lambert Welling, Managing Director
e-mail: bert.welling@gmail.com
Education: MBA, Columbia Business School; BA, Middlebury College
Background: Pace Consulting Group; VP, Federal Street Capital Corporation
Edward B Marsh, MD, Managing Director
e-mail: emarsh@medtechcapital.com
Education: AB, Princeton University; MD, Johns Hopkins University
Robert W Macleod, Managing Director
e-mail: bmacleod@medtechcapital.com
Education: BA, Trinity College; Harvard Business School
Background: Kendall Company; Eliot Bank; CFO, Foster Medical Supply

1199 MEIDLINGER PARTNERS
3401 Market Street
Suite 200
Philadelphia, PA 19104
Phone: 215-701-3299 Fax: 215-557-0912
e-mail: kmeidlinger@meidlingerpartners.net
web: www.meidlingerpartners.net

Mission Statement: A private equity firm with operational expertise in the water and wastewater sectors.

Geographic Preference: United States, Western Europe
Investment Criteria: Later-Stage, Growth Equity
Industry Group Preference: Water
Portfolio Companies: ANDalyze, Environmental Operating Solutions, Liberty Hydro, RedZone Robotics, Triton Water

Key Executives:
Karen Meidlinger, Principal
e-mail: kmeidlinger@meidlingerpartners.net
Education: BSc, Marine Biology, University of Liverpool; MBA, University of Cape Town
Background: University City Science Center, Johnson & Johnson
Michael Lynch, Senior Associate
Education: Cornell University, Pennsylvania State University Dickinson School of Law
Background: Contract Attorney

1200 MEKETA INVESTMENT GROUP
80 University Avenue
Westwood, MA 02090
Phone: 781-471-3500
web: www.meketagroup.com

Mission Statement: Investment partners who think strategically and execute with integrity to secure the future for institutions and individuals

Founded: 1978
Industry Group Preference: Finances, Healthcare
Key Executives:
James E Meketa, Managing Principal/Chairman
Education: AB, Harvard University

1201 MENDOZA VENTURES
359 Newbury Street
5th Floor
Boston, MA 02115
Phone: 617-505-6070
web: mendoza-ventures.com

Mission Statement: Mendoza Ventures is a Fintech, AI, and Cybersecurity venture capital. It is both woman and minority

Venture Capital & Private Equity Firms / Domestic Firms

owned and is the first latinx founded venture on the east coast.
Key Executives:
Adrian Mendoza, Founder/General Partner
Education: University of Southern California; Harvard University
Background: Co-Founder and CTO, Apptient
Senofer Mendoza, Founder/General Partner
Education: University of Massachussetts; Suffolk University
Background: Investor, Listo Unlimited; Investor, Senso.ai

1202 MENLO VENTURES
2884 Sand Hill Road
Suite 100
Menlo Park, CA 94025

Phone: 650-854-8540 Fax: 650-234-5449
e-mail: marketing@menlovc.com
web: www.menlovc.com

Mission Statement: Seeking combinations of talented management, superior products or services, and market opportunities that create the potential for exceptional returns on their investment, typical investment ranges from $4 million to $10 million.
Geographic Preference: United States
Fund Size: $3 billion
Founded: 1976
Average Investment: $10 million
Minimum Investment: $250K
Investment Criteria: All Stages
Industry Group Preference: Communications, Internet Technology, Semiconductors, Data Services, Computer Hardware & Software, Infrastructure, Information Technology, Enterprise Software, Mobile & Internet, Networking, Storage & Computing, Security
Portfolio Companies: 3T Biosciences, 6 River Systems, AeroScout, Aisera, Alloy, AppDome, Aquera, Aevere Systems, AVI Networks, Benchling, Betterment, BeyondCore, BitPay, BitSight Technologies, BlueVine, Bread, Breather, Carbonite Inc., Carta, Cellfire, Chime Bank, Cyras Systems, Cinemagram, Clarifai, Clear Labs, Cofactor Genomics, CouchSurfing, Credit Sesame, DataXu, Encoded Therapeutics, Envoy, Epiodyne, Everclaw, Fleetsmith, Getaround, Gilead Sciences Inc., Glide, Harness, HomeLight, Indio, INVIDI Technologies, JUMP, Kalpana, Keaton Row, Kidaptive, LiveOps, Livingly Media, Lumosity, MailFrontier, MealPal, Minted, NCircle Entertainment, Open Solutions, PillPack, Pixable, Platform9, Pliant Therapeutics, Pluribus Networks, Qualia, Recursion Pharmaceuticals, RightHand Robotics, Roku, Rover.com, Scality, Sellpoints, Scenti Bio, ShipBob, Signifyd, Spinnaker Networks, STANCE, StrataCom Inc., Synthego, Talari Networks, tCell, Telenav, The Black Tux, Uber, Unravel Data, UrbanSitter, Usermind, Veriflow, Vidyo, Voltage Security, Warby Parker, Waterline Data, Yellowbrick, YuMe, Zylo

Key Executives:
Douglas C. Carlisle, Partner Emeritus
Education: BS, Electrical Engineering, University of California, Berkeley; MBA, Stanford University Graduate School of Business; JD, Stanford University Law School
Background: Design Engineer, ROLM Corporation
Directorships: Cellfire, Check, LiveOps, Lytx, Nexxo, Nlight Photonics, Readyforce, RF Surgical, Vidyo
John W. Jarve, Partner Emeritus
Education: BS/MS, Electrical Engineering, MIT; MBA, Stanford University
Background: Charles Stark Draper Laboratory at Harvard Medical School; Booze Allen and Hamilton; Intel Corporation
Directorships: Avere Systems, Betterment, BeyondCore, Coraid, Credit Sesame, DataXu, Livingly Media
Mark A. Siegel, Partner
e-mail: mark@menloventures.com
Education: BS, Physics/Electrical Engineering, Massachusetts Institute of Technology; MBA, Stanford Graduate School of Business
Background: Oracle Corporation, Netscape Communications Corporation.
Directorships: Dropcam, Dstillery, eXelate, Invidi, Pluribus Networks, Tintri, Voltage Security
Venky Ganesan, Partner
Education: Reed College, California Institute of Technology
Background: Vice President, JAFCO Ventures, Program Manager, Encarta Group, Microsoft
Directorships: Avi Networks, BitSight, Dedrone, Machine Zone, OverOps, Rover, UpCounsel, Waterline Data Science
Shawn T. Carolan, Partner
e-mail: shawn@menloventures.com
Education: MBA, Stanford University Graduate School of Business; BS, MS, Electrical Engineering, University of Illinois
Background: Management Consultant, Booz-Allen & Hamilton; Open Port Technology; Motorola's Cellular Infrastructure Group; Wireless Data Group; Sprint PCS; University of Illinois' Center for Computational Electromagnetics
Directorships: IMVU, PlayPhone, Roku, TeleNav, Uber, YuMe
J.P. Sanday, Partner
e-mail: jp@menlovc.com
Education: Carroll School of Management, Boston College; MBA, Stanford Grad. School of Business
Background: Summit Partners; VP of Growth, CreativeLive; VP of Growth, Kiwi; Product Manager, Amazon
Nate Quinn, Venture Partner
e-mail: nate@menlovc.com
Education: BS, Accounting, Brigham Young University
Background: Associate, Silver Lake Partners; Investment Banker, Greenhill
H. DuBose Montgomery, Founder/Partner Emeritus
e-mail: dubose@menlovc.com
Education: MIT; Harvard Business School
Background: Bell Labs
Matt Murphy, Partner
e-mail: matt@menlovc.com
Education: Tufts University; Stanford Graduate School of Business
Background: Kleiner Perkins Caufield & Byers
Steve Sloane, Partner
e-mail: steve@menlovc.com
Education: Princeton University
Background: Oliver Wyman; Insight Venture Partners
Tyler Sosin, Partner
e-mail: tyler@menlovc.com
Education: Stanford University
Background: Accel Partners
Jordan Ormont, Talent Partner
e-mail: jordan@menlovc.com
Education: Bloomsburg University
Background: Century Associates; Howard Fischer Associates; Kleiner Perkins Caufield & Byers
Grace Ge, Venture Partner
e-mail: grace@menlovc.com
Education: BA, Rice University
Background: Associate, RRE Ventures; Consultant, Accenture
Kirsten A. Mello, Chief Financial Officer
Education: Santa Clara University
Background: Ernst and Young
Croom Beatty, Principal
Education: BA, History, Princeton University
Background: Payoneer; Susquehanna Growth Equity
Naomi Pilosof, Partner
e-mail: naomi@menlovc.com
Education: BSc, Industrial Engineering, Northwestern

Venture Capital & Private Equity Firms / Domestic Firms

University; MBA, Stanford University Graduate School of Business
Background: Vice President of Growth, Invoice2go; Product Lead, Evernote

1203 MENTOR CAPITAL PARTNERS LTD
PO Box 560
Yardley, PA 19067

Phone: 215-736-8882 **Fax:** 215-736-8882
e-mail: sager@mentorcapitalpartners.com
web: www.mentorcapitalpartners.com

Mission Statement: Engaging with management in a leadership role by leveraging operations to create sustaining value.
Fund Size: $50 million
Founded: 1994
Investment Criteria: Early Stage, Mezzanine Expansion, Leveraged Transactions
Industry Group Preference: Business Products & Services, Distribution, Financial Services, Healthcare, Industrial Technology, Information Technology
Portfolio Companies: Collect America, CoreCare Systems, JADE Equipment Corporation, KNF Corporation, Neoware Systems, North America Cable Equipment, PeerView, Veltek Associates

Key Executives:
Edward F Sager Jr, Co-Founder/President
215-736-8882
Fax: 215-736-8882
Education: BS, Mechanical Engineering, Lafayette College; MBA, Finance & Marketing, New York University Graduate School of Business
Background: VP, Sprout Group; Officer, CoreStates/First Pennsylvania Bank; Westinghouse Electric Corporation; Duriron Company; Colgate-Palmolive Company

1204 MERCATO PARTNERS
2750 E. Cottonwood Pkwy.
Suite 500
Cottonwood Heights, UT 84121

Phone: 801-220-0055 **Fax:** 801-220-0056
e-mail: info@mercatopartners.com
web: www.mercatopartners.com

Mission Statement: Mercato invests growth capital and brings world-class sales and marketing execution to emerging technology companies.
Investment Criteria: Later Stage, Growth Stage
Industry Group Preference: Technology, Consumer
Portfolio Companies: Alliance Health, Altitude Digital, Central Logic, Control4, CradlePoint, Cymphonix, Domo, Ephesoft, Fusio-Io, Gailileo Processing, Goal Zero, MediConnect Global, ObservePoint, Primary Data, SaltStack, Skullcandy, Sphero, Stance, SteelHouse, Untangle, upwell, Venafi

Key Executives:
Greg Warnock, Managing Director
Education: PhD, Entrepreneurship & Venture Finance, University of Utah
Background: Co-Founder, vSpring Capital
Directorships: Altitude Digital, Cymphonix, DOMO, Skullcandy, Stance
Ryan Sanders, Director
Education: BS, Brigham Young University; MBA, University of Texas
Background: Escalate Capital Partners
Directorships: ObservePoint, Galileo, Central Logic, Altitude Digital
Joe Kaiser, Director
Education: BSBA, Saint Louis University; MBA, Kellogg School of Management
Background: Director of Capital Markets, Vivint Solar; Blackstone Group; Analyst, A.G. Edwards & Sons

1205 MERCK GLOBAL HEALTH INNOVATION FUND
One Merck Dr.
Whitehouse Station, NJ 08889

Phone: 908-423-6551
web: merckghifund.com

Mission Statement: To identify new business models and adjacency opportunities in healthcare.
Fund Size: $125 million
Founded: 2011
Industry Group Preference: Healthcare, Diagnostics
Portfolio Companies: AdvanDx, AsuraGen, Cleveland HeartLab, Daktari, ElectroCore, GenomDx, Healthsense, MedCPU, PatientSafe Solutions, Preventice, VirtualScopics, WellDoc, ClearDATA Networks, eHealth Technologies, Humedica, Liaison, Medivo, Prophecy, Remedy Informatics, TelerX

Key Executives:
Bill Taranto, President
e-mail: william.taranto@merck.com
Education: BBA, St. Bonaventure University
Background: Johnson & Johnson
David Rubin, Managing Director
e-mail: david.m.rubin@merck.com
Education: BA, Biology, Binghamton University; PhD, Molecular Biology, Temple University
Background: CEO, Cognia Corporation
Dave Stevenson, Managing Director
e-mail: david.stevenson@merck.com
Education: BA, Washington University; MBA, Vanderbilt University
Background: Sanofi-Aventis; Ernst & Young
Joe Volpe, Managing Director
e-mail: joseph.volpe@merck.com
Education: BS, University of South Florida
Background: J&J Corporate Innovations
Joel Krikston, Managing Director
Education: BA, Fairfield University; MBA, NYU Stern School of Business
Background: Johnson & Johnson Development Corporation; JP Morgan

1206 MERCURY FUND
3737 Buffalo Speedway
Suite 1750
Houston, TX 77098

Phone: 713-715-6820
e-mail: info@mercuryfund.com
web: www.mercuryfund.com

Mission Statement: Mercury Fund is a seed-stage venture capital firm that makes equity investments in compelling and novel software and science-based startup opportunities. Mercury partners with extraordinary entrepreneurs to build globally competitive businesses, focusing on technology innovation originating in the U.S. Midcontinent. Our firm has a particular interest in startups associated with seed accelerators, incubators and universities. We frequently invest prior to the formation of a business plan or complete management team.
Geographic Preference: United States
Founded: 2005
Average Investment: $50,000 - $1.5 million
Investment Criteria: Seed-Stage, Early-Stage
Industry Group Preference: Software, Digital Media & Marketing, Mobile, Internet, SaaS, Cloud Computing, Life Sciences
Portfolio Companies: Ambiq Micro, Ambyint, Apto, Benson Hill Biosystems, BlackThorn Therapeutics, Datical, Deep Imaging, DNAtrix Therapeutics, GameSalad, Graylog, Koupon, Label Insight, Lisnr, Mobify, Optimizely, PactSafe, Resonant, ShareThis, Sight Machine, Sinopsys Surgical, Swift Biosciences, TrackX, Trendkite, Vistarmedia

437

Venture Capital & Private Equity Firms / Domestic Firms

Other Locations:
303 Detroit St.
Suite 100
Ann Arbor, MI 48104

Key Executives:
Blair Garrou, Managing Director
Education: BS, Management, Washington & Lee University
Background: CEO, Intermat; Principal, Genesis Park
Directorships: Alert Logic, GameSalad, Graphicly, Koupon Media, ShareThis

Dan Watkins, Managing Director
Education: BS, Materials Science, Engineering, Rice University; MS, PhD, Materials Science, Engineering, Carnegie Mellon University
Background: Founder & Managing Partner, A3 Associates; Co-Founder, Nanospectra Biosciences
Directorships: Deep Imaging, DNAtrix, GlycosBio, Illumitex

Aziz Gilani, Managing Director
Education: BBA, University of Texas; MBA, Kellogg School of Management
Background: Senior Enagagement Leader, Infosys Consulting; ABB Performance Services
Directorships: Black Locus, Datical, Epic Playground, GameSalad, Infochimps, Koupon Media, ShareThis

Adrian Fortino, Managing Director
Education: BSE, Mechanical Engineering, University of Michigan; MBA, Ross School of Business, University of Michigan
Background: Managing Director, Detroit Innovate; Managing Director, First Step Fund
Directorships: Ambiq Micro, Ambyint, Benson Hill, Lisnr, Sight Machine

1207 MERIDA CAPITAL PARTNERS
641 Lexington Avenue
18th Floor
New York, NY 10022

e-mail: info@meridacap.com
web: www.meridacap.com

Mission Statement: Invests in several aspects of the cannabis industry, including cultivation technology, products and services associated with cannabis as a agriculture product, medicinal cannabis, and recreational consumer products.

Founded: 2009
Industry Group Preference: Cannabis
Portfolio Companies: Grow Generation, Canndescent, Kush Bottles, Lumigrow, Manna Molecular Science LLC, Mainstem, New Frontier Data, Simplifya, Steep Hill, Valley Agriceuticals

Key Executives:
Mitch Baruchowitz, Managing Partner
Education: BA, History, Brandeis University; JD, Boston University School of Law
Background: Managing Director, Boo Trade; Attorney, Incloode; CCO, MarketAxess; Corp. counsel, Axiom Legal; Deputy General Counsel, Pali Capital; Sr. Managing Director, ACGM Inc.; Sr. Managing Director, Cavu Securities

Kevin Gibbs, Partner
Education: Old Dominion University
Background: Palace Investment Company; Principal, Grow West

David Goldburg, Partner
Education: BA, History, Brown University
Background: M&A Analyst, First Boston Corp.; Portfolio Manager, Oak Hill Advisors; Manager, Morgan Stanley; Manager, Bear Steams; Managing Director, Goldman Sachs

Peter Rosenberg, Partner
Education: BBA, University of Colorado Boulder
Background: Director, Salomon Brothers; Managing Director, Barrington Associates; Managing Director, Wells Fargo Securities; Managing Director, Duff & Phelps

Jeff Monat, Partner
Education: University Of Pennsylvania; Wharton School
Background: Analyst, Goldman Sachs; Sr. Analyst, Rockbay Capital; Sr. Analyst, Seven Locks Capital; Investment Professional, Sage Rock Capital
Directorships: Steep Hill

Daisy Mellet, Partner
Education: BA, International Relations, St. Joseph's University; MA, New School for Social Research
Background: Sr. Guide, Venture Europe GmbH; Operations Associate, FrontPoint Partners; Client Advisory Associate, Massif Partners; Operations Analyst/Investor Relations Manager, Seawolf Capital

Howard Glynn, Director of Investor Relations
Education: Tulane University
Background: Account Manager, Sony Signatures; OTC Trader, Cowen & Co.; Equity Sales Trading, Pali Capital; Sr. VP Institutional Sales Trading, Maxim Group; VP, Business Development, The Araca Group; Managing Director, Managing Director, Connecticut Family Office Association

Robert Swartz, Director of Relationship Management
Education: BS, Finance/Investment Management, Duquesne University; MS, Accounting, Saint Vincent College
Background: Officer & Securities Trader, PNC; VP/Investment Advisor, PNC; VP/Portfolio Advisor, FNB Corp.

Steven Ritterbush, Operating Partner
Education: BS, Engineering/BA, Political Science, Union College; MS, Oceanography, University of Hawaii; MA, Law & Diplomacy, Fletcher School Of Law and Diplomacy, Tufts University; PhD, International Economics, Harvard University
Background: Founder/Managing Partner, Fairfax Partners; Founder, HealthASPex Inc.; Founder, APACHE Medical Systems Inc.

1208 MERIDIAN MANAGEMENT GROUP
826 E Baltimore Street
Baltimore, MD 21202

Phone: 410-333-2548 Fax: 410-333-2552
web: mmgcapitalgroup.com

Mission Statement: Professional asset manager for economic development and private equity funds.

Geographic Preference: Mid-Atlantic
Fund Size: $75 million
Average Investment: $1 million
Minimum Investment: $500,000
Investment Criteria: First-Stage, Second-Stage, Mezzanine
Industry Group Preference: Computer Related, Healthcare, Communications
Portfolio Companies: EEC Incorporated, EZCertify.com, MidAtlantic Broadband, Odyssey Technologies, Stella May Contracting, The Great Gourmet

Key Executives:
Stanley W Tucker, President/CEO/Co-Founder
Education: BA, Science, Morgan State University; MA, Science, Carnegie-Mellon University
Background: Executive Director, Maryland Small Business Development Financing Authority; Vice President, Park Heights Development Corporation; Credit Analyst, The Equitable Trust Company

R Randy Croxton, Senior VP/Chief Information Officer
Education: BS, Morgan State University
Background: VP, Developing Systems Limited; Baltimore Economic Development Corporation

Timothy L Smoot, Senior VP/CFO
Education: BS, Morgan State University
Background: Deputy Director, Maryland Small Business Development Financing Authority

Venture Capital & Private Equity Firms / Domestic Firms

Anthony L Williams, VP Senior Investment Officer
Education: BA, University of California
Background: Capital Fund; Syndicated Communications; Fulcrum Venture Capital Corporation

1209 MERIT CAPITAL PARTNERS
303 West Madison Street
Suite 2100
Chicago, IL 60606

Phone: 312-592-6111 Fax: 312-592-6112
e-mail: mcp@meritcapital.com
web: www.meritcapital.com

Mission Statement: Formerly William Blair Mezzanine Capital Partners, Merit Capital invests alongside management and shareholders to effect a change in company's ownership structure, to provide capital for growth or acquisitions, or to sponsor and provide capital to effect a buyout of a business.

Geographic Preference: United States
Fund Size: $612 million
Founded: 1993
Average Investment: $15 million - 30 million
Minimum Investment: $15 million
Investment Criteria: Middle-market companies with consistent earning and healthy cash flow
Industry Group Preference: Manufacturing, Distribution, Business to Business, Logistics
Portfolio Companies: Active Minerals International, Advanced H2O, Advantaged Sintered Metals & Contact, Alliance, Bakewise Brands, B.E.T. - er Mix, Bluegrass Dairy and Food, Carex Health Brands, Carter-Waters, Choice Brands Adhesives, Cobra Waire & Cable, Crown Products & Services, Design Space, Digney York Associates, Dr. Comfort, E-Conolight, Engendren Corporation, Ferrara Fire Apparatus, Flunt Industries, Gartner, Glunt Industries, Green Creative, Icon Identity Solutions, Identity Group Holdings Corporation, ISI Detention Contracting Group, Kinex Medical Company, Kinex R&M Rehabilitation, Knights Apparel, Manistique Papers, Manitowoc Tool & Machining, Nedway Air Ambulance, Midwest Iron & Metals, Midwestern Manufacturing Company, Monarch Industries Limited, MTI International, Nester Hosiery, PVI Industries, Reliant Home Health, Rose Paving, RSA Engineered Products, Sales Performance International, Skyline Windows, Slocum Adhesives, Steele Solutions, Structural and Steel Products, TGR Industrial Services, U.S. Minerals, Versatile Processing Group, VTI Instruments

Key Executives:
Thomas F Campion, Managing Director
Education: BBA, Accountancy, St. Norbert College; MBA, University of Wisconsin, Madison
Background: Director, Prudential Asset Management Asia; Vice President, Prudential Capital Corporation
Directorships: MTI International, The Plastics Group, Active Minerals International, Ferrara Fire Apparatus, Bluegrass Dairy and Food, U.S. Minerals, Crown Products & Services, Engendren
David M Jones, Managing Director
Education: BBA, University of Notre Dame; MBA, University of Chicago
Background: Senior Consultant, Peterson Consulting
Timothy J MacKenzie, Managing Director
Education: BA, Northwestern University; MBA, University of Illinois
Background: SVP, Fiduciary Capital; Prudential Capital Corporation
Directorships: Digney York, Skyline Windows, Alden Industries, RSA Engineered Products, Structural and Steel Products
Daniel E Pansing, Managing Director
Education: BS, Political Science, Miami University, Ohio; MBA, Anderson School, UCLA
Background: First National Bank of Omaha; LaSalle Bank
Directorships: Knights Apparel, Skyline Windows, Monarch Industries Limited

Terrance M Shipp, Managing Director
Education: BS, University of Colorado; MBA, Kellogg School of Management, Northwestern University
Background: Partner, LaSalle Capital Group; Prudential Capital Corporation
Directorships: MTI International, The Plastics Group, Bakewise Brands, Versatile Processing Group, Carex Health Brands
Marc J Walfish, Managing Director
Education: BS, Business Administration, MBA, Boston University
Background: Prudential Insurance Company of America; SVP, Prudential Capital Corporation
Directorships: AAR Corporatin, B.E.T.-er Mix, VTI Instruments, Bakewise Brands, WeCare
Evan R Gallinson, Managing Director
Education: BBA, University of Michigan; MBA, Northwestern University Kellogg School of Management
Background: M&A Group, BMO Capital; Corporate Finance, William Blair & Company
Directorships: Digney York, Glunt Industries, RSA Engineered Products
Benjamin W Yarborough, Managing Director
Education: BA, Economics, University of Pennsylvania; MBA, University of Chicago Graduate School of Business
Background: Consultant, Marakon Associates
Directorships: Ferrara Fire Apparatus, Carex Health Brands, Knights Apparel, WeCare, Monarch Industries, Structural and Steel Products

1210 MERIT ENERGY COMPANY
13727 Noel Road
Suite 1200
Tower 2
Dallas, TX 75240

Phone: 972-701-8377 Fax: 972-960-1252
e-mail: info@meritenergy.com
web: www.meritenergy.com

Mission Statement: A private firm specializing in direct investments in mature oil and gas assets. Merit acquires, operates and develops producing oil and gas properties on behalf of equity-based, reinvestment oriented limited partnerships.

Geographic Preference: United States, Canada, Gulf of Mexico
Fund Size: $4 billion
Founded: 1989
Average Investment: $10 million
Minimum Investment: $5 million
Industry Group Preference: Industrial Equipment, Energy, Oil & Gas

1211 MERITAGE FUNDS
1530 Blake Street
Suite 200
Denver, CO 80202

Phone: 303-352-2040 Fax: 303-352-2050
e-mail: info@meritagefunds.com
web: meritagefunds.com

Mission Statement: Meritage is a Denver-based manager of private investment funds. Contributes both capital and expertise to every investment, working as a partner with entrepreneurs to accelerate the growth of their businesses.

Geographic Preference: U.S.
Fund Size: $600 million
Founded: 1998
Average Investment: $500K
Minimum Investment: $100K
Investment Criteria: Growth Equity
Industry Group Preference: Technology-Enabled Services
Portfolio Companies: Brooks Fiber Properties Inc., Cencom Cable, Completel, Conner Perphirals, Crown Castle International, Crisp Media, Datavail, Digital Fortress, Diveo,

Venture Capital & Private Equity Firms / Domestic Firms

Newpath Network, Edgeconnex, Faction, Masergy, McCaw Cellular, P2Binvestor, Nuvox, Smartsky, Verio

Key Executives:
David Solomon, Founder/Managing Director
Background: Executive Chairman, NuVox; CFO, Brooks Fiber Properties; KPMG
Directorships: NuVox

1212 MERITECH CAPITAL PARTNERS
245 Lytton Avenue
Suite 125
Palo Alto, CA 94301

Phone: 650-475-2200 Fax: 650-475-2222
e-mail: info@meritechcapital.com
web: www.meritechcapital.com

Mission Statement: Meritech is a late-stage venture capital firm dedicated to building technology companies of lasting value.
Geographic Preference: United States
Fund Size: $2.6 billion
Founded: 1999
Average Investment: $25 million
Minimum Investment: $10 million
Investment Criteria: Late Stage, Buy-outs, Spin-offs
Industry Group Preference: Information Technology, Communications, Enterprise Software, Internet Technology, Semiconductors, Infrastructure, Consumer Internet, Digital Media & Marketing, Wireless Technologies, SaaS, Medical Devices
Portfolio Companies: 10X Genomics, 2Wire, Acclarent, Alteryx, Amplitude, Anaplan, Ancestry, Ariosa Diagnostics, Auth0, BigFix, Box, Braze, Broadsoft, Bromium, CAN Capital, Cloudera, CloudHealth Technologies, CloudPassage, Cornerstone OnDemand, Coupa, Danger, DataDog, Datastax, DealerSocket, Duo, Evernote, ExtraHop, Facebook, Force10, ForeScout, Forgerock, Fortinet, Fusion-io, Glaukos, Glint, GoDundMe, Greenplum, GuideSpark, Icertis Applied, iMPERVA, Ionic, Kinetica, Lifesize, Looker, Lucid, Lynda.com, Model N, MuleSoft, Netezza, NetSuite, Nextdoor, Niantic, Panzura, Pendo, Pop Cap, Presidio, Proofpoint, Prosper, Rally Software, Riverbed, Roblox, Ruckus Wireless, Salesforce, Servicemax, Simplivity, Snapchat, Sonedo, Sourcefire, Spring by Pivetal, Tableau Software, Tele Atlas, Tensilica, UiPath, Veracode, Wonga.com, Yammer, Yapstone, Zipcar, Zulily

Key Executives:
Paul Madera, Managing Director
Education: MBA, Stanford Graduate School of Business; BS, US Air Force Academy
Background: Managing Director, Montgomery Securities; Morgan Stanley; US Air Force Pilot/Congressional Liaison to Senate/House Armed Services Committees
Michael Gordon, Partner Emeritus
Education: BA Economics/Public Policy, Stanford University
Background: Managing Director/Communications Equipment Analyst, Deutsche Bank Alex.Brown; Principal, Montgomery Securities Communications Research Group; Salomon Brothers Telecommunications Services Corporate Finance Group
Robert Ward, Managing Director
Education: BA, Williams College; MS, MIT
Background: VP/Private Equity Placement Group, Montgomery Securities; Corporate Finance Department, Smith Barney
George Bischof, Managing Director
Education: BA, Stanford University; MBA, Kellogg School of Management, Northwestern University
Background: General Partner, Focus Ventures; Robertson Stephens
Joel Backman, Chief Operating Officer
Education: BS, Business Administration, University of Arizona
Background: Senior Director of Business Development, IPWireless; Co-Founder, Ultimate Inc.; Sunterra Corporation
Craig Sherman, Managing Director
Education: Princeton University
Background: CEO, Gaia Interactive; Entrepreneur-in-Residence, Benchmark Capital; COO, Ancestry.com; American International Group; CEO, Cendant Japan

1213 MERITURN PARTNERS
234 Fayetteville Street
6th Floor
Raleigh, NC 27601

Phone: 919-821-1550
web: www.meriturn.com

Mission Statement: Meriturn invests in control-oriented stakes in middle-market companies experiencing financial or operational challenges. In addition, we pursue minority investments in undercapitalized financial institutions. Our mission is to enhance value for our investors and portfolio companies by utilizing our experience, relationships, and resources to deliver the best solutions to complex middle-market corporate problems.

Investment Criteria: Restructurings, Turnarounds, Special Situations, Chapter 11 Bankruptcy, 363 Asset Purchases, Stalking Horse Bidder, Reorganizations, Out-of-Court Restructurings, Distressed Debt Purchases
Industry Group Preference: Agriculture, Chemicals, Consumer Products, Distribution, Energy, Financial Services, Forestry, Mining, Life Sciences, Manufacturing, Metals, Packaging, Paper, Processing, Publishing
Portfolio Companies: Barnacle Seafood, Captain Ed's Lobster Trap, Cudahy Tanning Co., Dunn Paper, Irving Tanning, Johnston Fabrics & Finishing, Madvapes, Prime Leather, SSI, Valentine Paper, Vermont Smoke & Cure

Other Locations:
One Montgomery Street
Suite 2500
San Francisco, CA 94104
Phone: 415-595-5000

Key Executives:
Lee C Hansen, Partner
e-mail: lee@meriturn.com
Education: BS, Business Administration, Bucknell University; MBA, J.L. Kellogg School, Northwestern University
Background: President, Stonepath Group; SVP Strategy & Corporate Development, Bank of America
Mark W Kehaya, Partner
e-mail: mark@meriturn.com
Education: MA, Economics, Cambridge University; Fuqua School, Duke University
Background: President, Eturn Communications; Stanard Commercial Corporation
Directorships: Standard Commerical Corporation

1214 MERITUS VENTURES
362 Old Whitley Road
PO Box 1738
London, KY 40743-1738

Phone: 606-864-5175 Fax: 606-864-5194
e-mail: questions@meritusventures.com
web: www.meritusventures.com

Mission Statement: To generate market-rate returns for its investors while promoting shared and sustainable business growth and wealth creation throughout its target region.

Geographic Preference: Rural Regions of Southern & Central Appalachia
Fund Size: $36.4 million
Founded: 2002
Average Investment: $250,000 - $2.5 million

Venture Capital & Private Equity Firms / Domestic Firms

Investment Criteria: Expansion-Stage
Industry Group Preference: Manufacturing, Technology, Software
Portfolio Companies: Arkansas Automatic Sprinklers, Gridsmart Technologies, Pinnacle Medical Solutions, SinglePipe Communications, Superior Fabrication, Virtulytix, Wazoo Sports, Zipit
Other Locations:
10426 Jackson Oaks Way
Suite 103
Knoxville, TN 37922
Phone: 865-220-1715 **Fax:** 865-220-1711
Key Executives:
Ray Moncrief, Fund Manager
Background: President, Eclipse Management
Grady Vanderhoofven, Fund Manager
Background: Executive Vice President, Eclipse Management

1215 MERIWETHER CAPITAL CORPORATION
30 Rockefeller Plaza
Room 5600
New York, NY 10112
Phone: 212-649-5890 **Fax:** 212-649-5615
web: www.meriwethercapital.net

Mission Statement: Providing equity and desire to be the controlling shareholder in mergers and acquisitions.
Geographic Preference: Eastern United States
Founded: 1976
Average Investment: $4 million
Minimum Investment: $1,000,000
Investment Criteria: Second Stage, LBO, MBO, Middle-Market companies, Revenues ranging from $10-$100 million
Industry Group Preference: Manufacturing, Distribution
Portfolio Companies: Custom Wholesale Floors, Segrest, Tonka Equipment Company, Wood Pro
Key Executives:
Robert W Petit, Partner
e-mail: rpetit@meriwethercap.com
Education: Boston College; MBA, Wharton School of the University of Pennsylvania
Background: Dyson-Kissner-Moran Corporation; President/CFO, Furigas International
George D O'Neill, Founder
Education: Harvard University
Background: Train-Cabot & Associates; Equity Corporation; Chase Manhattan Bank

1216 MERLIN NEXUS
424 West 33rd Street
Suite 330
New York, NY 10001
Phone: 646-227-5270
e-mail: invest@merlinnexus.com
web: www.merlinnexus.com

Mission Statement: Merlin Nexus invests globally in private and public healthcare companies, and is among the most successful healthcare investment companies in the US.
Geographic Preference: Worldwide
Fund Size: $200 million
Founded: 2001
Investment Criteria: Late-Stage Private Companies, Private Investments in Public Equity (PIPEs), Long-Term Open Market Investments
Industry Group Preference: Healthcare, Life Sciences
Key Executives:
Dominique Semon, Chief Investment Officer
Education: Master in Economics, New York University; License in Science, Molecular Biology, University of Neuchatel, Switzerland; CFA
Background: Head, Healthcare Private Capital Markets Group, Robertson Stephens; Portfolio Manager, New York Life; Biotechnology Research Analyst, Citibank; Head of Sequencing Lab, Biogen
Alberto Bianchinotti, Chief Financial Officer
Education: BS, Accounting, Binghamton University; CPA
Background: Healthcare Analyst, Merlin BioMed Group; Audit & Tax Supervisor, Anchin Block & Anchin LLP

1217 MERRILL LYNCH VENTURE CAPITAL
2 World Financial Center
New York, NY 10281
web: www.ml.com

Mission Statement: Provides capital markets services, investment banking and advisory services, wealth management, asset management, insurance, banking and related products and services on a global basis. Merrill Lynch has over 14,000 advisors in offices across the United States and internationally.
Geographic Preference: Global
Fund Size: $1.1 billion
Founded: 1914

1218 MERUS CAPITAL
505 Hamilton Avenue
Suite 315
Palo Alto, CA 94301
e-mail: info@meruscap.com
web: www.meruscap.com

Mission Statement: We partner with founders who have the passion and ability to build lasting, dynamic businesses. Merus invests in seed and Series A stage iEnterprise startups in Silicon Valley. Our typical investment ranges from $200K to $2.5M. As a company's first institutional investor, we play an active role and believe in a deeply collaborative approach to business-building.
Geographic Preference: Silicon Valley
Average Investment: $200,000 - $2.5 million
Investment Criteria: Seed-Stage, Series A
Industry Group Preference: Software
Portfolio Companies: AdRoll, Alice, Alucid Technologies, Amplitude, Apptimize, Arch, Aromyx, Authentic8, Chai Labs, Corona Labs, Fixed, Indio, IOTurbine, Iterable, Kamcord, Modewalk, Natero, Nuvoloso, Omnity, Omny, Outward, Parabola, Periscope, Runa, SensorTower, Shelter Luv, Silexica, Splashtop, Symphony, TerrAvion, Womply, Xcalar
Key Executives:
Sean Dempsey, Managing Partner
Education: Claremont McKenna College
Background: Principal, Corporate Development, Google; Corporate Development, Microsoft; M&A, Deutsche Morgan Grenfel
Peter Hsing, Managing Partner
Education: BS, Industrial Engineering, Columbia University; MBA, Wharton School
Background: Managing Director, Corporate Strategy Group, Microsoft; Associate, JP Morgan Telecom
Directorships: Authentic8
Salman Ullah, Managing Partner
Education: BS, Physics, University of Oxford; PhD, Theoretical Physics, Stanford University
Background: Vice President, Corporate Development, Google; General Manager, Corporate Strategy, Microsoft
Directorships: Corona Labs, Runa

1219 MESA CAPITAL PARTNERS
3060 Peachtree Road, NW
Suite 970
Atlanta, GA 30305
Phone: 678-904-3223 **Fax:** 678-904-3226
web: www.mesacp.com

Venture Capital & Private Equity Firms / Domestic Firms

Mission Statement: Mesa Capital Partners invests in high-potential small businesses in industries and geographic areas underserved by other capital providers.
Founded: 2003
Average Investment: $500,000 - $2 million
Investment Criteria: Early-Stage
Industry Group Preference: Manufacturing, Services
Portfolio Companies: 555 Mansell, 860 South, 900 Dwell, 1322 North, Ansley Commons, Ansley at Roberts Lake, Bentley Place, Canopy at Belford Park, Cobblestone Fayette, Crestmark, Edgemont, Legacy at Sandhill, Legacy Ridge, Liv Riverale, Majestic Oaks, Montage Embry Hills, Palmetto Exchange, Riverstone, Sea Island Lake Cottages, Skyland Exchange, Spring Lake, Terramar, The Ace, The Gallery, The Mill at New Holland, The Overlook, The Paramont, The Phoenix at James Creek, The Retreat at Grand Lake, Town Place, Vista Ridge

Key Executives:
Thomas D. Bell, Jr., Chairman
e-mail: tbell@mesacp.com
Background: Cousins Properties
Directorships: Regal Entertainment Group, AGL Resources, Norfolk Southern Corporation, Emory University, Grady Memorial Hospital Corporation, Metro Atlanta Chamber of Commerce
Jeff S Tucker, Managing Partner
e-mail: jtucker@mesacp.com
Background: Land South Development
Zach E Schaumburg, Partner
Education: Bachelors Journalism & Advertising, University of Colorado; Masters Massachusetts Institute of Technology
Background: Vice President, J. Tucker Development Partners

1220 MESA GLOBAL
85 Fifth Avenue
Sixth Floor
New York, NY 10003

Phone: 212-792-3950

Mission Statement: Offers full-service investment banking capabilities and strategic advisory services to an international roster of clients
Fund Size: $4.3 billion
Industry Group Preference: Digital Media & Marketing

1221 MESA VERDE PARTNERS
4225 Executive Square
Suite 600
La Jolla, CA 92037

Phone: 619-289-7428
e-mail: info@mesaverdevp.com
web: www.mesaverdevp.com

Mission Statement: To invest in a diversified portfolio of early-stage biotechnology and medical technology companies in the Southwest.
Geographic Preference: Southwestern United States
Fund Size: $40 million
Founded: 2006
Average Investment: $1.5 million
Minimum Investment: $250,000
Investment Criteria: Seed, Startup, Early
Industry Group Preference: Life Sciences, Drug Development, Medical Devices, Diagnostics, Healthcare Information Technology
Portfolio Companies: Biomatrica, Elevation Pharma, Exagen Diagnostics, Independa, Lineagen, Mediapacs, Retrosense, Satiogen, Tokalas

Key Executives:
Carey Ng, Managing Director
Education: MBA, Rady School, UCSD; PhD, UCLA
Background: Abbott Laboratories
Directorships: Satiogen Pharmaceuticals, Medipacs, Biomatrica, Exagen Diagnostics, Tokalas, Independa, Retrosense Therapeutics
Fred A Middleton, Managing Director
Education: BS, MIT; MBA, Harvard Business School
Background: CFO, Genentech; Morgan Stanley Ventures; Sanderling; McKinsey & Co.

1222 MESA+
85 Fifth Avenue
6th Floor
New York, NY 10003

Phone: 212-792-3950
e-mail: sayhi@mesa.vc
web: www.mesa.vc

Mission Statement: MESA+ is an early stage venture fund focused on e-commerce, advertising technology and digital content. We co-invest between $50,000 and $250,000 in Seed and Series A rounds alongside established early stage venture firms (we never lead a financing). We concentrate on the New York digital media market but are able to invest in companies headquartered in other cities across the country and around the world.
Geographic Preference: New York
Investment Criteria: Seed-Stage, Series A
Industry Group Preference: Digital Media & Marketing, E-Commerce & Manufacturing, Advertising
Portfolio Companies: Abra, Basno, BetterDoctor, Bezar, BitVault, Bread, Button, Carmera, Clique Media Group, Codefights, Consumr, Culinary Agents, DJZ, EasyPost, Emissary, FEM, FitStar, Fuisz Media, Gem, Grand st., Hopscotch, Hungry Root, InVenture, Iodine, Keychain Logistics, KISI, MakersKit, Moonfrye, Nativo, Navdy, Panjo, Parachute, Pickie, Plan Vanilla, QuizUp, Republic Project, Ringly, Rinse, Seedling, Shake, Skift, Snowshoe, Soma, The Noun Project, Triage, TripleLift, Tution.io, Vrideo, Wedgies, Who What Wear, Yoshirt, Zillabyte

Key Executives:
Mark Patricof, Special Advisor
Education: BA, Emory University
Background: Co-Founder/CEO, Creative Arts Agency
Directorships: Rockwell Group, New York Cruise Lines, New Heights
Andrew Montgomery, Managing Partner
Education: BA, Georgetown University
Background: Analyst, Merrill Lynch; Co-Founder, New York Code & Design Academy
Directorships: Nonprofit Management Systems

1223 METAFUND
2545 S Kelly Avenue
Edmond, OK 73013

Phone: 405-949-0001 **Fax:** 405-949-9005
e-mail: info@metafund.org
web: www.metafund.org

Mission Statement: MetaFund is engaged in private equity, tax credits, credit enhancement, and portfolios of mortgage loans for Habitat for Humanity. Its private equity investments are targeted towards businesses with the goal of creating financial, social and environmental returns on investment.
Geographic Preference: Oklahoma, Arizona, Nebraska, Kansas, Colorado
Founded: 1999
Portfolio Companies: Custom Composites, Geophysical Research Company, Ideal Crane

Key Executives:
A. Thomas Loy, Founder, Chair & CEO
e-mail: tloy@metafund.org
Education: BA, Master of Liberal Studies, University of Oklahoma
Background: Oklahoma City University; U.S. Treasury Department; KPMG

442

Directorships: First Bethany Bank, Community Development Venture Capital Alliance
Blake Trippet, President
e-mail: btrippet@metafund.org
Education: University of Oklahoma
Background: Goldman Sachs

1224 METAPOINT PARTNERS
Three Centennial Drive
Peabody, MA 01960-7906

Phone: 978-531-1398
web: www.metapoint.com

Mission Statement: Focused primarily on acquiring new platform or stand-alone portfolio companies.
Geographic Preference: United States, Canada
Fund Size: $25 million
Founded: 1988
Average Investment: $2.4 million
Minimum Investment: $1.5 million
Investment Criteria: $8-$30 million in revenues, $750m in EBITDA, Inductrial/Commercial;Low-Medium Tech Products, Leadership in niche markets, Differentiated, Management Continuity preferred
Industry Group Preference: Industrial Equipment, Manufacturing
Portfolio Companies: Kochek, Nickson Industries, Northeastern Nonwovens, Nylon Corporation of America, Spaulding Composites, Stone Panels

Key Executives:
Keith C Shaughnessy, Chairman/CEO
978-531-4444
e-mail: keith@metapoint.com
Education: BS, Management, Boston College
Background: VP, Bank of Boston
Stuart I Mathews, President
978-531-1398 ext 4
e-mail: stuart@metapoint.com
Education: BA, Political Science, Tufts University
Background: Assistant VP, Bank of Boston

1225 METROPOLITAN PARTNERS GROUP
70 East 55th St.
19th Floor
New York, NY 10022

Phone: 212-561-1250 **Fax:** 212-561-1201
e-mail: info@metpg.com
web: www.metpg.com

Mission Statement: Metropolitan Venture Partners is a private equity investment manager with offices in New York and London. Our experienced team works in partnership with our portfolio companies and takes an active role in helping entrepreneurs create value and build their businesses.
Geographic Preference: United States, United Kingdom
Average Investment: $3 million
Minimum Investment: $500,000
Investment Criteria: Seed, First, Recapitalizations, High Growth companies
Industry Group Preference: Software, Communications, Internet Technology, Technology, Infrastructure

Key Executives:
Paul Lisiak, Managing Partner
Education: BA, Economics, University of Pennsylvania
Background: Lazard Asset Management; Metropolitan Venture Partners
Directorships: Playbox Corp., New Credit America, Next Level Finance Partners
Arvind Krishnamurthy, Managing Director
Education: BA, Harvard College; MBA, Harvard Business School
Background: Principal, Paragon Outcomes; Principal, CAM Capital; Goldman Sachs

1226 MHS CAPITAL
333 Bush Street
Suite 2250
San Francisco, CA 94104

Phone: 415-655-2800
e-mail: info@mhscapital.com
web: www.mhscapital.com

Mission Statement: We are early-stage investors backed by tech entrepreneurs. We work closely with visionary founders building the next-generation of category defining companies.
Investment Criteria: Early-Stage
Industry Group Preference: Advertising, Consumer Products, Digital Media & Marketing, Distribution, E-Commerce & Manufacturing, Education, Energy, Enterprise Software, Financial Services, Marketing, Mobile, SaaS, Social Media
Portfolio Companies: Applifier, Bizible, Bridge, Candex, Combatant Gentlemen, Convertro, CourtTrax, Fonality, GiftCertificates.com, Guidebook, HandShake, HowAboutWe.com, IndieGoGo, Julep, LifeShield Security, Magnify360, Mind Lab, MOAT, Nexleaf Analytics, OPOWER, Out of Milk, Ownza, Platfora, Pulpo Media, ShiftPlanning, Simply Measured, Thumbtack, Udemy, VentureBeat, WeHeartIt

Key Executives:
Mark Sugarman, Founder/Managing Partner
Background: Internet Capital Group, VerticalNet
Directorships: Applifier, Candex, Indegogo, Opower, Pulpo Media, Simply Measured, Thumbtack, Udemy
Vijay Nagappan, Principal
Education: BS, Economics, Wharton School
Background: Evercore Partners, Wired Gamez
Directorships: Simply Measured

1227 MID-ATLANTIC VENTURE FUNDS
Ben Franklin Technology Center
Lehigh University
125 Goodman Drive
Bethlehem, PA 18015

Phone: 610-865-6550 **Fax:** 610-865-6427
e-mail: info@mavf.com
web: www.mavf.com

Mission Statement: Primary investment interest is in purchasing the equity securities of new, young, or growing businesses located in the Mid-Atlantic, although we can invest elsewhere, and have.
Geographic Preference: Mid-Atlantic Region
Fund Size: $200 million
Founded: 1984
Average Investment: $8 million
Minimum Investment: $500,000
Investment Criteria: Seed, Start-Up, Turnarounds, Small Leveraged Buy-outs
Industry Group Preference: Biotechnology, Retailing, Construction, Natural Resources, Real Estate
Portfolio Companies: Access Health, Advanced Software Applications, AEP Networks, Anytime Access, Artifact Software, Axeda Systems, BDS, Brightside Academy, Aviom, Axicon Technologies, Calan, CareGain, Career Rewards, CarrierChoice.com, CEMA Technologies, Centra, Cigital, Colubris Networks, CorePROFIT Solutions, Elastomeric Technologies, GeoVue, Innovative Solutions & Support, InPhonic, Integrated Chipware, International Quantum Epitaxy, Medtrex, MicroE Systems, Midas Vision, Mindmatters, National Packaging Systems, Net2000 Communications, Netilla Networks, NexTone Communications, OpenServices, PackExpo.com, Pactolus Communications Software, Provox Technologies, RealWinWin, Response Networks, Scoreboard, Sentito Networks, Sentori, Softrax, Storeroom Solutions, TechTrader, Trinity Convergence, Turtle Beach Systems, UltraCision, Visual Networks, Wisor Telecom, Xycom Automation

Venture Capital & Private Equity Firms / Domestic Firms

Other Locations:
1850 K Street NW
Suite 1075
Washington, DC 20006
Phone: 202-223-7574 **Fax:** 202-293-8850

Key Executives:
Marc F Benson, Partner
703-904-4125
Fax: 703-904-4124
e-mail: Marc@MAVF.com
Education: BA, Virginia Commonwealth University
Background: Managing Director, AMF European Division
Directorships: Advanced Software Applications, CEM Technologies, Cendex, Cigital, Integrated Chipware, Open Service, Sentori, Wisor Telecom
Glen R Bressner, Partner
610-865-6550
Fax: 610-865-6427
Education: BSBA, Boston University; MBA, Babson College
Background: Key Venture Capital Corp.; Chairman, Greater Philadelphia Venture Group
Directorships: GeoVue, Innovative Solutions & Support, Mic Systems, RealWinWin, CorePROFIT Solutions

1228 MIDATLANTIC FUND

e-mail: info@midatlanticfund.com
web: www.midatlanticfund.com

Mission Statement: The MidAtlantic Fund seeks start-up opportunities that are producing innovative technologies.
Investment Criteria: Seed-Stage, Early-Stage
Industry Group Preference: Mobile Technology, Healthcare, Healthcare Services
Portfolio Companies: 5Medical Marketing, Acton Pharmaceuticals, Axiom CME, HLine Digital Media, Hudson Medical Communications, Performax Physical Therapy, Propel Orthodontics, QED, SNDR, TechDerm, Teladoc, Vertos Medical

Key Executives:
Richard Johnson, Managing Director
Education: BA, New York University; MD, Mount Sinai School of Medicine; Columbia University
Directorships: Propel Orthodontics

1229 MIDDLEBURG CAPITAL DEVELOPMENT
Liberty House
7 South Liberty Street
Middleburg, VA 20117

Phone: 540-687-7134
web: www.mcapd.com

Mission Statement: Middleburg Capital Development is a private equity investment firm. We partner with entrepreneurs, growing businesses, private banking groups, university incubation centers, funds, and other private equity groups. We are involved with new technologies, data and information sectors, the service sectors, core manufacturing and natural resources. Our partners and our Advisory Board members support interest in global opportunities.
Industry Group Preference: Information Technology, Big Data, Consumer Services, Business Products & Services, Manufacturing, Natural Resources
Portfolio Companies: CargoSense, Emu Technology, Horizon Packaging, Horizon Systems, Inovateus Solar, Ionic Liquid Solutions, MyBurger, SCP Ltd., Thermalin Diabetes, Trion Coating, Vagabond

Key Executives:
Timothy F. Sutherland, Chairman/CEO
540-687-7134
e-mail: tfsutherland@mcapd.com
Education: BA, Knox College; MBA, New York University
Background: Founder/Chairman/CEO, Pace Global Energy Services
David Sutherland, President
540-687-7314
e-mail: dsutherland@mcapd.com
Education: BA, MBA, University of Notre Dame
Background: Deputy Director, Operations, Pace Global Energy Services

1230 MIDMARK CAPITAL LP
177 Madison Avenue
Morristown, NJ 07960

Phone: 973-971-9960 **Fax:** 973-971-9963
e-mail: info@midmarkcapital.com
web: www.midmarkcapital.com

Mission Statement: Combines financial resources and business capabilities to acquire significant ownership positions and strategic buy-outs in privately and publicly owned middle-market companies with the objective to increase the value of those positions over the long term.
Geographic Preference: United States, Europe, Latin America, Asia
Fund Size: $300 million under management
Founded: 1989
Average Investment: $10 million
Minimum Investment: $5 million
Investment Criteria: Strong management team, businesses which do not involve very high rapidly changing technology, revenues from $20 to $150 million
Industry Group Preference: Manufacturing, Distribution, Service Industries, Retailing, Industrial Services
Portfolio Companies: AVO Carbon Holdings, Avista Oil, Cinedigm Digital Cinema, Fetco Home Decor, General Products, MRI Flexible Packaging, Pediatria, The PromptCare Companies, Strategic Legal Solutions, TCR

Key Executives:
Wayne L Clevenger, Managing Director
e-mail: wclevenger@midmarkcapital.com
Education: BBA, Case Western Reserve University; Executive MBA, Columbia University
Background: Lexington Investment Company, DLJ Capital Corporation
Denis Newman, Managing Director
e-mail: dnewman@midmarkcapital.com
Education: BA, Yale University; MBA, Harvard Business School
Background: Managing Director, First Boston; President, The Dunmore Group; Financial Officer, International Bank for Reconstruction & Development-World Bank
Joseph R Robinson, Managing Director
e-mail: jrobinson@midmarkcapital.com
Education: BA, Cornell University; Wharton School of Finance
Background: President, CEO Vendex International's Brazilian; Vice President, Lexington Investment Company
Matthew W Finlay, Managing Director
e-mail: mfinlay@midmarkcapital.com
Education: BA, Philosophy, Yale University; MBA, Columbia Business School
Background: Juno Partners; Mille Capital; Southport Partners
Larry A Colangelo, Director
e-mail: lcolangelo@midmarkcapital.com
Education: BA, Rowan University; MBA, Xavier University
Background: President/CEO, SPD Technologies; Executive Positions, RCA/Rockwell Internatioinal
Douglas A Parker, Managing Director
e-mail: dparker@midmarkcapital.com
Education: BA, Electrical Engineering & Economics, Yale University; MBA, Columbia Business School
Background: Regent Capital Partners LP; Sales, Thomson Financial Services/Truesdell Company

Venture Capital & Private Equity Firms / Domestic Firms

1231 MIDOCEAN PARTNERS
320 Park Avenue
Suite 1600
New York, NY 10022

Phone: 212-497-1407
web: www.midoceanpartners.com

Mission Statement: A private investment firm that specializes in middle market investments in the US and Europe. MidOcean targets control investments with minimum equity contribution of $25 million.

Geographic Preference: United States, Europe
Minimum Investment: $25 million
Industry Group Preference: Business Products & Services, Consumer, Media & Telecommunications, Niche Manufacturing, Industrial Services
Portfolio Companies: Affinity Dental Management, Agilex Fragrances, Alpha Guardian, Allant, BH Cosmetics, Fairway, Florida Food Products, Freshpet, Global Knowledge, Grandpoint, Hanley Wood/Meyers Research, Hunter Fan, Image Skincare, Jones & Frank, KidKraft, LegalShield, Noranco, Nutrabolt, Penton Media, The Planet Group, Questex, South Beach Diet, System One, Travelpro Group, Water Pik

Key Executives:
Ted Virtue, CEO
e-mail: tvirtue@midoceanpartners.com
Education: Middlebury College
Background: Chief Executive Officer, DB Capital Partners; President, BT Alex Brown Inc; Bankers Trust
Steve Miller, Chairman
e-mail: rsmiller@midoceanpartners.com
Background: Chairman, Delphi Corporation; Federal Mogul; Bethlehem Steel; Waste Management; Morrison Kudson; Ford Motor Company
Deborah Hodges, Managing Director, Chief Operating Officer
e-mail: dhodges@midoceanpartners.com
Education: BA, Princeton University; MBA, Kellogg Graduate School of Mangement
Background: Chief Operating Officer, DB Capital Partners; Capital Management Group, Bankers Trust
Andrew Spring, Managing Director, Chief Financial Officer
e-mail: aspring@midoceanpartners.com
Education: BS, The Wharton School; JD, Cornell Law School
Background: Director, DB Capital Partners; Associate, White & Case
Frank Schiff, Managing Director
e-mail: fschiff@midoceanpartners.com
Education: BS, University of Colorado; JD, Cornell Law School
Background: Managing Director, DB Capital Partners; Partner, White & Case LLP
Elias Dokas, Managing Director
e-mail: edokas@midoceanpartners.com
Education: BA, Economics, Columbia University; MBA, Harvard Business School
Background: Managing Director, Blackstone Group; Investment Professional, Merrill Lynch Capital Partners

1232 MIDWEST MEZZANINE FUNDS
55 West Monroe Street
Suite 3650
Chicago, IL 60603

Phone: 312-291-7300 Fax: 312-345-0665
e-mail: info@mmfcapital.com

Mission Statement: Since its inception, Midwest Mezzanine has partnered with private equity sponsors, fundless sponsors, and management teams by providing junior capital to U.S. and Canadian companies in the lower-end of the middle-market.

Geographic Preference: United States, Canada
Fund Size: $450 million
Founded: 1992
Average Investment: $15 million
Minimum Investment: $5 million
Investment Criteria: Buyouts, Acquisition, Recapitalizations, Growth Capital
Industry Group Preference: Manufacturing, Distribution, Business Products & Services, Consumer Products, Industrial Services, Food & Beverage, Education
Portfolio Companies: Allied 100 All Island Media, Apex Microtecnology, Driven Performance Brands, Capsa Solutions, Currie Medical, Denion Pharmaceuticals, FB Brands, Fiber Composites, Hughes, Premium Franchise Brands, Kadel's Auto Body, LeadingResponse, Merit Service Solutions, Microdynamics Group, Packaging Concepts & Design, Potter Electric, The RapcoHorizon Company, Sentient Medical Systems, OneTouchPoint, TS3 Technology, Uncle Milton, Vapor Power, Appied Adhesives, Water Co. Holding

Key Executives:
David A Gezon, Senior Managing Director
e-mail: david.gezon@abnamro.com
Education: MBA, Northwestern University; BS, Miami University
Background: GE Capital; Kleinwort Benson Limited
J Allan Kayler, Senior Managing Director
e-mail: allan.kayler@abnamro.com
Education: BA, DePaul University; MBA, Indiana University
Background: MNC Capital Corporation, Sherry Lane Partners, Midwest Mezzanine
Directorships: Hunter's Specialties, Potter Electric Signal, EB Brands
C Michael Foster, Senior Managing Director
e-mail: michael.foster@abnamro.com
Education: MBA, DePaul University; BS, Georgetown University
Background: Senior VP, LaSalle Bank; VP, Bank of Boston
Paul Kreie, Managing Director
e-mail: paul.kreie@abnamro.com
Education: BS, Finance, Marquette University; MBA, University of Chicago
Background: Longterm Credit Bank of Japan; Heller Financial
Ana M Winters, Principal
312-291-7302
e-mail: awinters@mmfcapital.com
Education: BS, Accounting, DePaul University; MBA, University of Chicago Graduate School of Business; CPA
Background: LaSalle Bank; Manager, Ernst & Young
Kristin K Lee, Principal
312-291-7307
e-mail: klee@mmfcapital.com
Education: BBA, Finance, University of Iowa; MBA, Kellogg School of Management, Northwestern University
Background: Investment Banking, Houlihan Lokey Howard & Zukin

1233 MILESTONE GROWTH FUND
401 Second Avenue South
Suite 1032
Minneapolis, MN 55401-2393

Phone: 612-338-0090
web: www.milestonegrowth.com

Mission Statement: Funds ethnic minority businesses to create wealth for their owners, generate jobs and contribute to improving the community. The goal is a permanent revolving investment fund that provides equity-type financing to facilitate and accelerate the formation of capital in minority-owned businesses.

Geographic Preference: United States
Fund Size: $200 million
Founded: 1990

Venture Capital & Private Equity Firms / Domestic Firms

Average Investment: $500,000
Minimum Investment: $200,000
Investment Criteria: Seed, Startup, Expansion, Minority-owned companies
Industry Group Preference: All Sectors Considered
Portfolio Companies: Armor Security, EMPO Corporation, Latino Communications Network, Manny's Tortas, Martinez Geospatial, Painting by Nakasone, Touching Lives Adult Day Services, Synico

Key Executives:
   Judy Romlin, President/CEO
   Education: University of Minnesota; Venture Capital Institute
   Background: National City Bank; Norwest Bank; Marquette Bank Minneapolis
   Directorships: St. Louis Park Dollars for Schools

1234 MILESTONE PARTNERS
555 East Lancaster Avenue
Suite 500
Radnor, PA 19087

Phone: 610-526-2700 **Fax:** 610-526-2701
web: www.milestonepartners.com

Mission Statement: Provides liquidity to non-management shareholders of family-owned businesses, facilitates the transition of ownership to key managers and capitalizes on growth opportunities while maintaining the legacy of the founding entrepreneurs.

Geographic Preference: United States, Canada
Fund Size: $360 million
Founded: 1995
Average Investment: $5 - $40 million
Minimum Investment: $5 million
Investment Criteria: LBO, MBO, Recapitalizations, Buy-and-Build Strategies
Industry Group Preference: Manufacturing, Distribution, Services
Portfolio Companies: Avure Food Processing, Black Letter Discovery, Blaschak Coal Corporation, Cafe Enterprises, CODi, Dydacomp, EB Brands, eCommission Financial Services, Eliason Corporation, EnterpriseDB, Freestyle Solutions, G5, Global Connection, Good Health Natural Products, H3 Sportgear, Higher Power Nutrition, Image API, Interconnect Devices, Knights Apparel, Learn It Systems, Machine Laboratory, Mariner Finance, Martex Fiber, mTAB, Neutronics, Occasion Brands, Outlook Group, Pancon, PayLink Payment Plans, Precision Partners Holding Company, Quintus Technologies, RedZone Robotics, Safemark Systems, Southern Management Corporation, Stravina, Trans-Trade, United Road Towing, US Auto Sales

Key Executives:
   Scott Warren, Co-Founder/Managing Partner
   610-526-2702
   e-mail: swarren@milestonepartners.com
   Education: BS, Finance, University of Virginia
   Background: Managing Director, Philadelphia First Group/Beacon Capital; VP Mergers Aacquisitions, Lehman Brothers; Private Placement, Philadelphia National Bank
   John P Shoemaker, Managing Partner
   610-526-2708
   e-mail: jshoemaker@milestonepartners.com
   Education: BA, University of Pennsylvania; JD, Boston College School of Law
   Background: Managing Director, Internet Capital Group; Managing Director, Mellon Ventures-Philadelphia Office; VP Corporate Development, RAF Industries; Corporate Attorney, Reed Smith Shaw & McClay-Philadelphia; Investment Banker, Morgan Stanley
   David G Proctor, Partner
   610-306-6590
   e-mail: dproctor@milestonepartners.com
   Education: BSc, Economics, Wharton School, University of Pennsylvania; MSE, EMTM Program, University of Pennsylvania
   Background: Senior Vice President, Wind River Holdings; VP, Sales & Marketing, Philadelphia Mixing Solutions
   Adam H Curtin, Partner
   610-526-2711
   e-mail: acurtin@milestonepartners.com
   Education: BS, Finance, Pennsylvania State University
   Background: Analyst, Merrill Lynch
   John J Nowaczyk, Partner
   610-526-2712
   e-mail: jnowaczyk@milestonepartners.com
   Education: BA, Harvard College
   Background: Financial Analyst, Kidder Peabody & Co.; Associate, Paine Webber; Legg Manson Wood Walker
   Pete Lloyd, Partner
   610-230-0580
   e-mail: plloyd@milestonepartners.com
   Education: BS, Villanova University; CPA
   Background: CFO, KTR Capital Partners; Keystone Property Trust; Morgan Stanley; TL Ventures; Arthur Andersen
   Dan Ryan, Partner
   610-526-2713
   e-mail: dryan@milestonepartners.com
   Education: BS, Finance, Georgetown University
   Background: PeakEquity Partners; Susquehanna International Group; Friedman Billings Ramsey
   Paul Slaats, Partner
   e-mail: pslaats@milestonepartners.com
   Education: BS, Purdue University; MBA, University of Chicago
   Background: Managing Director, Internet Capital Group; Co-Founder, Spyglass Partners; Associate, Safeguard Scientifics

1235 MILLENIUM TECHNOLOGY VALUE PARTNERS
60 East 42nd St.
Suite 1365
New York, NY 10165

Phone: 646-521-7800 **Fax:** 646-521-7878
e-mail: info@mtvlp.com
web: www.mtvlp.com

Mission Statement: Invests primarily in communications infrastructure, systems, tools and enabling technologies. Currently emphasizing later-stage investments and a range of promising new technologies and businesses with strong revenue growth and customer traction. Ready to commit not only our capital but our time, advice and relationships to build sound, successful businesses.

Fund Size: $1 billion
Founded: 2000
Investment Criteria: Growth Equity, Secondary & Alternative Liquidity, Venture Debt & Permanent Capital
Industry Group Preference: Communications, Networking, Enabling Technology, Infrastructure, Internet, Digital Media & Marketing, Fintech, Software
Portfolio Companies: 1st Virtual Communications, Acronis, Airvana, Agility, Alfresco, Alibaba Group, ArcSight, Art.com, Aventail, Axsun Technologies, BeachMint, BetterCloud, Bigcommerce, Chef, Chegg, Cloudreach, Datapipe, eHarmony, Epocrates, ETF Securities, Facebook, Fonality, Glam Media, Good, Green Dot, Hautelook, HootSuite, ID Analytics, Inspirato, iPass, Iron Planet, Janrain, Jumio, Kik, LegalZoom.com, LifeLock, LiveOps, Lookout, MarkLogic, NetSpend, Ning, OnX, Pentaho, Pinterest, Playspan, Precision Hawk, Rearden Commerce, Reply.com, Requisite Technology, RigNet, Spotify, SugarCRM, Surun, Telaria, TellMe, Tumblr, Twitter, Verilume, WatchDox, Wayport, WildTangent, Yodle, Zappos

Venture Capital & Private Equity Firms / Domestic Firms

Key Executives:
Daniel L Burstein, Founder/Managing Partner
e-mail: burstein@mtvlp.com
Background: CIO, Ps Capital Holdings; PS Capital Ventures; Senior Advisor, Blackstone Group; Consultant, Sony; Toyota; Microsoft; Sun Microsystems; Author
Samuel L Schwerin, Founder/Managing Partner
e-mail: schwerin@mtvlp.com
Education: BS, Lehigh University; MBA, Wharton School
Background: VP Finance, StorageApps; Blackstone Group; M&A, Salomon Brothers; Founder, OpenPeak
Ray Cheng, Partner
Education: BS, Economics, Wharton School; BS, Electrical Systems Engineering, University of Pennsylvania
Background: Rho Ventures
Directorships: Pentaho, PrecisionHawk, Blackmore Sensor & Analytics, Phantom AI, BigCommerce
Jonathan Glass, Chief Financial Officer
e-mail: glass@mtvlp.com
Education: BS, Boston University; MBA, Fordham University
Background: Vice President, Finace, Venrock; Controller, Greenbriar Equity Group; Tax Manager, Deloitte & Touche

1236 MINDFULL INVESTORS
2 Mallard Rd.
Belvedere, CA 94920

Phone: 415-847-2949
e-mail: connect@mindfullinvestors.com
web: www.mindfullinvestors.com

Mission Statement: Mindful Investors is the leading private equity fund which invests exclusively in companies providing sustainable and healthy living focused products to consumers.
Investment Criteria: Invests exclusively in the natural, organic and sustainable consumer products and consumer services marketplace.
Industry Group Preference: Consumer Products, Consumer Services, Clean Technology, Environment, Renewable Energy, Sustainability
Portfolio Companies: Atheer Labs, BINA, CleanFish, Marketwired, Next Thing Co., Retailigence, Scanadu, SOL Republic, Soma, Yerdle
Key Executives:
Stuart L Rudick, Founding Partner
Education: BS, Business Administration, University of Colorado
Background: Founding Partner, Uplift Equity; Associate Director, Bear Stearns; Partner, Shearson Lehman/Davis Skaggs

1237 MIRAMAR VENTURE PARTNERS
2101 E Coast Highway
Suite 300
Corona del Mar, CA 92625

Phone: 949-760-4450 Fax: 949-760-4451
web: www.miramarvp.com

Mission Statement: Miramar invests in early-stage information technology opportunities, with an emphasis on projects based in Southern California. We partner with leading entrepreneurs to transform game changing ideas into capital efficient, profitable businesses.
Geographic Preference: Southern California
Investment Criteria: Early-Stage
Industry Group Preference: Information Technology, Data Storage, Semiconductors, Networking, SaaS, Internet
Portfolio Companies: AccelOps, Aktino, Arradiance, Azuro, Berkana Wireless, Brand Affinity Technologies, Cirro, Coradiant, Factual, FastSoft, HyperQuality, Independa, Innovative Micro Technology, Jeda Networks, Load Dynamix, Matrix Sensors, OptionEase, Predixion Software, Protego Networks, Rachio, RealPractice, Scopely, Silicon Systems, Solarflare Communications, Tarari, Tempo AI, Veritone, Welltok
Key Executives:
Bruce Hallett, Managing Director
949-760-4455
e-mail: bhallett@miramarvp.com
Education: BA, University of California, Irvine; JD, UCLA
Background: Managing Partner, Brobeck Phleger & Harrison
Directorships: OCTANe
Sherman Atkinson, Managing Director
Education: BA, Purdue University
Background: CEO-In-Residence, Austin Ventures; COO, Intermix Media

1238 MISSION BAY CAPITAL
953 Indiana St.
San Francisco, CA 94107

Phone: 415-347-8287
e-mail: info@missionbaycapital.com
web: www.missionbaycapital.com

Mission Statement: Mission Bay Capital LLC uses capital and expertise to help entrepreneurs emerging from the University of California change the world. Its success will address social challenges, replenish future funds, and ultimately build a research and educational endowment the California Institute of Quantitative Biosciences will drive the development of the next generation of innovations.
Geographic Preference: California
Fund Size: $11.3 million
Founded: 2009
Investment Criteria: Seed, Startups
Industry Group Preference: Biotechnology, Healthcare
Portfolio Companies: Alector, Applaud Medical, Atreca, Avexegen, Bell Biosystems, Bolt Threads, Calithera, Caribou Biosciences, Cell Design Labs, Chrono Therapeutics, Circle Pharma, Droplet, eFFECTOR Therapeutics, Epiodyne, Fluxion, Graphwear, Invenio Imaging, Logic.ink, Magnamosis, Magnap, Mammoth Biosciences, Mitokinin, Ocular Dynamics, Perlara, Photoswitch Biosciences, Pionyr Immunotherapeutics, Principia, SiteOne Therapeutics, Sound Agriculture, Symicbio, Tangible Science, TrueNorth Therapeutics, Viewpoint Therapeutics, Vivace Therapeutics, Wild Type, Zephyrus, Zymergen
Key Executives:
Douglas Crawford PhD, Managing Partner
e-mail: douglas.crawford@missionbaycapital.com
Education: PhD, Biochemistry, University of California, San Francisco
Directorships: Redwood Biosciences, Delpor, BayBio Institute
Robert Blazej, PhD, Partner
e-mail: robert.blazej@missionbaycapital.com
Education: PhD, Bioengineering, University of California
Background: Director, Novozyme's Digital Biotechnology Unit; CEO, Allopartis Biotechnologies
Regis B Kelly PhD, Senior Advisor
Education: University of Edinburgh; PhD, Biosciences, California Institute of Technology
Background: Executive Vice-Chancellor, University of California, San Francisco
Directorships: Bay Area Scientific Innovation Consortium

1239 MISSION VENTURES
9255 Towne Centre Dr.
Suite 350
San Diego, CA 92121

Phone: 858-350-2100 Fax: 858-350-2101
e-mail: donna@missionventures.com
web: www.missionventures.com

Venture Capital & Private Equity Firms / Domestic Firms

Mission Statement: Mission Ventures helps build successful enterprises in Southern California and creates superior returns on investment for its investors. This is accomplished by investing in the most promising early stage companies in high growth emerging markets and providing significant assistance to those companies as they develop.

Geographic Preference: Southern California
Fund Size: $225 million
Founded: 1997
Average Investment: $10 million
Minimum Investment: $2 million
Investment Criteria: Early, Startup
Industry Group Preference: Communications, E-Commerce & Manufacturing, Enterprise Software, Infrastructure, Internet Technology, Technology, Software
Portfolio Companies: CalAmp, Enevate, Entropic Communications, MaxLinear, Networks in Motion, TransChip, Verimatrix, Wildcomm, Zyray Wireless, EVEO, ID Analytics, MarginPoint, Sitematic, Alpine Data Labs, Digital Island, Greenplum, Ortiva Wireless, 3E Company, Access Sports Media, BMS Reimbursement, Cogent Healthcare, Image Metrics, LeisureLink, NetSeer, RockeTalk, Slacker, SodaHead, Transaction Wireless, VMIX, WorkWell Systems, Zui.com

Key Executives:
Robert Kibble, Co-Founder/Managing Partner
Education: BA, Natural Sciences, Univ. of Oxford; MBA, Darden School, University of Virginia
Background: Founder/General Partner, Paragon Venture Partners; VP, Citicorp Venture Capital; VP, Citicorp Merchant Banking Group; Investment Banking, Wall Street
Directorships: Eveo, Nexiant, SodaHead
David Ryan, Managing Partner
e-mail: DavidR@missionventures.com
Education: BA, Northeastern University; MBA, Case Western Reserve University
Background: General Partner, Copley Venture Partners; Medusa Corporation
Directorships: Access360 Media, Active Storage, BMS Reimbursement Management, NetSeer, Nirvanix, WorkWell Systems
Ted Alexander, Managing Partner
e-mail: ted@missionventures.com
Education: MBA, Duke Uiversity; BS Engineering, United States Naval Academy
Background: Business Development/Market Analysis, Sandpiper Networks; GE Information Services
Directorships: Enevate, ID Analytics, Ortiva Wireless, Rocketalk, Verimatrix, LeisureLink
Leo Spiegel, Managing Partner
e-mail: leo@missionventures.com
Education: BA, Management Services, University of California, San Diego
Background: President, Digital Island; CEO, Sandpiper Networks; Senior VP/CTO, Donnelley Enterprise Solutions; Co-Founder/CTO, LANSystems
Directorships: Alpine Data Labs, Eveo, Zui.com, MaestroDev, RotoHog, Slacker, Transaction Wireless
Caroline Barberio, Chief Financial Officer
Education: BS, Business Adminstration, San Diego State University
Background: Auditor, Deloitte & Touche; Gray Cary Ware & Freidenrich; Sisthe Energies; Applied Molecular Evolution; Vice President, Finance, Sorrento Associates

---

1240 **MISSIONOG**
1760 Market St.
Suite 902
Philadelphia, PA 19103

e-mail: info@missionog.com
web: www.missionog.com

Mission Statement: We partner with high-growth businesses in segments where we have had prior success as operators, including financial services and payments, data platforms, and software. We apply our experience and capabilities to a group of highly skilled and passionate entrepreneurs whose businesses are on the cusp of exponential growth.

Minimum Investment: $100,000 - $500,000
Industry Group Preference: Enterprise Software, Technology, Business Products & Services, Software, Data & Analytics, Financial Services, Payments & Financial Services
Portfolio Companies: Accurate Group, Alkami, Behalf, Bento for Business, Bridge, Clip, Cloudamize, Deko, DemystData, DivvyCloud, Factor Trust, Frontline Selling, GAN Integrity, Ingo Money, Journey Sales, OneTwoSee, Revolution Credit, Solovis, Syncapay, Tethr, Venminder, Zibby

Key Executives:
Andy Newcomb, Managing Partner
e-mail: andy@missionog.com
Education: BA, History, Trinity College
Background: Co-Founder, Relay Network; Group Head of Sales and Corporate Development, Citi Prepaid Services; Founding Team Member, Ecount; Portfolio Manager, Chartwell Investment Partners
Directorships: PeopleLinx, Softgate Systems, RewardsNOW, OneTwoSee
Gene Lockhart, Chairman and Managing Partner
e-mail: gene@missionog.com
Education: BS, University of Virginia; MBA, The Darden School at the University of Virginia
Background: Special Advisor, General Atlantic; Venture Partner, Oak Investment Partners; President and CEO, MasterCard International; CEO, Midland Bank Plc; President of the Global Retail Bank of BankAmerica Corporation; President of Consumer Services, AT&T
George Krautzel, Managing Partner
e-mail: george@missionog.com
Education: BS, Finance, Villanova University
Background: Co-Founder, ITtoolbox

1241 **MITSUI GLOBAL INVESTMENT**
535 Middlefield Road
Suite 100
Menlo Park, CA 94025

Phone: 650-234-5000 **Fax:** 650-323-1516
e-mail: mgicontactsjfvz@mitsui.com
web: www.mitsui-global.com

Mission Statement: Mitsui Global Investment is committed to helping entrepreneurs build businesses from the early stages through global expansion. We wish to partner with exceptional individuals who are reinventing industries while improving human welfare all over the world.

Portfolio Companies: 4info, Actimis, AdBrite, Aeluros, Anaeropharma Science, ArmaGen, ArraVasc, ASA Foodnesia, Asthmatx, Autotalks, Axikin Pharma, Beceem Firetide, BioAmber, Bioelectron, Boingo Wireless, Boston Biomedical, Broncus Technologies, Calypso Medical Technologies, Cappella, Cardeus Pharmaceuticals, Cardiovascular Systems, Change Healthcare, ContinuumRx, Convenient Power HK Limited, CounterTack, Cylene Pharmaceuticals, Ekos Corporation, EnerVault, Etonenet, EyeSight Mobile Technologies, Fewmo Tech Limited, Garapon, Glamour Sales Holding, Global Consumer Products, GMZ Energy, goBalto, GTI Capital, Hainan Hailing Chemipharma Corporation, Halation Photonics, HelloSoft, IAT Automobile Technology, Infomart International, InnoPath Software, Inventys Thermal, Kaiima Bio Agritech, Kaltura, Kaminario, Kineto Wireless, Kovio, Laszlo Systems, LensVector, Leyou, Life Media, Location Labs, Marrone Bio Innovations, MC10, MoBeam, Mo'Minis, NanoGram, NapaJen Pharma, NetMotion Wireless, Neul, NovoStent Corporation, NxThera, On-Chip Biotechnologies, OpenX Software, OptiScan Biomedical, Palamida, Panacos, Pica 8, Pinnacle Energies, Promethera Biosciences, Protein Simple, Proterra, Prudent Energy, QD Laser, Redwood Systems, Rive

Venture Capital & Private Equity Firms / Domestic Firms

Technology, RGB Networks, Ruckus Wireless, S*BIO Pte., SenSage, Shanghai Global Baby Products, Shanghai Yi Shang Network Information Company, Sirrus, Six Rooms Holdings, Solaria Corporation, Spire Global, Symic, Valens Semiconductor, Virident Systems, YPX Caman Holdings

Other Locations:
Nippon Life Marunouchi Garden Tower 11F
1-3, Marunouchi 1-Chome
Chiyoda-Ku
Tokyo 100-8631
Japan
Phone: 81-3-3285-3166 **Fax:** 81-3-3285-9156

Room 810, China World Tower A
1 Jian Guo Men Wai Avenue
Beijing 100004
China
Phone: 86-10-5965-3560 **Fax:** 86-10-6505-3128

5F Asia House
4 Weizman St.
Tel Aviv 6423904
Israel
Phone: 972-3-696-0503 **Fax:** 972-3-696-0423

Key Executives:
Shinya Imai, President & CEO
Education: Bachelor of Law, Waseda University
Kenichi Kimura, Managing Director
Education: Bachelor of Mechanical Engineering, University of Tokyo

1242 MK CAPITAL
40 Skokie Blvd
Suite 430
Northbrook, IL 60062
Phone: 312-324-7700
e-mail: kris@mkcapital.com
web: www.mkcapital.com

Mission Statement: Offers multi-stage growth equity and venture capital to companies. MK Capital assists management teams in developing corporate strategy, generating business development opportunities and raising additional capital.

Investment Criteria: All Stages
Industry Group Preference: Digital Media & Marketing, Data Center, Software, Education Technology
Portfolio Companies: ADAR IT, Apex Learning, AwesomenessTV, BidPal, Bladelogic, Brightmont Academy, Carbon Media Group, CellTrak, Datapop, DramaFever, eSpark, Eved, GameFly, HealthiNation, Junction Solutions, Kollective, Kontiki, LLamasoft, Machinima, Multicast Media, Nerdio, Netuitive, OneCause, Passport, PECO Pallet, Playcast, Poptent, Quark Games, ReachForce, SimpleReach, Smoothstone, Unitas Global, Wellspring Worldwide, Zefr

Other Locations:
535 W. William
Suite 303
Ann Arbor, MI 48103
Phone: 734-663-6500

Key Executives:
Bret Maxwell, Managing General Partner
e-mail: bmaxwell@mkcapital.com
Education: McCormick School of Engineering, Northwestern University; Kellogg Graduate School of Management
Background: Co-Founder, First Analysis' Venture Capital Practice
Mark Koulogeorge, Managing General Partner
e-mail: mark@mkcapital.com
Education: Dartmouth College; Stanford Graduate School of Business
Background: Managing Director, First Analysis Corporation; Booz Allen Hamilton
Karen Buckner, Partner/COO
e-mail: kbuckner@mkcapital.com

Education: University of Michigan; Kellogg School of Management
Background: VP, Operations, I-Works
Directorships: TopSchool, Apex Learning, Smoothstone Communications, Retention Education, Enhancescape
Kirk Wolfe, Partner
e-mail: kwolfe@mkcapital.com
Education: BS, Industrial & Operations Engineering, University of Michigan; MBA, Stanford University
Background: Field Operations, Ariba; Motorola

1243 MOBILE FOUNDATION VENTURES
137 Forest Avenue
Palo Alto, CA 94301
e-mail: contact@MFVPartners.com
web: www.mfvpartners.com

Mission Statement: A venture capital fund focused on tech-based companies, such as AI, neural computing, big data, and shared mobility.

Founded: 2017
Investment Criteria: Pre-Series A, Series A
Industry Group Preference: Artificial Intelligence, Computing, Big Data, Data Analytics, Automotive, Mobility
Portfolio Companies: Analog Inference, Summary Analytics, TwentyBN

Key Executives:
Karthee Madasamy, Managing Partner
Education: BS, College of Engineering, Guindy; MS, University of Michigan; MBA, University of Chicago
Background: Managing Director/VP, Qualcomm Ventures

1244 MOBILITY VENTURES
P.O. Box 1597
Addison, TX 75001
Phone: 972-991-9942 **Fax:** 972-669-7873
e-mail: email@mobilityventures.com
web: www.mobilityventures.com

Mission Statement: Mobility Ventures focuses on early-stage, cutting edge companies that enable Mobility and promote a mobile lifestyle. We define Mobility as solutions that leverage the convergence of wireless infrastructures, the Internet, applications and services which result in anytime, anywhere connectivity. Ours franchise is Mobility. We invest across the Wireless Ecosystem in technologies, applications, services and medias that enable and promote a mobile society. These include areas such as, mobile marketing, mobile health, mobile commerce, location based services and energy/ power management.

Investment Criteria: Early-Stage
Industry Group Preference: Mobile, Wireless, Internet
Portfolio Companies: 10C Technologies, AdMarvel, Alereon, Always Market, B2X, Bakcell, Blue Calypso, Caribe, Command Audio, EnerAge, EntegraBlu, Genesis, GoldStar, Haxiot, Indoor Atlas, IndoTraq, Inner Wireless, InnoPath, Liquidmetal Technologies, Magnolia Broadband, Mobiserve, Mobixell, Navini Networks, Neonode, Now Public, Orpiva, Phenometrix, PulseWave, PWRF, Renren, Santerra, Sirific, Solarwinds, Tele Atlas, TelRock, Uniscon, VeriSign, VMX, Zebek

Key Executives:
Roman Kikta, Founder/Managing Partner
Education: BA, Rutgers University
Background: Nokia, Panasonic, GoldStar, OKI; Founder, Global Wireless Holdings
Mark Fruehan, Venture Partner
Education: BS, Economics, Pennsylvania State University
Background: Vice President, VeriSign
Arlan Harris, Partner
Education: BS, University of Texas, Dallas
Background: Austin Ventures, Genesis Campus Funds, LifeGate Ventures

Venture Capital & Private Equity Firms / Domestic Firms

1245 MOBIUS VENTURE CAPITAL
1050 Walnut Street
Suite 210
Boulder, CO 80302

e-mail: jill@mobiusvc.com
web: www.mobiusvc.com

Founded: 1996
Investment Criteria: Early-Stage
Industry Group Preference: Communications Software, Communications, Components & IoT, Consumer Services, Enterprise Applications, Healthcare Information Technology, Infrastructure, Infrastructure Software, Professional Services
Portfolio Companies: Bloom Energy, deCarta, Impinj, Rally Software, ReaMetrix, Return Path, Sitrion, Techorati
Key Executives:
   Brad Feld, Co-Founder, Managing Director
   Education: BS, MS, Management Science, MIT
   Background: Chief Technology Officer, AmeriData Technologies; Feld Technologies
   Directorships: National Center for Women & Information Technology
   Seth Levine, Principal
   Education: Macalester College
   Background: FirstWorld Communications; Business Development Group, ICG Communications

1246 MODERNE VENTURES
410 N Michigan Avenue
Suite 740
Chicago, IL 60611

web: www.moderneventures.com

Mission Statement: Moderne Ventures invests in early stage companies centering in and around real-estate, insurance, finance, hospitality and home service industries.
Key Executives:
   Constance Freedman, Founder/Managing Partner
   Education: BS, Boston University; MBA, Harvard University
   Background: Head, Strategic Investments, National Association of Realtors; Founder, REach; Investor, Cue Ball

1247 MOHR-DAVIDOW VENTURES
777 Mariners Island Blvs.
Suite 550
San Mateo, CA 94404

Phone: 650-854-7236 Fax: 650-854-7365
e-mail: info@mdv.com
web: www.mdv.com

Mission Statement: We are committed to helping new companies build great teams, devise winning product and marketing strategies, run smooth operations, establish effective distribution strategies, and create successful business models.
Geographic Preference: United States
Fund Size: $2 billion
Founded: 1983
Average Investment: $3 million
Minimum Investment: $500,000
Investment Criteria: Early Stage
Industry Group Preference: Software, Infrastructure, Life Sciences, Communications, Semiconductors, Information Technology, Clean Technology
Portfolio Companies: Actuate, Adamas, Agile, AirPR, Aryaka, Analyte Health, Aryaka, Audience Science, Balance Therapeutics, BandPage, Brickstream, Broadbase Software, Brocase, BuildDirect, CardioDX, Carrier IQ, Cenzic, Corventis, Coupa, Crescendo Biosciences, Critical Path, Doxo, DS-IQ, DVS Sciences, Echelon, Employee Channel, Epigram, Figs, Finsphere Corporation, FormFactor, Gain Credit, Genius Genomatics, Gordon Murray Design, Healthtap, Honest Buildings, Hotchalk, Infusionsoft, Ipsilon, iRhythm, Kabbage, Lagrange Systems, Marble, Massive, Medio, Neon, nLight, Numerical Technologies, One Spot, ONI Systems, Opxbio, Pacific Biosciences, Panasas, ParAllele, PB Works, People Pattern, Personalis, Pluribus Networks, Proofpoint, PunchTab, RainDance, Rally, RainDance, Rambus, Recurrent Energy, ReSci, Retention Science, Reverb, Rocketfuel, Ruby Ribbon, Sabrix, Sensity, Sequenta, Shutterfly, Simbol Materials, Sipx, SodaHead, Splice Machine, Ticketfly, Tuition.io, Verinata Health, Virtuoz, Visible Measures, Vitesse, WebScale, WorkFusion, Xambala, Xicato, ZeaChem, Zebit, Zip2
Key Executives:
   William Ericson, General Partner
   e-mail: bericson@mdv.com
   Education: BSFS, Georgetown University of Foreign Service; JD, Northwestern University School of Law
   Background: Managing Partner, Founder, Venture Law Group's Pacific Northwest office
   Jim Smith, General Partner
   Education: PhD, Electrical Engineering, MA, Industrial Management, BA, Computer Systems Engineering, MA, Electrical Engineering, Stanford University
   Background: Silicon Graphics; Researcher, Computer Systems Laboratory-Stanford University
   Jon Feiber, General Partner
   e-mail: jdf@mdv.com
   Education: BS, Computer Science & Mathematics, University of Colorado
   Background: Senior Engineer, Amdahl; Sun Microsystems
   Josh Green, General Partner
   e-mail: jgreen@mdv.com
   Education: UCLA; UCLA School of Law
   Background: Brobeck, Phleger & Harrison LP
   Bryan Stolle, General Partner
   e-mail: bstolle@mdv.com
   Education: BA, Business Administration; MBA, University of Texas, Austin
   Background: Co-Founder, Agile Software; Sherpa Corporation
   Nancy Schoendorf, General Partner
   Education: BS, Iowa State University; MBA, University of Santa Clara
   Background: Hewlett-Packard; Software Publishing Corp.
   Phyllis Whiteley, Venture Partner
   Education: PhD, Pharmacology, Washington University
   Background: 5AM Ventures; Co-Founder, Anaphore; Perlegen Sciences
   Geoffrey Moore, Venture Partner
   e-mail: gmoore@mdv.com
   Education: BA, Literature, Stanford University; Doctorate, Literature, University of Washington
   Background: Founder, The Chasm Group; Managing Director, TCG Advisors; Principal & Partner, Regis McKenna

1248 MONITOR CLIPPER PARTNERS
116 Huntington Avenue
9th Floor
Boston, MA 02116

Phone: 617-638-1100 Fax: 617-638-1110
e-mail: mcp@monitorclipper.com
web: www.monitorclipper.com

Mission Statement: Seeks to make private equity investments in middle-market companies to which we can add significant value through the combined skills of our principals and our privileged access to the proprietary resources of The Monitor Group.
Geographic Preference: United States, Western Europe
Fund Size: $2 billion
Founded: 1998
Average Investment: $20 - $200 million
Investment Criteria: Management Buyouts, Recapitalizations, Growth Equity Investments
Portfolio Companies: The Access Group, CMC Biologics, Colford Capital, Higher Education Partners, Kanetix,

Venture Capital & Private Equity Firms / Domestic Firms

LaserShip, Market Force Information, Merrick Pet Care, Microgame, MyEyeDr., National Entertainment Network, Palladium Group, Pharmetics, Reverse Logistics GmbH, Roger Garments, W2 Group, WoodPellets.com

Other Locations:
C/O Kendris
Wengistrasse 1
Zurich 8021
Switzerland

75, Parc d'activités
L-8303 Capellen
Luxembourg
Luxembourg
Phone: 352-20-33-2731 **Fax:** 352-20-33-2731-99

Key Executives:
Michael A Bell, Managing Partner
Education: BS, Finance & Accounting, Wharton School; MBA, Harvard Graduate School
Background: Senior Consultant, Bain & Company
Directorships: Access Communications, Medical Services Company
Travis R Metz, Managing Partner
e-mail: tmetz@monitorclipper.com
Education: AB, Harvard College
Background: Principal, Jupiter Partners
Directorships: Colford Capital, Higher Education Partners, Kanetix, LaserShip, Market Force, National Entertainment Network, Palladium, Paradigm Tax Group, W2 Group
Mark T Thomas, Managing Partner
Education: Queen's University; MBA, Harvard Business School
Background: Senior Consultant, Bain & Company
Directorships: LaserShip, Microgame, MyEyeDr., Palladium, Roger Garments
Adam S Doctoroff, Partner
617-252-2390
Fax: 617-252-2211
e-mail: adoctoroff@monitorclipper.com
Education: AB, Harvard College
Background: Consultant, Monitor
April E Evans, Partner & CFO
e-mail: aevans@monitorclipper.com
Education: BA, Duke University; MA, Boston University; MBA, Simmons College
Background: Partner & CFO, Advanced Technology Ventures; Founding Partner, Squillace & Evans
Peter S Laino, Managing Partner
41-44-389-7159
Fax: 41-44-389-7151
e-mail: plaino@monitorclipper.com
Education: BA, Williams College; MBA, Harvard Graduate School of Business Administration
Background: Director, K-III Communications Corporation; Associate, Dillon Read & Co.
Stephen A Lehman, Principal
41-44-389-7158
Fax: 44-44-389-7151
e-mail: slehman@monitorclipper.com
Education: BA, Economics & Mathematics, Williams College
Background: Consultant, Monitor Group

1249 MONITOR VENTURES
5050 El Camino Real
Suite 228
Los Altos, CA 94022
Phone: 650-475-7300
web: www.monitorventures.com

Mission Statement: We are committed to creating value by identifying strong entrepreneurs and building successful companies from the ground up.

Average Investment: $250,000 - $1 million

Investment Criteria: Early-Stage
Industry Group Preference: Software, Networking, Communications, Consumer Products
Portfolio Companies: Adaptive Planning, Greystripe, HydroPoint Data Systems, Limelife, Local Response, Media Platform, Meru, Verdezyne

Key Executives:
Neal Bhadkamkar, Co-Founder & Managing Partner
Education: Indian Institute of Technology; MBA, Harvard Business School; PhD, Electrical Engineering, Stanford University
Background: VP Manufacturing, Zowie Intertainment; Interval Research
Teymour Boutros-Ghali, Co-Founder & Managing Partner
Education: Electrical Engineering, Cambridge University; PhD, Physics, SM, Management, MIT
Background: AllBusiness; Zowie Intertainment; Thrive Online; Pubisher, Time International
Jerry Engel, General Partner
Education: Bachelors, Penn State; Masters, Wharton School
Background: Founder, Entrepreneurial Services Group, Arthur Young; General Partner, Kline Hawkes
Fern Mandelbaum, Partner
Education: BA, Economics, Brown University; MBA, Stanford Graduate School of Business
Background: Co-Founder, Skyline; SRI International

1250 MONTLAKE CAPITAL
1200 Fifth Avenue
Suite 1800
Seattle, WA 98101
Phone: 206-956-0898
e-mail: montlake@montlakecapital.com
web: www.montlakecapital.com

Mission Statement: Montlake Capital is a leading growth equity form dedicated to delivering superior returns for our investors by partnering with private companies that have solid growth potential.

Geographic Preference: Northwestern United States
Fund Size: $100 million
Founded: 1999
Industry Group Preference: Consumer Products, Healthcare, Retailing, Technology, Financial Services, Business Products & Services
Portfolio Companies: AA Asphalting, Blue Dog Bakery, Coastal Community Bank, Fresca Mexican Foods, HerbPharm, i4cp, Intrepid Learning Solutions, SmartRG, SOG Specialty Knives & Tools, Specified Fittings, Wellpartner

Key Executives:
Andy Dale, Managing Director
Education: AB, Harvard College; MBA, Harvard Business School
Background: M&A Group, Smith Barney; First Century Partners
Directorships: Coastal Community Bank, i4cp, Intrepid Learning Solutions, PayScale, SmartRG, WellPartner
Noel de Turenne, Managing Director
Education: BA, University of Washington; MBA, Foster School of Business
Directorships: AA Asphalting, Specified Fittings, SOG Specialty Knives & Tools, Herbpharm, i4cp

1251 MONTREUX EQUITY PARTNERS
Four Embarcadero Center
Suite 3720
San Francisco, CA 94111
Phone: 650-234-1200 **Fax:** 650-234-1250
e-mail: info@mepvc.com
web: www.mepvc.com

451

Venture Capital & Private Equity Firms / Domestic Firms

Mission Statement: A private equity firm focused o building great life science and healthcare companies. The goal is to generate significant long-term capital gain by investing in superior businesses with high quality management teams.
Fund Size: $250 million
Founded: 1993
Average Investment: $5 million
Minimum Investment: $2 million
Investment Criteria: All stages
Industry Group Preference: Life Sciences, Healthcare, Biopharmaceuticals, Medical Devices
Portfolio Companies: Asthmatx, Avantis Medical Systems, Best Health, Cerexa, Coalescent Surgical, Colore Science, Crown Laboratories, Enteric Medical Technologies, Epirus Biopharmaceuticals, GC Aesthetics, Glaukos, Great Lakes Health Plan, Integrated Biosystems, Kareo, KFX Medical, Know Better Foods, Mako Surgical Corp., MindBody, Moksha8, Nova Cardia, Novostent, Orexigen, Paymap, Peninsula, Percsys, Pivot Medical, Product Health, PulmonX, Pure Life Renal, Questcor Pharma, Renal Care Partners, Si-Bone, Skin Medica, Somaxon Pharma, Sonoma Pharma, Tiger Connect, Tobira Therapeutics, Transcept

Key Executives:
Daniel K Turner III, Managing Director
e-mail: dan@mepvc.com
Education: BS, Sacramento State University; MBA, Haas School of Business, University of California, Berkeley
Background: Turnaround Group Manager, Berkeley International; Founding CFO, Oclassen Pharmaceuticals; High Technology Group, Price Waterhouse
Directorships: GC Aesthetics, Moksha8, Epirus, Glaukos, Tobira Therapeutics
Michael Matly, MD, Managing Director
Education: BS, Cornell University; MD, Mayo Clinic; MBA, Harvard Business School
Background: Mayo Clinic
Directorships: Tiger Connect, Kareo, Pure Life Renal, Pulmonx
Michael Mayer, Managing Director
Education: BA, Washington State University
Background: Partner, PricewaterhouseCoopers

1252 MONUMENT ADVISORS
255 North Alabama
Suite 333
Indianapolis, IN 46204

Phone: 317-656-5065 **Fax:** 317-656-5060
e-mail: request@monument-capital.com
web: www.monumentadv.com

Mission Statement: A private equity firm focused on management buyins, management buyouts, leveraged buyouts and recapitalizations in the microcap market. We partner with management teams to acquire and help build companies within niche service, distribution and manufacturing industries with enterprise values between $8 and $20 million.
Geographic Preference: Midwestern United States
Fund Size: $22.5 million
Average Investment: $1 - $3 million
Industry Group Preference: Industrial Services, Distribution, Niche Manufacturing
Portfolio Companies: Citadel Architectural Products, CT Acquisition Corp., Dronen Consulting, Instrument Development Corporation, Insurance Auto Auctions, Felins USA, Foam Rubber Products, HETSCO, Lake City Acquisition, Mountain Muffler, Nationwide Distribution, New Polar, Presidential Holdings, Presidential, Separators, Service Design Associates

Key Executives:
Joseph P Schaffer, Managing Director
e-mail: jschaffer@monumentadv.com
Education: BS, Finance, Butler University; MBA, Indiana University
Background: Assistant Vice President, First Chicago Capital Markets
Directorships: Foam Rubber, Felins USA, Instrument Development Corporation

1253 MOORE VENTURE PARTNERS
La Jolla, CA

web: www.moorevp.com

Mission Statement: MVP Funds is a group of entrepreneurs and seasoned investors that are passionate about building the next generation of companies related to human longevity, high technology and life sciences.

Key Executives:
Terry Moore, Founder/Managing Partner
Education: MBA
Background: Founder/Chair, VC Roundtable; Founder/Executive Director, Morrison & Forrester Venture Network; Managing Director, HamiltonTech Capital Partners

1254 MORADO VENTURE PARTNERS
web: www.moradoventures.com

Mission Statement: Morado Venture Partners provides the resources entrepreneurs need to launch successful enterprises. Our partnership with our portfolio companies goes far beyond simply offering seed funding. We offer companies insights gained from experience, share their passion, and connect them to industry leaders who can help them.
Geographic Preference: San Francisco Bay Area, West Coast, New York City Area
Founded: 2011
Average Investment: $150,000
Investment Criteria: Seed-Stage
Industry Group Preference: Internet, E-Commerce & Manufacturing, Consumer Internet, Mobile, SaaS
Portfolio Companies: Active Mind Technology, Amitree, Apportable, Apsalar, Arterys, August Lock, Bagcheck, Betable, Betabrand, BitYota, BoarwalkTech, Boostable, Breakthrough, Bunndle, Cardspring, Cargomatic, Citrine Informatics, Class Dojo, Clef, Clover, Colingo, Colourlovers, Context Logic, CPUsage, Dasher, DataTorrent, Dot & Bo, Emmerge, eVenues, Evernote, Getaround, Gobble, GraphSQL, GreenGoose, Grid, Hiku, HipGeo, Impermium, Jetpac, JustOne, Layer, LitBit, Livestar, Local Motion, Lumo, ModBot, NeuMitra, Nuzzel, Onswipe, Openbucks, Opsclarity, Opsmatic, Optimus Ride, Osaro, Pen.io, Pepperdata, Polar, Proven.com, Puddle, Rainforest, RewardsPay, Rigetti, Romotive, Sano, Sapho, Savioke, Science Exchange, ShoCard, Sourcery, Space Monkey, Stackhut, Story Magic, Sunshine, Talech, ThinAir, Thislife, Tinfoil Security, Tomfoolery, Trnql, Trumo, Trusted Insight, Viewics, VIMOC, Watchsend, Wello, Whitetruffle, Wholeshare, Wittlebee, Xockets, Yozio

Key Executives:
Ash Patel, Founding Partner
Education: BSc, Computer Science, Kings College, University of London
Background: Senior Vice President, Platform Engineering, Yahoo!
Michael Marquez, Founding Partner
Education: BS, Managerial Economics, University of California, Davis; MBA, University of North Carolina, Chapel Hill
Background: Co-Founder, CODE Advisors; EVP, CBS Interactive

1255 MORGAN STANLEY EXPANSION CAPITAL
555 California Street
35th Floor
San Francisco, CA 94104

Phone: 415-984-6500 **Fax:** 415-984-6596
Toll-Free: 800-289-9060
e-mail: Expansion.Capital@morganstanley.com

Venture Capital & Private Equity Firms / Domestic Firms

Mission Statement: Our goal is to use the experience of our team and the strength of Morgan Stanley to help build successful companies, generate superior returns for our investors and create wealth for entrepreneurs.

Geographic Preference: United States, Western Europe
Fund Size: $1.2 billion
Founded: 1986
Average Investment: $30 million
Minimum Investment: $5 million
Investment Criteria: Expansion Stage, Late, Growth Buyout
Industry Group Preference: Information Technology, Healthcare, Enterprise Software, Communication Technology, Infrastructure, Semiconductors, Healthcare Information Technology, Healthcare Services, Biopharmaceuticals
Portfolio Companies: Airespace, Allscripts, Anasazi, Arcadian Management, Aurum Software, Avamar, Bachman Information Systems, Benefit Mall, Biex, BizBuyer.Com, Blaze Software, Blue Star Solutions, Bowstreet, Business Engine, Buzzsaw.com, CallFire, Cambridge Heart, Cardiac Pathways, ChemConnect, Children's Discovery Center, Chip Express Corporation, Chromatic Research, Ciphergen Biosystems, Clinipace Worldwide, Cohesity, Comergent, Commerce One, Compucare, Concentra, Connect South, Constant Contact, Control Delivery Systems, Core Security Technologies, DicoverRx, DocuWare, eCentria, EcoIntense, Elevate, Eska, Ethertronics, Fuhu, Global Custom Commerce, Good Technology, GumGum, High Q, Instapage, Integral, Internap, iRise, Mojo, Mondee, Motionpoint, Motive Medical Intelligence, NanoString Technologies, Nutanix, Perceptive Software, Plateau, Rocket Lawyer, Sendmail, Smart Pants Vitamins, Socialware, Southern Care Hospice Services, Spinal Kinetics, Sprout, ThruPoint, Tiff's Treats Cookie Delivery, VBrick Systems, Vigilant Solutions, VizExplorer, Voices.com, XSInc

Other Locations:
1585 Broadway
39th Floor
New York, NY 10036

Key Executives:
Peter Chung, Head of Expansion Capital
Education: Dartmouth College, Stanford Graduate School
Background: Investment Banking Professional, Morgan Stanley
Melissa Daniels, Managing Director
Education: BA, Economics, University of North Carolina at Chapel Hill; MBA, Haas School of Business at the University of California at Berkeley
Background: Product/Software Development Manager, National Director of Fulfillment Operations, Southeast Regional Manager at Commerce Clearing House; Staff of Aviation Subcommittee, U.S. House of Representatives and University of North Carolina.
Directorships: Arcadian Management Services, Clinipace Worldwide, Discoverx, EKOS, IDeas, National Healing, PeopleClick, SouthernCare
Bill Reiland, Managing Director
Education: BA, Economics, Yale University; MBA, Tuck School of Business
Background: Leerink Swann
Robert Bassman, Managing Director
Education: University of Pennsylvania
Directorships: Docuware, Vigilant Solutions, EcoIntense, GumGum, Voices.com, High Q, Blinds.com, Mitel, Digital Globe
Lincoln Isetta, Managing Director
Education: Boston College

1256 MORGAN STANLEY PRIVATE EQUITY
e-mail: private.equity@morganstanley.com
web: www.morganstanley.com

Mission Statement: Morgan Stanley Private Equity is the firm's primary business for investing in large and middle-market private equity transactions globally on behalf of its clients.

Geographic Preference: Worldwide
Average Investment: $100 million - $500 million
Portfolio Companies: McKechnie Aerospace, Tops Markets, Learning Care Group, Breitenfeld, Triana Energy, Trinity CO2, Zenith, ReachOut Healthcare America, EmployBridge, Sterling Energy, Access Cash, Creative Circle

Key Executives:
Mark Bye, Managing Director
Education: BS & MS, MIT
Background: President & CEO, Dystar GmbH; Group Vice President, Air Products & Chemicals
Directorships: Carus Chemical Corporation, Breitenfeld AG, Trinity CO2
James Howland, Managing Director
Education: BA, Bucknell University; MBA, Stanford University Graduate School of Business
Background: President, Dun & Bradsteet International; CEO, Edison Schools Educational Services Group; CEO, Regus Business Center; American Express; McKinsey & Company
Directorships: Learning Care Group, EmployBridge, Access Cash, ReachOut
Gary S Matthews, Managing Director
Education: BA, Princeton University; MBA, Harvard Business School
Background: Simmons Bedding Company; Sleep Innovations; Derby Cycle Corporation; Worldwide Consumer Medicines, Bristol Myers Squibb; Managing Director, UK, Diageo/Guinness Limited
Directorships: Van Wagner, Lagunitas, Learning Care Group
John Moon, Managing Director
Education: AB, Harvard College; AM & PhD, Business Economics, Harvard University
Background: Managing Director, Riverstone Holdings
Directorships: Sterling Energy, Triana Energy Investments, Trinity CO2
Aaron Sack, Managing Director
Education: Dartmouth College; MBA, Wharton School, University of Pennsylvania
Background: Vice President, Goldman Sachs
Directorships: EmployBridge, Learning Care Group, Access Cash, Creative Circle

1257 MORGENTHALER VENTURES
2710 Sand Hill Road
Suite 100
Menlo Park, CA 94025

Phone: 650-388-7600 Fax: 650-388-7601
e-mail: ching@morgenthaler.com
web: www.morgenthaler.com

Mission Statement: To partner with industry leading management teams and provide them with the highest possible level of support as they build their companies and create long term shareholder value.

Geographic Preference: United States
Fund Size: $3 billion
Founded: 1968
Average Investment: $5-$15 million
Minimum Investment: $500,000
Investment Criteria: Early-Stage
Industry Group Preference: Life Sciences, Information Technology, Internet, Enterprise Software, Biotechnology, Medical Devices
Portfolio Companies: Adara Media, Amati, Apple Computers, Aptis, Atria, Big Switch Networks, BilltoMobile, BlueAc, BlueGill Technologies, Brion Technologies, Catena Networks, Check, Chrysalis, CLK Design Automation, Convo, Cortina Systems, Crossbow Technology, Doximity,

453

Venture Capital & Private Equity Firms / Domestic Firms

Endwave, Evans and Sutherland, Evernote, Fiber Optic Network Systems, FiveStar, Force 10 Networks, Fundly, Illustra, Imeem, Intelleflex, Jaspersoft, KnowledgeNet, LendingClub, Microchip, MuleSoft, NBX Corporation, Netli, New Foxus, NEXTEL, Nominum, Nuance Communications, NuoDB, OneChip Photonics, Orb Networks, Overture Networks, Paratek Microwave, PeopleMater, Peregrine Semiconductor, Planet Soho, Practice Fusion, Premiys, QuickLogic, R2 Semiconductor, Rhythm NewMedia, Siri, Socrata, Sonatype, Synopsys, TimesTen, Unity Semiconductor, VeriFone, Vitesse, Voltage Security, Volterra Semiconductor, Webspective, Wize Commerce

Key Executives:

Gary Morgenthaler, Partner
e-mail: gmorgenthaler@morgenthaler.com
Education: BA, International Studies, Harvard University
Background: Co-Founder/CEO, Illustra Information Technologies; Director, Catena Networks; Nuance; Premisys Communications; Co-Founder/CEO/Chairman, Ingres Corporation; Management Consultant, Tymshare
Directorships: Nominum, NuoDB, OneChip Photonics, Overture Networks

Gary Little, Partner
e-mail: glittle@morgenthaler.com
Education: MBA, Harvard University; BSEE, UCLA
Background: Senior VP, Apple Computer; VP, Channel Sales; Director of Product Marketing, Sun Microsystems
Directorships: Adara Media, Evernote, Jaspersoft, MuleSoft, Wize Commerce, PeopleMatter, Rhythm NewMedia, Voltage Security

Rebecca Lynn, Partner
e-mail: rlynn@morgenthaler.com
Education: BS, Chemical Engineering, University of Missouri; JD, UC Berkeley School of Law; MBA, Haas School of Business, UC Berkeley
Background: Procter & Gamble; Vice President, Marketing, NextCard
Directorships: Check, Convo, Doximity, LendingClub, Socrata

Bob Pavey, Partner
e-mail: bpavey@morgenthaler.com
Education: BS, Physics, College of William & Mary; MS, Metallurgy, Columbia University; MBA, Harvard Business School
Background: Foseco
Directorships: CLK Design Automation, Cortina Systems, OmniPV, Peregrine Semiconductor Corporation, R2 Semiconductor

1258 MOTIV PARTNERS
755 Sansome Street
Suite 450
San Francisco, CA 94111

e-mail: info@motivpartners.com
web: www.motivpartners.com

Mission Statement: MOTIV is an ecosystem built to support leaders and company founders. MOTIV sources high quality deal flow, conduct diligence, make investments, and provide expertise to portfolio companies. MOTIV brings a network of aligned family offices and capital providers, many of whom also have deep industry insights and customer and supplier relationships.

Founded: 2016
Industry Group Preference: Clean Technology, Finance, Application Software, Food Services, Technology, Data Analytics, Healthcare
Portfolio Companies: Community Investment Management, The Cranemere Group Ltd., Good Eggs, Lending Club, Lyft, Peer IQ, Uprising, Virta, XL Hybrids

Key Executives:

Oliver Guinness, Co-Founder/Managing Director
Education: BS, Economics, Cornell University; MS, International Affairs & Business, Emerging Markets, Columbia University
Background: Merril Lynch; Greyrock Capital; Co-Founder, Clearpoint Ventures

Bill Tarr, Co-Founder/Managing Director
Education: BA, Dartmouth College
Background: Co-Founder, Aquillian Investments; Management Consultant, Origo Global Business Partners
Directorships: New Sector Alliance

1259 MOTLEY FOOL VENTURES
Alexandria, VA 22314

web: foolventures.com

Mission Statement: A venture capital fund seeking to invest in Early Stage Fintech companies.
Fund Size: $150 million
Founded: 2018
Average Investment: $1-$2 million
Minimum Investment: $500,000
Investment Criteria: Early Stage, Annual Revenue between $500,000 to $5 million
Industry Group Preference: Fintech, Artificial Intelligence, Information Technology
Portfolio Companies: Affectiva, Bitwise, Blockable, Eyrus, HomeCare.com, HUNGRY Marketplace, InHerSight, LegalMation, Microshare, MotoRefi, MyWallSt, PostProcess, RoundTrip, tEquitable, Territory Foods, Upskill, UrbanStems, WealthForge, YouEarnedIt, Runpath

Key Executives:

Olleb Douglass, Managing Director
Education: BA, Accounting, University of Baltimore
Background: CFO, The Motley Fool Holdings Inc.; Auditor, KPMG
Directorships: Eyrus; InHerSight; Young Artists of America

Brendan Mathews, Vice President
Education: BA, Economics, University of Virginia; MBA, University of California, Berkeley
Background: Accenture

Rob Runett, Vice President
Education: BA, Journalism, University of Maryland
Background: Director of Retail Operations, Motley Fool Asset Management LLC

1260 MOTOROLA SOLUTIONS VENTURE CAPITAL
500 West Monroe Street
Suite 4400
Chicago, IL 60661-3781

Phone: 847-576-5000
web: www.motorolasolutions.com

Mission Statement: As part of the Chief Technology Office of Motorola, Motorola Solutions Venture Capital invests in applications and technologies that complement and enhance the fund's ability to keep public safety personal safe and effective at their jobs, by letting them focus on the mission, not the technology.

Geographic Preference: United States
Fund Size: $11.3 billion
Founded: 1999
Average Investment: $5 million
Minimum Investment: $3 million
Investment Criteria: Startup, Growth, Expansion
Industry Group Preference: Entertainment, Information Technology, Communications, Electronic Components, Security, Healthcare, Wireless Technologies, Telecommunications, Digital Media & Marketing, Government, Networking, Mobile Broadband, Social Media
Portfolio Companies: Agent, BlueLine Grid, Boundless, Cyphy, Devmynd, Neurala, Nok Nok Lab, Nubo, Orion, Pellion, SceneDoc, Seamless Docs, RapidSOS, TRX Systems, VocalZoom, SST

Venture Capital & Private Equity Firms / Domestic Firms

Key Executives:
Eduardo Conrado, Chief Strategy & Innovation Officer
Background: VP, Marketing/IT, Motorola Solutions

1261 MOUNTAIN GROUP CAPITAL
3835 Cleghorn Avenue
Suite 300
Nashville, TN 37215

Phone: 615-843-9100 Fax: 615-313-9996
web: mtngp.com

Mission Statement: Mountain Group Capital is an investment firm dedicated to investing in and actively guiding transformational businesses in the Life Sciences and Technology sectors. Founded in 2002, MGC principals have invested in more than 20 companies in these sectors.

Founded: 2002
Investment Criteria: Seed-Stage, Early-Stage
Industry Group Preference: Life Sciences, Medical Devices, Diagnostics, Nutraceuticals, Technology, Business Products & Services, Consumer Services, Healthcare Services
Portfolio Companies: Apire Health, Castle Biosciences, Cerebrotech, Clearside Biomedical, Diabetes Care Group, Diagnovus, G1 Therapeutics, MedCenterDisplay, Myomo, NeuroTronik Limited, NuSirt, Cyber Physical Systems, ABT Molecular Imaging Evermind, Industrial Ceramic Solutions, InvisionHeart, Just A Pinch Recipe Club, OnFocus, Pathfinder Therepeutics, SwingPal, Streamweaver, VenX, Concept Therapeutics, DirectVetMarketing, Clinical Products, DeviceFidelity, Ironwood Pharmaceuticals, Panopto, PharmMD, Value Payment Systems

Key Executives:
Joe Cook Jr, Managing Director
Education: BS, Engineering, University of Tennessee
Background: Founder, Ironwood Pharmaceuticals; Group Vice President, Eli Lilly & Company
Directorships: Ironwood Pharmaceuticals, Corcept Therapeutics, Amylin Pharmaceuticals
Byron Smith, Managing Director
Education: MBA, University of Chicago
Background: Procter & Gamble, Pepsico, GTE Wireless, AT&T, EVP/CMO, Excite @ Home
Directorships: NuSirt Sciences, MedCenter Display, Value Payment Systems, Streamweaver
Joe Cook III, Managing Director
Education: BA, Economics, Davidson College
Background: Director, Private Placements, Robert W Baird & Co.; Vice President, JC Bradford & Co.
Directorships: Pathfinder Therapeutics, VenX Medical, Industrial Ceramic Solutions, DPS Healthcare
Steven D Singleton, Managing Director
Education: BS, Finance, University of South Florida; Stetson University College of Law
Background: Corporate Law, Trenam Kemker

1262 MOUNTAINEER CAPITAL
107 Capitol Street
Charleston, WV 25301

Phone: 304-347-7519 Fax: 304-347-0072

Mission Statement: To provide venture capital to promising new and existing businesses located in West Virginia and surrounding states.

Geographic Preference: West Virginia
Average Investment: $250,000 - $1 million
Investment Criteria: Early-Stage
Industry Group Preference: Technology, Information Technology, Communication Technology, Specialty Chemicals, Environmental Science, Forensic Science, Advance Polymers, Toxic Materials Handling, Hardwood Products, Coal Processes, Natural Gas, Medical Devices, Software, Education Technology
Portfolio Companies: Aero Corporation, Frontier Firewood, Game Plan, JBLCo, MetalWood Bats, New Carbon, Plethora, ThinOptX, Threewide, Troy, Vandalia Research, Vested Health

Key Executives:
William H Taylor II, Managing General Partner
Education: BS, Engineering Science, Johns Hopkins University; MS, Princeton University; PhD, Princeton University
Background: Partner, Taylor & Turner Associates; Founder & Vice President, Data Science Ventures
J Rudy Henley, Partner
e-mail: jrhenley@mtncap.com
Education: BS, Business Administration, West Virginia University
Background: Senior Managing Director, McCabe-Henley Properties
Patrick A Bond, General Partner
e-mail: pabond@mtncap.com
Education: BS, MS, Industrial Engineering, West Virginia University
Background: Managing Director, McCabe Henley LP, Consulting, Growth Management Group

1263 MOUSSE PARTNERS
9 West 57th St.
Suite 4605
New York, NY 10019-2701

Mission Statement: Mousse Partners specializes in venture capital investments.

Investment Criteria: Growth-Stage
Portfolio Companies: Beautycounter, Everplans, Harmless Harvest, Mavin, Memebox Corporation, Paddle8, SeatGeek, Teforia, WHOOP

Other Locations:
Beijing
China

Key Executives:
Charles Heilbronn, Founder & President
Education: Master in Law, Universite de Paris V, Law School; LLM, New York University Law School
Background: Chanel Inc.; Willkie Farr & Gallagher

1264 MOZART VENTURE PARTNERS
web: www.linkedin.com/in/rainerdechet

Mission Statement: Mozart Venture Partners is US-American seed venture capital company (in formation) that invests in tech startups.

Founded: 2014
Investment Criteria: Seed-Stage
Industry Group Preference: Technology

Key Executives:
Rainer Dechet, Founder

1266 MPE PARTNERS
Fifth Third Center
600 Superior Ave. East
Suite 2500
Cleveland, OH 44114

Phone: 216-416-7500
web: www.mpepartners.com

Mission Statement: Morgenthaler Private Equity (MPE) Partners focuses on the lower middle market, specifically on industry-leading companies with transaction values from $25 million to $150 million.

Geographic Preference: North America
Industry Group Preference: Manufacturing, Commercial Services, Industrial
Portfolio Companies: B&E Group, Bettcher Industries, dlhBowles, DreamLine, Plastic Components, Trachte, United Pipe & Steel Corp.

Venture Capital & Private Equity Firms / Domestic Firms

Other Locations:
One Liberty Square
Suite 620
Boston, MA 02109
Phone: 617-587-7800
Key Executives:
Peter Taft, Partner
e-mail: ptaft@mpepartners.com
Education: BA, Amherst College; MBA, Harvard Business School
Background: McDonald & Company Securities
Directorships: B&E Groups, Bettcher Industries, dlhBowles, Plastic Components
Karen Tuleta, Partner
e-mail: ktuleta@mpepartners.com
Education: BA, Baldwin-Wallace College
Background: Carnegie Capital Management Company
Directorships: Bettcher Industries, dlhBowles, Plastic Components, Trachte
Joe Machado, Partner
e-mail: jmachado@mpepartners.com
Education: BA, Princeton University; MBA, Harvard Business School
Background: American Capital Strategies; HCI/Thayer Capital Partners
Directorships: DreamLine, Trachte, United Pipe & Steel
Matt Yohe, Partner
e-mail: myohe@mpepartners.com
Education: BA, Washington & Lee University; MBA, Harvard Business School
Background: American Capital Strategies; HCI/Thayer Capital Partners
Directorships: Bettcher Industries, Plastic Components, Trachte
Graham Schena, Partner
e-mail: gschena@mpepartners.com
Education: BA, Colgate University; MBA, MIT Sloan School
Background: Windjammer Capital; Sentinel Capital Partners; HIG Capital
Directorships: DreamLine

1267 MPG EQUITY PARTNERS
17 East Monroe Street
#219
Chicago, IL 60603

Phone: 630-334-8131
e-mail: mgoy@mpequity.com
web: www.mpgequity.com

Mission Statement: MPG Equity Partners is seeking to acquire profitable, privately held businesses in the Midwestern US where owners are seeking liquidity and a transition out of daily management.
Geographic Preference: Midwest
Investment Criteria: Ownership Transitions
Industry Group Preference: Healthcare, Information Technology, Business Products & Services, Consumer Services, Niche Manufacturing, Value-Added Distribution
Portfolio Companies: BrainBits, Clear Contract, Clear NDA, Health iPASS, MedService Repair, MouseHouse, Power Hour Fitness
Key Executives:
Michael Goy, Managing Partner
630-334-8131
e-mail: mgoy@mpgequity.com
Education: BS, Finance, Kelley School of Business, Indiana University; MBA, Booth School of Business
Background: Founding Member, Foros Group; Associate, Sterling Partners

1268 MPM CAPITAL
450 Kendall St.
Cambridge, MA 02142

Phone: 617-425-9200
web: www.mpmcapital.com

Mission Statement: We seek to maximize value creation by focusing on inflection points in the development of companies, such as the achievement of clinical proof-of-concept data, the achievement of early commercial success, and by reinvigorating commercial platforms with potentially high growth assets.
Geographic Preference: United States, Europe
Fund Size: $900 million
Average Investment: $1 million
Minimum Investment: $500,000
Investment Criteria: All Stages
Industry Group Preference: Biotechnology, Healthcare, Medical Devices, Pharmaceuticals, Medical Technology
Portfolio Companies: 23andMe, 28-7, Alnara Pharmaceuticals, Amphivena Therapeutics, Anthera Pharmaceuticals, Aratana Therapeutics, Astute Medical, Biomarin, Blade, Celladon, Cerecor, Chiasma, Coda, Conatus Pharmaceuticals, CoStim Pharmaceuticals, Cullinan Oncology, DigiTx Partners, EKR Therapeutics, Endologix, Entrada, Epizyme, FortéBio, Harpoon, Iconic Therapeutics, Idenix, IOMX, iPerian, iTeos, Maverick, Mitokyne, Naked Biome, Nevro, Oncorus, Oxagen, Pacira Pharmaceuticals, Peplin, Pharmasset, Potenza Therapeutics, Proteon Therapeutics, Radius, Raze Therapeutics, Repare, Rhythm, Sai, Selexys Pharmaceuticals, Semma, Sideris Pharmaceuticals, Solasia, Syndax, TCR2, Tetherex, Tizona, Trieza, TriNetX, Trivascular, True North Therapeutics, Valeritas, Vascular Pharmaceuticals, Verastem, Werewolf

Other Locations:
2000 Sierra Point Pkwy.
Suite 701
Brisbane, CA 94005
Phone: 650-533-3300 **Fax:** 650-553-3301
Key Executives:
Luke B Evnin, Managing Director
650-553-3300
Fax: 650-553-3301
e-mail: levnin@mpmcapital.com
Education: PhD, University of California; BA, Princeton University
Background: Accel Partners
Directorships: Epic Therapeutics; Metabasis; PiMedical; Venturi Group
Todd Foley, Managing Director
617-425-9200
Fax: 617-425-9201
Education: BS, Chemistry, MIT; MBA, Harvard Business School
Background: Business Development, Genentech; Management Consulting, Arthur D Little
Directorships: Chiasma, CombinatoRx, Rhythm Pharmaceuticals
Ansbert K Gadicke MD, Managing Director
617-425-9200
Fax: 617-425-9201
Education: MD, JW Goethe University
Background: Boston Consulting Group; Research positions in Biochemistry and Molecular Biology, Whitehead Institute/MIT, Harvard University, German Cancer Research Center
Directorships: Cerimon Pharmaceuticals, Dragonfly Sciences, Elixir Pharmaceuticals, Radius Health, Solasia Pharma KK

1269 MS&AD VENTURES
2730 Sand Hill Road
Menlo Park, CA 94025

web: msad.vc

456

Venture Capital & Private Equity Firms / Domestic Firms

Mission Statement: MS&AD Ventures is funded by MS&AD Insurance Group Holdings. The firm seeks to invest in tech-based innovations.
Industry Group Preference: Technology, Insurance, FinTech, Mobility, Cyber Security, Security, Automation, IoT, Data Mangement, Healthcare
Portfolio Companies: Akinova, Averon, ClearedIn, Dathena Science, Element, FinLeap, Geosite, i2X, Jupiter Intelligence, Lucideus, Node, Qunomedical, Rubrick, SkopeNow, Skycatch, Socotra, Spot, Taiger, Tide, Tomorrow, Vdoo, Voyage, WorldCover

Key Executives:
Jon Soberg, Managing Partner
Education: BS, Harvey Mudd College; MS, Robotics, Northwestern University; MBA, Wharton School
Background: Managing Director, Blumberg Capital; Managing Partner, Expansive Ventures; COO, REEF Technology; Co-Founder/Partner, Early Impact Ventures; Venture Partner, CerraCap Ventures; Co-Founder, FlexCap Partners; Lecturer, The Wharton School
Directorships: Lucideus; WorldCover; True Link Financial
Tak Sato, Managing Partner
Education: MBA, Chuo University Graduate School
Background: General Manager, Cholamandalam MS General Insurance Co.; Head of Investment, MS&AD Insurance
Tiffine Wang, Partner
Education: BA, University of California, Davis
Background: Marketing Manager, Alchemist Accelerator; HACKcelerator Program Manager, AngelHack; Co-Founder/Marketing, Akiva Health Systems; Co-Founder, Entrepreneurcareer.com; Head of Mentoring Program, European Innovation Academy; Sr. Investment Manager, Singtel Innov8 Ventures

---

1270 MSOUTH EQUITY PARTNERS
Two Buckhead Plaza
3050 Peachtree Road NW
Suite 550
Atlanta, GA 30305

Phone: 404-816-3255 **Fax:** 404-816-3258
e-mail: info@msouth.com
web: www.msouth.com

Mission Statement: Provides equity capital and expertise to support management teams in acquisitions and recapitalizations of lower middle market companies.
Geographic Preference: Southern United States
Fund Size: $1 billion
Founded: 1984
Investment Criteria: Acquisitions, Recapitalizations
Industry Group Preference: Distribution, Business Products & Services, Manufacturing
Portfolio Companies: BC Technical, Building Products & Services Company, Capstone Logistics, Children & Teen Dental Group, Coastal Companies, Coastal Sunbelt, Community & Southern Bank, Crom, Diversified, Eagle Quest International, Eco-Site, Education Networks of America, Employ Bridge, EnergyCo. Holdings, Fischben, GaiaTech, Hire Dynamics, Interior Logic Group, One Path, PetroLiance, Signal Outdoor Advertising, Southern HVAC, Tachyon, Technical Innovation, The Intersect Group, Thompson Industrial Services, The Right People Construction Group, United Telephone Company, USA Television Holdings, Vectorply

Key Executives:
Mark L Feidler, Partner
e-mail: mfeidler@msouth.com
Education: BA, Economics, Duke University; JD, Vanderbilt Law School
Background: President & COO, BellSouth Corporation; COO, Cingular Wireless; Head of Corporate Development, BellSouth; Investment Banking, The Robinson-Humphrey Company
Michael D Long, Partner
e-mail: mlong@msouth.com
Education: BS Finance/Accounting, MBA, Oklahoma State University
Background: CEO, Pac Pizza LLC; NationsBank
Bart A McLean, Partner
e-mail: bmclean@msouth.com
Education: BS, University of Delaware; MBA, Indiana University
Background: Principal, Allsop Venture Partners; VP, Republic Venture Group; Lending Officer, Republic Bank
Peter S Pettit, Partner
e-mail: ppetit@msouth.com
Education: BS, Commerce, McIntire School of Commerce, University of Virginia; MBA, Kellogg School of Management, Northwestern University
Background: Vice President, Code Hennessy & Simmons; The Robinson-Humphrey Company
Wanda R Morgan, Chief Financial Officer
e-mail: wmorgan@msouth.com
Education: BS, Accounting, University of Alabama; CPA

1271 MTS HEALTH INVESTORS
623 Fifth Avenue
14th Floor
New York, NY 10022

Phone: 212-887-2100 **Fax:** 212-887-2111
e-mail: info@mtspartners.com
web: www.mtspartners.com

Mission Statement: A principal investor that partners with seasoned, highly motivated management teams to significantly enhance the overall equity value in the companies in which it invests; believes firmly in equity-based incentives for management teams; builds discernible value through both the experienced guidance of its principals and investing in operating companies with sound fundamentals.

Founded: 2000
Investment Criteria: LBO, Corporate Divestitures, MBO, Growth Financing, Recapitalizations
Industry Group Preference: Healthcare Services, Outsourcing & Efficiency, Medical Devices
Portfolio Companies: Activate Healthcare, Acorda Therapeutics, Addex Therapeutics, Adynxx, AeroCare Holdings, Alliance Healthcare Services, Ameritox, Apollo Global Management, Aprecia Pharma, Arbutus Biopharma, ARCA Biopharma, Arizona Center for Cancer Care, Arsenal Capital Partners, Baxter International, Bloom Health, Boston Children's Hospital, Caladrius Biosciences, Celator Pharma, Celerion Holdings, Celsus Therapeutics, Champions Oncolody, Churchill Pharma, Cold Spring Harbor Laboratory, CoLucid Pharma, Cyteir Therapeutics, Dana-Farber Cancer Institute, Data Driven Delivery Systems, Diffusion Pharma, Dimension Therapeutics, DNA Diagnostics Center, Envisia Therapeutics, Examination Management Services, Health Diagnostic Laboratory, HealthHelp, Horizon Pharma, IASIS Healthcare Corporation, Immunogen, ImmusanT, Ipsen, Jazz Pharma, Keryx Biopharma, Laurel Health Care Co., Ligand Pharma, Loving Care Agency, Madrigal Pharma, myNEXUS, Novozymes, Ocera Therapeutics, Ocular Technologies, OncoGenex Pharma, Otsuka Pharma, PathGroup, Physicians Dialysis, Poxel, Promise Healthcare, pSivida, Psyadon Pharma, Protalix Biotherapeutics, Realm Therapeutics, Shionogi & Co., Shire, Signature Hospice and Home Health, Starmount, StrataDx, Strongbridge Biopharma, Synta Pharma, Tarveda Therapeutics, TeamHealth, Tripex Pharma, Universal American, University of Massachusetts Medical School, Velicept Therapeutics, Verona Pharma, Vital Decisions, Walter and Eliza Hall Institute, Woodbury Health Products, Zymeworks

Key Executives:
Curtis S Lane, Founding Partner
e-mail: lane@mtspartners.com

Venture Capital & Private Equity Firms / Domestic Firms

Education: MBA, Wharton School
Background: Evercore Capital Partners; Manager Healthcare Investment, Bear Stearns & Co; Corporate Finance, Smith Barney, Harris Upham & Co
Directorships: Lifeline Center for Child Development
Mark E Epstein, Managing Partner
e-mail: epstein@mtspartners.com
Education: BS, Wharton School
Background: Managing Director, Banc of America Securities' Private Equity Placements Group; VP, Private Equity Placements, Merrill Lynch & Co.
Andrew J Weisenfeld, Managing Partner
e-mail: weisenfeld@mtspartners.com
Education: BS, Cornell University; MBA, Wharton School
Background: Managing Director, Banc of America Securities' Corporate and Investment Banking Healthcare Group; Managing Director, JP Morgan; Merrill Lynch

1272 MUNICH REINSURANCE AMERICA, INC
555 College Road E
PO Box 5241
Princeton, NJ 08543

Phone: 609-243-4200 **Fax:** 609-243-4257
e-mail: slevy@munichreamerica.com
web: www.munichreamerica.com

Mission Statement: Offers stability, financial security, and expertise to clients; as a member of Munich Re Group, investments are backed by Munich Re's financial strength and commitment to reinsurance.

Geographic Preference: United States
Fund Size: $3.5 billion
Founded: 1917
Average Investment: $2.5 million
Investment Criteria: Second Round
Industry Group Preference: Insurance

Key Executives:
Anthony J Kuczinski, President & CEO
M Steven Levy, President, Reinsurance
609-243-4806
Education: AB Mathematics, Dartmouth College; MBA, Wharton School
Background: Manager Business Development, Swiss Re America
Philip Roeper, SVP/Chief Information Officer
609-243-4711
Education: BSEE, University of Southampton, UK
Background: Director Global Network Services, DHL Systems; Comtext; ITT; Marconi Communications

1273 MURPHREE VENTURE PARTNERS
1221 Lamar
Suite 1136
Houston, TX 77010

Phone: 713-655-8500 **Fax:** 713-655-8503
web: www.murphreeventures.com

Mission Statement: Privately owned investment company that makes very early stage direct equity investments into entrepreneurial enterprises, and aligns itself with entrepreneurs and management groups, acting in concert with them as an owner and investor. In all instances, the company will operate to the highest standards of professionalism and ethical behavior. Quality of service and reputation will ultimately define the success of the firm's endeavors and the goal is to be worthy of the highest.

Geographic Preference: Southeastern United States
Fund Size: $60 million
Founded: 1987
Average Investment: $5 million
Minimum Investment: $250,000

Investment Criteria: Seed, Early-Stage, Quality management team, national or international market scope, definable exit within 3-7 years
Industry Group Preference: Business to Business, E-Commerce & Manufacturing, Semiconductors, Photonics, Life Sciences, Medical Devices, Telecommunications, Energy, High Technology
Portfolio Companies: Anark Corporation, Accello, Aldis, Dowley Security, Intrinergy, Object Reservoir, Smart Furniture, Square 1 Bank

Other Locations:
1 Swiftwater Trail
The Hills, TX 78738

3104 Blue Lake Drive
Suite 120
Birmingham, AL 35243

Key Executives:
Dennis E Murphree, Managing General Partner
e-mail: dmurphree@murphreeventures.com
Education: BA, Southern Methodist University; MBA, Wharton School
Background: President/CEO, Murphree & Company; Faculty, Jones Graduate School, Rice University; Founder, Vail National Bank
Directorships: Avent Networks, Unico Corporation, FiberDynamics, Journee Software
John White, General Partner
e-mail: jwhite@murphreeventures.com
Education: BS, Political Science, Texas A&M University; JD, University of Texas School of Law
Background: Private Law Practice; Co-Founder, Standard Renewable Energy Group; Managing Director, The Wind Alliance

1274 MURPHY & PARTNERS FUND LP
708 Third Avenue
Suite 1910
New York, NY 10017

Phone: 212-209-3879 **Fax:** 212-209-7148
e-mail: john@murphy-partners.com

Mission Statement: A private equity fund that, when fully invested, expects to hold a diversified portfolio of privately owned equity securities in profitable manufacturing, distribution and service companies. The fund typically invests in circumstances where it is the lead or controlling investor, where debt can be used along with equity to maximize growth, and where management seeks to have a significant equity share of the business.

Geographic Preference: United States
Founded: 1988
Average Investment: $1 - $10 million
Minimum Investment: $1 million
Investment Criteria: LBO, MBO, Growth, Early Stage
Industry Group Preference: Education, Healthcare, Media, Business Products & Services
Portfolio Companies: Mosaica Education Inc., N B Education

Key Executives:
John J Murphy Jr, Managing General Partner
212-209-3879 x1129
Fax: 212-209-7148
e-mail: john@murphy-partners.com
Education: MBA, Amos Tuck School of Business Administration; AB, College of the Holy Cross College
Background: 25-year investment track record with a lifetime IRR of over 30%; substantial investment experience in media/healthcare/education; Founder Fund I and II; Founding General Partner, Adler & Shaykin
Directorships: Board position on all M&P portfolio companies

Venture Capital & Private Equity Firms / Domestic Firms

1275 MVP CAPITAL PARTNERS
259 N. Radnor-Chester Road
Suite 130
Radnor, PA 19087

Phone: 610-254-2999 **Fax:** 610-254-2996
e-mail: info@mvpcap.com
web: www.mvpcap.com

Mission Statement: Private equity investment firms that provide capital for later-stage growth companies and to finance acquisitions and recapitalizations.

Geographic Preference: Central & Eastern United States
Fund Size: $150 million
Founded: 1987
Average Investment: $3-10 million
Minimum Investment: $1 million
Investment Criteria: Later-Stage, Buy-Outs, Recapitalizations, Roll-Ups
Industry Group Preference: Publishing, Database Services, Media, Retailing, Distribution, Niche Manufacturing, Computer Hardware & Software, Life Sciences, Infrastructure, Business Products & Services, Healthcare Services, Consumer Products, Aviation
Portfolio Companies: Air Chef, Air Medical Group Holdings, American Bath Group, Andrews International Holdings, ANI Pharmaceuticals, Cadence Capital Management, Coffin Turbo Pump, Compass Water Solutions, Composite Technologies, Comprehensive Addiction Programs, Destination Maternity, Dorland Health, Expert Plan, GCA Service Solutions, Implex Corporation, Index Stock Imagery, Keystone Ranger Holdings, Legal Communications, MCMC, Mothers Work, Northern Contours, Omega Health Systems, Planalytics, Professional Press, Saxbys Coffee, Soft-Switch, SupplyOne Holding, Swiss Farm Stores, The Fairways Group, The Praxis Companies, York Risk Services

Key Executives:
Robert E Brown Jr., Managing General Partner
Education: Princeton University; MBA, Wharton Graduate School; JD, University of Pennsylvania
Background: Principal, Venture Capital firm; Founding Member, Greater Philadelphia Venture Group; Founding Director, Penn Venture Fund
Thomas A Penn, Partner
Education: BS, MIT; MBA, Stanford University
Background: Partner, Boston Millennia Partners; President/CEO, Tektagen; President, Independence Ventures

1276 McCARTHY CAPITAL
1601 Dodge Street
Suite 3800
Omaha, NE 68102

Phone: 402-932-8600 **Fax:** 402-991-0020
e-mail: info@mccarthycapital.com
web: www.mccarthycapital.com

Mission Statement: McCarthy Capital uses its disciplined investment strategy to focus on investing in businesses in partnership with established management teams. This philosophy has enabled our portfolio companies to exceed their growth expectations for more than two decades.

Fund Size: $475 million
Founded: 1999
Minimum Investment: $10 million
Portfolio Companies: 365 Retail Markets, Advantor Systems Corporation, Altair Global, Alpha Comm Enterprises, AmeriSphere, Bamboo Rose, Bearence Management Group, Benaissance, Bigger Pockets, DSCI, Environmental Planning Group, Guild Mortage Company, HHA eXchange, Honey Smoked Fish, Life Care Services, Medical Solutions, Prospect Brands, Quantum Workplace, Remi, Rx Savings Solutions, SAFE Boats International, Scooter's Coffee, Seven10, Signal 88 Security, SKC Communication Products, Southwest Value Partners, The Remi Group, Triage Staffing, TriMech, United Real Estate Group

Other Locations:
20 William St.
Suite 160
Wellesley, MA 02481
Phone: 617-330-9700

Key Executives:
Michael R McCarthy, Partner
402-991-8414
e-mail: mmccarthy@mccarthycapital.com
Education: BA, St. John's University
Background: Founder, McCarthy Organization
Directorships: Cabela's Incorporated, Election Systems & Software, SAFE Boats
Patrick J Duffy, President and Managing Partner
402-991-8405
e-mail: pduffy@mccarthycapital.com
Education: BS, University of Southern California; JD, Creighton University School of Law
Background: Partner, Fraser Stryker
Directorships: Bearence Management Group, Benaissance, CoSentry.net, Life Care Services
Robert Y Emmert, Managing Partner
617-330-9710
e-mail: bemmert@mccarthycapital.com
Education: BA, Georgetown University
Directorships: NRG Media, Advantor Systems Corporation

1277 NASSAU CAPITAL
12 Vanderventer Avenue
PO Box 1475
Princeton, NJ 08542

Phone: 609-430-9700
e-mail: rspowell@nassaucap.com
web: www.nassaucap.com

Mission Statement: Specializes in real estate financial strategies.

Founded: 1997

Key Executives:
Robert S Powell Jr, Managing Director
e-mail: rspowell@nassaucap.com
Education: University of North Carolina; MA, PhD, Economics, Princeton University
Background: President/CEO, DKM Properties; New Jerseye Economic Development Authority
Gerry Doherty, Senior Associate
Education: BA, Economics, University of Connecticut; MBA, Economics, University of Delaware
Ian J Mount, Senior Associate
Education: Vanderbilt University; MBA, Finance, American University
Background: Director of Development, Hekemian Kasparian Troast Group; Project Manager, Nassau HKT Urban Renewal Associates

1278 NATURAL GAS PARTNERS
2850 N Harwood Street
19th Floor
Dallas, TX 75201

Phone: 972-432-1440
e-mail: inquiries@ngptrs.com
web: www.naturalgaspartners.com

Mission Statement: Invests in the energy and related industries, with particular emphasis on young companies that acquire and exploit producing oil and gas properties. Natural Gas Partners will generate superior risk-adjusted investment returns while forming and maintaining the highest quality industry relationships and will conduct its business according to the highest standards of honesty, integrity and fairness.

Geographic Preference: North America

Venture Capital & Private Equity Firms / Domestic Firms

Fund Size: $7.3 billion
Founded: 1988
Average Investment: $50 million
Minimum Investment: $10 million
Investment Criteria: Startup, First Stage, Mezzanine
Industry Group Preference: Oil & Gas, Natural Gas, Energy
Portfolio Companies: 89 Energy, Aspen Energy Partners, Avad Energy, Axia Energy, Black Mountain Sand, Blackbeard Operating LLC, Boaz Energy LLC, Caltex Resources, Camino Natural Resources, Castlerock Exploration, Catapult Services, Centennial Resource Development LLC, CH4 Energy, Colgate Energy, Conexus Energy, Confluence Resources, Crimson Pipeline LP, Enlink Midstream, Fifth Creek Energy, Hibernia Energy, Infinity Natural Resources, Iron Horse Midstream, Luxe Energy, Luze Minerals, Mallard Exploration, Massif Oil & Gas, Mettle Midstream Partners, Outrigger Energy, Petrus Resources, Prairie Storm Energy Corp., Rebllion Energy, Springbok Energy, Switchback Energy Acquisition, Tap Rock Resources, Teal Natural Resources, Titus Oil & Gas LLC, Torrent Oil, Trilogy Midstream, World Energy Partners

Other Locations:
1266 East Main Street
6th Floor
Stamford, CT 06902
Phone: 203-504-5072 **Fax:** 203-504-5073

100 North Guadalupe Street
Suite 205
Santa Fe, NM 87501
Phone: 505-983-8400 **Fax:** 505-983-8120

1279 NAUTIC PARTNERS
50 Kennedy Plaza
Providence, RI 02903

Phone: 401-278-6770
web: www.nautic.com

Mission Statement: Nautic's mission is to achieve superior long-term investment returns for investors while preserving a strong culture that is based on partnership, humility and respect.
Geographic Preference: United States
Fund Size: $2.5 billion
Founded: 1986
Average Investment: $75 - $250 million
Minimum Investment: $50 million
Investment Criteria: Buyouts, Recapitalizations, Consolidations, Growth Financiings
Industry Group Preference: Business Products & Services, Manufacturing, Healthcare, Communications
Portfolio Companies: 1105 Media Holdings, All Metro Health Care Services, Applied Consultants, CCD Holdings, Curtis Industries Holdings, Custom Window Systems, Design/Craft Fabric Holdings, HB Performance Systems Holdings, HPS Holding Company, Milestone Aviation Group, NLS Holdings, Oasis Outsourcing, PEP Industries, QoL Meds, Reliant Hospital Partners, Respond2 Communications Holdings, Simonds Industries, Superior Vision Holding Company, Theorem Clinical Research Holdings

Key Executives:
Bernie Buonanno, Managing Director
401-278-5670
e-mail: bbuonanno@nautic.com
Education: AB, Brown University; MBA, Harvard Business School
Background: Fleet Equity Partners; Prudential-Bache Capital Funding
Habib Y Gorgi, Managing Director
401-278-6770
e-mail: hgorgi@nautic.com
Education: AB, Brown University; MBA, Columbia University
Background: Fleet Equity Partners; BankAmerica; Fleet Bank
Chris J. Crosby, Managing Director
401-278-6770
e-mail: ccrosby@nautic.com
Education: BS, Boston College; MBA, Harvard Business School
Background: McCown De Leeuw & Co., Kidder Peabody & Co.
Scott Hilinski, Managing Director
401-278-6770
e-mail: shilinski@nautic.com
Education: AB, Harvard University
Background: Fleet Equity Partners; TA Associates; Deloitte & Touche
Chris F. Corey, Managing Director
e-mail: ccorey@nautic.com
Education: BA, Assumption College; MBA, Columbia Business School
Background: JH Whitney & Co., Lehman Brothers
James A. Beakey, Managing Director, Business Development
e-mail: jbeakey@nautic.com
Education: BA, Trinity College; MBA, Northwestern University
Background: Capstone Partners, Adams Harkness & Hill
Chris A. Pierce, Managing Director
e-mail: cpierce@nautic.com
Education: BA, Yale University; MBA, Stanford Graduate School of Business
Background: Greenhill Capital Partners, Saloman Smith Barney/Citigroup Global Markets

1280 NAVIGATION CAPITAL PARTNERS
1175 Peachtree Street NE
10th Floor
Atlanta, GA 30361

Phone: 404-264-9180 **Fax:** 404-264-9305
e-mail: deals@navigationcapital.com
web: www.navigationcapital.com

Mission Statement: Works in close collaboration with the senior management of our portfolio companies, providing the benefit of our operating experience, insight and relationships.
Geographic Preference: United States
Fund Size: $2 billion
Founded: 2006
Average Investment: $10 - $40 million
Investment Criteria: $20 to $200 million in revenue
Industry Group Preference: Distribution, Business Products & Services, Financial Services, Healthcare Services, Transportation, Logistics, Automotive, Building Materials & Services, Manufacturing, Infrastructure, Media, Food & Beverage, Government
Portfolio Companies: Brightwell Payments, Brown Integrated Logistics, Computex Technology Solutions, Definition 6, Exeter Finance Corporation

Key Executives:
Lawrence Mock, Managing Partner, Co-Founder
404-583-0425
e-mail: lmock@navigationcapital.com
Education: BA, Harvard College; MS, Florida State University; London School of Economics
Background: President & CEO, Mellon Ventures; Co-Founder, River Capital; COO, Hangar One
Directorships: Brown Integrated Logistics, Exeter Finance, Definition 6, Brightwell Payments, Computex Technology Solutions
John Richardson, Managing Partner, Co-Founder
Education: BA, Princeton University; MBA, University of Pittsburgh
Background: Managing Director, Mellon Ventures; CFO, Unibev
Directorships: Pecora Corp.

Mark Downs, Partner, Co-Founder
Education: BA, University of Pittsburgh; MBA, Northwestern University, JL Kellogg School of Management
Background: Senior Vice President, Mellon Ventures
Directorships: AH Harris, Brightwell Payments, Definition 6, Five Star Food Service, Quantapoint
Eerik Giles, Partner, Co-Founder
Education: BS, Economics, Pennsylvania State University
Background: Vice President, Mellon Ventures; Legg Mason
Directorships: Pecora Corporation, Computex Technology Solutions, Technical Innovation
Dennis Lockhart, Partner
Education: BA, Economics and Political Science, Stanford Universy; MS, International Economics and American Foreign Policy, Johns Hopkins University
Background: CEO, President, Federal Reserve Bank of Atlanta; Managing Partner, Zephyr Management; President of Heller International Group, Heller International; Citibank
Directorships: Metro Atlanta Chamber of Commerce, Georgia Research Alliance

1281 NAVIGATOR PARTNERS LLC
P.O. Box 159
Summit, NJ 07901

Phone: 908-273-7733 Fax: 908-273-5566
e-mail: info@navigatorpartners.com
web: www.navigatorpartners.com

Mission Statement: Navigator is a private equity firm, a related entity is the manager for Navigator Growth Partners LP, a private equity investment fund organized as an SBIC, which created a diversified portfolio with a focus on manufacturers and marketers of basic consumer products and services.

Geographic Preference: Mid-Atlantic
Fund Size: $100 million
Founded: 1999
Average Investment: $2 million
Minimum Investment: $500,000
Investment Criteria: Later-Stage, Acquisitions, Growth Capital
Industry Group Preference: Diversified
Portfolio Companies: Compass Water Solutions, Crestcom, FirstLight HomeCare, Jon M Hall Company, K9 Resorts, Molecular Imaging Technology, Nelson Pipeline, Revere

Key Executives:
W Joseph Imhoff, Co-Founder/Managing Partner
Education: Northwestern University
Background: Chairman, Hebi Health Care AB; Founder/CEO, Hagemeyer Foods; VP/CIO, Jim Walter Corp; VP, W.R. Grace & Co; Senior Marketing/Operations Officer, Borden
Directorships: Nelson Pipeline, K9 Resorts
Bernard B Markey, Co-Founder/Managing Partner
Education: Villanova University; MM, Kellogg School of Management Northwestern University
Background: Chairman, Greater Philadelphia Venture Group
Directorships: CK Franchising, Universal Envrionmental Services, Lumeta Corporation
William H Stewart, Co-Founder/Managing Partner
Education: BS, Villanova University; MBA, New York University
Background: Managing Director, Nassau Captical; CFO, KMC Telecom; KDC Solar; KDC Agribusiness
Directorships: FirstLight HomeCare, K9 Resorts, Nelson Popeline, Jon M Hall Company

1282 NAVITAS CAPITAL
1111 Broadway Avenue
Oakland, CA 94607

web: www.navitascap.com

Mission Statement: Navitas Capital is a cleantech venture capital firm focused on investing in next generation energy efficiency and green building technology companies.

Founded: 2008
Industry Group Preference: Clean Technology, Building Materials & Services, Software
Portfolio Companies: Aquicore, Bowery, Cherre, Comfy, Gridium, HappyCo, Harbour, Honest Buildings, HqO, Katerra, Livly, Matter Port, OpenSpace, Orchard, PeerStreet, PiinPoint, Powermat, Procore, Ravti, Sweeten, Truss, View Dynamic Glass

Other Locations:
9460 Wilshire Boulevard
Suite 850
Beverly Hills, CA 90212

Key Executives:
Travis Putnam, Co-Founder/Managing Partner
Education: BS, Economics, Wharton School
Background: Founder, Genesis Management Group; Murphy & Associates Capital
Jim Pettit, Co-Founder/Managing Partner
Education: BS, Haas School of Business, University of California, Berkeley
Background: Principal, Bancroft Capital; Managing Director, JP Morgan
Directorships: Optimum Energy, Gridium, Enmetric Systems, Lunera Lighting
Gary Dillabough, Managing Partner
Education: BS, Civil Engineering, California Polytechnic State University, San Luis Obispo
Background: Managing Partner, Westly Group; EBay; Vistro Corporation; Improvenet; Media Arts Group
Directorships: View Dynamic Glass, Lunera Lighting, Building Robotics, Honest Buildings, MyHealthTeams

1283 NAVY CAPITAL
575 Lexington Avenue
4th Floor
New York, NY 10022

Phone: 646-512-8748
e-mail: ir@navycapital.com
web: www.navycapital.com

Mission Statement: Invests in new opportunities within the legal cannabis industry, including consumer, healthcare and agriculture.

Founded: 2017
Industry Group Preference: Cannabis, Consumer Products, Healthcare, Technology, Agriculture
Portfolio Companies: CLS Holdings USA, GrowGeneration, MariMed, PLUS

Key Executives:
Kevin Gahwyler, President/Chief Financial Officer
Education: BS, Biology, Fairfield University; MIM, International Finance, Thunderbird School of Global Management
Background: Investment Analyst, GM Asset Management; Director of Investor Relations, Sagamore Hill; SVP, Pequot Capital; Managing Director, CDG Holdings; President, KenCole Capital LLC; COO/Director, Business Development, Twin Capital Management
Directorships: A Little Hope Foundation; Team Racing for Veterans (RV4)
Jeffrey Schultz, General Counsel/Chief Compliance Officer
Education: BA, English, University of Michigan; JD, Cardozo School of Law
Background: Legal & Compliance, K2 Advisor; Legal Counsel, BNP Paribas Investment Partners; Chief Legal/Compliance Officer, Phoenix Investment Advisor; Managing Director/Sr. Counsel/CCO, GPB Capital; Sr. Advisor, GPB Capital

Venture Capital & Private Equity Firms / Domestic Firms

Sean Stiefel, Principal
Education: University of St. Gallen (Switzerland); BBA, Marshall School of Business, University of Southern California
Background: Analyst, Barclays Capital; Associate, Millenium Management; Trader, Northwoods Capital
John T. Kaden, Principal
Education: AB, Harvard University; JD, Yale Law School
Background: Founder/Chief Investment Officer, Cynthion Partners; Co-Manager/Chief Investment Officer, Northwoods Capital; Manager/Chief Investment Offer, Navy Capital Green Fund LP

1284 NAXURI CAPITAL
425 Broadway St.
Redwood City, CA 94062

Mission Statement: Naxuri Capital is the premier seed fund investing in early stage companies at the intersection of fashion, retail, and technology. The Naxuri Capital Investment strategy is focused on early stage companies in the fashion and technology market. We are very selective when choosing our investment opportunities and we are very confident that we can add significant value to the companies we invest in.

Investment Criteria: Early Stage
Industry Group Preference: Fashion, Retail, Consumer & Leisure

Key Executives:
Enrico Beltramini, Managing Director
Background: Corporate Executive and Global Advisor at Gucci, Fiat, Rinascente Group, and PA Consulting Group
Patrick Chung, Managing Director
Background: Co-Founding Managing Director, SK Telecom Ventures; Corporate Attorney, Wilson Sonsini Goodrich & Rosati; Advior, Kim & Chang; Director of Business Development, Dialpad Communications

1285 NAYA VENTURES
222 W Las Colinas Boulevard
Suite 755E
Irving, TX 75039

e-mail: info@nayaventures.com
web: www.nayaventures.com

Mission Statement: Naya Ventures invests in companies located in the US and India in technology, focusing on mobile and cloud services.

Geographic Preference: United States, India
Average Investment: $250,000 - $3 million
Investment Criteria: Early-Stage
Industry Group Preference: Mobile, SaaS, Cloud Computing, Big Data, Business to Business, B2B, AI, Emerging Technology
Portfolio Companies: Altia Systems, Appnique, autoGraph, Boxfish, DocSynk, GlobalOutlook, Glympse, HyperVerge, KeepTrax, Kore.ai, Motivity Labs, PDHI

Other Locations:
710 Second Avenue
Suite 400
Seattle, WA 98104

Floor-3, Block-1
My Home Hub
Madhapur
Hyderabad 500081
India

Key Executives:
Dayakar Puskoor, Co-Founder/General Partner
Education: Stephen F. Austin University; MS, Computer Science, Nova University
Background: Hosting & Mobility Solutions, Microsoft; Founder & CEO, JP Mobile
Directorships: Altia Systems, SnapOne, Zoomingo
Pabhakar Reddy, Co-Founder/Managing Partner
Education: BS, Engineering, Andhra University; MBA, Booth School of Business
Background: Managing Director, ANSR Group; CIO, Risesmart.com
Directorships: GlobalOutlook, Motivity Labs

1286 NCT VENTURES
One Marconi Place
274 Marconi Boulevard
Suite 400
Columbus, OH 43215

e-mail: info@nctventures.com
web: www.nctventures.com

Mission Statement: NCT incvests in early-stage businesses, and they focus on helping entrepreneurs build lasting buisness.

Geographic Preference: Midwestern United States
Industry Group Preference: Marketing, Logistics, Research, Industrial Products, Economics
Portfolio Companies: 10X Engineered Materials, Aver, Azoti, Buzz Solutions, Data Inventions, DOmedia, Ethex, Exacter, FactGem, HAAS Alert, Healthy Roster, Heureka Software, Impact Economics, Imperva Bot Management, inTouch, iUNU, JadeTrack, LevelEleven, Mentored, Nikola Labs, Nimia, Olive, OnSeen, OROS, PopCom, PriorAuthNow, SHARE

Key Executives:
Rich Langdale, Managing Partner
Education: Ohio State University
Background: Co-Founder, Digital Storage
Bill Frank
Background: United States Army; Co-Founder, Prometheus Group; Co-Founder, MuniNET
Lindsay Karas, Partner
Education: BA, Political Science, Canisius College; JD, MBA, Ohio State University
Michael Butler, Partner
Education: BS, Accounting, Ohio State University; MBA, Ashland University; CPA
Background: President, Nationwide Fund Distributors; CFO, Ernst & Whinney

1287 NDI MEDICAL
22901 Millcreek Boulevard
Suite 110
Cleveland, OH 44122

Phone: 216-378-9106 Fax: 216-378-9116
e-mail: info@ndimedical.com
web: www.ndimedical.com

Mission Statement: NDI is a leading venture capital and commercialization firm that focuses on innovative neurodevice technologies to address significant unmet health conditions.

Founded: 2002
Industry Group Preference: Medical Devices
Portfolio Companies: Checkpoint Surgical, Deep Brain Innovations, MEDSTIM, SPR Therapeutics

Other Locations:
308 W Rosemary Street
Suite 308
Chapel Hill, NC 27516
Phone: 919-928-8005 Fax: 919-928-8006

601 Carlson Parkway
Suite 1050
Minneapolis, MN 55305
Phone: 612-770-0390 Fax: 216-378-9116

Key Executives:
Geoffrey B Thrope, Founder/CEO
Education: BS, Biomedical Engineering, Case Western Reserve University
Background: Vice President, New Business Development, NeuroControl Corporation

Venture Capital & Private Equity Firms / Domestic Firms

Leonard M Cosentino, Managing Director
Education: JD, Case Western Reserve University School of Law
Robert Strother, Vice Presiden of Engineering/CTO
Education: BEng, Electrical Engineering, Case Western Reserve University
Background: Research Instrumentation Associates

1288 NEEDHAM CAPITAL PARTNERS
250 Park Avenue
New York, NY 10177
Phone: 212-371-8300 Fax: 212-705-0411

Mission Statement: Provides private equity capital for the expansion of private and smaller public growth companies; liquidity for longer-term shareholders in private and smaller public growth companies; strategic acquisitions and management-led buyouts of growth companies.

Geographic Preference: United States
Fund Size: $1 billion
Founded: 1985
Average Investment: $2-$10 million
Investment Criteria: Mezzanine, LBO, Special Situations, Expansion, MBO, Recaps
Industry Group Preference: Computer Related, Consumer Services, Information Technology, Medical Devices, Software, Semiconductors, Retailing, Technology, Telecommunications, Clean Technology, Communications, Infrastructure, Financial Services
Portfolio Companies: Agile Software, Alacritech Inc., Athena Semiconductors, Atherotech, Auust Technology Corporation, Bay MicroSystems, Biocept, Blue Pumpkin Software/Witness Systems, Boxer Cross, Capital SLI Group, CenterRun, Ceon Corporation/Convergys Corporation, Ceradyne, Chip X Corp (Chip Express), Clarity Visual Systems/Planar Systems, Collectors Universe, College Enterprises/Blackboard, Color Kinetics, Conventor, CoWare, diCarta/Emptoris, Displaytech, ePartners, Fatbrain.com/Barnesandnoble.com, Favrille, Hot Rail/Conexant/Skyworks, Innovion, Kanisa/Knova, Lara Networks, Loadstar Sensors, Logic Vision, Nascentric, Neophotonics, Nextest/Teradyne, Obsidian/Applied Materials, Peregrine Semiconductor, Persistence Software, Pharsight, Rebar, Sensis, Silicon Metrics, SOFTEK Storage Solutions, Southwall Technologies, SpaceClaim, Stanford Microdevices/Sirenza, TestQuest, Trinity Convergence, ViewLogic Systems, Wind River Systems/Rapid Logic

Other Locations:
One Federal Street
Boston, MA 02110
Phone: 617-457-0910 Fax: 617-457-5777

3000 Sand Hill Road
Building 1
Menlo Park, CA 94025
Phone: 650-854-9111

535 Mission Street
San Francisco, CA 94105
Phone: 415-262-4860 Fax: 650-854-9853

180 North LaSalle
Suite 3700
Chicago, IL 60601
Phone: 312-981-0412 Fax: 312-377-0278

Key Executives:
Kevin McGrath, Principal/Head of Corporate & Venture Services
e-mail: corporateservices@needhamco.com
Education: BA, Southern Connecticut University
Background: JP Morgan; Merrill Lynch; Smith Barney; Banc of America Securities
Jack Iacovone, President/Heaf of Investment Banking
212-705-0297
e-mail: jiacovone@needhamco.com
Education: BS, Accounting, Pace University
Background: KPMG Peat Marwick LLP

1289 NEMO CAPITAL PARTNERS
28819 Franklin Road
Southfield, MI 48034
Phone: 248-213-9899
web: www.nemohealth.com

Mission Statement: NEMO Capital Partners is a private equity firm that targets companies in the medical technology sector.

Industry Group Preference: Healthcare, Healthcare Information Technology, Medical Technology
Portfolio Companies: Collaborative Practice Solutions, DirectEHR, SmartSheet10 Technology, TRAKnet
Key Executives:
Ali Safiedine DPM, Chief Executive Officer
Education: BA, Biology, Wayne State University; DPM, Barry University; MBA, University of Michigan
Background: President, Michigan Podiatric Medical Association
John Guiliana DPM, Executive Vice President
Education: BS, Pharmacy, St. John's University; MS, Healthcare Management, College of Saint Elizabeth; DPM, Temple University
Background: Owner, Foot Care Associates
Jeff Frederick DPM, Executive Vice President
Education: Michigan State University
Background: President, Michigan Podiatric Medical Association; American Academy of Podiatric Practice Management

1290 NEST VENTURES
3104 Camelback Road
Suite 144
Phoenix, AZ 85016-4595
Phone: 602-315-9550
e-mail: info@nestventures.com
web: www.nestventures.com

Mission Statement: A consulting boutique that offers customized solutions to its client companies. The company was formed with the purpose of advising both public and private companies focusing on capital formation, strategic alliances, mergers and acquisitions, and other operational issues.

Geographic Preference: International
Fund Size: $600 million
Founded: 1997
Average Investment: $7-$8 million
Minimum Investment: $5 million
Investment Criteria: Later Stage
Industry Group Preference: Biotechnology, Software, Communications, Digital Media & Marketing, Wireless Technologies, Energy
Key Executives:
Glenn Williamson, Managing Partner
Background: Founder/CEO, Canada Arizona Business Council; Director, Obsidian Strategies

1291 NEW ATLANTIC VENTURES
11911 Freedom Drive
Suite 1080
Reston, VA 20190
Phone: 703-563-4100 Fax: 703-563-4111
web: www.navfund.com

Mission Statement: To make seed and early-stage investments in businesses targeting high-growth emerging mass markets.

Fund Size: $117 million
Founded: 2006
Average Investment: $500,000 - $5 million
Investment Criteria: Seed-Stage, Early-Stage

Venture Capital & Private Equity Firms / Domestic Firms

Industry Group Preference: Mobile, New Media, Online Services, Technology, SaaS, Advertising, Software, Consumer, Entertainment, E-Commerce & Manufacturing
Portfolio Companies: AppTap, Bambecco, BlockScore, Brand Yourself, CivicScience, CrashMob, Crossboard Mobil, EveryScape, ExecOnline, HealthWarehouse.com, Invincea, Moda Operandi, Nantero, PokitDok, PulsePoint, Qliance, Quad Learning, Scoutmob, Solve Media, Spotflux, Tap 'n Tap, Truveris, TVU Networks, YieldBot, Zady, Zerve

Other Locations:
One Mifflin Place
Suite 400
Cambridge, MA 02138

Key Executives:
John Backus, Founder/Managing Partner
703-563-4101
e-mail: john@navfund.com
Education: BA, Economics, MBA, Stanford University
Background: President & CEO, InteliData Technologies
Directorships: AppTap, Invincea, Spotflux, PokitDok
Thanasis Delistathis, Founder/Managing Partner
703-563-4106
e-mail: thanasis@navfund.com
Education: BSE, Electrical Engineering, Princeton University; BCert, Public Policy, Princeton University Woodrow Wilson School; MBA, Harvard Business School
Background: Investment Banking, Thermo Electron Corp.; McKinsey & Co.
Todd Hixon, Founder/Managing Partner/Chief Financial Officer
617-758-4213
e-mail: todd@navfund.com
Education: BA, Princeton University; MBA, Harvard Business School
Background: Managing Partner, DFJ New England Fund; SVP, The Boston Consulting Group
Directorships: Qliance, CivicScience, Tap-n-Tap, EveryScape
Scott Johnson, Founder/Managing Partner
617-758-4234
e-mail: scott@navfund.com
Education: BS, Operations Research, Cornell University; MBA, MIT Sloan School of Management
Background: DFJ New England; East Coast Partner, Cambridge Technology Capital Fund
Directorships: Fashion Playtes, Solve Media, Truveris, Yieldbot, Spotflux

1292 NEW CAPITAL FUND
2100 Freedom Road
Suite A
Little Chute, WI 54140

web: www.newcapitalfund.com

Mission Statement: Focused on making early-stage life and material science, information technology and growth-stage niche/advanced manufacturing investments.

Geographic Preference: Wisconsin
Fund Size: $45 million
Founded: 2006
Average Investment: $500,000 to $1.5 million
Minimum Investment: $500,000
Investment Criteria: Early-Stage, Growth Stage
Industry Group Preference: Niche Manufacturing, Information Technology, Life Sciences
Portfolio Companies: Aurizon Ultrasonics, Magma Flooring, Phoenix Nuclear Labs, Ro-Flow Compressors, Simply Incredible Foods, Forte Research Systems, Hopster, Huterra, Optimine, TrafficCast International, Invenra, Rapid Diagnostek, Renovar, Silatronix, Swallow Solutions, Xolve

Key Executives:
Robert DeBruin, Managing Director
e-mail: bob.debruin@newcapitalfund.com
Education: BBA, Accounting, University of Wisconsin, Madison
Background: President, Schenck Corporate Finance Group; Arthur Young & Co.
Directorships: NEW Capital Fund, Master Mold, National Tissue Company, Werner Electric
Charlie Goff, Managing Director
e-mail: charlie@newcapitalfund.com
Education: Math & Computer Science, University of Wisconsin, Oshkosh; MBA, University of Wisconsin, Madison
Background: Staff Accountant, Arthur Anderson LLP; Founder, Forward Enterprises
Directorships: Azco, Keller, Inc., HuTerra, De Pere, Rapid Diagnostek, Xolve, Renovar, Aurizon Ultrasonics
David Gitter, Managing Director
e-mail: dave.gitter@newcapitalfund.com
Education: BBA, MBA, University of Wisconsin, Oshkosh
Background: M&I Marshal & Isley Corporation
Directorships: Azco, Network Health Plan, Valley Packaging, Fox Valley Residency Clinic, Community Real Estate, Personal Property Foundation
Steve Predayna, Managing Director
e-mail: steve.predayna@newcapitalfund.com
Education: BBA, Accounting, University of Wisconsin, Oshkosh
Background: Vice President, Schenck Corporate Finance Group; Great Northern Corporation

1293 NEW CAPITAL PARTNERS
2101 Highland Avenue South
Suite 700
Birmingham, AL 35205

web: www.newcapitalpartners.com

Mission Statement: To acquire and/or partner with businesses and management teams who are focused on building sustainable businesses of exceptional value.

Geographic Preference: Texas, Southeastern United States
Fund Size: $225 million
Founded: 2001
Investment Criteria: Buyouts, Acquisitions, Recapitalizations, Growth Equity
Industry Group Preference: Healthcare Services, Healthcare Information Technology, Financial Services, Insurance, Business Products & Services
Portfolio Companies: ACES Quality Management, Care Services LLC, Collect Rx, ControlCase, Dotcom Therapy, GeoVera Insurance, Healthfuse, Medsurant Health, P&R Dental Strategies, Precision, Sequence Health, Sprout, Telehealth Solutions, Volly

Other Locations:
2101 Cedar Springs Road
Suite 1200
Dallas, TX 75201
Phone: 214-871-5408 **Fax:** 214-871-5401

Key Executives:
Jim Little, Managing Partner & Founder
Education: BS, Engineering, Auburn University
Directorships: Cogent Partners, Safe Harbour Underwriters
James Outland, Managing Partner
Education: BA, Political Science, BFA, Advertising, Southern Methodist University
Background: Officer, UnitedHealth Group
Directorships: Repay Holdings, MDnet Solutions, Medsurant Holdings, Teladoc Medical Services
Adam Cranford, Managing Director
Education: BS/MS, Georgia Institute of Technology; MBA, Booth School of Business, University of Chicago
Background: Executive Group Analyst, Dollar General Corporation
Directorships: Collect Rx; Medsurant Holdings; P&R

Dental; Volly; ACES Quality Management; Precision; Healthfuse

Key Executives:
John Whorf, Managing Director
781-799-9474
Education: BS, Massachusetts Maritime Academy; MBA, FW Olin Graduate School of Business, Babson College

1295 NEW ENGLAND BUSINESS EXCHANGE
Wellesley, MA 02481

Phone: 781-801-4429
e-mail: jwhorf@nebex.com
web: www.nebex.com

Mission Statement: Focus on building strong relationships, paying attention to detail, recognizing value, delivering excellent service, and negotiating from a position of strength.

Founded: 1988
Average Investment: $500,000
Minimum Investment: $100,000
Investment Criteria: Open
Portfolio Companies: Accumeter Labs, Adams Brush Manufacturing, Aerovox, AET, American Candy, American Felt & Filter, Avista, BancBoston Capital, BAI Global, CLT Research, CML Group, Commonwealth Sprague, Contact East, Creative Solutions Group, General Electric, Geo Mcquesten, Goldner Hawn, Guideline Research, Harmony Toy, Infrasoft, Interlacken Capital, Jilcraft, Judson Technologies, The Langley Corporation, Language Management, International, The Leather Shop, Merlin Metalworks, Missouri Metals, New England Envelope, New England Growth Fund, Norsun Foods, Opticon, Pentzer Corporation, Perkin Elmer, Rad Locks, Retail Associated Mgt., Safeguard America, Standex International, The Stanley Works, Store Fixtures Group, Syon, Tech Pak, TEK Supply, Teradyne, Tra-con, Tripifoods, Westcoast Entertainment, Whistler, Williams Healthcare, Wilton Corporation, Worcester Brush, Xtra-Vision PLC, Videosmith, Voltarc

1296 NEW ENGLAND CAPITAL PARTNERS
One Gateway Center
Suite 405
Newton, MA 02458

Phone: 617-964-7300 **Fax:** 617-964-7301
web: www.necapitalpartners.com

Mission Statement: A private equity investment firm focused on acquiring lower middle-market operating companies. NECP is a successor to and affiliate of New England Capital Management.

Geographic Preference: Northeastern United States
Founded: 1991
Average Investment: $10 - 30 million
Minimum Investment: $2 million
Industry Group Preference: Manufacturing, Distribution, Business Products & Services, Consumer Products

Key Executives:
Aevin M McCafferty, Chairman
e-mail: kevin@necapitalpartners.com
Education: AB, Harvard College; MBA, University of Chicago
Background: General Partner, Madison Dearborn Partners; Vice President, First Chicago Venture Capital; Partner, Catalyst Health; Partner, Technology Partners
Robert D Winneg, President
e-mail: rwinneg@necapitalpartners.com
Education: BA, Economics, Tufts University; MBA, Tuck School of Business Administration, Dartmouth College
Background: Principal Investor, BancBoston Capital
Directorships: Wild Planet
Brendan McCafferty, Principal
e-mail: bmccafferty@necapitalpartners.com
Education: AB, Harvard University
Background: President, Dustless Floor Sanding

1297 NEW ENTERPRISE ASSOCIATES
1954 Greenspring Drive
Suite 600
Timonium, MD 21093

Phone: 410-842-4000 **Fax:** 410-842-4100
web: www.nea.com

Mission Statement: A leading venture capital firm investing in information technology, energy technology and healthcare companies. Practicing classic venture capital for over 25 years, NEA focuses on early stage investments, playing an active role in assisting management to build companies of lasting value. With $6 billion under management, NEA's experienced management team has invested in over 500 companies, of which more than 135 have gone public and more than 150 have been acquired. NEA has offices in across the U.S.

Geographic Preference: Global
Fund Size: $18 billion
Average Investment: $10 million
Minimum Investment: $200,000
Investment Criteria: All Stages
Industry Group Preference: Electronics, Consumer Technology, Enterprise Mobility, Virtualization, Technology-Enabled Services, SaaS, Cloud Computing, Biopharmaceuticals, Healthcare Devices, Healthcare Services
Portfolio Companies: 23andMe, 3-V Biosciences, 42Floors, 51offer, Acquia, Adaptimmune, Addex Therapeutics, Aera, Aerohive Networks, Aerospike, Aetion, Affirmed N.V., Air Works, Akari Therapeutics, Akouos, Alien Technology Corp., Alimera Sciences, Allakos, American Patholoy Partners, Amicus Therapeutics, Annexon, Antenna Software, Appian, AppSheet, Apropose, Aquabyte, Aquantia, Ardelyx, AstroWatt, Aurinia Pharmaceuticals, Automation Anywhere, Availink, AVEO Oncology, Baihe Holding Corp., Banjo, Barkly, BedRocket Media, Belly, Benchprep, BetterDoctor, Bitglass, Blend, Blispay, BlockCypher, Bloom Energy, BloomReach, Blue Jeans Network, BlueShift, Boku, BoxC, Branch Metrics, Branless, Bridge International Academies, Bright Health, Broadly, Broadview Network Holdings, Built Robotics, Burrow, Buzzfeed, Bytedance, Canopy, Cape, Cardionomic, Cardioxyl Pharmaceuticals, CareZone, Carticept Medical, Cascadian Therapeutics, Casper, Catalog, Catalytic, Cathay Industrial Biotech Ltd., CenterBeam, Centrexion Therapeutics, Cerecor Inc., Champions Oncology, Chelsio Communications, China Gtel Limited, Choosy, ChromaCode, Cista, ClearMetal, ClearMotion, Cleave Bioscience, Clementia, CloudFare, Clovis Oncology, Code42, CoEdition, Cohere Technologies, Collective Health, Conviva, Coursera, CrowdMed, CTi Biopharma, Cuponation, Curalate, Curisium, CVRx, Cydan, Dandelion, Databricks, DataRobot, Datavisor, Datrium, Dermira, Desire2Learn, Desktop Metal, Didi Chuxing, Docent Health, DOTS Technology Corp,

Other Locations:
5425 Wisconsin Avenue
Suite 800
Chevy Chase, MD 20815
Phone: 301-272-2300 **Fax:** 301-272-1700

2855 Sand Hill Road
Menlo Park, CA 94025
Phone: 650-854-9499 **Fax:** 650-854-1854

104 5th Avenue
19th Floor
New York, NY 10001
Phone: 646-677-2777

2 South Park Street
2nd Floor

Venture Capital & Private Equity Firms / Domestic Firms

San Francisco, CA 94107
Phone: 415-653-3850 **Fax:** 415-495-4506

700 Technology Square
3rd Floor
Cambridge, MA 02139

Key Executives:
Peter Barris, Chairman
Education: MBA, Dartmouth College; BSEE, Northwestern University
Background: President/COO, LEGENT; Senior VP/General Manager, UCCEL; VP/General Manger, GE
Forest Baskett, General Partner
Education: BA, Mathematics, Rice University; PhD, Computer Science, University of Texas, Austin
Background: Senior Vice President of R&D, Silicon Graphics; Founder, Western Research Laboratory; Professor of Computer Science & Electrical Engineering, Stanford University
Tony Florence, General Partner
Education: AB & MBA, Economics, Dartmouth College
Background: Managing Director, Morgan Stanley
Mohamad Makhzoumi, General Partner
Education: BS, International Relations, University of Pennsylvania
Background: UBS Investment Bank; Associate, Summitt Partners
Directorships: Aetion, American Pathology Partners, Bright Health, Collective Health, Curisium, Docent Healths, Nuvolo, Pager, Paladina Health, Radiology Partners, SCI Solutions, etc.
Josh Makower, General Partner
Education: BS, Mechanical Engineering, MIT; MBA, Columbia University; MD, NYU School of Medicine
Background: ExploraMed
Scott Sandell, Managing General Partner
Education: MBA, Stanford University; AB, Engineering Sciences, Dartmouth College
Background: Boston Consulting Group; C-ATS Software; Microsoft
Directorships: Bloom Energy. Branch Metrics, CareZone, Cloudflare, Coursera, Datrium, Enigma, Hello Alfred, One Concern, Qadium, Robinhood, Transfix, UnifyID
Peter Sonsini, General Partner
Education: BA, Political Economy, University of California, Berkeley; MBA, Kellogg School of Management, Northwestern University
Background: VMware; Mirapoint; Hewlett-Packard; Montgomery Securities
Directorships: Conviva, Databricks, GuideSpark, Instabase, Lattice Engines, MapR Technologies, Matroid, Nefeli, Nginx, Splashtop, Yubico

1298 NEW LEAF VENTURE PARTNERS
420 Lexington Avenue
Suite 408
New York, NY 10170

Phone: 646-871-6400 **Fax:** 646-871-6450
e-mail: info@nlvpartners.com
web: www.nlvpartners.com

Mission Statement: A leading healthcare technology investor, our goal is to build strong companies by supporting exceptional teams in the development of clinically important and commercially attractive products.

Fund Size: $1.3 billion
Founded: 2005
Industry Group Preference: Biopharmaceuticals, Medical Devices, Diagnostics
Portfolio Companies: Afferent Pharmaceuticals, Calchan Holdings, Calithera Biosciences, Chimerix, Concert Pharmaceuticals, Convergence Pharmaceuticals, Intarcia Therapeutics, Karos Pharmaceuticals, Karus Therapeutics, MEI Pharma, Principia Biopharma, Relypsa, Sopherion Therapeutics, Tioga Pharmaceuticals, VaxInnate, Versartis, Awarepoint, Irhythm Technnologies, Kit Check, QPID Health, Tigertext, Treato, Truveris, Altura Medical, Cardiokinetix, Direct Flow, Illuminoss Medical, Intrinsic Therapeutics, Neuronetics, Reshape Medical, Spine Wave, Spiracur, Advanced Cell Diagnostics, Caredx, Labcyte, Oxord Immunotec

Other Locations:
1200 Park Place
Suite 300
San Mateo, CA 94403
Phone: 650-234-2700 **Fax:** 650-234-2704

Ron Hunt, Managing Director
646-871-6400
e-mail: ron@nlvpartners.com
Education: BS, Cornell University; MBA, Wharton School
Background: Sprout Group; Consultant, Coopers & Lybrand Consulting; Johnson & Johnson; SmithKline Beecham Pharmaceuticals
Directorships: Durata Therapeutics, Spine Wave, IlluminOss Medical, Relypsa
Vijay Lathi, Managing Director
650-234-2700
e-mail: vijay@nlvpartners.com
Education: BS, Chemical Engineering, MIT; MS, Chemical Engineering, Stanford University
Background: Sprout Group; Analyst, Healthcare Venture Capital Group, Robertson Stephens & Co.; Cornerstone Research
Directorships: Expression Diagnostics, iRhythm Technologies, Kit Check, Oxford Immunotec, TigerText
James Niedel, Managing Partner
646-871-6400
e-mail: jim@nlvpartners.com
Education: MD, PhD, Biochemistry, University of Miami; Fellow, Royal College of Physicians
Background: Venture Parter, Sprout Group; Chief Science & Technology Officer, GlaxoSmithKline; Board Member, Glaxo Wellcome plc; Professor of Medicine & Chief of the division of Clinical Pharmacology, Duke Medical School
Directorships: Intarcia Therapeutics, Tioga Pharmaceuticals, Chimerix
Rebecca Luse, Principal
e-mail: rebecca@nlvpartners.com
Education: BS, Biochemistry & Mathematics, Indiana University
Background: Research Senior Associate, Biotechnology, Jefferies; Research Associate, Specialty Pharmaceuticals, Piper Jaffray; Analyst, Bay City Capital; Healthcare Investment Banking Analyst, Bank of America Securities
Craig Slutzkin, Chief Operating Officer/Chief Financial Officer
e-mail: craig@nlvpartners.com
Education: BA, Accounting, Queens College; MBA, Columbia Business School
Background: CFO, Sprout Group; Senior Manager, Ernst & Young

1299 NEW MARKETS VENTURE PARTNERS
8161 Maple Lawn Blvd
Suite 350
Fulton, MD 20759

Phone: 301-362-5511 **Fax:** 301-362-5517
web: www.newmarketsvp.com

Mission Statement: New Markets Venture Partners is a leading early stage venture capital firm that invests in and actively assists innovative information technology, education and healthcare companies.

Geographic Preference: Mid-Atlantic United States
Investment Criteria: Early-Stage
Industry Group Preference: Information Technology, Education, Healthcare

Venture Capital & Private Equity Firms / Domestic Firms

Portfolio Companies: American Honors, Authntk, BetterLesson, BioSet, Calvert Education Services, Civitas Learning, CSA Medical, eCoast Marketing, Fishtree, Graduation Alliance, Innovative Biosensors, K2 Intelligence, Kickboard, Kroll BondRatings, Mashable, MediaSolv, Orchestro, Overture Technologies, PresenceLearning, Questar Assesment, Regent, Snappcloud, Starfish Retention Solutions, StraighterLine, Think Through Learning, Three Ring, Videology, Workspace.com

Key Executives:
  Robb Doub, General Partner
  e-mail: rdoub@newmarketsvp.com
  Education: University of Vermont; MBA, Georgetown University
  Background: Managing Director, Small Enterprise Assistance Funds; Associate, Calvert Group
  Directorships: eCoast Sales Solutions, PresenceLearning
  Mark Grovic, General Partner
  e-mail: mgrovic@newmarketsvp.com
  Education: University of California, Berkeley; JD, Georgetown University
  Background: Portfolio Manager, Small Enterprise Assistance Funds; Director, Baltic Small Equity Fund; Co-Founder & Principal, Templeton Emerging Europe Fund; Principal, Templeton Direct Advisors; Portfolio Manager, Calvert Group
  Directorships: Graduation Alliance, Innovation Biosensors, Lightningcast, Moodlerooms, Workspace.com
  Donald Spero, Founding Partner
  e-mail: dspero@newmarketsvp.com
  Education: Cornell University; PhD, Physics, Columbia University
  Background: Director, Dingman Center for Entrepreneurship; Founder, Spero Quality Strategies; Founder, President & CEO, Fusion Systems Corporation

1300 NEW MEXICO COMMUNITY CAPITAL
801 University Blvd SE
Suite 102
Albuquerque, NM 87106

Phone: 505-924-2820 Fax: 505-213-0333
Toll-Free: 866-222-1552
e-mail: info@nmccap.org
web: nmccap.org

Mission Statement: Through targeted financial investments and entrepreneurial support, NMCC produces two primary results: positive social returns as the direct consequence of new job opportunities and a well-trained, well-compensated workforce in the local community; along with solid financial returns for our investors.

Geographic Preference: New Mexico
Fund Size: $14.65 million
Founded: 2004
Investment Criteria: At least 5 employees; in operation for more than 2 years; at least $500,000 in sales; pattern of sustained revenue growth; cash flow postive for at least one year; strong management team
Industry Group Preference: Manufacturing, Consumer Products, Energy, Environment, Food & Beverage, Tourism, Consumer Services, Business Products & Services
Portfolio Companies: Aspen Avionics, IntelliCyt, American Clay, Wellkeeper, Armed Response Team, MIOX Corporation, Aero Mechanical Industries, TruTouch Technologies

Key Executives:
  Elizabeth Gamboa, Executive Director
  e-mail: liz@nmccap.org
  Education: BS, San Francisco State University; MBA, Presidio Graduate School
  Background: Morgan Stanley; Project Manager, Quokka Sports
  J Michael Schafer, Managing Director
  e-mail: michael@nmccap.com
  Education: BS, Davidson College; MBA, University of Michigan
  Background: General Partner & Principal, Tullis-Dickerson & Company; Founder & President, Ventures UNC

1301 NEW MOUNTAIN CAPITAL
787 7th Avenue
49th Floor
New York, NY 10019

Phone: 212-720-0300 Fax: 212-582-2277
web: www.newmountaincapital.com

Mission Statement: To acquire the highest quality leaders in key growth industries and seek companies which are characterized by: market leadership in sustainable growth niches; high barriers to competitive entry, as demonstrated by high operating margins; strong 'downside' protection in all reasonable worst-case scenarios; and the opportunity for extraordinary returns due to rapid growth or to special factors existing at the time of investment.

Fund Size: $5.1 billion
Founded: 2000
Average Investment: $100 - $500 million
Minimum Investment: $50 million
Investment Criteria: Mid-Market with enterprise value of $100-500 million, LBO, Buildups, Recapitalizations, MBO, Growth Equity Transactions
Industry Group Preference: Education, Communications, Media, Healthcare, Business to Business, Power Technologies, Capital Goods, Consumer Products, Software, Logistics, Business Products & Services, Financial Services, Infrastructure, Energy
Portfolio Companies: Strayer Education, Surgis, Overland Solutions, Apptis Holdings, National Medical Health Card Systems, MailSouth, Validus Holdings, Connextions, Paris Re Holdings, Ikaria, Inmar, Deltek, Valet Waste, Intermarine, EverBank Financial Corporation, Camber, JDA Software Group, Avantor Performance Materials Holdings, Stroz Friedberg, NuSil Technology, IRI, SNL Financial, AmWINS Group, ABB Optical Group, Western Dentral, ACA Compliance Group, Medical Specialties Distributors, Alexander Mann Solutions, Bellerophone Therapeutics

Key Executives:
  Steven B Klinsky, Founder & CEO
  Education: BA Economics, University of Michigan; MBA, Harvard Business School; JD with Honors, Harvard Law School
  Background: Co-Founder LBO Group, Goldman, Sachs & Co; Associate Partner/General Partner, Forstmann Little & Co
  Vignesh M. Aier, Managing Director
  Education: BA, Economics-Mathematics, Columbia University
  Background: McKinsey & Company; Value Equities Group, OppenheimerFunds Inc.
  Directorships: Alteon Health; Intermarine; Western Dental; Signify Health; Overland Solutions
  Andrew D. Barous, Managing Director
  Education: BA, Economics, Hamilton College
  Matthew M. Bennett, Managing Director
  Education: AB, Political Science, Princeton University; JD, Villanova University School of Law
  Background: CEO, CIOX Health; EVP, Global Medical Operations; Chief Legal Officer, Ikaria Inc.; EVP/CAO/Chief Business Officer, VIASYS Healthcare Inc.; Litigator, Stradley Ronon Stevens & Young
  Directorships: CIOX Health; Gelest; Cytel; Sparta Systems; Bellerophon Therapeutics
  Prasad Chintamaneni, Managing Director
  Background: Oresident, Global Industries; Consultant, Cognizant
  David C. Coquillette, Managing Director
  Education: BA, DePauw University; MBA, Wharton School, University of Pennsylvania

467

Venture Capital & Private Equity Firms / Domestic Firms

Background: Oak Hill Advisors; Goldman Sachs; Lehman Brothers
Directorships: Goodwill Industries of Greater New York; Goodwill Industries of New Jersey
Robert A. Hamwee, Managing Director
Education: BBA, Finance & Accounting, University of Michigan
Background: President, GSC Group; Greenwich Street Capital Partners; The Blackstone Group
Directorships: Purina Mills; Envirosource; Viasystems
Laura C. Holson, Managing Director & Head of Capital Markets
Education: BS, Economics, Wharton School, University of Pennsylvania
Background: Healthcare Investment Banking, Morgan Stanley
Teddy Kaplan, Managing Director
Education: BS, McIntire School of Commerce, University of Virginia; MBA, Columbia Business School
Background: Managing Director, Angelo Gordon & Co.; W.P. Carey Inc.; Meyer Duffy & Associates; Brown Brothers Harriman
Lewis S. Klessel, Managing Director
Education: BS, Wharton School, University of Pennsylvania; MBA, Harvard Business School
Background: Bain Capital; Home Depot; McKinsey & Company; Ernst & Young
Matthew J. Lori, Managing Director
Education: BS, University of Windsor; MBA, JL Kellogg School of Management, Northwestern University
Background: Managing Director, CCMP Capital Advisors
John R. Kline, Managing Director
Education: MS, Mechanical Engineering, Polytechnic Institute of New York; PhD, University of Illinois, Urbana-Champaign; MBA, University of Chicago
Background: JP Morgan Partners; Managing Director, CCMP Capital Advisors; McKinsey & Company; AT Kearney
Peter N. Masucci, Managing Director
Education: BA, University of Iowa; MBA, Stanford Grad. School of Business
Background: M&A Analyst, Goldman Sachs
Directorships: Deltek; InComm Holdings; Inmar; Valet Waste
Matthew S. Holt, Managing Director & Deputy Head of Private Equity
Education: AB, English & American Literature, Harvard College
Background: M&A Group, Lehman Brothers
Directorships: Avantor Performance Materials Holdings, Ikaria Holdings, NuSil Technology
Andre V. Moura, Managing Director
Education: AB, Computer Science, Harvard College; MBA, Harvard Business School
Background: ABC Group, Goldman Sachs & Co.
Directorships: Aceto; Alteon Health; Avantor; Bellerophon; Gelest; Sparta Systems; Topixs Pharmaceuticals; ACA Compliance Group; Medical Specialties Distributors; NuSil
Robert W. Mulcare, Managing Director
Education: AB, Woodrow Wilson School, Princeton University; MA, Economics, National University of Ireland
Background: McKinsey & Company
Directorships: OneDigital; MAG Aerospace; ACA Compliance Group; AmWINS Group; Alight Solutions
Albert A. Notini, Managing Director
Education: AB, Boston College; MA, Boston University
Background: President & Chief Operating Officer, Sonus Network Inc.; CFO, Manufacturers' Services Ltd.; Senior Partner, Hale and Door LLP; Law Clerk to the Chief Justice of the Massachusetts Supreme Judical Court
Jack W. Qian, Managing Director
Education: BA, Economics & Mathematics, Yale University

Background: Global Technology Group, Morgan Stanley
Directorships: Ciox Health; Convey Health; Quian; IRI; JDA Software; Sparta Systems; DRB Systems; Revint Solutions

1302 NEW RHEIN HEALTHCARE INVESTORS
100 n 18th street
Two Logan Square, Suite 1930
Philidelphia, PA 19103

Phone: 215-419-7830
web: newrhein.com

Mission Statement: New Rhein is a venture capital fund manager focused on healthcare therapeutics and medical devices. Their investment strategies focus on proven molecules used in new ways.

Geographic Preference: Global
Average Investment: $10-30 Million
Investment Criteria: Unmet Medical Need; Proof of Scientific Concept; Health-Economic Value; Clear Clinical and Regulatory Plan; IP/Market Exclusivity
Other Locations:
Blokhuisstraat 47J
B-2800
Mechelen
Belgium
Phone: 32 15-48-08-00

Birch House, Fairfield Avenue
Staines upon Thames
Middlesex TW18 4AB
England
Phone: 44 1279-755-775

Key Executives:
Ivan Gergel, Founder/Managing Partner
Education: MD, University of London
Background: Chief Medical Officer, Nektar Therapeutics Inc.; EVP/Chief Scientific Officer, Endo Health Solutions; President, Forest Research Institute
Greg Parekh, Founder/Managing Partner
Education: PhD, Northwestern University
Background: CEO, Biocartis NV
Subhanu Saxena, Managing Partner
Education: MBA, INSEAD; MA, Oxford University
Background: Managing Director, Cipla; CEO, Novartis UK

1303 NEW SCIENCE VENTURES
299 Park Avenue
41st Floor
New York, NY 10171

Phone: 212-688-5100 Fax: 212-308-9196
e-mail: info@newscienceventures.com
web: www.newscienceventures.com

Mission Statement: New Science Ventures, LLC (NSV) is a New York-based venture capital firm which invests in companies using novel scientific approaches in the Life Sciences sector and the Information Technology sector.

Geographic Preference: United States, Europe, India, China
Fund Size: $300 million
Founded: 2004
Investment Criteria: Early-Stage, Later-Stage
Industry Group Preference: Information Technology, Life Sciences, Biotechnology, Pharmaceuticals, Medical Devices, Therapeutics
Portfolio Companies: Achronix, Alexar Therapeutics, Ario Pharma, BioScale, Caringo, CEGX, Celleration, Dali Wireless, Dezima Pharma, DirectedSensing, Ferric Semiconductor, GTxcel, iCAD, Juventas Therapeutics, Kateeva, Mangstor, Oxyrane, PerceptiMed, Resolve Therapeutics, RFArrays, Seahorse Bioscience, Silicon Space Technology, SoliCore, Svelte, Symphogen, Therox, Tigertext, Trellis Bioscience, Vaultive

Venture Capital & Private Equity Firms / Domestic Firms

Key Executives:
   Somu Subramaniam, Managing Partner
   212-661-3497
   e-mail: somu@newscienceventures.com
   Education: BTech, Indian Institute of Technology; MBA, Harvard Business School
   Background: Director, McKinsey & Company
   Directorships: Achronix Semiconductor, Silicon Space Technology, Dali Wireless, Oxyrane, Juventas Therapeutics, Resolve Therapeutics, Dexima Pharma, Vaultive, TigerText, iCAD
   Tom Lavin, Partner
   212-661-3498
   e-mail: tom@newscienceventures.com
   Education: AB, Government, Wesleyan University; MBA, Harvard Business School
   Background: Head, Real Estate Investment Banking, First Boston, Smith Barney; Head, Commercial Mortgage Lending, MetLife
   Directorships: Achronix Semiconductor, Celleration, RF Arrays Systems
   Andrew Abrams, Partner
   e-mail: andrew@newscienceventures.com
   Education: BA/MA/MS, Natural Sciences & Biochemistry, University of Cambridge; MBA, Harvard Business School
   Background: Associate, JP Morgan
   Directorships: Paradigm Diagnostics
   Brenda Marex, Chief Financial Officer
   e-mail: brenda@newscienceventures.com
   Education: BA, Accounting/Information Systems, Queens College; CPA
   Background: Controller, Cerberus Capital; Controller/VP, Citigroup Alternative Investments

1304 NEW VANTAGE GROUP
1616 Anderson Road
McLean, VA 22102

Phone: 703-255-4930
web: www.newvantagegroup.com

Mission Statement: Managers of five angel funds and angel groups for early-stage venture funds for active investors.

Geographic Preference: District of Columbia, East Coast
Founded: 1997
Average Investment: $ 500,000-1 million
Minimum Investment: $500,000
Investment Criteria: Seed, Early Stage
Industry Group Preference: All Sectors Considered

Key Executives:
   John May, Founder/Managing Partner
   e-mail: john@newvantagegroup.com
   Education: BA, Earlham College; MPA, Maxwell School, Syracuse University
   Background: Co-Founder, Investors' Circle; Co-Founder/Executive Director, Private Investors Network; General Partner, Calvert Social Venture Partners; Author
   Jeremy Bauman, Associate
   e-mail: mba@newvantagegroup.com
   Education: BA, Kenyon College; International MBA, University of South Carolina

1305 NEW VENTURE PARTNERS
PO Box 881
New Providence, NJ 07974

Phone: 908-464-0900 Fax: 908-655-9142
web: www.nvpllc.com

Mission Statement: Establishes close, long-term relationships with global technology corporations to commercialize innovations through spin-out ventures.

Geographic Preference: North America, Asia
Founded: 1997
Investment Criteria: Spin-Outs
Industry Group Preference: Networking, Communications, Software, Semiconductors, Hardware, Clean Technology, Nanotechnology, Storage, Bioinformatics
Portfolio Companies: @Roads, AetherPal, Airclic, Alverix, Andrew, AraLight, Azure Solutions, BLiNQ Networks, brisbane Materials, Celiant, CrossFiber, DAFCA, Elemedia, Everspin Technologies, Flarion, GainSpan, GeoVideo Networks, GlobalCast, iBiquity Digital, iCRTec, Intelleflex, Internet Photonics, ISPsoft, Liquavista, Lucent Digital Video, Lumeta, Maps on Us, Microwave Photonics, Neohapsis, NextG Networks, Novinda, NVMdurance, Own Products, Procelerate Technologies, PsyTechnics, Real Time Content, SavaJe Technologies, ShopWell, Silicon Hive, SiPort, Subex, SyChip, Valent, Vasona Networks, Vidus, VPI Systems

Key Executives:
   Andrew Garman, Managing Partner
   Education: AB, Engineering & Applied Physics, Harvard College; MS, Mechanical Engineering, Stanford University; MBA, Stanford University
   Background: Vice President, Lucent Technologies; Managing Director, BT Ventures; Vice President, Xerox New Enterprise Group
   Stephen Socolof, Managing Partner
   Education: BA, Economics, BS, Mathematical Sciences, Stanford University; MBA, Amos Tuck School, Dartmouth College
   Background: Lucent Technologies; Booz Allen & Hamilton
   Directorships: Center for the Study of Private Equity at the Tuck School
   Tom Uhlman, Managing Partner
   Education: BA, Political Science, University of Rochester; PhD, Political Science, University of North Carolina, Chapel Hill; Masters Degree, Stanford University School of Business
   Background: President, Lucent Technologies New Venture Group; AT&T; Director, Corporate Development, Hewlett-Packard
   Directorships: iBiquity Digital, Lumeta, AetherPal
   Marc Rappoport, Chief Financial Officer/Partner
   Education: BS, Economics, New York University; MBA, Columbia Business School
   Background: CFO/General Partner, Lucent Venture Partners

1306 NEW YORK ANGELS
1216 Broadway
2nd Floor
New York, NY 10001

web: www.newyorkangels.com

Mission Statement: An independent consortium of individual accredited angel investors. Incorporated by the former members of NYNMA Angel Investor Program to provide opportunities for its members to obtain outstanding financial returns by investing in early-stage technology and new media companies in the New York city area and accelerating them to market leadership.

Founded: 1997
Average Investment: $250,000 - $750,000
Minimum Investment: $250,000
Investment Criteria: Seed, Early Stage
Industry Group Preference: Technology, Media
Portfolio Companies: Adapt Media, SignStorey, Linkstorm, MediaTile, Good Health Advertising, uKnow, Sociocast, C3 Metrics, Ministore, Crowdly, Rockerbox, Snakblox, eJammingAudiiO, Synergy Beverages, DesignBuddy, Cookstr, Pinterest, AudioVroom, 1000 Museums, Brain Sentry, Sportsvite, Happy Toy Machine, Movio Network, Zenplaya, Antengo, Tripshare, 72Lux.com, Mouth, HeTexted, AllTheRooms, Concert Window, Librify, Slyce, Nito, PhotoKharma, Authorea, School Loop, Aristotle Circle, Timbuktu, CourseHorse, Citelighter, Metaphor, Zero G, Koolspan, GridPlex Networks, Email Data Source, Anvato,

Venture Capital & Private Equity Firms / Domestic Firms

Magnify.net, TalkShoe, innRoad, Pond5, MPoint, StandoutJobs, Viddler, FastTrac, Live Look, SalesconX, Localytics, Altruik, PublicStuff, Greenhouse, Field Lens, Carnegie Speech, WhiteSource, Critical Mention, SureDone, Dash, CrowdTangle, Seamless Docs, iSpeech, Meddle, StoryVine, SocialSign.in, CreativeWorx, Minds'Eye, Better Mobile Security, Keaton Row, Style for Hire, Tommy John, The RunThrough, Beauty Booke, Payoneer, Recognia, Transactis, EasyCopay, Payperks, PEX Card, Moven, Vestorly, Kasisto, DIGIT Wireless, Chromis Fiberoptics, Ambient, Clear Align, Senscient, SocialBicycles, goTenna, Vital Herd, Canary, ImagineAir, BioScale, UROValve, CogRx

Key Executives:
David S Rose, Founder
Education: BA, Yale University; MBA, Finance, Columbia University
Background: Chairman/CEO, Angelsoft; Co-Founder/Chairman, The Computer Classroom; Rose Associates
Brian Cohen, Chairman Emeritus
Education: BS, Biology & Speech Communications, Syracuse University; MS, Science Communications, Boston University School of Public Communications
Background: Founder, iFluence; Founder, Good Cause Communications

1307 NEW YORK CITY ENTREPRENEURIAL FUND New York City Economic Development Corporation
One Liberty Plaza
New York, NY 10006

web: www.nycedc.com

Mission Statement: To provide capital to promising New York City-based technology startup companies.

Fund Size: $22 million
Average Investment: $750,000
Minimum Investment: $100,000
Investment Criteria: Early Stage, New York City based companies
Industry Group Preference: Internet Technology, Biotechnology, Software, Telecommunications

Key Executives:
James Patchett, President/CEO
Education: BA, Economics, Amherst College; MBA, Stanford University
Background: VP, Urban Investment Group, Goldman Sachs

1309 NEW YORK LIFE CAPITAL PARTNERS
51 Madison Avenue
New York, NY 10010

web: www.nylinvestments.com/investmentsgroup

Mission Statement: An integrated asset management enterprise serving a variety of sectors. Manages two private equity co-investment funds and a mezzanine fund, by concentrating investments around Core Partners, a select group of veteran LBO sponsors with a history of strong performance, discipline across market cycles, a proven ability to create value, the co-investment funds are well positioned across all market cycles.

Fund Size: $8 billion
Founded: 1984
Average Investment: $15 - $25 million
Minimum Investment: $500,000
Investment Criteria: Leveraged Acquisitions, Recapitalizations, Growth Capital, Mezzanine
Industry Group Preference: Biotechnology, Communications, Computer Related, Electronic Technology, High Technology, Medical & Health Related, Software

Key Executives:
Yie-Hsin Hung, Chief Executive Officer
Education: BS, Mechanical Engineering, Northwestern University; MBA, Harvard University
Background: Bridgewater Associates; Morgan Stanley Investment Management

1310 NEW YORK VENTURE PARTNERS
New York, NY

e-mail: t@nyvp.com
web: www.nyvp.com

Mission Statement: A venture capital firm seeking to invest in tech-based companies in New York.

Founded: 2014
Industry Group Preference: Technology, Artificial Intelligence, Software, Health & Wellness, Applications
Portfolio Companies: 1000 Museums, AllTheRooms, Authorea, Bandwagon, Bon Voyaging, Boundless Mind, BrandYourself, Collectively, ComiXology, CourseHorse, Fi Smart Dog Collar, FutureStay, GameCo, goTenna, Gust, HeTexted, Heymama, Imagine Air, Journey Meditation, Media Armor, Peel Away Labs, Pinterest, PublicStaff, Rogue, Salido, School Loop Inc., Secfi, Tommy John, Uizard, VincePair Inc., Visual Vocal

Key Executives:
Brian Cohen, Founding Partner
Education: BS, Syracuse University; MS, Boston University
Background: CEO, TSI Communications Worldwide; CEO, Mindstorm Communications; CEO, Focus Technology; CEO, Globalcomm; Co-Founder/CEO, Launch.it; Founder/President, Good Cause Communications
Trace Cohen, Managing Director
Education: BW, Syracuse University; MBA, Columbia Business School
Background: Founder/CMO, Brand-Yourself.com; Co-Founder/SVP, iFluence PR; Advisor, Pivot; Co-Founder/Head of Product, Launch.it

1311 NEWBURY VENTURES
600 Menlo Avenue
Menlo Park, CA 94025

web: www.newburyven.com

Mission Statement: Newbury Ventures specializes in identifying opportunities for significant capital appreaciation, by investing in promising entrepreneurial companies at early stages of their corporate development.

Fund Size: $500 million
Founded: 1992
Average Investment: $5-10 million
Minimum Investment: $2 million
Investment Criteria: High Growth in technology, communications and IT industries
Industry Group Preference: Telecommunications, Data Communications, Information Technology, Internet Technology, Technology, Wireless Technologies, IT Security
Portfolio Companies: Clourdera, Quanergy, Womply, DeliveryAgent, Skully Helmets, AdStage, Fuel Powered, Wishabi, Lucibel, B DNA, Xtera, Zozi

Other Locations:
255 Shoreline Drive
Suite 520
Redwood Shores, CA 94065
Phone: 650-486-2444

Key Executives:
Ossama Hassanein, Senior Managing Director
e-mail: ossama@newburyven.com
Education: BSc, Electrical Engineering, University of Alexandria; MSc, Electrical Engineering & MBA, University of British Columbia

Venture Capital & Private Equity Firms / Domestic Firms

Background: EVP, Berkeley International; Chairman, Technocom Ventures; President, Newbridge Holdings
Joe Kell, Chief Financial Officer
e-mail: joe@newburyven.com
Education: BS, Business Admnistration, Saint Mary's College; CPA
Background: Audit Manager, Technology Assurance & Advisory Group

1312 NEWBURY, PIRET & COMPANY
One Boston Place
Suite 2600
Boston, MA 02108

Phone: 617-367-7300 Fax: 781-268-5081
web: www.newburypiret.com

Mission Statement: To provide investment banking services to middle market growth companies. Clients often have a technology focus which differentiates their products and services.

Geographic Preference: US and Europe
Founded: 1981
Average Investment: $3-$100 million
Minimum Investment: $3 million
Industry Group Preference: Business to Business, Healthcare, Manufacturing, Technology

Key Executives:
Marguerite A Piret, President/CEO
e-mail: mpiret@newburypiret.com
Education: MBA, AB, Harvard University
Background: Managing Director, Kridel Securities Corporation; Commercial Loan Officer, New England Merchants National Bank
Marvin W Ritchie, Managing Director, Valuations
e-mail: mritchie@newburypiret.com
Education: BS, West Virginia University; MBA, Wharton School
Background: Principal, Real Estate Investments Group, Northfield Capital; Vice President, Adams, Harkness & Hill; Vice President, Bear, Stearns
John Piret, Managing Director
e-mail: jpiret@newburypiret.com
Education: DSc, Physical Sciences, Ecole des Mines de Paris; MS, Chemical Engineering, MIT; AB, Applied Mathematics, Harvard College
Background: President/Founder, Corion Technologies

1313 NEWFIELD CAPITAL
555 5th Avenue
14th Floor
New York, NY 10017

Phone: 212-599-5000
e-mail: gcamp@newfieldcapital.com
web: www.newfieldcapital.com

Geographic Preference: United States, Canada, United Kingdom, France, Germany, Europe
Founded: 1991
Minimum Investment: $10 million
Investment Criteria: LBO, MBO
Industry Group Preference: Consumer Services, Financial Services, Media, Telecommunications, Real Estate, Consumer Products

Key Executives:
Gregory T. Camp, Managing Director

1314 NEWLIGHT MANAGEMENT
500 N Broadway
Suite 144
Jericho, NY 11753

Mission Statement: The Newlight Management family of funds seeks to achieve consistently superior returns for its stakeholders through investments in public and private technology companies.

Geographic Preference: United States
Fund Size: $120 million
Founded: 1997
Average Investment: $1 - $4 million
Minimum Investment: $1 million
Investment Criteria: High growth potential, strong management
Industry Group Preference: Semiconductors, Communications, Software, Services, Internet Technology, Business to Business, Infrastructure, E-Commerce & Manufacturing
Portfolio Companies: Acrodyne Communications, AuthenTec, CareGain, etrials, FatWire, GigOptix, Invision, Massive, NetOps, Newpoint Technologies, Parago, Peregrine Semicondutor, Raketu, SilverCarrot, Sonics, VideoNext, VitalStream

Key Executives:
Robert M Brill, Managing Partner
516-433-0090
Fax: 516-433-0412
e-mail: brill@nlventures.com
Education: PhD, Nuclear Physics, Brown University
Robert F Raucci, Managing Partner
e-mail: raucci@nlventures.com
Education: MBA, Columbia University

1315 NEWLIGHT PARTNERS
320 Park Avenue
25th Floor
New York, NY 10022

Phone: 212-205-2660
e-mail: info@newlightpartners.com
web: www.newlightpartners.com

Mission Statement: Partners with founders and management teams to build and grow businesses, providing them with the capital and support needed to execute on their vision. Unlike traditional private equity, Newlight invests over time with the flexibility to start with a platform buyout or de novo.

Founded: 2018
Average Investment: Up to $200 million
Industry Group Preference: Digital Infrastructure, Insurance, Specialty Lending, Energy, Healthcare, B2B
Portfolio Companies: APR Energy, Aurigen, Bay Tech, Bioenergy Development Company, Crystal Financial, Essent Group, Extenet Systems, Hyperoptic, Leyline, Liberty Pressure Pumping, Narragansett Bay, Oak Street Health, OneWest Bank, Pondurance, Propeller Industries, RITC, Sail Internet, Syndicate, TowerCo, Waypoint Leasing, Zenium

Key Executives:
David Wassong, Co-Managing Partner
Education: BA, University of Pennsylvania; MBA, Wharton School
Background: Co-Head of Strategic Investments Group, Soros Fund Management; Partner, Soros Private Equity Partners; VP, Lauder Gaspar Ventures
Ravi Yadav, Co-Managing Partner
Education: BS, Rutgers University; MBA, Harvard Business School
Background: Co-Head of Strategic Investments Group, Soros Fund Management; Managing Partner, Sunaria Group; VP, Warburg Pincus
Ruairi Grant, Managign Director/Chief Financial Officer
Education: LLB, Queen's University of Belfast; Postgrad in Accounting, University of Ulster
Background: Financial Controller/SVP, EIG Global Energy Partners; Manager of Assurance Services, Pricewaterhouse Coopers
Joshua Ho-Walker, Managing Director
Education: BS, Leonard N Stern School of Business, New York University

Venture Capital & Private Equity Firms / Domestic Firms

Background: Principal, Soros Fund Management; Analyst, Investment Banking, Merrill Lynch

1316 NEWSCHOOLS VENTURE FUND
1616 Franklin Street
2nd Floor
Oakland, CA 94612

Phone: 415-615-6860 **Fax:** 415-615-6861
e-mail: info@newschools.org
web: www.newschools.org

Mission Statement: NewSchools invests in both non-profit and for-profit organizations that are working to improve public education in a variety of ways. Our venture portfolio includes more than 100 highly effective organizations working to change the lives of low-income children across the country.
Geographic Preference: United States
Investment Criteria: Early-Stage, Seed-Stage
Industry Group Preference: Education
Portfolio Companies: 100Kin10, Academy for Urban School Leadership, Achievement Preparatory Academy, Alliance for College-Ready Public Schools, Appletree Institute for Education Innovation, Aspire Public Schools, AspireU, BetterLesson, Beyond 12, Blendspace, BrightBytes, Camelback Ventures Fellowship Program, Capital Teaching Residency, Center to Support Excellence in Teaching, Character Lab, Charter Board Partners, City on a Hill, ClassDojo, ClassWallet, CodeHS, CodeNow, Concentric Educational Solutions, CoreSpring, Crescent City Schools, Curriculet, Dc Preparatory Academy, DC Public Charter School Board, DC School Reform Now, Democrcy Prep Public School, District of Columbia International School, DSST Public Schools, E.L. Haynes Public Charter School, Edcamp Foundation, EdSurge, Education Elements, Educreations, Edward W. Brooke Charter School, Ellevation, EnCorps, Engrade, Equal Opportunity Schools, eSpark, Excel Academy Charter Schools, The Expectations Project, Explore Schools, Families for Excellent Schools, Fellowship for Race and Equity in Education, FreshGrade, Friends of Choice in Urban Schools, Friendship Public Charter Schools, Future Is Now Schools, Goalbook, Great Oakland Public Schools Leadership Center, GreatSchools, Grockit, Hapara, Ingenuityprep, Inspired Teaching Demonstration School, Junyo, Khan Academy, Kidaptive, KIPP DC, KIPP MA, Leadership Public Schools, Leading Educators, Learning Games Network, LearnZillion, Lighthouse Community Charter School, Listen Current, Locomotiv

Key Executives:
 Stacey Childress, Chief Executive Officer
 Background: Faculty Member, Harvard Business School
 Frances Messano, Senior Managing Partner
 Education: AB, Harvard College; MBA, Harvard Business School
 Background: VP, Teach for America; Associate Partner, Monitor Institute
 Scott Benson, Managing Partner
 Education: BSBA, University of North Carolina; MBA, Harvard Business School
 Background: Sr Program Officer, Gates Foundation; Director of Strategic Academic Initiatives, DC Public Schools

1317 NEWSPRING CAPITAL
Radnor Financial Center
555 East Lancaster Avenue
3rd Floor
Radnor, PA 19087

Phone: 610-567-2380 **Fax:** 610-567-2388
e-mail: aveverka@newspringcapital.com
web: www.newspringcapital.com

Mission Statement: NewSpring Capital's experienced and skilled investment professionals aim to partner with outstanding entrepreneurial management teams to build companies that are leaders in their fields.
Geographic Preference: Mid-Atlantic Region
Fund Size: $600 million
Investment Criteria: NewSpring Growth: Equity Capital for Growth & Expansion Stage; NewSpring Healthcare: Equity Capital; NewSpring Mezzanine: Mezzanine Capital for Expansion Stage & Buyout Opportunities
Industry Group Preference: Business Products & Services, Enabling Technology, Information Technology, Healthcare, Pharmaceuticals, Healthcare Services, Medical Devices, Specialty Manufacturing
Portfolio Companies: 3Pillar Global, Bluenog, BCG, Clutch, Dstillery, Enterprises DB, Exegy, Exelate, FirstBest, Ifbyphone, iPipeline, Market Street Advisors, Message Systems, Mobiquity, Open Road, Raritan, Relay, Smart Destinations, Star2Star Communications, Velocidata, VidSys, XOS Digital

Other Locations:
 575 5th Avenue
 18th Floor
 New York, NY 10017
 Phone: 610-567-2380 **Fax:** 610-567-2388

 120 S Riverside Plaza
 Chicago, IL 60606
 Phone: 312-342-2700 **Fax:** 610-567-2388

 100 West Road
 Suite 325
 Towson, MD 21204
 Phone: 410-832-7586 **Fax:** 610-567-2388

Key Executives:
 Michael DiPiano, Managing General Partner
 e-mail: mdipiano@newspringcapital.com
 Education: BS, Penn State University; MBA, Stern School of Business
 Background: Safeguard Scientifics; CEO, Chemical Leaman Corporation; Baxter Healthcare Corporation
 Marc Lederman, General Partner, NewSpring Growth
 e-mail: mlederman@newspringcapital.com
 Education: BS, Accountancy, Villanova University; MBA, Wharton School
 Background: Manager, Business Assurance & Advisory Services Group, Deloitte & Touche
 Glenn Rieger, General Partner, NewSpring Growth
 e-mail: grieger@newspringcapital.com
 Education: Colby College; MBA, Wharton School
 Background: Co-Founder & Managing Director, Cross Atlantic Partners
 Brian G. Murphy, General Partner, NewSpring Healthcare
 e-mail: bmurphy@newspringcapital.com
 Education: BS, Science, State University of New York, Cortland
 Background: Founder, Acquisition Management Services; NovaCare; Heritage Health Systems; Partners National Health Plans
 Bruce Downey, Advisory Partner
 e-mail: bdowney@newspringcapital.com
 Education: Miami University; Law Degree, Ohio State University
 Background: Chairman & CEO, Barr Pharmaceuticals; Capital Partner, Winston & Strawn
 Steven Hobman, General Partner, NewSpring Mezzanine
 e-mail: shobman@newspringcapital.com
 Education: AB, Franklin & Mashall College; MBA, West Chester University
 Background: Meridian Bank, Progress Bank, Comerica Bank; Founder, TechBanc; Co-Founder, Ben Franklin/Progress Capital Fund
 Greg Barger, General Partner, NewSpring Mezzanine
 e-mail: gbarger@newspringcapital.com
 Education: BS, Finance, University of Connecticut; MBA, Loyola College

Venture Capital & Private Equity Firms / Domestic Firms

Background: Managing Director, Calvert Street Capital Partners; SVP, Mercantile Bank

1318 NEXT VENTURES

e-mail: info@nextventures.com
web: nextventures.com

Mission Statement: Next Ventures is a venture capital firm created to grow opportunities in rising sports, fitness, nutrition and wellness markets.

Key Executives:
Lance Armstrong, Founder/Managing Partner
Background: Cyclist; Athlete; Host, THEMOVE Podcast; Host, THE FORWARD Podcast
Lionel Conacher, Managing Partner
Background: Co-Founder, Westwind Partners Inc.; CEO, Westwind; President, Thomas Weisel Partners; Senior Advisor/Operating Partner, Altramont Capital Partners
Melanie Strong, Managing Partner
Background: VP/General Manager, Nike Skateboarding; Nike

1319 NEXT WORLD CAPITAL
836 Montgomery Street
San Francisco, CA 94133

Phone: 415-202-5450 Fax: 415-358-8233
e-mail: businessplan@nextworldcap.com
web: www.nextworldcap.com

Mission Statement: Next World Capital is an international expansion-stage venture capital firm with $200 million of assets. Headquartered in San Francisco, NWC is the only Silicon Valley VC managing a sales and business development platform to help its companies expand in Europe.

Geographic Preference: Worldwide
Fund Size: $200 million
Investment Criteria: Expansion Stage
Industry Group Preference: Software, Internet, Mobile
Portfolio Companies: AgilOne, BrightRoll, Datameer, Datastax, DynamicOps, GoodData, Host Analytics, iDeeli, Nexgen Storage, Virtual Instruments, Zuora

Other Locations:
11 Avenue Myron Herrick
Paris 75008
France
Phone: 33-155359920 Fax: 33-145636098

The Stanley Building
7 Pancras Square
London NIC 4AG
United Kingdom
Phone: 44-2037145102

Craig Hanson, Co-Founder/General Partner
Education: BA, Carleton College; MS, Stanford Graduate School of Business
Background: Vice President, FTV Capital; Pricipal, Vista Ventures; Vice President, Berenson Minella & Company; Credit Suisse First Boston
Ben Fu, General Partner
Education: BS, Electrical Engineering & Computer Science, MEng, MIT
Background: Principal, Scale Venture Partners; Senior Sales Engineer, Symantec, IMlogic, Akamai
Frederic Halley, Operating Partner
Education: MS, Telecommunication Engineering, Telecom Paris; MBA, Kellogg School of Management
Background: Managing Partner, Tioga Venture; COO, Netsize; GM, Pertinence; Sales Director, SLP Infoware; Consultant, Boston Consulting Group

1320 NEXTGEN ANGELS
5404 Wisconsin Avenue
Suite 1000
Chevy Chase, MD 20815

e-mail: nextgenangels@gmail.com
web: www.nextgenangels.com

Mission Statement: Companies considered will have at least a few of the following characteristics: seed or early-stage with opportunity for explosive growth; web, mobile, SAAS; located in Greater Washington, DC region.

Geographic Preference: Greater Washington, DC Region
Investment Criteria: Seed, Early Stage
Industry Group Preference: Web Related, Mobile, SaaS
Portfolio Companies: Disruption Corporation, Socialradar, Speek, APX Labs, Spinnakr, uKnow, EncoreAlert, Nvite, Revmetrix, Avizia, CustomVine

1321 NEXTSTAGE CAPITAL
2570 Boulevard of Generals
Building 100, Second Floor
Audubon, PA 19403

Phone: 610-539-2297
web: nextstagecap.com

Mission Statement: NextStage Capital focuses on finding undiscovered early stage investment opportunities in the Mid-Atlantic region. With an emphasis on technology, software, hardware and services, our goal is to find talented entrepreneurs with a compelling and validated technology offering and help them build company value.

Geographic Preference: Mid-Atlantic Region
Fund Size: $175 million
Investment Criteria: Early-Stage
Industry Group Preference: Technology
Portfolio Companies: HigherNext, Lumesis, Sidecar, Certes Networks, Ticketleap, Savana, Evident Software, Dayak, Anysource Media, MODA Technology Partners, Orbius, Agilence, HX Technologies, Waywire (Magnify Networks), Hardmetrics, Visinex

Key Executives:
Terry Williams, Co-Founder/Managing Partner
e-mail: terry@nextstagecapital.com
Education: Indiana University of Pennsylvania
Background: Founder, TWC Group; Strategic Consultant, Dialogic Corporation
Directorships: Movitas, Cross X Platform
Dan McKinney, Co-Founder/Managing Partner
e-mail: dan@nextstagecapital.com
Education: University of Cincinnati
Background: Officer, Safeguard Scientifics; Sales & Marketing, IBM
Directorships: TicketLeap, Savana, Sidecar, Magnify Networks, Ben Franklin Technology Investment Advisory Committee, New Jersey Technology Advisory Board
Rob Adams, Co-Founder/Managing Partner
e-mail: rob@nextstagecapital.com
Education: BS, Economics, Skidmore College; MBA, University of Michigan
Background: VP & Officer, Safeguard Scientifics; Co-Founder, Ascendigm; Rascoff/Zysblatt; Entrepreneurial Services, Ernst & Young

1322 NEXTVIEW VENTURES
179 Lincoln Street
Suite 404
Boston, MA 02111

web: www.nextviewventures.com

Mission Statement: Dedicated seed stage investors building transforming internet businesses.

Geographic Preference: East Coast US
Average Investment: $250,000 - $500,000
Investment Criteria: Seed-Stage

473

Venture Capital & Private Equity Firms / Domestic Firms

Industry Group Preference: Internet
Portfolio Companies: Alignable, BookBub, Boundless, Bridj, Change Collective, Cloze, Code Climate, CustomMade, Dunwello, Emissary, Farmeron, Goodsie, Insight Squared, Mojo Motors, Objective Logistics, Paintzen, Platiq, Shareaholic, Skillz, SkyVu, Sunrise, Swipely, TaskRabbit, Thred Up, TripleLift, Turning Art, YesGraph

Key Executives:
Rob Go, Co-Founder/Partner
Education: Duke University; MBA, Harvard Business School
Background: Spark Capital; Business Product Leader, Ebay; Consultant, The Parthenon Group
Lee Hower, Co-Founder/Partner
Education: BAS, Systems Engineering, University of Pennsylvania; BS, Economics, Wharton School
Background: PayPal; Co-Founder, LinkedIn; Principal, Point Judity Capital
David Biesel, Co-Founder/Partner
Education: AB, Economics, Duke University; MBA, Stanford Graduate School of Business
Background: Vice President, Venrock; Co-Founder, Sombasa Media; Vice President, Marketing, About.com

1323 NFX
604 Mission Street
Suite 200
San Francisco, CA 94105

e-mail: qed@nfx.com
web: www.nfx.com

Mission Statement: NFX approach early-startup investments through the eyes of founders.
Geographic Preference: Silicon Valley, Isreal
Average Investment: $500,000 - 5 million
Minimum Investment: $250,000
Industry Group Preference: Technology, Software, Travel, Entertainment, Healthcare, Commercial Software, Big Data & Analytics, Retail, Social Media
Portfolio Companies: Lyft, Patreon, Doordash, Trulia, Poshmark, Houseparty, Honeybook, Outdoorsy, SmilarWeb, Good Readers, Wanelo, LiveRamp, Path, Playtika, 3DR, Feedly, Crackle, Flickr, Second Life, Life 360, Tickle, Lastminute.com, Wonderhill, Solv, Stella, Plenty, Honor, Virta Health, Ivy, Grabr, Ozzy, Mammoth Diagnostics, Fitmob, AngelList, Mapillary, Amino, Friend.ly, Splacer, Circle Up, Skout, Crossrider, iAngel, MyHeritage, Plarium, MyThings, Fuse.it, Worthy, Graduway, R2Net, Zula, Bizzabo, NanoRep, Tradeo, Kenshoo, Ava, Riptide, Hippo, Chatalytic, SweetIM, Viv, Saltside, Storyhunter, Peekk Travel, Gogo Bot, Swell, Iron Pearl, Red Bubble, Leap, Jiff, Branchout, Zinch, Affinity Labs, Maya's Mom, Zeus, Motivate, Rooster, MarketMan, Wheelhouse, LiquidSpace, Genome Compiler, Crowdcast, The Hotels Network, Cricket Health, Wheelwell, Jet Insight, Blueberry, KimKim, Kwik, Finrise, Leaders, Headnote, Mission Mark, Brightcrowd, Travel Joy, Golden Key, Fairly, Hipdot, Incredible Health, Materialist, Crater

Other Locations:
400 Florence Street
Palo Alto, CA 94301

8 Hachoshlim Street
Herzliya 1369377
Isreal

Key Executives:
James Currier, Managing Partner
Education: BA, Political Economics, Princeton University; MBA, Harvard Business School
Background: Co-Founder/CEO, Tickle; Co-Founder, Wonderhill; Co-Founder, IronPearl; Co-Founder, Jiff
Pete Flint, Managing Partner
Education: MS, Physics, University of Oxford; MBA, Stanford Grad. School of Business
Background: Co-Founder/CEO, Trulia; Co-Founder, lastminute.com

Gigi Levy-Weiss, Managing Partner
Education: MBA, Kellogg School of Management, Northwestern University
Background: CEO, 888 Holdingsl Division President, Amdocs
Directorships: EMEA Client Advisory Council, Facebook

1324 NGEN PARTNERS
733 Third Avenue
New York, NY 10017

Phone: 212-450-9700
web: www.ngenpartners.com

Mission Statement: NGEN Partners is a pioneering investor in the cleantech sector. They invest in businesses that offer economically valuable products and services that positiviely affect the environment.
Geographic Preference: United States, Canada
Fund Size: $500 million
Founded: 2001
Average Investment: $5 - $25 million
Investment Criteria: Early-Stage to Late-Stage
Industry Group Preference: Clean Technology, Environment, Alternative Energy, Energy Efficiency, Pollution, Advanced Materials, Green Technology, Energy Storage
Portfolio Companies: Adura Technologies, Alterra Power Corp., Artificial Muscle, Bare Snacks, Brightfarms, Catalytic Solutions, Choose Energy, DIRTT Environmental Solutions, eIQ Energy, ENXSuite, Enzymedica, eRecyclingCorps, evandtec, Fallbrook Technologies, Greengate, Hycrete, MokaFive, Nanosphere, Native Foods Cafe, nlyte Software, Powerspan, Pure Energies Group, Rayne, REGEN Energy, Renaissance Lighting, Renewable Funding, Sensicore, Solaria, SolFocus, Soraa, Textronics, Threshold Power, Tioga Energy, Two Moms in the RAW, Zevia

Other Locations:
1114 State Street
Suite 247
Santa Barbara, CA 93101
Phone: 805-564-3156 **Fax:** 805-564-1669

733 Third Avenue
18th Floor
New York, NY 10017
Phone: 212-450-9700

Key Executives:
Peter S.H. Grubstein, Founder/Managing Member
Education: Yale University
Directorships: Renewable Funding, BrightFarms, Native Foods Cafe
Shay Murphy, Partner
Education: BA, Columbia University; MBA, NYU Stern School of Business
Background: DG Energy Partners; Citigroup
Directorships: Encycle
Rosemary Ripley, Managing Director
Education: BA, MBA, Yale University
Background: Corporate Business Development, Altria Group; Managing Director, Furman Selz; Co-Founder, Circle Financial Group
Directorships: MokaFive, nlyte, Zevia, Bare Snacks, Two Moms in the Raw

1325 NGN CAPITAL
60 Long Ridge Road
Suite 402
Stamford, CT 06902

Phone: 212-972-0077 **Fax:** 212-972-0080
e-mail: investorrelations@ngncapital.com
web: www.ngncapital.com

Mission Statement: NGN Capital is a venture capital firm dedicated to healthcare investing, focusing on ventures with the potential to achieve above average private equity returns with an emphasis on later stage investments.

Geographic Preference: United States, Europe
Investment Criteria: Early-Stage to Later-Stage
Industry Group Preference: Healthcare, Biotechnology, Medical Devices
Portfolio Companies: Aerovance, Artisan Pharma, BeneChill, BioArray Solutions, EKOS, Horizon Pharma, Javelin Pharmaceuticals, Jerini AG, KIKA Medical, Micromet, MultiPlan, PIN Pharma, OptiScan Biomedical, Power Medical Interventions, Santhera Pharmaceuticals AG, Sightline Technologies, Small Bone Innovations, Tigris Pharmaceuticals, ACT Biotech, Cerapedics, Endosense SA, Exosome Diagnostics, Medrium, NOXXON Pharma AG, Resverlogix, SpineView, Valtech Cardio, Vivaldi Biosciences

Other Locations:
c/o Oracle Partners
200 Greenwich Avenue
Greenwich, CT 06830
Phone: 203-862-7900 **Fax:** 203-862-1613

Bergheimer Str. 89a
Heidelberg 69115
Germany
Phone: 49-6221893760 **Fax:** 49-62218937625

Key Executives:
Kenneth S Abramowitz, Co-Founder/Managing General Partner
Education: BA, Columbia University; MBA, Harvard Business School
Background: Managing Director, The Carlyle Group; Analyst, Sanford C Bernstein & Co.
Directorships: Valtech Cardio, Small Bone Innovations, Akorn
John R Costantino, Managing General Partner
Education: BS, JD, Fordham University; CPA
Background: Partner, Walden Partners; Partner, Constantino Melamede & Geenberg; EVP, COO, Director, Conair
Directorships: ACT Biotech, Vivaldi Biosciences
Peter Johann PhD, Managing General Partner
Education: PhD, Technical University of Munich
Background: Division Head, Corporate Development, Boehringer Ingelheim; Global Business Leader, F. Hoffman-La Roche
Directorships: Horizon Pharma, Exosome Diagnostics
Alexander Cuomo, Chief Financial Officer
Education: BA, Ithaca College; MS, Finance, Lubin School of Business, Pace University

1326 NGP
2850 North Harwood Street
19th Floor
Dallas, TX 75201

Phone: 972-432-1440
e-mail: inquiries@ngptrs.com
web: ngpenergycapital.com

Mission Statement: Energy sector investment fund.

Fund Size: $17 billion
Founded: 1988
Industry Group Preference: Oil & Gas
Portfolio Companies: 89 Energy, Aspen Energy Partners, Avad Energy, Axia Energy, Blackbeard Operating LLC, Black Mountain Sand, BlueStone Natural Resources, Bravo Natural Resources LLC, Caltex Resources, Castell Oil Company, Castlerock, Catapult, CH4 Energy, Colgate Energy, Conexus Energy, Confluence Resources, Crimson Pipeline LP, Crossing Rocks Energy, Fifth Creek Energy, Hibernia Energy, Highmark Energy, Iron Horse Midstream, Juniper Resources, Infinity Natural Resources, Luxe Energy, Mallard Exploration, Massif Oil & Gas II, Mettle Midstream Partners, Oilfield Water Logistics, Outrigger Energy, Petrus Resources, Prairie Storm Energy Corp, Rebllion Energy, Remora Petroleum, Springbok Energy, Steppe Resources Inc., Titus Oil & Gas LLC, Torrent Oil, Trilogy Midstream, World Oil Properties Inc.

Other Locations:
717 Texas Avenue
Suite 1650
Houston, TX 77002
Phone: 713-579-5700

Chris G. Carter, Managing Partner
Education: BBA & MPA, University of Texas; MBA, Stanford University
Background: Associate, McKinsey & Company; Analyst, Deutsche Bank
Tony R. Weber, Managing Partner
Education: BBA, Finance, Texas A&M University
Background: CFO, Merit Energy Company; SVP & Division Head of Energy, Union Bank of California

1327 NGP CAPITAL
418 Florence Street
Palo Alto, CA 94301

web: www.ngpcap.com

Mission Statement: Focusing exclusively on the mobile industry, NGP Capital brings a global perspective and deep understanding of global trends to every engagement. NGP are active investors adding value through strategic insight, operational excellence and its vast network of contacts in the mobile industry.

Geographic Preference: Worldwide
Fund Size: $250 million
Founded: 2005
Industry Group Preference: Mobile Technology
Portfolio Companies: Adknowledge, Babbel, Cloudmark, Dealsandyou.com, Digital Lumens, Fashion and You, Fyber, Ganji, Gigwalk, Grand Cru, Gridsum, Heptagon, Hipmunk, Innovis, Inside Secure, Intermedia, InVisage, Kaltura, MVD House, MAG Interactive, Meican, PubMatic, Quikr, RetailNext, Rocketfuel, SolarVista Media, TechProcess, Verve, Vizury, Wei Chai Shi, YPlan, Zubie
No. 1 Jianquomenwai Avenue
Room 710, Office Tower II
China World Trade Centre
Beijing 100004
China

1328 NJTC VENTURE FUND
1001 Briggs Road
Suite 280
Mount Laurel, NJ 08054

Phone: 856-273-6800 **Fax:** 856-273-0990
e-mail: info@njtcvc.com

Mission Statement: Catalytic seed, startup, and early stage venture capital investments. The firm actively partners with entrepreneurs to build unique, leading-edge businesses that drive superior returns for investors and economic growth in the community. NJTC Venture Fund is fully invested and closed to new investment opportunities.

Fund Size: $80 million
Founded: 2001
Investment Criteria: Fully Invested
Portfolio Companies: Achieve3000, Archive Systems, InstaMed, IntegriChain, RightAnswers, V12 Group, Andrew Technologies, Colby Pharmaceuticals, CytoSorbents, Intra-Cellular Therapies, Redpoint Bio, Sword Diagnostics, Power Survey

Key Executives:
Jim Gunton, General Partner
856-273-6800 x233
e-mail: jim@njtcvc.com
Education: BS, Stanford University; MBA, Fuqua School of Business
Background: Promoter Manager, Oracle Corporation; VP/Principal, Edison Venture Fund

Venture Capital & Private Equity Firms / Domestic Firms

Joseph Falkenstein, General Partner
856-273-6800 x 226
e-mail: joe@njtcvc.com
Education: CPA, Temple University
Background: Partner, Andersen's Growth Company and Technology Practice
Directorships: Archive Systems, V12 Group, Sword Diagnostics, Power Survey, Cylex
Robert Chefitz, General Partner
973-994-0606
e-mail: robert@njtcvc.com
Education: Northwestern University; Columbia University
Background: General Partner, Apax Partners; Golder Thoma Cressey

1329 NKM CAPITAL
Boston, MA

e-mail: info@nkmcap.com
web: www.nkmcap.com

Mission Statement: A venture capital firm that focuses on early stage tech-based companies across the US. NKM Capital has offices in Boston, New York, and Silicon Valley.

Founded: 2012
Investment Criteria: Early Stage
Industry Group Preference: Technology, Artificial Intelligence, Consumer, Software, Applications
Portfolio Companies: Analytical Space, Astranis, Bluesmart, Boom, Carta, Copia, Cruise, Deepgram, Eight Sleep, Flirtey, Hyperloop One, Instavest, Interviewed, Lyft, Mogul, Numerai, Relativity Space, Revlo, Ripple, Robinhood, Smarking, Tesorio, Truebill, Wakie Inc., WorldCover, Zenysis, ZoomCar India

Key Executives:
Nurzhas Makishev, Partner
Education: BS, MIT; MS, John F. Kennedy School of Government, Harvard University; MBA, Wharton School
Background: Researcher, MIT Media Lab; Investment Banker, Banc of America Securities; Investment Banker, JP Morgan; Software Engineer, Oracle; Angel Investor

Other Locations:
Maria 01
Lapinlahdenkatu 16
Building 3
Helsinki 00180
Finland

12, Avenue des Morgines
1213 Petit-Lancy
Geneva
Switzerland

Key Executives:
John Gardner, Venture Partner
Education: MBA, University of Chicago; JD, University of Cincinnati
Background: BlueRun Ventures; Senior Business Development, Nokia
Directorships: Adknowledge, Cloudmark, PubMatic, RetailNext, Rocketfuel, Verve Wireless, Vizury
Paul Asel, Partner
Education: BA, Dartmouth College; MBA, Stanford Graduate School of Business
Background: International Finance Corporation; General Partner, Telos Ventures; Senior Vice President, Delta Capital
Directorships: Intermedia, Luminate, Gangi.com, Gridsum, KongZhong, Madhouse, Network 18, SolarVista Media, Techprocess Solutions, UC Web
Bo Ilsoe, Partner
Education: MS, Electronics Engineering, Aalborg University, Denmark
Background: Alcatel, Nokia, Vertex Management
Directorships: Heptagon, Innovis, Inside Secure, InVisage, Pelican Imaging, Sponsorpay, Voddler

Upal Basu, Partner
Education: BS, Engineering, Imperial College, London; MS, Engineering, Stanford University; MBA, Harvard Business School
Background: Founder & CEO, Mformation Technologies; McKinsey & Company
Directorships: Deals and You, Fashion and You, Innovis, Kaltura, Network 18, Quikr

1331 NORO-MOSELEY PARTNERS
Medici Building
3284 Northside Parkway NW
Suite 525
Atlanta, GA 30327-2337

Phone: 404-233-1966
web: www.noromoseley.com

Mission Statement: Helps emerging and growth companies realize their long-term vision by providing the appropriate financial resources, experience and foresight to take them to the next level. It's mission is to create strong relationships with our portfolio companies and entrepreneurs and to add value where needed to produce superior returns for the company, its employees and shareholders.

Geographic Preference: Southeastern US
Fund Size: $580 million
Founded: 1983
Average Investment: $3-$5 million
Minimum Investment: $2 million
Investment Criteria: Startup, First-Stage, Second-Stage
Industry Group Preference: Technology, Fintech, Broadband, Security, Digital Media & Marketing, Logistics, Healthcare, Healthcare Services, Information Technology, Business Outsourcing, Financial Services, Technology-Enabled Services
Portfolio Companies: Array Health, Appia, Change Healthcare, ClearLeap, Diabetes Care Group, Direct General, FrontStream Payments, Hospice Link, Liaison, Navitas Lease, nCrowd, Outbound Engine, PeopleMatter, PlayOn, Pure Life Renal, PureWRX, RemitDATA, SalesFusion, Streamline Health, Tower Cloud, Virtustream, Wellcentive

Key Executives:
Mike Elliott, Venture Partner
Education: BS, Mathematics, MBA, University of North Carolina
Background: Managing Director, The Wakefield Group; Managing Director, NationsBank Capital
Directorships: Appia, Frontstream Payments, PeopleMatter, TowerCloud
Allen S Moseley, General Partner
Education: BA, University of North Carolina; MBA, Harvard Business School
Background: Associate, Robinson-Humphrey Company; Bowles Hollowell Conner & Company; Merrill Lynch; James River Corporation
Alan J Taetle, General Partner
Education: BA, Economics, University of Michigan; MBA, Harvard University
Background: Executive VP Marketing & Business Development, MindSpring
Spence McCelland, General Partner
Education: BA, Vanderbilt University; MBA, Kellogg School of Management at Northwestern University
William L Hudson, Administrative Partner/Chief Financial Officer
Education: CPA, BS, University of Virginia
Background: Equifax; nBank.com; Arthur Andersen

Venture Capital & Private Equity Firms / Domestic Firms

1332 NORTH AMERICAN FUND
135 S LaSalle Street
Suite 3225
Chicago, IL 60603

Phone: 312-332-4950 Fax: 312-332-1540
e-mail: dbergonia@northamericanfund.com
web: www.northamericanfund.com

Mission Statement: North American's perspective is long term. Its goal is to build companies through internal growth and/or additional acquisitions into significantly larger enterprises that are leading participants in their market niches.

Geographic Preference: Midwestern, Southeastern
Fund Size: $115 million
Founded: 1989
Average Investment: $5-$15 million
Investment Criteria: Buyouts or Growth Capital
Industry Group Preference: Manufacturing, Food & Beverage, Medical Products & Services, Consumer Products, Distribution, Business Products & Services, Education, Financial Services
Portfolio Companies: ACR Electronics, Actown-Electrocoil, Amtec Precision Products, Culinary Standards, Gateway Healthcare, Minnesota Educational Computing, Polymer Corporation, Valley Meats

Other Locations:
312 SE 17th Street
Suite 300
Fort Lauderdale, FL 33305
Phone: 954-463-0681 Fax: 954-527-0904

Key Executives:
  Charles L Palmer, Managing Partner
  954-463-0681
  Fax: 954-527-0904
  Education: BSBA, Georgetown University; MBA, Northwestern University
  Background: Co-founder/VP, Heizer Corporation; Director, National Venture Capital Association; Managing Partner, North American Company
  Robert L Underwood, Managing Partner
  312-332-4950
  Fax: 312-332-1540
  e-mail: runderwood@northamericanfund.com
  Education: BS in Mechanical Engineering, MS, PhD in Engineering Sciences, Stanford University; MBA, Santa Clara University
  Background: General Partner, ISSS Ventures; President, Northern Trust Venture Capital; VP, Heizer Corporation
  R David Bergonia, Managing Partner
  312-332-4950
  Fax: 312-332-1540
  e-mail: dbergonia@northamericanfund.com
  Education: JD, Harvard University; BBA, University of Notre Dame
  Background: VP Corporate Finance, Chicago Corporation; VP, Legal Administration, Heizer Corporation

1333 NORTH ATLANTIC CAPITAL CORPORATION
Two City Center
Fifth Floor
Portland, ME 04101

Phone: 207-772-4470 Fax: 207-772-3257
e-mail: ccoyne@northatlanticcapital.com
web: www.northatlanticcapital.com

Mission Statement: A later-stage fund manager that provides risk capital to privately owned businesses in the Northeastern United States. Through active board participation, annual executive education for CEOs and complimentary strategic advisory services, North Atlantic Capital Corporation helps entrepreneurs amplify their competitive advantages and grow their businesses.

Geographic Preference: East Coast
Fund Size: $100 million
Founded: 1986
Average Investment: $4 - 8 million
Minimum Investment: $1 million
Investment Criteria: To fund the expansion of existing growth businesses and management buyouts of established companies
Industry Group Preference: Computer Related, Financial Services, Wholesale, Health Related, Information Services, Internet Technology, Materials Technology, Software, Retailing, Telecommunications, Waste & Recycling, Business Products & Services, Technology-Enabled Services
Portfolio Companies: Academic Management Systems, Appia, Autotask Corporation, iContact, KickApps (KIT Digital), OnForce, Synacor, Triggit, Voxeo, Zmags

Key Executives:
  David M Coit, Managing Director
  207-772-4470
  Fax: 207-772-3257
  e-mail: dcoit@northatlanticcapital.com
  Education: BA, Yale University; MBA, Harard Business School
  Background: President, Maine Capital Corporation; First National Bank Boston
  Mark J Morrissette, Managing Director
  207-772-4470
  Fax: 207-772-3257
  e-mail: mark@northatlanticcapital.com
  Education: BA, Dartmouth; MBA, Harvard Business School
  Background: Strategic Consulting, CSC Index;

1334 NORTH BRIDGE VENTURE PARTNERS
60 William Street
Suite 350
Waltham, MA 02481

Phone: 781-290-0004 Fax: 781-290-0999
e-mail: info@northbridge.com
web: www.northbridge.com

Mission Statement: North Bridge invests in exceptional people whose ideas have the potential to disrupt the way we live and work. Its Seed, Venture and Growth Equity strategies help transform those ideas into companies and those companies into market leaders.

Geographic Preference: East Coast
Founded: 1994
Average Investment: $20 million
Minimum Investment: $100-$200,000
Investment Criteria: Early Stage; Special Situations
Industry Group Preference: Communications, Healthcare, Distribution, Electronic Components, Genetic Engineering, Software, Infrastructure, Digital Media & Marketing
Portfolio Companies: O3b Networks, 1366 Technologies, 45M, 480 Biomedical, A123 Systems, Acquia, Actifio, Active Endpoints, Active.com, Aeropost, Akiban Technologies, Akorri, Allegro, Antenna Software, Apperian, AppIQ, Aquto, Archivas, Argon Networks, Arris, ArrowPoint Communications, Arsenal Medical, Aushon Biosystems, Authentica, Awareness, Aylus Networks, Azimuth, Belmont Technology, Bigfoot Networks, Black Sand Technologies, BlueShift, Bluespec, Bright Tiger Technologies, BrightTalk, Broadband Access Systems, Cadia Networks, Camiant, Centra, Clarity Health, Clothia, Cognio, Compass EOS, Connance, Contact Solutions, CoolPlanet, Couchbase, Currensee, Demandware, Disqus, DYM, DYN, Embrane, eRoom Technology, Excelligence, Firm 58, FirstSense Software, Foro Energy, Fring, Gridco Systems, Healthrageous, Humedica, I-Logix, Idiom, IMN, Infineta, Infomedics, IP Mobile, Jive, kSaria, Leapfrog, LiveRamp, Lumigent, Lytro, Macheen, Mavenir Systems, Mc10, MessageBus, MFormation, Mitotix, Moasis, Movik, Mozes, My Perfect Gig, Nasuni, NaviNet, NetCore, New Oak, Newforma, NOCpulse, Notifymd, ID, Paydiant, PHARMetrics, Oracle, Philo, Plexxi, Proto Labs, QD Vision,

Venture Capital & Private Equity Firms / Domestic Firms

Quallaby, Quora, Qvidian, Radview, RagingMobile, Ravel, Redstone Communications, Reva Systems, Reval, Revit Technology, Revolution Analytics, Rpath, RuffaloCODY, Salsify, SambaCloud, Seniorlink, SensAble, Sharethrough, Signiant, Silverback Technologies, SilverStream, Smartassel, SmartPark Equine, SolidWorks, Sonus Networks, SoundBite, Spaceclaim

Key Executives:

Ed Anderson, Managing Director
Education: University of Denver, Columbia University Graduate School of Business
Richard A D'Amore, General Partner
Education: Northeastern University; Harvard University Graduate School of Business Administration
Background: Consultant, Bain and Company; CPA, Arthur Young & Company
Mikel Pehl, Managing Director
Background: Partner, Advent International; President & COO, Razorfish; Chairman & CEO, i-Cube
Paul A Santinelli, Partner
Education: BS, Emerson College
Background: Director, Red Hat Network; Founder & CEO, NOCpulse; Chief Technology Officer, Global Crossing

1335 NORTH CASTLE PARTNERS
183 East Putnam Avenue
Greenwich, CT 06830

Phone: 203-862-3200
web: www.northcastlepartners.com

Mission Statement: A leading smallcap consumer private equity firm focused on consumer-driven product and service businesses in the health, wellness and active living sector.

Geographic Preference: North America
Industry Group Preference: Consumer Products, Consumer Services, Nutrition
Portfolio Companies: Flatout Flatbread, Ibex, Jenny Craig, Palladio, Doctor's Best, Octane Fitness, Curves, Performance Bicycles, Red Door Spa, Mineral Fusion

Key Executives:

Charles F Baird Jr, Founder & Managing Director
Education: AB, Harvard College; MBA, Harvard Business School
Background: Managing Director, AEA Investors; Bain & Company
Directorships: Ignite, International Fitness, Red Door Spas
Jon Canarick, Managing Director
Education: B.B.A. University of Michigan, M.B.A. Columbia Business School
Background: Financial Sponsors Coverage and Leveraged Finance groups, Bear, Stearns, & Co.
Directorships: Curves, Mineral Fusion, Flatout, Palladio Beauty Group, International Fitness, Performance Bicycle
Alison Minter, Managing Partner
Education: A.B. Economics, Princeton University
Background: Evolution Global Partners, Insurance and Leveraged Finance groups at Donaldson, Lufkin & Jenrette
Directorships: Ignite, Doctor's Best, Ibex, Red Door Spas, Octane Fitness
Alyse Skidmore, Partner/Chief Financial Officer/Chief Operating Officer
Education: L.L.M. Taxation, New York University School of Law; Juris Doctorate, Hofstra University School of Law; Bachelor of Science Accounting, University of Massachusetts Amherst
Background: Senior Manager, Ernst & Young

1336 NORTH COAST TECHNOLOGY INVESTORS LP
300 Rodd Street
Suite 201
Midland, MI 48640

Phone: 734-662-7667
e-mail: partners@northcoastvc.com
web: www.northcoastvc.com

Mission Statement: Backs entrepreneurs who seek to build major enterprises in the Midwest. North Coast welcomes the opportunity to meet with entrepreneurs and discuss their business plans.

Geographic Preference: Midwest
Fund Size: $100 million
Founded: 1999
Average Investment: $4 million
Portfolio Companies: Advanced Material Process Corporation, Approach Software, Arbortext, Avidimer Therapeutics, BalaDyne, Camile Products, Chromatic Research, Colorbok, CytoPherx, Everex Systems, Excera Materials Group, Fulcrum Composites, Gema Diagnostics, Intelligence Controls, MaxFunds.com, Mechanical Dynamics, Nematron Corporation, Open Networks Engineering, Procite, RenaMed Biologics, Shertrack, Solidica, Virtela Communications

Other Locations:
206 S Fifth Avenue
Suite 550
Ann Arbor, MI 48104
Phone: 734-662-7667 Fax: 734-662-6261

Key Executives:

Lindsay Aspegren, Co-Founder
e-mail: lindsay@northcoastvc.com
Education: MBA, Harvard Business School; Graduated magna cum laude with distinction, BA in History, Yale University
Hugo Braun, Co-Founder
e-mail: hugo@northcoastvc.com
Education: MS, Management, Sloan School of Management at MIT; Graduated cum laude with distinction, BA in Economics, Yale University

1337 NORTH COVE PARTNERS
17 State Street
New York, NY 10004

Mission Statement: North Cove Partners was established to continue the successful investment strategy developed and implemented by the firm's investment professionals as members of Merrill Lynch Global Private Equity and subsequently BAML Capital Partners.

Fund Size: $3 billion
Founded: 2011
Average Investment: $20 - $75 million
Investment Criteria: Expansions, Management Buyout, Recapitalizations
Industry Group Preference: Energy, Power, Financial Services, Healthcare, Industrial Services, Media, Communications

1338 NORTH DAKOTA DEVELOPMENT FUND
1600 E. Century Avenue
Suite 2
PO Box 2057
Bismarck, ND 58503

Phone: 701-328-5300
web: www.business.nd.gov

Mission Statement: A statewide, non-profit development corporation, the Fund provides flexible gap financing through debt and equity investments for new or expanding primary sector businesses.

Geographic Preference: North Dakota

Fund Size: $25 million
Founded: 1991
Average Investment: up to $300,000
Investment Criteria: Based in North Dakota the entrepeneur must have generally a minimum of 15% equity in the project. Loans must be secured with a 1st or 2nd mortgage in fixed assets, equipment, inventory, collateral.
Industry Group Preference: Manufacturing, Business to Business, Information Technology, Processing, Consumer Services

Key Executives:
 James Leiman, Director
 701-328-5388
 e-mail: jleiman@nd.gov

1339 NORTH HILL VENTURES
535 Boylston Street
6th Floor
Boston, MA 02116

Phone: 617-835-9719
e-mail: brettj.rome@northhillventures.com
web: www.northhillventures.com

Mission Statement: Focused exclusively on early-stage financial technology and marketing technology investments.

Fund Size: $125 million
Founded: 1999
Investment Criteria: Early-Stage
Industry Group Preference: Fintech, Marketing
Portfolio Companies: Exchange Solutions, Smart Destinations, Simple Tuition, Interactions, Tervela, Live Well Financial, CashStar, MX, Saylent

Key Executives:
 Brett J Rome, General Partner
 e-mail: brettj.rome@northhillventures.com
 Education: AB, Princeton University; MBA, Amos Tuck School, Dartmouth College
 Background: Principal, Westbury Capital Partners; Principal, The Parthenon Group

1340 NORTHERN LIGHT VENTURE CAPITAL
2855 Sand Hill Road
Menlo Park, CA 94025

Phone: 650-585-5450 **Fax:** 650-585-5451
web: www.nlightvc.com

Mission Statement: Northern Light Venture Capital is a leading China-focused venture capital firm targeting early and growth stage opportunities. We partner with select entrepreneurs with groundbreaking ideas and exceptional vision to build world-class companies.

Geographic Preference: China
Fund Size: $1 billion
Founded: 2005
Industry Group Preference: Technology, Media, Telecommunications, Clean Technology, Healthcare, Manufacturing, Consumer Products, Consumer Services, Wireless Technologies
Portfolio Companies: AbMart, Advanced Solar Power, Aerohive, Anji, Anquanbao, Austri, Baihe, BGI, C-Platform, Caerphilly, Chukong Technologies, City Media, Crossbar, CSALC, Daojia, Denovo, DerbySoft, Dianrong, DinoDirect, Dream Square, EpiTop, GigaDevice, Gogo, Grandoil, Green Bio, Halathion, Hengxin Electric, Hillstone, Hoodong, iAppPay, iFreecomm, Kaixin001, Keduo, Koowo, LianLian, LineKong, M15, Macrosan, Masa Maso, Meituan, Micropoint, Nuovo Film, Pearl Hydrogen, Pipilu, Prudent Energy, Sentons, SGE, Shanghai iRay, Shineon, Sinldo, Solarvista, Spreadtrum, SPS, Starrino, Sunlit, TalkingData, Telegent Systems, ThunderSoft, Tidal Systems, TimesLED, TrustGo, Velo, Viatime, Xixun, Zamplus Technology, Zonton

Other Locations:
 Two Pacific Place
 88 Queensway Admiralty
 Suite 2210
 Hong Kong
 Phone: 852-2281-6200 **Fax:** 852-2537-3299

 China Central Place
 32F, Tower 2
 No. 79 Jianguo Road, Chaoyang District
 Beijing 100025
 China
 Phone: (8610) 57696500 **Fax:** (8610) 5969185

 1539 Nanjing West Road
 Unit 1702, Tower 2
 Kerry Centre
 Shanghai 200040
 China
 Phone: (8621) 61034800 **Fax:** (8621) 60671991

 Room 302, Building 13
 Sandlake VC/PE Community
 183 East Suhong Rd., Suzhou Industrial Park
 Jiangsu 215026
 China
 Phone: (86512) 66969911 **Fax:** (86512) 6699916

 Unit 1407
 East Block, Coastal Building
 Hai De San Dao, Nanshan District
 Shenzhen 518054
 China
 Phone: (86755) 36992780 **Fax:** (86755) 36882155

Key Executives:
 Feng Deng, Founding Managing Director
 Education: BS, MS, Electrical Engineering, Tsinghua University; MS, Computer Engineering, University of Southern California; MBA, Wharton School
 Background: Co-Founder, NetScreen Technologies
 Yan Ke, Founding Venture Partner
 Education: BS, Electrical Engineering, Tsinghua University; MS, PhD, Computer Science, Johns Hopkins University
 Background: Co-Founder, NetScreen Technologies; Senior Software Engineer, Cisco Systems
 Lixin Li, Managing Director
 Education: BS, Electrical Engineering, MA, School of Economics & Management, Tsinghua University
 Lei Yang PhD, Managing Director
 Education: BS, Chemistry, Peking University; MS, Computer Science, PhD, Chemistry, University of Wisconsin, Madison
 Background: Principal, VantagePoint Venture Partners; Associate Partner, McKinsey & Company
 Jeffrey Lee, Managing Director/CFO
 Education: BA, Economics, Harvard College; MBA, Wharton School
 Background: Strategic Marketing Manager, Agilent Technologies Wireless Semiconductor Division; Director, US Operations, Wavics; Founding Partner, Newton Technology Partners
 Zhi Tan PhD, Venture Partner
 Education: Computer Science & Technology Department, Jilin University; PhD, Computer Science, Worcester Polytechnic Institute of Massachusetts
 Background: President, Shanghai Framedia Advertising Development Ltd; Senior Advisor, Tom Group Limited; CEO, 8848.net; Vice President, Microsoft China; Senior Vice President, UTStarcom
 He Huang PhD, Partner
 Education: BS, Thermal Engineering & Environmental Engineering; MS, PhD, Thermodynamics, Tsinghua University
 Background: Vice President, Hina Group; US Department of Energy
 Tony Wu, Senior Partner
 Education: ME, Power Engineering, Huazhong University of Science & Technology; MBA, Cheung Kong Graduate School of Business
 Background: DFJ China, Shanda Strategic Investment

479

Venture Capital & Private Equity Firms / Domestic Firms

1341 NORTHGATE
649 San Ramon Valley Blvd
Danville, CA 94526

Phone: 925-820-9970 Fax: 925-820-9994
e-mail: info@northgate.com
web: www.northgatecapital.com

Mission Statement: Northgate's proven investment approach is predicated on the fact that tremendous investment opportunities exist within the alternative asset arena, specifically within sub-classes like private equity and venture capital, where the recognition of market changing innovation and active management dictates exceptional returns. To identify and gain access to the highest performing funds, Northgate capitalizes on its proprietary and rigorous processes, in addition to its deep industry relationships. Northgate's investment focus includes a mix of investments in funds operating in both developed markets and emerging markets.

Geographic Preference: North America, Europe, Asia, Latin America
Founded: 2000
Industry Group Preference: Technologies
Portfolio Companies: Ambarella, Adams Pharma, AdMob, Aoptix, Arresto Biosciences, Bloom Energy, Clearwell, Drobo, eMeter, FourSquare, Jive Software, Meraki, Palo Alto, Proofpoint, RingCentral, Rocketfuel, Root Music, Silver Peak, Silverspring Networks, Stoke, Tethys Bioscience, Verinata Health, Visible Measures, Xoom, Yelp, Zazzle.com

Other Locations:
Paseo de las Palmas 405
18th Floor
Mexico DF 11000
Mexico
Phone: 52-55-5202-3200

150 California Street
San Francisco, CA 94111
Phone: 415-417-6000 Fax: 415-417-3978

Key Executives:
Casey Gordon, Managing Partner
Education: BA, Sociology, Johns Hopkins University; MBA, Sloan School of Management, MIT
Background: Head, Private Investments, The Capital Partnership Group of Companies
Directorships: Atia Vision; Supira Medical; NuVera Medical
Brent Jones, Co-Founder/Managing Director
Education: BS, Economics, University of Santa Clara
Background: National Football League
Directorships: Zazzle
Allan Chou, Partner
Education: MBA, Amos Tuck School of Business, Dartmouth College; CFA
Background: Analyst, Cambridge Associates
Oscar Alvarado, Partner
Education: MBA, Kent Business School, University of Kent
Background: Managing Director, Diversified & Private Equity LatAm Coverage Group, Scotiabank Global Banking; Division Head, Banamex
Thomas Vardell, Co-Founder/Managing Director
Education: BS, Industrial Engineering, Stanford University
Background: National Football League
Jana Vazé, Chief Financial Officer
Education: MS, Accounting, University of Illinois; MBA, University of Pune, India
Background: Acountant, Shea Labagh Dobberstein; Finance Operations, Standard Chartered Mutual Fund, Mumbai, India

1342 NORTHPOND VENTURES
7500 Old Georgetown Road
Suite 850
Bethesda, MD 20814

Phone: 240-800-1200
web: northpondventures.com

Mission Statement: Northpond Ventures funds companies and management teams creating solutions for some of society's greatest needs in life sciences and technology.

Other Locations:
4 Brattle Street
3rd Floor
Cambridge, MA 02138

Key Executives:
Michael Rubin, Founder/CEO
Education: Harvard University; MBA, University of Massachusetts, Amherst; CFA
Background: Co-Founder/Managing Partner, Sands Capital Ventures
Sharon Kedar, Co-Founder/Partner
Education: BA, Rice University; MBA, Harvard University; CFA
Background: CFO, Sands Capital Management; Consultant, McKinsey & Co.

1343 NORTHSTAR CAPITAL
2310 Plaza Seven
45 South 7th Street
Minneapolis, MN 55402

Phone: 612-371-5700 Fax: 612-371-5710
web: www.northstarcapital.com

Mission Statement: Focused on junior capital lending.

Geographic Preference: United States, Canada
Founded: 1993
Average Investment: $5 - $30 million
Industry Group Preference: Distribution, Manufacturing, Business Products & Services, Financial Services, Education, Healthcare
Portfolio Companies: Advanced Duplication Services, KP Holdings, Techno-Aide, Keystone Retaining Wall Systems, Security American Financial Enterprises, LA Fitness International, CanGen Holdings, Bix Produce Company, MBH Settlement Group, Integrated Turf Solutions, Lucent Polymers, Paradigm Group, Synteract, Continental Structural Plastics, Comm-Works Holdings, Spectrum Lubricants, A&D Environmental Services, EMS Management & Consultants, RollEase, JL Darling, Bioreclamation, Clowe & Cowan of El Paso, JMH International, Accurate Component Sales, Trim Parts, Citadel Outsource Group, Control Device, Quick Attach Attachments, Indo-European Foods, Receivables Management Partners, Gary Platt Manufacturing, Persante, Industrial Magnetics, Omega Environmental Technologies, Huskie Tools, Union Tractor, GPA Acquisition Company, Pyramid Healthcare, SP Industries, ShurCo Acquisition, Lifesafer, Vectorply, All Tech/IESCO, Cash Management Solutions, United Rotary Brush Corporation, Kieffer & Co., Stant Corporation, World Wide Packaging, Contract Land Staff, Intelliteach, Mosquito Control Services, TMI International, Workhorse Rail, Specified Fittings, Atronix, Windy City Wire, St. Croix Hospice

Other Locations:
216 N Broadway
Suite 203
Fargo, ND 58102

Key Executives:
Douglas E Mark, Managing Partner
612-371-5703
e-mail: dmark@northstarcapital.com
Education: BBA, University of North Dakota
Background: Churchill Capital; Charles Bailly & Company

Venture Capital & Private Equity Firms / Domestic Firms

Scott L Becker, Founder/Advisory Partner
612-371-5704
e-mail: sbecker@northstarcapital.com
Education: BA, St. John's University; MBA, University of Minnesota; JD, William Mitchell College of Law
Background: Manager of Investments, Adler Management; General Mills; Control Data Business Centers
Charles L Schroeder, Founder/Advisory Partner
612-371-5706
Education: BA, Reed College; MA, Tufts University
Background: Investment Manager, Churchill Capital; Salomon Brothers

1344 NORTHWOOD VENTURES
485 Underhill Boulevard
Suite 205
Syosset, NY 11791

Phone: 516-364-5544 Fax: 516-364-0879
e-mail: pschiff@northwoodventures.com
web: www.northwoodventures.com

Mission Statement: Private equity firm which invests in venture capital opportunities, management buyouts and industry consolidations.
Geographic Preference: United States
Fund Size: $200 million
Founded: 1983
Average Investment: $2-10 million
Minimum Investment: $2 million
Investment Criteria: Wide Range Industries, Management Buyouts, Industry Consolidations
Industry Group Preference: Telecommunications, Consumer Services, Internet Technology, Manufacturing, Retailing, Broadcasting, Financial Services, Health Related, Service Industries, Wireless
Portfolio Companies: abc Financial, Air Waves Inc., Celebration Restaurant Group, Centerline Communications, Charge Point, Community Broadcasters LLC, Designer Protein, DSG, Gifnote, Jack Rogers, JVC, Man Crates, pdv Wireless, Red Built, Rudy's Barbershop, Spectrum Five, Stone Goff Partners, Tstar 600, Zevia
Key Executives:
  Paul Homer, Managing Director
  Education: MBA, Zarb School of Business at Hofstra University; BS Finance, Bentley College
  Background: Financial Analyst
  James G. Schiff, Managing Director
  Education: BA, History, Trinity College; Masters, Real Estate, Columbia University
  Background: Acquisitions group, HFZ Capital; Groton Partners
  Peter G. Schiff, Managing Partner/Founder
  Education: Lake Forest College; MBA, University of Chicago, Booth School of Business
  Background: Warburg Pincus Co.; Chemical Bank (JPMorgan Chase & Co.)

1345 NORWEST EQUITY PARTNERS
80 South 8th Street
Suite 3600
Minneapolis, MN 55402

Phone: 612-215-1600
web: www.nep.com

Mission Statement: Norwest Equity Partners (NEP) is a leading private equity firm focused on building companies into industry leaders. NEP manages $4.6 billion of capital through a series of equity and mezzanine funds. The firm is currently investing in NEP IX, a $1.2 billion fund.
Fund Size: $1.2 billion
Founded: 1961
Investment Criteria: Management Buyouts, Recapitalizations, Growth Financing
Industry Group Preference: Industrial Services, Business to Business, Healthcare, Consumer Services, Consumer Products, Distribution, Financial Services, Manufacturing, Technology
Portfolio Companies: Apothecary Products, Arteriors, Actex, Bailiwick, Bix Produce, Bowtech, Clover Imaging Group, Edge Fitness Clubs, Eyebobs, Focal Point Data Risk, GoHealth, Institute For Integrative Nutrition, Marco, Movati Athletic, Old Hickory Smokehouse, Pentec Health, Ramsey Industries, Surgical Information Systems, Unitah Engineering & Land Serveying, Wahoo Fitness, Welocalize, West Star Aviation
Key Executives:
  Tim DeVries, Managing Partner
  612-215-1679
  Fax: 612-215-1601
  e-mail: tdevries@nmp.com
  Education: BA, Bethel College; MBA, Cornell University
  Background: Churchill Companies
  Directorships: BowTech, Gopher Resource, Minnesota Rubber & Plastics
  Timothy Kuehl, Partner
  612-215-1668
  Fax: 612-215-1601
  e-mail: tkuehl@nep.com
  Education: BBA, University of Notre Dame; MBA, Wharton School of the University of Pennsylvania
  Background: Investment Advisors Inc.; Professional Hockey Player (Sweden)
  Directorships: Momentum Group, Pentec Health, Shock Doctor, Surgical Information Systems
  John Lindahl, Chairman
  612-215-1659
  Fax: 612-215-1601
  e-mail: jlindahl@nep.com
  Education: BS, BA, University of Minnesota
  Background: Norwest Bank
  Directorships: Pentec Health
  Todd Solow, Partner
  612-215-1671
  e-mail: tsolow@nep.com
  Education: BBA, University of Michigan; MBA, Kellogg School of Management Northwestern University
  Background: First Union Securities; Jacobson Companies
  Directorships: Actagro, Jacobson Companies, Shock Doctor, Stanton Carpet Corp., Trilliant Food & Nutrition, Wealth Enhancement Group

1346 NORWEST VENTURE PARTNERS
525 University Avenue
Suite 800
Palo Alto, CA 94301

Phone: 650-321-8000
web: www.nvp.com

Mission Statement: Norwest Venture Partners (NVP) is a global venture and growth equity investment firm that manages more than $3.7 billion in capital and has funded over 450 companies since inception. It has offices in Palo Alto, California, Mumbai and Bangalore, India and Herzelia, Israel.
Fund Size: $3.7 billion
Founded: 1961
Average Investment: $10-$15 million
Minimum Investment: $1-$5 million
Investment Criteria: Multi-Stage
Industry Group Preference: Software, Services, Internet, Systems & Hardware, IT Infrastructure, Information Technology, Technology-Enabled Business, Business Products & Services, Financial Services, Consumer Products, Healthcare
Portfolio Companies: 6 River Systems, ACL, ActOn, Agari, Alma Campus, American Endovascular, Aporeto, Appnomic, Appriss, Attune, Avetta, Bailey 44, Birdies, Bitglass, BlueJeans, Boost Insurance, Brite, Button, Capillary, CareCloud, Casper, ClearDATA, CognitiveScale, Common,

481

Venture Capital & Private Equity Firms / Domestic Firms

Copper, Cority, CRMnext, CyberX, Cynet, Dremio, Dtex Systems, ElasticRun, Angagio, Ess Kay Finance, Exabeam, Extole, Five Star Finance, Gong.io, Grove Collaborative, Health Catalyst, Hobnob, HoneyBook, IFTTT, Impel NeuroPharma, Infutor, Jolyn, JoyRun, Karat, Kendra Scott, Kishlay Snacks, Knotel, Kwik, Leanplum, Legion, Lending Club, Lumosity, Madison Reed, Manthan Systems, Minted, Mist, MobileIron, Modsy, Motif Investing, National Stock Exchange of India, NationWide Healthcare, NextHealth Technologies, Ninth Decimal, Nueclear, Omada Health, Onsite Dental, Opendoor, Ovum Hospitals, Owler, PCH International, Pepperfry, Perfint, Personali, Phiar, Plaid, Policygenius, Prevedere, Propel, Qubole, Quikr, Qventus, Rainmaker, RevX, Ritual, RiverMend Health, Sadbhav, Science Exchange, Second Measure, Shape Security, Silk Road Medical, Simppli, Singular, SlashNext, Smilo, SnapRoute, Socrates AI, Sojern, Spotify, StellaService, Sulekha, SundaySky, Suvidhaa, Swiggy, Talkspace, Target PharmaSolutions, Thyrocare, TigerConnect, Topo Athletic, Turnitin, Uber, Udemy, Vast, Veritas Finance, VisitPay, WekaIO, Wiliot, Wine Access, World View, Zenoti

Other Locations:
Two South Park St.
3rd Floor
San Francisco, CA 94107
Phone: 415-918-5010

6 Hachoshlim Street
7th Floor
PO Box 12242
Herzliya 46724
Israel
Phone: 972-774107090

15th Floor, Express Tower
Nariman Point
Mumbai 400021
India
Phone: 91-2261501111

Key Executives:
Promod Haque, Senior Managing Partner
Education: BS, Electrical Engineering, University of Delhi, India; PhD Electrical Engineering, Northwestern University; MBA, Northwestern Kellogg Graduate School of Management
Background: COO/CEO, Siemens International, Thorn EMI, Emergent Technologies, Dimensional Medicine
Jon Kossow, Managing Partner
Education: BA, Harvard College
Background: Goldman Sachs
Directorships: ACL, Appriss, Avetta, Cority, Infutor, Rainmaker, Topo Athletic, Turnitin, Wine Access
Matthew D Howard, General Partner
Background: VP Marketing, Vertical Networks; Digital Equipment Corporation; BDM International; Bolt, Beranek
Jeffrey M Crowe, Managing Partner
Education: MBA, Stanford Graduate School of Business; BA, Dartmouth College
Background: DoveBid, Edify Corporation, ROLM Corporation, Siemens, IBM,
Dror Nahumi, General Partner
Education: BSc, Electrical Engineering, Technion-Israel Institute of Technology, Haifa
Background: EVP & Chief Strategy Officer, ECI; CEO, Axonlink; Senior Research Engineer, AT&T Bell Labs
Directorships: Pontis, SolarEdge, SundaySky
Dr. Ryan A Harris, General Partner
Education: BA, Psychology, Stanford University; MS, Health Research & Policy, Stanford University; MD, University of California, San Francisco School of Medicine
Background: Principal, The Carlyle Group; Industry Ventures
Casper de Clercq, General Partner
Education: BA, Biochemistry, Dartmouth College; MS, Biological Science, Stanford University; MBA, Stanford University Graduate School of Business
Background: Partner, U.S. Venture Partners; Vice President, Business Development, Sales & Marketing, Aerogen; Co-Founder, Epicor; Marketing, Heartpoint
Directorships: Basis, Simpirica Spine
Sonya Brown, General Partner
Education: BS, Northwestern University; MBA, Harvard Busienss School; CFA
Background: Summit Partners
Directorships: Aramsco, Airborne Health, Central Security Group, Physicians Formula Holdings, Snap Fitness, Sparta Systems
Niren Shah, Managing Director, NVP India

1347 NORWICH VENTURES
1210 Broadcasting Road
Suite 201
Wyomissing, PA 19610
Phone: 610-373-5320 **Fax:** 610-373-5520
web: www.norwichventures.com

Mission Statement: Norwich Ventures is a venture capital firm committed to helping entrepreneurs, healthcare professionals and inventors build innovative medical device companies.

Investment Criteria: Early-Stage
Industry Group Preference: Medical Devices
Portfolio Companies: Affera, Arterys, Daktari Diagnostics, Intelligent Bio-Systems, Lexington Medical, Pelvalon, Podimetrics, ReThink Medical, Rhythmia Medical, Soffio Medical, Svelte Medical Systems, Syncro Medical Innovations, Vaxess Technologies

Other Locations:
303 Wyman Street
Suite 300
Waltham, MA 02451
Phone: 781-890-2161 **Fax:** 781-207-8526

Key Executives:
Philip Fleck, Director
e-mail: phil@norwichventures.com
Education: BS, Mechanical Engineering, Lehigh University; University of Pennsylvania
Background: President/COO, Arrow International
Marlin Miller, Co-Founder/Senior Advisor
e-mail: mm@norwichventures.com
Education: MBA, Harvard Business School; BS, Ceramic Engineering, Alfred University
Background: Chairman/CEO, Arrow International; VP, Connors Investor Services
Aaron Sandoski, Co-Founder/Managing Director
e-mail: aaron@norwichventures.com
Education: AB, Chemistry & Economics, Dartmouth College; MBA, Harvard Business School
Background: DEKA; Consultant, McKinsey & Company

1348 NOVAK BIDDLE VENTURE PARTNERS
PO Box 341877
Bethesda, MD 20827
Phone: 240-497-1910
e-mail: info@novakbiddle.com
web: www.novakbiddle.com

Mission Statement: To provide equity financing and assistance to the management of young, information technology companies.

Geographic Preference: East Coast
Fund Size: $580 million
Founded: 1997
Minimum Investment: $100,000
Investment Criteria: Early Stage through First Round, will consider Later Stage & Spinouts
Industry Group Preference: Communications, Computer Related, Education, Electronic Components, Instrumentation,

Internet Technology, Optical Technology, Information Technology, Consumer Internet, Security, Software
Portfolio Companies: 2U, AddThis, AnswerLogic, Appfluent Technology, Appian, Approva, Blackboard, Capital Education Group, Centice, Cetrifuge Systems, Clear Standards, Command Information, Copiun, CorasWorks, CounterStorm, Digital Signal, DigitalBridge Communications, Educational Initiatives, Emotive Communications, Entevo, FiberZone Networks, Fidelis Education, Giga Information Group, Infoblox, Intelliworks, LifeMinders, LifeShield Security, LogicLibrary, Luna Technologies, Matrics, N.E.W. Customer Service, ObjectVideo, Optinel Systems, Orchestro, Panasas, Paratek, Parchment, PlaySay, Previstar, Princeton Optronics, ReverbNation, SafeView, Shoeboxed, Simplexity, Social Gaming Network, SolidFire, Spectrum K12 School Solutions, SS8, Starfish Retention Solutions, Synchris, Tantivy Communications, Telogy Networks, Torrent Systems, Triumfant, Trusted Computer Solutions, Trusted Edge, UniversityNow, Vubiquity, WealthEngine, Webs, Woodwing Communications Systems, XtremeSpectrum, Ztar Mobile

Key Executives:
    A.G.W. Biddle III, Co-Founder/General Partner
    e-mail: jack@novakbiddle.com
    Education: University of Virginia
    Background: InterCAP; Partner, Vanguard Atlantic; Executive Assistant, Gartner Group; Business Development Partners
    E. Rogers Novak, Jr., General Partner
    Background: Co-Founder, Grotech Partners; Investment Banking, Baker, Watts & Co
    Directorships: Blackboard, SpectrumK12, Trusted Computer Solutions, Digital Signal Corporation, Intelliworks, Centrifuge Systems
    Philip L. Bronner, General Partner
    Education: BS, Computer Science, Carnegie Mellon University; JD, University of Pennsylvania School of Law; MBA, The Wharton School
    Background: Management Consultant, McKinsey & Co
    Directorships: Approva, Vision Chain, InGrid, Netcordia, Freewebs, Clearspring, Social Gaming Network, 2Tor
    Tom Scholl, General Partner
    e-mail: tom@novakbiddle.com
    Education: Purdue University
    Background: Founded Telogy Networks; VP, Hughes Network Systems; Co-Founder, Cognio; Author of 'Packet Switching' in McGraw Hill's Communications Handbook
    Simita Bose, Partner
    Education: BS, Northwestern University; MBA, Harvard Business School
    Background: The Boeing Company; Booz Allen Hamilton
    Joy E. Binford, Chief Financial Officer
    e-mail: joy@novakbiddle.com
    Education: BA, American University; Certified Public Accountant
    Background: CFO, InterCAP Graphics
    Prashanth V. Boccasam, General Partner
    Education: Computer Science, University of Pune; University of Cincinnati; Executive Management Program, Sloan School, MIT
    Background: Founder & CEO, Approva Corporation
    Directorships: Copiun, Approva, Appfluent, Appian, Centrifuge Systems

1349 NOVAQUEST CAPITAL MANAGEMENT
4208 Six Forks Road
Suite 920
Raleigh, NC 27609

Phone: 919-459-8620 **Fax:** 919-516-0580
e-mail: NQinfo@nqcapital.com
web: www.nqcapital.com

Mission Statement: NovaQuest Capital Management manages private equity and other investments in the global biopharmaceutical sector, where its principal focus is investing in late-stage clinical assets and commercial phase biopharmaceutical products. NovaQuest contracts with global biopharmaceutical corporations to invest side-by-side in their most strategic development and commercialization programs. Side-by-side investing means that NovaQuest invests in the products that biopharmaceuticals intend to develop and commercialize while the biopharmaceutical continues to invest its own capital in the same products.

Founded: 2000
Industry Group Preference: Biopharmaceuticals
Portfolio Companies: Allergan, Azurity, california Cryobank, Catalyst Clinical Research, Clinical Ink, Eisai, Global european Pharma, Hospira, Informed DNA, Lilly, Pfizer Inc., Pharmaxis, ProStrakan, sanofi, Shionogi Inc., Takeda

Key Executives:
    Ron Wooten, Founder/Managing Partner
    Education: BS, Chemistry, University of North Carolina; MBA, Boston University
    Background: EVP, Quintiles; First Union Securities
    John Bradley, Founder/Partner/Chief Operating Officer
    Education: BBA, MBA, Wake Forest University; CPA
    Background: SVP, Quintiles' Corporate Development Group
    Jonathan Tunnicliff, Founder/Partner/Chief Investment Officer
    Education: BS, Mathematical Statistics, University of Liverpool; MS, Medical Statistics, University of Newcastle; MBa, Sheffield Hallam University
    Background: Director of Operations, S-Cubed
    Robert Hester, Chief Financial Officer
    Education: BA, Accounting, North Carolina State University; CPA
    Background: Sr Finance Director, NovaQuest unit, Quintiles; Director/Controller, Misys Healthcare; Public Accountant, KPMG

1350 NOVARTIS VENTURE FUNDS
100 Technology Square
Cambridge, MA 02139

Phone: 617-871-3536
e-mail: claire.mcnulty@nvfund.com
web: www.nvfund.com

Mission Statement: Investing in innovative life science concepts for patient benefit creating attractive returns for entrepreneurs and investors.

Geographic Preference: United States, Canada, Europe, Switzerland, Asia/Pacific
Fund Size: $800 million
Founded: 1996
Average Investment: $15-30 million
Minimum Investment: $100,000
Investment Criteria: Seed Stage, All Stages Considered
Industry Group Preference: New Therapeutics & Platforms, Medical Devices & Implants, Diagnostics, Drug Delivery, Life Sciences, Healthcare, Biopolymers
Portfolio Companies: Aelin Therapeutics, AAD, Adicet Bio, Akouos, Artios, Annexon Bioscience, Anokion, AGL, Bicycle Therapeutics, Cavion, eFFECTOR, Enterprise Therapeutics, E-Scape Bio, Expansion Therapeutics, Forendo Pharma, Forma Therapeutics, Galera Therapeutics Inc., Genedata, ImaginAb, Inflazome, Kanyos Bio, LemonAid Health, Macrolide Pharmaceuticals, Myopowers, Oculis, Rox, Selenity Therapeutics, Scan Therapeutics, Twentyeight Seven, Vivet Therapeutics

Other Locations:
    Novartis International AG
    Postfach CH-4002
    Basel
    Switzerland

Venture Capital & Private Equity Firms / Domestic Firms

Phone: 41-61-324-37-14
Simone Forrer, Office Manager

Key Executives:
Dr. Markus Goebel, Managing Director, Cambridge
Education: MD, PhD, Ludwig Maximilians University in Munich; MBA, Henley Management College
Background: Pharmaceutical Corporate M&A; Head Nervous System Business Development & Licensing; Farmitalia Germany; Roche
Michal Silverberg, Managing Director, Cambridge
Education: BA, Economics & Business Management, Haifa University; MBA, Tel Aviv University; MA, Biotechnology, Columbia University
Background: Senior Partner, Takeda Ventures; Novo Nordisk; MGVS; OSI Pharmaceuticals
Dr. Campbell Murray, Managing Director, Cambridge
Education: MPP, John F. Kennedy School of Government; MBA, Harvard Business School
Background: Novartis Institutes for BioMedical Research; Auckland Hospital
Dr. Anja König, Global Head, Basel
Education: PhD, Cornell Univeristy
Background: Associate Partner, McKinsey and Company
Florent Gros, Managing Director, Basel
Education: MA, Biotechnology Engineering, in France
Background: Nestlé; Pasteur Merieux Connaught

1351 NOVELTEK CAPITAL CORPORATION
521 5th Avenue
Suite 1700
New York, NY 10175

Phone: 646-244-0098 Fax: 212-370-0925
e-mail: info@noveltek.com
web: www.noveltek.com

Mission Statement: Synergistic services revolving around emerging growth strategic business development and financing, exit strategies in the US and Europe (including dual listings), and post exit financial strategies.

Founded: 1983
Minimum Investment: $1 million
Investment Criteria: Emerging Growth
Industry Group Preference: Information Technology, Telecommunications, Healthcare, Energy, Transportation, Consumer Services, Biotechnology

Key Executives:
Gabor (Gabe) Baumann, President
212-286-1963
Fax: 212-661-7606
Background: Mitsubishi, Pfizer, Asahi, American Optical, ITW, Solomon Smith Barney, Natexis Banque Populaire, Gruntal and National Securities, President's White House Task Force

1352 NOVENTI VENTURES
Newark, CA 94560

web: noventi.net

Mission Statement: An early-stage venture capital firm focused on building successful companies through the partnership we establish with our entrepreneurs. By leveraging our decades of operating experience, a global network of resources, and a proven approach to venture investing, we help guide our companies through the many seen and unseen challenges of growth.

Founded: 2002
Investment Criteria: Early-Stage
Industry Group Preference: Technology, Clean Technology
Portfolio Companies: Active Optical MEMS, Auror Algae, Bitfone, Celltick, Dishcarft, Easy Market, Ercio, IrisCube, Kasenna, M7, Minerva Networks, Neato Robotics, Nextlabs, Sygate, Velomat Assembly Automation, Waterguru

Key Executives:
Giacomo Marini, Founder & Managing Director
Background: Chairman, Marini Investments; Chairman, TES Automation; Chairman, Cosmo Industrie; CEO, FutureTel; President & CEO, Common Ground Software; Co-Founder, Logitech; IBM; Olivetti
Directorships: Marini Investments, Velomat, PCTEL

Other Locations:
15 Bonnie Way
Allendale, NJ 07401
Phone: 610-254-4286 Fax: 610-254-4240

1354 NOVUS VENTURES LP
Cupertino, CA 95014

Mission Statement: To provide funding for promising early-stage companies and contribute Novus resources and participation to these ventures to help them grow and flourish in the dynamic, challenging high-tech business world.

Geographic Preference: Western United States
Fund Size: $150 million
Founded: 1994
Minimum Investment: $200,000
Investment Criteria: Early-Stage
Industry Group Preference: Information Technology, Enterprise Software, Infrastructure, Semiconductors
Portfolio Companies: ADECN, Encirq, FlyteComm, Inapac Technologies, expresso, Invivo Data, mBlox, Rainmaker Systems, PropertyView Solutions, Pathwork Diagnostics, Tidal Software, Venturi Wireless, Toolwire, Zantaz

Key Executives:
Shirley Cerrudo, General Partner
e-mail: scerrudo@novusventures.com
Background: Burr Egan Deleage & Company, Wells Fargo Investment Company, McKinsey & Company
Daniel Tompkins, Managing Partner
e-mail: ddtompkins@novusventures.com
Education: BA & BSEE, Rice University; MBA Stanford University
Background: Fairchild Semiconductor, DSC Ventures, Wells Fargo Investment Company
Stewart Schuster, Managing Director
e-mail: eschuster@novusventures.com
Education: B.Math, Washington University; M.Math, PhD, Computer Science, University of Illinois
Background: Vice President, Sybase Incorporated; Technical and Marketing Management at Ingres; Tandem Computers; and Intel

1355 NTH POWER TECHNOLOGIES
555 Mission Street
Suite 3300
San Francisco, CA 94105

Phone: 415-983-9983
e-mail: info@nthpower.com
web: www.nthpower.com

Mission Statement: Focusing on investment opportunities derived from the transition to competitive and global energy service markets.

Geographic Preference: United States
Fund Size: $420 million
Founded: 1997
Average Investment: $1-$2.5 million
Minimum Investment: $500,000
Investment Criteria: First-Stage, Second-Stage, Energy Sector
Industry Group Preference: Distribution, Utilities, Consumer Services, Power Technologies, Energy, Outsourcing & Efficiency, Storage, Business to Business, Information Technology, Energy Technology
Portfolio Companies: Accelergy, AllConnect, ARXX, BPL Global, Calstar, Capstone Turbine, Comverge, Evergreen Solar, FirstFuel Software, Glasspoint Solar, Hara, Nanogram

Venture Capital & Private Equity Firms / Domestic Firms

Devices, Nexant, Northern Power Systems, Precursor Energetics, Propel Biofuels, Proton Energy Systems, RSI, Rive Technology, Silicon Energy, SmartSynch, SpectraSensors, SynapSense, Terrapass, Tempronics, Thetus, Topanga, Tioga Energy

Key Executives:
Nancy C Floyd, Founder/Managing Director
Education: MA, Political Science, Rutgers University; BA, Political Science, Franklin and Marshall College
Background: Founder, NFC Energy Corporation; Co-Founder, Pac Tel Spectrum; Launched Spectrum Services
Directorships: Silicon Energy, Evergreen Solar, Smartsynch, Serveron, SpectraSensors, Propel Biofuels, Thetus
Tim Woodward, Managing Director
Education: MBA, UCLA; BS, Resource Economics, Berkeley University
Background: Liberty Environmental Partners; Chairman, Monitoring Technology Corporation; Senior Management, First Source
Bryant J Tong, Managing Director
Education: BS, Accounting, University of California at Berkeley
Background: Co-Founder, ReSourcePhoenix Inc.; Senior Management, Phoenix American; Ernst & Young
Directorships: Accelergy, Arxx, Calstar
Matt Jones, Partner
Education: Duke University's Fuqua School of Business; BA, Mechanical Engineering, University of California at Davis
Background: Accenture (Andersen Consulting)
Directorships: Tempronics, Topanga, REEl Solar, Precursor Energetics

1356 NUVEEN
730 Third Avenue
New York, NY 10017

e-mail: contact@nuveenglobal.com
web: www.nuveen.com

Mission Statement: Managing assets across diverse asset classes, geographies, and investment styles, offers solutions for a range of investors including pension funds, insurance companies, sovereign wealth funds, banks and family offices.

Geographic Preference: Worldwide
Fund Size: $989 billion
Founded: 1898

Key Executives:
Vijay Advani, Chief Executive Officer
Education: BA, University of Mumbai; MBA, University of Massachusetts
Background: Co-President, Franklin Templeton Investments; Advisor, World Bank
Jose Minaya, President & Chief Investment Officer
Education: BS, Finance, Manhattan College; MBA, Amos Tuck School of Business, Dartmouth College
Background: President, TIAA Global Real Assets; Merrill Lynch; JP Morgan

1357 NVIDIA INCEPTION
2788 San Tomas Expressway
Santa Clara, CA 95051

Phone: 408-486-2000
web: www.nvidia.com

Mission Statement: NVIDIA looks for partners that are using their GPU platforms to pursue breakthroughs in data analytics, self-driving cars, healthcare, Smart Cities, high performance computing, virtual reality and more.

1358 NYC SEED
Six MetroTech Center
Brooklyn, NY 11201

Phone: 707-469-3669
e-mail: apply@nycseed.com

Mission Statement: NYC Seed was formed to provide deserving New York City seed stage entrepreneurs with the capital and support they need to move from idea to product launch. NYC Seed has brought together many New York organizations to provide funding and support for young companies in New York City. The NYC Seed Partners include ITAC, The New York City Economic Development Corporation, The New York City Investment Fund, NYSTAR, and Polytechnic Institute of NYU.

Investment Criteria: Seed stage
Industry Group Preference: Software, Technology
Portfolio Companies: Magnetic, Valign, Ticketfly, SeatGeek, Enterproid, How About We, Datadog, ToutApp, Zipmark, Eachscape, Contently, Silver Lining, Amicus, See.me, Singly, Fieldiens, Powhow, Zeel, SoMoLend, Ufora, 10sheet, CourseHorse, Clothes Horse, Little Borrowed Dress, Bounce Exchange, Enigma

Key Executives:
Owen Davis, Managing Director
Education: BA, Brown University; MBA, Columbia Business School
Background: General Partner, Contour Venture Partners; Adjunct Professor, Columbia Business School; Private Equity Consultant, PC LLC; CEO, Petal Computing; CEO, Sonata; CEO, Thinking Media

1359 O'REILLY ALPHATECH VENTURES
1 Lombard Street
Suite 303
San Francisco, CA 94111

Phone: 415-693-0200
e-mail: plans@oatv.com
web: www.oatv.com

Mission Statement: As seed investors, our focus is to help founders find clarity around their product and market in the most cash efficient way possible. This is a critical stage of development and one that can easily be misguided should a company raise too much or too little capital.

Average Investment: $250,000 - $2 million
Investment Criteria: Seed Stage
Industry Group Preference: Internet, Big Data, Mobile, Networking
Portfolio Companies: 3D Robotics, Cquia, Amee, Artists Wanted, Betabrand, Bitly, Bloom, Chairish, Chartbeat, Chumby, Codeacademy, Cover, Devver, Fastyl, Fidelis, Fitnesskeeper, Foursquare, Gamelayers, Get Satisfaction, Good Data, Grouply, Instructables, Jirafe, Learnzillon, littleBits Electronics, Localdirt, Maker Meia, Makespace, Misfit Wearables, Openx, Opensignal, Parakey, Path Intelligence, Peerj, Planet Labs, Science Exchange, Seeclickfix, Sherpaa, Sight Machine, Signal Sciences, Sonicliving, Spark, Strobe, Sweetlabs, Timehop, Tripit, Wesabe

Key Executives:
Bryce Roberts, Managing Director
Education: Brigham Young University
Directorships: 3D Robotics, Bit.ly, Bloom, Chartbeat, Codeacademy, Cover, Devver, Fidelis, FitnessKeeper, Foursquare, Gamelayers, Get Satisfaction, Kirafe, OpenX, Parakey
Mark Jacobsen, Managing Director
Education: BA, St. Olaf College; JD, Georgetown University Law Center
Background: Executive VP, New Ventures, O'Reilly

Venture Capital & Private Equity Firms / Domestic Firms

Media; Business Affairs Director, Colossal Pictures
Directorships: AMEE, Betabrand, CollabNet, Planet Labs, Fast.ly, LocalDirt, LearnZillion, OpenSignal, Path Intelligence, SeeClickFix

1360 OAK HILL CAPITAL PARTNERS
One Stamford Plaza
263 Tresser Boulevard
15th Floor
Stamford, CT 06901

Phone: 203-328-1600
e-mail: hr@oakhillcapital.com
web: www.oakhillcapital.com

Mission Statement: Oak Hill Capital Partners is a leading private equity firm with a unique family-office heritage. Oak Hill targets opportunities to partner with exceptional entrepreneurs, management teams and corporations who share the firm's vision for value creation and philosophy of aligning interests.
Fund Size: $8 billion
Founded: 1985
Industry Group Preference: Business Products & Services, Financial Services, Distribution, Healthcare, Media, Telecommunications, Technology
Portfolio Companies: Ability, AccentCare, Align Technology, American Skiing Company, Anchor Media Investors, Arder Holdings, Atlantic Broadband Group, Avolon Aerospace Limited, Berlin Packaging, Blackboard, Butler Schein Animal Health, Caribbean Restaurants, Cincinnati Bell, Dave & Buster's, Duane Reade, Earth Fare, eGain Communications, Exl Services, Financial Engines, Firth Rixson, FNB United, GATX Logistics, Genpact Limited, Hillman Group, Intermedia.net, IPWireless, Jacobson Companies, Local TV, MeriStar Investment Partners Lesee, Metrika, Monsoon Commerce, NSA International, OH Aircraft Acquisition, Oversee.net, Primus International, Progressive Moulded Products, Pulsant Limited, RSC Holdings, Security Networks, SmartPak Equine, Southern Air Holdings, SVTC Technologies, SWS Group, Telecity Group, The Container Store, TravelCenters of America, Vantage Oncology, Vertex Data Science, ViaWest, WaveDivision Holdings, WideOpenWest

Other Locations:
2775 Sand Hill Road
Suite 220
Menlo Park, CA 94025
Phone: 650-234-0500

65 East 55th Street
32nd Floor
New York, NY 10022
Phone: 212-527-8400

Key Executives:
J. Taylor Crandall, Managing Partner
Education: BA, Bowdoin College
Background: Vice President, First National Bank of Boston
Tyler Wolfram, Managing Partner & CEO
Education: AB, Brown University; MBA, Wharton School, University of Pennsylvania
Background: Managing Director, J.H. Whitney & Co. LLC; Managing Director, Cornerstone Equity Investors LLC; VP, Donaldson Lufkin & Jenrette Inc.
Brian Cherry, Managing Partner
Education: AB, Princeton University; MBA, Wharton School, University of Pennsylvania
Background: Senior Managing Director, J.H. Whitney & Co. LLC; Merchant Banker, Donald Lufkin & Jenrette Inc.
Steven Puccinelli, Managing Partner
Education: BS, University of California, Berkeley; MBA, Harvard Business School
Background: Investcorp International Inc.; Donaldson Lufkin & Jenrette Inc.

1361 OAK INVESTMENT PARTNERS
Three Pickwick Plaza
Suite 302
Greenwich, CT 06830

Phone: 203-226-8346 **Fax:** 203-846-0284
web: www.oakvc.com

Mission Statement: OAK invests in rapidly growing companies that address large or expanding markets. These companies ideally can establish a leading market position in an equity-efficient manner, and protect that position once established.
Geographic Preference: United States, Worldwide
Fund Size: $5.8 billion
Founded: 1978
Average Investment: late stage $30-75 million; early $10-25 million
Minimum Investment: $5 million
Investment Criteria: Invest across a spectrum, in proven management teams, source deals from a refined referral network.
Industry Group Preference: Enterprise Services, Telecommunications, Storage, Financial Services, Outsourcing & Efficiency, Healthcare, Retailing, Infrastructure, Software, Information Technology, Internet, Consumer Products, E-Commerce & Manufacturing, Healthcare Information Technology, Energy
Portfolio Companies: Acculynk, Airspan Networks, Aspect Software, Attivio, Aurora Algae, Benefitfocus, Boston-Power, Brit Media, Catlight Health, Centric Software, Chamate, Cheddars, Circle Internet Financial Limited, Cloud Technology Partners, CommVerge Solutions, Deem, Demand Media, Dot & Bo, Duedil, Enjoy Technology, eSolar, FirstRain, FreshBooks, FRS, Gazillion Entertainment, GENBAND, Geotrace Technologies, Giosis, Good Technology, Great Gate Network, GTS CE Holdings, Hipmunk, IMI Exchange, Independent Living Solutions, iZENEtech, Keep Holdings/AdKeeper, Kinetic Social, Kratos Defense & Security Solutions, Kuaipay, Lianlian Pay, Limelight Networks, LumaSense Technologies, Major League Gaming, Milyoni, Mimosa Networks, MobiTV, Mojix, Movik Networks, Moxie Software, MyLife.com, NeoPhotonics Corporation, Nexant, NextNav, nLight Photonics, Nomorerack.com, Norse, NowThisMedia, One Medical Group, Photonic Devices, Photobucket, Plastic Logic, Precision fOr Medicine Holdings, Protean Electric, Radisphere National Radiology Group, RazorGator, Rebel Mouse, SmartDrive Systems, Solarflare Communications, sovrn Holdings, Sunrop Fuels, SunSun Lighting, Thrillist Media Group, Tikona Digital Networks, U.S. Auto Parts Network, Vesta, Wonga.com, xG Health Solutions, XIO, Ybrant, YoYi Media, Zayo Group, Zumobi

Other Locations:
901 Main Avenue
Suite 600
Norwalk, CT 06851

525 University Avenue
Suite 1300
Palo Alto, CA 94301
Phone: 650-614-3700 **Fax:** 650-328-6345

3890 Wells Fargo Center
90 South Seventh Street
Minneapolis, MN 55402
Phone: 612-339-9322 **Fax:** 612-337-8017

Key Executives:
Edward F. Glassmeyer, Managing Partner
e-mail: ed@oakvc.com
Education: MBA, The Tuck School; Princeton University
Background: Managing Director, Citicorp Venture Capital; Managing Director, The Sprout Capital Group
Directorships: Collabera, Enterprist Sourcing Services, Geotrace, Major League Gaming, Xiotech
Bandel L. Carano, Managing Partner
e-mail: bandel@oakvc.com

Education: BS/MS Electrical Engineering, Stanford University
Background: Morgan Stanley
Directorships: Stanford Engineering Venture Fund
Fred Harman, Managing Partner
650-614-3700
e-mail: fred@oakvc.com
Education: BS & MS, Electrical Engineering, Stanford University; MBA, Harvard Graduate School of Business
Background: Morgan Stanley's Venture Capital Group
Directorships: AdKeeper, Aspect Software, Demand Media, Federated Media, FRS, Knowledge Networks, Limelight Networks, MyLife.com, RazorGator, Rearden Commerce, Shop.com, Sutherland Global
Ann Lamont, Managing Partner
203-226-8346
e-mail: annie@oakvc.com
Education: BA, Political Science, Stanford University
Background: Research Associate, Hambrecht & Quist
Directorships: Acculynk, Argus Information & Advisory Services, Benefitfocus, Castlight Health, iHealth Technologies, NetSpend, PayFlex, PharMEDium Healthcare, Radisphere, TxVia, Vesta
Grace Ames, General Partner & Chief Operating Officer
e-mail: grace@oakvc.com
Education: BA Government, Smith College
Background: Harvard Management Company; VP, Barclay Investments
Ren Riley, Venture Partner
650-614-3700
e-mail: ren@oakvc.com
Education: BA, Government, Dartmouth College
Background: Senior Associate, Robertson Stephens
Directorships: Centric Software, Gazillion Entertainment, MyLife.com, Moxie Software, Sutherland Global Services, YoYi Media
Andrew Adams, General Partner
Education: BA, History, Princeton University
Background: Senior Associate, Capital Resource Partners
Directorships: iHealth Technologies, NetSpend, Radisphere, National Radiology Group, XG Health Solutions

1362 OAKTREE CAPITAL MANAGEMENT LLC
333 South Grand Avenue
28th Floor
Los Angeles, CA 90071

Phone: 213-830-6300 **Fax:** 213-830-6293
e-mail: contactus@oaktreecapital.com
web: www.oaktreecapital.com

Mission Statement: Seeks to purchase senior and secured debt and make short and long term investments.

Geographic Preference: United States, Canada, Western Europe
Fund Size: $13.3 billion
Founded: 1995
Average Investment: $100 million
Minimum Investment: $5 million
Investment Criteria: Mezzanine, Acquisition, Recapitalization, Special Situations, Distressed Debt
Industry Group Preference: All markets considered

Other Locations:
Oaktree Capital Management LP
1301 Avenue of the Americas
34th Floor
New York, NY 10019
Phone: 212-284-1900 **Fax:** 212-284-1901

Oaktree Capital Management LP
680 Washington Blvd
6th Floor
Stamford, CT 06901
Phone: 203-363-3200 **Fax:** 203-363-3210

Oaktree Capital Management LP
11611 San Vincente Blvd
Suite 700
Los Angeles, CA 90049
Phone: 310-442-0542 **Fax:** 310-442-0540

Oaktree GmbH
Frankfurter Welle
An Der Welle 3, 9th Floor
Frankfurt am Main 60322
Germany
Phone: 49-692443393000 **Fax:** 49-692443393199

Oaktree Capital Management (UK)
10 Bressenden Place
London SW1E 5DH
United Kingdom
Phone: 44-2072014600 **Fax:** 44-2072014601

Oaktree Capital Management Pte Ltd
80 Raffles Place #51-03
UOB Plaza 1
Singapore 048624
Singapore
Phone: 65-63056550 **Fax:** 65-63056551

Oaktree Japan Inc
Atago Green Hills Mori Tower
37th Floor, 2-5-1 Atago, Minato-ku
Tokyo 105-6237
Japan
Phone: 81-357766760 **Fax:** 81-357766761

Barbara Strozzilaan 201
1083 HN
Amsterdam 1083 HN
Netherlands
Phone: 31-205792128 **Fax:** 31-205792129

Oaktree France SAS
39, rue de Courcelles
Paris 75008
France
Phone: 33-142991515 **Fax:** 33-142991511

Oaktree Capital (Seoul) Limited
Suite 2203, 22/F Trade Tower
511 Yeongdong-daero, Gangnam-gu
Seoul 06164
Korea
Phone: 82-221918000 **Fax:** 82-221918080

Suite 2001, 20/F, Champion Tower
3 Garden Road
Hong Kong
China
Phone: 852-36556800 **Fax:** 852-36556900

26A Boulevard Royal
7th Floor
Luxembourg L-2449
Luxembourg
Phone: 352-2663254700 **Fax:** 352-26632599

Suite 8, 14th Floor
China World Office 1
No. 1 Jianguomenwai Avenue, Chaoyang District
Beijing 100004
China
Phone: 86-1065350208 **Fax:** 86-1065350209

Key Executives:
Howard Marks, Co-Chairman
Education: BSEc, Cum Laude, Wharton School at the University of Pennsylvania; MBA, University of Chicago
Background: TCW Group; CIO, Domestic Fixed Income of Trust Company; President, TCW Asset Management Company; Citicorp Investment Management
Bruce Karsh, Co-Chairman & Chief Investment Officer
Education: AB, Economics summa cum laude, Duke

Venture Capital & Private Equity Firms / Domestic Firms

University; JD, University of Virginia School of Law
Background: Managing Director, TCW; Associate, O'Melveny and Myers; Judicial Clerk, Honorable Anthony M Kennedy

Jay Wintrob, Chief Executive Officer
Education: BA & JD, University of California, Berkeley
Background: President & CEO, AIG Life & Retirement; President, SunAmerica Investments Inc.; O'Melveny & Myers

Sheldon Stone, Principal/Portfolio Manager
Education: BA, Bowdoin College; MBA, Accounting & Finance, Columbia University
Background: Citibank; Prudential Insurance Company

1363 OBVIOUS VENTURES
220 Halleck Street
Suite 120
San Francisco, CA 94129

e-mail: info@obvious.com
web: obvious.com

Mission Statement: Obvious Ventures seeks to work with companies dedicated to solving universal problems such as health and wellness and clean energy.

Founded: 2014
Industry Group Preference: Energy, Mobility, Healthcare, Wellness, Agriculture, Fintech, Education
Portfolio Companies: Amply, Bakpax, Beam, Beyond Meat, Block Renovation, Boon Supply, CareZone, Change.org, Computable, Corvus Insurance, DarwinAI, Devoted Health, Diamond Foundry, Enbala, Enervee, Fair, Good Eggs, Gusto, Happiest Baby, Hedvig, Incredible Health, Inspire, Joy, Keyo, LabGenius, Lilium, Long Game, Long-Term Stock Exchange, Lyric, Magic Leap, Medium, Mixt, Miyoko's Kitchen, Mosaic, Myro, Octave, Olly, Planet, Plant Prefab, Proterra, Recursion Pharmaceuticals, RenoRun, Seriforge, Sighten, Tentrr, Urban Remedy, Virta, Visor, VSCO, Welly, Workpop, XpertSea, Zymergen

Key Executives:

Ev Williams, Co-Founder
Background: Co-Founder of several companies including: Pyra Labs; Odeo; Obvious Corp; Twitter; CEO, Medium

James Joaquin, Co-Founder/Managing Director
Education: Brown University
Background: Co-Founder, Clearview Software; Co-Founder, When.com; President/CEO, Ofoto; President/CEO, Xoom.com

Vishal Vasishth, Co-Founder/Managing Director
Education: MS, North Carolina State University; MBA, Anderson School of Management
Background: Founding Partner, SONG Investment Advisors; Senior Executive, Steve Case's Revolution LLC; Chief Strategy Officer, Patagonia

Andrew Beebe, Managing Director
Education: BA, Dartmouth College
Background: Chief Commercial Officer, Suntech; VP of Distributed Generation, Nextera Energy; Co-Founder, Bigstep.com

Nan Li, Managing Director
Education: BS, Computer Science Engineering, University of Michigan
Background: Investment Manager, Innovation Endeavors; Head of Product/Operations/Finance, Gigwalk; Venture Capitalist, Bain Capital Ventures; Management Consultant, Bain & Company; PM, Microsoft

---

1364 OCA VENTURES
351 West Hubbard Street
Suite 600
Chicago, IL 60654

Phone: 312-327-8400 Fax: 312-542-8952
web: www.ocaventures.com

Mission Statement: OCA Ventures is a venture capital firm focused on investments in companies with dramatic growth potential, primarily in technology, financial services, for-profit education and technology-enabled services businesses.

Geographic Preference: United States
Founded: 2001
Average Investment: $3 - $5 million
Investment Criteria: Seed-Stage to Expansion-Stage
Industry Group Preference: Technology, Mobile Commerce, Financial Services, Education
Portfolio Companies: 71lbs, Alert Logic, Apparel Media Group, Automated Insights, Base, Base-2 Capital, BrightNest, Brill Street, Campus Explorer, Cartavi, Cleversafe, CohesiveFT, Ed Map, Excelerate Labs, FeeFighters, Fitocracy, Healthfinch, Iris Mobile, Javlin Capital, Midi Compliance & Ethics Solutions, Net-Hopper, National Billing Partners, OpenMarkets, Pangea, Pinpoint Care, Power 2 Switch, Red Foundry, Safe Shepherd, Sales Beach, Snapsheet, SpotHero, Sumridge Partners, Supplyhog, SwipeSense, TechSkills, TradeKing, Univa, WedPics, Whittl

Key Executives:

Jim Dugan, CEO/Co-Founder/Managing Partner
Education: BA, Economics, University of Rochester; MBA, JL Kellogg Graduate School of Management
Background: Continental Bank; Illinois Venture Capital Association

John Dugan, Chair Emeritus/Co-Founder
Education: BA, Business Administration, Pace College; US Naval Academy
Background: Americas for Swiss Bank Corporation; Purcell, Graham & Company; Controller, Baker, Weeks & Company

Peter Ianello, Chair/Co-Founder
Education: BA, Mount St. Mary College
Background: President & CEO, SBC Capital Markets; General Partner & Member, O'Connor & Associates

Mark Berman, Special Advisor
Education: BA, Accounting, Baruch College; JD, Brooklyn Law School
Background: Partner, O'Connor Partners Investment Office; Managing Director, Swiss Bank Corporation
Directorships: Techskills, Cohesive FT

1365 OCEANSHORE VENTURES
1350 Bayshore Highway
#920
Burlingame, CA 94010

Phone: 415-309-6752

Mission Statement: Oceanshore Ventures helps private companies get the early stage operating capital and access to world-class, international networks of suppliers, technologists and business leaders that they need to develop successfully. We are committed to making investments in early stage companies that develop breakthrough advanced materials-based technologies in renewable energy, energy storage, and energy efficiencies, and that hold the promise of delivering highly competitive solutions to the global market.

Investment Criteria: Early-Stage
Industry Group Preference: Technology, Energy Storage
Portfolio Companies: Confluence Solar, Skyline Solar, Lumiette, EnerVault, Crystal Solar

Key Executives:

Ken Pearlman, Founding Partner/Managing Director
e-mail: ken@oceanshorevc.com
Education: BS, Biology, University of California, Riverside; MBA, Santa Clara University
Background: Firsthand Capital; Executive Director, CIBC World Markets; Dean Witter Reynolds, Robertson Stephens & Company
Directorships: Crystal Solar, EnerVault, Lumiette

Eva Bjorseth, Founding Partner/Managing Director
e-mail: eva@oceanshorevc.com
Education: BBA, MBA, California State University

Venture Capital & Private Equity Firms / Domestic Firms

Background: Trade Commissioner, Innovation Norway; Presdio Ventures Partners

1366 OCTANe
65 Enterprise
Aliso Viejo, CA 92656

Phone: 949-330-6569 **Fax:** 949-330-6561
e-mail: info@octaneoc.org
web: www.octaneoc.org

Mission Statement: OCTANe connects people and ideas with capital and resources to fuel technology growth in Orange County. Our members represent Orange County technology executive leaders, entrepreneurs, investors, venture capitalists, academicians, and strategic advisors.

1367 ODEON CAPITAL PARTNERS
750 Lexington Avenue
27th Floor
New York, NY 10022

Phone: 212-257-6970 **Fax:** 212-504-3012
web: www.odeoncap.com

Mission Statement: To fund private and select public growth and expansion stage companies with established business franchises and solid financial metrics. The fund seeks to take either control or significant minority positions and to obtain board representation or board observer rights in each company in which it invests.

Fund Size: $250 million
Founded: 1999
Average Investment: $8 million
Industry Group Preference: Enterprise Services, Business to Business, Manufacturing, Distribution, Healthcare Services, Outsourcing & Efficiency

Key Executives:
   Evan Schwartzberg, Managing Partner
   Background: Merrill Lynch & Co., Louis Dreyfus Corporation, Pursuit Parners, Solomon Smith Barney, Bank of America Securities
   Matthew Van Alstyne, Co-Founder/Managing Partner
   Background: Ore Hill Partners LLC, Royal Bank of Scotland, Deutsche Bank, DebtTraders

1368 ODYSSEY INVESTMENT PARTNERS
590 Madison Avenue
39th Floor
New York, NY 10022

Phone: 212-351-7900
web: www.odysseyinvestment.com

Mission Statement: Odyssey makes majority, controlled investments primarily in established middle-market companies in a variety of industries.

Fund Size: $2 billion
Founded: 1998
Investment Criteria: Leveraged Acquisitions, Growth Financings, Recapitalizations
Industry Group Preference: Industrial Manufacturing, Business Products & Services, Insurance, Aerospace, Defense and Government, Energy, Supply Chain Management
Portfolio Companies: 4Wall Entertainment Inc., Addison Group, AeroPrecision, Aramsco, Aviation Technologies, Barcodes, BarrierSafe Solutions International, Cross-Country Infrastructure Services Inc., Dayton Superior Corporation, Dresser, Duravant, EAG Laboratories, Evergreen Tank Solutions, Integrated Power Services, Integro, Monarch Marking Systems, Montpelier Re Holdings, Neff Corp., Norcross Safety Products, One Call Medical, Peninsula Packaging Company, Pexco, Pro Mach, Ranpak, Safway Group Holding, SM&A Holdings, Testek Inc., TNT Crane & Rigging, TransDigm, TrialCard, tri-Star Aerospace, United Site Services, Wastequip, Wencor, Williams Scotsman, York Insurance Services

Other Locations:
   21650 Oxnard Street
   Suite 1650
   Woodland Hills, CA 91367
   Phone: 818-737-1111

Key Executives:
   Stephen Berger, Chairman
   Education: Brandeis University; University of Chicago
   Background: Executive Vice President, GE Capital Corporation; Chairman & CEO, Financial Guaranty Insurance Company
   Brian Kwait, Co-President, Managing Principal
   Education: University of Michigan; MBA, Wharton School
   Background: Associate, Bear Stearns & Co.; CPA, Ernst & Whinney
   William Hopkins, Co-President, Managing Principal
   Education: University of California, San Diego; MBA, University of Southern California
   Background: Merchant Banking Group, GE Capital Corporation; Wells Fargo Bank
   Doug Hitchner, Managing Principal
   Education: Bucknell University
   Background: Vice President, Goldman Sachs & Co.; Marine Midland Bank
   Doug Rotatori, Managing Principal
   Education: Bucknell University; MBA, Kellogg Graduate School, Northwestern University
   Background: Partner, Wellspring Capital Management; Bear Stearns & Co.; Andersen Consulting Group
   Randy Paulson, Managing Principal
   Education: BSB, Accounting, University of Minnesota; MBA, Kellogg Graduate School, Northwestern University
   Background: Executive Vice President, National Financial Partners; Bear Stearns & Co.; GE Capital Corporation
   Jeffrey McKibben, Managing Principal
   Education: BS, Economics, Wharton School; MBA, Harvard Business School
   Background: Associate, Saugatuck Capital; Associate, Marakon Associates
   Craig Staub, Managing Principal
   Education: BA, Economics, MPP, Public Policy, College of William & Mary
   Background: Vice President, Westbury Equity Partners; Vice President, The Shattan Group; Associate, Marakon Associates

1369 OEM CAPITAL
2507 Post Road
Southport, CT 06890

Phone: 203-254-0200 **Fax:** 203-259-4041
e-mail: rjk@oemcapital.com
web: www.oemcapital.com

Mission Statement: Specializes in sale or divestiture of electronics, communications and computer companies. Also secure capital to complete an acquisition or restructure a company and secure merger acquisition candidates.

Geographic Preference: United States
Fund Size: $50 million
Founded: 1985
Average Investment: $5-50 million
Minimum Investment: $500,000
Investment Criteria: Smaller Size, Technical Orientation
Industry Group Preference: Electronic Components, Computer Related, Communications, Information Technology

Other Locations:
   1875 Century Park E
   Suite 1220
   Los Angeles, CA 90067
   Phone: 310-432-8585 **Fax:** 310-432-8576

Key Executives:
   Ronald J. Klammer, President/Managing Director
   e-mail: rjk@oemcapital.com

489

Venture Capital & Private Equity Firms / Domestic Firms

Education: MBA, Harvard Business School; MS, University of Pennsylvania; BA, Electrical Engineering, Villanova University
Background: Corporate VP, Gulton Industries; VP, Cross River Products Inc; Management/Technical, General Electric's Missile and Space Division
Michael Cohen, Managing Director
e-mail: mc@oemcapital.com
Education: MSc, Electrical Engineering, Drexel University; MBA, Wharton School of Business, University of Pennsylvania
Background: Diamond Capital Advisors; Johnson & Johnson; Hewlett Packard; General Electric; Honeywell International; Norwest Equity Partners; 3i Capital; Kulicke & Soffa
Shawn Thompson, Managing Director
e-mail: st@oemcapital.com
Education: BS, Economics, Wharton School of Business, University of Pennsylvania
Background: Diamond Capital Advisors; Barrington Associates
Tom Kastner, Managing Director
e-mail: tk@oemcapital.com
Education: BA, University of California at Berkeley; MBA, Yale University
Background: GP Ventures
Steve Klammer, Managing Director
e-mail: jsk@oemcapital.com
Education: BSc, Economics, Northeastern University; MBA, Booth School of Business, University of Chicago
Background: OEM Capital; Highbar Capital Management; Whitebox Advisors; Walleye Trading
Lori L. Murphree, Managing Director
e-mail: lm@oemcapital.com
Education: BA, California State University; MBA, International Management, Thunderbird Graduate School of Global Management
Background: Diamond Capital Advisors; Sapient; WPP; IBM; CACI; GXS; Silicon Valley Bank; Grant Thornton UK; Results International; McCracken Advisory Partners; Bacchus Capital Management
Mike Brunell, Managing Director
e-mail: mjb@oemcapital.com
Education: BA, University of California San Diego; MBA, Finance, Wharton School of Business, University of Pennsylvania
Background: Diamond Capital Advisors; Natworks; Celgene; Abraxis Bioscience; American BioScience; Dillon, Read & Co.
Mark R. Ross, Managing Director
e-mail: mrr@oemcapital.com
Education: BSc, Finance, Lehigh University
Background: Diamond Capital Advisors; Mosaic Capital; Cogito Capital Partners; Chatsworth Securities
Directorships: Autobytel Inc.; AutoWeb; On Word Information
Chris Whitcomb, Managing Director
e-mail: cjw@oemcapital.com
Education: Economics, Lawrence University
Background: OEM Capital; Oppenheimer; Dain Bosworth; Piper Jaffray; William Blair; ThinkEquity Partners
Kristopher Prakash, Managing Director
e-mail: kp@oemcapital.com
Education: BS, Accounting, University of Southern California; Master's, Business Taxation, London School of Business
Background: Diamond Capital Advisors; Federal Reserve Bank of San Francisco
Wayne Platt, Managing Director
e-mail: wp@oemcapital.com
Education: MBA, Wharton School of Business, University of Pennsylvania; Finance, University of Cape Town

Background: Diamond Capital Advisors; Cappello Global; Houlihan Lokey

1370 OFF THE GRID VENTURES
2nd Street
San Francisco, CA 94111
e-mail: info@otgventures.com
web: www.otgventures.com

Mission Statement: Seeks to invest in "off the grid" entrepreneurs such as women and minority founders.

Founded: 2016
Investment Criteria: Seed, Early Stage
Industry Group Preference: Enterprise Tech, Fintech
Portfolio Companies: Aingel, Alchemy, AON3D, Barrel Park Investments, Base Venture, Bitesize, CreditStacks, DevCon Detect, Flexport, Fr8, OneKloud, OptionWay, Presence.ai, RankMyApp, Savitude, Skylights, Swarm Vision, Voxeet, Walnut Algorithms, WittyCircle, Zerply

Key Executives:
David Mes, General Partner
Education: Wharton School; La Sorbonne
Ben Orthlieb, General Partner
Education: Wharton School
Background: Tech Executive, LinkedIn; Boston Consulting Group
Mat Peyron, Co-Founder/Advisor
Education: MS, Imperial College; MBA, Wharton School
Background: Senior Director, Quinstreet; CEO, Wheelhouse Enterprises; VP of Venture Development, Aegon
Amber Caska, Advisor
Education: BS, University of Sydney
Background: Audit Senior, KPMG; GAAP Technical Lead, GE Capital; Controller, Safeco Insurance; Treasurer, Vulcan Inc.; VP of Private Banking, JP Morgan; CFO, Hillspire LLC; Leadership Council, Cinequest; Co-Founder/Venture Partner, Portfolia; CEO/Managing Partner, NEXT Family Office
Directorships: Portland Trail Blazers; The Hospital Club

1371 OKAPI VENTURE CAPITAL
1590 S Coast Highway
Suite 10
Laguna Beach, CA 92651
Phone: 949-715-5555 Fax: 949-715-5556
web: www.okapivc.com

Mission Statement: Okapi Venture Capital provides long-term capital and management support to start-ups. We take pride in partnering with exceptionally talented entrepreneurs and operational executives to develop their emerging businesses.

Geographic Preference: Southern California, Orange County
Investment Criteria: Seed-Stage, Early-Stage
Industry Group Preference: Life Sciences, Information Technology, Biotechnology, Diagnostics, Internet, Healthcare Information Technology, Healthcare Services, Materials Technology, Medical Devices, Semiconductors, Software, Wireless
Portfolio Companies: OmniVision Entertainment, Helixis, Transaction Wireless, OrthAlign, Obalon Therapeutics, WellTok, SignNow, BabyList, CrowdStrike, BioTrace Medical, Qualaroo, Pegasus Solar, Focal Therapeutics

Key Executives:
B Marc Averitt, Co-Founder/Managing Director
949-715-5555
e-mail: averitt@okapivc.com
Education: Philosophy & Business Administration, University of Southern California; JD, Pepperdine University School of Law
Background: Managing Director, Strategic Business Development, Intel Corporation; Sun Microsystems

490

Directorships: My Damn Channel, RF Nano Corporation, Transaction Wireless, SecondVoice
Sharon Stevenson DVM, PhD, Co-Founder/Managing Director
949-715-5557
e-mail: stevenson@okapivc.com
Education: MS, Veterinary Pathology, DVM, Ohio State University; PhD, Comparative Pathology, University of California, Davis; MBA, UCLA Anderson Graduate School of Management
Background: SVP, Technology & Planning, SkinMedical; Principal, Domain Associates; President & CFO, Volcano Therapeutics
Directorships: MicroVention, Neuropace, NuVasive, Santarus, SkinMedica, GenVault

1372 OLYMPUS PARTNERS
Metro Center
One Station Place
4th Floor
Stamford, CT 06902

Phone: 203-353-5900
web: www.olympuspartners.com

Mission Statement: To build a diversified portfolio by making investments in growth companies, acquisitions, financings and restructurings.

Geographic Preference: United States
Fund Size: $1.7 billion
Founded: 1988
Average Investment: $75 million
Minimum Investment: $25 million
Investment Criteria: Growth Capital to LBO and Restructuring
Industry Group Preference: Healthcare, Software, Financial Services, Business to Business
Portfolio Companies: 3D Corporation Solutions, American Residential, AMN Healthcare, AmSpec, Ann's House of Nuts, Ariel Re, Aspen Re, Centerplate Inc., Churchill Financial Group, Client Distribution Services, Club Staffing, CountryBanc, Eldorado Bancshares, Ennis-Flint, Foodware Group, FrontierVision Partners LP, Global Link Logistics, Heniff Transportation Systems LLC, Homax, IXS, K-MAC, Liqui-Box, Lyft, Meridian Rail Services, Nebraska Book Company, Norwesco, NPC International, Pennant Foods Corp., Pepper Dining, Petmate, Pharma Marketing Ltd., Phoenix Services LLC, PLZ Aeroscience Corporation, Pregis, Prime Advantage, The Princeton Review, PSAV, Professional Service Industries, Rise Baking Company, The Ritedose Corporation, Shemin, Siffron, Snyder Industries Inc., Soliant, Symmetry Medical, Talbot Underwriting, Tanenbaum-Harber Insurance Group, Tempest Re, TravelCenters of America, The Waddington Group, Woodcraft Industries

Key Executives:
Rob Morris, Managing Partner
Education: AB, Hamilton College; MBA, Tuck School of Business
Background: Senior VP, General Electric Investment Corporation; Management, GE, Manufacturing and Financial Service
Directorships: Churchill Financial, The Ritedose Corporation, Tank Holding Corp., Homax Products, Professional Service Industries, Woodcraft Industries
Lou Mischianti, Managing Partner
Education: BS, Yale University
Background: The Clippergroup, Odyssey Partners, First Boston
Directorships: The Ritedose Corporation, Tank Holding Corp., Homax Products, Pepper Dining, Professional Service Industries, Woodcraft Industries
Jim Conroy, Managing Partney
Education: BA, University of Virginia; MBA, Tuck School of Business
Background: Bain & Company, Goldman Sachs, General Elecrtic Investment Corporation
Directorships: The Ritedose Corporation, Ariel Re

1373 OMEGA FUNDS
185 Dartmouth St.
Boston, MA 02116

web: omegafunds.net

Mission Statement: Omega Funds focuses on addressing severe, unmet medical needs by investing in biotechnology and medical device companies, therapeutics, and disruptive technologies.

Geographic Preference: North America, Western Europe
Investment Criteria: Early-, Mid-, and Late-Stage
Industry Group Preference: Healthcare, Biotechnology, Medical Devices, Therapeutics

Key Executives:
Richard Lim, Managing Director
Education: AB, MBA, Harvard University
Background: General Partner, MVM Life Science Partners; Vice President, Saunders Karp & Megrue; Manager, LEK Consulting
Claudio Nessi, Managing Director
Education: MBA, Erasmus University; PhD, Genetics, University of Pavia
Background: Managing Partner, NeoMed Management
Anne-Mari Paster, Managing Director/CFO
Education: BS, Engineering, Turku Institute of Technology; Boston University
Background: CFO, Third Rock Ventures; CFO, MPM Capital; Founder & CFO, APS Material Services
Otello Stampacchia, Managing Director
Education: MS, Genetics, University of Pavia; PhD, Molecular Biology, University of Geneva
Background: AlpInvest Partners; Portfolio Manager, Lombard Odier Immunology Fund; Goldman Sachs; Index Securities

1374 OMIDYAR NETWORK
1991 Broadway Street
Suite 200
Redwood City, CA 94063

Phone: 650-482-2500
web: www.omidyar.com

Mission Statement: Omidyar Network is a philanthropic investment firm dedicated to harnessing the power of markets to create opportunity for people to improve their lives. We invest in and help scale innovative organizations to catalyze economic, social and political change.

Geographic Preference: Worldwide
Minimum Investment: $1 million
Industry Group Preference: Consumer Internet, Mobile, Government
Portfolio Companies: Alliance for Affordable Internet, Amicus, Change.org, Couchsurfing, DoSomething.org, GSMA Mobile for Development Intelligence, HealthKart, Linden Lab, Meetup, Mimoni, NationBuilder, Neoteny Labs, Quikr, Range Networks, sovrn, Versé, Wikia, African Leadership Academy, Akshara Foundation, Anudip Foundation, Aspiring Minds, Bridge International Academies, EnglishHelper, IkamvaYouth, Kalibrr, RLabs, Teach for India, Tree House, Better Than Cash Alliance, BRAC, Center for Financial Services Innovation, Cignifi, Consultative Group to Assist the Poor, Core Innovation Capital, Elevar Equity, GSMA Mobile Money for the Unbanked, IntelleGrow, Kiva, LeapFrog Investments, Lenddo, MFX Solutions, MicroEnsure, MicroSave, Off.Grid:Electric, Paga, Prosper, Rev, Ruma, SOLIDUS Investment Fund, Vistaar Finance, Zoona, Africa Check, African Media Initiative, Association for Democratic Reforms, BudgIT, Center for Global Development, Center for Research and Teaching in Economics, Center on Democracy, Development and the Rule of Law, Code for America, Committee to Protect Journalists, ePanstwo Foundation, Fundacion Ciudadano Inteligente,

Venture Capital & Private Equity Firms / Domestic Firms

Pundar, Global Integrity, Global Voices, IMCO, Instituto Cidade Democratica, International Budget Partnership, Janaagraha, Livity Africa, Media Development Investment Fund, Meu Rio, Mideast Youth, Myanmar Innovation Greenhouse, mySociety, New Citizen (Centre UA), ONE Campaign, Open Data Institute, Open Government Partnership, Open Knowledge, Praekelt Foundation, Proj

Other Locations:
1333 New Hampshire Avenue SW
Suite 730
Washington, DC 20036
Phone: 202-448-4505

61B, 2 North Avenue
Maker Maxity, Bandra-Kurla Complex
Bandra (E), Mumbai
Mumbai 400 051
India
Phone: 91-02261187300

Charlotte House, 1st Floor
47-49 Charlotte Road
London EC2 3QT
United Kingdom
Phone: 44-02077299997

Key Executives:
Pierre Omidyar, Co-Founder/Managing Partner
Education: BS, Computer Science, Tufts University
Background: Founder, eBay; Co-Founder, Ink Development Corp.

1375 OMNICAPITAL GROUP
800 West Main Street
Suite 204
Freehold, NJ 07728

Phone: 908-497-6807 **Fax:** 908-502-0424
web: theomnicapitalgroup.com

Mission Statement: A venture capital firm dedicated to helping entrepreneurs build the best next-generation communication and information technologies for rapidly growing markets.
Portfolio Companies: Catheter Robotics, Personalized Media, Veveo, One On One Ads, eZuce, Flowonix Medical
Key Executives:
Dr. Arun Netravali, Managing Partner
908-497-6807
Background: President, Bell Laboratories
Directorships: Level 3 Communications, LSI, Sezmi, Knewco
JD Gardner, General Partner
908-497-6807
e-mail: jdgardner@omnivc.com
Background: Telecom
John Harrington, Venture Partner
Background: Managing Partner, Accenture Communication
Doug Eby, General Partner
908-497-6807
Directorships: Level 3 Comminications, Markel

1376 ONE EQUITY PARTNERS
510 Madison Avenue
19th Floor
New York, NY 10022

Phone: 212-277-1500
web: www.oneequity.com

Mission Statement: To combine the strengths of an independent global private equity firm with the resources of a leading global bank.
Geographic Preference: Worldwide
Fund Size: $2 billion
Founded: 2001
Average Investment: $150 million
Minimum Investment: $50 million
Investment Criteria: MBO, Growth Capital
Industry Group Preference: Chemicals, Healthcare, Manufacturing, Technology, Travel & Leisure, Energy, Food & Beverage, Media
Portfolio Companies: Aligned Energy/Inertech, Allied S/A, AnexBusiness, Celltrion Healthcare, China Medicine, Cless Cosméticos, Constantia Flexibles, Duropak, East Balt Bakeries, Engineering Ingegneria Informatica, Expert Global Solutions, Genband, Grupo Phoenix, Library Solutions, M*Modal, Merfish Pipe and Supply and Pipe Exchange, Netas, Portal de Documentos, Schoeller Arca Systems, Smartrac Technology, Sonneborn Refined Products, Unicoba, Voltyre-Prom, Wilbanks Trucking and Wilbanks Leasing, Wow! Nutrition

Other Locations:
330 N Wabash Avenue
Suite 3750
Chicago, IL 60611
Phone: 312-517-3750

Herengracht 466
Amsterdam CA 1017
Netherlands
Phone: 31-204203000

Neue Mainzer Str. 84
Frankfurt am Main 60311
Germany
Phone: 49-6950607470

Chater House, 20/F
8 Connaught Road Central
Hong Kong
China
Phone: 852-28000185

One Equity Partners Austria GmbH
Opernring 17
Vienna 1010
Austria

Key Executives:
Brad Coppens, Managing Director
Education: BBA, Stephen M Ross School of Business, University of Michigan
Background: JP Morgan
Directorships: Cless Cosmetics; Ernest Health; OneLinke; The Results Company; Simplura Health Group; Unicoba; Wow! Nutrition; Allied; Portal de Documentos; Prodigy Health Group; X-Rite
David Lippin, Managing Director/Head, Investor Relations
Education: BA, Economics, Harvard College
Background: Sun Capital Partners; GoldPoint Partners; First Manhattan Consulting Group
Carlo Padovano, Managing Director
Education: BS, Engineering & Management Systems, Columbia University
Background: GP Investimentos; JP Morgan
Directorships: Cless Cosmetics; Orion; Rizing; Wow! Nutrition; Portal; Unicoba; Allied
Steve Rappaport, Director of Research
Education: BA, Colby College; MA & MPhil, Columbia University; Executive Certificate In Management & Technology, Sloan School of Management, MIT
Background: SVP, Lazard Frères & Co.; SVP, Prudential Securities; Captain, US Air Force
Joseph Huffsmith, Managing Director
Education: BS, Mathematics & Economics, Duke University; MBA, University of Chicago
Background: Asia Capital Markets, JPMorgan
Directorships: GENBRAND, Netas, Precision Gear Holdings
Brad Coppens, Managing Director
Education: BBA, Accounting & Finance, Ross School of Business, University of Michigan
Background: JPMorgan Chase

Venture Capital & Private Equity Firms / Domestic Firms

Directorships: Prodigy Health Group, Systagenix Wound Management, X-Rite
Andrew Dunn, Managing Director
Education: BA, Modern History, University of Oxford; MPP, International Trade & Finance, Harvard Kennedy School of Government
Background: Boston Consulting Group

1377 ONONDAGA VENTURE CAPITAL FUND
241 West Fayette Street
Syracuse, NY 13202

Phone: 315-478-0157
web: www.ovcfund.com

Geographic Preference: Northeast, Middle Atlantic
Fund Size: $2.5 million
Founded: 1985
Average Investment: $200,000
Minimum Investment: $100,000
Portfolio Companies: Accuracy Microsensors, AnAerobics, Appro Healthcare, Bioworks, Impact Technologies, Kiomix, UStec

Key Executives:
Michael Schattner, President
315-478-0157
Fax: 315-478-0158
Education: BS, University of Virginia; MBA, Syracuse University

1378 ONSET VENTURES
2490 Sand Hill Road
Menlo Park, CA 94025

Phone: 650-529-0700 **Fax:** 650-529-0777
e-mail: mp@onset.com
web: www.onset.com

Mission Statement: Focuses on seed and early-stage investing in medical technology and information technology markets.
Geographic Preference: Silicon Valley
Fund Size: $205 million
Founded: 1984
Average Investment: $5 million
Minimum Investment: $1 million
Investment Criteria: All Stages
Industry Group Preference: Medical Technology, Information Technology, New Media, Mobility, Infrastructure Software, Medical Devices, Drug Delivery, Diagnostics, Healthcare Information Technology
Portfolio Companies: Accelerated Networks, Access Closure, Adaptive Insights, Adara, Ads Native, Alteon WebSystems, AneuRx, APX, Arcot, Baronova, Buysight, Callidus Software, Clarify, ClariPhy, Cloud Cruiser, Conceptus, Corvita Corporation, Curon Medical, CytoPherx, Eloquent, Embollic Protection, Endocardial Solutions, Endotex, Ensim, EnteroMedics, Euphonix, Fleux Pine, Gadzoox Networks, Gale Technologies, Glimmerglass, Gridstore, Hotspur Technologies, Invarium, Nektar, NetSeer, Neuronetics, Nok Nok Labs, Novasys Medical, Obopay, Packeteer, Pancetera, Penederm, Placecast, Presidio Systems, Relievant, SS8, Sadra Medical, Securent, Sentilla, Spinal Concepts, Trilogy, Truviso, Uptake Medical, Valeritas, Vertos Medical, Vidder, Vindicia, VisionCare

Key Executives:
Terry Opdendyk, Founder/Partner, Information & Medical Technologies
e-mail: terry@onset.com
Education: BS, Michigan State University; MS, Stanford University
Background: VP, VisiCorp; Technical Manager, Hewlett-Packard; Intel Corporation
Directorships: Adaptive Planning, APX, Arcot Systems, Callidus Software, Nektak Therapeutics (formerly Inhal Therapeutics), NetSeer, Sentilla, Truviso

Robert Kuhling, Partner, Information & Medical Technologies
e-mail: rob@onset.com
Education: BA, Hamilton College; MBA, Harvard Business School
Background: Director Marketing, Sun Microsystems, VP, Manager, General Electric-Calma's, Team Leader, Bostons Consulting Group
Directorships: Access Closure, Aperion, BARNova, Hotspur Technologies, Uptake Medical
David Lane, Partner, Information Technology
e-mail: lane@onset.com
Education: BSEE, University of Southern California; MBA, Harvard Business School
Background: Diamondhead Ventures; Harvard Management Company; IBM
Directorships: Truviso, UPEK, Vindicia
Shomit Ghose, Partner, Information Technology
e-mail: shomit@onset.com
Education: BS, Computer Science, University of California, Berkeley
Background: SVP Operations, Tumbleweed Communications; VP, Worldwide Professional Services Organization, BroadVision
Steve LaPorte, Venture Partner, Medical Technology
e-mail: slaporte@onset.com
Education: BS, Mathematics & Computer Science, University of Wisonsin, Stevens Point; MBA, University of Minnesota
Background: VP, NeuroVentures; Business Development, Medtronic
David Pann, Venture Advisor, Information Technology
e-mail: dpann@onset.com
Education: Computer Science, Business Administration, University of Vermont
Background: General Manager, Microsoft's Search Business Group
Rick Schell, Venture Partner, Information Technology
e-mail: rick@onset.com
Education: BA, Mathematics & Computer Science, MS & PhD, Computer Science, University of Illinois
Background: Chief Technologist, NetIQ; Founder, iSharp; Intel; Sun Microsystems; Borland

1379 OPEN PRAIRIE VENTURES
400 East Jefferson
Effingham, IL 62401

Phone: 217-347-1000
e-mail: info@openprairie.com
web: www.openprairie.com

Mission Statement: An Illinois based venture capital firm that invests in early stage, technology companies in the midwest region.
Geographic Preference: Midwest Region
Founded: 2000
Average Investment: $3 million
Investment Criteria: Early Stage
Industry Group Preference: Biotechnology, Technology
Portfolio Companies: Infoblox, TomoTherapy, iNest, MedVenture, Vestaron, Compact Particle Acceleration, Metactive, NewLeaf Symbiotics, iCyt, Innara Health, FlowForward Medical, Axonia Medical, Metabolic Solutions Development Company, Monteris, Tolera, Vestaron

Key Executives:
Jim Schultz, Founder/Managing Partner
e-mail: jim@openprairie.com
Education: BA, Business Administration, Southern Methodist University; JD, DePaul University College of Law; MBA, J.L. Kellogg Graduate School of Management at Northwestern University
Background: Founder/Chairman, Telemind Captial Corporation; Chairman, Prime Banc Corporation; Chairman/CEO, Physicians Clinical Laboratories;
Directorships: Vestaron

Venture Capital & Private Equity Firms / Domestic Firms

Dennis Beard, General Partner
217-819-5202
e-mail: dennis@openprairie.com
Education: BS, Accounting, Millikin University, Decatur; MBA, University of Illinois, Urbana-Champaign
Background: Adjunct Lecturer, College of Business, University of Illinois; EPL BioAnalytical Systems; Controller, SLM Instruments
Mike Peck, General Partner
913-492-3636
e-mail: mike@openprairie.com
Education: BS, Mechanical Engineering, University of Kansas; MBA, Kellogg School, Northwestern University
Background: Fund Manager, Kansas Technology Enterprise Corporation; Manager, Accenture
Directorships: Cernium, Infoblox, KCBioMediX

1380 OPENVIEW VENTURE PARTNERS
303 Congress Street
7th Floor
Boston, MA 02210

Phone: 617-478-7500
e-mail: info@openviewpartners.com
web: www.openviewpartners.com

Mission Statement: An expansion-stage venture capital fund, with a focus on high-growth software, internet and technology-enabled companies. Much of the team's success has been driven by its active role in providing its portfolio companies with strategic value-add services and highly practical operating expertise.

Geographic Preference: Worldwide
Fund Size: $240 million
Founded: 2006
Average Investment: $5 to $15 million
Minimum Investment: $5 million
Investment Criteria: Expansion-Stage
Industry Group Preference: Technology, Software, Internet, Digital Media & Marketing, Technology-Enabled Services
Portfolio Companies: SwiftStack, DataDog, Field Lens, Signpost, Pantheon, Smashfly, FieldAware, Socrata, Spredfast, Sonian, UnboundID, Xtium, Nextdocs, Monetate, Canvas, Skytap, Kareo, uSamp, Balihoo, Intronis, Open-E, VersionONe, AtTask, Exinda

Key Executives:
Scott Maxwell, Founder/Senior Managing Director
e-mail: smaxwell@openviewpartners.com
Education: BS, MS, Mechanical Engineering, University of California, Davis; PhD, Mechanical Engineering, MIT; MBA, MIT Sloan School of Management
Background: Senior Managing Director, Insight Venture Partners; Partner, Putnam Investments
George Roberts, Venture Partner
e-mail: groberts@openviewpartners.com
Education: BA, Marketing & Finance, University of Wisconsin
Background: EVP, North American Sales, Oracle Corporation; System5; Applied Data Research

1381 OPUS CAPITAL
2730 Sand Hill Road
Suite 150
Menlo Park, CA 94025

Phone: 650-543-2900 Fax: 650-543-2901
e-mail: info@opuscapital.com
web: www.opuscapital.com

Mission Statement: Opus Capital works to accelerate growth, helping entrepreneurs build strong, sustainable enterprises. Aims to facilitate key relationships, provide access to critical resources and offer counsel on strategy, finance and operations.

Geographic Preference: Central United States
Fund Size: $1 billion
Founded: 1993
Average Investment: $5-$10 million
Minimum Investment: $5 million
Investment Criteria: Early Stage, Seed
Industry Group Preference: Communications, Software, Technology, Enterprise Software, Infrastructure, Internet, Semiconductors, Wireless
Portfolio Companies: AlertEnterprise, Cloud4Wi, Devpost, Dome9, Edunav, Jivox, Panzura, Payfone, Sequent Software, Sisense, SolarEdge, TrapX Security, Workboard

Key Executives:
Dan Avida, General Partner
e-mail: dan@opuscapital.com
Education: BSc, Computer Engineering, Technion, The Israel Institute of Technology
Background: President/CEO, Decru Inc.; Officer, Israel Defense Force
Gill Cogan, General Partner
e-mail: gill@opuscapital.com
Education: MBA, UCLA
Background: Founding General Partner, LightSpeed Venture Partners; Managing Partner, Weiss-Peck & Greer Venture Partners Fund; Adler & Company; CEO, Formtek
Directorships: EFI; Exigen; Personeta; Royalty Services; Softier; Telespree; Transparency
Joseph Cutts, Administrative Partner/CFO
e-mail: joe@opuscapital.com
Education: BS, Finance, Pennsylvania State University; MS, Finance/Marketing/International Business, Kellogg School of Management
Background: Executive Officer, Electronics for Imaging; CFO/COO, EFI; Hills Bros. Coffee; Nestle Beverage Company
Phil Greer, Special Limited Partner
e-mail: phil@opuscapital.com
Education: AB, Princeton University; MBA, Harvard Business School
Background: Founding Partner, Weiss, Peck & Greer
Serge Plotkin, Venture Partner
e-mail: serge@opuscapital.com
Education: BSc, MSc, Electrical Engineering, Ben Gurion University; PhD, Computer Science, MIT
Background: Associate Professor, Computer Science, Stanford University; Co-Founder, Decru

1382 ORBIMED HEALTHCARE FUND MANAGEMENT
601 Lexington Avenue
54th Floor
New York, NY 10022-4629

Phone: 212-739-6400
web: www.orbimed.com

Mission Statement: An asset management firm focused exclusively on the global health sciences industry with a family of private equity funds, hedge funds and other investment vehicles.

Fund Size: $5 billion
Founded: 1993
Average Investment: $15 million
Minimum Investment: $5 million
Investment Criteria: All Stages with emphasis on Mid-Later Stage private companies
Industry Group Preference: Life Sciences, Medical Devices, Drug Development
Portfolio Companies: Acutus, Adaptimmune, Adimab, Aerocrine AB, Aerpio, Affirmed, AIMS, Alector, Amarin, Ambit Biosciences, arGEN-X, ARMO Biosciences, Arsanis Biosciences, Audentes Therapeutics, Avitide, Bacterin, Bharat Serums and Vaccines, BioLineRx, Bonovo Orthopedics, CardiAQ, Cardioxyl, CCAM Biotherapeutics, Cerapedics, Cerenis Therapeutics, Cleave Biosciences, Clementia, Crown Bioscience, DFine, Dimension Therapeutics, Domain Surgical, EA, Ecron Acunova,

Venture Capital & Private Equity Firms / Domestic Firms

Eddingpharm, GC Aesthetics, GC-Rise Pharmaceutical, Glaukos, Good Start Genetics, Igenica, Inspire Medical Systems, Intercept, Invitae, Iroko Pharmaceuticals, Keystone Heart, KIMS GCC, KIMS India, Loxo Oncology, Medigus, MID Labs, Mirati Therapeutics, Natera, OmniGuide Surgical, Ornim Medical, Otic Pharma, Otonomy, OxOnc Development, PharmAcbine, Pieris AG, Practice Fusion, Principia Biopharma, ProNAi, RDD Pharma, Realton Corporation, Redhill Biopharma, Relypsa, Response BioMedical, Roka BioScience, Sage Therapeutics, Selecta Biosciences, Shasun, SI-Bone, Sientra, Ingulex, Sonnendo, Surya, Symbiomix Therapeutics, TELA Bio, TigerText, Treato, Unilife, ViewRay, Waterstone Pharmaceuticals, Whale Imaging

Other Locations:
1700 Owens Street
Suite 540
San Francisco, CA 94158
Phone: 415-294-8740

Suite F 27, Grand Hyatt Plaza
Santacruz East
Mumbai 400055
India
Phone: 91-2261403000

89 Medinat HaYehudim St.
Building E, 11th Floor
Herzliya 4614001
Israel
Phone: 972-732822600

Unit 4706, Raffles City
Shanghai Office Tower
268 Xizang Middle Road
Shanghai 200001
China
Phone: 86-2163351700

Key Executives:
Sven H. Borho, Managing Partner
Education: Univ. of Bayreuth; MSc Economics, London School of Economics
Background: Senior Analyst, Mehta and Isaly
Carl L. Gordon PhD, Managing Partner
Education: Harvard College; Fellow, Rockefeller University; PhD Molecular Biology, MIT; CFA
Background: Senior Biotechnology, Mehta and Isaly
Jonathan T. Silverstein, Managing Partner
Education: BA Economics, Denison University; JD, MBA, University of San Diego
Background: Director Life Sciences, Sumitomo Bank; Associate, Hambro Resource Development
Directorships: Given Imaging; DOV Pharmaceuticals; Emphasys Medical; Predix Pharmaceuticals; Avanir Pharmaceuticals
W. Carter Neild, General Partner
Education: BA Economics, Emory University; CEP, Institute D'Etudes Politiques, Paris; MBA, University of Chicago; CFA
Background: Director, UBS Alternative Investments Group; Investment Management, First Chicago Bank
Geoffrey C. Hsu, General Partner
Education: Harvard Medical School; MBA, Harvard Business School
Background: Financial Analyst, Lehman Brothers; Manager, Business Development, Veritas Medicine

1383 OREGON ANGEL FUND
760 SW 9th Avenue
Suite 2380
Portland, OR 97205

Phone: 503-727-2197

Mission Statement: The Oregon Angel Fund (OAF) is a community supported, professionally managed, investor driven angel fund. The fund provides investors privileged access to the most promising startups and early-stage growth companies in Oregon and SW Washington. OAF is the most active local venue for funding startups in terms of both participants and dollars invested.

Geographic Preference: Oregon, Southwest Washington
Founded: 2007
Average Investment: $100, 00 - $2 million
Minimum Investment: $100,000
Investment Criteria: Early-Stage
Industry Group Preference: All Sectors Considered
Portfolio Companies: AbSci, ActionSprout, BigLeaf, Networks, Brandlive, Bright.md, Cascade Prodrug, Celly, Chinook Book, ClearAccess, ClearFlow, Columbia Power Technologies, CrowdCompass, Customer.io, Daverci, DesignMedix, Diabetomics, Elemental Technologies, Farmhouse Culture, Giftango, GlobeSherpa, Green Zebra Grocery, Hubb, Inpria, IOTAS, Jama Software, Little Bird, Lumen Learning, Lumencor, Meridian, MobileRQ, Muut, Northshore Bio, Notion, Opal, Outdoor Project, Pacific Light Technologies, Paydici, Perfect Company, Poached Jobs, RNA Networks, RYNO Motors, Second Porch, Senrio, SmartRG, The Clymb, Veelo, Wicked Quick, Wild VR, Wildfang

Key Executives:
Eric Rosenfeld, Co-Founder
Education: Stanford Univ.; Institute for Management Development, Switzerland
Background: Co-Founder, Capybara Ventures; Principal Owner, Second Story Interactive Studios; Director, Corporate Development, Mentor Graphics; Analyst, SRI International; Research Fellow, Stanford Graduate School of Business
Scott Sandler, Fund Manager
Education: BS, Computer Systems Engineering, University of Massachusetts, Amherst
Background: CEO, Novas Software; Intel

1384 ORIGIN VENTURES
549 W Randolph Street
Suite 601
Chicago, IL 60061

Phone: 312-644-6449
e-mail: inquire@originventures.com
web: www.originventures.com

Mission Statement: Origin looks for companies in large, growing categories which have demonstrated product/market fit. They also back exceptional entrepreneurs in earlier stages who disrupt or create markets through unconventional, innovative approaches.

Geographic Preference: U.S.A., Canada
Fund Size: $80 million
Founded: 1999
Average Investment: $0.5-4 million
Investment Criteria: Early-Stage and Series A
Industry Group Preference: Technology, Marketplaces, SaaS, Business to Business
Portfolio Companies: 15Five, Ahalogy, Aisle50, AppDetex, Apptentive, Archer Education, Atavium, Avant, Backlot Cars, Bottlenose, Bound, Cameo, Cityscan, ClaimForce, Curiosity, DialogTech, DirectScale, Doggyloot, Fountain, Gamer Sensei, GrubHub, Idelic, Inest, Kidizen, Measured, Mighty, MyAlerts, Persio, Neat Work, Shoutlet, Teem, Tock, Tovala, Trala, ViralGains, Voxpopme, Whittl, Windsor Circle, Wove

Other Locations:
Salt Lake City, UT

Key Executives:
Steven N. Miller, Founding Partner
Education: BS, Business Administration/Marketing, University of Illinois, Urbana-Champaign
Background: Quill Corporation
Directorships: Backlot Cars, Impact Engine, VHT
Bruce N. Barron, Founding Partner
Education: BS, Accounting, University of Illinois, Urbana-Champaign; CPA
Background: Board Member, Applied NeuroSolutions;

495

Venture Capital & Private Equity Firms / Domestic Firms

CEO, APNS
Directorships: DialogTech, MyAlerts, Bound, Tock
Brent Hill, Managing Partner
Education: BS, Finance, Bradley University; MBA, Booth School of Business
Background: Leader, Central Region Sales Organization, Twitter; Head of Financial Services, Google; FeedBurner
Directorships: Ahalogy, Apptentive, Bound, Curiosity, Fountain, Kidizen, AppDetex, DirectScale, Teem
Jason Heltzer, Managing Partner
Education: BS, Computer Science, University of Michigan; MBA, Booth School of Business, University of Chicago
Background: Partner, OCA Ventures; Software Engineer, Deloitte Consulting
Directorships: Ahalogy, Atavium, Base, MyAlerts, Tock, Tovala
Alex Meyer, Managing Partner
Education: BS, Mechanical Engineering, University of Illinois; MBA, Harvard Business School; Theater, Second City Conservatory
Background: Vice President, Global Business Development, SAP; Senior roles with Deloitte and House of Blues
Directorships: Founder and Chair, Harvard Business School Alumni Angels and Entrepreneurship Council of Chicago; HBS Alumni Angels Association; HBSCC Charitable Fund

1385 ORIGINATE VENTURES
205 Webster Street
Bethlehem, PA 18015

Phone: 610-866-5588 Fax: 610-866-5688
e-mail: shannon.morin@originateventures.com
web: www.originateventures.com

Mission Statement: Originate Ventures is a venture capital investment firm, targeting early stage product and services companies located in Pennsylvania and the Mid-Atlantic region.

Geographic Preference: Pennsylvania, Mid-Atlantic Region
Average Investment: $500,000 - $4 million
Investment Criteria: Early-Stage
Industry Group Preference: Medical Devices, Healthcare, Consumer, Information Technology, Internet
Portfolio Companies: Adhezion Biomedical, BA Insight, Care Kinesis, Clickpay Services, CMP.LY, Collections Marketing Center, FSA Store, Holganix, Medallion Analytics, Micro Interventional Devices, NaturalInsight, Proton Media, RightsFlow, TB Biosciences

Key Executives:
Mike Gausling, Managing Partner
Education: BS, Mechanical Engineering, Rensselaer Polytechnic Institute; MBA, Finance, Miami University, Ohio
Background: Co-Founder & CEO, OraSure Technologies; Proctor & Gamble
Glen R Bressner, Managing Partner
Education: BSBA, Boston University; MBA, Babson College
Background: Partner, Mid-Atlantic Venture Funds
Eric Arnson, Managing Partner
Education: University of Michigan
Background: Founder, ENVISION; Proctor & Gamble

1386 ORIX
1717 Main Street
Suite 1100
Dallas, TX 75201

Phone: 214-237-2000
web: www.orix.com

Mission Statement: ORIX provides equity capital to lower middle market and middle market companies throughout the United States. Investments are made from $5-25 million for a variety of growth strategies, buyouts, recapitalizations, and strategic acquisitions. ORIX typically targets minority interests (10-49% ownership), allowing existing owners or sponsors to retain control.

Geographic Preference: United States
Average Investment: $5 - $25 million
Investment Criteria: Buyouts, Acquisitions, Co-Investments, Management-led Buyouts, Recapitalizations

Key Executives:
Terry Suzuki, President and CEO
Education: Keio University; MBA, University of Chicago
Background: Co-CEO, Cerberus Japan; Partner, KPMG
Jorge Jaramillo, Chief of Staff/Managing Director
Education: Butler University; MBA, Washington University
Background: Highland Capital Management; Wells Fargo, Capital Markets

1387 OSAGE PARTNERS
50 Monument Road
Suite 201
Bala Cynwyd, PA 19004

Phone: 484-434-2255 Fax: 484-434-2256
web: osageventurepartners.com

Mission Statement: Osage Partners is a family of venture capital funds that includes Osage Venture Partners and Osage University Partners. Each fund has a dedicated professional staff and a distinct investment strategy. We seek to invest in determined and creative entrepreneurs and assist them in building high growth businesses with consistent revenue streams.

Geographic Preference: Mid-Atlantic Region
Fund Size: $100 million
Founded: 1990
Average Investment: $1 - $2 million
Investment Criteria: Early-Stage
Industry Group Preference: Enterprise Applications, Healthcare Information Technology, Software, SaaS, Internet, Business Products & Services, Healthcare Services, Information Technology
Portfolio Companies: Automated Insights, BA-Insight, Canvas, Ceptaris, CMC, Earnest Research Company, ExecOnline, FieldView Solutions, Halfpenny Technologies, HardMetrics, Identropy, InstaMed, Medallion Analytics, Moda Technology Partners, PeopleLinx, Pneuron, ProtonMedia, RackWare, SevOne, Sidecar

Other Locations:
10 County Line Road
Branchburg, NJ 08876
Phone: 484-434-2255 Fax: 484-434-2256

Key Executives:
Robert S Adelson, Managing Partner
Education: Yale University, Yale University Law School
Background: Clerk, Third Circuit Court of Appeals; Corporate Law, Wolf Block Schorr & Solis-Cohen
Directorships: Melior Discovery, SevOne
Nathaniel V Lentz, Managing Partner
Education: Brown University, Stanford Graduate School of Business
Background: President & CEO, Verticalnet; Partner, Mercer Management Consulting
Directorships: Carnegie Speech, Landslide Technologies, InstaMed, Hard Metrics, Proton Media, FieldView
David Drahms, Principal
Education: Mechanical Engineering, University of Rochester; MBA, Wharton School
Background: Teradyne
Directorships: Halfpenny Technologies, Yaupon Therapeutics

Venture Capital & Private Equity Firms / Domestic Firms

1388 OUTCOME CAPITAL
11911 Freedom Drive
Suite 1010
Reston, VA 20190

Phone: 703-225-1500 Fax: 703-225-1515
web: www.outcomecapital.com

Mission Statement: Outcome Capital's investment strategy is to invest in sectors where we have knowledge, experience and a successful track record. These sectors are driven by fundamental economic and business trends that create attractive investment opportunities and are often supported by proprietary technology.

Average Investment: $1 - $3 million
Investment Criteria: All Stages
Industry Group Preference: Government, Aerospace, Defense and Government, Homeland Security, Communications, Internet, New Media, Technology, Life Sciences, Healthcare, Financial Services
Portfolio Companies: Alltrust Networks, Brightdoor, DoublePositive, Earth Networks, Genesis Financial Solutions, Preferred Systems Solutions, RFID Global Solutions, Saylent Technologies, Social Solutions

Other Locations:
80 William Street
Suite 250
Wellesley, MA 02481
Phone: 703-225-1500 Fax: 703-225-1515

Key Executives:
Jonathan R Wallace, Managing Director
e-mail: jwallace@outcomcapital.com
Education: BS, Commerce, University of Virginia McIntire School of Commerce; MBa, Darden School of Business
Directorships: Double Positive, RFID Global, AllTrust, Saylent, PerformLife
Michael J Cromwell III, Managing Director
e-mail: mcromwell@outcomecapital.com
Education: BA, Yale University; JD, Georgetown University
Directorships: BrightDoor Systems, Social Solutions, Preferred Systems
Oded Ben-Joseph PhD, Managing Director
e-mail: oben-joseph@outcomecapital.com
Education: Imperial College of Science, Technology & Medicine (UK); PhD, University of Cambridge
Background: Managing Director, Boston Equity Advisors
Arnie Freedman, Managing Director
e-mail: afreedman@outcomecapital.com
Education: University of Massachusetts
Background: Co-Founder/Principal, Boston Equity Advisors; Founder & CEO, Rustel

1389 OUTLOOK VENTURES
3000F Danville Boulevard
Suite 110
Alamo, CA 94507

Phone: 415-547-0000

Mission Statement: Actively invests in promising early and growth stage industry-transforming information technology companies.

Geographic Preference: West Coast United States
Fund Size: $140 million
Founded: 1996
Investment Criteria: Early-Stage, Growth-Stage
Industry Group Preference: Consumer Internet, Business to Business, Information Technology, Infrastructure, Internet
Portfolio Companies: The Active Network, ClairMail, Digital Chocolate, Echopass, Loyalty Lab, nSite Software, Overture, Reply, Soundview Technology, Toolwire, Vantos, Xactly

Key Executives:
Randy Haykin, Managing Director
Education: BA, Organizational Studies, Brown University; MBA, Harvard Business School
Background: Senior Sales & Marketing Positions at Yahoo!, Viacom, Paramount, BBN, IBM, Apple Computer
Directorships: Digital Chocolate, Reply.com, Reconnex, Loyalty Lab, Bridgestream, NetBrowser Communications, nSite Software, Impulse Network, eTeamz, Voquette, Obiquity, Logilent
Carl Nichols, Managing Director
Education: BS, Computer Science, Brown University; MBA, Harvard Business School
Background: SBC/Pacific Bell, Scrivner, Booz Allen & Hamilton
Directorships: ClairMail, Lasso Logic, Epicentric, MarketHome, Arthas, Toolwire, Vantos, Kinecta

1390 OUTPOST CAPITAL
355 Berry Street
San Francisco, CA 94158

web: outpostvc.com

Mission Statement: Outpost Capital is a venture vapital fund focused on Virtual Reality and Artificial Intelligence, as well as blockchain technology.

Geographic Preference: US, China
Founded: 2016
Investment Criteria: Early Stage
Industry Group Preference: Artificial Intelligence, Virtual Reality, Blockchain, Technology, Robotics
Portfolio Companies: Aconite, Big Box, Fable, Humense, Jido, Jingtum, Kite & Lightning, MOAC, Modal, Natilus, Pingpad, The Rogue Initiative, Supermedium, TheWaveVR, UploadVR, Visby

Key Executives:
Ryan Wang, Co-Founder/General Partner
Background: Venture Partner, CLI Ventures; Investment Banker, Citigroup
Sha Zhou, Co-Founder/General Partner
Background: HP; Alteon; NetScaler; NetScreen; Juniper
Cherie Liu, Vice President, Investment
Education: MS, Columbia University

1391 OVP VENTURE PARTNERS
Kirkland, WA

Phone: 425-889-9192
e-mail: hoban@ovp.com

Mission Statement: Makes equity investments in early stage technology-based companies primarily in the Western third of North America, while maintaining a leading market share position in the Pacific Northwest.

Fund Size: $185 million
Founded: 1983
Average Investment: $1-$5 million
Minimum Investment: $100,000
Investment Criteria: Seed, Startup, First-stage, Second-stage
Industry Group Preference: Software, Communications, Life Sciences
Portfolio Companies: Adapx, Cradlepoint Technology, Datsphere Technologies, EnerG2, Fate Therapeutics, GenoLogics, NanoString Technologies, Novomer, OncoFactor, RedSeal, Talyst, Tigo Energy, Verdezyne

Other Locations:
One SW Columbia
Suite 1675
Portland, OR 97258
Phone: 503-697-8766

Key Executives:
Gerry Langeler, Managing Director
Education: AB Chemistry, Cornell University; MBA, Harvard University

Venture Capital & Private Equity Firms / Domestic Firms

Background: Co-Founder & President Mentor Graphics, Author 'Vision Trap'
Directorships: Advanced Inquiry Systems, Carbonflow, Collaborative Software Initiative, EnerG2, GainSpan, Max-Viz, Viral Logic Systems Technology
Bill Funcannon, Managing Director
Background: Venture Fund Controller, Hambrecht & Quist
Directorships: LeMond Fitness, M2E

1392 OWL VENTURES
400 Pacific Avenue
3rd Floor
San Francisco, CA 94133
    Phone: 415-277-0300
    web: owlvc.com

Mission Statement: Owl Ventures is a global venture capital firm focused on the merger of K-12 education and technology.

Founded: 2014
Industry Group Preference: Software, Applications, Education, Healthcare, Technology, Child Care
Portfolio Companies: Abl, Accelerate Learning, Amira Learning, Bakpax, Benchprep, BetterLesson, Byju's, Degreed, Dreambox, Hazel Health, Imbellus, Kiddom, Kuali, Labster, LearnZillion, Lele Ketang, Lingo Live, Newsela, Noodle Partners, Panorama Education, Piper, Quizlet, Raftr, RaiseMe, Remind, Securly, SV Academy, Swing Education, Thinkful, Tinkergarden, Whitehat Jr.

Other Locations:
  300 Sand Hill Road
  Building 3
  Suite 180
  Menlo Park, CA 94025

Key Executives:
  Ian Chiu, Managing Director
  Education: BS/MS, Industrial Engineering, Stanford University; MBA, Stanford Grad. School of Business
  Background: Warburg Pincus; Silver Lake Partners; Bain & Company
  Directorships: Liaison International; Dude Solutions; Civitas Learning
  Tom Costin, Managing Director
  Education: BA, Bowdoin College; MBA, Stanford Grad. School of Business
  Background: Private Investment Specialist, Cambridge Associates; Managing Director, SoleTech; Associate, FLAG Capital
  Amit A. Patel, Managing Director
  Education: BA, Mathematical Economic Analysis, Rice University; MBA, Stanford Grad. School of Business; MA, Education, Stanford Grad. School of Education
  Background: Founder, Perfonal Academic Trainers; Director of Technology, Success Academy Charter Schools
  Tory Patterson, Co-Founder/Managing Director
  Education: BA, Economics, Williams College; MBA, Stanford Grad. School of Business
  Background: Partner, Catamount Ventures
  Jed Smith, Co-Founder/Advisor
  Education: BA, Middlebury College; MBA, Harvard Business School
  Background: Founder/Managing Partner, Catamount Ventures; Fouunder, Drugstore.com
  Directorships: Linden Labs; Revolutions; Abl.; Piper; RaiseMe; Amour Vert; Banyan Water; Plum Organics; Seventh Generation

1393 OXANTIUM VENTURES
2600 Virginia Ave NW
Suite 512
Washington, DC 20037
    e-mail: info@oxantium.com
    web: www.oxantium.com

Mission Statement: Oxantium Ventures invests worldwide in a diversified range of companies, distributed across three stages of enterprise development - seed, early stage, and growth. This is done for two primary reasons. One is to follow a balanced portfolio strategy and minimize risk. The other is to offer a 'lifecycle' of support to promising companies and to have the capacity to fund them from the early idea stage to well after they are out of incubation and require financing to sustain growth

Geographic Preference: Worldwide
Investment Criteria: Seed-Stage, Early-Stage, Later-Stage
Industry Group Preference: Software, Hardware, Wireless, Information Technology, Enabling Technology, Advanced Materials, Nanotechnology, Power
Portfolio Companies: Anvato, RFnano, EnerTech Environmental, iMove, E.A.R.T.H., Make a Mind Co., Solar Array Ventures, Wireless World Net

Key Executives:
  Newton Howard, Managing Director
  Education: PhD
  Background: Chairman, Center for Advanced Defense Studies
  Richard Wirt, Managing Director
  Education: PhD
  Background: Vice President/General Manager, Intel Corporation Software & Solutions Group; Chief Scientist & EVP, In-Q-Tel

1394 OXFORD BIOSCIENCE PARTNERS
535 Boylston Street
Suite 402
Boston, MA 02116
    Phone: 617-357-7474 Fax: 617-357-7476

Mission Statement: To generate long-term capital gains for both the investors in the Fund and the entrepreneurs that we support. To meet this goal, we invest in businesses capable of improving the diagnosis and treatment of disease, as well as the companies with technologies that accelerate drug discovery and development. We have achieved considerable success and above average returns in the bioscience field.

Geographic Preference: United States, Europe
Fund Size: $850 million
Founded: 1992
Average Investment: $5 million
Minimum Investment: $1 million
Investment Criteria: Healthcare
Industry Group Preference: Biotechnology, Genomics, Medical Devices, Research & Development, Therapeutics, Life Sciences
Portfolio Companies: Gene Logic, Human Genome Sciences, Exelixis, Genset S.A., ACADIA Pharmaceuticals, Inc., AVEO Pharmaceuticals, Cardiome Pharma, Ceres, Dicerna Pharmaceuticals, Enata Pharmaceuticals, ExonHit Therapeutics, Genetic Therapy, Geron Corporation, Glori Energy, Illumina, Inkine Pharmaceutical Company, Inverness Medical Innovations, Orchid BioSciences, QuadraMed, Salix Pharmaceuticals, Santhera Pharmaceuticals, Sosei, Targacept, VIVUS, Xencor

Other Locations:
  30765 Pacific Coast Highway
  Suite 370
  Malibu, CA 90265
  Phone: 310-589-0025 Fax: 310-589-0099

1395 OYSTER VENTURES
1355 Market Street
Suite 488
San Francisco, CA 94103
    e-mail: partners@oyster.vc
    web: oyster.vc

Mission Statement: Oyster Ventures invests in exceptional new-frontier technology companies. Targets companies that bring liquidity and efficiency to antiquated industries, companies that enable globalization, and with the leverage to massively scale.

Geographic Preference: North America, Asia
Fund Size: $30MM
Founded: 2016
Average Investment: $250K
Minimum Investment: $100K
Industry Group Preference: Fintech, Vertical, SaaS, Marketplace, Blockchain
Portfolio Companies: Blockstack, Equipmentshare, Forge Global, LogDNA, MasterClass, Postmates, Republic.co

Key Executives:
Sophie Liao, General Partner
Background: Managing Director, Rothenberg Ventures; Venture Partner, Draper Dragon; M&A Manager, Eight Solutions; M&A Manager, FFD Labs; Anchor, CCTV; Anchor, Travel Channel; Head of Business Development, Cameron Pace Group
Kenneth Ballenegger, Managing Partner
Background: Co-Founder/Chief Strategy Officer, Republic Crypto; Co-Founder/CTO, FreshPay; Architect/Head of Mobile Engineering, Chartboost; Engineer, Tapulous

1396 PACIFIC COMMUNITY VENTURES
51 Federal Street
San Francisco, CA 94107

Phone: 415-442-4300 Fax: 415-442-4313
e-mail: info@pcvmail.org
web: www.pacificcommunityventures.com

Mission Statement: Focused exclusively on growing small businesses in California. We seek to invest in and build companies in partnership with experienced and entrepreneurial managers who share our vision and passion for growth.

Geographic Preference: California
Founded: 1999
Average Investment: $1-4 million
Investment Criteria: Growth Equity, Management Led Buy-Outs, Liquidity for Family-Owned or Closely-Held Companies, Recapitalizations/Restructurings
Industry Group Preference: Specialty Food Products, Ethnic Products & Services, Health Related, Low-Capital Intensity Manufacturing, Environment Products & Services
Portfolio Companies: Adina, Beacon Fire & Safety, Bentek Corporation, Evergreen Lodge, Fresh Dining, Galaxy Desserts, Mercados SUVIANDA, Moving Solutions, New Leaf Paper, Niman Ranch, Pacific Pharmacy Group, SABEResPODER, Timbuk2

Other Locations:
2448 Historic Decatur Road
Suite 200
San Diego, CA 92106
Phone: 619-818-6872 Fax: 619-516-2295

Key Executives:
Bulbul Gupta, President and CEO
Education: George Washington University; University of Michigan
Background: Global Entrepreneurship Advisor, Clinton Campaign; Founding Advisor, Socos Labs; Adjunct Lecturer, NYU
Patrick Teixeira, Chief Financial Officer
Education: BSBA, Sonoma State University
Background: CEO, Abilene Partners; Managing Director, PCV Finance

1397 PACIFIC CORPORATE GROUP
Phone: 619-522-0100 Fax: 619-522-0099
e-mail: info@pcgfunds.com
web: www.pcgfunds.com

Mission Statement: A research driven investment management firm focused solely on private equity.

Geographic Preference: United States, Western Europe, Japan
Fund Size: $350 million
Founded: 1979
Investment Criteria: All Stages
Portfolio Companies: Armonix, Spectrawatt, SolarReserve, Allied Resource Corporation, ReliOn, Range Fuels, Odersun, Fat Spaniel Technologies

Key Executives:
Christopher J Bower, CEO/Founder
Education: BS, University of Colorado; JD, University of San Diego
Background: Arthur Young & Company

1398 PACIFIC HORIZON VENTURES
500 Union Street
Suit 835
Seattle, WA 98101

Phone: 206-682-1181 Fax: 206-682-8077
e-mail: phv@pacifichorizon.com
web: www.pacifichorizon.com

Mission Statement: A Seattle based venture capital firm with national presence, focused on the life science and healthcare industries. With a successful track record of over ten years, as demonstrated in our first two funds, we invest in validation phase, early and mid stage private companies across North America with a particular focus on the Pacific Northwest region.

Geographic Preference: North America, Northwest Region
Fund Size: $75 million
Founded: 1993
Minimum Investment: $250,000
Investment Criteria: Early Stage
Industry Group Preference: Health Related, Life Sciences
Portfolio Companies: Koronis Pharma, ViaCyte, Argos Therapeutics, AtheroGenics, CareWise, CellPathways, Diametrics Medical, Focal, Health Systems Technologies, Illumigen Biosciences, Inhibitex, iScience Interventional, NeoPath, Norian Corporation, Orquest, Rasiris, Sapient Health Networks, SleepMed, Tandem Medical, Therion Biologicals Corporation, Tissue Repair Company, Transmolecular, Trimeris, VirtGen, Coral Systems, Creative Multimedia, Edmark Corporation, Innova Corporation, Proxim, RTIME

Key Executives:
Donald J Elmer, Managing General Partner
206-682-1181
Fax: 206-682-807
e-mail: elmer@pacifichorizon.com
Education: MA, Economics, University of Pennsylvania; BA, Economics, Western Washington University
Directorships: ViaCyte, Koronis Pharmaceuticals
David A Krekel, Principal
Education: BS, Chemistry, Harvey Mudd College; MBA, University of Washington
Background: Virginia Mason Medical Center
William Robbins, Business Relations Principal
e-mail: phv@pacifichorizon.com
Education: BA, Catholic University of America

1399 PACIFIC VENTURES GROUP
Los Angeles, CA 90015

Phone: 310-800-4556
e-mail: info@pacvgroup.com

Mission Statement: Privately held venture capital partnership focused exclusively on investments in food, beverage and alcohol related industries.

Geographic Preference: United States
Fund Size: $100 million
Founded: 1995

499

Venture Capital & Private Equity Firms / Domestic Firms

Average Investment: $2-$5 million
Minimum Investment: $250,000
Investment Criteria: Seed, Startup, First-Stage, Second-Stage, Mezzanine, LBO, Special situations, Buy-ins, Consolidations, Recapitalization
Industry Group Preference: Food & Beverage Related
  Shannon Masjedi, CEO and President
  Education: Arizona State University

1400 PALADIN CAPITAL GROUP
2020 K Street NW
Suite 620
Washington, DC 20006

Phone: 202-293-5590
e-mail: info@paladincapgroup.com
web: www.paladincapgroup.com

Mission Statement: Paladin Capital Group is a leading multi-stage private equity firm that provides funding to growing companies. Across the globe, from Silicon Valley to Brazil, Paladin invests in best-of-breed companies with technologies, products, and services that meet the challenging demands of commercial, federal, and international customers.

Geographic Preference: North America, Brazil
Fund Size: $950 million
Founded: 2001
Average Investment: $10-$30 million
Minimum Investment: $5 million
Investment Criteria: Up to $250 million in annual sales, Small to mid-size, Consolidations, Restructurings, Growth Equity
Industry Group Preference: Homeland Security, Security, Alternative Energy, Technology
Portfolio Companies: 10x Technologies, Accubuilt, Adapx, Application Security, Arxan, BAInsight, BugCrowd, BuildingIQ, Clearcube, Cloudshield, Command Information, Courion, Crossbow, CyberCore Technologies, Damballa, DigitalBridge Communications, Digital Signal Corporation, Endgame, Fixmo, FPMI Solutions, HealthTell, HelioVOlt, Initiate, Luminus, Modius, Neohapsis, Newlanis, Nexidia, Orchestria, Paladin Ethanal Acquistion, PerspecSys, PhishMe, Previstar, Quantalife, Racemi, Renewable Energy Products, Royalty Pharma, SafeView, Shadow Networks, SOA Software, ThreatStream, TOMA Biosciences, Twist Bioscience, UniTrends, VREC, White Ops., WiSpry

Other Locations:
  295 Madison Avenue
  12th Floor
  New York, NY 10017
  Phone: 202-293-5590

  3000 Sand Hill Road
  Suite 2-145
  West Menlo Park, CA 94025

  20 North Audley Street
  London W1K 6WE
  United Kingdom
  Phone: 44-0203-931-9704

Key Executives:
  Michael Steed, Founder/Managing Partner
  Education: Loyola Marymount University; JD, Loyola University School of Law
  Background: Senior VP of Investments, Washington, DC Financial Company
  Mark Maloney, Founder/Managing Director/Chief Compliance Officer
  Education: BS, Towson University
  Directorships: Adaptx, FPMI Solutions
  Dr. Alf L. Andreassen, Global Security Expert
  Education: PhD, Physical Chemistry, Cornell University
  Background: Founding Member, AT&T Solutions; Technical Advisor, Naval Warfare; Bell Laboratories
  Directorships: AgION, CloudShield, Digital Signal, Oryxe Energy, Previstar

  Kenneth A. Minihan, Managing Director
  Education: BA, Florida State University; MA, Naval Postgraduate School
  Background: Lt. General (Ret), United States Air Force; Director, National Security Agency/Central Security Service; Chairman & President, Security Affairs Support Assocition
  Directorships: Arxan, Command Information, GlassHouse, Neohapsis, Nexidia
  E. Kenneth Pentimonti, Principal
  Education: BA, Economics & Political Science, Stanford University; MBA, Anderson School at UCLA
  Background: Investment Banker, JP Morgan Chase; Senior Consultant/Auditor, Arthur Andersen & Co.
  Paul Conley, Managing Director/Venture Studio Director
  Education: BS, MS, Mechanical & Aerospace Engineering, University of Virginia; PhD, Computational Physics, MS, Bioengineering, University of California, San Diego
  Background: Founding CEO, BrightScale; Los Alamos National Laboratory
  Philip Eliot, Venture Partner
  Education: AB, Physics, Harvard University
  Background: FBR Technology Venture Partners

1401 PALISADE CAPITAL MANAGEMENT
One Bridge Plaza
Suite 695
Fort Lee, NJ 07024

Phone: 201-585-7733
Toll-Free: 800-330-9966
web: www.palisadecapital.com

Mission Statement: Provide investment management services to large institutions through our Small-Cap Equity and Convertible Security strategies. Through the proper balancing of risk and reward we endeavor to provide meaningful returns while preserving clients' capital.

Fund Size: $400 million
Founded: 1997
Average Investment: $5 to $30 million
Minimum Investment: $2 million
Investment Criteria: All Stages
Portfolio Companies: Brickell Biotech, Everlaw, Neurologix, Send Word Now, RAD Technologies

Other Locations:
  251 Royal Palm Way
  Suite 601
  Palm Beach, FL 33480
  Phone: 561-832-3558

Key Executives:
  Alison Berman, President and CEO/Chair
  e-mail: aberman@palcap.com
  Education: Brown University; JD, Benjamin N. Cordozo School of Law
  Background: Attorney, Skadden, Arps, Slate & Flom LLP
  Jack Feiler, Vice Chair
  Education: BA, City College of New York; JD, Brooklyn Law School
  Background: Account Executive, Burnham & Co.; Senior Executive VP, Broad Street Investment Management; Senior VP of Investments, Smith Barney
  Steven E Berman, Vice Chair
  Education: BA, Syracuse University; JD, Brooklyn College Law School
  Background: Executive Vice President, Drexel Burnham; Attorney/CEO, Manufacturing Company; Senior Vice President, Smith Barney
  Jeffrey D Serkes, Chief Operating Officer
  Education: BBA, Accounting, George Washington University
  Background: Senior Vice President & CFO, Allegheny Energy; Vice President & Treasurer, IBM Corporation; RJR Nabisco

Venture Capital & Private Equity Firms / Domestic Firms

Dennison T Veru, Chief Investment Officer
Education: Franklin & Marshall College
Background: President & Director of Research, Awad Asset Management; Drexel Burnham Lambert; Smith Barney Harris Upham

1402 PALISADES VENTURES
11726 San Vicente Blvd
Suite 450
Los Angeles, CA 90049

Phone: 310-571-6214
web: www.palisadesgrowth.com

Mission Statement: A Los Angeles-based VC firm making growth stage investments in systems, services, software, and hardware companies that are driving the adoption of leading edge IT, communications, and media technologies.

Average Investment: $2.5 - $7 million
Investment Criteria: Growth-Stage
Industry Group Preference: Information Technology, Software, Media, Communications
Portfolio Companies: Apacheta Corporation, Language Weaver, Lucix, MegaPath Networks, Micro Power, Omneon, Peregrine Semiconductor, Polaris Wireless, SOA Software, xAD, Visage Mobile, Zinio Systems

Key Executives:
Paul D'Addario, Co-Founder, Partner
Education: BA, Boston College; MSc, London School of Economics, JD, Villanova Law School
Background: Managing Director, Donaldson Lufkin & Jenrette
Anders Richardson, Co-Founder, Partner
Education: BA, Harvard College; MBA, Harvard Business School
Background: Investment Banking, Donaldson Lufkin & Jenrette
Directorships: SOA Software, V-Enable

1403 PALLADIUM EQUITY PARTNERS
Rockefeller Center
1270 Avenue of the Americas
31st Floor
New York, NY 10020

Phone: 212-218-5150 Fax: 212-218-5155
web: www.palladiumequity.com

Mission Statement: Provides equity to companies seeking to grow, restructure or provide liquidity for shareholders. Palladium principals have invested more than $2 billion of equity in over 60 companies in the last two decades while developing a distinguished track record of successful partnerships with management teams.

Fund Size: $1 billion
Founded: 1997
Average Investment: $15 - 75 million
Investment Criteria: Leveraged Buyouts, Recapitalizations, Corporate Spin-Outs, Growth Financing, Restructurings
Industry Group Preference: Business Products & Services, Financial Services, Consumer Products, Food Services, Healthcare, Manufacturing, Media, Retail, Consumer & Leisure
Portfolio Companies: ABRA Auto Body & Glass, American Gilsonite, BankUnited, Cannella Media, Capital Contractors Inc., Castro Cheese, CircusTrix, Clarion Industries, DailyMe, Daniel's Jewelers, Del Real Foods, DolEx Dollar Express Inc., Fora Financial, GoodWest Industries Inc., HealthSun, Hy Cite Enterprises LLC, Jordan Health Services, Kar's Nuts, Kymera International, Mission Community Bank, Prince International Corporation, Pronto Insurance, QMax, Quirch, Raben Tire, Regional Management Corp., Sahale Snacks, Spice World, Taco Bueno, Teasdale Foods Inc., TransForce Inc., Wise Foods Inc.

Other Locations:
11726 San Vincente Blvd
Suite 300
Los Angeles, CA 90049
Phone: 310-820-4009

Key Executives:
David Perez, President/COO
Education: BS & MS, Dresden University of Technology; MEng, Cornell University; MBA, Harvard Business School
Background: General Atlantic Parnters; Atlas Ventures, Chase Capital Partners
Directorships: Aconcagua Holdings, American Gilsonite, Prince Minerals, Regional Management, Remesas Quisqueyana, Herald National Bank
Chris Allen, Managing Director
Education: BS, Mathematics, Morehouse College; BS, Electrical Engineering, Georgia Institute of Technology; MBA, Harvard Business School
Background: Arlon Capital Partners; GenNx360 Capital Partners; Windjammer Capital Investors; Bain & Co.
Directorships: Del Real; Kar's Nuts
Luis Zaldivar, Senior Managing Director
Education: BS, Finance, New York University, Stern School of Business; MBA, Harvard Business School
Background: Vice President, Coporate Development, Univerision; Lehman Brothers
Erik A. Scott, Managing Director
Education: BA, Economics, Vanderbilt University; MBA, Darden Graduate School of Business, University of Virginia
Background: Principal, FDG Associates; Principal, Parthenon Capital; Bowles Hollowel Conner & Co.

1404 PALMS & COMPANY
Palms Bayshore Building
West Wing Penthouse #408
6421 Lake Washington Boulevard NE
Kirkland, WA 98033-6876

Phone: 425-828-6774 Fax: 425-827-5528
e-mail: palms@peterpalms.com
web: www.peterpalms.com

Mission Statement: Transition from resources that will become seriously devalued due to Global Economic Meltdown of 2011 including hyper inflation, soaring gold prices, collapse of banking industry, collapse of real estate market, oil priced in other than dollars, other currencies becoming gold backed, etc.

Geographic Preference: Europe, Russia, China, Eastern Europe, United States, Canada, Mexico
Founded: 1934
Average Investment: $30 million
Minimum Investment: $1 million
Investment Criteria: Management team in place, simple solution for a big problem, defined exit strategy
Industry Group Preference: Pharmaceuticals, Agriculture, Mining, Construction, Oil & Gas, Machinery
Portfolio Companies: Congress Inns, Deltona Corporation, Eastern Elevator, Golf In Corporation, Gulf American Land Corporation, JSC Krasalkor Aluminiystroi Krasnoyarsk, Lummi Indian Nation, Mackle Brothers, Mechanical Rubber Products, Riva Boats

Other Locations:
1001 Oakwod Boulevard
Fairfield, IA 52556
Phone: 641-472-0262 Fax: 641-469-6360

Key Executives:
Dr. Peter J Palm IV, President
425-828-6774

Venture Capital & Private Equity Firms / Domestic Firms

1405 PALO ALTO VENTURE PARTNERS
300 Hamilton Avenue
4th Floor
Palo Alto, CA 94301

Phone: 650-462-1221
e-mail: judy@pavp.com
web: www.pavp.com

Mission Statement: An early stage, information technology, venture capital firm producing stellar returns by helping entrepreneurs lead new markets in enterprise communications and computing into proven companies.

Geographic Preference: United States, West Coast
Fund Size: $150 million
Founded: 1996
Investment Criteria: Seed, Early Stage, First Stage, Mezzanine, Second Stage, Seed, Startup
Industry Group Preference: Information Technology, Enterprise Services, Computer Related, Online Content, Software
Portfolio Companies: Adforce, Aspectrics, AGIS, AvantGo, CareerBuilder, Gemandforce, Empolyease, Esurance, More.com, Nextance, PostX, Semagtx, Vicinity, When.com
   Peter Ziebelman, Founding Partner
   Education: MSC Computer Science, Yale Unversity
   Background: Marketing Executive, Texas Instruments; Ryan McFarland

1406 PALO ALTO VENTURE SCIENCE
501 Forest Ave
Palo Alto, CA 94301

Phone: 650-530-0040
e-mail: info@venture-science.com
web: www.venture-science.com

Mission Statement: We invest in leading startups using model based approaches to venture capital. Our objective is to achieve a superior rate of return by following a systematic approach to investing and applying proprietary analytical models.

Investment Criteria: Early Stage
Industry Group Preference: Mobile, E-Commerce & Manufacturing, Consumer Technology, Education Technology, Healthcare Information Technology
Portfolio Companies: Appetas, Safe-Guard, Zipmark, Olapic, The Visual Revenue Platform, Vipit, TIO Networks Corporation, Clinipace Worldwide, KnowledgeTree, Lineagen, Quantenna Communcations, Ooma, Luxtera, Aggregate Knowledge

Key Executives:
   Matt Oguz, Founding Partner
   e-mail: matt@venture-tech.com
   Education: MBA, Decision Science, GSU
   Selahattin Onen, Managing Partner
   Education: BSEE, University of Denver; Stanford University
   Background: CEO, G101; CEO, AGE Energy Group

1407 PALOMAR VENTURES
1881 Von Karman Avenue
Suite 220
Irvine, CA 92612

Phone: 949-475-9455 Fax: 949-475-9456
e-mail: jgauer@palomarventures.com
web: www.palomarventures.com

Mission Statement: Focuses on early stage information technology companies that demonstrate the potential for exceptional growth and market leadership.

Fund Size: $225 million
Founded: 1999
Average Investment: $5 million
Minimum Investment: $2-$5 million
Investment Criteria: Early-Stage
Industry Group Preference: Broadband, Infrastructure, Business to Business, Telecommunications, Software, Technology
Portfolio Companies: Ace Metrix, Akonix Systems, AlterPoint, Applimation, Attensite Corporation, Biscotti, Bubbly, Cerebra, Composite Software, Continuous Computing, CoreObjects, Damballa, DATAllegro, Dorado, Edgewater Networks, Entone Technologies, Efficient Networks, ExteNet Systems, Fulcrum, Gluecode Software, Incuity Software, Inovys Corporation, Interperse, Lombardi Software, Mixed Signals, MyBuys, Netcontinuum, Netork Physics, Paymetrics, Predixion Software, Ravenflow, RealOps, Silver Creek Systems, Strix Systems, Utique, Virtela, Voxify

Other Locations:
   18881 Von Karman Avenue
   Suite 960
   Irvine, CA 92612
   Phone: 949-475-9455 Fax: 949-475-9456

   1200 Park Place
   Suite 300
   San Mateo, CA 94403
   Phone: 650-566-1100 Fax: 650-510-6836

Key Executives:
   Jim Gauer, Managing Director
   Education: BA, Mathematics, UCLA; PhD Candidate, Mathematics & Philosophy, Johns Hopkins University
   Background: General Partner, Enterprise Partners Venture Capital
   Directorships: Ace Metrix, Composite Software, CoreObjects, Dorado, Lombardi Software, Paymetric
   Lisa Riedmiller, Chief Financial Officer
   Education: BA, California State University
   Background: OSCCO Ventures

1408 PALOMINO CAPITAL
14881 Quorum Drive
Suite 525
Dallas, TX 75254

Phone: 214-269-3400
web: www.palominocap.com

Mission Statement: Palomino Capital partners with management teams to invest in middle-market buyouts, industry consolidations, and recapitalizations.

Geographic Preference: United States
Fund Size: $2 billion
Investment Criteria: Buyouts, Industry Consolidations, Recapitalizations
Industry Group Preference: Niche Manufacturing, Distribution, Building Materials & Services, Business Products & Services

Key Executives:
   Chuck Butler, Partner
   Education: BA, University of Texas, Dallas
   Background: Barrier Advisors, Convergent Communications, PricewaterhouseCoopers Corporate Finance
   John Toomay, Partner
   Education: BA, Economics, Brown University; AVA
   Background: Associate, Mercer Management Consulting; United Airliens

1409 PAMLICO CAPITAL
150 North College Street
Suite 2400
Charlotte, NC 28202

Phone: 704-414-7150 Fax: 704-414-7160
e-mail: contactus@pamlicocapital.com
web: www.pamlicocapital.com

Mission Statement: To generate exceptional investment returns by providing talented managers and growing companies with capital, ideas and encouragement. Formerly Wachovia

Capital Partners and First Union Capital, Pamlico Capital provides flexible capital and strategic advice to companies whose management teams have a vision for their business and operating expertise to implement their strategies.

Geographic Preference: United States
Fund Size: $1.1 billion
Founded: 1988
Average Investment: $15 million - $100 million
Minimum Investment: $1 million
Investment Criteria: Management or Leveraged Buyouts, Recapitalziations, Growth or Acquisition Financings, Mezzanine Financings, Special Situations
Industry Group Preference: Communications, Consumer Products, Distribution, Industrial Services, Medical & Health Related, Information Technology, Media, E-Commerce & Manufacturing, Manufacturing, Energy, Financial Services, Business Products & Services, Healthcare
Portfolio Companies: 10th Magnitude, A4 Health Systems, ACIST Medical Systems, Airwavz Solutions, American Community Newspapers, American Renal Associates, ATX Networks, BeckerBs Healthcare, BNI, Cartegraph, Clearlink, Coastal Drilling, Comsys, Constella, Daxko, DayNine, Dexter + Chaney, Digitech, excellRx, GreatAmerica, Greenway, Healthcare First, HelioCampus, Hosting, Inner City Broadcasting, iBBS, IntraLinks, JAG-ONE, Lightower, Mactec, MedCap, MetaMetrics, MetroPCS, NewWave Communications, NuVox, Office Practicum, Personify, Physicians Endoscopy, PrizeLogic, Prometheus, Randall-Reilly, Securadyne Systems, Secure-24, Service Express, Silverline, Sonitrol Corporation, Symplr, T2 Systems, TekLinks, Three Eagles Communications Company, TNW Systems, TRG Screen, USA Compression Partners, US Eye, US Radiosurgery, VRI, Vast Broadland, Veston Nautical, Veterinary Practice Partners, Wilcon, Winsight, World 50, WorldStrides

Key Executives:

Scott B. Perper, Partner
704-383-0000
Fax: 704-374-6711
Education: Undergraduate Degree, Bowdin College; MBA, Harvard Business School
Background: VP, Kidder, Peabody & Company
Directorships: HOB Entertainment; NuVox Communications; US Salt Holdings; VIVAX

Frederick W. Eubank II, Partner
704-383-0000
Fax: 704-374-4709
Education: Undergraduate Degree, Wake Forest University; MBA with honors, Duke University
Background: CIO, First Union's Specialized Industries
Directorships: CapitalSource; COMSYS IT Partners; Constella Group

L. Watts Hamrick III, Partner
704-383-0000
Fax: 704-383-6538
Education: Undergraduate Degree; MBA, Duke University;
Background: Tax Consultant, Price Waterhouse
Directorships: American Community Newspapers; Piedmont Television; Three Eagles Communications; BullsEye Telecom; Uticom Networks; Heartland Publications; NewWave Communications; MACTEC

Brian F. Chambers, Partner
704-414-7177
e-mail: brian.chambers@pamlicocapital.com
Education: BBA, University of Wisconsin; MBA, Booth School of Business
Background: Principal, Beecken Petty O'Keefe; Analyst, Piper Jaffray
Directorships: JAG-ONE; US Eye; Veterinary Practice Partners

Arthur C. Roselle, Partner
Education: Undergraduate Degree, MS Mathematics, University of Virginia
Background: EVP, R-H Capital Partners, VP, The Robinson-Humphrey Company
Directorships: COMSYS IT Partners; NewWave Communications; Worldstrides Holdings

Walker C. Simmons, Partner
Education: BS Commerce, University of Virginia; Masters of Management, JL Kellogg Graduate School
Background: VP, Bruckmann, Rosser, Sherrill & Company; Associate, The Robinson-Humphrey Company; Chartered Financial Analyst
Directorships: American Community Newspapers; Heartland Publications; Sonitrol; Three Eagles Communications; TMW Systems; MetroPCS; NuVox Communications

Scott R. Stevens, Partner
Education: Undergraduate, University of North Carolina, MB, Stanford University
Background: Analyst, First Union Securities' Communications And Media Finance Group

Eric J. Wilkins, Partner
704-715-4554
e-mail: eric.wilkins@wachovia.com
Education: BA, University of North Carolina, Chapel Hill; MBA, Columbia Business School
Background: Associate, DLJ Merchant Banking Partners; Associate, McCown De Leeuw & Company; Analyst, Bowles Hollowell Conner & Company
Directorships: Integrated Broadband Services

R. Scott Glass, Jr., Principal
701-414-7121
e-mail: scott.glass@pamlicocapital.com
Education: BS, Wake Forest University; MBA, Wharton School
Background: Associate, Tailwind Capital Partners; Associate, American Capital; Analyst, Wachovia Securities
Directorships: Digitech; Office Practicum; Veterinary Practice Partners

Jay R. Henry, Principal
704-414-7184
e-mail: jay.henry@pamlicocapital.com
Education: BS, West Virginia University; MBA, Kellogg School of Management
Background: Senior Associate, Saw Mill Capital; Analyst, Edgeview Partners
Directorships: Becker's Healthcare; BNI; HelioCampus; PrizeLogic; TRG Screen; Winsight; World 50

Andrew B. Tindel, Principal
704-414-7180
e-mail: andrew.tindel@pamlicocapital.com
Education: BE, Vanderbilt University; MBA, Harvard Business School
Background: Associate, GTCR LLC; Analyst, Goldman Sachs
Directorships: 10th Magnitude; Airwavez Solutions; Silverline; Vast Broadband

1410 PANORAMA CAPITAL
1999 S. Beascom Avenue
Suite 700
Campbell, CA 95008

Phone: 650-234-1420
web: www.panoramacapital.com

Mission Statement: Panorama Capital invests in passionate entrepreneurs building leading companies in life sciences and technology.

Industry Group Preference: Life Sciences, Technology
Portfolio Companies: Alvine Pharmaceuticals, Axiom, Auspex, Belair Networks, Beyond the Rack, CardioKinetix, Federated Media Publishing, Fixmo, Hyperion Therapeutics, Itero, NinthDecimal, Neoconix, NextWave Pharmaceuticals, Powervision, Presidio Pharmaceuticals, Shoedazzle, Skyfire, Syncapse, Tynt, Validity, Vyatta, World Golf Tour, Zoove

Venture Capital & Private Equity Firms / Domestic Firms

Key Executives:
Christopher J Albinson, Managing Director
Education: BS, MBA, University of Western Ontario
Background: General Partner, JP Morgan Partners
Directorships: Federated Media, Jiwire, Belair Networks, Tynt, Vyatta
Shahan D Soghikian, Managing Director
Education: BA, Pitzer College; MBA, UCLA Anderson School of Management
Background: Chemical Venture Partners, Bankers Trust, Prudential Equity Group
Directorships: Narus, Tagsys RFID, Squaretrade
Rod Ferguson, Managing Director
Education: BS, University of Illinois; PhD, State University of New York; JD, Northwestern University
Background: Partner, InterWest Partners; Genentech Inc.; Mccutchen, Doyle, Brown, & Enersen
Damion Wicker, Managing Director
Education: BS, Massachussets Institute of Technology; MD, Johns Hopkins School of Medicine; MBA, Wharton School
Background: President, Adams Scientific; MBW Venture Partners; Alexon Inc.

1411 PANTHEON VENTURES (US) LP
600 Montgomery Street
23rd Floor
San Francisco, CA 94111

Phone: 415-249-6200
e-mail: san.francisco@pantheon.com
web: www.pantheon.com

Mission Statement: Pantheon is a pioneer in private equity with a history of consistent performance and client service reflected in our continued success and reputation as an industry leader.
Geographic Preference: United States, Europe, Asia
Fund Size: $2.2 Billion
Founded: 1982
Investment Criteria: Leveraged Buyouts, Early-Stage & Later-Stage Venture Capital, Special Situations, Distressed Debt, Turnaround, Mezzanine Funds
Industry Group Preference: Manufacturing, Services, Information Technology, Healthcare, Energy, Communications, Consumer Products

Other Locations:
10 Finsbury Square
4th Floor
London EC2A 1AF
United Kingdom
Phone: 44-02033561800

33 Des Voeux Road
21st Floor
Central
Hong Kong
Phone: 85-237189600

11 Times Square
35th Floor
New York, NY 10036
Phone: 212-205-2000

Key Executives:
Brian J. Buenneke, Partner
Education: AB, Government, Dartmouth College; MBA, Kellogg School of Management, Northwestern University
Background: HarbourVest Partners; Duke Street Capital; Paul Capital Partners; Lehman Brothers Investment Banking Division
Dennis McCrary, Partner
Education: BA, Michigan State University; MBA, University of Michigan
Background: Adams Street Partners; Bank of America; Continental Bank
Kevin Dunwoodie, Partner
Education: University of Notre Dame; MBA, Harvard Business School
Background: Associate, Morgan Stanley; Private Equity Analyst, Pacific Corporate Group
Matt Garfunkle, Partner
Education: BA, History & Economics, Brown University
Background: Cambridge Associates
Jeff Miller, Partner
Education: BA, Economics & Mathematics, Gustavus Adolphus College; MBA, Northwestern University
Background: Vice President, Lehman Brothers; Associate, Wells Fargo
Kathryn Leaf, Partner
Education: BA, Modern Languages, Oxford University; MA, Modern Languages, Oxford University
Background: GIC Special Investments; Centre Partners; Morgan Stanley's Investment Banking Division
Evan Corley, Partner
Education: BS, Business Administation, Boston University
Background: Polaris Venture Partners; JPMorgan

1412 PAPPAS VENTURES
2520 Meridian Parkway
Suite 400
Durham, NC 27713

Phone: 919-998-3300 Fax: 919-998-3301
web: www.pappasventures.com

Mission Statement: Pappas Ventures invests exclusively in the life sciences sectory - biotechnology, specialty pharmaceuticals, drug delivery, diagnostics, medical devices, and related ventures - across the United States and Canada. Pappas Ventures has more than $350 million in capital under management, and has guided the launch and/or development of 56 companies.
Geographic Preference: Southeast, Mid-Atlantic Region
Fund Size: $350 million
Founded: 1994
Minimum Investment: $100,000
Investment Criteria: Seed, Early-Stage, Mezzanine
Industry Group Preference: Biopharmaceuticals, Biotechnology, Medical Devices, Drug Development, Health Related, Life Sciences, Technology
Portfolio Companies: Achillion, Aclara Biosciences, Afferent Pharmaceuticals, Anthera Pharmaceuticals, Arena, ArgoMed, Athersys, Balance Therapeutics, Barosense, Bayhill Therapeutics, Biosyntech, BrainCells, Calyx Therapeutics, CadrioDx, CeNeRx, Cequent Pharmaceuticals, Cerexa, Chimerix, Cognetix, CoLucid, Dynogen, EBM Solutions, Elitra, Emerald, Envisia, FlowCardia, Gentis, IlluminOss, LEAD, LipoScience, Liquida Technologies, Lumena, Marina, Milestone Pharmaceuticals, Mirati, Nereus, NuVasive, Optherion, Panacos, Peninsula Pharmaceuticals, Plexigen, Plexxikon, Reprogenesis, Rotation Medical, Selventa, Sensys, Signase, Spherics, Syndax, Syntonix, TargeGen, TESARO, Thrasos, TYRX, Ultragenyx, Variagenics, X-Ceptor

Key Executives:
Ford Worthy, Partner
919-998-3300
Education: BA Interdisciplinary Studies, University of North Carolina; JD, University of Chicago
Background: Corporate and securities attorney, Womble Carlyle Sandridge & Rice. Writer and associate editor, Fortune Magazine

1413 PAR CAPITAL MANAGEMENT
One International Place
Suite 2401
Boston, MA 02110

web: www.parcapital.com

Mission Statement: PAR Capital Management manages a private investment fund. The firm was founded in 1990 and is located in Boston, Massachusetts. Our philosophy is based on the belief that long term investment success can be achieved through narrowly focused and rigorous fundamental research, disciplined portfolio management, and the alignment of incentives between manager and client.

1414 PARADIGM CAPITAL LTD
155 North Wacker Drive
Suite 4400
Chicago, IL 60606

Phone: 312-474-1901 Fax: 312-277-2011

Mission Statement: Paradigm seeks to reconcile the dilemma that often occurs between investors and entrepreneurs. Entrepreneurs seek to retain the ownership, control and capital appreciation of the firm they operate. To achieve this goal entrepreneurs will need assistance in evaluating the capital raising alternatives and negotiating with institutional investors. Investors seek to control and maximize thee returns on each transaction. They have highly sophisticated financial talent and frequently must review many transactions to find investments that meet their criteria. By serving as a strategic conduit between these two parties, Paradigm Capital creates an optimal situation for both the company and potential investors.

Geographic Preference: United States
Founded: 1996
Investment Criteria: Seed Stage, Early Stage
Industry Group Preference: Business to Business, Logistics

Key Executives:
  Edward J Condon Jr, Founder
  Education: College of the Holy Cross
  Background: Vice President, Sears Roebuck & Company

1415 PARALLEL INVESTMENT PARTNERS
3889 Maple Avenue
Parkland Hall, Suite 220
Dallas, TX 75219

Phone: 214-740-3610 Fax: 214-740-3630
web: www.parallelip.com

Mission Statement: Parallel Investment Partners is an institutional private equity firm focused exclusively on investing in North American middle-market growth companies.

Geographic Preference: North America
Fund Size: $400 Million
Founded: 1992
Investment Criteria: Lower Middle-Market
Industry Group Preference: Business to Business, Consumer Products, Education, Energy, Healthcare, Specialty Consumer Products
Portfolio Companies: Marmalade Café, Mealey's Furniture, Moosejaw Mountaineering, Superior Automotive Group, Superior Automotive Group, The Fragrance Outlet, USA Discounters, Accelerated Companies, Offshore Inland Marine & Oilfield Services

Key Executives:
  F. Barron Fletcher III, Managing Director
  e-mail: bfletcher@parallelip.com
  Education: BA in Mathematics & Economics, Yale University
  Background: Merchant Banking & Mergers and Acquisitions, Wasserstein Perella & Co.
  Jared L. Johnson, Managing Director
  e-mail: jjohnson@parallelip.com
  Education: BA in American Studies, Stanford University
  Background: Vice President, Summit Partners

1416 PARTECH INTERNATIONAL
200 California Street
San Francisco, CA 94111

Phone: 415-788-2929
e-mail: media@partechpartners.com
web: partechpartners.com

Mission Statement: To provide financing for startup and emerging growth companies in the US and Europe, mostly in the field of infrastructure software, E-business, solutions and wireless communication.

Geographic Preference: United States, Europe
Fund Size: $1 billion
Founded: 1982
Average Investment: $1 million
Minimum Investment: $500,000
Investment Criteria: Early-Stage, Mid-Stage
Industry Group Preference: Communications, Software, Electronic Components, Medical & Health Related, Environment Products & Services, Industrial Equipment, Internet, E-Commerce & Manufacturing, Digital Media & Marketing, Information Technology, Energy
Portfolio Companies: Acco, Akimbi, Alephd, Alltricks.com, Attune, Atlantis Computing, Auxmoney, BugCrowd, Bolt, BrandsforFriends.com, Cartesis, Caarbon, Dailymotion, Dymant, DemanderJustice.com, Evergig, Fluxus, EverTeam, Getinsured.com, HeartThis, Goom Radio, Intalio, Leara, LED Engin, Lima, Meninvest Kantox, Moodbyme, OpenSesame, NovaSparks, Plae, PricingAssistant, PriceMatch, Prysm, Qapa.fr, Pulse.io, Riplay, Scoop.it, Rockyou, SecretSales.com, Sensopia, Sensee, Sigfox, Tapfwd, Fketchfab, Teads.tv, Touch Commerce, Total Immersion, TouchOfModern, TVTY, TVtrip, Ventealapropriete.com, Voxeet, Vodkaster, WunderCar, Yieldr

Other Locations:
18 Ave de Messine
Paris 75008
France
Phone: 33-153656553

Gipsstrasse 3
Berlin 10119
Germany

442 Rue de Kaolack
Point E
Dakar
Senegal

Key Executives:
  Jean-Marc Patouillaud, General Partner
  Education: BA, Public Policy, Stanford University
  Background: SPO Partners; Goldman, Sachs & Company
  Philippe Collombel, General Partner
  Education: Northwestern University; Masters, Law & Economics, University of Paris
  Background: Carrefour; Andersen Consulting
  Directorships: Netsize, Pertinence, Semagix/Protege
  Mark Menell, General Partner
  Education: BA, Economics, University of Pennsylvania; BS/MBA, Wharton School
  Background: SVP of Business Development, Wanderful Media; Founding COO/CFO, ShopRunner; Founding Partner, Rustic Canyon; Investment Banker, Morgan Stanley
  Directorships: FreedomPop; The Bouqs
  Nicolase El Baze, General Partner
  Education: MBA, Ecole Des Hautes Etudes Commerciales; Graduate Degree in International Management, UC Berkeley & University of Cologne, Germany
  Background: Co-Founder, Softway International; ISDnet; Bigstep.Com; MultiMania
  Jai Choi, Partner
  Education: BS, Finance & Business Economics, Marshall School of Business, University of Southern California
  Background: Principal, IGNITE Group; OnePage Software; Co-Founder, On-Air Networks; PA Consulting Group
  Karen Noel, General Partner, Legal & Operations
  Education: LLM, University Panthéon Assas; ESSEC Business School
  Background: Partner, Gide Loyrette Nouel

Venture Capital & Private Equity Firms / Domestic Firms

1417 PARTHENON CAPITAL
One Federal Street
21st Floor
Boston, MA 02110

Phone: 617-961-4000
web: www.parthenoncapital.com

Mission Statement: A private equity investment firm with $1.1 billion of capital under management. The firm focuses on investing in select middle market companies with revenues of $50-$500 million.

Fund Size: $2.2 billion
Founded: 1998
Average Investment: $60 million
Minimum Investment: $20 million
Investment Criteria: Leveraged Recapitalizations, MBO, Growth Capital
Industry Group Preference: Business Products & Services, Financial Services, Food & Beverage, Consumer Products, Consumer Services, Distribution, Manufacturing, Healthcare, Logistics, Technology-Enabled Services
Portfolio Companies: Abeo, Altegra Health, Ascension Insurance, ASG Security, BlueSnap, Bracket, Bryant & Stratton College, Coastal Credit, Eliza Corporation, Enyvision, eSecLending, HD Vest, loanDepot, Merchant Warehouse, Performant Financial Corporation, Periscope Holdings, Seaside National Bank & Trust, Social Service Coordinators, Triad Isotopes

Other Locations:
Four Embarcadero Center
Suite 3610
San Francisco, CA 94111
Phone: 415-913-3900

114 West 7th Street
Suite 1230
Austin, TX 78701
Phone: 512-813-4900

Key Executives:
Dave Ament, Managing Partner/Co-CEO
617-960-4088
Education: BA, Harvard University
Background: Princiapl, Audax Group; Apollo Advisors; Financial Analyst, Morgan Stanley & Company
Brian P Golson, Managing Partner/Co-CEO
415-913-3960
e-mail: bgolson@parthenoncapital.com
Education: BS with Honors and Distinction, University of North Carolina; MBA with High Distinction, Harvard Business School
Background: CFO/VP Operations, Everdream; Prometheus Partners; GE Capital Strategic Planning and Acquisition
Directorships: Rackable Systems; Arrow Financial Services
William C. Kessinger, Chief Investment Officer
415-913-3990
Education: BS, MS, Industrial Engineering, Stanford University; MBA, Harvard Business School
Background: Partner, GTCR Golder Rauner; Golder, Thoma, Cressey, Rauner; Parthenon Group; AnswerThink Consulting Group; National Equipment Services; Global Imaging Systems; Cambridge Protection Industries; Transaction Network Services; Associate, Prudential Asset Management Asia
Bill Winterer, Partner, Capital Markets
617-960-4060
e-mail: williamw@parthenoncapital.com
Education: BA, Williams College; MBA, New York University; CPA
Background: Director, FleetBoston Debt Capital Markets; Audit/M&A, KPMG; SPP Capital
Andrew C. Dodson, Managing Partner
e-mail: andrewd@parthenoncapital.com
Education: BA, Duke University; MBA, Harvard Business School
Background: Consultant, Bain & Company; Financial Analyst, Enron Corp.; Trilogy
Zachary Sadek, Partner
617-960-4083
e-mail: zachs@parthenoncapital.com
Education: BA, History, MS, Social Sciences, University of Chicago
Background: Investment Banking, Dresdner Kleinwort Wasserstein
Directorships: Restaurant Technologies, Tier Technologies
Kurt A. Brumme, Principal
617-960-4059
Education: BA, Economics/Mathematics, Williams College; MBA, Harvard Business School
Background: Finance/Corporate Development Manager, Grupo Qualicorp; General Atlantic; Morgan Stanley
Directorships: RedCard Systems; Trinity Partners; Zelis Health
Anthony J. Orazio, Principal
617-960-4066
Education: BA, Economics, Swarthmore College
Background: Oak Hill Capital Partners; Blackstone
Jim Chappell, Vice President
415-913-3920
Education: BA, Economics, Stanford University
Background: Senior Associate, Technology Crossover Ventures; Analyst, Thomas Weisel Partners
G. Thomas Hough, Vice President
617-960-4043
Education: BS/MS, Wake Forest University
Background: Analyst, BlackArch Partners
Steven Bressler, Vice President
617-960-4015
Education: BA, Duke University; MBA, Wharton School
Background: Principal, Varsity Healthcare Partners; VP, Riverside Partners; Associate Frazier Healthcare Partners; Senior Analyst, Shattuck Hammond Partners

1418 PARTISAN MANAGEMENT GROUP
293 Pearl St.
Boulder, CO 80302

Phone: 303-589-0019
web: www.partisanmgmt.com

Mission Statement: Partisan Management Group identifies unmet medical needs and invests in medical device and drug delivery companies that will meet those needs.

Investment Criteria: Early Stage
Industry Group Preference: Medical Devices, Drug Delivery
Portfolio Companies: Ash Access, Enable Injections, Neuronetics, Ponce de Leon Pharmaceuticals, Preceptis Medical, Surefire Medical

Other Locations:
6 Ocean Club Dr.
Amelia Island, FL 32034
Phone: 904-491-8619

Key Executives:
Karen Cassidy, Principal
e-mail: kjcassidy@partisanmgmt.com
Norman Weldon, Principal
e-mail: nrweldon@partisanmgmt.com

1419 PARTNERS HEALTHCARE RESEARCH VENTURES
101 Huntington Avenue
4th Floor
Boston, MA 02199

Phone: 617-954-9500
web: innovation.partners.org

Mission Statement: Partners HealthCare Research Ventures & Licensing is advancing commercialization of new medical technologies from Partners' academic medical centers. Bringing together specialists in medical technology licensing, research contracts, ventures and business development, we partner with investigators, scientists and clinicians to translate new medical technology into healthcare practice. Representing Brigham and Women's Hospital, Massachusetts General Hospital, and McLean Hospital, Partners HealthCare is the largest academic biomedical research enterprise in the US. We are committed to a creative, solutions-oriented approach to licensing, ventures and research that delivers opportunities to improve patient care around the world.

Geographic Preference: United States
Investment Criteria: Early-Stage
Industry Group Preference: Healthcare, Life Sciences, Diagnostics, Medical Devices, Pharmaceuticals
Portfolio Companies: Alopexx Pharmaceuticals, Annovation Biopharma, BIND Biosciences, BioBehavioral Diagnostics, CoStim, Daktari Diagnostics, Editas Medicine, Exosome Diagnostics, Fate Therapeutics, Life Image, MoMelan Technologies, NinePoint Medical, NKT Therapeutics, Provasculon, QPID, RaNA, Spero Therapeutics, Resolvyx, Sebacia, Selecta Biosciences, Synovex, T2 Biosystems, TargAnox, VisionScope Technologies, ZELTIQ

Key Executives:
 Chris Coburn, Chief Innovation Officer
 Background: Executive Director, Cleveland Clinic Innovations; Vice President/General Manager, Battell Memorial Institute
 Directorships: Automatic Technologies, Explorys, U.S. Enrichment Corporation
 Trung Q. Do, Vice President, Business Development
 Education: BS, University of California, Irvine; MA, MBA, Boston University
 Background: Director of Operations, PharMetrics; Consultant, Arthur Andersen; Boston Biomedical Consultants
 Roger Kitterman, Vice President, Venture
 e-mail: rkitterman@partners.org
 Education: AB, Harvard College; MBA, Finance, Columbia Business School
 Background: Founder, Mass Medical Angels; General Partner, Mi3 Venture Partners; Managing Director, Lee Munder Venture Partners

1420 PARTNERSHIP FUND FOR NEW YORK CITY
One Battery Park Plaza
5th Floor
New York, NY 10004

web: partnershipfundnyc.org

Mission Statement: A private fund with a civic mission in the vision of Henry R Kravis, to mobilize the city's financial and business leaders to help build a stronger and more diversified local economy, identifying and supporting New York City's most promising entrepreneurs in both the for-profit and nonprofit sectors.

Fund Size: $95 million
Founded: 1996
Average Investment: $1.5 million
Minimum Investment: $500,000
Investment Criteria: All Stages, Job Creation, Revitalization
Industry Group Preference: Healthcare, Retailing, Tourism, Information Technology, Media, Entertainment, Communications, Clean Technology
Portfolio Companies: Bien Cuit, Bionic Sight, Centripetal, Cureatr, Digital Reasoning, Dual Therapeutics, Freelancers Union, Grameen America, Hot Bread Kitchen, Independence Care System, Intra-Cellular Therapies, Karos Pharmaceuticals, Kasisto, Kings County Distillery, Marketing Technology Solutions, NY Accelerator Corp., New York Genome Center, OwnEnergy, PIN Pharma, Red Rabbit, Repairogen, Scratch Music Group, Trey Whitfield School, trueEx, True Office, Vivaldi Biosciences, Voxy

Key Executives:
 Maria Gotsch, President & CEO
 Education: BA, Wellesley College; MBA, Harvard Business School
 Background: Managing Director, BT Wolfensohn; LaSalle Partners; Merrill Lynch Capital Markets, NY and London

1421 PATHBREAKER VENTURES
San Francisco, CA

web: www.pathbreakervc.com

Mission Statement: Pathbreaker Ventures seeks to invest in tech companies with a specialization and a common goal to solve problems.

Founded: 2016
Investment Criteria: Early Stage
Industry Group Preference: Artificial Intelligence, Machine Learning, Deep Learning, Language Processing, Virtual Reality, Robotics
Portfolio Companies: Addressable, Apprente, Beyond View, Biobot Analytics, Catalog Technologies, Cinchapi, CryptoMove, Diligent Robotics, Difter Entertainment, Edify, Esper, Fathom Computing, Iron Ox, Limbix Health, Ono Food Co., OptimoRoute, Orderful, Reliable Robotics, Rheo, Safely You, Simbe Robotics, Spiketrap, Superhuman, Text IQ, Vergesense, Visby

Key Executives:
 Ryan Gembala, Managing Partner
 Education: BBA, University of Georgia; MBA, Booth School of Business
 Background: Co-Founder/Executive Director, H.E.R.O. for Children; Lead Associate, Hyde Park Angels; VP of Business Development, Telly; Early Stage Investor, Azure Capital Partners; Deal Lead, Corporate Development, Facebook

1422 PATRIOT CAPITAL
509 S Exeter Street
Suite 210
Baltimore, MD 21202

Phone: 443-573-3010 Fax: 443-573-3020
web: www.patriot-capital.com

Mission Statement: A leading source of growth capital for middle-market companies seeking to finance business expansion, acquisitions, management buyouts or balance sheet recapitalizations.

Fund Size: $270 million
Average Investment: $3 - $15 million
Investment Criteria: Business Expansion, Acquisition Financing, Major Capital Expenditures, Recapitalizations, Management Buyouts
Portfolio Companies: Vita Nonwovens, Metaltec Steel Abrasive, MetroGistics, Carthage Specialty Paperboard, Horizon Mud Comapny, AAA Slaes & Engineering, PCN Network, Red River Waste, The Sandbox Group, Food Distributor, McCubbin Hosiery, Orbital Tool Technologies, ErgoGenesis, Custom Control Concepts, Inspection Oilfield Services, Auburn Armature, CSP Business Media, ALON and XL Associates, GroupAero, Vantage Media, Mimeo.com, Chandler Industries, R&D Circuits, PPI-Time Zero, Cutex, Cyalume Technologies, STx Healthcare Services, The Motley Fool, Southeast Directional Drilling, Terracare Associates, CommutAir, International Development, R&H Supply, Instrument Sales and Service, AWS Convergence Technologies, eServices, Home Health Holdings, Fairfield Collectibles, PRI Group, Controlled Contamination Services, Expert Janitorial Services, D&S Residential Services, Dedicate Transport

Other Locations:
 225 West Washington
 Suite 2200

Venture Capital & Private Equity Firms / Domestic Firms

Chicago, IL 60606
Phone: 847-867-1299 **Fax:** 847-574-1285
Key Executives:
Thomas O Holland Jr, Managing Partner
e-mail: tholland@patriot-capital.com
Education: BA, University of Florida
Background: Founder, Allegiance Capital; Banc of America Corporation
Charles P McCusker, Managing Partner
e-mail: cmccusker@patriot-capital.com
Education: BS, Engineering, Virgina Tech; MBA, University of Chicago
Background: General Partner, ServiceMaster Venture Fund
Directorships: Dedicated Transport, Terminal Transportation, ExpertJMS, PRI Group
Daniel Yardley, Managing Director
e-mail: dyardley@patriot-capital.com
Education: Mount St. Mary's College; MBA, Johns Hopkins University
Background: Associate, Allegiance Capital; Analyst, M&A Group, Allegis Group
Charles A Bryan, Senior Principal & Adviser
e-mail: cbryan@patriot-capital.com
Education: BS, University of North Carolina; Harvard Business School; CPA
Background: Co-Founder & President, Bengur Bryan & Co.; VP, Alex. Brown & Sons
Directorships: PJPA LLC
Tom Kurtz, Managing Director - Midwest
e-mail: tkurtz@patriot-capital.com
Education: BS, Accounting, Western Michigan University
Background: Textron Financials Business Credit Division; GE Capital, Citicorp, Bank oF America, Chase/JP Morgan
Patrick Hamner, Managing Director - Southwest
e-mail: phamner@patriot-capital.com
Education: Southern Methodist University; BS, MBA, University of Texas
Background: Capital Southwest Corporation; Founding Chair, Heelys Inc.
Directorships: NASBIC
David Christopher, Managing Director - Southeast
e-mail: dchristopher@patriot-capital.com
Education: BBA, University of Michigan; MBA, University of Chicago
Background: Co-Founder/Partner, Peachtree Equity Partners; VP, Wachovia Bank; CIVC Partners; Kidder, Peabody & Co.; JP Morgan

---

1423 PEACHTREE EQUITY PARTNERS
1230 Peachtree Street NE
Suite 1900
Atlanta, GA 30309
Phone: 404-870-8900 **Fax:** 404-870-8191
e-mail: info@peachtreeequity.com
web: www.peachtreeequity.com

Mission Statement: Provides junior capital for small businesses.
Geographic Preference: United States
Fund Size: $60 million
Founded: 2002
Average Investment: $3 - $10 million
Minimum Investment: $3 million
Investment Criteria: Subordinate Debt with Cash Interest & Warrants
Industry Group Preference: Manufacturing, Healthcare, Business Products & Services, Consumer Products, Consumer Services, Government, Education, Financial Services, Media, Communications
Portfolio Companies: CV Holdings, Imagimed, Marlin Business Services Corp., Mertz Manufacturing, National P.E.T., American BioCare, Butler, Conger & Elsea, Convergent, DTl Transportation, Emtec, Expert NJS, FutureTech Holdings, Technical Innovation, Tech Rentals, The Roof
Key Executives:
David Christopher, Partner
Education: BBA, University of Michigan; MBA, University of Chicago
Background: Vice President, Wachovia Capital Associates; Continental Illinois Venture Corporation; Investment Banking Analyst, Kidder Peabody & Co.
Wendell Reilly, Partner
Education: BA, English, Emory University; MBA, Finance, Vanderbilt University
Background: Founder, Grapevine Communications; CFO, Lamar Advertising Company
Matt Sullivan, Partner
Education: University of Pennsylvania; Harvard Business School
Background: Managing Director, Wachovia Capital Associates; Corporate Finance, Kidder Peabody & Co.
John McCarty, Partner
Education: BS, Wharton School
Background: Senior Investment Officer, Roswell Capital Partners; Investment Banking, Banc of America Securities

---

1424 PEGASUS CAPITAL GROUP
3250 Ocean Park Blvd
Suite 203
Santa Monica, CA 90405
Phone: 310-392-9100 **Fax:** 310-392-9101
e-mail: info@pegasuscapgroup.com
web: www.pegasuscapgroup.com

Mission Statement: We invest in simple businesses with proven track records and clear opportunities for growth. Acquisition candidates include privately-held companies and divisions of larger corporations that are currently, or have the potential to become, leaders in their industry niche.
Geographic Preference: North America
Founded: 1997
Average Investment: $5 million
Minimum Investment: $2 million
Investment Criteria: Leveraged Buyouts, Management Buyouts, Corporate Divestitures, Recapitalizations, Growth Equity
Industry Group Preference: Low Technology, Manufacturing, Distribution, Specialty Services
Portfolio Companies: Midwest Automotive Designs, Jackrabbit, SANTIER, SPG International, American Piping Products
Key Executives:
Patrick F Whelan, Managing Partner
310-392-0100
e-mail: pwhelan@pegasuscapgroup.com
Education: Economics/Computer Science, Vanderbilt University; MBA, Wharton School
Background: Co-Managing Director Mergers/Acquisitions, Broadview International; Abacus Ventures; InterFirst Ventures; Co-Founder/Board Member, TranSwitch Corporation; Teleos Communications; Board Member, TelWatch Corporation; Quality Components
Directorships: WeatherGuard Building Products, Shield Pack, SPG, Design Space
Luke Sage, Partner
e-mail: lsage@pegasuscapgroup.com
Education: BS, Western Michigan University; MBA, Saint Louis University
Background: President, Health Capital Group

1425 PELION VENTURE PARTNERS
2755 E Cottonwood Parkway
Suite 520
Salt Lake City, UT 84121
Phone: 801-365-0262 Fax: 801-365-0233
e-mail: info@pelionvp.com
web: www.pelionvp.com

Mission Statement: We look constantly to discover innovative opportunities with visionary entrepreneurs who have a strong desire to succeed and the discipline to execute, and we help them launch their great ideas and achieve exciting new journeys in the marketplace.

Geographic Preference: Western U.S.
Fund Size: $200 million
Founded: 1986
Investment Criteria: Early stage
Industry Group Preference: Information Technology, Digital Media & Marketing, Software, Infrastructure, Communications, Medical Devices, Nanotechnology, Networking, Wireless, Internet
Portfolio Companies: 33across, Adapx, AngioScore, Bitcasa, Bloxr, CloudFlare, CloudVelocity, CONVIVA, Domo Technologies, DotNetNuke, Formation Data Systems, gazillion, Integral, Keen IO, MetaCloud, Mojiva, Moki Mobility, Primary Data, Skylight Healthcare Systems, Soasta, Stormpath, Venafi

Key Executives:
  Jeff Kearl, General Partner
  Education: BA, Bringham Young University
  Background: Logoworks; vSpring Capital
  Directorships: Scopely; Just Water
  Matt Mosman, General Partner
  Background: Founder, College Heights Partners; SVP, Oracle Corporation; CEO, Unifi Software
  Blake Modersitzki, General Partner
  Education: BS, Brigham Young University
  Background: Novell, WordPerfect
  Chris Cooper, General Partner
  Education: University of Utah, University of Phoenix
  Background: Director, Partner Engineering & Developer Services, Novell
  Ben Lambert, General Partner
  Education: BA, MBA, Bringham Young University
  Background: Jefferies Financial Group; Sears Holding Co.
  Chad Packard, General Partner
  Education: BA, Brigham Young University; JD, Santa Clara University; MBA, Brigham Young University
  Background: Director, Marich Confectionary

1426 PENINSULA CAPITAL PARTNERS LLC
One Detroit Center
500 Woodward Avenue
Suite 2800
Detroit, MI 48226
Phone: 313-237-5100 Fax: 313-237-5111
e-mail: campbell@peninsulafunds.com
web: www.peninsulafunds.com

Mission Statement: An investment company specializing in subordinated debt and structured equity investments in superior middle market companies.

Fund Size: $390 million
Founded: 1995
Minimum Investment: $4 million
Investment Criteria: MBO, LBO, Growth Capital
Industry Group Preference: Industrial Services, Consumer Products, Retailing, Food & Beverage, Distribution

Key Executives:
  William Y Campbell, Chairman/Founder
  e-mail: campbell@peninsulafunds.com
  Education: BA, Albion College; MBA, Bowling Green State University
  Background: Campbell & Company; First of Michigan Corporation; Standard Federal Bank; Michigan National Corporation & W.Y.
  Scott A Reilly CFA, President/CIO/Founder
  e-mail: reilly@peninsulafunds.com
  Education: BBA, University of North Dakota; MBA, Fuqua School of Business at Duke University
  Background: Churchill Capital; Northstar Capital Ltd.; Security Pacific Bank
  William F McKinley, Executive VP/Founder
  e-mail: mckinley@peninsulafunds.com
  Education: BS, Babson College; MBA, Fuqua School of Business at Duke University
  Background: WY Campbell & Company; First of Michigan Corporation
  James A Illikman CFA, Partner
  e-mail: illikman@peninsulafunds.com
  Education: BBA/MBA, University of Michigan
  Background: Talon Equity Partners LLC; Freudenberg-NOK General Partnership; United Technologies; Delphi Corporation
  Karle E LaPeer PE CFA, Partner
  e-mail: lapeer@peninsulafunds.com
  Education: BS, Mechanical Engineering, Michigan Technological University; MBA, University of Michigan
  Background: First of Michigan Corporation; Harrell & Associates; GMFanuc Robotics Corporation
  Steven S Beckett, Partner
  e-mail: beckett@peninsulafunds.com
  Education: BA, California Polytechnic State University; MBA, Fuqua School of Business At Duke University
  Background: Commercial Banking, Societe Generale; Citibank

1427 PENINSULA VENTURES
1500 Fashion Island Boulevard
Suite 102
San Mateo, CA 94404
Phone: 650-517-1900 Fax: 650-517-1999
e-mail: info@peninsulaventures.com
web: www.peninsulaequity.com

Mission Statement: At Peninsula Ventures, we believe in creativity, innovation, and the entrepreneurial spirit. Because the ones who matter most are the entrepreneurs whose ideas keep moving the world ahead. We're constantly searching for the next great market. We leverage our experience with past investments and the insights we gain from working with different companies to help identify these markets and the new technologies that emerge. To us, being and investor means being an active part of an ecosystem that is changing right before our eyes.

Geographic Preference: United States
Investment Criteria: Early-Stage
Industry Group Preference: Software, Infrastructure, Technology
Portfolio Companies: Axcient, Alianza, Basis, BroadHop, Flint, Lucid, Lumenetix, Marketo, Net Power & Lighting, Plastc Card, Pramata, Radius Intelligence, Response Analytics, Ribbit, Scinfiniti, SeeControl, Keyssa

Key Executives:
  Greg Ennis, Partner
  Education: BA, Economics & Political Science, Stanford University; MBA, Anderson School of Management
  Background: Managing Director, Thompson Clive & Partners
  Ryan Keating, Partner
  Education: Boston University
  Background: Microsoft; Salomon Smith Barney; PricewaterhouseCoopers

Venture Capital & Private Equity Firms / Domestic Firms

1428 PENN VENTURE PARTNERS
132 State Street
Suite 200
Harrisburg, PA 17101

Phone: 717-236-2300 Fax: 717-236-2350
web: www.pennventures.com

Mission Statement: Penn Venture Partners is focused on growth and expansion stage venture capital investment within certain underserved markets located in the Commonwealth of Pennsylvania.

Geographic Preference: Central & Northern Pennsylvania
Average Investment: $500,000 - $1.25 million
Investment Criteria: Growth-Stage, Expansion-Stage
Industry Group Preference: Agribusiness, Manufacturing, Biotechnology, Life Sciences, Computer Hardware & Software, Software, Media, Education, Business Products & Services, Energy, Environmental Technology, Marketing, Distribution, Networking, Telecommunications
Portfolio Companies: BioHitech America, Benten Bio Services, The Corporate University Xchange, Cyber-Patrol, NanoHorizons, Probity Medical Transcription, The Harrisburg Senators, Thermacore

Key Executives:
Thomas A Penn, Managing Director
Education: BS, Metallurgy & Materials Science, MIT; MBA, Stanford; JD, University of Pennsylvania
Background: Senior Partner, Meridian Capital Partners; Partner, Boston Millennia Partners; President & CEO, Tektagen
Dean M Kline, Managing Director
Education: MPhil, Cambridge University; BA, Wheaton College
Directorships: Journal Publications, Corporate University Xchange, Probity Medical Transcription, Senators Partners, Thermacore
Robert Graham, Managing Director
Education: BA, LaSalle University; MBA, Saint Joseph's University
Background: President, RG Consulting; President and CEO, Dorland Healthcare Information; EVP and CFO, Broadreach Consulting; VP and COO, Legal Communications Ltd.
Directorships: CyberPatrol Inc.

1429 PENNELL VENTURE PARTNERS LLC
332 Bleecker Street
#K-67
New York, NY 10014

Phone: 718-855-7087
e-mail: info@pennell.com
web: pennell.com

Mission Statement: An early-stage venture investor formed to meet the need for professional early-stage risk capital in New York and help bridge the gap in the investor marketplace between angel investors and institutional venture capital funds. PVP backs exceptional entrepreneurs who demonstrate the ability, creativity and drive necessary to develop leading companies.

Geographic Preference: New York
Fund Size: $5 million
Founded: 1996
Average Investment: $750,000
Investment Criteria: Early-Stage
Industry Group Preference: Software, Business to Business, Information Technology

Key Executives:
Thomas B Pennell, President
e-mail: thomas@pennell.com
Education: BA, University of Pennsylvania; MBA, New York University
Background: Chase Manhattan Bank; Endeavor Capital Management; Access Capital

1430 PENTA MEZZANINE FUND
20 N Orange Avenue
Suite 1550
Orlando, FL 32801

Phone: 407-648-5097 Fax: 407-650-3311
web: www.pentamezz.com

Mission Statement: Penta Mezzanine Fund is a private investment firm providing customized growth capital solutions to profitable, lower-middle-market companies nationwide. We look to invest our funds in established companies operated by experienced and proven management teams with a history of building enterprise value. Penta Mezzanine Fund was created by former industry executives and experienced investors who place a high value on their relationships with management teams.

Geographic Preference: United States
Average Investment: $2 - $25 million
Investment Criteria: Lower Middle Market, Growth Capital
Industry Group Preference: All Sectors Considered
Portfolio Companies: Twinlab Consolidated Holdings, Alexander Tank, Level Four Orthotics and Prosthetics, Green Distribution, Organic Holdings, Aviaion Inflatables, Method Holdings, Margaritaville, Orion Technologies, The Pub, KBP Foods, Great HealthWorks, Association Financial Services

Key Executives:
John Morgan, Founding Partner/Senior Advisor
e-mail: jmorgan@pentamezz.com
Education: BA, JD, University of Florida
Background: Principal, Florida Mezzanine Fund; WonderWorks Attractions; Morgan & Morgan
Rebecca Irish, Managing Partner
e-mail: rirish@pentamezz.com
Education: BS, Accounting, Mississippi College; CPA
Background: Co-Founder, RVR Consulting Group; CFO, Arcadia Resources; CFO, Rotech Medical Corporation
Jeff Black, Managing Partner
e-mail: jblack@pentamezz.com
Education: Goizueta Business School
Background: Managing Director, Cantaro Capital; Financial Network Investment Corporation; CEO, MidCap
Grant Hill, Senior Advisor
e-mail: ghill@pentamezz.com
Education: BA, History, Duke University
Background: Founder, Hill Ventures
Seth Ellis, Senior Advisor
e-mail: sellis@pentamezz.com
Education: BS, Accounting, University of Florida; CPA
Background: Principal/Co-Founder, Florida Mezzanine Fund; CEO, Digital Imaging; Co-Founder, Florida Regional Emergency Services

1431 PERFORMANCE EQUITY MANAGEMENT, LLC
5 Greenwhich Office Park
3rd Floor
Greenwich, CT 06831

Phone: 203-742-2400
e-mail: info@peqm.com
web: www.peqm.com

Mission Statement: Performance Equity Management is a leading global private equity firm with approximately $9 billion in AUM, as of December 2018. The firm's mission is to provide high quality private equity investment access, both partnership and direct, to institutional clients worldwide.

Geographic Preference: United States, Europe, Asia
Fund Size: $9 billion
Founded: 2005
Investment Criteria: Buyouts, Venture Capital, Asset/Portfolio Restructuring, Distressed For Control, Distressed Trading, Equity-Oriented, Mezzanine Debt
Industry Group Preference: All markets considered

Venture Capital & Private Equity Firms / Domestic Firms

Key Executives:
John Clark, President
Education: BA & MBA, Brigham Young University
Background: MetLife; KPMG Peat Marwick
Jeffrey Barman, Chief Investment Officer
Education: BA, Stanford University; MBA, Columbia University
Background: Portfolio Manager, General Motors Investment Management (GMIMCo) Private Equity Group; Operations Manager, Oracle Corporation
Marcia Haydel, Managing Director
Education: BA, Louisiana State University; MBA, Tulane Freeman School of Business
Background: VP of Fixed Income, Alliance Capital Management; Director of Investments, MetLife Investments Ltd.
Frank Brenninkmeyer, Managing Director
Education: BBA, University of Notre Dame; MBA, Anderson School of Management
Background: VP, GE Asset Management
Jeffrey Reals, Managing Director
Education: BA, Colgate University
Background: Portfolio Manager, General Motors Investment Management (GMIMCo) Private Equity Group; Advent International; Liberty Mutual Insurance
Lawrence Rusoff, Managing Director
Education: BA, Cornell University; MBA, Kellogg School of Management, Northwestern University
Background: Portfolio Manager, General Motors Investment Management (GMIMCo) Private Equity Group; Salomon Brothers, Inc.; Chairman, Private Equity Subcommittee, Cornell University Endowment
James Tybur, Managing Director
Education: Systems Engineering degree, University of Virginia; MBA, Harvard Business School
Background: Principal, Trinity Ventures; VERITAS Software; Boston Consulting Group

1432 PERMAL CAPITAL MANAGEMENT
The Prudential Tower
800 Boylston Street
Suite 1325
Boston, MA 02199-7610

Phone: 617-587-5300 **Fax:** 617-587-5301
web: www.permalcapital.com

Mission Statement: Established to formalize the US private equity activities of Permal Group to enhance risk/return investment profile versus other public and private equity alternatives.

Fund Size: $900 million
Founded: 1994
Minimum Investment: $500,000
Investment Criteria: Second-Stage, Mezzanine, LBO, MBO
Industry Group Preference: Communications, Computer Related, Consumer Products, Distribution, Electronic Components, Genetic Engineering, Industrial Equipment, Medical & Health Related

Other Locations:
900 Third Avenue
28th Floor
New York, NY 10022
Phone: 212-418-6500 **Fax:** 212-418-6510

Key Executives:
Redington Barrett III, Senior Managing Partner, Investment Committee
e-mail: rbarrett@permal.com
Education: Princeton University; MBA, Amos Tuck School of Business, Dartmouth
Background: Managing Director, Gemini Investors; Analyst, Fidelity Management & Research; Keefe, Bruyette & Woods
Robert Di Geronimo, Managing Director, Investment Committee
e-mail: rdg@permal.com
Education: BS Accounting, University of Delaware
Background: Senior Associate, Price Waterhouse
Benjamin Marino, Managing Director/CFO/CCO
e-mail: bmarino@permal.com
Education: BS Accounting, University of Massachusetts; MBA, Northeastern University; CPA
Background: Assistant Controller, Summit Partners; Accounting Manager, Real Estate Company; Senior Associate, Price Waterhouse
Michael D'Agostino, Managing Partner, Investment Committee
Education: BA, Economics, Colby College; MBA, Case Western Reserve University
Background: COO, Andesite LLC; President, Hartland & Co.
Aaron Bright, Principal
Education: BS, Accounting, Washington University; MBA, MSF, Boston College, Carroll School of Management
Background: Kendall Investments; Senior Associate, Cambridge Associates

1433 PEROT JAIN
8235 Douglas Avenue
Suite 200
Dallas, TX 75225

web: www.perotjain.com

Mission Statement: Perot Jain's mission is to provide timely capital and resources and high quality strategic advice to assist companies in achieving their maximum potential.

Geographic Preference: US-Based
Founded: 2014
Average Investment: Up to $500,000
Investment Criteria: Technology critical to Scalability; Leadership; Early Stage/Seed Focused; B2B/Business Services/Mobility/Healthcare

Key Executives:
Ross Perot, Jr., Co-Founder
Education: Vanderbilt University
Background: Captain, United States Air Force
Anurag Jain, Co-Founder/Managing Partner
Education: MBA, University of Michigan
Background: Founder, Brigade Corporationl VP, Dell; Director, WorldHaus

Other Locations:
1325 Avenue of the Americas
25th Floor
New York, NY 10019
Phone: 212-651-6400 **Fax:** 212-651-6399

4350 East-West Highway
Suite 202
Bethesda 20814
Germany
Phone: 301-6523200 **Fax:** 301-6523800

1435 PFINGSTEN PARTNERS LLC
300 N LaSalle Street
Suite 5400
Chicago, IL 60654

Phone: 312-222-8707 **Fax:** 312-222-8708
e-mail: pfingstenpartners@pfingsten.com
web: www.pfingstenpartners.com

Mission Statement: Provides equity capital to acquire and grow Midwest and Mid-Atlantic based middle market companies in partnership with management. Pfingsten Partners was formed on the concept of blending senior operating management and financial transaction expertise in its investment activities. Pfingsten Partners operates under four guiding principals: creation of shareholder value; responsible ownership; integrity; and professional conduct.

Geographic Preference: United States, China, India

511

Venture Capital & Private Equity Firms / Domestic Firms

Fund Size: $525 million
Founded: 1989
Average Investment: $15-$100 millionn
Minimum Investment: $15 million
Investment Criteria: Acquisition of growth companies, consolidations, leveraged buyouts, management buyouts, and recapitalizations
Industry Group Preference: Manufacturing, Distribution, Business Products & Services
Portfolio Companies: 4Wheel Drive Hardware, Allied Reliability Group, AllPoints, American Academic Suppliers, Ap+m, Arrowhead Electrical Products, Bailey International, Barjan, Burton Saw & Supply, Closet Works, Crane 1, CURT Manufacturing, Des-Case Corporation, Diamond Assets LLC, Dynapower, Environmental Lights, FireKing Security Group, Full Spectrum, Garretson Resolution Group, Hallcrest, Hy-Bon Engineering Company, Industrial Lighting Products, Kith Kitchen, Lumenier, Marlen International, MPE, Norcraft Companies, Oliver Printing & Packaging Co., Park Foods, Pfingsten Publishing, Premiere Global Sports, Powervar, Quality Valve, RapidAir, Rx Label Technology, Sign-Zone, South-Tek Systems, Suzo-Happ, SpeeCo, Superior Recreational Products, Technibus, TPC Wire & Cable, Tropitone, Unified Power, WoodallBs, ZSi-Foster

Other Locations:
5th Floor, Block A
Lucky Commercial Building
Second Road, Zhendi District
Changan Town, Dongguan, Guangdong 523850
China
Phone: 86-76981663655

335, Udyog Vihar, Phase IV
Near Delhi International Airport
Gurgoan
Haryana 122012
India
Phone: 91-1244308204

Key Executives:
Thomas S. Bagley, Founder/Senior Managing Director
e-mail: tbagley@pfingsten.com
Education: BA, North Park College; DePaul University
Background: Citicorp North America; Continental Bank
James J. Norton, Senior Managing Director
e-mail: jnorton@pfingsten.com
Education: University of Illinois
Background: Director, Cooper Lybrand
John H. Underwood, Senior Managing Director
e-mail: junderwood@pfingsten.com
Education: BBA, MBA, University of Wisconsin
Background: Heller Equity; VP, Citicorp North America
Denio R. Bolzan, Managing Director
e-mail: dbolzan@pfingsten.com
Education: BS, DePaul University
Background: Operations VP, Ryerson Tull; Washington Steele; Lukens; Coopers & Lybrand
Scott A. Finegan, Managing Director
e-mail: sfinegan@pfingsten.com
Education: BS, Marquette University; MBA, Northwestern University
Background: VP, American National Bank and Trust Company; Analysis, Horizon Partners Ltd
John J. Starcevich, Managing Director
e-mail: jstarcevich@pfingsten.com
Education: BS, DePaul University
Background: Lukens; Jupiter Mechanical Construction; Jupiter Industries; Lybrands
Phil D. Bronsteatter, Managing Director
Education: BBA, Finance, Economics & Mathematics, Marquette University
Background: Analyst, Investment Banking Group, Lazard Middle Market; Analyst, Investment Banking Group, Cleary Gull; Associate, American Appraisal Associates

1436 PFIZER VENTURE INVESTMENTS
235 East 42nd Street
New York, NY 10017

Phone: 212-733-2323
web: www.pfizer.com/partners/venture-investments

Mission Statement: Pfizer Venture Investments, the venture capital arm of Pfizer, Inc., invests for return in areas of current or future strategic interest to Pfizer. PVI seeks to remain at the forefront of life science advances, looking to identify and invest in emerging companies that are developing compounds and technologies that have the potential to enhance Pfizer's pipeline and shape the future of our industry.

Geographic Preference: United States
Fund Size: $50 million
Founded: 2004
Investment Criteria: All Stages
Industry Group Preference: Healthcare, Life Sciences, Therapeutics, Diagnostics, Drug Delivery, Pharmaceutical Services, Healthcare Information Technology
Portfolio Companies: Ablexis, Aquinox, Autifony, Biodesy, Celladon, Clovis Oncology, Cydan, DVS Sciences, Epic Sciences, Flexion Therapeutics, HD Biosciences, M2S, Merus, Mersana Therapeutics, MIRNA Therapeutics, MISSION Therapeutics, Neuronetics, Nodality, NovoCure, Rhythm Pharmaceuticals, TetraLogic

Key Executives:
Barbara J Dalton PhD, Vice President/Senior Management Partner
Education: Penn State University; PhD, Microbiology & Immunology, The Medical College of Pennsylvania
Background: Research Scientist, Immunology, SmithKline & Frenh Laboratories; SR One; General Partner, EuclidSR Partners
Bill Burkoth, Executive Director/Senior Partner
Education: BS, Chemistry, Whitman College
Background: Business Development, Galileo Pharmaceuticals; Analyst, Bay City Capital

1437 PHILQUO VENTURES
PO Box 721
Palo Alto, CA 94302-0721

e-mail: info@philquo.com
web: www.philquo.com

Mission Statement: Founded, funded and managed by a team of seasoned executives from Wall Street, Silicon Valley and Hollywood, we strive to bring financing, mentoring and managerial guidance to bright minds with relevant and timely new products or services.

Investment Criteria: Early-Stage
Industry Group Preference: Consumer Products, Consumer Services
Portfolio Companies: Anchange Productions, Cliptone, Crimson Hexagon, Fab, Fido Labs, Loudr, Mobile Commons, My Damn Channel, Parallel Geometry, Pixelux Entertainment, Ribbit, The Plunge, Wello

Key Executives:
Philip Engelhardt, Managing Partner
Background: Senior Advisor/Angel Investor, Plug and Play Tech Center

1438 PHYSIC VENTURES
200 California Street
5th Floor
San Francisco, CA 94111

Phone: 415-354-4901 **Fax:** 415-354-4915
e-mail: info@physicventures.com
web: physicventures.com

Mission Statement: Physic Ventures provides capital and support to entrepreneurs focused on building exceptional sci-

512

ence-based, consumer-directed health and sustainable living companies.
Geographic Preference: United States, Canada
Investment Criteria: Seed-Stage to Growth-Equity Stage
Industry Group Preference: Enabling Technology, Consumer Products, Sustainable Living
Portfolio Companies: Alliance Health, Chromatin, Elixir, EnergyHub, Gazelle, GoodGuide, HalSource, HealthLoop, Impinj, Merrimack, Novomer, Pharmaca, Rayne, Recyclebank, Revolutions Foods, Surface Logix, T2 Biosystems, Textronics, WaterSmart, Yummly

Key Executives:
Dion Madsen, Co-Founder/Managing Director
Education: BComm, Finance, University of Saskatchewan
Background: Managing Director, Unilever Technology Ventures; Partner, RBC Capital Partners
Directorships: Elixer Pharmaceuticals, HaloSource, On-Q-Ity, Pharmaca, SurfaceLogix
William Rosenzweig, Co-Founder/Managing Director
Background: Founding CEO, Republic of Tea; Faculty, Haas School of Business
Andy Donner, Director
Education: Duke University; MBA, Haas School of Business, UC Berkeley
Background: Senior Associate, Great Spirit Ventures; Technology M&A Group, Wasserstein Perella
Andrew Williamson PhD, Director
Education: BA, PhD, Physics, University of Cambridge; MBA, Haas School of Business, UC Berkeley
Background: National Renewable Energy Laboratory, Department of Energy
Directorships: Chromatin, EnergyHub, Gazelle, Halosource, Impinj, Novomer
Stacy Feld, Director
Education: BA, Sociology, University of Pennsylvania; JD, Vanderbilt Law School
Background: Associate Director, Business Development, Genentech; Director, Licensing & Corporate Development, Third Wave Technologies
Directorships: T2 Biosystems

1439 PHYTO PARTNERS
2080 NW Boca Raton Blvd.
Suite 6
Boca Raton, FL 33431

Phone: 561-542-6090
e-mail: larry@phytopartners.com
web: www.phytopartners.com

Mission Statement: Invests in companies within the cannabis industry focused on business solutions and services, including grow technology, packaging, data analytics, testing, research & development, distribution logistics, and consulting services.
Geographic Preference: US
Investment Criteria: Early-Stage; Companies not directly exposed to supply/demand/pricing; 6-9 months monitoring of management/operations; Visible exit strategy
Industry Group Preference: Cannabis, Technology, Data Analytics, Infrastructure
Portfolio Companies: New Frontier Data, Steep Hill, Leaf, Grownetics, Gatekeeper Innovation Inc., Baker Technologies, Flow Hub, Leaf Link, Würk, Front Range Biosciences, Marijuana Doctor, Vangst, Sail, Green Flower, Lucid Green

Key Executives:
Larry Schnurmacher, Managing Partner
Education: BBA, George Washington University
Background: Financial Advisor, Shearson Lehman Brothers; Financial Advisor, Oppenheimer & Co.; Financial Advisor, Morgan Stanley Wealth Management; Founder/CEO, Phyto Advisors
Directorships: New Frontier Data
Brett Finkelstein, Managing Director
Education: BBA, University of Hartford
Background: Managing Director, Skywest Partners

1440 PI CAPITAL GROUP LLC
6507 Wilkins Avenue
Pittsburgh, PA 15217

e-mail: info@picapitalgroup.com
web: www.picapitalgroup.com

Mission Statement: Pi capitalizes those early-stage ventures who create unique technology in the areas of Internet, software, information technologies, telecommunications, life sciences, advanced materials, and semiconductor.
Geographic Preference: Western Pennsylvania, Eastern United States
Founded: 2001
Investment Criteria: Early-Stage
Industry Group Preference: Technology, Internet, Software, Information Technology, Telecommunications, Life Sciences, Advanced Materials, Semiconductors
Portfolio Companies: Ondotek, CompAS Controls, Aethon, medSage Technologies, mSpoke, NewCare Solutions, CastGrabber

Key Executives:
John R Hammer, Chairman
Background: Chief Investment Officer & CFO, Innovations Works; President & Director of Corporate Finance, Capital Access Partners; VP, Weatherly Private Capital; VP, MMC Group; Gulf Oil Corporation

1441 PIDC PHILADELPHIA
1500 Market Street
Suite 2600
Philadelphia, PA 19102

Phone: 215-496-8020 **Fax:** 215-977-9618
web: www.pidc-pa.org

Mission Statement: PIDC plans and implements economic development initiatives which enhance the competitive environment, generate jobs and produce higher tax ratables throughout the city of Philadelphia.
Geographic Preference: Philadelphia, PA
Founded: 1957
Average Investment: $200,000
Industry Group Preference: Aerospace, Defense and Government, Biotechnology, Communications, Computer Related, Electronic Components, Natural Resources, Environment Products & Services, High Technology, Medical & Health Related, Energy

Key Executives:
Anne Bovaird Nevins, President
Education: MBA, Wharton School; University of Pennsylvania
Background: Director, Development, Historic Philadelphia; White House Office of Cabinet Affairs
Thomas Queenan, Chief Operating Officer/ Senior Vice President
Education: Syracuse University; Columbia University; MBA, Wharton School
Background: City Treasurer, Rendell Administration; Temple University Health System; Dickenson College

1442 PIEDMONT ANGEL NETWORK
243 S Marshall Street
Winston-Salem, NC 27101

e-mail: dgrein@piedmontangelnetwork.com
web: www.piedmontangelnetwork.com

Mission Statement: An angel investment group managed by its own members and operates on a fund resource for investments. The group focuses on investment opportunities with companies in the early stage of development and has a high potential for rapid growth.
Geographic Preference: North Carolina, South Carolina, Virginia
Investment Criteria: Early-Stage

Venture Capital & Private Equity Firms / Domestic Firms

Industry Group Preference: Life Sciences, Software, Technology
Portfolio Companies: Guerilla RF, Entigral Systems, Virtual Event Bags, ClearEdge 3D, Phthisis Diagnostics, Southeast TechInventures, Raw Essentials, Protochips, Pique Therapeutics, Bioptigen, Arbovax, Sensory Analytics, Sandbox Learning, Piedmont Pharmaceuticals, Optivia Medical, SpermCheck, Batanga, AvidXchange, Aldagen

Key Executives:
Andy Dreyfuss, Fund Executive
e-mail: adreyfuss@piedmontangelnetwork.com

1443 PINE BROOK ROAD PARTNERS
60 East 42nd Street
50th Floor
New York, NY 10165

Phone: 212-847-4333 Fax: 212-847-4334
e-mail: info@pinebrookpartners.com
web: www.pinebrookpartners.com

Mission Statement: To make business building and growth capital investments.

Founded: 2006
Industry Group Preference: Energy, Financial Services
Portfolio Companies: Brigham Resources, Comet Ridge Resources, Common Resources III, Elevation Resource Holdings, Forge Energy, GR Energy Services Holdings, High Ground Energy, Saguaro Resources, Serafina Energy, Source Energy Partners, Stonegate Production Company, Stonegate Production Company II, Wagon Wheel Exploration, AloStar Bank of Commerce, Amedeo Capital Limited, Aurigen Capital Limited, Community Trust Financial Corp., Essent Group, Global Atlantic Financial Group, Green Bancorp, NBIC Holdings, Strategic Funding Source, Third Point Reinsurance, United PanAm Financial Corporation

Key Executives:
Howard H Newman, Managing Partner
Education: Cambridge University; PhD, Business Economics, Harvard University
Background: Vice Chairman, Warburg Pincus; Morgan Stanley
Richard Aube, Managing Partner
Education: BA, Dartmouth College
Background: DE Shaw & Company; Partner, JP Morgan Partners; Beacon Group
Joseph M Gantz, Executive Advisor
Education: BA, History, University of Pennsylvania; MBA, Columbia University Business School
Background: Chairman & CEO, Empire Brushes; Fitz & Floyd; Seymour Housewares Corp.; Founding Partner, Walnut Investment Partners

1444 PINEBRIDGE INVESTMENTS
Park Avenue Tower
65 East 55th Street
New York, NY 10022

Phone: 646-857-8000
e-mail: insights@pinebridge.com
web: www.pinebridge.com

Mission Statement: Seeks to provide mezzanine and private equity capital to middle market and emerging growth companies based in North America and Western Europe. Funding is provided to facilitate leveraged buyouts, recapitalizations, consolidations, acquisition growth, and growth capital requirements. The firm manages $96.9 billion in global assets as of September 2019.

Geographic Preference: North America, Western Europe
Fund Size: $83 billion
Founded: 1960s
Average Investment: $50 million
Minimum Investment: $10 million

Investment Criteria: Second Stage, Mezzanine, Consolidations, Acquisition, LBO, MBO, Recapitalization, Privatizations
Industry Group Preference: All markets considered
Key Executives:
Gregory A. Ehret, Chief Executive Officer & Executive Director
Education: BA, Economics, Bates College; MBA, Boston University
Background: President, State Street Global Advisors (SSGA)
Tracie E. Ahern, Chief Financial Officer
Education: BS, Accounting, Manhattan College; MBA, Finance & International Business, NYU Stern School of Business
Background: CFO, Soros Fund Management; VP of Capital Markets Accounting, Freddie Mac; Lord Abbett & Co.; Beutsche Bank; Goldman Sachs
Kamala Anantharam, Chief Risk Officer & Head of Investment Operations
Education: MA, Accounting, University of Bombai, India
Background: Global Director of Internal Audit for the Financial & Retirement Services Segment, AIG
John Blebins, Global Chief Compliance Officer
Education: BS, Accounting, Oklahoma State University
Background: Managing Director & Deputy CCO, BlackBlock Inc.; Director & Global CCO, Lazard Asset Management LLC; SSB Citi Asset Management; AIG Global Investment Group

1445 PINNACLE VENTURES
160 El Camino Real
Suite 250
Palo Alto, CA 94025

Phone: 650-926-7800
web: www.pinnacleven.com

Mission Statement: A private venture capital fund focused on providing debt and equity financing to early-stage companies across information technology, cleantech and healthcare. Pinnacle differentiates itself through the strength and diversity of its team, its creative and flexible financing alternatives and its unique approach to helping its portfolio companies achieve success.

Investment Criteria: Early-Stage
Industry Group Preference: Information Technology, Clean Technology, Healthcare
Portfolio Companies: 1Life Healthcare, AcelRx Pharmaceuticals, Access Closure, APT Pharmaceuticals, Aquantia Corporation, Avnera Corporation, Baxano, BlueKat, Broadbus Technologies, Calistoga Pharmaceuticals, Cameron Health, Chegg, Cobalt Technologies, Confluent Surgical, Conformative Systems, eBureau, Farecast, Flixster, Gilt Groupe, Glu Mobile, Intersect ENT, Jasper Wireless, JBoss, Kaai, Kazeon Systems, Kerberos Proximal Solutions, Kontiki, Lanzatech NZ, LifeSize Communications, LipoSonix, Lotame Solutions, Lutonix, M-Factor, Mascoma Corporation, Miasole, Movius, MySpace, Newport Media, Ocular Therapeutix, Pandora Media, Pluck Corporation, Quidsi, Quorum Systems, Qumranet, Reliant Technologies, RGB Networks, Right Media, SentreHEART, Siliquent Technologies, Silver Peak Systems, SiPort, Solyndra, Spiracur, StumbleUpon, SVNetwork, The Fanfare Group, Topanga Technologies, Trapeze Networks, TriVascular, Troux Technologies, Visiogen, Vocalocity, WiChorus, Zazzle.com, Ze-Gen, ZeaChem, Zecter, ZING Systems, ZipCar

Key Executives:
Kenneth R Pelowski, Founder & Managing Partner
650-926-7802
e-mail: kpelowski@pinnacleventures.com
Education: BSE, Electrical Engieering, MBA, University of Michigan
Background: Redpoint Ventures; Founder & Board Member, Currenex; COO, CFO & Board Member,

514

GetThere; EVP & CFO, Preview Travel; Corporate Vice President, General Instruments; Sun Microsystems; Intel
Robert H Savoie, Partner, Chief Operating Officer
650-926-7805
e-mail: rsavoie@pinnacleventures.com
Education: BBA, University of Michigan; CPA
Background: VP, Finance, Comdisco Ventures; CFO, H&Q Fund Management; Access Technology Partners; Arthur Anderson
Arun Ramamoorthy, Principal
650-926-7811
e-mail: aramamoorthy@pinnacleventures.com
Education: BTech, Indian Institute of Technology; MS, Electrical Engieering, University of Michigan; MBA, Haas School of Business, University of California, Berkeley
Background: Corporate Branding & Strategic Marketing, Intel

1446 PIONEER CAPITAL
Five Tower Bridge
300 Barr Harbor Drive
Suite 280
West Conshohocken, PA 19428

Phone: 610-862-2100 Fax: 610-862-2120
web: www.pioneercapital.com

Founded: 2000
Portfolio Companies: Seattle Shellfish, MIM-Hayen, Evol Foods, WineCare Storage, Relay
Key Executives:
 J Peter Pierce, Founder & Chief Executive Officer
 Education: University of Pennsylvania
 Background: President & CEO, Pierce Leahy
 J Peter Pierce Jr, Partner
 Education: Tulane University
 Background: Cross Atlantic Capital Partners

1447 PITTSBURGH EQUITY PARTNERS
6507 Wilkins Avenue
Pittsburgh, PA 15217

Phone: 412-265-1325
e-mail: info@pghpep.com
web: www.pghpep.com

Mission Statement: Pittsburgh Equity Partners is a venture capital fund specifically formed to grow Western Pennsylvania's most promising early-stage companies in the life sciences and information technology industries.
Geographic Preference: Western Pennsylvania
Investment Criteria: Early-Stage
Industry Group Preference: Life Sciences, Information Technology
Portfolio Companies: Encentiv Energy, Intelligent Mobile Support, Industry Weapon, ShowClix, StatEasy, Voci Technologies, Wombat, Wright Therapy Products
Key Executives:
 Edward R Engler, Managing Partner
 e-mail: ed@pghpep.com
 Education: BS, Applied Mathematics & Computer Science, Carnegie Mellon University
 Background: Transarc Corporation; Founder, Summa Technologies
 Directorships: JumpStart Wireless, mSpoke, Brainstage, Summa Technologies
 Stephen G Robinson, Managing Partner
 e-mail: steve@pghpep.com
 Education: Political Science, University of Pittsburgh
 Background: Managing General Partner, Robinson Properties; Director, Gateway Travel Management
 Directorships: mSpoke, BitArmor, Webmedx, Automated Cell, Precision Therapeutics

1448 PITTSBURGH LIFE SCIENCES GREENHOUSE
2403 Sidney Street
Suite 285
Pittsburgh, PA 15203

Phone: 412-201-7370 Fax: 412-770-1276
e-mail: info@plsg.com
web: www.plsg.com

Mission Statement: The Pittsburgh Life Sciences Greenhouse provides capital investments and customized company formation and business growth services to our region's life sciences enterprises.
Geographic Preference: Western Pennsylvania
Founded: 2002
Investment Criteria: Seed-Stage, Early-Stage
Industry Group Preference: Life Sciences, Biotechnology, Diagnostics, Healthcare Information Technology, Medical Devices, Therapeutics
Portfolio Companies: Applied Isotope Technologies, Celsense, Crystalplex, Falcon Genomics, Immunetrics, MS2 Array, SpectraGenetics, Advanced Technology Healthcare Solutions, Cernostics, Intelomed, NanoLambda, ReddPath Integrated Pathology, Almadtrac, Blenderhouse, Caliber Infosolutions, Chronic Health Metrics, Health Monitoring Systems, Iagnosis, MedRespond, MedSage Technologies, Mymedcoupons.com, NewCare Solutions, PHRQL, Well Bridge Health, ALung Technologies, BioSafe, Carmell Therapeutics, ChemDAQ, Circadiance, ClearCount, Cohera Medical, Flexicath, Medrobotics, Quantum Ops, ReGear Life Sciences, Renal Solutions, Rinovum, Rubitection Separation Design Group, Spinal MetRX, Starr Life Sciences, Vytrace, Wright Therapy Products, ATRP Solutions, Cognition Therapeutics, Complexa, Knopp Biosciences, Launchcyte, Lipella Pharmaceuticals, Washburn Therapeutics
Key Executives:
 John W Manzetti, President & CEO
 e-mail: jwmanzetti@plsg.com
 Education: BSBA, Geneva College; MBA, University of Akron
 Background: President & CEO, NOMOS Corporation; EVP & CFO, Carnegie Group
 James Jordon, Vice President, Chief Investment Officer
 e-mail: jjordon@plsg.com
 Education: BS, Business Administration, Merrimack College; MBA, Boston University
 Background: SVP, McKesson Corporation; VP, Marketing, Johnson & Johnson

1449 PIVA
4 Embarcadero Center
Suite 3950
San Francisco, CA 94111

Phone: 650-420-7800 Fax: 650-209-8266
web: www.piva.vc

Mission Statement: Piva is an independent vC firm that makes big bets and has the perserverance to turn big ideas into reality.
Investment Criteria: Future Industries (AI, Automation); Future Materials/Production (Specialty Chemicals, Alternative Materials; Future Energy (Decarbonization, Electrification, Digitilization)
Key Executives:
 Ricardo Angel, CEO/Managing Partner
 Education: BS, MS, PhD, University of Illinois; MBA, Northwestern University
 Background: SVP, GE Energy Financial; Managing Director, GE Ventures
 Adzmel Adznan, Partner/Operating Manager
 Education: MBA, Harvard University
 Background: Chief of Staff, Petronas

515

Venture Capital & Private Equity Firms / Domestic Firms

Bennett Cohen, Partner
Education: BA, Columbia University; Oxford University
Background: Venture Principal, Shell; Investor, Aurora

1450 PIVOTNORTH CAPITAL
Palo Alto, CA

web: twitter.com/pivotnorth

Mission Statement: An early-stage capital fund for extraordinary founders.

Fund Size: $35 million
Founded: 2011
Investment Criteria: Seed-Stage, Series A
Industry Group Preference: Consumer Services, Business Products & Services

Key Executives:
Tim Connors, Founder/General Partner
Background: Sequoia Capital, US Venture Partners

1451 PLATINUM EQUITY
360 N Crescent Drive
Beverly Hills, CA 90210

Phone: 310-712-1850
web: www.platinumequity.com

Mission Statement: Platinum Equity specializes in mergers, acquisitions and operations of companies that provide mission-critical products, services and solutions in diverse industries.

Other Locations:
3 Allied Drive
Suite 109
Dedham, MA 02026
Phone: 781-461-8888

1 Greenwich Office Park
N Building, 2nd Floor
Greenwich, CT 06831
Phone: 203-930-2010

52 Vanderbilt Avenue
21st Floor
New York, NY 10017
Phone: 212-905-0010

5 Hanover Square
1st Floor
London W1S 1HQ
United Kingdom
Phone: 44 20-3535-0899

12 Marina View #21-05
Tower 2, Asia Square
Singapore 018961
Singapore
Phone: 65 6709-4090

Key Executives:
Tom Gores, Founder and CEO
Education: BSc, Michigan State University
Mary Ann Sigler, Partner and CFO
Education: BA, California State University; MA, University of Southern California
Background: Senior Partner, Ernst & Young LLP

1452 PLEXUS VENTURES
1701 Waterford Way
Maple Glen, PA 19002

Phone: 215-542-2727 **Fax:** 215-542-2288
e-mail: bob_moran@plexusventures.com
web: www.plexusventures.com

Mission Statement: Consulting services to the Life Sciences industry. Our vision is to provide a global network of professional consultants to augment the internal capabilities of Life Science companies. Our team consists of pharmaceutical industry trained and experienced entrepreneurs.

Founded: 1990
Investment Criteria: Seed, Startup, First-Stage
Industry Group Preference: Industrial Equipment, Biotechnology, Genetic Engineering, Medical
Portfolio Companies: ACADIA Pharmaceuticals, Inc., Advanced Scientifics, Albany Molecular Research, Angelini Group, Ansaris, Antares Pharma, ArBlast, AstraZeneca, Auden McKenzie, BioControl Limited, Bentley Pharmaceuticals, BRAINcoBiopharma, Britannia Pharmaceuticals Limited, Can-Fite BioPharma, Thermo Fisher Scientific, Celon Pharma, Cephalon, Consilient Health, Cubist Pharmaceuticals, Derma Sciences, Destiny Pharma, Diasome, Eisai, Elan, Elona Bio Technologies, Elusys Therapeutics, EUSA Pharma, Ferring Pharmaceuticals, GlaxoSmithKline, Jelfa SA, HRA Pharma, Kirin Pharmaceutical, Kun Wha Pharmaceutical, Kyowa Hakko Kirin, Labormed, Locus, Lorus Therapeutics, Mabion, MDM, Meda Pharmaceuticals, Mocuis, Nanjing Kingfriend Biochemical Pharmaceutical Co., Nektar Therapeutics, Neuronyx, Nosan, Noscira, NovaDel Pharma, Noscira, NovaDel Pharma, Novartis, NPS Pharmaceuticals, Opocrin, Orbona, Par Pharmaceutical, Permatec, West Pharmaceuticals, Pierre Fabre, Primus Pharmaceuticals, Polfa Kutno SA, Reckitt Benckiser, Recordati S.p.A., Salix Pharmaceuticals, Seikagaku, Sigma-Tau Pharmaceutical, Taisho Pharmaceutical Co., Teva, Becton, Dickinson and Company, Traslational Cancer Drugs Pharma, US Pharmcia, Xoma

Other Locations:
1223 Wilshire Boulevard
Suite 941
Santa Monica, CA 90403
Phone: 310-584-7480 **Fax:** 310-388-5572

Hancocks Mount
Sunningdale
Berkshire SL5 9PQ
United Kingdom
Phone: 44-1344873077 **Fax:** 44-1344624903

Via Stephenson 94
Milan 20157
Italy
Phone: 39-02-390-30807 **Fax:** 39-02-390-30820

Kompanii Kordian 38
Warsaw 02-495
Poland
Phone: 48-228391199 x 104 **Fax:** 48-228825194

Voltastrasse 35
Zurich CH-8044
Switzerland
Phone: 41-432680155 **Fax:** 41-432680155

Ahornweg 16
Oberursel D61440
Germany
Phone: 49-6172-32110 **Fax:** 49-3172-32129

Alameda Venezuela 69
Jandira SP 06648-040
Brazil
Phone: 55-1146180504 **Fax:** 55-1146175419

7F Toranomon 40MT Building
5-13-1, Toranomon
Minato-ku
Tokyo 105-0001
Japan
Phone: 81-05058068475 **Fax:** 81-367451759

Key Executives:
Robert P Moran, President
215-542-2727
e-mail: bob_moran@plexusventures.com
Education: BBA, Villanova University; CPA
Background: Corporate Development Consultant,

Venture Capital & Private Equity Firms / Domestic Firms

Hybridon; Business Development, SmithKline Beecham; Deloitte, Haskins & Sells
Michael P O'Sullivan, Managing Partner
44-1344-873-077
e-mail: michael_osullivan@plexusventures.com
Background: CFO, Ethical Holdings; VP Finance, SmithKline Beecham
Pino N Modica, Managing Partner
310-315-7106
e-mail: pino_modica@plexusventures.com
Background: International Marketing Manager, Recordati SA; A Menarini Srl; Product Manager, American Cyanamid Corporation/Lederle; Lawyer; Financial Consultant, Sanpaolo Bank of Italy
Richard A Brown, Partner & Head, Tokyo Office
81-3-6279-3570
e-mail: richard_brown@plexusventures.com
Background: Business Development, Eli Lilly & Company
John F Chappell, Founder, Special Advisor
e-mail: john_chappell@plexusventures.com
Education: BA, Harvard University
Background: SmithKlineBeecham
Directorships: Salix Pharmaceuticals

1453 PLUG AND PLAY VENTURES
Silicon Valley, CA

web: www.plugandplaytechcenter.com/ventures

Mission Statement: Plug and Play Ventures funds the teams that build defensible businesses of the future. Each investment is a case-by-case basis.
Fund Size: $30 Million
Average Investment: $114,000

1454 PLUM ALLEY
New York, NY

Phone: 347-348-7901
e-mail: info@plumalley.co
web: plumalley.co

Mission Statement: Plum Alley invests in advanced technology and healthcare that will improve our lives and the planet.
Fund Size: $25 million
Average Investment: $500,000-$1.5 million
Investment Criteria: Early Stage; Advanced Tech and Medical Breakthroughs; Women Founders or Women and Men Founders in STEM; Massive Impact at Scale Business Models
Key Executives:
Deborah Jackson, Founder and CEO
Education: MBA, University of Columbia
Background: Founder, Women Innovate Mobile
Andrea Turner Moffitt, Co-Founder and General Partner
Education: BA, Tulane University; MBA, University of Columbia
Background: Founder, Wealthrive Inc.; Author
Avantika Daing, Managing Director and Partner
Background: Senior Director, Global Marketing, Bristol-Myers Squibb; Senior Global Director, Marketing, Eyetech Pharmaceuticals; Co-Founder/CEO, SquareKey.com; Chief Revenue Officer, Jopwell

1455 PLYMOUTH MANAGEMENT COMPANY
555 Briarwood Circle
Suite 210
Ann Arbor, MI 48108

Phone: 743-747-9401
e-mail: info@plymouthvc.com
web: www.plymouthvc.com

Mission Statement: To realize superior returns through the long term appreciation of investments. Funds managed by PMC invest in small growth companies. We generally invest in revenue producing companies with the potential for growth through a defined, catalytic event or milestone whose achievement will be financed, at least in part, by PMC managed funds.

Geographic Preference: Michigan, Great Lakes Region
Founded: 2003
Average Investment: $500,000 - $2 million
Portfolio Companies: Certified Security Solutions, CloudOne, InContext Solutions, 365 Retail Markets, XanEdu, IDV Solutions, Lynx Network Group, UICO, FutureNet Group, Weathershield, Solulink, Neuromonics, Janeeva, Eagle River Homes
Key Executives:
Ian Bund, Chairman/Senior Advisor
e-mail: ibund@plymouthvc.com
Education: Bachelor of Economics, University of Sydney; MBA, Harvard University
Mark Horne, Operating Partner
e-mail: mhorne@plymouthvc.com
Education: BA, Business Administration, Cedarville University; MBA, Wharton School
Jeff Barry, Partner
e-mail: jbarry@plymouthvc.com
Education: BA, Economics, Trinity College; MBA, Finance, Vanderbilt University
Background: Senior Economist, Overseas Private Investment Corporation; Consultant, Oakland University Incubator

1456 PNC ERIEVIEW CAPITAL
1900 East 9th Street
17th Floor
Cleveland, OH 44114

Phone: 216-222-3763
web: www.pnc.com

Mission Statement: PNC Erieview Capital, formerly National City Equity Partners, is a Cleveland, Ohio-based investment firm that is currently managing approximately 50 investments. PNC Erieview Capital has actively invested junior capital in over 160 middle market transactions alongside successful private equity sponsors.

Geographic Preference: North America
Fund Size: $1 billion
Founded: 1979
Average Investment: $5 - 20 million
Minimum Investment: $1 million
Investment Criteria: Leverage Buyouts, Recapitalizations, Growth Capital, Aquisition Capital, Shareholder Liquidity
Industry Group Preference: Distribution, Food & Beverage, Healthcare, Manufacturing, Services
Portfolio Companies: Abrisa Industrial Glass, Accessories Marketing, Altech Inspections, Arrow Tru-Line, Associated Materials, ATI, Atrium Companies, Autosplice, Burton Flower & Garden, Connor Bros, CorePharma Holdings, Cumming Acquisition, DSI Holding Company, Eatem Foods, Energy Manufacturing, Excelsior Medical, Experient, Fasteners for Retail, FCX Performance, Franklin Energy Services, Gila, Group Dekko, Harden Manufacturing, Hardware Resources, Healthcare Management Systems, HealthTech Holdings, HGI Holdings, Hilite Industries, Hoffmaster Group, Home Decor Holdings, Hopkins Manufacturing, Hospitality Mints, Hygenic, Infiltrator Systems, Innerpac, Juice Tyme Acquisition Corp, LDiscovery, Liberty Safe & Security Products, Manhattan Beachwear, MicroGroup, Moss Holding Company, NeuroTherm, Nielsen & Bainbridge, Olon Industries, Paradigm Packaging, Radiac Abrasives, Royal Adhesives, Royal Baths Manufacturing, Savage Sports, SmartSource Holdings, Spartan Foods of America, Standadyne Corporation, Stanton Carpet Corp, The ServiceMaster Company, The Tranzonic Co, Titan Fitness, Transpac Imports, Transtar Industries, Tronair Holdings, Truck Bodies & Equipment International, Truck-Lite, US Foodservice,

Venture Capital & Private Equity Firms / Domestic Firms

U-Line Corporation, UMA Enterprises, Vendormate, Veritext Holding Company, Vitex Packaging Group, Wellborn Forest Products, Whitcraft Group

Key Executives:
Edward S. Pentecost, Managing Director/President
e-mail: ed.pentecost@pncerieview.com
Education: BA, Economics & Management, Albion College; MBA, Case Western University
Background: Investment Banking, McDonald Investments; National City Corporation
Carl E. Baldassarre, Managing Director
e-mail: carl.baldassarre@pncerieview.com
Education: BS, Finance, John Carroll University
Background: National City Corporation
David A. Sands, Director
e-mail: david.sands@pncerieview.com
Education: BSBA, Ohio State University
Background: Brown Gibbons Lang & Company
Eric C. Morgan, Managing Director
e-mail: eric.morgan@pncerieview.com
Education: BS, Finance, Boston College; London School of Economics
Background: Investment Banking, Saloman Smith Barney
Steve G. Pattison, Managing Director
e-mail: steve.pattison@pncerieview.com
Education: BS, Business Administration, Miami University; MBA, University of Chicago
Background: Investment Banking, McDonald Investments; Ernst & Young
Jason R. Cornacchione, Principal
e-mail: jason.cornacchione@pncerieview.com
Education: BSBA, Miami University; MBA, Case Western Reserve University
Background: Public Accounting, PricewaterhouseCoopers

1457 PNC RIVERARCH CAPITAL
Two PNC Plaza
620 Liberty Avenue
22nd Floor
Pittsburgh, PA 15222

web: www.pncriverarch.com

Mission Statement: A private equity firm with over $500 million of capital under management. We make investments to provide growth capital or to assist in ownership transitions such as leveraged buyouts or recapitalizations.
Geographic Preference: Eastern two-thirds of the United States
Fund Size: $500 million
Founded: 1982
Average Investment: $10-$30 million
Minimum Investment: $10 million
Investment Criteria: Growth Equity, Buyouts
Industry Group Preference: Telecommunications, Business Products & Services, Manufacturing, Distribution
Portfolio Companies: Custom Molded Products, Environmental Express, Goldco, LawLogix, Precision Aviation Group, The Cleaning Authority, Women's Marketing

1458 POINT B CAPITAL
300 East Pine Street
Seattle, WA 98122

Phone: 206-577-7221
e-mail: info@pointbcap.com
web: www.pointbcap.com

Mission Statement: In addition to decades of diverse investment experience, we provide proven strategic, operational and leadership skills that come from being part of Point B. Companies that we invest in know they have a partner that understands their industry and shares the practical business know-how to get things done. Only Point B Capital provides the connections that come with being part of the Point B brand and having Point B as our parent company. Our network of client and industry relationships includes hundreds of companies and strategic partners that value Point B's business perspective and track record of creating mutually beneficial relationships among our portfolio companies and Point B clients.

Portfolio Companies: appAttach, Calico Energy Services, Carrum Health, Cartavi, ClearEdge Partners, Earshot, Inovus Solar, Post.Bid.Ship., QwikCart, RoundPegg, Sales Portal, Telnyx

Other Locations:
1637 Wazee Street
Suite 200
Denver, CO 80202

Key Executives:
Mike Pongon, Chief Executive Officer
Education: Harvard University; University of Chicago; BA, University of Washington
Background: Business Analyst; Project Leader; Program Manager
EJ Blanchfield, Chief Operating Officer
Education: BA, University of Washington

1459 POINT JUDITH CAPITAL
211 Congress Street
Suite 210
Boston, MA 01220

Phone: 617-600-6260
e-mail: info@pointjudithcapital.com
web: pjc.vc

Mission Statement: At Point Judith Capital, we seek to unite innovative founders with serial entrepreneurs to build world class companies.

Founded: 2001
Industry Group Preference: Internet, Mobile Technology, Healthcare Information Technology, Clean Technology
Portfolio Companies: Coachup, Sittercity, Retroficiency, Tesora, Anover.net, SnapGear, TicketManager.com, Evergage, Envista, Ve24, Medical Metrix Solutions, Rndex, Nexamp, Curoverse, Kitsy Lane, Multiply, MyEnergy, GetWellNetwork, Nest, 3Tier, Powerhouse Dynamics, Pixability, AetherPal, Taqua, Antenna, Nabsys, MedOptions, FSA Store, Ozon.ru, Optasite, Expensify, Novare, Fidelis, Kalpan Hydro, Tower Ventures, Spirus Medical

David Martirano, Co-Founder, General Partner
e-mail: david@pointjudithcapital.com
Education: BS, University of Rhode Island; MBA, Columbia Business School
Background: Co-Founder, Rex Capital; Investment Banking, Cowen & Company
Directorships: Antenna Software, Envista, FanIQ, Fidelis Security Systems, GetWellNetwork, MedOptions, NABsys, Optasite, Taqua
Zaid Ashai, Venture Partner
e-mail: zaid@pointjudithcapital.com
Education: AB, International Relations & Economics, Brown University; MBA, Harvard Business School; MPA, JFK School of Government, Harvard University
Background: Good Energies; Associate, HarbourVest Partners; Investment Banking, Credit Suisse
Directorships: Nexamp, Power Assure
Rob May, General Partner
e-mail: dmixer@pointjudithcapital.com
Education: BA, Union College; MBA, Harvard Business School
Background: Founding Partner, Columbia Capital; Founder, Rex Capital; President, Providence Cellular

1460 POLARIS VENTURE PARTNERS
One Marina Park Drive
Boston, MA 02210

Phone: 781-290-0770
e-mail: partnership@polarispartners.com
web: www.polarispartners.com

518

Venture Capital & Private Equity Firms / Domestic Firms

Mission Statement: To indentify and invest in seed, first round, and early stage technology and life sciences businesses with exceptional promise and help them grow into sustainable, market-leading companies.
Geographic Preference: United States, Europe
Fund Size: $4.3 billion
Founded: 1996
Investment Criteria: Seed-Stage, First Round, Early-Stage
Industry Group Preference: Technology, Life Sciences, Information Technology, Digital Media & Marketing, Consumer Services, Business Products & Services, Healthcare
Portfolio Companies: 1366 Technologies, 480 Biomedical, Acceleron Pharma, Adimab, Advion, Aepona, Aerodesigns, Alimera Sciences, Antenna Software, Aria, Arsanis, Arsenal Medical, Art.com, Athletes' Performance, Atyr Pharma, Automattic, Balconytv, Barkbox, Best Doctors, Bind Therapeutics, Blackarrow, Botanical Labs, Bridgepoint Medical, Calorics, Cardiac Dimensions, Cardlytics, Cerulean Pharma, Confluence Technologies, Data Sciences, deCODE Genetics, Digicert, Doctrakr, Earth Networks, Egnyte, Ella Health, Erewards, Fancy Hands, Fate Therapeutics, Focus Financial, Follica, Formspring.Me, Genocea Biosciences, Hydra Biosciences, Ice.Com, Impinj, Imprivata, Infinian Corp, Infinite Power Solutions, InMobi, Inseal Medical, Iora, Ironwood Pharmaceuticals, Jibe, Jibjab, Kala Pharmaceuticals, Kissmetrics, Legalzoom, Liaison International, Life Line Screening, Living Proof, Localytics, Logentries, LogMeIn, Medvantx, Message Bus, Microchips, Mixel, Nanosys, Nea, Neuronetics, Noetix, Ocular Therapeutix, Partssource, Phreesia, Phytel, Postrocket, Promedior, Pulmatrix, Qualaroo, Quantcast, Readyforzero, Receptos, Recurly, Remedy Health, Respicardia, Roundbox, Selecta Biosciences, Seventh Sense Biosystems, Shoedazzle.Com, Sionyx, Six Waves, Snappcloud, Sosh, Space Monkey, Spindle Labs, Sun Catalytix, Sustainx, T2 Biosystems, Taris Biomedical, Teeology, Trevena, Trulia, Turntable.Fm, Vets First Choice, Visterra, Wantful, Wikicell, Xactly, Xpressdocs, Xtuit Pharmaceuticals

Other Locations:
150 W 28th Street
Suite 904
New York, NY 10001

One Letterman Drive
Building C
The Presidio of San Francisco
San Francisco, CA 94129
Phone: 855-787-3500

Key Executives:
Dave Barrett, General Partner
e-mail: dbarrett@polarisventures.com
Education: BS, University of Rhode Island
Background: COO, Calico Commerce; SVP, Worldwide Operations, Pure Atria
Directorships: Confluence, Egnyte, FREEjit, Imprivata, LogMeIn, MarkMonitor, Phytel, VKernel
Brian Chee, General Partner
e-mail: bchee@polarisventures.com
Education: BS, United States Military Academy, West Point; MBA, Amos Tuck School of Business, Dartmouth College
Background: Captain, US Army Corps of Engineers; Baxter Healthcare
Directorships: Apnex Medical, Ascend Health, Botanical Laboratories, BridgePoint Medical, Cardiac Concepts, Data Sciences International, MedVantx
Jon Flint, General Partner
e-mail: jflint@polarisventures.com
Education: BA, Hobart College; JD, University of Virginia Law School
Background: Partner, Burr Engan Deleage & Co; Associate, Testa Hurwitz & Thiebault; Watergate Special Prosecution Force
Directorships: Athlete's Performance, JibJab Media, Living Proof
Alan Crane, General Partner
e-mail: acrane@polarisventures.com
Education: BA, MA, MBA, Harvard University
Background: Co-Founder & CEO, Cerulean Pharma; Co-Founder, Visterra; President & CEO, Momenta Pharmaceuticals; Senior Vice President, Corporate Development, Millennium Pharmaceuticals
Directorships: Momenta Pharmaceuticals, T2 Biosystems, Hydra Biosciences, Seventh Sense Biosystems, Vaccinex, Cerulean Pharma, Visterra
Terry McGuire, General Partner
e-mail: tmcguire@polarisventures.com
Education: BS, Physics & Economics, Hobart College; MS, Engineering, Thayer School, Dartmouth College; MBA, Harvard Business School
Background: Burr Egan Deleage & Co.; Golder Thoma & Cressey
Directorships: Acceleron Pharma, Adimab, Arsenal Medical, Ironwood Pharmaceuticals, Life Line Screening, MicroCHIPS, Pulmatrix, Trevena
Amir Nashat, General Partner
e-mail: anashat@polarisventures.com
Education: BS, Mechanical Engineering, MS, Materials Science, University of Califnornia, Berkeley; PhD, MIT
Directorships: aTyr Pharmaceuticals, Avila Therapeutics, BIND Biosciences, Fate Therapeutics, Living Proof, Pervasis Therapeutics, Promedior Pharmaceuticals
Bryce Youngren, General Partner
e-mail: byoungren@polarisventures.com
Education: BA, Economics, University of Illinois, Urbana-Champaign; MBA, Wharton School
Background: Senior Associate, Great Hill Parnters; Analyst, Willis Stein & Partners; Bear Stearns & Co.
Directorships: Alimera Sciences, Cardlytics, e-Rewards, National Electronic Attachment, Xpressdocs

1461 POLESTAR CAPITAL
180 N Michigan Avenue
Suite 1905
Chicago, IL 60601
Phone: 312-984-9090 **Fax:** 312-984-9877
e-mail: dkcollins@polestarvc.com
web: www.polestarvc.com

Mission Statement: To bring technologies/innovations developed in the finance and capital markets to Tenant Improvement financing, focusing on commercial lease transactions.
Founded: 1970
Minimum Investment: $250,000
Investment Criteria: Startup, Early-Stage, First-Stage, Second-Stage
Industry Group Preference: Communications, Computer Related, Consumer Services, Education, Electronic Components, Instrumentation, Information Technology
Portfolio Companies: Adamation, BridgeStream, Bayview Systems, Kids123.com, Kinetic Computer Corporation, NetNoir, Network Commerce, Unisource Network Services, ViaNovus

Key Executives:
Derrick K Collins, General Partner
Education: BS, Texas A&M University; MBA, University of Chicago
Background: President of Shorebank Capital Corporation; South Shore Bank ; Ameritech Illinois
Directorships: Currently on Board of Directors of ViaNovus, Bridgestream, Adamation, National Association of Investment Companies
John W Doerer, General Partner
Education: BBA, University of Michigan, MBA, Indiana University
Background: Vice President of Amaco Venture Capital
Directorships: Curently serves on the Board of Directors off Vianovus, Adamation and Kids123.com

519

Venture Capital & Private Equity Firms / Domestic Firms

Wally Lennox, General Partner
Education: BS, Citadel; MBA, Ohio State University
Background: President, Amoco Venture Capital

1462 POMONA CAPITAL
780 Third Avenue
New York, NY 10017-7076

Phone: 212-593-3639
web: www.pomonacapital.com

Mission Statement: A global private equity investment firm focused on the purchase of primary, secondary interests in top performing venture capital and buyout funds.
Geographic Preference: United States, Europe, Israel
Fund Size: $6.7 billion
Founded: 1994
Minimum Investment: $10 million
Investment Criteria: Seed, Startup, First-Stage, Second-Stage, Mezzanine, LBO, MBO, Secondaries, Co-Investments
Industry Group Preference: Communications, Computer Related, Consumer Services, Equipment, Information Services, Media, Medical & Health Related, Industrial Services

Other Locations:
15 Portland Place
London W1B 1PT
United Kingdom
Phone: 44-2072686350 Fax: 44-2072062060

30 Queen's Road
Suite 28A, 28/F Entertainment Building
1 Connaught Place
Central
Hong Kong
Phone: 852-36283629 Fax: 852-25225191

Lvl. 21, 83 Clarence Street
Sydney, NSW 2000
Australia
Phone: 61-292992900 Fax: 618-6461-5880

Key Executives:
Michael D. Granoff, President & CEO
Education: JD, Georgetown University; BA, University of Pennsylvania
Background: Golodetz Ventures, TEI Industries
Frances N. Janis, Senior Partner
Education: MBA, Northeastern University; BS, State University of New York
Background: General Partner, Hambro International Equity Partners
Steve Futrell, Senior Advisor
Education: BA, Accounting, Northwestern State University
Background: CFO, Schroder Venture International Life Sciences Inc.; Controller, Schroder Capital Management International; Touche Ross & Company
Lorraine Hliboki, Partner
Education: BS, Fairfield University; MBA, NYU Stern School of Business
Background: Senior Managing Director, GE Equity, General Electrical Company; Senior Financial Analyst, Financial Guaranty Insurance Company
Jim Rorer, Partner
Education: BA, Duke University; MBA, Harvard Business School
Background: U.S. Trust; Bain & Co.; Credit Suisse

1463 PORTLAND SEED FUND
805 SW Broadway
Suite 2440
Portland, OR 97205

Phone: 503-419-3007
e-mail: info@portlandseedfund.com
web: www.portlandseedfund.com

Mission Statement: We find and surround the most promising seed-stage companies with capital, mentoring and contacts to nurture vigorous economic growth in Oregon.
Geographic Preference: Oregon
Average Investment: $25,000
Industry Group Preference: Diversified
Portfolio Companies: 4Tell, Appthwack, Auth0, Brandlive, Bright.md, Cloudability, Droplr, Energy Storage Systmes, Glider, GraphAlchemist, Hone Comb, Measureful, Minettabrook, MUUT, NurseGrid, Opal, PrestoBox, SERPs.com, Simple Emotion, Smart Mocha, Snapflow, Tellagence, Vadio, Cel.ly, Geoloqi, Globe Sherpa, Mobilitus, Alum.ni, Beeminder, Comic Rocket, Show Kicker, Surefield, Vizify, Better Bean, Homeschool, Indow Windows

Key Executives:
Jim Huston, Founder/Managing Director
503-780-1952
e-mail: jim@portlandseedfund.com
Education: MBA, Kellogg School of Management
Background: Managing Director, Blueprint Ventures; Intel Capital
Angela Jackson, Managing Director
e-mail: angela@portlandseedfund.com
Education: BA, English & History, Boston University; MA, Environmental Studies, University of Oregon
Background: AB Jackson Group, Portland State University Business Accelerator; Principal, Emergent

1464 POSEIDON ASSET MANAGEMENT
330 Fell Street
San Francisco, CA

Phone: 617-571-7114
web: poseidonassetmanagement.com

Mission Statement: Invests in seed, early-stage companies within the cannabis industry.
Founded: 2013
Industry Group Preference: Cannabis
Portfolio Companies: Ascend Wellness, Baker Technologies, Flow Kana

Key Executives:
Emily Paxhia, Managing Partner
e-mail: epaxhia@poseidonassetmanagement.com
Education: BA, Psychology, Skidmore College; MA, Psychology, New York University
Background: Market Research Analyst, Houghton Mifflin; Sr. Research Consultant, Sachs Insights; Research Consultant, Miner & Co. Studio
Directorships: Marijuana Policy Project, Athletes for CARE
Morgan Pahxia, Managing Partner
Education: BS, Applied Mathematics, University of Rhode Island
Background: Financial Advisor Associate, UBS Wealth Management; Investment Counselor, Providence Based Investment Advisor; Principal/Managing Director, Paxhia Investment Management
Directorships: Baker Technologies, Wurk, Surna Inc.
Michael Boniello, Managing Director
Education: BA, Marketing, Miami University
Background: Bond Analyst/Assist Portfolio Manager, Hunterview; Associate, Thomas Weisel Partners; Assistant VP, Barclays Wealth & Investment Management; Analyst, Merrill Lynch
Andy Roche, Investment Analyst
Education: BS, Accounting, SUNY Geneseo
Background: Associate, Deloitte

Venture Capital & Private Equity Firms / Domestic Firms

1465 POST CAPITAL PARTNERS
805 Third Avenue
8th Floor
New York, NY 10022

Phone: 212-888-5700 Fax: 206-222-2518
e-mail: mpfeffer@postcp.com
web: www.postcp.com

Mission Statement: A private investment firm that invests in small and lower middle-market businesses with solid fundamentals and a history of stable cash flow and/or attractive growth prospects.

Geographic Preference: North America
Investment Criteria: Leveraged Buyouts, Recapitalizations, Corporate Divestitures, Consolidations, Acquisitions, Growth Capital
Industry Group Preference: Business Products & Services, Financial Services, Consumer Products, Healthcare Services, Media, Publishing, Manufacturing, Transportation, Logistics
Portfolio Companies: EC Waste, Invo Healthcare, TBA Global, BHS Specialty Chemicals, DTT Surveillance, Amigo Insurance Holding Corporation, Agent Media Corporation, American Disposal Services, Abra, United Road Services, StatementOne

Key Executives:
 Mitchell Davidson, Managing Director
 Education: BA, Tufts University; JD, New York University School of Law
 Background: Financial Sponsors Group, Merrill Lynch; M&A, Skadden Arps Slate Meagher & Florn LLP
 Michael S Pfeffer, Managing Director
 Education: BSEE, Tufts University; MBA, Finance, Columbia University
 Background: Managing Director & Partner, Charterhouse Group International; Senior Vice President, GE Capital
 Christopher PH Cheang, Director, Head of Business Development
 Education: BA, Middlebury College; MBA, Stern School of Business, New York University
 Background: Cabot China Limited; Adams Harkness

1466 POUSCHINE COOK CAPITAL MANAGEMENT LLC
375 Park Avenue
Suite 3408
New York, NY 10152

Phone: 212-784-0620 Fax: 212-784-0621
web: www.pouschinecook.com

Mission Statement: A private equity firm whose mission is to transition companies to significantly higher growth and profitability, and to generate superior returns for investors and management-team partners.

Geographic Preference: United States
Fund Size: $175 million
Founded: 1997
Average Investment: $5-$25 million
Minimum Investment: $5 million
Investment Criteria: EBITDA $5 Million
Industry Group Preference: Business Products & Services, Consumer Products, Consumer Services, Education, Environment Products & Services, Manufacturing, Media, Restaurants, Specialty Chemicals, Financial Services, Retail, Consumer & Leisure, Healthcare Services
Portfolio Companies: Griswold, Latex International, SDI, Financial Health Services

Key Executives:
 John L Pouschine, Founder/Managing Director
 212-784-0624
 Fax: 212-784-0621
 e-mail: jpouschine@pouschinecook.com
 Education: Princeton University, Harvard Business School
 Background: Senior VP, Electra; VP, Ventures Ltd
 Directorships: MedPay Corproation, Latex Foam International, MasterCraft Boat Company, Spring Air Partners, Doc & Ingalls, Great Lakes Home Health & Hospice
 Everett R Cook, Founder/Managing Director
 212-784-0622
 Fax: 212-784-0621
 e-mail: ecook@pouschinecook.com
 Education: Dartmouth College; Tuck School of Business at Dartmouth
 Background: Managing Director, Ampton Investments; Chairman/CEO, Bake Rite Foods; Vice President/Director, Cook International; Vice President/Director, Terminix International; Director, PBCM; Chairman, Cook Flexner; Mortgage Securities Professional, First Pennco Securities
 Directorships: MedPay Corporation, Interplan Corporation, Ampac Packaging, Harlem Furniture
 Robert Jenkins, Principal
 212-784-0625
 Fax: 212-784-0621
 e-mail: rjenkins@pouschinecook.com
 Education: Middlebury College, New York University Leonard N Stern School of Business
 Background: Senior VP, S.N. Phelps; Principal, Head & Company; Senior Auditor, KPMG Peat Marwick
 Directorships: Latex Foam International, Spring Air Partners, Harlem Furniture, Doc & Ingalls
 Brian Harrison, Principal
 212-784-0627
 Education: BS, Vanderbilt School of Engineering
 Background: Brown Brothers Harriman's Merchant Banking Group; VP, Altpoint Capital Partners; Associate, MacQuarie's Industrials

1467 PPM AMERICA CAPITAL PARTNERS
225 W Wacker Drive
Suite 1200
Chicago, IL 60606

Phone: 312-634-2500
web: www.ppmamerica.com

Mission Statement: Providing private equity capital for co-investments in buyouts with equity sponsors, management buyouts, recapitalizations, industry build-ups and growth equity.

Geographic Preference: Worldwide
Fund Size: $2.2 billion
Founded: 1982
Minimum Investment: $5 million
Investment Criteria: MBO, Recapitalizations, Build-Ups, Growth Equity
Industry Group Preference: Diversified

Other Locations:
 750 Lexington Avenue
 10th Floor
 New York, NY 10022-1228
 Phone: 212-583-7300 Fax: 212-583-7311

 300 N Martingale Road
 Suite 440
 Schaumburg, IL 60173
 Phone: 847-413-8500 Fax: 847-413-3240

Key Executives:
 Bruce Gorchow, EVP/Head of Private Equity
 Education: MBA, Wharton School; BA, Economics, Haverford College
 Background: Equitable Capital Management; EF Hutton, TIAA
 Directorships: Elizabeth Arden Red Door Salon & Spas; Racal Acoustics; Sterigenics International; EMSI; Capital H Group; Packaging Advantage Corp; B2B Solutions
 Champ Raju, Partner
 Education: MBA, Kellogg Graduate School of Management; BS, Accounting and Finance, Indiana University

Venture Capital & Private Equity Firms / Domestic Firms

Background: PricewaterhouseCoopers LP; Audit Group
Directorships: Capital H Group, HCG Holdings, LLC
Austin Krumpfes, Partner/Head of Co-Investments
Education: BA, Political Sciences, Duke University; MBA, Kellogg School of Management; JD, Harvard Law School
Directorships: Echo Bridge Entertainment LLC
Scott Rooth, Executive Partner
Education: BA, American History, Yale University; MBA, Finance & Marketing, Kellogg School of Management
Background: Managing Director, Equitable Capital Management; Senior Vice President, GE Capital; Continental Bank
Directorships: Sterigenics International; Stergenics Holdings; Wirestone
Claudia Baron, Partner/Head of Fund Investments
Education: BA, Political Science & Economics, University of Michigan; MBA, Finance/MIS, University of Illinois
Craig Radis, Partner
Education: BS, Finance, University of Illinois, Champaign/Urbana; MBA, DePaul University Charles A Kellstade Graduate School of Business
Background: GE Capital/Heller Financial
Kevin Keefe, Partner
Education: BBA, Accounting, University of Notre Dame; MBA, Booth School of Business
Background: Director, FTI Consulting; International Truck & Engine; Danaher; Topco Associates; Lamina
Mark Staub, Partner
Education: BBA, Accounting, University of Notre Dame; MBA, Kellogg Graduate School of Management
Background: Middle Market Leveraged Finace Group, Dresdner Kleinwort Wasserstein
Ray Zhang, Partner
Education: Graduate Diploma, McGill University; MA, Economics, Concordia University; MBA, Booth School of Business
Background: Senior Auditor, Ernst & Young; Auditor, Glenn Ingram & Company

1468 PRAESIDIAN CAPITAL
419 Park Avenue South
New York, NY 10016

Phone: 212-520-2600 Fax: 212-520-2601
e-mail: info@praesidian.com
web: www.praesidian.com

Mission Statement: Praesidian Capital is an innovative private investment firm focused on providing senior and subordinated debt along with growth capital to private lower middle market businesses in the United States.

Geographic Preference: United States
Average Investment: $5 - $20 million
Investment Criteria: Growth & Acqusition Financings, Management & Sponsored Buyouts, Recapitalizations, Refinancings

Key Executives:
Jason D Drattell, Founder/Managing Partner
212-520-2620
e-mail: jdrattell@praesidian.com
Education: BBA, Finance, Pace University
Background: Founding Partner, The Blackstone Group; Heller Financial; Chemical Bank
Glenn C Harrison, Partner
212-520-2612
e-mail: gharrison@praesidian.com
Education: BA, Economics, Rutgers University
Background: Vice President, Merrill Lynch Middle Market Finance; Assistant Vice President, Fleet National Bank

1469 PRAIRIE CAPITAL
191 North Wacker Drive
Suite 800
Chicago, IL 60606

Phone: 312-360-1133 Fax: 312-360-1193
web: www.prairie-capital.com

Mission Statement: To facilitate ownership transitions for companies in the lower middle market.

Fund Size: $300 million
Founded: 1997
Industry Group Preference: Niche Manufacturing, Business Products & Services, Financial Services, Education, Consumer Products, Industrial Services
Portfolio Companies: Captek Softgel, Industrial Water Treatment Solutions, Swiss-American Products, Damac Products, Messenger, Riverchase Dermatology, TeacherMatch, DRB Systems, Forthfield, StyleCraft Home Collection, Specialized Education Services, FCA Packaging, Pioneer Metal Finishing, Statlab Medical Products, Chicago Deferred Exchange, Insource Contract Services, R3 Education, ProVest, Regency Beauty Institute

Key Executives:
C Bryan Daniels, Founding Partner
e-mail: bdaniels@prairie-capital.com
Education: BA, Mathematics & Chemistry, Wabash College; MBA, University of Chicago; MS, Computer Science, University of Chicago
Background: SVP, Commercial Banking, American National Bank & Trust Company; Investment Committee, ANB Mezzanine
Directorships: Chicago Deferred Exchange Corp., Creditors Interchange, ProVest, R3 Education, Security Technologies, Taylor Capital Group, Titanium Solutions
Stephen V King, Founding Partner
e-mail: sking@prairie-capital.com
Education: BS, Finance, University of Illinois; MBA, Finance, University of Chicago; JD, Loyola University
Background: President, ANB Mezzanine Corporation; VP, American National Bank & Trust Company
Directorships: FCA Packaging Products, Insource Contract Services, Pioneer Metal Finishing, R3 Education, Specialized Education Services
Darren M Snyder, Partner
e-mail: dmsnyder@prairie-capital.com
Education: BA, Economics, Drake University; MBA, University of Chicago
Background: VP, American National Bank & Trust Company
Directorships: Fortis, GPA, Messenger, Pioneer Metal Finishing, Plastimayd
Christopher T Killackey, Partner
e-mail: ckillackey@prairie-capital.com
Education: BS, Finance, University of Illinois; MBA, University of Chicago
Background: Director, Banc One Mezzanine Corporation; VP, American National Bank
Directorships: ProVest, Titanium Solutions, Plastimayd, Navman, Double E, StatLap
Nathan J Good, Vice President
e-mail: ngood@prairie-capital.com
Education: BA, Accountancy, University of Illinois; MBA, University of Chicago Booth School of Business
Background: Senior Analyst, BMO Nesbitt Burns Equity Partners; Analyst, Credit Suisse First Boston
Directorships: Messenger, StatLab, FCA, Fortis, Navman Wireless
Sean M McNally, Vice President
e-mail: smcnally@prairie-capital.com
Education: BS, Finance, University of Illinois; MBA, University of Chicago Booth School of Business
Background: Analyst, William Blair & Company
Directorships: Chicago Deferred Exchange, Double E

Venture Capital & Private Equity Firms / Domestic Firms

1470 PRAIRIEGOLD VENTURE PARTNERS
5708 South Remington Place
Suite 600
Sioux Falls, SD 57108

Phone: 605-275-2999
e-mail: info@pgvp.com
web: www.pgvp.com

Mission Statement: We prefer to invest in early-stage opportunities in the Midwest; this allows us to take meaningful ownership positions with less capital and play an active role in formulating company strategy. we seek to add value through our network of contacts and our experience.

Investment Criteria: Early-Stage
Industry Group Preference: Biotechnology, Clean Technology, Industrial, Life Sciences, Medical Devices and Equipment, Technology, Energy
Portfolio Companies: PrarieGold Solar, Virtual Incision Corporation, Lineagen, tenKsolar, ZeaChem, General Compression, Augusta Systems, Agrivida, Chronix Biomedical, Game Plan Technologies, iCentera

Key Executives:
Paul Batcheller, Partner
Education: B.A. Economics, Macalester College
Background: Advisor to Senator Tom Daschle
Directorships: tenKsolar, ZeaChem, Agrivida, General Compression, South Dakota Rural Enterprise
Mike Jerstad, Partner
e-mail: jerstad@pgvp.com
Education: B.A. Tufts University; J.D. Georgetown University; M.B.A. University of Chicago
Background: Pip Jaffray Healthcare Investment Banking Group, Attorney, Briggs and Morgan, P.A.
Directorships: Grand Prairie Goods, Chronix Biomedical, Orasi Medical, Virtual Incision, Lineagen
Susan Simko, Chief Financial Officer
e-mail: simko@pgvp.com
Education: B.B.A. Finance, University of Iowa; M.B.A. University of South Dakota
Background: Director of Planning, Verio; Finance Manager, Andersen Consulting

1471 PRECURSOR VENTURES
170 Grant Avenue
4th Floor
San Francisco, CA 94108

e-mail: hello@PrecursorVC.com
web: precursorvc.com

Mission Statement: Precursor Ventures believes that all entrepreneurs benefit from having an institutional investor to help them scale their company from the beginning.

Geographic Preference: San Francisco Bay Area, New York and Toronto
Average Investment: $100,000-$250,000
Investment Criteria: First Institutional Round of Investment; First-Time Entrepreneurs; Diversity

Key Executives:
Charles Hudson, Managing Partner/Founder
Background: Partner, SoftTech VC

1472 PRELUDE VENTURES
1 Ferry Building
San Francisco, CA 94111

Phone: 415-729-1270
web: www.preludeventures.com

Mission Statement: Prelude Ventures is a VC firm seeking to address climate change. They have a long-term commitment to the sector and accept well-informed risks.

Founded: 2013

Key Executives:
Nat Simmons, Co-Founder
Education: BA, MA, University of California, Berkeley
Background: Co-Founder, Sea Change Foundation; Principal, Renaissance Technologies
Laura Baxter-Simmons, Co-Founder
Education: BA, MA, University of California, Berkeley; JD, Stanford University
Background: Co-Founder, Sea Change Foundation; General Counsel/Chief Compliance Officer, Meritage Group LP

1473 PRESENCE CAPITAL
e-mail: hello@presencecap.com
web: www.presencecap.com

Mission Statement: Virtual and Augmented Reality venture fund.

Fund Size: $10 million
Industry Group Preference: Virtual Reality & Augmented Reality
Portfolio Companies: Baobab Studies, BeyondView, Bigscreen, Blue Vision, Byte, Camera IQ, Drifter Entertainment, Escher Reality, Experiment 7, Floreo, Harmonix, Lightform, Limbix, Loom.AI, Nomadic, Osso VR, The Rogue Initiative, Sandbox VR, Scope AR, Simbe, SkyLights, Thalmic Labs, TRIPP, Upload, Visbit, Wave VR

Key Executives:
Amitt Mahajan, Managing Partner
Education: University of Illinois - Urbana/Champaign
Background: Epic Games; Toro; MyMiniLife
Paul Bragiel, Managing Partner
Education: BS, University of Illinois
Background: Managing Partner, i/o Ventures; Co-Founder, GameFounders; Founding Partner, Sisu Game Ventures; Savannah Fund; Golden Gate Ventures; Managing Partner, Bragiel Brothers; CEO, Paragon Five; CEO, Meetro; CEO, Lefora
Phil Chen, Managing Partner
Education: UCSD; Fuller Seminary
Background: Alex eReader; Glo Bible; HTC

1474 PRESIDIO VENTURES
3979 Freedom Circle
Suite 340
Santa Clara, CA 95054

Phone: 408-845-9458
e-mail: info@presidio-ventures.com
web: www.presidio-ventures.com

Mission Statement: As an investor and a partner, we assist outstanding technology and media companies in expanding their business throughout Japan and Asia by leveraging our best assets: technology expertise, international business development experience, and a cross-industry network.

Geographic Preference: United States
Founded: 1998
Investment Criteria: Early-Stage
Industry Group Preference: Software, Consumer Internet, Media, Clean Technology, Semiconductors, Advanced Materials
Portfolio Companies: Adknowledge, Agrivida, Alta Devices, Appcelerator, Arbor Networks, ArcSight, Aryaka, Atheros Communications, Aurora Networks, Axxana, Azul Systems, BitTorrent, BlueLane, BlueStacks, Calient Technologies, Cambrios, Carrier IQ, Catalytic Solutions, Cleversafe, Cloudmark, CommVerge Solutions, Coskata, Cotendo, Embrane, Enevate, Engine Yard, ExtendMedia, Extensity, Extreme Networks, Fortinet, Fusion-io, Glympse, GreatPoint Energy, Ikanos Communications, Intermatix, Intrinsa, Karmasphere, Lastline, Liquid Audio, LiveScribe, Locamoda, mCube, Movius Interactive, MySQL, NetScreen, Nexenta, Nominum, Ocarina Network, ONI Systems, OpenX, Prism Skylabs, Revolution Analytics, RightScale, SEEO, Siara Systems, Siluria, SINA Corporation, Solantro, SoonR, Splashtop, Spring Tide Networks, Stoke, Tealium, Terracotta, Topspin Communications, VA Linux Systems, View Point, Vina Technologies XenSource, Xsigo Systems, Zimbra

523

Venture Capital & Private Equity Firms / Domestic Firms

Key Executives:
Doug Kuribayashi, CEO
Education: MBA, University of Virginia
Background: President and CEO, Sumisho E-Commerce

1475 PRIMARY VENTURE PARTNERS
48 West 21st Street
4th Floor
New York, NY 10010

e-mail: info@primary.vc
web: www.primary.vc

Mission Statement: Primary Venture Partners, formerly High Peaks Venture Partners, makes early-stage investments in industry transforming technology companies.

Geographic Preference: Northeast United States
Founded: 2004
Average Investment: $500,000 - $2 million
Investment Criteria: Early-Stage
Industry Group Preference: SaaS, E-Commerce & Manufacturing, Information Technology
Portfolio Companies: Accela, Allworx, Amicus, Apprenda, Auterra, Bench, Bounce Exchange, Clothes Horse, Coupang, CredSimple, DerbyJackpot, Divide, Drawbridge Networks, Fashion Project, FieldLens, FlatWorld Knowledge, Greats, Handshake, iQ License, Jet, Keychain Logistics, Kohort, MakeSpace, Maple, PS Dept, Pump Audio, RealDirect, Reonomy, ReQuest, Routehappy, SimpleReach, Synaptic Digital, TheSquareFoot, Ticketfly, Vnomics, VYou, WhoSay, Widetronix, Yipit, Zipmark

Key Executives:
Brad Svrluga, General Partner
e-mail: brad@primary.vc
Education: Williams College
Background: The Berkshires Capital Investors; Strategy Consultant, Monitor Group
Ben Sun, General Partner
e-mail: ben@primary.vc
Education: University of Michigan
Background: Co-Founder, LaunchTime

1476 PRIMUS CAPITAL
5900 Landerbrook Drive
Suite 200
Cleveland, OH 44124-4020

Phone: 440-684-7300 Fax: 440-684-7342
e-mail: info@primuscapital.com
web: www.primuscapital.com

Mission Statement: Primus Capital is a venture capital firm committed to funding private companies with exceptional growth potential.

Geographic Preference: United States, Canada
Fund Size: $620 million
Founded: 1983
Average Investment: $10 million
Investment Criteria: Proprietary Product Advantage, Seasoned Management, Early-Stage to Mature
Industry Group Preference: Business to Business, Education, Communications, Healthcare
Portfolio Companies: AOD Software, Cardinal Commerce, EMMI Solutions, G2 Web Services, Hyperwallet Systems, Medhost, PartsSource, PathGroup, SkillSurvey, Vondormate

Key Executives:
Phillip C Molner, Managing Partner
e-mail: pmolner@primuscapital.com
Education: BA, Economics & Mathematics, Yale University; JD, Yale Law School
Background: McKinsey & Company; Boston Consulting Group
Directorships: Encore Legal Solutions, Focus Receivables Management, Healthcare Management Systems, MedHost, Passport Health Communications, PathGroup

Jonathan E Dick, Managing Director
e-mail: jdick@primuscapital.com
Education: Bs Mathematics and Economics, Brown University, MBA Harvard University
Background: Sales Management, Lotus Development; IBM; McKinsey & Company
Directorships: Carrier International, Entek IRD International, Ingredients.Com, Paycor Inc, PlanSoft Corp, Wireless
Ronald C Hess Jr, Managing Director
e-mail: rhess@primuscapital.com
Education: BA, Economics & History, Middlebury College
Background: Investment Banking Analyst, Global M&A Group, Lehman Brothers
Directorships: G2 Web Services, Vendormate
William C Mulligan, Senior Advisor
e-mail: bmulligan@primuscapital.com
Education: BA, Economics, Denison University; MBA, University of Chicago
Background: McKinsey & Company; Deere and Company; First National Bank of Chicago
Directorships: Bioanalytical Systems, Brulin Corporation, HUEBCORE Communications, Isolab

1477 PRISM CAPITAL
444 North Michigan Avenue
Suite 1910
Chicago, IL 60611

Phone: 312-464-7900 Fax: 312-464-7915
e-mail: robert@prismfund.com
web: www.prismfund.com

Mission Statement: Prism Capital provides subordinated debt to lower middle market companies through the Prism Mezzanine Fund and expansion capital to smaller growing companies through the Prism Opportunity Fund. We partner with superior management teams and private equity professionals to finance growth, recapitalizations and buyouts.

Fund Size: $50 million
Average Investment: $2 - $15 million
Investment Criteria: Growth Equity, Recapitalizations, Buyouts
Industry Group Preference: Information Technology, Healthcare, Manufacturing, Services
Portfolio Companies: Banner Services, Celleration, Newser, Trustwave, 3-D Machining, Angie's List, Bell Automotive Products, Private Company, Craftsmen Industries, Destination Cinema, EZE Trucking, FCA, Fusion, Hill & Valley, Hi-Tech Manufacturing, McCoy Sales, Optical Experts Manufacturing, Ott-Lite, TCI, Vandor, VIA, Violet Packing

Key Executives:
Robert Finkel, Managing Partner
e-mail: robert@prismfund.com
Education: BA, Social & Behariorial Sciences, Johns Hopkins University; MBA, Harvard Business School
Background: Investment Manager, Wind Point Partners; Corporate Associate, Paine Webber
Directorships: Artromick Internationa, SteriMed Holdings
Steve Vivian, Partner
e-mail: steve@prismfund.com
Education: BS, General Engineering, MBA, University of Illinois
Background: Associate, BancAmerica Securities; Territory Manager, Parker Hannifin Corporation
Directorships: Fitzroy Dearborn Publishing, ClearSource
John Hoesley, Partner
e-mail: john@prismfund.com
Education: BS, Chemistry, University of Illinois; MBA, Kellogg School of Management
Background: CFO, Legato Partneres; Co-Founder & CEO, eVincio Corporation
Directorships: SteriMed Holdings, ISD Holdings, Trustwave, Celleration

Venture Capital & Private Equity Firms / Domestic Firms

Blaine Crissman, Partner
e-mail: blaine@prismfund.com
Education: BA, Economics & Finance, Augustana College; MBA, Fuqua School of Business, Duke University
Background: Principal, Bank of America Capital Investors; BancAmerica Securities; VP, First Bank Systems
Directorships: Optical Experts Manufacturing, VIA, Fusion Specialties, Violet Packing
Bill Harlan, Partner
e-mail: bill@prismfund.com
Education: BA, Economics & Political Science, University of Notre Dame; MBA, University of Chicago
Background: Golub Associates Incorporated; Principal, CID Equity Partners
Directorships: Braxton-Bragg Corporation, 3-D Machining, Craftsmen Industries, Bell Automotive Products, McCoy Sales Corporation

1478 PRISM VENTUREWORKS

Mission Statement: The goal at Prism VentureWorks is a simple one: to work with talented entrepreneurs and management teams to develop new technologies disruptive to the status quo and build substantial business enterprises around them. Office is based in Massachusetts.

Geographic Preference: New England, West Coast, Mid-Atlantic/Southeast
Fund Size: $1.25 billion
Founded: 1996
Average Investment: $5-$10 million
Minimum Investment: $5 million
Investment Criteria: Startup, First-Stage, Second-Stage. Companies with potential To achieve annual revenues in excess of $100mm and provide a substantial investment return within five years.
Industry Group Preference: Communications, Infrastructure, Healthcare, Software, Life Sciences, Digital Media & Marketing, Medical Devices, Therapeutics, Diagnostics
Portfolio Companies: Atritech, Avedro, Connotate, Entrigue Surgical, Expo, LifeCrowd, Proteon Therapeutics, Receivables Exchange, Sonian, Trius Therapeutics, WhiteSky, Xlumena

Key Executives:
Jim Counihan, General Partner/Managing Directpr
Education: BA, University of Massachusetts at Amherst; JD, Suffolk University Law School
Background: Legal Counsel, EPiCON; Corporate Legal Counsel, Sapient Corporation; Legal Counsel, Bell Atlantic Network
Brendan O'Leary, General Partner
Education: BA, Chemistry & Economics, Middlebury College; PhD, Organic Chemistry, MIT
Background: Meso Scale Discovery

1479 PRITZKER GROUP PRIVATE CAPITAL
111 South Wacker Drive
Suite 4000
Chicago, IL 60606
Phone: 312-447-6000
web: www.pritzkergroup.com/private-capital/

Mission Statement: Pritzker Group Private Capital acquires middle-market companies based in North America, and focuses primarily on businesses in the manufactured products, services and healthcare sectors. The firm seeks to create long-term value through its permanent capital base, which brings such advantages as flexibility with transaction structure, efficiency in decision-making, and partnership with management teams. Pritzker Group provides resources and expertise with the objective of helping to build companies, and is a potential partner for family- and entrepreneur-owned businesses.

Geographic Preference: United States, Canada
Founded: 2002
Investment Criteria: Middle Market, Mature Companies, Buyouts, Recapitalizations, Growth Capital, Industry Consolidations, Corporate Divestitures, Enterprise Value $100 - $500 million, EBITDA $15 million or greater
Industry Group Preference: Manufacturing, Services, Healthcare
Portfolio Companies: Clinical Innovations, ENTACT, Entertainment Cruises, LBP Manufacturing, Milestone AV Technologies, PECO Pallet, PLZ Aeroscience, Signicast, Technimark

Other Locations:
11150 Santa Monica Blvd
Suite 1500
Los Angeles, CA 90025
Phone: 310-575-9400

Key Executives:
JB Pritzker, Co-Founder/Managing Partner
Education: AB, Political Science, Duke University; JD, Northwestern University School of Law
Background: Founding Member, Illinois Venture Capital Association
Tony Pritzker, Co-Founder/Managing Partner
Education: BA, Engineering, Dartmouth College; MBA, University of Chicago
Background: Chairman, AmSafe Partners; President, Baker Tanks; Regional VP, Operations, Getz Bros & Co.; Group Executive, Marmon Group
Directorships: Heal The Bay
Paul Carbone, Managing Partner, Private Capital
Education: University of Chicago; MBA, Harvard Business School
Background: Director & Managing Partner, Private Equity Group, Robert W. Baird & Co.; Senior VP, Investment Banking Group, Kidder, Peabody & Co.
Directorships: Lyric Opera of Chicago, Misericordia Endowment Fund, Shedd Aquarium, University of Chicago Medical Center

1480 PRITZKER GROUP VENTURE CAPITAL
1 North Wacker Drive
Suite 2404
Chicago, IL 60606
Phone: 312-447-6001
web: www.pritzkergroup.com/venture-capital/

Mission Statement: Pritzker Group Venture Capital is a premier, early-stage venture capital firm investing in a broad range of technology and telecommunications companies that combine innovation and experience to take advantage of unique market opportunities. The firm dedicates all its resources to the pursuit of excellence.

Geographic Preference: United States
Fund Size: +$106 million
Founded: 1996
Average Investment: $500,000 - $50 million
Minimum Investment: $500,000
Investment Criteria: Early Stage, US-based
Industry Group Preference: Technology, Telecommunications, Enterprise Software, Healthcare, Energy, Emerging Technology, Consumer
Portfolio Companies: Active Network, AiCure, Aircell, Air Map, Analyte Health, Apervita, Apprentice, Augury, Avia, Away.com, Awesomeness TV, Baselayer, Big Frame, Bird, Bright.md, Built In, Cameo, Cartavi, Casper, Catalytic, Cleversafe, Cloud Technology Partners, CultureiQ, Curiosity.com, Dollar Shave Club, DroneBase, eCollege, egreetings.com, eSpark, Eved, Everdream, EverTrue, Firm58, FleetMatics, G2 Crowd, FreightWaves, Good Uncle, GraphicIQ, HelloGiggles, HopSkipDrive, Hollar, HqO, HyperQuest, Industrial Toys, Interior Define, InterOptic, IO,

525

Venture Capital & Private Equity Firms / Domestic Firms

Iris, Journera, Kollective, LeftHand Networks, Level Ex, Maisonette, Mapbox, Mindshow, Lightstream, OpenPath, Opternative, Outcome Health, Pin Drop Security, Playdom, Plus One Robotics, Pluto.TV, PreparedHealth, project44, PureWow, Red Balloon Security, Retention Science, Retrofit, Scopely, Seebo, SevenFifty, Shiftgig, Signal, SilverVue, SinglePlatform, Sittercity, Smartvid.io, SMS Assist, Snap Sheet, Sportvision, SpotHero, Spring Labs, SwipeSense, The Honest Company, Tock, Tovala, TicketsNow, Upserver, Vettery, Viv, Vow to be Chic, VTS, Wander Beauty, Wise Apple, X.ai, Zinch

Other Locations:
11150 Santa Monica Boulevard
Suite 1500
Los Angeles, CA 90025
Phone: 310-575-9400

Key Executives:
Tony Pritzker, Co-Founder/Managing Partner
Education: BA, Engineering, Dartmouth College; MBA, University of Chicago
Background: Chairman, AmSafe Partners; President, Baker Tanks; Regional VP, Operations, Getz Bros & Co.; Group Executive, Marmon Group
Directorships: Heal The Bay
J.B. Pritzker, Co-Founder/Managing Partner
Education: AB, Political Science, Duke University; JD, Northwestern University School of Law
Background: Founding Member, Illinois Venture Capital Association; Chicago Ventures
Chris Girgenti, Managing Partner
Education: BS, Applied Mathematics & Economics, Brown University; MBA, Finance & Accounting, Columbia Business School; CFA
Background: Corporate Finance, Chicago Corporation; Kemper Securities; Mergers & Acquisitions Group, KPMG Peat Marwick
Directorships: Advantage Optics, BASELAYER Technology, IO Data Centers; Chicago Botanic Garden; The Brown University Sports Foundation; National Venture Capital Association
Adam Koopersmith, Partner
Education: BS, Economics, Wharton School, University of Pennsylvania; MBA, Kellogg School of Management, Northwestern University
Background: Sportvision; Berkshire Partners; Investment Banker, Alex Brown
Directorships: Analyte Health, Apervita, G2 Crowd, Interoptic, Kollective, SilverVue
Matt McCall, Partner
Education: BA, Economics & History, Williams College; MBA, Kellogg School of Management, Northwestern University; McCormick School of Engineering, Northwestern University
Background: Boston Consulting Group; Bankers Trust; Merrill Lynch; US Trust
Gabe Greenbaum, Partner
Education: BA, Washington University in St. Louis; MBA, Kellogg School of Management, Northwestern University; JD, Northwestern University School of Law
Background: Investor, OCA Ventures; Consultant, AlixPartners; Financial Analyst, ABN AMRO Bank; Co-Founder, StudentSpace LLC

1481 PRIVATEER HOLDINGS
2701 Eastlake Avenue East
Seattle, WA 98102

Phone: 206-432-9325
web: www.privateerholdings.com

Mission Statement: Invests in the cannabis industry.

Founded: 2010
Industry Group Preference: Cannabis
Portfolio Companies: Tilray, Leafly, High Park, Marley Natural, Goodship, Irisa, Grail, Head Light

Key Executives:
Brendan Kennedy, Executive Chairman
Education: BA, University of California, Berkeley; MS, Engineering, University of Washington; MBA, Yale School of Management
Background: President/CEO, Mindability Inc.; COO, SVB Analytics
Michael Blue, Managing Partner
Education: BBA, Harding University; MBA, Yale School of Management
Background: VP, de Visscher & Co.; Principal, Herrington Inc.
Christian Groh, Partner
Background: Director of Sales, SVB Analytics
Directorships: Nextel Communications

1482 PRO-RATA OPPORTUNITY FUND
11911 Freedom Drive
Suite 1080
Reston, VA 20190

Phone: 703-563-4100 **Fax:** 703-563-4111
web: proof.vc

Mission Statement: PROOF invests strategic capital alongside early stage VC firms.

Founded: 2015

Key Executives:
John Backus, Co-Founder/Managing Partner
Education: BA, MBA, Stanford University
Background: Co-Founder, US Order; Bain & Co.; Bain Capital
John Burke, Co-Founder/Managing Partner
Education: BA, University of California, Santa Cruz; BS, University of California, Berkeley; MBA, Harvard Business School
Thanasis Delistathis, Co-Founder/Managing Partner
Education: BSE, Princeton University; MBA, Harvard Business School
Background: Mckinley & Co.

1483 PROCYON VENTURES
14/F, One Broadway
Cambridge, MA 02142

e-mail: contact@procyonventures.com
web: www.procyonventures.com

Mission Statement: Procyon Ventures focuses on early stage technology companies, with particular interest in innovations involving data, analytics and IT infrastructure.

Geographic Preference: North America, Asia
Fund Size: $10 million
Founded: 2014
Average Investment: $50,000 - $500,000
Investment Criteria: Startups, Seed, Series A, Series B, Early Stage
Industry Group Preference: Big Data, Analytics & Analytical Instruments, IT Infrastructure, SaaS, Networking
Portfolio Companies: APX Labs, Contastic, Essess, Infinite Analytics, Oculii, Reniac, Seven Bridges Genomics, Smarking, Speedy Packets, Weft

Key Executives:
Malcolm Sweeney, Partner
Drew Volpe, Partner
Education: AB, Computer Science, Harvard University
Background: VP, Product Development, Semantic Machines; Co-Founder & CTO, Locately; Director, Product Development, Endeca Technologies

1484 PROGRESS EQUITY PARTNERS
2200 Ross Avenue
Suite 3838
Dallas, TX 75201
Phone: 214-978-3838 Fax: 214-978-3848
web: www.progressequity.com

Mission Statement: A private equity investment firm that acquires majority control of well-managed, entrepreneurial, service-based businesses.

Industry Group Preference: Healthcare, Pharmaceuticals, Food & Beverage, Communications, Marketing

Portfolio Companies: American Exteriors, COCAT, Crestcom International, Diversified Machine Systems, D&S Residential Services, EnAqua Solutions, Oncology Molecular Imaging, Terracare Associates, Revere Packaging

Other Locations:
7887 E Belleview Avenue
Suite 1100
Englewood, CO 80111
Phone: 303-297-1701 Fax: 303-228-1638

Key Executives:
Michael L Bailey, Founding Partner
Education: BS, Business Administration, University of Chattanooga; MS, Management, Georgia State University
Background: Partner, Transition Capital Partners; Co-Founder, Specialty Dessers LLC
Directorships: American Exteriors, Cambridge Home Healthcare Holdings, COCAT, D&S Residential Holdings, Diversified Machine Systems Holdings, Revere Packaging Holdings

Stephen N Sangalis, Founding Partner
Education: BS, Business Administration, University of Colorado, Boulder; MBA, Finance, Indiana University Kelley School of Business
Background: Founding Partner, Rocky Mountain Capital Partners; Hanifen Imhoff Capital Partners
Directorships: Diversified Machine Systems, Terracare Associates, Westcon, American Exteriors, COCAT

Paul A Yeoham, Founding Partner
Education: BS, Business Administration & Finance, University of Texas, Arlington; MS, Business, Southern Methodist University
Background: Senior Partner, Transition Capital Partners; Westcott Communications
Directorships: Terracare Associates, Westcon, Oncology Molecular Imaging

Carolina B Hensley, Principal
Education: BS, Business Administration, University of Denver
Background: Guaranty Bank & Trust, Highline Equity Partners

1485 PROGRESS INVESTMENT MANAGEMENT COMPANY
33 New Montgomery Street
19th Floor
San Francisco, CA 94105
Phone: 415-512-3480 Fax: 415-512-3475
e-mail: info@progressinvestment.com
web: www.progressinvestment.com

Mission Statement: Create diversified, risk controlled multi-manager investment funds in a variety of asset classes for institutional clients. Specializing in working with smaller, entrepreneurial money management firms with innovative investment strategies.

Fund Size: $6.7 billion
Founded: 1990
Investment Criteria: Emerging firms that are independently owned and have less than $2 billion in assets under management, Minority-and-Woman owned firms, Short track record; a niche focus or a low marketing profile
Industry Group Preference: All markets considered

Other Locations:
445 Park Avenue
10th Floor
New York, NY 10022
Phone: 212-836-4842 Fax: 212-836-4843

Key Executives:
Thurman V White, CEO
Education: Undergraduate Degree, Public & International Affairs, Woodrow Wilson School, Princeton University; MA, Communications, Stanford University; JD, Boalt Hall, University of California, Berkeley
Patricia Gerrick, Chief Investment Officer
Background: Chief Investment Officer, Howard University

1486 PROGRESS VENTURES
One Broadway
14th Floor
Cambridge, MA 02142
Phone: 617-401-2711
web: www.progressventures.com

Mission Statement: Progress Ventures seeks to finance early-stage business-to-business platforms, with exclusive focus on media and marketing technology companies.

Fund Size: $20 million
Founded: 2008
Average Investment: $2 - $4 million
Investment Criteria: Startups, Early Stage
Industry Group Preference: Business to Business, Media Technology, Marketing Technology, Data & Analytics, Analytics & Analytical Instruments, Online Advertising, Mobile

Portfolio Companies: Crave Labs, Dstillery, Integral Ad Science, Iris.TV, Lisnr, Localytics, MediaMath, Pixability, Qualia, Simpli.fi, Skyword, Tru Optik, Trust Metrics

Other Locations:
245 Park Avenue
27th Floor
New York, NY 10167
Phone: 212-609-6914

Key Executives:
Sam Thompson, Founding Partner
Education: BA, Lewis & Clark College; MBA, FW Olin Graduate School of Business, Babson College
Background: Pod Consulting; Procter & Gamble; Phoenix Media/Communications Group; IGN Entertainment; Snowball.com
Directorships: MassBike

Nick MacShane, Founding Partner
Education: BA, Government & History, Skidmore College
Background: Virtual Access Networks; MyWay.com; Scotia Pharmaceuticals

Adriaan Zur Muhlen, Managing Partner
Education: BS, Miami University; MBA, Harvard Business School
Background: Partner, Glouston Capital Partners; Procter & Gamble

Chris Legg, Partner
Education: BCom, Queen's University; MBA, Harvard Business School
Background: Tandem Expansion Fund; Argo Global Capital; Credit Suisse; Merrill Lynch

Rick Gallagher, Managing Partner/Chief Financial Officer
Education: BBA, Accounting, Isenberg School of Management, University of Massachusetts, Amherst
Background: EVP, COO & CFO, Phoenix Media Group; CFO, WebGen Systems

Venture Capital & Private Equity Firms / Domestic Firms

1487 PROJECT 11 VENTURES
Boston, MA

web: www.project11.com

Mission Statement: Project 11 Ventures is a seed stage fund aiming to partner with entrepreneurs and work alongside them to build great software and technology businesses.
Fund Size: $30 million
Investment Criteria: Startups, Seed Stage
Industry Group Preference: Software, Technology
Portfolio Companies: Airmada, Alchemista, Alpha Sheets, Dataquest, DipJar, LibertyX, MoveWith, Sentenai, TVision Insights, Volta Networks
Key Executives:
　Bob Mason, Managing Director
　e-mail: bob@project11.com
　Education: BS, Worcester Polytechnic Institute
　Background: Co-Founder & CTO, Brightcove; Software Architect, ATG; Program Manager, Microsoft
　Katie Rae, Managing Director
　e-mail: katie@project11.com
　Background: Managing Director, Techstars Boston; Microsoft; Co-Founder, Startup Institute
　Reed Sturtevant, Managing Director
　e-mail: reed@project11.com
　Background: Managing Director, Techstars Boston; Microsoft; Managing Director & VP, Technology, Idealab; CTO, Eons; Co-Founder, Startup Institute

1488 PROLOG VENTURES
7701 Forsyth Boulevard
Suite 1095
St Louis, MO 63105

Phone: 314-743-2400
e-mail: prolog@prologventures.com
web: www.prologventures.com

Mission Statement: Venture Capital Firm specializing in life sciences.
Founded: 2001
Industry Group Preference: Life Sciences
Portfolio Companies: Divergence, IntelliCyt, Moleculera Labs, Plum Organics, Singulex, Spindrift, Zeel, AirXpanders, Attune, EndoStim, EraGen, Neurolutions, NxThera, ShopWell, TOMA Biosciences, Veniti, Veran
Key Executives:
　Brian Clevinger, Founder/Managing Director
　Education: Washington University
　Background: Alafai Capital
　Ilya Nykin, Founder/Managing Director
　Education: Odessa University
　Gregory Johnson, Founder/Managing Director
　Education: MIT
　Teddy Shalon, Managing Director
　Education: BA, BS, MS, Washington University
　Background: Co-Founder, Ivy Technologies; Co-Founder, Metaphase; Founder, ThinOptics, Waterpods, Airxpanders, Osteogenix and BioPolymetrix

1489 PROMUS VENTURES
Chicago, IL

e-mail: info@promusventures.com
web: www.promusventures.com

Mission Statement: Investing in early-stage software companies that are changing the world.
Investment Criteria: Early-Stage
Industry Group Preference: Software
Portfolio Companies: Virool, NewHound, BackOps, Storify, Kahuna, Getable, Prism Skylabs, YourMechanic, Chromatik, Owner Listens, Airware, First Opinion, Prizeo, Embarke, Solve Media, Audiodraft, Binpress, Sqwiggle, Layer, AngelList, Seamless Toy Company, Kensho, Vires Aero, Kurbo Health, Vaurum, Ambition, See Me, Bellabeat, Whoop, Tulip Retail, Gauss Surgical, Standard Treasury, Spire, Navdy
Key Executives:
　Mike Collett, Managing Partner/Founder
　e-mail: mcollett@promusventures.com
　Education: BS, BA, Vanderbilt University; MBA, Washington University
　Background: VP, Merrill Lynch M&A Group; Analyst, Masters Capital Management; Co-Founder/Managing Director, Masters Capital Nanotechnology Fund

1490 PROQUEST INVESTMENTS
2430 Vanderbilt Beach Road
Unit 108-190
Naples, FL 34109

Phone: 609-919-3560 Fax: 609-919-3570
web: www.proquestvc.com

Mission Statement: ProQuest Investments invests in healthcare companies ranging from seed stage to late-stage. The company is devoted to the advancement of developing businesses in the healthcare industry.
Geographic Preference: United States, North America, Europe
Fund Size: $900 million
Founded: 1998
Average Investment: $250,000 - $25 million
Investment Criteria: Seed to Late-Stage
Industry Group Preference: Healthcare
Portfolio Companies: Achillion Pharmaceuticals, Agile Therapeutics, Clarus Therapeutics, Eagle Pharmaceutical, Immune Design, Mast Therapeutics, Mersana Therapeutics, NovaDel Pharma, Revision, SomaLogic, Sopherion Therapeutics, TeLoRmedix, Tragara Pharmaceuticals, Zosano Pharma
Other Locations:
　12626 High Bluff Drive
　Suite 325
　San Diego, CA 92130
　Phone: 858-847-0315 Fax: 858-847-0316

　380 Rue St-Antoine Ouest
　Bureau 2020
　Montreal, QC H2Y 3X7
　Canada
　Phone: 514-842-1625 Fax: 514-842-1379
Key Executives:
　Jay Moorin, Partner
　609-919-3565
　Education: BA, Economics, University of Michigan
　Background: Chairman & CEO, Maganin Pharmaceuticals; Managing Director, Healthcare Banking, Bear Stearns & Co. Inc.; VP, Marketing & Business Development, ER Squibb Pharmaceutical Company
　Directorships: ACMI, Acurian, Aires Pharmaceuticals, Eagle Pharmaceuticals, Epic Therapeutics, Gloucester Pharmaceuticals, Guava Technologies, Mersana Therapeutics, MethlyGene, Novacea
　Alain Schreiber, MD, Partner
　609-919-3568
　Education: BS, MD, Free University of Brussels
　Background: President & CEO, Vical; Senior VP, Research, Rhone-Poulenc Rorer
　Directorships: Eagle Pharmaceuticals, Immune Design Corporation, Revision Optics, Telormedix, Tragara Pharmaceuticals
　Pasquale DeAngelis, CFO/Administrative Partner
　609-919-3567
　Education: BS, Accounting, St. Peter's College; MS, Taxation, Pace University; CPA
　Background: Partner, KPMG; Co-Founder/Managing Partner, DeAngelis & Higgins, Adjunct Professor, Seton Hall University & Rider University

Venture Capital & Private Equity Firms / Domestic Firms

Stuart Holden, MD, Chairman, Scientific Advisory Board
Education: University Of Winsconsin-Madison; MD, Cornell University
Background: Surgeon, Cedars-Sinai Medical Center; Assistant Professor of Surgery, Georgetown University School of Medicine
Directorships: Louis Warschaw Prostate Cancer Center, Prostate Cancer Foundation

1491 PROSPECT CAPITAL CORPORATION
10 E 40th Street
42nd Floor
New York, NY 10016

Phone: 212-792-2095
e-mail: investorrelations@prospectstreet.com
web: www.prospectstreet.com

Mission Statement: An mezzanine debt and private equity firm that manages a publicly-traded, closed-end, dividend-focuses investment company.

Fund Size: $1 billion
Founded: 1988
Average Investment: $10-50 million
Investment Criteria: Mezzanine Debt, Acquisitions, Growth, Development, Financings, Recapitalizations
Industry Group Preference: All sectors considered
Portfolio Companies: Adernant, Aircraft Fasteners, ALG USA Holdings, Allied Defense Group, American Broadband, American Gilsonite, AMU Holdings, APH Property Holdings, Apidos CLO, Arctic Glacier, Arctic Oilfield Equipment, Ark-La-Tex Wireline Services, Armor Holding II, ARRM Holdings, Atlantis Healthcare Group, Babson CLO, Blue Coat Systems, BNN Holdings, Broder Bros., Brookside Mill CLO, Byrider Systems, BXM Holding Company, Caleel and Hayden, Capston Logistics, Cargo Airport Services, CCPI Holdings, Cent 17 CLO, Cinedigm DC, Coverall, CP Well Testing, Credit Central, Crossman Corporation, CRT Midco, Deltek, Diamondback, Echelon Aviation, Edmentum, Learning, Empire Today, Energy Solutons, First Tower, Fischbein, Fleetwash, Focus Brands, FPG, Galaxy II, Global Employment Solutions, Grocery Outlet, GTP Operations, Gulf Coast Machine and Supply, Halcyon Loan Advisors, Harbortouch Holdings of Delaware, Harley Marine Services, ICON Health & Fitness, IDQ Holdings, Ikaria, Injured Workers Pharmacy, Instant Web, Interdent, JAC Holding Corporation, Laserhip, LCM XIV CLO, LHC Holdings, Madison Park Funding IX, Manx, Matrixx Initiatives, Maverick Healthcare, MITY Holdings of Delaware, Mountain View CLO, Nationwide Acceptance Holdings, NCP Finance, New Century Transportation, Nixon, NPH Property Holdings, Octagon Investment Partners, Onyx Payments, Pacfic World, Pelican Products, Photonic Technologies SAS, Pinnacle Treatment, PrimeSport, Prince Mineral Holding Corporation, Progrexion Holdings, Rocket Softwa

Key Executives:
John F. Barry III, Chairman/CEO
Education: AB History, Princeton University; JD Degree, Harvard Law School
Background: VP, Corporate Finance, Merrill Lynch; Chairman & CEO, BondNet Trading Systems; Managing Director, LF Rothschild & Company; Director, Prudential Securities
Directorships: CT Financial Developments, Prospect St. NYC Discovery Fund, Prospect St. NYC Vp-Investment Fund
Michael G. Eliasek, President/COO
Education: MBA, Harvard Business; BS, University of Virginia
Background: Bain & Company
David L. Belzer, Managing Director
Education: MBA, Washington University; BA, Indiana University
Background: Fieldstone Private Capital Group; Blaylock & Partners, GE Capital; Wheelabrator Technologies

Daria Becker, Chief Administrative Officer
Education: BA, Wellesley College; Massachusetts Institute of Technology
Background: CitiBank NA
David Moszer, Managing Director
Education: BA, University of Virginia; MBA, Columbia University
Background: GSO Capital Partners; Principal, FriedbergMilstein; Principal, GarMark Partners; Bear Stearns
Jason Wilson, Managing Director
Education: BS, Mechanical Engineering, University of Notre Dame; MBA, University of Chicago Graduate School of Business
Background: Investment Banking, Lehman Brotherse; UBS Investment Bank
Directorships: Yatesville Coal Holdings; Ajax Rolled Ring & Machine; Veterans Securing America

1492 PROSPECT PARTNERS LLC
200 W Madison Street
Suite 2710
Chicago, IL 60606

Phone: 312-782-7400 Fax: 312-782-7410
web: www.prospect-partners.com

Mission Statement: Manages two funds totaling $270 million focused exclusively on management-led leveraged acquisitions of lower middle market companies with niche strategies; partnering with management teams to acquire and help build companies whose base revenue is typically between $10 and $30 million at the time of our investment, and pursue add-on acquisitions with as little as $2 million in revenue.

Geographic Preference: United States
Fund Size: $270 million
Founded: 1998
Average Investment: $1-$7 million
Minimum Investment: $1 million
Investment Criteria: MBO, Recapitalizations in the lower middle market
Industry Group Preference: Household Goods, Consumer Products, Leisure, Food & Beverage, Education, Automotive, Marine Services, Sports, Information Technology, Health Related, Packaging
Portfolio Companies: Absolutely Custom Group, Codel Holding Company, Cyclonaire Holding Corporation, Education Futures Group, ESI Lighting, ICI Holding Company, Knight Packaging Group, Kronos Foods, Landmark Irrigation Holding Services, Navix Holdings Corporation, Owen Equipment Holdings, Polymer Holding, Prospect Pools Group, Prospect Water, Summit Fire Protetcion, Superior Tool Holding Company, SurePoint Holdings, Tender Products, Velocity Aerospace Holding Group, Velvac Holdings, WDP Holdings Corporation, Wedgewood Hospitality Group

Louis W Kenter, Partner
e-mail: lkenter@prospect-partners.com
Education: BS Mechanical Engineering, University of Illinois; MBA University of Chicago
Background: Kenter & Company; Marquette Venture Partners; McKinsey & Company; Skidmore, Owings & Merrill
Directorships: Education Corporation of America, GameMark Products, V4 Group, John Boos Company, Revere Group, Kifco
Richard C Tuttle, Partner
e-mail: rtuttle@prospect-partners.com
Education: BA Economics, Stanford University; MBA Stanford Graduate School of Business
Background: Health Care & Retirement Corporation; Golder, Thoma & Cressey; McKinsey & Company
Directorships: Office Resources, Excello Products LLC, Optronics Products, Remuda Ranch Company, Cobler Origin Technologies

529

Venture Capital & Private Equity Firms / Domestic Firms

Erik E Maurer, Partner
e-mail: emauer@prospect-partners.com
Education: BA, Stanford University; MBA, Northwestern JL Kellogg Graduate School of Management
Background: Northern Trust Company; Inroads Capital Partners
Directorships: PAC Holding Company, First Texas Products Company, Optronics Products, Wrap Pack Products Corporation, V4 Group
Brett P Holcomb, Partner
e-mail: bholcomb@prospect-partners.com
Education: BA, Kenyon College; MBA, Kellogg School of Management, Northwestern University
Background: Associate, American Capital; Analyst, Bear Stearns & Co
Bradley C O'Dell, Partner
e-mail: bodell@prospect-partners.com
Education: BS, University of Richmond; MBA, Kellogg School of Business, Northwestern University
Background: Vice President, Silver Oak Services Partners; Associate, Willis Stein & Partners
Directorships: Kronos Foods, Gold Star Food Service, Summit Fire Protection, Tender Products

1493 PROSPECT VENTURE PARTNERS
525 University Avenue
Suite 1350
Palo Alto, CA 94301

Phone: 650-327-8800
web: www.prospectventures.com

Mission Statement: Prospect Venture Partners is dedicated to investing in outstanding biopharmaceutical and medical device companies. Prospect targets commercially attractive biomedical enterprises with outstanding entrepreneurial management teams, proprietary products, and innovative technologies with the potential for significant investment returns.

Fund Size: $1 billion
Average Investment: $10 - $20 million
Investment Criteria: New Company Incubations, First and Second Financing Rounds, Late-Stage
Industry Group Preference: Biopharmaceuticals, Medical Devices
Portfolio Companies: Alvine Pharmaceuticals, Amicus Therapeutics, Amira Pharmaceuticals, AVEO Pharmaceuticals, Baxano Surgical, Cabochon Aesthetics, CHG Healthcare, Complete Genomics, DFine, Gloucester Pharmaceuticals, Hansen Medical, Idun Pharmaceuticals, Infinity Pharmaceuticals, Jazz Pharmaceuticals, Kythera Biopharmaceuticals, Nanosys, Neomend, NGM Biopharmaceuticals, NinePoint Medical, Nora Therapeutics, Novacept, Novavax, Opus Medical, Pamira, PCI Holding Corporation, Portola Pharmaceuticals, Rinant Neuroscience, ROXRO Pharma, Sapphire Therapeutics, Senomyx, SentreHEART, SGX Pharmaceuticals, Somaxon Pharmaceuticals, SurgRx, Tercica, Tinea Pharmaceuticals, Topica Pharmaceuticals, Transave, Trubion Pharmaceuticals, Vanda Pharmaceuticals, Visiogen, Vitae Pharmaceutcals

Key Executives:
Russell Hirsch MD, PhD, Managing Director
Education: BA, Chemistry, University of Chicago; MD & PhD, Biochemistry, University of California, San Francisco
Background: General Partner, Mayfield; Biomedical Research, University of California, San Francisco
Directorships: Intuitive Surgial, Hansen Medical, Opus Medical, Orquest, AVEO Pharmaceuticals, Visiogen, Baxano, Dfine, SentreHEART, Portola Pharmaceuticals
David Schnell MD, Managing Director
Education: BS, Biological Sciences, Stanford University; MA, Health Services Research, Stanford University School of Medicine; MD, Harvard Medical School
Background: Partner, Kleiner Perkins Caufield & Byers; Sandoz Pharmaceuticals; Co-Founder & CEO, Healtheon Corporation

1494 PROVCO GROUP
795 E Lancaster Avenue
Suite 200
Villanova, PA 19085

Phone: 610-520-2010 Fax: 610-520-1905
web: www.provcogroup.com

Mission Statement: Provco facilitates early-stage and mature financing on a select basis.

Average Investment: $1,000,000-$10,000,000
Minimum Investment: $100,000
Investment Criteria: First-Stage, Second-Stage
Industry Group Preference: Communications, Computer Related, Consumer Products, Distribution, Electronic Components, Instrumentation, Genetic Engineering, Medical & Health Related
Portfolio Companies: Integra Life Sciences, Prime Bank, Ballard Leasing, Interactive Investor International, Hooters Restaurants, HAL Trust, Medicus Technologies

Key Executives:
Richard E Caruso PhD, Founder
Education: BS, Susquehanna University; MSBA, Bucknell University; PhD, London School of Economics, University of London
Background: Principal, LFC Financial Corp.; Pricewaterhouse & Co.
Directorships: Integra Life Sciences Corporation
Gary R DiLella, Vice President
Education: BS, Pennsylvania State University; MS, Villanova University
Background: Finance Department, LFC Financial Corp.
Gerald Holtz, Vice President
610-520-2010
Fax: 610-520-1905
Education: MBA, Duke University; BS, Villanova University
Background: Co-Founder, Hoot Owl Restaurants LLC; PepsiCo; Price Waterhouse & Company

1495 PROVENANCE VENTURES
e-mail: bbiniak@yahoo.com
web: www.provenanceventures.com

Mission Statement: A venture capital firm focused on developing seed and early-stage social technology companies. The firm places value on the building of sustainable, high growth businesses through partnerships with entrepreneurs and operational execution.

Geographic Preference: United States
Fund Size: $10 million
Founded: 2006
Investment Criteria: Seed-Stage, Early-Stage
Industry Group Preference: Media, Digital Media & Marketing, Communications

Key Executives:
Bryan Biniak, Founder/Managing Director
Education: BA, International Relations, Business & Economics, Boston University
Background: Senior Vice President, AG Interactive Gem M Division; COO, Vivendi Universal Moviso Division; Founding Member, Harmonix Music Systems

1496 PROVIDENCE EQUITY PARTNERS
50 Kennedy Plaza
18th Floor
Providence, RI 02903

Phone: 401-751-1700 Fax: 401-751-1790
e-mail: info@provequity.com
web: www.provequity.com

Mission Statement: A private investment firm specializing in equity investments in communications and media companies around the world. To create value by building lasting partnerships with talented entrepreneurs and by providing them with the capital, industry expertise and broad network of relation-

Venture Capital & Private Equity Firms / Domestic Firms

ships necessary to build companies that will shape the future of the communications and media industries.
Fund Size: $22 billion
Founded: 1989
Average Investment: $75 million
Minimum Investment: $10 million
Investment Criteria: Growth capital
Industry Group Preference: Telecommunications, Media, Entertainment, Information Services
Portfolio Companies: ABTL, AcadeMedia, Altegrity, Ambassador Theatre Group, Ascend Learning, Asurion, Blackboard, CDW, Chernin Group, CSDVRS, Digiturk, EDMC, Galileo Global Education, GlobalTranz, Grupo TorreSur, Hathway, HSE24, Idea Cellular, ikaSystems, Ironman, ITT Educational Services, KIN, Learfield Sports, M7 Group, Miller Heiman, MLS Media, OpenSky, Q Networks, RentPath, SRA International, Star CJ, Study Group, SunGard, Survey Sampling International, Trilogy International Partners, TVB, UFO Movies India, Univision Communications, VectorLearning, VendorSafe Technologies, Volia, vRad, Wize Commerce, ZeniMax Media

Other Locations:
31 West 52nd Street
Suite 2400
New York, NY 10019
Phone: 212-588-6700 **Fax:** 212-588-6701

401 Park Drive
Suite 204
Boston, MA 02215

28 St. George Street
London W1S 2FA
United Kingdom
Phone: 44-2075148800 **Fax:** 44-2076292778

Providence Equity Asia Limited
9th Floor, Suite 902
15 Queen's Road
Central
Hong Kong
Phone: 852-36533800 **Fax:** 852-36533900

Birla Tower
25 Barakhamba Road
6th Floor
New Delhi 110 001
India
Phone: 91-1130419000 **Fax:** 91-1130419090

Key Executives:
Glenn M. Creamer, Senior Managing Director Emeritus & Senior Advisor
Education: MBA, Harvard Business School; BA, Brown University
Directorships: Transwestern Publishing
Paul J. Salem, Senior Managing Director Emeritus
Education: MBA, Harvard Business School; BA, Brown University
Directorships: eircom ltd
Lori B. Ali, Managing Director/Head of Talent
Education: Massachusetts School of Professional Psychology; BA, Hobart & William Smith Colleges
William J. Aliber, Managing Director
Education: BA, Brown University; MBA, University of Chicago
Background: CFO, Ascend Learning; CFO, Hallmark Cards
Directorships: OpusCapita
Skip Besthoff, Managing Director
Education: BA, Hamilton College; MBA, Johnson Grad. School of Management, Cornell University
Background: Chief Strategy Officer, Verizon Connect; CEO, InboundWriter; General Partner, Castile Ventures; Principal, Rho Ventures
Michael J. Dominguez, Managing Director
Education: MBA, Harvard Business School; BA, Bucknell University
Directorships: Bresnan Communications; F&W Publications
Edward A. Chestnut, Managing Director, Business Development
Education: BA, University of Notre Dame
Background: Managing Director, Fortress; Founder, Atlantic-Pacific Capital Chicago Office; Northern Trust Company
John P. Clancy, Managing Director/Head of Portfolio Operations
Education: BA, Assumption College
Background: President, Radius Worldwide; CEO, Azuki Systems; President, Iron Mountain Digital; COO, Connected Corporation
Patrick D. Dunn, Managing Director
Education: BA, Bowdoin College
Background: Portfolio Manager, Northern Pines; Raptor Group; Tudor Investment Corporation; Morgan Stanley
John C. Hahn, Senior Managing Director
Education: MBA, Anderson School of Management; BA, University of Notre Dame
Joshua C. Empson, Managing Director
Education: BA, Princeton University
Background: Partner, NantCapital; Managing Director, Forstmann Little & Co.; United Online; NBC
Directorships: Influence Media Partners; Learfield Sports; MLS Media
Rick Essex, Managing Director
Education: BS, Washington & Lee University; MBA, Columbia University
Background: CFO, Blackboard Inc.; CFO, Survey Sampling International
Marco J. Ferrari, Managing Director
Education: BA, Harvard University; MBA, Harvard Business School
Background: Principal, BV Investment Partners; Partner, Siemens Venture Capital
Directorships: Abacus Next; Government Brands; Impact; NXTsoft; Pineapple Payments; Propertybase; Snap!; Raise; Sovereign Sportsman Solutions; Therapy Brands; Tribute Technology
Jonathan M. Nelson, Chief Executive Director
Education: MBA, Harvard Business School; BA, Brown University
Directorships: Bresnan Broadband, eircom ltd., Language Life Services, Western Wireless Corp., Yankees Entertainment and Sports Network LLC, VoiceStream Wireless Corp.
Michael N. Gray, Managing Director
Education: BS & MS, University of North Carolina; MBA, Stanford Grad. School of Business
Background: First Union Capital Partners
Directorships: Grupo TorreSur; Univision Communications
William S. Hughes, Managing Director
Education: BA, Dartmouth College; MBA, Harvard Business School
Background: Associate, Summit Partners; CEO, Netdecisions Group; Analyst, Lehman Brothers
Directorships: KPa; n2Y; TimeClock Plus; Vistage
Edward FL. Hughes, Managing Director
Education: BS, Durham University
Background: VP, JP Morgan
Directorships: Imaweb-IDF; Mapal; OpusCapita; TES
Lisa M. Lee, Managing Director
Education: BA, Stanford University; MBA, Harvard University
Background: Managing Director, CVC Capital Partners; Merrill Lynch; A.T. Kearney
Karim A. Tabet, Managing Director
Education: Ecole Polytechnique; MBA, Wharton School
Background: Associate, Goldman Sachs
Directorships: Catalpa
Andrew A. Tisdale, Managing Director
Education: BA, Vanderbilt University; MBA, University

Venture Capital & Private Equity Firms / Domestic Firms

of North Carolina
Background: Morgan Stanley
Scott M. Marimow, Managing Director
Education: BS, Wharton School, University of Pennsylvania
Background: Analyst, Deutsche Bank
Directorships: RentPath; TAIT; Topgolf; EZLinks Golf; ZeniMax Media; AutoTrader Group; Hulu; Learfield Sports; MLS Media; Newport Television
Peter O. Wilde, Managing Director & Chairman, PSG
Education: BA, Colorado College; MBA, Harvard Business School
Background: General Partner, BCI Partners
Directorships: Archipelago Learning, Ascend Learning, Decision Resources, Edline, Education Management Corp., NEW Asurion, Study Group

1497 PRUDENTIAL CAPITAL GROUP
180 North Stetson Avenue
Suite 5600
Chicago, IL 60601

web: www.prudentialcapitalgroup.com

Mission Statement: Prudential Capital Group structures creative financial solutions that meet a variety of client needs.

Fund Size: $60 billion
Average Investment: $10 - $75 million
Investment Criteria: Recapitalizations, Growth Capital, Buyouts, Acquisitions
Industry Group Preference: All markets considered

Key Executives:
Allen A Weaver, Senior Managing Director
e-mail: allen.weaver@prudential.com
Education: BS, Stanford University; MBA, Wharton School
Jeffrey L. Dickson, Managing Director
e-mail: jeffrey.dickson@prudential.com
Education: BS, Babson College; MS, MIT Sloan School of Management
Mark A. Hoffmeister, Managing Director, Corporate Mezzanine
e-mail: mark.hoffmeister@prudential.com
Education: BA, MS, University of Wisconsin, Madison
Albert Trank, Executive Managing Director & Portfolio Manager
Education: BA, Rutgers University; MBA, Rutgers University's Business School

1498 PSILOS GROUP
165 Broadway
Suite 2301
New York, NY 10006

Phone: 212-242-8844
web: www.psilos.com

Mission Statement: Seeks to investment time, energy and relationships into each opportunity, helping entrepreneurial partners to put in place operating capital structures that will support and enhance the quality and value of the businesses over the long-term and navigate through the normal ups and downs.

Geographic Preference: United States
Fund Size: $580 million
Founded: 1998
Average Investment: $20 - $25 million
Minimum Investment: $8 million
Investment Criteria: Revenue Stage, Later Stage
Industry Group Preference: Healthcare, Medical Technology, Healthcare Services, Healthcare Information Technology
Portfolio Companies: AngioScore, Caregiver Services, Gamma Medica-Ideas, HealthEdge, Mauna Kea Technologies, OmniGuide, PatientSafe Solutions, SeeChange Health

Other Locations:
21 Tamal Vista Boulevard
Suite 194
Corte Madera, CA 94925
Phone: 415-945-7010 **Fax:** 415-945-7011

100 N Guadalupe Street
Suite 203
Santa Fe, NM 87501
Phone: 505-995-8500 **Fax:** 505-995-8501

Key Executives:
Stephen M. Krupa, Managing Partner/CEO/COO
Education: BS, Mechanical Engineering, University of South Florida; MBA, Wharton School
Background: VP, Wasserstein Perella & Co; Associate, Kidder Peabody & Co; Mechanical Engineer/Manager New Business, Johnson Controls
Directorships: Active Health Management; ARTISTdirect.com; HealthScribe; Caregiver Services
David Eichler, Managing Partner
Education: MBA, Darden Graduate School of Business Administration, University of Virginia; MA, National Security, Georgetown University; Undergraduate, Government & International Relations, Cornell University
Background: Investment Banker, Wasserstein Perella & Company; Defense Policy Analyst, DynCorp

1499 PSL VENTURES
240 2nd Avenue South
Suite 300
Seattle, WA 98104

Phone: 206-202-2227
web: www.psl.com/ventures

Mission Statement: Aims to invest in early-stage, pre-seed, seed, and series A companies in the area of technology.

Geographic Preference: Pacific Northwest, United States
Fund Size: $80 Million
Average Investment: $500,000 - $2,000,000
Minimum Investment: $500,000
Investment Criteria: Technology, Pacific Northwest, Early Stage, Seed, Series A
Industry Group Preference: Technology
Portfolio Companies: Canotic, Inspo Network, JetClosing, Shukinko, StopDDoS, Taunt

Key Executives:
Greg Gottesman, Managing Director/Co-Founder
Education: Stanford University; Harvard Busines School; Harvard Law School
Background: Managing Director, Madrona Venture Group; Co-Founder, Madrona Venture Labs
Directorships: Board Member, Rover.com; Board Member, Mighty Ai; President Evergreen Venture Capital Association
Julie Sandler, Managing Director
Education: BA, MA, Psychology, Stanford University; MBA, Harvard Business School
Background: Partner, Madrona Venture Group; Senior Product Manager, Amazon; Product Management, Accenture; TechStreet.com
Directorships: University of Washington Foster School of Business; Washington Roundtable; Washington State Opportunity Scholarship
Geoff Entress, Managing Director/Co-Founder
Education: University of Michigan Law School; Tepper School of Business, Carnegie Mellon University; University of Notre Dame
Background: Voyager Capital; Madrona Venture; Perkins Coie; Jones Day; UrbanEarth.com; Salomon Brothers; The Prudential Home Mortgage Company; Mellon Bank; Priority Investment Management; Dusquesne Capital Management
Directorships: JettClosing; Hiya; Meritage Soups; Bonanza; Foodee; LiquidPlanner; Alliance of Angels

1500 PTV SCIENCES
3600 N. Capital of Texas Highway
Suite B180
Austin, TX 78746

Phone: 512-872-4000
e-mail: bplans@ptvsciences.com
web: www.ptvsciences.com

Mission Statement: PTV Sciences is a healthcare venture capital and growth equity firm focused on enabling healthcare entrepreneurs and global innovation.

Geographic Preference: United States
Fund Size: $191 million
Founded: 2003
Industry Group Preference: Healthcare, Life Sciences, Medical Devices, Biotechnology, Pharmaceuticals, Diagnostics
Portfolio Companies: Apollo Endosurgery, AsuraGen, Bioform Medical, Biomimetic, Cameron Health, Cardiva Medical, Corventis, GlycoMimetics, IDEV, Intersect, LDR, Mirna Therapeutics, Osteobiologics, On-X Life Technologies, Ortho Kinematics, Tryton Medical

Other Locations:
1000 Main
Suite 3250
Houston, TX 77002
Phone: 713-209-7555 **Fax:** 713-209-7599

Matthew S Crawford, Founding Managing Director
Education: BA, MBA, Wake Forest University
Background: Partner, Academy Funds; First Union Capital Markets Corporation
Directorships: Apollo Endosurgery, IDEV Technologies, LDR Spine, On-X-Life Technologies

1501 PURETECH VENTURES
500 Boylston Street
Suite 1600
Boston, MA 02116

Phone: 617-482-2333 **Fax:** 617-482-3337
web: www.puretechhealth.com

Mission Statement: Focuses on major unmet medical needs that have yet to be addressed by emerging science, and looks for cutting edge discoveries and technologies that have the potential to yield products with considerable market differentiation.

Investment Criteria: Early-Stage
Industry Group Preference: Therapeutics, Medical Devices, Diagnostics

Daphne Zohar, Founder/CEO
e-mail: dzohar@puretechventures.com
Directorships: Enlight Biosciences, Follica, Libra Biosciences, Vendanta Bioscience, Mandara Sciences, Karuna Pharmaceuticals, Tal Medical, Satori Pharmaceuticals
Stephen Muniz, COO
e-mail: smuniz@puretechventures.com
Education: BA, Economics & Accounting, College of the Holy Cross; JD, New England School of Law
Background: Partner, Edwards Angell Palmer & Dodge LLP
Eric Elenko, CIO
e-mail: eelenko@puretechventures.com
Education: BA, Biology, Swarthmore College; PhD, Biomedical Sciences, University of California, San Diego
Background: Consultant, McKinsey & Company; President, Technology Evaluation Group

1502 QED INVESTORS
web: www.qedinvestors.com

Mission Statement: QED Investors actively supports high-growth businesses that use information to compete - and win. While our support is tailored to the specific needs of each portfolio company, we typically provide a combination of both capital and capability. With operationally-oriented skills that we believe are both fundamentally applicable and broadly transferable, we enjoy working closely with a small set of carefully selected companies that range in size and style. But common to all of our partnerships is a shared conviction that information plays a decisive role in the success of the company, a mutual desire for a high degree of direct engagement, and a shared enthusiasm for experimentation and learning.

Industry Group Preference: Information Technology
Portfolio Companies: 2U, 33across, AddThis, ApplePie Capital, Audience Partners, Avant Credit, BlueYield, Borro, Can Capial, Card.com, China Rapid Finance, Credit Karma, Drive Factor, Fundera, Future Finance, Global Analytics, GreenSky, Klarna, L2C, LendUp, MediaMath, Mobile Posse, OnSwipe, Optoro, NU Bank, Orchard, peerTransfer, Privlo, Propane Taxi, Prosper, Red Ventures, Remitly, Signifyd, SoFi, Spruce Media, The Americas Card, Valen Analytics, Video Blocks, Videology, Vubiquity, WealthEngine

Key Executives:
Nigel Morris, Partner
Education: MBA, London Business School
Background: Co-Founder, Capital One Financial Services
Frank Rotman, Founding Partner
Education: BS, MS, University of Virginia
Background: Capital One

1503 QUABBIN CAPITAL
160 Federal Street
Boston, MA 02110

Phone: 617-330-9041
e-mail: info@quabbincapital.com
web: www.quabbincapital.com

Mission Statement: Is a privately held firm, concentrating, since 1990, in the private equity market. Boston Projects develops investment opportunities directly and through affiliated sponsors and intermediaries that include investment bankers, attorneys, and co-investor partners.

Portfolio Companies: Advanced Duplication Services, Ascendant Advisors Group, Archon Woodworks, Dan-Loc Bolt & Gasket, Inventus, Library Systems & Services, Mozido, Porter Group, RIMCO Royalty Partners, SAMBASafety, Southwaste Serivces, SPC TelEquip, Upper Crust

Key Executives:
John I Snow III, President/Managing Director
Education: BA, Economics, Amherst College; MS, Accounting, New York University
Background: Auditor, KPMG Peat Marwick
Directorships: Advanced Duplication Services, Hoffco, Inc., Purater Group Library Systems & Services, Remco Royalty Partners
Steven A Leese, Managing Director
Education: BA Economics, Amherst College; MBA, Harvard University
Background: Investment Banking, Merrill Lynch
Directorships: Dan-Lol; Bolt & Gasket; SPL Telegroup; Southwaste, Inc.; Onecare, Inc.

1504 QUAD PARTNERS
570 Lexington Avenue
36th Floor
New York, NY 10022

Phone: 212-724-2200
web: www.quadpartners.com

Mission Statement: Quad Partners was founded to make value-added private investments in the education industry.

Fund Size: $200 million
Founded: 1999
Industry Group Preference: Education
Portfolio Companies: B&H Education, Beckfield College, Blue Cliff College, Dorsey Schools, Noel-Levitz, Pacific

Venture Capital & Private Equity Firms / Domestic Firms

College of Oriental Medicine, Stratford School, Swedish Institute, TargetX, The Learning Experience, Trillium College, ILSC Education Group, Inside Higher Ed, RuffaloCODY

Key Executives:

Lincoln E Frank, Managing Partner
Education: LL.M, Cambridge University; JD, University of Pennsylvania Law School; BA, Wesleyan University
Background: COO, JP Morgan; Banker, Goldman, Sachs & Company; Skadden Arps

Thomas H Kean, Advisory Partner
Education: MA, Columbia University Teachers College; BA, Princeton University
Background: President, Drew University; Governor, New Jersey

Daniel P Neuwirth, General Partner
Education: MBA, Amos Tuck School, Dartmouth; BA, Williams College
Background: Donaldson, Lufkin & Jenrette; Goldman, Sachs & Company

Stephen H Spahn, General Partner
Education: PhD, Columbia University; Univ. of Oxford; BA, Dartmouth College
Background: Headmaster/Owner, Dwight School; Founder, International School of London; John Catt Education Ltd.

Russell S Dritz, Principal
Education: BS, The Wharton School, University of Pennsylvania
Background: Banker, Credit Suisse First Boston

1505 QUAD-C MANAGEMENT
200 Garrett Street
Suite M
Charlottesville, VA 22902

Phone: 434-979-2070
e-mail: info@qc-inc.com
web: www.quadcmanagement.com

Mission Statement: To invest in profitable middle market companies with attractive growth opportunities where the firm can add value by providing capital and supporting the company's management and employees.

Geographic Preference: North America
Fund Size: $1 billion
Founded: 1989
Average Investment: $75 million
Minimum Investment: $25 million
Investment Criteria: LBO, Growth Capital
Industry Group Preference: Manufacturing, Distribution, Services
Portfolio Companies: @properties, A Stucki Company, Accoustical Material Services, AIT Worldwide Logistics, Asset Acceptance Capital Corp., Augusta Sportswear Group, Balboa Water Group, Behavioral Interventions, Boulder Scientific Company, Capital Tool & Design, Caribeean Restaurants, Century Graphics Corporation, Cloverhill Bakery, Colibri, Compassion-First Pet Hospitals, Curvature, Dental Care Alliance, Document Technologies, Durcon, EFC International, Galleher, Generation Brands, Heartland Automotive Services, Huddle House, Inmark, InterWrap, Joerns Healthcare, Krayden, Lexicon Marketing, MW Industries, Network Global Logistics, NuSil Technology, Pharm-Olam, Polaris Pool Holdings, Prism Vision Group, Rainbow Early Education, Red Robin Gourmet Burgers, Royal Adhesives & Sealants, Service Partners, Staff Leasing, Stanton Carpet, Stauber, Stimsonite Corporation, Tandus Flooring, TDS Logistics, Technimark, Transport Labor Contract, United Piece Dye Works, Universal Fiber Systems, Vaco, VMG Health, Wolf, Worldwide Express

Key Executives:

Terry Daniels, Chairman
Education: BA, University of Virginia; MBA, Colgate Darden School, University of Virginia
Background: Vice Chairman, WR Grace & Co; President, Western Publishing; Senior Vice President, Matel

Tony Ignaczak, Managing Partner
Education: BS, Wharton School; MBA, Harvard Business School
Background: Merrill Lynch; Bacus Communications

Steve Burns, Managing Partner
Education: BS, Boston College; MBA, Wharton School

Thad Jones, Partner
Education: BS, McIntire School of Commerce, University of Virginia
Background: Corporate Finance, Robinson-Humphrey; Croft & Bender
Directorships: Augusta Sportswear Group; Spa & Bath Holdings; Assset Acceptance Capital Corp

Tim Billings, Partner
Education: BS, Business Administration, Georgetown University
Background: Principal, MidOcean Partners
Directorships: Classic Party Rentals, Document Technologies, Generation Brands

Frank Winslow, Partner
Education: AB, Princeton
Background: Consultant, Quantitative Strategies Group, Public Financial Management

Tom Hickey, Partner
Education: BA, Economics & English, University of Virginia; MBA, Harvard Business School
Background: Managing Director, Castle Harlan
Directorships: TLC Companies, Heartland Automotive Services

Michael Brooks, Partner
Education: BA, Bucknell University
Background: Leveraged Finance Group, Bear Stearns & Co.

1506 QUADRANGLE GROUP
345 Seventh Avenue
Suite 1900
New York, NY 10001

Phone: 212-418-1700 Fax: 212-418-1701
e-mail: info@quadranglegroup.com
web: www.quadranglegroup.com

Mission Statement: Quadrangle is a private investment fund that specializes in the global media and communications industry.

Geographic Preference: United States, Asia
Fund Size: $3 billion
Founded: 2000
Industry Group Preference: Information Services, Communications, Media
Portfolio Companies: Access Spectrum LLC, Bresnan Broadband, Cequel Communications, Cinemark, DataNet Communications, DHI Group Inc., Get AS, Grupo Corporativo Ono, Hargray Holdings, Lumos Networks, Mobilicity, NTELOS Holdings, NuVox Communications, PMC, Protection One, Publishing Group of America, Tower Vision, US LEC, West Corporation

Key Executives:

Michael Huber, President/Managing Principal
Education: BA magna cum laude Mathematics, Macalester College; MBA, Sloan School of Management
Background: Media and Communications, Donaldson, Lufkin & Jenrette; BellSouth
Directorships: Access Spectrum, Cequel Communications, DAVE Holdings, Hargray Holdings, NTELOS Holdings

Brian Bytof, Advisor
Education: MBA & BS, Finance/Risk Management, Temple University
Background: CFO, Stillwater Capital Partners; Director of Operations, Axiom International Investors; Senior Finance Analyst, Towers Perrin

Venture Capital & Private Equity Firms / Domestic Firms

1507 QUAKE CAPITAL PARTNERS
100 Congress Avenue
Suite 2000
Austin, TX 78701

web: www.quakecapital.com

Mission Statement: A venture capital fund and startup accelerator seeking to build startup ecosystems and enhance innovation across multiple industry verticals and geographies.

Geographic Preference: US, Europe
Average Investment: $100K - $150K
Industry Group Preference: Blockchain, AdTech, AgTech, Virtual Reality, Artificial Intelligence, Cellular Communications, Cyber Security, Energy, Robotics, Infrastructure, SaaS, Social Media, Logistics, Machine Learning, Manufacturing
Portfolio Companies: 17TeraWatts, 70 Millions Staffing, A la Carte Delivery, Abravax, Axle.AI, Adventr, Adway, AimSteady, Alteria Automation, Ampathy, AptivIO, AquaSprouts, BBy Inc., BC3 Technologies, Baarb, Baby Quip, CarServ, Cartogram, CatapultX, ChatQuery, CitySmart, CityGrowsm Contentplace, Data Gram, Dentidesk, Digital Claim, Doctors, Dripkit, Drofika, Elliegrid, Endorsify, EsportsOne, Everlasting Wardrobe, Family Plan, FenSense, Five to Nine, Flatlay, Gluetech, GoTRIBE, Good Boy Studies, Good Company, Hava Health, Health Hero, Informu, Junkless, Kericure, Kittery, Lilu, Locus Insights, Love Goodly, Man Outfitters, Marquii, Mickey Forest, MicroEra Power, Mirow, Morbax, Node Capital, Open Health Network, Ormigga, Partify, Pebby, QuickBRCare, Randian, Radial3D, Rain Systems, Ranked Media & Technologies, Rebus, Recoup Fitness, RideKleen, Saasuma, SeaProducts, SeeRoseGo, Socionado, SolePower, Sonic Sleep, Steereo, Stemless, ToMarket, Tracks N Teeth, Trainers Vault, University Beyond, Upside Health, Versusgame, Vetty, ViaHero, Voiceitt, VueBox, WearWorks, Whoseyourlandlord, Yip Yap

Key Executives:
Glenn Argenbright, Founder/General Partner
Education: LLB, University of San Diego
Amy Coveny, Managing Partner
Jason Fernandez, Managing Partner
Dr Kai Buehler, Managing Partner

1508 QUAKER BIOVENTURES
Cira Centre
2929 Arch Street
Philadelphia, PA 19104-2868

Phone: 215-988-6800 Fax: 215-988-6801
e-mail: info@quakerpartners.com
web: www.quakerbio.com

Mission Statement: A venture capital firm dedicated to investing in life science companies located in the Mid-Atlantic region.

Geographic Preference: United States, Mid-Atlantic
Fund Size: $420 million
Founded: 2003
Average Investment: $5-$20 million
Minimum Investment: $2.5
Investment Criteria: All Stages, Superior Technology, Large market attraction
Industry Group Preference: Life Sciences, Medical Devices, Healthcare, Biopharmaceuticals, Healthcare Services
Portfolio Companies: Achillion, Amicus Therapeutics, Bioleap, Biolex, BioRexis, Celator Pharmaceuticals, Cellatope, Cempra, CorridorPharma, Diasome, DiscoveryLabs, Durata Therapeutics, EKR Therapeutics, Eximias, Horizon Pharma, Insmed, Intact Vascular, MedMark, NB Therapeutics, Neotropix, Neuronetics, NovaSom, NuPathe, New York Digital Health Accelerator, Optherion, Precision Dermatology, Precision Therapeutics, Protez Pharmaceuticals, RainDance Technologies, Regado, RapidMicro Biosystems, Semprae, TargetRx, Tarsa Therapeutics, TearScience, Tengion, TetraLogic, TransEnterix, Tranzyme Pharma

Key Executives:
Brenda D Gavin, Founding Partner
Education: Biology, Baylor University; DVM, University of Missouri; MBA, University of Texas
Background: President, S.R. One; Director of Business Development, SmithKline Beecham Animal Health Products; Epidemiologist, Centers for Disease Control and Prevention
Ira M Lubert, Founding Partner
Education: BS, Pennsylvania State University;
Background: Safeguard Scientifics; Founder, Radnor Venture Partners; Chairman/President, CompuCom Systems; IBM; Principal/Co-Founder, Independence Capital Partners
P Sherrill Neff, Founding Partner
Education: Wesleyan University; University of Michigan Law School
Background: President/CEO/Director, Neose Technologies; Senior VP Corporate Development, U.S. Healthcare; Managing Director, Alex-Brown & Sons; Attorney, Morgan-Lewis & Brockius
Directorships: Amicus Therapeutics; BioRexis; Regado Biosciences; Resource Capital Corporation; Greater Philadelphia Venture Group
Richard S Kollender, Partner
Education: BA, Franklin and Marshall College; MBA, Health Administration & Policy, University of Chicago
Background: GlaxoSmithKline; CPA, KPMG Peat Marwick
Directorships: Transport Pharmaceuticals; TargetRx
Adele C Oliva, Partner
Education: BSc, Finance, St. Joseph University; MBA, Marketing, Cornell University
Background: Partner, Apax Partners; Baxter Healthcare; CoreStates Financial Corp.
Directorships: EKR Therapeutics, NovaSom, Prometheus Labs, Semprea Laboratories

1509 QUALCOMM VENTURES
5775 Morehouse Drive
San Diego, CA 92121-1714

web: www.qualcommventures.com

Mission Statement: Qualcomm Ventures is the investment arm of Qualcomm Inc., a Fortune 500 company with operations across the globe.

Geographic Preference: Worldwide
Fund Size: $100 million
Founded: 2000
Investment Criteria: Early- to Late-Stage
Industry Group Preference: Artificial Intelligence, Automotive, Data Center, Enterprise, Digital Health, IoT, Mobile
Portfolio Companies: Accuvally Inc., AirMap, Airspace Technologies, Airspan, Airstrip, AliveCor, Alo7, Amec, Amionx, Anteryon, Any Vision, AttackIQ, Attune Technologies, Bell Robotics, Bitbar, Bluestacks, Boohee, Borqs, Brain Corporation, Cambridge Wowo, Capillary Technologies, Carbon Robotics, CargoX, Cavendish Kinetics, Chukong Technologies, Clarifi, ClearMotion, Clinitron, CloudFare, Cohesity, Common Sensing, Creatcomm, Cyanogen, Doctor On Demand, Dover Microsystems, Dunamu, Earn, Elevoc, Enovix, Eques, Even, Excelero, FabHotels, Farmeasy, Flirtey, Foneric, Formula E, Gift Talk, Gizwits, goBalto, GouKW, GWC, Hi Technologies, Housejoy, ideaForge, IguanaFix, Ineda Systems, Ingresse, InnoMake, Innovium, inPlug, Jana, JobPlanet, Kaleo, Kneron, Loggi, Lookout, M87, Magic AI, Magic Leap, Magisto, Maketion, Manda^, MangoPlate, Mantis Vision, MapMyIndia, MapR, Matterport, Medisafe, Memblaze, Memed, Meus Pedidos, Microduino, MindTickle, MoveInSync, NeoBear, Ninjacart, Noom, OneWeb, OpenSignal, Particle, Pitch Deck, Portea, PropTiger, Prospera, QuintoAndar, Reach Robotics, RetailNext, Reverie Language Technologies, Ridlr, ScyllaDB, Sense360,

Venture Capital & Private Equity Firms / Domestic Firms

SenseTime, SevenInvensun, SEWORKS, Shadowfax, Siklu, SJ Semi, Skycatch, Sparta Science, Spire, Splacer, Spyce, Steelhouse Stellapps Technologies, Stratoscale, Swift Navigation, TabTale, Tango, Team 8, thatgamecompany, The Void, Tonbo Imaging, Toss Lab, Unisound, Verve, Viva Republica, Voluntis, WebRadar, weka.io, Welltok, Wha Tap, Wiliot, Workspot, XHoogee, XIMMERSE

Other Locations:
Sao Paulo
Brazil

Beijing
China

London
United Kingdom

Bangalore
India

Haifa
Israel

Seoul
Korea

Key Executives:
Quinn Li, Senior Vice President/Global Head
Education: MBA, Cornell University; BS, MS, PhD, Electrical Engineering, Washington University, St. Louis
Background: IBM Systems; Lucent Technologies
Directorships: Airspan, Cohesity, Eero, Innovium, OneWeb, RetailNext, Verve, Zoom
Carlos Kokron, Vice President/Managing Director, North America
Education: BS, MS, Chemical Engineering; MBA, Haas School of Business, UC Berkeley
Background: Director, Intel Capital; Unilever; Unocal 76; Partner, Stratus Group
Directorships: Matterport, Spire, Particle, CargoX, Loggi, Ingresse, WebRadar
James Shen, Vice President/Managing Director, China
Education: BS, Electrical Engineering, Zhejiang University; MS, Communication Management, University of Southern California
Background: Head of QIS China, Qualcomm; GM, Tiani-BREW; Co-Founder, NeTrue Communications; VP, General Photonics
Alexandre Villela, Managing Director, Latin America
Education: BS, Electrical Engineering, UNICAMP; MBA, INSEAD
Background: Intel Capital; Stratus Investimentos; Gradiente Eletr"nica
Jason Ball, Managing Director, Europe/UK
Education: BS, Chemistry, Mississippi College; MBA, ESADE
Background: Investment Director, London Seed Capital
Merav Weinryb, Managing Director, Israel
Education: BSc, Information Systems Engineering, the Technion; MBA, INSEAD
Background: Director, Intel Capital; Principal, Pitango Venture Capital
Directorships: Excelero, Magisto, Mantis Vision, Medisafe, ScyllaDB, Splacer, Stratoscale, Tab Tale, Tapingo, Weka.io, Zeek
Varsha Tagare, Managing Director, India
Education: MS, Electrical Engineering, University of Wisconsin, Madison; BE, Electrical Engineering, University of Bombay
Background: Intel Capital

1510 QUANTUM CAPITAL PARTNERS
1511 North Westshore Blvd.
Sutie 700
Tampa, FL 33607

Phone: 813-280-1720
e-mail: information@quantumcapitalpartners.com
web: www.quantumcapitalpartners.com

Mission Statement: Provides capital for privately owned, rapidly-growing businesses, primarily in the Southeastern United States.
Geographic Preference: Southeastern United States
Founded: 1998
Average Investment: $1 - $5 million
Minimum Investment: $500,000
Investment Criteria: Experience, laterstage, mezzanine
Industry Group Preference: Technology, Retailing, Manufacturing, Service Industries, Hospitals, Financial Services, Wholesale, Business to Business
Key Executives:
Stuart G Lasher, Managing Director
Background: CPA, KPMG Peat Marwick; CFO, Silk Greenhouse Inc; Co-Founder, National Business Solutions
Tyler Lasher, Partner
Education: University of South Florida
Background: Fitlife Foods; Co-Founder, Positive Lifestyle International
William J Schifino Jr, Director
Background: Williams, Reed, Weinstein, Schifino & Mangione P.A.

1511 QUARRY CAPITAL MANAGEMENT
2 Pleasant Street
Natick, MA 01760

Phone: 508-655-3540
web: www.quarrycapital.com

Mission Statement: A private investment firm that specializes in providing capital and/or advisory services to lower middle-market companies.
Geographic Preference: North America
Industry Group Preference: Manufacturing, Distribution, Business Products & Services, Retailing, Healthcare
Portfolio Companies: Royal Pet Supplies
Key Executives:
Brent P Johnstone, Managing Director
e-mail: bjohnstone@quarrycapital.com
Education: BA, Harvard College; MBA, Harvard Business School
Background: Thomson Financial; General Manager, TheMarketsPro; Founder, BulldogResearch.com

1512 QUEEN CITY ANGELS
4555 Lake Forest Drive
Suite 650
Cincinnati, OH 45242

Phone: 513-373-6972
e-mail: info@qca.com
web: www.qca.com

Mission Statement: The Queen City Angels (QCA) is the first group of experienced, accredited investors committed to accelerating the growth of outstanding early-stage businesses in the Cincinnati area and the surrounding region, via smart investments capable of producing a substantial return.
Geographic Preference: Cincinnati & Surrounding Region
Average Investment: $200,000 - $1 million
Investment Criteria: Early-Stage
Industry Group Preference: All Sectors Considered
Portfolio Companies: Akebia Therapeutics, Alliance Business Lending, AssureRx, Bioformix, Business Backers, CHMack, Collabornet, Copper Mountain Beverages, CoupSmart, EndoSphere, Define My Style, Ischemia Care, Miminally Invasive Devices, OnTrak Software, RhinoCyte, Safeway Safety Step, SoMoLend, SonarMed, Spine Form

1513 QUEST VENTURE PARTNERS
Menlo Park, CA

web: www.questvp.com

Venture Capital & Private Equity Firms / Domestic Firms

Mission Statement: Quest Venture Partners believes in entrepreneurism and the magnificent achievements the right team of individuals can accomplish.
Founded: 2007
Average Investment: $100,000 - $1.5 million
Investment Criteria: Early-Stage
Portfolio Companies: 500friends, App.ic, Crowdbooster, CrodFlower, Expect Labs, Genwi, HighlightCam, Ifeelgoods, iSocket, PicCollage, Retailigence, Sociable Labs Stipple, Testmunk, theBouqs.com, Tripping, Whodini
Key Executives:
  Andrew Ogawa, Managing Partner
  e-mail: andrew@questvp.com
  Education: BA, Economics & East Asian Studies, University of California, Santa Barbara; MBA, International Management, Thunderbird
  Background: Manager, Daimler AG
  Directorships: Highlightcam, Fididel
  Marcus Ogawa, Managing Partner
  e-mail: marcus@questvp.com
  Education: BS, Computer Information Systems, Bentley University
  Directorships: Qik, Retailigence, Fididel
  Maarten 't Hooft, Managing Partner
  Background: Google; Android Team, Google; Mercury Software

1514 QUESTA CAPITAL
1156 15th Street NW
Suite 1101
Washington, DC 20005

e-mail: info@questacapital.com
web: www.questacapital.com

Mission Statement: Questa Capital invests and supports outstanding healthcare leaders who are striving to build the next generation of growth companies.
Founded: 1996
Average Investment: $15-40 million
Investment Criteria: Sectors: Healthcare Services, Healthcare Technology and Medical Devices
Other Locations:
  274 Brannan Street
  San Francisco, CA 94107
Key Executives:
  Ryan Drant, Founder/Managing Partner
  Education: BA, Stanford University
  Background: General Partner, New Enterprise Associates; Health Care Investment Banking Group
  Bradley Sloan, Founder/Managing Partner
  Education: BA, University of North Carolina
  Background: Senior Investment Professional, Parthenon Capital; Broadlane Inc.; Evercore Partners; MTS Health Partners

1515 QUESTMARK PARTNERS LP
2850 Quarry Lake Drive
Suite 301
Baltimore, MD 21209

web: www.questm.com

Mission Statement: Invest in emerging growth companies with exceptional management teams and proven products and services.
Geographic Preference: United States
Fund Size: $750 million
Founded: 1998
Average Investment: $5 - $15 million
Minimum Investment: $5 million
Investment Criteria: Late Stage growth companies in emerging markets
Industry Group Preference: Software, Medical Devices, E-Commerce & Manufacturing, Healthcare, Consumer Services
Portfolio Companies: Adara, Applause, Courion, Discover Books, Guavus, IntegenX, iStreamPlanet, Kodiak Networks, NComputing, Overture Networks, ServiceMax, Taulia, Teladoc, TrialPay, Vapotherm, Vidyo, Virtustream, Xirrus
Key Executives:
  Benjamin Schapiro, Founder/Partner
  410-895-5811
  Fax: 410-895-5808
  e-mail: bschapiro@questm.com
  Education: Economics, Randolph-Macon College
  Background: Alex Brown & Sons
  Directorships: Align, Aspect Medical, eHealthinsurance, Tisslink, Zaplet
  Mike Ward, Partner
  Education: Northwestern University; MBA, Harvard Business School
  Background: Management Consultant, Boston Consulting Group
  Directorships: Vapotherm, MedManage Systems

1516 QUILVEST PRIVATE EQUITY
527 Madison Avenue
11th Floor
New York, NY 10022

Phone: 212-920-3800 **Fax:** 212-920-3850
web: www.quilvestprivateequity.com

Mission Statement: Quilvest Private Equity, with nearly 100 seasoned professionals, offers sd independent, and global private equity and real estate solutions to private investors, families, and institutions around the world. During the past four decades, Quilvest Private Equity has invested approximately $5B in over 300 private equity and real estate funds and 150 direct investments and remains dedicated to leveraging the experience, insights, and resources of the Quilvest Group to achieve superior returns.
Geographic Preference: Worldwide
Fund Size: $5 billion
Founded: 2002
Industry Group Preference: Real Estate, Emerging Markets, Sectors & Technologies
Portfolio Companies: Alliant Group, Metro Franchising, SMI, Aminoagro, Gamo, BCI Broadband, Poof-Slinky, FCI, Towry, The Chia Co., BuzzParadise, Deltek, P.F. Chang's, Acrotec, Wholesome Sweetners, Schur Flexible, ThermaSys, Anthony's Pizza, Tortilla, Photobox, Appirio, STP, Del Monte Foods, Findis, Matthews, Tiway Oil, Multiplan, Net4, Vanksen, Neotract, Laney Drilling, Performance Food Group, Royalty Pharma, Yo! Sushi, RTS, 5aSec, Pay-O-Matic, SKS, Marco Aldany, Ubique, Intrinsic, OSI, BJB Education/Jade, IGPS, Intarcia, Masterskill, Nocibe, Kadent/Landau, Hill and Valley, Command Alkon, Innate Pharma, Tiendas 3B, Myriad, Pashas
Key Executives:
  Benton Cummings, Partner
  Education: BA, History, Dartmouth College; MBA, Kenan-Flagler Business School
  Background: Managing Director, Prospect Capital; Managing Director, Allied Capital
  Henrik Falktoft, Partner
  Education: MBA, Harvard Business School
  Background: Morgan Stanley, ZS Fund, Deutsche Bank
  Carlos Heneine, Partner/Senior Executive Officer, Quilvest Dubai
  Education: BS, Aeronautical Engineering, Imperial College of Science & Technology, London University; MBA, INSEAD
  Background: British Aerospace/BAE Systems; Consultant, Booz Allen & Hamilton; Mercer Management; Head of Strategy, Banque Sarador

Venture Capital & Private Equity Firms / Domestic Firms

Michele Kinner, Partner
Education: AB, Economics & Psychology, Smith College; MBA, Whittemore School, University of New Hampshire
Background: Royal Bank of Canada; JPMorgan Chase; Chase Alternative Asset Management
Marc Manasterski, Partner
Education: HND, Marketing, College of the Distributive Trades; MBA, INSEAD
Background: CEO, Alliance Hospitality Group; Real Estate Development
Lawrence Neubauer, Partner
Education: AB, Woodrow Wilson School, Princeton University; JD, MBA, University of Chicago
Background: Centre Partners; Founding Member, Malakand Capital; SG Capital Partners; White & Case; Bankers Trust Company; U.S. Department of Commerce, The White House
Jean-Francois Le Ruyet, Partner
Education: HEC; MBA, Columbia Business School
Background: Senior Associate Consultant, Bain & Company; Junior Engagement Manager, McKinsey & Company
Maninder Saluja, Partner
Education: BBA, Finance, University of Michigan; MBA, Harvard Business School
Background: Alvarez & Marsal; DLJ

1517 QUINBROOK INFRASTRUCTURE PARTNERS
1330 Post Oak Blvd
Suite 1350
Houston, TX 77056

web: www.quinbrook.com

Mission Statement: Investors in low carbon and renewable energy infrastructure.
Geographic Preference: North America, UK, Australia
Average Investment: $25-150 million
Industry Group Preference: Low Carbon and Renewable Energy Infrastructure
Portfolio Companies: Cape byron Power, Energy Trade, Gemini Solar and Battery Storage Project, Glidepath Power Solutions, Lockyer, Scout Clean Energy, Velox Power

Other Locations:
53/54 Grosvenor Street
5th Floor
London W1K 3HU
United Kingdom
Phone: 44 207 818 8600

Suite 1.303
15-21 Via Roma
Isle of Capri, Queensland 4217
Australia
Phone: 61 7 5592 6669

Key Executives:
David Scaysbrook, Co-Founder & Managing Partner
Education: University of Sydney
Rory Quinlan, Co-Founder & Managing Partner
Education: Queensland University of Technology

1518 QUOTIDIAN VENTURES
New York, NY 10010

e-mail: hi@quotidian.co
web: www.quotidianventures.com

Mission Statement: Quotidian Ventures is a seed to early-stage investment fund that invests in great visionaries building global companies whose services we want to incorporate into our everyday life.
Founded: 2010
Average Investment: $100,000 - $200,000
Investment Criteria: Early-Stage, Seed-Stage
Industry Group Preference: Digital Media & Marketing, Entertainment, Advertising, Mobile, E-Commerce & Manufacturing, Publishing
Portfolio Companies: Admitted.ly, Artsicl, Amicus, Adcade, August, Bench, Brass Monkey, BringMeThat, Circa, Clip, Clothia, Comprehend, Disruption, Docracy, FaithStreet, FieldLens, Idea.me, IMRSV, Keychain Logistics, Knodes, Launchrock, Loverly, Matchbook, Memoir, Moveline, Nestio, PaintZen, SmartAsset, SmileBack, SponsorHub, SupplyHog, Tagstand, Tapad, Thinkful, Thinkup, Versa, Videolicious, Wallaby, WePow, YesGraph, Zerply

Key Executives:
Pedro Torres Picon, Managing Director

1519 RA CAPITAL MANAGEMENT
20 Park Plaza
Suite 1200
Boston, MA 02116

Phone: 617-778-2500
web: www.racap.com

Mission Statement: RA Capital Management invests in public and private healthcare and life science companies that are developing medications, devices, and diagnostics. RA Capital has a flexible approach and invests at multiple stages.
Industry Group Preference: Healthcare, Drug Development, Life Sciences, Medical Devices, Diagnostics
Portfolio Companies: 89bio, Aclaris Therapeutics, Adeo Health Science, Aeglea Biotherapeutics, Aimmune Therapeutics, Agrimetis, Akouos, Arvinas, Ascendis Pharma, Attune Pharmaceuticals, Audentes, Avexis, Bellicum Pharmaceuticals, Biohaven Pharmaceuticals, Black Diamond Therapeutics, BlueBirdBio, Blueprint Medicines, Braeburn, CalmImmune, Carnot, Cidara Therapeutics, Civitas Therapeutics, Clementia, Coherus Biosciences, Collegium Pharmaceutical, Crinetics, Dicerna, Dimension Therapeutics, Eidos, Eiger Biopharmaceuticals, Expansion Therapeutics, G1 Therapeutics, Galera Therapeutics, GBT, Imbria Pharmaceuticals, InflaRx, InhibRx, Intarcia, Ivantis, Juno Therapeutics, Kala Pharmaceuticals, KalVista, Lantos Technologies, Lumena Pharmaceuticals, Lyra Therapeutics, Medeor Therapeutics, Merus, Mitra Biotech, Moderna, Natera, Nivalis, Orchard Therapeutics, Ova Science, Precision Biosciences, Prevail Therapeutics, Protagonist Therapeutics, RaPharma, Reneo, RxSight, Satsuma, SeluxDx, Seres Therapeutics, Shockwave Medical, Sierra Oncology, Solid Biosciences, Sojournix, Spero Therapeutics, Stoke Therapeutics, SynthOrx, Taris, Terapore, Theriana Pharmaceuticals, Vella, Versartis, ViaCyte, Wave Life Sciences, WhiteSwell, Xenikos, Zafgen, ZS Pharma

Key Executives:
Peter Kolchinsky, Portfolio Manager/Managing Director
Education: BS, Cornell University; PhD, Virology, Harvard University
Directorships: Dicerna Pharmaceuticals, Wave Life Sciences
Rajeev Shah, Portfolio Manager/Managing Director
Education: BA, Cornell University
Background: Senior Project Leader, Altus Pharmaceuticals
Andrew Levin, Managing Director
Education: BSE, Princeton University; PhD, MIT; MD, Harvard Medical School
Background: Vice President, H.I.G. BioVentures
Josh Resnick, Managing Director
Education: BA, Williams College; MD; University of Pennsylvania; MBA, Wharton School
Background: President & Managing Partner, MRL Ventures Fund; Venture Partner, Atlas Venture; Partner, Prism Venture Partners

Venture Capital & Private Equity Firms / Domestic Firms

1520 RADIUS VENTURES
680 Fifth Avenue
Suite 1202
New York, NY 10019

web: www.radiusventures.com

Mission Statement: Radius Ventures is a venture capital firm that invests exclusively in leading edge healthcare companies. Radius searches for the winners of tomorrow - entrepreneurs whose ideas and talents qualify them to pursue large market opportunities successfully.

Fund Size: $200 million
Founded: 1997
Average Investment: $5-10 million
Investment Criteria: Mid-Late Stage
Industry Group Preference: Healthcare
Portfolio Companies: Aethon, Ambit Biosciences, Amicus Therapeutics, Athersys, BioStorage Technologies, Carekinesis, EndoGastric Solutions, Esionic, Healthsense, Management Health Solutions, Minimally Invasive Devices, Nugen Technologies, Tactile Systems Technology

Key Executives:
  Jordan S Davis, Managing Partner
  Education: MBA, JL Kellogg Graduate School; BA, State University of New York
  Background: Managing Director, KBL Healthcare Acquisition Corporation; Private Client Services, Morgan Stanley;
  Directorships: Health Language
  Daniel C Lubin, Managing Partner
  Education: BS Foreign Service, Georgetown University; MBA, Harvard Business School
  Background: Director/Investment Banking Division, Schroder Wertheim & Company; Co-Founder/Managing Director, KBL Healthcare; Lending Officer, International Division, Manufacturers Hanover Trust
  Directorships: Management Health Solutions, Healthsense
  George M Milne, Jr. PhD, Venture Partner
  Education: BS, Yale University; PhD, MIT
  Background: Executive Vice President, Pfizer
  Directorships: Mettler-Toledo, Inc.; MedImmune, Inc.; Charles River Laboratories, Inc.; Athersys, Inc.; Mystic Aquarium-Institute for Exploration; New York Botanical Gardens; BioStorage Tech
  Vincent S Conti, Venture Partner
  Background: President & CEO, Maine Medical Center; Board of Trustees, Dartmouth-Hitchcock Medical Center & Health System
  Directorships: Healthscan
  James M Mead, Venture Partner
  Education: BS & MA, Penn State University
  Background: Vice Chairman, BOD BlueCross Blue Shield Association; President & CEO, BlueCross Blue Shield Association
  Directorships: Hershey Trust, Vitality Group LLC, Lebanon Valley College, Management Health Solutions, Milton Hershey School, Milton S Hershey Foundation, Greater Harrisburg Foundation
  Neenah Jain, Chief Financial Officer
  Education: BA, Southern Methodist University
  Background: Senior Associate, Pricewaterhouse Coopers LLP; Controller, Capital Analytics

1521 RAF INDUSTRIES
50 Momentum Road
Suite 303
Bala Cynwyd, PA 19004

Phone: 215-572-0738 Fax: 215-576-1640
e-mail: acquisitions@rafind.com
web: www.rafind.com

Mission Statement: Acquires and operates a diversified group of middle market manufacturing companies located across the United States. Our acquisition focus is on Giftware and Promotional Products, Industrial Products and Building and D-I-Y Products. RAF Ventures invests in early-stage companies with unique niche products.

Geographic Preference: United States
Founded: 1979
Average Investment: $500,000-$5 million
Minimum Investment: $250,000
Investment Criteria: Early-stage, Unique products, Strong management
Industry Group Preference: Computer Related, Consumer Products, Electronic Components, Instrumentation, Industrial Equipment, Equipment, Medical & Health Related, Manufacturing
Portfolio Companies: Earth Tech, Geo-Solutions, American Millwork Corporation, Ferche Millwork, Materials Marketing, Steamist, U.S. Tape, Freedom Medical, Pine Environmental Services, Technical Gas Products, Campania International, Lazart Production, Cool Gear International, Thirstystone Resources, Bar-Plate Manufacturing, Disston Precision, MILSPRAY Military Technologies

Key Executives:
  Robert A Fox, Chairman/CEO
  Education: BS, Economics, University of Pennsylvania
  Background: CEO, Warner Company
  Directorships: InPhonic, Inc.; Wistar Institute; Foreign Policy Research Institute
  Richard M Horowitz, President/COO
  Education: JD, Harvard Law School; BA, Economics & Political Science, University of Pennsylvania
  Background: Wolf, Block, Schorr and Solis-Cohen Law Firm
  Directorships: Children's Crisis Treatment Center; Wistar Institute; UPenn's Center for Community Partnerships
  Michael F Daly, VP/CFO
  Education: MBA, BS, Business Management, Temple University
  Background: CPA, Laventhol & Horwath
  Andrew Souder, VP, Acquistions
  Education: JD, Villanova University; MM, JL Kellogg Graduate School of Management; BBA, University of Notre Dame
  Background: Corporate Law, Reed Smith Shaw McClay; Corporate Banking, Continental Bank NA

1522 RALLY VENTURES
702 Oak Grove Avenue
Menlo Park, CA 94025

Phone: 650-854-1200
web: www.rallyventures.com

Mission Statement: Rally Ventures is a venture capital firm focused on investing in early-stage companies in the business technology industry.

Fund Size: $100 million
Founded: 2012
Investment Criteria: Early Stage
Industry Group Preference: Business Technology, Enterprise Software
Portfolio Companies: 9Lenses, Appboy, Atlantis Computing, Backtrace, Badgeville, Beckon, Bugcrowd, Cloud Elements, Corvil, Coupa, DecisionNext, Edgewater Networks, Elevate, GutCheck, HiveIO, InsideTrack, Joyent, Kapta, Lithium, LockPath, Qubell, ReadyPulse, Sport Ngin, Sqrrl, VentureBeat, VisiTrend, Zipongo

Other Locations:
  100 Washington Avenue S
  Suite 1310
  Minneapolis, MN 55401
  Phone: 952-995-7450

Key Executives:
  Charles Beeler, Managing Director
  e-mail: charles@rallyventures.com
  Education: BA, Colby College; MBA, Wharton School, University of Pennsylvania
  Background: General Partner, El Dorado Ventures;

Venture Capital & Private Equity Firms / Domestic Firms

Scripps Ventures; Piper Jaffray
Directorships: Atlantis Computing, Backtrace, Bugcrowd, Coupa, Joyent, Luxury Link, Qubell, Ready Pulse, Camp Chippewa Foundation
Jeff Hinck, Managing Director
e-mail: jeff@rallyventures.com
Education: BA, Economics, Northwestern University; JD, Harvard Law School
Background: General Partner, El Dorado Ventures; McKinsey & Company; Crescendo Ventures; CEO, Sistina Software
Directorships: Cloud Elements, Elevate, GutCheck, LockPath, Sport Ngin
Zenas Hutcheson, Venture Partner
e-mail: zenas@rallyventures.com
Background: Co-Founder, Vesbridge Partners; Co-Managing Partner, SPVC; CEO, Vivo Networks; CAECO; Control Automation
Directorships: Corvil, Kwicr, TA Labs, Visitrend, SaltDNA
Tom Peterson, Venture Partner
e-mail: tom@rallyventures.com
Background: Union Venture Corp.; El Dorado Ventures
Directorships: Appboy, Badgeville, Edgewater Networks, InsideTrack
Stephanie McCoy, Chief Financial Officer
e-mail: stephanie@rallyventures.com
Education: BA, Business & Accounting, University of St. Thomas
Background: PricewaterhouseCoopers; Crescendo Ventures; Decathlon Capital Partners

1523 RAND CAPITAL CORPORATION
2200 Rand Building
Buffalo, NY 14203

Phone: 716-853-0802 **Fax:** 716-854-8480
web: www.randcapital.com

Mission Statement: The primary focus of our investment strategy is to provide venture capital funds to small- to mid-sized companies headquartered in the Western and Upstate New York region.
Geographic Preference: Western & Upstate New York
Fund Size: $20 million
Founded: 1969
Average Investment: $50,000-$5 million
Investment Criteria: Private held companies, Unique or possess proprietary right (s), Membership on the company's Board of Directors, Duration of investment from 3-5 years
Industry Group Preference: Healthcare, Technology, Communications, Industrial Services
Portfolio Companies: BinOptics, Carolina Skiff, Chequed.com, First Wave Products Group, Gemcor II, G-TEC Natural Gas Systems, Knoa Software, Mercantile Adjustment Bureau, Mezmeriz, Microcision, QuaDPharma, Rheonix, SocialFlow, Somerset Gas Transmission Company, SOMS Technologies, Synacor
Key Executives:
  Allen F Grum, President & CEO
  Education: BA, Eisenhower College; MBA, Rochester Institute of Technology
  Background: Executive VP, Hamilton Financial Corporation; Senior VP, Marine Midland Mortgage Corporation
  Margaret Whalen Brechtel, Vice President, Finance
  Education: BS, MBA, State University of New York, Buffalo
  Background: Operations Finance Manager, Cellular One
  Daniel P Penberthy, CFO/Executive Vice President
  Education: MBA, State University of New Yor, Buffalo
  Background: CFO, Greater Buffalo Partnership; Greater Buffalo Convention and Visitors Bureau; Senior Associate, Greater Buffalo Development Foundation; KPMG

1524 RAPTOR GROUP
401 W 14th Street
4th Floor
New York, NY 10014

Phone: 212-266-6900
web: www.raptorgroup.com

Mission Statement: Raptor Group is the venture capital arm of Raptor Capital Management LP. Partners with and deploy capital to early-stage, market disrupting technology and media companies to build the next generation of market leaders.
Investment Criteria: Early-Stage
Industry Group Preference: Technology, Media, Music, Advertising, Branded Goods, E-Commerce & Manufacturing, Digital Media & Marketing, Broadcasting, Sports, Gaming, Social Media, Travel & Leisure, Hospitality, Entertainment
Portfolio Companies: AS Roma, Boston Celtics, Raptor Sports Properties, Blue Bottle, FIGS, Hulafrog, Julep, Moven, Narragansett Beer, Nic and Zoe, Normal, Quirky, Room77, Reebok Spartan Race, Twine Health, Unreal Candy, Yasso, Zhena's, Airbnb, Artsy, Backplane, Biobeats, Bluefin Labs, Datapop, Depict, E 1023, The Echonest, Fliptop, General Assembly, GraphScience, IfOnly, Krush, Layer Vault, Magnitude Software, Matter, Media Spike, Metamarkets, NumberFire, Openbay, Open Sky, PlaceIQ, Qualia, Securitypoint Media, Velos, Sonic Notify, Spongecell, Spotify, Fancy, Ticket Evolution, Twitter, Uber, Workpop
Other Locations:
  280 Congress Street
  12th Floor
  Boston, MA 02210
  Phone: 617-772-4600
Key Executives:
  James J Pallotta, Chairman/Managing Director
  Education: BBA, Finance, University of Massachusetts; MBA, Northeastern University
  Background: Essex Investment Management Company, Tudor Investment Management
  Directorships: Boston Celtics, AS Roma
  Harry DeMott, Managing Director
  Education: BS, Economics, Princeton University; MBA, Stern School of Business
  Background: Founder, Gothic Capital Management; King Street Capital Management; Knighthead Capital Management

1526 RAYMOND JAMES CAPITAL
Phone: 727-567-5066
e-mail: cindy.ford@raymondjames.com
web: www.raymondjames.com/ecm/rjcapital

Mission Statement: Raymond James Capital is the private equity subsidiary of Raymond James Financial.
Average Investment: $15 - $50 million
Investment Criteria: Recapitalizations, Management-Led Buyouts
Industry Group Preference: Consumer Products, Energy, Financial Services, Healthcare, Manufacturing
Portfolio Companies: Albion Medical Holdings, Event Photography Group, Sirchie Fingerprint Laboratories, Gabriel Logan, HVT Group, Southern Assisted Living, Souther Lithoplate
Key Executives:
  David E Thomas Jr, Managing Director
  Education: University of Richmond; JD, MBA, Emory University
  Background: Chairman & CEO, Safety-Kleen Corp.; Head of Investment Banking, Raymond James Financial
  Directorships: Albion Medical Holdings, Event Photography, Sirchie Acquisition Company
  Gene J Ostrow, Managing Director
  Education: University of Albany
  Background: CFO, NationsRent; CFO, OHM Corp.; Senior Manager, KPMG

Venture Capital & Private Equity Firms / Domestic Firms

Directorships: Albion Medical Holdings, Event Photography Group, Sirchie Acquistion Company

1527 REACH CAPITAL
Palo Alto, CA

web: reachcapital.com

Mission Statement: Reach Capital invests in technology that helps improve classroom learning, digital learning, and takes education to new heights.

Founded: 2015
Industry Group Preference: Technology, Applications, Software, Education, Digital Learning
Portfolio Companies: Abl, AdmitHub, Atlas, Aura, Betterlesson, Bitwise Industries, BookNook, Breathe for Change, ClassDojo, Collegebacker, Crash, Desmos, Ellevation, Epic, eSpark Learning, Frank, Freshgrade, Future Fuel, Gradescope, GradeSlam, Handshake, Holberton, Hone, InClassToday, Kaymbu, Kickup, LAB4U, Lightneer, Lingokids, Lovevery, Mathpix, Mrs Wordsmith, Mystery Science, Nearpod, Newsela, Outschool, Padlet, PeopleGrove, Piper, Replit, Riipen, SchoolMint, Schoolzilla, Stellic, Sunlight, TeachFX, The Podcast App, Tinkergarten, Tynker, Winnie, WriteLab

Key Executives:
Jennifer Carolan, General Partner
Education: BA, Loyola University of Chicago; MA, Stanford University
Background: Managing Director of Seed Fund, NewSchools Ventures Fund
Directorships: Equal Opportunity Schools; Education Elements; Bullis Charter School; WriteLab; Nearpod; EdSurge; BetterLesson; FreshGrade; PeopleGrove; Outschool; Ellevation Education
Shauntel Garvey, General Partner
Education: BS, Chemical Engineering, MIT; MEd, Stanford Grad. School of Education; MBA, Stanford Grad. School of Business
Background: Senior Engineer, Procter & Gamble; Partner, NewSchools Venture Fund
Directorships: Tales2Go; Schoolzilla; Abl; Holberton School; Riipen
Wayee Chu, General Partner
Education: BA, University of Michigan
Background: Financial Analyst, Morgan Stanley; Assistant VP, Merrill Lynch; Director of Finance, Lifestyle Media; Co-Founder, NewSchools Seed Fund
Directorships: Wishbone.org
Esteban Sosnik, General Partner
Education: BA, University of Virginia
Background: Analyst, JP Morgan; Associate, Innova Capital; CEO, Penguin Holdings; Co-Founder/CEO, Wanako Games; VP of Business Development, Vivendi; Co-Founder/CEO, Atakama Labs; VP, DeNa; Executive Director, co.lab
Directorships: Farmacity SA

1528 RECIPROCAL VENTURES
100 Crosby Street
Suite 605
New York, NY 10012

e-mail: info@recinv.com
web: recvc.com

Mission Statement: A venture capital fund interested in tech-based companies.

Geographic Preference: US, Canada, UK
Average Investment: Up to $3 million
Investment Criteria: Seed, Early Stage
Industry Group Preference: Infrastructure, Software, Technology, Consumer, FinTech
Portfolio Companies: Baton, Extend, Fanbank, The Graph, Mindbridge, Qwil, Radar Relay, Tallarium, TradeIt

Key Executives:
Michael Steinberg, Managing Partner
Education: BA, University of Wisconsin
Background: Portfolio Manager, SAC Capital Management
Josh Kuzon, Managing Partner
Education: BS, Lehigh University
Background: Silicon Valley Bank; JP Morgan
Craig Bural, Partner
Education: Lafayette College
Background: FiscalNote; Morgan Stanley

1529 RED CLAY CAPITAL HOLDINGS
1401 Peachtree Street
Suite 500
Atlanta, GA 30309-3142

Phone: 615-697-9144
e-mail: info@redclaycapital.com
web: redclaycapital.com

Mission Statement: A private investment firm focused on investing in and supporting the long-term development of growth-stage companies.

Geographic Preference: Southeastern US
Investment Criteria: Large Business (Fortune 1000); Government (Federal, State or Local; Revenue of $10 million to $50 million
Industry Group Preference: Manufacturing, Transportation, Infrastructure, B2B, Distribution Services
Portfolio Companies: Gray Line of Tennessee, Knowledge Architechts

Other Locations:
3200 West End Avenue
Suite 500
Nashville, TN 37203
Phone: 615-212-9136

Key Executives:
C Mark Arnold, Partner
e-mail: marnold@redclaycapital.com
Education: BA, Brown University; MM, Finance, Northwestern University
Background: VP of Operations, Gray Line of Tennessee; Founder/Chair, Nuestro Bano; Exec Dir. of Corp Development, BellSouth Corporation
H Beecher Hicks, III, Partner
e-mail: hhicks@redclaycapital.com
Education: BA, Marketing, Morehouse College; MBA, Finance, University of North Carolina
Background: Operating Principal, Onyx Capital Ventures; Investment Banker, Bank of America; Former White House Fellow
H Bryan Britt, Principal
e-mail: bbritt@redclaycapital.com
Education: BBA, Clark Atlanta University
Background: Analyst, Wachovia Securities; Member, Loan Syndications Group, Regions Capital Markets

1530 RED SEA VENTURES
120 East 23rd Street
New York, NY 10010

e-mail: hello@redseaventures.com
web: redseaventures.com

Mission Statement: A venture capital firm investing in early-stage startups focused on innovative technology.

Geographic Preference: New York
Founded: 2013
Investment Criteria: Early-Stage
Industry Group Preference: Technology
Portfolio Companies: Allbirds, Alwaysprepped, Ample Hills Creamery, Back To The Roots, Buster, Casetext, Convoy, Eargo, Elite Daily, Fabric, Fancy, FeVo, Fly, Genies, Goby, Insidehack, JanusRV, Joor, LeagueApps, Nest, Nucleus, Outdoor Voices, The Outline, Paintzen, Get Point, Prose,

541

Venture Capital & Private Equity Firms / Domestic Firms

SkySafe, Smart Vision Labs, Solid X Partners Inc., Sweet Green, Tracksmith, Splash, Universal Standard, Violet Grey, Way Up, Zipdrug

Key Executives:
   Scott Birnbaum, Founder
   Education: Georgetown University; Fordham University Law School
   Background: Co-Founder, EPOL; Corporate Attorney, White & Case; Strategy & Business Development, CBS Local
   Directorships: Peace
   Jason Fiedler, Principal
   Education: BA, Economics, University of Pennsylvania
   Background: Co-Founder, Splash.FM; Uber
   Paul Strachman, Venture Partner
   Education: BS, MS, Engineering, Ecole des Points et Chausees, France; MS, Finance & Economics, London School of Economics; MBA, Stanford Grad. School of Business
   Background: Bain & Co.; Equinox

1531 RED SWAN VENTURES

Mission Statement: Red Swan invests in entrepreneurs who delight customers, create culture, and disrupt industries.

Portfolio Companies: Bonobos, Oscar, Birchbox, Warby Parker, Hailo, Wanelo, Floored, Scopely, Coinbase, RJMetrics, Harry's, Chloe + Isabel, TaskRabbit, 42 Floors, Matterport, Days, Grovo, Sunglass, Weddington Way, ID.me, Modern Meadow, AidIn, Thanx, RelayRides, SeatGeek, Help, OrderAhead, Betterment, Keychain Logistics, Whistle, Nomi, Cabify, Trumaker, Artivest, Cover, LayerVault, Evertrue, Spree Commerce, Hinge, Cambrian Genomics, PolicyMic, Building Robotics, Hightower, AltSchool

Key Executives:
   Andy Dunn, Managing Director
   Dave Eisenberg, General Partner
   Chris Travers, General Partner

1532 REDHILLS VENTURES
PO Box 370369
Las Vegas, NV 89137-0369

Phone: 702-233-2160
e-mail: info@redhillsventures.com
web: www.redhillsventures.com

Mission Statement: To work with healthcare companies that clearly exhibit high growth potential.

Average Investment: $250,000 - $7 million
Industry Group Preference: Healthcare
Portfolio Companies: Adore Me, Communication Science, Global Medical Isotope Systems, Health Data Insights, Health Data Vision Inc., Intellicare, ItsMyNews, Ozonator, SimSuite, Trustifi, Velos

Key Executives:
   Victor Chaltiel, Founder
   e-mail: vchaltiel@redhillsventures.com
   Education: Ecole Superieure des Sciences Economiques et Commercials; MBA, Harvard Business School
   Background: Chairman & CEO, Total Renal Care Holdings; Chairman & CEO, Total Pharmaceutical Care; Baster International
   Antoinette "Toni" Chaltiel, Founder/Manager
   Education: Dublin City University
   Background: President, Total Insurance and Planning Corporation

1533 REDMONT VENTURE PARTNERS
820 Shades Creek Parkway
Suite 1200
Birmingham, AL 35209

web: www.redmontcapital.com

Mission Statement: A private equity firm providing capital for early-stage and expansion stage opportunities.
Geographic Preference: Southeastern United States
Investment Criteria: Early-Stage, Expansion-Stage
Industry Group Preference: Business Products & Services, Financial Services, Healthcare, Information Technology, Industrial Manufacturing
Portfolio Companies: Aero-Mark MRO, America Rotor Company, Atherotech, Chlorogen, ContinuumRx, Emageon, Entegreat, FreeTextbooks.Com, High Ground Solutions, Hoffman Media, Locox, Ocera Therapeutics, Optimal IMX, Pennant Sp, PeopleTec, Reliant Medical Products, Source Medical, Vaxin, Wadley Crushed Stone Company, Water Science Technologies

Key Executives:
   Roddy JH Clark, Partner Emeritus
   e-mail: rclark@redmontvp.com
   Education: BA, Political Science & History, Mercer University
   Background: American Hospital Supply Corporation, Medfusion, Norell Healthcare, Horizon Medical Products, Myelotec, Gynecare
   Directorships: Emageon, Folia, Reliant Medical Products, Chlorogen
   Philip L Hodges, Managing Partner
   e-mail: phodges@redmontvp.com
   Education: BS, Business Administration, Samford University
   Background: HealthSouth, Tubular Products Corporation, Atherotech
   Directorships: American Legal Search, EnteGreat, Vaxin
   Doug Sellers, Partner
   Education: BS, Commerce & Business Administration, University of Alabama
   Background: Co-Founder/EVP/CFO, Merchant Capital
   Directorships: Children's Harbor; Brantwood Children's Home; American Red Cross of Central Alabama

1534 REDPOINT VENTURES
3000 Sand Hill Road
Building 2
Suite 290
Menlo Park, CA 94025

Phone: 650-926-5600 Fax: 650-854-5762
web: www.redpoint.com

Mission Statement: Redpoint Ventures takes a three-tiered approach to starting businesses that bring value to young companies at every level.
Founded: 1999
Investment Criteria: Early Stage
Industry Group Preference: Communications, Enterprise Services, Storage, Mobile Communications Devices, Internet Technology, Infrastructure, Wireless Technologies, Software
Portfolio Companies: LaunchDarkly, Light Step, AppZen, TruSignal, Gigster, Bright Health, Essential Products, Cockroach Labs, RaiseMe, Astro, Chorus, Sentinel One, Nubank, Brandless, Sourcegraph, HashiCorp, Guild, Clara, Flexe, Justworks, Lifesize, Eero, Dremio, Duo Security, Collective Health, Nextdoor, Spring Path, Button Inc., Tenor, LuxeValet, Snowflake Computing, Vurb, Platform9, Victorious, Yunshan Networks, BitGo, RenRench.com, Just Eat, DraftKings, PocketGems, Qwilt, Caspida, RelateIQ, Pindrop Security, Apus, Tact.ai, Memoir, Acompli, Arista, Igneous, Refresh, 9Tong, Jauni, Bangcle, Looker, 117go.com, Lastline, Scripted, Twilio, Wochit, Curious.com, Bingdian, PSafe, Artic Wolf, Cyanogen, Pulse, Big Switch Networks, Zendesk, Tastemade, Sonos, IDreamSky, Open English, Stripe, Electric Imp, Axial, LoopNet, QuantiFind, Yixia, Moogsoft, Apple Toon, Trip.com, Intent Media, Mapr, Pure Storage, ThredUp, IntoNow, Viajanet.com.br, MMC Networks, Concur, Zuora, Xango, BlueFin Labs, Kabam, Machinima, Peel, Expensify, Miaozhen Systems, Posterous Spaces, Erply, Extole, Datameer, Tantalus, CouchDB Relax,

Venture Capital & Private Equity Firms / Domestic Firms

2U, Storsimple, NextG Networks, Gravity, Auditude, Internet Brands, Clicker, Cloud.com, Answers.com, Impact Radius, Heroku, BlueKai, True X Media, Hark, eBureau, FraudSciences, Adap.tv, Scribd., Innofidei, Qihoo 360, Fan.tv, KaDang, Gaia Online, Clearwell, Cgen, Jumptap, WiChorus, Right Media, Myspace, HomeAway, Intermolecular, Amec, Lead Point, Mobitv Inc., Zimbra, BCD Semiconductor, EfficientFrontier,

Other Locations:
21 South Park
Suite 100
San Francisco, CA 94107

1539 Nanjin Road West
Kerry Center, Tower 2
Suite 1801
Shanghai 200040
China
Phone: 86-21-6288-7757 **Fax:** 86-21-6288-7797

79 Jianguo Road
Hua Mao Center, Tower 2
9th Floor
Beijing 100025
China

Diamond Tower, Rue Joaquim Floriano
1120A, cj.92
Itaim Bibi
Sao Paulo, SP 04534-004
Brazil

Key Executives:
Allen Beasley, Partner
Education: BA, Stanford University; MBA, Stanford Graduate School of Business
Background: Ipsilon Networks; Synopsys; Alex Brown & Sons
Directorships: Amp'd Mobile; OuterBay; Orbital Data; AirPlay; eNet
Jeff Brody, Founding Partner
Education: BS Engineering, University of California; MBA, Stanford School of Business
Background: General Partner, Brentwood Venture Capital; Comdisco Venture Leasing; Associate, Crosspoint Venture Partners; Schlumberger
Directorships: Anger, ePeople, Lets Talk, Loopnet, KMV, Kodiak
Tim Haley, Founding Partner
Education: BA, Philosophy, Santa Clara University
Background: Principal, Haley Associates
Directorships: Homestead Technologies, Movaris, M7, Netflix, Reflect.com
Tom Dyal, Founding Partner
Education: BS Electrical Engineering, Georgia Institute of Technology; MS Electrical Engineering, Stanford University
Background: Product Management, Bay Networks; Systems Engineer, AT&T Bell Laboraotories;
Directorships: Cortina Systems, Santera Systems, TopSpin Communications, Velio Communications, Vivace Network Tellabs
Chris Moore, Partner
Education: BA, Mathematics/Economics, Dartmouth College; MBA, Stanford School of Business
Background: IVP, Business Development, wine.com; Management, Peapod; Ameritech; Financial Analyst, Wasserstein Perella & Co
Scott Raney, Partner
Education: BSEE, Duke University; MBA, Harvard Business School
Background: Senior Managing Partner, New Products/NorthPoint; Management Consultant, Bain & Company; Director Engineering, VideoPort Technologies; Advanced Technology Group, Andersen Consulting
John Walecka, Founding Partner
Education: BS, MS Engineering, Stanford University; MBA, Stanford University Graduate School of Business
Background: Director, Western Association of Venture Capitalists; Director, Stanford Business School Venture Capital Trust; Atherton Education Foundation; Management, Stanford University Smart Product Design Laboratory
Directorships: Stanford Business School Venture Capital Trust; Menlo Park Atherton Education Foundation
Geoff Yang, Founding Partner
Education: BSE Engineering/Management Systems/AB Economics, Princeton University; MBA, Stanford Graduate School of Business
Background: General Partner, IVP; Associate, First Century Partners; IBM
Directorships: Ask Jeeves, TiVo, Turnstone, Azul, BigBand Networks, Procket Networks, SyStream, Tahoe Networks, President's Information Technology Advisory Committee
Satish Dharmaraj, Partner
Education: BS, MS, Computer Science, Harvard University
Background: Founder/CEO, Zimbra; VP, Messaging Products Division, Openwave Systems
David Yuan, Partner, Head of Redpoint China
Education: BS, Electrical Engineering, MIT
Background: CEO, iTelco Communications
Annie Kadavy, Partner
Education: BA, MA, Biology & Organizational Business, Stanford University; MBA, Stanford Graduate School of Business
Background: Charles River Ventures; Bain & Company; Warby Parker; Uber Freight

1535 REDWOOD CAPITAL CORPORATION
PO Box 475668
San Francisco, CA 94147
Phone: 415-397-3800 **Fax:** 415-563-2127

Mission Statement: A family owned business that is well acquainted with the challenges facing the early stage company and its entrepreneurs, and is skilled at how to go about addressing those challenges.

Geographic Preference: San Francisco Bay Area
Founded: 1982
Average Investment: $10 - $25MM
Minimum Investment: $100,000
Investment Criteria: Early Stage
Industry Group Preference: Consumer Products
Portfolio Companies: eKnitting, GetRelevant, Airtreks, LeaseExchange, Native Minds, nextResort, ProClarity Corporation, TrueSAN Networks, Inc.

Key Executives:
Krist Jake, Founder/President
Education: BSE, Princeton University; MBA/MSE, Stanford University
Background: Co-Founder/Chairman, Denali National Park; Founder, San Francisco Ocean Film Festival

1536 REDWOOD CAPITAL GROUP
1 East Wacker Drive
Suite 1600
Chicago, IL 60601
Phone: 312-995-7300
web: redwoodcapgroup.com

Mission Statement: To be the foremost choice of institutional and private equity in pursuit of strategic multifamily investments.

Industry Group Preference: Real Estate, Property Management

Key Executives:
David Carlson, Co-Founder/Managing Director
Education: BS, Finance, University of Illinois; MBA, DePaul University

Venture Capital & Private Equity Firms / Domestic Firms

Background: Equity Residential; Onyx Capital International; Draper & Kramer
Mark Isaacson, Co-Founder/Managing Director
Background: EVP/CFO, Alliance Holdings; EVP/CFO, The Laramar Group; National Real Estate Division, Altschuler Melvoin and Glasser; Auditor, Deloitte and Touche
Bob Flannery, EVP/Chief Operating Officer
Education: BS, Northern Illinois University; MBA, Wayne State University
Background: President/COO, CA Residential; COO, JRG Capital Partners; Partner/CFO, Jameson Sotheby's International Realty

1537 REEFI CAPITAL
555 West 5th Street
Los Angeles, CA 90013

Phone: 323-406-6892
e-mail: SBlumenthal@ReeFi.com
web: www.reefi.com

Mission Statement: ReeFi is a private equity firm specializing in real estate financing for the cannabis industry. ReeFi clients including greenhouse facilities, processing, warehouse, testing, & distribution facilities, and retail & dispensary locations.
Geographic Preference: US
Average Investment: $500,000-$10 million
Minimum Investment: $500,000
Industry Group Preference: Cannabis, Real Estate
Other Locations:
  5727 South Lewis Avenue
  Suite 210
  Tulsa, OK 74105
  Phone: 918-392-3200 Fax: 918-392-2861

1539 RELATIVITY CAPITAL
1040 Founders Row
Suite D
Greensboro, GA 30642

Phone: 706-352-4112 Fax: 706-453-0042
e-mail: info@relativitycap.com
web: relativitycap.com

Mission Statement: An independent fee-only registered investment advisory firm focused on providing portfolios constructed from its top down review process to seek out superior returns while striving to reduce portfolio risk along the way.
Industry Group Preference: Diversified
Other Locations:
  85 Third Avenue
  36th Floor
  New York, NY 10022
  Phone: 212-350-1540
Key Executives:
  G Thomas Lackey, Jr, Managing Partner/Portfolio Manager
  Education: BBA, University of Georgia
  Background: Partner, Presidium Capital; Partner, Barber Lackey Financial Group
  Jennifer D Lackey, Founder/Chief Compliance Officer
  Education: Terry College of Business, University of Georgia
  Background: Chief Compliance Officer, Barber Lackey Financial Group

1540 REMBRANDT VENTURE PARTNERS
San Francisco, CA 94111

Phone: 415-528-2900 Fax: 415-528-2901
web: www.rembrandtvc.com

Mission Statement: Rembrandt focuses on early stage technology companies, where it plays an active role in helping entrepreneurs grow companies.
Geographic Preference: Silicon Valley
Fund Size: $230 million
Founded: 2004
Investment Criteria: Early-Stage
Industry Group Preference: Technology, Internet, Infrastructure, Applications Software & Services, Communications, Wireless, New Media
Portfolio Companies: Allegiance, Appcelerator, Autopilot, Avaamo, Cavium Networks, CloudOn, Concurrent, Convio, Coveroo, Dynamic Signal, Electric Cloud, Good Technology, InsideView, IronPort, LiveRamp, LotLinx, Lytics, MetaLINCS, Needle, Netuitive, Ooyala, Pipedrive, Proximetry, Quark Games, RadialPoint, Rhythm NewMedia, SensorTower, Skybox Security, Smart Recruiters, Xactly Corporation, Zenprise
Key Executives:
  Douglas Schrier, General Partner
  Education: Economics/Pre-Med, DePauw University; MBA, Columbia Business School
  Background: Senior Partner, Argo Global Capital; Senior Vice President, Acquisitions, SAIC
  Directorships: Solect Technology Group, Multium Information Systems, VocalDAta, ODS Networks, Ceon, Narad Networks, Digital Bridges, World Wide Packets, Cosmocom, uReach
  Gerald S Casilli, General Partner
  Education: BS, Electrical Engineering, University of Pittsburgh
  Background: Chairman, IKOS Systems; General Partner, Trinity Ventures; Founder & General Partner, Genesis Capital
  Directorships: InsideView, Xactly Corporation
  Scott Irwin, General Partner
  Education: B.S., Systems Engineering, University of Virginia; MBA, UCLA Anderson School of Management
  Background: General Partner, El Dorado Ventures
  Directorships: Allegiance, Convio, InsideView, Lytics, Pipedrive, SensorTower, Tower Cloud, Webtrends
  Pauline Duffy, Chief Financial Officer
  Education: BS, Accounting, San Jose State University
  Background: Controller, Prospero Ventures; Controller, CAD Solutions; Controller, Celtrix Pharmaceuticals

1541 RENAISSANCE VENTURES
33 South 13th Street
3rd Floor
Richmond, VA 23219

Phone: 804-643-5500
e-mail: info@renventures.com
web: www.renventures.com

Mission Statement: Renaissance Ventures and its affiliates invest in special situations across classes including mis-priced equity and debit securities and buy-out in both public and private markets.
Geographic Preference: Mid-Atlantic Region
Founded: 1997
Investment Criteria: Mis-priced equity and debt securities in the public markets.
Key Executives:
  Herbert W Jackson, Managing Director
  Education: BS, Business Administration, UNC-Chapel Hill
  Background: Avanti Partners

1542 RENEWABLETECH VENTURES
Salt Lake City, UT 84111

e-mail: info@renewablevc.com
web: www.renewablevc.com

Venture Capital & Private Equity Firms / Domestic Firms

Mission Statement: RenewableTech Ventures is an early stage and growth stage venture fund investing in renewable energy, clean technology, energy conservation, green materials and other technologies. Entrepreneurs with innovative technology and green solutions should seek financing from RenewableTech Ventures.

Geographic Preference: Rocky Mountain Region of United States & Canada
Industry Group Preference: Renewable Energy, Clean Technology, Energy Efficiency, Information Technology, Life Sciences
Portfolio Companies: ACTR (GeoStrut), Ashtech, Consolidated Energy Systems, Solid Carbon Products, Waterton Polymer Products

Other Locations:
301 North End East
Suite 113
Rexburg, ID 83440

301 Main Street
Cardston, AB T0K 0K0
Canada

Key Executives:
Todd Stevens, Managing Director
Education: BS, Accounting & Management, University of Utah; MBA, Harvard Business School
Background: Founder & Managing Director, EPIC Ventures; Manager, Zions Bank Venture Capital Department
Directorships: Netcentives, i-Central, O'Currance, Vertical Technologies, MyFamily/The Generations Network, Cirque, ZARS Pharma
Dal Zemp, Venture Partner
Education: BA, Educational Psychology, MA, Brigham Young University; MBA, NYU Stern School of Business
Background: Founder, Ashtech Industries; Founder, Kodiak Mountain Stone; Founder, Whisper Creek Log Homes; Founder, Paradise Canyon Golf Resort & Land Corporation
Directorships: ACTR, Kodiak Mountain Stone, Whisper Creek Log Homes, Paradise Canyon Land Corporation, Recycle Wear USA
Robert Pothier, Venture Partner
Education: BS, Finance, Brigham Young University; Executive Program, Stanford University
Background: Venture Partner, EPIC Ventures; Partner, Wasatch Venture Fund III
Directorships: Rockford Corporation, CopperKey, Exagen Diagnostics, Lumidigm, Lytek, MyGeek, Yellowstone Hotel Systems

1543 RESEARCH CORPORATION TECHNOLOGIES
6440 N Swan Road
Suite 200
Tucson, AZ 85718

Phone: 520-748-4400 **Fax:** 520-748-0025
e-mail: communique@rctech.com
web: www.rctech.com

Founded: 1987
Investment Criteria: Early-Stage
Industry Group Preference: Biotechnology, Life Sciences, Medical Devices, Therapeutics
Portfolio Companies: APT Pharmaceuticals, BioCision, Catalyst Biosciences, Cylene Pharmaceuticals, Esperance Pharmaceuticals, Jenrin Discovery, OncoGenex Technologies, ParinGenix, Peptech, Sertoli Technologies, Spirogen, Therapeutic Human Polyclonals, Alerion Biomedical, Clear Catheter Systems, Kerberos Proximal Solutions, Option 3, OrthAlign, Varix Medical Corp., Vasonova

Key Executives:
Chad W Souvignier, Vice President
520-748-4400
e-mail: csouvignier@rctech.com
Education: BS, Chemistry, University of Wisconsin, Eau Claire; MS, Polymer Science, University of Akron; MBA, PhD, Materials Science & Engineering, University of Arizona
Background: Manager, International Marketing, Guilford Pharmaceuticals; Product Development, Proctor & Gamble

1544 RESERVOIR VENTURE PARTNERS
735 Ceramic Place
Suite 120
Westerville, OH 43081

Phone: 614-846-7241

Mission Statement: Reservoir Venture Partners is a Columbus, Ohio based venture capital firm bringing capital, business building acumen, and a strong network of advisors to entrepreneurs and their teams. RVP supports portfolio companies with dynamic guidance to our entrepreneurs in all key aspects of operations, governance and strategy. We genuinely believe that teams succeed.

Average Investment: $500,000 - $1 million
Investment Criteria: Early-Stage
Industry Group Preference: Information Technology, Healthcare, Clean Technology
Portfolio Companies: AxioMed Spine, Juventas Therapeutics, Imalux, Minimally Invasive Devices, Cine-tal Systems, iSqFt, Manta Media, Scale Computing, Nextumi, WebLinc, Xcelerate Media

Key Executives:
Curtis D Crocker, Managing Partner
e-mail: ccrocker@reservoirvp.com
Education: BS, Olivet Nazarene University; MBA, Indiana University
Background: Partner, Alpha Capital Partners; Partner, Northwest Ohio Venture Fund

1545 RESILIENCE CAPITAL PARTNERS
25101 Chagrin Boulevard
Suite 350
Cleveland, OH 44122

Phone: 216-292-0200 **Fax:** 216-292-4750
web: www.resiliencecapital.com

Mission Statement: A merchant banking firm focused on principal investing/investment banking services for companies in distressed and restructuring situations.

Geographic Preference: Midwest, Great Lakes Regions
Fund Size: $300 million
Founded: 2001
Average Investment: $25 million - $250 million
Industry Group Preference: Automotive, Manufacturing, Capital Goods, Chemicals, Plastics, Metals, Retailing, Transportation, Packaging, Distribution
Portfolio Companies: Aero Communications, Aerospace Products International, Affinity Specialty Apparel, ASC Signal, CR Brands, Flight Options, Hynes Industries, North Coast Minerals, PendaForm, Thermal Product Solutions, Thermal Solutions Manufacturing, WT Hardwoods Group

Key Executives:
Bassem A Mansour, Co-CEO
216-292-4748
Fax: 216-292-4750
e-mail: bmonsour@resiliencecapital.com
Education: MBA, Case Western Reserve University; BS, University of Dayton
Background: SVP, McDonald Investments Restructuring Group; Operations Manager, Northwest Micrographics
Steven H Rosen, Co-CEO
216-292-4535
Fax: 216-292-4750
e-mail: srosen@resiliencecapital.com
Education: BS, University of Maryland; MBA, Case

Venture Capital & Private Equity Firms / Domestic Firms

Western Reserve University
Background: Management, Merrill Lynch & Company
David Glickman, Partner
e-mail: dglickman@resiliencecapital.com
Education: BA, Political Science, Washington & Jefferson College; MBA, University of Southern California
Background: Partner, Edgewater Capital
Ki Mixon, Partner
216-292-0503
Fax: 216-292-4750
e-mail: kmixon@resiliencecapital.com
Education: History, Wittenberg University; MBA, Weatherhead School of Management, Case Western Reserve University
Background: Associate, McDonald Investments; Management, KeyBank
Directorships: Penda Corporation, ASC Signal Corporation, ChemDesign Products

1546 RESOLUTE.VC
San Francisco, CA

web: www.resolute.vc

Mission Statement: Resolute is focused on finding extraordinary entrepreneurs and helping them succeed over the course of their career. Resolute invests as little as $50K and as much as $750K in a company's initial financing. Resolute guides entrepreneurs to the key milestones for a successful venture round.

Portfolio Companies: BarkBox, Bitium, Blippy, Card.com, DJZ, DocRun, EidoSearch, Fancy Hands, Greenhouse, Gympact, Happier, Homejoy, Hopscotch, Influitive, iSocket, Kissmetrics, MessageMe, OKpanda, People.co, Reonomy, Rollbar, Runnable, Shop Hers, Signifyd, Webshots, Sunrise, TidePool, Vayable, Yardsale, Zenbox

Key Executives:
   Mike Hirshland, Founder

1547 RESONANT VENTURE PARTNERS
Ann Arbor, MI 48104

web: www.resonantvc.com

Mission Statement: Resonant Venture Partners is a venture capital firm focused on investing in seed stage companies in the software, services, and cloud infrastructure sectors.

Geographic Preference: United States
Founded: 2010
Average Investment: $500,000
Investment Criteria: Seed Stage, Early Stage
Industry Group Preference: Information Technology, Cloud Infrastructure, Software, Services
Portfolio Companies: Accio Energy, Bitfusion, Cargo, Deepfield, Duo Security, Filament, Orchestrate, Precog, Search Lateral, Sookasa, Stratos, Virta Labs, ZeroVM

Key Executives:
   Michael Godwin, Managing Director
   e-mail: michael@resonantvc.com
   Education: Berklee College of Music; MBA, University of Michigan
   Background: Managing Director, Wolverine Venture Fund, University of Michigan; Consultant & Software Engineer, Menlo Innovations; Independent Online Distribution Alliance; WebCrawler
   Directorships: Accio Energy, Pinoccio
   Jason Townsend, Managing Director
   e-mail: jason@resonantvc.com
   Education: BS, Computer Engineering, MBA, University of Michigan
   Background: Managing Director, Wolverine Venture Fund, University of Michigan; CEO, Life Magnetics; Founder & CEO, Ikanos Power; CEO, Townsend Investments; ITT Automotive; Chrysler
   Directorships: Protean, ZeroVM

1548 RESOURCE CAPITAL FUNDS
1400 Sixteenth Street
Suite 200
Denver, CO 80202

Phone: 720-946-1444
web: www.resourcecapitalfunds.com

Mission Statement: Resource Capital Funds is a private equity firm specializing in the mining industry. RCF seeks to build successful companies with the ability to generate strong returns.

Geographic Preference: Worldwide
Fund Size: $2 billion
Founded: 1998
Average Investment: $10 - $300 million
Minimum Investment: $1 million
Industry Group Preference: Mining, Minerals, Metals, Energy
Portfolio Companies: AlloyCorp Mining, Ascot Resources, Atico Mining, Ausenco, Bannerman Resources, Blast Movement Technologies, Buffalo Coal, Coastal Ventures, Drummond Gold Limited, Firestone Diamonds, First Bauxite, First Nickel, Geopacific Resources, Global Advanced Metals, Gold Road Resources, IC Potash, India Resources Limited, Jolimont Global Mining Systems, Kingsgate Consolidated, Lighthouse Resources, Metalicity, MZI Resources, New Age Exploration, Noront Resources, NovaCopper, Nyota Minerals, Peninsula Energy, Piney Woods Resources, ProVale, Riversdale Resources, TMAC Resources, Toro Gold Limited, Uranium Resources, Vendetta Mining, Vimy Resources Limited, Wolf Minerals Limited

Other Locations:
RCF Management LLC
2 Jericho Plaza
Suite 103
Jericho, NY 11753
Phone: 631-692-0043

Resource Capital Funds Management Pty Ltd
24 Kings Park Road
Level 1
West Perth WA 6004
Australia
Phone: 61-0864761900

RCF Management (Toronto) Inc.
25 York Street
Suite 610
Toronto, ON M5J 2V5
Canada
Phone: 647-726-0640

RCF Management LLC
Oficina de Representacion en Chile
Nueva Costanera 4040, #31
Vitacura, Santiago 7630000
Chile
Phone: 56-222454361

RCF Management (UK) Ltd.
33 St. James's Square
St. James
London SW1Y 5JS
United Kingdom
Phone: 44-2081327672

Key Executives:
   James McClements, Managing Partner
   e-mail: jtm@rcflp.com
   Education: University of Western Australia
   Background: NM Rothschild; Standard Chartered Bank
   Directorships: Global Advanced Metals Pty Ltd
   Ryan Bennett, Partner/Senior Advisor
   e-mail: rbennett@rcflp.com
   Education: University of Wisconsin; Colorado School of Mines
   Background: NM Rothschild; US Bureau of Mines;

Caterpillar Inc.
Directorships: Coastal Ventures, Riversdale Resources
Ross Bhappu, Partner/Head of Fund
e-mail: rbhappu@rcflp.com
Education: BS, MS, Metallurgical Engineering, University of Arizona; PhD, Mineral Economics, Colorado School of Mines
Background: Director, Business Development, Newmont Mining Corporation; Cyprus Minerals Company
Directorships: Lighthouse Resources, Piney Woods
Russ Cranswick, Partner/Head of Fund
e-mail: rcranswick@rcflp.com
Education: BSc, Geology, University of British Columbia
Background: Freeport McMoRan Gold Company; Kennecott Canada Inc.
Directorships: Coastal Ventures, TMAC Resources Inc.
Mason Hills, Partner/General Counsel
e-mail: mhills@rcflp.com
Education: BEc, University of Western Australia; LLB, Murdoch University
Directorships: Global Advanced Metals, First Bauxite Corporation, First Drilling Group
Peter Nicholson, Partner, MD Australia, Investment Team Leader
e-mail: pnicholson@rcflp.com
Education: BEng, Mining, University of Queensland
Background: LionOre Australia; WMC Resources
Michele Valenti, Partner/COO
e-mail: mvalenti@rcflp.com
Education: BS, Accounting & International Business, New York University
Background: COO, Deutsche Bank; Nomura Securities; Merrill Lynch; Mahoney Cohen & Company

1549 RETAIL & RESTAURANT GROWTH CAPITAL LP
11700 Preston Road
Suite 660 PMB 411
Dallas, TX 75230

Phone: 214-766-8173 Fax: 469-533-1982
e-mail: rrgc@rrgcsbic.com
web: www.rrgcsbic.com

Mission Statement: Provides debt capital and strategic counsel to businesses operating in the retail and restaurant industry that have exhibited a potential for accelerated growth and expansion. The four general partners collectively have over 60 years of private investment, management, consulting and operating experience in the retail and restaurant industries.

Geographic Preference: United States
Fund Size: $60 million
Founded: 1996
Average Investment: $1-$3 million
Investment Criteria: Growth, Acquisition, Recapitalization, Buyouts
Industry Group Preference: Retailing, Restaurants, Services
Portfolio Companies: Quizno's, Elizabeth Arden, Texas Land & Cattle, Left at Albuquerque, The Art Store, Le Gourmet Chef, Walking Co., Cafe Express, Progressive Concepts, Beauty First, Uncle Julio's

Key Executives:
Raymond C Hemmig, General Partner
e-mail: rhemmig@rrgcsbic.com
Background: Chairman, ACE Cash Express; Executive, Hickory Farms; JC Penny; Grandy's Restaurant; Founding Partner, Hemmig & Martin
Directorships: Restoration Hardware; Elizabeth Arden Holdings; NASC Enterprises
J Eric Lawrence, General Partener
e-mail: elawrence@rrgcsbic.com
Background: Senior Consultant, Arthur Andersen, LLP; VP, Strategic Retail Ventures; Director Quizno's, Blue Cafe and Advisory Director, NASC Enterprises
Directorships: Progressive Concepts, Beauty First

Mark L Masinter, General Partner
e-mail: mmasinter@rrgcsbic.com
Education: BS, Political Science, Southern Methodist University
Background: Harber Masinter Company; Strategic Retail Ventures
Directorships: Le Gourmet Chef, Beauty First, The Walking Company, Shoes.com
Joseph L Harberg, President
e-mail: jharberg@rrgcsbic.com
Education: JD, University of Houston; BA, Business Administration, University of Texas
Background: Licensed Attorney; Harberg Masinter Company; Strategic Retail Ventures
Directorships: The Art Store, NASBIC, SoRASBIC

1550 RETHINK COMMUNITY
707 Westchester Ave.
Suite 401
White Plains, NY 10604

Phone: 914-269-0921
e-mail: info@rethink.vc
web: rethink.vc/community

Mission Statement: Rethink Community is focused on reinvigorating American communities through investments in real estate that maximize economic and civic growth. Investments center on improving education, housing, healthcare, and workforce opportunities.

Industry Group Preference: Housing, Education, Healthcare, Industry

Key Executives:
Michael Walden, Managing Partner
Education: BS, University of Richmond
Background: COO, Seavest Investment Group; Managing Director, Potomac Media Partners
Directorships: EverFi, Neverware

1551 RETHINK EDUCATION
707 Westchester Ave.
Suite 401
White Plains, NY 10604

Phone: 914-269-0921
e-mail: info@rethink.vc
web: rethink.vc/education

Mission Statement: Our education system is one of the last places to be remade by technology. That's about to change. We are investing in the people, ideas and companies that are rethinking the way we learn and teach. Rethink Education seeks to invest in progressive growth-stage companies that are at the forefront of the education technology industry and have the capacity to make positive impacts on our communities.

Investment Criteria: Growth-Stage
Industry Group Preference: Education
Portfolio Companies: 2U, Abl, Ace Learning, AdmitHub, AllHere, Allovue, American Prison Data Systems, Bridge International Academies, Bear, Bridge International Academy, BrightBytes, Burning Glass, CareAcademy, Civitas Learning, Clark, Cognitive Toy Box, Course Report, Crehana, Degreed, Edmit, Education Elements, Ellevation, Engrade, Entangled Ventures, EverFi, Flocabulary, Formative, General Assembly, Guild, Hapara, Hickory, Intellus Learning, Invibed, Kenzie Academy, KiraKira3D, Knowledge to Practice, Lessonly, McGraw-Hill, MedAux, MissionU, Neverware, NoodleMarkets, NoRedInk, Pathbrite, PathStream, Plianced, Pluralsight, Rethink, Rethink Autism, Second Accent, Sixup, Smarterer, StraighterLine, Student Opportunity Center, SV Academy, Trilogy Education Services, Toot, Upswing, VidCode, Voxy, Wonda VR, Wonderschool

Venture Capital & Private Equity Firms / Domestic Firms

Key Executives:
Rick Segal, Managing Partner
Education: BA, English, Wesleyan University
Background: Founder, Seavest
Directorships: Advanced Prison Data Systems, Flocabulary, Knowlege to Practice, Noodle Markets, Voxy, Civitas, Speakaboos
Matt Greenfield, Managing Partner
Education: BA, MA, PhD, English, Yale University
Background: Founder, Stonework Capital; Associate, ABS Ventures
Directorships: Allovue, Brightgytes, CareAcademy, Kenzie Academy, NoRedInk
Michael Walden, Managing Partner, Rethink
Background: COO, Seavest Financial Group; Managing Director, Potomac Media Partners; EVP, InPhonic
Directorships: EverFi, Neverware
Brandon Avrutin, Venture Partner
Education: BA, Philosophy & Economics, Middlebury College
Background: Investment Associate, Seavest Capital Partners; Investmant Banking Analyst, Lazard

1552 RETHINK IMPACT
707 Westchester Ave.
Suite 401
White Plains, NY 10604

Phone: 914-269-0921
e-mail: info@rethink.vc
web: rethink.vc/impact

Mission Statement: Rethink Impact is a venture capital firm that invests in female leaders in technology.

Industry Group Preference: Technology
Portfolio Companies: Aclime, Angaza, Catchafire, Change.org, Classy, Everfi, Evidation, Ketos, Neurotrack, Purpose, Sempre Health, Spring, Univfy, Winnie

Key Executives:
Jenny Abramson, Founder/Managing Partner
Education: BA, MA, Stanford University; MBA, Harvard Business School
Background: CEO, LiveSafe
Heidi Patel, Partner
Education: AB, Princeton University; MBA, Stanford Graduate School of Business
Background: Director, Pacific Community Ventures; Founding Member, AOL Time Warner Ventures; Credit Suisse First Boston
Kate Castle, Partner/Chief Marketing Officer
Education: BA, Wheaton College
Background: Marketing Partner, Flybridge Capital Partners; Co-Founder/Operating Partner, XFactor Ventures

1553 REV1 VENTURES
1275 Kinnear Road
Columbus, OH 43212

Phone: 614-487-3700
e-mail: info@rev1ventures.com
web: www.rev1ventures.com

Mission Statement: Rev1 Ventures provides investment capital for commercialization of innovations in information technology, advanced materials and medical technology. Supports early-stage, Ohio-based entities by facilitating risk sharing on opportunities with high upside potential.

Geographic Preference: Ohio
Industry Group Preference: Information Technology, Advanced Materials, Medical Technology
Portfolio Companies: 7signal Solutions, Acceptd, AircraftLogs, AquaBlok, AssureRx Health, Brand Thunder, BringShare, Capture Education, CardiOx, Clarivoy, ClearSaleing, Cryothermic Systems, Ecolibrium Solar, EndoSphere, Exacter, Great Lakes Pharmaceuticals, HTP, I2C Technologies, IncludeFitness, inmobly, Intelligent Mobile Support, Midwest MicroDevices, Minimally Invasive Devices, NanoStatics, nChannel, Neuros Medical, PreEmptive Solutions, SageQuest, SeeMore Interactive, Seen Digital Media, SironRx Therapeutics, SparkBase, T-Pro Solutions, TheraVase, Traycer Systems, Znode

Other Locations:
Rev1 Gateway
1590 North High Street
Columbus, OH 43201

Key Executives:
Tom Walker, President/CEO
Education: BS, University of Oklahoma; MBA, Oklahoma City University
Background: Business Development Manager, Battelle; CEO/Executive Director, Oklahoma Investment Forum; Founder, SeedStep Angels; President/CEO, i2E Inc.
Kristy Campbell, Chief Operating Officer
Education: BS, Ohio University; MBA, Ashland University
Background: Marketing Manager, Logica; EC Outlook Inc.; Evolving Systems; Director of Marketing, Title First Agency; Saama; Director of Digital Marketing, Manta; Chief Marketing Officer, Rev1 Ventures
David Dillman, Chief Financial Officer/Chief Compliance Officer
Education: BS, University of Montana
Background: Accounting Manager, Boone and Crockett Club; Controller, Enterprise Holdings

1554 REVEL PARTNERS
110 Greene Street
Suite 703
New York, NY 10012

web: www.revelpartners.com

Mission Statement: Revel Partners is a team of experienced entrepreneurs and investors that provides growth capital to exceptional management teams and helps them build leading digital media businesses.

Average Investment: $500,000 - $3 million
Investment Criteria: Early-Expansion Stage
Industry Group Preference: Digital Media & Marketing, Internet, Software, Consumer Services, Social Media
Portfolio Companies: Acre Trader, Akorda, Augmented Radar Imaging, Cadence, Curacity, Fetcher, Instnt, Lawmatics, Lawyaw, Lending Front, MarketMuse, Native Voice, Nexosis, Omnichain, Populus, Sourcify, STAQ, SupplyAI, Tenovos, Zylo Tech, Zype

Key Executives:
Joe Apprendi, Partner
Education: BA, Economics, Oberlin College
Background: Founder & CEO, Collective; K2 Digital; CLIQNOW! Sales Group, 24/7 Media, Eyeblaster; Klipmart; Falk eSolutions
Thomas Falk, Partner
Background: CEO, eValue Group; Founder, Falk & Partners
Chris Young, Partner
Education: BS, Business, Skidmore College; MBA, Rensselaer Polytechnic Institute
Background: Chairman & CEO, Digital Broadcasting Group; Co-Founder, Klipmart
John Vincent, Partner
Education: BA, Psychology, Vanderbilt University
Background: CEO/Co-Founder, EyeWonder; Leap Online; Magellan TSA; Place Space Media; Captive Concepts

1555 REVOLUTION LLC
1717 Rhode Island Avenue NW
Suite 1000
Washington, DC 20036

Phone: 202-776-1400
web: www.revolution.com

Venture Capital & Private Equity Firms / Domestic Firms

Mission Statement: Revolution invests in companies attacking traditional industries on the brink of disruptive change.
Geographic Preference: Eastern U.S.
Fund Size: $200 million
Average Investment: $4-8 million
Investment Criteria: Startups; Early Stage
Industry Group Preference: Education, Financial Services, Sports, Media & Entertainment, Marketplaces, Software & Services, Transportation, Hospitality & Travel, E-Commerce & Manufacturing, Health
Portfolio Companies: Aura, BenchPrep, Bloomscape, Bright Cellars, Busbud, eSUB Construction Software, Good Buy Gear, Homesnap, Member Suite, Mint House, Paro, Policy Genius, Resolute AI

Key Executives:
   Tige Savage, Managing Partner
   Education: BBA, James Madison University; MBA, University of Michigan Ross School of Business
   Background: Vice President, Time Warner Ventures; Founding Team, Riggs Capital Partners
   Directorships: AddThis, Homeshap, Booker, Flexcar, HelloWallet, LivingSocial, NewBrand Analytics, Personal, Revolution Money, Snagfilms, UberMedia
   David Golden, Managing Partner
   Education: AB, Harvard University; JD, Harvard Law School
   Background: JPMorgan, Hambrecht & Quist, Code Advisors
   Directorships: Barnes & Noble, Blackbaud, Everyday Health, Vinfolio
   Clara Sieg, Partner
   Education: Stanford University
   Background: UBS Investment Bank; Probitas Partners
   Directorships: Busbud; Framebridge; PolicyGenius

1556 REX HEALTH VENTURES
310 S Harrington Street
Raleigh, NC 27603

web: www.rexhealthventures.com

Mission Statement: Rex Health Ventures is part of Rex Healthcare's groundbreaking innovation platform, Rex Strategic Innovation. RHV features an early stage venture fund, a team of healthcare and investment professionals and a commitment to improving patient care.
Average Investment: $250,000 - $2 million
Investment Criteria: All Stages Considered
Industry Group Preference: Healthcare Information Technology, Healthcare Services, Medical Devices, Biopharmaceuticals
Portfolio Companies: Aerial Biopharma, Arrive BioVentures, Awarepoint, Baebies, BardyDX, Emergo Therapeutics, Gauss Surgical, Kit Check, Midnight Pharma LLC, Phononic, Phynd Technologies, Target Pharmasolutions, Veran Medical Technologies

Key Executives:
   Bobby Helmedag, Managing Director
   Education: BS, Finance, University of Notre Dame
   Background: BlueCross BlueShield of Tennessee, Citigroup, KPMG
   Directorships: Aerial BioPharma
   Anita Watkins, Director, Strategic Innovation
   Education: MS/JD, University of North Carolina
   Background: VP, Government Relations, University of North Carolina
   Ray Jang, Associate
   Education: BS, Biochemistry & Economics, University of California San Diego; MBA, University of North Carolina

1557 RFE INVESTMENT PARTNERS
36 Grove Street
New Canaan, CT 06840

Phone: 203-966-2800
e-mail: info@rfeip.com
web: www.rfeip.com

Mission Statement: A private equity investment firm focusing on smaller middle-market service, manufacturing and distribution businesses.
Geographic Preference: United States
Fund Size: $300 million
Founded: 1979
Average Investment: $10-$25 million
Minimum Investment: $5 million
Investment Criteria: Partner with management to acquire majority interests in smaller middle market companies, that passes leading marketShare positions in their care niche market.
Industry Group Preference: Manufacturing, Distribution, Services
Portfolio Companies: AbelConn Holdings, Advanced Technology Services, Baxter Manufacturing, Brooks & Whittle Limited, Camino Modular Systems, Cattron Group, CBT Technology, Commonwealth Business Media, ConsoliDent, DelStar Technologies, Flow Solutions, Great Clips, Hastings Holdings Corporation, Health Watch Holdings, HTI Technologies Holding Corporation, iMedX Holdings, JSI Store Fixtures, Kenan Advantage Group, Lectrus Corporation, McKenzie Sports Products, Metalico, Nudo Products, OK Indutries, PCX Aerostructures, Pro Active Therapy, PureRed Integrated Marketing, Rescare, Scandura Holdings, Seed Holdings, ShelterLogic Investment, Sun Healthcare, Washington Inventory Service

Key Executives:
   Michael J Foster, Senior Managing Director/Chief Compliance Officer
   e-mail: mfoster@rfeip.com
   Education: BS, Doctor of Jurisprudence, Cornell University
   Background: Partner, O'Sullivan Graev & Karabell
   Directorships: Brook & Whittle Ltd, Extrusion Technology Inc., iMedX Inc, Lectrus, Plantation Products Inc.
   James A Parsons, Senior Managing Director
   e-mail: jparsons@rfeip.com
   Education: MBA, University of Michigan; BA, Williams College
   Background: Michigan Capital; NBD Bancorp, Inc.
   Directorships: AbelComm LLC, Brook & Whittle Ltd, iMedX Inc., Lectrus Corp., Plantation Products
   Donald A Juricic, Managing Director/Chief Financial Officer
   e-mail: djuricic@rfeip.com
   Education: BS, Villanova University; MBA, New York University
   Background: Control Data Corporation
   Ned Truslow, Managing Director
   e-mail: ntruslow@rfeip.com
   Education: MA, University of St Andrews, Scotland; MBA, University of Texas
   Background: Columbia Naples Capital
   Directorships: AbelConn LLC, Nudo Products, TradeSource Inc.
   R Peter Reiter, Jr, Managing Director, Business Development
   e-mail: preiter@rfeip.com
   Education: BBA, Iona College; MBA, New York University
   Background: KPMG Peat Marwick
   Directorships: Extrusion Technology Inc., iMedX Inc., Lectrus Corp, Plantation Products Inc.
   Michael W Rubel, Managing Director
   e-mail: mrubel@rfeip.com
   Education: BBA, James Madison University; MBA, Duke

Venture Capital & Private Equity Firms / Domestic Firms

University
Background: Weston Presido
Directorships: iMedX Inc., Plantation Products Inc.

1558 RHO VENTURES
Carnigie Hall Tower
152 W 57th Street
23rd Floor
New York, NY 10019

Phone: 212-751-6677 **Fax:** 212-751-3613
web: www.rhoventures.com

Mission Statement: Rho Ventures invests in innovators that redefine the status quo. RhoBs investment philosphy does not fit a conventional model. Rho believes that formulaic approaches to investing lead to risk adverse strategies that stifle innovation. As a result, Rho is not bound by a particular stage of investment and do not shy away from contrarian ideas.

Fund Size: Rho Ventures VI: $510 million
Founded: 1981
Average Investment: $10 million
Minimum Investment: $1 million
Investment Criteria: All stages
Industry Group Preference: Electronic Technology, Internet Technology, Telecommunications, Computer Hardware & Software, Biotechnology, Healthcare, New Media, Healthcare, New Energy, Information Technology, Biopharmaceuticals, Medical Devices, Communications
Portfolio Companies: 3DP, Active Power, AddThis, Advancis/Middle Brook, Airspan Networks, Alibre, Alien Technology, AlleWin Technologies, Amp'd Mobile, Ample Communications, Anacor Pharmaceuticals, Ansa, AnswerSoft, Applied Science Fiction, AqueSys, Archemix, Archimede Technology Group, Aristacom, Aristotle Circle, August, Auto Data Network, Avolent, BioTransplant, Bluefly, BroadLogic, Calera, Capstone Turbine Corporation, Cara Therapeutics, Carparts/ADN, Celtro, Celunol, Cesura, ChaCha, Channel Insight, ChargePoint, Chiaro Networks, Chorum Technologies, Ciena, Ciris Energy, Claremont, Clear Urban Energy, CloudPay, COM21, Commerce One, Compaq, ComSpace, Constellar, Convercent, Convex, Convey Computer, Copper Mountain, Coral Network, Corton Precision Optical Company, CRB Innovations, Crosstrees Medical, Crystal Semi, Cypress Semiconductor, CytoMed, Dashlane, Delsys Pharmaceutical, Dendreon, diaDexus, Differential Diagnostics, Dyax, EAI-Vista, Eclat, Effective Measure, eMachines, Emerald Solutions, EndoMedix, Enerkem, enherent, Enmass, Eracom, eTang, Everdream, Everyday Health, Excara, Eziba, Fintech Lab, Fractal Systems, Feneral Paramterics, Genetic Therapy, GenVec, GetGlue, Global Exchange Services, Gloucester Pharmaceuticals, GynoPharma, Health Allies, HealthSynq, Human Genome Science, IdenTrust, Ingenuity, InnerWireless, Innova Dynamics, Inotek, inPowered, Integral Wave, IntraLinks, Intransa, Ipsum Networks, ItzBig, iVillage, JustFav, Kana Software, KD 1, Landmark Graphics, LeukoSite, LifetecNe

Other Locations:
525 University Avenue
Suite 1350
Palo Alto, CA 94301
Phone: 650-463-0300 **Fax:** 650-463-0311

Rho Canada
1800 McGill College Avenue
Suite 840
Montreal, QC H3A 3J6
Canada
Phone: 514-844-5605 **Fax:** 514-844-9004

Key Executives:
Habib Kairouz, Managing Partner
Education: BS, Engineering, BA, Economics, Cornell University; MBA, Finance, Columbia University
Background: Reich & Co., Jesup & Lamont
Directorships: Bluefly, Everyday Health, InnerWireless, IntraLinks, Public Mobile, ReachLocal, Travel Ad Network, Verified Person
Mark Leschly, Managing Partner
212-848-0414
Fax: 212-751-3613
e-mail: mleschly@rhomanagement.com
Education: MBA, Stanford Graduate School of Business
Background: General Partner, Healthcare Ventures; Consultant, McKinsey & Company
Directorships: Anacor, Diversa, Memory Pharmaceuticals, MPV, NitroMed, Orametrix, Orquis, Senomyx, Tercica, Vicuron
Joshua Ruch, Managing Partner
Education: MBA, Harvard Business School
Background: Investment Banker, Salomon Brothers
Directorships: 3-D Pharmaceuticals, Applied Science Fiction, Diacrin, Diversa, Human Genome Sciences, Sionex, TechSmart, Yantra
Martin Vogelbaum, Partner
Education: AB, Biology and History, Columbia University
Background: General Partner, Apple Tree Partners; General Partner, Oxford Bioscience Partners
Directorships: Gloucester Pharmaceuticals, Nuvelo
Doug McCormick, Venture Partner
Education: MBA, Columbia University School of Business
Background: NBC Universal ; CEO, Lifetime Entertainment Services
Directorships: Marketwatch, Lin Television, Wayport, Waterfront Media
Patrick Wack, Venture Partner
Education: BSE, Princeton University
Background: CEO, IntraLinks; COO, Professional Sports Care Management
Directorships: IntraLinks, MPV, Patersons, Xora
Mark Roehrenbeck, Principal
Education: BS, Fisher College of Business, Ohio State University
Background: PricewaterhouseCoopers
Peter Kalkanis, Chief Financial Officer
Education: BS, Accounting, Lehman College
Background: CPA, Eisner LLP

1559 RHYTHM VENTURE CAPITAL
1350 6th Avenue
New York, NY 10019

e-mail: info@rhythmvc.com
web: rhythmvc.com

Mission Statement: Rhythm invests in and partners with early stage companies taking transformational appraoches to healthcare.

Other Locations:
1350 6th Avenue
Palo Alto, CA 94022

Key Executives:
Jordan Ryan, Founder/Managing Partner
Education: BA, Stanford University
Background: Partner, Avalon Capital; Strategic Partner, Hardee Brothers
Anwar Hussain, General Partner
Education: AB, MHA, Cornell University; MD, Stony Brook University
Background: Physician; Chief Medical Information Officer, UHS Hospitals; Chief Medical Information Officer, Community Health Systems; Venture Advisor, New Leaf Venture Partners

1560 RIBBIT CAPITAL
Palo Alto, CA 94301

web: www.ribbitcap.com

Mission Statement: Ribbit Capital, a Silicon Valley-based venture capital firm with its sights on raising a significant amount of venture funding that will be aimed singularly at driving innovation around the world in lending, payments, insurance, accounting, tax preparation and personal financial management. Ribbit targets disruptive, early stage companies that leverage technology to reimagine and reinvent what financial services can be for people and businesses.

Fund Size: $100 million
Founded: 2013
Industry Group Preference: Financial Services
Portfolio Companies: Activehours, Borro, BTC Jam, CAN Capital, Coinbase, Comparaonline.com, ContaAzul, CreditKarma, Funding Circle, Invoice2go, Parasut, Policy Bazaar.com, Robinhood, Wealthfront, Xapo, Zest

Key Executives:
  Meyer Malka, Founder
  Background: Co-Founder/Chairman, Lemon
  Directorships: Wonga, Peixe Urbano
  Nick Shalek, General Partner
  Education: BA, Yale University; MA, Stanford University School of Education; MBA, Stanford Graduate School of Business
  Background: Senior Analyst, Yale Investment Office; Director of Business Operations, Verne Capital; Founding Member, Sutter LLC

1561 RICHMOND GLOBAL
20 W 55th Street
New York, NY 10019

e-mail: peter.kellner@rglobal.com
web: www.rglobal.com

Mission Statement: Ricmond Global are active, early stage investors in the U.S. and active, growth stage investors in global markets. Managing partners Peter Kellner and David Frazee have worked together for a decade growing companies that span five continents. Their strategy has permitted them to be diversified by sector and geography, achieving strong returns throughout cycles.

Geographic Preference: United States, Global
Investment Criteria: Early stage, Growth stage
Industry Group Preference: All Sectors Considered

Key Executives:
  Peter Kellner, Managing Partner
  e-mail: peter.kellner@rglobal.com
  Education: BA, Princeton University; JD, Yale Law School; MBA, Harvard Business School
  Background: Co-Founder, Endeavor; Founder, EMLA Association; Co-Founder, Richmond Global Sciences
  Directorships: Richmond Global Sciences
  David Frazee, Managing Partner
  e-mail: david.frazee@rglobal.com
  Education: AB, Stanford University; JD, University of Michigan Law School
  Background: Equity Partner, K&L Gates; Founder/CEO, Demystifying Silicon Valley

---

1562 RIDGE CAPITAL PARTNERS LLC
107 W Federal Street
Unit 4
PO Box 2056
Middleburg, VA 20118

Phone: 540-687-8161 Fax: 540-687-8164
e-mail: bdavis@ridgecapital.com
web: www.ridgecapital.com

Mission Statement: A private equity investment firm focused on partnering with outstanding managers to pursue platform build-ups and growth investments in companies in the smaller end of the middle market.

Geographic Preference: United States
Founded: 1992
Average Investment: $3-$8 million
Minimum Investment: $1 million

Investment Criteria: Recapitalizations, Management-Led Platform Build-Ups, Management-Led Buyouts, Take-Private Transactions, Growth Equity
Industry Group Preference: Niche Manufacturing, Distribution, Business Products & Services, Consumer Products
Portfolio Companies: Cavalier Fire Protection LLC, Equibrand Holding Corporation, LAT Apparel, Pumps and Controls, Wincore Window Company, Zamma Corporation

Key Executives:
  J. Bradley Davis, Managing Partner
  Education: BA, Pennsylvania State University
  Background: Trivest; LaSalle Partners; Chemical Bank
  Directorships: LAT Apparel, Wincore Windows and Doors, Cavalier Fire Protection, HELLEN Systems
  Clark F. Davis, Managing Partner
  Education: BS, Finance & Marketing, University of Richmond
  Background: Trivest
  Directorships: LAT apparel, Wincore Windows and Doors, Pumps and Controls, Equibrand Holdings, Zamma Corporation

---

1563 RIDGE VENTURES
One Letterman Dr.
Building D, Suite P100
San Francisco, CA 94129

Phone: 415-439-4420
e-mail: info@ridge.vc
web: ridge.vc

Mission Statement: Ridge Ventures is an early stage venture capital fund that invests in founders who redefine software using advanced technologies, new distribution models, and innovative user experience.

Investment Criteria: Early Stage
Industry Group Preference: Software, SaaS, Technology
Portfolio Companies: AlphaDraft, Andromedia, Babycenter, BandPage, BlueBox, Braze, cClearly, Chubbies, Datanyze, Discord, Espresa, F5, Fastly, Flowdock, FreeRange Games, FreeForm, FreshPlanet, Funzio, Grabango, GuideSpark, HeyMarket, IndieGoGo, JumpCloud, Jyve, Kixeye, Krux, Leaplife, Loup, MindMeld, Minted, Next Games, Nuzzel, nWay, Orion Labs, Outlier, ParkMe, Phoenix Labs, Plain Vanilla, Prism, Revcascade, SafeGraph, Sapho, Sense, Service Metrics, Simply Hired, Smartling, Soothe, Spinner, Splitwise, Super Bit Machines, Survata, Telltale, Tempered Networks, The League, Thirdlove, Tinfoil Security, Trifacta, Triller, UpLift, UpOut, UXPin, VA Linux, Vidible, WatchGuard, WeHeartIt, Yesware, YouEarnedIt

Key Executives:
  Alexander Rosen, Co-Founder/Managing Director
  Education: BS, MIT; MBA, Stanford University Graduate School of Business
  Background: Analyst, Credit Suisse; General Partner, Sprout Group
  Directorships: Minted, ThirdLove, Smartling, Braze, UpLift, Chubbies, Fastly, Tempered Networks, YouEarnedIt, SafeGraph
  Pat Kenealy, Co-Founder/Managing Director
  Education: BA, Economics, Harvard University
  Background: Managing General Partner, IDG Ventures San Francisco
  Gil Penchina, Partner
  Education: BS, University of Massachusetts; MBA, Kellogg School of Management
  Background: Vice President and General Manager, eBay
  Directorships: Fastly, Civic, Ripple, Brave

1564 RIDGEWOOD CAPITAL
14 Philips Parkway
Montvale, NJ 07645

Phone: 201-447-9000
e-mail: support@ridgewoodcapital.com

551

Venture Capital & Private Equity Firms / Domestic Firms

Mission Statement: Was formed to take advantage of the dramatic growth in the technology sector.
Fund Size: $2.7 billion
Founded: 1998
Average Investment: $7 million
Minimum Investment: $3 million
Investment Criteria: Expansion
Industry Group Preference: Semiconductors, Communications, Software, Energy, Wireless Technologies, Energy Technology, Renewable Energy, Oil & Gas

11700 Katy Freeway
Houston, TX 77079

Key Executives:
Robert Gold, President/CEO
e-mail: bgold@ridgewoodcapital.com
Education: JD, New York University School of Law; BA, Colgate University
Background: Corporate Attorney, Cleary, Gottlieb, Steen & Hamilton
Directorships: The FeedRoom; Orbcomm; SavaJe Technologies
Jeffrey H Strasberg, Chief Financial Officer
Education: BS, University of Florida
Background: Corporate Officer, NERCO; Divisional CFO, PacifiCorp; Price Waterhouse
Daniel Gulino, SVP/Legal & Corporate Secretary
Education: Farleigh Dickinson University; Rutgers University School of Law
Background: In-House Counsel, GPU; PPL Resources; Alumax
Matthew E. Swanson, Senior Managing Director
Education: BA, Harvard University; JD, Harvard Law School
Background: Investment Management Division, Securities & Exchange Commission; Tax Department, Chadbourne & Parke
Domenic Salvemini, Chief Information Officer
Background: Eizo Nanao Corporation

1565 RIDGEWOOD ENERGY
1254 Enclave Parkway
Houston, TX 77077

Fax: 201-447-0474
Toll-Free: 800-942-5550
e-mail: info@ridgewoodenergy.com
web: www.ridgewoodenergy.com

Mission Statement: Houston private equity firm focused on energy.
Geographic Preference: Gulf of Mexico
Founded: 2008
Industry Group Preference: Energy

Key Executives:
Robert Gold, Senior Managing Director

1566 RINCON VENTURE PARTNERS
803 Chapala Street
Santa Barbara, CA 93101

Phone: 805-969-5484
web: www.rinconvp.com

Mission Statement: Rincon Venture Partners seeks to partner with extraordinary entrepreneurs and assist them as they build world class businesses. Rincon Venture Partners serve in supporting roles, helping entrepreneurs achieve success.
Geographic Preference: Southern California
Average Investment: $500,000 - $1 million
Investment Criteria: Early-Stage
Industry Group Preference: Internet
Portfolio Companies: Campus Explorer, Connectivity, Datapop, Digital Performance, Divshot, Earnest, ElephantDrive, HGData, Invoca, Keen IO, Launchpad.la, Local Market Launch, Promt.ly, Ranker, The Resumator, Rentlytics, Shift, Sideqik, Steelhouse, Tradesy, Worksteady

Other Locations:
1217 2nd Street
Santa Monica, CA 90401

Key Executives:
Jim Andelman, Managing Partner
Education: BS, Economics, Wharton School; MBA, Amos Tuck School of Business, Dartmouth
Background: Broadview Capital Partners; Technology Investment Banking Group, Deutsche Banc Alex Brown; Symmetrix
Ryan A Smiley, Managing Director
e-mail: rsmiley@rlhequity.com
Education: BS, Finance, Wharton School; MBA, UCLA Anderson School of Management

1568 RITTENHOUSE VENTURES
Building 100 Innovation Center
4801 South Broad Street
Suite 340
Philadelphia, PA 19112

Phone: 215-972-1502
web: www.rittenhouseventures.com

Mission Statement: Rittenhouse Ventures invests in early stage companies across a range of technology sectors, and primarily seeks opportunities in Pennsylvania and the Mid-Atlantic region. Rittenhouse Ventures was formerly known as Emerald Stage2 Ventures.
Geographic Preference: Pennsylvania, Mid-Atlantic Region, Washington to New York Corridor
Founded: 2006
Average Investment: $500,000 - $750,000
Investment Criteria: Early-Stage
Industry Group Preference: Technology, Technology-Enabled Services, Healthcare Information Technology, Pharmaceuticals, Outsourcing & Efficiency, Financial Services, Fintech
Portfolio Companies: AlignAlytics, Core Solutions, GSI Health, Halfpenny Technologies, Kynectiv, Life.io, Miria Systems, Noble Biomaterials, Tabula Rasa Healthcare, Take the Interview, Vcopious

Key Executives:
Saul Richter, Managing Partner
Education: BA, Economics, Columbia University; MBA, Columbia Business School
Background: Principal, Himalaya Capital; Lucent Technologies; Softbank Ventures; Jerusalem Global Ventures; Flatiron Partners; Founder, US Operations, Zapper Technologies
Directorships: Take the Interview, Miria Systems, Vcopious
Bruce Luehrs, Managing Partner
Education: BA, Economics, Duke University; MBA, Kellogg School of Management, Northwestern University
Background: General Partner, Edison Venture Fund; VP, Columbia Capital; Principal, PNC Equity Management; President, SBIC Unit, Fidelcor Capital; Officer, United States Air Force
Directorships: Tabula Rasa Healthcare, Miria Systems, Core Solutions
Britton Murdoch, Principal
Education: BS, University of Pennsylvania; MBA, New York University
Background: Founder/Managing Director, Strattech Partners LLC
Directorships: Fiberlink; Internet Capital Group; Airgas; V-Span

Venture Capital & Private Equity Firms / Domestic Firms

1569 RIVER ASSOCIATES INVESTMENTS LLC
633 Chestnut Street
Suite 1640
Chattanooga, TN 37450

Phone: 423-755-0888 Fax: 423-755-0870
e-mail: ccudd@riverassociatesllc.com
web: www.riverassociatesllc.com

Mission Statement: Exclusively focused on control buyouts of lower middle market companies in the United States and Canada.

Geographic Preference: United States, Canada
Fund Size: $222 million
Founded: 1989
Average Investment: $10-$30 million
Minimum Investment: $10 million
Investment Criteria: Buyouts, Recapitalizations, Divestures
Industry Group Preference: Manufacturing, Distribution, Industrial Services, Business Products & Services, Select Retail
Portfolio Companies: Boxercraft, CMS Management Solutions, Industrial Magnetics, National Deli, Omega Environmental Technologies, Rose City Printing and Packaging, TrueNet Communications

Key Executives:
Jim Baker, Managing Partner
e-mail: jbaker@riverassociatesllc.com
Education: MBA/BS, University of Tennessee, Knoxville
Background: President/COO, CONSTAR International; President, Baker Dixon Packaging; Arthur Andersen & Company
Mike Brookshire, Managing Partner
e-mail: mbrookshire@riverassociatesllc.com
Education: BS, University of Tennessee, Chattanooga
Background: Arthur Andersen & Company
Mark Jones, Partner
e-mail: mjones@riverassociatesllc.com
Education: BA, Economics, Vanderbilt University; MBA, Samford University
Background: South Trust Bank
Directorships: Several Private companies and charitable organizations
Patten Pettway, Partner
e-mail: pprettway@riverassociatesllc.com
Education: BA, University of Colorado; MBA, The Wharton School
Background: Joseph Decosimo & Company
Craig Baker, Partner
e-mail: cbaker@riverassociatesllc.com
Education: MBA, Emory University; B.ChE., Georgia Institute of Technology
Background: Finance Manager, General Chemical Corporation; Operations Manager, Marsulex
Blake Lewis, Vice President
e-mail: blewis@riverassociatesllc.com
Education: BS, Finance & Accounting, University of Tennessee
Background: Avondale Partners
Stuart Vyule, Vice President
e-mail: svyule@riverassociatesllc.com
Education: BS, Finance, Virginia Tech.
Background: Bank of America Merrill Lynch

1570 RIVER CAPITAL
4200 Northside Parkway
Building 14
Suite 250
Atlanta, GA 30327

Phone: 404-873-2166
e-mail: info@river-capital.com
web: www.river-capital.com

Mission Statement: An Atlanta based private investment firm which provides capital for management buy-outs, recapitalizations and growth capital needs of well-established middle market companies.

Geographic Preference: South, Midwest, Mid Atlantic
Fund Size: $600 million
Founded: 1983
Average Investment: $10-$50 million
Minimum Investment: $10 million
Investment Criteria: Recapitalizations, Management Buy-outs, Growth Capital
Industry Group Preference: Distribution, Manufacturing, Business Products & Services
Portfolio Companies: American Threshold Industries, Blue Wave, Can-Do National Tape, DéCor Gravure, Five Start Manufacturing, Hometown Communications, New Image Group, Piedmont Aviation Services, Tronair, Winston Furniture Company

Key Executives:
Jerry D. Wethington, President
e-mail: jwethington@river-capital.com
Education: BA, Economics, University of Kentucky; MA, Economics, Western Kentucky University; MBA, University of Louisville
Background: COO, Mitchell Steel; Senior Manager, Fuqua Industries, Teledyne
Directorships: Blue Wave Products, Inc., CDNT, Five Star Manufacturing, New Image Group
Bryan M. Wethington, Vice President
e-mail: bwethington@river-capital.com
Education: BS, Managerial Finance, University of Mississippi
Background: Founder, Southern Setup; Founder, Rebel Yell Inc.
Directorships: Five Star Manufacturing

1571 RIVER CITIES CAPITAL FUNDS
221 East Fourth Street
Suite 2400
Cincinnati, OH 45202-4151

Phone: 513-621-9700
web: www.rccf.com

Mission Statement: A family of three venture capital funds based in Cincinnati, Ohio, with an office in Raleigh, NC. Invests primarily in early stage to middle stage companies, located in the Midwest and Southeast, that operate in a variety of high growth industries.

Geographic Preference: Midwest, Southwest
Fund Size: $300 million
Founded: 1994
Average Investment: $2 million
Minimum Investment: $2 million
Investment Criteria: First-stage, Second-stage
Industry Group Preference: Diversified
Portfolio Companies: Advanced Biomarker, Canvas, Continuity Control, EndoChoice, Health Integrated, Ifbyphone, Intradiem, Knowledge Tree, MedPlast, NICO, NineSigma, Orthalign, PerfectServce, SIM Partners, StepLeader, Surgiquest, Tissuetech, Trax, Univa, Urgent Team

Other Locations:
2501 Blue Ridge Road
Suite 220
Raleigh, NC 27607
Phone: 919-374-5600

Key Executives:
R Glen Mayfield, Co-Founder
Education: BA, DePauw University
Background: Founder, Mayfield & Robinson; VP, First National Bank
Edwin T Robinson, Co-Founder
Education: AB, Thomas More College; JD, University of Cincinnati College of Law

553

Venture Capital & Private Equity Firms / Domestic Firms

Background: Mayfield & Robinson; Arthur Andersen & Company
Daniel T Fleming, Managing Director
Education: BSME, Ohio State University; MBA Harvard University
Edward C McCarthy, Managing Director
Education: BSEE, Northeastern University; MSEE, Florida Institute of Technology; MBA, Stetson University
Background: Harris Corporation
J Carter McNabb, Managing Director
Education: BA, Trinity College; MBA, Owen School at Vanderbilt
Background: JC Bradford & Company; Paine Webber Group
Robert A Heimann, Managing Director
Education: BS, Accounting, University of Virginia; MBA, J.L. Kellogg School of Business at Northwestern University
Background: VP Corporate Development, Intelliseek, Inc.
Rurik G Vandevenne, Managing Director
Education: BE, Mechanical Engineering, Vanderbilt University
Background: Scient, Accenture

1572 RIVERSIDE COMPANY
45 Rockefeller Center
630 Fifth Avenue
Suite 400
New York, NY 10111

web: www.riversidecompany.com

Mission Statement: Private equity firm investing in premier companies at the smaller end of the middle market, focusing on industry-leading companies.
Fund Size: $1.3 billion
Founded: 1988
Minimum Investment: $3 million
Investment Criteria: LBO, MBO
Industry Group Preference: Business Services, Consumer, Education, Healthcare, Software & IT, Technology, Manufacturing, Retail
Portfolio Companies: ActiveStyle, Alchemy, Alcholo Monitoring Systems, American Hospice, American Stock Transfer & Trust Company, Anitox, ARCOS, Avatar International, Be Green Packaging, BeneSys, Blue Microphones, Bohemia Interactive Simulations, Brandmuscle, Brookson, Camelot Education, Censis, CorporateRewards, Crioestaminal, :DentalPlans, Diatron Group, DMA, DPA Microphones, Drex-Chem Malaysia, The Dwyer Group, Eemax, Emergency Communications Network, Fisher/Unitech, G&H Orthodontics, Global Orthopaedic Technologies, Grace Hill, Harvey Tool, H-D Manufacturing, HRA Pharma, iAutomation, IDOC, Insurance Claims Management, It's Just Lunch, Keycast, Keymile, Kyjen, Learning Seat, Lexipol, MEC3, Medical Payment Exchange, Mintra Trainingportal, MNX, Orliman, Paradigm Tax Group, PharmMD, Physicians Pharmacy Alliance, Polar Windows, PPS, ProSites, Rameder, Reima, Rutland Plastics, SAFEbuilt, SIGG, Simcro, Specialized Medical Services, Spectrio, Summit Medical Group, Sunless, Sunrise Windows, Tate's Bake Shop, Team Technologies, Tensator, Transporeon, Tropikal Pet, Uinta Brewing Company, Water-Jel, WhatCounts, Wiz Korea, Y International, YourMembership.com

Other Locations:
455 Market Street
Suite 1520
San Francisco, CA 94105
Phone: 415-348-9560 **Fax:** 415-348-9561

3131 McKinney Avenue
Suite 160
Dallas, TX 75204

Terminal Tower
50 Public Square
29th Floor
Cleveland, OH 44113

Alter Hof 5
Munich 80331
Germany

London
United Kingdom

Los Angeles, CA

Lloyd Georgelaan 7
Brussels 1000
Belgium

Stockholm
Sweden

46A, Avenue J.F. Kennedy
Luxembourg L-1855
Luxembourg
Phone: 352-2717291 **Fax:** 352-27172999

Serrano 120-3o dcha
Madrid 28006
Spain
Phone: 34-915901337 **Fax:** 34-915611606

Vaclavske namesti 832-19
Prague 1 110 00
Czech Republic
Phone: 420-224890166 **Fax:** 420-224890164

ul. Zielna 37/c
Warsaw 00-108
Poland
Phone: 48-223204820 **Fax:** 48-223204828

Level 9, Kamiyacho Prime Place
4-1-17, Toranomon, Minato-ku
Tokyo 105-0001
Japan
Phone: 81-354081230 **Fax:** 81-354081231

Riverside Asia Partners Ltd.
Times Square, Room 2912 Tower Two
1 Matheson Street
Causeway Bay, Hong Kong
China
Phone: 852-2159-7492 **Fax:** 852-2159-7493

Level 35, 140 William Street
Melbourne VIC 3000
Australia
Phone: 61-3-8672-2000 **Fax:** 61-3-8672-2001

31F. One IFC
10 Gookjekeumyoong-ro
Seoul 150-945
South Korea
Phone: 82-2-6137-9880 **Fax:** 82-2-6137-9889

Riverside Asia Partners Pte. Ltd.
9 Raffles Place, #58-27
Republic Plaza
Singapore 048619
Singapore
Phone: 65-9116-0772 **Fax:** 65-6823-1377

Key Executives:
Béla Szigethy, Co-CEO, New York
Education: BA, Oberlin College; Masters of International Affairs, Columbia University
Background: Citibank, NA
Stuart Baxter, Managing Partner, San Francisco
Education: BA, Economics, Stanford University
Background: Director of Crimson Capital's Czech Restructuring and Privatization Group; President, AI International Corporation; Credit Suisse First Boston
Suzanne Kriscunas, Managing Partner, Dallas
214-871-9640
Fax: 214-871-9620
e-mail: skriscunas@riversidecompany.com
Education: BA, French, Denison University; MA, MBA,

Venture Capital & Private Equity Firms / Domestic Firms

Indiana University
Background: Managing Director & Co-Founder, Legacy Private Capital Partners; Managing Director, Banc One Capital Corporation
Ron Sansom, Managing Partner, Cleveland
216-344-1040
Fax: 216-244-1330
Education: BS, Industrial Engineering, Auburn University; MS, Management, Krannert Graduate School of Management, Purdue University
Background: President, Sensing & Control, Honeywell Automation & Control Products; President & CEO, Kinetek
Loren Schlachet, Managing Partner, Los Angeles
310-499-5080
Fax: 310-499-5090
e-mail: lschlachet@riversidecompany.com
Education: BA, History, University of Pennsylvania; MBA, Finance, Stern School of Business, New York University
Background: Associate, Claremont Capital Corporation; Associate, TCW Capital
Timothy Gosline, Partner, Cleveland
216-344-1040
Fax: 216-344-1330
e-mail: tgosline@riversidecompany.com
Education: BBA, Business Administration, Kent State University; MBA, Finance, Case Western Reserve University
Background: Sea-Tech; Manager of Financial Analysis, Midland Ross Corporation; Senior Accountant, Deloitte & Touche

1573 RIVERSTONE
712 Fifth Avenue
36th Floor
New York, NY 10019

Phone: 212-993-0076 **Fax:** 212-993-0077
web: www.riverstonellc.com

Mission Statement: Since 2000 Riverstone has pursued a four-sector approach within the energy and power industry, targeting investments in the exploration & production, midstream, energy services and power & coal sectors. The Firm believes that a strategic allocation across the energy industry's main sectors results in superior rick-adjusted returns for Limited Partners.
Geographic Preference: North America, Latin America, Europe, Africa, Asia
Fund Size: $27 billion
Founded: 2000
Investment Criteria: Buyout, Growth Capital
Industry Group Preference: Conventional Energy, Renewable Energy
Portfolio Companies: 4Gas Holding B.V., Abasco Energy Technologies, AG Global, Bara Energia do Brasil Petróleo e Gás, Belden & Blake Corporation, Bottle Rock Power, Bridger, Buckeye Partners, C/R Energy Jade, CanEra Resources, Carrier Energy Partners, CDM Resource Management, CNDAA, Coastal Carolina Clean Power, Cobalt International Energy, CODA Holdings, Cuadrilla Resources Holdings, Davenport Newberry Holdings, Dresser, Dynamic Industries, Dynamic Offshore Resources, Eagle Energy Company of Oklahoma, Eagle Energy Exploration, Emerald Clean Power, Enduro Resource Partners II, Enduro Resource Partners, Ensus Ethanol, Enviva Holdings, EP Energy, Fairfield Energy, Fieldwood Energy, Foresight Reserves, Frontier Drilling, Gibson Energy, Green Earth Fuels, Heysta Energy, HongHua Co., Hudson Products Corporation, ILX Holdings, ILX Holdings II, InTANK, International Logging, Kerogen Energy Holdings, Kinder Morgan, Kramerk Junction, Legend Natural Gas, Legend Production Holdings, Liberty Oilfield Services, Liberty Resources, Liberty Resources II, Magellan Midstream Services II, Mistral Energy, Niska Gas Storage, Northern Blizzard Resources, Patagonia BioEnergia, Patriot Storage, Pattern Energy Group, Permian Tank & Manufacturing, Petroplus Holdings, Phoenix Exploration Company, PVR Partners, Quintana Shipping, Quorum Business Solutions, R/c Sugarkane, Raven Power Holdings, Red Technology Alliance, ReEnergy Holdings, Ridgebury Tankers, Sage Midstream, Sapphire Power Holdings, Seabulk International

Other Locations:
3 St. James' Square
London SW1Y 4JU
England
Phone: 44 20 3206 6300 **Fax:** 44 20 3206 6301

1000 Louisiana
Suite 1450
Houston, TX 77002
Phone: 713-357-1400 **Fax:** 713-357-1399

Javier Barros Sierra 540 Torre 2
Piso 2 Colonia Lomas de Santa Fe
Mexico City, DF 01210
Phone: 52-55-9177-2030

Herengracht 450
Amsterdam 1017 CA
The Netherlands
Phone: 31-20-240-4447

Key Executives:
Stephen S. Coats, Partner
Education: BA, Government, University of Texas at Austin; JD, University of Texas Law School
Background: Partner, Vinson & Elkins LLP
James T. Hackett, Partner (Based In Houston)
Education: BS, University of Illinois; MBA, Harvard Business School
Background: Chairman of the Board and CEO, Andarko Petroleum Corporation; President and Chief Operating Officer, Devon Energy Corporation; Chairman, President and Chief Executive Officer, Ocean Energy; Seagull; Duke Energy; Pan Energy; NGC Corp; Burlington Resources; Amoco Oil Corp.
D Thomas Healey Jr., Partner
Education: BA, Boston College; MBA, NYU Stern School of Business
Background: Roundtable Investment Partners; Merrill Lynch's Private Banking and Investments Group; Morgan Stanley's Private Wealth Management Group; Co-Founder, Gates Capital
N. John Lancaster, Jr., Partner
Education: BBA, University of Texas; MBA, Harvard Business School
Background: Director, The Beacon Group; Bankers Trust; CS First Boston
Directorships: Abaco Energy Technologies, Barra Energia, Cuadrilla Resources, Dynamic Industries, Enduro Resource Partners, Fieldwood Energy, Hudson Products, Kerogen Exploration
Christopher B Hunt, Partner/Managing Director
Education: BA, Wesleyan University; MBA, Columbia University
E Bartow Jones, Partner
Education: BS, McIntire School of Commerce, University of Virginia
Background: JP Morgan
Mark G Papa, Partner
Education: Petroleum Engineering degree, University of Pittsburgh; MBA, University of Houston
Background: Chairman and CEO, EOG Resources
Kenneth Ryan, Partner
Education: University of Dublin, Trinity College
Background: Gleacher & Company
Baran Tekkora, Partner
Education: BA, Hamilton College
Background: Goldman Sachs
Robert M Tichio, Partner
Education: AB, Dartmouth College; MBA, Harvard

555

Venture Capital & Private Equity Firms / Domestic Firms

Business School
Background: Goldman Sachs; JP Morgan

1574 RIVERVEST VENTURE PARTNERS
101 S. Hanley Road
Suite 1850
St Louis, MO 63105

Phone: 314-726-6700
e-mail: info@rivervest.com
web: www.rivervest.com

Mission Statement: Focuses exclusively on innovations in life sciences, a field in which our team has significant research, clinical, operational and investment expertise.
Geographic Preference: United States
Fund Size: $75 million
Founded: 2000
Average Investment: $500,000 - $6 million
Minimum Investment: $500,000
Industry Group Preference: Life Sciences
Portfolio Companies: Accumetrics, Allakos, CGI Pharmaceuticals, Cabrellis Pharmaceuticals, Calypso Medical Technologies, Cameron Health, Centerre Healthcare, Conforma Therapeutics, CyDex Pharmaceuticals, Excaliard Pharmaceuticals, IDev Techologies, Kaperio, Kereos, Lumena Pharmaceuticals, Luminous Medical, Lutonix, MacroGenics, Mpex Pharmaceuticals, Neuros Medical, Otonomy, Salient Surgical Technologies, Securus Medical Group, Tryton Medical, Velocimed, Xcyte, Xoft, ZS Pharma

Other Locations:
11000 Cedar Avenue
Suite 100
Cleveland, OH 44106
Phone: 212-658-3982

Key Executives:
Thomas C Melzer, Co-Founder/Managing Director
Education: BS, Stanford University; MBA, Stanford Graduate School of Business
Background: Managing Director, Morgan Stanley; President/CEO, Federal Reserve Bank of St. Louis
Jay W Schemelter, Co-Founder/Managing Director
Education: BA, Michigan State University; MBA, Booth School of Business, University of Chicago
Background: Sr Financial Analyst, General Mills; Marketing Manager, Medtronic; Equity Research Analyst, Piper Jaffray; Principal, Cresendo Ventures
John McKearn PhD, Managing Director
Education: BS, Biology, Northern Illinois University
Background: GD Searle & Co.; EI Dupont de Nemours and Company
Niall A O'Donnell PhD, Managing Director
Education: MA, University of Oxford; PhD, University of Dundee; MBA, Rady School of Management, University of California San Diego
Background: Interim Chief Medical Officer, Lumena Pharmaceuticals Inc.; President/Interim CEO, Reneo Pharmaceuticals; Principal, Rivervest Venture Partners
Karen Spilizewski, Vice President
Education: BS/MS/MBA, Case Western Reserve University
Background: Business Development Manager, Avery Dennison; VP, Business Development, BioEntreprise
Directorships: Neuros Medical Inc.; Securus Medical Group; Standard Bariatrics Inc.

1575 RLH EQUITY PARTNERS
10900 Wilshire Blvd
Suite 850
Los Angeles, CA 90024

Phone: 310-405-7200 Fax: 310-405-7222
web: www.rlhequity.com

Mission Statement: To be the preferred private equity partner of exceptional high growth middle-market companies. Formerly known as Riordan, Lewis & Haden.
Geographic Preference: United States
Fund Size: $265 million
Founded: 1979
Average Investment: $15M - $40M
Minimum Investment: $10 million
Investment Criteria: Equity growth financing, MBO, Recapitalization
Industry Group Preference: Business Products & Services, Healthcare, Government Services
Portfolio Companies: Avella Specialty Pharmacy, Bluewolf, Clarity Solution Group, Mondo, RGM Group, Silverado Senior Living, Siteworx, The Chartis Group, Total Woman

Other Locations:
18300 Von Karman Avenue
Suite 730
Irvine, CA 92612
Phone: 949-428-2200 Fax: 949-428-2210

300 East 5th Avenue
Suite 390
Naperville, IL 60563
Phone: 312-281-7987

Key Executives:
J Christopher Lewis, Co-Founder/Managing Director
310-405-7200
e-mail: clewis@rlhinvestors.com
Education: BS, Finance, MBA, University of Southern California
Murray E Rudin, Managing Director
Education: BS, Electrical Engineering, University of Rochester; JD, Harvard Law School
Michel Glouchevitch, Managing Director
e-mail: mg@rlhequity.com
Education: BA, Political Science, Swarthmore College; MBA, Hautes Etudes Commerciales, Paris
Michael J Orend, Managing Director
e-mail: morend@rlhequity.com
Education: BA, University of Virginia
Background: Sales Executive, Digital Equipment Corportation; Business Development Manager, PricewaterhouseCoopers
Directorships: Arthur Andersen & Co.; Lake Capital
Robert Rodin, Managing Director
e-mail: rrodin@rlhequity.com
Education: University of Connecticut
Background: CEO, Marshall Industries; Vice Chairman, CommerceNet; CEO/Chairman, RND Group Inc.
Directorships: Napster; CyberCoders; Collabrx; CareerBliss; ALS Therapy Development Institute; Siteworx LLC; Clarity Insights; Inspirage; Biorasi; SupplyFrame
Kevin D Cantrell, Managing Director
e-mail: kcantrell@rlhequity.com
Education: BS, Finance, Auburn University; MBA, Kellogg School of Management, Northwestern University

1576 ROARK CAPITAL GROUP
1180 Peachstreet Street NE
Suite 2500
Atlanta, GA 30309

Phone: 404-591-5200
web: www.roarkcapital.com

Mission Statement: Roark Capital Group is an Atlanta-based private equity firm that specializes in consumer, business and environmental services companies with attractive growth prospects and revenues ranging from $20 million to $1.0 billion. Roark focuses on middle-market investment opportunities through family-owned business transfers, management and corporate buyouts, recapitalizations, going-private transactions and corporate divestitures. Roark has acquired 20

franchise/consumer brands that operate in 50 states and 43 countries.
Geographic Preference: Worldwide
Fund Size: $1.5 billion
Average Investment: $25-$250 million
Investment Criteria: Family-Owned Business Transfers, Management & Corporate Buyouts, Recapitalizations, Going-Private Transactions, Corporate Divestitures
Industry Group Preference: Consumer Services, Business Products & Services, Environment Products & Services
Portfolio Companies: 1-800 Radiator, Anytime Fitness, Arby's, Auntie Anne's, Basecamp Fitness, Batteries Plus Bulbs, Bosley's, Buffalo Wild Wings, CARSTAR, Carvel, Cinnabon, CKE Restaurants, Corner Bakery Cafe, Culver's, Driven Brands, Drybar, Fitness Connection, FOCUS Brands, Great Expressions Dental Centers, Inspire Brands, Installation Made Easy, International Car Wash Group, Jamba Juice, Jim 'N Nick's Bar-B-Q, Jimmy John's, Maaco, Massage Envy, McAlister's Deli, Meineke, Miller's Ale House, Moe's Southwest Grill, Naf Naf, Orangetheory Fitness, Pet Supermarket, Pet Valu, Primrose Schools, R Taco, Schlotzsky's, Seattle's Best International, Self Esteem Brands, Solterra Recycling Solutions, Sonic, Take 5 Oil Change, Waxing the City

Key Executives:
Neal K. Aronson, Founder/Managing Partner
404-591-3333
e-mail: nealaronson@roarkcapital.com
Background: Co-Founder/CFO/Executive VP, US Franchise Systems; Principal, Odyssey Partners LP; Principal/General Partner, Acadia Partners LP
Directorships: FOCUS Brands, Money Mailer, FastSigns, McAlisters, Batteries Plus
Paul D. Ginsberg, President
404-591-3331
e-mail: pginsberg@roarkcapital.com
Education: BA, Union College; JD, University of Chicago Law School
Background: Paul Weiss Rifkind Wharton & Garrison LLP
Stephen D. Aronson, Managing Director/General Counsel
404-591-5210
e-mail: saronson@roarkcapital.com
Education: BA, Government, Lehigh University; JD, University of Chicago Law School
Background: SVP, General Counsel, Executive Committee, US Franchise Systems
Timothy B. Armstrong, Managing Director
212-518-0712
e-mail: tarmstrong@roarkcapital.com
Education: Undergraduate Degree, Yale University
Background: Saunders Karp & Megrue
Ezra S. Field, Senior Managing Director/Co-CIO
404-591-3337
e-mail: efield@roarkcapital.com
Education: BA, Wesleyan University; JD & MBA, Columbia University
Background: Managing Director, ACI Capital; Entrepreneur & Venture Capitalist; Co-Founder, TeachScape
Directorships: Cybercore, Pet Valu, Peachtree Business Products
Erik O. Morris, Senior Managing Director/Co-CIO
404-591-5205
e-mail: emorris@roarkcapital.com
Education: BS, Business Administration, University of North Carolina, Chapel Hill
Background: Partner, Grotech Capital Group, Deutsche Bank
Directorships: Primrose Schools, Waste Pro, Wingstop
Steve Romaniello, Senior Advisor
404-591-5215
e-mail: stever@roarkcapital.com
Education: Tufts University
Background: President & CEO, FOCUS Brands; President & COO, US Franchise Systems; VP, Holiday Inn Worldwide
Directorships: FOCUS Brands, FastSigns
Geoff A. Hill, Managing Director
404-591-3330
e-mail: ghill@roarkcapital.com
Education: BA, Cornell University School of Hotel Administration
Background: President, Cinnabon; VP, USFS; Director of Sales, Bristol Hotel Company
Directorships: FOCUS Brands
Kevin Hofmann, Managing Director
404-591-3322
e-mail: khofmann@roarkcapital.com
Education: BS, Computer Science, Central Michigan University
Background: President/Chief Marketing Officer, Home Depot; CIO/CTO, GE; Dow Chemical

1577 ROBIN HOOD VENTURES
3675 Market Street
Philadelphia, PA 19104

Phone: 215-839-6256 **Fax:** 484-214-0114
e-mail: info@robinhoodventures.com
web: www.robinhoodventures.com

Mission Statement: Robin Hood Ventures consists of Greater Philadelphia Region entrepreneurs/investors who have joined together to fund and aid the development of local companies through their collective business experience and contacts. Skill sets include depth in all functional areas, including general management, marketing, sales, product development, marketing communications, and finance.

Investment Criteria: Seed-Stage
Industry Group Preference: Energy, Information Technology, Business Products & Services, Financial Services, Insurance, Entertainment, Real Estate, Manufacturing, Healthcare, Consumer Products, Restaurants, Biopharmaceuticals, Medical Devices, Diagnostics
Portfolio Companies: ATRIN Pharmaceuticals, AlphaPoint, Biologics, Biomeme, Burrow, ChargeItSpot, Core Solutions, Document Depository Corp., ExpressCells, GenPro, FemSelect, Grassroots Unwired, Illumine Radiopharmaceuticals, Immunome, Inpensa, Intrommune, LIA Diagnostics, LoanLogics, Luxtech, NanoPack Inc., Ophidion, OWIT Global, Peeractive, Proscia, ReturnLogic, Sidecar, Simply Good Jars, TASSL, Thermalin, Thrupore, Virion Therapeutics, Wash Cycle Laundry, WizeHive, Yellowdig

Key Executives:
Ellen Weber, Executive Director
Education: BS, Economics, Wharton School, University of Pennsylvania
Background: Executive Director, Fox School of Business Innovation, Temple University; COO/Co-Founder, VisionMine; Managing Director/Founder, Antiphony Partners LLC; Sr Consultant, Andersen Consulting

1578 ROCK ISLAND CAPITAL
1415 W 22nd Street
Suite 1250
Oak Brook, IL 60523

Phone: 630-413-9136 **Fax:** 630-574-0213
web: www.rockislandcapital.com

Mission Statement: Rock Island Capital LLC is a private equity fund that provides equity and mezzanine capital to middle market companies. Rock Island has over $150 million in committed capital under management and makes majority and minority investments in leading middle market manufacturing, distribution or service companies with enterprise values up to $100 million. Our firm is focused on building long-term relationships with business owners, management teams, investors, lenders and referral sources. These relationships are

Venture Capital & Private Equity Firms / Domestic Firms

the cornerstones of our firm and are built on honesty, loyalty and fairness.

Fund Size: $150 million
Investment Criteria: Middle Market
Industry Group Preference: Manufacturing, Distribution, Business Products & Services
Portfolio Companies: Advanced Industrial Devices, Atlas Connectivity, Baker Manufacturing, Central Power, Continental Services, DGS Retail, Environmental Recovery Corporation, Esmark, Excel Engineering, ERC midwest, Kemco Systems, Lake Shore Group, Mascara Sales & Marketing, Piedmont Candy Company, Pumps and Controls, Runyon Equipment Rental, Thorco, Valley Fastener Group, Venture Sales Group, Welch ATM

Key Executives:
   Alfred M. Mattaliano, Partner
   e-mail: mattaliano@rockislandcapital.com
   Education: BBA, Finance, University of Notre Dame; MM, Finance & Accounting, Northwestern University Kellogg Graduate School of Management
   Background: Principal, Catalyst/Hall; Founder & Partner, Vine Street Partners; Vice President, Corporate Finance, Bankers Trust Company; Second Vice President, American National Bank
   Michael E. Nugent, Partner
   e-mail: nugent@rockislandcapital.com
   Education: BBA, Accounting, University of Notre Dame; CPA
   Background: Vice President, Dresner Capital; Director, Vine Street Partners; KPMG Peat Marwick LLP
   Daniel K. Alport, Vice President
   e-mail: alport@rockislandcapital.com
   Education: BS, Finance, University of Illinois
   Background: Vice President, Deloitte Corporate Finance
   Brian Bastedo, Vice President
   e-mail: bastedo@rockislandcapital.com
   Education: BBA, Accounting, University of Notre Dame; MBA, Finance, Indiana University; CPA
   Background: Managing Director, RedRidge Finance Group; Associte Director, Bridge Finance Group; Manager, PriceWaterhouseCoopers LLP

1579 ROCKPORT CAPITAL
160 Federal Street
18th Floor
Boston, MA 02210-1700

web: www.rockportcap.com

Mission Statement: A leading venture capital firm that partners with cleantech entrepreneurs around the world. Collaborates with management teams to foster growth and create value, building innovative companies that bring disruptive technologies and products to the 21st century.

Geographic Preference: Worldwide
Average Investment: $500,000 - $25 million
Minimum Investment: $500,000
Investment Criteria: All Stages
Industry Group Preference: Clean Technology, Energy, Resource Efficiency, Transportation, Advanced Materials, Green Building
Portfolio Companies: Achates Power, Aspen Aerogels, Clean Diesel Technologies, Comverge, Deerpath Energy, drillMap, EcoFactor, EcoSMART Technologies, Eka Systems, Enki Technology, Enlightened, Enovix, Enphase Energy, Evergreen Solar, Exclara, FirstFuel Software, Flywheel Software, GaN Systems, Gazelle, GlassPoint, Gridco Systems, Honest Buildings, Hycrete, HydroPoint Data Systems, InVisage, Luxim, MicroSeismic, NanoGram Devices, Nectar Power, NeoPhotonics, NewLeaf Symbiotics, Northern Power Systems, Project Frog, Qnovo, Rayne Water, Recurve, Renaissance Lighting, Renovate America, Solar Universe, Soliant, Southwest Windpower, Streetline, SustainX

Key Executives:
   William E James, Managing General Partner
   Education: BA, History, Colorado College
   Background: Chairman & CEO, Citizens Corporation; Founder, Citizens Lehman Power
   Directorships: MicroSeismic, Think Holdings AS
   Alexander Ellis III, General Partner
   Education: BA, Political Science, Colorado College; MBA, Yale School of Management
   Background: Knoll International; Kenetech Corporation
   Janet James, General Partner/COO
   Education: BA, Govenment, Dartmouth College; MBA, Columbia Business School
   Background: EVP, Citizens Corporation; CEO, Citizens Gas Supply Corporation
   Stoddard M Wilson, General Partner
   Education: BA, Economics & History, Brown University; MBA, Harvard Business School
   Background: AT&T; Director External Affairs, Wilbraham & Monson Academy

1580 RODA GROUP
2217 5th Street
Berkeley, CA 94710

Phone: 510-649-1900
e-mail: info@rodagroup.com
web: www.rodagroup.com

Mission Statement: Provides entrepreneurs the resources, environment, and guidance to launch and grow their high technology businesses.

Founded: 1997
Investment Criteria: Seed Stage
Industry Group Preference: High Technology
Portfolio Companies: Axine, Game Ready, Gridtential, Inventys, mOasis

Key Executives:
   Roger A Strauch, Chairman
   e-mail: roger@rodagroup.com
   Education: BS, Electrical Engineering, Cornell University; MS, Electrical Engineering, Stanford University
   Background: CEO, Chairman, Ask Jeeves; Board Member, CEO, Symmetricom; Co-Founder, TCSI Corp.
   Directorships: Cool Systems
   Daniel H Miller, Managing Director
   e-mail: dan@rodagroup.com
   Education: BS, Electrical Engineering, Cornell University; MS, Electrical Engineering, Stanford University
   Background: President, Board Member, Ask Jeeves; EVP, TCSI Corp.
   Directorships: Solazyme

1581 ROMULUS CAPITAL
101 Arch Street
Boston, MA 02110

web: www.romuluscap.com

Mission Statement: Romulus Capital invests in seed-stage technology companies that seek to become industry leaders. The firm is young, entrepreneurial, and global, while retaining deep experience at the earliest stages of company formation.

Founded: 2008
Average Investment: $50,000 - $500,000
Investment Criteria: Seed-Stage
Portfolio Companies: Aidin, Allurion Technologies, Bombfell, Classpass, Cohealo, Crocodoc, DashBin, Disrupt Beam, Docphin, ElaCarte, Estify, Fitocracy, Giner.io, Gyft, Placester, Scholar Locker, Smart Lunches, Soundtracker, TheTapLab, Zigfu

Venture Capital & Private Equity Firms / Domestic Firms

Key Executives:
Neil Chheda, Co-Founder/General Partner
Education: BA, Political Science, Yale University; MBA, Harvard Business School
Background: Product Manager, Zynga; McKinsey & Company; Kleiner Perkins
Krishna K Gupta, Co-Founder/General Partner
Education: BS, Materials Science & Engineering, MIT
Background: Management Consultant, McKinsey & Company; JPMorgan

1582 ROOT CAPITAL
130 Bishop Allen Drive
2nd Floor
Cambridge, MA 02139

Phone: 617-661-5792
web: www.rootcapital.org

Mission Statement: Root Capital is a non-profit social investment fund that is pioneering finance for grassroots businesses in rural areas of developing countries. Provides capital, delivers financial training and strengthen market connections for small and growing businesses that build sustainable livelihoods and transforms rural communities.

Geographic Preference: Latin America, Africa
Founded: 1999
Industry Group Preference: Food & Beverage, Agriculture
Other Locations:
225 metros Norte del BCR
Paseo Colon
San José
Costa Rica
Phone: 506-2258-7094

Methodist Ministries Centre
Oloitoktok Road
Lavington, Nairobi
Kenya
Phone: 254-736-864892

Ma. Adelina Flores No. 20
Zona Centro
San Cristobal de las Casas
Chiapas
Mexico
Phone: (52) 967-674-0465 **Fax:** (52) 967-631-5615

Key Executives:
William F Foote, Founder & CEO
Education: BA, Yale University; MSc, Development Economics, London School of Economics
Background: Financial Analyst, Latin American Corporate Finance Group, Lehman Brothers

1583 ROPART ASSET MANAGEMENT
3 Greenwich Office Park
2nd Floor
Greenwich, CT 06831

Phone: 203-552-6697
e-mail: contact@ropart.com
web: www.ropart.com

Mission Statement: The Ropart Asset Management Funds is a private equity firm that invests directly in small to midsize companies. The firm pursues a flexible strategy, investing throughout the capital structure and in multiple industries, including Business Services, Healthcare Services, Consumer Products, Financial Services, and Software/Technology.

Average Investment: $3 - $15 millin
Investment Criteria: Control Investments, Mezzanine Lending, Growth Capital, Distressed or Special Situations
Industry Group Preference: Business Products & Services, Healthcare Services, Consumer Products, Financial Services, Software, Technology
Portfolio Companies: ALC Concierge Service, Crexendo, Digital Traffic Systems, Elite Daily, Fragmob, iCentris, Liftoff Mobile, Protein Sciences, QCL Holdings, Root Wireless

Key Executives:
Todd A Goergen, Managing Partner
e-mail: tgoergen@ropart.com
Education: BA, Economics & Political Science, Wake Forest University
Background: M&A, Donaldson, Lufkin & Jenrette; Director, M&A, Blyth
Directorships: QCL Holdings, Digital Traffic Systems, Crexendo, FragMob, ViSalus

1584 ROSE TECH VENTURES
158 West 29th Street
11th Floor
New York, NY 10001

web: www.rose.vc

Mission Statement: Rose Tech Ventures is an early stage investment fund, incubator, and all-around support infrastructure dedicated to finding, nurturing and launching the next generation of world class ventures.

Investment Criteria: Early-Stage
Portfolio Companies: Ambient Devices, Bioscale, Catalist, Challenge Post, Chromis Fiberoptics, CircleUp, Comixology, Crimson Hexagon, Concierge Choice, Critical Mention, Domdex, eJamming, Email Data Source, FASTTAC, GridPlex, Gust, iGuitar, Inn Road, Instinctiv, Kidzui, KoolSpan, LearnVest, LinkStorm, LiveLOOK, Luxology, Magnify Networks, Mashery, MediaTile, Metaphor Solutions, Monetate, Nimbit, Panjiva, Performline, Pond5, Por ti, Familia, Postling, Rocket Racing League, School Loop, Senscient, SetJam, SocialBomb, Space Adventures/Zero-G, TalkShoe, Trazzler, Vidler, Say Media, 33across, Wellgood

Key Executives:
David S Rose, Managing Director
Education: BA, Yale University; MBA, Finance, Columbia Business School
Background: Chairman & CEO, Angelsoft; Chairman, New York Angels, Chairman, Egret Capital Partners
Directorships: KoolSpan, Pond5, Comixology, Magnifiy Networks

1585 ROSECLIFF VENTURES
245 Fifth Avenue
14th Floor
New York, NY 10016

Phone: 212-492-3000 **Fax:** 212-586-7695
e-mail: contact@rosecliffvc.com
web: www.rosecliffvc.com

Mission Statement: A venture capital firm interested in startup and early stage companies with substantial growth potential.

Founded: 2010
Average Investment: Up to $250,000
Investment Criteria: Seed, Series A Round
Portfolio Companies: Allbirds, Banza, Brad's Raw Foods, Brewpublik, Cargo, Create1, CYC Fitness, Edufii, FanAI, Goby, Heyday, Homer, Jack Threds, Juice Press, Leo Health, Lyon and Post, Neutun, Nuzzel, Open Sponsorhip, Ollie, Petal, Pure Growth Organics, Raden, RecoverX, RTS, Riide, Roomi, SelfMade, Sidedolla, Tout, TraceME, Trustify, Twist, Wheels Up, Viyet, Voyajoy, WSC, YellowDig, Youstake

Key Executives:
Michael P. Murphy, Founder/Managing Partner
Education: Hofstra University; D'Amore-Mckim School of Business, Northeastern University
Directorships: Ample Hills Creamery, KARR Group of Companies, Cargo,
Michael V. Caso, Principal
Education: BS, Mathematics & Economics, Gabelli School of Business, Fordham University

Venture Capital & Private Equity Firms / Domestic Firms

Background: Sales & Trading Division, Merrill Lynch; Investment Banker, Rosecliff Ventures

1586 ROSER VENTURES LLC
1105 Spruce Street
Boulder, CO 80302

Phone: 303-443-6436
e-mail: roserventures@roserventures.com
web: www.roserventures.com

Mission Statement: A venture firm established to invest in private offerings of companies that exhibit the potential for superior long term returns.

Geographic Preference: Rocky Mountain
Fund Size: $75 million
Founded: 1987
Average Investment: $2 million
Minimum Investment: $250,000
Investment Criteria: Early Stage
Industry Group Preference: Communications, Electronic Technology, Software, Manufacturing, Low Technology, Information Technology

Key Executives:
Christopher W Roser, Partner
303-443-7935
Education: University of Colorado; MBA, New York University
Background: Main Hurdman KMG; Equity Research Associates; Associate, Ladenburg
James LD Roser, General Partner
303-443-7924
e-mail: jroser@roserventures.com
Education: BA, Economics, Bucknell University; MBA, Harvard University
Background: Smith, Barney & Company; Brown Brothers Harriman; Cyrus J Lawrence & Company

1587 ROSEWOOD CAPITAL
One Maritime Plaza
Suite 1575
San Francisco, CA 94111

Phone: 415-362-5526 Fax: 415-362-1192

Mission Statement: Rosewood invests exclusively in a small number of high-quality, consumer-oriented, growth companies.

Fund Size: $80 million
Founded: 1985
Average Investment: $10 - $40 million
Minimum Investment: $3 million
Investment Criteria: Small-Medium size businesses, Experienced Management, Superior Market, Strong Growth, Proven Profitability
Industry Group Preference: Consumer Products, Consumer Services, Restaurants, Retail, Consumer & Leisure, Outsourcing & Efficiency, Financial Services
Portfolio Companies: Cobalt Boats, Jamba Juice, 3 Day Blinds, Noah's Bagels, New York Sports Clubs, Anna's Linens, Alternative, CapitalSource, Under Armour

1588 ROTH CAPITAL PARTNERS
888 San Clemente Drive
Newport Beach, CA 92660

Fax: 949-720-7215
Toll-Free: 800-678-9147
web: ww.roth.com

Mission Statement: Roth Capital Partners is dedicated to the micro-cap marketplace. Provides institutional quality investment banking, research and distribution services to high quality micro-cap companies and offers investment guidance and current market information to their investors. Professional investment counselors have the experience to help clients identify and achieve financial goals through solid investments that include an array of proprietary and third-party products.

Founded: 1984
Minimum Investment: $2 million
Industry Group Preference: Business Products & Services, Clean Technology, Consumer Products, Gaming, Healthcare, Technology, Media

Other Locations:
730 Fifth Avenue
25th Floor
New York, NY 10019

470 Atlantic Avenue
4th Floor, Office #4062A
Boston, MA 02210
Phone: 949-720-5745

11150 Santa Monica Boulevard
Suite 480
Los Angeles, CA 90025 Fax: 310-445-5864

6183 Paseo del Norte
Carlsbad, CA 92011
Phone: 858-509-2500 Fax: 858-509-0790

155 North Wacker Drive
Suite 1900
Chicago, IL 60606
Phone: 312-564-8100

888 San Clemente Drive
Suite 3103-04, K Wah Centre, 1010 Huai Hai Zhong Road
Xuhui District
Newport Beach, CA 92660
Phone: 86-21-6141-5757 Fax: 949-7207215

Hong Kong Limited
Two International Finance Centre
8 Finance Street, 19/F
Central
Hong Kong
Phone: 852-22518585

Key Executives:
Bryon C Roth, Chairman/CEO
949-720-5721
Fax: 949-720-7223
e-mail: broth@rothcp.com
Education: Undergraduate Degree, University of San Diego; MBA, Cornell University
Gordon Roth, Chief Operating Officer & CFO
949-720-5774
e-mail: groth@roth.com
Education: WM Penn University, Drake University
Background: Deloitte & Touche
Ted Roth, President/Head of Institutional Sales
858-509-2502
e-mail: troth@roth.com
Education: Iowa Wesleyan College; JD, Washburn University; LLM, University of Missouri Kansas City
Background: Biotech R&D, Plastics Manufacturing
Aaron M Gurewitz, Managing Director, Equity Capital Markets
949-720-5703
e-mail: agurewitz@roth.com
Education: San Diego State University
Background: Friedman Billings Ramsey; Wedbush Morgan Securities; Prudential Securities; Wells Fargo Bank

1589 ROUGH DRAFT VENTURES
20 University Road
4th Floor
Cambridge, MA 02138

web: www.roughdraft.vc

Venture Capital & Private Equity Firms / Domestic Firms

Mission Statement: Student-led fund backs student founders in Boston, Mass.
Geographic Preference: Greater Boston Area Colleges and Universities
Average Investment: $5,000 - $25,000
Investment Criteria: Early Stage
Industry Group Preference: Financial Services, Software, E-Commerce & Manufacturing
Portfolio Companies: Beepi, Bowery, Charitweet, Cloudstitch, DeskConnect, Downtyme, Findit, Grove Labs, Healogram, INDICO, Life Guard Games, Lilypad Scales, Local Lift, Mark43, Mercaux, Nightingale, Pegasense, Pluto Mail, Request Now, Sand Hill Exchange, Smarking, Speech4Good, Technical Machine, Valet.io, Valued Investing, Vaska Tech, WatchSend

1590 ROUNDTABLE HEALTHCARE PARTNERS
272 East Deerpath Road
Suite 350
Lake Forest, IL 60045

Phone: 847-739-3200 **Fax:** 847-482-9215
web: www.roundtablehp.com

Mission Statement: RoundTable Healthcare Partners seeks to leverage its healthcare industry knowledge, operational experience, and financial expertise to generate outstanding investment returns.
Geographic Preference: United States, Canada, Europe
Fund Size: $650 million
Founded: 2001
Investment Criteria: Buyouts, Acquisitions, Consolidations
Industry Group Preference: Healthcare, Medical Devices, Medical Products, Pharmaceuticals
Portfolio Companies: Advantice Health, AMI Holdings Inc., Aqua Pharmaceuticals, Ascent Healthcare Solutions, Argon Medical Devices, Aspen Surgical, Avalign Technologies, Beaver Visitec, Bioniche Pharma, Clinical Innovations, Core Pharma, Deerland, Excelsior Medical, MedAssist, Renaissance Pharma, Revision Skincare, Sabex, Salter Labs, Santa Cruz Nutritionals, Symmetry Surgical, TIDI, Vesta
Key Executives:
  Lester B. Knight, Founding Partner
  Education: BS, Industrial Engineering, MBA, Cornell University
  Background: Vice Chairman, Cardinal Health; Chairman & CEO, Allegiance
  Directorships: AdvaMed
  Joseph F. Damico, Founding Partner/Senior Advisor
  Education: MBA, James Madison University
  Background: Executive VP, Cardinal Health; President & COO, Allegiance; Baxter; American Hospital Supply Corporation
  Directorships: Renaissance Pharma, Salter Labs, Santa Cruz Nutritionals
  R. Craig Collister, Managing Partner
  Education: University of Michigan; MBA, Harvard University Graduate School of Business Administration
  Background: Credit Suisse First Boston
  Directorships: Argon Medical Devices, Salter Labs, TIDI Products
  David J. Koo, Senior Advisor
  Education: BBA, Accountancy, University of Notre Dame; CPA
  Background: VP, US Healthcare Investment Banking Group, Credit Suisse First Boston; KPMG Peat Marwick
  Directorships: Renaissance Acquisition Holdings, Santa Cruz Nutritionals
  Pierre FréChette, Managing Partner
  Education: BS, Mechanical Engineering & Diploma in Business Administration, University of Sherbrooke
  Background: VP of Marketing/Business Development, Baxter; President/COO, Sabex; Vice-Chair, Canadian Generic Pharmaceutical Association; President/CEO, Sandoz Canada Inc.; CEO, Renaissance Acquisition Holdings
  Andrew B. Hochman, Senior Partner
  Education: BS, Economics, Wharton School, University of Pennsylvania
  Background: VP, Business Development, Graceway Pharmaceuticals
  Directorships: Santa Cruz Nutritionals

1591 ROYALTY CAPITAL MANAGEMENT
Royalty Capital Management LLC
Lexington, MA 02420

Phone: 781-861-8490
e-mail: alf@royaltycapital.us
web: www.royaltycapital.us

Mission Statement: Actively seeking new investments where a royalty against gross revenue can return original capital within 18 months.
Founded: 1994
Average Investment: $200,000
Minimum Investment: Less than $100,000
Investment Criteria: All Stages
Industry Group Preference: Communications, Computer Related, Consumer Products, Electronic Components, Energy, Genetic Engineering, Industrial Equipment, Medical & Health Related, Natural Resources
Key Executives:
  Arthur L Fox, President
  Education: BSEE, University of Maryland; MSEE, Massachusetts Institute of Technology
  Background: Hewlett Packard Co., Westinghouse Corporation; Co-founder, Octek, Inc., Lexidata Corporation, Medicel, Inc.

1592 RPM VENTURES
320 N Main Street
Suite 400
Ann Arbor, MI 48104

Phone: 734-332-1700
web: www.rpmvc.com

Mission Statement: Provides sound guidance and support to entrepreneurs and technology startups, helping transform their ideas into the next generation of new economy companies. Investments concentrates on IT or Software firms selling to the Midwest Manufacturing or Automotive customer Base and Midwest University spin-outs.
Geographic Preference: Midwest, California
Fund Size: $275 million
Founded: 2000
Average Investment: $2 million
Minimum Investment: $250,000
Investment Criteria: Seed, Early Stage, Startup
Industry Group Preference: Wireless Technologies, Infrastructure, Technology, Software, Semiconductors, Manufacturing, Materials Technology, Energy
Portfolio Companies: ArborMetrix, Automatics, BountyJobs, Deepfield, Deliv, Eden Park Illmination, Glyde, Janrain, Mojo Motors, Oxlo Systems, ShareThis, Social Finance, BlueLeaf, Boom! Studios, Bloud Tecnology Partners, Filament Labs, Getaround, Giftly, Gobbler, Karmic Labs, Navdy, QZZR, SupportPay, Collabrify
Key Executives:
  Marc Weiser, Managing Director
  Education: BS, Aerospace Engineering, University of Michigan; MBA, University of Michigan Business School
  Background: Founder, QuantumShift; MessageMedia; Associate, Arbor Partners
  Tony Grover, Managing Director
  Education: BS, Mechanical Engineering, University of Michigan; MS, Industrial Engineering, Purdue University; MBA, Kellogg Graduate School of Business
  Background: VP, White Pines Ventures

Venture Capital & Private Equity Firms / Domestic Firms

Directorships: Performix, Arbor Photoics, Eden Park, JanRain

1593 RRE VENTURES
130 E 59th Street
New York, NY 10022

Phone: 212-418-5100
e-mail: info@rre.com
web: www.rre.com

Mission Statement: RRE Ventures is an early-stage venture capital firm headquartered in New York City. Partners with extraordinary entrepreneurs who seek to disrupt and transform industries. RRE is a long-term lead investor.

Fund Size: $850 million
Founded: 1994
Average Investment: $5-10 million
Investment Criteria: Seed-Stage, Early-Stage
Industry Group Preference: Internet Technology, Software, Communications, Information Technology, Financial Services, Mobile, Enterprise Software, Consumer Products, Media
Portfolio Companies: AvantCredit, Bark & Co., Base, Betaworks, Bitly, Bitpay, Boom, Breather, Business Insider, BuzzFeed, Chain, CoverHound, Crossboard Mobiel, Drobo, Electric Cloud, Floored, HYLA, imIX, K2 Global, Kik, Kroll BondRatings, Mod Operandi, Netsertive, Noom, Odyssey, Ojo, OnDeck, Open Peak, Palantir Technologies, Paperless, PayFone, PrimeRevenue, Quirky, Rave Mobile Safety, Recyclebank, Roundbox, Sailthru, Shake, Socialflow, Spire, Tendril, Tinybop, Trumaker & Co., VigLink, YieldBot, Yipit

Key Executives:
Stuart Ellman, Founder/General Partner
e-mail: sje@rre.com
Education: BA Economics, Wesleyan University; MBA, Harvard University
Background: Advisory Capital Partners; Associate, Morgan Stanley & Company; Analyst, Dillon, Read & Company; McKinsey & Company
James Robinson, Founder/General Partner
e-mail: jim@rre.com
Education: MBA, Harvard University
Background: Hambrecht & Quist Venture Capital
James Robinson, III, Founder/General Partner
e-mail: jdriv@rre.com
Education: MBA, Harvard University; BS Industrial Management, Georgia Institute of Technology
Background: Computer Entrepreneur; Investment Banking; Venture Capital
Directorships: On Deck Capital, Prime Revenue, SkyGrid, Visprise
Will Porteous, General Partner/COO
e-mail: will@rre.com
Education: BA, Stanford University; MSc, London School of Economics, MBA, Harvard University
Background: SupplyWorks, NetMarket
Directorships: BuzzFeed, Data Robotics, HowAboutWe, Peek, Skyhook Wireless, Xobni
Raju Rishi, General Partner
Education: BS & MS, MIT
Background: Venture Partner, Sigma Prime Ventures; Executive, AT&T; Executive, Lucent
Jay Hass, Partner
Education: BA, Politics, Princeton University; Completed CFA Institute's Investment Management Program, Harvard Business School
Background: Managing Director, Brown Brothers Harriman; Advisor to the M. Night Shyamalan Foundation
Directorships: Cheetah Korea Value Fund
Maria Palma, Principal
Education: BS, Industrial Engineering, University of Wisconsin, Madison; MBA, Harvard Business School
Background: Chief of Staff/Executive Director of Business Development, Eyeview; Operations Management, General Electric

Jason Black, Principal
Education: BA, Psychology, Harvard University

1594 RTP VENTURES
885 Third Avenue
24th Floor
New York, NY 10022

Phone: 646-568-7206
e-mail: info@rtp.vc
web: www.rtp.vc

Mission Statement: Building companies takes time and resources. Having experienced investors who, instead of watching from the sidelines, built companies themselves can make all the difference.

Geographic Preference: United States, Israel, Turkey
Investment Criteria: Seed-Stage, Early-Stage, Later-Stage
Industry Group Preference: Big Data, Cloud Computing, E-Commerce & Manufacturing, Automation, SaaS
Portfolio Companies: Datadog, Fab, GridGain, Koding, Lidyana, Liftopia, RichRelevance, SiSense, Techstars, Tinfoil Security, Tutum, WorkFusion, Zerto

Key Executives:
Kirill Sheynkman, Co-Founder/Partner Emeritus
Education: Electrical Engineering & Computer Science, Stanford University; MBA, Haas School of Business

1595 RUBICON VENTURE CAPITAL
One Little West Twelfth Street
3rd Floor
New York, NY 10014

e-mail: info@rubicon.vc
web: rubicon.vc

Mission Statement: The mission of Georgetown Angels is to invest in high potential early stage disruptive technology companies while leveraging our network and relationships to accelerate the growth of our portfolio companies.

Investment Criteria: Later Stage Seed, Series A & B Rounds Co-Investing
Industry Group Preference: Fintech, Human Resource Technology, Marketplaces, New Service Models, Transformational Businesses, SaaS, Big Data, Cloud Computing, Advertising Technology, Media Technology, Mobility, Consumer Internet, Commerce, Social Services
Portfolio Companies: AgentIQ, Boom Fantasy, Canvs, Carpe, Daily Harvest, Dealflicks, Domio, Easyship, Honeycommb, Iotera, Lenda, LISNR, Maestro, Navdy, NodePrime, Nylas, One Page, Partender, Percolata, PremFina, Privus, Sourcery, Student Loan Genius, Superhuman, Tackk, The Block, Today Tix, True Anthem, Trumaker & Co., Unikrn, Zylotech

Other Locations:
44 Tehama St.
San Francisco, CA 94105

Key Executives:
Joshua B. Siegel, General Partner - New York
Education: BA, Boston University; MBA, Georgetown University
Background: Managing Member, Fantastia Partners; Manager, Eastern European Banking Systems, Citibank; Director of Market Intelligence, Citicorp Debt Capital Markets
Andrew C. Romans, General Partner - San Francisco
Education: BA, UVM; MBA, Georgetown University
Background: General Partner, The Founders Club; Director, Rainmaker Securities; Founder & President, The Global TeleExchange

Venture Capital & Private Equity Firms / Domestic Firms

1596 RUNTIDE CAPITAL
250 Park Avenue
7th Floor
New York, NY 10177

Phone: 212-572-4857
web: www.runtidecapital.com

Mission Statement: RunTide invests in growth stage businesses addressing the connected digital economy.

Geographic Preference: North America, Europe
Average Investment: $15 - $35 million
Minimum Investment: $15 million
Investment Criteria: Early-Stage, Revenues of a minimum $5 million, Operating History of 3 to 10 years
Industry Group Preference: Digital Media, Mobile Services, Data Analytics, Digital Marketing, E-Commerce, Communications, Cloud Computing
Portfolio Companies: Adaptix, Antenna, Binwise, Canal+, Interxion, Mobile Embrace, Model Metrics, Intent, PlusTV, Wine.com

Key Executives:
   Charles Auster, Partner
   e-mail: causter@runtidecapital.com
   Education: Tufts University; JD, National Law Center George Washington University
   Background: Partner/Managing Director, One Equity Partners; Founder, Auster Capital Partners
   Directorships: Global Packaging Corporation
   Robert Manning, Partner
   e-mail: rmanning@runtidecapital.com
   Education: Williams College
   Background: Partner, Baker Capital; Founding Executive, DMX Inc.L CFO, Intermedia Communications Inc.; Director, Digex Inc.
   Directorships: Interxion, Wine.com, Adaptix Inc., CoreValue Software, Canal+, Broadview Networks, Turin Networks
   Kerri Ford, Partner
   e-mail: kford@runtidecapital.com
   Education: MBA, Wharton School, University of Pennsylvania
   Background: Baker Capital; Cabletron Systems
   Directorships: Canal+, Adaptix, Broadview Networks, MediaNet
   Matt Auster, Principal
   e-mail: mauster@runtidecapital.com
   Education: Colgate University
   Background: Auster Capital Partners; Carl Marks Advisory Group; Citigroup
   Directorships: Assure Space LLC, Binwise Inc., Wilcoms Ltd.

1597 S3 VENTURES
6300 Bridgepoint Parkway
Building One, Suite 405
Austin, TX 78730

Phone: 512-258-1759
web: www.s3vc.com

Mission Statement: To help talented entrepreneurs take their technology and market knowledge and form valuable businesses.

Geographic Preference: Texas, Southwest United States
Fund Size: $60 million
Investment Criteria: Early-Stage
Industry Group Preference: Technology, Infrastructure, Software
Portfolio Companies: Alkami, Bluecava, Complex Media Network, Gravitant, Invodo, Kimbia, Metal Networks, OrthoAccel Technologies, Packet Design, Phunware, Pivot3, Pristine, Tango, TVA Medical, VUV Analytics

Key Executives:
   Brian R Smith, Managing Director
   Education: BSEE, University of Cincinnati; MSEE, Purdue University
   Background: Co-Founder, Convergent Investors Fund; Managing Director, Convergent Investors; Founder, Chairman & CEO, Crossroads Systems; Product Development, IBM Corporation
   Directorships: Callvine, Digby, Invodo, LibreDigital, OrthoAccel, Sipera, StoredIQ, Tango Health
   Charlie Plauche, Partner
   Education: BS, Finance, University of Mississippi; MBA, Red McCombs School of Business, University of Texas
   Background: Commercial Portfolio Manager, Regions Bank; Associate, Private Equity Group, Harbert Management Corporation;
   Directorships: Pristine Inc.; Kimbia; Favor; TVA Medical Inc.; Tango Health Inc.; BrainCheck; Atmosphere; LevelSet; OutboundEngine; Interplay Learning; LeanDNA; IFM Restoration; Alkami Tech

1598 SABAN CAPITAL GROUP

Phone: 310-557-5100
web: www.saban.com

Mission Statement: Through its private equity activitites, the firm makes both controlling and minority investments in public and private companies. The firm looks to drive growth, profitability and significant shareholder value of its investments through its solid track record and a unique blend of hands-on operating success with private equity investment expertise. SCG takes and active role in its portfolio companies in partnership with strong management.

Founded: 2001
Industry Group Preference: Media, Entertainment, Communications
Portfolio Companies: Celestial Tiger Entertainment, ironSource, Media Nusantara Citra, MNC Sky Vision, Partner Communications, Saban Brands LLC, Saban Films, Taomee, Univision Communications

Key Executives:
   Haim Saban, Chairman and Chief Executive Officer
   Adam Chesnoff, President and Chief Operating Officer
   Education: MBA, Anderson School of Management; BA, Economics and Management, Tel Aviv University's Recanatl School of Business Administration
   Joel Andryc, Managing Director, Private Equity
   Education: BA, Marquette University
   Philip Han, Senior Vice President and Chief Investment Officer
   Education: BA, Economics/Business, UCLA; MBA, Anderson School
   Sumeet Jaisinghani, Managing Director, Private Equity
   Education: BS, Finance and Management, Kelley School of Business, Indiana University

1599 SACHS CAPITAL

web: www.sachscapital.com

Mission Statement: Sachs Capital is a patient and value-add investor that acquires equity positions in private operating companies in the Mid-Atlantic region. Sachs Capital targets private investment opportunities that are too small or do not meet the investment criteria for, or are otherwise overlooked by, larger, institutional venture capital and private equity funds.

Geographic Preference: Mid-Atlantic United States
Founded: 2007
Average Investment: $1 - $5 million
Industry Group Preference: Diversified
Portfolio Companies: Highline Wealth Management, The Cleaning Authority, Motista, Empire Petroleum Holdings, Source 4 Teachers, TLK Group, Interaction Laboratories, BizTel One, Core Commnications, Bluemercury, Community of Science, Congressional Bank, Corus Health Realty, Cvent, eGain, Underground Solutions, LifeLinkMD, Lucidmedia, Matrics, P&A, Skye Chesapeake Bay Roating Company, Viztec

563

Venture Capital & Private Equity Firms / Domestic Firms

Key Executives:
Andrew Sachs, Managing Member
Education: BS, Foreign Service, Georgetown University; MBA, Georgetown University's McDonough School of Business
Background: Analyst, Morgan Stanley; Co-Founder, KMS Investments; President, Capital Investors II; Co-Founder, Bethany Partners
Directorships: Chesapeake Bay Roasting, Cleaning Authority, Empire Petroleum Holdings, Frontier Strategy Group, Source 4 Teachers, 1A Labs
Stuart Bassin, Managing Partner
Education: BS, Accounting & Finance, Washington University
Background: Auditor, KPMG; Portfolio Analyst, The Zitelman Group; Co-Founder, Valuation Services Inc.; Arbitrator, American Arbitration Association

1600 SACRAMENTO ANGELS
Sacramento, CA

web: www.sacangels.com

Mission Statement: The Sacramento Angels and their Venture Capital strategic members believe in the journey of the entrepreneur and startups; the journey to make the world a better place, to create jobs and to keep America strong, competitive and at the forefront of innovation. We believe in this journey because we have traveled the path ourselves, either as entrepreneurs, working as executives in onetime startup companies, or as investors in the venture capital industry.

Geographic Preference: Northern California
Average Investment: up to $2 million
Portfolio Companies: Clinovo, ReovoRX, Revolights, Dynaoptics, TranscribeMe, Phyllom Bioproducts, On Farm Systems, Ecotensil, iSnap, Clean World Partners, LifeWave, Aperia, WellDog, Vokle, Glue Networks, Cloud Cruiser, Critical Perfusion, Reframe It, Vinperfect, Enkata Technologies, Freepath, NexGen Medical Systems, Visicon Technologies, Alter G, Clario Medical, Idapted, Revionics, Kovars, Prolacta Bioscience, Regenemed, Uptake Medical, American LegalNet, Novostent, PatientSafe Solutions, Mobius Technologies

1601 SAFEGUARD SCIENTIFICS
170 North Radnor-Chester Rd.
Suite 200
Radnor, PA 19087

Phone: 610-293-0600
e-mail: webmaster@safeguard.com
web: www.safeguard.com

Average Investment: $5-25 million
Investment Criteria: Seed Stage, Series A, Series B
Industry Group Preference: Technology, Healthcare, Financial Services, Digital Media
Portfolio Companies: Aktana, Clutch, Flashtalking, Hoopla, InfoBionic, Lumesis, Medcrypt, MediaMath, Mequilibrium, Moxe, NovaSom, Prognos, Quantic Mind, Sonobi, Syapse, T-Rex, The One Health Company, Transactis, Trice Medical, Velano Vascular, Vitaltrax, WebLinc, Zipnosis

Key Executives:
Gary J Kurtzman, SVP & Managing Director
Education: MD
Steven J Grenfall, SVP & Managing Director
Education: CPA

1602 SAGEVIEW CAPITAL
245 Lytton Ave.
Suite 250
Palo Alto, CA 94301

Phone: 650-473-5400
e-mail: info@sageviewcapital.com
web: www.sageviewcapital.com

Mission Statement: Sageview Capital combines active ownership, industry experience, and a partnership approach to provide growth capital to small and mid-size companies involved in the technology, financial services, and business services sectors.

Founded: 2005
Investment Criteria: Small and Mid-Sized Companies
Industry Group Preference: Technology, Financial Services, Business Services
Portfolio Companies: 360insights, Aceable, Avalara, Brandwatch, CallRail, Demandbase, DMT, Elastic Path, Exaro Energy III, MetricStream, NAM, Reflexis, Sageview-Wolff Real Estate, United Capital, Womply

Other Locations:
55 Railroad Ave.
Greenwich, CT 06830
Phone: 203-625-4200

Key Executives:
Ned Gilhuly, Co-Founder/Managing Partner
650-473-5410
e-mail: christine@sageviewcapital.com
Education: BA, Duke University; MBA, Stanford University
Background: Partner, KKR; Merrill Lynch Capital Markets
Directorships: Avalara, Elastic Path, Demandbase, Exaro Energy III, MetricStream
Scott Stuart, Co-Founder/Managing Partner
203-625-4255
e-mail: kathy@sageviewcapital.com
Education: AB, Dartmouth College; MBA, Stanford University
Background: Partner, KKR; Lehman Brothers Kuhn Leob
Directorships: NAM, Reflexis, United Capital, DMT Development Systems Group
Jeff Klemens, Partner
650-473-5430
e-mail: jeff@sageviewcapital.com
Education: BS, Business Administration, University of Southern California
Background: Associate, SPO Partners & Co.; Analyst, Goldman Sachs
Directorships: Avalara, Elastic Path, MetricStream, Reflexis, Sageview-Wolff Real Estate, DMT Development Systems Group
Andrew Korn, Partner
203-625-4217
e-mail: korn@sageviewcapital.com
Education: BA, Economics, Yale University
Background: Consultant, Boston Consulting Group
Directorships: Brandwatch, 360insights
Dean Nelson, Partner
Education: BS, Purdue University; MBA, University of Chicago
Background: Founder, KKR Capstone; Partner, Boston Consulting Group
Directorships: Reflexis, Brandwatch, 360insights, Womply, CallRail, Aceable

1603 SAIL VENTURE PARTNERS
3161 Michaelson Drive
Suite 750
Irvine, CA 92612

Phone: 949-398-5100 Fax: 949-398-5101
web: www.sailcapital.com

Mission Statement: A national venture capital firm specializing in early-stage companies.

Founded: 2002
Investment Criteria: Early Stage
Industry Group Preference: Clean Technology, Energy, Water
Portfolio Companies: Enerpulse, Ener-core, Ice Energy, SN Tech, Xtreme Power, Dow Kokam, Paragon, Kokam,

Venture Capital & Private Equity Firms / Domestic Firms

WaterHealth International, M2 Renewables, Cleantech Group, CNS Response, Clean Technology Solutions

Other Locations:
2900 S Quincy Street
Suite 410
Arlington, VA 22206
Phone: 703-379-2713

1441 Canal Street
Suite 324
New Orleans, LA 70112
Phone: 504-598-5244

79 Wellington Street West
PO Box 37, 21st Floor
Toronto, ON M5K 1B7
Canada

1604 SAINTS CAPITAL
2020 Union Street
San Francisco, CA 94123

Phone: 415-773-2080
web: saintscapital.com

Mission Statement: Saints is a leading direct secondary acquirer of venture capital and private equity investments in emerging growth companies around the globe.

Geographic Preference: United States
Fund Size: $1 billion
Founded: 2000
Industry Group Preference: Technology, Healthcare, Consumer, Industrial, Communications, Consumer Services, Retail, Consumer & Leisure, Semiconductors, Software, Internet
Portfolio Companies: Acsis, Actelis Networks, Art.com, AtTask, Bay Microsystems, Beta O2, Blurb, Capella Photonics, CardioFocus, Cascade, Cidra, Coloredge, Conviva, Deem, Factual, Fulcrum Bioenergy, Gem, Genband, GigaComm, GigaTrust, GlassPoint, Illumina, Imgur, Infra, InnoGraft, InnoPath, Innovative Technology, Innovia, Interactive Media Holdings, Into Networks, Kaleo, Kik, Kona Medical, Linden Lab, Lithium, Medallia, Microchip, Minerva, Mitralign, Nanomix, ON24, One Medical, OrSense, Porch, Radisys, Reunion, RibX, Siano, SnugMug, Thinkwell, Tissuemed, Toolwire, Trion, TVU Networks, Verance, Viron, VivaReal, Webroot, Zazzle

Key Executives:
Kenneth B Sawyer, Managing Director
Education: BS, Industrial Engineering, Stanford University; MBA, Stanford Graduate School of Business
Background: Head of M&A, Prudential Volpe Technology Group; Head, Strategic Advisory Services, Volpe Brown Whelan & Co.
Directorships: Clearguage, Continuous Computing, HK Systems, Travel Intelligence, Laureate Pharmaceuticals, Acsis, Alliance
David P Quinlivan, Managing Director
Education: BA, Physics, Harvard University; MBA, Stanford University
Background: SVP, Finance, Insweb; Investment Banking, Credit Suisse First Boston

1605 SALEM HALIFAX CAPITAL PARTNERS
1225 Johnson Ferry Rd.
Suite 630-A
Marietta, GA 30068

Phone: 770-790-5034 **Fax:** 770-790-5104
web: www.salemhalifax.com

Mission Statement: Seeks long-term capital appreciation with privately held companies. SHCP bridges the gap between pure equity funds and traditional senior bank financing by providing companies with subordinated, mezzanine debt and equity investments.

Geographic Preference: United States
Fund Size: $105 million
Founded: 2007
Average Investment: $2 to $10 million
Investment Criteria: Management & Leveraged Buyouts, Acquisition Financing, Growth Funding
Portfolio Companies: Bowlin Group, eCoast Sales Solutions, Environmental Services Provider, Focus Technology Consulting, Future Tech Holdings, Good Health Natural Foods, Industrial Services Group, Inland Container Express, K2 Industrial Services, LA Digital Post, Marianna Industries, Murray Supply Company, NeoSystems Corp., Nutrition Physiology Corporation, Panhandle Oilfield Service Companies, Premier Performance Products, Private Label Cosmetics, Professional Systems, S&R Cabinets, Salt Lake Brewing Company, Scent Air Technologies, Service Champ, Treasure Valley Business Group, Tulsa Inspection Resources, VSM Management

Other Locations:
1133 Connecticut Ave NW
Suite 700
Washington, DC 20036
Phone: 301-588-9442

Key Executives:
W Spalding White Jr, Partner
e-mail: swhite@salemcapital.com
Education: BS, Business Administration, The Citadel; MBA, Babcock Graduate School of Management, Wake Forest University
Background: SunTrust Bank, SunTrust Equity Partners
Virginia G Rollins, Partner
e-mail: vrollins@salemcapital.com
Education: BA, University of North Carolina, Chapel Hill; MS, International Management, American Graduate School of International Management/Thunderbird
Background: Managing Director, Gladstone Companies; Vice President & Principal, American Capital Strategies; Managing Director, Bulgarian American Enterprise Fund; Overseas Private Investment Corporation

1606 SALEM INVESTMENT PARTNERS
4064 Colony Rd.
Suite 430
Charlotte, NC 28211

Phone: 704-684-4700
web: www.salemip.com

Mission Statement: Provides mezzanine debt and equity capital to lower middle-market companies.

Geographic Preference: Southwest & Mid-Atlantic Regions
Founded: 1999
Investment Criteria: Growth Financing, Acquisitions, Buyouts, Recapitalizations, Ownership Transitions
Industry Group Preference: Business Products & Services, Information Services, Communications, Media, Consumer Products, Distribution, Manufacturing, Healthcare Services
Portfolio Companies: A Touch of Country Magic, Acme Finishing Company, Apogee Translite, BW Manufacturing, Catalyte, Century Resources, ClassOne Group, Connectivity Wireless, Data Display Systems, DeWayne's Quality Metal, Dewey's Bakery, Edge Technologies, Global Value Commerce, Himalayan Handmade Candles, Honor Medical Staffing, Independent Imaging, Insight 2 Design, Instadium, Lamination Services, Linuxx Global Solutions, Mason Steel, Protochips, PSA Worldwide, Quality Aluminum Products, Reeves Extruded Products, Rugs Direct, Southeast Guardrail, Sunbelt Medical, US Tarp, Village Realty

Other Locations:
7900 Triad Center Dr.
Suite 333
Greensboro, NC 27409
Phone: 336-245-4747 **Fax:** 336-768-6471

Key Executives:
David M Faris, Partner
e-mail: dfaris@salemip.com

Venture Capital & Private Equity Firms / Domestic Firms

Education: BA, International Studies, University of South Carolina; MBA, University of South Carolina Moore School of Business
Background: SVP, Commercial Banking Group, RBC Bank; Principal, Banc of America Securities
Kevin B Jessup, Partner
e-mail: kjessup@salemip.com
Education: BS, Finance, University of North Carolina, Greensboro
Background: Partner, Blue Ridge Investors II; M&A, Wachovia Corporation
Philip W Martin, Partner
e-mail: pmartin@salemip.com
Education: Lenoir-Rhyne University
Background: Founder, Salem Capital Partners; VP Finance/CFO, Central Air Conditioning Distributros; Corporate Treasurer, Douglas Battery Manufacturing Company

1607 SALESFORCE VENTURES
Salesforce Tower
415 Mission Street
3rd Floor
San Francisco, CA 94105

Toll-Free: 800-667-6389
e-mail: salesforceventures@salesforce.com
web: www.salesforce.com/company/ventures/

Mission Statement: Salesforce Ventures, the venture capital arm of Salesforce, is dedicated to investing in and building the next generation of enterprise technology companies.
Geographic Preference: United States, Europe, Japan, Global
Fund Size: $100 million
Founded: 2009
Investment Criteria: Startups, Early Stage, Late Stage
Industry Group Preference: Enterprise Applications, Enterprise Software, Mobile Apps, Mobile Communications Devices, Cloud Computing
Portfolio Companies: 6Sense, 7Summits, A-SaaS, Abeja, AirPR, Aislelabs, All Turtles, Amplero, Andela, Andpad, Angaza, Appiphony, Arxxus, Astadia, AttackIQ, Augment, Automile, Autopilot, Bizer, BizReach, Bloomreach, Bringg, Bugcrowd, Carto, ChatBook, Classy, CloudSense, Cogito, Conga, Cooladata, Crunchbase, Crystal, Cydas, DEG, DemandBase, Devenson, Digital Genius, Dispatch, Empaua, Ellevest, Evariant, Evernote, Figure Eight, FinancialForce, Flect, FollowAnalytics, Forter, Free, Full Circle Insights, Fullstory, Gainsight, GetFeedback, GoCo, Goodpatch, Gospel, Govini, Guild, Guru, Gusto, HelpShift, HighSpot, Hoopla, Hustle, IFTTT, Informatica, Innova, InsideSales.com, InsightSquared, Introhive, Invoca, Janrain, Jazz, Jitterbit, Kakehashi, Kapost, Kitalive, Kooltra, Kyruus, Layer, LeadSift, LevelEleven, Loop & Tie, Madaket, MapAnything, Measurabl, Moneytree, Msg.ai, Narvar, Ncino, Novidea, NS1, Nymi, neMob, Onfido, PenDataSoft, Optimizely, OSF Commerce, OwnBackup, Pendo, Pieberry, Privitar, Propel, Pymetrics, Qubit, Quovo, RaiseMe, Relationship Science, Resilinc, Revup, Rootstock Software, RoundCorner, Runa, Samanage, Saucelabs, ScopeAI, SessionM, Sigfox, Silverline, Simplus, Simpplr, Sitetracker, Skuid, Smart Recruiter, SocialSafeGuard, , Splice, Squirro, Stripe, Tact.aI, Talkdesk, TechSee, Tectonic, TierlCRM, Thousand Eyes, Torchlite, Traction Guest, Tulip, Unbabel, Universal Avenue, Up Skill, Vidyard, Viridis, Virsys12, Vlocity, Voicea, VSee, Wefox, Westbrook, Workato, Wootric, Wyng, Zylo

Key Executives:
Marc Benioff, Chairman/Co-CEO
Education: BS, Business Administration, University of Southern California
Background: Oracle Corporation; Founder, Liberty Software; Apple Computer
Keith Block, Co-CEO
Education: BS, Information Systems, MS, Management & Policy Analysis, Carnegie Mellon University
Background: Executive VP, North America Sales & Consulting, Oracle Corporation; Consultant, Booz Allen Hamilton
Parker Harris, Co-Founder
Education: BA, English Literature, Middlebury College
Background: Left Coast Software; Metropolis Software

1608 SALMON RIVER CAPITAL
1345 Avenue of the Americas
31st Floor
New York, NY 10105

Phone: 646-291-8831
e-mail: requestforinformation@salmonrivercapital.com
web: www.salmonrivercapital.com

Mission Statement: We have a single objective: working in active partnerships with entrepreneurial teams to build exceptional technology-enabled enterprises across a set of industries we know well.
Minimum Investment: $1 million
Industry Group Preference: Education, Healthcare Information Technology, Fintech, Online Media, Information Technology
Portfolio Companies: Axioma, Big Fish Games, Capella Education Company, eVestment, Moldflow Corporation, Netsmart Technologies, Parchment, PeriGen

Key Executives:
Joshua Lewis, Founder and Managing Principal
Education: PhD, Univ. of Oxford; AB, Princeton University
Background: General Partner, Warburg Pincus; General Partner, Forstmann Little

1609 SALT CREEK CAPITAL
2055 Woodside Road
Suite 250
Woodside, CA 94061

Phone: 415-238-4876
e-mail: info@saltcreekcap.com
web: www.saltcreekcap.com

Mission Statement: A private equity firm focused on lower middle market companies.
Geographic Preference: United States
Investment Criteria: Recapitalizations, Growth Capital, Buyouts, Management Led Buyouts, Corporate Divestitures
Industry Group Preference: Business Products & Services, Distribution, Energy Services, Franchising, Logistics, Specialty Finance
Portfolio Companies: Aquamar Holdings, Blue Ribbon Dispatch, Boyd Industries, Drake Equipment, Electro-Motion Inc., Extranomical Tours, The Flavor of california LLC, Four Wheel Campers, Garrison Manufacturing, Griplock Systems, IT Assist Inc., King Tester Corporation, michigan Landscape Professionals, Network Distributors, Pacific Paper, Pacific Shoring, Roman Products LLC, Safe In Sound Hearing, Sound Building Supply, Sperry & Rice, Warne Scope Mounts, WorkWell Medical Group

Key Executives:
Dan Phelps, Founder & Managing Director
e-mail: dan@saltcreekcap.com
Education: BSBA, Ohio State University; MBA, University of Chicago; CPA
Background: General Partner, Duchossois Technology Partners; Pritzker Family
Dan Mytels, Founding Member & Managing Director
Education: B.S. Management Science, University of California San Diego

Venture Capital & Private Equity Firms / Domestic Firms

1610 SALVEO CAPITAL
2100 Sanders Road
Suite 170
Northbrook, IL 60062

Phone: 312-260-1125
web: www.salveocapital.com

Mission Statement: Invests in companies serving the cannabis industry, including software & technology, support services, dispensaries, and cultivation centres.

Industry Group Preference: Cannabis
Portfolio Companies: Headset, Front Range Biosciences, Würk, Tokyo Smoke, Treez, Purissima, Flow Kana, PathogenDx, Harborside Health Center, Ascend Wellness, Baker Technologies

Key Executives:
  Michael C. Gruber, Managing Partner
  Education: BA, Enconomics/International Relations, University of Pennsylvania; MBA, Finance/Accounting/Marketing, Kellogg School of Management, Northwestern University
  Background: Mentor, The Founder Institute; Manager Partner, VentureLab; Investor/Mentor, TechStars Chicago; Founder/Managiner Partner/CEO, Cornerstone Opportunity Partners; Partner, Independence Equity
  Directorships: Front Range Biosciences, Algal Scientific, KitoTech Medical
  Jeffrey Howard, Managing Partner
  Education: BA, Philosophy, Westminster College; MBA, Charles H. Kellstadt Graduate School of Business, DePaul University
  Background: Managing Director/Head of Americas Futures & Options, Merrill Lynch; Managing Director/Global Head of Prime Services, Royal Bank of Scotland
  Sean Doyle, Senior Associate
  Education: BBA, Eller College of Management, University of Arizona; MBA, Booth School of Business, University of Chicago
  Background: Co-Founder, InsightDrive; Sales Analyst, Vestas

1611 SAMSUNG NEXT
2 Embarcadero Center
San Francisco, CA 94111

web: samsungnext.com

Mission Statement: Samsung NEXT is the venture capital arm of Samsung Group.

Geographic Preference: US, Canada, Europe, Israel, Korea
Founded: 2012
Industry Group Preference: Artificial Intelligence, Virtual Reality, Blockchain, Data Analytics, Digital Health, Robotics, IoT, Mobility, Security, Cryptocurrency
Portfolio Companies: 2sens, 8i, After School, Baobab Studios, Bayshore Networks, Beekeeper, BioBeats, BlazingDB, Branch, Brodmann17, Cohero Health, Converge, Covariant AI, Cylera, Dapper Labs, Dashbot, Data.World, Dataguise, Directly, Edgeworx, Eko Studio, Entrypoint VR, Famous, Figure 1, Filament, FloydHub, Glooko, Grover, HealthifyMe, Healthy.io, Home.is, HYPR, Intezer, Intuition Robotics, Juvo, Life360, LiquidSky, Mobidoo, Nexar, Packet, PlayVS, Puls, RapidDeploy, SafeDK, SignalWire, Sixense, Sliver.tv, Sorenson Media, Spatial Stae, StreamElements, Survios, Swiftly, Terapede, Tetrate, Unbabel, Unikey, VeeR, Vicarious, Vidrovr, Vinli, Virtru, WeVR, Zimperium

Other Locations:
  30 West 26th Street
  New York, NY 10010

  Neue Schonhauser Street 3-5
  Berlin 10178
  Germany

  129 Samsung-ro
  Yeongtong-gu
  Suwon
  Gyeonggi-do
  Korea

  Tel Aviv
  Israel

Key Executives:
  Gary Coover, General Manager/Head of Operations
  Education: BA, Santa Clara University; MBA, Haas School of Business
  Background: Consultant, Navigant Consulting
  Gus Warren, Managing Director, New York
  Education: BA, Cornell University
  Background: Venture Partner, FirstMark Capital; Co-Founder/COO, Disconnect; SVP/GM, Spot Runner; Portfolio Manager, Granite Ventures; Time Warner Ventures; Product Manager, Internet Profiles
  Jamie Choi, VP/Head of Samsung NEXT Korea
  Education: BA, Syracuse University; MBA, Yonsei University
  Background: VP, Goldman Sachs
  Eyal Miller, VP/Managing Director, Israel
  Education: MBA, Recanati School of Business, Tel Aviv University
  Background: Co-Founder, Google Cample, Tel Aviv; Head of New Business & Corporate Development, Google Israel

1612 SAN DIEGO VENTURE GROUP
10996 Torreyana Road
Suite 285
San Diego, CA 92121

Phone: 858-558-8750
e-mail: info@sdvg.org
web: www.sdvg.org

Mission Statement: To provide a networking forum for entrepreneurs, venture capitalists and advisors in an informal atmosphere where human expertise can foster new ventures.

Founded: 1986

Key Executives:
  Mike Krenn, President
  Background: DLA Piper; Founder, Venture Pipeline Group; Founder, Tech Coast Angels; Founder, CommNexus

1613 SAND HILL ANGELS
Mountain View, CA 94043

web: www.sandhillangels.com

Mission Statement: Makes early stage investments in promising startups and provides expertise and assistance in fledgling enterprises.

Geographic Preference: San Francisco Bay Area
Founded: 2000
Average Investment: $100,000 - $500,000
Investment Criteria: Early stage
Industry Group Preference: Information Technology, Software, Communications, Networking, Semiconductors, Life Sciences, Bioinformatics, Medical Devices, Pharmaceuticals, Diagnostics, Clean Technology
Portfolio Companies: Aligned Carbon, Ampaire, Apponboard, Arcadia, Archer Aviation, Armory, Ashvatta, Astra Augmedix, Axiom Space, Banzai, Beast Brands, Bryte, Carbon 38, Carbon Health, Carta, Chooch AI, ClearFlame Engines, ClearLaw AI, Connected Signals, Diatomix, EquipmentShare, FiscalNote, Front Range Biosciences, Greenlight Guideline, HitRecord, Hungry, HyperScience, IDbyDNA, Imprint Energy, Inhalon Biopharma, Invenia, Isabl, Jackpocket, KidsToPros, LeaseLock, Lex Markets, Lottery Now, madison Reed, Masterclass, Mati, Matrix Industries, Mission Bio, Mojo Vision, MycoTechnology, Nanomedical Diagnostics, New Age Meats, New Wave Foods, Nines, OnScale, Orbit Fab, Overtime, Owl AI, Parsley Health, Peloton Technology, Petal, Philo, PlusPlus, Prodigy,

Venture Capital & Private Equity Firms / Domestic Firms

PROFUSA, Quip, Qurasense Relativity Space, Samba TV, ShellHound, Senti Biosciences, Sentinel Healthcare, Shiprocket, Skillz, Sonavi Labs, Subspace, The Guild, Thirty madison, Trash Warrior, Volumetric Biotechnologies, WaterSmart Software, Xplore

1614 SANDALPHON CAPITAL
111 W Illinois Street
WeWork River North, 5th Floor
Chicago, IL 60654

e-mail: info@sandalphoncapital.com
web: sandalphoncapital.com

Mission Statement: Sandalphon seeks to be a helpgul partner to entrepreneurs to maximize the probability of a good outcome for all stakeholders.
Geographic Preference: Chicago and Midwest US
Founded: 2016
Average Investment: $100,000-300,000

Key Executives:
Jonathan Ellis, Founder/Managing Director
Education: BSc, University of Manchester; INSEAD
Background: SVP, MacQuarie Principal Finance Group

1615 SANDBOX INDUSTRIES
1000 West Fulton Market
Suite 213
Chicago, IL 60607

Phone: 312-243-4100
e-mail: info@sandboxindustries.com
web: www.sandboxindustries.com

Mission Statement: Sandbox Industries creates, invests in and explores new businesses. The firm pursues early-stage investment opportunities and aims to leverage its experience, expertise, and resources to drive the success of its portfolio companies. Sandbox Industries has partnered with Cultivian Ventures through the venture capital firm Cultivian Sandbox Ventures, which invests in agricultural technology companies.
Fund Size: $18.8 million
Average Investment: $50,000 - $2 million
Investment Criteria: Seed-Stage, Early Stage
Industry Group Preference: Software, Technology-Enabled Services
Portfolio Companies: 71LBS, Fresh Squeeze, Aavya Health, AbioGenix, Allituition, Allylix, Aquaspy, Aratana, Babbaco, BFF GEMZ, Bloom Health, Bluelight, Bon'App, Bookyap, Buzz Referrals, CakeStyle, Capson, Cara Health, CareCentrix, CareHubs, CareSimply, CareWire, Change Healthcare, Connection Brands, Cookitfor.us, Corengi, Cureeo, Defy, Dermlink, Desktop Geneti, Divergence, Doggyloot, Embodi, Eosi, Essence Group, EveryMove, Fango, Feefighters, Fibroblast, Food Genius, Foodini, Frintit, GeckoCap, Get Fresh Kit, Getafive, GiveForward, Goshi, Gweepi Medical, Harvery Automation, HealthClinicPlus, Healthspring, HealthDelivery, HeartFlow, HomeTouch, Initiate, IntroFly, Invivolink, iquartic, Lab42, Lasso, Lost Crates, Marbles, Mathzee, Medopad, Mira Rehab, Morgan Street, MoxieJean, My Coupon Doc, Myca, NaviHealth, Nexidia, Noblivity, Orbeus, Orggit, PatientCo, Phreesia, Pictarine, Portable Medic, Power2Switch, Push Wellness, PVPower, Readeo, ScholarPro, Shortlist, Smart Scheduling, Soma Analytics, Spothero, SwiftPay MD, SwipeSense, Exchangery, United Preference, Uprise Medical, WeGather, WhimseyBox, Yosko, Zeomega

Other Locations:
444 Townsend Street
Suite 3
San Francisco, CA 91407
Phone: 312-243-4100

Key Executives:
Robert Shapiro, Chairman/Managing Director
Education: AB, Harvard College; JD, Columbia University School of Law
Background: Chairman & CEO, Monsanto Agriculture Group; CEO, The NutraSweet Company; VP & General Counsel, GD Searle & Co.
Directorships: Chromatin, Elevance Renewable Sciences, Intrexon Corporation, Conservis Corp., Advanced Animal Diagnostics
Nick Rosa, Co-CEO
Education: BS, Political Science, Northern Illinois University; MBA, DePaul University
Background: CEO, NutraSweet Company; Senior Executive, Monsanto
Matt Downs, Co-CEO
Education: BA, Brigham Young University; MBA, Stanford Graduate School of Business
Background: Associate, Highland Capital Partners; Analyst, M&A, Morgan Stanley
Directorships: Aspire Health, Capson, Essence Group, Lumiata, Medsave, Myca
Anna Haghgooie, Managing Director
Education: BBA, University of Michigan Ross School of Business; MBA, University of Chicago Booth School of Business
Background: Financial Management Program, General Electric; Associate Director, Fitch Ratings; General Manager, Pulling Down the Moon
Steve Engelberg, Managing Director
Education: BA, University of Michigan; MA, Georgetown University; JD, Harvard Law School
Background: SVP, Monsanto Company; Managing Partner, Keck, Mahin & Cate; Legislative Council, Senator Walter F. Mondale

1616 SANDERLING VENTURES
1300 S El Camino Real
Suite 203
San Mateo, CA 94402

Phone: 650-401-2000 Fax: 650-375-7077
e-mail: info@sanderling.com
web: www.sanderling.com

Mission Statement: To be the partner of choice for entrepreneurs and investors in building biomedical companies that improve the treatment of human diseases.
Fund Size: $318 million
Founded: 1979
Average Investment: $1 million
Minimum Investment: $250,000
Investment Criteria: Seed, Early-Stage, Later-Stage
Industry Group Preference: Biotechnology, Medical & Health Related, Pharmaceuticals, Therapeutics
Portfolio Companies: Altor BioScience, Artielle, Asteres, Axikin Pharmaceuticals, CalciMedica, CoMentis, Cylene Pharmaceuticals, Dynatherm Medical, InfraReDx, LineaGen, Naviscan, NovoStent, Pulsar Vascular, Sotera Wireless, Tenex Greenhouse, TheraVida, Theregen Corporation, Tomophase, Torax, ViaCyte, Atherogenics, CardioNet, Chimerix, Dendreon, Digirad, Dynavax Technologies, Endocyte, InterMune Pharmaceuticals, ISTA Pharmaceuticals, Pacira Pharmaceuticals, ReGen Biologics, Regeneron Pharmaceuticals, SkyePharma, Stereotaxis, Vical, Xoma

Other Locations:
1010 Sherbrooke Street W
Suite 408
Montreal, QC H3A 2R7
Canada
Phone: 515-564-6474

Key Executives:
Fred A Middleton, Managing Director
Education: BS Chemistry, MIT; MBA, Harvard Business School
Background: Consultant, McKinsey & Company; Vice President, Chase Manhattan Bank; President Finance/Administration, Genentech; Co- Founder, Morgan Stanley Ventures

568

Venture Capital & Private Equity Firms / Domestic Firms

Robert G McNeil PhD, Managing Director
Education: PhD, Molecular Biology, Biochemistry, Genetics, University of California, Irvine
Background: Portfolio Manager, Shuman Agnew & Co; Co-founder/CEO, CoCensys; Chairman/CEO, Acea; Chairman, Peregrine Pharmaceuticals
Paulette Taylor, General Counsel/Principal
Education: JD, University of California Hastings College of Law; BA, University of Washington
Background: Counsel, Alumax; Associate, Farella, Braun & Martel; Executive VP, National Insurance Group
Timothy C Mills PhD, Managing Director
Education: BSEE, University of Colorado; MSEE and Computer Science, PhD Bioengineering, University of California, Berkeley; San Francisco School of Medicine
Background: Corporate VP New Business/Chief Scientific Officer, Target Therapeutics; Director, Prograft Medical; Director Interventional Cardiology, Baxter Healthcare
Directorships: Artifical Heart Program, Irvine Medical Center
Timothy Wollaeger, Managing Director Emeritus
Education: BA Economics, Yale University; MBA, Stanford Graduate School of Business
Background: VP/General Manager Mexico, Baxter International; VP/CFO, Hybritech; Founding General Partner, Biovest; Co-Founder, Columbia Hospital Corporation; Founder, Kingsbury Capital Partners
Peter C McWilliams PhD, Venture Partner
Education: PhD, MA, Chemistry, Princeton University; BA Natural Sciences, Cambridge University; MBA, Columbia Business School
Background: Product Manager, Genentech, Associate, Booz, Allen & Hamilton; Oxford Molecular

1617 SANDLER CAPITAL MANAGEMENT
711 5th Avenue
15th Floor
New York, NY 10022

Phone: 212-754-8100 **Fax:** 212-826-0280/0281
web: www.sandlercap.com

Mission Statement: To identify, invest and create value in companies that operate in the communications industries.
Geographic Preference: United States, Europe
Fund Size: $750 Million
Founded: 1990
Average Investment: $5 - $60 million
Minimum Investment: $5 Million
Investment Criteria: Early Stage, Growth Stage, Established
Industry Group Preference: Communications, Media, Entertainment
Key Executives:
  Michael Marocco, Managing Director/Head, Private Equity
  Education: BA, University of Southern Maine; MBA, New York University
  Background: Research Analyst, Morgan Stanley
  John Kornreich, Senior Advisor
  Education: BA, University of Pennsylvania; MBA, Columbia Business School
  Background: Investment Analyst, CBWL Hayden Stone; Portfolio Manager, Neuberger & Bermain
  William Bianco, Managing Director
  Education: BA, Brown University; JD, Harvard Law School
  Background: Associate/Partner, Akin Gump Strauss Hauer & Feld LLP
  Directorships: Farelogix; Modulant Solutions; Wizmo
  Andrew Sandler, Managing Director/Portfolio Manager, Head of Hedge Funds
  Education: B.S. Finance, University of Wisconsin at Madison

1618 SANOFI-GENZYME BIOVENTURES
50 Binney Street
Cambridge, MA 02142

web: www.sanofigenzymebioventures.com

Mission Statement: SGBV is different from traditional venture capital firms. SGBV provies portfolio companies with guidance and advice by leveraging established expertise in science, preclinical and clinical development, regulatory, manufacturing, market access, commercialization, and more. In return, SBV expects an ongoing window into the company's progress and future products, through advisory committee membership, technical update meetings, board observers and/or director positions.

Investment Criteria: Private early-stage
Industry Group Preference: Biotechnology, Healthcare Innovation, Oncology, Vaccines, Integrated Health Solutions, Life Sciences
Portfolio Companies: Unum Therapeutics, LTI, Immune Design, Common Sensing, Edimer, Ultrageny Pharmaceutical, Esperance, Kahr Medical, Fate Therapeutics, GlycoMimetics, KaloBios, Proteostasis, Valerion Therapeutics

Other Locations:
  54-56 Rue La Boétie
  Paris 75008
  France

  Jason P Hafler, Managing Director
  Education: BA, Bowdoin College; PhD, University of Cambridge
  Background: Director of Corporate Development, RaNA Therapeutics; Associate, Life Sciences Group, Atlas Ventures; Entrepreneurial Fellow, Flagship Ventures; Analyst, JSB Partners LP
  Directorships: Escient Pharmaceuticals; Icosavax; Expansion Therapeutics; Amathus Therapeutics
  Jim Tenkle, Head of Investments
  Education: BS, University of Michigan; PhD, Organic Chemistry, MIT; MBA, University of California Berkeley
  Background: VP of Investments, Pivotal bioVenture Partners; Gilead Sciences

1619 SANTE VENTURES
300 West 6th Street
Suite 2300
Austin, TX 78701

Phone: 512-721-1200
e-mail: press@santeventures.com
web: www.santeventures.com

Mission Statement: Focused on developing lasting, well-aligned partnerships with exceptional entrepreneurs and executives to build valuable companies. In addition to capital, Sante Ventures provides deep healthcare domain expertise and extensive background of industry contacts and resources.

Geographic Preference: United States
Fund Size: $14.5 million
Founded: 2006
Average Investment: $4 - $12 million
Investment Criteria: Early-Stage, Seed-Stage
Industry Group Preference: Life Sciences, Medical Technology, Healthcare Services, Healthcare Information Technology
Portfolio Companies: BARonova, BetaCat Pharmaceuticals, BioStable Science & Engineering, Claret Medical, Endo Stim, Iowa Approach, Lumos Pharma, Lyric Pharmaceuticals, Millipede, Mirna Therapeutics, Molecular Templates Inc., Terapio, TVA Medical, Healthcare Highways, HNI Healthcare, AbVitro, Accuro, Emageon, Explorys Medical, Healthspring, LDR Spine, Rise Health, Stereotaxis, TomoTherapy

Other Locations:
  4203 Montrose Boulevard
  Suite 300

569

Venture Capital & Private Equity Firms / Domestic Firms

Houston, TX 77006
Phone: 713-904-1926
Key Executives:
Kevin M. Lalande, Managing Director
Education: BS, Electrical & Computer Engineering; MBA, Harvard Business School
Background: Austin Ventures; Management Consultant, McKinsey & Company; Co-Founder, Netopia; Co-Founder, TimeMarker
Joe Cunningham MD, Managing Director
Education: BS, MD, Texas A&M University; MBA, Baylor University
Background: Healthcare Venture Partner, Austin Ventures; Vice Chair, Ascension Health Venture Investment Committee; Chief Medical Officer, Providence Health System; Executive Director, Providence Health Alliance
Douglas D. French, Managing Director
Background: President & CEO, Ascension Health System; Venture Partner, Austin Ventures
Directorships: Herman Miller, Emageon, Ascension Health, Diginity Health
Casey Cunningham, MD, Chief Scientific Officer
Education: MD, University of Texas Southwestern Medical School; Fellowship, Oncology & Hematology; Harvard Medical School
Background: Chief Medical Officer, Terapio; Chief Medical Officer, Molecular Templates; Founding Member, Division of Experimental Medicine, Brigham & Women's Hopsital; Associate Director, Mary Crowley Cancer Research Center
Billy Cohn, MD, Venture Partner
Education: Oberlin College; Baylor College of Medicine
Background: Associate Professor, Harvard Medical School; Director, Minimally Invasive Surgical Technology, Texas Heart Institute; Associate Professor, Surgery, Baylor College of Medicine; Adjunct Professor, Bioengineering, University of Houston
James Eadie, MD, Partner
Education: BS, Bioengineering, University of Michigan; MBA, University of Texas McCombs School of Business; MD, Harvard Medical School
Background: Air Force, Medical Director & Vice-Chair of Emergency Medicine, Wilford Hall Medical Center

1620 SAPPHIRE VENTURES
3408 Hillview Avenue
Building 5
Palo Alto, CA 94304

Phone: 650-382-1110
e-mail: info@sapphireventures.com
web: www.sapphireventures.com

Mission Statement: Sapphire Ventures is focused on helping today's most innovative expansion-stage technology companies become global category-defining leaders.
Geographic Preference: United States, Europe, Israel
Fund Size: $353 million
Founded: 1996
Average Investment: $5 - $12 million
Investment Criteria: Early- and Growth-Stage
Industry Group Preference: Information Technology
Portfolio Companies: Alfresco Software Alteryx, Apigee, Black Duck, Box, Convercent, DocuSign, Fitbit, GroundWork, iovation, iTAC Software AG, iYogi, Jibe, Kaltura, Krux, Lavante, Lithium Technologies, Mirantis, MuleSoft, Narrative Science, Newgen Software, Nutanix, OnDeck, One97, Onventis, OpenX, Ping Identity, Recommind, Retail Solutions, Return Path, SAVO, Scytl, Socrata, Splashtop, Spring Mobile, Square, Ticketfly, Zend
Key Executives:
Nino Marakovic, CEO and Managing Director
Education: Williams College; Stanford Grad. School of Business
Background: meVC Draper Fisher Jurvetson

Directorships: Inkling; Integral Ad Science; OpenX; Tidalscale

1621 SARATOGA PARTNERS
535 Madison Avenue
4th Floor
New York, NY 10022

Phone: 212-906-7800 Fax: 212-750-3343
e-mail: saratoga@saratogapartners.com
web: www.saratogapartners.com

Mission Statement: Saratoga partners has achieved attractive rates of return by consistently following a three-pronged investment strategy: add value through partnership with outstanding management; invest for growth in middle market companies; and customize capital structures to minimize risk and optimize return. Saratoga believes that its disciplined investment approach, based on time honored principals, will continue to provide the superior returns it has historically achieved.
Geographic Preference: United States
Fund Size: $750 million
Founded: 1984
Average Investment: $10-$400 million
Minimum Investment: $5 million
Investment Criteria: LBO, MBO, Recaps
Industry Group Preference: Communications, Distribution, Natural Resources, Financial Services, Industrial Equipment, Publishing, Energy
Portfolio Companies: Advanced Lighting Technologies Inc., Atlantic Cellular Company LP, The Bowery Saving Bank, CapMAC, Cannell Communications LP, Commsoft, Data Return LLC, Datavantage Corporation, Emeritus Corporation, Equality Specialties Inc., EUR Systems Inc., Formica Corporation, Gulf Coast Coca-Cola Bottling Company, Hawaiian Wireless Inc., Hi-Lo Automotive Inc., J&W Scientific Inc., James Communications, Koppers Inc., NAT Inc., Scovill Fasteners Inc., Sericol Inc., STC Wireless Resources Inc., USI Insurance Services Corp., Viking Office Products
Key Executives:
John P. Birkelund, Senior Advisor
Education: AB, Princeton University; Northwestern University
Background: Dillon Reed & Company; Co-Founder New Court Securities Corporation; Chief Executive Officer of N.M. Rothschild & Sons; Past Director New York Stock Exchange
Charles P. Durkin, Jr., Senior Advisor
Education: BS, Princeton University; MBA, Columbia University
Background: Director of the following companies, Atlantic Cellular; Datavantage Corporation, Koppers, Inc; Scovill Fasteners; USI Holdings; CapMSC, Formica Coproration, Hi-Lo Automotive; Viking Office Products
Christian L. Oberbeck, Managing Director
Education: BS in Physics and BA in Mathematics, Brown University; MBA, Columbia University
Background: Corporate Development Group of Arthur Young; Blyth Eastman Paine Webber; Castle Harlan
John F. MacMurray, Managing Director
Education: AB, Princeton University; MBA, Columbia Business School
Background: EuroConsult
Charles G. Phillips, IV, Managing Director
Education: AB, Harvard College; MBA, Harvard Business School
Background: Dillon Read's; McCown De Leeuw & Company; Equality Specialties; Datavantage Corporation
Richard A. Petrocelli, Managing Director
Education: BS, Georgetown University; MBA, New York University
Background: Gabelli; BDO Siedman
Maria F Costanzo, Controller
Education: BS, Iona College

Venture Capital & Private Equity Firms / Domestic Firms

Background: Compass Global Group; Gabelli Asset Management; Tax Consultant for Arthur Andersen
David W. Niemiec, Senior Advisor
Education: Graduated Harvard College; MBA, Harvard Business School
Background: Vice Chairman of Dillon, Read & Company;

1622 SATORI CAPITAL
2501 North Hardwood Street
20th Floor
Dallas, TX 75201

Phone: 214-390-6270
Toll-Free: 888-972-8674
e-mail: info@satoricapital.com
web: www.satoricapital.com

Mission Statement: Satori is the preferred partner for companies that are building significant long-term value through a sustainable approach.
Geographic Preference: Southwestern United States
Investment Criteria: Middle Market: Revenues from $25 to $200 million
Industry Group Preference: Business Products & Services, Consumer Products, E-Commerce & Manufacturing, Financial Services, Manufacturing, Software, Information Technology, Telecommunications
Portfolio Companies: 24 Hour Fitness, Aspen Heigths, Gibraltar Capital Holdings, Hodges Ward Elliott, Longhorn Health Solutions, The Lovesac Company, Nomacorc, Purple Land Management, Ranger Wireless Solutions, SunTree Snack Foods, Zorch International
Other Locations:
2821 West 7th Street
Suite 285
Fort Worth, TX 76107
Key Executives:
Sunny Vanderbeck, Managing Partner
Background: Co-Founder/CEO, Data Return; Team Leader, Microsoft; U.S. Special Operations Command
Randy Eisenman, Managing Partner
817-200-7805
Education: BS, Business Administration, University of Texas
Background: Partner, Q Investments; Financial Analyst, Goldman Sachs & Co.
Rugger Burke, Principal
214-390-6274
Education: BS, JD, Southern Methodist University
Background: Master in Chancery; FINRA Arbitrator
John Grafer, Principal
214-390-6284
Education: BBA, Accounting, University of Notre Dame; MBA, Finance, University of Chicago Booth School of Business
Background: Senior Vice President, Giuliana Partners; M&A Group, Credit Suisse First Boston; Proprietary Trading Group, JP Morgan Chase & Co.

1623 SATURN PARTNERS
75 Federal Street
Suite 1320
Boston, MA 02110

Phone: 617-574-3330 Fax: 617-574-3331
e-mail: saturnasset@saturnpartnersvc.com
web: www.saturnasset.com

Mission Statement: A venture capital and private equity firm committed to generating significant returns for its investors.
Geographic Preference: Northeastern United States
Founded: 1994
Investment Criteria: Early-Stage
Industry Group Preference: Biotechnology, Information Technology, E-Commerce & Manufacturing, Fintech, Advanced Materials
Portfolio Companies: 3form, Alignable, American Made, Applied CleanTech, Axioma, BioWish Technologies, Bodymedia, Boston Duck Tours, Chirpify, Constant Contact, CORE Outdoor Power, Express KCS, FreeMarkets, Good Technology, Knopp Biosciences, Marathon, Mismi, Omaze, Pavève, Panopto, SureLogic, The Ride, Think Through Math, Twin Rivers Technologies, Xpress Natural Gas
Key Executives:
Jeffrey S McCormick, Chairman/Managing Partner
Education: BS, Biology; MBA, Finance, Syracuse University
Background: Bariston Associates
Directorships: MooBella, American Made, SureLogic, Knopp Neurosciences, Applied Clean Tech, NHXS
Bill Guttman, Partner
Education: MA/PhD, Oxford University
Background: Co-Founder, CyLab; CEO, Printcafe; CEO, Axioma
Directorships: American Made LLC; Express KCS; Panopto; Trunomi; YieldStree
Edward A Lafferty, Partner/Chief Financial Officer
Education: BS, Business Administration, Northeastern University; MBA, Bentley College
Background: Controller, Berkshire Partners
Directorships: Applied CleanTech, ModelGolf

1624 SAUGATUCK CAPITAL COMPANY
4 Armstrong Road
Suite 230
Shelton, CT 06484

Phone: 203-348-6669 Fax: 203-324-6995
e-mail: saugatuck@saugatuckcapital.com
web: www.saugatuckcapital.com

Mission Statement: Private investment firm specializing in middle market acquisitions and growth equity investments.
Geographic Preference: United States, Canada
Fund Size: $126 million
Founded: 1982
Average Investment: $6 million
Minimum Investment: $3 million
Investment Criteria: Later-Stage, LBO, MBO, Consolidation, Growth, Recaps; Companies with prominent positions in niche markets, proprietary products and services or high-engineering and/or service content
Industry Group Preference: Diversified
Portfolio Companies: American Pipe & Plastics, APCT, Exocor, FEMCO Machine Co., Floor & DéCor Outlets of America, Lunada Bay Corp., Pharmaceutic Litho & Label Company, PPI/Time Zero Inc., The TharpeRobbins Company, TradeSource, Tulip Corporation
Key Executives:
Gary L Goldberg, Managing Director
e-mail: ggoldberg@saugatuckcapital.com
Education: BA, Philosophy, Colgate University; MBA, Cornell University Johnson Graduate School of Management
Background: Founder & Managing Partner, Arch Investment Management; VP Operations, Priceline.com
Stuart W Hawley, Managing Director
e-mail: shawley@saugatuckcapital.com
Education: BS, University of North Carolina; MBA, Kenan-Flagler Business School, University of North Carolina, Chapel Hill
Background: VP, Prudential Securities, Fidelity Investments
Frank J Hawley Jr, Senior Advisor
Education: Phi Beta Kappa, BS, Physics, University of North Carolina; MBA, Harvard Business School
Background: General Partner, Foster Management Company; Executive Vice President, Laidlaw-Coggeshall, Inc., Lazard Freres, Eaton & Howard, Inc.

Venture Capital & Private Equity Firms / Domestic Firms

1625 SAVANO CAPITAL PARTNERS
6 East Eager St.
Suite 4A
Baltimore, MD 21202

Phone: 443-873-3561
e-mail: info@savanocapital.com
web: www.savanocapital.com

Mission Statement: Savano Capital partners with private shareholders and exceptional growth companies.

Portfolio Companies: Actifio, Clarabridge, DrFirst, Endgame, Everquote, Hearsay, Ignition One, JobCase, Kaltura, Lotame, Nintex, Parallels, Silver Peak, UpWork, Vestmark

Other Locations:
1775 Tysons Blvd.
5th Floor
Tysons, VA 22102
Phone: 443-873-3561

Key Executives:
Tom Smith, Managing Partner
e-mail: tom@savanocapital.com
Education: BS, Elizabethtown College; MBA, University of North Carolina, Chapel Hill
Background: General Partner, Edison Ventures; General Partner, Mid-Atlantic Venture Funds

1626 SCALE VENTURE PARTNERS
950 Tower Lane
Suite 1150
Foster City, CA 94404

Phone: 650-378-6000 Fax: 650-378-6040
e-mail: businessplan@scalevp.com
web: www.scalevp.com

Mission Statement: A venture capital fund for all stages of a company's growth with a focus on innovative technologies.

Fund Size: $25 million
Founded: 1960
Average Investment: $5 - $15 million
Minimum Investment: $3 million
Investment Criteria: Early-Stage, Mid-Stage, Late-Stage
Industry Group Preference: Broadband, Enterprise Services, Semiconductors, Optical Technology, Software, Biotechnology, Medical Devices, Networking, Technology, Healthcare, Media, Marketing
Portfolio Companies: Actiance, Agari, Alimera Sciences, Applause, Apteligent, Arena, Ascenta Therapeutics, Aurum, Aviso, Bill.com, Obizible, Boundary, Box, BrightRoll, Chef Code Can, Circle Ci, Cloud Health Technologies, Connect, E-Data Sift, Datastax, Demand Base, DiaDexus, DocuSign, Drone Deploy, eGroups, Entone, Everyday Health, Exact Target, Extole, Forter, Front Bridge, Glu, Good, Healogics, Horizon Pharma, Hubspan, Hubspot, Imt, Jasper Soft, JFrog, Katch, Keep Truckin, Lever, Liaison, Livescribe, LivHome, Locus, Lumension, MBlox, Namely, Net6, NetGenesis, New Century Hospice, Omniture, Onelogin, Oraya Therapeutics, Orexigen, OuterBay, Pentheon, People Matter, Real-Time Collaboration Solutions By PlaceWare, PubNub, Realm, Ring Central, SailTthru, Scale Computing, ScanSafe, Solvvy, Sonexa, Speechworks, Spinal Kinetics, Stormpath, Sylantro, TalkIQ, Teros, Textio, Threat Stack, Treasure Data, Tripwire, Unifi, Vitrue, Walk Me, Wayport, Wrike, Zogenix, Zone Labs

Key Executives:
Mark Brooks, Venture Partner
e-mail: mark@scalevp.com
Education: BA, Economics, Dartmouth College; MBA, Finance & Entrepreneurial Managment, Wharton School
Background: Senior Associate, Mercer Management Consulting; Loan Officer, Media Group, Manufacturers Hanover Trust Company
Directorships: Alimera Sciences, Century Hospice, In-Patient Consultants Management, LivHome, National Healing Holding Corporation, Oraya Therapeutics, Spinal Kintetics

Kate Mitchell, Partner
e-mail: kate@scalevp.com
Education: BA, Stanford University; MBA, Executive Program, Golden Gate University
Background: Senior Vice President, Bank of America

Rory O'Driscoll, Managing Director
e-mail: rory@scalevp.com
Education: BSc, London School of Economics
Directorships: Arena Solutions, Box.net, DocuSign, ExactTarget, Hubspan, Innovion, LiveScribe, Lumension Security, Vantage Media

Stacey Bishop, Partner
e-mail: stacey@scalevp.com
Education: BA, University of Michigan; MBA, Columbia Business School
Background: M&A, Bank of America's Corporate Development Group; Account Manager, Syntel

Sharon Weinbar, Venture Partner
e-mail: sharon@scalevp.com
Education: BA, MA, Engineering, Harvard University; MBA, Stanford Graduate School of Business
Background: Critical Path, Amplitude Software, Adobe Systems, Bain & Company
Directorships: Actiance, Everyday Health, MerchantCircle, PlayPhone, Reply!Com, uTest

Andy Vitus, Partner
e-mail: andy@scalevp.com
Education: MS, Electrical Engineering, Stanford University; BS, Electrical Engineering;, University of Cape Town
Background: Hardware Engineer, Electronics for Imaging
Directorships: Entone, Innovion

Rob Herb, Venture Partner
e-mail: rob@scalevp.com
Education: BS, Electrical Engineering, University of Illinois
Background: Executive Vice President/Chief Marketing Officer, AMD
Directorships: Enpirion, NComputing, Siimpel Corporation

1627 SCHOONER CAPITAL LLC
Two Financial Center
60 South Street
1th Floor
Boston, MA 02111

Phone: 617-963-5200 Fax: 617-963-5201
e-mail: info@schoonercapital.com
web: www.schoonercapital.com

Mission Statement: Seeks growth equity investments and alternative assets with a long-term perspective.

Geographic Preference: United States
Fund Size: $300 million
Founded: 1971
Minimum Investment: $250,000
Investment Criteria: Startup, First-Stage, Second-Stage, Mezzanine
Industry Group Preference: Communications, Education, Training, Business to Business, Leisure, Consumer Services
Portfolio Companies: Best Doctors, Custom Made, COLO, Emerald Therapeutics, Exithera Pharmaceuticals, Fashion Project, F&B Asias, IndoStar Capital Finance, iiWisdom, Millstone, Mediasilo, Mimetogen, Moonshine Farms, Nanoscale Powders, Orthocare Innovations, Railcomm, StyleFeeder, SRS Medical, Seventh Generation, Topokine, Zixi

Key Executives:
Vin Ryan, Founder/Chairman
Education: Boston University
Background: Founder, National Hydro; Founder, Arch Mobile Communications
Directorships: Iron Mountain, Continental Cablevision

Venture Capital & Private Equity Firms / Domestic Firms

Peter Binas, Managing Director
Education: AB, Harvard University; JD, Harvard Law School; MBA, Harvard Business School
Background: Management Consultant, McKinsey & Company
Directorships: RailComm, Colo Railroad Builders, Orthocare Innovations
Ted Henderson, Managing Director
Education: Dartmouth College; MBA, Harvard Business School
Background: General Manager, The Washington Post Company
Directorships: Best Doctors, Orthocare Innovations, Seventh Generation, SRS Medical, Millstone Medical Outsourcing

1628 SCHRODER VENTURES HEALTH INVESTORS
One Boston Place
201 Washington Street
Suite 3900
Boston, MA 02108

Phone: 617-367-8100 Fax: 617-367-1590
web: www.svhealthinvestors.com

Mission Statement: SV Health Investors is a venture capital adviser and manager that makes selected investments in businesses with experienced entrepreneurs and management teams.

Geographic Preference: United States, Europe
Fund Size: $2.0 billion
Founded: 1993
Average Investment: $4-$15 million
Minimum Investment: $1 million
Investment Criteria: Seed, Startup, First-Stage, Second-Stage, Late-Stage, Buyouts, Turnarounds, Expansion
Industry Group Preference: Biotechnology, Pharmaceuticals, Medical Devices, Healthcare Information Technology, Life Sciences, Healthcare Services
Portfolio Companies: Accelecare Holdings, AcuFocus, Adimab, AeroCare, Alba Therapeutics, Aligned Telehealth, Alinea Pharma, Allegiance Hospice Group, AllianceCare, Aptiv Solutions, Arsais, Artios, Autifony Therapeutics, Avitide, AvroBio, BardyDx, Bicycle Therapeutics, BioCore Holdings, Broadlane, Cadent Technologies, Calchan Holdings, CardioFocus, Catabasis, Celerion, Centauri Health Solutions, Cibiem, Coral Therapeutics, CoreLab Partners, CRI Worldwide, CSA Medical, Deciphera, EBR Systems, Endotronix, ErVaxx Limited, Evidation, Jet Health, Juvaris BioTherapeutics, Kalvista Pharma, Karus Therapeutics, Kesios Therapeutics, Leiters, NKT Therapeutics, Nordic Consulting Partners, Ocular Therapeutix, Oxagen Limited, PanOptica, Pionyr Immunotherapeutics, Pulmocide, Remita Health, ReShape, Ribometrix, Schweiger Dermatology Group, Sitryx Therapeutics, Soffio Medical, Solsys Medical, Spectrum Professional Services, Spinal Kinetics, Stim Wave, Sun Behavioural Health, Sutro Biopharma, Thesan Pharma, TopiVert, TransEnterix, UrgentTeam, US Renal Care, ValenTx, Vantia Pharma, VHSquared, Ximedica, Zarodex

Other Locations:
71 Kingsway
London WC2B 6ST
United Kingdom
Phone: 44-2074217070 Fax: 44-2074217077

Key Executives:
James M Garvey, Chairman Emeritus
Education: BS, Northern Illinois University
Background: Managing Director, Allstate Venture Capital Division; Kendall & Millipore; President/CEO, Allegheny International Medical Technology; National Teledata
Directorships: AcuFocus, CardioFocus, Ocular Therapeutic, Cellutions, CHF, LaserVision Centers, Orthovita, Shire Pharmaceuticals, Sunrise Assisted Living

Eugene Hill, Chairman
Education: BA, Middlebury College; MBA, Boston University
Background: President, United Healthcare Behavioral Division; President/Chairman, Sierra Health and Life Insurance Company
Directorships: Accelecare Wound Centers, Cadent, ISG Holdings, Medifacts, Patient Care, Socios Mayores, US Renal Care
Kate Bingham, Managing Partner, Biotechnology
44-20-7421-7071
Education: Biochemistry, Univ. of Oxford; MBA, Harvard Business School
Background: Business Development, Vertex Pharmaceuticals; Monitor Company
Directorships: Alantos, Auxillium, ESBATech, Hexagen, Kinetix, KuDos, Leukosite, Mednova, Micromet, PowderMed, Bicycle, EUSA, RespiVert
Michael Ross PhD, Managing Partner, Biotechnology
Education: AB, Dartmouth College; PhD, Chemistry, Caltech, Post Doctorate, Molecular Biology, Harvard University
Background: Vice President Development, Genetech; Founding CEO, Arris Pharmaceutical; Managing Partner, Didyma LLC
Directorships: Aderis Pharmaceuticals, Arris Pharmaceutical, Carta Proteomics, CyThera, Glycofi, Epimune, Genencor, MetaXen, Rinat, Xenova
Paul LaViolette, COO/Managing Partner, Medical Devices
Education: BA, Psychology, Fairfield University; MBA, Boston College
Background: COO, Boston Scientific Corporation; CR Bard; Kendall/Tyco
Directorships: Urolgix, Percutaneous Valve Technologies, Advarned; Cameron Health, Conceptus, DC Devices, Direct Flow Media, DJO Global, Thoratec, Trans1, ValenTx
Michael Balmuth, Managing Partner, Healthcare
Background: General Partner, Summit Partners; General Partner, Edison Partners
Directorships: AeroCare, Aligned Telehealth, Cantauri Health Solutions, Evidation, Ximedica
Houman Ashrafian, Managing Partner, Biotechnology
Background: Co-Founder, Cardiac Report; Co-Founder, Heart Metabolics; VP, Clinical Science Group, UCB
Directorships: ErVaxx, TRexBio
Tom Flynn, Managing Partner, Healthcare
Background: Partner, Ferrer Freeman & Co.; GE Capital; Prudential Investment Corporation
Directorships: AeroCare, Jet Health, Leiters, Nordic, Remita Health, Schweiger Dermatology Group, Sun Behavioural Health, Urgent Team

1629 SCHULTZE ASSET MANAGEMENT
800 Westchester Ave
Suite 632
Rye Brook, NY 10573

Phone: 914-701-5260 Fax: 914-701-5269
e-mail: info@samco.net
web: www.samco.net

Mission Statement: Special situation investing in financially troubled and distressed credits.

Geographic Preference: United States
Fund Size: $170 million

Key Executives:
George J Schultze, Managing Member/Portfolio Management
e-mail: schultze@samco.net
Education: BA, Rutgers College; MBA/JD, Columbia University
Background: Resurgence Asset Management, MD Sass; Mayer Brown & Platt

573

Venture Capital & Private Equity Firms / Domestic Firms

1630 SCIENCEVEST

e-mail: info@sciencevest.com
web: www.sciencevest.com

Mission Statement: ScienceVest is a venture capital fund investing in tech-based companies. Special interests include biotechnology, batteries, drones, sensors, and bacteriphages.

Founded: 2016
Average Investment: $125,000
Industry Group Preference: Biotechnology, Robotics, Green Technology, Blockchain, Artificial Intelligence
Portfolio Companies: Avro Life Science, Advano, Calyx, ExplORer Surgical, Filecoin, Greensight Agronomics

Key Executives:
  Javier Noris, Partner
  e-mail: javier@sciencevest.com
  Education: BS, California State University
  Background: Venture Partner, Deep Science Ventures; Founder, NorisTalent
  Directorships: Life Extension Advocacy Foundation
  Ramphis Castro, Partner
  e-mail: ramphis@sciencevest.com
  Education: University of Puerto Rico
  Background: Software Engineer, Rock Solid Technologies; President/Chief Software Engineer, Simple Engineer Corporation; Principal Technology Advisor, Relisc Corporation; Co-Founder, TainoApp Inc.; Global Facilitator, Techstars; Co-Founder/Managing Partner, Mindchemy

1631 SCIFI VC
San Francisco, CA

e-mail: info@scifi.vc
web: scifi.vc

Mission Statement: SciFi invests in early-stage data-related projects.

Founded: 2017
Investment Criteria: Pre-Seed, Seed
Industry Group Preference: Data & Analytics, Technology
Portfolio Companies: Artivest, Blend Labs, Ellevest, Glow and Affirm, Gusto, OpenDoor, True Accord

Key Executives:
  Max Levchin, Founder
  Education: BS, Computer Science, University of Illinois
  Background: VP, Engineering, Google; Co-Founder/CTO, PayPal; Founder/CEO, Slide; Founder/CEO, Affirm; Chairman, Yelp
  Directorships: Yahoo!; Kaggle; Evernote
  Nellie Levchin, Partner
  Education: BA, Business Admin., California State University
  Background: Chief Risk Officer, Clarium Capital Management; Financial Systems Product Manager, PayPal; Financial Planning Analyst, eBay
  Directorships: Glow Inc.

1632 SCOUT VENTURES
New York, NY 10007

web: www.scoutventures.com

Mission Statement: Scout Ventures works with transformational technologies that disrupt an established business model. BHV's primary focus is where media and entertainment companies (content distribution hubs) impact consumers and their rapidly evolving tech-enhanced lifestyle. BHV's secondary focus is content creation. By analyzing consumer behavior through proprietary technology platforms, BHV understands the challenges brands have connecting and communicating with their increasingly fragmented and unfocused audience. At this intersection, BHV leverages operational experience and strategic relationships to aggregate audience and/or monetization.

Investment Criteria: Early-Stage
Industry Group Preference: Media, Entertainment, Consumer Internet, Mobile, Advertising Technology
Portfolio Companies: Borer City Media, FreshTemp, Local Motors, Circa, Cody, Olapic, Sverve, Kanvas, rFactr, BlackBook, Fliptu, Flow, TIDBT, Adcade, bContext, Signpost, inSparq, Villagize, Free Awesome, Plyfe, 1000 Museums, LeagueApps, Brainscape, GateGuru, Everplans, Legacy Connect, Zipmark, ClearServe, RedOwl Analytics, Bespoke Post, HealthyOut, Scoot, SeedInvest, Assurely, Speakr, IML, Portalarium, Hullabalu, NetPlenih, BuyFi, Vengo, Plexus Entertainment, SocialWeekend, Nestio, CirrusWorks, VOYAT, Unite US, ID.me, Mayvien, Virtuix

Key Executives:
  Bradley C Harrison, Managing Partner
  e-mail: brad@bhv.vc
  Education: BSE, Quantitative Economics, United State Military Academy, West Point; MBA, Sloan School of Management, MIT
  Background: Partner, ITU Ventures; Business Affairs, AOL; United States Army
  Wes Blackwell, Partner
  Education: BS, United States Naval Academy; MBA, Darden School of Business, University of Virginia
  Background: Aviator, US Navy; Director of Marketing, US Navy Academy; VP of Business Development & Strategy, Jacksonville JetPort; Sr Implementation Manager, LiveSafe; Angel Investor
  Directorships: DataTribe

1633 SCP PARTNERS
7 Great Valley Parkway
Suite 190
Malvern, PA 19355

Phone: 610-995-2900 Fax: 610-975-9546
e-mail: info@scppartners.com
web: www.scppartners.com

Mission Statement: A multi-stage venture capital firm focused on investments in Information and Communication Technology, Life Sciences, Services, Defense and Security.

Geographic Preference: United States
Fund Size: Over $1 Billion
Founded: 1996
Average Investment: $2 - 10 million
Minimum Investment: $2 million
Investment Criteria: Expansion Stage, Early Stage, Later Stage Middle Market Buyout Opportunitites
Industry Group Preference: Information Technology, Telecommunications, Financial Services, Medical Devices, Media, Life Sciences, Aerospace, Defense and Government, Security, Communications, Pharmaceuticals, Diagnostics
Portfolio Companies: Amkor Technology, Echo 360, FourthWall Media, GiftCertificates.com, Gigared, Grab Networks, Magnolia Broadband, Q Group, Software Technology, Deep Breeze, Trig, Vitalife, Pentech, Tammac, DVTel, XVIONICS, AMG, Hospitality Associates, Selway Partners, Vertex Management Israel

Other Locations:
  74 Grand Avenue
  Englewood, NJ 07631
  Phone: 201-541-1080 Fax: 201-541-1084

  74 Grand Avenue
  Engelwood, NJ 07631
  Phone: 201-541-1080 Fax: 201-541-1084

Key Executives:
  Wayne B Weisman, Partner
  Education: BA, cum laude, University of Pennsylvania; MBA, New York University Graduate School of Business Administration
  Background: Managing Director, Churchill Investment Partners; CIP Capital Management; Executive VP, Affinity Biotech; Saul, Ewing, Remick & Saul
  Directorships: Grab Networks; Echo 360; Deap Breeze, Ltd.

Thomas G Rebar, Partner
Education: BS, summa cum laude, University of Scranton; MBA, New York University Graduate School of Business
Background: Senior VP, Cvharterhouse; Bankers Trust Company
Directorships: Pentech Financial Services; DVTel, Inc.
Yaron Eitan, Partner
Education: MBA, Wharton School of Business, University of Pennsylvania
Background: Co-Founder/President/CEO, Selway Partners LLC
Directorships: DVTel, Magnolia Broadband, Cyalumax Technology, Inc.
Winston J Churchill, Managing General Partner
Education: BS in Physics, Fordham University; MA in Economics, Univ. of Oxford; JD, Yale Law School
Background: Founded Churchill Investment Partners; Bessemer Securities Corporation; Practiced Law at Saul Eqing LLP
Directorships: Trustee of Immaculate University, American Friends of New College Oxford, England and the Gesu School; AkmerTechnology, Inc.; Cylumax Technology, Inc.
Roger Carolin, Venture Partner
Education: BBE, Duke University; MBA, Harvard Business School
Background: Co-Founded CFM Technologies; Honeywell Inc; General Electric Company
Directorships: Chairman of Franklin Fuel Cells
Robert G Yablunsky, Venture Partner
Education: BS, Saint Vincent College; MS, Penn State
Background: Director of Native American CYF; Intelligent Electronics
Directorships: Serves on the Boards of BIAP Systems, DVIRC, STI, Penn State Great Valley Alumni and is a Trustee of the Young Scholars Charter School (Philadelphia)
Charles C Freyer, General Counsel & Chief Administrative Officer
Education: AB, Princeton University; JD, Yale Law School
Background: Miller Investment Management; Saul Ewing, LLP; Lieutenant Colonel, Retired in the US Army Judge Advocate General's Corps
Directorships: Admitted to practice in Pennsylvania and New York, has completed his Series 65
Richard L Sherman, Venture Partner
Education: University of Nebraska; JD, New York University School of Law
Background: Deputy General Counsel, SmithKline Beckman Corporation; Founder & Managing Officer, QED Technologies
Directorships: CytoMed, IBAH, Kenna Technologies, Mera Pharmaceuticals, Sparta Pharmaceuticals
Gen. John M Keane, Venture Partner
Education: BS, Fordham University; MA, Philosophy, Western Kentucky University; Army War College; Command & General Staff College
Background: Vice Chief of Staff, US Army
Directorships: MetLife, General Dynamics, MacAndrews & Forbes, Cyalume Technologies Holdings

1634 SCRUM VENTURES
575 Marsket Street
PO 1600
San Francisco, CA 94105

web: scrum.vc

Mission Statement: Scrum Ventures is an early stage venture capital based in Silicon valley. We invest in entrepreneurs who are creating startups in the high growth mobile sector. We help companies accelerate growth with our expertise and powerful network in Asia.

Average Investment: $100,000 - $1MM
Investment Criteria: Early Stage
Industry Group Preference: Mobile
Portfolio Companies: Kidaptive, App.io, Prizeo, Aarki, First Opinion, Binpress, SharePractice, Spire, Le Tote, Lob, Mobileworks, Placemeter, Koemei, Noom, Boostable, Panna, Vidpresso, Focus Motion, LivBlends, Pantry, Altitude

Key Executives:
Tak Miyata, Founding Partner
Education: Master's Degree in nano Science from Waseda University

1635 SCULPTOR CAPITAL MANAGEMENT
9 West 57th Street
39th Floor
New York, NY 10019

Phone: 212-790-0000
web: www.sculptor.com

Mission Statement: Alternative asset manager serving global base of institutional investors.

Fund Size: $33 billion
Founded: 1994
Industry Group Preference: Real Estate

Other Locations:
Sculptor Capital Management Europe Limited
2nd Floor
London W1F 7EB
United Kingdom
Phone: 44 207 758 4400

Sculptor Capital Management Hong Kong Limited
20th Floor
2 Queen's Road Central
Hong Kong
China
Phone: 852 2297 2580

Sculptor (Shanghai) Overseas Investment Fund Mgmt Co., Ltd.
Shanghai International Finance Center Tower II
8 Century Avenue, Pudong New Area
Shanghai 200120
China
Phone: 86 21 6062 6186

Key Executives:
Robert Shafir, Chief Executive Officer
Education: BA, Economics, Lafayette College; MBA, Columbia Business School
Background: Chairman & CEO, Credit Suisse Americas; Head of Global Equities, Lehman Brothers; Morgan Stanley
Wayne Cohen, President & Chief Operating Officer
Education: BA, International Relations, Tulane University; JD, New York University School of Law
Background: Attorney & General Counsel, Sculptor Capital Management; Attorney, Schulte Roth & Zabel LLP
Thomas Sipp, Chief Financial Officer
Education: BA, Finance, Alfred University; MBA, University of Pittsburgh
Background: Managing Partner, Magis Partners; CFO/COO of Asset Management Division, Credit Suisse; COO, Institutional Investment Division of Fidelity Investments; CFO & Head of Product Development, Gartmore Global Investments

1636 SEACOAST CAPITAL CORPORATION
55 Ferncroft Road
Suite 110
Danvers, MA 01923

Phone: 978-750-1300 Fax: 978-750-1301
web: www.seacoastcapital.com

Venture Capital & Private Equity Firms / Domestic Firms

Mission Statement: Invests mezzanine and equity capital in small, growing companies led by strong, entrepreneurial management teams.
Geographic Preference: United States
Fund Size: $200 million
Founded: 1990
Average Investment: $2-$10 million
Minimum Investment: $500,000
Investment Criteria: Second-Stage, Mezzanine, LBO, Special Situations
Industry Group Preference: Communications, Computer Related, Consumer Products, Distribution, Electronic Components, Industrial Equipment, Medical & Health Related, Electronic Components, Manufacturing, Business Products & Services
Portfolio Companies: BISCO Environmental, Cinetopia, ElectroCraft, FAPS, Frank Entertainment Group, The Jay Group, Matlet Group, Mearthane Products, Mountain Alarm, Northwest Cascade, Patriot Environmental Services, QK Holdings, QuVis, UX Specialized Logistics, Walden Behavioral Health

Other Locations:
One Bush Street
Suite 650
San Francisco, CA 94104
Phone: 415-956-1400

Key Executives:
Timothy P Fay, Partner
e-mail: tfay@seacoastcapital.com
Education: BA, Economics, University of Texas, Dallas; MBA, University of Chicago
Background: Co-Founder, Key Mezzanine Fund, Key Principal Partners; The Barclasy Group; The Federal Reserve Bank
Thomas W Gorman, Partner
e-mail: tgorman@seacoastcapital.com
Education: AB, Holy Cross College; MBA, Amos Tuck School of Business Administration
Background: General Motors Corporation; Lending Officer, Shawmut Bank of Boston
Jeffrey J Holland, Partner
e-mail: jholland@seacoastcapital.com
Education: BS, Stanford University; MBA, Harvard Business School
Background: Consultant, MAC Group; Andersen Consulting
Eben S Moulton, Senior Advisor
e-mail: emoulton@seacoastcapital.com
Education: BS, Colorado College; PhD, Vanderbilt; MBA, Columbia University Trustee of Colorado College
Background: Bank of New England
Directorships: Unitil Corporation
James T Donelan, Principal
e-mail: jdonelan@seacoastcapital.com
Education: BA, Economics, Middlebury College
Background: Analyst, Investment Banking, Adams Harkness & Hill

1637 SEAPOINT VENTURES
777 108th Ave. NE
Suite 1895
Bellevue, WA 98004

Phone: 425-455-0879
e-mail: info@seapointventures.com

Mission Statement: To generate unique insights that help portfolio companies lead market trends and build value in early stage companies. Seapoint stays focused on solid business models, intelligent fundraising, assembling exceptional teams and staying collaborative with our internal and external partners.
Founded: 1997
Investment Criteria: Early-Stage

Industry Group Preference: Communications, Wireless, Broadband, Network Infrastructure
Portfolio Companies: Airspan, aQuantive, BridgeWave Communications, Dantz, Entomo, Hubspan, Internap, Kineto, Modiv Media, Mojix, NetMotion, Ontela, PhoneSpots, PocketThis, PowerTech Group, Qpass, SinglePoint, SNAPin Software, Talisma, Tegic, Telecom Transport Management, Trumba, Vayusa, Wireless Services Corporation, Zumobi

Key Executives:
Thomas S Huseby, Managing Partner
Education: BS, Economics, BS, Industrial Engineering, Columbia University; MBA, Stanford University
Background: Co-Founder & CEO, Metawave Communications Corporation; President & CEO, Innova Corporation; Raychem Corporation
Directorships: Airspan, Ground Truth, Zumobi, Hubspan, Kineto Wireless, Modiv Media, Mojiz, Photobucket, SinglePoint
Melissa Widner, General Partner
Education: Bachelor's Degree, University of Washington; MA, Stanford University
Background: Co-Founder, 7Software; CEO, Northwest Supply
Directorships: Hubspan, Powertech, PhoneSpots, NetMotion

1638 SEAPORT CAPITAL
40 Fulton Street
27th Floor
New York, NY 10038

Phone: 212-847-8900 **Fax:** 212-320-0270
e-mail: info@seaportcapital.com
web: www.seaportcapital.com

Mission Statement: Works with talented management teams to create valuable companies that are leaders in their market segments.
Geographic Preference: United States
Fund Size: $400 million
Founded: 1991
Average Investment: $10-35 million over the life of the investment
Minimum Investment: $5 million
Investment Criteria: Late Stage. Growth, Recapitalizations, Buy-Outs
Industry Group Preference: Business to Business, Communications, Media, Technology, Information Services, Business Products & Services
Portfolio Companies: All Traffic Data, Atmosera, B Media Group, EoStar, Exacom, Filmwerks LLC, i3 Broadband, Keg Logistics, Linen King, Municipal Communications II, Quality Uptime Services, Quatris Healthco

Key Executives:
Bill Luby, Founding Partner
e-mail: bluby@seaportcapital.com
Education: BA Economics, Trinity College; MBA, Fuqua School of Business, Duke University
Background: CEA Capital Partners; Managing Director, Chase Capital; Managing Director LBO, Chase Merchant Banking Group
Jim Collis, Founding Partner
e-mail: jcollis@seaportcapital.com
Education: BSEE, Rensselaer Polytechnic Institute; MBA, Columbia Business School
Background: CEA Capital Partners; Principal, Chase Capital Partners; Associate/VP, Chase Merchant Banking Group; Principal Engineer, National Teleconsultants
Scott McCormack, Partner
e-mail: smccormack@seaportcapital.com
Education: AB, Economics, Harvard College
Background: BancBoston Capital
Directorships: Independence Media, SCDC Holdings, Peak 10

Venture Capital & Private Equity Firms / Domestic Firms

Bob Tamashunas, Partner
e-mail: btamashunas@seaportcapital.com
Education: BS, Science, Georgetown University; MBA, Columbia Business School
Background: Leveraged Bank Loan Group, Prudential Capital Group
Directorships: Bay Communications, Municipal Communications, Worley Claim Service
Howard Kaufman, Chief Financial Officer
e-mail: hkaufman@seaportcapital.com
Education: BS, Accounting, University of Scranton
Background: SVP & CFO, Lynch & Mayer; Financial Vice President, Carteret Financial Group

1639 SEAWAY VALLEY CAPITAL CORPORATION
10 Park St., Fl. 2
Gouverneur, NY 13642-1052

Phone: 315-287-1122 Fax: 302-636-5454

Mission Statement: Seaway Valley Capital Corporation was formed to provide companies access to capital for growth, expansion and restructuring. Seaway Valley has a particular, but not exclusive, focus of providing capital solutions to the underserved region of Northern New York.

Geographic Preference: Northern New York
Investment Criteria: Early-Stage, Mid & Later-Stage, Management Buyouts
Industry Group Preference: Manufacturing, Technology, Agriculture, Restaurants, Real Estate, Consumer Products
Portfolio Companies: Patrick Hackett Hardware Company, Altieri Bakery, Sackets Harbor Brewing Company, Seaway Restaurant Group

Key Executives:
Thomas W Scozzafava, President & CEO
Education: BA, Economics & Mathematics, Hamilton College
Background: Co-Founder, GS AgriFuels Corporation; Director, Prudential's Merchant Banking Group; Lehman Brothers' Merchant Banking Group; GE Capital Corporation
Directorships: New York State Power Authority

1640 SECOND ALPHA
276 Fifth Avenue
Suite 204
New York, NY 10001

Phone: 212-446-1600
web: www.secondalpha.com

Mission Statement: Second Alpha crafts innovative capital solutions that allow founders, managers and investors in private companies to achieve liquidity prior to company sales or IPOs. Second Alpha buys shares and convertible securities on a secondary basis and also invests capital directly into growth companies.

Geographic Preference: United States, Canada
Investment Criteria: Growth Stage
Industry Group Preference: Technology, Media, Telecommunications
Portfolio Companies: 23andme, AccessData, Artful Home, Avst, Bolt Insurance, Buffer, Code42, Coursera, DailyPay, Everbridge, Everquote, Healthcare.Com, Netmotion Wireless, On24, OpenX, Prove Inc., Sixth Sense Media, Sportvision, Terago, Touch Commerce, UserTesting

Key Executives:
Richard Brekka, Co-Founder/Managing Partner
e-mail: rbrekka@secondalpha.com
Education: BS, University of Southern California; MBA, University of Chicago
Background: President/Managing Partner/Founder, Dolphin Equity Partners; Managing Director, CIBC; Chase Capital

Jim Sanger, Co-Founder/Managing Partner
e-mail: jim@secondalpha.com
Education: BS, University of Pennsylvania
Background: General Partner, ABS Ventures; Managing Director, Deutsche Bank's DB Capital Venture Partners
Directorships: June Media, Terago Networks
Eugene Galantini, Chief Financial Officer
e-mail: egalantini@secondalpha.com
Education: BS, Accounting, University of Scranton; CPA
Background: CFO, Dolphin Equity Partners; Assistant Controller, New York Life Capital Partners

1641 SECOND AVENUE PARTNERS
1301 Second Avenue
Suite 2850
Seattle, WA 98101

Phone: 206-332-1200 Fax: 206-332-1201
web: www.secondave.com

Mission Statement: Second Avenue Partners is a Seattle-based provider of management, strategy, and capital for early stage companies. The partners invest their own money, typically directed at emerging Internet businesses in the high-tech field. Second Avenue Partners' investment approach is to make early-stage investments in promising ventures and build long-term relationships, actively assisting its portfolio companies in becoming market leaders.

Investment Criteria: Early-Stage
Industry Group Preference: High Technology
Portfolio Companies: AudienceScience, Azaleos, CoolSpotter, Essention, FanNation, Fantasy Moguls, FLEXE, Front Desk, Glassnetic Inc., HealthSlate, Inkd, Insitu Group, JeNu, Locationlabs, Market Leader, Modumetal, Newsvine, Qliance, RealSelf, Seeq, Slope, TreeRing, WISErg

Key Executives:
Mike Slade, Founding Partner
Education: BA, Economics, Colordo College; MBA, Stanford Graduate School of Business
Background: Director, Corporate Marketing, Microsoft; Starwave; NeXt Computer
Nick Hanauer, Founding Partner
Education: BS, Philosophy, University of Washington
Background: Board Advisor, Amazon; Founder & CEO, aQuantive; Founder, Gear.com
Pete Higgins, Founding Partner
Education: BS, Economics, History, MBA, Stanford University
Background: Microsoft
Directorships: Ice Energy, Modumetal, Rubicon Interactive, Insitu Group, Market Leader

1642 SECOND CENTURY VENTURES
Chicago, IL 60611

e-mail: hello@secondcenturyventures.com
web: www.secondcenturyventures.com

Mission Statement: Second Century Ventures is the strategic investment arm of the National Association of Realtors. We build companies using our extensive industry knowledge and experience, vast membership base and the power of the Realtor brand. We are a catalyst for building relationships among new technologies, new opportunities and new talent to help deliver the future of the industry.

Industry Group Preference: Real Estate
Portfolio Companies: Back At You Media, BombBomb, Deduct, Desktime, DocuSign, EndHub, EPropertyData, FundWell, Ifbyphone, Lumentus, Move, NAR REach, Planwise, Reach150, SeaSuite By Goby, SentriLock, SmartZip, Treater, Updater, WeVideo, Workface, xceligent, Ziplogix

Key Executives:
Tyler Thompson, Managing Partner
Education: BA, Brigham Young University; MS, Real Estate Development, MIT

577

Venture Capital & Private Equity Firms / Domestic Firms

Background: Director of Metrics, Business Software Alliance; CEO, CaptureQuest Inc.; CEO/Director, Avalon Digital Marketing Systems Inc.; VP of Business Development, Deductr; Managing Partner, Black Shamrock
Mark Birschbach, Managing Director
Education: BBA, Finance, University of Notre Dame
Background: VP of Banking Investments, Citigroup; President/COO, Active Radius LLC; COO, Monthlys; Managing Director REach; SVP of Strategic Business, Innovation & Technology, National Association of Realtors

1643 SECTION 32

e-mail: info@section32.com
web: www.section32.com

Mission Statement: Section 32 invests in a wide range of projects from robotics and digital currencies to medical research and agriculture to the music industry and more.

Fund Size: $150 million
Founded: 2016
Industry Group Preference: Robotics, Technology, Medical Research, Medical Equipment, Music, Health
Portfolio Companies: Arsanis, Auris, BloomAPI, Celularity, Coinbase, Dave, Dialpad, Eatsa, Embark, Freenome, Kobalt, LimeBike, Neocis, Norquin, Teckro, Vir

Key Executives:
  Bill Maris, Founder
  Education: Middlebury College
  Background: Investor AB, Burlee.com, Web.com, Google Ventures, Calico
  Mike Pellini, Managing Director
  Education: BA, Boston College; MBA, Drexel University; MD, Jefferson Medical College
  Background: CEO/Chairman, Foundation Medicine; President/COO, Clarient

1644 SEED MILESTONE FUND
1 Ferry Building
Suite 201
San Francisco, CA 94111

Phone: 415-479-6080
e-mail: contact@seedmilestone.com
web: www.seedmilestone.com

Mission Statement: Seed Milestone Fund is a new fund dedicated to core technology, B2B, foundational tech, platforms, IoT, information systems, SaaS, logistics and digital transformation.

Founded: 2020
Key Executives:
  Peter Henry, Founder/General Partner
  Education: Stanford University
  Background: Managing Partner, Perspectrum LLC; Managing Director, Canard Sauvage LLC; Founder/Managing Partner, Act 5 Ventures LLC
  Neal Strickberger, Founder/General Partner
  Background: Principal, Dangerous Knowledge, Applied; Angel Investor, Keiretsu Forum

1645 SEIDLER EQUITY PARTNERS
4640 Admiralty Way
Suite 1200
Marina del Rey, CA 90292

Phone: 213-683-4622 Fax: 213-624-0691
e-mail: info@sepfunds.com
web: www.sepfunds.com

Mission Statement: A private equity investment firm that partners with visionary executives to grow their businesses.

Founded: 1992
Investment Criteria: Growth Capital Financing, Management or Partner Buyouts, Recapitalizations
Industry Group Preference: Education, Specialty Retail, Distribution, Gaming, Railroad Services, Medical Products, Mobility
Portfolio Companies: LA Fitness International, Aden & Anais, Sportsman's Warehouse, Tonoga, Korvis, Sunny Sky Products, Emergency Essentials

Key Executives:
  Peter Seidler, Managing Partner
  Education: BS, Finance, University of Virginia; MS, Business Administration, University of California, Los Angeles
  Robert Seidler, Managing Partner
  Education: BA, Georgetown University; MBA, University of California, Los Angeles
  Eric Kutsenda, Managing Partner
  Education: BS, Accounting, University of Illinois; MS, Taxation, DePaul University

1646 SELBY VENTURE PARTNERS
3500 Alameda De Las Pulgas
Suite 200
Menlo Park, CA 94025

Phone: 650-854-7399 Fax: 650-854-7039
web: www.selbyventures.com

Mission Statement: To invest in passionate entrepreneurs who want to build the next generation of category defining companies.

Geographic Preference: West Coast
Fund Size: $135 million
Founded: 1998
Average Investment: $1-$2.5 million
Minimum Investment: $250,000
Investment Criteria: Early, Expansion, Seed
Industry Group Preference: Communications, Electronic Technology, Software, Manufacturing, Wireless Technologies, Hardware, Semiconductors, Internet, Sustainable Technologies, Digital Media & Marketing, Information Technology
Portfolio Companies: Attributor, BigFix, BigStage, Blue Pumpkin Software, ConsumerReview, Coremetrics, LiveCapital, ModViz, Pandora Media, Panopticon, SugarSync, Size Technologies, Tempo Payments, Visage Mobile, 3ware, 4INFO, Active-Semi, Bay Microsystems, Clairvoyante, HotRail, Intelleflex, Silicon Packets, SkyPilot Networks, Triformix, Active Semiconductors, Clairvoyante, Ecohaus

Key Executives:
  Bob Marshall, Managing Director
  e-mail: bob@selbyventures.com
  Education: BEE, Heald Engineering; MBA, Pepperdine University
  Background: Tandem Computers; Diablo Systems; InfoGear Technology
  Directorships: 3Ware, Bay Microsystems, Blue Pumpkin Software, Quicksilver Technology, Sierra Monitor Corp., Wytec
  Jim Marshall, Managing Director
  e-mail: jim@selbyventures.com
  Education: BS, Finance, Santa Clara University; MBA, Pepperdine University
  Background: VP, Commercial Software Practice
  Directorships: Live Capital, ConsumerReview, Panopticon, SkyPilot Network, Zenasis Technologies
  Doug Barry, Managing Director
  e-mail: doug@selbyventures.com
  Education: BS, UC Berkeley; MBA, Harvard University
  Background: Co-Founder, CobaltCard; Senior Executive, Electronic Arts; Mavio Communications; Turner Broadcasting
  Directorships: BigFix, Clairvoyante Laboratories, Cranite Systems, Size Technology, SkyPilot Network, Visage Mobile

Venture Capital & Private Equity Firms / Domestic Firms

1647 SELWAY CAPITAL
38 Ridge Road
Tenalfy, NJ 07670

web: www.selwaycapital.com

Mission Statement: To provide companies with a unique blend of capital, expertise, commitment and operational management at the earliest stages to a select number of promising ideas and projects within information technology and telecommunication markets.
Investment Criteria: Early Stage
Industry Group Preference: Information Technology, Telecommunications
Portfolio Companies: DVTEL, STI, Magonlia Broadband
Key Executives:
  Yaron Eitan, Founder
  Education: BA, Economics, Haifa University; MBA, Wharton School
  Background: Co-Founder, Reshef Technologies; Founder/CEO, Geotek Communications; Co-Founder/Chairman, Marpai Health; Co-Founder/Chairman, DeepCube; Co-Founder/Chairman, Emporus Technologies
Key Executives:
  Michael C Skaff, Co-Founder/Managing Director
  e-mail: mikes@senecapartners.com
  Education: BS, Economics & Mathematics, MBA, University of Michigan
  Background: Managing Director, Manchester Capital; VP, Home Care Operations, MedMax
  Anthony W Zambelli, Co-Founder/Managing Director
  e-mail: tonyz@senecapartners.com
  Education: Ross School of Business, University of Michigan
  Background: Managing Director, Manchester Capital; Great Lakes Region Corporate Finance, Deloitte & Touche

1649 SENECA PARTNERS
Two Towne Square
Suite 810
Southfield, MI 48076

Phone: 248-723-6650
e-mail: info@senecapartners.com
web: www.senecapartners.com

Mission Statement: A venture capital fund focused on providing growth capital to companies in the healthcare industry that are located in Middle America.
Geographic Preference: Midwest United States
Founded: 2002
Average Investment: $500,000 - $2.5 million
Investment Criteria: Early-Stage to Later-Stage
Industry Group Preference: Healthcare Services, Healthcare Information Technology, Medical Devices

1650 SENTIENT VENTURES
11412 Bee Caves Road
Suite 300
Austin, TX 78738

Phone: 512-402-1717 Fax: 512-402-1616
e-mail: info@senven.com
web: www.sentientventures.com

Mission Statement: Sentient Ventures is a private equity firm that invests in seed, early, and expansion stage companies using the following fund types: early stage venture capital, middle market private equity and subordinated debt.
Geographic Preference: Texas
Average Investment: $500,000 - $7.5 million
Investment Criteria: Seed-Stage, Early-Stage, Expansion Stage
Portfolio Companies: Austin Entrepreneurs Foundation, Texchange (Austin), Austin Technology Incubator, Venture Fellows, College of Natural Sciences Advisory Council, School of Management and Business Advisory Council, TXEntre
Key Executives:
  David Lee, Managing Partner
  Background: Managing Partner, Murphree Venture Partners; Viasoft; Tivoli Systems
  Jonathan Ring, Venture Partner
  Background: Founder & President, Caringo; VP, Engineering, Siebel Systems; Comdisco
  James Wells, Venture Partner
  Background: VP, Sales, RealNetworks; Dazel Corporation; Apple Computer
  Mansoor Ghori, Venture Partner

1651 SENTINEL CAPITAL PARTNERS
330 Madison Avenue
27th Floor
New York, NY 10017

Phone: 212-688-3100 Fax: 212-688-6513
e-mail: info@sentinelpartners.com
web: www.sentinelpartners.com

Mission Statement: To generate superior investment returns by enabling talented executives to build great businesses.
Geographic Preference: United States
Fund Size: $200 million
Founded: 1995
Average Investment: $20 million
Investment Criteria: MBO, Late Stage, Recapitalizations, Growth Financing
Industry Group Preference: Aerospace, Defense and Government, Industrial Manufacturing, Business Products & Services, Consumer Products, Consumer Services, Food Services, Franchising, Healthcare Services
Portfolio Companies: Checkers Drive-In Restaurants, Colson Group, Credit Infonet Group, Critical Solutions International, Hollander Sleep Products, Hospice Advantage Holdings, Huddle House, IEP Technologies, National Spine & Pain Centers, Newk's Eatery, North American Rescue, Northeast Dental Management, PlayCore, Power Products, RotoMetrics, Spinrite, TGI Fridays, Vintage Holdings, WellSpring Pharmaceutical Corporation
Key Executives:
  Eric D Bommer, Partner
  e-mail: Bommer@sentinelpartners.com
  Education: BA, Brown University
  John F McCormack, Co-Founder/Senior Partner
  e-mail: McCormack@sentinelpartners.com
  Education: BS, Boston College
  David S Lobel, Co-Founder/Managing Partner
  Education: MBA, MS, Stanford University; BS, University of Witwatersrand
  Background: Office Depot, Entre Computer Center, Rocky Mountain Saving Bank, Smith Barney, Bain and Company
  Paul F Murphy, Partner
  Education: MBA, Georgetown University; BS, US Military Academy
  Background: Vice President at NationsBanc Capital Markets; Merchant Banking Group, Chase Manhattan Bank
  Thomas P Fitzpatrick, Operating Partner
  Education: BBA, St. John's University; Certified Public Accountant
  Background: Coopers & Lybrand; Senior Vice President, Englehard Corp
  James D Coady, Partner
  Education: BA, Harvard University; MBA, Northwestern University
  Background: First Chicago Equity Capital, Analyst at Alex, Brown & Sons
  Sidney J Feltenstein, Operating Partner
  Education: BA, Boston University

579

Venture Capital & Private Equity Firms / Domestic Firms

Background: EVP, Worldwide Marketing, Burger King Corporation; Operations & Marketing, Dunkin' Donuts
Directorships: Interim Healthcare, Inscape Publishing, Massage Envy, Southern California Pizza Company
Edward L Kuntz, Operating Partner
Education: BA, JD, Master of Law, Temple University
Background: CEO, Kindred Healthcare; CEO, Living Centers of America; Associate General Counsel, ARA Services
Directorships: Kindred Healthcare, Rotech Healthcare

1652 SENTRY FINANCIAL CORPORATION
201 S Main Street
Suite 1400
Salt Lake City, UT 84111

Phone: 801-596-9600
e-mail: info@sentry.financial
web: www.sentryfinancial.com

Mission Statement: Invest growth capital with businesses under $10 million in revenue. Add value to portfolio companies through hands-on counsel in areas of marketing, finance, accounting and information systems processing. Provide in-house capability to finance sales to portfolio company customers where appropriate.

Geographic Preference: United States
Fund Size: $15 million
Founded: 2002
Average Investment: $500,000
Minimum Investment: $200,000
Investment Criteria: Second Stage, Mezzanine, MBO
Industry Group Preference: Financial Services, Conservation, Distribution, Health Related, Outsourcing & Efficiency, Energy, Entertainment, Internet, Healthcare Information Technology

Key Executives:
Jonathan M Ruga, Founder/CEO
801-303-1108
e-mail: jruga@sentryfinancial.com
Education: Graduated, magna cum laude, University of Utah with Undergraduate Degress in Accounting, Finance; MBA, Obtained a Law Degree
Background: Chairman, Sentry's Investment Committee; Attorney, Parr, Waddoups, Brown, Gee & Loveless; Lease Education/Consulting, Amembal, Deane & Associates
Scott F Young, COO
Education: Graduated Finance Degree, Obtained a Law Degree, University of Utah
Background: Partner, Parr, Waddoups, Brown, Gee & Loveless; Judicial Clerkship, Utah Supreme Court
G Stephen Browning, Chief Accounting Officer/Chief Information Officer
Education: BA Accounting, Masters in Information Systems, Brigham Young University
Background: Senior Manager, Browning, Creer & Associates; Accounting/Consulting, KPMG Peat Marwick

1653 SEQUEL VENTURE PARTNERS
4430 Arapahoe Avenue
Suite 220
Boulder, CO 80303

Phone: 303-546-0400
web: www.sequelvc.com

Mission Statement: Seeks to provide exceptional return to investors by combining knowledge, experience, and relationships to enhance the likelihood of substantial success for portfolio companies.

Geographic Preference: Rocky Mountain Region
Fund Size: $400 million
Average Investment: $3 million
Minimum Investment: $2 million
Investment Criteria: Seed, Early-stage
Industry Group Preference: Health Related, Information Technology, Telecommunications, Computer Related, Genetic Engineering, Internet Technology, Technology, Clean Technology, Healthcare

Key Executives:
Dan Mitchell, Partner
Education: BS, University of Illinois; MBA, University of California, Berkeley
Background: Founder, Capital Health Management; Institutional Venture Capital Fund, First National Bank of Chicago
Directorships: GlobeImmune, Kalypto Medical
Tom Washing, Partner
Education: BA, Dartmouth College; JD, University of Michigan Law School
Background: Founding General Partner, Horsley Keogh Associates; General Partner, Hill Carman & Washing
Directorships: SkyeTek, YieldEx
John Greff, Partner/CFO
Education: BS, Business Administration, Colorado State University; MBA, University of Denver
Background: CFO, Allos Therapeutics; CFO, Somatogen
Kinney Johnson, Partner
Education: BA, Mathematics/Business Administration, Augsburg College; MS, Mathematical Computer Science, University of Iowa
Background: Founder, Capital Health Management; Founder/President, Fischer Imaging Corporation
Directorships: Evolutionary Genomics, HomeSphere, Intio
Tim Connor, Partner
Education: BA, Washington College; MBA, Harvard Business School
Background: Managing Director, Lehman Brothers Technology Investment Banking Group; Senior VP Operations/CFO, Access Health
Directorships: Aztek Networks, Datalogic, InfoNow Corporation, Quova
Chris Scoggins, Venture Partner
Education: BS, Trinity University; MBA, Stanford Graduate School of Business
Background: Associate, The Sprout Group; Co-Founder, Internet Reports
Directorships: YieldEx

1654 SEQUOIA CAPITAL
2800 Sand Hill Road
Suite 101
Menlo Park, CA 94025

Phone: 650-854-3927
web: www.sequoiacap.com

Mission Statement: Provides start-up venture capital funding for seed-stage, early-stage and growth companies.

Geographic Preference: United States, Israel, China, India
Fund Size: $400 million
Founded: 1972
Average Investment: $5 million
Minimum Investment: $50,000
Investment Criteria: Seed Stage, Early Stage, Growth Stage
Industry Group Preference: Electronic Technology, Components & IoT, Software, Energy, Financial Services, Healthcare Services, Internet, Mobile, Outsourcing & Efficiency
Portfolio Companies: 100 Thieves, 23andMe, 3Com, [24]7.ai, ActionIQ, AdMob, Against Gravity, Agile Software, AgilOne, Airbnb, AirStrip, Altiscale, AMCC, Ameritox, Amplitude, Amylin, App Annie, Appirio, Apple, Arbor/Hyperion, Aruba, Aspect Development, Assurex Health, Aster Data, Atari, Athelas, Avanex, Barefoot Networks, Barracuda Networks, bebop, Berkeley Lights, Bird, Blue Danube Systems, Brud, Cafepress, Carbon, Carbon Black, CEGX, CenterRun Software, Charlotte Tillbury, Chartboost, Cisco, Citizen, Clari, Clearwell Systems, Clever, Clickatell, Clover Health, Clutter, Cobalt

Venture Capital & Private Equity Firms / Domestic Firms

Robotics, Cohesity, Comprehend, Confluent, Cortexyme, Crew, Cumulus Networks, Cypress, Decolar, Dia&Co, Docker, Domino Data Lab, DoorDash, Drawbridge, Drift, Dopbox, Druva, Electronic Arts, Elevate, Elevate Credit, Embark Trucks, EndoChoice, Ethos, Eventbrite, Evernote, Everwise, Faire, FireEye, First Republic Bank, Flex, Front, FutureAdvisor, GameFly, GenEdit, GitHub, Good Eggs, Google, Graphcore, Green Dot, Guardant Health, Hayneedle, Health Catalyst, Hearsay Sustems, HireVue, Houseparty, Houzz, HubSpot, Humble Bundle, Infoblox, Inkling, INS, Inside.Com, Instacart, Instagram, IPG, Isilon Systems, Jasper, Jawbone, Jive, Kahuna, KAYAK, Kenshoo, Kiwi, Klarna, Lattive Engines, Lifecode, LightStep, Lilt, Limbix, Linear Technology, LinkedIn, LitePoint, LSI Logic, Luminate, Mapillary, MarkLogic, Maven, Medallia, MedExpress, Mellanox, Meraki, Merlin Securities, Metanautix, MetaStable, Metaswitch Networks, Microchip Technology,

Other Locations:
Room 3606
China Central Place Tower 3
77 Jianguo Road Chaoyang District
Beijing 100025
China
Phone: 86 10 8447 5668 **Fax:** 86 10 8447 5669

Suite 3613, 36/F
Two Pacific Place
88 Queensway
Hong Kong
China
Phone: 852 2501 8989

Room 3006
Plaza 66 Tower 2
1366 Nanjing West Road
Shanghai 200040
China
Phone: 86 21 6288 4222

Sequoia Capital India Advisors
6th Floor, East Wing, Block B
77§ Town Centre, Off Hal Airport Road, Yemlur
Bengaluru 560037
India
Phone: 91 0 80 412 458 80

Sequoia Capital India Advisors
Peninsula Corporate Park
Ganpatrao Kadam Marg, Lower Parel
Mumbai 400013
India
Phone: 91 0 22 4074 7272

Sequoia Capital India Advisors Pvt. Ltd.
JW Marriott, Asset Area 4
Delhi Aerocity
New Delhi 110037
India
Phone: 91 0 11 4956 7200

Sequoia Capital India Advisors
26-12 South Beach Tower
Singapore 189767
Singapore
Phone: 65 6812 9162

50 Eli Landau Boulevard
Orchid Oceanus Hotel
Herzelia 4685150
Israel
Phone: 972 9 9579440

Key Executives:
Donald Valentine, Founder & Partner
Background: Founder, National Semiconductor; Senior Sales/Marketing, Fairchild Semiconductor
Directorships: Chairman, Network Appliance; Vice Chairman, Cisco; Chairman, diCarta; Traiana
Roelof Botha, Partner
Education: BS, Actuarial Science/Economics/Statistics, University of Cape Town; MBA, Stanford Graduate School of Business
Background: CFO, PayPal; Management Consultant, McKinsey & Company
Directorships: Luxim
Jim Goetz, Partner
Education: BSEE, University of Cincinnati; MSEE, Stanford University
Background: General Partner, Accel Partners; Entrepreneur, VitalSigns; VP/GM, VitalSoft/Lucent, VP Network Management, Bay Networks; SynOptics; Marketing, AT&T; AT&T Bell Labs; Digital Equipment
Douglas Leone, Partner
Education: BS, Mechanical Engineering, Cornell University; MS, Industrial Engineering, Columbia University; MS, Management, MIT
Background: Sales Management, Sun Microsystems; Hewlet-Packard; Prime Computer
Michael Moritz, Partner
Background: Time Warner; Founder, Technologic Partners
Alfred Lin, Partner
Education: BA, Applied Mathematics, Harvard University; MS, Statistics, Stanford University
Background: Chairman/COO/CFQ, Zappos.com; VP, Finance, Tellme Networks; Co-Founder & General Manager, Venture Frogs
Bryan Schreier, Partner
Education: BS, Computer Science, Princeton University
Background: Senior Director, International Online Sales & Operations, Google; Technology Banking Group, Morgan Stanley
Bill Coughran, Partner
Background: Bell Labs; Google; Entrisphere
Jess Lee, Partner
Education: Stanford University
Background: Google; Polyvore
Mike Vernal, Partner
Background: Facebook
Stephanie Zhan, Partner
Education: BS, Stanford University
Directorships: Sunday; Linear; Middesk; Rec Room Inc.; Brud; PicsArt; Ethos Life

---

1655 SERAPH GROUP
e-mail: paul@seraphgroup.net
web: www.seraphgroup.net

Mission Statement: Founded in 2005, Seraph Group is a super angel fund that invests between $50,000 and $1,000,000 in high-growth start-ups, bridging the funding 'gap' left by individual angels and institutional VCs. Our growing network of 180 members offers an unparalleled breadth of expertise and a unified passion for helping founders build great companies. As dedicated early-stage investors, we understand how a compelling product becomes a powerful business and commit strategic guidance from the Seraph members best suited to help our companies grow. We also understand the value of time: Seraph Group manages funds and operates with a single Managing Partner that makes quick investment decisions, eliminating the challenge of syndicating angel investors.

Founded: 2005
Average Investment: $50,000 - $1 million
Investment Criteria: Seed-Stage, Early-Stage
Industry Group Preference: Information Technology, Web Services, Communications, Life Sciences, Mobile, Consumer Internet, Consumer Products, Enterprise Software, Industrial Products, Mobile Apps
Portfolio Companies: Aarki, AfterSteps, Appbistro, Alsalar, Asankya, BringIt, Catch, Cc:Betty, Charles Chocolates, Creative Market, Digital Health Department, Fliggo, Fundly, Life360, Marble, Midverse Studios, Mixrank, Neurotic Media, nVision, Gopago, PBWorks, People Power, Primeloop, Prompt.ly, Qwiki, RallyOn, Second Genome, SendHub, SilverTail, Site Jabber, Stem Cell Theranostics,

Venture Capital & Private Equity Firms / Domestic Firms

Suddenly Social, TalentBin, Tasting Room, Trip Trotting, UCT Coatings, Urbantag, Victrio, Wakemate, Wifi Slam

Key Executives:
Tuff Yen, Founder/CEO
Education: BA, University of California, Berkeley; MBA, Yale School of Management
Jake Moilanen, General Partner
Education: BS, University of Michigan; MBA, University of Texas

1656 SEVEN PEAKS VENTURES
1001 Southwest Emkay Drive
Suite 140
Bend, OR 97702

e-mail: contactus@sevenpeaksventures.com
web: www.sevenpeaksventures.com

Mission Statement: Seven Peaks Ventures seeks to invest in innovative technology companies with the potential to make an impact on the world.

Fund Size: $15 million
Founded: 2013
Average Investment: $50,000 - $500,000
Investment Criteria: Early Stage
Industry Group Preference: Technology, Consumer Software, Cloud Computing, Digital Health Technology
Portfolio Companies: Amplion, Bright.md, ClientSuccess, CodeHS, Cozy, Cricket Health, CrowdStreet, Crowd Supply, Customer.io, Droplr, Enlitic, Kindara, Manzama, Opal, Scratch-it, SlamData, Upstream Health, Vungle, ZapInfo, Zembula

Key Executives:
Dino Vendetti, Managing Director
Education: BSEE, San Diego State University; MSEE, MBA, University of Washington
Background: Managing Director, Formative Ventures; General Partner, Bay Partners; Vulcan Ventures
Corey Schmid, General Partner
Education: BA, Human Development & Psychology, Boston College; MBA, Business Administration & Management, Portland State University School of Business
Background: Respironics; Invizeon Corporation; Invivodata
Directorships: Oregon Bioscience Association
Tom Gonser, General Partner
Education: BA, Economics, University of Washington
Background: Channel Development, Mccaw Cellular; VP of Business Development, Point.com; Founder/President, NetUPDATE; Founder, GPSflight Inc.; Managing Partner, TMD Ventures; Investment Partner, Seven Peaks Ventures; Founder, DocuSign Inc.
Directorships: Metricstory; Amitree; Trusona; Liveoak Technologies Inc.; NAVIS
Sara Leggat, Chief Financial Officer
Education: BComm., University of British Columbia; MBA, MIT
Background: Sr Research Analyst, Thomas Weisel Partners; Partner/Ressearch Analyst, Longwood Investment Advisor; Head of Business Development, Galt Investment Partners; Chief Marketing Officer, Longwood Investment Advisors; Founder/Managing Partner, BayPeak Partners LLC

1657 SEVENTYSIX CAPITAL
375 E Elm Street
Suite 100
Conshohocken, OA 19428

web: www.seventysixcapital.com

Mission Statement: SeventySix Capital invests in entrepreneurs who have 're-imagined' how we eat, play, drive, entertain, date, search, and stay healthy.

Geographic Preference: Eastern Corridor

Fund Size: $90 million
Average Investment: $4 million
Minimum Investment: $500,000
Industry Group Preference: Technology, Healthcare
Portfolio Companies: BBox, C360 Live, Diamond Kinetics, FORTE, Maestro, Nerd Street Gamers, Play By Play Sports Broadcasting Camps, ShotTracker, Swish Analytics, U.S. Intergrity, Vigtory Sportsbook, VSIN

Key Executives:
Wayne D Kimmel, Managing Partner
610-825-0250
Fax: 610-825-0205
Education: University of Maryland College Park; LLD, Widener University School of Law
Background: Founder/Manager, atPhilly Internet Email Newsletter; CEO, KimmelCorp.com; Attorney, Kimmel/Carter/Roman & Peltz
Directorships: OrganizedWisdom, Ryzing, meetMoi, KGRA Energy, SeamlessWeb
Jon Powell, Managing Partner
Education: BA, University of Maryland; JD, Delaware Law School
Background: Co-Founder, Microsoft Reactor Philadelphia; Strategic Partner, Rubicon Talent

1658 SEVIN ROSEN FUNDS
PO Box 192128
Dallas, TX 75219

Phone: 972-702-1100 Fax: 972-702-1103
web: www.srfunds.com

Mission Statement: Focused on early-stage investing for information sciences and life sciences companies.

Fund Size: $1.9 billion
Founded: 1981
Average Investment: $2 million
Minimum Investment: $500,000
Investment Criteria: Research and Development, Seed, Startup, First-Stage
Industry Group Preference: Internet, Media, Software, Technology, Communications, Infrastructure, Life Sciences, Healthcare, Advanced Materials, Energy
Portfolio Companies: Alder Biopharmaceuticals, BioBehavioral Diagnostics, Cube Optics, Ethertronics, Extennet, GENBAND, HexaTech, Hightail, Invodo, Luminescent, Luxtera, Market6, Metabolon, NetSocket, Scintera, Verified Person, Vidyo, Xtera

Key Executives:
Jon W Bayless, General Partner
Education: BSEE, University of Oklahoma; MEE, University of Alabama; PhD, Electrical Engineering, Arizona State University
Background: Arthur A Collins, E-Systems, Motorola
Stephen M Dow, General Partner
Education: BA, MBA, Stanford University
Background: Booz Allen and Hamilton
John Jaggers, General Partner
Education: BA, MEE, Rice University, MBA, Harvard University
Background: Rotan Mosle
Jackie Kimzey, General Partner
Dave Mclean, General Partner
e-mail: djm@srfunds.com
Background: IBM
Directorships: BioBehavioral Diagnostics, HexaTech, Market6, MetaCarta, SensorLogic
John Oxaal, General Partner
e-mail: jto@srfunds.com
Background: Co-Founder & CEO, Volumetrics Medical Imaging
Directorships: Astute Networks, Cadtel, Ethertronics, Luminescent, Luxtera, Metabolon, Scintera

582

Venture Capital & Private Equity Firms / Domestic Firms

Charles Phipps, General Partner
Education: BSEE, Case; MBA, Harvard University
Background: Texas Instruments
Nick Sturiale, General Partner
e-mail: nick.sturiale@carlyle.com
Education: BS, California State University, Chico; MBA, University of California, Berkeley
Background: Jafco Ventures, The Carlyle Groupo, Co-Founder, Timbre Technologies
Directorships: Bill.com, Groundwork Open Source, RedSeal Systems, ReputationDefender, SocialVibe, Vuclip

1659 SEYMOUR ASSET MANAGEMENT
150 East 58th St.
17th Floor
New York, NY 10155

Phone: 212-341-4030
e-mail: admin@seymourasset.com
web: seymouram.com

Mission Statement: Seymour Asset Management is a team of professionals who have managed allocations and assets for some of the worlds largest institutions. They offer clients a tailored investment strategy that aligns with best industry practices.

Key Executives:
  Tim Seymour, Chief Investment Officer
  Background: CIO, Triogem Asset Management; Managing Partner, Red Star Asset Management; Managing Director, Troia Dialog

1660 SHAMROCK CAPITAL ADVISORS
1100 Glendon Avenue
Suite 1600
Los Angeles, CA 90024

Phone: 310-974-6600 Fax: 310-734-4540
e-mail: contact@shamrockcap.com
web: www.shamrockcap.com

Mission Statement: Shamrock Capital Advisors is a private equity firm with over $700 million of capital under management. Investing exclusively in the media, entertainment, and communications sectors, Shamrock partners with strong management teams and takes an active, collaborative approach to creating value in each investment.

Fund Size: $700 million
Founded: 1978
Average Investment: $15 - $50 million
Investment Criteria: Growth Equity, Management & Leverage Buyout, Leveraged Recapitalizations
Industry Group Preference: Media, Entertainment, Communications
Portfolio Companies: FanDuel, Giant, Isolation Network, Mobilite, PGOA Media, Questex, Screenvision, T3Media

Key Executives:
  Stephen D. Royer, Partner
  Education: Stanford University; MBA, Anderson School of Management
  Background: Investment Banking, Lehman Brothers
  Directorships: Mobilitie, Learfield Communications, Screenvision, INgrooves
  Michael A. LaSalle, Partner
  Education: University of Notre Dame; MBA, Anderson School of Management
  Background: Associate, Putnam Lovell Securities
  Directorships: Harlem Globetrotters, INgrooves, Mojiva
  William J. Wynperle, Partner
  Education: Dartmouth College; MBA, Anderson School of Management
  Background: M&A Group, Smith Barney
  Directorships: MarketCast, Learfield Communications, Mojiva
  Andrew J. Howard, Partner
  Education: Stanford University
  Background: Vice President, Clarity Partners
  Directorships: Screenvision, MarketCast, Mobilitie
  Alan H. Resnikoff, Partner
  Education: Stanford University; MBA, Stanford Graduate School of Business
  Background: Associate Consultant, Bain & Company
  Directorships: Learfield Communications, Screenvision

1661 SHAMROCK HOLDINGS
3500 West Olive Avenue
Suite 700
Burbank, CA 91505

Phone: 818-845-4444
web: www.shamrock.com

Mission Statement: Shamrock Holdings, Inc. was founded by the late Roy E. Disney in 1978 and serves as the investment vehicle for certain members of the Roy E. Disney Family. Shamrock's tenet's are straightforward - invest and act with integrity, responsibility, and transparency. In addition to investing and providing services to the Disney Family, Shamrock, through a subsidiary, manages several real estate investment programs.

Founded: 1978

1662 SHARESPOST
555 Montgomery Street
Suite 1400
San Francisco, CA 94111

Fax: 650-492-6871
Toll-Free: 800-279-7754
e-mail: info@sharespost.com
web: sharespost.com

Mission Statement: The SharesPost marketplace makes it easy to explore private growth companies, access investment opportunities and find liquidity.

Founded: 2009
Investment Criteria: Late-Stage
Industry Group Preference: Diversified
Portfolio Companies: 23andMe, Circle Internet Financial, DoorDash, Getaround, Grab, instacart, Nextdoor, Planet, Postmates, Ripple, Robinhood, Virgin Hyperloop One

Key Executives:
  Nick Grabowski, Chief Technology Officer
  Education: BS, Florida State University
  Background: VP of Application Architecture, Charles Schwab & Co.; Managing Director, Software Architecture
  Erika McKiernan, Chief Financial Officer
  Education: BS, Califronia Polytechnic State University
  Background: CFO, PENSCO Trust Company
  Chris Setaro, Global Chief Compliance Officer
  Education: BS, Syracuse University
  Background: CCO, Nasdaq Inc.; CCO, Instinet LLC

1663 SHASTA VENTURES
2440 Sand Hill Road
Suite 300
Menlo Park, CA 94025

Phone: 650-543-1700
e-mail: info@shastaventures.com
web: www.shastaventures.com

Mission Statement: Shasta was formed to back brilliant entrepreneurs with an unwavering commitment to the customer experience. They seek passionate, hardworking entrepreneurs of early stage companies in the areas of enterprise, consumer, and emerging platforms.

Geographic Preference: United States
Investment Criteria: Early-Stage, Seed, Series A
Industry Group Preference: Software, Infrastructure, Business to Business, Wireless Technologies, Marketing, E-Commerce & Manufacturing, Semiconductors, Consumer Services, Internet

Venture Capital & Private Equity Firms / Domestic Firms

Portfolio Companies: 6D.ai, 8th Wall, ACC Systems, Adometry, Airspace, Aloha, Anaplan, Apptio, Apteligent, Aquera, Archrock, Athelas, Atrium, Aviso, Beautiful AI, Big Box, Bloc, Boomerage Commerce, Brandcast, Camera IQ, Canva, Caring.com, Cequence Security, Chartcube, ClassDojo, CloudPassage, Color, Cover, Data.World, Deep Sentinal, Demdex, Digital Air Strike, Dr. On Demand, Dollar Shave Club, Eero, Elroy Air, Entelo, Extole, Fable Studio, Fetch Robotics, Flyhomes, FogLogic, Frame.io, Glint, Grin, Highspot, Hinge, Hobo Labs, iConclude, Imperfect Produce, Isara, Jack Erwin, Kapwing, Leaftail Labs, LeanData, Leanplum, LearnUp, Let's Do This, Lightbend, Liquidspace, Lithium, LiveIntent, Logoworks, Lucidworks, Macro Meta, Makara, Mint, Mocana, Mochi, Needle, Nest, Neumob, Nextdoor, NodeFly, Noon, Numina, Octi, Outright, Path, Plays.tv, Poppin., Rd.Md, Resilinc, Rosie, SayNow, Scalyr, Second Measure, SendBird, Simple, Skilljar, Skycure, SlamData, Smule, Snap Strat, Socratic, Spiceworks, Spire, Squelch, Stance, Starship, Starsky Robotics, Steel Brick, StrongLoop, Suplari, Survios, Tally, TaskRabbit, The Farmer's Dog, The Pill Club, Tiger Connect, Timehop, Tonal, Tumri, Turn, Turo, Umuse, Unblockable, Upserve, Vailmail, Vector, vFunction, VoloMetrix, WatchDox, Whisper, Zefr, Zenprise, Zuora, Zwift

Other Locations:
27 South Park Street
Suite 101
San Francisco, CA 94107

Key Executives:
Robert Coneybeer, Founder/Managing Director
Education: BS, Mechanical Engineering, University of Virginia; MS, Mechanical Engineering, Georgia Institute of Technology; MBA, Wharton School
Background: General Partner, New Enterprise Associates; Lead Integration/Test Engineer Astro Space, Martin Marietta
Tod Francis, Managing Director
Education: BA, Economics, Northwestern University; MBA, Kellogg School of Management
Background: General Partner, Trinity Ventures; Partner, Ram Group Marketing Management; Product Manager, Johnson & Johnson
Ravi Mohan, Managing Director
Education: BS, Operations Research/Industrial Engineering, Cornell University; MBA, University of Michigan School of Business
Background: General Partner, Battery Ventures; Transaction Processing Systems, Accenture; Software Applications, Hyperion Software Corp; MIC; Co-Founder, Silicon Valley Chapter Indian Venture Capital Association; McKinsey & Company
Directorships: The Indus Entrepreneurs
Jason Pressman, Managing Director
Education: BS, Finance, University of Maryland; MBA, Stanford Graduate School of Business
Background: VP Strategy/Business Development/Operations, Walmart.com; Associate, Selby Venture Partners; Associate, Alex.Brown
Doug Pepper, Managing Director
Education: BA, Dartmouth College; MBA, Stanford University
Background: General Partner, InterWest Partners; Financial Analyst, Goldman Sachs; Amazon.com
Nikhil Basu Trivedi, Managing Director
Education: AB, Molecular Biology, Princeton University
Background: Artsy; Insight Venture Partners
Directorships: ClassDojo, Fram.io, Hinge, Imperfect Produce, Plays.tv, Tally, The Farmer's Dog, The Pill Club

1664 SHEPHERD VENTURES
11696 Sorrento Valley Road
Suite F
San Diego, CA 92121

Phone: 858-509-4744
e-mail: info@shepherdventures.com
web: www.shepherdventures.com

Mission Statement: A venture capital fund that generates significant capital appreciation through carefully selected and wisely shepherded investments. As an SBIC, Shepherd Ventures partners with the US Small Business Administration to help fund and grow America's small businesses.

Geographic Preference: Southern California, San Diego, Southwest
Investment Criteria: First Stage/Disruptive Technology; Later Stage
Industry Group Preference: Information Technology, Life Sciences, Software, Enterprise Applications, Wireless, Mobile Computing, Networking, Infrastructure, Medical Devices, Biotherapeutics, Diagnostics, Healthcare Information Technology
Portfolio Companies: Andigilog, CEYX Technologies, Digital Orchid, Emergent Respiratory Products, Lighting Technologies International, Lucix Corporation, MedManage Systems, NP Photonics, OCULIR, Planet ATE, Quickoffice, Revance Therapeutics, Sendio, SiliconSystems, Skylight Healthcare Systems, SpecificMEDIA, Voyager Systems, wiSpry

Key Executives:
George C Kenney, Managing Partner
Education: BSEE, Rensselaer Polytechnic Institute; MSEE, Stanford University; MBA, Columbia University; Optic's Program, London Imperial College; Industrial Management Program, Harvard University
Background: CTO/Partner, Nicholas-Applegate; CTO/Managing Director, Kidder Peabody; Swiss Bank; Salomon Brothers; American Stock Exchange; Director Research, North American Philips; Co-Founder, Digital Measurements Corp; Patentholder; Keynote Speaker
Tom W Siegel, Managing Director
Education: BA Economics, MBA, University of Illinois; CPA; CFA
Background: Senior VP, Advantage Capital Partners; Founder, National Association of Venture Forums; Publisher, Dealmaker's Digest; Founder, software/systems integrator; Management Consultant, KPMG Peat Marwick
Richard P Kuntz, Managing Director
Education: BS, MS, MIT; MBA, JL Kellogg Graduate School of Management at Northwestern University
Background: Senior Managing Director, Premier Medical Partner Fund; Principal, Senmed Medical Ventures; 3i Group; Prudential Insurance Company of America
John R Nelson, Venture Partner
Education: BA, University of Wisconsin; MA Economics, Washington State University; PhD work, doctoral skill certification in computer sciences, University of Oregon
Background: Managing Director: California Capital Partners, Terra Nova Capital Can-Am Fund, Consortium Capital Partners, Ventana Global Funds Technology Gateway, Venture Management Group; Investment Director, Commonwealth of Australia; Senior VP Marketing, National Computer Systems

1665 SHERBROOKE CAPITAL

e-mail: info@sherbrookecapital.com
web: www.sherbrookecapital.com

Mission Statement: Dedicated exclusively to providing growth and expansion capital to emerging companies in the health and wellness industry.

Founded: 1999
Average Investment: $1 - $4 million
Industry Group Preference: Food & Beverage, Healthcare, Medical Devices

Venture Capital & Private Equity Firms / Domestic Firms

Portfolio Companies: Advanced BioNutrition, Affinnova, Angie's, Boathouse Sports, Ciao Bella, Farmigo, Food Should Taste Good, Halfpops, HeartBar, Immaculate Baking Co., IZZE, Kill Cliff, Outside The Classroom, oregon Chai, TransMedics, VetCentric

Key Executives:
John K Giannuzzi, Managing General Partner
e-mail: giannuzzi@sherbrookecapital.com
Education: West Virginia University, American University
Background: Managing Director, BankBoston
Directorships: Outside The Classroom, Advanced BioNutrition, VetCentric, Polymerix, Affinnova, Boathouse Sports, FoodShouldTasteGood, Adina, Ciao Bella

1666 SHERPALO VENTURES
Menlo Park, CA 94025

e-mail: info@sherpalo.com
web: www.sherpalo.com

Mission Statement: Sherpalo guides and mentors exceptional entrepreneurs as they take their innovative ideas and disruptive technologies and turn them into successful businesses.

Founded: 2000
Investment Criteria: Early-Stage
Industry Group Preference: Consumer Internet
Portfolio Companies: Abacus.AI, AbCellera, Aisera, Alphabet Inc., Antheia, CaaStle, EasyPost, Filecoin, Flexport, GoForward Inc., Gusto, Hexagon Bio, Hypersonix, InMobi, Metabase Inc., Mix, Mosaic, Next Jump, Notion, Paperless Post, Protocol Labs, Robust Intelligence, Scalyr Inc., Stripe, Upwork, WishFin, Yubico

Key Executives:
Ram Shiriam, Founder/Managing Partner

1667 SHORE CAPITAL PARTNERS
1 East Wacker Drive
Suite 2900
Chicago, IL 60601

Phone: 312-348-7580 Fax: 312-348-7669
web: www.shorecp.com

Mission Statement: Shore Capital Partners is a private equity firm aiming to provide capital, business development guidance, and industry insight to lower middle market healthcare companies.

Geographic Preference: North America
Fund Size: $112.5 million
Investment Criteria: Management Buyouts, Leveraged Buyouts, Successions, Consolidations, Recapitalizations, Corporate Divestitures
Industry Group Preference: Healthcare
Portfolio Companies: Chicagoland Smile Group, ClearPath Diagnostics, Cumberland Therapy Services, Fast Pace Urgent Care, Florida Autism Center, My Therapy Company, RapidCare Clinic, Shippert Medical, Southern Veterinary Partners, Specialdocs Consultants, Summit Medical

Key Executives:
Justin Ishbia, Managing Partner
e-mail: jishbia@shorecp.com
Education: BA, Accounting, Michigan State University; JD, Vanderbilt University Law School
Background: Valor Equity Partners; Kirkland & Ellis
Directorships: Fast Pace Urgent Care, Pediatric Therapy Services, Southern Veterinary Partners, Summit Medical, Florida Autism Center, Specialdocs Consultants
Ryan Kelley, Partner
e-mail: rkelley@shorecp.com
Education: BA, Accounting, Honors College, Michigan State University; MBA, Kellogg School of Management, Northwestern University
Background: Water Street Healthcare Partners; Bank of America
Directorships: ClearPath Diagnostics, Fast Pace Urgent Care, Pediatric Therapy Staffing

Mike Cooper, Partner
e-mail: mcooper@shorecp.com
Education: BSBA, Finance & Management, McDonough School of Business, Georgetown University
Background: Wind Point Partners; UBS Investment Bank
Directorships: Southern Veterinary Partners, Specialdocs Consultants
John Hennegan, Partner
e-mail: jhennegan@shorecp.com
Education: BS, University of Illinois; MBA, Kellogg School of Management, Northwestern University
Background: Henry Crown & Company; Citigroup
Directorships: ClearPath Diagnostics, Fast Pace Urgent Care, Pediatric Therapy Services
Don Pierce, Partner
e-mail: dpierce@shorecp.com
Education: BBA, Finance, University of Notre Dame
Background: Baxter International; RoundTable Healthcare Partners; UBS Investment Bank
Directorships: Summit Medical Products, Shippert Medical Technologies

1668 SI VENTURES
12600 Gateway Boulevard
Fort Myers, FL 33913

Phone: 239-561-4760 Fax: 239-561-4916

Mission Statement: Provides strategic direction, operating advice, and business contacts through years of operational experience.

Geographic Preference: Southeastern United States
Fund Size: $125 million
Founded: 1998
Average Investment: $2 - $5 million
Minimum Investment: $2 million
Investment Criteria: Beyond Seed prior to Mezzanine (Rounds A-C)
Industry Group Preference: Wireless Technologies, Optical Technology, Infrastructure, Technology, Information Technology, Communications
Portfolio Companies: Appian Communications, Authentor Systems, Brainshark, Click Commerce, Cognet, Convergent Group, DoubleTrade.com, eAngler.com, eDoc Architects, eVu, FamilyTime, Graviton, Healinx, RelayHealth, RealVue, Inceptor, OpenNetwork Technologies, Sitara Networks, Skillsoft, TruSecure Corporation, USADATA.com, WebCriteria

Key Executives:
Manny Fernandez, Managing Director
941-561-4225
Fax: 941-561-4916
Education: BS, Electrical Engineering, University of Florida; BS, Business Administration, Florida Institute of Technology
Background: President/CEO, Gartner Group; President/CEO, Dataquest; President/CEO, Gavilan Computer Corporation; President/CEO, Zilog
Directorships: Black & Decker Corporation, Open Network Technology, RealVue Simulation Technology, eAngler
John Halligan, Co-Founder/Managing Director
239-561-4810
Fax: 239-561-4916
e-mail: john.halligan@siventures.com
Background: Executive VP/CFO/Treasurer, Gartner Group; Staff VP Finance, GE Communication Services; Manager Marketing/Sales, GE Appliances
Directorships: Top of the Tree Baking Company, TruSecure Corporation, eVu, Authentor, WebCriteria, IMDiversity
Randy Glein, Managing Director
Education: MBA, University of California, LA; MSEE, University of Southern California; BSEE, University of Florida

Venture Capital & Private Equity Firms / Domestic Firms

Background: Tribune Ventures; CID Equity Partners; Screenz; GM Hughes Electronics
Minette L La Croix, CFO
239-561-4716
Fax: 239-561-4916
Education: Florida Southern University
Background: Gartner Group; Coopers & Lybrand

1669 SIERRA ANGELS
PO Box 3215
Incline Village, NV 89450

web: www.sierraangels.com

Mission Statement: As a result of the extensive operational experience of our members, many entrepreneurs have found our high value-added model to be enormously helpful in both their strategic and operational development. Our thoughtful selectivity of companies in which to invest combined with our proactive collaboration with other funding and partnering entities helps to ensure that the chosen companies get the focus, support and funding required for success.

Geographic Preference: Northern Nevada, Northern California
Industry Group Preference: Clean Energy, Green Technology, Computing, Communications, Healthcare, Mobile, Software, Technology
Portfolio Companies: Animated Speech Corporation, Aperia Technologies, Cloud Cruiser, DynaOptics, Gatekeepr Innovation, Glue Networks, Jopari Solutions, Marrone Organic Innovators, OptiComp Corporation, Reframe It, RevoLights, Sierra Nevada Solar, TranscribeMe, Up Out, Vokle, Zippy App

1670 SIERRA VENTURES
1400 Fashion Island Boulevard
Suite 1010
San Mateo, CA 94404

Phone: 650-854-1000
e-mail: info@sierraventures.com
web: www.sierraventures.com

Mission Statement: Works with entrepreneurs and management teams to originate and build new companies into large, profitable businesses. Seeks to find the right combination of investment and expertise to help companies grow and deliver on their promise.

Geographic Preference: United States, India, China
Fund Size: $600 million
Founded: 1982
Average Investment: $10-$15 million
Minimum Investment: $1 million
Investment Criteria: Seed to Mid Stage
Industry Group Preference: Internet Technology, Communications, Computer Related, Consumer Services, Electronic Technology, Financial Services, High Technology, Information Technology, Service Industries, Software, Consumer Technology, Semiconductors
Portfolio Companies: Agent IQ, Appcues, Applitools, Astronomer, CNEX Labs, Core Tigo, Deep Lens, Drop, Falcon Computing, Headspin, Hired, Interplay Learning, K4Connect, Kinnek, Krisp, LeadGenius, Movandi, NextInput, Omniex, Phenom TRM Cloud Platform, Q-CTRL, Qeexo, Quadratic 3D, Radius, Regulus, Shape Security, Sikka Software Corporation, SiSense, SK Spruce, SkyDeck Accelerator, SkyDrop, Sliver.tv, Support Logic, Text IQ, VeeR, Yalo, Zaloni, Zeta Global, Zimperium, Zycada Delivery Network

Key Executives:
  Peter Wendell, Founder/Advisor
  e-mail: peter@sierraventures.com
  Education: BA, Princeton University; MBA, Harvard University
  Background: Executive Manager, IBM; McKinsey & Company; Faculty, Stanford University
  Directorships: Centex Telemanagement
  Tim Guleri, Managing Director
  e-mail: tim@sierraventures.com
  Education: BS, Electrical Engineering, Punjab Engineering College; MS, Robotics/Industrial Engineering, Virginia Polytechnic Institute
  Background: LSI Logic; VP Technical Field Operations/Product Marketing, Scopus Technology; Co-Founder/CEO, Octane Software; Vice Chairman/Executive VP, Epiphany
  Directorships: Approva, CodeGreen Networks, DotNetNuke, Everest Software, Greenplum, MakeMyTrip, Sourcefire, CarWale
  Mark Fernandes, Managing Director
  e-mail: mfernandes@sierraventures.com
  Education: BS Mechanical Engineering, Bangalore University; MS Mechanical Engineering, University of California, Berkeley; MBA, Harvard University
  Background: Director Infrastructure Software, Merrill Lynch; Research Analyst, Robertson Stephens; Product Manager, Cisco Systems; Product Manager, Seagate Technology; Founding Team, PanoCorp Displays
  Directorships: Ooyala, Opalis Software, Spotzer Media Group
  Ben Yu, Managing Director
  e-mail: byu@sierraventures.com
  Education: BSEE, University of Western Australia; MA, PhD, Princeton University
  Background: Managing Engineer/Corporate R&D, 3Com Corporation; Business Development, Merz Australia
  Directorships: AuthenTec, MicroPower, Paracer, SyChip

1671 SIGHTLINE PARTNERS
8500 Normandale Lake Boulevard
Suite 1070
Bloomington, MN 55437

Phone: 952-641-0300 Fax: 952-641-0310
e-mail: buzz@sightlinepartners.com
web: www.sightlinepartners.com

Mission Statement: SightLine Partners manages venture funds that invest in promising emerging growth companies in the medical technology sector and the healthcare industry.

Geographic Preference: United States
Founded: 1992
Average Investment: $2 - $8 million
Investment Criteria: Later Stage
Industry Group Preference: Medical Devices, Medical Technology, Healthcare

Key Executives:
  Buzz Benson, Managing Director
  Education: St. Johns University; CPA
  Background: Piper Jaffray, Partner, Stonebridge Capital; Investment Officer, Cherry Tree Ventures
  Directorships: Acorn Cardiovascular, Anulex, Broncus, LipoScience, Verax Biomedical
  Kunal Paymaster, Managing Director
  Background: Scientific Cardiac Rhytm Management, Boston

1672 SIGMA PARTNERS
2105 S. Bascom Ave.
Suite 370
Campbell, CA 95008

Phone: 650-853-1700 Fax: 650-853-1717
web: www.sigmapartners.com

Mission Statement: To identify, invest in, and provide support and constructive counsel to companies with exceptional management strength and growth prospects. We seek to combine our capital, experience, and active involvement with the ideas and capabilities of outstanding entrepreneurial teams to develop substantial and profitable businesses.

Geographic Preference: United States
Fund Size: $1 billion
Founded: 1984
Average Investment: $2 to $8 million
Minimum Investment: $2 million
Investment Criteria: Early-Stage
Industry Group Preference: Computer Related, Electronic Technology, Software, Communications, Clean Technology, Semiconductors, Wireless Technologies, Data Storage, Mobile Computing, Electronics, Internet, SaaS, Business Products & Services, Enterprise Software
Portfolio Companies: Acquia, Aprimo, aPriori, Arasys Technologies, Atrributor, AutoVirt, Azuik, Birthday Express, Blackwave, Blue Agave Software, Broadware Technologies, CallMiner, CaseNET, Centrify, Certeon, CiRBA, CrownPeak Technology, Damballa, Demandbase, Dexterra, Digital Fuel Technologies, Digital Music Network, DocuSign, EasyAsk, Emagia, Encover, EndWave, Enkata Technologies, EqualLogic, Envis Corp, Everspin Technologies, ExaGrid Systems, Expressor Software Corp, FieldCentrix, Fogbreak Software, Fortify Software, GainSpan Corp, GlassHouse Technologies, Idiom Technologies, Incipient, Initiate Systems, Inovis, Instill, Intacct Corporation, Interactions, iWatt, Jellyvision, Kana Software, Kateeva, Laser Diagnostic Technology, Leyden Energy, MarketLive, Menara Networks, Nasuni Corporation, Nexx Systems, Nimblefish Technologies, Noetix, Nucore Technology, O-In Design Automation, oDesk Corporation, OnExchange, OpenPages, OpenSpan, OutStart, Oversight Systems, POET Software, Quantenna Communications, QuickSilver Technology, R2 Semiconductor, Rave Wireless, RecycleBank, Reflectent Software, Replay Solutions, Responsys, Retica Systems, Savantis Systems, ScanCafe, Sequence Design, Silverlink Communications, SkillSoft, Soladigm, Solaria, Steelwedge, SugarSync, Sunchron, SupplySolution, Svaya Nanotechnologies, Tervela, Toolwire, Topio, Tradebeam, Trustwave, Vendavo, Vericept, Versata, Vettro, Vicom Systems, Vignette, Vinusa, Visual Mining, Vormetric, World Power Technology Senasis Technologies

Other Locations:
20 Custom House Street
Suite 830
Boston, MA 02110
Phone: 617-330-7872 **Fax:** 617-330-7975

Key Executives:
Lawrence G Finch, Managing Director
e-mail: lgf@sigmapartners.com
Background: President and CEO, Paradise Systems, Inc.; Founder, President and CEO, Shasta General Systems, Inc.; Singer Business Machines; Friden, Inc.
Directorships: Acumos, Global Village Communications, International Network Services IPNet Solutions, iWatt, Nimblefish, Nucore, Paradis Tech, Phoenix Tech, Quicksilver Tech, Ray Dream
Clifford L Haas, Managing Director
e-mail: haas@sigmapartners.com
Education: BS, California Polytechnic State University; MBA, Stanford University Graduate School of Business
Background: Cresap, McCormick and Paget; American Pacific Corporation; Engineer, 3M Corporation; Engineer, US Navy's Pacific Missile Test Center
Directorships: Clarify, Datasonix, Edify, FieldCentrix, Hypertrace, Kofax Image Products, Novellus, OnStream Networks, SalesLogix, Saratoga, Short Sycles, SupplySolution, Tencor Instruments
Gardner C Hendrie, Special Limited Partner
e-mail: hendrie@sigmapartners.com
Education: AB Physics, Harvard; MS Physics, University of Pennsylvania
Background: Co-Founder, Stratus Computer; Hardware Design Engineer, Data General; Computer Control Company; Honeywell; Engineer, Advanced Development, Foxboro Corporation; RCA
Directorships: Argon Networks, Atria Software, Cascade Comm, Cerulean, Chipcom, Course Tech, Epoch Systems, GeoTel Comm, Iris Graphics, LANart, Roll Systems, Synernetics, Wellfleet Comm
Paul Flanagan, Managing Director
e-mail: paul@sigmapartners.com
Education: BS, Accounting, Bentley College
Background: Executive Vice President, VistPrint; StorageNetworks; Vice President, Finance, Lasertron
Fahri Diner, Managing Director
e-mail: fahri@sigmapartners.com
Education: BS, Electrical Engineering, Florida Institute of Technology
Background: Founder & President, Qtera Corporation; Siemens; Founder, Concept Ventures
Wade Woodson, Managing Director
e-mail: woodson@sigmapartners.com
Education: BS, Electrical Engineering, Stanford University; JD, Harvard Law School; MBA, University of California Haas School of Business
Background: Emerging Companies Department, Cooley Godward

1673 SIGMA PRIME VENTURES
20 Custom House Street
Suite 830
Boston, MA 02110

Phone: 617-330-7872
web: www.sigmaprime.com

Mission Statement: Our first-hand experience allows us to give early-stage companies both tactical and strategic guidance and access to a powerful business network. Our team has founded or cofounded 10 companies, helped run 10 companies, and collectively been responsible for exits worth over $4.2B in companies where we were operators. We invest in early stage technology companies focusing on SaaS, Cloud, Mobile, disruptive technologies and technology-enabled service companies.

Geographic Preference: East Coast
Investment Criteria: Early-Stage
Industry Group Preference: SaaS, Cloud Computing, Mobile, Technology-Enabled Services
Portfolio Companies: Acquia, aPriori, BiOM, BlueConic, CallMiner, Ceros, Cirba, CloudHealth Technologies, Codeship, Coherent Path, Contently, Damballa, eCommHub, ExaGrid Systems, Interactions, Kwicr, Mobiquity, Nasuni, OpenSpan, Oversight Systems, Paradigm4, RAVE, Recyclebank, Rethink Robotics, Silverlink, Tervela, VoltDB, Wordstream

Key Executives:
Robert E Davoli, Managing Director
Education: BA, History, Ricker College
Background: President & CEO, Epoch Systems; Founder, SQL Solutions
Paul Flanagan, Managing Director
Education: BS, Accounting, Bentley College
Background: EVP/CFO, VistaPrint; President/CEO, StorageNetworks
John Mandile, Managing Director
Education: BSE, Engineering Science & Mathematics, Tufts University; MS, Computer Science, Worcester Polytechnic University
Background: President/CEO, Vermeer Technologies; Principal, SQL Solutions
Jere Doyle, Managing Director
Education: BS, Boston College; MBA, Harvard Business School
Background: Founder, Prospectiv; Oyster Angel Fund; Doyle Enterprises
John Simon, Managing Director
Education: BA, History & Science, Harvard University; MA, Politics, Univ. of Oxford

587

Venture Capital & Private Equity Firms / Domestic Firms

Background: Co-Founder/Managing Director, General Catalyst Partners; Founder/CEO, UroMed Corporation

1674 SIGNAL EQUITY PARTNERS
805 Third Avenue
Suite 1202
New York City, NY 10022

Phone: 860-479-1186 Fax: 212-208-4433
web: www.signal-equity.com

Mission Statement: Signal Equity Partners invests in capital, time and effort to grow our portfolio companies into enduring, large scale businesses.

Founded: 1996
Investment Criteria: Leveraged Buyouts, Roll-Ups, Restructurings, Secondary Purchases of Investment Portfolios
Industry Group Preference: Communications, Media, Technology

Key Executives:
 Timothy P Bradley, Co-Founder/Managing Director
 Education: BA, Yale University, JD, New York University, MBA, Columbia Business School
 Background: Partner, Exeter Group
 Charles T Lake II, Managing Director
 Education: BS, Trinity College, MBA, Northwestern University
 Background: Director Of Budget & Finance, Telular Corporation, Transworld Communications
 Malcolm C Nolen, Managing Director
 Education: BA, Yale University, MBA, Columbia Business School
 Background: Director, Evoke Software Corporation, Overseer Of Securities, Bank Of New York

1675 SIGNAL FIRE

e-mail: press@signalfire.com
web: www.signalfire.com

Mission Statement: A venture capital firm funding startup data companies.

Fund Size: $375 million
Average Investment: Seed, $1-5 million; Breakout, up to $15 million
Industry Group Preference: Data & Analytics, Entertainment, Technology, Applications, Retail, Consumer & Leisure
Portfolio Companies: ClassDojo, Zume Pizza, Yodas, Frame.io, Rocksbox, SmartSpot, TextRecruit, Jyve, PropelPLM, Ledger Investing, ScopeAR, SafeGraph, Grabr, Grammarly, Lighthouse, Hawthorne Effect, Osso VR, Juvo, OneSignal, Color Genomics

Key Executives:
 Chris Farmer, Managing Director/CEO
 Education: BA, International Relations/Business, Tufts University & the Fletcher School of Diplomacy
 Background: Cowen & Company; Venture Partner, General Catalyst Partners; VP, Bessemer Venture Partners; Consultant, Bain & Company
 Ilya Kirnos, Managing Director/CTO
 Education: BSE, Computer Science, Princeton University
 Background: Software Engineer, Google; Technical Lead, Gmail Ads; Technical Lead, AdWords Performance and Scalability; Founder/Technical Lead, Google Prediction Markets; CardSpring; Bell Labs; Oracle
 Walter Kortschak, Managing Director & Executive Chairman
 Education: BS, Engineering, Oregon State University; MS, Engineering, California Institute of Technology; MBA, University of California, LA
 Background: Co-Founder, EndCue; Managing Partner, Summit Partners; VP/Associate, Crosspoint Venture Partners
 Directorships: National Venture Capital Association

Tony Huie, Managing Director
Education: BS, MS, Electircal Engineering, Stanford University
Background: Executive, Dropbox; Investor, Technology Crossover Ventures; Consultant, McKinsey & Company

1676 SIGNAL LAKE
606 Post Road East
Suite 667
Westport, CT 06880-4549

Phone: 203-454-1133 Fax: 203-454-7142
e-mail: info@signallake.com
web: signallake.com

Mission Statement: To generate significant capital growth through early stage investments in the broadband telecom and networking infrastructure being built for the global economy over the next several decades.

Industry Group Preference: Broadband, Telecommunications, Networking, Infrastructure
Portfolio Companies: RemoTV, HVault Storage, InPhase, RFMD, Cradle Techologies, SLT Logic, Hermois, GlobalSoft, Force10, Corredge Networks, SeraStar, Oracle/Skywire, NET Technologies, Intellectual Ventures, Avail Media

Other Locations:
 50 Commonwealth Avenue
 Suite 504
 Boston, MA 02116
 Phone: 617-267-5205 Fax: 617-262-7037

Key Executives:
 Bart Stuck, Founder/Managing Director
 e-mail: bartstuck@signallake.com
 Education: BS, MS, Doctorate, Electrical Engineering & Computer Science, MIT
 Directorships: CorEdge Group, CorEdge Networks, Hermios, SeraStar, SLT Logic
 Michael Weingarten, Director
 e-mail: mikew@signallake.com
 Education: BS, MS, Columbia University; MBA, Harvard Business School
 Background: Boston Consulting Group, Monitor Group
 Directorships: CorEdge Networks, SLT Logic

1677 SIGNAL PEAK VENTURES
2755 E Cottonwood Parkway
Suite 520
Salt Lake City, UT 84121

Phone: 801-942-8999 Fax: 801-942-1636
e-mail: info@vsp.com
web: www.vsp.com

Mission Statement: To help passionate entrepreneurs build leading companies with enduring value.

Fund Size: $400 million
Average Investment: $2 - $3 million
Investment Criteria: Seed-Stage, Early-Stage, Later-Stage (under special circumstances)
Industry Group Preference: Enterprise Software, Networking, Communications, Security, Internet, Mobile Computing, Drug Delivery, Diagnostics, Medical Devices, Information Technology, Life Sciences
Portfolio Companies: Agilix, Alianza, Altiris, Alpha Bay, Ancestry.com, Aspen Avionics, Athena Feminine Technologies, BDNA, C7, Cerberian, Coherex Medical, ComScore, Control4, EFileCabinet, Experticity, Fat Pipe, Footnote, GlobalSim, Graduation Alliance, Helius, Infusionsoft, iTOKiNET, LANDesk Software, Lingotek, Luxul, MaxStream, MediConnect Global, Mirabilis Medica, Nano MR, Netaphor Software, NetVision, Numira, Penguin Computing, Power Innovations, PublicEngines, Q Therapeutics, Radiate Media, Senforce, Smile Reminder, Solera Networks, Solutionreach, Symbiot Business Group, True Fit, Verismic, Viawest, Voonami, Wildworks, ZARS Pharma

588

Key Executives:
Ben Dahl, Managing Director
Education: AB, Princeton University; JD, University of California Berkeley; MBA, Columbia Business School
Background: Partner, Pelion Venture Partners
Brandon Tidwell, Managing Director
Education: BS/MS, Accounting, Brigham Young University; JD, Columbia Law School
Background: Managing Director, Canopy Ventures
Scott Petty, Managing Director
Education: BS, Economics, Brigham Young University; MBA, Harvard Business School
Background: COO, Board Director, Zuka Juice; Consultant, Bain & Company

1678 SIGNIA VENTURE PARTNERS
2055 Woodside Road
Suite 270
Redwood City, CA 94061

Phone: 650-614-5800
web: www.signiaventurepartners.com

Mission Statement: To be the most helpful investor an entrepreneur will ever have.

Founded: 2012
Industry Group Preference: Blockchain, E-Commerce, Fitness, Transportation, Virtual Reality, Data Security, Fintech, Health, SaaS
Portfolio Companies: Alibaba.com, Boxed Wholesale, Cruise, Fun+, Kurbo Health, PepperData, Playdom, Super Evil Megacorp

Key Executives:
Ed Cluss, Managing Director
Education: BS/MS, Engineering, MIT; MBA, Harvard Business School
Background: VP of Marketing, Aspect Telecommunications; President/COO/CEO, Aveo; President/CEO, InfoGear Technology; VP/GM, Cisco; President/CEO, NextHop Technologies
Directorships: Schoop Technologies Inc.; ApplePie Capital; Pensa Systems; Fortem Technologies; Nativo; MomentFeed; Pepperdata; BlueTalon; Kauna Ventures
Sunny Dhillon, Managing Director
Education: BS, University of Oxford; MS, London School of Economics & Political Sciences; MBA, Kellogg School of Management, Northwestern University
Background: Investment Banking Analyst, Rothschild; VC Associate, Pritzker Group; Co-Founder/Head of Product, BarSchool
Directorships: GBx
Rick Thompson, Managing Director
Education: MBA, Wharton School
Background: Program Manager, Octel; Founding CEO/Chair, Flycast; Founding Chairman, Dogtime Media; Funzio; Idle Games; Wild Needle Inc.; Playdom; Adify

1679 SIGULER GUFF & COMPANY
200 Park Avenue
23rd Floor
New York, NY 10166

Phone: 212-332-5100 Fax: 212-332-5120
web: www.sigulerguff.com

Mission Statement: To generate high absolute rates of return by capitalizing on the inefficient allocations of capital that regularly occur in the financial markets.

Fund Size: $1.3 billion
Founded: 1995
Investment Criteria: Multi-strategy (distressed, venture, LBO, mezzanine, energy)
Industry Group Preference: Diversified

Other Locations:
One International Place
Suite 2710
Boston, MA 02110
Phone: 617-648-2100 Fax: 617-648-2121

2205 CITIC Square
1168 Nanjing Road West
Shanghai 200041
China
Phone: 86-2152925256 Fax: 86-2152925575

Siguler Guff India Advisers Private Limited
Suite 8FB, Grand Hyatt Plaza
Santacruz East
Mumbai 400 055
India
Phone: 91-2242154830

Stoleshnikov Per., 14
2nd Floor
Moscow 107031
Russia
Phone: 495-2343095 Fax: 495-2343099

160 Horacio Lafer Avenue
Suite 42, 4th Floor
Sao Paulo 04538-000
Brazil
Phone: 555-1134769992

Key Executives:
Drew Guff, Managing Director/Founding Partner
212-332-5108
Fax: 212-332-5120
e-mail: drewg@sigulerguff.com
Education: AB, Harvard University
Background: Principal, Paine Webber Merchant Banking Group; Assistant to the President, Paine Webber; Founder, Pacific Media KK
Directorships: Eurasia Foundation, Phillips Academy Institute for the Recruitment of Teachers, NPV Russia
George W. Siguler, Founding Principal/Managing Director
212-332-5111
Fax: 212-332-5120
Education: BA, Amherst College; MBA, Harvard Business School
Background: Founding Partner, Harvard Management Company; Founder, Paine Webber's Private Equity Group; Chief of Staff, US Department of Health and Human Services
Directorships: Board of Oversees Visiting Committee of the Harvard Medical School, Trustee of the Bement School
Donald Spencer, Managing Director/Founding Partner/COO
212-332-5105
Fax: 212-332-5120
e-mail: donalds@sigulerguff.com
Education: BA, Wesleyan University; JD, New York University School of Law
Background: First VP/Associate General Counsel, Mitchell Hutchins; Sr VP/General Counsel, Atalanta/Sosnoff Capital Corporation; Sullivan & Cromwell; Shereff Friedman, Hoffman & Goodman
Kenneth Burns, Managing Director
212-332-5102
Fax: 212-332-5120
e-mail: kenb@sigulerguff.com
Education: BS, State University of New York at Oneonta; MBA, St. Johns University
Background: CFO, Odyssey Investment Partners; Controller, Odyssey Partners; Controller, Buffalo Partners
Directorships: Frowen Holdings Limited (a Cyprus holding company)
James Corl, Managing Director
Education: BA, Quantitative Economics, Stanford University; MBA, Finance & Real Estate, Wharton School, University of Pennsylvania
Background: Chief Investment Officer, Cohen & Steers;

Venture Capital & Private Equity Firms / Domestic Firms

Associate, Real Estate Investment Banking Group, Credit Suisse First Boston
Kevin Kester, Managing Director
Education: BA, Government, Hamilton College; MBA, Finance, University of Colorado, Boulder
Background: Investment Division, Colorado Public Employees' Retirement Association
Cesar Collier, Managing Director
Education: Law Degree, Universidade Catolica de Pernambuci; MBA, Funacao Getulio Vargas
Background: SVP, Standard Bank Private Equity; Senior Management Positions Wal-Mart, Carrefour, Royal Ahold, Bompreco
Anthony Corriggio, Managing Director
Education: BS, Economics, Wharton School; BS, Enginnering, University of Pennsylvania School of Engineering & Applied Science; MBA, Wharton School
Background: Senior Analyst, Coeus Capital Management; CFO, The St. Joe Company; VP, Morgan Stanley Real Estate

1680 SILICON ALLEY VENTURE PARTNERS
300 Park Avenue
18t Floor GCP
New York, NY 10022

web: www.savp.com

Mission Statement: Founded 1998 in NYC by Steve Brotman, the successful Web 1.0 founder of AdOne, SAVP is entrepreneur centric. SAVP is making early and growth stage investments in its fourth fund. SAVP was the among the first institutional investors in two successful IPOs - Live Person and Medidata - and has many profitable exits in its portfolio. SAVP's investment focus continues to be on East Coast, post-revenue early and growth stage ventures in business software and information services, health care, e-commerce, and new networks enabled by mobile, social and data. SAVP makes a handful of North East, early stage investments per year, mostly as a co-investor.

Geographic Preference: East Coasts
Founded: 1998
Average Investment: $25,000 - $1 million
Investment Criteria: Early-Stage, Growth Stage
Industry Group Preference: Business Software, Information Services, Health Care, E-Commerce & Manufacturing, Mobile, Networking
Portfolio Companies: Critical Mention, Data Synapse, GameTrust, Headliner, Knovel, Live Person, Medidata, Navtrck, PartStore, Rewind.me, Ugo, You Now

Key Executives:
Steve Brotman, Managing Partner
Education: Duke University; JD/MBA, Washington University
Background: Founder, AdOne; Advisor, New World Ventures

1681 SILKROAD EQUITY
Chicago, IL 60654

e-mail: info@silkroadequity.com
web: www.silkroadequity.com

Mission Statement: SilkRoad Equity is a global private investment firm with interests in a diversified portfolio of public and private companies. SilkRoad Equity invests its own capital in companies with strong market positions, recognized brands and enormous growth potential. SilkRoad Equity's investment philosophy centers around a core set of principles focused on partnering with management to execute strategies for long term value creation.

Geographic Preference: Worldwide
Founded: 2003
Investment Criteria: Start-ups, Buy-outs, Build-ups, Spin-offs, Privatizations and Industry Consolidations

Industry Group Preference: Technology, Gaming, Media & Entertainment, Healthcare, Energy, Real Estate
Portfolio Companies: AffiliateShop, CardZee, ChatBlazer, ExpressCoin, GoCoin, InterAct911, MissionMode, MooMee, Onramp Branding, Pendulab, SilkRoad Technology, SolidSpace, TrueLook, Viwawa, Barefoot Landing, Harbourgate Resort & Marina, Liberty Plaza, SilkRoad Realty Capital, Jimmy Buffet's Margaritaville, Levy Acq., ONE Group, Sunda, EBOOST, Primo Water, Alabama Theater, House of Blues, Cryo-Cell

Key Executives:
Andrew "Flip" Filipowski, Co-Founder & Executive Chairman
e-mail: flip@silkroadequity.com
Background: COO, Cullinet; CEO, PLATINUM Technology
Directorships: SilkRoad Technology, InterAct 911, SilkRoad Realty Capital
Matthew Roszak, Co-Founder & Vice Chairman
e-mail: matt@silkroadequity.com
Education: BA, Economics, Lake Forest College
Background: Co-Founder & CFO, SilkRoad Technology; Principal, Advent International; Keystone Capital Partners

1682 SILVER CREEK VENTURES
5949 Sherry Lane
Suite 1515
Dallas, TX 75225

Phone: 214-265-2020 Fax: 214-692-6233
web: www.silvercreekfund.com

Mission Statement: Invests in companies and markets where there is industry expertise and opportunity for significant value. Areas of concentration are telecommunications carrier infrastructure, Internet, data networking, wireless services, infrastructure.

Geographic Preference: Texas, California
Fund Size: $75 million
Founded: 1989
Investment Criteria: Early Stage
Industry Group Preference: Communications, Computer Related, Electronic Components, Instrumentation, Information Technology
Portfolio Companies: Aktino, Alteon WebSystems, Bivio, Bloomfire, Cellfire, Centennial Communications, Corsair Communications, Credence Systems, Crystal Semiconductor, Diamond Lane, Egnyte, Gazzang, MetroPCS, NetSocket, Nimbix, OneSpot, ONI Systems, OpenConnect Systems, Optical Data Systems, Pivot3, Powerfile, ProNet, Sensity, Shomiti Systems, Talari Networks, Theatro, Traxo, WaferScale Integration, Xillinx, Yvolver

Key Executives:
Mark C Masur, General Partner
Education: BS, Weber State University; MBA, University of Denver
Background: General Partner, Trailhead Ventures/Sherry Lane Partners/O'Donnell & Masur; InterFirst Venture Corporation
Michael T Segrest, General Partner
Education: Undergraduate Degree/MBA Finance, University of Texas Austin
Background: General Partner, Trailhead Ventures; O'Donnell & Masur; Sherry Lane Partners

1683 SILVER LAKE
2775 Sand Hill Road
Suite 100
Menlo Park, CA 94025

Phone: 650-233-8120
web: www.silverlake.com

Mission Statement: Invests in leading technology businesses around the world.

Geographic Preference: North America, Europe, Asia

Fund Size: $10.3 billion
Founded: 1999
Industry Group Preference: Technology, Technology-Enabled Businesses
Portfolio Companies: Alibaba Group, Avago, Avaya, AVI-SPL, BlackLine, Cast & Crew, Dell, Fanatics, ForeFlight, Global Blue, GoDaddy, Influence Health, Intelsat, Locaweb, Motorola Solutions, Opera Solutions, Qunar, Quorum Business Solutions, Red Ventures, Sabre, SMART Modular, Talend, Vantage Data Centers, Velocity Technology Solutions, WME/IMG

Other Locations:
220 Halleck Street
Suite 100
San Francisco, CA 94129

55 Hudson Yards
550 W 34th Street
40th Floor
New York, NY 10001
Phone: 212-981-5600

10080 North Wolfe Road
Suite SW3-190
Cupertino, CA 95014
Phone: 408-454-4732

Silver Lake Europe LLP
Broadbent House
65 Grosvenor Street
London W1K 3JH
United Kingdom
Phone: 44-2032058400

Silver Lake Asia Limited
33/F Two IFC
8 Finance Street
Central
Hong Kong
Phone: 852-36643300 **Fax:** 852-36643456

Key Executives:
Kenneth Hao, Chairman/Managing Partner
Education: AB, Economics, Harvard College
Background: Managing Director, Hambrecht & Quist
Directorships: Avago Technologies Limited, SMART Modular Technologies
Mike Bingle, Vice Chairman
Education: BSE, Biomedical Engineering, Duke University
Background: Principal, Apollo Advisors; Investment Banker, Leveraged Finance Group, Goldman Sachs & Co.
Directorships: Fanatics, Gartner
Egon Durban, Co-CEO
Education: BS, Finance, Georgetown University
Background: Investment Banking Division, Corporate Finance Technology Group & Equity Capital Markets Group, Morgan Stanley
Directorships: Dell, Intelsat SA, Motorola Solutions
Greg Mondre, Co-CEO
Education: BS, Economics, Wharton School, University of Pennsylvania
Background: Principal, Texas Pacific Group; Investment Banker, Communications, Media & Entertainment Group, Goldman Sachs & Co.
Directorships: Avaya, Fanatics, GoDaddy, Motorola Solutions, Red Ventures, Sabre Holdings, Vantage Data Centers
Joe Osnoss, Managing Partner/Managing Director
Education: AB, Harvard College
Background: Goldman Sachs & Co.; Coopers & Lybrand Consulting; Bracebridge Capital
Directorships: Cegid; Cornerstone OnDemand; EverCommerce; First Advantage; Global Blue; LightBox; Sabre

1684 SILVER OAK SERVICES PARTNERS
1560 Sherman Avenue
Suite 1200
Evanston, IL 60201
Phone: 847-332-0400 **Fax:** 847-492-1717
e-mail: info@silveroaksp.com
web: www.silveroaksp.com

Mission Statement: Silver Oak Services Partners is a lower middle market private equity firm focused exclusively on services businesses. We seek to partner with exceptional management teams to build industry leading businesses, consumer and healthcare service companies.

Geographic Preference: United States
Average Investment: $10 - $30 million
Investment Criteria: Control Investments in Leveraged Acquisitions, Recapitalizations, Build-Ups and Growth Transactions
Industry Group Preference: Business Products & Services, Healthcare Services, Consumer Services
Portfolio Companies: Accent Ood Services, Altura Communication Solutions, Construction Labor Contractors, Direct Tavel, Glazer-Kennedy Insider's Circle, iSystems, National Distribution & Contracting, Physical Rehabilitation Network, Tranzonic, VASA Fitness

Key Executives:
Daniel M Gill, Managing Partner
847-332-0410
e-mail: dgill@silveroaksp.com
Education: BA, Economics, Bucknell University; MBA, University of Chicago Graduate School of Business
Background: Founding Partner & Managing Director, Willis Stein & Partners; CIVC/Bank of America; Corporate Finance Department, Kidder Peabody & Co
Directorships: Physicians Endoscopy, Convergent Resources, CompuPay, Education Corporation of America, Merit Health Systems Corporation
Gregory M Barr, Managing Partner
847-332-0401
e-mail: gbarr@silveroaksp.com
Education: BA, Economics & English, Wesleyan University; MBA, Harvard Business School
Background: Managing Director, Nautic Partners; Fleet Equity Partners; Management Consultant, McKinsey & Company
Directorships: VeriClaim, Accent Food Services, National Distribution & Contracting
Andrew S Gustafson, Partner
Education: BA, Middlebury College; MBA, Kellogg School of Management, Northwestern University
Background: VP, Thoma Bravo LLC; Boston Consulting Group; Associate, Wind Point Partners; Investment Banker, Goldman Sachs & Co.
Directorships: Convergent Resources; Direct Travel; iSystems; Porter & Chester Institute
Wade D Glisson, Partner
847-332-0408
e-mail: wglisson@silveroaksp.com
Education: BS, Finance, University of Illinois, Urbana-Champaign; MBA, Northwestern University Kellogg School of Management
Background: Private Equity Investments, Lake Capital; Associate, Advent Internaitonal; Investment Banking, AG Edwards
Directorships: Physicians Endoscopy, National Distribution & Contracting

1685 SILVERTON PARTNERS
600 W 7th Street
Austin, TX 78701
Phone: 512-476-6700 **Fax:** 512-477-0025
e-mail: businessplans@silvertonpartners.com
web: www.silvertonpartners.com

Venture Capital & Private Equity Firms / Domestic Firms

Mission Statement: An early-stage venture capital firm focused on Texas-based companies. Aspires to partner with exceptional entrepreneurs who are committed to attacking growth markets with proprietary products or services.

Geographic Preference: Texas
Average Investment: $200,000 - $1 million
Investment Criteria: Early-Stage
Industry Group Preference: Semiconductors, Advanced Materials, Consumer Internet, Mobile, Enterprise Software, Technology-Enabled Services
Portfolio Companies: 360pi, Boundless Network, Equipboard, Famigo, Favor, FibeRio, Nuve, OutboundEngine, Pingboard, PureWRX, Sailpoint, Silicon Laboratories, Socialware, SpareFoot, StackEngine, StepOne, Tk20, TrendKite, TurnKey, UnboundID, uShip, WP Engine, The Zebra

Key Executives:
Roger Chen, Partner
Education: BS, University of Michigan; MBA, Wharton School
Background: Principal, Genacast Ventures
Directorships: Apprentice; Billie; Cooper Cow Coffee; Fetch; Kronologic; Literati; Living Security; Mobile Tech RX; Novo Labs; OneDay; Popspots; Restream; RouteFusion; Wheel
Morgan Flager, Partner
Education: BS, Stanford University
Background: FTV Capital, Ingrian Networks, Kintana
Directorships: BlackLocus, CopperEgg, Famigo, Socialware, UnboundID
Kip McClanahan, Partner
Education: BS, Electrical Engineering, University of Texas
Background: BroadJump, TippingPoint, NetSpeed
Directorships: CopperEgg, OutboundEngine, Socialware, Sparefoot, WPEngine

1686 SIMON SCHOOL VENTURE CAPITAL FUND

e-mail: ssvcf@simon.rochester.edu

Mission Statement: The purpose of the Simon School Venture Capital Fund is to create unique and experiential learning opportunities for students with respect to entrepreneurship and venture capital investment. The Fund will provided a unique educational experience for Simon students through hands-on due diligence, interaction with entrepreneurs, presentations to advisory board members, direct participation in investment decisions based on comprehensive due diligence and investment analysis with the intent to perpetuate the life of the fund. The SSCVF will serve as a hallmark activity for the Simon School and increase the School's visibility and participation in Rochester's entrepreneurial ecosytem.

Investment Criteria: Early Stage
Portfolio Companies: StormBlok, Forsake, FINsix, FastCAP Systems

1687 SINEWAVE VENTURES
18th Street
South Arlington, VA

web: sinewave.vc

Mission Statement: A venture capital firm interested in early-stage investments in commercial companies with a focus on technology.

Founded: 2014
Industry Group Preference: Cloud, Cybersecurity, Big Data, Networking, Infrastructure, SaaS, Preventative Health and Services, Finance, Education, Technology
Portfolio Companies: APX Labs, SentinelOne, Tamr

Key Executives:
Yanev Suissa, Founding General Partner
Education: BA, Yale University; JD, Harvard Law School; MBA, Oxford Said School of Business; MA, Sydney Law School
Background: Investor, NEA; Senior Investment Officer, Bush & Obama Administrations
Christopher Gaughan, General Partner
Education: BA, Economics & Political Science, Yale University; CFA
Background: Co-Founder/President, Big Sky Capital; CEO, Condesa Financiera; Co-Founder/President, Illumination Asset Management; Principal, Matlin Patterson Asset Management
Vivek Ladsariya, Partner
Education: BA, Electrical Engineering, University of Mumbai; MBA, Yale University
Background: Partner, Fenox VC; Founder, GameGarage; Founder, Moyyer Research
Patricia Muoio, Venture Partner
Education: BA, Philosophy, Fordham University; PhD, Philosophy, Yale University
Background: National Security Agency
Karen Evans, Venture Partner
Education: BS, Chemistry; MBA, West Virginia University
Background: Administrator for E-Goverment/IT, Office of Management & Budget; Chief Information Officer, Department of Energy
Directorships: US Cyber Challenge
Oliver Libby, Venture Partner
Education: Harvard College
Background: Founding Partner/Managing Director, Hatzimemos/Libby; Consultant, Guiliani Partners LLC; Co-Founder, The Resolution Project Inc.
Eric Hatzimemos, Venture Partner
Education: New York Law School
Background: Co-Founder, Giuliani Partners LLC; Assistant Counsel to Mayor Giuliani; Assistant Criminal Justice Coordinator in the Mayor's Office; Associate, Weg and Myers; Assistant District Attorney
Brian Hibblen, Venture Partner
Education: BS, Physics, United States Airforce Academy; MS, Engineering Physics, US Air Force Institute of Technology
Background: Chairman, US Government Cyby S&T Working Group; Assistant Deputy Undersecretary of Defense
Directorships: Remote Sensing Center, Naval Postgraduate School

1688 SIXTHIRTY
911 Washington Avenue
Suite 816
St. Louis, MO 63101

Phone: 314-669-6803
e-mail: hello@sixthirty.co
web: www.sixthirty.co

Mission Statement: SixThirty provides fintech startups with $100K in funding, mentors, and connections to the top financial services companies in the country. Backed by the St. Louis Regional Chamber and venture capital firm Cultivation Capital, SixThirty selects eight financial-based technology startup companies each year, four for the Fall class and four in the spring. Those companies selected to take part in the four-month accelerator program will receive hands-on training, mentoring, and networking opportunities with the top financial services companies in the region.

Geographic Preference: St. Louis
Founded: 2013
Average Investment: $100,000
Investment Criteria: Start-Up, Seed-Stage
Industry Group Preference: Financial Services
Portfolio Companies: Davo Technologies, Gremlin, Hedgeable, Lending Standard, MiiCard, MyMoneyButler, New Constructs, PromisePay, Public Funds Investment Tracking and Reporting, Upside, Wealth Access, XY Verify

Venture Capital & Private Equity Firms / Domestic Firms

Key Executives:
Atul Kamra, Managing Director
Education: MComm., Bombay University; MBA, Duke Fuqua School of Business
Background: Partner, Booz & Company; President, First Clearing; Sr Managing Director, Wells Fargo Advisors

1689 SJF VENTURES
200 N Magnum Street
Suite 203
Durham, NC 27701

Phone: 919-530-1177 **Fax:** 919-530-1178
web: www.sjfventures.com

Mission Statement: SJF Ventures invests and assists high-growth companies that positively impact the world.

Fund Size: $17 Million; $28 Million
Founded: 1999
Average Investment: $1 - $10 Million
Minimum Investment: $1 Million
Investment Criteria: Expansion Stage
Industry Group Preference: Clean Technology, Web-Enabled Services, Premium Consumer Products, Sustainability, Business Products & Services
Portfolio Companies: YieldBot, Ayla Networks, Validic, EnTouch Controls, Easy Metrics, Think Through Learning, Versify, Vital Farms, Aseptia, BioSurplus, Living Earth Technology, Optoro, Community Energy, HYLA Mobile, FieldView, MediaMath, ServiceChannel, Truist, CleanScapes, Rustic Crust, MedPage Today, Telkore, Intechra, groSolar, Preclick, B.B. Hobbs, ED MAP, Home Bistro, Sun & Earth, Salvage Direct, Ryla, Evco Research, DDF, RealWinWin, Spectral Dimensions, CitySoft, Foxfire, Brightside Academy, SelecTec, R24 Lumber, Zap, Delta Systems

Other Locations:
85 Broad Street
28th Floor
New York, NY 10004
Phone: 917-693-4858

700 Larkspur Landing Circle
Suite 199
Larkspur, CA 94939
Phone: 415-646-4965

Key Executives:
Rick Defieux, Founder/Investment Committee Chair
Education: BA & MA, Boston University; MBA, Columbia University
Background: Venture Partner, Batelle Ventures; General Partner, Allegra Partners IV; General Partner, Edison Venture Funds I, II & III
Directorships: Silicon Power
David Griest, Managing Director
Education: MBA, Yale School of Management; BBA, Finance, University of Georgia
Background: Croft & Bender; C&B Capital
Alan Kelley, Managing Director
415-659-8277
e-mail: akelley@sjfventures.com
Education: MBA, Emory University; BA, Public Policy, Duke University
Background: Milestone Venture Partners; Program Director, Hands On Atlanta; Project Manager, The Landmarks Group in Berlin, Germany
Directorships: ServiceChannel, Ryla
David Kirkpatrick, Founder/Managing Director
919-530-1177 x407
e-mail: dkirk@sjfventures.com
Education: BA, Physics & History, Duke University; MBA, UNC Kenan Flagler School of Business
Background: Founder, KirkWorks; Founder, SunShares
Directorships: Community Energy, groSolar, B.B. Hobbs, EdMap
Arrun Kapoor, Managing Director
212-209-3063
e-mail: akapoor@sjfventures.com
Education: BA, New York University; Master's, International Political Economics, London School of Economics
Background: Bain & Company
Directorships: FieldView Solutions, ServiceChannel
Cody Nystrom, Managing Director
919-530-1177 x406
e-mail: cnystrom@sjfventures.com
Education: BS, Systems & Information Engineering, University of Virginia
Background: Ewing Bermiss & Co.
Directorships: Community Energy

1690 SK TELECOM VENTURES
310 De Guigne Drive
Sunnyvale, CA 94085

Phone: 408-328-2900 **Fax:** 408-328-2931
web: www.skta.com

Mission Statement: A dedicated venture capital fund that looks to make financial returns on investments through funding internet, mobile and digital media companies that can leverage the funds sole limited partner, SK Telecom.

Geographic Preference: Worldwide
Fund Size: $100 million
Investment Criteria: Seed-Stage, Early-Stage, Growth Stage
Industry Group Preference: Internet, Mobile, Digital Media & Marketing
Portfolio Companies: Skyera, Argyle Data, ChartBoost, Kabam, Tsumobi, deCarta, English Central, RockYou

Key Executives:
Min H. Park, General Partner
Background: Motorola
David Kim, Vice President/CFO

1691 SKYLINE VENTURES
525 University Avenue
Suite 1350
Palo Alto, CA 94301

Phone: 650-462-5800 **Fax:** 650-329-1090
web: www.skylineventures.com

Mission Statement: Specializes in investing in outstanding product-focused healthcare companies.

Geographic Preference: United States
Fund Size: $350 million
Founded: 1997
Average Investment: $15 - $35 million
Investment Criteria: Seed-Stage, Startup
Industry Group Preference: Industrial Equipment, Medical, Biotechnology, Medical Devices, Healthcare, Medical & Health Related
Portfolio Companies: AcelRx Pharmaceuticals, Advion BioSciences, Avidia, Collegium Pharmaceutical, Crescendo Biosciene, Concert Pharmaceuticals, Dicerna Pharmaceuticals, DiscoveRx, Dow Pharmaceutical Sciences, Genocea Biosciences, Hansen Medical, iBalance Medical, Intuitive Surgical, KAI Pharmaceuticals, MAKO Surgical, MAP Pharmaceuticals, Medivance, NimbleGen, NovaCardia, Theravance, Proteon Therapeutics, SI-BONE, Sirtris Pharmaceuticals, SpinalMotion, Sutro Biopharma, Tetraphase Pharmaceuticals, XenoPort

Key Executives:
John F Freund, Partner
Education: BA, Harvard College, MD, Harvard Medical School, MBA, Harvard Business School
Background: Partner, Morgan Stanley Venture Partners, Executive Vice President, Acuson Corporation
Eric M Gordon, Partner
Education: PH.D & MS, University of Wisconsin
Background: Director Of Medicinal Chemistry At The Squibb Institute For Medical Research, Bristol Myers Squibb Pharmaceutical Institute In Princeton,

593

Venture Capital & Private Equity Firms / Domestic Firms

Stephen J Hoffman MD, Partner
Education: MD, University of Colorado; PhD, Chemistry, Northwestern University
Background: General Partner, TVM Capital; Founding President, Allos Therapeutics
Yasunori Kaneko MD, Partner
Education: MD, Keio University School of Medicine; MBA, Stanford Graduate School of Business
Background: Genetech; Paribas Capital Markets; SVP/CFO, Isis Pharmaceuticals

1692 SKYTREE CAPITAL PARTNERS
1980 Festival Plaza Drive
Suite 425
Las Vegas, NV 89135

e-mail: info@skytreepartners.com
web: www.skytreepartners.com

Mission Statement: Invests in various sectors including technology, healthcare, energy, agriculture, and cannabis.

Industry Group Preference: Healthcare, Cannabis, Technology, Energy, Agriculture

Other Locations:
15260 Ventura Boulevard
Suite 1700
Sherman Oaks, CA 91403

Key Executives:
Matthew Neely, Co-Founder/Managing Partner
Education: Lee Business School, University of Nevada Las Vegas
Background: Owner, Matthew Neely Insurance Agency; Owner, Asher Macrae Insurance Services; Owner, Cannabis Risk Management; Founder, paTh.Media
Erik Allison, Co-Founder/Managing Partner
Education: William Woods University; University of Missouri-Columbia
Background: Financial Advisor, Morgan Stanley Smith Barney; Investment Advisor, United Capital Financial Partners; Investment Advisor, Cambridge Investment Research; Sr. Financial Advisor, Fountainhead Wealth; Founder/CEO, EA Wealth Management
Luke K. Stanton, Managing Director
Education: BA, Political Science, University of Notre Dame; JD, Pepperdine University School of Law
Background: Co-Founder/Principal, Frontera Entertainment; Founder/Executive Chairman, Frontera Law Group; Executive Director/US Operations, Sunniva Inc.

1693 SLATER TECHNOLOGY FUND
3 Davol Square
Providence, RI 02903

e-mail: info@slaterfund.com
web: www.slaterfund.com

Mission Statement: Focuses on the support of entrepreneurs who have the vision, leadership and commitment to build substantial business enterprises.

Geographic Preference: Rhode Island
Founded: 1997
Investment Criteria: Seed-Stage
Industry Group Preference: Life Sciences, Information Technology
Portfolio Companies: Illuminoss, Lucidux, Mnemosyne, Nabsys, ProThera Biologics, Neurotech, MyOmics, Cytosolv, EpiVax, Medrobotics, Dominion Diagnostics, Selva Medical, Concordia Fibers, Sentient Biosciences, Slater Technology Fund, Vitrimark, Cyberkinetics, Absolute Commerce, Care Thread, Andera, RxVantage, Mobile Fusion, Dynadec, GeneSpectrum, Location, Far Sounder, MTI Film, Tizra, Insight Health Solutions, Traction Software, Swyx, Advanced Image Enhancement, Enhanced Energy Group, VoltServer, vCharge, Alektrona, eGO, Modular Energy Devices, WeatherPredict, Bioprocess H2O

Key Executives:
Thorne Sparkman, Managing Director
Education: BA, Biological Anthropology, Harvard University; MBA, University of California, Berkeley, Haas School of Business
Background: Founder & CEO, Incubator, Inc.; CEO, EScribe Corporation
Bob Chatham, Director
Education: BA, Colgate University
Background: Industry Analyst, Forrester Research

1694 SLOW VENTURES
1006 Kearny Street
San Francisco, CA 94133

web: www.slow.co

Mission Statement: Dedicated to helping innovative projects reach their potential.

Founded: 2009
Industry Group Preference: Technology, Applications, Digital Media, Cannabis
Portfolio Companies: Breather, Wag, Eaze, Cadre, Meadow, Common, Verge Genomics, Collective Retreats, Phylos, Tile, WayUp, uBiome, Nexar, Brandless, allbirds, Boosted, Brain.fm, Domino Data Lab, Dwell, Eero, Gusto, Bloom Farms, Honor, Livongo Health, Perlara PBC, Airtable, Ro, Tempest, Angellist, Nextdoor, Postmates, Wealthfront, Everlane, Blue Bottle Coffee, Nest, Xapo, Amplitude, Evernote, Percolate, Pinterest, Codecademy, Managed by Q, Casper, Hipcamp, Resy Network, Slack, PillPack, ClassPass, Accion Systems, Front, Giphy, Robinhood, Houseparty

Key Executives:
Dave Morin, Founder/Partner
Education: BA, Economics, University of Colorado at Boulder
Background: Product & Marketing, Apple; Platform & Connect, Facebook; Special Partner, Kleiner Perkins Caufield & Buyers; Co-Founder/CEO, Path; Co-Founder/CEO, Sunrise Bio
Directorships: Dwell Media; Evenbrite
Sam Lessin, Partner
Education: AB, Social Studies, Harvard University
Background: Associate Consultant, Bain & Co.; CEO, Drop.io; VP of Product Management, Facebook; Co-Founder, Fin
Will Quist, Partner
Education: University of California, Berkeley
Background: Editor, AlwaysOn Network; Analyst, Banc of America Securities; VP/Managing Director, Industry Ventures
Scott Marlette, Partner
Education: BS EE, Networks/Security/Communications, Georgia Institute of Technology; MS EE, Networks/Distributed Systems, Stanford University
Background: Engineer/Product Manager, Facebook; Co-Founder, GoodRx
Kevin Colleran, Managing Director
Education: BA, Management & Marketing, Babson College
Background: Global Advertising Sales, Facebook; Columnist, The Wall Street Journal; Venture Partner/Advisor, General Catalyst Partners

1695 SMARTINVEST VENTURES
1007 North Orange Street
Wilmington, DE 19801

e-mail: gerry@smartinvestventures.com
web: www.smartinvestventures.com

Mission Statement: SmartInvest Ventures is an Early Stage accelerator fund.

Founded: 2015
Investment Criteria: Early Stage

Venture Capital & Private Equity Firms / Domestic Firms

Industry Group Preference: Artificial Intelligence, Technology, Software

Key Executives:
Fred Hosaisy, Co-Founder/General Partner
Education: BS, Accounting/Finance, Temple University; MBA, Wharton School
Background: CEO, CFL-LLC E-Commerce; Director of Operations, NLdH Law; CFO/Controller, Hotwire Communications & Business Solutions LLC; Assistant COO/Director, Fox Chase Cancer Center
Gerry Moan, Managing Partner
Charles Kerrigan, General Partner
Education: MBA, Fox School of Business & Management, Temple University
Background: VP, Jefferson Bank; CFO, Archdiocese of Philadelphia; VP/Manager, Allied Irish Bank; SVP, Wells Fargo Private Bank; Director of Marketing, Legacy Adivsor; SVP/Financial Consultant, First Cornerstone Bank

1696 SOCIAL CAPITAL
120 Hawthorne Avenue
Palo Alto, CA 94301

Phone: 650-521-9007
e-mail: inbox@socialcapital.com
web: www.socialcapital.com

Mission Statement: Company seeks to advance humanity by harnessing technology to address human needs.

Fund Size: $1.2 Billion
Founded: 2011
Investment Criteria: Lifecycle
Industry Group Preference: Consumer, Education, Enterprise, Financial Services, Frontier, Healthcare
Portfolio Companies: Aclima, AIRMAP, Athos, Autonomic, Base, Bitoya, Bluenose Analytics, Box, Breakthrough, Brilliant, Bustle, Captricity, Carta, ClearSide, CloudOn, CollectiveHealth, CommonBond, Confer Health, Coolan, Cover, Cozy, CreativeLIVE, Cryptomove, Datacoral, Descomplica, Digital Currency Group, DroneSeed, Ezetap, Forge, Fresno, Front, Glooko, Greenhouse, Groq, Harvey, HubHaus, Hustle, InstaEDU, Intercom, Lema21, LotusFlare, Lumity, Mango Games, MeMed, mParticle, MPHARMA, NetSkope, Neurotrack, NiYO, OneLogin, Penny, Premise, Propeller Health, Relativity, Remind, Replicon, SAILDRONE, Secret Cinema, SEMRE, SFOX, Simplee, Slack, Slang, SurveyMonkey, Swarm, Swing Education, Syapse, Treehouse, UrbanFootprint, Wave, Wealthfront, WeeCare, Yammer

Key Executives:
Chamath Palihapitiya, Founder & CEO
Education: BA, Electrical Engineering, University of Waterloo
Background: Facebook; BMO Nesbitt Burns; AOL; Mayfield Fund

1697 SOCIAL SECTOR VENTURES
855 East Collins Boulevard
Richardson, TX 75081

Phone: 972-852-2411
e-mail: connect@socialsectorventures.com
web: www.socialsectorventures.com

Mission Statement: The mission of Social Sector Ventures is to support the entrepreneurial activity most likely to benefit Nonprofit Organizations (NPOs) in initiating and developing the relationships needed to create a better world. Social Sector Ventures believes that entrepreneurship and technology innovation must be directed at the problems of the changing world within the context of private funding and investment. Capital funding and entrepreneurship are necessary if organizations are to unlock 21st century giving opportunities and guide donor relationships in a world of rapidly changing technology.

Portfolio Companies: 2DIALOG, Affinaquest, Call2Action

Key Executives:
John E Walvoord, Chief Executive Director
Education: PhD, Columbua University

1698 SOFINNOVA VENTURES
3000 Sand Hill Road
Building 4
Suite 250
Menlo Park, CA 94025

Phone: 650-681-8420 Fax: 650-322-2037
e-mail: info@sofinnova.com
web: www.sofinnova.com

Mission Statement: Seeks to create value by providing entrepreneurs with the resources, experience, and network necessary to grow early stage companies into profitable businesses.

Geographic Preference: San Francisco Bay Area, San Diego, Seattle, Europe
Fund Size: $1 billion
Founded: 1974
Average Investment: $5 - $7 million
Minimum Investment: $500,000
Investment Criteria: Seed, Early Stage, Startup
Industry Group Preference: Information Technology, Life Sciences, Therapeutics, Pharmaceuticals
Portfolio Companies: Aclaris Therapeutics, Aerie Pharmaceuticals, Alimera Sciences, Alvine, Amarin, Anthera Pharmaceuticals, Ascendis Pharma, Ascenta Therapeutics, Audentes Therapeutics, Auris Medica, Catalyst Biosciences, Cebix, Civitas Therapeutics, Coherus Biosciences, Durata Therapeutics, First Aid Shot Therapy, Histogenics Hyperion Therapeutics, Innocoli, KaloBios, Marinus Pharmaceuticals, Mirna Therapeutics, NuCana, ObsEba, Ocera, Ophthotech Corporation, Principia Biopharma, Prothena Corporation, Salveo, Spark Therapeutics, TESARO, Versartis, ZS Pharma

Other Locations:
1250 Prospect Street
Ocean Level-4
La Jolla, CA 92037
Phone: 858-551-4880

1000, rue de la Gauchetière Ouest
Suite 2400
Montreal, QC H3B 4W5

Key Executives:
James Healy, General Partner
415-228-3396
Fax: 415-228-3390
e-mail: jim@sofinnova.com
Education: BA, Molecular Biology, Scandinavian Studies, University of California, Berkeley; MD, PhD, Immunology, Stanford University
Background: Partner, Sabdering Ventures; Miles (Bayer) Pharmceuticals; Lawrence Berkeley Laboratory; Howard Hugh Medical Institute
Directorships: InterMune Pharmaceuticals, BioSpace.com
Michael Powell, General Partner
415-228-3387
Fax: 415-228-3390
e-mail: powell@sofinnova.com
Education: PhD, Physical Chemistry, University of Toronto; Postdoc'd, Bio-Organic Shemistry, University of California
Background: Group Leader, Drug Discovery at Genentech; Director of Product Development, Cytel; Scientist and Project Team Leader, Syntex Research
Directorships: Seattle Genetics, InterMune Pharmaceuticals
Eric Buatois, General Partner
415-228-3391
Fax: 415-228-3390
e-mail: eric@sofinnova.com
Education: MS, Computer Science, Communications Engineering, Ecole Nationale Superieure des Telecommunications (France)

595

Venture Capital & Private Equity Firms / Domestic Firms

Background: General Manager, Hewlett-Packard's Communications Business Unit; Vice President and Chief Operation Officer, both Ericson and HP; Texas Instruments
Directorships: HelloSoft, Volubill, Network Physics
Anand Mehra, General Partner
415-287-1885
e-mail: anand@sofinnova.com
Education: University of Virginia; MD, Columbia Medical School
Background: JP Morgan Private Equity
Directorships: Marinus Pharmaceuticals
Garheng Kong MD PhD, General Partner
Education: BS, Chemical Engineering & Biological Sciences, Stanford University; MD, PhD, Biomedical Engineering, MBA, Duke University
Background: General Partner, Intersouth Partners
Directorships: Serenex, Novamin Technologies
Alan Colowick, Partner
Education: BS, Molecular Biology, University of Colorado
Background: EVP, Celgene Corporation; CEO, Gloucester Pharmaceuticals Inc.; President of Oncology, Geron Corporation; Chief Medical Officer, Threshold Pharmaceuticals; VP of Medical Affairs Europe, Amgen
Directorships: Chairman, Velos Biopharma Inc.; Exec Chairman, Principia Biopharma, InCarda Therapeutics Inc.; XyloCor Therapeutics; Human Longevity Inc.
Maha Katabi, Partner
Education: BS, Biology/PhD, Pharmacology, McGill University
Background: Managing Partner, Oxalis Capital; Partner, Sectoral Asset Management; VP, Ventures West Management; T2C2 Capital Bio
Directorships: Chair, Exactis Innovation; BIOQuéBec
David Kabakoff, Executive Partner, Private Equity
858-550-0959 x101
e-mail: david@sofinnova.com
Education: BA, Case Western Reserve University; PhD, Yale University
Background: Co-Founder, Salmedix; CEO, Spiros Development Corp
Directorships: Trius Therapeutics, Amplimmune, InterMune, Avalon Pharmaceuticals, Alylix
Lars Ekman, Executive Partner, Private Equity
858-405-1653
Education: PhD & MD, University of Gothenburg, Sweden
Background: President of Research & Development, Elan
Directorships: ARYx Therapeutics, InterMune

1699 SOFTBANK CAPITAL
38 Glen Avenue
Newton, MA 02459

Phone: 617-928-9300 Fax: 617-928-9304
e-mail: contactus@softbank.com
web: www.softbank.com

Mission Statement: An independent venture capital firm focused on early stage high growth technology based businesses benefiting from the rapid deployment and adoption of broadband and mobile technologies.

Geographic Preference: United States
Founded: 1995
Average Investment: $2 million
Minimum Investment: $500,000
Investment Criteria: Early-Stage
Industry Group Preference: Digital Media & Marketing, E-Commerce & Manufacturing, Business to Business, Media, Networking
Portfolio Companies: Action X, Associated Content, Betaworks, Bigcommerce, Bluefin Labs, Boxee, Buddy Media, Burstly, BuzzFeed, Celtra, Cheezburger, Chloe + Isabel, Criteo, CrowdTwist, Dering Hall, Desktone, Echo360, EdCast, FieldLens, Fitbit, Flashnotes, FlightCar, Genius, Gilt Groupe, GLAMSQUAD, Grab Media, Grind Networks, The Huffington Post, Hyperpulic, IgnitionOne, Interactions, Jump Ramp Games, Kabbage, Keychain Logistics, KickApps, Kony, Lerer Ventures, LiteScape, Loverly/Dubblee Media, MobileDay, Moat, Mobile Posse, MocoSpace, NatureBox, Nellymoser, NowThis News, OMGPOP, Paper.li/Smallrivers, Pivot, Pogoplug/Cloud Engines, Popdust, Poptip, RebelMouse, Reonomy, Rivermine, Schematic Labs, SellerCrowd, Sermo, Shake, Shareablee, Sherpaa, Sidecar, SocialFlow, Spanfeller Media Group, Swirl Networks, Synaptic Digital, Talkspace, Taykey, TechStars, The Dodo, Thumb, True & Co., Updater, Vertical Performance Partners, Wildcard, X.ai, xAd, YouAre.TV, Zady, ZipList, Zynga

Other Locations:
One News Plaza
Suite 10
Buffalo, NY 14203
Phone: 716-845-7520 Fax: 716-845-7539

130 West 25th Street
8th Floor
New York, NY 10001
Phone: 617-558-6770 Fax: 617-928-9304

1 Circle Star Way
4th Floor
San Carlos, CA 94070
Phone: 617-928-9300 Fax: 617-928-9304

Key Executives:
Ronald D Fisher, Vice Chair
e-mail: ron_fisher@softbank.com
Education: MBA, Columbia University; Bachelor of Commerce, University of Witwatersand in South Africa
Background: CEO, Phoenix Technology; Interactive Systems Corporation; Visicorp; TRW; ICL
Directorships: ETrade Group, GSI Commerce, InsWeb Corporation, Terabeam Corporation, Vie Financial Group

1700 SOFTTECH VC
Palo Alto, CA 94301

web: www.softtechvc.com

Mission Statement: An early stage venture capital firm managing seed stage funds.

Average Investment: $200,000 - $750,000
Investment Criteria: Seed-Stage, Early-Stage
Industry Group Preference: Consumer Internet, Social Media, Mobile, Infrastructure
Portfolio Companies: 6SensorLabs, 8tracks, About.me, ADstruc, Animoto, August, Better Finance, BetterDoctor, Bit.ly, Blekko, Breezy, Chartbeat, ClassDojo, Clever, Coin, Curse, DNANexus, Docsend, DroneDeploy, Estately, Fab, FanBridge, Farmeron, Fitbit, FounderDating, FreshPlanet, Front, Get Satisfaction, Gigwalk, Grovo, Halo Neuroscience, Handshake, Hired, Kahuna, KissMetrics, Lantern, Mission Motors, MobileDay, Next Big Sound, Niche, Nuzzel, Panorama Education, Poshmark, PostMates, RedCap, Reputation.com, RJ Metrics, Sapho, SendGrid, Shippo, SmartShoot, SocialWire, Soldsie, Songkick, Stitch, StrikeAd, StyleSeat, Survata, TakeLessons, Teads, Thanx, Top Hat, True&Co., Tulip Retail, Ustream, Vidyard, VigLink, Visual.Ly, Vungle, YourMechanic, ZEFR

Key Executives:
Jeff Clavier, Founder/Managing Partner
Education: MS, Computer Science; Research Degree, Distributed Computing
Background: President, RVC Capital
Stephanie Palmeri, Partner
Education: BS, Villanova University; MBA, Columbia Business School

1701 SOGAL VENTURES
New York, NY

e-mail: hello@sogalventures.com
web: www.sogalventures.com

596

Mission Statement: SoGal Ventures is a female-led millennial venture capital firm investing in early stage startups in the US and Asia with diverse founding teams.
Geographic Preference: US, Asia
Investment Criteria: Seed-Stage
Portfolio Companies: AK Valley, Archer Rppse, ASAY, birdi, ClassTracks, emocha, Everly Well, Function of Beauty, Girls Labs, GiveCampus, Glidian, GuavaPass, Helium, HelloAva, Hidrate Spark, Insilico Medicine, Kairos, Kids on 45th, Kitt.ai, Kylie.ai, Little Spoon, Lovevery, Mindshare Medical, Moby Mart, Mogul, Motiva, NailSnaps, Nebulab, Negotiatus, Osmosis, Progressly, Proscia, Refresh Body, Siren Care, Sonavex Surgical, SWAAY, The Right.Fit, Torigen, Trustify, Tueo Health, Unbound, Voga Coffee, Werk, Wheelys, Winky Lux, Wisebanyan, Yet Analytics

Key Executives:
  Pocket Sun, Founding Partner
  Education: MS, University of Southern California
  Elizabeth Galbut, Founding Partner
  Education: MBA/MA Johns Hopkins University and Maryland Institute college of Art; Georgetown University; London School of Economics
  Background: Founder, A-Level Capital

1702 SOLSTICE CAPITAL LP
81 Washington Street
Suite 303
Salem, MA 01970

Phone: 617-523-7733
e-mail: info@solcap.com
web: www.solcap.com

Mission Statement: Seeks superior venture capital returns for limited partners through investments in seed and early-stage companies in the industry areas of alternative energy, education, environment, life science, and information technology; demonstrates commitment to provide both capital and expert guidance to assist portfolio companies as they deal with the challenges and opportunities of growth. Not currently making investments in new companies.
Geographic Preference: Northeast, Southwest
Fund Size: $85 million
Founded: 1995
Minimum Investment: $500,000
Investment Criteria: Seed, Startup, First-Stage, Second-Stage
Industry Group Preference: Information Technology, Alternative Energy, Life Sciences, Environment Products & Services, Education, Clean Technology
Portfolio Companies: Abuzz Technologies, Archivas, Arzan, Carefx, CodeRyte, Connected, MetaCarta, Okena, Optimax Systems, Pharsight, Q1 Labs, Angstrom Pharmaceuticals, CellzDirect, HTG Molecular Diagnostics, Regenesis Biomedical, Evergreen Solar, Proton Energy Systems, Protonex, StrionAir, Active Control eXperts, E Ink, Lipton Corporate Child Care Centers, Lumidigm, OutStart

Key Executives:
  Harry A George, Managing General Partner
  Education: AB, Bowdoin College
  Background: Co-Founder/Director/VP Finance, Interleaf; Co-Founder/Director/VP Finance, Kurzweil Computer Products
  Directorships: ImaRx Therapeutics, Lumidigm, High Throughput Genomics, CellzDirect, Regenesis Biomedical
  Henry W Newman, General Partner
  Education: Bowdoin College; MBA, Wharton School
  Background: VP, BancBoston Ventures; Financial Management, Bank of Boston; CPA, Coopers & Lybrand
  Directorships: CodeRyte, Quelsys, Lipton Corp Childcare, Intrak Wireless

1703 SONY INNOVATION FUND
1730 N 1st Street
San Jose, CA 95112

web: www.sonyinnovationfund.com

Mission Statement: The venture capital branch of Sony Corporation, Sony Innovation Fund actively invests in the technology industry.
Geographic Preference: US, Japan, Europe, Israel
Founded: 2016
Investment Criteria: Seed, Early Stage, Middle-Stage
Industry Group Preference: Technology, Artificial Intelligence, Entertainment, Gaming, Health & Wellness, Industry, Logistics, Manufacturing, Mobility, Fintech, Robotics, IoT, Virtual Reality, Security
Portfolio Companies: Activ Surgical, AdHawk, Adrich, Agility Robotics, AirMap, AWAKENS, DefinedCrowd, Digilens, Embodied, Exo Imaging, Little Star Media, Matternet, Miles, Ridecell, Shimmur, Sight Machine, sliver.tv, StrongArm Technologies

Other Locations:
  2207 Bridgepointe Parkway
  San Mateo, CA 94404

  6 Ha'harash Street
  Central District
  Hod Hasharon 45240
  Israel

  1-7-1 Konan Minato-ku
  Tokyo 108-0075
  Japan

Key Executives:
  Joseph Tou, Managing Director
  Education: BS, University of Michigan; MS/MEng, Northwestern Univesity; MBA, Kellogg School of Management
  Background: Software Engineer, Ford Motor Company; Sr. Marketing/Product Manager, Intel; Sr. Research Analyst, Pacific Crest Securities; VP, Bertram Capital; Managing Director, Mavent Partners; VP of Corporate Development, Sony Corporation of America

1704 SONY STRATEGIC TECHNOLOGY PARTNERSHIPS
1730 North 1st Street
San Jose, CA 95112

Phone: 408-352-4636 **Fax:** 408-352-4640
e-mail: austin.noronha@am.sony.com

Mission Statement: Provides a window into emerging technology and business opportunities and helps establish strategic partnerships with innovative startups.
Geographic Preference: Worldwide
Founded: 1998
Average Investment: $3-5 million
Investment Criteria: Differentiated Core Enabling Technologies
Industry Group Preference: Infrastructure, Internet Technology, Audio & Video Distribution, Advanced Data Compression Technologies, Digital Rights Management, Image-Recognition, Reconfigurable Processors, Display Technologies, Wireless Technologies, Video Gaming
Portfolio Companies: ACCESS, ArrayComm, Digital Founatin, IP Unity, Internet Number Corporation, NTRU Cryptosystems, Oren Semiconductor, Reflectivity, SecureMedia, Sandcraft, Tao, TeraLogic, Time Domain, Transmeta, 727 Solutions, Equator Technologies, i3 Mobile, IFILM, Intrinsic Graphics, Lightspan, Montavista, PacketVideo, TiVo, WildTangent

Key Executives:
  Austin Noronha
  408-352-4636
  Fax: 408-352-4640
  e-mail: austin.noronha@am.sony.com

Venture Capital & Private Equity Firms / Domestic Firms

Shoichi Osawa
408-352-4779
Fax: 408-352-4640
e-mail: shoichi.osawa@am.sony.com

1705 SORENSON CAPITAL
3400 N Ashton Blvd
Suite 400
Lehi, UT 84043

Phone: 801-407-8400
e-mail: info@sorensoncapital.com
web: www.sorensoncapital.com

Mission Statement: Sorenson Capital is a private equity firm headquartered in Salt Lake City, Utah. Provides small to middle-market buyout and growth equity investments, with a particular focus on opportunities in selected states in the Mountain and Western regions of the United States.

Geographic Preference: Mountain & Western United States
Average Investment: $3 - 25 million
Portfolio Companies: Pluralsight, Zerbee's, Excel Manufacturing, AtTask, Nexmo, Empathica, Suncrest Solar, JWD Machine, Wilson Electronics, AccessData, CustomControl Concepts, Roberts Tool Company, HealthCatalyst, Tru Hearing, Bamboo HR, Mindshare Technologies, Goal Zero, NCS Energy Services, Imagine Learning, MM Pipeline Services, Southeast Directional Drilling, HGB, Jetset Sports, IDC, MITY Enterprises, RWI Construction, LifePort, Omniture, Vitron, Atlas Aerospace, WASI, Provocraft, LS, Dickson Construction

Key Executives:
Fraser Bullock, Founder/Managing Director
Education: BA, Economics, MBA, Brigham Young University
Background: Partner, Bain Capital; Founder, Alpine Consolidated
Tim Layton, Founder/Managing Director
Education: BS, Statistics, MBA, Brigham Young University
Background: Co-Founder, InStar Services; Managing Director, Alpine Consolidated
Ron Mika, Founder/Managing Director
Education: BS, Chemical Engineering; Brigham Young University; MBA, Harvard Business School
Background: Bain Capital, Bain & Company
Luke Sorenson, Managing Director
Education: BS, Accounting, Brigham Young University; MBA, Wharton School
Background: Director, Sorenson Media; Vice President, Sorenson Real Estate
Mark Ludwig, Managing Director
Education: BA, Russian, Brigham Young University; MBA, Wharton School
Background: Associate, Bain & Company
Legrand Lewis, Advisor
Education: BS, Accounting, Brigham Young University; MBA, Harvard Business School
Background: Consultant, Bain & Company; Capmark Financial Group

1706 SORRENTO VENTURES
2211 Encinitas Boulevard
Suite 200
Encinitas, CA 92024

Phone: 858-792-2700 Fax: 858-792-5070
e-mail: aking@sorrentoventures.com
web: www.sorrentoventures.com

Mission Statement: Sorrento Ventures is committed to providing strategic capital and vision to promising emerging growth companies.

Geographic Preference: Southern California
Fund Size: $115 million
Founded: 1985
Average Investment: $1 to $5 million
Minimum Investment: $500,000
Investment Criteria: Startup, First-Stage, Second-Stage, Mezzanine, LBO
Industry Group Preference: Healthcare, Medical Devices, Biotechnology, Technology, Communications, Enterprise Software, Electronics, Internet, Internet Technology, E-Commerce & Manufacturing, Retailing, Consumer Products, Distribution
Portfolio Companies: Cameron Health, Digirad, Idun Pharmaceuticals, Neurogenetics, Perlan Therapeutics, A-Life Medical, Idetic, IP MobileNet, SeatAdvisor, V-Enable, Catheter Innovations, CombiChem, Corvas International, DepoTech, Endonetics, Gensia Pharmaceuticals, IDEC Pharmaceuticals, Infrasonics, La Jolla Pharmaceutical Company, Laser Diagnostic Technologies, Medication Delivery Devices, Mikotor, Mycogen Corporation, Viagene, Vical, ESI Software, FieldCentrix, Keylime Software, LAM Research Company, Pacific Communications Sciences, Primary Access Corporation, University Netcasting, Garden Fresh Restaurant, Hot Topic

Key Executives:
Robert M Jaffe, Co-Founder/President
Education: MBA, Harvard Business School; MS Electrical Engineering, California Institute of Technology; BS Electrical Engineering/Computer Science, University of California Berkeley
Background: Merrill Lynch Capital Markets; Salomon Brothers; Goldman Sachs; Hughes Aircraft Company; McKinsey & Co
Directorships: A-Life Medical, Bebe Stores, Digirad, IPMobileNet, Perlan Therapeutics

1707 SOURCE CAPITAL GROUP
276 Post Road West
Westport, CT 06880

Phone: 203-341-3500 Fax: 203-241-3515

Mission Statement: Offers equity and other debt financing to help further the growth of companies that are often overlooked by the larger investment banking firms.

Geographic Preference: Arizona, California
Fund Size: $17.2 million
Founded: 1992
Average Investment: $250,000
Minimum Investment: $50,000
Investment Criteria: First-stage, Second-stage, Mezzanine, Special situations
Industry Group Preference: Communications, Computer Related, Consumer Products, Distribution, Electronic Components, Electronic Technology, Energy, Natural Resources, Genetic Engineering, Industrial Equipment, Forestry, Medical & Health Related, Financial Services, Oil & Gas

Other Locations:
7377 East Doubletree Ranch Road
Suite 290
Scottsdale, AZ 85258
Phone: 480-368-1488 Fax: 480-368-1319

790 East Colorado Blvd
Pasadena, CA 91101
Phone: 626-240-0872 Fax: 626-240-0882

433 South Main Street
Suite 117
West Hartford, CT 06110
Phone: 866-433-0600 Fax: 860-313-0319

3170 North Federal Highway
Suite 103A

Lighthouse Point, FL 33064
Phone: 954-785-1990 **Fax:** 954-785-6579

98-1277 Kaahumanu Street
Aiea, HI 96701
Phone: 808-483-5005 **Fax:** 808-483-5020

632 Adams Street
Suite 210
Bowling Green, KY 42101
Phone: 270-843-8985 **Fax:** 270-842-3028

211 Main Street
Marlborough, MA 01752
Phone: 508-480-8383 **Fax:** 508-485-8161

708 Third Avenue
5th Floor
New York, NY 10017
Phone: 212-286-0890 **Fax:** 212-286-0891

245 Park Avenue
24th Floor
New York, NY 10167
Phone: 212-372-8840 **Fax:** 212-372-8839

2130 Headquarters Plaza
East Tower 2nd Floor
Morristown, NJ 07960
Phone: 973-590-2650 **Fax:** 973-590-2649

Key Executives:
David W Harris, President
Education: BA, University of Pennsylvania
Background: Smith Barney Harris Upham & Company; Oppenheimer & Company
Bruce C Ryan, Vice Chairman
Education: BS, Northeastern University
Background: Vice President, Private Capital Investment Group, Chemical Bank

1708 SOUTH ATLANTIC VENTURE FUNDS
614 W Bay Street
Tampa, FL 33606-2704

Phone: 813-253-2500 **Fax:** 813-253-2360

Mission Statement: We believe we are most successful when we have the opportunity to build long term relationships with outstanding entrepreneurs. By partnering with outstanding entrepreneurs with experience, vision and integrity, we can invest across a broad range of industries and generate an above average rate of return for our limited partners.

Geographic Preference: Mid-Atlantic, Southeast, Texas
Fund Size: $173 Million
Founded: 1983
Average Investment: $1.5-$7.5 million
Minimum Investment: $1, 500,000
Investment Criteria: First-stage, Second-stage, Mezzanine
Industry Group Preference: Broadcasting, Communications, Computer Related, Consumer Products, Electronic Technology, Natural Resources, Financial Services, Food & Beverage, High Technology, Industrial Equipment, Information Technology, Insurance, Manufacturing, Medical & Health Related, Energy
Portfolio Companies: Alphatronix, Applied Automation, Arbor Health Care, Async, AvData Systems, BMR Financial Group, BancWest Bancorp, Bitec Southeast, Centennial HealthCare, ClearSource, COIN, Computer Science Innovations, CooperSmith, Cryogenic Services, Cybex Computer Products, DEKA Medical, DgR, Digital Transmission Systems, Ganymede Software, ITC Cellular Holdings, ITC Holding Company, ITC DeltaCom, Innovative Healthcare Systems, InterCall, InterServ Services Corporation, JRL Systems, K&G Men's Center, Knology, KNOLOGY Holdings, Major Leasing, MainBancorp, Masada Security Holdings, Medsouth Health Care, MTL, National Laboratory Center, NF Holding Company, NLynx Systems, O.K. 4U KIDDO, Outback Steakhouse, Phoenix Microsystems, Powertel, Primis, Premiere Cinemas Corporation, PriCare, Regal Cinemas, Regent Communications, Sawtek, Silk Greenhouse, Henry Silverman Jewelers, Southeast Health Plan, Southeast Venture Capital Limited II, Ballard Medical Products, Data Net Corporation National Health Care Systems, Redgate Communications, Southern Systems, Symbion, Tasnet, Telecom USA, TowerCom Limited, TowerCom Development L.P., TxPort, United Dental Care

Other Locations:
6395 S Mitchell Manor Circle
Miami, FL 33156-4884
Phone: 305-250-4681 **Fax:** 305-250-4682

Key Executives:
Donald W Burton, Founder, Chairman
e-mail: dwburton@southatlantic.com
Education: BA American Studies, Yale University; MBA, Harvard Business School
Background: Fidelity Venture Associates
Directorships: National Venture Capital Association
Sandra P Barber, Managing Director
e-mail: spbarber@southatlantic.com
Education: Indiana University

1709 SOUTHEAST INTERACTIVE TECHNOLOGY FUNDS
1500 Perimeter Park Drive
Suite 310
Morrisville, NC 27560

Phone: 919-558-8324 **Fax:** 919-655-0541

Mission Statement: A venture stage investor who focuses exclusively on information technology and communications investments across industry verticals.

Geographic Preference: Southeast
Fund Size: $180 million
Founded: 1995
Average Investment: $4 million
Minimum Investment: $2 million
Investment Criteria: Early Stage
Industry Group Preference: Services, Technology, Telecommunications, Infrastructure, Enterprise Software, Business Products & Services, Software, Information Technology, Media
Portfolio Companies: Allconnect, BuildCraft Homes, BuildLinks, Nitronex, TerraServer, XS, OpenSite Technologies, Accipiter, Wave Systems, iEntertainment Network, ChanneLogics, GadgetSpace, Red Storm Entertainment, HAHT Commerce, Chatfish, HowStuffWorks, Pixel Magic Imaging, Arsenal Digital Studios, Waveguide Solutions, VisionAIR, MediaSpan Group

Key Executives:
Norvell E Miller IV, Managing General Partner
919-558-8324
Education: MBA/BA, Duke University
Background: EMS Financial; Triangle Assets Consulting; Mobius Group; Dental Care Partners;
Directorships: AllConnect, Arsenal, Digital Solutions, MediaSpan Group, Pixel Magic Imaging, VisionAIR, WaveGuide, Elumens
Steve Rakes, General Partner/CFO
Education: BA, English & Radio/Television Production, MS, Accounting, University of North Carolina, Chapel Hill
Background: Ernst & Young; Sloan Financial Group
Rami Elkhatib, Venture Consultant
Education: BS, Purdue University; MIT Sloan School
Background: Senior Director, Oneworld Software; Proctor & Gamble; UBS Warburg; Merrill Lynch

Venture Capital & Private Equity Firms / Domestic Firms

1710 SOUTHERN CAPITOL VENTURES
100 E Six Forks Road
Suite 200
Raleigh, NC 27609

Phone: 919-858-7580
web: www.southcap.com

Mission Statement: Southern Capitol Ventures is dedicated to helping outstanding entrepreneurs build market-leading companies.
Geographic Preference: Southeast, Mid-Atlantic United States
Founded: 2000
Average Investment: $500,000 - $1.5 million
Minimum Investment: $35,000
Investment Criteria: Early-Stage
Industry Group Preference: Software, E-Commerce & Manufacturing, Digital Media & Marketing, Mobile, Healthcare Information Technology
Portfolio Companies: Art.com, ArtusLabs, AZVIcode, AudienceFUEL, Batanga, BrightContext, ChannelAdvisor, DoublePositive, ETix, FullSeven Technologies, Global Value Commerce, Motricity, ReverbNation, Synthematix, WeddingWire, Zift Solutions

Key Executives:
Ben Brooks, Founding Partner
e-mail: ben@southcap.com
Education: University of North Carolina, Chapel Hill; MBA, Fuqua School of Business, Duke University
Background: Director, Strategy, Capital Investment Group; SVP, Josephthal & Co.; CEO, Marion Bass Securities
Directorships: FullSeven Technologies
Jason Caplain, General Partner
e-mail: jason@southcap.com
Education: BS, Finance, Bentley College
Background: Red Hat, Harrison Hurley & Company
Directorships: ReverbNation, Zift Solutions
David Jones, Partner
e-mail: david@southcap.com
Education: BS, Electrical Engineering, US Naval Academy; MS, Management Information Systems, University of Virginia; MBA, UNC Chapel Hill
Background: Deloitte Consulting; Co-Founder, CTO, Orthocopia.com
Directorships: ArtusLabs

1711 SOUTHERN CROSS VENTURE PARTNERS
420 Florence Street
Suite 210
Palo Alto, CA 94301

web: www.sxvp.com

Mission Statement: Assists early stage companies that demonstrate the potential for exceptional growth and market leadership.
Founded: 2006
Average Investment: $2 to $5 million
Industry Group Preference: Software Services, Telecommunications, Advanced Materials, Semiconductors, Digital Media & Marketing, Internet, Security, Nanotechnology, Environment, Energy, Mining, Water, Agriculture
Portfolio Companies: Autopilot, Brandscreen, CrossFiber, Effective Measure, Mantara, Mesaplexx, Mocana, Nitero, Pygg, Quantenna Communications, RIO, RMSS, SBA Materials, Shoes of Prey, Virsto, Wave Semiconductor, Woodboard, Precise Light Surgical, Brisbane Materials, Hydrexia, Boulder Ionics, Sunverge

Other Locations:
PO Box 5084
Elanora Heights NSW 2101
Australia
Phone: 61-0283147400

Key Executives:
Bob Christiansen, Managing Director
Education: Bachelor of Economics, Diploma of Information Processing, University of Queensland
Background: General Partner, Allen & Buckenridge
John Scull, Managing Director
Education: Bachelor's Degree, University of Oklahoma; MBA, Harvard University
Background: Venture Partner, Allen & Buckenridge
Directorships: Aurema, ekit, Wedgetail/Vintela, Fultec Semiconductor, Fiberom, VaST Systems
Mark Bonnar, Managing Director
Education: BS/PhD, Heriot-Watt University
Directorships: Sunman Energy; Wattwatchers; Greensync; BenAn Energy; Octillion Energy; Hydrexia; Mojo Power; Ecoult

1712 SOUTHPORT PARTNERS
2425 Post Road
Southport, CT 06490

Phone: 203-292-0019
e-mail: dm@southportpartners.com
web: www.southportpartners.com

Mission Statement: Southport Partners is a technology investment banking firm, specializing in mergers and acquisitions, as well as raising equity from institutional sources with over $2 billion of transactions completed over the last ten years.
Geographic Preference: United States
Founded: 1986
Average Investment: $12 million
Minimum Investment: $5 million
Investment Criteria: Second-Stage, Mezzanine, LBO, MBO
Industry Group Preference: Communications, Computer Related, Education, Electronic Components, Instrumentation, Financial Services, Insurance, Medical & Health Related, Internet Technology, Publishing, Transportation

Key Executives:
Dale McIvor, Founding Partner
Education: BSEE, University of Michigan; MSEE, University of Maryland; MBA, Harvard Business School
Background: Boston Consulting Group; Mitre Corp.; Research Engineer, National Security Agency
Katherine Watts, Founding Partner
Education: BA, Washington University, MBA, New York University
Background: Manager, Norton Simon; Merrill Lynch
Mathew Veedon, Affiliate
Education: BCom, Syndenham College, University of Mumbai; MBA, Yale University
Background: Consultant, Redding Consultants; Principal, NGV Partners Fund; Senior Consultant, Accenture

1713 SOUTHWEST MICHIGAN FIRST LIFE SCIENCE FUND Southwest Michigan First
2700 Stadium Drive
Kalamazoo, MI 49008

Phone: 269-553-9588
web: www.southwestmichiganfirst.com

Mission Statement: The Southwest Michigan First Life Science Fund is a limited partnership venture fund interested in early stage life science opportunities in the Kalamazoo Region that have demonstrably viable technologies.
Geographic Preference: Kalamazoo Region
Fund Size: $50 million
Investment Criteria: Early-Stage
Industry Group Preference: Life Sciences
Portfolio Companies: Axonia Medical, Metabolic Solutions Development Company, Monteris Medical, NephRx, Toera Therapeutics, Vestaron

Venture Capital & Private Equity Firms / Domestic Firms

Key Executives:
Ron Kitchens, Senior Partner
e-mail: rkitchens@southwestmichiganfirst.com

1714 SPACEVEST

web: www.spacevest.com

Mission Statement: Provides new business initiatives, strategic development, capital resource planning and investment management.

Geographic Preference: United States
Fund Size: $300 million
Founded: 1991
Average Investment: $3-$5 million
Minimum Investment: $500,000
Investment Criteria: Second Round or Later
Industry Group Preference: Components & IoT, Equipment, Software, Satellite Communications, Cable, Optical Technology, Copper, Applications Software & Services, Networking, Enterprise Services, Aerospace, Defense and Government

Key Executives:
John B Higginbotham, Founder/Chairman/Managing Director
703-904-9800
Fax: 703-904-0571
e-mail: jbh@spacevest.com
Education: BS Civil Engineering with Honors, Virginia Tech; MBA, Harvard Business School
Background: Co-Founder, Director, Sr VP, International Technology Underwriters; Satellite Systems Analyst, Corroon, Black/Inspace; President, Marketing Manager, Hewlett Packard
Directorships: Space Foundation, Virginia Tech Alumni Association

1715 SPARK CAPITAL
137 Newbury Street
8th Floor
Boston, MA 02116

Phone: 617-830-2000
e-mail: info@sparkcapital.com
web: www.sparkcapital.com

Mission Statement: Spark Capital is a venture capital firm that partners with exceptional entrepreneurs seeking to build disruptive, world-changing companies. Spark works to leverage their experiences, honed product & business instincts and extensive networks to help entrepreneurs build great companies.

Geographic Preference: Worldwide
Fund Size: $3 billion
Founded: 2005
Average Investment: $25,000 - $25 million
Investment Criteria: Early Stage
Industry Group Preference: Interactive Media, Mobile, Online Applications, Web Platforms, Infrastructure, Advertising, Cloud Computing, Social Media
Portfolio Companies: 1stdibs, 5minMedia, 8D World, Academia.edu, Accelera, Adap.TV, Adkeeper, Admeld, AltiusEd, Aviary, Benu, BloomNation, Boxee, Bug Labs, Close.io, Consumerunited, Contextin, Covestor, DIY, Etoro, Exfm, Fitorbit, Foursquare, Frontier Strategy Group, FundersClub, GDGT, Getyourguide, Hey, Inc., Intune Networks, IP Wireless, i-Wireless, JANA, Jelly in the News, Kateeva, KickApps, Kik, Kitchen Surfing, Lexity, Lift, LinkWell Health, Mark43, Enara Networks, Nextnew Networks, Nimble Commerce, Oculus VR, OMGPOP, OneRiot, Onswipe, Orchard, Panjo, peerTransfer, Picturelife, Plaid, Priceonomics, Qriously, Quantopian, RunKeeper, Sendme, Senr.net, Singpost, Sincerely, Skillshare, Socratic, StackExchange, StoreNVY, SuperPedestrian, Svpply, Thalmic Labs, thePlatform, Timehop, Triggit, tumblr, Twitter, Upworthy, VeriVue, Warby Parker, Wayfair, WorkMarter, Zazma

Other Locations:
165 Mercer Street
New York, NY 10012
Phone: 917-243-4200

332 Pine Street
Floor 7
San Francisco, CA 94104
Phone: 415-593-9002

Key Executives:
Alex Finkelstein, General Partner
Education: BA, Political Science, Middlebury College
Background: Principal, Seed Capital Partners; Associate, GrandBanks Capital; Cambridge Associates
Directorships: 5min, 8D World
Bijan Sabet, General Partner
Education: BS, Boston College
Background: Senior Vice President, Corporate Development, GameLogic; Entrepreneur-in-Residence, Charles River Ventures; Business Development, WebTV
Directorships: Tumbler, ThePlatform, Twitter, Sendme
Jeremy G. Philips, General Partner
Education: University of New South Wales; Harvard Kennedy School
Background: News Corporation; Photon Group
Directorships: TripAdvisor
Kevin Thau, General Partner
Education: UC, Santa Barbara
Background: Silicon Graphics; Software.com; Twitter
Nabeel Hyatt, General Partner
Education: Maryland Institute; Purdue University
Background: Conduit Labs; Zynga
Directorships: Cruise; Fig; Harmonix; Postmates; Proletariat; DIY; Sonder; Thalmic Labs
Santo Politi, Co-Founder & General Partner
Education: BS, Physics, Bogazici University, Istanbul; MS, Electrical Engineering, NJIT; MBA, Finance, Wharton School, University of Pennsylvania
Background: yPartner, Charles River Ventures; President, New Media, Blockbuster Entertainment; Co-Founder, BT Venture Partners; Matsushita Electric Industrial
Directorships: KickApps, OneRiot, IWireless Home
Todd Dagres, Co-Founder & General Partner
Education: BS, Psychology, Trinity College; MBA, Boston University
Background: General Partner, Battery Ventures; Senior Lecturer, MIT Sloan School of Management; Principal & Senior Technology Anaylst, Montgomery Securities; Senior Technology Anaylst, Smith Barney/Robinson Humphrey; Business Development Manager, Networks & Communications, Digital Equipment Corporation
Directorships: Verivue, Akamai Technologies, Covestor

1716 SPARKLABS GLOBAL VENTURES
Palo Alto, CA

web: www.sparklabsglobal.com

Mission Statement: Business is now truly global. Exceptional entrepreneurs, that are building strong, category defining companies at highly advantageous valuations - can be found anywhere.

Geographic Preference: Worldwide
Investment Criteria: Seed-Stage
Industry Group Preference: Enterprise Software, Consumer Internet
Portfolio Companies: Andela, Blend, Good.co, Codekingdoms, Flow State Media, Hullabalu, Iodine, Knowre, LawPal, Lifesum, Mango Plate, Memebox, My GO Games, The Orange Chef Co., Parko, PayByGroup, Payoff, Petnet, Quarterly, SelfScore, Soundwave, Stitch, Timecast, WOO, Zanbato, 42

Key Executives:
Frank Meehan, Co-Founder/General Partner
Background: Horizons Ventures; Founder, Kuato Studios; Ericsson; Hutchison Whampoa

601

Venture Capital & Private Equity Firms / Domestic Firms

Bernard Moon, Co-Founder/General Partner
Education: BA, English & Psychology, University of Wisconsin-Madison; MPA, Telecom & New Media Policy, Columbia University
Background: Co-Founder, SparkLabs; Co-Founder & CEO, Vidquik; Managing Director, Lunsford Group; Co-Founder, GoingOn Networks; Director, IRG
John Lee, Co-Founder/Partner
Education: BA, Biology, University of Chicago
Background: Co-Founder, Hostway

1717 SPECTRUM EQUITY INVESTORS LP
One International Place
35th Floor
Boston, MA 02110

Phone: 617-464-4600 Fax: 617-464-4601
web: www.spectrumequity.com

Mission Statement: Provide equity capital to companies in the communications, information, media, entertainment and interactive industries; with each investment our goals are the same, to build premier businesses and achieve substantial long term capital appreciation for shareholders.

Geographic Preference: North America, Western Europe, Australia
Fund Size: $4.7 billion
Founded: 1994
Average Investment: $25-$100 million
Minimum Investment: $1 million
Investment Criteria: Seed, First-stage, Second-stage, Mezzanine; Leveraged Buyouts, Recapitalizations, Acquisition Financings, Secondary Share Purchases
Industry Group Preference: Communications, Entertainment, Information Technology, Media, Business Products & Services, Online Advertising, Software, Internet, Digital Media & Marketing
Portfolio Companies: AllTrails, Ancestry, Animoto, Bats, Bitly, Business Monitor International, B-Stock, Choice, DataCamp, Definitive Healthcare, Digital Marketing Institute, EagleView Technologies, Ethoca, Exactbid, ExamSoft, Extreme Reach, Finalsite, GoodRx, Grubhub, Headspace, HealthMedX, Ibfx.com, iPay Technologies, iSelect.com.au, Ita Software, Jagex Games Studio, Jimdo, Lead Group, Litmus, Lucid, Lynda.com, MedHok, Mortgagebot, Net Health, NetQuote, NetScreen, Offensive Security, Origami Risk, Passport Health Communications, Payer Compass, PicMonkey, Prezi, QTC Medical Services, RainKing, RCN, Rightside, RiskMetrics Group, Seisint, Survey Monkey, Teachers Pay Tachers, Tenstreet, The Expert Institute, Trintech, Verafin, Verisys, Weddingwire, World-Check

Other Locations:
140 New Montgomery
20th Floor
San Francisco, CA 94105
Phone: 415-464-4600 Fax: 415-464-4601

Key Executives:
Brion B Applegate, Founder & Senior Managing Director
e-mail: brion@spectrumequity.com
Education: BA, Colgate University; MBA, Harvard Business School
Background: TA Associates
William P Collatos, Founder & Senior Managing Director
e-mail: bill@spectrumequity.com
Education: AB Economics, Harvard College
Background: General Partner, TA Associates; Founding General Partner, Media Communications Partners
Directorships: Access Television Network, CBSI, Egenera, Surebridge
Ronan Cunningham, Managing Director
Education: BComm, University College Dublin; MBA, INSEAD
Background: SVP, Capital Partnering, General Atlantic; Partner, Adam Street Partners
Directorships: Institutional Limited Partners Association

Mike Farrell, Managing Director
Education: BA, Bowdoin College; MBA, Harvard Business School
Background: Tudor Investment Corporation
Chris Mitchell, Managing Director
e-mail: chris@spectrumequity.com
Education: AB, Princeton University
Background: TA Associates; Monitor Clipper Partners; SG Warburg;
Directorships: Chartered Marketing Services; RiskMetrics Group, Seisint; Surebridge, Inc; United Asset Coverage
Jeff Haywood, Managing Director
Education: BA, Duke University
Background: Thoma Cressey Equity Partners; Goldman Sachs
Brian Regan, Managing Director
Education: BS, Bucknell University
Background: PricewaterhouseCoopers
Victor E Parker, Managing Director
e-mail: vic@spectrumequity.com
Education: BA, Dartmouth College; MBA, Stanford Graduate School of Business
Background: Summit Partners; Product Manager, ONYX Software; Consultant, Andersen Consulting
Benjamin M Spero, Managing Director
e-mail: bspero@spectrumequity.com
Education: AB, History & Economics, Duke University
Background: Consultant, Bain & Company; Co-Founder, TouchPak
Peter T Jensen, Managing Director
e-mail: pete@spectrumequity.com
Education: BA, Stanford University; MBA, Wharton School
Background: Technology, Media & Telecom Investment Banking Group, JPMorgan
Stephen M LeSieur, Managing Director
e-mail: steve@spectrumequity.com
Education: BA, Princeton University; MBA, Dartmouth College
Background: Associate, Trident Capital; Analsyst, Media & Communications Group, Thomas Weisel Partners
Adam J Margolin, Managing Director
e-mail: adam@spectrumequity.com
Education: AB, Harvard University
Background: Vice President, Media & Telecom Investment Banking Group, Citigroup

1718 SPEKTRA CAPITAL
620 Kirkland Way
Suite 204
Kirkland, WA 98033

Phone: 425-307-1299
e-mail: info@spektracapital.com
web: www.spektracapital.com

Mission Statement: Interested in companies operating in large markets or traditional segments underserved by emerging technologies. Prefers defined revenue models, a short path to profitability and straightforward value propostions.

Founded: 2012
Investment Criteria: Early Stage
Industry Group Preference: Mobile Apps, SaaS, Platform As A Service

1719 SPELL CAPITAL PARTNERS LLC
222 South Ninth Street
Suite 2880
Minneapolis, MN 55402

Phone: 612-371-9650 Fax: 612-371-9651
e-mail: info@spellcapital.com
web: www.spellcapital.com

Venture Capital & Private Equity Firms / Domestic Firms

Mission Statement: To sponsor a strong management team with a proven track record in a LBO situation. Focuses on industrial businesses and help industries to achieve goals.

Geographic Preference: Midwest
Fund Size: $75 million
Founded: 1988
Average Investment: $3 - $12 million
Minimum Investment: $2 million
Industry Group Preference: Chemicals, Manufacturing, Plastics, Metals
Portfolio Companies: American Card Services, Tech Cast Holdings, Animal Adventure, Valley Vessel Fabricators, Midwest Plastic Products, NPI Medical, Thermoforming Technology Group, Falls Fabricating, Filter Minder, Norshield Security Products, Premier Precision Group, Smartlink, Apartment Data Services, AC Busines Media, Las Vegas Color Graphics, Arandell, Learn It Systems, Alliance Steel Service, Adler Hot Oil Service, All Safe, Sellars

Key Executives:
   William H Spell, President
   612-371-9650
   Fax: 612-371-9651
   e-mail: williamspell@spellcapital.com
   Education: BS, University of Minnesota; MBA, Carlson School of Management, University of Minnesota
   Background: Former Investment Banker
   Directorships: A number of private/public companies and non-profits
   Darren Brathol, Managing Director
   e-mail: darren@spellcapital.com
   Education: BS, University of Wisconsin; MBA, Carlson School of Business, University of Minnesota
   Background: Investment Banking Analyst, Lazard Middle Market
   James W Rikkers, Senior Managing Director
   Education: BA, Economics & Finance, University of St. Thomas
   Background: Mezzanine Capital Group, Wells Fargo
   Andrea R Nelson, Chief Operating Officer/Chief Financial Officer
   Education: BSB, Carlson School of Management, University of Minnesota, CPA
   Background: Tax Director, PricewaterhouseCoopers LLP

1720 SPENCER TRASK VENTURES
1140 Avenue of the Americas
New York, NY 10036

Toll-Free: 800-622-7078
web: spencertraskco.com

Mission Statement: Spencer Trask is a leading private equity firm discovering idea to shape the 21st century. With our network of co-investors and business leaders, we provide visionary entrepreneurs with both financial and intellectual capital to transform bright ideas into world-changing companies.

Geographic Preference: United States
Founded: 1991
Investment Criteria: Startup, Early-Stage
Industry Group Preference: Healthcare, Life Sciences, Software, Media, Information Technology, Telecommunications, Mobile Communications Devices, Genomics, Optical Technology, Stem Cell Therapy
Portfolio Companies: Fastcase, Casemaker, El Super, Sessions.edu, Aperture, Innocentive, Ciena, Myriad, Health Dialog

Other Locations:
1700 East Putnam Avenue
Suite 306
Old Greenwich, CT 06870

1721 SPERO VENTURES
1991 Broadway Street
Suite 110
Redwood City, CA 94063

web: spero.vc

Mission Statement: Spero Ventures invests in late Seed tech companies.

Founded: 2018
Average Investment: $3 million - $12 million
Investment Criteria: Late Seed, Series A
Industry Group Preference: Artificial Intelligence, Technology, Applications, Software, Consumer, Health & Wellness
Portfolio Companies: Anchor, Base, Bunker, Core, Crew, DroneSeed, Fathom, Gencove, Huckleberry, Hustle, Indus, Jopwell, Koko, Markov, RevUp, Roam Robotics, SafeTraces, Shelfmint, Skillshare, Tortuga AgTech

Key Executives:
   Shripriya Mahesh, Partner
   Background: Omidyar Network; eBay; NextCard
   Rob Veres, Partner
   Education: MBA, Kellogg School of Management
   Background: Omidyar Network
   Ha Nguyen, Partner
   Education: BS, Wharton School; MBA, Harvard Business School
   Background: eBay; Oodle; Co-Founder, Product Leader Summit

1722 SPINDLETOP CAPITAL
7000 N Mopac Expy
Suite 315
Austin, TX 78731

Phone: 512-961-4633
e-mail: admin@spindletopcapital.com
web: www.spindletopcapital.com

Mission Statement: Spindletop Capital is a private equity and venture capital firm specializing in the healthcare industry.

Geographic Preference: United States
Founded: 2011
Average Investment: $10 - $50 million
Investment Criteria: Late Stage, Growth Equity, Expansion Capital
Industry Group Preference: Life Sciences, Healthcare Services, Healthcare Information Technology, Pharmaceuticals, Biopharmaceuticals, Medical Devices, Diagnostics
Portfolio Companies: Avanzar Medical, Bioventus, Castle Biosciences, Hospitalists Now, Navigating Cancer, QSpex Technologies

Key Executives:
   Dr Evan Melrose, Founding Managing Director
   Education: BA, University of Pennsylvania; MD, Indiana University School of Medicine; MBA, Wharton School
   Background: Founding Managing Director, PTV Sciences; Director, Burrill & Company
   Directorships: Texas Business Hall of Fame Foundation
   Steve Whitlock, Managing Director
   Education: BS, Mechanical Engineering, Texas A&M University; MBA, Embry-Riddle Aeronautical University
   Background: Co-Founder, Path4 Ventures; Operating Venture Partner, PTV Sciences; Co-Founder, Spinal Restoration; President, LDR Spine USA; Centerpulse Orthopedics
   Directorships: Spinal Restoration, Ortho Kinematics

Venture Capital & Private Equity Firms / Domestic Firms

Dr Robert McDonald, Venture Partner
Education: MD, University of Texas Southwestern Medical School; MBA, Wharton School of Business, University of Pennsylvania
Background: President & Founder, Aledo Consulting; Anthem Blue Cross and Blue Shield; Eli Lilly & Company
Shannon Rothschild, Venture Partner
Education: BA, Tulane University; MBA, MHA, Indiana University
Background: Venture Partner, Heron Capital; Manager, Product Design & Development, Humana Inc.; RealMed; Anthem Alliance

1723 SPINNAKER CAPITAL PARTNERS
Southport, CT 06890

Phone: 203-255-8828
web: www.spinnakercapital.com

Mission Statement: Spinnaker Capital Partners LLC is a private equity fund investing in various equity and debt instruments in non-public small and middle market consumer oriented businesses.
Geographic Preference: Northeast Corridor, Boston to Washington DC
Investment Criteria: Leveraged Buyouts, Management Buyouts, Expansion Financing, Early-Stage Venture Rounds, Distressed Situations

1724 SPIRE CAPITAL PARTNERS
1500 Broadway
Suite 1811
New York, NY 10036

Phone: 212-218-5454 Fax: 212-218-5455
web: www.spirecapital.com

Mission Statement: An active and experienced private equity firm with an investment focus in small market companies within the business services, information services, media and communications sectors.
Geographic Preference: United States
Fund Size: $600 milion
Founded: 2000
Average Investment: $20 million
Minimum Investment: $15 million
Investment Criteria: Seed, Growth, Expansion, Later
Industry Group Preference: Media, Communications, Business Products & Services, Information Services, Education
Portfolio Companies: American Community Newspapers, Ariston Global, AssetNation, Carpathia Hosting, Certiport, Dynamic Quest, Encoda Systems, ERI Solutions, Highline Financial, Highline Media, Inflow Inc., iNNERHOST, Just Marketing International, Lighthouse, Nassau Broadcasting Partners LP, NetFortris, O2B Kids, On Campus Marketing, Patriot Media, Performance Assessment Network Inc., Professional Bull Riders, Rainbow Child Care Centre, SkyMall, Sonitrol Inc., Surgent Professional Education, Tarpon Towers, Trax Group, Vector Media, Velocity, Vivax
Other Locations:
Five Tower Bridge
300 Barr Harbor Drive
Suite 400
Conshohocken, PA 19428
Phone: 610-397-1700
Key Executives:
Andrew J. Armstrong. Jr., Partner
Education: AB, Economics, Duke University
Background: Co-Founder, Waller-Sutton Media Partners; President, Waller Capital Corporation; Philadelphia National Bank and Manufacturers Hanover Trust
Bruce M. Hernandez, Partner
e-mail: bhernandez@spirecapital.com
Education: BS, University of Vermont; MBA, New York University
Background: Co-Founder & CEO, Waller-Sutton Media Partners; CFO, Horizon Cellular Group
Directorships: Certiport, Just Marketing International, Nassau Broadcasting Partners
Sean C. White, Partner
e-mail: swhite@spirecapital.com
Education: BS, Binghamton University; MBA, New York University
Background: Vice Presdient, Waller-Sutton Media Partners; Waller Capital Corporation
Directorships: Carpathia Hosting, SalvageSale, Certiport, SkyMall
David K. Schaible, Partner
e-mail: dschaible@spirecapital.com
Education: BS, Indiana University
Background: Financial Analyst, Bear Stearns & Co
Directorships: Ariston Global, Just Marketing International, PBR
Donald E. Stewart, Chief Financial/Compliance Officer
e-mail: dstewart@spirecapital.com
Education: BS, Accounting, Widener University
Background: CFO, Iron Oak Development; CFO/COO, Specialty Brands; Regional Controller, Wawa Food Markets
Directorships: On Campus Marketing

1725 SPLIT ROCK PARTNERS
16526 West 78th St.
Suite 504
Eden Prairie, MN 55346

Phone: 952-995-7474 Fax: 952-995-7475
web: www.splitrock.com

Mission Statement: A venture capital firm dedicated to building productive partnerships with entrepreneurs who have the vision and ability to create companies of enduring value.
Geographic Preference: West Coast
Fund Size: $750 million
Founded: 1988
Average Investment: $1-$10 million
Minimum Investment: $1 million
Investment Criteria: Seed, First-stage, Second-stage, Mezzanine
Industry Group Preference: Information Technology, Healthcare, Consumer Services, Retailing, Service Industries, Manufacturing, Life Sciences, Software, Internet, Medical Devices, Enterprise Software, Business Products & Services
Portfolio Companies: Acquia, Adaytum, AmCom, Anuluex Technologies, Ardian, Aritech, Auxilium, Bigcommerce, Bigfix, Black Duck, BlueKai, Calabrio, Calix, Caring.com, Cayenna Medical, Code42, Colorescience, Compete, DemandBase, DexCom, DFine, EBR Systems, eBureau, Entellus Medical, Evalve, Flycast, ForSight Newco II, Gravie, Guardian Analytics, Help Systems, HighJump, HireRight, Histogenics, Holaira, Ideas, InsideView, Intacct, Internet Broadcasting, Janrain, Kspine, Lawson, LowerMyBills, MyNewPlace, Net Perceptions, NextCard, Novologix, Nuvaira, Prometheus Laboratories, Quin Street, RF Surgical, Santarus, Sentillion, SkinMedica, Snagajob, Sonoma Orthpedic, Spanlink, Sparkcentral, Spine-Tech, SPS Commerce, Tarsus Medical, Tornier, Transcend Medical, TruSignal, Twelve, Vendavo, Volo Metrix, Vormetric, Xora, Zyga Technology
Key Executives:
Michael Gorman, Managing Partner
e-mail: michael@splitrock.com
Education: BA Economics/Public Policy, Duke University; MBA/JD, Harvard University
Background: Harvard Management Company; Bain & Co
Directorships: Adaytum Software, Auxilium, Bravanta, HighJump Software, IDeaS, Information Advantage, Lawson Software, Net Perceptions, Optical Solutions, SPS Commerce, Vendavo, XIOtech
Dave Stassen, Managing Director
e-mail: dave@splitrock.com

Education: Graduate, University of St. Thomas
Background: Spine-Tech; North Star Ventures; IBM
Directorships: Ancillary Care Management, Atritech, Avecor, Avera Pharmaceuticals, Converge Medical, DexCom, Disc Dynamics, Evalve, GeoDigm MiraMedica, Myocor, Sinus Rhythm Technologies
James R Simons, Managing Director
952-995-7488
e-mail: jim@splitrock.com
Education: BA, Economics, History, Stanford University; MBA, JL Kellogg Graduate School of Management of Northwestern University
Background: General Partner, Marquette Venture Partners; Associate, Trammell Crow Compnay; Analyst First Boston Corporation
Directorships: Aleri, BigFix, CarParts Technologies, Command Audio, Compete, Ecast, firstRain, Flycast Communications, HireRight, Internet Broadcasting, Lexar Media, LowerMyBills, NEW
Josh Baltzell, Venture Partner
e-mail: josh@splitrock.com
Education: St. Olaf College; MBA, University of Minnesota Carlson School of Management
Background: Principal, St. Paul Venture Capital; Vice President, Piper Jaffray
Steve Schwen, Chief Financial Officer
e-mail: steve@splitrock.com
Education: BA, Business Administration/Accounting, University of St. Thomas
Background: CFO, St. Paul Venture Capital; KPMG LLP

1726 SPP CAPITAL
550 Fifth Avenue
12th Floor
New York, NY 10036

Phone: 212-455-4500
web: www.sppcapital.com

Mission Statement: Dedicated to the proposition that every client is entitled to the highest standard of service: to execute every transaction in a diligent, comprehensive manner; to demonstrate integrity and vigilance in representing the best client interests; to exercise leadership and promote ethical standards in the securities industry; to assure clients achieve terms and conditions which reflect aggressive pricing and flexible structures.

Founded: 1989
Portfolio Companies: ACCT Holdings, Ambient Air, Angelle, Blueberry Broadcasting, EServices, Industrial Piping, Island Oasis, TCSC, Tulsa Inspection Resources, Wholesale Floors
Key Executives:
  Robin Ellis Busch, Managing Partner
  212-455-4504
  e-mail: rbusch@sppcapital.com
  Education: Graduate, New York University
  Background: Bankers Trust
  Stefan L Shaffer, Co-Founder/Managing Partner
  212-455-4502
  e-mail: sshaffer@sppcapital.com
  Education: JD, Cornell Law School; Graduate, Colgate University
  Background: Bankers Trust Company; White & Case; White House Intern
  Amy S Lazarus, Chief Operating Officer
  212-455-45115
  e-mail: alazarus@sppcapital.com
  Education: MBA Finance, Columbia Graduate School of Business; BS Business Administration, University of Vermont
  Background: Bankers Trust Company; CPA, Arthur Andersen
  C Todd Kumble, Managing Partner
  212-455-4508
  e-mail: tkumble@sppcapital.com

Education: BA, Yale University; MBA, Wharton School
Background: Home Box Office; Allen Group Inc; Manufacturers Hanover
John Cable, Partner
Education: BA, Economics & Art History, Stanford University; MBA, Amos Tuck School of Business Administration
Background: Corporate Finance Positions at Nike, Coach; Investment Banking Analyst,

1727 SPRING CAPITAL PARTNERS LP
The Foxleigh Building, Suite 340
2330 W Joppa Road
Lutherville-Timonium, MD 21093

Phone: 410-685-8000 Fax: 410-545-0015
web: www.springcap.com

Mission Statement: Spring Capital's mission is to contribute to the success of small and medium-sized businesses by providing mezzanine financing, and critical component of investment capital for growing companies.

Geographic Preference: Eastern United States
Fund Size: $75 million
Founded: 1999
Average Investment: $2 - $7 million
Minimum Investment: $2 million
Investment Criteria: Expansion, Acquisition, LBO, MBO, Recapitalization
Industry Group Preference: Technology, Communications, Business to Business
Portfolio Companies: Cybera, Cyberpoint, Dermatology Associates of Tyler, Enefco, eServices, GI Plastek, HomeCentric Healthcare, iPacesetters, Jawbone, MC MC, Monster Media, Numet Machining Techniques, Portadam, PSS, Quantem, QuantumClean, Swiss Farms, Tzetzo Bros., Xand

Other Locations:
170 N Radnor Chester Road
Suite 101
Radnor, PA 19087
Phone: 610-964-7972

Key Executives:
  Robert M. Stewart, Co-Founder/General Partner
  e-mail: rms@springcap.com
  Education: Graduate, Hampden-Sydney College; MBA, Wake Forest University
  Background: Armata; Cross Hill Financial; Legg Mason; Board Service, DIGEX/Cidera/Network Technologies Group
  Michael F. Donoghue, Co-Founder/General Partner
  e-mail: mfd@springcap.com
  Education: Graduate, Georgetown University; MBA, University of Virginia
  Background: Corestates
  Directorships: MathSoft Engineering and Education, Vocollect
  John C. Acker, General Partner
  e-mail: jca@springcap.com
  Education: Gettysburg College
  Background: Vice President, Capital Markets Group, Allfirst Bank
  Peter B. Orthwein, Jr., General Partner
  e-mail: pbo@springcap.com
  Education: BS, MBA, Cornell University
  Background: Priceline.com, Starwood Hotels & Resorts Worldwide, Brooks, Houghton & Company
  Brian C. McDaid, General Partner
  e-mail: bcm@springcap.com
  Education: Haverford College; CFA
  Background: Navigant Capital Advisors, KPMG Corp. Finance

Venture Capital & Private Equity Firms / Domestic Firms

1728 SPRING LAKE EQUITY PARTNERS
125 High St.
Suite 2211
Boston, MA 02110

Phone: 617-391-6300 **Fax:** 617-391-6390
e-mail: info@springlep.com
web: springlakeequitypartners.com

Mission Statement: Spring Lake Equity Partners is a Boston-based private equity firm. We invest equity capital primarily in later-stage, technology-oriented companies. Our investment philosophy is simple and has remained consistent over time - we seek to partner with great management teams to take their businesses to the next level, creating value for all stakeholders. Spring Lake strives to add value to our portfolio companies through active Board participation and accessing our network of contacts which includes our own and those of our key strategic partners, WestRiver Equity Partners, Tudor Investment Corp., and the George Kaiser Family Foundation.

Founded: 2013
Average Investment: $7-$15 million
Investment Criteria: Later-Stage Growth Equity, Recapitalizations, Acquisitions
Industry Group Preference: Software, Digital Media & Marketing, Mobile, Data Center, Healthcare Information Technology, Business & Financial Services
Portfolio Companies: Adaptive Computing, Advanced Fibre Communication, Allegro Development Corp, Arcsoft, Art Technology Group, Aspect Ratio, Assistive Technologies, Astadia, Avici Systems, Batanga, Benu Networks, Brio Technology, Captura Software, Chordiant Software, Classic Sports Network, Crossbeam Systems, Digital Island, Dorado, Fidelis Security Systems, Force10 Networks, Gain Capital Group, Global Cash Access, Gravy Analytics, Gray Peak Technologies, Icom Cmt, InsideView, Intelligrated, International Components, Lightspeed Financial, Matrixx, Mediamath, Mediaplatform, Meteor Learning, N2 Broadband, N2K, Neocera, Netbase Solutions, Netprospex, Observeit, One Door, Plated, Remedy Partners, Roberts Radio, Shoebuy, Single Digits, SmarterHQ, Sqrrl, Switch & Data Facilities, Thorne Research, TractManager, Transmeta Corporation, Transwitch, Turbine, Vantage Media, Vantrix Corporation, Velocity Technology Solutions, Virtify, Vurv Technology, Wavelink Corporation, Wimba, Wired Ventures

Key Executives:
Bob Forlenza, Managing Partner
Education: BS, Accounting & Business Administration, Washington & Lee University; MBA, Harvard Business School
Background: Managing Partner, Tudor Investment Corporation; Vice President, Carlisle Capital; Executive, American Management Company; Management Consultant, Bain & Company
Directorships: Virtify, Allegro Development, Thorne Research
Carmen Scarpa, Managing Partner
Education: BA, Economics, Harvard University; MBA, Harvard Business School
Background: Partner, Tudor Investment Corporation; Associate, Triumph Capital Group; Corporate Finance Analyst, Drexel Burnham Lambert
Directorships: Batanga
Dan MacKeigan, Partner
Education: BS, Biology, Trinity College
Background: Partner, Tutor Investment Corporation; Vice President and Senior Public Equity Research Analyst, Friedman, Billings, Ramsey; Financial Consultant, Zurich Investments
Directorships: Vantage, Vantrix, ArcSoft
Jeff Williams, Partner
Education: BA, History, Yale University; MBA, MIT Sloan School of Management
Background: Partner, Tudor Investment Corporation; Associate, Downer & Company; Strategic Consultant, Oplab; Financial Analyst, Fox-Pitt, Kelton Ltd.
Directorships: Single Digits, Thorne Research, Virtify

1729 SPRING LANE CAPITAL
50 Milk St.
16th Floor
Boston, MA 02109

Phone: 514-761-4150
e-mail: info@springlanecapital.com
web: www.springlanecapital.com

Mission Statement: Spring Lane Capital partners with strong management teams who are involved in creating sustainable solutions in the energy, water, food and waste sectors.
Industry Group Preference: Environment, Sustainability, Water, Waste & Recycling, Food & Beverage, Energy, Renewable Energy
Other Locations:
1200 Ave. McGill College
Sutie 1100
Montreal, QC H3B 4G7
Canada

Key Executives:
Christian Zabbal, Managing Partner
Education: MBA, McGill University
Background: Managing Partner, Black Coral Capital; Partner, ghSMART & Company
Rob Day, General Partner
Education: BA, Swarthmore College; MBA, Kellogg School of Management
Background: Consultant, Bain & Company
Directorships: New England Clean Energy Council
Nikhil Garg, General Partner
Education: BS, Stanford University; MBA, MIT Sloan School of Management
Background: Partner, Black Coral Capital; Climate Change Capital; Core Carbon Group; Bain & Company

1730 SPRING MOUNTAIN CAPITAL
650 Madison Avenue
20th Floor
New York, NY 10022

Phone: 212-292-8300
web: www.springmountaincapital.com

Mission Statement: Spring Mountain Capital's private equity group focuses on providing growth capital to small companies in both active co-investment and lead capacities.
Founded: 2001
Investment Criteria: All Stages
Industry Group Preference: All Sectors Considered
Portfolio Companies: Applied Genetics, Alphatec, Aton Pharma, BAWAG, BHS Specialty Chemical Products, Chrysler Holdings, Cleaire Advanced Emissions Control, Coolerado Corporation, Eletrobras, Foresight Reserves, Giga-Tronics, GlucoVista, GreenMan Technologies, IRON Solutions, MedAvante, Outrigger Media, Patriot National Bancorp, Perquest, Powermat, Perffered Pet Care, Whip Tail Technologies

Key Executives:
Raymond L.M. Wong, Managing Director/Head of Growth Equity
Education: BA, Political Science, Yale College; MBA, Harvard Business School
Background: Managing Director, Merrill Lynch & Co.; Managing Member, DeFee Lee Pond Capital
Directorships: Alleghany Corporation, Merrill Lynch Ventures
Jamie Weston, Managing Director
Education: BA, Economics, Drew University; MBA, Fordham University
Background: Partner, The Wicks Group of Companies; IBJ Whitehall Bank & Trust; National Wesmnister Bancorp

Venture Capital & Private Equity Firms / Domestic Firms

John L Steffens, Founder/Senior Managing Director
Education: BA, Economics, Dartmouth College
Background: President, Consumer Markets, Merrill Lynch & Co.
Directorships: Colony Financial, Cicero
Gregory P Ho, President
Education: BS, Administrative Science, Yale College; JD, Columbia Law School
Background: Principal/CFO, McKinsey & Company; Donovan Leisure Newton & Irvine

1731 SR ONE LTD
161 Washington Street
Suite 500
Eight Tower Bridge
Conshohocken, PA 19428

Phone: 610-567-1000 Fax: 610-567-1039
web: www.srone.com

Mission Statement: Invest globally in early-stage healthcare companies pursuing innovative, breakthrough science. Their expanded remit also focuses on maximizing the value of GSK technological innovation to establish new businesses and revenue opportunities.

Geographic Preference: North America, Europe
Fund Size: $560 million
Founded: 1985
Average Investment: $5-8 million
Minimum Investment: $100,000
Investment Criteria: Seed, Startup, First-Stage, Second-Stage, Mezzanine, LBO
Industry Group Preference: Medical & Health Related, Biotechnology
Portfolio Companies: AGTC, Aileron, Arcellx, Asceneuron, Ato Bio, AvhanaHealth, Bicycle Therapeutics, Bird Rock Bio, CalciMedica, Constellation Pharmaceuticals, Crispr Therapeutics, Decibel Therapeutics, Dicerna Pharmeceuticals, eFFECTOR, F-Star, Genocea, Gladius Pharmaceuticals, Gotham Therapeutics, HTG, Illuminoss, Macrolide Pharmaceuticals, Mission Therapeutics, Morphic Therapeutic, Navitor Pharmaceuticals, Nimbus Therapeutics, Nkarta Therapeutics, Palleon Pharmaceuticals, Pandion Therapeutics, Princepa Biopharma, Princeps Therapeutics, Progyny, Propeller, PSIOxus, Pulmocide, Scynexis, Second Genome, Spero Therapeutics, TP Therapeutics, Tranquis Therapeutics Inc., TranslateBio, VHsquared, ZappPx

Other Locations:
One Broadway
Cambridge, MA 02142
Phone: 610-567-1000

29 Farm Street
Office # 3.10
London W1J5RL
United Kingdom
Phone: 44-2080472610

1700 Owens Street
San Francisco, CA 94158
Phone: 610-567-1000

Key Executives:
Rajeev Dadoo, Partner
Education: BA, Chemistry & Mathematics, Knox College; PhD, Chemistry, Stanford University; MBA, The Wharton School of Business
Background: Genentech; BioRad; Unimicro Technologies
Simeon J. George, Partner
Education: BA, Neuroscience, Johns Hopkins University; MBA, Wharton School of Business; MD, University of Pennsylvania, School of Medicine
Background: Consultant, Bain & Company; Investment Banking, Goldman Sachs; Merrill Lynch
Directorships: Anaphore
Matthew Foy
Education: BA, Molecular Biology/Genetics/Statistics, Univeristy of Oxford; Corporate Finance, London Business School; Drug Discovery, University College London
Background: Greenhill & Co

1732 SSM PARTNERS
Triad III Building
6070 Poplar Avenue
Suite 560
Memphis, TN 38119

Phone: 901-767-1131
web: www.ssmpartners.com

Mission Statement: To invest in private companies distinguished by exceptional management, a unique business model and prospects for high growth: We view each investment as a partnership with management in developing a successful business. SSM invests in Internet businesses, typically software solutions and business-to-business e-commerce, high technology, telecommunications and other business service companies.

Geographic Preference: Southeastern United States, Texas
Fund Size: $250 million
Founded: 1973
Average Investment: $5-$20 million
Minimum Investment: $3 million
Investment Criteria: High growth companies with proven business models. Companies typically have $10 million of revenue and are profitable at the point of investment.
Industry Group Preference: Technology-Enabled Businesses, Healthcare Services, Business Products & Services, Consumer Services
Portfolio Companies: Bulldog Solutions, Complete Holdings Group, Connecture, FrontStream Payments, HealthTeacher, Ifbyphone, New Era Portfolio, OpinionLab, RemitDATA

Key Executives:
James D Witherington Jr, Advisory Partner
Education: BA Economics, Vanderbilt University; MBA, University of Chicago
Background: SSM Since 1973
Directorships: Plan Express; DataCert
R Wilson Orr III, Managing Partner
Education: BA Economics/Business Administration, Vanderbilt University
Background: JP Morgan
Directorships: Kirkland's, All Web Leads; Bulldog Solutions; Chronicity
Casey West, Managing Partner
Education: BA, History, Virginia Military Institute; MBA, Harvard Business School
Background: Petra Capital; Donaldson, Lufkin & Genrette (DLJ)
Directorships: FrontStream Payments; RemitDATA
Hunter Witherington, Managing Partner
Education: BA, Economics, Vanderbilt University
Background: Stephens, Inc.

1733 STAENBERG VENTURE PARTNERS
308 9th Avenue N
Seattle, WA 98109

Phone: 206-264-0784
e-mail: info@staenberg.com
web: www.staenberg.com

Mission Statement: Staenberg Ventures is a Seattle-based firm focused on venture capital funding, strategic consulting and entrepreneurship in the technology, business social media, and consumer products arenas. By leveraging an extensive partner network in the Silicon Valley, the Pacific Northwest, New York and South America, our firm provides a unique and important bridge between these business centers.

Geographic Preference: Silicon Valley, Pacific Northwest, New York, South America

Venture Capital & Private Equity Firms / Domestic Firms

Industry Group Preference: Communications, Network Infrastructure & Security, Business Products & Services, Software, Consumer Services, Medical Technology
Portfolio Companies: Airbiquity, Aprimo, Business.com, Care2, CaseCentral, Command Audio, Corrigo, ENA, ezboard, Lydian Trust, Mimio, mInfo, NapaStyle, New Vine Logistics, PAR3, Prime Advantage, Revenue Science, Salu, Seagate, SquareTrade, StubHub, Syncronex, Time Domain, VetCentric, Vista

Key Executives:
Jon Staenberg, Managing Partner
e-mail: jon@staenberg.com
Education: BS, MS, MBA, Stanford University
Directorships: Hand of God Wines

1734 STAGE 1 VENTURES
890 Winter Street
Suite 208
Waltham, MA 02451

Phone: 781-772-1010 **Fax:** 941-847-7121
e-mail: info@stage1ventures.com
web: www.stage1ventures.com

Mission Statement: Stage 1 Ventures works hard every day to earn its reputation as a quality partner for visionary entrepreneurs who date to innovate, challenge and fundamentally change the dynamics of new and existing markets.

Geographic Preference: Mid-Atlantic Region
Investment Criteria: Early-Stage
Industry Group Preference: Mobile, Internet, SaaS, Internet Technology, Marketing, Advertising, Security
Portfolio Companies: Paydiant, Marxent, AdelaVoice, OnePIN, Connect Towers, dondeEsta, xPeerient, Veloxum, Innerpass, Carbonite, Nimbit, Myxer, Zapoint, Interactive Television, Magnify.net, Parelastic, Deep, Dashbell, Vivox, Flashnotes, Nexercise, PhantomAlert, Autonet Mobile, Openbay, PureCars, Carvoyant, Maple Farm Media, InStream Media, OwnerIQ, Myxer, Promoboxx, Ditto, Mobee, Sitewit, Coherent Path, shareThat, LocusPlay, Delfigo Security, DropFire, Wing Power Energy, Banshee Wines, Newburyport Brewing Company, Glanola

Other Locations:
5580 La Jolla Boulevard
Unit 80
La Jolla, CA 92037
Phone: 650-336-3778

2F 242 Yang-Guang Street
NeiHu, Taipei 11491
Taiwan
Phone: 886-975726772

Key Executives:
David William Baum, Managing Director
e-mail: dwbaum@stage1ventures.com
Education: BS, Computer Science, Drexel University; MBA, Harvard Business School
Background: Founder, Pensoft Corporation; Manager, Prism Venture Partners
Jonathan Gordon, Managing Director
e-mail: jgordon@stage1ventures.com
Background: Founder, Ametron Technologies; CEO, mGen; CEO & Founder, EndPoints

1735 STARBOARD CAPITAL PARTNERS
30 Jelliff Lane
Southport, CT 06890

Phone: 203-259-8855 **Fax:** 203-259-8287
web: www.starboardcapital.net

Mission Statement: A financial sponsor that initiates, finances and partners with management and private equity investors in the acquisition of companies with enterprise values of $20 million to $250 million.

Fund Size: $85 million
Founded: 2004
Average Investment: $1,750,000
Minimum Investment: $500,000
Industry Group Preference: Biotechnology, Computer Related, Electronic Technology, Energy, Industrial Equipment, Real Estate, Natural Resources, Automotive, Consumer Products, Building Materials & Services, Construction, Distribution, E-Commerce & Manufacturing, Manufacturing, Healthcare
Portfolio Companies: Apothecare LLC, CV Properties LLC, JPC Holdings LLC, PureRED, PursueCare LLC, TheraPlay

Key Executives:
Dean E Fenton, Managing Member/Chairman
Education: Harvard College; Graduate School of Business at Columbia University; Officer, USAF
Background: Founding Partner, Prime Capital Management Company; General Partner, Sprout Group
Marc C Bergschneider, Managing Member
Education: AB, Brown University; MBA, University of Chicago
Background: CEO/Chairman, National Fairways; Managing Partner, New Charleston Capital; Managing Director, Lehman Brothers
Directorships: Brown University Sports Foundation; National Rowing Foundation
Peter H Smith Jr, Managing Director
e-mail: pjs@starboardcapital.net
Education: Middlebury College
Background: President & Founder, Canwell Capital; Birinyi Associates, Vice President, Bear Stearns
Brian E Stern, Operating Partner
e-mail: brians@starboardcapital.net
Education: University of East Anglia, Norwich England; Harvard University Graduate School of Business
Background: Director, ESP; Director, HNI Corporation; Senior Vice President, Xerox Corporation; Chief Strategy Officer, President, Office Document Products; President, Xerox Technology Enterprisees

1736 START GARDEN
e-mail: hello@startgarden.com
web: www.startgarden.com

Mission Statement: Start Garden invests $5,000 in a new idea each week. At the $50,000-$500,000 level of an investment, Start Garden works closely with their entrepreneurs to help identify new business models and develop their people and network. Start Garden offers an alternative experience to the traditional venture capital firms.

Fund Size: $15 million
Founded: 2012
Average Investment: $5,000
Minimum Investment: $5,000
Industry Group Preference: Diversified
Portfolio Companies: Hip Shot Dot, Varsity News Network, GinkgoTree, GreenLancer, IMSRV, Local Orbit, FetchNotes, NxtMile Sports Insoles, Blue Medora, Chalkfly, Breakup Goods, Benefit, Ambassador, Sol, EXO, Conpoto, Xcess Able, Alsentis, Eidex Education Analytics, VerifyValid, Silikids

Key Executives:
Rick DeVos, Founder & CEO
e-mail: rick@startgarden.com
Paul Moore, Director
e-mail: paul@startgarden.com
Mike Morin, Director
e-mail: mike@startgarden.com

1737 STARTUP CAPITAL VENTURES
535 Middlefield Road
Suite 280
Menlo Park, CA 94025

Phone: 650-461-8100
web: www.startupcapitalventures.com

Venture Capital & Private Equity Firms / Domestic Firms

Mission Statement: To build a supportive partnership around an outstanding entrepreneurial team, with a clear market vision for its product or service. To focus on investing in strong management teams, not just technologies. To strive to help build companies based on proven principals of integrity, patience and flexibility.

Geographic Preference: Silicon Valley, Hawaii, Texas, Oklahoma, China
Average Investment: $250,000 - $1 million
Investment Criteria: Early-Stage
Industry Group Preference: Software
Portfolio Companies: Adama Materials, AGIS, Attainia, Central Pacific Bank, Dali Wireless Systems, DeviceVM, Switchfly, TagArray, Think Finance, TuneIn, WhiteHat Security, Winery Exchange, Xignite, Zero2IPO

2800 Woodlawn Drive
Suite 156
Honolulu, HI 96822
Phone: 808-202-2538

Key Executives:
John C Dean, Managing Partner
Background: CEO, Silicon Valley Bank; Managing Director, Tupetele Ventures Fund; Investment Director, Advanced Technology Ventures; Walden International; Authosis Capital
Timothy Dick, Managing Partner
Education: BS, Electrical Engineering, University of California, Irvine; MBA, Stanford University
Background: Founder, Hawaii Superferry; Co-Founder, Grassroots.com; Founder, WorldPages.com; Principal, Boston Consulting Group
Directorships: Adama Materials, Dali Wireless, TRUSTe, Silvertail Systems, TagArray, RadioTime, Hawaii Superferry
Bob Rees, Venture Partner
Education: BA, Business, Principia College; MBA, New York University Stern School of Business
Background: Special Limited Partner, Woodside Fund; Access Venture Partners
Directorships: WhiteHat Security, Xignite

1738 STARVEST PARTNERS
650 Madison Avenue
20th Floor
New York, NY 10022
Phone: 212-863-2500 **Fax:** 212-863-2520
e-mail: info@starvestpartners.com
web: www.starvestpartners.com

Mission Statement: To invest in technology-enabled business services companies at the expansion stage.

Geographic Preference: United States
Fund Size: $150 million (Fund I) and $245 million (Fund II)
Average Investment: $5 million
Minimum Investment: $2 million
Investment Criteria: 2nd, 3rd, 4th Institutional Rounds
Industry Group Preference: Electronic Technology, Business to Business, Enterprise Services, Software
Portfolio Companies: Accept Software, AppDirect, Bluestreak, Ceros, Connected, CrowdTwist, Fieldglass, Host Analytics, iCrossing, Ideeli, Insurance.com, Iron Solutions, Mazu Networks, MessageOne, NetSuite, NewComLink, Newgistics, Outrigger, PeopleMatter, Perquest, PivotLink, PrecisionDemand, RAMP, Receivables Exchange, RetailNet, Switchfly, Take the Interview, Transactis, Travora Media, UrbanBound, Veracode, Xignite

Key Executives:
Laura Belle Sachar, Co-Founder/Managing Partner
e-mail: laura@starvestpartners.com
Education: BA, Barnard College; Columbia University; MBA, Columbia University Graduate School of Business
Background: Gabelli Securities; Founder, Sachar Capital; Founding Chairman, NYNMA Angel Investors Program; Associate Editor, Financial World magazine; Financial Analyst, Prudential Securities
Directorships: Newgistics, Ideeli, Veracode
Jeanne Mariani Sullivan, Co-Founder
212-863-2530
e-mail: jeanne@starvestpartners.com
Education: BS, University of Illinois; JD, Creighton University
Background: Managing Director, Olivetti Ventures; Managing Director, 4C Ventures; AT&T; Product Director, Bell Laboratories; Business Marketing/Production Director, Bozell Worldwide
Directorships: Iron Solutions, Transactis
Deborah A Farrington, Co-Founder/Managing Partner
Education: Smith College; MBA, Harvard Business School
Background: President/CEO, Victory Ventures; Senior Executive, Asian Oceanic Group; Merrill Lynch & Co
Directorships: NetSuite, Fieldglass, Insurance.com, Pivot Link, Host Analytics
Robert E Kelly, Chief Financial Officer
e-mail: bob@starvestpartners.com
Education: BBA, Manhattan College; MBA, Baruch College; CPA
Background: Senior VP Strategic Planning, Paradyme Human Resources Corporation; CFO, Hertz Corporation; Audit Manager, PricewaterhouseCoopers

1739 STARWOOD CAPITAL GROUP LLC
1601 Washington Avenue
Suite 800
Miami Beach, FL 33139
Phone: 305-695-5200
web: www.starwoodcapital.com

Mission Statement: Starwood Capital Group is a privately held investment management firm that specializes in real estate related investments on behalf of select private and institutional investor partners. It aligns its interests with those of its investment partners, placing its own capital at risk on every transaction and receiving returns only when its partners receive theirs.

Fund Size: $6.5 billion
Founded: 1991
Average Investment: $10-$100 million
Minimum Investment: $5 million
Investment Criteria: Seed, First-stage, Second-stage, Mezzanine
Industry Group Preference: Real Estate, Hotels, Property Management, Industrial Equipment

Other Locations:
100 Pine Street
Suite 3000
San Francisco, CA 94111
Phone: 415-247-1220

One East Wacker Drive
Suite 2600
Chicago, IL 60601-1927

Starwood Asset Management
400 Galleria Parkway
Suite 1450
Atlanta, GA 30339
Phone: 770-541-9046

1255 23rd Street NW
Suite 650
Washington, DC 20037
Phone: 202-507-6710

11601 Wilshire Blvd
Suite 420
Los Angeles, CA 90025
Phone: 310-893-2781

1 Eagle Place
2nd Floor
London SW1Y 6AF

Venture Capital & Private Equity Firms / Domestic Firms

United Kingdom
Phone: 44-2070163650

2-4, rue Eugene Ruppert
Luxembourg L-2453
Luxembourg
Phone: 352-26645121

Beechavenue 54
Schiphol-Rijk 1119 PW
The Netherlands
Phone: 31-206586520

Starwood Capital Asia
Somptueux Central, 20/F
52-54 Wellington Street
Hong Kong
Phone: 852-3792-0349

Key Executives:
Barry S. Sternlicht, Chairman & CEO
Education: BA, Brown University, MBA, Harvard Business School
Background: i Star Financial
Jeffrey G. Dishner, Senior Managing Director/Global Head, Real Estate Acquisitions
e-mail: dishner@starwood.com
Education: BA Economics, Wharton School; MBA, Amos Tuck School, Dartmouth
Background: Commercial Mortgage Finance Group JP Morgan; JMB Realty Corporation
Madison F. Grose, Senior Managing Director/Co-General Counsel
e-mail: grosem@starwood.com
Education: BS, Stanford University; JD, University of California, LA
Background: Senior Partner, Pircher Nichols & Meek
Directorships: i Star Financial
Christopher D. Graham, Managing Director/Head, Real Estate Acquisitions for the Americas
Education: BBA, Finance, James Madison University; MBA, Harvard Business School
Background: Director, Financial Consulting Group, CB Richards Ellis
Ellis F. Rinaldi, Senior Managing Director/Co-General Counsel
e-mail: rinaldi@starwood.com
Education: JD, Georgetown University; BA Accounting, University of Massachusetts
Background: Winthrop Stimson Putnam & Roberts; Pircher Nichold & Meeks
Directorships: RFF
Laura M. Rubin, Managing Director/Head, Portfolio Management
Education: BS, Economics, Wharton School; MBA, Kellogg School of Management
Background: VP, Goldman Sachs; JMB Realty; Urban Development Corp.

1740 STATELINE ANGELS
Rockford, IL

web: www.statelineangels.com

Mission Statement: Stateline Angels is an Angel investor organization that provides investment capital to start-up and early stage companies. Members who choose to invest may also lend their operational experience to enhance the chance of success to the ventures. We are dedicated to fostering growth in the Stateline area and upper Midwest region by assisting individuals in the development of successful businesses.

Geographic Preference: Midwest
Founded: 2004
Investment Criteria: Early-Stage
Industry Group Preference: Biotechnology, Business Products & Services, Computers & Peripherals, Peripherals, Consumer Products, Electronics, Financial Services, Energy, Information Technology, Medical Devices, Networking, Retailing, Distribution, Semiconductors, Software
Portfolio Companies: 10X, LiftSeat Corporation, Bias Power, Advanced Diamond Technologies, Ratio, Traycer Systems, Lumec Control Products, IMCO Technologies, Akoya

1741 STEELPOINT CAPITAL PARTNERS
215 S Highway 101
Suite 211
Solana Beach, CA 92075

e-mail: info@steelpointcp.com
web: www.steelpointcp.com

Mission Statement: Steelpoint Capital invests in growing consumer companies in the health, wellness and fitness sectors. Headquartered in San Diego, CA, Steelpoint looks to partner with companies that possess authentic brands and clear opportunities for growth. Steelpoint's team draws on extensive operating and investment experience to provide value-added support to portfolio companies and their management teams.

Geographic Preference: Southern California
Industry Group Preference: Health & Wellness, Fitness
Portfolio Companies: Acorns, Bag Borrow or Steal, Boingo Wireless, GreatCall, Hookit, Hylete, Kidrobot, Matuse, Orion Telescopes & Binoculars, Sealand Natural Resources, Tasti D-Lite, SKLZ, X-1 Audio

Key Executives:
James Caccavo, Founder/Managing General Partner
Education: BS, Economics & Finance, University of Scranton
Background: Managing Director, Moore Capital Management's Private Equity Group

1742 STERLING PARTNERS
650 S Exeter Street
Suite 1000
Baltimore, MD 21202

Phone: 443-703-1700 **Fax:** 443-703-1750
web: www.sterlingpartners.com

Mission Statement: Sterling Partners focus is on distinctive or products, favorable prospects for growth, a sustainable advantage, predictable cash flow and low inventories that turn quickly. Favor non-cyclical industries that are least vulnerable to recession. Focuses on buyouts, venture capital and real estate.

Geographic Preference: United States, Northeast, Mid-Atlantic, Midwest
Fund Size: $700 million
Founded: 1983
Investment Criteria: EBITDA $5-25mm; majority ownership opportunity; strong fit with Sterling's industry experience; competitive advantage; distinctive product/service; superior industry fundamentals
Industry Group Preference: Direct Marketing, Education, Distribution, Manufacturing, Healthcare, Business Products & Services, Technology
Portfolio Companies: Adeptus Health, Ameritox, Ashworth, Brace Industrial Gorup, Conversant, Educate Online, Educate, Foundation Partners Group, Gem Mobile Treatment Services, Infilaw, Innotrac, IO, Kids Care Dental Group, Laureate International Universities, Livingston International, Longitude Licensing, Meritas, Optimer, Pingora Asset Management, Plattform Advertising, Progressus Therapy, Prospect Mortgage, Q-Centrix, Remedi Seniorcare, Results Physiotherapy, Savo, School of Rock, Spartan College of Aeronautics and Technology, Surgical Solutions, Susiecakes, Tribeca Flashpoint Media Arts Academy

Other Locations:
401 North Michigan Avenue
Suite 3300

Venture Capital & Private Equity Firms / Domestic Firms

Chicago, IL 60611
Phone: 312-465-7000 **Fax:** 312-465-7001

701 Brickell Avenue
Suite 1700
Miami, FL 33131
Phone: 305-808-2970 **Fax:** 305-808-2900

Key Executives:
Eric Becker, Co-Founder
e-mail: ebecker@sterlingpartners.com
Education: University of Chicago
Background: Tango Communications
Directorships: Ashworth, Avectra, Connections Academy, Optimer Brands, Progressus Therapy
Steven Taslitz, Co-Founder/Chairman
e-mail: staslitz@sterlingpartners.us
Education: BS Accountancy, University of Illinois
Directorships: Many Boards in which Sterling has invested, as well as Sterling Venture Partners (a venture capital fund) and Sterling Real Estate Partners
Christopher Hoehn-Saric, Co-Founder/Managing Director
e-mail: choehn-saric@sterlingpartners.com
Directorships: Connections Academy, Educate Online, Educate, i/o Data Centers, The InfiLaw System, Livingston International, Meritas, Smarterville
Doug Becker, Co-Founder/Managing Director
Background: Founder, Laureate Education Inc.; Chairman/CEO, Sylvan Learning Systems
Jeff Elburn, Managing Director
Education: BBA, Salisbury University
Background: Finance Principal, ABS Capital Partners
Alv Epstein, Managing Director
Education: BA, Political Science, Ohio State University; JD, Harvard Law School
Background: General Counsel/VP of Business Affairs, Kaplan Inc.; Corporate Attorney, Katten Michin Rosenman LLP
Jason Rosenberg, Managing Director
Education: BA, Northwestern University; JD, Northwestern University School of Law; MBA, Kellogg School of Management
Background: Found, Inc.
Directorships: Ashworth, Cornerstone, The Leman International School
Shoshana Vernick, Managing Director
Education: BS, Indiana University
Background: One Equity Partners, Razorfish
Directorships: School of Rock, Securenet, Progressus
Rick Elfman, Managing Director
Education: BA Economics/Political Science, Tufts University; MBA Finance, University of Chicago
Background: Institutional Sales, Goldman Sachs; Owned/Operated Chain of Pharmacies-Boston; Founder, Little Elves
Directorships: Numerous portfolio companies
Jeff Schechter, Senior Advisor
e-mail: jschechter@sterlingpartners.com
Education: BS, Accounting, University of Maryland; MS, Finance, Loyola University
Background: Grotech Capital Group, Ernst & Young

1743 STONE POINT CAPITAL LLC
20 Horseneck Lane
Greenwich, CT 06830

Phone: 203-862-2900
web: www.stonepointcapital.com

Mission Statement: Stone Point Capital is a private equity firm that makes investments in the global financial services industry.
Geographic Preference: United States
Fund Size: $3.5 billion
Founded: 1993
Average Investment: $50-250 million
Minimum Investment: $50 million
Investment Criteria: Startup, LBO, MBO
Industry Group Preference: Insurance, Financial Services
Portfolio Companies: Access Point Financial, AloStar Bank of Commerce, The ARC Group, Atrium Underwriting Group, C3/CustomerContactChannels, Citco III, Duff & Phelps, Eagle Point Credit Management, Enhanced Capital/Tree Line, Enstar Group, Freepoint Commodities, First Data Holdings, HCBF Holding Company, Hodges-Mace, Lancaster Pollard Holdings, LTCG, Merchant Capital Solutions, NEBCO Insurance Services, New Point IV/V/VI, New Ocean Capital Management, NXT Capital, Prima Capital Advisors, Standcard Bancshares, SKY Harbor Capital Management, SCS Financial Serices, Sedgwick, Torus Insurance Holdings, Trident V Credit Holdings, Verisight, Amberst Holdings, Asset Allocation & Management Company, Atlantic Capital Bancshares, Auction.com, Automobile Protection Coporation, Carlile Bancshares, Cunningham Lindsey Group Limited, Edgewood Partners Holdings, Grandpoint Capital, Higginbotham Insurance Agency, NXT Capital, OneWest Bank Group, Pierpoint Securities, StoneRiver Holdings, Symbion, Yadkin Financial, Preferred Concepts, Privilege Unerwriters, Vanbridge

Other Locations:
919 Third Avenue
30th Floor
New York, NY 10022
Phone: 203-862-2900

Key Executives:
Charles A. Davis, Chief Executive Officer
e-mail: CDavis@stonepoint.com
Education: BA, University of Vermont; MBA, Columbia University
Background: Investment Banking Services, Goldman, Sachs & Company
Directorships: AMS Services, AXIS Capital Holdings Limited, Sedgwick CMS Holdings, Media General, Merchants Bancshares, Progressive Corporation, MMC Capital Foundation
Kurt E. Bolin, Principal
e-mail: KBolin@stonepoint.com
Education: BS, Wake Forest University; MBA, Wharton School
Background: Managing Director, GE Capital
Directorships: BLC Holdings LLC
Stephen Friedman, Chairman
e-mail: SFriedman@stonepoint.com
Education: BA, Cornell University; LLB, Columbia Law School
Background: Goldman-Sachs & Co., Law Clerk
Directorships: Goldman-Sachs & Company
James D. Carey, Senior Principal
e-mail: JCarey@stonepoint.com
Education: BS, Boston College; JD, Boston College Law School; MBA, Duku University Fuqua School of Business
Background: Associate, Merrill Lynch & Co.; Corporate Attorney, Kelley Drye & Warren LLP
Directorships: Asset Allocation & Management Company, Cunningham Lindsey Group Limited, Lane McVicker, Locton International Holdings Limited, Privilege Underwriters
David J. Wermuth, Senior Principal & General Counsel
e-mail: DWermuth@stonepoint.com
Education: BA, Yale University; MBA, New York University Stern School of Business; JD, Cornell Law School
Background: Corporate Attorney, Cleary Gottlieb Steen & Hamilton LLP; Auditor, KPMG Peat Marwick
Directorships: Amherst Holdings, Asset Allocation & Management Company, Edgewood Partners Holdings, OneWest Bank Group, StoneRiver Holdings
Nicolas D. Zerbib, Senior Principal
e-mail: nzerbib@stonepoint.com
Education: BA, Amherst College; MBA, Harvard Graduate School of Business Administration

Venture Capital & Private Equity Firms / Domestic Firms

Background: Analyst, Goldman Sachs & Co.; Catamount Capital Management; Boston Consulting Group
Darran A. Baird, Principal
e-mail: dbaird@stonepoint.com
Education: BA, Stanford University
Background: Deputy Head of Strategic Development, Marsh & McLennan Companies; Managing Director, Securitas Capital; Associate, Smith Barney
Christopher M. Doody, Principal
e-mail: Cdoody@stonepoint.com
Education: BA, Middlebury College; MBA, Columbia University Graduate School of Business
Background: Analyst, Merrill Lynch & Co.
Directorships: GENEX Services
Richard A. Goldman, Principal & Chief Financial Officer
Education: BS, State University of New York, Binghamton; CPA
Background: Director of Financial Analysis, Marsh & McLennan Companies; United Cable Television Corporation
Michael D. Gregorich, Principal
e-mail: Mgregorich@stonepoint.com
Education: BA, Middlebury College; MBA, New York University Leonard N Stern School of Business
Background: Senior Vice President, Donaldson Lufkin & Jenrette
Directorships: APCO Holdings, Cyprexx Services, NOVA Group Services, Real Estate Disposition Corporation
Agha Khan, Senior Principal
e-mail: AKhan@stonepoint.com
Education: BA, Cornell University
Background: Analyst, Salomon Smith Barney
Directorships: The ARC Group, Cyprexx Services, Real Estate Disposition Corporation
Peter M. Mundheim, Principal & Counsel
e-mail: Pmundheim@stonepoint.com
Education: AB, Duke University; JD, University of Pennsylvania Law School
Background: Attorney, Cleary Gottlieb Steen & Hamilton LLP; Law Clerk, Chancellor William T Allen, Delaware Court of Chancery; Assistant Product Manager, Commerce Clearing House
Directorships: APCO Holdings, Cunningham Lindsey Group Limited, Cyprexx Services, NOVA Group Services, Privilege Underwriters, Real Estate Disposition Corporation
Sally A. DeVino, Principal & Finance Director
Education: BS, Manhattan College; CPA
Background: Senior Manager, BDO Seidmen
Fayez S. Muhtadie, Senior Principal
e-mail: Fmuhtadie@stonepoint.com
Education: BSBA, Ohio State University; MBA, Columiba University Graduate School of Business
Background: Analyst, Credit Suisse First Boston; Financial Analyst, Aon Capital Markets
Directorships: NOVA Group Services
Eric L. Rosenzweig, Principal
e-mail: Erosenzweig@stonepoint.com
Education: BS, Wharton School, University of Pennsylvania
Background: Analyst, UBS Investment Bank

1744 STONEBRIDGE PARTNERS
81 Main Street
Suite 505
White Plains, NY 10601

Phone: 914-682-2700 Fax: 914-682-0834
e-mail: info@stonebridgepartners.com
web: www.stonebridgepartners.com

Mission Statement: Provides returns through leveraged recapitalizations of smaller, privately held companies or divisions of public companies.

Fund Size: $500 million
Founded: 1986
Average Investment: $10 million
Minimum Investment: $7 million
Investment Criteria: LBO, MBO
Industry Group Preference: Industrial Services, Specialty Packaging, Niche Manufacturing, Specialty Manufacturing, Building Materials & Services, Infrastructure
Portfolio Companies: American Dryer Corporation, BrandFX, Exal Group, Hydraulex Global, Safety Infrastructure Solutions, Specialty Bakers
Key Executives:
  Michael S Bruno Jr, Managing Partner
  e-mail: msb@stonebridgepartners.com
  Education: BS, Economics, Allegheny College; MBA, Columbia Business School
  Background: Mergers/Acquisitions, Salomon Brothers
  Andrew A Thomas, General Partner
  Education: BS, Engineering, Purdue University; MS, Engineering, Illinois Institute of Technology; MBA, University of Chicago Business School
  Background: Partner, Hawthorne Partners; Senior Member, Bank America; Managerial/Engineering, Inland Steel Company/Airco Industrial Gases
  William G. Connors, Manaing Director
  e-mail: wconnors@stonebridgepartners.com
  Education: BA, Business Administration, State University of New York; CPA
  Background: Manager, Accounting/Auditing Group, Prince Waterhouse, LLP
  Stephen A. Hanna, Managing Director
  e-mail: shanna@stonebridgepartners.com
  Education: BA, Economics, Lafayette College; MBA, Finance & Accounting, Stern School of Business, New York University
  Background: Director, Corporate Finance Group, IBJ Whitehall
  David R Schopp, Operating Partner
  Education: MS, Engineering, Rensselaer Polytechnic Institute
  Background: President & CEO, Orbis Corporation; General Manager, Promo Edge
  Directorships: American Dryer Corporation, Attica Hydraulic Exchange, Specialty Bakers
  Michael A Steinbeck, Operating Partner
  Education: Indiana University, DeVry Institute of Technology
  Background: CEO, CII Technologies; EVP, Sales & Marketing Operations, CP Clare
  Directorships: BondCote Corporation

1745 STONEHENGE GROWTH CAPITAL
236 Third Street
Baton Rouge, LA 70801

Phone: 225-408-3000 Fax: 225-408-3090

Mission Statement: Stonehenge Growth Capital manages the venture capital, private equity and mezzanine investment activities of Stonehenge Capital Company. Stonehenge is a perfect match for companies with a long-term vision focused on pursuing new, exciting and high growth opportunities, and for entrepreneurs with a passion for innovation and achievement.

Geographic Preference: Southeast, Northeast, Texas
Fund Size: $80 million
Founded: 1999
Average Investment: $4 million - $6 million
Minimum Investment: $1 million
Investment Criteria: Growth Equity
Industry Group Preference: Technology, Business Products & Services, Healthcare, Life Sciences, Manufacturing, Distribution
Portfolio Companies: 7thOnline, AuthenTec, Bulldog Solutions, Critical Mention, DataSynapse, eHealth Global Technologies, iCardiac Technologies, In.vision Research, Knovel, Lorica Solutions, Lumetrics, Medidata Solutions, Partsearch Technologies, Payformance, Pilgrim Software,

Venture Capital & Private Equity Firms / Domestic Firms

PixFusion, SensorTran, TouchPay Holdings, Alinean, Dowley Security Systems, Electronic Data Resources, Integrated Portfolio Management Services, Proficient Auto, Red Vector, Health Integrated, Image-Guided Neurologics, ZetrOZ, Dixie Southern, Environmental Lighting Concepts, Iron Horse Tools, T&K Machine, Twin Vee, American Scholar, COCAT, Moran Printing, Classic Events, Evolve, Oxford Collection Agenecy, AXIS Industrial Services, Coastal Drilling Company, Dolphine Marine International, Edgen Corporation, Florida Marine Group, Genesis Offshore, Gulfstream Services, H2X, Kim Susan, Louisiana Crane Company, Louisiana Tuggs, Rotorcraft Leasing Company, Technical Compression Services, Astro Electroplating, Avanti Marble & Granite, Barvista Homes, Col-Met Spray Booths, D'Lisi Food Systems, Ecoboard Holdings, Hornet Group, MB Industries, Millennium Outdoors, MilMar Food Group, Niagara Thermal Products, PECO Pallet, Petersen Pet Provisions, Sasun, Sunbelt Steel, The Metropolitan Switch Board Company, Trans American Rubber, Filco Carting, Rocky Mountain Portable Storage

Other Locations:
707 West Azeele Street
Tampa, FL 33606
Phone: 813-221-4413 **Fax:** 813-221-6453

152 W 57th Street
20th Floor
New York, NY 10019
Phone: 212-265-9380 **Fax:** 212-656-1344

7887 E Belleview Avenue
Suite 1100
Denver, CO 80111
Phone: 720-956-0235 **Fax:** 720-956-0209

191 W Nationwide Boulevard
Suite 600
Columbus, OH 43215
Phone: 614-246-2456 **Fax:** 614-246-2461

3424 North Shepard Avenue
Milwaukee, WI 53211
Phone: 414-906-1702 **Fax:** 414-906-1703

2001 Park Place
Suite 320
Birmingham, AL 35203
Phone: 205-458-2778 **Fax:** 866-539-9881

3625 N Hall Street
Suite 520
Dallas, TX 75219
Phone: 214-599-8850 **Fax:** 214-442-5626

8000 Maryland Avenue
Suite 1190
St. Louis, MO 63105
Phone: 314-721-5707 **Fax:** 314-721-5135

1020 Highland Colony Parkway
c/o Matt Thornton
Ridgeland, MS 39157
Phone: 601-985-4251 **Fax:** 601-985-4500

Brent T Sacha, Director, Growth Capital
e-mail: btsacha@stonehengegc.com
Education: BA, Economics, University of Virginia; MBA, Kellogg School of Management, Northwestern University
Background: Manager, M&A and Corporate Finance, AGL Resources; Townsend Frew & Company
Stephen A Bennett, Managing Director
Dallas Office
e-mail: sabennett@stonehengegc.com
Education: MBA, JL Kellogg Graduate School; BBA, University of Texas
Background: Banking Officer, Bank One; Manager Telecommunications/Media Practice, Deloitte Consultting
Directorships: Bulldog Solutions, TouchPay Holdings, Alinean, T&K Machine

1746 STONEWOOD CAPITAL MANAGEMENT
209 4th Avenue
Pittsburgh, PA 15222

Phone: 412-391-0300 **Fax:** 412-391-0500
e-mail: info@stonewoodcapital.com
web: www.stonewoodcapital.com

Mission Statement: To act as institutional angel investors, providing not only capital, but business expertise and advice to companies that are in the early phase of their development.
Geographic Preference: Eastern United States, Canada
Fund Size: $100 million
Founded: 1994
Average Investment: $2 million
Minimum Investment: $1 million
Investment Criteria: Seed, First Round Equity Capital, LBO, MBO
Industry Group Preference: Manufacturing, Distribution, Technology, Healthcare, Drug Development, Media, Business Products & Services
Portfolio Companies: Addressograph-Bartizan, C-K Composites Co., NewBold, Tank Services, Ardica Technologies, Demegen, Plan4Demand, Precision Therapeutics, ReGear, TimeSys

Key Executives:
J. Kenneth Moritz, President
Education: BS, University of Pennsylvania; JD, University of Pittsbugh School of Law; MSIA, Carnegie Mellon University
John Tippins, Managing Director
Education: BE, Electrical Engineering, Vanderbilt University; MBA, University of Pittsburgh Katz School of Business
Background: Director, Tippins Incorporated
Peter J Muth, Senior Vice President
Education: BS, Business, University of Dayton; MBA, University of Pittsburgh Katz School of Business
Background: Birchmere Capital; PNC Bank

1747 STORM VENTURES
3000 Sand Hill Road
Building 4, Suite 210
Menlo Park, CA 94025

Phone: 650-926-8800
web: www.stormventures.com

Mission Statement: Storm Ventures was founded by a seasoned group of industry veterans with the common vision of sharing a collective experience, passion and energy to help talented and driven entrepreneurs build great companies of enduring value.

Fund Size: $500 million
Founded: 1997
Industry Group Preference: Information Technology, Networking, Semiconductors, Software, Wireless, Security, Enterprise Applications, Hardware, Virtualization
Portfolio Companies: Acces 360, AdMobius, Airespace, AirPlug, Algolia, Amber Networks, Appcelerator, Asoka, AtScale, Averail, Berkana Wireless, BlackStratus, Catamaran, Cellfire, Cloudwords, Com2uS, Crowd Factory, DVDO, EchoSign, Flint Mobile, Greenlight Technologies, GuideSpark, HubPages, iML, JetCell, Kidaro, Kineto, Lightera, Marketo, Mcube Works, MetaCloud, Micel, MobileIron, Modo Labs, NetScaler, OSA Technologies, Parklet, Pipedrive, Qumu, Rafter, RainStor, Restorando, RiseSmart, SandForce, Sanera Systems, Sierra Monolithics, Silego, Splashtop, SwiftStack, TalkDesk, Telera, Transera, TrueSpan, Venturi Wireless

Key Executives:
Ryan Floyd, Managing Director
e-mail: ryan@stormventures.com
Education: BS, MS, Earth Systems, Stanford University
Background: Business Development, E-TEK Dynamics; Summit Partners

613

Venture Capital & Private Equity Firms / Domestic Firms

Directorships: 3Crowd, Appcelerator, Crowd Factory, HubPages, NetForensics, SandForce, Splashtop
Josef Friedman, Venture Partner
e-mail: josef@stormventures.com
Education: MS, Electrical Engineering, San Diego State University; MBA, National University
Background: Co-Founder & CEO, Expression; Apple Computers
Directorships: Anchor Bay Technologies, TrueSpan, Nuelight, Auvitek, Kidaro, Inovys

1748 STRIPES GROUP
402 West 13th Street
New York, NY 10014

Phone: 212-823-0720
e-mail: info@stripesgroup.com
web: www.stripesgroup.com

Mission Statement: Stripes Group delivers more than capital. By leveraging their resources, contacts and experience, their partner companies are able to increase profitability to grow faster and maximise value while maintaining the independence that defines an entrepreneul's success.

Founded: 2003
Average Investment: $10 - $100 million
Minimum Investment: $10 million
Industry Group Preference: Business to Business, Consumer Internet, SaaS, Consumer Products
Portfolio Companies: Art.com, Audio Network, Blue Apron, Craftsy, Elance ODek, EMarketer, Folica, GrubHub, Kareo, Kinetic Social, MyWebGrocer, Netbiscuits, NetQuote, Pond5, Refinery29, Sandata, SilverSky, SmartWool, Stella & Chewy's, Turtle Beach

Key Executives:
  Ken Fox, Managing Partner
  22-823-0730
  Education: BS, Economics, Pennsylvania State University
  Background: Managing Director, Internet Capital Group; Director, Safeguard Scientifics; Co-Founder, A-10 Capital; Co-Founder, Sentinel Fund
  Karen Kenworthy, Vice President, Consumer Investments
  212-823-0725
  Education: BS, Biomedical Engineering, BA, Economics, Yale University; MBA, Stanford Graduate School of Business
  Background: Bain & Company, UBS
  Ron Shah, Vice President
  212-823-0724
  Education: BA, Philosophy, Duke University
  Background: Co-Founder, Endgame Capital; M&A Group, Citigroup Global Markets
  Jason Santiago, Partner/Chief Technology Officer
  212-823-0731
  Education: BA, Architecture & Planning, Columbia University; MBA, Columbia Business School
  Background: Investment Banking, Cowen & Company; Director, Primedia
  Wayne Marino, Partner/Chief Financial Officer
  212-823-0733
  Education: BS, Finance, Rutgers University; MS, Accountancy, Mendoza College of Business, University of Notre Dame
  Background: Controller, Veronis Suhler Stevenson; Vice President, Aetos Capital; Ernst & Young

1749 STRUCTURE CAPITAL

e-mail: info@structure.vc
web: structure.vc

Mission Statement: Invests in entrepreneurs who desire to pass on their wealth, wisdom, and expertise as they grow over time.

Industry Group Preference: Waste & Recycling

Portfolio Companies: Uber, Shyp, MoviePass, SurfAir, Chicory, KangaDo, Gigit, PogoSeat, Boatbound, Peerspace, The Dating Ring, DJZ, Vessel, MakeSpace, Neighbor.ly, Stitch, Zaranga, DOZ, Popexpert, Willcall, Noble Transmission, Equidate, GoGoGab, Partnered, Mattermark, Lovely, Bohemian Guitars, AirHelp, ProductBIO, Beyond, Mavatar, Zootrock, Feastly, Totspot, Laurel & Wolf, Cross Fader, 15Five, Sumazi, Honk, Fixed, Ongig, Cambly, Breathometer, Cargomatic, Poliogg, Merchbar, Near Me, Knotch

1750 SUCSY, FISCHER & COMPANY
799 Central Avenue
Suite 350
Highland Park, IL 60035

Phone: 312-554-7575

Mission Statement: Frequently, situations arise where companies can use the skills, judgment and seasoned objectivity developed through our investment banking and corporate finance activities. Serving as financial advisor, the firm can assist management in the strategy and implementation of its capitalization plan and can assist in the process of selecting an underwriter for a public offering.

Geographic Preference: United States
Fund Size: $1 billion
Founded: 1972
Average Investment: $3-300 million
Minimum Investment: $3 million
Investment Criteria: Seed, First-stage, Second-stage, Mezzanine
Industry Group Preference: Communications, Software, Medical Devices, Manufacturing, Consumer Products, Energy, Food & Beverage, Financial Services, Business Products & Services, Healthcare Services

Key Executives:
  Rick Heyke, Investment Banker
  Education: BS, Physics, Yale University; MBA, Harvard Business School; JD, University of Chicago
  Background: Senior Counsel, Board of Governors of the Federal Reserve System; Counsel, Winston & Strawn LLP; Managing Director, Focus LLC; Managing Director, The Chicago Corporation; EVP, Aliier LLC; Senior Advisor, Eastgate Capital Advisors LLC

1751 SUMMER STREET CAPITAL PARTNERS
60 School Street
Suite 1420
Orchard Park, NY 14127

Phone: 716-566-2900 Fax: 716-566-2910
web: www.summerstreetcapital.com

Mission Statement: In addition to offering the capital companies need, Summer Street Capital Partners provides expertise, vast resources, and hands-on approach, all aimed at helping companies thrive like never before.

Geographic Preference: United States
Founded: 1997
Investment Criteria: Buyouts, MBO, Growth Financing, Family Transition, Corporate Divestiture, Recapitalization
Industry Group Preference: Education, Environment Products & Services, Healthcare, Niche Manufacturing
Portfolio Companies: Commonwealth Sprague Capacitor, UStec, IWS, Palladian, USA Datanet, Action, Graphic Controls, Pacific Pools, Praxis, Reichert, Belmont Meat Products, WillCare, ICE, Healthtrax, Sarolina Staff, la Madeline, Tulsa Welding School, RSI, Apple Valley Waste, Curtis Bay Medical Waste Services, New England Orthotic & Prosthetic Systems, Midwest Technical Institute, Multisorb Technologies, FSL 3D

Key Executives:
  Michael P McQueeney, Managing Partner
  e-mail: mmcqueeney@summerstreetcapital.com
  Education: MBA, Amos Tuck School of Business,

Bowdoin College
Background: Founder & President, Buffalo Ventures
Brian D'Amico, Managing Partner
e-mail: bdamico@summerstreetcapital.com
Education: BS, Finance, Cansius College
Background: Vice President, Buffalo Ventures
Jennifer Chalmers Balbach, Partner
e-mail: jbalbach@summerstreetcapital.com
Education: Harvard College; MBA, Amos Tuck School of Business
Background: Vice President, Buffalo Ventures; Management Consultant, Bain & Company
John Collins, Partner
Education: BA, Economics, Cornell University
Background: Investment Banking Analyst, Deutsche Bank's Leveraged Finance Group

1752 SUMMIT PARTNERS
222 Berkley Street
18th Floor
Boston, MA 02216

Phone: 617-824-1000 **Fax:** 617-824-1100
e-mail: financing@summitpartners.com
web: www.summitpartners.com

Mission Statement: Summit Partners provides growth equity for exceptional companies. Founded in 1984, Summit has raised more than $11 billion in capital and has provided growth equity, recapitalization and management buyout financing to more than 300 companies across a wide range of industries and geographies. The firm supports outstanding management teams that have self-financed their companies to market leadership. Summit Partners enhances the value of these companies through infrastructure development, executive and board recruiting, and strategic and operational advice. The firm also brings extensive experience in helping companies navigate the complex process of public offerings or strategic sales or mergers.

Geographic Preference: United States, Canada, Europe, Asia
Fund Size: $11 billion capital base
Founded: 1984
Average Investment: $25 million-$75 million
Minimum Investment: $5 million
Investment Criteria: Growth Equity, Recapitalizations, Management Buyouts
Industry Group Preference: Business Products & Services, Communication Technology, Communications, Consumer Products, Education, Energy, Financial Services, Healthcare, Life Sciences, Industrial Products, Internet, Information Services, Media, Entertainment, Semiconductors
Portfolio Companies: 3 Day Blinds, 360T Group, A+ Network, A10 Networks, ABILITY Network, Acacia Communications, Academic Management Services, Accedian Networks, Access Information Management, Active Voice, Actix, Acturis, AdvaCare, Advancce Health, Advance Medical, Advanced Cell Diagnostics, Aehr Text Systems, Aeryon Labs, Alert 360, Alpha Smart, AltoCom, Answers, ApoCell, Associa, Aurora Diagnostics, AVAST Software BV, AvePoint, Belkin International, Bigpoint GmbH, CareCentrix, Casa Systems, Central Security Group, Champion Windows, Clarabridge, Clearwater Analytics, Cloudmark, Commercial Defeasance, COMS Interactive, Continuum, Delphix, Empower RF Systems, FleetCor Technologies, Flow Traders BV, Focus Financial Partners, Fortegra Financial, Gainsight, Globe Wirelss, Heart to Heart Hospice, Help/Systems, Hiperos, Infor Global Solutions, JAMF Software, Logi Analytics, M/A-COM Technology Solutions Holdings, MEDITECH, Modernizing Medicine, Multifonds (IGEFI Group Sarl), National Veterinary Associates, Nomacorc, Paris Town, Peak Well Systems, PeerApp, PeopleAdmin, Philz Coffee, Progressive Finance, RiskIQ, Rocket Fuel, RuffaloCODY, Salient Partners, Solid State Equipment, Solutionreach, Sparta Systems, Systems Maintenance Services, Telerik, TeleSign Holdings, Tivoli Audio, Trident University International, Ubiquiti Networks, Vente-Privee, Visier, WebAction, Welltec International, Winshuttle Holdings, Wowza Media Systems, Zenoss

Other Locations:
200 Middlefield Road
Suite 200
Menlo Park, CA 94025
Phone: 650-321-1166 **Fax:** 650-321-1188

11-12 Hanover Square
London W1S 1JJ
United Kingdom
Phone: 44-02076597500 **Fax:** 44-02076597550

Summit Luxembourg S.a.r.l.
33, rue du Puits Romain
Bertange L-8070
Luxembourg
Phone: 352-2648-0048 **Fax:** 352-2736-5159

Key Executives:
John R Carroll, Managing Director-Boston
617-824-1052
e-mail: john@summitpartners.com
Education: AB, Dartmouth College; MM, Kellogg School of Management, Northwestern University
Background: Bain & Company; BayBank
Directorships: Associa, Cetero Research, ComPsych, FleetCor Technologies, Fortegra Financial
Matthias G Allgaier, Managing Director-London
44-0-20-7659-7505
e-mail: mallgaier@summitpartners.com
Education: MBA, Mannheim University; PhD, Business Administration, Karl Franzens University
Background: Managing Director, H.I.G. Capital Europe; Apax Partners, General Atlantic Partners
Directorships: Elatec, Market Logic, Signavio, Zahneins
David W Averett, Managing Director-Boston
617-824-1021
e-mail: daverett@summitpartners.com
Education: BS, US Military Academy at West Point; MBA, Goizueta Business School, Emory University
Directorships: MedOptions, NetBrain Technologies, Parts Town
Darren M Black, Managing Director-Boston
617-824-1011
e-mail: dblack@summitpartners.com
Education: AB, Harvard College; MBA, Wharton School
Background: Managing Partner, SV Life Sciences
Directorships: ABILITY Network, Advance Health, DMG Practice Management Solutions, HealthSun, Paradigm Outcomes, PharmScript, Sound Physicians
Andrew J Collins, Managing Director-Menlo Park
650-614-6652
e-mail: acollins@summitpartners.com
Education: BS, Finance, Miami University
Background: Banc of America Securities; ABN Amro Financial Services
Directorships: Arista, Delphix, Gainsight, InfoArmor, NetWitness, Podium, Reverb.com, RiskIQ, Striim, Uber, Ubiquiti, Wildfire Interactive, Winshuttle, Wowza Media Systems
Peter Y Chung, Managing Director-Menlo Park
650-614-6701
e-mail: pchung@summitpartners.com
Education: AB, Harvard University; MBA, Stanford University
Background: Goldman, Sachs & Company; Patagonia
Directorships: Coast Asset Management, Empower RF Systems, M/A-COM Technology Solutions Holdings, Trident University International (TUI), Ubiquiti Networks
Scott C Collins, Managing Director-Boston
617-824-1012
Education: AB, Harvard University; JD, Harvard Law School
Background: McKinsey and Company; US Department of Justice; The White House

Venture Capital & Private Equity Firms / Domestic Firms

Directorships: B&W TEK, My Dentist Holdings, NetWitness, OB Hospitalist Group
Christopher J Dean, Managing Director-Boston
617-824-1067
e-mail: cdean@summitpartners.com
Education: BA, University of Notre Dame; MBA, Harvard Business School
Background: Morgan Stanley; JH Whitney & Co; Sun Microsystems
Directorships: Aurora Diagnostics, Champion Windows, Commercial Defeasance, Focus Financial Partners, Salient Partners, Sun Trading
C.J. Fitzgerald, Managing Director-Menlo Park
650-614-6603
e-mail: cfitzgerald@summitpartners.com
Education: BS, Georgia Institute of Technology; MBA, Harvard Business School
Background: Founder & CEO, North Systems
Directorships: Trident University International (TUI), Ubiquiti Networks
Craig D Frances MD, Managing Director-Menlo Park
650-614-6602
e-mail: cfrances@summitpartners.com
Education: BA, Cornell University; MD, Cornell University Medical College
Background: Chief Medical Resident, University of California, San Francisco
Directorships: HealthCare Partners, National Veterinary Associates
Robin W Devereux, CAO/CCO/Managing Director-Boston
617-824-1606
e-mail: rdevereux@summitpartners.com
Education: BS, Accounting, Northeastern University
Background: National Development; Property Capital Trust; RM Bradley & Co.; Deloitte & Touche
Leonard C Ferrington, Managing Director-Menlo Park
650-614-6643
e-mail: lferrington@summitpartners.com
Education: BS, Accounting, Leventhal School of Accounting, University of Southern California
Background: Celerity Partners; Baxter Healthcare International
Directorships: A10 Networks, Access Information Management, Aeryon Labs, Ascentis, Heald College, Ruffalo Noel Levitz, Smartsheet, Teaching Strategies, Trident University Int'l, Ubiquiti
Greg S Goldfarb, Managing Director-Menlo Park
650-614-6653
e-mail: ggoldfarb@summitpartners.com
Education: AB, Harvard University
Directorships: Clearwater Analytics, Cloudmark, Gainsight, IntelliChem, Jamf, LiveOffice, onXmaps, PatSnap, Philz Coffee, ProClarity Corp., RiskIQ, Rocket Fuel, TeleSign, Tiny Prints, Visier
Thomas H Jennings, Managing Director-Boston
617-824-1053
e-mail: tj@summitpartners.com
Education: AB, Boston College
Background: Andersen Consulting (now Accenture)
Directorships: Accedian Networks, ApoCell, AvePoint, Hiperos, NameMedia, Teleik
Mark A deLaar, Managing Director-Boston
617-824-1027
e-mail: mdelaar@summitpartners.com
Education: BS, United States Military Academy; MBA, MIT Sloan School of Management
Background: DB Alex Brown, Banc of America Securities & Public Financial Management, United States Army
Directorships: IMMCO Diagnostics, My Dentist Holdings, OB Hospitalist Group
Matthew G Hamilton, Managing Director-Boston
617-824-1073
e-mail: mhamilton@summitpartners.com
Education: BA, Economics, Colby College

Directorships: Flow Traders, Focus Financial Partners, Invoice Cloud, Patriot Growth Insurance Services, Progressive Finance, Salient Partners, Telerik, Vestmark
Jay D Pauley, Managing Director-Boston
617-824-1070
e-mail: jpauley@summitpartners.com
Education: BS, Ohio State University; MBA, Wharton School
Background: Apax Partners; GE Capital
Directorships: Alert 360, FineLine Technologies, Grand Design RV, Harvey Performance Co., Parts Town, Vivint, Vivint Solar
Alexander D Whittemore, Managing Director-Boston
617-824-1025
e-mail: awhittemore@summitpartners.com
Education: BA, Carleton College; MBA, University of Virginia Darden School
Background: Morgan Stanley, Chase Manhattan Corporation, Chemical Banking Corporation
Peter L Rottier, Managing Director-Menlo Park
650-614-6624
e-mail: prottier@summitpartners.com
Education: BS, Carlson School of Management, University of Minnesota; MBA, Stanford Grad. School of Business
Background: KSL Capital Partners; Stone Arch Capital; RBC Capital Markets
Directorships: Answers, Ascentis, Healthline Media, HelpSystems, Infor, ISH, MercuryGate, Perforce Software, Rocket Fuel, Salient Partners, Snap Fitness, Solid State Equipment, Trintech
Hans Sikkens, Managing Director-London
44-0-20-7659-7500
e-mail: hsikkens@summitpartners.com
Education: BS, MSc, University of Groningen; MSc, CERAM Graduate School of Management & Technology
Background: Scotia Capital; IBM Corporation
Directorships: 360T Group, Acturis, Avast, Darktrace, Flow Traders, Masternaut, Multifonds, OnRobot, RELEX Solutions, SafeBoot, Siteimprove, Syncron, Welltec International
Christian R Strain, Managing Director-London
44-0-20-7659-7504
e-mail: cstrain@summitpartners.com
Education: BA, Yale University; MBA, Harvard Business School
Background: Apax Partners
Directorships: Normec, Ogone, Peak Well Systems, Sézane, Sipartech, vente-privee.com, Westwing Group
Thomas M Tarnowski, Managing Director-London
44-0-20-7659-7503
e-mail: ttarnowski@summitpartners.com
Education: BBA, Valdosta State University; MBA, Harvard Business School
Background: Triton; Credit Suisse First Boston; Citigroup
Directorships: Advance Medical, DentalPro, Independent Vetcare, zahneins

1753 SUN CAPITAL PARTNERS
5200 Town Center Circle
4th Floor
Boca Raton, FL 33486

Phone: 561-394-0550
web: www.suncappart.com

Mission Statement: Our mission is consistent, top decile returns for our LPs, to protect and enhance our reputation, continued growth & improvement, to provide outstanding people with great careers, and allow our stakeholder partners to share in our success.

Founded: 1995
Investment Criteria: Control Equity Investments, Leveraged Buyouts, Bank Debt, Trade Claims, Seller Notes, High Yield Securities

Venture Capital & Private Equity Firms / Domestic Firms

Industry Group Preference: Automotive, Business Products & Services, Distribution, Flexible Packaging, Manufacturing, Natural Resources, Restaurants, Retailing, Technology, Transportation, Food & Beverage, Financial Services, Healthcare, Media, Communications
Portfolio Companies: Aclara, ADTI, AlbéA, America Golf, American Rec, Ames, Arrow Tru-Line. Bar Louie, Bonmarché, Boston Market, BTX Group, Bundy Refrigeration, BWGS, C&K, Clear Choice, Coveris, Creekstone Farms, Demilec, Dreams, ELIX Polymers, Esim Chemicals, Famosa, Fazoli's, FFO Home, Flabeg, Flamingo Horticulture, Flavor1, Flexitech, Franchise, Freshpak, Friendly's Garden Fresh Restaurant Corp., Gem Shopping Network, Gordmans, Hanna Anderson, Heartland, Hickory Farms, Horizon Services, Hweden, Innocor, Jacques Vert Group, Johnny Rockets, Kellwood Company, Kraco, La Place, Lexington Home Brands, LOUD Technologies, Marsh, NextPharma, NFP Automotive, O&S Doors, PaperWorks, Parker, PEMCO, Perfect Timing, Performance Fibers, Point Blank Enterprises, Polestar, Pop Displays, Rebecca Taylor, Restaurants Unlimited, Robertshaw, Rowe, S&N Communications, Scotch & Soda, Sofa Carpet Specialist, Sharps, Shopko, Smokey Bones, Spectralink, Stake Center, Stone Point Materials, The Limited, Tier One Relocations, True, Trulite, Unico, V&D, Vari-Form, VPS, Vince, Windsor
Other Locations:
11111 Santa Monica Blvd
Suite 1050
Los Angeles, CA 90025
Phone: 310-473-1116

100 Park Avenue
Suite 2900
New York, NY 10017
Phone: 212-588-9156

Sun European Partners LLP
2 Park St.
1st Floor
London W1K 2HX
United Kingdom
Phone: 44-0-207-318-1100

Sun Capital Partners Sourcing LLC
Block A, World Finance Center
4003 Shennan East Road
Luohu District, Shenzhen 518001
China
Phone: 86-75525981628
Key Executives:
 Rodger R Krouse, Co-CEO
 Education: BS, Economics, The Wharton School
 Background: Senior Vice President, Lehman Brothers
 Marc J Leder, Co-CEO
 Education: BS, Economics, The Wharton School
 Background: Senior Vice President, Lehman Brothers
 M Steven Liff, Senior Managing Director
 Background: NationsBank; Bank of America Commercial Finance
 Bruce Roberson, Senior Managing Director
 Tim Stubbs, Senior Managing Director
 Education: BA, Oxford University; MBA, London Business School
 Background: Sapa Group
 C Deryl Couch, Managing Director & General Counsel
 Education: BA, Political Science, Furman University; JD, Cornell Law School
 Background: White & Case, Partner, Greenberg Traurig
 Scott W Edwards, Managing Director
 Education: BS, Finance, Georgetown University; MBA, Tuck School of Business
 Background: Principal, Henderson Private Capital; Associte, GE Equity
 Matthew N Garff, Managing Director
 Education: BS, Finance, University of Utah; MBA, Finance, University of Chicago
 Background: The Carlyle Group, KSL Fairways

 Aaron P Wolfe, Managing Director
 Education: BA, Economics, University of Virginia
 Background: Harris Williams & Co.
 Paul Daccus, Managing Director
 Education: Dundee University
 Background: Director, Deloitte & Touche; Arthur Andersen
 Kevin J Calhoun, Managing Director & CFO
 Education: BS, Accounting, University of Florida
 Background: Ernst & Young; Chief Financial Officer, Atlas Companies

1754 SUN MOUNTAIN CAPITAL
527 Don Gasper Avenue
Santa Fe, NM 87505
Phone: 505-780-4218
e-mail: info@sunmountaincapital.com
web: sunmountaincapital.com

Mission Statement: A private equity and venture capital investment firm that provides fund investment advisory services for public and private entities as well as manages direct investment funds.

Geographic Preference: Rocky Mountain & Southwest Regions
Fund Size: $500 million
Founded: 2006
Average Investment: $300,000 - $10 million
Investment Criteria: Venture Capital, Mezzanine Debt, Growth Equity
Industry Group Preference: Diversified
Key Executives:
 Brian Birk, Managing Partner
 Education: BS, Economics, Carleton College; MBA, Kellogg School of Management
 Background: VP & Director, Fort Washington Capital Partners; Founder, MetaWeb
 Directorships: Aspen Avionics, American Clay, Exagen Diagnostics, Lumidigm, Puente Partners
 Sally Corning, Partner
 Education: BSBA, Finance, Georgetown University; MBA, Columbia University Graduate School of Business
 Background: Investment Banking, Dean Witter Reynolds; Morgan Stanley; Credit Suisse First Boston
 Directorships: nanoMR
 Lee Rand, Partner
 Education: BA, Computer Science & Mathematics, Cornell University; MBA, Harvard Business School
 Background: Founder, Knogee; Ernst & Young
 Directorships: Skorpios Technologies, JackRabbit Systems

1755 SUNBRIDGE PARTNERS
3659 Green Road
Suite 100
Beachwood, OH 44122
Phone: 216-360-0151
web: www.sunbridgepartners.com

Mission Statement: To make a difference with entrepreneurs, by sharing their vision to change the world.

Geographic Preference: United States, Japan
Investment Criteria: Early-Stage
Industry Group Preference: Information Technology, SaaS, Cloud Computing, Wireless, Open Source, Clean Technology, Enterprise Software, Digital Media & Marketing, Semiconductors, Business Products & Services
Portfolio Companies: Accela Technology, Alien Technology, AucSale, Avec Lab, BeTrend, Bloom Energy, Blue Spark Technologies, bydsign, Class Technology, Concur Japan, e-Medical System, FAOPEN, FiBest, Fun-Life, G-Mode, GaiaX, Hamster, Horizon Digital Enterprise, istyle, ITMedia, LT Solutions, MacroMill, Miracle Linux, Net Asia, New IT Venture, OKWave, Roonets, RouteLambda,

Venture Capital & Private Equity Firms / Domestic Firms

Salesforce Japan, Salesforce.com, Shicoh Engineering, SilkRoad Japan, Smarts Japan, VistaPoint Technology, Yap, Zipit Wireless

Other Locations:
179 Jefferson Drive
Menlo Park, CA 94025
Phone: 650-353-5401

11f, JR Ebisu Building
1-5-5 Minami, Ebisu
Shibuya-ku
Tokyo 150-0022
Japan

222 South Church Street
Suite 100
Charlotte, NC 28202
Phone: 704-443-8369

Key Executives:
Allen Miner, Founder/General Partner
Education: Computer Science, Asian Studies, Brigham Young University
Background: CEO, SunBridge Corporation; Oracle Corporation; Founder, Oracle Japan
Directorships: Salesforce Japan
John Gannon, Founder/General Partner
Education: BS, Aerospace Engineering, Penn State University; MBA, University of Chicago
Background: Co-Founder, Equitek Capital; Engineer, General Electric Astro-Space Division; Associate, Merrill Lynch; SVP, NationsBank
Directorships: Embedded Planet, Blue Spark Technologies
Ken Ehrhart, Founder/General Partner
Education: University of California, Berkeley
Background: Co-Founder, Equitek Capital; Director of Research, Forbes' Gilder Technology Report; Founder, E-Consulting
Directorships: Alien Technology, NITV
Paul Grim, Founder/General Partner
Education: BSc, Mechanical Engineering, MIT; MBA, MIT Sloan School of Management
Background: Co-Founder, Equitek Capital; Gemini Consulting; Coopers & Lybrand
Directorships: Zipit Wireless, Yap

1756 SUNRISE CAPITAL PARTNERS
16950 Via de Santa Fe
Suite 5060-153
Rancho Santa Fe, CA 92067

Phone: 858-259-8911
e-mail: info@sunrisecapital.com
web: www.sunrisecapital.com

Mission Statement: Sunrise Capital Partners is a Systematic Global macro trading firm found in 1980. Sunrise brings an informed, long-term perspective, an adaptive and evolutionary research platform and responsive client-focused delivery to investors seeking the best opportunities in today's global financial markets. For more than 30 years, Sunrise has followed a thorough, methodical and highly risk-attuned course in developing and applying dynamic insights and innovations.

Key Executives:
Rick Slaughter, Founding Partner
Education: B.S. Finance San Diego State University, Systems Management University of Southern California
Background: Founder of Commodity Monitors, Inc.
Jason Gerlach, Managing Partner/CEO
Education: M.A. Public Policy Analysis and Public Administration University of Wisconsin; B.A. Government Cornell University
Background: Attorney with Hale and Dorr LLP and Howard Rice Nemerovski Canady Falk & Rabkin

1757 SUPPLY CHAIN VENTURES
Boston, MA

Phone: 207-286-6464
e-mail: dave@supplychainventure.com
web: supplychainventure.com

Mission Statement: Invests in marketing, sales, and supply chain innovators.

Industry Group Preference: Manufacturing, Marketing, Media, Robotics, Industry

Portfolio Companies: ActualMeds, Blank Label, Bow & Drape, CabinetM, Cohealo, Crimson Hexagon, Descartes Systems Group, Foxtrot, Jebbit, LevaData, Little Passports, Llamasoft, Logistics Marketplace, NBD, NextShift Robotics, Paradigm4, Placester, Resilinc, Sandymount Technologies, Shipmonk, SupplyAI, Supply Shift, Transporeon, Work Truck Solutions

Key Executives:
David L. Anderson, Managing General Partner
Education: BA, University of Connecticut; PhD, Boston College
Background: Managing Partner of Supply Chain Consulting, Accenture; VP of Logistics Consulting, Temple Barker & Sloane Inc.; VP, Data Resources Inc.
Directorships: Placester; NextShift Robotics; NBD Nanotechnology
Dan Dershem, General Partner
Directorships: Transplace; Transporeon; Llamasoft

1758 SUSA VENTURES
Mission District
San Francisco, CA

web: susaventures.com

Mission Statement: Seeks to invest in tech-based companies with a focus on proprietary data.

Founded: 2013
Investment Criteria: Seed
Industry Group Preference: Big Data, Technology, Consumer, Industry, Virtual Reality, Artificial Intelligence
Portfolio Companies: AMI, Andela, Aquera, Avro Life Science, Bright, Casetext, Chatdesk, Clutch, Cortex, CrowdAI, Drivezy.com, Elliot, Expanse, Flexport, Fourpost, Fuzzbuzz, Guilded, Hodinkee, Honeybee, Human Interest, Humble Dot, HYAS, Interviewing.io, Intricately, Juvena Therapeutics, LendUp, Locale, Lyst, Mashgin, Merit, Modsy, Mux, MycoWorks, Naborly, Namo Media, Newfront, Outlier, Pachyderm, Parachute, People Data Labs, Percolata, Periscope, Persephone Biome, Pex, Plan, PolicyGenius, Rigetti, Roam, Robin Care, Robinhood, Rockbot, RunaHR, Scalyr, Scope AR, SimpleLegal, Smile Identity, Spring Discovery, Stedi, Stord, Sundae, TigerGraph, Tortuga AgTech, Treasury Prime, TrendMD, Troops, Union Crate, VeriSIM Life, Viz, Wurb, Whisper, WorkRamp

Key Executives:
Chad Byers, Co-Founder/General Partner
Education: BA, Environmental Science, University of Colorado
Directorships: Robinhood; Flexport
Leo Polovets, Partner
Education: BS, California Institute of Technology
Background: Software Engineer, LinkedIn; Software Engineer, Google; Sr. Software Engineer, Factual; Angel Investor
Seth Berman, General Partner
Education: BS, University of Colorado
Background: VP of Strategic Marketing, Richmont; Angel Investor
Natalie Fleming Arora, Head of Operations
Education: BA, Arizona State University
Background: Director of Partnerships, JUST; Director of Business Development, Juicero

Venture Capital & Private Equity Firms / Domestic Firms

1759 SUSQUEHANNA GROWTH EQUITY
401 City Avenue
Bala Cynwyd, PA 19004

Phone: 610-617-2600
e-mail: info@sgep.com
web: www.sgep.com

Mission Statement: SGE is the US-based private equity arm of The Susquehanna International Group of Companies (SIG), a global financial institution still owned and operated by several of its founders. The culture they established drives our management-centric approach to private equity. We support operators, not run their businesses. Working behind the scenes, we reach new customers, introduce key partnerships, and recruit executive talent. We are open to a wide variety of transaction structures and are not subject to the vagaries of the private equity fundraising cycle.

Geographic Preference: North America, Europe, Israel
Average Investment: $5 - $50 million
Investment Criteria: Growth Capital, Buyouts, Recapitalizations, Divestitures, Acquisition Financing
Industry Group Preference: SaaS, E-Commerce & Manufacturing, Financial Services, Internet
Portfolio Companies: BoomTown, B-Stock Solutions, CallApp, Clearleap, Credit Karma, ETF Securities, Global Tranz, HMP, iCims, JK Group, MMIT, Netformx, Offers.com, Payoneer, PaySimple, Skybox Security, The Logic Group, Zyme

Key Executives:
Scott Feldmen, Director
e-mail: scott.feldman@sgep.com
Education: BS, Finance, Boston College
Background: Co-Founder, Superior Street Capital Markets
Directorships: Credit Karma, HMP Communications, iCIMS, JK Group, MMIT
Amir Goldman, Director
e-mail: amir.goldman@sgep.com
Education: BS, Economics, University of Pennsylvania; MBA, Harvard Business School
Background: TL Ventures, BRM Capital
Directorships: iCIMS, JK Group, MMIT, Netformx, PaySimple, Zyme
Jonathan Klahr, Director
e-mail: jonathan.klahr@sgep.com
Education: BA, War Studies, Kings College; MBA, Hebrew University
Background: BRM Capital
Directorships: iCIMS, Netformx, Offers.com, Skybox, The Logic Group, Versafe

1760 SUTTER HILL VENTURES
755 Page Mill Road
Suite A-200
Palo Alto, CA 94304-1005

Phone: 650-493-5600
e-mail: shv@shv.com
web: www.shv.com

Mission Statement: We invest in technology based start-ups that pioneer important products/services and devote our time, money and expertise to building these companies into industry leaders.

Fund Size: $200 million
Founded: 1962
Average Investment: $100,000 - $5 million
Minimum Investment: $100,000
Investment Criteria: Seed, startup, First-stage, Second-stage, Management buy-out
Industry Group Preference: Biotechnology, Computer Related, Education, High Technology, Medical & Health Related
Portfolio Companies: @Mobile.com, AAC Acoustic, ACACIA Venture Partners, Acceleron Pharma, Actiance, AkaRx, Aksys, AllBusiness, Alteon WebSystems, AmberPoint, Amerigroup Real Solutions, Ameritox, Amira, Amylin, Apollo Computers, Artisan Partners, Aspect Medical Systems, Avant!, Avid, Barrx Medical, Benu, Biovest International, Bix, Blue Ridge Pharmaceuticals, Boxer, Brierley + Partners, BroadVision, C3 Energy, Cardica, Celeritek, Chengwei Capital, Clarus, Closedloop Solutions, Clover, Connection Engine, Consorte Media, Copper Mountain, COR, Corcept Therapeutics, Corixa, Costanoa Venture Capital, Data Domain, DemandBase, Digidesign, Digital Chocolate, Dionex, Drais, Drobo, e-Rewards, Farecast, FeedBurner, Forte Tools, Foundation DB, Free Monee, Glassdoor.com, GLMX, Golden Gate Capital, Grain Communications Group, Grand Junction, Guardian Analytics, Helion, Horizon Pharma, Hybritech, Idexx, iDun, Infinera, Inflection, InQuira, Instart Logic, Intacct, Ideas Revenue Organization, ISIS, Interventional Technologies, Kalypto Medical, Kineto Wireless, Legato, Lifescan, LifeSize, Line 6, Linear Technology, LinkSmart, LSI Logic, Lucky, Lynk, Makena Capital, Mattersight, Mentor Graphics, Merced Systems, Metronome Therapeutics, Mips, Molecular Devices, MyNewPlace, Network Appliance, Networks in Motion, Neurex, Nexxo, Nimsoft, NuGen, nVidia, Omnicell, OnStream Networks, OpenDNS, Pacific Biosciences, Palm, PINC Solutions, Platfora, PMC-Sierra, Portola, Primary Access, PureStorage, Pyxis, QuinStreet,

Key Executives:
David L Anderson, Managing Director
Education: BS Electrical Engineering, MIT; MBA, Harvard University
Background: Watkins-Johnson; Past Board Seats: Palm Computing/Appollo Computing/Neurex/Hybritech; Responsible for start-up funding for LSI Logic/Quantum Corporation/Mentor Graphics/Linear Technology
Directorships: Dionex, Brierley & Partners, E-Rewards, Concept Shopping
Jeff Bird, Managing Director
Education: Biology Degree, Stanford; PhD Cancer Biology/MD, Stanford Medical School
Background: Senior Vice President, Gilead Sciences
Directorships: Artemis Health, Drais Pharmaceuticals, Horizon Therapeutics, MacuSight, NuGen Technologies, Portola Pharmaceuticals, Restoration Robotics, Roxro Pharma, Threshhold Pharma
Mike Speiser, Managing Director
Education: BA, University of Arizona; MBA, Harvard Business School
Background: Vice President, Community Products, Yahoo!; President & CEO, Bix; Vice President, Symantec; Vice President, Product Management, Veritas; Co-Founder, Epinions.com
David E Sweet, Chief Financial Officer
Education: BS, Civil Engineering, Stanford University; MBA, Harvard Business School
Background: International Tax Partner, PricewaterhouseCoopers
James N White, Managing Director
e-mail: jwhite@shv.com
Education: BS, Industrial Engineering, Northwestern University; MBA, Harvard University
Background: Vice President, Marketing, Macromedia; Vice President, Marketing, Silicon Graphics; Hewlett-Packard
Directorships: Digital Chocolate, Glassdoor.com, Inquira, Object Reservoir, Right Hemisphere, Satmetrix, Shutterfly, SilverRail Technologies, Streetline Networks, WebVisible

1761 SV ANGEL
San Francisco, CA 94102

web: svangel.com

Mission Statement: Angel investor in San Francisco offers advice on business development, financing and M&A.

Geographic Preference: California
Fund Size: $20 million
Investment Criteria: Seed-Stage, Early-Stage

619

Venture Capital & Private Equity Firms / Domestic Firms

Industry Group Preference: Information Technology, E-Commerce & Manufacturing, Consumer Internet, Gaming, Enterprise Software, Social Media
Portfolio Companies: Airbnb, Amplitude, Coinbase, Databricks, DoorDash, Dropbox, Gusto, Headspace, Instacart, Opendoor, Pagerduty, Pinterest, Slack, Square Space, TransferWise, Twilio, Twitch, Warby Parker

Key Executives:
Ron Conway, Founder & Co-Managing Partner
Education: BS, Political Science, San Jose State University
Background: National Semiconductor Corporation, Altos Computer Systems, Personal Training Systems
Topher Conway, Co-Managing Partner
Education: UCLA
Background: eCost; EQAL
Brian Pokorny, Advisor
Education: Santa Clara University
Background: Airbnb
Kevin Carter, Advisor
Education: Santa Clara University
Background: Silicon Valley Bank
Robert Pollak, Advisor
Education: University of Virginia
Background: Morgan Stanley

1762 SV HEALTH INVESTORS
One Boston Place
201 Washington St.
Suite 3900
Boston, MA 02108

Phone: 617-367-8100 **Fax:** 617-367-1590
web: svhealthinvestors.com

Mission Statement: SV Health Investors seeks to transform healthcare by investing in entrepreneurs who create disruptive companies and treatments.

Industry Group Preference: Biotechnology, Medical Devices, Healthcare, Digital Health
Portfolio Companies: AcuFocus, Adimab, AeroCare, Aligned Teleheath, Arsanis, Artios, Autifony, Avitide, Avrobio, BardyDx, Bicycle Therapeutics, CardioFocus, Catabasis, Centauri Health Solutions, Cibiem, CSA Medical, EBR Systems, Endotronix, Evidation, Deciphera, Jet Health, Leiters, Nordic, Ocular Therapeutix, Remita Health, ReShape, Schweiger Dermatology Group, Solsys Medical, Spectrum, Stim Wave, Sun Behavioural Health, Urgent Team, US Renal Care

Other Locations:
71 Kingsway
London WC2B 6ST
United Kingdom
Phone: 44-20-7421-7070 **Fax:** 44-20-7421-7077

Key Executives:
Houman Ashrafian, Managing Partner, Biotechnology
Education: University of Cambridge; BM BCh, DPhil, University of Oxford
Background: Co-Founder, Cardiac Report, Heart Metabolics; VP, Clinical Science Group, UCB Pharma
Directorships: Ervaxx, Sitryx
Michael Balmuth, Managing Partner, Healthcare
Education: AB, Dartmouth College; MBA, Harvard Business School
Background: General Partner, Summit Partners; General Partner, Edison Parters
Directorships: Aerocare, Aligned Telehealth, Centauri Health Solutions, Evidation, Ximedica
Kate Bingham, Managing Partner, Biotechnology
Education: First Class Degree, Biochemistry, Oxford University; MBA, Harvard Business School
Background: Vertex Pharmaceuticals; Monitor Company
Directorships: Artios, Autifony, Bicycle, Calchan, Delenex, Arvaxxm KalVista, Karus, Pulmocide, Sitryx, TopiVert, Vantia, VHsquared, Zarodex

Tom Flynn, Managing Partner, Healthcare
Education: AB, Economics, Holy Cross College; MBA, Harvard Business School
Background: Partner, Ferrer Freeman & Co.; GE Capital; Prudential Investment Corporation
Directorships: AeroCare, Jet Health, Leiters, Nordic, Remita Health, Schweiger Dermatology Group, Sun Behavioural Health, UrgentTeam
Paul LaViolette, COO & Managing Partner, Medical Devices
Education: BA, Psychology, Fairfield University; MBA, Boston College
Background: COO, Boston Scientific; CR Bard; Kendall
Directorships: BardyDx, CardioFocus, Cibiem, CSA Medical, EBR Systems, Endotronix, Soffio Medical, Solsys Medical, Stim Wave, TransEnterix, ValenTx, Ximedica
Mike Ross, Managing Partner, Biotechnology
Education: AB, Dartmouth College; PhD, Caltech; Post-Doctoral Fellowship, Harvard
Background: Genentech; Managing Partner, Didyma
Directorships: Adimab, Alba, Alinea, Archemix, Arsanis, Avitide, AvroBio, Catabasis, Deciphera, Juvaris, NKTT, Pionyr, Ribometrix, Sutro Biopharma, Thesan Pharmaceuticals

1763 SV INVESTMENT PARTNERS
1700 East Putnam Avenue
Greenwich, CT 06870

Phone: 212-735-0700 **Fax:** 203-990-0714
e-mail: nsomers@svip.com
web: www.svip.com

Mission Statement: SV Investment Partners, formerly known as Schroder Ventures US, is a private equity firm specializing in buyouts and buildups of business services companies.

Geographic Preference: United States
Fund Size: $270 million
Founded: 1999
Average Investment: $25 million
Minimum Investment: $10 million
Investment Criteria: Later Stage
Industry Group Preference: Business Products & Services
Portfolio Companies: International Decision Systems

Other Locations:
500 West Putnam
Suite 400
Greenwich, CT 06830
Phone: 203-987-3021 **Fax:** 203-738-1138

Key Executives:
Nicholas Somers, Partner
212-735-0700
Fax: 212-735-0702
e-mail: nsomers@svip.com
Education: MBA, University of Chicago; BA, Washington University, St. Louis
Background: Founder/Partner, Greenwich Street Capital Partners; Travelers; Morgan Stanley
Directorships: Mesa Communications, ThoughtWorks, Market Place Media
Philip Cole, Principal
Education: BA, Kingston University
Background: CFO, PrecisionIR
Will Sale, Vice President
Education: BA, Yale University
Background: Investment Banking Analyst, Bank of America Merrill Lynch

1764 SVB CAPITAL
3003 Tasman Drive
Santa Clara, CA 95054

web:
www.svb.com/gaining-traction/capital-strategies-solutions

620

Venture Capital & Private Equity Firms / Domestic Firms

Mission Statement: SVB Capital's deep industry knowledge and multi-faceted industry relationships provide us with extensive access to and knowledge of private equity at both the firm and portfolio company levels. SVB Capital's investment expertise allows us to leverage this unrivaled access, insight and proprietary deal flow to create a unique competitive advantage and superior investment selection ability.

Geographic Preference: United States
Fund Size: $1 Billion
Founded: 1983
Average Investment: $200,000
Minimum Investment: $50,000
Industry Group Preference: Biotechnology, Communications, Electronic Technology, Information Technology, Medical, Software, Clean Technology, Hardware, Life Sciences, Internet
Portfolio Companies: Adore, AtlEn Opportunity, Brickwood NYC, CAMSIE Leasing, Card Compliant, Clinical Research Investments, iLight, Muzik, Orange Groves/OCP Holding Company, Orbis Biosciences, Paradise Rentals, Ridgewood Energy Fund, SelectQuote, StoreFinancial, Spectrum Motors, The Wireless Stores, Worldwide Wireless

Key Executives:
Aaron Gershenberg, Managing Partner
Education: BA, Economics, Wesleyan University; MA, Finance, John F Kennedy School of Government, Harvard University
Background: FirstCorp; Investment Banking, Union Bank of California
Sulu Mamdani, Managing Partner
Education: BA, Applied Mathematics, Harvard College; MBA, Harvard Business School
Background: Co-founder of Mazu Networks, manager of venture capital investments at The Carlyle Group

1765 SVOBODA CAPITAL PARTNERS
One North Franklin Street
Suite 1500
Chicago, IL 60606
Phone: 312-267-8750 Fax: 312-267-6025
e-mail: info@svoco.com
web: www.svoco.com

Mission Statement: A private equity firm that invests in and helps build value-added distribution, business services and consumer products businesses.

Fund Size: $250 million
Average Investment: $10 - $25 million
Investment Criteria: Management Buyouts, Leveraged Recapitalizations, Growth Equity Investments
Industry Group Preference: Distribution, Business Products & Services, Consumer Products
Portfolio Companies: SWC Technology Partners, Reliable Parts, Blake & Pendleton, Strategic Marketing, MEI Labels Holdings, GPA, Monroe Engineering, DataBank, Applied Adhesives, Cape Electrical Supply, Border Construction Specialties

Key Executives:
John A Svoboda, Senior Managing Director
e-mail: jas@svoco.com
Education: BA, Williams College; MBA, Stanford Graduate School of Business
Background: Corporate Finance Department, William Blair & Company
Directorships: Glover Park Group, OPT Holdings, Cape Electrical Supply, GPA Holdings
Andrew B Albert, Managing Director
e-mail: aalbert@svoco.com
Education: BA, Washington University; MBA, University of Wisconsin
Background: CEO, Nashua Corporation; Chairman/CEO, Rittenhouse
Directorships: Border Construction Specialties, Forsythe Technologies, Transco

1766 SWAN & LEGEND VENTURES
P.O. Box 6247
Leesburg, VA 20178
web: www.swanandlegend.com

Mission Statement: Swan & Legend invests in tech-enabled consumer brands and the business-to-business companies that support them.

Industry Group Preference: Consumer Brands, Restaurants, Digital Commerce, Retail Services, Wellness
Portfolio Companies: Airbnb, Allegro Venture Partners, Anonymous Content, Bedrock, Beefsteak, Big Teams, Capital Sports Ventures, Cava, China Senior Care, Custom Ink, Duratap, Echo360, Evergreen Transport, Framebridge, Fyrfly, Glidr, Gwynnie Bee, Ideeli, José Andrés ThinkFoodGroup, Kind, La Lumière, MusiCapital, MyOwnMed, Noodle, Optoro, OrderGrove, Pinterest, Quad Learning, Revsite, Showfields, Soapbox, Social Radar, Square, Sugar23. SV Angel, Tango Card, Urbanstems, Veritonic, Wthn

Other Locations:
154 Grand St.
New York, NY 10013

Key Executives:
Fredrick D. Schaufeld, Co-Founder & Managing Director
Education: BA, Government, Lehigh University
Background: Partner, Monumental Sports and Entertainment; Founder, NEW Corp.
Directorships: Noodle, CustomInk, Frambridge, KIND Healthy Snacks, Quad Learning, José Andrés' ThinkFoodGroup, Cava, UrbanStems, DuraTap
Anthony Nader, Co-Founder & Managing Director
Education: John Carroll University; MBA Weatherhead School of Management at Case Western Reserve University
Background: Partner, Monumental Sports and Entertainment; Senior Management, NEW Corp.
Directorships: Cranemere Group; Optoro, BigTeams, DuraTap, KIND Healthy Snacks
David Strasser, Managing Director
Education: BS, Hotel Administration, Cornell University; MBA, Fuqua School of Business at Duke University
Background: Salomon Brothers; Citigroup; Bank of America Securities; Janney Montgomery Scott; Andor Capital
Directorships: Seeds of Peace

1767 SWANDER PACE CAPITAL
101 Mission Street
Suite 1900
San Francisco, CA 94105
Phone: 415-477-8500 Fax: 415-477-8510
e-mail: info@spcap.com
web: www.spcap.com

Mission Statement: Focuses on management-led buyouts, company recapitalizations, industry consolidation, changes of ownership, growth companies needing capital, turnarounds in select situations.

Fund Size: $600 million
Founded: 1996
Minimum Investment: $3 million
Investment Criteria: Second-Stage, LBO
Industry Group Preference: Consumer Products, Food & Beverage, Food Services, Retailing, Hardware, Health Related, Leisure, Sports, Consumer Services
Portfolio Companies: Kicking Horse Coffee, Lavo, Recochem, Frozen Specialties, Applegate, Branch Brook Holdings, Oregon Ice Cream, Clarion Brands, Aden & Anais, Incase Deigns, Kooba, Raj Manufacturing, Gilchrist & Soames, gloProfessional, Merrick Pet Care, Wholesome Pet Care, Bravo Sports

621

Venture Capital & Private Equity Firms / Domestic Firms

Other Locations:
550 Hills Drive
Suite 106
Bedminster, NJ 07921
Phone: 908-719-2322 Fax: 908-719-9311

81273 North Service Road East
Oakville, ON L6H 1A7
Canada
Phone: 416-573-6098

Andrew Richards, Co-Founder/CEO
e-mail: andrew@spcap.com
Education: AB Fine Arts, Harvard University; MBA, Harvard Business School
Background: VP, William E Simon & Sons; Investment Banker, PaineWebber
Directorships: Nonni's Food Company, Frozen Specialties, S T Specialty Foods
Mark Poff, Managing Director, San Francisco
Education: BA, University of California, Davis; MSc, London School of Economics
Background: Bain & Co; Consultant, LEK Consulting
Directorships: Bravo Sports, Incase Designs, Kooba, Fresh Food Concepts, Insight Pharmaceuticals, Lavo, Liberty Brand Products, Pineridge Bakery, Raj Manufacturing, ReNew Life Formulas
Corby Reese, Managing Director, New Jersey Office
Education: BA, Yale University; MBA, Harvard Business School
Background: BancBoston Capital
Directorships: Bravo Sports, Frozen Specialities, Ideal Snacks, Insight Pharmaceuticals Corporation, ReNew Life Formulas, Santa Cruz Nutritionals
C Morris Stout, Managing Director, San Francisco
Education: BA, Vanderbilt University; MBA, Stanford Business School
Background: Vice President, Lonbard Investments
Directorships: Gilchrist & Soames, Good Source Solutions, Insight Pharmaceuticals, Border Foods, International Fiber Corporation, Lavo, Prepared Meal Holdingds, Santa Cruz Nutritionals
Robert DesMarais, Managing Director
Education: BS, Michigan State University; MBA, Northwestern University
Background: Principal, Banc of America Secruties' Consumer & Retail Group
Directorships: Lavo, Marketfare Foods, Raj Manufacturing
Tyler Matlock, Managing Director
Education: BA, University of Wisconsin-Madison

1768 SWITCH VENTURES
San Francisco, CA

e-mail: pitch@switch.vc
web: www.switch.vc

Mission Statement: A venture capital fund seeking to invest in companies based in the software and internet sector.

Founded: 2016
Investment Criteria: Seed, Early Stage
Industry Group Preference: Software, Applications, IoT, Technology
Portfolio Companies: Aaptiv, Allay, Altostra, The Athletic, Audm, Bulk MRO, Coinbunble, Floravere, Goodpath, Instaread, Jupiter, Luxuery Presence, NewtonX, NextRequest, PolicyGenius, SketchDeck, Tolemi, Unbound
Key Executives:
Paul Arnold, Founder/Partner
Education: BS, University of Utah; JD, University of Michigan Law School
Background: Consultant, McKinsey & Co.; Senior Director, AppDirect; Founder/Partner, Arnold Capital

1769 SYCAMORE VENTURES
731 Alexander Road
Suite 303
Princeton, NJ 08540

Phone: 609-759-8888 Fax: 609-759-8900
web: www.sycaventures.com

Mission Statement: Sycamore Ventures is a team of dedicated investment professionals with a broad range of industry experiences in communication, software, and life sciences.

Geographic Preference: US, the greater China region, India
Fund Size: $550 Million
Founded: 1995
Average Investment: $10-25 Million
Minimum Investment: $5 Million
Industry Group Preference: Semiconductors, Telecommunications, Internet Technology, Software, Healthcare, Media, Financial Services, Networking, E-Commerce & Manufacturing, Biotechnology, Broadcasting
Portfolio Companies: Acer Group, ACM Research Corporation, Advanced Analogic Technologies, AirCell, Airspan Networks, Applied Optoelectronics, ASUSTek Computer, Avalent Technologies, BizLink Holdings, Brightcord Investment, CapMAC Holdings, Cardiva Medical, Cellink, Clear Technology, Corrigo, Co-Tech Copper Foil, C-Pro, DVN Holdings, eAccess, EASYLINK, Epitomics, Equity Broadcasting, Exclaim, FloNetwork, Global Sun Technology, Hayes Medical, HOLA Home Furnishing, Home Inns & Hotel Management, International Media Group, IPCore Tecnologies, Juno Online Services, Landune International, LogicVision, MAKO Surgical, Marketech International, Net263 Holdings, NWP Services, Ortodisc Technology, Ortega InfoSystems, OSA Technologies, Osteotech, Outlast Technologies, People's Motor International, Premier Pacific Pharmaceutical Industries, Ralink Technology, Redgate Media, RIM China Company, RxHope, Sakura Enterprises, Semiconductor Manufacturing International Corporation, Shin Kong Mitsukoshi Department Store, SOURCEBYNET, StemCyte, Taiwan IC Packaging, TeleNav, United Platform Technologies, Universal Media Group, Univision Technology, U-Systems, Wistron NeWeb, Xin Hua Media Coldings, Xylos, z-kat

Other Locations:
19925 Stevens Creek Boulevard
Cupertino, CA 95014-2358
Phone: 408-973-7861 Fax: 408-973-7261

3 Columbus Circle
Suite 1402
New York, NY 10019
Phone: 212-247-4590 x 5 Fax: 212-247-4801

Key Executives:
Stephen Chiao, Managing Partner
e-mail: sschiao@sycaventures.com
Education: Masters Degree in Electrical Engineering from Princeton University, and an MBA from the Wharton School at The University Pennsylvania
Background: Philips Electronics, RCA Corporation, AT&T Corporatio
Peter Gerry, Managing Partner
e-mail: pgerry@sycaventures.com
Kilin To, Managing Partner
e-mail: kto@sycaventures.com

1770 SYMMETRIC CAPITAL
950 Winter Street
Suite 2500
Waltham, MA 02451

Phone: 781-419-1100 Fax: 781-419-1101
web: www.symmetriccapital.com

Mission Statement: Symmetric Capital focuses on established businesses led by proven management teams, to create real partnerships to help them reach even greater success.

Geographic Preference: United States, Canada

Venture Capital & Private Equity Firms / Domestic Firms

Average Investment: $5 - $20 million
Investment Criteria: Growth-Stage, Expansion-Stage
Industry Group Preference: Business Products & Services, Consumer Products, Healthcare Services, Applied Technology, Industrial Products, Financial Services, Software
Portfolio Companies: Academic Management Services, Acurex, Air Serv, Appro Systems, Astech, Belkin, Biomedical Structures, BioRx, CBS Payroll Services, ChanTest, Cido, Complete Innovations, EMED, First Marketing, The Galtney Group, Gryphon Networks, Hemophelia Resources of America, Insperity, K-Tek, NewStar Financial, P&H Solutions, Pacer Electronics, Poorman-Douglas, Quote.com, Sanitors, School Imrpovement Network, Somero Enterprises, TekLinks

Key Executives:
  Daniel K Doyle, Managing Partner
  781-419-1120
  e-mail: ddoyle@symmetriccapital.com
  Education: AB, Economics, Harvard College
  Background: Managing Partner, Shawmut Capital
  Directorships: AirServ, Complete Innovations, Gryphon Networks
  Rob Walsh, General Partner
  e-mail: rwalsh@symmetriccapital.com
  Education: BS, Yale University; MBA, Harvard Business School
  Background: Principal, Texas Growth Fund

1771 SYNCOM VENTURE PARTNERS
4800 Hampden Lane
Suite 200
Bethesda, MD 20814

Phone: 301-608-3203 Fax: 301-608-3307
e-mail: info@syncom.com
web: www.syncom.com

Mission Statement: Syncom Venture Partners is aggressively focused on creating the next generation of market leaders within the rapidly growing sectors of digital media, mobile technology, and web based services.

Fund Size: $400 million
Founded: 1977
Average Investment: $5 - $15 million
Investment Criteria: Growth Stage
Industry Group Preference: Multimedia, License Communications, Digital Business Services
Portfolio Companies: AppTap, LikeList, Dub, Heatwave Interactive, Indoor Direct, Maya Entertainment Group, Outspark, Proclivity Systems, ShowUHow, Thought Equity Motion, V-ME Media, Voyages, WDT
  Terry L. Jones, Managing Partner
  Education: BS, Electrical Engineering, Trinity College; MS, Electrical Engineering, George Washington University; MBA, Harvard University Graduate School of Business Administration
  Background: Co-Founder and Vice President, Klambere Savings and Loan; Senior Electrical Engineer, Westinghouse Aerospace and Litton Industries
  Directorships: V-me Media, Weather Decisions, TV One
  Kateri Jones, Analyst
  Education: BA, English and Economics, Spelman College
  Roy Kosuge, Principal
  Education: BA, Harvard University
  Background: Vice President of International Strategy and Operations, Faith Inc; Director of Business Development, Universal Music Group; Strategy Analyst, AT&t Broadband
  Stanley T. Smith, Principal
  Education: BA, History, Dartmouth College
  Background: Director of Corporate Development, Yahoo!'s Search Marketing Group; Director of Mergers and Acquisitions, Overture Inc.; Vivendi Universal; Paine Webber; Merrill Lynch
  Directorships: Alikelist; Heatwave Interactive; Outspark; Proclivity Systems

Herbert P. Wilkins, Jr., General Partner
Education: BS, Marketing, University of Maryland; MBA, F.W. Olin School of Business at Babson College
Background: IVT; SI-TV; TMX Interactive
Tyrone Wilson, Chief Financial Officer
Education: BBA, Temple University

1772 SYNERGY LIFE SCIENCE PARTNERS
PO Box 22489
San Francisco, CA 94122

Phone: 650-854-7155 Fax: 650-332-1581
web: www.synergylsp.com

Mission Statement: Focused on investing in private, early-stage medical device companies or emerging companies who are combining a medical device with a therapeutic payload.

Geographic Preference: United States
Investment Criteria: Early-Stage
Industry Group Preference: Life Sciences, Therapeutics, Medical Devices
Portfolio Companies: Aptus Endosystems, Inspire Medical Systems, iRhythm Technologies, Oraya Therapeutics, Synecor

Key Executives:
  Richard Stack MD, Managing Director
  e-mail: rstack@synergylsp.com
  Background: President, Synecor; Professor Emeritus of Medicine in Cardiology, Duke University
  Directorships: BaroSense
  William Starling, Managing Director
  e-mail: wstarling@synergylsp.com
  Education: BS, University of North Carolina, Chapel Hill; MBA, University of Southern California
  Background: CEO, Synecor; American Edwards Laboratories; Founding Management Team, Advanced Cardiovascular Systems; Vice President, Ventritex; President/CEO, Cardiac Pathways Corporation
  Directorships: iRhythm Technologies
  Mudit Jain PhD, Partner
  e-mail: mjain@synergylsp.com
  Education: BE, Electrical Engineering, Regional Engineering College; PhD, Biomedical Engineering, Duke University; MBA, Wharton School
  Background: Executive Director, Johnson & Johnson Development Corporation; Chief Science Officer, Johnson & Johnson; Cardiac Rhythm Management Division, Guidant Corporation
  Directorships: Inspire Medical Systems
  Tracy Pappas, Chief Financial Officer
  e-mail: tpappas@synergylsp.com
  Education: BA, Economics, University of California, Berkeley; CPA
  Background: CFO, Scale Venture Partners; CFO, Saints; KPMG

1773 SYNERGY VENTURES
545 Middlefield Road
Suite 205
Menlo Park, CA 94025

Phone: 650-322-3475
web: www.synergyventures.net

Mission Statement: Synergy Ventures invests in medical device companies in the United States.

Geographic Preference: United States
Fund Size: $25 million
Founded: 1996
Average Investment: $250,000 - $1 million
Minimum Investment: $250,000
Industry Group Preference: Medical Devices
Portfolio Companies: Breathe Technologies, C2 Therapeutics, Chestnut Medical, CV Ingenuity, Promethean Surgical Devices, RetroVascular, Spiracur, Uptake Medical

623

Venture Capital & Private Equity Firms / Domestic Firms

Key Executives:
  Allan Johnston PhD, Co-Founder & Managing Director
  Education: PhD, Bioinorganic Chemistry, University of Guelph
  Background: Program Manager, Center for Medical Technology, SRI International
  Directorships: Three Oaks Innovations
  Robert Okun MIM, Co-Founder & Managing Director
  Education: BA, Japanese, MA, International Management, American Graduate School of Management
  Background: Director, Berkeley/NED Development Capital Limited

1774 SYNGENTA VENTURES
629 Davis Drive
Research Triangle Park
Durham, NC 27709

Phone: 919-226-7302
web: www.syngentaventures.com

Mission Statement: Syngenta Ventures, the venture capital arm of Syngenta, is seeking to indentify early stage companies with a strong technology base or new business model, or both, where our team of investment professionals, together with the support of our 26,000 colleagues across the world, can help build valuable businesses benefitting both Syngenta and the investee company stakeholders.

Geographic Preference: North America, Europe, Asia, South America
Average Investment: $500,000 - $5 million
Investment Criteria: Early-Stage
Portfolio Companies: Agrinos, Agrivida, Biognosys, BioLeap, BoMill, Brandtone, Edenspace, EuroFem, Illumitex, Marrone Bio Innovations, Metabolon, Nemgenix, Population Genetics
Key Executives:
  Shiri Ailons, Head
  Education: MBA, Oxford Business School; LLB, Tel Aviv University
  Background: ADAMA Agricultural Solution
  Jason Gabriel, Managing Director
  Education: MBA, University of Virginia
  Background: Managing Director, Third Security LLC
  David Pierson, Managing Director
  Education: BS, United States Military Academy; MBA, Duke University
  Background: Lieutenant, 82nd Airborne Division, Carolina; Captain, 2nd Infantry Division, Korea; Eneral Partner, Intersouth Partners
  Michael Lee, Managing Director
  Education: BSc, PhD, University of Durham; MBA, RSM Erasmus, Rotterdam
  Background: Unilever
  Shubhang Shankar, Managing Director
  Education: Indian Institute of Technology, New Delhi; MBA, Indian Institute of Management, Ahmedabad
  Background: Management Consultant, Boston Consulting Group

1775 SYNTHESIS CAPITAL
184 High Street
4th Floor
Boston, MA 02110

Phone: 857-366-8456 Fax: 857-366-8466
web: www.synthesis.capital

Mission Statement: Synthesis Capital is a Boston-based firm led by a team of investment professionals who previously managed the healthcare venture practice within Advent International for over 14 years. Collectively, the Synthesis Capital Team has led or helped manage over 35 private equity and venture investments in biotechnology, medical device companies and healthcare services at all stages of development.

Geographic Preference: United States, Europe
Average Investment: $10 - $15 million
Investment Criteria: Growth Financing, Special Situations, Spin Outs
Industry Group Preference: Biotechnology, Medical Technology, Medical Devices, Healthcare Services, Healthcare Information Technology, Biopharmaceuticals
Portfolio Companies: Achillion Pharmaceuticals, Aegerion Pharmaceuticals, Alcala Farma, Ampla Pharmaceuticals, Anadys Pharmaceuticals, Anesiva, Array BioPharma, Artemis Pharmaceuticals, Astex Therapeutics, Cellzone, Crucell, Cubist Pharmaceuticals, CV Therapeutics, deCODE Genetics, Enanta Pharmaceuticals, Exelixis, GPC Biotech, ILEX Oncology, Nereus Pharmaceuticals, Pharming, Prexa Pharmaceuticals, Raptor Pharmaceuticals, ReVision Therapeutics, Sirion Therapeutics, Spear Therapeutics, Tecan, Telik, Trident Pharmaceuticals, Variagenics, Viatris
Key Executives:
  Jason Fisherman, Co-Founder
  Education: BA, Molecular Biophysics & Biochemistry, Yale University; MD, University of Pennsylvania; MBA, Wharton School
  Background: Managing Director, Advent International; National Cancer Institute
  Directorships: Achillion Pharmaceuticals, Ampla Pharmaceuticals, Cellzome, Nereus Pharmaceuticals, Prexa Pharmaceuticals, Spear Therapeutics
  Charles Cohen, Co-Founder
  Education: BA, University of New York, Buffalo; PhD, New York University School of Medicine; Post Doctoral Fellowship, University of Virginia
  Background: Partner, Advent International; Co-Founder, Creative BioMolecules
  Directorships: Ampla Pharmaceuticals, Cellzome, Exelixis, Prexa Pharmaceuticals, Trident Pharmaceuticals, ReVision Therapeutics, Sirion Therapeutics
  Tom Needham, Co-Founder
  Education: BA, Bowdoin College; MBA, Olin Graduate School of Business
  Background: Principal, Advent International; Vice President, GPC Biotech
  Directorships: Prexa Pharmaceuticals, Spear Therapeutics, Trident Pharmaceuticals

1776 TA ASSOCIATES
200 Calrendon St.
56th Floor
Boston, MA 02116

Phone: 617-574-6700 Fax: 617-574-6728
web: www.ta.com

Mission Statement: TA Associates invests in private companies in growth industries to help management teams build significant value. During our over 40-year history, we have invested in and supported more than 400 companies as a long-term partner through a variety of economic and financial market cycles. In addition to providing financial support, we offer strategic guidance, industry knowledge and contacts in the financial community.

Fund Size: $16 billion
Founded: 1968
Minimum Investment: $60 million
Investment Criteria: Seeks investment opportunities in growing profitable, private companies. We will also provide capital for management-led buyouts and recapitalization of growth companies.
Industry Group Preference: Technology, Financial Services, Healthcare, Business Products & Services, Consumer
Portfolio Companies: 5.11, Accruent, Aicent, Amann Girrbach AG, Answers, Arxan Technologies, AVG Technologies, BATS Global Markets, Bigpoint GmbH, BluePay Processing, Cath Kidston, CMOSIS, Cosentry, Dealer Tire, DigiCert, DNCA Finance SA, Dr Lal PathLabs, Dutch, e-Rewards, Evanston Capital Management, First Eagle Investment Management, Flashtalking, Forgame Holdings

Venture Capital & Private Equity Firms / Domestic Firms

Limited, Fotolia Holdings, Fractal Analytics Private Limited, FreeWave Technologies, Full Sail University, Indialdeas.com, Internationella Engelska Skolan, IntraLinks, ION Investment Group, Jupiter Fund Management, Keeley Asset Management, Kinetic Social, M and M Direct, Med Solutions, Micromax Informatics Limited, MicroSeismic, Millenium Laboratories, MIS Implants Technologies, Nintex Group, Numeric Investors, Onlineprinters GmbH, Professional Warranty Service, Prometheus Group, Radialpoint, RGM Advisors, Senior Whole Health, SoftWriters, SpeedCast, Stadion Money Management, Tega Industries, TEOCO, The Los Angeles Film Schook, The Rocky Mountain School of Design, Towne Park, Twin Med, Vatterott Educational Centers, Viewpoint, Zadig & Voltaire

Other Locations:
64 Willow Place
Suite 100
Menlo Park, CA 94025
Phone: 650-473-2200 **Fax:** 650-473-2235

TA Associates Ltd
3rd Floor, Devonshire House
1 Mayfair Place
London W1J 8AJ
United Kingdom
Phone: 44-2078320200 **Fax:** 44-2078230201

TA Associates Advisory Pvt. Ltd.
13th Floor, Birla Aurora
Dr. Annie Besant Rd.
Worli, Mumbai 400 030
India
Phone: 91-2261443100 **Fax:** 91-2261443101

TA Associates Asia Pacific Ltd.
One Exchange Square
16th Floor, 8 Connaught Place
Central
Hong Kong
Phone: 852-3656-6300 **Fax:** 852-3656-6301

Key Executives:
Jeffrey S Barber, Managing Director
617-574-6795
e-mail: jbarber@ta.com
Education: BA Political Science, Johns Hopkins University; MBA, Columbia Business School
Background: Weiss Peck & Greer; Vestar Capital Partners; Financial Analyst/Global Power Utilities, Morgan Stanley & Co

Michael S Berk, Managing Director
617-574-6709
e-mail: mberk@ta.com
Education: AB, East Asian Studies, Harvard College; MBA, Harvard Business School; JD, Harvard Law School
Background: Joseph Littlejohn & Levy, Frontenac Company

Jeffrey T Chambers, Senior Advisor
650-473-2201
e-mail: jchambers@ta.com
Education: BA, Harvard University; MBA, Stanford University
Background: Meredith Associates

Todd R Crockett, Managing Director
650-473-2227
e-mail: tcrockett@ta.com
Education: BA, Princeton University; MBA, Harvard Business School
Background: Salomon Brothers

Brian J Conway, Managing Partner
617-574-6705
e-mail: bconway@ta.com
Education: BA, Amherst College; MBA, Standford University
Background: Merrill Lynch

Johnathan M Goldstein, Senior Advisor
617-574-6773
e-mail: jgoldstein@ta.com
Education: SB Biology/Chemical Engineering, SM Biochemical Engineering, MIT; MBA, Harvard Business School
Background: Biogen

Kurt R Jaggers, Managing Director
650-473-2203
e-mail: kjaggers@ta.com
Education: BS/MS Electrical Engineering, Stanford University; MBA, Stanford University Graduate School of Business
Background: Network Equipment Technologies; ROLM Corporation; Business Computer Corporation; Boston Consulting Group

A. Bruce Johnston, Advisor
617-574-6706
e-mail: bjohnston@ta.com
Education: BS, Electrical Engineering, Duke University; MBA, Pennsylvania State University
Background: President, idealab! Boston; General Manager, Lotus Development Corporation; Research Analyst, First Boston Corporation; Sales & Engineering, AT&T Communications

Roger B Kafker, Managing Director
617-574-6785
e-mail: rkafker@ta.com
Education: BA, History, Haverford College; MBA, Harvard Business School
Background: Bakers Trust Company

Kenneth T Schiciano, Managing Director
617-574-6768
e-mail: kts@ta.com
Education: BS, Electrical Engineering & Computer Science, Duke University; MS, Electrical Engineering, Stanford University; SM Management, MIT Sloan School of Management
Background: AT&T Bell Laboratories

Richard D Tadler, Senior Advisor
617-574-6708
e-mail: rtadler@ta.com
Education: BS, Finance, University of Virginia; MBA, Wharton School, University of Pennsylvania
Background: General Partner, Investments Oraange Nassau; ARMCO

Jonathan W Meeks, Managing Director
650-473-2238
e-mail: jmeeks@ta.com
Education: BS, Mathematics, Yale University
Background: Robertson Stephens

Jennifer M Mulloy, Managing Director
650-473-2229
e-mail: jmulloy@ta.com
Education: AB, Economics, Stanford University; MBA, Harvard Business School
Background: Robertson Stephens

Ajit Nedungadi, Managing Partner
011-44-20-7823-0210
e-mail: ajit@ta.com
Education: BS, Electrical Engineering & Economics, Yale University; MBA, Harvard Business School
Background: Trilogy Software, Investcorp International, Credit Suisse First Boston

M Roy Burns, Managing Director
617-574-6732
e-mail: rburns@ta.com
Education: BS, Business Administration, Washington & Lee University; MBA, Stanford Graduate School of Business
Background: Equity Investments, Davidson Kempner Partners; Leveraged Finance, Banc of America Securities

Mark H Carter, Managing Director
617-574-6739
e-mail: mcarter@ta.com
Education: BE, Mechanical Engineering, Vanderbilt University; MBA, Columbia Business School

Venture Capital & Private Equity Firms / Domestic Firms

Background: Parthenon Capital, FdG Associates, The Halifax Group, Lehman Brothers
Hythem T El-Nazer, Managing Director
617-574-6776
e-mail: hte@ta.com
Education: London School of Economics; AB, Economics, Brown University; MBA, Columbia Business School
Background: McKinsey & Company; Investment Banking, Donaldson Lufkin & Jenrette
Harry D Taylor, Managing Director
617-574-6767
e-mail: htaylor@ta.com
Education: AB, Economics, Hamilton College; MBA, Harvard Business School
Background: Associate, Stone Point Capital; Financial Analyst, Goldman Sachs & Co.
Directorships: e-Rewards, IntraLinks, Numara Software
William D Christ, Managing Director
617-574-6769
e-mail: bchrist@ta.com
Education: BS, Business Administration, Washington & Lee University; MBA, Tuck School of Business, Dartmouth College
Background: Global Real Estate Group, Lehman Brothers

1777 TAILWIND CAPITAL
485 Lexington Avenue
New York, NY 10017

Phone: 212-271-3800
e-mail: info@tailwind.com
web: www.tailwind.com

Mission Statement: Tailwind focuses on growing middle market companies in the healthcare and business & communications sectors.

Fund Size: $775 million
Founded: 2000
Average Investment: $25 million - $100 million
Investment Criteria: Enterprise Value of Up to $300 Million; EBITA of $10 Million to $50 Million
Industry Group Preference: Healthcare, Business Products & Services, Telecommunications
Portfolio Companies: Adobe Healthcare, Acertus, Anvil International, Apex Companies, Archway Marketing Services, AST, Banner Solutions, Benevis, Brawler Industries, Colony Hardware, Core BTS, Cumberland Consulting Group, Cumming Group, DermaRite, Diamondback Drugs, Diversified, Edenbridge, Freedom Innovations, Hamilton State Bancshares, HMT, Lieberman Research Worldwide, Loenbro, Lone Peak, Invatron Systems, Longs Pharmacy Solutions, National HME, Nautilus Neurosciences, Nsight, Oceus Networks, Optimal Solutions Integration, PetMedicus Laboratories, Pillar Processing, PremierXD, RANDYS Worldwide Automotive, ReTrans, SDI Health, Stratix, TowerCo, Transit Wireless, Ventiv Technology, VersaPharm

Key Executives:
Lawrence B. Sorrel, Managing Partner
e-mail: lsorrel@tailwind.com
Education: Brown University, Harvard Law School, Harvard Business School
Background: Welsh Carson Anderson & Stowe, Morgan Stanley
James S. Hoch, Partner
e-mail: jhoch@tailwind.com
Education: Williams College, Harvard Business School
Background: Morgan Stanley Capital Partners
Frank V. Sica, Partner
e-mail: fsica@tailwind.com
Education: Wesleyan University, Amos Tuck School of Business, Dartmouth College
Background: President, Soros Private Funds Management
Brian S. Berkin, Partner
e-mail: bberkin@tailwind.com
Education: University of Michigan; Wharton School

Background: Pacific Founders; LLR Partners; RoundTable Healthcare Partners; Credit Suisse
Jeffrey M. Calhoun, Partner
e-mail: jcalhoun@tailwind.com
Education: Tufts University, University of California, Berkeley Haas School of Business
Background: Montgomery Securities, Thomas Weisel Partners
Geoffrey S. Raker, Partner
e-mail: graker@tailwind.com
Education: Brown University; Harvard Business School
Background: Warburg Pincus, Morgan Stanley, Bain & Company
Adam F. Stulberger, Partner
e-mail: astulberger@tailwind.com
Education: Lafayette College, New York University School of Law
Background: SpectraSite Communications, Morgan Stanley, Credit Suisse
David S. Gorton, Partner
e-mail: dgorton@tailwind.com
Education: Vanderbilt University; Emory University School of Law
Background: Investment Banker, Lehman Brothers; Lawyer, Skadden Arps Slate Meagher & Flom
Andrew R. Mayer, Partner
e-mail: amayer@tailwind.com
Education: Dartmouth College; Wharton School
Background: Thomas H. Lee Partners; Deutsche Bank
Sanjay Swani, Partner
e-mail: sswani@tailwind.com
Education: Princeton University; Harvard Law School; MIT Sloan School of Management
Background: Welsh Carson Anderson & Stowe; Morgan Stanley

1778 TAKEDA VENTURES
435 Tasso St.
Suite 300
Palo Alto, CA 94301

Phone: 650-328-2900 Fax: 650-328-2922
e-mail: contact@tri-takeda.com
web: www.takedaventures.com

Mission Statement: Takeda Ventures, Inc. is the corporate venture arm of Takeda Pharmaceutical Company Ltd. that supports therapeutic innovation in the biopharmaceutical sector and academic sectors.

Founded: 2001
Investment Criteria: Early Stage, Late Stage
Industry Group Preference: Biopharmaceuticals, Healthcare, Pharmaceuticals
Portfolio Companies: Ambys Medicines, Cortexyme, Crescendo Biologics, Hookipa Biotech AG, Obsidian, Outpost Medicine, Palleon Pharmaceuticals, Presage Biosciences, Ribon Therapeutics, StrideBio

Key Executives:
Michael Martin, Head of Takeda Ventures
Education: PhD
Background: Takeda Pharmaceuticals
Karen Hong, Senior Partner
Education: BS, Chemistry, BA, Molecular Biology, University of California, Berkeley; PhD, Biology, MIT
Background: Partner, ProQuest Investments
Directorships: Agile Therapeutics, Mersana Therapeutics, Clarus Therapeutics
David A Shaywitz, Senior Partner
Education: MD, Harvard Medical School; PhD, MIT
Background: Chief Medical Officer, DNAnexus; Merck; Boston Consulting Group; Theravance
Robbie Woodman, Senior Partner
Education: MSc, Biochemistry, University of Oxford; PhD, Oncology, University of Cambridge
Background: Principal, Sofinnova Partners

Venture Capital & Private Equity Firms / Domestic Firms

1779 TALLWOOD VENTURE CAPITAL
325 Lytton Avenue
Suite 4A
Palo Alto, CA 94301

Phone: 650-473-6750
e-mail: information@tallwoodvc.com
web: www.tallwoodvc.com

Mission Statement: Focuses on investments in differential technologies and products that will have a significant impact on the semiconductor industry.
Fund Size: $600 million
Industry Group Preference: Semiconductors
Portfolio Companies: Accent, Alphion Corp., Audience, Axiom Microdevices, Calypto Design Systems Inc., Cavendish Kinetics, Crossing Automation Inc., Cyras Systems, Iknaos, Inphi Corp., Marvell Technology Group, NewPort Communications, Ozmo Devices, Pixim Inc., Qspeed Semiconductor, Quintic, Redfern Integrated Optics, Sandbridge Technologies Inc., SiRF Technology Holdings Inc., Silicon Clocks, Stream Machine, TrueSpan, Wave Computing, Wilocity

Other Locations:
Tallwood (WuXi) Venture Capital
#1002, #21-1 Chang Jiang Road
WuXi New District, WuXi
JiangSu Provice 214028
China
Phone: 86-051081816335 Fax: 86-051081814997

Key Executives:
Luis Arzubi, General Partner
Education: BS/MS, Electrical Engineering, National University of Littoral, Argentina
Background: VP/GM, Microelectronics Division, IBM; Lab Director, General Technology Division, IBM
Directorships: Cavendish Kinetics
Dado Banatao, Managing Partner
Education: BEng, Mapua Institute of Technology, Philippines; MS, Electrical Engineering, Stanford University
Background: Partner, Mayfield Fund; Co-Founder, Chips & Technologies; Co-Founder, Mostron; GM, National Semiconductor, GM, Seeq Technologies; GM, Intersil; GM, Commodore International

1780 TAO VENTURE CAPITAL PARTNERS
e-mail: info@taovp.com
web: www.taocap.com

Mission Statement: TAO Venture Capital Partners provides capital and advisory services to entrepreneurs pursuing global market opportunities in Information Technology, Internet, Media, and Consumer Services.
Industry Group Preference: Information Technology, Internet, Media, Consumer Services, Clean Technology, Security, SaaS
Portfolio Companies: Active.com, Active Network, BrightCloud, EcoATM, Par Accel, TradeBeam

1781 TAYRONA VENTURES
8411 Market Street
San Francisco, CA 94103

web: tayronaventures.wordpress.com

Mission Statement: Tayrona Ventures is a hands-on fund that invests in and works closely with early stage startups in Colombia and throughout Latin America. We take a Silicon Valley approach to venture capital, with a team of seasoned mentors and partners in the region. Our ultimate mission is to create and accelerate the next generation of technology companies in Latin America's rapidly emerging markets.
Geographic Preference: Latin America
Investment Criteria: Early-Stage
Industry Group Preference: Technology

Key Executives:
Paul Bragiel, General Partner
Alan Colmenares, General Partner
William Hsu, General Partner

1782 TDF
2 Wisconsin Circle
Suite 920
Chevy Chase, MD 20815

Phone: 240-483-4286 Fax: 301-907-8850
web: www.tdfventures.com

Mission Statement: To partner with talented entrepreneurs and build competitive and innovative technology and services companies.
Geographic Preference: North America
Average Investment: $500,000 - $5 million
Investment Criteria: Early-Stage, Later-Stage
Industry Group Preference: Communications, Media, Technology
Portfolio Companies: American Honors, AppMesh, Arxan Technologies, Aztek Networks, Booker, Colubris Networks, Cyan, EdgeConneX, HelloWallet, IEX Group, Inlet Technologies, Insightpool, Mindshift Technologies, Ooma, Punchh, Quantance, Spectrum Bridge, SpinMedia, Stellar Loyalty, Valencell, Virtustream

Key Executives:
Jim Pastoriza, Partner
Education: BS, Columbia University; MS, MIT
Background: Partner, JP Morgan Communications Partners LP; Partner, AT&T Ventures; AT&T; Lucent Technologies
Randall Brouckman, Operating Partner
Education: BS, University of Michigan; MS, Electrical Engineering, Stanford University
Background: CEO, EdgeConneX; Founder, Wade Capital Group

1783 TEAKWOOD CAPITAL
8226 Douglas Avenue
Suite 355
Dallas, TX 75225

Phone: 214-750-1590 Fax: 214-750-1468
e-mail: contact@teakwoodcapital.com
web: www.teakwoodcapital.com

Mission Statement: Teakwood Capital is a Dallas, Texas private equity firm. We make equity investments in profitable companies and strong management teams seeking growth.
Geographic Preference: Texas, Arizona, Arkansas, New Mexico, Louisiana, Oklahoma, Tennessee
Average Investment: $2 million
Investment Criteria: Growth, Buyouts, Recapitalization, Corporate Divestitures
Industry Group Preference: Technology-Enabled Services, Software
Portfolio Companies: Prodagio Software, SigmaFlow, Long Range Systems, Clockwork Solutions, MyOpenJobs, InReach, TWG Plus
Ed Olkkola, Managing Director
Education: University of Massachusetts; MBA, Northeastern University
Background: SVP, A.H. Belo Corporation; General Partner, Austin Ventures; Compaq
Vinse Davidson, Managing Director, Finance/CFO/COO
Education: BS, Accounting, University of Tennessee, Martin; MPA, University of Texas, Austin
Background: Partner & CFO, STARTech Early Ventures

1784 TECH COAST ANGELS
Santa Monica Blvd
Los Angeles, CA 90034

web: www.techcoastangels.com

627

Venture Capital & Private Equity Firms / Domestic Firms

Mission Statement: Tech Coast Angels is an angel investment organization consisting of over 300 members in five networks across California. TCA focuses on funding startups in a number of industries, including life sciences, information technology, media, consumer products, financial, software, retail and Internet.
Geographic Preference: Southern California
Founded: 1997
Investment Criteria: Startups, Early Stage
Industry Group Preference: Life Sciences, Biotechnology, Information Technology, Services, Retail, Consumer & Leisure, Internet, Software, Media, Consumer Products, Technology, Industrial, Clean Technology
Portfolio Companies: Accuscore, Active Live Scientific, Adventrx Pharmaceuticals, Aggregage, AgileNano, Airborne1, Airsis, Akiva, Allylix, Althea, AnaBios Corporation, Angstrom, AnyMeeting, Apeel Sciences, Ascendant Spirits, Atlas Apps, Avaxia Biologics, Axitron, Banshee Bungee, Beacon Healthcare, Benchmark Revenue Management, BikeStation, Bitvore Corporation, Bizbuyer, Bluebeam Software, Brain X, BrandAmerica, Business Backers, CardioCreate, CargoTech, CaseStack, Cashie Commerce, Cognition Therapeutics, Continental Windpower, Controltec, Cosemi Technologies, Crisi Medical Systems, Cyber Rain, Dax Solutions, DealCurrent, DermTech International, Dispatch Tracking Solutions, Docufide, EDN, Edufii, Eefoof, eGuardian, ElephantDrive, Enstigo, eTeamz, Etronica, ExtendCredit, EZ Apps, Fitn, Garden Organics, GazelleLab, Gemmus Pharma, GetThis, Ginni Designs, Gremln, GroundMetrics, H2O Audio, H2Scan, Heartland Resources, HitFix, Image Searcher, Immuno Gum, InfoBionic, Inhance Media Audiolife, Inlustra, Innozen, IPourIt, ISpeech, Iyia Technologies, JobSync, JointlyHealth, Kalyra, Landroller, Language Weaver, Larada Sciences, Leaselock, LeisureLink, Lendamend, Liquid Grids Swarmology, Luxim, Make It Work, Makucell, Mamoca, Masher Media, Media Matchmaker, Micropower, Mindbody Software, Mobile Cause, MobileXL, Mogl, MojoPages, Molecular Detection, MyShape, Neural Analytics, Nine Star, Ninja Metrics, Numira Biosciences, Olfactor Laboratories, Olive Medical, Ombitron, One Stop Systems, Opposing Views, Opticon M

1785 TECHNOLOGY CROSSOVER VENTURES
250 Middlefield Road
Menlo Park, CA 94025

Phone: 650-614-8200
web: www.tcv.com

Mission Statement: Technology Crossover Ventures (TCV) invests in public companies through private and public transactions. In evaluating technology companies, TCV looks for proven business models, demonstrated revenue traction and a solid path to profitability.
Geographic Preference: United States, Canada
Fund Size: $3.3 billion
Founded: 1995
Average Investment: $35 million
Minimum Investment: $15 million
Investment Criteria: Expansions, Late Stage
Industry Group Preference: Information Technology, Internet, Software, Fintech, Infrastructure
Portfolio Companies: Act-On, Actifio, Adknowledge, Alarm.cOm, Appnexus, Dollar Shave Club, Dough.com, eBags, eHarmony, Electronic Arts, Elevate Credit, ExtraHop Networks, Facebook, Genesys, Go Daddy, iPipeline, IQMS, Just Fabulous, K12, kgb, Merkle Group, Minted, Netflix, New Voice Media, NexTag, Open English, Origin Holdings, OSIsoft, Rapid7, Rent the Runway, Sitecore Corporation, SiteMinder, Spotify, Swagbucks, Tastytrade, TechTarget, TheStreet.com, Think Finance, ThinkingPhones, TradingScreen, Travelport, VICE Media, Webroot Software

Other Locations:
280 Park Avenue
East Building, 26th Floor
New York, NY 10017
Phone: 212-808-0200

11 Charles II Street
1st Floor
London SW1Y 4QU
United Kingdom
Phone: 44-2070042620

Key Executives:
Jay Hoag, Founding General Partner
650-614-8200
Fax: 650-475-1229
Education: BA, Economics and Political Science, Northwestern University; MBA, University of Michigan
Background: Managing Director, Chancellor Capital Mangement
Rick Kimball, Founding General Partner
650-614-8200
Fax: 650-475-1229
Education: Cum Laude, AB degree History, Dartmouth College; MBA Finance, University of Chicago
Background: Managing Director, Montgomery Securities
Kapil Venkatachalam, General Partner
Education: MS, Electrical Engineering, Dartmouth College
Background: CIO, Goldman Sachs
Directorships: EtQ; Rave Mobile Safety
John Drew, General Partner
650-614-8200
Fax: 650-475-1229
Education: BS, United States Military Academy; MS, Columbia University
Background: President, CEO, International Network Services
Woody Marshall, General Partner
Education: BA, Hamilton College; MBA, JL Kellogg Graduate School of Management, Northwestern University
Background: Trident Capital; Associate, Leveraged Capital Group, Banque Paribas; Financial Analyst, Chase Manhattan Bank
Jake Reynolds, General Partner
650-614-8200
Fax: 650-475-1229
Education: AB, Dartmouth College; MBA, Columbia Business School
Background: Associate, General Atlantic Partners
Robert Trudeau, General Partner
Education: BAH, Political Science, Queen's University; MBA, University of Western Ontario
Background: Principal, General Atlantic Partners; Managing Director, iFormation Group
Tim McAdam, General Partner
Education: BA, Dartmouth College; MBA, Stanford Graduate School of Business
Background: Trinity Ventures, GTCR
Susan Clark, General Partner
Education: BS, Kettering University; MBA, Oakland University
Background: VP Operations/Chief of Staff, Vista Equity Parnters
David Yuan, General Partner
Education: AB, Harvard University; MBA, Stanford Graduate School of Business
Background: JPMorgan Partners; Management Consultant, Bain & Company

Venture Capital & Private Equity Firms / Domestic Firms

1786 TECHNOLOGY PARTNERS
550 University Avenue
Palo Alto, CA 94301

Phone: 650-289-9000 Fax: 650-289-9001
e-mail: admin@technologypartners.com
web: www.technologypartners.com

Mission Statement: Technology Partners teams with visionary entrepreneurs to create successful new companies.
Geographic Preference: Western United States
Fund Size: $300 million
Founded: 1980
Average Investment: $1-$25 million
Minimum Investment: $100,000
Investment Criteria: Seed, Startup, First-stage
Industry Group Preference: Clean Technology, Energy Technology, Water Technology, Advanced Materials, Life Sciences, Consumer Medicine, Cost-Effective Medicine, Neurotechnology
Portfolio Companies: Accelergy, Akeros Silicon, G2X Energy, IMERGY Power Systems, Imperium Renewables, KAIAM Corporation, NYSE Blue, Ogin, PolyFuel, PowerGenix Systems, Sensicore, Solexel, Tesla Motors, Benvenue Medical, BrainCells, Cadence Pharmaceuticals, Calypte Biomedical, Cardax Pharmaceuticals, Cell Pathways, Cereve, Cholestech, Corcept Therapeutics, CryoCor, Cryogen, Ekos, Neura, Elcely Therapeutics, Essentialis, ForSight VISIONS, HeartStent, Incline Therapeutics, Inncercool Therapies, Iomai, Iridex, Leptos Biomedical, Mewave, NeuroPace, Nfocus Neuromedical, PercuSurge, Revance Therapeutics, Rinat Neuroscience, Saegis Pharmaceuticals, Scioderm, Solta Medical, Spinal Dynamics, TONIX Pharmaceuticals, Transcend Medical, Tria Beauty, Ventritex, Visiogen

Other Locations:
100 Shoreline Highway
Building B, Suite 282
Mill Valley, CA 94941
Phone: 415-332-9999 Fax: 415-332-9998

Key Executives:
Roger J Quy PhD, General Partner
e-mail: roger@technologypartners.com
Education: MBA, Hass School of Business, UC Berkeley; PhD, University of Keele; BA, Psychology, Law, University of Keele
Background: Hewlett-Packard Corporation, Oxford Instrument Group
Ted Ardell, Partner
e-mail: ted@technologypartners.com
Education: Graduate with Distinction, United States Naval Academy
Background: Impell Corporation, Bechtel Corporation
Ira M Ehrenpreis, General Partner
e-mail: ira@technologypartners.com
Education: JD, MBA, Stanford Graduate School of Business; Stanford University Law School; Graduate, UCLA
Background: Goldman, Sachs & Company, Juniper Partners
Jim Glasheen, General Partner
e-mail: jim@technologypartners.com
Education: BS, Duke University; MA/PhD, Harvard University; Deutsche Akademische Austauschdienst fellow at Universitaet des Saarlandes, Germany
Background: McKinsey & Company's Pharmaceutical and Medical Products Practice
Sheila Mutter, General Partner/CFO
e-mail: sheila@technologypartners.com
Education: BS in Accounting, University of Akron; Certified Public Accountant
Background: Coopers & Lybrand

1787 TECHNOLOGY VENTURES CORPORATION
1115 University Boulevard SE
2nd Floor
Albuquerque, NM 87106-4320

Phone: 505-246-2882
e-mail: contactus@techventures.org
web: www.techventures.org

Mission Statement: To facilitate the commercialization of technology in New Mexico, primarily from the national laboratories, and the research universities in the region. A primary focus of Technology Venture Corporation (TVC) is attracting risk investment money, and it assists technology-based companies by facilitating technology transfer and coordinating management and business assistance.
Geographic Preference: California, Nevada, New Mexico
Founded: 1993
Minimum Investment: Less than $100,000
Industry Group Preference: Technology

Key Executives:
John Freisinger, President & CEO
505-246-2882
Bob McCarty, CFO/Director of Operations
Background: GE, Avery Denison, Arthur Andersen, Sandia National Labs

1788 TECHOPERATORS
One Buckhead Plaza
3600 Peachtree Road NW
Suite 720
Atlanta, GA 30305

Phone: 404-537-2525
e-mail: info@techoperators.com
web: www.techoperators.com

Mission Statement: The TechOperators mission is straightforward: Helping seriously smart people turn game-changing ideas into great companies. We love taking a role in that rocket launch from early stage to widespread adoption, accelerated growth, and serious market share in a seriously competitive world. Today's software climate is ripe for innovation, and customers are ready to discover and purchase next-generation solutions. TechOperators makes smart investments that help innovative solutions reach those customers at scale. Our difference? Decades of hard-fought operating success and experience running at venture speed to keep you from being left in the dust. Because we're not just VCs, and great companies aren't built on just cool ideas and money.
Geographic Preference: Southeast United States
Fund Size: $450 million
Founded: 2008
Investment Criteria: Early-Stage
Industry Group Preference: Technology, Cloud Computing, Social Media, Technology-Enabled Software, Business to Business
Portfolio Companies: Vorstack, Siftit, Predikto, Hire IQ, Immunet, Endgame, Vocalocity, Joulex, Interactive Advisory Software, Ionic Security, Springbot

Key Executives:
Dave Gould, Operating Partner
Education: BS, Economics, University of Pennsylvania; MBA, Emory University
Background: Chairman & CEO, Witness Systems
Glenn McGonnigle, General Partner
Education: BS, Mechanical Engineering, University of Virginia
Background: CEO, VistaScape Security Systems; Co-Founder, Internet Security Systems
Said Mohammadioun, Managing Partner
Education: BS, MS, Electrical Engineering, Georgia Institute of Technology; MBA, Georgia State University
Background: CEO & Chairman, Synchrologic; Founder & CEO, Samna Corporation

Venture Capital & Private Equity Firms / Domestic Firms

Tom Noonan, Operating Partner
Education: Mechanical Engineering, Georgia Tech; MBA, Harvard University
Background: Chairman, President & CEO, Internet Security Systems; Senior Management, Dun & Bradstreet Sotware; National Infrastructure Advisory Council

1789 TECHSTARS
1050 Walnut Street
Boulder, CO 80302

web: www.techstars.com

Mission Statement: International network of startup accelerator programs.

Average Investment: $100K
Investment Criteria: Seed
Portfolio Companies: Digital Ocean, Localytics, Sendgrid, Contently, Occipital, Next Big Sound, Kapost, Orbotix, FullContact, Simple Energy, Mocavo, GrabCAD, Kinvey, Placester, Crowdtwist, OnSwipe, Everymove, Remitly, Remotive, Cloudability, Distil Networks, Moveline, Pivotdesk, Revolv, Coachup, Pillpack, Plated

Key Executives:
David Cohen, Founder/Chairman
Background: Pinpoint Technologies; earFeeder.com
Brad Feld, Co-Founder
Education: MIT
Background: Intensity Ventures; Mobius Venture Capital
David Brown, Co-Founder
Education: McGill University
Background: Pinpoint Technologies

1790 TEDCO
5565 Sterrett Place
Suite 214
Columbia, MD 21044

Phone: 410-740-9442 Fax: 410-740-9422
Toll-Free: 800-305-5556
e-mail: info@tedco.md
web: www.tedco.md

Mission Statement: TEDCO is a resource of mentoring, funding and networking for entrepreneurs and start-ups that need guidance as they bring innovative concepts to the market.

Fund Size: $550 million
Founded: 1998
Investment Criteria: Startup/Seed, Early State, Expansion, Later Stage Funding
Troy LeMaile-Stovall, CEO and Executive Director
Education: BS, Southern Methodist University; MS, Stanford University; MBA, Harvard University
Background: COO, University of the District of Columbia; Founder, LeMaile-Stovall LLC; Founder, GTMS Partners LLC
Stephen Auvil, Executive Vice President, Programs
e-mail: sauvil@tedco.md
Education: BS Biology & Engineering Science, Loyola College; MBA Administration, University of Baltimore; Masters of Science in Biotechnology, Johns Hopkins University
Background: Co-Principal Investigator, National Science Foundation; Director, UMBC Office of Technology Development; Assistant Director, Office of Technology Licensing at the Johns Hopkins University

1791 TEL VENTURE CAPITAL
3100 West Warren Avenue
Fremont, CA 94538

Phone: 510-624-3450 Fax: 510-624-3451
web: www.tel.com/about/tel_vc

Mission Statement: Our investments cover a range of technologies from those impacting Tokyo Electron's core semiconductor, flat panel display and PV businesses, to renewable energy, energy storage, water treatment, life science, healthcare, medical electronics, lighting, photonics, printable electronics and other areas of emerging innovation.

Geographic Preference: United States, Japan
Industry Group Preference: Semiconductors, Renewable Energy, Energy Storage, Water, Life Sciences, Healthcare, Electronics
Portfolio Companies: Molecular Imprints, Liola, Genalyte, MIOX, EnterVault, Luxtera, Crystal Solar, Vista Therapeutics, Quantum14, NanoGram, Unidym, Invarium

Other Locations:
Akasaka Biz Tower
3-1 Akasaka 5-Chome
Minato-ku
Tokyo 107-6325
Japan
Phone: 81-355617270 Fax: 81-355617066

Key Executives:
Kay Enjoji, President
Education: BA, Economis, Keio University
Background: Director, MEMS Division, TEL; TEL Corporate Marketing
Ted Hirose, Group Director
Education: BA, Keio University; MBA, New York University

1792 TELEGRAPH HILL PARTNERS
360 Post Street
Suite 601
San Francisco, CA 94108

Phone: 415-765-6980 Fax: 415-765-6983
e-mail: info@thpartners.net
web: www.thpartners.net

Mission Statement: A private equity firm dedicated to helping life science, medical device and healthcare companies achieve their growth objectives

Investment Criteria: Growth Equity
Industry Group Preference: Healthcare, Life Sciences, Medical Devices, Chemistry, Reagent Suppliers, Healthcare Services, Information Services
Portfolio Companies: Accumetrics, AcroMetrix, Agena Bioscience, Althea Technologies, AltheaDx, Ambion, AngioScore, Apppplied Precision, Asuragen, Aurora Discovery, BioVentrix, Confirma, Dharmacon, Estech, Freedom Innovations, Interface, Kinetikos Medical, LDR, MedPricer, NEXUS Biosystems, PneumRx, RareCyte, SAGE, SwitchGear, VidaCare

Key Executives:
J Matthew Mackowski, Chairman, Managing Director
e-mail: jmm@thpartners.net
Education: BA, Duke University; MBA, The Wharton School
Background: Citicorp Venture Capital; Roberton, Stephens & Co
Directorships: Kinetikos Medical, Ambion, Aurora Discovery, Interface Associates, Asuragen, Althea Technologies, AltheaDx, MedPricer
Thomas A Raffin MD, Venture Partner
e-mail: tar@thpartners.net
Education: BA, Stanford University; MD, Stanford University School of Medicine
Background: Faculty, Stanford Univeristy School of Medicine; Co-Founder, Stanford University Center for Biomedical Ethics
Deval A Lashkari PhD, Senior Partner
e-mail: dal@thpartners.net
Education: BA, University of California, Berkeley; PhD, Stanford University
Background: Research Director, Synteni; Operon Technologies
Jeanette M Welsh JD, Partner, COO
e-mail: jmw@thpartners.net
Education: BA, Philosophy & France, Hunter College,

Venture Capital & Private Equity Firms / Domestic Firms

City University of New York; JD, Fordham University School of Law
Background: Three Cities Research; Practiced Law, Epsten, Becker & Green PC
Rob C Hart CFA, Partner
e-mail: rch@thpartners.net
Education: BS, University of Califorina, Santa Barbara; JD/MBA, Northwestern University School of Law/Kellogg School of Management
Background: Citigroup's Financial Entrepreneurs & Healthcare Investment Banking Groups

1793 TELESOFT PARTNERS
601 California Street
19th Floor
San Francisco, CA 94111

Phone: 415-757-5650
web: www.telesoftvc.com

Mission Statement: Telesoft provides value-added capital for technology, communications and energy value chain companies, including wireless, software, systems, applications, services and components companies.

Geographic Preference: United States, Europe, Israel, India
Fund Size: $625 million
Founded: 1996
Average Investment: $1-15 million
Minimum Investment: $500,000
Investment Criteria: Seed, Startup, First-stage, Second-stage, Mezzanine
Industry Group Preference: Technology, Communications, Energy, Software, Information Technology, Wireless
Portfolio Companies: Aarohi Communications, AmberWave, BayPackets, BPL Mobile Comunications, Calient Networks, Calix, Catamaran, Cerent, ConvergeNet, CoSine Communications, CreekPath Systems, Education.com, empowertel, Ikanos Communications, Internet Photonics, iWitness/Zantaz, Jungo, Knowledge Adventure, Kymata, Lara Networks, LiteScape, LogLogic, Lynx Photonic Networks, Matrix Semiconductor, Nexant, Omnipoint, OnFiber, Promatory, Provide Commerce, Sierra Design, SigmaTel, Tele Atlas, Triton, Validity Sensors, Versatile, Vina Technologies, VoiceObjects, VxTel, Xambala, Xpedion Design Systems

Key Executives:
 Arjun Gupta, Chief Executive
 e-mail: arjun@telesoftvc.com
 Education: BS, MS, Washington State University; MBA, Stanford University
 Background: Strategy Consultant, McKinsey & Company; Software Engineer, Tektronix Inc
 George Schmitt, Managing Director
 e-mail: georges@telesoftvc.com
 Education: BA, Saint Mary's College; MS, Stanford University
 Background: Chairman/CEO, Espire Communications; President/Director, Omnipoint Communication Services
 Alan Howard, Chief Financial Officer
 Education: BS, Colorado State University
 Background: CFO, Creative Communications, Vice President Finance/Administration, Hydro Agri
 Alan Foster, Managing Director
 Education: BS, MS, Mechanical Engineering, Stanford University, MBA, The Anderson School, UCLA
 Background: Principal, Berkeley International Capital Corporation; Silicon Graphics; Apple Computer
 Chris LeBlanc, Industry Research
 Education: BS, Mechanical Engineering, San Jose State University; MBA, Santa Clara University
 Background: Vice President, Banc of America; Senior Research Analyst, RHK; Intel; Hewlett Packard
 Gary Cuccio, Operating Partner
 e-mail: garyc@telesoftvc.com
 Education: BA, Political Science, California State University Los Angeles; MBA, St. Mary's College; AMP, Harvard University
 Background: CEO, ATG; CEO, LHS Group; COO, Omnipoint; VP, Airtouch Europe & Asia; President, Airtouch Paging; Pacific Tel
 Paul Unruh, Managing Director
 e-mail: paulu@telesoftvc.com
 Education: BSBA, MS, Accounting, University of North Dakota
 Background: Vice Chairman, Bechtel Group; Founding President, Oracle Applications Users Group

1794 TEN ELEVEN VENTURES
250 Northern Avenue
Suite 300
Boston, MA 02210

Phone: 617-986-5040
web: www.1011vc.com

Industry Group Preference: Artificial Intelligence, Software, Applications, Technology, Cyber Security
Portfolio Companies: BlackHorse Solutions, CyberGRX, Cylance, Darktrace, Digital Shadows, GoSecure, Hexadite, Ionic Security, JASK, KnowBe4, Offensive Security, Optiv, Ordr, Ping Indentity, Sonrai Security, Twistlock, Verodin, Vulcan Cyber

Other Locations:
 345 Lorton Avenue
 Suite 401
 Burlingame, CA 94010
 Phone: 855-910-1011

 777 Pearl Street
 Suite 211
 Boulder, CO 80302
 Phone: 303-909-8873

Key Executives:
 Alex Doll, Founder/Managing General Partner
 Education: BS, Financial, Wharton School; BS, Systems Engineering, Moore School, University of Pennsylvania; MBA, Stanford Grad. School of Business
 Background: PGP Corporation; Embark; PeopleSoft; OneID; Investment Banker, Robertson Stephens & Co.
 Mark Hatfield, Founder/General Partner
 Education: BA, McMaster University; MBA, York University
 Background: Partner, Fairhaven Capital; Managing Director, Motorola Ventures; Various Corporate Business Development Roles, Bell Canada Enterprise; Bank of Montreal
 Brian Draves, Partner/COO
 Education: JD, University of California, Los Angeles
 Background: General Counsel, Techstars

1795 TENASKA CAPITAL MANAGEMENT
14302 FNB Parkway
Omaha, NE 68154-5212

Phone: 402-691-9700 Fax: 402-691-9727
e-mail: info@tenaskacapital.com
web: www.tenaskacapital.com

Mission Statement: Private equity investor in the power and energy sectors.

Founded: 2003
Industry Group Preference: Energy
Portfolio Companies: Armstrong Energy, Big Sandy Peaker, Calumet Energy, Commonwealth Chesapeake, Crete Energy, High Desert Power, Holland Energy, Lincoln Generating, New Covert Generating, Pleasants Energy, Rio Nogales Power, Rolling Hills Generating, Troy Energy, US Power Generating, University Park Energy, Wolf Hills Energy

Key Executives:
 Paul G Smith, Senior Managing Director

631

Venture Capital & Private Equity Firms / Domestic Firms

1796 TENAYA CAPITAL
3280 Alpine Road
Portola Valley, CA 94028

Phone: 650-687-6500
e-mail: deals@tenayacapital.com
web: www.tenayacapital.com

Mission Statement: Tenaya Capital is a leading venture capital firm that invests in early growth venture-backed technology companies. Tenaya Capital is an equal partnership and work as a team to evaluate investments and support their portfolio companies.

Fund Size: $1 billion
Founded: 2009
Average Investment: $5 - $10 million
Investment Criteria: Second or Third Instioutional Round; Early or Later-Stage
Industry Group Preference: Software, Consumer Internet, Communications, Semiconductors, Electronics, Clean Technology, Consumer Internet, Information Technology
Portfolio Companies: Acquia, Active-Semi, AgilOne, Avere Systems, Baihe, Baixing, Bigcommerce, Bluebox Security, Brighter, CareCloud, CastIron, CloudPassage, Composite Software, Contendo, Cyan, Digium, Druva, eBureau, Edmodo, Empirix, Endeca Technologies, Eventbrite, ExaGrid Systems, GameFly, GoodData, Green Dot, GupShup, Health Language, Hortonworks, HubSpot, Infoblox, Inkling, Instart Logic, Isilon Systems, ItsOn, Kaminario, Kayak.com, Kenshoo Kodiak Networks, Kontera, LifeSize Communications, Lithium Technologies, Lucky Pai, Lyft, Mark Logic, Maxta, Meru Networks, Mobilygen, Navini Networks, New Relic, Overture Networks, Palo Alto Networks, Platfora, PowerReviews, Qunar, Raptr, ResearchGate, Righscale, ShoreTel, SideStep, SilkRoad Technology, Smartling, Spiceworks, Storwize, Taykey, Tealium, TeleNav, ThreatMATRIX, Tidemark, Valere Power, VeriSilicon, VideoIQ, Wintegra, Wooga, Zappos.com, Zuora

Other Locations:
572 Washington Street
Suite 8
Wellesley, MA 02482
Phone: 781-663-0220

Key Executives:
Tom Banahan, Partner
Education: BA, University of California, Santa Barbara
Background: VP, Business Development, Marimba; VP, Worldwide Sales, Spyglass; Comdisco
Stewart Gollmer, Partner
Education: BA, Johns Hopkins University; JD, Brigham Young University; MBA, University of Chicago Graduate School of Business
Background: Technology Investment Banking Group, Lehman Brothers
Brian Melton, Partner
Education: BS, Wake Forest University; MBA, Stanford University
Background: Merchant Banking Group, Lehman Brothers
Brian Paul, Partner
Education: BS, Economics, Wharton School, University of Pennsylvania; MBA, Northwestern University Kellogg School of Management
Background: Global Technology & Healthcare Investment Banking Groups, Lehman Brothers; First Boston
Dorian Merritt, Chief Financial Officer
Education: BA, Economics, University of California; MS, Accountancy, San Jose State University
Background: PricewaterhouseCoopers; Lightspeed Venture Partners; Sierra Ventures; ONSET Ventures

1797 TENNESSEE COMMUNITY VENTURES
3841 Green Hills Village Drive
Suite 400
Nashville, TN 37215

e-mail: bizplan@tncvfund.com
web: www.tncvfund.com

Mission Statement: TNCV is focused on technology transfer, seed and early stage investment opportunities. TNCV seeks to identify technologies, products and/or services that offer a unique solution to a specific point of pain or opportunity for their respective industries, lend themselves to business models that offer a clear path to profitability with modest capital needs and promote scalable cost structures that create competitive advantages. Each investment opportunity will be evaluated based on an ability to deliver exceptional financial returns while transforming and diversifying Tennessee's economic base through the creation of quality jobs and community wealth.

Average Investment: $50,000 - $750,000
Investment Criteria: Seed-Stage, Early-Stage
Industry Group Preference: Technology-Enabled Products, E-Commerce & Manufacturing, Digital Media & Marketing, Manufacturing, Advanced Materials, Food & Beverage, Business Products & Services, Retailing
Portfolio Companies: Pro Player Connect, VoicesHeard Media

Key Executives:
William Guttman, Partner
Education: PhD
Background: Founding Group, Carnegie Mellon CyLab; Co-Founder, Printcafe; Partner, Saturn Asset Management, TL Ventures
Directorships: Alphacet, Axioma, ExpressKCS, Panopto, Mismi, Northstar

1798 TENONETEN VENTURES
Los Angeles, CA

web: www.tenoneten.net

Mission Statement: We are technologists who believe technology can make the world a better place. We are decision makers who believe 'having the data' leads to the best decisions. We live in Los Angeles and believe L.A. is a world-class technology hub that's getting stronger every day. And we believe in audacious ideas and the people with the conviction to make them happen.

Geographic Preference: Southern California
Investment Criteria: Early-Stage
Industry Group Preference: Technology
Portfolio Companies: Curbide, Connectivity, Wit.AI, Kixer, Second Spectrum, Honk, ConnectHQ, Mapsense, Zirtual, Misfit Wearables, Pipeline DB, Alation, Burner, Weotta, Divshot, Ranker, Cambrian Genomics, SRCH2, Nearwoo, Vurb, Bottlenose, StrikeAd, Kaggle, Kaleo, Wavii, Trippy, Triggit, Goodreads, SurfAir, The Climate Corporation, Zest Finance, Prismatic, Wish, Scopely, SodaHead, ProCore, PLYmedia, Movato, MomentFeed, Locu, Howcast, Expect Labs, eXist db

Key Executives:
David Waxman, Managing Partner
Education: MS, MIT Media Lab
Background: Co-Founder, Firefly; Co-Founder, PeoplePC; Co-Founder, SpotRunner
Gil Elbaz, Founding Partner
Education: BS, Engineering/Applied Science & Economics, Caltech
Background: IBM, Sybase, SGI; Co-Founder, Applied Semantics; Google

Venture Capital & Private Equity Firms / Domestic Firms

1799 TEXADA CAPITAL CORPORATION
62 Greenwood Shoals
Suite A
Grasonville, MD 21638

Fax: 443-782-0248
Toll-Free: 866-595-6224
e-mail: info@texada.com
web: www.texada.com

Mission Statement: An investment banking firm serving direct marketing companies: telemarketing, direct mail, printing, fulfillment, data base management and e-commerce. We assist the owners and officers of such companies to achieve their corporate development objectives. We offer a broad range of merger and acquisition services overseen by its principal who have extensive experience in investment banking. We maintain and constantly update its database on direct marketing companies.

Fund Size: $9 million
Founded: 1996
Average Investment: $2 million
Minimum Investment: $1 million
Investment Criteria: LBO, MBO, Acquisitions
Industry Group Preference: Database Services, Direct Marketing, Outsourcing & Efficiency, E-Commerce & Manufacturing

Key Executives:
Laurie G. Kolbeins, Managing Director
e-mail: lkolbeins@texada.com
Education: University of British Columbia; Harvard Business School
Background: Officer, Compass Capital Advisors; Manager of Business Advisory Services, Mellon Bank Corporate Finance Group
Bluette N. Blinoff, Managing Director
e-mail: bblinoff@texada.com
Education: Cornell University; University of Denver College of Law
Background: VP of Corporate Finance, EF Hutton & Company; Acting President, Patten Mortgage Company; Partner, Kutak, Rock & Huie; Practiced Law, Holme, Roberts & Owen

1800 TEXAS EMERGING TECHNOLOGY FUND
17919 Waterview Pkwy.
Suite 1.50
Dallas, TX 75252

Phone: 972-883-4920 Fax: 972-883-4919

Mission Statement: The Texas Emerging Technology Fund (TETF) was created by the 79th Texas Legislature in 2005 at the urging of Gov. Perry to provide Texas with an unparalleled advantage in the research, development, and commercialization of emerging technologies.

Geographic Preference: Texas
Founded: 2005
Investment Criteria: Early Stage
Industry Group Preference: Emerging Markets, Sectors & Technologies

Key Executives:
Laurie M. Rich, Special Advisor on Higher Education
512-936-8434
e-mail: laurie.rich@gov.texas.gov
Jonathon W Taylor, Director
Robert Crisalis, Investment Manager
Patrick Boswell, Investment Manager
David Morrow, Investment Manager

1801 TEXO VENTURES
6101 W Courtyard Drive
Suite 2-225
Austin, TX 78730

Toll-Free: 877-488-8396
web: www.texoventures.com

Mission Statement: Dedicated to investing in and building innovative healthcare companies. We work side-by-side with entrepreneurs, providing both the capital and collaboration needed for successful commercialization.

Geographic Preference: United States
Fund Size: $300 million
Investment Criteria: Early-Stage
Industry Group Preference: Healthcare, Healthcare Information Technology, Technology-Enabled Services, Medical Devices, Diagnostics
Portfolio Companies: Wenzel Spine, Televero Health, Ortho Kinematics, PrecedentHealth, EmployerDirect, AlaFair, IsoStem, SwipeSense, OpenMarkets

Key Executives:
Jerry DeVries, Partner
Education: BS, Mechanical Engineering, Louisiana State University; MBA, Baylor University
Background: General Partner, Path4 Ventures
Directorships: Wenzel Spine, OrthoKinematics, Alafair, IsoStem
Philip Sanger MD, Partner
Education: BA, Political Science, University of Texas, Austin; MD, Texas Tech; Internal Medicine Internship & Residency, Baylor School of Medicine; Chief Pulmonary Fellow, University of California, San Francisco
Background: Chief of Pulmonary Medicine, Texas Tech School of Medicine
Randall Crowder, Partner
e-mail: crowder@texoventures.com
Education: BS, General Management & Environmental Engineering, United States Military Academy; MBA, McCombs School of Business, University of Texas, Austin
Background: CEO, Texas Venture Labs

1802 TGAP VENTURES
7117 Stadium Drive
Kalamazoo, MI 49009

Phone: 269-217-1999 Fax: 269-381-7620
e-mail: pete@farner.net
web: tgapvcfunds.com

Mission Statement: TGap Ventures serves entrepreneurs through the Midwest by assisting them define, develop, grow and build value in their businesses.

Geographic Preference: Midwest Region
Average Investment: $500,000 - $1 million
Industry Group Preference: Software, Life Sciences, Internet Infrastructure, Specialty Manufacturing, Plastics, Communication Technology
Portfolio Companies: HistoSonics, Inspire Medical Systems, InStadium, Interrad Medical, MedVantx, NeoChord, Regesis Biomedical, ValenTx

Key Executives:
Jack K Ahrens II, General Partner
269-760-4570
Fax: 413-832-4838
e-mail: jahrens620@aol.com
Education: Indiana University
Background: President, United Capital Corporation of Illinois; General Partner, Parthfinder Venture Capital Funds
Peter W Farner, General Partner
269-217-1999
Fax: 269-381-7620
e-mail: pete@farner.net
Education: Duke University; MBA, University of Michigan
Background: Senior VP, Ryan Partnership; Stroh Brewery

Venture Capital & Private Equity Firms / Domestic Firms

1803 TGF MANAGEMENT
111 Congress Avenue
Suite 2900
Austin, TX 78701

Phone: 512-322-3100

Mission Statement: One of the largest and most active middle market buyout firms in the Southwest.
Geographic Preference: Southwest United States
Fund Size: $700 million
Founded: 1992
Average Investment: $25-$100 million
Investment Criteria: Later Stage
Industry Group Preference: Manufacturing, Distribution, Construction, Industrial Services, Outsourcing & Efficiency, Food & Beverage, Consumer Products
Portfolio Companies: ENTACT, M&M Manufacturing, Sterling Foods

1804 TH LEE PUTNAM VENTURES
1120 Avenue of the Americas
Suite 1807
New York, NY 10036

Mission Statement: TH Lee Putnam Ventures is a technology-focused private equity firm affiliated with Thomas H. Lee Partners, a leading buyout firm, and Putnam Investments, a leading global money management firm.
Fund Size: $1.1 billion
Founded: 1999
Average Investment: $20 - 50 million
Investment Criteria: Later-Stage, Public Entities, Middle Market Buyouts, Recapitalizations, Spinouts
Industry Group Preference: Technology, Financial Services, Retail, Consumer & Leisure, Consumer Products, Distribution, Logistics, Business Outsourcing
Portfolio Companies: Symphony Services, 4R Systems, LN Holdings, Parago

1805 THAYER STREET PARTNERS
41 Madison Ave.
34th Floor
New York, NY 10010

Phone: 212-256-8740
web: www.thayerstreet.com

Mission Statement: A boutique private investment firm with an emphasis on the specialty finance, technology, media and business services industries.
Founded: 2011
Average Investment: $5-50 Million
Investment Criteria: Middle-Market, Late Stage, Growth Stage
Industry Group Preference: Business Products & Services, Technology, Media, Technology-Enabled Services, Financial Services, Insurance
Key Executives:
  Alexandra Prima, Vice President
  212-253-3942
  e-mail: alexandrap@thayerstreet.com
  Education: BBA, Finance, Southern Methodist University; MBA, NYU Stern School of Business
  Background: Associate, Silver Point Capital; Senior Associate, Cedar Street Capital

1806 THAYER VENTURES
PO Box 7775
San Francisco, CA 94120

Phone: 415-782-1414
web: www.thayerventures.com

Mission Statement: Thayer Ventures partners with entrepreneurs to create, develop and build technology companies that will revolutionize the hospitality industry.
Founded: 2009
Industry Group Preference: Hospitality, Restaurants, Lodging, Gaming, Airlines
Portfolio Companies: Liftopia, TripBam, Traxo, Sphere, Hipmunk, Nor1, SocialTables, ID90, Posiq, Groupize, Duetto, Viridis, New Brand Analytics, Adara, Switchfly
Key Executives:
  Christopher R Hemmeter, Managing Director
  e-mail: chris@thayerventures.com
  Education: Cornell University, Harvard Business School
  Background: Founder & CEO, Dynamic Payment Ventures; Founder & CEO, CriticalArc Technologies
  Directorships: Capton
  Mark E Farrell, Managing Director
  e-mail: mark@thayerventures.com
  Education: BA, Loyola Marymount University; MA, University College Dublin; JD, University of Pennsylvania Law School
  Background: Investment Banker, Thomas Weisel Partners; Lawyer, Wilson Sonsini Goodrich & Rosati
  Jeff Jackson, Managing Director
  e-mail: jeff@thayerventures.com
  Education: Dartmouth College; MBA, Kellogg Business School
  Background: American Airlines, Sabre Inc.
  Directorships: Rent-A-Center
  Lee Pillsbury, Managing Director
  Education: BS, Cornell University; MBA, Northwestern University

1807 THE ARCVIEW GROUP
169 11th Street
San Francisco, CA 94103

Toll-Free: 855-892-1951
e-mail: info@arcviewgroup.com
web: arcviewgroup.com

Mission Statement: Invests in the cannabis industry.
Founded: 2010
Investment Criteria: Seed, Early-Stage
Industry Group Preference: Cannabis
Portfolio Companies: Tokyo Smoke, 4Front, Aqualitas, Eaze, Ebbu, Gatekeeper Innovation, Green Flower, Meadow, MJ Freeway, Chooze, Toke With, MJardin, SPARC, Mirth, Flowhub, Leaf, Würk, Medicine Man, The Goodship, Steep Hill, Growcentia
Key Executives:
  Troy Dayton, Chief Executive Officer
  Education: American University
  Background: Associate Director, Interfaith Drug Policy Initiative; Director of Development, Multidisciplinary Association for Psychedelic Studies; Co-Founder, Students for Sensible Drug Policy; Sr. Development Officer, Marijuana Policy Project; Partner, Canopy Boulder
  Directorships: Marijuana Policy Project; National Cannabis Industry Association
  Steve DeAngelo, President
  Education: University of Maryland
  Background: Co-Founder/Executive Director, Harborside; Co-Founder, Steep Hill
  Jeanne M. Sullivan, General Partner
  Education: BS, Marketing/Advertising, University of Illinois at Urbana-Champaign; JD, Creighton University School of Law
  Background: Product Management, AT&T/Bell Labs; Managing Director, Olivetti Ventures; Chief Inspiration Officer, Sullivan Adventures; Co-Founder, StarVest Partners
  Directorships: Astia; Women's Leadership Board, Harvard Kennedy School
  Brian Sheng, General Partner
  Education: Princeton University
  Background: Founder, IvyBound; Analyst, Shenzhen Capital Group Co.; Partner, DreamTech Ventures; Foreign

Venture Capital & Private Equity Firms / Domestic Firms

Investment Advisor, URI Investment Fund; Co-Founder/Managing Partner, Fresh VC
Directorships: Eaze
Michael Brosgart, VP, Sales & Marketing
Education: George Washington University
Background: Executive Director, LatinFinance; Director of Sales/Special Projects, Luxury Brand Partners
Directorships: Frecuencia Latinoamerica Publications

1808 THE CHANNEL GROUP
576 Fifth Avenue
Suite 903
New York, NY 10036

Phone: 212-330-8076 **Fax:** 212-627-8877
e-mail: info@thechannelgroup.com
web: www.thechannelgroup.com

Mission Statement: A New York-based life sciences venture development and management firm, that engages in two types of activities, venture formation and venture transactions.

Geographic Preference: North America, Europe, Pacific Rim
Founded: 2001
Industry Group Preference: Life Sciences, Biotechnology, Pharmaceuticals, Diagnostics, Medical Devices, Reagent Suppliers, Biologicals

Other Locations:
Pacific Channel Ltd.
101 Customs Street E
PO Box 106818
Auckland 1143
New Zealand
Phone: 64 9 377 9689 **Fax:** 64 9 337 0710

Key Executives:
Robert J. Beckman, Co-Founder/Managing Partner
e-mail: rbeckman@thechannelgroup.com
Education: BS, Pharmaceutical Sciences, Columbia University
Background: Co-Founder, Intergen Company; VP, Marketing Services, Revlon Health Care Group
Directorships: Lesanne Life Sciences, LLC
Allan R. Goldberg, PhD, Co-Founder/Partner Emeritus
e-mail: agoldberg@thechannelgroup.com
Education: BA, English & Mathematics, Cornell University; PhD, Biochemistry/Biology, Princeton University
Background: Co-Founder, Innovir Laboratories, Professor of Virology, The Rockefeller University
Directorships: Astex Pharmaceuticals
Philip N. Sussman, Managing Partner
e-mail: psussman@thechannelgroup.com
Education: BS, Physics, SUNY Stony Brook; MS, Biotechnology, Manhattan College; SM, Management, Sloan School of Management, MIT
Background: Senior Management, Perlegen Sciences; Memory Pharmaceuticals; Cadus Pharmaceutical Corp; Director, Strategy & Business Development, Ciba-Gelgy Corp's Pharmaceuticals Division
Directorships: Lesanne Life Sciences, Thar Pharmaceuticals
Vijay Aggarwal, PhD, Managing Partner
Education: BA, Chemistry, Case Western Reserve University; PhD, Pharmacology/Toxicology, Medical College of Virginia
Background: CEO, VaxiGenix; President & CEO, Aureon Laboratories; President, AAI Development Services
Directorships: AccuGenomics, Genisphere, Hycor Biomedical, Mitomics, Targeted Diagnostics and Therapeutics, Viracor-IBT Laboratories
Shmuel Einav, PhD, Advisory Partner
Education: BSc, MSc, Mechanical & Nulcear Engineering, Technion; PhD, Biomechanical Engineering, Stony Brook University
Background: Professor, Biomedical Engineering, Stony Brook University; Director, Medical Technologies, Center of Excellence for Wireless & Information Technology

1809 THE HIVE
720 University Avenue
Suite 200
Palo Alto, CA 94301

e-mail: info@hivedata.com
web: hivedata.com

Mission Statement: The Hive is a venture capital fund and co-creation studio working with AI-based companies.

Average Investment: $1.5 million - $2 million
Investment Criteria: Seed, Early Stage
Industry Group Preference: Artificial Intelligence, Industry, Finance, Insurance, Health & Wellness, Blockchain
Portfolio Companies: 8 Security, Astound, Augmented Pixels, Blockstream, Colabot, Decision Engines, Deep Forest Media, Dojo Madness, FogHorn, Geminus, Jobr, Lightning Network, Live Objects, Nurego, Percolata, Perspica, Peritus AI, Snips, Staq, Trusted Insight, TruU, Xage Security

Key Executives:
T.M. Ravi, Co-Founder/Managing Director
Education: PhD, University of California, Los Angeles
Background: President/CEO, Media Blitz Inc.; VP, Cheyenne Software; VP, Computer Associates; President/CEO, Peakstone Corporation; Founder/President/CEO, Mimosa Systems; CMO, Iron Mountain Digital; Co-Creator, FogHorn Systems Inc.
Sumant Mandal, Co-Founder
Education: Michigan State University; MBA, Kellogg School of Management
Background: Managing Director, Clearstone Venture Partners; Co-Founder, The Fabric; Managing Director, March Capital Partners
Directorships: BillDesk; 8 Security; Rubicon Project

1810 THINKTIV VENTURES
1011 San Jacinto Blvd
Suite 202
Austin, TX 78701

Phone: 512-745-8100 **Fax:** 512-857-7751
web: www.thinktiv.com

Mission Statement: Thinktiv revolutionizes the process of building businesses that win. In a world where the cost of launching products and companies continues to plummet, we believe lethal talent is more valuable than cash capital. Like most people investing in early-stage businesses, we also believe that finding and hiring the right talent represents the greatest risk factor to an early-stage company's ultimate success.

Founded: 2007
Investment Criteria: Early-Stage
Industry Group Preference: SaaS, E-Commerce & Manufacturing, Social Media, Digital Media & Marketing, Internet
Portfolio Companies: Adlucent, Affinergy, AlertTech, Attivio, BP3, Bazaarvoice, BlackLogus, Bloodbuy, Boundless Network, Bulldog, Burst, College Portfolio, Collider Media, Common Assets, CopperEgg, Democracy.com, Energytics, Experts Exchange, GasBuddy, Icon.me, LookNook, OnPulse, OtherInbox, PayGo, Prysm, QuickGifts, SharePost, Shopatron, Socialware, Spredfast, Stylefy, TrueCar, Vast

Other Locations:
111 N Whitfield Street
Third Floor
Pittsburgh, PA 15206
Phone: 412-404-2745

Key Executives:
Jonathan Berkowitz, Chief Executive Officer
Education: BS, MS, Information Systems, Carnegie Mellon University

635

Venture Capital & Private Equity Firms / Domestic Firms

Background: Vice President, Product Strategy, B-Side Entertainment; Director, Product Stategy, Trilogy
Justin B. Petro, Chief Product Officer/Co-Founder
Education: BFA, Carnegie Mellon University
Background: Director, User Experience, Design Edge; Trilogy Software
Paul Burke, Managing Partner/Co-Founder
Education: BFA, Carnegie Mellon University
Background: Design Director, Trilogy Software; Creative Director, CollegeHire.com; Founder, Inkwell Studios
Steve Waters, Chief Ventures Officer
Education: BA, Organizational Behavior, Stanford University
Background: Founder/CEO, Triggerbox; Trilogy; Firepond; RightNow Technologies; BetweenMarkets; B-Side Entertainment; M&A Analyst, Bear Stearns

1811 THIRD ROCK VENTURES
29 Newbury Street
3rd Floor
Boston, MA 02116

Phone: 617-585-2000
web: www.thirdrockventures.com

Mission Statement: Building of valuable and transformational life science companies that show high growth potential and are well-positioned to make a difference in the marketplace.

Fund Size: $800 million
Founded: 2007
Industry Group Preference: Life Sciences, Therapeutics, Diagnostics, Medical Devices
Portfolio Companies: Ablexis, Afferent Pharmaceuticals, Agios Pharmaceuticals, Alcresta, Allena Pharmaceutials, Alnara Pharmaceuticals, Bluebird Bio, Blueprint Medicines, Cibiem, Constellation Pharmaceuticals, CytomX Therapeutics, DC Devices, Edimer, Editas, Element Science, Eleven Biotherapeutics, Foundation Medicine, Global Blood Therapeutics, Ingenica, Jounce Therapeutics, Kala Pharmaceuticals, Lotus Tissue Repair, MyKardia, NinePoint Medical, Nurix, PanOptica, Rhythm, Sage Therepeutics, SeventhSense Biosystems, Taris Biomedical, Topica Pharmaceuticals, Voyager Therapeutics, WarpDrive Bio, Zafgen,

Other Locations:
499 Illinois Street
Suite 110
San Francisco, CA 94158
Phone: 415-766-3600

Key Executives:
Mark Levin, Partner
e-mail: mark@thirdrockventures.com
Education: MS, Chemical & Biomedical Engineering, Washington University
Background: Co-Founder, Mayfield Funds' Life Sciences effort; Founding CEO of Tularik, Cell Genesys/Abgenix, Focal, Stem Cells, Millennium Pharmaceuticals
Directorships: Blueprint Medicines, Constellation Pharmaceuticals, DC Devices, Eleven Biotherapeutics, Foundation Medicine, NinePoint Medical, Warp Drive
Kevin Starr, Partner
e-mail: kevin@thirdrockventures.com
Education: BA, Mathematics & Business, Colby College; MS, Corporate Finance, Boston College
Background: COO & CFO, Millennium Pharmaceuticals; Millennium BioTherapeutics; Biogen; Digital Equipment Corporation
Directorships: SAGE Therapeutics, Afferent Pharmaceuticals, Agios Pharmaceuticals, Global Blood Therapeutics, MyoKardia, PanOptica, Zafgen Pharmaceuticals
Robert Tepper, MD, Partner
e-mail: bob@thirdrockventures.com
Education: AB, Biochemistry, Princeton University; MD, Harvard Medical School
Background: President of R&D, Millennium Pharmaceuticals; Co-Founder, Cell Genesys/Abgenix
Directorships: Jounce Therapeutics, Alcresta, Allena, Bluebird.bio, Constellation Pharmaceuticals, Kala Pharmaceuticals
Abbie Celniker, Partner
Education: BA, Biology, University of California, San Diego; PhD, Molecular Biology, University of Arizona
Background: CEO, Eleven Biotherapeutics; CEO, Taligen Therapeutics Inc.; SVP of Pharmaceutical Sciences & Operations, Millennium Pharmaceuticals Inc.; Associate Director of Biological Assay Development, Genentech
Directorships: MassBio
Neil Exter, Partner
e-mail: neil@thirdrockventures.com
Education: BS, Cornell University; MS, Stanford University; MBA, Harvard Business School
Background: CBO, Alantos Pharmaceuticals; VP, Millennium Pharmaceuticals
Directorships: CytomX Therapeutics, Cibiem
Kevin Gillis, Partner/COO
e-mail: kgillis@thirdrockventures.com
Education: BA, Brandeis University; MBA, Bentley University
Background: VP, Finance, Coley Pharmaceutical Group; Millennium Pharmaceuticals, The Coca-Cola Company
Craig Muir, Partner, San Francisco
e-mail: craig@thirdrockventures.com
Education: BS, Animal Physiology, University of California, Davis
Background: SVP, Technical Operations, Codon Devices; Millennium Pharmaceuticals
Cary Pfeffer MD, Partner
e-mail: cary@thirdrockventures.com
Education: BA, Biochemistry, Columbia University; MD, University of Pennsylvania; MBA, Wharton School
Background: Founder, The Pfeffer Group; Biogen
Charles Homcy, MD, Partner
Education: AB/MD, John Hopkins University
Background: Professor of Medicine, San Francisco Medical School, University of California; Attending Physician, San Francisco VA Medical Center; Co-Founded, Portola Pharmaceuticals
Christoph Lengauer, PhD, Partner
Education: MS, Human Genetics, University of Salzburg; PhD, Biology, Heidelberg University; MBA, Medical Services Management, John Hopkins University

1812 THIRD SECURITY
The Governor Tyler
1881 Grove Avenue
Radford, VA 24141

Phone: 540-633-7900 **Fax:** 540-633-7939
web: www.thirdsecurity.com

Mission Statement: Third Security is a venture capital firm characterized by an expanding global perspective and a distinctively patient approach. We evaluate opportunities in a wide range of industries, but principally focus on emerging through late-stage investments in life-sciences and communications technology.

Investment Criteria: Expansion, Later Stage
Industry Group Preference: Life Sciences, Communication Technology
Portfolio Companies: Heyo, OvaScience, Agilis, Soligenix, AmpliPhi, Genopaver, Synethic Biologics, Oragenics, Intrexon, Halozyme, Fibrocell Science, Avexis, Persea Bio, Fitnet

Other Locations:
735 Market Street
3rd Floor

San Francisco, CA 94103
Phone: 415-644-5365 **Fax:** 415-344-0677

2875 South Ocean Boulevard
Suite 214
Palm Beach, FL 33480
Phone: 561-855-7831 **Fax:** 561-355-0627

Key Executives:
Randal J. Kirk, Senior Managing Director/Chief Executive Officer
Education: B.A. Business, Radford University; J.D., University of Virginia
Background: New River Pharmaceuticals
Directorships: Halozyme Therapeutics, ZIOPHARM Oncology, Intrexon
Marcus Smith, Senior Managing Director/General Counsel/Chief Compliance Officer
Education: B.B.A./J.D., University of Georgia
Background: Senior Vice President/General Counsel/Secretary, New River Pharmaceuticals; Attorney, The Southland Corporation and Occidental Oil & Gas Corporation
Directorships: Fibrocell Science

1813 THIRD WAVE DIGITAL

web: thirdwavedigital.vc

Mission Statement: Los Angeles company invests in early-stage media and technology entrepreneurs.

Investment Criteria: Early-Stage
Industry Group Preference: Media, Mobile
Portfolio Companies: 88Rising, All Def Digital, BeautyCon, Canvas, DanceOn, DigiTour, Drone Racing League, FameBit, Greenfly, Gunslinger Studios, Hello Giggles, Immortals, IndMusic, Insurrection Media, IRIS.TV, Jukin Media, Merry Jane, Mitu, Mondo Media, Naritiv, Pluto.TV, Rocket Jump, Stem, TasteMade, Tubular Labs, Vessel, VideoAmp, WeVR, ZEFR

1814 THOMA BRAVO LLC
300 North La Salle Street
Suite 4350
Chicago, IL 60654

Phone: 312-254-3300
web: www.thomabravo.com

Mission Statement: Thoma Bravo targets control investments in companies with strong business franchises led by experienced executives who aspire to achieve industry leadership.

Geographic Preference: United States
Fund Size: $2 billion
Founded: 1990
Average Investment: $60 million
Minimum Investment: $5 million
Investment Criteria: LBO, MBO, Later Stage
Industry Group Preference: Business Products & Services, Healthcare, Consumer Products, Software, Financial Services, Education, Technology
Portfolio Companies: Attachmate, Blue Coat Systems, Compuware Corporation, Deltek, Dynatrace, Edmentum, Embarcadero Technologies, Empirix, Flexera Software, Global Healthcare Exchange, Hyland Software, InfoVista S.A., Keynote Systems, LANDESK Software, Local Media of America, Mediware Information Systems, Porter & Chester Institute, SailPoint Technologies, Segall Bryant & Hamill, Sirius Computer Solutions, Sparta Systems, SRS Software, Telestream, TravelClick, Tripwire, Vision Solutions

Other Locations:
600 Montgomery Street
32nd Floor
San Francisco, CA 94111
Phone: 415-263-3660 **Fax:** 415-392-6480

Key Executives:
Carl D Thoma, Managing Partner/Founder
312-777-4420
e-mail: cthoma@thomabravo.com
Education: Graduate, Oklahoma State University; MBA, Stanford Graduate School of Business
Background: Implemented Growth, First Chicago Equity Group; Founder, Golder, Thoma & C
Orlando Bravo, Managing Partner/Founder
415-263-3665
e-mail: obravo@thomabravo.com
Education: BA, Brown University; MBA, Stanford Graduate School of Business; JD, Stanford Law School
Background: Mergers/Acquisitions, Morgan Stanley
Directorships: Embarcadero Technologies, Sirius Comuter Solutions, LANDesk Software, Blue Coat Systems, Deltek, Digital Insight, Keynote Systems
Lee M Mitchell, Managing Partner
312-777-4450
e-mail: lmitchell@thomabravo.com
Education: Wesleyan University; University of Chicago Law School
Background: Principal, Golder; Partner, Sidley & Austin; CEO, Field Enterprises
Directorships: Porter & Chester Institute, Local Media of America
Scott Crabill, Managing Partner
415-263-3662
e-mail: scrabill@thomabravo.com
Education: BS, Industrial Engineering, Stanford University; MBA, Stanford University
Background: Summit Partners, Hewlett-Packard, JH Whitney & Co., Alex Brown & Sons
Directorships: Attachmate Corporation, Vision Solutions, Edmentum, Tripwire, Mediware Systems, SRS Software
Seth Boro, Managing Partner
415-249-6719
e-mail: sboro@thomabravo.com
Education: BComm, Queen's University School of Business; MBA, Stanford Graduate School of Busienss
Background: Summit Partners, ServiceSource, CreditSuisse, First Marathon Securities
Directorships: Hyland Software, Vision Solutions, LANDesk Software, Tripwire, Blue Coat Systems, InfoVista S.A., Mediware Systems, Keynote Systems, Empirix
Holden Spaht, Managing Partner
415-263-3667
e-mail: hspaht@thomabravo.com
Education: BA, Economics, Dartmouth College; MBA, Harvard Business School
Background: Morgan Stanley Capital Partners, Thomas H Lee Partners, Morgan Stanley
Directorships: Embarcadero Technologies, Sirius Computer Solutions, Edmentum, Telestream, Deltek, Digital Insight

1815 THOMAS H LEE PARTNERS
100 Federal Street
Boston, MA 02110

Phone: 617-227-1050 **Fax:** 617-227-3514
e-mail: mbenson@sardverb.com
web: www.thl.com

Mission Statement: It only pursues companies that want to be pursued with a leveraged buyout. Typical acquisitions are middle market companies with growth potential, which are revamped and either sold or are taken public.

Fund Size: $12 billion under management
Founded: 1974
Investment Criteria: Growth Buyouts
Industry Group Preference: Business Products & Services, Financial Services, Consumer, Healthcare, Media, Information Services
Portfolio Companies: 1-800-CONTACTS, Agencyport Software, Aramark, Black Knight Financial Services, Ceridian, CompuCom Systems, CTI Foods, Cumulus Media, First Bancorp, Fogo De Chao, Hawkeye Renewables,

Venture Capital & Private Equity Firms / Domestic Firms

iHeartMedia, Intermedix, inVentiv Health, MoneyGram International, Party City, Phillips Pet Food & Supplies, Prime Risk Partners, ServiceLink, Systems Maintenance Services, The Nielsen Company, Umpqua Holdings Corporation, Univision Communications, West Corporation

Key Executives:

Scott M. Sperling, Co-President
Education: BS, Purdue University; MBA, Harvard Business School
Background: Managing Partner, The Aeneas Group; Senior Consultant, Boston Consulting Group

Anthony J. DiNovi, Co-President
Education: AB, Harvard College; MBA, Harvard Graduate School
Background: Corporate Finance, Goldman Sachs & Company; Wertheim Schroeder & Company

Todd M. Abbrecht, Head of Private Equity
Education: BSE, Finance, Wharton School; MBA, Harvard Business School
Background: M&A, Credit Suisse First Boston
Directorships: Aramark, Fogo de Chao, Intermedix, inVentiv Health, Party City

Michael A. Bell, Managing Director
Education: BS, Wharton School; MBA, Harvard Business School
Background: Exec. Chairman, Syneos Health; President, Commercial Division, INC Research, Syneos Health
Directorships: Agiliti Health Inc.; Centria Healthcare; Healthcare Staffing Services; Professional Physical Therapy

Mark L. Benaquista, Managing Director
Education: BS, Management Science Information Systems, Rutgers University; MS, Management Systems Analysis, Kean University
Background: SVP & Co-CIO Warner Music Group; Senior Director, Merck & Co.; JP Morgan; Chelsea Consulting

Henry J. Boye, Managing Director
Education: BA, International Studies, Dickinson College; MBA, Wharton School
Background: Managing Director, Blue Ridge Partners; Publisher, Harvard Business Review; COO & SVP of Corporate Development, Mass Insight

Thomas M. Hagerty, Managing Director
Education: BBA, University of Notre Dame; MBA, Harvard Business School
Background: M&A, Morgan Stanley & Co
Directorships: Fidelity National Financial, Fidelity National Information Services, Black Knight Financial Services, ServiceLink H9oldings, MoneyGram International, First Bancorp, Ceridian

Laura A. Grattan, Managing Director
Education: AB, Economics, Dartmouth College; MBA, Harvard Business School
Background: Goldman Sachs & Co.
Directorships: Alfresco Software Inc.; Juvare; Nextech; iHeartMedia; Syneos Health; West Corporation; Aramark Corporation; GrubHub Seamless Holding Corporation; Warner Chilcott Plc.

Douglas A. Haber, Managing Director
Education: BA, Economics & History, Middlebury College; MBA, Harvard Business School
Background: Goldman Sachs & Co.; Citadel Investment Group
Directorships: 8th Avenue Food & Provisions; Art Van Furniture; Bargain Hunt; Give & Go Prepared Food Corp.; CTI Foods; Fogo de Chao; Party City

Vincente Piedrahita, Managing Director
Education: BA, Sociology, Princeton University; MBA, Harvard Business School
Background: Director of Strategic Projects, Clear Channel Outdoor; Consultant, Monitor Group

James C. Carlisle, Managing Director
Education: BSE, Operations Research, Princeton University; MBA, Harvard Business School
Background: Financial Institutions Group, Goldman Sachs & Co.
Directorships: Univision Communications, Clear Channel Outdoor Holdings, Agencyport Software

Joshua M. Nelson, Managing Director
Education: AB, Politics, Princeton University; MBA, Harvard Business School
Background: JPMorgan Partners; McKinsey & Co; The Beacon Group
Directorships: 1-800-CONTACTS, inVentiv Health, Party City, Hawkeye Energy Holdings

Soren L. Oberg, Managing Director
Education: AB, Applied Mathematics, Harvard College; MBA, Harvard Business School
Background: Morgan Stanley & Co; Hicks Muse Tate & Furst Inc
Directorships: Ceridian Corporation, CompuCom Systems, Grupo Corporativo Ono, S.A., Systems Maintenance Services, West Corporation

Kent R. Weldon, Managing Director
Education: BA, Economics, University of Notre Dame; MBA, Harvard Business School
Background: Morgan Stanley & Co; Wellington Management Company

Gregory A. White, Managing Director
Education: BNE, Georgia Insitute of Technology; MBA, Harvard Business School
Background: Thomas Weisel Partners; TA Associates; Morgan Stanley & Co; Smith Barney; UNC Ventures

Daniel G. Jones, Managing Director
Education: BA, Dartmouth College; MBA, MIT Sloan School of Management
Background: Management Consultant, Monitor Group; Financial Project Manager, Deputy to CFO, Lan Airlines

Shari H. Wolkon, Managing Director & General Counsel
Education: AB, Economics, Princeton University; MBA, Johnson Graduate School of Management, Cornell University; JD, Cornell Law School
Background: Corporate Partner, Ropes & Gray LLP

Ganesh B. Rao, Managing Director
Education: BA, Economics, Duke University; MBA, Harvard Business School
Background: M&A, Morgan Stanley & Co.; Greenlight Capital
Directorships: Black Knight Financial Services, Ceridian HCM Holding, Comdata, MoneyGram International, ServiceLink Holdings, The Nielsen Company

Jeff T. Swenson, Managing Director
Education: BA, Economics, Northwestern University; MBA, Harvard Business School
Background: Private Equity Group, Bain Capital; Management Consultant, Bain & Company
Directorships: 1-800-CONTACTS, Acosta, CTI Foods, Fogo de Chao, Intermedix Corporation, Phillips Pet Food & Supplies and Seamless Holdings

1816 THOMAS WEISEL VENTURE PARTNERS
One Montgomery Street
Suite 3700
San Francisco, CA 94104

Phone: 415-364-2500 Fax: 415-364-2695
Toll-Free: 888-267-3700
web: www.tweisel.com

Mission Statement: An early-stage venture capital firm that invests in emerging information technology companies. As a partner with a long-term perspective, TWVP plays an active role in helping entrepreneurs turn ideas into sustainable businesses.

Industry Group Preference: Information Technology

Venture Capital & Private Equity Firms / Domestic Firms

1817 THOMAS, MCNERNEY & PARTNERS
One Landmark Square
Suite 1920
Stamford, CT 06901

Phone: 203-978-2000 Fax: 203-978-2005
web: www.tm-partners.com

Mission Statement: A healthcare private equity firm with over 60 years combined healthcare private equity and venture capital experience.
Geographic Preference: East Coast, Midwest, West Coast
Fund Size: $375 million
Average Investment: $20 million
Minimum Investment: $5 million
Investment Criteria: All Stages
Industry Group Preference: Healthcare, Life Sciences, Pharmaceuticals, Medical Devices, Biotechnology, Diagnostics
Portfolio Companies: Apptec Laboratory Services, Altair Therapeutics, Cebix, Coley Pharmaceutical Group, Invitae, SGB, Tranzyme Pharma, Virdante Pharmaceuticals, Arkal Medical, Asante Solutions, Atritech, AxioMed Spine, Bausch & Lomb, CAS Medical Systems, Galil Medical, Intuity Medical, Keystone Dental, Osteobiologics, Softscope Medical Technologies, Torax Medical, Vertiflex, Amarin, Auspex Pharmaceuticals, Celator Pharmaceuticals, Clarus Therapeutics, CNS Therapeutics, InnoPharma, Neurotherapeutics Pharma, Ocera Therapeutics, Oriel Therapeutics, Packaging Coordinators, Quinnova Pharmaceuticals, Solstice Neurosciences, Tioga Pharmaceuticals, Zogenix

Other Locations:
60 South 6th Street
Suite 3620
Minneapolis, MN 55402
Phone: 612-465-8660 Fax: 612-465-8661

3366 N. Torrey Pines Court
Suite 220
La Jolla, CA 92037
Phone: 858-373-5800 Fax: 858-228-5751

Key Executives:
James E Thomas, Partner
Education: BS, Wharton School; MS, London School of Economics
Background: Leader Healthcare Technology, Warburg Pincus; VP, Goldman Sachs International, London
Directorships: CAS Medical Systems, Clarus Therapeutics, Galil Medical, InnoPharma, Keystone Dental, Packaging Coordinators
Peter H McNerney, Partner
Education: BA, Yale University; MBA, Stanford University; CPA
Background: Co-Founder, Thomas, McNerney & Partners; Co-Founder/Managing Partner, Kensington Group; Founder/CEO, Memtec North America; Baxter Healthcare Corporation; President, Minnesota Venture Capital Association
Directorships: Asante Solutions, Torax Medical
Alex Zisson, Partner
Education: Brown University
Background: Managing Director/Health Care Strategist, Hambrecht & Quist
Directorships: Auspex Pharmaceuticals, Clarus Therapeutics, InnoPharma
Kathleen A Tune, Partner
Education: MS, Microbiology, University of Minnesota; MBA, University of Minnesota Carlson School of Management
Background: Health Care Analyst, Piper Jaffray; Solvay, SA; Senior Scientist, Molecular Biology, University of Minnesota
Directorships: AxioMed Spine, CAS Medical Systems, VertiFlex

1818 THOMVEST VENTURES
203 Redwood Shores Parkway
Suite 680
Redwood City, CA 94065

Phone: 350-965-4700 Fax: 350-618-1509
e-mail: info@thomvest.com
web: www.thomvest.com

Mission Statement: Our focus is working with entrepreneurs to make every company we invest in a success. We deliberately invest in a smaller number of select companies, making perhaps three to four new investments per year. We then bring the diverse talents of our team to bear, helping entrepreneurs in everything from strategy to marketing, sales, business development, to structuring and financing transactions. We are long-term partners with the companies we invest in, and encourage you to get in touch with us if you think our firm might be a good fit for yours.
Geographic Preference: Silicon Valley
Fund Size: $250 million
Investment Criteria: Early-Stage to Growth-Stage
Portfolio Companies: Apsalar, Axcient, DataXu, Kabbage, LendingClub, LendUp, Milyoni, NetBase, SoFi, Tactus, Virool, Vungle, YottaMark, Avalanche Technology, Inxent, SoonR

Key Executives:
Don Butler, Managing Director
Education: BA, Chinese, UCLA; MA, East Asian Studies & Political Science, Stanford University
Background: Asia Pacific Ventures; Analyst, Lehman Brothers
Directorships: Apsalar, Avalanche, Axcient, Kabbage, Milyoni, Netbase, Vungle, YottaMark

1819 THREE ARCH PARTNERS LP
19 South B Street
Suite 14
San Mateo, CA 94401

Phone: 650-529-8000 Fax: 650-529-8039
e-mail: threearchpartners@threearchpartners.com
web: www.threearchpartners.com

Mission Statement: Established and positioned to integrate the traditional roles of venture capitalist and entrepreneur. Assists physicians and inventors in establishing companies.
Fund Size: $1 billion
Founded: 1993
Average Investment: $15 million
Minimum Investment: $100,000
Investment Criteria: Seed, Early Stage, Development
Industry Group Preference: Life Sciences, Biopharmaceuticals, Healthcare, Medical Devices
Portfolio Companies: AcelRx Pharmaceuticals, Baxano, Centerre Healthcare, Concert Pharmaceuticals, Inova Labs, LipoScience, MEI Pharma, Neuronetics, Nevro, Respicardia, Salveo Specialty, SpinalMotion, Tibion, TriReme Medical, VisionCare Opthalmic Technologies

Key Executives:
Wilfred Jaeger, Co-Founder/Partner
e-mail: wj@threearchpartners.com
Education: BS Biology/MD, University of British Columbia School; MBA, Stanford Grad. School of Business
Background: General Partner, Schroder Ventures; Management, Chec Medical
Mark Wan, Co-Founder/Partner
e-mail: mwan@threearchpartners.com
Education: BS Engineering/BA Economics Summa cum laude, Phi Beta Kappa, Yale University; MBA, Stanford Grad. School of Business
Background: General Partner, Brentwood Associates

639

Venture Capital & Private Equity Firms / Domestic Firms

1820 THREE CITIES RESEARCH
135 East 57th Street
Suite 15-103
New York, NY 10022

Phone: 212-838-9660 Fax: 212-980-1142
e-mail: info@tcr-ny.com
web: www.tcr-ny.com

Mission Statement: Focused on businesses that are substantially underperforming their potential. To deploy dedicated resources to deeply understand the value proposition and competitive environment of its portfolio companies, and partner with management teams to develop and execute winning strategies.

Fund Size: $700 million
Founded: 1976
Minimum Investment: $10 million
Investment Criteria: Unexploited Growth, Underperforming companies, Complicated transactions
Industry Group Preference: Manufacturing, Service Industries, Distribution, Industrial Equipment, Retailing, Publishing
Portfolio Companies: Agrileum, Bluefish Holdings LLC, Finn Corp, Parallel Products

Key Executives:
   J. William Uhrig, Partner
   212-605-3206
   e-mail: uhrigb@tcr-ny.com
   Education: Purdue University, University of Chicago
   Christopher Erickson, Partner
   e-mail: christopher.erickson@tcr-ny.com
   Education: BS, University of Wisconsin, Madison; PhD, Physics, Princeton University
   Background: McKinsey & Co
   Jason Stein, Partner
   e-mail: jason.stein@tcr-ny.com
   Education: BA, University of San Diego; MBA, UC Berkeley
   Background: Vendio Corporation; Quantum Corporation
   Christian Schwartz, Principal
   e-mail: schwartzc@tcr-ny.com
   Education: BA, Duke University; MBA, Wharton School
   Background: Associate, Unisphere

1821 THRIVE CAPITAL
New York, NY

e-mail: info@thrivecap.com
web: www.thrivecap.com

Mission Statement: Thrive Capital is a venture capital investment firm focused on media and internet investments.

Founded: 2009
Industry Group Preference: Media, Internet
Portfolio Companies: Twitch, Tutorspree, Summly, Spree Commerce, Simple, Shift, Reddit, OnSwipe, Memoir, Maple, Jet, Instagram, Hyperpublic, Hot Potato, Hightower, GroupMe, Flatiron School, FabFitFun, Fab, Dispatch, Cue, Baby.com.br,

Key Executives:
   Joshua Kushner, Founder/Managing Partner
   Education: Harvard University
   Background: Co-Founder, Oscar Health
   Directorships: VTS, Hightower
   Kareem Zaki, Investor
   Education: AB, Economics & Healthcare Policy, Harvard University
   Background: Private Equity Invest, The Blackstone Group; Business Analyst, McKinsey & Company; Investment Banking Analyst, JP Morgan

1822 THUNDERBIRD ANGEL NETWORK
Phoenix, AZ

Phone: 385-232-4226
e-mail: z.c.mckinney@global.t-bird.edu

Mission Statement: The Thunderbird Angel Network (TAN) is a dynamic group of accredited investors who are affiliated with the Thunderbird School of Global Management. Our members are Tbird alumni, professors, friends and members of the Phoenix startup community. TAN serves as a source to its members for early-stage companies that have the potential to grow rapidly. The Network is based at the Thunderbird School of Global Management, a hotspot for global business; thus, its members are interested in both domestic and international deals. TAN members typically seek to invest between $50,000 and $500,000.

Minimum Investment: $50,000
Investment Criteria: Early-Stage
   Tanaha Hairston, Managing Director
   Lacey Yoder, Managing Director

1823 TI VENTURE CAPITAL Texas Instruments Incorporated
12500 TI Boulevard
Dallas, TX 75243

Phone: 972-995-2011
e-mail: ti_venture@list.ti.com
web: www.ti.com/tiventures

Mission Statement: To provide Texas Instruments with strategic awareness of new technologies and markets, allow close partnering with our business teams and external venture capital firms on investment and alliance opportunities, and provide financial return for TI.

Founded: 1996
Investment Criteria: Startup, Early-Stage
Industry Group Preference: Emerging Markets, Sectors & Technologies, Semiconductors, Wireless Architectures, Power Management, Medical Devices, Networking, Wireless Technologies, Energy Management

Key Executives:
   Jean-Louis Trochu, Managing Director
   Tom Shackelford, Managing Director

1824 TICONDEROGA PRIVATE EQUITY
2305 Broadway Street
Boulder, CO 80304

Phone: 303-938-3768 Fax: 650-384-5811
e-mail: craig@ticcap.com
web: www.ticcap.com

Mission Statement: Focus on private equity investments in SaaS and healthcare services.

Fund Size: $20 million
Founded: 2010
Average Investment: $500K
Minimum Investment: $400K
Investment Criteria: LBO, MBO, Later
Industry Group Preference: Enterprise Software, SaaS, Healthcare Services
Portfolio Companies: The Neck and Back Clinics, National Research Institute, Construction Software Technologies, FastSpring, Damac, Park Place Technologies, Aileron Solutions, Memorial MRI & Diagnostic, Samba Safety

Other Locations:
25 Braintree Hill Park
Suite 200
Braintree, MA 02184
Phone: 781-930-3142

Key Executives:
   Craig A.T. Jones, Co-Founder/Managing Partner
   e-mail: craig@ticcap.com
   Education: BA, California State University; JD Magna Cum Laude, Harvard Law School
   Background: Co-Founder, Ticonderoga Capital; Partner, Dillon Read Venture Capital and Advent International; Associate, Centennial Funds; Management Consultant, Bain & Company

Venture Capital & Private Equity Firms / Domestic Firms

Directorships: eStudySite; National Research Institute; CloudXPartners; InnoCentive; Blue Sky Networks; TransXSystems
James E Vandervelden, Co-Founder/Partner
e-mail: james@ticcap.com
Education: BA Economics/Organizational Behavior & Management, Brown University
Background: Principal, Dillon Reed; T A Associates; APM Inc
Robert M. Hannon, Administrative Director
781-416-3409
e-mail: bob@ticcap.com
Education: BA, Economics, Harvard College; MBA, Finance, Wharton School, University of Pennsylvania
Background: Treasurer, Town & Country Corporation; Data General Corporation; Ford Motor Company; Leesona Corporation

1825 TIE ANGELS GROUP SEATTLE
PO Box 821
Redmond, WA 98073

web: www.tieangels.com

Mission Statement: TiE Angels Group Seattle or TAGS is an angel investment group formed by Charter Members of TiE Seattle to cater to the funding needs of startups primarily in Seattle and the Northwest region. The mission of TAGS is to act as an intermediary to provide entrepreneurs a means to raise funds for their ventures. TAGS provides strategic early stage investment and support, by leveraging the invaluable experience and network of TiE Charter Members. TAGS will provide a high quality deal flow, and early stage, typically seed or Series A round, funding and investment opportunities to its members, and access to funds, mentorship and guidance from an elite group of TAGS members and TiE Seattle Charter Members.

Geographic Preference: Seattle, Northwest
Investment Criteria: Seed-Stage, Early-Stage
Industry Group Preference: Software, Infrastructure, Internet, Mobile, Clean Technology, Healthcare, Education, Medical Devices
Portfolio Companies: Byndl, Exponential Entertainment, Movie Pong, Minettabrook, Knewsapp, Unify2, Versium, TrueFacet

Key Executives:
Kumar Sripadam, Chair

1826 TIGER GLOBAL MANAGEMENT
9 West 57th St.
35th Floor
New York, NY 10019

Phone: 212-843-8030
web: www.tigerglobal.com

Mission Statement: Tiger Global Management is an investment firm that deploys capital globally. The firm launches and manages hedge funds and manages private equity.

Founded: 2001
Investment Criteria: Early-Stage, Growth-Stage
Industry Group Preference: Technology, Internet, Industrial, Consumer, Media, Telecommunications
Portfolio Companies: GaiaWorks, Guidelines, Ola, Olo, Postmastes, Procore, Roposo, Stripe, Taimei Medical Technology, Yaoshibang

Key Executives:
Charles P Coleman III, Co-Founder/Managing Partner
Education: BA, Williams College
Anil L Crasto, Chief Operating Officer
Background: Sr Accountant, Ernst & Young; Sr Manager, Price Waterhouse Coopers; Partner/COO/CFO, Compass Group; Partner/CFO, R6 Capital Management; Managing Director/COO, Mount Kellett Capital Management
Scott Schleifer, Partner
Education: BS, Wharton School

Background: Private Equity Investor, The Blackstone Group

1827 TIME WARNER INVESTMENT CORPORATION
1 Time Warner Center
New York, NY 10019-8016

Phone: 212-484-7819
e-mail: ir@timewarner.com
web: www.timewarner.com/our-company/tw-investments/

Mission Statement: The Time Warner Investments group focuses on investment opportunities that directly enhance Time Warner's ability to meet specific strategic goals. These strategic goals include the delivery of new services, enhancement of an existing product, entry or expansion into a key strategic market, completion of a strategic partnership, and critical research and development.

Geographic Preference: United States, Western Europe
Fund Size: $100 million
Founded: 2001
Average Investment: $10 million
Minimum Investment: $2 million
Investment Criteria: All Stages
Industry Group Preference: Broadcasting, Cable, Radio, Computer Hardware & Software, Internet Technology, Networking, Publishing, Telecommunications, Networking, Advertising
Portfolio Companies: Adaptly, BroadLogic, Bustle, Conviva, CrowdStar, Double Fusion, Dynamic Sinal, Epoxy, Exent, Gaia Online, Hammer & Chisel, Joyus, Krux, Nuvo TV, Simulmedia, Trion, Visible World, WeHeartIt, YieldMo
Jason Kilar, CEO

1828 TL VENTURES
435 Devon Park Drive
700 Building
Wayne, PA 19087

Phone: 610-971-1515
e-mail: info@tlventures.com
web: www.tlventures.com

Mission Statement: Focused on venture investing in category-defining, early-stage companies in software, communications, information infrastructure and business services, TL Ventures provides portfolio companies with operational, entrepreneurial and financial expertise and a global network of resources and contacts. Actively seeking new investments.

Geographic Preference: United States, Worldwide
Fund Size: $1.5 billion
Founded: 1988
Average Investment: $3 - 10 million
Minimum Investment: $3 million
Industry Group Preference: Biotechnology, Information Technology, Communications, Software, Networking, Business Products & Services
Portfolio Companies: Axiom, Celator Pharmaceuticals, Donuts, Finite Carbon, FIRE Solutions, Global Education Learning Holdings, iSpot, Noble BioMaterials, OEwaves, Pivotal Systems, QuatRx Pharmaceuticals, Salem International University, Schiller International University, SkyCross, Sopherion Therapeutics, Translarity

Key Executives:
Mark DeNino, Managing Director
e-mail: mdenino@tlventures.com
Education: BA, Finance, Accounting, Boston College; MBA, Harvard Business School
Background: President, CMS Corporate Finance
Directorships: Celarix; Coastal Security Systems; aRealty.com; Hire.com; MediaBrians.com; Mobility Technologies
Robert Keith, Managing Director
e-mail: rkeith@tlventures.com
Education: BS, American History, Amherst College; JD,

Venture Capital & Private Equity Firms / Domestic Firms

Temple University
Background: Managing Director, Radnor Venture Partners; Fidelity Bank
Robert N. Verratti, Operating Partner
Education: US Naval Academy
Background: CEO, Nationa; Media; CEO, Total Core Systems; CEO, Great Western Cities; CEO, Global Ticket; EDS
Robert J. McParland, Financial Partner
Education: BS, Accountancy, University of North Carolina, Chapel Hill
Background: Safeguard Scientifics; Senior Manager, PricewaterhouseCoopers
Janet L. Stott, Chief Financial Officer
Education: BS, Accounting, Philadelphia University; CPA
Background: Controller, Katalyst LLC; Senior Manager, KPMG LLP

1829 TOBA CAPITAL
San Francisco, CA

e-mail: hello@tobacapital.com
web: www.tobacapital.com

Mission Statement: Toba Capital is a venture firm founded by Vinny Smith. We are a small team with twice the per capita operating experience of traditional VCs, investing in the markets we know firsthand: business applications and IT & internet infrastructure. Our background enables us to provide portfolio companies with unique operational support. We know what it takes to build a billion dollar software company and have seen both sides of over a hundred investments and M&A transactions.

Industry Group Preference: Business Products & Services, Information Technology, Internet, Infrastructure
Portfolio Companies: Clear Slide, Alteryx, Catavolt, Cirro, Codenvy, Dataguise, Directly, FloQast, Liquidware Labs, Maven Link, Parsec, Paxata, Predixion, Stratos, Quorum, Reach150, Sauce Labs, Seal, Secureauth, SHIFTMobility, Smarsh, Smartbear, Speakr, Stealthbits, Synoptek, Team Snap, Transifex, WSO2

Key Executives:
Vinny Smith, Founder

1830 TOMORROW VENTURES

e-mail: info@tomorrowvc.com
web: www.tomorrowvc.com

Mission Statement: A hybrid, opportunistic venture capital firm developing innovative ideas with the power to change the way we live.

Geographic Preference: Worldwide
Industry Group Preference: Technology
Portfolio Companies: Legend Pictures, Humin, Maskd, Bitsqr, Doctor on Demand, Beautycounter, Shape Security, Remitly, LYFE Kitchen, Relay Foods, biNu, Stamped, Sharecare, Maker Studios, HealthLoop, Events.com, Remedy Systems, Sightly, Forbes Travel Guide, The Backplane, Prism Skylabs, Newhound, PowerGen Renewable Energy, Instructure, Appia, Ness Computing, DailyWOrth, Cortera, The BondFactor Company, Signal, Fanaticall, Prosper, Ciqual Limited, EverFi, Fullbridge, Scientific Media, Playsino, News Distribution Network, TomorrowInnovations, Welcu, Intern, Xfire, Cx, GTI Capital Group, GTI Medivenures

1831 TONIIC
901 Mission Street
Suite 205
San Francisco, CA 94103

Phone: 415-746-9925
web: www.toniic.com

Mission Statement: Toniic is an international impact investor network promoting a sustainable global economy by investing in entrepreneurs addressing the fundamental needs of people and planet.

Geographic Preference: Worldwide
Industry Group Preference: Healthcare, Education, Environment, Housing

Key Executives:
Adam Bendell, Chief Executive Officer
Education: Cornell University; University of Chicago Law School
Background: FTI Consulting

1832 TOPSPIN PARTNERS
Three Expressway Plaza
Suite 100
Roslyn Heights, NY 11577

Phone: 516-625-9400 Fax: 516-625-9499
e-mail: info@topspinpartners.com
web: www.topspinpartners.com

Mission Statement: To generate superior returns by partnering with management to build great companies.

Fund Size: $213 million
Average Investment: $1 - $15 million
Portfolio Companies: Patch Products, Brighter Dental, Care, GHS Interactive, Security, Hart Systems, HCOA Fitness, New Whey Nutrition, Pulse Veterinary Technologies, Stagnito Business Information, 2-20 Records Management, Utrecht Manufacturing

Key Executives:
Leo Guthart, Founding Partner
Education: AB, Physics, Harvard College; MBA, Harvard Business School; Doctorate, Corporate Finance, Harvard Business School
Background: President, CEO & Chairman, Ademco
Directorships: Aptar Group
Leigh Randall, Managing Partner
Education: AB, Duke University; JD, Harvard Law School
Background: CFO, Stonewater Spas; vP, Corporate Development, Small World Media; Consultant, McKinsey & Company

1833 TORNANTE COMPANY

Phone: 212-981-5216
web: tornante.com

Mission Statement: Founded in 2005 by Michael Eisner, The Tornante Company is a privately-held company that invests in, acquires and operates companies in media and entertainment.

Founded: 2005
Industry Group Preference: Media, Entertainment
Portfolio Companies: Airtime, Omaze, TaskRabbit, Topps, Tornate Animation, Vuguru, Who What Wear

Key Executives:
Michael Traub, Media Contact

1834 TOYOTA AI VENTURES
4440 El Camino Real
Los Altos, CA 94022

e-mail: info@toyota-ai.ventures
web: toyota-ai.ventures

Mission Statement: A subsidiary of the Toyota Research Institute, this venture capital firm seeks to invest in entrepreneurs committed to innovation in the AI sector. Toyota AI Ventures focuses on autonomous mobility, robotics, and data.

Founded: 2017
Minimum Investment: $100 million
Industry Group Preference: Artificial Intelligence, Autonomous Mobility, Robotics, Data Analytics
Portfolio Companies: Apex.AI, Blackmore, Boxbot, Bumblebee Spaces, Cartica AI, Cobalt Robotics, Connected

Signals, Elementary Robotics, Embodied, Freedom Robotics, Intuition Robotics, Joby Aviation, May Mobility, Metawave, Moodify, Nauto, Parallel Domain, Perceptive Automata, Realtime Robotics, Recogni, Revel, Sea Machines Robotics, SLAMcore, Skip, Third Wave Automation

Key Executives:
Jim Adler, Managing Director
Education: BS, Electrical Engineer, University of Florida; MS, Electrical/Computer Enginerring, University of California, San Diego
Background: VP of Data & Business Development, Metanautix; VP of Data Systems & Chief Privacy Officer, Intelius; Founder, VoteHere; Engineer, Lockheed Martin
Natalie Fonseca Licciardi, Operating Partner/VP, Platform & Marketing
Education: BComm, University of California, Los Angeles
Background: Consultant, Toyota Research Institute; Founder/CEO, SageScape; Co-Founder, Tech Privacy Summit; Executive Producer, Privacy Identity Innovation; Head of Conference Development & Marketing, Vox Media; Head of Marketing & Audience Development, Recode

1835 TPG CAPITAL
345 California St
Suite 3300
San Francisco, CA 94104

Phone: 415-743-1500 **Fax:** 415-743-1501
web: www.tpg.com

Mission Statement: TPG Capital is one of the largest private equity investment firms in the world.
Geographic Preference: Global
Fund Size: $75 Billion
Founded: 1992
Investment Criteria: Leveraged buyouts, growth capital, fund management
Industry Group Preference: Consumer/Retail, Media & Telecommunications, Industrials, Technology, Travel/Leisure, Healthcare
Portfolio Companies: Adare Pharmaceuticals, Advent Software, Alinta Energy, ALLTELL, American Beacon, Aptalis Pharma, Armstrong, Axip Energy Services, Beaver-Visitec International, Beringer, Diomet, Burger King, Catellus, CCC Information Services, Chobani, Cirque Du Soleil, Continental Airlines, Copano Energy, Creative Artists Agency, Cushman & Wakefield, Ducati Motor Holding Spa, Ellucian, Enlink Midstream, Enlivant, EnvisionRX, Exactech, Eze Software Group, Fenwal, Fidelity National Financial Services, Fleetpride Inc., Gelson's Market, Grohe, Healthscope, Hotwire.com, Iasis Healthcare, Immucor, Ims Health, Intergraph, J. Crew, Jonah Energy LLC, Kindred Healthcare, Kudu, Lenta, Life Time, Llamasoft, LPL Financial, Lynda.com, McAffee, Memc Electronic Materials, Mey Alcoholic Beverages, Neiman Marcus, Nexeo Solutions, Northern Tier Energy, Norwegian Cruise Line, Ontex International, Oxford Health Plans, P3 Logistic Parks, Par Pharmaceutical, Parkway Properties, Petco Animal Supplies, Petro Harvester, Poundworld Retail LTD, Prezzo, Prosight Specialty Insurance, Quintiles, RCN Grande, Rentpath Inc., Sabre, Saxo Bank, Seagate Technology, St Residental, Sungard, Surgical Care Affiliates, Taylor Morrison Home Corporation, TES Global, Texas Genco, The Warranty Group, Transplace, Transporeon, Univision Communications, Vertafore, Vice, Viking Cruises, WellSky, Wind River

Other Locations:
Two International Place
Suite 2230
Boston, MA 02110
Phone: 617-793-2000

816 Congress Avenue
Suite 1130
Austin, TX 78701

2100 McKinney Avenue
Suite 1500
Dallas, TX 75201
Phone: 469-621-3001 **Fax:** 469-621-3002

301 Commercial Street
Suite 3300
Fort Worth, TX 76102
Phone: 817-871-4000 **Fax:** 817-871-4001

1301 McKinney
9th Floor
Houston, TX 77002
Phone: 713-457-5510

888 7th Avenue
(between 56th & 57th Sts.)
35th Floor
New York, NY 10106
Phone: 212-601-4700 **Fax:** 212-601-4701

20th Floor, Parnas Tower
521 Teheran-ro, Gangnam-gu
Seoul 06164
Korea
Phone: 82 2 6944 7888

Suite 3801, China World Tower 3
No.1, Jianguomenwai Avenue
Chaoyang District
Beijing 100004
China
Phone: 86-10 5965-3888 **Fax:** 86-10 5965-3999

Units 1201-1204
Level 12, Cyberport 1
100 Cyberport Road
Hong Kong
China
Phone: 852 3515-8888 **Fax:** 852 3515-8999

1004, The Capital
Plot No. C-70, G-Block
Bandra Kurla Complex, Bandra (E)
Mumbai 400 051
India
Phone: 91-22 6136-1900 **Fax:** 91-22 6136-1901

80 Raffles Place
15-01 UOB Plaza 1
Singapore 048624
Singapore
Phone: 65 6390-5000 **Fax:** 65 6390-5001

The Goldbell Centre
5 rue Eugene Ruppert
Luxembourg L-2453
Luxembourg
Phone: 352 2700-41251 **Fax:** 352 2700-412599

5th Floor, Park House
116 Park Street
London W1K 6AF
United Kingdom
Phone: 44 0 20 7544 6500 **Fax:** 44 0 20 7544 6565

Regus, Smolensky Passage
Smolenskaya Square 3
Offices 728, 730, 731
Moscow 121099
Russia
Phone: 7 495 660-8600 **Fax:** 7 495 660-8601

Level 31
101 Collins Street
Melbourne 3000

Venture Capital & Private Equity Firms / Domestic Firms

Australia
Phone: 61-3 9664-4444 **Fax:** 61-3 9663-7005
Key Executives:
David Bonderman, Chairman
Education: Harvard Law School; University of Washington
Background: Co-Founder, Hotwire.com; Co-Founder, CoStar Group Inc.; Chairman, Continental Airlines Inc.; COO, Robert M. Bass Group Inc.; Partner, Arnold & Porter; Special Assistant to the U.S. Attorney General in the Civil Rights Division; Assistant Professor, Tulane University School
Directorships: Kite Pharma Inc.
Karl Peterson, President & CEO
Education: BBA, University of Notre Dame
Background: Director/President/CEO, Pace-I; Managing Partner, TPG Europe LLP
Directorships: Sabre; Caesars Acquisition Company; Playa Hotels & Resorts; Saxo Bank; TES Global; Pace-I

1836 TRANSCENDENT CAPITAL
447 Broadway
New York, NY 10002

e-mail: hello@transcendent.capital
web: www.transcendent.capital

Mission Statement: Transcendent Capital focuses on tech-based companies across all sectors.
Geographic Preference: North America
Founded: 2017
Investment Criteria: Early Stage, Growth Stage
Industry Group Preference: Technology
Key Executives:
Tarik Abbas, Managing Partner
Education: BA, Fordham University
Background: FinTech Mentor, Startupbootcamp; Venture Partner, NextGen Venture Partners

1837 TRANSITION PARTNERS LTD
1942 Broadway
Suite 314
Boulder, CO 80302

Phone: 303-938-6834 **Fax:** 303-938-6850
e-mail: terry@transitionpartnersltd.com
web: www.transitionpartnersltd.com

Mission Statement: We provide senior level transitional support to companies requiring capital, management, and or planning to achieve targeted business objectives. At our very essence, we provide transition to firms which find themselves at a crossroads.
Geographic Preference: United States, Worldwide
Fund Size: $98 million
Founded: 1994
Average Investment: $7 million
Minimum Investment: $500,000
Investment Criteria: Healthcare/High Technology Fields
Industry Group Preference: Biotechnology, Computer Related, Software, Financial Services, Medical & Health Related, Pharmaceuticals
Portfolio Companies: WAVi, Signal Storage Innovations, iSatori, X-COM, Lucid Dimensions, NavStar, Adaptive Ozone Solutions, FiberForge, Omni, TechPubs, 3QMatrix, Trimac Industries, One Cavo, PureTech Systems, WhiteDove Herbals, Adventure Sports Products, BSI2000, Crystal Packaging, Royal Sign Supply, TeamMates, comCables, Networth Services, Amorfix Life Sciences, dataQorp, Polar Molecular Corporation, Subscription Services, Aspen Laser & Technologies, Deciphera Pharmaceuticals, LAB InterLink, SimplyWell, BeyondNow Technologies, Concepts Direct, INF Tech Enterprises, International Medical Group, ZymeTx, Amarillo Biosciences, e-infoda.com, LANtech, US Medical, Cannect Communications, Corgenix, Integrated Spatial Information Solutions, Dataview Solutions, eSfot, NovaDx, Vidatron, Care Concepts, COMgroup International, Command Security Corporation, Conception Technology, CST Images, EnviroSolutions, Healthcare Funding Corp., H.J. Meyers & Co., Lifestream Diagnostics, Reaads, Ryan Murphy Inc., Dennis Conncer Sports, The Village Green Bookstore, Reality Female Condom, Hippocrates Associates, Hospital Therapy Services, Lutheran Family Services, Children's Cable Network, Primus, Biostar, DCX, Ferrell Companies, 1Mage Software, MainTech, NEON, OMNI Design, Jade Solutions, H.C. Berger Brewing Company
Key Executives:
W Terrence Schreier, President/Managing Director
303-938-6834
Fax: 303-938-6850
e-mail: terry@transitionpartnersltd.com
Background: Corporate Counsel, Hoechst Roussel AG(Marion Laboratories); Director/COO, Continental Healthcare Systems; Director/CEO, Cell Technology; Director/CEO, Air Methods; Outside Director, Recontek(PS Group)
Charles Holcomb, Managing Director
303-882-2425
Fax: 303-973-5020
e-mail: cnhol@aol.com
Gene Copeland, Managing Director
970-547-1879
Fax: 970-453-0773
e-mail: copelandcgi@aol.com

1838 TRANSLINK CAPITAL
228 Hamilton Avenue
Suite 210
Palo Alto, CA 94301

Phone: 650-330-7353 **Fax:** 650-330-7351
e-mail: info@translinkcapital.com
web: www.translinkcapital.com

Mission Statement: Build strong, long-lasting relationships between high technology start-ups in the United States and industry leaders in the technology markets of Japan, Korea and Greater China.
Geographic Preference: United States, Japan, Korea, Greater China
Industry Group Preference: Technology
Portfolio Companies: Adwo, AirPlug, Appcelerator, Carbonite, Chartboost, CloudOn, deCarta, Enterprise DB, Eye-Fi, Guavus, HZO, Kamcord, Livescribe, Luxul Technology, Memo Right, Montage Technology, MusicShake, Nexenta, Noom, nWay, Peel, Quixey, SandForce, SoundHound, Tango, Ubooly, Wildfire, Winking Entertainment, Workspot, Xsigo Systems, YuMe
Other Locations:
2fl, Ilsin Bldg
714 Hannam 2-dong
Yangsan-gu
Seoul 140-894
Korea
Phone: 82-25685029 **Fax:** 82-25685013

14/F, T2, China Central Place
No. 79 Jian Guo Road
Chaoyang District
Beijing 100020
China
Phone: 86-10-8588-9000 x667 **Fax:** 86-10-8588-9001

5th Floor, Tokio Marine Nichido Building
Shinkan 1-2-1 Marunouchi
Chiyoga-ku
Tokyo 100-0005
Japan
Phone: 81-3-3284-1711 **Fax:** 81-3-3284-1885

Toshi Otani, Co-Founder/Managing Director
Education: MBA, Stanford Business School
Background: Senior VP, Everypath

Venture Capital & Private Equity Firms / Domestic Firms

Jackie Yang, Co-Founder/Managing Director
Education: MBA, University of Missouri; BS, Mechanical Engineering, National Tsinghua University
Background: Founding Investor, Maxlin Montage Technology Group, Parade Technologies

1839 TRANSMEDIA CAPITAL
717 Market Street
Suite 100
San Francisco, CA 94103

web: www.transmediacapital.com

Mission Statement: Transmedia Capital helps build digital media and marketing businesses, bridging the gap between new and traditional media. We've started companies, raised venture capital, taken companies public, sold companies, and mentored many young entrepreneurs. We have a tremendous network of advisers and venture partners that can provide our portfolio companies the assistance to help accelerate their growth. Transmedia Capital is the only seed fund investing in specifically the new media and online advertising sector providing deep domain expertise, operating experience, and expert advisory relationships for entrepreneurs.

Average Investment: $250,000 - $2 million
Investment Criteria: Seed-Stage
Industry Group Preference: Digital Media & Marketing, Marketing, Advertising
Portfolio Companies: AngelList, Ark, Bottlenose, Buddy, Clypd, DOMO, Genius, Kiip, LevelUp, Lover.ly, Merchant Atlas, MyLikes, Optilly/Install Monitizer, Percolate, Rally, Relevvant, RolePoint, Traction, TrialPay, Two Tap, Wish, LinkedIn, Share This, Snapchat, Tagged, Twitter Urban Airship

Key Executives:
Chris Redlitz, General Partner
Background: Managing Partner, Kicklabs; Co-Founder, AdAuction; Co-Founder, OnVillage; Reebock Int'l
Peter Boboff, General Partner
Education: BS, Mathematics, Western Australia Institute of Technology
Background: Founder, Axis Consulting; Charles Schwab & Co.

1840 TRASK INNOVATIONS FUND Purdue Research Foundation
1801 Newman Road
Purdue Technology Center Aerospace
West Lafayette, IN 47906

Phone: 765-588-3475 **Fax:** 765-463-3486
e-mail: otcip@prf.org
web: www.prf.org/otc

Mission Statement: The Purdue Research Foundation-managed Trask Innovation Fund (TIF) is a Purdue University development mechanism to assist faculty with work to further commercial potential of technologies disclosed to the Office of Technology Commercialization (OTC). The fund's objective is provide financial support designed to provide an individual technology portfolio up to $50,000 for a period of six months. Formerly known as the Emerging Innovations Fund.

Geographic Preference: Indiana
Founded: 2008
Average Investment: $20,000 - $500,000
Investment Criteria: Early-Stage/Pre-Series A
Industry Group Preference: Life Sciences, Technology

Key Executives:
Brooke Beier, Executive Director
765-588-3464
e-mail: blbeier@prf.org
Education: BS, MS, PhD, Biomedical Engineering, Weldon School of Biomedical Engineering, Purdue University

1841 TRELLIS PARTNERS
138 Trinity Street
Cedar Creek, TX 78612

Phone: 512-330-9200
e-mail: businessplans@trellis.com
web: www.trellis.com

Mission Statement: Venture capital professionals whose focus is on helping build leading technology companies through early-stage investment.

Geographic Preference: Texas
Founded: 1997
Portfolio Companies: WiseGate, Other Inbox, Debix, Genband, Xtera, FRH Consumer Services, Encoding.com, CPO Commerce, Zilliant, Ziften, TabbedOut

Key Executives:
John L Long Jr, General Partner
Education: BS Electrical Engineering, Georgia Institute of Technology; MBA, University of Texas
Background: Partner, Dakota Venture Management; General Partner, Southwest Venture Partners
Directorships: Zilliant, Ziften
Alexander C Broeker, General Partner
Background: Director, Ernst & Young; Management, Deloitte & Touche; Director, Works; CPA
Directorships: Debix, TabbedOut

1842 TRELYS FUNDS
PO Box 5066
Cary, NC 27512-5066

Phone: 919-459-4650 **Fax:** 919-459-4670
web: www.trelys.com

Mission Statement: To invest in entrepreneurial teams who combine vision and creativity in addressing opportunities in growing markets.

Geographic Preference: South Carolina
Founded: 2001
Average Investment: $500,000 - $3 million
Investment Criteria: Early-Stage, Middle-Stage
Industry Group Preference: Information Technology, Communication Technology, Biotechnology, Life Sciences, All Sectors Considered
Portfolio Companies: Aldagen, Biolex Therapeutics, Metabolon, MiMedx, Ometric, TriVirix, UniTrends

Key Executives:
Adrian Wilson, Managing General Partner
e-mail: awilson@trelys.com
Education: JD, MBA, University of North Carolina
Background: Fund Manager, Coastal Growth Partners; Private Practice, Helms Mulliss & Johnston

1843 TRESS CAPITAL LLC
3 Columbus Circle
15th Floor
New York, NY 10019

e-mail: invest@tresscapital.com
web: www.tresscapital.com

Mission Statement: A venture capital and private equity firm investing in companies focused on the cannabis industry.

Founded: 2013
Industry Group Preference: Cannabis
Portfolio Companies: Baker Technologies, Cannabis Now, Headset, Infusion Biosciences, SC Labs, Grownetics, Northburd

Key Executives:
Asher Troppe, Co-Founder/CEO
e-mail: asher@tresscapital.com
Background: Founder/Managing Director, Capital Objectives; Founder/Managing Director, Capital Objects Alpha Balance
David Hess, President
e-mail: dhess@tresscapital.com

Venture Capital & Private Equity Firms / Domestic Firms

Background: Director of New Client Services, MetTel; VP, Business Property Finance Corp.; Director of Business Development, OccuNomix International; President/Founder, Luminosity International
Jonathan Eisenberg, Partner
e-mail: jeisenberg@tresscapital.com
Steven Peterson, Partner, Solutions
e-mail: speterson@tresscapital.com
Education: BS, Accounting, Villanova University; MBA, Golden Gate University
Background: VP of Finance, Rovi Corp.; SVP of Finance, Access Information Management; Chief Financial Officer, Borelli Investment Co.; Co-Founder, webKPI; VP of Marketing/Sales, CellarStone Inc.; General Manager, Elemental Wellness Center; Co-Founder, Turning Points Global; Partner, Cukierman & Co.
Anthony Davis, Operating Partner
Education: Silver Lake All Nations Bible College
Background: VP of Operations, Mactus Group; Co-Founder/Managing Partner, Anslinger Capital; Advisor/Investor, DOPE Magazine; Advisor/Investor, Headset; Investor/Partner, Saint Marie Records; Co-Owner/Advisor, Quantum Power Munich; Co-Founder/Managing Partner, Monition Partners; CEO, ALTO

1844 TREVI HEALTH CAPITAL
600 Madison Avenue
15th Floor
New York, NY 10065

Phone: 212-813-9201
e-mail: info@trevihealth.com
web: www.trevihealth.com

Mission Statement: Trevi Health Capital is a specialist investment firm that provides healthcare-focused alternative asset management through private equity and hedge funds on a global scale. The investment team combines experienced investment professionals and senior-level executives and entrepreneurs with proven track records.

Investment Criteria: Growth Stage
Industry Group Preference: Healthcare, Medical Devices, Biopharmaceuticals, Healthcare Services
Portfolio Companies: AGI Dermatics, Flynn Pharma, Manhattan Physicians Laboratories, MedAvante, Omeros, Optovue, Paradigm Spine, Small Bone Innovations, Salient Surgical Technologies, CareWell Urgent Care, US HealthVest, Home Skinovations, EasyLap

Other Locations:
52 Conduit Street
3rd Floor
London W1S 2YX
United Kingdom
Phone: 44-02072922570

Key Executives:
David Robbins, Co-Founder/CIO
Education: Wharton School, New York University School of Law
Background: Corporate Law, Cahill Gordon & Reindel; Strategic Advisor, Elan Corporation; Advisor, Barr Pharmaceuticals
Directorships: Paradigm Spine, Optovue, Home Skinovations, Bally Technologies
Andrew Fink, Co-Founder
Education: AB, Columbia College; JD, Columbia School of Law
Background: Healthcare & Life Sciences Group, Dresdner Kleinwort Wasserstein; Corporate Law, Paul Weiss Rifkind Wharton & Garrison

1845 TRIANGLE ANGEL PARTNERS
PO Box 110062
Research Triangle Park, NC 27709

Phone: 919-904-4565
web: www.triangleangelpartners.com

Mission Statement: Triangle Angel Partners (TAP) is an experienced group of angel investors who invest their time, analysis and money into early life cycle companies in the high tech and life services industries. Our members are executives, PhDs, successful entrepreneurs and professional investors. With TAP's exclusive network, we get the first look at the best new ideas coming our of the Raleigh, Durham, Chapel Hill and the Research Triangle Park areas.

Geographic Preference: North Carolina
Investment Criteria: Early-Stage
Industry Group Preference: High Technology, Life Sciences
Portfolio Companies: Adzerk, Entigral Systems, Physcient, SEAL, Stealz, WedPics, Windsor Circle

1846 TRIANGLE PEAK PARTNERS
505 Hamilton Avenue
Suite 300
Palo Alto, CA 94301

Phone: 650-561-4415
web: www.trianglepeakpartners.com

Mission Statement: Triangle Peak Partners conducts private investments in companies where we can work with management and help create value. We have a deep background in venture capital and private equity investing in private and public technology, energy, and alternative energy companies.

Minimum Investment: $2 - $15 million
Investment Criteria: Early-Stage, Later-Stage, Public
Industry Group Preference: Technology, Energy, Alternative Energy
Portfolio Companies: Achates Power, Agent Ace, Astroboundary, Bunchball, Coupons.com, FineLine Technologies, Fliaz, Framehawk, Fusion-io, Getaround, Guardian Analytics, Kurtosys, LibreDigital, Lytx, Machinima, Marlin Software, Optify, PCH International, Ping Identity, Prism Skylabs, Puppet Labs, SCIenergy, Send Me Mobile, Sojern, snapLogic, TakeLessons, Tremor Video, Vidyo, Yieldex, Aereon, American Energy Partners, Arc Terminals, Brawler, Chesapeake Energy, Copano Energy, Crestwood, Eclipse Resources, Endeavour, Plains GP Holdings, PXP, Regency, SandRidge, Seven Generations, Sunnova, Tallgrass Energy, Teekay, WireCo

Other Locations:
11 Greenway Plaza
Suite 2000
Houston, TX 77046
Phone: 713-439-1097

Key Executives:
Dain F DeGroff, Co-Founding Partner
Education: BS, Mechanical Engineering, Stanford University; MBA, Wharton School
Background: Managing Director, Fort Mason Capital; Investment Banking, Hambrecht & Quist; JP Morgan
Directorships: Yieldex
Michael C Morgan, Co-Founding Partner
Education: BA, Economics, MA, Sociology, Stanford University; MBA, Harvard Business School
Background: President/CEO, Portcullis Partners; President, Kinder Morgan
Directorships: Bunchball, DriveCam, SCIenergy
David L Pesikoff, Co-Founding Partner
Education: BA, Mathematics, Williams College; MBA, Stanford University
Background: Principal, Fayez Sarofim & Co.; Management Consultant, Gemini Consulting, Bain & Company
Directorships: Guardian Analytics, Optify

Venture Capital & Private Equity Firms / Domestic Firms

1847 TRIATHLON MEDICAL VENTURES
300 East Business Way
Suite 200
Cincinnati, OH 45241

Phone: 513-247-6122
web: www.tmvp.com

Mission Statement: Triathlon Medical Ventures is a Midwest-based venture capital firm that invests exclusively in the life sciences. We provide equity capital to early and expansion state companies with proprietary biomedical technology platforms or products addressing significant human healthcare needs.

Geographic Preference: Midwest United States
Founded: 2004
Average Investment: $500,000 - $7 million
Investment Criteria: Early-Stage, Expansion-Stage
Industry Group Preference: Life Sciences, Healthcare, Biopharmaceuticals, Medical Devices
Portfolio Companies: Aerpio Therapeutics, Akebia Therapeutics, Biovex, CoLucid Pharmaceuticals, Endocyte, Juventas Therapeutics, Kereos, SironRx Therapeutics, Tolera Therapeutics, Cellleration, Expanding Orthopedics, Hydrocision, Lonestar Heart, Mitralighn, Remon Medical Technologies, Renal Solutions, Suturtek

Other Locations:
201 North Illinois Street
16th Floor
South Tower
Indianapolis, IN 46204
Phone: 317-280-8233 Fax: 317-328-9743

222 South First Street
Suite 200
Louisville, KY 40202
Phone: 502-410-1652 Fax: 502-584-6335

Key Executives:
Dennis B Costello, Co-Founder/Managing Partner
Education: BS, United States Naval Academy; MBA, Harvard Business School
Background: Senmed Medical Ventures, American Crital Care, Clonetics, Regent Hospital Products, Hana Biologics
Suzette Dutch, Managing Partner
Education: BA, Economics, Case Western Reserve University; MBA, Wharton School
Background: Senmet, Sentron
Directorships: Tolera Therapeutics, Akebia, BioVex
John M Rice PhD, Co-Founder/Managing Partner
Education: BS, MS, PhD, Microbiology & Virology, Ohio State University
Background: Managing Director, Senmed Medical Ventures
Directorships: Akebia Therapeutics, Syntherix, Kereos
Carrie Bates, Managing Partner
317-280-8233
Fax: 317-328-9743
Education: BS, Finance, BS, Computer Science, MBA, Stanford University
Background: Guidant Corporation, Eli Lilly
Directorships: CS-Keys, Mitralign, Pradama

1848 TRIBE CAPITAL
Menlo Park, CA

web: www.tribecap.co

Mission Statement: Investments focus on internet and software leveraging data and technology.

Geographic Preference: United States
Fund Size: $22.7 Million
Founded: 2018
Investment Criteria: Seed, Series A
Industry Group Preference: Software & Internet
Portfolio Companies: Applied Intuition, Carta, Cover, Dataform, Front, GiveLegacy, Sfox, Snark.ai, Toko

Key Executives:
Arjun Sethi, Co-Founder/Partner
Education: BA, Economics, Boston University; BA, BS, University of Maryland College Park
Background: 6waves; MessageMe; Yahoo!; Social Capital LP
Directorships: Carta; Cover; Sfox
Jonathan Hsu, Co-Founder/Partner
Education: BS, Engineering Physics, University of California, Berkeley; MS, PhD, Stanford Univeristy
Background: Microsoft; SuperPoke; Slide, Inc.; Facebook; Social Capital LP
Directorships: Insight Data Science
Ted Maidenberg, Co-Founder/Partner
Education: BSBA, Finance, Washington University in St. Louis
Background: Credit Suisse; Time Warner Ventures; Warner Bros; USVP; Social Capital LP
Directorships: Simplee

1849 TRIBECA VENTURE PARTNERS
13-17 Laight Street
Suite 606B
New York, NY 10013

Phone: 212-966-9333
web: www.tribecavp.com

Mission Statement: TVP is an early-stage venture capital firm that partners with world class entrepreneurs in the NYC area leveraging emerging technologies and business models to create and disrupt huge markets.

Average Investment: $100,000 - $4 million
Investment Criteria: Early-Stage, Seed-Stage
Industry Group Preference: Digital Media & Marketing, E-Commerce & Manufacturing, Financial Services, Advertising, Mobile, Software
Portfolio Companies: AppNexus, Backtrace I/O, BetterCloud, clypd, Cognical, Coinsetter, CommonBond, Crowdtap, Flat World Knowledge, Forever, FTRANS, HomeSphere, LeadiD, Lendio, Live Gamer, MakersKit, Maxwell Health, Opternative, RealDirect, Shopkeep, Spanfeller Media, Truveris, Virsex, Vook

Key Executives:
Brian Hirsch, Co-Founder/Managing Partner
212-389-1601
e-mail: brian@tribecavp.com
Education: BA, Economics & American Studies, Brandeis University
Background: Founder & Managing Director, GSA Venture Partners; Principal, Sterling Venture Partners
Directorships: Coinsetter, CommonBond, CrowdTap, Flat World Knowledge, FTRANS, HomeSphere, Just Sing It, Lendio, Mobile Commons, Pontiflex, RealDirect, ShopKeep, Spanfeller Media Group, Vook
Chip Meakem, Co-Founder/Managing Partner
212-389-1604
e-mail: chip@tribecavp.com
Education: BA, Cornell University; MBA, Columbia Business School
Background: Managing Partner, Kodiak Venture Partners; DFJ Gotham; Founding Employee, Interactive Imaginations
Directorships: Appnexus, Ideeli, LiveGamer, TRA Global

1850 TRIDENT CAPITAL
400 S. El Camino Real
Suite 300
San Mateo, CA 94402

Phone: 650-289-4400 Fax: 650-289-4444
e-mail: info@tridentcap.com
web: www.tridentcap.com

647

Venture Capital & Private Equity Firms / Domestic Firms

Mission Statement: A venture capital firm founded to invest in information and business services companies.
Fund Size: $1.5+ billion
Founded: 1993
Average Investment: $3-20 million
Investment Criteria: Multi-Stage Venture Capital
Industry Group Preference: Information Technology, Enterprise Software, SaaS, Business Products & Services, Information Services, Consumer Services, Digital Media & Marketing, Social Media
Portfolio Companies: 2CheckOut, 8thBridge, Acclaris, AccountNow, Advanced ICU Care, Advanced Payment Solutions, Aethon, AirTight Networks, AlienVault, Amprius, Appia, Arxas Technologies, BlueCat Networks, BrightRoll, Bytemobile, Chamberlin Edmonds & Associates, CSG Systems International, Datatel, eGistics, Epicor Software, eXelate, Extole, Fruition Partners, HealthMEDX, Hip Digital, HomeAway, Host Analytics, HyTrust, Iconic Labs, Infotrieve, Internet Profiles, JiWire, Jobvite, Kayak, Mapquest.com, mBlox, Medicode, MedSave, MegaPath Networks, Merchant eSolutions, Microland, Mocana, Mustang Ventures, Neilsoft, Neohapsis, Odyssey Logistics & Technology, PAL, PeriGen, PivotLink, Profex, Prolexic, Qualys, Resolution Health, RezSolutions, RoyaltyShare, Sabre Holdings, Sidestep, Signio, Siva Power, Sojern, Solera Networks, Sygate Technologies, Tablus, Teladoc, Thismoment, THOR Technologies, Tiandi Energy, Turn, Voltage Security, XRS, Xunlight

Key Executives:
Donald R. Dixon, Co-Founder/Senior Managing Director
e-mail: ddixon@tridentcap.com
Education: BSE, Princeton University; MBA, Stanford Graduate School of Business
Background: Co-President, Partech International; Managing Director, Alex Brown & Sons; VP, Morgan Stanley & Company; Sr Account, Citibank NA
Directorships: 2Checkout, AccountNow, Advanced Payment Solutions, Amprius, eGistics, Infotrieve, Neohapsis, Odyssey Logistics, Qualys, RoyaltyShare, SivaPower, Tiandi Energy, XRS
John H. Moragne, Co-Founder/Senior Managing Director
e-mail: jmoragne@tridentcap.com
Education: BA, Dartmouth College; MS, Stanford University
Background: Principal, Bain Capital; Principal, Information Partners Capital Fund
Directorships: Turn, Sojern, Appia, JiWire, Perigen, ArrayPower, Jobvite
Arneek Multani, Managing Director
e-mail: amultani@tridentcap.com
Education: BS, Wharton School of Business, BAS Moore School of Engineering, University of Pennsylvania; MBA, Stanford Graduate School of Business
Background: Product Management, Network Storage Software Products Group, Sun Microsystems; Health & Fitness Industries, McCown De Leeuw & Co.; Media & Telecommunications, M&A Group, Morgan Stanley & Co.
Directorships: MedSave, HealthMEDX, Acclaris, Teladoc, Neilsoft, Microland
John Reardon, Managing Director
e-mail: jreardon@tridentcap.com
Education: BS, History, BS, Economics, Arizona State University; MBA, University of California
Background: President & CEO, CliniComp International; Operating Partner, JP Morgan Partners; Regional VP, Strategic Planning & Business Development, St. Joseph Health System; Co-Founder, Value Health Management & Health Economics Corp.
Directorships: PeriGen, Advanced ICU Care, HealthMEDX, TelaDoc, Aethon
J. Alberto Yepez, Managing Director
e-mail: ayepez@tridentcap.com
Education: BS, Kellogg School of Management, Northwestern University; BS, University of San Francisco
Background: VP, Indentity Management & Security, Oracle; Chairman, President & CEO, Thor Technologies; EIR, Warburg Pincus; Co-CEO, Entrust; Chairman & CEO, enCommerce; Senior Management Positions, Apple Computer
Directorships: AlientVault, Mocana, Neohapsis, AirTight Networks, BlueCat Networks, HyTrust, Mocana
Howard S. Zeprun, Chief Administrative Officer & General Counsel
e-mail: hzeprun@tridentcap.com
Education: BS, Systems Engineering, University of Pennsylvania School of Engineering & Applied Science; BS, Finance, Wharton School of Commerce & Finance; JD, Harvard Law School
Background: Corporate & Securities Partner, Wilson Sonsini Goodrich & Rosati; Corporate Counsel, Apple Computer
Michael Biggee, Managing Director
e-mail: mbiggee@tridentcap.com
Education: MS, Engineering, Cornell University; BS, Chemical Engineering, Cornell University
Background: Dolphin Equity Partners; Global Technology Banking, Merrill Lynch; Chemical Engineer, Procter & Gamble & General Mills

1851 TRILANTIC CAPITAL PARTNERS
399 Park Avenue
39th Floor
New York, NY 10022

Phone: 212-607-8450
e-mail: linda.due@trilanticpartners.com
web: www.trilantic.com

Mission Statement: Trilantic Capital Partners was formed by the former principals of Lehman Brothers Merchant Banking. Trilantic Capital Partners seeks to partner with management teams with a compelling strategy, a well-developed framework for execution, extensive industry and operating experience and an established performance record.

Geographic Preference: North America, Western Europe
Fund Size: $7 billion
Founded: 2009
Average Investment: $50 - $180 million
Investment Criteria: Management Buyouts, Recapitalizations, Growth Equity, Corporate Divestitures, Generational Transitions
Industry Group Preference: Business Products & Services, Consumer Services, Energy Services, Financial Services
Portfolio Companies: 24-7 Intouch Inc., Asset Living, Djr Energy LLC, Elephant Oil & Gas, Fluid Delivery Solutions LLC, Highgate Hotels, Indigo Natural Resources LLC, M5 Midstream LLC, Ortholite Holdings LLC, Solaris Midstream Holdings LLC, Sunbelt-Solomon Solutions, Sunrise Strategic Partners LLC, Taymax Group Holdings LLC, Traeger Pellet Grills LLC, TRP Energy LLC, Velvet Energy LTD, Ward Energy Partners

Other Locations:
301 Congress Avenue
Suite 2050
Austin, TX 78701
Phone: 512-362-6260

Heritage Hall
PO Box 225
Le Marchant Street, St Peter Port
Guernsey GY1 4HY
United Kingdom
Phone: 44 14 8173 7400

26 Bd Royal
Luxembourg L-2449
Luxembourg
Phone: 352 22 99 99 52 16

Key Executives:
Charles Ayres, Founding Partner & Chairman
212-607-8440

Venture Capital & Private Equity Firms / Domestic Firms

e-mail: cayres@trilanticpartners.com
Education: BA, Economics, Duke University; MBA, Amos Tuck School, Dartmouth College
Background: Founding Partners, MidOcean Partners; Head, DB Capital Partners North America
Daniel James, Founding Partner, Head/North America
212-607-8410
e-mail: djames@trilanticpartners.com
Education: BA, Chemistry, College of the Holy Cross
Background: Lehman Brothers M&A Group
Directorships: Angelica Corporation, Blount International, Houston International Insurance Group, VantaCore Partners
Christopher Manning, Partner
212-607-8484
e-mail: cmanning@trilanticpartners.com
Education: BBA, University of Texas, Austin; MBA, Wharton School
Background: Head, Lehman Brothers' Investment Management Division
Charles Fleischmann, Partner
212-607-8466
e-mail: cfleischmann@trilantic.com
Education: BA, Colgate University
Background: Investcorp International Inc.; JP Morgan; Shearman and Sterling; Chairman, Home Franchise Concepts Parents
Directorships: Sunbelt-Solomon Solutions; United Subcontractors Inc.
Jeremy Lynch, Partner
212-607-8448
e-mail: jlynch@trilanticpartners.com
Education: BS, Applied Mathematics, Union College
Background: Principal, Lehman Brothers Merchant Banking; Analyst & Associate, Lehman Brothers
Directorships: Addison Group; MicroStar Logistics; 24-7 InTouch Inc.; Asset
James Manges, Partner & Head of Consumer
212-607-8424
e-mail: jmanges@trilanticpartners.com
Education: BA, Yale University; MBA, Columbia Business School
Background: Principal, Lehman Brothers Merchant Bankingl Chairman, Sunrise Strategic Partners; President, Vice; Lazard Alternative Investments; Leveraged Finance Group; Merrill Lynch
Directorships: Kodiak Cakes; Ortholite Holdings; Taymax Group Holdings; Traeger Pellet Grills; Implus Corporation; Fortitech; Home Franchise Concepts Parents; SRAM
Grant Palmer, Partner
212-607-8415
e-mail: gpalmer@trilantic.com
Education: BA, Economics & History, Duke University; MBA, Columbia Business School
Background: Senior Associate, Lehman Brothers Merchant Banking
Directorships: Ortholite Holdings; Sunrise Strategic Partners; Traeger Pellet Grills; Implus Corporations
Elliot Attie, Partner & CFO
212-607-8423
e-mail: elliot.attie@trilanticpartners.com
Education: BS, Accounting, State University of New York
Background: VP, Lehman Brothers Merchant Banking; Senior Manager, PricewaterhouseCoopers
Directorships: New York Chapter of the Private Equity CFO Association
Andrew Hopping, Principal
512-362-6250
e-mail: andrew.hopping@trilantic.com
Education: BS & BA, University of Colorado
Background: Analyst, Lehman Brothers Merchant Banking
Directorships: DJR Energy; Elephant Oil & Gas

Glenn Jacobson, Partner
212-607-8420
e-mail: gjacobson@trilantic.com
Education: Dartmouth College
Background: Lehman Brothers

1852 TRILOGY PARTNERSHIP
155 108th Avenue NE
Suite 400
Bellevue, WA 98004

Phone: 425-458-5900
web: trilogyequity.com

Mission Statement: Trilogy Partnership seeks high growth opportunities in both developed and emerging countries.
Industry Group Preference: Wireless Technologies, Communications, Technology
Portfolio Companies: Alert1, Asurion, Farmstr, FireApps, GameChanger, Globys, Haiku Deck, Hola, Jobaline, Lookout, Mits, PrePlay, Red Tricycle, Remitly, SignalSense, Tellwise, Viva Bolivia, Viva Dominican Republic, 2degrees

1853 TRINITY VENTURES
2480 Sand Hill Road
Suite 200
Menlo Park, CA 94025

Phone: 650-854-9500 **Fax:** 650-854-9501
e-mail: info@trinityventures.com
web: www.trinityventures.com

Mission Statement: Trinity invests in companies where the business experience of its professionals can add significant value to the entrepreneur and the company, early stage companies, and more established businesses with high growth potential.

Fund Size: $300 million
Founded: 1986
Average Investment: $1-$5 million
Minimum Investment: $250,000
Investment Criteria: Seed, Startup, First-stage, Second-stage
Industry Group Preference: E-Commerce & Manufacturing, Communications, Software
Portfolio Companies: 21vianet.com, 24/7 Real Media, Act-On Software, Affinity Jobs, Ankeena, Aruba Networks, Aryaka, Aventail, BabyCenter, BackWeb, Badgeville, BeachMint, Biba, Bix, Blue Nile, BlueStripe, BlueTarp Financial, Bonfaire, Bright Horizons, Care.com, Clearleap, Cloudability, Cloudscaling, Connected, Conner, Crescendo Communications, CrowdFlower, CubeTree, Deliv, Digital Market, Digital Research, Docker, Dot & Bo, Dot Loop, DynamicSignal, EggDrop, Enovix, Exalt, Extreme Networks, Fitstar, Forté, Fuego, Getinsured.com, Gigi Hill, Green Patch, GreenThrottle, GridIron, Hoopla, ID Analytics, IKOS, Illustra, Infoblox, IntruVert Networks, Jama, Jamba Juice, Kiva Software, KIXEYE, Likewise, Loggly LoopNet, Marmot, MaxPoint, Mobile Messenger, Modulus Video, mSpot, MyNewPlace, Net Effect Systems, NetFlip, Network Alchemy, New Relic, NextGreatPlace, NextCard, Orative, Owler, P.F. Chang's, PayScale, PerfectMarket, Photobucket, PlayFirst, Posterous, RadiumOne, Red Aril, RiverMuse, RJMetrics, Ruby Ribbon, Sabrix, ScaleArc, SciQuest, ServiceMax, SevenSpace, ShopIgniter, Skyfire, Speedera Networks, StackMob, Starbucks Coffee, Sygate, Taulia, ThredUp, Torbit, Trion, Truaxis, TrustID, TubeMogul, Uptake, Virage, Wall Data, WeddingChannel.com, Weddington Way

Other Locations:
One Market Plaza
Steuart Tower, #1208
San Francisco, CA 94105

Key Executives:
Noel J Fenton, Founding General Partner
e-mail: noel@trinityventures.com

649

Education: BS Chemistry, Cornell University; MBA, Stanford Graduate School of Business
Background: Chief Executive Officer, Acurex and Covalent Systems
Directorships: BlueStripe Software, Blue Tarp Financial, DotLoop, SciQuest, ServiceMax, Taulia, TrustID
Patricia Nakache, General Partner
e-mail: patricia@trinityventures.com
Education: MBA, Stanford Graduate School of Business, AB, Harvard University
Background: McKinsey & Company
Directorships: BeachMint, Care.com, KIXEYE, Owler, PayScale, Ruby Ribbon, thredUP, Weddington Way, Whisper
Ajay Chopra, General Partner
e-mail: ajay@trinityventures.com
Education: BSEE, Birla Institute of Technology & Science, India; MSEE, Stony Brook University
Background: Co-Founder, Pinnacle Systems; Mindset Corporation; Atari Corporation; Unisys Corporation
Directorships: Bonfaire, CrowdFlower, Dynamic Signal, FitStar, Mobile Messenger, RadiumOne, TubeMogul, White Sky
Larry Orr, General Partner
e-mail: larry@trinityventures.com
Education: AB, Mathematics, Harvard University; MBA, Stanford Graduate School of Business
Background: Hewlett-Packard; Neiderhoffer Cross & Zeckhauser
Directorships: GetInsured, Perfect Market, ShopIgniter, ProtectWise, Hoopla Software
Dan Scholnick, General Partner
e-mail: dan@trinityventures.com
Education: AB, Computer Science, Dartmouth College; MBA, Harvard Business School
Background: SVB Capital; Wily Technology
Directorships: Aryaka Networks, Blue Stripe Software, Cloudscaling, CrowdFlower, Docker, Loggly, MongoHQ, New Relic
Gus Tai, Venture Partner
e-mail: gus@trinityventures.com
Education: AB, Applied Mathematics, Harvard University; MS, Materials Science & Engineering, MIT; MBA, MIT Sloan School of Management
Background: Digital Equipment Corporation, Bain & Company
Directorships: Callisto Media, Dot & Bo, MaxPoint Interactive, Moovweb, PlayFirst, Trion Worlds, WetPaint, Zulily

1854 TRIPLETREE LLC
3600 Minnesota Drive
Suite 200
Edina, MN 55435

Phone: 952-223-8400
web: www.triple-tree.com

Mission Statement: TripleTree is led by a team of former operating executives, bankers, entrepreneurs, and venture capitalists. Our services include mergers & acquisitions, principal investing and strategic advisory.

Industry Group Preference: Healthcare, Technology
Kevin R Green, Founding Managing Director
e-mail: kgreen@triple-tree.com
Education: BA, MBA, University of San Diego
Background: CEO, Summit Medical; CEO, Integrated Medical Systems
David A Henderson, Founding Managing Director
e-mail: dhenderson@triple-tree.com
Education: Morehead State University; CPA
Background: Arthur Andersen

1855 TRITON VENTURES
6300 Bridge Point Parkway
Building 1
Suite 500
Austin, TX 78730

Phone: 512-795-5820 Fax: 512-795-5828
e-mail: laura@tritonventures.com
web: www.tritonventures.com

Mission Statement: Established with the belief that significant opportunities exist to transfer technology from corporate or institutional development environments into new entrepreneurial companies focused on rapid growth.

Investment Criteria: Spinouts, Early Stage
Industry Group Preference: Enterprise Services, Information Technology, Communications, Advanced Materials, Software
Portfolio Companies: Applied Science Fiction, ClearOrbit, Exterprise, Gallery Watch, Charitygift, Greenmountain, Hart InterCivic, Innovalight, MindFlow Technologies, Vincera

Key Executives:
Laura J Kilcrease, Managing Director
e-mail: laura@tritonventures.com
Education: MBA, University of Texas; Chartered Management Accountant
Background: Director, Center for Commercialization & Enterprise; Founding Director, Austin Technology Incubator; Capital Network; Austin Software Council
Directorships: Women's Leadership Advisory Board; Beyster Institute
Scott Collier, Managing Director
e-mail: scott@tritonventures.com
Education: BS Engineering, Texas A&M University; MBA, University of Texas; Engineering Management Program, Cailfornia Institute of Technology
Background: VP, Capital Southwest Corporation; Aircraft Engineer/Project Manager, Northrop Grumman

1856 TRIVE CAPITAL
2021 McKinney Avenue
Suite 1200
Dallas, TX 75201

Phone: 214-499-9715 Fax: 469-310-9961
e-mail: info@trivecapital.com
web: www.trivecapital.com

Mission Statement: Trive Capital is a Dallas, Texas-based private equity firm investing in equity and debt securities with approximately $900 million in capital under management.

Geographic Preference: North America
Fund Size: $900 million
Average Investment: $10-150 million
Investment Criteria: Lower Middle Market
Industry Group Preference: Diversified
Portfolio Companies: AGM Automotive, Chicago Miniature Lighting, Valence Surface Technologies, Huron, Precise Packaging, Southern Towing Company

Key Executives:
Conner Searcy, Managing Partner
e-mail: connersearcy@trivecapital.com
Education: BA, Vanderbilt University; MBA, Harvard Business School
Background: Partner, Insight Equity; Stonegate; Bain & Company
Chris Zugaro, Partner
e-mail: chriszugaro@trivecapital.com
Education: BS, Computer Engineering, Texas A&M University; MBA, Stanford Graduate School of Business
Background: Principal, Insight Equity; Bain & Company
David Stinnett, Partner
e-mail: davidstinnett@trivecapital.com
Education: BA, Economics & Philosophy, Vanderbilt University

Venture Capital & Private Equity Firms / Domestic Firms

Background: Insight Equity; Associate, Pamlico Capital; Analyst, M&A Group, McGladrey Capital Markets
Desmond Henry, Managing Director
e-mail: desmondhenry@trivecapital.com
Education: BS, Finance, University of Southern California
Background: Managing Director, Black Canyon Capital; Vice President, Merrill Lynch European M&A Group
Blake Bonner, Partner
e-mail: blakebonner@trivecapital.com
Education: BBA, Finance & Entrepreneurial Management, Neeley School of Business, Texas Christian University
Background: Insight Equity; Analyst, Houlihan Lokey
Shravan Thadani, Managing Director
e-mail: shravanthadani@trivecapital.com
Education: MPA, McCombs School of Business, University of Texas
Background: VP, Sequel Holdings; Associate, Goldman Sachs; Analyst, Houlihan Lokey

1857 TRIVEST PARTNERS
550 South Dixie Highway
Suite 300
Coral Gables, FL 33146

Phone: 305-858-2200 Fax: 305-285-0102
e-mail: info@trivest.com
web: www.trivest.com

Mission Statement: A leading provider of equity for middle market corporate acquisitions, recapitalizations and growth capital financings, always co-investing with company management and pursues transactions which are supported by the management and Boards of Directors of the investee companies.

Geographic Preference: Southeast, Midwest, United States
Fund Size: $325 million
Founded: 1981
Minimum Investment: $5 million
Investment Criteria: Middle Market Acquisitions, Recapitalizations, Growth Financing
Industry Group Preference: Niche Manufacturing, Business Products & Services, Consumer Products
Portfolio Companies: Advanced Discovery, AM Conservation Group, Columbus Recycling, Ellery Homestyles, Endeavor, HandStands, National Auto Care, North Star Seafood, Northfield Industries, OnePath Systems, Pelican Water Systems, Ryko, SRS, Take 5, Twin-Star International, Wise Company

Key Executives:
Troy D Templeton, Managing Partner
e-mail: ttempleton@trivest.com
Education: BBA, MBA, Stetson University
Background: Southeast Bank, NA
Directorships: Endeavor Telecom
Jamie E Elias, Partner
e-mail: jelias@trivest.com
Education: BS, Boston College; MBA, Harvard Business School; CPA
Background: Audit/Advisory Group, Price Waterhouse, Miami
Directorships: Twin-Star, DirectBuy, Ryko Solutions, AM Conservation
David Gershman, Partner & General Counsel
e-mail: dgershman@trivest.com
Education: BA, Union College; JD, New York University School of Law; NY and Florida Bar
Background: Akerman, Senterfitt & Edison, PA; M&A Counsel, Automatic Data Processing; Practicing Lawyer, Morgan Lewis, NY
Directorships: Onepath Systems, Hazmasters, Endeavor, Onepath, Group III, Take 5
Russ Wilson, Partner
e-mail: rwilson@trivest.com
Education: BA, Business Management & Economics, Eckerd College

Background: Associate, PNC Equity; Associate, Raymond James' Investment Banking Division
Directorships: Twin-Star International, Ryko Solutions, Take 5 Oil Change, Ellery Homestyles
Forest Wester, Partner
e-mail: fwester@trivest.com
Education: Dartmouth College; MBA, Harvard Business School
Background: Associate, Lehman Brothers' Private Equity Division
Directorships: Group III International, Endeavor Telecom, Onepath Systems
Jorge Gross Jr, Partner
e-mail: jgross@trivest.com
Education: BA, Economics, Columbia University; MBA, Wharton School, University of Pennsylvania
Background: Associate, Credit Suisse First Boston
Directorships: AM Conservation, Hazmasters

1858 TRU MANAGEMENT
141 South 6th Avenue
Suite 1025
Tucson, AZ 85702-1025

Phone: 520-328-7443
web: www.trugroup.com

Mission Statement: To help build successful companies through fine tuning business strategies, building the right management team, finding resources, and introducing portfolio companies to corporate alliances to expand internationally. Tru Management provides their portfolio companies with services to help them succeed in a competitive and rapidly changing tech environment.

Geographic Preference: United States, Canada, Mexico, Europe, Middle East, China
Fund Size: $1 billion
Average Investment: $1 million - 10 million
Investment Criteria: Early, Expansion, Late
Industry Group Preference: Communications, Electronic Technology, Information Technology, Software

Other Locations:
95 Prince Arthur Avenue
Suite 117
Toronto, ON M5R 3P6
Canada
Phone: 416-935-1754

Key Executives:
Edward R. Anderson, President & CEO
e-mail: anderson@trugroup.com
Education: BSc, Dpl, Marketing Research, MBA

1859 TRUE NORTH VENTURE PARTNERS
205 North Michigan Avenue
Suite 2930
Chicago, IL 60601

Phone: 312-574-1700
web: www.truenorthvp.com

Mission Statement: True North Venture Partners invests in and supports early stage businesses that have the potential to transform, expand and lead global industries. Our goal is to identify exceptionally talented entrepreneurs with the vision, drive and business potential to significantly improve the world and help them realize their dreams by providing capital and expertise.

Average Investment: $100,000 - $25 million
Minimum Investment: $100,000
Investment Criteria: Early-Stage
Industry Group Preference: Energy, Water, Agriculture, Waste & Recycling

Other Locations:
2390 E Camelback Road
Suite 203

Venture Capital & Private Equity Firms / Domestic Firms

Phoeniz, AZ 85016
Phone: 602-476-5800
Key Executives:
Michael J Ahearn, Founder
Education: BS, JD, Arizona State University
Background: Co-Founder, First Solar; Partner & President, True North Partners
Matthew S Ahearn, Founder
Education: BS, Political Science & Economics, Northwestern University
Background: BDT Capital Partners, Goldman Sachs & Co.
Steven D Kloos PhD
Education: BS, Chemistry, University of Wisconsin, River Falls; PhD, Chemistry, North Dakota State University
Background: Advanced Technolgy Leader, GE Water & Porocess Technologies

1860 TRUE VENTURES
575 High Street
Suite 400
Palo Alto, CA 94301

web: www.trueventures.com

Mission Statement: True is a venture firm for very early stage entrepreneurs that partners with promising entrepreneurs at the earliest stages in the highest-growth segments of the technology market, where history demonstrates the best rates of return.

Investment Criteria: Seed-Stage, Early-Stage, Later-Stage, Private Equity, Debt Financing

Industry Group Preference: Digital Media & Marketing, Online Publishing, Internet Communications, Mobile Technology, Mobile Entertainment, Internet Advertising, Software, Gaming, E-Commerce & Manufacturing, SaaS, Media, Internet, Enterprise Software, Infrastructure, Mobile Services

Portfolio Companies: 3D Robotics, 410 Labs, 9GAG, About.me, Academia.edu, Adku, Airstone Labs, Always Prepped, AOptix, Apcera, Appconomy, Applauze, Apply Financial, appssavvy, Automatic, B-Stock Solutions, Bandcamp, Betable, bLife, Blue Bottel Coffee, BraceAbility, BrightRoll, Concurrent, Datacraft Solutions, Dinamundo, Directly, DJZ, Duo Security, EdgeConnex, Evident.io, Finderly, Fitbit, Flint, GigaOM, Ginger.io, Hedvig, Helpshift, High Fidelity, Inventables, Keep Holdings, Kicksend, Kiip, KISSmetrics, Kurtosys, littleBits Electronics, Loggly, Madefire, Madison Reed, Message Bus, Metamarkets, Mindbites, MobileSpan, MoviePass, Namely, Narrative, Nearstream, Neighborland, Neon, Orabrush, Orchestrate.io, Ovelin, PayNearMe, Piston Cloud, POSE, Puppet Labs, Qualaroo, Quarterly, RescueTimy, Runscope, SaveUp, Schematic Labs, Showyou, Sifteo, Singly, Smarterer, SocialPandas, Socrative, Soundhawk, Sparked, Spectrum Bridge, Splice, Spree Commerce, Stitch Labs, StockTwits, Streetline, TastemakerX, Technical Machine, tenXer, TerraEchos, ToyTalk, TripleLift, Urban Airship, Valencell, Webshots, WhoBet

Other Locations:
501 3rd Street
San Francisco, CA 94107

Phil Black, Founder
Education: AB, Economics, Stanford University
Background: Founder, Blacksmith Capital; General Partner, ABS Ventures; General Partner, Weiss Peck & Greer; General Partner, Greer Venture Partners
Jon Callaghan, Founder
Education: BA, Government, Dartmouth College; MBA, Harvard Business School
Background: Summit Partners; AOL Greenhouse; Managing Partner, @Ventures; Managing Director, Globespan
Tony Conrad, Partner
Education: BS, Telecommunications, Indiana University; BA, Economics, Indiana University
Background: Sphere; about.me
Toni Schneider, Founder
Education: BS, Computer Science, Stanford University
Background: Yahoo!; Automattic

1861 TSG CONSUMER PARTNERS
600 Montgomery Street
Suite 2900
San Francisco, CA 94111

Phone: 415-398-2300 **Fax:** 415-421-2350
web: www.tsgconsumer.com

Mission Statement: The leader in the U.S. in building and investing in leading middle-market branded consumer companies.

Geographic Preference: United States
Founded: 1987
Average Investment: $15-$100 million
Investment Criteria: Internal Growth & Acquisitions, Full or Partial Liquidity, Mangement Buyouts, Corporate Divestitures
Industry Group Preference: Consumer Products, Distribution, Industrial Equipment, Beauty & Personal Care, Food & Beverage, Restaurants
Portfolio Companies: Alexis Bittar, Paige, REVOLV, Alterna, Dentek, e.l.f. Cosmetics, IT Cosmetics, Kenra, Perricone MD, Pevonia, Sexy Hair, Cytosport, Gardein, Raybern's, thinkThin, Dogswell, My Fit Foods, Planet Fitness

Other Locations:
712 Fifth Avenue
46th Floor
New York, NY 10019
Phone: 212-265-4111 **Fax:** 212-265-4845

Key Executives:
Charles H Esserman, Founder/Managing Director, President & CEO
Education: BS, MIT; MBA, Stanford University
Background: Bain & Company

1862 TSG EQUITY PARTNERS
636 Great Road
Stow, MA 01775

Phone: 978-461-9900 x116
e-mail: tns@tsgequity.com
web: www.tsgequity.com

Mission Statement: A private equity investment firm providing growth and acquisition financing to expansion stage and middle market companies.

Geographic Preference: Mid-Atlantic, Northeast
Fund Size: $250 million under management
Founded: 1996
Average Investment: $1 to $2.25 million
Minimum Investment: $1 million
Investment Criteria: Growth Capital, Expansion Stage, Middle Market, Recapitalizations
Industry Group Preference: Communications, Consumer Services, Electronic Technology, Information Technology, Manufacturing, Software
Portfolio Companies: VA Linux Systems, Tower Ventures, Vermont Teddy Bear, SolarOne Solutions, Katahdin Inc., Optasite, Marketmax, 4R Systems

Key Executives:
T Nathanael Shepherd, Co-Founder, Principal
Education: MBA, Clark University Graduate School of Management
Background: Associate Director, PCS; Director Development, Perkins
Directorships: Katahdin Industries, Vermont Teddy Bear Co., SolarOne Solutions
Thomas R Shepherd, Co-Founder, Principal
Education: BA Economics, Washington & Lee University; Master of Industrial and Labor Relations, Cornell

Venture Capital & Private Equity Firms / Domestic Firms

University; Executive Program, Amos Tuck School, Dartmouth College
Background: Managing Director, Thomas H Lee Company; President, GTE Lighting Products Group; President NA, Phillips Commercial Electronics Corporation
Directorships: 4R Systems, Amerace, General Nutrition Companies, Optasite, PNC - New England, Thermoscan, Vermont Teddy Bear Co.

1863 TTV CAPITAL
1230 Peachtree Street
Suite 1150
Atlanta, GA 30309

Phone: 404-347-8400 Fax: 404-347-8420
e-mail: info@ttvcapital.com
web: www.ttvcapital.com

Mission Statement: TTV Capital is an Atlanta-based investment firm focused on providing capital to early-to-late stage privately held companies in the financial services industry and IT driven businesses with products that serve the financial services industry.

Founded: 2000
Investment Criteria: Early-Stage to Later-Stage
Industry Group Preference: Financial Services, Information Technology
Portfolio Companies: 3V, ALI Solutions, Bill.com, Bitpay, Bluepoint Solutions, Cardlytics, Connecture, ControlScan, CRESecure, EquityLock Solutions, eWise, EXACTUALS, Financelt, Ftrans, FX Bridge, Green Dot, Interactive Advisory Software, IP Commerce, KnowledgeStorm, Lendkey, Magnet Banking, MicroBilt, moneydesktop, Neovest, PayCycle, Perimeter eSecurity, ShopKeep, Silverpop, Springbot

Key Executives:
Gardiner W Garrard III, Founder/Partner
Education: BA, University of North Carolina, Chapel Hill; MBA, Goizueta Business School, Emory University
Directorships: Bluepoint Solutions, EquityLockSolutions, FTRANS, FX Bridge, Perimeter Security, ShopKeep
W Thomas Smith Jr, Founder/Partner
Education: BS, Industrial Management, Georgia Institute of Technology
Background: Vice President, IBM
Directorships: 3V, eWise, Silverpop, IP Commerce
Mark A Johnson, Partner
Education: Miami University; MBA, Ohio State University
Background: Founder, CheckFree Corporation; Founder, e-RM Ventures
Directorships: Bill.com, Cardlytics, ControlScan, Fleetcor, FX Bridge
Sean Banks, Partner
Education: BS, Economics, United States Naval Academy; JD, University of San Diego; MBA, Emory University
Directorships: ControlScan

1864 TUATARA CAPITAL
New York, NY

e-mail: info@tuataracap.com
web: www.tuataracapital.com

Mission Statement: Invests in companies across the supply chain for the cannabis industry, including research & testing, cultivation, processing, and retail.

Founded: 2014
Industry Group Preference: Cannabis
Portfolio Companies: Teewinot Life Sciences, Willie's Reserve, Green Dot, Enlighten, CanAscen Group

Key Executives:
Mark Zittman, Partner/Chairman
Education: BBA, University of Florida
Background: Sr. Managing Director, Guggenheim Partners

Al Foreman, Partner/Chief Investment Officer
Education: BS, Finance, University of Connecticut; JD, Arizona State University; MBA, W.P. Carey School of Business, Arizona State University
Background: Associate/VP, Citigroup; Sr. Business Development Manager, Virtual Growth Inc.; Managing Director, JP Morgan
Directorships: Vitech Systems Group
Marc Riiska, Partner/Chief Operating Officer
Education: BS, Finance, University of Connecticut
Background: Partner, Ilios Partners; Director of Business Development, SS&C Technologies
Richard Taney, Managing Director
Education: BA, History/Biology, Tufts University; JD, James E. Beasley School of Law, Temple University; JD, Boston University School of Law
Background: Managing Partner, Sandpiper Capital Partners; President/CEO, Delcath Systems Inc.; President/CEO, Curaleaf Inc.; Managing Partner, T2 Capital
Directorships: Veridian Capital Advisors, MGT Capital Investments, Medicsight, Delcath Systems Inc.
Adrienne Foo, Managing Director
Education: BS, Accounting, Northern Illinois University
Background: Sr. Auditor, Arthur Andersen; Sr. Auditor, KPMG; Accounting Supervisor, Spectrum Global Fund Administration; VP, Deutsche Asset Management; VP, JPMorgan Chase & Co.; Managing Director, Pinebridge Investment
Young Yeo, Vice President
Education: BS, Chemistry, Carnegie Mellon University
Background: Associate, China Momentum Fund; Scientist/Researcher, Carnegie Mellon University

1865 TUGBOAT VENTURES
306 Cambridge Avenue
Palo Alto, CA 94306

Phone: 650-470-1400
web: www.tugboatventures.com

Mission Statement: To help the highest potential entrepreneurs bring their dreams to life.

Investment Criteria: Seed-Stage, Early-Stage
Industry Group Preference: SaaS, Enterprise Software, Consumer Internet, Internet, Advertising
Portfolio Companies: Alminder, Amazon, Applied Silver, Business Signatures, Citrus Lane, Cranium, Drugstore.com, E.Piphany, Education Elements, Five Apes, Good, Google, Hapara, healthTap, HoneyApps, Ifeelgoods, Mahoot, Mamapedia, Matrixx, NewSchools Venture Fund, Peloton, Red Herring, RepairPal, RichRelevance, Risk I/O, SayNow, Savvymoney, Shop It To Me, Stella & Dot, SuccessFactors, Tapjoy, Wikia, Nine Plus

Key Executives:
Dave Whorton, Founder
Education: BS, Mechanical Engineering, University of California, Berkeley; MBA, Stanford Graduate School of Business
Background: Kleiner Perkins Caufield & Byers; Texas Pacific Group Ventures; Founding CEO, Good Technology; Co-Founder, Drugstore.com

1866 TULLIS HEALTH INVESTORS
55 Old Field Point Road
Stamford, CT 06830

Phone: 203-629-8700
web: www.thi-funds.com

Mission Statement: Provides capital to healthcare companies at all stages of growth with creative, committed management teams.

Geographic Preference: United States
Fund Size: $350 million
Founded: 1986

653

Venture Capital & Private Equity Firms / Domestic Firms

Average Investment: $500,000 - $10,000,000
Minimum Investment: $250,000
Investment Criteria: All Stages
Industry Group Preference: Biotechnology, Life Sciences, Healthcare, Medical Devices, Information Technology, Pharmaceuticals
Portfolio Companies: VidaCare, Impulse Monitoring, Physician Sales & Service, QuadraMed, BioRexis
Other Locations:
  11760 U.S. Highway 1
  Suite 502W
  North Palm Beach, FL 33408
  Phone: 561-799-7762
Key Executives:
  Jim Tullis, Founder/General Partner
  Education: BA, Stanford University; MBA, Harvard Business School
  Background: Morgan Stanley
  John Tullis, Managing General Partner
  Education: DePauw University; University of Virginia; MBA, University of Miami
  Background: Senior Director, Ryder System Inc.; Associate, MJ Meehan & Co.
  Neil Ryan, Venture Partner
  Education: BA, University of Ottawa; MBA, Wharton School
  Background: Co-Founder, Oxford Partners; Co-Founder, Oxford Bioscience Partners; Co-Founder & President, Randolph Computer Corporation; President, GTE New Ventures Corporation; SVP, GTE Corporation

1867 TULLY & HOLLAND
20 William Street
Suite 135
Wellesey, MA 02481
Phone: 781-239-2900 Fax: 781-239-2901
web: www.tullyandholland.com

Mission Statement: Tully & Holland specializes in highly complex transactions, custom designing financial solutions for the unique needs of each client.
Geographic Preference: United States
Founded: 1992
Minimum Investment: $5 million
Investment Criteria: Mezzanine, LBO, MBO
Industry Group Preference: Consumer Products, Distribution, Medical & Health Related, Food & Beverage, Retail, Consumer & Leisure
Key Executives:
  Timothy Tully, President, Food & Consumer Groups
  e-mail: ttully@tullyandholland.com
  Education: BA, Harvard University
  Background: Advising, Proctor & Gamble, General Mills Inc, Management Positions At H.J.Heinz, RJR Nabisco, Marketing, Dancer, Fitzgerald & Sample Inc
  Jamie Lane, Managing Director
  e-mail: jlane@tullyandholland.com
  Education: BA, Colgate University; JD, Northwestern University
  Background: Strategic Advisor, Merrill Lynch; Director, William Blair & Co.

1868 TUSK VENTURES
251 Park Avenue S
8th Floor
New York, NY 10010
e-mail: info@tusk.vc
web: tusk.vc

Mission Statement: TVP invests in early stage tecnology startups operating in heavily regulated markets or new businesses where no regulatory framework exists. They provide regulatory, political and media support to their founders.
Key Executives:
  Bradley Tusk, Co-Founder/Managing Partner
  Education: BA, University of Pennsylvania; JD, University of Chicago
  Background: Deputy Governor, Illinois; Communications Director, US Senator, Chuck Schumer; Author; Adjunct Professor, Columbia Business School
  Jordan Nof, Co-Founder/Managing Partner
  Education: BS, Florida State University; MBA, Rollins Graduate School of Business
  Background: Director, Blackstone; AllianceBernstein

1869 TVC CAPITAL
11260 El Camino Real
Suite 220
San Diego, CA 92130
Phone: 858-704-3261 Fax: 858-523-9560
web: www.tvccapital.com

Mission Statement: TVC Capital is a private equity firm focused on investments in and acquisitions of software companies and software-enabled service firms. We target a wide spectrum of software sectors and industry verticals that are poised for growth and consolidation. Our Partners have 60+ years of experience in technology leadership, executive management, public and private board participation, and strategic transaction advisory. In partnering with exceptional management teams, we work 'in the trenches' with our portfolio companies to accelerate growth, maximize value and position for a profitable M&A exit.
Geographic Preference: United States
Investment Criteria: Growth Equity, Recapitalizations, Buyouts
Industry Group Preference: Software
Portfolio Companies: Centage, EdgeWave, LiquidPlanner, ReverseVision, Levels Beyond, Limeade, Mercent, Halo Business Intelligence, MeetingSense Software, Digital Map Products, LocationSmart
Key Executives:
  Steven J Hamerslag, Co-Founder/Managing Partner
  Education: BA, Economics, University of California, Berkeley
  Background: President & CEO, J2 Global Communications; Founder, MTI Technology
  Jeb S Spencer, Co-Founder/Managing Partner
  Education: Boston College; MBA, Harvard Business School
  Background: Co-Founder/President, Backwire; Finance Division, Republican National Committee
  Directorships: Ellie Mae, ReverseVision, Levels Beyond, TechnoCom, Halo Business Intelligence

1870 TVV CAPITAL
201 Fourth Avenue North
Suite 1250
Nashville, TN 37219
Phone: 615-256-8061 Fax: 615-256-7057
web: www.tvvcapital.com

Mission Statement: A value-oriented, lower middle-market focused private equity firm that makes control leveraged buyout investments in established, private and profitable companies with strong management teams and enterprise values in the range of $10-100 million.
Geographic Preference: Southeastern United States
Fund Size: $10 million
Founded: 1998
Average Investment: $20 - 100 million
Minimum Investment: $5 million
Investment Criteria: Acquisition, LBO, MBO, Expansion, Recaps

Venture Capital & Private Equity Firms / Domestic Firms

Industry Group Preference: Telecommunications, Niche Manufacturing, Distribution, Industrial Services, Food & Beverage
Portfolio Companies: Design Molded Plastics, Critical Solutions International, IDI, Bigham Brothers, Indco, Big 3 Precision Products
Key Executives:
  Andrew Byrd, Founder/President
  615-256-8061
  Fax: 615-256-7057
  Education: BA, Vanderbilt University; JD, Vanderbilt University; Master of Taxation, Georgetown University
  Background: Director & EVP, GenCap America
  Andrew Byrd, Jr., Managing Director
  Education: BS, MS, Cornell University; JD, Vanderbilt University
  Background: National Security Agency

1871 TWIN BRIDGE CAPITAL PARTNERS
30 South Wacker Drive
Suite 1740
Chicago, IL 60606
Phone: 312-284-5600 Fax: 312-284-5599
e-mail: bgallagher@twinbridgecapital.com
web: www.twinbridgecapital.com

Mission Statement: Investor in LBO funds and co-investments.
Geographic Preference: North America
Fund Size: $1 billion
Founded: 2005
Average Investment: $20 Million
Minimum Investment: $10 Million
Investment Criteria: LBO Funds in North America
Industry Group Preference: All Sectors Considered
Portfolio Companies: Blue Coat, Bumble Bee Seafoods, American Industrial Partners, Carousel Capital, DrivenBrands, EN Engineering, Civic Partners, Lovell Minnick Partners, Gilchrist & Soames, LANDesk Software, Odyssey Investment Partners, Sentinel Capital Partners, Matthews, RenewLife, Swander Pace Capital, Thoma Bravo
Key Executives:
  F. Matthew Petronzio, Partner
  Education: BA, Bucknell University; MBA, Vanderbilt University
  Background: Partner, Five Points Capital; SunTrust Equity Partners
  Brian Gallagher, CFA, Partner
  312-284-5602
  e-mail: bgallagher@twinbridgecapital.com
  Education: MBA, Northwestern University; BA Accounting, University of Notre Dame
  Background: Principal, UIB Capital; Partner, PPM America Capital Partners
  Directorships: Renew Life, Grosvenor Registered Multi-Strategy Fund, HFS Chicago Scholars
  Joe Dimberio, Partner
  312-284-5605
  e-mail: jdimberio@twinbridgecapital.com
  Education: BA, Marketing, University of Notre Dame; MBA, University of Notre Dame
  Background: Senior Partner, PPM America Capital Partners
  Directorships: Gilchrist & Soames
  Pat Lanigan, Partner
  312-284-5606
  e-mail: planigan@twinbridgecapital.com
  Education: BA, Mechanical Engineering, University of Notre Dame; MBA, University of Chicago
  Background: Senior Partner, PPM Capital Partners
  Directorships: Pace Corporation

1872 TWIN CITIES ANGELS
web: tcangels.com

Mission Statement: To achieve an outstanding financial return on members' time commitment and invested capital.
Geographic Preference: Minneapolis/St. Paul. Minnesota, Wisconsin, Iowa, the Dakotas
Founded: 2006
Average Investment: $25,000 - $2 million
Investment Criteria: Seed-Stage, Early-Stage
Industry Group Preference: Medical Technology, Medical Devices, Diagnostics, Pharmaceuticals, Biotechnology, Veterinary Medicine, Information Technology
Portfolio Companies: Alvarri, Amphora Medical, Ativa Medical, Bard's Tale Beer, Cardia Access, Cardialen, EcoEnvelopes, Engineered Propulsion Systems, MainStay Medical, Marner, Once Innovations, Perk Health, PlaCor, ReconRobotics, TST Media, UnityWorks Media, Vixar

1873 TWJ CAPITAL
Six Landmark Square
Suite 404
Stamford, CT 06901
Phone: 203-359-5610 Fax: 203-359-5810
e-mail: twjones@twjcapital.com
web: www.twjcapital.com

Mission Statement: TWJ Capital makes growth equity investments in expansion stage companies which need 'acceleration capital' to achieve growth inflection, and venture capital investments in start-up and early stage investments.
Average Investment: $500,000 - $5 million
Investment Criteria: Start-Up, Early-Stage, Expansion-Stage
Industry Group Preference: Telecommunications, Internet Technology, Business Products & Services, Specialty Retail
Portfolio Companies: Acoustic Technologies, eData Source, Floor & Decor Outlets of America, Tango Networks, KoolSpan, NetNumber, Game Trust, MVP Group International
Other Locations:
  7272 Wisconsin Avenue
  Suite 300
  Bethesda, MD 20814
  Phone: 301-941-1959 Fax: 301-941-1265
Key Executives:
  Thomas W Jones, Founder/Senior Partner
  e-mail: twjones@twjcapital.com
  Education: BA, MS, Cornell University; MBA, Boston University
  Background: Chairman & CEO, Citigroup Asset Management; Vice Chairman & Director, TIAA-CREF; SVP, John Hancock Mutual Life Insurance Company
  Nigel W Jones, Partner
  e-mail: nigel@twjcapital.com
  Education: BA, Harvard University; MBA, Stanford University Graduate School of Business
  Background: Principal, Carlyle Group; Associate, Goldman Sachs & Co.; Communications Officer, Captain, Force Reconnaissance Company, United States Marine Corps

1874 TWO SIGMA VENTURES
100 Avenue of the Americas
16th Floor
New York, NY 10013
e-mail: ventures@twosigma.com
web: www.twosigmaventures.com

Mission Statement: Two Sigma Ventures, a division of Two Sigma Investments, LLC, invests in companies run by highly driven people with potentially world-changing ideas. We seek out people using technology, computing, mathematics, or data to tackle hard problems, and we aim to help them thrive.
Founded: 2001
Investment Criteria: All Stages
Industry Group Preference: Technology, High Technology

Venture Capital & Private Equity Firms / Domestic Firms

Portfolio Companies: 3DRobotics, Anki, Floored, Kickboard, littleBits Electronics, Rethink Robotics, Symcat.com, Experiment, Placed, Renthop, Tinybop, Ufora, Canary

1875 TXV PARTNERS
Austin, TX 75201

e-mail: connect@txvpartners.com
web: txvpartners.com

Mission Statement: TXV Partners is dedicated to the collaborative process with its portfolio companies.

Founded: 2015
Industry Group Preference: Healthcare, Enterprise Software, Consumer
Portfolio Companies: Future.Fit, Kambr, NameCoach

Key Executives:
  Brandon Allen, Founding Partner
  Education: Princeton University
  Background: Consultant, Stax; Consultant, Chartic
  Marcus Stroud, Founding Partner
  Education: Princeton University
  Background: Analyst, MarketAxess; Vida Capital; Clubhouse Investment Club
  Directorships: Trey Athletes

1876 TYLT LAB
1158 26th Street
Suite 325
Santa Monica, CA 90403

Phone: 310-331-8797 Fax: 310-870-7039
web: www.tyltlab.com

Mission Statement: Our focus is identifying, capitalizing, and building innovative, high growth companies. We are entrepreneurs ourselves, and have a hands-on approach to working with founders. Put simply, we believe in adding value, not just adding capital.

Investment Criteria: Early-Stage
Industry Group Preference: Consumer Electronics, Technology, Telecommunications, Consumer Products, Clean Technology, Healthcare, Entertainment, Fashion
Portfolio Companies: Cargomatic, Flexport, Moveline, Normal Ears, Paper Battery Company, PogoSeat, Tixr, Toguh, VNTANA, TodayTix

Key Executives:
  Rami Rostami, Chairman/Co-Founder
  Education: BS, Managment, California State University, Northridge
  Background: Founder/CEO, Technocel Wireless Products; American Investment Group; Information Control Company
  Gerard N. Casale, Managing Director/Co-Founder
  Education: BA, Economics, Fairfield University; JD, Pepperdine University School of Law
  Background: Founder, X-Laboratories

1877 UBIQUITY VENTURES
Palo Alto, CA 94301

e-mail: sunil@ubiquity.vc
web: www.ubiquity.vc

Mission Statement: A venture capital fund investing in machine learning and smart hardware companies.

Founded: 2017
Industry Group Preference: Machine Learning, Artificial Intelligence
Portfolio Companies: Diligent Robotics, Eclypsium, Elementary Robotics, Esper, Halter, Jargon, Loft Orbital, Parallel Domain, Windborne

Key Executives:
  Sunil Nagaraj, Founder/Managing Partner
  Education: BS, University of North Carolina; MBA, Harvard Business School
  Background: Bessemer Venture Partners; Bain & Company; Cisco; Microsoft
  Directorships: Diligent Robotics; Esper; Halter; Jargon; Levl; Parallel Domain

1878 UBS GLOBAL ASSET MANAGEMENT
One North Wacker Drive
Chicago, IL 60606

Phone: 312-525-5000
web: www.ubs.com

Mission Statement: UBS Global Asset Management believes that value-added investment returns are primarily function asset management decisions made within an integrated view of global capital markets, world economies and financial markets. Thus, investment management both within and across global stock markets, must be based upon comprehensive knowledge and analyses of integrated investment fundamentals.

Geographic Preference: North America, Asia Pacific, Switzerland, Europe
Fund Size: $10 billion
Founded: 1972
Average Investment: $1- $30 million
Minimum Investment: $1 million
Investment Criteria: Early-stage, Growth Equity Financings, MBO, Restructurings
Industry Group Preference: Global Industries

Key Executives:
  Sergio P. Ermotti, Group Chief Executive Officer
  Education: Oxford University
  Background: Group Deputy CEO, UniCredit; Merrill Lynch
  Kirt Gardner, Group Chief Financial Officer
  Education: BS, Economics, Williams College; MBA, Wharton School
  Background: CFO, Citigroup; Global Head of Financial Services Strategy, BearingPoint; Managing Director, Barents Group

1879 UNCORK CAPITAL
Palo Alto, CA

web: uncorkcapital.com

Mission Statement: Founded under the name SoftTech VC, Uncork Capital is a lead investor in the micro-VC market.

Fund Size: $100 Million
Founded: 2004
Average Investment: $1.2 million
Minimum Investment: $750,000
Investment Criteria: Seed
Industry Group Preference: Artificial Intelligence, Robotics, Information Technology, Applications, Software, Data Analysis
Portfolio Companies: ClassDoko, DroneDeploy, Fountain, Front, LaunchDarkly, Joya Communications Inc., Molekule, Panorama Education, Poshmark, Postmates, Shippo, Tempo Automation, Top Hat, Widyard, Zefr

Key Executives:
  Jeff Clavier, Founder/Managing Partner
  Education: MS, Computer Science, Université Paris Descartes
  Background: Head of Development, Effix Systems; Head of Development, Reuters Plc.; Co-Producer, RVC SoftEdge Conference; Partner, RVC Capital
  Directorships: Curse Inc.; Pathfire; Tacit; UltraDNS
  Stephanie Palmeri, Partner
  Education: BS, Marketing/Management Information Systems, Villanova University; MBA, Columbia Business School
  Background: NYC Seedl Accenture; Estee Lauder
  Directorships: ClassDojo

Venture Capital & Private Equity Firms / Domestic Firms

Andy McLoughlin, Partner
Education: BA, Economics, University of Sheffield
Background: Intercom; Pipedrive; Bugsnag; Apiary; Buffer; Postmates
Ashley Cravens, Director of Operations
Education: BS, Business Administration/Marketing, University of Oregon
Background: Securities Assistant, Rosenbaum Financial; Licensed Broker, Morgan Stanley; Associate, Smith Barney

1880 UNDERDOG VENTURES
23 Route 105, E Brighton Road
PO Box 443
Island Pond, VT 05846

Phone: 802-723-9909 Fax: 802-723-9933
e-mail: info@underdogventures.com
web: www.underdogventures.com

Mission Statement: Underdog Ventures creates innovative and customized investments to meet the specific needs of each of our investors, each of whom has a dedicated fund that invests in areas that they choose.

Investment Criteria: Socially Responsible Companies
Industry Group Preference: Environment, Conservation, Consumer Products, Food & Beverage

Key Executives:
David Berge, Founder/President/Managing Partner
e-mail: david@underdogventures.com
Background: Director, Vermont National Bank's Socially Responsible Banking Fund

1881 UNION CAPITAL CORPORATION
445 Park Avenue
14th Floor
New York, NY 10022

Phone: 212-832-1141 Fax: 212-832-0554
e-mail: ucc@unioncapitalcorp.com
web: www.unioncapitalcorp.com

Mission Statement: Union pursues a highly selective investment policy and as a general rule, will only invest in companies which combine an active, highly capable management team with a healthy business that is characterized by stable and modestly growing cash flow. We will also consider turn-around situations that could be combined with our existing portfolio companies.

Geographic Preference: United States
Founded: 1968
Average Investment: $5 - $50 million
Minimum Investment: $3 million
Investment Criteria: Leveraged Buyouts, Management Buyouts, Corporate Divestitures, Recapitalizations, Lower and Middle Markets
Industry Group Preference: Advertising, Commercial Services, Household Goods, Direct Marketing, Tourism, Distribution, Business Products & Services, Printing, Food & Beverage, Marketing, Printing, Manufacturing
Portfolio Companies: Caps Visual Communications, MKTG, MultiAd, Ventura Associates

Key Executives:
James Marlas, Founding Partner
Education: JD, University of Chicago; MA, Univ. of Oxford; BA, Harvard University
Background: CEO, Mickelberry Food Products, Associate, Baker & McKenzie
Directorships: New York City Opera, The Young Presidents Organization, The Chairman's Council of The Metropolitan Museum of Art, Commanderie De Bordeaux
Gina E. Molano, Director of Administration
Education: BA Advertising/Marketing, Universidad de Bogota Jorge Tadeo Lozano, Columbia
Arthur G Murray, Operating Partner
Background: President/CEO, Salerno-Mcgowan; Sunshine Biscuits
Directorships: Factset Research Systems
Jay F Laudauer, Managing Partner
Education: BBA, Baruch College; MBA, MIT Sloan School
Background: Ortech International
Kevin Delaplane, Finance Partner
Education: BBA, University of Notre Dame; MBA, DePaul University
Background: Asset Based Lending, Harris Bank/Bank of Montreal
William Ogden, Managing Partner
Education: BA, Dartmouth College; MBA, University of Virginia
Background: Granite Capital Partners; Prudential Financial; Inter-Atlantic Capital Partners
Reis L Alford, Managing Partner
Education: BA, Dartmouth College
Background: Management Consulting

1882 UNION SQUARE VENTURES
915 Broadway
19th Floor
New York, NY 10010

Phone: 212-994-7880 Fax: 212-994-7399
e-mail: info@usv.com
web: www.usv.com

Mission Statement: Union Square Ventures is an early stage venture capital fund focused on web services. Seeks to invest in passionate, experienced entrepreneurs who are focused on creating highly scalable services and significant value propositions for their end users.

Geographic Preference: United States, Europe
Fund Size: $1 billion
Founded: 2003
Average Investment: $250,000 - $25 million
Investment Criteria: Early-Stage
Industry Group Preference: Internet, Internet Technology
Portfolio Companies: Abridge, Algorand, Amino, Arweave, Assembly, Autonomous Partners, Auxmoney, Blockstack, Blocktower Capital, Cloudflare, CoverWallet, Codecademy, Code Climate, Coinbase, CrowdRise, Dapper Labs, Dronebase, DuckDuckGo, Duolingo, Etsy, Foursquare, GoTenna, Indeed, Kickstarter, Marley Spoon, MetaStabble Capital, Modern Fertility, Multicoin Capital, Onefootball, Payjoy, Placeholder, Polychain Capital, Protocol Labs, Quizlet, RealtyShares, Recount Media, Science Exchange, Shippo, ShopShops, Simscale, Sofar Sounds, SoundCloud, Top Hat, Twitter, Tucows, Veniam, Wattpad, YouNow, Zynga

Key Executives:
Brad Burnham, Partner
Education: BA, Political Science, Wesleyan University
Background: AT&T; Executive-in-Residence, AT&T Ventures
Directorships: Indeed, Pinch Media, Tumblr, Wesabe, Adaptive Blue, SimulMedia, Tracked.com, Meetup, Bug Labs
Fred Wilson, Partner
Education: BS, Mechanical Engineering, MIT, MBA, Wharton School
Background: Founder, Flatiron Partners
Albert Wenger, Partner
Education: Harvard College; PhD, Information Technology, MIT
Background: Founder, DailyLit; President, del.icio.us
John Buttrick, Partner
Education: American Studies, Northwestern University; JD, Villanova University School of Law
Background: Corporate Law, Davis Polk & Wardwell; Partner, Livewire; Board of Directors, Agfa-Gevaert NV; Advisor, Eckford Group
Directorships: Environmental Advocates of New York, Hirondelle USA

Venture Capital & Private Equity Firms / Domestic Firms

Andy Weissman, Partner
Education: BA, Wesleyan University; JD, Georgetown University
Background: AOL, Dawntreader Ventures
Rebecca Kaden, Partner
Education: BA, English & American Literature, Harvard; MBA, Stanford University
Background: Partner, Mavreon

1883 UNITED TALENT AGENCY VENTURES
9336 Civic Center Drive
Beverly Hills, CA 90210

Phone: 310-273-6700
e-mail: utaventures@unitedtalent.com
web: ventures.unitedtalent.com

Mission Statement: The early-stage and startup investment arm of United Talent Agency with an interest in media, sports, entertainment, and technology.

Founded: 2013
Investment Criteria: Seed, Early-Stage, Startup
Industry Group Preference: Media, Communications, Sports, Entertainment, Technology
Portfolio Companies: Art19, Awesomeness TV, Captiv8, Chorus, Cloud9, CrowdRise, Dreamscape, Fatherly, Figtagram, Hello Giggles, Houseparty, Lyft, MasterClass, MikMak, Pocket Watch, One Up Sports, Pluto, Patreon, The Players Tribune, Radish, Raze, Rex, Splash, Statmuse, Stem, Thrive Market, True Anthem, Uproxx, Victorious, Waggle

Other Locations:
888 7th Avenue
New York, NY 10106
Phone: 212-659-2600

Key Executives:
Brent Weinstein, Head of Digital Media
Education: University of Southern California; University of San Diego School of Law
Background: Corporate Law
Sam Wick, Head of Ventures
Background: MySpace, AOL, Mp3.com, Sony
Kosha Shah, Executive
Education: BA, Economics & Political Science, Stanford University
Background: Management Consulting/Strategic Planning, Mattel

1884 UNIVERSITY VENTURE FUND
299 South Main Street
Suite 310
Salt Lake City, UT 84111

Phone: 801-326-3590 Fax: 801-326-3598
e-mail: info@uventurefund.com
web: www.uventurefund.com

Mission Statement: University Venture Fund invests in compelling new technologies, high growth opportunities and stable cash flow businesses across a broad range of industries and sectors. This opportunistic approach allows UVF to take advantage of the latest trends and market dynamics, and leverage the diverse backgrounds of our students. UVF only co-invests alongside our other reputable institutional investors.

Geographic Preference: United States
Industry Group Preference: Consumer Products, Consumer Services, Internet, Technology, Healthcare
Portfolio Companies: Alianza, American Achievement Corporation, Ancora, Barosense, Catheter Connections, Coherex Medical, Control4, CompleteXrm, Daz3d, Handi Quilter, Infinera, Instructure, Intelisum, Lineagen, Merrimack Pharmaceuticals, Omniture, Socialtext, Transpond, TrustedID, Veritract

Key Executives:
Paul Brown, Managing Director

1885 UNSHACKLED VENTURES
435 Hamilton Avenue
Palo Alto, CA 94301

web: www.unshackledvc.com

Mission Statement: Unshackled is a venture capital fund providing capital, support and resources to immigrant entrepreneurs.

Geographic Preference: United States
Fund Size: $3.5 million
Founded: 2014
Average Investment: $300,000
Investment Criteria: Startups, Early Stage
Industry Group Preference: Diversified
Portfolio Companies: Geospago, Bluefield, OnTarget, Pluto, Shortlist, SensiHub, Togg, Gridraster, Lily, Sporple, Starskyrobotics, Brite Health, Pod Foods, CaaScade, Sote Logistics, Immediately

Key Executives:
Manan Mehta, Founding Partner
Education: BS & BA, Engineering & Economics, University of California, Los Angeles
Background: Co-Founder, Fanery; Head, Marketing, Kno; RBC Capital Markets
Nitin Pachisia, Founding Partner
Education: BComm, Finance & Accounting, Delhi University
Background: VP, Finance, Kno; Manager, Deloitte & Touche; ABB Limited

1886 UPDATA VENTURE PARTNERS
2099 Pennsylvania Avenue NW
8th Floor
Washington, DC 20006

Phone: 202-618-8750 Fax: 202-315-2668
web: www.updatapartners.com

Mission Statement: To invest in leading companies with outstanding management operating in large markets with an ascertainable technological advantage.

Geographic Preference: East Coast
Fund Size: $100 million
Founded: 1987
Average Investment: $5 - $20 million
Minimum Investment: $5 million
Investment Criteria: Growth Capital, LBO
Industry Group Preference: Enterprise Services, Information Technology, Financial Services, Healthcare, Business Products & Services, Outsourcing & Efficiency, Software, Internet
Portfolio Companies: Acclaris, Alert Logic, Amber Road, Appfluent, Bradford Networks, BRIDGE Energy Group, CMWare, Collective Bias, CoreStreet, DataCore Software, e-Security, Everest Software, ForeSee, GETPAID, Harmony Information Systems, iContact, Interactions, iSheriff, jobs2web, July Systems, The Kernel Group, LendKey, Logi Analytics, M86 Security, Mashable, Merlin Technologies, NetKey, Nimaya, Nintex, Numara Software, ObjectVideo, OrderMotion, OTG Software, Pet360, PulsePoint, RedVision Systems, RES Software, Secure Software, Softek, Spectrum K12, Trustwave, V3 Systems, Video Blocks, Viewpoint, XebiaLabs

Key Executives:
John Burton, Operating Partner
e-mail: jburton@updata.com
Education: Boston College
Background: President, Legent Corporation
Barry M Goldsmith, General Partner
Background: CGA Computer, Updata Software,
Carter Griffin, General Partner
e-mail: cgriffin@updata.com
Education: BS, Business Administration, University of North Carolina, Chapel Hill; MBA, JL Kellog School of Management

Venture Capital & Private Equity Firms / Domestic Firms

Background: Co-Founder, Brivo Systems; Senior Vice President, Kaiser Associates
James Socas, General Partner
e-mail: jsocas@updata.com
Education: University of Virginia; Harvard Business School
Background: Senior Vice President, Symantec
Ira D Cohen, Venture Partner
e-mail: icohen@updata.com
Education: BS, Accounting, City University; MS, Banking & Financial Services, Boston University; Executive Education Program, Harvard Business School
Background: CFO/CGA Computer; CFO/Tridex; Director of Internal Audit/MetPath;
Directorships: Director and Chair/Audit Committee Datastream Systems, Inc.
Jon Seeber, Principal
e-mail: jseeber@updata.com
Education: BA, Computer Science & History, Duke University; MBA, Harard Business School
Background: Busines Development, IBM Global Services
Kevin Zhang, Partner
Education: Harvard College
Background: The Boston Consulting Group; Verscend Technologies

1888 UPFRONT VENTURES
1314 7th Street
Suite 600
Santa Monica, CA 90401

web: www.upfront.com

Mission Statement: Formerly known as GRP Partners, UpFront Ventures invests in innovative technologies in relation to digital media, commercial and consumer goods and services.
Geographic Preference: United States, Europe
Fund Size: $300 million
Founded: 1996
Average Investment: $3 - $12 million
Minimum Investment: $3 million
Investment Criteria: First-Stage, Second-Stage
Industry Group Preference: Consumer Services, Retailing, Financial Services, Mobile Infrastructure, Distribution, Digital Media & Marketing, Marketing, SaaS, Cloud Computing, Mobile Apps
Portfolio Companies: 11 Honore, Adly, Adore Me, Alpha Draft, Apeel Sciences, Awe.sm, BillMeLater, Burstly, ChowNow, Comparably, Copilot, Cordial, CyberSource, DailyLook, eData Sift, Dealertrack Technologies, Deliv, Density, Digital Air Strike, Draft, Drone Base, Eagle Crest Energy, Emida, Envestnet, Epoxy, FabFitFun, Factual, Fame and Partners, Ferris, Goat, GoodRx, Gravity, Grove, Gumgum, Happy Returns, Health Data Insights, Health Data Vision Inc., HelloTech, HopSkipDrive, Imbellus, Inboard, Infosum, Invoca, Jiko, Kyriba, Lastminute.com, Luxe, Maker, MakeSpace, Mitu, MongoLab, Mytime, Nanit, Navdy, Nexkey, Nextplus, Nima, NuOrder, Osmo, Overture, Parachute, Pathmatics, Qualys, ReScie, Ring, Ritual, Rubica, Seedling, Seriously, Shots, Silversheet, Skurt, Skyline Home Loans, Stem, Tact.ai, Territory, The Mighty, The Wave VR, Thred Up, Token, Troopwork, TrueCar, uBeam, GUD, Ulta Beauty, Vemba, Vidme, Vreal, Waldo, Walker & Co., Zest Finance

Key Executives:
Mark Suster, Managing Partner
Education: BA, Economics, University of California, San Diego; MBA, University of Chicago
Background: VP, Product Management, Salesforce.com; Founder/CEO, Koral; Founder/CEO, BuildOnline; Accenture
Directorships: Density, Imbellus, Invoca, MakeSpace, Mitu, MyTime, Nanit, Osmo, Skurt, Tact, uBeam, Vidme, InfoSum, Vemba, Burstly, Gravity, Maker Studio

Yves Sisteron, Managing Partner
Education: JD/LLM, University of Law-Lyon France; LLM, New York University School of Law
Background: Fourcar BV, Carrefour SA
Directorships: Adore Me, Apeel Sciences, DailyLook, Fame and Partners, GumGum, Health Data Vision, Jiko, Kyriba, Nima, Health Data Insights, Ugo, Ulta
Greg Bettinelli, Partner
Education: BA, Political Science, University of San Diego; MBA, Graziadio School of Business & Management, Pepperdine University
Background: Chief Marketing Officer, HauteLook; EVP, Business Development & Strategy, Live Nation; Sr. Director, Business Development, StubHub
Directorships: 11 Honore, Deliv, DroneBase, Goat, Happy Returns, HopSkipDrive, Rention Science, Ring, Ritual, Rubica, Sense360, Silversheet, ThredUp, Walker and Company
Kara Nortman, Partner
Education: BA, Politics, Princeton University; MBA, Stanford University
Background: Co-Founder, Moonfrye, SVP/General Manager, Urbanspoon/Citysearch; M&A, IAC
Directorships: Hatch Labs, Parachute, Qordoba, Seddling, Stem, Territory, Waldo
Aditi Maliwal, Partner
Education: BA, Stanford University
Background: Product Manager, Next Billion Users Team, Google; Crosslink Capital; Deutsche Bank
Kobie Fuller, Partner
Education: Harvard College
Background: Investor, Accel; Chief Marketing Officer, REVOLVE; Co-Founder, OpenView Venture Partners; Investor, Insight Venture Partners
Michael Carney, Partner
Education: BS, University of California, Santa Barbara
Background: Editor, Pandoldaily; Founding Team Member, Worldvest

Key Executives:
Steven Florsheim, Partner
Education: Yale University; University of Michigan Law School
Background: Founder/Partner, Byron Marsh Capital; Managing Partner, Sperling & Slater; Chief Acquisitions Officer, Levy Acquisition Corp.

1890 UPHEAVAL INVESTMENTS
444 W Lake Street
Chicago, IL 60606

web: upheavalinvestments.com

Mission Statement: An early-stage venture capital fund focused on the tech industry.

Founded: 2018
Investment Criteria: Seed, Early Stage, Growth Stage
Industry Group Preference: Technology, Infrastructure
Portfolio Companies: Aktive, Atomos Nuclear and Space, Chowly, HaptX, LiveMetric, Passbase, Reniac, SpaceX
Riley Florsheim, Partner
Background: CIO, Byron Marsh Capital; CEO, RF School Tech; Analyst, Levy Family Partners

1891 UPS STRATEGIC ENTERPRISE FUND
55 Glenlake Parkway NE
Building 1, 4th Floor
Atlanta, GA 30328

e-mail: sef@ups.com

Mission Statement: The Strategic Enterprise Fund (the "SEF") is the private equity strategic investment arm of UPS. The Fund is a corporate venture capital group which focuses on developing critical partnerships and acquiring knowledge returns from its investments in information technology companies and emerging market-spaces. The Fund invests in companies that are strategically relevant to UPS, and reflects

659

Venture Capital & Private Equity Firms / Domestic Firms

the strong emphasis that UPS places on becoming the leading provider of technologically advanced services in the transportation and logistics industry.
Geographic Preference: United States and select foreign locations.
Founded: 1997
Average Investment: $250,000-1,500,000
Investment Criteria: Strategic Relevance and Knowledge Returns, Co-Investment and Early Stage Investing, Strong Management, Board Meeting Observation Rights, Investment Range and Geographic Location.
Portfolio Companies: Cold PackSystem, DemandPoint, Deposco, Docufree, Impinj, Kabbage, Liaison Technologies, Shutl, Skytree, United Villages

1892 UPWELLING CAPITAL GROUP
2800 Fifth Street
Suite 120
Davis, CA 95618

Phone: 530-758-7888
e-mail: contact@upwellingcapital.com
web: upwellingcapital.com

Mission Statement: The Principals have cumulatively overseen over $50 billion in global private equity commitments and have successfully managed over $5 billion in legacy, tail-end commitments, transfers and workouts for leading institutional investors.
Fund Size: $50 billion
Founded: 2011
Industry Group Preference: All markets considered
Key Executives:
  Joncarlo Mark, Founder
  Education: UC, Davis; UC, San Diego
  Background: California Public Employees Retirement System

1893 URBAN INNOVATION FUND
e-mail: info@urbaninnovationfund.com
web: www.urbaninnovationfund.com

Mission Statement: Urban Innovation Fund is a venture capital firm that invests in seed capital and entrepreneurs shaping the future of cities.
Investment Criteria: Seed-Stage
Industry Group Preference: Energy, Sustainability, Renewable Energy, Housing, Transportation, Education, Financial Services, Arts, Recreation, Health
Portfolio Companies: APANA, BookNook, Bumblebee Spaces, Catch, codeSpark, curbFlow, DropCountr, Ethic, Local Bushel, Milk Stork, Ride Report, Stop Breathe & Think, The Town Kitchen, udelv, Valor Water Analytics, Visage, Voatz
Key Executives:
  Julie Lein, Managing Partner
  Education: BA, Stanford University; MBA, MIT Sloan School
  Background: Co-Founder, Tumml
  Directorships: Tumml, Empower Work
  Clara Brenner, Managing Partner
  Education: BA, New York University; MBA, MIT Sloan School
  Background: Co-Founder, Tumml
  Directorships: Tumml

1894 URBAN US
29 Norman Avenue
Brooklyn, NY 11222

web: urban.us

Mission Statement: The Urban Us fund is focused on early stage investments to help businesses go from concept to reality.
Geographic Preference: US, Canada, Europe, Israel

Founded: 2013
Investment Criteria: Seed, Pre-Series A
Industry Group Preference: Real Estate, Energy, Finance, Fintech, GovTech, Infrastructure, Industry, Public Health & Safety, Transportation, Mobility, Workforce Development
Portfolio Companies: 3AM Innovations, Architizer, Avvir, BlocPower, Blockable, Blueprint Power, Borrow, Bowery, BRCK, Build Stream, Bumblebee, Circuit, ClearRoad, CityMart, CoInspec, Coord, Cove.tool, Dash, GreenQ, Evolve Energy, Ecomo, Flair, Food For All, Haas Alert, Hubster, KIWI, LiveStories, LogCheck, Lunewave, Mark43, Miles, One Concern, Onewheel, Open Data Nation, Park & Diamond, Perl Street, Pi Variables, Quicit, Rachio, Radiator Labs, Revivn, RoadBotics, Sapient Industries, SeamlessDocs, Skycatch, Social Construct, Starcity, Swell Energy, Swiftera, Thrilling, Toggle, Treau, Upshift, Urbint, Varuna, Versatile Natures, Wright Electric

Other Locations:
  Ferry Building, One
  Suite 201
  San Francisco, CA 94111

  2747 Glendon Avenue
  Los Angeles, CA 90064

Key Executives:
  Shaun Abrahamson, Managing Partner
  Education: BS, University of Cape Town; MS, MIT; MBA, Berlin School of Creative Leadership
  Background: Angel Investor
  Stonly Baptiste, Partner
  Background: Founder, Veddio Cloud Solutions
  Mark Paris, Partner
  Education: BA, Johns Hopkins University; MA, Public Policy, Harvard University
  Background: Managing Director, Citigroup Urban Innovation Initiative

1895 US RENEWABLES GROUP
2425 Olympic Boulevard
Suite 4050 West
Santa Monica, CA 90404

web: www.usregroup.com

Mission Statement: US Renewables Group is one of the largest investment firms focused exclusively on the renewable energy industry.
Fund Size: $750 million
Founded: 2003
Average Investment: $30 to $70 million
Investment Criteria: Early-Stage to Acquisitions of Operating Assets
Industry Group Preference: Renewable Energy, Energy, Power Generation, Biofuels
Portfolio Companies: ASAlliances Biofuels, Bottle Rocket Power, Free Flow Power, Fulcrum Bioenergy, General Compression, Integral Energy Management, Newberry Geothermal, Niagara Generation, NOVO Energy, OPX Biotechnologies, Oski Energy, Penrose Landfill Gas Conversion LLC, Pipestem Energy Group, Recovery Technology Solutions, Renewable Energy Group, SolarReserve, ThermaSource, Tracy Biomass, Westerly Wind

Other Locations:
  10 Bank Street
  Suite 580
  White Plains, NY 10606
  Phone: 914-390-9610

Key Executives:
  Lee Bailey, Managing Director
  Education: BA, St. Lawrence University; MS, Northwestern University; Law Degree, Washington University School of Law
  Background: Partner, Rustic Canyon Partners; Energy Conversion Devices; White House Director for

Venture Capital & Private Equity Firms / Domestic Firms

International Science & Technology Commercialization
Directorships: Bottle Rock Power, SolarReserve
James McDermott, Managing Director
Education: BA, Philosophy, Colorado College; MBA, Anderson School, UCLA
Background: Municipal Finance Group, First Boston; Private Capital Group, Prudential; Allen & Company
Directorships: BioEnergy, General Compression, Novo Development Corporation, Oski Energy, SolarReserve

1896 US VENTURE PARTNERS
1460 El Camino Real
Suite 100
Menlo Park, CA 94025
Phone: 650-854-9080 Fax: 650-854-3018
e-mail: contact@usvp.com
web: www.usvp.com

Mission Statement: USVP is active in all aspects of a young company's development including strategy, recruiting, partnerships, financing and operational advice. Works as a partnership to make initial investment decisions to make every investment successful in their portfolio. Primarily interested in helping a company make the decisions and investments it needs to become a leader in its industry. Increasing competitiveness and aggressiveness of mature companies requires knowledge and access at high levels in order to avoid head on collisions with market leaders. Comfortable making an initial $500,000 seed investment to a $10 million later stage investment.

Geographic Preference: California
Fund Size: $1.1 billion
Founded: 1981
Average Investment: $4-$5 million
Minimum Investment: $500,000
Investment Criteria: Seed, Startup, First-Stage, Second-Stage, LBO, Market Opportunity, Geography
Industry Group Preference: Internet Technology, Communications, Software, Semiconductors, Health Related, Consumer Products, Life Sciences, Energy, Web-Enabled Services, Data Storage, Wireless Technologies, Agriculture, Medical Devices, Drug Development
Portfolio Companies: Akros Silicon, AltoBeam, Adify, Accelops, Act On, Aerogen, Applied Biosystems, Applied Micro, Appthority, Aptus Endosystems, Articulinx, Artisan Components, Ascenta Therapeutics, Asempra, Ask, Astute Networks, AtheroMed, AtriCure, Avenue A Razorfish, Axiom, Bayhill Therapeutics, Bevocal, Blekko, Blue Coat, Box, Calithera Biosciences, Callaway Golf, CardioKinetix, Castlight Health, Centillium Communications, Check Point, Chute, Cipher Trust, Clear Shape Technologies, Cleave Biosciences, Clustrix, Comilion, Commerce 5, Compugen, Contour Energy Systems, Crescendo Communications, CryoVascular Systems, Determina, Devax, Diablo Technologies, DMO Systems, Dotomi, Dstillery, Dune Networks, EasilyDo, eFFECTOR Therapeutics, Elentec Semiconductor, Electric Cloud, Ensure Medical, Exablox, Force 10, Fresh Choice, Genta, Genus, Glycomed, GoPro, Grokr, Guidewire, Harmonic, Headway Technologies, HeartFlow, Hooked Media Group, Hotel Tonight, IC Works, Ilypsa, iMPERVA, Inadco, Inceptus, Insidesales.com, Inspire Medical Systems, Instantis, Integrated Vascular Systems, Intellikine, InterMolecular, Intersect Enterprises, Intransa, Intuity Medical, Iomega, Jeda Networks, Kaiam Corporation, Karma Sphere, Kilopass Klocwork, Lasso, LineStream Technologies, Livefyre, Living Social, Lutonix, LVL7, M-Factor, Matritech, MaxLinear, MegaPath, Mellanox Technologies, Micro Linear, MicroHeart, Microvention, Military Advantage, Minerva Networks, MMC Networks, Mobbles, Montavista, MyYearbook, Nanostim, Neoconix

Key Executives:
Irwin Federman, Advisor
e-mail: federman@usvp.com
Education: Honorary Doctorate, Engineering Science, Santa Clara University; BS, Economics, Brooklyn College
Background: CEO, Monolithic Memories; Chariman, Seniconductor Industry Association
Directorships: Check Point, Centillium, Nuance Communications, Lightspeed Semiconductor, ON24, Astute Networks, Mellanox
Alan L Kaganov ScD, Advisor
e-mail: akaganov@usvp.com
Education: MBA, New York University; MS, ScD, Biomedical Engineering, Columbia University; BS, Mechanical Engineering, Duke University
Background: Business Development & Strategic Planning, Boston Scientific Corporation; CEo, EP Technologies; Vice President, Technology & Business Development, Baxter International; General Manager, Fenwell; CEO, EMBOL-X; CEO, A-Med Systems
Directorships: A-Med Systems, Conway Stuart, Eclipse Surgical, Endocare, MicroHeart, Odyssey Technologies
Philip M Young, Advisor
e-mail: pyoung@usvp.com
Education: BME, Cornell University; MS in engineering Physics, George Washington University, MBA, Harvard University
Background: President & CEO, Oximetrix, Inc.; Concord Partners; Venture Capital & Corporaate Finance, New Court Securities; Management Consultant, McKinsey & Company; Boards: CoCensys, Penederm, Cardiovascular Imaging Systems
Directorships: Aerogen, Zoran, Bayhill Therapeutics, Caspian Networks, Gator, Healink, MicroHeart, RelayHealth, St. Francis Medical, Synarc, Time3
Steven M Krausz, General Partner
e-mail: skrausz@usvp.com
Education: MBA, Stanford Graduate School of Business; BS, Electrical Engineering, Stanford University
Background: NASA Ames; BTI Computers; Direct; Daisy Systems; Boards: EPIC Design Technologies, Photon Dynamics
Directorships: Agility Communications, New Focus, Exponent, Megapath, Sierra Monolithics, Object Reservoir, StrataLight, Vontu, Gluon Networks, Performance Retail, Kasenna, Notiva, WebCohort
Paul Matteucci, Operating Partner
Education: BA, University of the Pacific; MA, International Studies, Johns Hopkins University; MBA, Stanford University
Background: CEO, HearMe; Advisor, Accel Partners; Redpoint Ventures; Sutter Hil Ventures
Jonathan D Root MD, General Partner
e-mail: jroot@usvp.com
Education: MBA, Columbia University; MD, College of Medicine, University of Florida; AB, Economics, Government, Darthmouth College
Background: Assistant Professor of Neurology & Director of the Neurosurgery Intensive Care Unit, New York Hospital-Cornell Medical Center;
Directorships: Altus Biologics, CryoVascular Systems, Integrated Vascular Systems, MicroVention, Raven Biotechnologies
Casey Tansey, General Partner
Education: BS & MBA, College of Notre Dame
Background: CEO & President, Heartpoint; Baxter Edward's Cardiovascular Division
Directorships: Epicor Medical, Heartport
Rick Lewis, General Partner
Education: BS, Computer Science & Engineering, University of California, Davis; MS, Computer Science, University of California, Berkeley; MBA, Harvard Business School
Background: Autodesk, Walt Disney Imagineering; Co-Founder, Design Variations; Co-Founder, Common Point Technologies; Sun Microsystems
Directorships: Act-On Software, Victrio, Yammer
Jacques Benkowski PhD, Partner
Education: BSc, Computer Engineering, Technion Israel Institute of Technology; MS & PhD, Computer

Venture Capital & Private Equity Firms / Domestic Firms

Engineering, Carnegie Mellon University
Background: CEO & President, Monterey Design Systems; Founder & General Manager, Epic Design Technology
Dafina Toncheva, Partner
e-mail: dafina.t@usvp.com
Education: BA, Harvard University; MBA, Stanford Grad. School of Business
Background: Bain & Co.; Venrock
Directorships: Apptimize, Arkose Labs, Insidesales.com, Luma Health, Prevoty, Raken

1897 VALAR VENTURES
915 Broadway
Suite 1101
New York, NY 10010

web: www.valarventures.com

Mission Statement: Valar Ventures welcomes ideas from start-ups globally that dare to push to great what others would only push to good enough. We're looking for those who go their own way - entrepreneurs outside of the United States with groundbreaking ideas and the determination to see them to reality. With your passion and our capital, we can build the next great global company.

Geographic Preference: Worldwide
Investment Criteria: Early-Stage
Industry Group Preference: Enterprise Software, Internet, Education, Consumer Internet, Cloud Computing, Software
Portfolio Companies: Xero, Transferwise, Vend, Dinda, Granify, Canopy Labs, ScriptRock

Andrew McCormack, Partner
Education: BA, Political Science, University of Pennsylvania
Background: eCount, Yahoo!, PayPal, Clarium Capital Management
James Fitzgerald, Partner
Education: JD, University of California, Los Angeles
Background: COO, Thiel Capital; Skadden, Arps, Slate, Meagher & Flom LLP

1898 VALENCE LIFE SCIENCES
500 Park Avenue
New York, NY 10022

Phone: 212-891-1100
web: www.valencefund.com

Mission Statement: Valence Life Sciences is a leading life sciences investment firm focused on late-stage private and micro-cap public drug development companies. Valence Advantage Life Sciences Fund II's targeted late-stage investment strategy - in conjunction with the team's experience, insight, and disciplined approach - has produced successful results for both its investors and portfolio companies.

Founded: 2012
Investment Criteria: Later-Stage
Industry Group Preference: Life Sciences
Portfolio Companies: Anthera Pharmaceuticals, ArQule, Celator Pharmaceuticals, Corthera, Geminx, Gentium, Invuity, Regado Biosciences, Sunesis, Vivus

Key Executives:
A. Rachel Laheny, Managing Director
Education: AB, Harvard College; PhD, Columbia University
Background: Head, Biotech Research Team & SVP, Lehman Brothers; Hambrecht & Quist
Eric Roberts, Managing Director
Education: BS, Wharton School, University of Pennsylvania
Background: Managing Director & Co-Head, Global Investment Group, Lehman Brothers; Managing Director, Partner & Founder, Life Sciences Department, Dillon, Read & Co. Inc.

1899 VALHALLA PARTNERS
8000 Towers Crescent Drive
Suite 1050
Vienna, VA 22182

Phone: 703-448-1400 Fax: 703-448-1441
e-mail: info@valhallapartners.com
web: www.valhallapartners.com

Mission Statement: To help talented entrepreneurs build world-class companies, by choosing to focus on business models and geographies that are well known.

Geographic Preference: United States
Fund Size: VP I: $177 million; VP II: $264 million
Founded: 2002
Average Investment: $10 million
Minimum Investment: $100,000
Investment Criteria: Seed to Later-Stage
Industry Group Preference: Information Technology, Infrastructure, Digital Media & Marketing, Education, SaaS
Portfolio Companies: Adaptly, App47, Automated Insights, BlueStripe, Custora, DomainHoldings, EnterpriseDB, Exchange Solutions, Fishbowl, Flat World, Geomagic, Getwell Network, Jumptap, KZO, LeftHand Networks, MiserWare, My Docket, Nirvanix, Parature, Place IQ, Qumulo, RealOps, Register.com, Rivermine, SafeNet, Sepaton, Shareablee, ShopSocial.ly, Solidfire, Speek, Swoop, Upfront Digital Media, Verical, Videology, Vistar Media, Vubiquity, WellAWARE Systems, Zonoff

Key Executives:
Arthur J Marks, Managing General Partner
e-mail: art@valhallapartners.com
Education: BS Industrial Engineering, University of Michigan; MBA with High Distinction, Harvard University Graduate School of Business
Background: General Partner, New Enterprise Associates; General Electric; Marketing/Sales, Baxter Laboratories
Directorships: Domain Holdings, EnterpriseDB, Jumptap, Parature, SafeNet, Sepaton, SolidFire, Videology, Vubiquity
Kiran Hebbar, Partner
e-mail: kiran@valhallapartners.com
Education: Bachelor's Degree, Indian Institute of Technology; MS, University of Maryland; MBA, Wharton School, University of Pennsylvania
Background: Director, Product Management, Siebel Systems; Software Engineer, Bentley Systems; Mellon Ventures
Directorships: Adaptly, Custora, Fishbowl, Flat World Knowledge, PlaceIQ, ShopSocially, Upfront Digital Media, Vistar Media, Vubiquity, Yelli, Zonoff
Harry D'Andrea, Administrative General Partner
e-mail: harry@valhallapartners.com
Education: BA Foreign Service, Pennsylvania State University; MBA, Drexel University
Background: CFO, Advanced Switching Communications; CFO, Call Technologies; CFO, Yurie Systems; CFO, American Communication Services
Directorships: ExaDigm, Exchange Solutions, Safenet, Qumulo

1900 VALIA
875 Washington Street
New York, NY 10014

web: www.valia.vc

Mission Statement: Valia is a venture capital firm that backs founders building futuristic and iconic companies.

Other Locations:
595 Pacific Avenue
Jackson Square
San Francisco, CA 94133

72-74 Dean Street
SoHo

662

Venture Capital & Private Equity Firms / Domestic Firms

London W1D 3SG
England
Key Executives:
Khaled Jalanbo, Managing Partner
Education: BS, Boston University; MS, Columbia University
Background: Entrepreneur; Angel Investor

1901 VALLEY VENTURES LP
1275 W Washington Street
Suite 101
Tempe, AZ 85281

Phone: 480-661-6600 **Fax:** 602-286-5284
web: valleyventures.org

Mission Statement: Focused on creating sustained high market-value companies that will dominate their industry niches while achieving fast-growing revenues and earnings.
Geographic Preference: Southwestern United States-Arizona, New Mexico, Southern California
Fund Size: $95 million
Founded: 1995
Average Investment: $5 million
Minimum Investment: $500,000
Investment Criteria: Second-Stage, Mezzanine, LBO
Industry Group Preference: Communications, Electronic Components, Electronic Technology, Medical & Health Related, Software, Industrial Equipment, Financial Services, Life Sciences, Information Technology, Microelectronics, Pharmaceuticals, Diagnostics
Portfolio Companies: Amplimed Corporation, Ascent Healthcare Solutions, Azerx, Cellzdirect, Delinea, HTG Molecular Diagnostics, Innovasic Semiconductor, Quasar, Regenesis Biomedical, Siverion, Vital Therapies

Other Locations:
PO Box 62798
Phoenix, AZ 85082

1902 VALOR EQUITY PARTNERS
875 North Michigan Avenue
Suite 3214
Chicago, IL 60611

Phone: 312-683-1900 **Fax:** 312-683-1881
e-mail: info@valorep.com
web: www.valorep.com

Mission Statement: A Chicago-based, middle market private equity firm dedicated to building great businesses in partnership with proven managers.
Founded: 1995
Average Investment: $10 - 30 million
Investment Criteria: New Platforms, Equity Investment, Add-On Investments, Special Situations
Industry Group Preference: Industrial Products, Specialty Distribution, Infrastructure, Manufacturing, Healthcare, Business Products & Services, Consumer Products, Energy Services
Portfolio Companies: Addepar, Family Home Health Services, Fooda, Marathon Pharmaceuticals, Renovate America, Sizzling Platter, Space Exploration Technologies
Key Executives:
Antonio Gracias, Chief Executive/Investment Officer
Education: BS & MSFS, International Finance & Economics, Georgetown University School of Foreign Service; JD, University of Chicago Law School
Background: Founder; MG Capital; Associate, Goldman Sachs
Juan Sabater, Partner
Education: A.B. History, Princeton University; J.D. Stanford Law School
Background: Managing Director, Goldman, Sachs & Co.
Jonathan K. Shulkin, Partner
Education: B.B.A. Accounting, University of Texas at Austin
Background: Investment & Portfolio team, MG Capital; President of Electronic Plating Service and Chief Operating Officer, Amax Plating, Electronic Plating Service, And Associated Plating Company
Timothy Watkins, Partner
e-mail: twatkins@valorep.com
Education: BS, Mechanical Engineering, Bradford University; MS, Industial Robotics, Cranfield Institute of Technology
Background: Vice President, MG Capital; Principal Consultant, Westworks Ltd
Bradley Sheftel, Managing Director
e-mail: bsheftel@valorep.com
Education: BA, Political Science, Tulane University
Background: JP Morgan Securities

1903 VALUEACT CAPITAL
One Letterman Drive
Building D, 4th Floor
San Francisco, CA 94129

Phone: 415-362-3700 **Fax:** 415-362-5727
e-mail: info@valueact.com
web: www.valueact.com

Mission Statement: Valueact Capital's overall investment strategy takes a buy-the-whole-business or private equity approach as it seeks to take advantage of increasing structural inefficiencies in the small-capitalization sector of the public markets.
Fund Size: $5 billion
Founded: 2000
Industry Group Preference: Information Technology, Industry, Energy, Finance, Consumer, Healthcare
Portfolio Companies: Adobe Systems Inc., Alliance Data Systems Corp., Allison Transmission Holdings Inc., Arcosa Inc., Armstrong Flooring Inc., Armstrong World Industries Inc., Baker Hughes Inc., CBRE Group Inc., Citigroup Inc., Dresser-Rand Group; Exterran Energy Corp., Element Fleet Management Corp., Equifax, Fidelity National Financial Inc., Gartner Inc., Gevity HR Inc., Gardner Denver Inc., Intergraph Corp., Invensys Plc., Halliburton Co., Insurance Auto Auctions Inc., Immucor Inc., Life Technologies Corp., Lifeline Systems Inc., Lincare Holdings Inc., MDS Inc., MedQuist Inc., Mentor Corp., MSC Software Corp., Martha Stewart Living Omnimedia Inc., Merlin Enterainments Plc., Moody's Corp., Morgan Stanley, Rockwell Collins Inc., Rolls-Royce Holdings Plc., Redwood Trust Inc., Rentokil Initial Plc., Reynolds & Reynolds Co., Siebel Systems Inc., Seagate Technology Plc., Sara Lee Corp., Snap-On Inc., SLM Corporation, Seitel Inc., Tektronix Inc., Trinity Industries Inc., Twenty-First Century Fox Inc., TriZetto Group Inc., Warner Chilcott Plc., Williams Scotsman International Inc., Willis Towers Watson Plc.

Key Executives:
Jeffrey W Ubben, Founder, Chief Executive Officer & Chief Investment Officer
e-mail: jubben@valueact.com
Education: BA, Duke University; MBA, JL Kellogg Graduate School of Management at Northwestern University
Background: Managing Partner, BLUM Capital Partners LP; Fidelity Management & Research
Bradley E. Singer, Partner & Chief Operating Officer
Education: BS, University of Virginia; MBA, Harvard Business School
Background: Senior EVP & CFO, Discovery Communications Inc.; CFO & Treasurer, American Tower Corp.; Investment Banket, Goldman Sachs
Directorships: Citizens Communications Corp.; Martha Stewart Omnimedia Inc.; Motorola Solutions Inc.; Rolls-Royce Holdings Plc.
G. Mason Morfit, President
Education: BA, Princeton University
Background: Credit Swisse First Boston

663

Venture Capital & Private Equity Firms / Domestic Firms

Kelly J. Barlow, Partner
Education: BS, California State University
Background: EGM Capital, Wells Capital Management
Gregory P. Spivy, Partner
Education: BA, Northwestern University
Background: Gruphon, Farallon Capital, Fremont Partners, Bridgeford Group
Brandon B. Boze, Partner
Education: BE, Mechanical Engineering, Vanderbilt University
Background: Lehman Brothers; Chair, CBRE Group Inc.
Directorships: Valeant Pharmaceuticals International; ValueAct Capital
Allison A Bennington, General Consel/Chief Compliance Officer/Partner
Education: BA, University of California, Berkeley; JD, University of California Hastings College of the Law
Background: General Counsel, Artriax Ltd; Managing Director, Robertson Stephans
Briana J. Zelaya, Partner
Education: BA, Loyola Marymount University
Background: Marketing, Blum Capital Partners

1904 VANCE STREET CAPITAL
11150 Santa Monica Blvd
Suite 750
Los Angeles, CA 90025

Phone: 310-231-7100
web: www.vancestreetcapital.com

Mission Statement: Invests in profitable middle market companies with enterprise values ranging from $50 to $200 million.
Geographic Preference: United States
Industry Group Preference: Aerospace, Defense and Government, Medical Products, Manufacturing
Portfolio Companies: Micronics Filtration Holdings, International Aerospace Coatings, Klune Industries, Micross Components, Process Fab, Semicoa

Key Executives:
Richard R Crowell, Founding Partner
Education: BA, University of California, Santa Cruz; MBA, Anderson School of Business
Background: Co-Founder & President, Aurora Capital Group; Managing Partner, Acadia Partners; Managing Director, Corporate Finance, Drexel Burnham Lambert
Michael Janish, Managing Partner
e-mail: mjanish@vancestreetcapital.com
Education: BS, MBA, Michigan State University
Background: President and CEO, Avalon Laboratories; President and CEO, Precitech
Brian D Martin, Managing Partner
Education: BS, Business Administration, Haas School of Business, University of California, Berkeley
Background: Vice President, Leveraged Buyouts Group, American Capital; Robertson Stephens

1905 VANDAELE CAPITAL
web: www.vandaelecapital.com

Mission Statement: At Vandaele Capital, we invest in startups, acquire and turnaround distressed companies, and advise businesses of all sizes on strategy and execution by forming partnerships. We also offer the expertise necessary to take any business to the next level. We focus on the challenges that emerging companies face, and we deliver proven, practical, customized solutions geared towards making companies more profitable. Our diverse portfolio of companies offers unique collaboration with businesses that demonstrates early success and high future potential.

Investment Criteria: Early-Stage
Portfolio Companies: EventReviews.com, Willa Skincare, Events.com, My Event Insurance, Qnary, Little Ducks Organics, Bump, Peeled Snacks

Key Executives:
Christophe Vandaele, Founder
Education: Masters Degree, Political Science & Military, Chateau d'Arenberg Military Academy
Background: CEO, Redline Diplomatic Relocation

1906 VANTAGEPOINT CAPITAL PARTNERS
1001 Bayhill Drive
Suite 220
San Bruno, CA 94066

Phone: 650-866-3100 Fax: 650-869-6078
e-mail: marketing@vpcp.com
web: www.vpcp.com

Mission Statement: One of the leading venture capital firms in the world. With an interest in companies ranging from start-ups to pre-IPO, we're an active multi-stage investor. Providing long-term capital, we have more than $4 billion under management and available for companies.

Founded: 1996
Average Investment: $20-$100 million
Investment Criteria: Multi-Stages
Industry Group Preference: Technology, Healthcare, Clean Technology, Information Technology, Energy, Energy Efficiency, Internet, Digital Media & Marketing
Portfolio Companies: 1366 Technologies, 3VR Security, Adura Technologies, AlertMe, Allbusiness.com, Allvoices, Amprius, Angstrom Power, Anthera Pharmaceuticals, Axsun Technologies, BlueWhale, Bridgelux, BrightSource Energy, Cbeyond Communications, CGI Pharmaceuticals, ChaCha, Chemrec AB, ChipX, Cobalt Technologies, Conceptus, CymaBay Therapeutics, Datran Media, Definity Health, Direct Flow Medical, DNS Services, E-One Moli, edo Interactive, EndPlay, Entrisphere, Evolv, FanIQ, GAIN Capital Group, Genomatica, glo AB, Global Financial Technology, Goldwind, Grocery Shopping Network, Healthline Networks, HengFu Logistics, Huga Optotech, iBAHN, Identified, InnoPath Software, Innovari, IntelePeer, InvestLab, Inxight Software, iWatt, Kagoor Networks, Klipsch Audio, Liquid Light, Liquid Robotics, Livescribe, Mascoma, Mayi, Meritron Networks, MiaSolé, Mobile 365, Multiply, MyFP, Myspace/Intermix Media, Neuraltus Pharmaceuticals, Nexsan Technologies, Next Step Living, Ogin, Ostara, OZ Communications, Phreesia, Pica8, Premium Power, PulsePoint, Pure Digital Technologies, ReachLocal, Safe Life, Santur, Savvion, Scribd, Serious Energy, Solarcentury, Solazyme, Spanfeller Media Group, Spatial Wireless, Switch, TargeGen, Tendril, Tesla Motors, TIDAL Software, TouchTunes Interactive Networks, TransMedics, Transport Technology Systems, Trilliant, VeriSilicon, Vook, WageWorks, Widevine Technologies, Xcellerex, YouMail, Zvents

Other Locations:
Unit 601, 6th floor, Tower 3
China Central Place
No. 77 Jian Guo Road, Chao Yang District
Beijing 100025
China
Phone: 86-1065989650 Fax: 86-1065989884

Key Executives:
Alan E Salzman, Chief Executive Officer, Managing Partner
Education: GC, London School of Economics; BA, University of Toronto; JD, Stanford Law School; lLM, Vrije Universiteit Brussel
Tom Bevilacqua, Managing Director
Education: BA, University of California, Berkeley; JD, University of California, Hastings College of the Law
Background: Executive Vice President, E*Trade; Founder, ArrowPath Venture Partners
David Fries, Managing Director
Education: BS, Florida Atlantic University; PhD, Physical Chemistry, Case Western Reserve University
Background: President, General Electric Ceramics

Venture Capital & Private Equity Firms / Domestic Firms

Bill Harding, Managing Director
Education: BS, MS, University of Arizona; PhD, Arizona State University; Officer, Military Intelligence Branch, United States Army Reserve
Background: Managing Director, Morgan Stanley & Co.; President, Morgan Stanley Venture Partners
Jim Marver, Managing Director
Education: BA, Williams College; MPP, PhD, University of California, Berkeley
Patricia Splinter, COO/Managing Director
Background: Intel Corporation
Richard Harroch, Managing Director
Education: BA, University of California, Berkeley; JD, University of California, Los Angeles
Background: Orrick, Herrington & Sutcliffe LLP

1907 VARDE PARTNERS
901 Marquette Avenue South
Suite 3300
Minneapolis, MN 55402

Phone: 952-893-1554 Fax: 952-893-9613
e-mail: investor.services@varde.com
web: www.varde.com

Mission Statement: Varde Partners has employed a diversity of event-driven investment strategies, earning its investors attractive risk-adjusted rates of return. Investments have centered on debt obligations of financially-troubled companies and, in more than 100 private transactions, nonperforming and sub-performing commercial real estate, commercial and industrial loans, residential mortgages, and consumer debt. Varde Partners manages several different investment funds that provide varying investment strategies and include multi-year lock up, annual redemption and offshore vehicles.

Fund Size: $300 million
Founded: 1993
Minimum Investment: $1 million
Industry Group Preference: Financial Services, Real Estate, Infrastructure, Mortgages

Other Locations:
Varde Partners Europe Limited
2 St. James's Market
London SW1Y 4AH
United Kingdom
Phone: 44-02078083370 Fax: 44-02078083371

Varde Partners Asia Pte Ltd
6 Battery Road
#21-01 049909
Singapore
Phone: 65-65790800 Fax: 35-65790801

510 Madison Avenue
12th Floor
New York, NY 10022
Phone: 212-321-3780 Fax: 212-321-3799

Key Executives:
Marcia L. Page, Co-Founder/Executive Chair
Education: BA, Economics, Gustavus Adolphus College; MBA, University of Minnesota
Background: VP, EBF & Associates; Portfolio Manager, Cargill
George G. Hicks, Co-Founder/Co-CEO
Education: BA, Gustavus Adolphus College; JD, University of Minnsota Law School
Background: SVP, Cargill Financial
Ilfryn Carstair, Partner/Chief Investment Officer/Co-CEO
Education: BC, University of Queensland, Australia; MBA, INSEAD, France
Background: Deutsche Bank London; Pacific Equity Partners
Dave Marple, Partner/General Counsel
Education: BA, Colgate University; JD, New York University School of Law
Background: Sr. Managing Director/General Counsel, Residential Capital; Lawyer, Structured Finance Department, Orrick Herrington & Sutcliffe

1908 VCFA GROUP
509 Madison Avenue
Suite 812
New York, NY 10022

Phone: 212-838-5577 Fax: 212-838-7614
e-mail: sharris@vcfa.com
web: www.vcfa.com

Mission Statement: VCFA Group provides liquidity to private equity investors. VCFA purchases, on a secondary basis, single interests or entire portfolios of interests in venture capital funds and venture backed companies. VCFA also purchases interests in other private equity funds, including mezzanine and buyout funds.

Geographic Preference: Worldwide
Fund Size: $230 million
Founded: 1982
Minimum Investment: $250,000
Investment Criteria: Existing limited partnership interests or existing interests in venture backed companies.

Other Locations:
One Sansome Street
Suite 3680
San Francisco, CA 94104
Phone: 415-296-0660 Fax: 415-296-0990

David B Tom, Managing Director
e-mail: dtom@vcfa.com
Education: MBA, Harvard Business School
Background: Investment Banker, Goldman Sachs High Technology Group
Steven J Taubman, Director - San Francisco
415-296-0660
e-mail: taubman@vcfa.com
Education: MBA, Leonard M Stern School of Business; MS, Meteorology, Pennsylvania State University; BS, Atmospheric Science, University of California
Background: Standard & Poors
Andrew Riley, Managing Director
e-mail: areilly@vcfa.com
Education: BS, Boston College
Background: Director, Business Development, KVH Industries; Managing Director, Accretive Exit Capital LLC; Managing Director, Thomas Keenan Ventures

1909 VEBER PARTNERS LLC
605 NW 11th Avenue
Portland, OR 97209-3235

Phone: 503-229-4400 Fax: 503-224-0949
e-mail: gveber@veber.com
web: www.veber.com

Mission Statement: Veber Partners' goal is to develop and maintain long-term relationships through quality service and a record of performance raising new capital, assisting in corporate strategic alliances, and successfully closing acquisitions and ownership transitions. Veber also purchases middle market companies using its own equity and the equity of its strategic investors.

Geographic Preference: Pacific Northwest
Founded: 1994
Average Investment: $5-10 million
Minimum Investment: $2 million
Investment Criteria: Mezzanine, Equity
Industry Group Preference: Manufacturing, Distribution, Technology, Business Products & Services, Consumer Retail, Healthcare
Portfolio Companies: Veber Solar I, NWPolymers, CRU-DataPort, Pony Lumber, Pacific Interpreters, Tradewinds Forest Products, Associated Chemists, Tactix

Venture Capital & Private Equity Firms / Domestic Firms

Key Executives:
Gayle L Veber, Managing Partner/CEO
e-mail: gveber@veber.com
Education: BS, Massachusetts Institute of Technology; MBA, Columbia University
Background: Founder & CEO Of Nova Northwest, Inc., Chairman & CEO of PacifiCorp Financial Services Group, Mobil Oil, Caltex Petroleum, Halcon Int
Directorships: CRU-Data Port, Pacific Interpreters
Rodger P Adams, Senior Partner
e-mail: radams@veber.com
Education: BA, Humboldt State University; MA, MBA, University of Oregon
Background: PacifiCorp Financial Services, Security Pacific Bank Oregon Bank
Directorships: NW Polymers, CrossCurrent, CRU-Data Port
Nicholas J Stanley, Senior Partner
e-mail: nstanley@veber.com
Education: B.A. Finance/Psychology, Georgetown University
Background: Fine Arts Graphics; Stanley Investment Management; Titan Group
Directorships: OHSU Foundation, St. Anthony Village Enterprise, Services for All Generations, Oregon Entrepreneurs Network

1910 VECTOR CAPITAL
One Market Street
Steuart Tower
23rd Floor
San Francisco, CA 94105

Phone: 415-293-5000 **Fax:** 415-293-5100
web: www.vectorcapital.com

Mission Statement: A private equity boutique specializing in spinouts, buyouts and recapitalizations of established technology businesses. Vector identifies and pursues these complex investments in both the public and private markets.
Geographic Preference: Mainly outside of Silicon Valley
Fund Size: $2 billion
Founded: 1997
Average Investment: $20-$100 million
Minimum Investment: $10 million
Investment Criteria: Buy-outs, Recapitalizations, Spin-outs
Industry Group Preference: Technology
Portfolio Companies: 2020, Aladdin, Allegro, Aspect, Cambium Networks, Certara, Cheetah Digital, ChyronHego, CloudSense, CollabNet VersionOne, Corel, Emarsys, Extricity, Gerber Scientific, Host Analytics, IPVALUE Management, iVita Financial, LANDesk, Meltwater, MoxiWorks, Niku, Open Solutions, ProcessClaims, RAE Systems, RealNetworks, Register.com, Saba, SafeNet, Savi Technology, SourceHOV, Synamedia, Technicolor, Tekelec, Teletrac, The Kela Group, Tidel, Triton Digital, Vesta, Vispero, WatchGuard, WinZip

Key Executives:
Alex Slusky, Managing Director/Founder
Education: BA, Economics, Harvard University; MBA, Harvard Business School
Background: ZiffBrothers; Partner, New Enterprise Associates; Consultant, McKinsey & Company; Product Manager, Microsoft Corporation
David Fishman, Managing Director
Education: BA, Economics, Duke University; MBA, JL Kellogg School of Management
Background: Managing Director, M&A, Goldman Sachs & Co.
David Baylor, Managing Director/COO
Education: BS, Arizona State University; JD, Berkeley School of Law, University of California
Background: COO/CFO, Thomas Weisel Partners Group; Managing Director, Montgomery Securities; Securities Attorney, Howard Rise Nemerovski Canady Falk & Rabkin; CPA, Deloitte & Touche

Robert Amen, Managing Director
Education: BA, History & Economics, Stanford University; MBA, Wharton School
Background: Business Development, Microsoft Corporation; Finance Analyst, Montgomery Securities
Directorships: Precise Software Solutions

1911 VEDANTA CAPITAL LP
540 Madison Ave.
30th Floor
New York, NY 10022

Phone: 212-710-5220 **Fax:** 212-710-5221
web: vedacap.com

Investment Criteria: Growth stage
Industry Group Preference: Information Technology, Life Sciences, Biotechnology, Medical Devices, Healthcare Services, Retail, Consumer & Leisure, E-Commerce & Manufacturing, Transaction Processing, Financial Services
Portfolio Companies: Litescape, Cast Iron, Consentry, Cortina Systems, Touchdown Technologies, Genband, Wayport, Omneon, Callidus, Arcot, Placeware, E2open

Key Executives:
Michael Patterson, General Partner
Education: BA, Latin American Studies, Wesleyan University; MBA, Columbia Business School
Background: Principal, Invesco Private Capital; Corporate Associate, AMVESCAP; Executive Recruiter, Russell Reynolds
Shrikant Sathe, General Partner
Education: BT, Engineering, The Indian Institute of Technology; Masters, Electrical Engineering, Virginia Polytechnic Institute; MBA, Wharton Business School, University of Pennsylvania
Background: Customer Marketing Manager, Daisy Systems; Director of Product Marketing and Director of Strategic Vendor Partnerships, Cadence Design Systems; Senior Vice President of Marketing, Infineon Technologies; Co-Founder and Vice President Of Marketing and Operations, SiNett Corporation
Directorships: Erasmic Ventures, Harbinger Systems
Parag Saxena, Co-Founder
Education: BT, The Indian Institute of Technology, Bombay; MS, Chemical Engineering, West Virginia College of Graduate Studies; MBA, Wharton School, University of Pennsylvania
Background: Citigroup Investment Management; Managing Partner and Founder, Invesco Private Capital (IPC); Product Manager, Becton Dickinson; Business Strategy Development, Booz, Allen, and Hamilton
Howard Goldstein, Venture & Operating Partner
Education: JD, Brooklyn Law School; BA, Sociology and Government, Clark University
Background: General Partner and Co-founder, Invesco Private Capita
Directorships: Make-A-Wish
Gonzalo Cordova, Partner
Education: BA and MA, Economics, University of Florida; Diplome d'Etudes Approfondies, Economic Policy, Institut d'Etudes Politiques
Background: Senior Portfolio Manager, Citigroup Asset Management
Andrew L. Dworkin, Partner
Education: JD, New York University's School of Law; MA, Clinical Psychology, New York University; BA, Clinical Psychology and International Relations, University of Pennsylvania
Background: Administrative Partner, INVESCO Private Capital; General Counsel, Chancellor Capital Management; Corporate Associate, Debevoise & Plimpton
Margaret Riley, Partner
Education: BS, Accounting, University of Wisconsin at Eau Claire

Venture Capital & Private Equity Firms / Domestic Firms

Background: CFO, Invesco Private Capital; Auditor, Carlson Companies

1912 VEGAS TECHFUND
Las Vegas, NV

web: www.vegastechfund.com

Mission Statement: VegasTechFund is a seed stage investment fund focused on empowering amazing founders and startups passionate about building community in downtown Las Vegas.

Geographic Preference: Las Vegas
Investment Criteria: Seed-Stage
Portfolio Companies: Walls 360, Fancred, Understory, Ticketbase, Bow & Drape, Zirtual, AdEspresso, CoolChip Technolgies, Primeloop, Travelnuts, Mizzen & Main, CultureIQ, Tealet, Freak'n Genius, CheckiO, Mouth, World View, OrderWithMe, Spree Commerce, Fluencr, Local Motors, Moveline, Banjo, True&Co., Ministry of Supply, Quarterly, SurfAir, Combat Gent, CrowdHall, Umba, RecordSetter, Hachi, iDoneThis, Wildfang, Skillshare, Original, teamly, LaunchKey, General Assembly, Bluefields, wedgies, Rolltech, The SPIRIT Project, Fandeavor, Digital Royalty, LaunchBit, Local Motion, Romotive

Key Executives:
Tony Hsieh, Partner
Background: CEO, Zappos.com
Fred Mossler, General Partner
Background: Zappos.com
Will Young, General Partner
Background: Director of Engineering, Zappos.com
Zach Ware, Managing Partner
Background: Zappos.com, Founder, WorkInProgress

1913 VELOCITY EQUITY PARTNERS LLC
10 Liberty Square
Boston, MA 02109

Phone: 617-338-2545 Fax: 617-261-3864
e-mail: info@velocityep.com

Mission Statement: Creates value by identifying and supporting outstanding entrepreneurs with unique innovations and a powerful drive to build market-leading companies; works with management teams to create premier companies in their field with the help of capital, expertise in building companies, and access to key networks.

Geographic Preference: New England, New York, Washington DC Corridor
Average Investment: $1 million - $5 million
Investment Criteria: Early Stage
Industry Group Preference: Information Technology, Enterprise Software, Communications, Infrastructure, Wireless Technologies, Software, Manufacturing, Industrial Products
Portfolio Companies: AccuRev, BEZ Systems, CiDRA, CyVera, Dotomi Direct Messaging, Exmplar, The Feedroom, InnoPad, LP Innovations, Metatomix, Nexaweb, ProFind, Reflectent, Retail Solutions, Sonexis, WebDialogs

1914 VENBIO
1700 Owens Street
Suite 595
San Francisco, CA 94158

Phone: 415-800-0800
e-mail: info@venbio.com
web: www.venbio.com

Mission Statement: A unique private equity firm formed from many different backgrounds, experiences and disciplines. Our common belief is that life science investing has changed dramatically over the past decade and so the investment platform needed to change. venBio is the culmination of our vision to integrate finance, science, commercial and clinical experiences into all stages and forms of life science investing.

Industry Group Preference: Life Sciences, Therapeutics, Medical Technology
Other Locations:
1350 Avenue of the Americas
20th Floor
New York, NY 10019
Phone: 212-937-4970

Key Executives:
Corey Goodman, Co-Founder/Managing Partner
Background: President, Biotherpeutics & Bioinnovation, Pfizer; Co-Founder, Exelisis, Renovis, Second Genome & Ossianix
Directorships: Solstice Biologics, Labrys Biologics, Oligasis, Ossianix, Second Genome
Robert Adelman, Co-Founder/Managing Partner
Background: Private Equity Partner, OrbiMed Advisors; Founder, Operon Technologies & Roka Bioscience
Directorships: Seragon Pharmaceuticals, Solstice Biologics

1915 VENCORE CAPITAL
4500 SW Kruse Way
Suite 350
Lake Oswego, OR 97035

Phone: 503-699-4997 Fax: 503-675-3136
Toll-Free: 800-890-4992
web: www.vencorecapital.com

Mission Statement: With our unique approach to venture debt financing, Vencore Capital helps early-stage, emerging growth companies extend their operating cash runway, and move towards profitability and increased valuation.

Geographic Preference: United States
Average Investment: $50,000 to $2 million
Minimum Investment: $50,000
Investment Criteria: Early-Stage Growth Capital
Industry Group Preference: Computer Related, Consumer Products, Life Sciences, Semiconductors, Business Products & Services, Software, Media, Telecommunications, Wireless Technologies
Portfolio Companies: Absorbent Technologies, AdventureLink, Afiniti Ventures, Agoura Technologies, Airborne 1, Apex Construction Systems, Audiomojo, Axcel Photonics, Axial Biotech, Be Jane, Bella Pictures, Black Rock Systems, Blink Twice, Blue Heron Technologies, Blue Lava Group, Bossa Nova Beverages Group, Brainshark, Cadforce, Calypte, CardioKinetix, Catalyst Oncology, Caveon, Chartone, Chockstone, Clupedia, Commrail, Confirma, Control Works, Criteria Labs, Dakota Arms, Dynamic Organic Light, Efficere, Endurance International, Engine Yard, Farralon Medical, Foundationworks, Galileo Processing, Health Carechain, iLinkMD, Intelligent Medical Devices, Inlustra Technologies, iSense, Isonics, IsoRay Medical, iWorlds Simulations, KBI Biopharma, Kimomex Markets, Kyma Technologies, Layered Technologies, LeisureLink, Lipomics, LensVector, Luxine, MEC Dynamics, Melior Discovery, Microphage, Missions Controls Automation, Morrone Organic Innovations, Motoczysz, MultiGEN Diagnostics, NBS Design, Neato Robotics, Neptune, Neuroptix, Nextreme Thermal Solutions, Northwave Technology, Novalux, NxGen Electronics, Ondax, Orphgen Pharmaceuticals, Oxysure Systems, Pacific GMP, Pathwork Diagnostics, Piedmont Pharmaceuticals, Prolacta Bioscience, Proteogenix, PTRx, Quantumsphere, Quick Study Radiology, Rogue Valley Microdevices, Rubicon Technology, S3C, SensAble, Sirigen, SMT Dynamics, Sword Diagnostics, Texas Advanced Optoelectronic, Thorley Industries, Touchdown Technologies, Trius Therapeutics, Vesta Therapeutics

Key Executives:
John Saefke, Chief Executive Officer
Education: BS, Finance & Management, University of

Venture Capital & Private Equity Firms / Domestic Firms

Oregon; Post-Baccalaureate Degree, Accounting, Portland State University
Background: Controller, FirstCorp
Jim Johnson, Chief Operating Officer
Education: BS, Finance, California State University; Defense Language Institute
Background: Venture Leasing Division, FirstCorp; Household International
David Dolezal, Managing Director, Rocky Mountain Region
303-410-4495
e-mail: dave@vencorecapital.com
Education: BS, Business Administration, Portland State University
Background: Vice President, Silicon Valley Bank

1916 VENROCK ASSOCIATES
7 Bryant Park
23rd Floor
New York, NY 10018
Phone: 212-444-4100 Fax: 212-444-4101
web: www.venrock.com

Mission Statement: Provides funding and services for entrepreneurs with breakthrough ideas in technology, healthcare, media and energy.
Geographic Preference: United States
Fund Size: $1+ billion
Founded: 1969
Minimum Investment: $5 million
Investment Criteria: Early Stage
Industry Group Preference: Technology, Healthcare, Media, Energy, Healthcare Information Technology, Social Media, Biofuels, Distributed Electricity, Vehicle Technology, Biopharmaceuticals, Diagnostics, Medical Devices, Advertising Technology, Consumer Technology
Portfolio Companies: 6sense, 10X Genomics, Acceleron Pharma, Achaogen, Adavium Medical, ADiFY, Adnexus, Aha, Aledadem Amino, Alimera Sciences, Anacor Pharma, Appia, Appthority, AppNexus, Aria Systems, Ariosa Diagnostics, Atom Computing, Avalanche Biotech, BCD, B-Hive, Bizo, Beckon, BlogHer, Boston Power, Boundless, Burner, Castlight Health, Celladon, Chisel, Ciclon Semiconductor, Cloudflare, CodeRyte, Constellation Pharma, CoreTrace, Crunchyroll, Ctera, Cygilant, Cymabay Therapeutics, Cyteir Therapeutics, Dapper, DATAllegro, Dataminr, Devoted Health, Doctor on Demand, Dollar Shave Club, Dstillery, Dynamic Signal, Encoded Genomics, Evident.io, Extend Media, Fate Therapeutics, FINsix, Gazelle, Grand Rounds, Happier, Hua Medicine, Hyper9, Ikaria, Impopharma, INRIX, Inscripta, Intuityy Medical, Jiff, Juno Therapeutics, Klout, Kwicr, Kyruus, Lavante, Lucid, Luxe, Lyra, Misty Robotics, Niara, Nest, Newport Media, Numerated, Optinuity, P.A. Semi, PEAK Surgical, Percipient.ai, Personal Capital, Phononic, PowerVision, Quantenna, QuatRx, Quip, Receptos, Redbeacon, RedSeal, RegenXBio, Reflexion, Renew, Retail Solutions, Salsify, Sapphire Energy, Semtek, Shape, Shockwave Medical, Simple Star, Skyryse, SlideShare, SmartBix, Smartling, SocialShield, Socrates.ai, Spirox, Stride, Suki, Targeted Genetics Corp., Threadbox, Transonic Combustion, Tri Alpha Energy, Trubion Pharma, Tudou, Twofish, Unity Biotechnology, VeloCloud, Virdante Pharma, Virta, Where, Workframe, World Heart Corp., YouNow, Zeltiq, ZoomInfo

Other Locations:
3340 Hillview Avenue
Palo Alto, CA 94304
Phone: 650-561-9580 Fax: 650-561-9580

34 Farnsworth St.
3rd Floor
Boston, MA 02210
Phone: 617-995-2000 Fax: 617-995-2001

Key Executives:
Brian Ascher, Partner
e-mail: bda@venrock.com
Education: BA, Magna Cum Laude, Princeton University; MBA, Stanford University
Background: Senior Product Manager, Intuit; Strategy Consultant, Monitor Group
Directorships: Awarepoint, Vocera
Nick Beim, Partner
e-mail: nick@venrock.com
Education: Stanford University; University of Oxford
Background: Associate, McKinsey; Associate, Goldman Sachs; General Partner, Matrix Partners
Directorships: Dataminr, Workframe, Quip Inc., Chisel.ai, Percipient.ai
Camille Samuels, Partner
e-mail: cami@venrock.com
Education: BA, Duke University; MBA, Harvard Business School
Background: Managing Director, Versant Ventures
Directorships: Spirox Medical, Unity Biotechnology
Tom Willerer, Partner
e-mail: tom@venrock.com
Education: BA, Indiana University; MA, DePaul University
Background: Chief Product Officer, Coursera
Bob Kocher MD, Partner
e-mail: bkocher@venrock.com
Education: University of Washington; MD, George Washington University
Background: Special Assistant to the President, Healthcare & Economic Policy, Obama Administration, Member, National Economic Council; Partner, McKinsey & Company
Directorships: Castlight Health
David Pakman, Partner
e-mail: dpakman@venrock.com
Education: BSE, Computer Science Engineering, University of Pennsylvania School of Engineering & Applied Science
Background: CEO, eMusic; Co-Founder, Myplay, Inc.; Vice President, N2K Entertainment
Bryan Roberts, Partner
650-475-3750
Fax: 650-561-9180
e-mail: broberts@venrock.com
Education: BA, Dartmouth College; PhD, Chemistry/Biology, Harvard University
Background: Investment Banking, Kidder Peabody & Company
Directorships: Achaogen, Castlight Health, Ironwood Pharmaceuticals
Mike Tyrrell, Partner
617-679-0365
Fax: 617-679-0301
e-mail: mft@venrock.com
Education: BS, University of New Hampshire
Background: Spyglass; Multiflow Computer; Celerity Computing; Prime Computing
Directorships: Appia, Aria Systems

1917 VENSANA CAPITAL
3601 W 76th Street
Suite 20
Minneapolis, MN 55435
Phone: 612-217-8680
e-mail: info@vensanacap.com
web: www.vensanacap.com

Mission Statement: Vensana Capital is a venture capital and growth equity investment firm that partbers with entrepre-

Venture Capital & Private Equity Firms / Domestic Firms

neurs who will trasnform healthcare with breakthrough innovations in medical technology.

Fund Size: $225 Million
Founded: 2019
Average Investment: $10-30 Million
Investment Criteria: Medical Devices; Diagnostics and Data Science; Digital Health and Tech-Enabled Services

Other Locations:
101 Church Street
Suite D
Vienna, VA 22180

Key Executives:
Justin Klein, Co-Founder/Managing Partner
Education: AB, BS, MD, Duke University; JD, Harvard Law School
Background: Partner, NEA
Kirk Nelson, Co-Founder/Managing Partner
e-mail: kirk@vensanacap.com
Education: BA, MBA, Harvard University
Background: Consultant, Bain & Co.; Pro Hockey Player

1918 VENTANA CAPITAL MANAGEMENT LP
22431 Antonio Parkway
Suite B160-1002
Rancho Santa Margarita, CA 92688

Phone: 949-766-4486 **Fax:** 949-766-4487
web: ventanainnovation.wordpress.com

Mission Statement: Ventana likes to fund global expansion, especially in regards to China. It also concentrates efforts on first and second stage enterprises, technology developed by the aerospace, quasi-governmental industries, university-based scientific spin-outs, institutional research and private entrepreneurial opportunities in the areas of the environment, health services and medical devices, biotechnology and biopharmaceutical and technology.

Geographic Preference: Southern California, Worldwide
Fund Size: $230 million
Founded: 1974
Average Investment: +$5 million
Minimum Investment: $2 million
Investment Criteria: First and Second-Stage Including Growth Stage
Industry Group Preference: Environmental Protection, High Technology, Biotechnology, Biopharmaceuticals, Technology, Telecommunications, Pollution, Energy, Hazardous Waste, Medical & Health Related, Therapeutics, Research & Development, Aerospace, Defense and Government, Wireless Technologies, Digital Media & Marketing
Portfolio Companies: Advanced Photonix, Aktino, Brooktree Corporation, California Linear Devices, Cymer, Fidelica Microsystems, Innovent Systems, Neophotonics, PairGain Technology, Pathlight Technologies, Proxima, Sequoia Communications, Soma Networks, Alliance Pharmaceutical, Agouron Pharmaceuticals, BioCryst Pharmaceuticals, Corvas International, GalaGen, Idun Pharmaceuticals, Integra Life Sciences, Maxim Pharmaceuticals, R-2solid to Warburg Pincus, La Jolla Pharmaceutical Company

Other Locations:
11673-202 Charter Oak
Reston, VA 20190
Phone: 405-824-5549

Key Executives:
Thomas O Gephart, Founder/Managing Partner
Education: BA, Engineering, University of Southern California
Background: Executive Positions: AMP Inc., Bunker-Ramo Corporation, Hughes Aircraft; Founder, Interlink Company; Chariman: Advantix Inc., APTA Group Inc., Cellnet Corporation, HemaCare Coroporation, Infrasonics Inc., QTRON Inc.

1919 VENTURE ASSOCIATES PARTNERS LLC
355 Sweetbriar Road
Memphis, TN 38120-2515

Phone: 901-763-1434 **Fax:** 901-763-1428
e-mail: email@venture-associates.com
web: www.venture-associates.com

Mission Statement: Primarily underperforming situations in growth industries, primarily manufacturing; looking for new platform company as well as synergistic acquisitions.

Geographic Preference: United States, Canada, Mexico
Founded: 1985
Average Investment: $5 - $15 million
Minimum Investment: $1 million
Investment Criteria: Revenue $20-$200 million; Underperforming situations in growth industry
Industry Group Preference: Components & IoT, Aerospace, Defense and Government, Plastics, Electronic Technology
Portfolio Companies: Applied Composites, Crown Fiberglass, Diversified Composites, Applied Aerospace Structures, Century Wheel @ Rim, Applied Molded Products, Agena Technologies

Key Executives:
Burton B Weil, Chairman
e-mail: bweil@venture-associates.com
Education: BS, University of Tennessee; MBA, University of Memphis; JD, Vanderbilt University; CPA

1920 VENTURE CAPITAL FUND OF NEW ENGLAND
30 Washington Street
Wellesley, MA 02481

Phone: 781-431-8400 **Fax:** 781-237-6578
e-mail: inquiries@vcfne.com
web: www.vcfne.com

Mission Statement: The Venture Capital Fund of New England's investment activities are characterized by: a focus on early stage companies; a geographic concentration in the New England region; an emphasis on technology based enterprises; and an additional interest in direct marketing - related businesses. VCFNE prefers New England-based companies in the early stage investment category, though it is also willing to consider on an occasional basis a seed or expansion stage investment and companies located outside the Northeastern US.

Geographic Preference: New England
Fund Size: $80 million
Founded: 1981
Average Investment: $500,000 - $1.5 million
Minimum Investment: $500,000
Investment Criteria: Early-Stage
Industry Group Preference: E-Commerce & Manufacturing, Broadcasting, Communications, Computer Related, Electronic Technology, High Technology, Industrial Equipment, Information Technology, Software, Cable, Radio, Direct Marketing
Portfolio Companies: Protonex, First Equity, Tibersoft, Nutfield Technology, Texterity, NextMark, Aircuity, ComBrio, Redtail Solutions, ExoGenesis, EMO Labs, LP Innovations, Cartera Commerce, Saylent Technologies, Air-Inc

Key Executives:
Carl Novotny, Managing Director
e-mail: cnovotny@vcfne.com
Education: B.A. Rice University; MBA, Harvard Business School
Background: First USA Partners; First USA Bank; Trans National Financial Services
Directorships: Associates in Internation Research, Saylent Technologies, Next Mark, EMO Labs
Gordon R Penman, Managing Director
e-mail: gordon.penman@wbd-us.com
Education: B.A., College of William and Mary; J.D.,

Venture Capital & Private Equity Firms / Domestic Firms

University of Virginia Law School
Background: Brown Rudnick; Boston Bar Association
E Jack Stewart, Managing Director
e-mail: jstewart@vcfne.com
Education: BS, Yale University; MBA, Harvard Business School
Background: Partner, Corning Venture Management; Founder, Kestral Venture Management
Chad Novotny, Managing Director
e-mail: chad.novotny@vcfne.com
Education: BA, Amherst College; MBA, Babson College
Background: Principal and CTO; The Support Group Inc.

1921 VENTURE INVESTORS LLC
University Research Park
505 South Rosa Road
Suite 201
Madison, WI 53719

Phone: 608-441-2700 Fax: 608-441-2727
web: www.ventureinvestors.com

Mission Statement: Although the Midwest is home to many of the nation's leading research institutions, it possesses just a small fraction of the nation's venture capital. Venture Investors is filling this void with patient capital and the experience of building companies. We are investors that are willing to become actively involved in building the team and organization that are necessary to lead a company to success.

Geographic Preference: Midwest
Fund Size: $118 million
Founded: 1982
Average Investment: $5-7 million
Minimum Investment: $250,000
Investment Criteria: Focus is on the stage of company development rather than specific industries. In general, Venture Investors looks to invest in companies with proprietary products that offer distinct competiveness.
Industry Group Preference: Healthcare, Technology, Clean Technology
Portfolio Companies: Aerpio Therapeutics, Akebia Therapeutics, Cellectar Biosciences, Celleration, Deltanoid Pharmaceuticals, EBI Life Sciences, Euthymics Bioscience, Gala Biotech, Great Lakes Pharmaceuticals, HistoSonics, IntraLase, Inviragen, Juventas Therapeutics, LenSx, Madison Vaccines Inc., NanoBio, Nerites, NeuMoDx, Neurovance, NeuWave, NimbleGen Systems, Procertus, Promega, ReShape Medical, Third Wave Technologies, Tissue Regeneration Systems, TomoTherapy, ZyStor Therapeutics, AlfaLight, Guild, NetSocket, Pattern Insight, Thalchemy, UpTo, Chromatin, Silatronix, Virent

Other Locations:
201 South Main Street
Suite 900
Ann Arbor, MI 48104
Phone: 734-274-2904 Fax: 734-214-3006

John Neis, Executive Managing Director
e-mail: john@ventureinvestors.com
Education: BS Finance, University of Utah; MS Marketing & Financing, University of Wisconsin
Background: Chartered Financial Analyst
Directorships: Deltanoid Pharmaceuticals, Virent Energy Systems
Scott Button, Managing Director
e-mail: scott@ventureinvestors.com
Education: BS Mechanical Engineering, University of Wisconsin; MBA, University of Chicago
Background: Sales Engineer Rockwell International; Operations Manager, McDonalds Corporation
Directorships: SoftSwitching Technologies, Inc., NeuWave Medical, Silatronix
Paul Weiss, Managing Director
e-mail: paul@ventureinvestors.com
Education: BS, Biochemistry, Carleton University, Ottawa; PhD, Biochemistry, MBA, University of Wisconsin, Madison
Background: President, Gala Biotech Division of Cardinal Health; VP, Business Development, 3-Dimensional Pharmaceuticals; Director of Licensing, Wyeth-Ayerst Pharmaceuticals
Directorships: Akebia Therapeutics, Euthymics Bioscience, Mithridion, ProCertus
Jim Adox, Managing Director
e-mail: jim@ventureinvestors.com
Education: BS, Mechanical Engineering, MS, Mechanical Engineering, MBA, University of Michigan
Background: RidgeLine Ventures; EDF Ventures
Directorships: HistoSonics, Incept BioSystems, Michigan Venture Capital Association, Tissue Regeneration Systems

1922 VENTURE TECH ALLIANCE
2585 Junction Avenue
San Jose, CA 95134

Phone: 408-382-7927 Fax: 408-382-8004
web: www.vtalliance.com

Mission Statement: A venture investment management company targeting early-stage business investments in the semiconductor industry and other emerging technology areas.

Fund Size: $165 million
Founded: 2001
Minimum Investment: $1-$3 million
Investment Criteria: Early to Mid-Stage
Industry Group Preference: Semiconductors, Emerging Markets, Sectors & Technologies
Portfolio Companies: 5V Technologies, Aiconn Technology, AMCC, Apache, Aquantia, Audience, Auramicro, Axiom, Beceem, Bridgelux, Exclara, Gemfire, Ikanos, Impinq, IvenSense, Leadtrend, LiquidLEDs, MediaTek, Mutual-Pak, Maxim, Eoconix, NetLogic, NextIO, Nvidia, Optichron, Pixim, Power Analog, Microelectronics, Powervation, QUALCOM, Quellan, RichWave, Sentelic, SiRF Technology, SVTC, Synopsys, Teknovus, POWERPRECISE, Reflectivity, Thales, Tilera, Touch Micro-System, Tech, Validity, Xceive, YoBon

Other Locations:
615 West Prospect Street
Seattle, WA 98119

No. 10, Li-Hsin 6th Road
Hsin-Chu Science-Based Industrial Park
Hsin-Chu
Taiwan 300
China
Phone: 03-6669980 Fax: 03-6669970

Key Executives:
Ron Norris, Managing Partner
206-441-8080
Fax: 206-441-7373
e-mail: morris@vtalliance.com
Education: BS, Physics, Sam Houston State University; MS, Physics, University of Arkansas
Background: SVP, Worldwide Marketing & Sales, TSMC; President, TSMC USA; VP & General Manager, Data I/O Corporation
Kai Tsang, Managing Partner
408-382-7927
Fax: 408-382-8004
e-mail: ktsang@vtalliance.com
Education: BS, Physics, National Taiwan University; PhD, Physics, University of Illinois
Background: Senior Director, Cypress Semiconductor Company; VP Operations, Galvantech; VP Technology/Development, IC Works; Director Technology Development, Paradigm Technology
Directorships: RichWave Technology, Sentelic, 5V Technologies, Power Analog Microelectronics, Aiconn Technology, LiquidLEDs
Christy Chou, Managing Partner
408-382-8086

Venture Capital & Private Equity Firms / Domestic Firms

Fax: 408-382-8004
e-mail: cchou@vtalliance.com
Education: BA, Finance, MBA, Finance & International Business, National Taiwan University
Background: Hewlett Packard Company; Finance Manager, TSMC North America

1923 VENTURESOUTH
225 S Pleasantburg Drive
Suite C-5
Greenville, SC 29607

web: venturesouth.vc

Mission Statement: VentureSouth is an Angel investment group that work to develop and manage various angel grounds and funds across the Southeast.
Geographic Preference: Southeastern United States, The Carolinas
Fund Size: $20 million
Portfolio Companies: Actived, ATW, Atlas Organics, Avadim Technologies Inc., Babies, Booster, Brightfield, CharlestonPharma, Cirtemo, Emrgy, Farmshots, Grow Journey, Kiyatec, Kwipped, New York Butcher Shoppe, Nirvana Science, OBMedical, Pandoodle, Pharmright, Physcient, Plum Print, Proaxion, ProctorFree, Rival Health, Sensory Analytics, Servosity, Southeast TechInventures, Target Pharma Solutions, TIO, Tip Hive, Uvision360, Vendor Registry, Work America, Zipit, The Iron Yard, Lien Nation, Sabal Medical, Selah Genomics, Verdeeco, Virtual Event Bags

Key Executives:
Matt Dunbar, Managing Director
Education: MBA, MA, Education, Stanford University; BSc, Chemical Engineering, Clemson University
Background: Management Consultant, Boston Consulting Group; Engineer, Eastman Chemical Company
Directorships: UCAN, Angel Capital Accosiation, Entegra Financial Corp.
Charlie Banks, Managing Director
Education: BS, Business Admin., Newberry College
Background: Portfolio Manager
Paul Clark, Managing Director
Education: MA, Medieval History, Fordham University; BA, History, Durham University
Background: Senior Vice President of M&A; Principal, BC Partners; M&A Advisory Experience, NM Rothschild & Sons

1924 VERGE FUND
317 Commercial Street NE
Albuquerque, NM 87102

Phone: 505-247-1038 **Fax:** 505-244-8040
e-mail: information@vergefund.com
web: www.vergefund.com

Mission Statement: Verge Fund is a highly motivated venture capital fund that invests in seed-stage, high-growth ventures in the Southwest.
Geographic Preference: New Mexico, Southwest United States
Investment Criteria: Seed-Stage
Industry Group Preference: Technology, Clean Technology, Electronics, SaaS
Portfolio Companies: Altela, AttachedApps, BoomTime, Exemplify, IntelliCyt, Nuvita, Nuvita Professional, Pajarito Powder, Sportxast, Trutouch, Vertical Power, Vibrant, Wellkeeper, ZTEC Instruments

Key Executives:
William F Bice, Founding Partner
Background: Founder & CEO, ProLaw Software; West km; Founder, BoomTime
Directorships: Vertical Power, Nuvita
Thomas J Stephenson, Managing Partner
Education: BA, Physics, Rice University; MBA, Information Management & Technology, McCombs School of Business, University of Texas, Austin
Background: General Parnter, Murphree Venture Partners
Directorships: Altaview, Altela, Metaphor, Nanocrystal, Wellkeeper
Ron J McPhee, Partner
Education: Computer Engineering, University of New Mexico
Background: Founder, HealthFirst Corporation; Founder, Nuvita
Directorships: AltaView Technologies, Boomtime
Larry Lujan, Partner
Education: BA, New Mexico State University
Background: Manuel Lujan Agencies; HUB International
Directorships: Santa Miria el Mirrador Foundation; Albuquerque Hispano Chamber of Commerce

1925 VERITAS CAPITAL FUND LP
9 West 57th St.
29th Floor
New York, NY 10019

Phone: 212-415-6700
e-mail: info@veritascapital.com
web: www.veritascapital.com

Mission Statement: Veritas Capital Fund is a private equity firm that partners with experienced and motivated management teams to acquire and develop middle market companies.
Geographic Preference: North America
Fund Size: Fund I - $175 million, Fund II - $200 milion
Founded: 1992
Minimum Investment: $1,000,000
Investment Criteria: Later Stage Growth, LBO, MBO
Industry Group Preference: Aerospace, Defense and Government, Consumer Products, Telecommunications, Electronic Technology, Manufacturing
Portfolio Companies: Abaco Systems, Aeroflex, Alion, Anaren, Aptim, Athena, BeyondTrust, Cambium Learning Group, Contintental Electronics Corp., Cotiviti, CPI International, DynCorp International, Enterprise Electronics Corporation, Excelitas Technologies, Global Tel Link, Guidehouse, Integrated Defense Technologies, KeyPoint Government Solutions, McNeil Technologies, Onsolve, Peraton, Perspecta, Salient CRGT, SolAero Technologies, Standard Aero, Trak Communications, Truven Health Analytics, Vangent, Vencore, Vertex Aerospace, Virence, Wornick Company

Key Executives:
Ramzi M Musallam, CEO/Managing Partner
212-688-0020
Fax: 212-688-9411
e-mail: rmusallam@veritascapital.com
Education: BA in Economics & Mathematics, Colgate University; MBA, University of Chicago Graduate School of Business
Background: Associate, Pritzker & Pritzker; Berkshire Partners; Chemical Bank
Hugh D. Evans, Managing Partner
Education: B.A. Harvard University; M.B.A. University of Chicago
Background: Partner/member of Investment Committee at Falconhead Capital; Principal at Stonington Partners
Directorships: Aeroflex Holding Corp., Excelitas Technologies, CPI International, Truven Health Analytics, The SI Organiztion Holding Corp., KepPoint Government Solutions, CRGT
Ashish Chandarana, Partner
Education: BA, Brown University; M.Phil, Cambridge University; MBA, University of Chicago Booth School of Business; CFA
Background: Partner, McKinsey & Co.; Investment Principal, Aureos Capital
James Dimitri, Partner
Education: BS, Vanderbilt University; MBA, Kellogg

671

Venture Capital & Private Equity Firms / Domestic Firms

School of Management
Background: Principal, Welsh Carson Anderson & Stowe
Brian Gorczynski, Partner
Education: BS, Boston College; MBA, Harvard Business School
Background: Managing Partner, North Cove Partners; Managing Director, BAML Capital Partners; Managing Director, Merrill Lynch Global Private Equity
Benjamin M. Polk, Partner
Education: J.D. Cornell Law School; B.A. Hobart College
Background: Senior Partner, Schulte Roth & Zabel LLP
Directorships: Aeroflex Holding Corp., CPI International, CRGT, Excelitas Technologies, KeyPoint Government Solutions, The SI Organization Holding Corp., Truven Health Analytics.
Daniel Sugar, Partner
Education: BSE, Princeton University; MBA, Wharton School
Background: Miller Buckfire & Co.

1926 VERIZON VENTURES
1 Verizon Way
Basking Ridge, NJ 07920

web: www.verizonventures.com

Mission Statement: A tech-based venture capital fund interested in various technology sectors, including: connected devices and hardware, media and entertainment, commerce and advertising, data and analytics, and infrastructure. Verizon is a long-term investor.

Founded: 2013
Industry Group Preference: Commerce, Advertising, Software, Data & Analytics, Infrastructure, Networking, Media, Entertainment, Technology, Information Technology, Artificial Intelligence, Virtual Reality, Security
Portfolio Companies: 4Home, 8i, ActionX, AdStage, AdTheorent, Airborne Entertainment, Airship, Beamr, Benbria, BL Healthcare, BlueKai, Brit + Co., Bug Labs, CardStar, Cellfire, CENX, Civis Analytics, ClipCall, CloudBees, Consert, ConteXtream, Edgybees, Entropic, Filament, Flash Networks, Globetouch, Glympse, Iguazio, Invidi, Jana, Kiip, Kinvey, Kumu Networks, Light Field Lab, Lumina Networks, Medio, MobileRQ, Networks in Motion, OmniSci, Open Garden, Optibus, Payfone, PlaySight, PrecisionHawk, Q-Sensei, Renovo, Sfara, SimplyTapp, SparkCognition, Swiftmile, The Fabric, The Hive, The VOID, Thumbplay Music, Urgent.ly, Veniam, Verdigris, Versa Networks, VOOM, YourMechanic, Zenverge

Other Locations:
1095 6th Avenue
New York, NY 10036

499 Hamilton Avenue
Palo Alto, CA 94301

201 Spear Street
San Francisco, CA 94105

Rothschild Boulevard 22
Tel Aviv-Yafo
Israel

Key Executives:
Samy Ben Aissa, Managing Director
Education: MS, université de Technologie de Compiègne; MS, Gannon University; MBA, NYU Stern School of Business
Background: AT&T; JP Morgan; GE Transportation Systems; K. Hovnanian Homes; Avaya
Jeffrey Black, Managing Director
Education: BBA, University of North Carolina; MBA, Goizueta Business School, Emory University
Background: JP Morgan; Delta Air Lines
Alex Khalin, Managing Director
Education: MBA, MIT
Background: HP; Boston Consulting Group; Schlumberger

Michelle McCarthy, Managing Director
Education: BA, American University; MBA, Georgetown University
Background: Verizon Capital
Kristina Serafim, Managing Director
Education: BEng, Kettering University; MBA, Harvard Business School
Background: Director, Intellectual Ventures; Corporate Development, IBM; NAGRA Innovations

1927 VERONIS SUHLER STEVENSON
390 Park Ave.
13th Floor
New York, NY 10022

Phone: 212-935-4990 Fax: 212-381-8168
e-mail: mehranl@vss.com
web: www.vss.com

Mission Statement: Veronis Suhler Stevenson is a leading middle-market private investment firm that makes private equity, mezzanine and senior credit investments within the information, education, media and communications and business services industries.

Geographic Preference: North America, Europe
Fund Size: $3.1 billion
Founded: 1981
Average Investment: $10 - $150 million
Investment Criteria: Buyouts, Recapitalizations, Growth Financings, Strategic Acquisitions
Industry Group Preference: Media, Communications, Business Products & Services, Education, Marketing
Portfolio Companies: Access Intelligence, Acrisure, Advanstar, Ascend Media, Avatar International, B&B Merger Corp., Berliner Verlag, Birch Telecom, Brand Connections, Broadcasting Partners, Cable Management Ireland, Cambium Learning Group, Cannella Response Television, Canon Communications, Caravan Health, Cast & Crew, Centaur Communications, Chemical Week, Clarion Events, Connexion Point, Contexo Media, Coretelligent, CSC Media Group, DeTelefoongids BV, DOAR Communications, DTN, Ebiquity, Executive Health Resources, Eyewitness News, Fonecta Oy, Gallo Holdings, Golden State Towers, Granada Learning Group, Greenslate, Hanley-Wood, Hostway, Hughes Broadcasting Partners, Infobase, International Media Partners, Ipreco, ITE Group, IT-Ernity, ITN Networks, Market Strategies International, MediaResponseGroup, Mediatel, MetSchools, Navtech, Pepcom GmbH, PJS Publications, Quadranet, Red 7 Media, Remedy Health Media, Rifkin Acquisition Partners, Riviera Broadcast Group, Sandow Media, Schofield Media Group, SHL, SNL Securities, Solucient, SourceMedical, Southern Theaters, Spectrum Resources Towers, Strata Decision, SureSource, System One, Tax Credit, The Official Information Company, Thomsons Online Benefits, TMP Worldwide Advertising & Communications, TRANZACT, Triax Midwest Associates, Triax Southeast Assocites, Trover Solutions, User Friendly Media, Vault.com, VKidz, Writtle, YBR Group, Yellow Book USA, Zed Group

Key Executives:
Jeffrey T Stevenson, Managing Partner
212-381-8122
e-mail: stevensonj@vss.com
Education: BA, Rutgers College
Background: Executive VP Corporate Finance, VSS
David Bainbridge, Managing Director
e-mail: bainbridged@vss.com
Education: Cornell University; Stern School of Business at New York University
Background: Investment Banking, Berkery Noyes & Co.; Scott-Macon
R Trent Hickman, Managing Director
212-381-8454
e-mail: hickmant@vss.com
Education: AB, History & French Literature, Duke University; MBA, Finance, Wharton School, University

of Pennsylvania
Background: First Union Securities
Directorships: Brand Connections, Market Strategies, Souther Theatres, TMP Worldwide, Tranzact
Patrick N.W. Turner, Managing Director
e-mail: turnerp@vss.com
Background: Managing Director, Crescent Capital Group LP; Crimson Capital; Managing Partner, Canterbury Capital Partners
Directorships: IT-Ernity; MRG

1928 VERSANT VENTURES
One Sansome St.
Suite 3630
San Francisco, CA 94104

Phone: 415-801-8100

Mission Statement: Partners with entrepreneurs to finance young medical device, bio-pharmaceutical, healthcare service, and e-Health companies, helping them grow to become pre-eminent companies in their field.

Geographic Preference: California
Fund Size: $1.6 billion
Founded: 1999
Average Investment: $1 - $10 million
Minimum Investment: $1 million
Investment Criteria: Early-Stage
Industry Group Preference: Medical Devices, Pharmaceuticals, Healthcare, Biotechnology, Healthcare Services, Healthcare Information Technology
Portfolio Companies: Adverum, Akero, Aligos, Alter G, Amira Pharma, Anokion, Aprea, Audentes, Biotie, Black Diamond, Blue Rock, Bright Peak, Cadence, CardiAQ Valve Technologies, Ceterix Orthopaedics, Clovis Oncology, Crispr, Crinetics, CymaBay, Ebb, Enterprise Therapeutics, FivePrime, Flexion, ForSight Vision 4, ForSight Vision 5, GenSight, Glaukos, Gotham Therapeutics, Gritston Oncology, Inari, Inception 4, Inception 5, Inception IBD, Intuity Medical, Jecure, Jnana, Kanyos Bio, Lava, Metavention, Minerva Surgical, Monteris Medical, Monte Rosa, NeuWave Medical, Northern Biologics, NousCom, Novira, Nuvaira, Oculeve, Okairos, Oyster Point Pharma, Pandion, Passage Bio, Pipeline, Piqur, Quanticel, Quentis, Repare, Sebacia, Sirocco, Tarveda, Tempest, Therachon, Turnstone, Twelve, VenatoRx, Veran, Vividion, WaveTec Vision

Other Locations:
6175 Nancy Ridge Dr.
San Diego, CA 92121
Phone: 858-224-7700

920 Broadway
16th Floor
New York, NY 10010
Phone: 646-357-1286

3601 W 76th St.
Suite 20
Edina, MN 55435
Phone: 612-254-1170

Aeschenvorstadt 36
Basel CH - 4051
Switzerland
Phone: 41-61-225-4600

887 Great Northern Way
Suite 210
Vancouver, BC V5T 4T5
Canada
Phone: 604-424-9913

Key Executives:
Brian Atwood, Managing Director
e-mail: brian@versantventures.com
Education: BA Biological Sciences, MA, University of California; MBA, Harvard Business School
Background: General Partner, Brentwood Venture Capital; President/CEO, Glycomed; Director, Perkin Elmer/Cetus Instruments
Ross Jaffe, Managing Director
e-mail: rjaffe@versantventures.com
Education: BA, Policy Studies, Dartmouth College; MD, Johns Hopkins University; MBA, Stanford University
Background: Analyst, Lewin & Associates; Research Associate, Dartmouth Medical School
William Link PhD, Co-Founder/Managing Director
Education: BA, MS, PhD, Mechanical Engineering, Purdue University
Background: Chairman/CEO, Chiron Vision; President, American Medical Optics; General Partner, Brentwood Venture Capital
Barbara Lubash, Managing Director
e-mail: barbara@versantventures.com
Education: BS, Tufts University; MS Health Policy & Management, Harvard University
Background: Venture Partner, Crosspoint Ventures; President, Pacific Review Services; Senior VP, Private Healthcare Systems
Don Milder, Managing Director
e-mail: don@versantventures.com
Education: BA in Economics, Union College; MBA, Harvard Business School
Background: General Partner, Crosspoint Venture Partners, CEO, Infusion Systems Corporation; President, TRIMED Corporation
Samuel D Colella, Managing Director
e-mail: scolella@versantventures.com
Education: BS, Business & Engineering, University of Pittsburgh; MBA, Stanford University
Background: President, New York Stock Exchange; President, Spectra-Physics
Rebecca B Robertson, Co-Founder/Managing Director
e-mail: brobertson@versantventures.com
Education: BS Chemical Engineering, Cornell University
Background: General Partner, Institutional Venture Partners; Director, Pro-Duct Health; and Appriva Medical; Advisor, The Innovation Factory; Senior VP, Chiron Diagnostics; Co-Founder/VP, Egis; Senior Management, Lifescan
Directorships: Benvenue, Intuity Medical, Novasys, Orametrix, Sebacia
Brad Bolzon, Managing Director
e-mail: brad@versantventures.com
Education: PhD, MS Pharmacology, University of Toronto; Post Doctoral Research training, Ottawa Heart Institute, Ottawa
Background: Executive VP, F. Hoffmann-La Roche; Management, Eli Lilly and Company
Charles M. Warden, Managing Director
e-mail: charles@versantventures.com
Education: Bachelors, Beloit College; MBA, Harvard Business School
Background: General Partner, Schroder Ventures Life Sciences; Investments, Boston Capital Ventures; Consultant, Monitor Company
Directorships: AcuFocus, Celula, Ceterix, ForSight Vision 4, ForSight Vision 5, Foundry Newco XII, Glumetrics, Halscion, Ocular Therapeutix, WaveTec Vision Systems
Robin Praeger, CFO/Managing Director
e-mail: robin@versantventures.com
Education: BS, Political Economics of Industrial Societies, University of California, Berkeley; MS, Taxation, Golden Gate University
Background: Tax Partner, Arthur Andersen
Kirk G Nielsen, Managing Director
e-mail: kirk@versantventures.com
Education: BS, Biology, Harvard College; MBA, Harvard Business School
Background: Sales, Medtronic
Directorships: Inceptus Medical, Holaira, Metavention, Respicardia, Sequent Medical, Zyga Technology

Venture Capital & Private Equity Firms / Domestic Firms

Jerel Davis, Managing Director
Education: PhD, Stanford University
Background: Associate Principal, McKinsey & Co.
Directorships: Quantical, Novira, Cripr, Inception 4, Inception 5, Northern, Turnstone, BlueRock, Repare, VenatoRx, Akero

Clare Ozawa, Managing Director
Education: BS, Stanford University; PhD, Stanford University Medical School
Background: Inception Sciences; Novartis Pharma; McKinsey & Co.
Directorships: Inception IBD, Oyster Point Pharma, Pipeline, Sirocco

Tom Woiwode, Managing Director
Education: PhD, Stanford University
Background: XenoPort
Directorships: Adverum, Aligos, Anokion, CODA, Crispr, Gritstone, Kanyos, Passage Bio, Tempest, Therachon, Vividion

1929 VERTICAL GROUP
106 Allen Road
Suite 207
Basking Ridge, NJ 07920

Phone: 908-277-3737
e-mail: info@vertical-group.com
web: www.vertical-group.com

Mission Statement: Acts as a venture capital firm focused on the fields of medical technology and biotechnology; principals act as founders, early-stage investors, major shareholders and executives of many of the medical technology industry's most successful companies; manages partnerships with a vertical range of investments including: early and late-stage venture companies; private operating companies of all sizes.

Geographic Preference: United States
Fund Size: $200 million
Founded: 1988
Average Investment: $500,000 - $10 million
Minimum Investment: $500,000
Investment Criteria: Seed, First-stage, Second-stage, Mezzanine
Industry Group Preference: Medical Devices, Technology, Biotechnology, Healthcare
Portfolio Companies: Atheromed, Biosurface Technologies, Flexuspine, Galil Medical, Home Dialysis Plus, Incumed, InPhenix, Meritage Pharma, Omada, Oncomed, ProteinSimple, Silk Road Medical, Singular BIO, Tepha, TetraLogic Pharmaceuticals, Tornier, ViaCyte

Other Locations:
530 Lytton Avenue
Suite 304
Palo Alto, CA 94301
Phone: 650-566-9060

Key Executives:
Richard B Emmitt, General Partner
e-mail: REmmitt@vertical-group.com
Education: BA, Economics, Bucknell University; MBA, Rutgers College
Background: Investment Analyst, Cyrus J Lawrence; F Eberstadt
Directorships: American Medical Systems, BioSet, ENTrigue Surgical, ev3 Inc., Galil Medical, Incumed, Tepha, Tornier

Jack W Lasersohn, General Partner
e-mail: JLasersohn@vertical-group.com
Education: JD, Yale Law School; MA, Fletcher School of Law & Diplomacy; BS, Physics, Tufts University
Background: F Eberstadt; Corporate Attorney, Cravath, Swaine & Moore
Directorships: Anova, Masimo Corporation, Oncomed, Phothera, Silk Road Medical

John E Runnells, General Partner
e-mail: JRunnells@vertical-group.com

Education: JD, Harvard Law School; BS, Business Administration, Pennsylvania State University
Background: Co-Founder, Paddington Partners; Partner, Wabster & Sheffield
Directorships: Anova, Dynamic Implants, Flexuspine, Incumed

Tony M Chou, General Partner
Education: BS, Physics & Electrical Engineering, Carnegie Mellon University; MD, Case Western Reserve University
Background: Abbott Vascular Division, Abbott Labotories; Vice President & General Manager, Vascular Closure; Director, Adult Cardiac Catheterization Laboratory

1930 VESEY STREET CAPITAL PARTNERS LLC
101 Avenue of the Americas
New York, NY 10013

Phone: 212-213-4156
web: www.vscpllc.com

Mission Statement: Vesey Street Capital Partners seeks to invest in businesses that can create value for hospitals, payors, and healthcare providers.

Geographic Preference: United States
Founded: 2014
Investment Criteria: Middle Market
Industry Group Preference: Healthcare Services
Portfolio Companies: Imedex, ScribeAmerica

Key Executives:
Adam Feinstein, Co-Founder/Managing Partner
Education: BS, Business Management, University of Maryland, College Park; CFA
Background: Senior VP, Corporate Development & Strategic Planning, Laboratory Corporation of America Holdings; Managing Director, Equity Research, Barclays Capital; Lehman Brothers

1931 VESTAR CAPITAL PARTNERS
245 Park Avenue
41st Floor
New York, NY 10167

Phone: 212-351-1600
e-mail: info@vestarcapital.com
web: www.vestarcapital.com

Mission Statement: Most successful opportunities are created by management teams, who respond positively to having increased operating autonomy and a meaningful ownership position in their companies.

Fund Size: $7 billion
Founded: 1988
Average Investment: $100 million - $3 billion
Minimum Investment: $50 million
Investment Criteria: LBO, MBO
Industry Group Preference: Consumer Products, Consumer Services, Financial Services, Healthcare, Media, Communications
Portfolio Companies: American Roland Foods, Big Heart Pet Brands, Civitas Solutions, DeVilbiss Healthcare, Gleason, Healthgrades, Hearthside Food Solutions, Institutional Shareholder Services, MediMedia USA, Press Ganey Associates, Radiation Therapy Services, St. John Knits, Sun Products, Tervita, Triton Container

Other Locations:
1555 Blake Street
#200
Denver, CO 80202
Phone: 303-292-6300

200 Clarendon Street
48th Floor

Boston, MA 02116
Phone: 617-247-1200
Key Executives:
  Daniel S. O'Connell, Founder & CEO
  Education: BA, Brown University, MBA, Yale Univeresity School of Management
  Background: Management Buyout Group, First Boston Corporation
  Robert L. Rosner, Founder & Co-President
  Education: BA, Economics, Trinity College; MBA, Wharton School
  Background: Management Buyout Group, The First Boston Corporation
  James P. Kelley, Founder
  e-mail: jkelley@vestarden.com
  Education: BS, University of Northern Colorado; JD, University of Notre Dame, MBA, Yale University School of Management
  Background: Senior Executive, Management Buyout Group, First Boston Corporation
  James L. Elrod Jr., Managing Director
  Education: AB, Colgate University; MBA, Harvard Business School
  Background: Executive VP Finance/Operations, Physicians Health Services; Managing Director/Partner, Dillon, Read & Company
  Nikhil J. Bhat, Managing Director
  Education: BS, Economics, Wharton School; MBA, Stanford Grad. School of Business
  Background: Advent International; Bain & Company
  Kevin A. Mundt, Managing Director
  Education: BA, Brown University; MBA, Harvard Business School
  Background: Consultant, Bain & Company; Managing Director, Marsh & McLennan; Mercer Oliver Wyman
  Roger C. Holstein, Managing Director
  Education: BA, Swarthmore College
  Background: CEO & President, WebMD Corporation; CEO, Consumer Health Services
  Winston H. Song, Managing Director
  Education: BS, Economics-Political Science, Columbia College; MBA, Wharton School
  Background: Global Leveraged Finance Group, Lehman Brothers; Strategic Partners Group At CSFB, Credit Suisse
  Directorships: Nonni's Foods; Presence Marketing; Woodstream; BRIC Arts Media
  Chris A. Durbin, Managing Director
  Education: BBA, University of Notre Dame; MBA, Kellogg Graduate School of Management
  Background: Managing Director, Strategy & Business Development, Bank of America's Global Wealth & Investment Management
  Kenneth O'Keefe, Managing Director & COO
  Education: AB, Economics, Brown University
  Background: Executive Vice President & CFO, Pyramid Communications; CEO & President, AMFM; President & COO, Clear Channel Radio Group
  Norman W. Alpert, Founder & Co-President
  Education: AB, Brown University
  Background: Senior Executive, Management Buyout Group, First Boston Corporation
  John B. Stephens, Managing Director
  Education: BA, Middlebury College
  Background: Leveraged Finance Group, Wachovia Securities; LEK Consulting

1932 VIDA VENTURES
Boston, MA

Mission Statement: A venture capital firm specializing in growth capital investments in the healthcare sector.
Fund Size: $255 million
Founded: 2017
Industry Group Preference: Healthcare, Biotechnology
Portfolio Companies: Homology Medicines, Pionyr Immunotherapeutics
Key Executives:
  Tefan Vitorovic, Co-Founder/Managing Director
  Education: BS, Biological Sciences, MS, Biology, Stanford University; MBA, Harvard Business School
  Background: Principal, Third Rock Ventures; Associate, TPG Capital; Investment Bankinf Analyst, Credit Suisse; Research Associate, Stanford University Medical Center
  Arie S. Belldegrun, Co-Founder/Managing Director
  Education: MD, Hebrew University of Jerusalem
  Background: Chairman/President/CEO, Kite Pharma; Chairman, Cougar Biotechnology; Chairman/Partner, Two River;
  Directorships: UCLA Institute of Urology Oncology; Cell Design Labs; Teva; SonaCare Medical; Talon Therapeutics; Paramount Aquisition; Chem Rx Corp.; Email Real Estate.com
  Fred Cohen, Co-Founder/Managing Director
  Education: MD, Stanford University School of Medicine
  Background: Senior Advisor, TPG Capital

1933 VILLAGE GLOBAL
440 Davis Street
San Francisco, CA 94111

web: www.villageglobal.vc

Mission Statement: Non-traditional venture capital network of successful founders providing capital to startups.
Investment Criteria: Early-Stage
Industry Group Preference: Digital Health, Fintech, SaaS, Consumer Internet
Portfolio Companies: ADDI, Airbase, Bumblebee Spaces, Certain Lending, Compound, Darkstore, Forethought, Kapwing, Ontic, Shipwell, Superplastic, Traptic
Key Executives:
  Ben Casnocha, Co-Founder & Partner
  Background: Co-Founder, New Anchor Foundation; Co-Founder & Partner, Allied Talent; Chief of Staff to Ried Hoffman; CEO, Start-Up of You; Partner, Wasabi Ventures; Co-Founder, Silicon Valley Junto; Founder & Chair, Comcate
  Anne Dwane, Co-Founder & Partner
  Education: BSBA, Georgetown University; MBA, Harvard Business School
  Background: Co-Founder & Partner, GSV Acceleration Fund; Chief Business Officer, Chegg; CEO, Zinch; General Manager, Monster Worldwide; Co-Founder, Military.com; Business Development, Interval Research
  Directorships: Harvard Business Publishing
  Peter Torenberg, Partner
  Education: BA, Economics & English Literature, University of Michigan
  Background: Founder & Chair, On Deck; Co-Founder & Chair, Token Daily; Community & Business Development, Product Hunt; Co-Founder & CEO, Rapt.fm; Product Marketing, Seelio; Business Development, Direct Brands

1934 VINE ST VENTURES
e-mail: info@vinestventures.com
web: www.vinestventures.com

Mission Statement: Vine Street Ventures is a venture capital investment firm dedicated to investing in internet and mobile businesses.
Industry Group Preference: Internet, Mobile, Consumer Internet
Key Executives:
  Dave Knox, Partner
  Background: Co-Founder, The Brandery; CMO, Rockfish; Brand Manager, P&G

Venture Capital & Private Equity Firms / Domestic Firms

Robert McDonald, Managing Member
Background: VC Attorney, Taft Stettinius & Hollister LLP; Co-Founder, The Brandery
JB Kropp, Founder
Background: Twitter, The Brandery
Marina Dedes Gallagher, Managing Member

1935 VINTAGE CAPITAL MANAGEMENT
4705 S Apopka Vineland Road
Suite 210
Orlando, FL 32819

Phone: 407-506-7085
web: www.vintagecapitalmanagement.com

Mission Statement: Vintage Capital Management is a private equity investor specializing in aerospace and defense, manufacturing and consumer sectors. They seek investment opportunities where they can project investment strategies that can be executed in a short amount of time.

Investment Criteria: Corporate Spinoffs; Consolidations and build-ups; Family Owned Businesses; Bankruptcy Acquisitions; Recapitalizations; Private Acquisitions; Management Buyouts; Toehold Public Company Investments

Other Locations:
627 Harland Street
Milton, MA 02186
Phone: 617-690-2580

Key Executives:
Brian Kahn, Founder/Managing Partner
e-mail: bkahn@vintcap.com
Education: BA, Harvard University
Background: Chair, White Electronic Designs Corporation; Chair, API Technologies Corporation; Director, Integral Systems Inc.; Director, Aarons Inc.
Directorships: Buddy Newco LLC; Good to Go Wheels and Tires; Flexi Compras
Andrew Laurence, Partner
e-mail: alaurence@vintcap.com
Education: BA, Harvard University
Background: Triumph Capital; Managing Director, Causeway Partners; Partner, Coral Reef Capital Partners

1936 VIRGINIA SMALL BUSINESS FINANCING AUTHORITY
101 N 14th Street
11th Floor
Richmond, VA 23219

Phone: 804-786-6585
e-mail: sbsd@sbsd.virginia.gov
web: www.sbsd.virginia.gov

Mission Statement: Ready to assist those businesses and non-profit organizations looking to grow in Virginia, the local economic development authorities and municipalities needing debt financing to attract businesses into their jurisdictions, as well as bankers seeking to find creative ways in which to make that next loan to a small business.

Investment Criteria: Fewer than 250 employees, less than $10 million in annual gross revenues for each of its last three fiscal years or has a net worth of $2 million or less

Other Locations:
851 French Moore, Jr. Boulevard
Suite 110
Abingdon, VA 24210
Phone: 276-676-3768

Key Executives:
Jennifer Mayton, Executive Director
804-593-2007
e-mail: jennifer.mayton@sbsd.virginia.gov
Anna Mackley, Chief Credit Officer & Operations Manager
804-371-8255
e-mail: anna.mackley@vdba.virginia.gov

Lawrence Wilder, Senior Policy Advisor
804-371-2064
e-mail: lawrence.wilder@sbsd.virginia.gov

1937 VISION CAPITAL
681 Fifth Avenue
14th Floor
New York, NY 10022

Phone: 212-303-6200
web: www.visioncapital.com

Mission Statement: Structured to provide investment and growth capital for companies with products and technologies appropriate for rapid expansion into global markets; targets European-based technology companies who are seeking to enter the US capital and product markets and US companies with premier venture backing seeking to enter the European market. Has an established network of partners and investors in Europe and the US to execute this Trans-Atlantic investment strategy. Seeks technology companies that have proven the innovation and commercial validity of their products by reaching a significant level of strength, recognition, market acceptance and material revenues, but have not yet been able to achieve their full international potential.

Geographic Preference: United States, Europe
Fund Size: $78 million
Founded: 1994
Average Investment: $3 million
Investment Criteria: Companies with expansion capital to accelerate the global expansion and growth process.
Industry Group Preference: Communications, Computer Related, Consumer Services, Distribution, Electronic Components, Instrumentation, Financial Services, Insurance, Industrial Services, High Technology, Software, Internet
Portfolio Companies: Education Corporation of America, Strategic Materials, Velocitel, Vitopel, United Initiators, Pantex International, Bormioli Rocco, New Evolution Ventures, ABL Technic, Metallwarenfabrik Gemmingen, Swisshaus, The Service Companies, Nordax Finans, JDR, BrightHouse, Pirtek Europe, Park Cake, Pork Farms, Portman Travel, DeltaRail, NuVision Engineering, Kinectrics, CPL Industries, Elegant Hotels Group

Key Executives:
William Wick, Managing Director & CFO
Education: AB, Economics, Stanford University; MBA, Kellogg Graduate School of Management
Background: CFO, ZoZa.com; CFO, QuickPower

1938 VISTA EQUITY PARTNERS
401 Congress Avenue
Suite 3100
Austin, TX 78701

Phone: 512-730-2400
web: www.vistaequitypartners.com

Mission Statement: Vista Equity Partners invests in enterprise software. They partner with organizations at every phase of growth to rise to the next level.

Other Locations:
180 North Stetson Avenue
Suite 4000
Chicago, IL 60601
Phone: 312-229-9500

55 Hudson Yards
Floor 23
New York, NY 10001
Phone: 212-804-9100

4 Embarcadero Center
Floor 20

San Francisco, CA 94111
Phone: 415-765-6500

1111 Broadway
Suite 1980
Oakland, CA 94607

Key Executives:
Robert Smith, Founder, Chair and CEO
Education: BS, Cornell University; MBA, Columbia Business School
Background: Co-Head, Enterprise Systems, Goldman Sachs
David Breach, COO/Chief Legal Officer
Education: BBA, Eastern Michigan University; JD, University of Michigan
Background: Senior Corporate Partner, Kirkland & Ellis

1939 VISTA VENTURE PARTNERS
306 Cambridge Avenue
Palo Alto, CA 94306

Phone: 650-252-0550
e-mail: info@vistavp.com
web: vistavp.com

Mission Statement: Vista VP is an early stage Venture Capital fund firm.

Key Executives:
Michael Spector, Founder
e-mail: michael@vistavp.com
Education: University of California; CPA; PFS
Background: Partner, Burr Pilger Mayer Inc.
Fern Mandelbaum, Managing Member
e-mail: fern@vistavp.com
Education: BA, Brown University; MBA, Stanford University
Background: Co-Founder and CEO, Skyline Products; Metcal, Bain and Co.; SRI International; Hewlett Packard
Aaron White
e-mail: aaron@vistavp.com
Education: University of San Francisco; CFP
Background: Consultant

1940 VITAL FINANCIAL LLC
7101 Wisconsin Avenue
Suite 1210
Bethesda, MD 20814

Phone: 415-297-6451
e-mail: casher@vitalfin.com
web: www.vitalfin.com

Mission Statement: To use our talents, insights, knowledge and experience to find, analyze and structure private equity and venture capital investments in companies so as to provide significantly above-market returns on our own capital and on the funds that co-investors entrust to our stewardship.

Founded: 2007
Average Investment: $1 - $5 million
Investment Criteria: Early-Stage, Later-Stage
Industry Group Preference: Software, Technology, Financial Services
Portfolio Companies: 10X Technologies, AxioMx, Booker Software, CD Dignostics, Certicom, Clinverse, Halfpenny Technologies, HealthTell, Lookingglass Cyber Solutions, NovaTract Surgical, Pervacio, QuantaLife, SchoolChapters, Shoefitr, Sparqd, Twist Bioscience, Spikes Security, TOMA Biosciences

Other Locations:
92 Hopmeadow Street
3rd Floor
Simsbury, CT 06809
Phone: 860-729-3247

Key Executives:
A Craig Asher, Principal
e-mail: casher@vitalfin.com

Education: Stanford University; MBA & MS, Industrial Engineering, Northwestern University
Background: Director, Product Management, Trigo Technologies; Consultant, Andersen Consulting
Nathaniel C Brinn, Principal
e-mail: nbrinn@vitalfin.com
Education: University of Delaware; MBA, Finance & Accounting, Fuqua School of Business, Duke University
Background: CEO, CR Certification Corporation; EVP, Corporate Development, Webster Bank; CEO, HSA Bank

1941 VIVO CAPITAL
505 Hamilton Ave.
Suite 207
Palo Alto, CA 94301

Phone: 650-688-0818 **Fax:** 650-688-0815
e-mail: info@vivocapital.com
web: www.vivocapital.com

Mission Statement: At Vivo Capital, we leverage our internal expertise in evaluating data to generate outsized returns for company founders and employees as well as for our investors. The majority of Vivo's investments are in U.S. based companies with therapeutic products in clinical development.

Geographic Preference: West Coast
Fund Size: $200 million
Founded: 1996
Average Investment: $2 million
Minimum Investment: $500,000
Investment Criteria: Seed, Start-Up, Later Stage, Mezzanine, PIPE
Industry Group Preference: Biotechnology, Health Related
Portfolio Companies: Aclaris Therapeutics, Agile Therapeutics, AirXpanders, Akari Therapeutics, Apellis Pharma, Ascendis Pharma, Aurinia, Biohaven Pharma, BioPharmX, Capnia, Carbylan Therapeutics, Durata Therapeutics, Eiger, Essentialis, Foamix, Harmony Biosciences, Impel NeuroPharma, Kadmon, Kala Pharmaceuticals, KalVista Pharma, MacroGenics, Medeor Therapeutics, MEI Pharma, Menlo Therapeutics, Minerva Surgical, Nabriva Therapeutics, Nora Therapeutics, Ocera Therapeutics, OncoGenex Pharma, Outpost Medicine, Palatin, ProNAi Therapeutics, REGENXBIO, Revance Therapeutics, Sagent Pharmaceuticals, Selecta Biosciences, Semnur Pharma, SentreHEART, Sierra Oncology, Soleno Therapeutics, Strongbridge Biopharma, Surgical Specialties, Synapse BioMedical, Trevena, TRIA Beauty, Tricida, Verona Pharma

Other Locations:
Suite 2504, Hong Yi Plaza
No. 288, Jiu Jiang Road
Huang Pu District
Shanghai 200001
China
Phone: 86-21-6888-0039 **Fax:** 86-21-6888-0095

Suite 1801, West Tower, Twin Towers
B12 Jianguomenwai Avenue
Chaoyang District
Beijing 100022
China
Phone: 86-10-5764-2288 **Fax:** 86-10-5764-2208

Rm B3, 5f, No.335, Sec.2, Dunhua S. Rd.
Da'an District
Taipei 10669
Taiwan
Phone: 886-2-2378-2268 **Fax:** 886-2-2378-2338

Key Executives:
Dr. Edgar G Engleman, Managing Partner
Education: BA, Harvard University; MD, Columbia University
Background: Cetus Immunie; Genlabs Technologies; National Medical Audit; Dendreon Corporation; CellGate Technologies

Venture Capital & Private Equity Firms / Domestic Firms

Dr. Frank Kung, Founding/Managing Partner
Education: BS, National Tsing Hua University; MBA, University of California
Background: Cetus Immune; Genlabs Technologies
Dr. Albert Cha, Managing Partner
Education: BS, MS, Electrical Engineering, Stanford University; MD, PhD, Neuroscience, University of California
Dr. Chen Yu, Managing Partner
Education: MD, MBA, Stanford University; BA, Biology, Harvard University
Shan Fu, Managing Partner
Education: BA, MA, Peking University
Background: Senior Managing Director, Blackstone

1942 VOLITION CAPITAL
111 Huntington Avenue
Suite 2700
Boston, MA 02199
Phone: 617-830-2100
e-mail: info@volitioncapital.com
web: www.volitioncapital.com

Mission Statement: Volition Capital is a growth equity firm that principally invests in high potential, founder-owned companies across different technology sectors. Our firm specializes in partnering with founders to help them achieve their fullest aspirations for their business.
Geographic Preference: United States & London
Founded: 2010
Average Investment: $5 - 10 million
Minimum Investment: $3 million
Investment Criteria: Growth Capital, Acquisition Capital
Industry Group Preference: Internet, SaaS, Information Services, Technology-Enabled Business, Infrastructure
Portfolio Companies: Chewy.com, Ensighten, G5, GlobalTranz, iPipeline, LoanLogics, The Resumator, Velocify, Visual IQ

Key Executives:
Larry Cheng, Managing Partner & Founder
617-830-2305
Fax: 617-203-1270
e-mail: lcheng@volitioncapital.com
Education: BA, Psychology, Harvard College
Background: Partner, Fidelity Ventures; Senior Associate, Battery Ventures; Associate, Bessemer Venture Partners
Directorships: Cortera, Ensighten, GlobalTranz, MFG.com
Roger Hurwitz, Managing Partner & Founder
617-830-2306
Fax: 617-203-1275
e-mail: roger@volitioncapital.com
Education: BS, Accounting, Syracuse University; MBA, The Wharton School
Background: Partner, Fidelity Ventures; Partner, Apax Partners; Vice President GE Equity, GE Capital
Sean Cantwell, Managing Partner & Founder
617-830-2318
Fax: 617-203-1269
e-mail: sean@volitioncapital.com
Education: BBA, University of Notre Dame; MBA, Harvard Business School
Background: Vice President, Fidelity Ventures; Summit Partners; Arthur Andersen, Principal, The Parthenon Group
Andy Flaster, Managing Partner & COO
Education: BS, Wharton School, University of Pennsylvania; Boston College
Background: CFO, Fidelity Ventures; VP, Thomas H. Lee Partners; Consultant, Coopers & Lybrand

1943 VOODOO VENTURES, LLC
643 Magazine
Suite 102
New Orleans, LA 70130
Phone: 504-298-8884
web: www.voodooventures.com

Mission Statement: Our core philosophy revolves around matching talented partners with great ideas to build businesses. By providing resources and expertise, we work with people wo make ideas into reality.
Portfolio Companies: Launchpad, Flatstack, Niko Niko, BarNotes, Federated Sample, Neighborland
Key Executives:
Chris Schultz, Founder

1944 VORTEX PARTNERS
2626 Cole Avenue
Dallas, TX 75204
Phone: 214-849-9806

Mission Statement: Venture capital firm committed to providing critical resources, contacts and capital to promising startups.
Founded: 1999
Investment Criteria: Startups
Industry Group Preference: Business Products & Services, Software
Portfolio Companies: OpsTechnology, Real Foundations, RealManage

Key Executives:
Christopher O'Neill, Founder/General Partner
e-mail: coneill@vortexpartners.com
Education: MBA, Stanford University; BS Chemical Engineering, BA Economics, Rice University
Background: General Partner, EFO Holdings; Investment Banking, Paine Webber
Tom Hedrick, Senior Partner
Education: BS, University of Notre Dame; MBA, Harvard Business School
Background: Senior Partner, McKinsey & Company; Co-Director, North American High Tech Practice; Texas Venture Capital & Private Equity Practice

1945 VOYAGER CAPITAL
719 Second Avenue
Suite 1400
Seattle, WA 98104
Phone: 206-438-1800 **Fax:** 206-438-1900
e-mail: joanne@smartconnectionspr.com
web: www.voyagercapital.com

Mission Statement: Voyager Capital is a leading West Coast information technology venture firm, providing entrepreneurs with the resources, experience, and connections to build successful companies. Voyager invests primarily in early-stage clean IT, digital media, software and services, wireless, and web infrastructure companies, where the firm's domain expertise and 'Go-to-Market' resources help build market leaders. Voyager Capital has $370 million under management with offices in Seattle, Washington; Menlo Park, California; and Portland, Oregon.
Geographic Preference: Pacific Northwest, Northern California
Fund Size: $370 million
Founded: 1997
Average Investment: $6 million over life of company
Minimum Investment: Early: $1-2.5 million; Growth: $3-5 million
Investment Criteria: Early-Stage, Growth
Industry Group Preference: Enterprise Services, Internet Technology, Business to Business, Wireless Technologies, Software, Infrastructure, Digital Media & Marketing

Portfolio Companies: Act-On Software, Alliance Health Networks, AnswerDash, aQuantive, Art2Wave, Attenex, Attensa, autoGraph, AutoGrid, Ayla Networks, Blue Box Group, Bonanza, Capital Stream, Captura Software, ChargePoint, Chirpify, ClearCare, ClearCommerce, Coolr, Covario, Elemental Technologies, Geoloqi, Global Market Insie, GoAhead Software, Kadiri, Kryptiq, Lighter Capital, Lytics, Medify, Melodeo, MindSumo, NetPodium, Nusym Technology, Photobucket, Placecast, Qsent, Rio SEO, SeeCommerce, Sensys Networks, Skyward, Tegic Communications, Tropos Networks, UBIX, Vidder, WellnessFX, Wise.io, Yapta, Zebra Imaging, Zettics

Other Locations:
3000 Sand Hill Road, 3-100
Menlo Park, CA 94025
Phone: 650-854-4300 **Fax:** 650-854-4399

1044 NW 9th Avenue
Portland, OR 97209
Phone: 503-621-6668

Key Executives:
Erik Benson, Managing Director
e-mail: benson@voyagercapital.com
Education: Graduate Pacific Lutheran University; Harvard Business School
Background: President, Mimix; JP Morgan Chase
Directorships: Act-On Software, Chirpify, Covario, Elemental Technologies, Lighter Capital, Lytics, UBIX, Zettics
Diane Fraiman, Managing Director
Education: Vanderbilt University; MBA, INSEAD
Background: Sequent Computer; Tektronix Video and Networking; Informix Software; Sanctum

1946 VULCAN CAPITAL

Phone: 206-342-2000
e-mail: press@vulcan.com
web: capital.vulcan.com

Mission Statement: A leading private equity firm that creates long-term value by applying extensive industry knowledge, operational expertise and flexible financial resources to attractive investment opportunities.

Founded: 2003
Investment Criteria: Early-Stage
Portfolio Companies: Asentium Capital, Enhanced Capital Partners, Makena Capital Management, Silvercrest, 4info, Audience, Avalanche Technology, Bizo, Flipkart.com, Gilt Groupe, Gist, Magic Leap, Redfin, Sand9, Scytl, SiOnyx, TrueCar, Zuora, Applied Proteomics, BiPar Sciences, Omeros, PTC Therapeutics, Charter Communications, DreamWorks Animation SKG, Laureate Education, Tower Co.

Key Executives:
Chris Orndorff, Chief Investment Officer
Education: BS, Miami University; MBA, University of Chicago; CFA
Background: Portfolio Manager, Western Asset; Portfolio Manager, Payden & Rygel; Portfolio Manager, Northern Trust

1947 W CAPITAL PARTNERS
400 Park Avenue
New York, NY 10022

Phone: 212-561-5240 **Fax:** 212-561-5241
web: www.wcapgroup.com

Mission Statement: W Capital Partners invests in companies to execute long-term growth plans.
Geographic Preference: USA and Europe
Fund Size: $2.3 Billion
Founded: 2001
Average Investment: $15 Million

Key Executives:
David Wachter, Co-Founder/Managing Partner
e-mail: dwachter@wcapgroup.com
Education: BS, Tufts University; MBA, New York University
Background: Investment Banker/Private Equity Investor, Lehman Brothers
Robert Migliorino, Co-Founder/Managing Partner
e-mail: migs@wcapgroup.com
Education: BS, Drexel University
Background: Founding Partner, Canaan Partners; GE Information Services
Stephen Wertheimer, Co-Founder/Managing Partner
e-mail: swertheimer@wcapgroup.com
Education: BS, Indiana University; MM, Northwestern University
Background: Head, Paine Webber Investments, Tokyo; Founder, Water Capital Management

1948 WACHTEL & CO. INC
1701 K Street NW
Suite 615
Washington, DC 20006

Phone: 202-898-1144
web: www.wachtelco.com

Geographic Preference: Greater Washington DC
Founded: 1961
Average Investment: $100,000 - $300,000
Investment Criteria: Startups, First Stage, Second Stage, Recapitalizations
Industry Group Preference: Technology

Key Executives:
Bonnie K Wachtel, CEO
Education: BA, MBA, University of Chicago; JD, University of Virginia
Background: Information Analysis; Intergrated Systems; VSE Corportaion

1949 WAFRA CAPITAL PARTNERS INC
350 Park Avenue
16th Floor
New York, NY 10022

Phone: 212-377-0030 **Fax:** 212-293-6345
web: www.wafracapital.com

Mission Statement: An affiliate of Wafra Inc., Wafra Capital Partners is a seperate operating entity and a US registered investment adviser. WCP specializes in structuring, leasing, finance and real estate products.

Founded: 2012

Key Executives:
Robert Toan, Chief Executive Officer
Education: JD, LLM, New York University
Background: Partner, Hughes Hubbard & Reed LLP; Partner, Baker & MacKenzie
Michael Gontar, Chief Investment Officer
Education: New York University
Background: Experienced Associate, KPMG LLP; President and Co-Founder, NY based real estate investment firm

1950 WAFRA INC
345 Park Avenue
41st Floor
New York, NY 10154-0101

Phone: 212-759-3700
web: wafra.com

Mission Statement: Wafra's private equity strategy targets middle-market investments, co-investments and club deals, seeking to leverage their network and partnerships. Their ven-

ture capital strategy seeks to invest in leading venture capital funds and companies where they have a strategic edge.
Fund Size: $14 billion
Founded: 1986
Average Investment: $300 million
Other Locations:
27 Knightsbridge
London SW1X 7LY
England
Phone: 44 203-966-9865

1703 W 5th Street
Suite 800
Austin, TX 78703
Phone: 212-759-3700

Al Soor Street
Twin Towers, 21st Floor, Block A
Mirqab
Kuwait
Phone: 965 222-663-52

Ideation House, 94 Pitts Bay Road
1st Floor
Pembroke HM 08
Bermuda
Phone: 441-824-3700

Key Executives:
Fawaz Al-Mubaraki, Chief Executive Officer
Education: BS, Kuwait University
Background: Portfolio Manager, Wafra; Analyst, Department of Public Institution, Kuwait
Russel Valdez, Chief Investment Officer
Education: BA, Stanford University; JD, Harvard Law School
Background: Corporate Associate, Covington & Burling; Chemonics International; Visa Europe

1951 WALDEN INTERNATIONAL
One California Street
Suite 1750
San Francisco, CA 94111
Phone: 415-765-7100 **Fax:** 415-765-7200
e-mail: walden@waldenintl.com
web: www.waldenintl.com

Mission Statement: Walden International looks to invest in early and expansion stage companies with an appreciation for leveraging talents and markets indepdenent of geography.
Geographic Preference: United States, China, India, Israel, Southeast Asia, Taiwan
Fund Size: +$1.6 Billion
Founded: 1987
Investment Criteria: Startup, Seed-Stage, Early-Stage, Expansion Stage
Industry Group Preference: Communications, Electronic Technology, Consumer Services, Software, Semiconductors, Digital Media & Marketing, Consumer Products, Clean Technology, Internet, Information Technology, Emerging Markets, Sectors & Technologies
Portfolio Companies: Aquantina Corp., Berkeley Lights Inc., Bolb Inc., Calysta Energy Inc., CNEX LABS Inc., DSP Concepts Inc., ETA Compute Inc., Innovium Inc., Inphi Corporation, InSense Inc., Lion Semiconductor Inc., LucidWorks Inc., MEMS Drive Inc., Mojo Networks, NOD Inc., Paxata Inc., Shakr Media Company, CugarCRM Inc., Synacor Inc., VeriSilicon Holdings Company Ltd., Volta Industries LLC
Other Locations:
World Financial Center, No. 1
DongSanHuan Zhong Road, Suite 1412, 14/F
West Tower
Chaoyang District, Beijing 100205
China
Phone: 86 10 8519 2519 **Fax:** 86 10 8519 2520

222 Yan An Road East
Suite 2501, Bund Center
Shanghai 200002
China
Phone: 86 21 3135 2488 **Fax:** 86 21 3135 2499

Walden International India
#20, 2nd Floor
Uniworth Plaza, Sankey Road
Bangalore 560 020
India
Phone: 91 80 2334 7000

36 Hashacham Street
Building D, 5th Floor
Petach-Tikva
Israel
Phone: 972 37 585 585 **Fax:** 972 3 535 0999

Walden International Singapore
71 Ayer Rajah Crescent #05-05
Singapore 139951
Singapore
Phone: 65 6272 3250 **Fax:** 65 6272 3251

No. 76, 18F-2, Tun Hua South Road
Sec. 2
Taipei
Taiwan
Phone: 866 2 2704 8018 **Fax:** 886 2 2704 2787

Key Executives:
Lip-Bu Tan, Chairman & Founder
Education: BS, Physics, Nanyang University, Singapore; MS, Nuclear Engineering, MIT; MBA, University of San Francisco
Background: Vice President, Chappell & Co.; EDS Nuclear; ECHO Energy
Brian Chiang, Managing Director, Taiwan
Education: BS, Electrical Engineering, California State University, Los Angeles; MBA, University of Southern California
Background: Marketing Director, New Idea Electronic Corporation; Senior Design Engineer, Toshiba Corporation
Andrew Kau, Managing Director, US
Education: BS, Electrical Engineering, Brown University; MBA, University of Virginia
Background: President, Chemical Technologies Ventures; Management Consultant, Strategic Planning Associates; Booz Allen Hamilton; Systems Planning Corporation; IBM
Bill Li, Managing Director, China
Education: BS, Computer Science, Huazhong University of Science & Technology; MS, University of San Francisco; MBA, Golden Gate University
Background: Venture Partner, GSR Ventures; Google
Hing Wong, Managing Director, China
Education: PhD, University of California Berkeley; SiChuan University; Chinese University of Hong Kong
Background: IBM; Chromatic Research; Silicon Access Networks
Yimin Zimmerer, Managing Director, China
Education: BA, Psychology, MS, Telecommunications, University of Colorado; MBA, University of California, Berkeley
Background: Director, Marketing, Ericsson Communications; Senior Manager, Business Development, Concert Communications; Senior System Engieer, MCI

Venture Capital & Private Equity Firms / Domestic Firms

1952 WALDEN VENTURE CAPITAL
750 Battery Street
Suite 700
San Francisco, CA 94111

Phone: 415-391-7225
web: www.waldenvc.com

Mission Statement: Walden Capital Partners L.P. is a Small Business Investment Company (SBIC) which targets companies in need of growth capital. Walden Capital invests in companies that have strong, proven management teams have passed the early stages of business development, and are positioned for expansion.

Geographic Preference: United States, Worldwide
Fund Size: $500 million
Founded: 1974
Average Investment: $1 million
Minimum Investment: $500,000
Investment Criteria: Seed, First-stage, Second-stage, Mezzanine
Industry Group Preference: Digital Media & Marketing, Cloud-Based IT Services, Software, Infrastructure
Portfolio Companies: Aarki, Blazent, Blue Lithium, BoomBotix, The Clymb, Comedy.com, Glam.com, Gump's, H5, Iconoculture, Image Vision Labs, Niku, Palamida, Pandora, PowerCloud Systems, SoundHound Inc., Telekenex, Terayon, VitalStream

Other Locations:
2105 Woodside Road
Woodside, CA 94062

Key Executives:
Arthur Berliner, Managing Director
Education: BA, University of California, Berkeley
Background: Founded, Walden Group, Sutro & Company
Larry Marcus, Managing Director
Education: BA, University of California, Berkeley
Background: Deutsche Bank Alex Brown, Roberston Stephens
Bill McDonagh, Venture Partner
Education: BBA, University of Notre Dame; MBA, Golden Gate University
Background: President & COO, Broderbund Software
Directorships: Apollo International
George Sarlo, Venture Partner
Education: BA, Harvard Graduate School of Business, BS, University of Arizona
Background: Vice President, William D Witter Inc, Portfolio Manager, Capital Research Inc
Matt Miller, Managing Director
Education: BA, Cornell University; MBA, Columbia University
Background: CEO, Moai Technologies; VP, Marketing, Remedy; Gupta Group
Directorships: H5 Technologies, Iconoculture, Ignite Technologies, Palamida, Market Insight
Robert Raynard, Chief Financial Officer
Education: BA, American University; MBA, Boston University
Background: Chief Financial Officer, Robertson Stephens Asset Management; Senior Manager, PricewaterhouseCoopers LLP

1953 WALL STREET VENTURE CAPITAL
110 Wall Street
11th Floor
New York, NY 10005

Phone: 877-748-4468 Fax: 800-860-9489
e-mail: wallstreetventurecapital@yahoo.com

Mission Statement: A venture capital firm dedicated to helping entrepreneurs realize their dreams of building world class companies that will become leaders in their field. We believe deeply in the value created by the entrepreneurial process and in the relentless pursuit of opportunity. We enjoy the challenge of aiming high and believe that by pursuing lofty goals, we will ultimately generate the highest returns of our investors.

Geographic Preference: Worldwide
Fund Size: $800 million
Founded: 1984
Average Investment: $1 - $5 million
Minimum Investment: $1 million
Investment Criteria: Business Plan, Board in Place
Industry Group Preference: Business to Business

Other Locations:
28 East Jackson Building
10th Floor
Chicago, IL 60604
Phone: 877-748-4468

75 State Street
Boston, MA 02109
Phone: 877-748-4468

23 Nanjing E Road
Shanghi 200002
China
Phone: 8621-63295787 Fax: 8621-63295787

1954 WALNUT GROUP
312 Walnut Street
Suite 1151
Cincinnati, OH 45202

Phone: 513-651-3300 Fax: 513-651-1084

Mission Statement: The Walnut Group makes capital investments across a broad range of industry sectors and also facilitates transactions throughout North America.

Geographic Preference: North America
Investment Criteria: Acquisitions, Growth Equity, Recapitalizations, Late-Stage Ventures, Mergers, Alliances
Industry Group Preference: Retail, Consumer & Leisure, Consumer Products, Media, Communications, Consumer Services, Business Products & Services, Manufacturing, Real Estate, Entertainment, Restaurants, Aerospace, Defense and Government, Security
Portfolio Companies: Adspace Networks, Ameristop, Argo Tea, Build-a-Bear Workshop, CAP (Children at Play) Toys, Changing Paradigms, Conserv, CWK Network, Deal$ Nothing Over a Dollar, Duke Realty, Empire Brushes, Goliath Solutions, Home Products International, Horizon Development, Imagitas (TMSI-Targeted Marketing Solutions), ITC, Logo Athletics, LoveSac, Marian Heath Greeting Cards, M Cubed Technologies, Medsite, Nelson Communications, North American Baking, PECO Pallet, Pinnacle Direct Marketing, Reborn Beauty, Renaissance Mark, Rookwood Pavillion, Seed Media Group, SimonDelivers, Sleek Medspa, Skylight.net, Sovereign Brands, Tapper Candies, Total Management & Earlybird Courier, Wild Things, WMI Holdings, Work 'n Gear

Key Executives:
Frederic H Mayerson, Chairman/Managing General Partner
Education: Miami University; University of Michigan Law School
Background: Chairman, United Sports Ventures; Principal, Frederic H Mayerson Group

1955 WAND PARTNERS
1 Union Square West
Suite 208
New York, NY 10003

Phone: 212-909-2620 Fax: 212-307-5599
web: www.wandpartners.com

Mission Statement: An active private equity sponsor and investor focused on specialty financial services. In all of our investments, database analysis and feed-back driven

Venture Capital & Private Equity Firms / Domestic Firms

decision-making are central to the management's approach to business.
Fund Size: $250 million
Founded: 1985
Minimum Investment: $3 million
Investment Criteria: Seed, First-stage, Second-stage, Mezzanine
Industry Group Preference: Distribution, Energy, Natural Resources, Financial Services, Food & Beverage, Insurance, Industrial Services
Portfolio Companies: American Independent Companies, Paraline Group

Key Executives:
   Bruce W Schnitzer, Managing Director & Chairman
   212-949-1729
   Education: University of Texas, Austin; MBA, University of Texas, Austin
   Background: Director, Marsh & McLennan Companies; President & CEO, Marsh & McLennan Incorporated; Vice President, JP Morgan/Morgan Guaranty Trust Company
   John S Struck, Managing Director
   212-909-2620
   e-mail: jstruck@wandpartners.com
   Education: BA, Economics, University of Rhode Island
   Background: Principal, Friday Holdings; President, BIS Strategic Decisions; Director, Prudential Bache Securities, Corporate Finance; General Electric Corporation

1956 WARBURG PINCUS LLC
450 Lexington Avenue
New York, NY 10017
Phone: 212-878-0600 **Fax:** 212-878-9351
e-mail: info@warburgpincus.com
web: www.warburgpincus.com

Mission Statement: Warburg Pincus' private equity investment activities combine human and capital resources to make long-term investments. The firm takes an active role in the development of its investments and employs its professional, financial, and business skills to enhance investment results. Warburg Pincus does not itself run businesses on a day-to-day basis; rather it works in partnership with managements and makes its knowledge, experience, and relationships available to the companies in which it invests in a positive and supportive manner. In every case in which the firm makes a direct equity investment, the portfolio company's management also holds a significant equity stake to ensure that its interests are parallel to those of Warburg Pincus.

Geographic Preference: Worldwide
Fund Size: $5 billion
Founded: 1939
Minimum Investment: $10 million
Investment Criteria: Late-Stage, Developing, Expanding, Startup, Early-Stage, Recapitalizations, Buy-Outs
Industry Group Preference: Information Technology, Healthcare, Media, Communications, Energy, Financial Services, Business Products & Services
Portfolio Companies: 58.com, A Place for Mom, AAG Energy Limited, ACB (India), Accriva Diagnostics, Aeolus Re, AmRest, Amtek Auto, Antero Resources, Aramark, Association of Certified Anti-Money Laundering Specialists, Au Financiers, AVTEC, Banco Indusval & Partners, Beijing Amcare Women's & Children's Hospital, Beijing Tianyu Communications Equipment, Biba Apparels, Black Swan Energy, Bridgepoint Education, Brigham Resources, Builders FirstSource, Canbriam Energy, Capital First Limited, Ceres, China Auto Rental, China Biologic Products, China Kidswant, Clondalkin, Competitive Power Ventures Holdings, ComplexCare Solutions, Consolidated Precision Products, Continental Warehousing, Coyote Logistics, Crossmark, CrowdStrike, Delonex Energy, Diligent Power Private, e-Sharing, Endurance Energy, Evidon, Explora Petroleum, Extant Components, FacilitySource, Fairfield Energy, First Green Partners, Franshion Properties, Gangavaram Port, GrubHub Seamless, GT Nexus, Gulf Coast Energy Resources, Hawkwood Energy, Home Dialysis, IMC Limited, InComm, INEA, Interactive Data, International Asset Systems, iParadigms, JHP Pharmaceuticals, Jida Pharmaceuticals, Keystone Dental, Kontron, Kosmos Energy, Koudai Shopping, Laredo Petroleum Holdings, Lemon Tree, Liaison International, MBIA, MEG Energy, Melinta Therapeutics, Metropolis Healthcare Limited, MultiView, National Penn Bancshares, New Breed Logistics, Omega Energia Renovael S.A., onTargetjobs, Osum Oil Sands, Pet Center Comercio and Participacoes S.A., Poundland,

Other Locations:
   One Market Plaza
   Spear Tower, Suite 1700
   San Francisco, CA 94105
   Phone: 415-796-5200 **Fax:** 415-659-0045

   4400 Post Oak Pkwy
   Suite 1900
   Houston, TX 77027
   Phone: 713-325-5360 **Fax:** 713-583-9309

   Warburg Pincus Investment Consulting Co Ltd
   9th Floor, China World Tower 1,
   1 Jianguomenwai Avenue
   Beijing 100004
   China
   Phone: 86-1059232533 **Fax:** 86-1065056683

   Warburg Pincus India Ptv Ltd
   7th Floor, Express Towers
   Nariman Point
   Mumbai 400021
   India
   Phone: 91-2266500000 **Fax:** 91-2266500001

   Warburg Pincus Asia LLC
   Suite 6703
   Two International Finance Center, 8 Finance Street
   Hong Kong
   Phone: 852-25366183 **Fax:** 852-25213869

   Almnack House
   28 King Street, St. James's
   London SW1Y 6QW
   United Kingdom
   Phone: 44-2073060306 **Fax:** 44-2073210881

   Warburg Pincus Shanghai Branch
   45/F, HKRI Center One, HKRI Taikoo Hui
   No. 288 Shimen Yi Rd.
   Shanghai 200041
   China
   Phone: 86-2160577388 **Fax:** 86-2160577310

   Warburg Pincus do Brasil Ltda.
   Av. Brig. Faria Lima 2277- 9 andar
   Jd. Paulistano
   Sao Paulo 01451-001
   Brazil
   Phone: +55 11 3096 3500 **Fax:** +55 11 3096 3509

   Warburg Pincus Singapore Pte Ltd.
   50 Collyer Quay
   #06-04, OUE Bayfront
   Singapore 049321
   Singapore
   Phone: +65 6320-7500 **Fax:** +65 6634-0119

Key Executives:
   Charles R Kaye, Co-CEO
   Education: University of Texas
   Directorships: Partnership for New York City
   Joseph P Landy, Co-CEO
   Education: BS, Economics, Wharton School; MBA, Leonard N Stern School of Business, New York University
   Julian Cheng, Managing Director, Co-Head of China
   Education: BA, Harvard University
   Background: Salomon Smith Barney; Bankers Trust

Venture Capital & Private Equity Firms / Domestic Firms

Mark M Colodny, Managing Director
Education: AB, Harvard University; MBA, Harvard Business School; JD, Harvard Law School
Background: SVP Corporate Development, Primedia
Directorships: Helix, Liaison International, MultiView
Steven G Glenn, Managing Director, CFO
Education: BS, Binghamton University; MS, SUNY Albany; JD, Fordham University
Background: Partner, Ernst & Young
In Seon Hwang, Managing Director
Education: BS, Wharton School; MBA, Harvard Business School
Background: GSC Partners; Goldman Sachs; Boston Consulting Group
Peter Kagan, Managing Director
Education: AB, Harvard College; JD & MBA, University of Chicago
Background: Investment Banking, Salomon Brothers
Directorships: Antero Resources, Broad Oak Energy, Fairfield Energy, Laredo Petroleum, MEG Energy, Targa Resources
Robert B Knauss, Managing Director, General Counsel
Education: Harvard University; University of Michigan Law School
Background: Partner, Munger Tolles & Olson LLP
Vishal Mahadevia, Managing Director, Head of India
Education: BS, University of Pennsylvania
Background: Principal, Greenbriar Equity Group
Michael Martin, Managing Director
Education: BS, Economics, Claremont Men's College; JD, Columbia University School of Law
Background: President, Brooklyn NY Holdings; Managing Director, UBS Investment Bank
Directorships: Sallie Mae, Aeolus Re, Cortview Capital, National Penn Bancshares, Primerica, The Mutual Fund Store
James Neary, Managing Director
Education: BA, Tufts University; MBA, Kellogg School of Management
Background: Managing Director, Chase Securities
John W Shearburn, Managing Director
Education: Vanderbilt University; University of North Carolina
Background: Managing Director, Goldman Sachs
Christopher Turner, Managing Director, CAO
Education: BS, Cornell University; MBA, Finance, Leonard N Stern School of Business, New York University
Background: Managing Director, Goldman Sachs; Bankers Trust Company
Frank Z Wei, Managing Director, Co-Head of China
Education: BS, University of Texas; MBA, Harvard Business School
Background: Morgan Stanley; McKinsey & Co.
Daniel Zilberman, Managing Director, Head of Europe
Education: BA, Tufts University; MBA, Wharton School
Background: Evercore Capital Partners; Lehman Brothers

1957 WARWICK GROUP
51 Locust Avenue
Suite 202
New Cannan, CT 06840

Phone: 203-966-7447 Fax: 203-966-2199
e-mail: info@warwickgroup.com
web: www.warwickgroup.com

Mission Statement: A private equity firm specializing in the acquisition and recapitalization of profitable businesses with revenues up to $100 million.

Founded: 1970
Investment Criteria: Mergers, Acquisitions, Leveraged Buy-outs, Recapitalization
Industry Group Preference: Proprietary Products, Services, Distribution, Manufacturing

Portfolio Companies: CMG Holdings, e-Government Solutions, Premier Kids Care

1958 WASABI VENTURES
San Mateo, CA

web: www.wasabiventures.com

Mission Statement: Wasabi Ventures is a venture capital, incubator, and consulting firm that specializes in building and advising early stage technology companies. In the last 10 years, Wasabi Ventures has built, financed, and advised over 200 start-ups including some wildly successful ventures like Right Now Technologies, PBworks, Ustream, and Etherpad.

Geographic Preference: United States
Industry Group Preference: Advertising, E-Commerce & Manufacturing, Energy, Gaming, Healthcare Information Technology, Media, Mobile, Social Media, Technology
Portfolio Companies: Caplinked, UserTesting, Statisfy, Vidfall, Motion Math, Appglu, Apply Kit, Canvs+, CreativeGig, Cube26, Funsherpa, Gizmo, Haystagg, Humanoid, inVino, LawPivot, LSAT, Lutebox, Monstrous, Mosaic, Motifworks, PathSource, PBWorks, PEKU Publications, Postling, Proven.com, QuickAirLink, RepairPal, SalesGoose, SocialToaster, Roomi, SpeakerText, Immediatelyapp.com, SwitchNote, 500friends, Takeoff, TestSoup, Trove, TrackR, TrustEgg, Uconnect, UStream, Vidstructor, Wanderu

Key Executives:
Tom Kuegler, Co-Founder/Managing Partner
e-mail: tk@wasabiventures.com
Background: Co-Founder, SNT & SpinBox
Chris Yeh, Co-Founder/Managing Partner
e-mail: chris@wasabiventures.com
Education: Stanford University, MBA, Harvard Business School
Background: Founding Team, United Online Services, Merrill Lynch Intelligent Technologies Group

1959 WASHINGTON CAPITAL VENTURES
PO Box 9929
McLean, VA 22102

Fax: 703-827-0522
e-mail: info@wcvonline.com

Mission Statement: Venture capital firm investing in early stage and Mid-Atlantic based technology companies.

Geographic Preference: East Coast
Founded: 2001
Investment Criteria: Early Stage
Industry Group Preference: Technology, High Technology, Networking, Communications

Key Executives:
Lev Volftsun, Co-Founder & Managing Partner
Background: General Manager/Vice President, Cisco Systems, Co-Founded Lightspeed International, MCI, Stratus, British Telecom And Concert

1960 WASSERSTEIN & CO.
1185 Avenue of the Americas
39th Floor
New York, NY 10036

Phone: 212-702-5602
e-mail: contact@wasserco.com
web: www.wasserco.com

Mission Statement: A leading independent private equity and investment firm focused on middle-market leveraged buyout investments and related investment activities.

Fund Size: $2 billion
Founded: 1996
Minimum Investment: $2 million
Investment Criteria: Leveraged Buy-outs, Middle-Market
Industry Group Preference: Communications, Computer Related, Consumer Services, Genetic Engineering, Internet

Venture Capital & Private Equity Firms / Domestic Firms

Technology, Medical & Health Related, Media, Consumer Products, Water
Portfolio Companies: ALM Media, Globecomm Systems, High Pressure Equipment Company, Paris Presents, Penton Media, Recorded Books
Other Locations:
  1999 Avenue of the Stars
  Suite 2840
  Los Angeles, CA 90067-6086
  Phone: 310-286-3315 **Fax:** 310-286-3325
Key Executives:
  Ellis Jones, Chairman
  Education: Yale School of Management; University of California at Berkeley
  Background: Wasserstein Perella & Co.; Managing Director, Salomon Brothers; Vice President Investment Banking, The First Boston Corporation
  Directorships: Element K; True Advantage; Phoenix House; Cate School
  Rajay Bagaria, President/CIO
  Education: BA, Individualized Study, New York University; London School of Economics
  Background: Partner, Apollo Investment Management; Goldman Sachs
  Directorships: LVI Services Inc.; Generation Brands; Playpower Inc.; The Manitou School
  Joseph Dutton, Chief Financial/Compliance Officer
  Education: MS, Economics, University College Dublin; Joint Honors degree, Business & Economics, Trinity College Dublin
  Background: Senior Product Manager, JP Morgan
  Andrew McLellan, Managing Director
  Education: BS, Finance & Government, University of Notre Dame
  Background: SVP, Sheffield Asset Management; Apollo Global Management; Analyst, Deutsche Bank
  Alex Kelsey, Vice President
  Education: BS, University of Wisconsin; CFA
  Background: Leveraged Credit Research Group, Jefferies LLC
  Ralph Montana, Controller
  Education: BS, Finance & Economics, City University of New York
  Background: State Street Investment Management Services
  Sean O'Keefe, Director
  Education: BBA, Western New England University
  Background: S&P Capitala

1961 WATER STREET HEALTHCARE PARTNERS
333 West Wacker Drive
Suite 2800
Chicago, IL 60606

Phone: 312-506-2900
e-mail: info@wshp.com
web: waterstreet.com

Mission Statement: A strategic private equity firm focused exclusively on healthcare. Our team of healthcare executives invest their experience and insight to build market-leading companies of lasting value.

Founded: 2005
Average Investment: $50 - $500 million
Investment Criteria: Middle-Market Companies
Industry Group Preference: Healthcare, Diagnostics, Medical Products & Services, Pharmaceuticals, Specialty Distribution, Life Sciences, Healthcare Services
Portfolio Companies: Access MediQuip, BioClinica, Breg, CareCentrix, Celerity Pharmaceuticals, HealthPlan Holdings, MarketLab, New Century Health, Orgentec, Premise Health, RTI Surgical, Sarnova, Temptime

Key Executives:
  Tim Dugan, Managing Partner
  Education: Stanford University; MBA, University of Chicago Graduate School of Business
  Background: Founder & Partner, First Chicago Equity Capital; Director, One Equity Partners
  Directorships: AAIPharma, HealthPlan Holdings, Sarnova
  Kevin Swan, Founding Partner
  Education: University of Southern Illinois
  Background: President & CEO, Health Alliance; Group President, McKesson Medical Distribution; President & CEO, Griffith Micro Science/Sterigenics; Operating Partner, One Equity Partners
  Directorships: Precision Dynamics Corporation, Sarnova
  Chris Sweeney, Founding Partner
  Education: Williams College
  Background: Principal, Cleary & Oxford
  Directorships: Precision Dynamcis Corporation, Sarnova
  Robert Womsley, Partner
  Education: Vanderbilt University; MBA, University of Chicago Graduate School of Business
  Background: Senior Partner, Citi Private Equity
  Directorships: Medical Specialties Distributors

1962 WATERMILL GROUP
One Cranberry Hill
750 Marrett Road
Suite 401
Lexington, MA 02421

Phone: 781-891-6660
e-mail: kurstell@watermill.com
web: www.watermill.com

Mission Statement: Invests in a variety of industries, with a preference for medium-growth companies which are experiencing structural change due to new competitive market dynamics, new technologies, consolidation or shifts in demand.

Geographic Preference: United States
Founded: 1978
Minimum Investment: $1,000,000
Investment Criteria: Middle-market, manufacturing and value-added distribution, moderate industry growth, reasonable industry margins, market or segment leadership
Industry Group Preference: Metals, Building Materials & Services, Manufacturing, Environmental Protection, Chemicals, Wood Industries, Transportation, Distribution, Business Products & Services
Portfolio Companies: Fine Tubes, Superior Tube, FutureMark Group Manistique, Multilayer Coating Technologies, C&M Corporation, Tenere, The Plastics Group

Key Executives:
  Steven E Karol, Managing Partner & Founder
  e-mail: skarol@watermill.com
  Education: BS, Tufts University, President's Program on Leadership, Harvard Business School
  Directorships: HMK Enterprises
  Julia Karol, President and COO
  e-mail: jkarol@watermill.com
  Education: BA, Tufts University; MA, Stanford University; Harvard Business School
  Background: Jumpstart; Partner, Social Venture Partners, Boston
  Dale S Okonow, Senior Partner
  e-mail: dokonow@watermill.com
  Education: BS, Cornell University; JD & MBA, Cornell University
  Background: Partner, President & COO, Sawyer Realty Holdings; General Counsel & CFO, HMK Enterprises
  Benjamin P Procter, Senior Partner
  e-mail: bprocter@watermill.com
  Education: BA, Economics, Trinity College; MS, Accounting, Northeastern University
  Background: Director Financial Planning, HMK Enterprises

Venture Capital & Private Equity Firms / Domestic Firms

Robert W Ackerman, Senior Partner
e-mail: backerman@watermill.com
Education: Yale University; MBA & DBA, Harvard Business School
Background: Chairman & CEO, Sheffield Steel Corporation; President & CEO, Lincoln Pulp & Paper Company; President, Premoid Corporation

1963 WAUD CAPITAL PARTNERS LLC
300 North LaSalle Street
Suite 4900
Chicago, IL 60654

Phone: 312-676-8400 **Fax:** 312-676-8444
e-mail: info@waudcapital.com
web: www.waudcapital.com

Mission Statement: Founded in 1993, Waud Capital Partners is a leading middle-market private equity firm that partners with exceptional management teams to create, acquire, and/or grow companies that address significant, inefficient, highly fragmented and underserved industry segments. We invest primarily through control-oriented growth equity investments, industry consolidations, buyouts, or recapitalizations and seek companies that generate strong cash flow and can be grown both organically and through add-on acquisitions.

Geographic Preference: United States
Fund Size: $1 billion
Founded: 1993
Average Investment: $20-100 million
Minimum Investment: $20-100 million
Investment Criteria: Exceptional Management Teams, Market Niches, Strong Market, Growth Potential, Record of Historical Profitability
Industry Group Preference: Manufacturing, Distribution, Services
Portfolio Companies: Acadia Healthcare, Adreima, Adult & Pediatric Dermatology, ASG Security, Aquion Water Treatment, CarePoint Partners, The Center for Vein Restoration, Chirotouch, Cogent Healthcare, Compex, Cordant, CyberGrants, Dimensional Dental, DS Medical, Heart & Paw, iOffice, Ivy Rehab, Jazz Pharmaceuticals, National Security Partners, Optimum Outcomes, Parish Publishing Solutions, Pharmacy Partners, Pilot Thomas Logistics, ProNerve, PSI, Regency Hospital Company, Sphere, The GI Alliance, True Partners, Unifeye Vision Partners

Key Executives:
Reeve B Waud, Founder/Managing Partner
312-676-8450
e-mail: rwaud@waudcapital.com
Education: BA, Economics, Middlebury College; MA, Management, JL Kellogg Graduate School, Northwestern University
Background: Founder, Sovereign Specialty Chemicals; Founder, Pacer Propane LP; Investment Professional, Golder, Thoma, Cressey & Rauner; Corporate Finance, Salomon Brothers
Directorships: Alarm Security Group LLC, Whitehall Products, Christiana Industries, Parish Publications
Matt Clary, Partner
312-676-8406
e-mail: mclary@waudcapital.com
Education: BA, Economics, University of Washington; MBA, Kellogg School of Management, Northwestern University
Background: Partner, Banc of America Capital Investors; Senior Associate, Corporate Banking Group, Bank of America
Directorships: Aquion Water Treatment Products, CarePoint Partners, Hospitalists Management Group
David Neighbors, Partner
312-676-8407
e-mail: dneighbours@waudcapital.com
Education: BBA, Finance, University of Notre Dame
Background: Citigroup Investments, Salomon Smith Barney
Directorships: Hospitalists Management Group, Regency Hospital Company, True Partners Consulting
Justin C Dupere, Partner
e-mail: jdupere@waudcapital.com
Education: BS, Wharton School; MBA, Kellogg School of Management
Background: GTCR; Morgan Stanley
Directorships: ChiroTouch, CuberGrants, iOffice, PSI Services, Sphere Payments
Christopher J Garber, Partner
e-mail: cgraber@waudcapital.com
Education: BA, Duke University; MBA, Kellogg School of Management
Background: Baird & Co.
Directorships: Cordant Health Solutions, Pharmacy Partners, Unifeye Vision Partners
Mark Flower, Chief Financial Officer
312-676-8425
e-mail: mflower@waudcapital.com
Education: BBA, Accounting & Finance, University of Wisconsin; CPA
Background: Vector Fund Management, Arthur Andersen, Kemper Financial Services, Kemper Asset Management, Iowa Grain Company

1964 WAVELAND INVESTMENTS LLC
900 North Michigan Avenue
Suite 1100
Chicago, IL 60611

Phone: 312-506-6450
web: wvlnd.com

Mission Statement: Waveland Investments targets lower middle market companies based in the United States, with focus on the manufacturing, distribution and service industries. Waveland pursues profitable businesses with talented management teams.

Geographic Preference: United States
Founded: 2000
Average Investment: $5 - $10 million
Investment Criteria: Buyouts, Growth Stage
Industry Group Preference: Manufacturing, Distribution, Business Products & Services, Consumer Services, Financial Services
Portfolio Companies: Better Things, CCS, Clark Brands, Daddies Board Shop, Doodad, Fluidmesh Networks, Hudson Lock LLC, Indiana Business Bank, Justice Design Group, NTE Aviation LLC, O2 Cool

Other Locations:
1850 Second Street
Suite 201
Highland Park, IL 60035

Key Executives:
Dennis Zaslavsky, Founder/Partner
312-506-6460
e-mail: dzas@wavelandinvestments.com
Education: BBA, University of Michigan; JD, Stanford University; CPA
Background: COO, Urban Shopping Centers; JMB Realty Corporation; Katten Muchin & Zavis
Meghan Otis, Partner
312-506-6470
e-mail: motis@wavelandinvestments.com
Education: BA, Mathematics, Northwestern University; MBA, Harvard Business School
Background: Goldman Sachs & Co.; LaSalle Partners
Phil Calian, Operating Partner
312-506-6490
e-mail: pcalian@wavelandinvestments.com
Education: BA, Chemistry, Brown University
Background: Founder & Managing Partner, Kingsbury Partners; American Classic Voyages Co.; CFI Industries Inc.

Venture Capital & Private Equity Firms / Domestic Firms

1965 WAVEMAKER PARTNERS
1333 Second Street
Suite 600
Santa Monica, CA 90401

Phone: 310-861-2100
Toll-Free: 800-875-0757
web: www.wavemaker.vc

Mission Statement: We invest in a broad range of technology-driven companies that are catalysts for change.

Industry Group Preference: Seed, Technology
Portfolio Companies: 500 Startups, Adly, Adomic, Advent, Affinity Neworks, Amplify, Art of Click, Ayannah, BeTheBeast.com, Breaker, Bridg, Buzzstarter, Caplinked, Card.com, Cloud Access, Club W, Craftyful, Dealflicks, DFR, DSTLD, East Club, Eko, Ellie, Exist, Fanbread, FGL, FloQast, Four Eyes, Frenzoo, Gem, Gimmie, Groupsite, Gushcloud, Healint, HipVan, Investedin, Kalibrr, Laurel & Wolf, Leagues, Lingia, Luxola, Maestrodev, Markkit, MCN, Morph Labs, My New Financial Advisor, Naritiv, Nativo, OpenX, P4RC, Phunware, PicoCandy, Pie, Playsino, Pollenizer, Praized, Prospect Medical, RadPad, Ranker, Rexter, Ribbon, RxVantage, Science, Shift, ShipHawk, ShopYourWorld.com, Shop Genius, Simple Reach, SKOut, Smove, SOA Software, SocialAnnex, Squabbler, Stack Commerce, StaffRanker, StrikeAd, Strong Ventures, Structo, SurfAir, Takelessons, Technorati, Telly, TheBouqs.com, Trade Gecko, Trade Sparq, TransferSoft, Twitmusic, Uncovet, Vator.tv, Viagogo, VideoAmp, Vow To Be Chic, Webtide, Whisk, Xyleme, YouMail, Zap, Zumata

Key Executives:
  Eric Manlunas, Founder/Managing Partner
  Education: BS, Communications, Florida International University; MBA, Pepperdine University
  Background: Frontera Group; Founder, Sitestar; Siemer Ventures

1966 WAVEPOINT VENTURES
535 Middlefield Road
Suite 280
Menlo Park, CA 94025

Phone: 650-331-7393 Fax: 650-331-7393
e-mail: info@wavepointventures.com
web: www.wavepointventures.com

Mission Statement: Wavepoint helps committed teams bring unique innovations to market faster and more efficiently, resulting in more wealth creation for entrepreneurs and investors.

Average Investment: $15 Million
Investment Criteria: Seed, Early-Stage
Industry Group Preference: Information Technology, Clean Technology, Medical
Portfolio Companies: Cloud Cruiser, dotFX, Marrone Bio Innovations, Second Genome, Sentilla, Sevenly, Vandolay, Velomedix, Vertascale Software

Other Locations:
  535 Middlefield Road
  Suite 280
  Menlo Park, CA 94025
  Phone: 650-331-7393 Fax: 650-331-7393

1967 WAYZATA INVESTMENT PARTNERS
One Carlson Parkway North
Suite 220
Plymouth, MN 55447

Phone: 952-345-0700
web: www.wayzatainvestmentpartners.com

Mission Statement: At Wayzata, we uncover and actively manage unique alternative investment opportunities, consistently delivering success for our investors.

Founded: 2004

Portfolio Companies: Perkins Restaurant & Bakery, MasterCraft, Grede Casting, Merisant, Star Tribune Media Holdings, Lazydays, Arrow Storage Products, Key Plastics, Majestic Star, Portola, SuperService, Tembec, Stallion, Propex, Topack Fittings, Caraustar, Anchor Glass, Hawkeye Renewables, SDI Special Devices, RathGibson, US Corrugated, Pliant, AMES, Smurfit-Stone, Guadalupe Power, Minnetonka Tankers, Sundevil Power, Midgard, Sea Transportation-Dry Bulk, East Shore Aircraft, Mint Farm Energy, Cascade Pacific Pulp, California Power, CityNorth, Cobalt Office Park

1968 WEBB INVESTMENT NETWORK
web: www.winfunding.com

Mission Statement: Our goal is to invest in companies that aim to change the world, particularly in the fields of cloud computing, enterprise software, mobile, marketplaces, e-commerce, crowdsourcing, and consumer internet.

Average Investment: $350,000
Minimum Investment: $250,000
Investment Criteria: Seed, Later Stage
Industry Group Preference: Information Technology
Portfolio Companies: Aero, AppLovin, Badgeville, Bitnet, BitYota, Boost CTR, CloudHelix, Diffbot, Epic, Everwise, Grubwithus, Hangtime, Hellosign, Hipmunk, Indiegogo, Ionic Security, LiveLoop, Local Response, Lockpath, Meteor, Nebula, Okta, Opscode, Pagerduty, Panorama, Pepperdata, Pindrop Security, Quixey, RelayRides, Respondly, RethinkDB, Science Exchange, StarMobile, Takelessons, Tapsense, Tenxer, TrueAccord, Upstream Commerce, Voxer, Vungle, Wavefront, We Pay, Workspot, Yozio, Zanbato, Zuora

Key Executives:
  Maynard Webb, Founder
  Education: Florida Atlantic University
  Background: COO, eBay; CEO, LiveOps; Co-Founder, Everwise; Author

1969 WEDBUSH CAPITAL PARTNERS
1000 Wilshire Boulevard
Suite 830
Los Angeles, CA 90017

Phone: 213-688-8018 Fax: 213-688-8095
web: www.wedbushcapital.com

Mission Statement: Our objective is to make sound investments in profitable companies that are rapidly growing or poised for growth.

Geographic Preference: Western United States
Fund Size: $120 million
Founded: 1980
Average Investment: $5-$10 million
Minimum Investment: $2 million
Investment Criteria: Growth Investments, Recapitalizations, Management-Led Buyouts
Industry Group Preference: Business to Business, Consumer Products, Manufacturing
Portfolio Companies: Criterion Brock, Critical Alert Systems, Passport Food Group, VCC Optoelectronics

Key Executives:
  Eric D Wedbush, Managing Director
  e-mail: eric.wedbush@wedbushcapital.com
  Education: MBA, Anderson School; BS, San Diego State University
  Background: Wedbush Morgan Securities
  Directorships: Reyn Spooner, BATS Trading, ONE Industries, Wedbush Inc., Wedbush Bank
  Geoff Bland, Managing Director
  e-mail: geoff.bland@wedbushcapital.com
  Education: BA in Economics, Stanford University; MBA, JL Kellogg Graduate School
  Background: Co-Founder ShareWave, a fabless wireless semiconductor company

Directorships: CriterionBrock, ONE Industries, Critical Alert Systems

1970 WELLS FARGO CAPITAL FINANCE
2450 Colorado Avenue
3rd Floor
Santa Monica, CA 90404
Phone: 310-453-7300 **Fax:** 310-453-7444
Toll-Free: 877-770-1222
web: www.wellsfargocapitalfinance.com

Mission Statement: We are a specialty secured lender with an entrepreneurial spirit and the backing of our parent company, Wells Fargo, one of the nation's strongest financial services companies.

Geographic Preference: North America
Fund Size: $50 million
Average Investment: $50-$750 million
Minimum Investment: $15 million
Investment Criteria: Recapitalizations, Turnarounds, Debtor-in-Possession Financings, Rediscount Lines, Leveraged Acquisitions and Middle-Market for Growth Companies
Industry Group Preference: Manufacturing, Retailing, Communications, Technology, Distribution, Transportation, Wholesale, Specialty Finance, Restaurants, Healthcare, Real Estate
Portfolio Companies: Affordable Interior Systems, Allied Alloys, Curtis Screw Company, Emcore, ES Robbins, Freedom Group, HomeCare, Marcegaglia, MEGA Brands, Milacron, National Spinning Company, PolyOne, Sage Automotive, Solar Plastics, Tree Island Industries, Alliance Tire Company, Building Material Distributors, Building Materials Holding Corporation, Delek Refining, Design Ideas, Goodmans, Knights Apparel, MMS - A Medical Supply Company, Nash Finch, TriMas, Wave Electronics, Wellman, Wythe Will Distributing, Alaska Airlines, Aquent, Douglas Steel Supply, GLS Companies, Nortech Sytems, Perkins & Marie Callender's, SecurAmerica, Stream Global Services, API Healthcare, Bullhorn, Ex Libris Global Holdings, Insurity, PROS, Telogis, BeyondTrust Software, Calypso Technology, FleetMatics USA, Network Instruments, BJ's Wholesale Club, Brookstone, City Sports, Destination Maternity, Dick's Sporting Goods, Floor & Décor, Gander Mountain, Harbor Freight, Kitchen Collection, Marvin's, Pet Smart, Raley's, Sears Canada, Advance Group, APF - WFCF, Alliance Business Lending, Axis Capital Funding II, Cavalry Investments, Continental Business Credit, Direct Capital, Fast Pay Partners, Gemcap Lending I, JFIN Business Credit Fund, Mackinac Commercial Credit, Marquette Business Credit SPE I, Marquette Transportation Finance, MidCap Funding IV, National Funding, NXT Capital Funding IV, Rapid Financial Services, Siena Funding, ABRH, Arby's Restaurant Group, Mastro's Restaurants, Orion Healthcorp, Infusystem, Remedi S

Other Locations:
1100 Albernathy Road
Suite 1600
Atlanta, GA 30328-5657

14241 Dallas Parkway
Suite 1300
Dallas, TX 75254

601 California Street
7th Floor
San Francisco, CA 94108
Phone: 415-403-1100

10 South Wacker Drive
13th Floor
Chicago, IL 60606-7453

One Boston Place
18th Floor
Boston, MA 02108

100 Park Avenue
3rd Floor
New York, NY 10017
Phone: 212-703-3500

22 Adelaide St. West
Toronto, ON M5H 4E3
Canada

5901 Priestly Dr.
3rd Floor
Suite 306
Carlsbad, CA 92008-8825

116 Inverness Dr. E
3rd Floor
Suite 375
Englewood, CA 80112-5149

301 South College Street
5th Floor
Charlotte, NC 28202
Phone: 704-715-5417

1000 Louisiana St.
3rd Floor
Houston, TX 77002-5027

1700 Lincoln Street
6th & 21st Floor
Denver, CO 80203

333 South Grand Avenue
Suite 4150
Los Angeles, CA 90071
Phone: 213-443-6000

110 East Broward Boulevard
11th Floor
Suite 1100
Ft. Lauderdale, FL 33301-3503

200 South Biscayne Boulevard
14th Floor
Miami, FL 33131
Phone: 305-789-6982

730 Second Avenue South
8th Floor
Minneapolis, MN 55402
Phone: 612-673-8500

1 South Broad Street
3rd Floor
Philadelphia, PA 19107
Phone: 267-321-6692

100 West Washington Street
15th Floor
Phoenix, AZ 85003
Phone: 602-378-2478

1300 SW 6th Avenue
14th Floor
Portland, OR 97201
Phone: 503-886-2664

601 California St.
7th Floor
San Francisco, CA 94108
Phone: 415-403-1100

999 3rd Avenue
10th Floor

Venture Capital & Private Equity Firms / Domestic Firms

Seattle, WA 98104
Phone: 206-343-6402

1753 Pinnacle Drive
6th Floor
McLean, VA 22102-3833
Phone: 703-760-6100

2200 N. Commerce Pkwy.
2nd Floor
Suite 206
Weston, FL 33326-3258

800 N. Magnolia Ave.
7th Floor
Orlando, FL 32803-3264

Key Executives:
James Marasco, Senior Managing Director
e-mail: jim.marasco@wellsfargo.com
Education: BA, Accounting, Michigan State University
Background: GE Capital, Citicorp
Holly Kaczmarczyk, Senior Managing Director
Education: Millikin University; Thunderbird School of Global Management
Background: CEO, Wells Fargo Bank, N.A.

1971 WELLSPRING CAPITAL MANAGEMENT LLC
605 Third Avenue
44th Floor
New York, NY 10158

web: www.wellspringcapital.com

Mission Statement: Aims to increase the profitability of promising companies which can benefit from the firm's extensive experience in management, investment strategies, and business productivity.

Fund Size: $3 billion
Founded: 1995
Minimum Investment: $25 million
Investment Criteria: Acquisition, LBO, MBO
Industry Group Preference: Aerospace, Defense and Government, Consumer Services, Distribution, Financial Services, Food & Beverage, Insurance, Industrial Services
Portfolio Companies: Airswift, API Heat Transfer Inc., Chemaid Laboratories, Checkers Drive-In Restaurants Inc., Cleaver Brooks Inc., Crosman Corporation, Dave & Buster's Inc., Diagnostic Imaging, Edwin Watts Golf Shops, Great Lakes Caring Home Health & Hospice, Help At Home Inc., Hess Print Solutions Inc., Hoffmaster Group Inc., JW Aluminum Company, Lucky Strikes Entertainment, National Seating & Molbility, Neucel Specialty Cellulose LTD., Omni Energy Services Corp., Paragon Films, Performance Food Group, Proampac, Prolamina Corporation, Qualitor, Resco Products Inc., Residential Services Group Inc., Stripes Holdings LLC, Tradesmen, Tube City IMS Corporation, Vatterott College, Vistar Corporation

Key Executives:
Greg S. Feldman, Co-Founder/Managing Partner
Education: BA, Hampshire College; JD, Benjamin N Cardoza School of Law
Background: President Acquisitions, EXOR America; VP/Co-Founder, Clegg Industries; Paul, Weiss, Rifkind, Wharton & Garrison
William F. Dawson, Jr., Managing Partner
Education: BS, St. Francis College; MBA, Harvard Business School
Background: Whitney & Company; Donaldson, Lufkin & Jenrette Securities Corporation; Managing Director, DLJ Merchant Banking
Alexander E. Carles, Partner
Education: BA, Economics, College of William & Mary
Background: Whitney & Company; Research Analyst, Lehman Brothers
Matthew G. Harrison, Partner
Education: BA, Economics, Hamilton College

Background: Bear Stearns & Co.
Directorships: Tube City IMS Corporation; Dave & Buster's; Crosman Corporation; Prolamina Corporation; Airswift; ProAmpac Corporation; Hoffmaster Group; SupplyOne
Seth R. Pearson, Partner
Education: BA, Social Studies, Harvard University
Background: Analyst, Wachovia Capital Markets
Directorships: Cleaver-Brooks; ThermaSys Corporation; API Heat Transfer; National Seating & Mobility; Great Lakes Caring; Help at Home; Resco Products

1972 WELSH, CARSON, ANDERSON & STOWE
599 Lexington Ave.
Suite 1800
New York, NY 10022-6815

Phone: 212-893-9500 **Fax:** 212-893-9575
web: www.wcas.com

Mission Statement: We focus our investment activity in information/business services and healthcare. Our strategy is to buy growth businesses, partner with outstanding management teams and build value for our investors through a combination of operational improvements, internal growth initiatives and strategic acquisitions.

Geographic Preference: United States
Fund Size: $20 billion
Founded: 1979
Average Investment: $50 to $100 million
Industry Group Preference: Healthcare, Information Technology, Business Products & Services
Portfolio Companies: Abzena, Accredo Health, Accuro, AGA Medical, AIM Software, Alert Logic, Alliance Data Systems, Amdocs Ltd., American Residential, AmeriPath, Aptuit, Ardent Health Services, Asurion, Avetta, Bausch & Lomb, BISYS Group, Card Establishment Services, CareSpot Express Healthcare, Ceridian, Clearwater, Cohesive Network Systems, Concentra, Decision One, Dex Media, Emerus, FISERV, GetWellNetwork, Global Knowledge Network, GlobalCollect, Hawk Medical, Headstrong, Identifix/SRS, InnovAge, Intoxalock, K2M, Kindred at Home, Kindred Healthcare, LabOne, Lytx, Magella, Matrix Medical Network, MedAssets America, MedCath, MedE America, MemberHealth, MMIT, MultiPlan, National Dentex, NaviHealth, Onward Healthcare, Oxford Finance, Paycom, Peak10, Quick Base, Quorum Health Group, Renal Advantage, Revel Systems, Ruesch Systems, SAVVIS, Select Medical, Simeio Solutions, Smile Brands, Solstas Lab Partners, Springstone, TransFirst, Triple Point Technology, United Surgical Partners International, Universal American, US Acute Care Solutions, US Anesthesia Partners, US Investigation Services, US Oncology, US Radiology Specialist, Valeritas, Westminster Healthcare

Other Locations:
580 California St.
Suite 1700
San Francisco, CA 94104
Phone: 415-375-4110

Key Executives:
Russell L Carson, Founder & General Partner
Education: Dartmouth College; MBA, Columbia Business School
Background: Chairman/CEO, Citicorp Venture Capital
Bruce K Anderson, Founder & General Partner
Education: University of Minnesota
Background: Executive VP, Automatic Data Processing
Patrick J Welsh, Founder & General Partner
Education: Rutgers University; MBA, University of California, Los Angeles
Background: President, Citicorp Venture Capital
Paul B Queally, Special Advisor
Education: BA, University of Richmond; MBA, Columbia Business School

Venture Capital & Private Equity Firms / Domestic Firms

Background: General Partner, Sprout Group; Investment Banking Analyst, DLJ
Anthony J de Nicola, President & Managing Partner
Education: DePauw University; MBA, Harvard Business School
Background: William Blair & Company; Goldman Sachs & Company
D Scott Mackesy, Managing Partner
Education: College of William & Mary
Background: Investment Research Department, Morgan Stanley Dean Witter
Brian T Regan, General Partner
Education: Yale College
Background: Investment Banking, Merrill Lynch
Eric J Lee, General Partner
Education: Harvard University
Background: M&A & High Technology, Goldman Sachs & Co
Jonathan M Rather, General Partner
Education: BS, Accounting, Boston College; MS, Taxation, Pace University
Background: COO & CFO, Goelet Investment Office
Thomas A Scully, General Partner
Education: BA, University of Virginia; JD, Catholic University
Background: Administrator, Centers for Medicare & Medicaid Services; President & CEO, Federation of American Hospitals
Sean M Traynor, General Partner
Education: Villanova University; MBA, Wharton School, University of Pennsylvania
Background: BT Alex, Coopers & Lybrand
Michael E Donovan, General Partner
Education: Yale College
Background: Windward Capital Partners
Christopher Hooper, General Partner
e-mail: chooper@wcas.com
Education: BA, Colgate University
Background: Golden Gate Capital
Directorships: Avetta, Clearwater Analytics, Quick Base, Revel Systems
Gregory G Lau, General Partner
Education: AB, Harvard College; MBA, Harvard Business School
Background: FFL Partners
Edward P Sobol, General Partner
e-mail: esobol@wcas.com
Education: BA, Stanford University; MBA, Harvard Business School
Background: FFL Partners
Directorships: Emerus, InnovAge, Kindred Healthcare, Kindred at Home, MMIT, National Dentex
Christopher W Solomon, General Partner
Education: BA, Wake Forest University; MBA, Ross School of Business, University of Michigan
Background: JP Morgan

1973 WEST HEALTH INVESTMENT FUND
10350 North Torrey Pines Road
La Jolla, CA 92037

Phone: 858-535-7000
Toll-Free: 855-937-8100
web: www.westhealth.org

Mission Statement: The West Health Investment Fund was established with a unique mission - to lower health care costs - by providing risk capital for companies with cutting-edge health care technologies and services.

Fund Size: $100 million
Industry Group Preference: Healthcare, Healthcare Information Technology

Key Executives:
Shelley Lyford, President and CEO
Education: University of San Diego

Zia Agha, Chief Medical Officer and EVP
Education: MS, Medical College of Wisconsin; MD, Aga Khan University
Background: Director, San Diego Healthcare System; Professor, University of California

1974 WESTERN STATES INVESTMENT GROUP
4025 Sorrento Valley Boulevard
San Diego, CA 92121

Phone: 858-678-0800 Fax: 858-678-0900
web: www.wsig.com

Mission Statement: Invests in a portfolio of companies involved in sectors of industry ranging from networking to software to life sciences, in the interests of producing beneficial financial returns. Not actively seeking investment opportunities.

Geographic Preference: West Coast
Fund Size: $30 million
Founded: 1976
Average Investment: $2 million
Minimum Investment: $1 million
Investment Criteria: Seed, First-Stage, Second-Stage, Mezzanine
Industry Group Preference: Communications, Computer Related, E-Commerce & Manufacturing, Electronic Components, Electronic Technology, Internet Technology, Medical & Health Related
Portfolio Companies: Lpath, DermTech International, Vaxiion Therapeutics

Key Executives:
Terry Trzcinka, Investment Liaison

1975 WESTERN TECHNOLOGY INVESTMENT
104 La Mesa Drive
Suite 102
Portola Valley, CA 94028

Phone: 650-234-4300 Fax: 650-234-4343
e-mail: info@westerntech.com
web: www.westerntech.com

Mission Statement: Focused on expanding the productive partnership between venture capital investors and venture lenders. Asset-based investments enable venture capital investors and management to maximize their equity investment through leverage.

Fund Size: $400 million
Founded: 1980
Average Investment: $250,000 to $30 million
Minimum Investment: $250,000
Investment Criteria: Experienced management, high growth potential
Industry Group Preference: Communications, Computer Related, Electronic Components, Instrumentation, Internet Technology, Genetic Engineering, Medical & Health Related, Life Sciences, Biotechnology, Medical Devices, Healthcare, Security, Semiconductors, Wireless Technologies
Portfolio Companies: 0-In Design, 3PARdata, 5Square Systems, Ablathion Frontiers, Abrizio, Access360, Accruent, Accuri Cytometers, Aceva, Actelis, Active Software, AcuFocus, Acusphere, Adaptive Planning, Adforce, Adomo, AdRoll, Advanced ICU Care, Aeluros, Aerogen, AeroScout, Aesgen, Afara Websystems, Agistics, Airgo Networks, Akimbo Systems, Alere Medical, Alopa Networks, Altierre, Amber Networks, Ample Communications, Ample Medical, Ampulse, Analogix Semiconductor, Anchor Intelligence, Andale, Andigilog, Apere, Arena Solutions, Aristos Logic, Arroyo Video Solutions, Asera, Askola USA Corporation, Aspire Medical, Astral Point Communications, Astro Gaming, Athena Design Systems, Athersys, Atlantis Computing, Atrica, Avamar, Azuro, Berkeley Design Automation, Bevocal, BigFix, BioAbsorbable Therapeutics, Biometrix, Bitwave Semiconductor, Bivio Networks, Biz360, Blackfoot, Blaze Entertainment, Blekko, BlueRoads,

Venture Capital & Private Equity Firms / Domestic Firms

BlueSocket, Bluestar Solutions, Bocada, Bridgespan, Brion Technologies, Broad Daylight, Brocade Communications, Broncus Technologies, Business Engine, BuzzLogic, Calico Commerce, Calient Networks, Calista Technologies, Calix Networks, Cameron Health, CancerVax, Cardica, Cardio Focus, CardioNOW, Cardiva Medical, Catamaran Communications, Causes, Caymas Systemts, Cellfire, CellGate, Cellscape, Cerent, Ceres, Chakshu Research, Chameleon Systems, Ciphergen Biosystems, CipherOptics, CiraNova, Circle of Moms, Cloudmark, CloudShield, Coalescent Surgical, Collarity, Commerce One, Confirma, ConforMIS

Key Executives:
Maurice Werdegar, Investment Partner/CEO
e-mail: mauricew@westerntech.com
Education: BA, MBA, Stanford Universtiy
Background: iMinds Ventures; CFO, MetaMarkets; Corporate Finance, Robertson Stephens
Jay Cohan, Investment Partner
e-mail: jayc@westerntech.com
Education: BS, MS, Electrical Engineering, MIT; MBA, Harvard Business School
Background: Puma Technology; Orcale Corporation; SoftMagic
David Wanek, Investment Partner
e-mail: davidw@westerntech.com
Education: BS, University of Kansas, MBA, University of Mexico, JD, Santa Clara University
Background: Marketing, Verisign, Wilson Sonsini Goodrich And Rosati, And Os Alamos National Laboratories
Dave Gravano, Investment Partner
e-mail: daveg@westerntech.com
Education: BA, Duke University
Background: Silicon Valley Bank, Fortress Investment Group, Meier Mitchell/GATX Ventures
Marty Eng, CFO/VP of Administration
e-mail: martine@westerntech.com
Education: BA, Political Science, University of California, Davis; MBA, Taxation, Golden Gate University; CPA
Background: CNF, Inc.; Applied Materials; Ernst & Young
Rudy Ruano, Investment Partner
e-mail: rudy@westerntech.com
Education: BS, Finance, San Jose State University
Background: CEO, ScanRx; VP, Business Development, iMeditation SA
Hagi Schwartz, Venture Partner
e-mail: hagi@westerntech.com
Background: Founder, Magnolia Capital; CFO, Check Point Software Technologies
Directorships: Silicon Graphics, BigFix, TUI University

1976 WESTLAKE SECURITIES
2700 Via Fortuna
Suite 250
Austin, TX 78746

Phone: 512-314-0711 Fax: 512-306-1651
web: www.westlakesecurities.com

Mission Statement: Promotes economic growth by matching promising ventures to potential investors, educating companies and investors on business financing issues, and linking emerging companies with appropriate professional business expertise.

Fund Size: $275 million
Founded: 1992
Average Investment: $25 million
Minimum Investment: $5 million
Investment Criteria: Seed, Research & Development, Start-Up, First-stage, Second-stage, Mezzanine, LBO
Industry Group Preference: Business Products & Services, Communications, Consumer Products, Consumer Services, Distribution, Logistics, Energy Services, Healthcare, Information Services, Insurance, Financial Services, Manufacturing, Oil & Gas, Semiconductors, Software

Other Locations:
6363 Woodway
Suite 1000
Houston, TX 77057
Phone: 713-590-9690 Fax: 713-590-9601

11676 US Highway One
North Palm Beach, FL 33408
Phone: 561-352-8815

2000 Kaliste Saloom Road
Suite 400
Lafayette, LA 70508
Phone: 337-291-1260 Fax: 337-291-1265

Key Executives:
Matt Anderson, CEO/Managing Director
e-mail: andersend@westlakesecurities.com
Education: MBA, Sam Houston State University; University of Chicago; Harvard University
Wilson Allen, Partner/Managing Director
e-mail: wilson@westlakesecurities.com
Education: BA, Economics, University of Texas; MBA, Pepperdine University
Background: President, Signature Capital Securities, LLC; Co-Founder, Wind River Capital Company; Online Editor, Hoover's; Sr Equity Trader/Member of Equity Asset Allocation Committee, Eagle Management & Trust Company
Jon D'Andrea, Managing Director
e-mail: jdandrea@westlakesecurities.com
Education: University of Texas
Grant Pritchard, Managing Director
e-mail: gpritchard@westlakesecurities.com
Education: BS, University of Southern California; MBA, Columbia Business School
Mark Austin, Managing Director
e-mail: maustin@westlakesecurities.com
Education: BBA, MBA, University of Texas, Austin
Kevin Brady, Managing Director
e-mail: kbrady@westlakesecurities.com
Education: BS, Texas A&M University
Brian Hawkins, Managing Director
e-mail: bhawkins@westlakesecurities.com
Education: CPA, MBA, Sam Houston State University

1977 WESTLY GROUP
2200 Sand Hill Road
Suite 250
Menlo Park, CA 94025

Phone: 650-275-7420 Fax: 650-362-2338
e-mail: plans@westlygroup.com
web: www.westlygroup.com

Mission Statement: The Westly Group is a clean technology-oriented venture capital firm. We focus primarily on companies with proven revenue streams but are open to investments in all stages of growth.

Founded: 2007
Investment Criteria: All Stages
Industry Group Preference: Clean Technology
Portfolio Companies: Building Robotics, Enerkem, Ioxus, Revolution Foods, Solexel, Calstar Products, Feastly, Lunera, SCIenergy, View, Clean Well, Good Eggs, My Health Terms, Sentinel, WaterSmart, Cooliris, GreenWave Systems, Recyclebank, Simple Energy, Yerdle, Edeniq, Honest Buildings

Key Executives:
Steve Westly, Managing Partner
Education: Stanford University; MBA, Stanford Graduate School of Business
Background: Controller & Chief Fiscal Officer, State of California; Senior Vice President of Marketing, eBay;

Office of Conservation and Solar, US Department of Energy
Timothy Wang, Partner
Education: BA, Brown University; MBA, USC Marshall School of Business
Background: Co-Founder, ChinaScope; Analyst, S&P Capital IQ
Dave Coglizer, Principal
Education: University of California, Davis; MBA, Stanford Graduate School of Business
Background: Bancomer; Senior Category Manager, eBay; CB Richard Ellis
Directorships: Amonix

1978 WESTON PRESIDIO
John Hancock Tower
200 Clarendon Street
50th Floor
Boston, MA 02116

Phone: 617-988-2500 **Fax:** 617-988-2515
web: www.westonpresidio.com

Mission Statement: To help companies grow and prosper using financial, strategic, and professional services intended to foster the opportunity for industry expansion and business development.

Geographic Preference: United States
Fund Size: $3 billion
Founded: 1991
Average Investment: $10 - $50 milion
Minimum Investment: $10 million
Investment Criteria: Second-Stage, Mezzanine, LBO, MBO
Industry Group Preference: Retailing, Business to Business, Manufacturing, Industrial Equipment, Technology, Media, Publishing
Portfolio Companies: Advisors Excel, Azul Brazilian Airlines, DYSIS, Edge Systems, Evenflo Company, Flynn Restaurant Group, Integro, Jimmy John's, Silego Technology, Snooze, SquareTrade, Too Faced Holdings, Vitria Technology, Wolf Holdings Organization, Xenon Arc

Other Locations:
One Harbor Drive
Suite 300
Sausalito, CA 94965
Phone: 415-944-6479

Key Executives:
Michael Lazarus, Co-Founder/CEO
e-mail: mlazarus@westonpresidio.com
Education: Accounting, Grove City College
Background: Managing Director/Director Private Placement Department, Montgomery Securities; Price Waterhous
Michael F. Cronin, Managing Partner
Education: AB, Harvard Business School, MBA, Harvard Graduate School of Business
Background: Senior Vice President, Security Pacific Venture Capital
Directorships: Xenon Arc; DISYS; ipCapital Group; dataCon Inc; Beth Israel Deaconess Medical Center

1979 WESTVIEW CAPITAL PARTNERS
125 High Street
High Street Tower
26th Floor
Boston, MA 02110

Phone: 617-261-2050 **Fax:** 617-261-2060
e-mail: cvs@wvcapital.com
web: www.wvcapital.com

Mission Statement: WestView Capital Partners is a Boston-based private equity firm focused exclusively on lower middle market companies.
Fund Size: $500 million
Founded: 1990
Average Investment: $5 - $30 million
Investment Criteria: Recapitalizations, Growth Equity, Buyouts, Consolidations
Industry Group Preference: Business Products & Services, Software, Information Technology, Healthcare Services, Logistics, Distribution, Industrial, Manufacturing, Consumer Products, Retail, Consumer & Leisure, Media, Publishing
Portfolio Companies: Abacus Group LLC, Accountabil IT, Advanced Technology Services UK Limited, Alku, Alpha II, Apex Revenue Technologies, Bell and Howell, Body Central, CloudWave, Collaborative Solutions, L'Anza, English Color, eSolutions, Executive Health Resources, Fitness Connection, Graphic Controls, Health Monitor Network, Jopari Solutions, KLDiscovery, Mintz Group, Northwest Plan Services, Nwestco, OneNeck IT Services, Park Place Technologies, Peerless Industrial Group, Providea Conferencing, Radiac Abrasives, Receivable Solutions, Resource Ammirati, RuffaloCODY, Snow Companies, The Paper Store, The Phia Group, The Shelby Group, Thorne Research, TriTech Software Systems, Unified Patents, VaultLogix, VC3, Veriato, Wavelink Corporation, Xtend Healthcare

Key Executives:
Carlo A. von Schroeter, Managing Partner
617-261-2051
Education: BS, Mechanical Engineering, Queen's University; MBA, Harvard Business School
Background: General Partner, Weston Presidio; Vice President, Security Pacific Capital; District Engineering Manager, Shell Canada Limited
Directorships: American Asphalt & Grading, Star International Holdings, Geosystems, Delstar, Lion Brewery, Medscape
Richard J. Williams, Managing Partner
617-261-2052
e-mail: rjw@wvcapital.com
Education: BS, Computer Science, Yale University; MBA, Wharton School
Background: Partner, Tudor Investment Corporation; Managing Director, Triumph Capigal Group; Associate, Drexel Burnham Lambert
Directorships: Ameridata Technologies, United Natural Foods, Hatten Communications, Claricom Holdings, Longview Group, International Computer Graphics, OutSource International
John H. Turner, General Partner
617-261-2053
e-mail: jht@wvcapital.com
Education: BA, Economics, University of New Hampshire; MBA, Wharton School
Background: General Partner, Norwest Mezzanine Partners; Managing Director, Triumph Capital Group; Heller Financial
Matthew T. Carroll, General Partner
617-261-2054
e-mail: mtc@wvcapital.com
Education: BS, Finance, Boston College
Background: VP, Corporate Development, LogistiCare; Associate, Triumph Capital Group; Analyst, Dean Witter Reynolds
Directorships: LogistiCare
Jonathan E. Hunnicutt, General Partner
e-mail: jeh@wvcapital.com
Education: AB, Government/Geography, Dartmouth College; MBA, Tuck School of Business
Background: Associate, Weston Presidio; Associate, Fleet Equity Partners; Analyst, Merrill Lynch

1980 WGI GROUP
New York, NY

e-mail: contact@wgifund.com
web: www.wgifund.com

Mission Statement: WGI Group provides early stage capital to internet entrepreneurs.
Average Investment: $500,000

Venture Capital & Private Equity Firms / Domestic Firms

Investment Criteria: Seed-Stage, Early-Stage
Industry Group Preference: Internet
Key Executives:
Michael Walrath, Partner
Education: BA, English, University of Richmond
Background: Founder & CEO, Right Media
Directorships: Meteor Games, MOAT, GuideMe, Yext, InAdCo
Noah Goodhart, Partner
Education: BA, Cornell University; MA, Yale University
Background: Founder, Colonize.com; Co-CEO, Ad Group; Founding Investor, Right Media
Jonah Goodhart, Partner
Education: BA, Cornell University
Background: Co-CEO, Smarter Ad Group; Founding Investor, Right Media

1981 WHEATLEY PARTNERS
80 Cuttermill Road
Great Neck, NY 11021

Phone: 516-773-1024 Fax: 516-773-0996
e-mail: info@wheatleypartners.com

Mission Statement: To work closely with entrepreneurs to build successful businesses and typically support portfolio companies at all stages of development.

Founded: 1992
Investment Criteria: All Stages
Industry Group Preference: Software, Business Products & Services, Information Technology, Life Sciences, Medical Devices, Communications, Networking, Education, Healthcare, Healthcare Information Technology

Other Locations:
747 Third Avenue
24th Floor
New York, NY 10017

1982 WHITE STAR CAPITAL
331 Park Avenue S
New York, NY 10010

e-mail: info@whitestarvc.com
web: www.whitestarcapital.com

Mission Statement: White Star Capital, is an investment vehicle that deploys between $250k and $2.5M in startups in North America, Western Europe and other selective markets.

Geographic Preference: Europe, North America
Average Investment: $250,000 - $2.5 million
Investment Criteria: Early-Stage
Industry Group Preference: Mobile, Social Media, Gaming, E-Commerce & Manufacturing
Portfolio Companies: Salesfloor, adglow, Echo, aire, Gymtrack, KeyMe, Red Sift, Borrowell, Hole 19, Dice, Vention, Freshly, drop, mnubb, digg, Klaxoon, TheGuarantors, Bloglovin', Safello, Meero

Other Locations:
407 McGill
Suite 808
Montreal, QC
Canada

37-41 Mortimer Street
Fitzrovia
United Kingdom

40 Rue Francois
1st Floor
Paris 75008
France

20th Floor On Building
158-164 Queen's Road Central
Hong Kong
Hong Kong

Level 3, Sanno Park Tower
2-11-1 Nagata-Cho, Chiyoda-Ku
Tokyo 100-6162
Japan

Key Executives:
Eric Martineau-Fortin, Founder/Managing Partner
Education: HEC Canada; MSc
Background: ABN AMRO, Paris; Merrill Lynch International, New York
Jean-Francois Marcoux, Co-Founder/Managing Partner
Education: HEC Montreal; MSc, University of Sherbrooke; CFA
Background: Co-Founder, Ludia; Senior M&A, Scotia Bank; Deutsche Bank; CDPQ; TC Transcontinental

1983 WI HARPER GROUP
50 California Street
Suite 2580
San Francisco, CA 94111

Phone: 415-397-6200 Fax: 415-397-6280
web: www.wiharper.com

Mission Statement: Seeks to help talented entrepreneurs, engineers and scientists create world-class technology companies by providing them with valuable resources and guidance.

Geographic Preference: United States, Asia, Central Europe
Fund Size: $225 million
Founded: 1993
Average Investment: $7 million
Minimum Investment: $500,000
Investment Criteria: Early Stage, Early-Expansion Stage
Industry Group Preference: E-Commerce & Manufacturing, Digital Media & Marketing, Wireless Technologies, Broadband, Optical Technology, Biotechnology, Clean Technology, Healthcare, Technology
Portfolio Companies: Aicent, Airy:3D, Alpha Ring, Avaamo, Blossom, Coffee Meets Bagel, Cold Genesys, Commerce One, Divx, Drop, DynoSense, Epic!, Flutter, GCT, Holor, Kloudless, Momentum Machines, nway, Ooma, PAVmed, Percolata, Playswell, PMC, Polly Portfolio, Poshly, Shots Studio, Signma, Synthego, Thunder, ViSenze, Vizio, Walla.by, Wonder Workshop, Wynd

Other Locations:
10F-2 Ruentex Banking Tower
76 Tun Hua South Road
Sec. 2
Taipei
Taiwan
Phone: 886-2-2755-6033 Fax: 886-2-2709-2127

806 Tower A
Pacific Century Place
Beijing 100027
China
Phone: 86-10-6539-1366 Fax: 86-10-6539-1367

Key Executives:
Paul Chau, Managing Director
e-mail: pchau@wiharper.com
Education: MS, Business Administration/Finance, University of California, Berkeley; BS, Electrical Engineering, University of Canterbury, New Zealand
Background: VP, Walden International; VP, GIC Special Investment Private Limited; Senior Consultant, BARRA
Norman Liang, Vice President
Background: Sungy Mobile
Jimmy Lu, Managing Director
e-mail: jlu@wiharper.com
Education: BA, Yale College; MBA, Harvard Business School; JD, UC Berkeley School of Law
Background: Co-Founder & General Partner, iD Ventures America
Directorships: Quixley, CNano Technology Limited,

Venture Capital & Private Equity Firms / Domestic Firms

China Diagnostics Medical Corporation, Kindstar Global, StemCyte
Shahi Ghanem, Managing Director
Education: BS, Economics, University of California, Irvine
Background: Chief Strategy Officer/EVP, Corporate Development, BitTorrent Inc.; President, DivX. Chairman/CEO, Brickfish; CEO, EmpoweHER; SVP, Technology, Greens.com

1984 WICKS GROUP OF COMPANIES, LLC
400 Park Avenue
New York, NY 10022

Phone: 212-838-2100 Fax: 212-223-2109
e-mail: info@wicksgroup.com
web: www.wicksgroup.com

Mission Statement: Focused private equity firm that specializes in selected segments of the communications, information and media industries in the United States.

Geographic Preference: United States
Fund Size: fund I $62m, fund II $383m, fund III $535m
Founded: 1989
Average Investment: $5-$25 million
Investment Criteria: LBO, MBO
Industry Group Preference: Business to Business, Publishing, Radio, Advertising, Cable, Communications, Media, Information Technology, Broadcasting, Education, Media
Portfolio Companies: New Mountain Learning, Wicks Educational Publishing, CFM Religion Publishing Group, NewBay Media, Northstar Travel Media, SCI Solutions, Southern Technical College, Verse Music Group, Wilks Broadcast Group, Mcmurry/TMG, Jobson Healthcare Information, Harris Connect, Bonded Services Group, Bendon, Antenna International

Key Executives:
   Craig B Klosk, Co-Founder/Managing Partner
   212-407-2202
   e-mail: craig.klosk@wicksgroup.com
   Education: BS, Labor Relations, JD, Cornell University
   Background: Attorney, Paul, Weiss, Rifkind, Wharton & Garrison; Senior Editor, Cornell Law Review
   Daniel L Black, Managing Partner
   212-407-2212
   e-mail: daniel.black@wicksgroup.com
   Education: AB, Dartmouth College
   Background: Managing Director/Co-head, Merchant Banking; Senior VP/Co-head, US Corporate Banking; Trustee, Bank Street College
   Matthew E Gormly III, Managing Partner
   212-407-2205
   e-mail: matt.gormly@wicksgroup.com
   Education: BA, Economics, Hampden-Sydney College; MBA, Babcock School of Management, Wake Forest University
   Background: Managing Director, BC Advisors
   Daniel M Kortick, Managing Partner
   212-407-2207
   e-mail: daniel.kortick@wicksgroup.com
   Education: MBA, Finance, Bryant College; BA, Hobart College
   Background: Fleet Bank; BankBoston
   Max von Zuben, Managing Partner
   212-407-2210
   Education: BA, English & American Literature, Harvard College; MBA, Columbia Business School
   Background: Associate, Dubiler & Company; Investment Banking, Donaldson, Lufkin & Jenrette Securities

1985 WILDCAT VENTURE PARTNERS
777 Mariners Island Boulevard
Suite 550
San Mateo, CA 94404

Phone: 650-234-4840
e-mail: ideas@wildcat.vc
web: wildcat.vc

Mission Statement: Wildcat Venture Partners invests in Business-to-Business startups emerging in the tech industry.

Founded: 2015
Industry Group Preference: Technology, Machine Learning, Artificial Intelligence, IoT, Cloud, Mobility, Digital Health, EdTech, Education, SaaS, Software, FinTech
Portfolio Companies: Aceable, Amplero, C3.ai, Carrum Health, Clover, Drum, Green Fig, Key, LeaseLock, Obo, Olono, Reach, Remarkable, Ritual, Tuition.io, Vlocity, What 3 Words, Zebit

Key Executives:
   Bill Ericson, Founding Partner
   Education: BS, Georgetown University School of Foreign Service; JD, Northwestern University School of Law
   Background: Managing Partner, Mohr Davidow Ventures
   Bryan Stolle, Founding Partner
   Education: BBA/MBA, University of Texas at Austin
   Background: General Partner, Mohr Davidow Ventures; Founder/CEO, Agile Software
   Jennifer Trzepacz, Partner/COO
   Education: BA, Bryant University; MBA, Simmons Grad. School of Management
   Background: EVP, RocketFuel; LivingSocial; Salesforce; Electronic Arts; Yahoo!
   Bruce Cleveland, Partner
   Education: BBA, California State University
   Background: Founder, GreenFig; Apple; AT&T; Oracle; Siebel Systems
   Geoffrey Moore, Partner
   Education: BA, Literature, Stanford University; PhD, Literature, University of Washington
   Background: Author; Speaker; Advisor
   Phyllis Whiteley, Partner
   Education: BA, Chemistry; PhD, Pharmacology, Washington University
   Background: Partner, Mohr Davidow Ventures; Officer/SVP of Business Development, Perlegen Sciences Inc.; VP of Strategic Portfolio Management, Roche; Senior Research Immunology, Merck
   Randall Ussery, Partner
   Education: BA, History, James Madison University; MBA, Babson College
   Background: Herman Miller

1986 WILLIS STEIN & PARTNERS LLC
1033 Skokie Boulevard
Suite 360
Northbrook, IL 60062-4137

Phone: 312-422-2400 Fax: 312-422-2424

Mission Statement: Willis Stein & Partners is dedicated to investing in companies that can benefit from the management team's extensive strategic, financial and operational experience.

Geographic Preference: United States
Fund Size: $1.2 billion
Founded: 1989
Average Investment: $30 - $500 million
Investment Criteria: LBO, MBO, Middle Market, Equity Buyouts, Build-Ups, Carve-Outs, Public to Private Transactions
Industry Group Preference: Business Products & Services, Consumer Products, Healthcare, Manufacturing, Media, Telecommunications, Consumer Services, Education
Portfolio Companies: AAVID, Advantage Payroll Service, Aurum Technologies, Baker & Taylor, CompuPlay, Donlar Corp., Education Corporation of America, Education

693

Venture Capital & Private Equity Firms / Domestic Firms

Partners, Falcon First Communications LP, FDH Velocitel, Home Technology Healthcare, Interlink Communications, Intervalv, Marks Bros. Jewelers, Merit Health Systems Corporation, New Vision TV LP, Orius Corporation, PersonalPath Systems, Petersen Companies, Plastic Engineered Components, Premiere Page, Racing Champions Corporation, RoundyBs Supermarkets, Saba Medical Group LP, SRDS Media Information LP, Strategic Materials, Sunbelt National Mortgage Corporation, Transwestern Publishing Company LP, Troll Communications LLC, US One Communications Corporation, Zeborg

Key Executives:
Avy H. Stein, Co-Founder/Managing Partner
e-mail: astein@willisstein.com
Education: Harvard Law School; BS, University of Illinois
Background: Managing Directro, CIVIC; CEO, NL Industries

1987 WILLOWRIDGE PARTNERS
122 East 42nd Street
37th Floor
New York, NY 10017
Phone: 212-369-4700 **Fax:** 212-369-5661
e-mail: info@willowridge.com
web: www.willowridge.com

Mission Statement: Willowridge Partners buys limited partnership interests in buyout and venture capital funds on a secondary basis.
Fund Size: $535 million
Founded: 1995
Average Investment: $20 million
Investment Criteria: Buyouts, Mezzanine
Industry Group Preference: Diversified

Key Executives:
Jerrold Newman, Partner
212-369-2888
e-mail: jnewman@willowridgeinc.com
Education: MBA, Amos Tuck School, Dartmouth; BS, Cornell University
Background: CPA, Price Waterhouse; CPA, Acquisitions, Booz, Allen & Hamilton
Luisa Hunnewell, Partner
212-369-1220
e-mail: lhunnewell@willowridge.com
Education: MBA, Amos Tuck School, Dartmouth; BA, University of Pennsylvania
Background: Insurance, Chemical Bank
James O'Mara, Partner
212-369-3211
e-mail: jomara@willowridge.com
Education: BA, Hamilton College
Background: Office of Investments, Hamilton College
Lawrence Fang, Partner
212-369-8922
e-mail: lfang@willowridge.com
Education: BBA, University of Michigan
Background: Principal, Pomona Capital; AIG Global Investment Group
Michael Kenny, Controller
212-369-8844
e-mail: mkenny@willowridge.com
Education: BS, Accountancy, St. John's University
Background: Vice President, Goldman Sachs & Co.; RSM McGladrey; Merrill Lynch

1988 WILMINGTON INVESTOR NETWORK
1802 South Churchill Drive
Wilmington, NC 28403
Phone: 910-538-6641
e-mail: info@wilmingtoninvestor.com
web: www.wilmingtoninvestor.com

Mission Statement: WIN is a private equity fund interested in high-growth companies from all areas of business.
Geographic Preference: Eastern North Carolina & Eastern South Carolina
Industry Group Preference: Technology, Biotechnology, Medical Devices
Portfolio Companies: 3Derm, ABK Biomedical, Affinergy, Arbovax, Axial Exchange, Basho, CARS, Chaologix, Ecolibrium Solar, Gemmus Pharma, Mobee, Oculis Labs, Onco Health, Pique Therapeutics, Physcient, Protochips, Public Relay, Respiratory Motion, Sensory Analytics, Stimwave, TranscribeMe, Trusted Metrics, Validic, Wilmington Pharmaceuticals, WindGap Medical

1989 WILSHIRE PRIVATE MARKETS
1299 Ocean Avenue
Suite 700
Santa Monica, CA 90401
Phone: 310-451-3051 **Fax:** 310-458-6936
web: www.wilshire.com

Mission Statement: Provides customized investment solutions to institutional clients worldwide.
Geographic Preference: Worldwide
Fund Size: $5.5 Billion
Founded: 1984
Investment Criteria: LBOs, Distressed, Special Situations, Growth Capital, Venture Capital
Industry Group Preference: All markets considered

Other Locations:
210 Sixth Avenue
Suite 3720
Pittsburgh, PA 15222
Phone: 412-434-1580 **Fax:** 412-434-1584

222 West Adams Street
Suite 1880
Chicago, IL 60606
Phone: 312-762-5500 **Fax:** 312-762-5501

Wilshire Associated Europe B.V.
World Trade Center - Tower H, 25th Floor
Zuidplein 204
Amsterdam 1077 XV
Netherlands
Phone: 31-203057530 **Fax:** 31-203057539

370 Interlocken Boulevard
Suite 620
Broomfield, CO 80021
Phone: 303-626-7444 **Fax:** 310-458-6936

525 Washington Boulevard
Suite 2410
Jersey City, NJ 07310
Phone: 201-984-4899 **Fax:** 310-458-6936

3 Pickering Street
#02-39 Nankin Row
China Square Central
Singapore 048660
Singapore
Phone: 65-6435-2169 **Fax:** 65-6538-1633

Wilshire Australia Pty Limited
470 Collins Street
Suite 3, Level 10
Melbourne VIC 3000
Australia
Phone: 61.3.9678.0300

Wilshire Associates Europe B.V.
World Trade Center - Tower H
25th Floor, Zuidplein 204
Amsterdam 1077 XV
Netherlands
Phone: 31.20.305.7530 **Fax:** 31.20.305.7539

1 Connaught Place
Suite 3711

Venture Capital & Private Equity Firms / Domestic Firms

37F Jardine House
Hong Kong
China
Phone: 852-2832-6601 **Fax:** 852-2832-6636

23 Austin Friars
Suite 4.13
London EC2N 2QP
United Kingdom
Phone: 44.20.7920.3100 **Fax:** 44.20.7920.3101

Key Executives:
Denis A. Tito, Founder/CEO/Chairman
Education: BS, Astronautics & Aeronautics, New York University College of Engineering; MS, Engineering Science, Rensselaer Polytechnic Institute; PhD, Finance, Anderson School of Management
Background: Rocket Scientist, Jet Propulsion Laboratory
John C. Hindman, President, Vice Chairman of the Board of Directors
Education: BS, Accounting & Economics, University of Michigan
Background: VP of Finance, Allianz Global Investors; CFO, Paul Hastings; CFO, eCloser, Director and CEO, Cypress Financial Services; VP of Finance, West Capital Financial Services

---

1990 WIND POINT PARTNERS
676 North Michigan Avenue
Suite 3700
Chicago, IL 60611
Phone: 312-255-4800 **Fax:** 312-255-4820
web: www.wppartners.com

Mission Statement: Acquires middle market businesses in partnership with outstanding management teams that possess a clear vision for creating value over a five year time period.

Geographic Preference: United States
Fund Size: $400 million
Founded: 1983
Average Investment: $30 - $150 million
Minimum Investment: $8 million
Investment Criteria: LBO, Recapitalizations, Industry Consolidations, Expansion Capital
Industry Group Preference: Business to Business, Healthcare, Industrial Services, Consumer Services
Portfolio Companies: Active Interest Media, America's PowerSports, Argotec, Dicom Transportation Group, Interface Solutions, Knape & Vogt, Nelson Global Products, Nonni's, Novolex, Pelss, Petmate, RailWorks, Rupari Foods, Shearer's Foods, Taylor-Wharton International, Vertellus Specialties

Key Executives:
Nathan Brown, Managing Director
Education: BA, Philosophy with distinction, Queen's University; MBA with honors, University of Chicago
Background: Analyst, Corporate Finance/Mergers & Acquisitions, ScotiaMcLeod
Directorships: America's PowerSports, Marshfield DoorSystems, United Subcontractors
Joe Lawler, Managing Director
Education: BS, Boston College; MBA, Kellogg School of Management, Northwestern University
Background: Analyst, William Blair & Company
Bob Cummings, Managing Director/Co-Founder
e-mail: rlc@wppartners.com
Education: BSME, Rensselaer Polytechnic Institute; MBA, Harvard Business School
Background: General Partner, Robertson, Colman & Stephens; Consultant, McKinsey & Company
Directorships: Bakery Chef, Procyon Technologies, VICORP Restaurants
Richard R Kracum, Managing Director/Co-Founder
e-mail: rrk@wppartners.com
Education: MBA, MS, Chemistry, University of Chicago; BA, Carleton College
Background: Principal, Booz, Allen & Hamilton; Chairman, Prange Way
Directorships: Pacific Cycle, Bushnell Performance Optics, America's PowerSports, Benchmark Medical, Ames True Temper, AIR-Serv Holdings
Alex Washington, Managing Director
Education: BA Finance, Morehouse College; MBA, Harvard Business School
Background: Senior Associate, Whitney & Company; Business Analyst, McKinsey & Company; Member, Class VI Kauffman Fellows
Directorships: Arr-Maz Custom Chemicals
Paul Peterson, Managing Director
Education: BBA Finance, University of Iowa; MBA, Harvard Business School
Background: Associate, Wind Point; Financial Analyst, Houlihan Lokey Howard & Zukin; Management, Harley-Davidson Motor Company
David Stott, Managing Director
Education: BBA, Finance & Accounting, University of Michigan; MBA, Kellogg School of Management, Northwestern University
Background: Financial Analyst, Investment Banking Division, Citigroup
Konrad Salaber, Managing Director
e-mail: kas@wppartners.com
Education: BA, English, Washington University, St. Louis; MBA, Booth School of Business
Background: Analyst, AG Edwards Capital Markets
Directorships: Knape & Vogt, Nonni's, Rupari Foods

1991 WINDCREST PARTNERS
750 Third Avenue
33rd Floor
New York, NY 10017
Phone: 212-257-6704
e-mail: info@windcrestpartners.com
web: www.windcrestpartners.com

Mission Statement: Through WINDCREST PARTNERS II, we invest in private companies at all stages of development and seek to partner with talented management teams and innovative entrepreneurs. We pride ourselves on providing the financial support and guidance that management teams require to build strong, sustainable businesses.

Geographic Preference: United States
Investment Criteria: All Stages
Portfolio Companies: GoodData, Offerpop, Violin Memory, Mobilize.me, Voxer, Micro Office, Axial, Appriss, eNNOV, Dalet, GSO, HigherOne, Metropolitan National Bank, Syncsort, uTest, Clementon Park Splash Worlld, Nasville Shores Water Park, Ocean Breeze Water Park, Regent, SmartRecruiters, Monark, Wavemark Technologies

Key Executives:
James Gellert, Partner
212-257-6704
e-mail: jgellert@windcrestpartners.com
Education: AB, Harvard College
Background: Partner, Windcrest Discovery Investments; Oakes Fitzwilliams & Co.
Michael Gellert, Partner
212-599-3630
e-mail: mgellert@windcrestpartners.com
Education: AB, Harvard College
Directorships: Dalet Technologies, Seacor Holdings, Devon Energy, Humana, Six Flags, Regal Cinemas
William Fitzgerald, Partner
212-257-6705
e-mail: wfitzgerald@windcrestpartners.com
Education: AB, Harvard College; CFA
Background: Analyst, JP Morgan Investment Management

Venture Capital & Private Equity Firms / Domestic Firms

1992 WINDFORCE VENTURES, LLC
40 West 25th Street
New York, NY 10010

web: www.windforceventures.com

Mission Statement: Windforce Ventures is a venture capital firm specializing in early-stage social media and mobile technology investments. Headquartered in NYC, the firm is spearheaded by investment wizards and social media technology entrepreneurs. We couple exceptional entrepreneurs and cutting edge technologies with in-house advisory to help them build thriving companies.

Investment Criteria: Early-Stage
Industry Group Preference: Social Media, Mobile Technology
Portfolio Companies: BetterCompany, Sightly, Navdy, Food Genius, Reactor Labs, Mobile Roadie, Mashwork, Social Chorus, Kloudless, Freak'n Genius

Key Executives:
  Mario Montoya, Founder & President
  Education: Wharton School of Business
  Background: Renaissance Technologies; BEA Associates
  Jason Stein, Founding & Managing Partner
  Education: New York University
  Background: Founder & President, Laundry Service
  Directorships: Reactor, Inc; Kloudless
  Michoel Ogince, Founding & Managing Partner
  Background: Director of Platform and Product Strategy, Big Fuel
  Directorships: Mashwork; Nexgate, Mass Relevance; Video Genie; Social Chorus
  Waiman Leung, Advising Partner
  Education: BA, Economics, New York University
  Background: Founding Partner, LyonRoss Capital Management; Portfolio Manager, BEA Associates; Equity Research Analsyt, Lehman Brothers
  Brian Sullivan, Advising Partner
  Education: St. Johns University
  Background: Founder and Executive Producer, Movie Loft Productions

1993 WINDHAM VENTURE PARTNERS
1325 Ave. of the Americas
27th Floor
New York, NY 10019

Phone: 212-763-8525
e-mail: info@windhamventures.com
web: www.windhamvp.com

Mission Statement: Windham Venture Partners takes advantage of its unique relationships to access and build disruptive life science companies that will change the healthcare industry.

Industry Group Preference: Healthcare, Medical Technology, Digital Health
Portfolio Companies: BehaveCare, Blueprint Health, Cartiva, ClarVista Medical, Coravin, CredSimple, CuraSeal, CureAtr, CVRx, Dots, Earlens, GlySens, Help Around, InSleep Technologies, Invuity, Locemia Solutions, mc10, Nebula Genomics, Neotract, Neuspera, NovellusDx, Novocure, Nuelle, Nuvaira, Personal Genome Diagnostics, Science Exchange, Tales2Go, VytronUs, WellDoc, Willow

Key Executives:
  Adam E Fine, General Partner & CEO
  Education: BA, Boston University; MBA, New York University
  Background: VP & General Manager, I-many Inc.; Analyst, Cordis Corp.; Analyst, Coopers & Lybrand
  Directorships: Coravin, GlySens, CuraSeal, HelpAround, SpineView, MC10, Holaira, VytronUS
  Roger S Fine, General Partner & Chairman
  Education: Columbia University; New York University School of Law
  Background: VP & General Counsel, Johnson & Johnson

1994 WINDSPEED VENTURES
52 Waltham Street
Lexington, MA 02421

Phone: 781-860-8888 Fax: 781-860-0493
e-mail: info@wsventures.com
web: www.windspeed.com

Mission Statement: Actively helps build high technology companies, communications, security, media and internet services industries.

Geographic Preference: Northeast United States
Founded: 1999
Investment Criteria: Early-Stage
Industry Group Preference: Communications, Security, Media, Internet
Portfolio Companies: Active Network, Bradford Networks, BurstPoint Networks, Future Point Systems, Zipit Wireless, Apps.com, Bitfone, Fidelia Technology, Gracenote, OnFiber Communications, THINQ Learning Solutions, VistaPrint

Key Executives:
  Daniel H Bathon Jr, General Partner/Chairman
  Education: Villanova University
  Background: Partner, Drexel Burnham Lambert; FINATECH Inc.
  Directorships: Future Point Systems, BurstPoint Networks
  John W Bullock, Managing Partner
  Education: BS, Computer Science, Fitchburg State College
  Background: Bay Networks; Wellfleet Communications; Development Engineer, Codex/Motorola Corp.
  Directorships: Bradford Networks, BurstPoint Networks
  Steven E Karlson, General Partner
  Education: BS, Electrical Engineer, Brown University
  Background: Co-Founder/President, Accordance Corporation; OpenWave; Data General Corporation
  Directorships: Zipit Wireless

1995 WINDWARD VENTURES
San Diego, CA 92101

Phone: 619-435-5600
web: www.windwardventures.com

Mission Statement: A classic venture capital partnership organized to produce superior investment returns by providing capital and management assistance to early-stage, high growth companies. The firm manages a dedicated pool of capital provided by a group of institutional investors, individuals, and successful entrepreneurs; in addition, the firm occasionally manages direct investments on behalf of its limited partners. No longer making new investments.

Geographic Preference: Southern California
Fund Size: $90 million
Founded: 1997
Average Investment: $3 - $5 million
Minimum Investment: $250,000
Investment Criteria: Seed, Startup, First-Stage, Second-Stage, Early Stage, High Growth
Industry Group Preference: Data Communications, Electronic Technology, Semiconductors, Software, Internet Technology, Infrastructure, Medical Devices, Telecommunications
Portfolio Companies: Proximetry, SynergEyes, Syntricity

Other Locations:
  PO Box 7688
  Thousand Oaks, CA 91359
  Phone: 805-499-7338

Key Executives:
  David Titus, Managing Director
  e-mail: titus@windwardventures.com
  Education: BA, University of California, Santa Barbara
  Background: General Partner/Managing Director Corporate Finance, Technology Funding; Co-Founder/Senior VP, Silicon Valley Bank

James A Cole, Managing Director
e-mail: cole@windwardventures.com
Background: Founding General Partner, Spectra Enterprise Associates; Partner, New Enterprise Associates; Co-Founder/Executive VP, Amplica
Directorships: Vitesse Semiconductor Corporation, Gigatronics

1996 WING VENTURE PARTNERS
2061 Avy Avenue
Second Floor
Menlo Park, CA 94025

Phone: 650-316-8300
e-mail: info@wing.vc
web: wing.vc

Mission Statement: A next generation venture capital firm. Our sole focus is the transformation of Business Technology. Businesses of all sizes are embracing Data, Mobile and Cloud. The DMC paradigm shift is reshaping every corner of IT.

Investment Criteria: Early-Stage
Industry Group Preference: Business Technology, Data & Analytics, Mobile Computing, Cloud Computing, Information Technology
Portfolio Companies: Blue Jeans Networks, Jasper Wireless, Cumulus Networks, Redback Networks, Opower, Nimble Storage

Key Executives:
Gaurav Garg, Founding Partner
Education: BS, MS, Electrical Engineering, BS, Computer Science, Washington University, St. Louis
Background: Partner, Sequoia Capital; Founder, Redback Networks; Synoptics; Bay Networks
Directorships: Ruckus Wireless, FireEye, Mobileiron, Jasper, Shape Security, Instart Logic, Cohesity, Netscaler
Peter Wagner, Founding Partner
Education: AB, Physics, Harvard College; MBA, Harvard Business School
Background: Managing Partner, Accel Partners; Line Manager, Silicon Graphics
Directorships: Blue Jeans Network, OPOWER, Qwilt, Cumulus Networks, Jut, Platfora, CloudPhysics, Primary Data

1997 WINGATE PARTNERS
750 N St. Paul
Suite 1200
Dallas, TX 75201

Phone: 214-720-1313 Fax: 214-871-8799
web: www.wingatepartners.com

Mission Statement: To purchase controlling equity interests in companies where there is the opportunity to create value through superior operational and strategic execution.

Fund Size: $200 million
Founded: 1987
Average Investment: $250 million
Minimum Investment: $25 million
Investment Criteria: Controlling equity investments in manufacturing, distribution and service businesses undergoing significant transition, with revenues between $50 million and $500 million
Industry Group Preference: Consumer Services, Distribution, Electronic Components, Electronic Technology, Industrial Equipment, Business to Business, Manufacturing
Portfolio Companies: Strata Worldwide, MPI Products, Nekoosa, Preferred Compounding, Western Marketing, Dunn Paper, Stein World, Sunrise Oilfield Supply, USA Environment, Cal Pacific

Key Executives:
Jay I Applebaum, Partner
Education: BBA, University of Texas
Background: Founded, Plexus Financial Services; Merger & Acquisitions, Salomon Brothers; Management, Arthur Andersen & Company
Directorships: Corrpro; Pro Parts Xpress; Loomis, Fargo & Company
James A Johnson, Partner
Education: BS Industrial Engineering, Stanford University; MBA, Stanford Grad. School of Business
Background: Principal, Booz, Allen & Hamilton
Directorships: Corrpro; AmerCable; S&N Communications; Redmand Building Products; Century Products; AmeriStat; United Stationers; Pro Parts Xpress; Kevco
Jason Reed, Partner
Education: BS Economics/Finance, Oklahoma State University; MS Finance, London School of Economics; MBA, Harvard Business School
Background: Case Leader, Boston Consulting Group
Directorships: ENSR; AmerCable/Corrpro

1998 WINKLEVOSS CAPITAL

e-mail: press@winklevosscapital.com
web: www.winklevosscapital.com

Mission Statement: At Winklevoss Capital, we believe in determined entrepreneurs. Risk-taking is just in their blood. By providing guidance, relationships and capital, we reinforce their pursuit of a frictionless world and a better human experience. Because those who dare to fail greatly, dare to achieve greatly.

Portfolio Companies: Addy, ALOHA, AngelList, Astro, August, Authy, Bitcoin, BoxC, Cabify, Cambrian Genomics, Carbon38, Cargomatic, Changetip, Fedora, FiscalNote, Flexport, Keepy, Kimono, Lenda, Matternet, Memebox, MeUndies, Minibar, One Month, Paddle8, Partender, People.co, Regalii, Shyp, Sumzero, Sunshine, Taptalk, Vero, Xapo, Zuli

Key Executives:
Tyler Winklevoss, Founder
Cameron Winklevoss, Founder

1999 WINONA CAPITAL MANAGEMENT
980 North Michigan Avenue
Suite 1950
Chicago, IL 60611

Phone: 312-334-8800 Fax: 312-223-9484
e-mail: info@winonacapital.com
web: www.winonacapital.com

Mission Statement: Winona Capital Management is a unique private investment firm. We create lasting value by investing in consumer driven businesses operating in the lower end of the middle market.

Fund Size: $125 million
Industry Group Preference: Consumer Products, Consumer Services
Portfolio Companies: Boloco, CIRCA, Fusion Education Group, Johnny's Fine Foods, KJUS, Petsense, Top Driver
Luke Reese, Managing Director
e-mail: lreese@winonacapital.com
Education: DePauw University, University of Michigan Law School
Background: Senior Manager, Amer Sports; Corporate Law, Lathan & Watkins
Directorships: Peter Millar, Dragon Alliance, Johnny's Fine Foods, Top Driver
Laird Koldyke, Managing Director
e-mail: lkoldyke@winonacapital.com
Education: Northwestern University; Kellogg Graduate School of Management
Background: Founding Partner, Triple Tree Capital; General Partner, Frontenac Company
Directorships: Chipolte Mexican Grille, Einstein's Bagels, Wild Oats Markets, Home Fashions, Marks Bros. Jewelers, Leewards Crafts

Venture Capital & Private Equity Firms / Domestic Firms

Jason Sowers, Director
e-mail: jsowers@winonacapital.com
Education: Amherst College; MBA, University of Chicago Booth School of Business
Background: Global Strategic & Commercial Intelligence Group, KPMG
Directorships: Dragon Alliance

2000 WIREFRAME VENTURES
San Francisco, CA

web: www.wireframevc.com

Mission Statement: Wireframe Ventures seeks mission-driven entrepreneurs emerging in constantly growing tech industry.

Founded: 2016
Industry Group Preference: Technology, Fintech, Healthcare, Wellness
Portfolio Companies: Assurex Health, Astronomer, DNAnexus, Full Harvest, Geneticure, Level 10 Energy, Mammoth Biosciences, Misty Robotics, Near Space Labs, OpenInvest, Palantir, Renew Financial, Reverie Labs, Xtelligent

Key Executives:
Harsh Patel, Co-Founder/Managing Partner
Education: BS, University of Illinois; MBA, Stanford Grad. School of Business
Background: Manager, Accenture; Co-Founder/CTO, Orbit Commerce Inc.; General Partner, RRE Ventures; President, Bina Technologies; General Partner, Claremont Creek Ventures; Affiliate, Webb Investment Network
Directorships: CareMessage; DNAnexus; Assurex Health; NuMedii

2001 WISCONSIN INVESTMENT PARTNERS
PO Box 45919
Madison, WI 53744

Phone: 608-692-7481
e-mail: info@wisinvpartners.com
web: www.wisinvpartners.com

Mission Statement: Wisconsin Investment Partners is a life science- and technology-focused angel investment firm.

Geographic Preference: Wisconsin
Founded: 2000
Investment Criteria: Early Stage
Industry Group Preference: Life Sciences, Technology
Portfolio Companies: AquaMost, Aver Informatics, BeeKeeper Labs, BellBrook Labs, Biolonix, Carson Life, Cellectar, ConjuGon, Deltanoid Pharmaceuticals, Forward Health Group, HarQen, Health eFilings, Invenra, iVMD, Kiio, Lumec, Madison Vaccines, Murfie, Needls, NeoClone, nPoint, OptiMine, Phoenix Nuclear Labs, Pinpoint Software, Quintessence Biosciences, SHINE Medical Technologies, Silatronix, Skin Analytics, Snowshoe Stamps, SOLOMO, Stemina Biomarker Discovery, Stratatech Corporation, Swallow Solutions, TrackIF, Virent, Xolve, Zurex Pharma Inc.

Key Executives:
Brad Bodden, Co-Manager
Education: University of Washington
Michael Thorson, Co-Manager
Education: BS, Economics, United States Military Academy; Brasenose College, Univ. of Oxford
Background: Founder & Managing Director, Inventure Capital; Bank of America, London; President, Banc of America Securities, Japan; Soros Funds Limited; Bankers Trust Company
Bob Wood, Co-Manager
Background: Space-Metrics; American Players Theatre
Andrea Dlugos, Co-Manager
Background: Project Manager; Business Analyst; Financial Analyst

2002 WL ROSS & CO.
1166 Avenue of the Americas
New York, NY 10036

Phone: 212-826-1100

Fund Size: $12 billion
Founded: 2000

2003 WOMEN'S VENTURE CAPITAL FUND
9720 Wilhire Boulevard
Fifth Floor
Beverly Hills, CA 90212

Phone: 323-496-6424
e-mail: monica@womensvcfund.com
web: www.womensvcfund.com

Mission Statement: The Fund capitalizes on the expanding pipeline of women entrepeneurs leading gender diverse teams and creating capital efficient, high growth companies in digital media and sustainable products and services. We believe that this unique investment strategy now provides the potential for extraordinary returns.

Industry Group Preference: Digital Media & Marketing, Environment, Mobile, Social Media
Portfolio Companies: OMNI Retail Group, EdSurge, NVoicePay, Proxio, Ivycorp
Edith Dorsen, Founder & Managing Director
e-mail: edith@womensvcfund.com
Education: BS, Economics, Wharton School; MBA, Harvard Business School; MPA, Kennedy School of Government
Background: Business Development, Children's Television Workshop; Investment Banking, Salomon Brothers; McKinsey & Company

2004 WOODBRIDGE GROUP
1764 Litchfield Turnpike
Suite 250
New Haven, CT 06525

Toll-Free: 800-567-1119
e-mail: headquarters@woodbridgegrp.com
web: www.woodbridgegrp.com

Mission Statement: To professionally represent middle market companies in the mergers and acquisitions arena.

Geographic Preference: Worldwide
Investment Criteria: Middle-market companies with $5 to $100 million in revenue
Industry Group Preference: Business Products & Services, Consumer Products, Distribution, Franchising, Logistics, Manufacturing, Software, Waste & Recycling

Key Executives:
Robert Koenig, Chief Executive Officer
e-mail: robert@woodbridgegrp.com
Background: President, Koenig Corporation
Donald A Krier, Senior Managing Director/Partner
e-mail: donald@woodbridgegrp.com
Education: BS in Business/Systems, Taylor University
Larry Reinharz, Senior Managing Director/Partner
Education: BA, Political Science & Economics, Manhattanville College
Background: Commercial Finance, JP Morgan Chase; Merrill Lynch

2005 WOODSIDE FUND
303 Twin Dolphin Rive
Suite 600
Redwood Shores, CA 94065

Phone: 650-610-8050 Fax: 650-610-8051
e-mail: info@woodsidefund.com

Mission Statement: Woodside Fund is a venture capital firm. The firm has grown to four funds and over $110 million under management. The Fund is distinctive in that each partner has founded, built and served as CEO in at least one company

Venture Capital & Private Equity Firms / Domestic Firms

prior to joining the Fund. As former entrepreneurs, we understand the difficulties of raising venture capital and the challenges of launching a new enterprise. Our practical knowledge and firsthand experience enable us to develop unusually close, long-term relationships with the founders and managers of our portfolio companies. As a result, we typically serve as the lead investor and have co-founded a number of our portfolio companies. We also balance our early-stage emphasis with selective investments in emerging companies.

Fund Size: $110 million
Founded: 1983
Average Investment: $5-10 million
Investment Criteria: Seed, Startup, First-stage, Second-stage
Industry Group Preference: Biotechnology, Software, Electronic Technology, Energy, Natural Resources, Industrial Services, Medical & Health Related, Networking, Telecommunications, Semiconductors, Enterprise Software
Portfolio Companies: Analogix Semiconductor, APX, Aristos Logic, Athena Design, Azaire Networks, BeFree, Berkeley Design Automation, Borderware, Conexant Systems, Evans & Sutherland, Firepond, Intalio, Intellefex, Intelligent Markets, InterTrust, Matisse Networks, Merant, Nanoconduction, New Era of Networks, Novell, Onsite Systems, SS8 Networks, DMC Stratex Networks, Stream Processors, Tacit Software, Veriware, Zenverge, PowerReviews

Key Executives:
  Vincent M Occhipinti, Co-Founder, Managing Director
  Education: Graduate, Stanford University and Graduate School of Business, University of California, Berkeley
  Background: Founder, President, & CEO, Logisticon Inc.; Vice President of Marketing, Mobility Systems
  Robert E Larson, Co-Founder, Managing Partner
  Education: BS, MIT; Master of Science and PhD Degrees, Electrical Engineering, Stanford Unviersity
  Background: Co-Founder, President, & CEO, Systems Control; President, International Institute of Electrical & Electronic Engineers
  Directorships: Consulting Professor, Stanford University - Engineering/Economic Systems Department

2006 WORK-BENCH
110 Fifth Avenue
5th Floor
New York, NY 10011

Phone: 646-494-6231
e-mail: hello@work-bench.com
web: www.work-bench.com

Mission Statement: A venture capital firm investing in early-stage startups in the field of enterprise software.

Founded: 2012
Investment Criteria: Series A & B
Industry Group Preference: Big Data & Analytics, Cloud Native Infrastructure, Data-Defined Security
Portfolio Companies: Algorithmia, Alluvium, Blacktrace, Cockroach Labs, Core OS, Dialpad, Merlon Intelligence, Metric Insights, RA EL, Socure, Tamr, Trapezoid, True, UpLevel, UpSkill, vArmour, Versive, VTS, X.

Key Executives:
  Jonathan Lehr, Co-Founder/General Partner
  Education: BSE, Bioengineering, University of Pennsylvania
  Background: Founder, NY Enterprise Technology Meetup; IT, Morgan Stanley
  Jessica Lin, Co-Founder/General Partner
  Education: BA, Government & African Studies, Harvard University
  Background: Learning & Development Manager, Cisco Systems

2007 WORLDVIEW TECHNOLOGY PARTNERS
99 S Almaden Boulevard
6th Floor
San Jose, CA 95113

Phone: 650-322-3800
e-mail: wvfinance@worldview.com
web: www.worldview.com

Mission Statement: Dedicated to helping build leading US information technology companies. To add significant value to its portfolio companies through active participation and by making the connections needed to help US entrepreneurs expand their businesses into the Asia-Pacific region.

Geographic Preference: Worldwide
Fund Size: $1.4 billion
Founded: 1996
Average Investment: $5 million
Minimum Investment: $1 million
Investment Criteria: Seed, First-stage, Second-stage, Mezzanine
Industry Group Preference: Telecommunications, Software, Semiconductors, Infrastructure, Communications, Internet, Digital Media & Marketing, Wireless Technologies, Enterprise Software
Portfolio Companies: 3PAR, AFC, Ciena, Cogent Communications, Corvis, Cyras, DigitalThink, MMC, NVIDIA, PostPath, Redstone, Silicon Spice, Simplex Solutions, Tellium, Tensilica, Tivoli, WFI

Other Locations:
  101 S. Ellsworth Avenue
  Suite 401
  Shibuya-ku
  San Mateo, CA 94401
  Phone: 650-3223800 Fax: 650-3223880

Key Executives:
  James Wei, Co-Founder, General Partner
  650-322-3800
  Fax: 650-322-3880
  e-mail: jameswei@worldview.com
  Education: BS, System Design Engineering, University of Waterloo
  Background: Fund Manager Jafco, Sony & IBM
  Directorships: Caly Networks, Commverge Solutions, Mainsail Networks, Object Automation, Silicon Spice, Tensilica, Cogent Communications, 3ParData, Movaz Networks
  Michael Orsak, General Partner
  650-322-3800
  Fax: 650-322-3880
  e-mail: morsak@worldview.com
  Education: MBA, BA, Economics, Stanford University
  Background: Fund Co-Manager Jafco, Glenwood Management, Robertson, Stephens & Company
  Directorships: Snowball.Com, Lexiquest, Lightwave Microsystems, eVoice, Upshot
  Pete Goettner, General Partner
  Education: MBA, University of California, Berkeley, BS, University of Michigan
  Background: Co-Founder/CEo, DigitalThink, Knowledge Revolution
  James N. Strawbridge, General Partner/COO
  Education: BS, Industrial Engineering, Virginia Tech; JD, University of Virginia
  Background: EVP, CFO, CAO, RealNames Corporation; Wilson Sonsini Goodrich & Rosati
  Susumu Tanaka, General Partner
  Education: BA, Business Administration, Hitolsubashi University
  Background: Jafco, King Kogyo, Tokai Bank
  Yasuharu Watanabe, Partner
  Education: BA, Economics, Hiroshima University
  Background: Business Development Manager, JAFCO

Venture Capital & Private Equity Firms / Domestic Firms

2008 WRF CAPITAL
2815 Eastlake Avenue E
Suite 300
Seattle, WA 98102

Phone: 206-336-5600
e-mail: info@wrfcapital.com
web: www.wrfseattle.org

Mission Statement: Manages Washington Research Foundation's seed venture fund by creating and investing primarily in technology-based start-up companies that have strong ties to the University of Washington and other non-profit research institutions in Washington State.

Geographic Preference: Washington
Founded: 1981
Average Investment: $1-$2 million
Minimum Investment: $500,000
Investment Criteria: Early Stage
Industry Group Preference: Biomedical, Biotechnology, Infrastructure, Information Technology, Advanced Materials, Healthcare, Industrial Services, Software, Internet
Portfolio Companies: AbSci, Accelerator Corp., Accium Biosciences, Acylin Therapeutics, Alder Biopharmaceuticals, AnswerDash, Apogen, AppAttach, Aqueduct, Arzeda Corp., Bellwether Bio, Cardeas Pharma, Cardiac Insight, Corensic, EnerG2, Epithany, Faraday, FlexMinder, GlobeImmune, Groove Biopharma, Group14, Hyperion Therpeutics, Ikaria, Juno Therapeutics, MicroGREEN Polymers, Mirador Biomedical, Mobisante, Modumetal, Nexgenia, Nimbic, NLIGHT, Nohla, Oncofactor, One Radio, Phase Genomics, Phytelligence, Protemo, Qazzow, Resolve Therapeutics, Rodeo Therapeutics, Shippable, Skytap, SNUPI Technologies, Targeted Growth, TransformativeMed, Uptake Medical, VLST, Wibotic

Key Executives:
  Ronald S Howell, CEO
  Education: BS, Biochemistry, Washington State University
  Background: Medical sales and operations
  Jeff Eby, CFO
  Education: AB/B.Arch, Rice University; MBA, Finance & Accounting, Northwestern University's Kellogg Graduate School of Management
  Background: CFO, Seattle Art Museum; Consultant, Arthur Andersen & Christopher J. Brown and Associates
  Loretta Little, Managing Director
  Education: AB, Zoology, Pomona College; MA, Business Administration, University of Arizona
  Background: Marketing Manager/Market Consultant
  William J Canestaro, Managing Director
  Education: AB, Dartmouth College; MSc, Oxford University; PhD, University of Washington
  Background: National Pharmaceutical Council; Genetech; AstraZeneca
  Directorships: Arzeda, Bellwether Bio, Phase Genomics, Icosavax, EpiThany, Wibotic

2009 WYNNCHURCH CAPITAL
6250 North River Road
Suite 10-100
Rosemont, IL 60018

Phone: 847-604-6100 Fax: 847-604-6105
Toll-Free: 877-604-6111
web: www.wynnchurch.com

Mission Statement: To partner with management by capitalizing on the company's strength to achieve revenue growth and profit improvement.

Geographic Preference: United States, Canada
Fund Size: $500 million
Founded: 1999
Investment Criteria: Buyouts, Corporate Carve-Outs, Recapitalizations, Joint Ventures, Restructurings, Growth Capital, Going Private, Bankruptcies
Industry Group Preference: Niche Manufacturing, Distribution, Transportation, Logistics, Energy, Power Technologies, Business Products & Services, Industrial Services
Portfolio Companies: Burtek Enterprises, Calyx Transportation Group, Fabco Automotive, Foss Manufacturing Company, Groupe Moreau, Henniges Automotice Holdings, Indiana Limestone Company, Ironform Holdings, JAC Products, Loadmaster Derrick & Equipment, Northstar Aerospace, Pro-Fab Group, Senco Brands, Surepoint Technologies Group, United States Pipe and Foundry Company, US Manufacturing Corporation, Vista-Pro Automotive, Wolverine Advanced Materials

Other Locations:
  2121 Rosecrans Avenue
  Suite 2370
  El Segundo, CA 90245
  Phone: 310-492-4068

  Wynnchurch Capital Canada LLC
  150 York Street
  Suite 801
  Toronto, ON M5H 3S5
  Canada
  Phone: 416-363-1423

Key Executives:
  John A. Hatherly, Managing Partner
  e-mail: jhatherly@wynnchurch.com
  Education: BA, University of Notre Dame; MBA, University of Wisconsin
  Background: Senior Executive, GE Capital; First National Bank of Chicago
  Directorships: Android Industries, Connection Concepts, SafeWorks, Calyx Transporation Group, 4Front Engineered Solutions, The Surepoint Group
  Duncan S. Bourne, Managing Director
  847-604-6104
  e-mail: dbourne@wynnchurch.com
  Education: BS, Chemical Engineering, Northwestern University; MBA, University of Chicago
  Background: Parter, BDO Seidman LLP; Senior Manager, Ernst & Young
  Steve M. Welborn, Managing Director
  847-604-6129
  e-mail: swelborn@wynnchurch.com
  Education: BSBA, Finance, University of Missouri; MBA, St. Louis University
  Background: COO, Gateway Marketing International; AT&T; Adams Harris Inc.
  Morty White, Managing Director
  416-363-1423
  e-mail: mwhite@wynnchurch.com
  Education: BComm, McGill University; MBA, University of Michigan
  Background: GE Capital

2010 XG VENTURES

e-mail: info@xg-ventures.com
web: www.xg-ventures.com

Mission Statement: XG Ventures was founded in March 2008 by ex-Googlers, who were early hires in strategic roles at Google. Pietro Dova and Andrea Zurek are the managing members of XG Ventures and are dedicated to advising and investing in supremely talented early stage teams. We learned a great deal at Google, including how its unique culture shaped a dynamic and fun enterprise. Together, with our complementary expertise, our goal is to help successfully guide the start-up teams, in which we invest and advise, to the next stage. We provide operational and strategic expertise, mentorship, global networking contacts, and access to seed capital and beyond.

Founded: 2008
Investment Criteria: Early-Stage

Venture Capital & Private Equity Firms / Domestic Firms

Industry Group Preference: Consumer Internet, Mobile, Gaming, Social Media, Digital Media & Marketing
Portfolio Companies: AdStage, AirHelp, Altitude, Apiary.io, Apptimize, Blend, Chartboost, Chobo Labs, Dealflicks, eShares, Euclid, Facecake, Glympse, Graffiti Labs, Kamcord, Keen IO, Kloudless, LivBlends, Mighty Meeting, MNectar, Mylikes, NoRedInk, nWay, OLSet, PicCollage, Piqora, Pogoseat, Prediction IO, Rapt Media, Rockbot, Science Exchange, Shift, Shots, Shyp, Small Demons, Starmaker, Tangible Play, Tapsense, Telly, Thanx, Thirdlove, Tok.tv, Tsumobi, Tynker, Verious, Wizeline, Wish, Yango.com, Zesta, Zuli

Key Executives:
  Pietro Dova, Partner
  Education: Civil Engineering, Imperial College; MS, Management, MIT Sloan School of Management
  Background: Corporate Controller & Finance Director, Google
  Andrea Zurek, Partner
  Background: Google, Computerworld

2011 XSEED CAPITAL MANAGEMENT
3130 Alpine Road
Suite 200
Portola Valley, CA 94028

Phone: 650-331-1230
e-mail: info@xseedcap.com
web: www.xseedcap.com

Mission Statement: Founded in 2006 as one of the pioneers of the new venture industry, XSeed Capital works with entrepreneurs to build differentiated technology startups that dramatically change markets. We are serial entrepreneurs who appreciate the dedication, passion, anxiety and sleepless nights it takes to build something valuable from scratch.

Fund Size: $110 million
Founded: 2006
Investment Criteria: Seed-Stage
Industry Group Preference: Information Technology, Clean Technology, Life Sciences
Portfolio Companies: StackStorm, Cirro Secure, Trifacta, Zooz, @Scale, Chatous, Lex Machina, Biota Technology, Citrine, Cape Productions, Dispatcher, Breezeworks, DropThought, Neon, BrightBox, Sipx, The League, Pixlee, Playnomics, GeneWeave, ZipLine Medical, HMicro, Allopartis, MuseAmi, OpxBio, Siva

Key Executives:
  Michael Borrus, Founding General Partner
  e-mail: mborrus@xseedcap.com
  Education: BA, Princeton University; MA, UC Berkeley; JD, Harvard Law School
  Background: Technology Banking, The Petkevich Group; Adjunct Professor, UC Berkeley's College of Engineering
  Rob Siegel, General Partner
  e-mail: rsiegel@xseedcap.com
  Education: BA, UC Berkeley; MBA, Stanford University
  Background: General Manager, GE Security; EVP, Pixim; Co-Founder & CEO, Weave Innovations
  Alan Chiu, Partner
  e-mail: dhanzel@xseedcap.com
  Education: BASc, Electrical & Computer Engineering, University of British Columbia; MS, Management, Stanford Graduate School of Business
  Background: Vice President, Product Marketing & Reagent Development, Pacific Biosciences; Principal Scientist, Molecular Dynamics
  Jeff Thermond, Venture Partner
  e-mail: jthermond@xseedcap.com
  Education: BA, Philosophy & Psychology, Yale University; MBA, Marketing, Indiana University
  Background: CEO, Woven Systems; CEO, Epigram; VP & General Manager, 3Com
  Damon Cronkey, Partner
  Background: SurveyMonkey; Yahoo

2012 Y COMBINATOR
335 Pioneer Way
Mountain View, CA 94041

web: www.ycombinator.com

Mission Statement: Y Combinator funds large numbers of startups in two batches each year, in winter and summer.

Founded: 2005
Average Investment: $120K
Investment Criteria: Seed
Industry Group Preference: Web/Mobile Applications
Portfolio Companies: Stripe, Vidyard, Optimizely, Checkr, Coinbase, PlanGrid, Weebly, Gusto, DoorDash, Clever, LendUp, Dropbox, Teespring, Mixpanel, Machine Zone, Segment, CoreOS, Twitch, Reddit, FiveStars, Genius, Tilt, Docker, Matterport, Airbnb, PagerDuty, Memebox, Heroku, WePay, Instacart

Key Executives:
  Jessica Livingston, Co-Founder
  Education: Bucknell University
  Background: Adams Harkness

2013 YELLOWSTONE CAPITAL
1177 West Loop S.
Suite 1425
Houston, TX 77027

Phone: 713-650-0065 Fax: 713-650-0055
e-mail: info@yellowstonecapital.com
web: www.yellowstonecapital.com

Mission Statement: A Houston-based, private equity and venture capital investment firm, focused on acquiring and/or investing in small to medium-sized businesses.

Geographic Preference: North America, Europe, Middle East, Asia
Founded: 1993
Investment Criteria: Buy-outs
Industry Group Preference: Energy Technology, Industrial Manufacturing, Healthcare, Life Sciences, Food & Beverage

Key Executives:
  Omar A Sawaf, Chairman/CEO
  Education: BA, Ohio State University; MBA, Harvard University
  Background: President, Capital Guidance Corporation
  Sami Sawaf, Principal
  Education: BBA, MBA, Methodist University
  Background: Director, FTI Corporate Finance; MENA Solar Energy; White River Energy

2014 YES VC
San Francisco, CA

e-mail: partners@yes.vc
web: yes.vc

Mission Statement: Yes VC is an pre-seed and seed-stage venture capital firm investing in infrastructure, internet, and other technologies.

Geographic Preference: United States, Europe
Fund Size: $50 million
Founded: 2018
Average Investment: $250,000 - $1 million
Minimum Investment: $250,000
Industry Group Preference: Technology, Infrastructure, Internet, Applications, Security, AI
Portfolio Companies: Gaze, Orchid, Spell

Key Executives:
  Caterina Fake, Co-Founder
  Education: BA, English, Vassar College
  Background: Co-Founder, Flickr; Co-Founder, Hunch
  Jyri Engestrom, Co-Founder
  Education: MA, University of Helsinki; PhD, Lancaster University
  Background: Senior Product Manager, Internet Handhelds, Nokia; Product Manager, Google;

Venture Capital & Private Equity Firms / Domestic Firms

Co-Founder/Chairman, Jaiku; Co-Founder/CEO, Ditto.me; Director of Product Management, Groupon; Head of Product, Boosted Inc.; Entrepreneur in Residence, True Ventures
Directorships: ICEYE

2015 YORK STREET CAPITAL PARTNERS LLC
Bedminster, NJ 07921

e-mail: golding@yorkstreetcapital.com

Mission Statement: An investment firm that provides mezzanine and equity capital to private equity sponsors for acquisitions, buyouts, growth capital and recapitalizations of middle market companies.

Geographic Preference: United States
Fund Size: $557 million
Founded: 2002
Average Investment: $10-$35 million
Minimum Investment: $10 million
Investment Criteria: Acquistions, Buyouts, Growth Capital, Recapitalizations, Mezzanine
Industry Group Preference: Healthcare, Manufacturing, Industrial Services, Consumer Products, Food & Beverage
Portfolio Companies: Bare Escentuals, Brickman Group, Easton-Bell Sports, Hudson Products, i2, Lexington Home Brands, Managed Health Care Associates, MD Beauty, Miller Heiman, Motorsport Aftermarket Group, Neptune Technology Group, Panther Expedited Services, Performance, Powermat, Prestige Brands International, River Ranch Fresh Foods, Sunshine Restaurant Partners, Targus Group International, World Health Club

Key Executives:
  Robert M Golding, Managing Partner
  908-658-3714
  e-mail: golding@yorkstreetcapital.com
  Education: BA, Trinity College
  Background: Managing Director, CIT's Corporate Finance Group; Salomon Brothers; Merrill Lynch; Irving Trust Company
  Directorships: Lexington Furniture, Easton-Bell Sports, Miller Heiman, Panther Expedited Services, Performance, Targus Group International
  Christopher A Layden, Managing Partner
  908-658-3713
  e-mail: layden@yorkstreetcapital.com
  Education: BA, Fairfield University; MBA, The George Washington University
  Background: Senior Director/Founding Member, CIT's Corporate Finance Group; Reuben H. Donnelly Corp.; Xerox Credit Corporation
  Directorships: Targus Group International
  Logan V. O'Connor, Vice President
  908-658-9944
  e-mail: logal@yorkstreetcapital.com
  Education: B.A. Economics, Trinity College
  Background: Targus Group International, Lexington Furniture, World Health Club

2016 YUCAIPA COMPANIES
Los Angeles, CA

Phone: 310-789-7200
e-mail: investorrelations@yucaipaco.com
web: www.yucaipaco.com

Mission Statement: A premier investment firm that has established a record of fostering economic value through the growth and responsible development of companies.

Founded: 1986

Key Executives:
  Ron Burkle, Managing Partner

2017 ZELKOVA VENTURES
667 Madison Avenue
New York, NY 10065

web: www.zelkovavc.com

Mission Statement: At Zelkova Ventures, we are passionate about assisting in the growth of businesses. We roll up our sleeves and partner with our portfolio companies for success. Zelkova Ventures is a venture capital firm committed to helping talented entrepreneurs build incredible companies. Primarily we look to invest in early stage companies, many times pre-revenue. In many instances we provide a company's first outside/institutional capital. As former entrepreneurs, we understand the highs and lows of launching a new company. We look to take an active role and partner with the companies we invest in. Along with our capital Zelkova brings expertise, insight and execution to all of our portfolio companies.

Investment Criteria: Early-Stage
Industry Group Preference: SaaS, Internet, Media, Green Technology
Portfolio Companies: Ribbit, Locus Energy, Crimson Hexagon, My Damn Channel, Fynaz, Altruik, Encoding.com, JIBE, Livefyre, Kapost, Fab.com, GameChanger, Kohort, Spring Metrics, GreenGoose, FullContact, HelpScout, RedRover, BrandYourself, Ambassador, Dispatch.io, Space Monkey, Lettuce, RJ Metrics, Reachli, Customer.io, Postmaster, Crowdly, FlyCleaners

Key Executives:
  Jay Levy, Partner
  Education: Rutgers University
  Background: Morgan Stanley; Founder, MPI Professionals; Founding Partner, Trueview Services
  Larry Scheinfeld, Partner
  Background: Principal, Quellos Group; Partner, Uproot Wines

2018 ZEPHYR MANAGEMENT LP
320 Park Avenue
New York, NY 10022

Phone: 212-508-9400 Fax: 212-508-9494
e-mail: zephyr@zmlp.com
web: www.zephyrmanagement.com

Mission Statement: Zephyr Management LP is a global private equity and marketable securities firm. The firm specializes in the creation and management of highly focused and value added investment funds. Since its founding, Zephyr has sponsored twenty-two investment funds representing approximately $1.8 billion in capital commitments. Each Zephyr fund has a discrete management team which has skills matched to the particular investment opportunity.

Geographic Preference: Asia, Africa, Latin America, Europe, Middle East
Fund Size: $1 billion
Founded: 1994
Investment Criteria: Consolidations, Management Buy-outs, Recapitaizations, Growth Capital
Industry Group Preference: Diversified

Other Locations:
  3rd Floor, IndiQube TownHub
  Indira Nagar 1st Stafe, H Colony
  Indiranagar, Bengaluru
  Karnataka 560038
  India
  Phone: 91-80-4681-8300

  No. 48/5/1 (West Wing)
  Parkway Building
  Park Street
  Colombo 2
  Sri Lanka
  Phone: 94-11-2303810 Fax: 94-11-2303811

  #201 Embassy Classic
  11 Vittal Mallya
  Bangalore 560001

Venture Capital & Private Equity Firms / Domestic Firms

India
Phone: 91-8042613300 **Fax:** 91-8042613400
Key Executives:
Thomas C. Barry, Founder/CEO
e-mail: zephyr@zmlp.com
Education: MBA, Harvard Business School; BA, Latin American Studies, Yale University
Background: President/CEO, Rockefeller & Company; President, T. Rowe Price; CFA, Institute of Chartered Financial Analysts
Mukul Gulati, Managing Partner
Education: BA, Economics, University of Maryland; MBA, Columbia Business School
Background: VP of Quantitative Research, Reuters
Directorships: Multex
Stephen E. Canter, Managing Director
Education: AB, Cornell University; MBA, Columbia University Graduate School of Business
Background: Chairman & CEO, The Dreyfus Corporation; Vice Chairman, Mellon Financial Corporation

2019 ZETTA VENTURE PARTNERS
473 Jackson Street
Suite 200
San Francisco, CA 94111

e-mail: info@zettavp.com
web: www.zettavp.com

Mission Statement: Zetta Venture Partners is a tech-based venture capital firm with a specialty in Artificial Intelligence.

Average Investment: $1-3 million
Minimum Investment: $1 million
Industry Group Preference: Artificial Intelligence, Technology
Portfolio Companies: Allure Security, Aptology, Clearbit, Constructor, Crate.io, Domino Data Lab, Domo, Dor, Falkonry, Finite State, Focal Systems, FollowAnalytics, Galley, InsideSales.com, Invenia, Kaggle, Lilt, Marketing Evolution, Myia, Opsani, OptiMine, Promethium, Rever, Test.ai, Tractable, Verusen, VideaHealth

Key Executives:
Mark Gorenberg, Managing Director
Education: BS, MIT; MS, University of Minnesota; MS, Standford University
Background: Sun Microsystems
Ash Fontana, Managing Director
Education: University of Sydney
Background: Co-Founded, Topguest; Private Equity Analyst, MacQuarie Capital
Jocelyn Goldfein, Managing Director
Education: BS, Stanford University
Background: Software Engineer, Facebook; Software Engineer, VMware

2020 ZM CAPITAL
19 West 44th Street
18th Floor
New York, NY 10036

Phone: 212-223-1383 **Fax:** 212-223-1384
web: zmclp.com

Mission Statement: ZM Capital is the private equity investment fund of ZelnickMedia. The fund invests in media companies in which the partnership's capital resources, industry contacts and operational experience can meaningfully enhance growth and value.

Industry Group Preference: Media, Software, Publishing, Advertising, Direct Marketing, Networking & Equipment, Marketing, Music
Portfolio Companies: 9 Story Limited, Airvana, Alloy, Cannella Response Television, Cast & Crew, ITN Networks, Take-Two Interactive

Key Executives:
Strauss Zelnick, Co-Founder
Education: BA, Wesleyan University; JD, Harvard Law School; MBA, Harvard Business School
Background: President & CEO, BMG Entertainment; President & CEO, Crystal Dynamics; President & CEO, 20th Century Fox
Directorships: Take Two Interactive Software
Karl Slatoff, Managing Partner
Education: BA, Kenyon College; MBA, Harvard Business School
Background: Vice President, New Media, BMG Entertainment; Strategic Planning, Walt Disney Company
Directorships: Cannella Response Television
Jordan Turkewitz, Managing Partner/Chief Investment Officer
Education: BA, Government, Cornell University; MBA, Columbia Business School
Background: Senior Director, Acquisitions, JupiterMedia Corporation; Associate, Merrill Lynch
Andrew Vogel, Managaing Partner/Chief Investment Officer
Education: BA, Mathematics & Economics, Wesleyan University; MBA, Harvard Business School
Background: Ripplewood Holdings; McCown De Leeuw & Co.; Lehman Brothers

2021 ZONE VENTURES
2882 Sand Hill Road
Suite 150
Menlo Park, CA 94025

Phone: 650-233-9000
web: www.zonevc.com

Mission Statement: A partnership funded by institutional investors for the purpose of providing equity capital to young, high growth companies, while achieving superior returns to its investors.

Geographic Preference: United States, California
Fund Size: $135 million
Founded: 1998
Average Investment: $1-$2 million
Minimum Investment: $1 million
Investment Criteria: Seed, First Stage
Industry Group Preference: Software, Communications, Information Technology, Manufacturing, Media, Wireless Technologies, Networking, Technology
Portfolio Companies: 3GA, Advanced, Akimbo Systems, Allpets.com, Biger Boat, Copper Key, Digital Campaigns, DivX, eStyle, hiwire, Lumexis, Microfabrica, Neven Vision, Showbizdata, Siimpel, Traffic Station, Vizional, Zkey.com, Zone Reactor

Key Executives:
Frank M. Creer, Founder/Managing Director
Education: Finance, University of Utah
Directorships: Akimbo; DivX; emWare; e-Style; Packet Air Networks; Vizional Technologies; ZKey
Dr. N. Darius Sankey, Partner
Education: BS, Physics & Electrical Engineering, MIT; PhD, Optical Engineering, The Institute of Optics at the University of Rochester
Background: Management Consultant, McKinsey & Company; Rand, At&T Bell Laboratories; Adju
William Lewis, Partner
Education: BS, Engineering Physics, University of California, Berkeley; MS, PhD, Materials Science & Engineering, Stanford University
Background: JP Morgan, Intevac
Timothy Draper, Founder/Managing Director
Education: BS, Electrical Engineering, Stanford University; MBA, Harvard Business School

Venture Capital & Private Equity Firms / Domestic Firms

2022 ZS FUND LP
1133 Avenue of the Americas
New York, NY 10036
Phone: 212-398-6200 Fax: 212-398-1808
web: www.zsfundlp.com

Mission Statement: A private equity firm engaged in making long-term investments in successful middle-market companies.

Geographic Preference: United States
Fund Size: $150 million
Founded: 1985
Minimum Investment: $5 million
Investment Criteria: LBO, MBO
Industry Group Preference: Business to Business, Consumer Products, Distribution, Retailing, Instrumentation, Medical & Health Related, Insurance, Industrial Equipment
Portfolio Companies: Casabella Holdings, ECS Refining, Industrial Air Tool, L.P., Research Horizons, SOS Security, Transervice Logistics

Key Executives:
  Ned Sherwood, Co-Founder
  e-mail: nsherwood@zsfundlp.com
  Education: Wharton School at the University of Pennsylvania
  Background: Principal, AEA Investors; VP, W.R. Grace & Company; Assistant to President, Hazeltine Corporation
  Shahzad Pirvani
  e-mail: spirvani@zsfundlp.com
  Education: BBA, University of Warwick; University of Georgia
  Background: Battery Ventures; Blackford Capital; Arctaris Impact Investors
  Bob Horne
  e-mail: bhorne@zsfundlp.com
  Education: BA, Harvard College; MBA, Stanford Graduate School of Business
  Background: Vice President, Salomon Brothers
  Nick Burger
  e-mail: nburger@zsfundlp.com
  Education: BA, Yale University
  Background: Analyst, Merrill Lynch; MLC Funds Management

2023 eLAB VENTURES
635 Mariners Island
Suite 204
San Mateo, CA 94404
Phone: 650-551-5000
web: elabvc.com

Mission Statement: eLab Ventures is an early stage venture capital fund investing in disruptive technology that will fuel the rise of autonomous and connected vehicles.

Geographic Preference: Silicon Vallet and Michigan

Other Locations:
  505 E Liberty Street
  Suite LL500
  Ann Arbor, MI 48104
  Phone: 734-926-5221

Key Executives:
  Rick Bolander, Managing Director
  e-mail: rick@elabvc.com
  Education: BS, MS, University of Michigan; MBA, Harvard Business School
  Background: Founder, Blue Sky Ventures; General Partner, Apex Venture Partners; Co-Founder, Gabriel Venture Partners
  Paul Brown, Managing Director
  e-mail: paul@elabvc.com
  Education: Ba, MBA, University of Michigan
  Background: VP, Capital Markets, Michigan Economic Development Corp.; Co-Founder, Front Foor Insights
  Scott Chou, Managing Director
  e-mail: scott@elabvc.com
  Education: Harvard University; Stanford University
  Background: Gabriel Venture Partners
  Doug Neal, Managing Director
  e-mail: doug@elabvc.com
  Education: Central Michigan University
  Background: Co-Founder, Mobile Automation; Managing Director, University of Michigan Center for Entrepreneurship
  Bob Stefanski, Managing Director
  Education: University of Michigan
  Background: EVP, TIBCO Software

2024 i2E
840 Researh Parkway
Suite 250
Oklahoma City, OK 73104
Phone: 405-235-2305
web: i2e.org

Mission Statement: i2E works directly with entrepreneurs, researchers and companies to help them commercialize their technologies.

Fund Size: $88 Million
Founded: 1999

Other Locations:
  618 E Third Street
  Suite 1
  Tulsa, OK 74120
  Phone: 918-582-5592

Key Executives:
  Scott Meacham, President and CEO
  405-813-2401
  e-mail: smeacham@i2E.org
  Education: BA, MBA, JD, University of Oklahoma
  Background: Partner, Meacham & Meacham; CEO and General Counsel, First National Bank & Trust, Elk City; 17th State Treasurer, Oklahoma

Canadian Firms

Venture Capital & Private Equity Firms / Canadian Firms

2025 32 DEGREES CAPITAL
635 8th Avenue SW
Suite 650
Calgary, AB T2P 3M3
Canada

Phone: 403-695-1069 Fax: 403-695-1069
e-mail: info@32degrees.ca
web: www.32degrees.ca

Mission Statement: Private equity firm focused on developing crude oil and natural gas reserves and production.

Geographic Preference: Canada, United States
Fund Size: $105 million
Founded: 2004
Average Investment: $5 - $25 million
Investment Criteria: Early-Stage
Industry Group Preference: Oil & Gas
Portfolio Companies: Sphere Energy, Corval Energy, Sitka Exploration, Canamax Energy, Western Oilfield Equipment Rentals, Core Line Pipe, HPC Energy Services, Vertex Resource Group, Artis Exploration, Rising Star Resources, Summerland Energy, Karve Energy

Key Executives:
  Larry Evans, Founder & Managing Partner
  Education: University of Manitoba
  Background: Glacier Energy; Ice Energy; Avalanche Energy; Colony Energy
  Directorships: Artis Exploration; Corval Energy; Vertex Resource Group
  Mitch Putnam, Founder & Managing Partner
  Education: University of Alberta
  Background: Glacier Energy; Ice Energy; Avalanche Energy; Colony Energy
  Directorships: Canamax Energy; Summerland Energy; Karve Energy; Rising Star Resources; Sitka Exploration; HPC Energy Services
  Trent Baker, Managing Partner
  Education: Queen's University
  Background: KPMG
  Directorships: Vertex Resource Group; CORE Linepipe; Sphere Energy
  Melissa Fabreau, Vice President
  Education: University of Calgary
  Background: Enerplus Corporation
  Directorships: Karve Energy; Sphere Energy
  Matt Bauer, Chief Financial Officer
  Education: University of Calgary
  Background: Korite International; Rothschild; Grant Thornton

2026 4FRONT CAPITAL PARTNERS
47 Colborne Street
Suite 303
Toronto, ON M5E 1P8
Canada

Phone: 416-861-1100
web: www.4frontcapitalpartners.com

Mission Statement: 4Front Capital Partners us an independent investment bank focused on the growth of their companies in knowledge-based industries.

Key Executives:
  John Travaglini, Chief Executive Officer
  Education: Wilfred Laurier University
  Raj Natarajan, Partner/Vice President
  Education: MBA, University of Toronto
  Mark Kennedy, Managing Director
  Education: Wilfred Laurier University; MBA, York University

2027 500 STARTUPS CANADA
Calgary, AB
Canada

web: 500canada.ca

Mission Statement: Seed stage venture capital fund.
Geographic Preference: Canada
Fund Size: $30 million
Founded: 2017
Investment Criteria: Early-Stage, Seed
Portfolio Companies: AmpMe, ApplyBoard, Attendease, Avidbots, BenchSci, Chatkit, Chatter Research, Creative Market, dot Blockchain Music, Element AI, Finaeo, Fluent.ai, Homigo, Humi HR, Hysko, Innerspace, Keatext, Knotet, Local Logic, Logojoy, Lumotune, Mejuri, Meya.ai, Motorleaf, NestReady, Obie.ai, Play the Future, reDock, Shoelace, Smart Reno, Synervoz, Swept, Unito, Urbanlogiq, WayPay, Welltrack

2028 7 GATE VENTURES
68 Water Street
Suite 401
Vancouver, BC V6B 1A4
Canada

e-mail: info@7gate.vc
web: 7gate.vc

Mission Statement: 7 Gate Ventures funds technical founders to help them grow into billion-user companies.

Founded: 2015

Other Locations:
  2 Embarcadero Center
  8th Floor
  San Francisco, CA 94111

Key Executives:
  Amir Vohooshi, Founding Managing Partner
  Background: Founder, Beeptunes.com; Founder/CEO, Rahnema
  Alireza Rahnema, Managing Partner
  Education: BSc, McGill University; MBA, Schulich School of Business
  Background: Co-Founder, ALCK Entertainment

2029 ACCES CAPITAL QUEBEC
1000 route de l'Eglise
Suite 2010
Quebec, QC G1V 3V9
Canada

Phone: 418-684-8161 Fax: 418-650-7666

Mission Statement: Acces Capital Quebec invests in small and medium-sized technology and distribution companies based in Quebec, Canada.

Geographic Preference: Quebec
Founded: 1997
Minimum Investment: $100,000
Investment Criteria: Seed/Startup, Early/Mid/Late Venture, Buyout, Growth, Small and medium-sized companies
Industry Group Preference: Commercial and Professional Services, Retailing, Medical Equipment and Instruments, Biotechnology, Information Technology
Portfolio Companies: Audisoft, Biopharmacopae, Chlorophylle, Coveo Solutions, Creaform, Cybiocare, Epiderma, Distribution Alimentaire, Gecko, Groupe Conseil, Granicor, GDG Environnement Groupe, Groupe J.L. Leclerc, Habitation Mgr Deschenes, Korem, Tactic, LeddarTech, Lambert Somec, Marotech, Medicago, Myca, Novik, Opsens, Optosecurity, Resiver, Prevtec, Silicycle, Souris Mini, TeraXion, XD3

Key Executives:
  Serge Olivier, Managing Partner
  Education: BBA, Higher Commercial Studies, HEC Montreal
  Background: Investment Manager; SOQUIA; Investment Manager, Desjardins Venture Capital; Portfolio Manager, Capidem
  Lise Lapierre, Managing Partner
  Background: Samson Belaire/Deloitte & Touche

707

Venture Capital & Private Equity Firms / Canadian Firms

2030 ACCESS CAPITAL CORPORATION
3080 Yonge St.
Suite 4070
Toronto, ON M4N 3N1
Canada

Phone: 416-366-4820 Fax: 416-366-5123
e-mail: robmcl@access-capital.com
web: www.access-capital.com

Mission Statement: Offers guidance to companies that are major buyers and sellers of electric power projects.

Geographic Preference: North America, Canada
Fund Size: $2.6 billion
Founded: 1990
Investment Criteria: Acquisitions, Divestitures, Expansion Capital, Management Buyouts
Industry Group Preference: Power Technologies, Financial Services, Engineering

Key Executives:
Robert S. McLeese, Founder & President
Education: BSc, University of Western Ontario; MBA, McMaster University
Directorships: ACI Energy
George H. Cholakis, Senior Vice President
Education: BSc, University of Toronto; MBA, York University
Background: Vice President, Corporate Finance, Midland Doherty (subsequently Midland Walwyn and later Merrill Lynch), Toronto; Manager Corporate Finance and Manager Merchant Banking, Bank of Montreal, Toronto; Manager, Financial Planning.
Directorships: Vice Chairman, Toronto Board of Trade Electricity Task Force;Executive Committee, Stakeholders Alliance For Competition and Customer Choice ("SAC").

2031 AIP PRIVATE CAPITAL
Royal Bank Plaza, South Tower
200 Bay Street
Suite 3240
Toronto, ON M5J 2J5
Canada

Phone: 416-601-0808 Fax: 888-900-4123
Toll-Free: 855-275-0868
e-mail: info@aipprivatecapital.com
web: aipprivatecapital.com

Mission Statement: AIP Private Capital is an investment firm focused on providing private equity and venture debt financing to emerging growth businesses.

Geographic Preference: Canada, United States, South America, Europe
Founded: 2010
Average Investment: $1 - $5 million
Investment Criteria: Emerging, Management Buyouts, Recapitalizations, Turnarounds, Corporate Divestitures, Acquisitions, Growth Capital
Industry Group Preference: Financial Services, Business Products & Services, Clean Technology, Information Technology, Transportation, Oil & Gas
Portfolio Companies: Arkados Group, BioGanix, Carl Data Solutions, Cannabix Technologies, Next Door Lending, Relevium Technologies, Smart Autonomous Solutions, SolBright Renewable Energy, Torino Power Solutions, West Point Resources

Other Locations:
Moscow Embankment Tower
10 Presnenskaya
Naberezhnaya Block C
Moscow 123317
Russia

Korea Teachers Pension, 9th Floor
Yeouido-dong
Yeongdeungpo-Gu
Seoul 150-742
South Korea

Dubai Trade, 10th Floor
Limitless Galleries Building 4
Downtown Jebel Ali
Dubai
United Arab Emirates

Key Executives:
Alex Kanayev, Managing Partner
Education: San Diego State University; MBA, York University; CPA
Background: Senior VP, Sprott Asset Management; Portfolio Manager, BMO Financial Group; Managing Partner, Goldman & Partners; Managing Director, RUS Communications
Directorships: Capital Guardian

2032 ALBERTA ENTERPRISE
Suite 1405, TD Tower
10088 102 Avenue
Edmonton, AB T5J 2Z2
Canada

Phone: 587-402-6601 Fax: 587-402-6612
Toll-Free: 877-336-3474
e-mail: info@alberta-enterprise.ca
web: www.alberta-enterprise.ca

Mission Statement: Alberta Enterprise partners with proven VC technology funds investing in Alberta.

Geographic Preference: Alberta
Fund Size: $440 million
Founded: 2008
Industry Group Preference: Software, Internet, Media, Manufacturing, Clean Technology, Energy, Medical Devices, Life Sciences, Pharmaceuticals, Electronics
Portfolio Companies: 32 Degrees Capital, Accelerate Fund, Avrio Capital, Azure Capital Partners, Builders VC, Chrysalix, EnrTech Capital, iNovia Capital, McRock Capital, Panache Ventures, Relay Ventures, Yaletown

Key Executives:
Kristina Williams, President & CEO
Education: Master of Laws, Uppsala University; MBA, University of Alberta
Background: Director of Marketing, Cevena Bioproducts; VP Marketing, Natraceutical Canada
Directorships: TEC Edmonton
Rebecca Giffen, Director of Investments
Education: BComm, Haskayne School of Business, University of Calgary
Background: Director of Fund Investments, BDC Venture Capital
Paul Godman, Director of Investments
Education: University of Waterloo; University of Calgary
Background: EnCana

2033 ALBERTA INVESTMENT MANAGEMENT CORP.
10250 101 Street NW
Suite 1600
Edmonton, AB T5J 3P4
Canada

Phone: 780-392-3600
web: www.aimco.alberta.ca

Mission Statement: Alberta Investment Management Corp. is one of the largest institutional investment managers in Canada. A Crown corporation of the Province of Alberta, AIMCo seeks to produce superior, long-term investment results through good governance and the pursuit of the best investment opportunities around the world.

Fund Size: $108.2 billion
Founded: 2008
Industry Group Preference: Real Estate, Infrastructure

Portfolio Companies: Axcan Pharma, CCS, Cengage, Ceridian, DGAM, Generac, GLM Industries, KMC Mining, RTL-Westcan, TransAlta Corp.

Other Locations:
100 King Street West
Suite 5120
PO Box 51
Toronto, ON M5X 1B1
Canada
Phone: 647-789-5700

72 Welbeck Street
4th Floor
London W1G 0AY
United Kingdom
Phone: 44 (0)20 3102 1909

Key Executives:
Kevin Uebelein, CEO
Education: BBA, Harding Univeristy; MBA, Rice University
Background: Chief Investment Officer, Prudential Financial; President & CEO, Pyramis Global Advisors
Dale MacMaster, Chief Investment Officer
Education: BComm, Concordia University; MBA, Richard Ivey School of Business, University of Western Ontario
Robin Heard, Chief Financial Officer
Education: BCom, Queen's Univ.; MBA, Schulich School of Business
Sandra Lau, Executive VP, Fixed Income
Background: Senior Portfolio Manager
Directorships: Co-Founder & Co-Chair, Edmonton Women in Finance
Peter Pontikes, Executive VP, Public Equities
Education: MBA, Finance, University of Alberta; CFA Institute
Background: Barclays Global Investors; Alberta Treasury

2034 ALTAS PARTNERS
79 Wellington Street West
Suite 3500
PO Box 357
Toronto, ON M5K 1K7
Canada

Phone: 416-306-9800
e-mail: contact@altaspartners.com
web: altaspartners.com

Fund Size: $5 billion
Founded: 2012
Average Investment: $150-750 million
Portfolio Companies: Tecta America, Hub International, PADI, Capital Vision Services, Medforth Global Healthcare Education, NSC Minerals

Key Executives:
Andrew Sheiner, Founder/Managing Partner
Education: McGill Univ.; Harvard Univ.
Background: Onex Corp.
Directorships: Hospital for Sick Children (Toronto); Canadian Advisory Board (Harvard Business School)
Scott Werry, Managing Partner
Education: Univ. of North Carolina; Harvard Business School
Background: McColl Partners
Directorships: Capital Vision Services; PADI
Christopher McElhone, Managing Partner
Education: Harvard University; MBA, Wilfred Laurier University
Background: Director, Husky Injection Molding Systems; Onex Corp.

2035 AMORCHEM
4 Westmount Square
Suite 160
Westmount, QC H3Z 2S6
Canada

Phone: 514-849-7696
e-mail: info@amorchem.com
web: amorchem.com

Mission Statement: AmorChem is an early stage venture fund dedicated to biotech companies and academic research.
Fund Size: $87 Million
Founded: 2011

2036 AMPLITUDE
3, Place Ville-Marie
Espace CDPQ, Suite 12350
Montreal, QC H3b 0E7
Canada

Phone: 514-298-4222
e-mail: info@amplitudevc.com
web: amplitudevc.com

Mission Statement: Amplitude is a venture capital firm dedicated to bringing the best healthcare innovations to market to help improve the lives of patients.

Other Locations:
180 John Street
Toronto, ON M5T 1X5
Canada

2015 Main Street
Vancouver, BC V5T 3C2
Canada

Key Executives:
Jean-Francois Pariseau, Partner
e-mail: jfpariseau@amplitudevc.com
Dion Madsen, Partner
e-mail: dmadsen@amplitudevc.com
Nancy Harrison, Venture Partner
e-mail: neharrison@amplitudevc.com

2037 ANCIENT STRAINS
2702 - 401 Bay Street
Toronto, ON M5H 2Y4

Phone: 416-545-7214
web: www.ancientstrains.ca

Mission Statement: Invests in the global cannabis industry.
Geographic Preference: Canada, USA, India
Founded: 2014
Industry Group Preference: Cannabis

Key Executives:
Daryl Hodges, Chairman/CEO
Education: HBSc, Enconomic Geology; MSc, Geochemistry, University of Waterloo
Background: Founder/Mining Analyst/CEO/Chairman, Jennings Capital Inc.; President, Ladykirk Capital Advisors Inc.
Directorships: Executive Chairman, Minera IRL Limited
Samir Biswas, President/Director
Education: BCom, Finance; MBA, Agriculture
Background: CFO, MedCann Access; Has served as VP, CFO, Strategic Advisor, Deputy to CEO, Treasurer, and GM to 12 private/public Canadian companies.

2038 ANNAPOLIS CAPITAL
1100, 110-9 Avenue SW
Calgary, AB T2P 0T1
Canada

Phone: 403-231-4430
e-mail: info@anncap.com
web: www.annapoliscapital.ca

Venture Capital & Private Equity Firms / Canadian Firms

Mission Statement: A creative, value-adding, and long-term investor of growth capital in the Canadian energy sector. From its head office in Calgary, the Annapolis team uses its interdisciplinary expertise, Canadian network of relationships, and track record of value-creation to help its investors and portfolio company management teams profit.
Geographic Preference: Canada
Fund Size: $650 million
Founded: 2006
Average Investment: $15-60 million
Investment Criteria: Early-Stage
Industry Group Preference: Energy, Oil & Gas

Key Executives:
   Peter Williams, Managing Partner & CEO
   403-231-4434
   e-mail: pwilliams@anncap.com
   Education: BA, LLB, Dalhousie University
   Background: CEO & Chairman, Krang Energy; CEO, Passage Energy; Governor, Canadian Association of Petroleum Producers
   Directorships: Avalanche Energy, Caltex Energy, Evolve Exploration, HighRock Energy, Bulldog Oil & Gas, Corintian Energy, Caltex Energy
   Jody Forsyth, Managing Partner
   403-231-4433
   e-mail: jforsyth@anncap.com
   Education: BSc, Dip.Eng., LLB, MBA, Dalhousie University; LLM, Osgoode Hall Law School
   Background: Vice President, Krang Energy; Vice President, Berland Exploration; Corporate Secretary, Avalanche Energy
   Directorships: Evolve Exploration
   Mark Poelzer, Managing Partner
   403-231-4431
   e-mail: mpoelzer@anncap.com
   Education: BComm, University of Saskatchewan
   Background: Vice President, Finance & CFO, Vigilant Exploration; CFO, Berland Exploration; CFO, Questor Technologies; CFO, Passage Energy
   Directorships: Breton Energy
   David Vetters, Managing Partner
   Background: BMO Capital Markets

2039 APECTEC
3911 Trasimene Cr. SW
Calgary, AB T3E 7J6
Canada

Phone: 403-685-1888 **Fax:** 403-685-1880
web: www.apectec.com

Mission Statement: To help oil and gas and petroleum entrepreneurs to joint venture, partner and start, grow and finance promising investment opportunities, promising early-stage companies and companies employing technologies to enhance oil and gas operations.
Geographic Preference: Global
Average Investment: $1 Million
Investment Criteria: Startups, Seed-Stage, Early-Stage, Joint Venture Funding
Industry Group Preference: Oil & Gas, Natural Gas
Key Executives:
   Barclay W. Hambrook, Chief Executive Officer
   Education: University of Calgary; University of Toronto
   Background: Enercana Capital

2040 ARC FINANCIAL
4300, 400 - 3 Avenue SW
Calgary, AB T2P 4H2
Canada

Phone: 403-292-0680
web: www.arcfinancial.com

Mission Statement: To invest in partnerships with outstanding management teams to grow energy companies and create shareholder value.
Geographic Preference: Canada
Fund Size: CDN $6 billion
Founded: 1989
Average Investment: CDN $25 - $100 million
Investment Criteria: Early stage
Industry Group Preference: Energy, Oilfield Services, Infrastructure, Power Generation, Oil & Gas
Portfolio Companies: Beringer Energy, BluEarth Renewables, C&C Energia, Canbriam Energy, Canyon Services Group, Capio Exploration, Cequence Energy, Chinook Energy, Global Tubing, Huron Energy Corporation, Nexterra Systems, Tesla Exploration Ltd., Seven Generations Energy, Sitka Exploration, Shiningstar Energy, STEP Energy Services, Tangle Creek Energy, Unconventional Gas Resources

Key Executives:
   Kevin Brown, Executive Chair & Director
   403-292-0687
   e-mail: kbrown@arcfinancial.com
   Education: BSc, Chemical Engineering; MA, Economics, University of Alberta
   Background: Canadian Energy Research Institute
   Directorships: Unconventional Resources Canada, Seven Generations Energy Ltd
   Lauchlan Currie, Chief Executive Officer & Director
   403-292-0431
   e-mail: lcurrie@arcfinancial.com
   Education: BSc, Geology, University of Calgary; MBA, Queen's University
   Directorships: Capio Exploration Ltd., Tangle Creek Energy Ltd.
   Brian Boulanger, President & Director
   e-mail: bboulanger@arcfinancial.com
   Education: University of Western Ontario
   Directorships: Modern Resources Inc.; Rifle Shot Oil Corp.
   Peter Tertzakian, Chief Energy Economist & Managing Director
   403-292-0809
   e-mail: ptertzakian@arcfinancial.com
   Education: BSc, Geophysics, University of Alberta; MSc, Management of Technology, Sloan School of Management, MIT
   Directorships: Nexterra Systems Corp.
   Tanya Causgrove, Chief Financial Officer & Managing Director
   Education: BComm, University of Alberta
   Nancy Smith, Director
   403-292-0695
   e-mail: nsmith@arcfinancial.com
   Education: BA, Economics, MBA, University of Alberta
   Directorships: Canbriam Energy, Corinthian Exploration Corp.
   Mac Van Wielingen, Founder & Director
   403-292-0686
   e-mail: mvanwielingen@arcfinancial.com
   Education: BA, Business, Richard Ivey School of Business, University of Western Ontario
   Directorships: BluEartch Renewables
   John Dielwart, Vice-Chair & Director
   e-mail: jdielwart@arcfinancial.com
   Education: University of Calgary
   Chris Seasons, Vice-Chair & Director
   e-mail: cseasons@arcfinancial.com
   Education: Queen's University

Venture Capital & Private Equity Firms / Canadian Firms

2041 ARCTERN VENTURES
101 College Street
Suite 155
Toronto, ON M5G 1L7
Canada

web: www.arcternventures.com

Mission Statement: Provides early-stage 'seed' funding to cleantech companies with significant growth potential.
Geographic Preference: Canada
Fund Size: $30 million
Founded: 2006
Average Investment: $1 - $3 million
Investment Criteria: Startup
Industry Group Preference: Clean Energy, Energy Storage, Mobility, Advanced Manufacturing & Materials, Resource Use & Efficiency, Foodtech
Portfolio Companies: CircuitMeter, Clir, GreenMantra, Hydrostor, MMB Networks, Morgan Solar, Parity, Polar Sapphire, Sheertex, Smart Energy Instruments, Smarter Alloys, Sparq, Terramera, Woodland

Other Locations:
407, Rue McGill
Montreal, QC H2Y 2G3
Canada

Key Executives:
Tom Rand, Co-Founder & Managing Partner
Education: BSc, Electrical Engineering, University of Waterloo; MSc, Philosophy of Science, University of London; MA, PhD, University of Toronto
Background: Founder, Voice Courier
Murray McCaig, Co-Founder & Managing Partner
Education: MBA, University of Western Ontario
Background: McKenna Group; RSL Investments

2042 ARDENTON
1021 West Hastings Street
Suite 2400
Vancouver, BC V6E 0C3
Canada

Phone: 833-416-1490
web: www.ardenton.com

Mission Statement: Ardenton is a private equity corporation focused on long term growth. They nurture management teams and expand into new markets.

Other Locations:
18 King Street E
Suite 515
Toronto, ON M5C 1C4
Canada
Phone: 416-304-9454

120 Research Lane
Suite 202
Guelph, ON N1G 0B4
Canada
Phone: 833-416-1490

100 Crescent Court
Suite 595
Dallas, TX 75201
Phone: 214-390-7455

3 Hardman Square
2nd Floor
Manchester
United Kingdom
Phone: 44 161-457-0117

2043 ARGOSY PARTNERS
141 Adelaide Street West
Suite 760
Toronto, ON M5H 3L5
Canada

Phone: 416-367-3617 Fax: 416-367-3895
e-mail: info@argosypartners.com
web: www.argosypartners.com

Mission Statement: Argosy Partners is a private equity firm that provides capital to successful entrepreneurs and institutional investors to deliver a range of effective financial solutions for tough business situations.
Geographic Preference: Canada
Founded: 1995
Minimum Investment: $2 Million
Portfolio Companies: Art For Everyday, Bayview Hospitality Group, Carego, Celtrade, CAST Software, Eratech, Gourmet Settings, iMarketing Solutions Group, Insception Lifebank, Level Platforms, Logistik Unicorp, TCDS.com, Westmount Storefront Systems

Key Executives:
Richard Reid, Founder & Partner
Background: Burn Fry; Gordon Capital Corp.; Wood Gundy
Larry Klar, Partner
Background: KPMG; Canadian General Capital

2044 ARVA LIMITED
4120 Yonge Street
Suite 310
Toronto, ON M2P 2B8
Canada

Phone: 416-222-0842 Fax: 416-222-6243
web: arva.ca

Mission Statement: Arva looks for long-term opportunities in companies whose owners are seeking an exit, or who require ongoing financial and strategic support.
Geographic Preference: Canada
Founded: 1956
Investment Criteria: Long-Term, Later-Stage
Industry Group Preference: Communications, Manufacturing, Telecommunications, Construction
Portfolio Companies: MLL Telecom, Normerica Building Systems, Trylon-TSF, Ultra-Fit Manufacturing

Key Executives:
Mike Stevens, President
Background: President, Waltec Components; President, S.W. Fleming
John Stevens, Executive Vice President
Background: Managing Partner, Osler, Hoskin & Harcourt
Bill Smith, Vice President, Finance & Corporate Secretary
Background: Cott Corporation; Molson Breweries; Apple Computer

2045 ASHBRIDGE PARTNERS
31 Wingold Avenue
Toronto, ON M6B 1P8

e-mail: info@ashbridgepartners.ca
web: www.ashbridgepartners.ca

Mission Statement: Ashbridge is a private, entrepreneurial investment firm that seeks to acquire and manage small to medium-sized businesses by partnering with existing management teams.
Geographic Preference: Canada
Founded: 2013
Investment Criteria: Early-Stage, Mid-Stage

Venture Capital & Private Equity Firms / Canadian Firms

Industry Group Preference: Personal Care, Packaging, Manufacturing
Portfolio Companies: Caryl Baker Visage, Bagwell Supply, Geroline

Key Executives:
  Nathan Tam, Partner
  Education: Richard Ivey School of Business, University of Western Ontario
  Background: Co-Founder, Offleash Media; Onex Corporation; Morgan Stanley
  Jordan Goodman, Partner
  Education: University of Western Ontario
  Background: VP, Authentic Brands Group; Hilco Consumer Capital
  Ryan DeCaire, Partner
  Education: Richard Ivey School of Business, University of Western Ontario
  Background: Onex Corporation; Bank of America Merrill Lynch

2046 ATLAS PARTNERS
79 Wellington Street W
Suite 3500
PO Box 357
Toronto, ON M5K 1K7
Canada

Phone: 416-306-9800
e-mail: contact@altaspartners.com
web: www.atlas.com

Mission Statement: Long-term capital partner of market-leading businesses.

Fund Size: $7 billion
Founded: 2012
Average Investment: $250 million - $1 billion
Portfolio Companies: Capital Vision Services, DuBois Chemicals, Hub International, Medforth Global Healthcare Education, NSC Minerals, PADI, Tecta America, University of St. Augustine for Health Sciences

Key Executives:
  Andrew Sheiner, Founder and Managing Partner
  Education: McGill; Harvard
  Background: Onex Corp.
  Directorships: York School; Urban Squash Toronto, Toronto's Hospital for Sick Children
  Christopher McElhone, Founder Partner
  Education: Wilfrid Laurier Univ.
  Background: Onex Corp.

2047 AUXO MANAGEMENT
3198 Orlando Drive
Mississauga, ON L4V 1J2

web: www.auxomanagement.com

Mission Statement: Auxo is a private, entrepreneurial investment firm focused on small to medium-sized businesses whose owners are considering retirement.

Founded: 2010
Investment Criteria: Later-Stage
Industry Group Preference: Video Surveillance, Security
Portfolio Companies: Meglan, Stealth Monitoring, Trask Contracting, UCIT

Key Executives:
  Robert Cherun, Co-Founder & Managing Partner
  Education: MBA, Stanford Graduate School of Business; HBA, Richard Ivey School of Business, University of Western Ontario
  Background: Morgan Stanley; McKinsey & Company
  Erik Mikkelsen, Co-Founder & Managing Partner
  Education: HBA, Richard Ivey School of Business, University of Western Ontario
  Background: President & SRO, Stealth Monitoring; Regent Properties; Barclays Capital; Ink Media

2048 AVAC
220, 6815-8 Street NE
Calgary, AB T2E 7H7
Canada

Phone: 403-274-2774
web: avacgrp.com

Mission Statement: AVAC Ltd. is an Alberta-based investment company investing in promising early-stage commercial ventures in value-added agri-business, information and communications technologies, life sciences, and other industrial technology sectors. AVAC also manages an active early-stage venture capital fund-of-funds investment pool, and the Accelerate angel co-investment Fund. AVAC's mandate is to help bridge the critical investment gap that exists between innovative ideas and commercial business success.

Geographic Preference: Alberta
Fund Size: $15 million
Founded: 1997
Investment Criteria: Early-Stage, Startup, Exit
Industry Group Preference: Agricultural Technologies, Technology
Portfolio Companies: Afinity Life Sciences, Antibe Therapeutics, Baby Gourmet, Botaneco, Business Infusions, Calgary Scientific, CanBiocin, Ceapro, CoolIT Systems, Decisive Farming, Enterprise Macay, Enthrill Distribution, eThor, Himark Bogas, iKingdom, InnerVision Medical Technologies, IntelliView Technologies, Lethbridge Biogas, Livestock Water Recycling, Mobovivo, Radient Technologies, SBI Fine Chemicals, Sustainable Produce Urban Delivery, Tynt Multimedia, Under the Roof Decorating, Userful, Waggers Pet Products, Wedge Networks

Key Executives:
  Warren Bergen, President
  e-mail: wbergen@avacltd.com
  Education: BComm, University of Saskatchewan; Pepperdine University
  Mark Carlson, Managing Director
  e-mail: mcarlson@avacltd.com
  Education: MBA
  Directorships: Accelerate Fund Limited Partnership
  Martin Vetter, Senior Investment Manager
  e-mail: mvetter@avacltd.com
  Education: Memorial University of Newfoundland; MBA, University of Calgary
  Background: Acceleware; Hemisphere GPS; Novatel Wireless; Nortel
  Jim Hardin, Senior Investment Manager
  e-mail: jhardin@avacltd.com
  Education: BSc, Zoology, PhD, Gastrointestinal Physiology, University of Calgary

2049 AVRIO CAPITAL
Crowfoot West Business Centre
500, 400 Crowfoot Cres. NW
Calgary, AB T3G 5H6
Canada

Phone: 403-215-5492 Fax: 403-215-5495
web: avriocapital.com

Mission Statement: Avrio Capital invests in food and agriculture companies that seek to make advancements in the areas of sustainability, health and wellness. A hands-on investor, Avrio offers its portfolio companies the resources necessary to succeed in the global market.

Geographic Preference: Canada
Fund Size: $91 million
Founded: 2002
Average Investment: $3 - $5 million
Investment Criteria: Growth Stage, Late-Stage
Industry Group Preference: Agriculture, Food & Beverage
Portfolio Companies: AgriBiotics, Allylix Canada, Ascenta Health, Atlantic Cedar Products, Axter Agroscience, Baby Gourmet, BareFruit, Bento Nouveau, Bento Sushi, Big Sky Farms, BioAmber, Bioniche Life Sciences, Biopharmacopae

Venture Capital & Private Equity Firms / Canadian Firms

Design International, Biox, Botaneco, Brookside, Commercial Solutions, Ensyn, Enterra Feed, FarmersEdge, Fresh Hemp Foods, Hortau, Houwelings Nurseries, Kinnikinnick Foods, La Petite Bretonne, MCN Bio-Products, MJ's Fine Foods, Mout de POM, Multi-Portions, Natunola Health Biosciences, Organic Meadow, Origin Biomed, Otter Valley Foods, Pellet Systems International, Poss Design, Sembiosys Genetics, Siamons International, SJ Irvine Fine Foods, Sterling Pork Farms, Sulvaris, Sun Select, Sunworks Farm, Terra Grain Fuels, VoloAgri Group, Walker Seeds, Wolf Trax

Other Locations:
1155 Rene Levesque Blvd W
Suite 2500
Montreal, QC H3B 2K4
Canada
Phone: 514-868-9904

850-36 Toronto St
Toronto, ON M5C 2C5
Canada
Phone: 416-364-8122

Key Executives:
Jim Taylor, Co-Founder & Chairman
Education: BA, Economics, University of Alberta; MBA, Rotman School of Management, University of Toronto
Background: Founder, FCC Ventures; Bank of Montreal Capital; Westcoast Energy
Aki Georgacacos, Co-Founder & Managing Partner
Education: BComm, University of Saskatchewan; CFA
Background: Vice President, Deloitte Corporate Finance
Michael McGee, Managing Director
Education: University of Western Ontario; MS, Finance, Loyola University, Maryland
Background: Managing Director, Investments, Werklund Capital Corp.; EVP, Investments, Cavendish Investing Ltd.; Managing Director, Bank of Montreal; VP & Director, Toronto-Dominion Bank
Directorships: Innovate Calgary
Steven Leakos, Managing Director
Education: BComm, BA, University of Saskatchewan
Background: Managing Director, Roynat Capital Inc.

2050 AZIMUTH CAPITAL MANAGEMENT
Centennial Place East
3110, 520 - 3rd Avenue SW
Calgary, AB T2P 0R3
Canada
Phone: 403-517-1500 **Fax:** 403-517-1515
e-mail: info@navigatingenergy.com
web: navigatingenergy.com

Mission Statement: Focused on building long-term franchise value through partnership relationships with Limited Partners, portfolio companies, service providers and members of the Firm.

Geographic Preference: Canada
Fund Size: $1.6 billion
Founded: 2003
Investment Criteria: Startup, Early-Stage
Industry Group Preference: Energy, Oil & Gas, Infrastructure
Portfolio Companies: Altex Energy, M-Flow, Magma, Monolith, Recover Energy Services, Steelhead LNG

Key Executives:
Jim Nieuwenburg, Operating Partner
Education: BS, Electrical Engineering; Executive Program, University of Western Ontario
Background: CEO, Petromet Resources; VP, Norcan Energy; Amoco Canada
Directorships: Amarone Oil & Gas, Fairborne Energy, Black Swan Energy, Legacy Oil & Gas, Rifco
Jeff Van Steenbergen, Co-Founder & Managing Partner
Education: Bachelor of Applied Science, Civil Engineering, Queen's University; MBA, Dalhousie University
Background: Co-Head, North American Oil & Gas, JP Morgan & Co.; Mobil; Hibernia; Sable Offshore Energy
Directorships: Aduro Resources, Altex Energy, Cobal International Energy, Fairfield Energy, Magma Global, Seven Generations Energy
Dave Pearce, Deputy Managing Partner
Education: BS, Mechanical Engineering, University of Calgary
Background: President & CEO, Northrock Resources; VP, Corporate Development, Fletcher Challenge Canada; Dome Petroleum
Directorships: Fairfield Energy, Black Swan Energy, Cutpick Energy, All Points Energy
Francesco Mele, Chief Operating Officer
Education: BS, MBA, Bachelor of Laws, University of Alberta
Adam Le Dain, Vice President
Education: BComm, Queen's University; CFA
Background: RBC Capital Markets; RBC Rundle
Ryan Sapieha, Vice President
Education: BComm, University of Calgary; CFA
Background: Investment Banking Analyst, Energy Group, National Bank Financial; Fund Manager, Industrials & Healthcare, Calgary Portfolio Management Trust
Jim Farnsworth, Operating Partner
Education: BSc, Geology, Indiana University; MSc, Geology, Western Michigan University
Background: Co-Founder & President, Cobalt International Energy; SVP, British Petroleum
Directorships: Indiana University Advisory Board; Jackson School of Geosciences, University Of Texas
Howard Mayson, Operating Partner & Board Member
Education: MSc, Mechanical Engineering, MIT; BEng, University of Sheffield; Advanced Management Program, Wharton Business School
Background: SVP, British Petroleum
Directorships: Corex Resources; Encana

2051 BANYAN CAPITAL PARTNERS
1400 - 130 King Street W
PO Box 240
Toronto, ON M5X 1C8
Canada

web: www.cclgroup.com/banyan/en

Mission Statement: Banyan Capital Partners is a boutique private equity firm investing in mid-sized companies in North America.

Geographic Preference: North America
Investment Criteria: Growth Stage, Mergers, MBO, LBO, Spin-Offs, Going Private, Recapitalizations, Succession
Industry Group Preference: Diversified
Portfolio Companies: Bevo Agro, Corix Group, Dental Technologies, Fios, Foundstone, Genoa Healthcare, GW Anglin Manufacturing, ISR, KOS Corp, MIP, Newcrete, Oakcreek Golf, Party Packagers, Premium Brands, Qmax Solutions, Purity Life Health Products, Q'Max Solutions, Rack Attack, Shanahan's, Syscon Justice Systems, Tartan Canada Corporation

Key Executives:
Jeff Wigle, Managing Director
416-216-7076
e-mail: jwigle@banyancp.com
Education: BA, Economics, University of Western Ontario
Background: Vice President, Richardson Capital Limited
Directorships: Party Packagers, GW Anglin Manufacturing
Simon Gelinas, Managing Director
416-364-2801
e-mail: sgelinas@banyancp.com
Education: BComm, McGill Univ.; MBA, University of British Columbia
Directorships: G.W. Anglin Mfg., Oakcreek Golf & Turf, Rack Attack

713

Venture Capital & Private Equity Firms / Canadian Firms

2052 BAYSHORE CAPITAL
Commerce Court W
199 Bay Street, Suite 2900
PO Box 459
Toronto, ON M5L 1G4
Canada

Phone: 416-214-6851 Fax: 416-214-9895
web: bayshore.com

Mission Statement: Bayshore finances and builds companies in real estate, financial services, and information technology.
Founded: 1995
Industry Group Preference: Real Estate, Financial Services, Information Technology
Portfolio Companies: Armel Corporation, RPM Technologies, Secure Key, Fenix Opportunity
Key Executives:
  Henry Wolfond, Chair & CEO
  Background: Osler Hoskin & Harcourt
  Directorships: Canadian Jewish Political Affairs Ctee, University Hospital Foundation, UJA Federation Community Advisory Council, Faculty of Law University of Alberta Advisory Ctee
  Andrew Brown, President & Co-Founder
  Education: BComm, Queen's University; LLB, University of Toronto
  Background: i-money; Osler, Hoskin & Harcourt

2053 BC RENAISSANCE CAPITAL FUND
PO Box 9800
Stn Prov Govt
Victoria, BC V8W 9W1
Canada

Toll-Free: 800-665-6597
web: bciif.ca

Mission Statement: Subsidiary of BC Immigrant Investment Fund invests in British Columbia's technology sector.
Geographic Preference: British Columbia, North America
Fund Size: $2 billion
Founded: 2008
Industry Group Preference: Digital Media & Marketing, Information Technology, Life Sciences, Clean Technology
Portfolio Companies: Angstrom Power, Boreal Genomics, CoolEdge Lighting, Delta-Q Technologies Corp., Endurance Wind Power, E-One Moli Energy, GrowLab Ventures, Indicee, LaCima, Light Based Technologies, Mingleverse Laboratories, Nexterra Systems, NGRAIN, Ostara Nutrient Recovery Techologies, Partnerpedia Solutions
Key Executives:
  David Mortimer, Chief Executive Officer

2054 BCF VENTURES
Vancouver, BC
Canada

e-mail: info@bcfventures.vc
web: bcfventures.vc

Mission Statement: BCF Ventures invests at the seed and series A stage of technology-based start-ups.
Geographic Preference: Canada, USA, Israel, China, Western Europe
Founded: 2018
Average Investment: $1-5 Million
Investment Criteria: Up to $10 Million Valuation; Technology-Based; Low Cash Burn; At Least 2 Full-time Founders, one technical
Key Executives:
  Sergio Escobar, Chief Executive Officer

2055 BDC CAPITAL
5, Place Ville Marie
Suite 400
Montreal, QC H3B 5E7
Canada

Fax: 877-329-9232
Toll-Free: 877-232-2269
web: www.bdc.ca

Mission Statement: Crown corporation supports Canadian entrepreneurs with a focus on small and medium-sized businesses.
Geographic Preference: Canada
Founded: 1944
Key Executives:
  Michael Denham, President & CEO
  Education: BA, Princeton Univ.; MSc, London School of Economics
  Background: AquaTerra Corp.
  Pierre Dubreuil, Executive Vice President, Financing
  Education: BBA, Laval Univ.
  Background: National Bank of Canada
  Peter Lawler, Executive Vice President, BDC Advisory Services
  Education: BA, Carleton Univ.
  Background: BDC Senior VP, Financing & Consulting - Ontario
  Directorships: Hong Kong-Canada Business Association
  Stefano Lucarelli, Executive Vice President & CFO
  Education: BComm, Concordia Univ.
  Background: Office of the Auditor General
  Jerome Nycz, Executive Vice President, BDC Capital
  Education: BA, Concordia Univ.; IMBA, Hartford Univ.
  Background: BDC Senior VP, Corporate Strategy & Subordinate Financing
  Directorships: Canadian Venture Capital and Private Equity Association
  Christopher Rankin, Executive Vice President & Chief Risk Officer
  Education: BComm, McMaster Univ.
  Background: Wells Fargo Equipment Financing

2056 BEDFORD CAPITAL
130 Adelaide St. West
Suite 2900
Toronto, ON M5H 3P5
Canada

Phone: 416-947-1492 Fax: 416-947-9673
web: www.bedfordcapital.ca

Mission Statement: Bedford partners with management teams to build industry leading companies. All investment decisions are made internally by the principals of Bedford Capital, with a team comprised diverse backgrounds and direct operating experience.
Geographic Preference: Eastern Canada
Founded: 1982
Average Investment: $5 - $15 million
Investment Criteria: Management Buyouts, Recapitalizations, Growth Capital
Portfolio Companies: B+H International LP, Champion Petfoods LP, Elmira Pet Products, IPD Global, L.B. Maple Treat Corporation, Noranco, Spring Air Sommex Corporation
Key Executives:
  Tim Bowman, Managing Director
  416-947-1492 x310
  e-mail: tbowman@bedfordcapital.ca
  Education: BEng, MBA, LLB
  Background: Corporate Lawyer, Davies Ward & Beck; Vice President, Corporate Dvelopment, Magna International; Co-Founder, Apex Capital; Managing Director, BMO Nesbitt Burns
  Elliott Knox, Managing Director
  416-947-1492 x238

Venture Capital & Private Equity Firms / Canadian Firms

e-mail: eknox@bedfordcapital.ca
Education: BMath, Certified Management Accountant
Background: Andersen Consulting; Co-Founder, Janna Systems; Co-Founder, Lealand Group
David Hass, Partner
416-947-1492 x312
e-mail: dhass@bedfordcapital.ca
Education: BA, MBA
Background: Senior Account Manager, Royal Bank; Vice President, Lenbrook; Managing Director, Venture Debt Fund; Managing Director, Small Business Venture Fund, Royal Bank Ventures
Sheila Murray-Tateishi, Senior Vice President & CFO
416-947-1492 x320
e-mail: sheilamt@bedfordcapital.ca
Education: BA, MBA
Background: CFO, Techbanc; SVP/CFO, Nalvana Limited; CFO, Security Pacific Bank

2057 BERINGER CAPITAL
141 Adelaide Street W
Suite 750
Toronto, ON M5H 3L5

Phone: 416-928-2166
e-mail: hello@beringercapital.com
web: www.beringercapital.com

Mission Statement: Beringer partners with growing technology companies that have strong management teams and where there is an opportunity to create value.
Investment Criteria: Mid-Stage
Industry Group Preference: Technology
Portfolio Companies: blue acorn iCi, Brandweek Adweek, Hyper Giant, Union Digital
Other Locations:
  261 Madison Avenue
  Floor 8
  New York, NY 10016
  Phone: 718-577-4984
Key Executives:
  Perry Miele, Chair & Managing Partner
  e-mail: pmiele@beringercapital.com
  Background: Chief of Staff to the Minister of International Trade; Gingko Group; DraftWorldwide
  Directorships: Andrew Peller Wines, Canadian Heart & Stroke Foundation, Trilliam Health Partners, LCBO, Match Marketing, Budco
  Bill Kostenko, Vice Chair & Managing Partner
  e-mail: bkostenko@beringercapital.com
  Education: MBA, McMaster University
  Background: CFO, Sherwood; Genesis Microchip; Mitel; Rolm Canada; Rockwell International
  Brian F. Martin, Vice Chair & Managing Partner
  e-mail: bmartin@beringercapital.com
  Background: Pfizer Consumer Care; Wal-Mart; Brand Connections; Social Media Link; Brandshare
  Directorships: Childhood Domestic Violence Association
  Gil Ozir, Managing Partner
  Education: JD, New York University School of Law; Lafayette College
  Background: Managing Director, AMR International; McKinsey & Company
  Directorships: SEED Impact

2058 BEST FUNDS
181 Bay Street
Suite 810
Toronto, ON M5J 2T3
Canada

Phone: 416-203-7331 Fax: 416-203-6630
Toll-Free: 800-795-2378
e-mail: info@bestfunds.ca
web: bestfunds.ca

Mission Statement: BEST Fund invests in traditional industries with the objective of generating interest income and long term capital.
Geographic Preference: Ontario
Fund Size: $80 million
Founded: 1996
Investment Criteria: Seed-Stage, Early-Stage, Later-Stage
Industry Group Preference: Software, Cloud Computing, Financial Services, Clean Technology, SaaS
Portfolio Companies: 01 Communique, Acuity, Agile Systems, AIM Health Group, Apeks, ArcticDX, ARXX ICF, Asset Matrix, Axentra Corporation, Azonic, BitHeads, BSM Wireless, CNSX Markets, Cognivue Corporation, ComPower Systems, ComponentArt, Cymat, Bulldog Group, ChangePoint, Choreo, Chrysalis, Claymore Capital Management, Canadian National Stock Exchange, Cognivue Corporation, Combat Networks, ComponentArt, Compower Systems, Cygnal Technologies, Cymat, Dejero Labs, Delego, DisclosureNet, DragonWave, Echoworx Corporation, Eco Logic, Electrovaya, ERMS Corporation, Evault, FileTrek, Garner, Geminare, Grantium, Hatsize, Impath Networks, Indigo, Industrios Software, Infonaut, IMS, Internet Secure, Iogen Corporation, Kaval Wireless, Kneebone, Life Imaging Systems, Momentum, MKS, N-Dimension Solutions, Necho Systems, Newstep Networks, Novus Health, OnX Enterprise Solutions, Optessa, PitchPoint Solutions, Pixelink, Polyphalt, Powerband Global, Protus IP Solutions, Questrade, Sand Tech, Sensory Technologies, Signifi, Skura, Soliton, Spectra Securities Software, T-Base Communications, Teambuy.ca, Telos Entertainment, Transgaming, Triple G Systems, Vision Max, X2O Media, XipLink, XPi
Key Executives:
  John Richardson, CEO & Director
  416-203-7331 x228
  Education: University of Western Ontario; State University of New York
  Tom Lunan, Chief Financial Officer
  416-203-7331 x230
  Education: Wilfrid Laurier University
  Background: Toronto Stock Exchange; Ontario Securities Commission
  Mark Donatelli, Vice President
  416-203-7331 x227
  e-mail: mdonatelli@bestfunds.ca
  Background: Wave Financial; Northbridge Financial; PricewaterhouseCoopers; OpenText

2059 BINGLEY CAPITAL
36 Lombard Street
Suite 503
Toronto, ON M5C 2X3
Canada

web: www.bingleycapital.com

Mission Statement: Bingley focuses on mid-market companies where the founder is seeking an exit, and where long-term value can be built. The firm also offers advisory services.
Investment Criteria: Mid-Market
Portfolio Companies: Mansour Mining Technologies, Gregg Drilling & Testing
Key Executives:
  Stephan Bey, Principal
  647-930-9556
  e-mail: stephan.bey@bingleycapital.com
  Education: BBA, Wilfrid Laurier University; MBA, London School of Business; CA
  Background: Managing Director, Investment Banking, Lehman Brothers; Corporate Controller, Tsubaki of Canada; Deloitte & Touche
  Andrew Bishop, Principal
  e-mail: andrew.bishop@bingleycapital.com
  Education: BA, Political Science & Economics, McGill University; MBA, Schulich School of Business, York

Venture Capital & Private Equity Firms / Canadian Firms

University; CFA
Background: HSBC Securities
Directorships: Willow Breat & Hereditary Cancer Support

2060 BIOENTERPRISE
The Jaral Corporate Center
120 Research Lane
Suite 200
Guelph, ON N1G 0B4
Canada

Phone: 519-821-2960 Fax: 519-821-2960
Toll-Free: 866-464-4524
e-mail: info@bioenterprise.ca
web: www.bioenterprise.ca

Mission Statement: A not-for-profit business accelerator. Bioenterprise provides commercialization services to help with the growth of agri-technology businesses ranging from early start-ups to expanding established companies.

Geographic Preference: Canada
Founded: 2003
Investment Criteria: Start-ups to well-established
Industry Group Preference: Agricultural Technologies
Other Locations:
The Exchange Tower
130 King Street West
18th Floor
Toronto, ON M5X 1E3
Canada

Innovacorp
1 Research Drive
Dartmouth, NS B2Y 4M9
Canada
Phone: 902-424-8670

Wavefront
1055 W Hastings St
Suite 1400
Vancouver, BC V6E 2E9
Canada

Key Executives:
Dave Smardon, President & CEO
Background: Co-Founder, Learning Connections; Co-Founder, Commcorp Technologies; Co-Founder, Nibiru Investments; Co-Founder, Capital Management Ltd.
Italo Cerra, Vice President, Finance
Background: Accountant, Deloitte & Touche; Vice President, Finance, Teltone Limited
Jessica Bowes, Vice President, Commercialization
e-mail: jessica.bowes@bioenterprise.ca
Education: BSc & MSc, University of Guelph
Background: Program Manager, Agri-Food for Healthy Aging, Schlegal-UW Research Institute for Aging; Project Coordinator & Communications, MaRSLanding

2061 BIOINDUSTRIAL INNOVATION CANADA
1086 Modeland Road
Sarnia, ON N7S 6L2
Canada

Phone: 226-778-0020
e-mail: info@bincanada.ca
web: www.bincanada.ca

Mission Statement: Sarnia-based business accelerator focused on industrial bioproducts.

Geographic Preference: Sarnia-Lambton
Founded: 2008
Industry Group Preference: Bioenergy, Biofuel, Biochemicals & Biomaterials
Portfolio Companies: 3E Nano, Benefuel, CO2 GRO, Cellulosic Sugar Producers Co-Operative, Comet Bio, EcoSynthetic, FireRein, Forward Water Technologies, GreenCore, GreenMantra Technologies, Greyter Water Systems, KMX, Li-Cycle, Origin Materials, Polar Sapphire, Renix, Ubiquity Solar, Vive Crop Protection, Woodland Biofuels

Key Executives:
A.J. (Sandy) Marshall, Executive Director
Education: BASc, MASc, Univ. of Waterloo
Background: Lanxess Canada
Directorships: Lambton College, Biorefinery Research Inst. at Lakehead Univ.

2062 BIRCH HILL EQUITY PARTNERS
100 Wellington Street West
Suite 2300, TD West Tower
PO Box 22
Toronto, ON M5K 1A1
Canada

Phone: 416-775-3800 Fax: 416-775-3859
e-mail: info@birchhillequity.com
web: www.birchhillequity.com

Mission Statement: Mid-market private equity firm focused on companies valued between $30 million and $600 million, across a range of industries.

Geographic Preference: Canada, United States
Fund Size: CDN $3 billion
Founded: 1994
Investment Criteria: Middle-Market Companies
Portfolio Companies: Bio Agri Mix, Campus Energy, CCM Hockey, Citron Hygiene, Cozzini Bros, FlexNetworks, GDI, Greenfield Global, HomeEquity Bank, Marsulex Environmental Technologies, Mastermind Toys, Motion Specialties, Softchoice, Terrapure Environmental, Tidewater Midstream and Infrastructure

Key Executives:
Stephen J. Dent, Partner
Education: BBA, Wilfred Laurier University; MBA, Richard Ivey School of Business, University of Western Ontario
Background: TD Capital; Founding Partner, Merchant Private Trust
Andrew J. Fortier, Partner
Education: HBA, Richard Ivey School of Business, University of Western Ontario; MBA, Harvard Business School
Background: Vice President, Audax Group; Analyst, Morgan Stanley
Matthew B. Kunica, Partner
Education: Bachelor of Applied Science, Mineral Engineering, University of Toronto
Background: TD Capital; Associate, Credit Suisse First Boston; Analyst, BMO Nesbitt Burns
Felix-Etienne Lebel, Partner
Education: BComm, McGill University; CFA
Background: CIBC World Markets
Directorships: Citron Hygiene; Softchoice Corporation
John Loh, Partner, Capital Markets
Education: HBA, Richard Ivey School of Business, Western University
Background: Director, Asian Media and Telecom Group, TD; TD Securities
Directorships: Bluewave Energy, Carson Dellosa Publishing, Cookie Jar Entertainment, DHX Media, Novadent, GlobeNet Communications Group, Vector Intermediaries, WNI Holdings
John B. MacIntyre, Partner
Education: BComm, Queen's University; Chartered Accountant
Background: President, TD Capital
Michael J. Salamon, Partner
Education: BS, Applied Science, Electrical Engineering, University of Toronto; MBA, University of Chicago
Background: TD Capital; Vice President, Harrowston Inc.
David G. Samuel, Partner
Education: HBA, Richard Ivey School of Business,

University of Western Ontario; MBA, Harvard Business School
Background: President, Rogers High Speed Internet Access; McKinsey & Company; Morgan Stanley
Pierre J. Schuurmans, Partner & COO
Education: MBA, Stanford University; HBA, Richard Ivey School of Business, Western University
Background: CFO & Vice President at various companies; Consultant, McKinsey & Company; Monitor Company
Directorships: Hanlan Boat Club
Thecla E. Sweeney, Partner
Education: BA, University of Western Ontario; MBA, Richard Ivey School of Business, University of Western Ontario
Background: TD Capital; Business Development, Deluce Capital; George Weston Limited

2063 BMO CAPITAL MARKETS
100 King Street W
Toronto, ON M5X 1H3
Canada

Phone: 416-359-4000
web: capitalmarkets.bmo.com

Mission Statement: Invests in and works closely with exceptional management teams in companies with defensible market positions and franchise characteristics which generate strong cash flow and operate in attractive growth markets. The primary goal is long-term value creation, thus partnering with experienced management in compelling industry segments to identify and develop platform companies. In 2015, BMO co-invested in OMERS Ventures Fund II, a venture capital fund managed by OMERS Ventures.

Geographic Preference: North America
Fund Size: $647 billion
Founded: 2000
Minimum Investment: $500,000
Investment Criteria: Middle-Market Leveraged Buyouts, Growth Equity, Structured Equity Investments

Other Locations:
151 W 42nd Street
New York, NY 10036

129 Saint-Jacques Street
Montreal, QC H2Y 1L6
Canada

115 S LaSalle Street
Chicago, IL 60603

Key Executives:
Dan Barclay, CEO & Group Head
Education: BSc(Hons.), Unversity of Alberta; MBA, University of Calgary
Chris Taves, Chief Operating Officer
Education: MBA, Richard Ivey School of Business, Western University; University of Waterloo; CPA
Directorships: Armagh

2064 BOND CAPITAL
1100 Melville Street
Suite 1160
Vancouver, BC V6E 4A6
Canada

Phone: 604-687-2663
web: www.bondcapital.ca

Mission Statement: Offers capital in the form of debt or equity to entrepreneurs.
Geographic Preference: Western Canada, Northwestern U.S.A.
Founded: 2002
Average Investment: $2 to $30 million
Investment Criteria: Later-Stage
Industry Group Preference: Oil & Gas Services, Manufacturing, Distribution, Wholesale, Transportation, Agriculture, Food & Beverage, Financial Services, Healthcare, Consumer Products, Private Education

Key Executives:
Davis Vaitkunas, President & Founder
e-mail: davis@bondcapital.ca
Education: Univ. of Alberta
Jim Elliott, CFO
Education: University of Alberta
Background: Mercer Intl., Westcoast Energy/Duke Energy, Ernst & Young
Corry J. Silbernagel, Managing Director, Originations
Education: University of British Columbia; INSEAD

2065 BONNEFIELD FINANCIAL
141 Adelaide Street W
Suite 510
Toronto, ON M5H 3L5

Phone: 613-230-3854
Toll-Free: 877-695-3854
e-mail: info@bonnefield.com
web: bonnefield.com

Mission Statement: Bonnefield provides land-lease funding exclusively to farmers.
Founded: 2009
Investment Criteria: Farm Land
Industry Group Preference: Farming, Agriculture

Other Locations:
14 Concourse Gate
Suite 100
Ottawa, ON K2E 7S8

Key Executives:
Tom Eisenhauer, President & CEO
Education: BA, University of King's College; Dalhousie University; MA, Queen's University; PDO, Canadian Securities Institute; ICDD, Institute of Corporate Directors; Rotman School of Business
Background: Managing Partner, Latitude Partners; Managing Director, TD Securities; Managing Director, Lancaster Financial
Directorships: University of King's College
Marcus Mitchell, Chief Investment Officer
Education: BA, University of Western Ontario; CFA; CAIA

2066 BRIGHTSPARK VENTURES
MaRS Centre, Heritage Building
101 College Street
Suite 320
Toronto, ON M5G 1L7
Canada

Phone: 416-488-1999
e-mail: info@brightspark.com
web: www.brightspark.com

Geographic Preference: Canada
Fund Size: $200 Million
Founded: 1999
Average Investment: $3 Million
Minimum Investment: $1 Million
Investment Criteria: Start-up, Seed-Stage, Early-Stage
Industry Group Preference: Information Technology, Wireless Technologies, Mobile, Software, Artificial Intelligence
Portfolio Companies: AdHawk Microsystems, AOMS, Buy Back Booth, Classcraft, Hopper, Hubba, InVivo AI, Jazinga, Jewlr, Nano Magnetics, nGUVU, Nudge Rewards, Potloc, Sabse Technologies, Wysdom AI

Other Locations:
Espace CDPQ
3 Place Ville-Marie
Bureau 12350

Venture Capital & Private Equity Firms / Canadian Firms

Montreal, QC H3B 0E7
Canada
Key Executives:
  Mark Skapinker, Co-Founder & Managing Partner
  e-mail: marks@brightspark.com
  Background: President, Delrina
  Directorships: Upside Fdn. of Canada
  Sophie Forest, Managing Partner
  e-mail: sophie@brightspark.com
  Education: BA, Finance, University of Sherbrooke
  Background: CDP Capital Technology
  Directorships: Jewlr Inc., Hopper, nGUVU

2067 BROOKFIELD ASSET MANAGEMENT
Brookfield Place
181 Bay Street
Suite 330
Toronto, ON M5J 2T3
Canada

Phone: 416-363-9491
web: www.brookfield.com

Mission Statement: Global alternative asset manager focused on property, renewable power, infrastructure and private equity.
Geographic Preference: Canada, United States, Europe, India, Australia, South America
Fund Size: $500 billion
Industry Group Preference: Real Estate, Infrastructure, Renewable Power, Private Equity
Portfolio Companies: Ainsworth Lumber, Armtec Limited, Brookfield Real Estate & Relocation Services, Concert Industries, CWC Well Services, Ember Resources, Grande Cashe Coal, Hammerstone Corp., Hudson Bay Company, Insignia Energy, Longview Fibre Paper & Packaging, MAAX, Norbord, Stelco, Tecumseh Products, Vicwest, Western Forest Products

Other Locations:
  Brookfield Place
  250 Vesey Street
  15th Floor
  New York, NY 10281-0221
  Phone: 212-417-7000

  One Canada Square
  Level 25, Canary Warf
  London E14 5AAD
  United Kingdom
  Phone: 44 20 7659 3500

  Avenida Antonio Gallotti s/n
  Edificio Pacific Tower, BL 2
  2§ andar - Barra da Tijuca
  Rio de Janeiro 22775-029
  Brazil
  Phone: 55 21 3725 7800

  Level 22
  135 King Street
  Sydney NSW 2000
  Australia
  Phone: 61 2 9158 5100

  Level 15
  Gate Building, DIFC
  PO Box 507234
  Dubai
  United Arab Emirates
  Phone: 971 4 401 9211

  8th Floor, A Wing, One BKC
  Bandra Kurla Complex
  Bandra East
  Mumbai 400 051
  India
  Phone: 91 22 6600 0700

  Suite 2101, Shui On Plaza
  No. 333 Huai Hai Road
  Shanghai 200021
  China
  Phone: 86 21 2306 0700

Key Executives:
  Bruce Flatt, Chief Executive Officer
  Justin Beber, Managing Partner, Head of Corporate Strategy, Chief Legal Officer
  Education: BEcon, McGill University; MBA/LLB, Schulich School of Business & Osgoode Hall Law School, York University
  Barry Blattman, Vice Chair
  Education: University of Michigan; New York University
  Background: Salomon Brothers; Merrill Lynch
  Jeff Blidner, Vice Chair
  Ric Clark, Managing Partner, Real Estate
  Education: Indiana University of Pennsylvania
  Joe Freedman, Senior Vice Chair, Private Equity
  Education: Schulich School of Business; Osgoode Hall Law School
  Harry Goldgut, Vice Chair, Infrastructure & Renewable Power
  Education: University of Toronto; Osgoode Hall Law School
  Brian Kingston, Managing Partner & CEO, Real Estate
  Background: CEO, Prime Infrastructure; CFO, Multiplex
  Brian Lawson, Managing Partner & CFO
  Directorships: Governing Council, University of Toronto; Community Food Centers Canada
  Richard Legault, Vice Chair, Renewable Power
  Directorships: Isagen; QG100
  Luiz Lopes, Executive Chair, Latin America
  Background: Magliano CTVM; Fiat Leasing; Banco Fiat
  Directorships: Brazilian Symphonic Orchestra; Brazil-Canada Chamber of Commerce; Fundacao Dom Cabral; Fundacao Getulio Vargas
  Cyrus Madon, Managing Partner & CEO, Private Equity
  Background: PricewaterhouseCoopers
  Craig Noble, Managing Partner & CEO, Alternative Investments
  Education: Mount Allison University; Schulich School of Business
  Background: Bank of Montreal
  Lori Pearson, Managing Partner & COO
  Directorships: Brookfield Foundation; Pathways to Education in Canada
  Sam Pollock, Managing Partner & CEO, Infrastructure
  Education: Queen's University
  Directorships: TWC Enterprises
  William Powell, Managing Partner, Real Estate
  Education: University of Richmond; Darden School of Business
  Anuj Ranjan, Managing Partner & CEO, Middles East & South Asia
  Education: BSc, University of Alberta; MBA, Richard Ivey School of Business
  Sachin Shah, Managing Partner & CEO, Renewable Power
  Education: University of Toronto
  Ben Vaughan, Managing Partner, Infrastructure
  Education: Queen's University

2068 BUILD VENTURES
1505 Barrington St
6th Floor
Halifax, NS B3J 3K5
Canada

web: www.buildventures.ca

Mission Statement: Build Ventures works with dedicated management teams to help build early stage technology companies in the Atlantic region.

Fund Size: $50 million
Founded: 2013
Investment Criteria: Early Stage
Industry Group Preference: Technology
Portfolio Companies: Affinio, Celtx, Introhive, Resson Aerospace, Smart Skin Technologies, Interaxon, AirVM, icejam, Fiddlehead, Dash Hudson, Spring Loaded, The Money Finder, Manifold, Radient 360, ProcedureFlow

Key Executives:
  Patrick Keefe, General Partner
  e-mail: patrick@buildventures.ca
  Education: MPhil, Univ. of Oxford; MBA, Harvard Business School
  Background: VP, Investment, Innovacorp; Founder, CVAI; Atlas Venture; The Boston Consulting Group
  Rob Barbara, General Partner
  e-mail: rob@buildventures.ca
  Education: Queen's University; MBA, Richard Ivey School of Business, University of Western Ontario
  Background: SVP, Burgundy Asset Management; Founder, Beaujolais Private Investment Management; TD Securities; President & Co-Founder, eSalveo

2069 CAISSE DE DEPOT ET PLACEMENT DU QUEBEC
Édifice Price
65, rue Sainte-Anne
14th Floor
Québec, QC G1R 3X5
Canada

Phone: 418-684-2334 **Fax:** 418-684-2335
e-mail: info@cdpq.com
web: cdpq.com

Mission Statement: Fund manager for pension and insurance plans.

Fund Size: $326.7 Billion
Founded: 1965

Key Executives:
  Michael Sabia, President & CEO
  Education: BA, University of Toronto; MA, Yale University
  Background: CNR, BCE

2070 CANADIAN BUSINESS GROWTH FUND
730-145 King Street West
Toronto, ON M5H 1J8
Canada

Toll-Free: 833-459-2243
web: cbgf.com

Mission Statement: Growth capital investor formed by Canada's leading banks and insurance companies.

Fund Size: $545 million
Minimum Investment: $3-20 million
Portfolio Companies: Lift Auto Group, paybright

Key Executives:
  George Rossolatos, Chief Executive Officer
  e-mail: george.rossolatos@cbgf.com
  Education: Queen's Univ.; Kellogg School of Management
  Background: Avante Logixx; TorQuest Partners
  Dale Ponder, Chair
  e-mail: dale.ponder@cbgf.com
  Education: LLB, Western University
  Background: Osler, Hoskin & Harcourt
  Directorships: Morneau Shepell

2071 CANOPY RIVERS
40 King Street W
Suite 2504
Toronto, ON M5H 3Y2

Phone: 855-227-8639
e-mail: info@canopyrivers.com
web: www.canopyrivers.com

Mission Statement: Venture capital firm specializing in cannabis.

Geographic Preference: Global
Founded: 2017
Investment Criteria: Market Size, Market Need, Traction, Return on Investment, Leadership Team
Industry Group Preference: Cannabis
Portfolio Companies: Agripharm, BioLumic, Canapar, Civilized, Greenhouse Juice, Headset, Herbert, High Beauty, James E. Wagner Cultivation Corporation, LeafLink International, PharmHouse, Radicle, TerrAscend, Tweed Tree Lot, Vert Mirabel, YSS, ZeaKal

Key Executives:
  Narbe Alexandrian, President & CEO
  Education: BBA, Shulich School of Business, York University; CPA
  Background: OMERS Ventures; TELUS Internet of Things Group; Firmex Inc.; Deloitte LLP
  Olivier Dufourmantelle, Chief Operating Officer
  Education: BEng, Electrical Engineering, McGill University; MBA, Harvard Business School
  Background: Project Manager, Essilor; General Manager, Michelin; Strategic Project Manager, Inergy Automotive Systems; Engagement Manager, McKinsey & Co.; COO, Canopy Growth Corp.
  Mary Dimou, Director of Business Development
  Education: BS, Biomedical Sciences; MSc, Human Health/Nutritional Sciences, University of Guelph; Business Analysis Certificate; PhD, Phylosophy, University of Toronto
  Background: Product Development Specialist, Dairy Farmers of Ontario; Director of Procurement, JJD Holdings Corp.; Founder/Inventor, AgRegKit; Sr. Business Analyst, Bioenterprise Corp. Canada; Sr. Business/Investment Analyst, Ontario Ministry of Agriculture; Business Dev. Manager, Ontario Centres of Execellence
  James Bok, Associate Director, Finance
  Education: Singapore Management University; Queen's University
  Background: Sr. Accountant, KPMG Canada; Assistant VP, Merrill Lynch

2072 CARPEDIA CAPITAL
75 Navy St.
Oakville, ON L6J 2Z1
Canada

Phone: 416-364-8842
web: www.carpediacapital.com

Mission Statement: Carpedia Capital manages various investments on behalf of founding shareholders, financial instituations, and individuals. The Carpedia approach focuses on identifiuing and implementing sustainable, financially accretive change without capital expenditure, examining changes to product, process, system and behaviour.

Geographic Preference: Canada
Average Investment: $8 to $20 million
Minimum Investment: $8 million
Investment Criteria: Succession Sales, Recapitalizations, Management Buy-Outs/Buy-Ins, Carve-Outs, Growth Capital
Industry Group Preference: Manufacturing, Food & Beverage, Transportation, Distribution, Consumer Services, Business Products & Services, Hotels, Restaurants, Retailing

Venture Capital & Private Equity Firms / Canadian Firms

Key Executives:
Gregoire Tremblay, Co-Founder
e-mail: tremblay@carpediacapital.com
Education: Concordia University
Glen Ampleford, Vice President
e-mail: ampleford@carpediacapital.com
Education: Queen's University School of Business; CFA

2073 CATALYST CAPITAL GROUP
181 Bay Street, Suite 4700
PO Box 762
Bay Wellington Tower, Brookfield Place
Toronto, ON M5J 2T3
Canada

Phone: 416-945-3000 Fax: 416-945-3060
e-mail: info@catcapital.com
web: catcapital.com

Mission Statement: Catalyst specializes in control and/or influence investments in distressed and undervalued Canadian situations.
Geographic Preference: Canada
Fund Size: $4.3 billion
Founded: 2002
Portfolio Companies: Advantage, Allstream, Brushstrokes, Cabovisao, Callidus Capital Corporation, Call-Net Enterprises Inc., Calpine Co., Canwest, Countryside Power Income Fund, Frontera Energy, Gateway Casinos & Entertainment, Geneba Properties N.V., Hollinger, Imax, Mobility, Natural Markets Food Group, Quad/Graphics, Royal Group Technologies Limited, Snowbear, Sonar Entertainment Inc., SR Telecom & Co., Stelco Inc., Therapure Biopharma Inc., YRC Worldwide

Key Executives:
Newton Glassman, Managing Partner
Education: MBA, Wharton School of the University of Pennsylvania
Directorships: FrontPoint Partners, LLC., Gateway Casinos & Entertainment Ltd., Cable Satisfaction International Inc., Natural Markets Restaurant Corp., Ceberus Capital Management LP
Gabriel de Alba, Managing Director & Partner
Education: BSc, NYU Stern School of Business; MBA, Columbia University
Background: Bank of American International Merchant Banking Group, Banker's Trust New York Merchant Brank Group
Directorships: Geneba Properties, Advantage Rent-A-Car, Gateway Casinos & Entertainment, Therapure Biopharma, World Color Press, Sonar Entertainment
Rocco DiPucchio, Managing Director & COO
Education: Osgood Hall Law School, York University
Background: Senior Partner, Lax O'Sullivan Lisus Gottlieb LLP; Associate, Blake, Cassels & Graydon LLP
James Riley, Managing Director
Education: Masters of Law, Harvard University; University of Toronto
Background: Banking and Finance Law Group, Goodmans LLP; Norton Rose Filbright Canada; Stikeman Elliott LLP
Steven Rostowsky, CFO
Education: Univ. of Cape Town
Background: Sprott Inc.

2074 CBI² CAPITAL
407 - 3rd Street SW
3rd Floor
Calgary, AB T2P 4Z2

Phone: 403-351-1779
e-mail: contact@cbi2.com
web: cbi2.com

Mission Statement: Formerly known as Target Capital, CBI² Capital invests in early-stage companies within the expanding cannabis industry.
Geographic Preference: Canada, Europe, US
Founded: 2017
Investment Criteria: Early-Stage
Industry Group Preference: Cannabis
Portfolio Companies: LivWell International Corp.

Key Executives:
Sonny Mottahed, Chairman/President/CEO
Education: University of Calgary
Background: Chairman/CEO, 51st Parallel Life Sciences; Business Development, Nexen Inc.; Institutional Sales, Salman Partners Inc.; Investment Banking, Canaccord Financial; Managing Director, Raymond James & Associates; CEO, Black Spruce Merchant Capital
Directorships: IR Optimizer; Iridium Risk Services; Razor Energy Corp.
Bill MacDonald, Executive VP/Director
Directorships: Grunewahl Organics; Inner Spirit Holdings
David Cheadle, Chief Financial Officer
Education: BCom, University of Manitoba
Background: VP, Canaccord Genuity Inc.; VP, Raymond James & Associates; Managing Partner, Black Spruce Merchant Capital
Gregory G. Turnbull, Director
Education: BA, Philosophy/English, Queen's University; LLB, Law, University of Toronto
Background: Sr. Partner, McCarthy Tetrault LLP
Directorships: Hawk Exploration; Online Energy Inc.; Heritage Oil Plc.; Sonde Resources Corp.; Porto Energy Corp.; Sunshine Oilsands; Marquee Energy; Crescent Point Energy; Storm Resources
Matteo Volpi, Director
Education: BA, International Management, Franklin College; London Business School
Background: Business Development, INTELS Nigeria Ltd.; Business Development Manager, Olrean Invest Africa; Business Development Manager, Ocean Alliance Consultancy; CEO, IOMS
Directorships: Gaia Consulting Ltd.

2075 CCEI
10 Adelaide Street E
Toronto, ON M5C 1J3
Canada

Phone: 416-572-8526
e-mail: info@cc-ei.ca
web: www.cc-ei.ca

Mission Statement: CCEI invests equity in renewable energy and infrastructure assets in oECD and developing, high-yield markets.
Founded: 2019

Key Executives:
Okan Altug, Managing Director
Education: BA, Bogazixi University, Istanbul; MBA, Pace University
Background: Founder, Daruma Corporate Finance
Sasha Jacob, Managing Director
Education: BA, Bishop's University; MBA, Sir Wilfred Laurier University; GP LLM, University of Toronto
Background: CEO, Jacob Capital Management
Axel Goldenberg, Managing Director
Education: Richmond University, London
Background: Co-Founder/Managing Partner, Dem-Al Autogas; Founder, Naturelgaz
Warren Smulowitz, Managing Director
Background: Bank of Montreal
Ugur Kilic, Managing Director
Education: MBA, Boston University
Background: Country Manager, Yingli Solar, Istanbul
Ruchan Hamamci, Managing Director
Education: BSc, MSc, PhD, Bosphorus University

Venture Capital & Private Equity Firms / Canadian Firms

Background: Eksim Investment Holding; Sancak Energy Holding

2076 CELTIC HOUSE VENTURE PARTNERS
239 Argyle Avenue
Suite 100
Ottawa, ON K2P 1B8
Canada

Phone: 613-569-7200 **Fax:** 613-569-7209
web: www.celtic-house.com

Mission Statement: Celtic House Venture Partners is an independent Canadian investment firm actively pursuing and investing in innovative technology businesses. The company works closely with management teams to produce successful results for its investors. From offices in Toronto and Ottawa, Celtic House manages three funds.
Geographic Preference: Canada, United Kingdom
Fund Size: $425 million
Founded: 1994
Investment Criteria: Early-Stage
Industry Group Preference: Communications, Networking, Information Technology, Infrastructure, SaaS
Portfolio Companies: Auvik, Canvaspop, Corsa, Envenio, FileFacets, Graphite Software, KodaCloud, Nuvyyo, Peraso Technologies, Rare, Raven, Vleepo
Key Executives:
  David Adderley, Partner
  Education: BA, Queen's University; LLB, University of Western Ontario
  Background: Gowlings LLP
  Directorships: Avvasi, Diablo Technologies, Graphite Software, Nuvyyo
  Roger Maggs, Founder
  Education: University of Wales; Warwick Business School
  Background: Alcan Aluminum
  Directorships: LTX-Credence, Sandvine
  Tomas Valis, Partner
  Education: PhD, University of Toronto; Postdoctoral Researcher, MIT
  Julie Fallon, Chief Financial Officer
  Education: BComm, Mount Allison University
  Background: Taral Networks, webPLAN

2077 CENTRESTONE VENTURES
7-1250 Waverley Street
Winnipeg, MB R3T 6C6
Canada

Phone: 204-453-1230 **Fax:** 204-453-1293
web: www.centrestoneventures.com

Mission Statement: CentreStone Ventures is a life sciences focused private venture capital fund investing primarily in companies developing early stage therapeutics, medical devices, diagnostics and new drug delivery methods.
Geographic Preference: Western Canada, Midwest United States
Investment Criteria: Early-Stage
Industry Group Preference: Life Sciences, Therapeutics, Medical Devices, Diagnostics
Portfolio Companies: Diamedica, Medicure, Verista Imaging, LED Medical Diagnostics, Orasi Medical, Sanommune, Ardeo Imaging, Marsala Biotech, Limestone Pharma
Key Executives:
  Albert D. Friesen, Chief Executive Officer
  Education: PhD, Protein Chemistry, University of Manitoba
  Background: President, Winnipeg Rh Institute
  Marcus Enns, Venture Partner
  Education: B.Comm, University of Manitoba
  Background: VP, Corporate Affairs, Genesys Venture Inc.
  Directorships: Miraculins, Kane Biotech
  James Kinley
  Education: BComm, University of Manitoba
  Background: Manitoba Telecom

2078 CHRYSALIX
1111 West Hastings St.
Suite 333
Vancouver, BC V6E 2J3
Canada

Phone: 604-659-5499 **Fax:** 604-659-5479
e-mail: info@chrysalix.com
web: www.chrysalix.com

Mission Statement: The Chrysalix Global Network is a premier alliance of independent, top-tier clean energy venture capital firms - globally linked but locally managed - with the primary goal to better address the global nature of the cleantech industry. Spanning three continents, the CGN firms discuss local deal flow, exchange knowledge, and share networks resulting in faster geographical expansion for their portfolio companies, lowered investment risk, and superior fund performance.
Geographic Preference: Global
Founded: 2001
Investment Criteria: Early-Stage
Industry Group Preference: Oil & Gas, Metals & Mining, Manufacturing, Logistics, Construction, Transportation, Chemicals & Advanced Materials, Agriculture, Utilities & Electric Power, Asset Management, Artificial Intelligence, Data Analytics, Internet of Things, Robotic Systems, Blockchain
Portfolio Companies: minesense, GlassPoint, GaN Systems, General Fusion, Axine Water Technologies, enbala, Inventys, NanoSteel, Primus Power
Key Executives:
  Fred van Beuningen, Managing Partner
  Directorships: Director of Innovation & Strategic Marketing, AkzoNobel
  Wal van Lierop, Executive Chair/Managing Partner
  e-mail: wvlierop@chrysalix.com
  Education: PhD, Economics, Vrije Universiteit, Amsterdam
  Background: VP Strategic Planning, Westcoast Energy; McKinsey & Company
  Richard MacKellar, Managing Partner
  e-mail: rmackellar@chrysalix.com
  Education: Metallurgy Degree, Sheffield University; MBA, Harvard Business School
  Background: Engineer, NEI Parsons; President & CEO, BrightSide Technologies; President & CEO, NxtPhase
  Charles Haythornthwaite, Senior Partner
  e-mail: chaythornthwaite@chrysalix.com
  Education: MBA, Berkeley; PhD, Laser Physics & Materials Science, University of Southampton
  Background: Soliant Energy

2079 CIBC CAPITAL MARKETS
161 Bay St.
Brookfield Place
Toronto, ON M5J 2S8
Canada

Phone: 416-980-2211
web: www.cibccm.com

Mission Statement: Focuses on growth-oriented businesses and looks to help founders and management teams take their company to the next level, committed to providing steady support through all economic cycles.
Geographic Preference: Canada
Fund Size: $200 million
Founded: 1989
Average Investment: $10-20 million
Minimum Investment: $2 million

Venture Capital & Private Equity Firms / Canadian Firms

Investment Criteria: Later-Stage, Growth Equity, Acquisitions, Management/Leveraged Buy-Outs, Recapitalizations
Industry Group Preference: Software, Energy, Financial Services, Technology, Manufacturing, Pharmaceuticals, Medical Devices, Healthcare, Hardware, Communications, Mining, Oil & Gas, Power, Real Estate, Telecommunications
Portfolio Companies: AKQA, Adaytum, Advanced Interactive Systems, Algorithmics, Almonde, Arriva Pharmaceuticals, Avere, B2eMarkets, Bell ActiMedia, Broadband Services, Cardikine, CashEdge, CCS, Chrysalis, Clean Air Partners, Cornice Corporation, Creation Technologies, Datawire Communication Networks, Definiens AG, DirectBuy, eAssist Global Solutions, Eontec Limited, Equator Technologies, Esurg Corporation, Everypath, Firm AS, First Asset Management, FreshDirect, FuelQuest, Groupe Lucien Barriere, GCAN Insurance Company, GT Nexus, HAHT Commerce, Herbal Magic, Hubspan, Hydrogenics Corporation, InfoTalk Corporation, InQuira, Interwise, iSuppli Corporation, iVillage, Juniper Financial, Kaval Wireless Technologies, Keystone Communications, Lavalife, MetricStream, MicroMed Technology, Molecular Staging, Multi-Channel Communications, NetByTel, Nextpage, Nursefinders, Nuvelo, OnePath Networks, Otis Spunkmeyer, PerformanceRetail, Persona, Points International, PortalPlayer, Prepaid Direct, Prior Data Sciences, Progressive Group, Proton Energy Systems, Qpass, QUMAS, Realstar Management, Seisint, SemperCare, Servicesoft Technologies, SiGe Semiconductor, Silicon Bandwidth, Silicon Energy Corp, Soltrus, Syrrx, THINQ Learning Solutions, TheBrain Technologies Corporation, Totality, Triversity, US HealthWorks, ValiCert, Venturion Limited Partnership, Vigilance, Visiprise, Vividence Corporation, Vytek Corporation, Western Forest Products, Wild Tangent, Workbrain, Wysdom, Yantra

Key Executives:
Harry Culham, Sr. Exec. VP and Group Head, CIBC Capital Markets
Education: Sauder School of Business, University of British Columbia
Directorships: CIBC Children's Foundation; Faculty Advisory Board, Saunder School of Business; Mount Sinai Hospital
Roman S. Dubczak, Managing Dir., Global Investment Banking, CIBC Capital Markets
Education: BComm, University of Toronto; MBA, Schulich School of Business
Directorships: Fraser Institut, CIBC Children's Foundation
Christian Exshaw, Managing Dir. and Head, Global Markets, CIBC Capital Markets
Education: Master of Science, Risk Management & Financial Instruments, Insitut d'Administration des Entreprise, France

2080 CIBC INNOVATION BANKING
Toronto, ON
Canada

e-mail: Mailbox.CIBCInnovationBanking@cibc.com
web: www.cibc.com/en/commercial/areas-of-specialization/innovation-banking.html

Mission Statement: This branch of CIBC invests in clients who are in the innovation economy, from startups to later-stage businesses.
Founded: 2018
Investment Criteria: Early Stage, Middle Stage, Later Stage, Startups, Mature Companies
Industry Group Preference: Technology, Software, Innovation
Portfolio Companies: Expensify, Geoforce, Hootsuite, Jane Software, Lightspeed, Parchment

Key Executives:
Mark McQueen, President/Executive Managing Director
e-mail: mark.mcqueen@cibc.com
Amy Olah, Executive Director
e-mail: amy.olah@cibc.com
Mark Usher, Managing Director/North American Market Leader
e-mail: mark.usher@cibc.com

2081 CLAIRVEST GROUP
22 St. Clair Avenue East
Suite 1700
Toronto, ON M4T 2S3
Canada

Phone: 416-925-9270 Fax: 416-925-5753
web: www.clairvest.com

Mission Statement: Clairvest partners with management to invest in profitable small and mid-sized North American companies with the goal of helping to build value in the business and generate superior long term financial returns for investors.
Geographic Preference: North America
Fund Size: $1 billion
Founded: 1987
Average Investment: $15 - 100 million
Minimum Investment: $5 million
Investment Criteria: Expansion, Acquisition or Buy-out, Turnaround
Industry Group Preference: All Sectors Considered
Portfolio Companies: Accel Entertainment, ace2three.com, Also Energy, Digital Media Solutions, Elements Casino, Meriplex Communications, Right Time Heating and Air Conditioning, Winter Bros. Waste Systems

Key Executives:
Jeff Parr, Vice Chair and Managing Director
Education: University of Western Ontario
Background: Partner, Canadian Mezzanine Fund; Coopers & Lybrand
Directorships: N-Brook Mortgage Group, Casino Marina del Sol, Casino New Brunswick, Midwest Gaming
Ken Rotman, CEO and Managing Director
Education: BA, Tufts University; MSc, London School of Economics; MBA, New York University
Background: EM Warburg Pincus & Co.
Directorships: Wellington Finanaical, Light Tower Rentals, PEER 1, Discovery Air
Michael Wagman, President and Managing Director
Education: HBA, Richard Ivey School of Business; CFA
Background: BMO Nesbitt Burns Equity Partners
Directorships: Casino Marina del Sol, Latin Gaming Osorno, KUBRA, Sonco Gaming
Michael Castellarin, Managing Director
Education: BComm, Queen's University; MBA, Northwestern University Kellogg School of Management
Background: Management Consultant, Monitor Company
Directorships: Light Tower Rentals, Sonco Gaming
Mitch Green, Managing Director
Education: BS, Cornell University; MBA, University of Michigan School of Business
Background: Leveraged Finance, BNP Capital Markets; Corporate Finance, Bank of America
Directorships: KUBRA, PEER 1
Robbie Isenberg, Managing Director
Education: MBA, Northwestern Univeristy's Kellogg School of Management; HBA, Richard Ivey School of Business
Background: Sr. Case Team Leader, Monitor Group; Investment Banking, Credit Suisse
Adrian Pasricha, Managing Director
Education: BA, International Studies, University of Pennsylvania
Background: Warburg Pincus LLC, Boston Consulting Group, IB Partners

Venture Capital & Private Equity Firms / Canadian Firms

Sebastien Dhonte, Managing Director
416-413-6026
e-mail: sdhonte@clairvest.com
Education: BComm, McGill University; MBA, INSEAD
Background: Consultant, McKinsey & Company

2082 CLEARSPRING CAPITAL PARTNERS
333 Bay Street
Suite 640
Toronto, ON M5H 2R2
Canada

Phone: 416-868-4900 Fax: 416-868-4910
e-mail: info@cscap.ca
web: www.cscap.ca

Mission Statement: A private equity team with a focus on creating value and success for middle market Canadian companies. Formerly known as Callisto Capital.
Geographic Preference: Canada
Fund Size: $600 million
Founded: 2002
Average Investment: $20 - $50 million
Investment Criteria: Middle Market, Acquisitions, Buyouts, Consolidations, Restructurings, Recapitalizations
Industry Group Preference: Technology, Healthcare, Manufacturing, Consumer Products, Business Products & Services
Portfolio Companies: Demers Ambulances, Diversified Metal Engineering, telecon, Homewood Health, Logistik, Medical Pharmacies, Spectrum Health Care, town shoes, CBI Health Group, Creation Technologies, Dynacare Kasper, Maxxam Analytics, Mini-Skool, Voyages Traditours
Other Locations:
Espace CDPQ
3 Place Ville-Marie
Bureau 12350, Suite 1-160, 1er étage
Montréal, QC H3B 0E7
Canada
Phone: 514-879-9666 Fax: 416-868-4910

Key Executives:
Joseph Shlesinger, Managing Director
416-868-4516
e-mail: jshlesinger@cscap.ca
Education: Ryerson Polytechnic University; MBA, Richard Ivey School of Business, University of Western Ontario
Background: Strategy Consultant, Bain & Company Canada
Directorships: Medical Pharmacies Group, Town Shoes, Alpine Canada Alpin
Lawrence Stevenson, Managing Director
416-868-4512
e-mail: lstevenson@cscap.ca
Education: Royal Military College; MBA, Harvard Business School
Background: CEO, Chapters; Co-Founder, Bain & Company Canada; CEO, Pep Boys
Marie-Claude Boisvert, Partner
e-mail: mcboisvert@cscap.ca
Education: Ecoles des Hautes Etudes Commerciales de Montreal; MBA, INSEAD
Background: Managing Partner, Kilmer Capital; CFO, Greiche & Scaff; Goldman Sachs; KPMG
Jim Probert, Chief Financial Officer
416-868-4911
e-mail: jprobert@cscap.ca
Education: BA, University of Toronto
Background: Director, Finance, CARGO Cosmetics Corp.; PricewaterhouseCoopers
John Veitch, Principal
e-mail: jveitch@cscap.ca
Education: BComm, Queen's University
Background: Scotiabank
Directorships: Logistik Unicorp, Demers Ambulances

2083 CM PARTNERS 1021 West Hastings Street
Suite 1200
Vancouver, BC V6E 0C3
Canada

Phone: 604-558-6168
e-mail: info@cm-canada.com
web: cmpartners.ca

Mission Statement: CM Partners is a private equity firm that invests in profitable, well-managed, small to medium sized businesses.
Geographic Preference: Canada, USA
Fund Size: $200 Million
Founded: 2017
Average Investment: $5-30 Million
Key Executives:
Kenny Zou, Founder and CEO
Education: BA, University of California, Berkeley
Background: Hana Financial Group
Regan Li, Co-Founder and Managing Partner
Education: BS, Duke University; MBA, University of Pennsylvania
Background: HIG Capital; Macquarie Capital

2084 COBALT CAPITAL
1464 Cornwall Rd.
Suite 7
Oakville, ON L6J 7W5
Canada

Phone: 905-815-9755
e-mail: pkeane@cobaltcapital.ca
web: www.cobaltcapital.ca

Mission Statement: Cobalt Capital is a boutique private equity firm made up of former business owners and operators seeking to help private companies grow and innovate by investing their capital and contributing their operating expertise. The partners of Cobalt Capital have significant business and entrepreneurial experience in a wide range of disciplines, sectors, and geographies and they work closely with the companies they invest in to help them achieve their goal of growth activities.

Geographic Preference: Canada, United States
Average Investment: $2 - $5 million
Minimum Investment: $2 million
Investment Criteria: Ownership Succession, Expansion Capital, Acquisition Financing, Management Buy-Out/Buy-In, Divisional Spin Off, Recapitalization
Industry Group Preference: Diversified
Portfolio Companies: Pyrotek Special Effects, Phoenix Innovations Corp.
Key Executives:
Patrick Keane, President & CEO
905-815-9755 x222
e-mail: pkeane@cobaltcapital.ca
Background: Keanall Group of Comanies
Scott Dunlop, Managing Director
905-815-9755 x231
e-mail: sdunlop@cobaltcapital.ca
Background: Vice President/General Manager, Specialty Home Products, CFM Corporation
Brian Hogan, Director & CFO
905-815-9755 x223
e-mail: bhogan@cobaltcapital.ca
Background: CFO, Iovate Health Sciences; Corporate Finance, CFM Corporation

2085 COPPERLION CAPITAL
2600 - 200 Granville Street
Vancouver, BC V6C 1S4

Phone: 604-637-1112 Fax: 604-637-1113
web: www.copperlioncapital.com

723

Venture Capital & Private Equity Firms / Canadian Firms

Mission Statement: CopperLion performs corporate development and special projects on behalf of the Washington Companies.

Industry Group Preference: Marine Transportation, Construction, Engineering, Environmental, Mining, Aviation, Rail Transportation

Portfolio Companies: Seaspan Marine corporation, Envirocon, Modern Machinery, Montana Resources, Montana Rail & Southern Railway of British Columbia, Aviation Partners

Key Executives:
  Kyle Washington, Executive Chair
  Directorships: Seaspan Corporation, Seaspan Marine Corporation, Envirocon, Modern Machinery, Montana Rail Link, Montana Resources, Southern Railway of British Columbia
  Byron Horner, President
  604-637-1115
  e-mail: bhorner@copperlioncapital.com
  Education: BA, Political Science, Carleton University; MBA, Finance & MA, Political Science, University of British Columbia; LLB, University of Toronto; ICDD, Canadian Institute of Corporate Directors
  Background: Merrill Lunch; CIBC Work Markets; Lawson Lundell LLP
  Directorships: President, Spirit Bear Entertainment; Washington Kids Foundation

2086 CORDIANT CAPITAL
1002 Sherbrooke Street West
Suite 2800
Montreal, QC H3A 3L6
Canada

Phone: 514-286-1142
e-mail: relations@cordiantcap.com
web: www.cordiantcap.com

Mission Statement: Focused on infrastructure debt in emerging markets.

Geographic Preference: Asia, Eastern Europe, Latin America, Africa
Fund Size: $1.5 billion
Founded: 1999
Portfolio Companies: Tecon Rio Grande SA, Real People Investment Holdings, SREI Infrastructure Finance Ltd, Latapack, ProCredit Group, Vicentin SAIC, Eleme Petrochemical

Key Executives:
  Benn Mikula, Co-CEO
  Education: BA & MA, McGill University
  Background: Coradiant; Fibermedia; CEO, CloudOps; Montreal Neurological Hospital & Research Institut; Montreal Children's Hospital; President, Acorn Society
  Jean-François Sauvé, Co-CEO
  Education: Business Administration, L'École des Hautes études Commerciales; MBA, INSEAD
  Background: Barclays Bank; President, Pictet Canada LP
  James T. Kiernan, Chairman
  Education: BA, Brown University; MBA, Harvard University
  Background: President, Goldman Sachs Canada Inc.
  Don McKelvie, Chief Financial Officer
  Education: BA, Bishop's University
  Background: Chartered Accountant, Ernst & Young; Cadbury Schweppes; Chanel; Stork

2087 COVINGTON CAPITAL CORP.
36 Distillery Lane
Suite 440
Toronto, ON M5A 3C4
Canada

Phone: 416-365-0060
Toll-Free: 866-244-4714
e-mail: info@covingtonfunds.com
web: www.covingtonfunds.com

Mission Statement: Covington Capital is a Canadian venture capital investment firm focused on supporting the growth and success of visionary entrepreneurs within Canada. Lead by a team of seasoned venture capitalists, Covington has invested in over 100 enterprises throughout Canada. Covington invests in small to medium sized Canadian enterprises that hold strong growth potential.

Geographic Preference: Canada
Fund Size: $300 Million
Founded: 1994
Average Investment: $500,000 to $7 million
Minimum Investment: $500,000
Investment Criteria: Mid to Later Stage
Industry Group Preference: Manufacturing, Distribution, Information Technology, Healthcare
Portfolio Companies: Clek Inc., Interface Biologics, MMIST, PowerBand Global, Wire IE

Key Executives:
  Scott Clark, Managing Partner
  e-mail: scott@covingtoncap.com
  Education: HBA, Richard Ivey School of Business
  Background: Vice President, Harrowston; Business Development Bank of Canada
  Phil Reddon, Managing Partner
  e-mail: phil@covingtoncap.com
  Education: HBA
  Background: Business Development, Bank of Canada
  Directorships: Bank of Montreal Capital Corporation
  Matt Hall, SVP, Investments
  e-mail: matt@covingtoncap.com
  Education: BACS, Business Administration, Huron College University; CBV
  Background: Great-West Life Co.
  Lisa Low, VP, Finance
  e-mail: lisa@covingtoncap.com
  Education: MA, BA, BSc, University of Waterloo
  Background: IBM Canada, Deloitte, Touche
  Stephen Campbell, CFO and Director, Valuations
  e-mail: steve@covingtoncap.com

2088 CREDIT MUTUEL EQUITY
600 de Maisonneuve W
Suite 2810
Montreal, QC H3A 3J2
Canada

Phone: 514-281-2286
web: www.creditmutuelequity.com

Investment Criteria: Seed, Start-up, Expansion

Other Locations:
  First Canadian Place
  100 King Street W
  Suite 5600
  Toronto, ON M5X 1C9
  Canada
  Phone: 647-699-7401

  10 Post Office Square
  Suite 800 South
  Boston, MA 02109
  Phone: 917-515-0974

  520 Madison Avenue
  37th Floor
  New York, NY 10022
  Phone: 917-515-0974

  28, Avenue de l'Opera
  Paris 75002
  France
  Phone: 33(0)1 53 48 53 00

  32, avenue Camus
  BP 50416
  Nantes 44004 Cedex 01

France
Phone: 33(0)2 40 35 75 31

23, parvis des Chartrons
Bordeaux 33058
France
Phone: 33(0)5 56 99 58 81

33, avenue Le Corbusier
Lille 59000
France
Phone: 33(0)3 20 12 65 97

Espace Cordeliers
2, rue du President Carnot
Lyon 69293 Cedex 02
France
Phone: 33(0)4 72 56 91 00

31, rue Jean Wenger-Valentin
Strasbourg 67000
France
Phone: 44(0)3 88 37 74 85

Avenue de Champel 29
Geneva CH-1206
Switzerland
Phone: 41 22 347 66 35

Schutzengasse 30
Zurich CH-8001
Switzerland
Phone: 41 43 543 64 27

c/o BECM
9-11 Wilhelm-Leuschner Strasse
Frankfurt 60329
Germany
Phone: 49 69 274 021 87

Key Executives:
Ludovic André, Managing Director
e-mail: ludovic.andre@creditmutuel.eu
Education: MS, Grenoble Inst. of Techology; MBA, HEC - Paris
Background: Air Liquide
Isabelle Lechasseur, Senior Principal
e-mail: isabelle.lechasseur@creditmutuel.eu
Education: BBA, HEC Montreal; Université du Québec à Montréal
Background: Investissement Quebec; Desjardins; Sipar Inc.
Raghu Bharat, Principal
e-mail: raghu.bharat@emerilloncapital.com
Education: MBA, McGill University
Background: Nokia Siemens Networks
Directorships: lvl Studio, CM Labs Simulations

2089 CROSBIE & COMPANY
150 King Street West
15th Floor
PO Box 95
Toronto, ON M5H 1J9
Canada

Phone: 416-362-7726 **Fax:** 416-362-3447
e-mail: info@crosbieco.com
web: www.crosbieco.com

Mission Statement: Crosbie excels at creating customized market-based solutions to help clients meet their objectives. They bring experience, expertise and knowledge of markets, as well as specialized professional resources. They're known for developing and aggressively implementing creative approaches that produced successful client outcomes.

Geographic Preference: Canada
Founded: 1971
Investment Criteria: Restructurings, Management Buyouts
Portfolio Companies: ACI, Belmont Meat Products, CDI Computer Dealers, CFN, Circuit World, Construction Control, HMR Foods, Quint, Rumble Automation, Wolf Medical Systems

Key Executives:
Allan Crosbie, Chairman Emeritus
416-362-4217
e-mail: acrosbie@crosbieco.com
Education: MBA, Harvard Business School; BA, University of Toronto
Background: Wood Gundy
Ed Giacomelli, Vice Chair
416-362-0020
e-mail: egiacomelli@crosbieco.com
Education: BA, MBA, Ivey School of Business, Western University
Background: Wood Gundy, Rothschild
Directorships: WIC Communications, Prostate Cancer Canada, St. Michael's Hospital Foundation
Ian Macdonell, Managing Director
416-362-1953
e-mail: imacdonell@crosbieco.com
Education: BSc, Chemical Engineering, Queen's University; MBA, Richard Ivey School of Business, Western University
Background: CIBC Wood Gundy; RBC Capital Market
Directorships: Zeton International
Colin Walker, Managing Director
416-362-7016
e-mail: cwalker@crosbieco.com
Education: BEng, Management degree, McMaster University; MBA, Michael G. DeGroote School of Business
Background: Portfolio Manager, First Ontario Fund; Vice President, Swiss Bank Corporation
Directorships: Toronto Chapter of the Turnaround Manager
Richard Betsalel, Managing Director
416-362-4882
e-mail: rbetsalel@crosbieco.com
Education: BSc, Biology, McMaster University; MBA, Schulich School of Business, York University
Background: Financial Analyst, Bank of Nova Scotia
M. Junaid Zia, Vice President
416-204-3919
e-mail: mjzia@crosbieco.com
Education: BSc, Financial Economics, University of Toronto
Background: Deloitte
Michael Duncan, Associate
e-mail: mduncan@crosbieco.com
Education: Richard Ivey Business School

2090 CROSSWINDS HOLDINGS INC.
365 Bay Street
Suite 400
Toronto, ON M5H 2V1
Canada

Toll-Free: 800-439-5136
web: www.crosswindsinc.com

Mission Statement: Crosswinds is a publicly traded private equity firm focused on the insurance industry.

Geographic Preference: Canada
Investment Criteria: Small-Cap, Mid-Cap
Industry Group Preference: Insurance, Asset Management
Portfolio Companies: Salbro Bottle Group, Digital Payment Technologies

Key Executives:
Colin King, Chief Executive Officer
Education: BSc, Finance, Concordia University
Background: Managing Director, Goldman Sachs; Hill Samuel & Co.; Chase Manhattan Bank

Venture Capital & Private Equity Firms / Canadian Firms

2091 CROWN CAPITAL PARTNERS
333 Bay Street
Suite 2730
Toronto, ON M5H 2R2
Canada

Phone: 416-640-6715
e-mail: chris.johnson@crowncapital.ca
web: crowncapital.ca

Mission Statement: A specialty investment manager providing alternative debt financing for private equity backed and non-sponsored middle market transactions from offices in Toronto and Calgary. Crown Capital was founded as a successor company of Crown Life Insurance Company and is wholly owned by its management partners. For its investors, Crown Capital provides a strong track record of effective investment management in the alternative debt space. In 2011, Crown Capital entered into a strategic partnership with Hesperian Capital Management Ltd., portfolio manager of Norrep Group of Funds, whereby Hesperian will, pending regulatory and other approvals, acquire an equity interest in Crown Capital.

Geographic Preference: Canada
Founded: 2000
Average Investment: $5 to $25 million
Minimum Investment: $5 million
Investment Criteria: Acquisitions, Management Buy-Outs, Growth Financings, Recapitalizations
Portfolio Companies: Genalta Power, Touchstone Exploration, Landdrill International, Contac Services, Petrowest Energy Services Trust

Other Locations:
888 3rd Street SW
10 Fl., West Tower
Calgary, AB T2P 5C5
Canada
Phone: 403-775-2554

Key Executives:
Christopher A. Johnson, President and CEO
Education: BComm, University of Guelph; CFA, CBV
Background: Investment Manager, Crown Life Insurance Company
Brent G. Hughes, Executive Vice President
e-mail: brent.hughes@crowncapital.ca
Education: BComm, University of Saskatchewan; MSc, Finance, Concordia University; CFA
Background: Investment Analyst, Saskatchewan Opportunities Corporation
Michael Overvelde, SVP, Finance and CFO
Education: BComm, Queen's University; CPA; CFA
Background: VP, Raymond James; roles at TD Securities

2092 CTI LIFE SCIENCES
1 Place Ville-Marie
Suite 1050
Montreal, QC H3B 4S6
Canada

Phone: 514-798-2333 Fax: 514-787-1620
web: www.ctisciences.com

Mission Statement: CTI Life Sciences invests in pre-clinical and clinical development stage life sciences companies.

Geographic Preference: Canada, USA
Fund Size: $245 million
Founded: 2006
Industry Group Preference: Life Sciences, Biopharmaceuticals
Portfolio Companies: XTUIT, Sutrovax, Phemi, Dalcor Pharmaceuticals, Immunovaccine Inc., Visterra, Ilkos Therapeutics, Profound Medical Corp., Cellaegis Devices, Zymeworks, Precithera

Key Executives:
Ken Pastor, General Partner
514-798-2333
e-mail: kpastor@ctisciences.com
Background: Merrill Lynch Canada; Porfolio Manager, Federation des Caisses Desjardins
Jean-Francois Leprince, Managing Partner
514-787-1619
e-mail: jfleprince@ctisciences.com
Background: President & CEO, Aventis Pharma Canada; Marion Merrell Dow
Directorships: Somnus Therapeutics Inc., IRICoR (Insititue for Research in Immunology and Cancer), AllerGen NCE Inc.
Shermaine Tilley, Managing Partner
e-mail: stilley@ctisciences.com
Education: MBA, University of Toronto; PhD, John Hopkins University
Laurence Rulleau, Partner
e-mail: lrulleau@ctisciences.com
Education: Universite du Quebec a Montreal; PhD, Montreal University

2093 CYCLE CAPITAL MANAGEMENT
1000 Sherbrooke St. W
Suite 1610
Montreal, QC H3A 3G4
Canada

Phone: 514-495-1022 Fax: 514-495-8034
e-mail: info@cyclecapital.com
web: www.cyclecapital.com

Mission Statement: A cleantech venture capital fund manager.

Geographic Preference: Canada
Founded: 2009
Investment Criteria: Seed-Stage, Early Stage
Industry Group Preference: Clean Technology, Renewable Energy
Portfolio Companies: Agrisoma Biosciences, Airex Energy, CVT Corp., Energate, Enerkem, Eocycle, GaN Systems, Greenmantra Technologies, Inocucor Technologies, Laboratoire M2, LED Roadway Lighting, Local Logic, Lufa Farms, MineSense, Polystyvert, Power Survey, ESS Inc.

Key Executives:
Andree-Lise Methot, Founder & Managing Partner
e-mail: amethot@cyclecapital.com
Education: MS, University of Montreal; BS, Geological Engineering, University Laval
Background: Founder, Fonds d'investissement en developpement durable/FIDD
Directorships: Ecotech Quebec, Reseau Capital, Natural Gas Technologies Centre
Claude Vachet, Managing Partner
e-mail: cvachet@cyclecapital.com
Education: Chemical Engineering, Ecole Polytechnique; MBA, Finance, HEC Montreal
Background: Innovatech, Kirchner, Multiple Capital

2094 DANCAP PRIVATE EQUITY
197 Sheppard Ave. W
Toronto, ON M2N 1M9
Canada

Phone: 416-590-9444 Fax: 416-590-7444
e-mail: elias@dancap.ca
web: www.dancap.ca

Mission Statement: Provides direct investments to Canadian mid-market businesses that require private equity financing in the form of equity or subordinate debt. Participates in co-investment partnerships in medium to large sized Canadian companies and international co-investment opportunities alongside private equity and institutional investors.

Geographic Preference: Canada
Fund Size: $50 Million
Founded: 2002
Average Investment: $1 to $10 million
Minimum Investment: $1 million

Venture Capital & Private Equity Firms / Canadian Firms

Investment Criteria: Acquisitions, Management Buyouts, Recapitalizations, Capital Expansion
Industry Group Preference: Manufacturing, Healthcare, Consumer Products, Technology, Consumer Services
Portfolio Companies: Cann Trust Direct, Flyp Technologies Inc., IOU Financial Inc., GreenField Ethanol, Key Brandon Entertainment Inc., Porter Aviation Holdings, Christmas Tradition, Millennium Care Inc., BC Decker Inc., Victess Capital Corp., Hetworth Corp., Gavel & Gown, Jancee Screw Products, Newbury Equity Partners LP, Portfolio Litigation Fund, Direct Marketing Company, Madison Dearborn Capital Partners VII LP, Landmark Equity Partners XV LP, Blue Point Capital Partners III(A) LP, Brentwood Associates Private Equity V LP, MHR Institutional Partners IV LP, CTP Offshore-C Feeder Fund Ltd., Court Square Capital Partners III LP, GC Partners Interational Ltd., Landmark Equity Partners XIV LP, LODH Private Equity Euro Choice III LP, CEREP II Mezzanine Loan Partners LP, NYLIM Jacob Ballas India Fund III LLC, Carlyle Asia Partners III LP, Madison Dearborn Capital Partners VI LP, PAI Erope V LP, Newbury Second Fund LP, European Secondary Development Fund IV LP, Clearview Capital Fund II LP, Primus Pacfic Partners I LP, Brentwood Associates Private Equity IV LP, Lyceum Capital Fund II, Rosemont Solebury Co-Investment Fund LP, Tenaska Poer Fund II LP, The Resolute Fund II, MatlinPatterson Global Opportunities Partners III LP, CVCI Growth Partnership II, MHR Institutional Partners III, GCM Grosvenor LS Power Equity Partners II, Excellere Capital Partners LP, LODH Private Euro Choice III, Eureka II LP, The Succession Fund LP, Quadriga Capital III, Terra Firma Capital Partners III,

Key Executives:
   Aubrey Dan, Principal
   e-mail: aubreydan@dancap.ca
   Education: University of Western Ontario; Honorary Doctorate of Laws, Assumption University
   Background: Wampole Canada, Dancap Productions
   Elias Toby, COO, CFO
   e-mail: elias@dancap.ca
   Background: Anderson Quick, Deloitte & Touche

2095 DESJARDINS CAPITAL
2, complexe Desjardins
bureau 1717
CP 760
Montreal, QC H5B 1B8
Canada

Phone: 514-281-7131
Toll-Free: 866-866-7000
web: www.desjardinscapital.com

Mission Statement: Desjardins Capital invests in dynamic and innovative businesses in diverse sectors across Quebec.
Geographic Preference: Quebec
Fund Size: $1.25 billion
Founded: 2001
Minimum Investment: $50,000 - $750,000
Investment Criteria: All stages and possible exit strategies
Industry Group Preference: Manufacturing, Business Products & Services, Information Technology, Telecommunications
Portfolio Companies: 20-20 Technologies, 3ci, A. & D. Prevost, A.T.L.A.S. Aeronautique, Acceo Solutions, Acema Importations, Acier Majeau, Action Mecanique, Agence De Securite Mirado, Albert Perron, Alimentation Francis Gravel, Alutrans Canada, Alyotech Canada, Amaya Gaming Group, Ambulance Medilac, Anderson Group, Andre Potvin Cuisine/Salle De Bain, Approvisionnement Populaire, Arbell Electronics, Ateliers Cfi Metal, Attraction Media, Autobus Dionne, Autobus Dufresne, Avjet Holding, Axesnetwork Solutions, Azentic, Balances M. Dodier, Batitech, Beaudry & Theroux, Behaviour Interactive, Boisaco, Bonneterie Richelieu, Bouffard Sanitaire Et Acier Bouffard, Boutique Le Pentagone, Budget Propane, C.R.O.I., C.R.S/Vamic, Cables Ben-Mor, Cactus Commerce, Camoplast Solideal, Cam-Trac Sag-Lac, Canmec Group, Cavalia, Centre De Tri, Centre Des Congres De Sept-Œles, Centre Medical Le Mesnil, Cervo-Polygaz, Charcuterie L. Fortin Ltee, Chariots Elevateurs Du Quebec, Cheq Fm, Chlorophylle, Chocolat Jean-Talon, Cif Metal Ltd, Clic, Climatisation Mixair, Clinique D'Optometrie Vu, Cls Info, Cogiscan, Collection Papillon Gemme, Comact Equipment, Complexe Funeraire Ste-Bernadette, Complexe Sportif Interplus, Concept Mat, Conception Gsr, Congebec, Construction L.F.G., Construction Leclerc Et Pelletier, Cooperative De Travailleurs Actionnaire De Negotium Technologies, Cooperative De Travailleurs Actionnaire De Tec, Cooperative Forestiere De Girardville, Cooperative Forestiere De L'Outaouais, Cooperative Funeraire De

Key Executives:
   Guy Cormier, Chair, President and CEO
   Education: Bachelors of Business Administration, MBA, École des Hautes Études Commerciales
   Yves Calloch, Chief Operating Officer
   Education: HEC Montreal; Universite de Montreal

2096 DIFFERENCE CAPITAL
200 Front St W
Suite 2504
Toronto, ON M5V 3L1
Canada

Phone: 416-649-5085
e-mail: info@differencecapital.com
web: www.differencecapital.com

Mission Statement: Difference Capital targets late-stage Canadian companies in technology and media.
Geographic Preference: Canada
Founded: 2012
Investment Criteria: Late-Stage
Industry Group Preference: Fintech, Internet, Media Technology, Healthcare
Portfolio Companies: Vision Critical Communications, BrainScope, Quickplay Media
Key Executives:
   Henry Kneis, Co-Founder & CEO
   Background: Maple Securities, Abria Financial Group
   Steven Russo, Vice President
   Education: JD, MBA, Queen's Univ.
   Tom Astle, Chief Investment Officer
   Background: Merrill Lynch
   Tom Liston, Managing Partner
   Education: BBA, Univ. of New Brunswick; MA, Queen's Univ.
   Background: Yorkton Securities

2097 DISCOVERY CAPITAL
43-1238 Eastern Drive
Port Coquitlam, BC V3C 6C5
Canada

Phone: 604-683-3000 **Fax:** 604-662-3457
e-mail: info@discoverycapital.com
web: www.discoverycapital.com

Mission Statement: Discovery Capital is one of Canada's most experienced technology venture capital firms. Discovery Capital focuses primarily on the enhancement of BC-based technology ventures, in the areas of information technology, communications, health & life sciences and environmental & energy technologies.
Geographic Preference: British Columbia
Founded: 1986
Investment Criteria: Early-Stage
Industry Group Preference: Information Technology, Healthcare Information Technology, Advanced Technologies, Communications, Life Sciences, Technology, Environment, Energy
Portfolio Companies: Asprevea Pharmaceuticals, ALI Technologies, Cardiocomm Solutions Inc, Circon Systems

Venture Capital & Private Equity Firms / Canadian Firms

Corp, Day4 Energy, Idelix Software, Photochannel Networks, Sierra Wireless, Tantalus Systems Corp, Texada Software Inc, TIR Systems, Tri-Link Technologies Inc, Vigil Health Management, Vision2Hire Solutions Inc

Key Executives:
John McEwen, Chief Executive Officer
Education: BComm, University of British Columbia
Background: Tantalus Systems Corp., IBM Canada Ltd.
Harry Jaako, President
Education: B.Eng., Lakehead University
Background: TSX Group, Inc., Vancouver Stock Exchange, DMR Group, TSX Venture Exchange, Toronto Stock Exchange, IBM Canada Ltd.
Directorships: Texada Software Inc., Leading Edge, TIR Systems Ltd., Exceptional Technologies Fund 5 Inc., Vigil Health Solutions Inc., NRC-IRAP & BC Discovery Fund Inc.
Charles Cook, Vice President/CFO
Education: MBA, University of British Columbia; CMA
Background: Director, Dundee Securities Corporation

2098 DISRUPTION VENTURES
Bay Adelaide Centre
333 Bay Street
Suite 1130
Toronto, ON M5H 2R2
Canada

e-mail: info@disruption-ventures.com
web: disruption-ventures.com

Mission Statement: Disruption Ventures funds companies with female-led businesses.

Investment Criteria: Seed-Stage; Companies must be female-led
Industry Group Preference: Digital Technology, Fintech
Key Executives:
Elaine Kunda, Managing Partner
Education: McMaster University
Background: President & CEO, b5media; President & CEO, ZipLocal; Managing Director, Toronto.com; Business Development Manager, Grey Interactive
Directorships: G(irls)20 Summit

2099 DISTRICT VENTURES CAPITAL
2540 Kensington Road NW
Calgary, AB T2N 3S3
Canada

e-mail: contact@districtventurescapital.com
web: www.districtventurescapital.com

Mission Statement: Provides VC funding for innovative Canadian companies in the food & beverage and health & wellness sectors.

Geographic Preference: Canada
Fund Size: $30 million
Average Investment: $150K
Industry Group Preference: Consumer Products
Portfolio Companies: Chickapea Pasta, Balzac's Coffee, RTHM, Nada Moo!, Bow Valley BBQ, Drizzle, One World Foods, Cook It, Healthy Pets, Torill's Table, Prairie Fava, Little Tucker, Farm Fresh Pet Foods, Culcherd

Key Executives:
Arlene Dickinson, President & CEO
Jason Berenstein, Partner & CFO
Education: Univ. of Toronto

2100 DOVENTI CAPITAL
1462 St. Paul Street
Unit C
Kelowna, BC V1Y 2E6

web: www.doventi.com

Mission Statement: Invests in companies serving the cannabis industry. Areas of focus include production, research, bio-pharmaceuticals, health sciences, and phytoceuticals.

Founded: 2015
Industry Group Preference: Cannabis
Portfolio Companies: Altaire, BC Naturals, Cannera Consulting, GreenTec Bio-Pharmaceuticals, Qstrios, Vitalis Extraction Technology, Zenalytic Laboratories

Key Executives:
Norton Singhavon, Founder/Managing Director
Education: Kwantlen Polytechnic University
Background: Investor/Advisor, Permanent Construction & Project Management LTD; President, Syndicate Ventures; Consultant, Cronos Group; Advisor to CEO/Business Development, Invictus MD Strategies Corp.; Founder/Chairman/CEO, GTEC Holdings

---

2101 DREAM MAKER VENTURES
16 McAdam Avenue
Toronto, ON M6A 0B9
Canada

Phone: 905-553-7326
e-mail: info@dreammaker.vc
web: www.dreammaker.vc

Mission Statement: Dream Maker Ventures is the investment segment of Dream Maker Corp., an asset management firm in Toronto. Their goal is to fund early stage companies that use technology to transform the way businesses operate.

2102 DRI CAPITAL
100 King Street W
Suite 7250
PO Box 62
Toronto, ON M5X 1B1
Canada

Phone: 416-863-1865 Fax: 416-863-5161
e-mail: info@dricapital.com
web: www.dricapital.com

Mission Statement: DRI Capital manages funds that purchase royalties from pharmaceutical and biotechnology companies, research institutions, universities, and inventors. It is an indirect subsidiary of Persis Holdings Ltd.

Fund Size: $2 billion
Founded: 1992
Industry Group Preference: Healthcare, Biopharmaceuticals, Drug Development
Portfolio Companies: Enbrel, Keytruda, Myozyme, Remicade, Sensipar, Simponi, Stelara, Tysabri, Zytiga

Key Executives:
Behzad Khosrowshahi, President & CEO
Education: BA, History, Reed College; CA
Background: Future Shop Ltd., Deloitte & Touche LLP
Andrea Sotak, Senior Managing Director & CIO
Education: BSc, Biochemistry, University of Waterloo; MBA, Queen's University
Background: Aventis Pasteur, Allelix Biopharmaceuticals
Chris Anastasopoulos, Chief Financial Officer
Education: BComm, Univ. of Toronto; MBA, Rotman School of Management
Background: Ontario Municipal Employees Retirement System
Adam Marcus, Managing Director
416-324-5706
e-mail: am@dricapital.com
Education: BComm, McGill Univ.
Background: Macquarie Capital

2103 EDGESTONE CAPITAL PARTNERS
175 Bloor St. E
Suite 801 North
Toronto, ON M4W 3R8
Canada

Phone: 416-860-3740 Fax: 416-860-9838
e-mail: info@edgestone.com
web: www.edgestone.com

Mission Statement: EdgeStone provides capital, strategic direction and business and financial advice to help promising mid-market and early-stage companies achieve their full potential. EdgeStone leverages the resources of its broad business network and ensures an alignment of interests to achieve superior returns for all stakeholders.

Geographic Preference: Canada
Fund Size: $2 Billion
Founded: 2000
Investment Criteria: Management Buyouts, Leveraged Buyouts, Recapitalizations, Expansion Capial
Industry Group Preference: Information Technology, Software, Telecommunications, Data Services, Internet Technology, Infrastructure, Energy, Manufacturing, Business Products & Services, Consumer Services
Portfolio Companies: Aurigen, Eurospect Manufacturing Inc., EZShield, Porter Aviation Holdings, Stephen's Rental Servies Inc., Specialty Commerce Corp.

Key Executives:
   Samuel L. Duboc, Partner
   Education: BS, Chemical Engineering, Tufts University; MBA, Harvard Business School
   Background: Deals Review Committee, CIBC Capital Partners; Co-Founder, Loyalty Group; COO, Holzman Jewellers
   Directorships: EZShield, New Food Classics, Porter Aviation Holdings, Stephenson's Rental Services, Bryker Techology Partners
   Gilbert S. Palter, Managing Partner and Chief Investment Officer
   Education: University of Toronto; MBA, Harvard Business School
   Background: Founder/CEO/Managing Director, Eladdan Capital Partners; Founder, Eladdan Enterprises; Morgan Stanley; Smith Barney; McKinsey & Company; Clairvest Group
   Directorships: Aurigen Capital Limited, Continental Alloys & Services, Specialty Catalog Corporation, Eurospec Manufacturing, Mitel Networks Corporation
   Stephen O. Marshall, Managing Partner and Chief Operating Officer
   Education: LLB, University of Western Ontario; MBA, MIT Sloan School of Management
   Background: EVP, MDC Corporation; Managing Partner, Torys
   Directorships: EZShield, Eurospec Manufacturing, Porter Aviation Holdings, Continental Alloys & Services

2104 ELGNER GROUP INVESTMENTS
3280 Bloor Street West
Suite 902
Toronto, ON M8X 2X3
Canada

Phone: 647-426-0380 Fax: 647-426-0376
e-mail: csinclair@elgnergroup.com
web: www.elgnergroup.com

Mission Statement: A privately held, self-funded investment group focused on small to medium sized fundamentally sound businesses that face operational, financial or business stress. Elgner Group will invest in fundamentally sound businesses that are either growing profitably or face operational, financial or business stress. We are particularly attracted to companies that offer significant opportunities to improve operating costs and markets that face substantial business change, foreign competition or industry consolidation.

Geographic Preference: Canada, United States
Founded: 1993
Average Investment: $2 to $25 million
Minimum Investment: $2 million
Investment Criteria: Distressed Situations, Corporate Divestitures, Recapitalizations, Family Successions, Unique Situations
Industry Group Preference: Manufacturing, Real Estate, Industrial Services, Automotive, Information Technology, Transportation, Capital Equipment, Distribution

Key Executives:
   Claude Elgner, Managing Director
   Education: P.Eng.
   Roger Elgner, Managing Director
   Education: P.Eng.
   Craig Sinclair, Investment Director
   Education: B.Comm.
   Tim Chapman, Investment Director
   Education: P.Eng.

2105 ELNOS
ELNOS Corporation for Business Development
31 Nova Scotia Walk
Suite 306, Third Floor
Elliot Lake, ON P5A 1Y9
Canada

Phone: 705-848-0229 Fax: 705-848-1539
Toll-Free: 800-256-7299
e-mail: welliott@elnos.com
web: www.elnos.com

Mission Statement: A full-service business development corporation that was established to stimulate economic growth in the ELNOS Region through new business development and investment.

Geographic Preference: Canada
Fund Size: $23 Million
Founded: 1993
Average Investment: Up to $250,000
Minimum Investment: $10,000
Investment Criteria: Start Up, Expansion, Financial Restructuring

Key Executives:
   William Elliott, General Manager
   705-848-0229 x237
   e-mail: welliott@elnos.com
   Sharon Farquhar, Director of Financial Services
   705-848-0229 x235
   e-mail: sfarquhar@elnos.com

2106 EMERALD TECHNOLOGY VENTURES
MaRS Centre, West Tower
661 University Ave.
Suite 445
Toronto, ON M5G 1M1
Canada

Phone: 416-900-3453 Fax: 416-900-3457
e-mail: info@emerald-ventures.com
web: www.emerald-ventures.com

Mission Statement: Global industrial technology investor.

Geographic Preference: Europe, North America
Fund Size: $450 million
Founded: 2000
Investment Criteria: Early-Stage, Expansion-Stage
Industry Group Preference: Clean Technology, Energy, Advanced Materials, Water
Portfolio Companies: Advanced BioNutrition, AlphaICs, EWT, Enocean, GeoDigital, HydroPoint, Identec Solutions, Librestream, Lucintech, Metgen, Open Mineral, P97, Powerhouse Dynamics, TaKaDu, Tropic Biosciences, Ushr

Venture Capital & Private Equity Firms / Canadian Firms

Other Locations:
Emerald Technology Ventures AG
Seefeldstrasse 215
Zurich 8008
Switzerland
Phone: 41-442696100 **Fax:** 41-442696101

Key Executives:
Gina Domanig, Managing Partner
Education: MBA, Thunderbird; ESADE
Background: Senior Vice President, Sulzer
Directorships: Identec Solutions, Inge, Pelamis
Markus Moor, Partner
Education: Mechanical Engineering, University of Applied Sciences Solothum, Switzerland; MS, Economics & Technology, University of St. Gallen
Background: Investment Director, SAM Private Equity; Miteco
Directorships: Xunlight Corp., Enocean GmbH, O-Flexx Technologies
Hans Dellenbach, Partner and CFO
Education: School of Business Administration, Zurich
Background: Financial Controller, Kuoni Trave
Directorships: Identec Solutions
Charles Vaslet, Partner
Education: Electrical & Electronics Engineering, University of Leeds; MBA, Henley Management College
Background: Vice President, ABB Equity Ventures; National Power LLC

2107 ENTREPRENEUR CAPITAL
1100 Boulevard Rene-Levesque W
25th Floor
Montreal, QC H3B 5C9
Canada

web: www.entrepreneurcapital.ca

Mission Statement: Investments are comprised of both majority and minority positions. Companies should have a solid management team, superior products/services, a long-term vision, with national/international reach and a wide network of contacts.
Investment Criteria: Lower Mid-Market
Industry Group Preference: Food Service, Apparel, Tourism, Logistics, Medical, Property Management
Portfolio Companies: BSF/HOME, Enjay Converters, Inter V Medical, Ovation Logistics, Spencer Supports Canada, Voyages Traditours

Key Executives:
Guy Bessette, Partner
e-mail: guy@entrepreneurcapital.ca
Background: Vag; UAP/NAPA; Fix Auto
Eric Doyon, Partner
e-mail: eric@entrepreneurcapital.ca
Background: Caisse de depot; PWc Corporate Finance

2108 EPIC CAPITAL MANAGEMENT
2 Toronto Street
4th Floor
Toronto, ON M5C 2B6
Canada

Phone: 416-703-4291
e-mail: info@epiccapitalmanagement.ca
web: epiccapitalmanagement.ca

Mission Statement: Boutique asset manager with a focus on Canada.
Geographic Preference: Canada
Founded: 2000

Key Executives:
David Fawcett
e-mail: dfawcett@epiccapital.ca
Background: Deutsche Bank Securities; First Marathon Securities

Scott Kaplanis
e-mail: skaplanis@epiccapital.ca
Education: HBA, Richard Ivey School of Business
Background: Macquarie Capital Markets
Directorships: Memex Inc.

2109 ESPRESSO CAPITAL
8 King St. E
Suite 300
Toronto, ON M5C 1B5
Canada

Phone: 877-604-7733
e-mail: info@espressocapital.com
web: www.espressocapital.com

Mission Statement: Espresso Capital is partnered with private investors from the high technology community. They have built relationships with institutional finance companies, venture capital groups and professional service firms. Espresso Capital was founded by veteran technology company executives who understand first-hand the challenges faced by founders and entrepreneurs in funding the growth of their businesses.
Geographic Preference: Canada
Founded: 2009
Average Investment: $200,000
Industry Group Preference: Digital Media & Marketing, High Technology
Portfolio Companies: Algolux, Centah, Colligo, Coreworx, Unbounce, Datacratic, HomeStars, OM Signal, Pressly, Grouby, Q4, Strongpoint, Statfl
  3 Place Ville Marie
  4th Fl.
  Montreal, QC H3B 2E3
  Canada

Key Executives:
Will Hutchins, Managing Director
e-mail: will@espressocapital.com
Background: TD Securities, Stikeman Elliott, Paul Weisse
Enio Lazzer, Chief Operating Officer & CFO
e-mail: enio@espressocapital.com
Background: CIBC World Markets, Northern Trust Company Cananda
Alkarim Jivraj, Chief Executive Officer
e-mail: alkarim@espressocapital.com
Background: Managing Partner, Intrepid Business Acceleration Fund; Yorkton Securities
Directorships: eSentire, SCI Marketview
Will Jin, Managing Director
Background: Covington Capital; Hathaway Corp.

2110 EVENTI CAPITAL PARTNERS
250 Yonge Street
Suite 1602
Toronto, ON M5B 2L7
Canada

Phone: 416-927-8887 **Fax:** 888-869-1045
web: www.eventi.com

Mission Statement: Toronto-based investment group specializing in SaaS, Internet infrastructure services and medical devices.
Founded: 2002
Investment Criteria: Early-Stage, Later-Stage
Industry Group Preference: SaaS, Internet Infrastructure Services, Medical Devices
Portfolio Companies: Tenzing, Kinetic Commerce, Base Pair Biotechnologies

Key Executives:
Bill Di Nardo, Managing Partner
Education: Richard Ivey School of Business
Background: President & CEO, Grocery Gateway
Directorships: Kinetic Commerce, Tenzing

Venture Capital & Private Equity Firms / Canadian Firms

Scott Bryan, Managing Partner
Background: General Counsel, Grocery Gateway; Miller Thomson; Star Data Systems
Derek Ruston, Co-Founder/Partner
Background: President, B&R Associates; General Partner, Catalina Southwest Investments; Management Consultant, McKinsey & Company; Senior Partner, Peter Barnard Associates

2111 EVOK INNOVATIONS
1410-1130 West Pender St.
Vancouver, BC V6B 2L3
Canada

web: www.evokinnovations.com

Mission Statement: Partnership between BC Cleantech CEO Alliance, Cenovus Energy and Suncor Energy invests in the commercialization of clean technology.

Fund Size: $100 million
Industry Group Preference: Clean Technology
Portfolio Companies: DarkVision Technologies, Ekona Power, Expeto, Harbo Technologies, Kelvin Inc., Metabolik Technologies, Mosaic Material, Opus 12, Osprey Informatics, Quidnet Energy, Rotoliptic, Syzygy Plasmonics

Key Executives:
Marty Reed, Chief Executive Officer
Background: The Roda Group
Mike Biddle, Managing Director
Education: BSc, University of Louisville; PhD, Case Western Reserve University
Background: Dow Chemical; Cummins Engine Company; Founder, MBA Polymers

2112 EXPORT DEVELOPMENT CANADA
150 Slater Street
Ottawa, ON K1A 1K3
Canada

Phone: 613-598-2500 **Fax:** 613-598-3811
Toll-Free: 800-229-0575
web: www.edc.ca

Mission Statement: Offers financial and risk management solutions to help Canadian businesses expand into the international market.

Geographic Preference: North America, South America
Founded: 1944
Industry Group Preference: Industrial Equipment, Transportation, Engineering, Information Technology, Manufacturing, Telecommunications, Energy

Key Executives:
Mairead Lavery, President and CEO
Education: Queen's University Belfast
Background: Bombardier
Carl Burlock, EVP and Chief Business Officer
Education: MBA, Dalhousie Univ.
Background: Nova Scotia Power
Lorraine Audsley, SVP and Chief Risk Officer, Global Risk Management
Education: Henley Business School; University of Reading
Ken Kember, SVP, Finance and Technology & CFO
Education: BA, Master of Accounting, University of Waterloo; CA; CMA
Background: Senior Manager, Accounting Group, PricewaterhouseCoopers
Mairead Lavery, SVP, Business Development
Education: Management & Accounting, Queen's Universiry; ICA
Stephanie Butt Thibodeau, SVP, People and Culture
Education: BComm, University of Ottawa; CFA
Catherine Decarie, SVP, Channels and Marketing
Education: BA, Mount Allison Univ.; LLB, Queen's Univ.

2113 EXTREME VENTURE PARTNERS
67 Yonge Street
Suite 1600
Toronto, ON M5E 1J8
Canada

e-mail: info@evp.vc
web: evp.vc

Mission Statement: Focuses on providing early stage venture capital and management expertise to startup businesses to help propel them into the big leagues. Beyond the financial resources, EVP takes a hands-on approach to supporting startups, bringing a depth of technical and business expertise to the project.

Geographic Preference: Canada, United States
Average Investment: $300K
Minimum Investment: $250K
Investment Criteria: Pre-seed/Seed Stage
Industry Group Preference: Mobile, Data & Analytics, Internet of Things
Portfolio Companies: Statflo, Mavencare, Crowdcare, Flixel, ThinkData Works, Zoom.ai, ACTO, Damon X Labs, Dot Health, Lokafy, RiverPay, Dentem, Linkett, Spently, D1G1T, Blanclink, Blanc Labs, Webware, CRG, Extreme Innovations, Hackworks, Palette, Granify, Beam Messenger, Influitive, National Prostaff, Nekso, Guardly, Pitstop, Play the Future, Sensorsuite, Revlo, Qualia, Minbox, Airstream, Stem Village, Ubique, Uken, Upsight, Wagepoint, Groupie, Eve Tab, World of Angus, Evree, Foxquilt Insurance, DirectedAI, Chatter Research

Key Executives:
Ian Ainsworth, Managing Partner
Directorships: Altamira, Fields Institute for Mathematical Science
Ray Sharma, Founding Partner/CEO
Education: Business Administration, Richard Ivey School of Business
Background: CSFB Technology Group, BMO Nesbitt Burns, GMP Capital Trust
Imran Bashir, Founding Partner/COO
Education: MS, Electrical Engineering, University of Toronto
Background: President & CEO, Envision Mobile; President & COO, Octanewave Software
Ken Teslia, Founding Partner/Chairman
Education: MBA, York University
Background: RBC Capital Markets, Credit Suisse First Boston, GMP Capital Trust

2114 FARM CREDIT CANADA
3700 Victoria Ave. E
Regina, SK S4Z 1A5
Canada

Phone: 306-780-5616 **Fax:** 306-780-5611
Toll-Free: 855-230-6821
e-mail: skregina@fcc-fac.ca
web: www.fcc-fac.ca

Mission Statement: Provides venture capital financing to small and medium-sized businesses in value-added food processing, manufacturing of agricultural equipment, commercial processing and ag biotech.

Geographic Preference: Canada
Fund Size: $36 billion
Founded: 2002
Average Investment: $2.75 Million
Minimum Investment: $0.5 Million
Investment Criteria: Early-Stage, Growth-Stage, Mature-Stage Companies
Industry Group Preference: Agriculture, Forestry, Fishing, Food & Beverage, Nutraceuticals, Life Sciences, Biotechnology
Portfolio Companies: Sembiosys genetics Inc., MCN Bioproducts, Agribiotics Inc., Poss, Ensyn Technologies,

Venture Capital & Private Equity Firms / Canadian Firms

A&A Trading, Walker Seeds, BIOX Corporation, Atlantic Horticulture

Key Executives:
Michael Hoffort, President/Chief Executive Officer
Education: P.Ag., University of Saskatchewan
Directorships: STARS Air Ambulance
Sophie Perreault, Executive Vice President/Chief Operating Officer
Education: P.Ag., Laval University
Directorships: Regina Food Bank

2115 FASTBREAK VENTURES
Toronto, ON
Canada

web: www.fastbreak.co

Mission Statement: Fastbreak ventures focuses on enterprise software opportunities across FinTech, PropTech, Digital Health, and other industries where there's a growing customer base.

Founded: 2008
Investment Criteria: Pre-Seed/Seed Stage

Key Executives:
Matt Saunders, Co-Founder and Partner
Education: BA, MBA, Northeastern University
Background: COO, Millennium Data Systems; Partner, DVG Consulting; President, Ryerson Futures Inc.; Partner, Zone Startups Ventures
Alan Lysne, Co-Founder and Partner
Education: BEng, Queen's University
Background: Co-Founder/CTO, Davinci Technologies; CEO, Cascada Mobile; COO, Grapple Mobile; COO/Managing Partner, Ryerson Futures Inc.

2116 FENGATE
77 King Street W
Suite 3410
Toronto, ON M5K 1H1
Canada

Phone: 416-488-4184
web: fengate.com

Mission Statement: Fengate invests in long-life, high-quality assets and businesses on behalf of their clients.

Founded: 2016
Average Investment: $20-75 Million

Other Locations:
2275 Upper Middle Road E
Suite 700
Oakville, ON L6H 0C3
Canada
Phone: 905-491-6599

PO Box 30540
Houston, TX 77229
Phone: 346-241-0648

Key Executives:
Justin Catalano, Managing Director/Group Head of Private Equity
Education: BBA, Wilfred Laurier University; CFA
Background: Birch Hill Equity Partners; TD Capital; TD Securities
Omar Khalifa, Managing Director/Head of Private Equity Investments
Education: BBA, Wilfred Laurier University; CFA
Background: Director, Private Markets Group, OPTrust; BMO Capital Markets

2117 FIBERNETICS VENTURES
605 Boxwood Drive
Cambridge, ON N3E 1A5
Canada

Phone: 416-477-0073
e-mail: info@fibernetics.ca
web: www.fibernetics.ca/fibernetics-ventures

Mission Statement: Fibernetics looks for unique start-ups and early stage companies with innovative approaches to fiberoptic technology and telecommunications.

Founded: 2004
Investment Criteria: Start-Up, Early Stage
Industry Group Preference: Telecommunications

Key Executives:
Jody Schnarr, Managing Partner
Education: University of Toronto

2118 FIRST ASCENT VENTURES
10 King Street E
Suite 900
Toronto, ON M5C 1C3
Canada

Phone: 416-306-3021
e-mail: celia@firstascent.vc
web: www.firstascentventures.com

Mission Statement: Invests in emerging Canadian technology companies.

Founded: 2015
Average Investment: $5 - 10 Million
Investment Criteria: Series A and later
Industry Group Preference: Machine Learning, Big Data, Cloud Computing, Analytics, Mobile, Artificial Intelligence
Portfolio Companies: ScribbleLive, Assent, Q4, Sensibill, rubikloud, UpChain, ThinkData Works, SportlogiQ, Dialogue, DailyPay

Other Locations:
3 Place Ville Marie
Suite 12350
Montreal, QC H3B 0E7
Canada

Key Executives:
Richard Black, Co-Founder & Managing Partner
Tony Van Marken, Co-Founder & Managing Partner
Mo Bazazi, Vice President
Nicole Vivaldi, Chief Financial Officer

2119 FONDACTION
2175, boul. De Maisonneuve Est
Bureau 103
Montreal, QC H2K 4S3
Canada

Phone: 514-525-5505
e-mail: investissement@fondaction.com
web: www.fondaction.com

Mission Statement: Labor-sponsored retirement savings management fund.

Geographic Preference: Quebec
Fund Size: $1.7 Billion
Founded: 1996

Other Locations:
125, boul. Charest Est
Office 501
Quebec, QC G1K 3G5
Canada
Phone: 418-522-8650

Key Executives:
Genevieve Morin, President & CEO
Education: BA, Concordia University; MBA, HEC Montreal
Background: Anges Quebec Capital

Venture Capital & Private Equity Firms / Canadian Firms

2120 FONDS DE SOLIDARITE FTQ
545 Crémazie Blvd E
Suite 200
Montreal, QC H2M 2W4
Canada

Phone: 514-383-8383 Fax: 514-850-4888
e-mail: comm@fondsftq.com
web: www.fondsftq.com

Mission Statement: Invests in companies impacting the Quebec economy and offer them services to further their development and create, maintain or protect jobs. Promotes economic training for workers so they can increase their influence on the economic development of Quebec. Stimulates the Quebec economy through strategic investments that benefit both Quebec workers and companies alike.

Geographic Preference: Quebec
Fund Size: $14.3 billion
Founded: 1983
Investment Criteria: Growing markets, Niches, Management buyouts
Industry Group Preference: All Sectors Considered
Portfolio Companies: A. & L. Pinard, A.S. Nettoyage, Abc Environnement, Abipa Canada, Acceo Solutions, Acier Fastech, Acier Majeau, Acquisio, Addenda Capital, Adelard Soucy, Adventure Gold, Aeroport International De Mont-Tremblant, AGF Group, Agora Communication, Agritibi R.H., Agro-100 Ltee, Agro-Bio Controle, Agrocentre Belcan, Alary, St-Pierre Et Durocher Arpenteurs Geometres, Alimentation Coop Port-Cartier, Alimentation L'epicier, Aliments Urbains, Amecci, Amh Canada Ltee, Andy Transport, Ani-Mat, Armeco, Asmacure, Atelier D'Usinage Quenneville, Atelier Progun, Atelier Tangente, Athos Services Commemoratifs, Atrium Innovations, Auberge Et Spa Le Nordik, Auberge Relais Lac Cache, Aurizon Mines Ltd, Aurvista Gold Corporation, Autobus Lion, Auvents W. Lecours, Avior Integrated Products, Azimut Exploration, B.M.B., Bercomac Limitee, Bertrand Ducks, Bestar, Bioniche Life Sciences, Bmi Canada, Bombardier, Boreal - Informations Strategiques, Boreal Drilling, Boutique La Vie En Rose, Brome Financial Corporation, BSL Wood Products, Cactus Commerce, Cafe Faro, Camoplast Solideal, Canada Moteurs Importations, Canadian Helicopters, Cape By The Sea, Carriere Neigette, Carrosserie Pro 2010, Cartier Resouces, Casavant Brothers, Centre De Peinture L.B.G., Centre Jardin Lac Pelletier, Ch Group Limited Partnership, Chateau Bonne Entente, Chateau M.T., Chemco

Key Executives:
Gaétan Morin, President and CEO
Education: BA, Finance, Geology, MBA, Economic Geology, University of Quebec
Background: Pemberton Securities, Saumier Morrisson et associés

2121 FOUNDATION EQUITY CORPORATION
237 - 200 Carnegie Drive
St. Albert, AB T8N 5A8
Canada

web: www.foundationequity.com

Mission Statement: Provides capital to entrepreneurs in the areas of energy services, manufacturing, and B2B software.

Industry Group Preference: Energy Services, Manufacturing, B2B Software
Portfolio Companies: Circle Cardiovascular Imaging, DriveAble Assessment Centres, Trajectory IQ, McCoy Global

Key Executives:
Kerry Brown, Founder & Chair
Education: University of Alberta; CA
Directorships: McCoy Global, DriveAble Assessment Centres, First Yellowhead Equities
Mike Cabigon, President
Education: BComm, University of Alberta

Background: VP & General Manager, Persona Communications

2122 FOUNDATION MARKETS
77 King Street West
Suite 2905
P.O. Box 121 Toronto Dominion
Toronto, ON M5K 1H1

Phone: 416-777-7300
e-mail: info@foundationmarkets.com
web: www.foundationmarkets.com

Mission Statement: A private merchant bank investing in early-stage public & private companies.

Geographic Preference: Canada
Founded: 2005
Investment Criteria: Early-Stage
Industry Group Preference: Cannabis, Technology, Food & Beverage, Natural Resources
Portfolio Companies: Nutritional High, Lineage Grow Co., Aura Health Corp., California Gold Inc., Irri-Al-Tal Ltd., Blockchain Innovations Inc., Aquamiel Tequilla, Harborside Inc., Platinex Inc., Snow Lakes Resources Ltd.

Key Executives:
Adam Szweras, Chairman
Education: LLB, Osgoode Hall Law School, York University
Background: Partner, Fogler Rubinoff
Directorships: Nutritional High; Aurora Cannabis
Peter Bilodeau, President/CEO
Education: MBA, Dalhousie University
Alex Storcheus, Senior Vice President
Education: BBA, Finance, Schulich School of Business, York University
Directorships: Capricorn Business Acquisitions Inc.; BlockChain Innovations Corp.
Alex Storcheus, Managing Director, Corporate Finance
Education: BBA, Shulich School of Business; CFA

2123 FOUNDERS GROUP OF FOOD COMPANIES
1111 West Hastings St
Suite 200
Vancouver, BC V6E 2J3
Canada

web: www.foundersfoodgroup.com

Mission Statement: Family-owned company solely focused on food businesses.

Geographic Preference: Canada; Midwest/Western US
Average Investment: $15-75 million
Investment Criteria: Mature
Industry Group Preference: Food
Portfolio Companies: Presteve Foods, Armand Agra, Ganache Brands, Freshstone Brands

Key Executives:
Rod Senft, Partner
e-mail: rod.senft@foundersfoodgroup.com
Education: Univ. of Manitoba
Background: Tricor Pacific Capital; Pender West Capital Partners
Richard Harris, Partner
e-mail: richard.harris@foundersfoodgroup.com
Education: Univ. of Oxford; Univ. of London
Background: Golden Boy Foods; Coca-Cola Drikker AS
Trevor Johnstone, Partner
e-mail: trevor.johnstone@foundersfoodgroup.com
Education: UC Berkeley
Background: Tricor Pacific Capital
Derek Senft, Partner
e-mail: derek.senft@foundersfoodgroup.com
Education: Dartmouth College; London Business School
Background: Pender West Capital Partners

Venture Capital & Private Equity Firms / Canadian Firms

Directorships: Pender West Capital Partners; Canada Film Capital; Overland Container Transportation Services

2124 FRAMEWORK VENTURE PARTNERS
47 Front Street E
Suite 400
Toronto, ON M5E 1B3
Canada

web: www.framework.vc

Mission Statement: Framework invests in software companies with a focus on re-imagining everyday financial services applications or appling AI solutions to industry-specific datasets.

Other Locations:
415 W Cordova Street
Suite 203
Vancouver, BC V6B 1E5
Canada

Key Executives:
Peter Misek, Co-Founder and Partner
Education: CA, CPA, Illinois University
Background: Venture Partner, DN Capital; Partner, BDC IT Venture Fund; Founder, SoundPays Inc.; Managing Director/Co-Head, Global Technology Research, Jefferies
Andrew Lugsdin, Co-Founder and Partner
Education: BSc, McGill University
Background: Partner, BDC IT Venture Fund; Founder and President; Software Engineer, Nortel Networks

2125 FREYCINET INVESTMENTS
47 Colborne Street
Suite 306
Toronto, ON M53 1P8
Canada

web: freycinetventures.com

Mission Statement: Freycinet Investments is a venture capital firm that invests in high potential technology companies, with particular focus on early stage ventures in the Toronto-Waterloo area.

Geographic Preference: Canada
Founded: 2013
Investment Criteria: Seed, Early Stage
Industry Group Preference: Technology, Water, Human Wellness, Artificial Intelligence
Portfolio Companies: Borrowell, Canopy Labs, Football For Good, GrowSumo, Hubba, Lucent Sky, Lucent Sky, Mosaic Manufacturing, Hashtag Paid, Proteocyte AI, PumpUp, PUSH, Sampler, Set Scouter, TrendMD, WatrHub

Key Executives:
James Appleyard, Founder/President
Education: BA, MBA, Rotman School of Management, University of Toronto; MSc, London School of Economics
Background: Artez Interactive

2126 FULCRUM CAPITAL PARTNERS
885 West Georgia St
Suite 1020
Vancouver, BC V6C 3E8
Canada

Phone: 604-631-8088 **Fax:** 604-408-8892
e-mail: info@fulcrumcapital.ca
web: fulcrumcapital.ca

Mission Statement: Fulcrum Capital Partners provides flexible private equity and mezzanine financing to the Canadian middle market. They have helped build and grow more than 120 mid-market companies while generating superior, consistent returns for investors.

Geographic Preference: Canada
Fund Size: $750 million
Founded: 2011
Average Investment: $5 to $30 million
Minimum Investment: $5 million
Investment Criteria: Succession Planning, Growth Equity, Consolidations, Acquisitions, Management or Leveraged Buy-Outs, Privitization, Recapitalization, Pre-IPO Financing
Industry Group Preference: Manufacturing, Services, Distribution & Logistics, Consumer Products
Portfolio Companies: Accucam Machining, Athletica Sport Systems, Canstar Restorations, G.I. Group, JNM Group, National Logistics Services, Verdant, Vitalus, Arctic Chiller Group, Dana Hospitality, Mobile Parts, Nilex, Tradesmen Enterprises, Weatherhaven, ACI Brands

Other Locations:
79 Wellington St W
Suite 3510
Toronto, ON M5K 1K7
Canada
Phone: 416-864-2761

Key Executives:
Graham Flater, Partner
604-631-8078
e-mail: graham.flater@fulcrumcapital.ca
Education: BComm, University of British Columbia; CFA
John Philp, Partner
416-864-2705
e-mail: john.philp@fulcrumcapital.ca
Education: BA, Economics, Queen's University; MBA, Finance & Accounting, McGill University; ICC.D
Background: Richardson Greenshields, TD Securities, HSBC Securities, Managing Director, HSBC Capital
Johan Lemmer, Partner & CFO
604-631-8060
e-mail: johan.lemmer@fulcrumcapital.ca
Education: BComm, Bachelor of Accountancy, University of Witwatersrand; Business Economics Postgraduate Degree, University of South Africa
Background: CFO, HSBC Capital; CFO/VP Finance, Vancity
Paul Eldridge, Partner
416-864-2709
e-mail: paul.eldridge@fulcrumcapital.ca
Education: BComm, University of Guelph; MBA, University of Toronto
Background: HSBC Securities, Clairvest
Directorships: Allied, ACI, Astley Gilbert, G Adventures
Paul Rowe, Partner
604-631-8093
e-mail: paul.rowe@fulcrumcapital.ca
Education: BBA, St. Francis Xavier University; CFA
Background: HSBC Bank Canada; HSBC Capital
Directorships: A&B Rail Services, JAG Flocomponents, Petrospec Engineering
Greg Collings, Partner
416-864-3194
e-mail: greg.collings@fulcrumcapital.ca
Education: BBA, Wilfrid Laurier University; CA
Background: Audit Division, Collins Barrow Toronto
Directorships: Alumicor
Klemens Wilhelm, Partner
604-631-8072
e-mail: klemens.wilhelm@fulcrumcapital.ca
Education: University of Kufstein; CPA; CBV; ICD.D
Directorships: President, Association for Corporate Growth of BC

2127 GARAGECAPITAL
Waterloo, ON
Canada

web: www.garage.vc

Mission Statement: GarageCapital is a Venture capital firm built by founders for founders.

Key Executives:
Mike McCauley, Founder/General Partner
Education: BASc, University of Waterloo

Background: Co-Founder, BufferBox; Product Manager, Google Fi; Product Manager, Google X
Devon Galloway, Co-Founder/General Partner
Education: BASc, University of Waterloo
Background: Co-Founder, Redwoods Media; Co-Founder/CEO, Vidyard
Devon Galloway, General Partner
Education: BASc, University of Waterloo
Background: Co-Founder, Redwoods Media; Co-Founder/CTO, Vidyard

2128 GCI CAPITAL
4789 Yonge Street
Unit 706
Toronto, ON M2N 0G3
Canada

Phone: 416-218-8828
e-mail: info@gci.vc
web: www.gci.vc

Mission Statement: Toronto-based early stage venture capital firm with two funds, including GCI Ventures.

Geographic Preference: Canada, China
Investment Criteria: Early Stage
Industry Group Preference: Information Technology, SaaS, Digital Health, B2B
Portfolio Companies: Alongside, ApplyBoard, C2RO, DreamPayments, ECO Technologies, Envenio, Eigen Innovations, EwayTech, Fantuan Delivery, FileFacets, Genecis, Graphite Software, GrubMarket, Insuranceforchildren.ca, Juix, MappedIn, O2 Canada, Peraso, Repable, Sinitic, Tacit Innovations, TritonWear

Other Locations:
Unit 1001, Bld. 5, EFC
Dist. Yuhang
Hangzhou City, Zhejiang Province
China

Key Executives:
Larry Y. Liu, Founding Partner
e-mail: larry@gciventures.com
Education: Rotman School of Management, University of Toronto; University of Portsmouth
Background: EffiSolar Energy Corporation

2129 GENESIS CAPITAL CORPORATION
8 King Street E
Suite 1410
Toronto, ON M5C 1B5

Phone: 416-214-2225
web: www.genesiscapitalcorp.com

Mission Statement: Genesis acquires and grows companies that can benefit from the firm's experience, in a range of industries and deal sizes.

Founded: 2010
Industry Group Preference: Manufacturing, Construction, Energy Services, Industrial Services, Environmental & Waste Management

2130 GENESYS CAPITAL
123 Front St W
Suite 1503
PO Box 34
Toronto, ON M5J 2M2
Canada

Phone: 416-598-4900 Fax: 416-598-3328
e-mail: info@genesyscapital.com
web: www.genesyscapital.com

Mission Statement: Genesys Capital is focused on building companies in the high-growth sectors of healthcare and biotechnology. Through its expertise and network, Genesys accelerates the development of commercially viable emerging companies that represent promising life science investment opportunities.

Geographic Preference: Canada
Fund Size: $200 million
Founded: 2000
Average Investment: $3 Million
Minimum Investment: $1 Million
Investment Criteria: Seed, Early, Expansion
Industry Group Preference: Biotechnology, Healthcare, Life Sciences
Portfolio Companies: Adapsyn Bioscience, Aptinyx, Fairhaven Pharmaceuticals, Flosonics Medical, Functional Neuromodulation, Fusion Pharmaceuticals, Impopharma, Inversago Pharma, Invitae Corp., Profound Medical, Therapeutic Monitoring Systems, Tioga Pharmaceuticals

Key Executives:
Kelly Holman, Managing Director
Education: BS, Biochemistry, MBA, Queen's University
Background: Senior Investment Manager, MDS Capital Corp.
Damian Lamb, Managing Director
Education: McMaster University; MS, Molecular Neurobiology, MBA, Queen's University
Background: Investment Manager, MDS Capital Corp.
Directorships: Affinium Pharmaceuticals, Profound Medical
Jamie Stiff, Managing Director
Education: BS, Queen's University; MBA, Rotman School of Management
Background: Samuel Lunenfield Research Institute, Mount Sinai Hospital
Directorships: glcare Pharma

2131 GENWEALTH VENTURES
51 Wolseley Street
Toronto, ON M5T 1A4
Canada

e-mail: info@genwealthlp.com
web: www.genwealthlp.com

Mission Statement: Genwealth's mission is to provide early stage capital to create long term value.

Geographic Preference: Canada
Founded: 2011
Investment Criteria: Early-Stage
Industry Group Preference: SaaS, Mobile, Digital Media & Marketing, Social Media
Portfolio Companies: Atomic Reach, Outside Intelligence, Sport Testing, Legacy Investments

Key Executives:
Mark Lozzi, Partner
Education: MBA, Entrepreneurship, San Diego State Univeristy
Background: Vice President, Corporate Finance, Boutique Investment Bank
Craig Wallace, Director
Education: BComm, University of Toronto; CA
Background: President/COO, Kaboose; President/CEO, AOL Canada; General Partner, IceAngels
Ken Nickerson, Director
Background: Founder/CEO, iBinary; CEO, OpenCola; CTO, TheDocSpace; General Manager, Microsoft Network Canada
Directorships: Kobo

2132 GEORGIAN PARTNERS
2 St Clair Ave West
Suite 1400
Toronto, ON M4V 1L5
Canada

Phone: 416-868-9696 Fax: 416-868-1514
e-mail: info@georgianpartners.com
web: georgianpartners.com

Venture Capital & Private Equity Firms / Canadian Firms

Mission Statement: Investors in growth-stage software companies.
Geographic Preference: North America
Founded: 2008
Investment Criteria: Expansion-Stage, Growth-Stage
Industry Group Preference: Enterprise Software, Digital Media & Marketing, Information Technology, Internet, Cloud Computing, Artificial Intelligence
Portfolio Companies: Aera, Beam Dental, Bidgely, Bluecore, Chorus.ai, Cority, DataCandy, DefenseStorm, DISCO, eSentire, Fiix, Flashpoint, FreshBooks, Glooko, IEX Group, Influitive, Integrate.ai, Polar, Reonomy, RiskIQ, Ritual, Scribble, SentientScience, Shipwell, Siemplify, SignPost, Stratifyd, Tealium, Top Hat, TotalExpert, TraceLink, TrackTik, True Fit, Vision Critical, Welltok, WorkFusion, Xanadu

Key Executives:
   John Berton, Managing Director
   Education: BA, Queen's University; Computer Science, University of Calgary; CFA
   Background: VRG Capital
   Justin Lafayette, Managing Director
   Background: Vice President, Information Platform & Solutions, IBM; Co-Founder, DWL
   Simon Chong, Managing Partner
   Education: MBA, Henley Management School
   Background: Worldwide Director of Sales, Information Solutions, IBM Software Group; DWL

2133 GIBRALTAR & COMPANY
100 Adelaide Street West
Toronto, ON M5H 1S3
Canada

e-mail: contact@gibraltarcompany.ca
web: www.gibraltarcompany.ca

Founded: 2013
Industry Group Preference: Consumer Products
Portfolio Companies: Blue Ant Media, CivicConnect, CrowdRiff, fanxchange, LXR and Co., Lunata Hair, Sheerly Genius, Tilley, VisionCritical

Key Executives:
   Cam Di Prata, CEO and Managing Partner
   Education: Concordia Univ.; Richard Ivey School of Business
   Background: Nesbitt Burns, Citigroup, Scotia Capital, National Bank of Canada
   Directorships: Crowdriff, FanXchange, LXRandCo
   Joe Mimran, Co-Founder and Chairman
   Background: Alfred Sung, Club Monaco, Joe Fresh
   Luigi Fraquelli, Co-Founder and Managing Director
   Education: McGill Univ.
   Background: BMO Capital Markets

2134 GLOBALIVE
48 Yonge Street
Suite 1200
Toronto, ON M5E 1G6
Canada

Phone: 416-204-7559
e-mail: info@globalive.com
web: www.globalive.com

Mission Statement: Startup studio and global investment firm.

Founded: 1998
Investment Criteria: Seed, Pre-Seed, Series A
Industry Group Preference: Telecommunications, Media, Real Estate, Artificial Intelligence, Healthcare
Portfolio Companies: Flexiti Financial, Pitchpoint Solutions, GlobaliveXMG, TouchBistro, time play, draganfly, zoocasa, nuuvera, Gibraltar, Founders Advantage Capital, Trilogy International Partners, Alignvest Management Corporation

Other Locations:
Carnegie Hall Tower
152 West 57th Street
47th Floor
New York, NY 10019

318 Spear St, #8G
San Francisco, CA 94105

Key Executives:
   Anthony Lacavera, Founder & Chairman
   e-mail: anthonylacavera@globalive.com
   Education: Univ. of Toronto
   Background: WIND Mobile
   Brice Scheschuk, Managing Partner
   e-mail: bricescheschuk@globalive.com
   Education: BComm, Dalhousie Univ.
   Background: WIND Mobile
   Simon Lockie, Partner
   e-mail: simonlockie@globalive.com
   Education: BA, University of Toronto; LLB, McGill University
   Background: Partner, Davies Ward Phillips & Vineberg LLP
   Directorships: WIND Mobile, Canadian Sea Turtle Network
   David Roff, Partner
   e-mail: davidroff@globalive.com
   Education: BA, University of Western Ontario

2135 GOAL HOLDINGS
1021 West Hastings St
9th Fl.
Vancouver, BC V6E 0C3
Canada

Phone: 604-662-3373
web: www.goalholdings.com

Mission Statement: Angel investors for early stage investments, PE and VC for later stage investments.

Average Investment: $500,000 - $2,000,000
Minimum Investment: $500,000
Investment Criteria: Seed, Early, Venture, Minority Equity, Expansion
Industry Group Preference: Information Technology, Digital Media, Telecommunications, Green Technology, Agricultural Technologies, Medical, Health & Wellness, Business Services, Real Estate

2136 GOLDEN OPPORTUNITIES FUND
830, 410 22nd Street East
Saskatoon, Sk S7K 5T6

Phone: 888-866-4494
e-mail: info@goldenopportunities.ca
web: goldenopportunities.ca

Mission Statement: Provincial retail venture capital fund invests in Saskatchewan companies.

Geographic Preference: Saskatchewan
Industry Group Preference: Cannabis, Infrastructure, Construction, Healthcare, Innovation, Technology, Hospitality
Portfolio Companies: Superior Group of Companies, Aurora Cannabis Inc., Performance Plants, Western Building Centres Limited, Warman Home Centre, P.M. Power Group Inc., Gold Health Cre, Cova, DynaIndustrial, Fluid Clarification, Dyna Crane Services, TORC Oil & Gas, Safety Seven, Fort Garry Brewing Co., Librestream Technologies Inc., Terra Grain Fuels Inc., Credence Resources, LEX Energy Partners, Avalon, The Goal Group

Key Executives:
   Grant J. Kook, President/CEO
   Background: President/CEO, Cheung On; President/CEO, Ramada Hotels

Venture Capital & Private Equity Firms / Canadian Firms

2137 GOLDEN VENTURE PARTNERS
20 Maud Street
Suite 306
Toronto, ON M5V 2M5
Canada

web: goldenvp.com

Mission Statement: Golden Venture Partners provides funding and support to early stage companies focused on developing mobile products and services. The firm seeks to foster the next generation of breakthrough mobile technologies.

Geographic Preference: North America
Fund Size: $40 million
Average Investment: $750,000
Investment Criteria: Seed, Early Stage
Industry Group Preference: Mobile, Technology, Artificial Intelligence, Fintech, Robotics, SaaS
Portfolio Companies: Action X, Alyce, AppHero, ApplyBoard, Apptentive, Avidbots, BenchSci, Brightwheel, Carbonated, ChefHero, Clearbanc, Delphia, Ecopackers, Faire, Gallop, Helpful, Infinity Quick, Influitive, Inkbox, Jiffy, Joist, KitchenMate, Lentil, mParticle, Medchart, Plooto, Properly, ProteinQure, ResQ, Ritual, RoadMunk, Set.fm, Skip the Dishes, SkyWatch, Snowball, SoapBox, Tempo, TimeHero, Top Hat, Toucan, TVision, Upverter, Wattpad, WAVE, Xanadu, Yesware

Key Executives:
Matt Golden, Managing Partner
Education: BA, Economics, York University; Law/MBA, University of Ottawa
Background: Partner, BlackBerry Partners; Director, New Ventures, BrightsparkVentures; Co-Founder, Tira Wireless; Osler
Ameet Shah, Partner
Education: BSc, Computer Science & Economics, University of Toronto
Background: Managing Director, Zynga; Co-Founder, Five Mobile; Director, Systems Engineering & Strategic Accounts, Tira Wireless; IBM; Grey Interactive
Bert Amato, Venture Partner
Education: BSc, Engineering, University of Toronto
Background: Co-Founder & CTO, Delrina Corporation; VP, Symantec Corporation; IBM Canada Research Laboratory; Co-Founder, Schematix Computer Systems
Jamie Rosenblatt, Principal
Education: BA, Univ. of Western Ontario; JD, MBA Univ. of Toronto
Background: Avid Life Media

2138 GOOD NEWS VENTURES
Toronto, ON
Canada

e-mail: info@goodnewsventures.com
web: goodnewsventures.com

Mission Statement: Early-stage investor in all sectors.

Investment Criteria: Early-Stage
Industry Group Preference: Artificial Intelligence, Internet of Things, Big Data, B2B, Cloud/SaaS, Mobile, Marketplaces, Finance, Healthcare, Applications, Infrastructure, Networking, Security, Space Technology, Storage
Portfolio Companies: ACTO, Axis, Bruha, Claim Compass, Cuboh, Darwin AI, Doorr, eleven-x, Envoi, Fleetops, GoWrench, Hockeystick, HTBASE, Intelocate, iRestify, KitchenMate, Hashtag Paid, Rally, Sampler, Stay22, Voiceflow, Zoom.ai

Key Executives:
Marat Mukhamedyarov, Founding Partner
Education: Gubkin Russian State University of Oil & Gas; Internaitonal Business School; Georgian College; George Brown College
Background: Masters Alliance; Alumoplast
Directorships: York Angel Investors

Mohan Markandaier, Managing Partner
Education: University of Toronto
Background: Pulse Voice
Directorships: York Angel Investors
Mona Kung, Partner
Education: BSS, University of Ottawa; MBA, University of Ottawa; Rotman School of Management, University of Toronto; MiF, London Business School
Background: External Panel Reviewer, Ontario Centres of Excellence; Teaching Assistant, York University; Bankers Trust
Directorships: York Angel Investors; East Gate Capital Management

2139 GRANITE PARTNERS
20 Eglinton Ave W
Suite 1501
Toronto, ON M4R 1K8
Canada

Phone: 416-364-5311 Fax: 647-729-1548
e-mail: reidbuchanan@granitepartners.ca
web: www.granitepartners.ca

Mission Statement: A Canadian private equity firm that targets profitable, well-managed manufacturing and service companies with sales in the $10 million to $100 million range. Granite's goal is to help entrepreneurs and owner-managers build upon and unlock the value they have created in their businesses.

Geographic Preference: Canada
Founded: 1996
Investment Criteria: Estate Planning Transactions, Management Buy-Outs, Shotguns
Industry Group Preference: Manufacturing, Business Products & Services
Portfolio Companies: Ecom Food Industries, Mike & Mike's Organics, SIM Digital, PS Production Services, Chainsaw, Tattersall Sound and Picture, Pixel Underground, Post Factory NY, Chair-man Mills, Event Rental Group

Key Executives:
Doug Buchanan, Managing Director
Education: MBA
Background: President & CEO, Granite Venture Partners; Leveraged Capital Group, Citicorp; Corporate Finance Unit, CIBC

2140 GREEN ACRE CAPITAL
2 Bloor St W
Suite 1805
Toronto, ON M4W 3E2
Canada

e-mail: info@greenacrecapital.ca
web: greenacrecapital.ca

Mission Statement: Investment fund focused on the Canadian medical and recreational cannabis industry.

Geographic Preference: Canada
Industry Group Preference: Cannabis
Portfolio Companies: Ample Organics, Aqualitas, Humble & Fume, Green Tank Technologies, Solo Growth Corp., The Friendly Stranger, Leaf Forward, Trait Biosciences, Tokyo Smoke, Anandia Labs

Key Executives:
Matt Shalhoub, Managing Director
Education: HBA, Richard Ivey School of Business
Tyler Stuart, Managing Director
Education: BComm, Univ. of Saskatchewan

Venture Capital & Private Equity Firms / Canadian Firms

2141 GREENSKY CAPITAL INC
6 Adelaide Street E
Suite 500
Toronto, ON M5C 1H6
Canada

Phone: 416-585-7850
e-mail: info@greenskycapital.com
web: greenskycapital.com

Mission Statement: GreenSky is a group of affiliated organizations based in Toronto working with entrepreneurs across North America.

Founded: 2010

Key Executives:
  Greg Stewart, Principal
  Education: BSBA, University of Florida; MBA, University of Toronto
  Background: Equity Analyst, Neuberger Berman; CFO, American Strategic Insurance
  Michael List, Principal
  Education: BAH, LLB, Queen's University

2142 GREENSOIL INVESTMENTS
Toronto, ON
Canada

e-mail: info@greensoil-investments.com
web: www.greensoil-investments.com

Mission Statement: Greensoil Building Innovation Fund invests in products, services and technologies related to real estate.

Geographic Preference: Canada; U.S.
Industry Group Preference: Building Innovation
Portfolio Companies: Goby, Amatis, Honest Buildings, electrIQ Power, Kaarta, Lunera, SensorSuite, illuma Drive, Carbon Cure

Key Executives:
  Alan Greenberg, Co-Founder and Chairman
  Education: Univ. of Toronto
  Background: Minto Group of Companies
  Directorships: BridgeGreen Capital; BioHarvest Inc.; Goby Inc.; Haldor Inc.
  Gideon Soesman, Co-Founder and Managing Partner
  Education: Hebrew Univ.; Boston Univ.; Ben Gurion Univ.
  Background: GMS Capital
  Dave Harris Kolada, Managing Partner
  Education: BComm., Queen's University
  Background: Oracle; Cognos; Jefferson Partners
  Directorships: Great West Lifeco; Investors Group; Power Financial Corp.
  Jamie James, Managing Partner
  Background: Tridel

2143 GROWTHWORKS
Box 11170, Royal Centre
1055 West Georgia Street
Suite 2080
Vancouver, BC V6E 3R5
Canada

Phone: 604-633-1418
e-mail: investment@growthworks.ca
web: www.growthworks.ca

Mission Statement: Regional venture capital management firm with a focus on technology.

Geographic Preference: British Columbia, Atlantic Canada
Fund Size: $170MM
Founded: 1999
Average Investment: $100,000 to $5 million
Minimum Investment: $100,000
Investment Criteria: Seed-Stage, Start-Up, First-Stage, Second-Stage, Mezzanine, Buyout

Industry Group Preference: Information Technology, Life Sciences, Clean Technology, Commercial Services, Advanced Materials
Portfolio Companies: Adfinitum, Azorus, Bootup Labs, Boreal Genomics, BuildDirect Technologies, CleanRisk, Cooledge Lighting, Copperleaf Technologies, D-Wave Systems, General Fusion, HIGHLINE Canada Accelerator, Impath Networks, INETCO Systems, IntroHive, LightHaus Logic, Methylation Sciences, Mixpo Portfolio Broadcasting, Redlen Technologies, Responsetek Networks, Smart Skin Technologies, Spinzo, Switch Materials, Teradici, Verold, Virtual Marine Technology, Vitrium Systems, Xenon Pharmaceuticals

Other Locations:
1959 Upper Water Street
Suite 1301, Tower 1
Halifax, NS B3J 3N2
Canada
Phone: 902-492-0423

Key Executives:
  Derek Lew, President & CEO
  e-mail: derek.lew@growthworks.ca
  Education: BA, Univ. of British Columbia; LLB, Univ. of Alberta
  Background: Initio Group
  Directorships: Frank and Joan Lew Charitable Trust
  Jim Charlton, Owner/Principal
  e-mail: jim.charlton@growthworks.ca
  Education: BSc, Physics/Astronomy, University of British Columbia; MBA, University of Western Ontario
  Background: Discovery Enterprises; Ventures West Management
  Directorships: Apparent Networks, Cellex Power, Cellfor, Chancery Software, fSONA Communications, Gemcom Software, HotHaus Technologies, LightHaus Logic, Mixpo, SFG Technologies, Teradici
  Peter Clark, President & CEO, GrowthWorks Atlantic Venture Fund
  e-mail: peter.clark@growthworks.ca
  Education: BA, Economics, Dartmouth College
  Background: VP, Finance & Corporate Development, TeleTech Holdings Inc.; VP & Treasurer, Covad International
  Directorships: Enovex Technology Ltd., Introhive Inc., Smart Skin Technologies Inc., Spinzo Corp.

2144 HARDY CAPITAL PARTNERS
510 Seymour Street
Suite 1020
Vancouver, BC V6B 3J5
Canada

Phone: 604-235-5550
e-mail: invest@hardycapital.com
web: www.hardycapital.com

Mission Statement: Hardy focuses on companies that are positioned for growth and threaten to disrupt existing major players.

Fund Size: $100 million
Founded: 2014
Average Investment: $500,000 - $5 million
Investment Criteria: High Growth
Industry Group Preference: Optical, Fintech, Real Estate, Insurance
Portfolio Companies: Clearly.ca, Coastal.com, Cotopaxi, Cymax, Flexday, Flexitive, Foodee, Indi, Jive Software, LD Vision Group, Lensway.com, Lensway.se, Liquidity Wines, Merrco Payments, Mogo, Naborly, Privé Revaux, RDM Corporation, Solink, Sonder, Surkus, Tangoe

Key Executives:
  Roger Hardy, CEO & Chair
  Background: Co-Founder & CEO, Coastal Contacts

Venture Capital & Private Equity Firms / Canadian Firms

2145 HEADWATER EQUITY PARTNERS
1890 - 1111 West Georgia Street
Vancouver, BC V6E 4M3
Canada

e-mail: info@headwaterequity.com
web: www.headwaterequity.com

Mission Statement: Headwater Equity Partners is a private equity fund that targets lower middle market companies based in Western Canada.

Geographic Preference: Canada
Investment Criteria: Lower Middle Market, Growth Capital, Buyouts, Acquisitions, Divestitures, Successions
Industry Group Preference: Manufacturing
Portfolio Companies: Interior Heavy Equipment Operator School, Frost Fighter, 911 Industrial Response, Mormak, Precision Mounting, Pumps & Pressure

Key Executives:
Dan Jacques, Managing Partner
604-694-8064
e-mail: dan_jacques@headwaterequity.com
Education: BBA, Simon Fraser University; MBA, Richard Ivey School of Business, University of Western Ontario; CA
Background: Senior Director, Merchant Banking, HSBC Capital; Morgan Stanley; Donaldson Lufkin & Jenrette; KPMG Corporate Finance
Simon Koch, Managing Partner
604-694-8063
e-mail: simon_koch@headwaterequity.com
Education: BA, English Literature, University of British Columbia; CA
Background: Senior Director & CFO, HSBC Capital; KPMG

2146 HIGHLAND WEST CAPITAL
1508-999 West Hastings St
Vancouver, BC V6C 2W2
Canada

Phone: 604-558-4925
e-mail: info@hwcl.ca
web: hwcl.ca

Geographic Preference: Western North America (Western Canada)
Industry Group Preference: Industry, Manufacturing
Portfolio Companies: AllWest Insurance Services, BID Group

Key Executives:
David Rowntree, Founder & Managing Director
David A. Schellenberg, Managing Director
Background: Jim Pattison Group
Dave Mullen, Managing Director
Education: BComm.; MBA
Background: HSBC
Directorships: Graycliff Partners

2147 HIGHLINE BETA
1 University Avenue
3rd Floor
Toronto, ON M5J 2P1
Canada

e-mail: info@highlinebeta.com
web: highlinebeta.com

Mission Statement: Highline BETA works with corporations in the areas of Corporate Innovation Programming, New Venture Development and Investment Funds.

Portfolio Companies: Andela, Breather, Drop, FameBit, Hurrier, LocalMind

Other Locations:
135 Madison Avenue
5th Floor
New York, NY 10016

555 Burrard Street
2nd Floor
Vancouver, BC V7X 1M8
Canada

Key Executives:
Marcus Daniels, Founding Partner
Education: BA, Psychology & Economics, McGill University; MBA, Smith School of Business, Queen's University
Background: Founder & Exec. Chair, MeshSquared Ventures; Co-Founder & CEO, HIGHLINE.vc; Managing Director, Extreme Startups; COO, Trend Hunter; VP, Operations, Frameworks; VP, AME Learning; Co-Founder & President, FLUID eNovations
Directorships: SDEVM
Ben Yoskovitz, CPO & Founding Partner
Education: BSc, Psychology, McGill University
Background: VP, Product, VarageSale; Director, Product Management, Salesforce.com; VP, Product, GoInstant; Founder & Publisher, NextMontreal; Founding Partner, Year One Labs; Co-Founder, Standout Jobs; Director, Operations, Grasshopper New Media; Director, Operations, Standpipe Studios
Directorships: Proposify, LocalMind
Lauren Robinson, General Partner
Education: BComm, Finance & Entrepreneurship, McGill University; General Assembly
Background: Executive Director, Female Funders; Global Operations Director, HIHLINE.vc; Head of Operations, Extreme Startups; National Bank Financial
Directorships: National Angel Capital Organization; Vancouver Entrepreneurs Forum; Canadian Acceleration and Business Incubation Association

2148 HILL AND GERTNER CAPITAL CORP.
162 Cumberland Street
Suite 300
Toronto, ON M5R 3N5

Mission Statement: Invests in inovative retailers, manufacturers, distributors, and service providers interested in expansion or re-design.

Geographic Preference: Canada
Industry Group Preference: Fashion, Architecture, Consumer Products, Food & Beverage, Cannabis
Portfolio Companies: Quadrangle Architects Limited, SBG Capital, Seven Continents, Midori Capital, Toronto Fashion Week, Hullmark Stafford

Key Executives:
Lorne Gertner, Chairman/CEO
Education: The John H. Daniels Faculty of Architecture, University of Toronto
Background: Co-Founder, PharmaCan Capital Corp.; Co-Founder/Director, Cannasat Pharmaceuticals Inc.;
Directorships: Chairman, Midori Capital; Vice-Chair, FDCC (Fashion Design Council of Canada)

2149 IGAN PARTNERS
60 Bloor Street W
9th Floor
Toronto, ON M4W 3B8
Canada

Phone: 416-925-2433
e-mail: info@iganpartners.com
web: iganpartners.com

Mission Statement: iGan Partners is an early-stage investor in health technology companies.

Geographic Preference: Canada
Fund Size: $26 million

Venture Capital & Private Equity Firms / Canadian Firms

Founded: 2011
Investment Criteria: Early-stage
Industry Group Preference: Internet, Software, Healthcare Information Technology, Artificial Intelligence
Portfolio Companies: Augur, Cosm Care, eSight, Exact Imaging, Finaeo, FlipGive, Flosonics Medical, Limelight, MolecuLight, Quandl, ResQ, RetiSpec, Rhythm Xience, Rna Diagnostics, SceneDoc, SomaDetect, Adracare, BrainFx, CBx, MedChart, Meta, Right Health, Think Research, Triage

Key Executives:
  Sam Ifergan, Founder & Managing Partner
  Education: BEng, McGill University; MBA, John Molson School of Business, Concordia University
  Background: Co-Founder, Visualsonics; Tri-Link Technologies; Brighter Minds; Strategy Consultant, Mercer Management Consulting
  Joel Finlayson, Partner
  Education: Dalhousie University; MBA, Cambridge University; Berkeley School of Public Health
  Background: Co-Founder & Managing Director, WellNovation; Middle East Healthcare Partner, PWc; MONITOR Group
  Directorships: Creative Destruction Lab; Royal College of Physicians & Surgeons of Canada
  Kuljeev Singh, Principal
  Education: University of Waterloo
  Background: Associate, High Park Capital; Setter Capital

2150 IMPERIAL CAPITAL
200 King Street W
PO Box 57
Suite 1701
Toronto, ON M5H 3T4
Canada

Phone: 416-362-3658 **Fax:** 416-362-8660
e-mail: icl@imperialcap.com
web: imperialcap.com

Mission Statement: A private fund manager that focuses on buy-out opportunities in the Canadian and American mid-market. Imperial Capital has earned a reputation for: (i) identifying recession-resistant industries; (ii) undertaking extensive due diligence; (iii) strategic value creation; and (iv) creative liquidity events.

Geographic Preference: Canada, United States
Founded: 1989
Investment Criteria: Management Buy-Out Opportunities, Take-Private Opportunities, Leveraged Recapitalizations
Industry Group Preference: Healthcare, Business & Consumer Services
Portfolio Companies: AIM Health Group, Beefeaters, Lise Watier, Schulman Associates, Associated Freezers Corporation, E.D. Smith & Sons, Kenra, Pacific Coast Publishing, Procaps, Stantec

Key Executives:
  Jeffrey Rosenthal, Managing Partner
  416-362-3658 x226
  e-mail: jr@imperialcap.com
  Education: BA, Commerce & Economics, University of Toronto; MBA, Finance & Entrepreneurial Studies, Schulich of Business, York University
  Directorships: Schulman Associates Institutional Review Board, AIM Health Group
  Justin MacCormack, Managing Partner
  e-mail: jmaccormack@imperialcap.com
  Education: BSc, Environmental Engineering, University of Guelph; MBA, Richard Ivey School of Business, University of Western Ontario
  Background: McKinsey & Cmopany; Trafalgar Securities
  Directorships: Onex Corporation
  Christopher Harris, Partner
  416-362-3658 x235
  e-mail: charris@imperialcap.com
  Education: BComm, Queen's University
  Background: Transaction Services, KPMG
  Gene Shkolnik, Partner
  416-362-3658 x245
  e-mail: gs@imperialcap.com
  Education: Shulich School of Business; CPA
  Background: KPMG; Canadian Army

2151 IMPRESSION VENTURES
2300 Yonge St
PO Box 2398
Toronto, ON M4P 1E4
Canada

Phone: 647-725-3355
e-mail: info@impression.ventures
web: impression.ventures

Mission Statement: Late-seed/early Series A Fintech investors.

Investment Criteria: Late-seed, Early Series A
Industry Group Preference: Fintech
Portfolio Companies: zoocasa, brim, Wealthsimple, Sensibill

Key Executives:
  Christian Lassonde, Founder & Managing Partner
  Education: BSc, BESc, Univ. of Western Ontario; MBA, Univ. of South Florida
  Background: Virtual Greats, Millions of Us
  Directorships: SickKids Foundation
  Maor Amar, Managing Partner
  Education: McGill Univ.; ESC Nice

2152 INDURAN VENTURES INC.
PO Box 26
Kingston, ON K7L 4V6
Canada

web: www.induranventures.com

Mission Statement: Induran Ventures invests in Canadian companies in the biotechnology sector.

Geographic Preference: Canada
Average Investment: $5-15MM
Investment Criteria: Seed-Stage, Start-Up, First-Stage, Second-Stage, Mezzanine, Buyout
Industry Group Preference: Biotechnology

Key Executives:
  J. Peter Blaney, Founder & CEO
  e-mail: peterblaney@induranventures.com
  Education: MBA, MPA, Queen's University
  Background: Founder & CEO, Dynex Capital Corp.; Founder & CEO, Tancho Advisors Group
  Barry Markowsky
  Education: BSc, MSc, Microbiology, MBA, University of Toronto
  Background: General Manager, ViiV Healthcare ULC; VP, Business Development & Director, Specialty Care Division, Glaxo Wellcome Inc.; GlaxoSmithKline
  Paul Lucas
  Education: Queen's University; Columbia University
  Background: President & CEO, GlaxoSmithKline

2153 INFORMATION VENTURE PARTNERS
1 University Ave
Suite 1901
Toronto, ON M5J 2P1
Canada

Phone: 647-479-8732
e-mail: info@informationvp.com
web: www.informationvp.com

Mission Statement: Venture capital investors focused on the FinTech market.

Geographic Preference: Canada, United States
Fund Size: $106 million
Founded: 2014

Investment Criteria: Early-stage
Industry Group Preference: Core Financial Applications, Financial Security & Crime Prevention, Financial Data Applications, Capital Markets, Payments & Financial Services, SaaS
Portfolio Companies: Adaptive Insights, BigID, Coconut Software, Esentire, Flybits, Infobright, Igloo, Knowtions Research, LendingFront, Placemark Investments, Procurifiy, PostBeyond, Q4, Sensibill, Thor Technologies, Thoughtexchange, Varicent, Verafin, Viigo, YayPay

Key Executives:
  Robert Antoniades, Co-Founder & General Partner
  Education: BBA, Wilfrid Laurier University; CFA
  Background: Managing Director, RBC Venture Partners; VP, BMO Nesbitt Burns Equity Partners; Executive Director, CIBC Capital Partners
  Directorships: Infobright Software, Adaptive Insights, Brickstream, Igloo Software
  David Unsworth, Co-Founder & General Partner
  Education: BA, Economics, Wilfrid Laurier University; MBA, Queen's University
  Background: RBC Venture Partners
  Directorships: Verafin, Igloo Software, eSentire, Jana Mobile
  Kerri Golden, Partner & Chief Financial Officer
  Education: HBA, Richard Ivey School of Business, University of Western Ontario
  Background: Director & Co-Owner, Urban Flats Toronto; CFO, Primaxis Technology Ventures; COO, SeaWell Networks; CFO, Infobright; Rogers Wireless; CFO, Alliance Atlantis Communications; Lorus Therapeutics; CEO, Paging Division, Bell Mobility

---

2154 INITIATIVE CAPITAL LIMITED
141 Adelaide Street West
Suite 1200
Toronto, ON M5H 3L5

Phone: 416-307-3271 Fax: 416-363-2010
web: initiativecapital.com

Mission Statement: Invests in the cannabis industry.

Investment Criteria: Seed, Early-Stage
Industry Group Preference: Cannabis, Technology, Biotechnology, Data Management

Key Executives:
  Hamish Sutherland, President/CEO
  Education: BEng, McMaster University; MBA, Schulich School of Business, York University
  Background: VP of Marketing, Strike Technologies; Director of Business Development, Research Now; President, Porcupine Goldor Mines; President/CEO, Hunter Porcupine Gold; Managing Partner, The Marketing Partners; COO, Kaypok Inc.; COO, Bedrocan Canada; COO, Asterio Cannabis Inc.; President/CEO, White Sheep Corp
  Directorships: Chair, Little Geeks Foundation
  Loudon Owen, Managing Partner
  Education: BA, University of Toronto; JD, Osgoode Hall Law School; MBA, INSEAD
  Background: Co-Founder, McLean Watson Capital

2155 INNOVACORP
400-1871 Hollis Street
Halifax, NS B3J 0C3
Canada

Phone: 902-424-8670 Fax: 902-424-4679
e-mail: info@innovacorp.ca
web: innovacorp.ca

Mission Statement: Innovacorp helps high potential early stage companies commercialize their technologies and succeed in the global marketplace.

Geographic Preference: Nova Scotia
Fund Size: $40 million
Founded: 1995
Average Investment: $100,000 - $3 million
Investment Criteria: Early-Stage
Industry Group Preference: Technology
Portfolio Companies: ABK Biomedical, Agada Bioscience, Aiotv, Alentic Miscroscience, Appili Therapeutics, Apptonomy Mobile Technologies, Atlantic Motor Labs, Aqualitas, Carboncure, Cellufuel, Clinical Logistics, Conquer Mobile, covina Biomedical, Dash Hudson, Daxsonics Ultrasound, Densitas, DeCell Technologies, DeNovaMed, DGI Clinical, DMF Medical, EagleBurgmann, Eosense, Emagix, Green Power Labs, Health QR, Health Outcomes Worldwide, InNetwork, Immunovaccine, Island Water Technologies, Jetasonic, Kivuto, LeadSift, Light Sail Energy, Livenlenz, Maritime Biologgers, Medusa Medical Technologies Inc., Metamaterial Technologies Inc., The Money Finder, MouseStats, Mimir Networks, Novonix, Ocean Executive, Photo Dynamic, Proposify, QRA, Rend, The Rounds, SabrTech Inc., Show Battery, Spring Loaded, Sky Squirrel Technologies, Skyline, Solid State Pharma Inc., SimplyCast, Swell Advantage, Swept, TrueLeaf, TitanFil, Tesla, Up My Game, Ubique Networks, Woodscamp

Key Executives:
  Malcolm Fraser, President & CEO
  Education: BComm, Mount Allison University
  Background: Founder, ISL Internet Solutions Ltd.,
  Directorships: Art Gallery of Nova Scotia, Dalhousie Medical Research Foundation, Sobeyart Foundation, Digital Nova Scotia
  Andrew Ray, Vice President, Investment
  Education: BSc, Saint Mary's Univ.; MSc, Intl. Space Univ.; MBA, Brigham Young Univ.
  Background: Bazari
  Dawn House, Vice President, Client Engagement & Communications
  Education: Mount Saint Vincent Univ.
  Background: Health Canada
  Donna Bourque, Vice President, Finance & Operations
  Background: Nova Scotia Power; Saint Mary's Univ. School of Business

---

2156 INNOVOBOT
4297-B Sherbrooke Street W
Westmount, QC H3Z 1H2
Canada

Phone: 514-487-5557
e-mail: info@innovobot.com
web: www.innovobot.com

Mission Statement: Innovobot helps companies use technology to build stronger businesses.

Key Executives:
  Zoya Shcuhpak, Managing Partner, Innovobot Fund
  Education: Concordia University; MBA, McGill University
  Background: CFO, Fairstone Financial; Desjardins Venture Capital; CIBC World Markets; Scotia Capital Markets
  Mario Venditti, CEO
  Education: MSc, MBA, McGill University
  Background: COO, Above Security

2157 INOVIA CAPITAL
3 Place Ville-Marie
Suite 12350
Montreal, QC H3B 0E7
Canada

web: www.inovia.vc

Mission Statement: Investors in early-stage technology companies.

Geographic Preference: Canada, United States
Fund Size: $110 million
Investment Criteria: Seed-Stage, Early-Stage

741

Venture Capital & Private Equity Firms / Canadian Firms

Industry Group Preference: Technology, Life Sciences, Artificial Intelligence
Portfolio Companies: 33Across, AlayaCare, Allocadia, AppDirect, Armored Things, Bench, BenchSci, Boosted, Busbud, CareGuide, Clearblanc, Clearpath, Community Sift, CoolIT Systems, Darwin AI, Drivewyze, Eideticom, Fellow, FutureFamily, LightSpeed, North, Peraso, PEX Card, Poka, RenoRun, Resonate Networks, Ross, Rubikloud, SnapTravel, Sonder, Spatial, Street Contxt, Swept, Top Hat, TrackTik, TripleLift, Tulip Retail, Vidyard, WorkFusion

Other Locations:
130 Bloor Street W
Toronto, ON M5S 1N5
Canada

168 South Park
San Francisco, CA 94107

15-19 Bloomsbury Way
London WC1A 2TH
United Kingdom

Key Executives:
Patrick Pichette, Partner
Education: MA, Philosophy, Politics, Economics, Oxford University; BBA, Université du Québec à Montréal
Background: Google; McKinsey; Sprint Canada
Shawn Abbott, Partner
Education: BS, Physics, University of Alberta
Background: CTO/President, Rainbow Technologies
Directorships: CoolIT Systems, Peraso, Top Hat, Drivewyze, WorkFusion, Solium
Karamdeep Nijjar, Partner
Education: MBA, Richard Ivey School of Business, University of Western Ontario; BMath, Computer Sciences, University of Waterloo
Background: RBC; Platform Solutions Inc.
Chris Arsenault, Partner
Background: Founder & CEO, SIT
Directorships: Fixmo, Gamerizon, Localmind, Reflex Photonics, Ryma, Well.ca, Woozworld
Todd Simpson, Partner
Directorships: Collective, PEX

2158 INSTARAGF
66 Wellington Street W
Toronto-Dominion Bank Tower, 31st Floor
Toronto, ON M5K 1E9
Canada

Phone: 416-815-6224
e-mail: info@instaragf.com
web: instaragf.com

Mission Statement: InstarAGF promotes an entrepreneurial, collegial environment built on open communication and transparency. They offer opportunities for professional grwoth and partnerships.

Founded: 2014
Key Executives:
Gregory Smith, President and CEO
Education: Queen's University
Background: Managing Partner, Brookfield Financial Global Infrasturcture Advisory Group; President, Macquarie Capital Funds Canada Ltd.; Managing Director, RBC Capital Partners
George So, Managing Partner
Education: University of Waterloo
Background: Founder/Managing Partner, Kindle Capital Group Inc.; Senior Member, Canada Pension Plan Investment Board

2159 INTEGRATED ASSET MANAGEMENT CORP
70 University Ave
Suite 1200
Toronto, ON M5J 2M4
Canada

Phone: 416-360-7667 Fax: 416-360-7446
e-mail: info@iamgroup.ca

Mission Statement: A public company, majority owned by management, IAM develops, distributes and manages alternative investments including private corporate debt, private equity, real estate, managed futures, global government bonds and retail alternative investments, that allow investors to reduce risk and enhance returns in their investment portfolios.

Fund Size: $2 billion
Founded: 2000
Investment Criteria: Mid-Market, Less Than 100 Employees, Revenues $10 to $20 million
Other Locations:
1188 Avenue Union
Suite 521
Montreal, QC H3B 0E3
Canada
Phone: 514-876-1170

Key Executives:
David Mather, Executive Vice President

2160 INTRINSIC VENTURE CAPITAL
37 Richard Way SW
Suite 301
Calgary, AB T3E 7M8
Canada

e-mail: info@intrinsicvc.com
web: www.intrinsicvc.com

Mission Statement: Intrinsic Ventures is an early-stage venture fund uniquely positioned to support international teams gain a place in North America.

Geographic Preference: International

2161 INVESTECO
70 The Esplanade
Suite 400
Toronto, ON M5E 1R2
Canada

Phone: 416-304-1750 Fax: 416-362-2387
e-mail: info@investeco.com
web: investeco.com

Mission Statement: InvestEco focuses on sustainable food and agriculture.

Geographic Preference: North America
Fund Size: $35 million
Founded: 2002
Investment Criteria: Expansion Stage
Industry Group Preference: Sustainable Food and Agriculture, Renewable Energy, Water Technologies, Resource Productivity Technologies, Transportation Solutions
Portfolio Companies: Maison Le Grand, Lesser Evil, Sol Cuisine, Nada Moo!, Kuli Kuli, MamaEarth Organics, 100KM Foods Inc., Vital Farms, Maple Hill Creamery, GeoDigital, miovision technologies, Woodland Biofuels, Ensyn, Rowe Farms

Key Executives:
Andrew Heintzman, Managing Partner
Education: BA, MA McGill University
Background: Co-Founder & Publisher, Shift Magazine
Directorships: Lotek Wireless, Triton Logging, Horizon Distributors
Alex Chamberlain, Managing Partner
Education: LLB, MBA, CFA
Background: Attorney, Smith Lyons; Corporate Finance, PricewaterhouseCoopers Securites

Directorships: UV Pure Technologies, EnerWorks, Rowe Farms
Michael Curry, Partner/Director
Education: BA
Directorships: 100km Foods Inc.
Charles Holt, Partner
Education: LLM, London School of Economics; JD, University of Ottawa
Background: Corporate Law

2162 INVICO CAPITAL CORPORATION
209 8th Avenue SW
Suite 600
Calgary, AB T2P 1B8
Canada

Phone: 403-538-4771 Fax: 403-538-4770
e-mail: info@invicocapital.com
web: www.invicocapital.com

Mission Statement: Alternative investment fund management firm.

Geographic Preference: Canada
Fund Size: $350 million
Founded: 2006
Industry Group Preference: Energy, Real Estate

Key Executives:
Jason Brooks, President
Education: BComm, Haskayne School of Business; CFA
Background: Vice President, Ernst & Young
Allison M. Taylor, Chief Executive Officer/Portfolio Manager
Education: BS, Actuarial Science & Statistics, University of Western Ontario; MBA, Finance, Haskayne School of Business
Background: Senior Associate, Ernst & Young

2163 IRONBRIDGE EQUITY PARTNERS
Bay Adelaide Centre - East Tower
22 Adelaide Street West
Suite 3520
Toronto, ON M5H 4E3
Canada

Phone: 416-863-0105
e-mail: info@ironbridgeequity.com
web: ironbridgeequity.com

Mission Statement: Ironbridge is a Toronto-based private equity firm focused exclusively on investing in companies in the Canadian lower middle-market. Ironbridge specializes on traditional industry businesses in the manufacturing, distribution, consumer products and services.

Geographic Preference: Canada
Fund Size: $400 million
Average Investment: $15 to $40 million
Minimum Investment: $15 million
Investment Criteria: Management Buyouts, Expansions, Recapitalizations, Restructurings
Industry Group Preference: Manufacturing, Distribution, Consumer Products, Consumer Services, Business Products & Services
Portfolio Companies: Canada Metal (Pacific), midland appliances, A.V. Gauge & Fixture, Brooklin Concrete, Avena Foods, Thermogenics, Back in Motion, Advance Engineered Products, Dumur Industries, Alliance Corp., M&M Resources, Hank's Maintenance, L&C Trucking, MBRP, Alumni Educational Solutions

Key Executives:
Alan G. Sellery, President/Managing Partner
Education: BBA, University of Western Ontario; MBA, Harvard Business School
Background: Partner, EdgeStone Capital Partners; Bain & Company
Directorships: Gesco Industries, Gaspard LP, Global Railway Industries

Peter Samson, Managing Partner
Education: BBA, University of Western Ontario
Background: Bain & Company
Peter Drowse, Partner/CFO
Education: BComm, BA, Queen's University; CFA
Background: VP, EdgeStone Capital Partners
Directorships: Gesco Industries
Jeffrey N. Murphy, Partner
Education: BS, Materials & Metallurgical Engineering, Queen's University; MS, University of British Columbia
Background: Co-Founder, Blackmore Partners; Marketing Executive, Noranda; Engineering Consultant, Hatch Associates
Andrew Walton, Partner
Education: BComm, University of Cape Town; Rotman School of Management, University of Toronto
Background: Partner, Signal Hill Equity Partners; Partner, EdgeStone Capital Partners; Partner, PWc Transaction Services Group; CEO, Westridge Cabinets Ltd.; CFO, New Food Classics Partnership
Directorships: Alliance Corporation, Midland Appliance, OEL Projects, Romet Limited, C&V Portable Accommodations, Westridge Cabinets, Continental Alloys & Services, Eurospec Manufacturing

2164 ISLAND CAPITAL PARTNERS
31 Queen Street
Charlottetown, PE C1A 4A4
Canada

e-mail: info@peislandcapitalpartners.com
web: peislandcapitalpartners.com

Mission Statement: Island Capital is an early stage VC Fund investing in high growth potential PEI companies.

Geographic Preference: PEI
Fund Size: $4.25 million
Average Investment: $100,000-500,000

Key Executives:
Alex MacBeath, Managing Partner
Education: BSc, University of Prince Edward Island; MBA, Dalhousie University
Background: CEO, Grant Thornton LLP

2165 InstarAGF
Toronto Dominion Bank Tower
66 Wellington Street West
31st Floor
Toronto, ON M5K 1E9
Canada

Phone: 416-815-6224
web: www.instaragf.com

Mission Statement: Manages alternative investments in the North American middle market.

Geographic Preference: North America
Founded: 2014
Industry Group Preference: Industry, Manufacturing
Portfolio Companies: AllWest Insurance Services, BID Group

Key Executives:
Gregory J. Smith, President & CEO
Education: Queen's Univ.
Background: Brookfield Financial; Macquarie Capital Funds Canada
Directorships: Canadian Council of Public-Private Partnerships; Lighthouse Equity Partners; Avrio Ventures
George So, Managing Partner
Education: Univ. of Waterloo
Background: Kindle Capital Group; Canada Pension Plan

Venture Capital & Private Equity Firms / Canadian Firms

2166 JOG CAPITAL
440 - 2nd Avenue SW
Suite 2370
Calgary, AB T2P 5E9
Canada

Phone: 403-232-3340 Fax: 403-705-3341
e-mail: info@jogcapital.com
web: jogcapital.com

Mission Statement: Calgary-based PE firm focused on light oil assets in Western Canada.

Geographic Preference: Western Canada
Fund Size: $350 million
Founded: 2002
Average Investment: C$75-150 million
Investment Criteria: Early-Stage
Industry Group Preference: Energy, Oil & Gas

Key Executives:
Ryan Crawford, Chair
Education: BComm, Finance, University of Saskatchewan; CFA
Background: Relationship Manager, ATB Financial; Associate, Bank of America
Craig Golinowski, President
Education: MBA, University of Western Ontario; BComm, Finance, University of Alberta; CFA
Background: Investment Banking, RBC Capital Markets
Daryl Gilbert, Managing Director
Background: President & CEO, GLJ Associates; Great Northern Oil Ltd.
Kel Johnston, Managing Director
Education: BSc, Univ. of Manitoba; Univ. of Calgary
Background: Alberta Clipper Energy
Directorships: Leucrotta Exploration
Jason White, Managing Director
Education: Haskayne School of Business; Univ. of Alberta
Background: CIBC World Markets
Directorships: Karve Energy

2167 KENSINGTON CAPITAL PARTNERS
95 St. Clair Avenue West
Suite 905
Toronto, ON M4V 1N6
Canada

Phone: 416-362-9000 Fax: 416-362-0939
Toll-Free: 855-362-9329
e-mail: info@kcpl.ca
web: www.kcpl.ca

Mission Statement: Employee-owned alternative investment fund focused on the North American market.

Geographic Preference: Canada, United States
Fund Size: $1.1 billion
Founded: 1996
Industry Group Preference: Technology, Retailing, Consumer Products, Financial Services, Manufacturing, Media, Telecommunications, Healthcare, Information Technology, Energy, Industrial Services
Portfolio Companies: CGL Manufacturing Inc., Oncap, Novacap, Prodomax Automation Ltd., Protenergy, Providence Equityt, Parallel49 Equity, Trrivest, TriWest Capital Partners, Turtle Island Recycling, White Swan Environmental Ltd.

Other Locations:
221-10th Avenue SE
Suite 203
Calgary, AB T2G 0V9
Canada
Phone: 587-351-4122

675 West Hastings St
Suite 200
Vancouver, BC V6B 1N2
Canada
Phone: 604-565-2188

Key Executives:
Thomas Kennedy, Chairman and Senior Managing Director
Education: BSc, Engineering, Queen's University; DBA, University of Edinburgh
Background: Consolidation Coal Co., Alberta Energy Company, Bunting Warburg, Lancaster, TD Securities
Directorships: Triax Growth Fund
Richard Nathan, Senior Managing Director
Education: BA, Computer Science, Dartmouth College; LLB, University of Toronto, Faculty of Law
Background: Founding Partner, Brightspark Ventures; Managing Director, Goodmans Venture Group; Corporate Law, Osler Hoskin & Harcourt LLP
Eamonn McConnell, Senior Managing Director/Chief Investment Officer
Education: MBA, McGill University & HEC France; CAIA
Background: Barclays Global Investors, Deutsche Bank, Merrill Lynch
Matthew Cross, Managing Director (Vancouver)
Education: BA, Queen's University; HBA, Richard Ivey School of Business; MBA, Harvard Business School
Background: VP, Parallel49 Equity; Deloitte Consulting; Teekay Corporation
Directorships: White Swan Environment; Horseshoe Power
Harold Huber, Managing Director (Calgary)
e-mail: hhuber@kcpl.ca
Education: LL.B., University of Saskatchewan College of Law; B.Admin, University of Regina]
Background: Infrastruture & Energy Group of Torys LLP, McCarthy Tétrault LLP
Martin Kent, Managing Director
Education: B.Admin, Harvard University; BComm, Queen's University
Background: CFO, Quantum Murray LP, ONCAP, EdgeStone, Morgan Stanley, J.P. Morgan
Directorships: Newport Partners, RBC Dominion Securities

2168 KILLICK CAPITAL
95 Water Street
2nd Floor
PO Box 5383, Stn. C
St. John's, NL A1C 5W2
Canada

Phone: 709-738-5513 Fax: 709-738-5578
e-mail: inquiries@killickcapital.com
web: killickcapital.com

Mission Statement: Killick Capital invests in venture businesses, aerospace businesses, and businesses located in Newfoundland & Labrador specifically.

Geographic Preference: Atlantic Canada
Founded: 2004
Industry Group Preference: Aerospace, Technology
Portfolio Companies: Canadian Northern Outfitters, Carta Worldwide, Celtx, Clockwork Fox, CoLab Software, Coloursmith, Firecraft Products, Harbr, HeyOrca, Killick Aerospace, MAX, Mysa, PathFactory, radient360, Rally, Seaformatics, Sequence Bio, St. John's Hop On Hop Off, SucSeed, Turbine Engine Specialists, Verafin

Key Executives:
Mark Dobbin, Founder & President
Background: CEO, Vector Aerospace Corporation
Directorships: CHC Helicopter Corporation; Innovation & Business Investment Corporation; Business & Arts NL
Tom Williams, Partner & Vice President, Investments
Education: CA; CBV
Background: CHC Helicopter Corporation; Vector Aerospace Corporation; Grant Thornton

744

Joe McKenna, Partner & CFO
Background: CFO, Research & Development Corporation; Deloitte

2169 KILMER CAPITAL PARTNERS
Scotia Plaza
Suite 2700
King Street West, Box 127
Toronto, ON M5H 3Y2
Canada

web: www.kilmercapital.com

Mission Statement: A leader in making private equity investments in small to mid-sized businesses undergoing periods of rapid growth, significant change or ownership transition.

Geographic Preference: Canada
Fund Size: $1 billion
Average Investment: $5 to $50 million
Minimum Investment: $5 million
Investment Criteria: Later-Stage, Growth Equity
Industry Group Preference: Electronics, Communications, Technology, Food & Beverage, Apparel, Healthcare, Consumer Products, Media, Entertainment
Portfolio Companies: Compact Power, Atelka, Altasciences, Coalision

Other Locations:
1002 Sherbrooke Street West
Suite 2240
Montreal, QC H3A 3L6
Canada

Key Executives:
Larry Tanenbaum, Chairman
Education: BS, Economics, Cornell University
Michael Griffiths, Vice Chairman
Education: BComm, Loyola College/Concordia University; MBA, York University
Background: President/COO, KVN; Manager, Clarkson Gordon Chartered Accountants
Anthony Sigel, President/Managing Partner
e-mail: amsigel@kilmercapital.com
Education: BA, University of Pennsylvania; MBA, Wharton School
Background: Bankers Trust Company
Eric Gottesman, Vice President
e-mail: egottesman@kilmercapital.com
Education: BComm, McGill University
Background: Ernst & Young, CIBC World Markets
Doug Peel, Vice Chairman/Managing Partner
e-mail: dpeel@kilmercapital.com
Background: President & CEO, KVN; Twin Dolphin Technologies; President, Newstar Technologies; Bryker Data Systems; Cygnet Storage Solutions
Directorships: Unisync, Algorithme
William Blackburn, Managing Partner
e-mail: wblackburn@kilmercapital.com
Education: BBA, Wilfrid Laurier University
Background: NewPoint Capital Partners
Directorships: Tribal Sportswear, Unisync Group, Altasciences

2170 KLASS CAPITAL
MaRS Centre, Heritage Building
101 College Street
Suite 145
Toronto, ON M5G 1L7
Canada

Phone: 674-494-9881
web: www.klass.com

Mission Statement: A growth equity investment company targeting small software or web enabled post revenue companies.

Geographic Preference: Canada, United States
Fund Size: $50 million
Founded: 2010
Average Investment: $1 to $5 million
Minimum Investment: $500,000
Investment Criteria: Early-Stage
Industry Group Preference: Software, Web Applications & Services, SaaS, Enterprise Software
Portfolio Companies: Plex, Resolver, TrackTik, Nulogy, 360 Insights, Condo Control Central, Docebo, AlayaCare, Method CRM, Vena Solutions, Granify

Key Executives:
Daniel Klass, Founder/Managing Director
e-mail: daniel@klasscapital.com
Education: BSc, Mathematics; MBA, Finance/Accounting; CPA
Background: TD Capital, EdgeStone Capital Partners

2171 KNIGHT'S BRIDGE CAPITAL PARTNERS
Toronto, ON
Canada

Phone: 416-866-3132
e-mail: info@kbcpartners.com
web: www.kbcpartners.com

Mission Statement: Family office and private equity manager in Toronto.

Founded: 2008
Average Investment: $6 - $10 million
Investment Criteria: Later-Stage
Industry Group Preference: Consumer Products, Retailing, Internet, New Media
Portfolio Companies: Polaroid, TubeMogul, The Works, Robert Graham, Authentic Brands Group, Ellen Tracy

Key Executives:
Kenny Finkelstein, Co-Founder & CEO
Background: Co-Founder, Gen-X Sports; Co-Founder, Lifestyle Brands

2172 LAURENCE CAPITAL
150 Caroline St South
Suite 403
Waterloo, ON N2L 0A5
Canada

Phone: 226-476-1374 Fax: 519-340-0325
e-mail: info@laurencecapital.com
web: www.laurencecapital.com

Mission Statement: Waterloo-based private capital firm invests in public and private Canadian companies and real estate.

Geographic Preference: Canada
Founded: 2004
Investment Criteria: Late stage
Portfolio Companies: Bauer Marketplace, Cellwand Communications, Charcoal Group, Clearpath Robotics, Deer Ridge Centre, Fiix, Kognitiv Corporation, Langhaus Financial, Onco-Screen, Oviinbyrd Forest, Oviinbyrd Golf Club, Relay Ventures, Waterloo Brewing, Wealthpoint Health Services, XMG Studio

Key Executives:
Peter Schwartz, Chair & Partner
Education: MBA, University of Western Ontario
Background: Descartes Systems Group
Directorships: Kognitiv Corp.
Paul Laufert, Managing Director
Education: BA, LLB, Queen's University

2173 LEX CAPITAL MANAGEMENT
2530 Sandra Schmirler Way
Regina, SK S4W 0M7
Canada

Phone: 306-790-8676
e-mail: info@lexcapital.ca
web: lexcapital.ca

Venture Capital & Private Equity Firms / Canadian Firms

Mission Statement: Private equity firm makes early-stage investments in the Canadian energy sector.
Geographic Preference: Western Canada
Fund Size: $90 million
Investment Criteria: Early-Stage
Industry Group Preference: Energy, Oil & Gas
Key Executives:
  E. Craig Lothian, Executive Chair
  306-790-4152
  Education: BA, LLB, University of Saskatchewan
  Background: President, Keystone Royalty Corp.; Founder, Villanova Oil Corp.; Chairman & CEO, Flatland Exploration
  Directorships: PetroBakken Energy, Smart Completions
  Dean Popil, Managing Partner & CEO
  306-790-8658
  Education: BAdmin, University of Regina; CBV; CFA
  Directorships: CanGas Solutions, Wyatt Oil + Gas
  Curtis Armstrong, Managing Partner & CFO
  306-790-8660
  Education: BS, Management & Finance, Minot State University; CFA

2174 LGC CAPITAL
800 rue du square-Victoria
Suite 3700
Montreal, QC H4Z 1A1

web: www.lgc-capital.com
Mission Statement: Invests in the global cannabis industry.
Geographic Preference: Canada, Jamaica, Europe, Australia
Founded: 2015
Industry Group Preference: Cannabis
Portfolio Companies: Tricho-Med Corp.; Global Canna Labs; Etea Sicurezza Ltd.; Viridi Unit SA; CLV Frontier Brands; Evolution BNK, Little Green Pharma
Key Executives:
  John McMullen, Chief Executive Officer
  Education: BA, Political Science, University of Western Ontario
  Background: Investment Advisor, Canaccord Genuity; Investment Banking, Stratigis Capital Advisors

2175 LIGHTHEART MANAGEMENT PARTNERS
1040 West Georgia Street
15th Floor
Vancouver, BC V6E 4H1
Canada

e-mail: info@lightheartmanagement.com
web: www.lightheartmanagement.com
Mission Statement: LightHeart management partners looks to preserve and grow the legacy, heritage and culture of every business that they invest in.
Key Executives:
  Laing Henshall, Partner
  Education: BA, University of Western Ontario; JD, University of Calgary
  Background: Principal, CPS Capital; General Counsel, Premier Exhibitions
  Wei Lin, Partner
  Education: University of British Columbia
  Background: Engagement Manager, McKinsey & Co.
  Shay Nulman, Partner
  Education: BBA, York University; MBA, Western University
  Background: CFO, Gibraltar Ventures

2176 LIGHTHOUSE EQUITY PARTNERS
1333 W Broadway
Suite 750
Vancouver, BC V6H 4C1
Canada

e-mail: info@lhequitypartners.com
web: www.lhequitypartners.com
Mission Statement: Lighthouse invests in Western-based businesses that are currently profitable, looking for full or partial stakeholder liquidity, and want an investment partner to drive growth.
Geographic Preference: Western Canada, Western United States
Fund Size: $500 million
Founded: 2012
Industry Group Preference: Technology, SaaS
Portfolio Companies: Adperfect, Primex Technologies
Key Executives:
  Steve Hnatiuk, Co-Founder & Managing Partner
  Background: Yaletown Venture Partners; TD Bank; Accenture; PricewaterhouseCoopers
  Directorships: Entrepreneurship@UBC, Canadian Venture Capital & Private Equity Association; CapitalRoad Foundation, Pacific Parklands Foundation
  Joe Lucke, Co-Founder & Managing Partner
  Background: Tricor Pacific Capital; Credit Suisse Private Equity; JP Morgan & Co.; Morgan Stanley & Co.; M.K. Wong & Associates
  Directorships: Canadian Private Equity & Venture Capital Association; Association for Corporate Growth; Young Presidents' Association

2177 LIONHART CAPITAL LTD
Canada

Phone: 404-620-3350 Fax: 1-888-287-7949
web: www.lionhartcapital.com
Mission Statement: Lionhart Capital invests in Canadian business in the primary sector: forestry, mining, transportation, construction. They are commited to flexible financing solutions for startups and established companies alike.
Geographic Preference: Canada
Fund Size: $300 million
Founded: 1990
Average Investment: $10,000 - $30 million
Minimum Investment: $10,000
Investment Criteria: Startup, Early Stage, Middle Stage, Later Stage
Industry Group Preference: Commercial Transportation, Construction, Mining, Forestry, Oil & Gas

2178 LONGBOW CAPITAL
421 7th Avenue SW
Calgary, AB T2P 4K9
Canada

Phone: 403-264-1888 Fax: 403-264-1855
e-mail: communications@longbowcapital.com
web: www.longbowcapital.com
Mission Statement: Longbow invests in the energy sector, specifically in oil and gas. Longbow is run by energy experts who partner with companies who are doing their business efficiently, effectively, and responibly for long-term, high-growth investments.
Geographic Preference: North America
Founded: 1997
Investment Criteria: High-Growth, Long-Term Investment
Industry Group Preference: Oilfield Services, Energy, Infrastructure, Oil & Gas
Key Executives:
  Larry Birchall, Executive Chairman
  403-767-7362

e-mail: lbirchall@longbowcapital.com
Education: University Of Calgary
Tyson Birchall, Managing Director
403-767-7367
e-mail: tbirchall@longbowcapital.com
Education: BBA, Business Administration, Acadia University; CFA
Background: VP of Investment Banking, Tristone Capital Inc.
Directorships: North West Refining, North 40 Resources
Art Robinson, Managing Director
403-767-7368
e-mail: arobinson@longbowcapital.com
Education: BMgt, University of Lethbridge; MBA, Queen's University
Background: VP of Corporate Development, EnerMax Services; Vice President, SCF Partners
Directorships: Air Drilling Asscoiates, Moore Pipe, Tecton Energy Services, Xoleum Services
Chandra Henry, CFO/CCO
403-767-7359
e-mail: chenry@longbowcapital.com
Education: BComm, University of Calgary; CPA; CFA
Background: CFO, FirstEnergy Captial Corp.
Directorships: Pengrowth Energy Corporation, Alberta Ballet Company
Matt Cunning, Vice President
403-767-7374
e-mail: mcunning@longbowcapital.com
Education: BComm, Sauder School of Business, University Of British Columbia
Background: Director of Commercial Strategy, Parkland Fuel Corporation
Directorships: Drillform Technical Services

2179 LUGE CAPITAL
3 Place Ville Marie
Espace CDPQ, Office 12350, Floor L
Suite 50
Montreal, QC H3B 0E7
Canada

web: www.luge.vc

Mission Statement: Luge Capital is a fintech focused venture capital fund looking to invest in Canadian companies in the areas of data security, insurtech, lending algorithms, robo advisors, next gen payments, blockchain, merchant services, wealth management tools, alternative lending solutions, process automation, bots, regtech, and more.
Geographic Preference: Canada
Fund Size: $75 Million
Founded: 2017
Minimum Investment: $250,000
Investment Criteria: Early Stage, Seed, Series A
Industry Group Preference: Fintech, Artificial Intelligence, Data Security, Insurance, Blockchain, Wealth & Asset Management
Portfolio Companies: Flinks

Other Locations:
439 University Avenue
5th Floor
Toronto, ON M5G 2H6
Canada

Key Executives:
David Nault, General Partner
Education: BCom, Marketing, Concordia University
Background: Investor, iNovia Capital; President, Callio Technologies; Pivotal Payments
Karim Gillani, General Partner
Education: BASc, Systems Design Engineering, University of Waterloo; MSc, Finance/Economic Policy, University of London; LLM Master of Laws, University of Toronto
Background: Xoom; BlackBerry; Redknee Solutions

2180 LUMIRA CAPITAL
141 Adelaide Street W
Suite 770
Toronto, ON M5H 3L5
Canada

Phone: 416-213-4223
web: www.lumiracapital.com

Mission Statement: LUMIRA invests in later stage biopharmaceutical and medical device companies.
Geographic Preference: United States, Canada
Average Investment: $5 - $10 million
Investment Criteria: Later-Stage
Industry Group Preference: Biopharmaceuticals, Therapeutics, Pharmaceuticals, Life Sciences
Portfolio Companies: AmacaThera, Antio Therapeutics, Antiva Biosciences, Aurinia Pharmaceuticals, Bardy Diagnostics, BARonova, Cardiac Dimensions, Celtaxsys, Corvia Medical, Edesa Biotech, Endotronix, Engage Therapeutics, enGene, Exact Imaging, Forbius, G1 Therapeutics, Gladius Pharmaceuticals, HistoSonics, KalGene Pharmaceuticals, KisoJi Biotechnology, Medexus Pharmaceuticals, Notch Therapeutics, Opsens, OsteoQC, Satsuma Pharmaceuticals, Swift Medical, Think Research, Zymeworks

Other Locations:
303 Wyman St
Suite 300
Waltham, MA 02451-1208
Phone: 781-530-3868

Espace CDPQ
3, Place Ville Marie
Bureau 12350, Niveau L
Montreal, QC H3B 0E7
Canada
Phone: 514-844-6927

1021 W Hastings St
9th Floor
Vancouver, BC V6E 0C3
Canada
Phone: 604-558-5156

Key Executives:
Peter van der Velden, Managing General Partner
Education: BSc, MSc, Queen's University; MBA, Schulich School of Business
Background: Co-founder Fusion Capital Partners; Vencap Equities Alberta Ltd as Vice President, Business Development
Beni Rovinski, Managing Director
Education: BSc, Biochemistry, Rice University; PhD, Biochemistry, McGill University
Background: Senior Scientist, Sanofi Pasteur
Directorships: Aegera Pharmaceuticals, Avalon Pharmaceuticals, Cervelo Pharmaceuticals, Health Hero Network, Immunicon, IMMC, Inovise Medical, KAI Pharmaceuticals, Morphotek, Protana
Daniel Hetu, Managing Director
Education: MD, University of Sherbrook Quebec; MBA, Ecole des Hautes Etudes
Gerry Brunk, Managing Director
Education: BA, University of Virginia; MBA, Stanford University Graduate School of Business
Background: Founder and COO of a private bioinformatics company, and earlier was an executive at two venture-backed health care technology firms; Engagement Manager, The Boston Consulting Group
Directorships: ActivBiotics, AdipoGenix, LaConner Technologies, Targanta Therapeutics, Pharmasset

Venture Capital & Private Equity Firms / Canadian Firms

2181 MACKINNON, BENNETT & CO.
1 Place Ville Marie
Suite 3670
Montreal, QC H3B 3P2
Canada

Phone: 514-876-3939 Fax: 514-876-3956
e-mail: info@mkbandco.com
web: www.mkbandco.com

Founded: 2007
Investment Criteria: Growth
Industry Group Preference: Clean Energy, Transportation, Smart Cities
Portfolio Companies: Miovision, Communauto, BBOXX, Meteo Protect, Potentia Renewables

Key Executives:
    Kenneth MacKinnon, Managing Partner
    Education: McGill Univ.; Ivey Business School
    Background: Merrill Lynch
    Directorships: Miovision Technologies

2182 MANTELLA VENTURE PARTNERS
488 Wellington Street West
Suite 304
Toronto, ON M5V 1E3
Canada

Phone: 416-479-0779
e-mail: info@mantellavp.com
web: mantellavp.com

Mission Statement: Early-stage investors in mobile and Internet software businesses.
Geographic Preference: Canada
Fund Size: $24 million
Average Investment: $500,000
Investment Criteria: Early-Stage
Industry Group Preference: Wireless Technologies, Consumer Internet, Information Technology, Software, Artificial Intelligence
Portfolio Companies: Brave Commerce, Chango, Chatkit, Flixel, Gallop, Joist, PebblePost, Pushlife, Ritual, Shopcaster, SurfEasy, Unata, Wisk, Wysdom

Key Executives:
    Robin Axon, Co-Founder & General Partner
    Education: BAS, Aerospace Engineering, University of Toronto; MBA, Queen's University
    Background: Partner, Ventures West; MD Robotics
    Directorships: Brave Commerce, Unata, HipSell
    Duncan Hill, Co-Founder & General Partner
    Education: BMath, Computer Science & Combinatronics/Optimization, University of Waterloo
    Background: Entrepreneur in Residence, Ventures West; Founder & Chief Technology Officer, Think Dynamics
    Directorships: Chango, SurfEasy, Brave Commerce, HipSell
    Chris Sukornyk, Venture Partner
    Background: Founder & CEO, Chango; BubbleShare; The X-tream Network
    Directorships: Selina, Ritual, Chatkit, PebblePost

2183 MANULIFE CAPITAL
200 Bloor Street East
NT-6
Toronto, ON M4W 1E5
Canada

web: www.manulifecapital.com

Mission Statement: Invests junior capital in Canada and the United States to support growing middle market businesses and specialty real estate opportunities.
Geographic Preference: North America
Fund Size: $1.5 billion
Founded: 1998
Average Investment: $15 - $50 million fund investments
Investment Criteria: MBO, M&A, LBO, Growth
Industry Group Preference: Manufacturing, Retailing, Life Sciences, Financial Services, Real Estate, Oil & Gas
Portfolio Companies: Bradshaw International, English Bay Batter, Envirosystems, Flynn Restaurant Group, GoodLife Fitness, HOMEQ Corp., Knowlton Development Corporation, Marketwired, NSC Minerals, Recochem, Shred-It, Sleep Country Canada, Softchoice

Key Executives:
    Vipon Ghai, Senior Managing Director
    416-852-8468
    Education: BBA, Wilfrid Laurier University; CMA, CFA
    Background: Bank of Montreal Capital, Bank of Nova Scotia
    Rajiv Bakshi, Managing Director
    416-852-5228
    Education: BComm, University of Toronto; CA, CBV, CFA
    Background: KPMG
    Liam Coppinger, Managing Director, Private Equity - Asia
    Rob Scully, Director, Venture Capital

2184 MAPLE LEAF ANGELS
47 Colborne Street
Suite 403
Toronto, ON M5E 1E3
Canada

Phone: 416-646-6235
e-mail: info@mapleleafangels.com
web: mapleleafangels.com

Mission Statement: Not-for-profit organization connects high net worth investors with seed and early stage technology companies.
Geographic Preference: Canada
Founded: 2007
Average Investment: $120K
Investment Criteria: Seed-Stage, Early-Stage
Industry Group Preference: Technology, Artificial Intelligence
Portfolio Companies: Acto, AlayaCare, Bus.com, Chalk, ChipCare, Cinnos, Cybeats, Cybernetiq, Encycle, ExpertFile, Film Monkey, Fluent.AI, Futurestate IT, GotGame, Hangry, Intelivote Systems, iRestify, Jaza, Kenzington Brewing Company, Koomi, LifeHive Systems, Locketgo, Madcap Learning Adventure, Moregidge, Nicoya Lifesciences, OMX, Orchard, Quench, Raven, Red Wolf Security, ReDeTec, Spartatn, SportlogiQ, Stdlib, SuitedMedia, Suncayr, Suometry, Top Hat, Transit Labs, TritonWear, Ubisoft, UCIC, Wealthsimple, Wisely

Key Executives:
    Prathna Ramesh, Managing Director & CCO
    Education: BComm, University of Toronto
    Background: About Communications

2185 MARIGOLD CAPITAL
366 Adelaide Street W
Suite 606
Toronto, ON M5V 1R9
Canada

Phone: 647-783-7725
e-mail: info@marigold-capital.com
web: marigold-capital.com

Mission Statement: Marigold Capital invests in overlooked and undervalued teams and companies in sectors, industries and communities that can tranform the future.

Key Executives:
    Jonathan Hera, Founder/Managing Partner
    Background: Sarona Asset Management; Royal Bank of Canada
    Narinder Dhami, Managing Partner
    Background: Managing Director, LEAP

2186 MARKET SQUARE EQUITY PARTNERS
36 Distillery Lane
Suite 440
Toronto, ON M5A 3C4
Canada

web: marketsquarepartners.ca

Mission Statement: Toronto-based private equity firm focused on buyouts in the lower middle market.
Geographic Preference: Canada
Investment Criteria: Buyouts
Industry Group Preference: Infrastructure Services
Portfolio Companies: Ontario Excavac, D.M. Robichaud, Clean Water Works, Intelligent Soil Recycling

Key Executives:
Matt Hall, Managing Partner
Background: Great-West Life; Marcus Evans; Covington Capital
Derrick Ho, Partner
Background: PricewaterhouseCoopers; Wolseley plc; VenGrowth Private Equity; Covington Capital

2187 MARS INVESTMENT ACCELERATOR FUND
MaRS Discovery District
101 College Street
Suite 125
Toronto, ON M5G 1L7
Canada

Phone: 647-255-1080
e-mail: iaf@marsdd.com
web: www.marsiaf.com

Mission Statement: Helps accelerate the growth of new technology companies being established in Ontario and positions them for further investments by angels and venture capitalists.
Geographic Preference: Ontario
Average Investment: $500,000
Investment Criteria: Seed-Stage, Early-Stage
Industry Group Preference: Life Sciences, Information Technology, Communications, Entertainment, Healthcare, Clean Technology, Advanced Materials
Portfolio Companies: ACTO, Chatter, Klashwerks, Maple, MedChart, Ecamion, Encycle, GreenMantra, MetaFlo, Peak Power, Polar Sapphire, Pond Biofuels, Si-Cat, SPARQ, Temporal, Client Outlook, Encycle Therapeutics, eSight, figure 1, Flosonics Medical, Forbius, Intellijoint, Nicoya Lifesciences, OpenCare, Profound Medical, Swift Medical, VitaSound

Key Executives:
Larry LaKing, Managing Director
Education: BA, University of Waterloo; Queen's University; University of Western Ontario
Background: Executive Chair, Granite Networks; President and CEO, BTI Systems

2188 MCCAIN CAPITAL PARTNERS
95 St. Clair Avenue W
Suite 200
Toronto, ON M4V 1N6
Canada

Phone: 416-643-0702
e-mail: info@mccaincapital.com
web: mccaincapital.com

Geographic Preference: North America
Key Executives:
Zac McIsaac
Education: Mount Allison Univ.; Queen's Univ.
James Dent
Education: Queen's Univ.
Background: CIBC Capital Markets

2189 MCKENNA GALE CAPITAL
100 King Street West
Suite 5600
Toronto, ON M5X 1C9
Canada

Phone: 416-364-8884
web: www.mckennagale.com

Mission Statement: A Canadian provider of mid-market mezzanine debt and common equity financing to public and private companies. The firm specializes in financing management buyouts, acquisitions, expansion, recapitalizations, and going-private transactions through equity, convertible debt, or subordinated debt.
Geographic Preference: Canada
Fund Size: $600 Million
Founded: 1995
Average Investment: $41 Million
Minimum Investment: $7 Million
Investment Criteria: Growth Capital, Middle Market, Buyout, Recapitalization, Industry Consolidation, Mezzanine/SubDebt

Key Executives:
Gary Wade, Managing Director

2190 MCROCK CAPITAL
219 Dufferin Street
Suite 303B
Toronto, ON M6K 3J1
Canada

Phone: 647-478-9337
web: www.mcrockcapital.com

Mission Statement: McRock Capital is an Industrial Internet of Things venture capital fund focused on investing in companies that intersect Internet-related technologies with large industrial markets.
Geographic Preference: Canada, United States
Fund Size: $65 million
Founded: 2012
Investment Criteria: Early Stage
Industry Group Preference: Power, Water, Oil & Gas, Transportation, Manufacturing, Software, Hardware
Portfolio Companies: Praemo, Miovision, Worldsensing, Decisive Farming, Serious Integrated, Invixium, Mnubo, RtTech Software

Other Locations:
2540 Kensington Road NW
Calgary, AB T2N 3S3
Canada
Phone: 587-885-1520

Key Executives:
Scott MacDonald, Co-Founder & Managing Partner
e-mail: scott@mcrockcapital.com
Background: Managing Director, Venture Capital Subsidiary, Ontario Power Generation
Directorships: RtTech Software, Invixium, Pure Technologies, SynapSense, Pressure Pipe Inspection Company, RuggedCom
Whitney Rockley, Co-Founder & Managing Partner
e-mail: whitney@mcrockcapital.com
Education: BComm, Ryerson University; MBA, University of Calgary
Background: Partner, Nomura New Energy Ventures; Partner, Emerald Technology Ventures; Encana; Revolve Technologies
Directorships: RtTech Software, Mnubo, Invixium
Ha Nguyen, Vice President
e-mail: ha@mcrockcapital.com
Education: BA, Foreign Trade Univ., Hanoi; MSc, Aston Business School
Background: IDG Ventures Vietnam
Siddharth Srivastava, Vice President
e-mail: siddharth@mcrockcapital.com

Venture Capital & Private Equity Firms / Canadian Firms

Education: BA, Economics, Grinnell College; MSc, Finance, London School of Economics
Background: EY; Rothschild

2191 MEDTEQ+
740 Notre-Dame Street W
Suite 1400
Montreal, QC H3C 3X6
Canada

Phone: 514-398-0896
e-mail: info@medteq.ca
web: www.medteq.ca

Mission Statement: MEDTEQ+ strives to accelarate innovation and position, on a global scale, Canadian medical technologies, services and products.
Fund Size: $63 Million
Key Executives:
Diane Cote, Chief Executive Officer

2192 MERCATOR INVESTMENTS
161 Bay St
Suite 4520
PO Box 201
Toronto, ON M5J 2S1
Canada

Phone: 416-865-0003 Fax: 416-865-9699
e-mail: info@mercatorinvest.com

Mission Statement: Offers a combination of venture capital and practiced business and financial expertise.
Geographic Preference: Canada
Industry Group Preference: Networking, Infrastructure, Hardware, Software
Key Executives:
Peter A. Allen, President

2193 MINK CAPITAL
120 Adelaide Street W
Suite 2500
Toronto, ON M5H 1T1
Canada

Phone: 416-939-4975
e-mail: info@minkcapital.ca
web: www.minkcapital.ca

Mission Statement: Mink Capital is a consulting firm for Family Offices, providing education on investing in Private Equity.
Geographic Preference: North America
Founded: 2011
Key Executives:
Steve Balaban, Founder & Chief Investment Officer
Education: University of Waterloo; Wilfrid Laurier University; CFA
Background: President, Stellar Outdoor Advertising
Bruce Yang, Private Equity Associate
Education: MBA, Rotman School of Management, University of Toronto
Background: Impulsivity; Tokyo Star Bank; Atos

2194 MIRALTA
51 York Street
Westmount, QC H3Z 1N7
Canada

Phone: 514-484-9806
e-mail: miralta@miralta.com
web: www.miralta.com

Geographic Preference: Ontario; Quebec
Average Investment: $2-10 million
Industry Group Preference: Technology
Portfolio Companies: Ignis Innovation

Key Executives:
Eric Baker
Education: Queen's Univ.; MIT
Background: Innocan; Union Carbide Canada
Christopher Winn, CFO
Education: McGill Univ.
Background: Innocan
Thomas Kaneb
Education: Queen's Univ.; Harvard Business School
Background: Universal Terminals

2195 MISTRAL VENTURE PARTNERS
Ottawa
Canada

web: www.mistralvp.com

Mission Statement: The company invests in startups that focus on business to business solutions.
Geographic Preference: Eastern Canada
Investment Criteria: Startup, Seed Stage, B2B
Industry Group Preference: B2B, Marketplace, Software, Blockchain, Artificial Intelligence, Online Marketplaces
Portfolio Companies: Banter, Better Software Company, BlocWatch, Blue J Legal, Buckzy, Ceipal, CENX, CloudCheckr, edly, Expeto, Foko, Klipfolio, OMsignal, Quidbit, Rare.io, Relogix, Ritual, Sensibill, Soundpays, Stockpile, Symend, Unito, Zepheira
Key Executives:
Code Cubitt, Managing Director
Education: BSc, University of Alberta; MBA, Robert H. Smith School of Business, University of Maryland
Background: COO, Zephyr Technology; Partner, Motorola Ventures; Principal, Gabriel Venture Partners
Bernie Zeisig, Managing Partner
Education: BA, Economics, Carleton University; BA, Economics, Université de Chambéry; MSc, Entrepreneurial Studies, Stirling Univerity
Background: Senior Managing Partner, Cycle Capital; Senior Partner, VIMAC Ventures
Mike Scanlin, Venture Partner
Education: BS, Management Science, University of California, San Diego
Background: Partner, Battery Ventures; Sierra Ventures
Directorships: Axentis, DBS Communications, Element Labs, Vykor, Zebra Imaging
Gordon Smythe, Venture Partner
Education: BA, International Business, California State University, Fullerton; MBA, Entrepreneurial Studies and Finance, Marshall School of Business, University of Southern California
Background: Founder, The VC Forum; Founder, Pelna Inc.; Toshiba
Tianpeng Wang, Venture Partner
Education: LLB, International Economic Law, University of International Business and Economics, Beijing; JD, Bradeis School of Law, University of Louisville
Background: Partner, Jingtian & Gongcheng; PE/VC Lawyer, Clifford Chance; PE/VC Lawyer, Morrison & Foerster; PE/VC Lawyer, Linklaters
Pablo Srugo, Principal
Education: BA, Economics, Carleton University
Background: Co-Founder/COO, Gymtrack

2196 MMV CAPITAL PARTNERS
370 King Street West
Suite 442
Toronto, ON M5V 1J9
Canada

Phone: 416-977-9718 Fax: 416-591-1393
web: www.mmvf.com

Mission Statement: MMV Capital Partners is focused on providing growth capital to emerging technology and life sciences companies throughout North America. It has financed over 200 companies that range from being very early stage to established enterprises. MMV's creative financing solutions have helped the entrepreneurs of these companies realize their growth potential and reach critical milestones at all stages of development.

Geographic Preference: North America
Fund Size: $400 million
Founded: 1998
Average Investment: $1.5 to $10 million
Minimum Investment: $1.5 million
Investment Criteria: Growth Capital
Industry Group Preference: Technology, Life Sciences, Communications, Software, Clean Technology
Portfolio Companies: Abridean, Acclaris, Agilence, Airband, Andrew Davidson & Company, AgnioChem, Antares Pharma, Arxx Building Products, Avisena, Axeda, Axela, BelAir Networks, BeliefNet, Beyond The Rack, Blueprint, BTI Systems, Camillion Solutions, Canadian Bureau of Investigations & Adjustments, Chancery Software, CheckPoint HR, Chronogen, CiRBA, Cita Neuro Pharmaceutical, Clickability, ClickSquared, CorrectNet, Datawire Communication Networks, Decision Dynamics, Device Anywhere, DFT Microsystems, Diablo Technologies, Digital Payment Technologies, DMTI Spatial, eChalk, Ellumniate, EM4, EnterpriseDB, Epocal, ESP Technologies, Espial Group, Exchange Solutions, Exclaim, Exposoft Solutions, FitLinxx, Five Star Technologies, Foresee Results, Frantic Films, FullTilt Solutions, Generation5, GeoCom TMS, Globalserve, Health Integrated, HighRoads, HNW, Hubspan, Icera, iJET Intelligent Risk Systems, iKobo, Innovectra Corporation, Insception Biosciences, Integral Development Corporation, Intelliworks, Invivodata, Laszlo Systems, LogicTree, LucidMedia, Maptuit, MarketingIsland.com, Maximum Throughput, Merlin Technologies, Mistral Pharma, Momentum Healthware, Nakina Systems, Natural Convergence, Neat Receipts, NeoEdge Networks, NetBase Solutions, NetKey, NileGuide, NineSigma, Nistica, NOVX Systems, Ooma, OrderMotion, Osprey, PacketMotion, Pivot, Portico Systems, PowerSteering Software, PrimeRevenue, Quickhit, Qumu, Razorsight, Redknee, Reflex Photonics, Resonant Medical, ResponseTek Networks

Key Executives:
 Minhas Mohamed, Co-Founder & CEO
 Education: University of Western Ontario, CA, CFA
 Background: Senior Partner, Quorum Funding Corporation; Ernst & Young

2197 MONTECO STRATEGIC CAPITAL
55 St. Clair Avenue W
Suite 408
Toronto, ON M4V 2Y7
Canada

Phone: 416-960-9968
Toll-Free: 866-960-9968
e-mail: info@monteco.com
web: monteco.com

Mission Statement: Provides management experience, technical and product development infrastructure, and capital resources to startups and acquired properties.

Portfolio Companies: AutoServe1, Good Harbour Laboratories, Imtex, Riptide Tek
Key Executives:
 Scott Monteith, President & CEO
 Education: Ryerson University
 Michael Brandt, Chief Financial Officer
 Education: University of Waterloo
 Background: Loews Cineplex Odeon Corp., Thomas Cook Financial Services

2198 MOSAIC CAPITAL PARTNERS
6300 Northam Drive
Mississauga, ON L4V 1H7
Canada

Phone: 416-367-2888 Fax: 416-367-8146
e-mail: info@mosaicvp.com
web: www.mosaicvp.com

Mission Statement: Mosaic Capital Partners is a Toronto-based private investment firm.

Geographic Preference: Canada, United States
Fund Size: $135 Million
Founded: 1997
Average Investment: $2 - $10 million
Investment Criteria: Seed, Early-Stage, Expansion
Industry Group Preference: Internet Technology, Information Technology

Key Executives:
 Vernon Lobo, Managing Director
 Education: BSc, Engineering, University of Waterloo; MBA, Harvard University
 Background: McKinsey & Company, Nortel Networks
 Directorships: Cyberplex, AirIQ, Silanis Technologies, Tecsys
 Ron Farmer, Managing Director
 Education: BA, MBA, University of Western Ontario
 Background: McKinsey & Company
 Directorships: Bank of Montreal, Valeant Pharmaceuticals

2199 McLEAN WATSON CAPITAL
141 Adelaide Street W
Suite 1002
Toronto, ON M5H 3L5
Canada

Phone: 416-363-2000 Fax: 416-363-2010
web: www.mcleanwatson.com

Geographic Preference: North America, Far East
Founded: 1992
Average Investment: $1 - $5 million
Investment Criteria: Seed-Stage, Early-Stage, Later-Stage
Industry Group Preference: Information Technology, Communications, Hardware Technology, Software Services, Energy Technology
Portfolio Companies: i4i, Signiant, Quantec

Key Executives:
 John Eckert, Partner
 e-mail: john@round13capital.com
 Education: BA, MBA, University of Western Ontario
 Background: Joint COO, Softimage; VP, Director, Corporate Finance, Wood Gundy; CIBC Wood Gundy
 Directorships: Echelon, SkyWave Mobile Communications, Sitebrand, Activplant, Fortiva
 Loudon Mclean Owen, Partner
 e-mail: lowen@mcleanwatson.com
 Education: BA, University of Toronto; LLB, Osgoode Hall, Toronto; MBA, INSEAD
 Background: Joint COO, Softimage
 Directorships: i4i, Vismand Exploration, Amplus Communications, Ntegrator International, Quantec

2200 NEW BRUNSWICK INNOVATION FOUNDATION
40 Crowther Lane
Suite 100
Fredericton, NB E3C 0J1
Canada

Phone: 506-452-2884 Fax: 506-452-2886
Toll-Free: 877-554-6668
e-mail: info@nbif.ca
web: nbif.ca

Venture Capital & Private Equity Firms / Canadian Firms

Mission Statement: Private, not-for-profit corporation invests in startups and R&D.
Geographic Preference: New Brunswick
Fund Size: $100 million
Founded: 2003
Average Investment: $25,000 to $1 million
Minimum Investment: $25,000
Investment Criteria: Early-Stage
Industry Group Preference: Energy, Environmental Technology, Information Technology, Life Sciences, Natural Resources, Manufacturing, Aerospace, Defense and Government, Food & Beverage
Portfolio Companies: Alongside, Anessa, Avrij, Beauceron Security, Eigen Innovations, Encore Interactive, Fiddlehead Technology, Flixel Cinemagraph, Gemba, HotSpot Merchants, Introhive, Inversa Systems, Kognitiv Spark, MycoDev Group, PatriotOne Technologies, Populus Global, Porpoise, Repable, Resson Aerospace, Rise, Scene Sharp, Selectbidder, SimpTek Technologies, Smartpods, Smart Skin, SomaDetect, Sonrai, Soricimed, Stash Energy, Total Pave, WellTrack

Key Executives:
  Jeff White, President & CEO
  e-mail: jeff.white@nbif.ca
  Education: BBA, St. Francis Xavier University; CPA
  Background: COO, East Valley Ventures; CFO, Radian6; CFO, Q1 Labs; CFO, Genesys Laboratories Canada; Interim CEO, Canada's Ocean Supercluster
  Laura Richard, Director of Research
  Education: BSc, University of New Brunswick; PhD, Inorganic Chemistry, University of Oxford
  Background: Procter & Gamble; Velocys

2201 NEXT CANADA
175 Bloor Street East
Suite 200
North Building
Toronto, ON M4W 3R8
Canada

Phone: 647-259-8943
web: www.nextcanada.com

Mission Statement: A national, non-profit organization that focuses on four main streams of startups: Next 36, for students and grads launching startups; Next Founders, for founders of high growth ventures; Next AI, for artificial intelligence-related ventures; and Next ED for Canadian business looking to utilize AI.
Geographic Preference: Canada
Founded: 2010
Investment Criteria: Student/recent grad startups, high growth ventures, AI-related ventures.
Industry Group Preference: Artificial Intelligence

Key Executives:
  Joe Canavan, CEO
  Education: BBA, Concordia University; OPM, Business, Harvard Business School
  Background: CEO, Assante Wealth Management; CEO, Synergy Asset Management; Founder, GT Global (Canada); VP, National Sales, Fidelity Investment Canada, CEO, Children's Aid Foundation
  Directorships: Jays Care Foundation; Singularity University
  Kyle Winters, Chief Development Officer
  Education: Omnium Global MBA, Rotman School of Management, University of Toronto; EMBA, University of St. Gallen; Executive Education Certificates, Harvard University
  Background: Executive Director, Corporate & Foundation Relations, University of Toronto; National VP, Corporate Partnerships, Heart & Stroke Foundation of Canada; President, Canadian Foundation for AIDS Research

2202 NEXT EQUITIES
1804 Oxford Tower
10025 102A Avenue NW
Edmonton, AB T5J 2Z2
Canada

Phone: 780-986-0095
web: nextequities.com

Mission Statement: Targets promising companies looking for funding and complementary expertise to accelerate growth and profitability.
Geographic Preference: North America
Investment Criteria: Growth
Industry Group Preference: Industrials
Portfolio Companies: Block 45, Doorstat, Henry The Dentist, Kepler Academy, Nuwest Communities, Fiberex, Most Oil, The Press Gallery, Troverie, Vytalize Health

Key Executives:
  Fred Atiq, Chair
  Sikandar Atiq, President
  Education: BComm, Univ. of Alberta; MBA, NYU Stern School of Business
  Background: Goldman Sachs
  Ahmed Kamar, Vice President
  Education: B.Comm, University of Alberta

2203 NIAGARA BUSINESS & INNOVATION FUND
55 Clarence St
PO Box 519
Port Colborne, ON L3K 5X7
Canada

Phone: 905-834-2173
web: www.niagarafund.com

Geographic Preference: Niagara Region/Southern Ontario
Founded: 2014
Average Investment: $150K

2204 NORTHLEAF CAPITAL PARTNERS
79 Wellington Street West
6th Floor, Box 120
Toronto, ON M5K 1N9
Canada

Toll-Free: 866-964-4141
e-mail: contact@northleafcapital.com
web: www.northleafcapital.com

Mission Statement: Founded as TD Capital, Northleaf is a global private equity, infrastructure and private credit manager.
Geographic Preference: North America, Europe, Asia
Fund Size: $13 Billion
Founded: 2009
Investment Criteria: Venture & Growth Equity, Buyouts, Special Situations, Infrastructure
Portfolio Companies: BLS Revecore, Can Art Aluminum Extrusion, Cushman & Wakefield, Ecobee, Emerald Textiles, FreshBooks, Lenskart, Mercer Advisors, Pinova, Polycor, Randall & Reilly, Refresco, Vision Critical

Other Locations:
  1250 René Lévesque Blvd West
  Suite 2200
  Montreal, QC H3B 4WB
  Canada
  Phone: 514-989-3120

  14 Waterloo Place
  3rd Floor
  London SW1Y 4AR
  United Kingdom
  Phone: 44 (0) 20 7321 5750

  One North Franklin Street
  Suite 3340

Venture Capital & Private Equity Firms / Canadian Firms

Chicago, IL 60606
Phone: 312-871-4832

228 Hamilton Avenue
3rd Floor
Palo Alto, CA 94301

12 East 49th Street
9th Floor
New York, NY 10017
Phone: 646-844-1784

35 Collins St
Level 30
Melbourne 3000
Australia
Phone: 61 3 9900 6229

Key Executives:
Rob MacLellan, Chairman
e-mail: rob.maclellan@northleafcapital.com
Education: BComm, Carleton University; MBA, Harvard University; CA
Background: Managing Director, Lancaster Financial Holding
Stephen Foote, Managing Director, Sales
e-mail: stephen.foote@northleafcapital.com
Education: BA, York Univ.
Background: UBS Global Asset Management
Jeff Lucassen, Chief Financial Officer & Chief Operating Officer
e-mail: jeff.lucassen@northleafcapital.com
Education: BComm, Univ. of Windsor; BA, Univ. of Western Ontario
Background: The Carlyle Group
Gavin Foo, Managing Director, Investor Operations
e-mail: gavin.foo@northleafcapital.com
Education: BComm, University of Toronto; CA
Background: TD Capital Private Equity; SVP/CFO, IA Clarington Investments; Trimark Financial Corporation; Coopers & Lybrand
Stuart Waugh, Managing Director & Managing Partner
e-mail: stuart.waugh@northleafcapital.com
Education: BA, Trinity College, University of Toronto; LLB, Faculty of Law, University of Toronto
Background: TD Capital Private Equity; Management Consultant, McKinsey & Company; BPI Financial Corporation; McCarthy Tetrault

2205 NOVA SCOTIA BUSINESS INC.
World Trade & Convention Center
1800 Argyle St
Suite 701
Halifax, NS B3J 3N8
Canada

Phone: 902-424-6650
Toll-Free: 800-260-6682
e-mail: info@nsbi.ca
web: www.novascotiabusiness.com

Mission Statement: Invests in companies seeking growth capital, and looks for venture capital investors as partners in Nova Scotia's knowledge-based economy.
Geographic Preference: Nova Scotia
Fund Size: $55 million
Founded: 2001
Average Investment: $1 to $3 million
Minimum Investment: $1 million
Investment Criteria: Mid- to Late-Stage
Industry Group Preference: Financial Services, Aerospace, Defense and Government, Manufacturing, Security, Gaming, Life Sciences, Clean Technology
Portfolio Companies: Azorus, DynaGen, Halifax Biomedical, Health Outcomes Worldwide, Impath Networks, Intellivote Systems, Kytogenics, LED Roadway Lighting, Origin BioMed, Oris4, Techlink Entertainment, Unique Ltd.

Key Executives:
Laurel C. Broten, President & CEO
Education: BA, BSc, McMaster Univ.; JD, University of Western Ontario
Peter MacAskill, Chief Operating Officer
Education: BSc, St. Francis Xavier University
Michael Branchflower, Vice President, Sales & Strategic Marketing
Background: Execution Specialists Group
Directorships: Embrace Hope

2206 NOVACAP
3400, rue de l'Eclipse
Bureau 700
Brossard, QC L4Z 0P3
Canada

Phone: 450-651-5000 **Fax:** 450-651-7585
e-mail: info@novacap.ca
web: www.novacap.ca

Mission Statement: Novacap Industries invests in middle-market companies within traditional industries that have the potential to become world leaders by developing their market, technology and operations or through industry consolidations. Novacap technologies invests in companies focusing on growth and market leadership in information and communications technologies sectors. It partners with first rate management teams and actively works with them to build leading organizations in their markets.
Geographic Preference: North America
Fund Size: $3.6 Billion
Founded: 1981
Average Investment: $5-50 Million
Minimum Investment: $5 Million
Investment Criteria: Growth, Buyout
Industry Group Preference: Industry, Technology, Media & Telecommunications
Portfolio Companies: Bestar, Foliot Furniture, GHP Group, GTI, Hallcon, Horizon, Intelerad, Joseph Ribkoff, Kingsdown, Leading Edge Geomatics, Malhot Industries, Master, Mobile Storage Systems, Mucci Farms, Nautilus Plus, Nitrex, Noble Foods, Nuvei, Octasic, Pkware, Royal Mat, Spectrum Health Care, Smyth, Synergx, Syntax, Windmill Farms

Other Locations:
1 University Avenue
Suite 1600
Toronto, ON M5J 2P1
Canada
Phone: 416-536-2222 **Fax:** 450-651-7585

Key Executives:
Marc Beauchamp, Founder
Education: MBA, Columbia University
Background: Westhill Industries
Directorships: Technomedia, PKWare
Pascal Tremblay, President & Managing Partner
Education: BBA, University of Sherbrooke; MBA, McGill University
Background: Partner, Argo Global Capital; CDP Capital
Directorships: Ryma Technologies Solutions, LiquidxStream Systems, Creaform, Stingray Digital, Tenrox, PKWare
Jacques Foisy, Chair & Managing Partner
Background: KPMG, Montreal; Olympia Group
Directorships: KDC, Octasic, Royal Mat, BGR Saws, Tradition Foods, Demers Ambulances, Metro Supply Group, Rosmar Packaging Corporation

753

Venture Capital & Private Equity Firms / Canadian Firms

2207 OMERS PRIVATE EQUITY
900 - 100 Adelaide Street W
Toronto, ON M5H 0E2
Canada

Phone: 416-369-2400 Fax: 416-369-9704
e-mail: infoprivateequity@omers.com
web: www.omersprivateequity.com

Mission Statement: Pension administrator for municipal employees in the province of Ontario invests in high-quality private equity and infrastructure assets.

Geographic Preference: Global
Fund Size: $85 billion
Founded: 1962
Industry Group Preference: Infrastructure, Energy, Transportation
Portfolio Companies: Alexander Mann Solutions, Caliber Collision, CBI Health Group, CEDA, Epiq, ERM, Forefront Dermatology, Inmar, Kenan Advantage, Lifeways, National Veterinary Associates, Paradigm, Premise Health, Trescal, V.Group, Vue International

Other Locations:
450 Park Avenue
9th Floor
New York, NY 10022
Phone: 646-376-3100

The Leadenhall Building
122 Leadenhall Street
29th Floor
London EC3V 4AB
United Kingdom
Phone: 44 (0)20 7822 8300

One Raffles Quay
#30-02, North Tower 048583
Singapore
Phone: 44 (0)20 7822 8300

Key Executives:
Mark Redman, Executive VP & Global Head, Private Equity
Education: MA, Univ. of Oxford
Background: Grant Thornton, 3i
Michael Graham, Senior Managing Director & Head of North America
Education: BComm, Queen's University; MBA, Schulich School of Business, York University
Background: HSBC
Directorships: Kenan Advantage Group, EPIQ, Great Expressions Dental Centers, United States Infrastructure Corporation, Nordco, CHG Healthcare, Marketwired

2208 ONCAP
161 Bay Street
48th Floor
Toronto, ON M5J 2S1
Canada

Phone: 416-214-4300
e-mail: info@oncap.com
web: www.oncap.com

Mission Statement: Invests in and builds shareholder value in North American small and mid-sized companies that are leaders in their defined market niche and possess meaningful growth potential.

Geographic Preference: North America
Fund Size: $1.1 billion
Founded: 1999
Average Investment: $20 - $200 million
Investment Criteria: Equity Capital, Going Private Transactions
Portfolio Companies: AutoSource Motors, Bradshaw Home, Chatters, Davis-Standard, Enertech, Englobe, Hopkins Manufacturing, ILAC, IntraPac, Laces Group, Pinnacle Renewable Energy, Precision Global, Pure Canadian Gaming, Venanpri Group, Walter Surface Technologies, Wyse Meter Solutions

Other Locations:
712 Fifth Ave
40th Floor
New York, NY 10019
Phone: 212-582-2211

Key Executives:
Michael Lay, Managing Partner & Co-Head
e-mail: mlay@oncap.com
Education: Richard Ivey School of Business
Background: Ontario Teachers' Pension Plan Board; Versus Technologies
Gregory Baylin, Managing Director & Co-Head
e-mail: gbaylin@oncap.com
Education: Queen's University
Background: Scotia Capital
Mark Gordon, Senior Director
e-mail: mgordon@oncap.com
Education: Boston College; MBA, Richard Ivey School of Business
Background: Goldman Sachs & Co., BMO Nesbitt Burns
Mark MacTavish, Senior Director
e-mail: mmactavish@oncap.com
Education: Queen's University; MBA, Harvard Business School
Background: Whitney & Co., Lehman Brothers Merchant Banking

2209 ONEX PARTNERS
161 Bay Street
Toronto, ON M5J 2S1
Canada

Phone: 416-362-7711
e-mail: info@onex.com
web: www.onex.com

Mission Statement: Onex is one of North America's oldest and most successful private equity firms committed to acquiring and building high-quality businesses in partnership with talented management teams. The Company is guided by an ownership culture focused on achieving strong absolute growth, with an emphasis on capital preservation. With an experienced management team, significant financial resources and no debt at the parent company, Onex is well-positioned to continue to acquire and build businesses.

Geographic Preference: North America
Fund Size: $6.9 billion
Founded: 1984
Investment Criteria: Acquisitions, Carve-Outs, Restructurings, Consolidations
Industry Group Preference: Aerospace, Defense and Government, Healthcare, Industrial Products, Entertainment
Portfolio Companies: AIT, AutoSource, BBAM, BradshawHome, BrightSpring, Carestream, Celestica, Chatters, Clarivate Analytics, Davis Standard, Emerald Expositions, Englobe, Hopkins, IntraPac, Jack's, Jeld-Wen, Laces, Parkdean Resorts, Pinnacle, PowerSchool, Precision, Pure Canadian Gaming, Ryan, RSG, Save a Lot Food Stores, Schumacher, SGS Co., SIG, SMG, Survitec, Tecta America, Venanpri Group, Walter Surface Technologies, WireCo, York

Other Locations:
712 Fifth Avenue
New York, NY 10019
Phone: 212-582-2211

8 St. James's Square
London SW1Y 4JU

Venture Capital & Private Equity Firms / Canadian Firms

United Kingdom
Phone: 44 (0)20-7389-1540

930 Sylvan Avenue
Englewood Cliffs, NJ 07632
Phone: 201-541-2121

Key Executives:
  Gerry Schwartz, Chairman/Chief Executive Officer
  Education: MBA, Harvard Business School; LLB, BComm, University of Manitoba
  Background: Co-Founder/President, CanWest Capital
  Ewout Heersink, Vice Chairman
  Education: MBA, Queen's University; BBA, Richard Ivey School of Business
  Background: CanWest Capital, KPMG
  Robert Le Blanc, President and Head
  Education: BS, Bucknell University; MBA, New York University
  Background: Berkshire Hataway, General Electric
  Directorships: Magellan Health Services, Emergency Medical Services, Res-Care, Center for Diagnostic Imaging, Skilled Healthcare Group, The Warranty Group, Cypress Insurance
  Chris Govan, Senior Managing Director and CFO
  Education: BA, MA, University of Waterloo
  Background: Senior Tax Manager
  Anthony Munk, Vice Chairman
  Education: BA, Queen's University
  Background: Vice President, First Boston Corporation; Portfolio Manager, Guardian Capital
  Directorships: Cineplex, Barrick Gold Corporation, RSI Home Products, Tomkins Building Products, JELD-WEN Holding

2210 ONPOINT VENTURES
Toronto, ON
Canada

Mission Statement: OnPoint Ventures supports the advancement of Canadian start-up and scale-up businesses relating to health, medtech and commercialization.

Geographic Preference: Canada

Key Executives:
  Paul Weber, Managing Director
  647-504-4260
  e-mail: weberpaul112c@gmail.com
  Background: Founder, Toronto Medtech CEO Round Table
  Susan So, Partner
  e-mail: susanso416@gmail.com

2211 ONTARIO CAPITAL GROWTH CORPORATION
700 Bay Street
Suite 2401
Toronto, ON M5G 1Z6
Canada

Phone: 416-325-6874
Toll-Free: 877-422-5818
web: www.ocgc.gov.on.ca

Mission Statement: A joint initiative between the Government of Ontario and leading institutional investors to invest primarily in Ontario-based and Ontario-focused venture capital and growth equity funds that support innovative, high-growth companies.

Geographic Preference: Ontario
Fund Size: $455 million
Founded: 2009
Industry Group Preference: Clean Technology, Life Sciences, Media, Communications, Information Technology, Digital Media & Marketing

Key Executives:
  Steve Romanyshyn, President & CEO
  Education: MA, Economics, University of Victoria
  Background: Government of Ontario

2212 PANACHE VENTURES
3 Place Ville Marie
Bureau 12350
Montreal, QC H3B 0E7
Canada

web: www.panache.vc

Mission Statement: Seed stage venture capital fund.

Geographic Preference: Canada
Investment Criteria: Seed
Portfolio Companies: ACTO, MasterpieceVR, harbr, dooly, vyrill, MarketMuse, Communo, Lexop, Securicy, MobSquad, CTO.ai, certn, orchard, Wisk Bar Inventory, Audible Reality, aon3D, flinks, Colab Software, reDock, evree, spocket, Fleetops, InVivo AI, Lane, Wize, FightCamp, Green-eye Technology, Medstack, HumanFirst, Fispan

Other Locations:
  100 6 Avenue SW
  Calgary, AB T2G 2C4
  Canada

  101 College Street
  Suite 320
  Toronto, ON M5G 1L7
  Canada

Key Executives:
  Mike Cegelski, Managing Partner
  Patrick Lor, Managing Partner
  Education: Univ. of Calgary
  Background: 500 Startups, iStockphoto, Adobe

2213 PANGAEA VENTURES LTD
1500 West Georgia Street
Suite 1520
Vancouver, BC V6G 2Z6
Canada

Phone: 604-800-0411
e-mail: info@pangaeaventures.com
web: www.pangaeaventures.com

Mission Statement: Advanced materials venture capital.

Geographic Preference: North America, Europe, Asia
Fund Size: $157 million
Founded: 2000
Average Investment: $3 million
Minimum Investment: $250K
Investment Criteria: Commercial Products Based on Physical Science Innovations, Early Commercial Stage, Strong Management Team
Industry Group Preference: Advanced Materials, Clean Technology, Energy, Electronics, Health, Sustainability, Agriculture
Portfolio Companies: Airborne Intl., ESS Inc., A2M, Tivra Corp., Aspect Biosystems, Correlia Biosystems, NewLeaf Symbiotics, Redlen Technologies, Vestaron, Calysta, CarbonCure, polySpectra, Switch Materials

Other Locations:
  390 Amwell Road
  Bldg 3, Suite 318
  Hillsborough, NJ 08844
  Phone: 908-751-1360 **Fax:** 908-874-3854

Key Executives:
  Chris Erickson, Founder & General Partner
  e-mail: cerickson@pangaeaventures.com
  Education: BComm, University of Calgary; JD, University of Toronto
  Background: Partner, Osler Hoskin & Harcourt
  Purnesh Seegopaul, General Partner
  e-mail: pseegopaul@pangaeaventures.com

755

Venture Capital & Private Equity Firms / Canadian Firms

Education: BSc, Chemistry, University of Guyana; PhD, Chemistry, University of New South Wales
Andrew Haughian, General Partner
e-mail: ahaughian@pangaeaventures.com
Education: Bachelor of Applied Science, Mechanical Engineering, University of Toronto; MBA, Sauder School of Business, University of British Columbia

2214 PARALLEL49 EQUITY
1055 West Hastings Street
Suite 1060
Vancouver, BC V6E 2E9
Canada

Phone: 604-260-9570
web: www.p49equity.com

Mission Statement: A leading private equity firm that invests in profitable, well-managed, middle-market companies in Canada and the United States.
Geographic Preference: Canada, United States
Fund Size: $1.2 Billion
Founded: 1996
Investment Criteria: Acquisitions, MBO, Recapitalizations, Sales of Subsidiaries
Industry Group Preference: Manufacturing, Business Products & Services, Distribution, Consumer Products, Food & Beverage, Consumer Services, Waste & Recycling, Education, Financial Services, Healthcare, Logistics
Portfolio Companies: Certified Recycling, Gold Standard Baking, Kinetrex Energy, Questco, Tiger Calcium, BFG Supply, CPI Card Group, MedTorque

Other Locations:
225 East Deerpath Road
Suite 200
Lake Forest, IL 60045
Phone: 847-295-4410 Fax: 847-295-4243

Key Executives:
Brad Seaman, Managing Partner
847-295-4427
e-mail: bseaman@p49equity.com
Education: BBA, Bowling Green State University; MBA, University of Dallas
Background: Senior Vice President, Merchant Banking Business, General Electric Company
Directorships: CPI Card Group, Keyes Packaging Group, Strong Precision Technologies
Rod Senft, Founder & Investment Committee Member
604-646-4363
e-mail: rsenft@p49equity.com
Education: BComm, LLB, University of Manitoba
Background: Tricor Pacific Capital; Macluan Capital Corporation; Hines Nurseries; SunGro Horticulture; Davis & Company; Cargill (Canada) Inc.; Thompson, Dorftman, Sweatman
Directorships: Golden Boy Foods
Michael Eisinger, Vice President
847-295-4417
e-mail: meisinger@p49equity.com
Education: BA, Univ. of St. Thomas; MBA, Booth School of Business
Background: Arbor Investments

2215 PARKVIEW CAPITAL PARTNERS
105 Bedford Road
Toronto, ON M5R 2K4
Canada

Phone: 416-947-0123 Fax: 416-947-1877
e-mail: info@parkviewcapital.com
web: parkviewcapital.com

Mission Statement: Mid-market private investment firm in Toronto.
Geographic Preference: Canada
Founded: 1993

Average Investment: $10 to $30 million
Minimum Investment: $10 million
Industry Group Preference: Manufacturing, Business Products & Services, Energy, Aerospace, Defense and Government, Transportation, Financial Services, Education, Marketing
Portfolio Companies: Active Industrial Solutions, KV Custom Window and Doors, Labelink

Key Executives:
Donald Jackson, Chair & Founder
Education: BA, University of Alberta; MBA, University of Western Ontario Ivey School of Business
Background: President & CEO, Laidlaw
Directorships: Vector Aerospace, Northstar, Laidlaw, ADT, Attwoods, Trimac Limited, Derlan Industries
Catherine Herring, Managing Director
Education: HBA, Business Administration, Richard Ivey School of Business; MBA, Harvard Business School
Background: Royal Bank Equity Partners, Bain & Company, Morgan Stanley
Robert Bramer, Partner
Education: BComm, Queen's Univ.
Background: Ernst & Young

2216 PELORUS VENTURE CAPITAL
30 Harvey Road
Suite 2
St. John's, NL A1C 2G1
Canada

web: www.pelorusventure.com

Mission Statement: Venture capital company dedicated to building the Atlantic Canada ecosystem.
Geographic Preference: Atlantic Canada
Founded: 2015
Portfolio Companies: Hey Orca!, Clockwork Fox, Sentinal Alert, Sequence Bio

Other Locations:
1959 Upper Water St
Suite 1502, Purdy's Wharf Tower One
Halifax, NS B3J 3N4
Canada

Key Executives:
Chris Moyer, Director
e-mail: chris@pelorusventure.com
Education: BComm, Dalhousie Univ.; MBA, Saint Mary's Univ.
Background: GrowthWorks
Peter Clark, Director
Education: BA, Dartmouth College
Background: GrowthWorks Atlantic
Derek Lew, Director
Education: BA, Univ. of British Columbia; LLB, Univ. of Alberta
Background: GrowthWorks Capital

2217 PELOTON CAPITAL MANAGEMENT
8 King Street E
Suite 1100
Toronto, ON M5C 1B5
Canada

Phone: 647-957-8320
e-mail: info@pelotoncapitalmanagement.com
web: www.pelotoncapitalmanagement.com

Mission Statement: Peloton Capital Management is a Private Equity firm with long-term capital and investment orientation.

Key Executives:
Steve Faraone, Managing Partner
Education: BComm, University of British Columbia
Background: Managing Director, OTPP; BMO Capital Markets

Mike Murray, Managing Partner
Education: BComm, Queen's University; MBA, Tuck School of Business, Dartmouth
Background: Managing Director, OTPP; Bain & Co.

2218 PENDER WEST CAPITAL PARTNERS
1177 W Hastings Street
Suite 488
Vancouver, BC V6E 2K3
Canada

Phone: 604-669-1500

Mission Statement: Pender West invests in small- to medium-sized businesses in Canada. The company partners with no set hold periods or investment horizons

Geographic Preference: Canada, Western United States
Founded: 2000
Investment Criteria: Small Business, Medium Business, Buyout, Co-Investment
Industry Group Preference: Transportation, Logistics, Packaging, Recycling, Business Services, Manufacturing & Distribution
Portfolio Companies: Base 10 Group, Canada Film Capital, Dinoflex, EP Canada Film Services, Overland Container Transportation Services, Premium Brands, Tapp Label Technologies

Key Executives:
Bruce Hodge, Managing Director
e-mail: bhodge@penderwest.com
Education: MA, Economics, Queen's University; MBA, University of Western Ontario
Background: Founding Partner, CWC Capital; Vice President/Director, Pemberton Securites
Directorships: Base 10 Group, Canada Film Capital, Dinoflex, EP Film Services, Overland Container Transportation Services, Tapp Label Technologies
Wade Flemons, Managing Director
e-mail: wflemons@penderwest.com
Education: BEng, Industrial Engineering, Stanford University; MBA, University of Western Ontario
Background: Partner, CWC Capital; Pemberton Securites; Price Waterhouse
Directorships: Base 10 Group, Canada Film Capital, Dinoflex, EP Film Services, Overland Container Transportation Services, Tapp Label Technologies
Derek Senft, Director
e-mail: dsenft@penderwest.com
Education: BA, Dartmouth College; MBA, London Business School
Background: Principal, Tricor Pacific Founders Capital; Senior Associate, Tricor Pacific Capital; CIBC World Markets
Directorships: Base 10 Group, Canada Film Capital, Dinoflex, EP Film Services, Overland Container Transportation Services, Tapp Label Technologies
Rod Senft, Director
Education: Law, Business Administration, University of Manitoba
Background: Founder/Principal, Tricor Pacific Capital; Davis & Co.; Cargill Canada; Thompson, Dorfman, Sweatman
John Zaplatynsky, Director
Education: BSc, University of Manitoba
Directorships: Retail Merchants Association of BC, BC Landscape and Nursery Association, Premium Brands Holdings Corporation, Contech International Inc.
Carsten Sorensen, Director
Education: BSc, Finance, University of California, Berkeley
Background: CEO, The Orphanage; Proxicom

2219 PENFUND
Bay Adelaide Centre
333 Bay Street
Suite 610
Toronto, ON M5H 2R2
Canada

Phone: 416-865-0707 **Fax:** 416-364-4149
web: penfund.com

Mission Statement: Provider of junior capital to mid-market companies in North America.

Geographic Preference: North America
Fund Size: $1.8 Billion
Founded: 1979
Investment Criteria: Acquisitions, Recapitalizations, MBO, LBO, Reorganizations
Industry Group Preference: Consumer, Business Services, Healthcare
Portfolio Companies: 24-7 Intouch, Aveanna Healthcare, Caliber Collision, CBI Health Group, Forefront Dermatology, Give & Go, GoodLife Fitness, Hopkins, Mevotech, Mister, Pet Supermarket, Plews & Edelmann

Key Executives:
John Bradlow, Partner & Chair
416-645-3799
e-mail: jbradlow@penfund.com
Background: Founder, Private Equity Management Corporation
Richard Bradlow, Partner
416-645-3794
e-mail: richard@penfund.com
Education: BA, University of Western Ontario; MBA, Harvard University
Background: Scotia Capital
Adam Breslin, Partner
416-645-3796
e-mail: abreslin@penfund.com
Education: BA, McGill University; MBA, Wharton School
Background: Boston Consulting Group, C Bernstein & Co., CEO, Excentia, Imperial Capital
Directorships: Gesco Industries
Jeremy Thompson, Partner
416-645-3790
e-mail: jthompson@penfund.com
Education: BA, Economics, Queen's University
Background: Leveraged Finance, Goldman Sachs & Co.; Oak Hill Capital Management
Nicole Fich, Partner
e-mail: nfich@penfund.com
Education: HBA, Richard Ivey School of Business
Background: Onex Partners, GRI Capital
Joe Mattina, Partner
e-mail: jmattina@penfund.com
Education: BComm, McMaster University; CPA
Background: Apollo Management; MacQuarie Canada; Fortress Investment Group; GE Capital; KPMG
Denis Allman, Vice President, Tax & Accounting
e-mail: dallman@penfund.com
Nancy Turnbull, Vice President, Operations
416-645-3793
e-mail: nturnbull@penfund.com
Education: Bsc, Lauentian University
Background: Private Equity Management Corporation

2220 PERSISTENCE CAPITAL PARTNERS
600 de Maisonneuve Boulevard W
Suite 2000
Montreal, QC H3A 3J2
Canada

Toll-Free: 866-379-5842
e-mail: info@persistencecapital.com
web: www.persistencecapital.com

757

Venture Capital & Private Equity Firms / Canadian Firms

Mission Statement: Private equity firm focused exclusively on healthcare.
Geographic Preference: Canada
Founded: 2008
Average Investment: $5 to $10 million
Minimum Investment: $5 million
Investment Criteria: MBO, Recapitalizations, Divestitures/Carve Outs, Distress Situations, Growth Equity, Consolidations, Roll-Ups
Industry Group Preference: Healthcare
Portfolio Companies: AnimaPlus, Anova Fertility & Reproductive Health, functionability, kDa Group, LMC Diabetes & Endocrinology, MCA Dental Group, mdBriefCase, Medspa Partners, Rx Drug Mart
Other Locations:
  181 Bay Street
  Suite 4260
  Toronto, ON M5J 2T3
  Canada
Key Executives:
  Dr. Sheldon Elman, Founding Partner
  Education: McGill University Faculty of Medicine
  Background: Founder, Medisys Health Group
  Stuart M. Elman, Managing Partner
  Education: HBA, Richard Ivey School of Business
  Background: President, Medisys Health Group; Trader Classified Media
  Adrianna Czornyj, Partner
  Education: HBBA, Business Administration & Accounting, Wilfrid Laurier University
  Background: Deloitte; BDO Dunwoody LLP
  Directorships: Canadian Women in Private Equity
  Sean Karamchandani, Partner
  Education: AB, Economics, Harvard University; MBA, Columbia's Graduate School of Business
  Background: Monitor Group; Monitor Clipper
  John Trang, Partner
  Education: BComm, Queen's University
  Background: TorQuest Partners; Lloyds Banking Group; UBS
  Directorships: Lift Investments

2221 PFM CAPITAL
2nd Fl., The Assiniboia Club Bldg.
1925 Victoria Ave
Regina, SK S4P 0R3
Canada

Phone: 306-791-4855 Fax: 306-791-4848
e-mail: pfm@pfm.ca
web: www.pfm.ca

Geographic Preference: Saskatchewan
Fund Size: $728 million
Founded: 1989
Average Investment: $5-20 million
Portfolio Companies: Steel Reef Infrastructure Corp., Prairie Soil Services, Hi-Tec Profiles, Harbour Landing Village
Key Executives:
  Randy Beattie, President & Founding Partner
  e-mail: randybeattie@pfm.ca
  Directorships: Factory Optical, Hospitality Network, Hi-Tec Profiles
  Rob Duguid, Chief Executive Officer & Founding Partner
  e-mail: robduguid@pfm.ca
  Background: Crown Capital Partners
  Directorships: Steel Reef Infrastructure Corp., Auctus Property Fund, StorageVault Canada

2222 PINNACLE MERCHANT CAPITAL
Brookfield Place, TD Canada Trust Tower
161 Bay Street, Suite 3930
Toronto, ON M5J 2S1
Canada

Phone: 416-601-2270 Fax: 416-601-2280
e-mail: info@pincap.com
web: www.pincap.com

Mission Statement: Independent investor and financial advisory firm invests at all stages of the company life cycle.
Geographic Preference: Canada
Founded: 1998
Average Investment: $1 million
Investment Criteria: All Stages
Industry Group Preference: Information Technology, Software, Digital Media & Marketing, Internet
Key Executives:
  Arif N. Bhalwani, Managing Director
  Education: MBA, Queen's University; CFA
  Background: Managing Director, Third Eye Capital
  Hussein K. Bawa, Managing Director, Western Canada
  403-966-6814
  Education: BA, York University

2223 PIQUE VENTURES
142-757 West Hastings Street
Vancouver, BC V6C 1A1
Canada

web: piqueventures.com

Mission Statement: Pique Ventures is an impact investment and management company.
Founded: 2012
Industry Group Preference: Fashion, Digital Content, Digital Media & Marketing
Portfolio Companies: Beanworks, Careteam, ePACT Network, FoodMesh, MuseFind, myBestHelper
Key Executives:
  Bonnie Foley-Wong, Founder
  e-mail: bonnie@piqueventures.com
  Education: BS, Mathematics, MS, Accounting, Univ. of Waterloo

2224 PLAZA VENTURES
10 Wanless Avenue
Suite 201
Toronto, ON M4N 1V6
Canada

Phone: 416-481-2222 Fax: 416-481-8000
web: plaza.ventures

Mission Statement: Plaza Ventures focuses on high-growth, seed-stage technology companies looking for value-added capital, and micro-cap public technology companies looking for a breakout strategy.
Average Investment: $500K to $1.5M
Investment Criteria: Seed-Stage
Industry Group Preference: Real Estate, Enterprise Software, Digital Media, Mobile Technology, Artificial Intelligence
Portfolio Companies: 411.ca, Busbud, CareGuide, CareWorx, Dejero, Drop, FanXchange, Findspace, Hubba, Iguazio, Key Living, LANDR, Miovision, MMB Networks, Mobify, PostBeyond, Q4, StackAdapt, SweetIQ
Key Executives:
  Daniel Brothman, General Partner
  e-mail: danielbrothman@plazacorp.com
  Education: BA, York University; JD, Osgoode Hall Law School; MBA, Schulich School of Business
  Background: Corporate M&A
  Rob Richards, General Partner
  e-mail: rrichards@plazacorp.com
  Education: Physics Degree, University of Waterloo

Background: Nortel Networks, eCruiter
Directorships: Cavet Technologies, Locationary
Matthew Leibowitz, General Partner
e-mail: matthew@plaza.ventures
Education: HBA, Univ. of Toronto; MSc, Univ. of New South Wales; LLM, Oxford Univ.
Daniel Israelsohn, Vice President
e-mail: dan@plaza.ventures
Education: HBA, MBA, Richard Ivey School of Business

2225 PORTAG3 VENTURES
Toronto, ON
Canada

e-mail: info@p3vc.com
web: p3vc.com

Mission Statement: Invests in early stage financial tech companies with a potential for global impact.

Geographic Preference: Global
Fund Size: $400 Million
Founded: 2016
Investment Criteria: Early Stage, Financial Technology, Global
Industry Group Preference: Fintech, Artificial Intelligence, Data, Insurance, Wealth, Personal Finance, Banking
Portfolio Companies: Alan, Albert, Borrowell, Clark, ClearBanc, Collage, D1g1t, Dialogue, Drop, Flybits, Hellas Direct, Integrate.ai, Kin, Koho, League, LimelightHealth, Loot, Multiple, Neat, Planto, Quovo, Seed, Street Contxt, Stride Health, Wave, Wealthsimple

Key Executives:
Paul Desmarais III, Partner
Education: BA, Economics, Harvard College; MBA, INSEAD
Background: Risk Management Group, Great-West Lifeco; Imerys; Goldman Sachs
Adam Felesky, Partner
Education: BEng, Civil Engineering, BA, Political Science, McMaster University
Background: Horizons Exchange Traded Funds; JPMorgan Canada; CIBC World Markets; JPMorgan Derivative's Group
Samuel Robinson, President
Education: MA, English, MPhil, Modern Middle Eastern Studies, Christ Church
Background: Goldman Sachs
Directorships: Sagard Capital
Stephan Klee, Chief Financial Officer
Education: BA, Wilfrid Laurier University; MBA, Richard Ivey School of Business; AMP, Harvard Business School
Background: SoFi Banking Division

2226 PRIVEQ CAPITAL FUNDS
1500 Don Mills Road
Suite 711
Toronto, ON M3B 3K4
Canada

Phone: 416-447-3330 Fax: 416-447-3331
web: www.priveq.ca

Mission Statement: Private equity portfolio manager invests in niche service, distribution and manufacturing companies within 5 hours travel of Toronto, Canada.

Geographic Preference: Toronto Area
Fund Size: $85 Million
Founded: 1994
Average Investment: $3 to $7 Million
Minimum Investment: $3 Million
Investment Criteria: Expansion, Acquisition, Buy-out
Industry Group Preference: Niche Manufacturing, Distribution, Business Products & Services
Portfolio Companies: Integracare, Kraus Global, Accipiter, Frantic Films

Key Executives:
Bradley W. Ashley, Managing Partner
Education: JD, Osgoode Hall Law School; MBA, Schulich School of Business
Background: Senior Manager, Ernst & Young Corporate Finance; Assitant Treasurer, JP Morgan
Lee M. Grunberg, Partner
Education: BA, Economics & Political Science, McGill University; MBA, Schulich School of Business
Background: Associate Director, Merchant Banking
Directorships: R Nicholls Distributors, Frantic Films Corporation

2227 PRIVITI CAPITAL
850, 444 5th Avenue SW
Calgary, AB T2P 2T8
Canada

Phone: 403-263-9943 Fax: 403-265-1134
Toll-Free: 855-333-9943
e-mail: info@priviticapital.com
web: www.priviticapital.com

Mission Statement: Private equity firm specializing in the Canadian energy market.

Geographic Preference: Canada
Fund Size: $360 Million
Founded: 2007
Industry Group Preference: Energy, Oil & Gas, Natural Gas

Key Executives:
Ward Mallabone, President & CEO
e-mail: wmallabone@priviticapital.com
Education: BComm, University of British Columbia; Law Degree, University of Calgary
Background: COO/VP Law, Enervest Management Ltd
Robert Vargo, Chief Operating Officer
e-mail: rvargo@priviticapital.com
Education: BA, Russian Language & International Studies, Trinity University, San Antonio; MBA, University of Texas, Austin
Background: Management Consultant
Dave Ritchie, Vice President & Portfolio Manager
e-mail: dritchie@priviticapital.com

2228 QUANTUM VALLEY INVESTMENTS
560 Westmount Road North
Waterloo, ON N2L 0A9
Canada

e-mail: contact@quantumvalleyinvestments.com
web: quantumvalleyinvestments.com

Mission Statement: Private fund focused on the commercialization of breakthroughs in Quantum Information Science.

Geographic Preference: Canada
Fund Size: $100 million
Founded: 2013
Investment Criteria: Early-Stage
Industry Group Preference: Communications, Information Technology

Key Executives:
Mike Lazaridis, Co-Founder & Managing Partner
Education: University of Waterloo
Background: Co-Chairman/Co-CEO, Research In Motion/BlackBerry
Doug Fregin, Co-Founder & Managing Partner
Education: Electrical Engineering, University of Windsor
Background: Co-Founder, Research in Motion/BlackBerry

Venture Capital & Private Equity Firms / Canadian Firms

2229 QUARK VENTURE
2500-1075 West Georgia Street
Vancouver, BC V6E 3C9
Canada

Phone: 604-262-8818
web: www.quarkventure.com

Mission Statement: Vancouver VC firm focused on biotechnology and health sciences companies.

Founded: 2015
Portfolio Companies: ARTMS, Biscayne Neurotherapeutics, Canary Medical, CathWorks, Eloxx Pharmaceuticals, Eyevensys, Iome, Keros Therapeutics, Lyndra, Microbion Corporation, Phemi, PhysIQ, Pi Therapeutics, ReSolutionTx, Sitka Biopharma, SQZ Biotech, V-Wave

Other Locations:
608-80 Renming Road
Segment 2
Chengdu 610012
China
Phone: 86-18280375337

103-19 Xiangshan Road
District of High-Tech Development
Guangzhou 510665
China
Phone: 86-20-32068328-512

814-101 Arch Street
Boston, MA 02110
Phone: 617-880-9458

2001 Addison Street
Suite 337
Berkeley, CA 94704
Phone: 510-560-3370

Key Executives:
Jesson Chen, Chair & Partner
Education: Sichuan University; Sichuan MBA College; Southwest University
Karimah Es Sabar, CEO & Partner
Education: BSc, University of Salford; MSc, University of London; Cert., Sloan School of Management
Directorships: Triumf Innovations; Health & Biosciences Economic Strategy Table, Govt. of Canada
Franklin Jiang, COO & Partner
Education: BSc, Shanghai Jiotong University; MSc, University of Regina; PhD, UBC
Directorships: Stealth Energy, Sun Oil
Zafrira Avnur, Chief Scientific Officer
Background: Roche Partnering
Kaley Wilson, Director, Business Development
Education: PhD, University of British Columbia
Background: Centre for Drug Research and Development
Neena Kadaba, Director, Science
Education: MIT; CalTech
Background: California Inst. for Quantitative Biosciences
Directorships: Educational Council (MIT)

2230 RADAR CAPITAL
150 King Street W
Suite 1720
PO Box 47
Toronto, ON M5H 1J9
Canada

Phone: 416-800-6733 Fax: 416-862-2498
e-mail: info@radarcapital.ca
web: www.radarcapital.ca

Geographic Preference: Canada
Investment Criteria: Pre-IPO
Portfolio Companies: Kognitiv, Metamaterial Technologies, Bonne O

Key Executives:
Mark Lerohl, President
Education: Univ. of Alberta; Ivey Business School
Background: Canaccord Capital Corp.
Directorships: Big Brother Big Sisters

2231 RBC CAPITAL MARKETS
Royal Bank Plaza
200 Bay Street
Toronto, ON M5J 2W7
Canada

Phone: 416-842-7575
web: www.rbccm.com

Mission Statement: RBC Capital Markets is an international corporate and investment bank, offering customized products and services to institutions, corporations, governments and high net worth clients around the world.

Geographic Preference: North America, the UK, Europe, Asia-Pacific
Average Investment: $10 - $20 million
Investment Criteria: Mezzanine financing to mid-market
Industry Group Preference: Life Sciences, Technology, Telecommunications, Manufacturing, Business Products & Services, Consumer Products, Information Technology, Restaurants, Retail, Consumer & Leisure, Oil & Gas, Artificial Intelligence

Key Executives:
Doug McGregor, Chair
Education: BA, MBA, Univ. of Western Ontario
Background: Marcil Trust
Derek Neldner, CEO & Group Head
Education: BComm, Finance, University of Alberta; CFA
Directorships: Hospital for Sick Children Foundation, United Way of Toronto & York Region

2232 REAL VENTURES
Notman House
51 Sherbrooke Street West
Montreal, QC H2X 1X2
Canada

web: realventures.com

Mission Statement: A seed stage Venture Fund investing in web, mobile and digital media.

Geographic Preference: Canada
Investment Criteria: Seed-Stage
Industry Group Preference: Internet, Digital Media & Marketing, Wireless Technologies, SaaS, Mobile
Portfolio Companies: ROSS Intelligence, Swift Medical, Canvass, Mejuri, MindBridge

Other Locations:
MaRS Centre
101 College Street
Suite 140
Toronto, ON M5G 1L7
Canada

Key Executives:
JS Cournoyer, Founding Partner
Background: Co-Founder, Montreal Startup
Alan MacIntosh, Founding Partner
Background: President, OSMO Foundation
Directorships: McCord Museum, Quartier de l'Innovation, Mobile Giving Foundation Canada
John Stokes, Founding Partner

2233 RECAPHEALTH VENTURES
210 - 415 West Cordova Street
Vancouver, BC V6B 1E2
Canada

Phone: 604-512-8718

Mission Statement: RecapHealth Ventures supports opportunities that provide innovative solutions to the challenges facing health and social care systems around the world.

Geographic Preference: Canada, United States, Europe
Founded: 2011

Venture Capital & Private Equity Firms / Canadian Firms

Industry Group Preference: Healthcare
Portfolio Companies: Medeo, tyze, ThoughtWire, CML HealthCare, QHR Technologies, Health Innovations Group, YYoga, CoPatient, Vision Critical, Change Heroes, Ethelo, HealthEJourney, AlayaCare, KLUE

Key Executives:
Richard Osborn, Managing Partner
Education: University of British Columbia; Queen's University
Background: Co-Founder & Partner, Greenstone Venture Partners; Business Development Bank of Canada; Multiactive; Founder, BC Social Venture Partners
Matthew Moore, Partner
Education: University of California, Los Angeles; MBA, International Business, University of Geneva
Background: Netscape Communications; Healtheon; WebMD
Janelle Goulard, Associate
Education: MBA, Entrepreneurship & Innovation, University of British Columbia
Background: GE Healthcare

2234 RED LEAF CAPITAL
441 - 100 Innovation Drive
Winnipeg, MB R3T 6G2
Canada

Phone: 204-451-5243
web: www.redleafcapital.ca

Mission Statement: Red Leaf Capital is the first CVCA member based in Manitoba. They are a hybrid venture capital and management consulting firm in Manitoba.

Founded: 2009

Key Executives:
Stuart Henrickson, Founder
Background: Managing Director, National Bank of Abu Dhabi; CEO, Standard Bank, Dubai
Candy Dong, Investment Manager
Education: MBA, University of Manitoba
Background: AstraZenca

2235 REGIMEN PARTNERS
1285 West Pender Street
Suite 570
Vancouver, BC V6E 4B1
Canada

Phone: 778-379-1000
e-mail: info@regimenpartners.com
web: www.regimenpartners.com

Mission Statement: Private equity firm focused on buying and holding small businesses.

Portfolio Companies: Radial Engineering, CRS CraneSystems, Plastifab Industries, Central Technology Services, All Gold Imports

Other Locations:
151 Yonge Street
Suite 1100
Toronto, ON M5C 2W7
Canada

10072 Jasper Avenue
Suite 239
Edmonton, AB T5J 1V8
Canada

Key Executives:
Cooper Seeman, Managing Director
Education: Univ. of British Columbia
Background: Abacus Private Equity; Highgate Holdings
Gerry Bellerive, Managing Director
Education: Simon Fraser University
Background: Capital West Partners

David Eisler, Managing Director
Education: Queen's Univ.; Univ. of British Columbia
Background: Stern Partners; Banyan Capital Partners

2236 RELAY VENTURES
Bay Adelaide Center
333 Bay Street, Suite 1130
Toronto, ON M5H 2R2
Canada

Phone: 416-367-2440
e-mail: toronto@relayventures.com
web: relayventures.com

Mission Statement: Relay Ventures makes early-stage investments in mobile technology and services.

Fund Size: $800 million
Founded: 2008
Investment Criteria: Early Stage
Industry Group Preference: Mobile Technology, Mobile, SaaS, Digital Media & Marketing, Enterprise Software
Portfolio Companies: 7shifts, AdmitHub, Alate Partners, AngelList, Automat, Bird, Blue Ant Media, Blue J Legal, Circle, ecobee, FreshGrade, Good Buy Gear, Greenlight, Influitive, inPowered, Kira Talent, MobSquad, Mojio, Nymi, Payfone, Populus, PubNub, Quid, Rally Rd., Sherpa, Swift Medical, theScore, TouchBistro, Ujet

Other Locations:
3000 Sand Hill Road
Building 2, Suite 180
Menlo Park, CA 94025
Phone: 650-627-7749

474 Bryant Street
San Francisco, CA 94107
Phone: 650-600-8236

Key Executives:
Geoff Beattie, Chair
Education: JD, Univ. of Western Ontario
Background: Torys LLP, Woodbridge Company, Thomson Reuters
Directorships: General Electric, Maple Leaf Foods, Acasta Enterprises
John Albright, Co-Founder & Managing Partner
Education: BBA, Schulich School of Business
Directorships: OCAD University, Centre for Aging and Brain Health Innovation
Kevin Talbot, Co-Founder & Managing Partner
e-mail: kevin@relayventures.com
Education: BA, Strategic Studies, Rotman School of Management, University of Toronto; MBA, York University
Background: Royal Bank of Canada
Directorships: Kiip, Xobni, Payfone, WorldMate, Appia
Jake Cassaday, Partner
e-mail: jake@relayventures.com
Education: BA, McGill University; MBA, Rotman School of Management, University of Toronto
Background: Rotman Entrepreneurship & Venture Capital Association; Spin Master
Alex Baker, Partner
e-mail: alex@relayventures.com
Education: Schulich School of Business
Background: Management Consultant, BearingPoint; PWC Consulting
Directorships: Influitive, ClearFit, TribeHR, Payfone, Wiewdle, Neuralitic
Jeannette Wiltse, Partner & CFO
e-mail: jeannette@relayventures.com
Background: Director of Finance & Administration, RBC Venture Partners; Secretary-Treasurer, Euro Brokers Canada

761

Venture Capital & Private Equity Firms / Canadian Firms

2237 RELENTLESS PURSUIT PARTNERS
Canada

web: www.relentlesspursuitpartners.com

Investment Criteria: Early-Stage
Industry Group Preference: Health Technology
Portfolio Companies: Canary Medical

Key Executives:
  Brenda Irwin, Managing Partner

2238 RENEWAL FUNDS
The Flack Block
500-163 West Hastings Street
Vancouver, BC V6B 1H5
Canada

Phone: 604-424-9930
e-mail: sheila@renewalfunds.com
web: www.renewalfunds.com

Mission Statement: Mission venture capital firm investing in companies producing social and environmental change.

Geographic Preference: Canada, USA
Investment Criteria: Early Stage
Portfolio Companies: Back to the Roots, Cascadia Windows & Doors, Farmhouse Culture, FoodLogiQ, Goddess Garden, Ian's Natural Foods, Lotek, Mama Earth Organics, Miovision, Opti, Opus One Solutions, Prana, Rustic Crust, Sensible Organics, SPUD, Swiftly, Terramera

Key Executives:
  Carol Newell, Co-Founder
  Education: St. Lawrence University
  Paul Richardson, Managing & Founding Partner
  Education: Queen's University; University of Toronto
  Background: Fasken Martineau, Strathy & Richardson, Renewal Partners
  Directorships: Mama Earth Organics
  Joel Solomon, Founding Partner
  Background: Renewal Partners, Endswell Foundation
  Directorships: RSF Social Finance, Social Venture Network, Business for Social Responsibility, Tides Canada Foundation, Hollyhock

2239 RHO CANADA VENTURES
1500 Stanley
Suite A
Montreal, QC H3A 1P7
Canada

Phone: 514-944-4177
web: www.rhocanada.com

Mission Statement: A division of Rho Capital Partners investing in Canadian technology companies.

Geographic Preference: Canada
Fund Size: $100 Million
Founded: 2006
Investment Criteria: Early Stage
Industry Group Preference: New Media, Mobile Apps, Wireless Infrastructure, Semiconductors & Materials, Software (incl. SaaS)
Portfolio Companies: Acalvio, Aislelabs, Auvik, BounceX, Confirm.io, Exact Media, Fevo, Figure 1, Frank & Oak, Highline, Hyalto, Karma Gaming, LiveBarn, Plotly, Resson Aerospace, Smart Skin, Sociable Labs, SportlogiQ

Key Executives:
  Sean Brownlee, Partner
  Education: BA, MBA, Carleton Univ.
  Background: JMH Capital, 3i Corporation
  Roger Chabra, Partner
  Education: BA, Univ. of Western Ontario; MBA, Richard Ivey School of Business
  Background: GrowthWorks Capital
  Jeff Grammer, Partner
  Education: BA, MA, Boston Univ.

Background: Intel, Chips and Technologies, N*Able Technologies, Ember Corp.
  Habib Kairouz, Managing Partner
  Education: BA, BS, Cornell Univ.; MBA, Columbia Univ.
  Background: Reich & Co., Jesup & Lamont
  Peter Kalkanis, Chief Financial Officer
  Education: BS, City Univ. of New York
  Background: Eisner LLP

2240 RICHARDSON CAPITAL
1220 One Lombard Place
Winnipeg, MB R3B 0X3
Canada

Phone: 204-953-7969
e-mail: info@richardsoncapital.com
web: www.richardsoncapital.com

Mission Statement: Richardson Capital is the private equity division of Richardson Financial Group.

Geographic Preference: Canada
Fund Size: $500 million
Founded: 2004
Average Investment: $20 to $75 million
Minimum Investment: $20 million
Investment Criteria: Expansion Capital, Transition Capital
  Dave Brown, President & CEO
  204-953-7916
  e-mail: dave.brown@richardsoncapital.com
  Education: University of Manitoba; CA
  Background: Corporate Secretary, James Richardson & Sons; Partner, Gray & Brown

2241 RIPPLE VENTURES
410 Adelaide Street West
Toronto, ON M5V 1S8
Canada

web: www.rippleventures.ca

Mission Statement: Early-stage venture fund focused on "frontier technologies" in North America.

Geographic Preference: Toronto, Waterloo, Montreal, Boston
Average Investment: $250-500K
Minimum Investment: $250K
Investment Criteria: Early-Stage
Industry Group Preference: Enterprise Software, Healthcare Technology, Industrial Technology, Enterprise Blockchain, Media Technology
Portfolio Companies: OnúCall, Tread, voiceflow, Pitstop, omelas, Cybeats

Key Executives:
  Matt Cohen, Managing Partner
  Background: Turnstyle Solutions
  Michael Garbe, General Partner
  Background: Accelerated Connections

2242 ROADMAP CAPITAL INC.
130 Bloor Street W
Suite 603
Toronto, ON M5S 1N5
Canada

Phone: 647-748-0052 Fax: 647-748-0059
e-mail: info@roadmapcapitalinc.com
web: roadmapcapitalinc.com

Mission Statement: Roadmap Capital pursues high growth investment opportunities and seeks to create partnerships with outstanding companies.

Geographic Preference: Canada, United States
Founded: 2013
Industry Group Preference: Technology, Information Technology, Clean Technology, Healthcare, Life Sciences
Portfolio Companies: Corsa Technology, LiquiGlide, MMB Networks, Peraso Technologies, Perimeter Medical Imaging

Venture Capital & Private Equity Firms / Canadian Firms

Key Executives:
Riadh Zine, Co-Founder & Principal
Education: MSc, Financial Engineering, Ecole des Hautes Etudes Commerciales, University of Montreal
Background: Managing Director, Global Investment Banking, RBC Capital Markets; Royal Bank of Canada
Hugh Cleland, Co-Founder & Principal
Education: BA, Harvard University; CFA
Background: Research Associate, Midland Walwyn Capital; Analyst & Associate Portfolio Manager, Interward Capital Corporation; Portfolio Manager, Northern Rivers Capital Management
Imed Zine, Principal
Education: MSc, PhD, Electrical & Computer Engineering, University of Calgary
Background: Senior Engineer & Technology Advisor, CMC Microsystems; Research Associate, TRTech

2243 ROUND 13 CAPITAL
100 Broadview Avenue
Suite 300
Toronto, ON M4M 3H3
Canada

e-mail: info@round13capital.com
web: www.round13capital.com

Mission Statement: VC firm invests in growth-stage Canadian companies.

Geographic Preference: Canada
Investment Criteria: Growth Stage
Portfolio Companies: Affinio, Aislelabs, Article, Bluerush, Bold, HiMama, Hubdoc, Kooltra, Limelight, RouteThis, Sourced, Statflo, ThoughtWire, TouchBistro

Key Executives:
Bruce Croxon, Co-Founder
Background: Lavalife
John Eckert, Co-Founder
Background: McLean Watson Capital
Craig Strong, General Partner
Education: MBA, Rotman School of Management
Background: Fitzii, Deloitte, Ethos

2244 RUSSELL SQUARE PARTNERS
2 St. Clair Avenue W
Suite 1004
Toronto, ON M4V 1L5
Canada

e-mail: dbaum@russellsquarepartners.com
web: www.russellsquarepartners.com

Mission Statement: Russell Square Partners invest in Canadian businesses with growth opportunities.

Geographic Preference: Canada
Investment Criteria: Buyout, Recapitalizations, Transitions, Succession Plans
Portfolio Companies: Bitmaker, Pluck Tea

Key Executives:
Dan Baum, Managing Partner
Education: BA, McGill University; MBA, Harvard Business School
Background: Birch Hill Equity Partners; McKinsey & Co.
Directorships: Sleep Country Canada
Andy Burgess, Managing Partner
Education: BA, Princeton University; MBA, INSEAD
Background: CEO/Co-Founder, Somerset Entertainment; McKinsey & Co.; Loblaws
Directorships: Upper Canada College, Repath Industries, Alasko Foods, Hamburg Honda

2245 RYERSON FUTURES
Toronto, ON
Canada

web: www.ryersonfutures.ca

Mission Statement: Network of accelerator programs under the brand name Zone Startups.

Portfolio Companies: Buy Properly, Chatter, Esports Tickets, Evichat, Flipd, Flyshot, Halp, Intellisports, Maple Assist, SnapScreen

Key Executives:
Matt Saunders, President
Education: BS, MBA, Northeastern University
Alan Lysne, COO & Managing Partner
Education: Queen's University
Background: Davinci Technologies
Jam Michael McDonald, Director, Marketing & Communications
Education: Memorial University
Background: RateHub, Zoocasa, Jobpostings

2246 SAF GROUP
1900 Dome Tower
333 7th Ave SW
Calgary, AB T2P 2Z1
Canada

Phone: 403-984-1941
e-mail: info@safgroup.ca
web: www.streamasset.ca

Mission Statement: The SAF Group is a private equity firm that provides financing to companies in the energy, metals & mining, and commodities & marketing industries.

Geographic Preference: Canada
Fund Size: $2 billion
Founded: 2014
Industry Group Preference: Energy, Metals & Mining, Commodities, Marketing

Other Locations:
3123 Three Bentall Centre
595 Burrard Street
Vancouver, BC V7X 1J1
Canada
Phone: 403-984-1941

Key Executives:
Ryan Dunfield, Principal & CEO
Education: BA, Economics, University of Calgary
Background: Principal, Second City Capital Partners; Gibralt Capital Corp.
Aaron Bunting, Principal, COO & CFO
Education: BComm, Haskayne School of Business, University of Calgary; CFA; CA
Background: VP, K2 & Associates Investment Management; Director, Funds Management, Canoe Financial; VP, Mustang Capital Partners; Analyst, KPMG Advisory
Wiz Khayat, Principal & General Counsel
Education: BComm, University of Toronto; JD, University of Western Ontario; MBA, Richard Ivey School of Business
Background: Trimaven Capital Advisors; McCarthy Tetreault; Norton Rose
Dan Tsubouchi, Principal & Chief Market Strategist
Education: Saint Louis University; MBA, Univ. of Toronto
Background: GMP Securities, Haywood Securities
Directorships: Petrowest
Brian Paes-Braga, Principal & President, SAF Merchant Banking
Education: Harvard Business School
Background: Founder & CEO, Lithium X Energy Corp.
Directorships: DeepGreen Metals; Thunderbird Entertainment
Ryan Haughn, Principal, Energy
Education: MBA, Carleton University; CFA
Kyle Hickey, Principal, Metals & Mining
Education: BComm, McGill University; MA, University of Oxford
Background: BMO; JPMorgan

Venture Capital & Private Equity Firms / Canadian Firms

2247 SANDPIPER VENTURES
Canada

e-mail: hello@sandpiper.vc
web: sandpiper.vc

Mission Statement: Sandpiper Ventures is focused on investing in initiatives developed and led by women.
Founded: 2020
Investment Criteria: Women-Led or Founded
Key Executives:
  Cathy Bennett, Founding and Managing Partner
  Background: CEO, Bennett Group; CEO, TaskForce NL
  Rhiannon Davies, Founding and Managing Partner
  Background: GrandVision NV
  Sarah Young, Founding and Managing Partner
  Background: Managing Partner, NATIONAL Public Relations; Avenir Global

2248 SARONA ASSET MANAGEMENT
55 Victoria Street N
Unit K
Kitchener, ON N2H 5B7
Canada

Phone: 519-883-7557
e-mail: sarona@saronafund.com
web: www.saronafund.com

Mission Statement: The company invests in businesses and markets that allow for profitable growth and sustainable development.
Geographic Preference: Africa, Asia, Latin America, Emerging Europe
Fund Size: 500 million
Founded: 2010
Investment Criteria: Growth Stage, Mid Market,
Industry Group Preference: Healthcare, Financial Services, Consumer Goods & Services, Light Manufacturing, Transportation, Logistics, Communication Technology, Energy, Education
Other Locations:
  46 Claude Debussylaan
  Amsterdam, MD 10825
  The Netherlands
  Phone: 31.207981311

  400 Madison Avenue
  Suite 9-D
  New York, NY 10017
Key Executives:
  Gerhard Pries, Managing Partner/CEO
  Education: CPA
  Background: MEDA; PricewaterhouseCoopers
  Directorships: Grand Challenges Canada, ImpactAssets
  Paulus J Ingram, Partner/Deputy CEO
  Education: BA, Amherst College; MSc, International Finance, University of Amsterdam; LLM, Vrije University; LLM, Univerity of Amsterdam; CFA
  Background: APG Asset Management; Opportunity Fund; Capricorn Investment Group; Skoll Foundation
  Menno Derks, Managing Director Fund Investments
  Education: MA, Business Engineering, University of Twente; CFA
  Background: Senior Investment Manager, Investment Committeee Member, PGGM; FMO; ABN AMRO Asset Management
  Serge LeVert-Chiasson, Managing Director Impact Investment Advisory/COO
  Education: MSc, Accounting and Finance, London School of Economics; MBA, Schulich School of Business; CFA
  Background: Export Development Canada; Crédit Lyonnais; Founding Chair, Argo Captial Management
  Deborah de Rooij, Managing Director Trade Finance
  Education: BA, Economics, Amsterdam Schoool of Economics; RBA
  Background: Head of Emerging Market Debt, Head of Global Manager Selection, APG Asset Management; Senior Portfolio Manager, Achmea Gloal Investors

2249 SCALEUP VENTURES
114-250 The Esplanade
Toronto, ON M5A 1J2
Canada

web: suv.vc

Geographic Preference: Canada
Fund Size: $106 million
Founded: 2016
Investment Criteria: Early-Stage
Industry Group Preference: Technology
Portfolio Companies: autograph, Coconut Calendar, dooly, Flexitive, FundThrough, fusebill, mavencare, naborly, plooto, Revlo, roserocket, SoLink, Sonder, SortSpoke, Splash, Wysdom AI
Other Locations:
  3450 W 27th Ave
  Vancouver, BC V6S 1P6
  Canada

  Kevin Kimsa, Managing Partner
  Education: Univ. of Waterloo
  Background: Omers Ventures

2250 SCOTIABANK PRIVATE EQUITY
Scotia Plaza, 64th Floor
40 King Street West
Toronto, ON M5H 3Y2
Canada

Phone: 416-866-6506

Mission Statement: Private investment arm of Scotiabank.
Geographic Preference: Global
Average Investment: $5 to $25 million
Minimum Investment: $5 million
Investment Criteria: Mid- to Late-Stage
Industry Group Preference: Manufacturing, Industrial Goods, Finance, Consumer Products & Services, Technology, Building Materials & Resources
Key Executives:
  Peter Adamek, Director & Head
  416-945-4890
  Thomas Choi, Director
  416-945-4881
  Benoit Lacelle, Associate Director
  416-860-1260

2251 SEAFORT CAPITAL
Suite 701
CIBC Building
1809 Barrington Street
Halifax, NS B3J 3K8
Canada

Phone: 902-407-3766
e-mail: info@seafortcapital.com
web: seafortcapital.com

Mission Statement: Halifax-based investment firm with a diverse portfolio.
Geographic Preference: Canada
Founded: 2012
Industry Group Preference: Manufacturing, Distribution, Infrastructure
Portfolio Companies: AW Leil, Cooper Equipment Rentals, Jardine Transport, Mecfor, Titanium Energy Services
Key Executives:
  Rob Normandeau, President
  Education: BA, University of Western Ontario; MBA, University of Toronto
  Background: President & CEO, Clarke Inc.
  Directorships: IWK Children's Hospital Foundation,

Canadian Venture Capital & Private Equity Association, Rocky Mountain Liquor
Matthew Towns, Vice President
Education: BBA, Wilfrid Laurier University; MBA, St. Mary's University
Background: RBC Capital Markets; Imperial Oil Limited
Stephen Denton, Director, Investments
Education: BBA, MBA, Dalhousie University; CFA
Background: Manager, Commercial Banking, CIBC; Director, Research, Clarke Inc.
Directorships: Phoenix Youth Programs

2252 SEARCHLIGHT
22 Adelaide Street West
35th Floor
Toronto, ON M5H 4E3
Canada

Phone: 416-687-6590
web: www.searchlightcap.com

Geographic Preference: North America; Europe
Investment Criteria: Leveraged buyouts, growth equity, recapitalizations
Portfolio Companies: Ardent Hire Solutions, Cengage Learning, EOLO, Global Eagle, Gymboree, Hemisphere Media Group, Hunter Boot, Liberty Latin America, M&M Food Market, Mitel, Octave Group, PatientPoint, RackSpace, Roots, Shift4 Payments, Uniti

Other Locations:
745 Fifth Avenue
27th Floor
New York, NY 10151
Phone: 212-293-3730

56 Conduit Street
4th Floor
London W1S 2YZ
United Kingdom
Phone: 44 (0)20 7290 7910

Key Executives:
Oliver Haarmaan, Founding Partner
Education: Brown Univ.; Harvard Business School
Background: KKR & Co.
Directorships: Hunter Boot, EOLO
Erol Uzumeri, Founding Partner
Education: Univ. of Toronto; London Business School
Background: Ontario Teachers' Pension Plan
Directorships: M&M Food Market, Roots
Eric Zinterhofer, Founding Partner
Education: Univ. of Pennsylvania; Harvard Business School
Background: Apollo Management
Directorships: Charter Communications

2253 SECOND CITY REAL ESTATE
666 Burrard Street
Suite 3210
Vancouver, BC V6C 2X8
Canada

Phone: 604-806-3350 Fax: 604-661-4873
e-mail: info@secondcityrealestate.com
web: www.secondcityrealestate.com

Mission Statement: Private equity partnership focused on mid-market commercial real estate transactions.

Geographic Preference: North America
Founded: 2011
Industry Group Preference: Commercial Real Estate
Key Executives:
James Farrar, Managing Director
Education: CPA; CFA
Greg Tylee, Managing Director
Education: CA
Background: President, Bosa Properties

Ryan Chan, Chief Financial Officer
Education: BS, State University of New York; CGA
Background: Real Estate Investment Manager, Gibralt; Anthem Properties & Parklane Homes

2254 SERRUYA PRIVATE EQUITY
210 Shields Court
Markham, ON L3R 8V2

web: www.serruyaprivateequity.com

Mission Statement: Invests in various including retail, food & beverage, and cannabis. Commonly known as SPE.

Founded: 2010
Investment Criteria: $5M-$1B revenue
Industry Group Preference: Retail, Food & Beverage, Cannabis
Portfolio Companies: Global Franchise Group, Yogen Früz, Pinkberry, Swensen's, Yogurty's, Second Cup Coffee Co., STK, The Dirty Bird, Hydrofarm, Things Engraved, The Canadian National Institute of Health Inc., Persian Acceptance Corp., Chip and Pepper, Promenade, The Templar Hotel, Blue Mountain Village, Édifice Aldred, Jamba Juice, Famoso, Milestones, CoolBrands International, Kahala Brands, Fairweather, Tivoli Audio, Freedom Mobile, Sani-Service, The King Edward, The Town of Wasaga Beach, Laredo Hospitality, Aleafia, Verano Holdings, F/ELD, PROHBTED, Isodiol International, PLUS, Aphria

Key Executives:
Michael Serruya, Managing Director
Education: Ryerson University
Background: Chairman/CEO, Kahala Brands
Aaron Serruya, Managing Director
Education: Western University
Background: CEO, SU&BU
Simon Serruya, Managing Director
Directorships: Yogurty's Froyo; Swensen's Ice Cream; Yogen Früz
Gurion De Zwirek, Managing Director
Education: BA, Business Admin./Political Science, University of Haifa; MA, International Relations/Business, University of Toronto
Background: Former Naval Officer; Interim CEO, Things Engraved Inc.
Directorships: Tivoli Audio
Patrick Chung, VP, Finance
Education: BAFM, Accounting/Financial Management; MAcc, University of Waterloo
Background: Associate, Fuller Landau; Experienced Associate, PwC Canada; Assistant Manager of Finance Advisory, Deloitte; Director of Finance, Inside Edge Properties

2255 SIGNAL HILL EQUITY PARTNERS
2 Carlton Street
Suite 1700
Toronto, ON M5B 1J3
Canada

Phone: 416-847-1168
e-mail: admin@signalhillequity.com
web: www.signalhillequity.com

Mission Statement: Private equity firm focused on Canadian mid-market companies.

Geographic Preference: Canada
Fund Size: $300 million
Average Investment: $5 to $20 million
Minimum Investment: $5 million
Investment Criteria: Management Transitions, Restructurings, Acquisitions, Growth Equity
Industry Group Preference: Business & Consumer Services, Specialty Manufacturing, Building Products, Food & Consumer Products, Resource Services

Venture Capital & Private Equity Firms / Canadian Firms

Portfolio Companies: City Wide Towing, McIntosh Perry, C&V Portable, Romet, Westridge Cabinets, Shnier, Orbit Garant

Key Executives:

Patrick W.A. Handreke, Chair
Education: BA, Commerce & Economics, University of Toronto
Background: President & CEO, Northam Realty Advisors Limited

James C. Johnson, Managing Partner
e-mail: jjohnson@signalhillequity.com
Education: BComm, MBA, LLB, University of Windsor
Background: Senior Executive, Newcourt Credit Group; Co-Founder, Ironbridge Equity Partners
Directorships: Westridge Cabinets, Construction Control, Gesco Industries

Imran Siddiqui, Partner
e-mail: isiddiqui@signalhillequity.com
Education: BComm, McGill University; MBA, Wharton School
Background: Merrill Lynch
Directorships: City Wide Towing, OEL Projects, CCI Group

Fred Creasey, Chief Financial Officer
416-847-1501

2256 SKYPOINT CAPITAL

1371 E Woodroffe Avenue
Nepean, ON K2G 1V7
Canada

Phone: 613-727-5073 Fax: 613-727-8768
e-mail: info@skypointcorp.com
web: www.skypointcorp.com

Mission Statement: Early-stage investor in telecommunications and information technology.

Geographic Preference: Canada
Industry Group Preference: Telecommunications, Wireless Technologies

2257 STANDUP VENTURES

101 College Street
MaRS Discovery District, Suite 125
Toronto, ON M5G 1L7
Canada

e-mail: info@standupvc.com
web: standupvc.com

Mission Statement: StandUp Ventures champions breakthrough companies led by women.

Investment Criteria: At least 1 woman in a C-Level Leadership position and an equitable amount of ownership; enterprise software and digital health; seed stage

Key Executives:

Michelle McBane, Managing Director
Education: University of Ottawa; MBA, McMaster University
Background: Principal, Michelle McBane Consulting; Sr. Investment Director, MaRS Investment Accelerator Fund

2258 STERN PARTNERS

650 W Georgia Street
Suite 2900
Vancouver, BC V6B 4N8
Canada

Phone: 604-681-8817 Fax: 604-681-8861
e-mail: inquiries@sternpartners.com
web: www.sternpartners.com

Mission Statement: Stern Partners invest in companies from North America that have the potential for growth.

Geographic Preference: North America
Investment Criteria: Long-Term, Growth
Industry Group Preference: Manufacturing, Publishing & Printing, Distribution, Retail, Services

Portfolio Companies: Alberta Newsprint Company, Auld Phillips, Bootlegger Clothing, cleo fashions, Comark Services, Derksen Printers, FP Newspapers, Greenstar Plant Products, McMynn Leasing, McRae's Environmental Services, National Energy Equipment, OUTtv Network, Parian Capital Corporation, Parian Logistics, Port Hawkesbury Paper, Ricki's Fashions, Silver Jeans Co., TerraLink Horticulture, The Portables Exhibit Systems, Thinkingbox, Urban Barn, Warehouse One Clothing, Weskey Graphics, Western Glove Works

Key Executives:

Ronald N Stern, President
Background: Corporate and Commercial Law
Directorships: Vancouver Airport Authority, Vancouver East Cultural Centre, Vancouver General Hospital, Canadian Council For Israel and Jewish Advocacy

Norm Drewlo, Vice President
Background: Controller, Gas Equipment Supplies; President, National Energy Equipment

Shamsh Kassam, CFO/Vice President
Education: BComm, University of British Columbia; CA
Background: Vice President/CFO, Western International Communications; CanWest Global Communications

Shahid Pannun, Vice President
Education: CPA; CA
Background: Director of Finance, Global Container Terminals; Director of Finance, PNI Digital Media

Caroline Sanche, Vice President
Education: BBA, Marketing and Finance, Simon Fraser University; CA; CPA
Background: Associate Partner, KPMG; Interim CFO, Vancouver Board of Trade; Vice President, Finance, Rick Hansen Foundation

Keith Van Apeldoorn, Vice President, Taxation
Education: BComm, University of Saskatchewan; CA
Background: Arthur Andersen & Co.

Peter Roberts, Vice President, Technology
Background: Methanex; SK Group; Senior Consultant, Spectra Energy; SAP Managing Consultant, ISM; Managing Director, SAP Services, TELUS; Director of Consulting, Sierra Systems

2259 SUMMERHILL VENTURE PARTNERS

22 St. Clair Avenue E
Suite 1010
Toronto, ON M4T 2S3
Canada

Phone: 416-408-0700
web: www.summerhillvp.com

Mission Statement: Early-stage investor focused on the wireless, digital media and information technology sectors.

Geographic Preference: North America
Fund Size: $175 million
Founded: 1993
Investment Criteria: Early-Stage
Industry Group Preference: Mobility, Digital Media & Marketing, Enterprise Applications, Cloud Computing, Social Media

Portfolio Companies: Vantrix, BLiNQ, ScribbleLive, Sonian, C2FO

Key Executives:

Gary Rubinoff, Managing Partner
e-mail: grubinoff@summerhillvp.com
Education: LLP, University of Western Ontario School of Law; MBA, Richard Ivey School of Business
Background: Partner, JL Albright Venture Partners; Jefferson Partners LP

Joe Catalfamo, Managing Partner
e-mail: jcatalfamo@summerhillvp.com
Education: University of Waterloo
Background: EVP, CFO & Director, Whitecastle

Venture Capital & Private Equity Firms / Canadian Firms

Investments; Managing Director, Whitecap Venture Partners; KPMG
Directorships: Vantrix, Blinq, Radian6

2260 TACTICO
486 Saint-Catherine Street W
Suite 409
Montreal, QC H3B 1A6
Canada

e-mail: info@tactico.com
web: www.tactico.com

Mission Statement: Tactico is a hands-on venture capital firm focusing on start-ups and post-seed through Series A stage deals in technology-focused verticals, including FinTech and SaaS.

Geographic Preference: Canada, United States
Founded: 2008
Average Investment: $1 - 3 million
Minimum Investment: $10,000
Investment Criteria: Startups, Seed, Series A
Industry Group Preference: Fintech, Financial Services, Technology, SaaS Businesses, MarTech, Real Estate Tech
Portfolio Companies: Auticon, IRYStec, Moka, Pointus Partners, Soundskrit, Sportlogiq, StoneLock, Willful

Key Executives:
 Rick Ness, Managing Partner
 Education: BA, Economics, McGill University
 Background: Director, Link Energy Supply; Director, Sportlogiq; CEO/Director, Fidelit Clearing Canada ULC; President, Embanet; President/CEO, Penson Financial Services
 Liam Cheung, Managing Partner
 Education: BMath, MSc, Management, PhD, Economics, McGill University
 Background: Exec. Chairman, Mylo; CEO/COO/PM, Tactex; Managing Partner/Founder, Pointus Partners; COO, Embanet; SVP of Strategic Development; COO, Penson; President/Founder, LOC Info; EVP of Fixed Income Trading, Marleau Lemire Securities; Actuarial Specialist/Expert System Tech Developer, Towers Perrin
 Philippe Leroux, Partner/Legal Counsel
 Education: BSc/LLB, University of Montreal; MBA, HEC Montreal
 Background: VP/Associate General Counsel, Penson Financial Services Canada

2261 TANDEM EXPANSION FUND
460 McGill St
Suite 500
Montreal, QC H2Y 2H2
Canada

Phone: 514-510-8900
e-mail: info@tandemexpansion.com
web: www.tandemexpansion.com

Mission Statement: A growth equity investor in Canadian technology companies.

Geographic Preference: Canada
Fund Size: $300 million
Founded: 2009
Average Investment: $10 - $30 million
Minimum Investment: $10 million
Investment Criteria: Later-Stage
Industry Group Preference: Information Technology, Clean Technology, Energy Technology, Advanced Materials, Life Sciences
Portfolio Companies: Anaergia, Averna, Blueprint Software Systems, Coveo Solutions, Densify, Solace, Vertex Downhole

Key Executives:
 André Gauthier, Managing Partner
 514-510-8909
 Education: BBA, HEC Montreal; CA
 Background: EVP/CFO, Telesystem International Wireless

 Brent Belzberg, Co-Founder
 Education: BComm, Queen's University; JD, University of Toronto
 Background: Founder & Senior Managing Partner, TorQuest Partners
 Charles Sirois, Co-Founder
 Education: BS, Finance, University of Sherbrooke; MS, Finance, Laval University
 Background: Founder, Chairman & CEO, Telesystem; Chairman, Enablis Foundation Canada
 Directorships: Zone3 Inc., Propulsion Ventures Inc., ID Capital Management Inc., Argo Global Capital Inc., Rogers Communications

2262 TECH CAPITAL PARTNERS
8 Erb Street West
Waterloo, ON N2L 1S7
Canada

Phone: 519-883-8255 Fax: 519-883-1265
web: techcapital.com

Mission Statement: Venture capital firm focused on technology.

Geographic Preference: Waterloo Region
Fund Size: $95 Million
Founded: 2001
Average Investment: $500K - $2MM
Minimum Investment: $500,000
Investment Criteria: Seed, Early-Stage
Industry Group Preference: Communications, Electronic Technology, Information Technology, Photonics, Semiconductors, Telecommunications, Video Industry, Wireless Technologies, Infrastructure, Technology
Portfolio Companies: Avvasi, Bering Media, Ecobee, Fongo, Overlay.tv, Sidense

Key Executives:
 Andrew Abouchar, Co-Founder & Partner
 519-883-8416
 Education: Bachelor of Applied Science, BA, University of Waterloo; CFA, CA
 Background: Working Ventures Canadian Fund; Founder, Waterloo Ventures
 Directorships: Avvasi, Coverity, Sidense
 Tim Jackson, Co-Founder & Partner
 519-883-0959
 Education: BA, University of Waterloo; CA
 Background: CEO, Accelerator Center; Associate Vice President Commercialization, University of Waterloo; CEO/CFO, PixStream
 Directorships: Bering Media, Ecobee, FibreTech Telecommunications, LiveHive Systems, Metranome, PostRank, Q9 Networks, Sandvine, VideoLocus

2263 TECHNOCAP
4028 Marlowe
Montreal, NS H4A 3M2
Canada

Phone: 514-483-6000
e-mail: cpedroso@technocap.com
web: www.technocap.com

Mission Statement: Venture capital firm has been investing in small businesses since 1993.

Geographic Preference: Quebec, Ontario, Western Canada
Fund Size: $250 million
Founded: 1993
Average Investment: $6.5 Million
Minimum Investment: $3 Million
Investment Criteria: Startup, Expansion Stages, Proven Management, Management Style, 100% Dedication
Industry Group Preference: Technology, Telecommunications, Computer Related, Software, Electronic Technology, Instrumentation, Energy, Environmental Protection, Health Related

Venture Capital & Private Equity Firms / Canadian Firms

Portfolio Companies: Kinaxis, FreeBalance, BiblioMondo, DreamWater, SpaceWatts, Hyperchip, Yotta Yotta, GlobalMedic, telweb

Key Executives:
Richard Prytula, Chair & Founder
Education: BSc, Electrical Engineering, University of Saskatchewan; MBA, University of Western Ontario
Background: Owner, LNS Group

2264 TELESYSTEM
460 McGill Street
5th Floor
Montreal, QC H2Y 2H2
Canada

Phone: 514-397-9797 Fax: 514-397-1569
e-mail: info@telesystem.ca
web: telesystem.ca

Mission Statement: Family-owned media and technology investor since 1972.

Geographic Preference: Worldwide
Founded: 1972
Industry Group Preference: Healthcare, Environment Products & Services, Media, Entertainment, Internet, Software, Industrial Services, Digital Media & Marketing
Portfolio Companies: Zone3, Stingray, OnMobile, Coveo, iPerceptions, CVTCORP, Prevtec microbia

Key Executives:
Francois-Charles Sirois, President & CEO
Background: Founder & President, Up2 Technologies, Microcell i5, Masq Inc.
Directorships: Stingray Digital, Plexo, iPerceptions, Zone3
Charles Sirois, Chair & Founder
Background: BCE Mobile Communications; Teleglobe; Telesystem International Wireless; Microcell Communications
Directorships: Rogers Communications; Fondation de l'entrepreneurship
Denis M. Sirois, Vice President, Investments
Background: President, BCCL; Exaclan
Directorships: Exaclan, Plexo, iPerceptions, Opsens

2265 TELUS VENTURES
Telus Garden
510 W. Georgia Street
Vancouver, BC V6B 0M3
Canada

Fax: 604-438-0325
web: ventures.telus.com

Mission Statement: Investment arm of TELUS invests in innovative network technologies.

Geographic Preference: Canada, United States
Founded: 2001
Average Investment: $1 to $3 million
Minimum Investment: $1 Million
Investment Criteria: Early- to Late-Stage, Post-Beta Development
Industry Group Preference: Data Services, Internet Technology, Wireless Technologies, Telecommunications, Digital Media & Marketing, Networking
Portfolio Companies: Alithya, Beacon, DOmedic, Enstream, Fathom, Fortius Sport & Health, Get Real Health, League, MDS, Mojio, PatientSafe, Right Health, SecureKey Technologies, Sprout, Taulia, Vigilent, Vox Mobile
Richard Osborn, Managing Partner
Education: UBC; Queen's University
Background: RecapHealth Ventures
Directorships: Continuum, Fortius, Mojio, Right Health, ScaleUp Ventures, Vision Critical

2266 TENX VENTURES
4623 West 8th Avenue
Vancouver, BC V6R 2A6

e-mail: peter@tenx.biz
web: www.tenx.biz

Mission Statement: Invests in various Canadian industries.

Investment Criteria: Early-Stage
Industry Group Preference: Software, Robotics, Fintech, Cannabis
Portfolio Companies: Allocadia, QxMD, InvestX, Tagga, Immersive Media, Jones Rail Industries, Light Integra Technology, Lyft, Digital Domain, Campaign Monitor, CareCru, InsureCert Systems, CANBank, Chain Bureau, First National Digital Currency, Poseidon, Alphablock

Key Executives:
Mahala McCullagh, Managing Partner

2267 TERA CAPITAL CORPORATION
36 Distillery Lane
Suite 440
Toronto, ON M5A 3C4
Canada

Phone: 416-368-8372 Fax: 416-368-1427
Toll-Free: 1-888-368-8372
e-mail: info@teracap.com
web: www.teracap.com

Mission Statement: The company focuses on small capital equities room for growth in natural resources, clean energy, biotechnology and financial services.

Founded: 1996
Investment Criteria: Early Stage, Growth Markets, Mid Stage, Later Stage
Industry Group Preference: Natural Resources, Industrials, Clean Energy, Biotechnology, Financial Services
Portfolio Companies: Astound Inc., Electrophotonics, embotics, MKS, Opentext Corporation, Sierra Wireless, Truearc, VIQ Solutions, Vivecrop

Key Executives:
Howard Sutton, President
Education: PEng; MBA; CFA
Background: Partner, Goodman and Company
Directorships: Tera Capital, PESA

2268 TERALYS CAPITAL
999 Boulevard de Maisonneuve Ouest
Suite 1700
Montreal, QC H3A 3L4
Canada

Phone: 514-509-2080
e-mail: info@teralyscapital.com
web: www.teralyscapital.com

Mission Statement: Teralys Capital finances venture capital funds investing in information technology, life sciences and industrial innovations.

Geographic Preference: Canada
Fund Size: $2 Billion
Founded: 2009
Investment Criteria: Early-Stage, Growth & Expansion Stage
Industry Group Preference: Life Sciences, Clean Technology, Information Technology

Key Executives:
Jacques Bernier, Senior Partner
e-mail: jbernier@teralyscapital.com
Background: Senior Vice President, Solidarity Fund QFL
Eric Legault, Senior Partner
e-mail: elegault@teralyscapital.com
Background: Venture Capital Program, Caisse de depot et placements du Quebec
Luc Couture, Associate
e-mail: lcouture@teralyscapital.com

Background: Senior Investment Advisor, Solidarity Fund QFL
Cédric Bisson, Associate
Education: MD, McGill University; JD, University of Montreal
Background: McKinsey & Company
Directorships: ProCure, Montreal InVivo, Montreal Biennale of Art

2269 THE WESTERN INVESTMENT COMPANY OF CANADA
1010 24 Street SE
High River, AB T1V 2A7
Canada

web: winv.ca

Mission Statement: Publicly traded private equity company based in Western Canada.

Geographic Preference: Western Canada
Founded: 2015
Portfolio Companies: GlassMasters Autoglass, Golden Health Care, Ocean Sales, Foothills Creamery

Key Executives:
Scott Tannas, President and Chief Executive Officer
Background: Western Financial Group
Shafeen Mawani, Chief Operating Officer
Education: Simon Fraser Univ.; Ivey Business School
Background: CIBC World Markets; UBS Securities Canada
Directorships: GlassMasters Autoglass, Golden Health Care, Ocean Sales, Foothills Creamery
Stacey Cross, Chief Financial Officer
Directorships: GlassMasters Autoglass

2270 THERILIA
1010 Sherbrooke Street W
Suite 408
Montreal, QC H3A 2R7
Canada

Phone: 514-564-6474 **Fax:** 514-564-6424
e-mail: info@therillia.com
web: therilia.com

Mission Statement: Therilia is an autonomous company of Sanderling Ventures. It aims to cost effectively develop novel drug candidates from preclinical to clinical stages.

Key Executives:
Michael Dixon, President and CEO
Education: BComm, University of Toronto
Background: Chief Financial Officer, Gemin X Pharmaceuticals; VP, Finance, Morphometrix Technologies
Pierre Beauparlant, Chief Business Officer
Education: PhD, McGill University
Background: Medical Therapeutic Head, Hematology, Novartis Pharmaceuticals Canada; VP, Research and Development, Gemin X Pharmaceuticals

2271 TOP RENERGY INC.
1111 West Hastings St
Suite 790
Vancouver, BC V6E 2J3
Canada

Phone: 778-379-2891
e-mail: bp@toprenergy.com
web: www.toprenergy.com

Mission Statement: Investor in start-ups and early- and middle-stage companies in a broad range of industries including clean energy, education and manufacturing.

Geographic Preference: Canada, China
Founded: 2010
Investment Criteria: Startups, Early-Stage, Middle-Stage
Industry Group Preference: Technology, IT & Software, Social Media, Clean Energy, Supply Chain Management, Education, Healthcare, Manufacturing
Portfolio Companies: Srckode, Atiti, EraPlay, Cyclo‹des, Hausway, XParcels, Tabcon, Top in Nature, Eco Digitec, Top Canventure, Quality HVAC

Key Executives:
Chris Xie, President & Chief Executive Officer
Education: Wenzhou University; MBA, Schiller International University, Germany; MS, Financial Engineering & Risk Management, New York University
Background: Deputy of Business Administration Manager, Siemens
Stephan Siegel, Advisor
Education: BSc, University of Bayreuth, Germany; PhD, Finance, Columbia University
Background: Associate Professor, Department of Finance & Business Economics, University of Washington; Project Manager & Consultant, GCI Management

2272 TORQUEST PARTNERS
Brookfield Place
161 Bay St
Suite 4240
Toronto, ON M5J 2S1
Canada

Phone: 416-956-7022 **Fax:** 416-956-7000
e-mail: brock@torquest.com
web: www.torquest.com

Mission Statement: Private equity firm focused on the middle market.

Geographic Preference: Canada
Fund Size: $1 billion
Founded: 2002
Average Investment: $20 to $80 million
Minimum Investment: $20 million
Investment Criteria: Middle-Market; Entrepreneur or Family Successions, Corporate Carve-Outs, Public to Private, Management Buyouts, Recapitalizations
Industry Group Preference: Financial Services, Business Products & Services, Chemicals, Food & Beverage, Consumer Products, Manufacturing
Portfolio Companies: A&W, Bartek, Can Art Aluminum Extrusion, Cando Rail Services, Joriki, Maviro, McKeil Marine, Polycor, Prepac, Rubicon Pharmacies, SCM Insurance Services, The TEAM Companies, Universal Rail Systems

Key Executives:
Brent Belzberg, Senior Managing Partner
416-956-7006
e-mail: belzberg@torquest.com
Education: BComm, Queen's University; JD, University of Toronto
Background: Founder, Harrowston
Directorships: CIBC, Tandem Expansion Fund
Eric Berke, Managing Partner
416-956-7034
e-mail: berke@torquest.com
Education: BA, University of Vermont; MBA, Boston University
Background: President/CEO, Gustin Kramer
Daniel Sonshine, Partner
416-867-2482
e-mail: sonshine@torquest.com
Education: AB, Economics, Harvard University; JD, MBA, University of Toronto
Background: CIBC Capital Partners, CIBC World Markets
Directorships: Associated Brands, Herbal Magic
Craig Rankine, Partner & CFO
416-867-2484
e-mail: rankine@torquest.com

Venture Capital & Private Equity Firms / Canadian Firms

Education: BComm, University of Toronto
Background: Deloitte & Touche LLP
Matthew Chapman, Partner
416-867-2480
e-mail: chapman@torquest.com
Education: BSc, MSc, McGill University; MBA, Rotman School of Management, University of Toronto
Background: Workbrain, RBC Capital Markets
Directorships: Pinova Holdings
Michael Hollend, Partner
416-867-2487
e-mail: hollend@torquest.com
Education: LLB, MBA, University of Toronto; BA, Economics, University of Western Ontario
Background: Partner, EdgeStone Capital Partners; Goodmans LLP; Investment Banking, Griffiths McBurney & Partners
Directorships: 4Refuel

2273 TRELLIS CAPITAL CORPORATION
333 Wilson Avenue
Suite 600
North York, ON M3H 1T2
Canada

e-mail: info@trelliscapital.com
web: www.trelliscapital.com

Mission Statement: Trellis invests in Canadian growth technology companies.
Geographic Preference: Canada
Fund Size: $10 Million
Founded: 2000
Average Investment: $500,000 to $2 million
Minimum Investment: $500,000
Investment Criteria: Early- to Mid-Stage
Industry Group Preference: Industrial Products, Manufacturing, Alternative Energy, Infrastructure, Advanced Materials, Clean Technology, Semiconductors, Robotics, Technology
Portfolio Companies: BioAstra Technologies, Datec Coating Corporation, Flybits, Funnel Cake, Handshake VR, iS5 Communications, Rank, Teraspan Networks, Think Data Works, TrendMD, Volante System
Key Executives:
  Sunil Selby, Founder & Managing Partner
  Education: Richard Ivey School of Business, University of Western Ontario, MBA
  Dominic Talalla, Managing Partner

2274 TRICOR PACIFIC CAPITAL
1111 West Hastings Street
Suite 200
Vancouver, BC V6E 2J3
Canada

Phone: 604-646-4365
e-mail: opportunities@tricorpacific.com
web: www.tricorpacific.com

Mission Statement: Tricor Pacific is a leading Canadian family office investing in manufacturing, distriction, business services, food, real estate and private equity.
Geographic Preference: Canada and Mid-West to Western US
Founded: 1996
Investment Criteria: Mature Business; Generating EBITDA of $3-25 million; Seasoned Partners
Key Executives:
  Shawn Lewis, President and Managing Director
  604-646-4370
  e-mail: slewis@tricorpacific.com
  Education: BSc, LLB, McGill University
  Background: VP/General Counsel, Stern Partners
  Derek Senft, Managing Director
  604-726-5051
  e-mail: derek.senft@tricorpacific.com
  Education: BA, Dartmouth College; MBA, London Business School
  Background: Co-Founder, Founders Group of Food Companies; Owner, Presteve Foods, Totally Chocolate and Armand Agra; Owner/Director, Frontline Real Estate Services

2275 TRIWEST
4600, 400 - 3rd Avenue
Calgary, AB T2P 4H2
Canada

Phone: 403-225-1144 Fax: 403-225-3547
e-mail: info@triwest.ca
web: triwest.ca

Mission Statement: Western Canadian private equity firm.
Geographic Preference: Western Canada
Fund Size: $1.25 Billion
Founded: 1998
Average Investment: $15 to $50 million
Investment Criteria: Buy-Outs, Growth Financings, Corporate Divestitures, Special Situations
Industry Group Preference: Manufacturing, Distribution, Business Products & Services
Portfolio Companies: Broda Group, Bull Moose Capital, California Trusframe, Coast Appliances, Colter Energy, Fraser River Pile & Dredge, International Fitness Holdings, Kayden Industries, Lithion Power Group, Northern Mat & Bridge, Peloton Computer Enterprises, Prostar Energy, PRT-Growing Services, Source Energy Services, Strike Group, Trimlite Manufacturing, Triple M Housing, Zytech Building Systems
Key Executives:
  Jeff Belford, Senior Managing Director
  Education: BComm, University of Toronto; CA
  Background: CFO, Swiss Water Decafeinated Coffee Company; Director of Finance & Operations, Descente North America
  Ron Jackson, Co-Founder
  Background: President, Burns Foods
  Lorne Jacobson, Co-Founder & Vice Chair
  Background: Vice President, Corporate Development, General Counsel, Burns Foods Limited; Partner, Bennet Jones
  Mick MacBean, Senior Managing Director
  Education: BComm, University of Saskatchewan; CA
  Background: CEO, Diamond Energy Services; ARC Financial Corporation
  Norman Rokosh, Senior Managing Director
  Education: Engineering Degree, University of British Columbia; MBA, London Business School
  Dino DeLuca, Chief Operating Officer
  Background: Burnet, Duckworth & Palmer
  Chad Danard, Managing Director
  Education: BComm, Queen's University School of Business
  Background: Global Energy Group, Morgan Stanley
  Ryan Giles, Senior Managing Director
  Education: Business Administration, Richard Ivey School of Business; AB, Economics & Mathematics, Bowdoin College
  Background: Associate, Onex Corporation

2276 TVM LIFE SCIENCE MANAGEMENT
2 Place Alexis Nihon
Suite 902
3500 Boulevard de Maisonneuve W
Montreal, QC H3Z 3C1
Canada

Phone: 514-931-4111
web: www.tvm-capital.com

Venture Capital & Private Equity Firms / Canadian Firms

Mission Statement: Founded in Germany in 1983, TVM is now an international affiliation of PE and VC firms.

Key Executives:
 Hubert Birner, Managing Partner
 Education: MBA, Harvard Business School; PhD, Ludwig Maximilian University
 Background: Zeneca Agrochemicals; McKinsey & Company
 Directorships: CENTOGENE AG, SpePharm Holdings BV, leon nanodrugs GmbH, AL-S Pharma AG, Proteon Therapeutics, Acer Therapeutics
 Luc Marengere, Managing Partner
 Education: PhD, University of Toronto
 Background: Managing Partner, VG Partners; La Caisse De Depot; MDS Capital; MedTech Partners; Amgen
 Directorships: Emovi, Acanthas Pharma, Occelaris Pharma, Ixchelsis, PRCL Pharma, Panthera Dental, FAAH Pharma, Kaneq Biosciences, Acer Therapeutics, Rapid Micro Biosciences

2277 VANCITY CAPITAL
PO Box 2120
Station Terminal
Vancouver, BC V6B 5R8
Canada

e-mail: kalen_stewart@vancity.com
web: www.vancity.com/BusinessBanking/Financing/GrowthCapital

Mission Statement: A branch of Vancouver City Savings Credit Union, Vancity Capital invests in small- to medium-sized companies that have a positive influence in BC.

Geographic Preference: British Columbia
Average Investment: $500,000 - $5 million
Minimum Investment: $500,000
Investment Criteria: Subordinated Debt, Mezzanine Financing, Convertible Debentures
Industry Group Preference: Social Impact, Environment, Innovation

Key Executives:
 Kalen Stewart, Investment Manager
 e-mail: kalen_stewart@vancity.com
 Education: BComm, University of Victoria; CFA
 Background: Analyst, Capital Street Group; Analyst, Trilogy Properties; ARC Resources

2278 VANEDGE CAPITAL PARTNERS
1333 West Broadway
Suite 750
Vancouver, BC V6H 4C1
Canada

Phone: 604-569-3883
e-mail: info@vanedgecapital.com
web: www.vanedgecapital.com

Mission Statement: Vanedge is a Vancouver-based, early-stage venture capital fund.

Geographic Preference: Canada, United States
Fund Size: $296MM
Founded: 2010
Investment Criteria: Early-Stage, Later-Stage
Industry Group Preference: Cloud Computing, Artificial Intelligence, Cyber Security, SaaS, Digital Media
Portfolio Companies: AVA, Bitfusion, Bridgit, Boundless, Canalyst, Echodyne, Femtosense, GO-JEK, Hytrust, Illusense, Mediacore, Metafor, Omnisci, Plantiga, Playnomics, Plotly, Privacy Analytics, Quantum Benchmark, Recon Instruments, Rigado, RoosterBio, SensorUp, SpaceX, vArmour, Vendasta, Vodasafe, Wurldtech, xCures

Key Executives:
 V. Paul Lee, Managing Partner
 Background: President, Electronic Arts (EA)
 Directorships: DigiBC
 Moe Kermani, Managing Partner
 Education: MSc, PhD, Physics, University of British Columbia
 Background: Vice President, NetApp
 Micah Siegel, Partner
 Education: PhD, California Institute of Technology
 Background: C2C Ventures, Stanford Univ.
 Todd Tessier, Vice President & CFO
 Education: BComm, Univ. of Saskatchewan
 Background: Recon Instruments, BC Renaissance Capital Fund

2279 VERDEXUS
55 King Street West
Suite 700
Kitchener, ON N2G 4W1
Canada

Phone: 519-957-2230 Fax: 519-957-2239
Toll-Free: 888-713-4090
e-mail: canada@verdexus.com
web: www.verdexus.com

Mission Statement: Boutique firm focused on management buyouts and corporate divestitures.

Geographic Preference: Canada, United States, Europe
Founded: 2001
Investment Criteria: Management buyouts, corporate divestitures
Industry Group Preference: Information Technology, New Media, Mobile, Cyber Security, Software

Other Locations:
 London
 United Kingdom
 Phone: 44 2071 00 97 70 Fax: 44 2071 00 97 80

 San Francisco, CA
 Phone: 415-376-7230 Fax: 415-376-7239

 Munich
 Germany
 Phone: 49 89 12 14 09 175 Fax: 49 89 12 14 09 176

 Toronto, ON
 Canada
 Phone: 416-548-4730 Fax: 416-548-4739

Key Executives:
 Randall Howard, General Partner
 e-mail: rhoward@verdexus.com
 Education: B.Math, University of Waterloo
 Background: Founder, MKS
 Directorships: iotum
 Ray Simonson, General Partner
 e-mail: rsimonson@verdexus.com
 Education: Systems Designs Engineering, University of Waterloo; Finance Program, Queen's University
 Background: Coreworx, Bluegill Technologies
 Suresh Patel, Senior Advisor, Europe
 e-mail: spatel@verdexus.com
 Education: Artificial Intelligence, University of Brighton
 Background: Head of European Investments, Compaq Computer Corp.; Director, Netscape Communications Europe

2280 VERSION ONE VENTURES
Vancouver, BC
Canada

web: versionone.vc

Mission Statement: Version One Ventures is an early-stage fund investing in consumer internet, SaaS and mobile entrepreneurs.

Geographic Preference: North America
Average Investment: $200,000 - $500,000
Investment Criteria: Early-Stage
Industry Group Preference: Consumer Internet, Mobile, E-Commerce & Manufacturing, SaaS

Venture Capital & Private Equity Firms / Canadian Firms

Portfolio Companies: Abstract, Ada Support, AngelList, Blockstack, Booster Fuels, Celo, Chefit, Citizen Hex, Coinbase, Clio, Dapper, Dolly, Drover, Figure 1, Frank & Oak, Gencove, Guesser, Headout, Indiegogo, Indochino, Jobber, Kobalt, Lolli, Manifold, MetaStable Capital, Nexus Mutual, Outreach, Placenote, Pickle Robot, Polychain Capital, Preemadonna, Qurasense, Roost, Scanwell, Shippo, Smore, Top Hat, Trim, Unbounce, Wattpad, Yapta, Zenput

Key Executives:
  Boriz Wertz, Founding Partner
  e-mail: boris@versionone.vc
  Education: PhD, Graduate School of Management, Koblenz
  Background: AbeBooks.com
  Directorships: Andreesen Horowitz
  Angela Tran, Principal
  e-mail: angela@versionone.vc
  Education: Univ. of Toronto
  Background: Insight Data Science
  Directorships: Computer History Museum

2281 VERTU CAPITAL
150 King Street W
Suite 212
Toronto, ON M5H 1J9
Canada

web: vertucapital.ca

Mission Statement: Vertu Capital seeks to collaborate with teams in the Canadian technology industry that are building to go global.

Geographic Preference: Canada
Investment Criteria: Less than $20M Revenue; Enterprise Value between $75-250M

Key Executives:
  Lisa Melchior, Founder/Managing Partner
  Education: BA, Western University; MBA, York University
  Background: CIBC World Markets; OMERS Private Equity
  Kim Davis, Partner and COO
  Education: BComm, York University
  Background: Co-Founder, David Cornfield Melanoma Fund; CFO, TorQuest Partners; Senior Manager, Deloitte

2282 VRG CAPITAL
145 Wellington Street W
Suite 900
Toronto, ON M5J 1H8
Canada

Phone: 416-581-8850 Fax: 416-581-0020
e-mail: info@vrgcapital.com
web: www.vrgcapital.com

Mission Statement: VRG Capital Corp. is a Toronto-based private equity firm focused on investing in companies needing capital for growth, buyouts and mergers.

Geographic Preference: Canada
Founded: 1982
Investment Criteria: Acquisitions, Financings, Roll-Ups, Public Offerings
Industry Group Preference: Healthcare, Financial Services, Information Technology, Logistics, Insurance, Marketing/Sales Services

Other Locations:
  609 Granville Street
  Suite 805
  Vancouver, BC V7Y IG5
  Canada

Key Executives:
  Gordon Feeney, Chair
  Directorships: Finance Corp. of Bahamas, Moneris Solutions, Royal Mutual Funds
  J.R. Kingsley Ward, Managing Partner
  Education: BA, BComm
  Background: President, VRG; Chairman, Pareto Corporation
  Brock Bundy, Managing Partner
  Education: CMA, B.Soc.Sc.
  Background: Royal Bank of Canada
  Merv Simpson, Managing Partner
  Background: Senior Manager, Chartered Accounting Firm
  Greg Cochrane, Managing Partner
  Background: Co-Owner, Mariposa Communications & Promotions
  Directorships: Wheels Group
  Rod Campbell, Managing Partner
  Education: MBA, Univ. of British Columbia
  Background: Clarus
  Directorships: Jones Brown, Clarus Securities
  Michael Egan, Family Office Partner
  Background: InSystems Technologies
  Directorships: Real Matters
  Kerry Shapansky, Family Office Partner
  Background: Pareto
  Deborah McDonald, Chief Financial Officer
  Background: Royal Bank of Canada

2283 WATERTON GLOBAL RESOURCE MANAGEMENT
Commerce Court West
199 Bay Street
Suite 5050
Toronto, ON M5L 1E2
Canada

Phone: 416-504-3505 Fax: 416-504-3200
e-mail: info@watertonglobal.com
web: www.watertonglobal.com

Mission Statement: Waterton Global Resource Management is a private equity firm that specializes in the mining and metals sectors.

Geographic Preference: Canada, United States, South America
Fund Size: $1.75 billion
Founded: 2009
Average Investment: $10 - $300 million
Industry Group Preference: Mining, Metals

Key Executives:
  Isser Elishis, Managing Partner & Chief Investment Officer
  Background: Senior VP & Director, HSBC
  James Hennessy, Chair
  Background: President & CEO, ING Mutual Funds
  Directorships: Allis Chalmers Oil & Gas Services
  Cheryl Brandon, Partner, Investment Management
  Education: CFA
  Background: Leeward Hedge Funds; Duff Capital Advisors
  Jack McMahon, Partner, Head of Mining Operations
  Background: Tethyan Copper
  Richard Wells, Partner & Chief Financial Officer
  Education: CA
  Background: Manager, Financial Reporting, Magna International; PricewaterhouseCoopers

2284 WESLEY CLOVER
390 March Road
Suite 110
Ottawa, ON K2K 0G7
Canada

Phone: 613-271-6305
web: www.wesleyclover.com

Venture Capital & Private Equity Firms / Canadian Firms

Mission Statement: Ottawa-based super angel investor focused on information and communications technologies, and real estate and leisure properties.
Geographic Preference: Worldwide
Founded: 2000
Investment Criteria: Seed, Early-Stage, Follow-On
Industry Group Preference: Information Technology, Telecommunications, Digital Media & Marketing, Real Estate, Entertainment, Networking, Leisure, Cloud Computing, Mobile, SaaS
Portfolio Companies: Aydanaya, Benbria Loop, Brookstreet, Career JSM, Celtic Manor, Certn, Cliniconex, Codeherent, CounterPath, CreatorDen, CulturVate, Diskyver, Ecosec, Encepta, Encore Networks, English Ninjas, Enjovia, Filefacets, Hut Six Security, Hyalto, Hyas, ICC Wales, Init Live, Iven, KRP Properties, Learnium, Lota.cloud, Martello, Mydoma Studio, Pisano, Pretio Interactive, ProntoForms, ReactEvent, Referral Saasquatch, Reliving, Segmentify, Solace, Solink, SumoShift, Surple, Talkative, Taraspan, Teldio, ThinkRF, Twentify, WCS Europe, Wesley Clover Solutions

Other Locations:
3800 Concorde Parkway
Suite 1500
Chantilly, VA 20151
Phone: 703-318-4355

475 Park Avenue S
Floor 8
New York, NY 10016
Phone: 212-561-1320

240 Richmond Street W
Toronto, ON M5V 1V6
Phone: 613-271-6305

24, rue Jean Duplessis
Versailles 78150 Le Chesnay
France
Phone: 33 1 8381.2880

Business Central Towers, Tower A
Office 1604A, Internet City
PO Box 500826
Dubai
United Arab Emirates
Phone: 97 1 50 5545824

Key Executives:
Terry Matthews, Chair
Education: University of Wales
Background: Mitel, Newbridge Networks
Paul Chiarelli, President & COO
Background: Director, Finance, Tundra Semiconductor Corporation; Deloitte
Greg Vanclief, Managing Director, Global Investments
Background: VP, Corporate Planning, March Networks; Newbridge Networks

2285 WESTCAP
830, 410 22nd Street East
Saskatoon, SK S7K 5T6
Canada

Phone: 306-652-5557 **Fax:** 306-652-8186
e-mail: info@westcapmgt.ca
web: westcapmgt.ca

Mission Statement: Manager of niche investment funds.
Geographic Preference: Canada
Fund Size: $500 million
Founded: 1991
Industry Group Preference: Agriculture, Healthcare, Hospitality, Infrastructure, Innovation, Management Buyouts, Resources
Portfolio Companies: CanPro Ingredients, Superior Group of Companies, Golden Health Care, Ramada Plaza, Aria, Parliament Pointe, Sequoia, Shangri-La, Daxton, The Cayman, The Brixton, Kensington Flats, DynaIndustrial, Dyna Crane Services, Tackpoint, Fluid Clarification, Prairie Meats, Warman Home Centre, HJR Asphalt, Jump.ca

Key Executives:
Grant J. Kook, President, CEO and Founder
Background: President & CEO, Cheung On; President & CEO, Ramada Hotels

2286 WESTERN AMERICA CAPITAL GROUP
10025-102A Avenue
Suite 1500
Edmonton, AB T5J 2Z2
Canada

Phone: 780-496-9171 **Fax:** 780-496-9172
web: www.wacapital.com

Mission Statement: Private management and corporate buyout firm focused on mid-market manufacturing, distribution and service companies.
Geographic Preference: Western United States, Canada
Founded: 1987
Average Investment: Up to $50 million
Investment Criteria: Succession, Leveraged Buyouts, Management Buyouts, Acquisitions
Industry Group Preference: Manufacturing, Distribution, Business Products & Services, Oil & Gas, Construction, Software
Portfolio Companies: Canadian Forestry Equipment, Custom Welding Services, United Roadbuilders, Commercial Bearing Service, Northland Material Handling, Garneau Welding and Fabricating, Bri-Chem Supply, Sodium Solutions

2287 WHITE SHEEP CORP
141 Adelaide Street West
Suite 1200
Toronto, ON M5H 3L5

web: whitesheepcorp.com

Mission Statement: Invests and operates facilities that cultivate, process, extract, package, and distribute cannabis for medicinal & recreational use.
Geographic Preference: Canada, US
Founded: 2013
Industry Group Preference: Cannabis
Portfolio Companies: Altopa Inc., Oblend, Ample Organics, Cannabis Big Data, Biomedican

Key Executives:
Hamish Sutherland, President/Co-CEO
Education: BEng, McMaster University; MBA, Schulich School of Business, York University
Background: VP of Marketing, Strike Technologies; Director of Business Development, Research Now; President, Porcupine Goldor Mines; President/CEO, Hunter Porcupine Gold; Managing Partner, The Marketing Partners; COO, Kaypok Inc.; COO, Bedrocan Canada; COO, Asterio Cannabis Inc.
Michael Siltala, Co-CEO and Chief Legal Officer
Education: Queen's University; JD, Dalhousie University
Background: Professional NHL Player; Torys LLP
Bharat Choudhary, Chief Financial Officer
Education: University of Waterloo; CPA, CA, KPMG
Background: VP, Finance, TerrAscend Corp.; Director, Finance, Novadaq Technologies Inc.

2288 WHITECAP VENTURE PARTNERS
22 St. Clair Avenue E
Suite 1010
Toronto, ON M4T 2S3
Canada

Phone: 416-961-5355 **Fax:** 416-961-3232
e-mail: info@whitecapvp.com
web: www.whitecapvp.com

Venture Capital & Private Equity Firms / Canadian Firms

Mission Statement: Early-stage venture capital fund focused on information and communications technologies, food tech, and med tech.
Geographic Preference: Canada
Fund Size: $100 million
Average Investment: $2 to $5 million
Minimum Investment: $2 million
Investment Criteria: Early-Stage
Industry Group Preference: Healthcare, Medical Technology, Information Technology, Communications, Food & Beverage
Portfolio Companies: Bold Commerce, Nicoya, Second Closet

Key Executives:
  Carey Diamond, Partner
  e-mail: carey@whitecapvp.com
  Education: BA, Economics, University of Western Ontario; LLB, Osgoode Hall Law School
  Directorships: Broadband Networks, PC Docs Group, iMagicTV, Loran International, Protenergy
  Blaine Hobson, Chair, Investment Committee
  e-mail: blaine@whitecapvp.com
  Education: Richard Ivey School of Business, University of Western Ontario
  Directorships: Qvella, Real Matters
  Steve Lau, Partner
  e-mail: steve@whitecapvp.com
  Education: BBA, University of Toronto; MBA, Wharton Business School
  Background: Co-CEO, FieldEdge; CPPIB; TD Securities
  Russell Samuels, Partner
  e-mail: russell@whitecapvp.com
  Education: HBA, Richard Ivey School of Business; JD, University of Western Ontario
  Background: Senior Manager, Corporate & Business Development, Freshbooks; Associate, Mantella Venture Partners; Analyst, Canada Pension Plan Investment Board
  Shayn Diamond, Partner
  e-mail: shayn@whitecapvp.com
  Education: BA, Philosophy, University of Western Ontario; MBA, JD, Queen's University
  Background: Wildeboer Dellelce LLP
  Kim Coote, Vice President, Finance
  e-mail: kim@whitecastle.ca
  Education: BA, Economics, York University; CPA; CGA

2289 WHITEHORSE LIQUIDITY PARTNERS
200 Wellington Street West
Suite 600
Toronto, ON M5V 3C7
Canada

web: www.whitehorseliquidity.com

Key Executives:
  Yann Robard, Managing Partner
  Education: Dalhousie Univ.
  Background: Canada Pension Plan Investment Board
  Michael Gubbels, Partner
  Education: Wilfrid Laurier Univ.
  Background: Ontario Teachers' Pension Plan; OMERS Private Equity
  Giorgio Riva, Partner
  Education: McGill Univ.
  Background: Scotiabank
  Rob Gavin, Partner
  Education: Ivey Buesiness School, Western University
  Background: Denham Capital Management; BMO Capital Markets

2290 XPV WATER PARTNERS
40 University Ave
Suite 801
Toronto, ON M5J 1T1
Canada

Phone: 416-864-0475 Fax: 416-864-0514
e-mail: info@xpvwaterpartners.com
web: www.xpvwaterpartners.com

Mission Statement: XPV invests in and advises water-related companies.
Geographic Preference: Canada
Fund Size: $400 Million
Average Investment: Up to $25 million
Industry Group Preference: Water, Semiconductors, Building Materials & Services, Oil & Gas, Food & Beverage
Portfolio Companies: Aquatic Informatics, Atlas-SSI, BCR Solid Solutions, EOSi, FATHOM, Isle Utilities, LuminUltra, Metasphere Ltd., Mobiltex, Natural Systems Utilities, Newterra, Nexom, Organica, Shenandoah Growers, SmartCover Systems

Key Executives:
  David Henderson, Founder & Managing Partner
  Education: Ryerson Univ.
  Background: Kinghaven Capital Corp.
  Directorships: FATHOM Water Holdings, Newterra Group
  Khalil Maalouf, Partner
  Education: BComm, Concordia Univ.
  Background: VenGrowth Capital Partners
  Directorships: BCR Environmental Corp., Organica Water
  Sam Saintonge, Partner
  Education: BBA, Bishop's University

2291 YALETOWN VENTURE PARTNERS
1122 Mainland Street
Suite 510
Vancouver, BC V6B 5L1
Canada

Phone: 604-688-7807
e-mail: info@yaletown.com
web: www.yaletown.com

Mission Statement: Yaletown leverages an extensive on-the-ground network to seek out the most promising cleantech and IT investment opportunities.
Geographic Preference: Western Canada, United States
Fund Size: $160 million
Founded: 2001
Average Investment: $2 - $4 million
Investment Criteria: Early-Stage, Seed-Stage
Industry Group Preference: Clean Technology, Information Technology, Artificial Intelligence
Portfolio Companies: Circle Cardiovascular Imaging, Chaordix, Charli, Columbia Green Techologies, Cooledge, CTO.ai, Elastic Path, ePact, Equicare Health, Good Natured, Highline, Finn AI, Fluids Inc., Food.ee, LoginRadius, Mixpo, Mover, Redlen Technologies, Phemi Health Systems, Pretio Interactive, Showbie, Sokanu, Tasktop, ThoughtExchange, ThoughtWire, Tutela, Vizimax

Other Locations:
  1100 - 1st Street SE
  Suite 700
  Calgary, AB T2G 1B1
  Canada
  Phone: 403-444-8300

  1250 Rene Levesque Boulevard W
  Suite 2200
  Montreal, QC H3B 4W8
  Canada
  Phone: 514-548-2084

  56 Temperance St
  Suite 700

Toronto, ON M5H 3V5
Canada

Key Executives:
Salil Munjal, Managing Partner
604-800-2209
Education: BSc, University of Toronto; Law Degree, Queen's University
Background: COO, Leitch Technology
Directorships: Vizimax
Hans Knapp, Partner
Background: Brigill Investments
Shyam Gupta, Partner
Education: PhD
Background: SDP Telecom, Somel Investments
Brad Johns, Partner
Background: Moneta Capital, Nortel
Eric Bukovinsky, Partner
Background: Jefferies & Company
Sophie Gupta, Principal, Operations
Education: BComm, University of Ottawa; LLB, Laval University
Background: McCarthy Tetrault

2292 YELLOW POINT EQUITY PARTNERS
1285 West Pender Street
Suite 1000
Vancouver, BC V6E 4B1
Canada

e-mail: admin@ypoint.ca
web: www.ypoint.ca

Mission Statement: Mid-market investor now on its fourth fund.

Geographic Preference: Western Canada, Pacific Northwest United States
Founded: 2004
Average Investment: $5 to $25 million
Minimum Investment: $5 million
Investment Criteria: MBO, Going Private Transactions, Growth Capital Funding, Recapitalizations, Spin-Offs, Succession Planning
Industry Group Preference: Manufacturing, Technology, Communications, Energy, Financial Services, Healthcare, Business Products & Services
Portfolio Companies: Bravo Target Safety, Canadian Appliance Source, CBI Health Group, CIMS, Cast Steel Products, Edo Japan, Foley's, MacKay CEO Forums, RAMMP Hospitality, Remcan, Securiguard, Seymour Investment Management, The State Group, Viper

Key Executives:
Brian Begert, Co-Founder & Managing Partner
e-mail: bbegert@ypoint.ca
Education: BS, Economics, University of Southern California; MBA, University of British Columbia
Background: Founding Partner, Goepel Shields & Partners; Managing Director, Raymond James
Directorships: Prism Medical, Shanahan's, RAMMP, Seymour, CIMS
Dave Chapman, Co-Founder & Managing Partner
e-mail: dchapman@ypoint.ca
Education: BComm, Finance, University of Calgary; MBA, University of Western Ontario
Background: CEO, Greenlight Power Technologies; SVP, Merrill Lynch
Directorships: Crossroads C&I, We Care, CBV Collection Services

International Firms

Venture Capital & Private Equity Firms / International Firms

2293 21 PARTNERS
Via G. Felissent, 90
Treviso 31100
Italy
Phone: 39-0422316611 Fax: 39-0422316600
e-mail: info@21investimenti.it
web: www.21investimenti.it

Mission Statement: European private equity group providing capital, support and expertise to mid-market companies.
Geographic Preference: France, Southern Europe
Fund Size: $730 million
Founded: 1992
Average Investment: $1.22 - $111.44 million
Investment Criteria: LBO, Expansion, Development and Growth, Middle Market
Industry Group Preference: All Sectors Considered
Portfolio Companies: Adesso, Assicom, Cleor, CMG Silhouette Sports Club, Daltys, Digital Virgo, DGF, EGB Investments, Ethical Coffee Company, Farnese Vini, Forma-Dis, Forno d'Asolo, Ligier-Microcar, Nadella, Oberthur, Palmers, PittaRosso, Poligof, Potel & Chabot, SIFI, Sirti, Stroili Oro Group, Synerlab, Viabizzuno

Other Locations:
Via Montenapoleone 8
Milan 20121
Italy
Phone: 39-0277121311 Fax: 39-0277121333

9 Avenue Hoche
Paris 75008
France
Phone: 33-0156883300 Fax: 33-0156883320

37 Route du Creux de Genthod
Geneva 1294
Switzerland

Aleje Jerozolimskie 65/79
Warsaw 00-697
Poland
Phone: 48-226307575 Fax: 48-226307576

Key Executives:
Alessandro Benetton, Founding Managing Partner
Education: BS, Business Administration, Boston University; MBA, Harvard University
Background: Goldman Sachs
Directorships: Benetton Group, Edizione Srl, Autogrill
Gérard Pluvinet, Founding Managing Partner
Education: Institut d'Etudes Politiques
Background: Managing Director & Chairman, Societe Centrale pour l'Industrie
Dino Furlan, Managing Partner
Education: Ca' Foscari University of Venice
Background: Finance Department, Fiat Auto
Cedric Abitbol, Managing Partner
Background: Director, Private Equity, Capstone Palomar; VP, Private Equity, Unigestion
Francois Barbier, Managing Partner
Education: Ecole Superieure de Commerce
Background: Executive, Societe Centrale pour l'Industrie; CFO, Siaco
Henry Huyghues Despointes, Senior Advisor
Background: Executive, Societe Centrale pour l'Industrie
Matteo Chieregato, Partner
Education: University of Bologna
Background: Paladin Capital Partners; Fincomit
Andrea Mazzucato, Partner
Education: University of Padova
Background: Private Equity Partners; ABN Amro
Caroline Giral, Principal
Education: EMYLON Business School; Paris-Dauphine University
Background: KPMG
Giovanni Bonandini, Principal
Education: Bocconi University; CA
Background: 3i Group; KPMG

2294 212 CAPITAL PARTNERS
Eglence Sokak, No. 19
Arnavutkoy, Besiktas
Istanbul 34345
Turkey
e-mail: info@212ltd.com
web: www.212ltd.com

Mission Statement: 212 Capital Partners is a venture capital fund committed to investing in early stage Internet and technology companies in Turkey.
Geographic Preference: Turkey
Average Investment: $500,000 - $3 million
Investment Criteria: Early-Stage
Industry Group Preference: Internet, Technology, Communications, Software, Digital Media & Marketing, Cloud Computing
Portfolio Companies: ArcadeMonk, Hazinem, Hemen Kiralik, HotelRunner, IyziCo, Parca Deposu, Solvoyo, VizeraLabs

Key Executives:
Numan Numan, Managing Director
Education: BSc, Computer Science, Ege University
Background: Vice President, Goldman Sachs; CS First Boston; Dun & Bradstreet, GTE
Directorships: HemenKiralik.com, HotelRunner, IyziCo
Ali H Karabey, Managing Director
Education: University of Michigan
Background: Arthur Andersen; Morgan Stanley Capital International; Deutsche Bank
Directorships: Solvoyo, Hazinem.com, Parcadeposu.com
Dilek Dayinlari, Vice President
Education: BS, Mechanical Engineering, Yildiz Technical University; MBA, Strategy, Johnson & Wales University
Background: Director, Strategy & Analysis, Groupon; Senior Management Consultant, Communications & High Technology, Accenture; Business Developer, Koc Holding
Emre Kurttepeli, Investment Committee Member
Education: Columbia University
Background: Founder, Mynet Group; Founder, Fornet
Directorships: Endeavor
Mahmut L Unlu, Investment Committee Member
Education: Georgia Institute of Technology; MBA, Rice University
Background: Associate, Iktisat Bankasi; Assistant General Manager, Yatirim Bank; Co-Founder, Dundas Unlu

2295 350 INVESTMENT PARTNERS
4th Floor
Dorset House
27-45 Stamford Street
London SE1 9NT
United Kingdom
Phone: 44-02078324601
e-mail: invest@ctip.co.uk
web: www.ctip.co.uk

Mission Statement: CT Investment Partners LLP actively engages with entrepreneurs to build successful clean energy businesses. We invest in innovative, high-growth companies early in their lifecycles. At CT Investment Partners, our team knows that it's difficult to grow a business on your own. Since 2001, we have completed investments in 27 UK-based cleantech businesses, which have raised nearly £200 million in venture capital, making us one of the most active cleantech investors in Europe.

Geographic Preference: United Kingdom
Fund Size: £200 million
Founded: 2006
Average Investment: £500,000 - £10 million

Venture Capital & Private Equity Firms / International Firms

Investment Criteria: Early-Stage
Industry Group Preference: Clean Technology
Portfolio Companies: 4 Energy, CamSemi, Arieso, New Earth Solutions, Open Energi, Intamac, Helveta, Oxsensis, Aero Thermal, Acal Energy, Pelamis, Green Biologics, Imperative Energy, Senselogix, Cable Sense, Placefirst, EcoLogicLiving, Ultromex, Acoustic Sensing Technology

Key Executives:
Peter Linthwaite, Managing Partner
Education: Oxford University
Background: Founding Director, Royal London Private Equtiy Limited; Managing Director, Murray Johnstone Private Equity

2296 360 CAPITAL PARTNERS 360 Capital Management SA
13 Avenue de l'Opéra
Paris 75001
France

Phone: +33-01-7118-2912
e-mail: info@360capitalpartners.com
web: www.360capitalpartners.com

Mission Statement: 360 Capital Partners is a Venture Capital firm, investing in Innovation at full scale, in Europe and more particularly in France and Italy.

Geographic Preference: Europe, France, Italy
Fund Size: 350 million Euro
Founded: 1997
Average Investment: 2 million Euro
Minimum Investment: 500K Euro
Investment Criteria: Early-Stage, Seed-Stage
Industry Group Preference: Internet, Telecommunications, Clean Technology, Medical Technology, Media, Entertainment, Financial Services, New Materials, Engineering, Industrial Services, E-Commerce & Manufacturing, Robotics, Information Technology
Portfolio Companies: 21 Buttons, Alci, Alsid, Arbe Robotics, Balyo, BeMyEye, Bergamotte, Birdly, Brainiac, Casavo, CharityStars, Chronocam, Cubyn, Doveconviene/Shopfully, EarthCube, Eatalynet, Enerbee, Exotec, Exotrail, EZ-WHEEL, Fotokyte, HeyCater, Hi Bruno, ID5, Innoviz, Jobdisabili, LeSlipFrançais, Milkman, Musement, Neurala, Neutrino, Newlisi, Otherwise, PIQ, Qapa, Qopius, Seedcamp, Sophia Genetics, Supermercato 24, Tediber, The Socialite Family, Tiller, Traefik, TVTY, Unilend

Other Locations:
Via Brisa 3
Milan 20123
Italy
Phone: 39-0236560950

Key Executives:
Fausto Boni, General Partner, Milan
Education: BA, Economics, Bocconi University; MBA, INSEAD
Background: Co-Founder, Net Partners Ventures; McKinsey & Co.; L'Air Liquide
François Tison, General Partner, Paris
Education: ENST; MBA, Columbia University
Background: France Telecom; Assocate Director, Nomura; SVP, Europ@web
Emanuele Levi, General Partner, Paris
Education: University of Turin
Background: Unicredito Italiano Group; Bain & Co.; Lazard Investment Banking
Cesare Maifredi, General Partner, Milan
Education: MBA, Darden School of Business Administration, University of Virginia; MEng, University of Brescia
Background: McKinsey & Co.; Bain & Co.
Dominique Rencurel, General Partner, Paris
Education: MA, Université de Paris Dauphine
Background: BNP Paribas; Co-Founder, Orkos Capital

Nader Sabbaghian, General Partner, Paris
Education: MEng, MIT
Background: Accenture; McKinsey & Co.; CEO, BravoSolution; Founder, Bakeca

2297 3I ASIA PACIFIC 3i Group
6 Battery Road
Level 42, Unit 07
Singapore 049909
Singapore

Phone: 65-62322937 Fax: 65-62322943
e-mail: singapore@3i.com
web: www.3i.com

Mission Statement: Provides a comprehensive range of private equity and venture capital solutions across all funding stages, from start-ups through growth capital to buyouts.

Geographic Preference: Singapore, Southeast Asia, Hong Kong, Japan, Korea, Taiwan, India
Fund Size: $1.18 Billion
Founded: 1945
Average Investment: $95.04 Million
Minimum Investment: $2.37 Million
Investment Criteria: Early Stage, Growth Capital, MBO, MB, IBO
Industry Group Preference: Leisure, Engineering, Healthcare, Software Services, Manufacturing, Telecommunications, Information Technology, Oil & Gas, Transportation
Portfolio Companies: Focus Media, GST Holdings Ltd, Asia Renal Care

Key Executives:
Lisa Johnson, Director
Oliver Wong, Director

2298 3I AUSTRIA BETEILGUNG GmbH 3i Group
16 Palace St
London SW1E 5JD
United Kingdom

Phone: 44-2079753131 Fax: 44-2079753232
e-mail: vienna@3i.com
web: www.3i.com

Mission Statement: Actively seeking new investments.

Geographic Preference: Austria, Germany, London
Fund Size: $11 Billion
Founded: 1945
Average Investment: $95.04 Million
Minimum Investment: $2.37 Million
Investment Criteria: Seed, Early Stage, Start-up, Growth Capital
Industry Group Preference: Communications, Computer Related, Software, Electronic Technology, Private Equity, Infrastructure, Debt Management
Portfolio Companies: Hyperwave

Key Executives:
Simon Borrows, Chief Executive

2299 3I DEUTSCHLAND GESELLSCHAFT FUR 3i Group
Bockenheimer Landstraáe 2-4
Frankfurt am Main
Frankfurt 60306
Germany

Phone: 49-697100000 Fax: 49-69710000113
e-mail: frankfurt@3i.com
web: www.3i.com

Mission Statement: Investment activities range from early phase financing up to the financing of buyouts.

Geographic Preference: Germany
Fund Size: £15 Million
Founded: 1984

Venture Capital & Private Equity Firms / International Firms

Average Investment: $95.04 Million
Minimum Investment: $2.37 Million
Investment Criteria: Concentrates on start up and early growth enterprises
Industry Group Preference: Communications, Healthcare, Software, Electronic Technology, Semiconductors, Information Technology
Portfolio Companies: Gries Deco, DTMS, Epigenomics, Kontron Embedded AG, Igeneon, Element 5, SR Technics

Key Executives:
  Ulf von Haacke, Partner, Managing Director, Head of Industrial
  e-mail: london@3i.com
  Education: Degree in economics, PhD
  Background: serving on the boards of MVC MobilVideoCommunication AG,
  Directorships: Member of the Josef A. Schumpeter Gesellschaft.
  Peter Wirtz, Partner, Managing Director

2300 3I EUROPE PLC 3i Group
16 Palace St
London SW1E 5JD
United Kingdom

Phone: 44-2079283131 Fax: 44-2079753232
e-mail: kathryn.vanderkroft@3i.com
web: www.3i.com

Mission Statement: Investment activities: private equity, infrastructure, debt management.
Geographic Preference: UK, North America, Asia, Continental Europe
Fund Size: o14 billion
Founded: 1945
Investment Criteria: Private Equity, Infrastructure, Debt Management
Industry Group Preference: Business Products & Services, Healthcare, Consumer, General Industrial
Portfolio Companies: ACR Capital Holdings, Norma Group, Foster + Partners, Memora Services Funerarias, Mayborn Group, Quntiles, Transnational Corporation

Key Executives:
  Menno Antal, Managing Partner, Private Equity
  Julia Wilson, Group Finance Director

2301 3I GERMANY GmbH 3i Group
Bockenheimer Landstraáe 2-4
Frankfurt am Main
Frankfurt 60306
Germany

Phone: 49-697100000 Fax: 49-69710000113
e-mail: frankfurt@3i.com
web: www.3i.com

Mission Statement: Investment activities range from early phase financing up to the financing of buyouts.
Geographic Preference: Germany, Switzerland, Austria
Fund Size: £15 Million
Founded: 1984
Average Investment: $95.04 Million
Minimum Investment: $2.37 Million
Investment Criteria: Expansion, Leveraged Buyout, Management Buyout
Industry Group Preference: Communications, Healthcare, Software, Electronic Technology, Semiconductors, Information Technology
Portfolio Companies: Gries Deco, DTMS, Epigenomics, Kontron Embedded AG, Igeneon, Element 5, SR Technics

Key Executives:
  Laura Boeck, Associate Germany

2302 3I GESTION SA 3i Group
3 rue Paul Cezanne
Paris 75008
France

Phone: 33-173151100 Fax: 33-173151124
e-mail: paris@3i.com
web: www.3i.com

Mission Statement: 3i is an international leader in Private Equity. We focus on Buyouts, Growth Capital and Infrastructure and invest across Europe, Asia and North America. Our competitive advantage comes from our international network and the strength and breadth of our business relationships. These underpin the value that we deliver to our portfolio, shareholders and fund investors.
Geographic Preference: France
Fund Size: £15 Million
Founded: 1984
Average Investment: $95.04 Million
Minimum Investment: $2.37 Million
Investment Criteria: Expansion, Development, Mid-Market Buyout
Industry Group Preference: Healthcare, Industrial Products, Business Products & Services, Financial Services, TMT, Consumer Products
Portfolio Companies: Galva Union, Goto Software, Grands Vins De Girande, Meristem Therapeutics, None Networks, Repetto International, Tartine et Chocolat

Key Executives:
  David Fewtrell, Director
  Remi Carnimolla, Partner, Managing Director
  Denis Ribon, Partner, Managing Director, Head of Healthcare
  e-mail: paris@3i.com
  Education: MBA, HEC; University Veterinary surgeon de Lyon.
  Background: Veterinary surgeon
  Directorships: Consulting
  Stéphane Duhr, Director

2303 3I ITALY 3i Group
16 Palace Street
London SW1E 5JD
United Kingdom

Phone: 44-2079283131 Fax: 44-2079753232
e-mail: milan@3i.com
web: www.3i.com

Mission Statement: Actively seeking new investments.
Geographic Preference: Italy
Fund Size: Euro 500 million
Founded: 1945
Average Investment: Euro 200 Million
Minimum Investment: $2.39 Million
Investment Criteria: Expansion & Development Capital, Replacement Capital, Buyout & Buy in, All Stages
Industry Group Preference: Business Products & Services, Consumer, Healthcare, Industrial

Key Executives:
  Andrew Cox, Director
  e-mail: london@3i.com
  Education: ME, MBA
  Background: Sambonet. TTED (Table Top Engineering and Design). FEME,
  Directorships: Board member of AIFI, the Italian Venture Capital Association.
  Jonathan Crane, Director
  e-mail: london@3i.com
  Education: Electronic Engineering, MBA from INSEAD
  Background: Andersen Consulting, dealt with planning and development of information systems, and later at Arthur D. Little,
  Michael Curtis, Director
  e-mail: london@3i.com

781

Venture Capital & Private Equity Firms / International Firms

Education: Electrical Engineering/Industrial Automation, ENSEEIHT; IT Degree, ENSAE; MBA, Bocconi University in Milan
Background: management consultant at Andersen Consulting for four years (in London and Milan) focusing on business processes engineering and post merger integration projects.
Directorships: he worked in applied research in France
Anna Dellis, Director
e-mail: london@3i.com
Education: Doctorate, Business Economy
Background: Worked near the office of Bristol in England
Directorships: Auditor near KPMG

2304 3I SPAIN 3i Group
Calle Ruiz de Alarcó n 12 - 20.BM
Madrid 28014
Spain

Phone: 34-915214419 Fax: 34-915219819
e-mail: madrid@3i.com
web: www.3i.com

Mission Statement: Actively seeking new investments.
Geographic Preference: Spain
Fund Size: $1.18 Billion
Founded: 1995
Average Investment: $95.04 Million
Minimum Investment: $2.37 Million
Investment Criteria: Invests in buyouts in all sectors
Industry Group Preference: Diversified

Key Executives:
   Javier Martin, Senior Associate
   Education: MBA
   Background: Booz Allen and Consulting Hamilton
   Maite Ballester, Partner, Managing Director
   Education: MBA, Engineer of Mines
   Background: Executive of Investments in the office of Birmingham
   Directorships: Member of the committee of direction of the Spanish Association of Capital Risk.

2305 3I TEUPSCHLAND GmbH 3i Group
Bockenheimer Landstraáe 2-4
Frankfurt am Main
Frankfurt 60306
Germany

Phone: 49-697100000 Fax: 49-69710000113
web: www.3i.com

Mission Statement: A private equity and venture capital enterprise, leading world-wide, investment activities from early phase financing up to the financing of buyouts.

Geographic Preference: Germany
Fund Size: £15 Million
Founded: 1984
Average Investment: $95.04 Million
Minimum Investment: $2.37 Million
Investment Criteria: Seed, Startup, Early-Stage, First-Stage, Second-Stage, Expansion and Development
Industry Group Preference: Chemicals, Communications, Computer Related, Distribution, Electronic Components, Industrial Equipment, Life Sciences, Information Technology, Healthcare
Portfolio Companies: Gries Deco, DTMS, Epigenomics, Kontron Embedded AG, Igeneon, Element 5, SR Technics

Key Executives:
   Laura Boeck, Associate
   Education: Degree in Business
   Background: Lukas Hydraulik GmbH.
   Directorships: Board member of bwcon (Baden-Württemberg Connected). He is member of Rotary Stuttgart and also a fellow of the Alumni of St. Gallen University

Heiko Geissler, Associate Director
Education: MBA , Phd
Background: Bertelsmann AG as Executive Vice President for Corporate Development

2306 3I UK 3i Group
16 Palace Street
London SW1E 5JD
United Kingdom

Phone: 44-2079283131 Fax: 44-2079753232
e-mail: london@3i.com
web: www.3i.com

Mission Statement: Actively seeking new investments.
Geographic Preference: United Kingdom, USA, Asia, Europe
Fund Size: $1.18 Billion
Founded: 1995
Average Investment: $95.04 Million
Minimum Investment: $2.37 Million
Investment Criteria: Start-up and Early-Stage
Industry Group Preference: All Sectors Considered
Portfolio Companies: National Car Parks, Fairline Boats Holdings Ltd, Sparrowhawk Media, Hobbs, Bowater Building Products Limited, Bowater Home Improvements Limited, Huntswood CTC Ltd, Fairways Group (UK), Adande Refrigeration, Variable Message Signs, PD Services Ltd, Pap

Key Executives:
   Masaaki Fudeuchi, Senior Director
   e-mail: london@3i.com
   Education: MBA , Degree in Politics, Philosophy and Economics
   Background: Financial and strategy consultant for Arthur Andersen, RSM Robson Rhodes and the Kalchas Group
   Rowena Gracey, Senior Associate
   e-mail: london@3i.com
   Education: Degree in Mathematics and Management, CPA
   Background: Birmingham
   Directorships: Member of the Growth Capital leadership team and UK Growth Capital management group.

2307 3M UNITEK
Hermeslaan 7
Diegem 1831
Belgium

Phone: 02-7225111 Fax: 02-7200225
e-mail: 3munitek.be@mmm.com
web: www.3m.com

Mission Statement: A diversified technology company serving customers and communities with innovative products and services. Each of our seven businesses has earned leading global market positions.

Industry Group Preference: Consumer Products, Electronics, Health Related, Industrial, Safety and Graphics, Energy

Key Executives:
   Inge G. Thulin, Chairman, President & Chief Executive Officer
   Education: MBA, Economics & Marketing, Gothenburg University/IHM Business School;
   David W. Meline, Senior Vice President & Chief Financial Officer

2308 3T CAPITAL
46, rue Barrault
Paris 75634
France

e-mail: contact@3tcapital.com
web: www.3tcapital.com

Mission Statement: Focusing on technology transfer and innovative companies within the Information Technology and

Venture Capital & Private Equity Firms / International Firms

Communication sector from their seed, start-up and early-stage phases, and a partner with Institut Mines Telecom, Telecom Technologies Transfert (3T) is funded by the European Investment Fund, CDC Entreprises, within the framework of FSI France Investissement program, and Institut Mines Telecom. Founded by seasoned entrepreneurs with strong track record launching and growing technology companies, including successful transaction sales, Telecom Technologies Transfert (3T) is an independently managed Investment Fund.

Investment Criteria: Seed-Stage, Startup, Early-Stage
Industry Group Preference: Information Technology, Communications
Portfolio Companies: Recommerce Solutions, Ubicast, Go2mo, Luceor Wimesh Systems, Skerou, MuteeGaming.com, Plan Me Up, Green Bureau, Izypeo, Innes

Key Executives:
Daniel Caclin, Managing Partner
e-mail: daniel.caclin@3tcapital.com

2309 3TS CAPITAL PARTNERS 3i Group plc
web: www.3tscapital.com

Mission Statement: 3TS Capital Partners identifies, evaluates and recommends investments for the Funds it is advising. After the investment is made, 3TS represents the Fund either directly and/or with non-executive directors with positions on the Board and works with the management to fully support the development of the investee companies. Investors in the Funds include 3i, Cisco, Sitra, EBRD, and KfW among others.

Geographic Preference: Central Europe, Eastern Europe
Fund Size: $330 million Euro
Average Investment: $2 - $10 million Euro
Investment Criteria: Expansion Capital, Buyouts
Industry Group Preference: Technology, Telecommunications, Media, Marketing, Business Products & Services, Financial Services, Healthcare Services, Environment, Energy, Retail, Consumer & Leisure, Clean Technology, Pharmaceuticals, Software, Information Technology
Portfolio Companies: Expander, TMS Brokers, Romprest Service SA, Mobiltel EAD, Orange Slovensko, Elit Teknoloji, BKS Cable, InternetCorp, STK, ClickAd, Avangate, SolveDirect Service Management, LogMeIn, Systinet Corporation, PXP Group, Centrul Medical Unirea, Cycleenergy, Netretail Holding, Komex

Other Locations:
Wahringer Strasse 3/15 A
A-1090 Vienna
Austria
Phone: +43 1 402 36 79

Americka 23
Prague 2 120 00
Czech Republic
Phone: +420 225 990 847 Fax: +420 225 990 857

ul.Sienna 72/7
00-833 Warsaw
Poland
Phone: +48 22 890 22 15

50-52 Putul lui Zamfir St.
Et.2, Ap.5
Bucharest 1, RO-011367
Romania
Phone: +40 3 1100 0259

Buyukdere Caddesi Ecza
Sokak Safter Is Merkezi
Kat:6
Levent 34430 Istanbul
Turkey
Phone: +90 212 325 7653

Key Executives:
Pekka Santeri Maki, Managing Partner, Budapest/Vienna
e-mail: pmaki@3tscapital.com
Education: Helsinki University of Technology; Universidad Cumplutense in Madrid; Wirschaftsuniversitat Vienna
Background: Managing Partner, Red Catalyst Ltd
Jiri Benes, Partner
e-mail: jbenes@3tscapital.com
Education: BA and MA, Prague School of Economics
Zbigniew Lapinski, Partner
e-mail: zlapinski@3tscapital.com
Education: M.Sc., Warsaw School of Economics
Mihai Sfintescu, Partner
e-mail: msfintescu@3tscapital.com
Education: MBA, University of Washington
Elbruz Yilmaz, Investment Manager
e-mail: eyilmaz@3tscapital.com
Education: Economics, Ege University (Turkey); MBA, Pittsburg State University

2310 3W VENTURES Latour & Zuberbuhler GmbH
Oberdorfstrasse 124
Herisau 9100
Switzerland

web: www.3wventures.com

Mission Statement: We are funding or co-funding international internet startups up to USD 250,000.

Geographic Preference: Switzerland
Average Investment: CHF50'000 - CHF500'000
Industry Group Preference: Healthcare, Information Technology, Telecommunications, Gaming, New Media
Portfolio Companies: ForAtable.com, Lunchgate.ch, Inverstiere.ch, Blankpage AG, UEPAA!!, Shadow Government, Youblisher.com, Nanotion, Quitt.ch, Domo Safety, Hyperweek.net, Fontself.com, Medudem.com, Touchtown.ch, Annularspace, Store-Locator.com,

Key Executives:
Yves Latour, Founding Partner
Arvin Zuberbuehler, Founding Partner

2311 3i GROUP PLC
16 Palace Street
London SW1E 5JD
United Kingdom

Phone: 44-2079753131 Fax: 44-2079753232
web: www.3i.com

Mission Statement: An international investor, 3i Group PLC works with talented management teams to develop businesses that have potential for significant growth.

Geographic Preference: Worldwide
Fund Size: $1.3 billion
Average Investment: $100 - $300 million
Investment Criteria: High Growth, Mid-Market
Industry Group Preference: Business Products & Services, Financial Services, Industrial Services, Energy, Consumer Products, Consumer Services, Healthcare, Technology, Media, Telecommunications, Infrastructure
Portfolio Companies: ACR Capital Holdings, Action, AESSEAL, Agent Provocateur Limited, Amor GmbH, Aspen Pumps, Basic-Fit, BVG India, Cerenicimo, Christ, Dynatect Manufacturing, Element Materials Technology, Eltel Networks Oy, ESG, Etanco, EURO-DIESEL, GEKA GmbH, GIF, GO Outdoors, Hobbs, JMJ Associates, Lekolar, Loxam, Mayborn Group, Memora Inversiones Funerarias, MKM Building Supplies, Navayuga Engineering Company, OneMed Group, Polycopelyt, Q Holding, Quintiles Transnational, Refresco Gerber, Scandlines, SLR Consulting Limited, UFO Movietz Pvt, Weener Plastic Packaging Group

Venture Capital & Private Equity Firms / International Firms

Calle Ruiz de Alarcon n 12-2-B
Madrid 28014
Spain
Phone: 34-915214419 **Fax:** 34-915219819

Cornelis Schuytstraat 72
Amsterdam 1071 JL
Netherlands
Phone: 31-203057444 **Fax:** 31-203057455

3 Rue Paul Cezanne
Paris 75008
France
Phone: 33-173151100

OpernTurm
Bockenheimer Landstrabe 2-4
Frankfurt 60306
Germany

PO Box 7847
Stockholm 10399
Sweden
Phone: 46-850610100 **Fax:** 46-850621130

6 Battery Road
Level 42, Unit 7
Singapore 049909
Singapore
Phone: 65-62322937 **Fax:** 65-62322943

3rd Floor, Nicholas Piramal Tower
Peninsula Park
Ganpatrao Kadam Marg
Mumbai 400 013
India
Phone: 91-22-66523131 **Fax:** 91-22-66523141

One Grand Central Place
60 East 42nd Street
Suite 4100
New York, NY 10165
Phone: 212-848-1400 **Fax:** 212-848-1401

Key Executives:
Simon Borrows, Chief Executive
Education: University of London; MBA, London Business School
Background: Founder/Co-President, Greenhill; CEO, Baring Brothers International Limited; Corporate Finance, Morgan Grenfell
Directorships: The British Land Company PLC
Julia Wilson, Group Finance Director
Background: Arthur Andersen; Harrison PLC; Tomkins PLC; Group Tax Director, Cable & Wireless PLC
Directorships: Legal & General Group PLC
Menno Antal, Managing Partner/Co-Head, Private Equity
Education: MSc, Electrical Engineering, Delft University of Technology; MBA, IMD Switzerland
Background: Managing Director, Benelux; Heineken
Jeremy Ghose, Managing Partner/Debt Management CEO
Education: BA, Business Administration
Background: Executive Officer, Mizuho Corporate Bank
Alan Giddins, Managing Partner/Co-Head, Private Equity
Background: Managing Director, Societe Generale; Accountant, KPMG
Phil White, Managing Partner, Infrastructure
Education: MBA, London Business School
Background: Division Director, Infrastructure Funds, MacQuarie Group; Barclays; WestLB
Directorships: Anglian Water Group, Elenia
Ben Loomes, Managing Partner, Infrastructure/Group Strategy Director
Education: BA, Masters of Science, Experimental & Theoretical Physics, University of Cambridge
Background: Goldman Sachs; Greenhill; Morgan Stanley

2312 AAC CAPITAL PARTNERS
ITO Tower, 21st Floor
Gustav Mahlerplein 106
MA Amsterdam 1082
Netherlands

Phone: 31-203331326
e-mail: info@aaccapitalpartners.com

Mission Statement: AAC Capital Partners Holding is an investment management company with 1.7 billion Euro under management and two specialized investment funds, dedicated to mid-market buyouts in North-Western Europe.

Geographic Preference: Europe
Fund Size: 1.7 Billion Euro
Investment Criteria: Middle-Market Buyouts
Portfolio Companies: Exie, iRex Technologies, PIERIS Proteolab, NexWave Solutions

Key Executives:
Gerben Kujiper, Chairman
e-mail: gerben.kuijper@aaccapitalpartners.com
Education: Masters, Business Economics, Erasmus University
Background: ABN AMRO
John de Die, CFO/COO
e-mail: john.de.die@aaccapitalpartners.com
Education: MS, Econometrics & Mathematical Economics, Tirburg University
Background: SVP, Finance, KLM Royal Dutch Airlines

2313 AAVISHKAAR
13B, 6th Floor, Techniplex II, IT Park
Off Veer Sarvarkar Fly Over, Goregaon West
Mumbai 400 062
India

Phone: 91-2261248900 **Fax:** 91-2261248930
e-mail: funds@aavishkaar.org
web: www.aavishkaar.in

Mission Statement: Aavishkaar is a pioneer in early stage investing in the country and has been active in the space for over a decade. We are guided by the fundamental belief that investing in early stage entrepreneurial ventures can not only deliver commercial returns, but also bring about significant efficiencies and developmental impact to rural and underserved communities. Over time, Aavishkaar has built a track record of high impact scalable enterprises in its portfolio that span across seven key sectors, namely Agriculture and Dairy, Education, Energy, Handicrafts, Health, Water and Sanitation, Technology for Development and Microfinance and Financial Inclusion.

Geographic Preference: India
Investment Criteria: Early-Stage
Industry Group Preference: Agriculture, Education, Energy, Healthcare, Water, Sanitation, Technology, Rural Innovations, Handicrafts, Agriculture
Portfolio Companies: Mantra Dairy, INI Farms, Zameen Organic, Vaatsalya, GV Meditech, Swas Healthcare, MeraDoctor, Waterlife, Saraplast, B2R Technologies, Net Systems Informatics, Shree Kamdhenu Electronics, Vortex Engineering, Butterfly Fields, Karadi Tales Company, Rangusutra, Desert Artisans, Servals Automation, Vana Vidyut Private Ltd, Share Microfin, BASIX Group, Equitas, Grameen Koota, Utkarsh Microfinance, Suryoday Micro Finance, Belstar Investment

Key Executives:
Vineet Rai, Partner/Managing Director
Education: Indian Institute of Forest Management
Background: Co-Founder, Intellecap
P Pradeep, Partner/Executive Director
Education: MBA, Finance, Bachelor of Applied Science
Directorships: Belstar, Vaatsayla, Grameen Koota, Servals Automation

Venture Capital & Private Equity Firms / International Firms

2314 AB CAPITAL & INVESTMENT CORPORATION The Phinma Group
Units 1401-1403, 14th Floor Tower One & Excha
Ayala Triangle, Ayala Avenue
Metro Manila
Makati City 1226
Philippines
Phone: 632-8987555 Fax: 632-8987596
e-mail: customerservice@abcapital.com.ph
web: www.abcapitalonline.com

Mission Statement: Actively seeking new investments.
Geographic Preference: Philippines
Fund Size: $990 Million
Founded: 1980
Investment Criteria: Early Stage, Expansion, Startup
Industry Group Preference: Computer Hardware & Software, Consumer Services, Telecommunications

Key Executives:
Frank S. Gaisano, Chairman & Chief Executive Officer
e-mail: customerservice@abcapitalonline.com
Education: ME
Background: Director Cebu Holdings, Inc., Mapfre Asian Insurance Corporation, Governor and EVP of the Phil. Assoc.
Directorships: Trustee and Treasurer of the Phil. Stock Exhange Foundation, Inc
Senen L. Matoto, President and Chief Operating Officer

2315 ABB TECHNOLOGY VENTURES
Affolternstrasse 44
PO Box 8131
Zurich CH-8050
Switzerland
Phone: 41-43 317 7111 Fax: 41-43317 4420
web: new.abb.com/us

Mission Statement: Headquartered in Zurich, with offices in Silicon Valley and Washington, D.C., ABB Technology Ventures (ATV) invests in companies of strategic interest to ABB at all stages and in all parts of the world. Comprised of ABB veterans and seasoned venture capitalist professionals, ATV invests in high potential energy technology companies that improve performance while lowering environmental impact and which can benefit from ABB's technology development resources and global market access.
Geographic Preference: North America, Switzerland
Founded: 1988
Average Investment: $1 - $20 million
Industry Group Preference: Energy, Clean Technology, Wind Power
Portfolio Companies: Trilliant, Industrial Defender, Power Assure, Pentalum, Aquamarine Power, ECOtality, Validus DC Systems, TaKaDu, GreenVolts

Key Executives:
Alanna Abrahamson, Head of Investors Relations
Education: University of Bombay; LLM, University of Virginia School of Law; MBA, Harvard Business School
Background: Prudential, GE Capital

2316 ABINGWORTH MANAGEMENT LIMITED
38 Jermyn Street
London SW1Y 6DN
United Kingdom
Phone: 44-02075341500 Fax: 44-02072870480
e-mail: info@abingworth.com
web: www.abingworth.com

Mission Statement: Active investor in biotechnology and healthcare.
Geographic Preference: US, UK and Europe
Fund Size: $ 700 Million
Founded: 1973
Average Investment: $20-$80 million
Minimum Investment: $ 1 - 20 Million
Investment Criteria: Seed, Startup, Other Early Stage, Expansion and Development, Purchase of Quoted Shares
Industry Group Preference: Biotechnology, Medical, Life Sciences
Portfolio Companies: Ablynx, Akubio, Alexza Molecular Delivery Corporation, Dynogen Pharmaceuticals, Fovea, Gynesonics, Novexel, Portola Pharmaceuticals, PowderMed, Syntaxin

Other Locations:
3000 Sand Hill Road
B1-145
Menlo Park, CA 94025
Phone: 650-9260600 Fax: 650-9269782

890 Winter Street
Suite 150
Waltham, MA 02451
Phone: 781-4668800 Fax: 781-4668813

Key Executives:
Stephen Bunting, Managing Partner
Education: Degree in Biological Chemistry
Background: Biotechnology Editor, PJB Publications
David Leathers, Special Partner
e-mail: leathers@abingworth.com
Education: Chartered Accountant
Background: Director, Rothschild Asset Management; Biotechnology Investments Limited, GeneMedicine, GenPharm International and Pharming
Jonathan MacQuitty, Partner
e-mail: abingwthus@aol.com
Education: MA, Chemistry, Oxford University; PhD, University of Sussex; MBA, Stanford University
Background: Board of the Biotechnology Industry Organisation and is a Director of a number of biotech companies
Directorships: President of US Location
James Abell, Partner and CFO
e-mail: abell@abingworth.com
Education: Biology Degree, Chartered accountant
Background: KPMA; Consultant, Medical Research Council; Director, Cambridge Genetics; Chief Financial Officer, Prolifix Limited
Directorships: CFO
David Mayer, Partner
Education: PhD in biochemistry from Aston University, Birmingham, and a BSc in biology from Queen Mary College, London
Background: Pan-European Pharmaceuticals Analyst at investment bank, Dresdner Kleinwort Benson, Head of the Policy Unit at the Wellcome Trust
John Heard, Executive Partner and General Counsel
e-mail: info@abingworth.com
Education: PhD in Biological Sciences
Background: N M Rothschild & Sons as Advisor to Investments Limited
Directorships: Astex Technology, Aurora Biosciences, Cantab Pharmaceuticals, Devgen, Genetic Therapy, Hexagen and 3-Dimensional Pharmaceuticals.
John Shields, Executive Partner, Science and Technology
Education: PhD in Immunology, University of Glasgow
Background: Senior VP, Research, Cantab Pharmaceuticals; Glaxo Institute for Molecular Biology; Research Positions, Institute of Child Health, the University of London

2317 ABM AMRO CAPITAL FRANCE ABN AMRO Group
9 Avenue Matignon
Paris 75008
France
Phone: 33-0153936900 Fax: 33-0153936925

Venture Capital & Private Equity Firms / International Firms

Mission Statement: Actively seeking new investments. All sectors considered except banking, defense, real estate.
Geographic Preference: France
Fund Size: $118 Million
Founded: 2001
Average Investment: $59 Million
Minimum Investment: $35.6 Million
Investment Criteria: LBO, MBI
Industry Group Preference: All Sectors Considered
Portfolio Companies: Acteon, Tergal, Fibers, Cotterlaz, Bonna Sabla, JEC, Retif, Groupe Doucet, Salins

2318 ABOA VENTURE MANAGEMENT OY
Kluuvikatu 5
Helsinki 00100
Finland

Phone: 020-7798620 **Fax:** 358-24107779
e-mail: info@aboaventure.fi

Mission Statement: Aboa Venture has established itself as Western Finland's leading venture capital company. Aboa Venture offers equity financing and financing solutions, and a commitment to development work, and the shared risk with the entrepreneur.
Geographic Preference: Finland
Fund Size: $100 Million
Founded: 1994
Average Investment: $1.18 Million
Minimum Investment: $0.23 Million
Investment Criteria: Invests in unlisted Finnish small and medium-sized companies
Industry Group Preference: Life Sciences, Electronic Technology, Metals, Engineering
Portfolio Companies: Bio-Nobile Oy, BioTie Therapies Oyj, FIT Biotech Oyj, Hormos Medical Ltd Oy, Juvantia Pharma Ltd Oy, Bitboys Oy, Sanako Corporation, Mios e-Solutions Oy, Nisamest Oy, TR-Tech. Int Oy, Dino Lift Oy, DWT-Engineering Oy, Finn Lamex Safety Glass Oy, Hydrovoima

2319 ABRIS CAPITAL
Grzybowska Park
ul. Grzybowska 5A
Warsaw 00-132
Poland

Phone: 48-225645858 **Fax:** 48-225645859
e-mail: warsaw@abris-capital.com
web: www.abris-capital.com

Key Executives:
Neil Milne, Managing Partner

2320 ABRT VENTURE FUND
5, Building 4, Bersenevskaya
emb. Golden Island
Moscow 119072
Russia

Phone: 7-812-335-5545
e-mail: project@abrtfund.com
web: www.abrtfund.com

Mission Statement: ABRT Venture Fund helps entrepreneurs build world-class software companies.
Investment Criteria: Seed, Startup, Early-Stage, Growth-Stage
Industry Group Preference: Software, Consumer Software, SaaS, Internet, New Media, Mobility
Portfolio Companies: HomeMe.ru, StarWind Software, Acronis, InvisibleCRM, OKTOGO, Drimmi, Veeam Software, KupiVIP, AutomationQA
Key Executives:
Andrei Baronov, Partner
Education: Master's Degree, PhD, Physics & Technology, Moscow Institute of Physics & Technology
Background: R&D Director, Microsoft Business Unit, Quest

2321 ABU DHABI INVESTMENT AUTHORITY
211 Corniche Street
P.O. Box 3600
Abu Dhabi
United Arab Emirates

Phone: 971-24150000 **Fax:** 971-24151000
web: www.adia.ae

Mission Statement: Actively seeking new investments.
Geographic Preference: UAE
Fund Size: $2 Billion
Founded: 1977
Investment Criteria: Leveraged Buyout, Management Buyout, Recapitalization, Second Stage
Industry Group Preference: Advertising, Broadcasting, Business to Business, Communications, Equipment, Computer Related, Computer Hardware & Software, Consumer Services, Diversified, Electronic Technology, Entertainment, Film, Financial Services, Food Services
Key Executives:
Sheikh Khalifa bin Zayed Al Nahyan, Chairman
Sheikh Hamed bin Zayed Al Nahyan, Managing Director

2322 ACACIA CAPITAL PARTNERS
CPCI, Capital Park
Fullbourn, Cambridge CB21 5XE
United Kingdom

Phone: 44-2072997399
e-mail: info@acaciacp.com
web: www.acaciacp.com

Mission Statement: Acacia Capital Partners is an independent management company made up of experienced venture capitalists with in-depth operational and investment management experience. We invest in later stage innovative technology companies both directly and indirectly.
Investment Criteria: Later-Stage
Industry Group Preference: Technology
Portfolio Companies: Skinkers, Mirics Semiconductor, Xmos, Lionhead Studios, Solarflame Communications, Shazam, Empower, Automsoft, Clariteam
Key Executives:
Christopher Smart, General Partner
Education: MSc, Physics, Durban University; MSc, Management, Imperial College, London University
Directorships: Automsoft International, Mirics Semiconductor, Shazam, Solarflare

2323 ACCEDE CAPITAL
Level 11, 1 Chifley Square
Sydney NSW 2000
Australia

Phone: 61-282330030 **Fax:** 61-282330031

Mission Statement: Accede Capital is an early stage focused venture capital firm committed to backing our entrepreneurs build great companies. Our team has over 60 years collective experience in venture capital and working with early stage technology companies, so we understand what it takes to build great technology companies and create significant shareholder value.
Investment Criteria: Early-Stage
Industry Group Preference: Technology
Portfolio Companies: Dilithium Networks, G2 Microsystems, Sensory Networks, ManageSoft, Finisar
Key Executives:
Chris Beare, Chairman/General Partner
Education: BSc, BE, PhD, Adelaide University; MBA,

Venture Capital & Private Equity Firms / International Firms

Harvard Business School
Background: CEO, Hambros; CEO, Radiata

2324 ACCELMED
6 Hachoshilm St
6 Floor
PO Box 2014
Herzliya Pituach 46120
Israel

Phone: 972-97885599 **Fax:** 972-99588594
e-mail: Amir@accelmed.com
web: www.accelmed.co.il

Mission Statement: Accelmed is a private equity investment firm focused on long-term value creation for medical device companies. Accelmed invests in small and mid-cap private and public companies.

Geographic Preference: Israel
Industry Group Preference: Medical Devices, Life Sciences
Portfolio Companies: Cardiapex, CariHeal, EndoSpan, Eximo Medical, MCS/Medical Compression Systems, NLT Spine, PeerMedical, Pi-R Squared, Valcare Medical

Key Executives:
Mori Arkin, Chairman
Education: Tel Aviv University
Background: Chairman, Agis Industries

2325 ACCENT EQUITY PARTNERS
Lime Grove House
Green Street, St Helier
Jersey JE1 2ST
Channel Islands

Phone: 46-8-545-07300 **Fax:** 46-8-545-07329
e-mail: info@accentequityfunds.com
web: www.accentequity.se

Mission Statement: Accent is a group of private equity funds focusing on investments in lower mid-market buyout and later-stage expansion capital transactions in the Nordic region.

Geographic Preference: Nordic Region
Founded: 1994
Investment Criteria: Mid-Market Buyouts
Industry Group Preference: Diversified
Portfolio Companies: AR Carton, Autotube, Aviator, Bergteamet, Candyking, Corvara, DJO, Hooks, Jetul, Mont Blanc, NSS, RenoNorden, ScandBook, Scandic Hotels, Troax

Key Executives:
Ian Lambert, Director
Education: BSc, English & Social Sciences, Stockholm University; BSc, Journalism & Communcation, Stockhold School of Journalism
Background: Vice President, KF Industri AB

2326 ACCENTURE TECHNOLOGY VENTURES
1 Plantation Place
30 Fenchurch Street
London EC3M 3BD
United Kingdom

Phone: 44-2078444000 **Fax:** 44-2078444444
web: www.accenture.com

Mission Statement: Accenture Technology Ventures is the venture capital unit of Accenture. Our mission is to help entrepreneurs build great companies that can transform entire industries, create new markets and generate superior economic returns.

Geographic Preference: Americas, Asia Pacific, Europe / Middle East / Africa (EMEA)
Fund Size: $1.5 Billion
Average Investment: $7.5 Million
Minimum Investment: $2 Million
Investment Criteria: Early Stage, Expansion/Development

Industry Group Preference: Consumer Services, Business to Business, Wireless Technologies, Technology, Infrastructure, Management, Marketing

Key Executives:
Pierre Nanterme, Chairman & CEO
Background: Managing partner of ventures and alliances in Accenture's Communications & High Tech operating group, managing partner of Accenture's outsourcing group in the Americas.
Directorships: Roup director-sales development, managing partner of Accenture's corporate development activities in the Americas.
Jo Deblaere, Chief Operating Officer
Background: HSBC Midland Montagu
Directorships: Marketing Director, Global Financial Markets.
Gianfranco Casati, Group Chief Executive-Growth Markets
Background: Group chief executive of the Communications & High Tech Operating group, Managing partner for Accenture's operations.
Directorships: Chief Operating Officer-Client Services.
Stephen J Rohleder, Group Chief Executive-Health & Public Service
Background: Managing partner - Accenture's Government Operating Group U.S , Accenture's U.S. Federal operating unit.
Directorships: Group Chief Executive of Accenture's global Government operating group.
Michael J. Salvino, Group Chief Executive-Business Process Outsourcing
Background: Managing partner-Practice Process and Quality, Country Managing Partner & Regional managing Partner for Italy, Greece and Turkey.
Directorships: Chief Financial Officer, capital risk officer, chief risk officer, treasurer and managing partner of corporate matters.
Shawn Collinson, Chief Strategy Officer
Education: Oxford University
Background: Managing Partner of the Products-Europe operating unit, global managing partner for our Automotive, Industrial and Travel & Transportation industry groups, Pharmaceuticals & Medical Products group in Europe.

2327 ACCERA AG
Weinheimer Str. 64a
Mannheim 68309
Germany

Phone: 49-6211815370 **Fax:** 49-62118153799
e-mail: info@accera.de
web: www.accera.de

Mission Statement: Specializes in investments in the renewable energy sector.

Founded: 2001
Industry Group Preference: Renewable Energy, Energy
Portfolio Companies: EPV Solar

Key Executives:
Marcus Rist, Executive Board Member
Education: MSc, Electrical Engineering
Background: MVV Energie AG

2328 ACCESS MEDICAL VENTURES
35 Windsor Road
North Haven, CT 06473-3045

Phone: 203-281-4585
e-mail: webinfo@accessmv.com
web: accessmv.com

Mission Statement: Access Medical Ventures is a U.S based venture capital fund that focuses specifically on investing and advancing medical device start-ups.

Geographic Preference: United States

Venture Capital & Private Equity Firms / International Firms

Investment Criteria: Early-Stage
Industry Group Preference: Medical Devices
Portfolio Companies: CartiHeal, MinInvasive Orthopedic Solutions, AVMedical Dialysis Access Management, Tradeo, E-Motion Medical Ltd., Nitiloop, Samson Neuro Sciences, Latrima Medical
Key Executives:
  Michael Tal, Partner
  Education: MD, Hadassah Medical School, MCP, Hahnemann University, Yale University; MBA, Yale University
  Background: Associate Professor of Radiology, Yale University School of Medicine
  Limor Sandach, Partner
  Education: BSc, Chemical Engineering, Master of Engineering, Technion, Israel Institute
  Background: Partner, 7health Ventures

2329 ACE & COMPANY
30 Rue du Rhone
Geneva 1204
Switzerland
Phone: 41-223113333 Fax: 41-223116666
e-mail: info@aceandcompany.com
web: www.aceandcompany.com

Mission Statement: ACE & Company Development Group Ltd., is a diversified investment and advisory group specialized in direct investments in emerging markets and emerging industries.
Geographic Preference: United States, Europe, Middle East
Founded: 2005
Investment Criteria: Angel, Growth-Stage, Buyout Stage, Private Equity Secondaries
Industry Group Preference: Consumer Products, Consumer Services, Technology, Financial Services
Portfolio Companies: Acunote, Alpha Networks, Adgrok, Aerofs, Airlease, Apportable, Carthage Agricultural Company, Carwoo!, DotCloud, Gazillion Entertainment, Etacts, FlightCaster, Genagro, GoCardless, Global Blue, HighlightCam, Inpulse, Libero, Lucidity Lights, MidNox, Minomonsters, Movity, PayPlug, Paystack, PlanGrid, Priceonomics, Rescale, StepStone, Philadelphia Energy Solutions, Tok & Stok, RethinkDB, Terra Firma, Skysheet, StudyEdge, Taptolearn, Vayable, Verbling, Virool, Sensible Organics, Seventh Generation, Union Agriculture Group, Y Combinator
Key Executives:
  Adam Said, Co-Founder
  Christopher Kile, Co-Founder
  Sherif Elhalwagy, Co-Founder

2330 ACE VENTURE CAPITAL LIMITED
Dongwoo B/D
Mirae Asset Venture Tower, 16th Floor
Kangnam-Gu
Seoul 135-280
Korea
Phone: 82-234522202 Fax: 82-234522566
web: www.acecapventures.com

Mission Statement: Actively seeking new investments.
Geographic Preference: Korea, Japan
Founded: 2000
Investment Criteria: Seed, Start-Up, Expansion, Buyouts
Industry Group Preference: Information Technology, Biotechnology, Services, Semiconductors, Telecommunications, Electronic Technology, Internet Technology
Key Executives:
  Howard Greenberg, President & Founder
  Background: Board of Director of KSIA (Korea Semiconductor Industry Association)
  Directorships: Chairman of SEMI (Semiconductor Equipment's and Materials International).

2331 ACELERADORA
Contour Avenue
6594-17 Floor
Savassi-Belo Horizonte/MG 30110-044
Brazil

Mission Statement: Aceleradora supports startups with seed capital and management, and help companies in their innovation strategy.
Founded: 2008
Investment Criteria: Seed-Stage, Startup
Portfolio Companies: Acessozero, Anuncie La, Crowdtest, Ningo, Pligus
Key Executives:
  Yuri Gitahy, Founder
  Background: CTO, Vetta Technologies; Systems Engineering Manager, UOL

2332 ACKERMANS & VAN HAAREN
Begijnenvest 113
Antwerpen 2000
Belgium
Phone: 32-32318770 Fax: 32-32252533
e-mail: info@avh.be
web: en.avh.be/home.aspx

Mission Statement: Actively seeking new investments.
Geographic Preference: Belgium, France, Luxembourg, Netherlands
Fund Size: ?3.1 Billion
Founded: 1994
Investment Criteria: Bridge, Expansion - development, Replacement, Small buyout (£m equity), Mid market buyout (15M-150m equity), Large buyout (150m-300m equity), Public to private, Privatisation
Industry Group Preference: All Sectors Considered
Portfolio Companies: Alural Group, Cindu International, Corn. Van Loocke, Hertel Holding, IDOC, IlloSpear, NMC, Oleon Holding, Synvest.
Key Executives:
  Luc Bertrand, Executive director, Chairman EC
  e-mail: marc.depauw@sofinim.be
  Education: Master of Economics
  Background: Societe Nationale d'Investissement (General Manager), Civil Service.
  Andre-Xavier Cooreman, Chief Operating Officer

2333 ACME LABS
Pauler utca 12
IV/1
Budapest H-1013
Hungary

Mission Statement: ACME Labs provides not just funding, but the advice, expertise, and relationships to help entrepreneurs shape and realize their vision. ACME Labs is not just an accelerator, but an integrated strategic advisory, corporate finance, and venture capital practice.
Geographic Preference: Europe
Investment Criteria: Early-Stage
Industry Group Preference: Digital Media & Marketing, Financial Services, Clean Technology, Life Sciences
Portfolio Companies: Secure Directory, Stereocake, Crossway Media Solutions, Shinrai
Key Executives:
  Gyuri Karady, Chairman
  Education: McGill University; Doctorate in Engineering, Harvard University
  Background: Baring Private Equity/Baring Crilius, Julius Baer Capital

Venture Capital & Private Equity Firms / International Firms

2334 ACONCAGUA VENTURES
Humboldt 1967
2§ Floor
Buenos Aires C1414CTU
Argentina

Phone: 54-1155562673
web: www.aconcaguaventures.com

Mission Statement: Aconcagua Ventures is an early-stage hi-tech venture capital firm investing in Argentina and Latinamerica. Our goal is to generate outstanding returns for our investors and, by developing our portfolio, to help transform the regional economical landscape towards a more competitive model generating value from knowledge.
Geographic Preference: Argentina, Latin America
Investment Criteria: Early-Stage
Industry Group Preference: High Technology, Software, Internet, Communications, Medical Devices
Portfolio Companies: Container Consultants & Systems, Core Security Technologies, Keepcon, Popego
Key Executives:
  Jonatan Altszul, Co-Founder/Managing Partner
  Background: Co-Founder, Core Security Technologies; Special Projects Group, Argentine Tax Agency

2335 ACRUX LIMITED
103-113 Stanley Street
West Melbourne VIC 3003
Australia

Phone: 61-383790100 Fax: 61-383790101
web: www.acrux.com.au

Mission Statement: Actively seeking new investments in specialty pharmaceutical business products.
Geographic Preference: Australia
Fund Size: $30 Million
Founded: 1998
Average Investment: $1-5 Million
Minimum Investment: $500,000
Investment Criteria: Early Stage, Expansion
Industry Group Preference: Biotechnology, Pharmaceuticals
Key Executives:
  Ross Dobinson Bbus, Executive Chairman
  e-mail: info@acrux.com.au
  Education: PhD
  Background: Research and teaching appointments at universities in England, Australia and the USA and was on the founding Board of Directors of the International Pharmaceutical Aerosol Consortium - Regulatory Science.
  Tony Di Pietro, Chief Financial Officer and Company Secretary

2336 ACT VENTURE CAPITAL LIMITED
Richview Office Park, Clonskeagh
Dublin 14
Ireland

Phone: 353-12600966 Fax: 353-12600538
e-mail: info@actvc.ie
web: www.actventure.com

Mission Statement: ACT Venture Capital is Ireland's leading independent venture capital company.
Geographic Preference: Ireland & the UK
Fund Size: $415 Million
Founded: 1994
Average Investment: $200,000 - $10 million
Minimum Investment: $890,000
Investment Criteria: Invests in growth-oriented companies led by exceptional entrepreneurs with strong management team
Industry Group Preference: Software, Communications, Internet Technology, Hardware, Life Sciences
Portfolio Companies: Raidtec Corporation, MDS Gateways, Intense Photonics, Massana, Kymata, Stockbyte, CR2, Cape Clear, ACRA Control, Piercom, Scietific Systems, QUMAS, ASH Technologies, TV Three, Life Style, ODENBERG
Key Executives:
  Niall Carroll, Managing Partner
  Education: BE, FMCA, FIMC, FIBI, Electrical Engineering, University College, Dublin; Fellow, Chartered Institute of Management Accountants; Fellow, Institute of Management Consultants
  Background: Consumer Electronics Division of General Electric of the USA and became Manager - Quality Control in the United States and Ireland, general management and financial divisions of PA Management Consultants in Ireland, Managing Director of AIB Venture Capital
  Directorships: Founder.
  John Flynn, Managing Director
  Education: Commerce, Chartered Accountant, Business Strategy
  Background: KPMG in Dublin from 1976 to 1987, Director of AIB Corporate Finance from 1987 to 1984,
  John O'Sullivan, Director of ACT Venture Capital
  Education: BE, Chemical Engineering, MIE
  Background: Director of AIB Venture Capital and Allied Combined Trust
  Debbie Rennick, Director of ACT
  Education: Communications, DPA, FCA, Chartered Accountant
  Background: Director of AIB Capital Markets Holdings (U.K.) and also acted as Operations and Finance Director of a large, AIB associated

2337 ACTIS
2 More London Riverside
London SE1 2JT
United Kingdom

Phone: 44-2072345000 Fax: 44-2072345010
e-mail: info@act.is
web: www.act.is

Mission Statement: Actively seeking new investments.
Geographic Preference: Africa, China, Malaysia, South Asia
Fund Size: $5.0 Billion
Founded: 1948
Average Investment: $100 Million
Minimum Investment: $5 Million
Investment Criteria: Early Stage, Expansion and Development Capital, Replacement Capital, Buyout and Buyin
Industry Group Preference: Energy, Information Technology, Financial Services, Chemicals, Transportation, Telecommunications, Leisure, Manufacturing, Logistics, Tourism
Portfolio Companies: Glenmark Pharmaceuticals, Globeleq, Grain Bulk Handlers, Grameenphone, Housing Development Finance Corporation, Jyothy Laboratories, Lenco, Mengniu Dairy, Nitrex Chemicals, Orascom Telecom Algeria, Pacific Rim Palm Oil, Persianas, Platmin, Powercom
Key Executives:
  Jonathon Bond, Partner
  e-mail: info@act.is
  Background: Head of HR for Citibank's commercial banking division in South Asia and Asia Pacific
  Directorships: Head of Actis's Operations Group.
  Torbjorn Caesar, Partner

2338 ACTIVA CAPITAL
203, Rue du Faubourg Saint-Honore
Paris 75008
France

Phone: 31-143125012 Fax: 31-143125013
web: www.activacapital.com

Venture Capital & Private Equity Firms / International Firms

Mission Statement: Activa Capital is an independent private equity company with a strong entrepreneurial spirit.
Fund Size: 500 million Euro
Average Investment: $30 Million - $200 Million
Investment Criteria: MBO, Spin-Off, Owner Buyout, Growth Capital, Build-Ups
Industry Group Preference: Consumer Products, Distribution, Business Products & Services, Healthcare, Pharmaceuticals, Media, Information Technology
Portfolio Companies: Armatis-Laser Contact, Privamista Group, Findis, Abrisud, Ergalis-Selpro-Plus RH, Albarelle, Bruno Saint Hilarie, Sport 2000, Creal, Logitrade, ProNatura
Key Executives:
  Charles Diehl, Partner
  Education: University of Geneva; MBA, Wharton School
  Background: Co-Founder, Barclays Private Equity France

2339 ACTIVE VENTURE PARTNERS
Paseo de Gracia 35
Atico
Barcelona 08007
Spain

Phone: 34-93-178-6868 Fax: 34-93-272-2436
web: www.active-vp.com

Mission Statement: ACTIVE was founded in Barcelona in 2002. We manage two funds, Molins Capital Inversion SCR SA and Amerigo Innvierte Spain Ventures FCR RS, whose vintage years are 2004 and 2010 respectively. Both are early stage venture capital funds that invest in technology related businesses.
Geographic Preference: Spain, Germany, Switzerland, Austria, Scandinavia
Founded: 2002
Average Investment: 500,000 - 4 million Euro
Investment Criteria: Early-Stage
Industry Group Preference: Technology, Tech Enabled Services, Enterprise Software, Consumer Internet, Consumer Media, Communications, Wireless, Security, Clean Technology
Portfolio Companies: Banebys, PackLink, Review Pro, SanaExpert, Uzerzoom, YD, Offerton Liveshopping, Restalo, Whisbi, Zyncro
Key Executives:
  Christopher Pommerening, Founding Partner
  Education: European Business School, London
  Background: Co-Founder, AutoScout24 Spain

2340 ACTOMEZZ Groupama Private Equity SA
49 avenue d'Iena
Paris 75116
France

Phone: 33-153935151 Fax: 33-153935154

Mission Statement: ActoMezz primarily acts as an arranger of mezzanine financing and sometimes as a minority shareholder in two areas: investment alongside private equity funds, and investment alongside management teams who wish to increase their ownership position following an initial successful LBO.
Fund Size: 187 million Euro
Average Investment: $5 and $30 million
Investment Criteria: Buyouts, Acquisitions, Later-Stage/Expansion Financing
Portfolio Companies: Emeraude International, Domidep, Lagarrique, Forma-Dis, Abrisud, Groupe Rougnon, Editions Oberthur, Sotralu, Marie-Laure PLV, Emeraude Chimie International, Ionisos, Faab-Fabicauto, World Freight Company International
Key Executives:
  Stephane Bergez, Head
  01-53-9351-71
  e-mail: sbergez@groupama-pe.fr

Education: Master's Degree, Essec; Engineering Degree, Sup'Meca
Background: Euler-Hermes SFAC

2341 ACUMEN VENTURES
Australia

web: www.acumenvc.com

Mission Statement: An early stage venture capital fund investing in world class startups emerging from South East Asia and Australia.
Geographic Preference: South East Asia, Australia
Average Investment: $100,000 - $2 million
Investment Criteria: Seed Stage, Series A
Industry Group Preference: Software, Internet, Mobile, E-Commerce & Manufacturing, Cloud Computing, Infrastructure, Enterprise Software, Technology-Enabled Services
Key Executives:
  Shane Cheek, Managing Partner
  Background: Founder, Method Advisory; Playford Capital

2342 ADARA VENTURE PARTNERS
Calle Jose Abascal, 58
Madrid 28003
Spain

Phone: 34-914517070 Fax: 34-91-451-7090
web: www.adaravp.com

Mission Statement: The creation of Adara was driven by our partners' belief that venture capital needs to bring more than money to the table. We have a strong focus on bringing in-house expertise to portfolio companies, helping them successfully develop and reach ambitious business objectives. We believe this results-orientated approach combined with strict opportunity selection optimizes success for our partners - both investors and entrepreneurs.
Industry Group Preference: Software Services, Mobile Services, Semiconductors, Telecommunications, Clean Technology
Portfolio Companies: ADD, AlienVault, Arque, Berggi, Cambridge Broadband Networks, Ecutronic, Elastix, Eyesquad, Genasys, Illuminate, OpenBravo, Polymita Technologies, Ring2Conferencing
Key Executives:
  Jesus Sainz, Chairman
  Background: CEO, Ogden Corp.; Parcque Tematico de Madrid SA

2343 ADASTRA
Schafflerstrabe 4
Munchen D-80333
Germany

Phone: 49-8971040850
e-mail: info@adastra.de
web: www.adastra.de

Mission Statement: AdAstra actively accompanies its portfolio companies towards the capital markets or other means of realizing their value potential. In this process, we see ourselves as a reliable and business-oriented investor. It is our aim to be integrated in the business concept as a genuine partner not only through our capital but also through active involvement, guidance and support.
Founded: 2000
Investment Criteria: Growth Capital
Industry Group Preference: Information Technology, Internet, E-Commerce & Manufacturing, Telecommunications
Portfolio Companies: Ask, Ask|Net, Baurer, Gomez, Suse, Trados

Venture Capital & Private Equity Firms / International Firms

Key Executives:
Ulrich Clemm, Founder/Managing Partner
Background: Managing Director, HVB Beteilgungs GmbH

2344 ADD VENTURE
Bersenevskaya Naberezhnaya 6
Resident Digital October, bg
Moscow
Russia

Phone: 8-9263398250
web: www.addventure.to

Mission Statement: AddVenture provides start-up investments for a quick launch, 'smart money' and business contacts. Internet grows fast as so does our appetite for web projects: AddVenture III fund will invest $50k to $1 mln, the most promising ones will get even more.

Geographic Preference: Russia
Founded: 2008
Minimum Investment: $50,000
Investment Criteria: Seed-Stage
Industry Group Preference: Internet, SaaS
Portfolio Companies: Delivery-club.ru, Pixonic, AlterGeo, Insales, Minibanda, Easyfinance.ru, Timetovisit.ru

Key Executives:
Maxim Medvedev, Founder'/Managing Partner
Background: Co-Founder, Pixonic
Directorships: Pixonic

2345 ADLEVO CAPITAL CIM Fund Services
Les Cascades Building
Edith Cavell Street
Port Louis
Mauritius

Phone: 230-2129800
e-mail: info@adlevocapital.com
web: www.adlevocapital.com

Mission Statement: Adlevo Capital is a Mauritius-based private equity fund manager founded on the conviction that meaningful development in sub-Saharan Africa will be driven by the increasing application of technology to business processes across all sectors.

Geographic Preference: Africa
Industry Group Preference: Infrastructure, Consumer Services, Business Products & Services
Portfolio Companies: InterSwitch Limited, Paga, Rancard Solutions

Key Executives:
Yemi Lalude, Managing Partner

2346 ADVANCE PROPERTY FUND
Level 5, 182 George Street
Sydney 2000
Australia

Phone: 61-894155655 **Fax:** 61- 292311673
Toll-Free: 1800-819935
e-mail: investorservices@advance.com.au
web: www.advance.com.au

Mission Statement: Actively seeking new investments.

Geographic Preference: Australia
Fund Size: $75 billion
Founded: 1999

Key Executives:
Patrick Farrell, Head of Advance Investment Solutions

2347 ADVANTAGE PARTNERS
12F Sanno Park Tower
2-11-1 Nagata-cho
Minato-ku Tokyo 105-0001
Japan

Phone: 81-351570183 **Fax:** 81-351-570187
e-mail: master@advantagegroup.co.jp
web: www.advantagegroup.co.jp

Mission Statement: Investing in acquisitions, buy-outs, buy-ins and other private equity opportunities.

Geographic Preference: Japan
Fund Size: $387 Million
Founded: 1992
Average Investment: $20.85 Million
Minimum Investment: $8.34 Million
Investment Criteria: Early Stage, Expansion and Development Capital
Industry Group Preference: All Sectors Considered
Portfolio Companies: BMB Corp, Fuji Machinery Mfg. & Electronics Co. Ltd., Polygon Pictures Inc., ICREO Co. Ltd., KISCO Solutions, BrainyWorks, Hiramatsu Inc., AiCO Technologies Co. Ltd, Actus Corporation, Keyport Solutions, Inc., Kokunai Shi

Key Executives:
Shinichiro Kita, Manager
e-mail: master@advantagegroup.co.jp
Education: BA in Economics
Background: McKinsey & Company (Tokyo)
Hideo Nagatsuyu, Partner

2348 ADVENT VENTURE PARTNERS
158-160 North Gower Street
London NW1 2ND
United Kingdom

Phone: 44-2079322100 **Fax:** 44-2079322174
e-mail: info@adventventures.com

Mission Statement: Maintains a close hands-on management style and seeks to form a strong working relationship with each of its investees.

Geographic Preference: United Kingdom, USA, Western Europe
Fund Size: $885 Million
Founded: 1981
Average Investment: $17 Million
Minimum Investment: $3.54 Million
Investment Criteria: Start-up, Early Stage, Expansion/Development, Secondary purchase/replacement capital, MBO, MBI
Industry Group Preference: Electronic Technology, Software, Communications, Biotechnology, Medical Devices
Portfolio Companies: Adeptra, AM-BEO, Ask, Axion, Casella, Cartesis , Celoxia, Citel Tech, EQOS, INCA, K2 Optronic, Netik, Pelican, Phyworks, Snell and Wilcox

Key Executives:
Fiona MacLaughlin, Associate
Education: Metallurgy, Oxford University
Background: Industrial Engineer, De La Rue; Manufacturing Operations, Formica International; After steering through a management buy-out of a Formica subsidiary in 1971, ran the resulting company for 10 years.
Directorships: Founding Chairman, British Capital Venture Association
Peter Baines, General Partner
e-mail: info@adventventures.com
Education: BSC, MSC, London University; MBA, INSEAD
Background: Picker International, PricewaterhouseCoopers, Investment Director Schroder Ventures France
Alain Huriez, Venture Partner
e-mail: info@adventventures.com

Venture Capital & Private Equity Firms / International Firms

Education: Electrical Engineer
Background: Honeywell, Case & Variany/Univac, Director of High Technology Unit 3i
Mike Chalfen, General Partner
e-mail: info@adventventures.com
Education: Software Engineer
Background: UNISYS; ICL/Managing Director, INSAC Group
Les Gabb, Finance Director
e-mail: info@adventventures.com
Education: Biochemistry, Oxford University; Chartered Accountant
Background: Credit Industrial et Commercial et UEI for 3 years. Head of Accounts, London Branch of French Bank; Managing Director, Bemuda International Investment Management (Europe); Chartered Accountant, KPMG Peat Marwick McClintock
Dale Pfost, General Partner
e-mail: info@adventventures.com
Education: BSC Economics, London School of Economics
Background: Black & Decker; Innotech Investment; 3i
Ian J. Nicholson, Operating Partner
e-mail: info@adventventures.com
Education: Chemical engineering, Biotechnology
Background: Director Venture Capital, Monsato Healthcare/Petrochemical
Directorships: Non-executive Director, Dura Pharmaceuticals, Oxford Glycosciences, Othofix International NV, Professional Staff plc, Vernalis Group plc
Kaasim Mahmood, Partner
e-mail: info@adventventures.com
Education: BA, Biology, Vassar; MBA, Stanford University
Background: Group VP M&A, Rhone Poulenc
Andrew J Wood, Venture Partner
e-mail: info@ventures.com
Education: Physics, Oxford University
Background: Managing Director, Mowlem; Technology Venture Capital Fund Manager, MTI
Raj Parekh, General Partner
Shahzad Malik, General Partner
e-mail: info@adventventures.com
Education: Oxford University; Cambridge University; Specialized in International Cardiology, while pursuing research in heart muscle disorders
Background: McKinsey & Company

2349 AEM CAPITAL
Av. Nilo Pecanha, 50/1512 Centro
Rio de Janeiro 20020-906
Brazil

Phone: 21-25321592 Fax: 21-22927538
web: www.aembr.com.br

Mission Statement: Invests in high-growth markets with a highly specialized team.
Industry Group Preference: Energy, Infrastructure, Oil & Gas
Portfolio Companies: Starfish Oil & Gas, Tridemensional Engenharia
Key Executives:
   Antonio E.F. Muller, Partner
   Education: BS, Engineering, State University of Rio de Janeiro
   Background: VP, Business Development, ABB Setal Lummus

2350 AESCAP VENTURE
Barbara Strozzilaan 101
Aescap Venture, Spaces
Amsterdam 1083 HN
Netherlands

Phone: 31-205702940 Fax: 31-206737846
e-mail: pkrol@asecap.com
web: www.aescap.com

Mission Statement: Aescap Venture is a venture capital company investing in private medical companies in Europe. We invest in high-potential companies with realistic product opportunities. This involves investments in all phases of development.
Geographic Preference: Europe
Industry Group Preference: Healthcare, Medical Devices
Portfolio Companies: ActoGeniX, Affectis Pharmaceuticals AG, Aquapharm BioDiscovery, Avantium BV, to-BBB BV, Biocartis SA, EOS SpA, f-Star GmbH, i-Optics BV, Orphazyme ApS, ProtAffin Biotechnologic AG, Vivendy Therpeutics
Key Executives:
   Patrick Krol, Managing Partner
   e-mail: pkrol@aescap.com
   Background: Founder & Managing Director, Firm United Healthcare; Co-Founder, Interactive Healthcare; Co-Founder, Healthcare Management School
   Directorships: Shire Pharmaceuticals, Aquapharm, i-Optics, to-BBB, f-Star

2351 AFC MERCHANT BANK
180 Cecil Street,
Bangkok Bank Building
Suite 17-00
Singapore 69546
Singapore

Phone: 65-622247155 Fax: 65-622250727
web: www.afcmerchantbank.com

Mission Statement: Finances projects and assists in promoting industrialisation and overall economic development in the Asian region.
Geographic Preference: Asia
Fund Size: $200 Million
Founded: 1981
Investment Criteria: Early Stage, Expansion, Startup
Industry Group Preference: Diversified
Key Executives:
   Jeronimo U Kilayko, Chairman
   Adilaksana Putranto, President Director

2352 AFTERDOX
7 Nachlieli Street
Kfar Sava 44246
Israel

Phone: 972-545511688
e-mail: info@afterdox.com
web: www.afterdox.com

Mission Statement: AfterDox is a 'smart' angels investment group, comprised of 50 present and former top executives, mostly from Amdocs. Smart - because our partners are involved in the management and strategic planning of its portfolio companies, supporting the management in the initial business development, building the company and marketing it, participate in decision making processes and daily management.
Founded: 2007
Investment Criteria: Pre-Seed, Seed-Stage, Startup
Industry Group Preference: Telecommunications, Internet, Advertising, Information Technology, Software
Portfolio Companies: Bizzabo, RingYa, Donaza, FlixWagon, IMScouting, Fenavic, TodaCell, Internet Is Fun

Venture Capital & Private Equity Firms / International Firms

Key Executives:
Menahem Shalgi, Chairman
Education: BA, Business Administration, New York Technology University
Background: President/CEO/Founder, cVidya Networks

2353 AGATE MEDICAL INVESTMENTS
Toyota Tower B, 7th Floor
67 Igal Alon St
Tel-Aviv 67443
Israel

Phone: 972-35652285 Fax: 972-35652284
e-mail: agate@agate-invest.com
web: www.agate-invest.com

Mission Statement: Agate Medical investments LP is a group of funds, specialized in providing growth capital to mature Medtech companies. Agate, as one of Israel's leading healthcare investors, has established a leading position in the healthcare VC industry, resulting in quality deal-flow and investor partnerships.

Geographic Preference: Israel
Founded: 2007
Investment Criteria: Later-Stage
Industry Group Preference: Healthcare, Health Related, Medical Technology, Medical Devices
Portfolio Companies: VisionCare, Tulip Medical, Navotek Medical, BrainsGate, Angioslide, Iscare AS, Lumenis, Sensimed, Valeritas

Key Executives:
Dani Haveh, Co-Founder/Managing General Partner
e-mail: danin@agate-invest.com
Education: LLB, Hebrew University
Background: Minister of Health, Israel

2354 AGF PRIVATE EQUITY Allianz Group
117, avenue des Champs-Élysées
Paris 75008
France

Phone: 33-0158185656 Fax: 33-158185689
e-mail: contact@agfpe.com

Mission Statement: Works with the best partnerships worldwide and invests in the best emerging companies in France.

Geographic Preference: France, Europe
Fund Size: $120 Million
Founded: 1995
Average Investment: Euro50 - Euro70 Million
Minimum Investment: $1.8 Million
Investment Criteria: Early Stage
Industry Group Preference: Software, Telecommunications, Infrastructure, Life Sciences
Portfolio Companies: A.S. Group, Arisem, Cosmosbay, Diatos, Eolring Dynamic Cell Network, Exonhit, Fluxus, Leacom, Mediapps, NetGraph Information Technology SA, Neurotech, NexGen, PS Soft, Sefas, StreamCore, Travelprice.com, iProgress, Aptanomics, Bmd, Celectis, Elbion, Faust Pharma, Integragen, Meristem Therapeutics, SpineVision, Zealand Pharma, Alchimer, Everbee, Valiosys, BVRP, Dalet, Ever, Grid Expert, AS Groupe, Vizelia, Cril Telecom Software, Lea com, ONE Access Networks, Stepmind, Telisma, Cosmosbay Vectis, Kiala, Meetic

Key Executives:
Christophe Bavaria, CEO & Managing Partner
e-mail: contact@agfprivatequity.com
Education: Diploma of Secretary
Background: Bank Clerk
Benoist Grossmann, Managing Partner
Luc Maruenda, Partner
e-mail: contact@agfprivatequity.com
Education: Master degree in Accounting and Finance, Master degree in Business Law, Nantes University
Background: Asset Mnagement; Head of Fixed Income portfolio, Allianz France
Directorships: Investment Manager, Member
Sophie Cadorel, Communication Manager
e-mail: contact@agfprivatequity.com
Education: Masters in Corporate Communication amd Information Research, Paris University
Background: Information Researcher, IT Firm, Corporate Communication

2355 AIB SEED CAPITAL FUND Dublin Business Innovation Centre
The Tower, Trinity Tech & Enterprise Centre
Pearse Street
Dublin 2
Ireland

Phone: 353-1-6713111 Fax: 353-1-6713330
web: www.aibseedcapitalfund.ie

Mission Statement: Invests in seed-stage companies across Ireland.

Geographic Preference: Ireland
Founded: 2007
Investment Criteria: Seed-Stage, Startup
Portfolio Companies: AccountsIQ, Almotech, Arann Healthcare, Benetel, Cambus Medical, Clevamama, CrescentDx, DataKraft, Davra Networks, Donseed, Endeco, Episensor, Eventovate, Fantom, Ferfics, ICAP Media, Ideal Binary, ImeeGolf, Insulcheck, Kemartek, Kidspotter, Marvaomedical, MicksGarage, Mingoa, Movidius, Nortev, Onformonics, OnlineTradesmen.ie, Openplain, MeaningMine, Phorest, Reading Bridges, Sensl, Swrve, Smartbin, TerminalFour, Tvrecheck, VisibleThread, Zartis

2356 AIG INVESTMENT CORPORATION (ASIA) LIMITED
Peninsula Corporate Park
Piramal Tower
9th Floor, G.K. Marg
Mumbai 400013

Phone: 852-28321200 Fax: 852-28939530
Toll-Free: 1800-2667780
web: www.aig.com

Mission Statement: Provides insurance and financial services.

Geographic Preference: Worldwide
Industry Group Preference: Insurance, Financial Services
Key Executives:
Martin S. Feldstein, President & Chief Executive Officer
Education: MBA, Bachelor of Arts, Accounting.
Background: Deputy Director General of the Economics Staff to the President of the Philippines
Directorships: Senior Vice President, Investments.
Richard C. Holbrooke, Vice Chairman

2357 AITEC
23 Duke of Avila Avenue
Lisbon 1000-138
Portugal

Phone: 351-213100013 Fax: 351-213526314
e-mail: info@aitec.pt

Mission Statement: Invests in new technology based companies.

Geographic Preference: Lisbon.
Founded: 1987
Investment Criteria: Seed, Startup, Early-stage, Expansion & Development
Industry Group Preference: Computer Related, Software, Electronic Technology
Key Executives:
Manuel Alves, Director

Venture Capital & Private Equity Firms / International Firms

2358 AJU CAPITAL COMPANY
1329 Seocho-dong Secho-gu
Kangnam-Gu
Seoul NV
South Korea
Phone: 82-234717546 **Fax:** 82-234843400
web: www.aju.co.kr

Mission Statement: Investment strategy focused on core industry segments including electricity and electronics and information technology.
Geographic Preference: South Korea
Founded: 1997
Industry Group Preference: Electronic Technology, Information Technology
Key Executives:
  Kyu Young Moon, Chairman

2359 AKSOY INTERNET VENTURES
Mill Sk. Nida Tower No. 18
Kat 5 34 742
Kozyatagi Kadikoy
Istanbul
Turkey

Mission Statement: Seeks to invest in companies producing consumer internet products.
Industry Group Preference: Consumer Internet
Portfolio Companies: MarketPage, Tinypay.me

2360 ALBEMARLE PRIVATE EQUITY LIMITED
1 Albemarle Street
London W1X 3HF
United Kingdom
Phone: 020-74919555 **Fax:** 020-74917245

Mission Statement: A private equity firm that has three funds that are managed on a discretionary basis. We invest in well established unquoted companies with current profits of $750,000 Euro per annual or more.
Geographic Preference: United Kingdom
Fund Size: $160 Million
Average Investment: $5 Million
Minimum Investment: $2.5 Million
Investment Criteria: Expansion and Development, Bridge finance, Refinancing bank debt, Secondary purchase/replacement capital, Rescue/turnaround, MBO, MBI
Industry Group Preference: Agriculture, Biotechnology, Chemicals, Communications, Computer Related, Consumer Services, Energy, Financial Services, Industrial Services, Industrial Products, Medical & Health Related, Materials Technology

2361 ALCHEMY PARTNERS
21 Palmer Street
London SW1H 0AD
United Kingdom
Phone: 44-2072409596 **Fax:** 44-2072409594
web: www.alchemypartners.co.uk

Mission Statement: Offers speed and flexibility in private equity.
Geographic Preference: United Kingdom, Austria, Germany, Republic of Ireland, Switzerland
Fund Size: $226 Million
Founded: 1997
Average Investment: Euro 2.7 Billion
Minimum Investment: $35.5 Million
Investment Criteria: Refinancing bank debt, Secondary purchase/replacement capital, Rescue/turnaround, MBO, MBI, Public-to-Private
Industry Group Preference: All Sectors Considered
Portfolio Companies: Paramount Hotels, Inspired Group Ltd, Anglian PLC, Four Seasons Health Care, Air-sea Survival Equipment, Alcentra, Anglian Group, ASSE, Blagden, Brooks Service Group, CedarCrestone, Centric, compare, Datapoint, ICS, Jacques Vert, Just Learning
Key Executives:
  Dominic Slade, Managing Partner
  e-mail: dslade@alchemypartners.co.uk
  Education: MBA, International Relations, Harvard University
  Background: Director, Apax; Managing Partner, Schroder Ventures; Citicorp Venture Capital
  Ian Cash, Partner
  Background: Senior Manager, Coopers & Lybrand
  Frits Prakke, Partner
  e-mail: pbridges@alchemypartners.co.uk
  Background: Associate Director, Lonrho Plc
  John Rowland, COO & CFO
  e-mail: jbostock@alchemypartners.co.uk
  Education: Chartered Management Accountant
  Background: Medical/Aerospace Division, Vickers plc; Perkins Diesels and Rolls Royce Motors
  Bob Hewson, Director
  e-mail: steve@bodger.net
  Education: Economics, Cambridge University; Chartered Accountant
  Background: Finance Director, EWS; Armour Group
  Thomas Boszko, Director
  e-mail: pcasey@alchemypartners.com
  Education: Business graduate, Chartered Accountant
  Background: Career Venture Capitalist and Entrepreneur with a special interest in the Irish market; Director, DCC; Director, Apax Partners
  Alex Leicester, Partner
  e-mail: jmoulton@alchemypartners.co.uk
  Background: Apax; Schroder Ventures; Citicorp Venture Capital

2362 ALCUIN CAPITAL PARTNERS LLP
2 Eaton Gate
London SW1W 9BJ
United Kingdom
Phone: 44-2031784089 **Fax:** 44-2031784090
e-mail: info@alcuincapital.com
web: www.alcuincapital.com

Mission Statement: Alcuin Capital Partners specialises in making growth capital, or development capital investments in profitable smaller-middle market companies.
Geographic Preference: United Kingdom
Average Investment: £2-10 million
Investment Criteria: Buyouts, Buy-Ins, Recapitalizations, Growth Capital
Portfolio Companies: AVM, AudioGo, Agrivert, Alpine Risk Services, Cafe Nero, CW Environmental, Domus, Krispy Kreme UK, Osprey Publishing, Tasker Ventures, TTA
Key Executives:
  Mark Storey, Partner
  Education: BA, History, Balliol College; MA, Birkbeck
  Background: BancBoston Capital

2363 ALFA CAPITAL Alfa Group
ul. Garden Kudrinskaya, 32
page 1 Bronnaya Plaza
Moscow 123001
Russia
Phone: 7-0957973152 **Fax:** 7-0957973151
e-mail: info@alfacapital.ru
web: www.alfacapital.ru

Mission Statement: Focuses on companies with potential to become market leaders.
Geographic Preference: Ukraine, Russia
Fund Size: $236 Million
Founded: 1996
Investment Criteria: Early to mid stage

Industry Group Preference: Biotechnology, Health Related, Medical Devices, Pharmaceuticals, Telecommunications, Oil & Gas

Key Executives:
  Irina Krivosheeva, Chairman of the Board
  e-mail: info@alfacapital.ru
  Education: BA, University of Michigan; Senior Executive Program, Columbia University
  Background: Founder and Principal of Troika Dialog, Director of both the US-Russia Business Council and Moscow's American Chamber of Commerce
  Yakov Galperin, Member of the Board, Deputy General Director, Head of Multifamily

2364 ALICE VENTURES SRL
1 Piazzale F Baracca
Milan 20123
Italy

Phone: 39-024998171 Fax: 39-0248517583
e-mail: info@aliceventures.it
web: www.aliceventures.it

Mission Statement: Multinational venture capital management team comprised of partners.

Geographic Preference: Italy, Israel, United Kingdom
Fund Size: $203 Million
Average Investment: Euro 170 Million
Minimum Investment: $1.2 Million
Investment Criteria: Early - Mid Stage, Seed Capital, Start-Up Capital
Industry Group Preference: Communications, Information Technology, Internet Technology, Life Sciences, Semiconductors, Medical

Key Executives:
  Ilaria Rajevich, Chief Financial Officer
  Background: 3C Communications, Cardcast,
  Elisa Candeloro, Financial Controller
  John Gonzalez, Life Sciences
  e-mail: john.gonzalez@aliceventures.it
  Background: Telcordia Technologies, Smithkline Beecham
  Edoardo Lecaldano, Information Technologies
  e-mail: edoardo.lecaldano@aliceventures.it
  Background: Bank of Italy; Mediobanca
  Francesco Torelli, General Counsel
  Background: Major Italian and international law firms.
  Directorships: In charge of legal affair.
  Hillel Milo, Medical Devices and Communication Technologies
  Background: Zoran Microelectronics; Walden Israel VC Fund, Clal Venture Capital, Infinity
  Elisa Candeloro, Financial Controller
  e-mail: elisa.candeloro@aliceventures.it
  Education: Degree in Accounting
  Background: Stanleyworks Group; Caterpillar Group
  Cesare Luigi Sironi, Telecommunication and Data Networking
  Education: Telecommunications, internet infrastructure
  Background: Cisco Systems, Iunet, Lucent Technologies, Zhone Technologies

2365 ALIVE IDEAS
27 rue de Charonne
Paris 75011
France

Phone: 33-184166258
e-mail: contact@aliveideas.fr
web: www.aliveideas.fr

Mission Statement: The mission of Alive Ideas is right there in our name: we bring ideas to life. To achieve this mission, we seek passionate teams with fun or revolutionnary ideas, and try to help them with some of the ingredients of success: business tips and smart money. We also develop our own ideas, gathering code-gurus and marketing genius together.

Portfolio Companies: Deolan, Doctrackr, Infinit, Recisio, Declicmedia, Groupement JV, Mapado, La Cuisine du Web

Key Executives:
  Jerry Nieuviarts, Partner
  Nicolas Rosset, Partner

2366 ALLEGRO INVESTMENT FUND
Research Park Haasrode
Esperantolaan 4
Heverlee, Leuven B-3001
Belgium

Phone: 32-485664650
e-mail: info@allegroinvestmentfund.com
web: www.allegroinvestmentfund.com

Mission Statement: Allegro Investment Fund (AIF) is a Leuven-based investment group that provides funding to early stage high-tech companies primarily in Flanders. We are looking for innovative, technology-driven spin-off companies addressing a significant world-wide market opportunity managed by skilled and highly motivated teams.

Average Investment: 200,000 - 1 million Euro
Investment Criteria: Early-Stage
Industry Group Preference: Technology
Portfolio Companies: ICsense, EconCore, Formac Pharmaceuticals, Visys, GreenPeak, Leuven Air, EqcoLogic, Rmoni, Excico, Triphase, Pharma Diagnostics, Elytra, @Mire, ICMS, Zenso, Vision++, MagCam, Mindcet

Key Executives:
  Geert Everaert, Founder
  Background: CFO, Pension Fund Manager, Tenneco Monroe

2367 ALLELE FUNDS
5-8 The Sanctuary
London SW1P 3JS
United Kingdom

Phone: 020-30110360 Fax: 020-30111288

Mission Statement: Allele Funds are investment funds which invest in high-growth healthcare and technology companies worldwide.

Geographic Preference: Worldwide
Industry Group Preference: Healthcare, Technology
Key Executives:
  Gail Lese, Founder/CEO/Portfolio Manager
  Education: MD, Cornell University; MBA, Harvard Business School
  Background: Founder, Lese Investments LLC

2368 ALLIANCE ENTREPRENDRE
5-7 rue de Monttessu
Paris 75007
France

Phone: 33-158193208 Fax: 01-53648765
web: www.allianceentreprendre.com

Mission Statement: An investment company set up by the French savings banks and Caisse des Depots Group, takes a minority share in bigger SMEs, especially in companies at the transfer stage.

Fund Size: $60.5 Million
Founded: 1995
Average Investment: $1.5-$2.7 Million
Industry Group Preference: All Sectors Considered
Key Executives:
  Lionnel Thomas, Chief Executive Officer
  Jean-Pierre Léger, Associate director

Venture Capital & Private Equity Firms / International Firms

2369 ALLIANCE VENTURE
Stranden 57, Aker Brygge
Oslo N-0250
Norway

Phone: 47-22944020 Fax: 47-22471221
e-mail: info@allianceventure.com
web: www.allianceventure.com

Mission Statement: Alliance Venture invests in emerging technology companies at an early stage and supports their global expansion through our international network.
Geographic Preference: Norway/Scandinavia
Fund Size: $75 million
Founded: 2001
Investment Criteria: Seed-Stage, Early-Stage
Industry Group Preference: Technology, Information Technology, Semiconductors, Software, Media, Mobile
Portfolio Companies: Capnia, FXI Technologies, HYPRES, Interagon, bMenu, Intergrasco, PagePlanner, poLight, 3D Perception, Encap, Never.no, MemfoACT, Novelda, Optosense, Phonofile, Ping Communications, Edvantage Group AS, TiFiC AB, Owera, Net4Call AS, Falanx AS, Network Electronics ASA
Key Executives:
Jan-Erik Hareid, Managing Partner
e-mail: hareid@allianceventure.com
Education: MSc, Physics & Industrial Engineering, Norwegian University of Science; IEP, INSEAD
Background: Head, Innovation Norway

2370 ALLIANZ CAPITAL PARTNERS GmbH
Theresienstr. 6-8
Munich 80333
Germany

Phone: 49-8938007010 Fax: 49-8938007586
e-mail: contact@allianzcapitalpartners.com
web: www.allianzcapitalpartners.com

Mission Statement: Allianz Capital Partners offers financing solutions to meet the diverse capital requirements of unlisted companies.
Geographic Preference: Western Europe, Africa, Americas, Europe, Germany
Fund Size: $1.01 Billion
Founded: 1998
Minimum Investment: $30 Million
Investment Criteria: Growth Capital, MBO, Management Buy-in, Shareholder Restructuring, Mezzanine
Industry Group Preference: All Sectors Considered
Key Executives:
Rainer Husmann, Executive manager
Education: Business Administration, Economics, Law and Social Sciences University of St. Gallen;Harvard Business School:ISP
Background: Bain & Co., Boston ;Goldman Sachs & Co., New York;Goldman Sachs International, London;Goldman Sachs & Co. OHG, Frankfurt

2371 ALMI FORETAGSPARTNER AB
Liljeholmsvägen 32, Box 47631
Stockholm 117 94
Sweden

Phone: 46-087098900 Fax: 46-840-60300
e-mail: info@almi.se
web: www.almi.se

Mission Statement: Actively seeking new investments.
Geographic Preference: Sweden
Founded: 1994
Industry Group Preference: All Sectors Considered
Key Executives:
Góran Lundwall, Chief Executive Officer/Koncernchef
Maroun Aoun, Chief Executive Officer

2372 ALOE PRIVATE EQUITY
34 Boulevard Malesherbes
Paris 75008
France

web: www.aloe-group.com

Mission Statement: A dynamic team of people with high integrity and a passion for investing in proven environmental technologies that have an end market focused on Asia.
Geographic Preference: Asia
Founded: 2003
Portfolio Companies: Allied Technologies, AgroGeneration, Environcom, Greenko Group Plc, Longmen Group, Maxsys Ltd, MBA Polymers, Polygenta, Recupyl, Vertaris
Other Locations:
8 High Street
Twyford RG10 9AE
United Kingdom

Executive Suite 2
International Business Park Westin
Oberoi Garden City
Goregaeon East, Mumbai
India

Huan Teng Edifice
Room 1808, Chaoyang
Beijing 100021
China

Key Executives:
Vivek Tandon, Co-Founder/General Partner
Education: BSc, Physics, Imperial College; PhD, University College, London
Background: Managing Director, Viventures

2373 ALPHA ASSOCIATES
Talstrasse 80, PO Box 2038
Zurich 2038
Switzerland

Phone: 41-432443100 Fax: 41-432443101
web: www.alpha-associates.ch

Mission Statement: Alpha Associates is an independent private equity fund-of-funds manager and advisor based in Zurich, Switzerland. We manage globally diversified and geographically focused private equity funds-of-funds and customized private equity accounts for a global institutional and private client base.
Founded: 1999
Investment Criteria: Early-Stage Growth Financing, Late Stage Expansion Financing, Buyout Transactions, Distressed/Turnaround Investments
Key Executives:
Peter Derendinger, CEO/Partner
Education: PhD, Law, University of Fribourg; Master of Laws, Northwestern University
Background: Swiss Life Private Equity Partners; Credit Suisse

2374 ALPHA BANK
105, Athinon Avenue
Maroussi
Athens 104 47
Greece

Phone: 801-113260000 Fax: 30-6199170
e-mail: complaints@alpha.gr
web: www.alpha.gr

Mission Statement: A group of companies with highly demanding goals and objectives in shoosing companies to invest in.
Geographic Preference: Greece
Founded: 1907
Investment Criteria: Early Stage, Expansion & Development Capital, Seed Capital, Start-Up Capital.

Venture Capital & Private Equity Firms / International Firms

Industry Group Preference: All Sectors Considered
Key Executives:
　Leonidas A Zonnios, General Manager
　Directorships: Banker, Executive Member
　Nicholas Beis, General Manager
　Directorships: Banker, Executive Member

2375 ALPHA BETEILIGUNGSBERATUNG GmbH
49 Avenue Hoche
Paris 75008
France
　　　　Phone: 33-156602020 Fax: 33-156601022
　　　　e-mail: secretariat@groupealpha.fr
　　　　web: www.alphagruppe.com

Mission Statement: Alpha specialises in mid-size LBOs and concentrates on well managed family-owned companies and fast growing companies with build-up opportunities in France, Germany and the Netherlands.
Geographic Preference: France, Germany, USA, Belgium, Netherlands, Switzerland, Austria
Fund Size: $1.5 Billion
Founded: 1985
Minimum Investment: $11.8 Million
Investment Criteria: Expansion and Development Capital, Buyout and Buyin
Industry Group Preference: All Sectors Considered
Portfolio Companies: Basler, BFM, CDC, Gortz & Schiele, Retif, Neuf Telecom, Histoire d'Or, Hyva, KP1, Loxam, Business Materis, Offset Gerhard Kaiser, Seloger, Protegys Group, RMC, Rue du Commerce, Safic Alcan, Salins du Midi, Stokomani, Tom Tailor, Trans-o-Flex, HarbourVest Partners
Key Executives:
　Alain Blanc-Brude, Chairman
　Thomas Mulliez, Managing Director

2376 ALPHAMUNDI GROUP LTD
Bahnhofstrasse 54
4th Floor
Zurich 8001
Switzerland
　　　　Phone: 41-44-5080-556 Fax: 41-44-5080-543
　　　　e-mail: info@alphamundi.ch
　　　　web: www.alphamundi.ch

Mission Statement: AlphaMundi Group Ltd is a commercial entity based in Switzerland and exclusively dedicated to Impact Investing: profitable investments that generate net benefits to society. AlphaMundi provides debt and equity financing to profitable and scalable ventures in strategic Sustainable Human Development sectors such as Microfinance, Affordable Education, Fairtrade Agriculture and Renewable Energy. AlphaMundi also contributes to the emergence of Impact Investing through education events, publications, and industry associations.
Founded: 2007
Industry Group Preference: Microfinance, Education, Agriculture, Renewable Energy
Key Executives:
　Tim Radjy, Founding CEO
　Education: Master of Arts, Political Science, University of Geneva
　Background: Morgan Stanley Capital International, UBS

2377 ALPINVEST GmbH Alpinvest
701 Citibank Tower
3 Garden Road
Hong Kong 60325
China
　　　　Phone: 85-228787099 Fax: 85-228787009
　　　　web: www.alpinvest.com

Mission Statement: AlpInvest Partners is a private equity investment manager with a global focus on a full spectrum of investment products.
Geographic Preference: Germany, Switzerland, Austria
Fund Size: $23.74 Billion
Founded: 1999
Investment Criteria: Buyouts, Fund to Fund Investment, Expansion Financing, Bridging Finance, Replacement, MBO, MBI, Takeover Financing
Industry Group Preference: Technology, Life Sciences
Portfolio Companies: Alfabet, Impress, Infitel, VPI Systems, Axxima, Brahms, co.don, Coley, Curacyte
Key Executives:
　Volkert Doeksen, Chairman, Managing Partner
　Education: MBA, Columbia University; Tax Law, University of Amsterdam; Civil Law, University of Utrecht
　Background: ABN AMRO
　Paul de Klerk, Chief Financial Officer & Chief Operating Officer
　e-mail: volkert.doeksen@alpinvest.com
　Education: MA, Law, University of Leiden
　Background: Dresdner Kleinwort Benson, Mezzanine Fund , US Buy-Out Fund, Dillon Read (Mergers & Acquisitions),
　Directorships: Managing Partner

2378 ALPINVEST HOLDING NV Alpinvest
Jachthavenweg 118
Amsterdam 1081 KJ
Netherlands
　　　　Phone: 31-205407575 Fax: 31-205407500
　　　　e-mail: wim.borgdorff@alpinvest.com
　　　　web: www.alpinvest.com

Mission Statement: Actively seeking new investments.
Geographic Preference: Europe, Worldwide
Fund Size: $100 Million
Founded: 1999
Investment Criteria: MBO/LBO mid-market, Venture Capital technology, Mezzanine and industrial holding on long-term
Industry Group Preference: Technology, Life Sciences
Portfolio Companies: Raet, ReMark, IMCD, FanoFineFood, Spring Flower, Itho, Krauthammer, Novagraaf, Driessen Aerospace, Vetus den Ouden, Halin, Euromate, Nijgh Periodieken, Avantium, Crucell, Galapagos, IsoTis
Key Executives:
　Volkert Doeksen, Chairman, Managing Director
　Education: MBA, Brunel University
　Background: Dresdner Kleinwort Benson Private Equity, Kleinwort Benson
　Directorships: Head of Investments
　Wim Borgdorff, Managing Partner
　Education: BA, MA , Science, Delft University of Technology; MBA, Erasmus University; MA, Real Estate, University of Amsterdam
　Background: ABP Investments, ING Asset Management
　Maarten Vervoort, Partner
　e-mail: maarten.vervoort@alpinvest.com
　Education: London Business School; MBE, Erasmus University
　Background: PricewaterhouseCoopers Management Consultants (PWC);Corporate & Operations Strategy team of PWC;NIB Capital Bank

2379 ALPINVEST PARTNERS B.V.
Jachthavenweg 118
Amsterdam 1081 KJ
Netherlands
　　　　Phone: 31 20 540 7575 Fax: 31 20 540 7500

Venture Capital & Private Equity Firms / International Firms

Other Locations:
AlpInvest U.S. Holdings, LLC
35th Floor
New York, NY 10171
Phone: 212-332-6240 **Fax:** 212-332-6241

701 Citibank Tower
3 Garden Road
Hong Kong
China
Phone: 852-28787099 **Fax:** 852-28787009

Key Executives:
Paul de Klerk, Managing Director
e-mail: paul.de.klerk@alpinvest.com
Education: MBA, Columbia University
Tatiana Chopova, Managing Director
e-mail: tatiana.chopova@alpinvest.com
Education: BS, University of Bristol; MBA, INSEAD
Background: Consultant, McKinsey & Co.
Peter Cornelius, Managing Director
e-mail: peter.cornelius@alpinvest.com
Education: London School of Economics; MD, Economics, University of Gottingen
Background: ING Asset Management
Rob de Jong, Managing Director
e-mail: rob.de.jong@alpinvest.com
Education: MSc, Business Economics, Erasmus University Rotterdam
Background: Senior Consultant, PricewaterhouseCoopers
Marek Herchel, Managing Director
e-mail: marek.herchel@alpinvest.com
Education: BS, Business Administration, MS, Finance, Suffolk University
Background: Senior Analyst, State Street
Wouter Moerel, Managing Director
e-mail: wouter.moerel@alpinvest.com
Education: MS, Business Administration, University of Groningen
Background: The Carlyle Group; Vice President, Corporate Finance, JPMorgan; Director, Corporate Finance, Lehman Brothers
Directorships: Lyceum Capital; Paragon Partners
Christophe Nicolas, Managing Director
e-mail: christophe.nicolas@alpinvest.com
Education: MBA, Ecole Superieure de Commerce de Paris
Background: Morgan Stanley
Chris Perriello, Managing Director
e-mail: chris.perriello@alpinvest.com
Education: BA, Economics, University of Pittsburgh; MBA, Georgia Institute of Technology
Background: Principal, Paul Capital Investments
Sander van Maanen, Managing Director
e-mail: sander.van.maanen@alpinvest.com
Education: MS, Chemical Engineering, Delft University of Technology; MBA, INSEAD
Background: Boston Consulting Group; Product Development Manager, Procter & Gamble
Maarten Vervoort, Managing Director
e-mail: maarten.vervoort@alpinvest.com
Education: Master, Business Economics, Erasmus University in Rotterdam
Background: PricewaterhouseCoopers Management Consultants; PWC; NIB Capital Bank
Directorships: Advent, Alpha, Atlas, Varclays, PE, B&S, Bain Capital Europe, Candover, CVC, Charterhouse, Cinven, Nordic Capital, Quadriga
George Westerkamp, Managing Director
e-mail: george.westerkamp@alpinvest.com
Education: MA, Economics, Erasmus University in Rotterdam
Background: Parnib; NIB Capital Bank
Directorships: Rayner Food Group, Baxi Group, Nycomed
Wendy Zhu, Managing Director
e-mail: wendy.zhu@alpinvest.com
Education: BS, Business Administration, University of Southern California; CFA
Background: Senior Vice President, Macquarie Funds Management

2380 ALTA BERKELEY ASSOCIATES
42 Berkeley Square
London W1J 5AW
United Kingdom
Phone: 44-2033931107 **Fax:** 44-2030700797
e-mail: tb@altaberkeley.com

Mission Statement: Actively seeking new investments.
Geographic Preference: US , Europe , Israel
Founded: 1982
Average Investment: $15.05 Million
Minimum Investment: $2.65 Million
Investment Criteria: Seed, Startup, Other Early Stage, Expansion and Development
Industry Group Preference: Components & IoT, Data Communications, Software Services, Technology, Biotechnology, Semiconductors
Portfolio Companies: Elantec Semiconductors, Frontier Silicon, Inside Contactless, Polatis, Siliquent, Synad, Syquest, Teradici, Xtellus, Cambridge Positioning Systems, Castify Networks, Dune Networks, Native Networks, Araccel, C-Dilla, Emme, Improveline, ioBox, M-Spatial, SBS Broadcasting, Scoo

Key Executives:
Bryan Wood, Partner
e-mail: bw@alta-berkeley.com
Education: MBA, Harvard Business School; BS, Industrial Engineering, Virginia Polytechnic Institute
Background: European Finance Vice President, Gould Inc; several other European and US finance and operating roles
Directorships: Founder
Tim Brown, Partner
Education: Degree in Physics, Manchester University; MBA, Cranfield School of Management
Background: Eight years technology venture capital, Alta Berkeley and 3i Cambridge; consultant project management in RF division of the JET European Nuclear Fusion programme; technical sales management, Leybold; product management, Surface Technology Systems; semicon
Hugh Smith, Partner
Education: Degree in Accountancy and Statistics, Southampton University
Background: Chartered Accountant with Arthur Young, managing client portfolio covering a wide range of industries
Directorships: Chief Operating Officer

2381 ALTA GROWTH CAPITAL
Bosque de Duraznos 127
4th floor
Bosques de las Lomas
D.F. 11700
Mexico
Phone: 52-5552543280
e-mail: info@agcmexico.com
web: www.agcmexico.com

Mission Statement: Alta Growth Capital manages a private equity fund focused on investments in middle market companies in Mexico. Our private equity, transactional, and operational experience, both in Mexico and internationally, makes us well-positioned to provide attractive returns for our investors and help our portfolio companies achieve success.

Geographic Preference: Mexico
Average Investment: $10-20 million

Venture Capital & Private Equity Firms / International Firms

Investment Criteria: Middle-Market Companies
Portfolio Companies: Amerimed, ARG, Bunker's Group, Medicus
Key Executives:
  Erik Carlberg, Managing Director
  Education: BA, MS, Business Administration, Ivey School of Business, University of Western Ontario
  Background: Partner, Baring Latin American Partners

2382 ALTA VENTURES MEXICO
Avenida Gomex Morin 955 Sur
Suite 315
Colonia Montbello
San Pedro Garza Garcia, Nuevo Leon 66279
Mexico

Phone: 52-8114779014
e-mail: info@altaventures.com
web: www.altaventures.com

Mission Statement: Alta Ventures Mexico is an early-stage venture capital fund. Based in Monterrey Mexico we provide seed, venture and growth capital to companies targeting high-growth markets. The Alta team has directly founded startups and as investors helped launch more than 80 companies.

Geographic Preference: Mexico
Fund Size: $70 million
Average Investment: $5 - $10 million
Minimum Investment: $50,000
Investment Criteria: Early-Stage
Industry Group Preference: Internet, SaaS, Mobile Computing, Consumer Services, Security, Communications, Healthcare
Portfolio Companies: AeroPRISE, Altiris, The American Academy, Amerimed, Ancestry.com, Grupo ARG, Bunker's, Certifacame.com, Convert.com, Dalus, Diverza, Energyn Corporation, Familylink, GlobalSIM, JSK Therapeutics, Juxta Labs, Kickstart Seed Fund, Knowlix, Master Financial Management, Murally, Panoptic Security, Public Engines, Reachable, Rhomobile, Senforce, Xtreme Cinemas

Other Locations:
  3315 Mayflower Avenue
  Suite 1
  Lehi, UT 84043
  Phone: 801-653-3926

Key Executives:
  Paul Ahlstrom, Managing Director
  Education: BA, Communications, Brigham Young University
  Background: Co-Founder, vSpring Capital

2383 ALTO INVEST
65, rue du Marechal Foch
Versailles 78000
France

Phone: 01-39543567 Fax: 01-39545376
e-mail: contact@altoinvest.fr
web: www.altoinvest.fr

Mission Statement: Alto Invest is a portfolio management company independently approved by the AMF, specializes in investing in SMEs. ALTO INVEST offers a range of FCIC, FIP and venture capital for private and institutional clients.

Geographic Preference: Europe, North America, Asia
Founded: 1994
Portfolio Companies: Akamedia, Cedip Infared Systems, Decalog, Dmailer, iORGA Group, Ma-Papaterie, Memobox, Netflective Technology, TalentSoft, TXCOM

2384 ALTOR EQUITY PARTNERS
Jakobsgatan 6
Stockholm 111 52
Sweden

Phone: 46-86789100 Fax: 46-86789101
e-mail: info@altor.com
web: www.altor.com

Mission Statement: Altor is a private equity firm focused on investing in and developing medium sized companies anchored in the Nordic region. Our ambition is to make a real difference as a valuable partner for owners and managers in building world class companies.

Geographic Preference: Nordic Region
Fund Size: 3.8 billion Euro
Founded: 2003
Portfolio Companies: AGR Group, Akers Group, Alo, Apotek Hjartat, Byggmax, Carnegie, Constructor, CTEK Creator Group, Dustin, ELIXIA, Eltek Group, Euro Carter, Ferrosan Medical Devices, Haarslev Industries, Helly Hansen, Lindorff Group, Max Matthiessen, Navico, Njorsk Gjenvinning, NorthStar, ONE, Orchid Orthopedic Solutions, Papyrus, Piab, Qmatic, Sonion, Wrist

Key Executives:
  Bengt Maunsbach, Partner

2385 ALVEN CAPITAL
1 Place Andre Malraux
Paris 75001
France

Phone: 33-155343838 Fax: 33-155343839
e-mail: contact@alvencapital.com
web: www.alvencapital.com

Mission Statement: Alven Capital assists companies and the leaders of its portfolio in the long term, particularly in terms of strategy, acquisitions and exit.

Geographic Preference: France
Fund Size: 100 million Euro
Founded: 2000
Average Investment: £1 Million - £5 Million
Industry Group Preference: Internet, Media, Information Technology
Portfolio Companies: AntVoice Group, Aquarelle.com, BirchBox, Commerce Guys, Coupling Wave Solutions, Digibonus, EBlink, EntropySoft, Ercom, Happyview.fr, iAdvise, Jobintree, Koala.ch, Lengow, Mailjet, Makemereach, MeilleursAgents.com, Metaboli, Mobiletag, MobPartner, Myfab, Novapost, Planetveo, Qosmos, Quelleenergie.fr, SimpleIT, Smallable, SoCloz, Splendia, Startingdot, TextMaster, Urban Rivals, Voiturelib

Key Executives:
  Guillaume Aubin, Managing Partner
  Education: Ecole Polytechnique
  Background: Banking Division, Paribas

2386 AMADEUS CAPITAL PARTNERS LIMITED
Mount Pleasant Housex
2 Mount Pleasant
Cambridge CB3 0RN
United Kingdom

Phone: 44-01223707000 Fax: 44-01223707070
e-mail: info@amadeuscapital.com

Mission Statement: Amadeus is a private venture capital firm specializing in high-technology firms who have global aspirations, defensible technology and a strong management team.

Geographic Preference: United Kingdom, Western Europe, Ireland
Fund Size: $489 million
Founded: 1997
Average Investment: $244 million
Minimum Investment: $17 million

Venture Capital & Private Equity Firms / International Firms

Investment Criteria: Seed, Start-up, Other early stage, Expansion and Development, Bridge finance, Secondary purchase/replacement capital, Rescue/turnaround, MBI
Industry Group Preference: Medical & Health Related, Chemicals, Communications, Internet Technology, Electronic Technology, Networking, E-Commerce & Manufacturing
Portfolio Companies: Cambridge Silicon Radio, Clearswift, Optos PLC, Southampton Photonics, Enigmatec, ArtimiCambridge Broadband, CSR, E14, Level 5 Networks, Nujira, PacketFrpont, Red-M, Xelerated, AePONA, Axiom, End2End, Orchestream, Smartner, Valista, Nanomagnetics, Plastic Logic, Power Paper, TeraView, Mediasurface, Quadstone, Ridgeway, Riskclick, Whereonearch, Lastminute, LeatherXchange, Leisure-Hunt, Silicon Media, Optos, Solexa

Key Executives:
  Anne Glover, Co-Founder & Chief Executive
  e-mail: info@amadeuscapital.com
  Education: Andrea holds a BSc in Economics from the London School of Economics and an MBA from Cambridge University
  Background: Financial Auditor, Executive Vice President of Villa Playa Dorada SA,
  Hermann Hauser PhD, Partner, Co-Founder
  e-mail: info@amadeuscapital.com
  Education: Vienna Univ.; Univ. of Cambridge
  Peter Wynn, Partner, Co-Founder
  e-mail: info@amadeuscapital.com
  Education: Chartered accountant
  Background: Director of Finance for Acorn Computers, International Computers.
  Directorships: co-founder
  Simon Cornwell, Partner
  e-mail: info@amadeuscapital.com
  Background: Apax Partners & Co. Ventures Ltd.

2387 AMALFI CAPITAL MANAGEMENT
Suite 804 No. 233 Weihai Road
Shanghai 200040
China

Phone: 8621-6165-9399

Mission Statement: Amalfi Capital is an investment fund focused on China with a long-short concentrated portfolio strategy. The fund offers differentiation in its approach to investing in Asia, its understanding of the impact and influence of technology and its assessment of the risks and opportunities associated with emerging markets.
Geographic Preference: Asia
Portfolio Companies: Qriously
Key Executives:
  Paul A Waide, Co-Founder/Chief Investment Officer
  Education: BA, Economics & Asian Studies, University of Melbourne
  Background: Vice President, Winnington Capital

2388 AMANAH VENTURES SDN BHD
19th Floor, Menara MIDF
82, Jalan Raja Chulan
21st Floor
Kuala Lumpur 50200
Malaysia

Phone: 603-21738888 Fax: 603-21738877
e-mail: gcc@midf.com.my
web: www.midf.com.my

Mission Statement: Promotes the development of the manufacturing industry in Malaysia through the provision of medium and long-term loans.
Geographic Preference: Malaysia
Fund Size: $1.58 Million
Founded: 1960
Average Investment: $1.32 Million
Minimum Investment: $0.8 Million

Investment Criteria: All Stages, including Expansion, Mezzanine
Industry Group Preference: Industrial Services, Pharmaceuticals, Biotechnology, Advanced Manufacturing, Brokering, Retailing, Property Management, Asset Management
Key Executives:
  Tan Sri Dato Mahmood Bin Taib, Chairman
  Foo Wei Hoong, Chief Financial Officer

2389 AMANET TECHNOLOGIES LIMITED
34 Iron Street
Tel Aviv 69710
Israel

Phone: 972-37659555 Fax: 972-36440125
e-mail: amanet@amanet.co.il
web: www.amanet.co.il

Mission Statement: Provides in-depth services, working together with customers to identify needs and identify solution options.
Geographic Preference: Israel, UK, France, Germany, Norway, Switzerland, Australia, Czech Rep
Founded: 1970
Industry Group Preference: Technology, Computer Related, Electronic Technology, Pharmaceuticals, Telecommunications, Financial Services, Insurance, Tourism, Oil & Gas, Life Sciences, Marketing
Portfolio Companies: Avgol (Plastics), Amcor, A.S.T. Soldering Technologies, A.A. Kachtan, Arit Optronics, Atifon (Packaging prod.), Ashot Ashkelon (metal), Brom compositions, Coca-Cola, Deutsch-Dagan (Elect.), Dead Sea Industries (Chemicals), Echtman Engineering Co., EL-OP (Optics), Elbi
Key Executives:
  Avraham Assaf, Investor Relations
  e-mail: amanet@amanet.co.il
  Prisma Finance, Market Maker

2390 AMBIENT SOUND INVESTMENTS
Tallinn
Estonia

e-mail: info@asi.ee
web: www.asi.ee

Mission Statement: We are a unique seed investment company, investing in people and ideas in technology and across the industry spectrum. Our team is made up of founding engineers at Skype and professionals with tech, operational and finance backgrounds.
Geographic Preference: Asia, Europe, United States
Fund Size: 100 million Euro
Founded: 2003
Investment Criteria: Seed-Stage, Startup
Industry Group Preference: Enterprise Software, Computer Hardware & Software, Healthcare, Life Sciences, Internet, Consumer Services, Networking, Communications, Semiconductors
Portfolio Companies: Armorize, Blaast, Blip.tv, Clifton, DailyPerfect, Drimki, EGeen, Eleutian, Evikon, Flowplay, Frenzoo, Guardtime, InkSpin1, Markit, Mendeley, My Heritage, Oskando, Progeniq, Senseg, Wahanda
Key Executives:
  Tauno Tats, Chief Executive Officer
  e-mail: tauno@asi.ee
  Education: MSc, Tallinn Technical University
  Background: Vice-Chancellor for the Ministry of Finance of Estonia

Venture Capital & Private Equity Firms / International Firms

2391 AMBIENTA ENVIRONMENTAL ASSETS
Piazza Fontana, 6
Milan 20122
Italy

Phone: 39-027217461
e-mail: info@ambientasgr.com
web: www.ambientasgr.com

Mission Statement: An independent growth private equity investor, focused on industrial growth investing.
Geographic Preference: Europe
Founded: 2007
Industry Group Preference: Environment, Energy, Waste & Recycling, Renewable Energy
Portfolio Companies: Tattile, Found Ocean, Tower Light, Amplio Filtration Group, MBA Polymers, Spig, Ravelli, Icq Holding, Ambienta Biomasse
Key Executives:
Nino Tronchetti Provera, Managing Partner
Education: Business Adminstration, Luiss University; MBA, INSEAD
Background: CEO, Finsiel; Founder, Cam Technolgie

2392 AMICUS CAPITAL PARTNERS
Stone Lodge, Clare Road
Ballycastle BT54 6DJ
Northern Ireland

Phone: 44-2820769322

Mission Statement: Amicus Capital Partners Ltd is a private equity network that specialises in unusual investment opportunities. Amicus Capital Partners have an appetite for MBO's, BIMBO's, unpopular sectors and tough turnaround situations.
Geographic Preference: United Kingdom, North America, Ireland, Turkey
Investment Criteria: MBO, Turnarounds
Industry Group Preference: Industrial Services, Media, Retail, Consumer & Leisure, Healthcare, Technology
Portfolio Companies: ACS, Adria, AP Technical Textiles, APW Yarn Technologies, Glenaden Shirts Limited, Global Armour, Origin Fertility Care, Rombah Wallace
Key Executives:
John Beddows, Partne5r
Background: Vice President, Worldwide, UK Managing Director, Kurt Salmon Associates

2393 AMMER PARTNERS
Schauenburgstrasse 27
Hamburb 20095
Germany

Phone: 49-40-2000-3960
e-mail: info@ammerpartners.vc
web: www.ammerpartners.vc

Mission Statement: Ammer Partners' multi-disciplinary team supports start-ups and established companies with capital, know-how and networks on the basis of long-standing experience as a CEO, investor and advisor. Our focus is on companies which offer security-relevant services or products. For us the term 'security' contains all areas in which persons, infomations or objects are protected - no matter whether in a private or commercial environment.
Geographic Preference: Germany
Industry Group Preference: Security, Consumer Services, Retail, Consumer & Leisure, Clean Technology, Communications, High Technology
Portfolio Companies: Netbreeze, Secusmart
Key Executives:
Dieter Ammer, Founder/Senior Partner
Background: Partner, Arthur Andersen & Co.; CEO, Zucker AG

2394 AMOREPACIFIC VENTURES
181, 2ga Hangang-ro
Yongsan-gu
Seoul 140-777
South Korea

web: ventures.amorepacific.com

Mission Statement: AMOREPACIFIC Ventures is the AMOREPACIFIC group's corporate venture capital arm. We invest in early and later stage opportunities which are strategically relevant to AMOREPACIFIC.
Founded: 2011
Investment Criteria: All-Stages
Industry Group Preference: Health & Wellness

2395 AMP PRIVATE CAPITAL NEW ZEALAND LIMITED AMP Capital
Level 14, HP Tower, 171 Featherston Street
Wellington NV
New Zealand

Phone: 64-449-42200 Fax: 64-449-42123
web: www.ampcapital.co.nz

Mission Statement: AMP Capital Investors (New Zealand) Limited is AMP's specialist fund manager; it identifies financial market opportunities that investment managers actively turn into enhanced returns for their clients.
Geographic Preference: Australia , New Zealand
Fund Size: $7.1 Billion
Key Executives:
Graham Law, Managing Director
Background: Treasury Manager, Natural Gas Corporation
Nick Dobson, Principal

2396 AMPEZZO PARTNERS
36 Upper Brook Street
London W1K 7QJ
United Kingdom

Phone: 44-2074999081
e-mail: info@ampezzo.co.uk
web: www.ampezzo.co.uk

Mission Statement: Ampezzo Capital is a private equity firm specialised in online growth stage businesses. Ampezzo I currently has a portfolio of 7 investments employing over 100 employees.
Founded: 2010
Investment Criteria: Growth Equity, Later-Stage
Industry Group Preference: Internet
Other Locations:
Ampezzo Capital PCC Ltd.
Ogier House, St. Julian's Avenue
St. Peter Port
Guernsey GY1 1WA
United Kingdom
Key Executives:
Henrik Ljung, Co-Founding Partner
Background: CEO/Partner, Siguiente Capital AB

2397 AMPHION CAPITAL PARTNERS
19 Buckingham Gate
London W1J 8DJ
United Kingdom

Phone: 44-2086303843 Fax: 44-2070-169100
e-mail: info@amphionplc.com
web: www.amphionplc.com

Mission Statement: Amphion creates, operates and finances life science and technology companies in partnership with corporations, governments, universities and entrepreneurs.
Geographic Preference: UK, USA, Asia, Western Europe
Fund Size: $1.6 Billion
Founded: 1998

Venture Capital & Private Equity Firms / International Firms

Average Investment: $20 Million
Minimum Investment: $15 Million
Investment Criteria: Public and private early-stage investments
Industry Group Preference: Life Sciences, Technology, Pharmaceuticals, Genetic Engineering
Portfolio Companies: Motif Biosciences Inc., WellGen Inc., Beijing Med-Pharm Co. Ltd., Beijing Med-Pharm Co. Ltd., Firestar Software Inc., AXCESS International Inc., Durham Scientific Crystals Limited (DSC), Supertron Technologies, Inc.

Key Executives:
R. James Macaleer, Non-executive Chairman
Robert J. Bertoldi, President and Chief Financial Officer

2398 AMWIN MANAGEMENT PTY LIMITED
66 Mamre Road
St Mary's
Level 4
New South Wales 2760
Australia

Phone: 02-98332100 Fax: 02-98337900
e-mail: melinda@asims.com.au
web: www.amwin.com.au

Mission Statement: AMWIN Management is an international partnership between CHAMP Ventures and the Walden International Investment Group.

Geographic Preference: Australia, New Zealand
Fund Size: $42 Million
Founded: 1997
Average Investment: $2.5 Million
Minimum Investment: $1 Million
Investment Criteria: Start-up, Mezzanine, Expansions
Industry Group Preference: Electronic Technology, Medical, Manufacturing, Internet Technology, Health Related, Semiconductors, Infrastructure
Portfolio Companies: Seek Communications Limited, Gekko Systems Pty Limited, Austal Ships, Medical Imaging Australasia Group Limited, Looksmar

Key Executives:
Chon C Tang, Director
Education: Bachelor of Business Accounting, University of Western Sydney
Background: Australian Mezzanine Investments
Hock Voon Loo, Director

2399 ANACACIA CAPITAL
Level 2, 4-10 Bay Street
Double Bay
Sydney NSW 2028
Australia

Phone: 612-93631222 Fax: 612-85804600
e-mail: contact@anacacia.com.au
web: www.anacacia.com.au

Mission Statement: Anacacia Capital is a leading Australian private equity firm that focuses on small-medium enterprises (SMEs) in the mid-market. Our business is investing private equity into established companies that are managing ownership change, succession, management buyouts and new acquisitions. We provide strategic insight and capital to outstanding management teams to help these businesses to grow.

Geographic Preference: Australia, New Zealand
Fund Size: $125 million
Founded: 2007
Portfolio Companies: Appen Butler Hill, Home Appliances, Lomb Scientific, Muir Engineering Group, Norwest Productions, Planet Services, Rafferty's Garden, Roofsafe

Key Executives:
Jeremy A Samuel, Founder/Managing Director
Education: BA, Bachelor of Law, University of New South Wales; MBA, Yale University School of Management

Directorships: Appen, Home Appliances, Rafferty's Garden

2400 ANGEL COFUND
Angel CoFund Foundry House
3 Millsands
Sheffield S3 8NH
United Kingdom

e-mail: info@angelcofund.co.uk
web: www.angelcofund.co.uk

Mission Statement: The fund has been designed and established by a consortium of private and public bodies with expertise in business angel investment. It is a private sector body with clear objectives to boost the quality and quantity of business angel investing in England, and to support long-term, high quality jobs in growing companies.

Geographic Preference: United Kingdom
Fund Size: £50 million
Founded: 2011
Average Investment: £100 Million
Minimum Investment: £100,000
Portfolio Companies: Phase Vision, Style-Passport.com, Future Drinks, Enval, PlayJam, Leanworks, Non-Linear Dynamics, CrowdVision, MoBank, Micrima, HipSnip, Ebury Partners, Advanced LEDs, Gcrypt, Sanona, Upad, LumeJet

2401 ANGELAB VENTURES
Via P. Mascagni 14
Milan 20122
Italy

e-mail: info@angelabventures.com
web: www.angelabventures.com

Mission Statement: Founded by Angelo Moratti, AngeLab's Group focuses on Value Investing and Building Companies. We seek innovative ventures in the areas of lifestyle, new media and life sciences.

Industry Group Preference: New Media, Life Sciences
Portfolio Companies: Applix, Dal Bolognese Ristorante, Desantis, Emjag Digital, Golazo, Kensington & Sons, Lovin' Scoopful, Privategriffe, Telecom Design, Tommie Cooper, Viagogo, Wat-Aah

Key Executives:
Angelo Moratti, Chairman/CEO
Background: Chairman, Saras SpA; Chairman, Sarlux
Lorenzo Pozza, Vice Chairman
Education: L Bocconi University
Background: Founding Partner, Partners CPA
Paolo Gualdani, Investment Director
Education: BS, MS, Business Administration, L Bocconi University

2402 ANGLO CHINESE INVESTMENT COMPANY LIMITED
40th Floor
Two Exchange Square
8 Connaught
Central
Hong Kong

Phone: 852-28454400 Fax: 852-28451162
e-mail: accf@anglochinesegroup.com
web: www.anglochinesegroup.com

Mission Statement: Provides advisory services for mergers and acquisitions, raising capital, corporate reorganisation and rescue, litigation support and regulatory compliance.

Geographic Preference: Hong Kong, China
Founded: 1988
Investment Criteria: Value driven or Event driven opportunities
Portfolio Companies: Melco International Development Limited, K.Wah International Holdings Limited, MediaNation Inc., Pacific Coffee (Holdings) Limited, RT Sourcing Asia

Limited, China Resources Cement Holdings Limited, Fandango Inc., Tse Sui Luen Jewellery Limited

Key Executives:
Stephen Clark, Managing director and co-founder
Background: Wardley Limited;Citicorp International Limited; First National Bank of Boston
Christopher Howe, Managing director & Co-Founder
Background: Hong Kong Securities Institute;Listing Committee of The Stock Exchange of Hong Kong;Wardley Limited;Citicorp International Limited;Standard Merchant Bank Limited

2403 ANNAPURNA VENTURES
Piazzale Biacamano 2
Milan 20121
Italy

e-mail: info@annapurnaventures.com
web: www.annapurnaventures.com

Mission Statement: The mission of Annapurna Ventures is to identify and support disruptive innovations in the digital media industry, creating great companies with a proactive investment process.

Founded: 2009
Investment Criteria: Seed-Stage, Early-Stage, First-Stage, Second-Round
Industry Group Preference: Consumer Internet, Enterprise Software, Mobile, Digital Media & Marketing, E-Commerce & Manufacturing
Portfolio Companies: Appsbuilder, Paperlit, Pharmawizard, Plugg, MoneyFarm

Key Executives:
Massimiliano Magrini, Founder/Managing Partner
Background: Publitalia, Rusconi, Sole 24 Ore, Altavista, Google Italy

2404 ANT FINANCIAL
Z Space
No. 556 Xixi Road
Hangzhou
China

Phone: 86 571-2688-8888 Fax: 86 571-8643-2811
web: www.antfin.com

Mission Statement: A technology company that aims to create inclusive financial services to the world through technology innovations and an open, shared credit system.

Geographic Preference: China, Global
Fund Size: $150 Billion
Founded: 2014
Investment Criteria: Financial Technology
Industry Group Preference: Financial, Technology
Portfolio Companies: Alipay, Ant Financial Cloud, Ant Fortune, MYbank, Zhima Credit

Key Executives:
Eric Jing, Executive Chairman/CEO
Education: MBA, Carlson School of Management, University of Minnesota; BEng, College of Economics & Management, Shanghai Jiao Tong University
Background: CFO, Guangzhou Pepsi Cola Beverage Co; Senior Finance Director/Vice President, Alibaba Group; Chief Financial Officer, Alipay
Simon Hu, President
Education: EMBA, China Europe International Business School
Background: China Construction Bank; China Everbright Bank
Leiming Chen, General Counsel
Education: JD, Osgoode Hall Law School, York University
Background: Partner, Simpson Thacher & Bartlett

2405 ANTERRA CAPITAL
Herengracht 450
Amsterdam 1017 CA
Netherlands

Phone: +31 202 051 034
e-mail: office@anterracapital.com
web: www.anterracapital.com

Mission Statement: Anterra Capital is an independent growth capital fund. We invest in fast growing companies that are working to make the global food supply chain safer, more efficient and more sustainable. Our focus is on supporting the growth of companies who are commercializing novel technologies and services. We invest across the food supply chain from novel agro inputs and precision farming through to smarter logistics and consumer safety. We do not invest in other funds, land, operating assets, or other capital intensive businesses.

Average Investment: EUR 2M to EUR 12M
Industry Group Preference: Agriculture, Farming
Portfolio Companies: Voltea, Food Freshness Technology, Ceradis, BluWrap

Key Executives:
Adam Anders, Managing Partner
Education: Bachelors Degree in Commerce, University of Adelaide, Australia; MBA, Cambridge University
Background: Rabobank; Ironbridge Capital; Bain & Co.
Koen van Engelen, Partner
Education: Masters, Financial Economics, University of Amsterdam
Background: Rabobank Private Equity; Alpinvest
Philip Austin, Partner
Education: Masters, Chemical Engineerng and Pharmaceutical Chemistry, Heriot Watt University in Edinburgh
Background: Rabo Ventures; Atlas Ventures; McKinsey & Company; ICI
Maarten Goossens, Principal
Education: Masters of Business Administration, Free University of Amsterdam
Background: Rabo Ventures

2406 ANTHEMIS GROUP
Spirella House
2nd Floor 266-270 Regent Street
London W1B 3AH
United Kingdom

Phone: 44-20-7067-9050
e-mail: info@anthemis.com
web: www.anthemis.com

Mission Statement: Anthemis Group is the leading digital financial services investment and advisory firm focused on re-inventing financial services through technology for the 21st century. We advise, transform and invest in businesses that are building better ways to design, consume and distribute financial services in the Information Economy.

Investment Criteria: Growth Stage
Industry Group Preference: Financial Services
Portfolio Companies: Afb, AGILEci, Automatic Betterment, Blueleaf, EToro, Fidor, FinanceAcar, Indix, Metamarkets, MoPowered, Moven, Payoff, PayPerks, PeerIndex, Premise, Seedcamp, Simple, Suprmasv, The Climate Corporation, The Currency Cloud, Trov, Visual.Ly, Xanapto, Zyfin

2407 ANTRAK CAPITAL
Marc House
13/14 Great Saint Thomas Aposlte
London EC4V 2BB
United Kingdom

Phone: 44-2071834858

Mission Statement: Antrak Capital contributes growth capital and our time, targeted at helping businesses address the

Venture Capital & Private Equity Firms / International Firms

barriers to expansion thereby speeding up the achievement of the common goal.

Geographic Preference: United Kingdom
Industry Group Preference: Internet, SaaS, Digital Media & Marketing, Mobile
Portfolio Companies: Cognitive Match, CommonTime, i-Nexus, PeerIndex, weComm

Key Executives:
Kevin Douglas, Partner
Directorships: CommonTime

2408 ANVAR
27-31, avenue du Général Leclerc
Cedex 09
Paris 94710
France

Phone: 33-141-798000 Fax: 33-142660220
web: www.bpifrance.fr

Mission Statement: Promoting and financing technological innovation, especially for small and medium-sized companies and research and development partnerships.

Geographic Preference: Europe
Investment Criteria: Small and Medium Enterprises

Key Executives:
Michael Guilbad, Delegate General Manager
Jean-Marie Sepulchre, General Secretary

2409 ANZ GRINDLAYS 31 INVESTMENT SERVICES LIMITED
15 Kasturba Gandhi Marg
New Delhi 110 001
India

Phone: 91-1123721232 Fax: 91-1123721249

Mission Statement: Actively seeking new investments.

Fund Size: $13.5 Million
Founded: 1835

2410 ANZ PRIVATE EQUITY Private Equity Media
Level 8, ANZ Centre, 23-29 Albert Street
Auckland
New Zealand

Phone: 64-800-151393 Fax: 64-937-44121
e-mail: anzprivatenz@anz.com
web: www.anz.com

Mission Statement: Actively seeking new investments.

Geographic Preference: New Zealand, Austrailia
Fund Size: $302 Million
Founded: 1835
Minimum Investment: $0.75 Million
Investment Criteria: Development and Growth, Expansion, Late-Stage, Management BuyOuts or Management Buy-Ins
Portfolio Companies: Argent (Ford Alloy Wheel Plant), Motion Industries (Saeco and Precision Bearings), Alto Plastics, Securimax, Pacific Print Group

Key Executives:
Michael Smith, Chief Executive Officer
Education: Dumfries Academy;MA from the University of Edinburgh;MBA- Cranfield School of Management;London Business School
Background: Ford of Europe;Citibank;Standard Chartered Plc.;International Monetary Conference;Business Council of Australia and the Australian Graduate School of Management; London Stock Exchange, Capital Radio Plc., the Auditing Practices Board, Cranfield School of Management
Directorships: Member of the Foreign Affairs Council & The Business Regulation Advisory Group
Shayne Elliott, Chief Financial Officer

2411 AON JAUCH & HUBENER GmbH Aon Corporation
Lyonerstrasse 15 (ATRICOM)
Frankfurt 60528
Germany

Phone: 49-69297270 Fax: 49-692-97276200
Toll-Free: 1877-3844276
web: www.aon.com

Mission Statement: AON Mergers & Acquisitions Group (AMAG) provides risk, insurance & human capital advisory services to private equity investors through due diligence leading to transaction solutions.

Geographic Preference: Worldwide
Founded: 1982

Key Executives:
Michael O'Halleran, Chairman
Education: Undergraduate, Kansas State University; MBA, Harvard Business School
Background: Head Financial Services Practice, McKinsey & Company; Investment Banker, Piper Jaffray and Hopwood; Investment Banker, Federal Reserve Bank of Kansas City
Directorships: International Insurance Society; Financial Services Roundtable; Economic Club of Chicago
Axel Heitkamp, Chief Executive Officer
Background: CEO, Aon Corporation
Directorships: Board of Trustees, Northwestern University; Life Trustee, Rush University Medical Center; Director, Chicago Bears Football Club
Michael O'Halleran, Senior Executive VP
Education: BA Accounting & Finance, University of Wisconsin-Whitewater
Background: Chairman/CEO, Aon Global Re and Wholesale; Senior Executive, Wausau Insurance; Senior Executive, General Reinsurance; Senior Executive, Alexander Re
Directorships: Economic Club of Chicago; World Presidents Organization; World Business Chicago; Cardinal Health Board of Directors;

2412 AON MERGERS & ACQUISITIONS GROUP
8 Devonshire Square
London EC2M 4PL
England

Phone: 44-2076235500 Fax: 33-158-777777
Toll-Free: 1877-3844276
web: www.aon.com

Mission Statement: Aon's merger and acquisition experts provide a range of services and access to a global network of integrated resources to help you manoeuvre safely through your transaction. By providing in-depth due diligence and transaction solutions, we will help enhance your value creation and enable your management to identify the hidden opportunities and financial value so crucial to your portfolio company or corporate acquisition.

Founded: 1982

Key Executives:
Gregory C. Case, President & Chief Executive Officer
Patrick G. Ryan, Executive Chairman

2413 AON RISK SOLUTIONS Aon Corporation
Rue Jules Cockxstraat 8-10
Brussels BE-1160
Belgium

Phone: 32-027309511 Fax: 32-27309888
Toll-Free: 1877-3844276
web: www.aon.com

Mission Statement: Aon Corporation is a leading provider of risk management services, insurance and reinsurance broker-

Venture Capital & Private Equity Firms / International Firms

age, human capital and management consulting, and specialty insurance underwriting.

Geographic Preference: Belgium
Founded: 1982
Industry Group Preference: Insurance Brokerage, Risk Management, Human Capital Consulting
Key Executives:
   Aon Benfield, Executive Chairman
   e-mail: herman_kerremans@aon.be

2414 APAX GLOBIS PARTNERS & COMPANY
Globis Capital Partners/Apax
Sumitomo Realty & Development Kojimachi Build
5-1 Nibancho
Chiyoda-ku
Tokyo 102-0084
Japan

Phone: 81-352753939 **Fax:** 81-352753825
e-mail: info-gcp@globis.co.jp
web: www.globiscapital.co.jp

Mission Statement: A joint venture between Globis and Apax Partners that targets companies residing in the technology, retail, and health care sectors.
Geographic Preference: Japan
Fund Size: $166 Million
Founded: 1996
Average Investment: $5 Million
Minimum Investment: $1.6 Million
Investment Criteria: Early Stage, Expansion Stage, Later Stage
Industry Group Preference: Technology, Software, Information Technology, Digital Media & Marketing, Retailing, Healthcare
Portfolio Companies: AcuteLogic Corporation, Embedded Linux Technology Inc., Link Evolution, Lumin-oZ Co. Ltd., Nozomi Photonics Co. Ltd., Optware Corporation, PhotoniXnet Corporation, e-trees Japan Inc., C-guys Inc, ZMP Inc., Digital Media Professionals Inc., Wide Corporat
Key Executives:
   Yoshito Hori, Representative partners, Globis President
   Education: BA, Economics, Hitotsubashi University; MBA, Harvard Business School
   Background: Canon Inc
   Shoichi Kariyazono, Partner
   Education: BA, Law, Keio University; MBA, University of Pittsburgh
   Background: Management Strategy Division of Sanwa Research Institute Corporation
   Yumiko Hatori, Senior Associate
   Education: BS, Engineering, Tokyo University
   Background: Arthur D. Little, Inc
   Keisuke Ide, Principal
   Education: BA, Economics, Keio University; MBA, Stanford University
   Background: Sumitomo Bank, NEC
   Tetshushi Kawaguchi, Partner
   Education: BS, MS, Tokyo University
   Background: Arthur D. Little
   Akihiro Higashi, Senior Associate
   Education: MBA, London Business School, Masters, Policy and Management, Doshisha Graduate Unversity
   Background: Management Strategy Division of Sanwa Research Institute Corporation
   Shinichi Takamiya, Partner, Chief Strategy Officer
   Education: BA, Economics, Sophia University; MBA, New York University; CPA
   Background: Worked with 5 big audit firms in New York and Tokyo
   Minoru Imano, Partner, Chief Operating Officer
   Education: BS, Engineering, University of Waterloo; MBA, Japan American Institute of Management Science
   Background: Turbolinux's Embedded Division, Metrowerks Corporation

2415 APAX PARTNERS ET CIE
33 Jermyn Street
Cedex 16
London SW1Y 6DN
United Kingdom

Phone: 44-2078726300 **Fax:** 44-2076666441
e-mail: partners@apax-partners.fr
web: www.apax.com

Mission Statement: Actively seeking new investments in fast growing sectors.
Founded: 1980
Investment Criteria: Start-up, Early Stage, Development, Expansion, LBO, LBI, Turnaround and Restructuring
Industry Group Preference: Information Technology, Telecommunications, Health Related, Biotechnology, Multimedia, Retailing, Financial Services, Business Products & Services, Healthcare, Media, Retail, Consumer & Leisure, Technology & Telecommunications
Portfolio Companies: Aigle, CCMX, Cyperus, Future Publishing/Edicorp, Gifi, Hybrigenics, Meca-Teno, Morgan International, Syntem, Tredi, iMediation
Key Executives:
   Martin Halusa, Chief Executive Officer
   e-mail: jl.rambaud@apax-partners.fr
   Education: Ecole des Hautes Etudes Commerciales
   Background: Assistant Controller/Associate/Manager Structured Finance, Citibank, Gifi, Lehmann
   Giancarlo Aliberti, Partner
   Background: Associate Professor of Finance, HEC; Institut de Développement Industriel (IDI), Paris; Co-Founder, Apax Partners, Aigle, Celio, Histoire d'Or, Kalamazoo, Groupe Plien Ciel
   Ellie Beare, Associate
   Background: Marketing/Sales Director/VP, American Express; CEO, CEPP, CEPP, Cyperus
   Arnaud Bosquet, Associate
   e-mail: p.degiovanni@apax-partners.fr
   Education: Ecole Polytechnique
   Background: Consultant at Cofror; Controller at Neiman Group; Consultant at Société Générale; Turnaround of Criss, Effik, Icare, Horis Group, French Venture Capital Association (AFIC)
   Hafiz Chagani, Senior Associate
   e-mail: r.lambert@apax-partners.fr
   Education: Ecole des Hautes Etudes Commerciales; Institut d'Etudes Politiques de Paris
   Background: Managing Director, Europcar; Managing Director, Renault, UK; Executive VP, Renault, North America, Gifi, Frans-Bonhomme, Cofinluxe, Dagard
   Gabriele Cipparrone, Partner
   e-mail: e.misrahi@apax-partners.fr
   Education: Ecole Polytechnique; Harvard Business School
   Background: IT Specialist, McKinsey & Company; VP Sales/Service, M/A-COM, Desk, Prosodie, IMédiation, Travelprice
   Fiona Cooper, Director of Tax
   e-mail: c.rosevegue@apax-partners.fr
   Education: Graduate ESLSCA; French Chartered Accountant
   Background: Financial Analyst at GE Information Systems; Accounting and Managment Information Systems Manager, Ford (France); Controller, Lawry's Foods, Inc. (France); European Director of Finance, Levi-Strauss; CFO, FNAC.Horis Group, Desk
   Directorships: Qualified French Chartered Accountant
   Simon Cresswell, Partner, General Counsel
   e-mail: l.ganem@apax-partners.fr
   Education: MD, Paris University of Medicine; Columbia Business School
   Background: Baxter International; Vice-Chairman, OVI; Consultant, Eurofinance; Consultancy practice specialising in licensing, regulatory matters and mergers

Venture Capital & Private Equity Firms / International Firms

& acquisitions for French and 23 American companies, Nicox, IDM, Syntem, Hybrigenics
Ellen de Kreij, Investor Relations
e-mail: b.pivin@apax-partners.fr
Education: Ecole Polytechnique; Ecole Nationale Superieure des Telecommunications; MBA, Harvard University
Background: Engineer, Alcatel Group, France; Project Director, Alcatel Network Systems, USA, Meca-Teno, Atlanmold, Dagard, CCMX

2416 APIDC-VENTURE CAPITAL LIMITED
8-2-546, Plot No.140, Sheesh Mahal
Road No 7
Banjara Hills
Hyderabad 500 034
India
Phone: 91-4023351044 Fax: 91-4023351047
e-mail: info@ventureast.net
web: www.ventureast.net

Mission Statement: Actively seeking new investments.
Fund Size: $300 million
Key Executives:
  Ramesh Alur, General Partner
  Sameer Sawarkar, Chief Executive Officer

2417 AQUAGRO FUND
6 Kaufman Street
Beit Gibor
14th Floor, PO Box 17
Tel Aviv 68012
Israel
Phone: 972-37954111 Fax: 972-37954122
web: www.aquagrofund.com

Mission Statement: AquAgro Fund, L.P. is a venture capital fund focused on Israel's innovative water and agriculture technologies, as well as other innovative clean technologies. The fundamental problems in the water, energy and food sectors globally are growing steadily in gravity and magnitude and present a series of challenges to all of us. Along with these challenges come very big opportunities to companies which will create new cost effective and groundbreaking technologies that will provide solutions on a global scale to these very real problems which will stay with us in decades to come.
Geographic Preference: Israel
Industry Group Preference: Water, Agriculture, Clean Technology
Portfolio Companies: AquAgro Lab, Desalitech, Computerized Electricity Systems, Evogene, Impel Microchip, Transbiodiesel, Tomaisins, Variable Wind Solutions, ZoOpt
Key Executives:
  Benjamin Gaon, Chairman
  Background: President/Chairman, B. Gaon Holdings Ltd.; President/CEO, Koor Industries

2418 AQUITAINE INVESTMENT ADVISORS LIMITED
Suite 1905 ING Tower, 308 Des Voeux Road
Far East Financial Centre
Central
Hong Kong
Phone: 852-25281600 Fax: 852-25281900
web: www.aquitaine.com.hk

Mission Statement: Aquitaine Investment Advisors Ltd, an investment management firm, specialising in alternative investments targeted to Asia and Japan on behalf of institutional investors.
Geographic Preference: US, Europe and Asia
Founded: 1999

Investment Criteria: Early Stages
Key Executives:
  Marlene R Wittman, Group Managing Director
  Education: AB International Economics & MBA International Finance, Princeton University's Woodrow Wilson School of International/Public Affairs; Fudan University; Institute of International Relations of National Chengchi University
  Background: Headed, Nikko Europe's Asian Equities; Director, Nikko Securities
  Directorships: Investment Advisor, Securities and Futures Commission
  Arthur E Yama, Managing Director
  Education: BS Economics, Dartmouth College; MAR (Real Estate), Harvard University
  Background: Director, Managing Partners Limited; Senior Regional Analyst, Nikko Securites; VP, Batterymarch Real Estate Advisors; VP, Liberty Properties
  Directorships: Investment Advisor, Securities and Futures Commission

2419 ARAVIS VENTURES
Merkurstrasse 70
Zurich CH-8032
Switzerland
Phone: 41-434992000 Fax: 41-434992001
e-mail: info@aravis.ch
web: www.aravis.ch

Mission Statement: Aravis is the first independent Swiss on-shore private equity house, an established investor in the renewable energy and life science spaces.
Fund Size: 250 million Swiss francs
Founded: 2001
Industry Group Preference: Renewable Energy, Life Sciences
Portfolio Companies: Ambrx, Athelas, Biotie Therapies, Borean Pharma, Donnadolce Service SRL, Energy Life One SRL, EntreMed, Evolva, HF2 SRL, Ikaria, IMVision, Kalypsys, LuciaWind AG, Marino Med, Merlion Pharma, Miikana Therpeutics, Mundus Energia SRL, NovImmune, Nura, Omeros, Panomics, RuiYi, S*Bio, SOGEM, Symetis, Synosia Therpeutics, Telormedix
Key Executives:
  Jean-Philippe Tripet, Founder/Managing Partner
  e-mail: jeanphillippe@aravis.ch
  Education: Business Administration, University of Geneva
  Background: Senior Executive Vice President, Head of Sector, Lombard Odier & Cie
  Directorships: Telormedix, Symetis, S Bio, Merlion, Maison Takuya Pte Ltd, Evolva, Synosia, Omeros

2420 ARCHER CAPITAL
13 Hickson Road
Suite 7, Pier 2/3
Dawes Point
Sydney NSW 2000
Australia
Phone: 61-282433333 Fax: 61-292413151
web: www.archercapital.com.au

Mission Statement: Leading private equity investment house in Australia.
Geographic Preference: Australia, New Zealand
Fund Size: $3 Billion
Founded: 1986
Investment Criteria: LBO, Middle Market
Portfolio Companies: Amart All Sports, Australian Geographics, Dome Coffees, Emeco, Hirequip Projex, John West Foods, MCK Group, Red Paper Group, Repco Group, Signature Security Group, SULO, Tasman Building Products

Venture Capital & Private Equity Firms / International Firms

Key Executives:
Andrew Gray, Managing Director
Education: BS Engineering, BS Economics, University of Queensland; MBA, IMD Switzerland
Background: General Manager, CSR Limited; Management Consultant, McKinsey & Co
Peter Gold, Managing Director
Education: Bachelor of Commerce, University of Melbourne
Background: Analyst, Greenchip Funds Management; Financial Analyst, Morgan Stanley & Co; Superannuation/Investment Actuarial Analyst, Sedgwick Noble Lowndes
Justin Punch, Senior Advisor
Education: Bachelor of Commerce, Bachelor of Laws, University of NSW; MBA, Harvard Business School
Background: Co-Founder/Manager, The Spot; Executive General Manager, Simplot; Executive General Manager, Shelf Stable Foods Division; Management Consultant, Boston Consulting Group
Craig Cartner, Managing Partner
Education: Bachelor of Commerce, Melbourne University; MBA with distinction, Harvard University
Background: Director, MacQuarie Direct Investment Ltd; Funds Manager, Platinum Asset Management; Retail, Just Jeans
Adam Foster, Investment Director
Education: Ecole Superieure des Sciences Economiques et Commerciales (ESSEC)
Background: Financial Analyst, Morgan Stanley
Ben Frewin, Investment Manager
Education: Commerce, University of Adelaide; MBA, Kellogg School of Management
Background: Business Development Manager, Network Ten; Equity Analyst, MacQuarie Equities; PricewaterhouseCoopers

2421 ARCIS GROUP
30 rue Galile
Paris 75116
France

Phone: 33-0147238862 Fax: 33-147238855
e-mail: mail@arcisgroup.com
web: www.arcisgroup.com

Mission Statement: ARCIS is an international asset management firm, and a member of the Association Française des Investisseurs en Capital (AFIC) and the European Private Equity & Venture Capital Association (EVCA).

Geographic Preference: Europe, Asia, USA
Fund Size: $836 Million
Founded: 1993
Investment Criteria: Early Stage, Development Capital, LBO, Secondary basis
Industry Group Preference: All Sectors Considered

Key Executives:
Romain Bouché, Co-Founder & Managing Partner
Henri Isnard, Co-founder & Managing Partner

2422 ARGAN CAPITAL
15-17 Grosvenor Gardens
London SW1W 0BD
United Kingdom

Phone: 44-2076476970 Fax: 44-2076476999
web: www.argancapital.com

Mission Statement: Argan Capital is a leading independent European private equity fund focused on acquiring and developing European mid-market companies.

Geographic Preference: Nordic Region, Europe, Italy and France
Investment Criteria: Mid-Market Companies
Portfolio Companies: AAT, Delsey, Faster, Gas Control Equipment, Hortex, Humana, Janton

Key Executives:
Wojciech Goc, Managing Partner
e-mail: wgoc@argancapital.com
Education: MA, Economics, Akademia Ekonomiczna; MBA, Texas Christian University
Background: Managing Director, Investment Advisory Firm; JMAI; IBM

2423 ARGOS SODITIC SA
Rue du Rhone, 118
Geneva CH-1204
Switzerland

Phone: 41-228496633 Fax: 41-228496627
e-mail: gsemmens@argos-soditic.com
web: www.argos-soditic.com

Mission Statement: Argos Soditic is an independent European private equity which focuses on investing in small to medium sized companies; acts as exclusive advisor to the Euroknights group of Funds

Geographic Preference: Italy, Portugal, France, Switzerland
Founded: 1989
Investment Criteria: Small to Medium sized companies, Strong position on its markets, Potential for growth
Industry Group Preference: Insurance, Pensions
Portfolio Companies: Ceramic/Apolo Group, Chabert-Duval, De Vecchi Group, Du Pareil Au Meme, Eau Ecarlate, Eider, Fillattice, Le Bronze Industriel, Serap, Starline, Tipico

Key Executives:
Cédric Bruix, Partner
e-mail: ebugnone@argos-soditic.com
Education: University of Geneva
Background: SG Warburg Soditic
Directorships: Chairman of the EVCA (European Venture Capital Association)
Guy Semmens, Partner
e-mail: gsemmens@argos-soditic.com
Education: Law, Durham University
Background: Clifford Chance,
Directorships: Member of EVCA working committee

2424 ARGOS SODITIC SPAIN
Piazza Diaz 5
Milan 20122
Italy

Phone: 39-0200660700 Fax: 39-0200660799
web: www.argos-soditic.com

Mission Statement: Actively seeking new investments.

2425 ARGUS CAPITAL LTD
33 Cavendish Square
36 Poland Street
London W1G 0PW
United Kingdom

Phone: 44-2071824620 Fax: 44-2071824150
e-mail: ali.artunkal@arguscapital.com
web: www.arguscapitalgroup.com

Mission Statement: We seek companies that have high quality management teams that posses the requisite managerial skills and an entrepreneurial approach. Our investee companies will have products or services with distinct competitive advantage and strong growth prospects.

Fund Size: £ 263 million
Founded: 1998
Average Investment: £10 - £40 million
Investment Criteria: Buyouts, Mergers, Acquisitions, Roll-Ups, Restructurings

Key Executives:
Ali Artunkal, Managing Partner
Background: Director, Chase Investment Bank

Venture Capital & Private Equity Firms / International Firms

2426 ARKAFUND MEDIA & ICT
Gossetlaan 30
1702 Groot-Bijgaarden
Belgium
Phone: 32-2464911 **Fax:** 32-24633706
web: www.arkafund.be

Mission Statement: Arkafund provides support to its portfolio companies, combining operational insight with entrepreneurial understanding. The fund provided growth capital to mainly early stage media and internet innovators.

Founded: 2006
Investment Criteria: Early-Stage
Industry Group Preference: Internet, Digital Media & Marketing, Media
Portfolio Companies: Adam Software, Arco, Domaininvest, European Directory Assistance, Larian Studios, Mifratel, Netmining, Nieuws.Be, One Agency, Oxynade, Papillon D'Or, Queromedia, Quick Sensor, Wataro, Xpertize, Yuntaa

Key Executives:
Luc De Vos, Chairman

2427 ARMADA INVESTMENT GROUP
Seestrasse 39
Kusnacht CH-8700
Switzerland
Phone: 41-449149000 **Fax:** 41-449149001
e-mail: office@armada.com
web: www.armada.com

Mission Statement: Armada Investment Group is committed to helping exceptional entrepreneurs build innovative technology companies that will change the way people work and communicate.

Fund Size: $120 million
Founded: 2000
Average Investment: $3 - $7 million
Minimum Investment: $750,000
Investment Criteria: Early Stage, Spin Outs, or Later Stage with early attributes.
Industry Group Preference: Technology, Diversified
Portfolio Companies: Alegra AG, GoingOn Networks Inc., Oanda Coorperation, Overture Networks, Skyway, Wave7 Optics Inc., Celeris AG, edocs, Inc., Helvetic.com AG,

Key Executives:
Daniel S Aegerter, Chairman
Education: BS Business Administration, Winterthur School, Switzerland
Background: DYNABIT AG; Swiss Bank Corporation; Chairman/CEO TRADEX
Directorships: Higher Markets, DYNABIT
Simon Koenig, Managing Director

2428 ARTS ALLIANCE
5 Young Street
London W8 5EH
United Kingdom
Phone: 44-0-20-7361-7720 **Fax:** 44-0-20-7361-7766
e-mail: info@artsalliance.co.uk
web: www.artsalliance.co.uk

Mission Statement: Arts Alliance is a venture capital organization dedicated to entrepreneurship in Europe. We advise on investments on behalf of the Hoegh family. All of Arts Alliance's activities focus on technology-enabled service companies. We are interested in companies that provide services to both consumers and business users, and we invest in a number of sectors including film, and online marketing & advertising.

Geographic Preference: Europe
Founded: 1996
Industry Group Preference: Technology-Enabled Services, Film, Online Marketing, Advertising
Portfolio Companies: Arts Alliance Media, Brainient, CreativeLIVE, Kebony, Kenshoo, Ledlight Group, Lucky Voice Private Karaoke, Metfilmschool, Mr Wolf, Mydeco.com, Povo, Shazam, We Are Pop Up, YCD Multimedia

Key Executives:
Thomas Hoegh, Founder & CEO
Education: BS, Fine Arts, Theatre, Northwestern University; MBA, Harvard Business School
Directorships: Kenshoo, Kebony, Arts Alliance Media

2429 ARX
Kronberg Building
Ehlenuv dum, 28. rijna 12
Praha 11000
Czech Republic
Phone: 420-224235399 **Fax:** 420-224239424
e-mail: praha@arxequity.com

Mission Statement: ARX can assist entrepreneurs in buy outs or buy ins.

Geographic Preference: Europe
Fund Size: $120 Million
Founded: 1996
Average Investment: $9 Million
Minimum Investment: $3.6 Million
Investment Criteria: Expansion and Development, Mezzanine and Bridge
Industry Group Preference: All Sectors Considered
Portfolio Companies: Flanco International, Ergis, Cenega N.V., Print Polska, Hungarocamion Rt., Czech On Line, Scientific Publishers

2430 ASAHI BANK INVESTMENT COMPANY LIMITED
1-3-1 Kyobashi, Chuo-ku
Tokyo 104-0031
Japan
Phone: 81-3-3270-3311 **Fax:** 81-3-3270-3315

Mission Statement: Investment and financing for small and medium sized businesses.

Geographic Preference: Tokyo, Northern Japan
Fund Size: $4.4 million
Founded: 1988
Industry Group Preference: Information Technology

2431 ASAHI LIFE CAPITAL COMPANY LIMITED
1-7-3 Nishi Shinjuku, Shinjuku ku
Tokyo 163-8611
Japan
Phone: 81-423-383111 **Fax:** 81-333468246
web: www.asahi-life.co.jp

Mission Statement: Provides investment trust products mainly consist of Japanese equity.

Founded: 1888

Key Executives:
Yuzuru Huzita, President & Chief Executive Officer

2432 ASCENSION VENTURES
14 Fulwood Place
Floral Street
Covent Garden
London WC1V 6HZ
United Kingdom
Phone: 44-2074301800
e-mail: info@ascensionventures.com
web: www.ascensionventures.com

Mission Statement: Ascension Ventures is the investment arm of Ascension Media Group, one of the UK's leading investment and business services groups in the creative industries and digital technology sectors. At Ascension Ventures

we invest behind entrepreneurs and talent in the creative industries and related digital technology sectors providing capital to help build businesses that own and exploit intellectual property rights in content and brands.
Industry Group Preference: Digital Media & Marketing, Creative Industries
Key Executives:
 Sanjay Wadhwani, Founder/CEO
 Education: BSc, Economics, University of Bristol

2433 ASCLEPIOS BIORESEARCH
10 Philpot Lane
5th Floor
London EC3M 8AA
United Kingdom
 Phone: 44-2073985680 **Fax:** 44-2073985681
Mission Statement: A life science venture capital business offering ethically driven investment opportunities in mid-stage pharmaceutical testing and technologies.
Founded: 2009
Investment Criteria: Early-Stage, Mid-Stage
Industry Group Preference: Pharmaceuticals, Life Sciences, Diagnostics
Portfolio Companies: Genmedica Therapeutics
Key Executives:
 Simon A Conder, Managing Director
 Background: Registered Securities Representative, London Stock Exchange

2434 ASIAN INFRASTRUCTURE FUND ADVISERS LIMITED AIF Capital
Suite 3401, Jardine House, 1 Connaught Place
Central
Hong Kong
 Phone: 852-29127888 **Fax:** 852-28450786
 e-mail: info@aifcapital.com
 web: www.aifcapital.com
Mission Statement: One of the largest Asia based independent private equity firms that provides growth capital for expansion, buy-outs or recapitalizations.
Geographic Preference: Asia, Australia
Fund Size: $1 billion
Founded: 1994
Investment Criteria: Buy-outs, Recapitalizations, Expansion
Industry Group Preference: Financial Services, Manufacturing
Portfolio Companies: Bayantel, Bharti Tele-Ventures, CNK Telecom, DeMaT TransAsia, Excelcom, GVK Power, Meiya Power Company, Olam International, PT Marga Mandalasaki, SeAH Besteel, Sichuan Tomorrow Fine Chemical Co., Wison Chemical Engineering, Yes Bank
Key Executives:
 Peter Amour, Chief Executive Officer

2435 ASIAN STRATEGIC INVESTMENTS CORPORATION
Fangyuan West Road
Chao Yang District
China Parkview Center on the 5th four
Beijing 100015
China
 Phone: 86-1064382750 **Fax:** 86-1064382734
 e-mail: general@asimco.com.cn
 web: www.asimco.com.cn
Mission Statement: Actively seeking new investments.
Geographic Preference: US, China, Europe
Founded: 1994
Key Executives:
 John F Perkowski, Chairman & Chief Executive Officer

 Gary Ding, Vice President

2436 ASIAVEST PARTNERS
11/F, 318 Ruei Guang Road
Nei Hu District
Taipei
Taiwan 114
China
 Phone: 886-227972989 **Fax:** 886-227978289
Mission Statement: AsiaVest Partners, TCW/YFY Ltd. is a leading venture capital firm investing in private companies in the Greater China Region, namely Taiwan, China, and Hong Kong. Since its founding in 1995, the Firm has been nurturing companies with innovative technologies, competitive market positions, and strong management teams to develop high growth business.
Geographic Preference: Taiwan, China, Hong Kong
Fund Size: $980 million
Founded: 1995
Industry Group Preference: Semiconductors, Information Technology, Wireless Technologies, Manufacturing, Consumer Products
Portfolio Companies: Acer, Amtran, Anyka, Askey, ATT, Basso, Bei Jing Lepro Seva, Cems, Champtek, Chipbond, Chipmore, CMI, CMW, Coretronic, Coxon, Dac, Egistec, Eva Airways, Falconstor, Formosa International, Fubon Financial, Grand Cathay Securities, Holiday Enterainment, Inapac, Infrant, Isoftstone, Lattice Power, Leyou, Montage, Monterey, Opulan, Parade, Princo, Rf Magic, Scientech, Silitech, Smic, Solargigia, Solomon Systech, Stic, Sundia, Superalloy, Tpo, Tsmc, ULi, UTAC, Wischip, Wistron, Wpg Holding, Yieh United Steel
Other Locations:
 865 South Figaroa Street
 Los Angeles, CA 90017
 Phone: 1213-2441065 **Fax:** 1213-2440821
Key Executives:
 T.J. Huang, Founder/Managing Parnter
 Education: National Taiwan University; PhD, Computer Sciences, University of Wisconsin, Madison
 Background: CFO/Managing Director, YFY Paper Mfg. Co.

2437 ASLANOBA CAPITAL
Saray Mah. Dr. Adnan Buyukdeniz Cad. No. 2
Akkom Ofis Park.3 Blok Kat. 4
34768 Umraniye
Turkey
 Phone: 0216-6921284 **Fax:** 0216-6921265
 e-mail: contact@aslanobacapital.com
 web: www.aslanobacapital.com
Mission Statement: Aslanoba Capital is responsible for the early stage technology investments of Hasan Aslanoba, the leading angel investor in Turkey. We invest in ambitious teams pursuing disruptive ideas in areas such as marketplaces, e-commerce, mobile, and SaaS. Following investment, we apply our domain knowledge, business experiences, and relationships to help grow our companies.
Geographic Preference: Turkey
Investment Criteria: Early Stage
Industry Group Preference: E-Commerce & Manufacturing, Mobile, SaaS
Portfolio Companies: Metrekare, Modanisa, InfoDif, Fitc&Color, OnlineMarket, Sopsy, Guvenrehberi, Lilakutu, Idemama, Hazinem Pirlanta, Dugun.com, CloudArena, BuldumBuldum.com, MailMag, Ininal, Vivense, Bitaksi, Tasit.Com, Hemen Kiralikm, Etohum
Key Executives:
 Hasan Aslanoba, Founder
 Education: Instanbul University Management Program; MBA, San Diego National University
 Background: CEO, Erikli Water

Venture Capital & Private Equity Firms / International Firms

Cankut Durgun, Managing Director
Education: Degrees in Economics and Management Science, Massachusetts Institue of Technology; MBA, Stanford Univeristy
Background: Co-Founder, Romulus Capital; McKinsey & Company; Bain & Company; Goldman Sachs; AT&T; Pfizer

2438 ASTELLA INVESTMENTS
Rua Gomes de Carvalho
1666-19 Walk
Sao Paulo SP 04547-006
Brazil

e-mail: site@astellainvest.com
web: www.astellainvest.com

Mission Statement: Astella invests capital, culture and capabilities in entrepreneurial daring and determined to change the world by building extraordinary companies.

Geographic Preference: Brazil
Industry Group Preference: Education, Healthcare, Financial Services, Business Products & Services, Technology
Portfolio Companies: Dualtec, HelpSaude, Imobox, Mobilife, Navegg, Portal Educacao, SmartKids, Tryoop, Tuilux

Key Executives:
  Edson Rigonatati, Partner
  Education: Business Administration, University Mackenzie; MBA, Columbia Business School
  Background: ICT Management

2439 ASTER CAPITAL
26 avenue de l'Opera
Paris 75001
France

Phone: 33-1-45613095
e-mail: contact@aster.com
web: www.aster.com

Mission Statement: Aster Capital is a leading cleantech venture capital fund, sponsored by Alstom, Rhodia and Schneider Electric. Aster's mission is to support innovative start-ups by accelerating their growth. We focus on highly promising companies that have developed superior solutions to solve global challenges in the energy and environment sectors.

Geographic Preference: Worldwide
Founded: 2000
Investment Criteria: Early-Stage, Late-Stage
Industry Group Preference: Clean Technology, Energy, Environment, Mobility, Transportation
Portfolio Companies: Digital Lumens, Airbnb, Cpower, Casnov@, Cosmotech, Solairdirect, FraudMetrix, Jet Metal, Sun Culture, OpenDataSoft, D.Light, PEG, Atlantium, Aventium, Worktile, Optireno, Iceotope, IronSource, Easy Bike, Uber, Ping++, Open Wide, InspiraFarms, Teem Photonics, Planet, Eficia, Habiteo, BuildingIQ, Paygo Energy, EcoFactor, Element Analytics, NetasQ, LinkDoc, Alauda.io, Docker, Aligence, ekWateur, Finalcad, ConnectBlue, ZingBox, Ioxus, Ordinal, Entouch, Lucibel, Customer Matrix, Tronics

Other Locations:
  7 bd Malesherbes
  4th Floor
  Paris 75008
  France
  Phone: 33-145613095 Fax: 33-145613450

  10th Floor, ChangFeng
  International Tower
  89 YunLing Road E
  Shanghai 200062
  China
  Phone: 86-2160656507 Fax: 86-2160768988

  Sagid House, Industrial Park Hasaron
  PO Box 1800
  Kadima 60920
  Israel
  Phone: 972-98305552 Fax: 972-98996105

Key Executives:
  Jean-Marc Bally, Managing Partner
  e-mail: jmbally@aster.com
  Education: MS, Business Management, Grenoble Graduate School of Business; INSEAD
  Background: Co-Founder, Investment Partner, Aster
  Directorships: SolaireDirect, Tronics Microsystems, ConnectBlue, Jet Metal Technologies, Optireno, Lucibel
  Todd Dauphinais, Investment Partner
  e-mail: tdauphinais@aster.com
  Education: BBA, Finance, Texas A&M University; MBA, University of Notre Dame
  Background: President, EFI Electronics
  Alexander Schlaepfer, Investment Partner
  e-mail: aschlaepfer@aster.com
  Education: BA, Sciences, University of St. Gallen; MSc, Finance, London Business School
  Background: BU Power Service
  Directorships: Ioxus
  Pascal Siegwart, Investment Partner
  e-mail: psiegwart@aster.com
  Education: MSc, Biotechnology, Ecole Polytechnique, Montreal
  Background: CO2 Operations Director, Rhodia & Orbeo; Energy Purchasing Director, Rhodia Energy

2440 ASTOR CAPITAL GROUP
Moscow City, Naberezhayna Tower
Block C, Floor 4, Office 404
10, Presneskaya, Nabrezhnaya
Moscow 123317
Russia

Phone: 7-4955077980 Fax: 7-495-926-7315
e-mail: info@astorcg.com

Mission Statement: Specializes in business turn-around, special situaltions, conflict resoluton and growth boosting investment strategies.

Investment Criteria: Special Situations, Turnarounds
Industry Group Preference: Real Estate, Oil & Gas, Manufacturing, Distribution, Retail, Consumer & Leisure, Construction, Financial Services, Transportation

Key Executives:
  Will Andrich, President
  Education: MSc, Finance, London Business School; International Business Degree, University of Copenhagen
  Background: HSBC, European Bank for Reconstruction

2441 ASTUTIA VENTURES
Maximilianstrasse 45
Munchen D-80538
Germany

Phone: 49-89189083880 Fax: 49-891890838888
web: www.astutia.de

Mission Statement: Founded in 2006, ASTUTIA is an owner-controlled, independent investment company with headquarters in Munich and an office in Berlin. The main focus of our investments lies in the areas of digital media and the internet in the early and growth stages. We offer venture capital, an outstanding international network, and industry-related know-how to support your growth.

Founded: 2006
Investment Criteria: Early-Stage, Growth Stage
Industry Group Preference: Digital Media & Marketing, Internet

Venture Capital & Private Equity Firms / International Firms

Portfolio Companies: Commercetools, Dreamlines, Fashionette, Flaconi, InterNations, Mornin' Glory, Mister Spex, Mysportbrands & Mysportworld, Pactas, Quest.ii, V-Bank

Key Executives:
Benedict Rodenstock, Founder/CEO
Education: MBA, University St. Gallen; University Bologna
Background: Hurbert Burda Media, WEB.DE, Roland Berger Strategy Consultants

2442 ATILA VENTURES
Par La Ville Place
14 Par-la-Ville Road
Hamilton HM08
Bermuda

Phone: 441-2956081 Fax: 441-2921373

Mission Statement: ATILAVENTURES was founded in 1999 with the goal of providing capital, operating and other value adding resources to entrepreneurs in Europe. Our experience gained in Silicon Valley, Europe and Asia in the high growth technology sector is used to provide entrepreneurs primarily in Switzerland, France, Germany, Austria and other European countries with venture capital, advice and networking.

Geographic Preference: Western Europe
Founded: 1999
Industry Group Preference: Information Technology, Telecommunications, Electronics, E-Commerce & Manufacturing

Key Executives:
James Keyes, Chairman

2443 ATLANTIC BRIDGE
31 Kildare Street
Dublin 2
Ireland

Phone: 353-16034450 Fax: 353-16425661
web: www.abven.com

Mission Statement: Atlantic Bridge is a growth equity fund focused on technology investments with offices in Dublin, London and Silicon Valley. We believe in the entrepreneur and support management teams that have the vision and ambition to exploit major growth opportunities. Our team of seasoned entrepreneurs, experienced managers, finance professionals and investment experts possess decades of experience growing successful technology businesses globally. This wealth of experience and extensive industry contacts adds value above and beyond a purely financial investment.

Geographic Preference: Ireland, United Kingdom, United States
Investment Criteria: Growth Stage
Industry Group Preference: Cloud Computing, Virtualization, Infrastructure, Semiconductors, Wireless Technologies, Information Technology
Portfolio Companies: Accuris, Acision, BioSensia, Envivio, Panda Security, Maginaatics, Metaio, Nero, Openmind, Ozmo Devices, Quixey, Swrve

Other Locations:
33 St James's Square
London SW1Y 4JS
United Kingdom
Phone: 44-2076619304 Fax: 44-2076619594

Key Executives:
Peter McManamon, Chairman
Education: Business Studies, Trinity College
Background: Co-Founder, Parthus Technologies

2444 ATLANTIC VENTURES
Sempacherstrasse 1
Luzern 6002
Switzerland

Phone: 550-0049010
web: www.atlanticventures.com

Mission Statement: Atlantic Ventures in a Berlin and Zurich based vehicle focused on building lean startups and fostering talented entrepreneurs. Leveraging our network and experience, we invest in media and technology companies from their early stages and we make them become market leaders.

Industry Group Preference: Technology, Consumer Internet
Portfolio Companies: A., Barcoo, Bonusbox, EyeEm, Gate5, Gidsy, Loopcam, MangirKart, Monoqi, Phonedeck, Plazes, Plista, Readmill, Soundcloud, StudiVZ, Too.Step, Txtr

Key Executives:
Christophe Maire, Partner
Background: CEO, Txtr; Co-Founder, Gate5

2445 ATLAS VENTURE: FRANCE
25 First Street
Suite 303
Cambridge, MA 02141

Phone: 617-5882600 Fax: 33-158365960
web: www.atlasventure.com

Mission Statement: Atlas Venture takes an integrated, international team approach to building success for portfolio companies on the world stage.

Geographic Preference: USA, UK, France, Germany
Fund Size: $2.1 Billion
Founded: 1980
Average Investment: $15 Million
Minimum Investment: $5 Million
Investment Criteria: Technology and Life Sciences companies in US and Europe
Industry Group Preference: Technology, Components & IoT, Software, Life Sciences, Drug Development, Medical Devices, Tools
Portfolio Companies: Achillion, Active Endpoints, AEB, Alnylam, Anadigm, Anadys, Archemix, Arqule, Aureon Labrotories, Bit9, BlueShift, Bluespec, LK DEsign Automation, Compund Therapeutics, Dynogen, Ellacoya, Gotuit Media, Helicos, Isilon, Ivrea Pharmaceuticals, Jaulna, Kalid

Key Executives:
Fred Destin, Partner
Education: MS, University of Toulouse; Ecoie Nationale Superieure de l'Aeronautique et de l'Espace
Background: Arthur Anderson, Credit Lyonnais, SED Ventures.
Dustin Dolginow, Principal
Education: PhD, University Rene Descartes; Masters in Strategic Management, Ecole des Hautes Etudes Commerciales
Background: CDP Capital, Deutsche Bank and Merrill Lynch.
Jeff Fagnan, Partner
Education: MD, Paris School of Medicine; Masters in Management, Sloan School at MIT
Background: BioServe Ltd, Genset, Ipsen Beaufour.
Barry Fidelman, Partner
Education: MS, EM Lyon, London Business School; Materials Physics and Advanced Chemistry, Ecole Centrale
Background: Credit Lyonnais Private Equity, Clinvest.

2446 ATOMICO
50 New Bond Street
London W1S 1BJ
United Kingdom

e-mail: contact@atomico.com
web: www.atomico.com

Venture Capital & Private Equity Firms / International Firms

Mission Statement: Atomico is an international technology investment firm, focused on helping the world's most disruptive technology companies reach their full potential on a global scale.
Geographic Preference: Europe, North America, South America, Asia
Fund Size: $1.5 billion
Founded: 2006
Industry Group Preference: Technology, Consumer Internet
Portfolio Companies: 6wunderkinder, Bitmovin, Bossa Studios, Chemist Direct, Drivetribe, Everything, Equal Media, FON, Farmdrop, GoEuro, Graphcore, Habito, Hail, Hem, Hinge Health, IMA, Jobandtalent, Klarna, Last.flicloud, Klarna, Kyte, Last.Fm, LendInvest, Lilium Aviation, Mapillary, MessageBird, Mydeco, Onetwotrip, OnTruck, Ostrovok, Pipdrive, Playfire, Quipper, Rovio, Scandit, Seesmic, Siine, Silk, Skype, Supercell, Teralytics, Truecaller, UniPlaces, Viagogo, Wrapp, Clutter, Compas, Deca, Fab, Heysan, Jawbone, Knewton, Memphis Meats, Power Reviews, Quid, Rdio, Stripe, Technorati, The Climate Corp., Xobni, ZocDoc, Bebestore, Cinemaki, Connect Part, S Gympass, Pedidos Ya, Restorando, Cmune, Gengo, SmartNews, iBoxPay, Ofo

Other Locations:
Av. Brigadeiro Faria Lima
3729, 5 Andar
Sao Paulo 04538-905
Brazil

Regeringsgatan 65
Stockholm 111 56
Sweden

#1015, 1-9-7
Kita-Shinagawa
Shinagawa-ku
Tokyo 104-0001
Japan

15/F China World Tower 3
1 Jiangumenwai Avenue
Chaoyang District
Beijing 100020
China

Key Executives:
  Niklas Zennstrom, CEO/Founding Partner
  Education: Business, MSc, Engineering Physics, Uppsala University
  Background: Co-Founder, Skype, Kazaa, Joltid, Joost
  Directorships: Fon, Jolicloud, Rovio
  Carter Adamson, Venture Partner
  Background: Head of Product, Skype; Senior Program Manager, ICQ; Director of Product Strategy, AOL
  Alexis Bonte, Venture Partner
  Background: CEO, eRepublik Labs; Lastminute.com
  Chris Barnes, Partner/Chief Operating Officer
  Education: Double First, Economics & History, Cambridge University; CFA
  Background: CFO, Terra Firma; Private Equity Group, Arthur Andersen

2447 ATP PRIVATE EQUITY PARTNERS
2 Sjaeleboderne, 1 Floor
Copenhagen K DK-1122
Denmark

Phone: 45-33193070 **Fax:** 45-33193071
e-mail: info@atp-pep.com
web: www.atp-pep.com

Mission Statement: Dedicated to global private equity investment management.
Geographic Preference: Europe, USA
Fund Size: $7 Billion
Founded: 2001
Average Investment: $500 Million
Minimum Investment: $5.9 Million
Investment Criteria: Early stage venture capital, Buyout
Industry Group Preference: Food Services, Heating, Automotive, Healthcare, Industrial Services, Transportation
Portfolio Companies: Nordic Capital IV, Symbion, Axel, Bank Invest, Novi, Polaris, Dansk Erhvervsinvestering, Health Cap, Nordic Mezzanine, IT Provider, Nordic Venture Partners, BC Partners VIII

Key Executives:
  Torben Vangstrup, Partner
  45 33 19 30 81
  e-mail: tva@atp-pep.com
  Education: MS Economics, Aarhus University
  Background: HealthCap IV, Nordic Capital V, Lindsay Goldberg & Abingworth IV
  Susanne Forsingdal, Partner
  45 33 19 30 77
  e-mail: sus@atp-pep.com
  Education: MS Economics, Finance, Accounting, Copenhagen Business School; Political Science, Luther College
  Background: Senior VP, Danske Bank
  Klaus Ruhne, Partner
  45 33 19 30 76
  e-mail: klr@atp-pep.com
  Education: MS Economics, Copenhagen University
  Background: Director at Danske Bank, Senior Equity Analyst at Erskilda Securities

2448 ATRIA CAPITAL PARTENAIRES
5-7, rue de
Monttessuy 75007
France

Phone: 33-158194581 **Fax:** 33-158192641

Mission Statement: LBO and development capital specialist which takes equity stakes in French middle market companies.
Geographic Preference: France
Fund Size: 496 million Euros
Founded: 1999
Average Investment: ?25 million
Minimum Investment: 15 million Euros
Investment Criteria: French mid-cap growth companies with EV of 30 million to 200 million Euros
Industry Group Preference: Industrial Services, Consumer Products, Retailing, Healthcare, Information Technology, Insurance
Portfolio Companies: Abcd, Abrisud, Altead, Cap Vert Finance, Ekkia, European Homes, FPEE, Ionisos, LPR, Mc2i, Parcours, Phythea, Shark, Trigo, Un Jour Aileurs

Key Executives:
  Dominique Oger, Chairman
  e-mail: atria@atria-partenaires.com
  Education: IEP Paris, DES Economy Paris
  Background: Sefinnova (Madrid) Founder & CEO; Sofinindex Chairman, Coparis Founder & CEO, Cfi Chairman
  Eric Aveillan, CEO
  e-mail: atria@atria-partenaires.com
  Education: Ecole Polytechnique Paris; MBA, Wharton School, University of Pennsylvania
  Background: Worms & Cie, Pechel Industries Co-Founder, Warburg Dillon Read Executive Director
  Patrick Bertiaux, Member Management Board
  e-mail: atria@atria-partenaires.com
  Education: MBA, Paris Dauphine, DECS
  Background: Director of SCR Vecteur, Investment manager of Cfi

2449 AUGMENTA
Zinkgatan 2
Lomma 234 21
Sweden

Phone: 46-705-94-84-76

812

Mission Statement: Augmenta invests in early stages in companies that have unique products and great growth potential. We focus on companies in southern Sweden.
Geographic Preference: Sweden
Founded: 2003
Investment Criteria: Early-Stage
Portfolio Companies: Exini Diagnostics, Emstone Engineering, All of It IT, Pastair, Adenovir Pharma, CanImGuide

Key Executives:
   Conny Bjarnram, CEO
   e-mail: conny.bjarnram@augmenta.se

2450 AUGMENTUM CAPITAL
27 St James's Place
London SW1A 1NR
United Kingdom

Phone: 44-2075141998
e-mail: info@augmentumcapital.com
web: www.augmentumcapital.com

Mission Statement: Augmentum Capital is an investor with a wealth of international entrepreneurial experience. We invest in growth stage businesses in the e-commerce and technology sectors worldwide. We are a fund run by entrepreneurs who want to work with entrepreneurs.
Geographic Preference: Worldwide
Founded: 2009
Investment Criteria: Growth Stage
Industry Group Preference: E-Commerce & Manufacturing, Technology
Portfolio Companies: Borro, BuillionVault.com, SRL Global, Persistent Sentinel, Bathrooms.com, Zopa

Key Executives:
   Tim Levene, Co-Founder

2451 AURA CAPITAL OY Auratum Group
Aurakatu 8
Southampton 20100
Finland

Phone: 358-265166600 Fax: 358-265166621
e-mail: forename.surname@auratum.com
web: www.auracapital.com

Mission Statement: Venture capital company that makes investments in internationalising high tech companies
Geographic Preference: Finland
Founded: 1997
Average Investment: 500K - $1.5Million
Investment Criteria: Start-ups and early-stage growth companies.
Industry Group Preference: High Technology, Software, Media, Telecommunications, Mobile Communications Devices, Internet Technology
Portfolio Companies: Emic, First Orange Contact, Commit, Avset, Delfoi, Agentum Technologies, Bluegiga Technologies, Mforma, Oplayp, Mobilemode, AdaptaMat, Incap, Chip-Man Technologies, Stick Tech

Key Executives:
   ARI Siponmaa, Managing Partner
   e-mail: ari.spionmaa@auratum.com
   Education: MS
   Background: Consultant at Andersen Consulting
   Petri Salonen, Partner
   e-mail: jukka.harju@auratum.com
   Education: MS, Helsinki University of Technology
   Background: Senior management positions at AtBusiness Communications and Hewlett Packard

2452 AURELIA PRIVATE EQUITY
Kurhessenstrasse 1-3
Frankfurt am Main 60431
Germany

Phone: 069-80900 Fax: 069-8090109
e-mail: info@aurelia-pe.de
web: www.aurelia-pe.de

Mission Statement: AURELIA participates in the funds it manages as a financier of innovative early-stage technology companies in Germany. We provide capital for research and development, launch of the products, the production structure and internationalization. Our engagement is in the order of 0.5 to 3 million euro. AURELIA is a partner in time, introduces the strategic know-how and capital to the company. With our experience and contacts we accompany the management and create the basis for further expansion. The aim is to develop our investments into successful companies with strong market positions.
Industry Group Preference: Life Sciences, Information Technology, Communications
Portfolio Companies: Cooee, EMBL Technology Fund, GILUPI, Hematris Wound Care, jCatalog Software, MovingIMAGE24, MerLion Pharmaceuticals, PC-Soft,

Key Executives:
   Jurgen Leschke, Managing Partner
   Background: Corporate Banking, Dresdner Bank AG; Founder, TFG Venture Capital Group

2453 AURIGA PARTNERS
18 Matignon Avenue
Paris 75008
France

Phone: 33-153300707 Fax: 33-153300700
e-mail: auriga@aurigapartners.com
web: www.aurigapartners.com/

Mission Statement: Independent Venture Capital firm managing several early stage funds specializing in Information Technology and Life Sciences
Geographic Preference: France, Western Europe, North America, Israel
Fund Size: $136 Million
Founded: 1998
Average Investment: $5.9 Million
Minimum Investment: $1.18 Million
Investment Criteria: Seed, Start-up, First Stage, invest primarily in the European Union, with a minor focus on North America and Israel.
Industry Group Preference: Information Technology, Medical & Health Related, Life Sciences

Key Executives:
   Bernard Daugeras, Chairman
   Education: Finance Mnaagement/Advanced Accounting, Institut Superieur de Gestion
   Background: Financial control for an industrial group
   Directorships: Analyzing business models & administrative and financial follow-up of portfolio companies
   Patrick Bamas, Founder, General Partner
   Education: Ecole Superieure d'Electricite; Institut d'Administration des Enterprises de Paris
   Background: IT and strategy consultant, Director of Finovelec
   Directorships: Information Technology, Scientific Instrumentation and Industrial Processes.
   Jacques Chatain, Founder, General Partner
   Education: Paris Chamber of Commerce and Industry
   Background: IDI Group, investor and Secretary General of Finovelec
   Directorships: Information Technology and the Internet
   Philippe Granger, Partner
   Education: Doctorate in Information Technology, Ecole Polytechnique

Venture Capital & Private Equity Firms / International Firms

Background: IT researcher, Professor
Directorships: Information Technology, Electronics and the Telecommunication
Philippe Peltier, Partner
Education: Masters in Molecular Biology, University of Paris; Masters in Finance, ESSEC
Background: Equity analyst at CCF Securities
Directorships: Life Sciences

2454 AURUM VENTURES MKI
16 Abba Hillel Silver Street
Aurec House
Ramat Gan 52506
Israel

Phone: 972-35762420 Fax: 972-35762605
e-mail: info@aurum.co.il
web: www.aurum.co.il

Mission Statement: Aurum Ventures MKI provides value added growth capital to exceptional entrepreneurs within the fields of life-sciences and clean-tech. While we focus on investing in unique, cutting edge technologies that will mature into successful business companies, our investments reflect our own values, so we prefer investing in companies that, through their sound commercial propositions, also contribute to the well-being of mankind.

Industry Group Preference: Life Sciences, Clean Technology
Portfolio Companies: Nephera, LifeBond, I20 Pharma, VBL Therapeutics, Vecta, Corassist, Fertiseeds, Proteologics, Alantium, N-Triq, Elcom Technologies, OnePath Networks, Dune

Key Executives:
Nili Lesnick, CEO
Education: BA, Economics, MSc, Industrial Engineering, Ben-Gurion University
Background: Elbit Sytems Ltd.

2455 AUSTRAL CAPITAL PARTNERS
El Bosque North 0123
Suite 601
Santiago
Chile

Phone: 56-2-246-0808 Fax: 56-2-246-0809
web: www.australcap.com

Mission Statement: Austral Capital Partners is a venture capital firm focused on indentifying globally scalable, high growth entrepreneurs and technologies.

Founded: 2007
Industry Group Preference: Technology, Life Sciences
Portfolio Companies: Andes Biotechnologies, Atakama Labs, BAL, Fiscalia Privada, Green Pacific Biologicals, Junar, Multicaja, Nimbic, Paperless, Producto Protegido, Scanntech, Scopix

Key Executives:
Gonzalo Miranda, Managing Partner
Education: BSc, MSc, Mechanical Engineering, Catholic University of Chile; MBA, MOT, Haas School of Business
Background: Managing Director, Endeavor Chile
Directorships: Scopix Solutions, Paperless, Multicaja, Producto Protegido
Matias Errazuriz, Managing Director
Background: Founding Partner, Genera4
Directorships: AEON Biogroup, Coaniquem

2456 AUSTRALIAN ETHICAL INVESTMENT LIMITED
130 Pitt Street
Level 8
Sydney NSW 2000
Australia

Phone: 61-262011988 Fax: 61-0262011987
Toll-Free: 1800- 021227

Mission Statement: Australian Ethical Investment Ltd is an independent funds manager based in Canberra specialising in environmental and socially responsible investment.

Geographic Preference: Australia
Fund Size: $350 Million
Founded: 1986
Average Investment: $5 Million
Minimum Investment: $2.5 Million
Investment Criteria: Invests in environmental and socially positive activities
Industry Group Preference: Education, Conservation, Energy, Food & Beverage, Healthcare, Financial Services, Telecommunications, Information Technology, Investment Analysis and Research, Sales and Marketing, Administration and Accounting, Superannuation, Efficient Transport, Biotechnology, Recycling
Portfolio Companies: ABC Learning Centres Ltd, Ansell Ltd, Australian Pipeline Trust, Adeliade Bank Ltd, Australian Central Credit Union, Alinta Ltd, Australian Education, Baldor Electric Co, Bank of Qeensland, Bank of Western Australia, Baxter Group Ltd, Bendigo Bank Ltd, Blackmores Ltd

Key Executives:
Phillip Vernon, Managing Director
Education: BS
Background: Trustee of an award superannuation fund for the credit union industry, Faculties of economics, environmental studies and geography at the University of New South Wales
Directorships: Director
David Barton, Chief Financial Officer

2457 AUTHOSIS VENTURES
Room 2101, 21st Floor Westlands Centre
20 Westlands Road
Quarry Bay Hong Kong
China

Phone: 852-29604611 Fax: 852-29600185
e-mail: info@authosisvc.com
web: www.authosis.com

Mission Statement: With our extensive operational background, we have both the breadth and depth of professional experience to nurture companies from an initial concept to healthy growth and, ultimate commercial success.

Geographic Preference: Silicon Valley, China
Founded: 2000
Investment Criteria: Seed-Stage, Early-Stage
Industry Group Preference: Information Technology, Software, Internet, E-Commerce & Manufacturing, Wireless Technologies, Mobile Technology, Fabless IC, Communication Technology
Portfolio Companies: Affinity Engiens, AssistGuide, BioImagene, BitAuto, Dali Wireless, Ensenta, Erlang Technology, EzRez Software, H5 Technologies, Inphi Corp., Kahala Code Factory, MyETone, PayDay One, Pericom Technology, Radio Time, Sitoa, Solus Biosystems, Telegent Systems, United Platform Technologies, Uniwave, Voicesoft, WhiteHat Security, Xi'an Supermicro, Zero2IPO

Key Executives:
Danny Lui, Chairman
Education: Bachelor's Degree, Computing Science, Imperial College, University of London
Background: Co-Founder, Legend Group; Founder, APTG Ventures

Venture Capital & Private Equity Firms / International Firms

2458 AVANTI CAPITAL
25 Harley Street
London W1G 9BR
United Kingdom

Phone: 44-2072991459 Fax: 44-2072991451
e-mail: richard.kleiner@avanticap.com
web: www.avanticap.com

Mission Statement: Avanti Capital is a private equity company, with a strategy of investing in businesses, using a combination of debt and equity.
Geographic Preference: Europe
Industry Group Preference: Consumer Products, Leisure, Retail, Consumer & Leisure
Portfolio Companies: Eclectic Bars Limited, Expresso Education Limited, mBlox, Medcenter
Key Executives:
  Richard Kleiner, Director
  Background: Founder, Odyssey Partners; Managing Partner, Gerald Edelman Chartered Accountants

2459 AVENIR TOURISME
32 Bld de
Strasbourg 75468
France

Phone: 33-144540391 Fax: 33-144540392
e-mail: avenir.tourisme@orange.fr

Mission Statement: Actively seeking new investments.
Fund Size: Ffr 38.9 million
Founded: 1986
Minimum Investment: Ffr1 million
Industry Group Preference: Tourism
Key Executives:
  Cécile Legeais, Manager

2460 AVIGO CAPITAL
503-504 DLF Place (Office Tower)
A4 District Center, Saket
New Delhi 110017
India

Phone: 91-1143683300 Fax: 91-1143683335

Mission Statement: Avigo Capital, a Private Equity Fund Manager was formed in Sep 2003 with a focus on Private Equity Investments in the SME, and emerging sectors in emerging markets, mainly India. The Investment Team at Avigo has a cumulative experience of over 200 years in Private Equity, Investment/Corporate Banking, Consulting, and Operations. AVIGO's philosophy is to be the first or amongst the early institutional investors primarily providing growth capital to fast growing SME companies in the industrial/ emerging sectors in India. AVIGO has built up and demonstrated extensive on-the-ground expertise as well as experience in building businesses in the growth stage and handling various investment related issues.
Geographic Preference: India
Founded: 2003
Investment Criteria: Growth Stage
Portfolio Companies: Tecpro Systems, Hythro Power Corporation, GET Power, Spykar, Bharat Box Factory, Rinac India, Aeroflex, Comat
Other Locations:
  355, NexTeracon Tower 1
  3rd Floor, Cybercity
  Ebene
  Mauritius
  Phone: 230-4647275 Fax: 230-4643290

  161/162 A Wing
  Mittal Court
  Nariman Point
  Mumbai 400 021
  India
  Phone: 91-2249154242 Fax: 91-22-4915-4242
Key Executives:
  Achai Ghai, Founder/Managing Director
  Education: BComm, MBA
  Background: Corporate & Investment Banking, American Express, HSBC, EBIL, Canadian Imperial Bank of Commerce

2461 AVISTA PARTNERS
78 Pall Mall
London SW1Y 5ES
United Kingdom

Phone: 44-207-193-6780 Fax: 44-207-691-7112
e-mail: info@avistapartners.com
web: www.avistapartners.com

Mission Statement: Avista Partners is an independent investment banking firm focusing on the digital media and luxury & lifestyle industries. We bring deep sector expertise, global relationships, and world class transaction experience. Our global network is based on strong relationships with founders and senior management, as well as investors including venture capitalists, private equity firms, hedge funds, family offices and institutional investors.
Founded: 2007
Industry Group Preference: Digital Media & Marketing, Luxury/Lifestyle
Key Executives:
  Paul Heydon, Managing Director
  e-mail: paul.heydon@avistapartners.com
  Education: MBA, HBA, Richard Ivey School of Business, University of Western Ontario
  Background: Partner, London Venture Partners; Managing Director, Unity Capital; Head of Interactive Entertainment, Commerzbank Securities
  Valerie Blin, Managing Director
  e-mail: valerie.blin@avistapartners.com
  Education: BA, Northwestern University; CEP, Insitut d'Etudes Politques, París
  Background: Morgan Stanley, JP Morgan, Deutsche Bank
  Marianne Okland, Managing Director
  e-mail: marianne.okland@avistapartners.com
  Education: MSc, Finance & Economics, Norwegian School of Economics & Business Administration
  Background: JP Morgan, UBS

2462 AVIV VENTURE CAPITAL
36 Shacham Street
Ram Building, 5th Floor
Petach Tikva 49517
Israel

Phone: 972-39761111 Fax: 972-39199300
e-mail: info@avivvc.com
web: www.avivvc.com

Mission Statement: Aviv invests in Israel related, revenue stage companies that bring breakthrough technologies to large established industries. We have a preference for companies offering 'Hi-Tech solutions for Low-Tech industries' such as security, clean-tech, automotive, printing, and medical devices.
Geographic Preference: Israel
Founded: 2001
Investment Criteria: Later-Stage
Industry Group Preference: Security, Clean Technology, Automotive, Printing, Medical Devices
Portfolio Companies: Actona, Bitband, DeepBreeze, MCS, M.G.V.S, BeInSync, FriCSo, Ozvision, BriefCam, Jettable, ScaleMP, Minicom Digital, Apos, Tipa, Optimal Test, Valens Semiconductor, LGC Wireless
Key Executives:
  Dov Tadmor, Chairman
  Background: Founder & Chairmain, Israel Equity Limited

Venture Capital & Private Equity Firms / International Firms

2463 AVLAR BIOVENTURES
Highfield Court
Church Lane
Madingley
Cambs CB23 8AG
United Kingdom

Phone: 44-1954211515 Fax: 44-1954211516
web: www.avlar.com

Mission Statement: Active investment in seed and early stage biotechnology and healthcare opportunities. The differentiating philosophy of Avlar is not only in the selection of excellent opportunities but in the active development and management of its ventures, particularly those in the embryonic stages of their growth.

Founded: 1999
Industry Group Preference: Healthcare, Medical Devices, Diagnostics
Portfolio Companies: Amura, Cambridge Biotechnology, CeNeS, Cozart, Crescendo Biologics, De Novo Pharmaceuticals, ImmunoBiology, Medical Device Innovation, PAION, Paradigm Therapeutics, Proteom, Purely Proteins, Sangamo Biosciences, Sterix Limited

Key Executives:
Alan Goodman, Co-Founder
Daniel Roach, Co-Founder

2464 AVONMORE DEVELOPMENTS
6 Snow Hill
London EC1A 2AY
United Kingdom

Phone: +44 20 7002 7118
e-mail: contactus@avonmoredevelopments.com
web: www.avonmoredevelopments.com

Mission Statement: Avonmore's investments cover a number of different areas and consideration is given to all investment opportunities we receive. However, it should be noted that we currently only invest in UK based businesses and generally those with sub £3 million pre-money valuations. Experienced management teams, with defendable technology and a proven market demand are also key investment criteria.

Geographic Preference: United Kingdom
Founded: 2000
Average Investment: £100,000 - £250,000
Investment Criteria: Seed and early stage equity capital financing
Industry Group Preference: All Sectors Considered
Portfolio Companies: Tagman, Specle, Socialbro, OC Robotics Ltd, Languagelabs.com, Groupspaces, Glow Digital Media, ByBox, Bac2 Ltd, Virtual IT

Key Executives:
Simon Blakey
Michael Blakey

2465 AWAY REALTY
3rd Syromyatnicheskiy lane, 3/9, page 6
Moscow 105120
Russia

Phone: 7-495-2588866 Fax: 7-499-6782182
web: www.away.ru

Mission Statement: Delta Capital Management is a leading private equity manager dedicated to developing and funding emerging growth companies.

Geographic Preference: Russia
Fund Size: $300 Million
Founded: 1994
Average Investment: $7.5 Million
Minimum Investment: $5 Million
Investment Criteria: Focuses on Emerging Growth and Long-term Companies

Industry Group Preference: Telecommunications, Media, Technology, Research & Development, Energy, Consumer Products, Financial Services, Utilities
Portfolio Companies: CompuLink, DeltaBank, DeltaCredit, DeltaLease-Far East, EGAR Technology, Independent Network Television Holdings, Lomonosov Porcelain Plant, National Cable Networks, Polygraformlenie, Saint Springs, SPAR Middle Volga, SPAR Moscow Holdings, StoryFirst Co

Key Executives:
Patricia Cloherty, Chairman & Chief Executive Officer
Education: B.A. from the San Francisco College, M.A. and M.I.A. from Columbia University.
Background: Apax Partners, Inc., National Venture Capital Association, Chairman of an Investment Advisory Council, Lexicon Genetics, Inc., Independent Network Television Holdings (Moscow), the U.S. Russia Center for Entrepreneurship, and the EastWest Institute.
Roman Simonov, Managing Director
Education: BA Economics with Honors from Stanford University; MBA from Harvard Business School
Background: Deputy General Director, IBS, Moscow; Investment Banking, Goldman Sachs; Consultant, McKinsey & Company, Los Angeles/Moscow/Prague
Paul Price, Managing Director
Education: Irish Institute of Chartered Accountants
Background: Russia Country Inns/Rezidor SAS; SPAR Moscow/Middle Volga; Senior Management, Tetra Pack; Coca-Cola
Natalie Polischuk, Vice President
Education: BA in Economics from the University of Kiev-Mohyla, MBA from Harvard University.
Background: Western NIS Enterprise Fund in Kiev, Ukraine, CIS.
Anton Titov, Vice President
Education: MD from St. Petersburg State Medical Academy, PhD in Cell and Molecular Biology from The Rockefeller University and MBA from Harvard Business School in Boston.
Background: Neurological Surgery resident at Children's Hospital in Boston, University in New York.

2466 AXA INVESTMENT MANAGERS PRIVATE EQUITY EUROPE
20 Vendome Place
75001 Paris 75001
France

Phone: 33-144459200 Fax: 33-144459300
e-mail: sylvie.deneubourg@axa-im.com
web: www.axaprivateequity.com

Mission Statement: Focuses on investment opportunities where we have a distinct competitive advantage and can deliver both product and service excellence for our clients

Geographic Preference: Europe, Asia, USA
Founded: 1994
Average Investment: $458 Billion
Investment Criteria: Seed, Start-up, LBO Distress
Industry Group Preference: Internet Technology, Information Technology, Electronic Technology, Software, Telecommunications
Portfolio Companies: ianet, Poliris, Axialog, ConsortNT, FRA/Business Interactif, MediaDev, Quatermove, Coronis Systems, Europe Technologies, Finsecur, Tagsys, iRoc, Venture/Life Sciences Agendia, Coletica, Cytheris, Innate Pharma, Mutabilis, Neuro 3D, Proteus, Catalliances, Ever

Key Executives:
Dominique Senequier, President
e-mail: vincent.gombault@axa-im.com
Education: MS, Financial Techniques, ESSEC; DESS, Banking and Finance; Degrees in Law and Economics
Background: French Trade Commission in Detroit (USA), Investment Managers at the M&A department of Societe Generale,
Directorships: Member of the Executive Committee

Dominique Gaillard, Managing Director
e-mail: dominique.gaillard@axa-im.com
Education: Ecole Polytechnique; Ecole Nationale des Ponts et Chaussées; Institut d'Administration des Entreprises; MS, UC Berkeley
Background: Péchiney group, Member of the Executive Board - Charterhouse (now Chequers)
Directorships: Member of the Executive Committee

2467 AXIS PARTICIPATIONES EMPRESARIALES
C/ Los Madrazo, 38 2a
Madrid 28014
Spain

Phone: 34-91523165437 Fax: 34-915321933
e-mail: axis@axispart.com
web: www.axispart.com

Mission Statement: Invests in SMEs with a profitable high growth potential
Geographic Preference: Spain
Founded: 1986
Average Investment: $6.28 Million
Minimum Investment: $0.6 Million
Investment Criteria: Profitable working companies - or those with potential profits in the short term.

Key Executives:
Guillermo Jimenez, General Director
Emilio Ramos Gorostiza, Operations Manager

2468 AXM VENTURE CAPITAL
57g Randolph Avenue
London W9 1BQ
United Kingdom

Phone: 5089856
e-mail: info@axmvc.co.uk
web: www.axmvc.co.uk

Mission Statement: Manages the Creative Capital Fund and Northwest Fund 4 Digital Creative.
Geographic Preference: United Kingdom
Investment Criteria: Early-Stage
Portfolio Companies: First Active Media, Autology World, Mydish

Key Executives:
Fred Mendelsohn, Investment Director

2469 AXON PARTNERS GROUP
Jose Ortega y Gasset, 25
Madrid 28006
Spain

Phone: 34-913102894
web: www.axonpartnersgroup.com

Mission Statement: Axon Partners Group (Axon) is an international firm dedicated to value creation through investing and consulting services in the broad technology sector, from ICT to Energy. We manage early to growth capital funds of over 130 Million USD in technology and innovation, supported by prestigious investors from all over the world.
Geographic Preference: Spain, Latin America, India
Average Investment: $100,000K to $25M
Portfolio Companies: Aqua Mobile, Captronic Systems, DocOnYou, Enigma, Nanobiomatters, Nice People At Work, Virgin Play, Wuaki.tv, Zinkia

Other Locations:
801 Brickell Avenue
9th Floor
Miami, FL 33131
Phone: 786-6001462

Calle 87 No. 10 - 93 Of 701
Piso 15
Edificio Av. Chile
Bogota
Chile
Phone: 571-6353007

Key Executives:
Francisco Velazquez de Cuellar, CEO/Managing Director

2470 AXVENTURES
Republica de Eslovenia 1970
Piso 8 B
Buenos Aires C1426CZH
Argentina

Phone: 54-91154517555
e-mail: lbril@axventures.com
web: www.axventures.com

Mission Statement: Ax Ventures SRL is the Local Manager of Pymar Fund LP, in Argentina. The aim of PYMAR is to invest in Argentine innovative and technology companies that target regional and global markets.
Geographic Preference: Argentina
Industry Group Preference: Technology, Software, Biotechnology, Clean Technology
Portfolio Companies: Bioscience, Keclon, Cupoint, Zauber

Key Executives:
Juan Jose Zaballa, General Partner

2471 AXXESS CAPITAL
33 Aviatorilor Blvd
Bucharest 011853
Romania

Phone: 4021-2077100 Fax: 4021-2228503
e-mail: office@axxesscapital.net
web: www.axxesscapital.net

Mission Statement: Investment Manager of Romanian-American Enterprise Fund and Balkan Accession Fund
Average Investment: $5 Million - $15 Million
Portfolio Companies: EDY International, EELF, Capa Finance, Iceline/Darko, Industrial Access, Frigotechnica, BitDefender, Noriel, Banca Romenesca, Ralfi/Estima Finance, Motoractive, Domenia Credit, Jet Finance, Domo Retail, Policolor

Other Locations:
3 Ohridskoezero Street
Floor 4
Sofia 1330
Bulgaria
Phone: 3592-9269743 Fax: 3592-944-1475

545 Fifth Avenue
Suite 300
New York, NY 10017
Phone: 212-6975766 Fax: 212-8180445

Key Executives:
Horia D Manda, Managing Partner
Education: MBA, University of Quebec
Background: CIO, RAEF

2472 AZINI CAPITAL PARTNERS
29 Farm Street
London W1J 5RL
United Kingdom

Phone: 44-2031783388
e-mail: paul.hill@azini.com
web: www.azini.com

Mission Statement: Azini Capital is a UK based private equity firm that specialises in acquiring portfolios of private and public technology companies from historical investors and shareholders. Azini Capital typically acquires significant minority stakes and prefers to hold investments for a number of years - providing additional funding if required - in order to

Venture Capital & Private Equity Firms / International Firms

maximize the growth, development and ultimate value of the companies.
Geographic Preference: United Kingdom
Founded: 2007
Industry Group Preference: Software, Technology, Materials Technology, High Technology
Portfolio Companies: Amino Technologies, Antenova, Bluearc, Aim Technology, Bolero, Centerbeam, Corvil, Crescendo Networks, Digital Fuel, Focus Solutions, Frontier Silicon, Iforce, Investis, Keronite, Mobixell Networks, Ob10, Oberon Media, Onespin, Picochip, Pond Ventures, Portrait Software, Raysat, Shazam, Sonim, Starhome, Streamserve, Transitive
Key Executives:
  Michael Bennett, Co-Founder
  Education: BSc, Electronic Engineering, Southampton University
  Background: British Telecom, IBM, LMS Capital

2473 AZIONE CAPITAL
46 East Coast Rd
#07-03, Eastgate
Singapore 428766
Singapore

Phone: 65-31121688
e-mail: startup@azionecapital.com
web: www.azionecapital.com

Mission Statement: An early stage venture capital investment company and startup incubator.
Geographic Preference: Asia
Founded: 2006
Investment Criteria: Early-Stage
Industry Group Preference: Digital Media & Marketing, Mobile Communications Devices, Wireless Technologies, Energy, Maritime Industry
Portfolio Companies: LocAsian Networks, Who Works Around You Pte Ltd, Hibernator, Events Core, myWobile Pte Ltd, e994, ClickingHouse Pte Ltd, Talenz, Fusion Ads, GameMo
Key Executives:
  Nicholas Chan, Executive Director
  Education: Dip., Ngee Ann Polytechnic

2474 B DASH VENTURES
Holland Hills Mori Tower
No. 11, No. 2, 5-chome
Toranomon, Minato-ku
Tokyo
Japan

e-mail: info@bdashventures.com
web: www.bdashventures.com

Mission Statement: B Dash Ventures invests in promising startups and leading Internet industry entrepreneurs.
Portfolio Companies: Enter Crews, Lindoc, Mr Taddy, (es) Corporation, ScaleOut, FCV, Fresvii, Cubie Messenger
Key Executives:
  Hiroyuki Watanabe, President/CEO

2475 B-TO-V PARTNERS
Blumenaustrasse 36
St. Gallen 9000
Switzerland

Phone: 41-71-242-2000 **Fax:** 41-71-242-2001
e-mail: info@b-to-v.com
web: www.b-to-v.com

Mission Statement: b-to-v is both venture capital firm and a leading investor network. To our members, we provide an incomparable deal flow, in the form of lead- and co-investment-opportunities, collaborative investment processes and access to a unique network of like-minded entrepreneurs. To companies we are a reliable partner when it comes to capital access, entrepreneurial intelligence and professional support.
Geographic Preference: Germany, Europe
Average Investment: 50,000 - 2 million Euro
Industry Group Preference: Advanced Technologies, Internet, Mobile
Portfolio Companies: ArmedAngels, IWAtech, Campanda, Fantasy Shopper, Winlocal, Cycleon, Sum Up, Qype, Highdef, Cellity, Hitmeister, Curefab, ONTOPx, Mobile City, Fab, Flaconi, Angela Bruderer, Happify, Urbanara, Spinelab, Sharewise, Orcamp, Blacklane Limiusines, Ondeso, Xing, Quanta, Linguee, Cod Farmers, Zynga, W.I.S.E., Immatics, Carsablanca, Facebook, CellEra, Luxodo, HengZhi, Studitemps, Reille24, Voss, Finanzchek, Ixigo, Loxi, RomoWind, Alatest, Massiv Konzept, Nanda Tech, Plazes, Mybet.com, eCift, TVSmiles
Other Locations:
  Barerstrasse 1
  Munich 80333
  Germany

  Meinekestrasse 5
  Berlin 10719
  Germany
Key Executives:
  Florian Schweitzer, Co-Founder/Partner
  Education: University of St. Gallen

2476 BAEKELAND FUNDS
Bollebergen 2 B
Gent-Zwijnaarde 9052
Belgium

Phone: 32-09-264-8987
e-mail: patrick.dhaese@ugent.be

Mission Statement: Invests in growing, innovative companies that are commercializing technology developed within Ghent University.
Fund Size: 3.6 million Euro
Founded: 1999
Average Investment: 500,000 Euro
Investment Criteria: Seed-Stage, Startup
Industry Group Preference: High Technology
Portfolio Companies: ActoGeniX, Arcarios, Artisto Music, Caliopa, Complix Alphabody Therapeutics, Pronota, Sigasi, Spartanova, Trinean
Key Executives:
  Patrick Dhaese

2477 BAF SPECTRUM
30 Biopolis Street
#09-02 Matrix
Singapore 138671
Singapore

Phone: 65-6777-7139
e-mail: info@bafspectrum.com

Mission Statement: We are a Singapore-based angel fund investing in Asia-based technology startups with a compelling value proposition and a global high-growth potential. We like to work with entrepreneurs who can demonstrate both creative fervor and execution flair. We look at the feasibility of their innovative ideas, review their execution skills and assess their commitment & competency to grow the company to a global brand with our experienced investment team.
Geographic Preference: Asia
Founded: 2006
Average Investment: $1.5 million
Minimum Investment: $75,000
Investment Criteria: Startup, Seed-Stage
Industry Group Preference: Digital Media & Marketing, Internet, Consumer Internet, Mobile, Information Technology
Portfolio Companies: Anacle, Anafore, Game Ventures, Healthtrends Medical Investments, IXIGO, Mozat, ProgenIQ

Key Executives:
  Sanjeev Shah, Managing Director
  Education: BS, International Business, Loyola Marymount University
  Background: Founder, Rollon Hydraulics

2478 BALDERTON CAPITAL
28 Britannia Street
The Stables
London WC1X 9JF
United Kingdom

Phone: 4 020 701 668 00
web: www.balderton.com

Mission Statement: An early stage venture capital investor that focuses on European technology comanies.

Geographic Preference: Europe, United States, Asia
Fund Size: $2.2 Billion
Founded: 2000
Average Investment: $5-15 million
Minimum Investment: $100,000
Investment Criteria: Early-Stage, Series A, Seed
Industry Group Preference: E-Commerce & Manufacturing, Consumer Internet, Software, Communications, Security, Semiconductors, Consumer Services, Media, Financial Services
Portfolio Companies: 3D Hubs, Adludio, Aircall, Andjaro, Appear [here], Banjo, Carwow, Citymapper, Cleo, Comply Advantage, Contentful, Credit Benchmark, Crowdcube, Curious AI Company, Dalia Research, Depop, Dinghy, Display Link, Dubsmash, Eqise, Ezoic, Funnel, Furhat Robotics, Globoforce, GoCardless, Healx, Hiya, Infarm, Instabridge, InterResolve, Kobalt, Kupivip.ru, Labaster, Lovecrafts, Luno, Lyst, Memrise, Mojoworks, MyTomorrows, Nlyte Software, Nutmeg, Openet, Patients Know Best, Pay With My Bank, Peakon, Prodigy Finance, Pusher, Qubit, Rebtel, Recorded Future, Rentify, Revolut, ROLI, Scytl, Simple Feast, Sketchfab, Sophia Genetics, Soundtrack Your Brand, Tapdaq, Tempow, Tessian, The Hut Group, The Tab, Thread, Tictail, Touch Surgery, Trademark Now, Vestiaire Collective, Virtuo, Vivino, VOI, Wooga, Workable, Zego, Zopa

Key Executives:
  Tim Bunting, Partner
  44 020 7016 6800
  e-mail: tim@balderton.com
  Education: University of Cambridge
  Background: Goldman Sachs
  Bernard Liautaud, Managing Partner
  44 020 7016 6800
  e-mail: bernard@balderton.com
  Education: MS, Engineering Management, Stanford University; Ecole Centrale de Paris
  Background: Dashlane; Business Objects
  Jerome Misso, Operating Partner
  44 020 7016 6800
  e-mail: contact_jerome@balderton.com
  Education: University of Hull
  Background: Nabarro; Eversheds

2479 BALLPARK VENTURES
159/165 Great Portland Street
5th Floor
Tennyson House
London W1W 5PA
United Kingdom

e-mail: info@ballparkventures.com
web: www.ballparkventures.com

Mission Statement: Ballpark Ventures is a small, boutique fund investing in early stage technology startups.

Geographic Preference: Europe
Industry Group Preference: Technology, Mobile, Retail, Consumer & Leisure, Media

Portfolio Companies: Blismedia, Eyequant, Tadaa, Dbvu, Sales Gossip, Loop Me, Future Ad Labs, Blink, Bluefields, On Device Research, Springboard, Pipe

Key Executives:
  Ollie Bishop
  e-mail: ollie@ballparkventures.com
  Background: Founder, STEAK

2480 BALTCAP MANAGEMENT LTD
Tartu mnt. 2
Tallinn 10145
Estonia

Phone: 372-6650280 Fax: 372-6650281
web: www.baltcap.com

Mission Statement: Delivers superior return on equity for investors via invetsment in unlisted advanced stage growth oriented Baltic companies.

Geographic Preference: Baltic Countries
Fund Size: $90 million
Founded: 1995
Average Investment: $3 million
Minimum Investment: $ 300,000
Investment Criteria: Expansion Stage companies with good grwoth capabilities
Industry Group Preference: Telecommunications, Toys, Clinical Development, Food & Beverage, Information Technology, Machinery, Electronic Technology, Automotive

Key Executives:
  Peeter Saks, Managing Partner
  e-mail: vygandas.juras@BaltCap.com
  Matts Andersson, Senior Adviser, Partner
  e-mail: martin.kodar@BaltCap.com
  Education: BA Economics, Tallinn Technical University
  Background: Administrator in a machinery trading company Nava.
  Directorships: supervisory board member in AS Vipex and AS Ecometal.
  Dagnis Dreimanis, Partner
  e-mail: dagnis.dreimanis@BaltCap.com
  Education: BSBA Finance and Economics, Slippery Rock University of Pennsylvania
  Background: Financial Advisory Services Manager in PricewaterhouseCoopers.
  Directorships: supervisory board member in SIA Hansa Electronics, INTRAC Group AB, SIA DT Mobile, SIA Adam Auto, SIA DEPO DIY, SIA V.L.T.
  Oliver Kullman, Investment Director
  e-mail: ruth.laatre@BaltCap.com

2481 BANEXI VENTURES PARTNERS
13-15 rue Taitbout
Paris 75009
France

Phone: 33-173028969 Fax: 33-140143896

Mission Statement: Focuses on emerging and early stage companies with a priority given to high growth companies with high technology.

Geographic Preference: France
Founded: 1983
Investment Criteria: Emerging and Early Stage companies
Industry Group Preference: Life Sciences, Information Technology, Optical Technology, Semiconductors, Electronic Technology, Medical Technology
Portfolio Companies: Avertec, Iroc, Inpact, LDL Technology, Lumilog, Novasic, WSI, Mesatronic, SI Auto, Humirel, TEEM PH, Coronis, Infusio, Kelkoo, Masa, Webdyn, Quotatis

Key Executives:
  Michel Dahan, Chairman
  Education: Ecole Polytechnique; ENSAE
  Background: CEO - SAARI
  Directorships: Chairman

Venture Capital & Private Equity Firms / International Firms

Philippe Mere, General Partner, Electronics
Education: MS Engineering, Ecole des Mines de Paris
Background: Genset, a French Biotech company
Sophie Pierrin-Lepinard, General Partner
Education: PhD, Pharmacy, Toulouse University; MA, Finance, ESCP
Background: Marketing, Proctor & Gamble Pharmaceuticals; Investment Manager, Credit Agricole
Philippe Herbert, Partner, Internet
Education: Graduate, SUPELEC
Background: Director of Marketing, Schlumberger

2482 BANK J VONTOBEL COMPANY AG
Gotthardstrasse 43
Zurich CH-8022
Switzerland

Phone: 41-0582837111 Fax: 4-0582837650
e-mail: vontobel.group@vontobel.ch
web: www.vontobel.com

Mission Statement: Actively seeking new investments.

Founded: 1924

Key Executives:
Herbert J. Scheidt, Chairman
Dr. Frank Schnewlin, Vice-Chairman of the Board of Directors, Chairman of the Risk and

2483 BARCELONA EMPREN
Gran Via de les Corts Catalanes
635 6th floor
1 Planta
Barcelona 08010
Spain

Phone: 34-902227237 Fax: 34-934019709

Mission Statement: Actively seeking new investments in the Barcelona VC market.

Geographic Preference: Spain
Founded: 1999
Average Investment: $3 million - $15 million
Minimum Investment: $350,000
Investment Criteria: Invests in innovative companies with a technological base
Industry Group Preference: Biotechnology, Internet Technology, Software, Telecommunications, Media
Portfolio Companies: Xcellsyz, Advancell, Era-plantech, Crystax, Isoco, Net Translations, Nonstopyacht, Agents Inspired, Amr Systems, Fractus, Voz Telecom

Key Executives:
Christian Fernández, Chief Executive Officer
Emilio Gómez, Director Operations

2484 BARCLAYS LEVERAGED FINANCE
1 Churchill Place
London E14 5HP
United Kingdom

Phone: 44-2476-842100 Fax: 44-02071167636
web: www.barclays.co.uk

Mission Statement: Actively seeking new investments.

Geographic Preference: United Kingdom, Western Europe
Investment Criteria: Expansion and Development, Bridge Finance, Refinancing Bank Debt, Secondary Purchase/Replacement Capital, Rescue/Turnaround
Industry Group Preference: All Sectors Considered

Key Executives:
John Varley, Chief Executive Officer
Bob Diamond, President

2485 BARCLAYS PRIVATE EQUITY FRANCE
34 / 36 Avenue de Friedland
Cedex 8
Paris 75383
France

Phone: 33-144583232 Fax: 33-0156694344
web: www.barcap.com

Mission Statement: Actively seeking new investments.

Geographic Preference: France
Founded: 1991
Investment Criteria: MBO, MBI, Capital Expansion

Key Executives:
Eric Bommensath, Co-Chief Executive, Corporate and Investment Banking
e-mail: julie-lorin.meurisse@barclayscapital.com
Education: Graduation at Dauphine University Paris
Justin Bull, Chief Operating Officer
e-mail: gonzague.deblignieres@barclayscapital.com
Background: Investor in capital in Banexi & Charterhouse
Patrick Clackson, Chief Executive
e-mail: laurent.chauvois@barclayscapital.com
Education: IEP
Background: Agricultural credit Indosuez
Justin Bull, Chief Operating Officer
e-mail: guillaume.jacqueau@barclayscapital.com
Education: Economics, Business, Finance Graduate.Masters in Finance
Patrick Clackson, Chief Executive
e-mail: cedric.sicard@barclayscapital.com
Education: MBA, University of Texas
Background: Banexi, BNP Kuwait

2486 BARCLAYS VENTURES Barclays
1 Churchill Place
1st Floor
London E14 5HP
United Kingdom

Phone: 1-02124124096 Fax: 44-2075-994691
web: www.barclayscorporate.com

Mission Statement: Invests as a strategic partner alongside management teams, working together to build and realise shareholder value.

Geographic Preference: United Kingdom, Republic of Ireland
Fund Size: $124 Million
Founded: 1997
Average Investment: $6.20 Million
Minimum Investment: $1.77 Million
Investment Criteria: Expansion and Development, Secondary purchase/replacement capital, MBO, MBI, Buy and Build, Roll-out
Industry Group Preference: Business to Business, Leisure, Media, Retailing, Education, Financial Services, Healthcare, Manufacturing, Technology, Telecommunications, Logistics
Portfolio Companies: Benlowe Group Ltd, Diesel Marine International Ltd, System C Healthcare Ltd, Le Monde Holdings Ltd, Esprit Holidays Ltd, VJ Technology, Sovereign Woodmet

Key Executives:
Khilan Dodhia, Director
Alex Brebbia, Director

2487 BARING CORILIUS PRIVATE EQUITY
ul. Wspolna 47/49
Warsaw 00-684
Poland

Phone: 48-226274000 Fax: 48-226274001

Mission Statement: Manages the Baring Central European Fund. A private equity fund manager focused on central Eu-

Venture Capital & Private Equity Firms / International Firms

rope. BCPE is a member of Baring Private Equity International.
Geographic Preference: Central Europe, Poland, Hungary, Romania, Bulgaria
Founded: 1997
Minimum Investment: $10 Million
Investment Criteria: Growth, Development, Consolidation
Portfolio Companies: Allami Nyomda, Baoya Estates, CR Media Group, Falcon-Vision, Infopress, Poligrafia SA, Topway Industries
Key Executives:
  György Karády, Managing Partner
  Education: PhD, Harvard University
  Background: Director, European Bank for Reconstruction & Development; Strategy Consultant, US/France
  Jacek Pogonowski, Partner
  Education: BS Finance, St. John's University
  Background: Managing Director, IB Austria Financial Advisors; Arthur Andersen, Warsaw
  William R Watson, Partner
  Education: MBA, INSEAD
  Background: Telecom Team, EBRD; Corporate Finance, Salomon Brothers

2488 BARING PRIVATE EQUITY PARTNERS ASIA
8 Finance Street
Two International Finance Centre
Suite 3801
Central
Hong Kong
Phone: 85-228439300 Fax: 852-28439372
e-mail: hongkong@bpeasia.com

Mission Statement: Actively seeking new investments.
Geographic Preference: India, Singapore, China, Hong Kong, Taiwan, Korea
Fund Size: $257 Million
Founded: 1997
Key Executives:
  Dar Chen, Managing Director
  e-mail: info@bpepasia.com
  Malcolm Lai, Managing Director

2489 BARING PRIVATE EQUITY PARTNERS ESPANA SA
Hermosilla
11-5a Planta
Madrid 28001
Spain
Phone: 34-917818870 Fax: 34-917818877
e-mail: bpepmadrid@bpep.es
web: www.bpep.es

Mission Statement: Provides equity to private Spanish and Portuguese companies, with the objective of financing and contributing to their expansion, shareholder restructuring or management-buy-out.
Geographic Preference: Spain, Portugal
Fund Size: $240 Million
Founded: 1987
Investment Criteria: Expansion, Consolidations, Restructuring, Middle Market
Industry Group Preference: Medical & Health Related, Construction, Heating, Engineering, Media, Automotive
Portfolio Companies: Losán, Aricam, Manuel, Iturmo, Climastar, Ingemas, Novatex, Socinser, Selenis, Sedal, Elite, Marcanet, Aguamur, Iberchem, Autoequip, Bioferma, Euro-atomizado.
Key Executives:
  José Angel Sarasa, Managing Partner

2490 BARING PRIVATE EQUITY PARTNERS INDIA
9th Floor, Infinity Tower A, DLF Phase II
Gurgoan 122002
India
Phone: 91-124-4321100 Fax: 91-124-4321155
e-mail: rahul.bhasin@bpepindia.com
web: www.bpepindia.com

Mission Statement: Partner with exceptional entrepreneurs to build outstanding businesses by providing growth capital and assistance in scaling up through access to relevant industry and management expertise.
Geographic Preference: India
Fund Size: $1 Billion
Founded: 1984
Average Investment: $100 Million
Minimum Investment: $15 million
Investment Criteria: Mid-market transactions, Management buy-out, Significant Minority, Minority
Industry Group Preference: Information Technology, Infrastructure, Banking, Financial Services, Healthcare, Telecommunications, Real Estate, Media, Education, Consumer Products
Portfolio Companies: Mphasis, Molecular Connections, JRG Securities, AuroMira Energy, Infrasoft Technologies, Integra Securities, Secova Services, PharmArc Analytics, Rea Metrix, Maples, Molecular Connections, Sphaera Pharma, Shilpa Medicare, Muthoot Finance, Cethar Vessels
Other Locations:
  1 Royal Plaza
  Royal Avenue
  St Peter Port
  Guernsey, Channel Island GY1 2HL
  United Kingdom
  Phone: 44-14817-35814
Key Executives:
  Gyuri Karady, Managing Partner
  e-mail: rahul.bhasin@bpepindia.com
  SM Sundaram, Partner, Director
  408-690-4014
  e-mail: sundaram@bpepusa.com
  Education: MBA, Indian Institute of Management, Ahmedabad
  Background: Partner & CFO
  Directorships: Infrasoft Technologies, Infrasoft Tech, Secova e-Services, Maples, Auro Mira Energy, Sphaera Pharma

2491 BARING VOSTOK CAPITAL PARTNERS
125047, Moscow, ul. Forest, 9
Business Center White Gardens, Building B, 6 fl.
Gasheka Str. 7, Building 1
Moscow 123056
Russia
Phone: 7-0959671307 Fax: 7-0959671308
e-mail: info@bvcp.ru
web: www.bvcp.ru

Fund Size: $400 Million
Founded: 1994
Investment Criteria: Medium sized
Industry Group Preference: Oil & Gas, Energy, Media, Services, Telecommunications, Branded Goods, Technology
Portfolio Companies: Airln Space, Burren Energy, DalRybProm, GCMW, Golden Telecom, Promopost Holding, Rostik Restaurants Ltd, ru-Net Holdings, riskdata, Sakhinterlesprom, StoryFirst, Syktyvkar, United Confectioneries
Key Executives:
  Arkady Volozh, CEO of Yandex
  Background: European Bank for Reconstruction & Development (EBRD); Salomon Brothers
  Directorships: NIS Fund

Venture Capital & Private Equity Firms / International Firms

Vyacheslav Zarenkov, Chairman
Education: BS, PhD, Moscow Power Engineering Institute
Background: Professor/Researcher, Moscow Power Engineering Institute; CEO, Alfa Asset Management; Director, Alfa Capital
Directorships: Tops BI, AirInSpace

2492 BASF VENTURE CAPITAL
4, Gartenweg
Gebaude Z 025
Ludwigshafen 67063
Germany

Phone: 49-6216076801 Fax: 49-6216076819
web: www.basf-vc.de

Mission Statement: The corporate venture capital company of BASF Group, investing globally in promising start-up companies and funds. BASF invests in start-up companies and venture capital funds worldwide. Its investments focus on innovative technologies with a high growth potential where chemistry plays an important role, as well as new materials and substances with significant market opportunities. BASF not only invests venture capital, but also supports its investments through targeted interaction between BASF Group's worldwide know-how and research network and its portfolio companies.
Geographic Preference: Worldwide
Investment Criteria: Startup, Early-Stage
Industry Group Preference: Chemicals, Plastics, Agriculture, Oil & Gas, Energy, Biotechnology, Nanotechnology
Portfolio Companies: Advanced BioNutrition, Allylix, Arcadia Biosciences, ARCH Venture Partners, Aspen Aerogels, Baseclick, Chrysalix, Clean Diesel Technologies, Datalase, Deutsche Rohstoff AG, Fintech, FloDesign, Heliatek, Luca Technologies, NanoMas Technologies, NGen Enabling Technologies Funds, Oxonica, Pangaea Ventures, Plastic Logic, Sciessent, SDC Materials, Solidia Technologies
Other Locations:
46820 Fremont Blvd
Fremont, CA 94538
Phone: 510-4456140

45th Floor, Jardine House
No. 1, Connaught Place
Central
Hong Kong
Phone: 852-27313755

Roppongi Hills Mori Tower 21F
6-10-1, Roppongi, Minato-ku
Tokyo 106-6121
Japan
Phone: 81-337964117 Fax: 81-337965947

Key Executives:
Dirk Nachtigal, Managing Director
49-621-60-76813
Education: University of Gottingen, University of Hamburg
Background: Head of Finance, Accounting & Control, BASF Schwarzheide GmbH

2493 BASIL PARTNERS Kross Border Trust Services Limited
St. Louis Business Centre
Onr Desroches & St. Louis Streets
Port Louis
Mauritius

Phone: 230-2031100 Fax: 230-2031150
e-mail: info@basilpartners.com
web: www.basilpartners.com

Mission Statement: Basil Partners is a venture capital fund focused on investing in either Indian / Asian companies which seek to expand into Global markets or US / European companies which have an India / Asia centric offshore based model. Basil's investment philosophy is to Partner with the Portfolio company and 'Actively Build' world class companies. Our capital comes from 'Basil Growth Corporation', a closed-end Venture Capital Fund incorporated in Mauritius.
Geographic Preference: India, Asia, United States, Europe
Industry Group Preference: Information Technology
Portfolio Companies: Cignex, Endeavour, GGVS, IT Convergence, Karmic, Netscribes, SDG
Key Executives:
Rajeev Srivastava, CEO/Managing Partner
Education: BS, Engineering, MBA, Mumbai University
Background: Founder, Apar Infotech

2494 BAY BG BAVARIAN VENTURE CAPITAL CORP
Queen Street 23
PO Box 1155
Munich 80539
Germany

Phone: 089-122280100 Fax: 089-122280101
e-mail: info@baybg.de
web: www.baybg.de

Mission Statement: Invests in medium-sized companies
Geographic Preference: Germany
Investment Criteria: Growth, Innovation, MBO, MBI, Bridging loans
Industry Group Preference: Consumer Products, Wholesale, High Technology, Industrial Services, Retailing, Life Sciences
Portfolio Companies: Baierl & Demmelhuber Innenausbau GmbH, Töging am Inn, Balnea Erlebnisbäder GmbH & Co. Chieming/Obb, Cottan Cosmetic GmbH, München, Dinghartinger Apfelstrudel Productions-UND Vertriebs, Landsham, Dobler Metallbau GmbH, München, ES-Plastic GmbH
Key Executives:
Guenther Henrich, Managing Director
Peter Pauli, Managing Director

2495 BAYERN KAPITAL
Landgasse 135 a
Landshut 84028
Bavaria

Phone: 49-8719232555 Fax: 49-8719232555
e-mail: info@bayernkapital.de
web: www.bayernkapital.de

Mission Statement: Bayern Kapital GmbH is a public Bavarian venture capital company and was founded as part of the 'Bavarian Future Initiative' as a wholly-owned subsidiary of the LfA Foerderbank Bayern (Bavaria's development bank) at the end of 1995. The objective of Bayern Kapital is to finance research and development and market launch of new products. In this effort Bayern Kapital usually acts as co-investor in cooperation with a private lead investor. The 'Bayern Kapital model' is unique in Germany. Bayern Kapital has now developed into an essential location factor and driver of private financing in Bavaria.
Geographic Preference: Bavaria
Founded: 1995
Average Investment: 250,000-500,000 Euro
Investment Criteria: Seed-Stage, Startup, Early-Stage
Industry Group Preference: High Technology
Key Executives:
Roman Huber, Managing Director
Rudolf Mayr, Managing Director

Venture Capital & Private Equity Firms / International Firms

2496 BB BIOTECH VENTURES
Seestrasse 16
Kusnacht 8700
Switzerland

Phone: 41-442676700 Fax: 41-442676701
e-mail: info@bellevue.ch

Mission Statement: BB Biotech Ventures is a healthcare-dedicated venture capital fund, focused on companies that develop and market drugs and medical devices. The Guernsey-based fund is advised by the Bellevue Asset Management Group, which has operations in Curaçao, Boston/USA and Kusnacht/Zurich, Switzerland.

Industry Group Preference: Healthcare, Medical Devices
Portfolio Companies: Aerovance, Aleva Neurotherpeutics, Alpex Pharma, AM Pharma, Anteis, Atlas Genetics, BioVascular, Cadence Pharmaceuticals, Calypso Medical Technologies, Cameron Health, Cervelo Pharmaceuticals, Lumavita, Molecular Partners, NEOSE Technologies, Natural Dental Implants, Optimer Pharmaceuticals, Orthocon, Palyon, Pevion Biotech, Radius Health, Sonetik, Swiss Smile, TargeGen, Tioga Pharmaceuticals, Vaximm

Key Executives:
Klaus Breiner, Senior Investment Advisor Private Equity
Background: Business Consultant, Booz Allen & Hamilton
Directorships: Agendia, Alpex Pharma, Cadence Pharmaceuticals, Cervelo Pharmaceuticals, Glycart Biotechnology, Orthocon
Jurg Eckhardt, Senior Investment Advisor Private Equity
Education: MBA, INSEAD; MD, University of Basel
Background: Associate Partner, McKinsey & Company
Directorships: Anteis, Calypso Medical Technologies, TargeGen, Swiss Smile Holding

2497 BC PARTNERS LIMITED
40 Portman Square
London W1H 6DA
United Kingdom

Phone: 44-2070094800 Fax: 44-2070094899
e-mail: london@bcpartners.com
web: www.bcpartners.com

Mission Statement: Actively seeking new investments.
Geographic Preference: United Kingdom, Western Europe
Fund Size: $87.2 billion
Founded: 1986
Average Investment: $264 Million
Minimum Investment: $21.6 Million
Investment Criteria: Secondary purchase/replacement capital, MBO, MBI, Institutional BO, Leveraged Build Up, Public-to-Private
Industry Group Preference: Technology, Healthcare, Heating, Publishing, Automotive, Hospitals
Portfolio Companies: Amadeus, Dometic, Picard, Centro Médico Teknon, Baxi Group, SEAT, Telecolumbus, Hirslanden Holdings, Elis II, Galbani, LD COM, Mark IV Industries, General Healthcare Group

Key Executives:
Fahim Ahmed, Partner
Education: MBA from Stanford University and an economics degree from Cambridge
Background: Boston Consulting Group
Justin Bateman, Senior Partner
Education: MBA from the University of Chicago, Graduate of both the Ecole Polytechnique and the Ecole Nationale Supérieure des Télécommunications
Background: Director, Finapol Sarl, Manager, Finapol Sarl, Vice Chairman, Wasserstein Perella & Co.
Directorships: Executive
Michael Chang, Partner
Education: MBA from The Wharton School in Pennsylvania and an economics degree from Cambridge.

Background: Bankers Trust, Bain & Co in Boston and London,

2498 BECO CAPITAL
web: www.becocapital.com

Mission Statement: Based in Egypt, BECO Capital gives companies the two vital ingredients that they most need in their early development stage: growth capital and hands-on operational mentorship. BECO tries to to strike a balance between the bottom line and benefiting local communities. BECO aspires to give VSMEs the boost they need to make giant leaps for the Middle East.

Geographic Preference: Middle East
Key Executives:
Dany Farha, Founder/CEO
Background: Co-Founder, Bayt.com

2499 BEIJING HIGH TECHNOLOGY INVESTMENT COMPANY
Center Gate Technologies Building
12th floor
Haidian District
Beijing 100081
China

Phone: 86-1062140588 Fax: 86-1062142499
web: www.bhti.com.cn

Mission Statement: Committed to investing in strong, growing companies.

Geographic Preference: China
Fund Size: $31 Million
Founded: 1998
Investment Criteria: Making investment in high-tech enterprises
Industry Group Preference: Information Technology, Life Sciences, Energy, Environmental Protection
Portfolio Companies: Altan China Co Ltd, Shenzhen Tsinghua Tongfang Co Ltd, Tsinghua Tongfang Artificial Environment Co Ltd, Beijing Ibase Software Co Ltd, Capital Biochip Corporation, Beijing Phylion Battery Co Ltd, Beijing King's Orient Hi-Tech Group Co Ltd

Key Executives:
Qi Rong, General Manager
Xing Hualou, Chairman

2500 BEIJING VENTURE CAPITAL COMPANY LIMITED
10th Floor, Haidian Science Technology Tower
Haidian District
No.3 Nada Street, Zhongguancun
Beijing 100081
China

Phone: 86-1068943739 Fax: 86-1068943779

Mission Statement: Committed to investing in strong, growing companies.

Geographic Preference: China
Fund Size: $465 Million
Founded: 1998
Average Investment: $40 million
Minimum Investment: $1 Million
Investment Criteria: Expansion Capital, Development Capital, Buyout
Industry Group Preference: Information Technology, Environmental Protection, Materials Technology
Portfolio Companies: Beijing International Trust and Investment Co, Beijing International Power Development & Investment Corp, China CYTS Tours Holding Co Ltd.,

Key Executives:
Xu Zhe, Chairman
Rongzi Wang, Vice President & Supervisor

Venture Capital & Private Equity Firms / International Firms

2501 BENCIS CAPITAL PARTNERS
World Trade Center Amsterdam
Zuidplein 76
Amsterdam 1077 XV
Netherlands
Phone: 31-205400940 Fax: 31-205400941
e-mail: info@bencis.com
web: www.bencis.nl

Mission Statement: Bencis Capital Partners is an independent private equity firm targeting medium sized companies in the Benelux countries. Bencis Capital Partners is fully independent and is owned by its partners. Bencis Capital Partners is responsible for the management of Bencis Buyout Fund I (established in 2000) and is fund manager of Bencis Buyout Fund II (2004), Bencis Buyout Fund III (2007) and Bencis Buyout Fund IV (2011).

Geographic Preference: Benelux
Industry Group Preference: Manufacturing, Food & Beverage, Leisure, Media, Wholesale, Retail, Consumer & Leisure
Portfolio Companies: AXA Stenman, Baert, CMI-Dutchview, Desso, Florimex Group, Itho Daalderop, Neroc, Royal Sanders, Shoeby - Lakeside, SK FireSafety Group, Smulders Group, Stork Prints, Tandvitaal, Teidem - Jomo, The Employment Group, Unlimited Sports Group, Verelst, Winsol

Key Executives:
Zoran van Gessel, Co-Founder
Education: MSc, Economics, University of Amsterdam
Background: Senior Executive, MeesPierson Corporate Finance
Directorships: Jomo, Teidem, Axa Stenman, Tandvitaal

2502 BERENBERG PRIVATE CAPITAL
Neuer Jungfernstieg 20
Hamburg 20354
Germany
Phone: 49-40350600 Fax: 49-4035060900
e-mail: info@berenberg.de
web: www.berenbergbank.de

Mission Statement: Actively seeking new investments.
Founded: 1590
Minimum Investment: 25,000 Euro
Investment Criteria: All Stages
Industry Group Preference: All Sectors Considered
Key Executives:
Claus-G. Budelmann, General Partner
49 4035060212
Hans-Walter Peters, General Partner
49 4035060214

2503 BERLIN TECHNOLOGIE
Unter den Linden 16
Berlin 10117
Germany
Phone: 49-0-30-408-173-214
e-mail: info@berlinholding.com
web: www.berlinholding.com

Mission Statement: Berlin Technologie Holding focuses exclusively on growth capital and special opportunity situations in technology and technology-enabled businesses. BTH was founded by successful entrepreneurs and investors who invest in companies with significant growth potential.

Investment Criteria: Growth Stage, Special Situations
Industry Group Preference: Technology, Technology-Enabled Services
Portfolio Companies: Sevenval, Sensorberg, Realytics, Europe Apotheek, Viagogo
Key Executives:
Joern-Carlos Kuntze, Founder/Managing Partner
e-mail: joern.kuntze@berlinholding.com
Education: BA, International Finance, Regents College; MBA, London Business School
Background: Senior Partner, Oliver Wyman; Venturepark AG

2504 BERRIER CAPITAL
Via Manzoni, 16
Milan 20121
Italy
Phone: 39-0236644120 Fax: 39-0236644129
web: private-equity.berriercapital.com

Mission Statement: The Company researches, selects and evaluates investment in both the majority and the minority in SMEs, manages the due diligence, negotiate the terms and conditions investments, supports the management of investee companies in developing strategies and processes of growth and value creation, manages the processes of disinvestment. corporate structure is that of a holding company independent under Italian law. The Company does not use, if only marginally and, in any case, very contained, of leverage in the operations of acquisition, in the conviction of the total alignment between creating value for its members and creating value for the subsidiaries.

Portfolio Companies: Greentech Innovation, Mediamo
Key Executives:
Alberto Craici, Founding Partner
Alessandro Marina, Partner
Francesco Saibene, Investment Manager

2505 BERTI INVESTMENTS
7 Cavendish Square
London W1G 0PE
United Kingdom
Phone: 44-02076129362
web: www.bertiinvestments.com

Mission Statement: Berti is an environmental impact investment company. We invest in innovative, growing, entrepreneurial businesses in the UK whose strategy focuses on reducing carbon emissions.

Geographic Preference: United Kingdom
Industry Group Preference: Energy, Clean Technology, Renewable Energy
Portfolio Companies: Ecovision Renewables, Firefly Solar Generators, Ecometrica, HomeSun

2506 BERYTECH FUND
Berytech Technological Pole
Mkalles
Lebanon
Phone: 961-4533040 Fax: 961-4533070

Mission Statement: Berytech fund is a Lebanese start up fund. Its mission is to invest in early growth Lebanese companies whose business is in the information and communication technology (ICT) in exchange for equity ownership. With over USD6 million under management, the Fund focuses on technology companies in Lebanon with proven commercial viability. We have the operational experience to nurture the right management team to make the vision a reality, helping fast growing companies avoid pitfalls. We offer vision, imagination, experience and a network of contacts across the globe through the Fund partners.

Geographic Preference: Lebanon
Founded: 2008
Average Investment: $100,000 - $1.2 million
Investment Criteria: Startup, Seed-Stage
Key Executives:
Maroun N Chammas, Chairman
Background: Director, Chammas Group; Co-Founder, Teleinvest Holdings

Venture Capital & Private Equity Firms / International Firms

2507 BESTPORT VENTURES
29 Gloucester Place
London W1U 8HX
United Kingdom

Phone: 44-2074872555 Fax: 44-2074875535
e-mail: asimmons@bestport.co.uk
web: www.bestport.co.uk

Mission Statement: Bestport draws on the strong track record and experience of the founders and our accomplished advisory board to invest in and assist fast-growing, ambitious companies through to profitable exits.

Geographic Preference: United Kingdom
Founded: 2005
Average Investment: £250,000 - 3 million
Investment Criteria: Growth/Expansion Capital, MBO, MBI
Industry Group Preference: Business Products & Services, Healthcare, Technology
Portfolio Companies: CreditCall Limited, Healthcall Optical Services, Hotelscene Limited, Intela Global Limited, Mfuse Limited, Oracle Care Limited

Key Executives:
Ole Bettum, Co-Founder
e-mail: obettum@bestport.co.uk
Education: BSc, Economics, London School of Economics; MBA, Columbia Business School
Background: Price Waterhouse, Close Brothers Group

2508 BI WALDEN MANAGEMENT SDN Walden International
One California St.
Suite 2800
San Francisco, California
San Francisco, CA 94111

Phone: 415-7657100 Fax: 415-7657200
e-mail: usa@waldenintl.com
web: www.waldenintl.com

Mission Statement: Actively seeking new investments.
Geographic Preference: China, Malaysia, Taiwan, India, Singapore, USA
Fund Size: $1.6 Billion
Founded: 1987
Investment Criteria: Start Up
Industry Group Preference: Communications, Electronic Technology, Software, Semiconductors, Digital Media & Marketing, Information Technology
Portfolio Companies: 2bSURE.com Pte Ltd, Actelis Networks, Inc, AirTight Networks, Inc, Archway Digital Solutions Inc, BeamReach Networks, Broadxent Pte Ltd, Cameo Communications, Inc., Celestial Semiconductor, Ltd., Centillium Communications, Inc., Centrum Communic

Key Executives:
Brian Chiang, Managing Director
e-mail: akau@waldenintl.com
Education: BS, Electrical Engineering, Brown University; MBA, University of Virginia
Background: President of Chemical Technologies Ventures, Management consultant at Strategic Planning Associates and Booz
Lip-Bu Tan, Chairman

2509 BIG SOCIETY CAPITAL
72-78 Fleet Street
London EC4Y 1HY
United Kingdom

Phone: 020-7186-2500
e-mail: enquiries@bigsocietycapital.com
web: www.bigsocietycapital.com

Mission Statement: Big Society Capital is the world's first social investment wholesaler. Big Society Capital was launched in April 2012 with up to £600 million of capital to develop the social investment market in the UK by improving access to finance for social sector organizations and by raising investor awareness of investment opportunities that provide a social as well as a financial return.

Geographic Preference: United Kingdom
Fund Size: £600 million
Founded: 2012
Minimum Investment: £500,000
Industry Group Preference: Social Enterprises, Education, Wellness, Conservation, Environment
Portfolio Companies: Iaam, Resonance, Big Issue Invest, Bridges Ventures, ClearlySo, Ethical Property, Francising Works, LGT, Nesta Impact Investments, Pure Leapfrog, Social Stock Exchange

Key Executives:
Nick O'Donohoe, Chief Executive Officer
Background: Global Head of Research, JP Morgan; Goldman Sachs
Directorships: Global Impact Investing Network

2510 BIG SUR VENTURES
Fdez. de la Hoz 33
5 cto-dcha
Madrid 28010
Spain

Phone: 34-916237731
e-mail: jm@bigsurventures.es
web: www.bigsurventures.es

Mission Statement: Big Sur, based in Madrid, is an investor in companies early stage companies and working with passionate teams that seek to transform their markets with great ideas.

Investment Criteria: Seed-Stage, Early-Stage
Industry Group Preference: Internet, New Media, Technology-Enabled Services, Information Technology, Clean Technology, Digital Media & Marketing, Cloud Computing

Key Executives:
Jose Miguel Herrero, Founder
e-mail: jm@bigsurventures.es
Education: BSEECS, MSEE, Santa Clara University; MBA, Berkeley's Haas School of Business
Background: LaNetro

2511 BIGFOOT VENTURES
13th Floor C. Wisdom Centre
37 Hollywood Road
Causeway Bay
Central
Hong Kong

Phone: 852-58083400 Fax: 852-30158536
e-mail: info@bigfootventures.com
web: www.bigfoot.com/oc-bigfoot-ventures.php

Mission Statement: Bigfoot Ventures is a wholly-owned international private venture capital subsidiary of the Bigfoot Group of Companies. With operations in Hong Kong, Singapore, Cebu (Philippines), New York, Los Angeles and Antwerpen (Belgium), the company manages and implements the Group's investment plans and strategies, focusing on sectors operating in communications, technology, education, entertainment, and new media.

Geographic Preference: Asia, Europe, United States
Founded: 2004
Industry Group Preference: Communications, Technology, Education, Entertainment, New Media
Portfolio Companies: Fashion One

Other Locations:
BigFoot Entertainment
1451 Ocean Drive
Suite 200

Venture Capital & Private Equity Firms / International Firms

Miami Beach, FL 33139
Phone: 305-5045000

2512 BIO FUND MANAGEMENT OY
4 Mikonkatu, 3rd Floor, PO Box 164
Helsinki 101
Finland

Phone: 358-92514460 **Fax:** 358-92514620
web: www.biofund.fi

Mission Statement: The company manages the Bio Fund I, II, III and BFV II

Geographic Preference: Worldwide
Fund Size: $ 234 Million
Founded: 1998
Minimum Investment: $1.2 Million
Investment Criteria: Early Stage, Expansion, Development Capital, Start-Up Capital, Turnaround, Restructuring, Buyout/Buyin
Industry Group Preference: Agriculture, Biotechnology, Chemicals, Medical & Health Related, Food & Beverage, Forestry, Fishing

Key Executives:
Kalevi Kurkijärvi, Senior Partner, Chairman & Chief Executive Officer
e-mail: erkki.pekkarinen@biofund.fi
Education: MBA, Helsinki School of Economics & Business Administration
Background: Director of finance at the Local Government Pensions Institution
Directorships: In charge of funding work and investor relations
Seppo Mäkinen, Senior Partner
e-mail: kalevi.kurkijarvi@biofund.fi
Education: PhD in Biochemistry and Molecular Biology, University of Turku
Background: Director of venture capital group in the Finnish National Fund of Research and Development Sitra, executive vice president at Wallac Oy and as president and CEO at Pharmacia Diagnostics Production Oy.
Directorships: Chairman of the board at BioTie Therapies Oy, MAP Medical Oy, Bio Orbit Oy, Admin Technologies Oy, FibroGen Europe Oy, Pribori Oy, Hormos Medical Oy and Rados Technology Oy

2513 BIO*ONE CAPITAL EDMI
250 North Bridge Road
#28-00 Raffles City Tower
179101
Singapore

Phone: 65-68326832 **Fax:** 65-68326838
e-mail: infoHQ@edbi.com
web: www.edbi.com

Mission Statement: Through EDBI's dedicated fund manager for Biomedical Sciences, Bio*One Capital invests in innovative healthcare IT, services, devices and therapeutics companies; and played an instrumental role in growing Singapore's Biomedical Sciences industry over the last 10 years. With over 40 portfolio companies globally, we continue to back innovative fast-growing companies that target significant market opportunities with a clear exit strategy. With our support, they are able to leverage on Singapore's position as the leading Biomedical Sciences center in Asia to access Asia's rapid-growing markets and competitive resources in fuelling their global growth.

Geographic Preference: Asia
Industry Group Preference: Healthcare Information Technology
Portfolio Companies: Adamas Pharmaceuticals, Addex Pharmaceuticals, Artisan Pharma, Cylacel Pharmaceuticals, Five Prime Therapeutics, FORMA Therapeutics, goBalto, Idenix, Invaragen, Ironwood, KaloBios Pharmaceuticals, Kalypsys, Lonza Biologics, Maccine, MerLion, Perlegen, Renovis, Revance, S*Bio, Sotera Wireless, Vanda Pharmaceuticals

2514 BIOGENERATION VENTURES
Gooimeer 2-35
Naarden 1411 DC
Netherlands

Phone: 31-356993000 **Fax:** 31-356993001
web: www.biogenerationventures.com

Mission Statement: BioGeneration Ventures manages funds that are actively investing venture capital in the next generation of successful life sciences companies in The Netherlands, Belgium and Germany.

Geographic Preference: The Netherlands, Belgium, Germany
Founded: 1995
Industry Group Preference: Healthcare, Therapeutics, Medical Devices, Diagnostics, Food & Beverage
Portfolio Companies: Arcarios, arGEN-X, BioCeros, Cristal Delivery, Dezima Pharma, EPD-visionk, FlexGen, Lanthio Pharma, Medisse, Mucosis, NovioGendix, Progentix Orthobiology, Revisios, Simibio

Key Executives:
Edward van Wezel, Managing Partner
31-35-699-3011
e-mail: edward@biogeneration.vc
Education: MSc, Chemistry, University of Utrecht; MSc, Biochemical Engineering, Delft University of Technology
Background: Process Engineer, Chiron; Project Manager, Johnson & Johnson
Directorships: Arcarios, NovioGendix, Progentix, Orthobiology, Cristal Delivery

2515 BIOMED PARTNERS
Elisabethenstr. 23
Basel CH-4051
Switzerland

Phone: 41-612703535 **Fax:** 41-612703500
e-mail: info@biomedvc.com
web: www.biomedvc.com

Mission Statement: BioMedPartners is one of the leading European venture capital firms providing private equity and mezzanine financing to early- and mid-stage healthcare and human life science companies. We target the entire industry with special focus on pharmaceuticals, biotechnology, diagnostics and medical technology.

Geographic Preference: Europe
Fund Size: CHF 250 million
Investment Criteria: Early-Stage, Mid-Stage
Industry Group Preference: Healthcare, Life Sciences, Pharmaceuticals, Biotechnology, Diagnostics, Medical Technology
Portfolio Companies: Activaero, Aleva, Anergis, Curetis, Evolva, Sequana Medical, Vaximm, Ventaleon

Key Executives:
Gerhard Ries, Co-Founder/General Partner
41-61-270-3580
e-mail: ries@biomedvc.com
Education: MS, PhD, Molecular Biology, University of Basel
Background: Partner, InterPharmaLink

2516 BIOPACIFIC VENTURES
Level 6
2 Kitchener Street
Auckland 1010
New Zealand

Phone: 64-93072562 **Fax:** 64-93072349

Mission Statement: BioPacificVentures concentrates on making selective investments in a small number of companies

that are exceptionally innovative, have a sound business model and possess an experienced management team. Portfolio companies are actively supported by BioPacificVentures at all development stages, from R&D and clinical trial design to product launch and international expansion.
Geographic Preference: New Zealand, Australia
Founded: 2005
Industry Group Preference: Nutrition, Pharmaceuticals, Cosmetics, Food & Beverage, Biotechnology, Life Sciences
Portfolio Companies: Anzamune, CoDa Therapeutics, Focus Genetics, Horizon Science, New Zealand King Salmon, New Zealand Pharmaceuticals, Vital Foods
Key Executives:
  Andrew Kelly, Co-Founder/Executive Director
  Education: PhD, Life Sciences
  Background: Founding Executive, Celentis; General Manager, Investment, AgResearch

2517 BIOPROCESS CAPITAL PARTNERS
Bldg 1, 8, Nauchny Proezd
Moscow 117246
Russia

Phone: 7-4954118594 **Fax:** 7-4956443797

Mission Statement: Bioprocess Capital Partners LLP mostly invests in venture projects in two areas of modern high-tech industry - Live Systems / Biotechnology and Fine Chemistry and in selected biotechnological and pharmaceutical start-up projects from Russia and other countries.
Geographic Preference: Russia
Fund Size: 3 billion rubles
Founded: 2001
Investment Criteria: Early-Stage
Industry Group Preference: High Technology, Biotechnology, Pharmaceuticals

2518 BIOVEDA CAPITAL
50 Cuscaden Road
#07-02 HPL House
249724
Singapore

Phone: 65-62389200 **Fax:** 65-6733383
e-mail: info@biovedacapital.com

Mission Statement: BioVeda is a Singapore based firm. We invest in companies in the healthcare sector with leading market positions, proprietary technologies, and outstanding scientific and management talent. We are a crucial business and scientific bridge between companies in the East and West, linking business and technology between two very diverse markets.
Investment Criteria: Early-Stage to Development Stage
Industry Group Preference: Healthcare, Life Sciences, Pharmaceuticals
Portfolio Companies: Agilix Corporation, ASLAN Pharmaceuticals, Clearbridge BioMedics, Dynavax Technologies, Idun Pharmaceuticals, Kiadis Pharma, Memory Pharmaceuticals, MerLion Pharmaceuticals, NeuroVision, NOD Pharmaceuticals, Paratek Pharmaceuticals, Renovis, Renovo, Singapore Advanced Biologics
Key Executives:
  Damien Lin, General Partner
  Background: PrimePartners, Vickers Ballas, Morgan Grenfell Asia

2519 BIRK VENTURE
Karenslyst alle 8b
Oslo 0278
Norway

Phone: 47-90871483
e-mail: post@birkventure.no
web: www.birkventure.no

Mission Statement: Birk Venture is a Scandinavian venture company exclusively focusing on the life science industry. The company was founded in 2010 by Hans Ivar Robinson. Our vision is to be a preferred business partner in the life science sector. We offer venture capital to young companies with significant growth prospects. Our broad industrial experience from the pharmaceutical and biotechnology industry and international network, are the foundation for our strategic and long-term investments in life science.
Geographic Preference: Scandinavia
Founded: 2010
Industry Group Preference: Life Sciences
Portfolio Companies: Algeta, APIM Therapeutics, BerGenBio, Nextera, Nordic Nanovector AS, PCI Biotech, Pronova BioPharma, Targovax
Key Executives:
  Hans Ivar Robinson, Managing Director/Chairman
  Background: AstraZeneca, Pfizer, Pronova BioPharma

2520 BLACKBIRD VENTURES
Level 5
80 Mount Street
North Sydney NSW 2060
Australia

Phone: 61-0-2-8314-7400
e-mail: contact@blackbird.vc
web: www.blackbird.vc

Mission Statement: Blackbird Ventures is a venture capital firm that invests in inherently global Internet businesses formed by Australians. We back world-class founders who are setting out to make a difference in the world. Blackbird Ventures itself is a collection of Australia's most successful startup founders and Silicon Valley's top investors who want to help you succeed on a global stage.
Geographic Preference: Australia
Investment Criteria: Seed-Stage, Series A, Later-Stage
Industry Group Preference: Internet, Consumer Internet, Social Media, SaaS, Mobile, E-Commerce & Manufacturing, Software
Portfolio Companies: Canva, Coinjar, Elto.com, Ninja Blocks, Safety Culture, Sessions, Shoes of Prey, Startmate
Key Executives:
  Niki Scevak, Managing Director
  Education: University of New South Wales
  Background: Founder, Startmate; Founder, Homethinking

2521 BLACKFIN CAPITAL PARTNERS
127, avenue des Champs Elysees
Paris 750008
France

Phone: 01-75000230 **Fax:** 01-75000239
web: www.blackfincp.com

Mission Statement: BlackFin is a private equity firm dedicated to financial services: distribution and brokerage of financial products, asset management, electronic banking, BPO, internet finance and capital markets.
Average Investment: 10-30 million Euros
Industry Group Preference: Financial Services
Portfolio Companies: Applicam, Chiarezza, Groupe Cyrus, Kepler Capital Markets, MisterAssur, Owliance
Key Executives:
  Sabine Mathis, Chief Financial Officer
  Education: Ecole Polytechnique, Ecole de la Statistique de l'Administration Economique
  Background: Aquiline Capital Partners, ProCapital

Venture Capital & Private Equity Firms / International Firms

2522 BLOOM EQUITY
25-27 Fitzwilliam Pl
Ballsbridge
Dublin 2
Ireland

Phone: 01-669-4700
e-mail: sarah@hban.org

Mission Statement: Experienced entrepreneurs investing in early stage Irish Technology companies.

Geographic Preference: Ireland
Investment Criteria: Early-Stage
Industry Group Preference: Technology
Portfolio Companies: Boxever, Phorest, ManageCO2, InishTech, Fantom, SourceDogg, Scrazzl, B-Sm@rk

Key Executives:
Anthony Bermingham, Group Chairperson
Education: Chartered Accountant
Background: Director, Atlanta International Ltd

2523 BLUE COVE VENTURES
60 Hawker Street
2607 Torrens
2607
Australia

Phone: 61-413227711
web: www.bluecoveventures.net

Mission Statement: Blue Cove Ventures invests in innovation focusing on early expansion opportunities. We love web and software opportunities and invest in entrepreneurs who have great, commercially viable ideas with significant global potential. We like entrepreneurs with passion and persistence who go that extra mile to get the job done.

Geographic Preference: Australia
Founded: 2007
Investment Criteria: Early-Stage
Industry Group Preference: Internet
Portfolio Companies: Simmerson Holdings, Windlab Systems

Key Executives:
Nick McNaughton, Chief Operating Officer
e-mail: nick@bluecoveventures.net

2524 BLUEGEM CAPITAL PARTNERS
16 Berkeley Street
London W1J 8DZ
United Kingdom

Phone: 44-02076479710 Fax: 44-02076811304
e-mail: enquiries@bluegemcp.com

Mission Statement: An independent London based private equity fund, BlueGem seeks to invest in sector specific mid-market companies based in Western Europe.

Geographic Preference: Western Europe
Fund Size: £200 million
Founded: 2006
Average Investment: £10-40 million
Industry Group Preference: Retail, Consumer & Leisure, Consumer Products, Distribution, Business Products & Services
Portfolio Companies: Enotria, Fintyre, Liberty, Management Consulting Group, Neomobile, Olicar, The Private Clinic Group

Key Executives:
Marco Capello, Founder/Managing Partner
Education: Politecnico di Torino; MBA, Columbia University
Background: Managing Director, Merrill Lynch Global Private Equity
Directorships: Olicar, The Private Clinic, Fintyre, Neomobile, Management Consulting Group, Libery, Ufi Filters, Enotria

2525 BLUESHIFT INTERNET VENTURES
Blueshift
21, Abdul Razack Street
Dignity Centre
Saidapet
Chennai 600 015
India

Phone: 91-4442272583 Fax: 91-4442272582
web: www.blueshift.com

Mission Statement: Blueshift's suite of services includes Offshore Software Development for diverse industries and verticals, Consulting and Business Solutions (which include Knowledge Discovery and technology driven Recruitment services) and IT services.

Geographic Preference: USA, India
Founded: 1993
Investment Criteria: Blueshift's mission is to provide quality solutions and services with scalable, cost-effective resources, to reduce time-to-market for clients worldwide
Industry Group Preference: Software, Information Technology

Key Executives:
Prashant Sankaran, Chief Executive Officer
e-mail: sankaran@sankaran.com
Education: Ph.D, Temple University; MBA, XLRI
Background: Information systems industry
Dr. Sankaran P. Raghunathan, Chief Operating Officer

2526 BLUME VENTURES
Blume Venture Advisors
Unit 4, Jetha Compound, Opp Nirmal Park
Byculla (East)
Mumbai
India

e-mail: jobs@blumeventures.com

Mission Statement: Blume Ventures provides seed funding in the range of $50K-$250K to early-stage tech-focused/tech-enabled ventures. We are proponents of a collaborative approach and like to co-invest with like-minded angels and seed funds. We then provide follow0on investments to our stellar portfolio companies, ranging between $500K and $1.5 million.

Geographic Preference: India
Fund Size: 100 Crore
Average Investment: $500,000 - $1.5 million
Investment Criteria: Seed-Stage, Early-Stage
Industry Group Preference: Technology, Technology-Enabled Services
Portfolio Companies: CallRecall, E2E Networks, Mettl, Moneysights, Proptec Renewables, Remma Consulting, Sparsha Learning, SportsNest, Trolly, Valgen

Key Executives:
Karthik Reddy, Managing Partner
Education: MBA, IIM Bangalore & Wharton School
Background: SSKI, Brand Capital/Private Treaties, Times Group
Sanjay Nath, Managing Partner
Education: MBA, UCLA Anderson School of Graduate Management
Background: IBM Global Services, Pricewaterhouse Coopers

2527 BM-T BETEILIGUNGS MANAGEMENT THURINGEN GmbH
Gorkistrasse 9
Erfurt 99084
Germany

Phone: 49-3617447601 Fax: 49-3617447635
e-mail: info@bm-t.com
web: www.bm-t.com

Venture Capital & Private Equity Firms / International Firms

Mission Statement: Strengthens Thüringen's Economy through targeted Investments in innovative and growth-oriented companies with high potential.
Geographic Preference: Germany
Fund Size: $0.3 Billion
Founded: 2003
Average Investment: $1 Million
Minimum Investment: $0.2 Million
Investment Criteria: Germany Based, All Stages Considered
Industry Group Preference: Life Sciences, Electronics, Information Technology, Media, Engineering, Automation, All Sectors Considered
Portfolio Companies: APPsolute Mobility, Axsol, BianoGMP, c-LEcta, Crowd Architects, Devie Medical, Enginsight, Ezono, FBGS, Hacker Automation, Hapila, Hasec, Heyfair, Ifesca, InflaRX, Intercept Technology, Intercus, JeNaCell, Jenetric, jenID Solutions, Jenoptik, KAHLA Porzellan, Lean Plastics, Leyhs Pharma, Lynatox, Magnitude Internet, Master PIM, Mi-Factory, MITEC Automotive, Music DNA, NovaPump, oncgnostics, Paketin, Pamyra, PDV-Systeme, Pflegeplatz-manager, Plazz Entertainment, Preventicus, Q-Sensei, QSIL, Redwave Medical, SAMAG Group, Scienova, SecondSol, siOPTICA, SmartDyeLivery, TrophpSYS, Ucandoo, Zeilenwert

Key Executives:
Rudolf Humer, Chairman

2528 BMP AKTIENGESELLSCHAFT BMP Venture Capital
Schlterstrae 38
Berlin 10629
Germany
Phone: 49-30203050 Fax: 49-3020305555
e-mail: bmp@bmp.com
web: www.bmp.com

Mission Statement: One of the leading venture capital companies, we specialise in start-up and expansion financing strong growing companies.
Geographic Preference: Germany, Western Europe, Osteuropa
Fund Size: $59.3 Million
Founded: 1997
Investment Criteria: Early Stage, High-growth markets
Industry Group Preference: Business to Business, Life Sciences, Financial Services, Marketing, Publishing, Software, Technology, Telecommunications
Portfolio Companies: Newtron AG, Bankier, eHedge AG, eprofessional GmbH, ergoTrade AG, European Telecommunication Holding E.T.H. AG, Gamigo AG, Heliocentris Energiesysteme GmbH, Jerini AG, K2 Internet S.A., Revotar Biopharmaceuticals AG, Salt of Life AG, Shotgun Picture

Key Executives:
Oliver Borrmann, Chief Executive Officer
e-mail: bmp@bmp.com
Gerd Schmitz-Morkramer, Chairman
e-mail: bmp@bmp.com

2529 BOCI DIRECT INVESTMENT MANAGEMENT LIMITED Bank of China
1 Garden Road
Bank of China Tower Suite 35F
Central
Seoul
Hong Kong
Phone: 852-22308888 Fax: 852-28109736
web: www.bocgroup.com

Mission Statement: BOCI is a wholly owned subsidiary of the Bank of China and aims to provide a full range of investment banking services to its clients.
Geographic Preference: Hong Kong, UK
Fund Size: $1 Billion
Founded: 1998
Investment Criteria: State-owned companies, Medium and Small size listed companies
Industry Group Preference: Energy, Transportation, Infrastructure, Real Estate, Manufacturing

Key Executives:
Kwok Leung Lee, Managing Director

2530 BOEHRINGER INGELHEIM VENTURE FUND
Binger Strasse 173
Ingelheim am Rhein 55216
Germany
Phone: 49-6132778740
web: www.boehringer-ingelheim-venture.com

Mission Statement: Our primary aim is to activate success for those companies and entrepreneurs we support and to earn a reputation as a long-term trusted partner. Beyond capital investment, we intend to take an active role with our portfolio companies - delivering significant added value through our own extensive drug discovery, scientific and managerial expertise and access to selected relevant experts and knowledge. Nevertheless, we also attach significant importance to confidentiality, establishing ethical walls to protect our portfolio companies and entrepreneurs.

Average Investment: 10-15 million Euros
Investment Criteria: Early-Stage
Industry Group Preference: Healthcare, Life Sciences, Pharmaceuticals
Portfolio Companies: AMP Therapeutics, ArmaGen Technologies, Inserm Transfert Initiative, Okairos, Promethera

Key Executives:
Frank Kalkbrenner, Vice President
Background: Senior Scientist, Director, Boehringer Ingelheim

2531 BONVENTURE
Pettenkoferstrasse 37
Munchen D-80336
Germany
Phone: 49-89200012531 Fax: 49-89-200-01-2539
e-mail: info@bonventure.de
web: www.bonventure.de

Mission Statement: BonVenture is a social venture capital fund that was established by comitted individuals willing to take responsibility for the community. They believe, that with individual prosperity comes a social obligation to improve society. Our investors dedicate their material and intellectual resources in order to leverage efficent social or ecological solutions that cannot be provided by the public sector.

Geographic Preference: German-Speaking Countries
Industry Group Preference: Education, Social Services
Portfolio Companies: Atempo Group, Abotic, Bettermarks, Chancenwerk, DialogMuseum, Flachsland Zukunftsschulen, Hand In Gag, Kunterbunt, Moving Image 24, Rock Your Life, Violence Prevention Network

2532 BOTTS & COMPANY LIMITED
2nd Floor
103 Mount Street
44 Davies Street
London W1K 2TJ
United Kingdom
Phone: 44-2070161202 Fax: 44-87 01343714
e-mail: postmaster@bottscompany.com

Mission Statement: Actively seeking new investments.
Geographic Preference: United Kingdom, Western Europe
Fund Size: $176 Million
Founded: 1987

Venture Capital & Private Equity Firms / International Firms

Average Investment: $17.6 Million
Minimum Investment: $48.82 Million
Investment Criteria: Expansion and Development, Bridge Finance, Refinancing Bank Debt, Secondary Purchase/Replacement Capital, Rescue/Turnaround, MBO, MBI, Institutional BO
Industry Group Preference: Communications, Media, Leisure, Financial Services, Industrial Services, Entertainment
Key Executives:
    John Botts, Non-Executive Director
    Education: Columbia University
    Background: Kuhn Loeb Lehman Brothers; Kidder Peabody; CSFB
    Andrew Haining, Managing Director
    Education: MA, Economics, Cambridge University
    Background: Bank of America; Natwest Markets
    Robin Black, Director
    e-mail: r.black@bottscompany.com
    Education: BA, Politics, Exeter University
    Background: Vice President In the Structured Debt and Private Equity Division, Bankers Trust Company

2533 BR OPPORTUNITIES
Av. Ibirapuera 2.907
Conj. 509
Sao Paulo 04029-200
Brazil
    Phone: 55-23377126 **Fax:** +55-1123727430
    web: www.bropportunities.com.br

Mission Statement: BR Opportunities - Growth Capital Investments is a private equity fund manager that drives emerging, high-impact companies for the improvement of Brazil. Its mission is to invest in high-impact organizations, accelerate their growth and transform them into effective leaders in their markets of operation. In pursuit of this goal, its strategy is to bring to these organizations management and professional governance, while enhancing their visibility, transparency, and network of relationships. Based on this approach, we implement successful models of high added value.

Geographic Preference: Brazil
Founded: 2010
Key Executives:
    Carlos Miranda, Founder
    Education: BA, Architecture & Urban Planning; MBA, Finance, IBMEC-RJ
    Background: Ernst & Young
    Vitor Horibe, Partner
    Education: BA, Business Administration EAESP/FGV; MBA, Finance UCLA Anderson School of Management
    Background: Roland Berger

2534 BRABANTSE ONTWIKKELINGSMIJ NV (BOM)
Goirlese Weg 15
5026 PB Tilburg
PO Box 3240
Tilburg 5003 DE
Netherlands
    Phone: 31-135311120 **Fax:** 31-135311121
    e-mail: bom@bom.nl
    web: www.bom.nl

Mission Statement: Actively seeking new investments.
Investment Criteria: Startup, Early-Stage, Expansion, Development, MBO, Management Buy-in
Industry Group Preference: All Sectors Considered
Key Executives:
    Matthijs Van Miltenburg, Project Foreign Investments
    Ben Engel, Senior project manager

2535 BRAINSPARK PLC
12/16 Laystall Street
The Lightwell
Clerkenwell
London EC1R 4PF
United Kingdom
    Phone: 44-2078436600 **Fax:** 44-2078436601
    web: www.brainspark.com

Mission Statement: Brainspark Plc is an AIM listed company, focusing on investments in best-of-breed Information & Communication Technology (I&CT) primarily in Europe and Israel.

Geographic Preference: Europe, Israel
Founded: 1998
Investment Criteria: New investments
Industry Group Preference: Information Technology, Communications
Portfolio Companies: Advanced Computer Systems, Easyart.com, Fortune Cookie, Geosim Systems, Kerb, MetaPack, San Vicente Group, TraderServe
Key Executives:
    Francesco Gardin, chairman
    David Meacher, Non-Executive Board Member
    e-mail: email@brainspark.com
    Education: MBA, INSEAD; Durham University
    Background: Director of Strategic and Financial Planning for Bass PLC
    Directorships: Partner
    Steward Dodd, Founder and CEO

2536 BRANDON CAPITAL PARTNERS
Level 9
278 Collins Street
Melbourne, Victoria 3000
Australia
    Phone: 61-396570700 **Fax:** 61-396570777
    e-mail: info@brandoncapital.com.au
    web: www.brandoncapital.com.au

Mission Statement: Brandon Capital Partners makes seed and venture capital investments to support the development and international growth of Australian life science companies. We work collaboratively with entrepreneurs to demonstrate the benefit of their technology, thereby creating value for them, their teams and our investors.

Geographic Preference: Australia
Fund Size: AUD$50 million, AUD$51 million
Industry Group Preference: Life Sciences, Drug Development, Medical Devices
Portfolio Companies: Elastagen, Fibrotech, Global Kinetics, Osprey Medical, PolyActiva, Signostics, Spinifex, Vaxxas, Verva

Other Locations:
Level 7
210 George Street
Sydney, NSW 2010
Australia
Phone: 61-292472577 **Fax:** 61-292477344

Key Executives:
    Chris Nave, Managing Director
    Education: PhD, Endocrinology & Physiology, University of Melbourne
    Background: Manager, Biotechnology Team, Melbourne Ventures
    Directorships: BACE Therapeutics, Fibrotech Therapeutics, Fluorotrop, Global Kinetics Corporation

Venture Capital & Private Equity Firms / International Firms

2537 BRIDGEPOINT CAPITAL GmbH
Neue Mainzer Straáe 28
Frankfurt 60311
Germany

Phone: 49-692108770 Fax: 49-6921087777
e-mail: Frankfurt@bridgepoint.eu
web: www.bridgepoint-capital.com

Mission Statement: Bridgepoint is a leading provider of private equity with a 25-year track record of investing in businesses that will achieve long-term capital growth.

Geographic Preference: Europe, UK, France, Sweden, Italy, Germany
Fund Size: $12 billion
Founded: 1980
Average Investment: $162.7 Million
Minimum Investment: $29.75 Million
Investment Criteria: Expansion Financing, Bridging Finance, Replacement, MBO, MBI
Industry Group Preference: Consumer Services, Financial Services, Healthcare, Media, Chemicals, Manufacturing, Services, Beverages, Software, Automotive, Materials Technology, Computer Related
Portfolio Companies: 1st Credit, Adams Childrenswear, All3Media, Alliance Medical, Arco Bodegas, Attendo, Aura Light International AB, Autinform GmbH, Betterware, Capula, CarPark, CESA, CFP Flexible Packaging, Clinical Assessment Services, CompuTrain Europe B.V, Concent

Key Executives:
Bernie Schuler, Diretor
Marc Zügel, Diretor

2538 BRIDGEPOINT CAPITAL LIMITED
95 Wigmore Street
London W1U 1FB
United Kingdom

Phone: 44-2074323500 Fax: 44-2074-323600
e-mail: London@bridgepoint.eu
web: www.bridgepoint-capital.com

Mission Statement: Bridgepoint is a leading provider of private equity with a 25-year track record of investing in businesses that will achieve long-term capital growth.

Geographic Preference: Europe, UK, France, Sweden, Italy, Germany
Fund Size: $6.17 Billion
Founded: 1980
Average Investment: $162.8 Million
Minimum Investment: $30 Million
Investment Criteria: Expansion Financing, Bridging Finance, Replacement, MBO, MBI
Industry Group Preference: Consumer Services, Financial Services, Healthcare, Media, Chemicals, Manufacturing, Services, Beverages, Software, Automotive, Materials Technology, Computer Related
Portfolio Companies: 1st Credit, Adams Childrenswear, All3Media, Alliance Medical, Arco Bodegas, Attendo, Aura Light International AB, Autinform GmbH, Betterware, Capula, CarPark, CESA, CFP Flexible Packaging, Clinical Assessment Services, CompuTrain Europe B.V, Concent

Key Executives:
Benoit Alteirac, Director
Background: Carnaud Group
Chris Bell, Partner, Head of Manufacturing & Industrials sector

2539 BRIDGES VENTURES
1 Craven Hill
London W2 3EN
United Kingdom

Phone: 020-72625566 Fax: 020-72626389
e-mail: info@bridgesventures.com
web: www.bridgesventures.com

Mission Statement: Bridges Ventures is a specialist fund manager, dedicated to using an impact-driven investment approach to create superior returns for both investors and society at-large. We believe that market forces and entrepreneurship can be harnessed to do well by doing good.

Fund Size: £340 million
Founded: 2002
Portfolio Companies: Carduus, CloudIQ, Historic Futures, Ardenham Energy, TEG, Aerothermal Group, Babington, Halo, New Career Skills, Credential, SealSkinz, The Gym, Bagnali Court, Triage, School Stickers, Chill Factor, Whelan Refining Ltd, Smart Storage, Holiday Inn Express, Action For Children, Teens and Toddlers, New Horizons Program, Community Links, Auto22, Casa, HCT Group, Callbritannia

Key Executives:
Philip Newborough, Co-Founder/Managing Partner
Education: BA, York University
Background: General Manager, Aiwa; Managing Director, MWB Business Exchange

2540 BRIGHT CAPITAL
6/2 Bersenevskaya Emb.
Moscow 119072
Russia

Phone: 7-4959898540 Fax: 7-4959823309
web: www.bright-capital.com

Mission Statement: Bright Capital is an independent venture capital firm that invests globally in a wide range of promising companies solving problems in energy efficiency and resource scarcity.

Industry Group Preference: Energy, Renewable Energy, Energy Efficiency, Advanced Materials
Portfolio Companies: Cardiodx, Epuramat, Fotoshkola, RRT Global, Suvolta, Quantenna Communications

Other Locations:
3000 Sand Hill Road
Bldg 2, Suite 180
Menlo Park, CA 94025
Phone: 650-6277750

Key Executives:
Boris Ryabov, Managing Partner
Education: International Institute of Economic Relations; MBA, Warwick University
Background: Deputy Director General, RU-COM

2541 BRM SEED
10 Nissim Aloni Street
Tzameret Park
Herzliya
Tel Aviv 6291924
Israel

Phone: 972-39715100 Fax: 972-39715101
e-mail: info@brm.com
web: www.brm.com

Mission Statement: BRM Capital is a venture capital firm that invests primarily in Israel-related seed and early stage companies in the Software, Communications and Components domains.

Geographic Preference: US, Israel
Founded: 1988
Investment Criteria: Israel-related seed and early stage companies
Industry Group Preference: Infrastructure Software, Communications, Components & IoT
Portfolio Companies: GigaSpaces, Human Eyes, NPX Technologies Ltd., Pando Networks, ProSight, Whale Communications, Oplus Technologies, Passave, Schema, Wavion

Key Executives:
Eli Barkat, Chairman and Co-Founder
e-mail: eli@brm.com

Venture Capital & Private Equity Firms / International Firms

Education: BS, Computer Science and Mathematics, Hebrew University of Jerusalem
Background: CEO of BackWeb Technologies Ltd.
Yuval Rakavy, Venture Partner and Co-Founder

2542 BROADLINE PRINCIPAL CAPITAL
360 Pudong Nan Lu
Suite 26C
Shanghai 200120
China

Mission Statement: Broadline Principle Capital is a leading multi-industry private equity firm with global capabilities and China expertise. BPC selectively invests in companies that are industry leaders and rising stars that can benefit from BPC's platform, relationships, and expertise to expand operations, gain efficiencies, and grow earnings.

Industry Group Preference: Diversified
Portfolio Companies: Xi'an Longi Silicon, Beijing Odyssey Chemicals, Befar Group, Shida Shenghua Chemical, Show Long Fashion Gourmet Co, Sunrain Energy, Billions Chemicals, Xinya Paper Group, Jinhe Industrial, MySteel.com, Trendzone Construction, Shanghai Chunge Glass Co., South Memory Restaurant Co., Shanghai Shen-Li High Tech, Hisoar Pharma, Crystal Optech, Yotrio Group, Taizhou Reflecting Materials, Haihong Hydraulic Science, Tadelon Holding Group, Jiangxi Guohong Group, Lier Chemical Co., Guangdong Yashii Group

Key Executives:
Lin-Lin Zhou, Founding CEO
Education: MBA, PhD

2543 BROOKLYN VENTURES
Nyenrode Business Universiteit
Straatweg 25
PO Box 130
Breukelen 3621
Netherlands

e-mail: info@brooklyn-ventures.com
web: www.brooklyn-ventures.com

Mission Statement: Brooklyn Ventures brings together seasoned executives with various backgrounds. We have a joint commitment to help companies with great potential and ideas to succeed. Each of us has a proven track record in our own field.

Portfolio Companies: RBN, IRM Systems, Blivio, SoSocio, Valuewait, Needs & Senses

Key Executives:
Hans Osnabrugge, Partner
Education: BA, MSc
Background: Relationship Manager, Schretlen & Co.

2544 BRYAN GARNIER & COMPANY
53 Chandos Place
London WC2N 4HS
United Kingdom

Phone: 44-2073322500 **Fax:** 44-2073322559
e-mail: bede@bryangarnier.com
web: www.bryangarnier.com

Mission Statement: Providing fast-growing, independent partnership of experienced finance professionals servicing the needs of large corporations, venture capitalists, institutional investors and private clients.

Geographic Preference: Europe
Founded: 1996
Investment Criteria: Growing European companies and growth-oriented investors.
Industry Group Preference: Technology, Media & Telecommunications, Life Sciences, Branded Goods, Retailing, Outsourcing & Efficiency, Media, Healthcare, Renewable Energy & Environment, Business Products & Services

Portfolio Companies: Transgene, Centrale Partners, Carrere Group, MAPI, 21 Centrale Partners, ASK, Telisma, CAST, SCORT, Job partners, OMNITICKET network, DOUBLE Trade, Reef, Attol, Stella, Reef, SCORT, ActiveCard.

Key Executives:
Greg Revenu, Corporate Contact

2545 BRZTECH
Av. das Nacoes Unidas, 11541
14 Andar CJ 141
Brooklin
Sao Paulo
Brazil

Phone: 55-11975255282

Mission Statement: BRZtech is an investment group oriented to developing tech solutions and support tech companies with a future vision.

Portfolio Companies: Realtime, Mobbit Systems, HIS

2546 BT FUNDS MANAGEMENT LIMITED
Level 7, Westpac on Takutai Square
16 Takutai Square
Auckland 1141
New Zealand

Phone: 649-3673300 **Fax:** 64-936-73302
Toll-Free: 0800-800661

Mission Statement: Helping New Zealanders create and manage their wealth since 1989. Providing a diverse range of investment options including funds managed by our teams as well as alliances with global investment managers.

Geographic Preference: New Zealand, Australia
Fund Size: $1.6 billion
Founded: 1989

Key Executives:
Fiona Oliver, Chief Operating Officer
Chris Caton, Chief Economist

2547 BULL VENTURES
TC Gulliver, 27 Floor
Sportivnaya, Square 1
Kiev 01023
Ukraine

Phone: 044-500-6868

Mission Statement: We are interested in building long-term relationships with experienced and active partners who can bring into the team not only money, but also a deep understanding of business processes.

Geographic Preference: Ukraine, Central & Eastern Europe
Fund Size: $10 million
Founded: 2013
Industry Group Preference: E-Commerce & Manufacturing, Media, Marketing, Logistics

Key Executives:
Dmitry Smirnov, Managing Partner
Background: Managing Partner, FlintCap; Deputy Director, Finam Investment Fund

2548 BULLNET
Parque Empresarial La Finca
Paseo del Club Deportivo, 1
1 - Edificio 3 - Pozuelo de Alarcón
Madrid 28223
Spain

Phone: 34-917997206 **Fax:** 34-917995372
e-mail: julecia@bullnetcapital.com
web: www.grupobullnet.com

Mission Statement: Bullnet Gestión is a Spanish independent venture capital firm specialized in technology projects.

Geographic Preference: Spain

Venture Capital & Private Equity Firms / International Firms

Average Investment: $2 - $4 Million
Investment Criteria: Early-Stage
Industry Group Preference: Information Services, Telecommunications, Media, Healthcare
Portfolio Companies: Anafocus, Onco Vision, Multiwave, NetSpira, Arvirago, Visure, Digital Legends, Zhilabs, Codice Software, UAV Navigation, POF

Key Executives:
  Javier Ulecia, Partner
  Education: Universidad Politecnica, Madrid; MBA, HEC
  Background: Co-Founder/CEO, Doing; Senior Manager, Bain & Company

2549 BURAN VENTURE CAPITAL
Khlebny Lane 8
Moscow 121069
Russia

Phone: 7-495-5404842
e-mail: info@buranvc.com
web: www.buranvc.com

Mission Statement: Buran Venture Capital is a venture fund founded in 2010 targeting to invest US$50m over the course of the next 4-5 years in Russia, CIS and Israel.
Geographic Preference: Russia, CIS, Israel
Fund Size: $50 million
Founded: 2010
Average Investment: $300,000 - $3 million
Industry Group Preference: E-Commerce & Manufacturing, Digital Media & Marketing, Mobile & Internet, Communications, SaaS
Portfolio Companies: EpistoGraph, JustEva.ru

Key Executives:
  Alexander Konoplyasty, Managing Partner

2550 BUSINESS GROWTH FUND
45 Church Street
Birmingham B3 2RT
United Kingdom

Phone: 0845-2668862
e-mail: enquiries@bgf.co.uk
web: www.businessgrowthfund.co.uk

Mission Statement: BGF provides long-term capital for fast growing British companies.
Geographic Preference: United Kingdom
Average Investment: £2-10 million
Industry Group Preference: High Technology, Software, Electronics, Leisure & Hospitality, Tourism, Retail, Consumer & Leisure, Renewable Energy, Clean Technology, Healthcare, Life Sciences, Business Products & Services, Outsourcing & Efficiency, Consumer Goods
Portfolio Companies: Bulitt, Celaton, Magma Global, Boost Juice Bars

Key Executives:
  Richard Bishop, Head of Investments
  e-mail: richard.bishop@bgf.co.uk
  Education: Birmingham University
  Background: 3i

2551 BUTLER CAPITAL PARTNERS FRANCE
30, cours Albert 1er
1st Floor
Paris 75008
France

Phone: 33-145615580 **Fax:** 33-145619794
e-mail: contact@butlercapitalpartners.com
web: www.butlercapitalpartners.com

Mission Statement: Butler Capital Partners is the leading independent private equity partnership in France.
Geographic Preference: France, Eastern Europe
Fund Size: 500 Million Euros
Founded: 1991
Investment Criteria: LBO and turnarounds
Industry Group Preference: Information Technology, Distribution, Logistics, Advertising, Publishing, Marketing
Portfolio Companies: 1001 Listes, Abrium, Atys, AutoDistribution, Cesar, Exlinea, Flo, France Champignon, Giraud International, Press Index, REP

Key Executives:
  Laurent Parquet, Director
  Education: ESSEC
  Background: Andersen Consulting
  Pierre Costes, Director
  Education: ESSEC, Chartered Accountant
  Background: Arthur Andersen
  Walter Butler, Partner and Chairman of BCP
  Education: Polytechnique X, Ecole Nationale des Mines de Paris
  Background: Advisor to the Minister of Economy and Finance, French Treasury; Energy/Telecommunications/Raw Materials Advisor, Minister of Industry
  Frédéric Favreau, Director
  Education: Ecole Centrale de Paris, Master of Science MII
  Background: Bankers Trust, Paribes
  Marc-Eric Flory, CFO
  Education: Master Degree in Tax and Business Law
  Background: Lawyer

2552 BUTZOW NORDIA ADVOCATES LTD
Fabianinkatu 29 B
Helsinki FI-00100
Finland

Phone: 358-106841300 **Fax:** 358-106841700

Mission Statement: A full service law firm with expertise in mergers and acquisitions among other areas. Providing competent and extensive services in various kinds of transactions; corporate acquisition, capital investment and outsourcing.
Geographic Preference: Finland, Russia, Sweden, Germany, France, United States
Founded: 1999
Industry Group Preference: Commercial Contracts, Private Equity, Property Transactions, Labour Law, Company Law, Financial Services, Corporate Insolvency, Restructuring, Litigation

Key Executives:
  Marja-Leena Kangasrääsiö, Office Manager

2553 CAIXA CAPITAL RISC
Av. Diagonal
613 3 Planta
Barcelona B 08028
Spain

Phone: 93-4094060
e-mail: info@caixacapitalrisc.es
web: www.caixacapitalrisc.es

Mission Statement: Through its area for entrepreneurs, 'la Caixa' has developed a combination of tools to support, finance and accompany new business initiatives with a high growth potential in Spain. Among the main ones, those that stand out are the unique set of venture capital tools that invest in the early stages of innovative projects through Caixa Capital Risc, and the creation of instruments that promote the entrepreneurial spirit and accompaniment in the development of new innovative business initiatives through Iniciativa Emprendedor XXI.

Fund Size: $73 million
Investment Criteria: Early-Stage
Portfolio Companies: Onmia Molecular, Laboratorios Sanifit, Sabimedical, Sagetis Biotech, Genmedica Therapeutics, Medlumics, Privalla, Groupalia, I-Neumaticos, Syncro, Good Deal, Apesoft

Venture Capital & Private Equity Firms / International Firms

Venture Capital Association
Directorships: CEO

2563 CAPRICORN VENTURE PARTNERS NV
Jonge St. Jacob, Lei 19/1 - B-3000
Leuven 3000
Belgium

Phone: 32-16284100 Fax: 32-16284108
e-mail: capricorn@capricorn.be
web: www.capricorn.be

Mission Statement: Capricorn Venture Partners was established in 1993 as an advisor of venture capital funds that invest in technology-based growth companies in Western Europe.
Geographic Preference: Belgium, France, Netherland, Finland, Germany, United Kingdom.
Fund Size: $22.3 Million
Founded: 1993
Investment Criteria: Seed, Start-up, Other early stage.
Industry Group Preference: Biotechnology, Energy, Environment Products & Services, Internet Technology, Medical, Electronic Technology, Healthcare
Portfolio Companies: BioAlliance Pharma, Omrix Biopharmaceuticals, Orthovita, 4AZA Bioscience, UroGene, TiGenix, Amplexor, i-merge, Ortec International, Xplanation International, EcoPhos, Orthovita.

Key Executives:
Philippe Haspeslagh, Chairman
Education: Ph.D. Solid State Physics, University of Leuven.
Background: Founder of Quest For Growth N.V., Co-Founder and Vice Chairman of EASDAQ, Managing Director of BeneVent Management, Managing Director, Belgian VC.
Directorships: Managing Director,
Paul Decraemer, Executive Director

2564 CAPVIS EQUITY PARTNERS
Grabenstrasse 17
Baar/Zug CH-6340
Switzerland

Phone: 41-433005858 Fax: 41-433005859
e-mail: pr@capvis.com
web: www.capvis.com

Mission Statement: Actively seeking new investments, concentrating on well established medium-sized companies.
Geographic Preference: Switzerland, Austria, Southern Germany.
Fund Size: $480 Million
Founded: 1999
Average Investment: EUR900 million
Minimum Investment: $7.7 Million
Investment Criteria: Invests in Medium-sized Companies, MBO's, Expansion and Fast-growing Companies
Industry Group Preference: Textiles, Chemicals, Automotive, Electronic Technology
Portfolio Companies: KCS, Polytec Holding AG, REMP AG, RMB SA, Soudsonic, Tobles AG, Phonak, Disetronic, Saia-Burgess, Komax, SIA Abrasives

Key Executives:
Daniel Flaig, Partner
e-mail: felix.rohner@capvis.com
Background: UBS AG ,
Directorships: Partner, Advisory Board (Beirat): Findlay Industries
Rolf Friedli, Partner
e-mail: rolf.friedli@capvis.com
Education: MBA
Background: Investment Banking bei Goldman Sachs, Clariden Bank
Directorships: RMB SA, REMP AG, Soudsonic, Melches

Felix Rohner, Partner
Education: HSG, PhD
Background: Swiss Private Equity & Venture Capital Association
Directorships: Komax, sia Abrasives, Tobler AG, Saia-Burgess Electronics
Ueli Eckhardt, Partner
Education: PhD, Attorney at Law
Background: Worked the legal division of STG
Directorships: Feintool, Freetraders, Sandherr
Stephan Lauer, Partner
e-mail: yves.dudli@capvis.com
Education: MBA, PhD
Background: SBC Warburg , Citibank and Swiss Bank Corporation/SBC, Corporate Finance/Investment Banking.
Directorships: Polytec Holding AG, Soudsonic, Sia Abraoives, Saia Burgess Electronics
Ricarda Demarmels, Investment Director
e-mail: daniel.flaig@capvis.com
Education: HSG, Master of Science in Management
Background: Arthur Andersen Business Consulting Zurich
Directorships: Board of directors mandates include: Clinique Bois Cerf, Uster Technologies
Marc Battenfeld, Associate Director
e-mail: marc.battenfeld@capvis.com
Education: HSG
Background: Phoenix Aktiengesellschaft
Directorships: Tobler AG, Polytec Holding AG
Boris Zoller, Investment Director
e-mail: info@capvis.com
Education: lic. oec. publ., University of Zurich, Switzerland
Background: Procter & Gamble SA in Geneva, Volkswagen de México S. A. de C. V. in Puebla/Mexico, Siemens Business Services AG in Zurich-Kloten and Heidrick & Struggles AG in Zurich

2565 CARLYLE ASIA INVESTMENT ADVISORS LIMITED Carlyle Group
2 Pacific Place
Suite 88
Queensway 88
Hong Kong

Phone: 852-28787000 Fax: 852-28787007
e-mail: inquiries@carlyle.com
web: www.carlyle.com

Mission Statement: Actively seeking new investments.
Geographic Preference: U.S., Europe, and Asia
Fund Size: $400 Million
Founded: 1987
Investment Criteria: Buyouts, venture capital, real estate and leveraged finance
Industry Group Preference: Aerospace, Defense and Government, Automotive, Consumer Services, Healthcare, Industrial Services, Real Estate, Technology, Telecommunications, Media, Transportation, Retailing, Business to Business
Portfolio Companies: Actelis Networks, Inc., AcuFocus, Adesso Systems, Inc., Aerostructures Corporation, Airport Technology Center, Ballston Plaza II, Belden & Blake Corporation, Beru AG, Bfinance, Blackboard, Inc., BNX Systems, Boto International, CAMECA, Canes.

Key Executives:
Tamotsu Adachi, Managing Director
Julia Adam, Associate Director

2566 CARMEL VENTURES
12 Abba Eban Avenue
Ackerstein Towers Bldg. D
Herzeliya 46725
Israel

Phone: 972-99720400 Fax: 972-99720401
e-mail: info@carmelventures.com
web: www.carmelventures.com

Mission Statement: Carmel Ventures helps build great ideas into exceptional companies and talented entrepreneurs into genuine leaders. As investors with a significant track record, we have individually and collectively gone through every stage of the company building lifecycle, and our perspective - drawn from both sides of the investment equation - is based on real life experiences.

Fund Size: $235 million
Founded: 2000
Investment Criteria: Early-Stage
Industry Group Preference: Semiconductors, Communications, Software, SaaS, Internet, Media, Wireless, Mobile
Portfolio Companies: Abe's Market, Amadesa, Axxana, bTendo, C2 Microsystems, Clarizen, cVidya Networks, DesignArt Networks, eXelate, Group Commerce, Imagine Communications, ironSource, Kampyle, Kontera Technologies, LiveU, Multiphy, MyThings, OpTier, Optimal Test, Outbrain, Oversi Networks, Payoneer, Perfecto Mobile, Personetics, RealMatch, Red Bend Software, SAManage, Shunra Software, Skybox Security, SundaySky, Tapingo, TradAir, Wanova, YCD-Multimedia

Key Executives:
Eylon Penchas, General Partner
e-mail: sdovrat@carmelventures.com
Background: Co-Founder, Viola Group
Directorships: Outbrain, GroupCommerce, cVidya, eXelate, ECI Telecom, Amadesa, Wanova

2567 CASS ENTREPRENEURSHIP FUND Cass Business School
106 Bunhill Row
London EC1Y 8TZ
United Kingdom

Phone: 44-02070408600
e-mail: jan.reoch.1@city.ac.uk
web: www.cass.city.ac.uk

Mission Statement: The Cass Entrepreneurship Fund is a £10 million venture capital fund, providing growth equity to start-up and early stage companies. Established in 2010, The Fund has already financed a number of Cass entrepreneurs, as well as providing general support and incubation facilities.

Geographic Preference: United Kingdom
Fund Size: £10 million
Founded: 2010
Average Investment: £50,000 - £500,000
Investment Criteria: Early-Stage, Startup
Portfolio Companies: Alva, Cloud Business, Contego Fraud Solutions, Accutrainee, BuildaBrand

Key Executives:
Cliff Oswick, Chairman
e-mail: jane.reoch.1@city.ac.uk

2568 CASTROL INNOVENTURES
Castrol Technology Centre, Whitchurch Hill
Pangbourne
Berkshire RG8 7QR
United Kingdom

Phone: 44-1189843311

Mission Statement: Building on Castrol's strengths and heritage we want to invest in and create material businesses beyond lubricants. Our focus is on developing innovative technologies and business models in: Smart Mobility, Responsible Castrol, Next Gen Engineering and Intelligent Operations.

Founded: 2010
Industry Group Preference: Mobility, Sustainable Energy, Technology

Key Executives:
Roy Williamson, Founder
Education: Herriott Watt University
Background: Global Market Space Manager, Castrol; Unilever

2569 CATAGONIA CAPITAL
Rosenthaler Str. 42
Berlin 10178
Germany

Phone: 49-30398313030 Fax: 49-30398213031
web: www.catagonia.com

Mission Statement: We invest in software and service companies that make use of online and mobile technologies. In so doing, we rely on disruptive business ideas with the potential to redefine established markets. We actively support our founding teams with resources and comprehensive knowledge. We also apply our experiences to founding our own new companies in the areas of mobile Internet, social and local network applications, as well as other online business models.

Founded: 2009
Investment Criteria: Start-Up, Early-Stage
Industry Group Preference: Internet, Mobile
Portfolio Companies: Tynec, Deutsche Messe Interactive, BeLocal, Jamii, Autoda, Ubertweek, Bio.Logis

Key Executives:
Ralph Eric Kunz, Founder/Managing Partner
Education: University of Chicago; PhD
Background: Nokia Corporation, Bertelsmann AG

2570 CATALANA D'INICIATIVES CR SA
Valencia, 225, Entlo. Int
Barcelona 8007
Spain

Phone: 34-933178161 Fax: 34-933189287
web: www.iniciatives.es

Mission Statement: The main goal is to foment investment in existing companies, promote new business projects and manage third party funds invested in business initiatives with remarkable growth potential.

Geographic Preference: Spain, Europe
Fund Size: $50 million
Founded: 1985
Average Investment: $1.5 million
Industry Group Preference: All Sectors Considered

Key Executives:
Antoni Trallero Vilar, Manager
Background: Economist
Josep-Ramon Sanroma Celma, Chief Executive Officer
e-mail: malbanell@iniciatives.es

2571 CATALYST FUND LP
3 Daniel Frish Street
Tel Aviv 64731
Israel

Phone: 972-36950666
e-mail: audreyg@catalyst-fund.com
web: www.catalyst-fund.com

Mission Statement: Catalyst Fund, LP is an Israel-based venture capital fund investing in maturing companies.

Geographic Preference: Israel
Founded: 1995
Average Investment: $2.5 Million
Minimum Investment: $1 Million

Venture Capital & Private Equity Firms / International Firms

Investment Criteria: Maturing companies, High-technology industry.
Industry Group Preference: Telecommunications, Information Technology, Medical Devices, Enterprise Services, Biopharmaceuticals, Software, Real Estate
Portfolio Companies: Omrix, Bos, Corex, On-set, PowerDsine, MTI Wireless Edge, Ltd., Surf Communication Solutions, Scopus, VCON.

Key Executives:
Edouard Cukierman, CEO & Managing Partner
e-mail: edouardc@catalyst-fund.com
Education: MBA, INSEAD; BS, Israel Institute of Technology
Background: President and CEO of the Astra Fund, Vice Chairman of Citec-Environment and Services.
Directorships: Partner
Boaz Harel, Senior Partner

2572 CATALYST FUND MANAGEMENT & RESEARCH LIMITED
4th Floor, 20 Old Street
London EC1V 9AB
United Kingdom

Phone: 44-02074909520 Fax: 44-2072-811873
e-mail: info@catfund.com

Mission Statement: Actively seeking new investments.
Geographic Preference: United Kingdom, Eastern Europe, Western Europe
Fund Size: $91.39 Million
Founded: 1997
Average Investment: $6.85 Million
Minimum Investment: $571,000
Investment Criteria: Seed, Start-up, Other early stage, Expansion and Development, Refinancing bank debt, Secondary purchase/replacement capital, Rescue/turnaround, MBO, MBI
Industry Group Preference: Financial Services
Portfolio Companies: Avanza, EPO.com, Firstquote Masson Financial Services, Knowledge Power, Propero, Safeonline, Spiritsoft

Key Executives:
Tim Farazmand, Non-Executive Director
e-mail: tim@catfund.com
Education: MBA
Background: Royal Bank Development Capital
Directorships: CEO
Rodney Schwartz, Chief Executive Officer
e-mail: rod@catfund.com
Education: MBA
Background: PaineWebber, Lehman Brothers, Paribas
Directorships: CEO

2573 CATALYST INVESTMENT MANAGERS PTY LIMITED PPM Capital
Level 9, 151-153 Macquarie Street
Sydney 2000
Australia

Phone: 61-292701200 Fax: 61-292701222
e-mail: enquiries@catalystinvest.com.au
web: catalystinvest.com.au

Mission Statement: Catalyst is a wholly owned subsidiary of PPM Capital, the global private equity investing arm of Prudential Plc.
Geographic Preference: Australia, New Zealand
Fund Size: $1 billion
Founded: 1989
Average Investment: $135 Million
Minimum Investment: $20.0 Million
Investment Criteria: MBO, MBI
Industry Group Preference: Information Technology, Healthcare, Industrial Services, Agribusiness, Distribution, Education, Entertainment, Financial Services, Food & Beverage, Manufacturing, Retailing, Contracting, Life Sciences, Transportation, Business to Business

Key Executives:
Brian Gatfield, Chairman
e-mail: justinryan@catalystinvest.com.au
Background: Lawyer
John Story, Managing Director
e-mail: gwindeyer@catalystinvest.com.au
Background: NRMA, Ciba-Gigy, BLE Capital

2574 CATALYST VENTURE PARTNERS
The Innovation Centre
Carpenter House
Bath BA1 1UD
United Kingdom

Phone: 44-0-1225-331498 Fax: 44-0-1225-318568
e-mail: hello@catvp.com
web: www.catvp.com

Mission Statement: Catalyst Venture Partners was founded in 1999 when a group of technology entrepreneurs got together to create a networked accelerator and specialist corporate finance boutique. The genesis of the company lay in the partners experience as private investors who regularly came across technology companies, frequently with great IP, who were seeking funds but who were lacking the necessary commercial expertise and management firepower to be credible to potential sources of finance.

Founded: 1999
Average Investment: £500,000 - 5 million
Investment Criteria: Early-Stage, Later-Stage
Portfolio Companies: OCM Print Management Solutions, Oilstudios.com, Green Motion, EVRS, Classwatch, Azure Films, Pedalite, FTL, Firebrand Media, The Business Software Center, Claritum, Realflair, Euroflow, Yellowtag, Iken, The Sceptre Group

Other Locations:
Paragon House
Lyncombe Vale Road
Bath BA2 4LS
United Kingdom

Key Executives:
Richard Turner, Founder
e-mail: rjt@catvp.com
Education: MSc, Economics, University of Reading
Background: World Bank, African Development Bank, UN, Partner, East European Consulantcy Practice, KPMG

2575 CATAPULT VENTURE MANAGERS
11 Burrough Court
Burrough on the Hill, Melton Mowbray
Leicestershire LE14 2QS
United Kingdom

Phone: 0116-2388200 Fax: 0116-239-6997
web: www.catapult-vm.co.uk

Mission Statement: Catapult specializes in providing equity capital for businesses.
Fund Size: £100 Million
Founded: 1999
Average Investment: £200,000 - £2 million
Investment Criteria: Early Stage, Development Capital, MBO/MBI

Other Locations:
11 Burrough Court
Burrough on the Hill, Melton Mowbray
Leicestershire LE14 2QS
United Kingdom
Phone: 0116-2388200 Fax: 0121-616-0181

Key Executives:
Rob Caroll, Managing Director
0116-238-8200

Venture Capital & Private Equity Firms / International Firms

e-mail: rob@catapult-vm.co.uk
Education: BA, Pharmacy, Kings College London; MBA, Bradford University Management School
Background: 3i PLC
Directorships: Charles Lawrence Group PLC
Ed Wass, Chief Investment Officer
0116-238-8200
e-mail: robin@catapult-vm.co.uk
Education: Chemical Engineering, Bath University
Background: BP, Blue Circle, 3i PLC
Directorships: Melton Mowbray Building Society
Graham Mold, Position Director
0116-238-8200
e-mail: graham@catapult-vm.co.uk
Background: KPMG
Ray Harris, Investment Director
0121-616-0180
Education: First Class Honours Degree in Economics, UEA
Background: Corporate Finance Advisor

2576 CATHAYA CAPITAL
2105B, Financial Square
333 Jiujiang Road
Shaghai
China

Phone: 8621-60452690

Mission Statement: Cathaya Capital is a Cross Border Private Equity Fund investing in Chinese companies in the area of Clean Tech and Health Care. The fund targets companies that can benefit from cross border alliances to gain access to international markets and advanced technologies. Cathaya Capital works closely with the companies to help strengthen its operational and financial team, and helps the companies develop strategic partnerships and international market presence.
Geographic Preference: China
Industry Group Preference: Clean Technology, Healthcare
Portfolio Companies: Jonway Automobile, APMG, Zap China JV, Better World
Key Executives:
 Priscilla M Lu, Managing Partner
 Education: BS, MS, Computer Science, University of Wisconsin, Madison; PhD, Electrical Engineering & Computer Science, Northwestern University
 Background: China Advisor, Mayfield Fund; Founder, Interwave Communications

2577 CAZENOVE PRIVATE EQUITY Cazenove Capital
12 Moorgate
London EC2R 6DA
United Kingdom

Phone: 44-02034791000 **Fax:** 44-02034790010
web: www.cazenoveprivateequity.com

Mission Statement: CPE operates as a division of Cazenove Capital Management Limited, with the sole objective of producing superior returns for its investors.
Geographic Preference: United Kingdom, Western Europe
Fund Size: $414.5 Million
Founded: 2000
Average Investment: $24.8 Million
Minimum Investment: $10.63 Million
Investment Criteria: Expansion and Development, Bridge finance
Industry Group Preference: Communications, Media, Information Technology, Software, Internet Technology, Electronic Technology, Hardware, Computer Related
Portfolio Companies: Axiom, Clearswift Corporation, Empower, iOra, K-Vault Software Ltd (KVS), Metapack, Callserve, Cityspace, European Telecommunications & Technology, Fluency Voice Technology, Imagine, Avantium International B.V., BlackSpider Technologies, Celoxica
Key Executives:
 Mary-Anne Daly, Head of Wealth Management
 e-mail: info@cazenoveprivateequity.com
 Education: Graduate of Dartmouth College
 Background: IPOs of hundreds of companies worldwide.
 Jeremy Hervey, Head of Charities

2578 CDC CAPITAL PARTNER CDC Group
123 Victoria Street
80 Victoria Street
London SW1E 6DE
United Kingdom

Phone: 44-2079634700 **Fax:** 44-2079634750
e-mail: enquiries@cdcgroup.com
web: www.cdcgroup.com

Mission Statement: Actively seeking new investments.
Geographic Preference: Africa, Asia, Latin America
Founded: 1948
Investment Criteria: Start-up, Early Stage
Key Executives:
 Graham Wrigley, Chairman
 e-mail: enquiries@cdcgroup.com
 Education: Bachelor of Science, MBA
 Background: Director On the Board of Directors, IPDC
 Ian Goldin, Non-executive Director

2579 CDH INVESTMENTS
China

e-mail: cdhpe@cdhfund.com
web: www.cdhfund.com

Mission Statement: CDH Private Equity was established in 2002 by an experienced team of senior investment professionals who have been working and investing together since 1995. During this period of time, the CDH founding partners have built a strong culture of transparency and rigorous discipline that has generated an enviable level of consistency of investment performance. Today, CDH Private Equity has more than US$4 billion assets under management and has invested in more than 50 portfolio companies, many of which are well-known brands and industry leaders in China. CDH Private Equity focuses on partnering with superior management teams who aspire to grow their companies into world-class, industry leaders in China's growing domestic market.
Geographic Preference: China
Fund Size: $900 million
Founded: 2002
Investment Criteria: Early-Stage, Growth Stage
Industry Group Preference: Information Technology, Healthcare, Education, Clean Technology, High Technology
Portfolio Companies: 360, CDG, Yoho.com, Ether Optronics, Blue Ocean Network, Xiron, LDK, GCL, AOSP, Joyoung, Kanchli, Alltech

2580 CEDAR (ISRAEL) FINANCIAL ADVISORS LIMITED Cedar Fund
9 Keren Hayesod Street, PO Box 505
Herzelia 46105
Israel

Phone: 972-99577227 **Fax:** 972-99577228

Mission Statement: A leading provider of investment and financial advice for high technology companies.
Geographic Preference: Israel
Fund Size: $225 Million
Founded: 1997
Average Investment: $10 Million
Investment Criteria: Early stage
Industry Group Preference: Telecommunications, Networking, Enterprise Services, Internet Technology,

Venture Capital & Private Equity Firms / International Firms

Software, Infrastructure, Communications, Wireless Technologies
Portfolio Companies: Animon, Appilog Inc., BigBand Networks, Celtro, ClickFox, e-Glue, Guardium Inc., MessageVine Montilio, Onaro, Orsus Solutions, PeerApp, Red-C, Silver Kite, WebCollage Inc., WiNetworks
Key Executives:
  Gal Israely, Co-Founder
  e-mail: info@cedar.co.il
  Education: MBA Finance, Tel Aviv University
  Background: Managing Director in the High Tech Investment Banking group of Bear Stearns in NY
  Directorships: Active Board Member
  Amnon Shoham, Co-Founder
  e-mail: info@cedar.co.il
  Education: CPA, BA, Tel Aviv University
  Background: Assistant Controller for Champion Motors,
  Motti Vaknin, CEO
  e-mail: info@cedar.co.il
  Education: BS, Computer Science, Ben-Gurion University
  Background: President, CEO and founder of Exactium Ltd
  Dorin Miller, Venture Partner
  e-mail: info@cedar.co.il
  Education: Bachelor's degree in computer science and MIS from from Tel Aviv University
  Background: member of the R&D team-BigBand Networks

2581 CEDRUS INVESTMENTS
Grand Pavilion
802 West Bay Road
Grand Cayman
Cayman Islands

Phone: 345-7697100
web: www.cedrusinvestments.com

Mission Statement: Cedrus Investments' Private Equity Group makes venture capital, growth capital and mezzanine capital investments in companies located in the Greater China Region, Southeast Asia, Korea, Indonesia, Japan and Australia or elsewhere but with their business focusing on these geographical areas, and these companies are engaged in the following industries: clean technology, biotechnology, energy, nanotechnology, nature resources, consumer and media.
Geographic Preference: Asia, Australia
Industry Group Preference: Clean Technology, Biotechnology, Energy, Nanotechnology, Natural Resources, Consumer, Media
Key Executives:
  Rani Jarkas, Chairman

2582 CELADON CAPITAL GROUP
Suite 22-7
Wisma UOA II
21 Jalan Pinang
Kuala Lumpur 50450
Malaysia

Phone: 60-327117211 Fax: 60-327155211
e-mail: celadon@celadon.asia

Mission Statement: Investment Banking, specializing in M&A, PE and VC.
Geographic Preference: Malaysia, Southeast Asia, India
Founded: 1996
Investment Criteria: All States
Industry Group Preference: Clean Technology, Biotechnology, Healthcare, Innovative Technology, Services, Manufacturing
Key Executives:
  Nicholas C. Ashby, Founder & CEO
  e-mail: nick@celadoncapital.com
  Education: University of Cambridge
  Background: Investment & Securities Research, Portfolio Management, M&A, Privitizations, Corporate Finance

2583 CENTRALWAY
Binzstrasse 18
Zurich
Switzerland

Phone: 41-44-578-4000
e-mail: info@centralway.com
web: www.centralway.com

Mission Statement: Every year, Centralway Ventures funds numerous early stage companies, which are redefining the future of their respective industry. Based in Zurich and London, Centralway Ventures partners with leading investors to identify, fund and support innovative ventures across the globe. For 15 years, Centralway has been investing in online companies, helping them to develop. Our experience shows that company value can only be generated through a strong product focus, operative excellence and constant innovation.
Founded: 1999
Investment Criteria: Early-Stage
Industry Group Preference: Internet
Portfolio Companies: Numbrs, Buttercoin, Standard Treasury, LendingClub, Sandbox, Securesafe
Other Locations:
  Somerset House
  New Wing
  Strand
  London WC2R 1LA
  United Kingdom
Key Executives:
  Martin Saidler, CEO/Founder
  Background: Founder, Jobinteractive.com; Management Group, Beisheim Holding AG
  Severin Jan Ruegger, Managing Partner, Investments
  Education: BA, University of St. Gallen; MSc, London School of Economics
  Background: Founder, Solosso; Co-Founder, Dealicious
  Nicolas Ruflin, Managing Partner, Technology
  Education: MS, Computer Science, University of Basel
  Background: Co-Founder, Technical Lead, useKit

2584 CEYUAN
Qiniao Hutong
Number 35
Dongcheng District
Beijing 50450
China

Phone: +86 10 84028800 Fax: +86 10 84020999
e-mail: info@ceyuan.com
web: www.ceyuan.com

Mission Statement: Ceyuan is a Beijing-based early stage venture capital firm focused on IT and emerging growth companies. We emphasize backing great teams, technology and business innovation. Our mission is to assist entrepreneurs in creating and building world-class businesses. Our conviction, network of relationships and grass roots culture give us the opportunity to discover the next big idea early.
Investment Criteria: Early-Stage
Industry Group Preference: Information Technology, Internet, Wireless
Portfolio Companies: 360 Safe, 3GPP, CVT, Douban, ETSolar, HaoDF, iSpeak, Jiayuan, Letao, Light In The Box, NetWin, PPS, R2G, TX, UC, Vancl, Venustech, WE Magazine, Wuhan Groce Nordic New Energy, Yicha, Zbird, Zhongdian Biotech, Zunlei
Key Executives:
  Bo Feng, Co-Founder/Partner
  Education: College of Marin, San Francisco State University
  Background: Founder/Partner, Chengwei Ventures; Chief Representative, ChinaVest; Vice President, Robertson Stephens & Co.

840

Venture Capital & Private Equity Firms / International Firms

2585 CHALLENGE FUNDS - ETGAR LP
20 Lincoln Street
Rubenstein House
20th Floor
Tel Aviv 67134
Israel

Phone: 972-35628555 Fax: 972-35621999
e-mail: etgar@challenge.co.il

Mission Statement: The Challenge Funds are two Delaware limited partnerships focused on equity investments in Israel-related privately held and publicly traded companies.

Geographic Preference: Israel
Fund Size: $250 Million
Founded: 1995
Investment Criteria: All stages
Industry Group Preference: Communications, Media, Medical Devices, Real Estate, Industrial Services, Software, Biotechnology, Semiconductors, Internet Technology, Healthcare
Portfolio Companies: Alvarion, Atrica, Comgates, Congruency, DSP Group Inc, Liberate, PowerDsine, Schema Ltd, FlashNetworks Ltd, Orckit Communications Ltd, Radware, MATE Ltd, Demantra Ltd., BitBand Ltd, RT-SET Ltd, Viryanet Inc., CBD Tech Ltd, D-Pharm, Sol-Gel, XTL, ASI, M.T.R.E, Smartlight Ltd

Key Executives:
Yossi Ciechanover, Founder and Consultant
e-mail: joseph@challenge.co.il
Education: Ph.D. in Philosophy from Boston University, L.L.M. from the University of California at Berkeley, Magister Juris degree from the Hebrew University of Jerusalem, member of the New York and Israeli Bar Associations
Background: Chairman of the Board of El Al Israel Airlines. President of PEC Israel Economic Corporation
Directorships: Bank of Israel Advisory Committee, Board of Israel Discount Bank
Yossi Pastel, Chief Financial Officer & Vice President

2586 CHARLOTTE STREET CAPITAL
20 Portman Square
City of Westminster
London W1H 6LW
United Kingdom

web: www.charlottestreetcapital.com

Mission Statement: Invests up to £200,000 in early stage UK technology businesses that have barriers to entry and 'market validation' usually by way of initial sales.

Geographic Preference: United Kingdom
Average Investment: £20k to £200k
Investment Criteria: Early-Stage
Industry Group Preference: Technology
Portfolio Companies: Appshed, Culturelabel.com, GoSquared, HybridCluster, Last Second Tickets, Likely, Loveholidays.com, Ondevice Research, Retronaut, Seedcamp, Simpletax

Key Executives:
Bo Pedersen, Partner
e-mail: bo@sharlottestreetcapital.com

2587 CHARTERHOUSE CAPITAL PARTNERS I
Charterhouse
7th Floor Paternoster Square
Warwick Court
Paternoster Square
London EC4M 7DX
United Kingdom

Phone: 44-2073345300 Fax: 44-2073345333
web: www.charterhouse.co.uk

Mission Statement: Actively seeking new investments.

Geographic Preference: United Kingdom, Europe
Fund Size: $26.1 Billion
Founded: 1980
Average Investment: $400 million and $4 billion
Minimum Investment: $356.5 Million
Investment Criteria: All stages
Industry Group Preference: All Sectors Considered
Portfolio Companies: Barracuda, Avent, Autobar, Saga, TDF, Coral Eurobet, Cegelec Holdings, PreCon, Lucite International

Key Executives:
Duncan Aldred, Partner

2588 CHASE CAPITAL PARTNERS
One Exchange Square
8 Connaught Place
Hong Kong

Phone: 852-82288030 Fax: 852-82288031
web: www.chase.com

Founded: 1984
Industry Group Preference: Life Sciences, Healthcare, Media, Telecommunications, Technology, Consumer Services, Financial Services

Key Executives:
Peter DeMaria, Senior Vice President
John Goldthorpe, Head
Education: Bsc in Physics from Bristol University
Background: Life Assurance Holding Company Limited, M&H Plastics Limited, TIW Czech NV, Mobifon SA, SiTeco, JPMorgan Italian Fund III, Pemco and Chase Mittel Fund II
Derek A. Holley, Senior Vice President / National Field Exam Manager
Dan Lane, Senior Vice President / West Region Head
Education: Language from university of paris, bachelors of arts, economics & finance form university of north london
Background: The Chase Manhattan Bank
Mary Reasoner, Senior Vice President / Southeast Region Head
Education: Nijenrode Bachelor, HEC Master
Background: Greenwich Technology Partners Incorporated , Apax Partners , Botts & Company , Bain & Company
Jeffrey A. Stern, Senior Vice President / South Region Head
Education: Founder of J.P. Morgan plc, New York, Founder of IndustriKapital
Joseph J. Virzi, Senior Vice President / Midwest Region Head
Peter York, Senior Vice President / ABL-IB Region Head
Education: Bachelor of arts from Oxford university
Background: jpmp

2589 CHELSFIELD PARTNERS
67 Brook Street
London W1K 4NJ
United Kingdom

Phone: 44-02072902388
e-mail: enquiries@chelsfield.com
web: www.chelsfield.com

Mission Statement: Chelsfield Partners LLP invests in real estate and related businesses in the UK and Europe. We bring together businesses and individuals with the financial weight, track record, industry network and vision to identify exceptional opportunities. We create significant added value and deliver large scale projects and corporate investments across the real estate sector.

Geographic Preference: United Kingdom, Europe
Fund Size: £1.5 billion
Industry Group Preference: Real Estate

Venture Capital & Private Equity Firms / International Firms

Key Executives:
Elliott Bernerd, Co-Founder/Chairman
e-mail: ebernerd@chelsfield.com
Background: Founder/Chairman, Chelsfield PLC; Co-Founder, Stockley PLC; Chairmain/CEO, Michael Laurie & Partners

2590 CHENGWEI VENTURES
Lane 672, Suite 33C, Changle Road
Shanghai 200040
China

Phone: 86-2154048566 Fax: 86-2154048766
e-mail: General@Chengwei.com
web: www.chengwei.com

Mission Statement: Chengwei Ventures seeks to create entrepreneurial returns on capital by investing in and helping build companies that have scalable business opportunities in the global Chinese economy.

Geographic Preference: China
Average Investment: $11 million
Minimum Investment: $1 Million
Investment Criteria: Early stages
Industry Group Preference: Communications, Enterprise Services, Branded Goods, Manufacturing, Healthcare, Media, Software, Consumer Products, Education, Oil & Gas
Portfolio Companies: OneWave Inc, BabyCare, AAC Acoustic, Huaya Technology, BMI Asia, Oval Technologies, Digital Chocolate, Agape Package Manufacturing, Antig Technology Co, HDT Inc, Shengtang Entertainment, CNC, Asia Info, InfoSec, IEI Technologies.

Key Executives:
Steve Xiangdong Zou, President & CEO
e-mail: General@Chengwei.com
Education: B.A. from University of California, Berkeley and his M.B.A. from Stanford Business School
Background: Partner of Orchid Asia Holdings, Perot Systems Corporation in Texas
Directorships: Managing Partner
Bo Feng, Special Partner & Co-Founder

2591 CHEUNG KONG INFRASTRUCTURE HOLDINGS LIMITED
12/F Cheung Kong Centre
2 Queen's Road Central
Central
Hong Kong

Phone: 852-21223133 Fax: 852-25014550
e-mail: contact@cki.com.hk
web: www.cki.com.hk

Mission Statement: Diversified infrastructure company with a focus in the development, investment and operation of infrastructure businesses.

Geographic Preference: Hong Kong, China, Australia, UK, Canada, Philippines
Fund Size: $300 Million
Industry Group Preference: Infrastructure, Power Technologies, Utilities
Portfolio Companies: North of England Gas Distribution Network, CitiPower I Pty Ltd, Envestra Limited, ETSA Utilities, Powercor Australia Ltd, Hongkong Electric, Zhuhai Power Plant, Qinyang Power Plants, Henan, Siping Cogen Power Plants, Fushun Cogen Power Plants,

Key Executives:
Canning FOK Kin Ning, Deputy Chairman
e-mail: contact@cki.com.hk
Education: BSc in Engineering and MBA
KAM Hing Lam, Group Managing Director

2592 CHINA DEVELOPMENT INDUSTRIAL BANK CDFH
10504 125 Nanjing East Road
Taipei 10570
Taiwan

Phone: 886-227638800 Fax: 886-227562144
e-mail: ir@cdibh.com

Mission Statement: Actively seeking investments.
Geographic Preference: US, Japan, Korea, Southeast Asia, Taiwan
Fund Size: $58 Billion
Founded: 1959
Investment Criteria: all stages
Industry Group Preference: Electronic Technology, Telecommunications, Semiconductors, Wireless Technologies, Biotechnology, Medical Devices, Automotive

Key Executives:
Mu-Tsai Chen, Chairman
Mr. Paul Yang, President & Chief Executive Officer

2593 CHINA ISRAEL VALUE CAPITAL
Room 801, Central Tower
No. 88 Fuhua First Road
Fultan District
Shenzhen
China

Phone: 86-75533359986 Fax: 86-75533359970
e-mail: steven@civcfund.com

Mission Statement: China-Israel Value Capital L.P., is a China-focused, Private Equity Fund headquartered in Shenzhen, China, with 13 offices in China and Herzeliya, Israel. CIVC mainly focuses on Medium sized Chinese companies with: Exceptional and experianced management teams; Established sales operations, typically with revenues between $30M-$100M; and a Rapidly growing market.

Geographic Preference: China, Israel
Founded: 2005
Industry Group Preference: Information Technology, Consumer Electronics, Healthcare, Clean Technology
Portfolio Companies: C2 Micro, KeenHigh Technologies, Vtion Wireless, JinkoSolar Holdings, LuHua Chemical Co., Celgen Biopharmaceutical Co., China Dredging, Juli, Huji

Other Locations:
4 Shenkar Street
Belt Graph 1st Floor
POB 12549
Herzeliya 46725
Israel
Phone: 972-99505478 Fax: 972-99505475

Key Executives:
Jin Haitao, Co-Founder/General Partner
Education: Huazhong University
Background: Chairman, Shenzhen-Hong Kong Investment Association

2594 CHINA MERCHANTS CHINA DIRECT INVESTMENTS LTD.
168-200 Connaught Place
1803 China Merchants Tower
Shun Tak Centre
Central
Hong Kong

Phone: 852-28589089 Fax: 852-28588455
web: www.cmcdi.com.hk

Mission Statement: China Merchants Group, the major shareholder of CMCIM, operated directly under the Ministry of Communications of China before the PRC implemented

Venture Capital & Private Equity Firms / International Firms

the policy of separation of enterprises from government organizations.
Geographic Preference: Hong Kong, Beijing, Nanjing, Bangkok
Fund Size: $33 Billion
Founded: 1993
Average Investment: $10 Million
Minimum Investment: $120,000
Investment Criteria: Bridge, Early Stage, Expansion & Development Capital, Buyout
Industry Group Preference: Financial Services, Brokering, Insurance, Banking, Management, Culture and Media, Manufacturing, Energy and Resources, Information Technology, Agriculture
Portfolio Companies: China Merchants Bank, Industrial Bank Co. Ltd, Industrial Securities Co. Ltd, Jutian Fund Management Co, Ltd. Jutian Securities Co. Ltd, China Merchants Securities Co. Ltd.

Key Executives:
Li Yinquan, Chairman

2595 CHINA MERCHANTS CHINA INVESTMENT MANAGEMENT
1803 China Merchants
Shun Tak Centre
168 - 200 Connaught Road
Central
Hong Kong
Phone: 852-28589089 Fax: 852-28588455
web: www.cmcdi.com.hk

Mission Statement: Specializes in investing in China based businesses. Its investment objective is to acquire quality investments in China principally in unlisted enterprises.
Geographic Preference: China
Fund Size: $100 Million
Founded: 1993
Average Investment: US$10 million
Minimum Investment: $10 Million
Investment Criteria: Start up seed, early stages
Industry Group Preference: Financial Services, Real Estate, Manufacturing, Infrastructure
Portfolio Companies: China Merchants Bank Co. Ltd, Industrial Bank Co. Ltd, Industrial Securities Co. LtdChina Merchants Securities Co. Ltd, Jutian Securities Co. LtdHoulder China Insurance Broker Ltd, Jutian Fund Management Co. Ltd, China Merchants Plaza (Shanghai) Property C

Key Executives:
Li Yinquan, Chairman
Hong Xiaoyuan, Executive Director

2596 CHINA VEST LIMITED
Beijing China Resources Building
5th Floor, No. 8 Jian Guo Men Bei Avenue
Suite 508B
Beijing 100005
China
Phone: 86-1085191535 Fax: 86-1085191530
e-mail: info@chinavest.com.cn
web: www.chinavest.com

Mission Statement: The firm functions as a bridge to Chinese companies and foreign multi-national corporations.
Geographic Preference: China
Founded: 1981
Average Investment: $212 Million
Minimum Investment: $25 Million
Investment Criteria: growing middle market
Industry Group Preference: Logistics, Healthcare, Media, Textiles, Machinery, Information Technology, Financial Services, Private Equity, Research Provider

Key Executives:
Robert A. Theleen, Chairman & Chief Executive Officer
Directorships: Vice President and Beijing Representative
Jenny Hsui, President

2597 CHINA WALDEN MANAGEMENT LIMITED Walden Group
Beijing China Resources Bldg.
No. 8 Jianguomenbei Avenue, Ste. 1702, 17/F
Dongcheng District
Beijing 100005
China
Phone: 86-1085192519 Fax: 86-1085192520
e-mail: chinahk@waldenintl.com
web: www.waldenintl.com

Mission Statement: Invests in entrepreneurs and companies that demonstrate an ability to gain a competitive advantage in the markets they serve.
Geographic Preference: China
Fund Size: $1.6 Billion
Founded: 1987
Investment Criteria: early stages
Industry Group Preference: Communications, Electronic Technology, Software, Semiconductors, Consumer Services, Information Technology
Portfolio Companies: Celestial Semiconductor, Ltd, ChannelSoft Holdings, China Motion Telecom International ltd, CommVerge Solutions, Accel Semiconductor Corporation

Key Executives:
Lip-Bu Tan, Chairman/Founder
Brian Chiang, Managing Director

2598 CHORD CAPITAL
Harston Mill
Harston
Cambridge CB22 7GG
United Kingdom
Phone: 440-1223875598
e-mail: info@chordcapital.co.uk
web: www.chordcapital.co.uk

Mission Statement: Chord Capital is a venture investment company based in Cambridge and London. We work with entrepreneurs to drive our portfolio companies from technology projects to commercial enterprises.
Geographic Preference: United Kingdom
Industry Group Preference: Energy, Advanced Materials, Environment, Renewable Energy, Energy Efficiency, Medical Technology, Biometrics
Portfolio Companies: Altraverda, ImmunoBiology, Metalysis, FreeHand Surgical, Sensortec, CIP Technologies

Key Executives:
John Townsend, Managing Director
Education: BA, Economics, University of Manchester
Background: CEO, Vesta Capital Partners
Directorships: Altraverda, Metalysis, Prosurgics

2599 CHRYSALIS CAPITAL ChrysCapital
Suit 504, St. James Court
Room 101
Port Louis 110003
Mauritius
Phone: 23-02115410 Fax: 23-02086413
e-mail: kenny.chryscapital@intnet.mu
web: www.chryscapital.com

Mission Statement: ChrysCapital is a principal investment firm with Mission Partnering with passionate leaders to build world-class companies.
Geographic Preference: India, USA, Mauritius
Fund Size: $2.5 Billion
Founded: 1999

Venture Capital & Private Equity Firms / International Firms

Average Investment: $50 Million - $1 Billion
Minimum Investment: $10 Million
Investment Criteria: Growth investments, carve-outs, joint ventures, buy-outs/buy-ins
Industry Group Preference: Outsourcing & Efficiency, Business to Business, Healthcare, Software Services, Information Technology, Financial Services, Business Products & Services, Manufacturing, Consumer Products, Infrastructure
Portfolio Companies: Balkrishna Industries, Gammon, Global Vantedge, ING Vysya Bank, Micro Inks, Moser Baer, New Path, The Shriram Group, Suzlon, Yes Bank

Key Executives:
  Brahmal Vasudevan, Director
  e-mail: ashish.dhawan@rediffmail.com
  Education: Dual Bachelor (Bachelor of Science and Bachelor of Arts), Yale University. Harvard University , MBA With Distinction
  Background: Goldman Sachs , McCown De Leeuw & Co.
  Ashish Dhawan, Senior Managing Director

2600 CHRYSCAPITAL MANAGEMENT COMPANIES ChrysCapital
IFS Court, TwentyEight, Cybercity
Les Cascades
3rd Floor
Ebene
Mauritius

Phone: 230-4673000 **Fax:** 230-4674000
e-mail: kenny.chryscapital@intnet.mu
web: www.chryscapital.com

Mission Statement: Supports passionate leaders in building world class companies.

Geographic Preference: India, USA, Mauritius
Fund Size: $450 Million
Founded: 1999
Average Investment: $2.5 Billion
Minimum Investment: $8 Million
Investment Criteria: Focuses on companies with defensible market positions and strong underlying organic growth potential including Management Buy-Outs, Recapitalization, Carve-outs, Joint Ventures, PIPEs
Industry Group Preference: Outsourcing & Efficiency, Business to Business, Healthcare, Software Services, Information Technology, Financial Services
Portfolio Companies: Balkrishna Industries, Gammon, Global Vantedge, ING Vysya Bank, Micro Inks, Moser Baer, New Path, The Shriram Group, Suzlon, Yes Bank

Key Executives:
  Ashish Dhawan, Senior Managing Director
  e-mail: info@chryscapital.com
  Education: MBA, IIM Bangalore, Bachelors degree in accounting from Delhi University
  Sanjiv Kaul, Managing Director
  e-mail: info@chryscapital.com
  Education: Pharmacy graduate with an M.B.A.-IIM Ahmedabad, AMP from Harvard Business School, Boston.
  Background: Managing Director of Ranbaxy, China
  Brahmal Vasudevan, Managing Director
  e-mail: info@chryscapital.com
  Education: M.B.A. from the Harvard Business School and graduated in aeronautical engineering from Imperial College, London
  Background: Director of Marketing at ASTRO
  Kunal Shroff, Managing Director
  Education: BA, Knox College; MBA, University of Chicago
  Background: Radiowave; McCown De Leeuw & Company
  Kushal Agarwal, Associate
  e-mail: info@chryscapital.com
  Education: Bachelors degree in accounting from Mumbai University, CA
  Background: KPMG
  Gulpreet Kohli, Principal
  e-mail: info@chryscapital.com
  Education: MBA, Clark University;B.A Delhi University
  Background: GE Capital
  Ashish Agarwal, Associate
  e-mail: info@chryscapital.com
  Education: M.B.A. in finance from Mumbai University, B.Com from Garhwal University
  Background: Global Research division of McKinsey & Company

2601 CIC FINANCE CIC Group
6 Avenue of Provence
Cedex 9
Paris 75452
France

Phone: 33-145969696 **Fax:** 33-145969666
e-mail: filbprod@cic.fr
web: www.cic.fr

Mission Statement: CIC delivers high quality and specialist services to expatriate communities in France.

Geographic Preference: France
Fund Size: $293.5 Million
Founded: 1940
Average Investment: $3.7 - 5.5 Million
Minimum Investment: $0.9 Million
Investment Criteria: Expansion and Development, LBO, MBO, Venture Capital
Industry Group Preference: Retailing, Media, Communications, Industrial Services, Medical & Health Related
Portfolio Companies: Adhersis, Chantemor, Coficern/Sagem, Cote Sud Invetissement, Esi Group SA, Fenwick, Frans Bonhomme, Groupe De Presse Michel Hommell, Le Figano, Nature et D'couvertes, Right Vision, Sebia, Sucriere De Bernevil, Tabur/Bricogite

Key Executives:
  Bruno Julien-Laferrière, Chief Executive Officer
  e-mail: arnouca@cic.fr
  Education: IEP Paris, Maitrise en droit
  Hubert Veltz, Chief Operating Officer
  e-mail: messagfr@cic.fr
  Education: IEP Paris, Maitrise d'economie
  René Pastant, Director of logistics and organisation
  Education: DEA de mathematiques

2602 CICLAD
22 Avenue Franklin Roosevelt
Roosevelt
Paris 75008
France

Phone: 33-156597733 **Fax:** 33-153762210
e-mail: info@ciclad.com
web: www.ciclad.com

Mission Statement: Actively seeking new investments.

Fund Size: $135 Million
Founded: 1988
Average Investment: $30 Million
Minimum Investment: $10 Million
Industry Group Preference: All Sectors Considered
Portfolio Companies: Arthus-Bertrand, Dalie, Garard Pasquier, IMV, ITM, Mogarde, Calectro, Satelec, Siraga, Terres, Aventure, VSD, Vermed

Key Executives:
  Lionel Lambert, Associate
  e-mail: llambert@ciclad.com
  Education: MBA Politics, Paris Institute of Politics
  Background: Boston Consulting Group
  Thierry Thomann, Associate
  e-mail: tthomann@ciclad.com

Venture Capital & Private Equity Firms / International Firms

Jean-Francois Vaury, Founder/Associate
e-mail: jtvaury@ciclad.com

2603 CID GROUP
19F, Tower B, CCIG International Plaza
333 Cao Xi North Road
Shanghai 200030
China

Phone: 86-21-3397-3678 **Fax:** 86-21-3397-3599
e-mail: inquiries@cidgroup.com
web: www.cidgroup.com

Mission Statement: Founded in 1998, The CID Group was established by a seasoned and professional team with more than 200 years of direct investment experiences. Since inception, the team has been fully committed to carrying out the mission of 'Integrating Global Resources to Create Synergistic Businesses'. Today, CID has become one of the fastest growing Asia-headquartered private equity firms.

Geographic Preference: Greater China
Fund Size: $1 billion
Industry Group Preference: Semiconductors, Wireless, Telecommunications
Portfolio Companies: Advanced Analogic Technologies, Advanced Power Electronics Corporation, eGalax, Global Mixed-Mode Technology, Prolific Technology, Richtek Technology, Semiconductor Manufacturing International Corporation, STATs ChipPac Taiwan Semiconductor Corporation, Techwell, Worldwide Semiconductor, Flexium Interconnect, Inpaq Technology, Kinsus Interconnect Technology Corporation, Mstar Semiconductor, Shun On Electronic, Solomon Systech, Taiflex Scientific, Young Fast Optoelectronics, Entire Technology, Formosa Epitaxy, Gamma Optical, Quanta Display, Wiseware Technology, WSE Corporation, Elite Advanced Laser Corporation, Quanta Storage, Skymedi Corporation, Topray Technologies, Alpha Networks, Meru Networks, Tainet Communcation Systems, Aiptek International, Ambow Education, Asia Vital Components, Brighton Best International, Chenming Mold Industrial Corporation, Fullterton Technology, Rotam Global AgroSciences, Super Dragon Technology, Univacco Technology

Key Executives:
Steven Chang, Managing Partner
Education: BS, Electrical Engineering, National Taipei Institute of Technology; BS, Management, National Chung Hsing University; MBA, National Cheng Chi University; PhD, Management, Shanghai Jiao Tong University
Background: Investment Manager, China Development Industrial Bank; Founder, Taiflex Scientific

2604 CINCO CAPITAL
Gänsemarkt 43
Hamburg 20354
Germany

Phone: 49-4044191700 **Fax:** 49-40228211699
e-mail: contact@cinco-capital.com

Mission Statement: Cinco Capital is building a portfolio of holdings in private companies. Currently Cinco Capital holds investments in Europe and the U.S. in different industries such as technology, financial services, telecommunications, wholesale, marketing, media and others.

Geographic Preference: Europe, United States
Industry Group Preference: Technology, Financial Services, Telecommunications, Wholesale, Marketing, Media
Portfolio Companies: Adconion Media Group, Agarrius, Brille24, Cliqz.com, Dopplr.com, Fab.com, Facebook Investment Fund LLC, Getmobile, Impossible Software, IWATech, Jameslist.com, Lifebond, Lofty, Mobileye.com, Nikoma, Numberfour AG, Offbeatguides, Pixsta, Prezi.inc, PublicStuff, Qype, Samedi.de, Supreme NewMedia, Xing AG, Zynga

2605 CINVEN LIMITED
Warwick Court
Paternoster Square
London EC4M 7AG
United Kingdom

Phone: 44-2076613333 **Fax:** 44-2076613888
e-mail: info@cinven.com
web: www.cinven.com

Mission Statement: Applies effective strategies to our businesses, creating value and long-term growth.

Geographic Preference: Europe
Fund Size: $9.02 Billion
Founded: 1977
Average Investment: $601 Million
Minimum Investment: $300 Million
Investment Criteria: All stages of funding
Industry Group Preference: Business to Business, Consumer Services, Healthcare, Industrial Services, Retailing, Leisure
Portfolio Companies: Approvia, Gala, MediMedia, NCP, Unique Pubs, Springer, Fitness First, Amadeus, Eutelsat, CBR, Foseco, Klöckner Pentaplast, Foseco, Newsquest, William Hill, General Healthcare

Key Executives:
Hugh Langmuir, Partner
e-mail: info@cinven.com
Education: Graduate of Glasgow University
Background: The Royal Bank of Scotland in their Leveraged Finance Group, Ernst & Young- worked in Boston and London
Adam Prindis, Associate
e-mail: info@cinven.com
Education: Degree in Economics from LUISS in Rome and an MBA from INSEAD
Background: Henderson Private Capital- Partner and Managing director
Yagnish Chotai, Director
e-mail: info@cinven.com
Education: Degree in Economics and Accountancy from Edinburgh University
Background: Director with Hill Samuel Development Capital
Jonathan Clarke, Partner
e-mail: info@cinven.com
Education: He has a degree in Physiology from Oxford University
Background: Advisor-KPMG
Guy Davison, Partner
e-mail: info@cinven.com
Education: Guy has a History degree from Cambridge University.
Background: Larpent Newton, KPMG
Andrew Joy, Senior Adviser
e-mail: info@cinven.com
Education: A degree in Politics, Philosophy and Economics from Oxford University
Background: Managing Director of Hill Samuel Development Capital, Chairman of the British Venture Capital Association.
Alex Leslie, Principal
e-mail: info@cinven.com
Education: Degree in History from Cambridge University and has a doctorate in Medieval Politics.
Background: Board Director of research and planning at Valin Pollen, Board Director of planning at Gavin Anderson.
Hugh Langmuir, Managing Partner
Education: Hugh is a graduate of Edinburgh University, Harvard and London Business School
Background: Bain & Co, Citicorp in London and Paris.
Directorships: partner
Brian Linden, Director
e-mail: info@cinven.com

Venture Capital & Private Equity Firms / International Firms

Education: Business Finance graduate
Background: Deloitte & Touche.
Andrew Joy, Senior Adviser
e-mail: info@cinven.com
Education: Degree in Politics, Philosophy and Economics from Oxford University
Background: Managing Director of Hill Samuel Development Capital, Chairman of the British Venture Capital Association.
Ben Osnabrug, Principal
e-mail: info@cinven.com
Education: Graduate of Oxford University -studied Politics, Philosophy and Economics.
Background: Bain & Co, - worked on numerous strategy projects across a variety of sectors in the UK and South Africa
Simon Rowlands, Senior Adviser
e-mail: info@cinven.com
Education: Degree in Engineering, is a chartered engineer, MBA from Cranfield School of Management
Background: Simon worked with an international consulting firm on multidisciplinary engineering projects in the UK and Southern Africa.

2606 CIPIO PARTNERS
Palais am Lenbachplatz
Ottostrasse 8
Munich D-80333
Germany

Phone: 49-895506960 **Fax:** 49-8955069699
e-mail: info@cipiopartners.com
web: www.cipiopartners.com

Mission Statement: Cipio Partners is known as a leading international investment management firm in the secondary direct market. We were founded in June 2003 and are managing several funds of early and later-stage venture capital and mid-market investments worldwide. Our staff is based in Munich and San Jose, CA. Cipio Partners pursues the acquisition of portfolios of direct private equity investments in the secondary market. We consider transactions ranging from single-company shareholdings to large and well diversified portfolios across all stages of the investing life-cycle, from early to late-stage venture capital through mid-market and smaller buy-out investments. Securities purchased may include equity, mezzanine and debt.

Geographic Preference: Worldwide
Founded: 2003
Investment Criteria: Early-Stage to Late-Stage

Other Locations:
560 S Winchester Blvd
Suite 500
San Jose, CA 95128
Phone: 408-2367654 **Fax:** 408-2367651

Key Executives:
Tom S Anthofer, Managing Partner
e-mail: tanthofer@cipiopartners.com
Education: MBA, Duke University, Fuqua School of Business
Background: Partner, Broadview Holdings

2607 CITA GESTION
11bis rue Balzac
Paris 75008
France

Phone: 01-42257676 **Fax:** 33-145012429
e-mail: info@cita.fr
web: www.cita.fr

Mission Statement: CITA invests side to side with a management team, to support a company plan.
Geographic Preference: France
Fund Size: $336 Million
Founded: 1985
Average Investment: 1 to 12 million Euros
Minimum Investment: $1 Million
Investment Criteria: Startup, Development, Buyout, Leveraged buy outs (LBO)
Industry Group Preference: Pharmaceuticals, Software Services, Biotechnology, Media, Advertising, Textiles
Portfolio Companies: Actelion, Etam, Freesbee, Infodustry, Partenaires Livres, Porcher, REP, Sidel, Solsoft, Actelioln, Adelior, Allocine, Arpida, CB News, Locamex, Synerway

Key Executives:
Philippe Queveau, Managing Director
e-mail: info@cita.fr
Education: Queveau graduated from the Ecole Polytechnique.
Background: Managing Director of the Société Financière Heuliez, CEO of the SA Henri Heuliez
Patrick Plouvier, Investments Manager
e-mail: info@cita.fr
Education: Graduated Ecole Nationale Supérieure des Mines de Saint-Etienne, MBA Degree from the Wharton School (Pennsylvania).
Background: Executive at Coparis

2608 CITY OF LONDON INVESTMENT GROUP PLC
77 Gracechurch Street
London EC3V 0AS
United Kingdom

Phone: 44-2077111566 **Fax:** 44-2077110772
e-mail: ukclientservicing@citlon.co.uk
web: www.citlon.co.uk

Mission Statement: Provides long term capital growth via active Country Asset Allocation and Stock Selection in emerging markets.
Geographic Preference: London, Europe, Africa, Middle East, USA, Latin America, Canada, Singa
Fund Size: $1.5 Billion
Founded: 1991
Investment Criteria: emerging market

Key Executives:
Glenn Lee, Marketing

2609 CLAL ELECTRONICS INDUSTRIES LIMITED
3 Azrieli Center, 45th Floor
The Triangular Tower
Tel Aviv 67023
Israel

Phone: 972-36075777 **Fax:** 972-36075778
e-mail: cii@cii.co.il
web: www.cii.co.il

Mission Statement: Actively seeking new investments.
Geographic Preference: Israel
Fund Size: $3149 Million
Founded: 1998
Investment Criteria: Early stage
Industry Group Preference: Electronic Technology, Communications, Semiconductors, Graphic Arts
Portfolio Companies: Mashav, Nesher1, Taavura1, American Israeli Paper Mills2, Kitan Consolidated, Jafora, Cargal, Scitex3, ECI, Nova, Saifun, Main Venture Capital Funds, CBI (ARTE), ECTel, Viryanet

Key Executives:
Gonen Bieber, Vice President Finance
e-mail: cbi@cbi.co.il
Education: Tel Aviv University, L.L.B. & Political Science
Background: Ganden Group - Founder and Chairman
Avi Fischer, CEO & Chairman of the Board
e-mail: cbi@cbi.co.il
Education: Tel Aviv University, L.L.B

Venture Capital & Private Equity Firms / International Firms

Background: IDB Holdings Corp. Ltd, Ganden Holdings Ltd, Fischer, Behar, Chen & Co

2610 CLARENDON FUND MANAGERS
8th Floor
City Exchange
11-13 Gloucester Street
Belfast BT1 4LS
Ireland
Phone: 028-90326465 **Fax:** 028-90326473
e-mail: info@clarendon-fm.co.uk
web: www.clarendon-fm.co.uk

Mission Statement: Clarendon Fund Managers Limited is venture capital fund manager based in Belfast, which is authorised and regulated by the Financial Services Authority. Clarendon manage £20m of regional VC Funds in Northern ireland including £13m of fully invested Funds (Viridian Growth Fund and Nitech Growth Fund) and the recently established Co-Fund NI, a £7.2m fund that will co-invest with business angel/private investor lead deals which when matched to the private investment on a deal by deal basis will equate to a £16m Fund.
Geographic Preference: Ireland
Fund Size: £16 million
Founded: 2001
Industry Group Preference: Medical Devices, Biotechnology, Communications, Food & Beverage, Waste & Recycling, Renewable Energy, Gaming
Portfolio Companies: Lagan Technologies, Bluechip Technologies, Bittware, Art Technology Group, Fusion Antibodies, Datacitics, TraceAssured, AxisThree, Heartsine Technologies, Dark Water Studios, Biomass CHP, Intelesens, Vertical Wind Energy, Kelsius Limited, Biznet Solutions
Key Executives:
Alan Mawson, Chairman
Education: MBA, MIT; PhD, University of Lancaster
Background: Founding Director, Electra Innvotec

2611 CLARITY CAPITAL
28 Old Brompton Road
Suite 256
South Kensington
London SW7 3SS
United Kingdom
Phone: 44-2075914438
e-mail: info@claritycapital.com

Mission Statement: Long-term investor, focusing on private investments in entrepreneurial companies with leading-edge technology and motivated management teams. The firm provides guidance and accelerated time to market.
Geographic Preference: Canada, Mexico, Brazil, Africa, United Kingdom
Founded: 1996
Average Investment: $5.0 million
Minimum Investment: $1 million
Investment Criteria: Seed, Startup, First-Stage
Industry Group Preference: Minerals, Life Sciences, Energy, Creative Industries
Portfolio Companies: Lobby7, Raindance
Other Locations:
6235B 86 Avenue
Southest
Calgary, AB
Canada
Phone: 403-258-3680

Box 9422, Sonpark
Nelspruit, Mpumalanga
Box 9422, Sonpark
Mpumalanga 1206
South Africa
Phone: 27-13-755-1892 **Fax:** 27-13-755-1994
105 Plumtree Road
Belmont
Bulawayo
Zimbabwe
Phone: 263-94603612 **Fax:** 263-99460376
Key Executives:
Allan Dolan, Managing Director, Founder
Background: Founder, African Minerals Limited

2612 CLEANTECH INVEST
Malminrinne 1 B
Helsinki 00100
Finland
Phone: 358-405015127
e-mail: lassi.noponen@cleantechinvest.com
web: www.cleantechinvest.com

Mission Statement: We are a private equity fund management company focusing on cleantech. We create success stories by combining capital, technology & sector know-how and access to key players in the cleantech sector, globally. Our Nordic presence gives us access to some of the world's most exciting deals.
Industry Group Preference: Clean Technology
Portfolio Companies: Savo-Solar, Netcycler, Enersize, MetGen, BT Wood, Ultranat, Enercomp, Matox, Onel
Key Executives:
Lassi Noponen, Chairman/Partner
Education: LLM, MBA
Background: Co-Founder/CEO, Proventia Group Oy

2613 CLEANTECH VENTURES
Level 2, 710 Collins Street
Docklands
Victoria 3008
Australia
Phone: 61-439268350

Mission Statement: Cleantech Ventures is a specialist venture capital fund manager focused on investments in companies developing clean technologies. Cleantech Ventures Pty Ltd is an Australian-owned and managed venture capital company. Our highly experienced investment team has an extensive track record in venture capital investing in companies from pre-seed to expansion stage and a deep understanding of the cleantech sector.
Investment Criteria: Pre-Seed to Expansion-Stage
Industry Group Preference: Clean Technology
Portfolio Companies: Ilum-A-Lite, Lang Technologies, Netsol, MIGfast, Nu Energy, Oceanlinx, Renex Holdings, Semitech Semiconductor, Active Reactor Company, Ecoult, Ember Technologies, Hardwear, Worldwide Coatings
Key Executives:
Jan Dekker, Managing Director
Education: Masters Degree, Environmental Law, Sydney University; Graduate Diploma, Environmental Studies, Macquarie University
Background: Founding Managing Director, Centre for Energy & Greenhouse Technologies

2614 CLIFFORD CHANCE PUNDER
46 Mainzer Landsrasse
Frankfurt 60325
Germany
Phone: 49-69719901 **Fax:** 49-6971994000
e-mail: daniela.weber-rey@cliffordchance.com
web: www.cliffordchance.com

Venture Capital & Private Equity Firms / International Firms

Mission Statement: Provides advice, technical expertise, and an understanding of the commercial environment in which our clients operate.
Geographic Preference: Americas, Asia, Europe, Middle East
Investment Criteria: All stages
Industry Group Preference: Air Transportation, Automotive, Beverages, Chemicals, Construction, Energy, Pharmaceuticals, Financial Services, Food Services, Healthcare, Restaurants, Household Goods, Insurance, Information Technology, Media
Portfolio Companies: Altria, Safeway plc, Merrill Lynch, Carrefour, China Netcom, Metro Group

Key Executives:
Andreas Dietzel, Regional Managing Partner
Sebastian Maerker, Partner

2615 CLIMATE CHANGE CAPITAL
3 More London Riverside
London SE1 2AQ
United Kingdom
Phone: 44-02073935000 Fax: 44-02079395030

Mission Statement: A pre-eminent European cleantech private equity fund which invests expansion capital in high growth, later stage companies and buy outs in the areas of clean power, clean transport, energy efficiency, waste recovery and water. Our goal is to back exceptional companies that contribute to a lower carbon economy, a more sustainable environment and generate attractive returns for our investors.

Fund Size: £200 million
Average Investment: £10 - 20 million
Minimum Investment: £5 million
Investment Criteria: Later-Stage, Expansion Capital, Buy-Outs
Industry Group Preference: Clean Technology, Power, Transportation, Energy Efficiency, Waste & Recycling, Water
Portfolio Companies: Climate Energy, Enecsys, Enerqos, Metallkraft, Neura, Nualight, Nujira, Orege, Power Plus Communications

Key Executives:
James Cameron, Chairman
Education: BA, University of London; MA, Oxford University
Background: Senior Partner, Graphite Capital

2616 CLOSE BROTHERS EQUITY MARKETS
Close Brothers Group
Neue Mainzer Str. 1
Frankfurt 60311
Germany
Phone: 49-699720040 Fax: 49-6997200415
e-mail: info@closebrothers.de
web: www.dcadvisory.com

Mission Statement: Close Brothers, a Frankfurt based Investment Bank, specializes in providing corporate finance advice for medium sized transactions in Germany and its neighboring countries.

Geographic Preference: Germany
Founded: 1991
Investment Criteria: Medium sized transactions
Portfolio Companies: Klockner Pentaplast, Equivest, Schneidersohne, ELAXY, Elektronik+Kabeltechnik Gmbh & Co., RedDot, Lisi group, PCl Group, FTE, SIG Holding, DIEL

Key Executives:
Stefan Jaecker, Chief Executive
Dr. Wolfgang Kazmierowski, Managing Director

2617 CLOSE BROTHERS PRIVATE EQUITY
Close Brothers Group
2 George Yard
London EC3V 9DH
United Kingdom
Phone: 44-2070651100 Fax: 44-2075886815
e-mail: enquiries@cbpel.com

Mission Statement: Invests in UK management buy-outs.
Geographic Preference: United Kingdom
Fund Size: $780.9 Million
Founded: 1984
Average Investment: $61 Million
Minimum Investment: $11.15 Million
Investment Criteria: Expansion and Development, Bridge finance, Refinancing bank debt, Secondary purchase/replacement capital, Rescue/turnaround, MBO, MBI, Institutional BO, Public-to-Private
Industry Group Preference: Business to Business, Transportation, Manufacturing, Leisure, Tourism, Consumer Services, Logistics
Portfolio Companies: Minova International, V Ships, Allied Glass Containers, Park Resorts, Hillary's Group, IDIS, Walton Garden Buildings, Aqualisa

Key Executives:
Ben Alexander, Investment Director
e-mail: mark.perryman@cbpel.com
Education: CA
Background: Manager, PricewaterhouseCoopers
Ted Bell, Partner
e-mail: richard.lott@cbpel.com
Education: CIMA
Background: 3i Plc, Unilever
Directorships: Aurigny Anglo Group, SP Systems
Iain Slater, Partner
Education: CA, BA(Maths);University of Warwick
Background: Senior Manager, The Cooperative Bank; Manager, KPMG
Directorships: Chance & Hunt, Capital Incentives
Simon Wildig, Partner
e-mail: simon.wildig@cbpel.com
Education: CA, Degree in Accountancy & Finance(Kingston University)
Background: Deloitte & Touche
Directorships: ATC Holdings, Hillarys Blinds
John Snook, Managing Director, Chairman
e-mail: john.snook@cbpel.com
Education: CA
Background: 3i Plc; Cinven; Deloitte Haskins & Sells
Directorships: Founder Director, senior partner,
Nick MacNay, Partner
e-mail: nick.macnay@cbpel.com
Education: MA
Background: Director, Rothschild Ventures; Investment Controller, 3i Plc
Directorships: Corpack Ltd., Chessington Computer Services, Abbseal Ltd.
Neil Murphy, Partner
e-mail: neil.murphy@cbpel.com
Education: Degree from the University of Birmingham
Background: Manager, Norwich Union Venture Capital
Directorships: quoted fund manager, private equity team manager
Sean Dinnen, Partner
e-mail: francesco.santinon@cbpel.com
Education: BACC, ACA
Background: Investment Manager, Clydesdale Bank Equity; Executive, RMD Corporate Finance; Manager, Price Waterhouse
John Fisher, Investment Manager
e-mail: john.fisher@cbpel.com
Education: CA
Background: Corporate Finance, NM Rothschild; Chartered Accountant, Arthur Andersen

Venture Capital & Private Equity Firms / International Firms

2618 CM CAPITAL
Level 8
379 Queen Street
Brisbane
Queensland 4000
Australia
Phone: 61-738382888 Fax: 61-738311256
e-mail: admin@taluventures.com
web: www.cmcapital.com

Mission Statement: CM Capital is a pioneer of the Australian Venture Capital industry and is regarded as one of the market leaders. Our team combines management experience, industry knowledge, technology and financial expertise to help our portfolio companies build upon and transform great ideas into great companies. At CM Capital, we partner with the management teams of innovative companies to help create market leaders in their respective fields.

Average Investment: $500,000 - $8 million
Investment Criteria: Early-Stage
Industry Group Preference: Life Sciences, Telecommunications, Information Technology, Renewable Energy
Portfolio Companies: Alchemia, Dilthium Networks, Altiris Therapeutics, Pharmaxis, Phenomix, Xumii, CathRx, DSpace, Sunshine Heart, Mesaplexx, Mantara, AdGent, Piedmont Pharmaceuticals, Threat Metrix, Ingenero, Datacastle, BCode, Anteo Diagnostics, Osprey Medical, Universal Biosensors

Key Executives:
  Andy Jane, Managing Partner, Life Sciences
  Education: BSc, Electrical Engineering, Cornell University
  Background: Co-Founder, Technology Concepts
  Directorships: Dilthium Networks, Mantara, Ingenero, BCode

2619 COACH & CAPITAL
West Higgins Road 37
Stockholm SE-111
Sweden
Phone: 46-701800800
e-mail: anders@ingestrom.se
web: www.coachandcapital.se

Mission Statement: Coach & Capital is a venture company in Sweden focusing on investing in emerging growth companies in the commercialisation phase. We are very active in the companies we invest. For instance, in addition to active board work, we also have a dedicated Project Leader that works at least one day a week in the company we have invested.

Geographic Preference: Sweden
Founded: 2008
Investment Criteria: Growth-Stage
Industry Group Preference: Information Technology, Telecommunications, Internet, Media, Energy, Environment, Healthcare, Manufacturing
Portfolio Companies: Axiomatics, Biometron, ClimaCheck, Gardio, Idevio, Infrafone, Minimarketsimasys, uTales

Key Executives:
  Anders Ingeström, Partner
  Education: BSc, Economics
  Background: IBM; CEO, Data Routine

2620 COFINEP
26, rue André Pingat
Rheims 51100
France
Phone: 03-51308157 Fax: 33-26833554
web: www.cofinep.fr

Mission Statement: Actively seeking new investments.
Fund Size: Ffr70 million
Founded: 1991
Minimum Investment: Ffr1 million
Investment Criteria: Revenues of more than 3 million Euros
Industry Group Preference: All Sectors Considered
Portfolio Companies: Cedrepa, Champagne Gardet, Malteurop International SA, Sucreries de Berneuil

Key Executives:
  Hans de Breda, CEO
  Yves Besset, director of investment

2621 COLLER CAPITAL LIMITED
33 Cavendish Square
London W1G OTT
United Kingdom
Phone: 44-2076318500 Fax: 44-2076318555
e-mail: Jeremycoller@collercapital.com
web: www.collercapital.com

Mission Statement: Coller Capital is dedicated to the worldwide purchase of secondary interests in venture capital, buyout and mezzanine fund investments.

Geographic Preference: Worldwide
Fund Size: $3.5 Billion
Founded: 1990
Average Investment: $1 million to $1 billion
Investment Criteria: Application of a proven bottom-up valuation methodology, alternative investments held by institutions
Industry Group Preference: Telecommunications, Information Technology, Internet Technology, Technology, Communications
Portfolio Companies: NVP Brightstar, British Telecom, Lucent Technologies, National Westminster Bank, Shell Oil

Key Executives:
  Jeremy Coller, Chief Executive Officer
  e-mail: jordan@collercapital.com
  Background: Chief Executive, Hansing Associates, Europe; Managing Director, Equitable Capital Management Corporation (New York and London); Executive Vice President, International Division, Bayerische Hypotheken und Wechsel-Bank (Munich and New York); Executive Direc
  Jonathon Freeman, Partner
  e-mail: jeremy@collercapital.com
  Education: MA Philosophy from Sussex University. BSc (Hons) Management Sciences from Manchester School of Management, UMIST. Diplome Cours de Civilisation from Sorbonne University.
  Background: Venture Capital and Buyout Manager at ICI Pension Plan; Investment Analyst at Fidelity International. Attended Carmel College
  David Platter, Partner
  e-mail: groen@collercapital.com
  Education: MBA from École des Hautes Études Commerciales (Montreal). Canadian Chartered Accountant. Fluent in English and French.
  Background: Director, Private Equity, for Caisse de Dépot et Placement du Québec
  Stephen Bull, Partner
  e-mail: springett@collercapital.com
  Education: MBA, Stanford Graduate School of Business. Graduate of HEC Paris
  Background: Founder and Chief Executive of Crédit National Group's private equity arm, Financière Saint-Dominique (FSD), and deputy CEO of Crédit National, co-founder of Euro Private Equity Partners.

2622 COLONIAL FIRST STATE PRIVATE EQUITY
Reply Paid 27
Sydney 2000
Australia
Phone: 61-2293033000 Fax: 02-93033200
e-mail: contactus@colonialfirststate.com.au
web: www.colonialfirststate.com.au

Venture Capital & Private Equity Firms / International Firms

Mission Statement: Formerly known as Hambro-Grantham Management, we are committed to funding high growth companies throughout Australia and New Zealand. Colonial First State Private has invested in over 70 companies and assisted them with the implementation of their growth plans.

Geographic Preference: Australia, New Zealand
Fund Size: $300 Million
Founded: 1988
Average Investment: $10 Million
Minimum Investment: $3 Million
Investment Criteria: Early Stage, Late Stage
Industry Group Preference: All Sectors Considered
Portfolio Companies: Agrilink Holdings, Amber Technology, AtCor Medical, Australian Kitchen Industries, Endeavour Healthcare, Integration Management, Mincom Limited, Penrice, Ruthinium Group, SG Fleet Services, Sigtec Pty, Space-Time Research, Speedscan, Technisyst

Key Executives:
 Brian Bissaker, Chief Executive Officer
 e-mail: privateequity@colonialfirststate.com.au
 Education: BE (Hons) MSci (Eng) MBA
 Background: Chief Engineer of the Commonwealth Bank of Australia
 Nicolette Rubinsztein, General Manager, Advocacy and Retirement
 e-mail: privateequity@colonialfirststate.com.au
 Education: Bachelor of Commerce (Honours) degree from the University of Cape Town
 Background: Price Waterhouse and director (and treasurer) of Australian Venture Capital Association Limited (AVCAL)
 Chris Stevens, General Manager Custom Solutions
 e-mail: privateequity@colonialfirststate.com.au
 Education: BSc from University of Sydney, with a major in Mathematics
 Peter Chun, General Manager, Product and Investments
 e-mail: privateequity@colonialfirststate.com.au
 Education: BComm, M.App.Fin, MBA, CPA
 Background: Worked with Australian National Industries Limited Group for 20 years.
 Directorships: Group Secretary
 Geoff Peck, General Manager, Marketing and Distribution
 e-mail: privateequity@colonialfirststate.com.au
 Education: B Acc, CA, ASIA
 Background: Tom had over 5 years experience in Corporate Recovery with Arthur Andersen
 Scott Durbin, General Manager, Strategy
 e-mail: privateequity@colonialfirststate.com.au
 Education: BComm, CA
 Background: Seven years experience at PricewaterhouseCoopers

2623 COMMERCE ASSET VENTURES Sdn Bhd
No. 6, Commerce House
Damansara Heights
Kuala Lumpur 50490
Malaysia

Phone: 60-327325577 Fax: 60-327321343
e-mail: enquiry@commerce-ventures.com.my
web: www.commerce-ventures.com.my

Mission Statement: Consistently generates superior returns by infusing value inputs and growth capital into outstanding business opportunities.

Geographic Preference: Malaysia
Fund Size: $80 Million
Founded: 1980
Average Investment: $23 Million
Minimum Investment: $6.6 Million
Investment Criteria: Business Start-Ups, Small and Medium-Sized Enterprises
Industry Group Preference: Information Technology, Communications, Life Sciences

Portfolio Companies: Dbix Systems, Insyncro, Nasioncom, Nexusedge Technologies, Radiant Range, Vector Holding, Good Way Rubber Industries, Malaysia Steel Works, Flex-P Industries

2624 COMMERZ BETEILIGUNGSGESELLSCHAFT
Commerzbank Ag
Frankfurt 60261
Germany

Phone: 49-6913620 Fax: 49-69285389
e-mail: info@commerzbank.com
web: www.commerzbank.com

Mission Statement: Maintains an on-going flow of communication with investors for successful outcomes.

Geographic Preference: Germany, Asia, USA
Fund Size: $500 Billion
Founded: 1940
Investment Criteria: Seed, Startup, First-Stage, Second-Stage, Mezzanine, Expansion And Development, Mbo, Management Buy-In, Lbo
Industry Group Preference: All Sectors Considered

Key Executives:
 Frank Annuscheit, Chief Operating Officer
 Martin Blessing, Chairman

2625 COMPAGNIE FINANCIERE E DE ROTHSCHILD BANQUE
47 rue Du Faubourg St. Honor
Cedex 08
Paris 75401
France

Phone: 33-140172525 Fax: 33-040172402
web: www.edmond-de-rothschild.fr

Mission Statement: Actively seeking new investments.

Geographic Preference: France, Europe, America, Japan
Fund Size: $357 Million
Average Investment: $89 Million
Minimum Investment: $60 Million
Investment Criteria: High-Growth, Pre-Ipo.
Industry Group Preference: Infrastructure, Applications Software & Services, Multimedia, Information Technology, Telecommunications, E-Commerce & Manufacturing, Manufacturing, Electronic Technology, Food & Beverage, Distribution, Tourism, Media, Environment Products & Services, Life Sciences, Medical
Portfolio Companies: Ceraver Osteal, Hybrigenics, Actelion, Seche/Tredi, Le Figaro, Oenalliance, Sensas, Plasticos, Gespac, Avenir Finance, Tradingcom Europe, Groupe Eurilogic, Make Music, Brainpower, Kaidara.

Key Executives:
 Joel Warschawski, President/CEO
 Victor Sasson, Vice Chairman

2626 COMPANHIA RIOGRANDENSE DE PARTICIPACOES
Soledad Avenue, 550 - Set 1001
8th Floor
Porto Alegre 90010 230
Brazil

Phone: 55-5132110777 Fax: 55-5132110777
e-mail: crp@crp.com.br
web: www.crp.com.br

Mission Statement: Manages venture capital and private equity funds at all stages.

Geographic Preference: Brazil, South America
Founded: 1981
Investment Criteria: Growth Oriented Companies
Industry Group Preference: Technology

Portfolio Companies: 3Di, Ag2, Apyon, Aquamundi, Brasilmobile, Chronos/Checkforte, Conectt, Digilab, Fk-Biotecnologia, Fulano, Gens, Grupos, Gesplan, Hotelbar.Com, Impacto, Nano Endoluminal, Plugar, Ponfac, Teikon, Uni5.Com, 3Di, Ag2, Apyon.

Key Executives:
  Clovis Benoni Meurer, Managing Partner and CEO
  Ricardo Hingel, Director

2627 CONCEPT FINANCIAL SERVICES
Level 10, 365 Little Collins Street
Melbourne 3000
Australia
  Phone: 61-386760581 **Fax:** 61-386760589

Mission Statement: Direct investor using proprietary funds building shareholder wealth and value.

Geographic Preference: Australia
Fund Size: $100 million
Founded: 1991
Average Investment: $10 million
Minimum Investment: $1 million
Investment Criteria: Development & Growth Capital for companies at various stages of maturation
Industry Group Preference: All Sectors Considered

Key Executives:
  Marcus H. Rose, Founder and Principal
  e-mail: mhr@concept.net.au
  Education: MBA, FFin, AREI, FAICD
  Background: Equity Capital and Property Markets, Henty Corporation.
  Directorships: Various

2628 CONCORD VENTURES
85 Medinat Hayehudim St.
4th Floor
PO Box 4011
Harzelia 46140
Israel
  Phone: 972-99602020 **Fax:** 972-99602022
  e-mail: office@concordventures.com

Mission Statement: Invests in early and later-stage companies.

Geographic Preference: Europe, North America, Israel
Fund Size: $260 Million
Founded: 1995
Average Investment: $4.5 Million
Minimum Investment: $100,000
Investment Criteria: Privately-held companies with leading edge technologies that satisfy needs in large and growing markets
Industry Group Preference: Communications, Computer Related, Information Technology, Internet Technology, Life Sciences, Medical & Health Related, Communications, Telecommunications, Applications Software & Services, Internet Technology, Medical, Semiconductors, Software, Infrastructure

Key Executives:
  Yair Safrai, General Partner
  e-mail: avi@concordventures.com
  Education: B.Sc. in Electrical Engineering from the Technion Institute of Technology and a M.Sc. in Business Management from the Boston/Ben Gurion joint program.
  Background: Founded and served as CEO of Seabridge Ltd., Senior Director at ECI Telecom
  Directorships: Focuses on the Data and Telecommunications sector.
  Matty Karp, Managing Partner
  e-mail: matty@concordventures.com
  Education: B.Sc. cum laude in Electrical Engineering from the Technion Institute of Technology and is a graduate of the Harvard Business School Advanced Management Program.
  Background: CEO of the Nitzanim Venture Fund and CEO of Kardan Technologies, Matty spent fifteen years at Elbit Computers Ltd. Matty served as jet fighter pilot in the Israeli Air Force.
  Yaron Rosenboim, General Partner and CFO
  e-mail: shai@concordventures.com
  Education: B.Sc. in Computer Science from the University of Maryland and an MBA in marketing and financial management from the University of Maryland
  Background: President & CEO of Emblaze Systems, Vice President at Comverse Technology, Co-founder and Vice President of Coni Communication
  Directorships: Focuses on information technology with a specialization in wireless and cellular networks.

2629 CONNECT VENTURES
Unit 11, Zeus House
16-30 Provost Street
London N1 7NG
United Kingdom
  web: www.connectventures.co.uk

Mission Statement: Connect Ventures is a venture capital firm investing in early stage Internet and mobile businesses. We're based in London and invest throughout Europe. We take a hands-on approach to investing by helping founders grow their startups into companies and provide our expertise on product, marketing, and financing strategy. As a small and focused fund, we are able to move quickly and give our portfolio companies the time and attention they deserve.

Geographic Preference: Europe
Average Investment: £200,000 - 1 million
Investment Criteria: Seed-Stage, Early-Stage
Industry Group Preference: Mobile, Internet, Digital Media & Marketing
Portfolio Companies: Citymapper, Ondango, Secret Sales, Space Ape Games, Teleportd, Urli.st, YourGrind

Key Executives:
  Pietro Bezza, Managing Partner
  Background: Founder, Neo Network
  Bill Earner, Managing Partner
  Education: BS, Engineering, Harvey Mudd College; MBA, London Business School
  Background: Investment Manager, Amadeus Capital Partners
  Sitar Teli, Managing Partner
  Education: Mechanical Engineering & Economics, Duke University
  Background: Investment Manager, Doughty Hanson Technology Ventures; Jefferies

2630 CONOR VENTURE PARTNERS OY
Innopoli 2
Tekniikantie 14
FI-02150 Espoo
Finland
  Fax: +358 9 812 7305
  e-mail: jari@conor.vc
  web: www.conor.vc

Mission Statement: Our mission is to spot the brightest enabling technologies and help in turning them into global winners. We believe in building businesses that grow and succeed as leaders in their categories. We value niche solutions for a specific gloval market over more general offerings with limited geographical reach. Our approach is best suited for ambitious entrepreneurs with a global mindset. As opposed to building references in neighborhoods close by, we will push you to go directly to the ideal customers, wherever in the world they are.

Geographic Preference: Nordic, Baltic
Founded: 2005
Minimum Investment: $500,000
Investment Criteria: Early Stage

Venture Capital & Private Equity Firms / International Firms

Industry Group Preference: ICT, Electronics, Embedded Systems, New Materials, Optics
Portfolio Companies: Aito Technologies, AnaCatum, BehavioSec, Crystalsol, Eniram, Fits.me, Imbera Electronics, Neo Technology, Omegawave, Plexpress, Scint-X, Scoopshot, Sensinode, Sticky, Supponor Systems, TactoTek

Other Locations:
Birger Jarlsgatan 2
SE-114 34 Stockholm
Sweden

Key Executives:
Jari Mieskonen, Managing Partner
+358 50 563 6992
e-mail: jari@conor.vc
Background: Founding Partner, Eqvitec Partners; Investment Director, Sitra
Manu Mäkelä, Partner
+358 400 442 873
e-mail: manu@conor.vc
Background: Investment Director, Holtron Ventures; Investment Director, Eqvitec Partners
Jarkko Penttilä, Partner
+358 50 516 6420
e-mail: jarkko@conor.vc
Background: Partner, Eqvitec; Manager, Ericsson Business Innovations
Chris Barchak, Partner
+44 7852 333 965
e-mail: chris@conor.vc
Background: Principal, Fidelity Growth Partners Europe; Associate, Index Ventures

2631 CONTINENTAL VENTURE CAPITAL LIMITED
Level 42, Suncorp Place, 259 George Street
Sydney 2000
Australia

Phone: 61-290878000 Fax: 61-290878088
e-mail: cvc@cvc.com.au
web: www.cvc.com.au

Mission Statement: Seeks investment opportunities in predominantly established, profitable, high growth companies across all industry sectors.
Geographic Preference: Australia
Fund Size: $130 Million
Founded: 1984
Average Investment: $1 Million - $5 Million
Minimum Investment: $.5 Million
Investment Criteria: Funding at all stages and for all sectors
Industry Group Preference: Renewable Energy, Biotechnology, Medical & Health Related, Property Management, Information Technology, Technology
Portfolio Companies: CVC Sustainable, CVC Private Equity

Key Executives:
Jason Ters, Non-Executive Director
Education: Bachelor of Commerce from the University of New South Wales.
Background: He was General Manager of Pacific Communications Holdings Limited from January 1997 until May 1998AND With Tetley Medical Limited.As managing director of an ASX listed environmental waste processing company
Directorships: Chief Executive Officer of CVC Limited and he is also a Director of Greens Foods Limited, Pro-Pac Group Limited, CVC Sustainable Investments Limited and CVC Investment Manager
Alexander Beard, Chief Executive Officer
Education: Bachelor of Commerce in Accountancy and Master of Commerce in Accounting and Financial Management (UNSW);
Background: Worked Chartered Accountant for Greenwood Challoner.Established Gould Ralph and Company in 1976

Directorships: Chairman of the listed public company Macarthur National Limited

2632 CONVEXA Tyveholmen AS
Tjuvholmen Alle 19
Oslo N-0252
Norway

Phone: 47-22-39-8900
e-mail: post@convexa.com
web: www.convexa.no

Mission Statement: Convexa is a leading Norwegian venture capital company investing in technology companies in various areas. We invest in early-stage/growth technology companies that promise to deliver high growth and exceptional returns. We seek companies which have developed breakthrough technologies. Convexa focuses on accelerating these technology companies to international markets. We bring first-class competence and high energy level in combining broad strategic and deep operational insights, business development skills, private and public financing and exit capabilities, and a broad network to talented entrepreneurs in growth companies. We strive to be a superior partner to build leading companies.

Geographic Preference: United States, Europe
Founded: 2000
Investment Criteria: Early-Stage, Growth Stage
Industry Group Preference: Technology, Consumer Internet, Enabling Software, Cloud Computing, Wireless, Telecommunications, Oil & Gas, Materials Technology
Portfolio Companies: Conflucence Solar, Innova Light, Solar Implant Techn9logies, Wirescan, Nordic Energy Services, Wellbore Solutions, Brogea, OnTime Networks, Axxessit, Metamerge, Apptix, Consorte, TeleComputing

2633 CORE PACIFIC - YAMAICHI CAPITAL LIMITED Core Pacific Securities Company Ltd
36th Floor, Cosco Tower
Grand Millennium Plaza
183 Queen's Road
Central
Hong Kong

Phone: 852-21663888 Fax: 852-29180409
e-mail: info@cpy.com.hk
web: www.cpy.com.hk

Mission Statement: Provides a broad range of investment banking services to the region
Geographic Preference: Beijing, Los Angeles, Shanghai, Shenzhen, Taipei
Fund Size: $128 Million
Founded: 1992
Industry Group Preference: Corporate Services, Technology, Communications, Biotechnology, Industrial Services, Media
Portfolio Companies: Core Pacific Group, Yuanta Financial Group, Chang Hwa Bank, Nanjing Sample Technology Co. Ltd., Sjtu Sunway Software Industry Ltd., Technologies Co. Ltd., Shaanxi Northwest New Technology Industry Co. Ltd., Powerleader Science & Technology Ltd.

Key Executives:
Mr. Shen Qingjing, Chairman
Education: Graduated from National Chung-Hsing University, Master of Science from University of Southern California U.S.A., Doctor degree in University of La Verne, MBA..
Background: Director of Global Securities Finance Corporation, Chung Hsing Bills Finance Company, Central Investment Holding Company & Jen Hwa Investment Holding Company throughout the years.
Mr. Chen Qisheng, Chief Executive Officer

2634 CORVINUS NEMZETKOZI BEFEKTETESI RT Corvinus International Investment Ltd.

Fehérvári út 24. IV/1
Budapest 1117
Hungary

Phone: 36-17890575 Fax: 36-17002627
e-mail: ps@ps.hu
web: www.siteset.hu

Mission Statement: Inests in Hungarian companies abroad and equipped to ensure sufficient financial resources for its partners' investment projects.

Geographic Preference: Hungary
Founded: 1997
Average Investment: $0.28 Million
Minimum Investment: $0.10 Million
Investment Criteria: Facilitates foreign investments by creating, acquiring and developing ventures abroad
Industry Group Preference: All Sectors Considered

Key Executives:
Zoltán Lex, Chairman
e-mail: info@corvinus.hu
Viktor Katona, Director

2635 COVENT INDUSTRIAL CAPITAL INVESTMENT COMPANY

27 Maros U
Budapest H-1122
Hungary

Phone: 36-13552493 Fax: 36-12022381

Mission Statement: Focuses on the rehabilitation of industrial real estate and park development.

Geographic Preference: Hungry
Fund Size: $2.9 Million
Founded: 1993
Investment Criteria: Early Stage, Turnaround
Industry Group Preference: Real Estate, Property Management, Marketing, Legal, Industrial Services
Portfolio Companies: Bicske-M1 Industrial Park And Logistic Centre, Ozd Industrial Park, Vivien Mineral Water And Beverage Company Ltd.

Key Executives:
János Antal Bolyky, Chief Executive Officer
Györgyi Bereczkei, Head of Secretariat

2636 CRB INVERBIO

Almagro 1
1 Dcha
Madrid 28010
Spain

Phone: 34-914467897 Fax: 34-917021018
e-mail: info@crbinverbio.com
web: www.crbinverbio.com

Mission Statement: Cross Road Biotech Inversiones Biotecnologicas is a venture capital management firm. CRB Inverbío manages venture capital firms that invest in the development of seed stage companies in life sciences that address unmet medical needs and have the potential to grow into successful businesses. To that end, the company selects innovative projects led by prestigious scientists and entrepreneurs, providing financing, management support and strategic advice.

Geographic Preference: Spain
Investment Criteria: Seed Stage
Industry Group Preference: Life Sciences, Biotechnology

Key Executives:
Enrique Castellon, President
Education: Universidad Complutense de Madrid
Background: Secretary of State, Spanish Ministry of Health & Consumer Affairs; Executive President, Spanish Drug Agency; CEO, Galician Health Service

2637 CREANDUM

Jakobsbergsgatan 18
Stockholm 103 86
Sweden

Phone: +46 8 524 636 30
web: www.creandum.com

Mission Statement: We help our investments with recruiting, advisory boards, office spaces and all sorts of great leads to help them build and grow their businesses. Our network covers the globe, which leaves us with the possibility of helping our investments with pretty much everything.

Industry Group Preference: Consumer Hardware, Consumer Software, Hardware, Software
Portfolio Companies: PlayRaven, Vivino, Spotify, Brisk.io, Autobutler, Edgeware, Appear TV, 13th Lab, Xeneta, Aito Technologies, Itslearning, Cint, Wrapp, Linas Matkasse, VideoPlaza, Nonstop Games, Jays, Tripbirds, iZettle, JustBook, TrustWeaver, Xtract, Norstel, Mitrionics, IPtronics

Other Locations:
470 Ramona St.
Palo Alto, CA 94301

Key Executives:
Erik Olofsson, Investment Team
e-mail: erik.olofsson@creandum.com
Education: M.S.c, Industrial Engineering, Linkoping Institute of Technology; MBA, Harvard Business School
Background: CEO, Fakturino; Founder, Klipster
Lasse Pilgaard, Investment Team
Education: M.S.c, Economics, Aarhus University
Joel Eriksson Enquist, Investment Team
e-mail: joel.eriksson@creandum.com
Education: M.S.c, Industrial Engineering, Chalmers School of Entrepreneurship
Daniel Blomquist, Investment Team
e-mail: daniel.blomquist@creandum.com
Education: M.S.c, Industrial Engineering and Management, Linkoping Institute of Technology; MBA, Stockholm School of Economics

2638 CREATHOR VENTURE

Marienbader Platz 1
Bad Hamburg 61348
Germany

Phone: 49-6172139720 Fax: 49-61721397229
web: www.creathor.de

Mission Statement: We are looking for entrepreneurs who address new markets and have the potential to turn their company into a global market leader. Decisiveness and speed of building your business is important to us. We invest in all venture capital situations, with our primary focus on seed and startup phases. As a lead investor we support our portfolio companies through active mentoring during all stages of development, including further financing rounds as well as trade sales or IPOs. We utilize our experience at building companies and developing them on an international scale. We also tap into our global industry, scientific and financial networks for the benefit of our portfolio companies.

Geographic Preference: Europe
Fund Size: 150 million Euro
Founded: 1984
Average Investment: 10 million Euro
Investment Criteria: Seed-Stage, Startup
Industry Group Preference: High Technology, Telecommunications, Information Technology, Internet, Media, Life Sciences, Nanotechnology, New Materials, Electronics, Clean Technology
Portfolio Companies: Accovion, Alrise Biosystems, Caprotec, Cevec, Cloud Control, Cube Biotech, Donato, Dedendo, Hojoki, ITN Nanovation, Insited, Joiz, Kigo, Mobiles Republic, Net Biscuits, Phenex, Purmeo, Room Beats, Shopgate, Sirion Biotech, Sivdon Diagnostics,

Venture Capital & Private Equity Firms / International Firms

Sofialys, Stylefruits.de, Tellja, Viewster, Wired Minds, Zadego, Zimory

Key Executives:
Gert Kohler, Chief Executive Officer
Education: Master degree in Mathematics, Physics, Operational Research & Business Administration, PhD, Mathematics
Background: Managing Director, Herbert Quandt Group; Founder, Technologieholding

2639 CRESCENDO VENTURE MANAGEMENT LLC
600 Hansen Way
Mayfair
Palo Alto, CA 94304

Phone: 001-6504701200 Fax: 001-6504701201
e-mail: investorservices@crescendoventures.com
web: www.crescendoventures.com

Mission Statement: The mission of being the best venture partner for emerging communication and enterprise infrastructure companies.

Geographic Preference: Europe, America
Founded: 1993
Investment Criteria: Early-stage funding and growth resources to high-potential companies.
Industry Group Preference: Software, Communications, Computer Related, Electronic Technology
Portfolio Companies: airBand Communications, Arteris, bDNA, Broadsoft, Cognima, Compellent Technologies, CoreOptics, Dust Networks, eSilicon Corporation, Lumenaré Networks.

Key Executives:
David Spreng, Managing General Partner
e-mail: dspreng@crescendoventures.com
Education: Graduate from University of Minnesota with a degree in Accounting
Background: IAI Ventures, Investment Advisers, Inc., Salomon Brothers, Dain Bosworth,
John Borchers, General Partner

2640 CROSBY ASSET MANAGEMENT
Unit 502, 5th Floor, AXA Centre
151 Gloucestor Road
Wan Chai
Hong Kong

Phone: 85-234762700 Fax: 852-21690008
web: www.crosbycapitallimited.com

Mission Statement: A leading independent investment banking and asset management firm in Asia.

Geographic Preference: Asia, Middle East, Europe
Fund Size: $600 Million
Founded: 2007
Investment Criteria: Expansion & Development
Industry Group Preference: Telecommunications, Natural Resources, Oil & Gas, Imports/Exports

Key Executives:
Clive Ng Cheang Neng, Chairman and Executive Director
e-mail: info@crosby.com
Background: British Foreign Service and Treasury, Chairman of Lloyds Bank Group, Worked with Hong Kong Government (Securities & Futures Commission), Nomura Asia Holdings, Techpacific Capital Ltd, International Securities Consultancy Ltd.
Liu Guang He, Executive Director

2641 CROSBY CAPITAL LIMITED
Unit 502, 5th Floor, AXA Centre
151 Gloucestor Road
Wan Chai
Hong Kong

Phone: 852-34762700 Fax: 852-21690008
web: www.crosbycapitallimited.com

Mission Statement: Asia's premier independent corporate finance and investment banking firm.

Geographic Preference: Hong Kong
Fund Size: $350 Million
Founded: 2007
Average Investment: $24 Million
Investment Criteria: Private equity firms, buy-out funds and corporate and institutional investors
Industry Group Preference: Banking

Key Executives:
Clive Ng Cheang Neng, Chairman and Executive Director
Background: Managing Director of Nomura International Plc, member of Nomura's European Board of Directors, Credit Suisse First Boston in London as its Managing Director of convertible Eurobonds at Yamaichi International (Europe) Ltd

2642 CSL INVESTMENT & FINANCE
Somkid Place, 6 Soi Somkid
Bangkok 10330
Thailand

Phone: 66-2-650-3172-4 Fax: 66-2-650-3175
web: www.csl.cc

Mission Statement: Advisors in Asia for venture capital, project finance, real estate investment funds, energy finance and privatization.

Key Executives:
Jonathan Price, Chief Executive Officer
66-265031724

2643 CVC ASIA PACIFIC LIMITED CVC Capital Partners
Suite 901-3, ICBC Tower
Citibank Plaza ICBI Tower
3 Garden Road
Central
Hong Kong

Phone: 852-35186360 Fax: 852-35186380

Mission Statement: CVC Asia Pacific is an investment and advisory company focusing on buy-out opportunities in the Asia Pacific Region.

Geographic Preference: Asia Pacific region
Fund Size: $50 Billion
Founded: 1999
Investment Criteria: Buy-outs
Industry Group Preference: Manufacturing, Construction, Food & Beverage, Chemicals, Automotive
Portfolio Companies: Pacific Brands, Haitai Confectionery and Foods

Key Executives:
Srdjan Dangubic, Investment Director, Pan Asia Team
Education: Bachelors from Monash University, Business Degree from the University of Newcastle, Australia, MBA from Stanford University
Background: Inchcape Plc, Fosters Brewing Group and Elders Investments, McKinsey & Company,
William Ho, Managing Director

Venture Capital & Private Equity Firms / International Firms

2644 CVC CAPITAL PARTNERS LTD
111 Strand
London WC2R 0AG
United Kingdom

Phone: 44-2074204200 Fax: 44-2074204231
web: www.cvc.com

Mission Statement: An independent investment and advisory company dedicated to European Private Equity.

Geographic Preference: United Kingdom, Asia, Western Europe
Fund Size: $18 Billion
Founded: 1981
Average Investment: $28 Billion
Minimum Investment: $180 Million
Investment Criteria: Focuses on companies in market-leading positions, with strong, motivated management teams
Industry Group Preference: Construction, Manufacturing, Food & Beverage, Chemicals, Automotive
Portfolio Companies: Acordis, Amatek, BSN Glasspack, Bols Royal Distilleries, Cartiere del Garda, Colomer Group, Dorna Promocion del Deporte, Dutton-Forshaw, Hozelock, Invensys Sealing Systems, Kappa Packaging, Parisa Group, Synstar International, Wavin, William Hill

Key Executives:
Jonathan Feuer, Managing Partner - Co-Head of UK Investments
e-mail: info@cvceurope.com
Education: BA Degree in Business Administration from Yonsei University in Korea.
Background: McKinsey & Company in Seoul.
Rob Lucas, Managing Partner - Co-Head of UK Investments
e-mail: cvc@cvcltd.com.au
Education: CA
Background: Solution 6 Holdings Limited and Star City Holdings Limited, Mobile Innovations Limited, G-Tek Limited,
Richard Blackburn, Director
e-mail: info@cvceurope.com
Education: Degree in English from Pennsylvania State University, Masters in International Management, American Graduate School of International Management
Background: VP/Credit Officer/Operations Head, Citibank AG, Foreign Service Officer, US State Department
Julia Agafonova Director, Fund Administration
e-mail: info@cvceurope.com
Education: MA, Economics, Columbia University, LLM, University of Utrecht, Holland
Background: Citicorp Corporate Finance
Nick Archer Partner, Fund Administration
e-mail: info@cvceurope.com
Education: Commercial Engineering, Catholic University of Louvain, AMP from Insead.
Background: BBL in Brussels, investment banking department
Marc Boughton, Managing Partner
e-mail: info@cvceurope.com
Education: BA, Middlebury College
Background: Citibank Mezzanine Finance
Graham Brooke, Managing Director
e-mail: info@cvceurope.com
Education: Masters Degree in Economics, Erasmus University, Rotterdam, CA
Background: CVC's European Business.
Directorships: Chief Investment Officer
Tony Clamp, Director
e-mail: info@cvceurope.com
Education: MBA, New York University
Background: Steniel Manufacturing, Asia Printers Group, and Yellow Pages Singapore. Previously, Mr. King headed Citicorp's Taiwan.
Calum Conway, Legal Counsel
e-mail: info@cvceurope.com
Education: BA in Economics, University of Stirling, Scotland
Background: Citigroup, M.D. of Citigroup China Investment Management Limited
Benjamin Edgar, Managing Director, London
e-mail: info@cvceurope.com
Education: BA from Duke University, MBA, University of California, Los Angeles
Background: Citicorp Investment Management Group; Citibank Mezzanine Finance Group
Iain Parham, Managing Partner, London
e-mail: info@cvceurope.com
Education: Degree in Economics, Manchester University, CA
Background: CIN Venture Managers, City Office of 3i Plc.
Donald Mackenzie, Co-Founder and Co-Chairman
e-mail: info@cvceurope.com
Education: LLB, University of Dundee, Scotland, CA
Background: Investment Director, 3i Plc, Deloitte Haskins & Sells
Alex Fotakidis, Senior Managing Director
e-mail: info@cvceurope.com
Education: MBA, Stockholm School of Economics
Background: Senior Partner of BPEP Internationa, Chairman of MphasiS BFL Limitedco
Sebastian Künne, Investment Director
e-mail: info@cvceurope.com
Education: PhD in Economics from University of Vienna
Background: CEO, Helarb Management SA; B Metzler Seel Sohn & Company; Co-Headed, M&A and Corporate Finance

2645 CVC INVESTMENT MANAGERS LIMITED
259 George Street
AAP Centre
Level 42
Sydney NSW 2000
Australia

Phone: 61-290878000 Fax: 61-290878088
e-mail: lmacklin@cvc.com.au
web: www.cvc.com.au

Mission Statement: CVC Limited is one of the pioneering venture capital firms in Australia and has evolved to be a significant player in the private equity market.

Geographic Preference: Australia
Founded: 1984
Average Investment: $10 Million
Minimum Investment: $1 Million
Investment Criteria: Start-up through expansion, mezzanine, mature.
Industry Group Preference: Environmental Protection, Bio Materials, Environment Products & Services, Transportation, Energy, Packaging
Portfolio Companies: PRO-PAC Packaging, Wind Corporation Australia, Traffic Technologies, Soilwise, Plantic Technologies, Biodiesel Producers.

2646 CYBERAGENT VENTURES
6-1 Shinjuku Sumitomo Building 25F
Shinjuku-ku, Nishi 2-chome
Minato-ku
Tokyo 163-0225
Japan

Phone: 81-359095536 Fax: 81-3-5772-1233
web: www.cyberagentventures.com

Mission Statement: Our main aim is to be a specialist in the internet-mobile business fields and find/develop start-up companies that are expected to prosper further. We play a role as a partner of a start-up company to which we invest money. We not only provide money but also support its development and

855

Venture Capital & Private Equity Firms / International Firms

management providing management know-hows necessary for the company to succeed.
Geographic Preference: China, Taiwan, Vietnam, Indonesia, United States
Fund Size: 360 million yen
Founded: 2006
Investment Criteria: Early-Stage
Industry Group Preference: Internet
Portfolio Companies: Revolver, Piece of Cake, A-Star, Tunnel, Best Teacher, Imonomi, CrowdWorks, Qrunch, Zawatt, Kaditt, Retty, FrogApps, Samurai International, Mind Palette Co., ONEofTHEM, Insight Plus, GCLOUD, KAYAC, Bank of Innovation, Fringe81, Sparcyz, Realworld.co, PhotoCreate, SANSAN, Valuedesign, Fillmore Advisory, Smile Maker, Pankaku
Key Executives:
   Soichi Tajima, President
   Education: Osaka University
   Background: Unoh, Synergy Marketing, Full Speed, CROOZ, VECTOR

2647 CYBERSTARTS
Mikhmoret, HaMerkaz
Israel
web: cyberstarts.com

Mission Statement: Aims to support entrepreneurs who are focused on identifying and solving cybersecurity problems.
Fund Size: $50 Million
Investment Criteria: Cybersecurity
Industry Group Preference: Cybersecurity
Key Executives:
   Gili Raanan, Founder/General Partner
   Education: BA, Computer Science, Tel Aviv University; MBA, Recanati School, Tel Aviv University
   Background: Sanctum; AppScan; NLayers; Sequoia Capital Israel

2648 CZECH VENTURE PARTNERS SRO K+
Venture Partners B.V.
Opletalova 41/1683
Praha 113 32
Czech Republic
Phone: 420-556701900 **Fax:** 420-556709123
web: cvp.czechtrade.us

Mission Statement: Czech Venture Partners is an investment advisory company that manages venture capital funds in the Czech Republic.
Geographic Preference: Czech Republic
Fund Size: $12.67 Million
Founded: 1999
Average Investment: $ 2.26 Million
Minimum Investment: $ 0.95 Million
Investment Criteria: Private Small and Medium-sized enterprises
Industry Group Preference: Manufacturing, Services
Portfolio Companies: Health and Fitness Central Europe (HFCE), Finance New Europe, AMTEX Radiátory

2649 DAHER CAPITAL
Arab Bank Building, 2nd Flor
Riad el Solh Street
Beirut Central District
Lebanon
web: www.dahercapital.com

Mission Statement: Daher Capital is a Beirut-based family office that was founded and is led by Michel Daher, a veteran entrepreneur with over 30 years of experience across several sectors including financial services, manufacturing, distribution and agriculture.
Founded: 2003
Industry Group Preference: Financial Services, Manufacturing, Distribution, Agriculture
Portfolio Companies: Big Frame. Bonds.com, Browz, Burstly, Chownow, DataSift, Digital Air Strike, Divshot, Eagle Crest Energy Company, FXCM, Grubwithus, Maker, Master, Master Capital Group, Momentfeed, Poppins, SteelHouse, Stonegate Mortgage, Text+, Tradesy, TrueCar, Victor, YieldMetrics
Key Executives:
   Michel Draher, Founder
   Background: Founder, Master Global Assets
   Directorships: Victor IB Holdings

2650 DAIMLERCHRYSLER VENTURE GmbH
DaimlerChrysler AG
Mercedesstrasse 137
Stuttgart 70327
Germany
Phone: 49-711170 **Fax:** 49-7111722244
e-mail: dialog@daimler.com
web: www.daimler.com

Mission Statement: Actively seeking new investments.
Geographic Preference: Germany, USA
Fund Size: $42.87 Billion
Investment Criteria: Early Stage, Expansion & Development Capital, Seed Capital, Start-up Capital, Bridge
Industry Group Preference: Communications, Electronic Technology, High Technology, Internet Technology, Information Technology, Transportation
Key Executives:
   Dieter Zetsche, Chairman
   Background: Board Member of Mercedes-Benz, EUCLID Inc., Daimler-Benz AG, Daimler-Benz Aerospace AG.
   Dr. Christine Hohmann-Dennhardt, Integrity and Legal Affairs

2651 DANSK KAPITALANLAEG A/S
Havnegade 39
PO Box 1080
Copenhagen K 1058
Denmark
Phone: 45-77993250 **Fax:** 45-33369444

Mission Statement: Actively seeking new investments.
Geographic Preference: Denmark
Fund Size: $240 Million
Founded: 1984
Average Investment: EUR 5-35 million
Investment Criteria: Start-up, Expansion and Development, Long-term Capital Growth, MBO, Replacement, Turnaround, Restructuring
Portfolio Companies: 7-Technologies, A2SEA, ACADIA Pharmaceuticals, Inc., Accent Equity 2003 Ltd, Active Sportswear International, Agramkow Fluid Systems, Arpida AG, Baltic Rim Fund Ltd., Bison, CAT Forsknings-og Teknologipark
Key Executives:
   Jesper Johansen, Partner
   Lars Dybkjær, Partner
   Arne J Gillin, Vice President
   e-mail: dankap@dankap.dk
   Education: Master of Science, Copenhagen Commercial College
   Background: Revision/KPMG C.Jespersen, Vølund A/S., Display Systems Biotech A/S, Innovision A/S.
   Peter B Kristensen, Investment Manager
   e-mail: dankap@dankap.dk
   Background: KPMG C.Jespersen, Combio A/S, Sophion Bioscience A/S, Structural Bioinformatics, Inc., Torsana Diabetes Diagnostics A/S.

Venture Capital & Private Equity Firms / International Firms

2652 DB CAPITAL PARTNERS (ASIA)
Deutsche Bank AG
Taunusanlage 12
Frankfurt am Main 60325
Germany

Phone: 49-6991000 Fax: 49-6991034225
web: www.db.com

Mission Statement: A private equity investment group of Deutsche Bank which targets growth capital investments and buyouts in technology, telecommunications and new media, as well as consumer products and industrial companies.

Geographic Preference: Asia Pacific region, Central and Eastern Europe, and Latin America
Fund Size: $1.5 billion
Investment Criteria: Buy-outs
Industry Group Preference: Telecommunications, Technology, Consumer Products, Industrial Services
Portfolio Companies: Displaytech, eTime Capital, Exult, GlobalSight, iLumin Corporation, Paradigm4, PC On Call

Key Executives:
Jürgen Fitschen, Co-Chairman
Stefan Krause, Chief Financial Officer

2653 DEFI GESTION SA Banque Cantonale Vaudoise
Bd de Grancy 1
Lausanne CH-1006
Switzerland

Phone: 41-216143444 Fax: 41-216143445

Mission Statement: Focuses on financing start-up companies within Initiative Capital SA.

Geographic Preference: Europe, France, Italy, Germany, Switzerland
Fund Size: CHF 115 million
Founded: 1990
Investment Criteria: Seed, Start-up, Expansion, Buyout.
Industry Group Preference: Electronic Technology, Services, Logistics, Automotive, Transportation, Distribution
Portfolio Companies: France Hélices SA, Bartech System Corp, Financière Fouquet II, Came Automatismes, Actar International SA, Groupe Emera SA, Vanguard A.G., Stradeblu Srl, Financière C.T. (Captain Tortue).

Key Executives:
Mohammed Diab, Managing Director and Partner
e-mail: mdiab@definvest.com
Education: Engineer EPFL, MBA Laussane University
Background: Private Equity
Claude Suard, CFO and Partner

2654 DELTA PARTNERS Delta Partners FZ-LLC
Media One, Level 29
PO Box 502428
Dubai Media City
India

Phone: 971-43692999 Fax: 971-43688408
e-mail: info@deltapartnersgroup.com
web: www.deltapartnersgroup.com

Mission Statement: Delta Partners is the leading Management Advisory and Investment Firm specialized in Telecoms, Media, and Technology within the Middle East, Africa, Eastern Europe, Emerging Asia and Latin America. Through our different businesses lines, we partner with C-level clients within telecom operators, vendors, and other TMT players to help them address their most challenging strategic issues in a fast-growing and liberalizing market environment.

Geographic Preference: Middle East, Africa, Eastern Europe, Asia, Latin America
Average Investment: $25 - $75 million
Investment Criteria: Growth-Stage
Industry Group Preference: Telecommunications, Media

Portfolio Companies: Aricent, Armenian Datacom Company, Karoui&Karoui World, Mobiserve, Vigin Connect, Vox Spectrum

Key Executives:
Javier Alvarez, Managing Partner
Education: BBA, BS, Psychology, MBA, IESE Business School
Background: Senior Principal, DiamondCluster

2655 DELTA VENTURES LIMITED
PO Box 163
PO Box 4033
Kibutz Glil Yam 46905
Israel

Phone: 972-99517755 Fax: 972-99517799
web: www.delta-ventures.com

Mission Statement: The fund investment focus on information technology that provide business solutions, internet infrastructure, and telecommunications.

Fund Size: $65 Million
Founded: 1999
Average Investment: $1-$3 million
Minimum Investment: $1 million
Investment Criteria: Seed, First or Second round
Industry Group Preference: Communications, Data Communications, Wireless Technologies, Information Technology, Internet Technology, Medical Devices, Software
Portfolio Companies: Appilog, BroadLight, Chiaro Networks, ClickFox, E4X, G.I. View, Medigus, MonaLiza, OpTun's, Provigent, Resolute

Key Executives:
Mark Chais, Managing Partner & Co-Founder
e-mail: ofer@delta-ventures.com
Education: BA, Business Administration & Economics, Haifa University
Background: Combat Pilot, Israeli Air Force; President, JACADA; Management, Western Systems
Ben Harel, Managing Partner & Co-Founder
e-mail: ben@delta-ventures.com
Education: BSc, Chemistry & Biology, Louisanna College; MBA, Management, Keller Graduate School
Background: Founder, Interlogic; CEO, Konami
Directorships: TDNet; Provigent; Resolute; MonaLiza Medical

2656 DEMETER PARTNERS
7-9 Rue de la Boetie
75008 Paris
France

Phone: +33 1 43 12 53 33 Fax: +33 1 43 12 53 30
e-mail: contact@demeter-partners.com
web: demeter-partners.com/en

Mission Statement: Demeter Partners positions itself as the largest Private Equity managemetn company devoted to "green" investments in Europe. Because of its sector positioning, it takes into account the concept of Sustainable Development within its investments and this for all the funds it manages. It selects companies based on the filter sector of eco-energy and environmental industries, companies whose business is to improve the protection of the environment, to save energy and to reduce greenhouse gas emissions.

Geographic Preference: Europe, France
Founded: 2005
Investment Criteria: Expansion Capital
Industry Group Preference: Eco-Industries, Eco-Energies, Energy Efficiency, Renewal Energy, Site Remediation, Water, Waste & Recycling

Other Locations:
C/ Jose Abascal 52 2izda
28003 Madrid

Venture Capital & Private Equity Firms / International Firms

Spain
Phone: +34 915 639 704 Fax: +34 915 619 506

Kurfurstendamm 58
10707 Berlin
Germany
Phone: +49 30 890 68 296-8 Fax: +49 30 890 68 296-1

Key Executives:
Sophie Paturle-Guesnerot, Partner
Education: Masters, Political Science, Insitut d'Etudes Politiques de Paris
Stephane Villecroze, Partner
Education: Charter Engineer, Ecole Polytechnique and Ecole des Ponts et Chaussees
Lionel Cormier, Partner

2657 DERBYSHIRE FIRST INVESTMENTS LIMITED
Bridge House, Riverside Village, Hady Hill
Chesterfield
Derbyshire S41 0DT
United Kingdom
Phone: 44-1246207390 Fax: 44-1246221080

Mission Statement: DFI has undertaken economic development and inward investment promotional activity for Derbyshire County Council.
Geographic Preference: East Midlands, Derbyshire
Fund Size: $4 Million
Founded: 1987
Average Investment: £50,000 to £250,000
Minimum Investment: $ 0.09 Million
Investment Criteria: Invests in Start-up Businesses with Established Profitability and Good Growth Prospects
Industry Group Preference: All Sectors Considered
Portfolio Companies: Advanced Composite Group, Bespoke Furniture Ltd., Cobb Slater Ltd., Peter Geeson Ltd.

Key Executives:
David Bookbinder, Chairman
e-mail: info@dfil.co.uk
Background: China Britain Investments Limited
Melvyn Faulkner, Director

2658 DEUTSCHE ASSET & WEALTH MANAGEMENT
Elsa-Brändström-Str. 10-12
Cologne 50668
Germany
Phone: 49-8954908580 Fax: 49-895-49085845
e-mail: dbpe-info@db.com
web: www.dbpe.com

Mission Statement: As a fund-of-funds manager, provides individuals and institutional investors access to the highest performing partnerships in the private equity sector.
Geographic Preference: USA, Europe
Founded: 1991
Investment Criteria: All Stages
Industry Group Preference: All Sectors Considered
Portfolio Companies: TA Associates Battery, Seven Rosen, Bqteicg, USPT

Key Executives:
Ferdinand Dalhuisen, Director, Europe Head Cologne
Education: Studied Business Administration at European Business School in Oestrich-Winkel, London and Paris
Background: Norddeutsche Landesbank, Matuschka GmbH
Directorships: CO-Founder
Andreas Schmidt, Managing Director, Global Head
Education: Law and Economics in Munich and Lausanne
Background: Partner Matuschka GmbH.Co-Founder TVM Techno Venture Management, Deutsche Entwicklungs Gesellschaft (DEG) and Munich Reinsurance Company
Directorships: CO-Founder

2659 DEUTSCHE ASSET MANAGEMENT (AUSTRALIA) LIMITED Deutsche Bank AG
Deutsche Bank Place
Level 16
Sydney 2000
Australia
Phone: 800-034-402 Fax: 61-28-258-1600
Toll-Free: 1800-034402
e-mail: client.services@ironbarkam.com
web: www.deawm.com

Mission Statement: Deutsche Asset Management is one of the world's largest fund managers.
Geographic Preference: Global
Fund Size: $722 Billion
Founded: 1974
Investment Criteria: Expansion and Development, Mezzanine and Bridge
Industry Group Preference: All Sectors Considered, Global Equities, Global Insurance Solutions
Portfolio Companies: BHP Billiton, Westpac Banking, ANZ Banking Corp, Commonwealth Bank, National Australia Bank, Woolworths, Rio Tinto, Orica, St George Bank, Coles Myer

Key Executives:
Michele Faissola, Head of Deutsche Asset & Wealth Management
Education: B.E.(Honours) in Chemical Engineering from the University of Sydney and from the University of Melbourne with a Masters of Business Administration.
Background: AIDC Limited, Optus, Statewide Roads and Wyuna Water, Australian Pacific Technology Limited.

2660 DEUTSCHE BETEILIGUNGS AG
Börsenstraáe 1
Frankfurt 60313
Germany
Phone: 49-699578701 Fax: 49-6995787199
web: www.deutsche-beteiligung.de

Mission Statement: Deutsche Beteilgungs AG is a highly experienced private equity company.
Geographic Preference: Austria, Eastern Europe, France, Germany, Switzerland, USA
Fund Size: s1.3 Billion
Founded: 1965
Average Investment: $180 Million
Minimum Investment: $60 Million
Investment Criteria: Invests in companies with a positive earnings position and potential to build additional value
Industry Group Preference: Automotive, Machinery, Printing, Industrial Services, Technology, Construction, Media, Packaging, Logistics
Portfolio Companies: Bauer AG, Clyde Bergemann Group, Coveright Surfaces GmbH, Harvest Partners III L.P., Harvest Partners IV L.P., Hochtemperatur Engineering GmbH, Homag Group AG, Otto Sauer Achsenfabrik GmbH, Preh GmbH, Quartus Capital Partners

Key Executives:
Andrew Richards, Chairman
e-mail: welcome@deutsche-beteiligung.de
Education: Studied business administration and economics at the Johann Wolfgang Goethe-University of Frankfurt/Main.
Background: 14 years of experience in private equity and corporate finance.
Jochen Baumann, Senior Vice President
Livio Zanotelli, Investment Manager
e-mail: welcome@deutsche-beteiligung.de
Education: Law in Hamburg and Lausanne
Background: Experience in Private Equity and Investment Banking, Finance Director for a major German retail chain.

Reinhard Loffler, Member Board of Management
e-mail: welcome@deutsche-beteiligung.de
Education: Studied business administration and engineering at the University of Karlsruhe.
Background: Filitz-Metzler Group, Papst Motoren GmbH & Company, St. Georgen, Wfg Deutsche Geseilischaft

2661 DFC LTD
Torrent d'en Vidalet 55, L3
Barcelona 08024
Spain

Phone: 34 657 96 65 34
e-mail: fwc-lot6@bcn.thedfcgroup.com
web: www.thedfcgroup.com

Mission Statement: Actively seeking new investments in medium-sized private companies.
Geographic Preference: Europe, Americas, Asia, Africa
Founded: 1980
Investment Criteria: Expansion and Development, Mezzanine and Bridge
Industry Group Preference: Information Technology, Pensions, Financial Services, Corporate Services, Processing, Insurance
Key Executives:
  José Luis Mombrú, Group Managing Partner
  e-mail: barcelona@thedfcgroup.com
  Education: Univ. of Barcelona; Harvard Business School
  Background: European Investment Bank, Commercial Banking and Development Finance Sector., EIB,

2662 DFJ ESPRIT
14 Buckingham Gate
London SW1E 6LB
United Kingdom

Phone: 44-20-7931-8800 **Fax:** 44-20-7931-8866

Mission Statement: At DFJ Esprit we believe that good venture capital begins with good judgement and good relationships. Our partners have a track record of helping entrepreneurs to make their companies successful. In today's world the best businesses have global ambitions from day one and the best venture funds have the networks to support those ambitions. DFJ Esprit is a member of the Draper Fisher Jurvetson Global Network, the largest venture capital network in the world with 140 investment professionals and over 600 portfolio companies.
Geographic Preference: Nordics, Germany, France, United Kingdom, Ireland, Spain
Average Investment: $500,000 - $15 million
Investment Criteria: Early-Stage, Later-Stage
Industry Group Preference: Electronics, Software, Internet, Medical Technology, Mobile
Portfolio Companies: Achica, Airweb, Alphamosaic, ApaTech, Arieso, Avantium, Aveillant, AwoX, Biotie Therapies, Bitbar, BIW, BlackSpider Technologies, Bookham Technology, Bottomline Technologies, Buy.at, Cambridge Positioning Systems, Cambridge Silicon Radio, CamSemi, Cast, Cerillion Technologies, Clearswift, CloudApps, Connectivity, Conversocial, Datahug, DiBcom, Digital Route, Displaydata, DisplayLink, DNA Research, Enteraction TV, European Telecommunications & Technology, EVE, FillFactory, Formscape Group, Foviance Group, Garlik, Graze, GreenPeak Technologies, Healthcare Brands International, Horizon Discovery, Icera, Imagine Communications, Intense, Ipanema, Kiadis, Kiala, KVS, Lagan, Light Blue Optics, Lime Microsystems, LOVEFiLM, Lyst, Message Pad, Metalysis, Microcosm Communications, MindMatrics, Mobile Commerce, Mobile Travel Technologies, Mobile2Win, Mobixell Networks, MXData, NeoPhotonics, Neteconomy, Netonomy, Netronome, Neul, Nimbus Partners, Nordnav Technologies, OneAccess, OverSi Networks, Oxford BioMedica, Oxford Immunotec, PacketExchange, Phyworks, Polatis, PortWise, Powerlase, Psytechnics, Pulmagen, Qosmos, Radium One, Redkite Financial Markets, Road Angel, Rock Mobile Corp, Silecs, Speech Recognition, SportPursuit, StrikeAd, SVOX, Tagsys RFID, Taptu, The Cloud, The Listening Co., Trace One, Tribold, Virata Corp, VirtualLogix, WAYN, Webify Solutions, Xaar, Xitec Software, Xmos, Zeus Technology
Other Locations:
  Building 1010
  Cambourne Business Park
  Cambourne
  Cambridge CB23 6DP
  United Kingdom
  Phone: 11-1223-307-770 **Fax:** 44-1223-307-771
Key Executives:
  Simon Cook, CEO
  Education: University of Manchester Institute of Science & Technology
  Background: Cazenove Private Equity; Partner, Elderstreet Investments; Director, 3i

2663 DIGITAL SKY TECHNOLOGIES
Hong Kong

e-mail: info@dst-global.com

Portfolio Companies: Virool, MemSQL, Klarna, Airbnb, Spotify, Facebook, Groupon, Nival, Zynga, Forticom

2664 DIRECT CAPITAL PRIVATE EQUITY LIMITED
Level 6, 2 Kitchener Street
Aukland
New Zealand

Phone: 64-93072562 **Fax:** 64-93072349
web: www.directcapital.co.nz

Mission Statement: Actively seeking new investments.
Fund Size: $141 Million
Founded: 1994
Average Investment: $7.1 Million
Minimum Investment: $.07 Million
Investment Criteria: Seed, Early, Expansion
Industry Group Preference: Education, Information Technology, Healthcare, Industrial Services, Life Sciences, Entertainment, Financial Services, Business to Business, Food & Beverage, Manufacturing, Retailing, Processing
Portfolio Companies: Airwork, Blue Star (Acquired By Us Office Products), Communicado (Now Screentime Communicado), Eftpos New Zealand, Ezibuy, Genesis (Gen), Image Centre, Moore, Moore Gallagher, Nobil, Noel Leeming, Open Networks, Pacificflight Catering, Palliser Estate, Pc Dir
Key Executives:
  Ross George, LLB, Managing Director
  e-mail: ross.george@directcapital.co.nz
  Directorships: Directorships :Blue Star, Nobilo Wines, Pacific Flight Catering, EMS, Communicado and Robinson Industries.
  Mark Hutton, BCom, Director

2665 DIRIGEANTS ET INVESTISSEURS
31 rue Des Poissonniers
Neuilly-Sur-Seine F-92200
France

Phone: 33-141920292 **Fax:** 33-146410025
web: www.di-groupe.com

Mission Statement: Invests in companies at all stages to help them become profitable
Geographic Preference: Europe
Industry Group Preference: Management
Key Executives:
  Martial Papineau, Président
  e-mail: martial.papineau@di-groupe.com

Venture Capital & Private Equity Firms / International Firms

2666 DISCOUNT INVESTMENT CORPORATION LIMITED
3 Azrieli Center, 44th floor
Tel Aviv 6702301
Israel
Phone: 972-36075888 Fax: 972-36075889
e-mail: Investor.Relations@dic.co.il
web: www.dic.co.il

Mission Statement: As one of Israel's most prominent investment companies for the past four decades, DIC has taken a substantial part in the major development of the Israel economy.

Geographic Preference: Israel
Founded: 1961
Industry Group Preference: All Sectors Considered
Portfolio Companies: Cellcon, Net Vision, Elron, Scitex,

Key Executives:
Ami Erel, President & Chief Executive Officer
e-mail: oren.lieder@dic.co.il
Education: Bachelor of Arts, University of Haifa.
Background: Elco Holdings, BEZEQ
Directorships: Board Member, Israeli enterprises.
Michel Dahan, Acting General Manager, Vice President & Chief Financial Officer
e-mail: Investor.Relations@dic.co.il
Education: Bachelors of science degree in electrical engineering from the Technion.
Background: The Israel Telecommunication Corp., Israel's Association of Electronics & Information Industries, ForSoft Ltd. & Formula Computer Technologies Ltd.
Directorships: Scitex Corporation Ltd. (Chairman).

2667 DJF DRAGONFUND CHINA
Unit 3102, Wheelock Square
No. 1717 West Nanjing Road
Shanghai 200040
China
Phone: 86-21-6280-0580 Fax: 86-21-6280-0585
e-mail: info@dfjdragon.com
web: www.dfjdragon.com

Mission Statement: Established in March of 2006, DFJ DragonFund is a leading venture capital firm in the People's Republic of China. It is the China affiliated fund of the internationally recognized venture capital firm Draper Fisher Jurvetson (www.dfj.com). As a joint venture between DFJ and DragonVenture, DFJ DragonFund leverages an unparalleled track record of experiences, knowledge, and successes in venture capitals both internationally and domestically. At DFJ DragonFund, we focus on China-centric early-stage companies in the technology market. We work closely with them in developing their business strategies as well as providing necessary operating guidance from time to time.

Geographic Preference: China
Founded: 2006
Investment Criteria: Early-Stage
Industry Group Preference: Technology
Portfolio Companies: AltoBeam, Crystechcoating, Donson, DraTek Technologies, EDDA Technology, FastWeb, Fountain Medical Development, GD Interactive, GridNt, Hudong, Jing Jin Electric, Luxul, Miartech, Mobim Technologies, Splashtop, Senodia Technologies, StreamOcean, Synacast, TongCard Holdings, Viewhigh Technologies, Vital Therapies, YeePay

Other Locations:
Unit 818, SOHO Building
Zhongguancun
Beijing 100080
China
Phone: 86-10-8286-8228 Fax: 86-10-8286-8205

2882 Sand Hill Road
Suite 150
Menlo Park, CA 94025
Phone: 650-233-9000 Fax: 650-233-9233

Key Executives:
Larry Guanxin Li, Founding Managing Director
Education: PhD, Applied Mechanics, Shanghai Jiaotong University
Background: Co-Founder, Managing Director, SHVC-Shanghai DJ Venture; Managing Director, Shanghai VC

2668 DN CAPITAL
2 Queen Anne's Gate Buildings
Dartmouth Street
London SW1H 9BP
United Kingdom
Phone: 44-02073401600 Fax: 44-02073401601
e-mail: info@dncapital.com
web: www.dncapital.com

Mission Statement: DN Capital's objective is to identify, invest in and actively support leading digital media, e-commerce, software and mobile applications companies on a global basis. The investment professionals at DN Capital bring more than 50 years of early stage and growth equity experience to their investments, and work with portfolio companies to guide their growth through the various stages of development. We help portfolio companies by leveraging our extensive global network of managers, investors, and intermediaries who are actively involved with DN Capital's portfolio companies.

Investment Criteria: Early-Stage, Growth-Stage
Industry Group Preference: Digital Media & Marketing, E-Commerce & Manufacturing, Software, Mobile
Portfolio Companies: Shazam, Apsmart, AirSense Wireless, Mobile Roadie, Just Book, Digital Chocolate, Windeln.de, Mister Spex,

Other Locations:
228 Hamilton Avenue
3rd Floor
Palo Alto, CA 94301
Phone: 650-7985424

Key Executives:
Nenad Marovac, Founder/CEO/Managing Partner
Education: BS, Business Administration, San Diego State University; MBA, Harvard Business School
Background: Partner, Advent International

2669 DOTCORP PRIVATE EQUITY FUND
125 Avenue du X Septembre
L-2551
Luxembourg
e-mail: info@dotcorp.lu

Mission Statement: At Dotcorp Private Equity we are entrepreneurs who dedicate our experience and expertise to growing companies and mentoring founding CEOs.

Geographic Preference: Europe, Israel
Founded: 2007
Investment Criteria: All Stages
Industry Group Preference: All Sectors Considered
Portfolio Companies: Deezer, Mythings, Primavista, Interplay, Covertix, Lot18mimesis Republic, Restopolitan, IFrameApps, Guidespromos.Com, My Social Book, Step-In

Key Executives:
Steve Rosenblum, Co-Founder
Education: La Sorbonne; BA, Economics, Concordia University
Background: Co-Founder, Pixmania.Com; Co-Founder, The Kase
Jean-Emile Rosenblum, Co-Founder
Background: Co-Founder, Pixmaxia.Com; Co-Founder, The Kase

Venture Capital & Private Equity Firms / International Firms

2670 DOUBLE IMPACT BUSINESS ADVISORY
12th Floor, Empire Tower
Bangkok 10120
Thailand

Phone: 66-0226701100 Fax: 66-0226701101

Mission Statement: A well established advisory group assisting businesses present in Thailand and their activities in Asia and around the world.

Industry Group Preference: Manufacturing, Retailing, Financial Services, Media, Publishing

Key Executives:
Bruce Darrington, Managing Director
Rob Hurenkamp, Deputy Managing Director

2671 DOUGHTY HANSON & CO.
45 Pall Mall
London SW1Y 5JG
United Kingdom

Phone: 44-20-7663-9300
e-mail: info@doughtyhanson.com
web: www.doughtyhanson.com

Mission Statement: We invest in ambitious entrepreneurs and help them build industry leading businesses in the mobile technology, internet software and cleantech sectors.

Geographic Preference: Europe
Industry Group Preference: Mobile Communications Devices, Internet Technology, Clean Technology
Portfolio Companies: Actionality, Alphamosaic, Adaptive Mobile, Everbridge, Forth Dimension Displays, Garlik, Gomez, Handmade, MBAPolymers, Mega Zebra, Mobango, Nscaled, Orchestria, Plazes, RainStar, Secretsales, Eguana Technologies, Soundcloud, Sube, SDLtridion, Ubidyne

Key Executives:
Nigel Grierson, Co-Head, Technology Ventures
Background: Group Director, Intel Capital; AT&T
George Powlick, Co-Head, Technology Ventures
Education: BS, Materials Science & Engineering, University of California, Berkeley; MBA, Anderson School of Business
Background: Intel Corporation

2672 DPIXEL
Via Filippo Turati 38
20121 Milan
Italy

e-mail: info@dpixel.it
web: www.dpixel.it

Mission Statement: We are a venture capital firm, we are looking for entrepreneurs who want to change the world.

Geographic Preference: Italy
Investment Criteria: Seed Stage
Industry Group Preference: Internet
Portfolio Companies: Mangatar, Eco4Cloud, Affare Del Giorno, Sardex.net, Ciceroos, CrowdEngineering, Cortilla, Iubenda, SmartRM, Sounday, Farman

Key Executives:
Gianluca Dettori, Partner & Chairman
Education: University of Turin
Background: Manager, Italia Online (Olivetti); General Manager, Lycos Bertelsmann; Founder, Vitaminic; Head of Mergers & Acquisitions, Buongiorno Group
Antonio Concolino, Partner & CEO
Education: Business Engineering, University of Calabria
Background: Process Analyst, Andersen Consulting; Consultant, IT Sistem at University "La Sapienza" in Rome; Italian Regional Telecommunication Operator at Lombardiacom Spa; Chief Financial Officer and Financial Controller, Elitel Telcom Spa

2673 DR NEUHAUS TECHNO NORD GmbH
30 Jungfernstieg
Hamburg 20354
Germany

Phone: 49-403552820 Fax: 49-403-5528239
e-mail: info@drneuhaus.de
web: www.drneuhaus.de

Mission Statement: Actively seeking new investments.

Geographic Preference: Germany, German speaking countries
Fund Size: $62 Million
Founded: 1998
Average Investment: $2.1 Million
Minimum Investment: $0.6 Million
Investment Criteria: Seed, Startup, Expansion
Industry Group Preference: Information Technology, Software, Telecommunications, Internet Technology
Portfolio Companies: 7d Software GmbH & Co., Agentscape, Blau Mobilfunk GmbH, ePrint Factory GmbH, EUTEX European Telco Exchange, Exit Games GmbH, Gentleware, Infitel International N.V., Intenium GmbH, Newtention Extended Networks GmbH, Micro Technology

Key Executives:
Gottfried Neuhaus, Managing Partner
Education: MBA
Matthias Grychta, Managing Partner
Education: Electrical engineering in Argentina, PhD in computer science at the Technical University in Berlin.

2674 DRAPER ESPRIT
20 Garrick Street
London WC2E 9BT
United Kingdom

Phone: 44 (0)20 7931 8800
e-mail: info@draperesprit.com
web: draperesprit.com

Mission Statement: Draper Esprit invests into visionary and growing companies, primarily focused on innovative technologies. As one of the largest VC firms in Europe, Draper takes on projects on a long-term and multi-stage basis.

Fund Size: $1 billion
Founded: 2006
Industry Group Preference: Technology
Portfolio Companies: Apatech, Areso, Aveillant, Bitbar, Black Spider Technologies, Bright Computing, Buyat, CPS, CamSemi, Clavis Insight, Clear Swift, Cloud Apps, Clue, KCom, Conversocial, Crate, Crowdcube.com, Data Hug, DiBcom, Display Data, DisplayLink, Episode 1, GTT, Eve, Fill Factory, Fluidic Analytics, Foviance, Garlik, GetBulb, Graphcore, Graze, Green Peak, Healthcare Brands International, Horizon, Icera, Intense, Ipanema, Kiadis Pharma, KVS, Lagan, Lifesum, Light Blue Optics, Lime Microsystems, LoveFilm.com, Lyst, M-Files, Metalysis, Mobile Commerce, Movidius, Moviepilot, MTT, Fiserv., Netronome, Neul, TIBC, Oxford Immunotec, Packetexchange, Perkbox, Phyworks, Pod Point, Polatis, PremFina, Psytechnics, Push Doctor, QOSMOS, Raven Pack, Red Kite, Resolver, Seedcamp, Sport Pursuit, Tails.com, Taptu, The Cloud, Serco, Transferwise, Trust Pilot, Unbound, Verve, Xmos, Zeus

Other Locations:
O'Connell Bridge House
8th Floor
D'Olier Street
Dublin D02 RR99
Ireland
Phone: 353 (0)1 881 8792

Building 1010
Cambourne Business Park
Cambourne
Cambridge CB23 6DP

United Kingdom
Phone: 44 (0)1223 307 770
Key Executives:
Simon Cook, Chief Executive Officer
Education: University of Manchester Institute of Science & Technology
Background: Partner, Cazenove Private Equity; Partner, Elderstreet Investments
Directorships: Investment Director, 3i Technology Europe
Stuart Chapman, Chief Operating Officer
Education: Loughborough University
Background: Partner, 3i Ventures
Directorships: Board Member, Loughborough School of Business and Economics

2675 DTA CAPITAL PARTNERS S/B
24A, Jalan Datuk Sulaiman
Taman Tun Drive Ismail
Kuala Lumpur 60000
Malaysia
Phone: 60-377222560 **Fax:** 60-377222570
e-mail: dtav@dtacapital.com
web: www.dtacapital.com

Fund Size: $16.3 Million
Founded: 1996
Average Investment: $1.08 Million
Industry Group Preference: Financial Services
Key Executives:
Dali Sardar, Chief Executive Officer
e-mail: dali@dtacapital.com
Directorships: Chairman
KC Tan, Chief Operating Officer
e-mail: naim@dtacapital.com
Background: Ex-Citicorp; Citibank
Directorships: Deputy Chairman

2676 DUKE STREET CAPITAL Duke Street
Nations House
103 Wigmore Street
London W1U 1QS
United Kingdom
Phone: 44-02076638500 **Fax:** 44-02076638501
e-mail: mail@dukestreet.com
web: www.dukestreetcapital.com

Mission Statement: Duke Street Capital is an independent private equity company which principally invests in established, mid-market UK and French businesses.
Geographic Preference: United Kingdom, Western Europe
Fund Size: $2.4 Billion
Founded: 1988
Average Investment: Euro 300 Million
Investment Criteria: Mid stage
Industry Group Preference: Business to Business, Retailing, Healthcare, Leisure, Financial Services, Outsourcing & Efficiency, Consumer Services
Portfolio Companies: Xafinity, Waste link, Leisure link, Navimo, Accantia, Marie Brizard, Focus, Groupe Proclif, Affinity Healthcare, Thornbury Nursing Services, Paragon, Cremascoli Ortho, Cox Insurance
Key Executives:
Peter Taylor, Managing Partner
Education: BSc. (Hons) from Durham University.
Background: County Bank,
Paul Adams, Investment Manager
Education: graduate of Ecole Supérieure des Sciences Commerciales
Background: Smith Barney in New York City
Elaine Fullerton, General Counsel
Education: graduate of Institut Commercial de Nancy,
Background: Donaldson Lufkin & Jenrette in London, Credit Suisse

Emmanuel Logan-Moll, Investment Executive
Education: BBA from Stockholm University & MSc in Engineering Physics and Financial Mathematics from the Royal Institute of Technology, Stockholm.
Background: AB Segulah
Christian Fellowes, Investment Executive
Education: MBA from Havard University
Background: Rhône Capital, Donaldson, Lufkin & Jenrette,
Jean Garbois, Operating Partner
Education: Graduate from Loughborough University of Technology & Chartered Accountant
Background: Cannons Group Plc. & NatWest Equity Partners
Crispin Goldsmith, Investment Director
Education: BA in economics from Duke University and a Masters in business administration from Harvard University.
Background: Celfin & Morgan Stanley
Johanna Waterous, Operating Partner
Education: Modern Languages degree from Durham University.
Charlie Troup, Partner
Education: Degree in economics from Durham University.
Background: Bankers Trust's leveraged buyout groups
Directorships: He is an Associate of the Institute of Investment Management & Research. He was Chairman of the British Venture Capital Association 2001-2002.
Ben Long, Investment Director
Education: Graduate from Bocconi University, Milan.
Background: Merrill Lynch - Advisor

2677 DUNEDIN CAPITAL PARTNERS LIMITED
Saltire Court
20 Castle Terrace
Edinburgh EH1 2EN
United Kingdom
Phone: 44-1312256699 **Fax:** 20-7292-2110
e-mail: info@dunedin.com
web: www.dunedin.com

Mission Statement: Dunedin Capital Partners provides equity finance for management buy-outs and management buy-ins with a transaction size of $10 million - $50 million.
Geographic Preference: United Kingdom
Fund Size: $531 Million
Founded: 1983
Average Investment: $38 Million
Minimum Investment: $5.3 Million
Investment Criteria: All stages
Industry Group Preference: Construction, Consumer Products, Financial Services, Healthcare, Leisure, Media, Manufacturing, Services, Building Materials & Services, Consumer Services
Portfolio Companies: CET, Practice Plan Group Ltd., Zenith Vehicle Contracts Ltd., New Horizons, Celtic Inns, Total Fitness, ABI (UK) Ltd., Supreme Imports, Simply Smart Group, Home & Legacy, Hickson & Welch, Jessops Ltd., Gardner Aerospace, Caledonian Building Systems Ltd.
Key Executives:
Simon Miller, Chairman
e-mail: brian.scouler@dunedin.com
Education: Graduate from Glasgow University and CA.
Background: Royal Bank Development Capital & Charterhouse Development Capital Limited.
Nicol Fraser, Director
e-mail: nicol.fraser@dunedin.com
Background: Bridgepoint Capital & Scott Oswald,
Ross Marshall, Managing Director
e-mail: ross.marshall@dunedin.com
Education: BCom from Edinburgh University and chartered accountant
Background: Price Waterhouse, 3i, UK private equity
Dougal Bennett, Partner
e-mail: dougal.bennett@dunedin.com

Education: Graduate in biochemistry Edinburgh University
Background: OSS Group & Gardner Aerospace,
Shaun Middleton, Managing Partner
e-mail: shaun.middleton@dunedin.com
Education: Graduate from University of Witwatersrand and Chartered Accountant
Background: ABI

2678 DUTCH GROUP
Soestdijkerstraatweg 27 B
Hilversum 1213 VR
Netherlands

Phone: 31-205038070 **Fax:** 31-0205038071
web: www.dutch.com

Mission Statement: Focuses on temporary management solutions.
Geographic Preference: Netherlands, Israel, Belgium, England
Founded: 1984
Key Executives:
  Anda Van Liere, Business Professional
  e-mail: mail@ws-transition.com
  Background: Dutch management consultancy
  Directorships: Non-executive board member and chairman

2679 DVC DEUTSCHE VENTURE CAPITAL
Munich
Germany

Phone: +49 89 452 352-352 **Fax:** +49 89 452 352-110

Geographic Preference: Europe
Fund Size: $300 million Euro
Founded: 1998
Average Investment: $1 - $10 million Euro
Industry Group Preference: Information Technology, Telecommunications, Semiconductor, Industrial Technology, Life Sciences, Medical Technology

2680 E-CAPITAL MANAGEMENT
Tervurenlaan 273 - 1150
1150 Brussels
Brussels 1030
Belgium

Phone: 32-26422000 **Fax:** 32-26422009
e-mail: info@e-capital.be
web: www.e-capital.be

Mission Statement: E-Capital is an investment fund dedicated to the funding and/or the take-over (MBO, MBI) of small and mid-sized unquoted companies.
Geographic Preference: Belgium
Fund Size: $95 Million
Founded: 1999
Average Investment: $2.4 Million
Minimum Investment: $1.2 Million
Investment Criteria: Start-up and Growth-stage
Industry Group Preference: All Sectors Considered
Portfolio Companies: Biocode-Hycel, Gevaert Bandweverij, Globe, Guillaume-Teco, Kapitol, Splen, Unibioscreen & Zetes
Key Executives:
  Jerome Lamfalussy, Investment Partner
  Yves Trouveroy, Investment Partner

2681 E.BRICKS DIGITAL
Avenida República do Líbano, 1214
Vila Nova Conceiçao
Sao Paulo 04502-001
Brazil

Phone: 21-30500750
web: www.ebricksdigital.com.br

Mission Statement: e.Bricks invests in companies that are in a stage of rapid growth, with excellence and entrepreneurs operating in markets with great growth potential. There are three main sectors: e-commerce segmented, mobile and digital media and technology. At the heart of the strategy are the technology and scalability of business.
Founded: 2012
Investment Criteria: Growth-Stage
Industry Group Preference: E-Commerce & Manufacturing, Mobile, Digital Media & Marketing, Technology
Key Executives:
  Fabio Bruggioni, Chief Executive Officer
  Background: Vice President, Telefonica Group

2682 EARLYBIRD
Maximilianstr. 14
Munchen 80539
Germany

Phone: 49-892907020 **Fax:** 49-8929070222
web: www.earlybird.com

Mission Statement: Adds value to our portfolio companies through active support – serving as a sparring partner in decision making processes.
Geographic Preference: Germany, Switzerland, Austria, Netherlands, UK, USA, Italy, France
Fund Size: 430 millin Euros
Founded: 1997
Average Investment: 3 million Euros
Minimum Investment: 1 million Euros
Investment Criteria: Early stage, Startup, Expansion
Industry Group Preference: Online Consumer Services, Internet, Cloud-Based IT Services, Information Technology, Software, Communication Technology, Clean Technology, Medical Technology
Portfolio Companies: Alantos Pharmaceuticals, Asyntis Gmbh, Biovalve, Europroteome AG, Graviton, Hemoteq Gmbh, IQ Labs, Identify Sotware, Intime Software, Internetwork AG/Q Inc
Other Locations:
  Maximilianstr. 14
  Munchen 80539
  Germany
  Phone: 49-892907020 **Fax:** 49-8929070222
Key Executives:
  Hendrick Brandis, Co-Founder and Partner
  04-0432-9410
  e-mail: nagel@earlybird.com
  Education: Dipl.Wi-Ing., Technical University of Hamburg; PhD in Management from St. Gallen University, Switzerland.
  Background: Co-Founder & Managing Partner, SMB Industrieholding Wildau GmbH; DH Industriholding Hohenthurm; Consultant, McKinsey & Company
  Directorships: Crowdpark, BridgeCo, Lumics, madvertise, Smava, Yoom
  Christian Nagel, Partner
  089-290-7020
  e-mail: brandis@earlybird.com
  Education: Dipl.-Ing, PhD, Aerospace Engineering, Technical University of Munich
  Background: Co-Founder, GMM; Project Manager, EADS; Partner, McKinsey & Company
  Directorships: B2X Care Solutions, conject, nfton, Mikini Media, Music Network
  Roland Manger, Partner
  089-290-7020
  e-mail: manger@earlybird.com
  Education: Dipl.Wi-Ing, University of Karlsuhle; MBA, Georgetown University
  Background: Co-Founder & Marketing Director, Cybernet AG; Director, Business Development, Ditec AG;

Venture Capital & Private Equity Firms / International Firms

Principal, Gemini Consulting
Directorships: OneShield, Scoreloop
Rolf Mathies, Partner
04-043-294-10
e-mail: mathies@earlybird.com
Education: Dipl.-Kfm. degree (MBA equivalent) specializing in information science from the University of Hamburg
Background: Co-Founder & Managing Partner, ConAction AG; Consultant, Bain & Company
Directorships: azeti Networks, Hemoteq, enTRUST & TITLE
Ciarán O'Leary, Partner
e-mail: jung@earlybird.com
Education: PhD, and Dipl.- Biol. (MS equivalent) from the Ludwig-Maximilians-University in Munich.
Thom Rasche, Partner
Wolfgang Siebold, Partner
Heiko Thiel, Head of Finance

2683 EAST FUND MANAGEMENT GmbH
GiroCredit
Somolickeho 1/b
Bratislava SK- 81105
Slovakia

Phone: 43-152-22285 Fax: 43-152-22285
e-mail: office@hkkpartners.com
web: www.eastfund.com

Mission Statement: EFM and its holding company HKK Partners is a Central European based private Equity Investor with operations in Vienna, Prague, Bratislava and Bucharest.

Geographic Preference: Europe, Austria
Fund Size: $50 Million
Founded: 1994
Investment Criteria: All stages
Industry Group Preference: Media, Food & Beverage, Automotive, Logistics, Chemicals, Financial Services, Information Technology, Distribution
Portfolio Companies: Mec.com, Sky Europe, X Radio Express, Bohemia Prints, Seibold, Komptech Farwicks, Steiger, Tovarnity, Sigus Slovakia, Monopoly Media, Terapia

Key Executives:
Roland Haas, Managing Partner
Education: Degree in Economics from Vienna University.
Background: Slovak Post Privatisation Fund & Investment Bank Austria's Research department
Mark Kaltenbacher, Managing Director
Education: BA in Economics from the University of California and an MBA in Finance from Columbia Business School
Background: Merrill Lynch

2684 EASTLABS
75 Zhylianska Street
4th Floor
Kyiv
Ukraine

Phone: 44 377 74 79
e-mail: info@eastlabs.co
web: www.eastlabs.co

Mission Statement: Eastlabs looks for talented teams with ideas that have the potential to change the world. We feel that just as important as having an innovative idea that can shake the internet/mobile space, is to have a team determined to execution excellence. We are open to acception teams from any international location as long as they meet our selction criteria.

Average Investment: $20,000
Investment Criteria: Start-Up
Industry Group Preference: Internet, Mobile, Digital Media & Marketing

Key Executives:
Eveline Buchatskiy, Managing Partner
Education: BS, Chemical Engineering, UC Berkeley; Master of Engineering, SUNY Buffalo; MBA, INSEAD
Background: CEO, Ekonomika; CEO, APCT; Engineering Associate, Praxair
Ken Leaver, Managing Partner
Education: BS, Cornell University; MBA, IESE Business School in Barcelona, Spain
Background: CEO, Groupon Ukraine; Co-Founder, uGift; Executive, Visa Inc; Senior Manager, Strategy Partners

2685 EC1 CAPITAL LTD
Rainmaking Loft
International House
1 St Katharine's Way
E1W 1UN London
United Kingdom

e-mail: info@ec1capital.com
web: www.ec1capital.com

Mission Statement: We provide capital, expertise and connections for web based tech startups that provides a firm footing to further develop the technology.

Geographic Preference: London, Dublin, Edinburgh
Founded: 2012
Minimum Investment: £50,000
Investment Criteria: Seed Stage, Early Stage
Industry Group Preference: Web Applications & Services, Mobile
Portfolio Companies: CitySocializer, TRULY, User Replay, HANDS HQ, SmartTrade, Toothpick, Hybrid Cluster, SimpleTax, Unifyo, CultureLabel, Glean.in, Highgate Labs, Lifecake, HouseBites, Retronaut

Key Executives:
Julian Carter, Co-Founder & Managin Director
Directorships: Lifecake, Highgate Labs, Glean.in, Culture Label, Unifyo, Truly, User Replay, CitySocializer
Badr AlSabban, Co-Founder & Director

2686 ECAPITAL ENTREPRENEURIAL PARTNERS AG
Hafenweg 24
Münster 48155
Germany

Phone: 49 0251-7037670 Fax: 49 0251-70376722
e-mail: info@ecapital.de
web: www.ecapital.de

Mission Statement: eCAPITAL is a venture capital firm that provides early to growth stage funding to technology companies in the fields of software & information technology, cybersecurity, industry 4.0, new materials and cleantech. Founded in 1999, eCAPITAL has a history of leveraging relationships and supporting entrepreneurs determined to build companies with lasting significance. Partnering with eCAPITAL means joining a unique network of entrepreneurs, business leaders, operators, investors and scientists.

Geographic Preference: Germany, Europe
Fund Size: $200 million
Founded: 1999
Average Investment: $3 million
Minimum Investment: $0.5 million
Investment Criteria: Early-Stage, Later-Stage
Industry Group Preference: Information Technology, Software, Cybersecurity, New Materials, Industry, Cleantech, Semiconductor
Portfolio Companies: 4JET Technologies, BrandMaker GmbH, CNM Technologies, CREPAPER GmbH, Cysal, Evodos, Ferroelectric Memory GmbH, Greenergetic, Heliatek, INMATEC Technologies GmbH, Jedox, Milk the Sun, Open-Xchange, Perora GmbH, Prolupin GmbH, Rhebo GmbH, RIPS Technologies, saperatec, Smarthouse, Smart Hydro Power, Sonnen GmbH, Subitec, temicon GmbH,

Venture Capital & Private Equity Firms / International Firms

THEVA DüNnschichttechnik GmbH, Variowell Development, Videantis GmbH, VMRay GmbH
Key Executives:
Dr. Paul-Josef Patt, Managing Partner/CEO
e-mail: patt@ecapital.de
Education: University of Tubingen
Background: Roland Berger & Partner; Kaufhof Holding AG; MBI Ernstings
Michael Mayer, Managing Partner
0251 703767 0
e-mail: m.mayer@ecapital.de
Education: University of Konstanz
Background: Founder, Technostart GmbH; Fraunhofer Institute; Transmedia Verlag GmbH & Co
Willi Mannheims, Managing Partner
e-mail: w.mannheims@ecapital.de
Education: Queen's College, UK; Henley Management College, UK; MBA, University of Houston
Background: Fond Dasa/Daimler Chrysler; CUBIS AG; Secunet AG; Escrypt GmbH

2687 ECI VENTURES
Brettenham House
Lancaster Place
London WC2E 7EN
United Kingdom
Phone: 44-2076061000 Fax: 44-2072405050

Mission Statement: ECI provides capital for UK unquoted and smaller quoted companies including finance for various transactions.
Geographic Preference: United Kingdom
Fund Size: $887 Million
Founded: 1976
Average Investment: $97.5 Million
Minimum Investment: $17.75 Million
Investment Criteria: MBO, MBI, Institutional Buy-Out, Expansion, Acquisition, Turnarounds, Refinancing. No Early-Stage
Industry Group Preference: All Sectors Considered, Chemicals, Distribution, Information Technology, Manufacturing, Outsourcing & Efficiency, Communications, Transportation, Financial Services, Publishing
Key Executives:
Sean Whelan, member of the investment committee
Education: Degree in Material Science and metallurgy from Cambridge University.
Background: PriceWaterhouseCoopers where he gained an ACA and spent a period in business regeneration, effectively acting as FD to various struggling companies
Tim Raffle, Dierctor
Education: Graduated from Cambridge University and qualified with KPMG.
Stephen Dawson, Non-Executive Director
Background: ECI, business management experience at Sema, Logica, Reuters and as managing director of a start-up company. A director of the computer and electronics division at British Technology Group.
Directorships: MD.
Janet Brooks, Manager, Investor Relations/Marketing
Education: Graduated from Cambridge University and has a MBA from INSEAD.
Background: member of the BVCA's Investor Relations Committee and was a member of the EVCA's Investor Relations Committee from 1999 to 2004, She was previously an investment manager at fund-of-funds group VenCap International.
Steve Tudge, Director
Education: Graduating from Warwick University in management sciences.
Background: PriceWaterhouseCoopers, gaining an ACA and specialising in advising small and medium sized businesses

Ken Landsberg, Director
Education: Graduated in computer sciences from Bristol University and qualified as an accountant with Deloitte & Touche in 1983.
Background: service sector investments and has held board seats at Highway Emergency Services, Guardian iT, Hoseasons and Data Entry International. & director Enviros and Omnipack.

2688 ECONA AG
Wöhlert street 12/13
3rd Inner Court
Berlin 10115
Germany
Phone: 49-309210640 Fax: 49-3092106431
web: www.econa.com

Mission Statement: Actively seeking new investments in Internet based companies
Geographic Preference: Berlin
Founded: 1999
Investment Criteria: MBI, MBO
Industry Group Preference: Internet Technology, Media
Key Executives:
Bernd Hardes, Founder Partner
Education: MA
Background: Banker; Management Consultant in the range strategy and marketing
Daniel Engelbarts, Managing Director

2689 ECUS PRIVATE EQUITY Ecus Private Equity/AXA Capital Chile
Magdalena 140, 5th Floor
Las Condes
Santiago 7550104
Chile
Phone: 56-2-25772200 Fax: 56-2-25772222
e-mail: desk@ecuscapital.com
web: www.ecuscapital.com

Average Investment: $3 Million - $6Million

2690 EDBI Pte LTD.
250 North Bridge Road
#28-00 Raffles City Tower
179101
Singapore
Phone: 65-6832-6832 Fax: 65-6832-6838
e-mail: infoHQ@ebdi.com
web: www.edbi.com

Mission Statement: Investing since 1991, EDBI is a Singapore-based global investor in select high growth technology sectors ranging from Information & Communication Technology (ICT), Emerging Technology (ET), Healthcare (HC), and other strategic industries. As a value creating investor, EDBI assists companies achieve their ambitious goals by leveraging our broad network, resources and expertise. With our patient capital, EDBI supports companies seeking to grow in Asia and globally through Singapore.
Geographic Preference: US, Europe, Asia
Founded: 1991
Investment Criteria: Growth & Late Stage
Industry Group Preference: Healthcare Information Technology, Medical Devices, Therapeutics, Information Technology, Communication Technology, Consumer Internet, SaaS, Cloud Computing, Telecommunications, Infrastructure
Portfolio Companies: Adamas Pharmaceuticals, Addex Pharmaceuticals, Ambiq Micro, Appier, Artisan Pharma, Bitmain, Bright Machines, Byte Dance, Carousell, Chevron Phillips, Codexis, Connexions Asia, CounterTack, Coursera, Cyclacel Pharmaceuticals, DocuSign, Druva, Enginge Biosciences, Five Prime Therapeutics, FORMA Therapeutics, GoBalto, Green Wave Systems, Hedvig, Idenix, Iflix, I-Mab

Venture Capital & Private Equity Firms / International Firms

Biopharma, Inviragen, Ironwood, Ivantis, Joby Aviation, KaloBios Pharmaceuticals, Kalpsys, Klook, Knewton, Leqee, Livongo, LogRhythm, Lonza Biologics, LucasFilm Animation, Maccine, Magic Leap, Mdaq, Meiban, MerLion Pharma, MetricStream, Moderna, NanoFilm, Patientsafe, Moka, OakNorth, Paxata, Pear Therapeutics, Perlegen, Pindrop, Puppet, QTVascular, Ramp, Rapid Micro Biosystems, Renovis, Retail Next, Revance Therapeutics, Rotimatic, S*Bio, Savioke, Shape, Singapore Suzhou Township Development, Sotera Wireless, Sprinklr, Taulia, Tessa Therapeutics, Vanda, Vobile, WalkMe, Welltok

Other Locations:
250A, Twin Dolphin Drive
Redwood City, CA 94065-1402
Phone: 650-591-9102 **Fax:** 650-591-1328

Key Executives:
Swee Yeok Chu, Chief Executive Officer/President
Background: CEO, Bio*One Capital; Singapore Economic Development Board
Directorships: Merlion Pharmaceuticals, Singapore Suzhou Township Development, Alexandra Health Endowment Fund

2691 EDEN VENTURES
14 Golden Square
London W1F 9JF
United Kingdom

Phone: 44-0-22077583440
e-mail: info@edenventures.co.uk
web: www.edenventures.co.uk

Mission Statement: Eden Venture's background is that of serial entrepreneurs with a strong seed investment track record. We offer our portfolio companies considerable operational management expertise in creating businesses of lasting value. Eden's investment strategy is to provide early stage funding (seed and Series A). However, we also reserve allocation within our funds to follow our successful investments through their lifetime, meaning that entrepreneurs can focus on getting on with business knowing they have a strong investment partner by their side.

Investment Criteria: Early-Stage
Industry Group Preference: Telecommunications, Software, Enterprise Software, SaaS, Digital Media & Marketing, E-Commerce & Manufacturing, Internet, Social Media, Gaming, Mobile
Portfolio Companies: Borro, Reevoo, The Filter, We7, BaseKit, UberVU, Greenman Gaming, Lookk, What's In My Handbag, VoiceVault, Acunu, Doccom, Huddle, Tru, Zemanta, Brightpearl, New Voice Media, AFrame, Response Tap, Ontology, Tribold, Voss, Evolved Intelligence

Other Locations:
1 Widcombe Crescent
Bath BA2 6AH
United Kingdom
Phone: 44-0-1225-472950

Key Executives:
Mark Caroe, Partner
Background: Finance Director, Apertio; CFO, Paragon Software

2692 EIRCOM ENTERPRISE FUND LIMITED
1 Heuston South Quarter
St. John's Road
Dublin 8
Ireland

Phone: 353-167-14444 **Fax:** 353-16797253
web: www.eir.ie

Mission Statement: Actively seeking new investments.
Geographic Preference: Ireland
Minimum Investment: $45, 500

Investment Criteria: Seed Capital, Start-Up Capital, Early Stage
Industry Group Preference: Communications
Key Executives:
Cathal Magee, Managing Director
Alfie Kane, Group Chief Executive

2693 ELAIA PARTNERS
54 rue de Ponthieu
Paris 75008
France

Phone: 33-176749250 **Fax:** 33-176749260
e-mail: contact@elaia.com
web: www.elaia.com

Mission Statement: An independent private equity boutique focused on Digital Economy. Our belief is twofold: digital economy-related technologies are increasingly driving innovation growth in every key sectors and our focus in this sector will keep us among the leading experts in this domain.

Fund Size: $45 Million
Founded: 2002
Industry Group Preference: Information Technology, Financial Services, Enterprise Software
Portfolio Companies: Agnito, Allmyapps, Climpact, Criteo, Digital Healthcare, ePawn, Goom Radio, Mirakl, Orchestra Networks, Scoop.it, Sensorly, Sigfox, Total Immersion, Wyplay, Ykone

Key Executives:
Philippe Gire, Partner
Education: Ecole Polytechnique
Background: Accenture, Valeo Ventures

2694 ELECTRA PARTNERS ASIA LIMITED SFC of Hong Kong
18/F, 8 Queen's Road
1 Connaught Place
Central
Hong Kong

Phone: 852-25308700 **Fax:** 852-25305525
web: www.electra-asia.com

Mission Statement: Concentrates on established but high growth international companies based in Asia.

Geographic Preference: Asia
Founded: 1995
Investment Criteria: Growth Capital, Significant Minority Shareholdings
Industry Group Preference: Cable, Internet Technology, Construction, Outsourcing & Efficiency, Ancillary Services, Chemicals, Storage, Packaging, Processing, Software Services, Optical Technology, Manufacturing, Tourism, Media
Portfolio Companies: Aksh Optifibre Ltd. (India), Asia Travelmart Ltd. (Malaysia), Convansys Inc (Us/India), Locus Corporation (Korea), Meghmani Organics Ltd. (India), Moser Baer India Ltd. (India), Spi Technologies Inc, Zensar Technologies Ltd

Key Executives:
John Levack, Managing Director
e-mail: info@electra-asia.com
Education: Degree in business administration from Bath University in the UK.
Background: Electra, 3i Pic in Asia and Europe
Jessica Mak, Associate

2695 ELECTRA PARTNERS EUROPE
Paternoster House
65n St Paul's Churchyard
London EC4M 8AB
United Kingdom

Phone: 44-2072144200 **Fax:** 44-2072144201
e-mail: info@electrapartners.com

Venture Capital & Private Equity Firms / International Firms

Mission Statement: Actively seeking new investments.
Geographic Preference: France, Belgium, Switzerland
Fund Size: £450 million
Average Investment: Euro 3 Billion
Minimum Investment: Ffr150 million
Investment Criteria: MBO, MBI, Replacement
Industry Group Preference: Financial Services, Healthcare, Industrial Services, Services, Consumer Services
Portfolio Companies: CPI, Covenant Healthcare, Global Solutions, KSM Castings, UK Support Services, Urbium

Key Executives:
   Shakira Adigun-Boaye, Investment Associate
   Education: Lyon Business School
   Background: VP, Europe@Web; Investment Director, Fonds Partnaires (Lazard Freres & Cie); Arthur Andersen
   Nicholas Board, Marketing Executive
   Education: Ecole Polytechnique; Ecole Nationale des Ponts
   Background: Principal, Apax; BNP Paribas; Arthur Andersen
   Alex Cooper-Evans, Investment Partner & Head of Investor Relations
   Education: BS, Queen's University
   Background: Director, Prudential Venture Managers; Corporate Finance, Coopers & Lybrand; Chartered Accountant
   Philip Dyke, Partner
   Education: BS Civil Engineering, University of London; MBA, Cranfield Business School
   Background: VP, Citibank Leveraged Buyout Department
   Alex Fortescue, Chief Investment Partner
   Education: Chemistry degree, Nottingham University
   Background: Managing Director, L&G Ventures GmbH; Investment Manager, 3i; Chemist, BP Chemicals

---

2696 ELEVEN
4 Gurko Street
2nd floor
Sofia 1000
Bulgaria

Phone: +35 9886852881
web: www.eleven.bg

Mission Statement: Eleven is a EUR 12 million venture fund that provides financing to early-stage startups using an incremental investment approach alongside iterative development - thereby, starting with many small experiments, filter out failures, and invest in successes.
Fund Size: EUR 12 million
Founded: 2012
Average Investment: 150,000 Euro
Investment Criteria: Seed-Stage, Early-Stage
Portfolio Companies: KeenSkim, Fh, Filement, Meister Plus, Olympix, Lakoteka, SoccerScout.com, VetCloud, Sponsia, Squee, Unioncy, Sensika, Eventyard, Playground Energy, SoundVamp

Key Executives:
   Daniel Tomov, Partner
   Dilyan Dimitrov, Partner
   Ivo Simov, Partner
   Jonathan Bradford, Mentor-in-chief

2697 EM WARBURG, PINCUS & COMPANY INTERNATIONAL
Almack House
28 King Street, St. James's
London SW1Y 6QW
United Kingdom

Phone: 44-2073060306 Fax: 44-2073210881
e-mail: info@warburgpincus.com
web: www.warburgpincus.com

Mission Statement: Actively seeking new investments.
Geographic Preference: United Kingdom, Central Europe, Western Europe
Fund Size: $40 Billion
Founded: 1966
Average Investment: $25 Million
Minimum Investment: $8.85 Million
Investment Criteria: Early Stage, Expansion And Development, Secondary Purchase/Replacement Capital, Rescue/Turnaround, MBO, MBI
Industry Group Preference: Technology, Consumer Services, Education, Communications, Energy, Financial Services, Real Estate, Information Technology, Business to Business, Industrial Services, Natural Resources
Portfolio Companies: Asia Ec, Campsystems, Cobalt, Globalspec, Gt Nexus, Mach, Rmi, Workscape, Ugs, Iss, Vodlee, Aicent, Fibernet, Lssi, Bharti Enterprise, Neustar, Mbi, Jarden, Knoll, Polypore, Transdigm, The Neiman Marcus Group, Ambuja Cement, Northpole, Karsen, 4Gl, Aspen

Key Executives:
   Charles R. Kaye, Co-Chief Executive Officer
   e-mail: cjoung@warburgpincus.com
   Education: A.B. in physics from Dartmouth College and an M.B.A. with High Distinction from the Amos Tuck School of Business, where he was an Edward Tuck Scholar.
   Background: head of the Americas Natural Resources Group (Energy and Power practice) in the Investment Banking Division of Goldman, Sachs & Co
   Joseph P. Landy, Co-Chief Executive Officer
   e-mail: sarenare@warburgpincus.com
   Education: B.A. in political science magna cum laude from the University of Pennsylvania.
   Background: attorney in the Corporate and Finance department
   Michael Clancy, Managing Director
   Education: B.A. in economics from Yale University and an M.B.A. from the Stanford University Graduate School of Business.
   Background: engagement manager with McKinsey & Company and was Executive Vice President of InfoUSA
   Directorships: Director.
   Steve Coates, Managing Director
   e-mail: scoates@warburgpincus.com
   Education: M.A. in Politics, Philosophy and Economics from Oxford University and is a Chartered Accountant.
   Background: a corporate finance director for Arthur Andersen & Co.& 3i

---

2698 EM WARBURG, PINCUS & COMPANY JAPAN
Hibiya Marine Bldg., 8th Floor
Cjoupda-ku
Tokyo 100-0006
Japan

Phone: 81-355216830 Fax: 81-355210066
web: www.warburgpincus.com

Mission Statement: Invests in worldwide opportunities, actively seeking new investments
Geographic Preference: Worldwide
Fund Size: $8 Billion
Founded: 1966
Average Investment: $40 Billion
Investment Criteria: Early stage, growth and late stage
Industry Group Preference: Business to Business, Communications, Consumer Services, Education, Energy, Financial Services, Healthcare, Life Sciences, Information Technology, Media, Real Estate, Technology, Industrial Services, Natural Resources
Portfolio Companies: AsiaEC.com, CAMP Systems, Cobalt, GlobalSpec, GT Nexus, InfoGenesis, Institutional

Venture Capital & Private Equity Firms / International Firms

Shareholder Services, Inc., MACH, Manugistics, AsiaInfo & Aicent
Key Executives:
Charles R. Kaye, Co-President
Education: B.S.E. from Princeton University
Background: Oliver , Wyman & Co. & IMPEX
Directorships: Director, UL Systems & Director, Resolution Property plc
Joseph P. Landy, Co-President

2699 ENDEAVOUR CAPITAL PTY LIMITED
Endeavour Capital
Level 1, 432 Kent Street
Sydney 2000
Australia
Phone: 61-0280969222 Fax: 61-0280969229
e-mail: pw@endeavourcapital.com.au
web: www.endeavourcapital.com.au

Mission Statement: Independent corporate advisory firm, focusing exclusively on smaller and mid-market companies.
Geographic Preference: Australia, New Zealand
Founded: 1998
Key Executives:
Peter Wallace, Founder & Managing Director
e-mail: pw@endeavourcapital.com.au
Background: Investment Director, Hambro-Grantham
Directorships: Ambertech Limited; The Executive Connection Pty Ltd.; Carte Blanche Australia Pty Limited

2700 ENERGY VENTURES
Kongsgaardbakken 1
Stavanger 4005
Norway
Phone: 47 51 84 12 95

Mission Statement: Energy Ventures is an independent venture capital firm dedicated to new upstream oil and gas technologies. From the initial investment to the exit, we take a hands-on approach. By truly partnering with our portfolio companies, we ensure the most effective use of capital and talent. Our method is proven by our record: since Energy Ventures' creation in 2002 we have reviewed more than 2500 deals, made thirty-two investments and successfully exited twelve companies.
Geographic Preference: North Sea, North America
Fund Size: $750 million
Average Investment: $5 - $35 million
Industry Group Preference: Oil & Gas, Energy
Portfolio Companies: Acoustic Zoom, ARKeX, Foster Findlay Associates, Fotech Solutions, Ingrain, Wireless Seismic, 2TD, Abrado Welbore Services, Cubility, Deep Casing Tools, Energy Drilling, IWC, Meta, Oxane Materials, READ Cased Hole, Ziebel, Zilift, DeepFlex, Energreen, HalfWave, OsComp Systems, PanGeo Subsea, Produced Water Absorbents, Reality Mobile, Sigma Offshore
Other Locations:
10777 Westheimer
Suite 1175
Houston, TX 77042
Phone: 281-768-6721 Fax: 281-768-6726
Key Executives:
Jim Sledzik, Senior Partner

2701 ENNOVENT
Neubaugasse 11/14
4910 Ried im Innkreis
Vienna 1070
Austria
Phone: 43-1236585920 Fax: 43-1236585921
e-mail: office@ennovent.com
web: www.ennovent.com

Mission Statement: Ennovent is a venture catalyst that accelerates innovations for sustainability at the base of the economic pyramid. We work with a global network of entrepreneurs, investors and experts to discover, finance and scale up the best innovations.
Geographic Preference: India
Industry Group Preference: Energy, Food & Beverage, Water, Healthcare, Education

2702 ENSO VENTURES
10-11 Park Place
London SW1A 1LP
United Kingdom
Phone: 020-71484499
e-mail: info@ensoventures.com

Mission Statement: CLS Capital is a private investment and project management company that specializes in making highly selective equity investments in US and European biomedical companies with potential for capitalizing on technology transfer and product development in Russia and the CIS.
Geographic Preference: United States, Europe
Industry Group Preference: Healthcare, Life Sciences, Biomedical
Portfolio Companies: Novelos Therapeutics, Egalet, Seres Health
Other Locations:
747 3rd Avenue
2nd Floor
New York, NY 10017
Phone: 1-646-6960056
Key Executives:
Andrey Kozlov, Partner
Education: BS, Economics, St. Petersburg State University; MBA, Booth School of Business
Background: HSBC Investment Global Banking

2703 ENSPIRE CAPITAL PTE LTD
317 Outram Road
#B1-07 Holida Inn Atrium
169075
Singapore
Phone: +65 6349 0836 Fax: +65 6234 0532
e-mail: admin@enspire-capital.com
web: www.enspire-capital.com

Mission Statement: Our investment philosophy is to identify entrepreneurs with vision, innovative technology, and a strong sense of commitment. In addition to providing companies with venture capital, we also assume an active role in offering strategic advice to, and sharing our management expertise, experiences, and business connections with our portfolio companies.
Geographic Preference: United States West Coast, China, Taiwan, Hong Kong, Singapore
Minimum Investment: $1 million
Investment Criteria: Various Stages
Industry Group Preference: Technology, Media, Telecommunications, Internet
Portfolio Companies: A10 Networks, Amplus Communication Pte Ltd, ArrowSpan, Create Electronic Optical Co, Cipherium Systems Co, Dnium Pte Ltd, DynaScan Technology Corp, Egis Technology, Emine Software, Ether Optronics Inc, FocalTech Sytems, Genie Network Resource Management Inc, Global Communication Semiconductors, Hoodinn Interactive Limited, MBA Polymers, Pixelmetrix Corporation, Solapoint, Transcast Media, Voltafield Technology,
Key Executives:
Chay Kwong Soon, Founder & Chairman
Education: BSc, Physics, National University of Singapore

Venture Capital & Private Equity Firms / International Firms

Background: Co-Founder and President, Creative Technology Ltd
Dr. Lung Yeh, Managing Director
Education: BSEE, Communication Engineering, National Chiao-Tung University, Hsin-Chu, Taiwan; PhD, Electrical and Computer Engineering, University of Wisconsin - Madison
Background: Senior Vice President of Marketing, Sales and Operation, Centrality Communications; Co-Founder and Presdient and CEO, Pico Communications; Vice President of the Internet and Communication Division at Creative Labs; Founder, ShareVision Technology; Apple Computer; Verizon; Eastman Kodak

2704 ENTERPRISE EQUITY (NI) LTD
78A Dublin Road
Belfast BT2 7HP
United Kingdom
Phone: 44-2890242500 Fax: 44-2890242487

Mission Statement: Enterprise Equity backs growth orientated companies at various stages of their development.
Geographic Preference: Northern Ireland, Ireland
Fund Size: $12.4 Million
Founded: 1987
Average Investment: $1.06 Million
Minimum Investment: $445,000
Investment Criteria: Start-up, Other early stage, Expansion and Development, Secondary purchase/replacement capital, Rescue/turnaround, MBO, MBI
Industry Group Preference: Biotechnology, Medical & Health Related, Chemicals, Materials Technology, Energy, Construction, Building Materials & Services, Industrial Services, Manufacturing, Transportation, Communications, Information Technology, Computer Hardware & Software, Internet Technology, Electronic Technology
Portfolio Companies: Balcas Ltd, Bluechip Technologies Holdings Ltd, EZ-DSP Ltd, FIN Engineering Group Ltd, Gendel Ltd, Toughglass Holdings Ltd, TriVirix
Key Executives:
  Aidan Langan, Chief Executive Officer
  e-mail: info@eeni.com
  Education: Doctor of Public Administration
  Background: Gaeltarra Éireann
  Brian Cummings, Director
  e-mail: bob@eeni.com
  Education: Chartered Accountant
  Background: Non-Executive Director, Board Member

2705 ENTERPRISE EQUITY IRELAND LIMITED
Dublin Road
Teagasc Building
Dundalk, Co. Louth
Ireland
Phone: 353-429333167 Fax: 353-429334857
e-mail: info@enterpriseequity.ie
web: www.enterpriseequity.ie

Mission Statement: Commercial providers of Venture Capital to new and expanding business.
Geographic Preference: Ireland
Fund Size: $53 Million
Founded: 1987
Average Investment: $1.5 Million
Minimum Investment: $10.7 Million
Investment Criteria: Expansion - development, Seed, Small buyout (£m equity), Start-up
Portfolio Companies: International Test Technologies, Datacare Software Group, Ansamed Ltd, Iontas Ltd, Merenda Limited, Avenue Ltd, Duolog Ltd, Duolog Ltd, Aimware Limited, Swift Fine Foods Limited, SigmaX Limited, Celtrak Ltd, Neutekbio Ltd, AMT3D Limited.

Key Executives:
  Conor O'Connor, Managing Partner
  e-mail: info@enterpriseequity.ie
  Education: A Chartered Accountant he completed his training with PriceWaterhouseCoopers in Dublin
  Background: Chairman of the Irish Venture Capital Association as well as representing Ireland on the Board of the European Venture Capital Association (EVCA)
  Directorships: Director
  Rory Hynes, Partner
  Background: Civil Service; Gaeltarra Eireann; Udaras na Gaeltachta
  Tom Shinkwin, Partner
  Education: Bachelor of Commerce degree; MBA
  Background: Expreience: construction, engineering, corporate finance, management, property, banking
  Directorships: Strategic Equity Partners

2706 ENTERPRISE INVESTORS
Warsaw Financial Center, Emilii Plater 53
Warsaw 00-113
Poland
Phone: 48-224588500 Fax: 48-224588555
e-mail: info@ei.com.pl
web: www.ei.com.pl

Mission Statement: Actively seeking new investments.
Geographic Preference: Poland, Central and Eastern Europe
Fund Size: $2 billion
Founded: 1990
Average Investment: $28.8 Million
Investment Criteria: Start-up, buyouts, restructuring, strategic joint ventures, expansion financing for fast-growing companies, equity increase followed by flotation on the stock exchange, privatization with management s
Industry Group Preference: Computer Related, Financial Services, Industrial Equipment, Manufacturing, Telecommunications, Industrial Services
Portfolio Companies: AB SA, Wroclaw, DGS SA, Wloclawek, Agros Nova Sp. z o.o., Warsaw, Artima SA, Romania, Gamet Sp. z o.o., Torun, Kruk SA, Wroclaw, Magellan Sp. z o.o., Lódz, Medycyna Rodzinna SA, Warsaw
Key Executives:
  Robert Faris, Chairman
  e-mail: info@ei.com.pl
  Background: Director Corporate Development, Amoco Chemical/Standard Oil, Indiana; President/General Partner, Alan Patricof Associates
  Directorships: CEO
  Jacek Siwicki, President
  e-mail: info@ei.com.pl
  Background: Polish Deputy Minister of Privatization and as adviser to the International Finance Corporation. Mr. Siwicki focuses on privatization
  Michael Rusiecki, Managing Partner
  e-mail: info@ei.com.pl
  Background: Director at the Polish Ministry of Privatization, negotiated transactions with International Paper, ABB, Philips,
  Robert Manz, Managing Partner
  e-mail: info@ei.com.pl
  Background: Financial Analyst, Dillon, Read and Co. Inc.
  Dariusz Pronczuk, Managing Partner
  e-mail: info@ei.com.pl
  Background: Financial Analyst, Multicraft and PDG Partners; Vice President, Hejka Michna Inc.
  Tod Kersten, Portfolio Manager
  e-mail: info@ei.com.pl
  Background: Polish-American Enterprise Fund, Finance and a Director at the investment bank
  Stanislaw Knaflewski, Portfolio Manager
  e-mail: info@ei.com.pl
  Background: he worked for The Boston Consulting Group in Warsaw and Paris

Venture Capital & Private Equity Firms / International Firms

2707 ENTERPRISE VENTURE LIMITED
23 Berkeley Square
London W1J 6HE
United Kingdom

Phone: 0845-0948886 Fax: 0845-0948887
e-mail: mail@equityventures.co.uk
web: www.evgroup.uk.com

Mission Statement: Actively seeking new investments.
Geographic Preference: United Kingdom
Fund Size: $35.4 Million
Average Investment: Euro 100 Million
Minimum Investment: $88, 500 Million
Investment Criteria: Expansion and Development, Refinancing bank debt, Secondary purchase/replacement capital, MBO, MBI, Mezzanine
Industry Group Preference: All Sectors Considered
Portfolio Companies: Acrohone Ltd., Jackson Vending Ltd.

Key Executives:
  Valerie Andrew, Investment Executive
  e-mail: david@equityventures.co.uk
  Education: London School of Economics with a BSc Honours degree in Economics and International Relations, Masters degree in Business Analysis at Lancaster Universit
  Background: Price Waterhouse, Ernst & Young
  Ian Atkinson, Investment Manager
  e-mail: robert@equityventures.co.uk
  Education: University of Oxford, Honours in Politics Philosophy and Economics, Institute of Business Administration in Fontainbleau(MBA)
  Background: First National Bank of Boston in London, Hoare Govett,

2708 ENTERPRISE VENTURES LIMITED
Preston Technology Management Centre
Marsh Lane
Preston PR1 8UQ
United Kingdom

Phone: 0845-0948886 Fax: 0845-0948887
e-mail: richard.bamford@enterprise-ventures.co.uk
web: www.evgroup.uk.com

Mission Statement: Actively seeking new investments.
Geographic Preference: United Kingdom
Fund Size: $79.7 Million
Founded: 1941
Average Investment: $0.62 Million
Minimum Investment: $0.04 Million
Investment Criteria: Seed, Start-up, Other early stage, Expansion and Development, Rescue/turnaround, MBO, MBI
Industry Group Preference: All Sectors Considered
Portfolio Companies: RisingStars Growth Fund, Lancashire Rosebud Fund, Coalfields Enterprise Fund, eXML, Femeda Ltd, Bio Futures PLC, Avanticare, Specialist Heating Components Ltd, Cliq Designs Ltd, Transport Models, Farmhouse Fare Ltd

Key Executives:
  Richard Bamford, Executive Chairman
  Education: MA, Solicitor
  Background: Chaired the BVCA Legal & Technical Committee for several years
  Jonathan Diggines, Chief Executive
  Education: ACIB
  Background: Richard has been a leading private equity practitioner for some twenty years, and is highly experienced in all aspects of private equity,
  Lisa Ward, Investment Manager
  Education: ACIB
  Background: He was previously a Senior Corporate Lending Manager for a major UK bank.
  Directorships: Senior Corporate Lending Manager
  Mark Wyatt, Investment Manager
  Education: MBA, BA (Hons)

Background: Spent five years with 3i plc as an early stage technology investor in its Northern Investor team. He has considerable experience in undertaking, managing and exiting venture capital investments from start-ups to MBOs/MBIs in a variety of industrial sectors.
  Julian Viggars, Head of Technology Investment
  Education: BSc, ACA
  Background: Director of BioProjects International, an AIM-listed early stage technology fund. Julian has particular expertise in the healthcare sector.
  John Charles, Investment Director
  Education: ACIB
  Background: Previously held a number of senior positions in corporate banking, including North West Regional Commercial Banking Director for a major high street bank
  John Simpson, Finance Director
  Education: MA, FCA
  Background: Head of UK Corporate Finance at strategy consultants, Arthur D Little.
  Directorships: Senior Investment Manager
  Melanie Lowe, Fund Administrator
  Education: BSc, ACA
  Background: Chartered Accountant with a broad range of financial experience at main board level in both listed and private equity backed companies

2709 ENTREE CAPITAL
124 Baker Street
London W1U 6TY
United Kingdom

web: www.entreecap.com

Mission Statement: Entree Capital provides multi-stage funding for innovative seed, early and growth companies all over the world. Entree Capital was founded by entrepreneurs with a track record of having successfully invested and exited many businesses on five continents in the past two decades. Our offices are located in London and Tel Aviv, yet we make investments in most countries.
Geographic Preference: Worldwide
Investment Criteria: Seed-Stage, Early-Stage, Growth Stage
Industry Group Preference: Enterprise Software, Consumer Internet, High Technology, Business Products & Services, Real Estate, Medical Devices
Portfolio Companies: Cura Software, Intec Telecom Systems, JustEnough Software, CQS, Coupang, Internet Sports Marketing, DragonPlay, Connected Backup, UltraDNS, Maestro Commerce, 365Media, Independent Commercial, Harvest Automation, Concillium, Automated Fuel Systems Group, Bandit Vehicle Security, Mondial Risk Management, Brightside, Insight Technologies Network Academy, IOCORE, Zenprop, Virtual Ports

2710 ENTREPRENEURS FUND
3rd Floor, Standbrook House
2-5 Old Bond Street
London W1S 4PD
United Kingdom

Phone: 44-02073551011 Fax: 44-02073556199
e-mail: info@entrepreneursfund.com
web: www.entrepreneursfund.com

Mission Statement: There is nothing average about us or our partners. We believe our attitude and experience represent a major opportunity to companies. Simply, we allow them to overcome any restrictions to their growth objectives more quickly and more easily. And importantly we do that together. By using the global presence of our group parent to strengthen the potential and status of young companies. By networking companies together. By playing an active role in our investments. New sectors offer new opportunities and different dynamics. We actively seek out these challenges.
Geographic Preference: Worldwide
Investment Criteria: Early-Stage

Venture Capital & Private Equity Firms / International Firms

Industry Group Preference: Life Sciences, Clean Technology
Portfolio Companies: CPT, Cytoo, D3O, Evolva, Exosect, Fits.me, FutureE, General Fusion, Lifeline Scientific, N-Tec, OptiNose, Prosonix, ProtAffin, Real Eyes, Sequana Medical, T2Cure, Technolas, The New Motion, VasoPharm, Xeros
Key Executives:
   Klass de Boer, Managing Partner
   Education: MSc, Physics; MBA, INSEAD
   Background: Vanenburg Group; Consultant, McKinsey & Company

2711 EPISODE 1 PARTNERS
Kingsbourne House
229-231 High Holborn
London WC1 V7DA
United Kingdom
Phone: 44-02074864841 Fax: 44-02079357963
e-mail: info@episode1.com
web: www.episode1.com

Mission Statement: Takes an active role in helping to build the businesses we invest in

Geographic Preference: United Kingdom
Founded: 1942
Investment Criteria: early stage investments in technology and information services
Industry Group Preference: Internet Technology, Banking
Portfolio Companies: Commerce Decisions, Magicalia, Moreover Technologies, Natural Motion, Shazam, Wall Street Transcript, Betfair.com, Online Partners, Openharbor.com, Clovis, FriendsAbroad.com, Video Island
Key Executives:
   Adrian Lloyd, Partner
   Simon Murdoch, Co-founder
   Education: BA in Physics and a PhD in Computer Science and Expert Systems
   Background: Vice President Europe of Amazon.com.Managing Director of a UK-based software house, Triptych Systems.
   Directorships: Vice President

2712 EQT PARTNERS AB
Hovslagargatan 3, PO Box 16409
Stockholm SE-111 48
Sweden
Phone: 46-850655300 Fax: 46-850655319
web: www.eqt.se

Mission Statement: Actively seeking new investments in Nordic medium-sized companies as investment adviser to EQT Scandinavian I and II, EQT Danmark and EQT Finland.

Geographic Preference: Denmark, Finland, Germany, Norway, Sweden
Founded: 1995
Average Investment: Euro 11 Billion
Investment Criteria: have significant potential for top-line and earnings growth, can retain or attract high-quality management, have well-defined realization alternatives.
Industry Group Preference: Chemicals, Consumer Services, Consumer Products, Industrial Equipment, Telecommunications, Materials Technology, Retailing, Industrial Services, Carriers
Portfolio Companies: AG Kühnle Kopp & Kausch, Aleris AB, BHS Getriebe GmbH, Brandtex Group A/S, Carl Zeiss Vision GmbH, Contex A/S, Eldon Holding AB, Metall Technologie Holding GmbH
Key Executives:
   Johan Bygge, Chief Operating Officer
   e-mail: juha.lindfors@eqt.fi
   Education: graduated with a M.Sc. (Econ.) from the Helsinki School of Economics in 1994
   Background: Cultor Group in investor relations, and with Strategic Analysis & Management Inc., a management consulting firm
   Marcus Brennecke, Partner
   e-mail: marcus.brennecke@eqt.de
   Education: Graduated from the University of St. Gallen, Switzerland
   Background: Managing Partner and entrepreneurial investor at German private equity company SMB, Founder/CEO of a tv-sport rights company.
   Directorships: Entrepreneurial investor
   Caspar Callerström, Director
   e-mail: caspar.callerstrom@eqt.se
   Education: M.Sc. at the Stockholm School of Economics with two majors (Financial Economics, and International Business).
   Bjorn Hoi Jensen, Director
   e-mail: bjorn.jensen@eqt.de
   Education: Graduated from Copenhagen University with a Master of Science in Economics in 1985
   Background: 10 years in investment banking and private equity in London and Copenhagen, with amongst others Citibank, SDS and Enskilda Securities
   Hakan Johansson, Director
   e-mail: hakan.johansson@eqt.se
   Education: Graduate of the University of Gothenburg with majors in Accounting and Finance.
   Background: Volvo Group Finance in Amsterdam, Electrolux, Senior Vice President and Head of Mergers and Acquisitions at Electrolux.
   Thomas Von Koch, Director
   e-mail: thomas.vonkoch@eqt.se
   Education: Graduated from the Stockholm School of Economics in 1992 with two majors (Financial Economics and Accounting & Finance
   Background: Investor AB, director of the boards of Com Hem AB, Plantasjen ASA, VTI Technologies and Duni AB.
   Jan Stahlberg, Director
   e-mail: jan.stahlberg@eqt.se
   Education: Graduated from the Stockholm School of Economics in 1985 with two majors (Economic Analysis and Accounting & Finance).
   Background: Ovako Steel as Senior Vice President of Finance and member of the Executive Management
   Vesa Koskinen, Partner
   e-mail: vesa.koskinen@eqt.fi
   Education: MSc degree with a major in Finance in the Helsinki School of Economics.
   Background: JPMorgan and Metso Corporation

2713 EQUINET VENTURE PARTNERS AG
97 Graefstrasse
Frankfurt 60487
Germany
Phone: 49-69589970 Fax: 49-695-8997299
e-mail: info@equinet-ag.de
web: www.equinet-ag.de

Mission Statement: Equinet Venture Partners AG is the VC specialist of Equinet AG, an investment bank focused on rapidly growing technology companies.

Geographic Preference: Germany
Fund Size: $18 Million
Founded: 1999
Investment Criteria: Expansion - development, Seed, Start-up, Other early stage
Industry Group Preference: Information Technology, Life Sciences, High Technology
Portfolio Companies: Phenex Pharmaceuticals AG, Nova Ratio AG, Mobotix, Sysgo, iTAC, Geneart, Nanogate Technologies, Euroimmun, Eisfeld Datentechnik, Ihr Partner Software, Newtron
Key Executives:
   Lutz Weiler, CEO
   e-mail: lutz.weiler@equinet-ag.de

871

Venture Capital & Private Equity Firms / International Firms

Background: IPO transactions and was responsonsible for the bank's leading position, member of the Primary Market Advisory Committee
Anita Prattki, CFO
e-mail: goetz.gollan@equinet-ag.de
Background: Mid-caps in particular on IPOs, pre IPO financing, M&As and stock option schemes.
Prof. Dr. Andreas Wiedemann, Chairman of the Supervisory Board
e-mail: farsin.yadegardjam@equinet-ag.de

2714 EQUISTONE
Condor House, St Paul's Churchyard
Canary Wharf
London EC4M 8AL
United Kingdom

Phone: 44-02075129900 Fax: 44-2076535301ÿ
e-mail: rob.myers@equistonepe.com
web: www.barcap.com

Mission Statement: Invests as a strategic partner alongside management teams, working together to build and realise shareholder value.
Geographic Preference: United Kingdom, France, Germany, Italy
Fund Size: $1.97 Billion
Average Investment: $164 Million
Minimum Investment: $30 Million
Investment Criteria: Expansion and Development, Refinancing bank debt, Secondary purchase/replacement capital, MBO, MBI, Institutional BO, Leveraged Build Up, Public-to-Private
Industry Group Preference: Engineering, Automotive, Consumer Services, Transportation, Healthcare, Household Goods, Construction, Retailing, Financial Services, Chemicals, Food & Beverage, Electronic Technology, Oil & Gas, Tourism, Logistics
Portfolio Companies: Médi-Partenaires, Laho Equipement, Jack Wolfskin, Kurt Geiger, Maisons du Monde, Neumayer Tekfor, CEME Group, Alstom Power Conversion
Key Executives:
  Eric Bommensath, Co-Chief Executive, Corporate and Investment Banking
  e-mail: brian.blakemore@barcap.com
  Background: Investor Relations Director at Midlands
  Tom King, Co-Chief Executive, Corporate and Investment Banking
  e-mail: paul.goodson@barcap.com
  Background: Director in 3i transaction team
  Directorships: Board Member, Special Director
  Justin Bull, Chief Operating Officer, Corporate and Investment Banking
  e-mail: olvier.jennings@barcap.com
  Background: Head of Infrastructure in Bank of America, PPP/PFI sectors, Director in Price Waterhouse
  Lee Guy, Co-Chief Risk Officer
  e-mail: mark.taylor@barcap.com
  Background: Chartered Accountant at Price Waterhouse
  Directorships: Non-Executive Director

2715 EQUITY PARTNERS PTY LIMITED
Level 12, 201 Kent Street
Sydney 2000
Australia

Phone: 61-282985100 Fax: 61-282985150

Mission Statement: Actively seeking new investments
Geographic Preference: Australia, New Zealand, South Africa, Asia, United Kingdom
Fund Size: $350 million
Founded: 1995
Investment Criteria: Global Expansion, MBO, Acquisitions
Industry Group Preference: Technology, Management, Enterprise Services

Portfolio Companies: BOSS (Business Operations & Software Solutions), TOWER Software Engineering, Energetics, Snowball Group Limited , Yambay Technologies Pty Limited , Protocom Development Systems Pty Limited , Portland Orthopaedics Pty Limited, Agrilink Holdings Pty Limited , Imm
Key Executives:
  Quentin Jones BA Ll.B, Partner
  e-mail: kim.durack@equitypartners.com.au
  Education: Bachelor of Science in Biochemistry, a Bachelor of Arts in Economics and Journalism, a Post Graduate Certificate in Technology Management, and is completing an MBA at MGSM
  Background: Sale and marketing arms of two blue-chip pharmaceutical companies, Hoffman La-Roche and Schering Plough
  Rajeev Dhawan BCom, CA, MBA, Partner
  e-mail: peterbj@equitypartners.com.au
  Education: BCom (Hons) CA(SA)
  Background: Manufacturing, health care and other service delivery businesses
  Greg Wang BCom, CA, MBA, Associate Director
  e-mail: rgregson@equitypartners.com.au
  Education: BSc (Hons I) PhD MBA
  Background: Telecommunications, on-line business, software and hardware systems, health care services, biotechnology, energy, and other services

2716 EQVITEC PARTNERS OY
8 Fabianinkatu
PO Box 65
Helsinki 00131
Finland

Phone: 358-5066563 Fax: 358-207-809801
e-mail: jukka.makinen@eqvitec.com

Mission Statement: Actively seeking new investments.
Geographic Preference: Denmark, Estonia, Finland, Lithuania, Norway, Sweden
Fund Size: $360 Million
Founded: 1998
Investment Criteria: Early-Stage, Expansion and Development Capital, Mezzanine, Startup Capital, Buyout and Buyin
Industry Group Preference: Communications, Computer Related, Electronic Technology, Industrial Products, Industrial Services, Chemicals, Materials Technology
Portfolio Companies: AffectoGenimap Group Oyj, Aidox Oy, Anilinker Oy, Codenomicon Oy, Codetoys Oy, DynaRoad Oy, Envox Group AB (publ.), Fastrax Oy, Fox Technologies, Inc, FRENDS Technology Oy, Navicore Ltd, Oy 4Pharma Ltd, Samstock Oy, Sanako Corporation, Saraware Oy, Selmic Oy, SEVEN
Key Executives:
  Jukka Mäkinen, Managing Partner
  Background: Vice Chairman, Finnish Venture Capital Association, Director in, SITRA
  Directorships: Managing Director, CEO
  Juha Mikkola, Senior Partner

2717 ESPIRITO SANTO VENTURES
Rue Alexandre Herculano
38, 5 piso
Lisboa 1250-011
Portugal

Phone: 351-213106490 Fax: 351-213106425
web: www.es-ventures.com

Mission Statement: Espirito Santo Ventures is a venture capital firm of Espirito Santo Group, focused on technology based companies and innovative business projects with high-growth potential.

Fund Size: 200 million Euros
Founded: 2000

Venture Capital & Private Equity Firms / International Firms

Average Investment: 1 - 10 million Euros
Industry Group Preference: Clean Technology, Healthcare, Information Technology
Portfolio Companies: A123 Systems, Advanced Cyclone Systems, Altraverda, AquaSpy, Banco Best, Chipidea, Clarity Payment Solutions, Contact, Coreworks, Global Active, IOSIL Energy, MagPower, Malo Clinic, Megamedia, Milcom Technologies, Multiwave, Nanosolar, Novabase, Nutrigreen, Oceanlinx, Opthalmopharma, OutSystems, Petra Solar, Prepaid Capital, Prepaid Media, SafetyPay, Spectrum Bridge, Sousacamp, Super Bac, TxVia, UltraCell, Vortal, Watson Brown, Ydreams

Key Executives:
Joaquim Servulo Rodriques, Chief Executive Officer and Executive Director
Education: BSc, MSc, Electrotechnical Engineering, IST; MBA, INSEAD
Background: Assistant Professor, IST; Research Project Leader, INSEC; General Manager, Direct Channels Department, BES; CEO, CrediFlash SA
Pedro Ribeiro Santos, Executive Director, Chief Financial Officer
Education: BSc, Economics, UCP
Background: Investment Banking, CISF; Sociedada Independente de Servicios Financeiros; BPI
Jose Guerreiro de Sousa, Principal
Education: BSc, Electrotechnical Engineering & Computers, UCP
Background: Researcher, INESC; Assistant Professor, ISEG; Novabase SA; BES Group
Pedro Ribeiro Santos, Principal
Education: BSc, Physics Engineering, IST; MBA & MSc, Economics, UNL
Background: Researcher, Physics, University of Oxford; Accenture
Duarte Mineiro, Principal
Education: BSc, Management & Industrial Engineering, IST; MBA, Tuck School of Business, Dartmouth College
Background: Boston Consulting Group

2718 ETHOS PRIVATE EQUITY LIMITED: SA
PO Box 9773
Johannesburg 2000
South Africa

Phone: 27-113287400 Fax: 27-113287410
e-mail: cwilkinson@ethos.co.za
web: www.ethos.co.za

Mission Statement: Participates in the development and financing of companies within the university college sphere.
Geographic Preference: South Africa
Fund Size: $0.46 Million
Founded: 1998
Average Investment: $78,000
Minimum Investment: $15,500
Investment Criteria: Seed
Portfolio Companies: C-Takt AB, Cellectricom AB, Elektron AB, Eutech Medical AB, Framespot AB, Geositian AB, LightUp Technologies AB, Medeikonos AB, MicVac AB, Nanofactory Instruments AB, Q-Sense AB, Radiaus Innova AB, Sauiba Sensors AB

Key Executives:
Bill Ashmore, Partner
e-mail: aroux@ethos.co.za
Education: B.com (University of Withwatersand)
Background: More than 20 yrs experience in investment banking.
Directorships: Serves on the Dunlop Board
Andre Roux, Deputy Chairman

2719 EURAZEO
32 rue de Monceau
Paris 75008
France

Phone: 33-144150111 Fax: 33147668441
e-mail: Eurazeo_investor_relations@eurazeo.com

Mission Statement: Formerly Gaz-et-Eaux. An investment company unlike conventional holding companies, it is highly proactive and forward-looking; actively seeks new investment opportunities and works to enhance the value of those already in its portfolio.
Geographic Preference: Europe
Minimum Investment: $1,000,000 EURO
Investment Criteria: LBO, Expansion & Development Capital, Replacement Capital
Industry Group Preference: Communications, Consumer Services, Electronic Technology, Information Technology, Industrial Services, Internet Technology, Multimedia
Portfolio Companies: Distacom, Eutelsat, Fraikin, Rexel, Sandinvest, Terreal

Key Executives:
Patrick Sayer, Chairman
Education: Ecole Polytechnique; Ecole des Mines
Background: Managing Director, Lazard Freres et Cie
Directorships: Fraikin, Ipsos, Eutelsat
Bruno Keller, Chief Operating Officer
Education: Ecole Polytechnique
Background: Technical Project Manager, French Ministry of Defense
Virginie Morgon, Chief Operating Officer
Education: HEC, Paris
Background: JP Morgan
Philippe Audouin, Chief Financial Officer
Education: Ecole Polytechnique

2720 EUROFUND LP
87 Hayarkon Street
Tel Aviv 63432
Israel

Phone: 972-35202555 Fax: 972-35270041
e-mail: info@eurofund.co.il

Mission Statement: Eurofund and Eurofund 2000 are venture capital funds with a strongly defined identity and distinct areas of operation. They were established in alliance with powerful strategic partners who are industry leaders in the global marketplace. Eurofund 2000 still is open to new investments.

Geographic Preference: Israel
Fund Size: $ 72 Million
Investment Criteria: Early Stage
Industry Group Preference: Telecommunications, Microelectronics, Information Technology, Internet Technology, Security
Portfolio Companies: ART Advanced Recognition Technologies, BeInSync, ColorChip, CyOptics, Eldat, Exactium, Foxcom, Hotbar.com, Idanit, MobileAccess Networks, Passave Technologies, Radwin, Schema, Silicon Value, TEVET Process Control Technologies, Verisity

Key Executives:
Michael Federmann, Chairman
Education: BA Economics, Hebrew University
Directorships: Chairman/CEO, Federmann Enterprises; Elbit Systems; Dan Hotels Corp
Aharon Beth-Halachmi, Managing Partner
e-mail: betha@eurofund.co.il
Education: BSEE, Technion Institute of Technology, Israel; MS Computer Science, Naval Postgraduate School, Monterey
Background: Head R&D/Chief of Defense, Israeli Airforce; Director/General, Ministry of Defense; President, TAHAL; President, Federman Enterprises-Industries & Technology

873

Venture Capital & Private Equity Firms / International Firms

Ron Hiram, Managing Partner
Education: MBA, Columbia University
Background: CEO/VP/Managing Director, Lehman Brothers; Managing Director, Soros Fund Management; TeleSoft Partners
Directorships: Comverse Technology, Ulticom, Systems Management ARTS, Hotbar.com, Tevet Process Control Technologies, ART Advanced Recognition Technologies
Moshe Price, Venture Partner
Education: BSEE, MS Management Sciences, West Coast University
Background: R&D Director, Tadiran Telecommunications
Directorships: Passave Technologies, Colorchip, Eldat Communication
Tzvika Kerner, CFO
e-mail: tzvika@eurofund.co.il
Education: BA Economics/Accountancy, Master degree Business Management, Hebrew University
Background: Federmann Group; Tadiran Communication

2721 EUROMEZZANINE CONSEIL
11 rue Scribe
Paris 75009
France
Phone: 33-153302330 Fax: 33-153302340
web: www.euromezzanine.com

Mission Statement: Actively seeking new projects.
Geographic Preference: European Countries
Fund Size: $38.81 Million
Founded: 2000
Average Investment: $2.75 Million
Minimum Investment: $0.27 Million
Investment Criteria: Mezzanine, Growth/Development Capital, Large Buyout/in, Replacement, Public-to-Private
Industry Group Preference: All Sectors Considered
Portfolio Companies: Alain Afflelou, Autodis, Ccmx, Cnn, Daher Lhotellier, Fianciere Felix, Hoffiges, Laho Equipment, Oberthur Smart Cards

Key Executives:
Thierry Raiff, President
e-mail: louis.vaillant@euromezzanine.com
Education: Institut d'Etudes Politiques
Background: Financiere BFCE, Director, LBO Investment, Ciclad, Director, LBO Investment, Credit Lyonnais, Vice President, Structured Finance
Ajit Jayaratnam, Associate Director
e-mail: guy.fabritius@euromezzanine.com
Education: HEC
Background: BNP Private Equity, Director, LBO & Mezzanine Investment, IRDI Director, Investment, Protex, Vice President, Administration & Finance

2722 EUROPEAN ACQUISITION CAPITAL LIMITED
14 Floral Street
London WC2E 9DH
United Kingdom
Phone: 44-2074208800 Fax: 44-2074208827
e-mail: info@milestone-capital.com

Mission Statement: EAC is a well-established and respected player in the European buy-in, buy-out and development capital sectors.
Geographic Preference: United Kingdom, Austria, Belgium, Denmark, Finland, France, Germany
Fund Size: $473.4 Million
Founded: 1991
Average Investment: Euro 454 Million
Minimum Investment: $5.9 Million
Investment Criteria: Start-up, development, turnaround, MBO, MBI
Industry Group Preference: All Sectors Considered
Portfolio Companies: The Eton Group Ltd, MW Group Ltd, IX Europe PLC, Renaissance BV, 5 à Sec BV, ADP Dental Company Ltd, Groupe d'Emballages Souples

Key Executives:
Bill Robinson, Managing Partner
Philip Conboy, Partner

2723 EUROPEAN FOUNDERS FUND
e-mail: businessplan@europeanfounders.com
web: www.europeanfounders.com

Mission Statement: We are intimately familiar with every stage of establishing a successful company: raising money, getting started, building and growing an organization into a very large business and realizing significant value for all stakeholders through a definition of exit strategies.

Investment Criteria: Early-Stage, Later-Stage
Industry Group Preference: Internet, Software, Wireless, Technology
Portfolio Companies: Facebook, HomeAway, Linkedin, Nasza-Klasa, Sport1

Key Executives:
Alexander Samwer, Partner
Background: Founder, Alando.de; Founder, Jamba! AG; Managing Director, Ebay

2724 EUROPEAN INVESTMENT FUND
15 avenue J.F. Kennedy
L-2968
Luxembourg
Phone: 352-24851 Fax: 352-248581200
e-mail: info@eif.org
web: www.eif.org

Mission Statement: An European institution committed to support the creation, growth and development of Small and Medium-sized Enterprises.

Geographic Preference: Europe
Fund Size: $3.06 Billion
Founded: 1994
Investment Criteria: Early Stage, Development and Expansion, Preferably Technology Oriented
Industry Group Preference: Technology, Information Technology, Biotechnology
Portfolio Companies: E-Capital, Euroventures III, UBF Mittelstandfinanzierungs AG, Genesis Private Equity Fund, SEEFT Ventures

Key Executives:
Dario Scannapieco, Chairman
Richard Pelly, Chief Executive
Francis Carpenter, CEO
Jean-Philippe Burcklen, Head of Division, Venture Capital Operations1
Marjut Santoni, Chief Executive
Dr. Matthias Ummenhofer, Deputy Head of Venture Capital Operations 2

2725 EUROVENTURES CAPITAL
Mártonhegyi út 61/A
Budapest H-1124
Hungary
Phone: 36-13097900 Fax: 36-13194762
e-mail: office@euroventures.hu
web: www.euroventures.hu

Mission Statement: Euroventures is one of the longest-established and leading independent private equity firms in Central Europe.

Geographic Preference: Hungary
Fund Size: $79 Million
Founded: 1989
Average Investment: $3.3 Million
Minimum Investment: $0.6 Million

Venture Capital & Private Equity Firms / International Firms

Investment Criteria: Early-stage, expansion/development, smaller buyouts
Industry Group Preference: Information Technology, Industrial Services, Consumer Services, Media, Logistics, Transportation, Food & Beverage, Automotive, Processing
Portfolio Companies: Alfa, AP Aqua, Avonmore Pásztó, Enigma Software, Euronet
Key Executives:
András Geszti, Founder
Péter Tánczos, Investment Analyst

2726 EVERGREEN VENTURE PARTNERS
25 Habarzel Street
Tel Aviv 69710
Israel
Phone: 972-37108282 **Fax:** 372-37108210
e-mail: info@evergreen.co.il

Mission Statement: Evergreen was established in 1987 by Jacob Burak as one of Israel's first Venture Capital firms, and has grown into a leader, generating successful exits with tangible rewards for investors and entrepreneurs.
Geographic Preference: Israel
Fund Size: $700 million
Founded: 1987
Investment Criteria: Early-Stage
Industry Group Preference: Communications, Internet, Media, Software, Healthcare
Portfolio Companies: Activiews, Amimon, AniBoom, Aquarius Technologies, CorAssist, eAsic, Flash Networks, Inneractive, Nephera, NiTi Surgical Solutions, Notal Vision, N-Trig, Optimal Test, Peer Medical, PeerApp, Pentalum, Pontis, Precede, Pythagoras, QualiSystems, Siklu, Siverge, Taboola, Varonis
Key Executives:
Boaz Dinte, General Partner
e-mail: bdinte@evergreen.co.il
Background: Corporate Business Development Manager, M-Systems; Senior Consultant, POC
Directorships: N-Trig, Pontis, Pythagoras Solar, Qualisystems

2727 EXCELSIOR CAPITAL ASIA
Units 1208-1209, Level 12
Core F, Cyberport 3
100 Cyberport Road
Hong Kong
Phone: 852-22309800 **Fax:** 852-22309898
e-mail: businessplans@excelcapasia.com
web: www.excelsiorcapitalasia.com

Mission Statement: Excelsior Capital Asia is an independent Asian-based direct investment firm which invests in companies throughout the Asian region.
Geographic Preference: China, Hong Kong, Taiwan, Korea
Fund Size: $324 million
Founded: 1998
Average Investment: $15 - $50 million
Investment Criteria: Acquisitions, Growth Capital
Industry Group Preference: Media, Consumer Products, Manufacturing
Portfolio Companies: CKH Food & Health Limited, CJ HelloVision Co., Ganzhou Dingsheng Water Technological Co., Lida Holdings Limited, Quanzhou Jinhua Edible Oil Co., SBM Co.
Other Locations:
9th Floor, 27 Yeouinaru-ro
Yeongdeungpo-gu
Seoul 07321
South Korea
Phone: 82-220881288 **Fax:** 82-220881387
Key Executives:
Gary Lawrence, Managing Partner
e-mail: gary.lawrence@excelcapasia.com
Education: BA, Yale University; MA, University of Oxford; LLB, McGill University
Background: Managing Director, Merchant Banking Group, Lehman Brothers; Managing Director, Tiger Management; Mergers & Acquisitions Department, Goldman Sachs; Attorney, White & Case
Directorships: CJ HelloVision, Tony Wear Fashion Co., Sanlih E-Television, Tainan Enterprises, Zest Health Clubs, Downer EDI, DC Chemical, Nation Multimedia Group
Junghyung Cho, Partner
e-mail: junghyung.cho@excelcapasia.com
Education: Seoul National University; MBA, Kellogg School of Management, Northwestern University
Background: Direct Investment Specialist, Merrill Lynch; Lehman Brothers; Bank of Korea
Thomas Frick, Partner
e-mail: thomas.frick@excelcapasia.com
Education: Kenyon College; CFA
Background: Founding Director, Odyssey Venture Group; Lehman Brothers
Michael Kent, Partner
e-mail: michael.kent@excelcapasia.com
Education: BA, Australian National University; MBA, University of New South Wales
Background: Consultant, Peregrine Direct Investments; Finance Director, Adelaide Steamship Company Group
Directorships: Ganzhou Dingsheng Water Technology Co.
Seungki Min, Partner
e-mail: seungki.min@excelcapasia.com
Education: BA, Business Administration, MA, Financial Engineering, Korea University
Background: Senior Managing Director, Keystone Private Equity Korea; CEO, HTC Asset Management; Senior Managing Director, Hyundai Securities; Senior Managing Director/CIO, Heungkuk Financial Group
John Yang, Partner
e-mail: john.yang@excelcapasia.com
Education: BA, University of Toronto; CFA
Background: Investment Director, PrimePartners Asset Management Group; Equity Analyst, Cazenove Asia Limited; PricewaterhouseCoopers; Ernst & Young
Directorships: Quanzhou Jinhua Edible Oil, China King-Highway, Gazhou Dingsheng Water, Sunrex Technology
Kihong Ryu, Managing Director
e-mail: kihong.ryu@excelcapasia.com
Education: BA, Business Administration, Yonsei University
Background: Managing Director, Keystone Private Equity Korea; Hyundai Securities; Heungkuk Life Insurance
Albert Chung, Principal
e-mail: albert.chung@excelcapasia.com
Education: BS, Computer Engineering, National Chiao Tung University; MBA, National Central University
Background: Senior Manager, Corporate Finance Advisory Group, KPMG
Dicken Chiu, Principal
e-mail: dicken.chiu@excelcapasia.com
Education: Imperial College of Science, Technology and Medicine, London
Background: Business Development Manager, Dairy Farm; Manager, Ernst & Young; MTR Corporation
James Yu, Senior Associate
e-mail: james.yu@excelcapasia.com
Education: BS, Economics, Duke University; MS, Finance, Imperial College of Science, Technology and Medicine, London; CFA
Background: Senior Associate, Corporate Financial Advisory Group, Deloitte & Touche

Venture Capital & Private Equity Firms / International Firms

2728 EXPIBEL BV
8C Arsenalsgatan
Stockholm 103 32
Sweden

Phone: 46-86142000 Fax: 46-86142150
e-mail: Stefan.Stern@investorab.com
web: www.investorab.com

Mission Statement: Investor contributes to the development of its holdings and focuses on the special circumstances and potential of each individual holding in order to contribute to healthy long-term value of
Geographic Preference: Northern Europe, USA, Asia
Fund Size: $1.8 Billion
Founded: 1916
Average Investment: $26.5 Million
Minimum Investment: $3 Million
Investment Criteria: Expansion and Development Capital
Industry Group Preference: Technology, Engineering, Healthcare, Financial Services
Portfolio Companies: Aerocrine, Affibody, Amkor Technology, Inc, Apollo International, Applied Sensor, Asia Renal Care Ltd, Atrica Axcan Pharma, AxioMed, Biotage, BMI Asia Inc, Cameron Health, Carmel Pharma, Cavidi Tech AB, Cellectricon, CHF Solutions, Endo Vasix, Epigenesis

Key Executives:
Stefan Stern, Head of Corp. Relations and Communications
Education: M.Sc. in Engineering(Royal Institute of Technology, Stockholm), M.B.A.(INSEAD)
Magnus Dalhammar, Head of Investor Relations

2729 EXPLORADOR CAPITAL MANAGEMENT
Rua Fidencio Ramos 101
Suite 61
Villa Olimpia
Sao Paulo 04551-010
Brazil

Phone: 55-11-4064-5300
e-mail: contact@explorador.net
web: www.explorador.net

Mission Statement: Our investment objective is to preserve capital under different market environments, while seeking to achieve above average returns on a risk-adjusted basis.
Geographic Preference: Latin America
Fund Size: $60 million
Founded: 1995
Average Investment: $4 million
Minimum Investment: $500,000

Key Executives:
Andrew H Cummins, President & CIO
e-mail: andy@explorador.net
Education: MBA, Corporate Strategy/Finance, Harvard Business School; BS, University of California, LA
Background: Management, Emerging Markets Management; JMB Realty Corporation
Fernando Jasnis, Portfolio Manager
Education: Industrial Engineering Degree, Instituto Tecnologico de Buenos Aires (ITBA); MBA, University of California, Berkeley
Background: Citigroup, Buenos Aires
Daniel Delabio, Portfolio Manger
Education: Bachelor's Degree, Business Administration, FGV-Brazil
Background: Dimaio Ahmad Capital

2730 FENNO MANAGEMENT OY
Toppelundintie 5 B 10
Espoo 2170
Finland

Phone: 358-400706072

Mission Statement: Specializing in generating value growth in the mid size companies. Fenno Management typically seeks acquisition and investment cases where there is need for strategic re-thinking, re-positioning, add on acquisitions or other clear growth strategies.
Fund Size: EUR 83 million
Average Investment: EUR 1 Million - 25 million
Investment Criteria: Re-positioning, add on acquisitions or other clear growth strategies.

Key Executives:
Aaro Cantell, Managing Partner

2731 FERD CAPITAL
Strandveien 50
PO Box 34
Lysaker N-1324
Norway

Phone: 47-67-10-80-00 Fax: 47-67-10-80-01
e-mail: post@ferd.no
web: www.ferd.no

Mission Statement: Ferd is a family-owned Norwegian industrial and financial group that is an active and long-term owner of strong companies with international potential and carries out financial activities through investments in a broad range of asset classes. Ferd Capital is an active and long-term investor in privately held and listed companies. This means that Ferd Capital assesses when to invest or sell its investments, as well as working actively with the companies in which it invests for the duration of its ownership in order to ensure the best possible value creation. Ferd Capital carries out its role as an active investor through collaboration with the management of its portfolio companies.
Geographic Preference: Nordic Countries
Fund Size: NOK 7 billion
Average Investment: NOK 100-1,000 million
Investment Criteria: Development Stage, Expansion Stage
Portfolio Companies: Aibel, Elopak, Interwell, Mestergruppen, Servi Group, Swix Sport, Telecomputing, Arkex, CFEngine, Eniram, Napatech, Vensafe, Wimp

Key Executives:
Peter Sunde, Investment Director/Co-Head
67-10-80-69
e-mail: jps@ferd.no
Education: MSc, Norwegian School of Management; CFA
Background: Senior Vice President, Telenor ASA; Vice President, Saga Petroleum
Directorships: TeleComputing, Mestergruppen
Morten Borge, Investment Director/Co-Head
67-10-80-86
e-mail: mb@ferd.no
Education: MSc, Norwegian School of Management; CPA
Background: CFO, Interwell; Audit & Transactions, PricewaterhouseCoopers
Directorships: Aibel, Interwell, Servi Group, Gladiator GT
Trond Solberg, Investment Director/Co-Head
67-10-80-39
e-mail: ts@ferd.no
Education: MSc, Norwegian School of Management; CEFA
Background: Project Leader, Norway Post; Analyst, Ferd Invest; Analyst, Accenture
Directorships: Elopak, Swix

2732 FERRANTI LIMITED
43 Rosary Gardens
London SW7 4NQ
United Kingdom

Phone: 44-02078351325 Fax: 44-02072448387
e-mail: mike@ferranti.com
web: www.ferranti.com

Venture Capital & Private Equity Firms / International Firms

Mission Statement: Provides firms with the business support and investment
Geographic Preference: United Kingdom, USA
Fund Size: $7.08 Million
Founded: 1982
Average Investment: $ 0.8 Million
Minimum Investment: $0.04 Million
Investment Criteria: Seed, Start-up, Other early stage, Expansion and Development, Bridge finance, Refinancing bank debt, Secondary purchase/replacement capital, Rescue/turnaround, MBO, MBI
Industry Group Preference: Communications, Information Technology, Energy, Internet Technology, Industrial Equipment, Electronic Technology, Computer Hardware & Software, Engineering, Pharmaceuticals, Financial Services, Industrial Services
Portfolio Companies: Ziani's, Post Impressions, Update Software, Plasmanet, Marlin, SSI, Carlton Corporate Finance, Chelford Group PLC
Key Executives:
  Howard Flight, Chairman
  e-mail: jane.weyman@ferranti.co.uk
  Background: over twenty years experience in banking and has worked for N.M. Rothschild and NatWest Bank in establishing a new merchant bank - Rothschild Intercontinental, which was later acquired by American Express.Mrs Weyman also worked for Banque de Paris et des P
  Directorships: finance controller
  Adrian De Ferranti, Managing Director
  e-mail: adrian@ferranti.co.uk
  Education: Degree in Engineering
  Background: Chairman of Technology and a Treasurer of the Conservative Party from 1991 to 2004., experience spans all aspects of corporate finance from venture capital and private equity through to M&A and public floatations.
  Michael Campbell, Director
  e-mail: mike.campbell@ferranti.co.uk
  Education: Degree in Electronic Engineering and an MBA.
  Background: Over fifteen years of international business consulting experience in the technology sector.
  Directorships: He is also a regular guest lecturer at Warwick University.

2733 FIDELITY GROWTH PARTNERS ASIA
Unit 2207, 22nd Floor, Tower 2
China Central Plaza
No. 79 Jianguo Road, Chaoyang District
Beijing 100025
China
Phone: 86-1065989336 Fax: 86-1065989335
e-mail: fgpa@fil.com

Mission Statement: Fidelity Growth Partners Asia (previously named Fidelity Asia Ventures) is the venture capital and private equity arm of Fidelity focused on investing in Greater China. We help companies accelerate growth by providing them with Fidelity's proprietary capital, expertise and access to global resources.
Geographic Preference: Asia
Average Investment: $5 - $30 million
Investment Criteria: Early-Stage, Growth-Stage
Industry Group Preference: Technology, Media, Telecommunications, Healthcare, Education, Logistics, Financial Services, Consumer Products
Portfolio Companies: Alibaba, Asianinfo, CDP, Crystal CG, Datou, Dianji, Hurray, Huaxun Technology, iSoftstone, Linktone, MFG.com, Mineloader, Netqin, UiTV, Wisers, Xunlei, Asia Renal Care, Hile Bio-pharma, Pharmanex, NovaMed, TCT, Wuxi AppTec
Key Executives:
  Daniel Auerbach, Managing Partner/Senior Managing Director
  Education: BA, Dartmouth College; MBA, Harvard Business School
  Background: Partner, Arral & Partners Ltd; Analyst, Fidelity Investments
  Directorships: Dianji Technology Holdings, MFG, CDP

2734 FIDELITY GROWTH PARTNERS EUROPE
25 Cannon Street
London EC4M 5TA
United Kingdom
Phone: 011-442070745610

Mission Statement: A venture capital firm that invests where it can make a difference, creating real, long term value.
Geographic Preference: Europe
Founded: 1969
Industry Group Preference: Technology, Software, Cloud Computing, Data Services, Energy Efficiency, Healthcare Information Technology
Portfolio Companies: Asset Control, Curam Software, Neverfail, Newbay, QUMAS, Seatwave,
Key Executives:
  Simon Clark, Managing Partner
  Education: MA, Politics, Philosophy & Economics, Wadham College, Oxford
  Background: Chief Financial Officer & General Manager, International, TheStreet.com; Reuters; Chartered Accountant, Pricewaterhouse
  Davor Hebel, Partner
  Education: BS, Angelo State University; MS, Information Systems Management, Carnegie Mellon University; MBA, Harvard Business School
  Background: Co-Founder, Experia; McKinsey & Company
  Florian Oettinger, Senior Associate
  Education: BA, Jurisprudence, St Edmund Hall, Oxford
  Background: Partner, DFJEspirit
  Directorships: FirstMe Limited

2735 FINADVANCE
Le Derby, 570, avenue du Club Hippique
Aix eu Provence 13090
France
Phone: 33-0442529130 Fax: 33-0442529139

Mission Statement: Private equity funds management.
Geographic Preference: France
Fund Size: $26 Million
Founded: 1988
Average Investment: $1.83 Million
Investment Criteria: Takes minority holding in new or recently created companies.
Industry Group Preference: Electronic Technology, Telecommunications, Software
Portfolio Companies: Metrix Systems, SEA, Infobjects, VRTV Studios

2736 FINAM GLOBAL
Nastasinsky Pereulok, 7, Bld. 2
Moscow 127006
Russia
Phone: 7-495-796-9388
e-mail: invest@finamglobal.com

Mission Statement: FINAM Global creates Private Equity funds and makes Direct Investments focused on growth capital and buy-outs in the global TMT sector. FINAM Global operates within FINAM Group, a leading Russian brokerage and asset management firm. FINAM Global is one of the largest and most successful investment funds in the TMT sector in Russia.
Geographic Preference: Russia
Average Investment: $1 - $50 million
Industry Group Preference: Technology

Venture Capital & Private Equity Firms / International Firms

Portfolio Companies: Badoo, Shape.AG, Moneymail, MGid

2737 FINANCE WALES
Oakleigh House
Park Place
Cardiff CF10 3DQ
Wales

Phone: 0800-5874140 Fax: 029-20338101
e-mail: info@financewales.co.uk
web: www.financewales.com

Mission Statement: Finance Wales makes commercial investments in Wales-based businesses with the potential to grow.
Geographic Preference: Wales
Founded: 2009
Average Investment: £50,000 - 1 million
Investment Criteria: Seed-Stage, Growth-Stage
Industry Group Preference: Technology
Portfolio Companies: Mesura, Asalus, Cymtec, Haemair, AssayMetrics, Q Chip, Calon Cardio, GeoVS, Acutas Medical, Orthos
Key Executives:
  Sian Lloyd Jones, Chief Executive
  Education: Somerville College
  Background: Chief Executive, Development Board for Rural Wales

2738 FINANCIERE DE BRIENNE FCPR
48 rue de Lisbonne
Paris 75008
France

Phone: 01 58 56 25 62 Fax: 01 58 56 25 63
web: www.bpifrance.fr

Mission Statement: Actively seeking new investments, specializing in aeronautics and defense industries
Geographic Preference: France
Fund Size: $122 Million
Founded: 1993
Minimum Investment: $3.6 Million
Investment Criteria: Early-stage, Expansion, Development
Industry Group Preference: Aerospace, Defense and Government, Computer Related, Software, Electronic Technology, Industrial Equipment
Key Executives:
  Yves Michot, Chairman & managing Director
  Jean-Pierre Rochard, Chairman & managing Director

2739 FINLOMBARDA SpA
2 Piazza Belgioso
Milan 20121
Italy

Phone: 39-027-60441 Fax: 39-027-80819
web: www.finlombarda.it/

Mission Statement: Finlombarda operates in the Region of Lombardy's local and economic planning to implement regional and local economic and social development.
Geographic Preference: Europe
Founded: 1971
Investment Criteria: Startup, Early-Stage, Expansion, Development, Bridge
Industry Group Preference: Consumer Services, Energy, Manufacturing, Industrial Equipment, Consumer Products
Key Executives:
  Marisa Bedoni, President

2740 FINNISH INDUSTRY INVESTMENT LIMITED
Mannerheimintie 14 A (9th floor)
PO Box 685
Helsinki 00101
Finland

Phone: 358-96803680 Fax: 358-96121680
e-mail: juha.marjosola@industryinvestment.com
web: www.industryinvestment.com

Mission Statement: Actively seeking new investments.
Geographic Preference: Finland
Fund Size: $395 Million
Founded: 1995
Average Investment: $100 million
Investment Criteria: Seed and growth stage enterprises together with private investors.
Industry Group Preference: All Sectors Considered
Portfolio Companies: MB Equity Fund Ky, Forenvia Venture I Ky, Telecomia Venture I Ky, Profita Fund I Ky, Fenno Rahasto Ky, MB Equity Fund II Ky, Wedeco Seed Fund I Ky Kb , Jutron Oy
Key Executives:
  Juha Marjosola, President & CEO
  e-mail: juha.marjosola@industryinvestment.com
  Anne Tamminen, Executive Assistant

2741 FINNVERA PLC
8 Etelesplanadi
PO Box 1010
Helsinki 00130
Finland

Phone: 358-2046011 Fax: 358-204607220
web: www.finnvera.fi

Mission Statement: Specialised financing company owned by the State of Finland, Finnvera plc provides services to supplement the Finnish financial market. Finnvera's task is to promote the development of enterprise, regions and the exports of Finnish companies.
Geographic Preference: Finland, Europe
Fund Size: $1.2 Million
Founded: 1999
Minimum Investment: $0.2 Million
Investment Criteria: Early Stage, Expansion and Development Capital, Privatisation, Start-up Capital, Buyout and Buyin
Industry Group Preference: Communications, Biotechnology
Key Executives:
  Pauli Heikkilä, Chief Executive Officer
  e-mail: kalle.korhonen@finnvera.fi
  Education: M.Sc. (Tech.)
  Background: Finnish Industry Investment Ltd(Board member), SME Foundation(Board member)
  Mr Topi Vesteri, Executive Vice President, Export Financing
  e-mail: Pekka.Laajanen@finnvera.fi
  Education: L.L.M.
  Background: Fide Ltd (Vice Chairman), Ministry of Finance (Governmental Counsellor, Director of Legislative Affairs)

2742 FIR CAPITAL PARTNERS
Praca Carlos Chagas, 49
7 Andar
ZIP: 30170-020
Belo Horizonte MG
Brazil

Phone: 55 31 3074 0020 Fax: 55 31 3074 0015
web: www.fircapital.com

Mission Statement: Achieve extraordinary profits in partnership with exceptional entrepreneurs and companies, following the Principle for Responsible Investment.
Geographic Preference: Brazil
Founded: 1999
Investment Criteria: Emerging
Portfolio Companies: Akwan, Biobras, Minar
  Andre Capistrano Emrich

2743 FIRST CORPORATE PTY LIMITED
Level 9, 105 St. George Terrace
Perth 6000
Australia
  Phone: 61-892260326 Fax: 61-892260327
  web: www.firstgroup.com.au

Mission Statement: Corporate advisory group specializing in transitioning private companies to public listed status. Also coordinates private equity funding for growth orientated companies in Asia / Pacific.
Geographic Preference: Asia Pacific, Australia
Founded: 1996
Investment Criteria: Mezzanine/pre-IPO stage projects, SME
Key Executives:
  Jeffrey C Broun, Director
  e-mail: jbroun@firstgroup.com.au
  Education: CA, ACA, BA
  Background: ERG Limited, Mayne Nickless, Guardian Royal Exchange Limited
  Kent B Burwash, Director
  e-mail: mslater@firstgroup.com.au
  Education: Fellow of the Institute of Chartered Accountants in Australia
  Background: Chartered Accountant, M&A, Governance
  Directorships: ERG Limited, Mayne Nickless, Guardian Royal Exchange Limited

2744 FIRST INVESTMENT CORPORATION LIMITED
Level 20, 300 Queen Street.
Brisbane City 2067
Australia
  Phone: 07-30235089 Fax: 61-284488101
  e-mail: peter.janssen@corporatefirst.com.au

Mission Statement: Provides investment banking and fund management services.

2745 FIRST ISRAEL MEZZANINE INVESTORS LIMITED
Electra Tower
98 Yigal Alon St
Tel Aviv 67891
Israel
  Phone: 972-35652244 Fax: 972-35652245
  e-mail: sec@fimi.co.il
  web: www.fimi.co.il

Mission Statement: Actively seeking new investments.
Geographic Preference: Israel
Fund Size: $215 Million
Founded: 1996
Investment Criteria: Leveraged Buy-Outs (LBOs), Management Buy-Outs (MBOs), Growth Capital Financing
Industry Group Preference: Computer Hardware & Software, Consumer Services, Communications, Automotive, Plastics, Textiles, Metals, Water, Food & Beverage, Electronic Technology
Portfolio Companies: Tadir-Gan, Tadiran Com Ltd., Tedea, Mer Group, Elco-Brandt Group, Lipman, R.H. Electronics, Medtechnica, Formula Systems, Ginegar Plastic Products Ltd, TAT Technologies Ltd.
Key Executives:
  Ishay Davidi, Founder & Chief Executive Officer
  e-mail: ishay@fimi.co.il
  Background: Tikvah Fund (CEO)
  Gillon Beck, Senior Partner

2746 FLANDERS' FOREIGN INVESTMENT OFFICE
Koning Albert-II laan 37
Brussels 1030
Belgium
  Phone: 32-25048871 Fax: 32-25048870
  e-mail: invest@fitagency.be
  web: www.investinflanders.be

Mission Statement: Provides confidential advice free of charge on all aspects of investing in the Flanders region of Belgium.
Geographic Preference: Flanders
Fund Size: $136 Million
Founded: 2005
Industry Group Preference: Automotive, Information Technology, Life Sciences, Logistics, Chemicals, Food & Beverage, Electronic Technology, Telecommunications, Transportation
Key Executives:
  Lucas Huybrechts, Account Manager
  e-mail: invest@fitagency.be
  Education: Bachelor's degree in business economics, Master's degree in law
  Background: Financial & Administrative Director(Commercial Advice center; Ghent)
  Rita Saeys, Director Business Development

2747 FONDINVEST CAPITAL
33 rue de La Baume
Paris 75008
France
  Phone: 33-158364800 Fax: 33-1-5836-4828
  e-mail: mailbox@fondinvest.com
  web: www.fondinvest.com

Mission Statement: Invests in new funds in Europe; acquires secondary interests in funds worldwide; has invested in over 210 private equity funds.
Geographic Preference: USA, Europe, Asia
Founded: 1994
Key Executives:
  Charles Soulignac, Managing Partner
  33-1-5836-4800
  e-mail: c.soulignac@fondinvest.com
  Education: Engineer (INSA), MBA (CPA; Paris)
  Background: CDC Participations, BRED, Maynard, ex EVCA Board of Directors
  Emmanuel Roubinowitz, Partner
  Catherine Lewis La Torre, Partner

2748 FORBION CAPITAL PARTNERS
Goolmeer 2-35
DC Naarden 1411
Netherlands
  Phone: 31-0-35-699-3000 Fax: 31-0-35-699-3001
  e-mail: info@forbion.com
  web: www.forbion.com

Mission Statement: At Forbion Capital Partners we invest in Life Sciences and Biomedical Technology companies developing world-class drugs and technologies, with a clear focus on product development. The Forbion team is specialized in the evaluation of late stage preclinical / early stage clinical development programs. We focus on companies that have innovative technologies and drug development programs with unique advantages over current treatments. Furthermore, we invest in medical device companies with a special focus on

Venture Capital & Private Equity Firms / International Firms

interventional devices in cardiology, gastroenterology and pulmonology that are close to market approval.
Fund Size: 450 million euro
Founded: 2006
Investment Criteria: Early-Stage
Industry Group Preference: Life Sciences, Biotechnology, Medical Devices
Portfolio Companies: Abiomed, ACADIA Pharmaceuticals, Inc., Accelerated Technologies, Acorda Therapeutics, Alantos Pharmaceuticals, Allecra Therapeutics, Amakem, Am-Pharma, Amt, Ardana, Argen-X, Argos Therapeutics, Ario Pharma, Bioceros, Biovex, Bluebird Bio, Borean Pharma, Cardoz, Cell Based Delivery, Cellnovo, Circulite, Crucell, Curetis, Cytheris, Dezima Pharma, Exosome Diagnostics, Flowmedica, Fovea, Galapagos, Gho Holding, Gicare Pharma, Glycart, Hookipa Biotech, Impella Cardiosystems, Insmed, Jari Pharmaceuticals, Mitralign, Ness, Neutec Pharma, Novogi, Oxyrane, Pangenetics, Pathway Medical Technologies, Pieris, Pneumrx, Promedior, Pulmagen Therapeutics, Rhein Biotech, Santaris Pharma, Transave, Unique, X-Cell Medical, Xention

Other Locations:
 Maximillanstrasse 36
 Munchen 80539
 Germany
 Phone: 49-89-41-6161-950 **Fax:** 49-89-41-6161-959

Key Executives:
 G-J Mulder MD, General Partner
 e-mail: greet-jan.mulder@forbion.com
 Education: MD, University of Utrecht
 Background: ABN AMRO Capital Life Sciences; Resident, Obstetrics & Cynecology, University Medical Center, Utrecht
 Directorships: Exosome Diagnostics, Promedior, Ario Pharma
 Sander Slootweg, Managing Partner
 e-mail: sander.slootweg@forbion.com
 Education: Business & Financial Economics, Free University of Amsterdam; Business Administration, Nijenrode University
 Background: Co-Founder, ABN AMRO Capital Life Sciences
 Directorships: Dezima Pharma, Xention Discovery, Ario Pharma, Pulmagen Therapeutics, Oxyrane, UniQure
 Holger Reighinger, General Partner
 e-mail: holger.reighinger@forbion.com
 Education: PhD, Biochemistry, Max-Planck Institute of Biophyciscs; BS, Molecular Biology, University of Heidelberg & University of Munich
 Background: Product Development, Biometra; Investment Manager, Technologieholding VC; Director, 3i Group
 Directorships: Curetis, Allecra Therapeutics

2749 FORESIGHT VENTURE PARTNERS
The Shard
32 London Bridge Street
London SE1 6PQ
United Kingdom

Phone: +44 (0) 20 3667 8100
e-mail: info@foresightgroup.eu
web: www.foresightgroup.eu

Mission Statement: Foresight strives to generate increasing dividends and capital appreciation for its investors over the long term.
Industry Group Preference: Solar Infrastructure, Biomass, Energy
Portfolio Companies: Birmingham BioPower, Wharfedale Hospital, Stobhill Hosptial, Lochgilphead Hospital, Bishop Auckland Hospital, Staffordshire Schools, Sandwell Schools, Stirling Schools, Drumglass High School

2750 FORMULA VENTURES LIMITED Formula Group
11 Galgalei Haplada, PO Box 2062
Herzliya 46120
Israel

Phone: 972-99601800 **Fax:** 972-99601818
web: www.formulaventures.com

Mission Statement: Formula Ventures was founded as the successor fund for Argotec, a Formula Group company. Formula Ventures manages two venture funds – FV-I and FV-II.
Geographic Preference: Israel
Founded: 1998
Investment Criteria: Seed-stage ventures, First round funding, Later stage investments.
Industry Group Preference: Data Communications, Telecommunications, Internet Technology, Enterprise Services, Storage, Semiconductors, Media, Infrastructure, Software
Portfolio Companies: Civcom Inc., Commil Ltd., Composit Ltd., Radiotel Ltd., Radlan Ltd., Radview Software Ltd., Demantra Ltd., Maincontrol, Earnix, Identify, Magink, Nanomagnetics Ltd., Transtech control, Phonetic Systems Ltd.

Key Executives:
 Shai Beilis, Managing Partner
 e-mail: shai@formulaventures.com
 Education: B.Sc. In Mathematics and Economics(Hebrew University), M.Sc. in Computer Science (Weizmann Institute of Science in Rehovot)
 Background: Argotec Ltd(CEO), Crystal Systems Solutions(Chairman), Wiztec Solutions(Chairman), Clal Computers and Technology (CEO), Yael Software and Services Ltd(CEO)
 Directorships: Chairman
 Nir Linchevski, Partner

2751 FORUM TECHNOLOGIES VENTURE CAPITAL COMPANY Forum Group
34 Jerusalem St.
Raanana 43501
Israel

Phone: 972-97754646 **Fax:** 972-97601551

Mission Statement: Forum Technologies is designed to offer investors a unique opportunity to benefit from the success of Israeli Start-ups in the HighTechnology sector.
Geographic Preference: Israel
Founded: 1993
Investment Criteria: Startup Companies
Industry Group Preference: High Technology, Cable
Portfolio Companies: Manov, Shacham, ContentWise, VersaMed

Key Executives:
 Amit Segal, President
 e-mail: amir@forum-group.com
 Education: BA in Economics, MBA in Finance and Management of Financial Institutions(Tel-Aviv University)
 Background: Dun & Bradstreet(Senior Analyst), The Israel General Bank(Head of Marketing and International Relations), The Maritime Bank of Israel Ltd(Managing Director & CEO),
 Ami Segal, President

2752 FORWARD PARTNERS
Floor 2, Centro 3
19 Mandela Street
Camden NW1 0DU
England

web: www.forwardpartners.com

880

Venture Capital & Private Equity Firms / International Firms

Mission Statement: We blend investment with access to a specialist team of experts who work full time with entrepreneurs and founders.

Portfolio Companies: Appear[Here], BlikBook, Captalis, Driftrock, Hailo, Hubbub, Loyalty Bay, Makers Academy, Somo, Squawka, Top10, Unbound, Wool And The Gang, Zopa

Key Executives:
   Carlos Vilhena, Senior Developer
   Chris O'Sullivan, Senior Developer
   Dharmesh Raithatha, Head of Product
   Ed Davidson, Strategic Marketer
   Emma Gresko, Operations Manager
   Emma Patricios, Senior Front-End Developer

2753 FOUNDATION CAPITAL LIMITED
Minshull House, 67 Wellington Road North
Stockport SK4 2LP
United Kingdom

e-mail: info@foundation-capital.com

Mission Statement: Operates an open ended fund which aims to support the commercialisation of exceptional entrepreneurial business ideas in return for an equity stake.

Geographic Preference: United Kingdom, Scandinavia
Average Investment: £20K and £100k
Investment Criteria: Early to growth stage investments, start-up capital and/or sales marketing expansion capital
Industry Group Preference: Consumer Products, Wholesale, Imports/Exports, Hotels, Consumer Services, Retailing, Construction

Key Executives:
   Kai Rothoff Svendsen, Board Director & Chairman
   Background: Tradifood A/S, H.I.K Football APS(Board Director), AV Center CPH. A/S; ALFA HOTEL Holding (France)- (Board Director)

2754 FOUR SEASONS VENTURE CAPITAL
Vika Atrium/Munkedamsveien 45F
Munkedamsveien 45F
PO Box 1216 Vika
Oslo NO-0250
Norway

Phone: 47-24137000 Fax: 47-24137001
web: www.verdanecapital.com

Mission Statement: Actively seeking new investments. Invests in the primary venture capital market as well as the secondary direct market. Entrepreneurs are assisted in building outstanding companies through a wealth of investment experience and a global network. Four Seasons Venture currently has six active funds.

Geographic Preference: Sweden, Norway, Finland
Fund Size: $415 Million
Founded: 1985
Average Investment: $3 Million
Investment Criteria: All Stages
Industry Group Preference: All Sectors Considered
Portfolio Companies: Abeo, Active 24 ASA, Advertising.com, Affitech, Ahhaaa!, AquaGen, Axlon International, Banqsoft, Biosensor, Biotec Pharmacon, Bozoka.com Sweden, Brendmoe & Kirkestuen, Chipcon, Coding Technologies, Colibria, Conoptica, DebiTech, Direct 2 Internet, Dynapel Systems, Elprint, Evolving Systems, Exie AS, Fact Based Communication Ltd, Fjord Marin, Genomar, Global Name Registry, Ikivo, Keytouch Corporation, Maritech International, Markland Technologies, Metronor, Minox Technology, Mobilaris, Nordisk Terapi, Odim, Omnia, Optinel Systems, PortWise, Prenax Global, Procaptura, Read ASA, ResLab Holding, Reslink, Scali, Scanbio, Scanrope, Scanvacc, Seabed Geophysical, Sicom, Spring Consulting, talk2me, Telitas US, Tertio Service Management Systems, Tordivel, TradeDoubler, Troux Technologies, TwoWay Media, Vector International, Viz Risk Management, Voss of Norway

Key Executives:
   Bjarne K. Lie, Co-Founder & COO
   Education: Masters of Economics, BI-Norwegian School of Management; MBA, INSEAD
   Background: McKinsey & Company; Sales/Support Manager, Guru Software
   Birger Nergaard, Founder
   Education: BS Finance, St. John's University; MBA, INSEAD
   Background: Senior Associate, Braxton Associates; Management Consultant, Deloitte Consulting

2755 FOURIERTRANSFORM
Sveavagen 17, 10th Floor
Stockholm SE-111 57
Sweden

Phone: 46-841040600 Fax: 46-8-410-40-640
web: www.fouriertransform.se

Mission Statement: Fouriertransform is a state-owned venture capital company tasked with strengthening the Swedish automotive cluster's international competitiveness on a commercial basis. The mission includes taking an active role as an owner in order to help to ensure the structured and successful commercialization and continued growth of the portfolio companies. Fouriertransform contributes expertise by placing qualified representatives on the boards of all the companies in which it holds an interest.

Geographic Preference: Sweden
Fund Size: SEK 3 billion
Industry Group Preference: Automotive, Transportation
Portfolio Companies: Alelion Batteries, Applied Nano Surfaces Sweden, ArcCore, CeDe Group, EELCEE, El-Forest, Jobro Platkomponenter, LeanNova Engineering, Max Truck, Norstel, Pelagicore, Powercell Sweden, Smart Eye, TitanX, Vicura

Key Executives:
   Per Nordberg, CEO
   e-mail: per.nordberg@fouriertransform.se

2756 FRANKLIN TEMPLETON INVESTMENT
Indiabulls Finance Centre, Tower 2, 12th Floo
Elphinstone Road
Mumbai 400013
India

Phone: 91-56325820 Fax: 91-22810923
Toll-Free: 1800-4254255
e-mail: service@templeton.com
web: www.franklintempletonindia.com

Mission Statement: Actively seeking new investments.

Geographic Preference: India
Fund Size: $3.62 Billion
Founded: 1947
Investment Criteria: Equity, Second Stage, Expansion

Key Executives:
   Jennifer J. Bolt, Executive Vice President - Operations & Technology
   Vijay C. Advani, Executive Vice President - Global Advisor Services

2757 FRESHWATER VENTURE PARTNERS
Laan van Niftarlake 54
Utrecht Tienhoven 3612 BT
Netherlands

Phone: 31-653935800 Fax: 31-346282613

Mission Statement: Established as a venture capital firm focused on software. It's goal is to provide startups with private equity financing, support them in developing winning visions

Venture Capital & Private Equity Firms / International Firms

and strategies and help them execute with operational excellence.

Minimum Investment: $200,000
Investment Criteria: Early Stage, Start-up
Industry Group Preference: Computer Hardware & Software, Internet Technology

2758 FRIULIA SpA
Via Locchi 19
Trieste 34123
Italy

Phone: 39-04031971 Fax: 39-040-3197400
e-mail: mail@friulia.it
web: www.friulia.it

Mission Statement: Developing the economy of the Friulia-Venezia Giulia region in Northeastern Italy.

Fund Size: $278 Million
Founded: 1967
Average Investment: $950,000
Minimum Investment: $60,000
Industry Group Preference: Chemicals, Industrial Products, Electronic Technology, Retailing, Distribution

Key Executives:
Sara Spogliarich, General Secretariat and Communication
e-mail: augusto.antonucci@friulia.it
Daniela Ziraldo, Human Resources
e-mail: federico.marescotti@friulia.it
Dear Mark, Finance and Control Manager
e-mail: michele.degrassi@friulia.it

2759 FRONTLINE VENTURES
17 Rosebery Ave.
London EC1R4SP
United Kingdom

e-mail: info@frontline.vc
web: www.frontline.vc

Mission Statement: Frontline Ventures invest in ambitious seed-stage B2B companies in Europe. We are a pioneering early stage venture capital firm, believing in ideas, and investing in passion. We offer capital, mentorship when needed and a network of people that will assist the Founder in building their company. We spend time working with companies to win reference customers, make key hires, and develop the strategy for gaining access to commercial partners. With our backing, Founders can focus on customer discovery and development from the outset and get to proof of performance within months, not years.

Geographic Preference: Europe
Fund Size: Fund I 50m Euro (2013); Fund II 60m Euro (2016)
Founded: 2012
Average Investment: 200k - 1m Euro
Minimum Investment: 200k Euro
Investment Criteria: Pre-Seed, Seed
Industry Group Preference: Business to Business, Enterprise, Machine Learning
Portfolio Companies: BrightFlag, Currencyfair, James, Logentrics, Qstream, Signal AI, Verve

Other Locations:
26-28 Lombard St. E
Dublin 2
Ireland

Key Executives:
Shay Garvey, Partner
Education: BSc, University College Dublin; MEng, University of New Brunswick; MBA, Harvard Business School
Directorships: Qstream, Roomex, Linked Finance, AQMetrics, TravelNest, Finbourne

Will Prendergast, Partner
Education: Chemical Engineering Degree, University College Dublin
Background: Partner, NCB Venture Capital; Consultant, Accenture UK
William McQuillan, Partner
Background: Co-Founder and CEO, Osmoda.com; Founding Employee, Ondra Partner

2760 FSE GROUP
Riverside House, 4 Meadows Business Park
Station Approach
Blackwater
Camberley, Surrey GU17 9AB
United Kingdom

Phone: 01276-608510 Fax: 02176-608539
e-mail: fundingenquiries@thefsegroup.com
web: www.thefesgroup.com

Mission Statement: The FSE Group invests in small and medium-sized enterprises (SMEs) that have the potential for significant growth. We understand the funding challenges facing emerging and mid-sized companies looking to expand, and we provide funds and support, including mentors where appropriate, to help bridge the funding gap. A newer area of focus is that of Social Impact Funding, where we are working alongside experienced partners to finance social enterprises and communities.

Geographic Preference: United Kingdom
Investment Criteria: Small & Mediuim Enterprises
Industry Group Preference: Social Enterprises, Renewable Energy
Portfolio Companies: Bowman Power Group, BritishEco, Datasift, DevelopIP, Duvas Technologies, Imaginatik Limited, Omega Ingredients, ParcelGenie, Plum Baby, Quotient Diagnostics, Redd & Whyte, Solution Builders Limited, Stokes Sauces, TeraView Limited, TBD Fusion, ToxiMet, UltraSoc Technologies, VerdEng Connectors

Key Executives:
Robert Spencer, Chairman
Background: Founder, Regional Venture Capital Funds
Kevan Jones, CEO
01276-608527
e-mail: kevan.jones@thefsegroup.com
Education: MBA, Warwick Business School
Background: Group Sales & Marketing Director, Ultimate Finance Group
Directorships: NatWest

2761 FUEL CAPITAL
Unit 721
Cyberport 1
100 Cyberport Road
Hong Kong

e-mail: inquiry@fuelcapitalpartners.com
web: www.fuelcapitalpartners.com

Mission Statement: Founded in 2009 by industry veterans. Collectively, the founding team has over 40 collective years of leading investments at top-tier, China-focused venture capital and private equity funds, including Intel Capital, Walden International, AIG, and First Eastern, invested and managed a portfolio of approximately US$1 billion and have over 70 exits, including more than 40 IPOs in various stock exchanges around the world.

Geographic Preference: China
Founded: 2009
Investment Criteria: Early-Growth Stage
Industry Group Preference: Clean Technology, Healthcare, Environment
Portfolio Companies: United Imaging Healthcare, DSM Green Power, PowerGenix, Waveguider Optical Telecom Technology, ZBest Technology Company

Venture Capital & Private Equity Firms / International Firms

Other Locations:
Suite 36B
118 Zihun Road
Shanghai 200051
China

Suite 1218-1219, Caohu Building
1 Yongchangjing Avenue
Xiangcheng Economic Development Zone
Suzhou, Jiangsu Province 215144
China

Key Executives:
Cadol Cheung, Founding Partner
Education: Engineering Degree, Hong Kong Polytechnic; MBA, Chinese University of Hong Kong
Background: Intel Capital

2762 FULL CIRCLE INVESTMENTS
Nassima Tower, Level 2, Office 205
Sheikh Zayed Road
Dubai
United Arab Emirates
Phone: 9714-3516122 Fax: 9714-3516123
e-mail: admin@fullcircleinvest.com
web: www.fullcircleinvest.com

Mission Statement: Full Circle Investments combines strategy consulting, corporate finance and execution capabilities to deliver integrated strategic, operational and financial solutions to corporate clients and investment groups.
Geographic Preference: Middle East
Founded: 2006
Industry Group Preference: Financial Services, Energy, Technology, Healthcare, Real Estate, Food & Beverage
Key Executives:
Ghassan Medawar, Founding Partner, Managing Director
Education: BS, Economics, Wesleyan University; Law Degree, University of London
Background: ING Barings; ABN Ambro
Laya Medawar, Partner
Education: Chemistry, Oxford University; MBA, INSEAD
Background: Consulting, Bain & Company; Greig Fester
Nessrine Salah, Director
Education: BS, Business Administration, American University, Cairo
Background: Consultant, McKinsey & Company; Sernior Associate, Korn Ferry International
Richard Maddison, Venture Partner
Education: MBA, INSEAD
Background: Wireline Engineer, Schlumberger; Chief Analyst, ARCO; Robert Flemings; Bankers Trust; Deutsche Bank
Claudio Gonzalez, Venture Partner
Education: Bachelor's Degree in Economics, London School of Economics
Background: West Merchant Bank; Scotiabank Sudamericano; Director, Latin American Sales, ABN Ambro

2763 FUTURE VENTURE CAPITAL COMPANY LIMITED
4th Floor Karasuma-Chuo Building
659 Tearaimizu-cho, Nishikikoji-agaru Karasuma-dori
Nakagyo-ku
Kyoto 604-8152
Japan
Phone: 81-752572511 Fax: 81-752111601
web: www.fvc.co.jp

Mission Statement: Actively seeking new investments.
Key Executives:
Keiji Imajo, President & Chief Executive Officer
Tomohisa Suzuki, Director

2764 G & H KAPITAL PARTNER AG
Schwarzenbergplatz 16
Vienna 1010
Austria
Phone: 43-1502200 Fax: 43-150220249
e-mail: mail@gutmann.at
web: www.gutmann.at

Geographic Preference: Austria, Central and Eastern Europe, Germany, Latin America
Fund Size: $15.3 Billion
Founded: 1922
Minimum Investment: $2.4 Million
Investment Criteria: Buyout & Buyin
Key Executives:
Alexander Kahane, Chairman
Matthias Albert, Partner

2765 GALILEO II
109, boulevard Haussmann
Paris 75008
France
Phone: 33-153594500 Fax: 33-153599200
web: www.galileo.fr

Mission Statement: Actively seeking new investments.
Founded: 1989
Average Investment: $1.82 Million
Minimum Investment: $1.2 Million
Investment Criteria: Startup, Early Stage; Expansion—Development
Industry Group Preference: Communications, Internet Technology, Telecommunications, Computer Related
Portfolio Companies: Alapage.com, Business_Doc, Canal Web, Consodata, Icm, Influe, Netgem, Pictoris, Protraining
Key Executives:
Yoann Le Berrigaud, Co-founder and Marketing Director
e-mail: jflichy@galileo.fr
Education: Engineering and Economics degrees, Ecole Centrale de Lyon
Background: Co-Founder of Galileo Partners, 1989; M&A and Investment Specialist with Corporate Finance Department of CIC Bank
François Duliège, Partner

2766 GAON ASSET MANAGEMENT
Gaon House, 6 Kaufman Street, 14th Floor
Tel Aviv 68012
Israel
Phone: 972-037954100 Fax: 972-037954103
e-mail: info@gaon.com
web: www.gaon.com

Mission Statement: Initiates and promotes investments in various areas in Israel and abroad.
Geographic Preference: Israel
Founded: 1998
Investment Criteria: All stages considered.
Industry Group Preference: Financial Services, Agribusiness, Retailing, Wholesale
Key Executives:
Moshe Gaon, Chairman
e-mail: info@gaon.com
Education: M.B.A.and L.L.B.
Background: Legal Counselor in Koor Industries Legal Department.
Directorships: Member of the Board of Companies.
Avi Hochman, Chief Executive Officer

Venture Capital & Private Equity Firms / International Firms

2767 GE ASIA PACIFIC CAPITAL TECHNOLOGY FUND
Building 7A, 6th Floor
Sector 25A, DLF Cyber City, Phase III
3A Charter Road
Gurgaon, Haryana 122002
India

Phone: 91-1244808000 Fax: 852-2530-5527
Toll-Free: 1800-4334480
e-mail: ashok@geapctechfund.com
web: www.gecapital.in

Mission Statement: A joint venture between GE and Asia Pacific Capital Group. Flexible as to size and range of investment.
Geographic Preference: China, India
Founded: 1992
Average Investment: $3-100 million
Industry Group Preference: Technology, Life Sciences, Consumer Products, Infrastructure
Key Executives:
  Anish Shah, President and CEO
  Education: BE Mechanical Engineering, MS University, India; MS Industrial Engineering, Stanford University
  Background: Strategy Consultant, Deloitte & Touche; CEO/Regional President, WR Grace; President, PPG Industries (Pittsburgh Plate Galss)
  Neeta Mukherji, SVP & Business Head
  Education: AB Government, Harvard University; JD, Columbia University School of Law
  Background: Co-Founder, Asia Pacific Capital Ltd; US State Department; Adjunct Professor, Saigon Law School; Coudent Brothers; Founding Partner, ChinaVest
  Satyanarayanan Eluri, Business Leader, Healthcare Financial Services
  Education: PGDM, Indian Institute of Management
  Background: VP Finance Sponsors Group, Kotak Investment Banking; GE Equity India; GE Structured Finance
  Raghuveer Kurada, Business Leader, Energy Financial Services
  Education: BS Economics, Wharton School; MA, Fletcher School of Law & Diplomacy (Tufts University)
  Background: Global Strategy Grp, Elan Pharmaceuticals; VP, Prudential Asia Mezzanine Fund; Founding Principal, NetFuel Ventures; Cap Gemini; Ernst & Young; Lend Lease; Air Touch International
  Directorships: One Ummah
  Anand Trivedi, Business Leader, Private Equity
  Education: Bachelor of Law, Fu-Jen University; JD, Columbia University School of Law
  Background: VP Investment Banking, Morgan Stanly Dean Witter
  Directorships: International Bank of Taipei; FWU-Sheng Investment Co
  Raghuveer Kurada, Business Leader, Energy Financial Services
  Education: BS Finance/Economics, California State University; CPA
  Background: Head Audit Division, CPA firm

2768 GE CAPITAL SERVICES INDIA LIMITED
Building 7A, 6th Floor, Sector 25A
DLF Cyber City, Phase III
Gurgaon 122002
India

Phone: 91-1244808000 Fax: 91-124-2358044
Toll-Free: 1800-4334480

Mission Statement: Provides access to the financial tools and services vital to businesses and individuals.
Key Executives:
  Anish Shah, President and CEO
  Ashish Sharma, Business Leader, Corporate Accounts Group

2769 GE EQUITY EUROPE
Clarges House
London NV
United Kingdom

Phone: 207-3026310 Fax: 207-3026810

Geographic Preference: United Kingdom, Central Europe, Western Europe
Fund Size: $310 Million
Average Investment: $10 Million
Minimum Investment: $1 Million
Investment Criteria: Early Stage, Expansion, Replacement Capital, MBO, MBI
Industry Group Preference: Data Communications, Computer Related, Financial Services, Consumer Services, Consumer Products
Portfolio Companies: Cell Networks, Cell Ventures, Group Trade, Intrinsic, Media Surface, SM Logistics, TravelPrice
Key Executives:
  Frank Ertl, Chief Financial Officer
  Ed Hrvatin, Chief Marketing Officer

2770 GEMINI ISRAEL VENTURE FUNDS LIMITED
9 Hamenotim Street
Herzliya Pituach 46725
Israel

Phone: 972-99719111 Fax: 972-99584842
e-mail: info@gemini.co.il
web: www.gemini.co.il

Mission Statement: A pioneer in Israel's venture capital industry, Gemini provides start-up financing and expert guidance to help talented entrepreneurs build successful companies.
Geographic Preference: Israel
Fund Size: $700 Million
Founded: 1993
Average Investment: $150 Million
Minimum Investment: $5 Million
Investment Criteria: Early stage, start up
Industry Group Preference: Telecommunications, Data Communications, Internet Technology, Semiconductors, Medical, Infrastructure, Technology
Portfolio Companies: D-Pharm, Mellanox, Diligent TechnologiesAllot, Atrica, Celletra, Ceragon Networks, Commil ltd, IXI Mobile Inc, Olista Software Corporation, Ornet Data Communication, Outsmart Ltd, Radnet Ltd, Riverhead Networks Inc, Schema Ltd, Starhome, Tdsoft
Key Executives:
  Ed Mlavsky, Founding Partner & Chairman
  e-mail: info@gemini.co.il
  Education: Bachelor of Science & MBA
  Background: Managing Partner of Gemini Funds, Vice President, Marketing of DSP Group.
  Directorships: Board Member of Adimos Inc & IXI Mobile Inc.
  Yossi Sela, Managing Partner

2771 GENERAL ATLANTIC PARTNERS
Suite 5815, 58/F, Two IFC, 8 Finance Street
International Finance Tower
Central, Hong Kong
China

Phone: 852-36022600 Fax: 852-36022611
e-mail: vfeng@gapartners.com
web: www.generalatlantic.com

Venture Capital & Private Equity Firms / International Firms

Mission Statement: For over 25 years, General Atlantic has provided equity financing to private and public companies globally.
Geographic Preference: Worldwide
Fund Size: $17 Billion
Founded: 1980
Average Investment: $75 Million - $400 Million
Minimum Investment: $25 Million
Industry Group Preference: Information Technology, Outsourcing & Efficiency, Communications
Portfolio Companies: A-Max, abaxx, aI METRIX, Altair engineering, Archipelago, Compugroup, computershare, Criticalpath, DiceInc, Digital China, eOne Globe, Genpact, Healthvison, Hewitt, insightexpress, IHSInc, Intec, IPValue, iSoft, Organosys, Lenovo, LHS
Key Executives:
  Steven A. Denning, Chairman
  Education: Degree in Economics, MBA.
  Background: Senior Associate, Technology Crossover Ventures, Senior Business Analyst, McKinsey & Company.

2772 GENERAL ENTERPRISE MANAGEMENT SERVICES
805 Citibank Tower, 3 Garden Road
Central
Hong Kong

Phone: 852-28380093 Fax: 852-28380292
e-mail: contact@gems.com.hk
web: www.gems.com.hk

Mission Statement: General Enterprise Management Services Limited (GEMS) is a private equity fund management group that manages the GEMS Funds (GEMS I, II and III) - these in turn make direct investments in the Asia Pacific region.
Geographic Preference: China, Japan, Thiland, Hong Kong, Singapore, South Korea
Fund Size: $600 Million
Founded: 1998
Average Investment: $15 Million
Minimum Investment: $10 Million
Investment Criteria: Invests in well-managed and well-positioned companies in need of equity for strategic growth, acquisitions, market expansion or balance sheet restructuring
Industry Group Preference: Energy, Electronic Technology, Transportation, Telecommunications, Software, Financial Services, Retailing, Real Estate, Natural Resources, Media
Portfolio Companies: Cape Energy, CNOOC, Compass, Crescendo, E-mice, eBANK, Eutech, Grace, Hi-Tech Wealth, IP Flex, NatSteel, Newlife, Sino-Forest, Taejin, The Executive Centre, Trisara, Yozan
Key Executives:
  Simon Murray, Executive Chairman
  e-mail: contact@gems.com.hk
  Education: Bachelor of Arts degree in Economics
  Background: Vice President of Morgan's Capital Markets Group in Hong Kong.
  David Van Oppen, Senior Partner
  e-mail: contact@gems.com.hk
  Education: Master of Arts degree.
  Background: Vice President of Lazard Asia Investment Management.

2773 GENERICS GROUP LIMITED Generics Group
Harston Mill
Harston
Cambridge CB22 7GG
United Kingdom

Phone: 44-1223875200 Fax: 44-1223875201
e-mail: info@sagentia.com
web: www.sagentia.com

Mission Statement: The Generics Group (Generics) is a leading integrated technology consulting, development and investment organisation.
Geographic Preference: Worldwide
Founded: 1987
Industry Group Preference: Engineering, Telecommunications, Medical, Physical Sciences, Materials Technology, Electronic Technology, Management, Life Sciences, Energy
Key Executives:
  Dr Alistair Brown, Executive Director, Sales & Marketing
  Background: PricewaterhouseCoopers, based in Stockholm, Sweden.
  Martin Frost, Group Managing Director
  Background: GEC-Marconi, where he served as Financial Controller.
  Directorships: Board of Scientific Generics and several of the Group's spin-out companies.
  Gordon Edge, Non-Executive Director
  Background: Founding members of Cambridge Consultants Ltd & founder of PA Technology.

2774 GENES GMBH VENTURE SERVICES
Koelner Strasse 27
PO Box 560
Frechen D-50226
Germany

Phone: 49-2234955460 Fax: 49-2234955464
web: www.genes-ventures.de

Mission Statement: Focuses on transnational deals and pre-IPO investments by divesting existing funds and setting up new international venture capital funds.
Geographic Preference: Germany
Fund Size: $72.5 Million
Founded: 1978
Average Investment: $3.6 Million
Industry Group Preference: Technology
Key Executives:
  Klaus Nathusius, General Partner
  Kfm Lutz Nathusius, Partner
  e-mail: service@genes-ventures.de
  Dr. Detlev Geiss, Sr Partner
  e-mail: service@genes-ventures.de
  Andy Klose, Partner
  e-mail: service@genes-ventures.de

2775 GENESIS PARTNERS
11 HaMenofim Street
Ackerstein Towers
Building B, 4th Floor
Herzliya Pituach NV
Israel

Phone: 972- 99729000 Fax: 972-99729001
e-mail: innovation@genesispartners.com

Mission Statement: Genesis Partners is one of Israel's largest and most experienced venture capital firms.
Geographic Preference: Israel
Fund Size: $600 Million
Founded: 1996
Average Investment: $3.5 Million
Minimum Investment: $2 Million

Venture Capital & Private Equity Firms / International Firms

Investment Criteria: All Stages
Industry Group Preference: Communications, Wireless Technologies, Storage, Internet Technology, Infrastructure Software, Hardware, Enterprise Software, Internet Applications and Services, Digital Media & Marketing, Consumer Services, Mobile Services
Portfolio Companies: Airsphere, Allot, Cloverleaf, Colbar, Commprize, Comsys, Comview, Elcom, Filesx, Foxcom Wireless, Fundtech, G Connect, Gonet, Harmonycom, Healinx, AG Associates, Agentics Inc., Appilog Inc., Audiocodes Ltd., Butterfly VLSI, Ltd., Celtro Inc., Clicksoftwar
Key Executives:
  Dr. Eyal Kishon, Founder & Managing Partner
  e-mail: eyal@genesisvp.com
  Education: PhD, Computer Science, Robotics, New York University; BA, Computer Science, Technion, Haifa
  Background: Associate Director, Polaris Fund; Chief Technology Officer, Yozma Venture Capital; Research Positions, IBM Research Center, At&T's Bell Laboratories
  Eddy Shaler, Managing Partner
  e-mail: eddy@genesisvp.com
  Education: MS in Information Systems, BA in Statistics, Tel Aviv University
  Background: Oscar Gruss and Son Inc.; Co-Founded, Mofet Israel Technology Fund; Large Systems Expert and Account Executive, IBM (Israel); Large Strategic Planner, IBM (United Kingdon)
  Directorships: CEO
  Yair Shoham, General Partner
  e-mail: yair@genesisvp.com
  Education: JD, Loyola University School of Law; BA, Haifa University, Israel
  Background: VP Business Development, Butterfly; Partner, Goldfarb, Levy, Eran & Company
  Gary Gannot, General Partner
  e-mail: gary@genesisvp.com
  Education: BSc in Computer Engineering, Technion - Israel Institute of Technology
  Background: Co-Founder and Chief Operating Officer, Healink Corporation; Vice President of Engineering, Exemplar Logic; Project Leader, Intel

2776 GENEZIS CAPITAL TECHNOLOGY
Bld 2-11
Ugreshskaja Str.
Moscow 115088
Russia

Phone: 7-495-225-58-09
e-mail: info@geneziscap.com
web: www.geneziscap.com

Mission Statement: We seek creative, smart and entrepreneurial spirited people whose ambition is to grow businesses and tap new markets. We prefer long-term investments of 3-7 years.
Geographic Preference: Russia, CIS, United States, Europe, Asia
Minimum Investment: $25,000
Investment Criteria: Seed, Venture, Growth
Portfolio Companies: Fleecs, Martmania, B-152, System Heat, Aknol
Key Executives:
  Maxim Shekhovtsov, Chairman, Managing Partner
  Background: Co-Founder, TexDrive; Founder and Head of Venture Capital Division, Allianz SE; Advisor, RTI-Systems
  Denis Burlakov, Managing Partner
  Background: Founder, Front Line Capital
  Directorships: AGIC Group

2777 GESTION DE CAPITAL RIESGO DEL PAIS VASCO
Alameda de Urquijo, 36 4TH Floor Plaza Bizkai
Bilbao 48011
Spain

Phone: 34-944037000 Fax: 34-944-037056
e-mail: info@spri.es
web: www.spri.es

Mission Statement: Actively seeking new investments. Acts on behalf of third parties, managing venture capital companies and funds. It was founded by the Basque Government in order to promote and develop activities relating to venture capital in Basque Country.
Geographic Preference: Basque
Fund Size: $155 Million
Founded: 1985
Minimum Investment: $8.4 Million
Industry Group Preference: All Sectors Considered
Key Executives:
  Alexander Arriola Lizarriturri, Director-General
  Background: Vice Secretary, Information Society
  Directorships: Shanghai Municipal People
  Alexander Arriola Lizarriturri, Director-General

2778 GET2VOLUME ACCELERATOR
67 Ayer Rajah Crescent Unit 03-20/22
Singapore 139950
Singapore

Phone: +65 6777 9750 Fax: +65 6777 9750
e-mail: info@g2vaccelerator.com
web: www.g2vaccelerator.com

Mission Statement: We believe that the right eco-system of capital, connections, and capabilities is critical to successfully growing a technology company in Singapore. At Get2Volume, our approach is to work alongside entrepreneurs as a part of their team. We bring the capital capabilities and connections to complement the entrepreneurial team. Our deep experience in successfully growing and exiting enterprise and microelectronics centric companies allows us to complement the companies that we work with, enabling faster growth. We believe these companies are global from day one. This means that we bring global capabilities to address focused growth needs. We leverage these capabilities across our portfolio of companies to improve the efficiency.
Geographic Preference: Singapore
Industry Group Preference: Technology
Portfolio Companies: Silicon Cloud, Mobicart, Eco Consumer Services, Tabsquare, gridComm, Sprooki, Plunify, Semitech Semiconductor, ConnectedHealth, DarbeeVision, Novelics
Key Executives:
  Mike Holt, Managing Partner

2779 GILDE INVESTMENT FUNDS
Herculesplein 104
3584 AA Utrecht
Utrecht 3508 AB
Netherlands

Phone: 31-882202600 Fax: 31-882202601
e-mail: info@gilde.nl
web: www.gilde.com

Mission Statement: Actively seeking new investments.
Geographic Preference: Europe, USA, Israel
Fund Size: $240.5 Million
Founded: 1982
Average Investment: $75 - $600 million
Minimum Investment: $120,000
Investment Criteria: Start-up, First stage and Growth stage.
Industry Group Preference: Communications, Computer Related, Software, Electronic Technology, Mobile Communications Devices

Venture Capital & Private Equity Firms / International Firms

Portfolio Companies: AtoBe, Cambridge Broadband, Application Networks, Augeo, Carmen Systems, Covast, Cyco Software, I-Logix, JobPartners, Mondosoft, Tridion, Truston, WebCollage and HSCG.

Key Executives:

Gerhard Nordemann, Managing Partner
Education: Masters Degree in business economics.
Background: Private equity.
Remko Jager, Managing Partner
Boudewijn T Molenaar, Managing Director
Education: Graduated with a degree in electronic engineering.
Background: ABN AMRO's private equity.
Directorships: Executive board member.
Ferry de Vries, Investment Director
Education: Business administration and business financing
Background: Rabobank International.

2780 GIMV GIMV
Karel Oomsstraat 37
Antwerp 2018
Belgium

Phone: 32-32902100 **Fax:** 32-32902105
e-mail: info@gimv.be
web: www.gimv.com

Mission Statement: Supports the economic development of the Kempen region

Geographic Preference: Europe
Fund Size: $1.19 Billion
Founded: 1980
Minimum Investment: $3 Million
Investment Criteria: Seed, Startup, Early-Stage
Industry Group Preference: Biotechnology, Communications, Electronic Technology, Energy, Industrial Equipment, Medical & Health Related
Portfolio Companies: 3mensio, Ablynx, AGY Therapeutics, Alfacam, Ambit, Arcomet, Arrow Therapeutics, Astex Therapeutics, Avalon Pharmaceuticals, Barco New

Key Executives:

Koen Dejonckheere, CEO
e-mail: receptie@gimv.be
Education: Degree in applied economics from the University of Antwerp
Dirk Boogmans, General Counsel - Executive Vice President
e-mail: receptie@gimv.be
Education: Degree in Applied Economics-State University of Ghent.
Background: Barco, various other non-quoted companies.

2781 GIMV NV
37 Karel Oomsstraat
Antwerp 2018
Belgium

Phone: 32-32902100 **Fax:** 32-32384193
e-mail: info@gimv.com
web: www.gimv.com

Mission Statement: GIMV is the only prominent investment company in Flanders specialised in private equity i.e. investing in the equity of unlisted companies.

Geographic Preference: Europe
Fund Size: $643 Million
Founded: 1980
Average Investment: $2.1 Billion
Minimum Investment: $3 Million
Investment Criteria: All Stages
Industry Group Preference: All Sectors Considered
Portfolio Companies: Cril Telecom Software, Interwise, Intuwave, Mediornet, ORMvision, Telenet, Voxtron, Ablynx, AGY Therapeutics, Ambit, Arrow Therapeutics, CareX, Crop Design, Tops Foods, Mondi Foods, EBT, UFO, Westerlund Group

Key Executives:

Koen Dejonckheere, Chief Executive Officer
e-mail: receptie@gimv.be
Education: Master Degree.
Background: PricewaterhouseCoopers in Brussel.

2782 GIZA VENTURE CAPITAL
Ramat Aviv Tower
12th Floor, 40 Einstein St.
PO Box 17672
Tel Aviv 61175
Israel

Phone: 972-36402323 **Fax:** 972-36402319
e-mail: zholtzman@gizavc.com
web: www.giza.co.il

Mission Statement: Giza has investment professionals with a wealth of expertise and experience in Communication, Information Technology, Enterprise Software and Life Sciences. The Fund has the highest ratio of professionals to capital managed of any VC fund based in Israel.

Geographic Preference: Israel, USA, Singapore
Fund Size: $500 Million
Founded: 1992
Average Investment: $500,000
Minimum Investment: $300,000
Investment Criteria: Early-stage
Industry Group Preference: Communications, Information Technology, Enterprise Services, Life Sciences, Software, Semiconductors, Internet/Mobile/Media
Portfolio Companies: Advasense, Altair Semiconductor, Butterfly, Envara, Flash Networks, Horizon Semiconductors, Iamba, Libit, Lucid, Mysitcom Ltd, Oplus Technologies, Resolute Networks, Smart Link Ltd, Surf Communication Solutions, Telegate, Telrad Connegy, TMT Coaxial Network

Key Executives:

Ori Kirshner, Managing Partner
e-mail: zholtzman@gizavc.com
Education: BA, Hebrew University; MBA, Tel Aviv University
Background: Executive VP, Leumi & Co Investment Bankers; Lehman Brothers; Advisor to: Scitex, Elscint, Koor, Discount Investment Corporation, Poalim Investments, Bezeq; Founding Member, Israel Venture Association
Zvi Schechter, Co-Founder/Managing Director
e-mail: zvi@gizavc.com
Education: BS, Technion; MBA, Tel Aviv University
Background: Leumi & Co Investment Bankers; Financial Advisor to major Israeli banks
Ezer Soref, Managing Director
e-mail: esoref@gizavc.com
Education: BA Management and Economics, MA Economics, Tel Aviv University
Background: Corporate Research, Franklin Mint Corporation
Tal Mizrahi, CFO
Education: MBA, MD, Tel Aviv University; postdoctoral, Columbia University
Background: Vice Chairman, Abarbanel Hospital; Head Residency Training, Tel Aviv University Medicine;
Directorships: Chief Editor, Israeli National Board Examination
Zeev Holtzman, Chairman & Founder
e-mail: zholtzman@gizavc.com
Education: MBA in Finance, from Columbia University
Background: Former Executive VP at Leumi & Co. Investment Bankers and worked at Lehman Brothers in New York
Directorships: founder
Eyal Niv, Managing Director USA
Education: BA in Economics from The Hebrew

Venture Capital & Private Equity Firms / International Firms

University of Jerusalem
Background: Bynet; Iscar; Economist, Giyo International

2783 GLOBAL EQUITY PARTNERS BETEILIGUNGS-MANAGEMENT
Mariahilfer Strasse 1/Getreidemarkt 17
Vienna 1060
Austria
Phone: 43-15818390 **Fax:** 43-18517611
e-mail: office@gep.at
web: www.gep.at

Mission Statement: Global equity partner is an internationally operating investment company head-quartered in Vienna.

Geographic Preference: Austria, Germany, Switzerland
Fund Size: $550 Billion
Founded: 1998
Average Investment: $6.6 Million
Minimum Investment: $1.20 Million
Investment Criteria: Seed and start up, expansion
Industry Group Preference: Biotechnology, Communications, Computer Related, Industrial Products, Industrial Services, Manufacturing
Portfolio Companies: Integriertes Resource Management, ABATEC Electronics AG, Ray Sono AG, VennWorks LLC, WS Beteiligungs AG, PaysafeCard.com, Wertkarten AG, Goldbach Media, Stage1 Beteiligungs Invest, Indian Dreams, BET and WIN.com

Key Executives:
  Michael Tojner, Founder/ CEO
  Education: Master's in Business Administration
  Background: Creditanstalt, WKBG, Teleperformance, and Siemens.
  Herbert Herdlicka, Management Board
  Education: Master's degree.
  Background: Private Customer Department at Deutsche Bank Capital.

2784 GLOBAL FINANCE
7 Fragoklissas Str, 15125
Global Finance SA
Athens 15125
Greece
Phone: 30-2108124500 **Fax:** 30-2108055430
e-mail: office@globalfinance.gr
web: www.globalfinance.gr

Mission Statement: Global Finance takes a proactive role in backing exceptional entrepreneurs and managers, providing growth capital to companies with a potential for significant expansion. Global Finance has offices in Greece, Romania and Bulgaria.

Geographic Preference: Europe, Russia
Fund Size: $300 Million
Founded: 1991
Investment Criteria: Expansion.
Industry Group Preference: Manufacturing, Information Technology, Retailing, Media, Telecommunications, Services
Portfolio Companies: Baring Hellenic Ventures SA (BHV), Euromerchant Balkan Fund (EBF), Goody's, Chipita, Germanos, Jumbo, Dodoni, Yioula, Nikas, NetMed, United Milk Company, Sicomed, Temenos, Corporation Dermoaesthetica (Spain), Mobiltel.

Key Executives:
  George Gondicas, Non-Executive Director
  Education: BA in Economic And Business Sciences, MBA.
  Angelos Plakopitas, Managing Partner
  Education: MS, MBA, INSEAD.
  Background: General Manager, Shelman (wood products company); 14 years experience in corporate banking with Citibank and Hellenic Industrial Development Bank.

Theodore Klakidis, Partner
Education: MSc in Mathematics, MPP in International Trade and Finance.

2785 GLOBAL LIFE SCIENCE VENTURES GmbH
Tal 26
Munchen D - 80331
Germany
Phone: 49-892881510 **Fax:** 49-8928815130
e-mail: mailbox@glsv-vc.com
web: www.glsv-vc.com

Mission Statement: Global Life Science Ventures (GLSV) is a leading, independent venture capital fund focusing exclusively on the life sciences.

Geographic Preference: Western Europe, USA
Fund Size: 200 Million Euros
Founded: 1996
Average Investment: 5 million Euros
Minimum Investment: 1 million Euros
Investment Criteria: Early Stage and Later stage.
Industry Group Preference: Biotechnology, Life Sciences, Medical Technology, Pharmaceuticals
Portfolio Companies: Pieris AG, Santaris A/S, IMI AG, Agendia B/V, Horizon Pharma, Nabriva Therapeutics AG, Zalicas Inc., Neurogesx Inc., Glycart AG, Intercell AG, Cyberkinetics Inc., Cytos Biotechnology AG, DeveloGen AG, Sequenom Inc., Memory Inc., Exelixis Pharmaceuticals Inc., Artemis Pharmaceuticals GmbH, Coley Pharmaceutical Group, MBT Ag

Other Locations:
  Postplatz 1
  PO Box 626
  Zug 6301
  Switzerland
  Phone: 41-4172719 40 **Fax:** 41-41-727-1945

Key Executives:
  Dr. Hans A Kuepper, Partner
  e-mail: ha.kuepper@glsv-vc.com
  Education: PhD, Biochemistry
  Background: Senior management positions in research and R&D managment with biotech and pharm companies, technology assessment, and corporate M&A
  Dr. Peter H Reinsich, Partner
  e-mail: p.reinisch@glsv-vc.com
  Education: PhD, Business & Engineering
  Background: Senior management positions in the life science industry and in particular for the strategic coordination and business development of diagnostics worldwide
  Dipl.-Kfm Hanns-Peter Weiss, Partner
  Education: MBA
  Background: Senior management positions in private equity and venture capital firms investing across a range of industries in Europe and the USA, and in particular the life sciences

2786 GLOBAL MARITIME VENTURES BERHAD
Leve 15, Menara Bank Pembangunan
Jalan Sultan Ismail
Level 11
Kuala Lumpur 50250
Malaysia
Phone: 60-326-988231 **Fax:** 60-326-940860
web: www.gmv.com.my

Mission Statement: Global Maritime Ventures Berhad (GMV) is a marine venture capital investment holding company.

Geographic Preference: Malaysia
Fund Size: RM500 million
Founded: 1993
Industry Group Preference: Marine Services

Venture Capital & Private Equity Firms / International Firms

Key Executives:
En. Ahmad Sharifuddin bin Abdul Kadir, Chief Executive Officer
En. Abdul Karim bin Ismail, Chief Operating Officer

2787 GLOBAL TECHNOLOGY VENTURES
#23/2 Coffee Day Square
Vittal Mallya Road
Suite 23/2
Bangalore 560 001
India

Phone: 91-8040012345
e-mail: info@gtvltd.com

Mission Statement: Global Technology Ventures Ltd. (GTV) is a venture capital firm specializing in early stage, start up, and late stage financing. The firm typically invests in the technology sector, and seeks to invest in companies located in India, with a specific focus on Bangalore.

Key Executives:
V.G. Siddhartha, Managing Partner

2788 GLOBAL VENTURES MANAGEMENT LIMITED
2-6 Granville Road, Suite 1508, Tsimshatsui
Kowloon
Hong Kong

Phone: 852-27241223 Fax: 852-27224373
web: www.galliance.com

Mission Statement: Asia's first venture investment bank.

Geographic Preference: Japan, Hong Kong, British Virgin Islands
Founded: 1994
Portfolio Companies: Pacific Mandarin Assets Ltd., Spellacy Universal Ltd., Infinity Finance Ltd.

Key Executives:
C.J. Wilson, Group Managing Director
Education: Bachelors Degree in Economics from University of Wisconsin and a Masters Degree from Harvard University School of Business Administration.
Background: Banker and venture finance specialist.
Directorships: Co-head of international M&A for Asahi Bank in Japan.
Roger W Mills, Executive Managing Director

2789 GMT COMMUNICATIONS PARTNERS LLP
21 Gloucester Place
London W1U 8HR
United Kingdom

Phone: 44-2072929333
e-mail: tim.green@gmtpartners.com
web: www.gmtpartners.com

Mission Statement: GMT Communications Partners LLP is an independent private equity firm focused on investments in European content, communications infrastructure and tech-enabled services in Europe.

Geographic Preference: United Kingdom, Continental Europe
Fund Size: 542 million Euros
Founded: 1993
Average Investment: 25-30 million Euros
Minimum Investment: 10 million Euros
Investment Criteria: Later stage
Industry Group Preference: Communications, Software Services, Internet Technology, Telecommunications, Media, Computer Related

Key Executives:
Timothy S. Green, Managing Partner
e-mail: tim.green@gmtpartners.com
Education: MSc, Sloan Fellow, London Business School; ACA
Background: Partner, Baring Communications Equity; Partner, Baring Private Equity Partners; Chartered Accountant; KPMG
Directorships: TES Media
Ashley Long, Partner
e-mail: ashley.long@gmtpartners.com
Education: BA, Univ. of Kent
Background: Triton Private Equity
Directorships: Primesight
Vikram Krishna, Partner
e-mail: vikram.krishna@gmtpartners.com
Education: BA, Univ. of Oxford
Background: PricewaterhouseCoopers
Directorships: MeetingZone; Primesight

2790 GOBI PARTNERS
Building 7, Zhangjiang Innovation Park
399 Keyuan Road
Shanghai 201203, PRC
China

Phone: 86-2151601618 Fax: 86-2152929730
web: www.gobivc.com

2791 GOGIN CAPITAL COMPANY LIMITED
71 Shirakata honmachi, Matsue shi
Shimane 690-0061
Japan

Phone: 81-852-28-7170 Fax: 81-852-28-7177
web: www.gogin.co.jp

Fund Size: 54, 259 one million Yen

Key Executives:
Makoto Kose, President

2792 GOLDMAN SACHS INTERNATIONAL UK
133 Fleet Street
Peterborough Court
London EC4A 2BB
United Kingdom

Phone: 44-1717741000 Fax: 44-2077-741181
web: www.goldmansachs.com

Mission Statement: Actively seeking new investments.

Geographic Preference: United Kingdom, Europe
Founded: 1995
Investment Criteria: Early stage to Expansion
Industry Group Preference: All Sectors Considered
Portfolio Companies: Alliance Hotelerie, Diamond Cable, GCR Holdings Ltd, Pears Portfolio, Stirling Cooke Browne, Suez Portfolio

Key Executives:
Lloyd C. Blankfein, Chairman & Chief Executive Officer
Gary D. Cohn, President & Co-Chief Operating Officer

2793 GORILLA VENTURES
Aleksanterinkatu 15 B
0100 Helsinki
Finland

web: www.gorillaventures.fi

Mission Statement: Gorilla Ventures is a business accelerator which helps entrepreneurs realize their dreams by making seed investments and participating in the operationsal running of the company - whether strategy and customer development, go-to-market execution or globalization.

Investment Criteria: Seed

Other Locations:
Väinä Linnan aukio 15
33210 Tampere
Finland

Key Executives:
Petri Lehmuskoski
e-mail: petri.lehmuskoski@gorillaventures.fi

889

Venture Capital & Private Equity Firms / International Firms

Risto Rautakorpi
e-mail: risto.rautakorpi@gorillaventures.fi
Reijo Syrjalainen
e-mail: reijo.syrjalainen@gorillaventures.fi
Timo Tiihonen
e-mail: timo.tiihonen@gorillaventures.fi

2794 GRANITE VENTURE CAPITAL CORPORATION
One Bush Street
Suite 1350
San Francisco, California 94104
South Korea

Phone: 415-5917700 Fax: 415-5917720
web: www.granitevc.com

Mission Statement: Actively seeking investments.

Fund Size: $625 Million
Founded: 1998
Industry Group Preference: Software, Industrial Services
Portfolio Companies: Sibley & Associates, General Donlee, King-Reed & Associates, Vignette

Key Executives:
Chris Mckay, Managing Director

2795 GRANVILLE BAIRD CAPITAL PARTNERS
Mint House, 77 Mansell Street
London E1 8AF
United Kingdom

Phone: 44-2076678400 Fax: 44-2076678481
e-mail: mproudlock@bcpe.co.uk
web: www.bairdcapital.com

Mission Statement: Actively seeking new investments. The European private equity arm of Robert W Baird & Co.

Geographic Preference: United Kingdom, Germany, Spain
Fund Size: $789 Million
Founded: 1971
Average Investment: £10 Million and £50 Million
Minimum Investment: $1.2 Million
Investment Criteria: MBO, MBI, Buy and Build, Growth Capital
Industry Group Preference: Business to Business, Healthcare, Industrial Equipment
Portfolio Companies: Alukon, Amann, Armor Group, Balzac Coffee, Berkenhoff, Capital Consulting, Castlecare, Cerillion, Controlex, Eisenworld, ETC, Hahl, Mentor, MI International, Mobile.de, Nobis, Public Recruitment Group, SSB, Team BS, TSL, Ultralase, Vistorm, Westfalia

Key Executives:
James Benfield, Managing Director
Background: County Bank; Chartered Accountant, Ernst & Young; GKN
Andrew Ferguson, Managing Director
Background: Chartered Accountant, KPMG; Grant Thornton; NatWest Ventures
David Barrass, Operating Partner
Education: BBA
Background: Founder/Managing Director, M&A consultancy; Angermann Consulting
Simon Havers, Director
Education: MBA
Background: ABN AMRO Capital; Planning/Rollout, BBC World Service Television; Strategy Consultant
Directorships: ArmorGroup; Cerillion

2796 GRAPHITE CAPITAL MANAGEMENT LTD
Berkeley Square House
Berkeley Square
London W1J 6BQ
United Kingdom

Phone: 44-2078255300 Fax: 44-2078255399
e-mail: info@graphitecapital.com
web: www.graphitecapital.com

Mission Statement: Graphite Capital has been a private equity investor since 1981 as F&C Ventures and became independent in 2001. Emphasis is put on rapid decision-making and deliverability for quality management teams with strong track records.

Geographic Preference: United Kingdom, Western Europe
Fund Size: £1.5 billion
Founded: 1981
Average Investment: £200 million
Minimum Investment: $3.5 Million
Industry Group Preference: Retailing, Consumer Services, Leisure, Property Management, Services, Distribution, Manufacturing, Financial Services, Healthcare, Consumer Products
Portfolio Companies: Alliance Medical, Aktrion, Applied Energy, Avery Haelth, Business Advirory Service, Clearminster, Clinovia, Computacenter, Denison, Denplan, Dewhurst/Angloarch, Equanet, Game, Go Plant, Golden Tulip, Hiscox, Huntress, JTF, Jane Norman, Kingsclear, Leading Edge Labels, Leaderflush, London & Henley, MMS, Maplin, Ottakar's, PIFC, PSD Group, Paperchase, Ridgmont, SBJ, Salt Union, Sealine, Sharelink, Sodastream, Stalwart, Streamline, Tesla, U Pol, Vardon, Wagamama

Key Executives:
Emma Osborne, Partner
Education: Oxford University; MBA, INSEAD
Background: McKinsey & Co; Bell & Howell Ltd
Rod Richards, Managing Partner
Education: Oxford University
Background: Hill Samuel Development Capital; Management Consultant, LEK
Andrew Gray, Partner
Education: Stirling University; MBA, Warwick Business School
Background: Morgan Grenfell Development Capital
Markus Golser, Partner
Education: Business degree, HEC Paris; MBA with distinction, Oxford University
Background: Morgan Grenfell Development Capital
Jeremy Gough, Partner
Education: Oxford University
Background: Director, Morgan Grenfell Development Capital; 3i; Close Brothers
John O'Neill, Investment Manager
Education: Business/Accounting degrees, University College, Dublin
Background: Finance Advisor, Hawkpoint Partners; antfactory; Chartered Accountant, Deloitte & Touche
Jenny Michelman, Investment Director
Education: Oxford University; MBA, Open Business School
Background: J Henry Schroder & Co Ltd; Manager International Distribution Center, Pitney Bowes; Development Manager, Boral UK
Mike Tilbury, Investment Director
Education: Nottingham University
Background: Deutsche Bank; NatWest Securities; NatWest Ventures
Mike Innes, Investment Director
Education: St Andrews University; MBA, London School of Business
Background: Integrated Finance Team, Bank of Scotland; Solicitor, Clifford Chance; Founder, internet-based legal recruitment consultancy
Mark Hudson, Investment Director
Education: Modern History degree, Oxford University;

Venture Capital & Private Equity Firms / International Firms

MBA, INSEAD
Background: Management Consultant, OC&C Strategy Consultants; East Africa Operations, Tilda Rice; Founder, internet software company
Anne Hoffmann, Investment Manager
Education: Queen's University; MBA, JL Kellogg Graduate School
Background: Strategy Consultant, McKinsey & Co; PPM Ventures

2797 GRAZIA EQUITY
Breitscheidstrasse 10
Stuttgart 70174
Germany

Phone: 49-711-90-710-90 Fax: 49-711-90-710-988
e-mail: info@grazia.com
web: www.grazia.com

Mission Statement: Grazia Equity, based in Stuttgart and Munich, is one of Europe's top names in venture capital. Grazia specializes in start-up or early-stage financing for innovative companies with market-changing potential and opportunities for superior returns. Our successful track record and expanding global network now enable us to fund selected start-ups elsewhere in Europe as well as in the US.

Geographic Preference: Europe, United States
Founded: 200
Portfolio Companies: 4-Antibody, Adconion, B2X Care Solutions, BeStylish, Delivery Agent, Immatics, Mister Spex, Moviepilot, Mysportgroup, Quantenna, Starboard, SiTime, Statista, StyleTread, Urbanara

Key Executives:
Jochen Kluppel, Partner
Background: McKinsey & Company
Directorships: Adconion, Moviepilot, Mister Spex, MySportGroup, Urbanara, Statista, Immatics

2798 GREE VENTURES
Roppongi Hills, Mori Tower
6-10-1 Roppongi
Minato-ku
Tokyo
Japan

e-mail: info@greeventures.com
web: www.greeventures.com

Mission Statement: At GREE Ventures, we leverage our successful experiences with Japan's fastest growing enterprises and the resulting industry know-how in addition to our exclusive network to invest in and support start-ups in the field of Internet and mobile services.

Geographic Preference: Southeast Asia
Founded: 2011
Average Investment: 30 million yen to 100 million
Investment Criteria: Early-Stage
Industry Group Preference: Internet, Mobile, E-Commerce & Manufacturing, Advertising, Social Media
Portfolio Companies: Aucfan, PT Pricearea Andalan Prestasi, Star Festival, Geniee, PT Bukalapak.com, Retty.com, PT Berrybenka, Luxola

Key Executives:
Naoki Aoyagi, Managing Partner
Education: BS, Policy Management, Keio University
Background: Deutsche Bank

2799 GRESHAM PRIVATE EQUITY LIMITED
Level 17, 167 Macquarie Street
Sydney 2000
Australia

Phone: 61-292215133 Fax: 61-292216814
e-mail: GPE@gresham.com.au
web: www.gresham.com.au

Mission Statement: Actively seeking new investments.
Geographic Preference: Australia, Europe, America, Asia, Africa
Fund Size: $200 Million
Founded: 1985
Average Investment: $11.16 Million to $14.8 Million
Minimum Investment: $7.4 Million
Investment Criteria: MBO, MBI and Development Capital. Generally Later Stage Deals in Established Companies
Industry Group Preference: Corporate Advisory, Private Equity, Property Development, Asset Finance
Portfolio Companies: Norcos

Key Executives:
David Feetham, Deputy Chairman
Directorships: Electronic Banking Solutions
Antony Breuer, Director
61-292215133
Fax: 61-292239072
Directorships: Norcos, Eurogestion, Raywood, Electronic Banking Solutions
Charles Graham, Managing Director
61-292215133
Fax: 61-292239072
Directorships: Eroc
Bruce McLennan, Head of Advisory and Managing Director
61-292215133
Fax: 61-29223-9072
Directorships: Raywood, Electronic Banking Solutions
Chris Stephenson, Chief Financial Officer

2800 GRUPO BISA
Recongquista 1166
11th Floor
Buenos Aires 1003
Argentina

Phone: 54-1143133830 Fax: 54-1143139030
web: www.grupobisa.com

Mission Statement: To make capital gains for investors as an active investor whose management skills contribute to create value in portfolio companies.

Fund Size: $150 Million
Founded: 1992
Average Investment: $15 Million
Minimum Investment: $5 Million
Investment Criteria: First Stage, Acquisitions, Recapitalizations, Special Situations, Consolidations, Privatization
Industry Group Preference: Broadcasting, Business to Business, Consumer Services, Entertainment, Financial Services, Food Services, Manufacturing, Retailing, Telecommunications, Wholesale, Cable, Radio, Distribution

Key Executives:
Nichollas Wollak, Director, Partner
Education: AB, Harvard University
Background: VP, Private Placement Department of Drexel Burnham Lambert, Executive Director, Invercapital

2801 GSR VENTURES
5620, China World Trade Center Tower III
No. 1 Jianguomenval Street
Chaoyang District
Beijing 100004
China

Phone: 86-10-5706-9898 Fax: 86-10-5706-9899
web: www.gsrventures.com

Mission Statement: GSR Ventures is a venture capital fund that invests primarily in early and growth stage technology companies with substantial operations in China.

Geographic Preference: China
Fund Size: $1 billion

Venture Capital & Private Equity Firms / International Firms

Industry Group Preference: Semiconductors, Internet, Wireless, Green Technology
Other Locations:
245 Lytton Avenue
Suite 350
Palo Alto, CA 94301
Phone: 650-331-7300 Fax: 650-331-7301
Golden Sand River (Hong Kong) Limited
18 Harbour Road
Wanchai
Hong Kong
Phone: 852-2201-6300 Fax: 852-2877-9833
Key Executives:
James Ding, Managing Director
e-mail: ding@gsrventures.com
Education: BS, Chemistry, Peking University; MS, Information Science, UCLA; Haas Business School
Background: Co-Founder, AsiaInfo-Linkage
Directorships: BORQS, China Rainbow, NQ Mobile

2802 GUANGDONG TECHNOLOGY VENTURE CAPITAL COMPANY
13F. Hi-Tech R&D Center, 100 Mid Xianlie Rd
Guangzhou
China
Phone: 020-87683662 Fax: 020-87684955
Geographic Preference: Guangdong Province, China
Fund Size: 1.2 billion RMB
Founded: 1998
Investment Criteria: Expansion Stage
Industry Group Preference: Electronic Technology, Physical Sciences, Medical, Bioengineering, Environmental Protection, Materials Technology, Optical Technology
Portfolio Companies: Zhuhai Yueke Tsinghua Electronic Ceramics, Guangdong Hongtu Technology, Guangdong Ronsen Super Micro-wire, Shenzhen Sunlord Electronics, Shenzhen Yinboda Telecommunication Technology, Haikou Qili Pharmaceutical, Shenzhen WuZhouLong Motors, Shenzhen Green Materials Hi-tech

2803 GUIDANT EUROPE SA
Green Square, Lambroekstraat 5D
Culliganlaan 2B
Diegem 1831
Belgium
Phone: 32-24167011 Fax: 32-27141665
web: www.bostonscientific.com
Mission Statement: Investing in new medical technologies.
Geographic Preference: Europe
Fund Size: $47.3 Billion
Founded: 1979
Average Investment: $895 million
Minimum Investment: $3.8áBillion
Investment Criteria: Design and development of cardiovascular medical products
Industry Group Preference: Medical & Health Related
Portfolio Companies: Johnson and johnson
Key Executives:
Michael F. Mahoney, President and Chief Executive Officer
Kevin Ballinger, Senior Vice President and Global President

2804 GUJARAT STATE FERTILIZERS COMPANY LIMITED
PO Fertilizernagar
Vadodara 391 750
India
Phone: 91-2652242451 Fax: 91-2652240966
e-mail: info@gsfcltd.com
web: www.gsfclimited.com

Mission Statement: Actively seeking new investments.
Geographic Preference: India
Fund Size: $11 Million
Founded: 1962
Key Executives:
Dr. Varesh Sinha, IAS, Chairman
Dr. Hasmukh Adhia, IAS, Director

2805 HALDER BETEILIGUNGSBERATUNG GmbH
Bockenheimer Landstraáe 98-100
Frankfurt am Main 60323
Germany
Phone: 49- 692425330 Fax: 49-69236866
e-mail: mail@halder.eu
web: www.halder.eu
Mission Statement: Invests private equity in mature, profitable and well-managed mid to large-size companies.
Geographic Preference: Germany, Penelopes
Fund Size: $1.32 Billion
Founded: 1991
Average Investment: $8.4 Million
Minimum Investment: $15.2 Million
Investment Criteria: MBO, Management Buy-In, Expansion and Development
Industry Group Preference: Industrial Equipment, Manufacturing, Industrial Services
Portfolio Companies: FMA France, Deka-Brushes
Key Executives:
Paul De Ridder, Partner
e-mail: mail@halder-d.com
Education: MBA, Business Administration
Background: Private Equity
Michael Wahl, Partner
e-mail: mail@halder-d.com
Background: Private Equity, Corporate Finance
Susanne Quint, Managing Director, Partner
e-mail: mail@halder-d.com
Education: Degree, Business Administration
Background: Private Equity(Halder)_
Michael Wahl, Managing Partner
e-mail: mail@halder-d.com
Education: Degree, Business Administration
Background: Private equity and Investment Banking

2806 HALDER HOLDINGS BV
Bockenheimer Landstraáe 98-100
Frankfurt am Main 60323
Germany
Phone: 49- 692425330 Fax: 49-69236866
e-mail: mail@halder.eu
web: www.halder.eu
Mission Statement: Invests private equity in mature, profitable and well managed companies mid to large-size companies.
Geographic Preference: Belgium, Europe, Germany, Netherlands
Founded: 1983
Minimum Investment: $150 Million
Investment Criteria: Expansion and Development, MBO, Management Buy-In, Bridge, Replacement
Industry Group Preference: Consumer Services, Industrial Equipment, Transportation, Industrial Services
Portfolio Companies: Arma Beheer BV, Badenia Bettcomfort GmbH & Company KG, Benefood NV, Bopack NV, Care4Data NV, Control Systems BV, Essanelle Hair Group AG, Euretco NV, FCS, Gealean Holding GmbH, Geka-brush GmbH, Goffin NV, Happich Fahzeug-und Industrieteile GmbH

Key Executives:
Thomas Fotteler, Partner
e-mail: mail@halder-d.com
Background: 14 years private equity experience (Halder)
Tanja Kilb, Office Manager
e-mail: info@halder.nl
Background: Risk capital (Halder, Oranje-Nassau Groep), Auditing (KPMG and Ernst & Young)
Magdalena Kijak, Office Manager
e-mail: info@halder.nl
Background: Private equity, Management Consultancy, Marketing and Sales

2807 HALLIM VENTURE CAPITAL
Kangnam-Gu Nonhyun-Dong 237-11
Dong Gang
Nam Gu
Seoul 135-010
South Korea

Phone: 82-2-511-6100 **Fax:** 82-2-511-6108

Geographic Preference: Korea
Founded: 1998
Industry Group Preference: Internet Technology, Biotechnology, Information Technology, Machinery
Portfolio Companies: Charm Engineering, Comware, Daewon Special Wire Co, ECtelecom, Integrant Technologies, JS Digitech, MEDIAI Co, PSIA, Sung Industrial, Tae-san Techno, Teltron Telecommunications & Electronics

Key Executives:
Kim Kwang, Chief Executive Officer
Education: BA Economics, MA Public Administration, Seoul National University; MS Finance, London Business School
Background: Assistant Planning Manager, Hansol Paper; President/CEO, Asia M&A Corp; President/CEO, A-One Venture Capital; Author; Director, Pan-Pacific Trading
Jung Dong Soo, Executive Director
Education: BBA, University of Korea
Background: Kookmin Venture Capital; Doobon Corp; Aztec Venture Capital Corp
Dong Soo Jung, Executive Director
Education: BA Chemical Engineering, Seoul National University; MBA, University of Washington
Background: Handysoft Corp; Deloitte Tohmatsu Japan; HP Consulting Corp; SUDO Pharm Corp
Jung Hoon Lee, General Manager
Education: BA Economics, Kyunghee University
Background: KICPA; Sinhan Accounting firm; AI Investment Management

2808 HAMBRO CAPITAL MANAGEMENT LTD
Ground Floor, Ryder Court, 14 Ryder Street
London SW1Y 6QB
United Kingdom

Phone: 44-2077475678 **Fax:** 44-2077-475647
e-mail: info@johcm.co.uk
web: www.johcm.co.uk

Mission Statement: JO Hambro's private equity funds invest in companies that are not listed on the stockmarket. Investments usually involve focused management by the team or fund managers and held for tww through five years before sale. The three funds are: Trident Private Equity Fund; Trident Private equity Fund II; and Leisure & Media VCT plc.
Fund Size: Euro 8.4 Billion
Industry Group Preference: Leisure, Media

Key Executives:
Jamie Hambro, Chairman
Background: Fund Manager, Kleinwort Benson; Citibank; Managing Director, Smith New Court Europe; Senior Fund Manager, Rowe Price Fleming International
Directorships: Northern Rock plc
Nichola Pease, Chief Executive
020-77475601
e-mail: slockyear@johcm.co.uk
Background: Samual Montagu Limited; Montagu Investment Management Limited; Director, Invesco MIM
Directorships: NASCIT; American Opportunity Trust
Gavin Rochussen, Chief Executive Officer
020-77475602
e-mail: jbrade@johcm.co.uk
Education: Science, Oxford University
Background: Diplomatic Officer, Foreign & Commonwealth Office
Maarten Hemsley, Fund Manager
020-77475604
e-mail: mhemsley@johcm.co.uk
Background: Founder, Bryanston Management Ltd; President/CFO of several companies
Directorships: Sterling Construction Company

2809 HAMON INVESTMENT GROUP
3510 - 3515 Jardine House, 1 Connaught Place
Central
Hong Kong

Phone: 852-25264268 **Fax:** 852-25267277
e-mail: enquiry@hamon.com.hk
web: www.hamon.com.hk

Mission Statement: Hamon Group is an independent asset management firm specializing in investing in the shares of regional Asian companies and emerging blue chip growth companies.
Geographic Preference: Hong Kong, China, South Korea, Taiwan, Singapore, Thailand, Malaysia
Founded: 1989

Key Executives:
Hugh Simon, Chief Executive Officer
e-mail: enquiry@hamon.com.hk
Background: he worked for Schroders in London, Australia and Hong Kong for five years. He has over 20 years of experience in Asian regional investments.
Raymond Chan, Managing Director & Chief Investment Officer

2810 HANNOVER FINANZ GmbH
Gunther-Wagner-Allee 13
Hanover 30177
Germany

Phone: 49-511280070 **Fax:** 49-5112800737
e-mail: mail@hannoverfinanz.de
web: www.hannoverfinanz.de

Mission Statement: Actively seeking new investments in growing companies, both for its own account and on behalf of five funds under its management.
Fund Size: $449 Million
Founded: 1979
Average Investment: $4.9 Million
Minimum Investment: $1.2 Million
Investment Criteria: Later Stage, Development, Buyout, Pre-IPO, Replacement
Industry Group Preference: Engineering, Service Industries, Telecommunications, Manufacturing, Financial Services, Media
Portfolio Companies: AIXTRON Semiconductor Technologie, Alt United Garment Service, AWECO, Biologische Analysensystem, BAG Med, BIG, Peter Butz, Commerz, Back-und Kondit, Display Design & Instore Marketing, Dittmers Korrosionsschutz, Wandel und Gotermann Management Holding, HL Leasing, Hanseatische Verlags-Beteiligung, Markant Sdwest Handel, Mecoswiss, Mechanische Componenten, MobilCom Holding

Key Executives:
Andreas Schober, Chief Executive Officer
Education: MBA

Venture Capital & Private Equity Firms / International Firms

Johannes Voss, Investment Manager
Education: MSEE
Steffen Frenzel, Investment Manager
Education: Diploma-Kfm

2811 HANSUTTAM FINANCE LIMITED
H-57, Connaught Circus
1st Floor
Suite 11-57
New Delhi 110001
India

Phone: 91-1123320876 Fax: 91-1123353944
e-mail: hfl@hansuttam.com
web: www.hansuttam.com

Mission Statement: A leading investment banking company headquartered in New Delhi
Geographic Preference: Malaysia, Singapore, Dubai, Turkey, UK, Israel
Founded: 1986
Investment Criteria: Sponsors, developers, investors, contractors, service companies, operators, financial institutions, governments
Industry Group Preference: All Sectors Considered

Key Executives:
  Dipti Chopra, Chairman
  e-mail: hfl@hansuttam.com
  Background: PHDCCI, FICCI, ASSOCHAM
  Shyam Kishore, Executive Director

2812 HANWHA VC CORPORATION
Hanwha Bldg., 15F # 1 Changgyo-Dong
Kangnam-Gu
Seoul NV
South Korea

Phone: 82-272-92836 Fax: 82-272-91447
web: www.hanwha.co.kr

Mission Statement: Actively seeking new investments.
Fund Size: $87.7 Billion
Founded: 1952
Industry Group Preference: Biotechnology

2813 HASSO PLATTNER VENTURES
PO Box 90 02 62
Potsdam D-14438
Germany

Phone: 49-033197992101 Fax: 49-033197992130
e-mail: info@hp-ventures.com
web: www.hp-ventures.com

Mission Statement: Our mission, instilled by our main investor, Prof. Dr. h.c. Hasso Plattner, founder and chairman of software giant SAP, is to support and inspire young software and IT entrepreneurs in the successful transformation of their ideas into sustainable and viable products and companies, in Germany and abroad.
Geographic Preference: Germany, Israel, Europe
Fund Size: 150 million Euro
Founded: 2005
Average Investment: 250,000 - 10 million Euro
Industry Group Preference: Information Technology, Software
Portfolio Companies: Monoqi, SponsorPay, ReBuy.de, Collax, Ujam, GoEuro, Panaya, D-Labs, Facton, Smeet, Senzari, Opensynergy, Dreamlines.de, Vioso, Diablo Technologies, Inchron, Kenesto, Vasco.de, My Heritage

Key Executives:
  Yaron Valler, Managing Partner
  Education: MBA, Tel Aviv University
  Background: ProSeed Capital Fund, Eurofund, Inventech

2814 HASTINGS FUNDS MANAGEMENT PTY LIMITED
Level 27, 35 Collins Street
Melbourne 3000
Australia

Phone: 61-386503600 Fax: 61-386503701

Mission Statement: Activelty seeking new investments.
Geographic Preference: Australia
Fund Size: A$7.2 Billion
Founded: 1994
Portfolio Companies: Integrated Packaging Group, Acme Fine Furniture Natra Group, Craigcare Group, MCS Property Group.

Key Executives:
  Andrew Day, CEO
  e-mail: hfm@hfm.com.au
  Education: Masters in Applied Statistics and a Masters in Mathematics from Oxford University.
  Background: Cargill's
  Colin Atkin, Executive Director
  e-mail: hfm@hfm.com.au
  Education: BCom, ACA
  Background: Director of the private equity group

2815 HBM PARTNERS
Bundesplatz 1
2454 West Bay Road
Zug CH-6300
Switzerland

Phone: 41-438887171 Fax: 41-438887172
e-mail: lesieur@hbmcayman.com
web: www.hbmpartners.com

Mission Statement: HBM Partners is among the global leaders in healthcare-focused investing. HBM focuses on development stage, growth and buy-out financings of private companies as well as investments in public companies. HBM Partners advises HBM Healthcare Investments AG, HBM BioCapital and further specialized private-equity and public-equity funds. HBM has a complementary team of experienced professionals to source, analyze, execute and exit investments in the pharma/biotech, medical devices and diagnostics industries. We have been an active contributor to value creation in our portfolio companies, generating over 40 trade sales and IPOs since inception.
Fund Size: $800 million
Investment Criteria: Development Stage, Growth-Stage, Buyout
Industry Group Preference: Healthcare, Pharmaceuticals, Biotechnology, Medical Devices, Diagnostics
Portfolio Companies: Barofold, Cathay Industrial Biotech, Delenex, Enanta, Koltan Pharmaceuticals, Lux Biosciences, Nabriva, Nereus, Odyssey Thera, Opththotech, Paratek, Probiodrug, PTC, Symphony Evolution

Key Executives:
  Andreas Wicki, CEO
  Education: MSc, PhD, Chemistry & Biochemistry, University of Berne
  Background: Co-Owner/CEO, ANAWA Holding, Clinserve

2816 HEALTHCAP Odlander, Fredrikson & Co AB
Strandvagen 5B
Stockholm SE-114 51
Sweden

Phone: 46-84425850 Fax: 46-84425879
e-mail: bjorn.odlander@ofco.se
web: www.healthcap.se

Mission Statement: HealthCap is a family of multi-stage venture capital funds, investing globally in life sciences, with the Odlander Fredrikson Group as their exclusive investments advisor. With committed capital exceeding 800 million Euros,

Venture Capital & Private Equity Firms / International Firms

HealthCap is one of the largest specialized providers of venture capital within life sciences in Europe.

Geographic Preference: Worldwide
Investment Criteria: Early State, Later Stage
Industry Group Preference: Life Sciences, Pharmaceuticals, Biotechnology, Medical Technology
Portfolio Companies: Aerocrine AB, Affibody AB, Alba Therapeutics, Algeta AS, Apoxis SA, Benechill Inc., BioStratum, Biotage AB, Bonesupport AB, Cardoz AB, Cebix, Cerenis Therapeutics, ChemoCentryx, Creative Peptides Sweden AB, Evotec, FerroKin Biosciences, Five Prime, Genzion BioSciences, IDEA AG, Immune Targeting Systems, Inion Ltd., LTB4 Sweden AB, Lumavita AG, MIPS AB, NeuroNova AB, Nexstim Ov, Nucleonics Inc., Odyssey Thera Inc., Oncos Therapeutics Ltd., Optuvt AB, Orexo AB, OxThera AB, PTC Therapeutics, PulmonX Corp., Renovis Inc., Sopherion Therapeutics Inc., SpineVision SA, Technolas Perfect Vision GmbH, Tengion Inc., TopoTarget A/S, Trigen Ltd., Ultrazonix DNT AB

Other Locations:
Odlander Fredrikson SA
18 Avenue D'Ouchy
Lausanne CH-1066
Switzerland
Phone: 41-21-614-3500 **Fax:** 41-21-601-5544

Key Executives:
Bjorn Odlander MD, Founding Partner
e-mail: bjorn.odlander@ofco.se
Education: PhD, Medical Chemistry
Background: Head, ABB Aros Health Care Equity Research Team
Peder Fredrikson, Founding Partner
e-mail: peder.fredrikson@healthcap.ch
Education: BSc, University of Lund
Background: Corporate Finance, ABB Aros; Managing Director, Dillon Read & Co., Inc.; Managing Director, Prudential-Bache Capital Funding
Staffan Lindstrand, Partner
e-mail: staffan.lindstrand@ofco.se
Education: MSc, Engineering, Royal Institute of Technology, Sweden
Background: Vice President, Aros Securities
Anki Forsberg, Partner
e-mail: anki.forsberg@ofco.se
Education: LLM, University of Helsinki; MBA, University of Uppsala
Background: Chief Administrative Officer, Odlander Fredrikson; President, Skandigen AB; Vice President, Industriforvaltnings AB Skandigen
Per Samuelsson, Partner
e-mail: per.samuelsson@ofco.se
Education: MSc, Engineering, Institute of Technology, Linkoping
Background: Director, Aros Securities
Johan Christenson, Partner
e-mail: johan.christenson@ofco.se
Education: MD, Karolinsak Institute
Background: SEB Foretagsinvest; Project Director, Astra Pain Control; Project Director, AstraZeneca
Marten Steen MD, Partner
e-mail: marten.steen@healthcap.eu
Education: BSc, Business Administration, Lund University School of Economics & Management; MD, Lund University; PhD, Clinical Chemistry
Background: Merck Serno
Jacob Gunterberg, Partner
e-mail: jacob.gunterberg@ofco.se
Education: MSc, Business Administration & Economics, University of Lund; University of St. Gallen
Background: Hjalmarsson & Gunterberg Corporate Finance; ABB Aros; Aros Securities
Eugen Steiner, Partner
e-mail: steiner.eugen@gmail.com
Background: CEO, Creative Peptides; CEO, Affibody AB; CEO, Calab Medical AB; CEO, Eurona Medical AB; CEO, Melacure Therapeutics AB; CEO, PyroSequencing AB; CEO, Visual Bioinformatics
Carl-Johan Dalsgaard, Partner
e-mail: carl-johan.dalsgaard@ofco.se
Education: PhD, Neurobiology, Harvard Medical School
Background: CEO, Biolipox AB; CEO, CePeP AB; CEO, Biofactor Therapeutics AB; CEO, Biocrine AB; VP Preclinical Research, Astra Pain Control AB

2817 HELIANT VENTURES
7/F, Kin On Commercial Building
49-51 Jervois Street
Sheng Wan
Hong Kong

Mission Statement: A Hong Kong based venture capital fund providing end-to-end support to its portfolio companies, leveraging its Asia/Australia relationships.

Geographic Preference: Asia, Australia
Investment Criteria: Early-Stage, Late-Stage
Industry Group Preference: Technology

Key Executives:
Ben Weiss, Managing Partner
Education: BCom, LLB, University of New South Whales; CFA; Sydney College of Law
Background: Salomon Smith Barney, Macquarie Bank, Shinsei Bank, AXA, CLSa, Baker & McKenzie

---

2818 HELION VENTURE PARTNERS, LLC
International Management (Mauritius) Ltd
Les Cascades Building
Edith Cavell Street
Port Louis
Mauritius

Phone: 230-212-9800 **Fax:** 230-212-9833
e-mail: contact.helion@gmail.com
web: www.helionvc.com

Mission Statement: Our mission is "Partnering with entrepreneurs to build world-class companies." We believe that companies are fundamentally built from inside, but as Board members we play an active role. Typically we help companies in making strategic choices in building and organization that can execute on strategy. We have access to world-class executives that we can bring to our portfolio companies. We also help in building a high quality Board of Directors/Advisors. We also team with the management and provide operational value in the area of finance, HR, technology, marketing and operations. In helping manage rapid growth, we participate in future rounds of financing in syndication with other venture partners.

Geographic Preference: India
Fund Size: $605 million
Investment Criteria: Early - mid Stage
Industry Group Preference: Clean Technology, Consumer Services, Education, Enterprise Software, Healthcare, Internet, Media, Mobile, Outsourcing & Efficiency, Technology-Enabled Products
Portfolio Companies: Azure Power, Brand Calculus, Qwikcilver, Hummingbird, YLG, Mast Kalandar, GTT, Attano, Vienova, Seclore, NetAmbit, IndiaHomes, Shubham, Eye-q, LifeCell, Jivox, Komli Media, TaxiForSure, MySmartPrice, ShopClues, 9.9 Media, GETiT, Ngpay, Kirusa, GupShup, Amba, Anantara, Hurix Systems, Mindworks, UnitedLex, Zmanda

Other Locations:
Helion Advisors Private Limited
Marathalli - Sarjapur Outer Ring Road
Bangalore 560 103
Karnataka

Venture Capital & Private Equity Firms / International Firms

India
Phone: +91 80 4018 3333 **Fax:** +91 80 4018 3456

Helion Advisors Private Limited
Vatika Towers, Sector 54
Gurgaon 122 002
Haryana
India
Phone: +91 124 461 5333 **Fax:** +91 124 461 5345

Key Executives:
Ashish Gupta, Senior Managing Director, Co-Founder
Education: BA, Indian Institute Of Technology Kanpur; Ph.D, Computer Science, Stanford University
Background: Co-Founder, Tavant Technologies; Co-Founder, Junglee; Woodside Fund; Oracle Corporation, IBM
Directorships: Baboye.com, Dhingana, InfoEdge, Jivox, Kirusa, Komli, MySmartPrice.com, Pubmatic, SMSGupshup
Sanjeev Aggarwal, Senior Managing Director, Co-Founder
Education: Bachelors degree in Electrical Engineering; MBA
Background: Founder & CEO, Daksh; Motorola India; Digital Equipment Corporation; CEO 3COM India
Directorships: IndiaHomes, Azure Power, Amba Research, Eye-Q, ShopClues
Sandeep Fakun, Member Board of Directors
Dourvesh Kumar (Vikas) Chumun, Member Board of Director

2819 HELIX INVESTMENTS
Corner St. Georges and de Chazel Streets
Port Louis
Mauritius

Phone: 230-2036600
web: www.helix-investments.com

Founded: 2007
Average Investment: $5-20 million

2820 HELMET CAPITAL FUND MANAGEMENT OY
Fredrikinkatu 48 A, 11th floor
Helsinki 00100
Finland

Phone: 358-96869220 **Fax:** 358-968692241
e-mail: info@helmetcapital.fi
web: www.helmetcapital.fi

Mission Statement: Helmet specializes in ownership arrangements and development of non-listed growth companies.

Geographic Preference: Finland
Fund Size: $24, 2 Million
Founded: 1995
Investment Criteria: Early Stage, Mid-Stage
Industry Group Preference: Biotechnology, Metals, Electronic Technology, Information Technology, Electronic Technology, Retailing

Key Executives:
Seppo Ahonen, Founding Partner
e-mail: pauli@helmetcapital.fi
Education: MSc, (Eng.), MBA
Background: Fortum Oyj & Tamro Group
Kalevi Puonti, Founding Partner

2821 HENDERSON PRIVATE CAPITAL
201 Bishopsgate
London EC2M 3AE
United Kingdom

Phone: 44-2078181818 **Fax:** 44-2078181819
web: www.henderson.com

Mission Statement: Henderson is a leading investor in a new and constantly growing area of the European infrastructure market — operational stakes in Private Finance Initiative (PFI) projects.

Geographic Preference: Europe, Asia Pacific
Fund Size: Euro 64, 825 Million
Founded: 1934
Industry Group Preference: Waste & Recycling, Education, Health Related, Leisure, Publishing
Portfolio Companies: Baydrive Limited, Boat International Publications, Leisure Link Holdings Limited, Redecam Group SpA, Vacant Property Security Limited, Homann Chilled Foods

Key Executives:
Andrew Formica, Chief Executive
e-mail: paul.woodbury@henderson.com
Education: BA (Hons) in Politics and Economics
Background: Member of Institute of Transport and Logistics
Roger Thompson, Chief Financial Officer
e-mail: roger.greville@henderson.com
Education: Bachelor of Agricultural Economics & Master of Commerce (Economics)
Directorships: Chairman of the Investment Committee.
Phillip Apel, Head of Fixed Income
e-mail: rahul.bhargava@henderson.com
Education: Bachelor of Science (Economics) from the University of Calcutta and an MBA from the Australian Graduate School of Management.
Background: Ion Global
Lesley Cairney, Chief Operating Officer
e-mail: matteo.perale@henderson.com
Education: MBA from Columbia University, a master degree in international business from HEC in Paris and has a summa cum laude degree in economics from Bocconi in Milan.
Background: Palamon Capital Partners, Warburg Pincus & McKinsey & Co
Jacqui Irvine, General Counsel
e-mail: guy.pigache@henderson.com
Education: BSc Honours degree in Maths and Physics from Kings College, London.
Background: HSBC
Graham Kitchen, Head of Equities
e-mail: steven.proctor@henderson.com
Education: Chartered Management Accountant & Economics Degree from St. Andrews University.
Background: Sumitomo Mitsui Banking Corporation

2822 HENQ
Herengracht 124-128
1015 BT Amsterdam
Netherlands

Phone: +31 10 452 1346
e-mail: info@henq.nl
web: www.henq.nl

Mission Statement: henQ helps its companies to build a strong international network, access high-level expertise and distribution power, attract the right people to grow the company, set ambitious goals and stick to them, apply a lean methodology for efficient growth, and maintain focus. henQ's founders have a considerable experience in both business and investing, and know how to make companies grow. Through their extensive network, they can also hook up entrepreneurs with other valuable people.

Geographic Preference: The Netherlands
Investment Criteria: Startup
Industry Group Preference: E-Commerce & Manufacturing, Mobile, Analytics & Analytical Instruments, Software Development
Portfolio Companies: Campalyst, CWR Mobility, IS enterprise, Libersy, Mads, Mendix, Monolith, Myngle, PlayToTV, Seedcamp, SEOshop, Studytube, Videostrip, Wakoopa, Xite

Venture Capital & Private Equity Firms / International Firms

Key Executives:
Herman Hintzen, Co-Founder
Background: Founder, Arpa Systems; Co-Founder, Great Idea Factory
Coen van Duiven, Co-Founder
Background: Unilever Investement Group

2823 HG CAPITAL
2 More London Riverside
Minerva House
3rd Floor
London SE1 2AP
United Kingdom
Phone: 44-2070897888 Fax: 44-2070897999
e-mail: info@hgcapital.com
web: www.hgcapital.net

Mission Statement: Hg Capital is the successor to Mercury Private Equity (founded 1985). The staff of MPE aquired the business from Merrill Lynch and renamed the company. It has funds under management of 1.4 billion euro and services over 200 institutional clients and manag

Geographic Preference: United Kingdom, Western Europe, Ireland, Germany, Benelux
Fund Size: $42.48 Billion
Founded: 2000
Average Investment: $177 Million
Minimum Investment: $70 Million
Investment Criteria: Expansion, Leveraged Buy-Out, Public-to-Private, Turnarounds, Divisions, Business Assets
Industry Group Preference: All Sectors Considered, Health Related, Consumer Services, Media, Leisure, Industrial Services, Technology, Renewable Energy, Consumer Products
Portfolio Companies: Addison Software, Alizyme, Allegro, Axiom, Ballygowan, Barracuda, Belfast International Airport, Bertram, Boosey & Hawkes, Braitrim, BrightReasons, Britt Allcroft Group, Burns e-Commerce Solutions, Castlebeck, Checkpoint, CityFlyer Express, Clarion Events

Key Executives:
Martin Block, Director
e-mail: frances.jacob@hgcapital.net
Education: Engineering degree, Durham University
Background: Production Engineer, 3i plc
Stephen Bough, Director, Finance
2070897982
e-mail: stephen.bough@hgcapital.net
Education: Stephen qualified as an accountant while at Prudential Assurance Company where he spent ten years.
Background: Accountant, Prudential Assurance Company
James Bath, Portfolio Management Team
2070897962
e-mail: lindsay.dibden@hgcapital.net
Education: Aeronautical Engineering, Imperial College
Background: Corporate Finance, Coopers & Lybrand
Tom Murley, Head Renewable Energy Team
e-mail: tom.murley@hgcapital.net
Background: Co-Head Renewable Energy Team, Allianz Private Equity; EIF Group; Corporate Lawyer
Martin Block, Portfolio Management Team
2070897950
e-mail: ian.armitage@hgcapital.net
Education: Politics, Philosophy, Economics, Oxford University
Background: 3i plc
Directorships: Chairman, Investor Relations Committee of the British Venture Capital Association; Orbiscom; ClinPhone; Comnitel; Profiad
Lisa Stone, Portfolio Management
2070897960
e-mail: lisa.stone@hgcapital.net
Education: Human Sciences, Oxford University
Background: Director Strategy/Business Planning, LucasVarity; Management Consultant, Kalchas; Management Consultant, Bain & Co

Directorships: IRIS Software; Remploy; Newchurch; Match; Tunstall; Profiad; Trados
Nic Humphries, Managing Partner
2070897987
e-mail: nic.humphries@hgcapital.net
Education: First Class degree Electronic Engineering; IEEE; National Engineering Council Scholar
Background: General Partner, Geocapital Partners; Telecom/IT Team Head, Barclay Private Equity; 3i plc
Directorships: Axiom; IRIS Software; Rolfe & Nolan; Xyratex
Rob de Laszlo, Renewable Energy Team
2070897892
Education: BA, MBA, London School of Business
Background: Strategy Consultant, Braxton Associates
Directorships: The Sanctuary Spa
Saad Islam, Renewable Energy Team
2070897940
Education: Psychology, Durham University
Background: Leveraged Finance, Bankers Trust; Chartered Accountant, Coopers & Lybrand; Corporate Finance, Charterhouse Bank

2824 HIGH-TECH GRUENDERFONDS
Schlegelstrasse 2
Bonn 53113
Germany
Phone: 0228-82300100 Fax: 0228-82300050
web: www.high-tech-gruenderfonds.de

Mission Statement: Since 2005, High-Tech Grunderfonds has been financing young technology companies on attractive terms and actively supporting their management teams with a strong network and entrepreneurial expertise. We are focused on investing in early stage companies in life science, materials science, and information technology. In our first 5 years we financed approximately 250 companies from the high-tech sector and successfully set them on their way.

Geographic Preference: Germany
Fund Size: 301 million Euro
Founded: 2005
Investment Criteria: Early-Stage
Industry Group Preference: Life Sciences, Materials Technology, Information Technology, Clean Technology, Consumer Products, Nanotechnology
Portfolio Companies: AdvanceCOR, Advanova, Algiax, Altruja, Amedo, Amedrix, Antispameurope, Audiocure, Autoaid, Autoloader, Anvendeo Designwelt, Avidal, AyoxxA, Babla, Baimos Technologies, Base Case Management, Biametrics, BioRob, Bohner-EH, Bomedus, Bubbles & Beyond, C-Lecta, C2Call, CA Customer Alliance, Capical, CargoGuard, Caterna, ChromoTek, Cliqloc, Collinor Software, Commercetools, Compositence, Conceptboard, Confovis, Contros, ConWeaver, Corrmoran, CorTec, Crealytics, Crossvertise, Cryotherpeutics, CrystAl-N, Cubical, Cuculus, Cumulocity, CureFab, Cysal, Deal United, Dilitronics, Divolution, DJTunes.com, DRDx, E-Senza Technologies, EBS Technologies, EcoIntense, eGym, Enercast, Enexion, Entellios, Evocatal, ExCentos, Eyefactive, Eyesight&Vision, Ezeep, FamPlus, Fiagon, Fidlock, Fos4x, Fruux, FTAPI SecuTransfer, Futalis, Galantos Pharma, GameGenetics, GeneQuine, Gestigon, Gfnmediber, Gilupi, Gimahot, GME, GrandCentrix, H.C. Carbon, Hapila, Heliatek, Hematris Wound Care, HiperScan, HMC+, HR New Media, Humangride, Humedics, IBK Bioanalytik, ILIAS-Medical, Immunservice, Implandata Opthalmic Products, InnoCyte, InnoMotix, Intana Bioscience, Intermed, IQ Evolution, JeNaCell, JenAffin, JobLeads, Keyrocket, Klmeta, Kiwigrid, KonTEM, Krohnert Infotecs, LaTherm, Lenimed, Limata, Lipocalyx, Livedome, Locr, Lophius Biosciences, Luceo Technologies, Luphos, M2p-Labs, Maxment, Mbm Systems, Medovent, MeinProspekt, MicroNet Automation, Microstim, MimoOn, MinCell, Mister Spex, Mivenion, ML-C,

Venture Capital & Private Equity Firms / International Firms

Key Executives:
  Alexander von Frankenberg, Managing Director
  e-mail: a.frankenberg@high-tech-gruenderfonds.de
  Education: Business Economics, University of Manheim; MBA, University of Texas, Austin
  Background: Andersen Consulting, Siements Management Consulting, Siemens Technology Accelerator

2825 HIGHGROWTH
Tuset, 20-24, 4 5
Barcelona 08006
Spain
  Phone: 34-933630386 Fax: 34-932183333

Mission Statement: Highgrowth is an independent financial company that invests in innovative companies with growth potential, providing them with support, advice and guidance, through two clearly differentiated business lines: management of venture capital funds aimed at companies in their initial launch phases, business consulting and training of entrepreneurs.

Key Executives:
  Ferran Lemus, President/Partner
  Education: Economics, Barcelona University; MA, European Studies, Reading University
  Background: Banco de Vizcaya, Argentaria/Banco Exterior

2826 HIKARI TSUSHIN CAPITAL
1-16-15 Toshima-ku, Minami-Ikebukuro
Tokyo 171-0021
Japan
  Phone: 81-359513718 Fax: 81-359513709
  e-mail: info@po.hikari.co.jp
  web: www.hikari.co.jp

Mission Statement: Hikari Tsushin has taken a leadership role in investing in the ever-changing world of communications and technology

Geographic Preference: Japan
Founded: 1988
Industry Group Preference: Internet Technology, Information Technology, Telecommunications
Portfolio Companies: Estore, Edge, MTI, Goodwill Group, Global Media Online, KBOS, SOTEC, Digital Arts, Nexus, Prime System, Emachines

Key Executives:
  Shigeta Yasumitsu, Chairman & Chief Executive Officer
  e-mail: info@po.hikari.co.jp
  Takeshi Tamamura, President & Chief Operating Officer

2827 HILKO UK LTD/VALCO CAPITAL PARTNERS
80 New Bond Street
London W1S 1SB
United Kingdom
  Phone: 44-02073172050 Fax: 44-02073172051
  e-mail: info@hilcouk.com

Mission Statement: Hilco is uniquely positioned to evaluate, recommend and implement the best course of action. We do this successfully because we are an independent, objective team with unique skills and substantial experience. We have been involved in many of the most notable retail restructuring projects in the last five years in the UK and continental Europe.

Geographic Preference: United Kingdom, Europe
Investment Criteria: Retail Acquisitions, Mergers, Divestitures, Restructurings, Asset Disposition
Industry Group Preference: Retailing

Key Executives:
  Paul McGowan, Principal and Senior Directors
  Background: KPMG; Operations Director, Jacqmar Plc; Leslie Fay Ltd
  Andrew Pepper, Principal and Senior Directors
  Background: Partner, Kroll & BDO; KMPG; PwC
  Howard Gunn, European Chief Financial Officer
  Background: Accountant, Peat Marwick Mitchell & Co; Finance Director, CHS Electronics Plc
  Mark O'Neill, Investment Analyst
  Background: Vice President, Lesco; Roses Discount Stores; Target Stores; Macy's Department Store
  Chris Emmott, Investment Director
  Henry Foster, Investment Director
  Steven Pell, Investment Director
  Background: Strategy Consultant, Kalchas Group; CRO Team, NTL

2828 HOLLAND VENTURE BV
Franz Zieglerstraat 24
Amsterdam 1087 HN
Netherlands
  Phone: 31-203119411 Fax: 31-206973326
  e-mail: info@hollandventure.com
  web: www.hollandventure.com

Mission Statement: Holland Venture is an independent private equity fund located in Amsterdam. Since 1981 Holland Venture has realized the growth potential of many of its investments and has proven to be a trustworthy partner.

Geographic Preference: Netherlands
Fund Size: $216 Million
Founded: 1981
Industry Group Preference: Business to Business, Medical, Security
Portfolio Companies: Sunday's Nederland BV, Brinkhof Group International NV, SigValue Technologies Inc., Bwise BV, Decell, Mr.Ted Ltd. Macaw BV, INS SA, Royal Mosa BV & Freecom Technologies BV

Key Executives:
  Rolf Deves, managing director
  e-mail: info@hollandventure.com
  Hubert Verbeek, Managing Partner
  e-mail: info@hollandventure.com
  Ewout Prins, Managing Partner
  e-mail: info@hollandventure.com

2829 HOLTZBRINCK VENTURES
Kaiserstrasse 14b
Munich 80801
Germany
  Phone: 49-89206070 Fax: 49-8920607742
  web: www.holtzbrinck-ventures.com

Mission Statement: Being one of the most successful venture capital firms, we have been supporting founders in developing their Internet companies for over a decade. During this time, we as a team have financed over 100 companies. We seek founders who share our passion for growth and innovation and who want to achieve excellence working as a team.

Founded: 2000
Average Investment: 250,000 - 5 million Euro
Investment Criteria: Early-Stage
Industry Group Preference: Internet
Portfolio Companies: Zalando, Dafiti, Wooga, Westwing, eDarling, Game Duell, Experteer, GlossyBox, Adscale, Lamoda, Home 24, 21Diamonds, Delivery Hero, Auctionata, BerryAvenue, Hello Fresh, DaWanda, Fashion for Home, Pippa Jean, Kiveda, Lazada, Linio, Namshi, Mindmatics, MeinAuto.de, Outfittery, YepDoc, MusicPlayr, DropGifts, BillPay, Payleven, Paymill, Ozon.ru, Goodbeans, Semasio, HitFox Group, Autoda, Care.com, Studitemps, Stylight, Seatwave, Lecturio, Classmarkets, Cafe Press, TrustYou, Kissnofrog, InterNations, VirtualNights, Rumble Media, Proximic, Restaurant-Kritik.de, Gute TV Laune, Newtron, Deutsche Startups, Innofact

Venture Capital & Private Equity Firms / International Firms

Key Executives:
Sven Achter, General Partner
e-mail: sven.achter@holtzbrinck.net
Education: Masters, Information Technology, Technical University of Munich
Background: Consultant, Hewlett Packard

2830 HONGKONG LAND INFRASTRUCTURE LIMITED
8th Floor, One Exchange Square
Central
Hong Kong

Phone: 852-28428428 Fax: 852-28459226
e-mail: gpobox@hkland.com
web: www.hkland.com

Mission Statement: Actively seeking new investments.
Geographic Preference: Hongkong, Singapore, Vietnam, China
Founded: 1889
Key Executives:
Simon Keswick, Chairman
e-mail: gpobox@hkland.com
Background: Jardine Matheson group,
Directorships: Chairman of Jardine Matheson Limited, and managing director of Dairy Farm International Holdings, Jardine Matheson Holdings, Jardine Strategic Holdings and Mandarin Oriental I
Y.K. Pang, Chief Executive

2831 HORIZONS VENTURES
Hong Kong

e-mail: general@horizonsventures.com
web: www.horizonsventures.com

Mission Statement: Horizons Ventures is Hong Kong based venture capital firm, focused on technology and disruptive ideas.
Geographic Preference: Hong Kong
Founded: 2006
Industry Group Preference: Hardware, Electronics, Artificial Intelligence, Financial Services, Mobile, Digital Media & Marketing, Social Media, Analytics & Analytical Instruments, Security, Data & Analytics
Portfolio Companies: Affdex, Aniways, Bitcase, Bitpay, Bitstrips, Core Photonics, Cortica, Crosswire, Deepmind, Desti, Everything.me, Facebook, Filip, Fixmo, Friendsurance, Genetic Finance, Ginger, Guardtime, Hampton Creek, Hola!, How.do, HzO, Interaxon, Invi, Kaiima, Kuato, Lock8, Magisto, Medial Cancer Screening, MeMed, Meteo-Logic, Misfit, Mishor, Nanoleaf, NanoSpun, NBA.com China, Nipendo, Onavo, Preen.me, Rubikloud, Secondmarket, Shine, Siri, Skype, Spotify, Stevie, Summly, Tempo, Traity, Trap!T, Union Mobile Pay, Waze, Wibbitz, Zoom
Key Executives:
Li Ka-Shing, Founder/Chairman

2832 HORIZONTE VENTURE MANAGEMENT GmbH
c/o Regus Opera
Kärntner Ring 5-7
Wien A-1010
Austria

Phone: 43-15335601 Fax: 43-153356014
e-mail: office@horizonte.at
web: www.horizonte.at

Mission Statement: Actively seeking investments in small and medium-sized enterprises which have the potential to achieve internationally important market positions
Geographic Preference: Austria, Central European countries
Fund Size: $8.4 Million
Founded: 1985
Average Investment: $1.2 Million
Minimum Investment: $600,000
Investment Criteria: Start-up
Industry Group Preference: Biotechnology, Information Technology
Portfolio Companies: Rudjer Boskovic Institute, Splonum, Styrotherm
Key Executives:
Martin Wodak, Managing Partner
Education: Physics at the Technical University in Vienna and obtained a doctorate in physics (Ph.D.) from the University of Pennsylvania, Philadelphia
Background: Dr. Krejs worked in the area of financing of technical innovations in Vienna (Innova, FGG
Directorships: participated in TVM-Techno Venture Management's start-up.
Alfred Matzka, Managing Partner
e-mail: dansco@horizonte.at
Education: Doctorate in business administration from the Wirtschaftsuniversität Wien
Background: Worked at the Austrian Ministry of Trade and subsequently as a consultant to small and medium sized companies
Directorships: After three years with an accounting and auditing firm he joined FGG in 1981 and led FGG's division for risk financing and turn-around management. Dr. Matzka joined Horizonte
Dr. Matej Penca, Managing Partner
e-mail: dansco@horizonte.at
Education: Ph.D. in chemistry of the University of Ljubljana and wrote his doctoral thesis on Decision Algorithms for Chemical Information Systems.
Background: Was an associate professor at the University of Ljubljana, and a Visiting Fellow at the US National Institutes of Health (NIH) design of IR search medule for the Chemical Information System (CIS) run by NIH and the Environmental Protection Agency (EPA).
Directorships: He later was director of the Informatics Department at SMELT global project management, Ljubljana and Counsellor to the Ministry of Science and Technology in the Government of

2833 HOSEO VENTURE CAPITAL
1603-54 Seocho-dong
Kangnam Telpia Building
13th Floor
Seoul 137-070
South Korea

Phone: 82-234-878400 Fax: 82-234-878500

Mission Statement: Actively seeking new investments.
Geographic Preference: South Korea
Fund Size: $69 Million
Founded: 2000
Investment Criteria: Early-stage and growth companies
Industry Group Preference: Telecommunications, Information Technology
Portfolio Companies: Uju Electronics, D-gate Semiconductor, CJ Entertainment, Innostream, Bellwave, MC Technology, Chips & Media, Gravity

2834 HOXTON VENTURES
1 Fore St.
London EC2Y 9DT
United Kingdom

e-mail: businessplans@hoxton.vc
web: www.hoxtonventures.com

Mission Statement: Hoxton Ventures partners with founders in early stage technology who are seeking to invent new market categories or transform existing ones.
Geographic Preference: United Kingdom, United States, India
Investment Criteria: Early-Stage

Venture Capital & Private Equity Firms / International Firms

Industry Group Preference: Technology, Software, Internet, Mobile
Portfolio Companies: Adazza, Algomi, Babylon, Behavox, DarkTrace, Deliveroo, Mainframe, Optimo Route, Raptor Supplies, Super Awesome, Tourradar, Vitesse, Yieldify
Key Executives:
  Hussein Kanji, Partner
  Education: Stanford University; MBA, London Business School
  Directorships: POPxo, bd4travel, Darktrace, TourRadar, Babylon, Behavox, Yieldify
  Rob Kniaz, Partner
  Education: Stanford University; BS, University of Maryland
  Directorships: Deliveroo, Raptor Supplies, Babylon

2835 HRL MORRISON & COMPANY LIMITED
Level 19, 1 Eagle Street, Waterfront Place
Brisbane
Queensland 4001
Australia

Phone: 61-733600295 Fax: 61-732200855
e-mail: info@hrlmorrison.com.au
web: www.hrlmorrison.com

Mission Statement: Actively seeking new investments.
Geographic Preference: Australia, New Zealand, Europe
Fund Size: $5 Billion
Founded: 1988
Industry Group Preference: Infrastructure, Energy, Aviation
Key Executives:
  Rob Morrison, Chairman
  Steven Fitzgerald, Executive Director Airports Group

2836 HSBC VENTURES UK LIMITED
78 St. James Street
London SW1A 1JB
United Kingdom

Phone: 44-2078605000 Fax: 44-2078605001
web: www.hsbcprivatebank.com

Mission Statement: Invests in British companies that are at least three years old and which offer potential for growth.
Geographic Preference: United Kingdom
Founded: 1853
Average Investment: $26.59 Million
Minimum Investment: $3.55 Million
Investment Criteria: Expansion and Development, Refinancing bank debt, Secondary purchase/replacement capital, MBO, MBI
Industry Group Preference: All Sectors Considered
Portfolio Companies: Comcen Computer Supplies Ltd, Connaught Group Ltd, Lady In Leisure Ltd, Reward Group Ltd, VFG Plc
Key Executives:
  Stephen K Green, Chairman
  Peter Widmer, Vice Chairman
  Paul Chambers, Director
  Tom Chaloner, Director
  Mike Barstow, Investment Manager
  Derek King, Investment Manager

2837 HUMMINGBIRD VENTURES
Hangar 26/27
Rijinkaai 98
Antwerp 2000
Belgium

Phone: 32-32923710
e-mail: info@hummingbird-ventures.com
web: www.hummingbirdventures.com

Mission Statement: Hummingbird Ventures is a venture capital fund for high-growth digital media and software companies. In addition to funding, Hummingbird Ventures leverages its extensive operational experience and worldwide network to actively help startups accelerate their growth.
Geographic Preference: Europe, Turkey, Middle East
Founded: 2000
Average Investment: 500,000 - 2 million Euros
Investment Criteria: Early-Stage
Industry Group Preference: Digital Media & Marketing, Software
Portfolio Companies: Amplidata, Avinity, CicekSepeti, Clear2Pay, CVWarehouse, Cybersports, Dacentec/Awingu, DataCenter Technologies, Dedigate, Digitouch, IS/Pins, iQu, Peak Games, PeopleCube, Q-layer, MarkaVIP, Ractivity, Shutl, Wakoopa
Other Locations:
  2nd Floor, White Bear Yard
  144A Clerkenwell Road
  London EC1R 5DF
  United Kingdom

  Esentepe Mah. Atom Sokak
  King Plaza 18, 6th Floor
  Levent
  Istanbul
  Turkey
Key Executives:
  Barend Van den Brande, Managing Partner
  e-mail: barend@hummingbird-ventures.com
  Education: MS, Economics, University of Louvain, Belgium
  Background: President, Benelux Tech Tour; Co-Founder, SwiftTouch
  Directorships: Clear2Pay, MMO Life, Wakoopa, Travel Intelligence Group, Cybersports, Shutl

2838 HV HOLTZBRINCK VENTURES
Kaiserstrasse 14b
Munich 80801
Germany

Phone: 49-89-20-60-770 Fax: 49-89-20-60-7742
e-mail: information@holtzbrinck.net
web: www.holtzbrinck-ventures.com

Mission Statement: Being one of the most successful venture capital firms, we have been supporting founders in developing their Internet companies for over a decade. During this time, we as a team have financed over 100 companies. We seek founders who share our passion for growth and innovation and who want to achieve excellence working as a team.
Investment Criteria: Seed Stage, Early-Stage
Industry Group Preference: Internet
Portfolio Companies: Zalando, Dafiti, Wooga, Westwing, eDarling, Game Duell, Experteer, GlossyBox, Lamoda, Home24, 21Diamonds, Delivery Hero, Aucionata, Outfittery, Hello Fresh, DaWanda, Fashion for Home, Pippa Jean, Kiveda, Paymill, Jabong, Lazada, Linio, Namshi, Flixbus, JetLore, Depop, HitFox Group, Mindmatics, MeinAuto, Springlane, Wonga, BillPay, Payleven, Ozon.ru, Goodbeans, Semasio, Care.com, L'ArcoBaleno, Studitemps, Stylight, Seatwave, Lecturi, Classmarkets, Cupo Nation, Trust You, Kiss No Frog, Smartlaw, InterNations, Virtual Nights, GlamLoop, Locafox, Funanga, MusicPlayr, BerryAvenue, Rumble Media, Proximic, Gute TV Laune, Newtron, Deutsche Startups, Innofact AG, Restaurant Kritic
Key Executives:
  Sven Achter, General Partner
  e-mail: sven.achter@holtzbrinck.net
  Education: Master Degree, Information Techology, Technical University of Munich
  Background: Immobileenscout, Hewlett-Packard

2839 HYUNDAI VENTURE INVESTMENT CORPORATION
National Information Society Agency Bldg.
4th Floor
Seoul
South Korea

Phone: 82-27288990 Fax: 82-27288999
e-mail: webmaster@hvic.co.kr
web: www.hvic.co.kr

Mission Statement: HVIC partners with companies who have innovative technology but weak finances and management.

Geographic Preference: South Korea
Fund Size: $39.6 Million
Founded: 1997
Investment Criteria: Small-stage and Mid-stage
Industry Group Preference: Information Technology, Biotechnology, Software, Internet Technology
Portfolio Companies: Dusan Co. LTD, Daum Communications corp, DB and SOFT, Ecoin Co Ltd, Em Teck, Econex, Gracel, GaeaSoft. ICO Inc. & Imas Co Ltd.

Key Executives:
Mong-il Chung, Chairman & Chief Executive Officer
e-mail: webmaster@hvic.co.kr
Education: Graduates Business Administration dept. of Yonsei University
Background: Daewoo Corp. & Hyundai International Merchant Bank
Jong-Sung Lee, Adviser
e-mail: webmaster@hvic.co.kr
Education: Graduates Bae-jae High School & MBA from George Washington University in U.S.A
Background: Hyundai International Merchant Bank & Hyundai Capital

2840 I-PACIFIC PARTNERS
6rd Floor, Hyundai Intellex Bldg
Samsung Dong Gang
Nam Gu
Seoul 135-832
Korea

Phone: 82-234-465861 Fax: 82-234-465864

Mission Statement: Invests in promising new ventures and provides hand-on management support. Manages three funds.

Fund Size: 46.5 Million
Founded: 2000
Industry Group Preference: Wireless Technologies, Telecommunications, Software, Electronic Technology, Media

Key Executives:
Youngmin Yune, President & Chief Executive Officer
Jerry Shim, Director

2841 IBB BETEILIGUNGSGESELLSCHAFT MBH
Bundesallee 210
10719 Berlin
Germany

Phone: +49 30 2125 3201 Fax: +49 30 2125 3202
e-mail: venture@ibb-bet.de
web: www.ibb-bet.de

Mission Statement: IBB Beteiligungsgesellschaft mbH provides venture capitalfor young Berlin-based technology-oriented companies and companies from the creative industries. We were founded in 1997 as a 100% subsidiary of Investitionsbank Berlin to support Berlin-based small and medium-sized enterprises. Since 1997, syndicates involving IBB Beteiligungsgesellschaft mbH have provided Berlin-based companies with more than 1, 430 m EUR.

Geographic Preference: Berlin
Fund Size: 100 Mio. EUR
Founded: 1997
Average Investment: 500 KEUR
Minimum Investment: 200 KEUR
Investment Criteria: Equity
Industry Group Preference: Creative Industries, Information Technology, Communication Technology, Life Sciences, Industrial Technology
Portfolio Companies: 21sportsgroup, ALRISE, Blinks Labs, blogfoster, CareerFoundry, Content Flow, CrossEngage, Crowd Guru, dailyme TV, Dalia Research, Dentolo, DiaMonTech, EMC (Emmy), Eternygen, Fairr.De, flexperto, Fliit, German Auto Labs, Getsurance, Hey Group, High-Mobility, Humedics, JobUFO, labfolder, Learnfield (Skoove), Lesson Nine (Babbel), LLS Internet (loopline), Lumenaza, Lunchio, machtfit, Media4Care, Meetrics, Myelo, MyGall, MYMORIA, Natural Dental Implants, Neonga, NursIT, Omeicos, ONO Labs, Outfittery, Paper and Tea, PictureTree, Qinous, R3 Communications, Realbest, Remerge, Selfapy, Seniovo, Smart Host, Sofatutor, Softgames, Spark Networks, Spontaneous Order, Store2be, SuitePad, Tausendkind, Thermondo, Travelcircus, Ubitricity, Vetevo, Viasto, Websitebutler, Wunderflats

Key Executives:
Roger Bendisch, Managing Director
Marco Zeller, Managing Director

2842 IBK CAPITAL CORPORATION Industrial Bank of Korea
702-22 Yoksam-dong
Seoul NV
South Korea

Phone: 82-25543131 Fax: 82-25683533
web: www.ibk.co.kr

Mission Statement: Focuses on promoting growth among Korea's small and medium-sized enterprises (SMEs).

Geographic Preference: Korea
Founded: 1961
Investment Criteria: Small and medium-sized enterprises (SMEs

2843 IBRIDGE CAPITAL CORPORATION
Stanley Street
5th & 17th Floor, Malahon Centre
Central
Hong Kong

Phone: 852-25263280 Fax: 852-25267299

Mission Statement: iBridge Capital Group is a pan-Asian group of companies with two principal business areas providing professional services to established businesses as well as young, growing companies.

Geographic Preference: Asia

2844 IBUSINESS CORPORATION
12/F Cheung Kong Center, 2 Queen's Road
Central
Hong Kong

Phone: 852-21263333 Fax: 852-21211111
web: www.ibusiness-hk.com

Mission Statement: iBusiness Corporation Limited invests in and builds profitable e-commerce, m-commerce, Internet and software technology infrastructure businesses.

Geographic Preference: Asia
Fund Size: $250 Billion
Investment Criteria: Start up and Eastablished companies
Portfolio Companies: AMTD, Excel Technology, mReferral

Key Executives:
Victor Li, Deputy Chairman & Managing Director
e-mail: contact@ibusiness-hk.com
Directorships: Executive Director, CEO - iBusiness Corporation Ltd.
Edmond Ip, Executive Director

Venture Capital & Private Equity Firms / International Firms

2845 ICAN ISRAEL-CANNABIS.COM
Hauman 5
Beit Shemesh
Israel

Phone: 972-545-604843
e-mail: info@israel-cannabis.com
web: www.israel-cannabis.com

Mission Statement: An Israel-based accelerator and incubator firm dedicated to the global medical cannabis inudstry.

Fund Size: $3.1M
Founded: 2015
Investment Criteria: Seed
Industry Group Preference: Cannabis, Healthcare, Biotech
Portfolio Companies: Cannabis Mercantile Trading Exchange, Yom Chai, CannRx Technology Inc., Cannabinit

Key Executives:
   Saul Kaye, Founer/CEO
   Education: BSc, Pharmacy, Curtin University of Technology; BPharm, University of Sydney
   Background: Founer, Pharma Shaul Pharmacy; Founder/Investor, Start Up Beit Shemesh; Co-Founder, CannaTech
   Reavis Daniel Moore, Managing Director
   Education: BS, Education, Ohio State University; MS, Human Services, Southern Illinois University Edwardsville
   Background: CEO/Founder, MBC Networks; Sr. Advisor, Higher Octave Music; Founder, CannabisReal; Partner, Deep Green Agency; Co-Founder, Earthdance Global
   Directorships: Chairman, Cannabics Pharmaceuticals Inc; YouLicense; iAlbums
   David Yahid, Director of Marketing
   Education: BA, Marketing, Yeshiva University
   Background: Marketing Manager, Applause; Sr. Marketing Consultant, Aquakef; Founder/Marketing Manager, Mobilized Marketing; Director of Marketing, Steven Land; CMO, Guiderr; Founder, Yahid Consulting; Consultant, Penguin Strategies; Co-Director, Startup Grind; Founder/Business Development, Sparkly

2846 ICF VENTURES PVT LTD
No. 205, Krishnaji, 3rd main, Defence Colony
Bangalore 560 038
India

Phone: 91-8051269191 Fax: 91-8051269393

Mission Statement: ICF Ventures has been founded US and European institutional investors and individuals with global contacts and experience in building highly innovative companies.

Geographic Preference: India
Fund Size: $16.51 Million
Founded: 2001
Average Investment: $1.65 Million
Minimum Investment: $1.1 Million
Investment Criteria: Start-up , Early Stage/Growth and Development/Expansion
Industry Group Preference: Computer Hardware & Software, Information Technology, Consumer Products, Biotechnology, Consumer Services, Media
Portfolio Companies: Linc Software, MatexNet, Sasken, Explocity, Gangagen

Key Executives:
   Robin Farkas, Chairman
   Background: Lazard Freres & Co, Citibank.
   Directorships: Managing Partner
   Vijay Angadi, Managing Partner

2847 IDG CAPITAL PARTNERS
6th Floor, Tower A
COFCO Plaza
8 Jianguomennei Avenue
Beijing 100005
China

Phone: 86-10-6526-2400 Fax: 86-10-6526-0700
e-mail: idgvc@idgvc.com.cn
web: www.idgvc.com

Mission Statement: IDG Capital Partners is a China-focused investment firm with over US$2.5B capital under management. With in-depth understanding of local market, we invest in high quality companies with long-term growth potential. We continuously dedicate ourselves to the growth of great Chinese companies.

Geographic Preference: China
Average Investment: $1 - $100 million
Investment Criteria: All Stages
Industry Group Preference: Consumer Products, Franchising, Internet, Wireless, New Media, Education, Healthcare, New Energy, Advanced Manufacturing
Portfolio Companies: Allyes Information Technology, Bus Online, DAC, Shanghai Framedia Advertisement, Impression-Show, Media China Corp, Mei Ah Entertainment, Ocean Butterflies, Wuzhen Tourism Development, Yadii

Other Locations:
   Room 1105, Aetna Tower
   No 107 Zunyi Road
   Shanghai 200051
   China
   Phone: 86-21-6237-5408 Fax: 86-21-6237-5409

   Rm 2506, South Tower, Poly International Plaza, No. 1, East Pazhoudadao, Haizhu District
   Guangzhou 510308
   China
   Phone: 86-20-8412-0357 Fax: 86-20-8412-0490

   Room 29018, Jinzhoughuan Business Bldg
   No. 3037 Jintian Road
   Futian District
   Zhenzhen 518048
   China
   Phone: 86-75-8280-5462 Fax: 86-755-8280-5475

   Unit 5505, 55th Floor, The Center
   99 Queen's Road
   Central
   Hong Kong
   Phone: 852-2529-1016 Fax: 852-2529-1619

2848 IDG TECHNOLOGY VENTURE INVESTMENT
6 Floor, Tower A, COFCO Plaza
8 Jianguomennei Ave
Jianguomem Nei Dajie
Beijing 100005
China

Phone: 86-1065262400 Fax: 86-1065260700
e-mail: idgvc@idgvc.com.cn
web: www.idgvc.com

Mission Statement: Provides venture capital to high tech start-up companies developing products or services in market sectors with the greatest potential for rapid growth.

Geographic Preference: China
Fund Size: $200 Million
Founded: 1992
Average Investment: $1 Million - $100 Million
Minimum Investment: $500,000
Investment Criteria: Start up
Industry Group Preference: High Technology, Internet Technology, Information Services, Software,

Telecommunications, Networking, Biotechnology, Life Sciences, New Energy, Healthcare

Key Executives:
Alexandre Quirici, Partners
e-mail: idgvc@idgvc.com.cn
Education: BS - China Science and Technology University, Ph.D. in fiber optics-Rutgers University.
Directorships: General Partner

2849 IDG VENTURES INDIA International Financial Services Limited
IFS Court
Twenty-Eight, Cybercity
Ebene
Mauritius

Phone: 230-4673000 Fax: 230-4674000
e-mail: contact@idgvcindia.com

Mission Statement: We offer years of experience in helping build world-class companies by leveraging the IDG Ventures India team and IDG global platform.

Industry Group Preference: Internet, Mobile, Software, SaaS, Enterprise Services, Medical Devices
Portfolio Companies: 3DSoc, Agile Financial Technologies, Apalya Technologies, Aujas Netowks, ConnectM, eShakti.com, Brainbees Technologies, Forus Health, iCreate Software, iProf Learning Solutions, iViZ Techno Solutions, Kreeda Games, Manthan Software Services, Myntra.com, Ozone Media Solutions, Perfint Healthcare, Sourcebits Technologies, Valyoo Technologies, vServe Digital Services, Zivame.com

Key Executives:
Sudhir Sethi, Founder/Chairman/Managing Director
Education: BTech, Engineering, MBA, FMS, Delhi
Background: Walden International India
Directorships: Aujas, ConnectM, iProf, iViZ, Manthan, Mynthra, Perfint, 3DSoC

2850 IDG-ACCEL
8 Jianguomennei Avenue
6th Floor, Tower A
COFCO Plaza
Beijing 100005
China

Phone: 86-10-6526-2400 Fax: 86-10-6526-0700
e-mail: idgvc@idgvc.com.cn

Portfolio Companies: 21ViaNet, 265.com, 39.net, 5173.com, 51edu.com, Tiange Technology, JiuDing China, Baidu, Baofeng.com, Colorme Info, Ctrip, China Finance Online, Ketai, Kkeye, L99, HiChina, Net Movie, Poco, Shenzhoufu.com, Sohu, SouFun, QQ, Toudou.com, Xunlei, Yesky, Yoka, Zhongsou, 798 Entertainment, 3G, A8 Music Group, App Annie, Archermind Technology, Hook Mobile, Ilink, Longcheer Holdings Limited, Beijing Yangpuweiye Technology Development, Simlife, Techfaith Wireless, Tengwu, Gbits Network Technology, Fuzhou Skyunion Digital, Linekong, Netdragon, G10 Entertainment Korea, Amlogic, Baud Data Communications, Shenzhen Guanri Telecom, Memsic, RDA Microelectronics, Royole, Sun & Sea, VeriSilicon, Bonson Inormation Technology, CAXA Technology, Double Bridge Technology, Shanghai Hintsoft Software, Shenzhen Kingdee Software, Shenzhen Kingsky, Longshine Information Technology, Mapbar, MobilePeak Systems, Goodview International, Superdata Technology, Supresoft, Sursen, Tongtech, Zhizhen Node, Tiantian Online, Emay, Great Wall, Kong.net, Longmaster Information & Technology, MIG, Beijing MMIM Technologies, Guangdong Fendhua High-Tech, Sate, Shanghai Superrfid Electronics Technology, Bosideng, Competitor Sports Technology, Doright Fashion, EVE NY, Tiannong, Shin Kong International, Chamate, Mansion Hotel, Home Inns, Hanting Inns & Hotels, Secoo, Wumart Group, Dangdang, Didatuan, Eachnet, iHaveU, SinoBnet, Vancl, Yeecare, 51edu, ChinaEdu, Elite Education Media Group, New Channel, Tarena International

Other Locations:
No. 107 Zunyi Road
Aetna Tower
Room 1105
Shanghai 200051
China
Phone: 86-21-6237-5408 Fax: 86-21-6237-5899

No. 1 East Pazhoudadao
Poly International Plaza
Room 2506-2508, South Tower, Haizhu District
Guangzhou 510308
China
Phone: 86-20-8412-0357 Fax: 86-20-8412-0490

No. 3037 Jintian Road
Jinzhounghuan Business Building, Room 2901B
Futian District
Shenzhen 518048
China
Phone: 86-755-8280-5462 Fax: 86-755-8280-5475

99 Queen's Road
The Center, Unit 5505, 55th Floor
Central
Hong Kong
China
Phone: 852-2529-1016 Fax: 852-2529-1619

Key Executives:
Suyang Zhang, Partner
Education: Bachelor's Electronics Engineering, Shanghai University; EMBA China Europe International Business School
Background: Central Programming Coordination Manager, Shanghai Bell; Deputy Director, Shanghai Factory 520 of Minister of Poster and Telecommunications; General Manager, Hainan Vantone Group
Dongliang Liu, Venture Partner
Education: Tsinghua University
Background: Senior Research Fellow, Development Research Center of the State Department of China; CitiBank New York
Drake Yu, Venture Partner
Education: MBA Cheung Kong Graduate School of Business; Jianxi University of Chinese Medicine
Background: Sinotrust Managerial Consulting Company; Jiangzhong Pharmaceutical Co., Ltd.
Quan Zhou, Managing Director
Education: Bachelor's China Science and Technology University; Master's Chinese Academy of Science; PhD Fiber Optics Rutgers University

2851 IDINVEST PARTNERS
117, avenue des Champs Elysees
Paris 75008
France

Phone: 33 0 1 58 18 56 56 Fax: 33 0 1 58 18 56 89
web: www.idinvest.com

Mission Statement: A private equity and venture capital firm that invests in small to medium sized European companies through venture and growth capital, private debt, and dedicated portfolios and funds.

Geographic Preference: Europe
Fund Size: $8.1 Billion
Founded: 1997
Investment Criteria: Small Sized, Medium Sized, European
Industry Group Preference: Internet Technology, All Sectors Considered
Portfolio Companies: 1000mercis, 21Buttons, Acces, Acta Groupe, Actility, Adocia, AlVest, Ammeraal Beltech, Amplitude, AMTrust, Appart City, Appsfire, Asarina, AS International Group, Assystem, Audisoft, Automic, Aveni,

Venture Capital & Private Equity Firms / International Firms

Averys, Axelliance, Back Werk, Bequam, bGroupe Berkem, Bimedia, Biogroup LCD, Biotie Therapies, Blink Biomedical, BreezoMeter, Boxtal, byTourexcel, Campanda, Cardiologs, Cast, CCM Benchmark, Cerelia, Clustree, Chereau, Colisee, Cooptalis, Concours Mania Groupe, Corti, Criteo, Curse, Dailymotion, Delpharm, Domainiac, Domain Therapeutics, Drive For Me, Dunlop, Dupont, Dynacure, EDH Groupe des Ecoles, Eolite, ER, Erytech, Euro Part, European Homes, Europe Snacks, Exxelia Magnetics, Famoco, Frichti, Genticel, GHD, Grand Cru, Grand Frais, Groupe Bertrand, Groupe Bio7, Groupe Segex, Grupo Terratest, Habx, Halex, Hensoldt, Homeperf, House of HR, Iberchem, Inseec, Integragen, Italmatch Chemicals, J&S, Kantox, Keesing, KEP Technologies, Kether, Kiala, Konecta, Lea, Leosphere, Lima Corporate, LSR Group, Lumapps, M2i, MAINtag, Maisons Babeau-Seguin, MDX Health, Median, Meetic, Meilleire Gestion, Meilleurmobile.com, Megadyne, Memora, Mentum, Minoryx, Mix.com, Molotov.tv, Mondo Minerals, MP Hygiene, NETASQ, Nexway, Neurala, NG Data, Nosto, October, Okko Hotels, OneAccess, ONXEO, Orbility, Organica, Ornikar, OxThera, Ouicar, Papernest, Parella, PathoQuest, Pharmacie Lafayette, Planday, Platform.sh, Plumble, Pretty Simple, Prosensa, Proxiserve, Pure People, Quadrimex, R2P, Reworld Media

Other Locations:
An der Welle 4
Frankfurt 60322
Amsterdam

22F Jing An Kerry Centre Tower 3
1228 Yan An Zhong Road
Shanghai 200040
China

Key Executives:
Christophe Baviere, CEO/Managing Partner
Education: MBA, University of Ottawa; ESLSCA
Background: AGF-Allianz Group; Caisse des Depots et Consignations; BNP Paribas
Directorships: President, Private Equity Commission, AFG
Benoist Grossmann, Managing Partner
Education: MBA, Institut d'Etudes Politiques; PhD, Universite de Paris VI
Background: Partner, Viventures; Investment Manager, La Financiere de Brienne; EDF; NASA; Thompson-CSF Optronique
Directorships: Criteo, Dailymotion, Deezer, Meetic
Matthieu Baret, Managing Partner
Education: CENTRALE-SUPELEC; MS, Electrical Engineering, Georgia Tech; MBA, INSEAD
Background: VP, Italtel; Europatweb; Cap Gemini Telecom; Bouygues Telecom
Directorships: Private Equity Steering Committee, UNPRI
Nicolas Chaudron, Managing Partner
Education: MBA, Wharton School, University of Pennsylvania; MBA, College des Ingenieurs; PhD, Mathematics, University of Paris VI; Peking University
Background: Europatweb
Francois Lacoste, Managing Partner
Education: MS, Banking/Finance, Paris-Dauphine University
Background: Fortis Bank; Banque Worms
Christophe Simon, Managing Partner
Education: MS, Corporate Finance/Financial Engineering, University of Paris-Dauphine
Background: Ernst & Young

2852 IFE CONSEIL (INTERMEDIATE FINANCE EUROPE)
41 George V Avenue
Paris 75008
France
Phone: 33-156520240 Fax: 33-147200694
web: www.ifemezzanine.com

Mission Statement: IFE Conseil is the investment adviser of IFE Fund (Intermediate Finance Europe Fund), a fund dedicated to mezzanine financing in continental Europe

Geographic Preference: Europe
Fund Size: $ 200 Million
Founded: 1999
Average Investment: $ 10 Million
Minimum Investment: $ 5 Million
Investment Criteria: Mezzanine, LBO, MBO and companies with experienced management team, and strong growth perspectives
Industry Group Preference: All Sectors Considered
Portfolio Companies: Global Garden Products, Fraikin, Center Parcs, BB Hotels, Eau Ecarlate, Gautier, CFP Flexible Packaging, Oberthur Card Systems, Allen Afflelou

Key Executives:
Michel Dupont, Chairman
e-mail: info@ifeconseil.com
Education: Graduate of ESC Rouen, with a major in Finance.
Background: Analyst with Société Générale's Asset Recovery Management department, Paribas' M&A team.
Directorships: No other Position held in the company
Jean-Pascal Ley, Director Associate
e-mail: info@ifeconseil.com
Education: A French business school and MBA graduate
Background: In charge of Acquistion Finance, Banque du Phénix, principal of Phénix Mezzanine
Directorships: No other Position held in the company
Christian Quets, Head of Management Control
e-mail: info@ifeconseil.com
Education: A graduate of HEC and of the Harvard Business School.
Background: Suez Group—- commercial and investment banking.
Julien Drie, Investment Director
e-mail: info@ifeconseil.com
Education: A graduate of IEP Paris, INSEAD, and the Harvard Business School.
Background: CII and then Olivetti —— Strategy and Planning department, Director in Management Consulting, notably with Hay and Solving International, Downer & Co., a US-based M&A boutique, as Director.
Directorships: No other Position held in the company

2853 IGLOBE PARTNERS
11 Biopolis Way
Helios #09-03
Singapore 138867
Singapore
Phone: +65 6478 9716 Fax: +65 6478 9717
e-mail: contact@iglobepartners.com
web: www.iglobepartners.com

Mission Statement: Seek global investment opportunities in high growth companies and assist these companies in their globalization strategy and ensure best of breed corporate governance practices, transparency and risk management in order to achieve superior returns for our investors.

Geographic Preference: United States, Europe, Asia
Founded: 1999
Industry Group Preference: Wireless Technologies, Mobile Apps, Digital Media & Marketing, Clean Technology, Next Generation Materials, Semiconductors, IT/BIO Convergence
Portfolio Companies: 3PAR, Aicent, Anacle, ASK, Celestry, Fortemedia, IntruGuard, Kilopass, Lypanosys Limited, Matterport, Projectpartner, Shop Your World, Silicon Blue, Sparky Animation, StarMaker Interactive, Telenav, uBlox, Unity Technologies, VeriSilicon, VKorus Pte Ltd, Wise Giant Enterprise, Xumii, Zephyr Technology

Other Locations:
5201 Great America Parkway
Suite 320

Venture Capital & Private Equity Firms / International Firms

Santa Clara, CA 95054
Phone: 408-982-2126 **Fax:** 408-982-2129

Unit 16
43D Apollo Drive
Mairangi Bay, Auckland 0632
New Zealand
Phone: +64 9 915 3401 **Fax:** +64 9 968 8431

Key Executives:
  Philip Yeo, Chairman
  Soo Boon Koh, Founder & Managing Partner
  Michel Birnbaum, Partner
  Joyce Ng, Partner

2854 IGNITE JAPAN KK Ignite Group
1F Place Canada
7-3-37 Akasaka
Minato-ku
Tokyo 107-0052
Japan
Phone: 81-368947680 **Fax:** 81-368947701
web: www.ignite.co.jp

Mission Statement: Ignite has been very successful in operating IT industry focused venture investment activities.
Geographic Preference: US, Japan, Asia
Fund Size: $20 Billion
Founded: 2000
Industry Group Preference: Software, Communications, Internet Technology, Computer Related, Printing, Graphic Arts
Portfolio Companies: Acca Networks, atmarkIT, Wine in style, Natural Communications, Realcom, E-Supportlink ltd, Axiom, Virtualex, Sitecare, Ariel Networks, Pacific Design, Fibest.

Key Executives:
  Natsuaki Sasaki, President
    e-mail: contact@ignite.co.jp
    Education: B.A.-Economics from Hitotsubashi University, MBA - Columbia Business School.
    Background: Lehman Brothers Tokyo, Pangaea Wireless.
  Hiroaki Yano, President

2855 ILE-DE-FRANCE
66 Sartrouville Road
3 Technological Park of Maples
Pecq Cedex 78232
France
Phone: 33-130156400 **Fax:** 33-130156409

Mission Statement: IDFD intervenes in own capital stocks and clean quasi-bottoms: ordinary actions or of priority, convertible, good obligations of subscription and actions.
Geographic Preference: France
Fund Size: $16.8 Million
Founded: 1995
Average Investment: $370,000
Minimum Investment: $180,000
Investment Criteria: MBOs
Industry Group Preference: Industrial Products, Technology, Services
Portfolio Companies: Abaxia, Hello Machines, Adventuer Ventures, Carlipa Systems, Square Gourmet, Coralog, DG Industries, Delia Systems, Deltamed, Multi-Media Digilab, E-printing Company, Euro Services Laboratory, Exentive F.B. Technology, GO Albert Group, Epsitech Group

2856 IMI.VC
Bolshaya Tulskaya, 44
Moscow 115191
Russia
Phone: 7495-9582862
e-mail: au@imi.vc
web: www.imi.vc

Mission Statement: IMI.VC is an investment company funding innovative mobile applications that are able to change the market and behavior of mobile device users.
Industry Group Preference: Internet, Mobile
Portfolio Companies: Game Insight, NARR8, Farminers Startup Academy, Social Insight, WeHeartPics, Planner5D, Monosnap, App in the Air, BeatTheBushes, Gipis, Inflow, Kloudpics, Cookwizme, Dish.fm, IPQ2, FreeBrie, My-apps, Cute Town, Kula, CoFoundit, Prognolic, Woodla

Key Executives:
  Igor Matsanyuk, Founder

2857 IMM INVESTMENT CORP HCI Private Equity Fund
110 Sokong-Dong
Chung-Gu
4F Hanwa Building
Seoul 100-755
South Korea
Phone: 82-027330540 **Fax:** 82-027331942
web: www.imm.co.kr

Fund Size: $200 million
Founded: 1999
Investment Criteria: Recapitalizations, Consolidations, Buyout
Portfolio Companies: 12Soft, AD Technology, ALBA 1, Allm, Altrium CNI, ArtLab, Bellwave, CD Networks, CD Park, CJ Entertainemnt, Cy World, D&F Solution, Daekyung Machinery & Engineering, Doum & Nanum, Dream Execution, EMLSI, enCross Partners, Enium, Ensiz Technology, Epivalley, Etoos, FCI, Funkyfunky, Geomind, Greek and Roman mythology, Green Cross Biotech, Hannetware, IHQ, Independence, Innochip Technology, Intvnet, Jinu, KING&I, Korea OTC, Lets, MLT, Magiceyes, Mediaflex, Modemore, Namotech, Nanum Technologies, Naviya Entertainment, Needs Entertainment, Ness Display, Net TV, Netinbiz, Next Instrument, Ninza Turtle, Nongshim, Peptron, Pipax Environment, Polimedia, Possmedia, SK Sinsegi Telecom, Sanyang Electronics, Secure Soft, Sysdaq, Taeyang 3C, Teradian, Thinkware, Xemi Interactive, Zen Holdings

Key Executives:
  Dong Woo Chang, Chief Executive Officer
  Jae Mo Jeon, Chief Executive Officer

2858 IMPERIAL INNOVATIONS
52 Princes Gate
Exhibition Road
London SW7 2PG
United Kingdom
Phone: 44-02075814949
e-mail: info@imperialinnovations.co.uk
web: www.imperialinnovations.co.uk

Mission Statement: Imperial Innovations builds and invests in technology and healthcare businesses based on research from the UK's four leading universities: Imperial College London, Cambridge, Oxford and University College London.
Geographic Preference: United Kingdom
Founded: 1986
Investment Criteria: All Stages
Industry Group Preference: Healthcare, Technology
Portfolio Companies: Circassia, Veryan, PsiOxus Therapeutics, Cell Medica, PolyTherics, Oxford Immunotec, Stanmore Implants, TopiVert, Abingdon Health, Autifony Therapeutics, Mission Therapeutics, Ixico, Nexeon, Cortexica Vision Systems, Plaxica, Evo Electric, Process Systems Enterprise, Permasense, FeatureSpace, Acunu, Econic Technologies, Fractal

Key Executives:
  Russ Cummings, Chief Executive Officer
    Education: MA, Chemistry, Oxford University

Venture Capital & Private Equity Firms / International Firms

Background: Montech, Signet Group, Bank of Nova Scotia, Shell Chemicals Limited
Directorships: Plaxica, Evo Electric, Thiakls

2859 INDASIA FUND ADVISORS PVT LTD
3, Scheherazade, Justice Vyas Road, Colaba
Justice Vyas Road
Colaba
Mumbai 400 005
India

Phone: 91-2222881301 Fax: 91-2222830376
e-mail: info@indasiafund.com
web: www.indasiafund.com

Mission Statement: Provides advisory services for mergers and acquisitions, joint ventures and strategic alliances, business development, and corporate finance matters to both domestic and multi-national corporations.

Geographic Preference: Worldwide
Founded: 1998
Average Investment: $25 million
Minimum Investment: $15 million
Investment Criteria: Growth, Development/Expansion, MBO, Joint Ventures
Industry Group Preference: Information Technology, Biotechnology, Media, Computer Hardware & Software, Pharmaceuticals, Information Technology, Distribution, Communications, Life Sciences, Logistics, Oil & Gas
Portfolio Companies: Associated Container Terminals Ltd, Enable M, ARSS Infrastructure Ltd, Innova B2B Logistics

Key Executives:
Pradip Shah, Founder/Chairman
Education: MBA (Harvard Business School), Bachelor of Commerce (Sydenham College)
Background: Housing Development Finance Corporation, Asian Development Bank, World Bank, Reserve Bank of India, Credit Rating and Information Services of India Limited

2860 INDEX VENTURES
3 Burlington Gardens
London W1S 3EP
United Kingdom

Phone: 44 20 7154 2020 Fax: 44 20 7154 2021
web: www.indexventures.com

Mission Statement: Index Ventures network has invested in 160 consumer and enterprise technology companies in 24 countries.

Geographic Preference: Europe, Israel, USA
Founded: 1996
Average Investment: $100,000 to $2 million
Investment Criteria: Seed to Growth
Industry Group Preference: Infrastructure, Entertainment, Business Products & Services, Fintech, Retail, Consumer & Leisure
Portfolio Companies: BlaBlaCar, Criteo, Dropbox, Etsy, Flipboard, Funding Circle, Hortonworks, King, Lookout, Nasty Gal, Pure Storage, SoundCloud, Squarespace, Supercell

Key Executives:
Neil Rimer, Co-Founder
e-mail: anete@indexventures.com
Education: Stanford University
Background: Montgomery Securities; Index Securities
Damir Becirovic, Principle
Education: BS, Business Admin., University of Southern California
Background: Goldman Sachs; Coatue; Activision Blizzard; Apple; Flextronics
Directorships: Glossier, Hollar

2861 INDIAN DIRECT EQUITY ADVISORS PVT LTD
1007, Raheja Centre, Nariman Point
Mumbai 400 021
India

Phone: 91-2222041140 Fax: 91-222818156
web: www.ideaequity.com

Mission Statement: The company approaches high risk investments with the philosophy of identifying promoters and ideas which can scale up significantly in a short period.

Geographic Preference: India
Fund Size: $34 Million
Founded: 1999
Average Investment: $2.3 Million
Minimum Investment: $1 Million
Investment Criteria: Mezzanine to High-Growth Companies
Industry Group Preference: Media, Building Materials & Services, Communications, Services, Software, Textiles, Entertainment
Portfolio Companies: Alok Textile Industries Limited, BrainGEM L.L.C, Delta Innovative Enterprises Limited, Drish Shoes Limited, Ecoboard Industries Limited, New World Application, Secure Meters Limited, Sun Earth Ceramics Limited, Time Packaging Limited, United Studios Ltd

Key Executives:
Sanjaya Kulkarni, Managing Director
Education: Engineering Degree from IIT Bombay, MBA - IIM Ahmedabad.
Background: Citibank N.A.'s Merchant Banking department, 20th Century Leasing Corporation.
Nimesh Grover, Vice President

2862 INDUFIN
Research Park
Interveuvenlaan 1515-D1
Heverlee 3001
Belgium

Phone: 32-016393040 Fax: 32-016393049
e-mail: evelyne.ackermans@indufin.be
web: www.indufin.be

Mission Statement: Indufin is a Private Equity investment company (not a fund) with the long term commitment of its shareholders. We provide capital and know-how to support (international) growth, buy-outs and buy-ins. We invest in medium-sized companies in Belgium and Luxembourg and have a selected approach towards investment opportunities in neighbouring countries. Talented and passionate people are key to the success of an enterprise. We partner with entrepreneurs and entrepreneurial managers based on a shared vision of the future and a relationship of trust. We are an active shareholder focused on strategic opportunities and value creation. We are not a substitute for management and do not interfere in day-to-day decisions.

Geographic Preference: Belgium, Luxembourg
Founded: 2001
Average Investment: 3 - 15 million Euro
Investment Criteria: Growth Financing, Buy-Outs, Buy-Ins
Portfolio Companies: All-Tag Security, Alphamin, Bartech, Herbalgem, Kyotec Group, Preflexibel, Rowies, SecureLink

Key Executives:
Guy Wygaerts, Partner
e-mail: guy.wygaerts@indufin.be
Education: Commercial Engineer, KU Leuven; INSEAD
Background: Managing Partner, Andersen Consulting; Deloitte
Directorships: Rowies, SecureLink

Venture Capital & Private Equity Firms / International Firms

2863 INDUSTRI KAPITAL SVENSKA AB
4 Birger Jarlsgatan
Stockholm 11434
Sweden

Phone: 46-086789500 Fax: 46-086780336
web: www.industrikapital.com

Mission Statement: Industri Kapital strives to build lasting value in businesses by effecting fundamental performance improvement.
Geographic Preference: Sweden, Finland, Norway, Denmark, Benelux countries, France, Germany
Fund Size: $4.8 Billion
Founded: 1989
Investment Criteria: Mid sized companies.
Industry Group Preference: Manufacturing, Services, Retailing, Food & Beverage, Processing, Building Materials & Services, Media, Wholesale, Distribution
Portfolio Companies: Addum, Amas, Crisplant Industries, Guldfynd Holding, Hjem Is Europa, Idesta, Lithells, Nobia, Nyge Aero, Nyge Aero, Idesta, Bonna Sabla, Tradeka Ltd., Kid Interiør, The SIA Group, Myresjöhus, Idex, Ekstrem Lavpris, CEVA Santé Animale, Welzorg, Gardena
Key Executives:
  Kristian Carlsson Kemppinen, Partner
  e-mail: bjorn.saven@industrikapital.com
  Education: Degree - Stockholm School of Economics, MBA - Harvard Business School
  Background: Esselte Group in Sweden, the UK and the US.
  Directorships: CEO
  Helena Stjernholm, Partner, Sweden
  e-mail: kim.wahl@industrikapital.com
  Education: University of San Diego, MBA - Harvard Business School.
  Background: Corporate Finance Department at Goldman Sachs in New York and in London.
  Helena Stjernholm, Partner, Benelux
  e-mail: kristiaan.nieuwenburg@industrikapital.com
  Education: M.Sc.(Chem Eng)-Delft University of Technology, MBA-Harvard Business School.
  Background: Investment banking at Lehman Brothers in London.
  Erik Ingemarsson, Director, Swedish
  e-mail: detlef.dinsel@industrikapital.com
  Education: MBA-INSEAD, MSc.- Mechanical Engineering from the Technical University of Munich.
  Background: Bain & Company, Schmidlin division of Hilti AG, Liechtenstein.
  Carl Jakobsson, Associate
  e-mail: samir.kamal@industrikapital.com
  Education: BSc.-Electrical & Electronic Engineering(Imperial College, University of London), MSc. in Business Administration and Economics(Stockholm School of Economics).
  Background: Investment Banking Division of Carnegie.
  Daniel Mogerud, Director, Manager Operations
  e-mail: gustav.ohman@industrikapital.com
  Education: MSc.(Econ)-Financial Economics and Business Administration(Stockholm School of Economics), with a major in Finance from Ecole des Hautes Etudes Commerciales (HEC) in Paris.
  Background: Corporate Finance Department of Enskilda in Stockholm
  Directorships: CEO (Region West-Benelux, France, Denmark/Norway)
  Christoffer Zilliacus, Director
  e-mail: michael.rosenlew@industrikapital.com
  Education: MSc.(Econ)-Corporate Finance and Accounting from Swedish School of Economics, Business Administration
  Background: Amer Group
  Directorships: CEO (Region East- Sweden, Finland, Germany)
  Kristian Larsen, Deputy Director
  e-mail: erik.larsson@industrikapital.com
  Education: MSc. in Economics and Business Administration(Stockholm School of Economics), CEMS Masters from Universität zu Köln, MBA from Harvard Business School.
  Thomas Ramsay, Partner, Finland
  e-mail: thomas.ramsay@industrikapital.com
  Education: MSc.(Econ)Major in Accounting from the Swedish School of Economics and Business Administration in Helsinki.
  Background: Corporate Finance Department of Salomon Brothers in London.
  Anders Peterson, Associate Director
  e-mail: anders.petersson@industrikapital.com
  Education: MSc. in Economics and Business Administration from the University of Uppsala.
  Background: Investment Banking Division of JP Morgan.

2864 INDUSTRIAL DEVELOPMENT BANK OF INDIA
IDBI Tower, WTC Complex, Cuffe Parade, Colaba
Mumbai 400005
India

Phone: 91-2266937000 Fax: 91-2222181294
Toll-Free: 1800-2001947
e-mail: customercare@idbi.co.in
web: www.idbi.com

Mission Statement: Actively seeking new investments.
Fund Size: $29.6 Billion
Founded: 1964
Investment Criteria: Expansion, diversification and modernisation of existing projects.
Key Executives:
  M. S. Raghavan, Chairman & Managing Director
  e-mail: vp.shetty@idbi.co.in
  B. K. Batra, Deputy Managing Director

2865 INDUSTRIALIZATION FUND FOR DEVELOPING COUNTRIE
Fredericiagade 27
Copenhagen K 1310
Denmark

Phone: 45-33637500 Fax: 45-33637599
e-mail: ifu@ifu.dk
web: www.ifu.dk

Mission Statement: IFU offers capital and advice to joint venture enterprises in developing countries.
Geographic Preference: Nordic countries, Europe, Beijing, Johannesburg, New Delhi, Cape Town,
Average Investment: $12.01 Million
Portfolio Companies: The Investment Fund For Central and Eastern Europe, The Investment Fund for Emerging Markets
Key Executives:
  Tommy Thomsen, Manging Director
  e-mail: ifu@ifu.dk
  Torben Huss, Deputy Managing Director
  e-mail: ifu@ifu.dk
  Alex Unsgaard, Senior Investment Manager
  e-mail: ifu@ifu.dk
  Anders Nellemose, Senior Investment Manager
  e-mail: ifu@ifu.dk

2866 INDUSTRIEBANK LIOF NV
Boschstraat 76, 6211 AX
PO Box 1310
Maastricht 6201 BH
Netherlands

Phone: 31-433280280 Fax: 31-433-280200
web: www.liof.com

Venture Capital & Private Equity Firms / International Firms

Mission Statement: Actively seeking new investments
Fund Size: $460,000
Founded: 1975
Minimum Investment: $48,000
Industry Group Preference: Communications, Consumer Services, Electronic Technology, Pollution, Industrial Equipment, Medical & Health Related, Life Sciences, Automotive, Mobile Communications Devices, Consumer Products, Data Communications

Key Executives:
  Mark Koppers, Project Manager Logistics, Agro-Food
  Jacques Mikx, Director Foreign Investments
  Jaap Heukelom, Senior Projectmanager High Tech Systems, Aerospace
  Sjoerd Boomsma, Senior Projectmanager LifeSciences & Health, Contact Centers

2867 INDUSTRIFONDEN
Vasagatan 11, Box 1163
Stockholm SE - 111 91
Sweden

Phone: 46-858791900 Fax: 46-858791950
web: www.industrifonden.se

Mission Statement: Industrifonden provides development capital, competence and networks for Swedish growth companies; offer various types of financing, both loans for specific projects and equity capital.

Geographic Preference: Sweden
Fund Size: $458 Million
Founded: 1979
Minimum Investment: $0.13 Million
Investment Criteria: Early stage, Start-up, medium sized enterprises
Industry Group Preference: Biotechnology, Computer Related, Semiconductors, Electronic Technology, Industrial Equipment, Industrial Services, Medical, Healthcare
Portfolio Companies: Småföretagsinvest, Emano, Investa Företagskapital, CIMON Medical, Malmöhus Invest, Lunova, KTH Seed Capital, Lumitec, SRK, Uminova Invest, Iteksa Venture.

Key Executives:
  Charlotte Brogren Karlberg, Chairman
  e-mail: lennart.samuelsson @industrifonden.se
  Education: B.Sc. in business administration
  Anders Schelin, Investment Manager Technology
  e-mail: claes.de.neergaard @industrifonden.se
  Education: M Sc in Economics ans Business Administration

2868 INDUSTRIO VENTURES
Via Ora del Garda, 97
Trento 38121
Italy

e-mail: info@industrio.co
web: www.industrio.co

Mission Statement: Industrio transforms teams into companies, and prototypes into products.

Geographic Preference: Italy
Average Investment: 50,000 euro
Investment Criteria: Early-Stage, Seed-Stage
Industry Group Preference: Technology, Medical Devices
Portfolio Companies: Meccatronicore, Melixa, Sinphoniq

Key Executives:
  Jari Ognibeni, CEO/Co-Founder
  e-mail: jo@industrio.com
  Alfredo Maglione, President/Co-Founder
  Background: President, Optio Group
  Directorships: Trentino Sviluppo
  Alberto Gasperi, Co-Founder
  Education: Chartered Accountant
  Background: Founder & President, CSI
  Alessio Romani, Co-Founder
  Background: Plant Manager, Zobele Group

2869 INFINITY VENTURE PARTNERS
Japan

web: www.infinityventures.com

Mission Statement: At Infinity Venture Partners, we strive to create venture companies with infinite possibilities. We bridge JAPAN - the second largest global economy and CHINA - the world's growth engine, to support the birth of new ventures. Infinity Venture Partners is a unique venture capital firm which combines industry platform with venture capital financing. Infinity Venture Partners not only provides venture capital, but also brings the vast network of experienced, international partners. We strive to maximize the value of young ventures with our strategic support. Furthermore, strategic investors in the IVP fund bring opportunities in business and technology partnerships and thus accelerate growth of our portfolio companies.

Geographic Preference: Japan, China
Founded: 2007
Investment Criteria: Early-Stage
Industry Group Preference: Internet, Mobile
Portfolio Companies: Groupon Japan, JMTY, Mlab, Muse & Co., The One Of Them, Rekoo Japan, Smart Education, App Annie, Daguu, Goyoo Networks, Jihua.fm, Mobcent, Moyo Game, Order With Me, Yeahka, DeNA China, DragonsMeet, Rekoo

Key Executives:
  Akio Tanaka, Co-Founder/Managing Partner
  Education: Master's Degree, University of British Columbia
  Background: Head of Venture Investments, Adobe; CTO, Macromedia Japan
  Hirofumi Ono, Co-Founder/Managing Partner
  Education: BS, Biological Science, MS, Molecular Biology, University of Tokyo
  Background: Co-Founder/COO, CA Mobile
  Masashi Kobayashi, Co-Founder/Managing Partner
  Education: BS, Naval Architecture & Ocean Engineering, University of Tokyo
  Background: Partner, Globis Capital Partners
  Directorships: RecycleOne, Interactive Brains, Interscope, Ariel Networks, VirtualeX

2870 INFOCOMM INVESTMENTS
10 Pasir Panjang Road #10-01
Mapletree Business City
117438
Singapore

Phone: 65-62110888
e-mail: info@infocomminvestments.com
web: www.infocomminvestments.com

Mission Statement: Infocomm Investments is the VC arm of Singapore's Infocomm Development Authority. As an investment fund, our main objective is to invest in innovative technology companies that complement our vision of building a competitive IT landscape in Singapore.

Geographic Preference: Singapore
Fund Size: $200 million
Industry Group Preference: Information Technology
Portfolio Companies: Moonshoot, JustCommodity, Bubble Motion, GuardTime, Data Security Systems Solutions, Sconce, Quid, Game Ventures, Twilo, Mobilewalla

Other Locations:
3 Twin Dolphin Drive
Suite 260
Redwood City, CA 94065
Phone: 650-5931716

Unit 1, Level 3
Explorer Block, International Tech Park
Whitefield Road

Venture Capital & Private Equity Firms / International Firms

Bangalore 560 066
India
Phone: 91-8051156400

1038 Nanjing West Road
Westgate Tower 18-01
Shanghai 200041
China
Phone: 86-2162178822

Key Executives:
Lee Kheng Nam, Chairman
Education: BS, MS, Doctorate, Electrical Engineering, MIT
Background: Senior Sales & Business Development Executive, Ancentuate; Reputation Technologies; Consultant, Boston Consulting Group

2871 INGENIOUS VENTURES
15 Golden Square
London W1F 9JG
United Kingdom
Phone: 44-02073194000 **Fax:** 44-02073194001
e-mail: generalenquiries@ingeniousmedia.co.uk

Mission Statement: We invest in media and entertainment companies. The finance and expertise we provide helps them keep growing. Our understanding of both the media and private equity sectors means we speak fluently to investors and media owners alike. We are active investors. Our deep knowledge of the media and entertainment industries adds significant value to the companies we invest in.

Geographic Preference: United Kingdom
Founded: 1998
Average Investment: £2 million
Investment Criteria: Expansion-Stage, MBO
Industry Group Preference: Music, Marketing, Television, Gaming, Entertainment, Media
Portfolio Companies: Digital Theatre, Property Network, Casabu, Whizz Kid Entertainment, DRG Limited, Brand Events Holdings, BrandRapport Group, Review Centre Limited

Key Executives:
Patrick Bradley, CEO/Director
e-mail: patrick.bradley@ingeniousmedia.co.uk
Education: King's College, Worcester College, Oxford University
Background: Lawyer

2872 INITIAL CAPITAL
Avenida Paulista
Sao Paulo 2073
Brazil
e-mail: hello@initial.vc
web: www.initial.vc

Mission Statement: Initial Capital is a firm, not a fund. This means we have neither limited partners, nor an investment committee taking part in our decision making process. Being focused on early-stage startups, our sweet-spot is the $100K-300K range, however, we do have the flexibility to invest higher amounts.

Geographic Preference: Brazil, Israel
Average Investment: $100,000 - $300,000
Investment Criteria: Early-Stage
Industry Group Preference: Internet, Business Products & Services
Portfolio Companies: Soluto, Glambox, Enprego Ligado, Samba Ads, Startupi.com.br, Pitzi, Evoz, Wibbitz, Shine, Parallel Universe, POSE

Other Locations:
Ehad Ha'am 72
Tel Aviv
Israel

Key Executives:
Roi Carthy, Managing Partner
e-mail: roi@initial.vc
Background: Zend Technologies, Head of Products, Soluto

2873 INNOFINANCE OY
Westendintie 99-101 A 28
Espoo 02160
Finland
Phone: 358-207-43-2500 **Fax:** 358-207-43-2501
e-mail: office@innofinance.fi

Mission Statement: A venture capital company that invests in small and medium sized Finnish companies. Actively seeking new investments.

Fund Size: $1.1 Million
Founded: 1997
Average Investment: $40,800
Minimum Investment: $10,200
Investment Criteria: Early Stage
Industry Group Preference: Electronic Technology, Security, Biotechnology, Energy, Chemicals, Consumer Services, Medical, Industrial Equipment, Industrial Services
Portfolio Companies: ABR Innova Oy, Absolute Engery, Acusto Oy, Addoz, B-Band, Bevesys Oy, Book-It Oy, Ch5 Finland Oy, Codetoys Oy, CWP Coloured Wood Products Oy, Delsitech, Deveinfo Oy, Eagle Filter, Ellibs Oy, Emillion Oy, Euroelektro International Oy, Futurice Oy, Granula, Greenvironment Oy, Group Intelligentia Oy, Heeros Systems Oy, Homesoft Oy, Hydrox Pipeline Oy, Ima Engineering, Imagetalk Oy, Karhu Sporting Goods, Kuusama Design Oy, Labgas Instrument Company, Liekki Oy, Mandrel Oy, On-Motion Oy, Openbit Oy, Oy Plusdial Ab, Oy Stinghorn, Oy Wireless Media Finland, Prewise Group Oy, Primet Oy, Remote Analysis, R.Rouvari Oy, Staselog Oy, Suomen Kuitulava Suvisoft Oy, Suomen Teollisuusosa Oy, Taipale Telematics, Viope Solutions Oy, Voxpoint Technologies Oy

Key Executives:
Martti Hintikka, President and CEO, Partner
358-400-302-081
e-mail: martti.hintikka@innofinance.fi
Juha Turunen, Investment Director, Partner

2874 INNOGEST CAPITAL
Via A. Locatelli 2
Milano 20124
Italy
Phone: 39 011 5091411 **Fax:** 39 011 590488
e-mail: info@innogest.it
web: www.innogestcapital.com

Mission Statement: A leading Italian seed- and early-stage venture capital fund with offices in Turin, Geneva and San Francisco.

Geographic Preference: Italy, Europe, USA
Fund Size: 200 million Euro
Founded: 2006
Average Investment: 200,000 - 2 million Euro
Investment Criteria: Seed-Stage, Early-Stage
Industry Group Preference: Healthcare, Fintech, Foodtech, Fashion/Lifestyle, Digital Health
Portfolio Companies: Cornerjob, GreenBone Ortho, Empatica, MedLumics, Diet to go, Digital Magics, Anaconda, CV Lab, BetaGlue Technologies, Supermercato24, Newronika, Sardex, Armadio Verde, D-Eye, Prestiamoci, Pi-Cardia, Angiodroid, Drexcode, Thron, Atricath, 40 South Energy, Agroils, Cuebiq, Beintoo, MBooster, Erydel

Venture Capital & Private Equity Firms / International Firms

Key Executives:
Claudio Giuliano, Founder and Managing Partner
Education: MS, Politecnico di Torino; MBA, INSEAD
Background: The Carlyle Group, Bain & Company, Hewlett Packard

2875 INNOVACOM SA
23 rue Royale
Paris 75008
France

Phone: 33-144941500 Fax: 33-144941515
e-mail: info@innovacom.com
web: www.innovacom.com

Mission Statement: Works with the most promising entrepreneurs whose ideas improve the ability of telecom carriers to deliver services.

Geographic Preference: France and Europe
Founded: 1988
Average Investment: $500,000 - $10 million
Investment Criteria: Expansion and Development Capital, Early Stage, Startup Capital
Industry Group Preference: Materials Technology, Telecommunications, Software, Enterprise Services, Content, Components & IoT, Computer Hardware & Software
Portfolio Companies: CyOptics, Defacto, Heptagon, HighWave, IFOTEC, Innova Card, Actelis, Aperto Networks, Astellia, Atrica, Avilinks, Danger, Appium, Active Circle, Air2Web, Assima, Envivio, FrontCall, Groupe SQLI, Highdeal, Kabira, Kimotion.

Key Executives:
Denis Champenois, Chairman
Education: Graduate of the French business school HEC and the École Nationale Supérieure des Postes et Télécommunications
Background: Boards of directors of many communications companies in France and Europe (Editions Glénat, Algety, Madrid Film), etc.
Jerome Lecoeur, CEO

2876 INNOVATION CAPITAL
57 Avenue Franklin Delano Roosevelt
Paris 75008
France

Phone: 33-1-40-76-99-00 Fax: 33-1-45-61-24-78
e-mail: businessplan@innovationcapital.fr
web: www.innovationcapital.fr

Mission Statement: Founded in 1996, Innovation Capital is an international venture capital firm with its head office in Paris and a local presence in the Silicon Valley. With over 415 M Euro currently under management, our focus is on venture investments at both the early and late stage, in two sectors: information technologies and life sciences.

Founded: 1996
Investment Criteria: Early-Stage, Later Stage
Industry Group Preference: Information Technology, Life Sciences, Telecommunications, Biotechnology
Portfolio Companies: 6 Wind, Anevia, Expway, Maeglin, One Access, Ask, Citilog, Crocus, EI Technologies, Linedata Services, Micropole Univers, Roctool, RSI, Stantum, Teem Photonics, TES, FAB Pharma, Genoway, Integragen, Scynexis, Txcell, Zealand Pharma, DMS, Kuros Biosurgery, Orthopaedic Synergy, Therodiag, Tronic's Micro Systems

Key Executives:
Valery Huot, Managing Partner
Education: MS, Electrical Engineering, Stanford University; Ecole Polytechnique, Paris
Background: Co-Leader, Fund of Fund Team, Caisse des Depotss; SME Financing Office, French Treasury; French Defense Procurement Agency; Telstra
Directorships: Expway, Anevia, Ask, 6 Wind, Stantum
Franck Noiret, General Partner
Education: Sciences-Po Paris; Masters in Corporate Finance, Paris-Dauphine University; MBA, Wharton School
Background: Director, Apax Partners; Principal Banker, EBRD
Directorships: Ei Technologies, Genoway, Maeglin, Tronic's
Michel Desbard, Venture Partner
Background: Financial Auditor, Thomson Group; Financial Controller, Fairchild Semiconductor; COO, Matra-Harris
Directorships: Crocus Technology, One Access, Teem Photonics, TES Electronics Solutions
Bertrand Limoges, Partner
Education: Sciences-Po Paris, HEC School of Management
Background: Viventures
Chantal Parpex, President/Managing Partner
Education: MD, Faculte de Medecine de Paris; International Program of General Management, INSEAD/CEDEP
Background: Founder/Managing Partner, Bioam Gestion; Rhone-Poulenc Rorer Group; Medical Director, Synthelabo
Directorships: IntegraGen
Florian Reinaud, Partner
Education: BA, Physiology, Oxford University; MD, Imperial College London
Background: CFO, DBV Technologies; Apax Partners; Equity Analyst, Schroder Salomon Smith Barney/Citigroup
Directorships: FAB Pharma, Orthopaedic Synergy, Zealand Pharma

2877 INNOVATION CAPITAL LIMITED
Suite 401, 35 Lime St
Sydney 2000
Australia

Phone: 61-282966000 Fax: 61-282966066
web: www.innovationcapital.net

Mission Statement: Innovation Capital focuses on Australian technology intensive businesses.

Geographic Preference: Australia, US
Fund Size: $100 Million
Investment Criteria: Seed, Early
Industry Group Preference: Wireless Technologies, Energy, Medical & Health Related, Biopharmaceuticals, Management, Environmental Protection, Media, Telecommunications, Information Technology, Engineering, Clean Technology, Biotechnology
Portfolio Companies: ActiveSky, cap-XX, Enterix, QRxPharma, Neuromonics, Micromet.

Key Executives:
Michael A Quinn, Managing Partner
e-mail: michaelquinn@innovationcapital.net
Education: Harvard University MBA University of Western Australia Bachelor of SciencePhysics and Applied Mathematics; Bachelor of Science BEc MBA
Background: Chief Executive Officer of Phoenix Scientific Industries Limited; Co-founded Memtec; active director of ResMed Inc
Directorships: QRxPharma Pty Ltd Board Member Warren Centre for Advanced Engineering at Sydney University Board Member (past); ATP Innovations Pty Ltd Chair of NSW Enterprise Workshop and
Robert Frater, Chief Technology Officer

2878 INNOVATIONSKAPITAL
1 Kungsportsplatsen
Gothenburg SE-411 10
Sweden

Phone: 46-31609190 Fax: 46-31609199
e-mail: info@innkap.se
web: www.innkap.se

Venture Capital & Private Equity Firms / International Firms

Mission Statement: To invest in start-up and early stage private companies in the Nordic region. The investment strategy is directed towards companies in the Information Sciences and Healthcare industry sectors, with special emphasis on the commercial development of leading

Geographic Preference: Sweden, Denmark, Finland, Norway
Fund Size: $323 Million
Founded: 1994
Average Investment: $1.27 Million
Minimum Investment: $0.12 Million
Investment Criteria: Startup, Early Stage, Expansion/development, Seed
Industry Group Preference: Information Technology, Health Related, Hardware, Software, Telecommunications
Portfolio Companies: Altitun, Appgate, Bioinvent, Carmen Systems, Comlase, Cureon, Firedoor, Formex, Heptagon, Mathcore, Medeikonos, Mitra, Nassko, Plexus, Radians Innova, Samba Sensors, Simtra Aerotech Spotfire

Key Executives:
Staffan Ingeborn, Managing Investment Director
e-mail: info@innkap.se
Education: MSc in European Accounting and Finance from an Erasmus Programme, MSc in Business Administration and Economics from the University of Göteborg
Background: Managing Director of Healthcare Division, SCA M'lnlycke; Technical Director and Executive Vice President, SCA M'lnlycke Group
Gunnar Fernström, Investment Director
e-mail: info@innkap.se
Education: MBA certificate from the University of North Carolina. He holds an Executive MBA from Stockholm School of Economics, an MSc in Business Administration and Economics from the University of Gothenburg and has studied engineerin
Gabriella Ohldin, Chief Financial Officer
e-mail: info@innkap.se

2879 INTEGRATED TECHNOLOGIES LIMITED
Viking House
Ellingham Way
Ashford, Kent TN23 6NF
United Kingdom

Phone: 44-1233638383 Fax: 44-1233639401
web: www.itl.co.uk

Mission Statement: A joint ownership by Israel Aircraft Industries (IAI) and a $1.6 billion conglomerate comprised of Israeli & US entrepreneurs, bankers and industrialists.

Geographic Preference: Germany, Europe, Israel, North America

2880 INTELLIGENT CAPITAL SDN BHD
18-2, Jalan 1/76C, Desa Pandan
Kuala Lumpur 55100
Malaysia

Phone: 60-392-816588 Fax: 60-3-9281-6598
web: www.intelligentvc.com

Fund Size: $16 Million
Founded: 2000
Average Investment: $3 Million
Minimum Investment: 500000
Investment Criteria: Focus on companies that can protect their margin or that have excellent management
Industry Group Preference: High Technology

2881 INTER-ASIA VENTURE MANAGEMENT LIMITED
141 Des Voeux Road
510, China Insurance Group Building,
Central
Hong Kong

Phone: 852-25285717 Fax: 85225279704
e-mail: iavm@iavmhk.com
web: www.iavmhk.com

Geographic Preference: America, Africa, Asia Pacific
Fund Size: $ 60 million
Founded: 1972
Average Investment: $ 8 Million
Minimum Investment: $ 1 million
Investment Criteria: Start-up, Early Stage
Industry Group Preference: Food & Beverage, Software, Environmental Protection, Logistics, Distribution, Healthcare, Health Related, Information Technology, Alternative Energy, Processing
Portfolio Companies: ACL Wireless, Asia Foods, Asia Renal Care, China Veg, Contech, Exsequor, Heart Center, IKEA, Jump, McDonald's, New Horizons, PNE/Ecogas, Ross Systems, Solarex Photovaltaic, Temenos

Key Executives:
Lewis P. Rutherfurd, Co-founder & Managing Partner
Education: BA East Asian Studies, Princeton University; MBA, Harvard Business School
Background: Governor/VP, American Chamber of Commerce in Hong Kong; Chairman, Honk Kong Venture Capital Association
Louis S. K. Wong, Executive Director
Education: Lingnan University
Background: Senior Accountant, Thomas Lee C Kuen & Co
Bolormaa Luvsandorj, Partner, Ulaanbaator
Education: MBA, Harvard Business School
Background: Director: Hong Kong Sheraton Hotel & Shopping Mall, IKEA, Five Pillars Indonesia Office Park, McDonald's of Singapore; US Navy Underwater Demolition Team; US Navy SEAL Team 2
Cyril Fung, Co-founder & Chairman
Education: BBA, University of Missouri
Background: Senior VP/CFO, GE Asia Pacific Capital Technology Fund; Finance/Administrative Manager, Sumitomo Metal Group; CPA

2882 INTER-RISCO: SOCIEDADE DE CAPITAL DE RISCO
284 rua Tenente Valadim
OPorto 4100-476
Portugal

Phone: 351-226073111 Fax: 351-226006488
web: www.bancobpi.pt

Mission Statement: Invests in Expansion, Development, Small buyout, Minority Equity opportunities.

Geographic Preference: Portugal
Industry Group Preference: All Sectors Considered

2883 INTERMEDIATE CAPITAL GROUP PLC
100 St Paul's Churchyard
Juxon House
London EC4M 8BU
United Kingdom

Phone: 44-02032017700 Fax: 44-02072482536
e-mail: terri.jasper@icgplc.com
web: www.icgplc.com

Mission Statement: Actively seeking new investments.

Geographic Preference: France, Germany, Italy, Netherlands, Spain, United Kingdom
Fund Size: Euro 12.1 Billion
Founded: 1989

Venture Capital & Private Equity Firms / International Firms

Average Investment: $8 Million
Minimum Investment: $2 Million
Investment Criteria: Bridge, Expansion, Management Buy-In, Management Buy-Out, Refinancing Bank Debt, Secondary Purchase and Replacement Capital, Mezzanine
Industry Group Preference: Consumer Products, Insurance, Manufacturing, Information Technology, Textiles, Biotechnology, Aviation
Portfolio Companies: Acova, Cartiere del Garda, Calvet, Coal Products, Convenience Food Systems, Electrokoppar, Elmville, Great Western Holdings, MTL, Thomson Directories, Unipart Rail Holdings
Key Executives:
  Christophe Evain, Managing Director and CEO
  Education: University of Hamburg
  Background: Citibank for five years in Frankfurt and New York and three years for Bankgesellschaft Berlin/Landesbank Berlin
  Philip Keller, Managing Director and Chief Financial Officer
  Education: Graduate from Oxford University & qualified as a chartered accountant.
  Background: for Price Waterhouse for seven years
  Andreas Klein, Associate Director - Credit Fund Management
  Education: MBA from the London Business School
  Background: he worked for Chemical Bank for seven years
  Andreas Mondovits, Senior Managing Director
  Education: MBA, Univ. of Southern California
  Background: UBS Global Asset Management
  Alan Carey, Associate Director - CFM Administration
  Background: Williams & Glyns, Chemical Bank & Specialist Finance Group
  Chris Connelly, Director of Operations
  Education: Oxford University and subsequently qualified as a chartered accountant
  Background: he worked for Coopers & Lybrand for seven years
  Benoit Durteste, Managing Director and Head of European Mezzanine
  Education: MBA from Heriot-Watt University Business School, graduate of Napier University and subsequently qualified as a Certified Accountant
  Background: he worked for The Royal Bank of Scotland for two years
  Alex Hone, Associate Director - Mezzanine Funds Administration
  Education: Vrije University
  Background: he worked for the private equity firm HAL Investments in the Netherlands for four year
  Amalia Formoso, Associate - Marketing and Client Relations
  e-mail: james.davis@icgplc.co.uk
  Education: Graduate from Oxford University & C.A.
  Background: Deloitte & Touche
  Ian Stanlake, Financial Controller
  Education: graduate of Copenhagen Business School and has an MBA from the European School of Management
  Background: he worked as a strategy consultant for Braxton Associates for three years

2884 INTERNATIONAL PRIVATE EQUITY SERVICES LIMITED Guernsey
1, Royal Plaza, Royal Avenue
St Peter Port
Channel Islands
Guernsey GY1 2HL
United Kingdom
Phone: 44-1481713843 Fax: 44-1481715219
web: www.ipes.com

Mission Statement: Independent provider offering services for private equity and venture capital funds and their related vehicles
Geographic Preference: United Kingdom
Fund Size: $50 Billion
Founded: 1998
Key Executives:
  Andrew Whittaker, Managing Director, Guernsey
  e-mail: ipesgsy@aol.com
  Education: Qualified banker and a Chartered Director.
  Background: 25 years administration, investment and management experience working with major international finance institutions in the offshore industry.
  Directorships: founder
  Sharon Alvarez, Director, Guernsey

2885 INVEMAX
ul. M. Reja 13/15
81-874 Sopot
Poland
e-mail: info@invemax.com
web: www.invemax.com

Mission Statement: The thing that a fresh idea needs the most is acceleration. Ideas should be constantly tested, modified and validated asap. Our specialty is seed investing. Beyond financial support we provided contact with the most important startup hot-spots in the world.
Investment Criteria: Seed
Portfolio Companies: 3HACK.PL, Startup Weekend Trójmiasto, ElimiDateapp.com, Coinbase, TeleportMe

2886 INVENTURE PARTNERS
Novinsky Boulevard 31, Office 8-20B
Floor 8
Moscow 123242
Russia
Phone: 7 495 641 3635 Fax: 7 495 641 3866
e-mail: info@inventurepartners.com
web: www.inventurepartners.com

Mission Statement: We are solely focused on investing in the equity of young technology companies in Russia. We seek investments with unique value propositions. We generally seek a representation on the board of the companies we invest in, as we believe we can make a valuable contribution in the strategic decision making process.
Geographic Preference: Russia
Investment Criteria: Early Stage
Industry Group Preference: Internet, Mobile, Software, E-Commerce & Manufacturing
Portfolio Companies: GetTaxi, Fogg, OnlineTours, Starcard, GetGoing, Smarfin, Happlink
Key Executives:
  Sergey Azatyan, Managing Partner
  Anton Inshutin, Managing Partner

2887 INVEST EQUITY MANAGEMENT CONSULTING GmbH
Garnisongasse 7/Top 22
Vienna 1090
Austria
Phone: 43-15320551 Fax: 43-15320551
e-mail: office@investequity.at
web: www.investequity.at

Mission Statement: INVEST EQUITY enjoys an excellent reputation as an active and reliable investor in unlisted companies with the focus on growth companies and mid-market buy-outs and is a strong local partner for both international investors and private equity players alike.
Geographic Preference: Czech Republic and Slovakia
Fund Size: $110 Million

Founded: 1998
Average Investment: $1.5 Million
Minimum Investment: $800,000
Investment Criteria: Seed, start-up, expansion, pre-IPO, buy-out
Industry Group Preference: Industrial Products, Industrial Services, Manufacturing
Portfolio Companies: Chemson, Infoniqa, Kolbe-Coloco, LMF, Logim, Steudle, Strohal

Key Executives:
  Jörgen Hausberger, Managing Partner
  Education: Graduate engineer from Vienna University of Technology
  Background: 15 year experience in PE/VC market, having previously worked in the area of corporate finance at Investkredit Bank AG and also for many years in the Austrian industry

2888 INVESTMENT AB BURE
Dawson Street 6
Stockholm 114 34
Sweden

Phone: 08-6140020 **Fax:** 08-6140038
e-mail: info@bure.se
web: www.bure.se

Mission Statement: Focuses on long-term ownership of un-listed companies with strong and stable earnings.

Geographic Preference: Sweden
Founded: 1993
Industry Group Preference: Communications, Computer Related, Medical & Health Related, Industrial Services
Portfolio Companies: Appelberg, Carl Bro, Celemi, Citat, Cygate, Mercuri International, Retea, Systeam, Textilia, Vittra Utbildning, Mitra Medical, Kreatel

Key Executives:
  Patrik Tigerschiöld, Chairman
  e-mail: info@bure.se
  Agneta Schein, Director secretary

2889 INVESTMENT FUND FOR CENTRAL & EASTERN EUROPE
Fredericiagade 27
Copenhagen K 1310
Denmark

Phone: 45-33637500 **Fax:** 45-33637599

Mission Statement: IFU participates as a partner in the joint ventures through committing equity capital and/or loans and through board membership.

Geographic Preference: Central, Eastern Europe
Founded: 1967
Average Investment: $1.5 Million
Minimum Investment: $100,000
Investment Criteria: Invests in profitible companies with Danish base
Industry Group Preference: Pharmaceuticals, Transportation, Chemicals, Beverages, Wood Industries, Construction, Consumer Products, Research & Development
Portfolio Companies: Camsavon, Aldaph, Camtainer, NOBRA, CITB, SAM, Sedan, Danilait, Dilaz, El Rayan Danfarm, EPL, African Lakes Ethiopia, Muk Air, Pako Bay, Volta Arkil

Key Executives:
  Tommy Thomsen, Managing Director
  Torben Huss, Deputy Managing Director

2890 INVESTOR AB
8C Aresenalsgatan
Stockholm SE-103 32
Sweden

Phone: 46-86141800 **Fax:** 46-86141809
e-mail: info@investorab.com
web: www.investorab.com

Mission Statement: The group focuses on being an active, value-added investor in technology and healthcare companies in North America and Europe.

Geographic Preference: China, South Korea
Fund Size: $1.8 Billion
Founded: 1916
Average Investment: $26.5 Million
Minimum Investment: $0.63 Million
Investment Criteria: Expansion stage companies with customers and revenue, buy-out and co-control deals, branded consumer goods and services, manufacturing business for outsourcing and export markets
Industry Group Preference: Healthcare, Information Technology, Communications, Manufacturing
Portfolio Companies: Aerocrine, Affibody, Amkor Technology, Inc., Apollo International, Applied Sensor, Asia Renal Care Ltd, Atrica, Axcan Pharma, Biotage, Cameron Health, Cavidi Tech AB, CHF Solutions, EDT Learning, eSilicon Corporation, Excosoft, Gyros, Info Talk, JP Mobil

Key Executives:
  Jacob Wallenberg, Chairman
  e-mail: info@investorab.com
  Education: B.Sc. Economics and M.B.A., Wharton School, University of Pennsylvania
  Background: President and CEO, SEB, Head of Enskilda Division, Advisor to the President and CEO, SEB, Executive Vice President and CFO, Investor
  Henry E Gooss, Managing Director
  e-mail: info@investorab.com
  Education: M.B.A. in Investments, New York University and B.A. in Economics, Rutgers University
  Background: Director of Mainstream Data, Inc. and Telegea, Inc
  Börje Ekholm, President and CEO
  e-mail: info@investorab.com
  Education: M.Sc. in Engineering, Royal Institute of Technology, Stockholm
  Background: President, CEO and Chairman AB Electrolux, Chairman Saab-Scania AB, Member of the Board The Federation of Swedish Industries
  Sune Carlsson, Vice Chairman
  e-mail: info@investorab.com
  Education: M.Sc. in Mechanical Engineering, Chalmers University of Technology, Gothenburg
  Background: Executive Vice President, ASEA AB and ABB Ltd, President and CEO, SKF
  Susanne Ekblom, Chief Financial Officer
  e-mail: info@investorab.com
  Education: D.Sc. (Econ.), Helsinki School of Economics
  Background: Economist and Head of Office, Bank of Finland, Director General, Economics Department, Finnish Ministry of Finance
  Susanna Sjödin, Communications Officer
  e-mail: info@investorab.com
  Education: M.Sc. in Business Administration and Economics, Stockholm School of Economics, M.B.A., Massachusetts Institute of Technology
  Background: Managing Director and member of Management Group, Portfolio Manager Öhman Fondkommission
  Gunnar Brock, Director
  e-mail: info@investorab.com
  Education: Sc.D. in Applied Biochemistry, Royal Institute of Technology, Stockholm
  Background: President and CEO, AB Marabou and Astra AB

Venture Capital & Private Equity Firms / International Firms

O. Griffith Sexton, Director
e-mail: info@investorab.com
Education: M.B.A., Stanford University Graduate School of Business and B.S.E., Princeton University
Background: Advisory Director, Morgan Stanley, Managing Director, Morgan Stanley

Marcus Wallenberg, Director
e-mail: info@investorab.com
Education: M.Sc. in Engineering, Royal Institute of Technology, Stockholm and The Management Development Institute (IMEDE), Lausanne
Background: CEO and Chairman, Ericsson, CEO, SEB

2891 INVEXCEL PATRIMONIO
Claudio Coelle 78
Madrid 28001
Spain
Phone: 34-915783676 Fax: 34-914319303
e-mail: info@invexcel.com
web: www.invexcel.com

Mission Statement: Excel Partners is an active investor in all companies in which it holds a stake, supporting its shareholders and managers with all our resources and ability in the design of the most appropriate strategy to be implemented by the company.

Geographic Preference: Europe, Latin America, Iberian Peninsula
Fund Size: $100 Million
Founded: 1991
Average Investment: $30 Million
Minimum Investment: $ 2 Million
Investment Criteria: Management buy-outs, buy-ins, buy-and-build, reorganizations and spin-offs, divestments, expansions, joint-ventures
Industry Group Preference: Software, Consumer Products, Information Technology, Distribution, Industrial Services, Electronic Technology, Telecommunications, Components & IoT
Portfolio Companies: Gas Gas, PrintOne, Real Musical, Rotographik, Unitronics

Key Executives:
José María López de Letona, Partner
Ramón Menéndez de Luarca, Partner
Background: Three Cities Research Fund
Ramon Menendez de Luarca, Partner
Education: Degree in Economic Science and Business(Pontifical University of Comillas - ICADE), MBA in Industrial Management (Carnegie Mellon University; Pittsburgh, USA)
Background: Arthur D. Little, Boston Consulting Group
Directorships: Principal

2892 IP GROUP
24 Cornhill
London EC3V 3ND
United Kingdom
Phone: 44-2074440050 Fax: 44-2079296415
web: www.ipgroupplc.com

Mission Statement: IP Group is a leading UK intellectual property commercialisation company, developing technology innovations primarily from its research intensive partner universities. The Group offers far more than traditional venture capital, providing its companies with access to business building expertise, networks, recruitment and business support.

Founded: 2001
Investment Criteria: Early-Stage to Later-Stage
Industry Group Preference: Energy, Renewable Energy, Medical Devices, Pharmaceuticals, Biotechnology, Information Technology, Communications, Chemicals, Advanced Materials
Portfolio Companies: Activiomics, Actual Experience, Amaethon, Arkivum, Asalus, Avacta, Azellon, Capsant, CCapture, Ceres Power, Ch4e, Chamelic, Crysalin, Durham Graphene, DyeCat, Emdot, Empiricom, Encos, Evocutis, FrontierIP, Gusion, Getech, Glythera, Green Chemicals, Icona, Iuka, Inhibox, IQur, Karus Therapeutics, Mode Diagnositics, Modern Water, Nanotecture, Overlay Media, Oxford Advanced Surfaces, Oxford Catalysts, Nanopore, Oxford RF Sensors, Oxtox, Oxyntix, Perpetuum, Pharminax, Photopharmica, Plexus, Polar Oled, Progenteq, Proximagen, Retroscreen Virology, Revolymer, RDR, RSI, Seren, Stratophase, Structure Vision, Surrey Nanosystems, Sustainable Resource Solutions, Synairgen, Tissue Regenix, Tracsis, Xeros

Key Executives:
Alan Aubrey, Chief Executive Officer
Education: BA, Economics, University of Leeds; MBA, University of Bradford
Background: Joint Founder, Chief Executive, Techtran Group; KPMG

2893 IPBM Group IDI
18 Matignon Avenue
Paris 75008
France
Phone: 33-155-278000 Fax: 33-140170444

Mission Statement: Actively seeking new investments.

Geographic Preference: Asia, Eastern Europe
Fund Size: $396 Million
Founded: 1970
Average Investment: $9.60 Million
Minimum Investment: $1.2 Million
Investment Criteria: Small-stage and Mid-stage
Industry Group Preference: All Sectors Considered

2894 IPG GROUP
24 Cornhill
Warwick Court
London ECV3 3ND
United Kingdom
Phone: 44-02074440050 Fax: 44-02079296415
e-mail: hatt@toptechnology.co.uk
web: www.ipgroupplc.com

Mission Statement: Top Technology Ventures is a UK-based venture capital company which specialises in providing equity funding for early stage technology based growth companies.

Geographic Preference: United Kingdom
Fund Size: $74 Million
Founded: 1986
Average Investment: Euro 49 Million
Minimum Investment: $708,000
Investment Criteria: Start-up, Other early stage, Expansion and Development
Industry Group Preference: Medical & Health Related, Communications, Information Technology, Computer Hardware & Software, Internet Technology
Portfolio Companies: nCipher, Focus Solutions Group, IP2IPO Group, Wire-e Limited, Commerce Decisions Ltd, One clickHR, Metapack Ltd, Webabcus Ltd, Infoucs Health Ltd, AP Benson Ltd, ANT, Nanotecture Ltd, Arieso Ltd, Netronome Systems Ltd, Oxford Immunotec Ltd

Key Executives:
Alan Aubrey, Chief Executive Officer
Mike Townend, Chief Investment Officer

2895 IPOSCOPE NV/SA
19 Jan van Boendalelaan, Tervuren
Brussels 3080
Belgium
Phone: 32-27672500 Fax: 32-27682994
e-mail: e.hallmann@iposcope.com
web: www.iposcope.com

Mission Statement: Global advisory for high growth companies on private equity and going public regardless of the clients geographic origins.

Industry Group Preference: Information Technology, Software, Life Sciences

2896 IRDI MIDI-PYRENEES
18 Dupuy Place
BP 808
Cedex 6
Toulouse 31080
France

Phone: 33-581317320 Fax: 33-581317339
e-mail: contact@irdi.fr
web: www.irdi.fr

Mission Statement: Actively seeking new investments.

Fund Size: $66.3 Million
Minimum Investment: $36,000
Industry Group Preference: Industrial Equipment, Industrial Services

Key Executives:
Thierry Letailleur, President
Dorothée Watine, Investment Manager

2897 IRIS CAPITAL
62 rue Pierre Charron
Paris 75008
France

Phone: 33-145627373 Fax: 33-145627370
e-mail: c.micoski@iriscapital.com
web: www.iriscapital.com

Mission Statement: A pan-European venture and development capital fund specializing in media and entertainment, communications and IT.

Geographic Preference: Europe, North America, Asia
Founded: 1986
Average Investment: $1.2 Million -$24 Million
Minimum Investment: $0.6 Million
Investment Criteria: Early Stage, Expansion and Development Capital
Industry Group Preference: Communications, Media, Information Technology, Entertainment
Portfolio Companies: 1-2-3.TV, Abry, Acapela Group, Alphanim, Altitude, Altitude, American Greetings Interactive, Apach Network, Atrica, Canal Guyane, Cirpack, Cityneo, DataDirect Networks, E-Net, Editions Montparnasse, Elitel, Everbee, Exception Wild Bunch, Fast Booking

Key Executives:
Antoine Garrigues, Managing Partner
e-mail: c.blanche@iriscapital.com
Education: Institut Superieur du Commerce de Paris
Background: PricewaterhouseCoopers Luxembourg
Pierre de Fouquet, Managing Partner
e-mail: p.defouquet@iriscapital.com
Education: Graduate PhD in Economics.
Background: Strategic Planning at CDC.
Denis Barrier, Partner
e-mail: a.garrigues@iriscapital.com
Education: Graduate of the French Ecole Polytechnique and Ecole des Ponts et Chaussees engineering schools
Background: The Director of International Affairs and Development for Dassault A.T.

2898 ISIS EP LLP F & C
2nd Floor, 100 Wood Street
London EC2V 7AN
United Kingdom

Phone: 44-2075065600 Fax: 44-2075065665
e-mail: leanne.metcalfe@isisep.com

Mission Statement: Centered on helping entrepreneurial management teams achieve substantial capital gain.

Geographic Preference: United Kingdom, Germany, Netherlands
Fund Size: £1.2 Billion
Founded: 1995
Average Investment: $8.8 Million
Minimum Investment: $3.5 Million
Industry Group Preference: Business to Business, Media, Consumer Services, Technology, Financial Services, Healthcare, Education, Communications

Key Executives:
James Bagan, Operating Partner

2899 ISOURCE GESTION
23 Avenue D'Iena
Paris 75116
France

Phone: 33-0-1-4501-4646 Fax: 33-0-1-4501-4660
e-mail: info@isourcevc.com
web: www.isourcevc.com

Mission Statement: These past few years, a certain number of capital risk players, including entrepreneur funds, have reinforced the market's capacity to initiate new start-ups. As a result, young companies have emerged with force, often with promising futures. But once their first goals are accomplished i.e. finalizing a product or completing a team, these enterprises must raise consequent funds during the 1st round. It is these companies, still in the early phase of development and that require significant funds (0.5 to 5 million euros), that iSource specializes in assisting. It is this momentum that capital investment players hesitate over and which iSource believes is the best time for creating value, therefore establishing a market opportunity.

Geographic Preference: France, Western Europe
Average Investment: 0.5 to 5 million euros
Investment Criteria: Early-Stage, First Round
Industry Group Preference: Business Software, Technology, Telecommunications, Internet, Embedded Systems, Managed Services, Green Technology, Information Technology, Software
Portfolio Companies: BeamExpress, Captain Dash, Commpario, Cyanide, DarQroom, Digital Media Solutions, E-Blink, EdXact, Expway, eYeka, Fluoptics, IDS, IJenko, IMinent, Jetchange.fr, LeddarTech, Link Care Services, Metablo, Movea, Rhapso, Sequans Communicatinos, Smartesting, Total Immersion

Key Executives:
Didier Moret, Managing Partner
Education: Centrale Paris Engineering School
Directorships: Captain Dash, Compario, IDS, JeChange.fr, LeddarTech, Link Care Services, Rhapso, Smartesting

2900 ISRAEL CLEANTECH VENTURES
Hakfar Hayorok Youth Village
Ramat Hasharon 47800
Israel

Phone: 972-36446611 Fax: 972-36493737
web: www.israelcleantech.com

Mission Statement: Israel Cleantech Ventures is the leading venture capital fund focused on backing Israel's emerging clean technology companies. We are dedicated to providing value added growth capital to exceptional entrepreneurs building Israel's energy, water and environmental technology leaders. Our geographical focus and market leadership enable us to take advantage of Israel's prominence as an innovative market leader in energy, water and agricultural technologies, as well as ancillary cleantech sectors including energy efficiency, smart-grid/communications, green IT, power electronics and capital equipment.

Geographic Preference: Israel

Venture Capital & Private Equity Firms / International Firms

Founded: 2006
Industry Group Preference: Clean Technology, Energy, Water, Agriculture, Energy Efficiency, Power
Portfolio Companies: AcousticEye, Aqwise, Better Place, Cellera, Emefcy, FRX Polymers, Metrolight, Panoramic Power, Pythagoras, Scodix, Tigo Energy
Key Executives:
  Jack Levy, Partner
  Education: BA, Harvard College; JD, Columbia Law School
  Background: Vice President & General Counsel, Register.com

2901 IT VENTURES LIMITED Digital Heritage Publishing Ltd.
29 Floor, EGL Tower, 83 Hung To Road
Kwun Tong
Kowloon
Hong Kong
Phone: 852-23023011 **Fax:** 852-27308686
web: www.itventuresltd.com
Mission Statement: Actively seeking new investments.
Fund Size: $700 Million
Founded: 1995
Industry Group Preference: Information Technology
Key Executives:
  Gabriel Chi Ming Yu, Founder & Chairman

2902 IT-PARTNERS NV
105 H. Henneaulaan
Zaventem 1930
Belgium
Phone: 32-27251838 **Fax:** 32-27214435
Mission Statement: Invests in companies in the ICT sector.
Geographic Preference: Belgium, USA, Netherlands
Fund Size: $79.4 Million
Founded: 1997
Investment Criteria: Early-stage, 2nd Round, Expansion.
Industry Group Preference: Information Technology, Telecommunications, Security
Portfolio Companies: Captor N.V., Coware Inc., EDS Docdata B.V., Encore Media Systems B.V., Fillfactory N.V., Hypertrust N.V., Lenel Systems International, Inc., Septentrio N.V., Target Compiler Technologies N.V.
Key Executives:
  Paul Verdurme, Investment Manager
  e-mail: info@it-partners.be
  Education: Master degree in electronics and applied mathametics.
  Background: GTE Sylyania.
  Stefaan Nicolay, Investment Manager
  e-mail: info@it-partners.be
  Education: Master degree in electronics.
  Background: General Banking.

2903 ITC VENTURES
Centro Empresarial Mourisco
Praia de Botafogo
Cep 22250-040
Brazil
Phone: 55-2193115200
web: www.itcventures.com
Mission Statement: ITC Ventures focuses exclusively on internet related businesses in Latin America in their early stages of business models and financing
Geographic Preference: Brazil, Latin America, US, Europe
Fund Size: $200,000
Founded: 1999
Average Investment: $450,000
Minimum Investment: $700,000

Investment Criteria: Medium sized international companies
Industry Group Preference: Internet Technology, Technology, Media, Financial Services
Key Executives:
  Indio Brasileiro Guerra Neto, General Partner
  e-mail: ben@itcventures.com
  Education: Graduated from Washington University, graduate of the University of Nebraska, College of Law.
  Background: KPMG International in Santiago de Chile.
  Ben Hormel Harris, Corporate Development Officer

2904 IXORA VENTURES
Ixora Ventures Pvt. Ltd.
Suite No. 28
The Lodhi Hotel, Lodhi Road
New Delhi 110003
India
Phone: 91-1124362424
Mission Statement: Ixora's strategy follows one of sector focused investing, looking for opportunities where capital, experience and insight can release the potential of businesses and lead to significant growth. The firm attempts to grow businesses by acting as a catalyst for change and we have established clear processes to maximize the value of each member of our portfolio.
Geographic Preference: ASEAN Region, India
Investment Criteria: Seed-Stage, Early-Stage
Industry Group Preference: Technology, Healthcare, Education, Aerospace, Defense and Government
Portfolio Companies: Learnpedia, AlmaConnect, Warranty Asia
Key Executives:
  Sunder Mulchandani, General Partner
  Background: Managing Director, Argus Systems Private Limted

2905 J-SEED VENTURES INCORPORATED
Isshin Building 9F
2-11-7 Yaesu
Chuo-ku
Tokyo 104-0028
Japan
Phone: 81-345205424 **Fax:** 81-362038466
e-mail: info@j-seed.com
web: www.j-seed.com
Mission Statement: International provider of management and technology consulting services and solutions.
Geographic Preference: Worldwide
Fund Size: 52.6 Million Yen
Founded: 2000
Industry Group Preference: Management, Technology
Key Executives:
  C. Jeffrey Char, President & Chief Executive Officer

2906 JAFCO COMPANY LIMITED JAPAN
Otemachi First Square, West Tower 11F
1-5-1 Otemachi, Chiyoda-ku
Tokyo 100-0004
Japan
Phone: 81-352237536 **Fax:** 81-352237561
e-mail: info@jafco.co.jp
web: www.jafco.co.jp
Mission Statement: Focuses on venture capital and buyout investment and management of related funds
Geographic Preference: Japan, USA, Asia, Europe
Fund Size: $3 Billion
Founded: 1973
Average Investment: $3 Million
Minimum Investment: $.19 Million

Venture Capital & Private Equity Firms / International Firms

Investment Criteria: Companies with long term profitablity and sustainable growth potential.
Industry Group Preference: Electronic Technology, Software, Information Technology, Restaurants, Medical, Manufacturing, Distribution, Retailing
Key Executives:
Shinichi Fuki, President & Chief Executive Officer
e-mail: info@jafco.co.jp
Directorships: CEO
Hiroshi Yamada, Executive Managing Director

2907 JAPAN ASIA INVESTMENT COMPANY LIMITED
Seiko Takebashi-Kyodo Building
3-11 Kandanishiki-cho, Chiyoda-ku
Tokyo 101-8570
Japan
Phone: 81-335048518 Fax: 81-335048511
web: www.jaic-vc.co.jp

Mission Statement: Independent venture capital company that invests in unlisted venture companies.
Geographic Preference: Japan
Founded: 1981
Industry Group Preference: Biotechnology, Medical, Computer Hardware & Software, Medical Devices, Information Technology, Internet Technology
Portfolio Companies: Inter Co., Ltd., Tay Two Co., Ltd., Nihon Eslead Corp, PC Depot Corp, MediaPlex, Inc, Procomp Informatics, Handsman Co., Ltd, Bell-Park Co., Ltd, Taiwan Cellular Corp, Design EXchange Co., Ltd, Nihon Trim Co., Ltd, Nextware Ltd., Prime Network Inc.
Key Executives:
Toyoji Tatsuoka, President & Chief Executive Officer
Directorships: CEO
Yoshiki Sasaki, Senior Managing Directors

2908 JAVELIN INVESTMENTS
Guang Cheng Yuan, Building 16, Suite 21A
Haidian District
Beijing 100088
China
Phone: 86-1062381066 Fax: 86-1062355459

Mission Statement: Full service investment company that invests in high-growth private sector companies in China.
Geographic Preference: China, Beijing, Shanghai, Dallas, Hong Kong
Average Investment: $5.5 Million
Minimum Investment: $1 Million
Investment Criteria: High-technology start-up companies and foreign investors including investment banks, private equity funds, venture capital companies.
Industry Group Preference: Wireless Technologies, Electronic Technology, Information Technology, Computer Related, Biotechnology, Industrial Equipment, Petrochemicals, Food & Beverage, Packaging, Consumer Products, Automotive, Telecommunications, Chemicals

2909 JC TECHNOLOGIES LTD
21 Havaad Haleumi Street
PO Box 16031
Jerusalem 91160
Israel
Phone: 972-2751123 Fax: 972-2751195

Mission Statement: Cultivates promising technology-based businesses by providing excellent conditions for business success.
Geographic Preference: Jerusalem
Industry Group Preference: Optical Technology, Microelectronics, Medical, Instrumentation, Electronic Technology, Software, Applied Mathematics

2910 JERUSALEM VENTURE PARTNERS
24 Hebron Road
Jerusalem 93542
Israel
Phone: 972-26409000 Fax: 972-26409001
e-mail: info@jvpvc.com
web: www.jvpvc.com

Mission Statement: Venture capital fund with a unique international network; focuses on building technology-based market leaders in the areas of enterprise software and media technologies, semiconductors and innovative materials and communications and networking.
Geographic Preference: North America, Europe, Israel and Asia
Fund Size: $680 Million
Founded: 1993
Investment Criteria: Early-stage technology companies in the Enterprise Software & Media Technologies, Semiconductors & Innovative Materials and Communications & Networking sectors.
Industry Group Preference: Components & IoT, Innovative Products & Services, Enterprise Services, Media, Communications, Networking, Semiconductors, Software
Portfolio Companies: Celltick Software Technologies, Chromatis Networks, Cogent Communications, ComSong Interactive Technologies, CyOptics, First Access, Fundtech, Geophysical, InLight Communications, Kerenix, Macada, MysticCom, Native Networks, Netro Corporation, Nuvisio
Key Executives:
Erel N. Margalit, Founder & Managing Partner
e-mail: info@jvpvc.com
Education: MBA from Columbia Business School, BS from Tel Aviv University.
Background: McKinsey & Company in London.
Gadi Tirosh, General Partner
Haim Kopans, Partner and CTO
e-mail: info@jvpvc.com
Education: BS in International Economics and Finance from Georgetown University.
Background: JVP's Israel office in 1996 as an analyst, President of the Stern Group.
Kobi Rozengarten, General Partner
Education: BS in Electrical Engineering from University of Cape Town, MBA from INSEAD.
Background: GE Capital in London, MAC Consulting Group.

2911 JTP CORPORATION
1-30-20, Kaminoge, Setagaya-ku
Yoga, Setagaya-ku
Tokyo 158-0097
Japan
Phone: 81-364322337 Fax: 81-364322338
e-mail: jtmerge@gmail.com
web: www.transaction.co.jp

Mission Statement: Advisors specializing in complex transactions: mergers and acquisitions, spin-offs, strategic alliances, and joint ventures.
Geographic Preference: Japan
Key Executives:
Nicholas E Benes, Founder & President
e-mail: nbenes@transaction.co.jp
Education: BA in Political Science from Stanford University, MBA and law degree (JD) from UCLA.
Background: Senior Managing Director in The Kamakura Corporation, Vice President at JP Morgan.

Venture Capital & Private Equity Firms / International Firms

2912 JUMPSEED VENTURES
PICO Jerusalem
2 Poalei Tzedek
4th Fllor
Talpiot, Jerusalem
Israel

Mission Statement: If a portfolio company wants us to take a more active, day-to-day role, we are available to work hand in hand with the founder(s), executing the company's business development and marketing strategy as active members of the team. Portfolio companies can, but are not required to, choose from a range of levels of hands-on support.

Geographic Preference: Israel
Average Investment: $50,000 - $150,000
Investment Criteria: Early-Stage
Industry Group Preference: Internet

Key Executives:
Ben Wiener, Managing Partner
Education: BA, Economics, Yeshiva University; JD, Columbia Law School
Background: Vice President, IDT Corp.; Corporate Lawyer; Clerk, Israel Supreme Court

2913 JUNGLE VENTURES
306 Tanglin Road
Phoenix Park Office Campus
247973
Singapore

Phone: 65-64239516 Fax: 65-64239516
e-mail: amit@jungle-ventures.com
web: www.jungle-ventures.com

Mission Statement: Jungle Ventures is a SIngapore native global venture capital firm that provides early stage investments and business building infrastructure to startups.

Geographic Preference: Singapore, India, South East Asia
Investment Criteria: Early-Stage
Portfolio Companies: Cinemacraft, Doc Doc, eBus.TV, Ekstop.com, Mobikon, One Animation, Sconce Solutions, Travelmob

Key Executives:
Peng T Ong, Fund Advisor
Background: Partner, GSR Ventures; President, Interwoven
Directorships: Singapore Telecommunications

2914 KAEDAN INVESTMENTS
6 Wallenberg Street
PO Box 13169
Ramat Hachayal
Tel Aviv 61131
Israel

Phone: 972-77-234-8890 Fax: 972-77-234-8880
e-mail: contact@kaedan.com
web: www.kaedan.com

Mission Statement: Kaedan Capital is a private investment firm engaged in seed to early stage ventures in focus areas of Internet, Mobile applications & services, Digital Media, On Demand Software (Saas), and Digital Marketing & Advertising. We view active investment involvement as our guideline in creating value. Therefore, one of Kaedan's team members, with the required skill set and ability to add value to the specific investment, will assume an active role in the invested company's board. Our strategy and motivation are well aligned with those of the entrepreneurs in which we invest, exemplified by taking a long investment horizon and participating in follow on investments when needed.

Geographic Preference: Israel
Investment Criteria: Early-Stage
Industry Group Preference: Internet, Mobile Apps, Digital Media & Marketing, Software, SaaS, Digital Marketing, Advertising, Consumer Products

Portfolio Companies: Playtika, 5minMedia, Tvinci, Somoto, Jelly Button, Bizzabo, Visualead, JoyTunes, Adience, Flayvr, Baligam, ONE, WhiteSmoke, YCD Multimedia, Mobile 1

Key Executives:
Yair Hamburger, Chairman
Education: BA, Economics & Social Sciences, Hebrew University
Background: Chairman, Harel Insurance Investments
Ron Tamir, Founder/Managing Partner
Education: LLB, Tel Aviv University; MBA, Kellogg School of Management
Directorships: Tvinci, Citynet
Ofer Lazovski, Director
Education: BSc, Computer Science, Technion
Background: Co-Founder, 888.com
Directorships: 5min
Ziv Yanous, Director
Background: Founder, Hydepark.co.il; Founding Team, eToro

2915 KALORI GROUP INVESTMENTS
131 Macquarie Street
Level 14
Sydney 2000
Australia

Phone: 61293864646 Fax: 61-29-386-4420
e-mail: cwitt@kalorigroup.com

Mission Statement: Develops and invests in young technology-intensive businesses. A single dedicated team takes a project from inception to implementation.

Founded: 1998
Investment Criteria: Early Stage
Industry Group Preference: Technology, Information Technology, Telecommunications, Software, Internet Technology, Medical Devices, Infrastructure, Retail, Consumer & Leisure, Oil & Gas, Fashion, Hospitality, Medical Technology
Portfolio Companies: Health Communications Network Limited

Key Executives:
Christopher Witt, Partner
e-mail: cwitt@kalorigroup.com
Education: BS Industrial Engineering/Economics, Northwestern University; MBA, Kellogg Graduate School of Management
Background: GM Radio Producst Group, Motorola; Telstra; Ameritech Corp; Professor, DePaul University
David Wright, Partner

2916 KARDAN LTD
154 Menachem Begin Road
Tel Aviv Yafo 64921
Israel

Phone: 972-36083444 Fax: 972-36083434
e-mail: info@kardan.nl
web: www.kardan.com

Key Executives:
Peter Sheldon, Chairman
Background: Israeli Defense Forces
Directorships: Tahal, Aeronautics Defense Systems

2917 KBL FOUNDER SA
2, boulevard Emmanuel Servais
L-2535
Luxembourg

Phone: 325-4730251 Fax: 352-479-773900
e-mail: luxembourg@puilaetco.com
web: www.kbl.lu

Mission Statement: Actively seeking new investments
Geographic Preference: Europe, Germany
Fund Size: $30 Billion

Venture Capital & Private Equity Firms / International Firms

Founded: 1949
Investment Criteria: Start-up, Expansion and Development
Industry Group Preference: Biotechnology, Communications, Computer Related, Software, Electronic Technology, Energy, Medical & Health Related
Key Executives:
  Jan Huyghebaert, Chairman
  e-mail: info@kbl-bank.com
  Education: Degree in Accounting and Fiscal studies and post graduate degree in computer.
  Background: CEO of Krefima NV and Concentra NV.
  George Nasra, Vice-Chairman
  e-mail: info@kbl-bank.com
  Education: Degree in Civil Engineering from University of Louvania, and MBA from University of Chicago.
  Background: Generale Bank,

2918 KERNEL CAPITAL
Rubicon Centre
Rossa Avenue
Bishoptown
Cork
Ireland
  Phone: 353-0214928974
  e-mail: boi_seedfund@kernelcapital.ie
  web: www.kernelcapital.ie

Mission Statement: Kernel Capital is one of Ireland's largest and most active venture capital funds. The firm has a portfolio of investee companies across, technology, life science and general industry.

Founded: 2002
Average Investment: 100,000 - 5 million Euro
Industry Group Preference: Technology, Life Sciences
Portfolio Companies: AES, AGI, Alimentary Health, BioAtlantis, Biocroi, Biosensia, Brightwork, ChipSensors, Crescent Diagnostics, DecaWave, Deerac Fluidics, Diabetica, Ely Medical Group, Farran Technology, Feedhenry, H2HCare, Hybrid Energy, Ikon Semiconductor, InishTech, Intune Networks, Medicom Medical, Merrion, Mini Storage Self Storage Center, MPStor, NeoSurgical, Nova Science, Novate, Opsona Therapeutics, Quanta Fluid Solutions, Qumas, Radisens Diagnostics, Resourcekraft, Service Frame, Smart Telecom, Sonru, Straatum, Stokes Bio, Teamer, Wavebreak Media, Xention, Zolk
Key Executives:
  Ger Goold, Partner
  Education: BComm, University College Cork
  Background: KPMG

2919 KFW-BANKENGRUPPE
5-9 Palmengartenstasse
Frankfurt 60325
Germany
  Phone: 49-6974310 **Fax:** 49- 6974312944
  e-mail: info@kfw.de
  web: www.kfw.de

Mission Statement: Focuses on improving the economy, society and ecology in Germany, Europe and the world over.
Geographic Preference: Worldwide
Fund Size: $395 Billion
Founded: 1948
Investment Criteria: SMEs, in home finance or housing modernization.
Key Executives:
  Günther Bräunig, Managing Director
  e-mail: peter.fleischer@kfw.de
  Education: Studies in Economics at the University of Münster; 1981 Doctorate in political science
  Background: Chairman of the Managing Board of DtA
  Dr Ulrich Schröder, Chief Executive Officer (CEO)
  e-mail: hans.riech@kfw.de
  Education: Bank training, Graduation form Bankfachwirt

  Background: Credit Secretariat of Dresdner Bank AG, Export Finance Department of KfW, Chief Export Finance Department, Special Export Finance Department.

2920 KIBO VENTURES
Suero de Qunones, 34-36
3 planta
Madrid 28002
Spain
  e-mail: info@kiboventures.com
  web: www.kiboventures.com

Mission Statement: Kibo Ventures invest in exceptional digital companies led by great teams and entrepreneurs. We invest in their earlier stages and look for exponential growth.
Average Investment: 250,000 - 750,000 Euro
Investment Criteria: Early-Stage
Industry Group Preference: E-Commerce & Manufacturing, Internet, Digital Media & Marketing
Portfolio Companies: PromocionesFarma.com, Nonabox, Ludei, Mimub, Blink, Jobandtalent, Stop&Walk, SinDelantal.com, Mediasmart, Visualnet, Super Truper, Smarty Content, Colingo, Ducksboard
Key Executives:
  Aquilino Pena, Founding Partner
  Education: MBA, Harvard Business School; Law & Business Administration, ICADE
  Background: CEO, MediaEdge
  Directorships: BaseKit, Acierto, Matrix, Bodeboca, PayCo, Virtual Contenidos, Alice

2921 KIZOO TECHNOLOGY CAPITAL
Amaliebadstrasse 41
Karlsruhe D-76227
Germany
  e-mail: ventures@kizoo.com
  web: www.kizoo.com

Mission Statement: KIZOO helps young start-up teams grow. We provide seed and early stage financing with a focus on SaaS, Internet & Mobile Services and Social Applications. Apart from our financial resources, we are happy to share our longtime experience in development, marketing and product management in those markets.
Investment Criteria: Early-Stage
Industry Group Preference: SaaS, Internet, Mobile, Social Applications
Portfolio Companies: Hijoki, Takyca, Mambu, Babbel, Umbono, Reposito, MegaZebra, Keebitz, Advertory, CatchApp
Key Executives:
  Michael Greve, Managing Partner
  Background: Founder, Flug.de; Founder, Lastminute.de
  Matthias Hornberger, Chief Financial Officer

2922 KK RESEARCH/KK SWISS VALUE INVESTOR
Forsterstreet 30
CH-8044
Zurich CH-8044
Switzerland
  Phone: 41-12679020 **Fax:** 41-1-267-9025
  e-mail: kern@kkresearch.com
  web: www.kkresearch.com

Mission Statement: Invests in a limited number of companies with above average prospects for long term growth.
Geographic Preference: Switzerland
Founded: 1986
Investment Criteria: Small - Medium sized companies
Industry Group Preference: All Sectors Considered
Portfolio Companies: Advanced Digital Broadcast, Also, Amazys, Arpida, Ascom, Austriamicrosystems, Barry Callebaut, Batigroup, Berna Biotech, Charles Voegele,

Venture Capital & Private Equity Firms / International Firms

Clariant, Converium, Dottikon, Dufry, Ems Chemie, Esmertec, Interroll, Mobimo, Oridion, OZ Holding, Panalpina, Quadrant, Saia Burgess, Saurer, Speedel, Wachstum, Winterthur Technologie

2923 KLEINWORT CAPITAL LIMITED
10 Slingsby Place
St. Martin's Courtyard
London WC2E 9AB
United Kingdom

Phone: 44-02076328200 Fax: 44-02076328201
web: www.augustequity.com

Mission Statement: Kleinwort Benson Development Capital leads private equity investments in medium sized growth companies.
Geographic Preference: United Kingdom, Ireland, Continental Europe
Fund Size: $402 Million
Founded: 1980
Average Investment: $ 17 Million
Minimum Investment: $ 8.85 Million
Investment Criteria: Expansion and Development, Refinancing Bank Department, Secondry Purchase/Replacement Capital, MBO, MBI, Medium sized companies
Industry Group Preference: Media, Manufacturing, Healthcare, Technology, Media
Portfolio Companies: Sona Group, Intermad, Discovery Group, Video Arts, Hat Tricks Group, Kangol, Rayner Foods, Hale Hamilton, Securistyle, Vivista Holdings
Key Executives:
  Richard Green, Chairman
  e-mail: richard.green@Dresdner-bank.com
  Background: the Chairman of the British Venture Capital Association.
  Directorships: Octopus Publishing Group, Tractiv, Hale Hamilton
  Ian Grant, Partner
  e-mail: andrew.hartley@Dresdner-bank.com
  Education: MBA, City University Business School
  Background: Worked in a finance company as a credit analyst, Kleinwort Benson Development Capital in 1995
  Directorships: Eye Clinic, Kangel, TBP Group, Octopus Publishing Group
  Aatif Hassan, Partner
  e-mail: anoosha.livani@Dresdner-bank.com
  Education: BA Arabic and Middle Eastern Studies, Durham University
  Background: Marketing Assistant, American Express
  Tim Clarke, Partner
  e-mail: tim.clarke@Dresdner-bank.com
  Education: BA Economics, University of Kent; Member, The Institute of Chartered Accountants in England and Wales
  Background: Merchant bank, Kleinwort Benson

2924 KOREA FIRST VENTURE CAPITAL CORPORATION
8F, Shinil bldg., 64-5 2ka, Chungmu-ro, Chung
Seoul 100-012
Korea

Phone: 82-27757302 Fax: 82-27757305
web: www.kfvc.co.kr

Mission Statement: Invests in core potential venture capital companies in all stages.
Geographic Preference: China, USA
Fund Size: $48 Million
Founded: 1990
Investment Criteria: Core Potential Venture Companies
Industry Group Preference: Information Technology, Environmental Protection, Manufacturing, Semiconductors, Internet Technology, Electronic Technology

Portfolio Companies: Hunger Computer, Natia, UBK, Sewon Telecom, Gold Bank Communications, Goldbook, Netian, Darks Club, Mimoatec Co. Ltd, Bit Computer, Moatech, Ed Laboratory, Humax, CTI Semiconductor, M.K Electron Co. Ltd, Prochips Inc., E&B Technology Co., GenoProt Ltd
Key Executives:
  Joong-Hyun Shin, chairman
  Young-Pan Hur, President & Chief Executive Officer

2925 KOREA INVESTMENT CORPORATION
100 State Tower Namsan-dong, Jung-gu
17, 18 toegyero floor
Seoul 100-768
South Korea

Phone: 82-221791000 Fax: 82-221-791065
e-mail: info_kic@kic.go.kr
web: www.kic.go.kr

Founded: 1986
Key Executives:
  Serck-Joo Hong, President & Chief Executive Officer
  Je Yeong Park, Chief Operating Officer

2926 KOREA TECHNOLOGY & BANKING (KTB) NETWORK CORP
Securities Building
23-3 Yeongdeungpo-gu
Seoul 150-709
South Korea

Phone: 82-0234662000 Fax: 82-0221842050
e-mail: webmaster@ktb.co.kr
web: www.ktb.co.kr

Mission Statement: KTBnetwork provides clients with financial support through direct capital investments plus a variety of services to help maximize corporate value.
Geographic Preference: China, Taiwan, South Korea, India, Southeast Asia
Fund Size: $230 Million
Founded: 1981
Average Investment: $30 Million
Investment Criteria: From startups to SMEs, MBOs or LBOs
Industry Group Preference: Aerospace, Defense and Government, Wireless Technologies, Broadband
Portfolio Companies: Airespace, Inc., Berkana Wireless, Inc., BitFone, GPE II LP., Inphi Corporation, Novera Optics, OnePath Networks, Polaris Networks, Terawave Communications
Key Executives:
  Won Ju, Chairman
  e-mail: webmaster@ktb.co.kr
  Education: Yonsei University, Business Administration, BA , University of Missouri, MBA
  Background: CEO, Korea M&A Corporation, CEO, The Will-bes Co. (formerly Kunja Industrials Co.)
  Han-Sup Kim, President & Chief Executive Officer

2927 KUBOTA CORPORATION
1-2-47 Shikitsu-higashi, Naniwa-ku
Osaka 556-8601
Japan

Phone: 06-6648-2111 Fax: 06-6648-3862
web: www.kubota.co.jp

Fund Size: $ 6.8 Billion
Founded: 1890
Industry Group Preference: Agriculture, Cement Roofing, Metals, Construction
Portfolio Companies: Mycogen

Venture Capital & Private Equity Firms / International Firms

Key Executives:
Ekihon Yasuo, Chairman of the Board and Chief Executive Officer
Tetsuji Tomita, Representative Director and Executive Vice President

2928 LAKESTAR
Zurich
Switzerland

web: www.lakestar.com

Mission Statement: A venture capital firm that invests in outstanding entrepreneurs worldwide.
Portfolio Companies: Skype, Spotify, Klarna, Facebook, Airbnb, KupiVIP, Markafoni, Algomi Ltd., Harry's, Angie's List, Maker Studios, Confide, GoEuro, Taulia, Lookback, Teralytics, Nu3
Key Executives:
Klaus Hommels, Founder
Education: PhD Finance, University of Fribourg; MBA University of Fribourg
Background: Venture Partner, Benchmark Capital; Freenet

2929 LANDSBANKI VENTURES
Austurstraeti 11
Reykjavik 155
Iceland

Phone: 354-410-4000
e-mail: info@landsbanki.is
web: www.landsbankinn.com

Mission Statement: Actively seeking new investments.
Geographic Preference: Europe, North America, Iceland, Scandinavia
Fund Size: $11.75 Billion
Minimum Investment: $100,000
Investment Criteria: Expansion and Development Capital, Mezzanine, Buyout and Buyin
Industry Group Preference: Communications, Computer Related, Industrial Equipment, Industrial Services, High Technology, Computer Related, Software
Key Executives:
Bjorn Sigurdsson, Correspondent Banking
Sigurður Erlingsson, Correspondent Banking

2930 LANTA DIGITAL VENTURES
Barcelona
Spain

e-mail: investors@lantacapital.com
web: www.lantacapital.com

Mission Statement: Lanta Digital Ventures is a Barcelona-based early stage venture capital fund focused in investing in innovative Spanish and European Startups with high potential growth.
Geographic Preference: Spain, Europe
Founded: 2015
Average Investment: 300,000 EUR
Investment Criteria: Seed, Early Stage
Industry Group Preference: Digital Media & Marketing, Mobile, Internet
Key Executives:
Angel Garcia, Founding Partner
Education: MBA, Stanford University

2931 LAUNCHPAD VENTURES
Knowledge House
6, Kasturirangan Road, Alwarpet
Chennai
Chennai 600 018
India

Phone: 91-44-3912-3456
web: www.launchpadventures.com

Mission Statement: Launchpad Ventures seeks to partner with entrepreneurs to build admirable companies and looks forward to a facilitating role in companies we invest in. We are not afraid of investing in pre-revenue companies and often provide a company's first outside capital. Though we are primarily seed-stage investors, we also engage with companies which are currently not realizing their full value potential. As a group, we are well connected with potential customers, service providers, partners and future sources of funding. Our members come from a variety of backgrounds and profiles, including former bureaucrats, technology experts, finance and other domain experts.
Founded: 2004
Investment Criteria: Early-Stage
Industry Group Preference: Energy, Technology, Food & Beverage, Education, Marketing
Portfolio Companies: I-Food Chains, Launchpad Global Consulting, Language Labs, DTX Studios, Uniq Investigation & Security Services
Key Executives:
Sriram Venkatasubramanian, Founder
Background: HCL, EAP Global

2932 LBBW VENTURE CAPITAL
King street
10C
Stuttgart D-70173
Germany

Phone: 49-71130589200 Fax: 49-711305892099
web: www.lbbw-venture.de

Mission Statement: We see ourselves as a partner who provides the economic framework for the growth of promising ideas and business models. Moreover, we stand with our extensive network and a lot of technical know-how at any time to advise you.
Investment Criteria: Startup, Expansion-Stage, Pre-IPO
Industry Group Preference: Information Technology, Software, Telecommunications, Innovative Products & Services, Life Sciences
Portfolio Companies: Biametrics, Bubbles & Beyond, CargoGuard, CheckMobile, Conceptboard, CorTec, Crealytics, Fludicon, Oxid Esales, Phenex Pharmaceuticals, Technolas,

2933 LBO FRANCE
148 University Street
Paris 75007
France

Phone: 33-140627767 Fax: 33-140627555
e-mail: radia.guria@lbofrance.com
web: www.lbofrance.com

Mission Statement: Seeks out leveraged buyout transactions in which it can acquire a majority stake.
Geographic Preference: France
Fund Size: 1 Billion Euros
Founded: 1985
Average Investment: 10 Million - 2, 500 Million Euros
Minimum Investment: Negotiable
Investment Criteria: Market leaders with growth potential, Subsidiaries of major groups or family-owned companies
Industry Group Preference: All Sectors Considered
Key Executives:
Robert Daussun, Président
e-mail: elizabeth.oreilly@lbofrance.com
Education: MA economics HEC
Background: Worked for four years at Arthur Anderson
Pascal Oddo, Chairman of the Supervisory Board
e-mail: elizabeth.oreilly@lbofrance.com
Education: Engineering degree Telecom paris, DESS postgraduate degree in bussiness and tax law
Background: specialized in M&A and Taxation at international law firm freshfields.

Venture Capital & Private Equity Firms / International Firms

2934 LEAD ANGELS
A-102, Neelam Center
S K Ahire Marg, Worli
Mumbai 400030
India

Phone: 022 65660023
e-mail: info@leadangels.in
web: www.leadangels.in

Mission Statement: The founding team at Lead Angels originally from IIT Bombay and its members include entrepreneurs who have built successful companies, angel investors who have invested in multiple startups, academics who have nurtured innovation and entrepreneurship and consultants who have been advisors to high growth companies.

Geographic Preference: India
Investment Criteria: Seed-Stage, Early-Stage

Key Executives:
Atul Pradhan, Director
Background: Founder, Transfolign Consulting; KPMG India; Managing Partner, KPMG Consulting

2935 LEGAL AND GENERAL VENTURES LIMITED
One Coleman Street
London EC2R 5AA
United Kingdom

Phone: 44-2031242900 Fax: 44-2031242546
e-mail: enquiries@ventures.landg.com

Mission Statement: LGV is a well established provider of private equity in the UK and has professionally managed funds on behalf of external investors.

Geographic Preference: United Kingdom, Ireland
Fund Size: $325 Million
Founded: 1986
Average Investment: $1.6 Billion
Minimum Investment: $ 35.4 Million
Investment Criteria: Expansion, MBO, Management Buy-In, Secondary Purchase, Replacement Capital, Infrastructure Project Financing
Industry Group Preference: Communications, Consumer Services, Industrial Equipment, Food & Beverage, Medical & Health Related, Consumer Products
Portfolio Companies: Air Energi, Novus Leisure, ABI, Amber Taverns, Snow+Rock, The Liberation Group, South Lakeland Parks, IDH, Classic Hospitals, Verna Group, Tragus, Kingfield Health, Club Company, LGC, Vue Cinemas, Jeyes, Unique Pub Company, Craegmoor, Bourne Leisure

Key Executives:
Zoe Clements, Director
James Dawes, Finance Director
e-mail: enquiries@ventures.landg.com
Education: Qualified as a Chartered Accountant
Background: 3i plc, where he spent six years, specialising in venture capital and project finance
Michael Mowlem, Managing Director
e-mail: enquiries@ventures.landg.com
Background: Hambros Bank-corporate finance division

2936 LEGEND CAPITAL
10F, Tower A
Reycom Infotech Park
No. 2 Kexueyuan South Road, Zhongguancun
Haidian District, Beijing 100190
China

Phone: 86-10-6250-8000 Fax: 86-10-6250-9100
e-mail: master@legendcapital.com.cn

Mission Statement: The core business of Legend Capital is early-stage Venture Capital and expansion-stage Growth Capital investment.

Investment Criteria: Early-Stage, Expansion Stage

Industry Group Preference: Healthcare, Clean Technology, Advanced Manufacturing, Consumer Products
Portfolio Companies: ASP, AutoNavi, Auto Radio, Access Medical, Berkana, Boloni, BitAuto, Bonck Education, Beauty in Fashion, BOC International Limited, Bonovo, Berrygenomics, BYJC, Chongqing Broadband, Covics, China SpeedNet, Chipsbank, China Search, CDIM, Cub Digital, Crystal CG, Chongqing New Standard, Cybrid, Careray, Car King, CCID, Calsys, ChinaInvent, Digital China Jinxin, Dianji, Dooland, Urachip, DENOVO, Eyang Holdings, Eedoo, Evercare, Evergreen Group, Fullhan, Fengkai Machinery, Ftuan, Golden Eye, BGE, HolyTax, Hiconics, Happy Elements, Huicheng Pectechnology, Hichain, HDR, iFLYTEK, ITS, innogreen, Oyo, Jolimark Holdings, Kaitone, Kawin Technology, Lakala, Life Express, Live By Touch, Luxin Evotech, Leepet, Linglong Tire, Lihua Group, LocoJoy, McAobao, Amcare, Mosh, Minsheng Energy, MobCrete, New Vision, Norel Systems, New China Life, Nouriz, Oak Pacific Interactive, Pod Inn, OPDA, Photonic Bridges, Precom, Phylion Battery, Power Genius, Parade, Pharmaron, PEAK Sports, PPA, PBA, Rock Mobile, Renren, Reach Surgical, Rye Studio, RenRui, Spreadtrum, Shanghai Huahong, Surekam, Sinocom, 7234, Sling Media, SolarFun, Sunshine Paper, Saturday Shoes, Sihe Wood, Sate Auto, ShopEx, Shenzhen Yuton, Suzhou Anjie Technology, Selavo Machinery, 16fun, Sportica, 7Gege, Tianya, Tengchuang, 21cake, Tianji New Materials, Tanyuan Tech, TeChen, Tongbanjie, Universe Media, Universal Education, Unicell, UStar, VanceInfo, VeriSilicon, Virtuos, Viscap, Wep, Watch Data, Weiyun, Wuxi Lead Auto Equipment, Wuhan B

Key Executives:
Zhu Linan, Founder/CEO
Education: MSEE, Shanghai Jiaotong University
Background: General Manager, Shenzhen Legend Computer
Directorships: Saturday Shoes, Peak Sports

2937 LEONIA MB GROUP/MB FUNDS
1 Boulvarde A
Helsinki 00100
Finland

Phone: 358-9131011 Fax: 358-913101310
web: www.mbfunds.fi

Mission Statement: Invests in buy-outs and privatizations to build transactions and expansion capital.

Geographic Preference: US
Fund Size: $240 Million
Founded: 1992
Average Investment: $132 Million
Minimum Investment: $28 Million
Investment Criteria: Expansion, Buyout, Bridge, Buy-outs, Privatizations, buy and build transactions and expansion capital.
Industry Group Preference: Machinery, Technology, Confectionery, Healthcare, Electronic Technology, Plastics, Components & IoT
Portfolio Companies: Makua Foods Oy, Parmaco Oy, Suomen Transval Oy

Key Executives:
Juhani Suomela, Chairman of the board
e-mail: juhani.suomela@leonia.fi
Education: MSc Econ
Background: Vice President of the Mortgage Bank of Finland Ltd and President of MB Corporate Bank
Directorships: President
Matti Mertsola, Partner
e-mail: matti.mertsola@leonia.fi
Education: Msc, Tech, CEFA
Background: Director at MB Corporate Bank

Venture Capital & Private Equity Firms / International Firms

2938 LETA CAPITAL
Derebenevskaya Naberezhnaya 7
Building 9
Moscow 115114
Russia

Phone: 7(495)-797-26-94
e-mail: info@leta.vc

Mission Statement: We believe that enthusiastic entrepreneurs are able to present the world with new values. The aim of our fund is to support innovative IT startup companies at their seed or early growth stage.

Minimum Investment: $400,000
Investment Criteria: Seed, Early Growth
Industry Group Preference: Information Technology
Portfolio Companies: Wakie, MSU Business Incubator, Displair, RedHelper, Hamstersoft, rollApp, RoboCV, Geeklist, iBinom, 365Scores, bright box

Key Executives:
Sergey Toporov, Principal
e-mail: stoporov@leta.ru
Education: Ural State University
Alex Chachava, Managing Partner
e-mail: alex@leta.ru
Education: Moscow National University

2939 LIFE SCIENCES PARTNERS BV
Johannes Vermeerplein 9
Amsterdam 1071 DV
Netherlands

Phone: 31-206645500 Fax: 31-206768810
web: www.lspvc.com

Mission Statement: A leading European venture capital fund, providing private equity capital to early stage life sciences companies.

Geographic Preference: Netherlands, Europe, America
Fund Size: $204 Million
Founded: 1996
Average Investment: $87 Million
Minimum Investment: $500,000
Investment Criteria: Early Stage, Expansion and Development Capital, Startup
Industry Group Preference: Life Sciences, Medical & Health Related, IT Services, Industrial Services, Food & Beverage, Bio Materials
Portfolio Companies: Illuminoss, Ventaleon, Rotation Medical, Atlas Genetics, Mint Solutions, Mendor, Merus, Sequana Medical, Curetis, Harvest Automation, Cobalt, IBI Biosensors, Seahorse Bioscience, ActoGeniX, Pronota, EyeSense, Vitromics, ISTO, Kiadis Pharma

Key Executives:
Martijn Kleijwegt, managing partner
e-mail: rkuijten@lspvc.com
Education: MBA degree from INSEAD in Fontainebleau, France., PhD studies at the University of Pennsylvania in the area of oncology,
Background: Worked at McKinsey & Company for eight years as a senior consultant and co-leader of the European Pharmaceuticals and Health Care Practice.
Directorships: he directed multiple teams of client executives on strategic and organizational assignments in Amsterdam, Brussels and Zurich
René Kuijten, general partner
e-mail: mkleijwegt@lspvc.com
Education: Masters degree in economics at Amsterdam University.
Background: He has gained extensive experience in all aspects of biotech venture capital. On behalf of LSP, Martijn served on the supervisory board of Crucell (NL)
Directorships: He served on the supervisory board of, amongst others, Rhein Biotech (G, NL), Qiagen (G) and Quadrant (UK). In 1998, Martijn co-founded the first Life Sciences Partners fund,
Joachim Rothe, Managing Partner
e-mail: jrothe@lspvc.com
Education: Masters degree in Biochemistry from the Free University in Berlin, and he earned his PhD degree from the University of Freiburg in Germany
Background: Was at McKinsey & Company where he worked as an engagement manager on assignments in the chemical and pharmaceutical industries
Directorships: as a scientist with Hoffmann-La Roche in Basel, Switzerland, and at the Imperial Cancer Research Fund in London, Joachim focused on molecular immunology and genomics.
Fouad Azzam, Partner
e-mail: tschwarz@lspvc.com
Education: Masters degree in pharmacy from the University of Utrecht.
Background: Interpharm, one of the largest pharmaceutical wholesalers in the Netherlands
Directorships: Tom played an important role at the start of BioPartner, a Dutch government agency supporting starting biotech companies in the Netherlands, and participated in the superviso
John de Koning, Partner
e-mail: mwegter@lspvc.com
Education: Masters degree in business economics from the Erasmus University of Rotterdam.
Background: ING Barings Investment Banking in Amsterdam and São Paulo, where he worked as a senior analyst on Global Risk Management
Directorships: served as the assistant to a member of the executive committee, with worldwide responsibility for risk management.

2940 LIFE.SREDA
Varshavskoye Shosse, 9-1 B
Moscow
Russia

web: www.lifesreda.com

Mission Statement: Life.SREDA is a venture capital firm focusing on mobile and online fintech startups.

Investment Criteria: Any Stage
Industry Group Preference: Finanical Mobile, Internet Applications and Services
Portfolio Companies: SumUp, Scorista, Settle, Anthemis Gropu, Fidor Russia, Simple, Instabank, LifePAD, LifePay, Moven, My-Apps, MyWishBoard,

Key Executives:
Vladislav Solodkiy, CEO, Managing Partner
Alexander Ivanov, CFO, Partner

2941 LINK TECHNOLOGIES LIMITED
3 Mallard Way
Strathclyde Business Park
Bellshill ML4 3BF
Scotland

Phone: 44-1698849911 Fax: 44-1698849922
web: www.linktech.co.uk

Mission Statement: To provide the unique link between scientists working in biological research, and the chemical tools and technologies that they require.

Geographic Preference: Scotland
Founded: 1989
Investment Criteria: All Stages
Industry Group Preference: Pharmaceuticals, Biotechnology, Global Industries, Diagnostics, Life Sciences

Key Executives:
Michael J. McLean, Ph.D., , Chairman
e-mail: support@linktech.co.uk
Background: Investment executive in the venture capital industryt
Dr Mike Gray, Managing Director

Venture Capital & Private Equity Firms / International Firms

2942 LION SELECTION GROUP LIMITED
Level 4/15 Queen Street
Melbourne 3000
Australia

Phone: 61-396148008 Fax: 61-396148009
web: www.lionselection.com.au

Mission Statement: Lion Selection Group Limited is a publicly listed resource investment company, providing patient equity capital to carefully selected Small and Medium Enterprises (SME's).
Geographic Preference: Australia, Africa, South East Asia
Fund Size: $100 Million
Founded: 1997
Average Investment: $12.5 Million
Minimum Investment: $5 Million
Investment Criteria: Small and Medium Enterprises
Industry Group Preference: Mining
Portfolio Companies: Doray Minerals, Rum Jungle Resources, Auricup Resources, Roxgold, Toro Gold, Kasbah Resources, One Asia Resources, Asian Mineral Resources, Sihayo Gold, Manas Resources

Key Executives:
 Peter Maloney, Chairman
 e-mail: lionselection@lsg.com.au
 Education: BComm, MBA (Roch)
 Background: senior executive-WMC Limited, FH Faulding & Co
 Directorships: CFO
 Chris Melloy, Non-Executive Director
 e-mail: lionselection@lsg.com.au
 Education: MSc, DIC, BSc (Eng), ARSM, FIMMM
 Background: Chief Executive Officer of Lihir Gold Limited
 Barry Sullivan, Non Executive Director
 e-mail: lionselection@lsg.com.au
 Education: BEc (Hons)
 Background: Chief Financial Officer and Company Secretary of Acacia

2943 LIONBIRD
HaBarzel 25
Tel Aviv 69710
Israel

Phone: 972-35333885 Fax: 972-35333995
e-mail: jonathan@lionbird.com
web: www.lionbird.com

Mission Statement: By harnessing cloud computing and crowd networking, companies are revolutionizing certain offline markets in ways never previously imagined. These technologies open endless opportunities to meaningfully improve healthcare delivery, retail processes and enterprise collaboration. LionBird invests in young companies capable of making it happen.
Average Investment: $200,000 - $500,000
Investment Criteria: Early-Stage
Industry Group Preference: Cloud Computing, Mobile, Internet
Portfolio Companies: Bento, Sweetch, amSTATZ, Tyto, PhysiHome, Genome Compiler, KitCheck, physIQ, Telesofia, Fundbox, CartCrunch, Ovuline, Marqueta, ShopClues

Other Locations:
 708 Church Street
 Suite 252
 Evanston, IL 60201
 Phone: 847-7212171 Fax: 847-3489161

Key Executives:
 Ed Michael, Managing Partner
 Education: BA, Politics & Government, JD, Indiana University
 Background: EVP, Diagnostic Products, Abbott Laboratories

2944 LLOYDS DEVELOPMENT CAPITAL LIMITED
One Vine Street
London W1J 0AH
United Kingdom

Phone: 44-02077583680 Fax: 44-02077583681
e-mail: churley@ldc.co.uk
web: www.ldc.co.uk

Mission Statement: We are private equity specialists with a 30 year history of supporting management buy-outs, equity release (cash out), development (DevCap) and acquisition finance transactions. With a current portfolio of 60+ businesses valued in excess of £2billion LDC's experience in the private equity arena is well known.
Geographic Preference: United Kingdom
Founded: 2000
Average Investment: £2 - 100 million
Investment Criteria: Management Buyouts, Equity Release, DevCap, Acquisition Finance
Industry Group Preference: Clean Technology, Renewable Energy, Construction, Financial Services, Healthcare, Industrial Services, Retailing, Travel & Leisure
Portfolio Companies: Waterfall Services, United House Developments, One Two Four, Capital Economics, Eley Group, Adler and Allen, Clifford Thames, Anite Travel, Stroma, Ministry of Cake, Connect Managed Servies, Prism Medical UK, CEL Procurement, Imagine Nation, Bluestone, Nexinto, The Property Software, Joules, Twofour Group, Express Engineering, The Training Room, Equiom, uSwitch, Angus Fire, Rimor, Node4, D&D London, NRS Healthcare, New World Trading, Validus IVC, Ramco Oil Services, Fever Tree, ATG Access, Blue Rubicon, MAMA & Company, Keoghs, Forest Holidays, Dale Power Solutions, Metronet, BigHand, Ocean Outdoor, Bifold Group, Showcard Print, Airline Services, Corporate Trael International, Best Kids (YeeHoo Baby World), Pertemps Network Group, Benson Group, PDJ Group, Kirona, Evander Group, Scottish Equity Partners, learndirect, WRG, Angel Springs, Original Additions, Driver Hire, UK2, A-Gas, OnApp, musicMagpie.co.uk, Kee Safety, The ComplEAT Food Group, United Legal Services, Easynet & MDNX, Mountain Warehouse, AIM Aviation, Antler, Exceed Midlands Advantage Fund, Unite House, Matrix, Vysionics, Integrated Dental Holdings, Marussia F1 Team, Avelo, Orion Media, The Independent Group, Cranswick Pet and Aquatics (Tropical Marine Center), Nuclear Engineering Services, Quantum Pharmaceuticals, Snell, Porterbrook, CNEI, Zenith-Leaerive, Eve, kidsunlimited, United Living Group, Davies Group, Omega Red, JCC, GVA, The Pallet Network, VSG, Direct Group, Epi-V, Kimberly Access Limited, British Salt,

Key Executives:
 Darryl Eales, Chief Executive Officer
 Candida Morley, Chief Operating Officer
 e-mail: deales@ldc.co.uk
 Education: Chartered Accountant
 Background: Ran the Birmingham office from 1994 to 1999, became Regional Managing Director for the Midlands
 Directorships: North in 1999 and was appointed Managing Director in January 2003.
 Jonathan Caswell, Investment Director
 e-mail: jandrew@ldc.co.uk
 Education: Graduated from Durham University with an honours degree in Molecular Biology and Biochemistry Jonathan
 Background: Price Waterhouse in the UK and Australia and at Arcadia Group, the high street fashion retailer
 Directorships: Jonathan was a founder member of PwC's Operations and Post Deal Services team where he specialised in working closely with private equity backed management teams to implement
 Jane Gilbert, Investment Director
 e-mail: mdraper@ldc.co.uk

Venture Capital & Private Equity Firms / International Firms

Background: ten years with PricewaterhouseCoopers,
Directorships: Grant became Regional Director for the North in August 2003 and became Head of New Business in August 2004 where he is now responsible for all new investment activity national
Daniel Sasaki, Marketing Director
e-mail: rpendleton@ldc.co.uk
Background: Previous new business and marketing roles were held with Lloyds Bowmaker (Corporate, Consumer, and Home Improvement Division) during an eleven-year term.
Directorships: Rob specialises in B2B and B2C financial services marketing.
Waqqas Ahmad, Investment Director
e-mail: aleach@ldc.co.uk
Education: Andy is a mathematics graduate of Oxford University, After qualifying as a Chartered Accountant with Coopers & Lybrand
Background: Andy joined Byvest, an Australian based private equity fund.
Directorships: he spent 10 years with 3i in Manchester. After two years with Montagu Capital Andy joined LDC in September 2004.
Gordon Hague, Investment Director
Background: Following six successful years with County he moved to LDC in 1990.
Directorships: Over the last four years he has specialised on working with portfolio companies.
Andrew McMurray, Portfolio Director
e-mail: amcmurray@ldc.co.uk
Education: Having completed a Law Degree at Kings College London, Andrew qualified as a Chartered Accountant with Ernst and Whinney
Background: He joined Hill Samuel in 1986
Directorships: and has specialised in portfolio work since 1991.
John Harper, Investment Director
e-mail: cmorley@ldc.co.uk
Education: Law Degree from Oxford and a Masters Degree in Small Business,
Background: Extensive experience in investment banking / M&A (with Barings), venture capital (at 3i)
Directorships: corporate development within a large plc (Harrisons & Crosfield)

2945 LMBO FINANCE
5 rue de Castiglione
Paris 75001
France

Phone: 33-171732020 Fax: 33-171732021
e-mail: lmbo@lmbo.com
web: www.lmbo.com

Mission Statement: By using resources that are varied and often well-spread, human, economic and financial, an LMBO amounts to the re-creation of a firm.
Geographic Preference: France
Fund Size: $240 Million
Founded: 1986
Average Investment: $132 Million
Minimum Investment: $24 Million
Investment Criteria: Mid market firms
Industry Group Preference: Retailing, Industrial Services, Telecommunications, Electronic Technology
Portfolio Companies: Groupe Caillé, Ora VéHicules Electriques, Technocer
Key Executives:
  Gerard Favarel, President
  e-mail: f.desmarest@lmbo.com
  Mary Kim Bennett, Secretary General
  Yvan Favarel, Investor
  e-mail: a.riss@lmbo.com
  Pierre Favarel, Compliance Officer and Internal Control
  e-mail: nc.macleod@lmbo.com

  Gérard Favarel, President
  Directorships: Chairmain

2946 LOMBARD/APIC (HK) LIMITED
Room 2202, 22/F
Tower 1, Lippo Centre
Queensway 89
Hong Kong

Phone: 852-28787388 Fax: 852-28787288
e-mail: info@lombardinvestments.com
web: www.lombardinvestments.com

Mission Statement: Lombard invests private equity capital in competitive enterprises needing financing for expansion or to complete financial restructuring.
Geographic Preference: San Francisco, Hong Kong, Bangkok
Founded: 1985
Average Investment: $25 Million
Minimum Investment: $10 Million
Investment Criteria: All Stages
Industry Group Preference: All Sectors Considered
Portfolio Companies: Asia Books Company, Asiasoft Corporation, Career Choices, Inc., Centara Hotels and Resorts, Central Pattana, Dakota, Minnesota & Eastern Railroad, Easy Buy, Fu Sheng Industrial, Good Morning Shinhan Securities, Hansol Gyoyook Company, Kantana Group, Krungthep Land, KSNET, Inc., MC Group PLC, Mega Lifesciences, Mermaid Maritime, Nok Airlines, Overseas Dragon China, Pruska Real Estate, Robinson Department Store, S. Pack & Print, San Shing Fastech Corporation, S&P Syndicate, SNC Former, Somboon Advance Technology, The Medical Cit, TICON Industrial, Trinity Watthana, Viet - UC Group
Key Executives:
  Kanchit Bunajinda, Director
  e-mail: tsmith@lombardinvestments.com
  Education: Mr. Smith graduated cum laude from Harvard College (A.B. 1975).
  Background: CEO and CFO of ACI, Inc.
  Directorships: Managing Director
  Anita Chik, Director

2947 LOOL VENTURES
Tushiya 2
4th Floor
Tel Aviv
Israel

e-mail: info@lool.vc
web: www.lool.vc

Mission Statement: Investor in early-stage startups based in Tel Aviv.
Geographic Preference: Israel
Industry Group Preference: Internet, Digital Media & Marketing, Social Media
Portfolio Companies: Zooz, Wibbitz, LawGeex, Brodmann17, MarketMan, MediSafe, Talenya, DBmaestro, Farm Dog, KIDOZ, SiteAware, Sensibo, ClipCall, MyPermissions, Mabaya
Key Executives:
  Avichay Nissenbaum, General Partner
  e-mail: avichay@lool.vc
  Yaniv Golan, General Partner
  e-mail: yaniv@lool.vc

2948 LOUGH SHORE INVESTMENTS
47 A Botanic Avenue
Belfast BT7 1JL
Northern Ireland

Phone: 0044-2890438510 Fax: 0044-2890436651
web: www.loughshore.co

Venture Capital & Private Equity Firms / International Firms

Mission Statement: Our mission is to invest in high potential management teams and partner with them to build great businesses. Our goal is to bring ten great companies to exit or IPO by 2025.
Geographic Preference: Ireland
Portfolio Companies: Geopii, The Shore, World Desk, Converser, SendbyBag, Profeshion

Key Executives:
  Danny Moore, Founder
  Background: COO, NYSE Euronext Trading; COO/CEO, Wombat Financial Software

2949 LRM - INVESTERINGSMAATSCHAPPIJ VOOR LIMBURG
555 Kempische Steenweg
Hasselt 3500
Belgium

Phone: 33-11246801 Fax: 32-011246850
e-mail: info@lrm.be
web: www.lrm.be

Mission Statement: LRM provides private equity to industrial and service companies which located in Limburg Province of Belgium. Further, LRM is also involved in Real Estate financing.
Geographic Preference: Belgium
Fund Size: $360 Milllon
Founded: 1994
Average Investment: $6 Million
Minimum Investment: $0.12 Milliom
Investment Criteria: All size companies, Minority shareholding, Start-up capital, Growth capital, MBO, MBI, Spin offs, Project financing
Industry Group Preference: Real Estate, Pharmaceuticals, Security, Carpet Yarn, Software, Biotechnology
Portfolio Companies: Cegeka, C-Mine Crib, Comm-Art International, Corda Campus, D Square, Doxis Lighting Factory, Elan Languages, Excico, Jordens DC, Ledlite, Maris Group, NASCOM, Niceberg Studios, Ontoforce, Pearlchain.net, Right Brain, Rmoni Wireless, Soulco, Sparkcentral, Thalento, TopSportLab, Zappware, 3DD Pharma, Amakem, Apitope, Arcarios, Bioville, Bocasa, Complix, FF Pharmaceuticals, Promethera, SEPS Pharma, Ter Hulst, Therasolve, Tigenix, 4HAMCOGEN, Bio Gas Bree, Bis-Technics 2000, Bruno Invest, Capricorn, Epigan, Fish2BE, HCJ, KEY/VISYS, Limburg Gas, Limburg Win (D) T, Limburgs Klimaatfonds, Machiels Building Solutions, Minerva, Punch Powertrain, Restore, Ridley - Race Productions, Visiomatics, Vivixtum, Zonnecentrale Limburg, Cavalę Steel Company, Different Hotels Group, Fremach Groep, Kristalpark III, MCGZ, Quinsis, Scana Noliko, Value Retail, Alro, Blue Line Logistics, Bosmans Graphics, Brouwerij Martens, Cobelguard CIT, Connect Group, D2E Capital, Diresco, Ducatt, ETG, Spaas Kaarsen, VCST, Veldeman Group

Key Executives:
  Hugo Leroi, Chairman
  Jean Claude Van Red, Vice President

2950 MACMILLAN DIGITAL EDUCATION
The MacMillan Building
4 Crinan St.
London N1 9XW
United Kingdom

Phone: 44-20-7418-5581
web: www.digital-education.com

Mission Statement: Launched in January 2012 by one of the world's leading educational publishers, Macmillan Digital Education captures opportunities in the consumer online education markets. A corporate venture capital investor and incubator, we are technology and service driven to make learning more effective and fun whilst embracing our user centric business understanding.
Geographic Preference: Global
Founded: 2012
Investment Criteria: Early-Stage
Industry Group Preference: Online Education
Portfolio Companies: Mobile Teacher, MacTrac, Maths Doctor, tutoria, EnglishUp, Easyaula, Veduca

Key Executives:
  Matthias Ick, Managing Director
  Sebastian Peck, Finance Director

2951 MACQUARIE DIRECT INVESTMENT LIMITED
50 Martin Place
Sydney 2000
Australia

Phone: 61-282323333
web: www.macquarie.com.au

Mission Statement: Macquarie Bank is a pre-eminent provider of investment banking and financial services.
Geographic Preference: Australia, New Zealand
Fund Size: $29.7 Billion
Founded: 1969
Average Investment: $22 Million
Minimum Investment: $7 Million
Investment Criteria: Expansion, Mezzanine Debit, Mezzanine Funding, Management Buyout, Leveraged Buyout, Recapitalization
Industry Group Preference: Broadcasting, Communications Equipment, Computer Hardware & Software, Electronic Technology, Energy, Food & Beverage, Components & IoT, Internet Technology, Manufacturing, Medical, Publishing, Retailing, Telecommunications, Wholesale, Cable
Portfolio Companies: Neverfail Water, Crevet Limited, Broadcast Media Group, Millers Self Storage, Hermes Precisa Australia, Millers Fashion Group, Com Tech Communications, Tower Technology, Volante, JB Hi Fi, Staging Connections, InvoCare, Repco, The Reject Shop

Key Executives:
  David S Clarke, Chairman
  e-mail: mdi@macquarie.com
  Education: BEcon Hons (Syd), MBA (Harvard), Hon DScEcon Sydney
  Background: Chairman of McGuigan Simeon Wines Limited, the Wine Committee of the Royal Agricultural Society of New South Wales, the Sydney Advisory Board of the Salvation Army and the Opera Australia Capital Fund, Member of the Investment Advisory Committee of the Australian Olympic Foundation, Royal Agricultur
  Directorships: Honorary life member of the Financial Markets Foundation for Children, Committee member of the NIDA Stage II Project and Governor of the Australian Ireland Fund and Vice Presi
  Allan E Moss, Managing Director
  e-mail: Roblee@Macquarie.Com
  Education: BS (Cornell), MBA (Harvard)
  Background: Macquarie Bank with 3 years investing bank funds, Experienced in structured finance, capital raisings and acquisitions and disposals, Appointed head of Macquarie Direct Investments and Director of Surf Hardware, Ringwood, Club Hotels, FNS and Helmsman Funds Management.
  Mark R G Johnson, Executive Deputy Chairman
  e-mail: mdi@macquarie.com
  Education: B Com (Hons) (Rhodes), CA
  Background: Joined Macquarie Financial Operations Division in 2003 and Macquarie Direct Investment in 2004, Extensive experience in general management, accounting and financial control.
  John G Allpass, Chairman of Board Audit & Compliance Committee
  e-mail: Riyna.Denett@Macquarie.Com

Venture Capital & Private Equity Firms / International Firms

Education: B Bus (UTS), MBA-Exec (AGSM), CA, ASIA
Background: Joined Macquarie Financial Operations Division in 2000 and Macquarie Direct Investment in 2001, Extensive experience working in accounting and financial control roles,
Directorships: Former Chief Financial Officer of Macquarie Direct Investment.

2952 MAGMA VENTURE PARTNERS
22 Rothschild Boulevard
25th Floor
Tel Aviv 6688218
Israel

Phone: 972-36967285 Fax: 972-36955960
e-mail: info@magmavc.com
web: www.magmavc.com

Mission Statement: Magma Venture Partners invests in early stage communication, semiconductor, internet and media companies and helps to build these companies to target global markets and create industry leading success stories. Our approach is based on an unrelenting commitment to quality and innovation and the courage to invest in ideas at their early stages. We concentrate on the fields we know best, seeking the brightest ventures in communication, semiconductors, internet and media. The fund invests in opportunities that have the potential to define and shape the industry. Our approach is active, integrative, and dynamic. We provide our portfolio companies with the contact networks, resources, advice, and tools needed to succeed.

Geographic Preference: Israel
Investment Criteria: Early-Stage
Industry Group Preference: Communications, Semiconductors, Internet, Media
Portfolio Companies: Applitools, Appreciate, AppsFlyer, Argus, Autotalks, CloudEndure, Core Photonics, DesignArt Networks, Forty Cloud, GreenSQL, Guesty, Hola!, Magisto, Nipendo, Oliver Solution, Onavo, Phonetic Systems, PhotoMania, Provigent, Sentrix, TabTale, Teridion, Trivnet, Valens Semiconductor, Waze, Wintegra, WireX, Xplenty

Key Executives:
Modi Rosen, Co-Founder/Managing Partner
e-mail: modi@magmavc.com
Background: Monitor Company, Shaldor Ltd
Directorships: Amdocs, Provigent, Crescendo Networks, Hola!, Nipendo

2953 MAKERS FUND
Hong Kong
China

web: www.makersfund.com

Mission Statement: Dedicated to supporting businesses in the area of interactive entertainment.

Geographic Preference: Global, United States, China, Europe
Fund Size: $180 Million
Founded: 2018
Average Investment: $1,000,000 - $10,000,000
Minimum Investment: $1 Million
Investment Criteria: Series A, Seed
Industry Group Preference: Gaming, Entertainment
Portfolio Companies: Active8, Bossa Studios UK, Facet, FRVR, Genvid, Klang, Medal Playlabs, Popdog, Superdata, Teacher Gaming, Tiny Build, TSM, Typhoon Studios

Key Executives:
Jay Chi, Founding Partner
Education: BA, Stanford University
Background: McKinsey & Company; Kowloon Nights
Michael Cheung, Partner
Education: BEng, University of Warwick
Background: Brynleigh Tech; dunnhumby; McKinsey & Company; Tencent
Directorships: Klang Games

2954 MARATHON VENTURE CAPITAL FUND LIMITED
85 Medinat Hayehudim Street
Herzlia 46766
Israel

Phone: 972-99602010 Fax: 972-99569081
web: www.marathonvc.com

Mission Statement: To finance Israeli Hi-Tech companies engaged in the development of highly innovative technologies based on firm patents.

Geographic Preference: Israel
Fund Size: $22 Million
Founded: 1993
Average Investment: $4 Million.
Minimum Investment: $2 Million
Investment Criteria: Seed, Start-up, First Stage
Industry Group Preference: Communications, Electronic Technology, Industrial Services, Medical Devices, Biotechnology, Artificial Intelligence, Software, Components & IoT
Portfolio Companies: Nanomotion Ltd., Optibase Ltd., Arel Communication and Software Ltd., Pegasus Technologies Ltd., Margan Business Development Ltd., Qronus Interactive Ltd., IRLan Ltd, Aisys Ltd., Bioview Ltd, Polygene Ltd, Optinex Inc, Metabogal Ltd.

2955 MARCEAU INVESTISSEMENTS
France

Phone: +44 (0) 20 7881 2990 Fax: +44 (0) 7866 030 464
e-mail: stasmichael@mergers-alliance.com
web: www.mergers-alliance.com

Mission Statement: Marceau Finance offers specialist advice covering strategy, corporate finance and negotiations.

Geographic Preference: France
Founded: 1987
Investment Criteria: Development, Restructuring
Industry Group Preference: Telecommunications, Information Technology, Electronic Technology, Construction, Engineering, Food & Beverage, Building Materials & Services

Key Executives:
Patrick Atzel, Senior Advisor
Background: CEO of Compagnie Générale d'Electricite, Principal Secretary of various French Ministers in France.
Nicolas Balon, Director

2956 MATI-HIGH-TECH
11 HaTassia Street
Ra'anana 4366107
Israel

Phone: 972-97602716 Fax: 972-97602245
e-mail: efrat@startup.org.il
web: www.matiran.org.il

Geographic Preference: Israel
Founded: 1994

2957 MATURO KAPITAL
Leirvollen 23
Skein 3736
Norway

Phone: 47-35505550 Fax: 47-35505555
web: www.maturo.no

Mission Statement: Invests in companies with unique a technology or which operates in business areas with rapid growth.

Geographic Preference: Nordic Region
Fund Size: NOK 330 millioin
Industry Group Preference: Energy, Environment

Venture Capital & Private Equity Firms / International Firms

Key Executives:
Leif Svarstad, Managing Partner
47-3550-5551
e-mail: leif.svarstad@maturo.no

2958 MAYBAN VENTURES
100 Jalan Tun Perak
Menara Maybank
26th Floor
Kuala Lumpur 50050
Malaysia

Phone: 60-320322188 Fax: 60-320312188

Mission Statement: Mayban Ventures manages several private equity funds which invest in companies at all stages.

Geographic Preference: Malaysia
Founded: 1993
Average Investment: $4.1 Million
Minimum Investment: $0.26 Million
Investment Criteria: Start-ups, Mezzanines, Pre-IPOs, and Specific purpose business.
Portfolio Companies: Picarda Holdings Sdn. Bhd, Proprietary Fund,

2959 MEDICAL RESEARCH COMMERCIALIZATION FUND
Level 9
278 Collins Street
Melbourne VIC 3000
Australia

Phone: 61-396570700 Fax: 61-396570777
e-mail: info@mrcf.com.au
web: www.mrcf.com.au

Mission Statement: The Medical Research Commercialisation Fund provides dedicated, investment funding to support the commercialisation of early-stage medical research discoveries that originate from its member institutes. The collaborative nature of the MRCF seeks to foster best practice in the commercialisation of medical innovations.

Founded: 2007
Investment Criteria: Early-Stage
Industry Group Preference: Healthcare, Medical Technology
Portfolio Companies: Auspherix, Fibrotech Therapeutics, GI-Therapies, Global Kinetics, Helmedix, miReven, OccuRx, Osprey Medical, Otifex, PolyActiva, Protego Medical, Q-Sera, University of South Australia - The Mawson Institute, Vaxxas, Verva Pharmaceuticals

Key Executives:
Alan Stockdale, Chairman
Background: Treasurer & Minister for IT & Multimedia; Investment Banker, Macquarie Bank

2960 MEDRA CAPITAL
60/2 Melita Street
Valetta VLT 1122
Malta

e-mail: info@medracapital.com
web: www.medracapital.com

Mission Statement: We are a private investment company providing seed and Series A funding for start-ups. As well as backing in-house ventures under our own direction, we are particularly interested in opportunities in technology, manufacturing, robotics, renewable energy, and sustainability, where our team's expertise adds most value.

Founded: 2013
Investment Criteria: Seed-Stage, Series A
Industry Group Preference: Technology, Manufacturing, Robotics, Software, Renewable Energy
Portfolio Companies: Appvance, Boatbound, Evvnt, Incrediblue, Knowledge Transmission, Mover, PocketFM, Sailogy, Scaled Networks, Sugru, Vantage Power

2961 MEKONG CAPITAL
Capital Place, 8th Floor
6 Thai Van Lung St.
District 1
Ho Chi Minh City
Vietnam

Phone: 84-88273161 Fax: 84-88273162
e-mail: info@mekongcapital.com
web: www.mekongcapital.com

Mission Statement: A private equity investment company that specializes in investing in the leading private companies in Vietnam.

Geographic Preference: Vietnam, Cambodia, Laos
Fund Size: $168.5 Million
Founded: 2001
Average Investment: $1.2 Million
Minimum Investment: $1 Million
Investment Criteria: Expansion, Restructuring, MBO
Industry Group Preference: Consumer Products, Retailing, Distribution
Portfolio Companies: Phu Nhuan Jewelry, Mobile World, Asia Chemical Corporation, FPT Corporation, Nam Long Investment Corporation, Intresco, Vietnam Australia International School, An Giang Plant Protection, Traphaco, Minh Hoang Garment

Key Executives:
Chris Freund, Partner
e-mail: info@mekongcapital.com
Education: Latin School of Chicago; BS Psychology, University of California, Santa Cruz
Background: VP/Portfolio Manager, Templeton Asset Management, Investment Research, Harris Associates, Consultant, Templeton Vietnam
Chad Ovel, Partner
Education: Dr. Economic Sciences & Capital Markets Theory, Vienna University of Economics, Vienna
Background: Executive Director, Templeton Asset Management in Singapore; Portfolio Manager, BIDV-Vietnam Partners Investment Management

2962 MERCAPITAL SA
Padilla 17
1 Edificio 14
28223 Pozuelo de Alarcon
Madrid 28006
Spain

Phone: 34-915578000 Fax: 34-913-449191

Mission Statement: Actively seeking new investments

Geographic Preference: Spain
Fund Size: $2 Million
Founded: 1982
Average Investment: ?25 and ?150 million
Minimum Investment: $36,000
Investment Criteria: Iberion Buyouts, LBO, MBO, MBI, Buy-And-Builds, Growth Capital Transactions, Middle Market
Industry Group Preference: All Sectors Considered
Portfolio Companies: ADL Technology, Blinker, Bodegas Lan, Broadnet, Cesa, Grupo Abaco Menorquin Yachts, Holmes Place, Jofel, KA International Group, Lasem, MSC Wellness Experts, Occidental Hotels Allegro Resorts, Piaggio/Derbi Record, Quiron Hospital Group, Recoletos, Saprogal, System, USP Hospitales, Xfera, Ydilo

Key Executives:
Gonzalo de Rivera, CEO
e-mail: mzurita@mercapital.com
Education: Degree Law & Business Studies, ICADE; MBA with Honors, INSEAD
Background: Project Director, MexCapital
Directorships: Wellness Experts; Bodegas Lan; Grupo Logistico Santos

Venture Capital & Private Equity Firms / International Firms

Federico Pastor, Chairman
e-mail: cbg@mercapital.com
Education: MBA, INSEAD; Degree Business & Economics, Universidad Pontificia Comillas (ICADE)
Background: Graduate Trainee, Airbus Industrie, Peugeot & Ernst & Young
Directorships: Quiron; Hospiten

2963 MERIFIN CAPITAL
Place Flagey 18
Brussels B-1050
Belgium

Phone: 32-26462580 **Fax:** 32-26463036
e-mail: enquiries@merifin.com
web: www.merifin.com

Mission Statement: Actively seeking new investments as a private international investment group.
Geographic Preference: Brussels, Geneva, New York
Founded: 1980
Investment Criteria: Early-Stage, Expansion and Development, Management Buyout, Management Buyin, Turn-Around and Restructuring
Industry Group Preference: All Sectors Considered
Key Executives:
  Simona Heidempergher, Director
  e-mail: enquiries@merifin.com

2964 MERRILL LYNCH (ASIA PACIFIC) LIMITED Merrill Lynch Group
15/F Citibank Tower, 3 Garden Road
Central
Hong Kong

Phone: 85-225363888 **Fax:** 85-225363789

Mission Statement: Leading financial management and advisory company.
Geographic Preference: Worldwide
Fund Size: $1.6 Trillion
Founded: 1914
Investment Criteria: Expansion, Restructuring, MBO
Industry Group Preference: Consumer Products, Electronic Technology, Information Technology, Leisure, Media, Medical, Retailing, Wholesale, Telecommunications, Transportation, Distribution, Consumer Services, Entertainment
Key Executives:
  John A Thain, Chairman & Chief Executive Officer
  Education: Juris Doctor degree from Yale Law School, Bachelor of Arts degree, summa cum laude, in economics from Colgate University.
  Background: co-head of the Global Financial Institutions Group, Global Investment Banking, Served as a Financial Advisor to Leading Banking.
  Rosemary Berkery, Vice Chairman & General Counsel
  Education: Master's of Business Administration with Finance from Harvard University, Graduate of Kettering University
  Background: Merrill Lynch's U.S. Private Client group, General Motors Corporation in New York and Madrid,
  Directorships: Chairman of the Board, Chief Executive Officer
  Ahmass Fakahany, Vice Chairman
  Education: Bachelor of Science degree from Boston University School of Management and an M.B.A from Columbia University.
  Background: Served as senior vice president and finance director, Global Chief Financial Officer and Chief Administrative Officer for the Corporate and Institutional Client Group.
  Directorships: Chief Administrative Officer

2965 MEZZANINE MANAGEMENT LIMITED
Mezzanine Management UK Ltd.
One Strand
1-3 Strand
London WC2N 5HR
United Kingdom

Phone: 44-2070242200 **Fax:** 44-2070242201
e-mail: info@mezzanine-management.co.uk
web: www.mmlcapital.com

Mission Statement: Actively seeking new investments
Geographic Preference: USA, Europe
Fund Size: $1 Billion
Founded: 1988
Average Investment: $10 million and $50 million
Minimum Investment: $10 Million
Investment Criteria: Expansion and Development, Refinancing bank debt, Secondary purchase/replacement capital, MBO, MBI, Institutional BO, Leveraged Build Up
Industry Group Preference: Aerospace, Defense and Government, Petrochemicals, Industrial Equipment, Media, Engineering
Portfolio Companies: Apache, Arena Group, Argyle Security, ATA Groiup, Carre Blanc, Clyde Bergemann, Coventya, EIC, FrontierMedEx, GlobeOp, Hawkpoint, IAC, Instant, Lomond, Nactis, Optionis Group, PAR, Precision, Regard, Tournus, TNT, Vanguard Healthcare, VIP Cinema Seating, Vulcanic, WSH, XServ, Yonkers
Key Executives:
  Rory Brooks, Founding Partner
  e-mail: info@mezzanine-management.co.uk
  Education: Bachelor's degree from the University of Michigan and an MBA degree in Finance from the University of Pittsburgh.
  Background: Toronto-Dominion Bank and Held numerous commercial and merchant banking positions in the United States and the United Kingdom.Much of his career has been spent as a cash flow lender and equity provider analyzing and arranging financings in New York and Lo
  Edward Baker, Investment Manager
  e-mail: info@mezzanine-management.co.uk
  Education: Bachelor's degree in Management from the University of Manchester Institute of Science and Technology
  Background: Bank of Boston, Director of BPC, Ferembal, Sicli, Century Inns, Eurofarad and Polestar.
  Gemma Chivers, Investor Relation Manager
  e-mail: info@mezzanine-management.co.uk
  Education: Masters of Science in International Banking and Finance from Herriot Watt University in Edinburgh.
  Background: Bank of Scotland, Director of Hallmark
  Robert Devonshire, Investment Manager
  e-mail: info@mezzanine-management.co.uk
  Education: BA and MA from Cambridge University
  Background: Private Equity Investor.in US and Europe.
  Parag Gandesha, Chief Operating Officer
  e-mail: info@mezzanine-management.co.uk
  Education: Parag has a BSc in Accounting and Finance and an MBA in International Management and is ACCA qualified.
  Background: Finance Director of Cdb Web Tech Group, BC Partners

2966 MIDINVEST LIMITED
Kauppakatu 31 C
Jyväskylä 40100
Finland

Phone: +358 50 539 9378
web: www.midinvest.fi

Mission Statement: Midinvest Management Oy is a venture capital company which manages seven regional venture capital funds.
Geographic Preference: Finland

929

Venture Capital & Private Equity Firms / International Firms

Fund Size: $70 Million
Founded: 2000
Average Investment: $1.83 Million
Minimum Investment: $42,000
Investment Criteria: Startup, Expansion, MBO/MBI, Seed
Industry Group Preference: Software, Manufacturing, Education, Healthcare
Portfolio Companies: A-Lab Oy, C2 SmartLight Oy, Flaaming Oy, Inka Oy, Intelle Innovations, Kilosoft Oy, Kotidata, Metcase Consulting Oy, Paytrail Oyj, Pisla Oy, Polarmatic Oy, Soikea Solutions Oy, Stafix Oy, Valttori Oy

Key Executives:
Jukka-Pekka Nikula, Managing Director

2967 MIDVEN
Cavendish House
39-41 Waterloo St.
Birmingham B2 5PP
United Kingdom

Phone: 0121-7101990 **Fax:** 0121-7101999
e-mail: enquiries@midven.com
web: www.midven.co.uk

Mission Statement: Midven is an owner managed, entrepreneurial, venture capital company located in the heart of Birmingham. We have been successfully investing in dynamic, small and medium sized businesses since we started in 1990 when six Midlands based entrepreneurs established the business.

Geographic Preference: Midlands
Founded: 1990
Average Investment: £1 million
Investment Criteria: Early-Stage
Industry Group Preference: Biotechnology, Environment, Digital Media & Marketing, Software, Hardware, Consumer Services, Manufacturing, Engineering
Portfolio Companies: 21Net, Abgentis, AccurIC, Activ8, Admedo, AerisTech, Aitua, Allinea, Amalyst, Amba Defence, Anaxsys, Anvil Semiconductors, Ardentia, BeGo, Big Button, BioSyntha, Breaking Free, Caperfly, Caption Data, Cellcentric, Cellfacts, Cipher Surgical, Claresys, Clearview, Cobalt Light Systems, Complyserv, Concurrent Thinking, Connexica, Consero Consulting, Contego Fraud, Corso UK, CPA, Craft Dragon, Crescendo Biologics, Crowd Technologies, Cytox, Diamond Software, Diverse World, Dynamic Change, E-Motion Ventures, Eagle Genomics, Edudo, Edududes Ltd., Etive Technologies, Everyclick, Fertility Focus, Foodient T/A Whisk, Formolgy, Fubar Radio, Gemba Solutions, GeoScience International, H4-Global, Health2works, I-Solutions Global, Igloo Education, Igloo Vision, Infinity CCS, Inscentinel, Ionic Polymer Solutions, Isys Interactive, Kallik, Keit, Kobus Services, L3 Technology, Learning Labs, Lontra, LumeJet, Meals & Media, Microbial Solutions, Microvisk, Midland Industrial Glass, Minivator, MVI Technology, Netmania, Novacta, Occam Systems, Orbital Optics, Orthogem, Oxsensis, P2i, Perfectus Biomed, Phasor Solutions, Phoenix Health & Safety, Playmob, Portal Entertainment, Prism Network, Procarta Biosystems, ProKyma, Prolojik, Quantum Compliance, SALT, Scriptswitch, Silver Lining Solutions, Simworx, Soshi Games, Sparcana, Spectral Edge, Speed Plastics, Talecom, Tokamak Energy, TR Fleet, Uni2 Hold Tight, WalkinWifi, Warwick Audio Technologies, Webmoco, Your Vets

Key Executives:
Tony Stott, Chief Executive Officer
0121-710-1990
Education: Economics & Politics, Manchester University
Background: Principal, HSBC Enterprise & Exceed Funds; Deloitte & Touche

2968 MINI VENTURES
Pakistan

e-mail: info@miniventures.com

Mission Statement: Mini Ventures is a seed fund for small sized ventures aiming to fund, mentor and help launch start-ups to create an entrepreneur-friendly eco-system in the Pakistan market.

Geographic Preference: Pakistan
Investment Criteria: Seed-Stage

Key Executives:
Faizan Laghari, Founding Partner
Education: Business & Information Technology Degree, Curtin University of Technology
Background: Founder, Suite401; Founder, Textualy; Founder, Viaduct

2969 MIRAE ASSET VENTURE ACCELERATOR
Mirae Asset Group
28/F Seoul Finance Center
84, Taepyungro 1-ka, Chung-ku
Seoul 100-768
South Korea

Phone: +82 2 3707 0400
web: www.miraeasset.com

Mission Statement: Mainly supports companies in the initial stages of business set-ups.

Geographic Preference: Asia, Korea
Fund Size: 53.85 Billionÿ
Founded: 1999
Investment Criteria: Small & medium-sized enterprises and venture start-ups.
Industry Group Preference: Multimedia, Internet Technology, Bioengineering, Information Technology, Security
Portfolio Companies: Softmax, Fi-on, Tmax soft, Geni Tech, J-Tell, Alpha vision tech, Dinalit System, Wow Tv, Tel-loin, Dae-in-Info sys, Hitech, Al-F-Hitech, Han net, Hans bio med.

Key Executives:
Hyeon Joo Park, Chairman
Background: Research Head of Mirae Asset Securities

2970 MITSUBISHI UFJ CAPITAL
1-7-17 Nihonbashi, Chuo-Ku
Tokyo 103-0027
Japan

Phone: 81-0-3-5205-8581 **Fax:** 81-0-3-3273-5570
web: www.mucap.co.jp/english

Mission Statement: Formed by the merger of Diamond Capital and UFJ Capital, Mitsubishi UFJ Capital have financed more than 1,000 companies, more than 290 of which have gone public.

Fund Size: 2.95 billion Yen
Founded: 2005
Industry Group Preference: Healthcare, Biotechnology, Information Technology, Electronics, High Technology
Portfolio Companies: Sucampo Pharmaceuticals, Affymax, OPKO Health, FivePrime Therapeutics, MacroGenics, FibroGen, Acologix, Acucela, BrainCells, Aveo, Inotek, iPerian, KaloBios, Cardiac Dimensions, AnGesMG, TransGenic, MediBic, MEDINET, Shin Nippon Biomedical Laboratories, Takara Bio, MediciNova, GNI, R-Tech Ueno, NanoCarrier, TMRC, GreenPeptide, Perseus Proteomics, CanBas, Y's Therapeutics, UMN Pharma, Dynavec, D.Western Therapeutics, Japan Tissue Engineering, CellSeed, ReproCELL, Carna Biosciences, Big Matrix Research Institute, MC Laboratory, ReqMed Company

Key Executives:
Kei Andoh, President

Venture Capital & Private Equity Firms / International Firms

2971 MITSUI SUMITOMO INSURANCE VENTURE CAPITAL CO
Yaesu Nagoya Bldg 3F
Yaesu 2-2-10
Chuo-Ku, Toky 104-0028
Japan

Phone: 81 3 3279 3672 Fax: 81 3 3242 3068
web: www.msivc.co.jp

Mission Statement: Our mission is to contribute to the technological advance and service enhancement that helps our society be sustainable. This is also our significance of existence as a venture capital which continues to be essential in our society. For the past two decades, we have supported a number of venture companies go public through investing into and connecting them to the right partners to realize their potential value. We support entrepreneurs according to the stages of their development. We offer entrepreneurs broad support such as leadership and entrepreneurship education in university as well as providing capital, management skills and networks to help early-stage R&D and commercialization.

Geographic Preference: Asia
Founded: 1990
Investment Criteria: Later Stage, Early Stage, Middle Stage, Start-Up
Industry Group Preference: Real Estate, Construction, Financial Services, Consumer Products, Web Applications & Services, Biotechnology, Healthcare, Electronics, Semiconductors, Telecommunications, Energy, Environment, Sustainability

Key Executives:
Hitoshi Igarashi, President

2972 MMC VENTURES
2 Kensington Square
London W8 5EP
United Kingdom

Phone: 020-79382220 Fax: 020-79382259
e-mail: jennifer.newall@mmcventures.com

Mission Statement: MMC invests in early stage, high growth companies. We give our investors access to a professionally managed fund, investing growth equity in dynamic young companies in the UK.

Geographic Preference: United Kingdom
Founded: 2000
Investment Criteria: Early-Stage
Industry Group Preference: Business Products & Services, Digital Media & Marketing, Consumer Internet, Healthcare, Financial Services, Clean Technology, E-Commerce & Manufacturing
Portfolio Companies: AlexandAlexa, Appear Here, Base79, Bottica.com, Breathing Buildings, Brightpearl, Creativity Software, Gousto, iJento, Immedia, Interactive Investor, Invenias, Knowledgemill, LoveHomeSwap, Masabi, MBA & Company, MoneyExpery, MUBI, Neoss, NewVoiceMedia, Obillex, OneClick HR, Pact, PayasUgym, Reevoo, SafeGuard, Small World, Somo Global, The Practice, TotalMobile, Tyres on the Drive, VC-Net, WeDo, Wool and the Gang

Key Executives:
Bruce Macfarlane, Managing Partner
e-mail: bruce.macfarlane@mmcventures.com
Education: BA, English, Leeds University
Background: Managing Director, Merrill Lynch; Securities Lawyer, Skadden Arps
Directorships: Neoss, Interactive Investor, Breathing Buildings

2973 MMT MILLENNIUM MATERIALS TECHNOLOGIES FUND LP
6 Kaufman St, Beit Gibor
14th Floor
Tel Aviv 68012
Israel

Phone: 972-35167674 Fax: 972-35167301
web: www.mmtfund.com

Mission Statement: Actively seeking new investments.
Geographic Preference: Israel
Fund Size: $40 Million
Founded: 1998
Investment Criteria: Early Stage
Industry Group Preference: Microelectronics, Pharmaceuticals, Biotechnology, Communications, Nanotechnology, Technology, Bio Materials, Energy
Portfolio Companies: Cima Nanotech, Cymbet Corp, Enzymotec, Glycominds Ltd, MeMPile Ltd, Nanolayers, Power Paper Ltd, Real-time Radiography Ltd, Sol-Gel Ltd, Triton BioSystems.

Key Executives:
Zwi Vromen, Senior Partner
e-mail: info@mmtfund.com
Education: Bachelor's degree in Social Sciences
Background: Astra Technological Investments Ltd
Nir Belzer, Senior Partner
e-mail: info@mmtfund.com
Education: MBA, Bachelor's degree in Mathematics and computers
Background: Business Development Manager at IDBH, Director of Marketing and Business Development at Globes.
Didi Kalaydzhiev, Public and Investor Relations
e-mail: info@mmtfund.com
Education: B.Sc. degree in Chemical Engineering and business diploma from the Hebrew University of Jerusalem.
Background: Vice President of Business Development at Koor Chemicals, a Director on the Board of Tambour Ltd., Agan Chemicals Ltd., as well as the Joint Managing Director of Plantex and Ikapharm and General Manager of SBRC Ltd
Oren Gafri, Senior Partner
e-mail: info@mmtfund.com
Education: B.Sc. and M.Sc. studies in Materials & Process Engineering at Ben-Gurion University.and Business Administration for Engineers program at the Hebrew University of Jerusalem
Background: CEO of Pulsar Welding Ltd, General Manager of Chemitas Ltd.and executive of the Israeli Aircraft Industries Ltd (IAI)
Dr. Ram Vromen, Partner
e-mail: info@mmtfund.com
Education: PhD in History, LLB in law and a BA in history
Background: Portfolio manager of the First IsraTech Fund, Partner in the law firm of Bach, Arad, Scharf & Co.

2974 MOBILE INTERNET CAPITAL
Jowa Akasaka 1-chome Building, 8th Floor
1-11-28 Akasaka
Minato-ku
Tokyo 107-0052
Japan

web: www.mickk.com

Mission Statement: Mobile Internet Capital Inc. is a corporate VC specializing in Japan-based mobile and internet technologies.

Geographic Preference: Japan
Fund Size: 100 Million Yen
Founded: 1999

Venture Capital & Private Equity Firms / International Firms

Investment Criteria: Technology, contents and services for mobile communications, the internet and related fields
Industry Group Preference: Wireless Technologies, Internet Technology
Portfolio Companies: Shanon, Monstar Lab, ReNet Japan Group, StreetAcademy, MINKABU, Music Securities, S-cubism Holdings, Techpoint, Tattva, SUVACO, Ruby Groupe, Skeed, FLENS, Accounting SaaS Japan Co., CredoRax, Remote Co., SAN Home Entertainment, WEIC, Showcase-TV, Ricmedia, sMedio, GainSpan, REAL SAMURAI, GoNet Systems, Jin-Magic, Audyssey Laboratories, Explay-Japan, Innofidei Corporation, Agile Media Network, Chelsio Communications, HEROZ, Mlog, Centrix, Net-Marketing Corporation, eflow, Japan Carlife Assist, C2cube

Key Executives:
   Hidemiÿ Horseback, President, Chief Executive Officer
   e-mail: micinfo@mickk.com
   Education: Masters in engineering
   Background: Sharp Corporation, Intel Japan as vice-president
   Directorships: CEO, CIO
   Takeshi Inada, Director, Investment Officer

2975 MOMENTUM FUNDS MANAGEMENT PTY LIMITED
Level 1, 230 Balaclava Rd, Caulfield
Melbourne 3162
Australia

Phone: 61-395089333 Fax: 61-395089343
e-mail: mail@momentumvc.com.au
web: www.momentumvc.com.au

Mission Statement: Invests in companies with high growth potential based on the commercialisation of Australian research and development.
Geographic Preference: Australia
Fund Size: $30 Million
Founded: 1999
Investment Criteria: High tech, Early stage
Industry Group Preference: Electronic Technology, Biotechnology, Biosciences, Manufacturing, Software, Communications
Portfolio Companies: EnGene IC, Benthic Geotech, Panviva, CR-X, Petrecycle, Retriever Communications, Biovend, Briter Electronics, Cerylid, DSP Holdings, Juswin Technologies

Key Executives:
   John Thompson, Chairperson
   Education: B.Comm, Melbourne University; MBA, Melbourne Business School
   Background: Arthur Andersen
   Directorships: Panviva Ltd., Benthic Geotech Ltd.
   Martha Cleary, Director
   Education: B.Sc (Summa Cum Laude) in Physics from University College Dublin & Ph.D in astronomy from ANU, Canberra
   Background: Marketing and sales manager of the new ICIA diagnostics & Director of Client Operations at Dendrite International
   Directorships: Director of Justwin Technologies Inc
   Ron Finkel, Principal and Executive Director
   e-mail: mail@momentumvc.com.au
   Education: Bachelor of Business

2976 MONASHEES CAPITAL
R. Samuel Morse
74 CJ 39
Sao Paulo 04576-060
Brazil

Phone: +55 11 5501 2032
e-mail: contact@monashees.com.br
web: www.monashees.com.br

Mission Statement: Monashees Capital is a venture capital firm that partners with outstanding entrepreneurs to build great companies. They have a long-term approach and a business model that is tailored to the Brazilian environment.
Geographic Preference: Brazil
Portfolio Companies: Algentis, Baby.com.br, Bidu.com.br, Boo-Box, Buzzerd.com, Dabee, Elo7, Getninjas, Keepcon, Madeira Madeira, Medicinia, Mind Lab, Olook, Oppa, Peixeurbano, Pet Love, Playlore, VivaReal

2977 MONTAGU PRIVATE EQUITY LIMITED
2 More London Riverside
Vinters Place
London SE1 2AP
United Kingdom

Phone: 44-02073369955 Fax: 44-02073369961
e-mail: investment@montagu.com
web: www.montagu.com

Mission Statement: Montagu is a leading private equity advisors.
Geographic Preference: UK, France, Germany, Poland, Nordic Region
Fund Size: Euro 2.5 Billion
Founded: 1968
Average Investment: $152 Million
Minimum Investment: $35 Million
Investment Criteria: Secondary purchase/replacement capital, MBO, MBI, Institutional BO, Leveraged Build Up
Industry Group Preference: Environment, Industrial Products, Business Products & Services, Industrial Services, Chemicals, Consumer Products, Consumer Retail, Consumer Services, Energy
Portfolio Companies: Visma, Arkopharma, Nemera, DORC, CliniSys, University of Law, St-Hubert, BSN Medical, Euromedic International, Maplin Electronics

Key Executives:
   Jason Gatenby, CEO
   e-mail: chris.masterson@montagu.com
   Education: Psychology at University College & MBA from Manchester Business School
   Chris Masterson, Chairman
   Simon Pooler, Director
   e-mail: vince.obrien@montaguequity.com
   Education: Graduate in Modern History & Chartered Accountant
   Background: Coopers & Lybrand
   Directorships: Chairman of the British Venture Capital Association

2978 MORNINGSIDE VENTURES
e-mail: enquiries@morningside.com
web: www.morningside.com

Mission Statement: Morningside Group was founded in 1986, by the Chan family of Hong Kong to make private equity and venture capital investments. The group is managed by investment professionals who are entrepreneurial, have deep industry knowledge and are effective in the local environment in which they operate. In addition to its investment activitites, Morningside Group is strongly committed to social responsibility.
Founded: 1986
Portfolio Companies: Alpha Therm, ANZ, CrestMarc, Dakota Bodies, Magnatech, PressPass, Southland Log Homes, The Tile Shop, Clearn Membranes, Combined Solar, Green Biologics, ZinniaTek, Advanced Cell Diagnostics, BioScale, Cancer Targeting Systems, Heuresis, Insilixa, RapidScan, Cognoa, Excera, Glysure, Knoa, Vioptix, Converd, HD Biosciences, HumanZyme, KBI, Kindstar, Microscreen, Origene, PHC, Synermore, Aduro, Apellis, Argo, Atea, Atreaon, CellCentric, Chimerix, CVI, Edison, Envisia, Genocea, Liquidia, Matatu, Matriavax, MicuRx, Nucana, OrienGene, Oxyrane, Pinteon, Procarta, Stealth

Venture Capital & Private Equity Firms / International Firms

Peptides, Sunbio, Synchroneuron, Vaccine Tech, Building For Good, China Homerun, CO Everywhere, Forensic Logic, Hailo, Idibon, NPIC, One Smart, Phoenix New Media, Proximiant, Skycredit, TTPOD, VoiceBox, Xiaomi

Key Executives:
  Richard Liu, Managing Director
  Education: B.A. Beijing University of Science and Technology; MBA China Europe International Business School

2979 MOUNTAIN PARTNERS
Unterer Leihof
Fuhrstrasse 12
Waedenswil CH-8820
Switzerland

Phone: 41-447838030 **Fax:** 41-447838040
e-mail: contact@mountain.partners
web: www.mountain-partners.ch

Mission Statement: We are a global investment holding headquartered in Switzerland with currently more than 100 corporate investments. Our shareholders and co-investors benefit from our long-time experience in the 'value creation' and the management of our strong portfolio. We are close to our affiliated companies - with the help of our unique network and thanks to intensive support. An active role is important to us. Globally operating divisions cover our strategic business areas. Through this worldwide interaction, we also promote technology transfer into emerging markets. It is our aim to create real 'value add' for all of our stakeholders.

Geographic Preference: Switzerland
Industry Group Preference: Clean Technology, Information Technology, Financial Services
Portfolio Companies: Bab.La, Biocell, Bio Gate, Crealytics, Customer Alliance, Datapine, ePetWorld GmbH, Exasol, FCF Fox Corporate Finance, GEPPERT, Global Group, Grunspar, GVO, Hetan Technologies, Identive Group, ITEMBASE, Lashou, LOCR, xishiwang.com, Mixxt, Motionet AG, MovingImage24, Pearfection, Rebuy, ReigoHelden, SCHUTZKLICK, Secusmart, Shirtinator, Sinosol AG, Smart Loyalty, Torqeedo, URBANARA, Ushi.cn, VIPSTORE, yasni

Key Executives:
  Jens-Jurgen Bockel, Chairman
  Background: Henkel, Bahlsen, Werhaha-Group, Schickdanz-Holding; COO/CFO, Tengelmann Group
  Directorships: CDU Wirtschaftsrat

2980 MVC CORPORATION
No. 3 No. 7 Nihon Keizai Shimbun headquarters
Chiyoda-ku
Tokyo 100-0004
Japan

Phone: 81-0332853124 **Fax:** 81-0332859156

Mission Statement: Provides early-stage venture capital to various types of technology firms.

Geographic Preference: US, China, Korea, Japan
Fund Size: $35 Million
Founded: 1984
Average Investment: $5.5 Million
Minimum Investment: $500,000
Investment Criteria: Early-Stage
Industry Group Preference: Information Technology, Healthcare, Consumer Services

Key Executives:
  Kenichi Kimura, President & Chief Executive Officer
  Education: MBA from the University of Chicago
  Background: Nippon Venture Capital Corporation
  Masashi Kiyomine, Investment Director

2981 MVM LIFE SCIENCE PARTNERS
6 Henrietta Street
London WC2E 8PU
United Kingdom

Phone: 44-02075577500 **Fax:** 44-02075577501
e-mail: hh@mvm.com
web: www.mvmlifescience.com

Mission Statement: MVM's approach focuses on the risk and return characteristics of an investment rather than those criteria that are often used to define investments (e.g. sector, therapeutic area, stage of asset development). Hence, MVM invests in both early stage and late stage companies, platforms and products, discovery and development, devices and drugs.

Geographic Preference: Europe, Israel, United States
Fund Size: $500 million
Founded: 1997
Investment Criteria: Early-Stage, Later-Stage
Industry Group Preference: Biopharmaceuticals, Diagnostics, Drug Delivery, Gene Therapy, Healthcare Information Technology, Medical Devices, Life Sciences, Healthcare
Portfolio Companies: eZono AG, Patient Connect Service Limited, Horizon Discovery Limited, AccuVein, Lombard Medical Technologies, Vascular Pathways, Solx, Cheetah Medical Holdings, Tarsa Therapeutics, Alliance Pharma, Vantia Limited, Heptares Therapeutics, Cara Therapeutics, Zention Limited, Pulmagen Therapeutics, Wilson Therapeutics

Other Locations:
  Old City Hall
  45 School Street
  Boston, MA 02108
  Phone: 617-3832101 **Fax:** 617-3832106

Key Executives:
  Stephen Reeders, Founder
  e-mail: sr@mvm.com
  Education: Cambridge University; MD, Oxford University
  Background: Saunders Karp & Megrue
  Directorships: Beacon Endoscopic, Biomedix, Cara Therapeutics, Cheetah Medical, Pulmagen Therapeutics

2982 NANYANG VENTURES PTY LIMITED
Level 5 NAB House, 255 George Street
Sydney 2000
Australia

Phone: 61-292474866 **Fax:** 61-292411087
web: www.nanyang.com.au

Mission Statement: To provide outstanding returns to investors by subscribing equity into mainly private companies that have the potential to develop into substantial, listable corporations.

Geographic Preference: Australia
Fund Size: $150 Million
Founded: 1996
Average Investment: $3 Million
Minimum Investment: $2 Million
Investment Criteria: MBO, MBI
Industry Group Preference: All Sectors Considered

2983 NAPKN VENTURES
Brazil

web: www.napkn.co

Mission Statement: Napkn Ventures invests in outstanding entrepreneurs who want to change the world.

Portfolio Companies: Dabee, 2Mundos, Everwrite, Conta Azul

Key Executives:
  Luciano Tavares, Partner
  e-mail: luciano@napkn.co

Venture Capital & Private Equity Firms / International Firms

Education: BS, Business Administration, Fundacao Getulio Vargas; MS, Financial Engineering, Escola Politecnica da Universidade de Sao Paulo
Background: VP, Equity Derivatives, Merrill Lynch

2984 NARANYA VENTURES
Lazaro Cardenas 2400 Pte
Garza Garcia
Nuevo Leon CP 66260
Mexico

Phone: 52-81-8044-4500

Mission Statement: Naranya Ventures is a seed capital fund for mobile tech startups. We fund teams in their early stages that are looking for distribution and monetisation platforms in emerging markets with business models that solve meaningful problems and we help them with strategic advice, business development, financing, distribution, marketing and M&A at inflection points throughout their life.

Geographic Preference: Latin America
Investment Criteria: Seed-Stage, Early-Stage
Industry Group Preference: Mobile
Portfolio Companies: Cotton Tracks, Oja.la, Bit Pagos, PingStamp, Hostspot, Kuona, String, Cine+, AlmaBox, Flipter, Twitt2go, Tic, Compro Pago, Cre Apps

Key Executives:
  Arturo Galvan, Founding Partner
  e-mail: arturo.galvan@naranya.com
  Pablo Salazar, Managing Partner/Director
  e-mail: pablo.salazar@naranya.com
  Education: BS, Marketing, MS, Entrepreneurship, London Business School
  Background: Co-Founder, Latinstocks.com; Partner, IGNIA
  Sergio Romo, Managing Partner
  e-mail: sergio.romo@naranya.com
  Background: Co-Founder, Miorden.com; Co-Founder, Ploombox.com
  Jonathan Lewy, Managing Partner
  e-mail: jonathan.lewy@naranya.com
  Background: Co-Founder, Wise Media Group; Drake Finance; Co-Founder, Investomex

2985 NATWEST VENTURES LIMITED
Fenchurch Exchange, 8 Fenchurch Place
London EC3M 4TE
United Kingdom

Phone: 44-1713743000 **Fax:** 44-1713743572
web: www.natwest.com

Mission Statement: Supplying private equity across a broad range of sectors as part of the NatWest Group

Fund Size: $1 Billion
Founded: 1969
Average Investment: $7 Million
Minimum Investment: $1 Million
Industry Group Preference: All Sectors Considered
Portfolio Companies: Abec Group, Alperton Ford & Truck, Artcraft, Charrington Fuels, Bodegas Campo Burgo, El Rancho, Financiere Orefi, Graphics Arts Equipment, Mercury Taverns, Porter Lancastrian, Rusts of Cromer, DBS Nationwide, Expocolour, Gibbons Refractories, Groupe Soloc, Industrias Y Fundiciones Iglesias, John Barker Group, Magnus, Morris Homes, PKL Group, Pelham Homes, Peterhouse Group, Robison and Davidson, Rodgers Plant Hire, Thomas Steelwork, Trevi Holdings, Victor Homes Charco 99, France Portes, Hill Leigh Group, Wade Building Services, Chemical Express, Chemical Manufacturing and Refining, HRP Refrigerants, Solrec, Sterling Technology, Victrex

2986 NAUSICAA VENTURES
Axisparc Business Center
Rue Fond Cattelain 2/1.2
Mont-Saint-Guibert B-1435
Belgium

Phone: 32-010485020 **Fax:** 32-010485021
Toll-Free: 21
web: www.nausicaa-ventures.be

Mission Statement: Nausicaa Ventures is an early stage investment fund organisation focused on investment rounds between EUR 1 and 4 million. Nausicaa Ventures was created in 2009 by bringing together 35 private investors and selected institutional investors, such as the European Investment Fund or ING Bank, under the management of an experienced investment team. The target size of Nausicaa Ventures is upwards of EUR 20 million. Nausicaa Ventures combines the best of institutional venture capital groups and individual investors. It aims to cover the equity gap faced by most, promising early stage companies on their path towards profitable growth.

Geographic Preference: Belgium
Average Investment: 1 - 4 million Euro
Investment Criteria: Early-Stage, Early Growth-Stage
Industry Group Preference: Information Technology, Communications, Medical Technology, Clean Technology, High Technology

Key Executives:
  Bart Luyten, General Partner
  Education: Applied Economics, University of Antwerp
  Background: Parter, Privast Capital Partners; Director, Partners@Venture

2987 NAUTA CAPITAL
Avda. Diagonal, 593 7th Floor
Barcelona 08014
Spain

Phone: 34-93-503-5900
e-mail: info@nautacapital.com
web: www.nautacapital.com

Mission Statement: Nauta Capital, founded in 2004 with presence in Barcelona (Spain), Boston (USA) and London (UK), is a Venture Capital firm specialized in early stage disruptive technology companies having a special focus on 3 segments: wireless/mobility, enterprise software/security, and ecommerce/internet. Nauta seeks to invest in companies that have developed highly disruptive technologies or business models, have strong potential to grow and a clear strategy to develop international markets. Nauta partners with highly committed and solvent executive teams in Europe and the USA.

Geographic Preference: Europe, United States
Fund Size: £170 million
Founded: 2004
Investment Criteria: Early-Stage
Industry Group Preference: Wireless Technologies, Mobile, Enterprise Software, Internet, E-Commerce & Manufacturing, Security
Portfolio Companies: Abiquo, Agnitio, AirSense, BaseKit, Brandwatch, CarrierIQ, Eyeview, Fizzback, Fractus, GCM, Nubera, Groupalia, Handmade, iJento, In Crowd, Jitterbug, Marfeel, Mobileaware, Mysportgroup, Privalia, Scytl, Socialpoint, Taptap, Yuilop

Other Locations:
  200 High Street
  Third Floor
  Boston, MA 02110
  Phone: 617-986-5060

  42-44 Grosvenor Gardens
  London SW1W 0EB

Venture Capital & Private Equity Firms / International Firms

United Kingdom
Phone: 44-0-203-553-5757

Key Executives:
Dominic Endicott, General Partner
Education: BS, Economics, London School of Economics; MBA, MIT Sloan School of Management
Background: TMT Practice, Diamond Cluster International; Booz Allen

2988 NBC CAPITAL PTY LIMITED
493 Ipswich Road
Level 1
Annerley Qld 4103
Australia

Phone: 61-732339200 **Fax:** 61-732339223
e-mail: info@nbccapital.com.au

Mission Statement: Equity capital for growing companies.

Fund Size: $100 Million
Founded: 1999
Average Investment: $5 Million
Minimum Investment: $2 Million
Investment Criteria: High Growth Sectors
Industry Group Preference: Manufacturing, Agribusiness, Health Related, Food & Beverage, Technology

Key Executives:
Bruce Scott, Managing Director
Education: Bachelor of Commerce
Background: Pioneer's Chief Executive Officer, Trinity Consolidated Group Limited, Northern Business Consultants
Bernard Stapleton, Director

2989 NEO TECHNOLOGY VENTURES
Australia

Mission Statement: Neo's investment model and expertise is based on identifying innovative and sustainable technology-based businesses through which it can help passionate entrepreneurs create the next market leaders.

Geographic Preference: Australia
Average Investment: Up to $5 million
Investment Criteria: Early And Expansion Stage
Industry Group Preference: Internet, Digital Media & Marketing, Communications, Clean Technology
Portfolio Companies: Open Kernel Labs, Genbook, SigNav, RPO

Key Executives:
Brett Morris, General Partner
+61 414 918 600
e-mail: brett.morris@ntfund.com
Education: BSc, University of Auckland
Marc Woodward, General Partner
+61 439 980 299
e-mail: marc.woodward@ntfund.com
Education: Georgetown University

2990 NEOMARKKA OYJ Neomarkka
Niinistönkatu 8 to 12
Helsinki 05800
Finland

Phone: 358-207-209190 **Fax:** 358-968446531
e-mail: info@neoindustrial.fi

Mission Statement: Invests in industrial companies with long term potential.

Geographic Preference: Finland
Fund Size: $115 Million
Founded: 1987
Average Investment: $6.62 Million
Minimum Investment: $1.2 Million
Investment Criteria: Synergic Industrial Investments
Industry Group Preference: Cable

Portfolio Companies: Aspocomp Group Oyj, Atria Yhtymä Oyj, Finnair Oyj, Finnlines Oyj, Fortum Oyj, HK Ruokatalo Oyj, Huhtamäki Oyj, Kemira Oyj, Kemira GrowHow Oyj, Kesko Oyj, M-Real Oyj, Okmetic Oyj, Osuuspankkien Keskuspankki Oyj, Olvi Oyj, Outokumpu Oyj, Pohjola-Yhtymä Oyj, Raisio Yhtymä Oyj, Rautaruukki Oyj, Stora Enso Oyj, Tecnomen Oyj, UPM-Kymmene Oyj

Key Executives:
Markku E. Rentto, Chairman
Education: Master of Science (Econ.)
Background: Kaupthing New York, Managing Director, Kaupthing Bank hf., Dep. CEO, Kaupthing hf., Dep. CEO
Directorships: CEO
Sari Tulander, Chief Financial Officer
Education: Master of Science (Econ.)
Background: Kaupthing Bank hf., Managing Director and CEO, Kaupthing hf., Deputy Managing Director
Directorships: Director

2991 NEOTENY COMPANY LIMITED
3F Plaza Mikado, 2-14-5 Akasaka Minato-ku
Tokyo 107-0052
Japan

Phone: 81-355492270 **Fax:** 81-355492271
e-mail: jito@neoteny.com
web: www.neoteny.com

Mission Statement: Invests in developing and supporting information technology-based businesses.

Geographic Preference: Silicon Valley, Japan
Fund Size: $86, 200
Founded: 2000
Investment Criteria: Early Stage, Seed
Industry Group Preference: Communications, Networking, Enabling Technology, Electronic Technology, Technology
Portfolio Companies: 3Dsolve, BeatCraft, Inc., Blockline, Inc. (e-Colle), BrainSellers.com, Contents Japan, Generation Create, fyto, IP Infusion Inc., Mediaprobe Inc., Neoteny Venture Development, Six Apart

Key Executives:
Joichi Ito, Chief Executive Officer & Founder
e-mail: jito@neoteny.com
Education: B.A. in Economics, MBA (Harvard Business School)
Background: Managing Director and Branch Manager of the Tokyo office of Goldman, Sachs & Co.
Jun Makihara, Chairman

2992 NESBIC INVESTMENT FUND II
Rozenburglaan 3
3503 RM
PO Box 8530
Groningen 9727 DL
Netherlands

Phone: 31-502110100 **Fax:** 31-502110119

Mission Statement: Value added Venture Capital Investors enabling, supporting and accelerating growth.

Geographic Preference: Europe, North America, South America
Fund Size: $144 Million
Founded: 1997
Average Investment: $14.4 Milllion
Minimum Investment: $2.4 Million
Investment Criteria: Invests in companies with Well Balanced Management Team, Predictable Cash Flow, Pan European Growth Opportunities, Realistic Business Plan, Springboard Position in their Market Segment
Industry Group Preference: Food & Beverage, Business to Business, Publishing, Media, Logistics, Healthcare
Portfolio Companies: Boekhandels Groep Nederland Holding BV, Boemer BV, Fair Information Services BV, Incotec Holding BV, JSI NV, Koninklijke Swets and Zeitlinger BV

Venture Capital & Private Equity Firms / International Firms

Key Executives:
Robert Wilhelm, Managing Partner
Education: Master Degree, Economics, University of Amsterdam
Background: Over five years of international venture capital experience at Atlas Venture in Amsterdam and Boston.
Directorships: Senior Executive Mergers & Acquisitions of the pan European telecommunications joint venture Unisource NV for four years
Willem Van Vark, Chief Financial Officer
Education: SPD degree next to a degree as Auditor for small and medium-sized business companies (AA).
Background: Financial controller at Amev
Directorships: Certified Public Auditor (CPA)

2993 NETROVE ASIA SDN BHD
140 One Pacific Place, Floor 17th, Unit 1703-
Sukhumvit Rd
Klongteoy
Bangkok 10110
Thailand
Phone: 60-380231360 Fax: 60-380231361
e-mail: ideas@netrove.com
web: www.netrove.com

Mission Statement: Generating net value through sharing.
Geographic Preference: Asia
Fund Size: $17 Million
Founded: 1999
Average Investment: $500,000
Minimum Investment: $100,000
Investment Criteria: Start-up, Growth
Industry Group Preference: Semiconductors, Agriculture, Biotechnology, Web Applications & Services
Portfolio Companies: Corpmart.com, MnEBay, V2 Technology, Deltaknot

Key Executives:
Teh Kim Seng, Chairman
Education: Graduated, Electrical and Electronics Engineering , MIS degree.
Background: NCR, AT&T and Bell Lab.
Bryan Chung, Partner
Education: L.L.B, L.L.M.
Background: Clarion Capital.

2994 NEUHAUS PARTNERS
Jungfernsteig 30
Hamburg 20354
Germany
Phone: 49-40-355-2820 Fax: 49-40-355-28239
web: www.neuhauspartners.com

Mission Statement: Founded in 1998, Neuhaus Partners is headquartered in the heart of Hamburg. The team is composed of 10 individuals who are mostly IT specialists with successful careers in the industry. Dr. Gottfried Neuhaus (Managing Partner) developed his hardware and software company into one of Germany's most successful telecommunications companies in the 1980's and 1990's. Dr. Neuhaus Computer KGaA produced a number of pioneering products in the field of data telecommunications.
Geographic Preference: European Union
Fund Size: 126 million euro
Founded: 1998
Industry Group Preference: High Technology, Information Technology, Hardware, Software, Infrastructure, Laser, Photonics, Microsystems, Telecommunications, Multimedia
Portfolio Companies: Antispameurope, Apprupt, Charismathics, Content Fleet, Exit Games, HR New Media, INTENIUM, Kaboa, MAZ Germany, MyHeritage, Next Kraftwerke, Propertybase, Searchmetrics, Smava, Sofatronic, Tellja, Testroom, Tolingo

Key Executives:
Gottfried Neuhaus, Managing Partner
Education: PhD
Background: Founder, Neuhaus Computer

2995 NEW MODEL VENTURE CAPITAL
58 Davies St.
London W1K 5JF
United Kingdom
Phone: 44-020-3538-5274
e-mail: info@newmodel.vc
web: newmodel.vc

Mission Statement: New Model Venture Capital is a team of experienced private equity and venture capital professionals who offer investors a pragmatic approach to venture capital, private equity, and corporate finance.
Portfolio Companies: EyeQuant, Live Better With, MOGO BankConnect, Property Detective, Radara, Wazoku, Xenomorph

Key Executives:
James King, Managing Director
Mark Hanington, Managing Director
Education: University of Leeds
Background: Managing Director, Fig
Robin McIlvenny, Managing Director
Background: Deutsche Bank; Security Pacific National Bank; Creditanstalt; JP Morgan
David Marshall, Managing Director

2996 NEW WORLD INFRASTRUCTURE LIMITED
17/F, New world tower, 18 Queens Road
Tower II
Central
Hong Kong
Phone: 852-21310600 Fax: 852-21310611
e-mail: nwsnews@nwsh.com.hk

Mission Statement: Committed to taking an instrumental role in incubating china dotcom companies.
Geographic Preference: Hong Kong
Fund Size: $2.4 Billion
Founded: 1995
Industry Group Preference: Infrastructure, Energy, Cargo Handling, Water

Key Executives:
Zheng Jiachun, Chairman
Background: Marriott international Inc.
Tsang Yam Pui, Executive Director

2997 NEWABLE VENTURES
140 Aldersgate Street
6th Floor
London EC1A 4HY
United Kingdom
e-mail: privateinvesting@newable.co.uk
web: www.newable.co.uk/private-investing

Mission Statement: The Fund targets the funding gap that exists for companies which have de-risked their technology, developed traction with customers and now seek funding to scale their commercial operations. The Fund aims to provide investors with a diversified portfolio of 7-10 Qualifying Companies.
Geographic Preference: United Kingdom
Fund Size: £2 Million
Founded: 1982
Average Investment: £250,000
Minimum Investment: £50,000
Investment Criteria: Early-Stage, Growth, Pre-Series A

Industry Group Preference: Space Technology, Downstream Technologies, Electronics, Automation, Medical Technology, Life Sciences
Portfolio Companies: BluWireless Technology, Contact Engine, Sphere Fluidics, Rezatec, Hummingbird Technologies, Jellagen, Hopster, Oxtex, City Pantry, Benivo
Key Executives:
  Alex Sleigh
  Education: MA, Economics/Modern History, University of St. Andrews; MA, General Management, Vlerick Ghent Management School, Belgium
  Background: Investor In Residence, King's College
  Anthony Clarke
  Background: Co-Founder/Director, Seraphim Capital VC Fund; Co-Founder/Chair, UK Business Angel Association; President Emeritus, European Business Angel Network; Chartered Accountant/Chartered Secretary, Deloitte Haskins & Sells

2998 NEWMARGIN VENTURE CAPITAL
Villa 11, Radisson Plaza, 78 Xing Guo Road
Shanghai 200052
China
Phone: 86-2162138000 **Fax:** 86-2162123900
e-mail: info@newmargin.com
web: www.newmargin.com

Mission Statement: Mission is to support China's emerging entrepreneurs to build world-class companies.

Geographic Preference: China
Fund Size: $120 Million
Founded: 1999
Average Investment: $1-$5 Million
Minimum Investment: $1 Million
Investment Criteria: Early Stage Investments
Industry Group Preference: Information Technology, Healthcare, Biotechnology, Environment Products & Services, Materials Technology
Portfolio Companies: Asiainfo, CNC, Chinalliances, E-Future, Geong, Infosec, Lanjing Technology, M&W, One Wave, Rongshu.com, Roxus, Shanghai Mining Software Company, Sinofusion
Key Executives:
  Feng Tao, Founder & CEO
  e-mail: info@newmargin.com
  Zhou Shuiwen, Managing Partner

2999 NEXIT VENTURES OY
Kaisaniemenkatu 2 b
Helsinki Fl-00100
Finland
Phone: 358 9 6818 910
e-mail: info@nexitventures.com
web: www.nexitventures.com

Mission Statement: Venture capital firm focused on mobile and wireless innovation.

Geographic Preference: Nordics, U.S. West Coast
Founded: 1999
Investment Criteria: Start-up, Growth
Industry Group Preference: Mobile, Wireless
Portfolio Companies: Bitfone, Futuremark, Hantro, HDmessaging, Hybrid Graphics, Mobile 365, Octoshape, Rightware, SkyPilot
Other Locations:
  Nexit Ventures Inc.
  14th Floor
  San Francisco, CA 94105
  Phone: 408-725-8400
Key Executives:
  Michel Wendell, General Partner
  e-mail: michel.wendell@nexitventures.com
  Background: Cadence Design Systems
  Artturi Tarjanne, General Partner
  e-mail: artturi.tarjanne@nexitventures.com
  Background: Solid Information Technology; AT Consulting
  Pekka Salonoja, General Partner
  e-mail: pekka.salonoja@nexitventures.com
  Education: Helsinki University of Technology
  Background: Nokia; Startupfactory
  Sami Karppinen, Investment Director
  e-mail: sami.karppinen@nexitventures.com
  Education: Helsinki University of Technology
  Risto Yli-Tainio, Chief Financial Officer
  e-mail: risto.yli-tainio@nexitventures.com
  Education: University of Vaasa
  Background: Sitra; Sonera Corp.; SmartTrust

3000 NEXTEC DEVELOPMENT CAPITAL LIMITED
Suite 4, Level 10
66 Hunter Street
Sydney 2000
Australia
Phone: 61-292378600 **Fax:** 61-29-237-8690
e-mail: richard.gibson@nextec.com.au
web: www.nextec.com.au

Mission Statement: Specializes in providing strategic capital and independent corporate advice for growth orientated companies.

Geographic Preference: Australia
Founded: 1996
Industry Group Preference: Media, Information Technology, Healthcare, Entertainment, High Value Added Manufacturing, Retail, Consumer & Leisure, Financial Services, Healthcare
Key Executives:
  Richard Gibson, Managing Director
  e-mail: mail@nextec.com.au
  Neil Bourne, Managing Director

3001 NEXUS VENTURE PARTNERS Nexus India Capital Advisors Pvt Ltd
G-2 Sarjan Plaza
100, Dr. Annie Besant Road
Worli
Mumbai 400018
India
Phone: 91-2266260000 **Fax:** 91-2266260001
web: www.nexusvp.com

Mission Statement: Nexus Venture Partners is India's leading Venture Capital fund. NVP invest in early and early growth stage companies across sectors in India and US. They are a team of successful entrepreneurs with extensive investing and operating experience, who love to get their hands dirty. They understand the unique challenges faced by entrepreneurs and know that it takes teamwork and exceptional execution capability for a company to succeed. Their partner companies have access to the entire Nexus team in India and Silicon Valley for help in recruiting talent, forging new alliances, opening doors to new customers, shaping strategy and connecting with best-of-breed executives, advisors, co-investors and board members.

Geographic Preference: India, United States
Average Investment: Up to $10 million
Investment Criteria: Early-Stage, Early Growth-Stage
Industry Group Preference: Internet, Media, Technology, Agriculture, Consumer Services, Consumer Products, Business Products & Services
Portfolio Companies: Altruist, Armor5, Aryaka, BSB, Cloud.com, CloudByte, Craftsvilla.com, Datagres, Dimdim, D.Light, Druva, Eka, EyeQ, Genwi, Gluster, GreyWater, Helpshift, ISFC, Kaltura, Kirusa, Komli, Map My India, MChek, Mistral, Netmagic, OLX, Prana, Pubmatic, Salorix,

Venture Capital & Private Equity Firms / International Firms

ScaleARc, Sedemac, ShopClues.com, Snapdeal.com, Sohan Lal Commodity, Suminter India Organics, Talent Sprint, Unicon, Unmetric, Vdopia, What's On India

Other Locations:
Nexus India Capital Advisors Pvt Ltd
Suite 1001, 10th Floor, Tower B, RMZ Millenia
No. 1&2, Murphy Road, Close to Ulsoor Lake
Bangalore 560 008
India
Phone: 91-8049456600

2200 Sand Hill Road
Suite 230
Menlo Park, CA 94025
Phone: 650-2330700

Key Executives:
Naren Gupta, Co-Founder
e-mail: naren@nexusvp.com
Education: BTech, Indian Institute of Technology; MS, California Institute of Technology; PhD, Stanford University
Background: Co-Founder, Integrated Systems
Directorships: Red Hat, Tibco

3002 NHN INVESTMENT
7th FL, KT&G Tower
416 Yeongdong-daero
Gangnam-gu
Seoul 135-549
Korea
Phone: 82-221364500
web: www.nhninv.com

Mission Statement: Provides investment, loan, management as well as technological guidance to new technology enterprises and venture businesses.

Industry Group Preference: Internet, Mobile, Gaming, Information Technology, Communications, Internet, Semiconductors, Medical Devices

Portfolio Companies: LTC, Dongwoon Anatech, M-Biz Global, Mekics Co., Dym Co., Nanoom Tech, Glosil, Smart Ace, Nepes Display, ATO Solution Co., Kostek Systems, SPM, Wonil Co., Saehwa IMC, Caffe Bene, Vessel Co., Solueta Co., DCG Systems, UGint, Doobic, Rekoo

Key Executives:
Jong-Seung Lee, Executive Director
Background: CEO, Korea Investment Partners

3003 NIELSEN INNOVATE FUND
PO Box 3113
15 Halamish St
Northern Industrial Park
Caesarea 30889
Israel
Phone: 972-722-700-790 **Fax:** 927-722-700-791
e-mail: info@nif.co.il
web: www.nielseninnovate.com

Mission Statement: Nielsen Innovate is an early stage technological incubator licensed by the Chief Scientist of Israel. It operates as an incubator and investment fund.

Geographic Preference: Israel
Founded: 2013
Investment Criteria: Early Stage
Industry Group Preference: Market Research, Consumer Behavior, Data & Analytics, Marketing, Big Data, Social Services, Mobile, New Media
Portfolio Companies: eDealya, Zollo, Revuze, Evolita, Adstrix, cValue, Mobilibuy

Key Executives:
Esther Barak-Landes, CEO
e-mail: esther@nif.co.il
Education: LL.b, Tel Aviv University; MBA, IDC Business School
Background: CEO, Partam Hightech; Founding Partner, Israel-Angels; Senior Business Development Executive, Cash U Mobile Technologies; Corporate Attorney, Kantor, Elhanni, Tal and Co
Dov Yarkoni, VP Business Development
e-mail: dov@nif.co.il
Education: Bachelor of Technology, Engineering and Management, Shenkar
Background: SVP, Business Development and Sales, Matomy Media Group; VP, Client Services, Amadesa; Director of Consumer Division, Deltathree

3004 NIF VENTURES COMPANY LIMITED
1-2-1, Kyobashi
Daiwa Yaesu Building Chuo-ku
5th Floor
Tokyo 104-0031
Japan
Phone: 81-352011570 **Fax:** 81-352011518
web: www.nif.co.jp

Mission Statement: Committed to developing worldwide opportunities for both investors and entrepreneurs.

Geographic Preference: Tokyo
Fund Size: 10 Million Yen
Founded: 2006

3005 NIPPON TECHNOLOGY VENTURE PARTNERS LIMITED
Ekimae Bldg. 4th Floor, 4-1-1
Todoroki, Setagaya-ku
Tokyo 158-0082
Japan
Phone: 81-357581311 **Fax:** 81-357581322
web: www.ntvp.com

Mission Statement: Invests in independent innovative individuals and institutions with incubating new businesses with international cooperation and investment incentives.

Geographic Preference: Japan
Fund Size: 14 Billion Yen
Founded: 1998
Investment Criteria: Venture Finance, Management Consultation
Industry Group Preference: Information Technology, Financial Services, Management, Marketing

Key Executives:
Kazutaka Muraguchi, Representative Director
Education: Bachelor in Economics from Keio University
Background: Investment Manager in JAFCO.
Directorships: Founder.

3006 NISSAY CAPITAL
No. 4 No. 8 Nissei Nagata-cho Building
8th Floor
Nagatacho, Chiyoda-ku
Tokyo 100-0014
Japan
Phone: 03-35016644 **Fax:** 03-35016640
web: www.nissay-cap.co.jp

Mission Statement: Responds to a wide range of on-stage capital policy. Makes a wide range of investment capital policy stance based on the medium-and long-term investment, an eye to the post-listing from the startup.

Fund Size: 3 billion yen
Founded: 1991
Portfolio Companies: Nippon Dry-Chemical, Morpho, Pharmaceutical SymBio, Berg Earth, Double-Scope, Chiome Bioscience, Startflyer, Tee Life

Venture Capital & Private Equity Firms / International Firms

3007 NOMURA PHASE4 VENTURES LTD
Nomura House
1 St Martins-le-Grand
London EC1A 4NP
United Kingdom

Phone: 44-20-7521-2386 Fax: 44-20-7521-1291
web: www.nomura.com

Mission Statement: To provide a premium rate of return for investors by creating, identifying and investing in development stage healthcare companies.

Geographic Preference: United States, Europe
Average Investment: $10 - $25 million
Industry Group Preference: Healthcare, Pharmaceuticals, Medical Devices
Portfolio Companies: ACADIA Pharmaceuticals, Inc., Albrieo, Altus Pharamceuticals, Arakis, Ark Therapeutics, ARYx Therapeutics, Atani, Avant Immunotherapeutics, Cerimon Pharmaceuticals, Chroma Therapeutics, Contec Medical, DeveloGen, DrugAbuse Sciences, Idenix, Immgenics, Intercell, Morphochem, Nabriva Therapeutics, OmniSonics Medical Technologies, OncoMed Pharmaceuticals, Paratek Pharmaceuticals, Pharmion, Phenomix, Proteolix, Sequenom, Targacept, Viacell, Weston Medical, Zosano Pharma

Key Executives:
Koji Nagai, Group CEO
Education: PhD & BSc, Birmingham University; University of California, Berkeley
Background: Investment Manager, Rothschild Asset Management
Directorships: Albireo, Cerimon, Indenix, Nabriva, OncoMed
Atsushi Yoshikawa, President and Group COO
Education: LLB, Hull University
Background: Corporate Lawyer, Freshfield
Naveed Siddiqi, Partner
Education: Medical Degree, Guy's Hospital, London
Background: EFG Group

3008 NORDIC CAPITAL
4A Stureplan
Stockholm SE-11435
Sweden

Phone: 46-84405050 Fax: 46-86117998
web: www.nordiccapital.se

Mission Statement: Actively seeking new investments.

Geographic Preference: Denmark, Finland, Norway, Sweden, Continental Europe
Fund Size: $0.19 Billion
Founded: 1989
Average Investment: $6.35 - 82.6 Million
Minimum Investment: $63, 500 - $0.5 Million
Investment Criteria: Focuses on companies with predictable cash-flows, strong market positions, turnarounds and development capital situations with a view to create long-term value rather than current profits
Industry Group Preference: All Sectors Considered
Portfolio Companies: Elmo-Calf, Eosex, Gislaved Folic, Hilding Anders, MóLnlycke Health Care, Nycomed Pharma, Wilson Logistics Group

Key Executives:
Mark Bulmer, Partner and Head of Banking
e-mail: cathrine.siwers@nordiccapital.com
Education: M. Sc. in Business Administration and Economics.
Background: Sifo Research International.
Jonas Agnblad, Partner
e-mail: robert.andreen@nordiccapital.se
Education: MSc, PhD in Industrial Management.
Background: SKF, Svenska Handelsebanken.
Bo Soderberg, Partner
e-mail: bo.soderberg@nordiccapital.se
Education: MSc in Economics.
Background: Industrivarden AB, Spira Invest, Forreningsbanken.
Robert Andreen, Partner
e-mail: christian.dyvig@nordiccapital.se
Education: LLM and MBA (Hons).
Background: Department at Morgan Stanley.
Anders Hultin, Partner
e-mail: lars.spongberg@nordiccapital.se
Education: MSc in Economics.
Background: Electrolux Group, Svenska Handelsbanken, Svenska Finans International, AB Handel & Industri, Autoliv Group, Spectra Physics.
Fredrik Näslund, Partner
e-mail: kent.stevens.larsen@nordiccapital.se
Education: MBA, INSEAD; MS, Engineering.
Background: McKinsey & Company.
Ulf Rosberg, Senior Adviser
e-mail: ulf.rosberg@nordiccapital.se
Education: MSc in Economics , Major in Finance.
Background: Corporate Finance at Enskilda Fondkommission, Leirndorfer Bernhardtson Westerberg & Partners.
Peter Hansson, Partner
e-mail: peter.hansson@nordiccapital.se
Education: MSc in Economics.
Background: Merrill Lynch in London.
Joakim Karlsson, Managing Partner
e-mail: joakim.karlsson@nordiccapital.se
Education: MS, Economics, Graduate Business School.
Background: JP Morgan in London, Swedish Embassy in Moscow.
Kristoffer Melinder, Managing Partner
e-mail: kristoffer.melinder@nordiccapital.se
Education: MSc in Economics and The University of Cologne.
Background: JP Morgan in London, UN-Officer Bosnia.
Morgan Olsson, Partner
e-mail: morgan.olsson@nordiccapital.se
Education: M.Sc.. Business Administration
Background: Svetab, Svenska Handelsbanken
Toni Weitzberg, Partner
e-mail: felix.bjorklund@nordiccapital.se
Education: M.Sc. in Economics and Business Administration.
Background: Fazer Group.
Kim Gulstad, Principal
e-mail: kim.gulstad@nordiccapital.com
Education: M.Sc. in Applied Economics and Finance and a B.Sc. in Economics and Business Administration.
Background: Investment Banking Division at Goldman Sachs in London.

3009 NORDIC MEZZANINE LIMITED
Mikonkatu 4 B
4th Floor
Helsinki 00100
Finland

Phone: 358-96840640 Fax: 358-968406410
e-mail: vesa.suurmunn@nordicmezzanine.com
web: www.nordicmezzanine.com

Mission Statement: Nordic Mezzanine provides mezzanine financing for buyouts, growth and capital restructuring.

Geographic Preference: Nordic Countries, Germany, Austria, Switzerland, the Netherlands, Belg
Fund Size: EUR 480 million
Founded: 1998
Average Investment: EUR 10 to 40 million
Minimum Investment: $6 Million
Investment Criteria: Buyouts, Buyins, Growth Capital
Industry Group Preference: All Sectors Considered
Portfolio Companies: Dyno Nobel A, Nycomed Pharma, Frigoscandia, pParoc, Dynapac, Global Garden Products, Jamo, Dometic, ANI Printing Inks

Venture Capital & Private Equity Firms / International Firms

Key Executives:
Vesa Surmunne, CEO
e-mail: pekka.hietaniemi@nordicmezzanine.com
Education: MSC, MBA.
Background: Hambro European Ventures, MB Corporate Finanace, Postidankki Limited.
Pekka Hietaniemi, Executive Director
e-mail: pekkasunila@compuserve.com
Education: MSC, MBA.
Background: Hambro European Ventures, MB Corporate Finance, Control Data.

3010 NORTH WEST FUND
The Maltings
98, Wilderspool Causeway
Warrington WA4 6PU
United Kingdom

Phone: 01925-418232
web: www.thenorthwestfund.co.uk

Mission Statement: The North West Fund provides debt and equity finance from £50,000 to £2 million to small and medium sized businesses based in, or relocating to, the North West of England to start, develop and grow.

Geographic Preference: North West United Kingdom
Founded: 1982
Average Investment: £50,000 to £2 million
Investment Criteria: Early-Stage, Start-Up
Industry Group Preference: Technology
Portfolio Companies: Compliance Control, BiOxyDyn, SenseLogix Limited, Molplex, Redtree People, Dot Medical

Key Executives:
Malcolm Edge, Chairman NWBF
Background: Vice Chairman, KPMG UK

3011 NORTHERN ENTERPRISE LIMITED
11 Waterloo Square
Newcastle upon Tyne
Gateshead NE1 4DP
United Kingdom

Phone: 44-8451111850 Fax: 44-8451111853
e-mail: enquiries@nel.co.uk
web: www.nel.co.uk

Mission Statement: Independent fund management organization that provides risk funding to growth businesses that are based in the North East Region.

Geographic Preference: United Kingdom
Fund Size: £90 Million
Founded: 1989
Average Investment: $0.31 Million
Minimum Investment: $0.04 Million
Investment Criteria: Seed, Start-up, Early Stage, Expansion and Development, MBO, MBI, Mezzanine
Industry Group Preference: Biotechnology, Chemicals, Industrial Services, Industrial Equipment, Consumer Services, Energy, Environment Products & Services, Leisure, Medical & Health Related, Electronic Technology, Manufacturing, Service Industries, Transportation, Materials Technology
Portfolio Companies: Non Linear Dynamics Ltd, Orchard Information Systems Ltd, Visitech International Ltd, Torque Tension Systems Ltd, Appleyards Plastics Ltd.

Key Executives:
Barrie Hensby, Chief Executive
e-mail: enquires@nel.co.uk
Background: Northern Enterprise Limited
Chris Parker, Investment Executive
e-mail: enquires@nel.co.uk

3012 NORTHSTAR VENTURES
Maybrook House, 5th Floor
27-35 Grainger Street
Newcastle upon Tyne NE1 5JE
United Kingdom

Phone: 44-0191-229-2770
web: www.northstarventures.co.uk

Mission Statement: Based in Newcastle, Northstar is a venture capital firm with over £80m under management. Northstar has been inspiring local entrepreneurs with financial backing and the expertise of a highly experienced team since 2004, investing in over 200 pioneering, high potential enterprises.

Geographic Preference: North East UK
Fund Size: £80 million
Founded: 2004
Investment Criteria: Early-Stage
Industry Group Preference: Biotechnology, Technology, Television, Film, Digital Media & Marketing, Music, Gaming, Healthcare, Energy, Environment
Portfolio Companies: Orangebus, Screenreach, Aframe, Low Carbon Lighting, Car 2 U, The Wood Heating Company, Mylearnadfriend, Applied Graphene Materials, Audacious, Biomass CHP, Komodo, Socialrel8

Key Executives:
Ian Richards, Director
0191-229-2778
e-mail: ian.richards@northstarventures.co.uk
Background: 3i, National Westminster Bank
Alasdair Greig, Director
0191-229-2775
e-mail: alasdair.greig@northstarventures.co.uk
Education: BA, Heriot Watt University; MBA, Ashridge
Background: The Cambridge Gateway Fund; Emerging Markets Credit Risk, CIBC World Markets

3013 NORTHZONE
Master Samuelsgatan 42, 16 tr
Box 7257
Stockholm 103 89
Sweden

Phone: 46-8-599-05-880
e-mail: info@northzone.com
web: www.northzone.com

Mission Statement: Northzone is a technology investment partnership. Over the past 17 years we have been chosen by some of Europe's most exceptional entrepreneurs as a long-term partner for growth. We have thus far invested in over 75 companies, injecting some 200 years of collective operational and investment experience into businesses that truly make a difference.

Geographic Preference: Nordics, United States, Europe
Founded: 1996
Investment Criteria: Early-Stage, Expansion-Stage
Industry Group Preference: Digital Media & Marketing, Media, E-Commerce & Manufacturing, Energy Efficiency, Cloud Computing
Portfolio Companies: Appear Networks, Artfinder, Avito, Asetek, Billian, Bilguiden, BraveNew Talent, ChapDrive, Climatewell, Colibria, Doubletwist, Edvantage Group, Energy Micro, Envox, EPiServer, EProspects, Fox Technologies, Fotango Ltd, Funcom, Global Name Registry, Hugin, Ibistic, Imbera, Innotech Solar, Intility, IZettle, Jasper, Lastminute, Mamut, Massmarket, MCP, Naptech, Nevion, NextGenTel, Nimsoft, Norstel, NYX Security, Photonyx, P1.CN, Playdo, PortIT, PriceRunner, Reisefeber, ReVolt Technology, Silex Microsystems, Soundrop, Spaceape Games, Spotify, Stepstone, Sticky, Supponor, Testfreaks, The Online Backup Company, Tinde, Tobii, Trolltech, Trustpilot, VideoPlaza, VisualDNA, Widespace, X5 Music Group, Xcerion

Venture Capital & Private Equity Firms / International Firms

Other Locations:
Bygdoy Alle 2
Pb. 573 Sentrum
Oslo 0105
Norway
Phone: 47-22-12-5010

Strandvejen 100, 4th Floor
Hellerup 2900
Denmark
Phone: 45-70-222-475

Key Executives:
Tellef Thorleifsson, Co-Founder
Education: MSc, Business Adminstration, Norwegian School of Economics, MSc, Economics, London School of Economics
Background: Founder, Western Bulk Shipping
Directorships: Innotech Solar, Online Backup Company, Chapdrive, Silex

3014 NOTION CAPITAL
8a Ledbury Mews North
London W11 2AF
United Kingdom
Phone: 44-08454989393
e-mail: info@notioncapital.com
web: www.notioncapital.com

Mission Statement: Notion is an entrepreneur-backed venture capital firm focused on Cloud Computing and Software-as-a-Service. We have a unique approach to investing that is founded on entrepreneurial empathy and a laser focus on a market that we know very well.

Geographic Preference: United Kingdom
Industry Group Preference: Cloud Computing, SaaS
Portfolio Companies: Brightpearl, Concentra, eSellerProf, New Voice Media, Norland Technology, Selfnet, Shutl, Star, The Currency Cloud, Tradeshift, Zattikka

Other Locations:
Suite 101
Eagle Tower
Montpellier Drive, Cheltenham
Gloucestershire GL50 1TA
United Kingdom
Phone: 44-1-845-498-9393

Key Executives:
Stephen Chandler, Managing Partner
Education: University of Exeter
Background: Deloitte, UBS Investment Bank
Directorships: SelfNet, Star, Tradeshift

3015 NOVO A/S
Tuborg Havnevej 19
Hellerup Dk-2900
Denmark
Phone: 45-35276500 **Fax:** 45-35276510
e-mail: ventures@novo.dk
web: www.novo.dk

Mission Statement: An active and independent company in its support of biotech ventures. The aspiration is to bring together the best of both worlds: industry insight and network from our pharma/biotech inheritance combined with a venture capital mindset that focuses on results and value creation.

Geographic Preference: Denmark, Europe, North America
Founded: 1999
Average Investment: 1 - 15 million Euro
Investment Criteria: Startups, Seed Stage, IPO, Public Companies
Industry Group Preference: Biotechnology, Life Sciences, Medical Devices
Portfolio Companies: 7TM Pharma, Alios BioPharma, AlloCure, Altheos, Amira Pharmaceuticals, AnaptysBio, Asante Solutions, BioMimetic Therapeutics, Cell Biosciences, Celltrix, Cytochroma, f-star GmbH, Funxional Therapeutics, Inogen, LifeCycle Pharma, Light Sciences Oncology, Logical Therapeutics, Lux Biosciences, MediQuest Therapeutics, Metabolex, NeoMend, NeuroTherapeutics Pharma, Nuevolution, Ophthotech Corporation, Otonomy, PTC Therapeutics, Reata Pharmaceuticals, Santaris Pharma, Symphogen, Synosia Therapeutics, Tarsa Therapeutics, Tobira Therapeutics, Vantia Therapeutics, Xenon Pharmaceuticals

Other Locations:
Novo Ventures US
1700 Owens Street
Suite 450
San Francisco, CA 94158

Key Executives:
Henrik Gürtler, Chief Executive Officer
Directorships: 7TM Pharma, PTC Therapeutics, Santaris Pharma, Arpida
Peter Bisgaard, Partner
Education: MSc, Technical University of Denmark
Background: General Consultant, McKinsey & Co.
Directorships: Altheos, Asante Solutions, Light Science Oncology, Otonomy
Kim L Dueholm, Partner
Education: MSc, Chemistry & Business Administration, Odense University; PhD, Organic Chemistry, University of Copenhagen
Background: Principal Scientific Analyst, Novo Nordisk A/S
Directorships: f-star GmbH, Neurokey
Thomas Dyrberg, Senior Partner
Education: DMSc, MD, University of Copenhagen
Background: Hagedorn Research Institute; Scripps Research Institute; International Clinical Project Manager, Novo Nordisk A/S
Directorships: AlloCure, LifeCycle Pharma, Lux Biosciences, Ophthotech Corporation
Martin W Edwards, Senior Partner
Background: CEO, ReNeuron Holdings; VP, Head of Drug Development, Novo Nordisk A/S; VP, Pharmacology & Medical Affairs, ZymoGenetics; Senior VP, Medical Affairs, Novo Nordisk
Directorships: Funxional Therapeutics, Logical Therapeutics, Tarsa Therapeutics
Heath Lukatch, Partner
Education: BA, Biochemistry, University of California, Berkeley; PhD, Neurosciences, Stanford University
Background: Managing Director, Piper Jaffray Ventures; SightLine Partners; Bench Scientist, Cetus Chiron & Roche Bioscience; McKinsey & Co.; Founder & CEO, AutoMate Scientifict
Directorships: Synosia, Amira, Anaptys, Inogen, Neurtherapeutics
Peter Moldt, Partner
Education: PhD, Medicinal Chemistry, Royal Danish School of Pharmacy
Background: Co-Founder, Curalogic; COO, 7TM Pharma; Clinical Drug Development, NeuroSearch
Directorships: Cytochroma
Jack B Nielsen, Partner
Background: R&D Strategy, Novozymes A/S
Directorships: Alios BioPharma, Cell Biosciences, MediQuest Therapeutics, NewMend, Reata Pharmaceuticals, Tobira Therapeutics

3016 NUTEK (NARINGS- OCH TEKNIKUTVECKLINGSVERKET) NUTEK
Götgatan 74
Stockholm 11786
Sweden
Phone: 46-086819100 **Fax:** 46-488196826
e-mail: tillvaxtverket@tillvaxtverket.se
web: www.tillvaxtverket.se

Venture Capital & Private Equity Firms / International Firms

Mission Statement: Actively seeking new investments
Geographic Preference: Sweden
Investment Criteria: Seed
Industry Group Preference: Manufacturing, Financial Services, Business to Business
Key Executives:
  Lars Nyberg, Director & politikområdesansvarig
  Sune Halvarsson, Director-General

3017 NVM PRIVATE EQUITY LIMITED
Rotterdam House
116 Quayside
Newcastle-Upon-Tyne NE1 3DY
United Kingdom

Phone: 44-1912446000 Fax: 44-1912446001
web: www.nvm.co.uk

Mission Statement: nVM is independently owned with 25 years experience of investing in UK businesses. Our executives live and work on the ground in regional business communities across the UK. NVM manages over £170 million of funds and is a generalist investor specializing in making equity investments in UK unquoted companies. We are focused on making equity investments of between £2 million and £10 million.
Geographic Preference: United Kingdom
Fund Size: Euro 170 million
Founded: 1984
Average Investment: Euro 5 Million
Minimum Investment: Euro 2 Million
Investment Criteria: Expansion and Development, MBO, MBI, Public-to-Private, Purchase of quoted shares
Portfolio Companies: Longhurst Group, DMN Installations, Keith Prowse, Stainton Metals, TJ Brent, John Laing Partnership, Omnico Plastics, I G Doors, Pivotal Laboratories

Other Locations:
  Forbury Court
  12 Forbury Road
  Reading RG1 1SB
  United Kingdom
  Phone: 44-01189517000 Fax: 44-01189517001

  82 King Street
  301 Deansgate
  Manchester M2 4WQ
  United Kingdom
  Phone: 44-01619358419

Key Executives:
  Mark R Dixon, CEO
  0118-951-7000
  e-mail: new@nvm.co.uk
  Education: MBA, Cranfield
  Background: Officer in the Royal Navy for ten years, he held line management positions with Shell UK and International Paints before becoming general manager of Tremco Limited, the specialist construction products subsidiary of B F Goodrich Inc. He joined Northern I
  Directorships: Northern 3 VCT PLC
  James Arrowsmith, Investment Team
  0118-951-7000
  Education: Banking & Finance, Loughborough University
  Background: HSBC London; 3i
  Directorships: Northern 3 VCT PLC
  Chris Mellor, Investment Team
  0191-244-6000
  e-mail: new@nvm.co.uk
  Education: FCA MSI, Physics, chartered accountant with Spicer & Pegler
  Background: Chartered accountant with Spicer & Pegler; Northern Investors Company PLC
  Norman Yarrow, Investment Team
  0162-081-0428
  Education: BCom, Edinburgh University; Chartered Accountant, Thomson McLintock
  Background: Investment Management; Advisor, Turcan Connell; Non-Executive Director, Dunedin Smaller Companies Investment Trust PLC
  Alastair Conn, Investment Team
  e-mail: new@nvm.co.uk
  Education: Philosophy, politics and economics.
  Background: Price Waterhouse in Newcastle
  Clive Austin, Investment Manager
  0845-272-7023
  Education: Read Applied Physics, Durham University; MBA, Warwick University
  Background: Consulting, Accenture; 3i; Catapult Venture Managers
  Mauro Biagioni, Investment Manager
  0191-244-6025
  Education: Chartered Accountant, KPMG
  Peter Hodson, Investment Manager
  0845-272-7014
  Education: Read Mechanical Engineering, University of Exeter
  Background: BMW Group; 3i

3018 OCTOPUS INVESTMENTS
33 Holborn
London EC1N 2HT
United Kingdom

Toll-Free: 800-316-2295
web: www.octopusinvestments.com

Mission Statement: The Ventures team at Octopus finds and supports talented individuals and exceptional businesses. We're straight-talking, human investors who back people, rather than specific sectors. We look for opportunities that are capable of creating, transforming or dominating an industry.
Portfolio Companies: 21Net, AdBrain, Affectiv, Aframe, Amplience, Artesian, BehavioSec, Vowman, Box-It, Calastone, CertiVox, Coal, Conversocial, CSL DualCom, e-Therapeutics, ECNlive, Ecrebo, Elliptic, Evi, GetLenses.co.uk, Graze.com, Iovox, ITM Power, Kabbee, KeTech, Lovefilm.com, Luther Pendragon, Mailcloud, Metrasens, Mi-Pay, Michelson Diagnostics, Phasor Solutions, Plum, Progility, Property Partners, Rangespan, Reading Room, Secret Escapes, Seedcamp, Semafone, Shopa, SmartKem, Sofar Sounds, StreetHub, Surrey Nanosystems, SwifyKey, Swoon Editions, T4 Media Group, Tails.com, The Faction Collective, The History Press, The Kendal Group, TrialReach, Tristar, Ultra SoC Technologies, UniPlaces, Vega-Chi, YPlan, Zoopla Property Group, Zynstra

Key Executives:
  Alan Wallace, Senior Investment Director
  Education: BA, Economics, Liverpool University; PhD, Business Administration, University of Manchester
  Background: Managing Director, Cambridge Nutrition, Dairy Crest, Premier Brands

3019 OJAS VENTURE PARTNERS
#772, 3rd Floor, 80ft
Peripheral Road
4th Block Koramangala
Bangalore 560 034
India

Phone: +91 80 4061 0300 Fax: +91 80 4142 5476
e-mail: pingus@ojasventures.com

Mission Statement: Ojas Venture Parners is a US $35 Million, India-focused early stage venture capital financing & investing firm investing in technology based businesses and other businesses that use technology in innovative ways to create high growth business opportunities. Typically, from our first fund corpus of US $35 Million, we make an initial investment of US $250,000 to US $1.5 Million and follow that by participating in subsequent rounds up to a maximum of US $3 Million per company over the life of the company.
Geographic Preference: India
Fund Size: $35 million

942

Investment Criteria: Early Stage
Industry Group Preference: Mobile Apps, Telecommunications, Embedded Software, Web Applications & Services, Consumer Internet, Low Capex Semiconductor, Enterprise Software, Technology-Enabled Business
Portfolio Companies: Tyfone, Ziva Software, Mango Technologies, Vizury, CoCubes.Com, Radiowalla, BrizzTV, Telibrahma, RiverSilica, Insieve, Cbazaar
Key Executives:
  Dr. Rajesh Srivathsa, Managing Partner
  e-mail: rajesh@ojasventures.com
  Education: BT, National Institute Of Technology Karnataka at Suratkal; MS, University of Texas at Austin; Ph.D, University of Illinois at Urbana-Champaign
  Background: Mobile Terminals Business Unit (MTBU), Aricent, Inc; CTO, Emuzed
  Pavan Krishnamurthy, Partner
  e-mail: pavan@ojasventures.com
  Education: BS, Mathematics, Economics, & Statistics
  Background: Nadathur Holdings; SRW Advisors; Syndicated Research Group; Ernst & Young; Price Waterhouse
  Gautam Balijepalli, Partner
  e-mail: gautam@ojasventures.com
  Education: BT, Indian Institute of Technology, Madras; MBA, London Business School
  Background: Nomura; Business Development, Sun Microsystems
  Raghu Batta, Partner
  e-mail: raghu@ojasventures.com
  Education: BE, Manipal Institute of Technology; MBA, Baruch College
  Background: VantagePoint Venture Partners; Madge Networks; Bay Networks; Assured Access; Alcatel; CopperCom

3020 OMNES CAPITAL
37-41 rue de Rocher
Paris 75008
France
Phone: 33-0180487900 **Fax:** 33-0142934855
web: www.omnescapital.com

Mission Statement: Omnes Capital, a leading name in private equity, is directly involved in financing the economy by providing companies with the equity needed to expand. It thus helps to drive growth, innovation and job creation. We play the role of an active shareholder, working with the managers of the companies in which we invest and sharing with them a single commercial and strategic vision of how best to pursue their expansion plans. As the leading equity investor in French SMEs, Omnes Capital works on a daily basis to support 160 businesses and infrastructure projects.

Investment Criteria: All Stages
Industry Group Preference: Energy, Life Sciences, Renewable Energy
Portfolio Companies: ACCO, AEMI, AT Internet, Abakus Solar, Abcia, Adamence, Adictiz, Amakem, Ameos, Annonay Productions France, Arcarios, Ariane Systems, Armatis, Bailtrand, CMR Group, COIFF'Idis, CPC, CaméRus, Cellnovo, Compin Group, Complix, Conexia Energy, Confortvisuel.com, Cooltech Applications, Cytheris, Daltys, Delete, Deny all, Diam, EA Pharma, ERA Biotech, Edagora, Elettrostudio Energia, Elettrostudio Energia Infrastructure, Enterome, Eptica, Eratome, European Games Group, ExaProtect, Exclusive Networks, Exosun, EyeTechCare, Fine Sounds Group, FlexGen, Fondis Electronic, France Géothermie, Futures, Gerard Darel, Gecko Biomedical, Greenbureau, Groupe BPS, Groupe Eyssautier, Groupe Hermès-Métal Yudigar, Roupe Pommier, Groupe Unafinance, HTI, Heidrich, Hermés Métal, Ikaros Solar, Ividence, Keldelice, Labco, Les Fréres Blanc, Lyonnaise de Garantie, METabolic EXporer, MONCLER, Medisse, Minimax Viking Group, Mister Bell, Multitec, Neoen Netzoptiker, Nomios, Novate Medical, Numericable, Opsona Therapeutics, Orexo, Oxatis, PanGenetics, Pixium, Pomme de Pain, Porcher Industries, Poste Imo, Poxel, Prodealcenter, Progexia, Qualtera, R&R Ice Cream, RAC, Regency Entertainment, SCT Telecom, SEVE, SIMP, SLG Recycling, SVP, Sateco, Scality, Solar Energies, Solar Participations, SpineGuard, Splendia, Stentys, SuperSonic Imagine, Temis, Tennis Point, Themis, Tiama, Titanobel, Tronic's Micro Systems, TrustYou, Trusted Shops, Turtle Entertainment GmbH, Urbasolar, Valorem, Visiware, Vivalto Santé, Weole Ene

Key Executives:
  Fabien Prevost, Chairman
  Education: Civil Engineering, Ecole Polytechnique, Ecole National des Ponts et Chaussees; MEng, University of California, Berkeley
  Background: Boston Consulting Group
  Directorships: AFIC

3021 ONO PHARMACEUTICALS COMPANY LIMITED
8-2, Kyutaromachi 1-chome, Chuo-ku
Chuo-ku
Osaka 541-8564
Japan
Phone: 81-0662635670
web: www.ono.co.jp

Mission Statement: Actively seeking new investments.
Geographic Preference: Japan
Fund Size: $17, 358 Million YEn
Founded: 1717
Industry Group Preference: Medical & Health Related
Key Executives:
  Gyo Sagara, President, Representative Director and CEO

3022 OYSTER INVEST
Denmark
Phone: +45 25 68 00 00

Mission Statement: Oyster Invest is a Danish based investment firm, dedicated to tech and startups with a global perspective. We bring entrepreneur expertise to all stages from angel investment to pre IPO, Our portfolio currently consists of a variety of companies engaged in both software, hardware and mobile.

Investment Criteria: Start-Up
Industry Group Preference: Technology, Software, Hardware, Mobile
Portfolio Companies: Meedor, Responsfabrikken, BlueTown, Axcess, A-Solutions
Key Executives:
  Peter Warnoe, Owner

3023 OneVentures
Suite 13.02
179 Elizabeth St.
Sydney NSW 2000
Australia
Phone: +62 2 8205 7379
e-mail: admin@one-ventures.com
web: www.one-ventures.com.au

Mission Statement: OneVentures is one of Australia's leading venture capital firms, with over $320M in funds under management. The OneVentures Team applies their years of experience, expertise, operational and executional excellence to accelerate the growth of OneVentures portfolio companies and launch them into global markets. Our Investment Team has helped create 5 Nasdaq and 3 ASX listed companies, and realised returns to investors of over $1 billion.

Geographic Preference: Australia
Fund Size: $330 million
Founded: 2010
Minimum Investment: $1.5 million

Venture Capital & Private Equity Firms / International Firms

Investment Criteria: Seed, Start Up, Early Expansion
Industry Group Preference: Telecommunications, Information Technology, New Media, Clean Technology, Life Sciences, Healthcare, SaaS
Portfolio Companies: 8i, BiVACOR, Blade Therapeutics, Clinical Genomics, Employment Hero, Find-Me Technologies, Hatchtech, Madorra, OVO Mobile, Paragen Bio, Prota Therapeutics, Smart Sparrow, Vaxxas

Other Locations:
The Precint, Level 2
315 Brunswick St.
Fortitude Valley QLD 4006
Australia

C/O FB Rice
Level 14
90 Collins St.
Melbourne VIC 3000
Australia

Key Executives:
Dr. Michelle Deaker, Managing Partner and Executive Director
Education: BS, University of Sydney; MS, University of Sydney; PhD, Applied Science, University of Canberra
Background: Founder, E Com Industries
Directorships: 8i, Smart Sparrow, Incoming Media, Employment Hero
Dr. Paul Kelly, General Partner & Executive Director
Education: MBBS, MD, University of New South Wales; FRACP
Background: CEO, Medcenter Holdings Inc; President and CEO, Orchid Cellmark; CEO, Gemini Genomics; Researcher and Physician at St. Vincent's Hospital, Sydney, Australia; Research Physician, Garvan Institute for Medical Research, Co-Founder, MEARS Technologies; Co-Founder, AgaMatrix
Directorships: Vaxxas, Clinical Genomics, Find-Me Technologies, Hatchtech, Agamatrix, Garvan Institute of Medical Research
Anne-Marie Birkill, General Partner & Executive Director
Education: BSc, Flinders University; MBA, The University of Queensland; FIML; GAICD
Background: CEO, i.lab Incubator; UniQuest
Directorships: Find-Me Technologies, Madorra, Paragen Bio, Creative Enterprises Australia, Advance Queensland Business Development Fund, AVCAL

3024 PAC-LINK MANAGEMENT CORP.
13Fl. 2. Tun Hwa South Road, Sec.2
Taipei
Taiwan

Phone: +866-2-2755-5000 **Fax:** +866-2-2755-2000
web: www.paclinkventure.com

Mission Statement: Pac-Link seeks to invest in companies in which our unique resources and insights can generate significant gains for all shareholders. We work closely with company managers to minimize risks, maximize opportunities, and help build rapidly growing businesses in Asia and North America. Pac-Link connects the best of emerging companies with the best business relationships to achieve maximum growth potential.

Geographic Preference: Asia, North America
Fund Size: $370 million
Founded: 1998
Industry Group Preference: Automotive, Semiconductors, Electronics, Communications, Optical, Software, Information Technology, Life Sciences

Other Locations:
1301 Shoreway Road
Ste 160
Belmont, CA 94002
Phone: 650-857-0686

Key Executives:
Allen Hsu
Education: BS, Managemnt Science, Chiao Tung University in Taiwan; MBA, Cheng-Chi University in Taiwan
Background: Current Vice Executive Officer, Yulon Group Headquarters
Directorships: Altek Technology Corp, Taiwan Mask Corp, Century-Myson Semiconductor Corp
Ming Hsu, President
Education: BS, Communication Engineering, Chiao Tung University in Taiwan; MS, Computer and Electrical Engineering, North Carolina State University in Raleigh
Background: Founder and President, Elite Group Computer Systems; Founder, APAQ
Bill Shelander, Managing Director
Education: BS, Systems Engineering, Georgia Institute of Technology; MSE, Chemical Engineering, West Virginia College of Graduate Studies; MBA, Stanford University
Background: Chairmand and CEO, Micronics Computers; Co-President, JAFCO America Ventures Inc; National Product Manager, Liquid Air Corporation; Systems Engineer, Union Carbide
Directorships: Wavesat, CrossFiber, GlobalLocate, BrightPlanet

3025 PACIFIC EQUITY PARTNERS PTY LIMITED
Level 31, 126 Phillip Street
Sydney 2000
Australia

Phone: 61-282382600
web: www.pep.com.au

Mission Statement: focusing on buyouts and late stage expansion capital

Geographic Preference: Australia, New Zealand
Fund Size: $2.5 Billion
Founded: 1998
Average Investment: $500 Million
Minimum Investment: $6 Million
Investment Criteria: Buy-outs, Late Stage, Expansions
Industry Group Preference: All Sectors Considered
Portfolio Companies: Spotless, Energy Developments, American Stock Transfer & Trust Company, Veda, Xtralis, Link Market Services

Key Executives:
Rickard Gardell, Managing Director
e-mail: information@pep.com.au
Education: Rickard received a BSc/MSc from the Stockholm School of Economics where he was awarded Carl Liljevalchs Scholar and an IMP Scholar attending McGill University Graduate School of Management.
Background: Founder PE, Director of Bain & Company
Directorships: Board of Link MS Group & A&R Whitcoulls
Cameron Blanks, Managing Director

3026 PAI MANAGEMENT
232, rue de Rivoli
Paris 75054
France

Phone: 33-143166300 **Fax:** 33-143166389
e-mail: pai.paris@paipartners.com
web: www.paimanagement.com

Mission Statement: PAI Management operates PAI LBO Fund, future funds to be created and Paribas direct investments (Paribas Affaires Industrielles) on a contractual basis.

Geographic Preference: Europe
Fund Size: $4.3 billion
Founded: 1994

Venture Capital & Private Equity Firms / International Firms

Average Investment: $100 and $300 million
Minimum Investment: $5 Million
Investment Criteria: Mid-sized companies with High Growth, LBO
Industry Group Preference: Media, Communications, Telecommunications, Information Technology, Agribusiness, Pharmaceuticals, Chemicals, Distribution, Engineering, Energy
Portfolio Companies: Custom Sensors & Technologies, DomusVi, EMG, Labeyrie Fine Foods, VPS, R&R Ice Cream, ADB Airfield Solutions, IPH, Marcolin, Kiloutou, Swissport, The Nuance Group, Hunkemoller, Cerba European Lab, Zella, Atos, Kaufman & Broad, Perstorp, Global Closure Systems, Grupo Cortefiel
Key Executives:
  Christopher Afors, Investment Director
  e-mail: cvarin@cobepa.be
  Education: Diploma, Institut d'Etudes Politiques; MBA, Wharton Graduate School of Business; PhD, Business Administration
  Background: Paribas-New York, Hong Kong, Singapore; COBEPA
  Lionel Zinsou, Partner
  Education: Graduate, Ecole des Hautes Etudes Commerciales; Graduate, Ecole Nationale d'Administration
  Background: Jean-Marie began his career in the Budget Department of French Ministry of Finance where he was Adviser to the Minister of Finance.
  Directorships: Head of Finance Department.
  Pauline Ammeux, Investment Officer
  Education: Graduate, Ecole des Hautes Etudes Commerciales
  Background: Banque Paribas; PAI
  Francesco Capurro, Investment Director
  Education: Graduate, Institut d'Etudes Politiques; Masters, Economics and Management
  Background: Paribas; PAI
  Edward Chandler, Partner
  Education: Graduate, CPA, Stanford Business School
  Background: A.B. Volvo; PAI
  Directorships: Chairman and Chief Executive Officer

3027 PAMA GROUP
Hong Kong

Phone: 852-97403373
e-mail: robert@pama.hk
web: www.pama.hk

Mission Statement: Utilizes experience and established working relationships in regional markets to make and support investments.
Geographic Preference: Asia Pacific Region
Fund Size: $500 Million
Average Investment: $30 Million
Minimum Investment: $10 Million
Investment Criteria: Development, Expansion, Buy-In/Buy-Out
Key Executives:
  Robert Suen, CEO
  Education: Brigham Young University; Harvard Graduate School of Business Administration
  Background: General Mills; Continental Grain Company; Richina Group; Asia Access Investment Company
  Timothy CM Chia, President
  Education: Fairleigh Dickinson University
  Background: American International Assurance Company Limited
  Cliff L Cheung, Chief Investment Officer/Managing Director
  Education: University of Hong Kong
  Background: Hamburgische Landesbank

  Tan Yong-Nang, Managing Director
  Education: Cambridge University
  Background: Hamburgische Landesbank

3028 PARKWALK ADVISORS
University House
11-13 Lower Grosvenor Place
London SW1W 0EX
United Kingdom

Phone: 44-2077592285
e-mail: enquiries@parkwalkadvisors.com
web: www.parkwalkadvisors.com

Mission Statement: Parkwalk is a truly independent investment management firm seeking to generate significant capital gains through venture capital investing, enhanced by the attractive tax relief provided by the Enterprise Investment Scheme. Parkwalk is dedicated to providing clients with access to some of the most exciting deal-flow emanating from British R&D intensive institutions and Universities. Parkwalk invests in, and raises capital for, innovative UK technology companies. Parkwalk portfolio companies all have deeply-embedded IP and commercial potential, and range from early stage seed capital, through development and commercial capital to AIM-listed investments.

Geographic Preference: United Kingdom
Founded: 2009
Industry Group Preference: Technology, Internet, Information Technology, Communications, Life Sciences, Clean Technology, Electronics, Semiconductors, Chemicals, Advanced Materials, Medical Technology, Energy, Renewable Power
Portfolio Companies: Fluidic Analytics, TheySay, Salunda, Nandi Proteins, Fuel 3D, Perpetuum, Brainomix, Oxtex, RoadMap, Tracsis, Jukedeck, Vocal IQ, Revise, AQDOT, Symetrica, Omega Diagnostics, Microsaic Systems, Horizon Discovery, Tangentix, Sphere Fluidics, DefiniGEN, Clean Air Power, YASA Motors, Inotec AMD, Cambridge CMOS Sensors, Arkivum, Mode DX, Arvia Technology, Surrey Nanosystems, Reinnervate, Lime Microsystems, Xeros, First Light Fusion, OxfordPV, Revolymer, Acal Energy, Eykona Technolgies
Other Locations:
  Atenas 2
  Pozuelo de Alarcon
  Madrid 28224
  Spain
  Phone: 34-91-709-1130
Key Executives:
  Alastair Kilgour, CIO
  44-20-7759-2290
  e-mail: akilgour@parkwalkavdisors.com

3029 PARTNERS GROUP
57 Zugerstrasse
Baar 6341
Switzerland

Phone: 41-417846000 **Fax:** 41-417846001
web: www.partnersgroup.ch

Mission Statement: Partners Group is a Private Equity Asset Manager that invests worldwide, both directly in portfolio companies and as a Limited Partner in more than 2000 Partnerships managed by some of the most renowned Private Equity Managers. We put our extensive multi-

Geographic Preference: Europe, North America, Israel, Asia, Latin America
Fund Size: $8.4 Billion
Founded: 1996
Average Investment: $1.2 Billion
Minimum Investment: $5 Million
Investment Criteria: Invests in companies with Strong Leadership and Growth Potential
Industry Group Preference: All Sectors Considered

945

Venture Capital & Private Equity Firms / International Firms

Key Executives:
Alfred Gantner, Co-Founder and Executive Chairman
Education: He holds a degree from the Swiss Banking School, Zurich, Switzerland.
Background: Partners Group in the private equity team with responsibilities in buyout partnerships selection and was a member of the private equity investment committee.
Directorships: Prior to joining Partners Group, Mr. Trommsdorff headed the asset management division at the Cantonal Bank of Zug and worked as a trader and investment manager at the Industri
Dr. Cyrill Wipfli, Chief Financial Officer
Education: He holds a degree in business administration from the University of Zurich, Switzerland.
Background: Was a member of the executive board of Bank Hofmann.
Directorships: he headed Credit Suisse Private Banking in Germany after assignments at Credit Suisse in Zurich and in the private banking department of Credit Suisse in New York.
Jürg Wenger, Chief Operating Officer and Head Resources
Education: He holds a master's degree in business administration from the University of St. Gallen (HSG), Switzerland
Background: Has held various private equity investment management positions at Partners Group and was instrumental in building Partners Group's portfolio of venture capital investments in Europe and the USA.
Directorships: Prior to joining Partners Group, Mr. Gysler worked for UBS Warburg (now UBS Investment Bank) in Zurich, where he advised institutional clients regarding equities, derivatives
Urs Wietlisbach, Co-Founder and Executive Member
Education: He holds a master's degree in business administration from the University of St. Gallen (HSG), Switzerland.
Directorships: He is a member of the private equity investment committee
Christoph Rubeli, Co-Chief Executive Officer and Head Private Equity Directs
Education: He holds an MBA degree from INSEAD, Paris, and a master's degree in industrial engineering from the Swiss Federal Institute of Technology (ETH), Zurich, Switzerland
Background: Was Head of the Private Equity Investment Management business group, where he was responsible for the firm's private equity partnership, direct and secondary investment activities.
Directorships: Prior to joining Partners Group, Mr. Rubeli spent 11 years at UBS, ultimately as a Singapore-based manager for Southeast Asia, with responsibility for all business units in th
Claude Angeloz, Co-Head Private Real Estate
Education: He holds a master's degree in business administration from the University of St. Gallen (HSG), Switzerland.
Background: Headed the firm's structuring business unit, where he was responsible for developing and structuring Partners Group's private equity transactions and products.
Directorships: Prior to joining Partners Group, Mr. Angéloz spent seven years with Credit Suisse Financial Products in Zurich and London and served as a Director with responsibility for Swis
Dr. Stephan Schali, Head Private Equity
Education: He holds an MBA degree from the University of Chicago and a doctorate and master's degree in business administration from the University of St. Gallen (HSG), Switzerland.
Background: He started in primary partnership investments before assuming responsibility for Partners Group's global secondaries business.
Directorships: Prior to joining Partners Group, Mr. Schäli worked for UBS, where he was a business and management associate with assignments in the firm's branch performance analysis and str
Walter Keller, Private Equity
Education: He holds a degree in economics and business administration from the Zurich University of Applied Sciences, and is a Certified Public Accountant (CPA).
Background: Significant experience in investment origination, valuation, execution and monitoring.
Directorships: Prior to joining Partners Group, Mr. Keller was a member of the transaction group at PriceWaterhouseCoopers with responsibilities in the field of IPOs, mergers & acquisitions

3030 PASSION CAPITAL
White Bear Yard
144a Clerkenwell Road
2nd Floor
London EC1R 5DF
United Kingdom

web: www.passioncapital.com

Mission Statement: We invest in ambitious entrepreneurs who have global ambition for their early stage digital media and technology startups.

Investment Criteria: Early-Stage
Industry Group Preference: Digital Media & Marketing, Technology
Portfolio Companies: Adzuna, Birdback, CarThrottle, Coinfloor, Digital Shadows, DueDil, DueGo, EyeM, Flattr, Future Ad Labs, GoCardless, GoSquared, Lazook, Limejump, Loopcam, Lulu, Mixlr, Narrative, On Device Research, OpenSignal, Pusher, Sho My Homework, Smarkets, Swipe, Thread, Toothpick, Tray.io, Trucktrack, ViCampo, WeDo, Wine In Black, WireWax, Zesty

Key Executives:
Eileen Burbidge, Founding Partner
Education: BS, Computer Science, University of Illinois at Urbana-Champaign
Background: Apple; Sun Microsystems; Skype; PalmSource; Yahoo!
Directorships: Chair, Tech City UK; Special Envoy, FinTech; Tech Ambassador, Mayor of London's Office

3031 PATHENA
Edificio Peninsula, sala 506
Praça do Bom Sucesso, No131
4150-456 Porto
Portugal

Phone: +351 225 430 707
e-mail: info@pathena.com
web: www.pathena.com

Mission Statement: Pathena is a specialized investment firm focused on boosting the success of Information Technology companies.

Investment Criteria: Late Early Stage, Growth Phase
Industry Group Preference: Information Technology, Applied Science, Digital Convergence
Portfolio Companies: Cardmobil, Exago, iMobileMagic, iM3MDICAL, NMusic, Stemmatters, Vortal, MedChronic, i2s

Key Executives:
António Murta, Managing Partner and Co-Founder
e-mail: antonio.murta@pathena.com
Education: Minho University; University of Porto
Background: Corporate Information Officer, Sonae Distribuiçfo; Founder and CEO, Enabler; VP of Retail Services, Wipro; Founder, Mobicomp; Founder, ITPeers; Founder, Profimetrics; Founder, QuiiQ; Founder, Cardmobili
Jorge Brás, Managing Partner and Co-Founder
e-mail: jorge.bras@pathena.com
Education: University of Minho
Background: Co-Founder and COO, Enabler; General

Venture Capital & Private Equity Firms / International Firms

Manager-Head of Delivery, Wipro; IT Director, Sonae Retail

3032 PENTECH VENTURES
One Alfred Place
London WC1E 7EB
United Kingdom

Phone: 44-2031287473
e-mail: info@pentechvc.com
web: www.pentechvc.com

Mission Statement: We invest in technology companies, including Internet, social media, e-commerce, digital media, mobile, SaaS, enterprise software, telecom software, and embedded applications companies. We are not prescriptive on quantum or stage, but rather focus on the opportunity, and whether there is a smart, passionate and energetic entrepreneurial team that possesses the determination to build a globally successful business.

Average Investment: £500,000 - 4 million
Investment Criteria: All Stages
Industry Group Preference: Internet, Social Media, E-Commerce & Manufacturing, Digital Media & Marketing, Mobile, SaaS, Telecommunications
Portfolio Companies: Acunu, CertiVox, Critical Blue, FanDuel, Flightman, Maxymiser, Nutmeg, Outplay Entertainment, SecretSales, Semetric/Musicmetric, Struq

Other Locations:
39 Melville Street
Edinburgh EH3 7JF
United Kingdom
Phone: 44-1312408280

Key Executives:
Craig Anderson, Partner
e-mail: craig@pentechvc.com
Background: Chartered Accountant, Arthur Andersen; Group Financial Controller, Kwik-Fit; CFO/COO, Voxar

3033 PERMIRA Permira Advisers LLP
80 Pall Mall
London SW1Y 5ES
United Kingdom

Phone: 44-2076321000 Fax: 44-2079303185
web: www.permira.com

Mission Statement: Offering a fresh approach to private equity with eighteen funds.

Geographic Preference: Worldwide
Fund Size: 11 billion euro
Founded: 1985
Average Investment: 50 million - 5 billion euro
Minimum Investment: 50 million euro
Investment Criteria: LBO, LBI, Turnarounds, Growth Buyouts, Acquisitions, Public to private transactions
Industry Group Preference: Business to Business, Chemicals, Consumer Products, Healthcare, Industrial Services, Technology, Industrial Equipment
Portfolio Companies: Akindo Sushiro, Ancestry.com, Rysta LifeScience, Asia Broadcast Satellite, Atrium Innovations, BakerCorp, CABB, Cortefiel, Creganna-Tactx Medical, Dr. Martens, Freescale, Genesys, Hugo Boss, iglo Group, Intelligrated, Just Retirement, LegalZoom, Maxeda DIY Group, MESA and Asteral, Metalogix, Netafim, New Look, OdigeO, Pharmaq, Saga (Acromas), Sisal, TeamViewer, Telepizza, Tilney Bestinvest

Other Locations:
Permira Beteiligungsberatung GmBH
Bockenheimer Landstrasse 33
Frankfurt am Main 60325
Germany
Phone: 49-699714660 Fax: 49-6997146699

Plaza del Marques de Salamanca, 10
Primero Izquierda
Madrid 28006
Spain
Phone: 34-914182499 Fax: 34-914261193

320 Park Avenue
33rd Floor
New York, NY 10022-4690
Phone: 212-3867480 Fax: 212-3867481

Permira Associati SpA
Via San Paolo 10
Milan 20121
Italy
Phone: 39-0276004740 Fax: 39-0276004706

Permira Advisers KB
Birger Jarlsgatan 12
Stockholm 114 34
Sweden
Phone: 46-850312200 Fax: 46-850312299

Permira Advisers KK
Akasaka Intercity Building 3F
1-11-44 Akasaka
Minato-ku, Tokyo 107-0052
Japan
Phone: 81-0362302051 Fax: 81-0362302052

Key Executives:
Kurt Björklund, Co-Managing Partner
212-386-7480
Fax: 212-386-7481
e-mail: allen.haight@permira.com
Education: BBA, Washington & Lee University; MBA, University of Virginia
Background: KPMG; Chemical Bank
Guido Paolo Gamucci, Chairman
39 02 76 00 47 40
Fax: 39 02 76 00 47 06
e-mail: guido.gamucci@permira.com
Education: Mechanical Engineering degree, University of Rome, Italy; MBA, INSEAD, France
Background: Founding Partner/Managing Director, UBS Capital, Italy; Deputy Head Investment Banking, Citicorp
Veronica Eng, Partner/Operating Committee
44 207 632 1000
Fax: 44 207 497 2174
e-mail: veronica.eng@permira.com
Education: BBA, University of Singapore
Background: Head Corporate Finance, Schroder Investment Bank, Singapore
Gianluca Andena, Partner
39 02 76 00 47 40
Fax: 39 02 76 00 47 06
e-mail: gianluca.andena@permira.com
Education: BBA, Bocconi University
Background: Sales/Marketing, Pirelli Group
Paolo Colonna, Partner
39 02 76 00 47 40
e-mail: paolo.colonna@permira.com
Education: Chemical Engineering degree, Politecnico di Torino; MBA, Harvard Business School
Background: Co-Founder, several small MBOs; VP Planning/Marketing, Italsider; McKinsey & Company, Chigao and Milan
Mike Garland, Partner
44 207 632 1000
e-mail: mike.garland@permira.com
Education: Mechanical Engineering degree, University of Southampton, England; Chartered Accountant
Background: Finance Director, Williams Holdings; Price Waterhouse, London
Paul Armstrong, Principal
46 8 503 122 00
e-mail: kurt.bjorklund@permira.com
Education: Economics degree, Swedish School of Economics and Business Administration, Finland; MBA, INSEAD; Graduate studies, Rensselaer Polytechnic Institute

Venture Capital & Private Equity Firms / International Firms

Background: Boston Consulting Group, Stockholm; IT reseller, Finland
Philip Bassett, Partner
44 207 632 1000
e-mail: philip.bassett@permira.com
Education: Classics degree, Oxford University; Chartered Accountant
Background: Fundraising/Investor Communications, Schroder Ventures
Martin Clarke, Partner
44 207 632 1000
e-mail: martin.clarke@permira.com
Education: MA, PhD History, Cambridge University
Background: Senior Director, PPMV
Fidel Baptista, Organisational Professional
44 207 632 1000
e-mail: guy.davies@permira.com
Education: BS Economics, London School of Economics; Chartered Accountant
Background: Price Waterhouse
Audinga Besusparyte, Investment Professional
49 69 97 14 66 0
Education: BBA, Frankfurt University; Programme for Management Development, Harvard Business School
Background: Audit/Corporate Finance, Arthur Andersen, Frankfurt
Robert Van Goethem, Partner
33 1 40 73 85 00
Education: BBA, University of Louvain-la-Neuve, Belgium; Law degree, Universities of Louvain and Antwerp; MBA, University of Chicago
Background: Director, Salomon Barney, London; Leveraged Finance, Citibank, London; Chase Manhattan Bank, NY
Uwe Kolb, Partner
49 69 97 14 66 0
e-mail: uwe.kolb@permira.com
Education: MBA, Saarbrucken University
Background: Managing Partner, PwC Transaction Services, Germany

3034 PHENOMEN VENTURES
Russia

web: www.linkedin.com/company/3258746

Mission Statement: Phenomen Ventures is a venture capital investment firm focused on internet and tech phenomenons.
Industry Group Preference: Internet, Technology

3035 PHILLIP MUTUAL BERHAD
B-2-7, Megan Avenue II
12, Jalan Yap Kwan Seng
Kuala Lumpur 50450
Malaysia

Phone: 603-27830300 Fax: 603-27113036
e-mail: phillipmutual@poems.com.my
web: www.phillipmutual.com

Mission Statement: The Malaysian unit trust management company of the Phillip Capital Group. It is approved by the Securities Commission to carry out unit trust management business.
Founded: 2002
Key Executives:
  En. Mohd Fadzli Bin Mohd Anas, Chief Executive Officer

3036 PHOENIX EQUITY PARTNERS LIMITED
25 Bedford Street
London WC2E 9ES
United Kingdom

Phone: 44-02074346999 Fax: 44-02030041496
e-mail: enquiries@phoenix-equity.com
web: www.phoenix-equity.com

Mission Statement: Formerly known as DLJ European Private Equity Limited, an independent provider of equity financing for UK, middle-market management buy-outs, buy-ins and expansion capital transactions.
Geographic Preference: United Kingdom
Fund Size: $619 Million
Founded: 2001
Average Investment: $88 Million
Minimum Investment: $1.7 Million
Investment Criteria: Buy-outs and Buy-ins, Expansion
Industry Group Preference: Transportation, Logistics, Consumer Services, Leisure, Retailing, Education, Healthcare, Industrial Services, Media
Portfolio Companies: Andrew Page, Ashtead Technology, Busaba Eathai, CloserStill, Edif Group, Global Navigation Solutions, Just Childcare, Karma Communications Group, Key Retirement, LK Bennett, Musto, Palletways, Porthaven Care Homes, Radley, Riviera Travel, Signum Technology, The Gym, Vivid Toy Group
Key Executives:
  Sandy Muirhead, Managing Partner
  Hugh Lenon, Chairman
  020-74346987
  e-mail: hugh.lenon@phoenix-equity.com
  Background: Chartered Accountant, Touche Ross
  Directorships: Palletways

3037 PHOSPHAGENICS
11 Duerdin Street
Clayton VIC 3168
Australia

Phone: 1300 354-942 Fax: 61-0395651151

Mission Statement: Phosphagenics is a pharmaceutical and neutraceutical comapny with a diversified portfolio of technologies encompassing drug delivery, drug enhancement, and active ingredients for dietary supplements, functional foods and personal care products.
Geographic Preference: Worldwide
Founded: 1993
Industry Group Preference: Plastics, Biotechnology
Key Executives:
  Harry Rosen, President & Chief Executive Officer
  e-mail: info@phosphagenics.com
  Education: B.A. Psychology, LLB
  Background: Attorney for 10 years, specializing in taxation and corporate law and Founders of Betatene Ltd and Denehurst Ltd , Vice-President, Corporate Development. President of Henkel Corporation
  Jonathan Addison, Chairman and Independent Director
  e-mail: info@phosphagenics.com
  Education: BVsc, MVPM
  Background: Director of, the Mackinnon Project at the University of Melbourne
  Directorships: Non-executive Director of Ridley Corporation Ltd, Animal Health Australia Ltd, Primesafe, the Australian Sheep Industry Cooperative Research Centre and the Zoological Parks an
  Sandra Webb, Independent Director
  e-mail: info@phosphagenics.com
  Education: BSc. (Hons), & PhD
  Background: Asia/Pacific Director in charge of the Nutrition and Health Division of Cognis, Managing Director of Betatene
  Directorships: Managing Director of Betatene
  Don Clarke, Independent Director
  e-mail: info@phosphagenics.com
  Education: BS, MD, FACP, FRACP
  Background: Director of the Macfarlane Burnet Institute for Medical Research
  Directorships: Managing Director of Advanced Diagnostic Concepts Ltd, a consulting physician at the Alfred and Austin Hospitals, a non-executive Director of GBS Venture Partners Ltd and Mana

Venture Capital & Private Equity Firms / International Firms

Stuart James, Independent Director
e-mail: info@phosphagenics.com
Education: BSc (Hons) PhD
Background: Dr Ogru conducted research at Monash University's Department of Biochemistry and Molecular Biology for Metabolic Pharmaceuticals Limited

3038 PINEHURST ADVISORS
Tokyo
Japan

e-mail: info@pinehurstadvisors.com
web: www.pinehurstadvisors.com

Mission Statement: Pinehurst Advisors is an early stage angel/seed fund management company with an investment focus in the internet media, mobile, and ecommerce space.

Founded: 2010
Investment Criteria: Seed Stage, Early-Stage
Industry Group Preference: Internet, Media, Mobile, E-Commerce & Manufacturing
Portfolio Companies: Cacafly, Cubie, Replaid, East District, Goodlife, Bosslady, e27, Viscovery, Gamelet, QLL, Cycle Taiwan, WritePath

Key Executives:
Mark Hsu, Partner
Background: Co-Founder, Sinanet; Co-Founder, KKBox; Co-Founder & Partner, TMIÆHolding
Kevin Chen, Partner
Background: COO, Laureate China; Managing Director, Ingram Micro Hong Kong; Head of M&A, Ingram Micro Asia
Munetaka Takahashi, Partner
Background: Managing Director, Hedgecafe.com; CFO, GABA Corp.

3039 PITANGO VENTURE CAPITAL
11 HaMenofim St. Building B
Herzliya 46725
Israel

Phone: 972-99718100 Fax: 972-99718102
e-mail: pitango@pitango.com
web: www.pitango.com

Mission Statement: Israel's largest venture capital firm and a lead investor in seed, early stage and expansion stage companies.

Geographic Preference: Israel
Fund Size: $1.3 Billion
Founded: 1993
Average Investment: $50 Million
Investment Criteria: Seed, Early-Stage, Expansion-Stage
Industry Group Preference: Communications, Software, Infrastructure, Wireless Technologies, Networking, Storage, Medical & Health Related, Semiconductors, Internet Technology, Mobile Communications Devices, Clean Technology

Other Locations:
Pitango Silicon Valley
540 Cowper St.
Suite 200
Palo Alto, CA 94301
Phone: 1-6503222201 Fax: 1-6504731347

Key Executives:
Rami Kalish, Managing General Partner & Co-Founder
Education: B.Sc. in Industrial Engineering and Information Science from the Technion Institute of Technology
Background: Garnered rich managerial experience at high-technology firms in the U.S., Europe and Israel. He previously held sales and marketing positions at IBM and senior executive roles at Orbotech
Directorships: Serves on the Board of Directors of Surf, CTI2, ForeScout, Comsys, and VCON (La Nouveau Marche).

Nechemia (Chemi) J Peres, Managing General Partner & Co-Founder
Education: MBA degree and a Bachelor of Science degree in Industrial Engineering & Management from Tel Aviv University
Background: Founded and managed the Mofet Israel Technology Fund, VP Marketing and Business Development at Decision Systems Israel (DSI), and a Senior Consultant to Israel Aircraft Industries (IAI). Mr. Peres served as a pilot in the Israeli Air Force for 10 years.
Directorships: Board of Dir: Olive Software; Provident; Speedbit; Voltaire; Precede Technologies. Founder & Chairman of IVA (Israel Venture Assoc.); serves on the Board of MOIT Seed Fund.
Aaron Mankovski, General Managing Partner
e-mail: aaron.m@pitango.com
Education: B.Sc. in Computer Science and Statistics from Tel Aviv University
Background: Co-founded Eucalyptus Ventures, and served as Managing Director; 16 years of experience in Executive Management (CEO, Sales and Marketing) in the high-technology sector in Israel and abroad he served as Corporate Vice President of Orbotech Ltd.
Directorships: Serves on the Board of Directors of Optimal-Test, Precede Technologies, Kilopass Technology Inc.; Compass-EOS; Kaminario and Jinko Solar in China
Isaac Hillel, General Managing Partner
e-mail: isaac.h@pitango.com
Education: B.Sc. in Electrical Engineering from Tel Aviv University and an M.B.A. from the Anderson School of Management at UCLA
Background: Executive Vice President at NEC Computers International, Board member of nine subsidiaries of NEC, a member of NEC's Executive Committee, and Chairman of its Worldwide Internet Strategy Committee; Casio PhoneMate.
Directorships: Serves on the Board of Directors of: AeroScout; 51 Global Ecommerce (formerly E4X); Winbuyer; Techtium; Celeno Communications; Discretix
Rami Beracha, General Managing Partner
e-mail: rami.b@pitango.com
Education: J.D. from Tel Aviv University, L.L.M. from Fordham University, NY, and M.B.A. from INSEAD, France
Background: Practiced law in New York at the corporate financing department of Fried, Frank, Harris, Shriver and Jacobson, a leading Wall Street law firm.
Directorships: Currently serves on the Board of Directors of Annobit; Convergin; dbMotion; Fixya; MobileAccess Newrworks; mySupermarket; Optier; Neebula
Zeev Binman, General Partner & Chief Financial Officer
Education: BA, Economics, MBA, Finance, Tel Aviv University
Background: Vice President, Finance, PazGas; Vice President, Finance, Fibronics International USA; referent for the defense industries in the Budget Department of the Israel Ministry of Finance
Directorships: Galil Medical

3040 PITON CAPITAL
Venture House
5th Floor
27-29 Glasshouse Street
London W1B 5DF
United Kingdom

Phone: 44-2074080451
e-mail: info@pitoncap.com
web: www.pitoncap.com

Mission Statement: Choosing network economics as the focus of our investments means that we contribute the most valuable part of our knowledge and experience to the right

Venture Capital & Private Equity Firms / International Firms

businesses. And this lets us continually learn and improve our input to the companies we invest in.
Industry Group Preference: Internet, E-Commerce & Manufacturing
Portfolio Companies: Watchfinder & Co., Quandoo, BundleTech, JamesEdition, Videdressing, 3Scale, MBA & Company, BullionVault, DaWanda, FanDuel, DocPlanner
Key Executives:
  Andrin Bachmann, Managing Director
  e-mail: andrin.bachmann@pitoncap.com
  Education: MSc, Computer Science, Swiss Federal Institute of Technology
  Background: Co-Founder, Glocalnet; Partner, M/C Venture Partners

3041 PLUS VENTURES
A 283, 1st Floor
Defence Colony
New Delhi 110024
India

Phone: 91-1141012350 Fax: 91-1141654689
web: www.plusventures.com

Mission Statement: Plus Ventures is an early-stage venture capital investment firm. We look to invest in extraordinary entrepreneurs and support them to build great teams that create superior companies. Plus Ventures investments are primarily focused on technology enabled products and services in sectors like Internet, Mobile, Education and Consumer Services.
Geographic Preference: India
Average Investment: $500,000 - $3 million
Investment Criteria: Early-Stage
Industry Group Preference: Technology-Enabled Services, Internet, Mobile, Education, Consumer Services
Portfolio Companies: Gridstone Research, Accela Media, Info Pro Solutions
Other Locations:
  1000, Route 9 North
  Suite 102
  Woodbridge, NJ 07095
  Phone: 732-8959432
Key Executives:
  Vivek Bansal, Founder/Managing Director
  Education: Engineering Degree, MS University, India; MS, Computer Science, Kansas State University
  Background: EVP/General Manager, GlobespanVirata

3042 PMV
Oude Graanmarkt 63
Brussels 1000
Belgium

Phone: 02-229-5230 Fax: 02-229-5231
e-mail: seed@pmv.eu
web: www.pmv.eu

Mission Statement: PMV provides risk capital to innovative starters and young companies in their initial growth phase. Through its sub-offer of risk capital in this phase, PMV plays a key catalytic role. At the same time, PMV mainly considers those businesses that can demonstrate a major potential for creating added value for their stakeholders in Flanders. In this sense, PMV wants to help create the future motors of Flemish prosperity.
Geographic Preference: Belgium
Investment Criteria: Seed Stage, Early-Stage
Industry Group Preference: Clean Technology, Information Technology, Life Sciences, Real Estate, Infrastructure, Renewable Energy
Portfolio Companies: 2Rivers/Yesplan, Absynthe Minded, AescAp Venture, Agrosavfe, Alvey, Amakem Therapeutics, Aminolabs, Any Media, Apitope, Arcarios, Arendsoog, Arkavund Media, Ark-Angels Fund, ARKimedes, Asia Pacific Carbon Fund, Baby Belle, Baekeland Fonds, Bedrijvencentrum Waasland, Belwind, Big Bang Ventures, Biocartis, Biofer, Biotech Fonds Vlaanderren, Boma International, Bout'chou, Bumba, Cafe Costume, Caliopa, Capital-E, Cartagenia, Choupettes, Citymesh, Clear2Pay, Cmosis, Complix, Dacentec, De Boelekes, Deborah Centrum, De Kleine Kikker, De Kleine Wereld, Deme Blue Energy, Den Berenboot, De Toverboom, De Zebra, Dink, Dou-Dou, Drie Pees, Dsquare, Ducatt, Duimelotje, Eastvillage, Eco Projects, Electrawinds, Engeltjes & Bengeltjes, Ensamblage, Esaturnus, Excico Group, Exuvis, Ffpharma, Fien En Mile, Filoukes, Flanders' Drive, Formac Pharmaceuticals, Fringilunch, GDM Electronics, Gigarant, Ginsenga, Goednavond, Grenslandhallen, Het Engeltje, High Wind, Ikaros Solar Fund, Iparc, ISPC, Intineris, Judas Theatreproducteies, Kabron, KBC Arkiv, Kelst, Kids Garden, Kids Kitchen, Kmofin Arkiv, La Luna, Larian Publishing, Layerwise, LRM, Madoc, Ma Maison Fleur, Michael Verheyden, Moeke, Morthier Catering, Multiplicom, Newtec, Niceberg Studios, NMDG Engineering, Novovil, Office Baroque Gallery, Okapi Sciences, Vof Clemence & Juliette, V2W Fun4kids, Waarborgeheer
Key Executives:
  Clair Ysebaert, Chairman

3043 POD INVESTMENT
Grev Turegatan 19
Stockholm 114 38
Sweden

Phone: 46-854506460 Fax: 46-854506469
e-mail: info@podinvestment.com
web: www.podinvestment.se

Mission Statement: We aim to build the next generation of internationally successful Nordic growth companies. We invest in companies with turnovers from 5 to 50 million Euros. As owners we add value by actively providing competence and capital.
Founded: 2000
Portfolio Companies: Adra Match, Birdstep, op5, STING Capital, Transmode

3044 POINT NINE CAPITAL
Germany

e-mail: info@pointninecap.com
web: www.pointninecap.com

Mission Statement: Like all good angel investors, we are a friendly source of capital with lots of additional value-add. We strive to become your mentors, someone who you can trust and who you're happy to call in good AND in bad times. At the same time you benefit from our ability to invest much larger amounts of capital, as well as the extensive expertise and network of all of our partners.
Geographic Preference: Europe, Germany, Poland
Average Investment: 100,000 - 500,000 Euro
Investment Criteria: Early-Stage
Industry Group Preference: Internet, SaaS, E-Commerce & Manufacturing, Mobile
Portfolio Companies: 15Five, Algolia, Bitbond, Brainly, Ciband, Clio, Combatant Gentlement, Contactually, Contentful, CouchSurfing, DaWanda, Delivery Hero, DigitaleSeiten, Docplanner.com, ePetWorld GmbH, Gengo, Handshake, Hipclub, inFakt, Infogr.am, Jobber, Kekemeke, Kreditech, Lieferheld, Mambu, Mention, Mister Spex, Mobilike, Oferteo.pl, Pomocni.pl, Positionly, PurMeo, Risk Methods, Roomorama, Scondoo, ShiftPlanning, Spinnakr, SponsorPay, StyleSeat, Typeform, Unbounce, Userfox, Vend, Westwing, Wirkaufens, Xeneta
Key Executives:
  Pawel Chudzinski, Co-Founder/Managing Partner
  Education: Leipzig Graduate School of Management
  Background: Co-Founder, Team Europe; Associate, Greenhill & Co.

Venture Capital & Private Equity Firms / International Firms

3045 POLYTECH VENTURES
Ecole Polytechnique Federale de Lausanne
Innovation Park
Batiment E
Ecublens CH-1015
Switzerland

Phone: 41-0-21-693-9210
e-mail: gdubray@polytechventures.ch
web: www.polytechventures.ch

Mission Statement: An early stage VC firm based in Switzerland with a strong international focus.

Geographic Preference: Switzerland
Founded: 2008
Investment Criteria: Early-Stage
Industry Group Preference: Information Technology, Digital Media & Marketing, Healthcare Information Technology
Portfolio Companies: Beam Express, Lotaris, Netguardians, Abionic, Slyde, Typesafe, Bugbuster, Paper.li, Seevibes

Key Executives:
Alexandre Cadosch, Chairman
e-mail: acadosch@eurofin.ch
Education: Hospitality Mangement, Ecole Hoteliere de Lausanne
Background: Vice President, Gestar SA; Tradition Financial Services

3046 POLYTECHNOS VENTURE PARTNERS GmbH
12 Promenadeplatz
Munich 80333
Germany

Phone: 49-0892422620 Fax: 49-08924226221

Mission Statement: PolyTechnos Venture-Partners is a leading independent European venture capital firm based in Munich, Germany, with a track record of building world class technology companies.

Geographic Preference: Europe
Fund Size: $240 Million
Founded: 1998
Average Investment: EUR 5 - 15 Million
Minimum Investment: $6 Million
Investment Criteria: Early to Expansion Stage
Industry Group Preference: Information Technology, Communications, Microelectronics, Life Sciences
Portfolio Companies: Cappella, IMI Intelligent Medical Implants AG, ColorChip, DBD Deutsche Breitband Dienste GmbH, Innolume GmbH, Media Lario Technologies, Nanotron Technologies GmbH, Panoratio Database Images, Power Paper, Vaioptic

Key Executives:
Tonio Barlage, Partner
Education: MBA, PhD Physics
Background: Monsanto, Product development manager at Zeneca, Senior research scientist at ICI Advanced Materials division
Knut Heitmann, Partner
e-mail: knut.heitmann@polytechnos.com
Education: Degree in electrical engineering from the Technical University of Darmstadt.
Background: Siemens, Proctor & Gamble, Baring, Managing director of Freiberger Compound Materials, Director of the technology monitoring division,
Dirk Kanngiesser, Founder, Managing Partner (IT)
Education: Electrical engineering from the Technical University of Dortmund, Germany, and his MBA from the University of Michigan.
Background: McKinsey, Bosch, Quandt, venture capital,
Directorships: Partner of Baring Private Equity Partners,
Dan Maher, Partner
Education: MBA from the Heriot-Watt University in Edinburgh, a graduate of the Harvard Graduate Business School's Advanced Management Program, a degree from the Basel School of Business & Economics.
Background: Monsanto, EuropaBio and the U.S.-China business council,
Dr. Lee Schalop, Partner
e-mail: eric.achtmann@polytechnos.com
Education: B.S. in mechanical engineering, M.S. in aeronautics & astronautics from MIT, post-graduate degree from the Von Karman Institute for Fluid Dynamics, Belgium, He received his MBA from the MIT.
Background: MS, MBA, McKinsey & Co., BMW, Daimler-Benz Aerospace, and McDonnell-Douglas, Petrotech International
Directorships: Board member or observer

3047 POND VENTURES
Grand Prix House
102-104 Sheen Road
Richmond
Surrey TW9 1UF
United Kingdom

Phone: 44-0-20-8940-1001

Mission Statement: Our team in Silicon Valley, London & Israel is dedicated to building technology into global success stories. We focus on investing in ideas which start in any of our geographies, but whose success is destined to be Worldwide.

Geographic Preference: United States, Europe, Israel
Investment Criteria: Early-Stage
Industry Group Preference: Energy, Water, New Media, Software, Consumer Products, Consumer Services
Portfolio Companies: 4Home, LiveRail, Broadway Networks, Gigle Networks, Nanotech Semiconductor, Microcosm Commnications, Transitive, PicoChip, ACCO, Mekanist, Swapit, Emefcy

Other Locations:
2033 Gateway Place
Suite 600
San Jose, CA 95110
Phone: 408-467-3806

Ackerstein Towers
Building B, 5th Floor
11, Hamenofim Street
Herzliya Pituach 46120
Israel
Phone: 972-2-971-6010

Key Executives:
Richard Irving, Co-Founder
e-mail: richard@pondventures.com
Education: BSc, MSc, Electrical Engineering, Manchester University
Background: Technical Staff, Bell Labs; Strategic Marketing Manager, AMD
Directorships: Acco Semiconductor, Emefcy
Charles Irving, Co-Founder
Education: Kingston University
Background: Glencore

3048 PORTUGAL CAPITAL VENTURES
Institutional Headquarters
Av. Dr. Antuens Guimaraes, 103
Porto 4100-079
Portugal

Phone: 351-226-165-390 Fax: 351-226-102-089
e-mail: contact@portugalventures.pt
web: www.portugalventures.pt

Mission Statement: We aim to improve the competitiveness of the Portuguese economy by investing in cutting edge industries and technologies.

Geographic Preference: Portugal
Fund Size: 600 million euros
Investment Criteria: All Stages

951

Venture Capital & Private Equity Firms / International Firms

Industry Group Preference: Industrial, Energy, Tourism, Transportation, Technology, Life Sciences, Creative Industries
Portfolio Companies: A. Silva & Silva, Abyssal, ACH BRITO & CIA, AJP Motos, Aldeia da Pedralva - Empreend. Turisticos, Alert Life Sciences Computing, Anusbisnetworks, Aptoide, Arlant, BERD, Biomode, Biosurfit, Biotrend - Inovacao e Engenharia Em Biotecnologia, BParts, C-Side, Catari, Chic by Choice, Coimbra Genomics, Critical Links, DuritCast, EDIGMA.com, Eneida, Epedal, Exponor Digital, Friday, Frissul, G3P, GenePreDiT, GebIBET, GetSocial, Girissima, Gleam, Greenfiber Tech, Grupo Salvador Caetano, Grupo Visabeira, Guestcentric Systems, iM3dical, JScrambler, Just in Time Tourist, Kinematix, Liquid Data Intelligence, Longevity, Luzitin, Lymphact, Magnomics, Marope Algarve, Marriott Praia D'El Rey, ME 3I, MediaOmics, Medical Port, Moneris, Muzzley, Desenvolvimento de Colucoes Digitais, MyChild, New Coffee Co. II, Nutri Ventures, Oasis Atlantico - Hotelaria e Turismo, Omniflow, Outsystems, Parkalgar, Passworks, Pastceram, Perceive 3D, Pestana Berlin, PETsys Electronics, Pharma 73, Process'ware, Quinta da Marinha Leisure, SABE Online, Sagrotel - Sociedade Imobilaria, Science4You, Serafim Silva - Atividades Hoteleiras, SGGHM - Soc. Geral Gestao Hoteis de Mocambique, ShiftForward, Shopitur, Skaphandrus, Somelos Tecidos, SPPTH, Steambolico, Taifas, Thelial Technologies, Travel Store, Treat U, TTR - Transactional Track Record, Tuizzi, Vista Alegre Atlantis, Whizztek, Windplus, Wizdee, Wizi to Find, Xhockware, Xtourmaker, youbeQ, Zaask

Key Executives:
Jose Franca, Chairman and CEO
Education: PhD, Imperial College of Science, Technology and Medicine; Degree in Electrical Engineering from the Technical University of Lisbon
Background: Professor, Technical University of Lisbon; CEO and Chairman, CHIPIDEA; State Secretary for Education, Portugal; Director, MIPS Technologies
Luis Filipe Lopes, Deputy CEO

3049 PRACTICA CAPITAL
Naurgarduko Street 3
Vilnius LT-03231
Lithuania

Phone: 370-5-260-3159
e-mail: info@practica.lt
web: www.practica.lt

Mission Statement: Practica Capital manages seed and venture capital funds established under JEREMIE initiative. The funds invest in early-stage development of high-potential business ideas (seed, startup) and expansion of established businesses in Lithuania.

Geographic Preference: Lithuania
Fund Size: 6 million Euro
Founded: 2011
Average Investment: 300,000 - 3 million Euro
Investment Criteria: Early-Stage
Portfolio Companies: Fast Goods Groups UAB, Tokia.It, MCT, TVC, Mano daktaras, TrackDuck, adtarget.me, CGTrader.Om, Cheap Data Communications, Trustribe, Trafi, Kurgyvenu.It, Dragdis, Mobassurance, ImpressPages, AdDuplex, GAUDRE, Gifty, TransferGo, TransferGo, Benjamin River Productions, Celi APS, Startup.Lt

Key Executives:
Anatoly Faktorovicius
370-699-28-655
e-mail: antolijus@practica.lt

3050 PREVIZ VENTURES
Ackerstein Towers
Building D, 10th Floor
12 Abba Eban Ave.
Herzeliya 46725
Israel

Phone: 972-99720467 Fax: 972-99520732
web: www.previzv.com

Mission Statement: Previz Ventures is a venture capital fund with an existing portfolio of investments in innovative technology companies addressing critical challenges primarily in the medical sector, with secondary focus on the information & communications technologies (ICT) sector. The fund invests in early stage firms, post proof of concept, at initial or approaching commercial stage, targeting large underserved markets with scalable solutions. The fund targets primarily Israeli based companies given the attractiveness of the technology and innovation landscape and the unique market access of the fund's management team.

Geographic Preference: Israel
Investment Criteria: Early-Stage
Industry Group Preference: Medical Devices, Information Technology, Communications, Mobile, Education, Security
Portfolio Companies: ReWalk, LunGuard, Clear-Cut Medical, Real Imaging, Profility, CellRox, Giraffic

Key Executives:
Dan Baruchi, Managing Partner
Education: BA, Economics, Haifa University; MBA, Tel-Aviv University
Background: Senior Partner, Monitor Group

3051 PRIME TECHNOLOGY VENTURES NV
Museumplein 5A
PO Box 51129, 1007 EC
Amsterdam 1071 DJ
Netherlands

Phone: 31-202050820 Fax: 31-202050819
e-mail: info@ptv.com

Mission Statement: Leading early stage venture capital firm.

Geographic Preference: Europe
Fund Size: $144 Million
Founded: 1999
Average Investment: Euro5 - 15 Million
Minimum Investment: $600, 500
Investment Criteria: Expansion, Development, Seed, Start-up, Other early stage, Small buyout
Industry Group Preference: Communications, Computer Related, Electronic Technology, Internet Technology, Telecommunications, Semiconductors, E-Commerce & Manufacturing, Digital Media & Marketing, Software, Mobile
Portfolio Companies: 3mensio Medical Imaging, AppLift, Bright Computing, Cint, Civolution, Codenomicon, Buddy, Eutechnyx, Genkey, Global Collect, Greetz, Human Inference, Intrinsic ID, Ipida, Layar, Liquavista, MarkaVIP, MarketXS, Mendix, Nedstat, Pairingo, Pulsic, Q-GO, SAAS, Service2Media, Silicon Hive, Takeaway.com, Tridion, ZeroLight, Watermark Inc.

Other Locations:
Wellington House
East Road
Cambridge CB1 1BH
United Kingdom
Phone: 44-1223-451-007 Fax: 44-1223-451-100

Key Executives:
Monish Suri, General Partner
e-mail: info@ptv.com
Education: Bachelor degree in Computer Engineering, MBA degree from Rotterdam School of Management and J.L. Kellogg Graduate School of Management.
Background: Held various commercial management positions with Baan Company(Channel Management

director, Business Development director and International Marketing Manager).
Directorships: Serves on the board of Codenomicon and Navicore as a board observer with MarketXS.
Jelto Kromwijk Smits, General Partner
e-mail: info@ptv.com
Education: B.Sc. and M.Sc. degrees in Physics from the University of Helsinki.
Background: Chairman of Solid (Finnish company).
Sake Bosch, Founder/Managing Partner
e-mail: sake@primeventures.com
Education: BA, Management Science, MSc, Business Administration
Background: Senior Principal, Holland Ventures
Directorships: 3mensio Medical Imaging, Civolution, MarkaVIP, MarketXS, Nedstat, Service2Media, SaaSPlaza, Tridion, Watermark

3052 PRINCIPIA SGR
Via Pietro Mascagnia
n.20
Milan 20122
Italy

Phone: 39-0236589750 **Fax:** 39-0236589779
e-mail: info@principiasgr.it
web: www.principiasgr.it

Mission Statement: Thanks to the institutional connections and a management with a history of success in business innovation, Principia SGR is one of the largest of the Italian venture capital, both for longevity and experience of its team for both the relevance of assets under management.
Geographic Preference: Italy
Founded: 2002
Investment Criteria: All Stages
Industry Group Preference: Internet, Mobile, E-Commerce & Manufacturing, Digital Media & Marketing, Entertainment
Portfolio Companies: Tacati, Eximia, Neodata Group, MoneyFarm, Bibutek, Bangbite, DoveConviene, Games Are Social, Altilia, Docebo, Emediamarketing, 4w MarketPlace, ITSworld Sicilia, Weekend Company, PharmaEste, JUSP, X2 TV, im3D Clinic South, Vivocha, Ciceroos, Zoorate, Simplicissius Book Farm, D-Share, Applix, CrowdEngineering, Sounday, Eco4Cloud, Rhysto, Banza, EOS SpA, Citynews, 6sicuro

Key Executives:
Roberto Mazzei, Chief Executive Chairman

3053 PRIVATE EQUITY PARTNERS SPA
Via degli Omenoni, 2
Milano 20121
Italy

Phone: 39-28052171 **Fax:** 39-28052321
e-mail: info@privateequitypartners.com
web: www.privateequitypartners.com

Mission Statement: Developed a unique experience and expertise in Italy as a fund manager in Eastern Europe.
Geographic Preference: Eastern Europe
Fund Size: $240 Million
Founded: 1989
Average Investment: $18 Million
Minimum Investment: $6 Million
Investment Criteria: Expansion, Buy-outs
Industry Group Preference: Pharmaceuticals, Medical, Ceramic Tiles, Food Services, Automotive, Household Goods, Software, Electronic Technology, Furniture, Logistics

Key Executives:
Fabio Lorenzo Sattin, Presidente & Chairman
e-mail: info@privateequitypartners.com
Giovanni Campolo, Amministratore Delegato & Managing Director
e-mail: info@privateequitypartners.com
Directorships: Founding Partner

Alessandra Stea, Investment Manager
e-mail: info@privateequitypartners.com
Directorships: Founding Partner
Pier Paolo Quaranta, Investment Manager
e-mail: info@privateequitypartners.com
Directorships: Chairman
Leonardo Bruzzichesi, Partner
e-mail: info@privateequitypartners.com

3054 PROCURITAS PARTNERS KB
Linnegatan 9-11
Stockholm SE-114 47
Sweden

Phone: 46-850614300 **Fax:** 46-850614344

Mission Statement: One of the leading private equity houses in Scandinavia.
Geographic Preference: Denmark, Sweden
Fund Size: $0.37 Billion
Founded: 1986
Average Investment: $75 Million
Minimum Investment: $32.1 Million
Investment Criteria: MBO's, Buyouts
Industry Group Preference: Manufacturing, Telecommunications, Data Communications, Electronic Technology, Water, Waste & Recycling, Education, Concrete, Logistics
Portfolio Companies: Global Scanning, Pierce, Farma Holding, Gram Equipment, Team Olivia, Oral Care, Osby Glas, Perimter Protection Group, Sonas, Wermland Paper AB, Expan, Lekolar, Ariterm, Disa Holding, Zone Holding, North Trade, KGH Customs Services

Key Executives:
Michael Ahlstrom, Founder and Partner
e-mail: andersen@procuritas.se
Education: MSc in Business Administration from the Business School in Aarhus.
Background: JPMorgan.
His Wikse, Managing Partner
e-mail: karlander@procuritas.se
Education: MSc in Economics and Business Administration from the Stockholm School of Economics.
Background: Board member of the private equity companies Företagskapital AB (1989-92) and Atle AB (1992-95).
Mattias Feiff, Partner
Education: MBA in Finance and International Business from the Stern School of Business at New York University and a BSc in Economics from Copenhagen Business School.
Background: NSG Logistics AB, Sandå Projekt AB, Axenti A/S, Expan Holding A/S and Thermia Holding AB.
Directorships: Senior Partner.
Björn Lindberg, Partner
e-mail: toyberg@procuritas.se
Education: MSc in Economics from Copenhagen Business School.
Background: Started his professional career with Procuritas In 1993.
Johan Conradsson, Investment Manager
e-mail: wiske@procuritas.se
Education: MBA from INSEAD and an MSc in Engineering Physics from the University of Uppsala.
Background: Vice President of ABB.
Directorships: Partner of Procuritas since 1998.
Daniel Schuss, Investment Manager
e-mail: rignell@procuritas.se
Education: MSc in Engineering Physics from the Royal Institute of Technology in Stockholm and an MSc in Finance and Business Administration from Stockholm School of Economics.
Background: Consultant at Andersen Consulting Strategic Services and at SIAR-Bossard.
Directorships: Partner

Venture Capital & Private Equity Firms / International Firms

3055 PROFOUNDERS CAPITAL
3 Cadogan Gate
Chelsea
London SW1X 0AS
United Kingdom

Phone: 44-02077666900
e-mail: rogan@profounderscapital.com
web: www.profounderscapital.com

Mission Statement: Our aim is to invest in and support new businesses with capital plus proactive advice and expertise. We believe that the combination of dynamic new entrepreneurs and PROfounders' experience leads to a strong base for new ventures to flourish. Our goal is to create long-term value and promote entrepreneurism.

Geographic Preference: Europe
Average Investment: £500,000 - 2.5 million
Investment Criteria: Early-Stage
Industry Group Preference: Digital Media & Marketing, Technology
Portfolio Companies: Cursogram, Small Giant Games, Compass, Festicket, Splash, Younity, busuu, GetYourGuide, easyCar, Lulu, Leap Motion, 9flats, onefinestay, CitySocializer, Mangahigh, Made.com

Key Executives:
 Rogan Angelini-Hurll, Partner
  e-mail: rogan@profounderscapital.com
  Background: Pan European Media Research Team, Citi; Salomon Brothers; Spectrum Strategy Consultants

3056 PROJECT A VENTURE GmBH & CO. KG
Julie-Wolfthorn-Straáe 1
Berlin 10115
Germany

Phone: 49-30-340-606-300 Fax: 49-30-340-606-399
e-mail: info@project-a.com
web: www.project-a.com/en

Mission Statement: Project A Ventures is a company builder focusing on Internet, Advertising Technology and Mobile. With our experts' operational know-how and our financial support, we help start-ups to build up competence in key areas such as IT, Performance Marketing, Business Intelligence and Organization Building, and thus contribute to their sustainable success. Our experts, based in Berlin and Sao Paulo, are among the best in their field and have been involved in building more than 50 market leading companies worldwide within the last 15 years.

Geographic Preference: Worldwide
Investment Criteria: Seed, Growth
Industry Group Preference: Internet, Advertising Technology, Mobile
Portfolio Companies: 42matters, Catawiki, Contorion, ESV Digital, Evino, Eyeota, Glow, Intelipost, Kouchzauber, Kyto, Loopline Systems, Metrigo, MiNodes, Natue, nu3, Procompra, Saatchi Art, Semasio, Spryker, Tictail, Tirendo, uberall, Wine in Black, Worldremit, ZenMate

Other Locations:
 Project A Ventures Latam
 775 cj 133
 Sao Paulo
 Brazil
 Phone: 55-11-4872-8008
 Olivier Raussin, Managing Director

Key Executives:
 Dr. Florian Heinemann, Co-Founder and Managing Director
  Education: MBA, WHU Koblenz
  Background: Managing Director, Rocket Internet; Co-Founder and Managing Director, JustBooks/AbeBooks; Co-Head, Online Marketing Department, Jamba!

3057 PROMETHEAN INVESTMENTS LLP
5 Old Balley
2nd Floor
London EC4M 7BA
United Kingdom

Phone: +44 20 7426 2590
web: www.prometheaninvestments.com

Mission Statement: Promethean Investments LLP is a special situations principal investment firm founded in 2005. We are an independent partnership providing innovative capital solutions in the UK lower mid-market.

Geographic Preference: United Kingdom
Founded: 2005
Investment Criteria: Special Situations

Other Locations:
 1 Hill Street
 3rd Floor
 Edinburgh EH2 3JP
 United Kingdom

Key Executives:
 Sir Peter Burt, Partner

3058 PROMETHYAN LABS
Portfolio Companies: Jabbit, BabaBoo, Prelert, Rivermuse
156 Blackfriars Road
London SE1 8EN
United Kingdom

3059 PROSEED
85 Yehuda Halevi Street
Tel Aviv 65796
Israel

Phone: 972-3-566-1284 Fax: 972-3-566-1285
e-mail: admin@proseed.co.il

Mission Statement: ProSeed, solidly positioned on the Israeli Venture Capital map since April 2000, has recently taken major steps in establishing itself in the forefront of the VC market, providing funding as well as hands-on managerial assistance and analytical support to capable technology-based enterprises.

Geographic Preference: Israel
Founded: 2000
Investment Criteria: Seed-Stage, Early-Stage
Industry Group Preference: Renewable Energy, Computer Hardware & Software, Healthcare
Portfolio Companies: PerfAction, EarlySense, Argo Medical Technologies, Gene Grafts, Regentis Biomaterials, Medic Vision, CorrelSense, VibeSec, Genieo, DataEssence, Attunity, Tehuti Networks, DigiFlex, Capital Nature

Key Executives:
 Shai Levy, CEO
  e-mail: shai@proseed.co.il
  Education: BS, Accounting, Tel Aviv University
  Background: CFO/CIO, Tahari Family; Director, Financial Reporting, Deutsch
 Adina Makover, Life Science Director
  e-mail: adina@proseed.co.il
  Education: PhD, Life Sciences, Columbia University; MBA, Bar-Ilan University
  Background: Post Doctoral Fellow, Weizmann Institute

3060 PROVENTURE AG
7101 Executive Center Drive
Suite 200
Brentwood, TN 37027

Phone: 615-3770909 Fax: 615-3776921
e-mail: info@proventure.com
web: www.proventure.com

Mission Statement: The Proventure companies are advisers to private equity fund-of-funds.
Geographic Preference: Europe
Fund Size: $ 215 Million
Founded: 1999
Average Investment: $5.4 Million
Minimum Investment: $2.4 Million
Investment Criteria: Seed, start-up, early stage or expansion financings.
Industry Group Preference: All Sectors Considered

3061 PT BHAKTI INVESTAMA TBK
MNC Tower 16th Floor
Jl. Kebon Sirih Kav 17-19
Jakarta Pusat 10340
Indonesia

Phone: 62-213922949 **Fax:** 62-213910454
Toll-Free: 01-8001262626

Mission Statement: Striving to become one of the largest and most successful investment banks in Indonesia.
Geographic Preference: Indonesia
Founded: 1989
Industry Group Preference: Electronic Components, Services, Logistics, Distribution, Cellular Service & Products
Portfolio Companies: Global Mediacom, Media Nusantara Citra, MNC Sky Vision, Infokom Elektrindo, MNC Kapital Indonesia, MNC Securities, MNC Asset Management, MNC Finance, MNC Life Assurance, MNC Asuransi Indonesia, MNC Bank, MNC Land, MNC Energy, Global Transport Services
Key Executives:
Hary Djaja, Director
Darma Putra, Director

3062 PT BNI NOMURA JAFCO MANAJEMEN VENTURA
Alexandra House
6th Floor
18 Chater Road
Central 10210
Hong Kong

Phone: 65-62246383 **Fax:** 65-62213690
e-mail: enquiry_hongkong@jafcoasia.com
web: www.jafcoasia.com

Mission Statement: Actively seeking new investments.
Fund Size: $100 Million
Founded: 1990
Portfolio Companies: Mobilewalla, Unmetric, Bubble Motion, Customer XPs Software Private Limited, Vriti Infocom, Consilium Software, Data Security Systems Solutions, Mozat, Si2 Microsystems, Apnapaisa Private, Tessolve Solutions, Mistral Solutions, Consistel, Microquai Techno, Avega Systems, Vignani Technologis, Microland Limited, RPO, Run Service, Dilithium Networks, Inzign Private, Merlion Pharmaceuticals, R&B Technology Holding Corporation, ShowWorld Holding, ByPay Information, Shezhen Shenzinlong Industry, Boqii, Lumi Holdings, IHAVEU.com, China Synthetic Mica Technology, Meize Energy Industries Holding Limited, M2 Holdings Limited, Athieva, UltiZen Games, Modjoy, JD Holding, Synerchip, Greatville Limited, iPeer Multimedia International, eHi Car Services, OptoTrace Technologies, Amsky Technology, Tarena, R & V, Global Market Group, First Point Holdings, hiu! Media, 51 Deco, Medsphere International Holding, Heguang International, Palm Commerce Holdings, Ether Optronics, GolferPass, LDK Solar, JRD Communication, Sungy Mobile, Tudou, Ambow Education Holding, Madhouse, Cgen Diital Media Company Limited, Leadtone Limited, Cash River, Canadia Solar, Agape Package Manufacturing, Arkmicro Technologies, BCD Semiconductor, China Wireless, Fiberxon, HiSoft Technology International, InterChina Network Software, Photonic Bridges Holdings, Pollex Mobile, China GrenTech Holdings Limited, Egis Tecnology, Gamemage Interactive, DSM-AGI Corporation, Sunlux Energy, Grandsys Technologies & Service
Key Executives:
Richard Uichel Joung, Chief Investment Officer & Managing Director

3063 PUILAETCO PRIVATE BANKERS KBL Group
46 Herrmann Debroux Avenue
Brussels 1160
Belgium

Phone: 32-26794511 **Fax:** 32-26794622
e-mail: private.banking@puilaetcodewaay.be

Mission Statement: Provides specialised services in asset management, investment funds, estate planning; specialises in active European equity management
Geographic Preference: Worldwide
Founded: 1868
Investment Criteria: Long Term, Bottom-up, Global approach
Key Executives:
Jacques Peters, President
Bettina Leysen, Administrator

3064 PWC
113-119 The Terrace
Wellington
New Zealand

Phone: 64-44627000 **Fax:** 64-44627001
Toll-Free: 0800 229 229
web: www.pwc.co.nz/lombard-finance/

Mission Statement: The Lombard Group of Companies is a New Zealand owned and operated financier providing an innovative approach to finance and investment options for its clients throughout New Zealand.
Geographic Preference: New Zealand
Founded: 1989
Minimum Investment: $1,000
Investment Criteria: Performance and risk management, Mortgage Backed Property, Unsecured Lending
Industry Group Preference: Machinery, Financial Services, Consumer Services, Property Management
Key Executives:
Jonathan Freeman, Chairman
Background: General manager with a Brierley owned subsidiary
Directorships: Director
Bruce Hassall, Chief Executive Officer and Senior Partner

3065 QBIC FUND
Gaston Crommelaan 8
Gent 9050
Belgium

web: www.qbic.be

Mission Statement: Qbic Fund seeks to invest in spin-off companies of the universities of Ghent, Brussels and Antwerp, leveraging the creativity of more than 8.500 researchers. This strategic alliance provides a sufficient level of critical mass to set up a sizeable, professionally managed fund. The fund mainly targets life sciences, new materials, cleantech and ICT start-ups.
Geographic Preference: Belgium
Investment Criteria: Seed-Stage, Early-Stage, Spin-Offs
Industry Group Preference: Life Sciences, New Materials, Clean Technology, Information Technology, Communications
Portfolio Companies: AgroSavfe, Multiplicom, Track4C, CoScale, PharmaFluidics, Biogazelle

Venture Capital & Private Equity Firms / International Firms

Key Executives:
Marc Zabeau, Founder/Managing Partner
Education: MSc, Zoology, PhD, Genetics, University of Ghent
Background: Plant Genetic Systems, KeyGene
Directorships: Trinean, Calicopa

3066 QIMING VENTURE PARTNERS
Room 3906
Jinmao Tower
88 Century Boulevard
Shanghai 200121
China

Phone: +86 21 6101 6522 Fax: +86 21 6101 6512
web: www.qimingventures.com

Mission Statement: We believe in helping companies succeed and we are committed to supporting them as they become sector leaders in China. With a portfolio featuring over 70 investments, Qiming captures market opportunities, choosing promising enterprises with great growth potential, undervalued enterprises, and high-tech enterprises with independent innovation technologies. Our entrepreneurs benefit from access to our portfolio of companies and our global network. While striving to be the investor of choice, Qiming also works closely with other leading venture capital firms in China to deliver the investor value that growing Chinese companies require.

Geographic Preference: China
Fund Size: $1.1 Billion
Founded: 2006
Investment Criteria: Early stage, Growth stage
Industry Group Preference: Information Technology, Consumer, Retail, Consumer & Leisure, Healthcare, Clean Technology

Qiming Shaghai Office
Shanghai 200121
China
Phone: +86 21 6101 6522 Fax: +86 21 6101 6512

Qiming Beijing Office
Jianguomenwai Street
Beijing 100004
China
Phone: +86 10 5961 1188 Fax: +86 10 5961 1288

Qiming Suzhou Office
Suzhou Industrial Park
Jiangsu
China
Phone: +86 21 6588 3308

Qiming Development HK Limited
Queens Road East
Hong Kong
Phone: +852 2855 6901

3067 QUADRAN GESTION Deutsche Beteiligungs AG
Börsenstraáe 1
Frankfurt 60313
Germany

Phone: 49-699578701 Fax: 49-6995787199
web: www.deutsche-beteiligung.de

Mission Statement: Actively seeking new investments.

Founded: 1965
Investment Criteria: MBO, Mid-market segment
Industry Group Preference: Automotive, Machinery, Printing, Construction
Portfolio Companies: Broetje-Automation GmbH Wiefelstede, Clyde-Bergemann-Gruppe Wesel/Glasgow/Delaware, DNS:NET Internet Service GmbH, FDG-Gruppe, Formel D GmbH, Grohmann GmbH Prum, Heytex Bramsche GmbH Bramsche, inexio Informationstechnologie und Telekommunikation KGaA, JCK KG, Plant Systems & Services PSS GmbH, Romanoco-Gruppe Karlsruhe, Schulerhilfe Gelsenkirchen, Spheros GmbH, Stephan Machinery GmbH, Unser Heimatbacker Holding GmbH

Key Executives:
Torsten Grede, Chief Executive Officer

3068 QUANTUM WAVE FUND
Tsvetnoy Bulvar, 11, Building 6
6th Floor
Moscow 127051
Russia

Phone: 404-537-2055

Mission Statement: Quantum Wave Fund is a venture capital firm focused on seeking out early stage private companies with breakthrough quantum technology. Our mission is to help these companies capitalize on their opportunities and provide a platform fo our investors to participate in the quantum technology wave.

Investment Criteria: Early Stage
Industry Group Preference: Security, Telecommunications, Military, Data Storage, Data Mining, Microprocessors, Microcontrollers, New Materials, Physical Sciences
Portfolio Companies: Centice, Clifton, ID Quantique, Nano-Meta Technologies, Lunera Lighting

Other Locations:
4105 Peachtree-Dunwoody Road NE
Atlanta, GA 30342
Phone: 678-999-4474

Key Executives:
Serguie Kouzmine, Managing and Founding Partner, Board Member
e-mail: sk@qwcap.com
Education: Master's Degree in Physics from Novosibirsk State University and PhD in Physics from Institute of Nuclear Physics in Russia. Degree in Business Administration from the University of Chicago Business School
Background: Founder, Nonolet; CEO, Ritzio Entertainment Group; General Partner, Solution Fund
Directorships: Nano-Meta Technologies, Inc
Frank Creer, Partner, Managing Director West Coast
e-mail: fc@qwcap.com
Education: Degree in Finance and Entrepreneurship from the University of Utah
Background: Founding Member, Stevens Wood Consulting Group; Co-Founder, Wasatch Venture Fund; Founder and Managing Director, Zone Venture Fund
Directorships: Lunera Lighting Inc, Centice Corp

3069 QUEST FOR GROWTH
Lei 19, Box 3
Leuven B-3000
Belgium

Phone: 32-0-16-28-41-28 Fax: 32-0-16-28-41-29
e-mail: quest@questforgrowth.com
web: www.questforgrowth.com

Mission Statement: Quest for Growth is a Privak that focuses on European growth companies covering a diversity of sectors. Quest for Growth focuses on European technology-based growth companies in sectors such as life sciences, information technology, software, semiconductors, telecom, electronics, new materials and special situations in other growth sectors.

Geographic Preference: Europe
Fund Size: 112 million euro
Investment Criteria: Growth Stage
Industry Group Preference: Life Sciences, Information Technology, Software, Semiconductors, Telecommunications, Electronics, New Materials
Portfolio Companies: Init Innovation, Nemetschek, SAP, USU Software, EVS Broadcast Equipment, LEM Holding,

TKH Group, Tomra Systems, Melexis, Fresenius, Gerresheimer, Nexus, Pharmagest Interactive, Sartorius, UDH Healthcare, Andritz, Arcadis, Bertrandt, Centrotec, Kendrion, Nibe, Saft Groupe, Schaltbau Holding, FMC, Umicore, Aliaxis, Anteryon, Capricorn Cleantech Co-Investments, Idea AG, Kiadis Pharma, Magwel, Mapper Lithography, Prosonix

Key Executives:
Rene Avonts, Chairman

3070 QUESTER CAPITAL MANAGEMENT LIMITED
5 St John's Lane
London EC1M 4BH
United Kingdom

Phone: 44-2081230665 Fax: 44-2078-517770
e-mail: enquiries@sparkventures.com
web: www.sparkventures.com

Mission Statement: Quester invests in the UK's best technology to create great companies. As well as capital, we bring a wealth of experience of developing high growth companies in a variety of technologies from early stage through IPO or trade sale.

Geographic Preference: UK, Western Europe
Fund Size: $380 Million
Founded: 1984
Average Investment: Euro 165 Million
Minimum Investment: $1.32 Million
Investment Criteria: Focuses on Start-ups and early stage companies seeking to raise their first or second round of venture capital, MBO, MBI
Industry Group Preference: Healthcare, Nanotechnology, Education, Electronic Technology, Security, Biotechnology, Software, Leisure, Media, Life Sciences, Communications, Environment Products & Services
Portfolio Companies: Academia, Antenova, Aspex Semiconductor, Celoxica Holdings, Cluster Seven, DEM Solutions, Firebox.com, Gambling Compliance, Haemostatix, IMImobile, Kobalt Music, Mind Candy, MyDeco, Nototehighstreet.com, OpenX, Oxford Immunotec, Perpetuum, Xention, Xtera Communications

3071 RABO BLACK EARTH Eagle Venture Partners
Str. Arbat street, 10
13-3 Building One
Moscow 119002
Russia

Phone: 7495-6204885 Fax: 7495-6204886
e-mail: info@evp.ru

Mission Statement: Actively seeking new investments.
Geographic Preference: Central and Eastern Europe
Fund Size: $31.7 Million
Founded: 1996
Investment Criteria: Early stage, Small and Medium Enterprises
Industry Group Preference: Confectionery, Cement Roofing, Construction, Beverages, Cosmetics, Ice Cream, Agribusiness, Telecommunications
Portfolio Companies: Polypack, Stroidetal, BEZRK, Kodotel, Lipetski Khladokombinat , Izorok , Tamak, TAKF, Kreker

Key Executives:
Yang Devingart, Managing Director
e-mail: valery@evp.ru
Casper Heijsteeg, Managing Director

3072 RAFAEL DEVELOPMENT CORPORATION (RDC) LIMITED
The Triangle Tower
42nd Floor
Tel Aviv 67023
Israel

Phone: 972-36075500 Fax: 972-36075529
e-mail: info@rdc.co.il
web: www.rdc.co.il

Mission Statement: Focuses on generating new businesses by applying the core technologies of RAFAEL.

Geographic Preference: Israel
Fund Size: $150 Million
Founded: 1993
Investment Criteria: Companies from inception to maturity
Industry Group Preference: Aerospace, Defense and Security, Information Technology, Software, Communications, Medical Devices, Advanced Weapons Systems, Electronic Technology
Portfolio Companies: Given Imaging, Galil Medical, Medingo, Starling, SELA, 3DV, Sync-Rx, Kyma, Smart Wave

Key Executives:
Avishai Friedman, President & Chief Executive Officer
e-mail: rbaron@rdc.co.il
Hezi Nahum, Vice President Business Development

3073 RED DOT VENTURES
Singapore

Phone: 65-63249730 Fax: 65-63241637
e-mail: contact@reddotventures.com
web: www.reddotventures.com

Mission Statement: Established in 2011, Red Dot Ventures is a seed-stage venture capital firm focused on Singapore-based high-tech startups in areas including ICT, Interactive Digital Media, MedTech, Nanotech, CleanTech, and Engineering.

Geographic Preference: Singapore
Founded: 2011
Investment Criteria: Early-Stage
Industry Group Preference: High Technology, Digital Media & Marketing, Medical Technology, Nanotechnology, Clean Technology, Engineering
Portfolio Companies: iCarsclub, Ascenz, aSpecial, The Stakeholder Company, Paywhere, Daylight Studios, Pirate3D, GCoreLab, Digify, Gnosis Analytics, Ractiv, I3 Precision, Pytheas, Intuitive Creations, Protag, Socialwalk, Taamkru, Algo Access

Key Executives:
Leslie Loh, Managing Director
Education: BComm, Finance, Saint Mary's University
Background: Founder/Chairman/CEO, System Access
Directorships: SPRING Singapore

3074 REED ELSEVIER VENTURES
1-3 Strand
London WC2N 5JR
United Kingdom

Phone: 44-20-7166-5500 Fax: 44-20-7166-5799
e-mail: london@reedelsevier.com
web: www.reedelsevier.com/aboutus/ventures/pages/home.aspx

Mission Statement: Founded in 2000, Reed Elsevier Ventures is a venture capital firm with offices in London and San Francisco. We are backed by one of the world's most successful media and information companies, Reed Elsevier. Our mission is to invest in entrepreneurs and management teams that have the vision to build great companies. We take an active role in the development of our companies and help our entrepreneurs to build value via our extensive network of industry contacts & business relationships.

Geographic Preference: United States, Europe, Israel

Venture Capital & Private Equity Firms / International Firms

Investment Criteria: All Stages
Industry Group Preference: Internet, Media, Technology, New Media, Mobile, Big Data, Healthcare Information Technology, Software
Key Executives:
  Luke Smith, Investment Analyst
  e-mail: luke.smith@reedelsevierventures.com

3075 REGENT PACIFIC PRIVATE EQUITY LIMITED Regent Pacific Group Ltd.
8th Floor, Henley Building
5 Queen's Road Central
Central
Hong Kong
  Phone: 852-25146111 **Fax:** 852- 28104792
  e-mail: info@regentpac.com
  web: www.regentpac.com

Mission Statement: Actively seeking new investments.
Geographic Preference: Asia Pacific Region
Key Executives:
  James Mellon, Non-Executive Co-Chairman
  Stephen Roland Dattels, Non-Executive Co-Chairman

3076 REITEN & CO STRATEGIC INVESTMENTS AS Reiten & Company
Haakon VIIs gt. 1, 3rd floor
Oslo 0161
Norway
  Phone: 47-23113700 **Fax:** 47-23113721
  e-mail: post@reitenco.no
  web: www.reitenco.no

Mission Statement: A leading Nordic Investment and Advisory firm specializing in private equity and corporate advisory.
Geographic Preference: Denmark, Finland, Norway, Sweden
Fund Size: $264 Million
Founded: 1992
Average Investment: EUR 10 and 40 Million
Minimum Investment: $12 Million
Investment Criteria: Expansion and Development Capital, Buyout and Buyin
Industry Group Preference: Computer Related, Medical & Health Related, Energy, Consumer Services, Financial Services, Real Estate, Business to Business, Industrial Services, Insurance
Portfolio Companies: Data Respons, Webstep, Grilstad, Con-Fom, Brubakken, Malthus, QuestBack, NEAS, Competentia
Key Executives:
  Narve Reiten, Founding Partner
  e-mail: an@reitenco.no
  Education: Masters of Science degree in Mathematics(Norwegian University of Science and Technology)
  Background: Bearingpoint(Adviser), Sensonor(R&D group)
  Kathryn M. Baker, Partner
  e-mail: nr@reitenco.no
  Education: Master of Business and Economics degree(Norwegian School of Management), CFA(Norwegian School of Economics and Business Administration)
  Background: I.M. Skaugen(M&A, Project development)
  Terje Bakken, Partner
  Education: Toronto
  Background: ON
  Brath Brath Ingero, Partner
  e-mail: bbi@reitenco.no
  Education: Degree in Economics(University of Oslo)
  Background: The Norwegian Association of Masters of Science in Business(Visiting Lecturer)
  Morten Viksoy, Partner
  e-mail: mv@reitenco.no
  Education: Master of Business and Economics degree(Norwegian School of Economics and Business Administration)
  Background: Telenor Broadcast(Project Director), McKinsey & Co(Management Consultant)
  John M. Bjerkan, Partner & CFO
  e-mail: jmb@reitenco.no
  Education: MBA, Master of Business and Economics(Norwegian School of Management)
  Background: Telenor(Project Manager), PA Consulting Group(Research Analyst)

3077 RENAISSANCE PARTNERS
44 Lowicka
Warszawa 02-551
Poland
  Phone: 48-228488777 **Fax:** 48-228568935
  web: www.rp.com.pl

Mission Statement: Renaissance Partners is the management company of the European Renaissance Capital venture capital funds. The mission is to seek and analyze potential investment opportunities, finance projects through purchase of shares and contribute to increasing the values.
Geographic Preference: Poland, Czech Republic, Solvakia, USA
Fund Size: $39.5 Million
Founded: 1994
Average Investment: $1 Million
Minimum Investment: $0.5 Million
Industry Group Preference: Broadcasting, Global Industries, Communications, Energy
Portfolio Companies: Bielsko Business Center, Pirios, Solgaz, Slovpack Bratislava, Ticketstream
Key Executives:
  Peter Bardadin, Partner
  Education: Graduated(Czech Technical University), Diploma from postgraduate studies(Sloan School of Management, MIT)
  Background: Bank of America, Victor Computers, Tandem Computers(Executive position)
  Marlena Czyzewska, Office Manager
  Witold Grabowski, 9 Canton Road
  Education: Kowloon
  Background: National and Pennsylvania Labor Relations Boards
  Radoslaw Czyrko, Partner
  Education: Graduated(Agricultural University), Financial management (Georgetown University, USA)
  Background: Czech-American Enterprise Fund(Investment Officer)

3078 REVO CAPITAL
Barbaros Mh. Halk Cd. Kardelen Sok.
Palladium Tower Kat:9
Ofis:36 Atasehir
Istanbul 34357
Turkey
  Phone: 90-212-327-2184
  web: www.revo.vc

Mission Statement: A venture capital fund investing in truly innovative, seed & early-stage B2B or B2C technology ventures in Turkey.
Geographic Preference: Turkey
Investment Criteria: Early-Stage, Seed-Stage
Industry Group Preference: Business to Business, Technology, Cloud Computing, Internet, E-Commerce & Manufacturing, Gaming

Venture Capital & Private Equity Firms / International Firms

Portfolio Companies: Fit Solutions, SkyAtlas, 8digits, Parasut, Onedio

Key Executives:
Ozcan Tahincioglu, General Partner
Background: Chairman/CEO, Tahincioglu Holding; Chairman, Endeavor Turkey; Chairman, Kent Gida

3079 RFC AMBRIAN RFC Group Ltd.
L14, 19-31 Pitt Street
Sydney NSW 2000
Australia

Phone: 61-292500000 Fax: 61-292500001
web: www.rfcambrian.com

Mission Statement: Resource Finance Corporation is a merchant and investment bank; provides world leading expertise in mining and other areas of specialised finance to private and public sector corporations, banks, institutional investors and government.

Geographic Preference: Australia, Canada, North America, South America, South Africa
Fund Size: $3.95 Million
Founded: 1985
Investment Criteria: Early Stage project development capital for natural resources and mining industry related projects and technology
Industry Group Preference: Mining, Oil & Gas

3080 RHB - H&F MANAGEMENT COMPANY SDN BHD RHB Capital
Level 5, Tower One, RHB Centre
Kuala Lumpur 50400
Malaysia

Phone: 60-392-802536 Fax: 60-321427573
e-mail: enquiry@rhb.com.my
web: www.rhb.com.my

Mission Statement: Actively seeking new investments.
Geographic Preference: Malaysia
Fund Size: $3.57 Million
Founded: 1997
Industry Group Preference: Consumer Services, Commercial Services, Corporate Services, Banking, Consumer Products

Key Executives:
Chay Wai Leong, Managing Director
Roslan Haji Tik, Senior Vice President

3081 RHODIUM
91 Medinat Hayehudium
St. Herteliya
Pituach 46140

Phone: 972-9-960-6900 Fax: 972-9-960-6910
web: www.rhodium.co.il

Mission Statement: Rhodium invests in early-stage ventures in Israel, New York, and Silicon Valley. We focus on identifying and partnering with the very best and most promising entrepreneurs and innovators with a view to building disruptive, world-changing companies.

Geographic Preference: Israel, New York, California
Investment Criteria: Early-Stage
Portfolio Companies: Switch, Outbrain, Zooz, Face.com, Yotpo, HopStop, Rounds, Captain Up, Compass, SambaAds, Chosen, Green SQL

Other Locations:
535 Madison Avenue
New York, NY 10022

Key Executives:
Daniel Recanati, Founder/CEO
Education: BA, LLB, Interdisciplinary Center, Herzliya
Directorships: Face.com, Hopstop, YieldMo, ZooZ, GreenSQL, Yotpo, Rounds.com

Yaron Kniajer, Managing Director
Education: MBA, London Business School; CPA
Background: Investment Banking, Lehman Brothers; CFO, Mediagate
Directorships: Rounds.com, GreenSQL, Yotpo, CaptainUp, Face.com

3082 RICHINA CAPITAL PARTNERS LIMITED
56 Jiang Xi Zhong Road
Shanghai 200002
China

Phone: 86-216-323-1200 Fax: 86-216-323-1511

Mission Statement: A China-centric investment firm with high ethics, performance and acumen.

Geographic Preference: China, New Zealand
Fund Size: $150 Million
Founded: 1993
Industry Group Preference: Real Estate, Financial Services, Manufacturing

3083 RMB VENTURES LIMITED RMB Australia
Level 13, 60 Castlereagh Street
Sydney NSW 2000
Australia

Phone: 61-292566200 Fax: 61-292566290
web: www.rmb.com.au

Mission Statement: Provides financing and strategic support for management buyouts and expansion capital as medium to long term investors.

Geographic Preference: Australia, New Zealand
Fund Size: $300 Million
Founded: 1988
Minimum Investment: $10 Million
Investment Criteria: MBOs, MBIs, IBOs
Industry Group Preference: All Sectors Considered

Key Executives:
Mark Habner, Director
Education: B.COM, LLB (Hons), MM (Kellogg), ASA
Background: Booz Allen and Hamilton

3084 ROAD KING INFRASTRUCTURE LIMITED
Suite 501, 5th Floor, Tower 6
9 Canton Road, Tsimshatsui
Kowloon
Hong Kong

web: www.roadking.com.hk

Mission Statement: Road King Infrastructure Limited is a leading Hong Kong publicly listed company with its core business in the investment, development, operation and management of toll roads and bridges in China.

Geographic Preference: China
Investment Criteria: Propert development
Industry Group Preference: Transportation, Bridges

Key Executives:
William Zen Wei Pao, Chairman
Education: Bachelor of Science degree in Physics & Master of Business Administration degree
Background: Member and a fellow member of Hong Kong Institution of Highways and Transportation

Ko Yuk Bing, Managing Director & Chief Executive Officer

3085 ROCHE VENTURE FUND F. Hoffman-La Roche AG
Grenzacherstrasse 124
Basel CH-4070
Switzerland

Phone: +41 61-688 1111 Fax: +41 61-691-9391
web: www.venturefund.roche.com

Venture Capital & Private Equity Firms / International Firms

Mission Statement: The Roche Venture Fund is a committed long-term stable investor with sufficient money reserved for follow-on financing rounds. As part of a multinational healthcare company, the Roche Venture Fund has access to considerable expertise both internally and externally. We co-invest with leading venture funds, including other corporate venture funds, on a regular basis.

Geographic Preference: Europe, North America, Pacific Region
Fund Size: CHF 500 million
Founded: 2002
Average Investment: CHF 1-5 million
Investment Criteria: Series B
Industry Group Preference: Life Sciences
Portfolio Companies: 23andMe, Afferent Pharmaceuticals, Aileron Therapeutics, Alios BioPharma, Allakos, Ambit Biosciences, Ambrx, Biodesy, Conatus Pharmaceuticals, Curetis, CytomX Therapeutics, Epic Sciences, Foundation Medicine, Horizon, LTO, Maclogix, Mission Therapeutics, Opsona Therapeutics, Proacta, Senseonics, Stratos, Symphogen, TiGenix, Xenon
Key Executives:
   Severin Schwan, Chief Executive Officer

3086 ROTHSCHILD AUSTRALIA - ARROW PRIVATE EQUITY Rothschild Group
Level 21, No. 120 Collins Street
Melbourne 3000
Australia

Phone: 61-396564600 Fax: 61-396564700
web: www.rothschild.com

Mission Statement: Rothschild provides leading financial advice and services to organisations worldwide.
Geographic Preference: Australia
Fund Size: 1 Billion AUD
Founded: 1992
Industry Group Preference: Manufacturing, Global Financial Advisory, Wealth Management & Trust, Merchant Banking, Institutional Asset Management, Specialist Financial Businesses
Key Executives:
   Baron David de Rothschild, Chairman
   Nigel Higgins, Chief Executive Officer

3087 RU-NET VENTURES
B.Ovchinnikovsky per., 16,
4th Floor, Office 402
Moscow 115184
Russian Federation

Phone: +7(495)797-97-63

Mission Statement: Driven by a passionate, principled and expert senior team, ru-Net's approach to investment is long term. Aiming not just to invest in, but also to partner with its target companies, ru-Net works to share knowledge, build capacity and develop expertise to help company teams achieve their growth ambitions. Combined with strict investment criteria, clear strategies and demonstrable investment goals, this approach is enabling ru-Net to shape a successful future for some of the world's most exciting technology companies.

Geographic Preference: United States, Europe, Russia, Southeast Asia
Founded: 1999
Investment Criteria: Early-stage, Energy, E-Commerce & Manufacturing, Outsourcing & Efficiency
Other Locations:
   RTP Ventures
   25th Floor
   New York, NY 10022
Key Executives:
   Leonid Boguslavsky, Chairman of the Board
   Oleg Sundukov, Vice-President, IT Business
   Maria Krayukhina, Director, Internet and IT Business
   Galina Chifina, Investment Director
   Alexander Pavlov, Investment Director

3088 RUNA CAPITAL
Russian Federation

Phone: 7-4959849703
e-mail: info@runacap.com
web: www.runacap.com

Mission Statement: Runa Capital is a technology-focused venture capital firm whose investments have created or incubated companies with more than US$10 billion in assets. It was established to seek growth opportunities in the rapidly growing areas of the tech sector, with specific focus on cloud computing and other hosted services, virtualization and mobile applications. The key execution point is to select promising teams and drive and support them in the global marketplace, turning them into international champions.

Fund Size: $135 million
Industry Group Preference: Cloud Computing, Internet, Software, Mobile
Portfolio Companies: Gninx, Ecwid, LinguaLeo, Acumatica, Jelastic, Jopa, Cellrox, B2B Center, Dhebhuk, Profi.ru
Key Executives:
   Serguei Beloussov, Founder/Senior Partner
   Education: BS, Physics, MS, Electrical Engineering, PhD, Computer Science, Moscow Institute of Physics & Technology
   Background: Venture Partner, Almaz Capital; Founder, Parallels; Founder, Acumatica
   Directorships: Acumatica

3089 RUSSELL INVESTMENT MANAGEMENT LIMITED
Level 29
135 King Street
Sydney NSW 2000
Australia

Phone: 02-92295111 Fax: 02-92214505
web: www.russell.com

Mission Statement: A global investment services firm, providing investment management, advisory and diversified funds to clients.

Geographic Preference: Australia, Canada, China, Spain, Finland, Hong Kong, US, Malaysia, UK
Fund Size: $3.2 Trillion
Founded: 1936
Industry Group Preference: All Sectors Considered
Key Executives:
   Alan Schoenheimer, Managing Director
   e-mail: info@russell.com
   Education: B.Sc., Mathematics, M.Sc., Mathematics, Ph.D., Business Administration
   Background: Professor in the Accounting and Finance Department at the University of Auckland; professor at the Australian Graduate School of Management; faculty member in the Statistics and Econometrics group at the Graduate School of Business, University of Chicago;
   Directorships: Board of Trustees of the National Provident Fund, Boards of a number of companies in the financial sector in Auckland
   Linda Elkins, Managing Director

3090 S-REFIT GmbH & COMPANY KG
15 Sedanstrasse
Regensburg 93055
Germany

Phone: 49-941695560 Fax: 49-9416955611
e-mail: info@s-refit.de
web: www.s-refit.de

Venture Capital & Private Equity Firms / International Firms

Mission Statement: Actively seeking new investments.
Founded: 1990
Key Executives:
Walter Paulus-Rohmer, Chairman
Peter Terhart, CEO

3091 SABIC VENTURES
Europa Boulevard 1
PO Box 5151
Sittard 6130 PD
Netherlands

Phone: 31-0-46-722-2479
e-mail: ventures@sabic.com
web: www.sabic.com/ventures

Mission Statement: SABIC Ventures is a wholly-owned subsidiary of SABIC that is focused on providing seed and early stage venture capital financing to innovative companies in the fund's sectors of interest on a global scale. We aim to invest in outstanding entrepreneurial teams who dare to challenge the status quo in their respective industries and who are seeking to build extraordinary businesses that can support SABIC's innovation and growth strategy. We seek to invest and co-invest with a broad network of VC partners, angel investors or investment groups that specialize in our targeted investment markets and geographies. Through collaborative innovation, we can leverage SABIC's global footprint and turn our strategic insights into market impact.
Geographic Preference: Middle East, North America, Europe, India, China
Average Investment: $2 - $20 million
Investment Criteria: Seed-Stage, Early-Stage, Later-Stage
Industry Group Preference: Advanced Materials, Alternative Energy, Renewable Energy, Clean Technology
Key Executives:
Hans Kolnaar, Managing Director

3092 SAFFRON HILL VENTURES
4/5 Park Place
London SW1A 1LP
United Kingdom

Phone: 44-02076938300
e-mail: contact@saffronhill.com
web: www.saffronhill.com

Mission Statement: Saffron Hill works with entrepreneurs and partners to transform disruptive ideas into world class companies.
Geographic Preference: Europe
Founded: 2000
Average Investment: £500,000 to £2 million
Investment Criteria: Seed Capital to Later-Stage Growth Equity
Industry Group Preference: Technology, Media, Clean Technology
Portfolio Companies: Agilyx, Coyuchi, Entuity, Flogit4u, Faceware, Image Metrics, InfraTrac, Optasia Medical, Tagsys Rfid
Key Executives:
Ranjeet Bhatia, Co-founder
e-mail: rbhatia@saffronhill.com
Education: BA, Environmental Science, Occidental College; MBA, UCLA Anderson School of Business; MA, International Relations & Economics, Johns Hopkins University School of Advanced International Studies
Background: Advisor, Loot Ltd.; Advisor, Lord Rothschild; Booz-Allen & Hailton; Dynacorp-Meridian
Shawn Luetchens, Co-founder
e-mail: sluetchens@saffronhill.com
Education: BS, Physical Sciences, University of Nebraska; MBA, Kellogg Graduate School of Management
Background: Principal, Tribune Ventures; Senior Project Manager, US Environmental Protechtion Agency

3093 SAIF PARTNERS
Suites 2516-2520
Two Pacific Place
88 Queensway
Hong Kong

Phone: 852-2918-2200 Fax: 852-2234-9116
web: www.sbaif.com

Mission Statement: SAIF Partners is a leading private equity firm that provides growth capital to companies in Asia.
Geographic Preference: Asia
Fund Size: $3.5 billion
Founded: 2001
Average Investment: $10 million - $100 million
Investment Criteria: Early-Stage, Growth Stage
Industry Group Preference: Information Technology, Internet, Mobile, Consumer Products, Consumer Services, Healthcare, Clean Technology, Education, Agriculture, Financial Services, Manufacturing
Portfolio Companies: Xiamen Orient Wanli Stone, Acorn International, Advision Media Holdings, Alchip Technologies, Appotronics, ATA, Beijing Hua Yu Network Technology Development, Beijing Jingeng Clean Energy, Beijing Lepro Seva Da Technologiy Development, Beijing Rising Technology Co., Beijing Ryzur Exiom Medical Investment Co., Beijing Yize Jianyuan Technology Co., Best Elite International, Biosensors International Group, Bona Film Group, Bros Catering, Careland International, ChannelSoft Holdings, China Broad Media Corp, China Digital TV Holding Co.
Other Locations:
18F Tower C, Central Intl Trade Center
6a Jianguomenwai Avenue
Chao Yang District
Beijing 100022
China
Phone: 86-10-6563-0202 Fax: 86-10-6563-0252

Villa +16, Shanghai Hong Qiao State Hotel
1591 Hong Qiao Road
Shanghai 200336
China
Phone: 86-21-6295-2768 Fax: 86-21-6295-2783

Unit 511, 5th Floor
Time Tower, MG Road
Gurgaon
Haryana 122002
India
Phone: 91-98-6646-1770 Fax: 91-22-6645-9581

Key Executives:
Andrew Y. Yan, Managing Partner
Education: BS, Engineering, Nanjing Aeronautic Institute; MA, Sociology, Peking University; MA, International Political Economy, Princeton University
Background: Managing Director, Emerging Markets Partnership; Director, Sprint International Corporation

3094 SAINT-GOBAIN NOVA EXTERNAL VENTURING
Les Miroirs
18, avenue d'Alsace
Courbevoie 92400
France

web: www.saint-gobain.com

Mission Statement: NOVA External Venturing is the Saint-Gobain unit dedicated to developing strategic partnerships between the Group and star-up companies all over the world.
Geographic Preference: United States, Europe, Asia
Investment Criteria: Early-Stage

961

Venture Capital & Private Equity Firms / International Firms

Industry Group Preference: Energy, Environment, Construction

3095 SALFORD CAPITAL PARTNERS
Bulevar Mihajla Pupina 115 G
Belgrade 11070
Yugoslavia

Phone: 381-11-2222-500 Fax: 381-11-2222-533

Mission Statement: A private equity firm investing primarily in developing markets.
Geographic Preference: Former Soviet Union, Central & Eastern Europe
Founded: 2001
Portfolio Companies: Adjara Hotel, Bambi/Banat, Borjomi, IDS/Morshinkaya, Imlek Group, Knjaz Milos, Standard Bank, Subotica, Telenet, United States Embassy Residential Community

Other Locations:
Salford Investment Limited
2-Ya Magistrinaya Street
8a, 4th Floor
Moscow 123290
Russia
Phone: 7-495-787-5314 Fax: 7-495-787-5316

Salford Old Georgia
44 Leselidze Street
Tbilisi 0105
Georgia
Phone: 995-32-505-400 Fax: 995-32-505-406

Salford (UK) Ltd
78 Pall Mall
London SW1Y 5ES
United Kingdom
Phone: 44-20-3178-4850 Fax: 44-20-3178-4851

3096 SAMBRINVEST SA
Avenue Georges Lema, tre, 62
Aéropole
Gosselies 6041
Belgium

Phone: 32-71259494 Fax: 32-71259499
e-mail: sambrinvest@sambrinvest.be
web: www.sambrinvest.be

Mission Statement: SAMBRINVEST and its subsidiaries is a source of venture capital to support the development of SME in the Charleroi and Thuin districts.
Founded: 1985
Investment Criteria: Start-up, Development stage, Transfer of ownership.
Industry Group Preference: Aviation, Building Materials & Services, Pharmaceuticals, Electronic Technology, Environment Products & Services, Food Services, Metals, Manufacturing, Wholesale, Services, Printing, Glass, Wood Industries

Key Executives:
Guy Paeau, President
Education: Engineering
Denis Tillier, Partner

3097 SAMOS INVESTMENTS
22 Charing Cross Road
London WC2H 0HS
United Kingdom

Phone: 44-0-2076322520
e-mail: contact@samos.uk.com

Mission Statement: Samos Investments is a private equity investor with a focus on high-growth European businesses. Samos takes a proactive approach with its portfolio companies, working alongside many of the US and Europe's top venture funds, family offices and private investors.
Geographic Preference: Europe
Industry Group Preference: Financial Services, Retailing, Clean Technology, Energy, Natural Resources, Transportation, Medical Technology, Digital Media & Marketing, E-Commerce & Manufacturing
Portfolio Companies: 3legs, Betfair, Business of Fashion, BytePlay, Carwow, Charlotte Tilbury, Cointerra, Coniq, Clenarm, Goal.com, Gridpoint, Ironstone Resources, Insightra Medical, Kabbee, Kincora Group, LDC, Nuji, Ocado, Second Home, Senhouse Capital, Seedcamp, Small World, Vouchedfor, WTG

Key Executives:
Charles Cecil, Chairman

3098 SAMSUNG VENTURE INVESTMENT CORPORATION Samsung Electronics
06620 Samsung Electronics 29F
Seocho-Daero 74-Gil
Seocho-Gu
Seoul
Korea

Phone: 02 2255-0299
web: www.samsungventure.co.kr

Mission Statement: Samsung Electronics (SEC) seeks to form strategic partnerships with start-ups are growing companies engaged in the development of new technologies.
Fund Size: $340 Billion
Founded: 1999
Average Investment: $10.2 Million
Minimum Investment: $500,000
Investment Criteria: Start-Up, Growth Capital
Industry Group Preference: Internet Technology, Information Technology, Semiconductors, Medical, Biotechnology, Telecommunication, Software, Bioengineering
Portfolio Companies: Cool Dry, Delta ID, HIMS, Kateeva, Kngine, Maluuba, MasterImage 3D, Mecatronix, Mindmeld, Mixaroo(Boxfish), nLight, Novasentis, nuTonomy, Philoptics, Power By Proxy, Scientific Magnetics, TeraView, YuMe

Other Locations:
2440 Sand Hill Road
Suite 302
Menlo Park, CA 94025

260 Franklin Street
Suite 510
Boston, MA 02110

Plot No. 2A
Sector 127
NOIDA
Utter Pradesh
India

Lidabashi Grand Bloom Sakura Terrace
2-10-2 Fujimi
Chiyoda-ku
Tokyo 102-0071
Japan

18F TaiYangGong Plaza
12A TaiYangGong Middle Road
Chaoyang District
Beijing
China

Crane Building 3F
22 Lavington Street
London SE1 0NX
England

1st Floor
Holland Building
Europark

962

Venture Capital & Private Equity Firms / International Firms

Yakum
Israel

Key Executives:
Yongbae Jeon, President/CEO
Background: Samsung Fire & Marine Insurance; Samsung Future Strategic Office; Samsung Electronics; Samsung President's Office Tream 2; Samsung Corporate Restructuring Office; Samsung Life Insurance

3099 SAUDI ARAMCO ENERGY VENTURES
9/F Al-Midra Tower
Dhahran 31311
Saudi Arabia

Mission Statement: Saudi Aramco Energy Ventures is the corporate venturing subsidiary of Saudi Aramco, the Saudi Arabian national oil company. Established in 2012 as a wholly-owned subsidiary of Saudi Aramco, our mission is to invest globally into start-up and high growth companies with technologies of strategic importance to Saudi Aramco and to accelerate their development and their deployment in the Kingdom.

Geographic Preference: Worldwide
Founded: 2012
Average Investment: $1 to $30 million
Investment Criteria: Seed Stage, Growth Venture Capital
Industry Group Preference: Oil & Gas, Renewable Energy, Energy Efficiency, Water
Portfolio Companies: Utildata, AnTech, inflow Control, Novomer, Rive Technology, Sekal, Zilift, Siluria, Wearable Intelligence

Other Locations:
Aramco Energy Ventures
Houston, TX 77096-1799
Phone: 713-432-5422
Cory Steffek

Key Executives:
Caroline Slind Svae
47-97-00-82-11
e-mail: caroline.svae@energycapital.no

3100 SB CHINA VENTURE CAPITAL
15A-C, HuaMin Empire Plaza
728 YanAn Road (West)
Suite 15 A-C
Shanghai 200050
China

Phone: 86-2152534888
e-mail: contact@sbcvc.com

Mission Statement: Actively seeking new investments in the China marketplace.

Geographic Preference: Shanghai
Founded: 2000
Industry Group Preference: TMT, Clean Technology, Healthcare, Consumer Retail, Advanced Manufacturing, New Materials
Portfolio Companies: Alibaba, Taobao, Focus Media, PPTV, OCJ, GDS, Linkage, Tianpin, Etrans, Easou, Hairun, Suninfo, Yooli, Edai.com, Shenwu, DKT, NYF, SRET, Hi-Tech, ECOSO, Jiangli, Di'an, EDAN, EYES, BGI, Panther, NANOMED, KingYee, Precise, Goodbaby, DMTG, Loncin, Deyu Agri, Glory, Jiahua, Yifang

3101 SBRC INVESTMENT CONSULTATION LIMITED
3 Daniel Frisch Street
Tel Aviv 64731
Israel

Phone: 972-36950666 Fax: 972-36950222
e-mail: Daniela.f@cukierman.co.il
web: www.cukierman.co.il

Mission Statement: The firm provides a full scope of European focused investment banking activities, including corporate finance, equity investment, strategic consulting and alliances, as well as capital market services to Israeli and European companies.

Geographic Preference: Europe
Fund Size: Euro 3.5 Billion
Founded: 1993
Average Investment: $2 Million
Minimum Investment: $1 Million
Investment Criteria: European focused investment banking activities, including corporate finance, equity investment, strategic consulting and alliances
Industry Group Preference: Telecommunications, Software, Medical Devices, Multimedia
Portfolio Companies: Tufin, Cyren, Dori Media, MobilEye, Harmon.ie, Omrix, Lamina Technologies, Miba Plast, Dot Hill, Better Online Solutions, PowerD, Orex Technologies

Key Executives:
Edouard Cukierman, Chairman
e-mail: info@cukierman.co.il
Education: BA from Tel-Aviv University in Accounting and Economics, Licence in CPA
Background: Corporate Finance Consultant at Ernst & Young, Israel
Haggai Ravid, Chief Executive Officer
e-mail: info@cukierman.co.il
Education: B.Sc from the Technion - Israel Institute of Technology, MBA - INSEAD(Fontainebleau, France).
Background: Citec-Environment and Services in Paris, Lamina Technologies.

3102 SCALE INVESTORS
Level 4
167 Flinders Lane
Melbourne VIC 3000
Australia

Phone: 61-3-9653-5314 Fax: 61-432-324-324
web: www.scaleinvestors.com.au

Mission Statement: Scale helps investors and entrepreneurial women to connect, invest and succeed. Scale is a female focused angel investor network. We were founded in Melbourne in March 2013 inspired by the US based organization Golden Seeds. Our founding members are women, but we welcome and include men who share our vision of maximizing returns by supporting early stage businesses that value gender diverse leadership.

Founded: 2013
Average Investment: $50,000 - $500,000
Investment Criteria: Female Founder; Early-Stage

Key Executives:
Susan Oliver, Founding Chairman
Directorships: Fusion Retail Brands, CNPR, Coffey International

3103 SCOTTISH ENTERPRISE
Atrium Court
50 Waterloo Street
Glasgow G2 6HQ
United Kingdom

Phone: 0845-6078787
e-mail: enquiries@scotent.co.uk
web: www.scottish-enterprise.com

Mission Statement: Actively seeking new investments in emerging growth companies in Scotland.

Geographic Preference: Scotland
Fund Size: $25 Million
Founded: 1982
Investment Criteria: Start-up
Industry Group Preference: Education, Aerospace, Defense and Government, Chemicals, Energy, Telecommunications, Optical Technology, Multimedia, Industrial Services

Venture Capital & Private Equity Firms / International Firms

Key Executives:
Anne MacColl, Chief Executive
Education: BSc, CA
Background: Corporate Finance, Venture Capital
Directorships: Bathgate Investment Fund Ltd, Edinburgh Technology Fund
Paul Lewis, Managing Director Operations - Sectors, Commercialisation and Inv

3104 SCOTTISH EQUITY PARTNERS
17 Blythswood Square
Glasgow G2 4AD
United Kingdom

Phone: 44-01412734000
web: www.sep.co.uk

Mission Statement: A leading venture capital and growth equity investor focused on the UK and other European countries. As well as investing in early stage companies, we invest in more established companies looking to build scale and momentum. All of the companies we partner with have the potential to build and strong and defensible competitive position in the global marketplace.

Geographic Preference: United Kingdom, Europe
Fund Size: Euro 200 Million
Founded: 1991
Investment Criteria: Early-Stage, Growth-Stage
Industry Group Preference: Information Technology, Energy, Healthcare, Life Sciences, Clean Technology, Digital Media & Marketing
Portfolio Companies: Anesco, Arakis Aridhia, Arkex, Atlantech, Biovation, BioVex, CamSemi, Carloan 4U, Clavis Insight, Cmed, Control Circle, Craneware, CSR, Cyberhawk, Cyclacel, Daysoft.com, Deep Casting Tools, Exco inTouch, Fotech Solutions, Gai Energy, Gigle Networks, Green Highland, Hetras, Indigo Vision, Indigo Pipelines, IntelligentReach, IP Access, Klala, Matches, Metaforic, Mister Spex, MTEM, Nallatech, Orbital, Picochip, Rhetorical, Searchspace, Silent, Skyscanner, Smarter Grid Solutions, SocialBro, Solar Century, Stentys, Sumerian, Tideway, TotallyMoney.com, Tryzens Group, Vital Energi, Virtensys, Voxar, Wayn, Wolfson, Workshare, Zeus, Zinwave

Other Locations:
29 St. George Street
London W1S 2FA
United Kingdom
Phone: 44-02077585900 Fax: 44-02077585901

Key Executives:
Adrian Pike, Founder and CEO
44-0-20-7758-5938
e-mail: contact_richard@sep.co.uk
Calum Paterson, Co-Founder, Managing Partner
44-0-20-7758-5930
e-mail: contact_calum@sep.co.uk
Background: Ernst & Young
Directorships: Skyscanner, Daysoft UV, Sumerian
Andrew Davison, Partner
44-0-20-7758-5938
e-mail: contact_andrewd@sep.co.uk
Directorships: IP Access, Kiala, Surfkitchen, Zeus
Brian Kerr, Partner
44-0-20-7758-5938
e-mail: contact_brian@sep.co.uk
Directorships: Cmed, Stensys
Gary Le Sueur, Partner
44-0-20-7758-5938
e-mail: contact_gary@sep.co.uk
Fearghal O Riordain, Partner
44-0-20-7758-5930
e-mail: contact_fearghal@sep.co.uk
Education: MEng Sc, BE, Electrical Engineering, National University of Ireland; MBA, INSEAD
Background: Founding Principal & Partner, Accel Partners; Ericsson
Directorships: Clavis Technology, Powervation
Stuart Paterson, Partner
44-0-20-7758-5938
e-mail: contact_stuart@sep.co.uk
Education: Venture Capital Executive Program, Harvard Business School
Directorships: Control Circle, Elonics, PicoChip, Virtensys, Gigle Networks
Jan Rutherford, Partner
44-0-20-7758-5930
e-mail: contact_jan@sep.co.uk
Background: Life Science team, Dresdner Kleinwort Capital
Directorships: Sosei, BioVex, Cmed
David Sneddon, Partner
44-0-20-7758-5938
e-mail: contact_david@sep.co.uk
Directorships: ARKeX, Atraverda, Deep Casingtools, Fotech
Gordon Beveridge, Principal
44-0-20-7758-5930
e-mail: contact_gordon@sep.co.uk
Background: Corporate Finance, Ernst & Young
Directorships: CamSemi
Andrew Buchan, General Counsel
44-0-20-7758-5938
e-mail: contact_andrewb@sep.co.uk
Education: Glasgow University
Background: Private Practice, Maclay Murray & Spens
Mark Gracey, Principal
44-0-20-7758-5930
e-mail: contact_mark@sep.co.uk
Background: European Director, Sensory Networks
Directorships: Zinwave
Fraser McLatchie, Associate
44-0-20-7758-5938
e-mail: contact_fraser@sep.co.uk
Education: MA, Social Science, University of Glasgow

3105 SEAYA VENTURES
Plaza de la Independencia 2, 3o Izda
Madrid 28001
Spain

Phone: 34-911-10-86-97
e-mail: info@seayaventures.com
web: www.seayaventures.com

Mission Statement: Seaya Ventures seeks to transform early and growth stage companies into category leaders. We look for innovative businesses that require growth or expansion capital and can build a lasting value. At Seaya we understand what being an entrepreneur means. We empower outstanding teams and businesses and help them navigate the path from early and growth stages into rapid growth and sustainable profitability with a focus on expansion in Latin America.

Geographic Preference: Spain
Investment Criteria: Early Stage, Growth Stage
Industry Group Preference: Computer Related, Consumer Internet, Consumer Mobile Media, Consumer Software, Internet Technology
Portfolio Companies: Plenum Media, Restalo, Sin Delental, Ticketea.com, Cabify

Key Executives:
Beatriz Gonzalez, Founder and Managing Partner
Education: Business Degree from CUNEF; MBA, Columbia Business School
Background: Head of Private Equity Program In Telefonica's Pension Fund; Darby Overseas Investments; Excel Partners; Equity Research Department, Morgan Stanley
Michael Kleindl, Founder and Managing Partner
Education: Oestrich-Winkel
Background: Co-Founder and CEO, AdLINK Internet

Venture Capital & Private Equity Firms / International Firms

Media AG
Directorships: Hi Media S.A.

3106 SEB VENTURE CAPITAL
Sweden

Phone: +4687639110
e-mail: press@seb.se
web: www.sebgroup.com

Mission Statement: SEB Venture Capital creates opportunities for entrepreneurs and innovators to build and develop successful companies. Our goal is sustainable, long-term value creation.

Fund Size: SEK 2.4 billion
Founded: 1995
Average Investment: SEK 20 - 80 million
Industry Group Preference: Life Sciences, Technology

3107 SEED CAPITAL LIMITED
Magdalen Centre, Oxford Science Park
Oxford Science Park
Oxford OX4 4GA
United Kingdom

Phone: 44-1865784466 Fax: 44-1865784430
e-mail: lucius@oxfordtechnology.com
web: www.oxfordtechnology.com

Mission Statement: Actively seeking new investments in early-stage technology companies in and around Oxford.

Geographic Preference: United Kingdom
Fund Size: $40 Million
Founded: 1983
Average Investment: Euro 2,000,000
Minimum Investment: $0.08 Million
Investment Criteria: Seed, Start-up, Other Early Stage
Industry Group Preference: Biotechnology, Medical & Health Related, Chemicals, Industrial Equipment, Instrumentation, Energy, Natural Resources, Genetic Engineering, Industrial Products, Medical & Health Related, Materials Technology

Portfolio Companies: Run 3D, BioMoti, Combat Medical, Message Missile, Ibexis Technologies, Lightpoint Medical, Metal Powders & Process, Powder OLEDs, Abgentis, Designer Carbon Materials, Sasets, Sime Diagnostics, BioCote, Dataflow, DHA, Equitalk, Getmapping, MET, Scancell, Select Technology, Valid Information Systems, Arecor, Commerce Decisions, DHA, ImmunoBiology, Inaplex, Insense, MET, OC Robotics, Orthogem, Oxis Energy, Plasma Antennas, Select Technology, Telegesis, Allinea Software, BioAnaLab, Concurrent Thinking, Glide Pharma, Invro, Ixaris, Metal Nanopowders, Promic, Superhard Materials, Warwick Effect Polymers, Bluewater Bio International, Dexela, Diamond Hard Surfaces, Dynamic Extractions Historic Futures, Imagineer Systems, Impact Applications, Meciria, MirriAd, Naked Objects, Novacta Biosystems, OxTox, Pharma Engineering, Select Technology

Key Executives:
Lucius Cary, Founder and Managing Director
Education: Degree in Cell and Molecular Biology, D.Phil in Biochemistry from Oxford University.
Background: Astra Zeneca, British Biotech subsidiary.
Jackson John, Chairman
Education: Degree in engineering and economics- Oxford University, MBA-Harvard Business School, was an engineering apprentice at the Atomic Energy Research Establishment, Harwell.
Background: Venture Capital Report.
Directorships: Founder

3108 SEEDCAMP
4-5 Bonhill Street
Shoreditch
London EC2A 4BX
United Kingdom

e-mail: info@seedcamp.com
web: seedcamp.com

Mission Statement: Seedcamp believes investing at the earliest stage is the best approach to building a successful company.

Geographic Preference: United Kingdom, EU
Fund Size: $1 billion
Founded: 2007
Portfolio Companies: Bunker Ex, Creative Labs, SeedLegals, CyberSmart, Heresy, Fraugster, The Engineering Company, Stupeflix, Gyant, Cuvva, Labstep, 9fin, Stowga, VChain, Legit Patents, Beagle, Wevat, Telleroo, Ai Build, Sunlight, Clause, Libryo, Viz.ai, Pollen, Weengs, TheWaveVR, Grocer, ThirdEye, CRU Kafe, Trail, Reposit, Thriva, Oratio, Juro, Splash, ActionBar, YodelTalk, Vinterior, KareInn, CharlieHR, ThingThing, SwiftShift, Repositive, Open Sensors, Propoly, Nevercode, Wefox, Cardlife, Buuldcon, Beeline, Authentiq, Alterest, Curve, Edgefolio, Pointy, Revolut, MagicTab, Data Smoothie, Pleo, Wombo, Evercontact, Land Insight, Hitch, Captini, GetAgent, Adventures, MyRecovery, Acasa, Spoke, Traderion, Talkpush, Trussle, UiPath, Priori Data, WealthKernel, Cymmetria, Monese, Rialto, Rienfer, Oinky, Kasko, Intelliment Security, Findify, Hubble, HOKO, MarcoPolo Learning, Queueco, JOBDOH, Twine, Car Quids, Lateral, Divido, Podo Labs, Cronofy, BranchTrack, Property Partner, EMoov, Wriggle, Shoprocket, Homeshift, Voyage Control, Teleport, FarmHopping, BridgeU, Oradian, Reedsy, Tanaza, GoWorkaBit, Interact.io, We Are Colony, Elliptic, Formisimo, Lodgify, Krak, Satago, Popcorn Metrics, BorrowMyDoggy, Winnow, Stamplay, ShareLaTeX, Saberr, Revision App, Apperio, Hype!, Ctrlio, Fishbrain, TruckTrack, Countly, Line-Up, Minubo, Maily, Codeship, SimpleTax, Codacy, Hole19, CrowdProcess, Poq, TRDATA, Rawstream, Try.com, Traity, Antavo, Sayduck, 24symbols, Audiense, Qminder, Blossom, Totems, Transferwise, Farmeron

Key Executives:
Reshma Sohoni, Co-Founder/Manager Partner
Carlos Eduardo Espinal, Managing Partner
Background: Doughty Hanson Technology Ventures, Advanced Communications Technologies Group of The New York Stock Exchange, PKI Developer, Cybertrust/Baltimore Technologies
Tom Wilson, Investment Partner
Background: King & Wood Mallesons
Sia Houchangnia, Investment Partner
Education: MSc, International Management, ESADE Business School

3109 SEEDFUND
3 Turf Estate
Shakti Mills Lane
Off. Dr. E. Moses Road, Mahalaxmi
Mumbai 400 011
India

Phone: +91 22 2490
e-mail: info@seedfund.in
web: www.seedfund.in

Mission Statement: SeedFund identifies market disrupters in different industries and backs them early to promote stable growth.

Portfolio Companies: Afaqs!, AxisRooms, Browntape, CarWale, Cumbak, DailyObjects, Done By None, EduSports, Fetise, Frontier Markets, Healthizen, Heckyl, Innoz, Ixsight, Jeevanti, Jeeves, Level10 Comics, Lifeblob, Technium Labs, My Dentist, Nearify, Nevales, Printo, RedBus, Rupeetalk, Sportskeeda, ThinkLabs, Uhuroo, Vaatsalya, ViralMint, Voonik, V Resorts

Venture Capital & Private Equity Firms / International Firms

3110 SENETAS CORPORATION LIMITED
Senatas Group
312 Kings Way
South Melbourne VIC 3205
Australia

Phone: 61-398684555 Fax: 61-398214899
e-mail: security@senetas.com
web: www.senetas.com

Mission Statement: Provides world-leading encryption products, the ability to tailor and implement whole-organisation security solutions, and innovative Enterprise Information Professional Services.
Geographic Preference: Australia, New Zealand, United Kingdom
Founded: 1999
Key Executives:
Francis W. Galbally, Non-Executive Chairman
e-mail: enquiries@senetas.com
Background: Finance Express Home Loans Pty Ltd, Barrister and Solicitor of the High Court of Australia and Supreme Courts of Victoria and New South Wales.
Directorships: Chairman
Lachlan Given, Director

3111 SERGE PUN & ASSOCIATES (MYANMAR) LIMITED
380 Bogyoke Aung San Street, Pebedan Township
10th Floor, FMI Centre
Yangon
Myanmar

Phone: 95-1240363 Fax: 95-1246881
web: www.spa-myanmar.com

Mission Statement: Actively seeking new investments.
Geographic Preference: Myanmar, Thailand, Hongkong
Founded: 1991
Industry Group Preference: Financial Services, Real Estate, Automotive, Healthcare
Key Executives:
Serge Pun, Chairman
e-mail: mail@spa.com.mm
Education: Doctorate in Business Administration.
Martin Pun, Non-executive Vice Chairman

3112 SEVEN SPIRES INVESTMENTS
33c Davenant Road
Oxford OX2 8BU
United Kingdom

Phone: 44-0-1865-302-909 Fax: 44-0-7966-892-335
web: www.sevenspires.co.uk

Mission Statement: Seven Spires Investments Ltd. (SSIL) is a private, off-shore investment company. SSIL was established in 2003 and invests around £5 million annually across the existing portfolio and new investments. We are actively seeking new investment opportunities in high-tech companies in the United Kingdom. We look for excellent management, defensible Intellectual Property, a well characterized route to market and global scalability to an expected market capitalization in excess of $100m.
Geographic Preference: United Kingdom
Founded: 2003
Investment Criteria: All States
Industry Group Preference: High Technology, Automotive, Energy
Key Executives:
Ian Page, Managing Partner
Background: Reader in Computation, Programming Research Group, University of Oxford; Founder, Celonica Ltd; Visiting Professor, Imperial College & Cass Business School

Edward McCabe, Managing Partner
Background: Investment Management

3113 SEVENTURE PARTNERS
5-7 rue de Monttessuy
Paris 75340
France

Phone: 33-0158192270 Fax: 33-0158192280
e-mail: contact@seventure.fr
web: www.seventure.fr

Mission Statement: Seventure Partners finance innovation and participate in the entrepreneurial adventure alongside our entrepreneurs. We share their passion to succeed. As an active partner of French and European technology firms with strong growth potential, we finance the development of innovative companies in two areas: Information and Communication Technology (ICT) and Life Sciences (LS).
Geographic Preference: Europe
Fund Size: 600 million Euro
Founded: 1997
Industry Group Preference: Information Technology, Communications, Life Sciences
Portfolio Companies: Airtag, Anevia, Anyware, Balyo, EBlink, Ipdia, Microwave Vision, Mootwin, MReadBooks, Netasq, Nexess, Parrot, Presto Engineering, Scaleo Chip, Scentys, Silkan, Swapcom, Transatel, Volubill, Web Geo Services, Xiring, Alsyon Technologies, Arlettie, AssurOne, Calednra, Conject, DailyCall, DSO Interactive, Easyvoyage, Efficity, Emailvision, Eodom, Footways, FromAtoB.com, Hi Media, imusic-school, IsCool, Kayentis, L4 Epsilon, LeGuide.com, Maximiles, MinuteBuzz, MLstate, Myobis, Navabi, Netino, Plinga, Praditus, PrestaShop, Recommerce Solutions, Retailo, Santessima, Sidetrade, SoFactory, SquareClock, Studitemps, TalentSoft, Testbirds, Tigerlily, Tradoria, Vistaprint, W4, WebInterpret, Acarix, Advanced Accelerator Applications, arGEN-X, BiancaMed, BioAlliance Pharma, Biomatlante, BioPhytis, Corwave, Domain Therapeutics, Endocontrol, Enterome, Fluxome Sciences, Global Bioenergies, Humedics, Impeto Medical, Implanet, Ipsogen, Kebony, LNC, Lucane Pharma, MaaT Pharma, Mainstay Medical, Mauna Kea Technologies, MDX Health, Metabolic Explorer, Middle Peak Medical, Mint Solutions, Nanobiotix, Noxxon, Nutrionix, OPi, Personal Medsystems, Phosphonics, Pixium Vision, Polaar, Polaris, ProTip, Quanta, Santaris Pharma, Syntaxin, Txcell, Vivostat
Key Executives:
Isabelle de Cremoux, CEO/Managing Partner
Education: Ecole Centrale, Paris
Background: Arthur Andersen, Pfizer, Fournier

3114 SHANGHAI INFORMATION INVESTMENT INCORPORATED
32nd floor, BEA Finance Tower
66 Huayuan Shiqiao Road
Lujiazui Financial Trade Zone, Pudong New Area
Shanghai 200120
China

Phone: 86-2133831700 Fax: 86-2133831724
web: www.sii.com.cn

Mission Statement: Makes strategic and exemplary investment in the city's major information projects; provides substantial coordinating efforts among different sectors and entities.
Geographic Preference: China
Founded: 1997
Industry Group Preference: Telecommunications, Internet Technology, Infrastructure, E-Commerce & Manufacturing, Services, Banking, Enabling Technology
Key Executives:
Yadong Liu, Chairman

Venture Capital & Private Equity Firms / International Firms

3115 SHANNON COMMERCIAL PROPERTIES
Shannon Commercial Properties
2nd Floor
Arrivals Building, Shannon Airport
Shannon
Ireland
Phone: +353 (0)61 710000 Fax: +353 (0)61 712859
web: www.shannonproperty.ie

Mission Statement: Pioneers Regional Development for the technical knowledge era.
Geographic Preference: Ireland
Founded: 1959
Investment Criteria: Seed, Start-up, Management Buyin, MBO, Expansion and Development, Early Stage
Industry Group Preference: Biotechnology, Communications, Computer Related, Software, Electronic Technology, Medical & Health Related
Key Executives:
Kevin Thompstone, Chief Executive
Sean Fitzgibbon, Corporate Development Director
John King, Director(Heritage & Tourism)
Eugene Brennan, Director(Knowledge Enterprise)
Martin McKeogh, Director(Spatial Development)

3116 SHAW KWEI AND PARTNERS
1601 Euro Trade Centre
13 Connaught Road
Central
Hong Kong
Phone: 852-31628479 Fax: 852-31628499
e-mail: info@shawkwei.com
web: www.shawkwei.com

Mission Statement: Invests in later-stage private companies.
Geographic Preference: Asia, Taiwan, China, Singapore, USA
Founded: 1999
Investment Criteria: Growth Capital, MBO, Buyouts
Industry Group Preference: Technology, Electronic Technology, Manufacturing, Food & Beverage, Medical & Health Related, Transportation, Materials Technology
Key Executives:
Kyle Shaw, Managing Director
e-mail: info@shawkwei.com
Education: Diplomas in Production Engineering and Management Studies from Hong Kong Polytechnic
Background: Flextronics International, National Semiconductor (HK) Ltd., GTE Sylvania Far East Ltd. and NCR (Mfg.) Hong Kong Ltd.
Tsui Sung Lam (S.L), Managing Director
e-mail: info@shawkwei.com
Education: BS Commerce, University of Virginia; MBA, Wharton School
Background: Flextronics International (Singapore), China Fangda Group (China), Suga International (Hong Kong), Abest Communication Corp. (Taiwan), SNP Leefung Holdings Ltd. (Hong Kong), B & B Natural Products Ltd. (Hong Kong), the University of Virginia Alumni Assoc

3117 SHENZHEN INTERNATIONAL HOLDINGS LIMITED
Rooms 2205-08, 22/F., Greenfield Tower
Concordia Plaza, No. 1 Science Museum Road
Tsimshatsui East
Kowloon NV
Hong Kong
Phone: 852-23660268 Fax: 852-27395123
e-mail: info@szihl.com
web: www.szihl.com

Mission Statement: Focuses on the provision of total logistics and transportation ancillary services, as well as investment, operation and management of related assets and projects.
Geographic Preference: Hong Kong, Bermuda
Key Executives:
Gao Lei, Chairman
Education: Bachelor's degree in engineering from Wuhan University of Technology
Background: Shenzhen Expressway Company Limited
Directorships: Chief Executive
Li Jing Qi, Chief Executive Officer

3118 SIEMENS VENTURE CAPITAL
Otto-Hahn-Ring 6
Munich 81739
Germany
Phone: 49-8963633585 Fax: 49-8963634884
web: finance.siemens.com

Mission Statement: Venture Capital team takes a hands-on approach to investments in all stages.
Geographic Preference: Europe, North America, Israel
Founded: 1999
Investment Criteria: First Class Management Team and Businessplan
Industry Group Preference: Communications, Information Technology, Industrial Equipment, Medical & Health Related
Portfolio Companies: Agilliance Group, Aglity Communications, Air2Web Asera, Alvarion, Apptitude, Band of Angels, BeamReach Networks, Blue Pumpkin Software, Caly Networks, Cambridge Positioning Systems Limited, Cambridge Silicon Radio, Carmel Ventures, Chiaro Networks
Key Executives:
Michael Aust, Senior Investment Associate
e-mail: eugene.yeh@siemens.com
Education: dual Bachelor's degrees in Molecular and Cell Biology and Business Administration, University of California
Background: Financial analyst at ChevronTexaco.
Eric Bielke, Senior Investment Associate
e-mail: thomas.kolbinger@seimens.com
Education: MBA
Background: Corporate Strategy & Development
Doris Blasel, Managing Partner Siemens Global Innovation Partners
Education: Doctorate, University of Stuttgart
Background: President of the Medical Engineering Group (now: Medical Solutions), Siemens Ltd. Bombay, India, Managing Director
Eric Emmons, Investment Partner Venture Capital
Education: Young Managers Programme, INSEAD Fontainebleau
Background: Member of the Group Executive Management of the Automation and Drives Group
Jackie Hoffmann, Investment Partner
e-mail: jackie.hoffmann@siemens.com
Education: University of California, Bachelor's in Mathematics, MBA UC Berkeley's Haas School of Business
Background: Intel.
Dr. Andrew Jay, Investment Partner Venture Capital
Education: Bachelor of Science degree in Computer Engineering, MBA from Southern Methodist University
Background: Director, Service Evolution within the Chief Technology Office of seimens
Madeline Song, Investment Partner
e-mail: madeline.song@siemens.com
Education: Bachelor's degree in Chemical Engineering, and a Master of Business Administration.
Background: Managing Director of First Group Holding, Ltd
Kathrin Fox, Executive Assistant
e-mail: kathrin.fox@siemens.com
Education: studied languages

Venture Capital & Private Equity Firms / International Firms

Background: administrative and executive Assistant in U.S.A., Italy and Luxembourg.
Mike Majors, Investment Partner Venture Capital
e-mail: alexander.rietz@siemens.com
Education: MBA (Dipl.-Kfm.) in finance from the Johann Wolfgang Goethe-University
Background: South African electricity monopolist Eskom, Junior Investment Manager for a Venture Capital firm in Cape Town
Gerd Goette, Partner
e-mail: gerd.goette@siemens.com
Education: masters degree in electrical engineering (Dipl. Ing.) from Technische Hochschule Darmstadt, Germany
Background: Investment Partner of Mustang Ventures ,
Svetoslav Simeonov, Head of Accounting & Controlling
Background: Luis held a variety of managerial jobs in research and development as well as product line management at the Siemens Carrier Division in Florida
Joyce E. Jordan, Executive Assistant
Education: Physics Diploma from Technical University Munich (TUM).
Background: Rohde und Schwarz, BMW, EADS Astrium and Siemens Venture Capital.

3119 SIF TRANSYLVANIA
2, Nicolae Iorga Street
Brasov 500057
Romania
Phone: 0268 419 460 Fax: 0268 473 215
e-mail: siftransilvania@siftransilvania.ro
web: www.transif.ro

Geographic Preference: Romania
Fund Size: $81.9 Billion
Founded: 1996
Average Investment: $5 Million
Minimum Investment: $50,000
Industry Group Preference: Chemicals, Financial Services, Tourism, Machinery, Agribusiness, Transportation, Food & Beverage, Banking

Key Executives:
Ec. Razvan Gavaneanu, President of the Supervisory Board
Education: Accounting
Background: Economist; Director, PRESCON Group Brasov
Ec. Stefan Szabo, Vice President of the Supervisory Board
e-mail: marketing@transif.ro
Education: Ph.D. in economics (business management)
Directorships: General Manager
Constantin Fratila, Member of the Supervisory Board
e-mail: marketing@transif.ro
Education: Economics
Ec. Gheorghe Lutac, Member of the Supervisory Board
e-mail: transif@transif.ro

3120 SIGNATURE CAPITAL LLC
76 Merrion Square
Dublin 2
Ireland
Phone: 353-16690700 Fax: 353-16760694
e-mail: info@signaturecapital.com
web: www.signaturecapital.com

Mission Statement: A results-oriented venture capital firm that leverages its insight, wisdom and proven track record to allow breakthrough technology-based startup businesses to reach their full potential.

Founded: 1997
Investment Criteria: Early, Seed
Industry Group Preference: Biotechnology, Communications, Electronic Technology, Information Technology, Software, Internet, Telecommunications, Semiconductors, Healthcare

Other Locations:
Savignyplatz 9-10
Berlin 10623
Germany
Phone: 49-3031804920 Fax: 49-30318049211

Berkely Square House
Berkely Square
London W1J 6BD
United Kingdom
Phone: 44-2078871517

Key Executives:
Ciaran McNamara, Co-Founder/Managing Director
Education: University College of Dublin
Enda Woods, Co-Founder/Director
Education: University of California, Davis

3121 SINGTEL INNOV8
71 Ayer Rajah Crescent
#02-22
139951
Singapore
Phone: 65-68384686 Fax: 65-68728456
e-mail: newsroom@singtel.com
web: innov8.singtel.com

Mission Statement: SingTel Innov8, a wholly-owned subsidiary of the SingTel Group, is a corporate venture capital fund, with its own set of decision making, approval and funding processes. Innov8 focuses its investments on technologies and solutions that lead to quantum changes in network capabilities, next generation devices, digital content services and enablers to enhance customer experience. It works closely with the ecosystem of leading innovators, developers, government agencies, R&D and capital providers to bring cutting-edge technologies and solutions to the various markets the SingTel Group operates in.

Geographic Preference: Asia Pacific, Africa
Fund Size: S$200 million
Average Investment: S$100,000 - S$30 million
Investment Criteria: All Stages
Industry Group Preference: Internet, Digital Media & Marketing
Portfolio Companies: Ninja Blocks, Bitglass, Pokkt, DemystData, TheNeura, Arista Networks, MobileIron, Maker Studios, Fab, Kai Square, Tempo.AI, TubeMogul, Net Power & Light, Yodo1, ShopSpot, Flocations, Everything.me, Vuclip, Venuemob, 121cast, Qvivo, Moment.me, General Moile, Jasper Wireless, Nexage, Ruckus Wireless, InGameAd, Le Kan, Sodacard, Bubble Motion, Massive Impact, Baynote, 2359 Media

Other Locations:
Shanghai Times Square
Unite 1210
93 Huai Hai Zhong Road
Shanghai 200021
China
Phone: 86-2161371258

100 Marine Parkway
Suite 450
Redwood City, CA 94065

Key Executives:
Edgar Hardless, Chief Executive Officer
Education: BSc, Business Administration, University of Bath
Background: VP, Strategic Investments, SingTel; British Telecommunications

Venture Capital & Private Equity Firms / International Firms

3122 SLOVAK AMERICAN ENTERPRISE FUND
58 Obchodna
PO Box 100
Bratislava 810 00
Slovakia

Phone: 421-257100200 Fax: 421-252731323
web: www.saef.sk

Mission Statement: Actively seeking new investments.
Geographic Preference: Slovakia, Czech Republic
Founded: 1991
Average Investment: $2.2 Million
Minimum Investment: $500,000
Investment Criteria: Expansion - development, Other early stage, Small buyout, Start-up
Industry Group Preference: All Sectors Considered
Portfolio Companies: Profesia, Gotive, MäsospiÜ, Slovlepex, Novomanip, Rabbit Farm, Esox s.r.o., Ameta s.r.o., ZIN s.r.o., Leader Gasket of Slovakia s.r.o., Gamma spol. s r.o., Bee-keeping Dedinsk[2].

Key Executives:
Martina Rosková, President
e-mail: chren@saef.sk
Education: MBA, Old Dominion University
Background: Investment Banking
Mary Hurajová, Director General, Stock Exchange
e-mail: graic@saef.sk
Education: Master Degree in Engineering
Background: Venture Capital
Directorships: Member of Boards in investee companies

3123 SMAC PARTNERS
Germany

web: www.smacpartners.com

Geographic Preference: Germany, Western Europe
Founded: 2001
Investment Criteria: Management Buyouts, Single and portfolio secondary direct transactions, Merger between two companies with additional operational funding needs, Distressed situations
Industry Group Preference: Technology, Telecommunications
Portfolio Companies: Actelis, Alchip, Exit Games, Flash Networks, nLight, Olive Software, Rock Mobile

Key Executives:
Dr. Dietrich Ulmer, Managing Partner and Co-Founder
Education: Technical University (RWTH) of Aachen; PHd, Sociology, Konstanz University
Background: CEO and President, Siemens Acceleration; Chief Strategist, O2 Germany
Oliver Kolbe, Managing Partner and Co-Founder
Education: University of Applied Sciences in Munich, Germany
Background: CFO, Simens Acceleration; Vice President Strategy and Marketing BA, Siemens Mobile

3124 SMART BUSINESS CONSULTING
85 Medinat Hayehudim Street
Herzliya Pituach 46851
Israel

Phone: 972-99710710 Fax: 972-99710711
web: www.smartandbetter.co.il

Mission Statement: Focuses on the high-tech market, with an Israeli emphasis, especially by partnering with start-ups, and using our global network to bring Israeli technology to the world.
Geographic Preference: Israel, USA, Europe
Fund Size: $500 Million
Founded: 1997
Investment Criteria: Start-up
Industry Group Preference: Wireless Technologies, Communications, Internet Technology, Enterprise Services, Infrastructure, Software
Portfolio Companies: Interwise, XOR Technologies, Pl-x, Vidius, BIS, Odimo, SpeedBit, Mobile Access, Memscap, Flash Networks, Prominence Networks

3125 SOCIALATOM VENTURES
Bogata
Columbia

web: www.socialatomventures.com

Mission Statement: An international team of entrepreneurs, investors and business professionals that invests in and partners with high-technology companies offering global solutions across the Americas. Our unique founder-centric services provide both capital and in-depth services across the entrepreneurial life cycle.
Geographic Preference: Latin America
Founded: 2005
Investment Criteria: Early-Stage
Industry Group Preference: High Technology
Portfolio Companies: Micarga.com, Gone App, Mortgage Hippo, Replica Labs, Socrex, PulsoSocial, Seahorse App, Agora, Viajala, Ustraap, Oppten, Genuisly, CodeRise, Authy, Entryless, Cambly, AllTheRooms, Play Vox, Oja.la, Bankity, Donortap, LetsLunch, Streem

Key Executives:
Andres Barreto, Managing Partner
Hernando Barreto, Managing Partner

3126 SOCIEDAD REGIONAL DE PROMOCION DEL PRINCIPADO
Parque Tecnológico de Asturias
Llanera 33428
Spain

Phone: 34-985980096 Fax: 34-985980222
e-mail: srp@srp.es
web: www.srp.es

Mission Statement: Its objective is the promotion of investments in the region, participating in the share capital in societies to constitute or already existing by means of the capital risk modality. Actively seeking new investments
Fund Size: $21.9 Million
Founded: 1984
Industry Group Preference: All Sectors Considered

Key Executives:
Víctor M. González Marroquín, President
María Callejón Fornieles, Vice President

3127 SOFTBANK VENTURES KOREA
Kyobo Tower
13th Floor, A-Wing
Seocho-Dong, Seocho-Gu
Seoul 1302-22
Korea

Phone: 02-34849000 Fax: 02-34849010
web: www.softbank.co.kr

Mission Statement: Goes beyond a mere financial investor, Softbank Ventures, aids in the creation and development of each company's value as a strategic partner.
Industry Group Preference: Internet, Mobile, Entertainment, Education
Portfolio Companies: Naldo, Aiara, Buzzbil, Chinada, Classting, Clipcomm, Cocone, Dadam Game, Doobic, Dramafever, Ender's Fund, Enermont, Enswers, FXGear, Smartots, Gretech, GSM, Healcerion, HelloNature, ID INCU, IMX, Infomark, ini3, IntelRa, Knowre, KNS, Korbit, LeisureQ, Mangoplate, Microsoftware, Mirageworks, MOS, NBIZ, Ngine, nPlatform, PenAndFree, Pishoniac, Phychips, Megaphone TV, Playnery, Pulsus, Qualson, RadioPulse, R-Square, Redmart, Seworks, Snaps, Standard Networks,

Venture Capital & Private Equity Firms / International Firms

Strong Hold, Systran, TeraSquare, Tokopedia, Jandi, TVU, Uway, Vaimi, Value Creators & Company, TVU Pack, Wave3Studio, Xavis

Key Executives:
Greg Moon, CEO/President
Education: BA, Spanish Literature, Korea University; MBA, Drexel University
Background: Business Development, Trigen Computers; Associate, Softbank Technology Ventures; CEO, Softbank Commerce Korea; Co-CEO, KeyEast

3128 SOLID VENTURES
1001 LH Amsterdam
Amsterdam 1001 LH
Netherlands

Phone: 31-655-32-58-73
e-mail: info@solidventures.nl
web: www.solidventures.nl

Mission Statement: Solid Ventures invests in young, innovative and fast growing companies in the Netherlands.

Geographic Preference: The Netherlands
Industry Group Preference: Internet, Telecommunications, Software, Digital Media & Marketing
Portfolio Companies: SoldPrint Europe, Sixpack Mobile Applications, Scense, Boostermedia, BackupAgent B.V., Immidio, Mirror 42, Respectance B.V., 24access Solutions B.V., Avinity Systems B.V.

Key Executives:
Floris van Alkemade, Partner
Herman DeLatte, Partner
Robert Wilhelm, Partner

3129 SONY EUROPE
Kemperplatz 1
Berlin 10785
Germany

Phone: 49-30585812345 Fax: 49-1805252587
e-mail: support.l@eu.sony.com
web: www.sony.de

Founded: 1946
Minimum Investment: $ 1000000 EURO
Investment Criteria: Early Stage, Expansion and Development Capital, Seed Capital, Startup Capital
Industry Group Preference: Communications, Computer Related, Electronic Technology, Financial Services, Internet Technology, Insurance, Real Estate

Key Executives:
Howard Stringer, Chairman and CEO

3130 SOVEREIGN CAPITAL
25 Victoria Street
London SW1H 0EX
United Kingdom

Phone: 44-2073408800 Fax: 44-2073408811
e-mail: info@sovereigncapital.co.uk
web: www.sovereigncapital.co.uk

Mission Statement: Formerly Nash, Sells & Partners.

Geographic Preference: United Kingdom
Fund Size: $794 Million
Founded: 1988
Average Investment: $3.5-17.6 Million
Investment Criteria: MBO, MBI, Development Capital, Refinancing, Restructuring, IBO, Acquisitions
Industry Group Preference: Leisure, Healthcare, Waste & Recycling, Education, Corporate Services, Environment Products & Services
Portfolio Companies: 8 Solutions, Alcumus Group, Axis Group Integrated Services, Cordium

Key Executives:
Andrew Hayden, Managing Partner
Education: BS Medical Applications, University of London
Background: Commercial Director, Industrial MBI
Monica Bergvall, Investment Manager
Education: BA History, Cambridge University
Background: Director, Gresham Trust

3131 SPARK VENTURES
5 St. John's Lane
London EC1M 4BH
United Kingdom

Phone: (0)20 8123 0665
e-mail: enquirie@sparkventures.com
web: www.sparkventures.com

Mission Statement: SPARK Ventures is a leading European early stage venture capital company. Across a range of funds, we invest in the UK's best technology to create great companies with world class potential.

Geographic Preference: Europe
Investment Criteria: Early-Stage
Industry Group Preference: Technology
Portfolio Companies: Academia, Aspex Semiconductor, DEM Solutions, Firebox.com, Gambling Compliance, IMImobile, Kobalt Music, Mind Candy, MyDeco, Notonthehighstreet.com, OpenX

Key Executives:
Charles Berry, Non-Executive Director
Education: C.A.(KPMG)
Background: Carnegie Group, Union Bank of Switzerland, the Bank of Tokyo-Mitsubishi, London
Andrew Carruthers, Director
Education: CA..(Moore Stephens)
Background: 3i plc, Investment Trust plc(non-executive director)
Directorships: Co-founder
Helen Sinclair, Non-Executive Director
Education: C.A., MA in Economics(Cambridge University)
Background: Advent Venture Partners(Finance Director), Coopers & Lybrand(Accountancy), Laurence Prust(Corporate Finance)

3132 SPINUP VENTURE
Ozerkovskaya Nab.
50/1 Office 512
Moscow 1150504
Russia

Phone: +7 916 665 71 48
e-mail: info@spinupper.com
web: www.spinupventure.com

Mission Statement: SpinUp Venture has been founded by professionals with vast experience in business consultancy, corporate banking, project management and executive search. We offer a hands-on and pragmatic approach to commercialization of new concepts, expanding the potential of original ideas and providing a sound platform to build a link between the talents, innovators and traditional venture capital.

Geographic Preference: Russia, Asia, United States, Europe
Investment Criteria: Early-Stage
Industry Group Preference: Internet, Mobile, Robotics, Alternative Energy, Clean Technology, New Materials, Nanotechnology, Biomedical, High Technology
Portfolio Companies: JFDI.Asia, HaxAsia, Displair

Key Executives:
Sergey Gorokhov, General Director/Partner
e-mail: sgorokhov@spinupper.com
Education: MBA, Open University Business School

Venture Capital & Private Equity Firms / International Firms

3133 SRIJAN CAPITAL
Sri Sai Complex, 1st Floor
Pampa Extension
Hebbal Kempapura
Bangalore 24
India

e-mail: ravi@srijancapital.com
web: www.srijancapital.com

Mission Statement: Srijan provides seed stage investments to technology startups. We target start-ups that are based out of India, or have India as a target market.
Geographic Preference: India
Investment Criteria: Early-Stage
Industry Group Preference: E-Commerce & Manufacturing, SaaS, Mobile, Social Media, Consumer Internet
Portfolio Companies: Explara, Tokitaki, Mech Mocha, Venturesity, CollateBox, CouponRani, AllConnect, Mediaspan, BuildLinks, Visionair

Key Executives:
   Ravi Trivedi, Founder
   Education: MS, Computer Science, Indian Institute of Technology; MBA, Fuqua School of Business
   Background: Principal, Southeast Interactive Technology Funds; Equity Analyst, Bank of America

3134 SRIW SA SRIW Group
13 Destenay Avenue
Liege 4000
Belgium

Phone: 32-42219811 Fax: 32-42219999
e-mail: info@sriw.be
web: www.sriw.be/en/

Mission Statement: Actively seeking new investments.
Industry Group Preference: Metals, Chemicals, Agribusiness, Wood Industries, Tourism, Services, Construction, Glass, Paper, Printing, Publishing
Portfolio Companies: Barthel Pauls, Comes Bois, Spacebel, Ateliers Jean Del'Cour, Cortigroupe, Bodymat, Belga-Films, Trendy Foods Finances, Briqueteries de Ploegsteert, Coprosain, ISIS, Grandes Distilleries de Charleroi, Equilis, Cap Energie II, Lampiris, TPF, Istar Medical, Cardio 3 Biosciences, Euroscreen, Icarus, Ronveaux

Key Executives:
   Jean-Claude Dehovre, Chairman
   Bernard Marchand, Vice Chairman

3135 SSE VENTURES
200 Dunkeld Road
Perth PH1 3AQ
United Kingdom

Phone: 44-0-1738-456-253
e-mail: ventures@sse.com

Mission Statement: SSE Ventures was established to develop and grow SSE's portfolio of investments in small and medium-sized businesses offering renewable, sustainable and energy efficiency products and services. The team is interested in products and services which support current activities within the SSE group or which we expect to play key roles in the future.
Geographic Preference: United Kingdom, Ireland, Europe, United States, Asia
Industry Group Preference: Energy, Energy Efficiency
Portfolio Companies: Aquamarine Power, BiFab, Wind Towers Ltd, ONZO, SSE Rogerstone, IE CHP, Intelligent Energy, Logan Energy, Premium Power

Key Executives:
   Alistair Phillips-Davies, Chief Executive

3136 STAGEONE VENTURES
89 Medinat HaYehudim Street
Building E, 11th Floor
Herzliya Pituach
Israel

Phone: 972-3-649-4000 Fax: 972-3-649-5000
e-mail: info@stageonevc.com
web: www.stageonevc.com

Mission Statement: StageOne Ventures provides financing and professional guidance to early-stage companies in order to help building exceptional enterprises. We invest primarily in early stage companies in the fields of Software, Communications, Internet and Media, The fund is committed to providing its portfolio companies with top value creation through the technological and financial strength of its team. By acting in synergy with the dominant trends in IT & Telecommunications, StageOne invests in start-ups whose exceptional technologies address market leaders' true needs.
Geographic Preference: Israel
Fund Size: $50 million
Investment Criteria: Early-Stage
Industry Group Preference: Software, Communications, Internet, Media
Portfolio Companies: AVANAN, cVidya Networks

Key Executives:
   Yuval Cohen, Managing Partner
   Education: LLB, MBA, Hebrew University
   Background: General Partner, Israel Infinity Fund; Vice President, ISAL
   Directorships: Traffix Systems, Trivnet, Guardium, Radwiz, Oridion Medical, Lab-One Innovations, cVidya Networks, Oversi Networks

3137 STAR VENTURES
Maximilianstr. 35a
Munich D-80539
Germany

e-mail: info@star-ventures.de
web: www.star-ventures.com

Mission Statement: Invests in private, emerging and later-stage companies.
Geographic Preference: Israel, USA
Fund Size: $1 Billion
Founded: 1992
Investment Criteria: Seed, start-up and late stage investments.
Industry Group Preference: Telecommunications, Enterprise Services, Wireless Technologies, Life Sciences
Portfolio Companies: Accord, Acopia Networks, AeroScout, Airspan, Aigotec, Alvarion, Answersoft, Applied Science Fiction, Armon, Aspect, Advanced Vision Technology, Be, Benchmarq Microelectronics, BigBand Networks, Bioline Rx, Brix Networks, Broadbus, Broadlight, C-Port, Cadent, Capstone, Cedar Point Communications, Celerica, Celletra, Ceragon Networks, Ciena, CigniTens, Creo Products, Cube Optics AG, cVidya, Decalog B.V., Decru, EFI Electronics for Imaging, Entrisphere, EveryDay Health, Evotec NeuroSciences GmbH, EZchip, Fuego Tech, Fundtech, GENBAND, Geotek, Groove Mobile, Identity Software, iloxx GmbH, Imedia, Intercell AG, Jacada, Kabira, PPU Maconomy, maincontrol, Mangrove, Medical Present Value, MediGene AG, Mercado, Mintera, NextNet Wireless, Nicecom, Nur, Odin, Omnia Communications, Onex Communications, OraMetrix, OrSense, OSHAP, Paradigm, Precise Software Solutions, Procognia, RADCOM, RAScom, RF Micro Devices, RiT, Sequenom, Sheer Networks, Siano, Sipera, Softcom, Summit, Technomatix, Proxim Wireless, Topio, TranSwitch, Trivnet, UltraCom, UPTI, Vidyo, Viryanet, Vizrt, Wayport, Xignal, Xtera

Other Locations:
   Ackerstein Towers Bldg. C
   10 Abba Eben Avenue

Venture Capital & Private Equity Firms / International Firms

PO Box 12600
Herzelia Pituach 4672528
Israel
Phone: 972-97662226 **Fax:** 972-97662227

Two Galleria Tower
13455 Noel Road
Suite 1670
Dallas, TX 75240
Phone: 972-776-1516 **Fax:** 972-702-1103

Key Executives:
Dr. Meir Barel, Managing Partner
e-mail: jb@star-ventures.com
Education: MS, University of Texas; BS, Texas A&M University
Background: Director of Strategic Investments for Intel Capital, Founder, CEO and President of AnswerSoft, Davox as VP Marketing, VP Marketing of NetBoost Corporation
Amit Barel, Investment Manager
e-mail: BAR@star-ventures.com
Education: Dr. Barel holds a Master's Degree and a Doctorate Degree (Dr.-Ing.) in Electrical Engineering from the Department of Data Communication at the Technical University in Aachen, Germany.
Background: Investment Manager & Managing Partner of TVM - Techno Venture Management GmbH & Co. KG
Petra Pornin, Assistant to Managing Partner
Education: Mr. Maher graduated Cum Laude with a Masters Degree in Electrical Engineering and Physics from the University of Illinois in 1969.
Background: Member of the Board of Directors for Siemens Information and Communication Networks Group from 1997 - 2002. Founded and chaired Mustang Ventures; President - Access; Director of Marketing for worldwide product planning within the Public Communication Netw
Directorships: Investment Manager

3138 STARFISH VENTURES
Level 1
120 Jolimont Road
East Melbourne VIC 3002
Australia
Phone: 61-3-9654-2121
e-mail: admin@starfishvc.com
web: www.starfishvc.com

Mission Statement: Starfish Ventures partners with talented entrepreneurs to build successful innovative global technology companies. Their team's proven expertise in venture capital investing, entrepreneurship and technology gives the firm the skills to navigate the challenges of seeding, building and managing high growth technology businesses from an Australian base.

Geographic Preference: Australia
Fund Size: AU $400 million
Founded: 2001
Average Investment: $1 - $5 million
Investment Criteria: All Stages
Industry Group Preference: Information Technology, Life Sciences
Portfolio Companies: Aktano, Armaron Bio, Audinate, Bubble Gum, DesignCrowd, dorsaVi, ImpediMed, MetaCDN, Mimetica, MuriGen Therapeutics, Myriax, Nitro Software, Protagonist

Key Executives:
John Dyson, Investment Principal
Education: BS, Monash University, Graduate Diploma, Finance & Investment, Securities Institute of Australia; MBA, RMIT University
Background: General Manager, JAFCO Investment; Schroders, Nomura Securities, KPMG, ANZ McCaughan
Directorships: Aruspex, Atmail, Audinate, Ausra, Distra, Holly Australia, Icix, Myriax, Quickcomm, Space-Time Research, Xelor, Zoom Systems
Michael Panaccio, Investment Principal
Education: BS, PhD, Medicine, University of Melbourne; MBA, RMIT University
Background: Investment Manager, JAFCO Investment; Head of the Department of Microbiology, Victorian Institute of Animal Science
Directorships: DorsaVi, Energy Response, Impedimed, Murigen, Neuprotect, Ofidium

3139 STARPHARMA POOLED DEVELOPMENT LIMITED
4-6 Southampton Crescent
Abbotsford 3067
Australia
Phone: 61-385322700 **Fax:** 61-395105955
e-mail: info@starpharma.com
web: www.starpharma.com

Mission Statement: An ASX listed company developed to invest in both pharmaceutical and non-pharmaceutical applications of dendrimer nanotechnology.

Geographic Preference: Australia
Founded: 1996
Industry Group Preference: Drug Delivery, Agrochemicals
Key Executives:
Peter T Bartels AO, FAISM, FRS, Chairman & Non-Executive Director
e-mail: john.raff@starpharma.com
Education: John Raff received a Ph.D. from Melbourne University in 1982 for molecular biology studies on cell recognition systems, under the supervision of Professor Adrienne Clarke
Background: General Manager of the Biomolecular Research Institute
Directorships: Executive Director
Jackie Fairley, BSc, BVSc (Hons), MBA, Chief Executive Officer

3140 STATE STREET GLOBAL ADVISORS
68th Floor, Two International Finance Centre
Hong Kong
China
Phone: 852-21030288 **Fax:** 852-21030200
web: www.ssga.com

Mission Statement: Established in Asia to service clients and develop new institutional business.

Geographic Preference: Worldwide
Fund Size: $1.4 Trillion
Founded: 1990

Key Executives:
Bernard P. Reilly, Global Head of Strategy
Education: BA Economics and Agricultural Economics, University of Exeter
Background: Private Client Portfolio Manager, KBIM; Research Team, KBIM UK; Senior Asian Fund Manager, KBIM
Scott F. Powers, President and CEO

3141 STATOIL TECHNOLOGY INVEST
Norway
web: innovate.statoil.com

Mission Statement: Statoil engages in projects with entrepreneurs and industrial companies in order to help new and emerging technologies reach the market. We have a particular focus on the development and commercialisation phases of new technology. This includes detailed product development, prototyping, testing and verification, and market planning. Our contribution to a project can include technical expertise, defining user requirements, project supervision, pilot tests, es-

tablishing networks, business/commercial advice, and financial support.
Geographic Preference: Norway
Investment Criteria: Seed-Stage, Early-Stage
Industry Group Preference: Oil & Gas, Energy
Portfolio Companies: AGR Enhanced Drilling Systems, Aptomar AS, Fisbones AS, Octio AS, Resman AS, Sekal AS, Silixa Ltd., TracID AS, Verdande Technology AS, Coreteq Systems, Ecotone AS, Gravitude AS, Hybond AS, Lux Assure, Neodrill AS, Numascale AS, Robotic Drilling Systems AS, Sofitech AS, TechInvent AS

3142 STEAMBOAT VENTURES
Unit 1002-1005
One Corporate Avenue
222 Hu Bin Road
Shanghai 200021
China
Phone: 86 (21) 2308 1800 **Fax:** 86 (21) 2308 1999
web: www.steamboatvc.com

Mission Statement: To help young companies successfully face the challenges of becoming leaders in their markets.
Geographic Preference: United States, China
Founded: 2000
Average Investment: $2 - $15 million
Investment Criteria: Early-Stage, Mid-Stage
Industry Group Preference: Technology, Digital Media & Marketing, Consumer Products
Portfolio Companies: 51Fanli.com, 56.com, Bokecc, Cocoa China, FunPlus, GoPro, Gridsum, Netmovie, Shangpin, Troodon, UUSee, Youxigu, Yoyi, YY.com

20/F Wellable Commercial Building
513 Hennessy Road, Causeway Bay
Hong Kong SAR
China
Phone: 852-35119276 **Fax:** 852-35119002

801 North Brand Boulevard
Suite 665
Glendale, CA 91203
Phone: 818-858-1890 **Fax:** 818-696-2686

Key Executives:
John Ball, Founder & Managing Director
e-mail: john.ball@steamboatvc.com
Education: BA, Biological Sciences, Tufts University; MBA, Harvard Business School
Background: Corporate Development Group, Walt Disney Company; Burr Egan Deleage & Co.
Directorships: RazorGator, Beijing NetMovie
Liping Fan, Chief Financial Officer
e-mail: liping.fan@steamboatvc.com
Education: MS, Accounting, MBA, Finance, Binghamton University
Background: CFO, RWI Ventures; Senior Financial Analyst, Merck & Company; Senior Associate, PricewaterhouseCoopers
Directorships: VCBC

3143 STEELHOUSE VENTURES
Sundgauer Strasse 105c
Berlin 14169
Germany
Phone: 49-030221608199

Mission Statement: Steelhouse Ventures Limited has been established to bring capital and expertise to new business start-ups in the areas of energy, telecommunications and advanced technology.
Geographic Preference: Europe
Average Investment: £500,000
Investment Criteria: Early-Stage
Industry Group Preference: Energy, Technology

Key Executives:
Peter Bryant, Founding Partner
e-mail: peter@steelhouse-ventures.com

3144 STEPSTONE
57-59 St James's Street
London SW1A 1LD
United Kingdom
Phone: 44 0 207 647 7550 **Fax:** 44 0 207 647 7599
web: www.stepstoneglobal.com

Mission Statement: A dedicated purchaser of secondary private equity interests and advises funds in excess of $700 million. The team has the capacity to manage deals in a broad range of sizes worldwide.
Geographic Preference: Europe, United States, Middle East, Far East
Founded: 2000
Investment Criteria: Discreet liquidity solutions, buyout, growth, mezzanine: Corporations, Financial Institutions, Family Offices

Key Executives:
Marleen Groen, Senior Advisor
e-mail: groen@greenparkcapital.co.uk
Education: BA, MA, Leiden University; MBA, Rotterdam School of Management
Zifri Baharudin, Performance Monitoring Manager
e-mail: jordan@greenparkcapital.co.uk
Education: MBA, Leicester Business School
Background: Strategic Acquisitions, international real estate company; Business Analyst, US family office
John Bohill, Senior Advisor
e-mail: french@greenparkcapital.co.uk
Education: BS, University of Southampton
Background: Chartered Accountant, KPMG
Nicole Chadwick, Executive Assistant
e-mail: topley@greenparkcapital.co.uk
Education: BS Biochemistry, Imperial College; MBA, INSEAD
Background: Partner, early stage venture capital fund; CSFB

3145 STIC VENTURES CORPORATION LIMITED
10 Fl. MSA Bldg., 12, Teheran-ro 78-gil
Gangnam-gu
Seoul 135-840
South Korea
Phone: 82-234047800 **Fax:** 82-234535188
web: www.stic.co.kr

Mission Statement: Actively seeking new investments.
Geographic Preference: South Korea, USA, Hong Kong, China
Fund Size: $333 Million
Founded: 1999
Average Investment: $2 Million
Minimum Investment: $500,000
Investment Criteria: Early-stage
Industry Group Preference: Information Technology
Portfolio Companies: LIG, CSL, Yusin, Daesung Eltec, Songwoo, Orion Technology, Wooyang HC, TacBright, Hyundai Oil Terminal, Posco Energy, RFHIC, Innorex Technologies, New Focus Auto, SaehWa, AccessBio, Soulbrain, Shinsung Solar Energy, Hy-Lok, MDS Technology, JNTC, TIB, JEL Hydraulics, YG, Medytox, Golfzon, Kona International, Genic, Vieworks, Sapphire Technology

Key Executives:
Yong Hwan Do, Founder and Chairman
e-mail: log@stic.co.kr
Education: BA. Business Administration from Yeungnam University and completed MBA course at Seoul National

Venture Capital & Private Equity Firms / International Firms

University.
Background: Dongsuh Securities
Byung Won Choi, Founding Member / Executive Partner & CEO
e-mail: log@stic.co.kr
Education: BSEE from Sogang University
Background: Samsung Electronics

3146 STRAND HANSON LIMITED
26 Mount Row
Mayfair
London W1K 3SQ
United Kingdom

Phone: 44-02074093494 Fax: 44-02074091761
e-mail: mail@strandhanson.co.uk
web: www.strandhanson.co.uk

Mission Statement: Provides financial advice to public and private UK corporates, private equity houses and qualified investors.
Geographic Preference: Europe
Founded: 1993
Investment Criteria: Mbos, Mbis
Industry Group Preference: Technology, E-Commerce & Manufacturing, Financial Services, Telecommunications, Biotechnology
Portfolio Companies: Education Overseas Ltd, European Investor Services, Federated Foods, Newsletter Publishing
Key Executives:
   Simon Raggett, Chief Executive
   e-mail: simonraggett@strandhanson.co.uk
   Background: Grieg Middleton & Co
   Hon. Robert Hanson, Chairman
   e-mail: roberthanson@strandhanson.co.uk
   Education: Oxford University
   Background: Associate Director, NM Rothschild & Sons
   Rory Murphy, Director
   e-mail: rorymurphy@strandhanson.co.uk
   Background: Accountant, KPMG; Grieg Middleton & Co; Charterhouse Securities Limited
   James Harris, Director
   e-mail: jamesharris@strandhanson.co.uk
   Background: Robert Fleming Securities; SG Securities; Arbuthnot Securities
   Stuart Faulkner, Director
   e-mail: stuartfaulkner@strandhanson.co.uk
   Education: St. Anne's College, Oxford University
   Background: Investment Banking, Barclays de Zoete Wedd; Merrill Lynch
   Matthew Chandler, Director of Corporate Finance
   e-mail: matthewchandler@strandhanson.co.uk
   Education: BS, Bath University
   Background: Capita Corporate Finance Ltd
   Angela Hallett, Director of Corporate Finance
   e-mail: angelapeace@strandhanson.co.uk
   Education: BA & BC, University of Melbourne
   Background: Accountant, Arthur Andersen
   Richard Tulloch, Director of Corporate Finance
   e-mail: richardtulloch@strandhanson.co.uk
   Education: Bristol University
   Background: Corporate Finance, ING Barings; Arbuthnot Securities
   Warren Pearce, Managing Director, Strand Hanson South Africa
   e-mail: warrenpearce@strandhanson.co.uk
   Education: Business Science, University of Cape Town
   Richard Evans, Chief Operating Officer and Compliance Director
   e-mail: paulcocker@strandhanson.co.uk
   Background: Day Investment Banking; Deloitte London
   James Spinney, Director of Corporate Finance
   e-mail: jamesspinney@strandhanson.co.uk
   Education: Durham University
   Background: Accountant, Pricewaterhousecoopers; Corporate Finance, Earnst & Young

   Andrew Emmott, Director of Corporate Finance
   e-mail: davidaltberg@strandhanson.co.uk
   Background: Corporate Dept, Rosenblatt Solicitor
   Naiem Hussain, Director - Strand Ventures
   e-mail: liambuswell@strandhanson.co.uk
   Education: University of Warwick
   Background: Investment Banking, Merrill Lynch; Inenco Group
   James Bellman, Analyst
   e-mail: rorychichester@strandhanson.co.uk
   Background: Kandahar Real Estate; Carphone Warehouse
   Scott McGregor, Analyst
   e-mail: williambarkes@strandhanson.co.uk
   Education: Newcastle University
   Background: Killik & Co Stockbrokers; Evolution Securities; Daniel Stewart; St Helen's Capital
   Simon Wharmby, Non-Executive Director
   e-mail: simonwharmby@strandhanson.co.uk
   Education: University of East Anglia
   Background: Corporate Stockbroker, Sheppards, Charles Stanley, Corporate Synergy

3147 SUMMIT BRIDGE CAPITAL
No. 7 East Third Ring Middle Road
Chaoyang District
Beijing 100020
China

Phone: +86 (10) 5979 7669 Fax: +86 (10) 6804 3607
web: www.summitbridgecapital.com

Mission Statement: Summit Bridge Capital is a growth technology fund co-managed by Atlantic Bridge Capital and WestSummit Capital. The Fund targets fast growing technology companies with a presence or strategic interest in Ireland and China.
Geographic Preference: Ireland, China
Fund Size: $100 million
Industry Group Preference: Technology, Software, Semiconductors, Cloud Computing, Big Data, Clean Technology, Food & Beverage, Medical Technology, Agriculture, Financial Services
Portfolio Companies: Accuris, Fieldaware

3148 SUNEVISION HOLDINGS LIMITED
52/F, Sun Hung Kai Centre
30 Harbour Road
Wanchai
Hong Kong

Fax: 852-25115388
e-mail: enquiry@sunevision.com
web: www.sunevision.com

Mission Statement: SUNeVision is the first company in China and Asia to integrate and leverage the entire Internet value chain to achieve critical mass with significant economies of scale.
Geographic Preference: China, Asia
Founded: 1972
Investment Criteria: Start-up
Industry Group Preference: Technology, Internet Technology
Other Locations:
   37/F, Shanghai Central Plaza
   381 Huai Hai Zhong Road
   Shanghai 200020
   China
   Phone: 86-21-6391-5123 Fax: 86-21-6391-5868

   Room 1117, 11/f, Office Tower 2, Sun Dong An
   Sun Dong An Plaza
   138 Wang Fu Jing Da Jie
   Beijing

China
Phone: 86-10-6528-1822 **Fax:** 86-10-6528-1823

Key Executives:
Ping Luen, Chairman

3149 SUNSTONE CAPITAL
Lautrupsgade 7
5th Floor
Copenhagen 2100
Denmark
Phone: 45-20126000 **Fax:** 45-39209898
web: www.sunstone.eu

Mission Statement: Headquartered in Copenhagen, Sunstone Capital is an early-stage Life Science and Technology venture capital company investing in European start-up companies with strong potential to achieve global success in their markets. Since our establishment in 2007, we have built a strong portfolio currently totaling 50 companies and have completed several successful trade sales and IPOs.

Geographic Preference: Europe
Fund Size: 700 million Euro
Founded: 2007
Investment Criteria: Early-Stage
Industry Group Preference: Life Sciences, Technology
Portfolio Companies: Acarix, Adenium Biotech, Alligator Bioscience, Amen, Anergis, Asante, Asetek, Atonomics, Biomonitor, Booztgroup, Cloud Made, Contrast, Egalet, Evolva, F2G, FBC Device, FlatFrog, Folicum, Freespree, Galecto Biotech, Gidsy, Imix, Ipt, Issuu, Jenavalve, Jurag Separation, Layar, MakieLab, Microtask, Neotechnology, Nsgene, Nuevolution, OrphaZyme, Paymill, Podio, Preview Networks, Prezi, Rovsing Dynamics, Santaris Pharma, Symphogen, Trunk Archive, Vaximm, Vivostat, Zealand Pharma, Zymenex

Other Locations:
1370 Willow Road
2nd Floor
Menlo Park, CA 94025
Phone: 650-5871518

Angelholmsvagen 28
Bastad 26931
Sweden
Phone: 46-431311740

Key Executives:
Jimmy Fussing Nielsen, Co-Founder/Managing Partner
45-27-12-8221

3150 SUPREMUM CAPITAL
10 Haymarket
London SW1Y 4BP
United Kingdom
Phone: 44-2071291061
web: www.supremum-capital.com

Mission Statement: Supremum Capital Partners have a broad and diversified investment mandate focused on VC investments in Cleantech, Internet & Digital as well as Innovative Technology sectors. Within those broad sectors we tend to prefer companies that offer a unique solution to real customer issues as well as products that offer a distinct and defensible technology advantage.

Geographic Preference: Europe, Israel, Russia
Average Investment: $500,000 - $10 million
Industry Group Preference: Clean Technology, Internet, Digital Media & Marketing, Technology
Portfolio Companies: Inplat, Atosho, CTRL, MRGK, Webbankir, Domfinans

Other Locations:
Donskaya str. 29/9, build. 1
Moscow 119049
Russia
Phone: 7-4955024780

Key Executives:
Ilya Belyaev, Co-Founder
Background: JP Morgan, Barclays Capital, VEB Capital

3151 SVI VEN CAPITAL
1 Raffles Place
#18-03 One Raffles Place
048616
Singapore
Phone: 65-6536-6123 **Fax:** 65-6536-6983

Mission Statement: SBI Ven Capital is a Singapore-based, leading private equity firm that invests in growth capital opportunities across Asia. We have a proven track record of partnering with growth-stage companies and assembling critical resources needed to grow businesses in Asia. Our investment team combines financial acumen, industry insight and operational expertise to enhance the value of the companies we invest in.

Geographic Preference: Asia
Investment Criteria: Growth-Stage
Portfolio Companies: Greenlots, Liqvid, HNB, Commercial Bank of Ceylon, Panviva

3152 SWISSCOM
Alte Tiefenaustrasse 6
Worblaufen 3048
Switzerland
web: www.swisscom.ch

Mission Statement: Swisscom Ventures seeks to acquire minority stakes in companies that operate in promising markets for information, communication and entertainment technologies. We invest in innovative areas that are strategic for Swisscom, in terms of revenue increase, quality improvements and cost reductions. As a value-creating investor, Swisscom is able to provide companies with the technical know-how and strategic experience of an established telecommunications provider.

Geographic Preference: Switzerland
Founded: 1852
Industry Group Preference: Telecommunications, Communications
Portfolio Companies: Amplidata, Asoka, ASSIA, Connect.me, Glass2Energy, I-Concerts, Matrixx, MVP, MyStrom, Piston Cloud Computing, Poken, Quantenna, Softbank Broadband Fund, Swiss VC/PE Investment, Vilant Systems, Firecomms, Kyte, LiberoVision, Sequans

Key Executives:
Hansueli Loosli, Chairman of the Board of Directors
Education: PhD, University of Saarland
Background: Google; Director Product Management & Engineering, YouTube

3153 SYDNEY SEED FUND
Level 2, 60 Clarence Street
Sydney NSW 2000
Australia
web: www.sydneyseedfund.com.au

Mission Statement: The Sydney Seed Fund is an early stage investment fund managed by experienced entrepreneurs looking to invest in Australia's most passionate tech founders.

Geographic Preference: Australia
Founded: 2013
Average Investment: $100,000
Investment Criteria: Early-Stage
Industry Group Preference: Technology
Portfolio Companies: Qwilr, CeeQTM, Rate Us, GoFar

Venture Capital & Private Equity Firms / International Firms

Key Executives:
Benjamin Chong, Co-Director
Education: BComm, University of New South Wales

3154 SYNERGO SGR
Via Campo Lodigiano, 3
Milan 20122
Italy

Phone: +39 02 859111 **Fax:** +39 02 72094122
e-mail: welcome@synergosgr.it

Mission Statement: Specializes in partnering with ambitious entrepreneurs in order to increase the value of their companies.

Average Investment: 35 million
Minimum Investment: 20 million
Portfolio Companies: Air Italy, allSystem, Arquati, Bozzetto Group, Building Energy, Cobra, Cast Futura, Cartonplast Group, Ducati, Glutinatus, E-Motion, IPC, Kinetika, Mediacontech, Redecam Group, Trei, Tecnowind Group, Unopiu, Valvitalia, V2, Waste Italia, Motovario, Fin Tyre, Lediberg, Riri, Roenest Group, Byte, Kiian Group, Optissimo, Selènia, Vending System, Teckal, Cemengal, TMCI Padovan, Raccortubi Group, Colony Sardegna

3155 T-VENTURE HOLDINGS GmbH Deutsche Telecom
156 Gotenstrasse
Bonn 53175
Germany

Phone: 49-228308480 **Fax:** 49-22830848819
web: www.t-venture.de

Mission Statement: T-Venture invests in the seed and early stages of growth and expansion of companies in the TIMES market.

Geographic Preference: Europe, USA, Asia
Founded: 1997
Average Investment: EUR0.5 - EUR10 million
Minimum Investment: $0.6 Million
Investment Criteria: Start-up
Industry Group Preference: Information Technology, Communications, Telecommunications, Wireless Technologies
Portfolio Companies: BelAir Networks, Bol.com, CoreMedia, Danger, Flarion Technologies, Flash Networks, Gamigo, High-Tech Grunderfonds, Kineto Wireless, MessageVine, MindMatics & Mobile Commerce

Key Executives:
Patrick Meisberger, Managing Director and Fund Manager Digital Services
Katharina Hollender, Managing Director / CFO

3156 TAISHAN CAPITAL CORPORATION
2906, Central International Trade Center
6A Jianguomenwai Avenue
Chao Yang District
Beijing 100022
China

Phone: 86-1058693440 **Fax:** 86-1084193495
e-mail: investbank@taishancapital.com
web: www.taishancapital.com

Mission Statement: Focuses on investment banking, primarily corporate finance, mergers and acquisitions, and project finance; works closely with some of the world's leading investment banks, direct investment funds, and accounting and legal firms.

Geographic Preference: United States, Europe, China & Hong Kong
Fund Size: $10 Million.
Founded: 1998
Investment Criteria: Small and Mid-Stage
Industry Group Preference: All Sectors Considered

Key Executives:
Po-Wen Huang, Chairman and CEO

3157 TALIS CAPITAL
Unit 4 Rowan Court
56 High Street
Wimbledon
London SW19 5EE
United Kingdom

Phone: 44-02035426260 **Fax:** 44-02089447264
web: www.taliscapital.com

Mission Statement: As a multi family office, Talis Capital offers a differentiated approach to traditional technology venture firms. We offer a flexible approach in deal structuring with long term and hands on support to management teams. We look to create long term value by not only providing capital, but with our networks, contacts, sector experience and on-going commitment to the management team.

Industry Group Preference: Digital Media & Marketing
Portfolio Companies: Navmii Holdings, FuelQuest, Iwoca, Queremos/WeDemand

Key Executives:
Bob Finch, Co-Founder
Background: Co-Founder, Finch Investments
Directorships: The Vitol Group

3158 TAMAR TECHNOLOGY VENTURES LIMITED
Okeanos
50 Ramat Yam
Herzliya Pituach 46851
Israel

Phone: 972-99543555 **Fax:** 972-99543423

Mission Statement: Tamar Ventures, a venture capital partnership headquartered in Israel, invests in Israeli technology companies in Israel.

Geographic Preference: Europe, USA, Israel
Founded: 1998
Investment Criteria: All stages consider
Industry Group Preference: Technology, Communication Technology, Software, Networks, Optical Networks and Components, Wireless Technologies
Portfolio Companies: Allot Communication Ltd., Cergaon Networks Ltd, RADVision, Ex Libris Ltd., Hotbar.com, Edge Medical Devices Ltd, Lenslet Ltd., Silicon Value Ltd, Wisair Inc.

Key Executives:
Zohar Gilon, Managing Partner
e-mail: zohar@tamarventures.com
Education: MBA from Tel Aviv University
Background: W.S.P. Capital Holdings,
Thomas I. Unterberg, General Partner

3159 TAMIR FISHMAN VENTURES
38 Habarzel St
Tel Aviv 69710
Israel

Phone: 972-36849333 **Fax:** 972-36853393
web: www.tamirfishman.com

Mission Statement: The Tamir Fishman Group is Israel's leading and fastest growing full-service financial group.

Geographic Preference: Israel
Fund Size: $275 Million
Founded: 1997
Average Investment: $6.5 Million
Minimum Investment: $3 Million
Investment Criteria: Early Stage, Seed, Late Stage
Industry Group Preference: Communications, Software, Internet Technology, Life Sciences

Portfolio Companies: Sagitta, Nova, Disksites, Voltaire, MindGuard, Allot Comm, Expand Network, Native Networks, Celight & Blade fusion

Key Executives:
  Eldad Tamir, President & Joint Chief Executive Officer
  Education: B.A. in Economics and an M.B.A. in Finance from Tel Aviv University.
  Background: Evergreen Group & Clal Financing & Investment
  Ilan Yanoshevsky, VP Finance

3160 TANK STREAM VENTURES
Level 10, 17-19 Bridge Street
Sydney NSW 2000
Australia

Phone: 61-2-9247-2232
e-mail: info@tankstream.vc
web: www.tankstream.vc

Mission Statement: Tank Stream Ventures is a technology focused fund investing in the brightest Australian early-stage startups.
Geographic Preference: Australia
Investment Criteria: Early-Stage
Industry Group Preference: Technology, Mobile, E-Commerce & Manufacturing, Software
Portfolio Companies: GoCatch, Spring.me, Pocketbook

Key Executives:
  Jonathan Lui, Director/Founding Member
  Background: Co-Founder/COO, Airtasker; Executive, IBM

3161 TARGET PARTNERS
Kardinal-Faulhaber-Strasse 10
Munich 80333
Germany

Phone: 49 (89)2070490 Fax: 49 (89)2070499
e-mail: info@targetpartners.de
web: www.targetpartners.de

Mission Statement: Target Partners invests in young technology companies in Germany, Austria and Switzerland.
Geographic Preference: Germany, Austria, Switzerland
Fund Size: 300 million Euro
Founded: 1999
Average Investment: 1 - 4 million Euro
Minimum Investment: 1 million Euro
Investment Criteria: Early-Stage
Industry Group Preference: Software, SaaS, Mobile, Green Technology, E-Commerce & Manufacturing, Internet
Portfolio Companies: Abusix, adjust, adsquare, ArangoDB, Datapath.io, Dedrone, Doo, Finanzchef24, German Auto Labs, Gpredictive, Instana, Locanis, Mercateo, NavVis, Quobyte, Scanbot (by Doo), Senic, Sicoya, Simplaex, So1, Suitpad, Swarm 64, tado§, Theva, TIS

Key Executives:
  Kurt Müller, Partner
  Education: Northwestern University; MBA, University of Chicago
  Directorships: Mercateo AG, tadoø, ArangoDB, Adjust, NavVis, Theva DÜNnschichttechnik
  Waldemar Jantz, Partner
  Directorships: Finanzchef24, Gpredictive, Locanis, Sicoya, Abusix, Quobyte, Dedrone
  Dr. Berthold von Freyberg, Partner
  e-mail: berthold@targetpartners.de
  Education: Diploma, Doctorate, Physics, ETH; MBA, INSEAD
  Background: Investment Manager, TVM Capital; Office Product Division, Microsoft
  Directorships: German Auto Labs, Simplaex, So1, SuitePad, Treasury Intelligence Solutions, Instana
  Dr. Michael Münnix, Partner
  Education: Technical University of Berlin; PhD,

University of Duisberg-Essen
Directorships: Adsquare, Datapath.io, Swarm64

3162 TAT CAPITAL PARTNERS LTD.
Sonnhalde 2
PO Box
Oberrohrdorf CH-5452
Switzerland

Phone: 41-628323262 Fax: 41-56-485-8985
web: www.tat.ch

Mission Statement: TAT capital partners is a sector focused transatlantic venture firm investing in early stage and established companies in U.S. and Europe.
Geographic Preference: Worldwide, United States, West Coast
Fund Size: $100 million
Average Investment: $1 million
Investment Criteria: Early Stage, Expansions, Seed
Industry Group Preference: Biotechnology, Communications, Electronic Technology, Manufacturing, Medical
Portfolio Companies: Actano Ltd, Applied Spectral Imaging, Applied Sensor AB, Colibrys Ltd, Diamedica Ltd, EndoArt Ltd, Inovise Medical Inc, Medizinaltechnik Ltd, Media-Streams.Com, Nextek Inc, nLine Systems Corp, Sunlight Ltd, Unitive, Vertis Neuroscience Inc, Xemics Ltd

Other Locations:
  Pletterjiweg Oost 1
  Ara Hill Top Building
  PO Box 6085
  Curacao
  Netherlands
  Phone: 599-97323200 Fax: 599-9723232

Key Executives:
  Dr. Thomas Egolf, Managing Director, Partner
  e-mail: mputney@tat.ch
  Mark Putney, Partner
  e-mail: tegolf@tat.ch
  Education: PhD Chemistry, MBA, University of Zurich
  Background: Managing Director, Cellpack; Chairman/CEO, Zevatech
  Johan Ekman, Partner
  e-mail: jekman@tat.ch
  Education: Masters Engineering Physics, Chalmers University of Technology; Masters Electrical Engineering, Swiss Federal Institute; Graduated, Business Information, IBO
  Background: Management, Erni & Company AG; Consultant, Datex; Invent Management AB;
  Rolf Haegler, Managing Director/Partner
  e-mail: rhaegler@tat.ch
  Background: Head of Sales, Ruegge Medical AG; Co-Owner/Managing Director, Schiller Ltd

3163 TECH TOUR
Place Flagey 7/7
Brussels 1050
Belgium

Phone: 32-26446580 Fax: 32-26446581
e-mail: info@e-unlimited.com
web: www.e-unlimited.com

Mission Statement: Profiles Europe's best technology companies through research, events and consulting.
Geographic Preference: Belgium
Fund Size: $200 Million
Founded: 1998

Key Executives:
  Piet Serrure, Chairman
  William Stevens, Chief Executive Officer

Venture Capital & Private Equity Firms / International Firms

3164 TECHNOLOGY PARK MALAYSIA CORPORATION SDN BHD
Level 5, Enterprise 4
Lebuhraya Puchong
Sg Besi
Kuala Lumpur 57000
Malaysia

Phone: 60-389982020 Fax: 60-389982110
e-mail: info@tpm.com.my
web: www.tpm.com.my

Mission Statement: Actively seeking new investments.
Geographic Preference: Worldwide
Founded: 1996
Investment Criteria: Various Stages
Industry Group Preference: Engineering, Biotechnology, Marketing, Communications, Property Management, Information Technology, Publishing
Portfolio Companies: Novozymes Malaysia Sdn Bhd, CCM Pharma Sdn Bhd, TT dotCom Sdn Bhd, Momentum Technologies Sdn Bhd, BERNAMA Systems And Solutions Advisor Sdn Bhd, MyStudyWeb Sdn Bhd, Intralink Concept Sdn Bhd, Datascan Berhad, Pilot Multimedia (M) Sdn Bhd
Key Executives:
  YBhg Dato' Hj. Mohd Azman Hj. Shahidin, President and Chief Executive Officer
  YB Dato' Nasarudin Hashim, Chairman

3165 TECNET
Niederosterreichring 2
Haus B
St. Polten 3100
Austria

Phone: 43-2742900019300 Fax: 43-2742900019319
web: www.tecnet.co.at

Mission Statement: Tecnet equity is a very experienced and open-minded contact for high technology firms in Lower Austria. Highly skilled in the fields of technology, and capital, engineering and business administration, our team provides a wide array of services for technology companies in Lower Austria. tecnet equity supports projects as they develop from innovative ideas to economically successful business ventures. tecnet's activities have created a strong economic stimulus for Lower Austria as a business location for technology companies.
Geographic Preference: Lower Austria
Fund Size: 38.3 million Euro
Average Investment: 300,000 - 3 million Euro
Investment Criteria: Seed-Stage, Startup, Early-Stage, Expansion Stage
Industry Group Preference: Technology
Portfolio Companies: Anagnostics Bioanalysis, Indoo.rs, Kinamu Business Solutions, NxtControl, SeaLife Pharma, Sipwise, Visocon, Wikitude
Key Executives:
  Georg Bartmann, Chairman

3166 TEKINVEST KK
3-17-14 Higashi 7F
Shibuya-ku
Tokyo 150-0011
Japan

Phone: 81-354669222
e-mail: info@tekinvest.com

Mission Statement: Actively seeking new investments.
Geographic Preference: Tokyo, North America
Fund Size: $10 Million
Founded: 1990
Investment Criteria: Direct Representation Service, Restructuring, Negotiating, Fundraising
Industry Group Preference: Information Technology, Banking, Distribution
Portfolio Companies: Mixx Entertainment Inc, Watchfire, XaQti Corporation, Vitesse Semiconductor Corporation
Key Executives:
  Ray Klein, President
  Education: Fluent speaker of English and a native speaker of Japanese. He graduated with a degree in Management and Economy from Hosei University
  Background: General Manager, OEM and channel management strategy
  Masahiro Kano, Executive Director

3167 TEKNOINVEST MANAGEMENT
Stranden 1A
Oslo 250
Norway

Phone: 47-22979000 Fax: 47-22979001

Mission Statement: Provides investors with attractive venture capital returns by assisting outstanding people building excellent companies based on innovative technologies.
Geographic Preference: Scandinavia, USA
Fund Size: $70 Million
Founded: 1984
Average Investment: NOK 5-50 million
Minimum Investment: $100,000
Investment Criteria: Seed, Start-up, First Stage, Second Stage
Industry Group Preference: Information Technology, Communications, Life Sciences, Medical & Health Related, Electronic Technology
Portfolio Companies: Affitech, AKVASmart, Angiogenix, BioForm
Key Executives:
  Rune Dybesland, Chief Financial Officer Oslo - Norway
  Education: M.Sc. degree in Computer Engineering(Norwegian Institute of Technology), MBA from INSEAD
  Background: McKinsey & Co, Scandinavian companies, R&D strategy
  Dr. Steinar J. Engelsen, Partner
  Education: M.Sc. degree in Control Engineering from The Norwegian Institute of Technology
  Background: Tandberg AS, AT Kearney, Norcontrol, The Norwegian Venture Capital Association, (EVCA),
  Directorships: Partner Oslo - Norway
  Andreas Mollatt, Partner
  Education: M.Sc. degree in Economics and Business Administration,
  Background: Amersham, Strategic Planning and Development, Thyssen Industrie AG,

3168 TELECOM VENTURE GROUP LIMITED
Unit A, 8th Floor, World Trust Tower
50 Stanley Street
Suite 4903
Central
Hong Kong

Phone: 852-21472080 Fax: 852-21473320

Mission Statement: International private equity firm that originates and structures transactions, and acts as a principal investor in companies involved in the Communications, Media, and Technology industries.
Geographic Preference: Asia Pacific
Fund Size: $600 Million
Industry Group Preference: Communications, Media, Technology
Portfolio Companies: Harbour Networks, Hanaro Telecom, PowerTel, Japan Telecom, Saehan Enertech, Neighborhood Cable, Request Broadband, Initech, 90East, SpeedCast, TransACT, inter-touch, Haansoft, Suntel, Usha Martin, BPL Communications, WorldxChange, PowerTel, Spectrum Network Systems, BayanT

Key Executives:
  Varun Bery, Managing Director & Co-Founder
  e-mail: contact@tvglp.com
  Education: Yale University Bachelor of Arts, summa cum laude, Harvard Business School MBA
  Background: AIFAL, Hanaro Telecom Inc, Newbridge Capital Korean Ltd.
  Directorships: Co-Founder
  John Troy, Managing Director & Co-Founder

3169 TELEFONICA VENTURES
20 Air Street
London W1B 5DN
United Kingdom

web: www.telefonica.com

Mission Statement: With offices in London, Silicon Valley and Madrid, Telefónica Ventures aims to maximise the VC portfolio value within the Telefonica Group, enhance Telefónica's relationship with start-ups and identify tomorrow's opportunities.
Geographic Preference: Europe, United States, Israel
Investment Criteria: Early-Stage, Mid-Stage, Late-Stage
Industry Group Preference: Technology, Communications, Digital Media & Marketing, Financial Services, Advertising, Cloud Computing, Healthcare, Security
Portfolio Companies: Amobee, Assia, Kit Digital, Eventful, Quantenna, Joyent, Boku

Other Locations:
  200 Evelyn Avenue
  Suite 120
  Mountain View, CA 94041

  Avenida das Nacoes Unidas 12901
  Torre Norte, 36th Floor
  Sao Paulo 04578-000 SP
  Brazil

  Rua Martiniano de Carvalho, 851
  Sao Paulo 01321-001 SP
  Brazil

  Distrito Telefonica
  Ronda de la Comunicadcion s/n
  Madrid 28050
  Spain

  Hadidhar 17
  Raanana
  Tel Aviv
  Israel

Key Executives:
  Matthew Key, Chief Executive Officer
  Education: Birmingham University
  Background: Chairman & CEO, Telefonica Europe; CEO O2 UK

3170 TENGELMANN VENTURES
Wissollstrasse 5-43
Mulheim an der Ruhr 45478
Germany

Phone: 49-0-208-5830 Fax: 49-0-208-583-2148
web: www.tev.de

Mission Statement: Since 2009, the Tengelmann Group's e-commerce strategy has involved investing in fast-growing, innovative e-commerce and internet companies. Indeed, since late 2009 Tengelmann-Ventures GmbH, a 100% subsidiary of the Tegelmann Group, has acquired shares in young, dynamic companies under the motto 'Funding your ideas'. Today, the company is already among the most important start-up companies in Germany. The focus of these investments is on e-commerce and social commerce concepts, market places, as well as on internet and web 2.0 technologies. Moreover, Tengelmann-Ventures GmbH not only offers financing expertise for start-ups, but also and management know-how and a useful infrastructure.
Founded: 2009
Investment Criteria: Seed-Stage, Early-Stage
Industry Group Preference: E-Commerce & Manufacturing, Social Media, Internet
Portfolio Companies: Baby-Mart.de, Brands4Friends, Canimix, Coffee Circle, Dafiti, Deal United, Delivery Hero, EKomi, Fab Furnish, High-Tech Grunderfonds, HitFox, Jumia, Lamoda, Lazada, Lieferheld, Linio, Mac IT Solutions, Mebelorama, Neonga, Olivenoel, Otto Gourmet, Selektessen, Stylight, Sum Up, Supreme, The Iconic, Trademob, Vinogusta, Zalando, Zalora, Zando, Zanui, Zitra

3171 TEUZA MANAGEMENT & DEVELOPMENT LTD
PO Box 25266
Haifa 31250
Israel

Phone: 972-48728788 Fax: 972-48729393
web: www.teuzafund.com

Mission Statement: To manage venture capital and to invest venture capital in Israel and abroad and also co-invest with the funds managed by it.
Geographic Preference: Israel
Fund Size: $300 Million
Founded: 1992
Average Investment: $500,000 -$4 million
Minimum Investment: $500,000
Investment Criteria: Start-up, Second Stage, Early Stage
Industry Group Preference: Telecommunications, Internet Technology, Biotechnology, Healthcare, Semiconductors, Software
Portfolio Companies: Botlex, Celtronix, Diagnostic Technology, Foxborn NMR, NESS, Nova, Oramir, Sagantea

Key Executives:
  Avi Kerbs, Chief Executive Officer
  Prof. Moshe Arens, Chairman

3172 TFG CAPITAL AG
Mainstra, 16
Marl 45768
Germany

Phone: 49-236597800 Fax: 49-236-5978033

Mission Statement: Actively seeking new investments.
Geographic Preference: Germany
Fund Size: $173 Million
Founded: 1994
Investment Criteria: Innovation, Management, IPO, Trade Sale
Industry Group Preference: Software, Biotechnology, Electronic Technology, Technology
Portfolio Companies: Eclerot and Ziegler AG, Oar AG, Power Automation AG, Viction AG

Key Executives:
  Detlef Geldmacher, Investment Manager
  Education: Banking background and is a business management graduate
  Background: Manager of a financial research institute
  Mechthild Obländer, Office Manager
  Background: Commercial employee in TFG

3173 THE ABRAAJ GROUP
1 Grafton Street
Sureste de Multiplaza Edificio
London W1S 4FE
United Kingdom

Phone: 44-02035401500 Fax: 44-02035401501

Mission Statement: The Abraaj Capital Group is a leading private equity manager investing in global growth markets. Founded in 2002 by Arif Naqvi, the group has raised over $8 billion and distributed $3.5 billion to investors. Employing over 300 people, the group has 33 offices spread across 7 regional hubs in Bogota, Dubai, Istanbul, London, Mumbai, Nairobi and Singapore.

Geographic Preference: Panama, Costa Rica, Nicaragua, Guatemala
Fund Size: $7.5 Billion
Average Investment: $10 Million - $100 Million
Industry Group Preference: Technology, Healthcare, Education, Community Engagement
Portfolio Companies: Viking, Saham Finances, Kuwait Energy, Network International, Karachi Electric Supply Company, Mediaquest, Man Infraconstruction, Ramky Infrastructure, ECI Engineering & Construction, Numarine
Other Locations:
   510 Madison Avenue
   Sureste de Multiplaza Edificio
   New York, NY
   Phone: 10022 **Fax:** 506 2015033

Key Executives:
   Arif Naqvi, Group Chief Executive
   Education: London School of Economics
   Background: Arthur Andersen, American Express Bank, Olayan Group, Cupola Group
   Ahmed Badreldin, Regional Managing Partner
   Education: BA, Political Science, California at Berkeley; MBA, Golden Gate University
   Background: Bank of America; Provident Group Ltd
   Ashish Dave, Partner
   Education: MA, Economics & Industrial Engineering, Texas Tech University
   Background: Privatization Manager, El Salvador Government; Finance Senior Consultant, KPMG Consulting
   Hanjaya Limanto, Partner
   Education: MBA, National University; BA, Universidad Autonoma CentroAmerica
   Background: Privatization Manager, El Salvador Government; Finance Senior Consultant, KPMG Consulting
   Sev Vettivetpillai, Partner
   Education: MB, Wharton School; MA, International Studies, University of Pennsylvania; BA, Economics, University of California at Berkeley
   Background: Provident Group Ltd

3174 THE MORPHEUS
India

            e-mail: neo@themorpheus.com
            web: www.themorpheus.com

Mission Statement: The Morpheus was started without any set agenda. It was simply for the joy of growing ourselves by working with smart young entrepreneurs & contributing to the eco-system. Today, The Morpheus is a 6 year old project that is made up of a strong community of 160+ entrepreneurs called the morpheusgang, who provide non-stop support to each other.

Geographic Preference: India
Founded: 2008
Investment Criteria: Startups
Portfolio Companies: CloudEngine, Dwll.in, MathHarbor, MotrPart, MyCodeSchool, Padhaaro, Pocket Science

Key Executives:
   Sameer Guglani
   Education: BE, Electrical Engineering, Thapar University
   Background: Co-Founder, Madhouse Media; Vice President, Corporate Strategy, Seventymm
   Nandini Hirianniah
   Education: MS, Communications, Bangalore University; Bachelors in Journalism, Mount Carmel College, Bangalore
   Background: Co-Founder, Madhouse Media

   Sarvjeet Ahuja
   e-mail: sa@themorpheus.com
   Education: IIT Roorkee
   Background: Microsoft; HP; PPI; Times of India; Shell

3175 THOMPROPERTIES OY
Fredrikinkatu 51-53 B
Helsinki 00100
Finland

        Phone: 358-9681661 **Fax:** 358-968166205
        e-mail: Pekka.Soikkeli@thominvest.fi
        web: www.thominvest.fi

Mission Statement: Actively seeking new investments.
Geographic Preference: Finland
Fund Size: $30 Million
Founded: 1911
Average Investment: $1.2 Million
Minimum Investment: $0.6 Million
Investment Criteria: Equity, Expansion Capital
Industry Group Preference: Real Estate, Financial Services, Banking, Information Technology, Environment Products & Services

Key Executives:
   Pekka Soikkeli, Chief Executive Officer
   e-mail: juha.jouhki@thominvest.fi
   Mats Söderström, Chief Investment Officer

3176 THOMSON-CSF VENTURES
45 rue de Villiers
Neuilly-sur-Seine Cedex 92526
France

        Phone: 33-157778000 **Fax:** 33-144-889969
        web: www.thalesgroup.com

Mission Statement: Actively seeking new investments.
Geographic Preference: Europe, USA
Fund Size: $13 Million
Founded: 1968
Average Investment: $8.6 million
Minimum Investment: $500,000
Investment Criteria: Expansion, Turnaround, Buyin
Industry Group Preference: Communications, Computer Related, Software, Consumer Services, Components & IoT, Electronic Technology, Consumer Products

Key Executives:
   Jean-Bernard Lévy, Chairman and Chief Executive Officer
   Bruno Bézard, Managing Director

3177 THROUNARFELAG ISLANDS PLC
Sudurlandsbraut 22
Reykjavik IS - 00108
Iceland

        Phone: 354-568-8266 **Fax:** 354-568-0191
        e-mail: andri.tf@skyggnir.is

Mission Statement: Actively seeking new investments, specializing in high-technology industries

Geographic Preference: Europe, Iceland
Minimum Investment: EUR50,000
Investment Criteria: Expansion & Development, MBO, MBI, Turnaround & Restructing, Replacement, Bridge, Mezzanine
Industry Group Preference: Transportation, Communications, Computer Related, Computer Hardware & Software, Electronic Technology, Industrial Equipment, Information Technology, Medical & Health Related

Key Executives:
   David Gudmundsson, Investment Manager

Venture Capital & Private Equity Firms / International Firms

3178 TIANGUIS LIMITED
5 Edwardes Place
London W8 6LR
United Kingdom

Phone: 44-2076037788 Fax: 807-7625734
e-mail: info@tianguis-ltd.com
web: www.tianguis-ltd.com

Mission Statement: Focuses on developing companies in the chemical industry.
Geographic Preference: Global
Founded: 1985
Investment Criteria: Mid market buyout;Small buyout;Turnaround - restructuring
Industry Group Preference: Chemicals, Allied Process Industries
Portfolio Companies: Calpulli Inc, European Colour plc, Finnish Chemicals, Brunner Mond, Magadi Soda, Penrice Soda Products, EuroChlor, CEFIC

Key Executives:
Steve Smith, Chairman
e-mail: info@tianguis-ltd.com
Education: Case Institute of Technology Davidson College
Background: Europe Independent Director; Chairman of European Colour plc; Managing Director and Chief Executive Officer of Erikem Luxembourg SA & Finnish Chemicals Oy; Managing Director and Chief Executive Officer of the Australian based Penrice Group & the Brunner
Directorships: President Pochteca Corporation United States; Director Calpulli Inc (USA); member of the Society of the Chemical Industry (SCI) and the American Chemical Society (ACS); on the

3179 TLCOM CAPITAL
188 Hammersmith Road
London W6 7DJ
United Kingdom

Phone: 44-0-208-23770-70 Fax: 44-0-208-23770-79
e-mail: info@tlcom.co.uk
web: www.tlcom.co.uk

Mission Statement: TLcom is dedicated to the success of entrepreneurs and investors. Success in technology ventures is created by teams of exceptional people working inside and around a company, focused on delivering on an ambitious, market driven business vision. We look for entrepreneurs with the ability to identify an innovative solution to a relevant need, and the humility to recognize the need to align multiple contributions in order to achieve tangible results. TLcom works for the success of the entrepreneur by providing, in addition to finance, deep company building expertise based on the experience and breadth of skills within our team.
Geographic Preference: Europe, Israel, Sub-Saharan Africa
Fund Size: 200 million Euro
Founded: 1999
Industry Group Preference: Telecommunications, Media, Technology
Portfolio Companies: Axerra, Beintoo, Cognima, CommProve, Eblana Photonics, Iobox, IXI Mobile, Media Lano, Movirtu, Netscalibur Limited, Noos, Packetfront, Runcom, Sphera, TheBlogTgv, Topica, Upstream, Userfarm, Xtempus, Xypoint

Other Locations:
1st Floor, Chaka Place
Argwings Kodhek Road
Nairobi
Kenya
Phone: 254-731-955-922

Key Executives:
Maurizio Caio, Founder/Managing Partner
Education: Business Adminitration, Bocconi Unveristy & New York University; MBA, Stanford University
Background: Founding Partner, Bain & Company
Directorships: Movirtu, PacketFront, TheBlogTV, Medial Lario, Topica

3180 TMG CAPITAL PARTNERS
Rua Joaquim Floriano, 72, CJ 93
Sao Paulo, SP 04534-000
Brazil

Phone: 55-1130795055 Fax: 55-1140645056
e-mail: tmg_capital@tmg.com.br
web: www.tmg.com.br

Mission Statement: To increase the value of investee companies through the injection of capital, modern management practices and scale in order to attain international levels of performance.
Fund Size: $100 Million
Founded: 1997
Average Investment: $15 Million
Minimum Investment: $5 million
Investment Criteria: Consolidation and Expansion of Medium Sized Companies in Segments that are still Fragmented
Industry Group Preference: Healthcare, Education, Food & Beverage, Information Technology, Telecommunications, Media, Cosmetics
Portfolio Companies: Cade (Dental Care), Clidec, Conductor (Credit Card Processing), Multiacao (Call Center), Odontoprev, Softway, Unident

Key Executives:
Luiz Francisco Novelli Viana, President & CEO
Peter André Dias, Investment

3181 TMI
11F-1, No. 159, Sec.1
Keelung Rd., Xinyi Dist.
Taipei 11070
Taiwan

Phone: 888-2-2769-1698

Mission Statement: Founded in 2012, TMI is a Taiwan-based company that looks to make early stage investments and also to incubate promising entrepreneurs. We are looking for entrepreneurs who want to tackle a global market. Through our assembled network of seasoned professionals, serial entrepreneurs and institutional investors from across the globe, we can allow a start-up to "soft land" in any major market. We are eager to work with entrepreneurs/start-ups looking at the Mobile, Internet and eCommerce spaces.
Geographic Preference: Taiwain
Founded: 2012
Average Investment: $100,000 - $300,000
Investment Criteria: Early-Stage
Industry Group Preference: Mobile, Internet, E-Commerce & Manufacturing
Portfolio Companies: Eumakh, KPop Stage, Re.mu, Roam & Wander, Citiesocial, Driving Curve, Codementor, 4Free WiFi, Swivi, 886 Food, Puman, Pagineer

Key Executives:
Lucas Wang, Chief Executive Officer / Partner
e-mail: lucas.wange@tmi.vc
Education: BA, Finance, National Taiwan University in Taiwan; MBA, National Sun Yat-Sen University
Background: Partner, WI Harper; Investment Manager, Corporate Venture Department, Microelectronics Technology
Kevin Ho, Chief Investment Officer / Partner
e-mail: kevin.ho@tmi.vc
Education: MS, Opto-Electronics Science Research, National Central University; BS, Physics, Chung Yuan Christian University in Taiwan
Background: Vice President, ITIC; ITRI USA

Venture Capital & Private Equity Firms / International Firms

3182 TOKIO MARINE CAPITAL COMPANY LIMITED
Tokio Marine Nichido Building Shinkan 6F
1-2-1, Marunouchi
Chiyoda-ku
Tokyo 100-0005
Japan

Phone: 81-352233516 Fax: 81-352233547

Mission Statement: Actively seeking new investments through partnering with companies in all stages, including sustained growth, business restructuring, and succession.

Geographic Preference: Japan
Fund Size: 400 million yen
Founded: 1991
Investment Criteria: Established companies located or having core operation in Japan that exhibit stable future cash flows will be targeted. Seed stage/early stage
Industry Group Preference: Information Technology
Portfolio Companies: Xymax, Angel food Systems, Sportsplex Japan, Weathernews Inc, Vehicle Trasportation Service, Intellasset, Japan Medical Data Centre, Business Service Corporatiom, Wanbishi Archives, Sweet Garden, Benex

Key Executives:
Hideaki Fukazawa, President and Managing Partner
e-mail: sasaki@tmcap.co.jp
Koji Sasaki, General Partner

3183 TONG YANG VENTURE CAPITAL CORPORATION Tong Yang Cement Corporation
19/F., High-Living Bldg, 890-16 Daechi-Dong
Seoul 135-280
Korea

Phone: 82-25610056 Fax: 82-25619191
web: www.tyvc.co.kr

Mission Statement: Tong Yang, as the largest merchant bank of Korea, is devoting all its energies for development and globalization of Korean financial market.Its affiliate is Tong Yang Venture Capital for establishing a cohesive marketing system which is exclusive of Tong.

Geographic Preference: South Korea
Fund Size: $1.69 Billion
Founded: 1989
Average Investment: $1 Million
Minimum Investment: $0.5 Million
Investment Criteria: All Stages
Industry Group Preference: Information Technology, Biotechnology
Portfolio Companies: Tatron, M.S Solutions

Key Executives:
Jae Hyun Hyun, Chairman
SeungIk Jang, Chief Executive Officer

3184 TPA CORPORATE FINANCE CONSULTING GMBH Horwarth International
62-64 Praterstrasse
Vienna 1020
Austria

Phone: 43-1588350 Fax: 43-158835500
e-mail: webmail@tpa-horwath.com

Mission Statement: Actively seeking new investments.

Geographic Preference: Austria
Founded: 2000
Investment Criteria: small and medium-sized enterprises (SMEs), associations, foundations, and individuals.
Industry Group Preference: Biotechnology, Winegrowing & Agriculture, Waste & Recycling, Transportation, Trade, Real Estate, Non-profit & Public Authorities, Hotel, Tourism & Leisure, Manufacturing, Information Technology & Media, Banking, Insurance, Financial Services, Energy, Pharmaceuticals

Key Executives:
Klaus Bauer-Mitterlehner, Partner
e-mail: janeba-hirtl.emilie@tpawt.com
Helene Bovenkamp, Partner
e-mail: klaus.bauer-mitterlehner@tpa-horwath.com
Education: Economist

3185 TRANS COSMOS INCORPORATED
3-25-18, Shibuya
Shibuya-ku
Tokyo 150-8530
Japan

Phone: 81-343631111 Fax: 81-343630111
e-mail: pressroom@trans-cosmos.co.jp
web: www.trans-cosmos.co.jp

Mission Statement: Actively seeking new investments.

Geographic Preference: Japan
Founded: 1985
Investment Criteria: Expansion, Mezzanine
Industry Group Preference: Information Technology, Software, Manufacturing, Machinery, Transportation

Key Executives:
Hideaki Fukazawa, President
Koji Funatsu, Chairman & Chief Executive Officer

3186 TRANSATLANTIC CAPITAL LTD
17 Devonshire Street
Suite 3
London W1N 2EY
United Kingdom

Phone: 44-2074361216 Fax: 44-2074361226

Mission Statement: Actively seeking new investments.

Geographic Preference: North America, Western Europe
Investment Criteria: Startup, Early-Stage, Development, Expansion
Industry Group Preference: Biotechnology, Environmental Protection, Medical
Portfolio Companies: Alliance Medical Ltd, Cardinal Medical Ltd, Ethical Pharmaceuticals Ltd, Micromed Technology

3187 TRANSYLVANIA FINANCIAL INVESTMENT COMPANY
2 Nicolae Iorga Street
Brasov 2200
Romania

Phone: 40-0268413752 Fax: 40-0268473215
e-mail: marketing@transif.ro
web: www.transif.ro

Mission Statement: Actively seeking new investments, using the latest state-of-the-art technology.

Geographic Preference: Romania
Fund Size: $819 Billion
Founded: 1996
Investment Criteria: Early Stage
Industry Group Preference: Chemicals, Financial Services, Machinery, Agribusiness, Building Materials & Services, Food & Beverage, Transportation
Portfolio Companies: Ludus, Upruc Tap-Sdv SA, Upruc Ctr SA, Marchim SA, Marasesti, IT-Pac Romania SA, Nitramonia SA, Rompetrol Rafinare SA, Constanta, Antibiotice, IASI, Armax Gaz SA

Key Executives:
Floriean Firu, Member of the Supervisory Board
e-mail: ffiru@transif.ro
Education: Graduate, Economics, Doctor Economics
Background: Financial Management

Venture Capital & Private Equity Firms / International Firms

Ec. Mihai Fercala, PhD, President of the Executive Board/Chief Executive Officer
e-mail: ctraian@transif.ro
Education: Graduate, Economics, Chartered Evaluator
Background: Macroeconomic analysis, valuations and audit
Ec. Ion Mihaila, Vice President of the Executive Board / Deputy C.E.O.
e-mail: pioan@transif.ro
Education: Graduate, Economics, Chartered Accountant
Background: Valuation and financial audit reports
Ec. Iulian Stan, PhD., Vice President of the Executive Board / Deputy C.E.O.
e-mail: paura@transif.ro
Education: Graduate, information Technology
Background: Co-ordination, development and maintenance of information and communication systems

3188 TRIANGLE VENTURE CAPITAL GROUP
Talstrasse 27e
Bensheim-Auerback D-64614
Germany

Phone: 49-6251-800-830 Fax: 49-6251-800-839
e-mail: triangle@triangle-venture.com
web: www.triangle-venture.com

Mission Statement: For more than 16 years Triangle has been focusing on research spin-offs to create outstanding and highly innovative companies.

Geographic Preference: Europe
Industry Group Preference: Technology, Information Technology, Medical Devices, Clean Technology
Portfolio Companies: FG Microtek, iOpener Media, IPCentury, iPharro Media, Takwak

Key Executives:
Bernd Geiger, Managing General Partner/Founder
e-mail: b.geiger@triangle-venture.com
Education: PhD, Natural Science, University of Heidelberg

3189 TRIGENTA CAPITAL GmbH
Kreuzstraáe 34
Duesseldorf 40210
Germany

Phone: 49-211-86289-0 Fax: 49-211-86289-455

Geographic Preference: German-Speaking Europe
Fund Size: EUR 500 million
Founded: 1999
Minimum Investment: EUR 1 million
Investment Criteria: Invests small & medium-sized companies with annual sales volume of EUR 20-200 million, operatinal profitability and positive cash flows; Late-State Venture; Portfolio Transactions
Industry Group Preference: All Sectors Considered

Other Locations:
Markgrafenstrasse 33
Berlin 10117
Germany

Schiffgraben 13
Hanover 30159
Germany

Key Executives:
Sybille Lutje, Chief Financial Officer
Peter Folle, Managing Partner
Dr. Anthony Bunker, Partner

3190 TRIGINITA CAPITAL
Kreuzstraáe 34
Triginta Capital GmbH
Dusseldorf 40210
Germany

Phone: 49-211862890 Fax: 49-21186289455
e-mail: info@triginta-capital.com
web: www.triginta-capital.com

Mission Statement: Actively accompanying the portfolio.

Geographic Preference: Europe
Founded: 1983
Minimum Investment: EUR 0.2 million
Investment Criteria: Seed, Startup, Early-Stage
Industry Group Preference: Information Technology, Telecommunications, Environment Products & Services, Communications, Life Sciences, Advanced Materials, Microelectronics
Portfolio Companies: Lenscare AG, TITUS AG, X VERLEIH, Analyticon Discovery GmbH, ATTO-TEC GmbH, Capsulation NanoScience AG, Chiracon GmbH, GenPat77 Pharmacogenetics AG, Getemed AG Medizin- und Informationstechnik, NOXXON Pharma AG, SEPIAtec GmbH, Zellwerk GmbH

Other Locations:
Kreuzstrade 34
Triginita Capital GmbH
Dusseldorf 40210
Germany
Phone: 49-211-862890 Fax: 49-211-86289455

Key Executives:
Sybille Lutje, Chief Financial Officer
Peter Folle, Managing Partner
Dr. Anthony Bunker, Partner
Johannes Rabini, Managing Director
Crsten Just, Authorized Officer

3191 TRINITY VENTURE CAPITAL TVC
Holdings plc
Block 2A, Richview Office Park
Clonskeagh
Clonskeagh
Dublin 4
Ireland

Phone: 353-12057700 Fax: 353-12057701
e-mail: info@tvc.com
web: www.tvc.com

Mission Statement: Trinity Venture Capital provides equity capital for early stage and expanding private technology companies, particularly in Ireland.

Geographic Preference: Ireland
Fund Size: $195 Million
Founded: 1997
Average Investment: $4.8 Million
Minimum Investment: $1.2 Million
Investment Criteria: Early and Growth Stage Technology Companies
Industry Group Preference: Communications, Computer Related, Consumer Services, Electronic Technology, Industrial Services, Industrial Products, Computer Related, Software
Portfolio Companies: AePONA, APT, ChangingWorlds, CR2, Havok, Nova Science, Rococo Software, Valista

Venture Capital & Private Equity Firms / International Firms

3192 TRIVENTURES
6 Hahoshilm St
1st Floor
PO Box 12006
Herzliya 46722
Israel

Phone: 972-99721080
e-mail: info@triventures.net
web: www.triventures.net

Mission Statement: TriVentures brings together the best attributes of a venture fund and a device accelerator. We have a unique approach to venture investing. We leverage our first hand knowledge and an international blend of clinical, technical and strategic expertise to successfully identify, invent and integrate new medical technologies. Our partners have years of accumulative experience in the fields of medicine, engineering, venture investing, founding start-ups, and working with strategic partners.

Geographic Preference: Israel
Investment Criteria: Early-Stage
Industry Group Preference: Medical Technology
Portfolio Companies: Angioslide, Apica, Assis Medical, Cardiva Medical, MST, Orthspace, Pop Medical, VasoStar

Key Executives:
Michal Geva, Co-Foudner/Managing Partner
Background: BgyPass, AST, GI View

3193 TROIKA CAPITAL PARTNERS
4, Romanov Perelok
Moscow 125009
Russia

Phone: 495-258-0500 Fax: 495-258-0547

Mission Statement: Troika Dialog is one of the oldest and largest investment houses in the CIS. Throughout our 20-year history, we have consistently demonstrated market leadership in our core lines of business: capital markets, investment banking, asset management, alternative investments, and personal investments and finance. We are an integrated securities firm that aims to bring the best global solutions and world-class service to clients.

Founded: 1991
Industry Group Preference: High Technology, Information Technology, Internet, Alternative Energy, Clean Technology, New Materials, Electronics

Key Executives:
Peter Derby, Partner

3194 TSING CAPITAL
Unit B23-B, BUP
No.10 Jiuxianqiao RD
Beijing 100084
China

Phone: 86-1056815700 Fax: 86-1056815788
e-mail: info@tsingcapital.com
web: www.tsingcapital.com

Mission Statement: Established in 2001, Tsing Capital is the pioneering and leading cleantech venture capital firm in China. Through its China Environment Fund and Yiyun Cleantech Fund series, Tsing Capital works intimately with its portfolio companies across China in areas of renewable energy, energy efficiency, environmental protection, new materials, sustainable transportation, smart grids, sustainable agriculture and cleaner production.

Founded: 2001
Industry Group Preference: Clean Technology, Renewable Energy, Energy Efficiency, Environment, Transportation, Agriculture
Portfolio Companies: Enevate, CCTM, CPCEP, Polyvera, Jinfengyuan, Golsun, Convertergy, Miartech, EEMCO, Anpute, Baichuan, Hybolic, Renle, BBS, InvenLux, Qinyuan, Tonys Farm, EcoMade, Hong Bang, Haocen, Devotion New Energy, Sunpreme, Atieva, BGB, Neo-Neon, Nobao, SureAuto, Fengguang Bio-Fan, Sound Fuhua, Longmen, Top Gain, Net Power, CHC, ET Solar, China Sunergy, TGBS, Haiyuan Group, LDK, Giant Hemu, ESG, PowerU, Dong Jiang

Other Locations:
B2102, Dawning Center
500 Hongbaoshi Road
Shanghai 201103
China
Phone: 86-2160907180 Fax: 86-2160907181

Unit 2301, 23/F
New World Tower 1
16-18 Queen's Road Central
Central
Hong Kong
Phone: 852-36283859 Fax: 852-36283854

Key Executives:
Don Ye, Founding Managing Partner

3195 TTP VENTURES
Melbourn Science Park
Melbourn
Hertfordshire SG8 6EE
United Kingdom

Phone: 44-1763-262626 Fax: 44-1763-262265
web: www.ttpventures.com

Mission Statement: TTP Ventures is a member of TTP Group, a leading technology development and services company. Through our investment and incubation activities we have supported over 75 companies.

Fund Size: £34 million
Investment Criteria: Early-Stage
Industry Group Preference: Technology
Portfolio Companies: Alphamosaic, Argenta Discovery, Azuro, Cambridge Semiconductor, Element 14, Ocuity, Oxford Diffraction, Pulmagen Therapeutics, TeraView, ZBD

3196 TVM CAPITAL
Ottostrabe 4
Munich 80333
Germany

Phone: 49 (89) 998 992-0
web: www.tvm-capital.com

Mission Statement: Particularly focuses on Trans-Atlantic opportunities where detailed understanding of the private equity markets in both Europe and the United States provides investors with added flexibility and value.

Geographic Preference: North America, Europe
Fund Size: Funds Raised Under Management: $1 billion
Founded: 1983
Average Investment: $10 million
Minimum Investment: $500,000
Industry Group Preference: Information Technology, Life Sciences, Communications, Healthcare
Portfolio Companies: Aspireo Pharmaceuticals, Wilex AG, Albireo, Altor BioScience, Anchor Therapeutics, Argos Therapeutics, Biovertis, Bluebird Bio, Cerenis Therapeutics, Concert Pharmaceuticals, DIREVO Industrial Biotechnology, Enanta Pharmaceuticals, Evotec, FAAH Pharma, F-Star, GLWL Research, Horizon Pharma, Invendo Medical, Lxchelsis, Kaneq Bioscience, MediGene, Newron Pharmaceuticals, NOXXON Pharma, PRCL Research, Precision Therapeutics, Pridenta, Probiodrug, Proteon Therapeutics, Rapid Micro Biosystems, SelectX Pharmaceuticals, Spepharm Holding, Bourn Hall International, Cambridge Medical & Rehabilitation Center, Manzil Health Care Services, ProVita International Medical Center

Venture Capital & Private Equity Firms / International Firms

Other Locations:
TVM Capital GmbH
Maximillanstr, 35, Entrance C
Munich D-80539
Germany
Phone: 49-89-998-992-0

TVM Capital MENA Ltd.
DIFC Gate Village
Building 4, PO Box 113355
Dubai
United Arab Emirates

Key Executives:
Helmut Schühsler, Managing Partner
Education: University of Vienna
Background: Investment Manager, Horizonte Venture Management
Directorships: SelectX Pharmaceuticals
Alexandra Goll, PhD, General Partner
Education: Freie Universitat Berlin; Phillips Universitat
Background: Roche Ltd
Directorships: Albireo; Biovertis AG; Cerenis Therapeutics
Hubert Birner, General Partner
Education: MBA, Harvard Business School; Ludwig-Maximilians University
Background: Head of Business Development, AstraZeneca; Consultant, McKinsey & Company's Healthcare and Pharmaceutical; Assistant Professor, Ludwig-Maximilians University
Directorships: Argos Therapeutics, Proteon Therapeutics, SpePharm Holding BV

3197 UCA UNTERNEHMER CONSULT AG
29 Stefan George Ring
Munich 81929
Germany
Phone: 49-899931940 **Fax:** 49-8999319444
e-mail: info@uca.de
web: www.uca.de

Mission Statement: U.C.A. provides equity capital to innovative and fast-growing companies while endeavouring to be more than just a money-lender.
Geographic Preference: Austria, France, Germany, Italy, Switzerland, United Kingdom
Founded: 1998
Investment Criteria: Small and mid-sized companies
Industry Group Preference: All Sectors Considered, Communications, Computer Related, Electronic Technology, Healthcare, Tourism, Biotechnology
Portfolio Companies: DeTeBe AG, aovo Touristik AG, MedLEARNING AG, My Blog Media GmbH, Sportnex GmbH

3198 UDD VENTURES
Av Las Condees 11287
3rd Floor Tower
Santiago
Chile
Phone: 56-223279266

Mission Statement: Promotes innovative ventures in early stages of development, through the continuous support of the entrepreneur, providing expertise, support tools, support, advice and links to relevant networks to create value, so that each project materialize his idea so successful. Our aspiration is to become the benchmark for value creation and support for enterprises generated in Chile, standing out for innovative businesses enhance high-impact social and economic development of the country.
Geographic Preference: Chile
Founded: 2010
Industry Group Preference: Environment, Healthcare

Key Executives:
Federico Valdes
Education: Civil Engineering, University of Chile; MS, Management, Stanford University

3199 UNILAZER VENTURES
75, Dr. Annie Besant Road
Nishuvi, 3rd Floor
Worli
Mumbai 400 018
India
Phone: 022-40983730 **Fax:** 022-40983722
e-mail: careers@unilazer.com

Mission Statement: Unilazer Ventures Ltd has morphed (originally called Unilazer Exports & Management Consultants Ltd) into a company spanning Treasure Operations on the one side, increasing Fixed Income and Debt Instruments to an active Equity Investor in the public markets space, to being active in the commodities market, to being a strategic investor in start ups, early stage and mature companies, to building an active business model in certain sectors.
Investment Criteria: Startup, Early-Stage
Portfolio Companies: Blume Ventures Fund, Himex Limited, INI Farms, Mera Career Guide, M.I.T.R.A, Oncontract.com, Valyoo Technologies

Key Executives:
Ronnie Screwvala, Founder/Advisor

3200 UNION BANK OF SWITZERLAND
45 Bahnhofstrasse
Zurich 8001
Switzerland
Phone: 41-44-234 11 11 **Fax:** 41-44-238 44 70
web: www.ubs.com

Mission Statement: Actively seeking new investments.
Geographic Preference: Switzerland, Europe, USA, Asia
Industry Group Preference: All Sectors Considered

Key Executives:
Marcel Ospel, Chairman
Stephan Haeringer, Executive Vice Chairman

3201 UNISON CAPITAL PARTNERS LP
The New Otani Garden Court 9F
4-1 Kioicho
Chiyoda-ku
Tokyo 102-0094
Japan
Phone: 81-335113901
web: www.unisoncap.com

Mission Statement: Our philosophy is to orchestrate all parties involved to work in unison to maximize corporate value.
Geographic Preference: Japan
Fund Size: 600 Billion Yen
Founded: 1998
Average Investment: $0.03 Billion
Minimum Investment: $0.02 Billion
Investment Criteria: Invests in Non-core or under-performing divisions or subsidiaries of large corporations
Industry Group Preference: Agriculture, Insurance, Real Estate, Media, Automotive, Retailing, Manufacturing
Portfolio Companies: Intelsat Holdings, ENOTECA, Minit Asia Pacific, Asahi Tec Corporation, Showa Yakuhin Kako, Nexcon, Dexerials

Key Executives:
John Ehara, Partner
Education: B.A. in Economics from Keio University and an M.B.A. from the Harvard Graduate School of Business Administration.

Venture Capital & Private Equity Firms / International Firms

Background: Director of Finance at NextCard and McKinsey and Goldman Sachs
Tatsuya Hayashi, Partner

3202 USHA MARTIN VENTURES LIMITED
2A Shakespeare Sarani
Mangal Kalash
Kolkata 700071
India

Phone: 91-3339800300 Fax: 91-3322829029
e-mail: contact@ushamartin.co.in
web: www.ushamartin.com

Mission Statement: Acts as a venture investor for expansion stage to consolidation stage equity financing.
Geographic Preference: India
Founded: 1961
Investment Criteria: expansion stage to consolidation stage
Industry Group Preference: Information Technology, Telecommunications, E-Commerce & Manufacturing, Media, Biotechnology
Key Executives:
   Prashant Jhawar, Chairman
   A. K. Somani, Chief Financial Officer and Company Secretary

3203 VAEKSTFONDEN
104A Stramdveaen
Hellerup 2900
Denmark

Phone: 45-35298600
e-mail: vf@vf.dk
web: www.vf.dk

Mission Statement: We provide funding to fast-growing Danish companies and act as a fund-of-funds investor in the private equity sector in the Nordic region.
Geographic Preference: Denmark
Fund Size: $360 Million
Founded: 1992
Average Investment: $8.05 Million
Minimum Investment: $16,000
Investment Criteria: Invests in Small- and medium-size businesses
Industry Group Preference: Biotechnology, Communications, Computer Related, Industrial Equipment, High Technology, Medical & Health Related, Pollution
Portfolio Companies: Abeo, Adenium Biotech, Advalight, Agilic, Akustikken, AnyBody Technology, API Maintenance Systems, Aporta Digital, Asetek, Autolog Systems, Bennedikthegaard, Bennedsgaard, Billetto, Blackwood Seven, Blueprinter, Borg & Bigum, Brdr. Sommer, Capevo, Carta Finana, CBIT, Celco, Cetrea, Christiansopigens Sild, CodeSealer, Cost:bart, CrossEyes, Dao Aviation, Deli'en, Deskwolf, DITA Exchange, Drivr, EffiMat, Ellipse, Energy Cool, ExpreS2ion Biotechnologies, Falby Design, Falcon Social, FBC Device, Fiberline, Hanegal, HeSaLight, Hjem-IS, Holmris, Iconfinder, ipvision, Jens Jorgensen, Jydsk Aluminum Industrial, Jydsk Planteservice, Jorn Ditlevsen, LeanEco, Leon Hansen Maskinfabrik, LogPoint, Lyngsaa, Merus Audio, Microlytic, Microshade, Milling Hotels, MT MembraTec, Multimac, Murermester Jon Rasmussen, Nanovi, Nocopo, Observe Medical, Oosterhof Dairy, Operator Systems, PF Group, Plast Team, Reapplix, Regal, RushFiles, Rodvig Kro & Badehotel, Sigma Estimates, Skansogaard, SmartShare, Sorbisense, Sticks'n'Sushi, Sumisura, SwipBox, Symphogen, Saelvigbugtens Camping, Tantaline, TeesuVac, Teklatech, Tier1Asset, Tresu, Trustpilot, UNO Danmark, Vivino, Volt, VoresVilla, watAgame, Water for Life, WorldTicket, Ostergard, Aavangs Fiskehus
Key Executives:
   Peter Bruun, Communications

3204 VALUE PARTNERS LIMITED
9th Floor, Nexxus Building
41 Connaught Road
Suite 3301
Central 89
Hong Kong

Phone: 852-28809623 Fax: 852-25648487
e-mail: vpl@vp.com.hk
web: www.valuepartners.com.hk

Mission Statement: Actively seeking new investments.
Geographic Preference: Greater China region
Founded: 1993
Investment Criteria: Bottom Up Stocks, Fund Investment Company
Industry Group Preference: Banking
Key Executives:
   Chean Cheng Hye, Chief Investment Officer & Chairman
   Background: Founder-Morgan Grenfell group in Hong Kong and financial journalist with The Asian Wall Street Journal and Far Eastern Economic Review,
   Directorships: Chairman
   So Chun Ki Louis, Deputy Chairman and Co-Chief Investment Officer
   Education: Bachelor's degree in finance from the University of British Columbia and is a CFA charterholder.
   Background: Director-Manulife Asset Management (Hong Kong) Limited

3205 VCN GROUP INCORPORATED
Kazusaya Bldg. 5F, 1-8-1, Ebisu Nishi
Shibuya-ku
Tokyo 150-0021
Japan

Phone: 81-0354571650 Fax: 81-0354571658
e-mail: info@vcn.co.jp
web: www.vcn.co.jp

Mission Statement: VCN assists spirited entrepreneurs in the Japanese market place.
Geographic Preference: Japan
Founded: 1996
Investment Criteria: Early stage
Key Executives:
   Hiroyuki Shibata, Representative Director
   e-mail: info@vcn.co.jp
   Education: Graduated from the Social Science Department, Waseda University
   Background: Joined JAFCO Co., Ltd. (formerly Japan Associated Finance Co., Ltd.) in April 1985 and was assigned to a post in the Investment Evaluation Division, Investment Evaluation Department.
   Hajime Sugiura, Director
   e-mail: info@vcn.co.jp
   Education: Graduated from the Chemistry Division, Department of Science and Engineering, Waseda University.
   Background: NIF Ventures Co., Ltd. (NIF) (formerly Nippon Investment & Finance Co., Ltd.), Office of Director - Pan-Asia Air Lines Co., Ltd.
   Nobuyuki Hata, Non-executive Director
   e-mail: info@vcn.co.jp
   Education: Obtained a master's degree in economics from Waseda University.
   Background: Nomura Research Institute, Ltd. in March 1974 and was assigned to a post in the Corporate Research Department.professor in the Economics Department, Kokugakuin University in April, and then a professor of the university's Economics Department in April 199

3206 VENCAP
King Charles House
Park End Street
Oxford OX1 1JD
United Kingdom

Phone: 44-1865799300 Fax: 44-1865799301
web: www.vencap.com

Mission Statement: Actively seeking new investments.

Geographic Preference: US, Europe, China and India
Fund Size: US$1.9 billion
Founded: 1987
Investment Criteria: All Stages

Key Executives:
Michelle Ashworth, Director of Fund Investments
e-mail: info@vencapintl.com
Education: B.Comm. from the University of Alberta and an MBA from Wharton
Background: Association of British Insurers as an economist and statistician
Tim Cruttenden, Chief Executive Officer
e-mail: info@vencapintl.com
Education: Chartered Accountant and a graduate of Cambridge University.
Background: Saatchi and Saatchi group
David Howells, Investment Manager
e-mail: info@vencapintl.com
Education: MBA with honours from the Anderson School at UCLA, a JD from UC Hastings College of Law, and a BA in Economics from UCLA.
Background: Executive Director in the Telecommunications Investment Banking Group at Bear, Stearns & Co

3207 VENISTA VENTURES
Erftstr. 19a
Cologne 50672
Germany

Phone: 49-0221933167700 Fax: 49-0221933167170
web: www.venista-ventures.com

Mission Statement: We are a Cologne, Germany-based mobile ventures group specializing in early-stage mobile entertainment and value products. We secure the seed-financing, technical expertise, marketing knowledge and international connectivity necessary to guide mobile media ideas from concept to market.

Geographic Preference: Germany
Investment Criteria: Early-Stage
Industry Group Preference: Communications, Marketing
Portfolio Companies: KissMyAds, Stylemarks, GTX Messaging, Spyke Media, Startupbootcamp, Secret Escapes, datapine, Need, Familonet, mjoy, Klash

Key Executives:
Olivier Wimmertoth, Owner
Christian Teichert, Owner

3208 VENTECH
47, Avenue de l'Opera
Paris 75002
France

Phone: 33-183798190 Fax: 33-183798200
e-mail: contact@ventechvc.com
web: www.ventech.fr

Mission Statement: Alongside the best entrepreneurs and managers, we fund ambitious companies seeking to create a major market break to generate quickly a leading position. Our industry expertise enables us to work closely with these projects in their product development and market creation.

Geographic Preference: Europe, China
Fund Size: 360 million Euro
Founded: 1998

Industry Group Preference: Information Technology, Digital Media & Marketing, Entertainment, Enterprise Software, Semiconductors, Infrastructure, Communications
Portfolio Companies: Adore Me, AnneLutfen.com, Altitude Telecom, Alapage.com, Arteris, AsGoodAsNew, Augure, Ateme, Ad Valem Technologies, Arkoon, Business & Decision, Blink, B-Process, Bonitasoft, Byecity.com, Believe, Calendra, Cyrano, Com6, Crocus Technology, Curse, Easou, Ekinops, Eyeka, Futureo, Genesys, Hassle.com, Internext, We Hostels, iBase, interCloud, Jimu Box, Jumei.com, K Mobile, Kai Yuan, Keopsys, Adikteev, myBlee, Musiwave, Meilleurtaux.com, Mamsy, Nineyu, Ogury, Orchestra, Oktogo, Picanova, Qarnot Computing, Qiandai.com, Racing-Live, SoJeans, Shopmium, Sinocampus, Secoo, Shenzhoufu, StickyADS.tv, TVSmiles, Trends for Friends Brands, Umanto, Virtools, Vestiaire Collective, Viadeo, Viva, Walkin, Withings, Wengo, Wise Media, Webedia, 21Diamonds, 3Guu.com, 51wan.com

Other Locations:
2140-05 Yintai Office Tower
Beijing Yintai Centre
No. 2 Jinaguomenwai Road, Chaoyang District
Beijing 100022
China
Phone: 86-10-8517-2122

Key Executives:
Alain Caffi, Founder/General Partner
Education: MS, University of Kansas
Background: Accor Group
Directorships: Omen, Webedia, Viadeo, Believe, Curse, Eyeka, WomenJournal

3209 VENTURE FUND ROTTERDAM BV Indofin Group
Westerkade 3
Rotterdam 3016 CL
Netherlands

Phone: 31-104144544 Fax: 31-104332879
e-mail: info@indofin.nl
web: www.indofin.nl

Mission Statement: Invests in strong, established, growing companies with excellent management, or in need of management support.

Geographic Preference: Europe, USA, Canada, Australia, Asia
Founded: 1968
Investment Criteria: Expansion and Development, MBO, Turnaround, Mezzanine, Bridge
Industry Group Preference: All Sectors Considered
Portfolio Companies: IHC Merwede Group, Technische Handelsmaatschappij Marchand-Andriessen N.V., HES Beheer, Net Display Systems, AND Automotive Navigation Data, Energia Zachod, Nordofin Resources, Vooruitgang Energie, DPW Van Stolk Holding, Mannesmann Plastics Machinery, Roosland

3210 VENTURE INVESTORS
Kremencova 17
Prague 1 110 00
Czech Republic

Phone: 420-224931600
e-mail: rm@vi.cz
web: www.ventureinvestors.cz

Mission Statement: Finds suitable solutions for the development of strong and growing companies in the Central and Eastern European region.

Geographic Preference: Europe, Czech Republic, Poland, Hungary, USA
Founded: 1999
Investment Criteria: Early-Stage, Expansion & Development Capital, Start-Up Capital, Buyout & Buyin

Venture Capital & Private Equity Firms / International Firms

Industry Group Preference: Communications, Computer Related, Biotechnology, Medical & Health Related, Consumer Services, Industrial Equipment, Financial Services, Real Estate, Insurance

Key Executives:
Michael Rostock, Founding Partner

3211 VENTUREAST
5B, Ramachandra Avenue, Seethammal
Colony, First Main Road, Alwarpet
Chennai 600 018
India

Phone: +91 44 2432 9864 **Fax:** +91 44 2432 9865
e-mail: info@ventureast.net
web: www.ventureast.net

Mission Statement: Ventures into new markets and provides cutting-edge ideas to help navigate the challenges of building a business related to India.
Geographic Preference: India
Investment Criteria: Seed Stage, Early Stage, Growth Stage
Industry Group Preference: Information Technology, Life Sciences, Healthcare, Clean Environment, Emerging Markets, Sectors & Technologies
Portfolio Companies: Atyati, Loyalty Rewardz, Sai Sudhir, Royalimages.in, Ad2pro, Goli, Bharat Light and Power (BLP), Central Parking Services, E2E Rail, Richcore, eYantra, Orca Systems, Si2, Vysr, Little Eye Labs, OneBreath, SmartRx, Stylecraze, Seclore, Vortex, Inopen, Mobien Technologies, Crederity, Desicrew, Intelizon Energy, Rope, Reviews 42, Polygenta, Sresta, Bioserve, Onconova Therapeutics, Evolva, Sapala, Elbit, iMedX, Naturol, Neurosynaptics, Mardil Medical, Melior Discovery, Comprehensive Prosthetics & Orthotics, Ocean Sparkle, Gland Pharma, EPI, Moschip, Itero Biopharmaceuticals, Dodla Dairy, Vibromech, Four Soft, VKS Farms

Key Executives:
Sarath Naru, Managing Partner
Ramesh Alur, General Partner
Raghuveer Mendu, General Partner
Bobba Venkatadri, General Partner

3212 VERITAS VENTURE PARTNERS
2A Hamelacha St., 3rd Floor
Ra'anana 43661
Israel

Phone: 972-99561621 **Fax:** 972-737146734
e-mail: info@veritasvc.com
web: www.veritasvc.com

Mission Statement: Actively seeking new investments.
Geographic Preference: USA, Israel
Founded: 1990
Investment Criteria: Invest primarily in technology-based companies at the seed and very early stages of their lives
Industry Group Preference: Genetic Engineering, Medical & Health Related, Enterprise Services, Networking, Software, Communications
Portfolio Companies: Polycom, Nuance, Asankya, Rumcom, Sandvine, Cisco Systems, fring, Gilat Satellite Networks, Trivnet, ClickFox, Guardium, IBM, WebLayers, Lumenis, UltraSPECT, Escape Rescuse Systems, Siemens AG, Sandisc

3213 VERSOVENTURES
Mikonkatu 6
Helsinki 00100
Finland

Phone: 358-505890520
e-mail: info@versoventures.com
web: www.versoventures.com

Mission Statement: VersoVentures is a new finance sector company that has developed a unique model for corporate spin-offs. The model offers a financially attractive way for corporations to enable new jobs to be created from non-strategic activities. Founded by Anssi Kariola in 2012, VersoVentures is currently investing into spin-offs via the first Verso Spin-off Fund, with first investments targeted in November 2012.
Geographic Preference: Finland
Founded: 2012
Investment Criteria: Spin-Offs
Portfolio Companies: Boftel Oy, Cumulocity GmbH, Dedicated Network Partners Oy, CloudStreet Oy, Atrinet Ltd.

Key Executives:
Ansii Karlota, Managing Partner

3214 VERTEX VENTURE CAPITAL
1 HaShikma Street
PO Box 89
Savyon 56530
Israel

Phone: 972-37378888 **Fax:** 972-37378889
e-mail: contact@vertexvc.com
web: www.vertexvc.com

Mission Statement: Actively seeking new investments.
Geographic Preference: Israel, UK, USA, Singapore, Japan
Fund Size: $600 Million
Founded: 1997
Average Investment: $10 Million
Minimum Investment: $1 Million
Investment Criteria: Invests in Israeli and Israel-related high tech companies, with significant and sustainable competitive advantages
Industry Group Preference: Digital Media & Marketing, Fixed & Mobile Broadband, Enterprise IT & Infrastructure, Green Technology
Portfolio Companies: Actelis Argus Cyber Security, Asocs, Aternity, ColorChip, Correlsense, Cyber-Ark, DigiFlex, Heptagon, InnoPath, Leadspace, Mediaboost, MoreCom, MultiPhy, Neuralitic, Perfecto Mobile, Sidense, Solar Edge, Vigilance Networks

Key Executives:
Yoram Oron, Founder & Managing Partner
e-mail: contact@vertexvc.com
Education: Degree in Electrical Engineering from Columbia University, New York, MBA program at Babson College, Massachusetts.
Background: Philips Electronics, President and CEO of MoreCom Inc
Ehud Levy, Managing Partner
Orit Einstein, Controller
e-mail: contact@vertexvc.com
Education: MA, Economics and Business Administration; BA Economics and Mathematics, Tel Aviv University
Background: President & CEO, Aryt Industries, Co-Founder, Geotek Communications, Co-Founder, President & CEO, Reshef Technologies, Co-Founder & Chairman, Telegate Ltd.
David Heller, Managing Partner
e-mail: contact@vertexvc.com
Education: LLB, Hebrew University; LLM, Kyoto University
Background: Partner, Yossi Avraham & Company, Wakabayashi & Watanabe, VP, Israel International Fund
Emanuel Timor, Managing Partner
e-mail: contact@vertexvc.com
Education: BA, LLB, Tel Aviv University
Background: Muscal, Shimonov, Barnea
Merav Shemesh, Controller
e-mail: contact@vertexvc.com
Education: B.Sc.in Electrical Engineering from the Technion - Israel Institute of Technology, MBA, cum laude, from Tel Aviv University.
Background: Partner at Formula Ventures, Vice President and Chief Technology Officer of the DSP Group

Venture Capital & Private Equity Firms / International Firms

Ran Gartenberg, Managing Partner and CFO
e-mail: contact@vertexvc.com
Education: BA, Accounting & Economics, Tel Aviv University; MBA, New York University
Background: Business Development Manager, Israel Corporation, Supervising Auditor, Price Waterhouse Coopers

Paula Trostchansky, Office Administrator
e-mail: contact@vertexvc.com
Education: DEC, Commerce, Marianopolis College; BA, Political Science & International Relations, Hebrew University; MSc, Boston University
Background: Corporate Marketing & Communications, 3M

Iris Elkayam, Office Manager
e-mail: contact@vertexvc.com
Education: MBA from Tel-Aviv University, B.A in Economics and Management (cum laude) from the Technion - Israel Institute of Technology
Background: Investment banker in the Global Technology, Media and Telecom Group at JPMorgan Chase & Co

3215 VICKERS FINANCIAL GROUP
1 Maritime Square
#09-28 Harbourfront Centre
Singapore 0099253
Singapore

Phone: 65-6339-0338
web: www.vickersventure.com

Mission Statement: Vickers Capital Group is an investment house with offices in Shanghai and Singapore. The group manages 3 funds and proprietary capital. Founded in 2004 by Dr. Finian Tan, the Group seeks to create long term value for our investors by investing in and building a stable of great companies focused primarily on the Asia Pacific market.

Geographic Preference: Asia
Founded: 2004
Industry Group Preference: Technology, Media, Healthcare, Energy, Automotive, Education, Real Estate
Portfolio Companies: Sammumed, Jing-Jin Electric, CalUniversity, Asian Food Channel, UUCun, Tenfen, Matchmove, Sunfun (iPart), Lotaris, Mobinex, Cambridge, The Wellness Group, Spicy Horse, RTG Asia, M-Daq, Hillstone, LL Games, Roomorama, Cardvalue, Appletoon, Delivering Happiness Group/Daredu, Chinaway, Skyroam, Alo7, Lumina Looue, Affordable Luxury Network, Luminaire, Babeeta, Playpeli, Netpower, Vitamin Research, Benchmark

Key Executives:
   Finian Tan, Chairman
   Education: BSc, Engineering, University of Glasgow
   Background: Partner & Managing Director, Draper Fisher Jurvetson Eplanet

3216 VIKING VENTURE
Nedre Bakklandet 77
Trondheim 7014
Norway

web: www.vikingventure.no

Geographic Preference: Norway, Nordic Countries
Fund Size: $200 million
Founded: 2001
Investment Criteria: Early-Stage
Industry Group Preference: Electronics, Software, Oil & Gas, Materials Technology, Clean Technology
Portfolio Companies: Enhanced Drilling, Evatic, ExproSoft, Gas Secure, MemfoACT, Meta, poLight, READ, Room Sketcher, Safetel, Signicat, Ziebel, Zilift, PetroStreamz, 4subsea, Eco Online

Key Executives:
   Erik Hagen, Managing Partner
   47-920-22-430
   Education: MSc, Computer Science, NTH; MBA, INSEAD
   Background: Partner, Arthur Andersen; CEO, Schibsted Nett; Marketing Director, NetCom ASA; Consultant, McKinsey & Company

   Harald Jeremiassen, Partner
   47-932-58-570
   Education: MSc, Business & Administration, NHH; Owen Graduate School of Managment, Vanderbilt University

   Jostein Vlk, Partner
   47-922-22-392
   Education: MSc, Business & Administration, Norwegian School of Management
   Background: Business Manager, Lilleborg; Business Controller, Carlsberg Breweries;
   Directorships: Safetel ASA, InvivoSense ASA, Iqua Oy, MyVR Technologies AS, Cinevation AS

   Joar Welde, Partner
   47-982-06-930
   Education: BA, Business & Administration, Norwegian School of Management; MBA, University of Warwick
   Background: Project Manager, Ernst & Young; Consultant, DnB Eiendom
   Directorships: Aqualyng AS, Ziebel AS, Ecowat, Signicat AS

   Eivind Bergsmyr, Partner
   47-920-99-010
   Education: MSc, Electronics Engineering, Norwegian University of Technology & Science; Norwegian School of Management
   Background: CEO, Nacre AS; Siemens Telecom; Siemens Electrical Heating

3217 VINACAPITAL GROUP
17th Floor, Sun Wah Tower
115 Nguyen Hue, Dist. 1
Ho Chi Minh City
Vietnam

Phone: 84-88219930 Fax: 84-88219931
web: www.vinacapital.com

Mission Statement: Invests in all stages of business in the Vietnamese market place.

Geographic Preference: Vietnam, China, Cambodia, Laos
Fund Size: $1.6 Billion
Founded: 2003
Investment Criteria: Expansion capital; Mid-Stage
Industry Group Preference: Real Estate, Insurance, Beverages, Telecommunications, Media, Materials Technology, Infrastructure

Key Executives:
   Dr. Jonathan Choi, Chairman
   e-mail: info@vinacapital.com
   Education: Holds a joint Masters degree in Engineering, Economics and Management from Oxford University
   Background: Engagement Manager, McKinsey & Co; Founder, two Greenfield companies, China; Restructuring of state-owned enterprise, Pritzker family

   Don Lam, CEO
   e-mail: info@vinacapital.com
   Education: BA Commerce and Political Science, University of Toronto
   Background: Partner-in-Charge, PricewaterhouseCoopers; Deutsche Bank; Coopers & Lybrand

3218 VINCERA CAPITAL
17th Floor
105 Tun-Hwa S Road
Sec.2
Taipei, Taiwan 106
China

Phone: 886-227540168 Fax: 886-227540169
web: www.vinceracapital.com

989

Venture Capital & Private Equity Firms / International Firms

Mission Statement: A top tier private equity firm that sponsors growth capital in Greater China.
Geographic Preference: China
Fund Size: $230 Million
Founded: 1997
Average Investment: $2 - $20 million
Investment Criteria: Early, Expansion & Mezzanine
Industry Group Preference: Consumer Products, Industrial, Technology
Portfolio Companies: Advanced Ceramic X Corp, Alcor Micro, Alltop Tech, Amigo Technology, Ampire Co, Arima Computer Corp., Aten International, Celxpert Energy Corp., Chip Hope Co., Cincon Electronics, Compal Communications, Divio, Enable Semiconductor, Entergy Industrial, Etronic, Epox Computer, Firich Enterprises, Formosa Epitaxy, Galaxy Far East, Genaissance Pharmaceuticals, Global Mixed-Mode Technology, Himax Technologies, Hold Jinn Electronics, Honghua Group Limited, Hsin Yung Chien Co., IC Media, Jarlltyec Co., KG Telecom, Largan Precision, Maxteck Technology, NAFACO, Nanya Technology, Palmax, Plotech, Polytronics, Rapidstream, Silicon Touch Technology, Uniscape, Verplex Systems, Worldwide Semicondctor, Xintec

Key Executives:
   John S.C.Tang, Chairman
   e-mail: sc.tang@vinceracapital.com
   Education: MS, PhD, Economics, Takushoku University; BS, Accounting, Soochow University
   Background: Chairman, Kuo Hua Life Insurance; President, Cathay Life Insurance
   Richard S. H. Chen, Chairman & CEO
   e-mail: richard.chen@vinceracapital.com
   Education: MA, International Studies, University of Pennsylvania; MBA, Wharton School
   Background: EVP, GFC Ltd; Huang & Chen Financial Services; Global Shearson Financial Services; Proctor & Gamble
   Dr In-Chyuan Ho, Vice Chairman & CTO
   e-mail: ic.ho@vinceracapital.com
   Education: PhD, Electrical Engineering, National Cheng Kung University
   Background: China Steel Corp; Ascentek Venture Capital Corp.; Vice President, Gains Investment Corp.
   Benjamin MS Cheng, CIO
   Education: BS, Control Engineering, National Chiao Tung University
   Background: Investment Manager, Gains Investment Corp.; ABB Taiwan

3219 VINTAGE INVESTMENT PARTNERS
12 Abba Eban Avenue
Ackerstein Towers, Bldg D, 10th Floor
Herzilyah Pituach 46120
Israel

Phone: 972-99548464 **Fax:** 972-99541012

Mission Statement: With over $500 million under management, Vintage Investment Partners is the only combined secondary, co-invest and fund of funds manager focused on Israel. The management team combined has over 100 years experience with Israeli companies in both the private and public equity markets as well as long-standing relationships with top-tier Israeli funds and foreign investors.
Geographic Preference: Israel, Europe
Fund Size: $500 million
Key Executives:
   Alan Feld, Founder/Managing Partner
   Education: BA, Commerce & Finance, University of Toronto; MBA, York University
   Background: General Partner, Israel Seed Partners, Vertex Ventures, Founding Chairman, StartUp Jerusalem

3220 VIOLA FINTECH
12 Abba Eban Avenue
Ackerstein Towers Bldg. D
Herzeliya 47625
Israel

Phone: 972 9 9720 400 **Fax:** 972 9 9720 401
e-mail: info@viola-group.com
web: www.viola-group.com

Mission Statement: Viola FinTech is a cross-stage venture fund that invests in financial institutions and startup projects focused on modernizing financial markets.
Geographic Preference: Israel, Europe, North America
Fund Size: $100 million
Founded: 2017
Average Investment: $3M-$7M
Investment Criteria: Startups
Industry Group Preference: Technology, Wealth & Asset Management, Finance, Commercial Real Estate, Insurance
Key Executives:
   Daniel Tsiddon, Founder/General Partner
   e-mail: danielt@violafintech.com
   Background: Deputy CEO, Bank Leumi; Chairman, Leumi Partners; Professor, Economics, Berglas School, Tel Aviv University
   Tomer Michaeli, General Partner
   e-mail: tomerm@violafintech.com
   Education: M.Eng, Biomedical Engineering, Israel's Institute of Technology; BSc, Physics, Mathematics & Chemistry, Hebrew University, Jerusalem; MBA, INSEAD
   Background: Co-Founder/Chief Operating Officer, FUNDBOX; Principal, Viola Ventures; Israeli Defense Forces
   Itzik Avidor, Partner
   e-mail: itzika@viola-group.com
   Education: BA, Accounding & Economics, MBA, Tel Aviv University
   Background: Senior Audit Manager, Oshap & Technomatix; CFO, Viola Group;

3221 VIOLA VENTURES
12 Abba Eban Avenue
Ackerstein Towers, Building D
Hertzliya 4672530
Israel

Phone: 972 9 9720 400 **Fax:** 972 9 9720 401
e-mail: info@viola-group.com
web: www.viola-group.com

Mission Statement: A venture capital firm whose mission is to invest in early stage Israeli tech companies.
Geographic Preference: Israel
Fund Size: $2.8 Billion
Founded: 2000
Investment Criteria: Growth Stage, Early Stage, Israeli
Industry Group Preference: All Sectors Considered
Portfolio Companies: Cellwize, Clarizen, Cloudyn Code Fresh, Cooladata, Coppergate, CrediFi, Deep, Design Art Networks, ECI The Elastic Network, Ensilo, Ever Compliant, Exelate, Followap Telecommunications, Iron Source, Kampyle, Kontera, Lightricks, LiveU, Lucky Fish, Maapilim, Mov.ai, MultiPhy, Nice Actimize, Nsknox, Optimal, Origami Logic, Oversi, Pagaya, Pando Logic, Parallel, Payoneer, Perfecto, Peronetics, PlainID, Playbuzz, ProteanTecs, Puls, Redbend, Redis Labs, Reduxio, Samanage, Seebo, Skybox Security, Snapt, SPlacer, Sunday Sky, Tapingo, Taranis, Tradair, Utbrain, Vaya Vision, VM Ware Wanova, Worthy
Key Executives:
   Shlomo Dovrat, Co-Founder/General Partner
   Background: Oshap; Tecnomatix; ECI Telecom; Wanova; Redbend; eXeleate;
   Avi Zeevi, Co-Founder/General Partner
   Background: MINT Technologies; Oshap; Actimize

Venture Capital & Private Equity Firms / International Firms

Directorships: Payoneer; SundaySky; Personetics; TradAir; Evercompliant; CrediFi; Pagaya; ParallelM; The Center for Educational Technology; Technion
Ronen Nir, General Partner
Education: BA, Economics/Middle-East History, Tel Aviv University; MSc, Technology Management, University of Maryland University College
Background: VP of Product Management, Verint Systems; Director of Product Management, ECtel; Israeli Defense Forces
Directorships: Samanage; ironSource; Perfecto Mobile; enSilo; Redis Labs; CodeFresh
Daniel Cohen, General Partner
Education: BA, Computer Science, Tel Aviv University; MBA, INSEAD
Background: Commtouch; Scitex; Gemini Israel Ventures
Directorships: Circle of Friends

3222 VIRGIN GREEN FUND
United Kingdom

Portfolio Companies: Gevo, Solyndra, Odersun, Metrolight, Wildcat Discovery Technologies, DuraTherm, Seven Seas, Quench USA, GreenRoad

Other Locations:
The Battleship Building
179 Harrow Road
London \W2 6NB
United Kingdom
Phone: 44-2073391500

Key Executives:
Evan Lovell, Partner
e-mail: evan.lovell@virgingreenfund.com
Education: University of Vermont
Background: Director, International Development, Culligan Water Technologies
Directorships: DuraTherm, Quench, Seven Seas Water
Shai Weiss, Partner
e-mail: shai.weiss@virgingreenfund.com
Education: MBA, Columbia University
Background: ntl:Telewest
Michael Odai, General Counsel & COO
e-mail: michael.odai@virgingreenfund.com
Education: BA, Economics, University of Rochester; JD, Albany Law School
Background: General Counsel, Virgin Money Australia
Mike Willis, Principal
e-mail: mike.willis@virgingreenfund.com
Education: BCom, Queen's University; MBA, INSEAD
Background: Virgin Management Limited; Bedford Capital

3223 VITAMINA K VENTURE CAPITAL
C/de La Botanica
Madrid 4 28028
Spain

Phone: 34-915613719
web: www.vitaminak.com

Mission Statement: Vitamin K is an SCR that invests in technology companies and internet in its early stages.

Average Investment: $200,000
Investment Criteria: Early-Stage
Industry Group Preference: Technology, Internet
Portfolio Companies: Otogami, Chicisimo, The Mad Video, Ludei, YPD Online, Promociones Farma, 8Fit, Mailtrack, Blinkfire, Cartodb, Icontainers, Selltag

Key Executives:
Rafael Garrido, Founder/CEO
Background: Co-Founder, Sequoias, Bubok, 737 Shaker, Kschool, Kaleidos, Experit, Mimub

3224 VITULUM VENTURES
Mediarena 7
Amsterdam 1114 BC
Netherlands

web: www.vitulumventures.com

Mission Statement: Vitulum Ventures BV is a Dutch micro VC based in Amsterdam. It was formed when 5 Dutch angel investors started to work together: Camiel Dobbelaar, Chang Ng, Erwin van der Veen, Jaap Visser and Ian Zein. We look for seed stage deals in promising internet/mobile startups. Our involvement is in the form of a mentoring shareholder.

Geographic Preference: The Netherlands
Average Investment: 50,000 - 100,000 Euro
Investment Criteria: Seed-Stage, Early-Stage
Industry Group Preference: Internet, Mobile
Portfolio Companies: Earlydoc, Human.co, Wercker, Karma, Nouncy, Gibbon

Key Executives:
Camile Dobbelaar, Partner

3225 VIVES
Chemin du Cyclotron 6
Louvain-la-Neuve B-1348
Belgium

Phone: 00-32010390021 **Fax:** 00-32010390029
e-mail: info@vivesfund.com
web: www.vivesfund.com

Mission Statement: Vives is a private seed capital that invests in high-technology companies. This multi-sectoral fund supports young companies in all technological sectors, with particular emphasis on eco-innovation projects. Vives invests in companies at all stages of maturity: seed, start-up and growth. The deal flow of Vives is ensured by UCL spin-offs as well as by technological start-ups located within a radius of 250km around Louvain-la-Neuve.

Geographic Preference: Belgium
Investment Criteria: All Stages
Industry Group Preference: High Technology
Portfolio Companies: Alterface, Cissoid, DELFMEM, GreenWatt, IntoPIX, Iteos, Keemotion, Novadip, Promethera, Viridaxis, Xylowatt

Key Executives:
Philippe Durieux, Chief Executive Officer
e-mail: p.durieux@sopartec.com
Education: Graduate Degree, Economics, Louvain-la-Neuve, Post-Graduate Degree, Finance, Hautes Etudes Commerciales Saint-Louis
Background: CEO, Sopartec SA; Senior Investment Manager, Dexia Private Equity

3226 VOLVO GROUP VENTURE CAPITAL
AB Volvo
Gothenburg SE-405 08
Sweden

Phone: 46-31-66-660000
web: www.volvogroup.com/venturecapital

Mission Statement: At Volvo Group Venture Capital, we dedicate ourselves to the success of each of our investments. We make the difference by contributing not only with capital but also with extensive investing experience coupled with the unique capabilities of the entire Volvo Group.

Industry Group Preference: Automotive, Consumer Electronics, Telecommunications

Other Locations:
425 Market Street
Suite 2200

Venture Capital & Private Equity Firms / International Firms

San Francisco, CA 94105
Phone: 415-691-5835

Key Executives:
Olof Persson, President and CEO
e-mail: johan.m.carlsson@volvo.com

3227 VON BRAUN & SCHREIBER PRIVATE EQUITY PARTNERS
Ottostrasse 1
Munich 80333
Germany

Phone: 49-892869520 Fax: 49-8928695210
e-mail: private.equity@braunschreiber.com
web: www.braunschreiber.com

Mission Statement: Leading independent European fund of funds managers for private equity.

Geographic Preference: Europe, USA
Founded: 1999
Investment Criteria: Venture capital, Buyout, Distressed
Industry Group Preference: Administration and Accounting, Legal and Compliance
Other Locations:
150 South US Highway One
Suite 305
Jupiter, FL 33477

Key Executives:
Emmeram von Braun, Managing Directors
e-mail: Private.Equity@BraunSchreiber.com
Education: Law degree from University of Augsburg & Master's degree in business administration from the Academy in Villingen-Schwenningen (Germany).
Background: Allianz AG
Alexander C Binz, Managing Director
Emmeram von Braun, Managing Director
Timothy J Reynolds, Managing Director

3228 VONTOBEL PRIVATE EQUITY MANAGEMENT CAYMAN
Third Floor
22 Sackville Street
London W1S 3DN
United Kingdom

Phone: 44-2072558300 Fax: 44-2072558301
web: www.vontobel.com

Mission Statement: Focused on asset management in the Swiss private.

Fund Size: $57.7 billion
Founded: 1984
Investment Criteria: Early-Stage, Expansion & Development Capital, Mezzanine & Bridge Finance, Replacement Capital, Start-up Capital, Turnaround & Restructuring, Buyout & Buyin

Key Executives:
Herbert J. Scheidt, Chairman
Dominic Brenninkmeyer, Member of the Risk and Audit Committee

3229 VTB CAPITAL
10, Presnenskaya Emb.
Block C
Moscow 123317
Russia

Phone: 7-495-725-5540 Fax: 7-495-725-5538
web: www.vtbcapital-im.com

Mission Statement: VTB Capital venture business leads the way in the venture capital market in Russia and the CIS. Investing in Russian innovative cutting-edge technology is among VTB Capital's priorities.

Geographic Preference: Russia
Fund Size: $320 million
Founded: 2007
Investment Criteria: Early-Stage
Industry Group Preference: Information Technology, Internet, Digital Media & Marketing, E-Commerce & Manufacturing
Portfolio Companies: Breeze Tecnhologies, Fab.com, Avalanche Technology, SmS Tnzotherm, Rolith, Fast Lane Ventures, Eccentex, Oktogo.ru, AiHit, Grid Dynamics, MOBI.Money, Russian Navigation Technologies

Key Executives:
Tim McCarthy, Managing Director, Chief of Staff
Teresa Smith, Chief Financial Officer
Education: BS, Accounting; CPA
Background: WebEx Communication

3231 WALDEN ISRAEL VENTURE CAPITAL
13 Zarchin Street
Building C, 8th floor
Raanana
Israel

Phone: 972-99605565 Fax: 972-35214587
e-mail: office@walden.co.il

Mission Statement: To be the leading quality early-stage venture capital firm in Israel.

Geographic Preference: Global
Fund Size: $185 Million
Founded: 1993
Average Investment: $2.5 Million
Minimum Investment: $1 Million
Investment Criteria: Invests in First-Stage
Industry Group Preference: Communications, Internet Technology, Software, Healthcare, E-Commerce & Manufacturing, Infrastructure
Portfolio Companies: Abirnet, Axeda Systems, ClearForest, Enigma Information Systems, Ex Libris, Informative, Mercado Software, nLayers, Safend, Sanctum, SintecMedia, Universal Ad, Zend Technologies, Camero, CogniTens, EPOS, D-Pharm, Odin Technologies, Peptor, Actelis, Allot Communications, Amimon, CableMatrix, Colorchip, Mellanox Technologies, Narus, Ornet, Passave Technologies, Radcom, Schema, Siano, Terayon

Key Executives:
Shirley Zakar Menda, Administrative Assistant
e-mail: noga@walden.co.il
Education: Economics and psychology
Background: Consortium International and Koor Communications.
Eyal Kaplan, General Partner
e-mail: eyal@walden.co.il
Education: MBA at the Wharton School of Business
Background: Geotek Communications
Roni Hefetz, General Partner
e-mail: moty@walden.co.il
Education: B.Sc. degree in Electronic Engineering & MBA degree from Tel Aviv University
Background: Radcom & Elisra

3232 WATERLAND PRIVATE EQUITY INVESTMENT
Nieuwe's-Gravelandseweg 17
Bussum 1405 HK
Netherlands

Phone: 31-356941680 Fax: 31-356970972
e-mail: info@waterland.nu
web: www.waterland.nu

Mission Statement: Waterland is an independent private equity investment group that supports entrepreneurs in realizing their growth ambitions. With substantial financial resources and committed relevant expertise.

Geographic Preference: Belgium, Germany, Netherlands
Fund Size: $1.7 billion
Founded: 1999

Average Investment: $10 - $200 million
Minimum Investment: $12 Million
Investment Criteria: Buyout and Buyin, Expansion and Development Capital, Replacement Capital
Industry Group Preference: Consumer Services, Industrial Products, Industrial Services, Medical & Health Related, Outsourcing & Efficiency
Portfolio Companies: A-ROSA, Actuera, Aevitae, Attero, BioMCN, Brouwerij Bosteels, Casino Royal, Didix, Diversi Foods, FleetPro, Infra Group/Verbraeken, Interbest, Ipcom, JVH Gaming, Mauritsklinieken, Omega Pharma, Ranger Marketing, RHM Klinik und Pflegeheime, Sarens, SENIOcare, U-Center, VeluwseBron, VivaNeo

Key Executives:
   Lex Douze, Principal

3233 WELLINGTON PARTNERS VENTURE CAPITAL GmbH
6 Theresienstr
Munich 80333
Germany

Phone: 49-892199410
e-mail: munich@wellington-partners.com
web: www.wellington.de

Mission Statement: To be a quality leader in the European early-stage venture capital industry.
Geographic Preference: Europe, US
Fund Size: $800 million
Founded: 1990
Average Investment: $15 million
Minimum Investment: $1.2 million
Investment Criteria: Focuses on Companies with Experienced Management Team, Large Market, and Strong Technology
Industry Group Preference: Medical Technology, Diagnostics, Therapeutics, Digital Media & Marketing, Resource Efficiency, Internet Technology
Portfolio Companies: ACG, Astaro, Cobion, Gardeners, Gten, Safe-id, Belenus, Collax, Covast, Meiosys, Nexwave, Reportive, SAF, SWYX, Voice Objects, WLAN, Enocean, Multiplex, Nawotec, WWNET, Immobilienscout24, Netmobile, Openbc, Truck24, Zopa, 1-2-3.TV, Alando, Ciao, Codetoys

Key Executives:
   Rolf Christof Dienst, General Partner
   e-mail: boehnke@wellington-partners.com
   Education: Business Administration from the University of Essen
   Background: J.P. Morgan, IBM
   Bart Markus, General Partner
   e-mail: dienst@wellington-partners.com
   Education: Law degree from Ludwig-Maximilians University of Munich
   Background: Munich-based Matuschka Group & Techno Venture Management

3234 WESTERN NIS ENTERPRISE FUND
4 Rayevskoho street
Kyiv 01042
Ukraine

Phone: 380-442475580 **Fax:** 380-2475589

Mission Statement: Investing in small and medium-sized enterprises operating in what are expected to be the fastest growing sectors in Ukraine, Moldova and Belarus, providing them with capital and the necessary management tools to evolve from entrepreneurial ventures into professionally managed companies. Arranging for experienced Western executives to work with local management in order to prepare and position them for growth, and seek to achieve long-term appreciation with a modest current return on its capital, which was initially provided by the United States government.

Geographic Preference: Ukraine, Moldova

Fund Size: $150 Million
Founded: 1995
Average Investment: $2.3 Million
Minimum Investment: $500,000
Investment Criteria: All sectors
Industry Group Preference: Agriculture, Communications, Construction, Ice Cream, Confectionery, Food & Beverage, Financial Services, Industrial Equipment, Management, Pharmaceuticals, Forestry, Fishing, Energy
Portfolio Companies: ProCredit Bank, AVK, International Mortgage Bank, Ecoprod, Glass Container Company (GCC), Troyanda, Shvydko, ProCredit Moldova, Vitanta-Intravest

Key Executives:
   Natalie A. Jaresko, President and Chief Executive Officer
   Education: B.A.Degree in International Business, Master's in Business Administration from New York University
   Background: Philip Morris International, National Demographics
   Directorships: Head of Marketing Department for Philip Morris Ukraine
   Mark A. Iwashko, Executive Vice President and Chief Investment Officer
   Education: Business Administration Degree at the Richard Ivey School of Business in London
   Background: Coopers & Lybrand & Ashurst Technology Corporation Ltd
   Lenna Koszarny, CA, Chief Financial and Administrative Officer
   Education: MBA) from the Fisher Business School at Ohio State University
   Background: BancOne Corporation
   Directorships: Chairperson of the Finance and Investment Committee of the American Chamber of Commerce in Ukraine

3235 WESTSUMMIT CAPITAL
A-3805 Fortune Centre, No.7
East Third Ring Middle Road
Chaoyang District
Beijing 100020
China

Phone: 86-1059797669 **Fax:** 86-1058043607
web: www.westsummitcap.com

Mission Statement: WestSummit Capital is a China-based technology investment firm with deep local expertise in China and a global approach to creating market leaders. We are the first growth capital firm sponsored by the most prestigious financial institution in China focused on growth-stage technology companies operating between China and the rest of the world. Our senior partners collectively bring over 100 years of success as entrepreneurs, public company executives and investors of many leading technology companies in China and the United States. Through our offices in Beijing and Silicon Valley, we closely partner with our companies to realize the full potential of developing their businesses in China to become global industry leaders.

Geographic Preference: China, United States
Average Investment: $10 - $30 million
Industry Group Preference: Technology, New Media, Clean Technology, Consumer Services, Mobile, Software, Enabling Technology
Portfolio Companies: Accent, Anji-Micro, Couchbase, GigaDevice, Inside-Secure, Maginatics, Mirantis, NetBase, Nexenta, Shanghai-Haier-IC, SilkRoad, Tilera, Twitch, Union-Optech, Unity, VeriSilicon, YuMe

Other Locations:
   720 University Avenue
   Suite 100

Venture Capital & Private Equity Firms / International Firms

Palo Alto, CA 94301
Phone: 650-847-1886 **Fax:** 650-887-1489
Key Executives:
Raymond Yang, Co-Founder/Managing Director
Education: BS, Tsinghua University; MS, Graduate School of China
Background: Managing Partner, Navi Capital Partner; CEO, Linktone
Directorships: Unity Technologies

3236 WESTTECH VENTURES
Saarbuucker Strasse 36
Berlin 10405
Germany

Phone: 49 (0)30-21 430 6613 **Fax:** 49 (0)30-21 280 6660
e-mail: info@westtechventures.com
web: www.westtechventures.com

Mission Statement: Pre-seed and seed-stage venture capital firm in Berlin.
Geographic Preference: Germany
Founded: 2012
Minimum Investment: 25K EUR
Investment Criteria: Pre-Seed, Seed-Stage, Early-Stage
Industry Group Preference: Business to Business, Developer Tools, Enterprise Software, Media Technology, Education
Portfolio Companies: Applause, Book A Tiger, Cookies, Craftrad, Dalia, Dailyme, Delivery Hero, Edition F, Familonet, Fliit, Itembase, Knotable, Knotel, Marley Spoon, Remerge, Semknox, Sensorberg, Softgames, Startup Bootcamp, Styla, Tab, Talent Wunder, Testhub, Test Object, Ubeeko, Vertical Techmedia, Volocopter, Wunderdata
Key Executives:
Masoud Kamali, Founder & Managing Director
Background: Founder, S&S Media Group
Alexander Kolpin, Partner & Managing Director
Background: Founder, German Startups Group

3237 WHEB GROUP
2 Fitzhardinge Street
London W1H 6EE
United Kingdom

Phone: 44-0-20-3219-3441 **Fax:** 44-0-20-3219-3451
e-mail: info@whebgroup.com
web: www.whebgroup.com

Mission Statement: WHEB is a specialist investor focused on the opportunities created by the global transition to more sustainable, resource efficient and energy efficient economies.
Investment Criteria: SME
Industry Group Preference: Energy Efficiency, Energy Storage, Sustainable Materials, Renewable Energy, Waste & Recycling, Recycling, Water
Other Locations:
Maximillanstrasse 36
Munchen 80539
Germany
Phone: 49-89-122-2808-20 **Fax:** 49-89-122-2808-11
Key Executives:
James McNaught-Davis, Managing Partner
Education: MA, University of Cambridge; MBA, Wharton School
Background: General Partner, Advent; Partner, Warburg Pincus
Directorships: Watson Brown, Green Energy Group, PassivSystems, Petainer, WEMS
Jorg Sperling, Partner
Education: MS, Electrical Engineering, RWTH Aachen
Background: Venture Partner, Targe Partners; Global VP Sales, ZMD
Directorships: FriedolaTech Hoffmeister, PvXchange, SensorTran, Torqeed, VIA Optronics, UBC GmbH

Rob Wylie, Partner
Education: MA, PhD, University of Cambridge
Background: Agrochemical Business, Shell; Bioscience Unit, Rothschild; KPMG
Directorships: AquaSpy, EVAP, Exosect, Steritrox
Alexander Domin, Partner
Education: MSc, Biological Sciences, Stanford University; PhD, Chemical Engineering, University of Cambridge
Background: Boston Consulting Group; Founder, Enval Ltd.
Directorships: Resysta, Torqeedo, VIA Optronics, Hoffmeister

3238 WINE INVESTMENT FUND
15 Clifford Street
London W1S 4JY

Phone: 44-2070430885
web: www.wineinvestmentfund.com

Mission Statement: The International Wine Investment Fund was created for the purpose of holding wine investment assets, in particular.
Geographic Preference: Australia
Founded: 1989
Key Executives:
Andrew Della Casa, Director

3239 XANGE PRIVATE EQUITY
Maximillianstrasse 45
Munchen D-80538
Germany

Phone: 49-89381699730 **Fax:** 49-89381699739
web: www.xange.fr

Mission Statement: We invest in innovation in the broadest sense, focusing on sectors where we have developed truly specialized expertise. We look for inspiring projects. We invest in growth companies, innovative ideas and outstanding people.
Geographic Preference: France, Germany
Fund Size: 375 million Euro
Founded: 2004
Average Investment: 500,000 - 5 million Euro
Industry Group Preference: Direct Marketing, Business Products & Services, Logistics, Printing, Mobile, Clean Technology, Telecommunications, Internet, Software, Electronics
Portfolio Companies: A Little Market, A/B Tasty, ABC Cosmétique, Altaven, Assima, Ateme, Au Forum du Batiment, Believe, Clinique Développement, Conexance, Dolead Dynadmic, European Homes, Evaneos, Exoplatform, Expé, Fidor, Groupe IP, H-Log, Harvest, IDS, Intent Technologies, ITL Canis, Kayentis, KissKissBankBank, Kxen, La Ruche qui dit Oui!, Luneau Technology, Marcel & Fils, Mein Auto, Mister Spex, Mobiles Republick, Mysportgroup, Naskeo, Neolane, Nexway, Novawatt, Odoo, Orolia, Pactas, Pixways, PrestaShop, Pret a changer, PrivateLot, Provendi, Qeep, Royal Cactus, Sculpteo, SequoiaSoft, Shopmium, SideTrade, Sinequa, SmartAngels, Snadec, Sparkow, Sport Universal Process, Studitemps, Tag Commander, Technoflex, The Currency Cloud, Travador, TVH, Ucopia, VOSS, Webedia, Wedia, Woman Journal
Other Locations:
12 rue Tronchet
Paris 75008
France
Phone: 01-53430530 **Fax:** 01-53300225

44 place de la Republique
Lyon 69002

Venture Capital & Private Equity Firms / International Firms

France
Phone: 04-37262530
Key Executives:
Herve Schricke, CEO
Education: Masters, International Law
Background: Managing Director, Financiere Natexis

3240 XENIA VENTURE CAPITAL
Igal Alon 76
Tel Aviv
Israel

Phone: 972-9-957-5259 **Fax:** 972-2-625-70-83
e-mail: info@xenia.co.il
web: www.xenia.co.il

Mission Statement: Xenia Venture Capital is an investment company publicly traded in the Tel-Aviv Stock Exchange that operates a technological incubator, and is engaged in the initiation and build-up of high-technology start up companies in Israel, in the fields of Information Technology and Life Sciences Medical Devices.
Geographic Preference: Israel
Founded: 2004
Investment Criteria: Early-Stage
Industry Group Preference: Information Technology, Life Sciences, Medical Devices, High Technology
Portfolio Companies: ActiVein, Bio Protect, Ninox, Medi Tate, Neat Stitch, Ortho Space, PolyPid, Xenolith, Saguna, Superfish, Playcast, LiveTune, Arcos, Correlix, SafePeak, Samanage, IntuView, BandWD, VCortex

Key Executives:
Anat Segal, Chief Executive Officer
Education: BS, Economics & Management, MBA, Finance, LLB, Tel Aviv University
Background: Managing Director, Tamir Fishman & Co.; VP Investment Banking, Robertson Stephens/Evergreen

3241 XT INVESTMENTS
Ramat Aviv Tower
40 Einstein Street
PO Box 11
Tel Aviv 69102
Israel

Phone: 972-37456060 **Fax:** 972-37604650
e-mail: xtht@xtholdings.com
web: www.xtholdings.com

Mission Statement: XT Investments is a leading investor in technology-based companies. XT Investments portfolio is diversified; concentrating mainly around the fields of information technologies and healthcare, from early-stage to publicly-traded companies.
Founded: 1956
Investment Criteria: Early-Stage
Industry Group Preference: Information Technology, Healthcare
Portfolio Companies: Lumenis, Enzymotec, RayV, Angioslide, Checkmarx, Intratech Medical, NanoPass, MGVS, PainReform, EndoCross, NextNine, YouLicense, Applied Spectral Imaging, dPharm, CorAssist

Key Executives:
Yoav Doppelt, CEO, XT Investments
Education: BS, Economics, Technion-Israel Institute of Technology; MBA, Haifa University
Background: CEO, XT Hi-Tech
Directorships: Israel Corporation, Lumenis, TowerJazz, Enzymotec, MGVS, Yozma, RayV, Angioslide

3242 YASUDA AND PAMA LIMITED
Shinwa Building
5/F, 2-9-11, Toranomon
Minato-ku
Tokyo 105-0001
Japan

Phone: 81-335970051 **Fax:** 81-335970053
e-mail: ymc@yasudamakoto.com
web: www.yasudamakoto.com

Fund Size: $540 million
Key Executives:
Makoto Yasuda, Chief Executive

3243 YASUDA ENTERPRISE DEVELOPMENT COMPANY
Marumasu Kojimachi Bldg. 8F
3-3-8 Kojimachi
Chiyoda-ku
Tokyo 102-0083
Japan

Phone: 81-368117100 **Fax:** 81-352133405
Geographic Preference: Japan, United States
Fund Size: $400 Million
Investment Criteria: Start-up/Early stage, Expansion/Development stage
Industry Group Preference: Information Technology, Medical Devices, Biotechnology

Key Executives:
Yuji Kawakami, President
Masanori Ando, Senior Managing Director

3244 YFM GROUP
5th Floor
Valiant Building
14 South Parade
Leeds LS1 5QS
United Kingdom

Phone: 0113 244 1000
e-mail: info@yfmep.com
web: www.yfmgroup.co.uk

Mission Statement: Meeting the demand for risk capital, consultancy and property services from entrepreneurially led small companies.
Geographic Preference: United Kingdom
Fund Size: £310 Million
Founded: 1982
Average Investment: £500,000
Minimum Investment: £100,000
Investment Criteria: Early-Stage, Later-Stage, MBO, Management Buy-In, Secondary Buy-Outs, Startup
Industry Group Preference: Business Products & Services, Retail, Consumer & Leisure, Healthcare, Software, Telecommunications
Portfolio Companies: Macro Art, Deep Secure, Mangar International, GO Outdoors, Leengate Valves, GTK UK, Gill, Harvey Jones, Seven Technologies, Intelligent Office, Bagel Nash, Harris Hill, PowerOasis, RMS Group, Selima, Insider Technologies, Dryden Human Capital, Caterplus, Displanplan, Callstream, Cambridge Cognition, President Engineering, Nanoco, Pressure Technologies, DataLase, Gentronix, ImmunoBiology, Intamac, K3

Key Executives:
David Hall, Managing Director, YFM Private Equity
Andrew Marchant, Chairman

Venture Capital & Private Equity Firms / International Firms

3245 YISSUM TECHNOLOGY TRANSFER
Hi-Tech Park, Edmond J. Safra Campus
Givat-Ram
PO Box 39135
Jerusalem 91390
Israel

Phone: 972-26586688 Fax: 972-26586689
e-mail: info@yissum.co.il
web: www.yissum.co.il

Mission Statement: Yissum Research Development Company of the Hebrew University of Jerusalem Ltd. Founded in 1964 to protect and commercialize the Hebrew University's intellectual property. Ranked among the top technology transfer companies, Yissum has registered over 7,000 patents covering 2,023 inventions; has licensed out 530 technologies and has spun-off 72 companies. Products that are based on Hebrew University technologies and were commercialized by Yissum generate today over $2 Billion in annual sales.

Geographic Preference: Israel
Founded: 1964
Industry Group Preference: Agriculture, Chemicals, Advanced Materials, Clean Technology, Environment, Computer Related, Engineering, Food & Beverage, Life Sciences, Biotechnology, Electronics, Nanotechnology
Portfolio Companies: Angiob, Atox Bio, Bactusense, Beelogics, Biocancell Therapeutics, Biosensor Application AB, Breedit, Briefcam, Chiasma, Collplant, Danziger Innovations, Eggdetect, En Gibton, Ex Libris, Futuragene, HIL Applied Medical, HumanEyes Technologies, Intec Pharma, Jexys Pharmaceuticals, Kovax, Maimonidex RA, Medgenics, MELODEA, MobilEye, Morflora, Morria Biopharmaceuticals, Nanonics Imaging, NasVax, Novagali Pharma SA, Novel Therapeutic Technologies, Novotyr Therapeutics, Paulee Cleantec, Pepticom, Phenome Networks, Protein Laboratories Rehovot, Qlight Nanotech, Rav Galai, Real-Time Radiography, SCT Stem Cell Technology, Sensotrade, Sol-Gen, TheraVir, Tiltan Pharma, TreaTec21, Valentis

Key Executives:
Yaacov Michlin, President/CEO
Education: Bachelor of Law & Economics, Master of law, Bar-Ilan University; MBA, Technion Israel Institute of Technology
Background: Partner, Tulchinsky Stern & Co. Law Offices

3246 YL VENTURES
PO Box 847
Grand Cayman KY1-1103
Cayman Islands

Phone: 415-3000039 Fax: 415-7237703
web: www.ylventures.com

Mission Statement: YL Ventures invests early in core technology software companies in and around the Internet space, and accelerates their evolution via value-added involvement and Silicon Valley-based business development. We then spearhead the exit process, with particular expertise in arranging strategic acquisitions by US-based corporations known to the firm.

Geographic Preference: Israel
Average Investment: $1M - $2M
Investment Criteria: Early-Stage
Industry Group Preference: Software, E-Commerce & Manufacturing, Infrastructure, Cloud Computing, Mobile Technology, Analytics & Analytical Instruments, Business Intelligence
Portfolio Companies: Hexadite, Seculert, BlazeMeter, FireLayers, Upstream Commerce, 6Scan

Other Locations:
San Francisco, CA
Phone: 415-300-0039 Fax: 415-723-7703

Tel Aviv
Israel
Phone: 972-9971-6021 Fax: 972-9777-0119

Key Executives:
Yoav Andrew Leitersdorf, Managing Partner
Education: MBA, Columbia University
Background: CEO/Co-Founder, Movota; Associate, DFJ Gotham Ventures
Directorships: ClickTale, Seculert, Upstream Commerce, BlazeMeter

3247 YLR CAPITAL MARKETS LTD
16 Beit Hashoeva Lane
Tel Aviv 65814
Israel

Phone: 972-35667339 Fax: 972-35605818

Mission Statement: YLR enables its clients create the foundation for a strong business, and a strong future, through a comprehensive offering of investment banking services.

Geographic Preference: North America, Europe, Asia
Founded: 1990
Investment Criteria: Start-up, Development.
Industry Group Preference: Internet Technology, Telecommunications, Healthcare, Marketing, Retailing, High Technology

3248 YUUWA CAPITAL
Enterprise Unit 3, Suite 4, Office 7
9 De Laeter Way
Bently WA 6102
Australia

Phone: 61-400605960 Fax: 61-8-9355-5694
e-mail: matthew@yuuwa.com.au
web: www.yuuwa.com.au

Mission Statement: Yuuwa Capital is a $40M early-stage venture capital firm based in Perth, Western Australia. We are actively seeking outstanding investment opportunities where Yuuwa can provide both capital and expertise to help founders, management and early investors to turn good ideas into great companies.

Geographic Preference: Australia
Fund Size: $40 million
Average Investment: $1,000,000 to $5,000,000
Investment Criteria: Early-Stage
Industry Group Preference: Software, Life Sciences, Biotechnology, Communications, Clean Technology
Portfolio Companies: GordianTec, OzSonotek, Adalta, iCetana, Agworld, Filter Squad, Dealised

Key Executives:
Liddy McCall, Managing Director
Education: LLB, BJuris, BCom
Background: Co-Founder, Tessitura Pty Ltd; Co-Founder, iCeutica Group; Associate Director, Macquarie Bank

3249 YVC - YOZMA MANAGEMENT & INVESTMENTS LIMITED
Ramat Aviv Tower
40 Einstein Street
Tel Aviv 69102
Israel

Phone: 972-36437766 Fax: 972-36437888
e-mail: keren@yozma.com
web: www.yozma.com

Geographic Preference: Israel
Fund Size: $170 Million
Founded: 1993
Average Investment: $1 million and $6 million
Minimum Investment: $1 Million

Venture Capital & Private Equity Firms / International Firms

Investment Criteria: Primary focus on Early-Stage, High-Growth.
Industry Group Preference: Communications, Information Technology, Technology, Life Sciences
Portfolio Companies: Brighthaul (Israel) Ltd., Clariton, Hywire Ltd., KaiLight Photonics, KiloLambda, Paragon, Pegasus, Radiotel, Telegate, CardonetCommtouch, eShip-4U, E-SIM, Ligature, Maincontrol, NextNine, Security 7, Ubique, ASI, Biosense, Can-Fite BioPharma, Collgard, CorAssist, Discote
Key Executives:
   Orli Disi Ben-Zion, Chief Financial Officer
   Education: B.Sc. and M.Sc. in Chemistry and an MBA from the Hebrew University of Jerusalem.
   Background: Founder of Gemini, JPV, Nitzanim (Concord), Polaris, STAR and Walden Israel.
   Yoav Sebba, Partner

3250 ZERNIKE SEED FUND BV
Paterswoldseweg 802
Groningen 9728 BM
Netherlands

Phone: +31 (0)50 30 50 600 **Fax:** +31 (0)50 30 50 601

Mission Statement: Actively seeking investments
Geographic Preference: Europe, Asia, North America
Fund Size: $150 million
Founded: 1992
Investment Criteria: Start-up, Development.
Industry Group Preference: Agriculture, Biotechnology, Computer Related, Forestry, Industrial Products, Medical & Health Related

3251 ZHENFUND
China World Trade Center
Tower 1
Jianguomenwai Dajie Beijing
Beijing 100004
China

e-mail: dream@zhenfund.com
web: www.zhenfund.com

Mission Statement: ZhenFund is a seed investment firm based in Beijing in collaboration with Sequoia Capital China.
Geographic Preference: United States, China
Founded: 2011
Industry Group Preference: TMT, IOT, Mobile Internet, Entertainment, Enterprise Software, O2O, E-Commerce, Education
Portfolio Companies: Jumei.com, LightInTheBox.com, Jiayuan.com, Zhaogang.com, Everstring, Miyabaobei, com, Nice, 51talk, Yongche.com, Melele, Ehang, Meicai.cn, KV Games, The ONE, Bobo, Jeepglint, Mobvoi, Super Evil Megacorp, NWay
Key Executives:
   Bob Xu, Founder
   Background: Co-Founder, New Oriental Education
   Victor Wang, Co-Founder
   Education: Foundation Fellow of Harris Manchester College, University of Oxford
   Background: Co-Founder/VP/Chairman, New Oriental Education

3252 ZOUK VENTURES
100 Brompton Road
London SW3 1ER
United Kingdom

Phone: 44-2079473400 **Fax:** 44-2079473449
web: www.zouk.com

Mission Statement: To leverage our established position, networks and partnerships to optimize the value created through investment in the cleantech market.
Geographic Preference: Europe, Asia, Middle East, the Americas
Fund Size: Euro 400 Million
Founded: 2000
Investment Criteria: Development Stage, Operational Stage
Industry Group Preference: Clean Technology, Renewable Infrastructure, Renewable Energy, Resource Efficiency, Environmental Infrastructure
Portfolio Companies: Anesco, Nanotron Technologies, Orb, Ozz Electric, SiC Processing, Solarcentury, Trilliant, Va-Q-Tec, LightingScience, The Mobility House, Space-Ime Insight, iZettle
Key Executives:
   Samer Salty, Founder and CEO
   Education: BS, Electrical Engieering, California Polytechnic; MS, Management & Finance, MIT
   Background: JP Morgan, Martin Lockheed, AT&T, Hughes Aircraft, US Federal Aviation Administration
   Directorships: Orb Energy, Solarcentury
   Erich Becker, Partner
   Education: MS, Economics, University of Cologne, Germany; CEP, Institut d'Etudes Politeques, Paris
   Background: JP Morgan, French Ministry of Finance, German Chamber of Commerce, Russia
   Anthony Fox, Partner
   Background: Chief Executive, Global Ecommerce, Kingfisher Pic; Managing Director, Kingfisher Asia Pacific Limited; CFO, Planning Sciences International/Gentia Software
   Alois Flatz, Partner
   Education: International Management, HEC; MBA, Vienna University of Economics; PhD, Business Administration, University of St. Gallen
   Background: Partner, Head of Research, Sustainable Asset Management; Managing Partner, BTS Investment Advisors; Austrian Ministry of the Environment
   Directorships: SiC Processing
   Colin Campbell, Partner
   Education: BSc, Chemical & Process Engineering
   Background: CEO, Killingholme Power Group Ltd; VP, Corporate M&A, TXU Europe; Project Finance Manager, Mitsui Babcock; FCA, Coopers & Lybrand
   Directorships: Enviromena Power Systems
   Richard Pereira, CFO
   Background: Ernst & Young; KPMG London

3253 ZURCHER KANTONALBANK
Stockerstrasse 33
Postfach 8010
Zurich 8010
Switzerland

Phone: 41-844-843823 **Fax:** 41-12928792
web: www.zkb.ch

Mission Statement: Actively seeking new investments
Geographic Preference: Switzerland
Founded: 1870
Investment Criteria: Expansion and Development, MBO
Industry Group Preference: All Sectors Considered
Key Executives:
   Urs Oberholzer, Chairman
   Liselotte Illi, Deputy-Chairman

3254 ZURMONT MADISON PRIVATE EQUITY
Eisengasse 15
PO Box 272
Zurich 8034
Switzerland

Phone: 41-0442675000 **Fax:** 41-0442675001
web: www.zurmontmadison.ch

997

Venture Capital & Private Equity Firms / International Firms

Geographic Preference: Switzerland, Southern Germany, Austria
Founded: 2006
Investment Criteria: Buyout of established mid-market industrial and consumer goods companies. MBO/MBI, Corporate spin-offs, succession solutions.
Industry Group Preference: Industrial Products, Medical Devices, Machinery, Consumer Products, Logistics, Business Products & Services
Key Executives:
   Guido Patroncini, Founding Partner
   Werner Schnorf, Founding Partner & Chief Executive Officer
   Dr. Björn Böckenförde, Founding Partner / CFO
   Kurt Hitz, Partner
   Andreas Ziegler, Partner / Investor Relations

National & State Associations

Venture Capital & Private Equity Firms / National & State Associations

3255 AMERICAN INVESTMENT COUNCIL
799 9th Street NW
Suite 200
Washington, DC 20001

Phone: 202-465-7700
e-mail: info@investmentcouncil.org
web: www.investmentcouncil.org

Mission Statement: Advocacy organization develops and provides information on the private equity investment industry.

Founded: 2007
Portfolio Companies: Members: ACON Investments, Adams Street Partners, Altamont Capital Partners, Alvarez & Marsal Capital, Apollo Global Management, ArcLight Capital Partners, The Blackstone Group, Brookfield Asset Management, The Carlyle Group, CCMP Capital Advisors, Clearlake Capital Group, Crestview Partners, CVC Capital Partners, The Edgewater Funds, EnCap Investments, Energy Capital Partners, Genstar Capital, Goldman Sachs, GTCR, HarbourVest Partners, Hellman & Friedman, Investcorp International, The Jordan Company, Kelso & Company, Kline Hill Partners, Kohlberg Kravis Roberts & Co., KPS Capital Partners, Madison Dearborn Partners, New Mountain Capital, Pantheon Ventures, Providence Equity Partners, The Riverside Company, Silver Lake, SoftBank Group, Sterling Partners, TA Associates, Thoma Bravo, TPG, Vector Capital, Vestar Capital Partnrs, Welsh, Carson, Anderson & Stowe

Key Executives:
Drew Maloney, President & CEO
Background: Principal Liaison between the Treasury and Congress
Emily Schillinger, Senior Vice President, Public Affairs
Education: BA, Clemson University
Background: Communications Director, House Ways & Means Committee; Press Secretary, Speaker of the House John Boehner; Communications Director, Senator John Barrasso and the Senate Republican Policy Committee; Press Secretary, Department of Commerce; Asst. Press Secretary, White House

3256 ANGEL CAPITAL ASSOCIATION
10977 Granada Lane
Suite 103
Overland Park, KS 66211

Phone: 913-894-4700
web: www.angelcapitalassociation.org

Mission Statement: Professional development organization for angel investors with more than 14,000 members.

Key Executives:
Pat Gouhin, Chief Executive Officer
e-mail: pgouhin@angelcapitalassociation.org
Education: Aerospace Engineering, Ohio State University; MA, George Washington Unviersity; Certificate, Stanford University Graduate School of Business; Certificate, Wharton School
Background: Association Advisor; Executive Director & CEO, ISA; COO, AIAA; VP, Operations & Technology Transfer, National Institute of Aerospace
Directorships: Past Chair, Council of Engineering & Scientific Society Executives; Ctte. Member, The Center for Association Leadership
Sarah Dickey, Membership Director
e-mail: sdickey@angelcapitalassociation.org
Education: BA, Northwest Missouri State University; MA, Communication, May Business School, Texas A&M University
Background: VP, Research, Angel Resource Institute

3257 CALIFORNIA COAST VENTURE FORUM
800 Anacapa Street
Suite A
Santa Barbara, CA 93101

Phone: 805-495-6962
web: www.ccvf.org

Mission Statement: Non-profit organization promotes tech companies in California.

Geographic Preference: California
Founded: 1996
Investment Criteria: Emerging Growth, Later Stage
Industry Group Preference: Software & Internet, Technology, Mechanical Products, Retail, Restaurants & Distribution, Food & Beverage, Utilities & Farming
Portfolio Companies: ACQI, Apeel Sciences, Channel Wind, ECO Products, Foxy's Pash, Gramercy Beverage, Harvest, Hope20, Kaibae, Kiwa, Locali, LyfeStart International, Maker Labs, Mica Sense, Necessity LLC, Next, Ojai Energy Systems, Re-Leash, Seaters, Sierra Lifestyle, Slightly Nutty, SweetSpring Salmon, T4 Spatial, Teecinno, Waiakea, Wash-it

Key Executives:
Jerry Knotts, President & CEO
e-mail: jeknotts@ccvf.org
Education: BSEE, Pennsylvania State University; MBA, Auburn University; Defense Systems Management College; Industrial College of the Armed Forces; Air War College
Background: VP & General Manager, Defense Electronics Division, California Microwave; VP, American Nucleonics Corporation

3258 CANADIAN VENTURE CAPITAL ASSOCIATION Canadian Venture Capital & Private Equity Association
372 Bay Street
Suite 1201
Toronto, ON M5H 2W9
Canada

Phone: 416-487-0519
e-mail: reception@cvca.ca
web: www.cvca.ca

Mission Statement: CVCA's mission is to help its members fuel the economy of the future by growing the businesses of today. They accomplish this by supporting and connecting the private capital industry with advocacy, research, and education. Please see www.cvca.ca for a complete list of member firms.

Founded: 1974
Industry Group Preference: Energy, Power, Hospitality, Healthcare, Life Sciences, Clean Technology, Media, Food & Beverage, Infrastructure, Consumer, Information Technology, Manufacturing, Industrial, Transportation, Business Products & Services
Portfolio Companies: 7 Gate Ventures, AIMCo, AIP Private Capital, Alberta Enterprise Corporation, Alberta Teachers' Retirement Fund, Atlas Partners LP, Amplitude Ventures, Anges Quebec Capital, Ardenton Capital Corporation, AVAC Ltd., Azimuth Capital Management, Azure Capital Partners, BC Tech Fund, BCF Ventures, BDC Capital, Bedford Capital Limited, Bioindustrial Innovation Canada, Birch Hill Equity Partners Management, BlueSky Equities, BMO Capital Partners, Bond Capital, Brightspark Ventures, British Columbia Investment Management Corporation, Brookfield Asset Management, CAI Capital Partners, Caisse de depot et placement du Quebec, Canada Pension Plan Investment Board, Canadian Business Growth Fund, Cathay Capital NA LLC, Cedarpoint Investments, Celtic House Venture Partners, CIBC Innovation Banking, CIC Capital Canada, CIC Capital Ventures, Clairvest Group, Clearspring Capital Partners, Coller Capital, Comerica Bank, CTI Life Sciences Fund, Cycle Capital Management, Dancap Family Investment

Venture Capital & Private Equity Firms / National & State Associations

Office, Dream Maker Ventures, EnerTech Capital, Espresso Capital, Evok Innovations, Export Development Canada, Extreme Venture Partners, FACIT, FirePower Debt GP, First Ascent Ventures, First West Capital, Fondaction, Fonds de soliderite FTQ, Framework Venture Partners, Freycinet Investments, Fulcrum Capital Partners, Genesys Capital Management, Georgian Partners, Globalive, Golden Ventures, Good News Ventures, GreenSoil Building Innovation Fund, Hamilton Lane, HarbourVest Partners, Headwater Equity

Key Executives:
Kim Furlong, CEO
Education: BA, American History, Mgill University; MA, Trade Policy & Global Finance, Norman Paterson School Of International Affairs, Carleton University
Background: Director, Federal Government Affairs, Amgen; VP, Federal Government Relations, Retail Council of Canada; Department of Foreign Affairs
Matt Ivis, Director, Government Relations & Policy
Education: BA, Carelton University; MA, Carleton University
Background: Independent Strategy & Business Consulting; VP, Business Development & Sales & Federal Public Sector Sales, MDA; Government Relations & Regulatory Affairs, IBM Canada Ltd.; Senior Analyst, Service Strategies, Treasury Board of Canada Secretariat, Policy Analyst, Canadian Chamber of Commerce
Elaine Bedell, Head, Talent & Operations
Jon Jackson, Head, Communications
Education: Broadcasting, Fanshawe College; Public Relations, Seneca College of Applied Arts & Technology
Background: Producer, Bell Media; Producer, Corus Entertainment; Producer, Newcap Radio
Fil Varino, Head, Development & Member Engagement
Education: BSc, University Of Ottawa; Certificate, Fundraising Management, Humber College; Executive Boardroom Education Program, Institute of Corporate Directors
Background: RightBlue Labs; Social Profit Partners; The DMZ at Ryerson University; Causeway Work Centre; Salvation Army
Karen Hung, International Trade Liaison Officer
Education: BAdmin, York University; Institute of Chartered Accountants of Ontario; MSc, London School of Economics
Background: Global Affairs Canada; KPMG
David Kornacki, Associate, Research & Product
Education: BA & Certificate in Project Management, University of Toronto
Background: GSK
Igli Panariti, Membership Coordinator
Education: BComm, Ryerson University; MOOC, Bocconi University; MOOC, Babson College
Background: B Lab; Canadian Sport Business Network; Starters.co; iBoost Canada, RightBlue Labs; Revera; Athletics Canada

3259 COUNCIL FOR ENTREPRENEURIAL DEVELOPMENT
600 Park Offices Drive
Suite 100
Triangle Park, NC 27709
Phone: 919-549-7500 Fax: 919-549-7405
web: cednc.org

Mission Statement: To promote high growth companies in North Carolina by providing education and capital formation resources to entrepreneurs in a broad range of industries, including the life sciences, technology and services sectors.

Geographic Preference: North Carolina
Founded: 1984
Investment Criteria: High Growth, Startups, Growth Stage
Industry Group Preference: Advanced Manufacturing & Materials, Clean Technology, Green Technology, Life Sciences

Portfolio Companies: 10 for Humanity, 3DFS Power Solutions, 8 Rivers Capital, Abbey Road Consulting, Acorn Applications, Adamas Nanotechnologies, Affinergy, Agile Sciences, Airwavz Solutions, Akili Software, Align Global Consulting, All Elements, Alston & Bird, Altaravision, Atmospheric Plasma Solutions, Aura Life, Axial Exchange, Bagchi Law, BBVA Compass, BCombs, BDO, Bernard Robinson & Company, BioKier, BioMASON, BioResource International, Bioventus, Blue Gas Marine, Bridge Bank, Bright View Technologies, Bull City Forward, Business Ready Solutions, C10 Connect, CAI, Candlescience, Canopy, Capitol Broadcasting Company, Cary Street Partners, CDS Outsourcing, CertifiGroup, ChannelAdvisor, Charlotte Research Institute, Chimerix, Chubb Insurance Group, Cii Technology, Cisco Systems, Cityzen, CivaTech Oncology, Clark Nexsen, Clarkston Consulting, Clinipace Worldwide, Cloud Pharmaceuticals, Code A Site, Concentrx Pharmaceuticals, Cooley, Cornerstone Medical & Technology Financial, Creas Carolinas, CrossComm, Cushman & Wakefield, DecisionPoint, Deloitte LLP, Diagnosoft, Dignify Therapeutics, Diposta, Divvy Investments, DNA Group, Dude Solutions, Eco-Site, EG Gilero, EmployUs, Enzerna Biosciences, Ever EdTech, Expion, FabSource, Fennebresque, Fidelity Investments, Financial Directions Group, FLAG Therapeutics, FM:Systems, Forecast Health, Forge Communications, Fuentek, Full Scale Solutions, GlaxoSmithKline, Goldhat Advisors, Grant Thornton LLP, HireNetworks, HQ Raleigh, Hughes Pittman & Gupton LLP, Ici

Key Executives:
Kelly Rowell, President and CEO
Education: BA, Marketing, Small Business Management and Entrepreneurship

3260 DIGITAL VENTURE CAPITAL ASSOCIATION
Techmart Center
5201 Great America Pkwy
Santa Clara, CA 95054
web: www.digitalvca.org

Mission Statement: The Digital Venture Capital Association is a not-for-profit organization focused on supporting entrepreneurship and venture capital development in the technology industry.

Founded: 2010

Key Executives:
Martin Bueno, President
Education: BA, Universidad Tecnologica Nacional
Background: Co-Founder & Investor, SmartCultiva Hydroponics; Mentor, Ohio University; Managing Digital Director, Havas Global; Venture Partner, Digital Innovation Capital Group; VP, Digital, JWT; Founder Investor & CEO, Fiera.com; Founder Investor & CEO, Los Pinos II BBS

3261 EMERGING MARKETS PRIVATE EQUITY ASSOCIATION
The Watergate Office Building
2600 Virginia Ave NW
Suite 500
Washington, DC 20037-1905
Phone: 202-333-8171
web: www.empea.org

Mission Statement: EMPEA's mission is to promote and support private capital investment in emerging markets.

Geographic Preference: Emerging Markets
Portfolio Companies: Members: 17 Asset Management, 3TS Capital Partners, 57 Stars, AA Consulting & Associates, ABC TEST, Abu Dhabi Investment Authority, Accion, Actis, Adams Street Partners, Adansonia Management Services Limited, Adenia Partners, ADM Capital, Advanced Finance & Investment Group LLC, Affirma Capital, Africa50, African

Venture Capital & Private Equity Firms / National & State Associations

Capital Alliance, African Infrastructure Investment Managers Pty (Ltd.), AfricInvest, Aif Capital Ltd, Akin Gump Strauss Hauer & Feld LLP, Albright Capital Management LLC, Alloy Merchant Finance LP, Alothon Group, Alpha Associates, Alta Growth Capital, Alta Semper Capital, Amadeus Capital Partners, Amethis Finance, APS Investments, Aqua Capital, ARM-Harith Infrastructure Investments Ltd, Artha Partners, Asante Capital Group, Ascent Capital Partners, Ashburton Investments, Asia Alternatives Management, Asia Grown Capital Advisors (S) Pte Ltd, Asia Partners, Asian Development Bank, Asian Infrasturcture Investments Bank, ATP-PEP, Austral Capital Partners, Avanz Capital, AZB & Partners, Baker McKenzie, Baltoro Capital, Baring Private Equity Asia Ltd, Baring Vostok Capital Partners, Barnellan Equity Advice Ltd, Bill & Melinda Gates Foundation, BIO - Belgian Investment Company for Developing Countries, Blackpeak Group, BlueOrchard Finance, BluePeak Private Capital, Brookfield Asset Management, Bull Capital Partners Pte Ltd, Caisse de Depot et Placement du Quebec, CalPERS, CalSTRS, Cambridge Associates LLC, Capital Dynamics, Capria Ventures LLC, Cartica Management LLC,

Key Executives:
Cate Ambrose, Chief Executive Officer
Education: Universidad Compultense de Madrid; BA, Saint Lawrence University; MPA, Columbia University - School of International & Public Affairs
Background: President & CEO, LAVCA; Chief of Advocacy, Commission on Legal Empowerment of the Poor, UN Development Programme; Executive Director, Programmes, The Economist
Directorships: Youth INC NYC; Girls Write Now
Holly Radel, Managing Director, Institutional Relations and Membership
e-mail: radelh@empea.net
Education: BA, Rice Univ.; MA, Johns Hopkins Univ.
Background: World Affairs Council (Houston)
Jeff Schlapinski, Managing Director, Research
e-mail: schlapinskij@empea.net
Education: Beijing Center for Chinese Studies; BSFS, Georgetown University
Background: English Program Manager, Beijing Fermat Edu; Intern, True Run Media; Business Development Associate, News Distribution Network Inc.; Teaching Assistant, Georgetown University; Intern, Jeffrey J. Kimbell Associates
Julie Ruvolo, Managing Director, Venture Capital
646-315-6735
e-mail: ruvoloj@empea.net
Education: BA, Stanford University
Background: Journalist, TechCrunch, Buzzfeed, GOOD Magazine, Advertising Age, atlanticCityLab.com and others
Directorships: LatinSF; Latin American Tech Growth Coalition

3262 FLORIDA VENTURE FORUM
707 W. Azeele Street
Tampa, FL 33606

Phone: 813-335-8116
web: www.flventure.org

Mission Statement: The Florida Venture Forum is a not-for-profit organization designed to provide financial advice and management assistance to entrepreneurs. The Forum organizes educational programs across the state that offer insight on a number of topics, including raising equity and debt capital, development, marketing, research and management. The goal of the Forum is to help drive the success of entrepreneurial enterprises.

Geographic Preference: Florida
Founded: 1984
Investment Criteria: Early Stage
Portfolio Companies: Aegis Business Credit, Agro Arms, Aim Above, Akerman LLP, Amzur Technologies, AON, AquaMelon Water, Arsenal Venture Partners, Auxadyne, AZZLY, Bairo, Ballast Point Ventures, Bank of America Merrill Lynch, BedaBox, Berger Singerman LLP, Bit Cauldron, Bridge Bank, Cambridge Solutions, CapitalSouth Partners, CareAngel, CarePredict, CBIZ, Cherry Bekaert LLP, Citrix Systems, CliftonLarsonAllen, Concentric Equity Partners, CoTech Ventures, Cross Fernandez & Riley, Crowe Horwath, DATIS HR Cloud, eNow, Enterprise Florida, Eonian Technology, Equastream, FFI Contracting Services, Florida Blue, Florida Funders, Florida Gulfshore Capital, Foley & Lardner LLP, Frontier Capital, Fulcrum Equity Partners, FVF, Grant Thornton LLP, Greenberg Traurig, Gretel, Harbert Management, Harbert Venture Partners, Harbor View Advisors, Hercules Technology Growth Capital, Hill Ward Henderson, Holland & Knight LLP, Hopkins Capital Group, Hub International, Hunter Business Law, Hyde Park Capital Partners, Hydrocore, iCare.com, InformedDNA, Innovatia Medical Systems, Insulo, Intrepid, Ioppolo Law Group, Johnson Biomedical Capital, Keiretsu, Key Associates, KynderMed, Laughlin & Associates, Lenley Holdings, LFE Capital, LifeNet Systems, Locke Lord LLP, LogZilla, Luma Sleep, MAJEC Ventures, MassInvestor, MedAffinity, Medical Tracking Solutions, My Senior Portal, Nawboi Technologies, New World Angels, Noro-Moseley Partners, Norstrem Associates, Nperspective, Oakstone Holdings, Ocean Current Energy, Offerdat, Oo

Key Executives:
Kevin Burgoyne, President & CEO
305-343-0617
e-mail: kevin@flventure.org
Education: BS, University of Florida; MBA, University of Chicago
Background: Walt Disney Company; PanAmSat; Global Crossing
Pat Schneider, Vice President
e-mail: pat@flventure.org
Education: BA, International Business, Florida International University
Background: Executive Assistant, The Florida Aquarium; Dominion Financial Group; Home Shopping Network

3263 HAWAII VENTURE CAPITAL ASSOCIATION
PO Box 4677
Honolulu, HI 96812

Phone: 808-371-9403
e-mail: admin@hvca.org
web: hvca.org

Mission Statement: The Hawaii Venture Capital Association seeks to promote entrepreneurial development and growth by serving as a platform for capital formation, network, education and entrepreneurship.

Geographic Preference: Hawaii
Founded: 1988

Key Executives:
Meli James, President
Education: BS, Cornell University
Background: Head, New Ventures, Sultan Ventures; Program Director & Entrepreneur in Residence, XLR8UH; Founder, HonNewTech; Founding Member, Startup Paradise

3264 HEALTHCARE PRIVATE EQUITY ASSOCIATION
2500 Williston Drive
Charlottesville, VA 22901

Phone: 312-650-9014
web: www.hcpea.org

Mission Statement: The Healthcare Private Equity Association's mission is to support and promote the healthcare private equity industry of the United States.

Founded: 2010
Industry Group Preference: Healthcare

Venture Capital & Private Equity Firms / National & State Associations

Portfolio Companies: Members: A&M Capital Partners, Advent International, Apax Partners, Archimedes Health Investors, Ares Management LLC, Arsenal Capital Partners, Audax Private Equity, Bain Capital, Beecken Petty O'Keefe & Company, Blackstone Group, BlueMountain Capital, Brookfield Asset Management, Century Equity Partners, Chicago Pacific Founders, Cinven, Clayton Dubilier & Rice, Comvest Partners, Concord Health Partners, Court Square Capital Partners, The Cranemere Group, Cressey & Company, CVC Capital Partners, Deerfield Management, DW Healthcare Partners, EQT, EW Healthcare Partners, FFL Partners, Flexpoint Ford, Formation Capital, Frazier Healthcare Partners, General Atlantic, GI Partners, Granite Growth Health Partners, Harren Equity Partners, Harvest Partners, HealthEdge Investment Partners, Health Enterprise Partners, HealthInvest Equity Partners, HealthQuest Capital, Hellman & Friedman, Heritage Group, HIG Capital, Kelso & Company, KKR, Lee Equity Partners, Leonard Green & Partners, Linden Capital Partners, LLR Partners, Madison Dearborn Partners, Martis Capital, MBF Healthcare Partners, Morgan Stanley Capital Partners, Mubadala Investment Company, Nautic Partners, Oak HC/FT, OMERS Private Equity, Ontario Teachers' Pension Plan, PPC Partners, Revelstoke Capital Partners, The Riverside Company, Spindletop Capital, Summit Partners, Sverica Capital Management, SV Health Investors, TA Associates, Thomas H. Lee Partners, TPG, Varsity Healthcare Partners, Vesey Street Capital Partners,

Key Executives:
Brian Miller, Founder
Education: BA, Economics, Princeton University; MBA, Harvard Business School
Background: Co-Founder & Partner, Linden Capital Partners; First Chicago Equity Capital; Salomon Brothers
Directorships: CORPAK MedSystems, SeraCare, Strata Pathology Services, Hycor BioMedical, Advamed Dx
Karen Kajmo, Executive Director
Education: BSBA, Bryant College; MA, Boston University
Background: VP, HBS Healthcare Alumni Association; Executive Director, HBS Real Estate Alumni Association; Independent Consultant; Senior Product Marketing Manager, AllVertical, Inc.; Art Technology Group, Product Manager; Senior Product Marketing Manager, SupplyWorks Inc.; Management Consultant, PWC

3265 ILLINOIS VENTURE CAPITAL ASSOCIATION
27 N Wacker Drive
Suite 405
Chicago, IL 60606

Phone: 312-241-1615 Fax: 312-241-1623
web: www.illinoisvc.org

Mission Statement: The Illinois Venture Capital Association seeks to foster the development and growth of the venture capital and private equity industry in Illinois by offering member networking opportunities and educational programs in private equity.

Geographic Preference: Illinois
Founded: 2000
Investment Criteria: Early Stage to Buyout Stage
Portfolio Companies: Adams Street Partners LLC, Anderson Pacific Corporation, Arbor Investments, ARCH Venture Partners, Baird Capital, Beecken Petty O'Keefe & Company, BlueCross BlueShield Venture Partners, CapX Partners, Chicago Ventures, Chrysalis Ventures, CHS Capital LLC, Cressey & Company, Duchossois Capital Management, Dundee Venture Capital, Dunrath Capital, Financial Investments Corporation, First Analysis, Frontenac Company, Golder Investment Management LLC, GTCR LLC, Harrison Street Capital, HIG Capital, High Street Capital, Hyde Park Venture Partners, IllinoisVENTURES LLC, LaSalle Capital, Limerick Investments, Linden Capital Partners, Liquidity Ventures, Madison Dearborn Partners, MATH Venture Partners, Mercury Fund, Mesirow Financial Private Equity, Mid Oaks Investments LLC, MK Capital, Monroe Capital, Motorola Solutions Venture Capital, MVC Capital, New Enterprise Associates, NIN Ventures, Ninth Street Advisors, Northern Trust Private Equity, OCA Venture Partners, Origin Ventures, Paradigm Capital, Patriot Capital, PPM America Capital Partners, Prairie Capital, Pritzker Group, Prospect Partners LLC, RCP Advisors, Romar Partners, RoundTable Healthcare Partners, Sandbox Industries, Shore Capital Partners, Sterling Partners, Svoboda Capital Partners, The Edgewater Funds, Thoma Bravo, Tribune Company, Victory Park Capital, Vistria Group, Water Street Healthcare Partners, Waveland Investments, Wind Point Partners, Winona Capital Management LLC, WP Global Partners, Wynnchurch Capital, Zeb

Key Executives:
Maura O'Hara, Executive Director
e-mail: mohara@illinoisvc.org
Education: BA, Economics, University of Illinois, Urbana-Champaign; MBA, Kellogg School of Management, Northwestern University
Background: VP, Customer Strategies & Consumer Research, Sears Roebuck & Co.; Operational Planning, Helene Curtis; Investment Banking, Stevenson & Company

3266 INSTITUTIONAL LIMITED PARTNERS ASSOCIATION
1800 M Street NW
Suite 825-S
Washington, DC 20036

Phone: 416-941-9393 Fax: 416-941-9307
e-mail: info@ilpa.org
web: ilpa.org

Mission Statement: Global organization of institutional private equity investors including public pensions, corporate pensions, foundations and sovereign wealth funds.

Other Locations:
55 York Street
Suite 1200
Toronto, ON M5J 1R7
Canada
Phone: 416-941-9393 Fax: 416-941-9307

Key Executives:
Steve Nelson, Chief Executive Officer
202-804-6617
e-mail: snelson@ilpa.org
Education: BS, Boston College
Background: Cambridge Associates
Directorships: Loudoun Country Day School; American Chamber of Commerce in Singapore
Jennifer Choi, Managing Director, Industry Affairs
e-mail: jchoi@ilpa.org
Education: BA, Augustana College; MA, Fletcher School, Tufts University
Background: Emerging Markets Private Equity Assoc.
Greg Durst, Managing Direcor, Corporate Development
647-325-2889
e-mail: gdurst@ilpa.org
Education: BS, Georgetown University; Certificate, New York University; MBA, Harvard Business School
Background: Co-Founder & Senior Advisor, The Imprint Group LLC; Head, Business Development & Launch COO, Marto Capital LLC; EVP & COO, Accommodations Plus International; Executive Director, Seabury Group; Principal, Horizon Equity Partners; Managing Director, Endeavor South Africa; Managing Director, Conscripti
Matt Kelly, Managing Director, Education
e-mail: mkelly@ilpa.org
Education: BA, University of Virginia; JD, Washington & Lee University
Background: CEB, Inc.

Venture Capital & Private Equity Firms / National & State Associations

3267 LONG ISLAND CAPITAL ALLIANCE
1111 Marcus Avenue
Lake Success, NY 11042
Phone: 516-592-5855
e-mail: info@licapital.org
web: www.licapital.org

Mission Statement: LICA connects investors with opportunities in the state of New York.
Geographic Preference: New York
Founded: 1984
Portfolio Companies: Abrams Fensterman, ActionCOACH, Ambrose, Applied Visions, Asset Enhancement Solutions LLC, BDO USA, The Berkman Law Firm, Blue Pixels Media, Breslow & Walker LLP, Broad Hollow Bioscience Park, Button Down Solutions LLC, Campolo Middleton & McCormick LLP, Capell Barnett Matalon & Schoenfeld, Chasella Capital Partners, Checks and Balances Bookkeeping, Collaborative Medical, CORE Interactive, Crystal & Company, Darrow Associates, EAA Inspection Services, Eagle Business Solutions, EisnerAmper LLP, Executive Strategies Group LLC, Farrell Fritz PC, Ferrera DeStefano & Caporusso, FranchiseKnowHow LLC, Fulwisdom Capital, Golden Seeds, Grassi & Co., GxG Management LLC, HJMT Communications LLC, Hoffman & Baron LLP, Insperity, iSine, Jaspan Schlesinger LLP, Jericho Capital Corp., Jove Equity Partners, JP Morgan Private Bank, Katz Sapper & Miller, Ken Taub, Kildare Capital, Marcum LLP, Northwood Ventures, NYIT, Oximeter Plus, Patient Innovations, Protegrity Advisors, Pryor Cashman LLP, Ringo, Riscica Associates, Rivkin Radler LLP, Ruskin Moscou Faltischek, Soundview Advice, Stony Brook University, Trident Group, TriNet

Key Executives:
Michael Lane, CEO
e-mail: mlane@licapital.com
Education: BA, University Of California, Los Angeles; MBA, Columbia Business School
Background: CEO, SteriLux Systems; President, Plum Logic; President, Real Content Media Group; President & CEO, Data Impact Inc.; General Manager & SVP, Bottomline Technologies; Managing Director, Pegasystems Inc.; Managing Director, Vitria Technology; CMO, Accenture
Directorships: Darrow Associates; Saint Matthew's Society; Broadlook Technologies; RingLead Inc.

3268 LOS ANGELES VENTURE ASSOCIATION
11301 Olympic Boulevard
Suite 376
Los Angeles, CA 90064
Phone: 866-466-5282 Fax: 866-537-4899
e-mail: info@lava.org
web: www.lava.org

Mission Statement: Learning and networking forum for Los Angeles entrepreneurs and investors.
Geographic Preference: Los Angeles
Founded: 1985
Portfolio Companies: Members: Applied Facts, Arizona Technology Enterprises, Bryant Stibel, Direct Health Delivery, Fine Line Services LLC, Fox Rothschild, Knobbe Martens, Knobbe Martens Olson & Bear, March Capital Partners, Moss Adams, Peate Institute for Entrepreneurs, Silver Regulatory Associates, Stubbs Alderton & Markiles LLP, Toronto Stock Exchange, Trade & Invest British Columbia, USC Stevens Center for Innovation

Key Executives:
Darren Eng, Executive Director
Education: BS, Yale University
Background: Executive Director, SoCal; Founder, The Sponsorship Group; CEO, Greenbelt Resources Corporation

3269 MICHIGAN VENTURE CAPITAL ASSOCIATION
39555 Orchard Hill Place
Suite 203
Novi, MI 48375
e-mail: info@michiganvca.org
web: michiganvca.org

Mission Statement: Association of the Michigan entrepreneurial and investment community.
Geographic Preference: Michigan
Founded: 2002
Portfolio Companies: 5AM Ventures, Allos Ventures, Amherst Fund, Ann Arbor Angels, Apjohn Ventures, Arbor Partners, Arboretum Ventures, Arsenal Venture Partners, Augment Ventures, Baird Capital, BELLE Michigan, Beringea, Capital Community Angels Investors, Chrysalis Ventures, Cultivian Sandbox, Detroit Innovate, Detroit Venture Partners, Dow Venture Capital, Draper Triangle Ventures, EDF Ventures, Flagship Ventures, Fletcher Spaght Ventures, Fontinalis Partners, GM Ventures, Grand Angels, Great Lakes Angels, Grosvenor Capital Management, Hopen Life Sciences Venture, Huron River Ventures, Hyde Park Venture Partners, IncWell, Invest Detroit, Invest Michigan, Ludlow Ventures, Mercury Fund, Michigan Accelerator Fund, Michigan Angel Fund, Michigan eLab, MK Capital, Muskegon Angels, North Coast Technology Investors, Northern Michigan Angels, Plymouth Ventures, Renaissance Venture Capital Fund, Resonant Venture Partners, River Cities Capital Funds, RPM Ventures, Start Garden, TGap Ventures, Three Leaf Ventures, Valenti Capital, Venture Investors, Wolverine Venture Fund

Key Executives:
Ara Topouzian, Executive Director
e-mail: Ara@MichiganVCA.org
Education: Marketing, Oakland Community College; BA, Wayne State University
Background: Musician; President & CEO, Troy Chamber of Commerce; Economic Development Director, City of Novi, Michigan; Owner, American Recording Productions; President, Farmington Chamber of Commerce
Directorships: Michigan Society of Association Executives; Michigan Council for Arts & Cultural Affairs; Creative Many Michigan; Troy Community Foundation
Angela Helfin, Associate Director
e-mail: Angela@MichiganVCA.org
Education: BA, Spring Arbor University; MBA, Liberty University
Background: Head Osoccer Coach, Ann Arbor Public Schools; Founder, Vaulted Foundations; Co-Founder & Executive Officer, Education for All; Business Development Strategist & HR Director, Employees Only; Director of Development, MI Association of Public Schools; Chief Academic Officer, K-12 School District
Directorships: Ann Arbor Public Schools; Early Childhood Initiatives; Northrock Church

3270 MID-ATLANTIC VENTURE ASSOCIATION
1400 K Street NW
Suite 1100
Washington, DC 20005
e-mail: mava@mava.org
web: mava.org

Mission Statement: Association serves the needs of innovators, venture capital and private equity in the Mid-Atlantic region.
Geographic Preference: Mid-Atlantic
Portfolio Companies: Investor Members: 3TS Capital Partners, ABS Capital Partners, Boulder Ventures, Camber Creek, CIT GAP Funds, Columbia Capital, Core Capital Partners, Fulcrum Equity Partners, Harbert Growth Partners, Inner Loop Capital, In-Q-Tel, JMI Equity, Kinetic Ventures, New Enterprise Associates, Osage Venture Partners, Paladin

Venture Capital & Private Equity Firms / National & State Associations

Capital Group, Revolution Growth, River Cities Capital Funds, Route 66 Ventures, Sands Capital Ventures, Squadra VC, TCP Venture Capital, TDF Ventures, Updata Partners, Vital Venture Capital

Key Executives:
Julia Spicer, Executive Director
Education: BA, Communications, University of North Carolina
Background: VP, Communications, Columbia Capital; President & COO, IntellEvents; GTE Corporation
Jason Waxberg, Senior Director, Strategic Services
Education: BA, Franklin & Marshall College; MBA, College of William & Mary
Background: Principal Consultant, Water's Edge Strategies; Founder, RoadFan; Founder & CEO, Receptive Mail; Strategic Markets Analyst, Holland & Knight LLP; Market Research Analyst, Waxberg Consulting Company

3271 MISSOURI VENTURE FORUM
123 S Spoede Rd
St. Louis, MO 63141

Phone: 314-241-2683
web: www.mvfstl.org

Mission Statement: The Missouri Venture Forum is a non-profit organization designed to provide a means for entrepreneurs to grow their companies through networking, education, information exchange and access to financial resources.

Founded: 1985
Portfolio Companies: Sponsors: BDO, Carmody MacDonald, Danna McKitrick PC, Evans & Dixon, Greensfelder, Mueller Prost, Regional Growth Capital, Schmersahl Treloar & Co., St. Louis Arch Angels

3272 NATIONAL VENTURE CAPITAL ASSOCIATION
25 Massachusetts Ave NW
Suite 730
Washington, DC 20001

Phone: 202-864-5920 **Fax:** 202-864-5930
web: nvca.org

Mission Statement: The National Venture Capital Association is a trade association that represents the venture capital community of the Unites States. The NVCA supports entrepreneurial activity by promoting policies that encourage innovation and investment, as well as providing data resources and professional services for its member firms.

Portfolio Companies: Industry Partners: Deloitte, Dentons, DLA Piper, Duff & Phelps, EY, First Republic Bank, Gunderson Dettmer, IHS Markit, KPMG, Latham & Watkins, Morgan Lewis, Morrison & Foerster, Nelson Mullins, Pacific Western Bank, Perkins Coie, Phoenix American Financial, PitchBook, Proskauer, Sensiba San Filippo, Shaerworks, Sidley Austin, Signature Bank, Sparkpr, SRS Acquiom, VMS Fund Administration, William Blair, WilmerHale, Wilson Sonsini Goodrich & Rosati, Withum

Other Locations:
T3 Advisors Studio
137 Forest Ave
Palo Alto, CA 94301

T3 Advisors Studio
140 Geary Street
Suite 1000
San Francisco, CA 94108

Key Executives:
Bobby Franklin, President & CEO
202-864-5925
e-mail: bfranklin@nvca.org
Education: BSBA, Finance & Banking, University of Arkansas, Fayetteville
Background: EVP, CTIA The Wireless Association; VP, Federal Government Affairs, ALLTEL; Legislative Director, AESOP Enterprises

3273 NEW ENGLAND VENTURE CAPITAL ASSOCIATION

e-mail: info@newenglandvc.org
web: newenglandvc.org

Mission Statement: The New England Venture Capital Association's mission is to promote venture capital investing and strengthen the entrepreneurial community in New England. NEVCA seeks to accelerate the growth of new businesses, help build partnerships between entrepreneurs and investors, and support innovation-friendly public policies.

Geographic Preference: New England
Portfolio Companies: Members: Abingworth, Ascent Venture Partners, Atlas Venture, Battery Ventures, Bessemer Venture Partners, Boston Seed Capital, Breakthrough Energy Ventures, Broadview Ventures, Connecticut Innovations, Converge Venture Partners, CRV, Dell Technologies, Echo Health Ventures, F-Prime Capital, Flare Capital Partners, Flybridge Capital Partners, Founder Collective, G20 Ventures, General Catalyst Partners, Highland Capital Partners, In-Q-Tel, Infinite Road, Innospark Ventures, Innouvo, Johnson & Johnson Innovation, LaunchCapital, LRV Health, LS Polaris Innocation Fund, MassCEC, MassDevelopment, MassVentures, Matrix Partners, MPM Capital, New Enterprise Associates, NextView Ventures, Novartis Venture Fund, Oak HC/FT, Omega Funds One Way Ventures, Optum Ventures, Orion Equity Partners, Point Judith Capital, Polaris Partners, Pulse Ventures, RA Capital, Romulus Capital, Schooner Capital, SR One, SV Health Investors, Tectonic Ventures, The Engine, Third Rock Ventures, Tiger Iron Capital, Underscore, Venrock, Victress Capital, Vida Ventures, Will Ventures, XFactor Ventures, Zaffre Investments

Key Executives:
Jody Rose, President
Background: SVP, Corporate Development & Digital Strategy, Blueprint; Swirl Networks; Rue La La; MTV Networks; The Food Network; HGTV
Directorships: My Sister's Keeper
Ari Fine Glantz, Director of Development & Strategic Initiatives
Education: Vassar College

3274 NJ TECH COUNCIL
96 Albany Street
New Brunswick, NJ 08901

Phone: 732-456-5700
e-mail: hello@njtc.org
web: njtc.org

Mission Statement: The New Jersey Technology Council represents New Jersey's technology-related businesses. The NJTC supports its member companies by providing access to a variety of resources, including business development, education and networking opportunities.

Geographic Preference: New Jersey
Founded: 1996
Portfolio Companies: Members: DLA Piper, ECI Technology, Edison Partners, Eisner Amper, EPIC Insurance Brokers & Conultants, Ernst & Young, GHO Ventures, Grant Thornton, Kirusa, KPMG, Mercer County Community College, Morgan Lewis, Optima Global Solutions, Phone.com, PNC, Radiant Systems, Rowan University, Rutgers University, SPHERE Technology Solutions, Stevens Institute of Technology, Synchronoss Technologies, The Harris Agency, Tierpoint, Valley National Bank, Verizon, Wayside Technology Group, Yorktel

Key Executives:
Aaron Price, President & CEO
Background: Founder, Propelify; Founder, NJ Tech Meetup

3275 PITTSBURGH VENTURE CAPITAL ASSOCIATION
700 Bursca Dr
Suite 706
Bridgeville, PA 15017

Phone: 412-228-5826 Fax: 412-228-5879
e-mail: information@thepvca.org
web: thepvca.org

Mission Statement: The Pittsburgh Venture Capital Association was formed in 1982 to promote venture capital investment and entrepreneurship in the western Pennsylvania region. The PVCA represents western Pennsylvania's private equity investors and advocates for the venture capital industry through various programs, including networking events and other promotional activities.

Geographic Preference: Western Pennsylvania
Founded: 1982
Portfolio Companies: Sponsors: Activate Venture Partners, Adams Capital Management, Baker Tilly, Birchmere Ventures, BlueTree Allied Angels, BNY Mellon Wealth Management, Buchanan Ingersol & Rooney, Burns Scalo Real Estate, Carnegie Mellon University, Cherin Law Offices, CliftonLarsonAllen, Cohen & Company, Cohen & Grigsby, Dinsmore, Donnelley Financial Solutions, Connelly-Boland and Associates, Draper Triangle, EY, Fox Rothschild, IdeaFoundry, Innovation Works, KPMG, Kuzneski Financial Group, Louis Plung & Company, The Lynch Law Group, Meyer Unkovic & Scott, Morgan Lewis, Pepper Hamilton, Pittsburgh Equity Partners, Pittsburgh Life Sciences Greenhouse, Pittsburgh Technology Council, Quaker Capital Investments, Reed Smith, Right Brain + Left Brain, Rivers Agile, Saul Ewing Arnstein & Lehr, Schnader Attorneys at Law, Sisterson, TJS Insurance Group, Tucker Arsenberg Attorneys, University of Pittsburgh Innovation Institute, UPMC Enterprises, West Allen Capital

Key Executives:
   Mike Stubler, Chairman
   Education: BBA, University of Notre Dame
   Background: Vice President, CFO, International Cybernetics Corp.; CFO, Draper Triangle; Touche Ross & Company
   Directorships: New Media, Ayalogic, Unitask, TOA Technologies, Landslide
   Kelly Szejko, President
   Education: University of Pittsburgh
   Background: Founder, Tikes; Association for Corporate Growth (Pittsburgh Chapter)

3276 ROCKY MOUNTAIN VENTURE CAPITAL ASSOCIATION
798 Pope Drive
Erie, CO 80516

web: www.rockymountainvca.com

Mission Statement: The Rocky Mountain Venture Capital Association is an association for venture capitalists and entrepreneurs in the Rocky Mountain region of the United States.

Geographic Preference: Rocky Mountain Region
Founded: 1999
Portfolio Companies: Members: 104 West, Access Venture Partners, Aegis Legal Consulting, Bigfoot Captial, Boulder Ventures, Bow River Capital, Break Trail Ventures, Bridge Bank, Bullish, Canal Partners, Carta, Catalyst Law Group, Catapult Growth, CCIG, CIBC, Cobre Capital, Colorado Technology Association, Cooley, Coplex, Cornerstone Fund Services, Crawley Ventures LLC, Crowe UK LLP, Deloitte & Touche, Delta-V Partners, Epic Ventures, First Hill Partners, Foundry Group, Grayhawk Capital LLC, Greylock Partners, Holland & Hart, HSBC, Invest Southwest, Iron Gate Capital, Jones Lang LaSalle, Kickstart Seed Fund, KPMG, Liberty Global Ventures, Mercato Partners, Moreton and Company, Peak Ventures, Pelion Venture Partners, Perpetual Ventures, Point B Capital LLC, Rockies Venture Fund, RSM US, Signal Peak Ventures, Signature Bank NY, Silicon Valley Bank, SRS Acquiom, Stout Street Capital, Sun Mountain Capital, Tahoma Ventures, Tango/High Country Venture, Techstars Ventures, TenEighty, TMX, Trinity Capital Investment, UAVenture Capital, University of Denver, Upslope Capital Management

Key Executives:
   Nanette Schunk, Executive Director
   e-mail: nanette@rockymountainvca.com
   Education: BA, German, Math, Rutgers University
   Background: Principal, Strategic Solutions Marketing and Events; Chapter Manager, Entrepreneurs' Organization

3277 SOCIAL VENTURE CIRCLE
1111 W. El Camino Real
Suite 109-273
Sunnyvale, CA 94087

e-mail: hello@svcimpact.org
web: www.svcimpact.org

Mission Statement: World's largest early-stage investing network, formerly known as Investors' Circle and Social Venture Network.

Geographic Preference: North America
Fund Size: $3 million
Founded: 1992
Average Investment: $250,000 - $500,000
Investment Criteria: Startup, Early-Stage
Industry Group Preference: Energy, Consumer Products, Agriculture, Healthcare, Biotechnology, Digital Media & Marketing, Software, Education, Health & Wellness
Portfolio Companies: Agora Fund, Alter Eco America, APDS, Aunt Bertha, Avancen, aWhere, AYZH, Big City Farms, Bioceptive, BlocPower, California Safe Soil, Cardinal Resources, Castlewood Surgical, Community Sourced Capital, CSRHub, DailyWorth.com, DR2, E3Bank, EcoTensil, Edthena, Emerge, Eniware, EnSolve Biosystems, Episencial, EV Connect, Farmland LP, First Light Hospitality, Food Matters Market, Genomic Expression, Goalbook, Gridtest, Grower's Secret, Indow Windows, Isidore Electronics Recycling, Jack and Jake's, Jail Education Solutions, Kickboard, KnipBio, LearnZillion, Listen Current, Locus Energy, Lomo Market, Mamma Chia, Medolac, MicroEnergy Credits, MovingWorlds, MPOWERD, Mytonomy, Natural Systems Utilities, Oliberte, OtoSense, Pact Apparel, Peepoople, Portapure, Querium, Relay Foods, Rezzcard, Rivertop Renewables, Runa, Scrible, Seal Innovation, Social Imprints, Sundolier, SunFunder, Sustainable Minds, Susty Party, Thread, Transparent Healthcare, United By Blue, Validic, VOZ, Wash Cycle Laundry, Waste Enterprisers, Zagster

Other Locations:
   4225 Solano Avenue
   Suite 709
   Napa, CA 94558

Key Executives:
   Isaac Graves, Executive Director
   e-mail: isaac@svcimpact.org

3278 TEXAS VENTURE CAPITAL ASSOCIATION
PO Box 476
Austin, TX 78767-0476

Phone: 512-477-1991
e-mail: info@taraontheweb.com
web: www.txvca.org

Mission Statement: The Texas Venture Capital Association is a non-profit association that represents venture capital firms in Texas. In addition to protecting venture capital firms from harmful legislation, the TxVCA also provides information resources to its members and promotes the venture capital industry in both public and political environments.

Founded: 2004

Venture Capital & Private Equity Firms / National & State Associations

Key Executives:
　Blair Garrou, President
　Background: Mercury Fund

3279 THE COLLABORATIVE
10 S 5th Street
Suite 415
Minneapolis, MN 55402

Phone: 612-338-3828
e-mail: info@collaborative.net
web: www.collaborative.net

Mission Statement: The Collaborative serves to support Minnesota's community of investors, entrepreneurs and innovators. The Collaborative works with a range of businesses and teams, including startups, CFOs and growth-company CEOs, angels, venture capitalists and veteran investors. The organization's goal is to assist building companies in Minnesota.

Geographic Preference: Minnesota
Founded: 1987
Portfolio Companies: 2020 Marketing, ABILITY Network, ABRA Auto Body, Advanced Circulatory Systems, Affinity Capital Management, American Medical Systems, Baker Tilly, Barnes & Thornburg, BFL Capital, Black Dog Investment, Cairn Ventures, Calabrio, Code 42 Software, Comerica Bank, Cresa, Datuit, DelaGet, Dorsey & Whitney, EarthClean, Electromed, EY, Field Solutions, Galil Medical, General Blood, Grant Thornton, HDH Advisors, HSIO Technologies, Infinite Graphics, Insignia Systems, JAMF Software, Jones Lang LaSalle, Key Investment, Kidblog, Lemhi Ventures, LFE Capital, Lifecore Biomedical, Medafor, MicroNet, MOCON, MRI Robotics, Nanocopoeia, Norwest Equity Partners, Oak Investment Partners, Osprey Medical, Preventice, ProfoundNano, Proto Labs, Qumu, Respircardia, RespirTech, Restaurant Technologies, ReUrban, SALO, Segetis, SetSight, Sport Ngin, SterilMed, Technology Village, TFF, Tornier, Twin Cities Business, UAS Laboratories, Venture Bank, Virteva, Vital Images, Winland Electronics, Wipfli, XRS, Zimmer Spine, Zivix

Key Executives:
　Dan Carr, Founder

3280 UPSTATE CAPITAL ASSOCIATION OF NEW YORK
180 South Street
Suite 200
Highland, NY 12528

Phone: 845-204-8090
e-mail: info@upstatecapital.org
web: www.upstatecapital.org

Mission Statement: Statewide network of investors and advisors helps to build businesses in Upstate New York.

Geographic Preference: Upstate New York
Founded: 2003

Key Executives:
　Noa Simons, Executive Director
　Education: BA, Politics, Brandeis University
　Background: Founding Manager, Hudson Valley Startup Fund; Co-Founder, Community Compost Company; TianDi Growth Capital; Executive Director, Mary Ferrell Foundation

3281 VENTURE CAPITAL ASSOCIATION OF ALBERTA
Canada

e-mail: info@vcaa.ca
web: www.vcaa.ca

Mission Statement: Focuses on the professional development of members of the VC industry in Alberta.

3282 VENTURE CLUB OF INDIANA
3656 Washington Boulevard
Indianapolis, IN 46205

Phone: 317-926-2723
e-mail: info@ventureclub.org
web: www.ventureclub.org

Mission Statement: The Venture Club of Indiana is a non-profit organization dedicated to assembling entrepreneurs and investors through networking opportunities and ensuring the success of emerging and established companies. The Venture Club provides programs, seminars, luncheons, and other networking and education resources for Indiana's professional community.

Founded: 1984

3283 VENTURE CONNECTORS
462 S Fourth Street
Suite 2600
Louisville, KY 40202

Phone: 502-552-2140
web: www.ventureconnectors.org

Mission Statement: The Venture Connectors was established to advance business and commercial investment activities in the Kentuckiana area. The organization participates in monthly luncheon meetings and other entrepreneurial events with the goal of uniting entrepreneurs and investors.

Geographic Preference: Kentucky and Indiana
Founded: 1995

Key Executives:
　Larry Horn, President
　Education: BSc, Marketing, MBA, Entrepreneurship, University of Louisville
　Background: Executive Director, Louisville Entrepreneurship Acceleration Partnership; Co-Founder, Roth River; Co-Founder, Director, TNG Pharmaceuticals; Director, Ecosystem Development, Techstar; President, Great Northern Building Products; Co-Founder, CEO, Derby City Cut & Sew

3284 WESTERN ASSOCIATION OF VENTURE CAPITALISTS
3041 schooner Drive
El Dorado Hills, CA 95762

web: www.wavc.org

Mission Statement: The Western Association of Venture Capitalists is a non-profit venture capital organization dedicated to bringing venture capitalists together to socialize and network.

Geographic Preference: West Coast
Founded: 1969
Portfolio Companies: Members: Abingworth, Acacia Venture Partners, Accel Partners, Acuity Ventures, Alloy Ventures, Almaz Capital Partners, Altos Ventures, Asset Management Company, August Capital, Battery Ventures, Bay Partners, Benchmark Capital, BlueRun Ventures, Canaan Partners, Charter Life Sciences, Claremont Creek Ventures, Comerica, Costella Kirsch, DeNovo Ventures, Doll Capital Management, Draper Fisher Jurvetson, Draper Richards, El Dorado Ventures, Financial Technology Ventures, Focus Ventures, Foundation Capital, Fremont Ventures, Gabriel Venture Partners, Globespan Capital Partners, Glynn Capital Management, Highland Capital Partners, Horizon Partners, Hummer Winblad Venture Partners, Icon Ventures, IDG Ventures SF, Inman Investment Management, Institutional Venture Partners, InterWest Partners, Javelin Venture Partners, Khosla Ventures LLC, Kleiner Perkins Caufield Byers, Labrador Ventures, Lauder Partners, Legacy Venture, Levensohn Venture Partners, Lexington Partners, Lighthouse

Capital Partners, Lightspeed Venture Partners, Longitude Capital, Matrix Partners, Mayfield Fund, MedVenture Associates, Menlo Ventures, Mission Ventures, Mohr Davidow Ventures, Montreaux Equity Partners, Morgenthaler Ventures, New Enterprise Associates, Norwest Venture Partners, Onset Ventures, Osprey Ventures, Partech International, Peninsula Ventures, Pinnacle Ventures, Pitango Venture Capital, Redpoint Ventures, Rembrandt Venture Partners, RockPort Capital Partners, SBV Venture Partners, Scale Venture

Key Executives:

Ira Ehrenpreis, Co-President
e-mail: ira@dblpartners.vc
Education: BA, University of California, Los Angeles; JD, Stanford Law School; MBA, Stanford Graduate School of Business
Background: Founder & Managing Partner, DBL Partners; Technology Partners

Philip Sanderson, Managing Director
Education: BA, Economics, Hamilton College; MBA, Harvard Business School
Background: Managing Director, IDG Ventures; Chairman, VCNetwork; General Partner, WaldenVC; Associate, Robertson Stephens; Financial Analyst, Goldman Sachs

---

3285 WOMEN'S ASSOCIATION OF VENTURE & EQUITY INC.
10 Winton Farm Road
Newtown, CT 06470

Phone: 203-763-9255
Toll-Free: 855-928-3606
e-mail: wavecoordinator@gmail.com
web: women-wave.org

Mission Statement: Women's Association of Venture and Equity is a non-profit association that represents professional women in the venture capital and private equity industries. The organization offers a network of industry contacts with the goal of creating opportunities for its members.

Founded: 2003

Portfolio Companies: Sponsors: ACG New York, Association of Asiona American Investment Managers, CAIA Association, Kayo Conference Series, Mergers & Acquisitions

Key Executives:
   Julie Gionfriddo, President

College/University Index / Auburn University

A.B. Freeman School of Business
Daniel Finkelstein, 845

Aalborg University
Bo Ilsoe, 1330

Academy of Economic Studies
Raluca Florea, 332

Acadia University
Tyson Birchall, 2178

Adelphi University
John S Schnabel, 716

Adrian College
Roger Goddu, 334

Aga Khan University
Zia Agha, 1973

Albert Einstein College
Carl Goldfischer, MD, 237
Doug Kelly MD, 87

Albion College
Eric V Bacon, 1132
William Y Campbell, 1426
Nicholas S. Christopher, 1093
Evonna Karchon, 981
Peter W Klein, 348
Edward S. Pentecost, 1456

Alfred University
Marlin Miller, 1347
Thomas Sipp, 1635

Allegheny College
Michael S Bruno Jr, 1744
Sean Ward, 290

Ambassador College
W. Jack Kessler Jr., 494

American Graduate School of Mgmt
Lou Gerken, 822
Richard Harding, 1011
JJ Healy, 848
Robert Okun MIM, 1773
Marshall W Parke, 1112
Phil Samper, 805
Arnold B Siemer, 606
Robert L. Zorich, 672

American International College
Joelle Marquis, 170

American University
Stephen S Beitler, 636
Joy E. Binford, 1348
John Brecker, 99
Amy Burr, 1035
Matt Cheney, 499
James Conlon, 358
Celia Daly, 392
Troy Dayton, 1807
Vin Fabiani, 938
Robert J Flanagan, 508
John K Giannuzzi, 1665
David Gladstone, 828
Michael P Hompesch, 632
Richard E Maybaum, 1134
Michelle McCarthy, 1926
Ian J Mount, 1277
Cindy Rose Quackenbush, 1139
Robert Raynard, 1952
Bob Shaw, 192

Robert Shaw, Jr., 160

American University of Beirut
Raymond Debbane, 1018

Amherst College
Michael Barach, 990
Samuel Bartlett, 456
George W. Carmany III, 697
Brian J Conway, 1776
Alex De Winter, 809
David Douglass, 604
Paul Ferris, 215
David A Fiorentino, 1049
Michael T. Fitzgerald, 521
John W. Flanigan, 461
Standish Fleming, 769
William E. Ford, 815
Paul Goodrich, 1158
Douglas C Grissom, 1156
H. Irving Grousbeck, 949
Gregory Grunberg, 1143
Paulus J Ingram, 2248
Jeff Jordan, 124
Robert Keith, 1828
Rich Lawson, 959
Steven A Leese, 1503
Glen Lewy, 954
Brent Nicklas, 1112
James Patchett, 1308
Chris Pike, 62
Jon D. Ralph, 783
Mark Rosen, 456
Lisa Schule, 834
Tim Shannon, 386
Rob Sherman, 312
George W. Siguler, 1679
John I Snow III, 1503
Andrew Snyder, 846
Jason Sowers, 1999
Christopher Spofford, 343
Peter Taft, 1266
Devin Talbott, 680
Richard Upton, 907
Barry Volpert, 559
Tyler Wick, 21
Nicolas D. Zerbib, 1743

Amherst University
Benjamin Santonelli, 597

Amos Tuck School of Business
Allan Chou, 1341

Amsterdam School of Economics
Deborah de Rooij, 2248

Anderson School of Management
Michael Banks, 870
Frank Brenninkmeyer, 1431
Mike Carlotti, 203
Adam Chesnoff, 1598
Grace Chui-Miller, 544
Richard R Crowell, 1904
Greg Ennis, 1427
Alan Foster, 1793
David C. Franklin, 951
Tammy Funasaki, 331
Randy Glein, 609
John C. Hahn, 1496
Philip Han, 1598
Derek Idemoto, 483
Don Jamieson, 374
Buck Jordan, 397
Brian Knitt, 467
Michael A. LaSalle, 1660
Arthur Levine, 1111

James McDermott, 1895
Dana Moraly, 502
Michael Morgan, 373
Brian R. Nelson, 869
Robin Nourmand, 225
Daniel E Pansing, 1209
Paula Robins, 126
Charles W. Roellig, 449
Mark Rosenbaum, 199
Stephen D. Royer, 1660
Chris Shipman, 427
Rick Shuart, 374
Ryan A Smiley, 1567
Shahan D Soghikian, 1410
Sharon Stevenson DVM, PhD, 1371
Anil Tammineedi, 126
Denis A. Tito, 1989
Cleve Tzung, 203
Vishal Vasishth, 1363
Eric D Wedbush, 1969
William J. Wynperle, 1660

Andhra University
Pabhakar Reddy, 1285

Aquinas College
John M. Goense, 838

Arizona State University
Michael J Ahearn, 1859
Larry L. Aschebrook, 802
Jon W Bayless, 1658
David Baylor, 1910
Brian N Burns, 856
Daley Ervin, 677
Bart Faber, 192
Natalie Fleming Arora, 1758
Al Foreman, 1864
Gregory J Forrest, 765
Bill Harding, 1906
Paul D Kestler, 606
Steve Kirby, 297
Shannon Masjedi, 1399
Raj Pai, 834
Joseph Piper JD, 1002
John Reardon, 1850
Greg Robinson, 10
Scot E Swenberg, 478

Art Center College of Design
Adam Bruss, 264

Ashland University
Michael Butler, 1286
Kristy Campbell, 1553
Richard M. Ferrari, 598
Vince Owens, 886

Assumption College
John P. Clancy, 1496
Chris F. Corey, 1279
John Lawrence, 1146

Aston Business School
Ha Nguyen, 2190

Auburn University
Kevin D Cantrell, 1575
Billy L. Harbert, 282
Raymond J. Harbert, 904
Jerry Knotts, 3257
Jim Little, 1293
Charles R Martin, 111
Charles D. Miller, 904
Ron Sansom, 1572

College/University Index / Augsburg College

Augsburg College
Kinney Johnson, 1653

Augustana College
Jennifer Choi, 3266
Blaine Crissman, 1477
Rafael Romero, 667

Australian National University
Nathan Campbell, 868
Richard Cawsey, 605
Jeremy Liew, 1121

Babson College
Brady Bohrmann, 206
Braden M (Brady) Bohrmann, 1175
Glen R Bressner, 52
Glen R Bressner, 1227
Glen R Bressner, 1385
Daniel Budde, 901
John Burns, 329
John Burns, 1161
Yumin Choi, 221
Kevin Colleran, 1694
Dan Corcoran, 1173
Bob Davis, 935
Christopher W. Dick, 178
Jeffrey L. Dickson, 1497
Michael J Dolce, 1156
Suzanne L Dwyer, 1173
Cory Eaves, 815
Brett Gordon, 909
Mark Jrolf, 926
Andrew H Kalnow, 90
Caitlyn MacDonald, 1104
Robert J. Maccini, 125
William F McKinley, 1426
James F Milbery, 468
Mike O'Malley, 989
Amanda Outerbridge, 909
Igli Panariti, 3258
Stacie Rader, 747
David B Ragins, 492
Roger Roche, 1021
Sam Thompson, 1486
Randall Ussery, 1985
Martha DiMatteo Vorlicek, 909
Scott Voss, 909
Karan Wadhera, 417
Paul Weinstein, 215
John D. White, 774
John Whorf, 1294
Herbert P. Wilkins, Jr., 1771
Caleb Winder, 703

Baldwin Wallace College
Will Lynn, 881
David Moll, 988
Jeff Morton, 48
Karen Tuleta, 1266

Ball State University
James L Smeltzer, 409

Bandung Institute of Technology
Helman Sitohang, 554

Bangalore University
Mark Fernandes, 1670
Ashish Kaul, 765

Bar Iian University
Iian Bunimovitz, 44

Barnard College
Laura Belle Sachar, 1738
Beth Seidenberg, 1075

Barry University
Ali Safiedine DPM, 1289

Baruch College
Walter Barandiaran, 161
Mark Berman, 1364
Iian Bunimovitz, 44
Steven Chrust, 448
Daniel Colon, Jr., 507
Matthew Croft, 1130
Warren H. Haber, 774
Robert E Kelly, 1738
Jay F Laudauer, 1881
Kathleen Thomas, 1033

Bates College
J Michael Chu, 1088
Patrick J Donnellan, 691
Gregory A. Ehret, 1444
Lori Lombardo, 683

Baylor College of Medicine
Billy Cohn, MD, 1619
Stephanie Kreml MD, 241
Philip Sanger MD, 1801

Baylor Law School
Kevin Green, 545

Baylor University
James G Benedict, 1071
Joe Cunningham MD, 1619
Jerry DeVries, 1801
Brenda D Gavin, 1508
Christopher K. Mirabelli, PhD, 919

Beijing Center for Chinese Studies
Jeff Schlapinski, 3261

Beijing Normal University
Ru-Guang Bal, 905

Beijing University
Ting Gootee, 658

Beirut University
Firas El Amine, 1017

Belmont University
Theresa Sexton, 493

Beloit College
Justin Benshoof, 373
Arthur Schneiderman, 833
Charles M. Warden, 1928

Bemidji State University
Dan Hodgson, 1131

Ben-Gurion University
Dror Berman, 996
Gideon Soesman, 2142

Benares Hindu University
Vish Mishra, 502

Benedictine University
Richard P Earley, 636

Benjamin N. Cordozo School of Law
Alison Berman, 1401
Greg S. Feldman, 1971

Bentley College
Jason Caplain, 1710
Paul Flanagan, 1672
Paul Flanagan, 1673

Kevin Gillis, 1811
Craig Gilmore, 414
Paul Homer, 1344
Edward J Keefe, 1153
Edward A Lafferty, 1623
Kelly Meldrum, CFA, 57
Marcus Ogawa, 1513
Kim Sichel, 1139
Bruce Tiedemann, 312
Richard Zannino, 433

Berea College
Mark Bolinger, 1064

Berkeley School of Law
David Baylor, 1910

Berkeley School of Public Health
Joel Finlayson, 2149

Berklee College of Music
Michael Godwin, 1547

Bernard Baruch College
Marta De La Cruz, 834

Berry College
Karen Houghton, 189

Bethany College
Dave Carlson, 685

Bethel College
Tim DeVries, 1345

Bilkent University
Murat Aktihanoglu, 684

Binghamtom University
Steven G Glenn, 1956

Binghamton University
Alberto Bianchinotti, 1216
Rich Levandov, 206
Richard W Levandov, 1175
David Rubin, 1205
Sean C. White, 1724
David Zilberman, 518

Birla Institute of Technology
Ajay Chopra, 1853
Vijay C Parikh, 833

Birmingham Southern College
Donald C. Harrison, 458

Bishop's University
Paul Bamatter CA, 109
Sasha Jacob, 2075
Don McKelvie, 2086
Sam Saintonge, 2290
Eric Schmadtke, 676

Bloomsburg University
Kimberly Kyle, 22
Vincent P. Menichelli, 53
Jordan Ormont, 1202

Boalt Hall School of Law
Anthony Patek, 253

Bob Jones University
Meredith Pflug, 213

Bocconi University
Luca Bassi, 220
Igli Panariti, 3258

College/University Index / Boston University

Emilio S Pedroni, 733

Bogazici University
Santo Politi, 1715

Bombay University
Sandeep D Alva, 716
Atul Kamra, 1688
Darshana Zaveri, 426

Booth School of Business
Sean Barrette, 468
Gale Bowman, 1019
Scott Brown, 654
Lauren K Bugay, 633
Brian F. Chambers, 1409
Ashish Chandarana, 1925
Joanne Chen, 770
Nicholas S. Christopher, 1093
Adam Cranford, 1293
Krisin Custar, 1045
Yizhen Dong, 4
Kaitlyn Doyle, 1019
Sean Doyle, 1610
Paul W. Drury, 1111
Michael Eisinger, 2214
Mark Emery, 1045
Paul Fishbin, 901
Ryan Gembala, 1421
Nathan J Good, 1469
Michael Goy, 1267
John Grafer, 1622
Thomas R. Groh, 104
Anna Haghgooie, 1615
Matthew Hankins, 928
Jason Heltzer, 1384
Brent Hill, 1384
Charlie Hipwood, 1172
Timothy Huang, 1112
Andy Jones, 1169
Kevin Keefe, 1467
Steve Klammer, 1369
Scott McConnell, 88
Sean M McNally, 1469
Drew Molinari, 577
Paul Purcell, 222
Pabhakar Reddy, 1285
Frank Reppenhagen, 529
Joseph R Rondinelli, 789
Douglas J. Rosenstein, 873
Ian Ross, 529
Konrad Salaber, 1990
Jay W Schemelter, 1574
Thomas P. Shaw, 900
Jason Sowers, 1999
Edwin Tan, 401
Guy Turner, 962
Kyle Veatch, 926
Ira Weiss, 962
Ray Zhang, 1467

Boston College
Rich Aldrich, 1145
David L. Anderson, 1757
Michael C. Ascione, 254
Darrell W Austin, 201
Tate Bevis, 1040
Anik Bose, 249
Aaron Bright, 1432
John Burns, 329
Steve Burns, 1505
John Burton, 1886
James D. Carey, 1743
Mike Carlotti, 203
Matthew T. Carroll, 1979
Amit Chandra, 220
Andrew Chang, 1115

Dan Colao, 808
Paul A. Colone, 77
William C Connell, 931
Dan Corcoran, 1173
Chris J. Crosby, 1279
Paul D'Addario, 1402
Mark DeBlois, 359
Mark DeNino, 1828
Joe Del Guercio, 508
Kenneth M. Doyle, 894
Jere Doyle, 1673
Scott Feldmen, 1759
David Fialkow, 816
Andy Flaster, 1942
Christopher S. Gaffney, 857
Wayne P. Garrett, 66
Bill Geary, 748
Anthony Giannobile, 359
Brian Gorczynski, 1925
Mark Gordon, 2208
Marshall Griffin, 528
Brendyn T Grimaldi, 897
David Harnisch, 484
D Thomas Healey Jr., 1573
Marty Hernon, 312
Tim Heston, 255
Erika Highland, 828
Jason Hill, 1195
Charlie Hipwood, 1172
Mary T Hornby, 18
Lincoln Isetta, 1255
Raymond J Jeandron III, 1144
Thomas H Jennings, 1752
Matthew E Keis, 812
Douglas L. Kennealey, 328
Charlie Kim, 1186
Paul LaViolette, 1628
Paul LaViolette, 1762
John Malloy, 296
TJ Maloney, 1127
Jack Manning, 309
Michael Marino, 200
Louis Marino, 818
Matthew McCooe, 530
John F McCormack, 1651
Ryan Milligan, 468
Eric C. Morgan, 1456
Steve Nelson, 3266
Albert A. Notini, 1301
Daniel Nova, 935
Tim O'Loughlin, 646
Frank J Pados Jr, 632
Mike Pellini, 1643
Joseph Pesce, 859
Barbara Piette, 1077
Brian Pryor, 1195
Jill C. Raker, 862
Jonathan M Rather, 1972
Michael Rawlings, 477
Andrew Riley, 1908
Bijan Sabet, 1715
Corey Schmid, 1656
Mary Shannon, 586
Mary M Shannon, 1175
Keith C Shaughnessy, 1224
Kyparissia Sirinakis, CPA, 689
Theodore J. Smith, 638
Jeb S Spencer, 1869
Geoffrey D. Spillane, 873
Brian Stansky, 1003
Kevin Starr, 1811
Greg Stupore, 14
Mark A. Tarini, 156
Lee J Tesconi, 1112
Mike Wong, 938
Steve Wood, 835
Caroline Yeager, 1019

Boston College Law School
James D. Carey, 1743
Frank Castellucci, 38
Joel Cutler, 816
Mary T Hornby, 18
Brian J. Knez, 421
James D. Leroux, 179
Christopher Mirabile, 1100
John P Shoemaker, 1234
Daniel Weintraub, 194

Boston College School of Management
Richard Joseph, 194

Boston University
Bruce Adams, 979
Matthew Ahern, 1077
Mitch Baruchowitz, 1207
Eric Berke, 2272
Bryan Biniak, 1495
Kevin Blank, 881
Chris Bodnar, 646
Mike Bologna, 860
Glen R Bressner, 52
Glen R Bressner, 1227
Glen R Bressner, 1385
Thomas E. Brew Jr., 66
Richard Burnes, 455
Keith Carlton, 886
Brian Cohen, 1306
Brian Cohen, 1310
Ira D Cohen, 1886
Evan Corley, 1411
Todd Dagres, 1715
Rick Defieux, 1689
Trung Q. Do, 1419
Joseph J. Downing Jr., 77
Gregory A. Ehret, 1444
Jamie E Elias, 1857
April E Evans, 1248
Dave Fachetti, 835
Sidney J Feltenstein, 1651
Adam E Fine, 1993
Hadley Ford, 966
Constance Freedman, 1246
A Leigh Fulmer, 647
Jonathan Glass, 1235
Brett Gordon, 909
Melanie Grace, 925
Jeff Grammer, 2239
Shai Greenwald, 380
Mark G. Hilderbrand, 949
Eugene Hill, 1628
George R. Hutchinson, 1032
Masa Isono, 602
Angela Jackson, 1463
Linda Jacobson, 32
Jeffrey R. Jay, MD, 859
Debbie Johnson, 21
Thomas W Jones, 1873
James Jordon, 1448
Karen Kajmo, 3264
Brandon M. Katz, 492
Ryan Keating, 1427
Ugur Kilic, 2075
John E Knutsen, 1156
Scott Kokones, 886
Peter Lamm, 722
Charles R Lax, 848
Renske Lynde, 8
Michael J Lyons, 1127
Robert MacInnis, 21
Ian B. MacTaggart, 357
Travis Macinnes, 38
Robert D Manchester, 1162
Rebecca Norlander, 976

College/University Index / Boston University School of Law

Albert A. Notini, 1301
Geoffrey S. Oblak, 178
Anne-Mari Paster, 1373
Gordon R Penman, 1920
Robert Raynard, 1952
Shari Redstone, 60
Manu Rekhi, 1013
Vin Ryan, 1627
Robert Savignol, 1153
Steven Schwartz, 239
Aydin Senkut, 720
Arjun Sethi, 1848
Chris Shipman, 427
Zubeen Shroff, 806
Joshua B. Siegel, 1595
R Adam Smith, 481
Gideon Soesman, 2142
Lou Volpe, 1080
Marc J Walfish, 1209
Paul Walsh, 368
Todd Warden, 907
James Westra, 62
Mike Wong, 938
Ron Wooten, 1349
Darshana Zaveri, 426
Jeffrey M. Zucker, 860

Boston University School of Law
Michael L. Gordon, 127
Randal A. Nardone, 767
Jonathan D. Salon, 242
Richard Taney, 1864

Bowdoin College
Frank Castellucci, 38
Tom Costin, 1392
J. Taylor Crandall, 1360
Brendan Dickinson, 386
Patrick D. Dunn, 1496
Mike Farrell, 1717
Harry A George, 1702
Ryan Giles, 2275
Thomas Groves, 64
Peter Grua, 938
Jason P Hafler, 1618
Paul A Howard, 1197
Julie Jubeir, 406
Michael P McQueeney, 1751
Tom Needham, 1775
Henry W Newman, 1702
Jake Odden, 20
Jared B Paquette, 359
Jeff Patterson, 515
Scott B. Perper, 1409
Peter R. Seaver, 139
Sheldon Stone, 1362
Joshua R. Weiner, 740
Tim Wilson, 174

Bowling Green State University
William Y Campbell, 1426
Kenneth Petrilla, 473
Maribeth Rahe, 766
Brad Seaman, 2214
Tom Shehab, 149

Bradeis School of Law
Tianpeng Wang, 2195

Bradford University
Steven Tang, 626
Timothy Watkins, 1902

Bradley University
Brent Hill, 1384
Nancy O'Leary, 1038
Robert Riemer, 175

Brandeis University
Nick Adams, 614
Mitch Baruchowitz, 1207
Stephen Berger, 1368
Kevin Gillis, 1811
Jonathan Ginns, 46
Matt Gorin, 533
Brian Hirsch, 1849
Jeffry S. Pfeffer, 407
Bruce Pollack, 447
Noa Simons, 3280
Eric D. Starr, 407
Scott Tobin, 235

Bridgewater State College
Suzanne L Dwyer, 1173

Brigham Young University
Peter Bodine, 84
G Stephen Browning, 1652
Fraser Bullock, 1705
Gavin Christensen, 1070
John Clark, 1431
Gary Crittenden, 959
Matt Downs, 1615
Nick Efstratis, 688
Paul K. Erickson, 462
John Fife, 470
Stewart Gollmer, 1796
Sid Krommenhoek, 79
Tim Layton, 1705
Rand Lewis, 441
Legrand Lewis, 1705
Ryan Lucero, 782
Mark Ludwig, 1705
Robert Lund, 999
John Mayfield, 79
Ron Mika, 1705
Allen Miner, 1755
Blake Modersitzki, 1425
Diogo Myrrha, 79
Chad Packard, 1425
Shane R. Peery, 462
Scott Petty, 1677
Robert Pothier, 1542
Nate Quinn, 1202
Andrew Ray, 2155
Trevor C Rich, 1147
Bryce Roberts, 1359
Colin Robinson, 470
Ryan Sanders, 1204
Sean Schickedanz, 498
Brian S Smith, 856
Scott L. Snow, 746
Luke Sorenson, 1705
Spencer Tall, 84
Tyler Thompson, 1642
Brandon Tidwell, 1677
Kenton S. Van Harten, 902
Kurt C. Wheeler, 495
Kirk Whickman, 127
Brandon C. White, 456
Steve Young, 959
Dal Zemp, 1542

Brighton Polytechnic University
Stephen K Smith, 1175

Bringham Young University
Jeff Kearl, 1425
Ben Lambert, 1425

Bristol Polytechnic
Peter Van Cuylenburg, 555

Bristol University
Mark Emery, 1045

Stuart Gent, 220
Tom Hulme, 889
Duncan Priston, 239

Brooklyn College
Harry Edelson, 651
Irwin Federman, 1896

Brooklyn College Law School
Mark Berman, 1364
Steven E Berman, 1401
Jack Feiler, 1401
Steven M. Friedman, 686
Howard Goldstein, 1911

Brooklyn Law School
Andrew Sturner, 557

Brooklyn Polytechnic Institute
Stephen Einhorn, 400

Brown University
William F Aikman, 882
William J. Aliber, 1496
Norman W. Alpert, 1931
C Mark Arnold, 1529
Zaid Ashai, 1459
Mark Attanasio, 556
Chris Baldwin, 455
Marc C Bergschneider, 1735
Alison Berman, 1401
Elizabeth Q Betten, 1156
William Bianco, 1617
Eric D Bommer, 1651
Orlando Bravo, 1814
Robert M Brill, 1314
Jeff Brodlieb, 448
Bernie Buonanno, 1279
James J. Burke Jr., 1023
C.A. Burkhardt, 953
Phil Calian, 1964
Rich Caputo, 1045
Ashish Chandarana, 1925
David Chao, 596
Robert A. Comey, 1016
Glenn M. Creamer, 1496
Duncan Davidson, 358
Owen Davis, 1358
Michael Dearing, 911
Lister Delgado, 971
Jonathan E Dick, 1476
Brendan Dickinson, 386
Hythem T El-Nazer, 1776
Karim Faris, 889
Timothy J Flynn, 1109
Scott Friend, 221
Matt Garfunkle, 1411
Chris Girgenti, 1480
David Goldburg, 1207
Ross Goldstein, 608
Bob Goodman, 260
Habib Y Gorgi, 1279
Theresia Gouw, 180
Anthony P. Green, PhD, 246
Oliver Haarmaan, 2252
Geoff Harris, 755
Randy Haykin, 1389
Ned Hazen, 1119
Blair Hendrix, 220
Troy Henikoff, 1178
Eric Hjerpe, 1065
Spencer P Hoffman, 1147
Ben Holbrook, 1171
James Joaquin, 1363
G. Kent Kahle, 888
Steven E Karlson, 1994
Andrew Kau, 1951

1014

Peter Keehn, 88
James T. Kiernan, 2086
John Kim, 1062
Richard C Klaffky, 739
Lauren Kolodny, 180
James Kondo, 820
Nathaniel V Lentz, 1387
Anthony Limberis, 744
Felix Lo, 839
Hambleton Lord, 1100
Fern Mandelbaum, 1249
Fern Mandelbaum, 1939
Saif Mansour, 330
Saif Mansour, 331
Paul Margolis, 1146
Christopher Masto, 787
Samuel M Mencoff, 1156
Anthony Moretti, 352
Kevin A. Mundt, 1931
Brian R. Nelson, 869
Jonathan M. Nelson, 1496
Carl Nichols, 1389
Daniel S. O'Connell, 1931
Kenneth O'Keefe, 1931
Christian L. Oberbeck, 1621
Michael B Persky, 80
Robert Petty, 504
Geoffrey S. Raker, 1777
Patrick Rea, 392
Andy Sack, 773
Paul J. Salem, 1496
Andrew Schiff, MD, 74
Mark Selcow, 547
Eric H. Sillman, 136
Brad Silverberg, 974
Lawrence B. Sorrel, 1777
Barry S. Sternlicht, 1739
Dickson Suit, 1021
Craig C. Taylor, 87
John Toomay, 1408
J Russell Triedman, 1129
James E Vandervelden, 1824
Timothy Wang, 1977
Donna Williamson, 452
Stoddard M Wilson, 1579
Tyler Wolfram, 1360
Naeem Zafar, 95
Alex Zisson, 1817
Alex von der Goltz, 310

Bryant College
Karen Kajmo, 3264
Scott Voss, 909

Bryant University
Jim Barra, 1021
Matthew J Hurley, 716
Jason King, 422
Daniel M Kortick, 1984
Christopher Quinn, CPA, 879
Jennifer Trzepacz, 1985
Walter Wiacek, 722

Bryn Mawr College
Karen Kerr, 809

Bucknell University
Mark Allsteadt, 401
Nathaniel P Bacon, 359
Michael Brooks, 1505
Frank Brown, 815
Richard E Caruso PhD, 1494
James Conlon, 358
Michael J. Dominguez, 1496
Richard B Emmitt, 1929
Daniel M Gill, 1684
Lisa Hagerman, 595

Lee C Hansen, 1213
Doug Hitchner, 1368
James Howland, 1256
Karen Kassouf, 437
Matt Kraus, 439
Mark Langer, 401
Robert Le Blanc, 2209
Jessica Livingston, 2012
James McLaughlin, 1127
Scott A Perricelli, 1136
F. Matthew Petronzio, 1871
Dennis G Prado, 1159
Brian Regan, 1717
John Reynolds, 1125
James LD Roser, 1586
Doug Rotatori, 1368
Gerald Saltarelli, 654
John Sinnerberg, 577
Robert M. Williams Jr., 1037
Ryan Ziegler, 655

Butler University
Jorge Jaramillo, 1386
Sean McGould, 1120
Joseph P Schaffer, 1252

Caleton University
Bernie Zeisig, 2195

California Institute of Technology
Dr Philippe H Adam, 186
Scott Chou, 805
Michael Ehlers, 143
Gil Elbaz, 1798
Ilya Fushman, 1075
Venky Ganesan, 1202
Karen Gilmore, 487
Bill Gross, 972
Dylan Hixon, 826
Wen Hsieh, 1075
Michael Hunkapiller, 87
Robert M Jaffe, 1706
Neena Kadaba, 2229
JJ Kang, PhD, 517
Regis B Kelly PhD, 1238
Walter Kortschak, 1675
Dr. David Lee, 494
Shaun Maguire, 889
Janis Naeve, PhD, 112
Leo Polovets, 1758
Mike Ross, 1762
Michael Ross PhD, 1628
Micah Siegel, 2278

California Polytechnic State Univ.
Craig Chrisney, 972
Daniel L. Delaney, 985
Clifford L Haas, 1672
Mark Lydon, 1004
Matthew McDonald, 227
Matthew T. Potter, 604
Carol Wong, 595

California State University
Bary Bailey, 558
Kelly J. Barlow, 1903
Gil Beyda, 518
Gil Beyda, 814
Eva Bjorseth, 1365
Brian Chiang, 1951
Bruce Cleveland, 1985
Gary Cuccio, 1793
John Earhart, 834
Doug Fahoury, 1020
Edward Hamati, 267
Kirby Harris, 229
R. Bryan Jadot, 925

Jim Johnson, 1915
Craig A.T. Jones, 1824
Leo Kim PhD, 214
Nellie Levchin, 1631
Claudia L. Llanos, 132
Jeff Low, 645
Sonja Markova, MBA, 226
William Miller, 126
Michelle Moreno, 629
Lori L. Murphree, 1369
Javier Noris, 1630
Lisa Riedmiller, 151
Lisa Riedmiller, 1407
Rami Rostami, 1876
Mary Ann Sigler, 1451
Gordon Smythe, 2195
Kevin T. Walsh, 946

California State University, Chico
Nick Sturiale, 1658

California State University, LA
Ana Quintana, 275

California Western School of Law
Bruce Taub, 190

Calvin College
Mike DeVries, 652

Cambridge University
Michael Chae, 277
Ashish Chandarana, 1925
Joel Finlayson, 2149
Wei Liu, 219

Campbell University
Michael S. Marr, 405

Canisius College
Brian D'Amico, 1751
Lindsay Karas, 1286

Cardozo School of Law
Sonia Gardner, 208
Jeffrey Schultz, 1283

Caregie Mellon University
Sreekar Gadde, 293

Carleton College
Brian Birk, 1754
Stephen Davis, 227
Craig Hanson, 1319
Laurence Lederer, 327
Matthew Strongin, 738
Alexander D Whittemore, 1752
Charles Yim, 641

Carleton University
Sean Brownlee, 2239
Patrick Edeburn, 850
Kim Furlong, 3258
Ryan Haughn, 2246
Byron Horner, 2085
Matt Ivis, 3258
Deepak Kamra, 386
Richard R Kracum, 1990
Peter Lawler, 2055
Rob MacLellan, 2204
Pablo Srugo, 2195
Paul Weiss, 1921

Carlson School of Business
Darren Brathol, 1719

1015

College/University Index / Carlson School of Management

Carlson School of Management
Kathleen A Tune, 1817

Carnegie Mellon University
Joel P. Adams, 56
Robert C. Ammerman, 402
Roger D Bailey, 606
Jacques Benkowski PhD, 1896
Jonathan Berkowitz, 1810
Keith Block, 1607
Jeff Branman, 937
Philip L. Bronner, 1348
Paul Burke, 1810
Jason Cahill, 408
Babs Carryer, 1098
Tony M Chou, 1929
Patrick J Donnellan, 691
Edward R Engler, 1447
Geoff Entress, 1499
Michael Farah, 1128
Edward Frank PhD, 59
Kim P. Goh, 954
Gregory T Hebrank MD, 1098
Peter Herz, 8
Larry Kaplan, 242
Raj Kapoor, 1184
Jay Katarincic, 628
Vinod Khosla, 1069
Manu Kumar, 1050
Eric Kwan, 1138
Rich Lunak, 998
J. Kenneth Moritz, 1746
Vince Owens, 886
Cindy Padnos, 976
Justin B. Petro, 1810
Randall E. Poliner, 131
Maryanna Saenko, 800
Tom Shehab, 149
Avie Tevanian, 659
Stanley W Tucker, 1208
Dan Watkins, 1206
Robert B. Wetzel, 196
Young Yeo, 1864

Carroll School of Management
J.P. Sanday, 1202
Steve Wood, 835

Carroll University
Daniel J. Greifenkamp, 240

Carson Newman College
Dell Larcen, 881

Case Western Reserve University
Vijay Aggarwal, PhD, 1808
Cindy Babbit, 577
Mike Biddle, 2111
Asheem Chandna, 872
Tony M Chou, 1929
Wayne L Clevenger, 1230
Jason R. Cornacchione, 1456
Leonard M Cosentino, 1287
Michael D'Agostino, 1432
Suzette Dutch, 1847
David Fries, 1906
Timothy Gosline, 1572
Brian Hersman, 1041
Karen Hodys, 747
David Jargiello, 756
David Kabakoff, 921
David Kabakoff, 1698
Byron Ling, 386
Frank Linsalata, 1132
Will Lynn, 881
Joe Mandato, 598
Bassem A Mansour, 1545

John McIlwraith, 86
Ryan Meany, 653
Shailesh Mehta, 851
Ki Mixon, 1545
Jon Pastor, 298
Edward S. Pentecost, 1456
Arvind Purushotham, 486
Steven H Rosen, 1545
David Ryan, 1239
Richard Schwarz, 653
Rachid Sefrioui, 729
Karen Spilizewski, 1574
Robert Strother, 1287
Geoffrey B Thrope, 1287

Catholic University of America
Jorge Aguilo, 522
Manuel Jose Balbontin, 522
William Robbins, 1398
Thomas A Scully, 1972
Jim Walker, 57

Catholic University of Eichstaett
Martin Beck, 222

Cedarville University
Mark Horne, 1455

Central Connecticut State Univ.
Alexander R Castaldi, 1039
Kristen Kosofsky, 925

Central Michigan University
Matthew Blevins, 503
Steven E Hall, 1124
Kevin Hofmann, 1576
Doug Neal, 2023

Central Washington University
Steve Bailey, 782
Denny Weston, 753

Chapman University
Doug Francis, 664
Steve Nelson, 473

Chiao-Tung University
C.K. Cheng, 905

Chicago-Kent College of Law
Maurice Doyle, 61
Daniel Norr, 203

China Europe Int. Business School
Dennis Wu, 290

Chinese University of Hong Kong
Hing Wong, 1951

Christian Brothers University
Ryan Schuler, 176
Russ Williams, 16

Chuo University
Michio Fujimura, 183

City College of New York
Steven Kotler, 827
William E. Macaulay, 740

City University London
James D.C. Pitt, 1112
Tim Wright, 848

City University of New York
Ira D Cohen, 1886
Peter Kalkanis, 2239

Donald B Marron, 1123
Ralph Montana, 1960
I. Donald Rosuck, 1093
Anthony J Veith, 503
Jeanette M Welsh JD, 1792

City of London College
Neil J. Taylor, 321

Claremont Graduate University
José Blanco, 573
P Frank Limbaugh, 759

Claremont McKenna College
Michael Arrington, 564
Kevin Baker, 368
Sean Dempsey, 1218
Patrick Gallagher, 564
Russell J. Greenberg, 104
E David Hetz, 572
Jeffrey Johnson, 276
Jeffrey W. Johnson, 827
Randy Moser, 200
Scott I. Oakford, 899
George Roberts, 1082

Claremont Men's College
Michael Martin, 1956

Clark Atlanta University
H Bryan Britt, 1529

Clark University
Larry Bohn, 816
Dan Devorsetz, 946
Sonia Gardner, 208
Howard Goldstein, 1911
Bob Hurst, 559
Marc Lasry, 208
John Morris, 909
T Nathanael Shepherd, 1862
Steven Swain, 440

Clarkson University
Thomas J. Buono, 263

Clemson University
Matt Dunbar, 1923
Pat Duncan, 213
Thomas L Greer, 794
Stuart McWhorter, 496
Emily Schillinger, 3255
Lane W Wiggers, 164

Cleveland Marshall College of Law
Peter W Klein, 348
Arnold B Siemer, 606

Colby College
Charles Beeler, 1522
Joel Cutler, 816
Michael D'Agostino, 1432
Michael L. Gordon, 127
Todd W. Halloran, 783
Matthew G Hamilton, 1752
Michael Henderson-Cohen, 845
Matt Lapides, 21
Alex Levental, 1021
Mike O'Malley, 989
Steve Rappaport, 1376
Glenn Rieger, 1317
Ned Scheetz, 138
Kevin Starr, 1811
Cal Wheaton, 22
Caleb Winder, 703

College/University Index / Columbia Business School

Colby-Sawyer College
Charlotte D. MacDonald, 949

Colgate University
Christopher J. Ackerman, 750
Will Adams, 92
Brion B Applegate, 1717
Matt Auster, 1596
John C. Bombara, 946
Lee E Bouyea, 786
Scott Brown, 654
Bob Chatham, 1693
Jean-Pierre L. Conte, 819
Brian Dovey, 621
James L. Elrod Jr., 1931
David Fialkow, 816
Charles Fleischmann, 1851
Andrew S. Gelfand, 355
Robert Gold, 1564
Gary L Goldberg, 1624
Jonathan Grad, 897
Christopher Hooper, 1972
David W Jahns, 806
Christian B. Johnson, 783
William Johnston, 909
Elliott Jones, 168
Jamie Lane, 1867
David Lincoln, 657
Christopher W. Lynch, 178
Dave Marple, 1907
John Mazzarino, 463
Edward McNulty, 573
Christopher Mirabile, 1100
Thomas Murphy, 815
Ramzi M Musallam, 1925
Gordon G. Pan, 222
Jean-Pierre Paquin, 240
Jeffrey Reals, 1431
Tyler Reeder, 675
Jonathan D. Salon, 242
Graham Schena, 1266
Stefan L Shaffer, 1726
Mayank Singh, 446
Eric Von Stroh, 1141
Bruce Wesson, 806

College des Ingenieurs
Nicolas Chaudron, 2851

College of Charleston
Richard Maclean, 790

College of Notre Dame
Nancy McCroskey, 183
Casey Tansey, 1896

College of Saint Elizabeth
John Guiliana DPM, 1289

College of St. Catherine
Ann Winblad, 956

College of William & Mary
Matthew P. Antaya, 985
Tom Benedetti, 288
Alexander E. Carles, 1971
James J Connors II, 1062
Ted Dintersmith, 455
Edmund J Feeley, 1134
Tim Komada, 600
D Scott Mackesy, 1972
Mark McFadden, 433
Stacey McKittrick, 142
James B Murray Jr, 551
Bob Pavey, 1257
Kelly Perkins, 1120
Scott Perkins, 1120

Lisbeth Poulos, 979
G Michael Stakias, 1116
Craig Staub, 1368
James W. Tucker, 546
Jason Waxberg, 3270

College of Wooster
David G. Arscott, 524
Tom Jones, 628
John Kneen, 244

College of the Holy Cross
Edward J Condon Jr, 1414
Kevin J. Curley, 1037
Bill Fitzgerald, 816
Thomas W Gorman, 1636
Michael Greene, 66
Daniel James, 1851
Jay Katarincic, 628
Jeffrey Keay, 909
Brian P Kelley, 1129
Robert J. Maccini, 125
Hank Mannix, 1062
Stephen Muniz, 1501
John J Murphy Jr, 1274
Matthew Schaefer, 714

Colorado College
Nicholas B Binkley, 765
Alexander Ellis III, 1579
Dave Furneaux, 1080
Craig Hart, 208
Eric Hender, 17
Pete Hudson, 94
William E James, 1579
James McDermott, 1895
Eben S Moulton, 1636
Mike Slade, 1641
Lucius H. Taylor, 156
Timothy Thompson Black, 1002
Peter O. Wilde, 1496

Colorado School of Mines
David Becker, 1194
Ryan Bennett, 1548
Ross Bhappu, 1548
Tom Glanville, 696

Colorado State University
Celia Daly, 392
Doug Fahoury, 1020
John Greff, 1653
Alan Howard, 1793
Brian Knitt, 467
Tracy Marshbanks, 732
John Ord, 542
Phil Parrott, 467
Timothy Reeser, 146
Ryan Williams, 542

Columbia Business School
Jeffrey S Barber, 1776
Jonathan P Barnes, 897
Luca Bassi, 220
Stacey Bishop, 1626
Stephen Bordes, 109
Timothy P Bradley, 1674
Michael S Bruno Jr, 1744
Jon Canarick, 1335
Michael Cardamone, 30
Russell L Carson, 1972
Mark H Carter, 1776
Eli Casdin, 419
Jerome A Chazen, 460
David F Chazen, 460
Alan Chen, 374
Ben Choi, 1106

Trace Cohen, 1310
Jim Collis, 1638
Elizabeth Colonna, 918
Stephen B. Connor, 899
Chris F. Corey, 1279
Ben Dahl, 1677
Owen Davis, 1358
James T. Denton, 343
A. Sinclair Dunlop, 689
Roger Ehrenberg, 965
Hythem T El-Nazer, 1776
Derek Eve, 673
Dorian Faust, 881
Alex Ferrara, 260
Matthew W Finlay, 1230
James Frischling, 878
Chris Girgenti, 1480
Liron Gitig, 793
Michael Goldberg, 99
Tom Groos, 488
Stewart KP Gross, 1123
Mukul Gulati, 2018
Timothy T. Hall, 476
Howard A. Halligan, 714
David Heidecorn, 1088
Michael Henderson-Cohen, 845
Daniel Hoffer, 204
Kevin M. Jackson, 873
Janet James, 1579
Jay Jordan, 1045
Teddy Kaplan, 1301
John Kim, 933
Matt Kinsey, 361
Roger Kitterman, 1419
John Kornreich, 1617
Roman Krislav, 239
Michael Lane, 3267
Eric Lauerwald, 1023
Amy S Lazarus, 1726
Jean-Francois Le Ruyet, 1516
Jeffrey A. Lipsitz, 546
Scott MacLeod, 834
John F. MacMurray, 1621
Marc Magliacano, 1088
James Manges, 1851
Carol Mao, 799
Lenard Marcus, 655
Edward W Martin, 492
David Martirano, 1459
Peter C McWilliams PhD, 1616
Chip Meakem, 1849
Ezra Mehlman, 918
Peter H Mills, 1
Frank Mora, 958
Malcolm C Nolen, 1674
Dennis O'Brien, 1131
Ting-Pau Oei, 644
Grant Palmer, 1851
Stephanie Palmeri, 1879
Douglas A Parker, 1230
Anil Patel, 502
Michael Patterson, 1911
Brian Peters, 933
Grant Pritchard, 1976
Paul B Queally, 1972
Jay Radtke, 1171
Marc Rappoport, 1305
Manu Rekhi, 1013
Anthony Ressler, 159
Jake Reynolds, 1785
Saul Richter, 1568
David S Rose, 1584
Devraj Roy, 1022
Laura Belle Sachar, 1738
Jason Santiago, 1748
Sandeep Sardana, 295
Douglas Schrier, 1540

1017

College/University Index / Columbia College

Bob Schulz, 918
Robert Shafir, 1635
Lawrence R Simon, 503
Vic Singh, 679
Craig Slutzkin, 1298
Robert Smith, 1938
Joshua Sobeck, 14
Jose M. Sosa del Valle, 1112
Dickson Suit, 1021
Patrick Sullivan, 220
Neil S. Suslak, 322
Steven Swartzman, 364
Hans Swildens, 986
Bob Tamashunas, 1638
Andrew C. Taub, 1088
Owen G. Tharrington, 873
James W. Tucker, 546
Jordan Turkewitz, 2020
Emily Turner, 486
Mark F Vassallo, 1123
W Lambert Welling, 1198
Robert J. Wenzel, 74
Ryan Wierck, 849
Eric J. Wilkins, 1409
Keith Zadourian, 1022
Gerard von Dohlen, 343
Max von Zuben, 1984

Columbia College
Andrew Fink, 1844
Winston H. Song, 1931

Columbia Law School
Thomas A Alberg, 1158
Rashid Alvi, 913
Hiram A. Bingham, 588
Kevin J. Curley, 1037
Andrew Fink, 1844
Brian P. Friedman, 1032
Stephen Friedman, 1743
Neil Garfinkel, 779
Liron Gitig, 793
Gregory P Ho, 1730
Lauren B Leichtman, 1111
Arthur Levine, 1111
Michael Martin, 1956
Ivar W. Mitchell, 123
Anil Patel, 502
Jon Rattner, 192
Bob Shapiro, 570
Robert Shapiro, 1615
Stephen C. Sherrill, 354
Dick Spalding, 1059
Brandon Tidwell, 1677

Columbia Medical School
Anand Mehra, 1698

Columbia Teachers College
Thomas H Kean, 1504

Columbia University
Kenneth S Abramowitz, 1325
Vignesh M. Aier, 1301
Cate Ambrose, 3261
Ed Anderson, 1334
Mark Attanasio, 556
Stuart A. Auerbach, 118
Gerald T. Banks, 101
Jeffrey Barman, 1431
Marc Beauchamp, 2206
Robert J. Beckman, 1808
Michael Bego, 1076
Christopher Behrens, 433
Michael C Bellas, 261
James G Benedict, 1071
Peter Bennett, 1116

Jay Bernstein, 1085
Len Blavatnik, 34
Christopher D. Brady, 457
Mike Brown Jr., 317
C.A. Burkhardt, 953
Kristina Burow, 153
Stephen E. Canter, 2018
Eli Casdin, 419
Mike Cataldo, 1142
Kevin Centofanti, 352
Duncan A Chapman, 1112
Robert Chefitz, 1328
John W Childs, 1049
Jonathan Y Chou, 698
Todd Clapp, 427
Gregory E. Clark, 946
Wayne L Clevenger, 1230
Vanessa Colella, 486
John Connor, 21
Sally Corning, 1754
Usama Cortas, 1109
Stephen Davis, 227
Charles A. Davis, 1743
Gabriel de Alba, 2073
Steven DeCillis II, 64
Rick Defieux, 1689
James R. Deitzer, 355
David N Deutsch, 589
Elias Dokas, 1231
Christopher M. Doody, 1743
George Doomany, 123
John Drew, 1785
Charles P. Durkin, Jr., 1621
Ron Eastman, 697
Dr. Edgar G Engleman, 1941
Rick Essex, 1496
Dean E Fenton, 1735
Paul J Ferri, 1181
Ezra S. Field, 1576
Roger S Fine, 1993
Ronald D Fisher, 1699
Steven Flyer, 193
Jean-Francois Formela, MD, 191
Joseph M Gantz, 1443
Andrew S. Gelfand, 355
Kim P. Goh, 954
Robert Goldberg, 536
Michelle Goldberg, 974
Edwin A Goodman, 52
Bob Goodman, 260
Habib Y Gorgi, 1279
Jorge Gross Jr, 1857
Peter Grua, 938
Oliver Guinness, 1258
Joshua L. Gutfreund, 494
Charles Gwirtsman, 1086
Seth L. Harrison, M.D., 143
Rob Hayes, 741
Michael Henderson-Cohen, 845
Charles Ho, 41
Ben Horowitz, 124
Joe Horowitz, 968
Timothy F Howe, 474
Peter Hsing, 1218
Mark Hsu, 892
Christopher B Hunt, 1573
Thomas S Huseby, 1637
Nikos Iatropoulos, 1051
Phil Jakeway, 1127
Don Jamieson, 374
J. Blair Jenkins, 462
Richard Johnson, 1228
Elliott Jones, 168
Alan L Kaganov ScD, 1896
Habib Kairouz, 1558
Habib Kairouz, 2239
Julius Kalcevich, 966

George C Kenney, 1664
Fred Kittler, 730
Richard C Klaffky, 739
Stephen Knight MD, 710
Henry R Kravis, 1082
Celine Kwok, 858
A. Rachel Laheny, 1898
Peter Lamm, 722
Mark Langer, 401
Philippe Le Houérou, 1007
Douglas Leone, 1654
Anton Levy, 815
Jeanne Li, 126
Richard Lipkin, 644
Robert W. Liptak, 495
Cherie Liu, 1390
James LoGerfo, 643
Paul Lucas, 2152
Megan Lundy, 1129
Patrick A. Maciariello, 523
Josh Makower, 1297
David Marquardt, 197
Matthew McCooe, 530
Doug McCormick, 1558
Edward McNulty, 573
Chip Meakem, 1080
Matt Miller, 1952
Sami Mnaymneh, 928
Jonathan Mo, 4
Bernard Moon, 1716
John Morris, 909
David Moszer, 1491
Eben S Moulton, 1636
Fayez S. Muhtadie, 1743
Shay Murphy, 1324
Eugene P. Nesbeda, 546
Christian L. Oberbeck, 1621
Arnie Oronsky, 1010
Carlo Padovano, 1376
Jim Pastoriza, 1782
Bob Pavey, 1257
James A. Pelusi, 211
Michael S Pfeffer, 1465
Cary Pfeffer MD, 1811
Brett L. Prager, 610
Thomas Queenan, 1441
Gary Ragusa, 408
Steve Rappaport, 1376
Robert F Raucci, 1314
Brian Rich, 427
Saul Richter, 1568
Jonathan D Root MD, 1896
David S Rose, 1306
Laura Belle Sachar, 1738
Rohan Saikia, 859
Jason Santiago, 1748
James G. Schiff, 1344
Andrew Schiff, MD, 74
Daniel Schultz, 608
George J Schultze, 1629
Rick Shuart, 374
Stephan Siegel, 2271
Ian Sigalow, 871
Michal Silverberg, 1350
Ajit Singh, 174
R Adam Smith, 481
Stephen H Spahn, 1504
Edson W. Spencer Jr., 68
Donald Spero, 1299
Sheldon Stone, 1362
Béla Szigethy, 1572
John L. Teeger, 774
John Trbovich, 171
Robert Tucker, 401
Gayle L Veber, 1909
Martin Vogelbaum, 1558
Gerard von Dohlen, 343

College/University Index / Cornell University

John E. Walvoord, 1697
Michael Weingarten, 1676
Joshua S. Weinstein, 403
Robert Weisskoff PhD, 710
Bruce Wesson, 806
Christoph Westphal, 1145
Bill Wiberg, 59
Alan Wilkinson, 64
Robert M. Williams Jr., 1037
Katherine Zamsky, 408

Concordia University
Joe Canavan, 2201
Cam Di Prata, 2133
Michael Griffiths, 2169
Brent G. Hughes, 2091
Colin King, 2090
Stefano Lucarelli, 2055
Khalil Maalouf, 2290
Dale MacMaster, 2033
Genevieve Morin, 2119
David Nault, 2179
Jerome Nycz, 2055
Daniel Pharand, 430
Zoya Shcuhpak, 2156
Amy Ssuto, 162
Gregoire Tremblay, 2072
Ray Zhang, 1467

Connecticut College
Seth W Alvord, 739
Tim Armstrong, 134
Andrew P. Bonanno, 1081
Michael J Dubilier, 631
Will Manuel, 110

Connecticut State University
Steven F. Wood, 1014

Copenhagen Business School
Jan Leschly, 412

Copenhagen College of Pharmacy
Jan Leschly, 412

Copenhagen University
Christian Borcher, 411

Cornell College
Chris Christoffersen PhD, 1122

Cornell Law School
John C. Bombara, 946
David Castle, 327
C Deryl Couch, 1753
Steven Flyer, 193
James McLaughlin, 1127
Jonathan H. Owsley, 1088
Frank Schiff, 1231
Stefan L Shaffer, 1726
Andrew Spring, 1231
David J. Wermuth, 1743
Shari H. Wolkon, 1815

Cornell University
Neeraj Agrawal, 235
Eric Aguitar, MD, 74
Sandeep D Alva, 716
Seth W Alvord, 739
Dr. Alf L. Andreassen, 1400
David Bainbridge, 1927
Dr John Baldeschwieler, 186
Dennis Baldwin, 329
John Balen, 386
Rajeev Batra, 1184
Eric Beckman, 330
Eric Beckman, 331

Michael Bego, 1076
Cécile Belaman, 220
Adam Bendell, 1831
Skip Besthoff, 422
Michael Biggee, 1850
Bluette N. Blinoff, 1799
Chris Bodnar, 646
David J Breazzano, 597
Frank W. Bruno, 451
Andrew M Bushell, 540
Andrew Byrd, Jr., 1870
Stephen E. Canter, 2018
J Michael Cline, 39
John Collins, 1751
Ed Colloton, 260
David D Croll, 1153
Tim DeVries, 1345
Karen Derr Gilbert, 793
Salil Deshpande, 221
Dan Devorsetz, 946
Omar Diaz, 629
Christopher W. Dick, 178
Jeffrey Diehl, 57
A. Barr Dolan, 458
Douglas M. Dunnan, 875
Park Durrett, 29
David Eichler, 1498
Stephen Einhorn, 400
Daniel Einhorn, 400
Neil Exter, 1811
Noel J Fenton, 1853
Paul J Ferri, 1181
Ari Fine, 148
Michael J Foster, 1557
Craig D Frances MD, 1752
Lizzie Francis, 342
Daniel Freyman, 1123
Stephen Friedman, 1743
Michael Fulton MD, 943
Quin Garcia, 204
Quin Garcia, 205
Benjamin D. Geiger, 783
David S. Gellman, 801
Jason Gerlach, 1756
Jim Gilbert, 747
Gary L Goldberg, 1624
Allan R. Goldberg, PhD, 1808
Noah Goodhart, 1980
Jonah Goodhart, 1980
Michael D Goodman, 849
Alissa Grad, 844
Mitch Green, 2081
Tom Groos, 488
Oliver Guinness, 1258
Eugene Hahn, 1039
Ammar H. Hanafi, 87
Leonard M. Harlan, 423
Christopher R Hemmeter, 1806
Sharlyn C. Heslam, 254
Geoff A. Hill, 1576
Eva Ho, 728
Stuart Holden, MD, 1490
Aaron Holiday, 13
Timothy Huang, 1112
Ron Hunt, 1298
Anwar Hussain, 1559
Meli James, 3263
Dave Johnson, 1004
Scott Johnson, 1291
Andy Jones, 1169
Thomas W Jones, 1873
Habib Kairouz, 1558
Habib Kairouz, 2239
Jonathan Kalman, 1025
Krishnamurty Kambhampati, 505
Agha Khan, 1743
William J Kidd, 1071

Ruben J King-Shaw Jr, 1165
Craig B Klosk, 1984
Lester B. Knight, 1590
Michael Koby, 5
Peggy Koenig, 21
Peter Kolchinsky, 1519
Mehmet Kosematoglu, 250
Marlene R. Krauss, 1058
Jennifer Krusius, 515
Samir Kumar, 1154
Dr. Anja König, 1350
Jeremy D. Lack, 188
Gerry Langeler, 1391
Cliff Lardin, 432
Jenny Lee, 823
Douglas Leone, 1654
Quinn Li, 1509
Michael Lynch, 1199
E Peter Malekian, 1189
Randy Maslow, 966
Michael Matly, MD, 1251
W. Christian McCollum, 1109
Scott A. McFetridge, 901
Kevin M. McGovern, 1191
Chip Meakem, 1080
Chip Meakem, 1849
Tony Miller, 1107
Daniel H Miller, 1580
Matt Miller, 1952
Ravi Mohan, 1663
Michael E. Najjar, 546
Jerrold Newman, 1987
Yi-Jian Ngo, 85
Scott Nolan, 775
Peter J Nolan, 1109
Nickie Norris, 926
Dale S Okonow, 1962
Adele Oliva, 5
Adele C Oliva, 1508
Douglas E. Onsi, 919
Peter B. Orthwein, Jr., 1727
Jeffrey P Parker, 848
Brian Peiser, 654
David Perez, 1403
Lee Pillsbury, 1806
Benjamin M. Polk, 1925
Bob Proctor, 285
Phil Proujansky, 432
John Raguin, 710
Lee Rand, 1754
Stan J Reiss, 1181
Meredith L Rerisi, 18
Rebecca B Robertson, 1928
Joseph R Robinson, 1230
Micah Rosenbloom, 771
Jonathan D Roth, 18
Bryon C Roth, 1588
Lawrence Rusoff, 1431
Bruce Sachs, 455
Doug Schillinger, 639
Raj Seth, 925
Sam Sezak, 288
Rajeev Shah, 1519
Saurabh Sharma, 1046
Bob Shaw, 192
Robert Shaw, Jr., 160
Thomas R Shepherd, 1862
Zachary Shulman, 432
Andrew Singer, 675
Robert Smith, 1938
Donald Spero, 1299
Gregory Stento, 909
David Stern, 502
John Stobo, 22
Gordon Stofer, 464
Richard Stokes, 928
Brent Stone, 21

College/University Index / Cornell University Medical College

David Strasser, 1766
Roger A Strauch, 1580
Thorsten Suder, 401
Ilya Sukhar, 1181
Scott Sweet, 1139
Jason R. Tagler, 383
Juliet Tammenoms Bakker, 1143
Larry Tanenbaum, 2169
Jennifer Tegan, 432
Ralph Terkowitz, 22
Bill Trenchard, 741
Jordan Turkewitz, 2020
Guy Turner, 962
Christopher Turner, 1956
Jeff Valentine, 705
Andrew W Verhalen, 1181
Carter A. Ward, 156
Gus Warren, 1611
Jeffrey M. Webb, 985
Andrew J Weisenfeld, 1271
Victor Westerlind, 809
Bill Wiberg, 59
Gred Widroe, 1195
Charles A. Wiebe, 263
L John Wilkerson, 806
Matthew L Witte, 1168
Josh Wolfe, 1151
Shari H. Wolkon, 1815
Eric Young, 386
Philip M Young, 1896
James W Young PhD, 12

Cornell University Medical College
Craig D Frances MD, 1752
Andrew Schiff, MD, 74

Cranfield School of Management, UK
Bill Kelsall, 681
Neil J. Taylor, 321

Creighton University
Mike Buttry, 464
Mark Hasebroock, 635
Jeanne Mariani Sullivan, 1738
S Edward Torres, 1124

Creighton University School of Law
Patrick J Duffy, 1276

Cumberland School of Law
Charles A Cox, 1144
John W. McCullough, 904

Curtin University, Australia
Bill Kelsall, 681

D'Amore-Mckim School of Business
Michael P. Murphy, 1585

Dalhousie University
Peter Bilodeau, 2122
Carl Burlock, 2112
Stephen Denton, 2251
Tom Eisenhauer, 2065
Joel Finlayson, 2149
Jody Forsyth, 2038
Alex MacBeath, 2164
Chris Moyer, 2216
Yann Robard, 2289
Brice Scheschuk, 2134
Michael Siltala, 2287
Jeff Van Steenbergen, 2050
Peter Williams, 2038

Daniels College of Business
Anders Bjork, 21

Darden School of Business
Wes Blackwell, 1632
Jonathan B. Blanco, 746
Douglas Burns, 551
Thomas A. Carver, 910
Gregory W. Cashman, 844
Randy Castleman, 551
C Taylor Cole Jr, 910
Terry Daniels, 1505
Christopher Delaney, 1023
Jonathan Ebinger, 296
S. Whitfield Edwards, 746
Sean Foote, 1089
Paul Johan, 224
Sean M. Kelley, 873
Robert Kibble, 1239
Joel Lanik, 790
Richard Maclean, 790
David M Maher, 352
Rajan Mehra, 502
Bob More, 94
William Powell, 2067
Jeffrey Schutz, 441
Erik A. Scott, 1403
William B. Thompson, 780
Richard Upton, 907
Jonathan R Wallace, 1388
Russ Williams, 16

Dartmouth College
Brent Ahrens, 386
Reis L Alfond, 1881
Alexei Andreev, 205
Alison Andrews Reyes, 7
Paul Asel, 1330
Richard Aube, 1443
Kathleen Bacon, 909
Michael Balmuth, 1762
Maren Thomas Bannon, 1026
Peter Barris, 1297
Andrew Beebe, 1363
Walter M (Jerry) Bird, 1172
Leon Black, 140
Daniel L Black, 1984
Stephen Bloch, 386
Graham Brooks, 2
Mark Brooks, 1626
Brian J. Buenneke, 1411
Bill Burgess, 23
Jon Callaghan, 1860
Dana Callow, 312
William J Canestaro, 2008
Baron Carlson, 64
John R Carroll, 1752
Russell L Carson, 1972
Eric Chin, 563
Allan Chou, 1341
William D Christ, 1776
Peter Chung, 1255
Peter Clark, 2143
Peter Clark, 2216
Doug Cole, 747
William E Conway Jr, 413
Everett R Cook, 1466
Marshall Cooper, 863
Jeffrey M Crowe, 1346
Benton Cummings, 1516
Sean L. Cunningham, 884
Diane M. Daych, 434
Gerard A Debiasi, 1071
Casper de Clercq, 1346
Liam Donohue, 2
Dana Donovan, 631
Chris Egan, 62
Timothy M. Evans, 156
Patrick Fallon, 29
Matt Fates, 178

Phil Ferneau, 308
Jim Feuille, 563
Michael Fisch, 110
Peter Fitzgerald, 1094
Walter C Florence, 789
Tony Florence, 1297
Andrew N. Ford, 903
Walter G. Freedman, 1093
Charlie Friedland, 820
Carolyn Galiette, 1021
Bob Geiman, 431
Steven Gillis, 153
Cliff Gilman, 72
Tom Goodrich, 581
Steven C. Graham, 846
Kenneth A. Graham, 1014
Laura A. Grattan, 1815
Jason Green, 665
Jonathan M Haas, 492
Beth Haas, 577
Kallie Hapgood, 873
John Henderson, 966
Ted Henderson, 1627
David Hodgson, 815
Alec Hufnagel, 1062
William S. Hughes, 1496
Jonathan E. Hunnicutt, 1979
Michael C. Jackson, 949
Jeff Jackson, 1806
Glenn Jacobson, 1851
Ross Jaffe, 1928
Janet James, 1579
Ross M. Jones, 254
Daniel G. Jones, 1815
Scott A. Kehoe, 1014
Yoo Jin Kim, 1104
Rick Kimball, 1785
Thies O Kolln, 17
Mark Koulogeorge, 1242
Jeffrey Kovach, 170
Mike Krupka, 221
Farouk Ladha, 777
Stephen M LeSieur, 1717
M Steven Levy, 1272
Morgan Livermore, 820
Bernardo H. Llovera, 706
Phil Loughlin, 220
Chris Lund, 899
David Mace, 824
Ben Magnano, 782
Rick Magnuson, 824
David M Maher, 352
John Maldonado, 62
Robert D Manchester, 1162
Andrew R. Mayer, 1777
Frederick Maynard, 909
Tim McAdam, 1785
Stephen McCormack, 521
Matt McIlwain, 1158
David McKenna, 62
Roger McNamee, 659
Nate Mitchell, 820
Brendan M. Moore, 686
Erik Moore, 229
Chris Moore, 1534
John H. Moragne, 1850
Mark J Morrissette, 1333
Rick Moss, 253
Richard Nathan, 2167
Joseph M. Niehaus, 949
John Nies, 1040
Nate Niparko, 28
Scott O'Hare, 594
Jake Odden, 20
William Ogden, 1881
Sandy Osborne, 1062
Jonathan W Osgood CFA, 572

College/University Index / Duke University

Bart D Osman, 1112
Bruce Ou, 879
John E. Palmer, 903
David J. Parker, 118
Victor E Parker, 1717
Marni F. Payne, 254
Tripp Peake, 1142
Doug Pepper, 1663
Dennis Phelps, 1001
Tony Pritzker, 1479
Tony Pritzker, 1480
Jake Reynolds, 1785
James T Rich, 812
Jeff Richards, 823
Matt Rightmire, 308
Ren Riley, 1361
Bryan Roberts, 1916
Greg Robinson, 10
Doug Roeder, 604
Jonathan D Root MD, 1896
Mike Ross, 1762
Michael Ross PhD, 1628
John G Rudge, 1112
Aaron Sack, 1256
John K. Saer Jr., 824
Enrique Salem, 221
Scott Sandell, 1297
Aaron Sandoski, 1347
Dan Sanner, 92
Dan Scholnick, 1853
Hondo Sen, 188
Derek Senft, 2123
Derek Senft, 2218
Derek Senft, 2274
Scott Silverman, 70
David Silverman, 563
Stanley T. Smith, 1771
Mark Soane, 142
Stephen Socolof, 1305
Stephen H Spahn, 1504
Holden Spaht, 1814
John L Steffens, 1730
Josh Stein, 609
Scott Stuart, 1602
Eric Swanson, 888
Timothy R Sweeney, 637
Dave Tabors, 235
Bill Tarr, 1258
Robert M Tichio, 1573
Michael Triplett, 1000
Emily Turner, 486
Kapil Venkatachalam, 1785
Tom Washing, 1653
Daniel Weintraub, 194
Forest Wester, 1857
T.J. Whalen, 786
Edward J. Whelan, 254
Kirk Whickman, 127
Elizabeth C Williamson, 789
Robert D Winneg, 1296
Chris Winship, 793
Alfred S Woodworth Jr, 647
William J. Wynperle, 1660
Royce G. Yudkoff, 21
Keith Zadourian, 1022

David Eccles School of Business
Brad Money, 869

Davidson College
Cathy Belk, 1047
Peter L. Clark, Jr., 415
Joe Cook III, 1261
William Dunbar, 538
Jacqueline Glynn, 836
Chris Holden, 551
Christopher N. Jones, 746

John Moore, 193
J Michael Schafer, 1300
Andrew J Schwab, 12
Gregg Smart, 722
Jennifer Steans, 529
Ben Wallace, 213
Adrian N. Wilson, 1842

DeGroote School of Business
Colin Walker, 2089

DePaul University
Thomas S. Bagley, 1435
Denio R. Bolzan, 1435
David Carlson, 1536
Kevin Delaplane, 1881
C Michael Foster, 1232
Jeffrey Howard, 1610
J Allan Kayler, 1232
Eric Kutsenda, 1645
Matt Leinauer, 399
Timothy W Maloney, 18
Lee J. Monahan, 910
Michael E Moran, 348
Jeffry S. Pfeffer, 407
Craig Radis, 1467
Robert Riemer, 175
Nick Rosa, 570
Nick Rosa, 1615
William H. Schaar, 945
Jim Schultz, 1379
John J. Starcevich, 1435
Tom Willerer, 1916
Ana M Winters, 1232

DePauw University
Steve A Cobb, 478
Thomas P. Cooper, MD, 136
David C. Coquillette, 1301
R Glen Mayfield, 1571
Peter Munson, 409
Luke Reese, 1999
Douglas Schrier, 1540
Michael L Smith, 409
John Tullis, 1866
Anthony J de Nicola, 1972

DeVry Institute of Technology
Wayne Cantwell, 555
Michael A Steinbeck, 1744

DeVry University
Michael Hara, 925

Defence System Management College
Thomas K Churbuck, 66

Defense Research Institute
Alexander Galitsky, 89

Dehli University
Alipt Sharma, 834

Delaware Law School
Jon Powell, 1657

Delhi College of Engineering
Raman Khanna, 603

Delhi University
Promod Haque, 1346
Nitin Pachisia, 1885

Denison University
Jason Allen, 1172
Michael Bevan, 657
Maddie Callander, 307

John A Canning Jr, 1156
Eugene P. Conese Jr., 873
Charlie Gifford, 926
Timothy D. Johnson, 843
Suzanne Kriscunas, 1572
Kenneth Mabbs, 711
William C Mulligan, 1476
Ralph Schlosstein, 699
Jonathan T. Silverstein, 1382
Jack Wyant, 287

Dickinson College
Henry J. Boye, 1815
W Ryan Davis, 1159
Jay Grossman, 21
John Paul Kirwin III, 164

Dominican College
Debra Guerin Beresini, 1011

Downing College
Jonathan Aberman, 119

Drake University
John C Aplin, 478
John Meilner, 338
Michael E Moran, 348
Stephen P Mullin, 629
Gordon Roth, 1588
Darren M Snyder, 1469

Dresden University of Technology
David Perez, 1403

Drew University
Joseph T. Sobota, MD, 139
Jamie Weston, 1730

Drexel University
Mel Baiada, 230
David William Baum, 1734
Michael Cohen, 1369
Harry D'Andrea, 1899
Alex Katz, 724
Charles Lewis, 258
Jesse Middleton, 754
Robert Migliorino, 1947
Richelle P. Parham, 383
Mike Pellini, 1643

Drury College
Joel Rommines, 1077

Dublin City University
Antoinette "Toni" Chaltiel, 1532

Duke Fuqua School of Business
Atul Kamra, 1688

Duke University
Matthew L. Altman, 166
Andrew J. Armstrong. Jr., 1724
Christopher Austen, 350
Chip Austin, 964
Merrick Axel, 558
Charles Ayres, 1851
Jeffrey Barnes, 270
Fouad Bashour, 477
Steven S Beckett, 1426
Cathy Belk, 1047
David Biesel, 1322
Mike Bingle, 1683
Dave Blivin, 549
Philip Borden, 806
Jan Bouten, 995
Larry Bradshaw, 695
Steven Bressler, 1417

1021

College/University Index / Duke University Law School

Kenneth S. Bring, 254
Steve Brotman, 91
Steve Brotman, 1680
Thomas A. Burger Jr., 873
Blake Byers, 889
Doug Cameron, 738
John A Canning Jr, 1156
Roger Carolin, 1633
Jack Carsten, 947
Gillis C Cashman, 1153
Scott E. Chappell, 263
Robert Cioffi, 80
Christopher L Collins, 1062
Richard H Copans, 1156
Jeffrey Craver, 61
Todd Creech, 921
David Cummings, 189
Daniel Dickinson, 917
Andrew C. Dodson, 1417
Andy Donner, 1438
Dana Donovan, 631
Dennis Dougherty, 1008
Kenneth M. Doyle, 894
Matt Edgerton, 1062
Frederick W. Eubank II, 1409
April E Evans, 1248
Peter W Farner, 1802
Mark L Feidler, 1270
Josh Felser, 784
David Fishman, 1910
David C. Franklin, 951
Christopher J Garber, 1963
Ned Gilhuly, 1602
Cliff Gilman, 72
Jim Glasheen, 1786
John Glushik, 1008
Rob Go, 1322
Michael Gorman, 1725
Dave Gravano, 1975
Marshall Griffin, 528
Gregory Grunberg, 1143
Steve Gullans PhD, 703
Lawrence S. Hamelsky, 254
L. Watts Hamrick III, 1409
Felda Hardymon, 260
Tom Hawkins, 768
Jeff Haywood, 1717
R Trent Hickman, 1927
Grant Hill, 1430
Gerald Holtz, 1494
Davis Hostetter, 894
Joseph Huffsmith, 1376
Andrew Humphries, 911
Jeffrey M. Hurst, 521
Mudit Jain PhD, 1772
A. Bruce Johnston, 1776
Matt Jones, 1355
Alan L Kaganov ScD, 1896
Azra Kanji, 21
Rishi Kapoor, 1017
Bruce Karsh, 1362
Aftab R. Kherani, MD, 74
David Kirkpatrick, 1689
Justin Klein, 1917
Garheng Kong, 921
Garheng Kong MD PhD, 1698
Trent Kososki, 675
Austin Krumpfes, 1467
Larry Kubal, 1089
Tatsuya Kubo, 909
Joel Lanik, 790
Jeremy Levine, 260
Dan Levitan, 1183
Regan Li, 2083
Rob Little, 839
Bill Luby, 1638
Bruce Luehrs, 1568

Joshua A. Lutzker, 254
Ian B. MacTaggart, 357
J Matthew Mackowski, 1792
Mike Marcantonio, 288
Norvell E Miller IV, 1709
Aaron Money, 787
Mitch Mumma, 1008
Peter M. Mundheim, 1743
Timothy M Murray, 468
Suzanne Niemeyer, 53
Neill Occhiogross, 547
Stephen Pagliuca, 220
Grant Palmer, 1851
Travis Pearson, 824
Douglas S. Perry, 588
Steven F. Piaker, 434
David Pierson, 1774
Todd T Pietri, 52
JB Pritzker, 1479
J.B. Pritzker, 1480
Diana Propper de Callejon, 706
Steven G Raich, 1134
Michael Ramich, 790
Leigh Randall, 1832
Scott Raney, 1534
Ganesh B. Rao, 1815
Geoffrey Rehnert, 194
Pamela L. Reiland, 888
Scott A Reilly CFA, 1426
Meredith L Rerisi, 18
Bruce Roberts, 414
Carmichael Roberts, 1177
Alex Rogers, 909
Bruce Rogers, 1086
Jim Rorer, 1462
Jonathan D Roth, 18
Michael W Rubel, 1557
David M Rubenstein, 413
Peter M. Rubin, 190
Camille Samuels, 1916
Kenneth T Schiciano, 1776
Sean Schickedanz, 498
Adam Schimel, 239
Michael Schnabel, 447
Andrew Schwab, 737
Eric Schwartz, 423
Christian Schwartz, 1820
Jon Seeber, 1886
Ron Shah, 1748
Adam Sharkawy, 1177
Ben Sheridan, 289
Raleigh A. Shoemaker, Jr., 254
Benjamin M Spero, 1717
W Brad Stephens, 283
Mark D. Taber, 857
Stephen C. Tardio, 953
Jeffrey W Ubben, 1903
Ted Wang, 552
Michael Weiss, 862
R Patrick Weston CFA, 213
Ken Widder, 1094
Jim Woody, 1094
James Zelter, 140
Bob Zipp, 114

Duke University Law School
William K. Richardson, 939

Duke University School of Medicine
John Kim, MD, 138

Dundee University
Paul Daccus, 1753

Duquesne University
Tom Eddy, 1027
Robert Swartz, 1207

Robert A Theleen, 473

Durham University
Paul Clark, 1923
Edward FL. Hughes, 1496

EAP European School of Management
Gabriel Caillaux, 815

ESADE Business School
Jason Ball, 1509
Gina Domanig, 2106

ESC Nice
Maor Amar, 2151

Earlham College
J. Russell Chapman, 172
John May, 1304

Eastern Illinois University
Jeffrey Holdsberg, 373
Robert A Ingram, 915

Eastern Kentucky University
Brenda McDaniel, 1064
Jerry Rickett, 1064

Eastern Michigan University
David Breach, 1938

Eckerd College
Russ Wilson, 1857

Ecole Centrale de Paris
Philippe Amouyal, 1018
Stefan Goetz, 924

Ecole Nationale des Mines de Paris
John Piret, 1312

Ecole Nationale des Ponts et Chauss
Dominique Gaillard, 2466

Ecole Polytechnique
Lionel Assant, 277
Dominique Gaillard, 2466
Claude Vachet, 2093

Ecole Speciale des Travaux Publics
Marcel Fournier, 423

Edinburgh University
Andrew Cleland, 518

Edith Cowan University
Simon Cresswell, 135

Eisenhower College
Allen F Grum, 1523

Elizabethtown College
James B Hoover, 587

Eller College of Management
Sean Doyle, 1610

Elon University
Ashton Newhall, 867

Embry-Riddle University
Steve Whitlock, 1722

Emerson College
Caitlyn MacDonald, 1104
Paul A Santinelli, 1334

College/University Index / Gabelli School of Business

Emory University
Cory S Anderson, 40
Craig Baker, 1569
Sean Banks, 1863
Stuart Barkoff, 834
Scott Bluestein, 925
Jeffrey B Bunder, 1129
Nathan R. Every, MD, MPH, 782
Doug Fisher, 821
Gardiner W Garrard III, 1863
Dave Gould, 1788
David Greenberg, 1041
Bahniman Hazarika, 855
Paul Johan, 224
Kim Kamdar, PhD, 621
Alan Kelley, 1689
Michael S. Marr, 405
Marc Michel, 525
Ashish H. Mistry, 282
Dave Munichiello, 889
W. Carter Neild, 1382
Grant A Patrick, 244
Mark Patricof, 1222
Isai Peimer, 1196
Douglas S. Perry, 588
Wendell Reilly, 1423
Charles Rim, 626
Cynthia Ringo, 595
Mark Swaine, 494
David E Thomas Jr, 1526
Neil A. Wizel, 740
Oren Yerushalmi, 354

Emory University School of Law
David S. Gorton, 1777
Michael Hyatt, 1022
Arthur Rogers, 152

Erasmus University
Claudio Nessi, 1373
Joost F. Thesseling, 476

Eton College
Sanjay Patel, 140

European University Brussels
Marc der Kinderen, 14
Jean-Edouard van Praet, 978

Exeter University
Dennis Atkinson, 690

FW Olin Graduate School of Business
Matthew Ahern, 1077
John Whorf, 1294

Fairfield University
Derek Blazensky, 411
Phil Cagnassola, 899
Mary Lincoln Campbell, 652
Gerard N. Casale, 1876
Scott Dupcak, 532
Kevin Gahwyler, 1283
Lorraine Hliboki, 1462
J. Ryan Kelly, 774
Joel Krikston, 1205
Paul LaViolette, 1628
Paul LaViolette, 1762
Christopher A Layden, 2015
John G Loverro, 1112
Owen G. Tharrington, 873

Fairleigh Dickinson University
Beth L. Bernstein, 686
James J. Dowling, 1032
Daniel Gulino, 1564
Tom Mac Mahon, 748

Constantine J. Rakkou, 900

Fanshaw College
Jon Jackson, 3258

Federal Institute of Technology
Francois Helou, 187

Fergusson College
Sonali Vijayavargiya, 195
Devdutt Yellurkar, 455

Fisher College of Business
Mark Roehrenbeck, 1558

Fitchburg State College
John W Bullock, 1994

Fletcher School of Law & Diplomacy
Jennifer Choi, 3266
Chris Farmer, 1675
Steven Ritterbush, 1207

Florida Atlantic University
David Fries, 1906
Maynard Webb, 1968

Florida Institute of Technology
Fahri Diner, 1672
Edward C McCarthy, 1571

Florida International University
Ruben J King-Shaw Jr, 1165
Eric Manlunas, 1965
Pat Schneider, 3262

Florida Southern University
Minette L La Croix, 1668

Florida State University
Nick Grabowski, 1662
Grant A Jackson, 550
Kenneth A. Minihan, 1400
Lawrence Mock, 1280

Fordham Graduate School of Business
Richard W. Gaenzle Jr., 827

Fordham University
Tarik Abbas, 1836
Ellen R. Alemany, 484
Geoffrey Baehr, 89
Jack Baron, 565
Michael V. Caso, 1585
Christopher Childres, 653
Winston J Churchill, 1633
Paul Clark, 1923
Robert A. Comey, 1016
John R Costantino, 1325
Ryan J. Faulkingham, 523
Charles Gedge, 290
Jonathan Glass, 1235
Steven G Glenn, 1956
Luke Gosselin, 446
Gen. John M Keane, 1633
Thomas Keaveney, 61
Kevin Lynch, 431
Patricia Muoio, 1687
Daniel J. O'Brien, 1037
Scott Powers, 53
Joseph Saviano, 223
Bruce K. Taragin, 301
Jamie Weston, 1730
James W Young PhD, 12

Fordham University School of Law
Scott Birnbaum, 1530
Dave Butler, 1045
TJ Maloney, 1127
Robert B Nolan Jr, 897
Alan G. Schwartz, 740
Andrew Tananbaum, 565
Jeanette M Welsh JD, 1792
David Wolmer, 1111

Foreign Trade University
Ha Nguyen, 2190

Foster School of Business
Noel de Turenne, 1250

Fox School of Business
Tyler Dautrich, 866
Timothy G. Fallon, 147
Dean Sciorillo, 676

Fox School of Business & Management
Charles Kerrigan, 1695

Franklin & Marshall College
Nancy C Floyd, 1355
Steven Hobman, 1317
Richard S Kollender, 1508
Dennison T Veru, 1401
Jason Waxberg, 3270
Matthew Young, 686

Franklin College
Matteo Volpi, 2074

Franklin College, Switzerland
Randall S. Fojtasek, 328

Free University of Brussels
Alain Schreiber, MD, 1490

Freie Universität Berlin
Thomas Korte, 128

Fu-Jen Catholic University
Ronald Han, 906

Fuller Seminary
Phil Chen, 1473

Fuqua School of Business
Christopher Austen, 350
Nathaniel C Brinn, 1940
Ben Brooks, 1710
James D. Carey, 1743
Blaine Crissman, 1477
Jim Duda, 582
Josh Felser, 784
Scott Garfield, 901
Jim Gunton, 1328
Mark W Kehaya, 1213
John Kim, MD, 138
Michael Miller, 443
Steven C Pierson, 1147
Ned Scheetz, 138
David Strasser, 1766
Paul Straub, 491
Tim Wilson, 174

Furman University
C Deryl Couch, 1753
Scott Hoch, 790

Gabelli School of Business
Michael V. Caso, 1585

1023

College/University Index / Garvin School of International Mgmt

Garvin School of International Mgmt
Michael J Dubilier, 631

General Assembly
Lauren Robinson, 2147

General Motors Institute
Thien-Ly Ngo, 526

Geneva College
John W Manzetti, 1448

George Brown College
Marat Mukhamedyarov, 2138

George Institute of Technology
AT Gimble, 189

George Mason School of Law
John Malloy, 296

George Mason University
Dave Armstrong, 770
E Peter Malekian, 1189
Thien-Ly Ngo, 526
Don Rainey, 876

George Washington University
Jonathan Aberman, 119
Charles Auster, 1596
Mel Billingsley PhD, 1117
Elon S Broms, 1097
Michael Brosgart, 1807
Kate Chhabra, 428
Evan DeCorte, 515
Kirk Fichtner, 1167
John Fletcher, 749
Sreekar Gadde, 293
Laura Gladstone, 828
Pat Gouhin, 3256
Bulbul Gupta, 1396
Ronald Han, 905
Ronald Han, 906
Terry L. Jones, 1771
John Paul Kirwin III, 164
David Kivitz, 155
Randy Klueger, 538
Bob Kocher MD, 1916
Christopher A Layden, 2015
Mark Levine, 538
Cyril L. Meduna, 63
Jonathan Murray, 642
William Osborn, 520
Marshall W Parke, 1112
Alex Radcliffe, 406
Ned J Renzi, 272
Michael S. Sarner, 403
Geoff Schneider, 431
Larry Schnurmacher, 1439
Jeffrey D Serkes, 1401
John W. Snow, 451
Oak Strawbridge, 875
Steven Swain, 440
Micah Tapman, 392
Peggy Wallace, 841
April Young, 925
Philip M Young, 1896

Georgetown University
John F Aiello, 1129
Roger Altman, 699
Joseph Baratta, 277
Jeffrey Bartoli, 447
Tom Benedetti, 288
Matt Bigge, 563
Tim Billings, 1505
Scott Birnbaum, 1530
Michael Brown, 235
Theodore D. Burke, 156
Curtis L Buser, 413
Andrew Byrd, 1870
David J Cooney, 244
Mike Cooper, 1667
Sally Corning, 1754
Fred Craves, PhD, 237
Michael J Cromwell III, 1388
Vahe A Dombalagian, 1156
Donald J Donahue Jr, 691
Michael F. Donoghue, 1727
Liam Donohue, 2
Robb Doub, 1299
James B. Dougherty, MD, 157
Egon Durban, 1683
Eliot Durbin, 305
Greg Durst, 3266
Anne Dwane, 1933
Scott W Edwards, 1753
David Eichler, 1498
Robert Y Emmert, 1276
Beth Engel, 635
Steve Engelberg, 1615
William Ericson, 1247
Bill Ericson, 1985
Jonathan Farber, 1125
Robert M. Feerick, 945
Adam Fisher, 260
Robert J Flanagan, 508
Dave Flanagan, 1004
Jennifer Fonstad, 180
C Michael Foster, 1232
Elizabeth Galbut, 1701
Joseph V. Gallagher, 125
Rupert Gerard, 888
Antonio Gracias, 1902
Stephen X Graham, 562
Michael D. Granoff, 1462
Mark Grovic, 1299
Donald L Hawks III, 353
Chad Heath, 673
Rick Heitzmann, 743
Marty Hernon, 312
Phil Jakeway, 1127
Dan Janney, 94
Mike Jerstad, 1470
Christopher M. King, 873
Michael Kosty, 333
Chris Kryder, 748
Pete Labbat, 675
Maja Lapcevic, 486
Kyle Largent, 828
Christopher Lee, 828
Joshua M. Levinson, 844
Daniel C Lubin, 1520
John Lyman, 889
Salvatore A Massaro, 656
Michelle McCarthy, 1926
John C McNamara II, 1144
Andrew Montgomery, 1222
Cheryl Moss, 788
Paul F Murphy, 1651
Oleg Nodelman, 709
Robert B Nolan Jr, 897
Charles L Palmer, 1332
Douglas S. Perry, 588
Richard A. Petrocelli, 1621
Thomas Pryma, 64
Michael Psaros, 1085
Ben Rabinowitz, 116
Benjamin J. Ramundo, 166
Anthony Ressler, 159
Ellis F. Rinaldi, 1739
Andrew C. Romans, 1595
Jason Rottenberg, 171
Noah Roy, 862
Dan Ryan, 1234
Chris Sacca, 1149
Andrew Sachs, 1599
Andrew Salenbier, 37
Claudi Santiago, 740
Zita Saurel, 924
Jeff Schlapinski, 3261
David Schroder, 17
David R. Schroder, 1016
Robert Seidler, 1645
Sam Sezak, 288
Judd Sher, 924
Brian J Siegel, 891
Joshua B. Siegel, 1595
Matthew M Smith, 18
Tammi Smorynski, 1004
Joseph T. Sobota, MD, 139
Michael Sotirhos, 277
McLain Southworth, 563
Nicholas J Stanley, 1909
Caroline Stout, 709
Matthew Strottman, 979
Devin Talbott, 680
Bob Tamashunas, 1638
Andrew Tichenor, 288
C. Bowdoin Train, 875
Stephanie Von Friedeburg, 1007
Fred Wakeman, 62
Andy Weissman, 1882
Marshall C. White, 746
David C. Wodlinger, 166

Georgetown University Law Center
Zachary Bogue, 585
Paul Diaz, 558
Daniel K Flatley, 1175
Mark Jacobsen, 1359
Suzanne Niemeyer, 53
Steve Oetgen, 839
Lisa Schule, 834
Bruce Taub, 190
Annie S Terry, 1156

Georgia Institute of Technology
Chris Allen, 1403
Craig Baker, 1569
Gregory Bloom, 48
Lee Bryan, 528
Mark Buffington, 271
Brook Byers, 1075
Robert Coneybeer, 1663
Adam Cranford, 1293
Michael DeRosa, 657
Steven Denning, 815
David Dullum, 828
Tom Dyal, 1534
C.J. Fitzgerald, 1752
Dick Hunter, 594
Ariel Jaduszliwer, 324
Anthony V Lando, 40
John L Long Jr, 1841
Scott Marlette, 1694
John Paul Milciunas, 32
Said Mohammadioun, 1788
Randall E. Poliner, 131
James Robinson, III, 1593
Randy Scott, 921
W Thomas Smith Jr, 1863
Gregory A. White, 1815

Georgia State University
Michael L Bailey, 1484
Brian Cayce, 855
James S Douglass, 794
Said Mohammadioun, 1788
Matt Oguz, 1406
Todd T Pietri, 52

College/University Index / Harvard Business School

David Reynolds, 960
Cynthia Ringo, 595

Georgia Tech
Mark G Miller, 1194
Tom Noonan, 1788

Georgian College
Marat Mukhamedyarov, 2138

Gettysburg College
John C. Acker, 1727
John Willert, 401

Ghent University
Sigrid Van Bladel, 20

Glasgow University
A. Sinclair Dunlop, 689

Goizueta Business School
David W Averett, 1752
Jeff Black, 1430
Jeffrey Black, 1926
David Greenberg, 1041
Billy L. Harbert, 282
Rimas Kapeskas, 380
Tory Rooney, 354

Golden Gate University
Marty Eng, 1975
Mark J Gill, 713
Richard Harding, 1011
Raman Khanna, 603
James A Kohlberg, 1081
Bill Li, 1951
Bill McDonagh, 1952
Kate Mitchell, 1626
Steven Peterson, 1843
Kenneth Petrilla, 473
Robin Praeger, 1928
Richard Stubblefield, 1119
Henry Wong, 612
Henry Wong, 807

Goldey Beacom College
Anna May L Trala, 884

Gonzaga University
Sean Cunningham, 763
Bridget Storm, 996

Graduate School of Mgmt, Koblenz
Boriz Wertz, 2280

Grand Valley State University
Gerry Boylan, 1141
Mike DeVries, 652
Turner Novak, 811
Mark Olesnavage, 943

Graziadio School of Business & Mngm
Greg Bettinelli, 1888

Grenoble Institute of Technology
Ludovic André, 2088

Grinnell College
Siddharth Srivastava, 2190

Grove City College
Sean Ammirati, 272
Michael Lazarus, 1978
Jennifer E. Parulo, 56

Gubkin State University
Marat Mukhamedyarov, 2138

Gujarat University
Gary Gauba, 574

Gustavus Adolphus College
Mik Gusenius, 464
George G. Hicks, 1907
Jeff Miller, 1411
Marcia L. Page, 1907

HEC
Pierre-Olivier Lamoureux, 844

HEC - Paris
Ludovic André, 2088

HEC Lausanne
Robert Fenwick-Smith, 146

HEC Montreal
Marie-Claude Boisvert, 2082
André Gauthier, 2261
Jean-Francois Le Ruyet, 1516
Isabelle Lechasseur, 2088
Philippe Leroux, 2260
Genevieve Morin, 2119
Serge Olivier, 2029
Claude Vachet, 2093

HEC Paris
Nicolas Massard, 21
Eamonn McConnell, 2167

Haas School of Business
Gavin Bates, 374
James Beck, 1184
Jeffrey M. Calhoun, 1777
Gary Coover, 1611
Melissa Daniels, 1255
Keval Desai, 1010
Gary Dillabough, 1282
Andy Donner, 1438
John Dougery, 1013
Tim Heston, 255
Danny Jaffe, 126
Jed Katz, 1028
Carlos Kokron, 1509
Steve Kuo, 925
Rebecca Lynn, 1257
Brian D Martin, 1904
Jim Pettit, 1282
Arun Ramamoorthy, 1445
Manu Rekhi, 1013
Steve Schuman, 895
Kirill Sheynkman, 1594
Thorne Sparkman, 1693
Daniel K Turner III, 1251
Ken Wallace III, 986
Andrew Williamson PhD, 1438

Hahnemann University
Matthew Naythons MD, 163

Haifa University
Michal Silverberg, 1350

Hamilton College
Andrew D. Barous, 1301
Skip Besthoff, 422
Skip Besthoff, 1496
Bob Delaney, 559
Richard T Dell'Aquila, 353
Edward I Dresner, 646
Matthew G. Harrison, 1971
Donald R Kendall Jr, 1063

Kevin Kester, 1679
Robert Kuhling, 1378
Woody Marshall, 1785
Rob Morris, 1372
James O'Mara, 1987
Geoffrey S. Oblak, 178
Arthur Rogers, 152
Philip Sanderson, 3284
Thomas W Scozzafava, 1639
Harry D Taylor, 1776
Baran Tekkora, 1573

Hampden-Sydney College
Matthew E Gormly III, 1984
Robert M. Stewart, 1727

Hampshire College
Jeff Davison, 989
Greg S. Feldman, 1971

Hampton University
Edwin Shirley, 714

Hanover College
Michael Miller, 443

Harding University
Michael Blue, 1481
Kevin Uebelein, 2033

Hartford University
Jerome Nycz, 2055

Hartwick College
Richard W. Gaenzle Jr., 827
Stephen Rossetter, 448

Harvard Business School
Todd M. Abbrecht, 1815
Kenneth S Abramowitz, 1325
Andrew Abrams, 1303
Jenny Abramson, 1552
Robert W Ackerman, 1962
Charles E Adair, 537
Samantha A. Adams, 254
Ajay Agarwal, 221
Neeraj Agrawal, 235
Payal Agrawal Divakaran, 2
Garrick Ahn, 373
Dmitry Alimov, 792
Chris Allen, 1403
Zaid F Alsikafi, 1156
Mark M. Anderson, 884
Frank Angella, 879
Brion B Applegate, 1717
Joe Aragona, 202
Thomas W. Arenz, 914
David Aronoff, 754
Michael C. Ascione, 254
Zaid Ashai, 1459
Lindsay Aspegren, 1336
Dennis Atkinson, 690
Brian Atwood, 1928
Stuart A. Auerbach, 118
Chip Austin, 964
Merrick Axel, 558
Charles F Baird Jr, 1335
John Baker, 223
Jeffrey L Balash, 527
Thomas J. Baldwin, 354
Perry O. Ballard, 750
Michael Balmuth, 1762
Michael Barach, 990
Paul Barber, 1041
Hayley Barna, 741
Gregory M Barr, 1684
Peter Barrett, 191

1025

College/University Index / Harvard Business School

Thomas C. Barry, 2018
Upal Basu, 1330
Rajeev Batra, 1184
Len Batterson, 234
Richard Bauerly, 850
David William Baum, 1734
Dan Baum, 2244
Josh Bekenstein, 220
Michael A Bell, 1248
Michael A. Bell, 1815
Kent Bennett, 260
Scott Benson, 1316
Erik Benson, 1945
Michael S Berk, 1776
Chaz Bertrand, 329
Neal Bhadkamkar, 1249
Matt Bigge, 563
Peter Binas, 1627
Kate Bingham, 1628
Kate Bingham, 1762
Hubert Birner, 2276
Leon Black, 140
Pete Blackshaw, 480
Len Blavatnik, 34
Rick Bolander, 805
Rick Bolander, 2023
John Borchers, 555
David C. Bordeau, 254
Philip Borden, 806
Simita Bose, 1348
Leslie Bottorff, 809
Martin Brand, 277
Greg Brenneman, 433
Peter C Brockway, 348
Jeff Brodlieb, 448
Matthew Bronfman, 42
Peter Brooke, 62
John Brooke, 350
Kenneth Brotman, 46
Sonya Brown, 1346
Terry Brubaker, 828
Kurt A. Brumme, 1417
Lee Bryan, 528
Charles A Bryan, 1422
Adam Bryant, 648
Roberto Buaron, 733
Bernie Buonanno, 1279
Bill Burgess, 23
David Burgstahler, 209
John Burke, 1482
James J. Burke Jr., 1023
Donald W Burton, 1708
Christopher M. Busby, 857
Jeffrey Bussgang, 754
Jon Callaghan, 1860
Joe Canavan, 2201
Sean Cantwell, 1942
Thomas J Caracciolo, 632
Paul Carbone, 1479
James C. Carlisle, 1815
Roger Carolin, 1633
Andrew Carragher, 639
Chris C Casciato, 1123
John K. Castle, 423
Todd C. Chaffee, 1001
Victor Chaltiel, 1532
James Cham, 284
Rishi Chandna, 839
J. Russell Chapman, 172
Drew Chen, 220
Jerry Chen, 872
Neil Chheda, 1581
Eric Chin, 563
Hoon Cho, 824
Arjun Chopra, 751
Tony Christianson, 464
Quentin Chu, 559

Nelson Chu, 1072
Jeff Chung, 107
Young Chung, 581
Patrick Chung, 708
Tom Clark, 528
Ryan Clark, 819
Tyson Clark, 889
Sam Clemens, 38
Miles Clements, 28
J Michael Cline, 39
Ed Cluss, 1678
David Coats, 544
Steve A Cobb, 478
Jay Cohan, 1975
Ira D Cohen, 1886
David M Coit, 1333
Jeffrey J Collinson, 474
Stuart Collinson, 769
R. Craig Collister, 1590
Mark M Colodny, 1956
John Connaughton, 220
William C Connell, 931
Tim Connor, 1653
Wayne Cooper, 863
Dennis B Costello, 1847
McCall Cravens, 957
Andrew Crawford, 815
Glenn M. Creamer, 1496
Bryan Cressey, 558
Gary Crittenden, 959
David D Croll, 1153
Michael F. Cronin, 1978
Allan Crosbie, 2089
Chris J. Crosby, 1279
Matthew Cross, 2167
Bob Cummings, 1990
Chip Cureton, 888
James Currier, 1323
Daniel A D'Aniello, 413
Scott A. Dahnke, 1088
Anupam Dalal MD, 1059
Andy Dale, 1250
John E Dancewicz, 619
John G Danhakl, 1109
Roanne Daniels, 924
Stuart Davidson, 1089
Timothy C Davis, 786
William F. Dawson, Jr., 1971
Michael B. DeFlorio, 914
Mark DeNino, 1828
Thompson Dean, 209
Christopher J Dean, 1752
Michael Dearing, 911
Gerard A Debiasi, 1071
Michael W Dees, 1129
Joe Del Guercio, 508
Bob Delaney, 559
Thanasis Delistathis, 1291
Thanasis Delistathis, 1482
Anthony J de Nicola, 1972
Sasha Dichter, 55
Jorge Dickens, 46
Chun Ding, 472
Andrew C. Dodson, 1417
Elias Dokas, 1231
Adam B. Dolder, 859
Michael J. Dominguez, 1496
Mark Dorman, 673
Edith Dorsen, 2003
Brian Dovey, 621
Jere Doyle, 1673
Tim Draper, 626
Timothy Draper, 2021
William H Draper III, 627
Samuel L. Duboc, 2103
Olivier Dufourmantelle, 2071
Kevin Dunwoodie, 1411

Greg Durst, 3266
Anne Dwane, 1933
Tom Eddy, 1027
Patrick Edeburn, 850
Donald J. Edwards, 750
Jamie E Elias, 1857
Michael G. Eliasek, 1491
Qian W. Elmore, 969
James L. Elrod Jr., 1931
Juan Enriquez, 703
Martin Escobari, 815
Timothy M. Evans, 156
Neil Exter, 1811
Bruce F Failing, 80
Henrik Falktoft, 1516
Michael Farah, 1128
Michael J. Farello, 1088
Karim Faris, 889
Brad Farkas, 964
Jim Farrell, 368
Mike Farrell, 1717
Deborah A Farrington, 1738
Brandon Farwell, 708
Jesse Feldman, 235
Robert Fenwick-Smith, 146
Marco J. Ferrari, 1496
John Fife, 470
Robert Finkel, 1477
David A Fiorentino, 1049
Mark L. First, 686
Michael T. Fitzgerald, 521
C.J. Fitzgerald, 1752
John W. Flanigan, 461
Raluca Florea, 332
Brian Flynn, 772
Tom Flynn, 1762
Norman A. Fogelsong, 1001
David I. Foley, 277
Todd Foley, 1268
Jennifer Fonstad, 180
Bob Forlenza, 1728
Andrew J. Fortier, 2062
Frank Foster, 791
Frank H Foster, 826
Michael J. Fourticq Sr., 902
David Frankel, 771
Robert Fraser, 200
Kris Fredrickson, 509
John F Freund, 1691
Scott Friend, 221
Jeffrey Frient, 654
Jeff S. Fronterhouse, 328
Dean Frost, 253
Eric T Fry, 1129
Max Gazor, 455
Bob Geiman, 431
Scott Gibaratz, 917
Jim Gilbert, 747
Steven J. Gilbert, 827
AT Gimble, 189
Marc A. Gineris, 982
Jonathan Ginns, 46
David Gladstone, 828
Rob Go, 1322
Roger Goddu, 334
David L Gold, 359
Marc Goldberg, 270
William J Golden, 1092
Andy Goldfarb, 835
Amir Goldman, 1759
Johnathan M Goldstein, 1776
Brian P Golson, 1417
Lawrence E. Golub, 844
Peter D Goodson, 631
Brian Gorczynski, 1925
Chris Gordon, 220
Benjamin Gordon, 380

Matt Gorin, 533
Maria Gotsch, 1420
Blake L. Gottesman, 254
Greg Gottesman, 1499
Drew Graham, 224
Christopher D. Graham, 1739
Laura A. Grattan, 1815
McComma Grayson III, 909
Michael Greeley, 748
Myles D Greenberg, 474
Michael Greene, 66
Phil Greer, 1381
Thomas G Greig, 1116
Rick Grinnell, 712
Rick Grinnell, 829
David Gross-Loh, 220
Jay Grossman, 21
H. Irving Grousbeck, 949
Harry Gruner, 1041
Alex Gruzen, 545
Arun Gupta, 515
Leo Guthart, 1832
Perry Ha, 626
Oliver Haarmaan, 2252
Douglas A. Haber, 1815
James T. Hackett, 1573
Thomas M. Hagerty, 1815
H H Haight, 162
Lawrence S. Hamelsky, 254
Mamoon Hamid, 1075
Philip Hammarskjold, 924
Leonard M. Harlan, 423
Steve Harrick, 1001
Joshua Harris, 140
Hendrik J. Hartong III, 357
Hendrik J. Hartong, Jr., 357
Jay Hass, 1593
John Hawkins, 818
Frank J Hawley Jr, 1624
John G. Hayes, 857
Randy Haykin, 1389
Chip Hazard, 754
Ned Hazen, 1119
Robert P Healy, 468
Patrick Healy, 924
Donald B. Hebb, Jr., 22
Tom Hedrick, 1944
Rick Heitzmann, 743
Christopher R Hemmeter, 1806
Ted Henderson, 1627
Patrick Heron, 782
Catherine Herring, 2215
Brian Hersman, 1041
E David Hetz, 572
Rick Heyke, 1750
Tom Hickey, 1505
John B Higginbotham, 1714
Mark G. Hilderbrand, 949
Todd Hixon, 1291
James S. Hoch, 1777
Steve Hochberg, 177
Benjamin A Hochberg, 1104
Ryan Hodgson, 109
Don Hofmann, 565
Jeffrey J Holland, 1636
David Horing, 110
Zachary Hornby, 487
Jim Hornthal, 192
Camilo E. Horvilleur, 928
Bob Howe, 9
Paul Hsiao, 396
Michael Hsieh, 796
Geoffrey C. Hsu, 1382
Eion Hu, 1045
Edward Huang, 277
Lydie Hudson, 554
William S. Hughes, 1496

Gregory Hulecki, 711
Tom Hulme, 889
Wende Hutton, 386
In Seon Hwang, 1956
Tony Ignaczak, 1505
Robert M Jaffe, 1706
Thomas Janes, 1067
Jeffrey R. Jay, MD, 859
Mark Jennings, 818
Jeffrey Johnson, 276
Jeffrey W. Johnson, 827
Brent P Johnstone, 1511
Terry L. Jones, 1771
Reginald L. Jones III, 862
TJ Jubeir, 406
Roger B Kafker, 1776
Julia Kahr, 277
Samantha Kaminsky, 552
Deepak Kamra, 386
Edward W Kane, 909
Thomas Kaneb, 2194
Raj Kapoor, 1184
Julia Karol, 1962
Joseph R Katcha, 932
Samir Kaul, 1069
Patrick Keefe, 2068
Brian P Kelley, 1129
Peter Kellner, 1561
Thomas L. Kelly II, 461
Douglas L. Kennealey, 328
William C. Kessinger, 1417
Trevor Kienzle, 544
Daniel Kim, 333
John Kim, 1062
Yoo Jin Kim, 1104
Chris Kitching, 933
Ronald J. Klammer, 1369
Stephan Klee, 2225
Adam Klein, 559
Michael I Klein, 1134
Lewis S. Klessel, 1301
Josh Klinefelter, 199
Steven B Klinsky, 1301
Ailliam Knoke, 913
Laurie G. Kolbeins, 1799
James Kondo, 820
Stephen Kraus, 260
Marlene R. Krauss, 1058
Dave Kreter, 824
Arvind Krishnamurthy, 1225
Jennifer Krusius, 515
Robert Kuhling, 1378
Ethan Kurzweil, 260
Farouk Ladha, 777
Peter S Laino, 1248
Christopher M Laitala, 1129
Kevin M. Lalande, 1619
Rachel Lam, 977
N. John Lancaster, Jr., 1573
David Lane, 1378
Michael S Langdon, 789
Gregory G Lau, 1972
Ron Laufer MD, 1196
Tom Lavin, 1303
Rich Lawson, 959
Matthew Laycock, 199
Laurence Lederer, 327
Peter Lee, 228
Kewsong Lee, 413
Aileen Lee, 552
Peter Lee, 663
Chris Legg, 1486
Paul Lehman, 1022
Dan Levitan, 1183
Legrand Lewis, 1705
Rick Lewis, 1896
Frank Linsalata, 1132

Peter Lipson, 909
C. Malcolm Little, 166
Simon Lonergan, 245
Greg Long, 1166
Ian Loring, 220
Phil Loughlin, 220
Jimmy Lu, 1983
Daniel C Lubin, 1520
Joshua A. Lutzker, 254
Christopher W. Lynch, 178
Richard MacKellar, 2078
Mark MacTavish, 2208
David Mace, 824
Joe Machado, 1266
Robert W Macleod, 1198
Paul Maeder, 935
John Maldonado, 62
Elliot Maluth, 928
Sulu Mamdani, 1764
Peter M. Manos, 166
John Mapes, 199
Mike Maples Jr., 751
Paul Margolis, 1146
Michael Marino, 200
Roger Marrero, 528
Kim Marvin, 109
Alex Mason, 416
Christopher Masto, 787
Michael Matly, MD, 1251
Alan Mattamana, 714
William Matthes, 245
Gary S Matthews, 1256
Rob May, 1459
John A. (Tony) Mayer, 706
Steve McConahey, 1020
Douglas McCormick, 917
Burton McGillivray, 505
Terry McGuire, 1460
Dale McIvor, 1712
Jeffrey McKibben, 1368
Marc McManus, 489
John C McNamara II, 1144
Scott Meadow, 654
Seth Meisel, 277
Prakash A. Melwani, 277
Frances Messano, 1316
Lloyd M. Metz, 969
Alex Meyer, 1384
Gerald A. Michaud, 946
Fred A Middleton, 1221
Fred A Middleton, 1616
Constantine S. Mihas, 884
Ron Mika, 1705
Don Milder, 1928
Brian C Miller, 1128
W Scott Miller, 1148
Marlin Miller, 1347
Brian Miller, 3264
Cory D. Mims, 969
Sami Mnaymneh, 928
Lee J. Monahan, 910
H. DuBose Montgomery, 1202
Dinesh Moorjani, 518
Michael C Morgan, 1846
Frederic H. Morris, 349
John L. Morrison, 843
Mark J Morrissette, 1333
Allen S Moseley, 1331
David Motley, 298
Andre V. Moura, 1301
Terrence Mullen, 170
Corey Mulloy, 935
Jennifer M Mulloy, 1776
Kevin A. Mundt, 1931
Dave Munichiello, 889
Tom Murphy, 559
Dr. Campbell Murray, 1350

College/University Index / Harvard Business School

Sunil Nagaraj, 1877
Ajit Nedungadi, 1776
Jonathan M. Nelson, 1496
Joshua M. Nelson, 1815
Denis Newman, 1230
Ha Nguyen, 1721
Carl Nichols, 1389
Joseph M. Niehaus, 949
Kirk G Nielsen, 1928
David W. Niemiec, 1621
John Nies, 1040
Charles E. Noell, 1041
William Nolan, 928
A. Bilal Noor, 166
Daniel Nova, 935
Carl Novotny, 1920
Ben Nye, 221
Soren L. Oberg, 1815
Jonathan T. Oka, 750
Nnamdi Okike, 13
Josh Olshansky, 839
Meghan Otis, 1964
Brian Paes-Braga, 2246
Stephen Pagliuca, 220
Eric Paley, 771
Maria Palma, 1593
Gilbert S. Palter, 2103
Greg J. Pappas, 254
Scott G Pasquini, 1156
Jon Pastor, 298
Manish Patel, 935
Bob Pavey, 1257
Marni F. Payne, 254
Marshall Payne, 477
James A. Pelusi, 211
Kevin S Penn, 42
Kevin Penn, 110
David Perez, 1403
Scott B. Perper, 1409
Justin J. Perreault, 521
William Perry, 988
Paul Peterson, 1990
Scott Petty, 1677
M Troy Phillips, 244
Joshua S. Phillips, 426
Charles G. Phillips, IV, 1621
Vincente Piedrahita, 1815
Barbara Piette, 1077
Randall E. Poliner, 131
Scott Pressly, 271
Diana Propper de Callejon, 706
Steven Puccinelli, 1360
Robert Puopolo, 687
Arvind Purushotham, 486
Mitchell Quain, 42
Jeffrey K. Quake, 740
William Quigley, 502
Ali Rahimtula, 567
Jill C. Raker, 862
Geoffrey S. Raker, 1777
Michael Ramich, 790
Lee Rand, 1754
Zeena Rao, 969
Ganesh B. Rao, 1815
Jason Reed, 1997
Corby Reese, 1767
Scott Requadt, 495
Roland Reynolds, 986
Matt Rice, 224
Andrew Richards, 1767
Anders Richardson, 1402
William L. Richter, 451
Randy O. Rissman, 1108
Collin E. Roche, 884
Steven C Rodger, 691
Jesse Rogers, 96
Alex Rogers, 909

Rafael Romero, 667
Jonathan Roosevelt, 986
Jim Rorer, 1462
T.J. Rose, 21
Mickie Rosen, 798
Rick Rosen, 928
Micah Rosenbloom, 771
Jason Rottenberg, 171
Joshua Ruch, 1558
Atul Rustgi, 37
Joseph A. Saldutti Jr., 873
Paul J. Salem, 1496
Wayne Sales, 981
Anthony Salewski, 819
Maninder Saluja, 1516
David G. Samuel, 2062
Camille Samuels, 1916
Philip Sanderson, 3284
Julie Sandler, 1499
Aaron Sandoski, 1347
Robert Savignol, 1153
Carmen Scarpa, 1728
Doug Schillinger, 639
Cas Schneller, 787
Dan Scholnick, 1853
Brian D. Schwartz, 928
Gerry Schwartz, 2209
Stephen A. Schwarzman, 277
Conner Searcy, 1856
Jon Seeber, 1886
Alan G. Sellery, 2163
Kristina Serafim, 1926
Rudina Seseri, 712
Rudina Seseri, 829
Dana Settle, 871
Andrew Sheiner, 2034
Rob Sherman, 312
Jack Shields, 310
Raleigh A. Shoemaker, Jr., 254
John Siegel, 515
George W. Siguler, 1679
Eric H. Sillman, 136
Neil P. Simpkins, 277
George L Sing, 1092
Bradley E. Singer, 1903
Karl Slatoff, 2020
Alex Slusky, 1910
Robert J. Small, 254
Jed Smith, 428
Stephen K Smith, 1175
Scott L. Snow, 746
Christopher Sobecki, 1018
Edward P Sobol, 1972
James Socas, 1886
Erica S. Son, 166
Lawrence B. Sorrel, 1777
Holden Spaht, 1814
Mike Speiser, 1760
Jeb S Spencer, 1869
Scott M. Sperling, 1815
Samuel W. Spirn, 254
Scott Stanford, 45
Ira Starr, 1141
Christopher Staudt, 667
Martin Stein, 276
Gregory Stento, 909
James A. Stern, 575
Barry S. Sternlicht, 1739
Todd Stevens, 1542
Lawrence Stevenson, 2082
E Jack Stewart, 1920
Gordon Stofer, 464
Rick Stowe, 918
Christian R Strain, 1752
Ned Stringham, 9
Santi Subotovsky, 665
Somu Subramaniam, 1303

Matt Sullivan, 1423
Jason D. Sutherland, 328
Ryan Sweeney, 28
David E Sweet, 1760
Jeff T. Swenson, 1815
Peter Taft, 1266
Dave Tamburri, 918
Tony Tamer, 928
Jo Tango, 1065
Thomas M Tarnowski, 1752
Jake Tarr Jr., 1072
Harry D Taylor, 1776
Jeffrey J Teschke, 1049
David Teten, 724
Mark T Thomas, 1248
Michael G. Thonis, 456
Allen Thorpe, 924
Ethan Thurow, 368
Robert M Tichio, 1573
Paul E. Tierney Jr., 136
Andrew B. Tindel, 1409
Tony Tjan, 567
David Tolmie, 654
David B Tom, 1908
Graves Tompkins, 815
John Toomey Jr., 909
John Trbovich, 171
Victoria Treyger, 720
Mitch Truwit, 135
Tenno Tsai, 928
Jim Tullis, 1866
David Tunnell, 924
James Tybur, 1431
Matthew T. Vettel, 857
Pote Videt, 1139
Tefan Vitorovic, 1932
Andrew Vogel, 2020
Barry Volpert, 559
Johan von der Goltz, 310
Carlo A. von Schroeter, 1979
James F Wade, 1153
Eliot Wadsworth II, 949
Peter Wagner, 1996
Rob Walsh, 1770
Mike Ward, 1515
Charles M. Warden, 1928
Jermaine L. Warren, 969
Alex Washington, 1990
Frank Z Wei, 1956
John Weinberg, 699
Michael Weingarten, 1676
Gregory M Weinhoff MD, 474
Kent R. Weldon, 1815
Richard Wells, 1000
Scott Werry, 2034
Ted West, 772
Casey West, 1732
Forest Wester, 1857
Victor Westerlind, 809
Edward J. Whelan, 254
Gregory A. White, 1815
Peter O. Wilde, 1496
Mark N. Williamson, 368
Elizabeth C Williamson, 789
Andrew Wilson, 200
Peter Wilson, 909
Stoddard M Wilson, 1579
Rob Wolfson, 928
Marc Wolpow, 194
Raymond L.M. Wong, 1730
Willie E. Woods Jr., 969
Christopher G. Wright, 556
Ravi Yadav, 1315
Chris Yeh, 1958
Krishna Yeshwant, 889
Matt Yohe, 1266
Gwill York, 1119

1028

Glenn A Youngkin, 413
Royce G. Yudkoff, 21
Guy Zaczepinski, 449
Luis Zaldivar, 1403
Jeff Zanarini, 928
Strauss Zelnick, 2020
Wan Li Zhu, 712
Eric Zinterhofer, 2252
Adriaan Zur Muhlen, 1486

Harvard College
Samantha A. Adams, 254
Charles F Baird Jr, 1335
Ben Ball, 779
Michael S Berk, 1776
Darren M Black, 1752
Peter Brooke, 350
John Brooke, 350
John Caddedu, 581
Brian Cassidy, 559
Caley Castelein MD, 1059
Michael Chae, 277
Anna H. Chen, PhD, 782
Larry Cheng, 1942
Quentin Chu, 559
Young Chung, 581
Patrick Chung, 708
Ryan Clark, 819
Robert Clark Jr, 359
Andy Dale, 1250
Michael W Dees, 1129
Paul Desmarais III, 2225
Adam S Doctoroff, 1248
David Dominik, 839
Daniel K Doyle, 1770
Alex Earls, 881
Martin Escobari, 815
Jeffrey A. Ferrell, 188
Andy Fillat, 1102
Christopher Finn, 413
John Fisher, 609
William Fitzgerald, 1991
Kobie Fuller, 1888
Neil Garfinkel, 779
Andrew Garman, 1305
James Gellert, 1991
Michael Gellert, 1991
Michael Gladstone, 191
Andy Goldfarb, 835
David Golob, 779
David B. Golub, 844
Chris Gordon, 220
Nicholas Green, 1099
Leo Guthart, 1832
John Hamel, 567
Robert M. Hannon, 1824
Kenneth Hao, 1683
Benjamin A Hochberg, 1104
Matthew S. Holt, 1301
Bob Horne, 2022
Greg Huff, 701
Jason Hurd, 359
David W. Jaffin, 321
Thomas Janes, 1067
Brent P Johnstone, 1511
Peter Kagan, 1956
Roger Kitterman, 1419
Adam Klein, 559
Blake Kleinman, 924
Jon Kossow, 1346
Arvind Krishnamurthy, 1225
Thomas Y. Kuo, 254
A. Rachel Laheny, 1898
Christopher M Laitala, 1129
Mitch Lasky, 248
Gregory G Lau, 1972
Kewsong Lee, 413

Thomas H Lee, 1104
Jeffrey Lee, 1340
Stephen Leibowitz, 1832
Oliver Libby, 1687
Jonathan E. Lim, MD, 487
Robert D Lindsay, 1129
David Lippin, 1376
Michael H. Lustbader, 166
Julian C. Mack, 1088
Sulu Mamdani, 1764
Benjamin Mao, 1081
Tom Mawhinney, 968
Kevin M. McCafferty, 426
Aevin M McCafferty, 1296
Scott McCormack, 1638
Burton McGillivray, 505
Ryan McNally, 427
Scott Meadow, 654
Frances Messano, 1316
Travis R Metz, 1248
Jonathan Miller, 60
Jeb Miller, 968
Lawrence G Miller, MD, 1197
Antonio Miranda, 1134
Lawrence Mock, 1280
John Moon, 1256
Andre V. Moura, 1301
Michael Mullany, 968
Kirk G Nielsen, 1928
John J Nowaczyk, 1234
Ben Nye, 221
Soren L. Oberg, 1815
Joe Osnoss, 1683
Robert Porell, 810
Bill Reichert, 721
Jon Rezneck, 820
Anders Richardson, 1402
William L. Richter, 451
Jonathan Roosevelt, 986
Alex Rose, 559
Charles E. Ryan, 89
Anthony Salewski, 819
Greg Sands, 547
Bob Shapiro, 570
Robert Shapiro, 1615
Carlyle Singer, 55
Dick Spalding, 1059
Samuel W. Spirn, 254
Scott Stanford, 45
Jonathan A. Stein, 546
Howard Steyn, 1088
Laela Sturdy, 578
Jason D. Sutherland, 328
Sam Teller, 1099
Tony Tjan, 567
Catherine Ulrich, 743
Max von Zuben, 1984
Peter Wagner, 1996
Peter Wallace, 277
Albert Wenger, 1882
James Westra, 62
Kevin Zhang, 1887

Harvard Divinity School
Jason Allen, 1172

Harvard Graduate School
Anthony J. DiNovi, 1815
Steven E Karol, 1962
Peter Roshko, 315
Harold R. Werner, 919

Harvard Graduate School of Business
Jean-Pierre L. Conte, 819
Leslie M Corley, 1137
Steve Crihfield, 899
Michael F. Cronin, 1978

Vahe A Dombalagian, 1156
Paul J Finnegan, 1156
Brian Fitzgerald, 401
Douglas C Grissom, 1156
Fred Harman, 1361
Stephen Holmes, 1010
Eugene P. Nesbeda, 546
Vikrant Raina, 361
George Sarlo, 1952
R. Scott Schafler, 546
Thomas S Souleles, 1156
Brian E Stern, 1735
Steve Tomlin, 206
Nicolas D. Zerbib, 1743

Harvard Kennedy School
Patrick Connelly, 1009
Jeremy G. Philips, 1715
Graves Tompkins, 815

Harvard Law School
Kevin Baker, 368
Jeffrey L Balash, 527
Andrew Banks, 21
Michael Barach, 990
John F. Barry III, 1491
Skip Baum, 1103
Michael S Berk, 1776
Jordan S. Bernstein, 476
William Bianco, 1617
Peter Binas, 1627
David Bonderman, 1835
Michael Borrus, 2011
Bruce C. Bruckmann, 354
Victor Budnick, 1021
Patrick Chung, 708
Scott C Collins, 1752
Ed Colloton, 260
Mark M Colodny, 1956
Bryan Cressey, 558
David Dominik, 839
Douglas M. Dunnan, 875
Bill Elkus, 502
Robert C Embry Jr, 19
Steve Engelberg, 1615
Alv Epstein, 1742
John F. Erhard, 156
Norman A. Fogelsong, 1001
Tully M. Friedman, 787
Francisco Garcia, 644
Steven J. Gilbert, 827
David Golden, 1555
Richard Goldstein, 65
Lawrence E. Golub, 844
Greg Gottesman, 1499
Donald B. Hebb, Jr., 22
Sharlyn C. Heslam, 254
Jeff Hinck, 1522
David Hornik, 197
Richard M Horowitz, 1521
David Jegen, 710
Craig A.T. Jones, 1824
Michael S Kaye, 501
Justin Klein, 1917
Steven B Klinsky, 1301
Austin Krumpfes, 1467
Jeffrey T Leeds, 1105
Andrew McLaughlin, 934
Sami Mnaymneh, 928
Nnamdi Okike, 13
Travis Pearson, 824
Leigh Randall, 1832
Edward Reitler, 150
Murray E Rudin, 1575
John E Runnells, 1929
John H. Simpson, 343
Rick Smith, 561

College/University Index / Harvard Medical School

Lawrence B. Sorrel, 1777
Thomas S Souleles, 1156
Avy H. Stein, 1986
Yanev Suissa, 1687
Sanjay Swani, 1777
Matthew E. Swanson, 1564
Russel Valdez, 1950
Barry Volpert, 559
Marc Wolpow, 194
Wade Woodson, 1672
Chris Yang, 879
Strauss Zelnick, 2020

Harvard Medical School
Eric Aguitar, MD, 74
David Berry, 747
Kevin Bitterman, PhD, 191
Casey Cunningham, MD, 1619
James Eadie, MD, 1619
John F Freund, 1691
Sen. William H. Frist, MD, 558
Nicholas Galakatos, PhD, 495
David Grayzel, MD, 191
David Hirsch MD, PhD, 1143
Geoffrey C. Hsu, 1382
Marlene R. Krauss, 1058
Andrew Levin, 1519
Lawrence G Miller, MD, 1197
James Nelson MD, 1002
Dr. Boris Nikolic, 268
Kush M Parmar, MD, PhD, 12
David Schnell MD, 1493
David A Shaywitz, 1778
Robert Tepper, MD, 1811
Gregory M Weinhoff MD, 474
Christoph Westphal, 1145
Krishna Yeshwant, 889
Brett Zbar, 762

Harvard University
Frank A. Adams, 876
Adzmel Adznan, 1449
William F Aikman, 882
Mohammed Alardhi, 1017
Thomas A Alberg, 1158
Dave Ament, 1417
David L Anderson, 1760
Matt Anderson, 1976
Dan Aquilano, 86
Joe Aragona, 202
Peter Arrowsmith, 1041
Jonathan Axelrod, 684
Roy Bahat, 284
John Baker, 223
Manuel Jose Balbontin, 522
Steven Baloff, 59
Amy Banse, 518
Jonathan P Barnes, 897
Doug Barry, 1646
Richard Bauerly, 850
David Becker, 1194
Gregory C. Belmont, 847
Hazem Ben-Gacem, 1017
R David Bergonia, 1332
Betsy Biemann, 438
Peter Binas, 1627
Ben Bisconti, 29
Peter Blacklow, 313
Stephen Bloch, 386
David J. Blumberg, 301
James J. Bochnowski, 604
Zachary Bogue, 585
Gaye Bok, 703
Ralph Booth, 760
Steve Bowsher, 979
Richard Bradlow, 2219
Sayles Braga, 80

Jim Breyer, 336
Peter Brooke, 62
Bruce C. Bruckmann, 354
Ethan A. Budin, 750
Ian Bund, 1455
Sylvester Burley, 332
Richard Burnes, 455
Luke Burns, 178
Jeffrey Bussgang, 754
Thomas R Callahan, 1127
James Carnegie, 277
Joseph Carrabino, Jr., 64
J. Ryan Carroll, 456
Tom Cervantez, 32
Jeffrey T Chambers, 1776
John F Chappell, 1452
Jean-Marc Chapus, 556
Chris Cheever, 760
Anna H. Chen, PhD, 782
Julian Cheng, 1956
Michael Choe, 456
Iris Choi, 751
Ben Choi, 1106
Scott Chou, 805
Scott Chou, 2023
Peter Y Chung, 1752
John Clarke, 410
Hugh Cleland, 2242
James D Coady, 1651
Ross Cockrell, 695
William P Collatos, 1717
Scott C Collins, 1752
Mark M Colodny, 1956
David Cowan, 260
Alan Crane, 1460
Catherine Crockett, 879
John Crumpler, 915
Gary Cuccio, 1793
Richard A D'Amore, 1334
Robert R. Davenport III, 340
Stuart Davidson, 1089
Kim G. Davis, 456
Ken DeAngelis, 202
Donald F. DeMuth, 610
Lawson DeVries, 876
Satish Dharmaraj, 1534
Anthony J. DiNovi, 1815
Sasha Dichter, 55
Jonathan E Dick, 1476
Jeffrey Diehl, 57
A. Barr Dolan, 458
Timothy Draper, 609
Ted Driscoll, PhD, 491
Olivier Dufourmantelle, 2071
William Dunbar, 538
Philip Eliot, 1400
Stuart Ellman, 1593
Dr. Edgar G Engleman, 1941
Juan Enriquez, 703
Hugh D. Evans, 1925
Patrick Fallon, 29
Brad Farkas, 964
Andrew Farquharson, 980
Brian Feinstein, 260
Dean E Fenton, 1735
Mark Fernandes, 1670
Marco J. Ferrari, 1496
Paul J Finnegan, 1156
Daniel T Fleming, 1571
Frank Foster, 791
Frank H Foster, 826
Constance Freedman, 1246
Bradford M. Freeman, 783
Mason Freeman MD, 12
John F Freund, 1691
Samuel P Frieder, 1081
Alexander A. Friend, 788

Francisco Garcia, 644
Luis E Garcia Garcia de Brigard, 141
Bob Gay, 959
Aaron Gershenberg, 1764
Flip Gianos, 1010
Michael W Gibbons, 713
Douglas H. Gilbert, 610
Walter Gilbert, PhD, 270
Tehinder Gill, 511
Jim Glasheen, 1786
Charles E. Glew, Jr., 750
Kim P. Goh, 954
Marc Goldberg, 270
Michelle Goldberg, 974
David Golden, 1555
Greg S Goldfarb, 1752
Lawrence E. Golub, 844
James J Goodman, 812
Carl L. Gordon PhD, 1382
Michael Gorman, 1725
John Patrick Grayken, 1140
Bruns Grayson, 23
McComma Grayson III, 909
Jason Green, 665
Brad Greiwe, 727
Stewart KP Gross, 1123
Drew Guff, 1679
Eric Gulve PhD, 267
William A. Hanna, 371
Felda Hardymon, 260
Drew Harman, 1010
Sam Hartwell, 201
John Hawkins, 818
Patrick Healy, 924
Gardner C Hendrie, 1672
George J Henry, 1127
Scott Hilinski, 1279
Jeff Himawan, PhD, 697
Eva Ho, 728
Thierry F Ho, 1123
Brian Hoesterey, 64
Daniel Hoffer, 204
Bob Hower, 59
Michael Hsieh, 796
Eion Hu, 1045
Yie-Hsin Hung, 1309
Dean Jacobson, 29
David Jaffe, 447
John Jaggers, 1658
Andrew S. Janower, 456
Michael Johnson, 61
John Johnston, 197
Nigel W Jones, 1873
John T. Kaden, 1283
Rebecca Kaden, 1882
Brian Kahn, 1935
JJ Kang, PhD, 517
Sean Karamchandani, 2220
Sharon Kedar, 1342
Pat Kenealy, 1563
James T. Kiernan, 2086
Philip Kim, 1127
John Kim, MD, 138
Charles F Kireker, 786
Jonathan I. Kislak, 131
Gil Kliman, 1010
Paul Klingenstein, 20
Robert B Knauss, 1956
Peter Kolchinsky, 1519
Mehmet Kosematoglu, 250
Roy Kosuge, 1771
Joshua Kushner, 1821
David Lane, 613
Lou Lange, MD, PhD, 181
Gerry Langeler, 1391
Andrew Laurence, 1935
Thong Q Le, 31

Troy LeMaile-Stovall, 1790
Lisa M. Lee, 1496
Eric J Lee, 1972
Steven A Leese, 1503
H Jeffrey Leonard, 834
Sam Lessin, 1694
Ping Li, 28
Richard Lim, 1373
Alfred Lin, 1654
Jessica Lin, 2006
Gary Little, 396
Gary Little, 1257
Vernon Lobo, 2198
Jim Long, 805
Rad Lovett, 1148
Jeff Low, 645
Barbara Lubash, 1928
Vishal Lugani, 49
Michael J Lyons, 1127
Kenneth Mabbs, 711
William I MacDonald, 1103
Rob MacLellan, 2204
Nurzhas Makishev, 1329
Adam J Margolin, 1717
Dorothy Margolskee, 762
Arthur J Marks, 1899
James Marlas, 1881
Salvatore A Massaro, 656
Russ Mayerfeld, 88
Brendan McCafferty, 1296
Christopher McElhone, 2034
Thomas McKinley, 410
Kevin W McMurchy, 629
James E Meketa, 1200
Samuel M Mencoff, 1156
Adrian Mendoza, 1201
David Michael, 133
David F Millet, 812
Charles Moldow, 770
John Moon, 1256
Gary Morgenthaler, 1257
Scott Murphy, 61
Patricia Nakache, 1853
Kirk Nelson, 1917
James Nelson MD, 1002
Jennifer Keiser Neundorfer, 1026
Howard H Newman, 1443
David W. Niemiec, 1621
Tom Noonan, 1788
George D O'Neill, 1215
Nnamdi Okike, 13
Larry Orr, 1853
Mark Paris, 1894
Kush M Parmar, MD, PhD, 12
Sanjay Patel, 140
Manish Patel, 935
Robert Paulson, 67
Seth R. Pearson, 1971
Ezra Perlman, 779
Charles G. Phillips, IV, 1621
Charles Phipps, 1658
Marguerite A Piret, 1312
John Piret, 1312
David B. Pittaway, 423
Mike Pongon, 1458
Will Porteous, 1593
Robert Puopolo, 687
Dennis Purcell, 74
Deborah Quazzo, 883
David P Quinlivan, 1604
Keith Rabois, 775
Eduardo Rallo, 324
Scott Raney, 1534
Bill Reichert, 807
Andrew Richards, 1767
Aaron Richmond, 673
James Riley, 2073

Steven Ritterbush, 1207
Bryan Roberts, 1916
James Robinson, 1593
James Robinson, III, 1593
Antonio Rodriguez, 1181
James LD Roser, 1586
Mike Ross, 1762
Michael Ross PhD, 1628
Steven J Rosston, 836
Michael Rubin, 1342
Jim Savage, 1146
Omar A Sawaf, 2013
Carmen Scarpa, 1728
Joseph L. Schocken, 346
Peter M. Schulte, 507
Evan M. Schwartz, 156
John Scull, 1711
Andrew Sheiner, 2046
Ben Sheridan, 289
Ed Sim, 305
John Simon, 1673
Andrew Singer, 675
Steven F. Skoler, 788
Alex Slusky, 1910
Robert A. Smith, 421
Thomas Smith, 1139
Stephen B Solomon MD, 572
Daniel Sonshine, 2272
Thorne Sparkman, 1693
Ronald P. Spogli, 783
Dimitri Steinberg, 772
Julie Sunderland, 268
Matthew E. Swanson, 1564
Steven R. Swartz, 922
Steven Swartzman, 364
Alan J Taetle, 1331
Gus Tai, 1853
Jim Tananbaum, 762
William N. Thorndike, 949
Clay B Thorp, 915
Ethan Thurow, 368
Esther Tian, 343
Keith Titan, 256
Dafina Toncheva, 1896
John Toomey Jr., 909
Tuan Tran, 1009
Timothy Tully, 1867
David Tunnell, 924
Adam Valkin, 816
Mark F Vassallo, 1123
Drew Volpe, 1483
John Vrionis, 1121
Robert Wadsworth, 909
Eliot Wadsworth II, 949
David Weiden, 1069
Sharon Weinbar, 1626
Ed Weinfurtner, 289
Gregory M Weinhoff MD, 474
Robert Weisskoff PhD, 710
Peter Wendell, 1670
Christoph Westphal, 1145
James N White, 1760
Steve Wiggins, 697
Greg Williams, 29
Edward C. Williams, III, 349
Kyle Winters, 2201
Daniel B. Wolfe, Ph.D, 6
Gordon H Woodward, 1081
Alfred S Woodworth Jr, 647
Gwill York, 1119
Brian D. Young, 686
Philip M Young, 1896
Janie Yu, 796
Dr. Chen Yu, 1941
David Yuan, 1785
Kareem Zaki, 1821
Darshana Zaveri, 426

Harvey Mudd College
David A Krekel, 1398
Hodong Nam, 100
Jon Soberg, 1269

Haskayne School of Business
Jason Brooks, 2162
Allison M. Taylor, 2162
Jason White, 2166

Hastings College of Law
Tom Bevilacqua, 1906
Elliot B Evers, 1195

Haverford College
Phin Barnes, 741
Steven L. Begleiter, 750
Bruce Gorchow, 1467
Roger B Kafker, 1776
Brian C. McDaid, 1727
Dave Stubbs, 380

Heald Engineering
Bob Marshall, 1646

Hebrew University
Jonathan Klahr, 1759
Ron Laufer MD, 1196
Gideon Soesman, 2142

Hebrew University of Jerusalem
Hagai Barlev, 669

Helsinki University of Technology
Petri Vainno, MD, PhD, 697

Hendrix College
Todd McIntyre, 870

Henley Business School
Lorraine Audsley, 2112

Henley Management College
Dr. Markus Goebel, 1350
Charles Vaslet, 2106

Herbrew University of Jerusalem
Arie S. Belldegrun, 1932

Heriot-Watt University
Mark Bonnar, 1711
Alan MacIntosh, 51

Hillsdale College
John McIlwraith, 86

Hiroshima University
Yasuharu Watanabe, 2007

Hitotsubashi University
Susumu Tanaka, 2007

Hobart & William Smith Colleges
Lori B. Ali, 1496

Hobart College
Jon Flint, 1460
David L Gold, 359
Daniel M Kortick, 1984
Terry McGuire, 1460
Trevor W. Pieri, 404
Benjamin M. Polk, 1925

Hofstra University
David Benyaminy, 193
Don Hofmann, 565
Michael P. Murphy, 1585

College/University Index / Hollins College

Joe Rubin, 150
John S Schnabel, 716
Alyse Skidmore, 1335
Jermaine L. Warren, 969

Hollins College
Martha P.E. Arscott, 524

Holy Cross College
Christopher Colecchi, 347
John Dean, 939
Tom Flynn, 1762
Mary M Shannon, 1175

Hong Kong International Law School
Diana Saca, 681

Hong Kong Polytechnic University
Anita Chik Lin Oi, 1139
Margaret Lee Lai Chu, 1139

Howard University
Cory D. Mims, 969
Laurence C. Morse PhD, 714
JoAnn H. Price, 714

Huazhong University of Science
Bill Li, 1951

Humber College
Fil Varino, 3258

Humboldt University
Rodger P Adams, 1909

Hunter College
Jeanette M Welsh JD, 1792

Huron University College
Matt Hall, 2087

IIT-Bombay
Shailesh Mehta, 851

INEAD
Andy Burgess, 2244

INSEAD
Nilanana Bhowmik, 534
Pavel Bogdanov, 89
Marie-Claude Boisvert, 2082
Roberto Buaron, 733
Eric Buatois, 249
Lionel Carnot, 237
Ilfryn Carstair, 1907
Andrew Cleland, 518
Ronan Cunningham, 1717
Paul Desmarais III, 2225
Sebastien Dhonte, 2081
Rutvik Doshi, 1013
Rodrigo Feitosa, 928
Rupert Gerard, 888
David Gussarsky, 1121
Drew Harman, 1010
Francois Helou, 187
Carlos Heneine, 1516
Daniel Hullah, 809
Evan Jaysane-Darr, 1015
Alan MacIntosh, 51
Marc Manasterski, 1516
Loudon Mclean Owen, 2199
Loudon Owen, 2154
James D.C. Pitt, 1112
Pal B Ristvedt, 1112
Claudi Santiago, 740
Subhanu Saxena, 1302
Corry J. Silbernagel, 2064

Andrew Sillitoe, 135
Raj Singh, 1035
Rick Stahl, 660
Alastair Tedford, 78
Tidjane Thiam, 554
Alexandre Villela, 1509
Merav Weinryb, 1509

Idaho State University
Hatch Graham, 183

Illinois Benedictine University
John M. Reher, 323

Illinois Institute of Technology
Bob Bode, 1022
Daniel Norr, 203
Andrew A Thomas, 1744

Imeperial College London
Raj Singh, 1035

Imperial College
Nick Adams, 107
Pietro Dova, 2010

Imperial College London
Upal Basu, 1330
Will Honeybourne, 740
Mohit Kaushal MD, 20

Imperial College of Science
Oded Ben-Joseph PhD, 1388

Indian Institute of Management
Parag Dhol, 1013
Ashu Garg, 770
Vishal Gupta, 260
Amit Gupta, 504
Hemant Khatwani, 690
Samir Kumar, 1013

Indian Institute of Technology
Neal Bhadkamkar, 1249
Parag Dhol, 1013
Rutvik Doshi, 1013
Ashu Garg, 770
Ramneek Gupta, 486
Amit Gupta, 504
Kiran Hebbar, 1899
Uttam Jain, 188
Krishnamurty Kambhampati, 505
Rishi Kapoor, 1017
Vinod Khosla, 1069
Samir Kumar, 1013
Sundeep Peechu, 720
Arvind Purushotham, 486
Ramesh Radhakrishnan, 174
Arun Ramamoorthy, 1445
Kanwal Rekhi, 1013
Shrikant Sathe, 1911
Parag Saxena, 1911
Bipul Sinha, 1121
Amit Srivastava, 682
Somu Subramaniam, 1303

Indian School of Business
Aditya Arora, 834
Alipt Sharma, 834

Indiana State University
Brad Muse, 71

Indiana University
Farraz Abassi, 443
Jack K Ahrens II, 1802
Jeff Akers, 57

Laura Albrecht, 1166
Blake Austin, 1022
Roger D Bailey, 606
Sandra P Barber, 1708
Brian Bastedo, 1578
David L. Belzer, 1491
Julie A Bender, 789
Julian L Carr, 244
John M. Carsello, 900
John Chambers, 1031
Chris Christoffersen PhD, 1122
Tony Conrad, 1860
Thomas P. Cooper, MD, 136
Curtis D Crocker, 1544
Kevin Culp, 1022
Omar Diaz, 629
John W Doerer, 1461
Scott Dorsey, 929
Rajat Duggal, 787
Christopher M. Eline, 900
Jim Farnsworth, 2050
Kathy Fields, 1041
Michael E Flannery, 633
Michael Gallagher, 928
Ting Gootee, 658
James B Hoover, 587
Sumeet Jaisinghani, 1598
David Jegen, 710
J Allan Kayler, 1232
Daniel Kessler, 577
Ted H. Kramer, 900
David Krane, 889
Suzanne Kriscunas, 1572
Jim Lim, 867
Rebecca Luse, 1298
Scott Lutzke, 443
Florence J. Mauchant, 953
Mark Maybell, 645
Bart A McLean, 1270
Dr Evan Melrose, 1722
Craig Overmyer, 944
Brent L Paris, 632
David E Pequet, 1156
Luke A. Phenicie, 900
Champ Raju, 1467
Andy Reed, 316
Douglas J. Rosenstein, 873
Shannon Rothschild, 1722
Stephen N Sangalis, 1484
Joseph P Schaffer, 1252
David K. Schaible, 1724
David R. Scholl, 187
Glenn Scolnik, 900
Thomas P. Shaw, 900
Harpinder Singh, 996
Brian S Smith, 856
Michael A Steinbeck, 1744
Jeff Thermond, 2011
Shoshana Vernick, 1742
William D. Waldrip, 671
Thomas D Weldon, 40
Stephen Wertheimer, 1947
Tom Willerer, 1916
William Young, 495
Darell E Zink Jr, 409

Indiana University School of Law
Glenn Scolnik, 900
James C. Snyder, 900

Indiana University of Pennsylvania
Ric Clark, 2067
Terry Williams, 1321

Indiana University, Bloomington
Angie Grimm, 967

College/University Index / Karl Franzens University

Indiduan Institute of Technology
Nilanana Bhowmik, 534

Inst. for Management Development
Eric Rosenfeld, 791
Eric Rosenfeld, 1383

Institut Commercial de Nancy
Florence J. Mauchant, 953

Institut d'Administration des Entre
Dominique Gaillard, 2466

Institut d'Etudes Politiques
Gonzalo Cordova, 1911
W. Carter Neild, 1382
Joern Nikolay, 815

Institute of Actuaries
Mark Arnold, 78

International Inst. of Mgmt Dev.
Jui Tan, 296

International Space University
Andrew Ray, 2155

International Technical University
David Tsang, 47

International University of Monaco
Matt Turner, 113

Iona College
Maria F Costanzo, 1621
Peter Polimino, 104
R Peter Reiter, Jr, 1557
Gregory P. Sullivan, 788

Iowa State University
Dan Broderick, 267
Frederick J Dotzler, 598
Spiros Liras, 143
Alan Marty, 1106
Vivek Mehra, 197
Nancy Schoendorf, 1247
James A Severson PhD, 840
Paul Spieker, 736
Anil Tammineedi, 126

Isenberg School of Management
Jeffrey Mark, 507

Ithaca College
Michael E Bogucki, 1163
Alexander Cuomo, 1325
Damien A. Dovi, 263
Matt Kinsey, 361
Peter H Mills, 1
Paul A. Scott, 269

Ivey Business School
Rob Barbara, 2068
Roger Chabra, 2239
Robert Cherun, 2047
Scott Clark, 2087
Ryan DeCaire, 2045
Stephen J. Dent, 2062
Bill Di Nardo, 2110
Cam Di Prata, 2133
Michael Duncan, 2089
Stuart M. Elman, 2220
Nicole Fich, 2219
Andrew J. Fortier, 2062
J Kristofer Galashan, 1109
Darrick Geant, 331
Ryan Giles, 2275
Kerri Golden, 2153
Mark Gordon, 2208
Ewout Heersink, 2209
Catherine Herring, 2215
Blaine Hobson, 2288
Robbie Isenberg, 2081
Daniel Israelsohn, 2224
Donald Jackson, 2215
Dan Jacques, 2145
Scott Kaplanis, 2108
Wiz Khayat, 2246
Stephan Klee, 2225
Michael Lay, 2208
Mark Lerohl, 2230
John Loh, 2062
Justin MacCormack, 2150
Kenneth MacKinnon, 2181
Ian Macdonell, 2089
Erik Mikkelsen, 2047
Anuj Ranjan, 2067
Gary Rubinoff, 2259
David G. Samuel, 2062
Russell Samuels, 2288
Pierre J. Schuurmans, 2062
Sunil Selby, 2273
Matt Shalhoub, 2140
Ray Sharma, 2113
Joseph Shlesinger, 2082
Thecla E. Sweeney, 2062
Nathan Tam, 2045
Chris Taves, 2063
Douglas B. Trussler, 274
Mac Van Wielingen, 2040
Michael Wagman, 2081

Ivey School of Business
Monica J. Holec, 1111

J. Reuben Clark Law School
Steve Young, 959

JL Kellogg School Of Management
Rebecca Lucia, CFA, 12

JW Goethe University
Ansbert K Gadicke MD, 1268

James E. Beasley School of Law
Richard Taney, 1864

James Madison University
Joseph F. Damico, 1590
Christopher D. Graham, 1739
Steve Guffey, 834
Paul Holland, 770
Mike Marcantonio, 288
Don Rainey, 876
Michael W Rubel, 1557
Michael S. Sarner, 403
Tige Savage, 1555
David A Stienes, 1136
Randall Ussery, 1985
Joshua Wilson, 846

Jawaharlal Nehru University
Eric Beckman, 331

Jefferson Medical College
Mike Pellini, 1643

John Carroll University
Carl E. Baldassarre, 1456
Anthony Nader, 1766
Arnold B Siemer, 606
Sean Ward, 290

John Molson School of Business
Sam Ifergan, 2149

Johns Hopkins University
Garrick Ahn, 373
Jeffrey Aronson, 442
Stephen Auvil, 1790
John Avirett, 867
Jeffrey S Barber, 1776
Nicholas B Binkley, 765
Keith Carlton, 886
Matt Cheney, 499
Tom Clark, 528
Emmett Cunningham Jr., 495
Michael Ehlers, 143
Robert Finkel, 1477
Elizabeth Galbut, 1701
Simeon J. George, 1731
Richard Gilmore, 825
Michael Goldberg, 337
Stewart Gollmer, 1796
Casey Gordon, 1341
David Hirsch MD, PhD, 1143
Charles Homcy, MD, 1811
Michael C. Jackson, 949
Ross Jaffe, 1928
Yan Ke, 1340
Christoph Lengauer, PhD, 1811
Dennis Lockhart, 1280
Edward B Marsh, MD, 1198
Paul Matteucci, 1896
Jessica Milano, 376
Chris Pacitti, 202
Mark Paris, 1894
Caroline Popper MD MPH, 241
Holly Radel, 3261
Greg Raiten, 743
R. Scott Schafler, 546
John W. Snow, 451
Megan Sparks, 532
Julie Sunderland, 268
William H Taylor II, 1262
Shermaine Tilley, 2092
Tim Weglicki, 22
Daniel Yardley, 1422

Johns Hopkins University School of Medicine
JH Bilenker, MD, 74
Dorothy Margolskee, 762
Vance Vanier, 469
Damion Wicker, 1410

Johnson Grad. School of Business
Karen Derr Gilbert, 793

Johnson Grad. School of Management
Skip Besthoff, 1496
Sven K. Grasshoff, 716

Jones Graduate School of Business
Stephanie Campbell, 950

Kalamazoo College
William J Oberholtzer, 932

Kansas State University
Dixon Doll, 596
Brian Lueger, 1053
Marshall D. Parker, 1053
Chris Traylor, 756

Karl Franzens University
Matthias G Allgaier, 1752

1033

College/University Index / Kean University

Kean University
Mark L. Benaquista, 1815

Keble College
Liz Birch, 268

Keio University
George Hara, 602
Yasunori Kaneko MD, 1691
James Kondo, 820
Koji Osawa, 833
Terry Suzuki, 1386

Kelley School of Business
Michael Goy, 1267
Blair Greenberg, 333
Angie Grimm, 967
Mark Hollis, 443
Chris LaMothe, 658
Jill Margetts, 443

Kellogg School of Business
Raj Seth, 925

Kellogg School of Management
John F Ackerman, 409
Christopher J. Ackerman, 750
Will Adams, 92
Laura Albrecht, 1166
Alexandre Alvim, 834
Brad Armstrong, 1147
Robert M Austin, 985
Keith Bank, 1056
Keith Bank, 1057
Hagai Barlev, 669
Derek Beaty, 834
Michael H. Beaumont, 985
Julie A Bender, 789
Stephen A Bennett, 1745
Kent Berkley, 782
Brian Birk, 1754
George Bischof, 1212
Geoff Bland, 1969
Robert D Blank, 468
Jason Booma, 515
Karen Buckner, 1242
Brian J. Buenneke, 1411
Andrew M Bushell, 540
Kevin D Cantrell, 1575
Virginia Cargill, 80
John R Carroll, 1752
John M. Carsello, 900
Michael Castellarin, 2081
Chris Cathcart, 894
Cheryl Cheng, 296
Rob Chesney, 471
Sach Chitnis, 1046
Gavin Christensen, 1070
Matt Clary, 1963
Michael Cohn, 883
Richard H Copans, 1156
Kelly A. Cornelis, 1093
Chuck Cullen, 876
D Patrick Curran, 364
Joseph Cutts, 1381
Albert DaValle Jr., 1038
Robert E Davis, 1134
Jordan S Davis, 1520
Rob Day, 1729
Brian Demkowicz, 960
Sunny Dhillon, 1678
James Dimitri, 1925
Mishone B. Donelson, 946
Robert Dreier, 359
Jim Dugan, 1364
Justin C Dupere, 1963
Chris A. Durbin, 1931

Park Durrett, 29
Steven A. Elms, 74
Thomas Erickson, 738
Jeff Farrero, 468
David Fishman, 1910
Andy Fligel, 1004
Walter C Florence, 789
Andrew N. Ford, 903
Tod Francis, 1663
Peter B Franz, 752
Marc-Henri Galletti, 1143
Evan R Gallinson, 1209
Christopher J Garber, 1963
David S. Gellman, 801
Charlie Gifford, 926
Aziz Gilani, 1206
John Glushik, 1008
Stefan Goetz, 924
Miki Granski, 536
Gabe Greenbaum, 1480
Blair Greenberg, 333
Carter Griffin, 1886
Tony Grover, 1592
Michael Gruber, 983
Michael C. Gruber, 1610
Andrew S Gustafson, 1684
Jonathan M Haas, 492
James N. Hallene, 407
Frederic Halley, 1319
Rob C Hart CFA, 1792
Tom Hawkins, 768
John Hennegan, 1667
Jay R. Henry, 1409
Deborah Hodges, 1231
John Hoesley, 1477
Beth Hoffman, 254
Brett P Holcomb, 1492
Ken Hooten, 529
Jim Huston, 1463
Grant A Jackson, 550
Jeff Jackson, 1806
David W Jahns, 806
Brian James, 489
Rich Jander, 1166
Stephen M. Johnson, 949
Gregory Jones, 654
Julie Jubeir, 406
Bill Kaczynski, 338
Joe Kaiser, 1204
Jonathan Kalman, 1025
Ashish Kaul, 765
Scott A. Kehoe, 1014
Ryan Kelley, 1667
Colton King, 1086
Demian Kircher, 1166
John Kneen, 244
Laird Koldyke, 1999
Adam Koopersmith, 1480
Austin Krumpfes, 1467
Ronald W Kuehl, 789
John Kuelper, 176
John LeMay, 290
Jenny Lee, 823
Kristin K Lee, 1232
Mark Leigh, 950
Gigi Levy-Weiss, 1323
Rand Lewis, 441
Alex Lieberman, 489
Bernardo H. Llovera, 706
Matthew J. Lori, 1301
Bruce Luehrs, 1568
Peter N Magas, 244
Sumant Mandal, 1809
Bernard B Markey, 1281
Woody Marshall, 1785
Alfred M. Mattaliano, 1578
Erik E Maurer, 1492

Bret Maxwell, 1242
Matt McCall, 1480
Michael McCullough, 983
Steve McKay, 772
John Meilner, 338
Ryan Milligan, 468
William H. Miltenberger, 984
Gregory Moerschel, 244
Anthony J. Moore, 822
Jason B Moskowitz, 633
James Neary, 1956
Bradley C O'Dell, 1492
Maura O'Hara, 3265
John E. Palmer, 903
Gordon G. Pan, 222
Thomas Parkinson, 944
Thomas Parkinson, 975
Steven W. Parks, 1093
Naimish Patel, 1141
Jeff Patterson, 515
Brian Paul, 1796
Randy Paulson, 1368
Mike Peck, 1379
Gil Penchina, 1563
Scott A Perricelli, 1136
Peter S Pettit, 1270
Matthew W Raino, 1156
Champ Raju, 1467
Thomas R. Raterman, 802
Chris Redmond, 399
Scott Rooth, 1467
Jason Rosenberg, 1742
George Rossolatos, 2070
Doug Rotatori, 1368
Sarah G Roth, 164
Laura M. Rubin, 1739
Lawrence Rusoff, 1431
Brent T Sacha, 1745
Neel Sarkar, 441
Adam Schimel, 239
David L. Schnadig, 546
Jodi Sherman Jahic, 83
Terrance M Shipp, 1209
Walker C. Simmons, 1409
James R Simons, 1725
Paul Smith, 830
Peter Sonsini, 1297
Andrew Souder, 1521
Mark Staub, 1467
Jennifer Steans, 529
Roderick Stephan, 99
Gary Stevenson, 1187
Mark Strauch, 92
Nancy Sullivan, 975
Eric Swanson, 888
Mark D. Taber, 857
Pete Tedesco, 918
Brian C. Tilley, 610
Joseph Tou, 1703
Jeffrey W Ubben, 1903
Rob Veres, 1721
Sona Wang, 452
Michael Watts, 1128
Reeve B Waud, 1963
William Wick, 1937
J. Alberto Yepez, 1850
Ari M. Zur, 348

Kenan-Flagler Business School
Brad Armstrong, 1147
Charles A Cox, 1144
Benton Cummings, 1516
Stuart W Hawley, 1624
Dan Rua, 990
Krishnan Varier, 151
Thomas H. Westbrook, 746

College/University Index / London School of Economics

Kennedy School of Government
Zaid Ashai, 1459
Catherine Crockett, 879
Edith Dorsen, 2003
Andrew Dunn, 1376
Dr. Campbell Murray, 1350
Juliet Tammenoms Bakker, 1143

Kent Business School
Oscar Alvarado, 1341

Kent State University
Timothy Gosline, 1572
Drew Molinari, 577
Joseph J. Zabik, 343

Kenyon College
Jeremy Bauman, 1304
Donald B. Hebb, Jr., 22
Brett P Holcomb, 1492
David Reynolds, 960
Karl Slatoff, 2020
John Tomes, 916

Kettering University
Susan Clark, 1785
Gregory Hulecki, 711
Kristina Serafim, 1926
Matt Tsien, 817

King's College
Jonathan Klahr, 1759
Chuck Parente, 669
Alan Wilkinson, 64

Kingston Business School
Malcolm Moss, 251

Kingston University
Philip Cole, 1763

Knox College
Rajeev Dadoo, 1731
Joseph H Heinen, 843
Timothy F. Sutherland, 1229

Kogod School of Business
Paul Diaz, 558

Kolping College
Eckard Weber, MD, 621

Krannert Business School
Stephen Can, 277

Krannert Grad. School of Management
Ron Sansom, 1572

Kuwait University
Fawaz Al-Mubaraki, 1950

Kwantlen Polytechnic University
Norton Singhavon, 2100

Kyoto University
Shunichiro Matsumoto, PhD, 182

LMU University
Ahim Kandler, 759

La Salle University
Raymond Larkin, 572
Kevin Provost, 866
Dean Sciorillo, 676
Brian J Siegel, 891
Raymond F Weldon, 353

La Sorbonne
David Mes, 1370

LaSalle University
Robert Graham, 1428
Dean Sciorillo, 676

Lafayette College
Craig Bural, 1528
Bruce A Eatroff, 897
Stephen A. Hanna, 1744
Hendrik J. Hartong III, 357
Robert Hinaman, 48
Andrew Mitchell, 325
Gil Ozir, 2057
Craig Pisani, 168
Daniel R. Revers, 156
Edward F Sager Jr, 1203
Robert Shafir, 1635
Adam F. Stulberger, 1777

Lake Erie College
Stephen B Perry, 1132

Lake Forest College
Mark Headrick, 536
Matthew Roszak, 1681
Peter G. Schiff, 1344

Lakehead University
Jim Boyle, 990
Harry Jaako, 2097

Lauder Institute
Stephanie Von Friedeburg, 1007
Dalton Wright, 1070

Laurentian University
Nancy Turnbull, 2219

Laval University
Pierre Dubreuil, 2055
Andree-Lise Methot, 2093
Sophie Perreault, 2114
Charles Sirois, 162
Charles Sirois, 2261

Lawrence University
George L. Buzzy, 289
Andrew H Kalnow, 90
Steve Mech, 566
Scott D. Roeper, 719
Chris Whitcomb, 1369

Lebanese American University
Firas El Amine, 1017

Lee Business School
Matthew Neely, 1692

Leeds University
Andy Bayliffe, 143

Lehigh University
William J. Amelio, 594
Stephen D. Aronson, 1576
Jack Baron, 565
Peter Bennett, 1116
Thomas A Berglund, 733
John Bolduc, 239
Steve Carpenter, 1117
Mike Carusi, 59
Mike Carusi, 1122
Kevin Clayton, 675
Diane M. Daych, 434
Ryan J. Faulkingham, 523
Stewart Fisher, 1086
Philip Fleck, 1347
Timothy T. Hall, 476
David Heidecorn, 1088
Kenneth J Heuer, 1071
Stephen Holmes, 1010
Bill Kirsch, 548
Josh Kuzon, 1528
Paul S. Levy, 1039
Paul Martino, 358
Vincent P. Menichelli, 53
Matthew Nicklin, 732
Greg J. Pappas, 254
David J Reuter, 1136
Mark R. Ross, 1369
Joseph Saviano, 223
Fredrick D. Schaufeld, 1766
Geoff Schneider, 431
Samuel L Schwerin, 1235
Mark Strauch, 92
Gordon T Wyatt, 40

Lehman College
Peter Kalkanis, 1558
Ruben Rodriguez, 360

Lenoir-Rhyne University
Kenneth B Lee, 915
Philip W Martin, 1606

Leonard N Stern School of Business
Joshua Ho-Walker, 1315

Lewis & Clark College
Mark Dorman, 673
Sam Thompson, 1486

Liberty University
Angela Helfin, 3269
Paul S. Williams, 734

Linkoeping University
Goran Ando, MD, 697

Loma Linda University
Wes Ferrari, 972
Jim Woody, 1094

Lomonosov Moscow State University
Anna Batarina, 143

London Business School
Gerald T. Banks, 101
Matthew Foy, 1731
Mona Kung, 2138
Matt Lee, 472
Derek Senft, 2123
Derek Senft, 2218
Tim Stubbs, 1753
Andrew Tarazid-Tarawali, 55
Erol Uzumeri, 2252
Matteo Volpi, 2074

London City University
Cécile Belaman, 220

London School of Business
Stephan Bey, 2059
Ravi Bhaskaran, 758
Kristopher Prakash, 1369
Norman Rokosh, 2275

London School of Economics
Jonathan Aberman, 119
James Appleyard, 2125
Rajay Bagaria, 1960
David Beecken, 244
Sven H. Borho, 1382

1035

College/University Index / London University

Justin Burden, 986
Paul D'Addario, 1402
Michael Denham, 2055
Hythem T El-Nazer, 1776
William F Foote, 1582
Elizabeth Galbut, 1701
Ralf Gruss, 135
Charles Holt, 2161
Karen Hung, 3258
Asad Jamal, 690
Arrun Kapoor, 1689
Serge LeVert-Chiasson, 2248
H Jeffrey Leonard, 834
Bernardo H. Llovera, 706
Jessica Milano, 376
Lawrence Mock, 1280
Quinn Morgan, 446
Rory O'Driscoll, 1626
Will Porteous, 1593
Jason Reed, 1997
Ken Rotman, 2081
Siddharth Srivastava, 2190
Paul Strachman, 1530
James E Thomas, 1817

London University
Mark Arnold, 78
Carlos Heneine, 1516

Long Beach City College
Russ Aldrich, 887

Long Island University
Charlotte Chapanoff, 305
Kim P. Goh, 954
Steven Insalaco, 369
Joe Mandato, 598
Joseph B Rotberg, 1104
Jeffrey M. Sauerhoff, 177

Louisiana State University
Jerry DeVries, 1801
Marcia Haydel, 1431
D. Martin Phillips, 672
Steven L. Soignet, MD, 157
S Somasegar, 1158
Martin Sutter, 697
W. Anthony Toups, 61

Louisiana Tech University
Jarett Carson, 676
William D. Waldrip, 671

Lowell Technological Institute
Peter Barrett, 191

Loyola College
Stephen Auvil, 1790
Greg Barger, 1317
David Freschman, 150
Eileen O'Rourke, 19
Nicholas J. Simon, 495
Jim Zucco, 505

Loyola Law School
Lloyd Greif, 869
Craig Gunther, 278

Loyola Marymount University
Elmer Baldwin, 464
Tom Cervantez, 32
Jim Demetriades, 1051
Mark E Farrell, 1806
Ted Fourticq, 902
Monty Lapica, 512
Michael Steed, 1400
Briana J. Zelaya, 1903

Loyola University
Chuck Cullen, 876
Michael T Dieschbourg, 987
Jeff Griffor, 1119
Donald W. Hughes, 383
Stephen V King, 1469
Rick Kohr, 701
Rocco J. Martino, 1093
Michael McGee, 2049
Omar Mejias, 63
William H. Miltenberger, 984
Annie Piotrowski, 234
Jeff Schechter, 1742
Michael Steed, 1400
Nancy Sullivan, 975
Eric Thompson, 867
Mary Tolan, 469
Kyle Welborn, 569

Loyola University of Chicago
Jennifer Carolan, 1527
Tracy Chadwell, 7
David Knoch, 1022
Paul A. Scott, 269

Lubin School of Business
Alexander Cuomo, 1325
Vincent D'Angelo, 240

Ludwig Maximilian University
Dr. Markus Goebel, 1350

Ludwig Maximilion University
Hubert Birner, 2276

Lycoming College
Donald W. Hughes, 383

M. Katz Grad. School of Business
Michael Beauregard, 960

METU University
Sensu Serpen, 239

MIT
Shaun Abrahamson, 1894
Noubar Afeyan, 747
Payal Agrawal Divakaran, 2
Yuval Almog, 536
Jorge Amador, 109
David L Anderson, 1760
Vikram Bajaj, 762
Henry G. Baker, 223
Eric Baker, 2194
Daria Becker, 1491
Gregory C. Belmont, 847
Stephen Berenson, 747
David Berry, 747
James J. Bochnowski, 604
Teymour Boutros-Ghali, 1249
Hugo Braun, 1336
Josh Breinlinger, 1024
Luke Burns, 178
Mark Bye, 1256
Brian Byun, 1069
Doug Cameron, 738
John K. Castle, 423
Brownell Chalstrom, 207
James Cham, 284
Wesley Chan, 720
Pierre Chao, 680
Richard A. Charpie, 118
Nelson Chu, 1072
Joyce Chung, 807
Ed Cluss, 1678
Jay Cohan, 1975
Vanessa Colella, 486

Dennis R. Costello, 322
Will Cowen, 1142
Gregory S Czuba, 691
Jeff Davison, 989
Stephen P DeFalco, 1129
Tom Dennedy, 174
Brian Dixon, 660
Mishone B. Donelson, 946
Rami Elkhatib, 41
Bill Elkus, 502
David O Ellis, 656
Chuck Esserman, 1861
Charles H Esserman, 1861
Saman Farid, 219
Brad Feld, 776
Brad Feld, 1245
Brad Feld, 1789
Andy Fillat, 1102
Todd Foley, 1268
Bill Ford, 760
Richard Fox, 971
Arthur L Fox, 1591
Richard H. Frank, 584
Ben Fu, 1319
Nicholas Galakatos, PhD, 495
Sameer Gandhi, 28
Shri Ganeshram, 785
Luis E Garcia Garcia de Brigard, 141
Shauntel Garvey, 1527
Max Gazor, 455
John Glushik, 1008
Jim Goldinger, 712
Johnathan M Goldstein, 1776
Carl L. Gordon PhD, 1382
Mark Gorenberg, 2019
Paul Grim, 692
Paul Grim, 1755
Rick Grinnell, 712
Rick Grinnell, 829
Alex Gruzen, 545
Greg Gunn, 488
Krishna K Gupta, 1581
Perry Ha, 626
Steven E Hall, 1124
Howard Hartenbaum, 197
Kamil Hassan, 851
William Heflin, 1072
Jeff Himawan, PhD, 697
David Hirsch MD, PhD, 1143
Janey Hoe, 483
Karen Hong, 1778
Larry Hootnick, 54
Jeff Horing, 1000
Paul Hsiao, 396
Maha Ibrahim, 386
Brian Jacobs, 665
Uttam Jain, 188
John W. Jarve, 1202
Gregory Johnson, 1488
Mark Jrolf, 926
Neena Kadaba, 2229
Alex Khalin, 1926
Kevin J. Kinsella, 206
Dave Kowalick, 887
Chris Kryder, 748
Richard P Kuntz, 1664
Philippe Laffont, 509
Vijay Lathi, 1298
Patrick Latterell, 1094
Kenneth Lau, 446
Jay F Laudauer, 1881
Derek Leck, 109
Peter Lee, 228
Aileen Lee, 552
Peter Lee, 663
Sara Leggat, 1656
Douglas Leone, 1654

Andrew Levin, 1519
Nurzhas Makishev, 1329
Josh Makower, 1297
Jill Margetts, 443
Kim Marvin, 109
Scott Maxwell, 1380
Howard Mayson, 2050
John Mazzarino, 463
Mark McDowell, 51
Mark McDowell, 1096
Fred A Middleton, 1221
Fred A Middleton, 1616
David S. Miller, 497
George M Milne, Jr. PhD, 1520
H. DuBose Montgomery, 1202
Amir Nashat, 1460
Brendan O'Leary, 1478
Jim Pastoriza, 1782
Thomas A Penn, 1275
Thomas A Penn, 1428
William Perry, 988
Mark Perutz, 595
John Piret, 1312
Serge Plotkin, 1381
Lisa Porter, 979
Tim Porter, 1158
Stan J Reiss, 1181
Raju Rishi, 1593
Scott M Rocklage PhD, 12
Alexander Rosen, 1563
Phil Samper, 805
Dave Samuel, 784
Dr. N. Darius Sankey, 2021
Neel Sarkar, 441
Christopher Schaepe, 1121
Zach E Schaumburg, 1219
Kenneth T Schiciano, 1776
Bob Schulz, 918
Stephen Shapiro, 59
Shantnu Sharma, 106
David A Shaywitz, 1778
Ben Shih, 968
Mark A. Siegel, 1202
Ian Sigalow, 871
Jeff Silverman, 70
Peter Sinclair, 1102
Greg Somer, 692
Bart Stuck, 1676
Katie Szczepaniak Rice, 688
Lip-Bu Tan, 1951
Jim Tananbaum, 762
Hemant Taneja, 816
Ralph Taylor-Smith, 809
Jim Tenkle, 1618
Yaniv Tepper, 126
Tyler Thompson, 1642
Michael G. Thonis, 456
Linda Tufts, 749
Tomas Valis, 2076
Gayle L Veber, 1909
Jim Walker, 57
Robert Ward, 1212
David Waxman, 1798
David Weiden, 1069
Robert Weisskoff PhD, 710
Albert Wenger, 1882
Andy Wheeler, 889
Damion Wicker, 1410
Fred Wilson, 1882
Rich Wong, 28
Chris Yang, 879
David Yuan, 1534
Wan Li Zhu, 712
Geoffrey von Maltzahn, 747
Johan von der Goltz, 310
Alex von der Goltz, 310

MIT Sloan School of Management
Sim Blaustein, 256
Prashanth V. Boccasam, 1348
Gaye Bok, 703
Clara Brenner, 1893
Justin Butler, 648
Chris Davis, 810
Stephen P DeFalco, 1129
Mark A deLaar, 1752
Jeffrey L. Dickson, 1497
Pietro Dova, 2010
Rami Elkhatib, 1709
Karimah Es Sabar, 2229
Nikhil Garg, 1729
Jeffrey P Gerson, 849
Jim Goldinger, 712
Bob Greene, 533
Paul Grim, 692
Paul Grim, 1755
Bradley C Harrison, 1632
Eric Hjerpe, 1065
Paul A Howard, 1197
Michael Huber, 1506
Scott Johnson, 1291
Daniel G. Jones, 1815
Amit Karp, 260
Ray Leach, 1047
Julie Lein, 1893
Stephen O. Marshall, 2103
Scott Maxwell, 1380
Bill McCullen, 1097
Preetish Nijhawan, 454
Zach Noorani, 770
Kola Olofinboba, 714
Mark Perutz, 595
Steve Rappaport, 1376
Andy Sack, 773
Graham Schena, 1266
Evan M. Schwartz, 156
Joel Serface, 253
Paul Spicker, 736
Brian Stansky, 1003
Philip N. Sussman, 1808
Sanjay Swani, 1777
Gus Tai, 1853
Peter Tertzakian, 2040
Lee J Tesconi, 1112
Linda Tufts, 749
Jeff Williams, 1728
Donna Williamson, 452
Paul Wu, 870
Chris Yang, 879
George Zachary, 455

MS University Baroda
Amit Shah, 174

Macalester College
Paul Batcheller, 1470
Beth Hoffman, 254
Michael Huber, 1506
Evis Hursever, 697
Seth Levine, 776
Seth Levine, 1245
TJ Mahony, 38
John L Ritter, 739
Steve Wiggins, 697

Manchester Business School
John W. Littlechild, 919

Manchester University
R. Patrick Forster, 985
John W. Littlechild, 919

Manhattan College
Tracie E. Ahern, 1444

Bob DeSena, 878
Sally A. DeVino, 1743
William Farrell, 170
Brian J. Girvan, 178
Robert E Kelly, 1738
Anthony V Lando, 40
Jose Minaya, 1356
Philip N. Sussman, 1808

Manhattanville College
Paula G. McInerney, 299
Larry Reinharz, 2004
Thorsten Suder, 401

Mannheim University
Matthias G Allgaier, 1752

Marietta College
Dean Didato, 995

Marquette University
Joel Andryc, 1598
Phil D. Bronsteatter, 1435
Chad M. Cornell, 843
Jim Domach, 1171
Scott A. Finegan, 1435
Paul Kreie, 1232
Lesya Kulchenko, 925
Mark McDonnell, 153
Greg Myers, 1171
Gregory J. Purcell, 147
Paul J. Raab, 719
Robert Shen, 892

Marriott School of Management
Ryan Lucero, 782

Marshall School of Business
Kevin T. Dugan, 869
Jerry Lotter, 664
Gordon Smythe, 2195
Sean Stiefel, 1283
Keith Wasserman, 811

Marshall University
David Becker, 1194
Barry B Conrad, 984
Joe Spratt, 737

Maryland Institute
Elizabeth Galbut, 1701
Nabeel Hyatt, 1715

Massachusettes Maritime Academy
John Whorf, 1294

Massachusetts College of Pharmacy
Argeris Karabelas, 412
Ronald P Thiboutot PhD, 1117

Mayo Clinic
Michael Matly, MD, 1251

Mays Business School
Ben Stanton, 888

McCombs School of Business
Randall Crowder, 1801
James Eadie, MD, 1619
Dwight Scott, 277
Ryan Shulz, 702
Shravan Thadani, 1856

McDaniel College
William J. Westervelt, Jr., 179

College/University Index / McDonough School of Business

McDonough School of Business
Cheryl Moss, 788
Matthew Ritchie, 48

McGill University
Maor Amar, 2151
Dan Baum, 2244
Pierre Beauparlant, 2270
Justin Beber, 2067
Raghu Bharat, 2088
Andrew Bishop, 2059
Keith Bisson, 438
Cédric Bisson, 2268
Adam Breslin, 2219
David Brown, 1789
Jake Cassaday, 2236
Matthew Chapman, 2272
Rob Chesney, 471
Liam Cheung, 2260
Dr Ronald Chwang, 970
Todd Clapp, 427
Thomas D'Halluin, 73
Marcus Daniels, 2147
Sebastien Dhonte, 2081
Andrea Drager, 215
Olivier Dufourmantelle, 2071
Dr. Sheldon Elman, 2220
Luigi Fraquelli, 2133
Kim Furlong, 3258
Eric Gottesman, 2169
Lee M. Grunberg, 2226
William A. Hanna, 371
Andrew Heintzman, 2161
Kyle Hickey, 2246
Sam Ifergan, 2149
Avak Kahvejian, 747
Julius Kalcevich, 966
Maha Katabi, 1698
Daniel H. Kosoy, MD, 187
David Lawee, 578
Felix-Etienne Lebel, 2062
Dr. David Lee, 494
Shawn Lewis, 2274
Jonathan E. Lim, MD, 487
Simon Lockie, 2134
Andrew Lugsdin, 2124
Kenneth MacKinnon, 2181
Adam Marcus, 2102
Shunichiro Matsumoto, PhD, 182
Eamonn McConnell, 2167
Benn Mikula, 2086
Rick Ness, 2260
John Philp, 2126
Alireza Rahnema, 2028
Scott Requadt, 495
Giorgio Riva, 2289
Lauren Robinson, 2147
Beni Rovinski, 2180
Zoya Shcuhpak, 2156
Andrew Sheiner, 2034
Andrew Sheiner, 2046
Imran Siddiqui, 2255
Pascal Tremblay, 2206
Mario Venditti, 2156
Morty White, 2009
Greg Williams, 581
Peter Wilson, 909
Christopher Winn, 2194
Ben Yoskovitz, 2147
Christian Zabbal, 1729
Ray Zhang, 1467

McIntire School of Commerce
Mark M. Anderson, 884
J.S. Gamble, 285
E Bartow Jones, 1573
Teddy Kaplan, 1301

Kristin Steen, 433
Jonathan R Wallace, 1388

McMaster University
Richard Betsalel, 2089
Jim Boyle, 990
Laurel C. Broten, 2205
Adam Felesky, 2225
Mark Hatfield, 1794
Bill Kostenko, 2057
Elaine Kunda, 2098
Damian Lamb, 2130
Joe Mattina, 2219
Michelle McBane, 2257
Robert S. McLeese, 2030
Christopher Rankin, 2055
Hamish Sutherland, 2154
Hamish Sutherland, 2287
Colin Walker, 2089

Medical College of Pennsylvania
Barbara J Dalton PhD, 1436

Medical College of Virginia
Vijay Aggarwal, PhD, 1808
Sandeep Naik, 815

Medical College of Wisconsin
Zia Agha, 1973

Meinders School Of Business
Craig Woodruff, 48

Memorial University
Jam Michael McDonald, 2245

Memphis College of Art
Gary Backaus, 16

Mercer University
Roddy JH Clark, 1533

Merrimack College
James Jordon, 1448
Robert MacInnis, 21

Methodist University
Sami Sawaf, 2013

Meyers College
Gary Graham, 736

Miami University
Robert D Blank, 468
Michael Boniello, 1464
Andrew J Collins, 1752
Daniel Colon, Jr., 507
Jason R. Cornacchione, 1456
Todd Creech, 921
Bruce Downey, 1317
David A Gezon, 1232
Stephen R Haynes, 831
Rich Jander, 1166
Mark A Johnson, 1863
Gregory Jones, 654
John LeMay, 290
Brian Leonard, 653
Peter N Magas, 244
Frederic H Mayerson, 1954
Scott McConnell, 88
Ryan Meany, 653
Patrick Meenan, 173
Peter E Mogk, 960
Mark Morris, 290
Lisa Ondrula, 1045
Chris Orndorff, 1946
Steve G. Pattison, 1456

Susan Sheskey, 594
Paul Smith, 830
Nelson Teng, 458
Bob West, 200
Adriaan Zur Muhlen, 1486

Miami University of Ohio
Mike Gausling, 1385
Peter Mogk, 960
Daniel E Pansing, 1209

Michigan Law School
Duncan Davidson, 358

Michigan State University
Deepak Advani, 924
Aohn Cambier, 971
Robert DesMarais, 1767
Linda Fingerle, 652
Kelly Ford Buckley, 655
Jeff Frederick DPM, 1289
Tom Gores, 1451
Steve Grizzell, 999
Michael Gross, 251
Justin Ishbia, 1667
Michael Janish, 1904
Ryan Kelley, 1667
Ted Lai, 970
Mike Letourneau, 1062
Travis Macinnes, 38
Sumant Mandal, 1809
James Marasco, 1970
Dennis McCrary, 1411
Lake McGuire, 925
John Melstrom, 981
Terry Opdendyk, 1378
Blake Robins, 1150
Ian Ross, 529
Jay W Schemelter, 1574
Chris Sugden, 655
Christopher G. Wright, 556
Yipeng Zhao, 663

Michigan Technological University
Kanwal Rekhi, 1013

Michigan Technology University
Wade Sheffer, 817

Middle Tennessee State University
Marshall Cole, 213

Middlebury College
Brandon Avrutin, 1551
Jared J. Bartok, 118
Christopher D. Brady, 457
C. Andrew Brickman, 222
James W. Brush, MD, 782
Christopher PH Cheang, 1465
Schuyler Coppedge, 675
David N Deutsch, 589
Chun Ding, 472
James T Donelan, 1636
Christopher M. Doody, 1743
Alex Finkelstein, 1715
Michael D. Gregorich, 1743
Andrew S Gustafson, 1684
Douglas A. Haber, 1815
Parker Harris, 1607
Justin Harrison, 361
Ronald C Hess Jr, 1476
Eugene Hill, 1628
Lydie Hudson, 554
Jeremy Janson, 782
Robert Jenkins, 1466
Samantha Kaminsky, 552
Bill Maris, 1643

College/University Index / National University of Singapore

Brian W Michaud, 1134
Bob More, 94
Tyler Newton, 427
Brendan O'Leary, 1478
Jonathan H. Owsley, 1088
Keith W. Pennell, 610
John G Rudge, 1112
Rick Scanlon, 996
Kathleen Schoemaker, 621
Jeffrey Schutz, 441
Jed Smith, 428
Peter H Smith Jr, 1735
Joshua Sobeck, 14
John B. Stephens, 1931
Gus Taylor, 719
Robert Tucker, 401
Ted Virtue, 1231
Reeve B Waud, 1963
W Lambert Welling, 1198

Millikin University
Dennis Beard, 1379
Holly Kaczmarczyk, 1970

Minnesota State University
Jane Bortnem, 464

Minot State University
Curtis Armstrong, 2173

Mississippi College
Jason Ball, 1509
Rebecca Irish, 1430

Missouri Univ. of Science & Tech.
Dennis F. Jaggi, 671
Brian Matthews, 569

Montana State University
Cairn G Cross, 786

Montclair State University
Thomas Girardi, 953
Gene Wolfson, 427

Monterey Institute of Int'l Studies
Wes Ferrari, 972

Montreal University
Laurence Rulleau, 2092

Moore School
Alex Doll, 1794

Moore School of Business
Amy Burr, 1035

Moore School of Engineering
Jeff Lieberman, 1000
Bret Pearlman, 659
Adam L Suttin, 1049

Morehead State University
David A Henderson, 1854

Morehouse College
Chris Allen, 1403
Qian W. Elmore, 969
Kirby Harris, 229
H Beecher Hicks, III, 1529
Aaron Holiday, 13
Ira L. Moreland, 969
David C Neverson, 1105
Alex Washington, 1990
Willie E. Woods Jr., 969

Morgan State University
R Randy Croxton, 1208
Timothy L Smoot, 1208
Stanley W Tucker, 1208
Anthony L Williams, 1208

Moritz College of Law
Eric Kaup, 937

Moscow Institute of Physics
Pavel Bogdanov, 89
Alexander Galitsky, 89

Moscow Institute of Steel and Alloy
Alexei Andreev, 204

Moscow State Technical University
Dmitry Grishin, 874

Moscow State University
Yuri Milner, 615

Moscow Steel And Alloys Institute
Alexei Andreev, 205

Mount Allison University
Catherine Decarie, 2112
Julie Fallon, 2076
Malcolm Fraser, 2155
Zac McIsaac, 2188
Craig Noble, 2067

Mount Holyoke College
Nissa Bartalsky, 80
Maria Cirino, 2

Mount Saint Vincent University
Dawn House, 2155

Mount St. Mary College
Peter Ianello, 1364
Daniel Yardley, 1422

Muhlenberg College
Matthew Naythons MD, 163

Murdoch University
Mason Hills, 1548

NYU School of Medicine
Josh Makower, 1297

NYU Stern School of Business
Tracie E. Ahern, 1444
Samy Ben Aissa, 1926
Sikandar Atiq, 2202
David Bainbridge, 1927
Sam Barthelme, 1033
Christopher PH Cheang, 1465
Chris Chung, 878
John Daileader, 862
Gabriel de Alba, 2073
Harry DeMott, 1525
Bob Delaney, 559
Michael DiPiano, 1317
Brendan Dickinson, 386
Donald J Donahue Jr, 691
Jeff Drazan, 257
Michael J Dubilier, 631
Tammy Funasaki, 331
Jeffrey M Goodrich, 931
Michael D. Gregorich, 1743
D Thomas Healey Jr., 1573
Matthew Hermann, 176
Kenneth J Heuer, 1071
Lorraine Hliboki, 1462
Matthew Kimble, 208

Eric R. Korsten, 327
Joel Krikston, 1205
Pierre-Olivier Lamoureux, 844
Peter A Lyons, 1105
Paula G. McInerney, 299
Thomas Murphy, 815
Shay Murphy, 1324
Alexandra Prima, 1805
John Raguin, 710
Bob Rees, 1737
Loren Schlachet, 1572
Steven Schwartz, 239
Mayank Singh, 446
Matt Smalley, 380
Eric D. Starr, 407
Scott Steele, 1040
Roy Thiele-Sardina, 933
Justin Topilow, 250
Christopher Turner, 1956
Anibal Wadih, 834
David J. Wermuth, 1743
Luis Zaldivar, 1403
Dal Zemp, 1542
Scott Zoellner, 64

Nanyang Technological University
Jui Tan, 296
Lip-Bu Tan, 1951

Nasson College
Joe Mandato, 598

National Cheng Chi University
Ted Lai, 970

National Cheng Kung University
Hsing Kung, 47
Robert Shen, 892
Ed Yang, 970

National Chiao Tung University
Sam Lee, 729
M.R. Lin, 905

National Sun Yat-Sen University
Lucas Wang, 519

National Taiwan University
Wu-Fu Chen, 47
T.C. Chou, 905
Christy Chou, 1922
William Chung, 892
Ta-Lin Hsu, 892
George J Lee, 117
M.R. Lin, 905
Woody Sing-Wood Yeh, 117
Kai Tsang, 1922
John Tzeng, 905
Lucas Wang, 519
Tzyy-Po Wang, 905

National Tsing Hua University
Dr. Frank Kung, 1941
Jackie Yang, 1838

National University
Josef Friedman, 1747

National University of Ireland
Robert W. Mulcare, 1301

National University of Singapore
Jixun Foo, 823
Kelvin Liu, 1015
Evelyn Sun, 148

College/University Index / Natl. Tech. University of Athens

Natl. Tech. University of Athens
Niko Bonatsos, 816

Naval Postgraduate School
Steven Denning, 815
Kenneth A. Minihan, 1400

New College, Oxford
John Frankel, 724

New England College
Chris Mathieu, 946

New England School of Law
John Fitzgerald, 467
Stephen Muniz, 1501

New Hampshire College
Cairn G Cross, 786

New Jersey Institute of Technology
Charles E Larsen, 40

New Mexico State University
Larry Lujan, 1924

New York Law School
Eric Hatzimemos, 1687
Marc Lasry, 208

New York Medical College
Paul Eisenberg, 143
Lawrence Howard MD, 954

New York State University
Rod Ferguson, 1410

New York University
Krishna K Agrawal, 1129
John F Aiello, 1129
Jeffrey Aronson, 442
Rajay Bagaria, 1960
Stephen A Baker, 766
Scott Barry, 697
Nicolas Berggruen, 250
Brett Berson, 741
Barry Blattman, 2067
Timothy P Bradley, 1674
Clara Brenner, 1893
Jeffrey B Bunder, 1129
Robin Ellis Busch, 1726
Andrew Chang, 1115
Wayne Cohen, 1635
Charles Cohen, 1775
Ao Ann Corkran, 841
Michael Dempsey, 525
Gerry Doherty, 1277
Jeff Drazan, 257
Greg Durst, 3266
Andrew L. Dworkin, 1911
Harry Edelson, 651
Bart Faber, 192
Peter Feinstein, 270
Adam E Fine, 1993
Michael J Fram, 1116
Thomas Giannetti, 1112
Jay N. Goldberg, 954
Alan E Goldberg, 1129
Michael Gontar, 1949
Michael D Goodman, 849
Mark K Gormley, 1104
Arthur P. Gould, 172
Andrew G Gould, 172
Thomas G Greig, 1116
Stephen A. Hanna, 1744
David Harnisch, 484
Charles Heilbronn, 1263

Bruce M. Hernandez, 1724
Ted Hirose, 1791
Eric Hixon, 826
Jerry Hobbs, 361
Charles B Hughes III, 644
David W. Jaffin, 321
Richard Johnson, 1228
Robert Johnston, 1044
Donald A Juricic, 1557
Alan L Kaganov ScD, 1896
Arrun Kapoor, 1689
Anita K. Kerr, 240
Brian Kinsman, 359
Peter W Klein, 348
Michael I Klein, 1134
James A Kohlberg, 1081
Mike Kwatinetz, 215
Robert Le Blanc, 2209
Matt Lee, 472
William D. Lese, 322
Waiman Leung, 1992
Basil Livanos, 78
Eric J. Lomas, 953
Timothy W Maloney, 18
Michael Marocco, 1617
Lauren M Massey, 18
Mark McAndrews, 645
Thomas McKinley, 410
Ivar W. Mitchell, 123
Britton Murdoch, 1568
Nader Naini, 782
Joshua Nussbaum, 525
Arnie Oronsky, 1010
Gil Ozir, 2057
Raja M. Parvez, 1057
Paolo Parziale, 18
Emily Paxhia, 1464
Thomas B Pennell, 1429
Peter Petrillo, 849
Richard A. Petrocelli, 1621
Craig Pisani, 168
John Poindexter, 1030
Robert Porell, 810
Jonathan Pulitzer, 809
Steven G Raich, 1134
Marc Rappoport, 1305
Thomas G Rebar, 1633
R Peter Reiter, Jr, 1557
Christopher W Roser, 1586
Ken Rotman, 2081
Kathleen Schoemaker, 621
Dominique Semon, 1216
David Shainberg, 225
J. Frederick Simmons, 783
Robert J. Simon, 321
Edward J Siskin, 937
Alyse Skidmore, 1335
John I Snow III, 1503
Joan Solotar, 277
Jason Stein, 1992
William H Stewart, 1281
Timothy F. Sutherland, 1229
David Tisch, 318
Denis A. Tito, 1989
Robert Toan, 1949
Jon Trauben, 99
Michele Valenti, 1548
David Wachter, 1947
Katherine Watts, 1712
David Weiden, 1069
Wayne B Weisman, 1633
Sean C. White, 1724
Bill Winterer, 1417
Chris Xie, 2271

New York University Business School
Joshua L. Gutfreund, 494

Joseph P Landy, 1956
Steven J Taubman, 1908

New York University School of Law
Jonathan Aberman, 119
Lawrence S. Atinsky, 177
Mitchell Davidson, 1465
Roger S Fine, 1993
David Gershman, 1857
Robert Gold, 1564
Greg Raiten, 743
David Robbins, 1844
David Rosenstein, 815
Richard L Sherman, 1633
Yves Sisteron, 1888
Donald Spencer, 1679
G Michael Stakias, 1116
Adam F. Stulberger, 1777

New York University of Law
Dave Marple, 1907

Newberry College
Charlie Banks, 1923

Nicholls State University
Corey Callais, 372

Nicholls University
Harold Callais II, 372

Nijenrode School of Business
Marc der Kinderen, 14

North Carolina School of Law
Dan Rua, 990

North Carolina State University
Robert Hester, 1349
Michael Marshall, 894
Jaime McMillan, 390
William B. Thompson, 780
Vishal Vasishth, 1363
Ken Woody, 995

North Dakota State University
Doug Burgum, 173
James Burgum, 173
John G. Cosgriff, 1016
Steven D Kloos PhD, 1859
Vish Mishra, 502
Gerald F Schmidt, 537
Matthew T. Vettel, 857

North Park College
Thomas S. Bagley, 1435

Northeastern University
Nick Adams, 614
Jason Allen, 1172
Peter Barrett, 191
Adam Bryant, 648
Alec Burger, 808
Dennis P Cameron, 646
Thomas J Caracciolo, 632
Paul Ciriello, 712
Richard A D'Amore, 1334
Bob Davis, 935
Robin W Devereux, 1752
Jeffrey H. Goldstein, 309
Frances N. Janis, 1462
Steve Klammer, 1369
Edward A Lafferty, 1623
Benjamin Marino, 1432
Edward C McCarthy, 1571
Gerald A. Michaud, 946
Michael P. Murphy, 1585

Ed Olkkola, 1783
James J Pallotta, 1524
Morgan Polotan, 814
Benjamin P Procter, 1962
David Ryan, 1239
Bruce C Ryan, 1707
Bruce Sachs, 455
Matt Saunders, 2115
Matt Saunders, 2245
Stuart Skinner, 316
Nina Stepanov, 30
Michael S Weissenburger, 597

Northeastern University, China
Lili Zhou, 540

Northern Arizona University
Brian Connors, 764
Jim Upchurch, 373
Jim Upchurch, 374

Northern Illinois University
John I Abernethy, 636
Bob Flannery, 1536
Adrienne Foo, 1864
James M Garvey, 1628
John McKearn PhD, 1574
Daniel Norr, 203
Nick Rosa, 570
Nick Rosa, 1615
Michael Siemplenski, 732

Northwest Missouri State University
Sarah Dickey, 3256

Northwestern Ohio University
Akhil Saklecha, 174

Northwestern Oklahoma State Univ.
H Lee Frost, 591

Northwestern State University
Steve Futrell, 1462

Northwestern Uniersity
Charlie Gifford, 926

Northwestern University
Matthew S Ahearn, 1859
Aaron C. Aiken, 903
Jeff Akers, 57
Alexandre Alvim, 834
Ricardo Angel, 1449
C Mark Arnold, 1529
A Craig Asher, 1940
Robert M Austin, 985
Lee Bailey, 1895
Keith Bank, 1057
Peter Barris, 1297
Bret Batchelder, 463
James A. Beakey, 1279
Derek Beaty, 834
Maurey J Bell, 619
Kent Berkley, 782
Terrence Berland, 1074
John P. Birkelund, 1621
Charles Birnbaum, 260
Jason Booma, 515
Simita Bose, 1348
Dennis C Bottorff, 550
Duncan S. Bourne, 2009
Matthew L. Brennan, 985
Sonya Brown, 1346
David M Browne, 1168
John Buttrick, 1882
John M. Carsello, 900
Robert Chefitz, 1328

Cheryl Cheng, 296
Christopher Childres, 653
Chris Chung, 878
James D Coady, 1651
Philippe Collombel, 1416
Anthony B Davis, 1128
Robert E Davis, 1134
Robert DesMarais, 1767
Mishone B. Donelson, 946
Scott Dorsey, 929
Mark Downs, 1280
Jim Duda, 582
Jeff Eby, 2008
William Ericson, 1247
Bill Ericson, 1985
Rod Ferguson, 1410
Scott A. Finegan, 1435
Brian Flucht, 278
David I. Foley, 277
Andrew N. Ford, 903
R. Patrick Forster, 985
Tod Francis, 1663
T. Bondurant French, 57
Michael Fulton MD, 943
Brian Gallagher, CFA, 1871
David A Gezon, 1232
Wade D Glisson, 1684
Stefan Goetz, 924
Rashmi Gopinath, 1154
James Gordon, 654
Gabe Greenbaum, 1480
Alex Gregor, 1078
Michael C. Gruber, 1610
Jonathan M Haas, 492
Lee C Hansen, 1213
Promod Haque, 1346
John Harris, 1029
Robert A Heimann, 1571
John Henderson, 966
Troy Henikoff, 1178
Jeff Hinck, 1522
James Ho, 64
Jay Hoag, 1785
Beth Hoffman, 254
Stephen J Hoffman MD, 1691
Yie-Hsin Hung, 1309
W Joseph Imhoff, 1281
Robbie Isenberg, 2081
Scott Jacobson, 1158
Brian James, 489
Peter Jarman, MBA, 560
Timothy D. Johnson, 843
Stephen M. Johnson, 949
Kim Kamdar, PhD, 621
Nagraj Kashyap, 1154
Peter Keehn, 88
Laird Koldyke, 1999
Richard P Kuntz, 1664
Charles T Lake II, 1674
Jamie Lane, 1867
Joe Lawler, 1990
Mark Leigh, 950
Gigi Levy-Weiss, 1323
Jack R. Luderer, MD, 139
Mark T Lupa PhD, 930
Timothy J MacKenzie, 1209
Robert Maeder, 766
Dan Malven, 10
Joe Mandato, 598
Bret Maxwell, 1242
Matt McCall, 1480
Spence McCelland, 1331
Ryan R. McKenzie, 147
Jeff Miller, 1411
Gregory Moerschel, 244
David Moll, 988
Dinesh Moorjani, 518

Stephen Natali, 654
Kenneth O'Keefe, 244
Meghan Otis, 1964
John E. Palmer, 903
Charles L Palmer, 1332
Gordon G. Pan, 222
Greg Parekh, 1302
Thomas Parkinson, 944
Thomas Parkinson, 975
Don Parsons, 142
Tom Petzinger, 1098
Lee Pillsbury, 1806
Naomi Pilosof, 1202
JB Pritzker, 1479
J.B. Pritzker, 1480
Jim Rauh, 839
John M. Reher, 323
Douglas Rescho, 1091
Joseph R Rondinelli, 789
Jason Rosenberg, 1742
David Scalzo, 1074
Jim Schultz, 1379
Jon Soberg, 1269
Todd Solow, 1345
Gregory P. Spivy, 1903
Michael Stark, 563
Roderick Stephan, 99
Chelsea Stoner, 235
David Stott, 1990
Nancy Sullivan, 975
Eric Swanson, 888
Jeff T. Swenson, 1815
Joseph Tou, 1703
Leda Trivinos, 747
Philip A Tuttle, 591
Ahmed Wahla, 1081
Mike Ward, 1515
Todd Warren, 618
John W Watkins, 1153
Stephen Wertheimer, 1947
Kurt C. Wheeler, 495
James N White, 1760
Ken Widder, 1094
Rob Wolfson, 928
Mark Wright, 287
Paul Wu, 870
Philip Yau, 824
Eric Young, 386
Ari M. Zur, 348

Northwestern University Law School
Rob C Hart CFA, 1792
Kevin P Kenealey, 1171
Jason Rosenberg, 1742

Norwich University
David Orfao, 816

Nottingham University
Steven Tang, 626

Nova University
Dayakar Puskoor, 1285

Oakland Community College
Ara Topouzian, 3269

Oakland University
Susan Clark, 1785

Oberlin College
Joe Apprendi, 1554
Billy Cohn, MD, 1619
Kevin M. Jackson, 873
Jim Petras, 642
Béla Szigethy, 1572

1041

College/University Index / Occidental College

Occidental College
Eric Gulve PhD, 267
Steven Hartanto, 463
Chris Howard, 974

Odessa University
Ilya Nykin, 1488

Ohio Northern University
Charlie Kim, 1186

Ohio State University
Michael Butler, 1286
Dennis R. Costello, 322
Bruce Downey, 1317
Alv Epstein, 1742
Daniel T Fleming, 1571
Christopher Fountas, 171
Pat Gouhin, 3256
Colleen Greenrod, 290
Mark A Johnson, 1863
Lindsay Karas, 1286
Anthony M Lacenere, 987
Rich Langdale, 1286
Sam Lee, 729
Wally Lennox, 1461
Fayez S. Muhtadie, 1743
Jay D Pauley, 1752
Dan Phelps, 1609
David W. Pidwell, 87
Michael Price, 450
Eric A Reeves, 633
John M. Rice, 479
John M Rice PhD, 1847
David A. Sands, 1456
Omar A Sawaf, 2013
David R. Scholl, 187
Richard Schwarz, 653
Sharon Stevenson DVM, PhD, 1371
Robert Unkovic, 1098
John Willert, 401

Ohio University
Kristy Campbell, 1553
John P. Gilliam, 299
Jeff Griffor, 1119
H Randall Litten, 348
Brian C. Tilley, 610

Ohio Wesleyan University
Darrell W Austin, 201
Charlie MacMillan, 642

Oklahoma Baptist University
Michael Hunkapiller, 87

Oklahoma Christian University
W Michael Partain, 591

Oklahoma City University
Tom Walker, 1553

Oklahoma State University
John Blebins, 1444
Dennis Dougherty, 1008
Richard Garman, 793
Michael D Long, 1270
Jason Reed, 1997
Carl D Thoma, 1814
James Thorp, 17
Anis Uzzaman, 721
Craig Woodruff, 48

Old Dominion University
Kevin Gibbs, 1207

Olin Business School
Stephen Broun, 399
Rick Holton Jr., 569
Kevin Malone, 1105

Olin Graduate School of Business
David Q. Anderson, 118
Michael Harden, 175
Tom Needham, 1775

Olivet Nazarene University
Curtis D Crocker, 1544

Oregon State University
John Becker, 109
Wesley R. Edens, 767
Maurice Gunderson, 204
Maurice Gunderson, 205
Utkarsh Kanal, 198
Walter Kortschak, 1675
Ali Shadman, 1038
Ed Yang, 970

Osgoode Hall Law School
Bradley W. Ashley, 2226
Justin Beber, 2067
Daniel Brothman, 2224
Rocco DiPucchio, 2073
Carey Diamond, 2288
Jody Forsyth, 2038
Joe Freedman, 2067
Harry Goldgut, 2067
Loudon Mclean Owen, 2199
Loudon Owen, 2154
Adam Szweras, 2122

Ottawa Heart Institute
Brad Bolzon, 1928

Oxford Said School of Business
Yanev Suissa, 1687

Oxford University
Kate Bingham, 1762
Trevor Burgess, 1125
William J Canestaro, 2008
Bennett Cohen, 1449
Sergio P. Ermotti, 1878
Bill Guttman, 1623
Whitney Haring-Smith, 133
Patrick Pichette, 2157
Subhanu Saxena, 1302
Andrew Scotland, 239
Tim Stubbs, 1753
Jonathan Victor, 225

PSG Tech
Anil Tammineedi, 126

Pace University
Roland V. Bernardon, 404
Alexander Cuomo, 1325
Pasquale DeAngelis, 1490
Gerry Doherty, 1277
Jason D Drattell, 1468
John Dugan, 1364
Thomas P (Todd) Gibbons, 303
Jack Iacovone, 1288
Shant Mardirossian, 1081
Steven J Morgenthal, 164
Jonathan M Rather, 1972
Stephen Rossetter, 448
Tony Shum, 39
Savitha Srinivasan, 967
Andrew H. Steuerman, 844
Gene Wolfson, 427
Richard Zannino, 433

Thomas de Jager, 118

Pacific Lutheran University
Erik Benson, 1945
Armen B Shanafelt, 1124

Pacific Union College
Clinton W. Walker, 494

Pacific University
Zachary C. Berk, 1058

Panthéon-Sorbonne University
Marcel Fournier, 423
Eric Hippeau, 1110

Paris University of Medicine
Jean-Francois Formela, MD, 191

Paul Merage School of Business
Justin Hartfield, 664

Peking University
Nicolas Chaudron, 2851
Shan Fu, 1941
Carol Mao, 799
Evelyn Sun, 148

Pennsylvania State University
Susan Adams, 23
Edward Anchel, 669
Jason S Barg, 1147
Bruce Booth, 191
John Burns, 1161
Steve Carpenter, 1117
Bryan Castillo, 44
Adam H Curtin, 1234
Joseph Cutts, 1381
Harry D'Andrea, 1899
Barbara J Dalton PhD, 1436
W Ryan Davis, 1159
J. Bradley Davis, 1562
Gary R DiLella, 1494
Michael DiPiano, 1317
James B. Dougherty, MD, 157
Greg Dracon, 2
Jerry Engel, 1249
Ken Fox, 1748
Mark Fruehan, 1244
John Gannon, 692
John Gannon, 1755
Eerik Giles, 1280
A. Bruce Johnston, 1776
Paul S. Kasper, 678
Jason Klein, 29
Jerry Knotts, 3257
Ira M Lubert, 1136
Ira M Lubert, 1508
Michael Lynch, 1199
David J Machlica, 1163
Jim Marra, 290
Michael McMahon, 1046
James M Mead, 1520
Kirk Morgan, 53
Scott Nissenbaum, 246
Steven G Park, 616
Ned J Renzi, 272
John E Runnells, 1929
Santosh Sankar, 640
Peter D. Schreiber, 616
Steven J Taubman, 1908
Lara J. Warner, 554
Robert G Yablunsky, 1633
Joseph Zanone, 581

Pepperdine University
Wilson Allen, 1976

Lisa Atia, 218
Warren Bergen, 2048
Greg Bettinelli, 1888
Dan Chiriaev, 861
Mark Fields, 93
Matt Fuller, 820
Joshua Mack, 501
Eric Manlunas, 1965
Bob Marshall, 1646
Jim Marshall, 1646
Chris Perry, 489
Dennis Podlesak, 621
Luke K. Stanton, 1692
Mark Swaine, 494

Pepperdine University School of Law
B Marc Averitt, 1371
Gerard N. Casale, 1876

Philadelphia University
RoseAnn B. Rosenthal, 246
Janet L. Stott, 1828

Philips International Institute
Ed Yang, 970

Pierce College
Michael Dunn, 693

Pitzer College
Shahan D Soghikian, 1410

Politecnico di Milano
Roberto Buaron, 733

Polytechnic Institute of Brooklyn
Ta-Lin Hsu, 892

Polytechnic Institute of New York
John R. Kline, 1301

Polytechnic University of New York
Paul J Ferri, 1181
Robert Humes, 1038

Pomona College
Steve Crihfield, 899
Marc A. Gineris, 982
Marcia Goodstein, 972
Wei Hopeman, 148
Kristin Johnson, 96
M. Scott Jones, 893
Loretta Little, 2008
Daniel I. Rubin, 87
Jodi Sherman Jahic, 83
Michael S Solomon, 1109
Christopher Staudt, 667
Brian Wheeler, 257

Portland State University
Steve Bailey, 782
David Dolezal, 1915
John Saefke, 1915
Corey Schmid, 1656

Princeton University
Andrew Adams, 1361
Joseph B. Alala III, 405
Brandon Allen, 1875
James G Andersen, 503
Robert Anderson, 793
Carl T Anderson, 836
Christopher Anderson, 1081
Merrick Andlinger, 123
Brian Ascher, 1916
Jeffrey L Balash, 527
Tom Barnds, 29

Redington Barrett III, 1432
John F. Barry III, 1491
Nikhil Basu Trivedi, 1663
Croom Beatty, 1202
Matthew M. Bennett, 1301
Betsy Biemann, 438
JH Bilenker, MD, 74
James G Binch, 1127
John P. Birkelund, 1621
Jim Blair, PhD, 621
David C. Bordeau, 254
Michael Borrus, 2011
Peter L. Briger Jr., 767
Graham Brooks, 2
Robert E Brown Jr., 1275
Steve Brownlie, 96
Terry Brubaker, 828
C.J. Brucato, 21
Andy Burgess, 2244
Kevin T. Callaghan, 254
James C. Carlisle, 1815
Randy Castleman, 551
David G Chandler, 468
Frank Chang, 755
Brian Cherry, 1360
Stephen Chiao, 1769
Hoon Cho, 824
Daniel Ciporin, 386
David Coats, 544
Brooke B Coburn, 413
Michael M Cone, 631
Ryan Cotton, 220
James Currier, 1323
Ben Dahl, 1677
Harry DeMott, 1525
Matt DeNichilo, 675
Thanasis Delistathis, 1291
Thanasis Delistathis, 1482
Michael Denham, 2055
John D Diekman PhD, 12
Donald Dixon, 763
Donald R. Dixon, 1850
Charles P. Durkin, Jr., 1621
Rory Eakin, 482
Ash Egan, 38
Joshua C. Empson, 1496
John F. Erhard, 156
Christopher Erickson, 1820
Luke B Evnin, 1268
Robert Faber, 224
Jim Farrell, 368
Stephen A. Feinberg, 451
Brian Fitzgerald, 401
Bill Ford, 760
Charles C Freyer, 1633
Sen. William H. Frist, MD, 558
Marc-Henri Galletti, 1143
John Garcia, 64
Edward F. Glassmeyer, 1361
Michael Goldberg, 337
Allan R. Goldberg, PhD, 1808
Andrew Grapkowski, 101
Gerald Greenwald, 862
Phil Greer, 1381
Thomas G Greig, 1116
Philip Hammarskjold, 924
Seth L. Harrison, M.D., 143
Jay Hass, 1593
Todd Hixon, 1291
Deborah Hodges, 1231
Adam Hopkins, 659
Jim Hornthal, 192
Charles B Hughes III, 644
John Hummer, 956
Krist Jake, 1535
John Johnston, 197
Robert Johnston, 1044

Tripp Jones, 197
Greg Kats, 398
Thomas H Kean, 1504
Peter Kellner, 1561
Jay Kern, 1066
John Kilgallon, 220
Charles F Kireker, 786
Ilya Kirnos, 1675
Fred Kittler, 730
Joshua A. Klevens, 456
John Kole, 1142
Paul Koontz, 770
Dave Kreter, 824
Stephen M LeSieur, 1717
Anthony Lee, 100
Scott Lenet, 791
H Jeffrey Leonard, 834
Andrew Levin, 1519
Joshua Lewis, 1608
Richard Lipkin, 644
John F. MacMurray, 1621
Joe Machado, 1266
Paul Maeder, 935
Edward B Marsh, MD, 1198
Paul Martino, 358
Alan Mattamana, 714
Gary S Matthews, 1256
John A. (Tony) Mayer, 706
Peter C McWilliams PhD, 1616
Sameet Mehta, 851
Seth Meisel, 277
Christian T Miller, 698
Brian C Miller, 1128
Brian Miller, 3264
Alison Minter, 1335
Chris Mitchell, 1717
Ryan Moore, 38
G. Mason Morfit, 1903
Laurence C. Morse PhD, 714
Robert W. Mulcare, 1301
Tom Murphy, 559
Nathan Myhrvold, 1005
Andriy Mykhaylovskyy, 727
Joshua M. Nelson, 1815
Kara Nortman, 1888
James D. O'Brien, 97
Standish O'Grady, 852
William Osborn, 520
Rob Palumbo, 29
Kush M Parmar, MD, PhD, 12
Scott G Pasquini, 1156
Heidi Patel, 1552
Vincente Piedrahita, 1815
Nic Poulos, 317
John L Pouschine, 1466
Robert S Powell Jr, 1277
Russell Pyne, 192
Deborah Quazzo, 883
David Ramsay, 412
Roland Reynolds, 986
John Richardson, 1280
Gordon Ritter, 665
Sarah Rogers, 836
Brett J Rome, 1339
Donald C. Roth, 670
Jared Ruger, 257
Juan Sabater, 1902
Jeff Samberg, 26
Eric Schmidt, 996
Bryan Schreier, 1654
Keoni Schwartz, 96
Jim Shapiro, 1059
Brian Sheng, 785
Brian Sheng, 1807
Craig Sherman, 1212
Edwin Shirley, 714
John Siegel, 515

1043

College/University Index / Princeton Universtiy

Steve Sloane, 1202
Bruce Smith, 414
Thomas S Souleles, 1156
Ira Starr, 1141
Wright Steenrod, 475
Dimitri Steinberg, 772
P Bart Stephens, 283
Marcus Stroud, 1875
Daniel Sugar, 1925
Peter Sullivan, 1139
Sanjay Swani, 1777
William H Taylor II, 1262
Ralph Taylor-Smith, 809
Pete Tedesco, 918
Robert Tepper, MD, 1811
Graves Tompkins, 815
Jesse Treu, PhD, 621
Scott Ungerer, 676
Tom Vander Schaaff, 655
Jonathan Victor, 225
Patrick Wack, 1558
Bradaigh Wagner, 673
Brendan Wallace, 727
Trevor Watt, 924
Graham Weaver, 92
Peter Wendell, 1670
Harold R. Werner, 919
Ted West, 772
Thurman V White, 1485
Andrew Wilson, 200
Frank Winslow, 1505
Shari H. Wolkon, 1815
Geoff Yang, 1534
Philip Yau, 824
Ben Yu, 1670

Princeton Universtiy
John Weinberg, 699

Principia College
Andy Reed, 316
Bob Rees, 1737

Pritzker School of Law
John Kuelper, 176

Punjab University
Vivek Mehra, 197

Purdue University
Mark Achler, 1178
Mike Asem, 1155
Sherman Atkinson, 1237
Brooke Beier, 1840
Thomas A Berglund, 733
Leslie Bottorff, 809
Eric J Bruun, 478
Jerome Camp, 385
Stephen Can, 277
Bob Curry, 1094
Albert DaValle Jr., 1038
Brian Demkowicz, 960
Rami Elkhatib, 41
Rami Elkhatib, 1709
Bill Elmore, 770
Ting Gootee, 658
Brian Graves, 629
Tony Grover, 1592
Mamoon Hamid, 1075
Robert Humes, 1038
Nabeel Hyatt, 1715
Rouz Jazayeri, 429
William Link PhD, 1928
Scott Lutzke, 443
Dan Malven, 10
Tracy Marshbanks, 732
Dean Nelson, 1602

Tim R. Palmer, 456
Tom Scholl, 1348
Paul Slaats, 1234
Brian R Smith, 1597
Christopher Sobecki, 1018
Scott M. Sperling, 1815
Sven Strohband, 1069
Scot E Swenberg, 478
Eric Terhorst, 732
Andrew A Thomas, 1744
John Tzeng, 905
J. William Uhrig, 1820
Thomas D Weldon, 40
William Young, 495

Queen's University
Angelo Acconcia, 277
David Adderley, 2076
Glen Ampleford, 2072
Robin Axon, 2182
Trent Baker, 2025
Eric Baker, 2194
Rob Barbara, 2068
Gregory Baylin, 2208
Brent Belzberg, 2261
Brent Belzberg, 2272
John Berton, 2132
Arif N. Bhalwani, 2222
J. Peter Blaney, 2152
James Bok, 2071
Seth Boro, 1814
Robert Bramer, 2215
Nathan Brown, 1990
Michael Castellarin, 2081
Matthew Cross, 2167
Lauchlan Currie, 2040
Chad Danard, 2275
Marcus Daniels, 2147
Chris Davis, 810
Catherine Decarie, 2112
James Dent, 2188
Shayn Diamond, 2288
Peter Drowse, 2163
Tom Eisenhauer, 2065
David Eisler, 2235
Michael Graham, 2207
Christopher Harris, 2150
Robin Heard, 2033
Ewout Heersink, 2209
Kelly Holman, 2130
Thomas Kaneb, 2194
Thomas Kennedy, 2167
Larry LaKing, 2187
Damian Lamb, 2130
Paul Laufert, 2172
Mairead Lavery, 2112
Adam Le Dain, 2050
Lars Leckie, 956
Chris Legg, 1486
Michael List, 2141
Tom Liston, 2096
Paul Lucas, 2152
Alan Lysne, 2115
Alan Lysne, 2245
John B. MacIntyre, 2062
Mark MacTavish, 2208
Ian Macdonell, 2089
Zac McIsaac, 2188
Salil Munjal, 2291
Anthony Munk, 2209
Jeffrey N. Murphy, 2163
Mike Murray, 2217
Richard Osborn, 2233
Richard Osborn, 2265
Michael Overvelde, 2091
Christopher Payne, 916
John Philp, 2126

Sam Pollock, 2067
Paul Richardson, 2238
Art Robinson, 2178
George Rossolatos, 2070
Steven Russo, 2096
Rob Rutledge, 819
Chris Seasons, 2040
Michael Siltala, 2287
Ray Simonson, 2279
Gregory Smith, 2158
Gregory J. Smith, 2165
Andrea Sotak, 2102
Jamie Stiff, 2130
Mark T Thomas, 1248
Jeremy Thompson, 2219
Robert Trudeau, 1785
Gregory G. Turnbull, 2074
David Unsworth, 2153
Peter van der Velden, 2180
Jeff Van Steenbergen, 2050
Ben Vaughan, 2067
John Veitch, 2082
Carlo A. von Schroeter, 1979

Queen's University Belfast
Ruairi Grant, 1315
Mairead Lavery, 2112

Queens College
Michael Falk, 528
Richard Goldstein, 65
Harris Landgarten, 172
Brenda Marex, 1303
Howard Matlin, 1062
Jordan Odinsky, 877
Sylvia F. Rosen, 423
Craig Slutzkin, 1298

Queensland University of Technology
Rory Quinlan, 1517

Questrom School of Business
Jeffrey M. Zucker, 860

Quinnipiac University
Kevin Crowley, 530
Daniel Wagner, 530

Radford University
Randal J. Kirk, 1812

Rady School of Management
Niall A O'Donnell PhD, 1574

Randolph-Macon College
Benjamin Schapiro, 1515

Red McCombs School of Business
Wesley Gottesman, 325
Matthew J. Nordgren, 151
Charlie Plauche, 1597

Reed College
Venky Ganesan, 1202
Behzad Khosrowshahi, 2102
Heather Redman, 755
Charles L Schroeder, 1343

Regis University
Dan Aweida, 210
Scott Morris, CPA, 736

Reims Management School
David Espitallier, 729

Rensselaer Polytechnic Institute
Jim Collis, 1638

College/University Index / SUNY Oneonta

Bob Cummings, 1990
John Daileader, 862
Peter Fitzgerald, 1094
Mike Gausling, 1385
George C Kenney, 1664
Richard Kiley, 287
Cyril L. Meduna, 63
Dennis O'Brien, 1131
Justin J. Perreault, 521
Elias J. Sabo, 523
David R Schopp, 1744
Sean Sebastian, 272
Wade Sheffer, 817
David Shen, 590
Amit Srivastava, 682
Rick Stowe, 918
Patrick Sullivan, 220
Denis A. Tito, 1989
Jason P Torres, 1165
Jesse Treu, PhD, 621
Mark Visser, 245
Chris Young, 1554

Rhodes College
Thomas Gieselmann, 641
David Lightburn, 189
James A. O'Donnell, 734

Rice University
Cliff Atherton Jr., 888
Forest Baskett, 1297
Jay Benear, 639
Stephanie Campbell, 950
Tony Di Bona, 87
Jeff Eby, 2008
Grace Ge, 1202
Barton Goodwin, 576
John Jaggers, 1658
Michael Kane, 374
Sharon Kedar, 1342
Carl Novotny, 1920
Christopher O'Neill, 1944
Howard Park, 824
Amit A. Patel, 1392
Sam H. Pyne, 893
Holly Radel, 3261
Leighton Read, 326
J. Leighton Read, MD, 87
Pamela L. Reiland, 888
Beni Rovinski, 2180
Richard Simoni, 181
Thomas J Stephenson, 1924
Daniel Tompkins, 1354
Philip A Tuttle, 591
Kevin Uebelein, 2033
Aamir Virani, 777
Dan Watkins, 1206
Brent Williams, 894
Daniel B. Wolfe, Ph.D, 6
Glenn A Youngkin, 413

Richard Ivey School of Business
Matthew Cross, 2167

Richmont Graduate University
Karen Houghton, 189

Ricker College
Robert E Davoli, 1673

Roanoke College
Jake Tarr Jr., 1072

Robert H. Smith School of Business
Code Cubitt, 2195
Randy Guttman, 1041
Meghan M. McGee, 383

Rochester Institute of Technology
Allen F Grum, 1523
Michael Stanek, 1040

Rockefeller University
Carl L. Gordon PhD, 1382

Rockhurst University
Peter Esparrago, 569
Kevin F. Mullane, 1016
Jared Poland, 364

Rockhust Jesuit University
Kevin Mullane, 17

Rollins College
Jennifer Dunham, 171

Rome Center for International Law
Bruce Rogers, 1086

Rose Polytechnic
Felda Hardymon, 260

Ross School of Business
Adrian Fortino, 1206
Anna Haghgooie, 1615
Dan Kidle, 149
Marcy Marshall, 149
Paul McCreadie, 149
Tige Savage, 1555
Christopher W Solomon, 1972
Ryan Waddington, 961

Rotman School of Management
Chris Anastasopoulos, 2102
Matthew Chapman, 2272
Tom Eisenhauer, 2065
Mona Kung, 2138
Larry Y. Liu, 2128
Jamie Stiff, 2130
Craig Strong, 2243
Kevin Talbot, 2236
Andrew Walton, 2163
Kyle Winters, 2201

Rowan University
Larry A Colangelo, 1230
Paul M Grassinger, 164

Royal Military College
Lawrence Stevenson, 2082

Rutgers Business School
Thomas Girardi, 953

Rutgers Grad. School of Business
Kevin P. Costello, 309

Rutgers Law School
Andrew M Bushell, 540
Gerry Doherty, 1277
Daniel Gulino, 1564
Randy Maslow, 966

Rutgers University
Mark L. Benaquista, 1815
Kevin Bitterman, PhD, 191
Donald F. DeMuth, 610
James T. Denton, 343
Richard B Emmitt, 1929
Mark Fields, 93
Nancy C Floyd, 1355
Glenn C Harrison, 1468
Sheldon Howell, 969
Mir Imran, 980
Andrew Intrater, 516

Murray Karp, CPA, 675
Roman Kikta, 1244
Jay Levy, 2017
Wayne Marino, 1748
Gerald A. Michaud, 946
Vineet Pruthi, 1127
Sandeep Sardana, 295
Thomas A Schlesinger, 244
George J Schultze, 1629
Nanette Schunk, 3276
Jeffrey T Stevenson, 1927
Tony Tamer, 928
Jim Thornton, 887
Keith Titan, 256
Albert Trank, 1497
Jon Trauben, 99
Patrick J Welsh, 1972
Ravi Yadav, 1315
Tomer Yosef-Or, 21
David W. Young, 434

Ryerson University
David Henderson, 2290
Scott Monteith, 2197
Igli Panariti, 3258
Whitney Rockley, 2190
Michael Serruya, 2254
Joseph Shlesinger, 2082

SUNY Albany
Paul Dibella, 768
Michael B Kaplan, 1134
Rocky Mountain, 594
Gene J Ostrow, 1526
Edward J Siskin, 937

SUNY Binghamton
Sean Barrette, 468
Richard A. Goldman, 1743
Ira D. Kleinman, 914
Lauren M Massey, 18
Devin Mathews, 468

SUNY Buffalo
Kevin Centofanti, 352
Paul Ciriello, 712
Dorian Faust, 881
Chris Kryder, 748
George J Lee, 117
Michael G. Levine, 356
Daniel P Penberthy, 1523
Frank Reppenhagen, 529
Brian Rich, 427
Robert A. Spass, 404
Patrick Tan, 865
William E Watts, 1049
Margaret Whalen Brechtel, 1523

SUNY College of Arts & Sciences
John P. Truehart, 954

SUNY College of Technology
Jennifer Dunham, 171

SUNY Cortland
Brian G. Murphy, 1317

SUNY Fredonia
Dennis R. Costello, 322

SUNY Geneseo
Andy Roche, 1464

SUNY Oneonta
John Fitzgerald, 467
Calvin A Neider, 503

1045

College/University Index / SUNY Oswego

SUNY Oswego
Juli Marley, 290

SUNY Stony Brook
Ajay Chopra, 1853
Larry Kaplan, 242
Philip N. Sussman, 1808

Sacramento State University
Skip Glass, 770
Daniel K Turner III, 1251

Saint Bonaventure University
Kevin P. Fahey, 299

Saint Edward's University, Texas
Atif Abdulmalik, 152

Saint Edwards University
Rudy Garza, 804

Saint Joe's University
Scott Nissenbaum, 246

Saint John's University
Bob DeSena, 878
Kevin M. McGovern, 1191

Saint Joseph's University
Robert Graham, 1428

Saint Louis University
Joe Kaiser, 1204
Luke Sage, 1424
Dan Tsubouchi, 2246
April Young, 925

Saint Mary's College
Joe Kell, 1311
Brad Triebsch, 573

Saint Mary's College of California
Steven Rea, 185

Saint Mary's University
Chris Moyer, 2216
Andrew Ray, 2155

Saint Michael's College
José Blanco, 573
Vincent D'Angelo, 240
Peter A Lyons, 1105

Saint Vincent College
Robert Swartz, 1207

Salem State College
John Fiato, 909
Elliot M. Katzman, 521

Salisbury University
Jeff Elburn, 1742

Salmon P Chase College
Jack Wyant, 287

Salve Regina University
R. Wade Aust, 77
Stephan C. Sloan, 125

Sam Houston State University
Matt Anderson, 1976
Brian Hawkins, 1976
Ron Norris, 1922

Samara State Aerospace University
Dmitry Alimov, 792

Samford University
Ted Alling, 640
Philip L Hodges, 1533
John W. McCullough, 904
R. Clayton McWhorter, 496

San Diego School of Law
David Stern, 502
Court R. Turner, J.D., 31

San Diego State University
Kristen Bailey, 769
Caroline Barberio, 1239
Christopher J Bower, 1397
Rich DeMartini, 559
Josef Friedman, 1747
Aaron M Gurewitz, 1588
Alex Kanayev, 2031
Mark Lozzi, 2131
Steven Rea, 185
Tighe Reardon, 206
Bryon C Roth, 1588
Jonathan T. Silverstein, 1382
Rick Slaughter, 1756
Court R. Turner, J.D., 31
Dino Vendetti, 764
Dino Vendetti, 1656
Eric D Wedbush, 1969

San Francisco State University
Kirsi Fontenot, 949
Elizabeth Gamboa, 1300
Stacy Huynh, 151
Carolyn Ticknor, 990
Gottfried P. Tittiger, 985
James Vaughan, 234

San Jose State University
Ron Conway, 1761
Pauline Duffy, 1540
Malcolm Finayson, 898
John E. Hall, 947
Lara Kwong, 994
Chris LeBlanc, 1793
Robert May, 986
Teresa McDaniel, 169
Christie Pitts, 218
Ven N. Reddy, 130
Rudy Ruano, 1975
Kirk Westbrook, 1011

Santa Barbara College of Law
Debra P Geiger, 826

Santa Clara University
George Arnold, 1077
Kevin Carter, 1761
Gianna Conci Orozco, 491
Gary Coover, 1611
Wayne Doiguchi, 214
Irwin Federman, 1896
Peter Fitzgerald, 1094
Tim Haley, 1534
John E. Hall, 947
Stephen Hyndman, 823
Hsing Kung, 47
Chris LeBlanc, 1793
Vivian Loh Nahmias, 836
Jim Marshall, 1646
Matthew McDonald, 227
Kirsten A. Mello, 1202
Matthew Miau, 905
Angela Nuttman, 770
Kevin Ober, 618
Chad Packard, 1425
Ken Pearlman, 1365
Brian Pokorny, 1761
Larry Randall, 94
Diana Saca, 681
Dana Stalder, 1181
Pete Thomas, 183
David Tsang, 47
Doug Tsui, 947
Robert L Underwood, 1332
David Wanek, 1975
Joseph Zanone, 581

Sarah Lawrence College
Carl Goldfischer, MD, 237

Schiller International University
Chris Xie, 2271

School
AT Gimble, 189

Schulich School of Business
John Albright, 2236
Narbe Alexandrian, 2071
Bradley W. Ashley, 2226
Alex Baker, 2236
Justin Beber, 2067
Richard Betsalel, 2089
Andrew Bishop, 2059
Daniel Brothman, 2224
Roman S. Dubczak, 2079
Joe Freedman, 2067
Michael Graham, 2207
Lee M. Grunberg, 2226
Robin Heard, 2033
Serge LeVert-Chiasson, 2248
Craig Noble, 2067
Alireza Rahnema, 2028
Gene Shkolnik, 2150
Alex Storcheus, 2122
Hamish Sutherland, 2154
Hamish Sutherland, 2287
Peter van der Velden, 2180

Seattle University
Steve Hooper, 974
Kent Johnson, 82
Joseph Piper JD, 1002
Mike Templeman, 887
Timothy Thompson Black, 1002

Seneca College
Jon Jackson, 3258

Seoul National University
Henry Chung, 626

Seton Hall University
Kenneth J. Kulaga, 725

Shanghai Jiao Tong University
Benson He, 892

Shanghai Jiotong University
Franklin Jiang, 2229

Shanghai University
Dennis Wu, 290
Eric Xu, 823

Sheffield Hallam University
Jonathan Tunnicliff, 1349

Sheffield University
Richard MacKellar, 2078

Shulich School of Business
Alex Storcheus, 2122

College/University Index / St. Olaf College

SiChuan University
Hing Wong, 1951

Sichuan MBA College
Jesson Chen, 2229

Sichuan University
Jesson Chen, 2229

Siena College
Thomas Iannarone, 277

Sienna College
Thomas J. Baldwin, 354

Simmons College
April E Evans, 1248
Jean George, 59
Jean George, 1122

Simmons Grad. School of Management
Jennifer Trzepacz, 1985

Simon Fraser University
Gerry Bellerive, 2235
Dan Jacques, 2145
Gursh Kundan, 997
Caroline Sanche, 2258

Simon School of Business
Brennan Mulcahey, 349
Kyle Stanbro, 349

Singapore Management University
James Bok, 2071

Skidmore College
Rob Adams, 1321
David Castle, 327
Nick MacShane, 1486
Emily Paxhia, 1464
Chris Young, 1554

Slippery Rock University
David Koegler, 1194

Sloan School of Management
Mike Bryant, 1078
Casey Gordon, 1341
Chris McLeod, 660

Smith College
Grace Ames, 1361
Deborah A Farrington, 1738
Joelle Kayden, 37
Michele Kinner, 1516
Jennifer Tegan, 432

Sonoma State University
Greg Lyon, 648
Patrick Teixeira, 1396

South Dakota School of Mines
Richard H. Frank, 584
Terry Rock, 444

South Dakota State University
Tyler J Stowater, 297

Southern Connecticut University
Kevin McGrath, 1288

Southern Illinois University
John Fletcher, 749
Herb Shear, 380
Jamie Wehrung, 176

Southern Methodist University
Rugger Burke, 1622
Jack Carsten, 947
A Baron Cass III, 364
Michael Coppola, 582
Jeff Davis, 48
Daniel Einhorn, 400
Randall S. Fojtasek, 328
Kevin Gabelein, 753
Lou Gerken, 822
Kevin Green, 545
Patrick Hamner, 1422
Bob Howe, 9
Peter Huff, 291
Neenah Jain, 1520
Brian Jolly, 957
Stuart Larkins, 471
Troy LeMaile-Stovall, 1790
Kevin L. Listen, 902
Jim Madden, 416
Clayton Main, 333
Charles R Martin, 111
Mark L Masinter, 1549
Felipe Mendoza, 165
David B. Miller, 672
Dennis E Murphree, 1273
Ryan K Nagim, 1144
James Outland, 1293
Alexandra Prima, 1805
Louis Rajczi, 768
Jason C. Schmidly, 415
Jim Schultz, 1379
Robert Shen, 892
Tim Storer, 9
Vik Thapar, 576
Paul A Yeoham, 1484
Jeff Zanarini, 928

Southwest Missouri State University
Richard Garman, 793
Joseph Zell, 876

Southwest University
Jesson Chen, 2229

Southwestern University
Victoria Dominguez-Edington, 445
Lauren B Leichtman, 1111
Alex Maleki, 972

Spelman College
Kateri Jones, 1771

Spring Arbor University
Angela Helfin, 3269

Spring Hill College
Stephanie Campbell, 950

St. Andrews University
David O Ellis, 656
Ned Truslow, 1557

St. Anselm College
David H Donabedian, 1145
JJ Healy, 848

St. Bonaventure University
Bill Taranto, 1205
David J. Zatlukal, 1037

St. Catherine University
Ann Winblad, 956

St. Edward's University
Bob Goodman, 392

St. Francis College
William F. Dawson, Jr., 1971

St. Francis Xavier University
Peter MacAskill, 2205
Paul Rowe, 2126
Jeff White, 2200

St. John Fisher College
Kyle Stanbro, 349

St. John's University
Richard Bauerly, 850
Scott L Becker, 1343
Buzz Benson, 1671
John Brecker, 99
Kenneth Burns, 1679
Tony Christianson, 464
Thomas P Fitzpatrick, 1651
John Guiliana DPM, 1289
Arnold J Hoegler, 1103
Steven Insalaco, 369
Joe Kaczorowski, 331
Michael Kenny, 1987
Ira D. Kleinman, 914
Emanuel Martinez, 865
Howard Matlin, 1062
Michael R McCarthy, 1276
Thomas E. McInerney, 299
John L. McInerney, 299
Dan Moorse, 917
Kevin Ober, 618
Paolo Parziale, 18
Sylvia F. Rosen, 423
Angela Santi, 35
Andrew H. Steuerman, 844
Brian Sullivan, 1992

St. Joseph's University
Kevin Clayton, 675
Timothy G. Fallon, 147
Chris Fralic, 741
Daisy Mellet, 1207
Adele Oliva, 5
Adele C Oliva, 1508

St. Lawrence University
Cate Ambrose, 3261
Lee Bailey, 1895
Keith L. Crandell, 153
William Ford, 853
Chris Lund, 899
Carol Newell, 2238

St. Louis University
Stephen Broun, 399
Bill Conley, 380
Charles Resnick, 990
Steve M. Welborn, 2009

St. Mary's College
Gary Cuccio, 1793
George Schmitt, 1793

St. Mary's University
Matthew Towns, 2251

St. Norbert College
Thomas F Campion, 1209
John Connolly, 221
Jim Domach, 1171

St. Olaf College
Josh Baltzell, 1725
Thomas Erickson, 738
Mark Jacobsen, 1359
B. Kristine Johnson, 68

College/University Index / St. Peter's College

Tony Miller, 1107

St. Peter's College
Pasquale DeAngelis, 1490
Tom Mac Mahon, 748
Kenneth J Mathews, 381

St. Vincent College
Robert G Yablunsky, 1633

Stanford Grad. School of Business
Krishna K Agrawal, 1129
Mark Allsteadt, 401
Matthew L. Altman, 166
William J. Amelio, 594
Steve Anderson, 231
Carl T Anderson, 836
Merrick Andlinger, 123
Martin Arzac, 500
Paul Asel, 1330
Stephen E. Babson, 673
John Backus, 1291
Ben Ball, 779
Steven Baloff, 59
Zach Barasz, 302
Tom Barnds, 29
William Barnum, 334
Carrie Bates, 1847
Allen Beasley, 1534
William Beckett, 810
David Bell, 325
Dror Berman, 996
Elizabeth Q Betten, 1156
Nikhil J. Bhat, 1931
David Biesel, 1322
Jeff Bird, 1760
Christian Borcher, 411
Seth Boro, 1814
Roelof Botha, 1654
Scott Brady, 996
Orlando Bravo, 1814
Jeff Brody, 1534
Doug Burgum, 173
M Roy Burns, 1776
John Caddedu, 581
Kevin T. Callaghan, 254
Paul D Carbery, 789
Douglas C. Carlisle, 1202
Brian Cassidy, 559
Todd C. Chaffee, 1001
Leon Chen, PhD, 517
Robert Cherun, 2047
Helen Chiang, 110
Ian Chiu, 1392
Joyce Chung, 807
Peter Chung, 1255
Lisa Coca, 809
Dave Coglizer, 1977
Christopher L Collins, 1062
Tom Costin, 1392
Ryan Cotton, 220
Ryan Craig, 257
Jeffrey M Crowe, 1346
Natalie D Cryer, 378
Scott Darling, 603
Paul L Davies III, 378
Ben DeRosa, 109
Dipanjan (DJ) Deb, 779
Raymond Debbane, 1018
Steven Denning, 815
Donald R. Dixon, 1850
Alex Doll, 1794
Matt Downs, 1615
David Dullum, 828
Ira Ehrenpreis, 595
Ira M Ehrenpreis, 1786
Ira Ehrenpreis, 3284

Peter Ehrich, 558
Bill Elmore, 770
Brian Fearnow, 368
Noel J Fenton, 1853
Brett Fisher, 744
Skip Fleshman, 181
Pete Flint, 1323
John Fogelsong, 836
William E. Ford, 815
Gene Frantz, 578
Sameer Gandhi, 28
Brian Garrett, 561
Shauntel Garvey, 1527
Eric Gevada, 1105
Charles E. Glew, Jr., 750
David Glynn, 836
Ross Goldstein, 608
David Golob, 779
David B. Golub, 844
Tom Goodrich, 581
Michael N. Gray, 1496
Maurice Gunderson, 204
Maurice Gunderson, 205
Russell B Hall, 1106
Craig Hanson, 1319
Chris Harris, 787
David Hodgson, 815
Adam Hopkins, 659
Bob Horne, 2022
James Howland, 1256
Peter Huff, 291
Jay Huffard, 531
Victor Hwang, 986
Dean Jacobson, 29
Scott Jacobson, 1158
Wilfred Jaeger, 1819
Kurt R Jaggers, 1776
Kristin Johnson, 96
James A Johnson, 1997
Ross M. Jones, 254
Leland Jones, 673
Nigel W Jones, 1873
Jeff Jordan, 124
Scott Jordon, 836
Steve Jurvetson, 800
Annie Kadavy, 1534
Yasunori Kaneko MD, 1691
Rimas Kapeskas, 380
Paul S. Kasper, 678
Joelle Kayden, 37
Karen Kenworthy, 1748
Vinod Khosla, 1069
Paul Klingenstein, 20
Lauren Kolodny, 180
Thomas Korte, 128
Mark Koulogeorge, 1242
Steven M Krausz, 1896
Larry Kubal, 1089
Thomas Y. Kuo, 254
Patrick Latterell, 1094
Gary Lauder, 1095
Lars Leckie, 956
Nathaniel V Lentz, 1387
Mark Leschly, 1558
Ping Li, 28
Anthony Limberis, 744
Robert D Lindsay, 1129
Casey Lynch, 96
Linda Lynch, 744
Paul Madera, 1212
Rick Magnuson, 824
Billy Maguy, 92
Fern Mandelbaum, 1249
Nino Marakovic, 1620
Peter N. Masucci, 1301
George E Matelich, 1062
Tom Mawhinney, 968

Tim McAdam, 1785
Thomas McKinley, 410
Mark A. McLaughlin, 949
David Michael, 133
Antonio Miranda, 1134
Chris Moore, 1534
John H. Moragne, 1850
Arneek Multani, 1850
Matt Murphy, 1202
Andriy Mykhaylovskyy, 727
Patricia Nakache, 1853
Tom Newby, 1112
Brent Nicklas, 1112
Nate Niparko, 28
Vincent M Occhipinti, 2005
Larry Orr, 1853
Toshi Otani, 1838
Victor E Parker, 1717
Sanjay Patel, 140
Harsh Patel, 491
Amit A. Patel, 1392
Heidi Patel, 1552
Harsh Patel, 2000
Tory Patterson, 428
Tory Patterson, 1392
Sundeep Peechu, 720
Thomas A Penn, 1428
Carol Pereira, 96
Ezra Perlman, 779
Michael B Persky, 80
Michal Petrzela, 1123
Nick Pianim, 581
Chris A. Pierce, 1279
Naomi Pilosof, 1202
Scott Plumridge, 894
Tim Porter, 1158
Jason Pressman, 1663
David P Quinlivan, 1604
Erik Ragatz, 924
David Ramsay, 412
Alan H. Resnikoff, 1660
Barry D. Reynolds, 949
Robin Richards Donohoe, 627
Aaron Richmond, 673
Antonio Rodriguez, 1181
Sarah Rogers, 836
Alexander Rosen, 1563
Peter L Rottier, 1752
Jared Ruger, 257
John K. Saer Jr., 824
J.P. Sanday, 1202
Greg Sands, 547
Kenneth B Sawyer, 1604
Christopher Schaepe, 1121
Eric Schwartz, 423
Chris Scoggins, 1653
Tasha Seitz, 1038
Mark Selcow, 547
Jim Shapiro, 1059
Jason Shideler, 1156
Ben Shih, 968
Greg Shove, 1083
Mark A. Siegel, 1202
Peter Sinclair, 1102
Harpinder Singh, 996
Mike Slade, 1641
Sam Smith-Eppsteiner, 996
Mark Soane, 142
Katie Solomon, 819
McLain Southworth, 563
C Morris Stout, 1767
Paul Strachman, 1530
Laela Sturdy, 578
Timothy P Sullivan, 1156
William P. Sutter Jr., 944
John A Svoboda, 1765
Gus Taylor, 719

1048

College/University Index / Stanford University

Nelson Teng, 458
Carl D Thoma, 1814
William N. Thorndike, 949
John Thornton, 202
Carolyn Ticknor, 990
Dafina Toncheva, 1896
Jason P Torres, 1165
Pavan Tripathi, 333
Richard C Tuttle, 1492
Tom Uhlman, 1305
Sigrid Van Bladel, 20
Sigrid Van Bladel, PhD, 20
Steve Vassallo, 770
John Walecka, 1534
Brendan Wallace, 727
Mark Wan, 1819
Trevor Watt, 924
Graham Weaver, 92
Sharon Weinbar, 1626
Eric Weiner, 291
Eli Weiss, 819
Steve Westly, 1977
Dave Whorton, 1865
Timothy Wollaeger, 1616
Geoff Yang, 1534
David Yuan, 1785
TX Zhuo, 1055
Chris Zugaro, 1856
Casper de Clercq, 1346

Stanford Grad. School of Education
Shauntel Garvey, 1527
Amit A. Patel, 1392

Stanford Law School
Michael Arrington, 564
Stephen E. Babson, 673
William Barnum, 334
Orlando Bravo, 1814
Tom Dennedy, 174
Ira Ehrenpreis, 595
Ira M Ehrenpreis, 1786
Ira Ehrenpreis, 3284
Kathy Fields, 1041
Michael Johnson, 61
Geoffrey Rehnert, 194
John Roos, 820
Lisa Y. Roskens, 71
Alan E Salzman, 1906
David Smolen, 824
Peter Thiel, 775
Daniel Weiss, 126

Stanford Medical School
Jeff Bird, 1760
Thomas A Raffin MD, 1792

Stanford University
Jenny Abramson, 1552
Frank A. Adams, 876
Ajay Agarwal, 221
Daniel Agroskin, 1039
Robert Amen, 1910
Alexei Andreev, 204
Alexei Andreev, 205
R. David Andrews, 881
George Arnold, 1077
Martin Arzac, 500
Brian Ascher, 1916
A Craig Asher, 1940
Stephen E. Babson, 673
John Backus, 1291
John Backus, 1482
Eric V Bacon, 1132
Darran A. Baird, 1743
Dado Banatao, 1779
Michael Banks, 870

Maren Thomas Bannon, 1026
Paul Barber, 1041
Jeffrey Barman, 1431
Jeffrey Barnes, 270
William Barnum, 334
Timothy A Barrows, 1181
Upal Basu, 1330
Carrie Bates, 1847
Stuart Baxter, 1572
Laura Baxter-Simmons, 1472
Allen Beasley, 1534
Nick Beim, 1916
David Bell, 325
Eric Benhamou, 249
Neal Bhadkamkar, 1249
George Bischof, 1212
Phil Black, 1860
Geoff Bland, 1969
David J. Blumberg, 301
Rick Blume, 703
Simon Boag, 981
Pavel Bogdanov, 89
Niko Bonatsos, 816
Steve Bowsher, 979
Phil Brady, 837
Sam Brasch, 1052
Jim Breyer, 336
Chris L Britt, 1168
Randall Brouckman, 1782
Gerry Brunk, 2180
Don Butler, 1818
Blake Byers, 889
Brook Byers, 1075
John Cable, 1726
Bandel L. Carano, 1361
Shawn T. Carolan, 1202
Jennifer Carolan, 1527
Chris G. Carter, 1326
Xavier Casanova, 772
Jane Castle, 208
Dr. Albert Cha, 1941
Navin Chaddha, 1184
John Chaisson, 681
Jeffrey T Chambers, 1776
Connie Chan, 124
William Chan, 1138
David Chao, 596
Jim Chappell, 1417
Jerry Chen, 872
Alice Chen, PhD, 31
Leon Chen, PhD, 517
Cheryl Cheng, 296
Ian Chiu, 1392
Alan Chiu, 2011
Scott Chou, 805
Scott Chou, 2023
Peter Y Chung, 1752
Tyson Clark, 889
John D Cochran, 1147
Fred Cohen, 1932
Samuel D Colella, 1928
Brian J Conway, 1776
Wayne Cooper, 863
James Corl, 1679
Everett Cox, 665
Scott Crabill, 1814
Ryan Craig, 257
David Cremin, 791
Todd R Crockett, 1776
Natalie D Cryer, 378
Ben Cukier, 440
Chip Cureton, 888
D Patrick Curran, 364
Rajeev Dadoo, 1731
Shivanandan A. Dalvie, 64
Dr. Kerry Dance, 898
Natalie L Davies, 378

Paul L Davies III, 378
Jerel Davis, 1928
Casper de Clercq, 1346
Elisa del Gaudio, 41
Alex De Winter, 809
Dain F DeGroff, 1846
Salil Deshpande, 221
Timothy Dick, 1737
John D Diekman PhD, 12
Ted Dintersmith, 455
Donald Dixon, 763
A. Barr Dolan, 458
Michael Dolbac, 809
David A. Donnini, 884
David Douglass, 604
Stephen M Dow, 1658
Ryan Drant, 1514
Timothy Draper, 609
Tim Draper, 626
Timothy Draper, 2021
Ted Driscoll, PhD, 491
Tim Dugan, 1961
Matt Dunbar, 1923
Tom Dyal, 1534
Randall Eason, 96
Barry Eggers, 1121
Omar El-Ayat, 563
Steven A. Elms, 74
Greg Ennis, 1427
Patrick Enright, 1143
Chuck Esserman, 1861
Charles H Esserman, 1861
Daniel Estes, PhD, 782
Neil Exter, 1811
Michael J. Farello, 1088
Brandon Farwell, 708
Brian Fearnow, 368
David S. Felman, 869
Peter Fenton, 248
Jim Feuille, 563
Michael Fisch, 110
Doug Fisher, 1010
Peter Fitzgerald, 1094
Morgan Flager, 1685
Jim Fleming, 515
Wade Flemons, 2218
Ryan Floyd, 1747
John Fogelsong, 836
Norman A. Fogelsong, 1001
Hadley Ford, 966
R. Patrick Forster, 985
Alan Foster, 1793
Adam J. Fountain, 346
Clinton Foy, 561
Edward Frank PhD, 59
Robert Fraser, 200
David Frazee, 1561
Bradford M. Freeman, 783
Tully M. Friedman, 787
Alexander A. Friend, 788
Leslie Frécon, 1113
Adam Fuller, 333
Ilya Fushman, 1075
Quin Garcia, 204
Quin Garcia, 205
Nikhil Garg, 1729
Andrew Garman, 1305
Brian Garrett, 561
Keith Geeslin, 779
Flip Gianos, 1010
Michael W Gibbons, 713
Ned Gilhuly, 1602
Richard Ginn, 548
John W. Glynn, 836
Jim Goetz, 1654
Jocelyn Goldfein, 2019
Daria Gonzalez, 890

College/University Index / Stanford University

Giles Goodhead, 863
Peter D Goodson, 631
Bing Gordon, 1075
Michael Gordon, 1212
Mark Gorenberg, 2019
Greg Gottesman, 1499
Pat Gouhin, 3256
Theresia Gouw, 180
David Grayzel, MD, 191
Madison F. Grose, 1739
Lauren Gross, 775
Jim Gunton, 1328
Ramneek Gupta, 486
Arun Gupta, 515
Arjun Gupta, 1793
Saar Gur, 455
Clifford L Haas, 1672
James Halow, 368
Mamoon Hamid, 1075
Ammar H. Hanafi, 87
George Hara, 602
Eric Hardgrave, 54
Fred Harman, 1361
Chris Harris, 787
John Harris, 1029
Dr. Ryan A Harris, 1346
Randy Hawks, 491
Chip Hazard, 754
Robert Headley, 974
James Healy, 1698
Shahram Hejazi, 266
Peter Henry, 1644
Dr. Steve Herrod, 816
Pete Higgins, 1641
Mark G. Hilderbrand, 949
Reid Hoffman, 872
Kirk Holland, 36
Jeffrey J Holland, 1636
Wei Hopeman, 148
Avshalom Horan, 337
Zachary Hornby, 487
David Hornik, 197
Andrew J. Howard, 1660
Jonathan Hsu, 1848
Tony Huie, 1675
John Hummer, 956
Andrew Humphries, 911
Thomas S Huseby, 1637
Wende Hutton, 386
Victor Hwang, 986
Maha Ibrahim, 386
Masazumi Ishii, 214
Brian Jacobs, 665
Asha Jadeja, 623
Wilfred Jaeger, 920
Ross Jaffe, 1928
Kurt R Jaggers, 1776
Krist Jake, 1535
David Jargiello, 756
John W. Jarve, 1202
Peter T Jensen, 1717
Jared L. Johnson, 1415
James A Johnson, 1997
TJ Jubeir, 406
Steve Jurvetson, 800
Annie Kadavy, 1534
Rebecca Kaden, 1882
Julia Karol, 1962
Jonathan Kaskow, 291
Greg Kats, 398
Mohit Kaushal MD, 20
Guy Kawasaki, 807
Michael S Kaye, 501
Doug Kelly MD, 87
George C Kenney, 1664
William C. Kessinger, 1417
Asad Khaliq, 49

Jennifer W Kheng, 1112
Han Kim, 100
Daniel Kim, 333
Doug Kimmelman, 675
Kirt Kirtland, 666
Chris Kitching, 933
Joshua A. Klevens, 456
Gil Kliman, 1010
Ailliam Knoke, 913
Garheng Kong, 921
Garheng Kong MD PhD, 1698
Paul Koontz, 770
Joe Kraus, 889
Steven M Krausz, 1896
Manu Kumar, 1050
Ethan Kurzweil, 260
Tim Kutzkey, PhD, 517
Eric Kwan, 1138
Ann Lamont, 1361
Robert E. Larson, 25
Robert E Larson, 2005
Deval A Lashkari PhD, 1792
Vijay Lathi, 1298
Troy LeMaile-Stovall, 1790
Lars Leckie, 956
Anthony Lee, 100
Lisa M. Lee, 1496
Jess Lee, 1654
Julie Lein, 1893
Alda Leu Dennis, 991
William Lewis, 2021
Jeremy Liew, 1121
Jonathan E. Lim, MD, 487
Alfred Lin, 1654
David S Lobel, 1651
Dennis Lockhart, 1280
Greg Long, 787
Steve Loughlin, 28
Trevor R Loy, 756
Casey Lynch, 96
Julian C. Mack, 1088
Paul Maeder, 935
David Magerman, 614
Shaun Maguire, 889
Billy Maguy, 92
Aditi Maliwal, 1888
Jules Maltz, 1001
Fern Mandelbaum, 1939
Peter M. Manos, 166
Mike Maples Jr., 751
Lenard Marcus, 655
Paul Mariani, 22
Scott Marlette, 1694
David Marquardt, 197
Alan Marty, 1106
Renee Masi, 269
Arun Mathew, 28
Paul Matteucci, 1896
William Matthes, 245
Erik E Maurer, 1492
Dirk McDermott, 98
Josh McFarland, 872
Ryan McIntyre, 776
Todd McIntyre, 870
Peter H McNerney, 1817
Sameet Mehta, 851
Richard Melmon, 358
Brian Melton, 1796
Thomas C Melzer, 1574
Lloyd M. Metz, 969
Ravi Mhatre, 1121
Sandy Miller, 1001
Daniel H Miller, 1580
Kate Mitchell, 1626
Ann Miura-Ko, 751
Andrew Moley, 1121
Geoffrey Moore, 1247

Geoffrey Moore, 1985
Brian Morfitt, 782
Michael C Morgan, 1846
Takeshi Mori, 837
Michael Mullany, 968
Jennifer M Mulloy, 1776
Hodong Nam, 100
Guido Neels, 697
Jennifer Keiser Neundorfer, 1026
Peter Nieh, 1121
Scott Nolan, 775
Zach Noorani, 770
Kara Nortman, 1888
Jacqueline Novogratz, 55
Scott O'Hare, 594
Christopher O'Neill, 1944
Vincent M Occhipinti, 2005
Selahattin Onen, 1406
Terry Opdendyk, 1378
Michael Orsak, 2007
Nick Orum, 881
T.C. Ostrander, 300
Clare Ozawa, 1928
Raquel Palmer, 1085
James Patchett, 1308
Anthony Patek, 253
Anil Patel, 502
Jean-Marc Patouillaud, 1416
Marshall Payne, 477
Thomas A Penn, 1275
E. Kenneth Pentimonti, 1400
Doug Pepper, 1663
Carlos Perea, 966
David L Pesikoff, 1846
George Petracek, 192
Nancy Pfund, 595
David W. Pidwell, 87
Scott Platshon, 709
Will Porteous, 1593
Lisa Porter, 979
Russell Pyne, 192
Keith Rabois, 775
Thomas A Raffin MD, 1792
Erik Ragatz, 924
Heather Redman, 755
Bill Reichert, 721
Bill Reichert, 807
Alan H. Resnikoff, 1660
Matt Rightmire, 308
Paula Robins, 126
Antonio Rodriguez, 1181
Charles W. Roellig, 449
Jesse Rogers, 96
John Roos, 820
Susie Roos, 820
Rick Rosen, 928
Eric Rosenfeld, 791
Eric Rosenfeld, 1383
Peter Roshko, 315
Steven J Rosston, 836
Stephen D. Royer, 1660
Rob Rutledge, 819
Julie Ruvolo, 3261
Jordan Ryan, 1559
Juan Sabater, 1902
Donald Sackman, 983
Neil Sadraranganey, 620
Kamil Saeid, 180
Rob Salvagno, 483
Jeff Samberg, 26
Scott Sandell, 1297
Julie Sandler, 1499
Kenneth B Sawyer, 1604
Kenneth T Schiciano, 1776
George Schmitt, 1793
Toni Schneider, 1860
David Schnell MD, 1493

College/University Index / Technion

Pierre J. Schuurmans, 2062
Kosha Shah, 1883
Nick Shalek, 1560
Bob Shaw, 192
David E. Shaw, 579
Robert Shaw, Jr., 160
David Shen, 590
Kirill Sheynkman, 1594
John F. Shoch, 87
Clara Sieg, 1555
Rob Siegel, 2011
David Silverman, 563
Bonny Simi, 1035
Richard Simoni, 181
James R Simons, 1725
Carlyle Singer, 55
Brian Singerman, 775
Steven F. Skoler, 788
Sarah Smith, 221
Jim Smith, 1247
Sam Smith-Eppsteiner, 996
David Smolen, 824
Ian Sobieski, PhD, 226
Edward P Sobol, 1972
Stephen Socolof, 1305
Katie Solomon, 819
Glenn Solomon, 823
Greg Somer, 692
Tyler Sosin, 1202
Pearson Spaght, 749
Ronald P. Spogli, 783
Jon Staenberg, 1733
Clancey Stahr, 837
Josh Stein, 609
Scott R. Stevens, 1409
Roger A Strauch, 1580
Sven Strohband, 1069
Scott Stuart, 1602
David E Sweet, 1760
David Sze, 872
Napoleon Ta, 775
Tony Tamer, 928
Garry Tan, 991
Bryan Taylor, 62
Craig C. Taylor, 87
Eric Terhorst, 732
Peter Thiel, 775
Allen Thorpe, 924
Daniel Tompkins, 1354
James N. Topper, MD, PhD, 782
Tommy Tsai, 1138
Matt Tsien, 817
Jim Tullis, 1866
Hans Tung, 823
Richard C Tuttle, 1492
Louie Ucciferri, 913
Salman Ullah, 1218
Robert L Underwood, 1332
Petri Vainno, MD, PhD, 697
Russel Valdez, 1950
Vance Vanier, 469
Vince Vannelli, 1084
Thomas Vardell, 1341
Steve Vassallo, 770
Jonathan Victor, 225
Paul R. Vigano, 1037
Eric Vishria, 248
Tefan Vitorovic, 1932
Andy Vitus, 1626
John Von Schlegell, 673
John Vrionis, 1121
John Walecka, 1534
Hunter Walk, 941
Sona Wang, 452
Samantha Wang, 563
Steve Waters, 1810
Allen A Weaver, 1497

Eckard Weber, MD, 621
Daniel Weiss, 126
Robert J. Wenzel, 74
Maurice Werdegar, 1975
Victor Westerlind, 809
Peter Westley, 300
Steve Westly, 1977
J.P. Whelan, 1066
Thurman V White, 1485
Bill Wiberg, 59
William Wick, 1937
Melissa Widner, 1637
Tom Woiwode, 1928
Kirk Wolfe, 1242
Wade Woodson, 1672
Chris Yeh, 1958
Krishna Yeshwant, 889
Kwan Yoon, 296
Bill Youstra, 1083
Dr. Chen Yu, 1941
Homan Yuen, 799
Lu Zang, 799
Dennis Zaslavsky, 1964
Stephanie Zhan, 1654
TX Zhuo, 728

State University of New York
Joel P. Adams, 56
Elliot Attie, 1851
Sid Banon, 460
Josh Bouk, 705
Kenneth Burns, 1679
Phil Carpenter III, 1022
Ryan Chan, 2253
William G. Connors, 1744
Jordan S Davis, 1520
Paul R DiBella, 537
Joe El Chami, 1022
Robert Frankel, 172
Steven G Glenn, 1956
Frances N. Janis, 1462
Peter Petrillo, 849
John Richardson, 2058
Joan Solotar, 277

Stephen F. Austin State University
John T Harkrider, 1063
Dayakar Puskoor, 1285

Stephen M. Ross School of Business
Brad Coppens, 1376
John Yang, 325

Stetson University
Peter C Brockway, 348
Edward C McCarthy, 1571
Bruce Rogers, 1086
Steven D Singleton, 1261
Troy D Templeton, 1857

Stevens Institute of Technology
David Kronfeld, 1038
Steven J Morgenthal, 164
George L Sing, 1092

Stirling University
Bernie Zeisig, 2195

Stockholm School of Economics
Mats Lederhausen, 567

Stonehill College
Kevin P. Costello, 309

Stony Brook University
Shmuel Einav, PhD, 1808

Stuart School of Business
Bob Bode, 1022

Suffolk University
Charles E. Ball, 123
Bill Fitzgerald, 816
Peter A. Hunter, 211
Edward J Keefe, 1153
Senofer Mendoza, 1201
Mike O'Malley, 989

Suffolk University Law School
Jim Counihan, 1478

Susquehanna University
Richard E Caruso PhD, 1494
William J Kennedy Jr, 716

Swarthmore College
Bruce Adams, 979
Rob Day, 1729
Eric Elenko, 1501
Michel Glouchevitch, 1575
Roger C. Holstein, 1931
Darby Kopp, 907
Corey Mulloy, 935
Anthony J. Orazio, 1417

Swiss Federal Inst. of Technology
George Arnold, 1077

Sydeham College
Rajan Mehra, 502

Sydney Law School
Yanev Suissa, 1687

Syracuse University
Steven Barnes, 220
Steven E Berman, 1401
Michael Cardamone, 30
Jamie Choi, 1611
Brian Cohen, 1306
Brian Cohen, 1310
Trace Cohen, 1310
Daniel A D'Aniello, 413
Stephen P DeFalco, 1129
A. Sinclair Dunlop, 689
Luke Gosselin, 446
Roger Hurwitz, 1942
Michael Hyatt, 1022
Peter Hébert, 1151
William Johnston, 909
Charles R Martin, 111
John May, 1304
Jeffrey S McCormick, 1623
Doug K. Mellinger, 492
Michal Petrzela, 1123
Thomas Queenan, 1441
Michael Schattner, 1377
Chris Setaro, 1662
Ajit Singh, 174
Michael G. Thonis, 456

Taylor University
Donald A Krier, 2004

Technical University (Karlsruhe)
Ralf Gruss, 135

Technical University of Munich
Peter Johann PhD, 1325

Technion
Dan Avida, 1381
Jacques Benkowski PhD, 1896
Shmuel Einav, PhD, 1808

1051

Miki Granski, 536
Amit Karp, 260
Itzik Parnafes, 235
Eyal Shaked, 536
Merav Weinryb, 1509

Technion Israel Institute of Tech
Elena Winefeld, 41

Tel Aviv University
Izhar Armony, 455
Adam Chesnoff, 1598
Yoni Chiefetz, 1121
Vered Digmy, 116
David Gussarsky, 1121
Mony Hassid, 1154
Eyal Miller, 1611
Shimrit Samuel, 116
Yafit Schwartz, 116
Eyal Shaked, 536
Shlomi Shiloni Shem Tov, 436
Michal Silverberg, 1350

Temple University
Steve Berman, 161
Brian Bytof, 1506
Michael F Daly, 1521
Tyler Dautrich, 866
Joseph Falkenstein, 1328
Saul A. Fox, 778
Anthony P. Green, PhD, 246
Karen Greene, 53
John Guiliana DPM, 1289
Fred Hosaisy, 1695
Edward L Kuntz, 1651
Scott Powers, 53
RoseAnn B. Rosenthal, 246
David Rubin, 1205
Dean Sciorillo, 676
Richard Taney, 1864
Tyrone Wilson, 1771

Temple University School of Law
Amy Banse, 518
Alex Katz, 724
Robert Keith, 1828

Tennessee Technological University
L Edward Wilson PE, 537

Tepper School of Business
Sreekar Gadde, 293
Ben T. Smith, IV, 32

Terry College of Business
Jennifer D Lackey, 1539

Terry School of Business
John Lee, 686

Texas A&M University
Kevin Brady, 1976
Gil Burciaga, 594
Clinton W. Bybee, 153
Sherman I Chu, 856
Scott Collier, 1855
Derrick K Collins, 1461
Joe Cunningham MD, 1619
Sarah Dickey, 3256
Heidi Hargrove, 702
Camilo E. Horvilleur, 928
William R. Lemmons, Jr., 671
David McWhorter, 425
Jeffrey R. Shannon, 546
Ben Stanton, 888
Matthew Van Alstyne, 1367
John White, 1273

Steve Whitlock, 1722
Bob Zipp, 114
Chris Zugaro, 1856

Texas Christian University
Roger D Bailey, 606
Blake Bonner, 1856
Brian Hoesterey, 64

Texas Tech University
Lynn Alexander, 1062
Paul W. Drury, 1111
Kirk Fichtner, 1167
E. Murphy Markham IV, 672
Felipe Mendoza, 165
Gary R. Petersen, 672
Art Reidel, 947
Philip Sanger MD, 1801
Meg Taylor, 984

Thayer School, Dartmouth College
Terry McGuire, 1460

The Citadel
Tim Komada, 600
Wally Lennox, 1461
W Spalding White Jr, 1605

The Darden School
Gene Lockhart, 1240

The London School of Economics
Jonathan Mo, 4

Thomas Jefferson University
Brian K. Halak, PhD, 621

Thomas M Cooley Law School
G Michael Stakias, 1116

Thomas More College
Edwin T Robinson, 1571

Thunderbird School of Management
Dave Carlson, 685
Gina Domanig, 2106
Holly Kaczmarczyk, 1970
Mark Mullen, 306
Mark Mullen, 624
Lori L. Murphree, 1369
Andrew Ogawa, 1513
Virginia G Rollins, 1605
Robert A Theleen, 473
Andy Unanue, 193
Gijs FJ Van Thiel, 14
Blue VanDyke, 9
Tom Whiteaker, 912

Tohoku University
Koji Osawa, 833

Tokyo Institute of Technology
Anis Uzzaman, 721

Tokyo Metropolitan University
Anis Uzzaman, 721

Towson University
Mark Maloney, 1400

Trinity College
Jeff Barry, 1455
James A. Beakey, 1279
Alec Burger, 808
Todd Dagres, 1715
Robert M Golding, 2015
Kyle Griswold, 793

John Howard, 1022
Terry L. Jones, 1771
Charles T Lake II, 1674
Ian Loring, 220
Bill Luby, 1638
Dan MacKeigan, 1728
Robert W Macleod, 1198
J Carter McNabb, 1571
Rick Moss, 253
Andy Newcomb, 1240
Logan V. O'Connor, 2015
Benjamin P Procter, 1962
Robert L. Rosner, 1931
James G. Schiff, 1344
David L. Schnadig, 546
C. Bowdoin Train, 875
Timothy Walsh, 433
Mimi Wolfe Strouse, 39
Scott Zoellner, 64

Trinity College Dublin
Laela Sturdy, 578

Trinity College, Hartford
Chauncey Hamilton, 622

Trinity Law School
Jaime McMillan, 390

Trinity University
Cam McMartin, 444
Chris Scoggins, 1653
John Thornton, 202
Robert Vargo, 2227

Tsinghua University
C.K. Cheng, 905
T Chester Wang, 47
Mingyao Wang, 519

Tuck School of Business
Rich Aldrich, 1145
Jim Andelman, 306
Jim Andelman, 1566
Charles Ayres, 1851
Kathleen Bacon, 909
Redington Barrett III, 1432
Marshall Bartlett, 744
Lee E Bouyea, 786
Thomas J. Buono, 263
John Cable, 1726
Mike Carusi, 59
Mike Carusi, 1122
Jennifer Chalmers Balbach, 1751
David G Chandler, 468
Brian Chee, 1460
Jim Conroy, 1372
Everett R Cook, 1466
Jeffrey G. Dishner, 1739
Dana Donovan, 631
Scott W Edwards, 1753
Robert Faber, 224
William Ford, 853
Walter G. Freedman, 1093
Thomas W Gorman, 1636
Kenneth A. Graham, 1014
Russell J. Greenberg, 104
Steve Halstedt, 441
John Henderson, 966
Bob Hower, 59
Luisa Hunnewell, 1987
Jonathan E. Hunnicutt, 1979
John Kilgallon, 220
Darby Kopp, 907
Jeffrey Kovach, 170
Nancy Lotane, 220
Chris Lund, 899

1052

College/University Index / Université de Chambéry

Devin Mathews, 468
Frederick Maynard, 909
Roger McNamee, 659
Michael P McQueeney, 1751
Richard S Melrose, 1163
Jose Minaya, 1356
Rob Morris, 1372
Rick Moss, 253
John J Murphy Jr, 1274
Daniel P Neuwirth, 1504
Jerrold Newman, 1987
Jeffrey T Newton, 812
John O'Connor, 1127
Standish O'Grady, 852
Jonathan W Osgood CFA, 572
Bruce Ou, 879
Howard Park, 824
Isai Peimer, 1196
Jonathan Perl, 315
Jonathan Pressnell, 290
Bill Reiland, 1255
Daniel R. Revers, 156
Brett J Rome, 1339
Thomas R Shepherd, 1862
Frank V. Sica, 1777
John W Watkins, 1153

Tufts University
Charles Auster, 1596
Sophie Bakalar, 511
Brad Bernstein, 793
Jeffrey M. Calhoun, 1777
Dana Callow, 312
Mitchell Davidson, 1465
Samuel L. Duboc, 2103
Stephen Eisenstein, 914
Rick Elfman, 1742
Jason Epstein, 516
Bruce F Failing, 80
Chris Farmer, 1675
Matthew Hermann, 176
Mike Jerstad, 1470
Steven E Karol, 1962
Julia Karol, 1962
Jack W Lasersohn, 1929
James D. Leroux, 179
Nancy Lotane, 220
Barbara Lubash, 1928
William I MacDonald, 1103
John Mandile, 1673
Stuart I Mathews, 1224
Yoni Meyer, 417
Matt Murphy, 1202
James Neary, 1956
Pierre Omidyar, 1374
Jonathan Perl, 315
Michael S Pfeffer, 1465
Nick Pianim, 581
Daniel Prawda, 834
Sam H. Pyne, 893
Shari Redstone, 60
Steven Ritterbush, 1207
Steve Romaniello, 1576
Ken Rotman, 2081
Tim Rotolo, 155
Charles L Schroeder, 1343
Nicholas Scola, 21
Andrew A. Silverman, 402
James A. Stern, 575
Richard Taney, 1864
Kathryn Taylor, 703
Lou Volpe, 1080
David Wachter, 1947
Paul Walsh, 368
Jeffrey M. Walters, 1093
Sebastian C. Widmann, 1130
Robert D Winneg, 1296

Daniel Zilberman, 1956
Kurt von Holzhausen, 343

Tulane Freeman School of Business
Marcia Haydel, 1431

Tulane University
Adit Abhyankar, 758
Cory S Anderson, 40
Stephen Bordes, 109
Mark Buffington, 271
Nicholas Callais, 372
Jarett Carson, 676
Urs Cete, 256
Wayne Cohen, 1635
Avantika Daing, 1454
Daniel Finkelstein, 845
Howard Glynn, 1207
Michael Goldberg, 99
Jeffrey M. Hurst, 521
Josh Klinefelter, 199
Omar Mejias, 63
David Mussafer, 62
J Peter Pierce Jr, 1446
Rick S Rees, 1144
Shannon Rothschild, 1722
David H. Rowe, 66
Bradley Sheftel, 1902
Joseph T. Sobota, MD, 139
Andrea Turner Moffitt, 1454

Tulane University Sch of Medicine
Gregory T Hebrank MD, 1098

Tulane University School of Law
Charles Booker, 61

Turku Institute of Technology
Anne-Mari Paster, 1373

UC Berkeley
Roy Bahat, 284
Dominique Gaillard, 2466
Charles Hamilton, 1086
Kamil Hassan, 851

UC Berkeley School of Law
Jimmy Lu, 1983

UC Hastings College of the Law
Allison A Bennington, 1903

UC Santa Barbara
Kristen Bailey, 769
Keval Desai, 1010
Andrew Ogawa, 1513
Hans Swildens, 986
Kevin Thau, 1715
Robert L. Zorich, 672

UC Santa Cruz
Richard R Crowell, 1904

UCLA Anderson School of Management
Gregory Bloom, 48

UCLA School of Law
Bob Brownell, 666
Josh Green, 1247

UIBE
Tianpeng Wang, 2195

UNC Business School
David Kirkpatrick, 1689

US Air Force Academy
Tom Dennedy, 174
Jeffrey Frient, 654
Michael C Giese, 1190
Brian Hibblen, 1687
Paul Madera, 1212

US Airforce Institute of Technology
Brian Hibblen, 1687

US Coast Guard Academy
Hans Lundin, 1002

US Military Academy
David W Averett, 1752
Chris C Casciato, 1123
Brian Chee, 1460
Phil Clough, 22
Patrick Connelly, 1009
Randall Crowder, 1801
John Drew, 1785
Russell B Hall, 1106
Bradley C Harrison, 1632
Robert P Healy, 468
Han Kim, 100
Douglas McCormick, 917
Paul F Murphy, 1651
David Pierson, 1774
Timothy R Sweeney, 637
Dave Tamburri, 918
Michael Thorson, 2001
Mark A deLaar, 1752

US Naval Academy
Ted Alexander, 1239
Ted Ardell, 1786
Thomas W. Arenz, 914
Sean Banks, 1863
Wes Blackwell, 1632
Dennis B Costello, 1847
David Jones, 1710
Bill Lyons, 488
Jeffrey R. Shannon, 546
Timothy P Sullivan, 1156
Michael Taylor, 909
Samit Varma, 132
Robert N. Verratti, 1828

Union College
Dennis Baldwin, 329
David J Breazzano, 597
William F Case Jr, 503
John Cozzi, 64
David Gershman, 1857
Steve Gullans PhD, 703
Eric Lauerwald, 1023
Jeffrey A. Lipsitz, 546
Jeremy Lynch, 1851
Rob May, 1459
Don Milder, 1928
Ting-Pau Oei, 644

Union University
Richard D. Parsons, 977

Universidad Compultense de Madrid
Cate Ambrose, 3261

Universidad de Bogota
Gina E. Molano, 1881

Universidad Tecnologica Nacional
Martin Bueno, 3260

Université de Chambéry
Bernie Zeisig, 2195

1053

College/University Index / Universite de Paris

Universite de Paris
Charles Heilbronn, 1263

Universite de Sherbrooke
Charles Sirois, 162

Université du Québec à Montréal
Isabelle Lechasseur, 2088
Patrick Pichette, 2157
Laurence Rulleau, 2092

Université Laval
André Dallaire, 473

Université Paris Dauphine
Carine Magescas, 128

Université Paris Descartes
Jeff Clavier, 1879

University British Columbia
Matt Cunning, 2178

University College
Alastair Tedford, 78

University College Dublin
Ronan Cunningham, 1717
Mark E Farrell, 1806
John O'Connor, 1127
John O'Neill, 1111

University College London
Matthew Foy, 1731

University of Aalborg
Joseph J. Downing Jr., 77

University of Aberdeen
David Q. Anderson, 118

University of Akron
Ray Leach, 1047
John W Manzetti, 1448
Sheila Mutter, 1786
Michael Price, 450
Chad W Souvignier, 1543

University of Alabama
Charles E Adair, 537
Yuval Almog, 536
Jon W Bayless, 1658
Jeff Demond, 154
Neeraj Gupta, 454
Donald C. Harrison, 458
Stuart McWhorter, 496
Wanda R Morgan, 1270
Doug Sellers, 1533
Toni F. Sikes, 375
Miller Welborn, 459

University of Alaska
Jeff Fagnan, 38

University of Alberta
Shawn Abbott, 2157
Sikandar Atiq, 2202
Dan Barclay, 2063
Kevin Brown, 2040
Kerry Brown, 2121
Mike Cabigon, 2121
Tanya Causgrove, 2040
Code Cubitt, 2195
Jim Elliott, 2064
Craig Golinowski, 2166
Donald Jackson, 2215
Ahmed Kamar, 2202

Mark Lerohl, 2230
Derek Lew, 2143
Derek Lew, 2216
Francesco Mele, 2050
Peter Pontikes, 2033
Mitch Putnam, 2025
Anuj Ranjan, 2067
Nancy Smith, 2040
Jim Taylor, 2049
Peter Tertzakian, 2040
Davis Vaitkunas, 2064
Jason White, 2166
Kristina Williams, 2032

University of Alexandria
Ossama Hassanein, 1311

University of Amsterdam
Paulus J Ingram, 2248
John R Jonge Poernik, 1130

University of Antwerp
Lode J Devlaminck, 637

University of Arizona
Dan Aquilano, 86
Joel Backman, 1212
Todd Belfer, 387
Ross Bhappu, 1548
Andrew Braccia, 28
Jerome Camp, 385
Abbie Celniker, 1811
Sherman I Chu, 856
Sean Doyle, 1610
Robert Dreier, 359
Skip Glass, 770
Bill Harding, 1906
Brian J. Knez, 421
Loretta Little, 2008
Loretta McCarthy, 841
Donald R. Parfet, 139
George Sarlo, 1952
Chad W Souvignier, 1543
Mike Speiser, 1760
Anthony J Veith, 503
Brian D Wallace, 36

University of Arkansas
Tyler A. Bozynski, 611
Jerome Camp, 385
Larry B. Carter, 611
Jeff Davis, 48
Bobby Franklin, 3272
Randy Hawks, 491
Joe T. Hays, 611
Ron Norris, 1922

University of Auckland
David Bell, 325

University of Baltimore
Frank A. Adams, 876
Stephen Auvil, 1790
Olleb Douglass, 1259
Kimberly Kyle, 22
William J. Westervelt, Jr., 179

University of Baltimore Law School
Steven B. Fader, 190
Peter M. Rubin, 190

University of Bangalore
Nupur Jalan, 834

University of Bath
David Atterbury, 909

University of Bayreuth
Sven H. Borho, 1382
Stephan Siegel, 2271

University of Behrain
Hisham Al Raee, 152

University of Bombay
Kamala Anantharam, 1444
Vikram Godse, 1184
Raj Pai, 834
Deepa Pakianathan, PhD, 604
Vineet Pruthi, 1127
Varsha Tagare, 1509

University of Boston
Khaled Jalanbo, 1900

University of Bradford
Daniel Docter, 603

University of Bridgeport
Ivar W. Mitchell, 123

University of Brighton
Suresh Patel, 2279

University of Bristol
Anthony W. Garton, 1112

University of British Columbia
Brian Begert, 2292
Rod Campbell, 2282
Alan Chiu, 2011
Charles Cook, 2097
Russ Cranswick, 1548
Harry Culham, 2079
David Eisler, 2235
Steve Faraone, 2217
Malcolm Finayson, 898
Graham Flater, 2126
Janelle Goulard, 2233
Ossama Hassanein, 1311
Andrew Haughian, 2213
Ashton Herriott, 365
Byron Horner, 2085
Wilfred Jaeger, 920
Wilfred Jaeger, 1819
Franklin Jiang, 2229
Shamsh Kassam, 2258
Moe Kermani, 2278
Simon Koch, 2145
Laurie G. Kolbeins, 1799
Sara Leggat, 1656
Derek Lew, 2143
Derek Lew, 2216
Wei Lin, 2175
Ward Mallabone, 2227
John McEwen, 2097
Tracey McVicar, 365
Arda M Minocherhomjee, 468
Jeffrey N. Murphy, 2163
Omkaram Nalamasu, Ph.D., 144
Richard Osborn, 2233
Richard Osborn, 2265
Norman Rokosh, 2275
Cooper Seeman, 2235
Corry J. Silbernagel, 2064
Akio Tanaka, 641
Kaley Wilson, 2229

University of Calcutta
Aditya Arora, 834

University of Calgary
Dan Barclay, 2063
Matt Bauer, 2025

College/University Index / University of California, Berkeley

John Berton, 2132
Larry Birchall, 2178
Aaron Bunting, 2246
Dave Chapman, 2292
Lauchlan Currie, 2040
John Dielwart, 2040
Ryan Dunfield, 2246
Chris Erickson, 2213
Melissa Fabreau, 2025
Rebecca Giffen, 2032
Paul Godman, 2032
Barclay W. Hambrook, 2039
Jim Hardin, 2048
Chandra Henry, 2178
Curtis Johansson, 365
Kel Johnston, 2166
Patrick Lor, 2212
Ward Mallabone, 2227
Sonny Mottahed, 2074
Dave Pearce, 2050
Whitney Rockley, 2190
Ryan Sapieha, 2050
Eric Schmadtke, 676
Martin Vetter, 2048
Imed Zine, 2242

University of California
Robert R. Ackerman, Jr., 84
Brian Atwood, 1928
Tom Banahan, 1796
Laura Baxter-Simmons, 1472
Walter Beinecke, 349
Pete Blackshaw, 480
Robert Blazej, PhD, 1238
Mike Brunell, 1369
John Burke, 1482
Justin Butler, 648
Jeff Carmody, 69
Michael Carney, 1888
Dr. Albert Cha, 1941
Brownell Chalstrom, 207
Daniel Corry, 69
Fred Craves, PhD, 237
Todd R Crockett, 1776
Kevin T. Dugan, 869
Luke B Evnin, 1268
Michael J Fram, 1116
Brett Gibson, 991
Mark J Gill, 713
Melanie Grace, 925
Chris Grant, 1052
Russell B Hall, 1106
Rob C Hart CFA, 1792
Justin Hartfield, 664
William Hopkins, 1368
Tamiko Hutchinson, 1004
Jeffrey Iverson, 277
Ray Jang, 1556
Leland Jones, 673
Tom Kastner, 1369
Hsing Kung, 47
Dr. Frank Kung, 1941
Anthony V Lando, 40
Michael Lane, 3267
Damian Langere, 811
Dr. Robert P Lee, 612
Will Lin, 763
Zack Lynch, 1029
Renske Lynde, 8
John Mapes, 199
David J Matlin, 1179
Dorian Merritt, 1796
Matt Moore, 92
Brian R. Nelson, 869
Niall A O'Donnell PhD, 1574
Robert Paulson, 67
Michael Powell, 1698

John Reardon, 1850
Barry D. Reynolds, 949
George Roberts, 1082
Charles W. Roellig, 449
Anhishek Shukla, 927
Mark Silverman, 428
Nat Simmons, 1472
Michael Spector, 1939
Richard Stubblefield, 1119
Robert Swan, 1120
Paulette Taylor, 1616
David Titus, 1995
Arthur Trueger, 252
Doug Tsui, 947
Fred Wakeman, 62
Brad Webb, PhD, 491
Gred Widroe, 1195
Wade Woodson, 1672
Kenny Zou, 2083

University of California, Berkeley
Dr John Baldeschwieler, 186
Kirby Bartlett, 45
Tom Beerle, 257
Christopher Behrens, 433
Amy Belt Raimundo, 1052
Mark Benham, 439
Allison A Bennington, 1903
Arthur Berliner, 1952
Tom Bevilacqua, 1906
Ravi Bhaskaran, 758
Richard C. Blum, 300
Michael Borrus, 2011
Jeff Branman, 937
David Brewer, 145
David Britts, 798
Jeff Brody, 1534
Bob Brownell, 666
Justin Burden, 986
Kristina Burow, 153
Douglas C. Carlisle, 1202
Rishi Chandna, 839
Clint Chao, 764
Paul Chau, 1983
Wu-Fu Chen, 47
Joanne Chen, 770
Alice Chen, PhD, 31
Leon Chen, PhD, 517
Jeff Chung, 107
William E Conway, 201
Ben Dahl, 1677
Anupam Dalal MD, 1059
John G Danhakl, 1109
Rahsaan Dean, 992
Alex De Winter, 809
Dipanjan (DJ) Deb, 779
Byron Deeter, 260
Michael Deleray, 343
John Dougery, 1013
Sean Doyle, 1004
Noah J. Doyle, 1028
Ken Ehrhart, 692
Ken Ehrhart, 1755
Nicolase El Baze, 1416
Elliot B Evers, 1195
Andrew Farquharson, 980
Mark Fernandes, 1670
Tami Flores, 229
Joe Floyd, 665
Gene Frantz, 578
Dean Frost, 253
Purvi Gandhi, 942
Jan Garfinkle, 149
Max Gazor, 455
Shomit Ghose, 1378
Pete Goettner, 2007
Nat Goldhaber, 491

Mark Grovic, 1299
Debra Guerin Beresini, 1011
H H Haight, 162
Steven J Hamerslag, 1869
James Hardiman, 585
Gregory Harriman, 266
Richard Harroch, 1906
Rob Hayes, 741
David Haynes, 793
Charles Haythornthwaite, 2078
James Healy, 1698
Dave Herron, 498
Cliff Higgerson, 976
Michael Hodges, 183
Janey Hoe, 483
Paul Holland, 770
Karen Hong, 1778
Herbert H. Hooper, 118
Ta-Lin Hsu, 892
Jonathan Hsu, 1848
Derek Idemoto, 483
Ariel Jaduszliwer, 324
Danny Jaffe, 126
David Jargiello, 756
Andrew Jensen, 1059
Trevor Johnstone, 2123
Ellis Jones, 1960
Scott Jordon, 836
Brendan Kennedy, 1481
Richard Kent MD, 1008
Rene Kern, 815
Eurie Kim, 761
Jason Krikorian, 596
Amit Kumar, 28
Tim Kutzkey, PhD, 517
Mark D. Kvamme, 630
Mike Kwatinetz, 215
Rachel Lam, 977
Leif Langensand, 129
Deval A Lashkari PhD, 1792
Rick Lewis, 1896
William Lewis, 2021
Darren Liccardo, 429
Anthony Lin, 1004
Jim Long, 805
John Lyman, 889
Rebecca Lynn, 396
Rebecca Lynn, 1257
Jeff Marcus, 559
Larry Marcus, 1952
Jim Marver, 1906
Brendan Mathews, 1259
Nancy McCroskey, 183
Ron Meeusen, PhD, 570
Richard Melmon, 358
Frank Mendicino III, 36
Jonathan Mi, 340
Matthew Miau, 905
Timothy C Mills PhD, 1616
Antonis Mistras, CFA, 637
Dan Mitchell, 1653
Cameron Myhrvold, 974
Amir Nashat, 1460
Thomas Neustaetter, 1038
Jessica Ngo, 472
David Nguyen, 126
Vincent M Occhipinti, 2005
Mimo Ousseimi, 810
Tracy Pappas, 1772
Elizabeth Park, 782
Lisa Parks, 229
Anu Pathria, 544
Rob Pomeroy, 946
Barry Porter, 494
Robin Praeger, 1928
Steven Puccinelli, 1360
Will Quist, 1694

College/University Index / University of California, Davis

Roger J Quy PhD, 1786
Jill A. Raimondi, 949
Pal B Ristvedt, 1112
Scott M Rocklage PhD, 12
Dennis D Ryan, 762
Phil Samper, 805
Eric Schmidt, 996
Jeffrey A. Schoenfeld, 240
Steve Schuman, 895
Armen B Shanafelt, 1124
Stephen Shapiro, 59
Rob Shurtleff, 618
Rob Siegel, 2011
Peter Sonsini, 1297
Carsten Sorensen, 2218
Jared Stasik, 607
Jason Stein, 1820
Nick Sturiale, 1658
Trey Sykes, 1014
Nelson Teng, 458
Jim Tenkle, 1618
Yaniv Tepper, 126
Ralph Terkowitz, 22
Bryant J Tong, 1355
Leda Trivinos, 747
Daniel Weiss, 126
Thurman V White, 1485
Dave Whorton, 1865
Randy Williams, 1061
Karen Wilson, 1010
Jay Wintrob, 1362
Hing Wong, 1951
Tim Woodward, 1355
Veronica Wu, 942
Tuff Yen, 1655
Peter Yi, 968
Homan Yuen, 799
Shelley Zhuang, 4
Yimin Zimmerer, 1951
Leo de Luna, 1154

University of California, Davis
Amira Atallah, 690
Dave Coglizer, 1977
Marty Eng, 1975
Skip Fleshman, 181
Edward Hamati, 267
John E Hamer PhD, 840
Matt Jones, 1355
Rick Lewis, 1896
Thomas E Mallett, 103
Joncarlo Mark, 1892
Michael Marquez, 1254
Scott Maxwell, 1380
Craig Muir, 1811
Richard Pardoe, 466
Mark Poff, 1767
Ben T. Smith, IV, 32
Sharon Stevenson DVM, PhD, 1371
Steven J Taubman, 1908
Tiffine Wang, 1269
Scott D. Winship, 888

University of California, Irvine
Timothy Dick, 1737
Trung Q. Do, 1419
Shahi Ghanem, 1983
Bruce Hallett, 1237
Michelle Kincanon, 126
Robert G McNeil PhD, 1616
Georganne Perkins, 744
Amit Shah, 174

University of California, LA
Fred Anderson, 659
Jim Armstrong, 502
Cristy Barnes, 1119

Ben Bisconti, 29
Gregory Bloom, 48
Greg Brackett, 373
Brett Brewer, 561
Chris L Britt, 1168
Brad J. Brutocao, 783
Don Butler, 1818
Lou Caballero, 274
Justin Camp, 385
Mike Carlotti, 203
Romeo Cerutti, 554
Walter Chung, 331
John D Cochran, 1147
Gill Cogan, 1381
Topher Conway, 1761
Richard Crosby, 898
Alda Leu Dennis, 991
Karen Derr Gilbert, 793
Wayne Doiguchi, 214
Ned Doubleday, 1152
Sean Doyle, 1004
Adam Draper, 307
Jesse Draper, 896
Brian Draves, 1794
Barry Eggers, 1121
Ira Ehrenpreis, 595
Ira M Ehrenpreis, 1786
Ira Ehrenpreis, 3284
David S. Felman, 869
James Fitzgerald, 1897
Standish Fleming, 769
Natalie Fonseca Licciardi, 1834
Kris Fredrickson, 509
Leslie Frécon, 1113
Jim Gauer, 1407
Richard Ginn, 548
Randy Glein, 1668
Kirsten Green, 761
Josh Green, 1247
Lloyd Greif, 869
Richard G. Grey, 939
Madison F. Grose, 1739
Alejandro Guerrero, 50
Craig Gunther, 278
Pamela Hagenah, 1003
Bruce Hallett, 1237
Philip Han, 1598
Richard Harroch, 1906
Travis Haynes, 225
Eric D. Heglie, 985
Ben Horowitz, 124
Mark Hsu, 892
Tamiko Hutchinson, 1004
John S. Hwang, 783
Scott Irwin, 1540
Dan Janney, 94
Buck Jordan, 397
Jed Katz, 1028
Guy Kawasaki, 807
Bill Kirsch, 548
Walter Kortschak, 1675
Christopher Lane, 1086
Kevin L. Listen, 902
Gary Little, 396
Gary Little, 1257
Christopher Lucas, 275
Susan Mason, 83
Manan Mehta, 1885
Matthew Moore, 2233
Dana Moraly, 502
Nathan Myhrvold, 1005
David Nagel, PhD, 768
Thomas Neustaetter, 1038
Carey Ng, 1221
Robin Nourmand, 225
Mimo Ousseimi, 810

Arrie Park, 924
Stuart Peterson, 175
T.M. Ravi, 1809
Marc Reich, 1021
Mark Rosenbaum, 199
Peter Seidler, 1645
Robert Seidler, 1645
Steve Simonian, 84
Tammi Smorynski, 1004
Scott Sweet, 1139
Pavan Tripathi, 333
Cleve Tzung, 203
Patrick J Welsh, 1972
Tim Woodward, 1355
Kevin Yamashita, 257

University of California, Riverside
Andrea Caoile, 494
Amy L. Laforteza, 949
Ken Pearlman, 1365

University of California, Santa Barbara
Richard G. Grey, 939
Alex Maleki, 972
William K. Richardson, 939

University of California, Santa Cruz
Scott Darling, 603

University of California, SF
Caley Castelein MD, 1059
Douglas Crawford PhD, 1238
Anupam Dalal MD, 1059
Mason Freeman MD, 12
Dr. Ryan A Harris, 1346
Russell Hirsch MD, PhD, 1493
Philip Sanger MD, 1801

University of California, San Diego
Jim Adler, 1834
Ashvin Bachireddy, 820
Abbie Celniker, 1811
Andy Chen, 509
Phil Chen, 1473
Grace Chui-Miller, 544
Paul Conley, 1400
Emmett Cunningham Jr., 495
Eric Elenko, 1501
David V. Goeddel PhD, PhD, 517
Gregory Harriman, 266
Doug Kelly MD, 87
Richard Kent MD, 1008
Michelle Kincanon, 126
Robert G. Leupold, 25
Peter Lipson, 909
Joncarlo Mark, 1892
Dayton Misfeldt, 237
Dan Mytels, 1609
Carey Ng, 1221
Eduardo Rallo, 324
Mickie Rosen, 798
Whitney Sales, 30
Mike Scanlin, 2195
Laura Siegal, 48
Leo Spiegel, 1239
John Stobo, 22
Mark Suster, 1888
Yipeng Zhao, 663
Geoffrey von Maltzahn, 747

University of Cambridge
Andrew Abrams, 1303
Houman Ashrafian, 1762
Oded Ben-Joseph PhD, 1388
Niko Bonatsos, 816
Teymour Boutros-Ghali, 1249

Roger Byford, 298
Lincoln E Frank, 1504
Walter Gilbert, PhD, 270
Giles Goodhead, 863
Jason P Hafler, 1618
David Hornik, 197
Mark W Kehaya, 1213
Dean M Kline, 1428
John Leibovitz, 515
Tim Lemmon, 134
Simon Lonergan, 245
Mike Majors, 586
David Mathers, 554
Peter C McWilliams PhD, 1616
Prakash A. Melwani, 277
Lawrence G Miller, MD, 1197
Anthony J. Moore, 822
Nathan Myhrvold, 1005
Khaled Nasr, 1010
Howard H Newman, 1443
Deep Shah, 779
Andrew Williamson PhD, 1438
Robbie Woodman, 1778

University of Campinas
Anderson Thees, 641
Alexandre Villela, 1509

University of Cape Town
Shaun Abrahamson, 1894
Roelof Botha, 1654
Joel R. Jacks, 507
Karen Meidlinger, 1199
Wayne Platt, 1369
Ryan Pollock, 1020
Steven Rostowsky, 2073
Andy Vitus, 1626
Andrew Walton, 2163

University of Chattanooga
Michael L Bailey, 1484

University of Chicago
William J. Aliber, 1496
Roger Altman, 699
Matt Anderson, 1976
Bernard Aronson, 46
Glenn W. Askew, 328
Michael E. Aspinwall, 434
Nicholas H Barker, 960
J.P. Bauman, 98
Eric Becker, 1742
David Beecken, 244
Robert M Belke, 1147
Mark Benham, 439
Stephen Berger, 1368
Marc C Bergschneider, 1735
Ravi Bhaskaran, 758
Mark Bounds, 316
Duncan S. Bourne, 2009
Richard Brekka, 1640
Matthew L. Brennan, 985
Nathan Brown, 1990
Lauren K Bugay, 633
Karla J Bullard, 1156
Kevin Burgoyne, 3262
Kristina Burow, 153
Scott Button, 1921
Clinton W. Bybee, 153
Philip A. Canfield, 884
Paul Carbone, 1479
Eric Carlborg, 197
Bill Carson, 954
Joanne Chen, 770
Charles Cherington, 1009
David Christopher, 1422
David Christopher, 1423

Derrick K Collins, 1461
John Compall, 489
John Connor, 21
William E Conway Jr, 413
Keith L. Crandell, 153
Adam Cranford, 1293
Kevin Culp, 1022
Krisin Custar, 1045
C Bryan Daniels, 1469
Anthony B Davis, 1128
Daniel L. Delaney, 985
Daniel Dickinson, 917
Frederick J Dotzler, 598
Sean Doyle, 1610
Steven M Dresner, 629
Tim Dugan, 1961
Douglas M. Dunnan, 875
Jon Edelson, MD, 177
Rick Elfman, 1742
Mark Emery, 1045
David S. Evans, 830
Hugh D. Evans, 1925
Timothy P Fay, 1636
Robert M. Feerick, 945
Paul Fishbin, 901
Robert J Fitzsimmons, 931
Marcel Fournier, 423
Steven M. Friedman, 686
John Gannon, 692
John Gannon, 1755
Rommel Garcia, 1166
John Gardner, 1330
Matthew N Garff, 1753
Daniel M Gill, 1684
Paul D. Ginsberg, 1576
John M. Goense, 838
Stewart Gollmer, 1796
Charles Gonzalez, 78
Stephen X Graham, 562
Terrence M. Graunke, 1091
Brian Graves, 629
Daniel J. Greifenkamp, 240
Greg Gunn, 488
Victor Gutwein, 1155
James Hardiman, 585
Bill Harlan, 1477
Rick Heyke, 1750
Russell Hirsch MD, PhD, 1493
Paul E Hoffman, 629
Joseph Huffsmith, 1376
Mike Jerstad, 1470
David M Jones, 1209
Peter Kagan, 1956
Louis W Kenter, 1492
Jay Kern, 1066
Karen Kerr, 809
Daniel Kessler, 577
Quintin Kevin, 57
Christopher T Killackey, 1469
John Kim, 933
Rick Kimball, 1785
Daniel Kimerling, 599
Stephen V King, 1469
Phil Kirk, 483
John R. Kline, 1301
Eric D Kogan, 492
Richard S Kollender, 1508
Thies O Kolln, 17
Richard R Kracum, 1990
Paul Kreie, 1232
Tom Lane, 675
Pat Lanigan, 1871
David Lawee, 578
Derek Leck, 109
John Lee, 1716
Kyle Lefkoff, 315
Karthee Madasamy, 1243

James Mahoney, 960
Howard Marks, 1362
James Marlas, 1881
Tracy Marshbanks, 732
Kevin M. McCafferty, 426
Aevin M McCafferty, 1296
Scott McConnell, 88
Charles P McCusker, 1422
Ryan R. McKenzie, 147
Michael W. Miller, 526
Peter Mogk, 960
Peter E Mogk, 960
Drew Molinari, 577
Ira L. Moreland, 969
William C Mulligan, 1476
Timothy M Murray, 468
Ramzi M Musallam, 1925
W. Carter Neild, 1382
Robert T. Nelsen, 153
Dean Nelson, 1602
Lawrence Neubauer, 1516
Matthew Nicklin, 732
Kenneth O'Keefe, 244
William J Oberholtzer, 932
Chris Orndorff, 1946
Peter Pacelli, 1078
Raj Pai, 834
Tim R. Palmer, 456
Jared B Paquette, 359
Brent L Paris, 632
Grant A Patrick, 244
Steve G. Pattison, 1456
Laura Pearl, 452
James N Perry, 1156
Stuart Peterson, 175
Dan Phelps, 1609
Luke A. Phenicie, 900
Greg Phillips, 343
Mike Pongon, 1458
Tony Pritzker, 1479
Tony Pritzker, 1480
Gregory J. Purcell, 147
Paul J. Raab, 719
Damon Rawie, 61
Scott Rogan, 675
Douglas J. Rosenstein, 873
Donald C. Roth, 670
David M Rubenstein, 413
Donald Sackman, 983
Zachary Sadek, 1417
Michael J. Salamon, 2062
William H. Schaar, 945
Jay W Schemelter, 1574
Peter G. Schiff, 1344
Thomas A Schlesinger, 244
David Seldin, 133
David Shapiro, 1085
Saurabh Sharma, 1046
Thomas P. Shaw, 900
Woody Sing-Wood Yeh, 117
Paul Slaats, 1234
Robert Smith, 364
Byron Smith, 1261
Darren M Snyder, 1469
Nicholas Somers, 1763
Vipul B. Soni, 357
Martin Stein, 276
Chelsea Stoner, 235
Mark Suster, 1888
Terry Suzuki, 1386
Scot E Swenberg, 478
Katie Szczepaniak Rice, 688
Immanuel Thangarai, 697
Andrew A Thomas, 1744
Nikhil Thukral, 1088
Mary Tolan, 469
John Tomes, 916

1057

College/University Index / University of Chicago Law School

Bradley Tusk, 1868
J. William Uhrig, 1820
Scott VanHoy, 1105
John Vrionis, 1121
Bonnie K Wachtel, 1948
Timothy Walsh, 433
Jeffrey M. Webb, 985
Jason Wilson, 1491
Ana M Winters, 1232
James D Witherington Jr, 1732
Robert Womsley, 1961
Ford Worthy, 1412
Benjamin W Yarborough, 1209
Paul G. Yovovich, 1091

University of Chicago Law School
Stephen D. Aronson, 1576
Adam Bendell, 1831
Antonio Gracias, 1902
Glen Lewy, 954
Lee M Mitchell, 1814
J Russell Triedman, 1129
J.P. Whelan, 1066
Adrian van Schie, 227

University of Cincinnati
Stephen A Baker, 766
Prashanth V. Boccasam, 1348
Laura Dotson, 1063
Thomas J Fogarty MD, 666
John Gardner, 1330
Jim Goetz, 1654
Hendrik J. Hartong, Jr., 357
Dan McKinney, 1321
Edwin T Robinson, 1571
Brian R Smith, 1597

University of Cologne
Nicolase El Baze, 1416

University of Colorado
Seth Berman, 1758
Christopher J Bower, 1397
Ryan Broshar, 1176
Chad Byers, 1758
Alan Colowick, 1698
Will Cowen, 1142
Jon Feiber, 1247
Dave Flanagan, 1004
Dietz Fry, 673
Debra P Geiger, 826
Jessica Geran, 638
David V. Goeddel PhD, PhD, 517
Jeffrey H. Goldstein, 309
Sven K. Grasshoff, 716
Stephen J Hoffman MD, 1691
Andrew Hopping, 1851
Pete Hudson, 94
Jeffrey Iverson, 277
Kevin Kester, 1679
Rand Lewis, 441
Jeffrey D Lovell, 1147
Hans Lundin, 1002
Jiong Ma, 322
Susan Mason, 83
Loretta McCarthy, 841
Timothy C Mills PhD, 1616
Dave Morin, 1694
Scott Morris, CPA, 736
Phil Parrott, 467
Patten Pettway, 1569
Daniel Pfeffer, 81
Joseph Piper JD, 1002
Peter Rosenberg, 1207
Christopher W Roser, 1586
Stuart L Rudick, 1236
Stephen N Sangalis, 1484

Scott Savitz, 586
Zach E Schaumburg, 1219
Frank Schiff, 1231
Terrance M Shipp, 1209
Frank Simon, 172
Napoleon Ta, 775
Ryan Williams, 542
Yimin Zimmerer, 1951

University of Colorado, Boulder
Ingrid Chiavacci, 956

University of Columbia
Bennett Cohen, 1449
Avantika Daing, 1454
Deborah Jackson, 1454
Khaled Jalanbo, 1900
Andrea Turner Moffitt, 1454

University of Connecticut
David L. Anderson, 1757
Greg Barger, 1317
Jim Barra, 1021
Nissa Bartalsky, 80
Derek Blazensky, 411
Nick Bologna, 646
Gregory E. Clark, 946
Al Foreman, 1864
Heidi M. Goldstein, 104
Rimas Kapeskas, 380
Peter Longo, 530
Deborah Magid, 967
Pauline Murphy, 530
Randal A. Nardone, 767
Calvin A Neider, 503
Dennis O'Brien, 881
Enrico Picozza, 938
Marc Reich, 1021
Marc Riiska, 1864
John L Ritter, 739
Robert Rodin, 1575
Mathias Rumilly, 503
Guy M. Russo, 386
Tim Shannon, 386
James Sidwa, 401
Michael S Weissenburger, 597

University of Costa Rica
Jorge Amador, 109

University of Dallas
Matthew J. Nordgren, 151
Brad Seaman, 2214

University of Dayton
Brent Ahrens, 386
Anthony M Lacenere, 987
Bassem A Mansour, 1545
Peter J Muth, 1746
Rick Ruffolo, 80
Steve Schuman, 895
Judd Sher, 924
Mike Venerable, 479
Daniel Wagner, 530

University of Delaware
James J Brinkman, 508
Nathaniel C Brinn, 1940
Daryl B Brown, 637
Jeff Davidson, 465
Robert Di Geronimo, 1432
David Freschman, 150
Michael Kelley, 150
Bart A McLean, 1270
Diane Messick, 989
Dennis Purcell, 74
David Rowley, 465

Eileen Sivolella, 62
David L. Warnock, 383

University of Delhi
Anik Bose, 249
Bahniman Hazarika, 855

University of Denver
Ed Anderson, 1334
Anders Bjork, 21
Mark K Gormley, 1104
Gregory L. Greenberg, 104
John Greff, 1653
Carolina B Hensley, 1484
Mark C Masur, 1682
James Minnick, 1147
Mark Mullen, 306
Mark Mullen, 624
Selahattin Onen, 1406
John Ord, 542
Christopher Quinn, CPA, 879
Tina Saxton, 470
Alex Suh, 371
Mike West, 467

University of Denver College of Law
Bluette N. Blinoff, 1799

University of Dublin
Kenneth Ryan, 1573

University of Dundee
Niall A O'Donnell PhD, 1574

University of Durham
Michael Lee, 1774

University of East Anglia
Brian E Stern, 1735

University of Edinburgh
Regis B Kelly PhD, 1238
Thomas Kennedy, 2167

University of Florida
Jim Adler, 1834
Andrew Banks, 21
Scott Brady, 996
Kevin Burgoyne, 3262
Kevin J Calhoun, 1753
Wu-Fu Chen, 47
Gonzalo Cordova, 1911
Seth Ellis, 1430
Manny Fernandez, 1668
Randy Glein, 609
Randy Glein, 1668
Michael B Goldberg, 1062
Melissa Guzy, 148
David Hellier, 257
Thomas O Holland Jr, 1422
Kevin J. May, 946
John Morgan, 1430
Scott Pressly, 271
Jonathan D Root MD, 1896
Dan Rua, 990
Bryan Simpson Jr., 826
Greg Stewart, 2141
Jeffrey H Strasberg, 1564
Mark Zittman, 1864

University of Fribourg
Romeo Cerutti, 554

University of Geneva
Lionel Carnot, 237
Matthew Moore, 2233
Otello Stampacchia, 1373

University of Georgia
Jon Birdsong, 189
Brian Cayce, 855
Scott E. Chappell, 263
Charles A Cox, 1144
Doug Fisher, 821
Ryan Gembala, 1421
David Griest, 1689
G Thomas Lackey, Jr, 1539
Michael A. Lonergan, 821
Melanie Martin, 768
Jeffrey S Muir, 794
Shahzad Pirvani, 2022
Marcus Smith, 1812
Jack Swan, 1120

University of Ghent
Sigrid Van Bladel, PhD, 20

University of Glasgow
James B. Walker, 554

University of Gothenburg
Lars Ekman, 1698

University of Guelph
Jessica Bowes, 2060
Paul Eldridge, 2126
Christopher A. Johnson, 2091
Allan Johnston PhD, 1773
Justin MacCormack, 2150

University of Guyana
Purnesh Seegopaul, 2213

University of Haifa
Gurion De Zwirek, 2254

University of Hartford
Brett Finkelstein, 1439
Douglas H. Leighton, 638
Peter Longo, 530

University of Hawaii
Richard D. Parsons, 977
Steven Ritterbush, 1207
Darell E Zink Jr, 409

University of Houston
Joseph L Harberg, 1549
Gayla W. Hightower, 328
James K. Lam, 893
E. Murphy Markham IV, 672
Mark G Papa, 1573
Jeffrey Sheldon, 485
Martin Sutter, 697
Jim P. Wise, 893
Timothy Zappala, 170

University of Hull, UK
Hisham Al Race, 152

University of Idaho
Carol Eckert, 782

University of Illinois
Collin Abert, 1091
Daniel K. Alport, 1578
Jonathan H Alt, 540
Ricardo Angel, 1449
Claudia Baron, 1467
Derek Beaty, 834
Paul Bragiel, 1473
Karla J Bullard, 1156
Eric Carlborg, 197
Barrett D. Carlson, 407
David Carlson, 1536
Shawn T. Carolan, 1202
Aaron D. Cohen, 884
John Compall, 489
David J Cooney, 244
Leslie M Corley, 1137
Bob Curry, 1094
John Dugenske, 88
Donald J. Edwards, 750
Jeff Farrero, 468
Rod Ferguson, 1410
Michael E Flannery, 633
Jacques V Galante, 1105
David Gervase, 529
Wade D Glisson, 1684
Charles Gonzalez, 78
Nathan J Good, 1469
James T. Hackett, 1573
James N. Hallene, 407
Laurence Hayward, 983
William Heflin, 1072
Kristina Heinze, 468
John Hennegan, 1667
Rob Herb, 1626
Cliff Higgerson, 976
John Hoesley, 1477
Ken Hooten, 529
Brian James, 489
Eric Keen, 550
Louis W Kenter, 1492
Quintin Kevin, 57
Christopher T Killackey, 1469
Matthew Kimble, 208
Stephen V King, 1469
John R. Kline, 1301
Eric Kutsenda, 1645
Mark Leigh, 950
Max Levchin, 1631
Christin Leybold, 641
Jay Lichter, PhD, 206
Timothy J MacKenzie, 1209
Jeanne Mariani Sullivan, 1738
Mark Maybell, 645
Russ Mayerfeld, 88
Sean M McNally, 1469
Alex Meyer, 1384
Constantine S. Mihas, 884
Michael W. Miller, 526
Tony Miller, 1107
Peter Misek, 2124
Dan Mitchell, 1653
Michelle Moreno, 629
Scott Mygind, 830
James J. Norton, 1435
Maura O'Hara, 3265
Steve Oetgen, 839
Bob Paluck, 444
Mike Parilla, 1166
Harsh Patel, 491
Harsh Patel, 2000
Chris Perry, 489
William Petty Jr, 244
Devin Quarles, 845
Craig Radis, 1467
Douglas Rescho, 1091
Rick Schell, 1378
Stewart Schuster, 1354
Raj Seth, 925
Jeffrey R. Shannon, 546
Tom W Siegel, 1664
Michael Siemplenski, 732
Rick Smith, 561
Sajid A. Sohail, 95
Christopher R Stalcup, 470
Avy H. Stein, 1986
John A. Strom, 893
Jeanne M. Sullivan, 1807
Stephen C. Tardio, 953
Steven Taslitz, 1742
Annie S Terry, 1156
Nikhil Thukral, 1088
Kai Tsang, 1922
Jana Vazé, 1341
Sriram Venkataraman, 209
Steve Vivian, 1477
Michelle A Waldusky, 633

University of Illinois, Urbana
Marc Andreessen, 124
Bruce N. Barron, 1384
Dennis Beard, 1379
Krisin Custar, 1045
Michael Hills, 1073
Bill Kaczynski, 338
Amitt Mahajan, 1473
Steven N. Miller, 1384
Mike Parilla, 1166
Laura Pearl, 452
Sundeep Peechu, 720
Bryce Youngren, 1460

University of Indiana
Chris LaMothe, 658

University of Iowa
Kenneth D. Anderson, 122
George Anson, 909
John C Aplin, 478
Bob Bode, 1022
Mark Bounds, 316
James H. Cavanaugh, PhD, 919
Cory Eaves, 815
Jodi Hubler, 1107
Kinney Johnson, 1653
Utkarsh Kanal, 198
Kristin K Lee, 1232
Jason Lettmann, 1122
Peter N. Masucci, 1301
Michael McCullough, 983
Greg Myers, 1171
Paul Peterson, 1990
Michael H. Reynoldson, 1016
Sarah Rogers, 836
Carol Sands Langensand, 129
Susan Simko, 1470

University of Johannesburg
Neil Ruthven, 775

University of Kansas
Chris Abshire, 721
David Burgstahler, 209
Fred Coulson, 745
Robert Ellsworth, 898
Patrick Healy, 364
Leo Kim, PhD, 214
Kendall Mohler, PhD, 31
Brett A Parr, 399
Mike Peck, 1379
David B. Pittaway, 423
Robert Smith, 364
David Wanek, 1975

University of Keele
Roger J Quy PhD, 1786

University of Kent
Stephen Cherington, 1009
John Garcia, 64

University of Kentucky
Christopher McCleary, 287
Jerry D. Wethington, 1570

College/University Index / University of King's College

University of King's College
Tom Eisenhauer, 2065

University of Kufstein
Klemens Wilhelm, 2126

University of La Laguna
Manuel Lopez-Figueroa, 237

University of Las Palmas
Manuel Lopez-Figueroa, 237

University of Law at Lyon
Yves Sisteron, 1888

University of Leeds
Charles Vaslet, 2106

University of Lethbridge
Art Robinson, 2178

University of Leuven
Guido Neels, 697

University of Liverpool
Karen Meidlinger, 1199
Jonathan Tunnicliff, 1349

University of London
Richard E Caruso PhD, 1494
Karimah Es Sabar, 2229
Ivan Gergel, 1302
Karim Gillani, 2179
Richard Harris, 2123
Donald O'Shea, 571
Ash Patel, 1254
Tom Rand, 2041
John Televantos, 170
Marcus Wood, 744
Jim Woody, 1094

University of Louisville
Charles W Beckman, 955
Mike Biddle, 2111
Larry Horn, 3283
Robert Nardelli, 667
Jerry D. Wethington, 1570

University of Lund
Mark T Lupa PhD, 930

University of Maine
John Burns, 1161
Kevin M. Crosby, 156
Michael A. Foisy, 900
Jean George, 59
Jean George, 1122
Edward J Keefe, 1153
Steve Salmon, 1094
Judd Sher, 924
Jeffrey G Wood, 900

University of Manchester
Eric Xu, 823

University of Manitoba
Dave Brown, 2240
David Cheadle, 2074
Candy Dong, 2234
Marcus Enns, 2077
Larry Evans, 2025
Albert D. Friesen, 2077
Kel Johnston, 2166
James Kinley, 2077
Gerry Schwartz, 2209
Rod Senft, 2123
Rod Senft, 2214

Rod Senft, 2218
John Zaplatynsky, 2218

University of Mannheim
Thomas Korte, 128

University of Maryland
G. Woodrow Adkins, 719
Rajeev Batra, 1184
Hope Brown, 376
Jerome Camp, 385
Steve DeAngelo, 1807
Scott Dupcak, 532
Adam Feinstein, 1930
Arthur L Fox, 1591
Mukul Gulati, 2018
Randy Guttman, 1041
Kiran Hebbar, 1899
Marty Hernon, 312
David Hirsch, 525
Larry Hootnick, 54
Greg Huff, 701
Samir Kaul, 1069
Wayne D Kimmel, 1657
Howard Kra, 190
Meghan M. McGee, 383
Dale McIvor, 1712
Jon Powell, 1657
Jason Pressman, 1663
Cindy Rose Quackenbush, 1139
Steven H Rosen, 1545
Rob Runett, 1259
Jeff Schechter, 1742
Curtis Schickner, 532
Mike Schuh, 770
Nicholas J. Simon, 495
Shounok Sinha, 532
Jack Slye, 1136
Joseph Statter, 701
Bruce Taub, 190
Katie Vasilescu, 834
Lane W Wiggers, 164
Herbert P. Wilkins, Jr., 1771
Bill Youstra, 1083
Natty Zola, 1176

University of Maryland College Park
Arjun Sethi, 1848
Megan Sparks, 532

University of Massachusetts
Vijay Advani, 1356
Dave Andonian, 580
Mark M Andrew, 1112
Stacey Bauer, 806
Larry Bohn, 816
Christopher Colecchi, 347
Jim Counihan, 1478
David H Donabedian, 1145
Dave Fachetti, 835
Arnie Freedman, 1388
Rick Gallagher, 1486
Steve Grizzell, 999
Ralf Gruss, 135
Paul A Howard, 1197
John Hunt, 21
Jeff Low, 645
David J Machlica, 1163
Benjamin Marino, 1432
Senofer Mendoza, 1201
Ed Olkkola, 1783
James J Pallotta, 1524
Gil Penchina, 1563
Ellis F. Rinaldi, 1739
Michael Rubin, 1342
Scott Sandler, 1383
Paul L. Schaye, 465

Alyse Skidmore, 1335
Prabakar Sundarrajan, 502
Edward C. Williams, III, 349

University of Melbourne
James Carnegie, 277
Simon Cresswell, 135

University of Memphis
Wally Rose, 16
Cynthia S Sheridan, 241
Burton B Weil, 1919

University of Mexico
David Wanek, 1975

University of Miami
Cindy Babbit, 577
Todd Boren, 557
Scott Broder, 993
Kevin T. Dugan, 869
Christopher Fountas, 171
Adam Kalish, 1151
James Niedel, 1298
J. Travis Prichett, 904
Beth Seidenberg, 1075
John Tullis, 1866
Andy Unanue, 193
Robert A. Vigoda, 426

University of Miami School of Law
Paul R DiBella, 537
Paul Dibella, 768

University of Michigan
John F Ackerman, 409
Rob Adams, 1321
Jim Adox, 1921
Lynn Alexander, 1062
David Armstrong, 195
Eric Arnson, 1385
David G. Arscott, 524
Perry O. Ballard, 750
Nicholas H Barker, 960
Claudia Baron, 1467
Michael Beauregard, 960
Michael C Bellas, 261
Steven T. Berg, 421
Brian S. Berkin, 1777
Casey Berman, 377
Jay Bernstein, 1085
Stacey Bishop, 1626
William Blake III, 251
Barry Blattman, 2067
David Bohnett, 228
Rick Bolander, 805, 2023
David Breach, 1938
Randall Brouckman, 1782
Paul Brown, 2023
Karen Buckner, 1242
Mary Lincoln Campbell, 652
Jon Canarick, 1335
Eric Ceresnie, 916
Roger Chen, 1685
David Christopher, 1422, 1423
Wayee Chu, 1527
Brian M Clark, 1153
Josh Cohen, 488
Jake Cohen, 607
Michael Cohn, 883
R. Craig Collister, 1590
Bradley E. Cooper, 404
Marshall Cooper, 863
Brad Coppens, 1376
Kevin Costantino, 864
Kelli Cullinane, 1106
Brian Dixon, 660

1060

College/University Index / University of Missouri

John W Doerer, 1461
Dixon Doll, 596
James Eadie, MD, 1619
Roger Ehrenberg, 965
Robert Ellsworth, 898
Steve Engelberg, 1615
Gary C Epstein, 937
Daniel Estes, PhD, 782
David S. Evans, 830
Lawrence Fang, 1987
Karim Faris, 889
Peter W Farner, 1802
Edmund J Feeley, 1134
Matthew S. Feldman, 492
Linda Fingerle, 652
Adrian Fortino, 1206
Evan R Gallinson, 1209
Michael Godwin, 1547
Pete Goettner, 2007
Mitch Green, 2081
Alex Gregor, 1078
Tony Grover, 1592
Bulbul Gupta, 1396
Robert A. Hamwee, 1301
Matthew Hankins, 928
Robert A Heimann, 1571
Jason Heltzer, 1384
Dave Herron, 498
John C. Hindman, 1989
Jay Hoag, 1785
Steve Hochberg, 177
Karen Hodys, 747
Seth H Hollander, 1081
Sheldon Howell, 969
Ernest D Humphreys, 1162
James A Illikman CFA, 1426
Anurag Jain, 1433
Christina D. Jamieson, 844
Michael Jandernoa, 943
David Kaplan, 159
Gabe Karp, 607
Samir Kaul, 1069
Brad Keywell, 1118
Dan Kidle, 149
Demian Kircher, 1166
Steven B Klinsky, 1301
Scott Kokones, 886
Ted H. Kramer, 900
David E. Kroin, 859
Brian Kwait, 1368
Karle E LaPeer PE CFA, 1426
Michael S Langdon, 789
John Leckrone, 58
Jason Lettmann, 1122
Nan Li, 1363
Roy Y. Liu, 925
Karthee Madasamy, 1243
Kent Madsen, 688
Arthur J Marks, 1899
Joelle Marquis, 170
Marcy Marshall, 149
Richard McClain, 932
Stephen McCormack, 521
Dennis McCrary, 1411
Paul McCreadie, 149
Lake McGuire, 925
Dale McIvor, 1712
Cam McMartin, 444
Jason Mendelson, 776
Ravi Mohan, 1663
Jake Moilanen, 1655
Steven Moore, 334
Jay Moorin, 1490
Mark Mullen, 624
Jonathan Murray, 642
P Sherrill Neff, 1508
Michael Ozechov, 543

Cindy Padnos, 976
Donald R. Parfet, 139
Vijay C Parikh, 833
John Park, 410
Don Parsons, 142
James A Parsons, 1557
Anthony Patek, 253
Naimish Patel, 1141
Brian Peiser, 654
Kenneth R Pelowski, 1445
Gretchen B Perkins, 960
Brian Peters, 933
Timothy Petersen, 149
Jim Petras, 642
Laura Petterle, 760
J. Travis Prichett, 904
Matthew W Raino, 1156
Louis Rajczi, 768
Arun Ramamoorthy, 1445
Milton K Reeder, 33
Eric A Reeves, 633
Randy O. Rissman, 1108
Sanford Robertson, 779
Eric Y Rogoff, 716
Charlie Rothstein, 251
Atul Rustgi, 37
Ali Safiedine DPM, 1289
Neal G Sahney, 789
Gerald Saltarelli, 654
Maninder Saluja, 1516
Martin A. Sarafa, 449
Robert H Savoie, 1445
J Michael Schafer, 1300
Greg Schulte, 886
Jeffrey Schultz, 1283
Evan Schwartzberg, 1367
David Shapiro, 1085
Christopher S Sheeren, 960
Kevin Shin, 878
M.G. Siegler, 889
Michael C Skaff, 1648
David S. Slackman, 953
Roman Sobachevskiy, 890
Todd Solow, 1345
Michael Stark, 563
Jared Stasik, 607
William Staudt, 667
Scott Steele, 1040
Bob Stefanski, 2023
Jason Stoffer, 1183
Kathryn J Stokel, 18
David Stott, 1990
Ben Sun, 1475
Alan J Taetle, 1331
Andrew Tananbaum, 565
Andrew C. Taub, 1088
Jim Tenkle, 1618
Keith Titan, 256
James N. Topper, MD, PhD, 782
Peter Torenberg, 1933
S Edward Torres, 1124
Joseph Tou, 1703
Jason Townsend, 1547
Brent Traidman, 721
Jonathon Triest, 1150
Matt Turner, 113
Amherst Turner, 113
Paul R. Vigano, 1037
Ryan Waddington, 961
Marc Weiser, 1592
Morty White, 2009
Evan Wildstein, 1081
Kirk Wolfe, 1242
David Wolmer, 1111
Austin Wright, 359
Victor L Wu, 1112
Dr. Lan Xeuzhao, 232

Anthony W Zambelli, 1648
Dennis Zaslavsky, 1964
Toby Zhang, 472
Brett deMarrais, 1150

University of Michigan Law School
Paul Arnold, 1768
Geoff Entress, 1499
Steven Florsheim, 1889
David Frazee, 1561
Ernest D Humphreys, 1162
Robert B Knauss, 1956
John Kole, 1142
Eric Lefkofsky, 1118
Frederic H Mayerson, 1954
Douglas E. Onsi, 919
Luke Reese, 1999
Tom Washing, 1653

University of Minnesota
Bruce K Anderson, 1972
Josh Baltzell, 1725
Greg Baszucki, 772
Scott L Becker, 1343
Justin Benshoof, 373
Greg Benson, 959
Darren Brathol, 1719
Ryan Broshar, 1176
Todd C. Chaffee, 1001
Daniel Docter, 603
Robin Dowdle, 68
Mark Gorenberg, 2019
Mik Gusenius, 464
Charles M. Hall, PhD, 139
Chad Johnson, 464
Kevin P Kenealey, 1171
Steve LaPorte, 1378
John Lindahl, 1345
Christopher S Meldrum, 840
Vish Mishra, 502
Michael Moe, 883
Andrea R Nelson, 1719
Marcia L. Page, 1907
Constance Paiement, 738
Randy Paulson, 1368
Greg Reichow, 648
Judy Romlin, 1233
Peter L Rottier, 1752
Gerald F Schmidt, 537
Jeffrey Sheldon, 485
Robert J. Simon, 321
William H Spell, 1719
David Spreng, 555
Kathleen A Tune, 1817
Naeem Zafar, 95

University of Minnesota Law School
George G. Hicks, 1907
Michael A.G. Korengold, 678

University of Minnesota Med. School
Ronald J. Shebuski, PhD, 139

University of Mississippi
Charlie Plauche, 1597
Bryan M. Wethington, 1570

University of Missouri
Dmitry Alimov, 792
Erik Allison, 1692
Charlie Bolten, 267
Andy Butler, 364
Robert Ehrhart, 220
Peter Esparrago, 569
Sean Foote, 1089
Brenda D Gavin, 1508
Rebecca Lynn, 396

College/University Index / University of Montana

Rebecca Lynn, 1257
Rod MacDonald, 594
Hank Plain, 1122
Douglas Reed MD, 915
Ted Roth, 1588
Gary Stevenson, 1187
Steve M. Welborn, 2009
Bill Witzofsky, 399
Jackie Yang, 1838
Shelley Zhuang, 4

University of Montana
John Connors, 974
David Dillman, 1553
Richard Harding, 1011

University of Montreal
Cédric Bisson, 2268
Philippe Leroux, 2260
Andree-Lise Methot, 2093
Riadh Zine, 2242

University of Mumbai
Vijay Advani, 1356
Keval Desai, 1010
Rashmi Gopinath, 1154
Nikhil Khattau, 1184
Vivek Ladsariya, 1687
Sandeep Naik, 815
Ashwini Sahasrabudhe, 855
Mathew Veedon, 1712

University of Mysore
Nagraj Kashyap, 1154

University of Nebraska
Eric M. Ball, 108
Barry Dunaway, 108
Thomas M Galvin, 940
Vinod Gupta, 700
David Guthrie, 108
Mark Hasebroock, 635
Steven King Neff, 993
George Krauss, 71
Christopher S Sheeren, 960
Richard L Sherman, 1633
Eli L. Thomssen, 139
Michael Yanney, 71

University of Neuchatel
Dominique Semon, 1216

University of Nevada
Thomas Bell, 512
Lucius H. Taylor, 156

University of Nevada Las Vegas
Matthew Neely, 1692

University of New Brunswick
Joe Allen, 674
Tom Liston, 2096
Laura Richard, 2200

University of New Hampshire
Janice Borque, 925
Daniel Budde, 901
Julie Eiermann, 909
Michael A. Foisy, 900
Lawrence Howard MD, 954
Michele Kinner, 1516
Robert Kirby, 839
Augustine Lawlor, 919
Alan G. Schwartz, 740
John H. Turner, 1979
Mike Tyrrell, 1916
Michael Van Vleck, 853

Timothy Zappala, 170

University of New Mexico
Ron J McPhee, 1924
Carlos Perea, 966
Chris Traylor, 756

University of New Orleans
Steven L. Soignet, MD, 157

University of New South Wales
Charles R Grant, 1112
Matt Lee, 472
Matthew Leibowitz, 2224
Jeremy G. Philips, 1715
Purnesh Seegopaul, 2213

University of New York
Charles Cohen, 1775

University of Newcastle
Jonathan Tunnicliff, 1349

University of North Carolina
Lee Ainslie, 1182
Bret Batchelder, 463
Matt Becker, 702
Scott Benson, 1316
Philip E Berney, 1062
Jeffrey Black, 1926
Jonathan B. Blanco, 746
Kenneth S. Bring, 254
Ben Brooks, 1710
Charles A Bryan, 1422
Walter W. Buckley III, 53
Christopher M. Busby, 857
Aohn Cambier, 971
Melissa Daniels, 1255
Tom Darden, 463
Lister Delgado, 971
David H Donabedian, 1145
Bruce B. Dunnan, 875
David Dupree, 894
S. Whitfield Edwards, 746
Charles Elliott, 656
Mike Elliott, 1331
Robert C. Eubanks Jr., 780
Alston Gardner, 794
Gardiner W Garrard III, 1863
Robert Girardi, 209
Brian P Golson, 1417
Michael N. Gray, 1496
Carter Griffin, 1886
Lisa Hagerman, 595
Seth Harward, 790
Stuart W Hawley, 1624
Frank J Hawley Jr, 1624
H Beecher Hicks, III, 1529
Ian A.W. Howes, 31
Herbert W Jackson, 1541
Ray Jang, 1556
Kevin B Jessup, 1606
David Jones, 1710
Victor Kats, 176
Greg Kats, 398
W. Brent Kulman, 746
Matthew Laycock, 199
Kenneth B Lee, 915
Steve Lerner, 1096
Michael Marquez, 1254
Michael S. Marr, 405
Tom McDermott, 656
Nannette McNally, 64
Robert J. McParland, 1828
Elizabeth Merritt, 463
Erik O. Morris, 1576
Allen S Moseley, 1331

Sunil Nagaraj, 1877
Tom Newby, 1112
Frank T Nickell, 1062
Charles E. Noell, 1041
Julie Ocko, 909
George A Parker, 1103
John Powell, 1003
Robert S Powell Jr, 1277
Steve Rakes, 1709
Robin Richards Donohoe, 627
Matthew Ritchie, 48
Virginia G Rollins, 1605
David Rosenstein, 815
Lloyd R. Sams, 263
Nelson Schwab III, 415
Dwight Scott, 277
John W Shearburn, 1956
Bryan Simpson Jr., 826
Bradley Sloan, 1514
Tom Smith, 1625
Julia Spicer, 3270
William Starling, 1772
Scott R. Stevens, 1409
James Stevenson, 22
Kathleen Thomas, 1033
Clay B Thorp, 915
Andrew A. Tisdale, 1496
David G Townsend, 746
Tom Uhlman, 1305
Scott VanHoy, 1105
Krishnan Varier, 151
Anita Watkins, 1556
Scott Werry, 2034
Thomas H. Westbrook, 746
Eric J. Wilkins, 1409
Adrian N. Wilson, 1842
Adrian Wilson, 1842
Ron Wooten, 1349
Ford Worthy, 1412
Phil Yates, 333

University of North Dakota
Douglas E Mark, 1343
Lauris Molbert, 173
Scott A Reilly CFA, 1426
Paul Unruh, 1793

University of North Texas
Tex Sekhon, 1167

University of Northern Colorado
Dan Aweida, 210
James P. Kelley, 1931

University of Northern Iowa
Joseph Galligan, 765
Dave Latzke, 464
Paul Rhines, 17

University of Notre Dame
Brian Bastedo, 1578
John M Baumer, 1109
R David Bergonia, 1332
Terrence Berland, 1074
Mark Birschbach, 1642
Christopher J Blum, 619
Gale Bowman, 1019
Jason T. Brass, 843
Frank Brenninkmeyer, 1431
Lauren K Bugay, 633
Dave Butler, 1045
Sean Cantwell, 1942
Bill Carson, 954
Charles Cascarilla, CFA, 1115
Edward A. Chestnut, 1496
Richard Conklin, 732
Kelly A. Cornelis, 1093

Catherine Crockett, 879
Dino Cusumano CFA, 109
Scott A. Dahnke, 1088
Christopher J Dean, 1752
Kevin Delaplane, 1881
Michael Denvir, 1045
Joe Dimberio, 1871
Maurice Doyle, 61
Kaitlyn Doyle, 1019
Kevin Dunwoodie, 1411
Chris A. Durbin, 1931
Richard P Earley, 636
Beth Engel, 635
Geoff Entress, 1499
Daniel K Flatley, 1175
Brian Flynn, 772
Shawn Foley, 208
Clinton Foy, 561
Brian Gallagher, CFA, 1871
Chris Geneser, 489
Eric Gevada, 1105
John W. Glynn, 836
David Glynn, 836
William J Golden, 1092
John Grafer, 1622
Doug Groh, 479
Brad Gurasich, 425
Thomas M. Hagerty, 1815
John C. Hahn, 1496
Bill Harlan, 1477
John A. Hatherly, 2009
Tom Hedrick, 1944
Bobby Helmedag, 1556
Jim Hunt, 285
Matthew A. Janchar, 254
David M Jones, 1209
Jay Jordan, 1045
Kevin Keefe, 1467
James P. Kelley, 1931
Colton King, 1086
David J. Koo, 1590
Ronald W Kuehl, 789
Timothy Kuehl, 1345
Michael A. LaSalle, 1660
Pat Lanigan, 1871
Ian Larkin, 1166
Joseph Linnen, 1045
Rob Little, 839
Greg Long, 1166
Patrick A. Maciariello, 523
Ben Magnano, 782
Wayne Marino, 1748
Rocco J. Martino, 1093
Alfred M. Mattaliano, 1578
Tom McCloskey, 542
Bill McDonagh, 1952
Jack McGlinn, 405
Steve McKay, 772
Andrew McLellan, 1960
Ed Mello, 576
Arthur Monaghan, 850
Jason B Moskowitz, 633
Terrence Mullen, 170
David Neighbors, 1963
Michael E. Nugent, 1578
Kevin O'Brien, 433
Karl Peterson, 1835
M Troy Phillips, 244
Don Pierce, 1667
Jonathan Pressnell, 290
Paul Purcell, 222
Chris Redmond, 399
Cas Schneller, 787
John W Sherman, 597
Andrew Souder, 1521
Luke K. Stanton, 1692
Mark Staub, 1467

Roderick Stephan, 99
Matthew Strottman, 979
Mike Stubler, 628
Mike Stubler, 3275
David Sutherland, 1229
Ryan Sweeney, 28
Dave Thomas, 839
Paul E. Tierney Jr., 136
James F Wade, 1153
Kent R. Weldon, 1815
Jason Wilson, 1491
David Wurzer, 530
Caroline Yeager, 1019
Douglas Zych, 1045

University of Nottingham
Gavin Bates, 374

University of Oklahoma
Jon W Bayless, 1658
Jay Benear, 639
Barry M Davis, 591
Brian Grigsby, 545
S Kim Hatfield, 553
Scott Meacham, 2024
Rick Nagel, 48
John Scull, 1711
Blake Trippet, 1223
Tom Walker, 1553
Ben West, 39

University of Oregon
Rodger P Adams, 1909
Ashley Cravens, 1879
Rocky Dixon, 673
Angela Jackson, 1463
John R Nelson, 1664
John Saefke, 1915
T Chester Wang, 47

University of Otago
Adrian van Schie, 227

University of Ottawa
Anne-Marie Bourgeois, 676
Stephanie Butt Thibodeau, 2112
Matt Golden, 2137
Charles Holt, 2161
Mona Kung, 2138
Michelle McBane, 2257
Gaétan Morin, 2120
Neil Ryan, 1866
Eric Schmadtke, 676
Fil Varino, 3258

University of Oxford
Shiri Ailons, 1774
George E. Aitken-Davies, 97
Houman Ashrafian, 1762
Roy Bahat, 284
Andrew Banks, 21
Nick Beim, 1916
Kate Bingham, 1628
Liz Birch, 268
Bruce Booth, 191
Martin Brand, 277
Winston J Churchill, 1633
Stuart Collinson, 769
Sunny Dhillon, 1678
Andrew Dunn, 1376
Spencer Fleischer, 787
Pete Flint, 1323
Matthew Foy, 1731
Keith Geeslin, 779
David B. Golub, 844
Bruns Grayson, 23
Richard Harris, 2123

Ryan Hemingway, 688
Kyle Hickey, 2246
Reid Hoffman, 872
Daniel Hullah, 809
Patrick Keefe, 2068
Robert Kibble, 1239
Paul Kusserow, 955
Jeremy D. Lack, 188
Thong Q Le, 31
Kathryn Leaf, 1411
Jeffrey T Leeds, 1105
Matthew Leibowitz, 2224
Joshua Lewis, 1608
James Marlas, 1881
Niall A O'Donnell PhD, 1574
Ryan Pollock, 1020
Mark Redman, 2207
Laura Richard, 2200
Ned Scheetz, 138
Andrew Sillitoe, 135
Scott Silverman, 70
John Simon, 1673
Neil P. Simpkins, 277
Stephen H Spahn, 1504
Michael Thorson, 2001
Salman Ullah, 1218
Roger Walton, 422
Mark N. Williamson, 368
Robbie Woodman, 1778

University of Paris
Marc-David Bismuth, 1088
Nicolas Chaudron, 2851
Philippe Collombel, 1416
Elliot B Evers, 1195
Laurent D. Hermouet, 188

University of Pavia
Claudio Nessi, 1373
Otello Stampacchia, 1373

University of Pennsylvania
Mike Ackrell, 44
Deepak Advani, 924
Sandip Agarwala, 1143
Rahul Aggarwal, 334
William F Aikman, 882
Ryan Anderson, 433
Izhar Armony, 455
Jon Auerbach, 455
Keith Bank, 1057
Robert Bassman, 1255
Josh Baumgarten, 127
David Bell, 325
Larry Benaroya, 247
Jordan S. Bernstein, 476
Charles Birnbaum, 260
Jim Blair, PhD, 621
Sam Brasch, 1052
Philip L. Bronner, 1348
Robert E Brown Jr., 1275
Frank W. Bruno, 451
Thomas A. Burger Jr., 873
Barbara Burns, 64
Tara Butler, MD, 176
Justin Camp, 385
David F Chazen, 460
Ray Cheng, 1235
Iris Choi, 751
Yee-Ping Chu, 274
Chris Chung, 878
Andrew B. Cohen, 510
Doug Cole, 747
Stephen B. Connor, 899
David C. Coquillette, 1301
Chad M. Cornell, 843
Anthony Corriggio, 1679

College/University Index / University of Pennsylvania

Ben Cukier, 440
Rahman D'Argenio, 675
Nicholas Daraviras, 1032
Tyler Dautrich, 866
Ken DeAngelis, 202
Ben DeRosa, 109
John Dean, 939
Peter Detkin, 1005
Randolph C Domolky, 1133
Ted Driscoll, PhD, 491
Andrew L. Dworkin, 1911
Loren Easton, 110
Yaron Eitan, 1633
Joe El Chami, 1022
Donald J Elmer, 1398
Nathan R. Every, MD, MPH, 782
Jonas Fajgenbaum, 1018
William Farrell, 170
Mark E Farrell, 1806
Stacy Feld, 1042
Stacy Feld, 1438
Alex Ferrara, 260
Beth Ferreira, 743
Jason Fiedler, 1530
Paul Fishbin, 901
Doug Fisher, 1010
Stewart Fisher, 1086
Jason Fisherman, 1775
Robert J Fitzsimmons, 931
Andy Flaster, 1942
Philip Fleck, 1347
Kerri Ford, 1596
Saul A. Fox, 778
Robert A Fox, 1521
Lincoln E Frank, 1504
Brian P. Friedman, 1032
J.S. Gamble, 285
Joseph M Gantz, 1443
Jan Garfinkle, 149
Wesley H.R. Gaus, 507
Simeon J. George, 1731
Jeffrey P Gerson, 849
Liron Gitig, 793
Newton Glassman, 2073
Amir Goldman, 1759
Jeffrey M Goodrich, 931
Dave Gould, 1788
Michael D. Granoff, 1462
Jonathan Gray, 277
Myles D Greenberg, 474
James H. Greene III, 949
Michael Gruber, 983
Michael C. Gruber, 1610
Sarah Guo, 872
Beth Haas, 577
Christopher J. Hadley, 254
Brian K. Halak, PhD, 621
Hadley Harris, 679
David W Harris, 1707
Brooke Hayes, 155
Eric D. Heglie, 985
Gardner C Hendrie, 1672
Andrew Hertzmark, 818
Justin Heyman, 834
Ryan Hinkle, 1000
Mitchell L Hollin, 1136
Laura C. Holson, 1301
David Horing, 110
Jeff Horing, 1000
Richard M Horowitz, 1521
Davis Hostetter, 894
Lee Hower, 1322
Luisa Hunnewell, 1987
Evis Hursever, 697
David Istock, 294
Joel R. Jacks, 507
Matthew Jacobson, 1096

Uttam Jain, 188
Amish Jani, 743
Craig N. Johnson, 832
Stephen M. Johnson, 949
Rick Jones, 266
Christopher N. Jones, 746
G. Kent Kahle, 888
Edward W Kane, 909
Jonathan D. Kelly, 404
Rene Kern, 815
Christopher M. King, 873
Ronald J. Klammer, 1369
Karin Klein, 284
Randal Klein, 208
Scott Kleinman, 140
Lewis S. Klessel, 1301
Gil Kliman, 1010
Eric D Kogan, 492
David P Kollock, 832
Michael Kopelman, 655
John Kornreich, 1617
Eric R. Korsten, 327
Krzysztof A. Kowal, CFA, 637
Roman Krislav, 239
Leon Kuan, 744
Monish Kundra, 515
Gary Lauder, 1095
Christopher Lawler, 846
Seth J Lehr, 1136
Jonathan Lehr, 2006
John Leibovitz, 515
Tim Lemmon, 134
Ben Lerer, 1110
Paul S. Levy, 1039
Regan Li, 2083
Jeff Lieberman, 1000
Ben Lin, 858
David Lincoln, 657
Paul Lisiak, 1225
Angus C Littlejohn Jr., 1134
Alexander Lloyd, 32
John Loftus, 53
Lori Lombardo, 683
Peter Macdonald, 274
Kent Madsen, 688
David Magerman, 614
Deborah Magid, 967
Stephen A. Magida, 123
Marc Magliacano, 1088
Vishal Mahadevia, 1956
Mohamad Makhzoumi, 1297
Scott M. Marimow, 1496
Howard Marks, 1362
Edward W Martin, 492
Arun Mathew, 28
Stephen McClean, 170
Andrew McCormack, 1897
Bill McKee Jr., 846
Marc McMorris, 416
Nihal Mehta, 679
Dr Evan Melrose, 1722
Mark Menell, 1416
Alex Millar, 294
Charles D. Miller, 904
Jeff Monat, 1207
Erik Moore, 229
Michael Morgan, 373
Christina Morin, 846
J. Kenneth Moritz, 1746
Michael B. Morrissey, 1014
Mira Muhtadie, 42
Peter M. Mundheim, 1743
Britton Murdoch, 1568
David Mussafer, 62
Nader Naini, 782
Michael E. Najjar, 546
Vas Natarajan, 28

Anne Bovaird Nevins, 1441
Robert Newbold, 846
James A. O'Donnell, 734
Josh Olshansky, 839
Jason Ostheimer, 60
Frank J Pados Jr, 632
David Pakman, 1916
Adrian Pasricha, 2081
Satya Patel, 941
Bret Pearlman, 659
Thomas A Penn, 1428
Thomas B Pennell, 1429
James N Perry, 1156
Joseph Pesce, 859
Robert W Petit, 1215
Cary Pfeffer MD, 1811
J Peter Pierce, 1446
Barry Porter, 494
Brett L. Prager, 610
David G Proctor, 1234
Mitchell Quain, 42
David B Ragins, 492
Boris Rapoport, 1123
Daniel Raynor, 161
Josh Resnick, 1519
Jon Rezneck, 820
Jason Rhodes, 191
Charles Rim, 626
Gregory A. Robbins, 844
Eric Roberts, 1898
Mark Rosenbaum, 199
Bennett Rosenthal, 159
Howard D Ross, 1136
Adam Rothenberg, 318
Judson Samuels, 926
Jim Sanger, 1640
Martin A. Sarafa, 449
Loren Schlachet, 1572
Ted Schlein, 1075
Adam Schwartz, 127
Scott Schwartz, 489
Brian D. Schwartz, 928
Andrew M. Schwartz, 1111
Jonathan Seiffer, 1109
David Seldin, 133
Aydin Senkut, 720
John Seung, 796
John P Shoemaker, 1234
Brian J Siegel, 891
Anthony Sigel, 2169
Vic Singh, 679
John Sinnerberg, 577
Geoffrey W. Smith, 177
David Stark, 877
Rob Stavis, 260
Keith Stimson, 881
Matt Sullivan, 1423
Adam L Suttin, 1049
Dov Szapiro, 557
Edwin Tan, 401
Dharmesh Thakker, 235
David Tisch, 318
Jason Turowsky, 1009
Bradley Tusk, 1868
Cleve Tzung, 203
Richard J Ulevitch PhD, 12
Marc A Utay, 492
Michael Van Vleck, 853
Roland Van der Meer, 798
Stephanie Von Friedeburg, 1007
David Wassong, 1315
Ellen Weber, 1577
Wayne B Weisman, 1633
Richard Wells, 1000
John D. White, 774
Tyler Wolfram, 1360
Dalton Wright, 1070

1064

Jeffrey Wu, 245
Benjamin W Yarborough, 1209
Tim Young, 679
Guy Zaczepinski, 449
Philip Zaorski, 782
Howard S. Zeprun, 1850
Toby Zhang, 472
Eric Zinterhofer, 2252
Andy Ziolkowski, 570
Ari M. Zur, 348
Charles H van Horne, 18

University of Peshawar
Raja M. Parvez, 1057

University of Phoenix
Chris Cooper, 1425
Gerald A. Michaud, 946
Christie Pitts, 218

University of Pittsburgh
Mel Billingsley PhD, 1117
Joseph P. Campolo, 147
Gerald S Casilli, 1540
Samuel D Colella, 1928
James R. Deitzer, 355
Mark Downs, 1280
Donald W. Grimm, 898
Jay Katarincic, 628
Rich Lunak, 998
Jim Marra, 290
Mark G Miller, 1194
J. Kenneth Moritz, 1746
David Motley, 298
Peter J Muth, 1746
Mark G Papa, 1573
Dennis G Prado, 1159
Jonathan Pressnell, 290
Ned J Renzi, 272
John Richardson, 1280
Stephen G Robinson, 1447
Ralph Schlosstein, 699
Thomas Sipp, 1635
Kelly Szejko, 3275
John Tippins, 1746
Anthony L Tomasello, 987
Ryan Walsh, 751

University of Pittsburgh, School of Law
Michael Beauregard, 960

University of Portsmouth
Larry Y. Liu, 2128

University of Pretoria
Thomas de Jager, 118

University of Prince Edward Island
Alex MacBeath, 2164

University of Puget Sound
Robert T. Nelsen, 153

University of Pune
Jana Vazé, 1341

University of Quebec
Anne-Marie Bourgeois, 676
Gaétan Morin, 2120

University of Queensland
Ilfryn Carstair, 1907
Bob Christiansen, 1711
Peter Nicholson, 1548

University of Reading
Lorraine Audsley, 2112
Paul A. Colone, 77

University of Redlands
Lou Gerken, 822
Carolyn Ticknor, 990

University of Regina
Harold Huber, 2167
Franklin Jiang, 2229
Dean Popil, 2173

University of Rhode Island
Michael Ashton, 21
Dave Barrett, 1460
Paul Caliento, 503
James S Gladney, 1114
Richard J Harrington, 567
David Martirano, 1459
Morgan Pahxia, 1464
Matt Pierson, 3
Nina Saberi, 422
Brian St. Jean, 21
John S Struck, 1955

University of Richmond
John Borchers, 555
Jeffrey Craver, 61
Clark F. Davis, 1562
Neil Q. Gabriele, 299
Mary Gay, 168
Kyle Grace, 897
Thomas B. Hoyt, 984
Christopher Lawler, 846
Bradley C O'Dell, 1492
William Powell, 2067
Paul B Queally, 1972
David E Thomas Jr, 1526
Andrew Tichenor, 288
Michael Walden, 1550
Michael Walrath, 1980

University of Rochester
Chris Baldwin, 455
Robert W. Bruml, 355
Sach Chitnis, 1046
George Doomany, 123
David Drahms, 1387
Jim Dugan, 1364
Jeff Fagnan, 38
Karen Greene, 53
Bruce Greenwald, 65
Abigail Hunter-Syed, 1101
Gregg E. Johnson, 263
Lou Lange, MD, PhD, 181
Rohit Makharia, 817
Richard E Maybaum, 1134
John Moore, 193
Brennan Mulcahey, 349
Dennis O'Brien, 1131
Steven F. Piaker, 434
Murray E Rudin, 1575
Dr. N. Darius Sankey, 2021
Neil S. Suslak, 322
Jeffrey J Teschke, 1049
Avie Tevanian, 659
Tom Uhlman, 1305
Robert A. Vigoda, 426
Nicole Vitullo, 621
Ralph R. Whitney Jr., 900

University of Salford
Karimah Es Sabar, 2229

University of San Diego
Glenn Argenbright, 1507

Sean Banks, 1863
Greg Bettinelli, 1888
Kevin R Green, 1854
Shelley Lyford, 1973
Jason Stein, 1820
Brent Weinstein, 1883

University of San Francisco
Kirby Bartlett, 45
Jackie Berterretche, 852
David Brewer, 145
Alexander Fries, 650
Bill Li, 1951
Mark E. Pearson, 130
Lip-Bu Tan, 1951
Aaron White, 1939
J. Alberto Yepez, 1850

University of Santa Clara
Brent Jones, 1341
Dennis D Ryan, 762
Nancy Schoendorf, 1247

University of Saskatchewan
Warren Bergen, 2048
Ryan Crawford, 2166
Aki Georgacacos, 2049
Michael Hoffort, 2114
Harold Huber, 2167
Brent G. Hughes, 2091
Steven Leakos, 2049
E. Craig Lothian, 2173
Mick MacBean, 2275
Dion Madsen, 1438
Mark Poelzer, 2038
Richard Prytula, 2263
Tyler Stuart, 2140
Todd Tessier, 2278
Keith Van Apeldoorn, 2258

University of Scranton
James Caccavo, 1741
Eugene Galantini, 1640
Howard Kaufman, 1638
Thomas G Rebar, 1633

University of Sheffield
David Q. Anderson, 118
Howard Mayson, 2050
Andy McLoughlin, 1879

University of Sherbrooke
Sophie Forest, 2066
Pierre FréChette, 1590
Charles Sirois, 2261
Pascal Tremblay, 2206

University of Singapore
Jenny Hsui, 473

University of South Alabama
Sonja J. Keeton, 904

University of South Carolina
Jeremy Bauman, 1304
Nilanana Bhowmik, 534
Frank X Dalton, 537
Frank X Dalton, 794
David M Faris, 1606
Martin P. Gilmore, 746
Chris Heivly, 192
Mark Rostick, 1004
R Patrick Weston CFA, 213

University of South Dakota
Sandy Horst, 297
Steve Kirby, 297

College/University Index / University of South Florida

Nikole Mulder, 297
Dave O'Hara, 173
Susan Simko, 1470

University of South Florida
Richard M. Ferrari, 598
Stephen M. Krupa, 1498
Tyler Lasher, 1510
Christian Lassonde, 2151
Michael A. Novielli, 638
Josh Richardson, 1143
Steven D Singleton, 1261
Joe Volpe, 1205

University of Southampton
Charles Haythornthwaite, 2078
Philip Roeper, 1272

University of Southern California
Amir Akhavan, 1033
David Aronoff, 754
B Marc Averitt, 1371
Eric Baroyan, 109
Brian Begert, 2292
Marc Benioff, 1607
Nilanjana Bhowmik, 1146
David Bohnett, 228
Richard Brekka, 1640
James W. Brush, MD, 782
Alan Chen, 374
Brian Chiang, 1951
Jai Choi, 1416
Dr Ronald Chwang, 970
Everett Cox, 665
William M. Custer, 571
Feng Deng, 1340
Patrick J Duffy, 1276
Leonard C Ferrington, 1752
Brian Flucht, 278
Gregory J Forrest, 765
Jeff Fox, 908
Kris Fredrickson, 509
Tammy Funasaki, 331
Thomas O Gephart, 1918
Randy Glein, 609
Randy Glein, 1668
David Glickman, 1545
Michael F. Gooch, 902
Lloyd Greif, 869
Craig Gunther, 278
Desmond Henry, 1856
William Hopkins, 1368
Greg Howorth, 374
Henry Huey, 171
Jerry Ilhuyn Cho, 690
Martin Irani, 902
W. Jack Kessler Jr., 494
Jeff Klemens, 1602
Brian Knitt, 467
David Lane, 613
David Lane, 1378
Huan Le, 951
J Christopher Lewis, 1575
Jerry Lotter, 664
Jeffrey D Lovell, 1147
Christopher Lucas, 275
Peter Macdonald, 274
Adrian Mendoza, 1201
Janis Naeve, PhD, 112
Preetish Nijhawan, 454
Eric Pakravan, 120
Kristopher Prakash, 1369
Grant Pritchard, 1976
William Quigley, 502
Stephen P. Rader, 494
Susie Roos, 820
James Shen, 1509

Mary Ann Sigler, 1451
Rick Slaughter, 1756
William Starling, 1772
Sean Stiefel, 1283
Timothy P Sullivan, 1156
Pocket Sun, 1701
Rob Ukropina, 275
Samit Varma, 132
Joshua S. Weinstein, 403
Brent Weinstein, 1883
William Woodward, 132
Simon Yu, 391
Adam Zacuto, 449

University of Southern Illinois
Kevin Swan, 1961

University of Southern Indiana
Mark Hollis, 443

University of Southern Maine
Michael Marocco, 1617

University of Southern Mississippi
Shane McCarthy, CPA, 678

University of St. Andrews
Christopher J Mairs, 1105

University of St. Cyril
Sonja Markova, MBA, 226

University of St. Francis
Mike Bryant, 1078

University of St. Gallen
Markus Moor, 2106
Mathias Schilling, 641
Kyle Winters, 2201

University of St. Thomas
Jason T. Brass, 843
Michael Eisinger, 2214
Chuck Gorman, 464
Stephanie McCoy, 1522
Constance Paiement, 738
Steve Polski, 1131
James W Rikkers, 1719
Steve Schwen, 1725
Dave Stassen, 1725
Ann Winblad, 956
Ann Winblad, 956

University of Stirling
James B. Walker, 554

University of Sussex
Mark T Lupa PhD, 930
David R Skok, 1181

University of Sydney
Ian Bund, 1455
Amber Caska, 1370
Ash Fontana, 2019
David Scaysbrook, 1517

University of Tennessee
Jim Baker, 1569
Mike Brookshire, 1569
Joe Cook Jr, 1261
Vinse Davidson, 1783
Joelle Fox, 677
Wilma Jordan, 1033
Dell Larcen, 881
Blake Lewis, 1569
Akhil Saklecha, 174
Christy Shaffer PhD, 915

Burton B Weil, 1919

University of Texas
Farraz Abassi, 443
Wilson Allen, 1976
Jorge Amador, 109
Jay I Applebaum, 1997
Glenn W. Askew, 328
Cliff Atherton Jr., 888
Charles W Beckman, 955
Stephen A Bennett, 1745
Jeffery P. Blanchard, 734
Craig A. Bondy, 884
Larry Bradshaw, 695
Daryl B Brown, 637
Duncan Butler, 441
Philip A. Canfield, 884
Chris G. Carter, 1326
Mike Chambers, 363
Stephen S. Coats, 1573
Ross Cockrell, 695
Scott Collier, 1855
Keith L. Crandell, 153
Lucas T. Cutler, 328
Jon D'Andrea, 1976
Jason M. DeLorenzo, 672
Bowen S. Diehl, 403
Victoria Dominguez-Edington, 445
David Druley, 379
Sean Ebert, 98
Randy Eisenman, 1622
Michael J. Fourticq Sr., 902
Jeff S. Fronterhouse, 328
Matt Fuller, 820
Rudy Garza, 804
Brenda D Gavin, 1508
Scott Gibaratz, 917
Aziz Gilani, 1206
Patrick Hamner, 1422
Joseph L Harberg, 1549
Thomas M. Hargrove, 888
Charles Ho, 41
David Hull, 441
Mark Jennings, 818
Nagraj Kashyap, 1154
Jonathan Kaskow, 291
Charles R Kaye, 1956
Douglas M. Kelley, 403
Bill Kennedy, 804
Laura J Kilcrease, 1855
N. John Lancaster, Jr., 1573
Huan Le, 951
John L Long Jr, 1841
Murray McCabe, 300
Richard McClain, 932
Kip McClanahan, 1685
Dr Robert McDonald, 1722
David McWhorter, 425
Jake Moilanen, 1655
David Moross, 717
Rocky Mountain, 594
Robert Newbold, 846
Ron Nixon, 425
Jonathan Pearce, 291
Charlie Plauche, 1597
J. Leighton Read, MD, 87, 326
Gary D. Reaves, 740
Scott Rogan, 675
Ryan Sanders, 1204
Tony Schell, 695
Dwight Scott, 277
Mike Sherman, 1187
Jason Shideler, 1156
Brooks Shugharts, 740
Jonathan K. Shulkin, 1902
Kevin Spain, 665
Bryan Stolle, 1985

Douglas E. Swanson Jr., 672
Dharmesh Thakker, 235
Ned Truslow, 1557
Elias "Lee" Urbina, 594
Frank Z Wei, 1956
Eric Weiner, 291
Brent Williams, 894
Leo de Luna, 1154

University of Texas Health Science
Tony Di Bona, 87
Kendall Mohler, PhD, 31

University of Texas School of Law
M. Scott Jones, 893
John White, 1273

University of Texas Southwestern
Casey Cunningham, MD, 1619

University of Texas, Arlington
Paul A Yeoham, 1484

University of Texas, Austin
Jim Armstrong, 502
Mark Austin, 1976
Jeff Baker, 702
Forest Baskett, 1297
Alan J. Blackburn, 888
Matthew Bryant, 557
Arjun Chopra, 751
Rob Cohen, 1020
Vinse Davidson, 1783
Lister Delgado, 971
Michael J. Fourticq Jr., 902
Chase Fraser, 781
James O. Futterknecht Jr., 900
Brad Gurasich, 425
Matt Hawkins, 557
Dr. Steve Herrod, 816
Bob Inman, 1126
Tom Inman, 1126
Brian Jolly, 957
J. Chris Jones, 893
Stephanie Kreml MD, 241
Colt Leudde, 888
Clark Lipscomb, 542
Brian J. Lobo, 888
Christopher Manning, 1851
Roger Marrero, 528
Jim McBride, 291
J.D. McCulloch, 514
Yatin Mundkur, 174
Matthew J. Nordgren, 151
Robert Norris, 425
Ryan Pollock, 1020
Philip Sanger MD, 1801
Bruce W Schnitzer, 1955
Michael T Segrest, 1682
Joel Serface, 253
Cynthia S Sheridan, 241
Ryan Shulz, 702
Thomas J Stephenson, 1924
Bryan Stolle, 1247
Paul Thurk, 153
Robert Vargo, 2227
Krishnan Varier, 151
Kenneth G. Walter Jr., 902
James Yang, 14

University of Texas, Dallas
Chuck Butler, 1408
Timothy P Fay, 1636
Arlan Harris, 1244
Vik Thapar, 576

University of Tokyo
Masazumi Ishii, 214
Kenichi Kimura, 1241
Kazunori Maruyama, PhD, 182
Takeshi Mori, 837

University of Toledo
Carmen Evola, 276
Roger Goddu, 334
Edward Kinsey, 1073
H Randall Litten, 348
John W. Snow, 451
Bryan J. Toth, 759

University of Toronto
Bert Amato, 2137
Chris Anastasopoulos, 2102
James Appleyard, 2125
Robin Axon, 2182
Rajiv Bakshi, 2183
Imran Bashir, 2113
Jeff Belford, 2275
Brent Belzberg, 2261
Brent Belzberg, 2272
Jason Berenstein, 2099
Simon Boag, 981
Brad Bolzon, 1928
Jake Cassaday, 2236
George H. Cholakis, 2030
Allan Crosbie, 2089
Gurion De Zwirek, 2254
Michael Dixon, 2270
Roman S. Dubczak, 2079
Paul Eldridge, 2126
Chris Erickson, 2213
Gavin Foo, 2204
Lorne Gertner, 2148
Karim Gillani, 2179
Newton Glassman, 2073
Harry Goldgut, 2067
Alan Greenberg, 2142
Barclay W. Hambrook, 2039
Patrick W.A. Handreke, 2255
Andrew Haughian, 2213
Michael Hollend, 2272
Byron Horner, 2085
Sasha Jacob, 2075
Wiz Khayat, 2246
David Kornacki, 3258
Mona Kung, 2138
Matthew B. Kunica, 2062
Anthony Lacavera, 2134
René Lajous, 378
Steve Lau, 2288
Matthew Leibowitz, 2224
Simon Lockie, 2134
Luc Marengere, 2276
Mohan Markandaier, 2138
Barry Markowsky, 2152
Loudon Mclean Owen, 2199
Arda M Minocherhomjee, 468
Salil Munjal, 2291
Raj Natarajan, 2026
Richard Nathan, 2167
Rob Normandeau, 2251
Loudon Owen, 2154
Gilbert S. Palter, 2103
Larry Porcellato, 289
Michael Powell, 1698
Jim Probert, 2082
Prathna Ramesh, 2184
Tom Rand, 2041
Craig Rankine, 2272
Scott Requadt, 495
Paul Richardson, 2238
James Riley, 2073
Jamie Rosenblatt, 2137
Jeffrey Rosenthal, 2150
Michael Sabia, 2069
Michael J. Salamon, 2062
Jody Schnarr, 2117
Sachin Shah, 2067
Ameet Shah, 2137
Brad Silverberg, 974
Daniel Sonshine, 2272
Greg Stewart, 2141
Jim Taylor, 2049
Shermaine Tilley, 2092
Angela Tran, 2280
Dan Tsubouchi, 2246
Gregory G. Turnbull, 2074
Erol Uzumeri, 2252
Tomas Valis, 2076
Craig Wallace, 2131
Stuart Waugh, 2204
Bruce Yang, 2193
M. Junaid Zia, 2089

University of Toulouse
Pierre Lamond, 648

University of Tsukuba
Shunichiro Matsumoto, PhD, 182

University of Tulsa
Julian L Carr, 244
Kyle Largent, 828

University of Twente
Menno Derks, 2248
Alain le Loux, 549

University of Ulm Medical School
Eckard Weber, MD, 621

University of Ulster
Ruairi Grant, 1315

University of Utah
Paul Arnold, 1768
Michael Ballard, 145
José Blanco, 573
Peter Bodine, 84
Chris Cooper, 1425
Frank M. Creer, 2021
Kamran Elahian, 833
Doug Folsom, 9
Matthew N Garff, 1753
Bob Gay, 959
Paul Goodrich, 1158
Steve Grizzell, 999
J. Blair Jenkins, 462
Len Jordan, 1158
Sid Krommenhoek, 79
Luke Mau, 225
Christopher S Meldrum, 840
Brad Money, 869
John Neis, 1921
Jonathan M Ruga, 1652
Lance Ruud, 639
Alex Soffe, 1070
Todd Stevens, 1542
Ned Stringham, 9
Pete Thomas, 183
Matthew Van Alstyne, 1367
Troy Wardrop, 9
Greg Warnock, 1204
Henry Wong, 612
Henry Wong, 807
Dalton Wright, 1070
Scott F Young, 1652

University of Vermont
David Aronoff, 754

1067

College/University Index / University of Victoria

Eric Berke, 2272
Theodore D. Burke, 156
Robert Cioffi, 80
Jackson Craig, 239
Timothy C Davis, 786
Charles A. Davis, 1743
Robb Doub, 1299
Konstantine Drakonakis, 1097
Sarah Fay, 829
Bruce M. Hernandez, 1724
Amy S Lazarus, 1726
Jeffrey T Newton, 812
Evan Nisselson, 1101
David Pann, 1378
Andrew C. Romans, 1595
Joseph Scharfenberger, 433
Todd Warden, 907
Steve Wood, 835
Caroline L. Young, 900

University of Victoria
Steve Romanyshyn, 2211
Kalen Stewart, 2277

University of Virginia
Lee Ainslie, 1182
Amir Akhavan, 1033
Frank Angella, 879
Martha P.E. Arscott, 524
Robert M Austin, 985
Mike Avon, 22
Tiki Barber, 878
Melissa Barry, 926
Kent Bennett, 260
Douglas Berman, 928
A.G.W. Biddle III, 1348
Wes Blackwell, 1632
Jonathan B. Blanco, 746
John Bolduc, 239
Gerry Brunk, 2180
Lee Buck, 286
Lee Buck, 1096
Frank K Bynum, Jr, 1062
Thomas A. Carver, 910
Gregory W. Cashman, 844
John H Chadwick, 493
Miles Clements, 28
Phil Clough, 22
C Taylor Cole Jr, 910
Elizabeth Colonna, 918
Robert Coneybeer, 1663
Paul Conley, 1400
John Connaughton, 220
James J Connors II, 1062
Jim Conroy, 1372
Mike Crothers, 702
Roanne Daniels, 924
Terry Daniels, 1505
Thompson Dean, 209
Christopher Delaney, 1023
Douglas Diamond, 693
Michael F. Donoghue, 1727
Steve Dutton, 1062
David A. Eagle, 357
Jonathan Ebinger, 296
Tom Eddy, 1027
S. Whitfield Edwards, 746
David Eichler, 1498
Michael G. Eliasek, 1491
Chad Ellis, 42
Jeffrey W Ferguson, 413
Andy Fligel, 1004
Jason Gabriel, 1774
David Gladstone, 828
Tom Glanville, 696
John W. Glynn, 836
Jacqueline Glynn, 836

Michael B Goldberg, 1062
Wesley Gottesman, 325
Andrew Grapkowski, 101
Bruns Grayson, 23
Kirk B Griswold, 164
Kevin T. Hammond, 1039
Dennis Henner, PhD, 495
George J Henry, 1127
Tom Hickey, 1505
Paul Holland, 770
Thomas B. Hoyt, 984
William L Hudson, 1331
Charles B Hughes III, 644
Scott Irwin, 1540
Gregg E. Johnson, 263
Thad Jones, 1505
David Jones, 1710
Teddy Kaplan, 1301
Bruce Karsh, 1362
Andrew Kau, 1951
Sean M. Kelley, 873
Matt Kelly, 3266
Robert Kibble, 1239
Trevor Kienzle, 544
Randal J. Kirk, 1812
Randal Klein, 208
Jason Krikorian, 596
Doug Kuribayashi, 1474
Chris Lanning, 815
Mitch Lasky, 248
Anton Levy, 815
Peter Lipson, 909
C. Malcolm Little, 166
Gene Lockhart, 1240
Frank J Loverro, 1062
John G Loverro, 1112
Laura L. Lukaczyk, 207
David M Maher, 352
Brendan Mathews, 1259
George McCabe, 910
Glenn McGonnigle, 1788
Chris McKay, 852
Anand Mehra, 1698
Sandy Miller, 1001
Church M Moore, 1062
Christina Morin, 846
David Moszer, 1491
James B Murray Jr, 551
A. Bilal Noor, 166
Christopher B. Norton, 405
Jacqueline Novogratz, 55
Cody Nystrom, 1689
Julie Ocko, 909
William Ogden, 1881
Michael J Orend, 1575
Tim R. Palmer, 456
Shaneel D. Patel, 1037
Robert Paull, 1151
Peter S Pettit, 1270
Kurt Pilecki, 274
Robert Pollak, 1761
John Powell, 1003
Brian Powers, 924
Alex Radcliffe, 406
Ramesh Radhakrishnan, 174
Matt Rice, 224
Josh Richardson, 1143
Tom Robertshaw, 1022
Steven C Rodger, 691
Arthur C. Roselle, 1409
Frank Rotman, 1502
Brent T Sacha, 1745
Andrew Salenbier, 37
Judson Samuels, 926
Michael Schattner, 1377
Barbara Schilberg, 266
Andrew Schwab, 737

Thomas A Scully, 1972
Peter Seidler, 1645
Timothy D Sheehan, 244
Walker C. Simmons, 1409
Bradley E. Singer, 1903
John W. Snow, 451
James Socas, 1886
Esteban Sosnik, 1527
Kristin Steen, 433
Paul Straub, 491
James N. Strawbridge, 2007
Richard D Tadler, 1776
William B. Thompson, 780
David Tolmie, 654
Mary Traer CPA, 909
John Tullis, 1866
James Tybur, 1431
Robbert Vorhoff, 815
Bonnie K Wachtel, 1948
Robert Wadsworth, 909
Ted Wang, 552
Scott Warren, 1234
Alexander D Whittemore, 1752
Russ Williams, 16
Greg Williams, 29
Aaron P Wolfe, 1753
Caroline L. Young, 900

University of Virginia Law School
Timothy P Agnew, 1175
Jon Flint, 1460
Van Zandt Hawn, 843
Gordon R Penman, 1920

University of Wales
Roger Maggs, 2076
Terry Matthews, 2284
Stu Phillips, 238

University of Warwick
Gautam Banerjee, 277
Ian A.W. Howes, 31
Roger Maggs, 2076
Shahzad Pirvani, 2022

University of Washington
Steve Anderson, 231
David L. Belzer, 1491
EJ Blanchfield, 1458
Brad Bodden, 2001
David Bonderman, 1835
William J Canestaro, 2008
Matt Clary, 1963
Bryan Cressey, 558
Neal Dempsey, 238
Noel de Turenne, 1250
Derek Eve, 673
Nathan R. Every, MD, MPH, 782
Clinton Foy, 561
Alan D. Frazier, 782
Kevin Gabelein, 753
Brad Gillespie, 965
Tom Gonser, 1656
Nick Hanauer, 1641
Scott Hardman, 82
Kirk Holland, 36
Chris Howard, 974
Simon James, 695
Kent Johnson, 82
Brendan Kennedy, 1481
Bob Kocher MD, 1916
David A Krekel, 1398
James LoGerfo, 643
Wendy Lung, 967
Elliot Maluth, 928
Alex Mason, 416
Pete McCormick, 1183

College/University Index / University of the Pacific

Geoffrey Moore, 1247
Geoffrey Moore, 1985
Elliot Parks, 898
Mike Pongon, 1458
Michael H. Reynoldson, 1016
Johnathan Roberts, 974
Joseph L. Schocken, 346
Stewart Schuster, 1354
Dana Settle, 871
Steven Stull, 61
Paulette Taylor, 1616
Mike Templeman, 887
Victoria Treyger, 720
Dino Vendetti, 764
Dino Vendetti, 1656
Katherine Watts, 1712
Denny Weston, 753
Melissa Widner, 1637
Jen Wolf, 991

University of Waterloo
Andrew Abouchar, 2262
Steve Balaban, 2193
Michael Brandt, 2197
Bharat Choudhary, 2287
Patrick Chung, 2254
Bonnie Foley-Wong, 2223
Devon Galloway, 2127
Devon Galloway, 2127
Karim Gillani, 2179
Paul Godman, 2032
Chris Govan, 2209
Duncan Hill, 2182
Daryl Hodges, 2037
Randall Howard, 2279
Tim Jackson, 2262
Arif Janmohamed, 1121
Ken Kember, 2112
Kevin Kimsa, 2249
Larry LaKing, 2187
Mike Lazaridis, 2228
Vernon Lobo, 2198
Lisa Low, 2087
A.J. (Sandy) Marshall, 2061
Mike McCauley, 2127
Kevin Negus, 385
Karamdeep Nijjar, 2157
Chamath Palihapitiya, 1696
Anu Pathria, 544
Tom Rand, 2041
Rob Richards, 2224
Neil Sadraraganey, 620
Ray Simonson, 2279
Kuljeev Singh, 2149
George So, 2158
George So, 2165
Andrea Sotak, 2102
Chris Taves, 2063
James Wei, 2007

University of West Florida
Tom Robertshaw, 1022

University of Western Australia
Mason Hills, 1548
James McClements, 1548
Ben Yu, 1670

University of Western Ontario
David Adderley, 2076
Christopher J Albinson, 1410
Geoff Beattie, 2236
Brian Boulanger, 2040
Richard Bradlow, 2219
Laurel C. Broten, 2205
Andrew Carragher, 639
Roger Chabra, 2239

Dave Chapman, 2292
Aubrey Dan, 2094
Christopher Darby, 979
Carey Diamond, 2288
Shayn Diamond, 2288
John Eckert, 2199
Ron Farmer, 2198
Wade Flemons, 2218
Rob Gavin, 2289
Craig Golinowski, 2166
Jordan Goodman, 2045
Bruce Hodge, 2218
Michael Hollend, 2272
Wally Hunter, 676
Wiz Khayat, 2246
Larry LaKing, 2187
Christian Lassonde, 2151
David Lawee, 578
Jeff Lucassen, 2204
Dale MacMaster, 2033
Stephen O. Marshall, 2103
Murray McCaig, 2041
Michael McGee, 2049
Doug McGregor, 2231
Robert S. McLeese, 2030
John McMullen, 2174
Marcus Mitchell, 2065
Minhas Mohamed, 2196
Jim Nieuwenburg, 2050
Karamdeep Nijjar, 2157
Rob Normandeau, 2251
Jeff Parr, 2081
Richard Prytula, 2263
John Richardson, 2058
David Roff, 2134
Jamie Rosenblatt, 2137
Gary Rubinoff, 2259
Peter Samson, 2163
Russell Samuels, 2288
Peter Schwartz, 2172
Alan G. Sellery, 2163
Allison M. Taylor, 2162
Robert Trudeau, 1785
Douglas B. Trussler, 274
Jeff Wigle, 2051

University of Westminster
Adam Kalish, 1151

University of Windsor
Doug Fregin, 2228
James C. Johnson, 2255
Matthew J. Lori, 1301
Jeff Lucassen, 2204
Tristan Velez, 926

University of Wisconsin
Andrew B Albert, 1765
David J. Anderson, 461
Lawrence S. Atinsky, 177
Robert M Belke, 1147
Ryan Bennett, 1548
Darren Brathol, 1719
Scott Button, 1921
Brian F. Chambers, 1409
Jerome A Chazen, 460
Mark Flower, 1963
Jason Gerlach, 1756
Eric M Gordon, 1691
Adam S. Gruber, 686
Christopher J. Hadley, 254
John A. Hatherly, 2009
Eric Hender, 17
Alex Kelsey, 1960
Steven D Kloos PhD, 1859
Steve LaPorte, 1378
Laura L. Lukaczyk, 207

Steve McConahey, 1020
Steve Mech, 566
John Neis, 1921
John R Nelson, 1664
Maria Palma, 1593
Timothy Petersen, 149
Margaret Riley, 1911
George Roberts, 1380
Arthur Schneiderman, 833
David R. Schroder, 17, 1016
Ronald J. Shebuski, PhD, 139
Sarah Smith, 221
Michael Steinberg, 1528
Paul A Stone JD, 12
John Streur, 376
John H. Underwood, 1435
Ryan Waddington, 961
David L. Warnock, 383
Michael Yanney, 71

University of Wisconsin, Eau Claire
Chad W Souvignier, 1543

University of Wisconsin, Madison
Andy Boszhardt, 858
Thomas F Campion, 1209
Robert DeBruin, 1292
Christopher Erickson, 1820
David Gitter, 1292
Charlie Goff, 1292
Saar Gur, 455
Kent C Haeger, 932
Mark A. Hoffmeister, 1497
Stuart Holden, MD, 1490
Joseph R Katcha, 932
Tyler Matlock, 1767
Bernard Moon, 1716
Judy M. Owen, 375
John Philosophos, 858
Andrew Sandler, 1617
Toni F. Sikes, 375
Tom Smith, 1171
Vipul B. Soni, 357
Varsha Tagare, 1509
Roy Thiele-Sardina, 933
Terrence R Wall, 583
Linda Watchmaker, 536
Paul Weiss, 1921
Leon R Wilkosz, 583
Lei Yang PhD, 1340

University of Wisconsin, Oshkosh
Charlie Goff, 1292
Steve Predayna, 1292

University of Witwatersrand
Michael H. Beaumont, 985
Grant Behrman, 245
Spencer Fleischer, 787
Sven M Jacobson, 662
David S Lobel, 1651
Caroline Popper MD MPH, 241
John L. Teeger, 774

University of Wyoming
Frank Mendicino II, 36

University of York
Nick Morriss, 834

University of Zagreb
Kresimir Letinic MD PhD, 644
Dr. Boris Nikolic, 268

University of the Pacific
James Beck, 1184
Rick Blume, 703

1069

College/University Index / University of the South

Paul Matteucci, 1896

University of the South
David Beecken, 244
Charles M. Hall, PhD, 139
W Scott Miller, 1148

University Panthéon Assas
Karen Noel, 1416

Uppsala University
Goran Ando, MD, 697
Kristina Williams, 2032

Utah State University
José Blanco, 573
Ryan Hemingway, 688
L John Wilkerson, 806

Valdosta State University
Thomas M Tarnowski, 1752

Valparaiso University
Steven W. Parks, 1093
Ben A Schnakenberg, 931

Vanderbilt Law School
Mark L Feidler, 1270
Stacy Feld, 1042
Stacy Feld, 1438

Vanderbilt School of Engineering
Brian Harrison, 1466

Vanderbilt University
Charles E Adair, 537
Jeff Barry, 1455
Michael Berolzheimer, 243
Erik W. Bloom, 838
Charles Booker, 61
Dennis C Bottorff, 550
Brandon B. Boze, 1903
Andrew Byrd, 1870
Andrew Byrd, Jr., 1870
Mark H Carter, 1776
Mike Collett, 1489
McCall Cravens, 957
Bowen S. Diehl, 403
James Dimitri, 1925
Yizhen Dong, 4
Craig Driscoll, 935
Ted Fourticq, 902
Diane Fraiman, 1945
Bryan C. Frederickson, 888
Neil Q. Gabriele, 299
John Gaffney, 363
Katie H Gambill, 550
David S. Gorton, 1777
Gregory T Hebrank MD, 1098
Patrick Hendy, 515
Chris Hollod, 15
Rick Holton Jr., 569
Justin Ishbia, 1667
Adam Jackson, 772
Dave Johnson, 1004
Mark Jones, 1569
Stephen A. Lasher, 888
Joshua M. Levinson, 844
Spence McCelland, 1331
Patrick K. McGee, 328
Marc McManus, 489
Robert McMullan, 277
J Carter McNabb, 1571
Eben S Moulton, 1636
Ian J Mount, 1277
Thiago Olson, 677
R Wilson Orr III, 1732

Ross Perot, Jr., 1433
F. Matthew Petronzio, 1871
Joshua S. Phillips, 426
Jay Radtke, 1171
Jon Rattner, 192
Wendell Reilly, 1423
Andrew Roche, 489
Ian Rountree, 395
Erik A. Scott, 1403
Conner Searcy, 1856
John W Shearburn, 1956
Dave Stevenson, 1205
David Stinnett, 1856
Tim Storer, 9
C Morris Stout, 1767
William Timmerman III, 846
Andrew B. Tindel, 1409
John Tippins, 1746
Andrew A. Tisdale, 1496
William Tomai, 447
Rurik G Vandevenne, 1571
John Vincent, 1554
Ben Wallace, 213
Burton B Weil, 1919
Patrick F Whelan, 1424
Jay Wilkins, 914
Hunter Witherington, 1732
James D Witherington Jr, 1732
Robert Womsley, 1961
Mark Wright, 287
J.D. Wright, 489
Darell E Zink Jr, 409

Vassar College
Timothy P Agnew, 1175
Stuart Barkoff, 834
Caterina Fake, 2014
Ari Fine Glantz, 3273
Jeffrey Goldstein, 924
Frederick H Hager, 1163
Michael A.G. Korengold, 678
Kyle Lefkoff, 315
Paul Lehman, 1022
Mitch Truwit, 135
Hunter Walk, 941

Villanova University
Daniel H Bathon Jr, 1994
Matthew M. Bennett, 1301
Steve Berman, 161
Joseph P. Campolo, 147
Matthew A Cook, 1071
Steven DeCillis II, 64
Gary R DiLella, 1494
Chris Fralic, 741
Christopher G Hanssens, 698
Joseph Heinmiller, 846
Gerald Holtz, 1494
Thomas Iannarone, 277
Donald A Juricic, 1557
Karen Kassouf, 437
Ronald J. Klammer, 1369
George Krautzel, 1240
Marc Lederman, 1317
Pete Lloyd, 1234
John Loftus, 53
James Mahoney, 960
Bernard B Markey, 1281
Paul Mehring, 35
Robert P Moran, 1452
William Nolan, 928
Stephanie Palmeri, 1879
John Park, 410
Steven Peterson, 1843
Philip Siuta, 530
Andrew Souder, 1521
William H Stewart, 1281

Steven Swain, 440
Daniel Terpak, 465
Sean M Traynor, 1972
Christine Vogt, 78
Robert Walsh, 699
Raymond F Weldon, 353

Villanova University School of Law
John Buttrick, 1882
Paul D'Addario, 1402
Anne-Marie Shelley, 39

Virginia Commonwealth University
Marc F Benson, 1227
Brenda Bracken, 855
Casey Jones, 203

Virginia Military Institute
Casey West, 1732

Virginia Polytechnic Institute
David Calhoun, 277
Nelson Chu, 1072
Jonathan Ebinger, 296
Steve Fredrick, 876
Tim Guleri, 1670
John B Higginbotham, 1714
Ashish Kaul, 765
William H. Kucheman, 269
Zach Malone, 628
Charles P McCusker, 1422
Steven C Pierson, 1147
Shrikant Sathe, 1911
Ian Sobieski, PhD, 226
James N. Strawbridge, 2007
Stuart Vyule, 1569
Pete Zippelius, 1109

Virginia State University
William H. Kucheman, 269

Virginia Tech
Dave Armstrong, 770
Raman Khanna, 603

Vrije Universiteit
Wal van Lierop, 2078

Vrije University
Paulus J Ingram, 2248

Vrunel University
Donald O'Shea, 571

W.P. Carey School of Business
Al Foreman, 1864
Kyle Hufford, 227

WHU Otto Beisheim School of Mgmt
Joern Nikolay, 815

WM Penn University
Gordon Roth, 1588

Wabash College
C Bryan Daniels, 1469
James C. Snyder, 900

Wagner College
Steven Leischner, 940

Wake Forest University
Joseph B. Alala III, 405
Kurt E. Bolin, 1743
John Bradley, 1349
Sean Britain, 239
M. Hunt Broyhill, 405

Chris Cathcart, 894
Matthew S Crawford, 1500
Adam B. Dolder, 859
David Dupree, 894
Frederick W. Eubank II, 1409
Thomas P (Todd) Gibbons, 303
R. Scott Glass, Jr., 1409
Todd A Goergen, 1583
Matthew E Gormly III, 1984
Thomas L Greer, 794
G. Thomas Hough, 1417
Chris Julich, 695
Sean M. Kelley, 873
Brian Melton, 1796
Deepa Pakianathan, PhD, 604
George A Parker, 1103
Scott Plumridge, 894
Christopher W Solomon, 1972
Robert M. Stewart, 1727
David I Wahrhaftig, 1062
Ken Wallace III, 986
W Spalding White Jr, 1605
Felix J Wong, 752

Walsh College
David Armstrong, 195

Waseda University
Shinya Imai, 1241
Masa Isono, 602
Tatsuya Kubo, 909
Tak Miyata, 1634

Washburn University
Greg Brenneman, 433
R Clayton Funk, 1195
Ted Roth, 1588

Washington & Jefferson College
David Glickman, 1545
Richard J Ulevitch PhD, 12

Washington & Lee University
Douglas Burns, 551
M Roy Burns, 1776
Brian Castleberry, 290
William D Christ, 1776
Andrew Crawford, 815
Louis Dubuque, 61
Bruce B. Dunnan, 875
David G. Ellison, 97
Rick Essex, 1496
Bob Forlenza, 1728
Blair Garrou, 1206
Michael Harden, 175
Cliff Holekamp, 569
Evan Jaysane-Darr, 1015
Matt Kelly, 3266
John W. McCullough, 904
Noah F. Rhodes III, 859
Lloyd R. Sams, 263
Thomas R Shepherd, 1862
Chris Stevenson, 722
Bennett Thompson, 1086
Thomas R Wall, IV, 1062
Michael Watts, 1128
Matt Yohe, 1266

Washington College
Tim Connor, 1653

Washington College of Law
James Conlon, 358

Washington State University
Roy C. Carriker, PhD, 832
Arjun Gupta, 1793

Ronald S Howell, 2008
Karin Lagerlund, 909
Michael Mayer, 1251
Ted Nark, 1086
John R Nelson, 1664
Bridget Storm, 996
Martin Tan, 152

Washington University
Andrew B Albert, 1765
Stuart Bassin, 1599
Andrew P. Bonanno, 1081
Aaron Bright, 1432
Steve Brotman, 91
Steve Brotman, 1680
Brian Clevinger, 1488
Mike Collett, 1489
Jeff Fox, 908
Sherri Haskell, 388
Jorge Jaramillo, 1386
John Kuelper, 176
Mark Levin, 1811
Philip Lewis, 794
Jim Lim, 867
Lisa Nelson, 1154
Brett A Parr, 399
Teddy Shalon, 1488
Dave Stevenson, 1205
Andrew Sturner, 557
Phyllis Whiteley, 1247
Phyllis Whiteley, 1985

Washington University School of Law
Lee Bailey, 1895
Jonathan Goldstein, 61

Washington University, St. Louis
Len Batterson, 234
Jeffrey Craver, 61
Jeremy Degenhart, 61
Louis Dubuque, 61
Gaurav Garg, 1996
Gabe Greenbaum, 1480
Cliff Holekamp, 569
Quinn Li, 1509
Ted Maidenberg, 1848
Jim McKelvey, 569
Rick Ruffolo, 80
Konrad Salaber, 1990
Ryan Schuler, 176
Nicholas Somers, 1763

Wasthington University, St. Louis
Ezra Mehlman, 918

Wayne State University
Bob Flannery, 1536
Gerald Greenwald, 862
Gabe Karp, 607
Ali Safiedine DPM, 1289
Tom Shehab, 149
Ara Topouzian, 3269

Weatherhead School
Brian Hersman, 1041

Weatherhead School of Management
Karen Hodys, 747
Anthony Nader, 1766

Weber State University
Mark C Masur, 1682
Scott Stenberg, 999

Webster University
Sherri Haskell, 388
Matt Turner, 113

Gijs FJ Van Thiel, 14

Weizmann Institute of Science
Yoni Chiefetz, 1121

Wellesley College
Daria Becker, 1491
Virginia Cargill, 80
Alisa Frederick, 374
Maria Gotsch, 1420
Melissa Guzy, 148
Maia Heymann, 534
Tasha Seitz, 1038
Rudina Seseri, 712
Rudina Seseri, 829

Wenzhou University
Chris Xie, 2271

Wesleyan College
Ted Roth, 1588

Wesleyan University
Gregory M Barr, 1684
Scott Barry, 697
Alex Benik, 235
Brad Burnham, 1882
Charles Cherington, 1009
Stu Dalheim, 376
Stuart Ellman, 1593
Jesse Feldman, 235
Ezra S. Field, 1576
James Frischling, 878
Aaron Gershenberg, 1764
Christopher B Hunt, 1573
Nicholas Iovino, 830
Paul Kusserow, 955
Tom Lavin, 1303
Christian Lawless, 535
Frederick Maynard, 909
Lee M Mitchell, 1814
P Sherrill Neff, 1508
Michael Patterson, 1911
Damon Rawie, 61
Rick Segal, 1551
Frank V. Sica, 1777
Donald Spencer, 1679
Andrew Vogel, 2020
Andy Weissman, 1882
Strauss Zelnick, 2020
TX Zhuo, 728
TX Zhuo, 1055

West Chester University
Jason M Cunningham, 164
Chris Heivly, 192
Steven Hobman, 1317

West Point
James M. Bannantine, 190

West Virginia State University
Joe Spratt, 737

West Virginia University
Patrick A Bond, 1262
John Chambers, 1031
Karen Evans, 1687
Gary Gauba, 574
John K Giannuzzi, 1665
J Rudy Henley, 1262
Jay R. Henry, 1409
Marvin W Ritchie, 1312

Western Illinois University
Robert Nardelli, 667
Dennis Podlesak, 621

1071

College/University Index / Western Kentucky University

Warren Weiss, 770

Western Kentucky University
Thomas C. Fitzgerald, 360
Gen. John M Keane, 1633
Jerry D. Wethington, 1570

Western Maryland College
Steven B. Fader, 190
David I Wahrhaftig, 1062
Jim Zucco, 505

Western Michigan University
Jim Farnsworth, 2050
Tom Kurtz, 1422
Luke Sage, 1424
Eli L. Thomssen, 139

Western New England College
Joelle Marquis, 170

Western New England University
Sean O'Keefe, 1960

Western University
Darrick Geant, 331
Ed Giacomelli, 2089
Dave Harris Kolada, 2142
Ian Macdonell, 2089
Lisa Melchior, 2281
Shay Nulman, 2175
Dale Ponder, 2070
Aaron Serruya, 2254

Western Washington University
Donald J Elmer, 1398

Westminster College
Jeffrey Howard, 1610

Westmont College
Lou Caballero, 274

Wharton
Stephen Chiao, 1769

Wharton Business School
Steve Lau, 2288
Howard Mayson, 2050

Wharton Group
Keval Patel, 928

Wharton School
Todd M. Abbrecht, 1815
Mike Ackrell, 44
Dr Philippe H Adam, 186
Deepak Advani, 924
Sandip Agarwala, 1143
Rahul Aggarwal, 334
Daniel Agroskin, 1039
Zaid F Alsikafi, 1156
Robert Amen, 1910
Jim Andelman, 306
Jim Andelman, 1566
James G Andersen, 503
Ryan Anderson, 433
Izhar Armony, 455
Keith Bank, 1056
Keith Bank, 1057
James M. Bannantine, 190
Jason S Barg, 1147
Phin Barnes, 741
John M Baumer, 1109
Josh Baumgarten, 127
Charles Beeler, 1522
Grant Behrman, 245

Michael A Bell, 1248
Michael A. Bell, 1815
Steven T. Berg, 421
Thomas A Berglund, 733
Brian S. Berkin, 1777
Douglas Berman, 928
Robert A Bernstein, 1105
Michael Bevan, 657
Nikhil J. Bhat, 1931
James G Binch, 1127
Charles Birnbaum, 260
Anders Bjork, 21
Darren M Black, 1752
Alan J. Blackburn, 888
Erik W. Bloom, 838
Michael E Bogucki, 1163
Kurt E. Bolin, 1743
Anne Bovaird Nevins, 1441
Henry J. Boye, 1815
Sam Brasch, 1052
Adam Breslin, 2219
Steven Bressler, 1417
Peter L. Briger Jr., 767
David Britts, 798
Philip L. Bronner, 1348
Mark Brooks, 1626
Kenneth Brotman, 46
Robert E Brown Jr., 1275
David M Browne, 1168
Robert W. Bruml, 355
Mike Brunell, 1369
Frank W. Bruno, 451
Thomas A. Burger Jr., 873
Steve Burns, 1505
Tara Butler, MD, 176
William F Case Jr, 503
A Baron Cass III, 364
John H Chadwick, 493
Nicolas Chaudron, 2851
Roger Chen, 1685
Ray Cheng, 1235
Brian Cherry, 1360
Kyce Chihi, 193
Iris Choi, 751
Jonathan Y Chou, 698
T.C. Chou, 905
Yee-Ping Chu, 274
John Clarke, 410
Lisa Coca, 809
Josh Cohen, 839
Michael Cohen, 1369
Robert Coneybeer, 1663
Richard Conklin, 732
Stephen B. Connor, 899
Schuyler Coppedge, 675
David C. Coquillette, 1301
James Corl, 1679
Anthony Corriggio, 1679
John Cozzi, 64
Sean L. Cunningham, 884
Rajeev Dadoo, 1731
Nicholas Daraviras, 1032
Ken DeAngelis, 202
Michael B. DeFlorio, 914
Dain F DeGroff, 1846
Michael DeRosa, 657
John Dean, 939
Feng Deng, 1340
Karl D Dillon, 940
Jeffrey G. Dishner, 1739
Michael Dolbac, 809
Alex Doll, 1794
Edith Dorsen, 2003
Greg Dracon, 2
David Drahms, 1387
Steven M Dresner, 629
Russell S Dritz, 1504

Justin C Dupere, 1963
Suzette Dutch, 1847
Shomik Dutta, 934
David A. Eagle, 357
Loren Easton, 110
Bruce A Eatroff, 897
Peter Ehrich, 558
Stephen Eisenstein, 914
Yaron Eitan, 1647
Joe El Chami, 1022
Martin Eltrich III, 64
Jerry Engel, 1249
Patrick Enright, 1143
Mark E Epstein, 1271
Jonas Fajgenbaum, 1018
William Farrell, 170
Beth Ferreira, 743
Robert J Fioretti, 717
Mark L. First, 686
Doug Fisher, 1010
Jason Fisherman, 1775
John Fletcher, 749
Joe Floyd, 665
Kerri Ford, 1596
Peter B Franz, 752
Brian P. Friedman, 1032
W Robert Friedman Jr, 629
Eric T Fry, 1129
Michael Gallagher, 928
J.S. Gamble, 285
John Garcia, 64
Kirt Gardner, 1878
Wesley H.R. Gaus, 507
Simeon J. George, 1731
Steven J. Gilbert, 827
Robert Girardi, 209
Liron Gitig, 793
R. Scott Glass, Jr., 1409
Bruce Gorchow, 1467
Pat Gouhin, 3256
Jonathan Gray, 277
Bob Greene, 533
Charles S. Grigg, 415
Kirk B Griswold, 164
Jorge Gross Jr, 1857
David Gross-Loh, 220
Aflalo Guimaraes, 1018
Sarah Guo, 872
Beth Haas, 577
Christopher J. Hadley, 254
Frederick H Hager, 1163
Eugene Hahn, 1039
Robert M. Hannon, 1824
Christopher G Hanssens, 698
Joshua Harris, 140
Hadley Harris, 679
Donald L Hawks III, 353
Brooke Hayes, 155
Joe T. Hays, 611
Kiran Hebbar, 1899
Eric D. Heglie, 985
Eric Hender, 17
Andrew Hertzmark, 818
Justin Heyman, 834
R Trent Hickman, 1927
Ryan Hinkle, 1000
Thierry F Ho, 1123
Andrew B. Hochman, 1590
Ryan Hodgson, 109
Spencer P Hoffman, 1147
Mitchell L Hollin, 1136
Laura C. Holson, 1301
Michael P Hompesch, 632
Osuke Honda, 596
Steve Hooper, 974
David Horing, 110
Jeff Horing, 1000

College/University Index / Wharton School

Mark Horne, 1455
Joe Horowitz, 968
Fred Hosaisy, 1695
Davis Hostetter, 894
Lee Hower, 1322
Peter Hsing, 1218
Ron Hunt, 1298
Bob Hurst, 559
Roger Hurwitz, 1942
In Seon Hwang, 1956
Tony Ignaczak, 1505
David Istock, 294
Joel R. Jacks, 507
Matthew Jacobson, 1096
Ariel Jaduszliwer, 324
David Jaffe, 447
Mudit Jain PhD, 1772
Amish Jani, 743
Arif Janmohamed, 1121
Andrew S. Janower, 456
Peter T Jensen, 1717
Craig N. Johnson, 832
Stephen M. Johnson, 949
Christopher N. Jones, 746
John R Jonge Poernik, 1130
G. Kent Kahle, 888
Victor Kats, 176
Jonathan D. Kelly, 404
Rene Kern, 815
Eurie Kim, 761
Doug Kimmelman, 675
Christopher M. King, 873
Phil Kirk, 483
Jason Klein, 29
Randal Klein, 208
Karin Klein, 284
Gentry S Klein, 1134
Scott Kleinman, 140
Lewis S. Klessel, 1301
Michael Koby, 5
Peggy Koenig, 21
Eric D Kogan, 492
David P Kollock, 832
Tim Komada, 600
Adam Koopersmith, 1480
Michael Kopelman, 655
Josh Kopelman, 741
David Kronfeld, 1038
Rodger R Krouse, 1753
Alex T. Krueger, 740
Stephen M. Krupa, 1498
Leon Kuan, 744
Timothy Kuehl, 1345
W. Brent Kulman, 746
C Todd Kumble, 1726
Monish Kundra, 515
Brian Kwait, 1368
Pete Labbat, 675
René Lajous, 378
Joseph P Landy, 1956
Curtis S Lane, 1271
Gary Lauder, 1095
Christopher Lawler, 846
Marc J Leder, 1753
Marc Lederman, 1317
Jeffrey Lee, 1340
Seth J Lehr, 1136
Tim Lemmon, 134
Scott Lenet, 791
Chris Leong, 161
Michael S. Levine, 1116
M Steven Levy, 1272
Jeff Lieberman, 1000
Ben Lin, 858
Byron Ling, 386
Kelvin Liu, 1015
Alexander Lloyd, 32

Scott Lopano, 677
Mark Ludwig, 1705
Melanie C Lyren, 164
Kenneth Mabbs, 711
William E. Macaulay, 740
Peter Macdonald, 274
J Matthew Mackowski, 1792
Kent Madsen, 688
Stephen A. Magida, 123
Marc Magliacano, 1088
Nurzhas Makishev, 1329
Christopher Manning, 1851
Scott M. Marimow, 1496
Renee Masi, 269
David J Matlin, 1179
Andrew R. Mayer, 1777
John McCarty, 1423
Stephen McClean, 170
Tom McCloskey, 542
W. Christian McCollum, 1109
Dr Robert McDonald, 1722
Bill McKee Jr., 846
Jeffrey McKibben, 1368
John McKinley, 1096
Marc McMorris, 416
Robert McMullan, 277
Kevin W McMurchy, 629
Dr Evan Melrose, 1722
Mark Menell, 1416
David Mes, 1370
Marc Michel, 525
Alex Millar, 294
Christian T Miller, 698
Yuri Milner, 615
Cory Moelis, 877
Charles Moldow, 770
Andrew Moley, 1121
Jeff Monat, 1207
Greg Mondre, 1683
Mario Montoya, 1992
Erik Moore, 229
Frank Mora, 958
Christina Morin, 846
Michael B. Morrissey, 1014
Randy Moser, 200
Mira Muhtadie, 42
Arneek Multani, 1850
Dennis E Murphree, 1273
David Mussafer, 62
Vijay Nagappan, 1226
Ryan K Nagim, 1144
Sandeep Naik, 815
Michael E. Najjar, 546
David C Neverson, 1105
Robert Newbold, 846
Henry W Newman, 1702
Ha Nguyen, 1721
Matthew W Norton, 1156
Kevin O'Brien, 433
James A. O'Donnell, 734
Brian O'Malley, 761
Neill Occhiogross, 547
Ben Orthlieb, 1370
Jason Ostheimer, 60
David B Outcalt, 1112
Jean-Pierre Paquin, 240
Deven Parekh, 1000
David J. Parker, 118
Brian Paul, 1796
Jay D Pauley, 1752
Christopher Payne, 916
Bret Pearlman, 659
Kevin S Penn, 42
Kevin Penn, 110
Joseph Pesce, 859
Robert W Petit, 1215
Patten Pettway, 1569

Cary Pfeffer MD, 1811
Wayne Platt, 1369
Dennis Podlesak, 621
Santo Politi, 1715
Barry Porter, 494
Brett L. Prager, 610
David G Proctor, 1234
Travis Putnam, 1282
Thomas Queenan, 1441
David B Ragins, 492
Rashad Rahman, 354
Zeena Rao, 969
Daniel Raynor, 161
Douglas Reed MD, 915
Eric Reiter, 334
Josh Resnick, 1519
Peter Restler, 365
Jon Rezneck, 820
Jason Rhodes, 191
Trevor C Rich, 1147
Glenn Rieger, 1317
Marvin W Ritchie, 1312
Gregory A. Robbins, 844
David Robbins, 1844
Joseph R Robinson, 1230
Frank J. Rodriguez, 1039
Alex Rose, 559
Mark Rosenbaum, 199
Bennett Rosenthal, 159
Eric L. Rosenzweig, 1743
Robert L. Rosner, 1931
John M. Roth, 783
Marc Rowan, 140
Laura M. Rubin, 1739
Neil Ryan, 1866
Aaron Sack, 1256
Neal G Sahney, 789
Judson Samuels, 926
Martin A. Sarafa, 449
Shrikant Sathe, 1911
Parag Saxena, 1911
Scott Schleifer, 1826
Ben A Schnakenberg, 931
Jeffrey A. Schoenfeld, 240
Richard R Schreiber, 616
Amanda Schutzbank, 120
Nelson Schwab III, 415
Scott Schwartz, 489
Andrew M. Schwartz, 1111
Christian Schwartz, 1820
Samuel L Schwerin, 1235
Stacey D. Seltzer, 74
Aydin Senkut, 720
Ned Sherwood, 2022
Zubeen Shroff, 806
Imran Siddiqui, 2255
Anthony Sigel, 2169
Lawrence R Simon, 503
David E Simon, 1134
Bipul Sinha, 1121
John Sinnerberg, 577
Jack Slye, 1136
Gregg Smart, 722
Ryan A Smiley, 1567
Andrew Snyder, 846
Jon Soberg, 1269
Erica S. Son, 166
Winston H. Song, 1931
Luke Sorenson, 1705
Kevin Spain, 665
Andrew Spring, 1231
Amit Srivastava, 682
Rob Stavis, 260
Howard Steyn, 1088
Keith Stimson, 881
Jason Stoffer, 1183
Kathryn J Stokel, 18

College/University Index / Wheaton College

Dave Stubbs, 380
Daniel Sugar, 1925
Julie Sunderland, 268
Trey Sykes, 1014
Dov Szapiro, 557
Karim A. Tabet, 1496
Richard D Tadler, 1776
Lucius H. Taylor, 156
Michael Taylor, 909
Dharmesh Thakker, 235
James E Thomas, 1817
Shawn Thompson, 1369
Rick Thompson, 1678
James Thorp, 17
Paul Thurk, 153
William Tomai, 447
Sean M Traynor, 1972
David W. Truetzel, 196
Daniel G. Tully, 97
John H. Turner, 1979
Marc A Utay, 492
Michael Van Vleck, 853
Roland Van der Meer, 798
Sriram Venkataraman, 209
Stephanie Von Friedeburg, 1007
Bradaigh Wagner, 673
Alyse Wagner, 1109
David Wassong, 1315
Allen A Weaver, 1497
Ellen Weber, 1577
Tim Weglicki, 22
Andrew J Weisenfeld, 1271
Richard Wells, 1000
Cal Wheaton, 22
Patrick F Whelan, 1424
John D. White, 774
Damion Wicker, 1410
Ryan Wierck, 849
Richard J. Williams, 1979
Fred Wilson, 1882
Tyler Wolfram, 1360
Marc Wolpow, 194
Emil Woods, 1115
Dalton Wright, 1070
Jeffrey Wu, 245
Victor L Wu, 1112
John Yang, 325
Cene Yoon, 333
Bryce Youngren, 1460
Guy Zaczepinski, 449
Philip Zaorski, 782
Howard S. Zeprun, 1850
Toby Zhang, 472
Daniel Zilberman, 1956
Andy Ziolkowski, 570
Ari M. Zur, 348

Wheaton College
Kate Castle, 1552
Stephen Cherington, 1009
Dean M Kline, 1428
Tom Lane, 675
Kathleen Schoemaker, 621

Whitman College
Bill Burkoth, 1436
Karl D Dillon, 940

Whittemore School of Business
Michael A. Foisy, 900

Whittier College
Fred Anderson, 659
William M. Wardlaw, 783

Widener University
Donald E. Stewart, 1724

Widener University School of Law
Wayne D Kimmel, 1657

Wilfrid Laurier University
Robert Antoniades, 2153
Steve Balaban, 2193
Stephan Bey, 2059
William Blackburn, 2169
Justin Catalano, 2116
Greg Collings, 2126
Adrianna Czornyj, 2220
Stephen J. Dent, 2062
Vipon Ghai, 2183
Michael Gubbels, 2289
Sasha Jacob, 2075
Mark Kennedy, 2026
Martin Kent, 2167
Omar Khalifa, 2116
Stephan Klee, 2225
Tom Lunan, 2058
Christopher McElhone, 2034, 2046
Matthew Towns, 2251
John Travaglini, 2026
David Unsworth, 2153

William College
Sarah G Roth, 164

William Mitchell College of Law
Scott L Becker, 1343
Mark Headrick, 536

William Paterson University
Jennifer Cerminaro, 168

William Woods University
Erik Allison, 1692

Williams College
Timothy A Barrows, 1181
Andrew Brennan, 501
Matthew Bronfman, 42
Kurt A. Brumme, 1417
Ed Cahill, 938
Charles P Coleman III, 1826
Charlie Crawford, 475
Christopher Delaney, 1023
Shomik Dutta, 934
Ron Eastman, 697
Michael R. Eisenson, 456
Robert C Embry Jr, 19
Kirt Gardner, 1878
Scott Garfield, 901
Douglas H. Gilbert, 610
Steven Gillis, 153
Steven C. Graham, 846
Michael Greeley, 748
Howard A. Halligan, 714
Matt Harris, 221
Van Zandt Hawn, 843
John G. Hayes, 857
Brian Higgins, 1045
James S. Hoch, 1777
Reginald L. Jones III, 862
Peter S Laino, 1248
Stephen A Lehman, 1248
Robert Manning, 1596
Nino Marakovic, 1620
Jim Marver, 1906
Matt McCall, 1480
Daniel P Neuwirth, 1504
Bruce Ou, 879
David B Outcalt, 1112
Todd G. Owens, 343
James A Parsons, 1557
Tory Patterson, 428
Tory Patterson, 1392

David L Pesikoff, 1846
Timothy Petersen, 149
Adam Piatkowski, 846
Jeffrey K. Quake, 740
Josh Resnick, 1519
Collin E. Roche, 884
Chris Seitz, 703
J. Frederick Simmons, 783
John H. Simpson, 343
Geoffrey W. Smith, 177
Jonathan Sokoloff, 1109
Edson W. Spencer Jr., 68
John A Svoboda, 1765
Brad Svrluga, 1475
Chris Sweeney, 1961
Martha Tracey, 553
Tenno Tsai, 928
Robert Ward, 1212
Wilson S Warren, 1112
Kara Weber, 342
Bill Winterer, 1417

Winona State University
Carl Nelson, 917

Wittenberg University
Anthony Eames, 376
Brian Leiber, 235
Ki Mixon, 1545

Wofford College
Thomas H. Westbrook, 746

Woodrow Wilson School
Robert W. Mulcare, 1301

Woodrow Wilson School, Princeton
Thanasis Delistathis, 1291
Michael A. Kumin, 857
John Locke, 28
Lawrence Neubauer, 1516
Edwin Shirley, 714

Worcester Polytechnic Institute
Michael E. Aspinwall, 434
Adam Bryant, 648
Steve Halstedt, 441
Jiong Ma, 322
John Mandile, 1673
Bob Mason, 1487
Bill McCullen, 1097
Sean Sebastian, 272
Jack Shields, 310
Zhi Tan PhD, 1340
Steve Vassallo, 770

Wright State University
Deepak Advani, 924

Xavier University
Larry A Colangelo, 1230
Thomas J Fogarty MD, 666
Betsy Hoover, 934

Xi'an Jiaotong University
Evelyn Sun, 148

Yale College
Michael E Donovan, 1972
Gregory P Ho, 1730
Jimmy Lu, 1983
Roger McNamee, 659
Brian T Regan, 1972
Raymond L.M. Wong, 1730

Yale Law School
Robert S Adelson, 1387

Eric Beckman, 330
Eric Beckman, 331
Michael Chae, 277
Winston J Churchill, 1633
Tom Darden, 463
Rajat Duggal, 787
Charles C Freyer, 1633
John H Friedman, 644
David Jones, Jr., 475
John T. Kaden, 1283
Peter Kellner, 1561
Jack W Lasersohn, 1929
John Leibovitz, 515
Phillip C Molner, 1476
Arrie Park, 924
Peter Sullivan, 1139
Matt Turck, 743

Yale School of Management
Rob Bettigole, 660
Michael Blue, 1481
Elon S Broms, 1097
Victor Budnick, 1021
Chris Cheever, 760
Alexander Ellis III, 1579
Craig Hart, 208
John Howard, 1022
Ellis Jones, 1960
Brendan Kennedy, 1481
Stephen Knight MD, 710
Nancy Pfund, 595
Peter M. Schulte, 507
Anderson Thees, 641
Tuff Yen, 1655

Yale School of Medicine
Mel Billingsley PhD, 1117
Stephen Knight MD, 710
Stephen B Solomon MD, 572
Robert J. Wenzel, 74

Yale University
Robert W Ackerman, 1962
Robert S Adelson, 1387
Timothy B. Armstrong, 1576
Michael Arougheti, 158
Lindsay Aspegren, 1336
Thomas C. Barry, 2018
Marshall Bartlett, 744
Anna Batarina, 143
Skip Baum, 1103
Eric Beckman, 331
Josh Bekenstein, 220
Michael C Bellas, 261
Amy Belt Raimundo, 1052
Rob Bettigole, 660
Evren Bilimer, 1018
Hiram A. Bingham, 588
Timothy P Bradley, 1674
Chris Brady, Jr., 457
Hugo Braun, 1336
Victor Budnick, 1021
Nick Burger, 2022
Donald W Burton, 1708
Ed Cahill, 938
Paul D Carbery, 789
Jane Castle, 208
Dorothy Jean Chang, 1115
Neil Chheda, 1581
Helen Chiang, 110
John W Childs, 1049
Daniel Ciporin, 386
Sam Clemens, 38
Matt Cohler, 248
David M Coit, 1333
Jeffrey J Collinson, 474
Michael M Cone, 631

William E Conway, 201
Matthew A Cook, 1071
Michael J Cromwell III, 1388
Shivanandan A. Dalvie, 64
John E Dancewicz, 619
Chris DeVore, 773
David A. Donnini, 884
Ned Doubleday, 1152
Chris Douvos, 72
Konstantine Drakonakis, 1097
William H Draper III, 627
John Earhart, 834
Jon Edelson, MD, 177
Michael R. Eisenson, 456
Darren Eng, 3268
Matt Fates, 178
Benjamin Felt, 1018
Matthew W Finlay, 1230
Brett Fisher, 744
Jason Fisherman, 1775
F. Barron Fletcher III, 1415
Steven Florsheim, 1889
William F Foote, 1582
Molly Fowler, 622
John H Friedman, 644
Christopher Gaughan, 1687
Jonathan Goldstein, 61
Jeffrey Goldstein, 924
Noah Goodhart, 1980
Edwin A Goodman, 52
Benjamin Gordon, 380
Bing Gordon, 1075
Andrew G Gould, 172
Myles D Greenberg, 474
Matt Greenfield, 1551
David Griest, 1689
Charles S. Grigg, 415
Peter S.H. Grubstein, 1324
Harry Gruner, 1041
Aflalo Guimaraes, 1018
David Hanson, 1152
Whitney Haring-Smith, 133
Steve Harrick, 1001
Sam Hartwell, 201
Rick Heyke, 1750
Dylan Hixon, 826
Edward Huang, 277
Jay Huffard, 531
Frederick J Iseman, 476
David Jones, Jr., 475
David Kabakoff, 921
David Kabakoff, 1698
John T. Kaden, 1283
Julia Kahr, 277
Tom Kastner, 1369
Eric Kaup, 937
James P. Kelley, 1931
Thomas L. Kelly II, 461
Karen Kenworthy, 1748
Brian Kinsman, 359
James Kondo, 820
Andrew Korn, 1602
Daniel H. Kosoy, MD, 187
Stephen Kraus, 260
C Todd Kumble, 1726
Vivek Ladsariya, 1687
Augustine Lawlor, 919
Roger Lee, 235
Jeffrey T Leeds, 1105
Kresimir Letinic MD PhD, 644
Daniel Levine, 28
Linda Lynch, 744
Scott MacLeod, 834
Jules Maltz, 1001
James Manges, 1851
Mark McAndrews, 645
Niall McComiskey, 862

Andrew McLaughlin, 934
Chris McLeod, 660
Peter H McNerney, 1817
Jonathan W Meeks, 1776
George M Milne, Jr. PhD, 1520
Lou Mischianti, 1372
Ann Miura-Ko, 751
Phillip C Molner, 1476
Frederic H. Morris, 349
John L. Morrison, 843
Patricia Muoio, 1687
Ajit Nedungadi, 1776
Denis Newman, 1230
Malcolm C Nolen, 1674
Daniel S. O'Connell, 1931
Matt Ocko, 585
Jonathan T. Oka, 750
Peter Pacelli, 1078
Douglas A Parker, 1230
Tripp Peake, 1142
Chris A. Pierce, 1279
Brian Powers, 924
Jack W. Qian, 1301
Vikrant Raina, 361
Corby Reese, 1767
Bill Reiland, 1255
Jason Rhodes, 191
Rosemary Ripley, 1324
John L Ritter, 739
Scott Rooth, 1467
David S Rose, 1306
David S Rose, 1584
Mark Rosen, 456
Devraj Roy, 1022
Michael Sabia, 2069
Will Sale, 1763
Stephen A. Schwarzman, 277
Stacey D. Seltzer, 74
Nick Shalek, 1560
J. Louis Sharpe, 64
Anne-Marie Shelley, 39
Stephen C. Sherrill, 354
Robert J. Small, 254
John Spinale, 1029
Jerry Sprole, 1103
Rick Stahl, 660
William Staudt, 667
E Jack Stewart, 1920
Christian R Strain, 1752
Yanev Suissa, 1687
William P. Sutter Jr., 944
David Sze, 872
Jim Tananbaum, 762
Jo Tango, 1065
David Teten, 724
Jeff Thermond, 2011
Steve Tomlin, 206
Justin Topilow, 250
Martha Tracey, 553
Kyle Veatch, 926
Mathew Veedon, 1712
Pote Videt, 1139
Rob Walsh, 1770
Mark Wan, 1819
Eli Weiss, 819
David J. Wermuth, 1743
Jeff Williams, 1728
Richard J. Williams, 1979
Timothy Wollaeger, 1616
Veronica Wu, 942
Brett Zbar, 762
Peter Ziebelman, 1405
Shivon Zilis, 284

Yeshiva University
Alan E Goldberg, 1129
Bruce K. Taragin, 301

1075

College/University Index / Yonsei University

Yonsei University
Jamie Choi, 1611

York University
Hussein K. Bawa, 2222
Daniel Brothman, 2224
George H. Cholakis, 2030
Kim Coote, 2288
Kim Davis, 2281
Stephen Foote, 2204
Matt Golden, 2137
Michael Griffiths, 2169
Mark Hatfield, 1794
Karen Hung, 3258
Alex Kanayev, 2031
Mark Kennedy, 2026
Lisa Melchior, 2281
Shay Nulman, 2175
Jeffrey Rosenthal, 2150
Alex Storcheus, 2122
Hamish Sutherland, 2154
Hamish Sutherland, 2287
Adam Szweras, 2122
Kevin Talbot, 2236
Ken Teslia, 2113

Zhejiang University
Erica Yu, 823

Zicklin School of Business
Marta De La Cruz, 834

Executive Name Index

A

Abassi, Farraz, 443
Abbas, Tarik, 1836
Abbott, Shawn, 2157
Abbrecht, Todd M., 1815
Abdulmalik, Atif, 152
Abele, Chris, 566
Aberman, Jonathan, 119
Abernethy, John I, 636
Abert, Collin, 1091
Abhyankar, Adit, 758
Abouchar, Andrew, 2262
Abrahamson, Shaun, 1894
Abram, Joshua, 539
Abramowitz, Kenneth S, 1325
Abrams, Andrew, 1303
Abramson, Jenny, 1552
Abshagen, Jonathan, 880
Abshire, Chris, 721
Acconcia, Angelo, 277
Acher, Mark, 1178
Acker, John C., 1727
Ackerley, Christopher, 43
Ackerley, Ted, 43
Ackerley Cleworth, Kim, 43
Ackerman, John F, 409
Ackerman, Christopher J., 750
Ackerman, Robert W, 1962
Ackerman, Jr., Robert R., 84
Ackrell, Mike, 44
Adair, Charles E, 537
Adam, Dr Philippe H, 186
Adamek, Peter, 2250
Adams, Susan, 23
Adams, Joel P., 56
Adams, Will, 92
Adams, Nick, 107
Adams, Samantha A., 254
Adams, Nick, 614
Adams, Frank A., 876
Adams, Bruce, 979
Adams, Rob, 1321
Adams, Andrew, 1361
Adams, Rodger P, 1909
Adderley, David, 2076
Addiego, Joe, 93
Adelman, Robert, 1914
Adelson, Robert S, 1387
Adkins, G. Woodrow, 719
Adler, Jason, 845
Adler, Jim, 1834
Adox, Jim, 1921
Advani, Deepak, 924
Advani, Vijay, 1356
Adznan, Adzmel, 1449
Afeyan, Noubar, 747
Agarwal, Ajay, 221
Agarwala, Sandip, 1143
Aggarwal, Rahul, 334
Aggarwal, PhD, Vijay, 1808
Agha, Zia, 1973
Agnew, Timothy P, 1175
Agrawal, Neeraj, 235
Agrawal, Krishna K, 1129
Agrawal Divakaran, Payal, 2
Agroskin, Daniel, 1039
Aguilo, Jorge, 522
Aguitar, MD, Eric, 74
Aharwal, Shradha, 731
Ahearn, Michael J, 1859
Ahearn, Matthew S, 1859
Ahern, Matthew, 1077
Ahern, Tracie E., 1444
Ahn, Garrick, 373
Ahrens, Brent, 386
Ahrens II, Jack K, 1802
Aiello, John F, 1129

Aier, Vignesh M., 1301
Aiken, Aaron C., 903
Aikman, William F, 882
Ailons, Shiri, 1774
Ainslie, Lee, 1182
Ainsworth, Ian, 2113
Aissa, Samy Ben, 1926
Aitken-Davies, George E., 97
Akers, Jeff, 57
Akers, Roger, 75
Akhavan, Amir, 1033
Aktihanoglu, Murat, 684
Al-Mubaraki, Fawaz, 1950
Alala III, Joseph B., 405
Alardhi, Mohammed, 1017
Alberg, Thomas A, 1158
Albert, Andrew B, 1765
Albinson, Christopher J, 1410
Albrecht, Laura, 1166
Albright, John, 2236
Aldrich, Russ, 887
Aldrich, Rich, 1145
Alemany, Ellen R., 484
Alexander, Lynn, 1062
Alexander, Ted, 1239
Alexandrian, Narbe, 2071
Alfond, Reis L, 1881
Ali, Lori B., 1496
Aliber, William J., 1496
Alimov, Dmitry, 792
Allan, Rob, 681
Allen, Christopher, 76
Allen, Joe, 674
Allen, Nancy S, 718
Allen, Jason, 1172
Allen, Chris, 1403
Allen, Brandon, 1875
Allen, Wilson, 1976
Allen, Peter A., 2192
Allgaier, Matthias G, 1752
Alling, Ted, 640
Allison, Erik, 1692
Allman, Denis, 2219
Allsteadt, Mark, 401
Almany, MD, Steven L., 269
Almog, Yuval, 536
Alpert, Norman W., 1931
Alport, Daniel K., 1578
Alsikafi, Zaid F, 1156
Alsop, Stewart, 93
Alt, Jonathan H, 540
Altman, Matthew L., 166
Altman, Roger, 699
Altug, Okan, 2075
Alva, Sandeep D, 716
Alvarado, Oscar, 1341
Alvi, Rashid, 913
Alvim, Alexandre, 834
Alvord, Seth W, 739
Amador, Jorge, 109
Amar, Maor, 2151
Ambrose, Cate, 3261
Amelio, William J., 594
Amen, Robert, 1910
Ament, Dave, 1417
Ames, Grace, 1361
Amidi, Rahim, 115
Amidi, Saeed, 115
Ammerman, Robert C., 402
Ammirati, Sean, 272
Amouyal, Philippe, 1018
Ampleford, Glen, 2072
Anantharam, Kamala, 1444
Anastasopoulos, Chris, 2102
Anchel, Edward, 669
Andelman, Jim, 306

Andelman, Jim, 1566
Andersen, James G, 503
Anderson, Cory S, 40
Anderson, David Q., 118
Anderson, Kenneth D., 122
Anderson, Steve, 231
Anderson, Ryan, 433
Anderson, David J., 461
Anderson, Fred, 659
Anderson, Robert, 793
Anderson, Carl T, 836
Anderson, Mark M., 884
Anderson, Christopher, 1081
Anderson, Ed, 1334
Anderson, David L., 1757
Anderson, David L, 1760
Anderson, Edward R., 1858
Anderson, Bruce K, 1972
Anderson, Matt, 1976
Andlinger, Merrick, 123
Ando, MD, Goran, 697
Andonian, Dave, 580
Andreassen, Dr. Alf L., 1400
Andreessen, Marc, 124
Andreev, Alexei, 204
Andreev, Alexei, 205
Andrew, Mark M, 1112
Andrews, R. David, 881
Andrews, Lawrence D, 1174
Andrews Reyes, Alison, 7
Andrianopoulos, Alex, 1051
Andryc, Joel, 1598
André, Ludovic, 2088
Angel, Ricardo, 1449
Angell, Suzanne, 419
Angella, Frank, 879
Anson, George, 909
Antaya, Matthew P., 985
Antoniades, Robert, 2153
Aplin, John C, 478
Applebaum, Jay I, 1997
Applegate, Brion B, 1717
Appleyard, James, 2125
Apprendi, Joe, 1554
Aquilano, Dan, 86
Aragona, Joe, 202
Ardell, Ted, 1786
Arenz, Thomas W., 914
Argenbright, Glenn, 1507
Armony, Izhar, 455
Armstrong, Tim, 134
Armstrong, David, 195
Armstrong, Jim, 387
Armstrong, Jim, 502
Armstrong, Dave, 770
Armstrong, Brad, 1147
Armstrong, Lance, 1318
Armstrong, Timothy B., 1576
Armstrong, Curtis, 2173
Armstrong. Jr., Andrew J., 1724
Arnold, Mark, 78
Arnold, George, 1077
Arnold, C Mark, 1529
Arnold, Paul, 1768
Arnson, Eric, 1385
Aronoff, David, 754
Aronson, Bernard, 46
Aronson, Jeffrey, 442
Aronson, Neal K., 1576
Aronson, Stephen D., 1576
Arora, Aditya, 834
Arougheti, Michael, 158
Arrington, Michael, 564
Arrowsmith, Peter, 1041
Arroyo, Damian, 1119
Arscott, David G., 524
Arscott, Martha P.E., 524

Arsenault, Chris, 2157
Arzac, Martin, 500
Arzubi, Luis, 1779
Aschebrook, Larry L., 802
Ascher, Brian, 1916
Ascione, Michael C., 254
Asel, Paul, 1330
Asem, Mike, 1155
Ashai, Zaid, 1459
Asher, A Craig, 1940
Ashley, Bradley W., 2226
Ashrafian, Houman, 1628
Ashrafian, Houman, 1762
Ashton, Michael, 21
Askew, Glenn W., 328
Aspegren, Lindsay, 1336
Aspinwall, Michael E., 434
Assant, Lionel, 277
Astle, Tom, 2096
Atallah, Amira, 690
Atherton Jr., Cliff, 888
Atia, Lisa, 218
Atinsky, Lawrence S., 177
Atiq, Fred, 2202
Atiq, Sikandar, 2202
Atkinson, Dax, 424
Atkinson, Dennis, 690
Atkinson, Fraser, 694
Atkinson, Sherman, 1237
Attanasio, Mark, 556
Atterbury, David, 909
Attie, Elliot, 1851
Atwood, Brian, 1928
Aube, Richard, 1443
Audsley, Lorraine, 2112
Auer-Welsbach, Christoph, 967
Auerbach, Stuart A., 118
Auerbach, Jon, 455
Aust, R. Wade, 77
Austen, Christopher, 350
Auster, Charles, 1596
Auster, Matt, 1596
Austin, Darrell W, 201
Austin, Chip, 964
Austin, Robert M, 985
Austin, Blake, 1022
Austin, Mark, 1976
Auvil, Stephen, 1790
Averett, David W, 1752
Averitt, B Marc, 1371
Avery, Tim, 952
Avida, Dan, 1381
Avirett, John, 867
Avnur, Zafrira, 2229
Avon, Mike, 22
Avrutin, Brandon, 1551
Aweida, Jesse, 210
Aweida, Dan, 210
Axel, Merrick, 558
Axelrod, Jonathan, 684
Axon, Robin, 2182
Ayres, Charles, 1851

B

Babbit, Cindy, 577
Babson, Stephen E., 673
Bachireddy, Ashvin, 820
Backaus, Gary, 16
Backman, Joel, 1212
Backus, John, 1291
Backus, John, 1482
Bacon, Nathaniel P, 359
Bacon, Kathleen, 909
Bacon, Eric V, 1132
Baehr, Geoffrey, 89
Bagaria, Rajay, 1960
Bagley, Thomas S., 1435

1077

Executive Name Index

Bahat, Roy, 284
Baiada, Mel, 230
Bailey, Bary, 558
Bailey, Roger D, 606
Bailey, Kristen, 769
Bailey, Steve, 782
Bailey, Michael L, 1484
Bailey, Lee, 1895
Bainbridge, David, 1927
Baird, Darran A., 1743
Baird Jr, Charles F, 1335
Bajaj, Vikram, 762
Bakalar, Sophie, 511
Baker, John, 223
Baker, Henry G., 223
Baker, Kevin, 368
Baker, Jeff, 702
Baker, Stephen A, 766
Baker, Jim, 1569
Baker, Craig, 1569
Baker, Trent, 2025
Baker, Eric, 2194
Baker, Alex, 2236
Bakshi, Rajiv, 2183
Bal, Ru-Guang, 905
Balaban, Steve, 2193
Balash, Jeffrey L, 527
Balbontin, Manuel Jose, 522
Baldassarre, Carl E., 1456
Baldeschwieler, Dr John, 186
Baldwin, Dennis, 329
Baldwin, Thomas J., 354
Baldwin, Chris, 455
Baldwin, Elmer, 464
Balen, John, 386
Ball, Eric M., 108
Ball, Charles E., 123
Ball, Ben, 779
Ball, Jason, 1509
Ballard, Michael, 145
Ballard, Perry O., 750
Ballenegger, Kenneth, 1395
Balmuth, Michael, 1628
Balmuth, Michael, 1762
Baloff, Steven, 59
Balter, Dave, 313
Baltzell, Josh, 1725
Bamatter CA, Paul, 109
Banahan, Tom, 1796
Banatao, Dado, 1779
Banerjee, Gautam, 277
Bank, Keith, 1056
Bank, Keith, 1057
Banks, Andrew, 21
Banks, Gerald T., 101
Banks, Michael, 870
Banks, Sean, 1863
Banks, Charlie, 1923
Bannantine, James M., 190
Bannon, Maren Thomas, 1026
Banon, Sid, 460
Banse, Amy, 518
Baptiste, Stonly, 1894
Barach, Michael, 990
Barandiaran, Walter, 161
Barasz, Zach, 302
Baratta, Joseph, 277
Barbara, Rob, 2068
Barber, Tiki, 878
Barber, Paul, 1041
Barber, Sandra P, 1708
Barber, Jeffrey S, 1776
Barberio, Caroline, 1239
Barclay, Dan, 2063
Barg, Jason S, 1147
Barger, Greg, 1317
Barker, Nicholas H, 960

Barker, CFA, Karey, 560
Barkoff, Stuart, 834
Barlev, Hagai, 669
Barlow, Kelly J., 1903
Barman, Jeffrey, 1431
Barna, Hayley, 741
Barnds, Tom, 29
Barnes, Steven, 220
Barnes, Jeffrey, 270
Barnes, Phin, 741
Barnes, Jonathan P, 897
Barnes, Cristy, 1119
Barnum, William, 334
Baron, Jack, 565
Baron, Claudia, 1467
Barous, Andrew D., 1301
Baroyan, Eric, 109
Barr, David, 821
Barr, Gregory M, 1684
Barra, Jim, 1021
Barrelet, Blaise, 121
Barrett, Peter, 191
Barrett, Ross P., 362
Barrett, Dave, 1460
Barrett III, Redington, 1432
Barrette, Sean, 468
Barris, Peter, 1297
Barron, Bruce N., 1384
Barrows, Timothy A, 1181
Barry, Scott, 697
Barry, Melissa, 926
Barry, Jeff, 1455
Barry, Doug, 1646
Barry, Thomas C., 2018
Barry III, John F., 1491
Bartalsky, Nissa, 80
Barthelme, Sam, 1033
Bartlett, Kirby, 45
Bartlett, Samuel, 456
Bartlett, Marshall, 744
Bartok, Jared J., 118
Bartol, Stopher, 731
Bartoli, Jeffrey, 447
Baruchowitz, Mitch, 1207
Bashir, Imran, 2113
Bashour, Fouad, 477
Baskett, Forest, 1297
Bassi, Luca, 220
Bassin, Stuart, 1599
Bassman, Robert, 1255
Bastedo, Brian, 1578
Basu, Upal, 1330
Basu Trivedi, Nikhil, 1663
Baszucki, Greg, 772
Batarina, Anna, 143
Batchelder, Bret, 463
Batcheller, Paul, 1470
Bates, Gavin, 374
Bates, Carrie, 1847
Bathon Jr, Daniel H, 1994
Batra, Rajeev, 1184
Batterson, Len, 234
Bauer, Stacey, 806
Bauer, Matt, 2025
Bauerly, Richard, 850
Baum, Skip, 1103
Baum, David William, 1734
Baum, Dan, 2244
Bauman, J.P., 98
Bauman, Jeremy, 1304
Baumann, Gabor (Gabe), 1351
Baumer, John M, 1109
Baumgarten, Josh, 127
Bawa, Hussein K., 2222
Baxter, Stuart, 1572
Baxter-Simmons, Laura, 1472
Bayless, Jon W, 1658

Bayliffe, Andy, 143
Baylin, Gregory, 2208
Baylor, David, 1910
Bazazi, Mo, 2118
Beakey, James A., 1279
Beard, Dennis, 1379
Beasley, Allen, 1534
Beaton, Kirk M., 1112
Beattie, Randy, 2221
Beattie, Geoff, 2236
Beatty, Croom, 1202
Beaty, Derek, 834
Beauchamp, Marc, 2206
Beaumont, Michael H., 985
Beauparlant, Pierre, 2270
Beauregard, Michael, 960
Beber, Justin, 2067
Beck, Martin, 222
Beck, James, 1184
Becker, John, 109
Becker, Matt, 702
Becker, David, 1194
Becker, Scott L, 1343
Becker, Daria, 1491
Becker, Eric, 1742
Becker, Doug, 1742
Beckett, William, 810
Beckett, Steven S, 1426
Beckman, Eric, 330
Beckman, Eric, 331
Beckman, Charles W, 955
Beckman, Robert J., 1808
Bedell, Elaine, 3258
Beebe, Andrew, 1363
Beecken, David, 244
Beeler, Charles, 1522
Beerle, Tom, 257
Begert, Brian, 2292
Begleiter, Steven L., 750
Bego, Michael, 1076
Behm, Denny, 171
Behrens, Christopher, 433
Behrman, Grant, 245
Beier, Brooke, 1840
Beim, Nick, 1916
Beinecke, Walter, 349
Beitler, Stephen S, 636
Bekenstein, Josh, 220
Belaman, Cécile, 220
Belfer, Todd, 387
Belford, Jeff, 2275
Belk, Cathy, 1047
Belke, Robert M, 1147
Bell, David, 325
Bell, Thomas, 512
Bell, Maurey J, 619
Bell, Michael A, 1248
Bell, Michael A., 1815
Bell, Jr., Thomas D., 1219
Bellas, Michael C, 261
Belldegrun, Arie S., 1932
Bellerive, Gerry, 2235
Belmont, Gregory C., 847
Belt Raimundo, Amy, 1052
Beltramini, Enrico, 1284
Belzberg, Brent, 2261
Belzberg, Brent, 2272
Belzer, David L., 1491
Ben-Gacem, Hazem, 1017
Ben-Joseph PhD, Oded, 1388
Benaquista, Mark L., 1815
Benaroya, Larry, 247
Bendele, Jenner, 725
Bendell, Adam, 1831
Bender, Julie A, 789
Benear, Jay, 639
Benedetti, Tom, 288

Benedict, James G, 1071
Benham, Mark, 439
Benhamou, Eric, 249
Benik, Alex, 235
Benioff, Marc, 1607
Benkowski PhD, Jacques, 1896
Bennett, Kent, 260
Bennett, Peter, 1116
Bennett, Matthew M., 1301
Bennett, Ryan, 1548
Bennett, Stephen A, 1745
Bennett, Cathy, 2247
Bennington, Allison A, 1903
Benshoof, Justin, 373
Benson, Greg, 959
Benson, Marc F, 1227
Benson, Scott, 1316
Benson, Buzz, 1671
Benson, Erik, 1945
Benyaminy, David, 193
Berenson, Stephen, 747
Berenstein, Jason, 2099
Berg, Steven T., 421
Berge, David, 1880
Bergen, Warren, 2048
Berger, Stephen, 1368
Berggruen, Nicolas, 250
Berglund, Thomas A, 733
Bergner, Richard F., 694
Bergonia, R David, 1332
Bergschneider, Marc C, 1735
Berk, Zachary C., 1058
Berk, Michael S, 1776
Berke, Eric, 2272
Berkin, Brian S., 1777
Berkley, Kent, 782
Berkowitz, Barak, 253
Berkowitz, Jonathan, 1810
Berland, Terrence, 1074
Berliner, Arthur, 1952
Berman, Steve, 161
Berman, Jeffrey, 377
Berman, Casey, 377
Berman, Douglas, 928
Berman, Dror, 996
Berman, Mark, 1364
Berman, Alison, 1401
Berman, Steven E, 1401
Berman, Seth, 1758
Bernardon, Roland V., 404
Berney, Philip E, 1062
Bernier, Jacques, 2268
Bernstein, Jordan S., 476
Bernstein, Beth L., 686
Bernstein, Brad, 793
Bernstein, Jay, 1085
Bernstein, Robert A, 1105
Berolzheimer, Michael, 243
Berry, David, 747
Berson, Brett, 741
Berterretche, Jackie, 852
Berton, John, 2132
Bertrand, Chaz, 329
Bessette, Guy, 2107
Besthoff, Skip, 422
Besthoff, Skip, 1496
Betsalel, Richard, 2089
Betten, Elizabeth Q, 1156
Bettigole, Rob, 660
Bettinelli, Greg, 1888
Bevan, Michael, 657
Bevilacqua, Tom, 1906
Bevis, Tate, 1040
Bey, Stephan, 2059
Beyda, Gil, 518
Beyda, Gil, 814
Bhadkamkar, Neal, 1249

Executive Name Index

Bhalwani, Arif N., 2222
Bhappu, Ross, 1548
Bharat, Raghu, 2088
Bhaskaran, Ravi, 758
Bhat, Nikhil J., 1931
Bhowmik, Nilanana, 534
Bhowmik, Nilanjana, 1146
Bianchinotti, Alberto, 1216
Bianco, William, 1617
Bice, William F, 1924
Biddle, Mike, 2111
Biddle III, A.G.W., 1348
Biemann, Betsy, 438
Biesel, David, 1322
Bigge, Matt, 563
Biggee, Michael, 1850
Bilenker, MD, JH, 74
Bilimer, Evren, 1018
Billings, Tim, 1505
Billingsley PhD, Mel, 1117
Bilodeau, Peter, 2122
Binas, Peter, 1627
Binch, James G, 1127
Binford, Joy E., 1348
Bingham, Hiram A., 588
Bingham, Kate, 1628
Bingham, Kate, 1762
Bingle, Mike, 1683
Biniak, Bryan, 1495
Binkley, Nicholas B, 765
Birch, Liz, 268
Birchall, Larry, 2178
Birchall, Tyson, 2178
Bird, Walter M (Jerry), 1172
Bird, Jeff, 1760
Birdsong, Jon, 189
Birk, Brian, 1754
Birkelund, John P., 1621
Birnbaum, Charles, 260
Birnbaum, Scott, 1530
Birner, Hubert, 2276
Birschbach, Mark, 1642
Bischof, George, 1212
Bisconti, Ben, 29
Bishop, Stacey, 1626
Bishop, Andrew, 2059
Bismuth, Marc-David, 1088
Bisson, Keith, 438
Bisson, Cédric, 2268
Biswas, Samir, 2037
Bitterman, PhD, Kevin, 191
Bjork, Anders, 21
Bjorseth, Eva, 1365
Black, Leon, 140
Black, Jeff, 1430
Black, Jason, 1593
Black, Darren M, 1752
Black, Phil, 1860
Black, Jeffrey, 1926
Black, Daniel L, 1984
Black, Richard, 2118
Blackburn, Alan J., 888
Blackburn, William, 2169
Blacklow, Peter, 313
Blackshaw, Pete, 480
Blackwell, Wes, 1632
Blair, PhD, Jim, 621
Blake III, William, 251
Blanchard, Jeffery P., 734
Blanchfield, EJ, 1458
Blanco, José, 573
Blanco, Jonathan B., 746
Bland, Geoff, 1969
Blaney, J. Peter, 2152
Blank, Robert D, 468
Blank, Kevin, 881
Blanton, Darren, 514

Blaszkiewicz, David, 742
Blattman, Barry, 2067
Blaustein, Sim, 256
Blavatnik, Len, 34
Blazej, PhD, Robert, 1238
Blazensky, Derek, 411
Blebins, John, 1444
Blevins, Matthew, 503
Blidner, Jeff, 2067
Blinoff, Bluette N., 1799
Blivin, Dave, 549
Bloch, Stephen, 386
Block, Keith, 1607
Bloom, Gregory, 48
Bloom, Erik W., 838
Blue, Michael, 1481
Bluestein, Scott, 925
Blum, Richard C., 300
Blum, Christopher J, 619
Blumberg, David J., 301
Blume, Rick, 703
Boag, Simon, 981
Boboff, Peter, 1839
Boccasam, Prashanth V., 1348
Bochnowski, James J., 604
Bodden, Brad, 2001
Bode, Bob, 1022
Bodine, Peter, 84
Bodnar, Chris, 646
Bogdanov, Pavel, 89
Bogucki, Michael E, 1163
Bogue, Zachary, 585
Bohn, Larry, 816
Bohnett, David, 228
Bohrmann, Brady, 206
Bohrmann, Braden M (Brady), 1175
Boisvert, Marie-Claude, 2082
Bok, Gaye, 703
Bok, Scott L., 864
Bok, James, 2071
Bolander, Rick, 805
Bolander, Rick, 2023
Bolduc, John, 239
Bolin, Kurt E., 1743
Bolinger, Mark, 1064
Bologna, Nick, 646
Bologna, Mike, 860
Bolten, Charlie, 267
Bolzan, Denio R., 1435
Bolzon, Brad, 1928
Bombara, John C., 946
Bommer, Eric D, 1651
Bonanno, Andrew P., 1081
Bonatsos, Niko, 816
Bond, Patrick A, 1262
Bonderman, David, 1835
Bondy, Craig A., 884
Boniello, Michael, 1464
Bonnar, Mark, 1711
Bonner, Blake, 1856
Booker, Charles, 61
Booma, Jason, 515
Booth, Bruce, 191
Booth, Ralph, 760
Borcher, Christian, 411
Borchers, John, 555
Bordeau, David C., 254
Borden, Philip, 806
Bordes, Stephen, 109
Boren, Todd, 557
Borhanu, Nabil, 854
Borho, Sven H., 1382
Boro, Seth, 1814
Borque, Janice, 925
Borrus, Michael, 2011
Borsum, Christina, 367

Bortnem, Jane, 464
Bose, Anik, 249
Bose, Simita, 1348
Boswell, Patrick, 1800
Boszhardt, Andy, 858
Botha, Roelof, 1654
Bottorff, Dennis C, 550
Bottorff, Leslie, 809
Bouk, Josh, 705
Boulanger, Brian, 2040
Bounds, Mark, 316
Bourgeois, Anne-Marie, 676
Bourne, Duncan S., 2009
Bourque, Donna, 2155
Bouten, Jan, 995
Boutros-Ghali, Teymour, 1249
Bouyea, Lee E, 786
Bovaird Nevins, Anne, 1441
Bower, Christopher J, 1397
Bowes, Jessica, 2060
Bowman, Gale, 1019
Bowman, Tim, 2056
Bowsher, Steve, 979
Boye, Henry J., 1815
Boylan, Gerry, 1141
Boyle, Jim, 990
Boze, Brandon B., 1903
Bozynski, Tyler A., 611
Braccia, Andrew, 28
Bracken, Brenda, 855
Brackett, Greg, 373
Bradley, John, 1349
Bradley, Timothy P, 1674
Bradlow, John, 2219
Bradlow, Richard, 2219
Bradshaw, Larry, 695
Brady, Christopher D., 457
Brady, Phil, 837
Brady, Scott, 996
Brady, Kevin, 1976
Brady, Jr., Chris, 457
Braga, Sayles, 80
Bragiel, Paul, 1473
Bragiel, Paul, 1781
Bramer, Robert, 2215
Branchflower, Michael, 2205
Brand, Martin, 277
Brand, Hanan, 543
Brandon, Cheryl, 2283
Brandt, Michael, 2197
Branman, Jeff, 937
Brasch, Sam, 1052
Brass, Jason T., 843
Brathol, Darren, 1719
Braun, Jeff, 253
Braun, Hugo, 1336
Bravo, Orlando, 1814
Breach, David, 1938
Breazzano, David J, 597
Brecker, John, 99
Breinlinger, Josh, 1024
Brekka, Richard, 1640
Brennan, Andrew, 501
Brennan, Matthew L., 985
Brenneman, Greg, 433
Brenner, Clara, 1893
Brenninkmeyer, Frank, 1431
Breslin, Adam, 2219
Bressler, Steven, 1417
Bressner, Glen R, 52
Bressner, Glen R, 1227
Bressner, Glen R, 1385
Brew Jr., Thomas E., 66
Brewer, David, 145
Brewer, Brett, 561
Breyer, Jim, 336
Bricault, Paul, 120

Brickman, C. Andrew, 222
Briger Jr., Peter L., 767
Bright, Aaron, 1432
Brill, Robert M, 1314
Bring, Kenneth S., 254
Brinkman, James J, 508
Brinn, Nathaniel C, 1940
Britain, Sean, 239
Britt, Chris L, 1168
Britt, H Bryan, 1529
Britts, David, 798
Brockway, Peter C, 348
Broder, Scott, 993
Broderick, Dan, 267
Brodlieb, Jeff, 448
Brody, Jeff, 1534
Broeker, Alexander C, 1841
Broms, Elon S, 1097
Bronfman, Matthew, 42
Bronfman Jr, Edgar, 39
Bronner, Philip L., 1348
Bronsteatter, Phil D., 1435
Brooke, Peter, 62
Brooke, Peter, 350
Brooke, John, 350
Brooks, Graham, 2
Brooks, Michael, 1505
Brooks, Mark, 1626
Brooks, Ben, 1710
Brooks, Jason, 2162
Brookshire, Mike, 1569
Brosgart, Michael, 1807
Broshar, Ryan, 1176
Broten, Laurel C., 2205
Brothman, Daniel, 2224
Brotman, Kenneth, 46
Brotman, Steve, 91
Brotman, Steve, 1680
Brouckman, Randall, 1782
Broun, Stephen, 399
Brown, Michael, 235
Brown, Hope, 376
Brown, Thomas P., 384
Brown, Daryl B, 637
Brown, Scott, 654
Brown, Jeffrey J., 765
Brown, Frank, 815
Brown, Sonya, 1346
Brown, Richard A, 1452
Brown, David, 1789
Brown, Paul, 1884
Brown, Nathan, 1990
Brown, Paul, 2023
Brown, Kevin, 2040
Brown, Andrew, 2052
Brown, Kerry, 2121
Brown, Dave, 2240
Brown Jr., Mike, 317
Brown Jr., Robert E, 1275
Browne, David M, 1168
Brownell, Bob, 666
Browning, G Stephen, 1652
Brownlee, Sean, 2239
Brownlie, Steve, 96
Broyhill, M. Hunt, 405
Brubaker, Terry, 828
Brucato, C.J., 21
Bruckmann, Bruce C., 354
Bruml, Robert W., 355
Brumme, Kurt A., 1417
Brunell, Mike, 1369
Brunk, Gerry, 2180
Bruno, Frank W., 451
Bruno Jr, Michael S, 1744
Brush, MD, James W., 782
Bruss, Adam, 264
Brutocao, Brad J., 783

1079

Executive Name Index

Bruun, Eric J, 478
Bryan, Lee, 528
Bryan, Charles A, 1422
Bryan, Scott, 2110
Bryant, Matthew, 557
Bryant, Adam, 648
Bryant, Mike, 1078
Buaron, Roberto, 733
Buatois, Eric, 249
Buatois, Eric, 1698
Bubnack, Tim, 958
Buchanan, Doug, 2139
Buck, Lee, 286
Buck, Lee, 1096
Buckley III, Walter W., 53
Buckner, Karen, 1242
Budde, Daniel, 901
Budin, Ethan A., 750
Budnick, Victor, 1021
Buehler, Dr Kai, 1507
Buenneke, Brian J., 1411
Bueno, Martin, 3260
Buffington, Mark, 271
Bugay, Lauren K, 633
Bukovinsky, Eric, 2291
Bullard, Karla J, 1156
Bullock, Fraser, 1705
Bullock, John W, 1994
Bund, Ian, 1455
Bunder, Jeffrey B, 1129
Bundy, Brock, 2282
Bunimovitz, Iian, 44
Bunting, Aaron, 2246
Buonanno, Bernie, 1279
Buono, Thomas J., 263
Bural, Craig, 1528
Burch, John R., 496
Burch, John, 718
Burciaga, Gil, 594
Burden, Justin, 986
Burger, Alec, 808
Burger, Nick, 2022
Burger Jr., Thomas A., 873
Burgess, Bill, 23
Burgess, Trevor, 1125
Burgess, Andy, 2244
Burgoyne, Kevin, 3262
Burgstahler, David, 209
Burgum, Doug, 173
Burgum, James, 173
Burke, Theodore D., 156
Burke, John, 1482
Burke, Rugger, 1622
Burke, Paul, 1810
Burke Jr., James J., 1023
Burkhardt, C.A., 953
Burkle, Ron, 15
Burkle, Ron, 2016
Burkoth, Bill, 1436
Burley, Sylvester, 332
Burlock, Carl, 2112
Burnes, Richard, 455
Burnham, Brad, 1882
Burns, Barbara, 64
Burns, Luke, 178
Burns, John, 329
Burns, Douglas, 551
Burns, Brian N, 856
Burns, John, 1161
Burns, Steve, 1505
Burns, Kenneth, 1679
Burns, M Roy, 1776
Burow, Kristina, 153
Burr, Amy, 1035
Burstein, Daniel L, 1235
Burton, Donald W, 1708
Burton, John, 1886

Busby, Christopher M., 857
Busch, Robin Ellis, 1726
Buser, Curtis L, 413
Bushell, Andrew M, 540
Bussgang, Jeffrey, 754
Buten, Matthew, 762
Butler, Andy, 364
Butler, Duncan, 441
Butler, Justin, 648
Butler, Dave, 1045
Butler, Michael, 1286
Butler, Chuck, 1408
Butler, Don, 1818
Butler, MD, Tara, 176
Butt Thibodeau, Stephanie, 2112
Button, Scott, 1921
Buttrick, John, 1882
Buttry, Mike, 464
Buzzy, George L., 289
Bybee, Clinton W., 153
Bye, Mark, 1256
Byers, Blake, 889
Byers, Brook, 1075
Byers, Chad, 1758
Byford, Roger, 298
Bynum, Jr, Frank K, 1062
Byrd, Andrew, 1870
Byrd, Jr., Andrew, 1870
Bytof, Brian, 1506
Byun, Brian, 1069

C

Caballero, Lou, 274
Cabigon, Mike, 2121
Cable, John, 1726
Caccavo, James, 1741
Caddedu, John, 581
Cagnassola, Phil, 899
Cahill, Jason, 408
Cahill, Ed, 938
Caillaux, Gabriel, 815
Caldbeck, Ryan, 482
Calhoun, David, 277
Calhoun, Kevin J, 1753
Calhoun, Jeffrey M., 1777
Calian, Phil, 1964
Caliento, Paul, 503
Callaghan, Kevin T., 254
Callaghan, Jon, 1860
Callahan, Thomas R, 1127
Callahan PhD, Jerry, 943
Callais, Corey, 372
Callais, Nicholas, 372
Callais II, Harold, 372
Callander, Maddie, 307
Calloch, Yves, 2095
Callow, Dana, 312
Cambier, Aohn, 971
Cameron, Dennis P, 646
Cameron, Doug, 738
Camp, Justin, 385
Camp, Jerome, 385
Camp, Gregory T., 1313
Campbell, Mary Lincoln, 652
Campbell, Alex, 731
Campbell, Nathan, 868
Campbell, Stephanie, 950
Campbell, William Y, 1426
Campbell, Kristy, 1553
Campbell, Stephen, 2087
Campbell, Rod, 2282
Campion, Thomas F, 1209
Campolo, Joseph P., 147
Can, Stephen, 277
Canarick, Jon, 1335
Canavan, Joe, 2201
Canestaro, William J, 2008

Canfield, Philip A., 884
Canning Jr, John A, 1156
Cannon, MD, Louis, 269
Canter, Stephen E., 2018
Cantrell, Kevin D, 1575
Cantwell, Wayne, 555
Cantwell, Sean, 1942
Canty, Ed, 226
Caoile, Andrea, 494
Caplain, Jason, 1710
Caputo, Rich, 1045
Caracciolo, Thomas J, 632
Carano, Bandel L., 1361
Carbery, Paul D, 789
Carbone, Paul, 1479
Cardamone, Michael, 30
Carey, James D., 1743
Cargill, Virginia, 80
Carlborg, Eric, 197
Carles, Alexander E., 1971
Carlisle, Douglas C., 1202
Carlisle, James C., 1815
Carlotti, Mike, 203
Carlson, Baron, 64
Carlson, Barrett D., 407
Carlson, Dave, 685
Carlson, David, 1536
Carlson, Mark, 2048
Carlton, Keith, 886
Carmany III, George W., 697
Carmody, Jeff, 69
Carnegie, James, 277
Carney, Michael, 1888
Carnot, Lionel, 237
Carolan, Shawn T., 1202
Carolan, Jennifer, 1527
Carolin, Roger, 1633
Carpenter, Steve, 1117
Carpenter III, Phil, 1022
Carr, Julian L, 244
Carr, Dan, 3279
Carra, Phillip C., 139
Carrabino, Jr., Joseph, 64
Carragher, Andrew, 639
Carriker, PhD, Roy C., 832
Carroll, J. Ryan, 456
Carroll, John R, 1752
Carroll, Matthew T., 1979
Carryer, Babs, 1098
Carsello, John M., 900
Carson, Jarett, 676
Carson, Bill, 954
Carson, Russell L, 1972
Carstair, Ilfryn, 1907
Carsten, Jack, 947
Carter, Larry B., 611
Carter, Chris G., 1326
Carter, Kevin, 1761
Carter, Mark H, 1776
Carusi, Mike, 59
Carusi, Mike, 1122
Caruso PhD, Richard E, 1494
Carver, Thomas A., 910
Casabona, Mario, 418
Casale, Gerard N., 1876
Casanova, Xavier, 772
Cascarilla, CFA, Charles, 1115
Casciato, Chris C, 1123
Casdin, Eli, 419
Case Jr, William F, 503
Cashman, Gregory W., 844
Cashman, Gillis C, 1153
Casilli, Gerald S, 1540
Caska, Amber, 1370
Casnocha, Ben, 1933
Caso, Michael V., 1585
Cass III, A Baron, 364

Cassaday, Jake, 2236
Cassidy, Brian, 559
Cassidy, Karen, 1418
Castaldi, Alexander R, 1039
Castelein MD, Caley, 1059
Castellarin, Michael, 2081
Castellucci, Frank, 38
Castillo, Bryan, 44
Castle, Jane, 208
Castle, John S., 327
Castle, David, 327
Castle, John K., 423
Castle, Kate, 1552
Castleberry, Brian, 290
Castleman, Randy, 551
Castro, Ramphis, 1630
Catalano, Justin, 2116
Cataldo, Mike, 1142
Catalfamo, Joe, 2259
Cathcart, Chris, 894
Cato, Jo, 430
Cato MD PhD, Allen, 430
Causgrove, Tanya, 2040
Cavanaugh, PhD, James H., 919
Cawsey, Richard, 605
Cayce, Brian, 855
Cecchetto, Marcelo, 928
Cegelski, Mike, 2212
Celniker, Abbie, 1811
Centofanti, Kevin, 352
Ceresnie, Eric, 916
Cerminaro, Jennifer, 168
Cerra, Italo, 2060
Cerrudo, Shirley, 1354
Cerutti, Romeo, 554
Cervantez, Tom, 32
Cete, Urs, 256
Cha, Dr. Albert, 1941
Chabra, Roger, 2239
Chaddha, Navin, 1184
Chadwell, Tracy, 7
Chadwick, John H, 493
Chae, Michael, 277
Chaffee, Todd C., 1001
Chaisson, John, 681
Chait, Jon, 580
Chalmers Balbach, Jennifer, 1751
Chalstrom, Brownell, 207
Chaltiel, Victor, 1532
Chaltiel, Antoinette "Toni", 1532
Cham, James, 284
Chamberlain, Alex, 2161
Chambers, Mike, 363
Chambers, John, 1031
Chambers, Brian F., 1409
Chambers, Jeffrey T, 1776
Chan, Connie, 124
Chan, Wesley, 720
Chan, William, 1138
Chan, Ryan, 2253
Chandarana, Ashish, 1925
Chandler, David G, 468
Chandna, Rishi, 839
Chandna, Asheem, 872
Chandra, Amit, 220
Chang, Frank, 755
Chang, Andrew, 1115
Chang, Dorothy Jean, 1115
Chao, David, 596
Chao, Pierre, 680
Chao, Clint, 764
Chapanoff, Charlotte, 305
Chapman, J. Russell, 172
Chapman, Duncan A, 1112
Chapman, Tim, 2104
Chapman, Matthew, 2272
Chapman, Dave, 2292

Executive Name Index

Chappell, Scott E., 263
Chappell, Jim, 1417
Chappell, John F, 1452
Chapus, Jean-Marc, 556
Charlton, Jim, 2143
Charpie, Richard A., 118
Chatham, Bob, 1693
Chau, Paul, 1983
Chazen, Jerome A, 460
Chazen, David F, 460
Cheadle, David, 2074
Cheang, Christopher PH, 1465
Chee, Brian, 1460
Cheever, Chris, 760
Chefitz, Robert, 1328
Chen, Wu-Fu, 47
Chen, Drew, 220
Chen, Alan, 374
Chen, Andy, 509
Chen, Joanne, 770
Chen, Jerry, 872
Chen, Jesse, 1180
Chen, Phil, 1473
Chen, Roger, 1685
Chen, Jesson, 2229
Chen, PhD, Alice, 31
Chen, PhD, Leon, 517
Chen, PhD, Anna H., 782
Cheney, Matt, 499
Cheng, Cheryl, 296
Cheng, C.K., 905
Cheng, Ray, 1235
Cheng, Larry, 1942
Cheng, Julian, 1956
Cherington, Charles, 1009
Cherington, Stephen, 1009
Cherkashin, Pavel, 890
Cherry, Brian, 1360
Chertok, Doug, 580
Cherun, Robert, 2047
Chesney, Rob, 471
Chesnoff, Adam, 1598
Chesse, Jean Pierre, 281
Chessick, Cary, 731
Chestnut, Edward A., 1496
Cheung, Liam, 2260
Chhabra, Kate, 428
Chheda, Neil, 1581
Chiang, Helen, 110
Chiang, Brian, 1951
Chiao, Stephen, 1769
Chiarelli, Paul, 2284
Chiavacci, Ingrid, 956
Chiefetz, Yoni, 1121
Chihi, Kyce, 193
Chik Lin Oi, Anita, 1139
Childres, Christopher, 653
Childress, Stacey, 1316
Childs, John W, 1049
Chin, Eric, 563
Chintamaneni, Prasad, 1301
Chiriaev, Dan, 861
Chitnis, Sach, 1046
Chiu, Ian, 1392
Chiu, Alan, 2011
Cho, Hoon, 824
Choe, Michael, 456
Choi, Yumin, 221
Choi, Iris, 751
Choi, Ben, 1106
Choi, Jai, 1416
Choi, Jamie, 1611
Choi, Thomas, 2250
Choi, Jennifer, 3266
Cholakis, George H., 2030
Chong, Simon, 2132
Chopra, Arjun, 751

Chopra, Ajay, 1853
Chou, Jonathan Y, 698
Chou, Scott, 805
Chou, T.C., 905
Chou, Allan, 1341
Chou, Christy, 1922
Chou, Tony M, 1929
Chou, Scott, 2023
Choudhary, Bharat, 2287
Chrisney, Craig, 972
Christ, William D, 1776
Christensen, Gavin, 1070
Christiansen, Bob, 1711
Christianson, Tony, 464
Christianson, MBA, Tyler, 560
Christoffersen PhD, Chris, 1122
Christopher, Nicholas S., 1093
Christopher, David, 1422
Christopher, David, 1423
Chrust, Steven, 448
Chu, Yee-Ping, 274
Chu, Quentin, 559
Chu, Sherman I, 856
Chu, Nelson, 1072
Chu, J Michael, 1088
Chu, Wayee, 1527
Chuang, Connie, 1180
Chui-Miller, Grace, 544
Chung, Jeff, 107
Chung, Walter, 331
Chung, Young, 581
Chung, Henry, 626
Chung, Patrick, 708
Chung, Joyce, 807
Chung, Chris, 878
Chung, William, 892
Chung, Peter, 1255
Chung, Patrick, 1284
Chung, Peter Y, 1752
Chung, Patrick, 2254
Churbuck, Thomas K, 66
Churchill, Winston J, 1633
Chwang, Dr Ronald, 970
Cioffi, Robert, 80
Ciporin, Daniel, 386
Ciriello, Paul, 712
Cirino, Maria, 2
Claassen, Robert, 384
Clancy, John P., 1496
Clapp, Todd, 427
Clark, Tom, 528
Clark, Ryan, 819
Clark, Tyson, 889
Clark, Gregory E., 946
Clark, Brian M, 1153
Clark, John, 1431
Clark, Roddy JH, 1533
Clark, Susan, 1785
Clark, Paul, 1923
Clark, Ric, 2067
Clark, Scott, 2087
Clark, Peter, 2143
Clark, Peter, 2216
Clark Jr, Robert, 359
Clark, Jr., Peter L., 415
Clarke, John, 410
Clary, Matt, 1963
Clavier, Jeff, 1700
Clavier, Jeff, 1879
Clayton, Kevin, 675
Cleland, Andrew, 518
Cleland, Hugh, 2242
Clemens, Sam, 38
Clements, Miles, 28
Cleveland, Bruce, 1985
Clevenger, Wayne L, 1230
Clevinger, Brian, 1488

Cline, J Michael, 39
Clough, Phil, 22
Cloyd, Malcolm, 186
Cluss, Ed, 1678
Coady, James D, 1651
Coats, David, 544
Coats, Stephen S., 1573
Cobb, Steve A, 478
Coburn, Brooke B, 413
Coburn, Chris, 1419
Coca, Lisa, 809
Cochran, John D, 1147
Cochrane, Greg, 2282
Cockrell, Ross, 695
Cocozza, Keith, 1827
Cogan, Gill, 1381
Coglizer, Dave, 1977
Cohan, Jay, 1975
Cohen, Josh, 488
Cohen, Andrew B., 510
Cohen, Jake, 607
Cohen, Josh, 839
Cohen, Aaron D., 884
Cohen, Rob, 1020
Cohen, Brian, 1306
Cohen, Brian, 1310
Cohen, Trace, 1310
Cohen, Michael, 1369
Cohen, Bennett, 1449
Cohen, Wayne, 1635
Cohen, Charles, 1775
Cohen, David, 1789
Cohen, Ira D, 1886
Cohen, Fred, 1932
Cohen, Matt, 2241
Cohler, Matt, 248
Cohn, Michael, 883
Cohn, MD, Billy, 1619
Coit, David M, 1333
Colangelo, Larry A, 1230
Colao, Dan, 808
Cole, Marshall, 213
Cole, Doug, 747
Cole, Philip, 1763
Cole, James A, 1995
Cole Jr, C Taylor, 910
Colecchi, Christopher, 347
Colella, Vanessa, 486
Colella, Samuel D, 1928
Coleman III, Charles P, 1826
Collatos, William P, 1717
Colleran, Kevin, 1694
Collett, Mike, 1489
Collier, Cesar, 1679
Collier, Scott, 1855
Collings, Greg, 2126
Collins, Christopher L, 1062
Collins, Derrick K, 1461
Collins, John, 1751
Collins, Andrew J, 1752
Collins, Scott C, 1752
Collinson, Jeffrey J, 474
Collinson, Stuart, 769
Collis, Jim, 1638
Collister, R. Craig, 1590
Collombel, Philippe, 1416
Colloton, Ed, 260
Colmenares, Alan, 1781
Colodny, Mark M, 1956
Colon, Jr., Daniel, 507
Colone, Paul A., 77
Colonna, Elizabeth, 918
Colowick, Alan, 1698
Comey, Robert A., 1016
Compall, John, 489
Conacher, Lionel, 1318
Conci Orozco, Gianna, 491

Condon Jr, Edward J, 1414
Cone, Michael M, 631
Conese Jr., Eugene P., 873
Coneybeer, Robert, 1663
Conklin, Richard, 732
Conley, Bill, 380
Conley, Paul, 1400
Conlon, James, 358
Connaughton, John, 220
Connell, William C, 931
Connelly, Patrick, 1009
Connolly, John, 221
Connor, John, 21
Connor, Stephen B., 899
Connor, Tim, 1653
Connors, Brian, 764
Connors, John, 974
Connors, Tim, 1450
Connors, William G., 1744
Connors II, James J, 1062
Conrad, Barry B, 984
Conrad, Tony, 1860
Conrado, Eduardo, 1260
Conroy, Jim, 1372
Conte, Jean-Pierre L., 819
Conti, Vincent S, 1520
Conway, William E, 201
Conway, Ron, 1761
Conway, Topher, 1761
Conway, Brian J, 1776
Conway Jr, William E, 413
Cook, Matthew A, 1071
Cook, Everett R, 1466
Cook, Charles, 2097
Cook III, Joe, 1261
Cook Jr, Joe, 1261
Cooney, David J, 244
Cooper, Bradley E., 404
Cooper, Wayne, 863
Cooper, Marshall, 863
Cooper, Chris, 1425
Cooper, Mike, 1667
Cooper, MD, Thomas P., 136
Coote, Kim, 2288
Coover, Gary, 1611
Copans, Richard H, 1156
Copeland, Gene, 1837
Coppedge, Schuyler, 675
Coppens, Brad, 1376
Coppens, Brad, 1376
Coppinger, Liam, 2183
Coppola, Michael, 582
Coquillette, David C., 1301
Corcoran, Dan, 1173
Cordova, Gonzalo, 1911
Corey, Chris F., 1279
Corkran, Ao Ann, 841
Corl, James, 1679
Corley, Leslie M, 1137
Corley, Evan, 1411
Cormier, Guy, 2095
Cornacchione, Jason R., 1456
Cornelis, Kelly A., 1093
Cornell, Chad M., 843
Corning, Sally, 1754
Corriggio, Anthony, 1679
Corry, Daniel, 69
Cortas, Usama, 1109
Corzine, Nicola, 226
Cosentino, Leonard M, 1287
Cosgriff, John G., 1016
Costantino, Kevin, 864
Costantino, John R, 1325
Costanzo, Maria F, 1621
Costello, Kevin P., 309
Costello, Dennis R., 322
Costello, Dennis B, 1847

Executive Name Index

Costin, Tom, 1392
Cote, Diane, 2191
Cotton, Ryan, 220
Couch, C Deryl, 1753
Coughran, Bill, 1654
Coulson, Fred, 745
Counihan, Jim, 1478
Cournoyer, JS, 2232
Couture, Luc, 2268
Coveny, Amy, 1507
Cowan, David, 260
Cowen, Will, 1142
Cox, Everett, 665
Cox, Charles A, 1144
Cozzi, John, 64
Crabill, Scott, 1814
Craig, Jackson, 239
Craig, Ryan, 257
Cramer, Yeon, 268
Crandall, J. Taylor, 1360
Crandell, Keith L., 153
Crane, Alan, 1460
Cranford, Adam, 1293
Cranswick, Russ, 1548
Crasto, Anil L, 1826
Cravens, McCall, 957
Cravens, Ashley, 1879
Craver, Jeffrey, 61
Craves, PhD, Fred, 237
Crawford, Charlie, 475
Crawford, Andrew, 815
Crawford, Matthew S, 1500
Crawford, Ryan, 2166
Crawford PhD, Douglas, 1238
Creamer, Glenn M., 1496
Creasey, Fred, 2255
Creech, Todd, 921
Creer, Frank M., 2021
Cremin, David, 791
Cressey, Bryan, 558
Cresswell, Simon, 135
Crihfield, Steve, 899
Crisalis, Robert, 1800
Crissman, Blaine, 1477
Crittenden, Gary, 959
Crocker, Curtis D, 1544
Crockett, Catherine, 879
Crockett, Todd R, 1776
Croft, Matthew, 1130
Croll, David D, 1153
Cromwell III, Michael J, 1388
Cronin, Michael F., 1978
Cronkey, Damon, 2011
Crosbie, Allan, 2089
Crosby, Kevin M., 156
Crosby, Richard, 898
Crosby, Chris J., 1279
Cross, Cairn G, 786
Cross, Matthew, 2167
Cross, Stacey, 2269
Crothers, Mike, 702
Crouthamel, Jamie, 731
Crowder, Randall, 1801
Crowe, Jeffrey M, 1346
Crowell, Bill, 93
Crowell, Richard R, 1904
Crowley, Kevin, 530
Croxon, Bruce, 2243
Croxton, R Randy, 1208
Crumpler, John, 915
Crussel, David, 787
Cruz, Brandon, 731
Cryer, Natalie D, 378
Cubitt, Code, 2195
Cuccio, Gary, 1793
Cukier, Ben, 440
Culham, Harry, 2079

Cullen, Chuck, 876
Cullinane, Kelli, 1106
Culp, Kevin, 1022
Cummings, David, 189
Cummings, Benton, 1516
Cummings, Bob, 1990
Cunning, Matt, 2178
Cunningham, Jason M, 164
Cunningham, Sean, 763
Cunningham, Sean L., 884
Cunningham, Ronan, 1717
Cunningham Jr., Emmett, 495
Cunningham MD, Joe, 1619
Cunningham, MD, Casey, 1619
Cuomo, Alexander, 1325
Cureton, Chip, 888
Curley, Kevin J., 1037
Curran, D Patrick, 364
Currie, Lauchlan, 2040
Currier, James, 1323
Curry, Bob, 1094
Curry, Michael, 2161
Curtin, Adam H, 1234
Custar, Krisin, 1045
Custer, William M., 571
Cusumano CFA, Dino, 109
Cutler, Lucas T., 328
Cutler, Joel, 816
Cutts, Joseph, 1381
Czarny, Samuel, 250
Czornyj, Adrianna, 2220
Czuba, Gregory S, 691

D

Daccus, Paul, 1753
D'Addario, Paul, 1402
Dadoo, Rajeev, 1731
D'Agostino, Michael, 1432
Dagres, Todd, 1715
Dahl, Ben, 1677
Dahnke, Scott A., 1088
Daileader, John, 862
Daing, Avantika, 1454
Dalal MD, Anupam, 1059
Dale, Andy, 1250
Dalheim, Stu, 376
Dallaire, André, 473
Dalton PhD, Barbara J, 1436
Dalton, Frank X, 537
Dalton, Frank X, 794
Dalvey, David, 341
Dalvie, Shivanandan A., 64
Daly, Celia, 392
Daly, Michael F, 1521
D'Amico, Brian, 1751
Damico, Joseph F., 1590
D'Amore, Richard A, 1334
Dan, Aubrey, 2094
Danard, Chad, 2275
Dance, Dr. Kerry, 898
Dancewicz, John E, 619
D'Andrea, Harry, 1899
D'Andrea, Jon, 1976
D'Angelo, Vincent, 240
Danhakl, John G, 1109
Dani, Nick, 625
D'Aniello, Daniel A, 413
Daniels, C Bryan, 1469
Daniels, Marcus, 2147
Daniels, Melissa, 1255
Daniels, Roanne, 924
Daniels, Terry, 1505
Daraviras, Nicholas, 1032
Darby, Christopher, 979
Darden, Tom, 463
D'Argenio, Rahman, 675
Darling, Scott, 603

Dautrich, Tyler, 866
DaValle Jr., Albert, 1038
Davenport III, Robert R., 340
Davidson, Duncan, 358
Davidson, Jeff, 465
Davidson, Mitchell, 1465
Davidson, Stuart, 1089
Davidson, Vinse, 1783
Davies III, Paul L, 378
Davies, Natalie L, 378
Davies, Rhiannon, 2247
Davis, Allan, 640
Davis, Anthony B, 1128
Davis, Anthony, 1843
Davis, Barry M, 591
Davis, Bob, 935
Davis, Charles A., 1743
Davis, Chris, 810
Davis, Clark F., 1562
Davis, J. Bradley, 1562
Davis, Jeff, 48
Davis, Jerel, 1928
Davis, Jordan S, 1520
Davis, Kim G., 456
Davis, Kim, 2281
Davis, Owen, 1358
Davis, Robert E, 1134
Davis, Stephen, 227
Davis, Timothy C, 786
Davis, W Ryan, 1159
Davison, Jeff, 989
Davoli, Robert E, 1673
Dawson, Jr., William F., 1971
Day, Rob, 1729
Daych, Diane M., 434
Dayton, Troy, 1807
de Alba, Gabriel, 2073
de Clercq, Casper, 1346
de Jager, Thomas, 118
De La Cruz, Marta, 834
de Luna, Leo, 1154
de Nicola, Anthony J, 1972
de Rooij, Deborah, 2248
de Turenne, Noel, 1250
De Winter, Alex, 809
De Zwirek, Gurion, 2254
Dean, Christopher J, 1752
Dean, John C, 1737
Dean, John, 939
Dean, Rahsaan, 992
Dean, Thompson, 209
DeAngelis, Ken, 202
DeAngelis, Pasquale, 1490
DeAngelo, Steve, 1807
Dearing, Michael, 911
Deb, Dipanjan (DJ), 779
Debbane, Raymond, 1018
Debiasi, Gerard A, 1071
DeBlois, Mark, 359
DeBruin, Robert, 1292
DeCaire, Ryan, 2045
Decarie, Catherine, 2112
Dechet, Rainer, 1265
DeCillis II, Steven, 64
DeCorte, Evan, 515
Dedes Gallagher, Marina, 1934
Deeb, George, 731
Dees, Michael W, 1129
Deeter, Byron, 260
DeFalco, Stephen P, 1129
Defieux, Rick, 1689
DeFlorio, Michael B., 914
Degenhart, Jeremy, 61
DeGroff, Dain F, 1846
Degroot, Seth, 341
Deitzer, James R., 355
del Gaudio, Elisa, 41

Del Guercio, Joe, 508
deLaar, Mark A, 1752
Delaney, Bob, 559
Delaney, Christopher, 1023
Delaney, Daniel L., 985
Delaplane, Kevin, 1881
Deleray, Michael, 343
Delgado, Lister, 971
Delistathis, Thanasis, 1291
Delistathis, Thanasis, 1482
Dell'Aquila, Richard T, 353
Dellenbach, Hans, 2106
DeLorenzo, Jason M., 672
DeLuca, Dino, 2275
deMarrais, Brett, 1150
DeMartini, Rich, 559
Demetriades, Jim, 1051
Demkowicz, Brian, 960
Demond, Jeff, 154
DeMott, Harry, 1525
Dempsey, Michael, 525
Dempsey, Neal, 238
Dempsey, Sean, 1218
DeMuth, Donald F., 610
Deng, Feng, 1340
Denham, Michael, 2055
DeNichilo, Matt, 675
DeNino, Mark, 1828
Dennedy, Tom, 174
Denning, Steven, 815
Denos, Kenneth I., 694
Dent, James, 2188
Dent, Stephen J., 2062
Denton, James T., 343
Denton, Stephen, 2251
Denvir, Michael, 1045
der Kinderen, Marc, 14
Derks, Menno, 2248
DeRosa, Ben, 109
DeRosa, Michael, 657
Derr Gilbert, Karen, 793
Dershem, Dan, 1757
DeRubertis, Jamie J., 299
Des Pallieres, Bertrand, 694
Desai, Keval, 1010
DeSena, Bob, 878
Deshpande, Salil, 221
Desmarais III, Paul, 2225
DesMarais, Robert, 1767
Detkin, Peter, 1005
Deutsch, David N, 589
Devereux, Robin W, 1752
DeVino, Sally A., 1743
Devita, Andrea, 371
Devitte, Jesse, 308
Devlaminck, Lode J, 637
DeVore, Chris, 773
Devorsetz, Dan, 946
DeVos, Rick, 1736
DeVries, Jerry, 1801
DeVries, Lawson, 876
DeVries, Mike, 652
DeVries, Tim, 1345
D'Halluin, Thomas, 73
Dhami, Narinder, 2185
Dharmaraj, Satish, 1534
Dhillon, Sunny, 1678
Dhol, Parag, 1013
Dhonte, Sebastien, 2081
Di Bona, Tony, 87
Di Geronimo, Robert, 1432
Di Nardo, Bill, 2110
Di Prata, Cam, 2133
Diallo, Vincent, 1006
Diamond, Carey, 2288
Diamond, Douglas, 693
Diamond, Shayn, 2288

Executive Name Index

Diaz, Omar, 629
Diaz, Paul, 558
DiBella, Paul R, 537
Dibella, Paul, 768
Dichter, Sasha, 55
Dick, Christopher W., 178
Dick, Jonathan E, 1476
Dick, Timothy, 1737
Dickens, Jorge, 46
Dickey, Sarah, 3256
Dickinson, Arlene, 2099
Dickinson, Brendan, 386
Dickinson, Daniel, 917
Dickson, Jeffrey L., 1497
Didato, Dean, 995
Diehl, Bowen S., 403
Diehl, Jeffrey, 57
Dickman PhD, John D, 12
Dielwart, John, 2040
Dieschbourg, Michael T, 987
Digmy, Vered, 116
DiLella, Gary R, 1494
Dillabough, Gary, 1282
Dillman, David, 1553
Dillon, Karl D, 940
Dimberio, Joe, 1871
Dimitri, James, 1925
Dimou, Mary, 2071
Diner, Fahri, 1672
Ding, Chun, 472
DiNovi, Anthony J., 1815
Dintersmith, Ted, 455
DiPiano, Michael, 1317
DiPucchio, Rocco, 2073
Dishner, Jeffrey G., 1739
Dixon, Brian, 660
Dixon, Donald R., 1850
Dixon, Donald, 763
Dixon, Michael, 2270
Dixon, Rocky, 673
Dlugos, Andrea, 2001
Do, Trung Q., 1419
Dobbin, Mark, 2168
Docter, Daniel, 603
Doctoroff, Adam S, 1248
Dodson, Andrew C., 1417
Doerer, John W, 1461
Doherty, Gerry, 1277
Doiguchi, Wayne, 214
Dokas, Elias, 1231
Dolan, A. Barr, 458
Dolbac, Michael, 809
Dolce, Michael J, 1156
Dolder, Adam B., 859
Dolezal, David, 1915
Doll, Alex, 1794
Doll, Dixon, 596
Domach, Jim, 1171
Domanig, Gina, 2106
Dombalagian, Vahe A, 1156
Dominguez, Michael J., 1496
Dominguez-Edington, Victoria, 445
Dominik, David, 839
Domolky, Randolph C, 1133
Donabedian, David H, 1145
Donaghy, Brian, 344
Donahue Jr, Donald J, 691
Donatelli, Mark, 2058
Donelan, James T, 1636
Donelson, Mishone B., 946
Doner, Chris, 253
Dong, Candy, 2234
Dong, Yizhen, 4
Donnellan, Patrick J, 691
Donner, Andy, 1438
Donnini, David A., 884

Donoghue, Michael F., 1727
Donohue, Liam, 2
Donovan, Dana, 631
Donovan, Michael E, 1972
Doody, Christopher M., 1743
Dooley, John, 1027
Doomany, George, 123
Dorman, Mark, 673
Dorsen, Edith, 2003
Dorsey, Scott, 929
Doshi, Rutvik, 1013
Dotson, Laura, 1063
Dotzler, Frederick J, 598
Doub, Robb, 1299
Doubleday, Ned, 1152
Dougery, John, 1013
Dougherty, Dennis, 1008
Dougherty, MD, James B., 157
Douglass, David, 604
Douglass, James S, 794
Douglass, Olleb, 1259
Douvos, Chris, 72
Dova, Pietro, 2010
Dovey, Brian, 621
Dovi, Damien A., 263
Dow, Stephen M, 1658
Dowdle, Robin, 68
Dowling, James J., 1032
Downey, Bruce, 1317
Downing Jr., Joseph J., 77
Downs, Mark, 1280
Downs, Matt, 1615
Dowty, Scott, 203
Doyle, Daniel K, 1770
Doyle, Jere, 1673
Doyle, Kaitlyn, 1019
Doyle, Kenneth M., 894
Doyle, Maurice, 61
Doyle, Noah J., 1028
Doyle, Sean, 1004
Doyle, Sean, 1610
Doyon, Eric, 2107
Dracon, Greg, 2
Drager, Andrea, 215
Drahms, David, 1387
Drakonakis, Konstantine, 1097
Drant, Ryan, 1514
Draper III, William H, 627
Draper, Adam, 307
Draper, Jesse, 896
Draper, Tim, 626
Draper, Timothy, 2021
Draper, Timothy, 609
Drattell, Jason D, 1468
Draves, Brian, 1794
Drazan, Jeff, 257
Dreier, Robert, 359
Dresner, Edward I, 646
Dresner, Steven M, 629
Drew, John, 1785
Drewlo, Norm, 2258
Dreyfuss, Andy, 1442
Driscoll, Craig, 935
Driscoll, PhD, Ted, 491
Dritz, Russell S, 1504
Drokova, Masha, 593
Drowse, Peter, 2163
Druley, David, 379
Drury, Paul W., 1111
Dubczak, Roman S., 2079
Dubilier, Michael J, 631
Duboc, Samuel L., 2103
Dubreuil, Pierre, 2055
Dubuque, Louis, 61
Duda, Jim, 582
Duffy, Patrick J, 1276
Duffy, Pauline, 1540

Dufourmantelle, Olivier, 2071
Dugan, Jim, 1364
Dugan, John, 1364
Dugan, Kevin T., 869
Dugan, Tim, 1961
Dugenske, John, 88
Duggal, Rajat, 787
Duguid, Rob, 2221
Dullum, David, 828
Dunaway, Barry, 108
Dunbar, Matt, 1923
Dunbar, William, 538
Duncan, Michael, 2089
Duncan, Pat, 213
Dunfield, Ryan, 2246
Dunham, Jennifer, 171
Dunlap, Kevin, 370
Dunlop, A. Sinclair, 689
Dunlop, Scott, 2084
Dunn, Andrew, 1376
Dunn, Andy, 1531
Dunn, Michael, 693
Dunn, Patrick D., 1496
Dunnan, Bruce B., 875
Dunnan, Douglas M., 875
Dunwoodie, Kevin, 1411
Dupcak, Scott, 532
Dupere, Justin C, 1963
Dupree, David, 894
Durban, Egon, 1683
Durbin, Chris A., 1931
Durbin, Eliot, 305
Durkin, Jr., Charles P., 1621
Durrett, Park, 29
Durst, Greg, 3266
Dutch, Suzette, 1847
Dutta, Shomik, 934
Dutton, Joseph, 1960
Dutton, Steve, 1062
Dwane, Anne, 1933
Dworkin, Andrew L., 1911
Dwyer, Suzanne L, 1173
Dyal, Tom, 1534

E

Eadie, MD, James, 1619
Eagle, David A., 357
Eakin, Rory, 482
Eames, Anthony, 376
Earhart, John, 834
Earley, Richard P, 636
Earls, Alex, 881
Eason, Randall, 96
Eastburn Jr., John S., 1083
Eastman, Ron, 697
Easton, Loren, 110
Eatroff, Bruce A, 897
Eaves, Cory, 815
Ebert, Sean, 98
Ebinger, Jonathan, 296
Eby, Doug, 1375
Eby, Jeff, 2008
Eckert, Carol, 782
Eckert, John, 2199
Eckert, John, 2243
Eddy, Tom, 1027
Edeburn, Patrick, 850
Edelson, Harry, 651
Edelson, MD, Jon, 177
Edgerton, Matt, 1062
Edwards, S. Whitfield, 746
Edwards, Donald J., 750
Edwards, Scott W, 1753
Efstratis, Nick, 688
Egan, Ash, 38
Egan, Chris, 62

Egan, Michael, 2282
Eggers, Barry, 1121
Ehlers, Michael, 143
Ehrenberg, Roger, 965
Ehrenpreis, Ira, 595
Ehrenpreis, Ira M, 1786
Ehrenpreis, Ira, 3284
Ehret, Gregory A., 1444
Ehrhart, Robert, 220
Ehrhart, Ken, 692
Ehrhart, Ken, 1755
Ehrich, Peter, 558
Eichler, David, 1498
Eiermann, Julie, 909
Einav, PhD, Shmuel, 1808
Einhorn, Stephen, 400
Einhorn, Daniel, 400
Eisenberg, Paul, 143
Eisenberg, Dave, 1531
Eisenberg, Jonathan, 1843
Eisenhauer, Tom, 2065
Eisenman, Randy, 1622
Eisenson, Michael R., 456
Eisenstein, Stephen, 914
Eisinger, Michael, 2214
Eisler, David, 2235
Eitan, Yaron, 1633
Eitan, Yaron, 1647
Ekman, Lars, 1698
El Amine, Firas, 1017
El Baze, Nicolase, 1416
El Chami, Joe, 1022
El-Ayat, Omar, 563
El-Nazer, Hythem T, 1776
Elahian, Kamran, 833
Elbaz, Gil, 1798
Elburn, Jeff, 1742
Eldridge, Paul, 2126
Elenko, Eric, 1501
Elfman, Rick, 1742
Elgner, Claude, 2104
Elgner, Roger, 2104
Elias, Jamie E, 1857
Eliasek, Michael G., 1491
Eline, Christopher M., 900
Eliot, Philip, 1400
Elishis, Isser, 2283
Elkhatib, Rami, 41
Elkhatib, Rami, 1709
Elkus, Bill, 502
Elliott, Charles, 656
Elliott, Mike, 1331
Elliott, Jim, 2064
Elliott, William, 2105
Ellis, Chad, 42
Ellis, David O, 656
Ellis, Seth, 1430
Ellis, Jonathan, 1614
Ellis III, Alexander, 1579
Ellison, David G., 97
Ellman, Stuart, 1593
Ellsworth, Robert, 898
Elman, Dr. Sheldon, 2220
Elman, Stuart M., 2220
Elmer, Donald J, 1398
Elmore, Bill, 770
Elmore, Qian W., 969
Elms, Steven A., 74
Elrod Jr., James L., 1931
Eltrich III, Martin, 64
Embry Jr, Robert C, 19
Emery, Mark, 1045
Emmert, Robert Y, 1276
Emmitt, Richard B, 1929
Empson, Joshua C., 1496
Emry, Deric, 867
Eng, Marty, 1975

1083

Executive Name Index

Eng, Darren, 3268
Engel, Beth, 635
Engel, Jerry, 1249
Engelberg, Steve, 1615
Engelhardt, Philip, 1437
Engestrom, Jyri, 2014
Engle, Bridget E, 303
Engleman, Dr. Edgar G, 1941
Engler, Edward R, 1447
Enjoji, Kay, 1791
Ennis, Greg, 1427
Enns, Marcus, 2077
Enright, Patrick, 1143
Enriquez, Juan, 703
Entress, Geoff, 1499
Epstein, Jason, 516
Epstein, Gary C, 937
Epstein, Mark E, 1271
Epstein, Alv, 1742
Erhard, John F., 156
Erickson, Paul K., 462
Erickson, Thomas, 738
Erickson, Christopher, 1820
Erickson, Chris, 2213
Ericson, William, 1247
Ericson, Bill, 1985
Ermotti, Sergio P., 1878
Ervin, Daley, 677
Es Sabar, Karimah, 2229
Escobar, Sergio, 2054
Escobari, Martin, 815
Esparrago, Peter, 569
Espitallier, David, 729
Esserman, Chuck, 1861
Esserman, Charles H, 1861
Essex, Rick, 1496
Estes, PhD, Daniel, 782
Eubank II, Frederick W., 1409
Eubanks Jr., Robert C., 780
Evans, Timothy M., 156
Evans, David S., 830
Evans, April E, 1248
Evans, Karen, 1687
Evans, Hugh D., 1925
Evans, Larry, 2025
Eve, Derek, 673
Evers, Elliot B, 1195
Every, MD, MPH, Nathan R., 782
Evnin, Luke B, 1268
Evola, Carmen, 276
Exshaw, Christian, 2079
Exter, Neil, 1811

F

Faber, Bart, 192
Faber, Robert, 224
Fabiani, Vin, 938
Fabreau, Melissa, 2025
Fachetti, Dave, 835
Fade, Richard, 974
Fader, Steven B., 190
Fagnan, Jeff, 38
Fahey, Kevin P., 299
Fahoury, Doug, 1020
Failing, Bruce F, 80
Fajgenbaum, Jonas, 1018
Fake, Caterina, 2014
Falk, Michael, 528
Falk, Thomas, 1554
Falkenstein, Joseph, 1328
Falktoft, Henrik, 1516
Fallon, Patrick, 29
Fallon, Timothy G., 147
Fallon, Julie, 2076
Fang, Lawrence, 1987
Farah, Michael, 1128
Faraone, Steve, 2217

Farber, Jonathan, 1125
Farello, Michael J., 1088
Farid, Saman, 219
Faris, Karim, 889
Faris, David M, 1606
Farkas, Brad, 964
Farmer, Chris, 1675
Farmer, Ron, 2198
Farner, Peter W, 1802
Farnsworth, Jim, 2050
Farquhar, Sharon, 2105
Farquharson, Andrew, 980
Farrar, James, 2253
Farrell, William, 170
Farrell, Jim, 368
Farrell, Mike, 1717
Farrell, Mark E, 1806
Farrero, Jeff, 468
Farrington, Deborah A, 1738
Farsht, Steve, 731
Farwell, Brandon, 708
Fassnacht, Michael, 731
Fates, Matt, 178
Faulkingham, Ryan J., 523
Faust, Dorian, 881
Fawcett, David, 2108
Fay, Sarah, 829
Fay, Timothy P, 1636
Fearnow, Brian, 368
Federman, Irwin, 1896
Feeley, Edmund J, 1134
Feeney, Gordon, 2282
Feerick, Robert M., 945
Feiber, Jon, 1247
Feidler, Mark L, 1270
Feiler, Jack, 1401
Feinberg, Stephen A., 451
Feinstein, Brian, 260
Feinstein, Peter, 270
Feinstein, Adam, 1930
Feitosa, Rodrigo, 928
Feld, Brad, 776
Feld, Stacy, 1042
Feld, Brad, 1245
Feld, Stacy, 1438
Feld, Brad, 1789
Feldman, Jesse, 235
Feldman, Matthew S., 492
Feldman, Greg S., 1971
Feldmen, Scott, 1759
Felesky, Adam, 2225
Felman, David S., 869
Felser, Josh, 784
Felt, Benjamin, 1018
Feltenstein, Sidney J, 1651
Fenton, Peter, 248
Fenton, Dean E, 1735
Fenton, Noel J, 1853
Fenwick-Smith, Robert, 146
Ferguson, Jeffrey W, 413
Ferguson, Rod, 1410
Fernandes, Mark, 1670
Fernandez, Jason, 1507
Fernandez, Manny, 1668
Ferneau, Phil, 308
Ferrara, Alex, 260
Ferrari, Richard M., 598
Ferrari, Wes, 972
Ferrari, Marco J., 1496
Ferreira, Beth, 743
Ferrell, Jeffrey A., 188
Ferri, Paul J, 1181
Ferrington, Leonard C, 1752
Ferris, Paul, 215
Feuille, Jim, 563
Fialkow, David, 816
Fiato, John, 909

Fich, Nicole, 2219
Fichtner, Kirk, 1167
Fiedler, Jason, 1530
Field, Ezra S., 1576
Fields, Mark, 93
Fields, Kathy, 1041
Fife, John, 470
Filipowski, Andrew "Flip", 1681
Fillat, Andy, 1102
Finayson, Malcolm, 898
Finch, Lawrence G, 1672
Fine, Ari, 148
Fine, Adam E, 1993
Fine, Roger S, 1993
Fine Glantz, Ari, 3273
Finegan, Scott A., 1435
Fingerle, Linda, 652
Fink, Andrew, 1844
Finkel, Robert, 1477
Finkelstein, Daniel, 845
Finkelstein, Brett, 1439
Finkelstein, Alex, 1715
Finkelstein, Kenny, 2171
Finlay, Matthew W, 1230
Finlayson, Joel, 2149
Finn, Christopher, 413
Finnegan, Paul J, 1156
Fiorentino, David A, 1049
Fioretti, Robert J, 717
First, Mark L., 686
Fisch, Michael, 110
Fishbin, Paul, 901
Fisher, Adam, 260
Fisher, Bob, 493
Fisher, John, 609
Fisher, Brett, 744
Fisher, Doug, 821
Fisher, Doug, 1010
Fisher, Stewart, 1086
Fisher, Mark, 1188
Fisher, Ronald D, 1699
Fisherman, Jason, 1775
Fishman, David, 1910
Fitzgerald, Thomas C., 360
Fitzgerald, Brian, 401
Fitzgerald, John, 467
Fitzgerald, Michael T., 521
Fitzgerald, Bill, 816
Fitzgerald, Peter, 1094
Fitzgerald, C.J., 1752
Fitzgerald, James, 1897
Fitzgerald, William, 1991
Fitzpatrick, Thomas P, 1651
Fitzsimmons, Robert J, 931
Flager, Morgan, 1685
Flanagan, Robert J, 508
Flanagan, Dave, 1004
Flanagan, Paul, 1672
Flanagan, Paul, 1673
Flanigan, John W., 461
Flannery, Michael E, 633
Flannery, Bob, 1536
Flaster, Andy, 1942
Flater, Graham, 2126
Flatley, Daniel K, 1175
Flatt, Bruce, 2067
Fleck, Philip, 1347
Fleischer, Spencer, 787
Fleischmann, Charles, 1851
Fleming, Jim, 515
Fleming, Standish, 769
Fleming, Daniel T, 1571
Fleming Arora, Natalie, 1758
Flemons, Wade, 2218
Fleshman, Skip, 181
Fletcher, John, 749
Fletcher III, F. Barron, 1415

Fligel, Andy, 1004
Flint, Pete, 1323
Flint, Jon, 1460
Florea, Raluca, 332
Florence, Walter C, 789
Florence, Tony, 1297
Flores, Tami, 229
Florsheim, Steven, 1889
Florsheim, Riley, 1890
Flower, Mark, 1963
Floyd, Joe, 665
Floyd, Nancy C, 1355
Floyd, Ryan, 1747
Flucht, Brian, 278
Flyer, Steven, 193
Flynn, Brian, 772
Flynn, Timothy J, 1109
Flynn, Tom, 1628
Flynn, Tom, 1762
Fogarty MD, Thomas J, 666
Fogel, Lawrence M, 759
Fogelsong, John, 836
Fogelsong, Norman A., 1001
Foisy, Michael A., 900
Foisy, Jacques, 2206
Fojtasek, Randall S., 328
Foley, Shawn, 208
Foley, David I., 277
Foley, Todd, 1268
Foley-Wong, Bonnie, 2223
Folk, M. Holly, 139
Folsom, Doug, 9
Fonseca Licciardi, Natalie, 1834
Fonstad, Jennifer, 180
Fontana, Ash, 2019
Fontenot, Kirsi, 949
Foo, Jixun, 823
Foo, Adrienne, 1864
Foo, Gavin, 2204
Foote, Sean, 1089
Foote, William F, 1582
Foote, Stephen, 2204
Ford, Bill, 760
Ford, William E., 815
Ford, William, 853
Ford, Andrew N., 903
Ford, Hadley, 966
Ford, Kerri, 1596
Ford Buckley, Kelly, 655
Foreman, Al, 1864
Forest, Sophie, 2066
Forlenza, Bob, 1728
Formela, MD, Jean-Francois, 191
Forrer, Simone, 1350
Forrest, Gregory J, 765
Forrest, Brady, 936
Forster, R. Patrick, 985
Forsyth, Jody, 2038
Fortier, Andrew J., 2062
Fortino, Adrian, 1206
Foster, Frank, 791
Foster, Frank H, 826
Foster, C Michael, 1232
Foster, Michael J, 1557
Foster, Alan, 1793
Fountain, Adam J., 346
Fountas, Christopher, 171
Fournier, Marcel, 423
Fourticq, Ted, 902
Fourticq Jr., Michael J., 902
Fourticq Sr., Michael J., 902
Fowler, Molly, 622
Fox, Joelle, 677
Fox, Saul A., 778
Fox, Jeff, 908
Fox, Richard, 971
Fox, Robert A, 1521

Executive Name Index

Fox, Arthur L, 1591
Fox, Ken, 1748
Foy, Clinton, 561
Foy, Matthew, 1731
Fraiman, Diane, 1945
Fralic, Chris, 741
Fram, Michael J, 1116
Frances MD, Craig D, 1752
Francis, Lizzie, 342
Francis, Doug, 664
Francis, Tod, 1663
Frank, Richard H., 584
Frank, Bill, 1286
Frank, Lincoln E, 1504
Frank PhD, Edward, 59
Frankel, Robert, 172
Frankel, John, 724
Frankel, David, 771
Franklin, David C., 951
Franklin, Will, 1125
Franklin, Bobby, 3272
Frantz, Gene, 578
Franz, Peter B, 752
Fraquelli, Luigi, 2133
Fraser, Robert, 200
Fraser, Chase, 781
Fraser, Malcolm, 2155
Frazee, David, 1561
Frazier, Alan D., 782
Frederick, Alisa, 374
Frederick DPM, Jeff, 1289
Frederickson, Bryan C., 888
Fredrick, Steve, 876
Fredrickson, Kris, 509
Freedman, Walter G., 1093
Freedman, Constance, 1246
Freedman, Arnie, 1388
Freedman, Joe, 2067
Freeman, Bradford M., 783
Freeman MD, Mason, 12
Fregin, Doug, 2228
Freisinger, John, 1787
French, T. Bondurant, 57
French, Douglas D., 1619
Freschman, David, 150
Freund, John F, 1691
Freyer, Charles C, 1633
Freyman, Daniel, 1123
Frieder, Samuel P, 1081
Friedland, Charlie, 820
Friedman, John H, 644
Friedman, Steven M., 686
Friedman, Tully M., 787
Friedman, Brian P., 1032
Friedman, Stephen, 1743
Friedman, Josef, 1747
Friedman Jr, W Robert, 629
Friend, Scott, 221
Friend, Alexander A., 788
Frient, Jeffrey, 654
Fries, Alexander, 650
Fries, David, 1906
Friesen, Albert D., 2077
Frischling, James, 878
Frist, MD, Sen. William H., 558
Fronterhouse, Jeff S., 328
Frost, Dean, 253
Frost, H Lee, 591
Fruehan, Mark, 1244
Fry, Dietz, 673
Fry, Eric T, 1129
FréChette, Pierre, 1590
Frécon, Leslie, 1113
Fu, Ben, 1319
Fu, Shan, 1941
Fujimura, Michio, 183
Fulgoni, Gian, 731

Fuller, Adam, 333
Fuller, Matt, 820
Fuller, Kobie, 1888
Fulmer, A Leigh, 647
Fulton MD, Michael, 943
Funasaki, Tammy, 331
Funcannon, Bill, 1391
Funk, Andy J., 797
Funk, R Clayton, 1195
Furlong, Kim, 3258
Furneaux, Dave, 1080
Fushman, Ilya, 1075
Futrell, Steve, 1462
Futterknecht Jr., James O., 900

G

Gabelein, Kevin, 753
Gabriel, Jason, 1774
Gabriele, Neil Q., 299
Gadde, Sreekar, 293
Gadicke MD, Ansbert K, 1268
Gaenzle Jr., Richard W., 827
Gaffney, John, 363
Gaffney, Christopher S., 857
Gahwyler, Kevin, 1283
Galakatos, PhD, Nicholas, 495
Galante, Jacques V, 1105
Galantini, Eugene, 1640
Galashan, J Kristofer, 1109
Galbut, Elizabeth, 1701
Galiette, Carolyn, 1021
Galitsky, Alexander, 89
Gallagher, Joseph V., 125
Gallagher, Patrick, 564
Gallagher, Michael, 928
Gallagher, Rick, 1486
Gallagher, CFA, Brian, 1871
Galletti, Marc-Henri, 1143
Galligan, Joseph, 765
Gallinson, Evan R, 1209
Galloway, Devon, 2127
Galloway, Devon, 2127
Galvin, Thomas M, 940
Gambill, Katie H, 550
Gamble, J.S., 285
Gamboa, Elizabeth, 1300
Gandhi, Sameer, 28
Gandhi, Koonal, 250
Gandhi, Purvi, 942
Ganesan, Venky, 1202
Ganeshram, Shri, 785
Ganguly, Raj, 216
Gannon, John, 692
Gannon, John, 1755
Gantz, Joseph M, 1443
Garbe, Michael, 2241
Garber, Christopher J, 1963
Garcia, John, 64
Garcia, Quin, 204
Garcia, Quin, 205
Garcia, Francisco, 644
Garcia, Rommel, 1166
Garcia de Brigard, Luis E Garcia, 141
Gardner, Sonia, 208
Gardner, Alston, 794
Gardner, John, 1330
Gardner, JD, 1375
Gardner, Kirt, 1878
Garff, Matthew N, 1753
Garfield, Scott, 901
Garfinkel, Neil, 779
Garfinkle, Jan, 149
Garfunkle, Matt, 1411
Garg, Ashu, 770
Garg, Nikhil, 1729
Garg, Gaurav, 1996

Garman, Richard, 793
Garman, Andrew, 1305
Garner, Jason, 553
Garrard III, Gardiner W, 1863
Garrett, Wayne P., 66
Garrett, Brian, 561
Garrou, Blair, 1206
Garrou, Blair, 3278
Garton, Anthony W., 1112
Garvey, Shauntel, 1527
Garvey, James M, 1628
Garza, Rudy, 804
Gauba, Gary, 574
Gauer, Jim, 1407
Gaughan, Christopher, 1687
Gaus, Wesley H.R., 507
Gausling, Mike, 1385
Gauthier, André, 2261
Gavin, Brenda D, 1508
Gavin, Rob, 2289
Gay, Mary, 168
Gay, Bob, 959
Gazor, Max, 455
Ge, Grace, 1202
Geant, Darrick, 331
Geary, Bill, 748
Gedge, Charles, 290
Geeslin, Keith, 779
Gehringer, Ryan, 861
Geiger, Benjamin D., 783
Geiger, Debra P, 826
Geiman, Bob, 431
Gelfand, Andrew S., 355
Geliebter, David M, 662
Gelinas, Simon, 2051
Gellert, James, 1991
Gellert, Michael, 1991
Gellman, David S., 801
Gembala, Ryan, 1421
Geneser, Chris, 489
Gent, Stuart, 220
Georgacacos, Aki, 2049
George, Jean, 59
George, Jean, 1122
George, Harry A, 1702
George, Simeon J., 1731
Gephart, Thomas O, 1918
Geran, Jessica, 638
Gerard, Rupert, 888
Gerber, Scott, 813
Gergel, Ivan, 1302
Gerken, Lou, 822
Gerlach, Jason, 1756
Gerrick, Patricia, 1485
Gerry, Peter, 1769
Gershenberg, Aaron, 1764
Gershman, David, 1857
Gerson, Jeffrey P, 849
Gertner, Lorne, 2148
Gervase, David, 529
Gevada, Eric, 1105
Gezon, David A, 1232
Ghaffary, Mike, 396
Ghai, Vipon, 2183
Ghanem, Shahi, 1983
Ghori, Mansoor, 1650
Ghose, Shomit, 1378
Giacomelli, Ed, 2089
Giannetti, Thomas, 1112
Giannobile, Anthony, 359
Giannuzzi, John K, 1665
Gianos, Flip, 1010
Gibaratz, Scott, 917
Gibbons, Thomas P (Todd), 303
Gibbons, Michael W, 713
Gibbs, Kevin, 1207
Gibson, Brett, 991

Gideon, Austin, 745
Giese, Michael C, 1190
Gieselmann, Thomas, 641
Giffen, Rebecca, 2032
Gifford, Charlie, 926
Gilani, Aziz, 1206
Gilbert, Dan, 607
Gilbert, Douglas H., 610
Gilbert, Jim, 747
Gilbert, Steven J., 827
Gilbert, Daryl, 2166
Gilbert, PhD, Walter, 270
Giles, Eerik, 1280
Giles, Ryan, 2275
Gilhuly, Ned, 1602
Gill, Tehinder, 511
Gill, Mark J, 713
Gill, Daniel M, 1684
Gillani, Karim, 2179
Gillespie, Brad, 965
Gilliam, John P., 299
Gillis, Steven, 153
Gillis, Kevin, 1811
Gilman, Cliff, 72
Gilmore, Craig, 414
Gilmore, Karen, 487
Gilmore, Martin P., 746
Gilmore, Richard, 825
Gimble, AT, 189
Gineris, Marc A., 982
Ginn, Richard, 548
Ginns, Jonathan, 46
Ginsberg, Paul D., 1576
Gionfriddo, Julie, 3285
Girardi, Robert, 209
Girardi, Thomas, 953
Girgenti, Chris, 1480
Girvan, Brian J., 178
Gitig, Liron, 793
Gitter, David, 1292
Gladney, James S, 1114
Gladstone, Michael, 191
Gladstone, David, 828
Gladstone, Laura, 828
Glanville, Tom, 696
Glasheen, Jim, 1786
Glass, Skip, 770
Glass, Jonathan, 1235
Glass, Jr., R. Scott, 1409
Glassman, Newton, 2073
Glassmeyer, Edward F., 1361
Glein, Randy, 609
Glein, Randy, 1668
Glenn, Steven G, 1956
Glew, Jr., Charles E., 750
Glickman, David, 1545
Glisson, Wade D, 1684
Glouchevitch, Michel, 1575
Glushik, John, 1008
Glynn, John W., 836
Glynn, Jacqueline, 836
Glynn, David, 836
Glynn, Howard, 1207
Go, Rob, 1322
Goddu, Roger, 334
Godman, Paul, 2032
Godse, Vikram, 1184
Godwin, Michael, 1547
Goebel, Dr. Markus, 1350
Goeddel PhD, PhD, David V., 517
Goense, John M., 838
Goergen, Todd A, 1583
Goettner, Pete, 2007
Goetz, Stefan, 924
Goetz, Jim, 1654
Goff, Charlie, 1292
Goggin, Peter, 163

1085

Executive Name Index

Goh, Kim P., 954
Gold, David L, 359
Gold, Robert, 1564
Gold, Robert, 1565
Goldberg, Michael, 99
Goldberg, Marc, 270
Goldberg, Michael, 337
Goldberg, Robert, 536
Goldberg, Jay N., 954
Goldberg, Michelle, 974
Goldberg, Michael B, 1062
Goldberg, Alan E, 1129
Goldberg, Gary L, 1624
Goldberg, PhD, Allan R., 1808
Goldburg, David, 1207
Golden, William J, 1092
Golden, David, 1555
Golden, Matt, 2137
Golden, Kerri, 2153
Goldenberg, Adam, 561
Goldenberg, Axel, 2075
Goldfarb, Andy, 835
Goldfarb, Greg S, 1752
Goldfein, Jocelyn, 2019
Goldfischer, MD, Carl, 237
Goldgut, Harry, 2067
Goldhaber, Nat, 491
Golding, Robert M, 2015
Goldinger, Jim, 712
Goldman, Richard A., 1743
Goldman, Amir, 1759
Goldsmith, Barry M, 1886
Goldstein, Jonathan, 61
Goldstein, Richard, 65
Goldstein, Heidi M., 104
Goldstein, Jeffrey H., 309
Goldstein, Ross, 608
Goldstein, Jeffrey, 924
Goldstein, Daniel, 996
Goldstein, Johnathan M, 1776
Goldstein, Howard, 1911
Golinowski, Craig, 2166
Gollmer, Stewart, 1796
Golob, David, 779
Golson, Brian P, 1417
Golub, Lawrence E., 844
Golub, David B., 844
Gonser, Tom, 1656
Gontar, Michael, 1949
Gonzalez, Charles, 78
Gonzalez, Daria, 890
Gooch, Michael F., 902
Good, Nathan J, 1469
Goodhart, Noah, 1980
Goodhart, Jonah, 1980
Goodhead, Giles, 863
Goodman, Edwin A, 52
Goodman, Bob, 260
Goodman, Bob, 392
Goodman, James J, 812
Goodman, Michael D, 849
Goodman, Corey, 1914
Goodman, Jordan, 2045
Goodrich, Tom, 581
Goodrich, Jeffrey M, 931
Goodrich, Paul, 1158
Goodson, Peter D, 631
Goodstein, Marcia, 972
Goodwin, Barton, 576
Gootee, Ting, 658
Gopinath, Rashmi, 1154
Gorchow, Bruce, 1467
Gorczynski, Brian, 1925
Gordon, Michael L., 127
Gordon, Chris, 220
Gordon, Benjamin, 380
Gordon, James, 654

Gordon, Brett, 909
Gordon, Bing, 1075
Gordon, Michael, 1212
Gordon, Casey, 1341
Gordon, Eric M, 1691
Gordon, Jonathan, 1734
Gordon, Mark, 2208
Gordon PhD, Carl L., 1382
Gore, Arun, 855
Gorenberg, Mark, 2019
Gores, Tom, 1451
Gorgi, Habib Y, 1279
Gorin, Matt, 533
Gorman, Chuck, 464
Gorman, Thomas W, 1636
Gorman, Michael, 1725
Gormley, Mark K, 1104
Gormly III, Matthew E, 1984
Gorton, David S., 1777
Gosline, Timothy, 1572
Gosselin, Luke, 446
Gotsch, Maria, 1420
Gottesman, Blake L., 254
Gottesman, Wesley, 325
Gottesman, Greg, 1499
Gottesman, Eric, 2169
Gouhin, Pat, 3256
Goulard, Janelle, 2233
Gould, Arthur P., 172
Gould, Andrew G, 172
Gould, Dave, 1788
Gouw, Theresia, 49
Gouw, Theresia, 180
Govan, Chris, 2209
Goy, Michael, 1267
Grabowski, Nick, 1662
Grace, Kyle, 897
Grace, Melanie, 925
Gracias, Antonio, 1902
Grad, Alissa, 844
Grad, Jonathan, 897
Grafer, John, 1622
Graham, Hatch, 183
Graham, Drew, 224
Graham, Stephen X, 562
Graham, Gary, 736
Graham, Steven C., 846
Graham, Kenneth A., 1014
Graham, Robert, 1428
Graham, Christopher D., 1739
Graham, Michael, 2207
Grammer, Jeff, 2239
Granoff, Michael D., 1462
Granski, Miki, 536
Grant, Chris, 1052
Grant, Charles R, 1112
Grant, Ruairi, 1315
Grapkowski, Andrew, 101
Grasshoff, Sven K., 716
Grassinger, Paul M, 164
Grattan, Laura A., 1815
Graunke, Terrence M., 1091
Gravano, Dave, 1975
Graves, Brian, 629
Graves, Isaac, 3277
Gray, Jonathan, 277
Gray, Michael N., 1496
Grayken, John Patrick, 1140
Grayson, Bruns, 23
Grayson III, McComma, 909
Grayzel, MD, David, 191
Greeley, Michael, 748
Green, Kevin, 545
Green, Jason, 665
Green, Kirsten, 761
Green, Nicholas, 1099
Green, Josh, 1247

Green, Kevin R, 1854
Green, Mitch, 2081
Green, PhD, Anthony P., 246
Greenbaum, Gabe, 1480
Greenberg, Russell J., 104
Greenberg, Gregory L., 104
Greenberg, Blair, 333
Greenberg, Myles D, 474
Greenberg, David, 1041
Greenberg, Alan, 2142
Greene, Karen, 53
Greene, Michael, 66
Greene, Bob, 533
Greene III, James H., 949
Greenfield, Matt, 1551
Greenhill, Robert F., 864
Greenrod, Colleen, 290
Greenwald, Bruce, 65
Greenwald, Shai, 380
Greenwald, Gerald, 862
Greer, Thomas L, 794
Greer, Phil, 1381
Greff, John, 1653
Gregor, Alex, 1078
Gregorich, Michael D., 1743
Greif, Lloyd, 869
Greifenkamp, Daniel J., 240
Greig, Thomas G, 1116
Greiwe, Brad, 727
Grenfall, Steven J, 1601
Gretsch, Greg, 1024
Grey, Richard G., 939
Griest, David, 1689
Griffin, Marshall, 528
Griffin, Carter, 1886
Griffiths, Michael, 2169
Griffor, Jeff, 1119
Grigg, Charles S., 415
Grigsby, Brian, 545
Grim, Paul, 692
Grim, Paul, 1755
Grimaldi, Brendyn T, 897
Grimm, Donald W., 898
Grimm, Angie, 967
Grinnell, Rick, 712
Grinnell, Rick, 829
Grishin, Dmitry, 874
Grissom, Douglas C, 1156
Griswold, Kirk B, 164
Griswold, Kyle, 793
Grizzell, Steve, 999
Groh, Thomas R., 104
Groh, Doug, 479
Groh, Christian, 1481
Groos, Tom, 488
Gros, Florent, 1350
Grose, Madison F., 1739
Gross, Michael, 251
Gross, Lauren, 775
Gross, Bill, 972
Gross, Stewart KP, 1123
Gross Jr, Jorge, 1857
Gross-Loh, David, 220
Grossman, Jay, 21
Grousbeck, H. Irving, 949
Grover, Tony, 1592
Groves, Thomas, 64
Grovic, Mark, 1299
Grua, Peter, 938
Gruber, Adam S., 686
Gruber, Michael, 983
Gruber, Michael C., 1610
Grubstein, Peter S.H., 1324
Gruenberg, Paul, 154
Grum, Allen F, 1523
Grunberg, Gregory, 1143
Grunberg, Lee M., 2226

Gruner, Harry, 1041
Gruss, Ralf, 135
Gruzen, Alex, 545
Gubbay, David, 717
Gubbels, Michael, 2289
Guerin Beresini, Debra, 1011
Guerrero, Alejandro, 50
Guff, Drew, 1679
Guffey, Steve, 834
Guiliana DPM, John, 1289
Guimaraes, Aflalo, 1018
Guinness, Oliver, 1258
Gulati, Mukul, 2018
Guldin, Andreas, 668
Guleri, Tim, 1670
Gulino, Daniel, 1564
Gullans PhD, Steve, 703
Gulve PhD, Eric, 267
Gunderson, Maurice, 204
Gunderson, Maurice, 205
Gunn, Greg, 488
Gunther, Craig, 278
Gunton, Jim, 1328
Guo, Sarah, 872
Gupta, Vishal, 260
Gupta, Neeraj, 454
Gupta, Ramneek, 486
Gupta, Amit, 504
Gupta, Arun, 515
Gupta, Vinod, 700
Gupta, Bulbul, 1396
Gupta, Krishna K, 1581
Gupta, Arjun, 1793
Gupta, Shyam, 2291
Gupta, Sophie, 2291
Gur, Saar, 455
Gurasich, Brad, 425
Gurewitz, Aaron M, 1588
Gusenius, Mik, 464
Gussarsky, David, 1121
Gustafson, Andrew S, 1684
Gutfreund, Joshua L., 494
Guthart, Leo, 1832
Guthrie, David, 108
Guttman, Randy, 1041
Guttman, Bill, 1623
Guttman, William, 1797
Gutwein, Victor, 1155
Guzman, Arlene, 391
Guzy, Melissa, 148
Gwirtsman, Charles, 1086

H

Ha, Perry, 626
Haarmaan, Oliver, 2252
Haas, Jonathan M, 492
Haas, Beth, 577
Haas, Clifford L, 1672
Haber, Warren H., 774
Haber, Douglas A., 1815
Hackett, James T., 1573
Hadley, Christopher J., 254
Haeger, Kent C, 932
Hafler, Jason P, 1618
Hagenah, Pamela, 1003
Hager, Frederick H, 1163
Hagerman, Lisa, 595
Hagerty, Thomas M., 1815
Haghgooie, Anna, 1615
Hahn, Eugene, 1039
Hahn, John C., 1496
Haight, H H, 162
Hairston, Tanaha, 1822
Halak, PhD, Brian K., 621
Haley, Tim, 1534
Hall, Timothy T., 476
Hall, John E., 947

Executive Name Index

Hall, Russell B, 1106
Hall, Steven E, 1124
Hall, Matt, 2087
Hall, Matt, 2186
Hall, PhD, Charles M., 139
Hallene, James N., 407
Hallett, Bruce, 1237
Halley, Frederic, 1319
Halligan, Howard A., 714
Halligan, John, 1668
Halloran, Todd W., 783
Halow, James, 368
Halstedt, Steve, 441
Hamamci, Ruchan, 2075
Hamati, Edward, 267
Hambrook, Barclay W., 2039
Hamel, John, 567
Hamelsky, Lawrence S., 254
Hamer PhD, John E, 840
Hamerslag, Steven J, 1869
Hamid, Mamoon, 1075
Hamilton, Arlan, 218
Hamilton, Chauncey, 622
Hamilton, Charles, 1086
Hamilton, Matthew G, 1752
Hammarskjold, Philip, 924
Hammer, Michael Christoph, 302
Hammer, John R, 1440
Hammond, Kevin T., 1039
Hamner, Patrick, 1422
Hamrick III, L. Watts, 1409
Hamwee, Robert A., 1301
Han, Ronald, 905
Han, Ronald, 906
Han, Philip, 1598
Hanafi, Ammar H., 87
Hanauer, Nick, 1641
Handreke, Patrick W.A., 2255
Hankins, Matthew, 928
Hankinson, Henry W., 694
Hanna, William A., 371
Hanna, Stephen A., 1744
Hannon, Robert M., 1824
Hansen, Lee C, 1213
Hanson, David, 1152
Hanson, Craig, 1319
Hanssens, Christopher G, 698
Hao, Kenneth, 1683
Hapgood, Kallie, 873
Haque, Promod, 1346
Hara, George, 602
Hara, Michael, 925
Harberg, Joseph L, 1549
Harbert, Billy L., 282
Harbert, Raymond J., 904
Harden, Michael, 175
Hardgrave, Eric, 54
Hardiman, James, 585
Hardin, Jim, 2048
Harding, Richard, 1011
Harding, Bill, 1906
Hardman, Scott, 82
Hardy, John A., 694
Hardy, Roger, 2144
Hardymon, Felda, 260
Hargrove, Heidi, 702
Hargrove, Thomas M., 888
Haring-Smith, Whitney, 133
Harkrider, John T, 1063
Harlan, Leonard M., 423
Harlan, Jason, 726
Harlan, Bill, 1477
Harman, Drew, 1010
Harman, Fred, 1361
Harnisch, David, 484
Harrick, Steve, 1001
Harriman, Gregory, 266

Harrington, Richard J, 567
Harrington, John, 1375
Harris, Joshua, 140
Harris, Matt, 221
Harris, Kirby, 229
Harris, Hadley, 679
Harris, Geoff, 755
Harris, Chris, 787
Harris, John, 1029
Harris, Arlan, 1244
Harris, Dr. Ryan A, 1346
Harris, Parker, 1607
Harris, David W, 1707
Harris, Richard, 2123
Harris, Christopher, 2150
Harrison, Justin, 361
Harrison, Donald C., 458
Harrison, Brian, 1466
Harrison, Glenn C, 1468
Harrison, Bradley C, 1632
Harrison, Matthew G., 1971
Harrison, Nancy, 2036
Harrison, M.D., Seth L., 143
Harroch, Richard, 1906
Hart, Craig, 208
Hart CFA, Rob C, 1792
Hartano, Steven, 463
Hartenbaum, Howard, 197
Hartfield, Justin, 664
Hartong III, Hendrik J., 357
Hartong, Jr., Hendrik J., 357
Hartwell, Sam, 201
Harward, Seth, 790
Hasebroock, Mark, 635
Haskell, Sherri, 388
Hass, Jay, 1593
Hass, David, 2056
Hassan, Kamil, 851
Hassanein, Ossama, 1311
Hassid, Mony, 1154
Hatch, Chad, 273
Hatfield, S Kim, 553
Hatfield, Mark, 1794
Hatherly, John A., 2009
Hatzimemos, Eric, 1687
Haub, Christian W.E., 668
Haug, Andreas, 641
Haughian, Andrew, 2213
Haughn, Ryan, 2246
Hawkins, Matt, 557
Hawkins, Tom, 768
Hawkins, John, 818
Hawkins, Brian, 1976
Hawks, Randy, 491
Hawks III, Donald L, 353
Hawley, Stuart W, 1624
Hawley Jr, Frank J, 1624
Hawn, Van Zandt, 843
Haydel, Marcia, 1431
Hayes, Brooke, 155
Hayes, David, 319
Hayes, Rob, 741
Hayes, John G., 857
Haykin, Randy, 1389
Haynes, Travis, 225
Haynes, David, 793
Haynes, Stephen R, 831
Hays, Joe T., 611
Haythornthwaite, Charles, 2078
Hayward, Laurence, 983
Haywood, Jeff, 1717
Hazard, Chip, 754
Hazarika, Bahniman, 855
Hazen, Ned, 1119
He, Benson, 892
Headley, Robert, 974
Headrick, Mark, 536

Healey Jr., D Thomas, 1573
Healy, Patrick, 364
Healy, Robert P, 468
Healy, JJ, 848
Healy, Patrick, 924
Healy, James, 1698
Heard, Robin, 2033
Heath, Chad, 673
Hebb, Elise, 1183
Hebb, Jr., Donald B., 22
Hebbar, Kiran, 1899
Hébert, Peter, 1151
Hebrank MD, Gregory T, 1098
Hedrick, Tom, 1944
Heersink, Ewout, 2209
Heflin, William, 1072
Heglie, Eric D., 985
Heidecorn, David, 1088
Heilbronn, Charles, 1263
Heimann, Robert A, 1571
Heinen, Joseph H, 843
Heinmiller, Joseph, 846
Heintzman, Andrew, 2161
Heinze, Kristina, 468
Heitzmann, Rick, 743
Heivly, Chris, 192
Hejazi, Shahram, 266
Helbing, Scott C., 594
Helfin, Angela, 3269
Hellier, David, 257
Helmedag, Bobby, 1556
Helou, François, 187
Heltzer, Jason, 1384
Hemingway, Ryan, 688
Hemmeter, Christopher R, 1806
Hemmig, Raymond C, 1549
Hender, Eric, 17
Henderson, John, 966
Henderson, Ted, 1627
Henderson, David A, 1854
Henderson, David, 2290
Henderson-Cohen, Michael, 845
Hendrie, Gardner C, 1672
Hendrix, Blair, 220
Hendy, Patrick, 515
Heneine, Carlos, 1516
Henikoff, Troy, 1178
Henley, J Rudy, 1262
Hennegan, John, 1667
Henner, PhD, Dennis, 495
Hennessy, James, 2283
Henrickson, Stuart, 2234
Henry, George J, 1127
Henry, Jay R., 1409
Henry, Peter, 1644
Henry, Desmond, 1856
Henry, Chandra, 2178
Henshall, Laing, 2175
Hensley, Carolina B, 1484
Hera, Jonathan, 2185
Herb, Rob, 1626
Hermann, Matthew, 176
Hermouet, Laurent D., 188
Hernandez, Bruce M., 1724
Hernon, Marty, 312
Heron, Patrick, 782
Herring, Catherine, 2215
Herriott, Ashton, 365
Herrod, Dr. Steve, 816
Herron, Dave, 498
Hersman, Brian, 1041
Hertzmark, Andrew, 818
Herz, Peter, 8
Heslam, Sharlyn C., 254
Hess, David, 1843
Hess Jr, Ronald C, 1476
Hester, Robert, 1349

Heston, Tim, 255
Hetu, Daniel, 2180
Hetz, E David, 572
Heuer, Kenneth J, 1071
Heyke, Rick, 1750
Heyman, Justin, 834
Heymann, Maia, 534
Hibblen, Brian, 1687
Hickey, Tom, 1505
Hickey, Kyle, 2246
Hickman, R Trent, 1927
Hicks, George G., 1907
Hicks, III, H Beecher, 1529
Higgen, Uwe, 302
Higgerson, Cliff, 976
Higginbotham, John B, 1714
Higgins, Ron, 939
Higgins, Brian, 1045
Higgins, Pete, 1641
Highland, Erika, 828
Hightower, Gayla W., 328
Hildebrandt, Joseph P, 583
Hilderbrand, Mark G., 949
Hilinski, Scott, 1279
Hill, Jason, 1195
Hill, Brent, 1384
Hill, Grant, 1430
Hill, Geoff A., 1576
Hill, Eugene, 1628
Hill, Duncan, 2182
Hills, Michael, 1073
Hills, Mason, 1548
Himawan, PhD, Jeff, 697
Hinaman, Robert, 48
Hinck, Jeff, 1522
Hindman, John C., 1989
Hinkle, Ryan, 1000
Hippeau, Eric, 1110
Hipwood, Charlie, 1172
Hirose, Ted, 1791
Hirsch, David, 525
Hirsch, Brian, 1849
Hirsch MD, PhD, David, 1143
Hirsch MD, PhD, Russell, 1493
Hirshland, Mike, 1546
Hitchner, Doug, 1368
Hixon, Dylan, 826
Hixon, Eric, 826
Hixon, Todd, 1291
Hjerpe, Eric, 1065
Hliboki, Lorraine, 1462
Hnatiuk, Steve, 2176
Ho, Charles, 41
Ho, James, 64
Ho, Eva, 728
Ho, Thierry F, 1123
Ho, Gregory P, 1730
Ho, Derrick, 2186
Ho-Walker, Joshua, 1315
Hoag, Jay, 1785
Hobbs, Jerry, 361
Hobman, Steven, 1317
Hobson, Blaine, 2288
Hoch, Scott, 790
Hoch, James S., 1777
Hochberg, Steve, 177
Hochberg, Benjamin A, 1104
Hochman, Andrew B., 1590
Hodge, Bruce, 2218
Hodges, Michael, 183
Hodges, Deborah, 1231
Hodges, Philip L, 1533
Hodges, Daryl, 2037
Hodgson, Ryan, 109
Hodgson, David, 815
Hodgson, Dan, 1131
Hodys, Karen, 747

Executive Name Index

Hoe, Janey, 483
Hoegler, Arnold J, 1103
Hoehn-Saric, Christopher, 1742
Hoesley, John, 1477
Hoesterey, Brian, 64
Hoffer, Daniel, 204
Hoffman, Beth, 254
Hoffman, Paul E, 629
Hoffman, Reid, 872
Hoffman, Spencer P, 1147
Hoffman MD, Stephen J, 1691
Hoffmeister, Mark A., 1497
Hoffort, Michael, 2114
Hofmann, Don, 565
Hofmann, Kevin, 1576
Hogan, Brian, 2084
Holbrook, Ben, 1171
Holcomb, Brett P, 1492
Holcomb, Charles, 1837
Holden, Chris, 551
Holden, MD, Stuart, 1490
Holdsberg, Jeffrey, 373
Holec, Monica J., 1111
Holekamp, Cliff, 569
Holiday, Aaron, 13
Holland, Kirk, 36
Holland, Paul, 770
Holland, Jeffrey J, 1636
Holland Jr, Thomas O, 1422
Hollander, Seth H, 1081
Hollend, Michael, 2272
Hollin, Mitchell L, 1136
Hollis, Mark, 443
Hollod, Chris, 15
Holman, Kelly, 2130
Holmes, Stephen, 1010
Holson, Laura C., 1301
Holstein, Roger C., 1931
Holt, Matthew S., 1301
Holt, Charles, 2161
Holton Jr., Rick, 569
Holtz, Gerald, 1494
Homcy, MD, Charles, 1811
Homer, Paul, 1344
Hompesch, Michael P, 632
Honda, Osuke, 596
Honeybourne, Will, 740
Hong, Karen, 1778
Hooper, Herbert H., 118
Hooper, Steve, 974
Hooper, Christopher, 1972
Hooten, Ken, 529
Hootnick, Larry, 54
Hoover, James B, 587
Hoover, Betsy, 934
Hopeman, Wei, 148
Hopkins, Adam, 659
Hopkins, William, 1368
Hopping, Andrew, 1851
Horan, Avshalom, 337
Horing, David, 110
Horing, Jeff, 1000
Horn, Larry, 3283
Hornby, Mary T, 18
Hornby, Zachary, 487
Horne, Mark, 1455
Horne, Bob, 2022
Horner, Byron, 2085
Hornik, David, 197
Hornthal, Jim, 192
Horowitz, Ben, 124
Horowitz, Joe, 968
Horowitz, Richard M, 1521
Horst, Sandy, 297
Horvilleur, Camilo E., 928
Hosaisy, Fred, 1695
Hostetter, Davis, 894

Hough, G. Thomas, 1417
Houghton, Karen, 189
House, Dawn, 2155
Howard, Chris, 974
Howard, John, 1022
Howard, Paul A, 1197
Howard, Matthew D, 1346
Howard, Newton, 1393
Howard, Jeffrey, 1610
Howard, Andrew J., 1660
Howard, Alan, 1793
Howard, Randall, 2279
Howard MD, Lawrence, 954
Howe, Bob, 9
Howe, Timothy F, 474
Howe, Timothy, 920
Howell, Sheldon, 969
Howell, Ronald S, 2008
Hower, Bob, 59
Hower, Lee, 1322
Howes, Ian A.W., 31
Howland, James, 1256
Howorth, Greg, 374
Hoyt, Thomas B., 984
Hsiao, Paul, 396
Hsieh, Michael, 796
Hsieh, Wen, 1075
Hsieh, Tony, 1912
Hsing, Peter, 1218
Hsu, Ta-Lin, 892
Hsu, Mark, 892
Hsu, Geoffrey C., 1382
Hsu, William, 1781
Hsu, Jonathan, 1848
Hsui, Jenny, 473
Hu, Eion, 1045
Huang, Edward, 277
Huang, Timothy, 1112
Huang PhD, He, 1340
Huber, Michael, 1506
Huber, Harold, 2167
Hubler, Jodi, 1107
Hudson, Pete, 94
Hudson, Lydie, 554
Hudson, L'Sheryl D, 694
Hudson, William L, 1331
Hudson, Charles, 1471
Huey, Henry, 171
Huff, Peter, 291
Huff, Greg, 701
Huffard, Jay, 531
Hufford, Kyle, 227
Huffsmith, Joseph, 1376
Hufnagel, Alec, 1062
Hughes, Donald W., 383
Hughes, William S., 1496
Hughes, Edward FL., 1496
Hughes, Brent G., 2091
Hughes III, Charles B, 644
Huie, Tony, 1675
Hulecki, Gregory, 711
Hull, David, 441
Hullah, Daniel, 809
Hullet, JK, 1090
Hulme, Tom, 889
Humes, Robert, 1038
Hummer, John, 956
Humphreys, Ernest D, 1162
Humphries, Andrew, 911
Hung, Yie-Hsin, 1309
Hung, Karen, 3258
Hunkapiller, Michael, 87
Hunnewell, Luisa, 1987
Hunnicutt, Jonathan E., 1979
Hunt, John, 21
Hunt, Jim, 285
Hunt, Ron, 1298

Hunt, Christopher B, 1573
Hunter, Peter A., 211
Hunter, Dick, 594
Hunter, Wally, 676
Hunter-Syed, Abigail, 1101
Hurd, Jason, 359
Hurley, Matthew J, 716
Hursever, Evis, 697
Hurst, Jeffrey M., 521
Hurst, Bob, 559
Hurwitz, Roger, 1942
Huseby, Thomas S, 1637
Hussain, Anwar, 1559
Huston, Jim, 1463
Hutcheson, Zenas, 1522
Hutchins, Will, 2109
Hutchinson, Tamiko, 1004
Hutchinson, George R., 1032
Hutton, Wende, 386
Huynh, Stacy, 151
Hwang, John S., 783
Hwang, Victor, 986
Hwang, In Seon, 1956
Hyatt, Michael, 1022
Hyatt, Nabeel, 1715
Hyndman, Stephen, 823

I

Iacovone, Jack, 1288
Iaffaldano, Paul, 271
Ianello, Peter, 1364
Iannarone, Thomas, 277
Iatropoulos, Nikos, 1051
Ibrahim, Maha, 386
Idemoto, Derek, 483
Ifergan, Sam, 2149
Ignaczak, Tony, 1505
Ilhuyn Cho, Jerry, 690
Illikman CFA, James A, 1426
Ilsoe, Bo, 1330
Imai, Shinya, 1241
Imhoff, W Joseph, 1281
Imran, Mir, 980
Ingram, Robert A, 915
Ingram, Paulus J, 2248
Inman, Bob, 1126
Inman, Tom, 1126
Insalaco, Steven, 369
Intrater, Andrew, 516
Iovino, Nicholas, 830
Irani, Martin, 902
Irish, Rebecca, 1430
Irvin, Thomas J., 885
Irwin, Scott, 1540
Irwin, Brenda, 2237
Isaacson, Mark, 1536
Iseman, Frederick J, 476
Isenberg, Robbie, 2081
Isetta, Lincoln, 1255
Ishbia, Justin, 1667
Ishii, Masazumi, 214
Isono, Masa, 602
Israelsohn, Daniel, 2224
Israely, Gal, 436
Issa, Natalie, 593
Istock, David, 294
Iverson, Jeffrey, 277
Ivis, Matt, 3258

J

Jaako, Harry, 2097
Jacks, Joel R., 507
Jackson, Grant A, 550
Jackson, Adam, 772
Jackson, Kevin M., 873
Jackson, Michael C., 949
Jackson, Deborah, 1454

Jackson, Angela, 1463
Jackson, Herbert W, 1541
Jackson, Jeff, 1806
Jackson, Donald, 2215
Jackson, Tim, 2262
Jackson, Ron, 2275
Jackson, Jon, 3258
Jacob, Sasha, 2075
Jacobs, Brian, 665
Jacobsen, Mark, 1359
Jacobson, Dean, 29
Jacobson, Linda, 32
Jacobson, Sven M, 662
Jacobson, Matthew, 1096
Jacobson, Scott, 1158
Jacobson, Glenn, 1851
Jacobson, Lorne, 2275
Jacques, Dan, 2145
Jadeja, Asha, 623
Jadot, R. Bryan, 925
Jaduszliwer, Ariel, 324
Jaeger, Wilfred, 920
Jaeger, Wilfred, 1819
Jaffe, Danny, 126
Jaffe, David, 447
Jaffe, Robert M, 1706
Jaffe, Ross, 1928
Jaffin, David W., 321
Jaggers, John, 1658
Jaggers, Kurt R, 1776
Jaggi, Dennis F., 671
Jahns, David W, 806
Jain, Uttam, 188
Jain, Anurag, 1433
Jain, Neenah, 1520
Jain PhD, Mudit, 1772
Jaisinghani, Sumeet, 1598
Jake, Krist, 1535
Jakeway, Phil, 1127
Jalan, Nupur, 834
Jalanbo, Khaled, 1900
Jamal, Asad, 690
James, Brian, 489
James, Simon, 695
James, William E, 1579
James, Janet, 1579
James, Daniel, 1851
James, Jamie, 2142
James, Meli, 3263
Jamieson, Don, 374
Jamieson, Christina D., 844
Janchar, Matthew A., 254
Jander, Rich, 1166
Jandernoa, Michael, 943
Janes, Thomas, 1067
Jang, Ray, 1556
Jani, Amish, 743
Janis, Frances N., 1462
Janish, Michael, 1904
Janmohamed, Arif, 1121
Janney, Dan, 94
Janower, Andrew S., 456
Janson, Jeremy, 782
Jaramillo, Jorge, 1386
Jargiello, David, 756
Jarman, MBA, Peter, 560
Jarve, John W., 1202
Jay, MD, Jeffrey R., 859
Jaysane-Darr, Evan, 1015
Jazayeri, Rouz, 429
Jeandron III, Raymond J, 1144
Jegen, David, 710
Jenkins, J. Blair, 462
Jenkins, Robert, 1466
Jennings, Mark, 818
Jennings, Thomas H, 1752
Jensen, Andrew, 1059

Executive Name Index

Jensen, Peter T, 1717
Jerstad, Mike, 1470
Jesselson, Michael, 1034
Jessup, Kevin B, 1606
Jiang, Franklin, 2229
Jin, Will, 2109
Jivraj, Alkarim, 2109
Joaquin, James, 1363
Johan, Paul, 224
Johann PhD, Peter, 1325
Johansson, Curtis, 365
Johns, Brad, 2291
Johnson, Debbie, 21
Johnson, Michael, 61
Johnson, B. Kristine, 68
Johnson, Kent, 82
Johnson, Kristin, 96
Johnson, Phil, 143
Johnson, Gregg E., 263
Johnson, Jeffrey, 276
Johnson, Chad, 464
Johnson, Christian B., 783
Johnson, Jeffrey W., 827
Johnson, Craig N., 832
Johnson, Timothy D., 843
Johnson, Stephen M., 949
Johnson, Dave, 1004
Johnson, Ken, 1060
Johnson, Richard, 1228
Johnson, Scott, 1291
Johnson, Jared L., 1415
Johnson, Gregory, 1488
Johnson, Kinney, 1653
Johnson, Mark A, 1863
Johnson, Jim, 1915
Johnson, James A, 1997
Johnson, Christopher A., 2091
Johnson, James C., 2255
Johnston, John, 197
Johnston, William, 909
Johnston, Robert, 1044
Johnston, A. Bruce, 1776
Johnston, Kel, 2166
Johnston PhD, Allan, 1773
Johnstone, Brent P, 1511
Johnstone, Trevor, 2123
Jolly, Brian, 957
Jones, Elliott, 168
Jones, Tripp, 197
Jones, Casey, 203
Jones, Charles S., 242
Jones, Ross M., 254
Jones, Rick, 266
Jones, Tom, 628
Jones, Gregory, 654
Jones, Leland, 673
Jones, Christopher N., 746
Jones, J. Chris, 893
Jones, M. Scott, 893
Jones, Andy, 1169
Jones, David M, 1209
Jones, Brent, 1341
Jones, Matt, 1355
Jones, Thad, 1505
Jones, Mark, 1569
Jones, E Bartow, 1573
Jones, David, 1710
Jones, Terry L., 1771
Jones, Kateri, 1771
Jones, Daniel G., 1815
Jones, Craig A.T., 1824
Jones, Thomas W, 1873
Jones, Nigel W, 1873
Jones, Ellis, 1960
Jones III, Reginald L., 862
Jones, Jr., David, 475
Jonge Poernik, John R, 1130

Jordan, Jeff, 124
Jordan, Buck, 397
Jordan, Wilma, 1033
Jordan, Jay, 1045
Jordan, Len, 1158
Jordon, Scott, 836
Jordon, James, 1448
Joseph, Richard, 194
Jrolf, Mark, 926
Jubeir, TJ, 406
Jubeir, Julie, 406
Julich, Chris, 695
Jung, Edward, 1005
Juricic, Donald A, 1557
Jurvetson, Steve, 800

K

Kabakoff, David, 921
Kabakoff, David, 1698
Kabbes, Scott R, 244
Kaczmarczyk, Holly, 1970
Kaczorowski, Joe, 331
Kaczynski, Bill, 338
Kadaba, Neena, 2229
Kadavy, Annie, 1534
Kaden, John T., 1283
Kaden, Rebecca, 1882
Kafker, Roger B, 1776
Kagan, Peter, 1956
Kaganov ScD, Alan L, 1896
Kahle, G. Kent, 888
Kahn, Brian, 1935
Kahr, Julia, 277
Kahvejian, Avak, 747
Kairouz, Habib, 1558
Kairouz, Habib, 2239
Kaiser, Joe, 1204
Kajmo, Karen, 3264
Kalcevich, Julius, 966
Kalish, Adam, 1151
Kalkanis, Peter, 1558
Kalkanis, Peter, 2239
Kalman, Jonathan, 1025
Kalnow, Andrew H, 90
Kamar, Ahmed, 2202
Kambhampati, Krishnamurty, 505
Kamdar, PhD, Kim, 621
Kaminsky, Samantha, 552
Kamra, Deepak, 386
Kamra, Atul, 1688
Kanal, Utkarsh, 198
Kanayev, Alex, 2031
Kandler, Ahim, 759
Kane, Michael, 374
Kane, Edward W, 909
Kaneb, Thomas, 2194
Kaneko MD, Yasunori, 1691
Kang, PhD, JJ, 517
Kanji, Azra, 21
Kapeskas, Rimas, 380
Kaplan, David, 159
Kaplan, Larry, 242
Kaplan, Michael B, 1134
Kaplan, Teddy, 1301
Kaplanis, Scott, 2108
Kapoor, Rishi, 1017
Kapoor, Raj, 1184
Kapoor, Arrun, 1689
Kapor, Mitchell, 1054
Kapor Klein, Freada, 1054
Karabelas, Argeris, 412
Karamchandani, Sean, 2220
Karas, Lindsay, 1286
Karchon, Evonna, 981
Karlson, Steven E, 1994
Karol, Steven E, 1962
Karol, Julia, 1962

Karp, Amit, 260
Karp, Gabe, 607
Karp, CPA, Murray, 675
Karsh, Bruce, 1362
Kashyap, Nagraj, 1154
Kaskow, Jonathan, 291
Kasper, Paul S., 678
Kassam, Shamsh, 2258
Kassouf, Karen, 437
Kastner, Tom, 1369
Katabi, Maha, 1698
Katarincic, Jay, 628
Katcha, Joseph R, 932
Kats, Victor, 176
Kats, Greg, 398
Katz, Brandon M., 492
Katz, Rami, 704
Katz, Alex, 724
Katz, Harold, 891
Katz, David A, 891
Katz, Jed, 1028
Katzman, Elliot M., 521
Kau, Andrew, 1951
Kaufman, Howard, 1638
Kaul, Ashish, 765
Kaul, Samir, 1069
Kaup, Eric, 937
Kaushal MD, Mohit, 20
Kawasaki, Guy, 807
Kayden, Joelle, 37
Kaye, Michael S, 501
Kaye, Charles R, 1956
Kayler, J Allan, 1232
Ke, Yan, 1340
Kean, Thomas H, 1504
Keane, Gen. John M, 1633
Keane, Patrick, 2084
Kearl, Jeff, 1425
Keating, Ryan, 1427
Keaveney, Thomas, 61
Keay, Jeffrey, 909
Kedar, Sharon, 1342
Keefe, Edward J, 1153
Keefe, Kevin, 1467
Keefe, Patrick, 2068
Keehn, Peter, 88
Keen, Eric, 550
Keeton, Sonja J., 904
Kehaya, Mark W, 1213
Kehoe, Scott A., 1014
Keis, Matthew E, 812
Keith, Robert, 1828
Kell, Joe, 1311
Kelley, Michael, 150
Kelley, Douglas M., 403
Kelley, Sean M., 873
Kelley, Brian P, 1129
Kelley, Ryan, 1667
Kelley, Alan, 1689
Kelley, James P., 1931
Kellner, Peter, 1561
Kelly, Jonathan D., 404
Kelly, J. Ryan, 774
Kelly, Robert E, 1738
Kelly, Matt, 3266
Kelly II, Thomas L., 461
Kelly MD, Doug, 87
Kelly PhD, Regis B, 1238
Kelsall, Bill, 681
Kelsey, Beth, 548
Kelsey, Alex, 1960
Kember, Ken, 2112
Kendall Jr, Donald R, 1063
Kenealey, Kevin P, 1171
Kenealy, Pat, 1563
Kennealey, Douglas L., 328
Kennedy, Danny, 367

Kennedy, Charles, 382
Kennedy, Bill, 804
Kennedy, Keith, 1189
Kennedy, Brendan, 1481
Kennedy, Mark, 2026
Kennedy, Thomas, 2167
Kennedy Jr, William J, 716
Kenney, George C, 1664
Kenny, Michael, 1987
Kent, Chelsea, 1099
Kent, Martin, 2167
Kent MD, Richard, 1008
Kenter, Louis W, 1492
Kenworthy, Karen, 1748
Kermani, Moe, 2278
Kern, Rene, 815
Kern, Jay, 1066
Kerr, Anita K., 240
Kerr, Karen, 809
Kerrigan, Charles, 1695
Kershisnik, Thomas, 745
Kertzman, Mitchell, 956
Kessinger, William C., 1417
Kessler, Daniel, 577
Kessler Jr., W. Jack, 494
Kester, Kevin, 1679
Kestler, Paul D, 606
Kevin, Quintin, 57
Kewalramani, Kabir, 250
Keywell, Brad, 1118
Keziah, Sanford, 1090
Khalifa, Omar, 2116
Khalin, Alex, 1926
Khaliq, Asad, 49
Khan, Agha, 1743
Khanna, Raman, 603
Khattau, Nikhil, 1184
Khatwani, Hemant, 690
Khayat, Wiz, 2246
Kheng, Jennifer W, 1112
Kherani, MD, Aftab R., 74
Khosla, Vinod, 1069
Khosrowshahi, Behzad, 2102
Kibble, Robert, 1239
Kidd, William J, 1071
Kidle, Dan, 149
Kienzle, Trevor, 544
Kiernan, James T., 2086
Kikta, Roman, 1244
Kilar, Jason, 1827
Kilcrease, Laura J, 1855
Kiley, Richard, 287
Kilgallon, John, 220
Kilic, Ugur, 2075
Killackey, Christopher T, 1469
Kim, Han, 100
Kim, Andrew, 232
Kim, Daniel, 333
Kim, Eurie, 761
Kim, John, 933
Kim, John, 1062
Kim, Yoo Jin, 1104
Kim, Philip, 1127
Kim, Charlie, 1186
Kim, David, 1690
Kim PhD, Leo, 214
Kim, MD, John, 138
Kimball, Rick, 1785
Kimble, Matthew, 208
Kimerling, Daniel, 599
Kimmel, Wayne D, 1657
Kimmelman, Doug, 675
Kimsa, Kevin, 2249
Kimura, Kenichi, 1241
Kimzey, Jackie, 1658
Kincanon, Michelle, 126
King, Jason, 422

1089

Executive Name Index

King, Matthew, 496
King, Matthew A, 718
King, Christopher M., 873
King, Colton, 1086
King, Stephen V, 1469
King, Colin, 2090
King III, Madding, 384
King Neff, Steven, 993
King-Shaw Jr, Ruben J, 1165
Kingston, Brian, 2067
Kinley, James, 2077
Kinner, Michele, 1516
Kinsella, Kevin J., 206
Kinsey, Matt, 361
Kinsey, Edward, 1073
Kinsman, Brian, 359
Kirby, Steve, 297
Kirby, Robert, 839
Kircher, Demian, 1166
Kireker, Charles F, 786
Kirk, Phil, 483
Kirk, Randal J., 1812
Kirkpatrick, David, 1689
Kirnos, Ilya, 1675
Kirsch, Bill, 548
Kirtland, Kirt, 666
Kirwin III, John Paul, 164
Kislak, Jonathan I., 131
Kitchens, Ron, 1713
Kitching, Chris, 933
Kitterman, Roger, 1419
Kittler, Fred, 730
Kivitz, David, 155
Klaffky, Richard C, 739
Klahr, Jonathan, 1759
Klammer, Ronald J., 1369
Klammer, Steve, 1369
Klapper, Paul, 506
Klapper, Brad, 506
Klar, Larry, 2043
Klass, Daniel, 2170
Klee, Stephan, 2225
Klein, Jason, 29
Klein, Randal, 208
Klein, Karin, 284
Klein, Peter W, 348
Klein, Adam, 559
Klein, Terry, 594
Klein, Michael I, 1134
Klein, Gentry S, 1134
Klein, Justin, 1917
Kleinhandler, Mitchell, 614
Kleinman, Scott, 140
Kleinman, Ira D., 914
Kleinman, Blake, 924
Klemens, Jeff, 1602
Klessel, Lewis S., 1301
Klevens, Joshua A., 456
Kliman, Gil, 1010
Kline, John R., 1301
Kline, Dean M, 1428
Klinefelter, Josh, 199
Klingenstein, Paul, 20
Klinsky, Steven B, 1301
Kloos PhD, Steven D, 1859
Klosk, Craig B, 1984
Klueger, Randy, 538
Knapp, Hans, 2291
Knauss, Robert, 694
Knauss, Robert B, 1956
Kneen, John, 244
Kneis, Henry, 2096
Knez, Brian J., 421
Knight, Lester B., 1590
Knight MD, Stephen, 710
Knitt, Brian, 467
Knoch, David, 1022

Knoke, Ailliam, 913
Knotts, Jerry, 3257
Knox, Dave, 1934
Knox, Elliott, 2056
Knutsen, John E, 1156
Koby, Michael, 5
Koch, Simon, 2145
Kocher MD, Bob, 1916
Kodde, Pieter, 1127
Koegler, David, 1194
Koenig, Peggy, 21
Koenig, Robert, 2004
Kogan, Eric D, 492
Kohlberg, James A, 1081
Kohlberg, James A., 1083
Kohr, Rick, 701
Kokones, Scott, 886
Kokron, Carlos, 1509
Kolada, Dave Harris, 2142
Kolbeins, Laurie G., 1799
Kolchinsky, Peter, 1519
Koldyke, Laird, 1999
Kole, John, 1142
Kollender, Richard S, 1508
Kolln, Thies O, 17
Kollock, David P, 832
Kolodny, Lauren, 49
Kolodny, Lauren, 180
Komada, Tim, 600
Kometz, MD, Avi, 177
Kondo, James, 820
Kong, Garheng, 921
Kong MD PhD, Garheng, 1698
König, Dr. Anja, 1350
Koo, David J., 1590
Kook, Grant J., 2136
Kook, Grant J., 2285
Koontz, Paul, 770
Koopersmith, Adam, 1480
Kopelman, Michael, 655
Kopelman, Josh, 741
Kopp, Darby, 907
Kopp, Tim, 962
Korengold, Michael A.G., 678
Korn, Andrew, 1602
Kornacki, David, 3258
Kornreich, John, 1617
Korsten, Eric R., 327
Korte, Thomas, 128
Kortick, Daniel M, 1984
Kortschak, Walter, 1675
Kosematoglu, Mehmet, 250
Kosofsky, Kristen, 925
Kososki, Trent, 675
Kosoy, MD, Daniel H., 187
Kossow, Jon, 1346
Kostenko, Bill, 2057
Kosty, Michael, 333
Kosuge, Roy, 1771
Kotler, Steven, 827
Koulogeorge, Mark, 1242
Kovach, Jeffrey, 170
Kowal, CFA, Krzysztof A., 637
Kowalick, Dave, 887
Kra, Howard, 190
Kracum, Richard R, 1990
Kramer, Ted H., 900
Krane, David, 889
Kraus, Stephen, 260
Kraus, Matt, 439
Kraus, Joe, 889
Krauss, George, 71
Krauss, Marlene R., 1058
Krausz, Steven M, 1896
Krautzel, George, 1240
Kravis, Henry R, 1082
Kraynak, Mark, 49

Kreie, Paul, 1232
Krekel, David A, 1398
Kreml MD, Stephanie, 241
Krenn, Mike, 1612
Kreter, Dave, 824
Krier, Donald A, 2004
Krikorian, Jason, 596
Krikston, Joel, 1205
Kriscunas, Suzanne, 1572
Krishnamurthy, Arvind, 1225
Krislav, Roman, 239
Kroin, David E., 859
Krommenhoek, Sid, 79
Kronfeld, David, 1038
Kropp, JB, 1934
Krouse, Rodger R, 1753
Krueger, Alex T., 740
Krumpfes, Austin, 1467
Krupa, Stephen M., 1498
Krupka, Mike, 221
Krusius, Jennifer, 515
Kryder, Chris, 748
Kuan, Leon, 744
Kubal, Larry, 1089
Kubo, Tatsuya, 909
Kucheman, William H., 269
Kuczinski, Anthony J, 1272
Kuegler, Tom, 1958
Kuehl, Ronald W, 789
Kuehl, Timothy, 1345
Kuelper, John, 176
Kuhling, Robert, 1378
Kulaga, Kenneth J., 725
Kulchenko, Lesya, 925
Kulman, W. Brent, 746
Kumar, Amit, 28
Kumar, Samir, 1013
Kumar, Manu, 1050
Kumar, Samir, 1154
Kumble, C Todd, 1726
Kumin, Michael A., 857
Kunda, Elaine, 2098
Kundan, Gursh, 997
Kundra, Monish, 515
Kung, Hsing, 47
Kung, Dr. Frank, 1941
Kung, Mona, 2138
Kunica, Matthew B., 2062
Kuntz, Edward L, 1651
Kuntz, Richard P, 1664
Kuo, Thomas Y., 254
Kuo, Steve, 925
Kuribayashi, Doug, 1474
Kurtz, Tom, 1422
Kurtzman, Gary J, 1601
Kurzweil, Ethan, 260
Kushner, Joshua, 1821
Kusserow, Paul, 955
Kutcher, Ashton, 15
Kutsenda, Eric, 1645
Kutzkey, PhD, Tim, 517
Kuzon, Josh, 1528
Kvamme, Mark D., 630
Kwait, Brian, 1368
Kwan, Eric, 1138
Kwatinetz, Mike, 215
Kwok, Celine, 858
Kwong, Lara, 994
Kyle, Kimberly, 22

L

La Croix, Minette L, 1668
LaKing, Larry, 2187
LaMothe, Chris, 658
LaPeer PE CFA, Karle E, 1426
LaPorte, Steve, 1378
LaSalle, Michael A., 1660

LaSorda, Tom, 981
LaViolette, Paul, 1628
LaViolette, Paul, 1762
Labbat, Pete, 675
Lacavera, Anthony, 2134
Lacelle, Benoit, 2250
Lacenere, Anthony M, 987
Lack, Jeremy D., 188
Lackey, Jennifer D, 1539
Lackey, Jr, G Thomas, 1539
Ladha, Farouk, 777
Ladsariya, Vivek, 1687
Lafayette, Justin, 2132
Lafferty, Edward A, 1623
Laffont, Philippe, 509
Laforteza, Amy L., 949
Lagerlund, Karin, 909
Laheny, A. Rachel, 1898
Lai, Ted, 970
Laino, Peter S, 1248
Laitala, Christopher M, 1129
Lajous, René, 378
Lake II, Charles T, 1674
Lalande, Kevin M., 1619
Lam, James K., 893
Lam, Rachel, 977
Lamb, Damian, 2130
Lambert, Ben, 1425
Lamm, Peter, 722
Lamond, Pierre, 648
Lamont, Ann, 1361
Lamoureux, Pierre-Olivier, 844
Lancaster, Jr., N. John, 1573
Landgarten, Harris, 172
Lando, Anthony V, 40
Landy, Joseph P, 1956
Lane, David, 613
Lane, Tom, 675
Lane, Christopher, 1086
Lane, Curtis S, 1271
Lane, David, 1378
Lane, Jamie, 1867
Lane, Michael, 3267
Langdale, Rich, 1286
Langdon, Michael S, 789
Lange, MD, PhD, Lou, 181
Langeler, Gerry, 1391
Langensand, Leif, 129
Langer, Mark, 401
Langere, Damian, 811
Lanier, Cam, 1072
Lanigan, Pat, 1871
Lanik, Joel, 790
Lanning, Chris, 815
Lapcevic, Maja, 486
Lapica, Monty, 512
Lapides, Matt, 21
Lapierre, Lise, 2029
Larcen, Dell, 881
Lardin, Cliff, 432
Large, Barry, 640
Largent, Kyle, 828
Larkin, Raymond, 572
Larkin, Ian, 1166
Larkins, Stuart, 471
Larsen, Charles E, 40
Larson, Robert E., 25
Larson, Robert E, 2005
Lasersohn, Jack W, 1929
Lasher, Stephen A., 888
Lasher, Stuart G, 1510
Lasher, Tyler, 1510
Lashkari PhD, Deval A, 1792
Lasky, Mitch, 248
Lasky, PhD, Larry, 517
Lasry, Marc, 208
Lassonde, Christian, 2151

Executive Name Index

Lathi, Vijay, 1298
Latterell, Patrick, 1094
Latzke, Dave, 464
Lau, Kenneth, 446
Lau, Gregory G, 1972
Lau, Sandra, 2033
Lau, Steve, 2288
Laudauer, Jay F, 1881
Lauder, Gary, 1095
Lauerwald, Eric, 1023
Laufer MD, Ron, 1196
Laufert, Paul, 2172
Laurence, Andrew, 1935
Lavery, Mairead, 2112
Lavery, Mairead, 2112
Lavin, Tom, 1303
Lawee, David, 578
Lawler, Christopher, 846
Lawler, Joe, 1990
Lawler, Peter, 2055
Lawless, Christian, 535
Lawlor, Augustine, 919
Lawrence, John, 1146
Lawrence, J Eric, 1549
Lawry, Richard V, 656
Lawson, Rich, 959
Lawson, Brian, 2067
Lawson-Johnston II, Peter O., 885
Lax, Charles R, 848
Lay, Michael, 2208
Laycock, Matthew, 199
Layden, Christopher A, 2015
Layton, Tim, 1705
Lazaridis, Mike, 2228
Lazarus, Amy S, 1726
Lazarus, Michael, 1978
Lazzer, Enio, 2109
Le, Thong Q, 31
Le, Huan, 951
Le Blanc, Robert, 2209
Le Dain, Adam, 2050
Le Houérou, Philippe, 1007
Le Loux, Alain, 549
Le Ruyet, Jean-Francois, 1516
LeBlanc, Chris, 1793
LeMaile-Stovall, Troy, 1790
LeMay, John, 290
LeSieur, Stephen M, 1717
LeVert-Chiasson, Serge, 2248
Leach, Ray, 1047
Leaf, Kathryn, 1411
Leakos, Steven, 2049
Lebel, Felix-Etienne, 2062
Lechasseur, Isabelle, 2088
Leck, Derek, 109
Leckie, Lars, 956
Leckrone, John, 58
Leder, Marc J, 1753
Lederer, Laurence, 327
Lederhausen, Mats, 567
Lederman, Marc, 1317
Lee, Nancy, 93
Lee, Anthony, 100
Lee, George J, 117
Lee, Peter, 228
Lee, Roger, 235
Lee, Kewsong, 413
Lee, Matt, 472
Lee, Dr. David, 494
Lee, Aileen, 552
Lee, Dr. Robert P, 612
Lee, Peter, 663
Lee, John, 686
Lee, Sam, 729
Lee, Jenny, 823
Lee, Christopher, 828
Lee, Kenneth B, 915

Lee, Thomas H, 1104
Lee, Cat, 1183
Lee, Kristin K, 1232
Lee, Jeffrey, 1340
Lee, Lisa M., 1496
Lee, David, 1650
Lee, Jess, 1654
Lee, John, 1716
Lee, Michael, 1774
Lee, Eric J, 1972
Lee, V. Paul, 2278
Lee Lai Chu, Margaret, 1139
Leeds, Jeffrey T, 1105
Leese, Steven A, 1503
Lefkoff, Kyle, 315
Lefkofsky, Eric, 1118
Legault, Richard, 2067
Legault, Eric, 2268
Legg, Chris, 1486
Leggat, Sara, 1656
Lehman, Paul, 1022
Lehman, Stephen A, 1248
Lehr, Seth J, 1136
Lehr, Jonathan, 2006
Leiber, Brian, 235
Leibovitz, Hila, 436
Leibovitz, John, 515
Leibowitz, Stephen, 1832
Leibowitz, Matthew, 2224
Leichtman, Lauren B, 1111
Leigh, Mark, 950
Leighton, Douglas H., 638
Leiher, Edina, 78
Leiman, James, 1338
Lein, Julie, 1893
Leinauer, Matt, 399
Leischner, Steven, 940
Lemmer, Johan, 2126
Lemmon, Tim, 134
Lemmons, Jr., William R., 671
Lenet, Scott, 791
Lengauer, PhD, Christoph, 1811
Lennox, Wally, 1461
Lentz, Nathaniel V, 1387
Leonard, Brian, 653
Leonard, H Jeffrey, 834
Leone, Douglas, 1654
Leong, Chris, 161
Leprince, Jean-Francois, 2092
Lerer, Kenneth, 1110
Lerer, Ben, 1110
Lerner, Steve, 1096
Lerohl, Mark, 2230
Leroux, James D., 179
Leroux, Philippe, 2260
Leschly, Jan, 412
Leschly, Mark, 1558
Lese, William D., 322
Lessin, Sam, 1694
Letinic MD PhD, Kresimir, 644
Letourneau, Mike, 1062
Lettmann, Jason, 1122
Leu Dennis, Alda, 991
Leudde, Colt, 888
Leung, Waiman, 1992
Leupold, Robert G., 25
Levandov, Rich, 206
Levandov, Richard W, 1175
Levchin, Max, 1631
Levchin, Nellie, 1631
Levental, Alex, 1021
Leventhal, Jeff, 305
Levin, Andrew, 1519
Levin, Mark, 1811
Levine, Daniel, 28
Levine, Jeremy, 260
Levine, Michael G., 356

Levine, Mark, 538
Levine, Seth, 776
Levine, Arthur, 1111
Levine, Michael S., 1116
Levine, Seth, 1245
Levinson, Joshua M., 844
Levitan, Dan, 1183
Levy, Anton, 815
Levy, Paul S., 1039
Levy, M Steven, 1272
Levy, Jay, 2017
Levy-Weiss, Gigi, 1323
Lew, Jacob J, 1129
Lew, Derek, 2143
Lew, Derek, 2216
Lewis, Charles, 258
Lewis, Rand, 441
Lewis, Philip, 794
Lewis, Clayton, 1183
Lewis, Blake, 1569
Lewis, J Christopher, 1575
Lewis, Joshua, 1608
Lewis, Legrand, 1705
Lewis, Rick, 1896
Lewis, William, 2021
Lewis, Shawn, 2274
Lewis II, Alan D., 1012
Lewy, Glen, 954
Leybold, Christin, 641
Li, Ping, 28
Li, Jeanne, 126
Li, Lixin, 1340
Li, Nan, 1363
Li, Quinn, 1509
Li, Bill, 1951
Li, Regan, 2083
Liang, Norman, 1983
Liao, Sophie, 1395
Libby, Oliver, 1687
Liccardo, Darren, 429
Lichter, PhD, Jay, 206
Lieberman, Alex, 489
Lieberman, Jeff, 1000
Liew, Henry, 1121
Liff, M Steven, 1753
Lightburn, David, 189
Lim, Jim, 867
Lim, Richard, 1373
Lim, MD, Jonathan E., 487
Limbaugh, P Frank, 759
Limberis, Anthony, 744
Lin, Will, 763
Lin, Ben, 858
Lin, M.R., 905
Lin, Anthony, 1004
Lin, Alfred, 1654
Lin, Jessica, 2006
Lin, Wei, 2175
Lincoln, David, 657
Lindahl, John, 1345
Lindner, Andrew, 790
Lindsay, Robert D, 1129
Ling, Byron, 386
Link PhD, William, 1928
Linn, Jaff, 1180
Linnen, Joseph, 1045
Linsalata, Frank, 1132
Lipkin, Richard, 644
Lippin, David, 1376
Lipscomb, Clark, 542
Lipsitz, Jeffrey A., 546
Lipson, Peter, 909
Liptak, Robert W., 495
Liras, Spiros, 143
Lisiak, Paul, 1225
List, Michael, 2141
Listen, Kevin L., 902

Liston, Tom, 2096
Litten, H Randall, 348
Little, C. Malcolm, 166
Little, Gary, 396
Little, Rob, 839
Little, Gary, 1257
Little, Jim, 1293
Little, Loretta, 2008
Littlechild, John W., 919
Littlejohn Jr., Angus C, 1134
Liu, Wei, 219
Liu, Roy Y., 925
Liu, Kelvin, 1015
Liu, Cherie, 1390
Liu, Larry Y., 2128
Livanos, Basil, 78
Livermore, Morgan, 820
Livingston, Jessica, 2012
Llanos, Claudia L., 132
Llovera, Bernardo H., 706
Lloyd, Alexander, 32
Lloyd, Pete, 1234
Lo, Felix, 839
LoGerfo, James, 643
Lobel, David S, 1651
Lobo, Brian J., 888
Lobo, Vernon, 2198
Locke, John, 28
Lockhart, Gene, 1240
Lockhart, Dennis, 1280
Lockie, Simon, 2134
Loftus, John, 53
Loh, John, 2062
Loh Nahmias, Vivian, 836
Loiacono, John, 183
Lomas, Eric J., 953
Lombardo, Lori, 683
Lonergan, Simon, 245
Lonergan, Michael A., 821
Long, Greg, 787
Long, Jim, 805
Long, Greg, 1166
Long, Michael D, 1270
Long Jr, John L, 1841
Longo, Peter, 530
Lopano, Scott, 677
Lopes, Luiz, 2067
Lopez, Alberto, 763
Lopez-Figueroa, Manuel, 237
Lor, Patrick, 2212
Lord, Hambleton, 1100
Lorenzen, Lee, 103
Lori, Matthew J., 1301
Loring, Ian, 220
Lotane, Nancy, 220
Lothian, E. Craig, 2173
Lotter, Jerry, 664
Loughlin, Steve, 28
Loughlin, Phil, 220
Louie, Gilman, 93
Lovell, Jeffrey D, 1147
Loverro, Frank J, 1062
Loverro, John G, 1112
Lovett, Rad, 1148
Low, Jeff, 645
Low, Lisa, 2087
Loy, Trevor R, 756
Loy, A. Thomas, 1223
Lozzi, Mark, 2131
Lu, Jimmy, 1983
Lubash, Barbara, 1928
Lubert, Ira M, 1136
Lubert, Ira M, 1508
Lubin, Daniel C, 1520
Luby, Bill, 1638
Lucarelli, Stefano, 2055
Lucas, Christopher, 275

1091

Executive Name Index

Lucas, Paul, 2152
Lucassen, Jeff, 2204
Lucero, Ryan, 782
Lucia, CFA, Rebecca, 12
Lucke, Joe, 2176
Luderer, MD, Jack R., 139
Ludwig, Mark, 1705
Lueger, Brian, 1053
Luehrs, Bruce, 1568
Lugani, Vishal, 49
Lugsdin, Andrew, 2124
Lujan, Larry, 1924
Lukaczyk, Laura L., 207
Lunak, Rich, 998
Lunan, Tom, 2058
Lund, Chris, 899
Lund, Robert, 999
Lundin, Hans, 1002
Lundy, Megan, 1129
Lung, Wendy, 967
Lupa PhD, Mark T, 930
Luse, Rebecca, 1298
Lustbader, Michael H., 166
Lutzke, Scott, 443
Lutzker, Joshua A., 254
Ly, Eric, 661
Lydon, Mark, 1004
Lyford, Shelley, 1973
Lyman, John, 889
Lynch, Casey, 96
Lynch, Christopher W., 178
Lynch, Kevin, 431
Lynch, Linda, 744
Lynch, Zack, 1029
Lynch, Michael, 1199
Lynch, Jeremy, 1851
Lynde, Renske, 8
Lynn, Rebecca, 396
Lynn, Will, 881
Lynn, Rebecca, 1257
Lyon, Greg, 648
Lyons, Bill, 488
Lyons, Peter A, 1105
Lyons, Michael J, 1127
Lyren, Melanie C, 164
Lysne, Alan, 2115
Lysne, Alan, 2245

M

Ma, Jiong, 322
Maalouf, Khalil, 2290
Mabbs, Kenneth, 711
Mac Mahon, Tom, 748
MacAskill, Peter, 2205
MacBean, Mick, 2275
MacBeath, Alex, 2164
MacCormack, Justin, 2150
MacDonald, Rod, 594
MacDonald, Charlotte D., 949
MacDonald, William I, 1103
MacDonald, Caitlyn, 1104
MacDonald, Bill, 2074
MacDonald, Scott, 2190
MacInnis, Robert, 21
MacIntosh, Alan, 51
MacIntosh, Alan, 2232
MacIntyre, John B., 2062
MacKeigan, Dan, 1728
MacKellar, Richard, 2078
MacKenzie, Timothy J, 1209
MacKinnon, Kenneth, 2181
MacLellan, Rob, 2204
MacLeod, Scott, 834
MacMaster, Dale, 2033
MacMillan, Charlie, 642
MacMurray, John F., 1621
MacShane, Nick, 1486

MacTaggart, Ian B., 357
MacTavish, Mark, 2208
Macaulay, William E., 740
Maccini, Robert J., 125
Macdonald, Peter, 274
Macdonell, Ian, 2089
Mace, David, 824
Machado, Joe, 1266
Machlica, David J, 1163
Maciariello, Patrick A., 523
Macinnes, Travis, 38
Mack, Joshua, 501
Mack, Julian C., 1088
Mackesy, D Scott, 1972
Mackley, Anna, 1936
Mackowski, J Matthew, 1792
Maclean, Richard, 790
Macleod, Robert W, 1198
Madasamy, Karthee, 1243
Madden, Jim, 416
Madera, Paul, 1212
Madon, Cyrus, 2067
Madsen, Kent, 688
Madsen, Dion, 1438
Madsen, Dion, 2036
Maeder, Robert, 766
Maeder, Paul, 935
Magas, Peter N, 244
Magerman, David, 614
Magescas, Carine, 128
Maggs, Roger, 2076
Magid, Deborah, 967
Magida, Stephen A., 123
Magliacano, Marc, 1088
Magnano, Ben, 782
Magnuson, Rick, 824
Maguire, Shaun, 889
Maguy, Billy, 92
Mahadevia, Vishal, 1956
Mahajan, Amitt, 1473
Maher, David M, 352
Mahesh, Shripriya, 1721
Mahoney, James, 960
Mahony, TJ, 38
Maidenberg, Ted, 1848
Main, Clayton, 333
Mairs, Christopher J, 1105
Majors, Mike, 586
Makharia, Rohit, 817
Makhzoumi, Mohamad, 1297
Makishev, Nurzhas, 1329
Makower, Josh, 1297
Maldonado, John, 62
Maldonado, Alejandro, 141
Maleki, Alex, 972
Malekian, E Peter, 1189
Maliwal, Aditi, 1888
Malka, Meyer, 1560
Mallabone, Ward, 2227
Mallett, Thomas E, 103
Mallios, Demetrios, 1012
Malloy, John, 296
Malone, Zach, 628
Malone, Kevin, 1105
Maloney, Timothy W, 18
Maloney, TJ, 1127
Maloney, Mark, 1400
Maloney, Drew, 3255
Maltz, Jules, 1001
Maluth, Elliot, 928
Malven, Dan, 10
Mamdani, Sulu, 1764
Manasterski, Marc, 1516
Manchester, Robert D, 1162
Mandal, Sumant, 1809
Mandato, Joe, 598
Mandelbaum, Fern, 1249

Mandelbaum, Fern, 1939
Mandile, John, 1673
Mandl, Ryan, 745
Manges, James, 1851
Manlunas, Eirc, 1965
Manlunas, Eric, 1965
Manning, Jack, 309
Manning, Robert, 1596
Manning, Christopher, 1851
Mannix, Hank, 1062
Manos, Peter M., 166
Mansour, Saif, 330
Mansour, Saif, 331
Mansour, Bassem A, 1545
Manuel, Will, 110
Manzetti, John W, 1448
Mao, Carol, 799
Mao, Benjamin, 1081
Mapes, John, 199
Maples Jr., Mike, 751
Marakovic, Nino, 1620
Marasco, James, 1970
Marcantonio, Mike, 288
Marcoux, Jean-Francois, 1982
Marcus, Jeff, 559
Marcus, Lenard, 655
Marcus, Larry, 1952
Marcus, Adam, 2102
Mardirossian, Shant, 1081
Marengere, Luc, 2276
Marex, Brenda, 1303
Margetts, Jill, 443
Margolin, Adam J, 1717
Margolis, Paul, 1146
Margolskee, Dorothy, 762
Mariani, Paul, 22
Mariani Sullivan, Jeanne, 1738
Mariel, Serafin, 360
Marimow, Scott M., 1496
Marini, Giacomo, 1352
Marino, Michael, 200
Marino, Louis, 818
Marino, Benjamin, 1432
Marino, Wayne, 1748
Maris, Bill, 1643
Mark, Jeffrey, 507
Mark, Douglas E, 1343
Mark, Joncarlo, 1892
Markandaier, Mohan, 2138
Markey, Bernard B, 1281
Markham IV, E. Murphy, 672
Markova, MBA, Sonja, 226
Markowsky, Barry, 2152
Marks, Howard, 1362
Marks, Arthur J, 1899
Marlas, James, 1881
Marlette, Scott, 1694
Marley, Juli, 290
Marocco, Michael, 1617
Marple, Dave, 1907
Marquardt, David, 197
Marques Oliveira, Fernando, 928
Marquez, Michael, 1254
Marquis, Joelle, 170
Marr, Michael S., 405
Marra, Jim, 290
Marrero, Roger, 528
Marron, Donald B, 1123
Marschmeyer, Carsten, 1170
Marsh, MD, Edward B, 1198
Marshall, Marcy, 149
Marshall, Michael, 894
Marshall, Bob, 1646
Marshall, Jim, 1646
Marshall, Woody, 1785
Marshall, A.J. (Sandy), 2061
Marshall, Stephen O., 2103

Marshbanks, Tracy, 732
Martin, Charles R, 111
Martin, Edward W, 492
Martin, Tim, 540
Martin, Melanie, 768
Martin, Philip W, 1606
Martin, Michael, 1778
Martin, Brian D, 1904
Martin, Michael, 1956
Martin, Brian F., 2057
Martineau-Fortin, Eric, 1982
Martinez, Ignacio, 747
Martinez, Emanuel, 865
Martino, Paul, 358
Martino, Rocco J., 1093
Martirano, David, 1459
Marty, Alan, 1106
Maruyama, PhD, Kazunori, 182
Marver, Jim, 1906
Marvin, Kim, 109
Masi, Renee, 269
Masinter, Mark L, 1549
Masjedi, Shannon, 1399
Maslow, Randy, 966
Mason, Susan, 83
Mason, Alex, 416
Mason, Bob, 1487
Massard, Nicolas, 21
Massaro, Salvatore A, 656
Massey, Lauren M, 18
Masto, Christopher, 787
Masucci, Peter N., 1301
Masur, Mark C, 1682
Matelich, George E, 1062
Mather, David, 2159
Mathers, David, 554
Mathew, Arun, 28
Mathews, Kenneth J, 381
Mathews, Devin, 468
Mathews, Stuart I, 1224
Mathews, Brendan, 1259
Mathieu, Chris, 946
Matlin, Howard, 1062
Matlin, David J, 1179
Matlock, Tyler, 1767
Matly, MD, Michael, 1251
Matsumoto, PhD, Shunichiro, 182
Mattaliano, Alfred M., 1578
Mattamana, Alan, 714
Matteucci, Paul, 1896
Matthes, William, 245
Matthews, Brian, 569
Matthews, Gary S, 1256
Matthews, Terry, 2284
Mattina, Joe, 2219
Mau, Luke, 225
Mauchant, Florence J., 953
Maurer, Erik E, 1492
Mawani, Shafeen, 2269
Mawhinney, Tom, 968
Maxwell, Bret, 1242
Maxwell, Scott, 1380
May, Kevin J., 946
May, Robert, 986
May, John, 1304
May, Rob, 1459
Maybaum, Richard E, 1134
Maybell, Mark, 645
Mayer, John A. (Tony), 706
Mayer, Michael, 1251
Mayer, Andrew R., 1777
Mayerfeld, Russ, 88
Mayerson, Frederic H, 1954
Mayfield, John, 79
Mayfield, R Glen, 1571
Maynard, Frederick, 909
Mayson, Howard, 2050

Executive Name Index

Mayton, Jennifer, 1936
Mazzarino, John, 463
Mazzullo, Theresa B, 704
McAdam, Tim, 1785
McAndrews, Mark, 645
McBane, Michelle, 2257
McBride, Jim, 291
McCabe, Murray, 300
McCabe, George, 910
McCafferty, Kevin M., 426
McCafferty, Aevin M, 1296
McCafferty, Brendan, 1296
McCaig, Murray, 2041
McCall, Matt, 1480
McCarthy, Loretta, 841
McCarthy, Michael R, 1276
McCarthy, Edward C, 1571
McCarthy, Michelle, 1926
McCarthy, CPA, Shane, 678
McCarty, John, 1423
McCarty, Bob, 1787
McCauley, Mike, 2127
McCelland, Spence, 1331
McClain, Richard, 932
McClanahan, Kip, 1685
McClean, Stephen, 170
McCleary, Christopher, 287
McClements, James, 1548
McCloskey, Tom, 542
McCollum, W. Christian, 1109
McComiskey, Niall, 862
McConahey, Steve, 1020
McConnell, Scott, 88
McConnell, Eamonn, 2167
McConoughey, Jim, 923
McCooe, Matthew, 530
McCormack, Stephen, 521
McCormack, Scott, 1638
McCormack, John F, 1651
McCormack, Andrew, 1897
McCormick, Douglas, 917
McCormick, Pete, 1183
McCormick, Doug, 1558
McCormick, Jeffrey S, 1623
McCoy, Stephanie, 1522
McCrary, Dennis, 1411
McCreadie, Paul, 149
McCroskey, Nancy, 183
McCullagh, Mahala, 2266
McCullen, Bill, 1097
McCulloch, J.D., 514
McCullough, John W., 904
McCullough, Michael, 983
McCusker, Charles P, 1422
McDaid, Brian C., 1727
McDaniel, Teresa, 169
McDaniel, Brenda, 1064
McDermott, Dirk, 98
McDermott, Tom, 656
McDermott, James, 1895
McDonagh, Bill, 1952
McDonald, Matthew, 227
McDonald, Dr Robert, 1722
McDonald, Robert, 1934
McDonald, Jam Michael, 2245
McDonald, Deborah, 2282
McDonnell, Mark, 153
McDowell, Mark, 51
McDowell, Mark, 1096
McElhone, Christopher, 2034
McElhone, Christopher, 2046
McEwen, John, 2097
McFadden, Mark, 433
McFarland, Josh, 872
McFetridge, Scott A., 901
McGee, Patrick K., 328
McGee, Meghan M., 383

McGee, Michael, 2049
McGillivray, Burton, 505
McGlinn, Jack, 405
McGonnigle, Glenn, 1788
McGould, Sean, 1120
McGovern, Kevin M., 1191
McGowan Sr, Gene, 1192
McGrath, Kevin, 1288
McGregor, Doug, 2231
McGuire, Lake, 925
McGuire, Terry, 1460
McIlwain, Matt, 1158
McIlwraith, John, 86
McInerney, Thomas E., 299
McInerney, Paula G., 299
McInerney, John L., 299
McIntyre, Ryan, 776
McIntyre, Todd, 870
McIsaac, Zac, 2188
McIvor, Dale, 1712
McKay, Samuel, 212
McKay, Steve, 772
McKay, Chris, 852
McKearn PhD, John, 1574
McKee Jr., Bill, 846
McKellar, Winston P., 1193
McKelvey, Jim, 569
McKelvie, Don, 2086
McKenna, David, 62
McKenna, Joe, 2168
McKenzie, Ryan R., 147
McKibben, Jeffrey, 1368
McKiernan, Erika, 1662
McKinley, Thomas, 410
McKinley, John, 1096
McKinley, William F, 1426
McKinney, Dan, 1321
McKittrick, Stacey, 142
McLaughlin, Andrew, 934
McLaughlin, Mark A., 949
McLaughlin, James, 1127
McLean, Bart A, 1270
McLeese, Robert S., 2030
McLellan, Andrew, 1960
McLemore, Don, 493
McLeod, Chris, 660
McLoughlin, Andy, 1879
McMahon, Michael, 1046
McMahon, Jack, 2283
McManus, Marc, 489
McMartin, Cam, 444
McMillan, Jaime, 390
McMorris, Marc, 416
McMullan, Robert, 277
McMullen, John, 2174
McMurchy, Kevin W, 629
McNabb, J Carter, 1571
McNally, Nannette, 64
McNally, Ryan, 427
McNally, Sean M, 1469
McNamara II, John C, 1144
McNamee, Roger, 659
McNeil PhD, Robert G, 1616
McNerney, Peter H, 1817
McNulty, Edward, 573
McParland, Robert J., 1828
McPhee, Ron J, 1924
McQueen, Mark, 2080
McQueeney, Michael P, 1751
McVicar, Tracey, 365
McWhorter, David, 425
McWhorter, Stuart, 496
McWhorter, R. Clayton, 496
McWilliams PhD, Peter C, 1616
Mclean, Dave, 1658
Mclean Owen, Loudon, 2199
Meacham, Scott, 2024

Mead, James M, 1520
Meadow, Scott, 654
Meakem, Chip, 1080
Meakem, Chip, 1849
Meany, Ryan, 653
Mech, Steve, 566
Meduna, Cyril L., 63
Meehan, Frank, 1716
Meeks, Jonathan W, 1776
Meenan, Patrick, 173
Meeusen, PhD, Ron, 570
Mehlman, Ezra, 918
Mehra, Vivek, 197
Mehra, Rajan, 502
Mehra, Anand, 1698
Mehring, Paul, 35
Mehta, Nihal, 679
Mehta, Shailesh, 851
Mehta, Sameet, 851
Mehta, Manan, 1885
Meidlinger, Karen, 1199
Meilner, John, 338
Meisel, Seth, 277
Mejias, Omar, 63
Meketa, James E, 1200
Melchior, Lisa, 2281
Meldrum, Christopher S, 840
Meldrum, CFA, Kelly, 57
Mele, Francesco, 2050
Mellet, Daisy, 1207
Mellinger, Doug K., 492
Mello, Ed, 576
Mello, Kirsten A., 1202
Melmon, Richard, 358
Melohn, Joseph, 707
Melohn, Ryan, 707
Melrose, Richard S, 1163
Melrose, Dr Evan, 1722
Melstrom, John, 981
Melton, Brian, 1796
Melwani, Prakash A., 277
Melzer, Thomas C, 1574
Mencoff, Samuel M, 1156
Mendelson, Alan, 212
Mendelson, Jason, 776
Mendicino II, Frank, 36
Mendicino III, Frank, 36
Mendoza, Felipe, 165
Mendoza, Adrian, 1201
Mendoza, Senofer, 1201
Menell, Mark, 1416
Menichelli, Vincent P., 53
Merritt, Elizabeth, 463
Merritt, Dorian, 1796
Mes, David, 1370
Messano, Frances, 1316
Messick, Diane, 989
Methot, Andree-Lise, 2093
Metz, Lloyd M., 969
Metz, Travis R, 1248
Meybaum, Hardi, 1181
Meyer, Yoni, 417
Meyer, Alex, 1384
Mhatre, Ravi, 1121
Mi, Jonathan, 340
Miau, Matthew, 905
Michael, David, 133
Michaud, Gerald A., 946
Michaud, Brian W, 1134
Michel, Marc, 525
Middleton, Jesse, 754
Middleton, Fred A, 1221
Middleton, Fred A, 1616
Miele, Perry, 2057
Migliorino, Robert, 1947
Mihas, Constantine S., 884
Mika, Ron, 1705

Mikkelsen, Erik, 2047
Mikula, Benn, 2086
Milano, Jessica, 376
Milbery, James F, 468
Milciunas, John Paul, 32
Milder, Don, 1928
Millar, Alex, 294
Miller, Jonathan, 60
Miller, William, 126
Miller, Michael, 443
Miller, David S., 497
Miller, Michael W., 526
Miller, Ken, 658
Miller, David B., 672
Miller, Christian T, 698
Miller, Charles D., 904
Miller, Jeb, 968
Miller, Sandy, 1001
Miller, Tony, 1107
Miller, Brian C, 1128
Miller, W Scott, 1148
Miller, Mark G, 1194
Miller, Steve, 1231
Miller, Marlin, 1347
Miller, Steven N., 1384
Miller, Jeff, 1411
Miller, Daniel H, 1580
Miller, Eyal, 1611
Miller, Matt, 1952
Miller, Brian, 3264
Miller IV, Norvell E, 1709
Miller, MD, Lawrence G, 1197
Millet, David F, 812
Milligan, Ryan, 468
Mills, Peter H, 1
Mills PhD, Timothy C, 1616
Milne, Jr. PhD, George M, 1520
Milner, Yuri, 615
Miltenberger, William H., 984
Mimran, Joe, 2133
Mims, Cory D., 969
Minaya, Jose, 1356
Miner, Allen, 1755
Minerd, B. Scott, 885
Minihan, Kenneth A., 1400
Minnick, James, 1147
Minocherhomjee, Arda M, 468
Minter, Alison, 1335
Mirabelli, PhD, Christopher K., 919
Mirabile, Christopher, 1100
Miranda, Antonio, 1134
Mischianti, Lou, 1372
Misek, Peter, 2124
Misfeldt, Dayton, 237
Mishra, Vish, 502
Mistras, CFA, Antonis, 637
Mistry, Ashish H., 282
Mitchell, Ivar W., 123
Mitchell, Andrew, 325
Mitchell, Nate, 820
Mitchell, Kate, 1626
Mitchell, Dan, 1653
Mitchell, Chris, 1717
Mitchell, Lee M, 1814
Mitchell, Marcus, 2065
Miura-Ko, Ann, 751
Mixon, Ki, 1545
Miyata, Tak, 1634
Mnaymneh, Sami, 928
Mo, Jonathan, 4
Moan, Gerry, 1695
Mock, Lawrence, 1280
Modersitzki, Blake, 1425
Modica, Pino N, 1452
Moe, Michael, 883
Moelis, Cory, 877
Moerschel, Gregory, 244

Executive Name Index

Mogk, Peter, 960
Mogk, Peter E, 960
Mohamed, Minhas, 2196
Mohammadioun, Said, 1788
Mohan, Ravi, 1663
Mohler, PhD, Kendall, 31
Moilanen, Jake, 1655
Molano, Gina E., 1881
Molbert, Lauris, 173
Moldow, Charles, 770
Moley, Andrew, 1121
Molinari, Drew, 577
Moll, David, 988
Molner, Phillip C, 1476
Monaghan, Arthur, 850
Monahan, Lee J., 910
Monat, Jeff, 1207
Moncrief, Ray, 1214
Mondre, Greg, 1683
Money, Aaron, 787
Money, Brad, 869
Montana, Ralph, 1960
Monteith, Scott, 2197
Montgomery, H. DuBose, 1202
Montgomery, Andrew, 1222
Montoya, Mario, 1992
Moon, John, 1256
Moon, Bernard, 1716
Moor, Markus, 2106
Moore, Ryan, 38
Moore, Matt, 92
Moore, John, 193
Moore, Erik, 229
Moore, Steven, 334
Moore, Brendan M., 686
Moore, Anthony J., 822
Moore, Church M, 1062
Moore, Geoffrey, 1247
Moore, Terry, 1253
Moore, Chris, 1534
Moore, Paul, 1736
Moore, Geoffrey, 1985
Moore, Matthew, 2233
Moorin, Jay, 1490
Moorjani, Dinesh, 518
Moorse, Dan, 917
Mora, Frank, 958
Moragne, John H., 1850
Moraly, Dana, 502
Moran, Michael E, 348
Moran, Robert P, 1452
More, Bob, 94
Moreland, Ira L., 969
Moreno, Michelle, 629
Moretti, Anthony, 352
Morfit, G. Mason, 1903
Morfitt, Brian, 782
Morgan, Kirk, 53
Morgan, Howard, 216
Morgan, Jonathan, 253
Morgan, Michael, 373
Morgan, Quinn, 446
Morgan, Wanda R, 1270
Morgan, John, 1430
Morgan, Eric C., 1456
Morgan, Michael C, 1846
Morgenthal, Steven J, 164
Morgenthaler, Gary, 1257
Mori, Takeshi, 837
Morin, Christina, 846
Morin, Dave, 1694
Morin, Mike, 1736
Morin, Genevieve, 2119
Morin, Gaétan, 2120
Moritz, Michael, 1654
Moritz, J. Kenneth, 1746
Moross, David, 717

Morris, Mark, 290
Morris, Frederic H., 349
Morris, John, 909
Morris, Rob, 1372
Morris, Nigel, 1502
Morris, Erik O., 1576
Morris, CPA, Scott, 736
Morrison, John L., 843
Morriss, Nick, 834
Morrissette, Mark J, 1333
Morrissey, Michael B., 1014
Morrow, David, 1800
Morse PhD, Laurence C., 714
Mortimer, David, 2053
Morton, Jeff, 48
Moseley, Allen S, 1331
Moser, Randy, 200
Moskowitz, Jason B, 633
Mosman, Matt, 1425
Moss, Malcolm, 251
Moss, Rick, 253
Moss, Cheryl, 788
Mossler, Fred, 1912
Moszer, David, 1491
Motley, David, 298
Mott, Catherine, 293
Mott, Catherine, 298
Mottahed, Sonny, 2074
Moulton, Eben S, 1636
Mount, Ian J, 1277
Mountain, Rocky, 594
Moura, Andre V., 1301
Moyer, Chris, 2216
Muhtadie, Mira, 42
Muhtadie, Fayez S., 1743
Muir, Jeffrey S, 794
Muir, Craig, 1811
Mukhamedyarov, Marat, 2138
Mulcahey, Brennan, 349
Mulcare, Robert W., 1301
Mulder, Nikole, 297
Mullane, Kevin, 17
Mullane, Kevin F., 1016
Mullany, Michael, 968
Mullen, Terrence, 170
Mullen, Mark, 306
Mullen, Mark, 624
Mullen, Dave, 2146
Mulligan, William C, 1476
Mullin, Stephen P, 629
Mulloy, Corey, 935
Mulloy, Jennifer M, 1776
Multani, Arneek, 1850
Mumma, Mitch, 1008
Munakata, PhD, Ryosuke, 182
Mundheim, Peter M., 1743
Mundkur, Yatin, 174
Mundt, Kevin A., 1931
Munichiello, Dave, 889
Muniz, Stephen, 1501
Munjal, Salil, 2291
Munk, Anthony, 2209
Munson, Peter, 409
Muoio, Patricia, 1687
Murdoch, Britton, 1568
Murphree, Dennis E, 1273
Murphree, Lori L., 1369
Murphy, Scott, 61
Murphy, Pauline, 530
Murphy, Tom, 559
Murphy, Thomas, 815
Murphy, Matt, 1202
Murphy, Brian G., 1317
Murphy, Shay, 1324
Murphy, Michael P., 1585
Murphy, Paul F, 1651
Murphy, Jeffrey N., 2163

Murphy Jr, John J, 1274
Murray, Timothy M, 468
Murray, Alan, 539
Murray, Jonathan, 628
Murray, Jonathan, 642
Murray, Dr. Campbell, 1350
Murray, Arthur G, 1881
Murray, Mike, 2217
Murray Jr, James B, 551
Murray-Tateishi, Sheila, 2056
Musallam, Ramzi M, 1925
Muse, Brad, 71
Mussafer, David, 62
Muth, Peter J, 1746
Mutter, Sheila, 1786
Myers, Greg, 1171
Mygind, Scott, 830
Myhrvold, Cameron, 974
Myhrvold, Nathan, 1005
Mykhaylovskyy, Andriy, 727
Myrrha, Diogo, 79
Mytels, Dan, 1609

N

Nader, Anthony, 1766
Naeve, PhD, Janis, 112
Nagappan, Vijay, 1226
Nagaraj, Sunil, 1877
Nagel, Rick, 48
Nagel, PhD, David, 768
Nagim, Ryan K, 1144
Nahumi, Dror, 1346
Naik, Sandeep, 815
Naimi, Ramtin, 24
Naini, Nader, 782
Najjar, Michael E., 546
Nakache, Patricia, 1853
Nalamasu, Ph.D., Omkaram, 144
Nam, Hodong, 100
Narayan, Sridhar, 834
Nardelli, Robert, 667
Nardone, Randal A., 767
Nark, Ted, 1086
Nashat, Amir, 1460
Nasr, Khaled, 1010
Natali, Stephen, 654
Natarajan, Vas, 28
Natarajan, Raj, 2026
Nathan, Richard, 2167
Nault, David, 2179
Naythons MD, Matthew, 163
Neal, Maria, 992
Neal, Doug, 2023
Neary, James, 1956
Nechiti, Ionel V., 997
Nedungadi, Ajit, 1776
Needham, Tom, 1775
Neels, Guido, 697
Neely, Matthew, 1692
Neff, P Sherrill, 1508
Negus, Kevin, 385
Neider, Calvin A, 503
Neighbors, David, 1963
Neild, W. Carter, 1382
Neis, John, 1921
Neldner, Derek, 2231
Nelsen, Robert T., 153
Nelson, Steve, 473
Nelson, Brian R., 869
Nelson, Carl, 917
Nelson, Lisa, 1154
Nelson, Jonathan M., 1496
Nelson, Dean, 1602
Nelson, John R, 1664
Nelson, Andrea R, 1719
Nelson, Joshua M., 1815
Nelson, Kirk, 1917

Nelson, Steve, 3266
Nelson MD, James, 1002
Nesbeda, Eugene P., 546
Ness, Rick, 2260
Nessi, Claudio, 1373
Netravali, Dr. Arun, 1375
Neubauer, Lawrence, 1516
Neundorfer, Jennifer Keiser, 1026
Neustaetter, Thomas, 1038
Neuwirth, Daniel P, 1504
Neverson, David C, 1105
Newbold, Robert, 846
Newby, Tom, 1112
Newcomb, Andy, 1240
Newell, Carol, 2238
Newhall, Ashton, 867
Newman, Bruce, 683
Newman, Denis, 1230
Newman, Howard H, 1443
Newman, Henry W, 1702
Newman, Jerrold, 1987
Newton, Tyler, 427
Newton, Jeffrey T, 812
Ng, Carey, 1221
Ngo, Yi-Jian, 85
Ngo, Jessica, 472
Ngo, Thien-Ly, 526
Nguyen, David, 126
Nguyen, Ha, 1721
Nguyen, Ha, 2190
Nichols, Carl, 1389
Nicholson, Peter, 1548
Nickell, Frank T, 1062
Nickerson, Ken, 2131
Nicklas, Brent, 1112
Nicklin, Matthew, 732
Niedel, James, 1298
Nieh, Peter, 1121
Niehaus, Joseph M., 949
Nielsen, Kirk G, 1928
Niemeyer, Suzanne, 53
Niemiec, David W., 1621
Nies, John, 1040
Nieuwenburg, Jim, 2050
Nijhawan, Preetish, 454
Nijjar, Karamdeep, 2157
Nikolay, Joern, 815
Nikolic, Dr. Boris, 268
Niparko, Nate, 28
Nisselson, Evan, 1101
Nissenbaum, Scott, 246
Nixon, Ron, 425
Noble, Craig, 2067
Nodelman, Oleg, 709
Nodine, Ralph, 1160
Noel, Karen, 1416
Noell, Charles E., 1041
Nof, Jordan, 1868
Nolan, Scott, 775
Nolan, William, 928
Nolan, Peter J, 1109
Nolan Jr, Robert B, 897
Nolen, Malcolm C, 1674
Nolen, Tom, 1788
Noonan, Tom, 1788
Noor, A. Bilal, 166
Noorani, Zach, 770
Nordgren, Matthew J., 151
Noris, Javier, 1630
Norlander, Rebecca, 976
Normandeau, Rob, 2251
Noronha, Austin, 1704
Norr, Daniel, 203
Norreri, Federica, 161
Norris, Robert, 425
Norris, Nickie, 926
Norris, Ron, 1922
Nortman, Kara, 1888

1094

Executive Name Index

Norton, Christopher B., 405
Norton, Matthew W, 1156
Norton, James J., 1435
Notini, Albert A., 1301
Nourmand, Robin, 225
Nova, Daniel, 935
Novak, Turner, 811
Novak, Jr., E. Rogers, 1348
Novielli, Michael A., 638
Novogratz, Jacqueline, 55
Novotny, Carl, 1920
Novotny, Chad, 1920
Nowaczyk, John J, 1234
Noy, Oded, 120
Nugent, Michael E., 1578
Nulman, Shay, 2175
Nussbaum, Joshua, 525
Nuttman, Angela, 770
Nycz, Jerome, 2055
Nye, Ben, 221
Nykin, Ilya, 1488
Nystrom, Cody, 1689

O

O'Brien, James D., 97
O'Brien, Kevin, 433
O'Brien, William, 661
O'Brien, Dennis, 881
O'Brien, Daniel J., 1037
O'Brien, Dennis, 1131
O'Connell, Daniel S., 1931
O'Connor, John, 1127
O'Connor, Logan V., 2015
O'Dell, Bradley C, 1492
O'Donnell, Charlie, 351
O'Donnell, James A., 734
O'Donnell PhD, Niall A, 1574
O'Driscoll, Rory, 1626
O'Grady, Standish, 852
O'Hara, Dave, 173
O'Hara, Maura, 3265
O'Hare, Scott, 594
O'Keefe, Kenneth, 244
O'Keefe, Kenneth, 1931
O'Keefe, Sean, 1960
O'Leary, Nancy, 1038
O'Leary, Brendan, 1478
O'Loughlin, Tim, 646
O'Malley, Brian, 761
O'Malley, Mike, 989
O'Mara, James, 1987
O'Neill, John, 1111
O'Neill, George D, 1215
O'Neill, Christopher, 1944
O'Rourke, Eileen, 19
O'Shaughnessy, Patrick, 341
O'Shea, Donald, 571
O'Sullivan, Michael P, 1452
Oakford, Scott I., 899
Ober, Kevin, 618
Oberbeck, Christian L., 1621
Oberg, Soren L., 1815
Oberholtzer, William J, 932
Oblak, Geoffrey S., 178
Occhiogross, Neill, 547
Occhipinti, Vincent M, 2005
Ocko, Matt, 585
Ocko, Julie, 909
Odden, Jake, 20
Odinsky, Jordan, 877
Oei, Ting-Pau, 644
Oetgen, Steve, 839
Ogawa, Andrew, 1513
Ogawa, Marcus, 1513
Ogden, William, 1881
Ogince, Michoel, 1992
Oguz, Matt, 1406

Oka, Jonathan T., 750
Okike, Nnamdi, 13
Okonow, Dale S, 1962
Okun MIM, Robert, 1773
Olah, Amy, 2080
Olesnavage, Mark, 943
Oliva, Adele, 5
Oliva, Adele C, 1508
Olivier, Serge, 2029
Olkkola, Ed, 1783
Olofinboba, Kola, 714
Olsen, Chris, 630
Olshansky, Josh, 839
Olson, Thiago, 677
Omidyar, Pierre, 1374
Ondrula, Lisa, 1045
Onen, Selahattin, 1406
Onofrio, Joe, 745
Onsi, Douglas E., 919
Opdendyk, Terry, 1378
Orazio, Anthony J., 1417
Ord, John, 542
Orend, Michael J, 1575
Orfao, David, 816
Ormont, Jordan, 1202
Orndorff, Chris, 1946
Oronsky, Arnie, 1010
Orr, Larry, 1853
Orr III, R Wilson, 1732
Orsak, Michael, 2007
Orthlieb, Ben, 1370
Orthwein, Jr., Peter B., 1727
Orum, Nick, 881
Osawa, Koji, 833
Osawa, Shoichi, 1704
Osborn, William, 520
Osborn, Richard, 2233
Osborn, Richard, 2265
Osborne, Sandy, 1062
Oseary, Guy, 15
Osgood CFA, Jonathan W, 572
Osman, Bart D, 1112
Osnoss, Joe, 1683
Ostheimer, Jason, 60
Ostrander, T.C., 300
Ostrow, Gene J, 1526
Otani, Toshi, 1838
Otis, Meghan, 1964
Ou, Bruce, 879
Ousseimi, Mimo, 810
Outcalt, David B, 1112
Outerbridge, Amanda, 909
Outland, James, 1293
Overmyer, Craig, 944
Overvelde, Michael, 2091
Owen, Judy M., 375
Owen, Loudon, 2154
Owens, Todd G., 343
Owens, Vince, 886
Owsley, Jonathan H., 1088
Owusu, George Y, 1164
Oxaal, John, 1658
Ozawa, Clare, 1928
Ozechov, Michael, 543
Ozir, Gil, 2057

P

Pacelli, Peter, 1078
Pachisia, Nitin, 1885
Pacitti, Chris, 202
Packard, Chad, 1425
Padnos, Cindy, 976
Padovano, Carlo, 1376
Paes-Braga, Brian, 2246
Page, Marcia L., 1907
Pagliuca, Stephen, 220

Pahxia, Morgan, 1464
Pai, Raj, 834
Paiement, Constance, 738
Pakianathan, PhD, Deepa, 604
Pakman, David, 1916
Pakravan, Eric, 120
Paley, Eric, 771
Palihapitiya, Chamath, 1696
Pallotta, James J, 1524
Palm IV, Dr. Peter J, 1404
Palma, Maria, 1593
Palmer, Tim R., 456
Palmer, John E., 903
Palmer, Raquel, 1085
Palmer, Charles L, 1332
Palmer, Grant, 1851
Palmeri, Stephanie, 1700
Palmeri, Stephanie, 1879
Palter, Gilbert S., 2103
Paluck, Bob, 444
Palumbo, Rob, 29
Pan, Gordon G., 222
Panariti, Igli, 3258
Pann, David, 1378
Pannun, Shahid, 2258
Pansing, Daniel E, 1209
Papa, Mark G, 1573
Pappas, Greg J., 254
Pappas, Tracy, 1772
Paquette, Jared B, 359
Paquin, Jean-Pierre, 240
Pardoe, Richard, 466
Parekh, Deven, 1000
Parekh, Greg, 1302
Parente, Chuck, 669
Parfet, Donald R., 139
Parham, Richelle P., 383
Parikh, Vijay C, 833
Parilla, Mike, 1166
Paris, Brent L, 632
Paris, Mark, 1894
Pariseau, Jean-Francois, 2036
Park, John, 410
Park, Steven G, 616
Park, Elizabeth, 782
Park, Howard, 824
Park, Arrie, 924
Park, Min H., 1690
Parke, Marshall W, 1112
Parker, David J., 118
Parker, Jeffrey P, 848
Parker, Marshall D., 1053
Parker, George A, 1103
Parker, Douglas A, 1230
Parker, Victor E, 1717
Parkinson, Thomas, 944
Parkinson, Thomas, 975
Parks, Lisa, 229
Parks, Elliot, 898
Parks, Steven W., 1093
Parmar, MD, PhD, Kush M, 12
Parnafes, Itzik, 235
Parr, Brett A, 399
Parr, Jeff, 2081
Parra, Ro, 594
Parrott, Phil, 467
Parsons, Don, 142
Parsons, Richard D., 977
Parsons, James A, 1557
Partain, W Michael, 591
Partlow, Ann, 643
Parulo, Jennifer E., 56
Parvez, Raja M., 1057
Parziale, Paolo, 18
Pascucci III, Vic, 1118
Pasquini, Scott G, 1156
Pasricha, Adrian, 2081

Paster, Anne-Mari, 1373
Pastor, Jon, 298
Pastor, Ken, 2092
Pastoriza, Jim, 1782
Patchett, James, 1308
Patek, Anthony, 253
Patel, Sanjay, 140
Patel, Harsh, 491
Patel, Anil, 502
Patel, Keval, 928
Patel, Manish, 935
Patel, Satya, 941
Patel, Shaneel D., 1037
Patel, Naimish, 1141
Patel, Ash, 1254
Patel, Amit A., 1392
Patel, Heidi, 1552
Patel, Harsh, 2000
Patel, Suresh, 2279
Pathria, Anu, 544
Patouillaud, Jean-Marc, 1416
Patrick, Grant A, 244
Patricof, Alan, 871
Patricof, Mark, 1222
Patterson, Tory, 428
Patterson, Jeff, 515
Patterson, Tory, 1392
Patterson, Michael, 1911
Pattison, Steve G., 1456
Patton, Blake, 677
Paul, Brian, 1796
Pauley, Jay D, 1752
Paull, Robert, 1151
Paulos, Joey, 512
Paulson, Robert, 67
Paulson, Randy, 1368
Pavey, Bob, 1257
Paxhia, Emily, 1464
Paymaster, Kunal, 1671
Payne, Marni F., 254
Payne, Marshall, 477
Payne, Christopher, 916
Peake, Tripp, 1142
Pearce, Jonathan, 291
Pearce, Dave, 2050
Pearl, Laura, 452
Pearlman, Bret, 659
Pearlman, Ken, 1365
Pearson, Mark E., 130
Pearson, Travis, 824
Pearson, Seth R., 1971
Pearson, Lori, 2067
Peck, Mike, 1379
Pecorini, Domenico, 352
Pedroni, Emilio S, 733
Peechu, Sundeep, 720
Peel, Doug, 2169
Peery, Shane R., 462
Pehl, Mikel, 1334
Peimer, Isai, 1196
Peiser, Brian, 654
Pellini, Mike, 1643
Pelowski, Kenneth R, 1445
Pelusi, James A., 211
Penberthy, Daniel P, 1523
Penchina, Gil, 1563
Penman, Gordon R, 1920
Penn, Kevin S, 42
Penn, Kevin, 110
Penn, Thomas A, 1275
Penn, Thomas A, 1428
Pennell, Keith W., 610
Pennell, Thomas B, 1429
Pentecost, Edward S., 1456
Pentimonti, E. Kenneth, 1400
Pepper, Doug, 1663
Pequet, David E, 1156

Executive Name Index

Perea, Carlos, 966
Pereira, Carol, 96
Perez, David, 1403
Perkins, Georganne, 744
Perkins, Gretchen B, 960
Perkins, Kelly, 1120
Perkins, Scott, 1120
Perl, Jonathan, 315
Perlman, Ezra, 779
Perot, Jr., Ross, 1433
Perper, Scott B., 1409
Perreault, Justin J., 521
Perreault, Sophie, 2114
Perricelli, Scott A, 1136
Perrier, Jean-Damien, 953
Perry, Chris, 489
Perry, Douglas S., 588
Perry, William, 988
Perry, Stephen B, 1132
Perry, James N, 1156
Persky, Michael B, 80
Perutz, Mark, 595
Pesce, Joseph, 859
Pesikoff, David L, 1846
Peters, Brian, 933
Petersen, Timothy, 149
Petersen, Gary R., 672
Peterson, Stuart, 175
Peterson, Tom, 1522
Peterson, Karl, 1835
Peterson, Steven, 1843
Peterson, Paul, 1990
Petit, Robert W, 1215
Petracek, George, 192
Petras, Jim, 642
Petrilla, Kenneth, 473
Petrillo, Peter, 849
Petro, Justin B., 1810
Petrocelli, Richard A., 1621
Petronzio, F. Matthew, 1871
Petrzela, Michal, 1123
Petterle, Laura, 760
Pettit, Peter S, 1270
Pettit, Jim, 1282
Pettway, Patten, 1569
Petty, Robert, 504
Petty, Scott, 1677
Petty Jr, William, 244
Petzinger, Tom, 1098
Peyron, Mat, 1370
Pfeffer, Daniel, 81
Pfeffer, Jeffry S., 407
Pfeffer, Michael S, 1465
Pfeffer MD, Cary, 1811
Pflug, Meredith, 213
Pfund, Nancy, 595
Pharand, Daniel, 430
Pharand, Daniel, 430
Phelps, Dennis, 1001
Phelps, Dan, 1609
Phenicie, Luke A., 900
Philips, Jeremy G, 1715
Phillips, Stu, 238
Phillips, M Troy, 244
Phillips, Greg, 343
Phillips, Joshua S., 426
Phillips, D. Martin, 672
Phillips, IV, Charles G., 1621
Philosophos, John, 858
Philp, John, 2126
Phipps, Charles, 1658
Piaker, Steven F., 434
Pianim, Nick, 581
Piatkowski, Adam, 846
Pichette, Patrick, 2157
Picozza, Enrico, 938
Pidwell, David W., 87

Piedrahita, Vincente, 1815
Pierce, Chris A., 1279
Pierce, J Peter, 1446
Pierce, Don, 1667
Pierce Jr, J Peter, 1446
Pieri, Trevor W., 404
Pierson, Matt, 3
Pierson, Steven C, 1147
Pierson, David, 1774
Pietri, Todd T, 52
Piette, Barbara, 1077
Pike, Chris, 62
Pilecki, Kurt, 274
Pillsbury, Lee, 1806
Pilosof, Naomi, 1202
Piotrowski, Annie, 234
Piper JD, Joseph, 1002
Piret, Marguerite A, 1312
Piret, John, 1312
Pirvani, Shahzad, 2022
Pisani, Craig, 168
Pitt, James D.C., 1112
Pittaway, David B., 423
Pittman, Sherri, 366
Pitts, Christie, 218
Plain, Hank, 1122
Platshon, Scott, 709
Platt, Wayne, 1369
Plauche, Charlie, 1597
Plotkin, Serge, 1381
Plumridge, Scott, 894
Podlesak, Dennis, 621
Poelzer, Mark, 2038
Poff, Mark, 1767
Poindexter, John, 1030
Pokorny, Brian, 1761
Poland, Jared, 364
Policy, Dan, 992
Polimino, Peter, 104
Poliner, Randall E., 131
Politi, Santo, 1715
Polk, Benjamin M., 1925
Pollack, Bruce, 447
Pollak, Robert, 1761
Pollock, Ryan, 1020
Pollock, Sam, 2067
Polotan, Morgan, 814
Polovets, Leo, 1758
Polski, Steve, 1131
Pomeroy, Rob, 946
Ponder, Dale, 2070
Pongon, Mike, 1458
Pontikes, Peter, 2033
Popil, Dean, 2173
Popper MD MPH, Caroline, 241
Porcellato, Larry, 289
Porell, Robert, 810
Porteous, Will, 1593
Porter, Barry, 494
Porter, Lisa, 979
Porter, Tim, 1158
Pothier, Robert, 1542
Potter, Matthew T., 604
Poulos, Nic, 317
Poulos, Lisbeth, 979
Pouschine, John L, 1466
Powell, John, 1003
Powell, Jon, 1657
Powell, Michael, 1698
Powell, William, 2067
Powell Jr, Robert S, 1277
Powers, Scott, 53
Powers, Brian, 924
Prado, Dennis G, 1159
Praeger, Robin, 1928
Prager, Brett L., 610
Prakash, Kristopher, 1369

Prawda, Daniel, 834
Predayna, Steve, 1292
Pressly, Scott, 271
Pressman, Jason, 1663
Pressnell, Jonathan, 290
Price, Michael, 450
Price, JoAnn H., 714
Price, Aaron, 3274
Prichett, J. Travis, 904
Pries, Gerhard, 2248
Prima, Alexandra, 1805
Priston, Duncan, 239
Pritchard, Grant, 1976
Pritzker, JB, 1479
Pritzker, Tony, 1479
Pritzker, Tony, 1480
Pritzker, J.B., 1480
Probert, Jim, 2082
Procter, Benjamin P, 1962
Proctor, Bob, 285
Proctor, David G, 1234
Propper de Callejon, Diana, 706
Proujansky, Phil, 432
Provost, Kevin, 866
Pruthi, Vineet, 1127
Pryma, Thomas, 64
Pryor, Brian, 1195
Prytula, Richard, 2263
Psaros, Michael, 1085
Puccinelli, Steven, 1360
Pulitzer, Jonathan, 809
Puopolo, Robert, 687
Purcell, Dennis, 74
Purcell, Gregory J., 147
Purcell, Paul, 222
Purushotham, Arvind, 486
Puskoor, Dayakar, 1285
Putnam, Travis, 1282
Putnam, Mitch, 2025
Pyne, Russell, 192
Pyne, Sam H., 893

Q
Qian, Jack W., 1301
Quackenbush, Cindy Rose, 1139
Quain, Mitchell, 42
Quake, Jeffrey K., 740
Quarles, Devin, 845
Quay, Ulrich, 302
Quazzo, Deborah, 883
Queally, Paul B, 1972
Queenan, Thomas, 1441
Quigley, William, 502
Quinlan, Rory, 1517
Quinlivan, David P, 1604
Quinn, Nate, 1202
Quinn, CPA, Christopher, 879
Quintana, Ana, 275
Quist, Will, 1694
Quy PhD, Roger J, 1786

R
Raab, Paul J., 719
Rabinowitz, Ben, 116
Rabois, Keith, 775
Radbod, Antony, 155
Radcliffe, Alex, 406
Radel, Holly, 3261
Rader, Stephen P., 494
Rader, Stacie, 747
Radhakrishnan, Ramesh, 174
Radis, Craig, 1467
Radtke, Jay, 1171
Rae, Katie, 1487
Raee, Hisham Al, 152
Raffin MD, Thomas A, 1792
Ragatz, Erik, 924

Ragins, David B, 492
Raguin, John, 710
Ragusa, Gary, 408
Rahe, Maribeth, 766
Rahimtula, Ali, 567
Rahman, Rashad, 354
Rahnema, Alireza, 2028
Raich, Steven G, 1134
Raimondi, Jill A., 949
Raina, Vikrant, 361
Rainey, Don, 876
Raino, Matthew W, 1156
Raiten, Greg, 743
Rajczi, Louis, 768
Raju, Champ, 1467
Rajwani, Suraj, 625
Raker, Jill C., 862
Raker, Geoffrey S., 1777
Rakes, Steve, 1709
Rakkou, Constantine J., 900
Rallo, Eduardo, 324
Ralls, Rawleigh, 1090
Ralph, Jon D., 783
Ramamoorthy, Arun, 1445
Ramesh, Prathna, 2184
Ramich, Michael, 790
Ramsay, David, 412
Ramundo, Benjamin J., 166
Rand, Lee, 1754
Rand, Tom, 2041
Randall, Larry, 94
Randall, Leigh, 1832
Raney, Scott, 1534
Ranjan, Anuj, 2067
Rankin, Christopher, 2055
Rankine, Craig, 2272
Rao, Zeena, 969
Rao, Ganesh B., 1815
Rapoport, Boris, 1123
Rappaport, Steve, 1376
Rappoport, Marc, 1305
Raterman, Thomas R., 802
Rather, Jonathan M, 1972
Rattner, Jon, 192
Raucci, Robert F, 1314
Rauh, Jim, 839
Ravi, T.M., 1809
Rawie, Damon, 61
Rawlings, Michael, 477
Ray, Andrew, 2155
Raynard, Robert, 1952
Raynor, Daniel, 161
Rea, Steven, 185
Rea, Patrick, 392
Read, Leighton, 326
Read, MD, J. Leighton, 87
Reals, Jeffrey, 1431
Reardon, Tighe, 206
Reardon, John, 1850
Reaves, Gary D., 740
Rebar, Thomas G, 1633
Reddon, Phil, 2087
Reddy, Ven N., 130
Reddy, Pabhakar, 1285
Redlitz, Chris, 1839
Redlitz, Chris, 1839
Redman, Heather, 755
Redman, Mark, 2207
Redmond, Chris, 399
Redstone, Shari, 60
Reed, Andy, 316
Reed, Jason, 1997
Reed, Marty, 2111
Reed MD, Douglas, 915
Reeder, Milton K, 33
Reeder, Tyler, 675
Rees, Rick S, 1144

Executive Name Index

Rees, Bob, 1737
Reese, Corby, 1767
Reese, Luke, 1999
Reeser, Timothy, 146
Reeves, Eric A, 633
Regan, Brian, 1717
Regan, Brian T, 1972
Reher, John M., 323
Rehnert, Geoffrey, 194
Reich, Marc, 1021
Reichert, Bill, 721
Reichert, Bill, 807
Reichow, Greg, 648
Reid, Richard, 2043
Reidel, Art, 947
Reiland, Pamela L., 888
Reiland, Bill, 1255
Reilly, Wendell, 1423
Reilly CFA, Scott A, 1426
Reinharz, Larry, 2004
Reiniger, Carissa, 813
Reininger, Barbara, 560
Reiss, Stan J, 1181
Reiter, Eric, 334
Reiter, Jr, R Peter, 1557
Reitler, Edward, 150
Rekhi, Kanwal, 1013
Rekhi, Manu, 1013
Rendino, Kevin M., 6
Renna, James, 1165
Renzi, Ned J, 272
Reppenhagen, Frank, 529
Requadt, Scott, 495
Rerisi, Meredith L, 18
Rescho, Douglas, 1091
Resnick, Charles, 990
Resnick, Josh, 1519
Resnikoff, Alan H., 1660
Ressler, Anthony, 159
Restler, Peter, 365
Reuter, David J, 1136
Revers, Daniel R., 156
Reynolds, Barry D., 949
Reynolds, David, 960
Reynolds, Roland, 986
Reynolds, John, 1125
Reynolds, Jake, 1785
Reynoldson, Michael H., 1016
Rezneck, Jon, 820
Rhines, Paul, 17
Rhodes, Jason, 191
Rhodes III, Noah F., 859
Rice, Matt, 224
Rice, John M., 479
Rice PhD, John M, 1847
Rich, Brian, 427
Rich, James T, 812
Rich, Trevor C, 1147
Rich, Laurie M., 1800
Richard, Laura, 2200
Richards, Jeff, 823
Richards, Andrew, 1767
Richards, Rob, 2224
Richards Donohoe, Robin, 627
Richardson, William K., 939
Richardson, Josh, 1143
Richardson, John, 1280
Richardson, Anders, 1402
Richardson, John, 2058
Richardson, Paul, 2238
Richmond, Aaron, 673
Richter, William L., 451
Richter, Saul, 1568
Rickett, Jerry, 1064
Riedmiller, Lisa, 151
Riedmiller, Lisa, 1407
Rieger, Glenn, 1317

Riemer, Robert, 175
Rightmire, Matt, 308
Riiska, Marc, 1864
Rikkers, James W, 1719
Riley, Ren, 1361
Riley, Andrew, 1908
Riley, Margaret, 1911
Riley, James, 2073
Rim, Charles, 626
Rimas, Tony, 781
Rinaldi, Ellis F., 1739
Ring, Jonathan, 1650
Ringo, Cynthia, 595
Ripley, Rosemary, 1324
Rishi, Raju, 1593
Rissman, Randy O., 1108
Ristvedt, Pal B, 1112
Ritchie, Matthew, 48
Ritchie, Marvin W, 1312
Ritchie, Dave, 2227
Ritter, Gordon, 665
Ritter, John L, 739
Ritterbush, Steven, 1207
Riva, Giorgio, 2289
Robard, Yann, 2289
Robbins, Gregory A., 844
Robbins, William, 1398
Robbins, David, 1844
Roberson, Bruce, 1753
Roberts, Bruce, 414
Roberts, Johnathan, 974
Roberts, George, 1082
Roberts, Carmichael, 1177
Roberts, Bryce, 1359
Roberts, George, 1380
Roberts, Eric, 1898
Roberts, Bryan, 1916
Roberts, Peter, 2258
Robertshaw, Tom, 1022
Robertson, Sanford, 779
Robertson, Rebecca B, 1928
Robins, Paula, 126
Robins, Blake, 1150
Robinson, Greg, 10
Robinson, Duwain, 354
Robinson, Colin, 470
Robinson, Joseph R, 1230
Robinson, Stephen G, 1447
Robinson, Edwin T, 1571
Robinson, James, 1593
Robinson, Lauren, 2147
Robinson, Art, 2178
Robinson, Samuel, 2225
Robinson, III, James, 1593
Roche, Andrew, 489
Roche, Collin E., 884
Roche, Roger, 1021
Roche, Andy, 1464
Rock, Terry, 444
Rocklage PhD, Scott M, 12
Rockley, Whitney, 2190
Rodger, Steven C, 691
Rodin, Robert, 1575
Rodriguez, Ruben, 360
Rodriguez, Frank J., 1039
Rodriguez, Antonio, 1181
Rodriguez Jr., Harold J., 864
Roe, Wayne, 980
Roeder, Doug, 604
Roehrenbeck, Mark, 1558
Roellig, Charles W., 449
Roeper, Scott D., 719
Roeper, Philip, 1272
Roeshkin, Nikolai, 661
Roff, David, 2134
Rogan, Scott, 675
Rogers, Jesse, 96

Rogers, Arthur, 152
Rogers, Sarah, 836
Rogers, Alex, 909
Rogers, Bruce, 1086
Rogoff, Eric Y, 716
Rokosh, Norman, 2275
Rollins, Virginia G, 1605
Romaniello, Steve, 1576
Romans, Andrew C., 1595
Romanyshyn, Steve, 2211
Rome, Brett J, 1339
Romero, Rafael, 667
Romlin, Judy, 1233
Rommines, Joel, 1077
Rondinelli, Joseph R, 789
Rooney, Tory, 354
Roos, John, 820
Roos, Susie, 820
Roosevelt, Jonathan, 986
Root MD, Jonathan D, 1896
Rooth, Scott, 1467
Rorer, Jim, 1462
Rosa, Nick, 570
Rosa, Nick, 1615
Rose, Wally, 16
Rose, T.J., 21
Rose, Alex, 559
Rose, David S, 1306
Rose, David S, 1584
Rose, Jody, 3273
Roselle, Arthur C., 1409
Rosen, Sylvia F., 423
Rosen, Mark, 456
Rosen, Mickie, 798
Rosen, Rick, 928
Rosen, Steven H, 1545
Rosen, Alexander, 1563
Rosen Wildstein, Amy, 304
Rosenbaum, Mark, 199
Rosenberg, Peter, 1207
Rosenberg, Jason, 1742
Rosenblatt, Jamie, 2137
Rosenbloom, Micah, 771
Rosenfeld, Eric, 791
Rosenfeld, Eric, 1383
Rosenfield, Andrew M., 885
Rosenstein, David, 815
Rosenstein, Douglas J., 873
Rosenthal, Bennett, 159
Rosenthal, RoseAnn B., 246
Rosenthal, Jeffrey, 2150
Rosenzweig, William, 1438
Rosenzweig, Eric L., 1743
Roser, Christopher W, 1586
Roser, James LD, 1586
Roshko, Peter, 315
Roskens, Lisa Y., 71
Rosner, Robert L., 1931
Ross, Ian, 529
Ross, Howard D, 1136
Ross, Mark R., 1369
Ross, Mike, 1762
Ross PhD, Michael, 1628
Rossetter, Stephen, 448
Rossolatos, George, 2070
Rosston, Steven J, 836
Rostami, Rami, 1876
Rostick, Mark, 1004
Rostowsky, Steven, 2073
Rosuck, I. Donald, 1093
Roszak, Matthew, 1681
Rotatori, Doug, 1368
Rotberg, Joseph B, 1104
Roth, Jonathan D, 18
Roth, Sarah G, 164
Roth, Donald C., 670
Roth, John M., 783

Roth, Bryon C, 1588
Roth, Gordon, 1588
Roth, Ted, 1588
Rothenberg, Adam, 318
Rothschild, Shannon, 1722
Rothstein, Charlie, 251
Rotman, Frank, 1502
Rotman, Ken, 2081
Rotolo, Tim, 155
Rottenberg, Jason, 171
Rottier, Peter L, 1752
Rountree, Ian, 395
Rovinski, Beni, 2180
Rowan, Marc, 140
Rowe, David H., 66
Rowe, Paul, 2126
Rowell, Kelly, 3259
Rowley, David, 465
Rowntree, David, 2146
Roy, Noah, 862
Roy, Devraj, 1022
Royer, Stephen D., 1660
Rua, Dan, 990
Ruano, Rudy, 1975
Rubel, Michael W, 1557
Rubenstein, David M, 413
Rubin, Daniel I., 87
Rubin, Joe, 150
Rubin, Peter M., 190
Rubin, David, 1205
Rubin, Michael, 1342
Rubin, Laura M., 1739
Rubinoff, Gary, 2259
Ruch, Joshua, 1558
Rudge, John G, 1112
Rudick, Stuart L, 1236
Rudin, Murray E, 1575
Ruffolo, Rick, 80
Ruga, Jonathan M, 1652
Ruger, Jared, 257
Rulleau, Laurence, 2092
Rumilly, Mathias, 503
Runett, Rob, 1259
Runnells, John E, 1929
Rusoff, Lawrence, 1431
Russo, Guy M., 386
Russo, Steven, 2096
Rustgi, Atul, 37
Ruston, Derek, 2110
Ruthven, Neil, 775
Rutledge, Rob, 819
Ruud, Lance, 639
Ruvolo, Julie, 3261
Ryan, Charles E., 89
Ryan, Dennis D, 762
Ryan, Dan, 1234
Ryan, David, 1239
Ryan, Jordan, 1559
Ryan, Kenneth, 1573
Ryan, Vin, 1627
Ryan, Bruce C, 1707
Ryan, Neil, 1866

S

Saban, Haim, 1598
Sabater, Juan, 1902
Saberi, Nina, 422
Sabet, Bijan, 1715
Sabia, Michael, 2069
Sabo, Elias J., 523
Saca, Diana, 681
Sacca, Chris, 1149
Sacha, Brent T, 1745
Sachar, Laura Belle, 1738
Sachs, Bruce, 455
Sachs, Andrew, 1599
Sack, Andy, 773

Executive Name Index

Sack, Aaron, 1256
Sackman, Donald, 983
Sadek, Zachary, 1417
Sadraranganey, Neil, 620
Saefke, John, 1915
Saeid, Kamil, 180
Saenko, Maryanna, 800
Saer Jr., John K., 824
Safiedine DPM, Ali, 1289
Sage, Luke, 1424
Sager Jr, Edward F, 1203
Sagisi, Patrick, 27
Sahasrabudhe, Ashwini, 855
Sahney, Neal G, 789
Saifee, Moiz, 544
Saikia, Rohan, 859
Saintonge, Sam, 2290
Saklecha, Akhil, 174
Salaber, Konrad, 1990
Salamon, Michael J., 2062
Saldutti Jr., Joseph A., 873
Sale, Will, 1763
Salem, Enrique, 221
Salem, Paul J., 1496
Salenbier, Andrew, 37
Sales, Whitney, 30
Sales, Wayne, 981
Salewski, Anthony, 819
Salmon, Steve, 1094
Salon, Jonathan D., 242
Saltarelli, Gerald, 654
Saluja, Maninder, 1516
Salvagno, Rob, 483
Salvemini, Domenic, 1564
Salvino, Mike, 416
Salzman, Alan E, 1906
Samberg, Jeff, 26
Samper, Phil, 805
Sams, Lloyd R., 263
Samson, Peter, 2163
Samuel, Shimrit, 116
Samuel, Dave, 784
Samuel, David G., 2062
Samuels, Judson, 926
Samuels, Camille, 1916
Samuels, Russell, 2288
Sanche, Caroline, 2258
Sanday, J.P., 1202
Sandell, Scott, 1297
Sanders, Ryan, 1204
Sanderson, Philip, 3284
Sandler, Scott, 1383
Sandler, Julie, 1499
Sandler, Andrew, 1617
Sandoski, Aaron, 1347
Sands, Greg, 547
Sands, David A., 1456
Sands Langensand, Carol, 129
Sangalis, Stephen N, 1484
Sanger, Jim, 1640
Sanger MD, Philip, 1801
Sankar, Santosh, 640
Sankey, Dr. N. Darius, 2021
Sanner, Dan, 92
Sansom, Ron, 1572
Santi, Angela, 35
Santiago, Claudi, 740
Santiago, Jason, 1748
Santinelli, Paul A, 1334
Santonelli, Benjamin, 597
Sapieha, Ryan, 2050
Sarafa, Martin A., 449
Sardana, Sandeep, 295
Sarkar, Neel, 441
Sarlo, George, 1952
Sarner, Michael S., 403
Sartre, Joseph, 1006

Sathe, Shrikant, 1911
Sato, Tak, 1269
Sauerhoff, Jeffrey M., 177
Saunders, Matt, 2115
Saunders, Matt, 2245
Saurel, Zita, 924
Sauvé, Jean-François, 2086
Savage, Jim, 1146
Savage, Tige, 1555
Saverin, Eduardo, 216
Saviano, Joseph, 223
Savignol, Robert, 1153
Saville, B Hagen, 1189
Savitz, Scott, 586
Savoie, Robert H, 1445
Sawaf, Omar A, 2013
Sawaf, Sami, 2013
Sawyer, Kenneth B, 1604
Saxena, Subhanu, 1302
Saxena, Parag, 1911
Saxton, Tina, 470
Scalzo, David, 1074
Scanlin, Mike, 2195
Scanlon, Rick, 996
Scarpa, Carmen, 1728
Scaysbrook, David, 1517
Schaar, William H., 945
Schaefer, Matthew, 714
Schaepe, Christopher, 1121
Schafer, J Michael, 1300
Schaffer, Joseph P, 1252
Schafler, R. Scott, 546
Schaible, David K., 1724
Schapiro, Benjamin, 1515
Scharfenberger, Joseph, 433
Schattner, Michael, 1377
Schaufeld, Fredrick D., 1766
Schaumburg, Zach E, 1219
Schaye, Paul L., 465
Schechter, Jeff, 1742
Scheetz, Ned, 138
Scheinfeld, Larry, 2017
Schell, Tony, 695
Schell, Rick, 1378
Schellenberger, David A., 2146
Schemelter, Jay W, 1574
Schena, Graham, 1266
Scheschuk, Brice, 2134
Schiciano, Kenneth T, 1776
Schickedanz, Sean, 498
Schickner, Curtis, 532
Schiff, Frank, 1231
Schiff, James G., 1344
Schiff, Peter G., 1344
Schiff, MD, Andrew, 74
Schifino Jr, William J, 1510
Schilberg, Barbara, 266
Schilling, Mathias, 641
Schillinger, Doug, 639
Schillinger, Emily, 3255
Schimel, Adam, 239
Schlachet, Loren, 1572
Schlapinski, Jeff, 3261
Schleifer, Scott, 1826
Schlein, Ted, 1075
Schlesinger, Thomas A, 244
Schlosstein, Ralph, 699
Schmadtke, Eric, 676
Schmid, Corey, 1656
Schmidly, Jason C., 415
Schmidt, Gerald F, 537
Schmidt, Eric, 996
Schmitt, George, 1793
Schnabel, Michael, 447
Schnabel, John S, 716
Schnadig, David L., 546
Schnakenberg, Ben A, 931

Schnarr, Jody, 2117
Schneider, Geoff, 431
Schneider, Stephanie, 745
Schneider, Toni, 1860
Schneider, Pat, 3262
Schneiderman, Arthur, 833
Schnell MD, David, 1493
Schneller, Cas, 787
Schnitzer, Bruce W, 1955
Schnurmacher, Larry, 1439
Schock, Paul, 273
Schocken, Joseph L., 346
Schoemaker, Kathleen, 621
Schoendorf, Nancy, 1247
Schoenfeld, Jeffrey A., 240
Schoettler, Jason, 370
Scholl, David R., 187
Scholl, Tom, 1348
Scholnick, Dan, 1853
Schopp, David R, 1744
Schraith, Jim, 791
Schreiber, Richard R, 616
Schreiber, Peter D., 616
Schreiber, MD, Alain, 1490
Schreier, Bryan, 1654
Schreier, W Terrence, 1837
Schrier, Douglas, 1540
Schroder, David, 17
Schroder, David R., 1016
Schroder, Marc, 1170
Schroeder, Charles L, 1343
Schuh, Mike, 770
Schule, Lisa, 834
Schuler, Ryan, 176
Schulte, Peter M., 507
Schulte, Greg, 886
Schultz, Daniel, 608
Schultz, Jeffrey, 1283
Schultz, Jim, 1379
Schultz, Chris, 1943
Schultze, George J, 1629
Schulz, Bob, 918
Schuman, Steve, 895
Schunk, Nanette, 3276
Schuster, Stewart, 1354
Schutz, Jeffrey, 441
Schutzbank, Amanda, 120
Schuurmans, Pierre J., 2062
Schwab, Andrew J, 12
Schwab, Andrew, 737
Schwab III, Nelson, 415
Schwartz, Keoni, 96
Schwartz, Yafit, 116
Schwartz, Adam, 127
Schwartz, Evan M., 156
Schwartz, Steven, 239
Schwartz, Eric, 423
Schwartz, Scott, 489
Schwartz, Alan G., 740
Schwartz, Alan D., 885
Schwartz, Brian D., 928
Schwartz, Andrew M., 1111
Schwartz, Christian, 1820
Schwartz, Hagi, 1975
Schwartz, Peter, 2172
Schwartz, Gerry, 2209
Schwartzberg, Evan, 1367
Schwarz, Richard, 653
Schwarzman, Stephen A., 277
Schwen, Steve, 1725
Schwerin, Samuel L, 1235
Sciorillo, Dean, 676
Sciorillo, Dean, 676
Scoggins, Chris, 1653
Scola, Nicholas, 21
Scolnik, Glenn, 900
Scotland, Andrew, 239

Scott, Paul A., 269
Scott, Dwight, 277
Scott, Randy, 921
Scott, Erik A., 1403
Scozzafava, Thomas W, 1639
Scull, John, 1711
Scully, Thomas A, 1972
Scully, Rob, 2183
Seaman, Brad, 2214
Searcy, Conner, 1856
Seasons, Chris, 2040
Seaver, Peter R., 139
Sebastian, Sean, 272
Seeber, Jon, 1886
Seegopaul, Purnesh, 2213
Seeman, Cooper, 2235
Sefrioui, Rachid, 729
Segal, Rick, 1551
Segrest, Michael T, 1682
Seidenberg, Beth, 1075
Seidler, Peter, 1645
Seidler, Robert, 1645
Seiffer, Jonathan, 1109
Seitz, Chris, 703
Seitz, Tasha, 1038
Sekhon, Tex, 1167
Selby, Sunil, 2273
Selcow, Mark, 547
Seldin, David, 133
Sellers, Doug, 1533
Sellery, Alan G., 2163
Seltzer, Stacey D., 74
Semon, Dominique, 1216
Sen, Hondo, 188
Senft, Rod, 2123
Senft, Derek, 2123
Senft, Rod, 2214
Senft, Derek, 2218
Senft, Rod, 2218
Senft, Derek, 2274
Senkut, Aydin, 720
Serafim, Kristina, 1926
Serena, Ottavio, 1127
Serface, Joel, 253
Serkes, Jeffrey D, 1401
Serpen, Sensu, 239
Serruya, Michael, 2254
Serruya, Aaron, 2254
Serruya, Simon, 2254
Seseri, Rudina, 712
Seseri, Rudina, 829
Setaro, Chris, 1662
Seth, Raj, 925
Sethi, Arjun, 1848
Settle, Dana, 871
Seung, John, 796
Severson PhD, James A, 840
Sexton, Theresa, 493
Seymour, Tim, 1659
Sezak, Sam, 288
Shackelford, Tom, 1823
Shadman, Ali, 1038
Shaffer, Stefan L, 1726
Shaffer PhD, Christy, 915
Shafir, Robert, 1635
Shah, Amit, 174
Shah, Deep, 779
Shah, Niren, 1346
Shah, Rajeev, 1519
Shah, Ron, 1748
Shah, Kosha, 1883
Shah, Sachin, 2067
Shah, Ameet, 2137
Shainberg, David, 225
Shaked, Eyal, 536
Shalek, Nick, 1560
Shalhoub, Matt, 2140

Executive Name Index

Shalon, Teddy, 1488
Shanafelt, Armen B, 1124
Shankar, Shubhang, 1774
Shannon, Tim, 386
Shannon, Jeffrey R., 546
Shannon, Mary, 586
Shannon, Mary M, 1175
Shapansky, Kerry, 2282
Shapiro, Stephen, 59
Shapiro, Craig, 511
Shapiro, Bob, 570
Shapiro, Jim, 1059
Shapiro, David, 1085
Shapiro, Robert, 1615
Sharkawy, Adam, 1177
Sharma, Shantnu, 106
Sharma, Alipt, 834
Sharma, Saurabh, 1046
Sharma, Ray, 2113
Sharpe, J. Louis, 64
Shaughnessy, Keith C, 1224
Shaw, Bob, 192
Shaw, David E., 579
Shaw, Thomas P., 900
Shaw, Jr., Robert, 160
Shaywitz, David A, 1778
Shcuhpak, Zoya, 2156
Shear, Herb, 380
Shearburn, John W, 1956
Shebuski, PhD, Ronald J., 139
Sheehan, Timothy D, 244
Sheeren, Christopher S, 960
Sheffer, Wade, 817
Sheftel, Bradley, 1902
Shehab, Tom, 149
Sheiner, Andrew, 2034
Sheiner, Andrew, 2046
Sheldon, Jeffrey, 485
Shelley, Anne-Marie, 39
Shen, David, 590
Shen, Robert, 892
Shen, Dave, 1097
Shen, James, 1509
Sheng, Brian, 785
Sheng, Brian, 1807
Shepherd, T Nathanael, 1862
Shepherd, Thomas R, 1862
Sher, Judd, 924
Sheridan, Cynthia S, 241
Sheridan, Ben, 289
Sherman, Rob, 312
Sherman, John W, 597
Sherman, Mike, 1187
Sherman, Craig, 1212
Sherman, Richard L, 1633
Sherman Jahic, Jodi, 83
Sherrill, Stephen C., 354
Sherwood, Ned, 2022
Sheskey, Susan, 594
Sheynkman, Kirill, 1594
Shideler, Jason, 1156
Shields, Jack, 310
Shih, Ben, 968
Shiloni Shem Tov, Shlomi, 436
Shim, Brian, 419
Shin, Kevin, 878
Shipman, Chris, 427
Shipp, Terrance M, 1209
Shiriam, Ram, 1666
Shirley, Edwin, 714
Shkolnik, Gene, 2150
Shlesinger, Joseph, 2082
Shoch, John F., 87
Shoemaker, John P, 1234
Shoemaker, Jr., Raleigh A., 254
Shoham, Amnon, 436
Shove, Greg, 1083

Shroff, Zubeen, 806
Shuart, Rick, 374
Shuchman, Salem, 683
Shugharts, Brooks, 740
Shukla, Anhishek, 927
Shulkin, Jonathan K., 1902
Shulman, Zachary, 432
Shulz, Ryan, 702
Shum, Tony, 39
Shurtleff, Rob, 618
Sica, Frank V., 1777
Sichel, Kim, 1139
Siddiqui, Imran, 2255
Sidwa, James, 401
Sieg, Clara, 1555
Siegal, Laura, 48
Siegel, John, 515
Siegel, Brian J, 891
Siegel, Mark A., 1202
Siegel, Joshua B., 1595
Siegel, Tom W, 1664
Siegel, Rob, 2011
Siegel, Stephan, 2271
Siegel, Micah, 2278
Siegler, M.G., 889
Siemer, Arnold B, 606
Siemplenski, Michael, 732
Sigalow, Ian, 871
Sigel, Anthony, 2169
Sigler, Mary Ann, 1451
Siguler, George W., 1679
Sikes, Toni F., 375
Sikkens, Hans, 1752
Silbernagel, Corry J., 2064
Sillitoe, Andrew, 135
Sillman, Eric H., 136
Siltala, Michael, 2287
Silton, Michael, 50
Silverberg, Brad, 974
Silverberg, Michal, 1350
Silverman, Scott, 70
Silverman, Jeff, 70
Silverman, Andrew A., 402
Silverman, Mark, 428
Silverman, David, 563
Silverstein, Jonathan T., 1382
Sim, Ed, 305
Simi, Bonny, 1035
Simko, Susan, 1470
Simmons, J. Frederick, 783
Simmons, Walker C., 1409
Simmons, Nat, 1472
Simon, Frank, 172
Simon, Robert J., 321
Simon, Nicholas J., 495
Simon, Lawrence R, 503
Simon, David E, 1134
Simon, John, 1673
Simoni, Richard, 181
Simonian, Steve, 84
Simons, James R, 1725
Simons, Noa, 3280
Simonson, Ray, 2279
Simpkins, Neil P., 277
Simpson, John H., 343
Simpson, Todd, 2157
Simpson, Merv, 2282
Simpson Jr., Bryan, 826
Sinclair, Peter, 1102
Sinclair, Craig, 2104
Sing, George L, 1092
Sing-Wood Yeh, Woody, 117
Singer, Carlyle, 55
Singer, Andrew, 675
Singer, Bradley E., 1903
Singerman, Brian, 775
Singh, Ajit, 174

Singh, Mayank, 446
Singh, Vic, 679
Singh, Harpinder, 996
Singh, Raj, 1035
Singh, Kuljeev, 2149
Singhavon, Norton, 2100
Singleton, Steven D, 1261
Sinha, Shounok, 532
Sinha, Bipul, 1121
Sinnerberg, John, 577
Sipp, Thomas, 1635
Sirinakis, CPA, Kyparissia, 689
Sirois, Charles, 162
Sirois, Charles, 2261
Sirois, Francois-Charles, 2264
Sirois, Charles, 2264
Sirois, Denis M., 2264
Siskin, Edward J, 937
Sisteron, Yves, 1888
Sitohang, Helman, 554
Siuta, Philip, 530
Sivolella, Eileen, 62
Skaff, Michael C, 1648
Skapinker, Mark, 2066
Skidmore, Alyse, 1335
Skinner, Stuart, 316
Skok, David R, 1181
Skoler, Steven F., 788
Slaats, Paul, 1234
Slackman, David S., 953
Slade, Mike, 1641
Slatoff, Karl, 2020
Slaughter, Rick, 1756
Sloan, Stephan C., 125
Sloan, Bradley, 1514
Sloane, Steve, 1202
Slodowitz, Mitchell, 416
Slusky, Alex, 1910
Slutzkin, Craig, 1298
Slye, Jack, 1136
Small, Robert J., 254
Smalley, Matt, 380
Smardon, Dave, 2060
Smart, Gregg, 722
Smeltzer, James L, 409
Smiga, Brian, 91
Smiley, Ryan A, 1567
Smith, Matthew M, 18
Smith, Geoffrey W., 177
Smith, Sarah, 221
Smith, Robert, 364
Smith, Michael L, 409
Smith, Bruce, 414
Smith, Robert A., 421
Smith, Jed, 428
Smith, R Adam, 481
Smith, Rick, 561
Smith, Theodore J., 638
Smith, Paul, 830
Smith, Brian S, 856
Smith, Adrian, 974
Smith, Thomas, 1139
Smith, Tom, 1171
Smith, Stephen K, 1175
Smith, Jim, 1247
Smith, Byron, 1261
Smith, Jed, 1392
Smith, Brian R, 1597
Smith, Tom, 1625
Smith, Stanley T., 1771
Smith, Paul G, 1795
Smith, Marcus, 1812
Smith, Vinny, 1829
Smith, Robert, 1938
Smith, Nancy, 2040
Smith, Bill, 2044
Smith, Gregory, 2158

Smith, Gregory J., 2165
Smith Jr, Peter H, 1735
Smith Jr, W Thomas, 1863
Smith, IV, Ben T., 32
Smith-Eppsteiner, Sam, 996
Smith-Maxwell, Andrew, 726
Smolen, David, 824
Smoot, Timothy L, 1208
Smorynski, Tammi, 1004
Smulowitz, Warren, 2075
Smythe, Gordon, 2195
Snow, John W., 451
Snow, Scott L., 746
Snow III, John I, 1503
Snyder, Pete, 617
Snyder, Andrew, 846
Snyder, James C., 900
Snyder, Darren M, 1469
So, George, 2158
So, George, 2165
So, Susan, 2210
Soane, Mark, 142
Sobachevskiy, Roman, 890
Sobeck, Joshua, 14
Sobecki, Christopher, 1018
Soberg, Jon, 1269
Sobieski, PhD, Ian, 226
Sobiloff, Peter, 1000
Sobol, Edward P, 1972
Sobota, MD, Joseph T., 139
Socas, James, 1886
Socolof, Stephen, 1305
Soesman, Gideon, 2142
Soffe, Alex, 1070
Soghikian, Shahan D, 1410
Sohail, Sajid A., 95
Soignet, MD, Steven L., 157
Sokol, Marc, 1038
Sokoloff, Jonathan, 1109
Solomon, Katie, 819
Solomon, Glenn, 823
Solomon, Michael S, 1109
Solomon, David, 1211
Solomon, Christopher W, 1972
Solomon, Joel, 2238
Solomon MD, Stephen B, 572
Solotar, Joan, 277
Solow, Mark G, 565
Solow, Todd, 1345
Solvik, Pete, 1024
Somasegar, S, 1158
Somer, Greg, 692
Somers, Nicholas, 1763
Son, Erica S., 166
Song, Winston H., 1931
Soni, Vipul B., 357
Sonshine, Daniel, 2272
Sonsini, Peter, 1297
Sorensen, Carsten, 2218
Sorenson, Luke, 1705
Sorrel, Lawrence B., 1777
Sosa del Valle, Jose M., 1112
Sosin, Tyler, 1202
Sosnik, Esteban, 1527
Sotak, Andrea, 2102
Sotirhos, Michael, 277
Souder, Andrew, 1521
Souleles, Thomas S, 1156
Southworth, McLain, 563
Souvignier, Chad W, 1543
Sowers, Jason, 1999
Spaght, Pearson, 749
Spahn, Stephen H, 1504
Spaht, Holden, 1814
Spain, Kevin, 665
Spalding, Dick, 1059
Sparkman, Thorne, 1693

1099

Executive Name Index

Sparks, Megan, 532
Spass, Robert A., 404
Spector, Michael, 1939
Speiser, Mike, 1760
Spell, William H, 1719
Spencer, Donald, 1679
Spencer, Jeb S, 1869
Spencer Jr., Edson W., 68
Sperling, Scott M., 1815
Spero, Donald, 1299
Spero, Benjamin M, 1717
Spicer, Julia, 3270
Spiegel, Leo, 1239
Spicker, Paul, 736
Spilizewski, Karen, 1574
Spillane, Geoffrey D., 873
Spinale, John, 1029
Spirn, Samuel W., 254
Spivy, Gregory P., 1903
Splinter, Patricia, 1906
Spofford, Christopher, 343
Spogli, Ronald P., 783
Spratt, Joe, 737
Spreng, David, 555
Spring, Andrew, 1231
Sprole, Jerry, 1103
Srinivasan, Savitha, 967
Sripadam, Kumar, 1825
Srivastava, Amit, 682
Srivastava, Siddharth, 2190
Srugo, Pablo, 2195
Ssuto, Amy, 162
St. Jean, Brian, 21
Stack MD, Richard, 1772
Staenberg, Jon, 1733
Stahl, Rick, 660
Stahr, Clancey, 837
Stakias, G Michael, 1116
Stalcup, Christopher R, 470
Stalder, Dana, 1181
Stampacchia, Otello, 1373
Stanbro, Kyle, 349
Stanek, Michael, 1040
Stanford, Scott, 45
Stanley, Nicholas J, 1909
Stansky, Brian, 1003
Stanton, Ben, 888
Stanton, Luke K., 1692
Starcevich, John J., 1435
Stark, Michael, 563
Stark, David, 877
Starling, William, 1772
Starr, Eric D., 407
Starr, Ira, 1141
Starr, Kevin, 1811
Stasik, Jared, 607
Stassen, Dave, 1725
Stata, Nicole M., 313
Statter, Joseph, 701
Staub, Craig, 1368
Staub, Mark, 1467
Staudt, William, 667
Staudt, Christopher, 667
Stavis, Rob, 260
Steans, Jennifer, 529
Steed, Michael, 1400
Steele, Scott, 1040
Steen, Kristin, 433
Steenrod, Wright, 475
Stefanski, Bob, 2023
Steffens, John L, 1730
Stein, Martin, 276
Stein, Jonathan A., 546
Stein, Josh, 609
Stein, Jason, 1820
Stein, Avy H., 1986
Stein, Jason, 1992

Steinbeck, Michael A, 1744
Steinberg, Dimitri, 772
Steinberg, Michael, 1528
Stenberg, Scott, 999
Stento, Gregory, 909
Stepanov, Nina, 30
Stephan, Roderick, 99
Stephens, W Brad, 283
Stephens, P Bart, 283
Stephens, John B., 1931
Stephenson, Thomas J, 1924
Stern, David, 502
Stern, James A., 575
Stern, Brian E, 1735
Stern, Ronald N, 2258
Sternlicht, Barry S., 1739
Steuerman, Andrew H., 844
Stevens, Scott R., 1409
Stevens, Todd, 1542
Stevens, Mike, 2044
Stevens, John, 2044
Stevenson, James, 22
Stevenson, Chris, 722
Stevenson, Gary, 1187
Stevenson, Dave, 1205
Stevenson, Jeffrey T, 1927
Stevenson, Lawrence, 2082
Stevenson DVM, PhD, Sharon, 1371
Stewart, William H, 1281
Stewart, Donald E., 1724
Stewart, Robert M., 1727
Stewart, E Jack, 1920
Stewart, Greg, 2141
Stewart, Kalen, 2277
Steyn, Howard, 1088
Stiefel, Sean, 1283
Stienes, David A, 1136
Stiff, Jamie, 2130
Stimson, Keith, 881
Stinnett, David, 1856
Stobo, John, 22
Stofer, Gordon, 464
Stoffer, Jason, 1183
Stokel, Kathryn J, 18
Stokes, Richard, 928
Stokes, John, 2232
Stolle, Bryan, 1247
Stolle, Bryan, 1985
Stone, Brent, 21
Stone, Sheldon, 1362
Stone JD, Paul A, 12
Stoner, Chelsea, 235
Storcheus, Alex, 2122
Storcheus, Alex, 2122
Storer, Tim, 9
Storm, Bridget, 996
Stott, Janet L, 1828
Stott, David, 1990
Stout, Caroline, 709
Stout, C Morris, 1767
Stowater, Tyler J, 297
Stowe, Rick, 918
Strachman, Paul, 1530
Strain, Christian R, 1752
Strasberg, Jeffrey H, 1564
Strasser, David, 1766
Straub, Paul, 491
Strauch, Mark, 92
Strauch, Roger A, 1580
Strawbridge, Oak, 875
Strawbridge, James N., 2007
Streur, John, 376
Strickberger, Neal, 1644
Stringham, Ned, 9
Strohband, Sven, 1069
Strom, John A., 893

Strong, Melanie, 1318
Strong, Craig, 2243
Strongin, Matthew, 738
Strother, Robert, 1287
Strottman, Matthew, 979
Stroud, Marcus, 1875
Struck, John S, 1955
Stuart, Scott, 1602
Stuart, Tyler, 2140
Stubblefield, Richard, 1119
Stubbs, Dave, 380
Stubbs, Tim, 1753
Stubler, Mike, 628
Stubler, Mike, 3275
Stuck, Bart, 1676
Stulberger, Adam F., 1777
Stull, Steven, 61
Stupore, Greg, 14
Sturdy, Laela, 578
Sturner, Andrew, 557
Sturtevant, Reed, 1487
Subotovsky, Santi, 665
Subramaniam, Somu, 1303
Suder, Thorsten, 401
Sugar, Daniel, 1925
Sugarman, Mark, 1226
Sugden, Chris, 655
Suh, Alex, 371
Suissa, Yanev, 1687
Suit, Dickson, 1021
Sukhar, Ilya, 1181
Sukornyk, Chris, 2182
Sullivan, Patrick, 220
Sullivan, Gregory P., 788
Sullivan, Nancy, 975
Sullivan, Peter, 1139
Sullivan, Timothy P, 1156
Sullivan, Matt, 1423
Sullivan, Jeanne M., 1807
Sullivan, Brian, 1992
Sun, Evelyn, 148
Sun, Ben, 1475
Sun, Pocket, 1701
Sundarrajan, Prabakar, 502
Sunderland, Julie, 268
Suri, Saurabh, 453
Susan, Lior, 648
Suslak, Neil S., 322
Sussman, Philip N., 1808
Suster, Mark, 1888
Sutherland, Jason D., 328
Sutherland, Timothy F., 1229
Sutherland, David, 1229
Sutherland, Hamish, 2154
Sutherland, Hamish, 2287
Sutter, Martin, 697
Sutter Jr., William P., 944
Suttin, Adam L, 1049
Sutton, Lynda, 430
Sutton, Howard, 2267
Suzuki, Terry, 1386
Svennilson, Peter, 517
Svoboda, John A, 1765
Svrluga, Brad, 1475
Swain, Steven, 440
Swaine, Mark, 494
Swan, Robert, 1120
Swan, Jack, 1120
Swan, Kevin, 1961
Swani, Sanjay, 1777
Swanson, Eric, 888
Swanson, Matthew E., 1564
Swanson Jr., Douglas E., 672
Swartz, Steven R., 922
Swartz, Robert, 1207
Swartzman, Steven, 364

Sweeney, Ryan, 28
Sweeney, Timothy R, 637
Sweeney, Malcolm, 1483
Sweeney, Chris, 1961
Sweeney, Thecla E., 2062
Sweet, Scott, 1139
Sweet, David E, 1760
Swenberg, Scot E, 478
Swenson, Jeff T., 1815
Swildens, Hans, 986
Sykes, Trey, 1014
Syversen, Jason, 3
Szapiro, Dov, 557
Szczepaniak Rice, Katie, 688
Sze, David, 872
Szejko, Kelly, 3275
Szigethy, Béla, 1572
Szweras, Adam, 2122

T

Ta, Napoleon, 775
Taber, Mark D., 857
Tabet, Karim A., 1496
Tabors, Dave, 235
Tadler, Richard D, 1776
Taetle, Alan J, 1331
Taft, Peter, 1266
Tagare, Varsha, 1509
Tagler, Jason R., 383
Tai, Gus, 1853
Talalla, Dominic, 2273
Talbot, Kevin, 2236
Talbott, Devin, 680
Tall, Spencer, 84
Tam, Nathan, 2045
Tamashunas, Bob, 1638
Tamburri, Dave, 918
Tamer, Tony, 928
Tammenoms Bakker, Juliet, 1143
Tammineedi, Anil, 126
Tan, Martin, 152
Tan, Jui, 296
Tan, Edwin, 401
Tan, Patrick, 865
Tan, Garry, 991
Tan, Lip-Bu, 1951
Tan PhD, Zhi, 1340
Tanaka, Akio, 641
Tanaka, Susumu, 2007
Tananbaum, Andrew, 565
Tananbaum, Jim, 762
Taneja, Hemant, 816
Tanenbaum, Larry, 2169
Taney, Richard, 1864
Tang, Steven, 626
Tango, Jo, 1065
Tannas, Scott, 2269
Tannenbaum, Jeff, 296
Tansey, Casey, 1896
Tapman, Micah, 392
Taragin, Bruce K., 301
Taranto, Bill, 1205
Tarazid-Tarawali, Andrew, 55
Tardio, Stephen C., 953
Tarini, Mark A., 156
Tarnowski, Thomas M, 1752
Tarr, Bill, 1258
Tarr Jr., Jake, 1072
Taslitz, Steven, 1742
Taub, Bruce, 190
Taub, Andrew C., 1088
Taubman, Steven J, 1908
Taves, Chris, 2063
Taylor, Bryan, 62
Taylor, Craig C., 87
Taylor, Lucius H., 156
Taylor, Neil J., 321

Executive Name Index

Taylor, Kathryn, 703
Taylor, Gus, 719
Taylor, Michael, 909
Taylor, Meg, 984
Taylor, Paulette, 1616
Taylor, Harry D, 1776
Taylor, Jonathon W, 1800
Taylor, Jim, 2049
Taylor, Allison M., 2162
Taylor II, William H, 1262
Taylor-Smith, Ralph, 809
Tedesco, Pete, 918
Tedford, Alastair, 78
Teeger, John L., 774
Tegan, Jennifer, 432
Teixeira, Patrick, 1396
Tekkora, Baran, 1573
Televantos, John, 170
Teller, Sam, 1099
Templeman, Mike, 887
Templeton, Troy D, 1857
Teng, Nelson, 458
Tenkle, Jim, 1618
Tepper, Yaniv, 126
Tepper, MD, Robert, 1811
Terhorst, Eric, 732
Terkowitz, Ralph, 22
Terpak, Daniel, 465
Terry, Annie S, 1156
Tertzakian, Peter, 2040
Teschke, Jeffrey J, 1049
Tesconi, Lee J, 1112
Teslia, Ken, 2113
Tessier, Todd, 2278
Teten, David, 724
Tevanian, Avie, 659
Thadani, Shravan, 1856
Thakker, Dharmesh, 235
Thangarai, Immanuel, 697
Thapar, Vik, 576
Tharrington, Owen G., 873
Thau, Kevin, 1715
Thees, Anderson, 641
Theleen, Robert A, 473
Thermond, Jeff, 2011
Thesseling, Joost F., 476
Thiam, Tidjane, 554
Thiboutot PhD, Ronald P, 1117
Thiel, Peter, 775
Thiele-Sardina, Roy, 933
Thoma, Carl D, 1814
Thomas, Pete, 183
Thomas, Harry, 251
Thomas, Dave, 839
Thomas, Kathleen, 1033
Thomas, Mark T, 1248
Thomas, Andrew A, 1744
Thomas, James E, 1817
Thomas Jr, David E, 1526
Thompson, William B., 780
Thompson, Eric, 867
Thompson, Bennett, 1086
Thompson, Shawn, 1369
Thompson, Sam, 1486
Thompson, Tyler, 1642
Thompson, Rick, 1678
Thompson, Jeremy, 2219
Thompson Black, Timothy, 1002
Thompson PhD, James, 880
Thomssen, Eli L., 139
Thonis, Michael G., 456
Thorndike, William N., 949
Thornton, John, 202
Thornton, Jim, 887
Thorp, James, 17
Thorp, Clay B, 915
Thorpe, Allen, 924

Thorson, Michael, 2001
Thrope, Geoffrey B, 1287
Thukral, Nikhil, 1088
Thurk, Paul, 153
Thurow, Ethan, 368
Tian, Esther, 343
Tichenor, Andrew, 288
Tichio, Robert M, 1573
Ticknor, Carolyn, 990
Tidwell, Brandon, 1677
Tiedemann, Bruce, 312
Tierney Jr., Paul E., 136
Tilley, Brian C., 610
Tilley, Shermaine, 2092
Timmerman III, William, 846
Tindel, Andrew B., 1409
Tippins, John, 1746
Tisch, David, 318
Tisdale, Andrew A., 1496
Titan, Keith, 256
Tito, Denis A., 1989
Tittiger, Gottfried P., 985
Titus, David, 1995
Tjan, Tony, 567
To, Kilin, 1769
Toan, Robert, 1949
Tobin, Scott, 235
Toby, Elias, 2094
Tolan, Mary, 469
Tolle, Steve, 938
Tolmie, David, 654
Tom, David B, 1908
Tomai, William, 447
Tomasello, Anthony L, 987
Tomes, John, 916
Tomlin, Steve, 206
Tompkins, Graves, 815
Tompkins, Daniel, 1354
Toncheva, Dafina, 1896
Tong, Bryant J, 1355
Toomay, John, 1408
Toomey Jr., John, 909
Topilow, Justin, 250
Topouzian, Ara, 3269
Topper, MD, PhD, James N., 782
Torenberg, Peter, 1933
Torres, S Edward, 1124
Torres, Jason P, 1165
Torres Picon, Pedro, 1518
Toth, Bryan J., 759
Tou, Joseph, 1703
Toups, W. Anthony, 61
Towns, Matthew, 2251
Townsend, David G, 746
Townsend, Jason, 1547
Tracey, Martha, 553
Traer CPA, Mary, 909
Traidman, Brent, 721
Train, C. Bowdoin, 875
Trala, Anna May L, 884
Tran, Tuan, 1009
Tran, Angela, 2280
Trang, John, 2220
Trank, Albert, 1497
Traub, Michael, 1833
Trauben, Jon, 99
Travaglini, John, 2026
Travers, Chris, 1531
Traylor, Chris, 756
Traynor, Sean M, 1972
Trbovich, John, 171
Tremblay, Gregoire, 2072
Tremblay, Pascal, 2206
Trenchard, Bill, 741
Trenk, Steve, 1135
Treu, PhD, Jesse, 621
Treyger, Victoria, 720

Triebsch, Brad, 573
Triedman, J Russell, 1129
Triest, Jonathon, 1150
Tripathi, Pavan, 333
Triplett, Michael, 1000
Trippet, Blake, 1223
Trivinos, Leda, 747
Trochu, Jean-Louis, 1823
Troppe, Asher, 1843
Trudeau, Robert, 1785
Trueger, Arthur, 252
Truehart, John P., 954
Truetzel, David W., 196
Truslow, Ned, 1557
Trussler, Douglas B., 274
Truwit, Mitch, 135
Trzcinka, Terry, 1974
Trzepacz, Jennifer, 1985
Tsai, Christine, 11
Tsai, Tenno, 928
Tsai, Tommy, 1138
Tsang, David, 47
Tsang, Kai, 1922
Tsien, Matt, 817
Tsubouchi, Dan, 2246
Tsui, Doug, 947
Tucker, Robert, 401
Tucker, James W., 546
Tucker, Stanley W, 1208
Tucker, Jeff S, 1219
Tufts, Linda, 749
Tuleta, Karen, 1266
Tullis, Jim, 1866
Tullis, John, 1866
Tully, Daniel G., 97
Tully, Timothy, 1867
Tune, Kathleen A, 1817
Tung, Hans, 823
Tunnell, David, 924
Tunnicliff, Jonathan, 1349
Turck, Matt, 743
Turk, Dr. Bernd, 952
Turkewitz, Jordan, 2020
Turnbull, Gregory G., 2074
Turnbull, Nancy, 2219
Turner, Matt, 113
Turner, Amherst, 113
Turner, Emily, 486
Turner, Guy, 962
Turner, Patrick N.W., 1927
Turner, Christopher, 1956
Turner, John H., 1979
Turner III, Daniel K, 1251
Turner Moffitt, Andrea, 1454
Turner, J.D., Court R., 31
Turner, PhD, Mervyn, 237
Turowsky, Jason, 1009
Tusk, Bradley, 1868
Tuttle, Philip A, 591
Tuttle, Richard C, 1492
Twiford, J. Rainer, 384
Tybur, James, 1431
Tylee, Greg, 2253
Tyrrell, Mike, 1916
Tzeng, John, 905
Tzung, Cleve, 203

U

Ubben, Jeffrey W, 1903
Ucciferri, Louie, 913
Uebelein, Kevin, 2033
Uhlman, Tom, 1305
Uhrig, J. William, 1820
Ukropina, Rob, 275
Ulevitch PhD, Richard J, 12
Ullah, Salman, 1218
Ulrich, Catherine, 743

Unanue, Andy, 193
Underwood, Robert L, 1332
Underwood, John H., 1435
Ungerer, Scott, 676
Unkovic, Robert, 1098
Unruh, Paul, 1793
Unsworth, David, 2153
Unterberger, Steve, 416
Upchurch, Jim, 373
Upchurch, Jim, 374
Upton, Richard, 907
Urbina, Elias "Lee", 594
Uribe, Juan, 141
Usher, Mark, 2080
Ussery, Randall, 1985
Utay, Marc A, 492
Uzumeri, Erol, 2252
Uzzaman, Anis, 721

V

Vachet, Claude, 2093
Vainno, MD, PhD, Petri, 697
Vaitkunas, Davis, 2064
Vaknin, Motti, 436
Valdez, Russel, 1950
Valenti, Michele, 1548
Valentine, Jeff, 705
Valentine, Donald, 1654
Valis, Tomas, 2076
Valkin, Adam, 816
Van Alstyne, Matthew, 1367
Van Apeldoorn, Keith, 2258
van Beuningen, Fred, 2078
Van Bladel, PhD, Sigrid, 20
Van Bladel, Sigrid, 20
Van Cuylenburg, Peter, 555
Van der Meer, Roland, 798
van der Velden, Peter, 2180
Van Harten, Kenton S., 902
van Horne, Charles H, 18
van Lierop, Wal, 2078
Van Marken, Tony, 2118
van Praet, Jean-Edouard, 978
van Schie, Adrian, 227
Van Steenbergen, Jeff, 2050
Van Thiel, Gijs FJ, 14
Van Vleck, Michael, 853
Van Wielingen, Mac, 2040
VanDyke, Blue, 9
VanHoy, Scott, 1105
Vanclief, Greg, 2284
Vandaele, Christophe, 1905
Vander Schaaff, Tom, 655
Vanderbeck, Sunny, 1622
Vanderhoofven, Grady, 1214
Vandervelden, James E, 1824
Vandevenne, Rurik G, 1571
Vanier, Vance, 469
Vannelli, Vince, 1084
Vardell, Thomas, 1341
Vardhana, Anarghya, 1183
Vargo, Robert, 2227
Varier, Krishnan, 151
Varino, Fil, 3258
Varma, Samit, 132
Varshneya, Rajeev, 278
Vasilescu, Katie, 834
Vasishth, Vishal, 1363
Vaslet, Charles, 2106
Vassallo, Steve, 770
Vassallo, Mark F, 1123
Vaughan, James, 234
Vaughan, Ben, 2067
Vazé, Jana, 1341
Veale, Stuart, 251
Veatch, Kyle, 926
Veber, Gayle L, 1909

1101

Executive Name Index

Veedon, Mathew, 1712
Veitch, John, 2082
Veith, Anthony J, 503
Velazquez, Louis, 725
Velez, Tristan, 926
Vendetti, Dino, 764
Vendetti, Dino, 1656
Venditti, Mario, 2156
Venerable, Mike, 479
Venkatachalam, Kapil, 1785
Venkataraman, Sriram, 209
Vere Nicoll, Neville, 542
Veres, Rob, 1721
Verhalen, Andrew W, 1181
Vermylen Jr, Paul A, 1068
Vernal, Mike, 1654
Vernick, Shoshana, 1742
Verratti, Robert N., 1828
Veru, Dennison T, 1401
Vettel, Matthew T., 857
Vetter, Martin, 2048
Vetters, David, 2038
Victor, Jonathan, 225
Victor, Skip, 225
Videt, Pote, 1139
Vigano, Paul R., 1037
Vigoda, Robert A., 426
Vijayavargiya, Sonali, 195
Villela, Alexandre, 1509
Vincent, John, 1554
Virani, Aamir, 777
Virtue, Ted, 1231
Vishria, Eric, 248
Visser, Mark, 245
Vitorovic, Tefan, 1932
Vitullo, Nicole, 621
Vitus, Andy, 1626
Vivaldi, Nicole, 2118
Vivian, Steve, 1477
Vogel, Andrew, 2020
Vogelbaum, Martin, 1558
Vogt, Christine, 78
Vohooshi, Amir, 2028
Volftsun, Lev, 1959
Volpe, Lou, 1080
Volpe, Joe, 1205
Volpe, Drew, 1483
Volpert, Barry, 559
Volpi, Matteo, 2074
von der Goltz, Alex, 310
von der Goltz, Johan, 310
von Dohlen, Gerard, 343
Von Friedeburg, Stephanie, 1007
von Holzhausen, Kurt, 343
von Maltzahn, Geoffrey, 747
Von Schlegell, John, 673
von Schroeter, Carlo A., 1979
Von Stroh, Eric, 1141
von Sydow, Ferdinand, 952
von Zuben, Max, 1984
Vorhoff, Robbert, 815
Vorlicek, Martha DiMatteo, 909
Voss, Scott, 909
Vrionis, John, 1121
Vyule, Stuart, 1569

W

Wachtel, Bonnie K, 1948
Wachter, David, 1947
Wack, Patrick, 1558
Waddington, Ryan, 961
Wade, James F, 1153
Wade, Gary, 2189
Wadhera, Karan, 417
Wadih, Anibal, 834
Wadsworth, Robert, 909
Wadsworth II, Eliot, 949

Wagman, Michael, 2081
Wagner, Daniel, 530
Wagner, Bradaigh, 673
Wagner, Alyse, 1109
Wagner, Peter, 1996
Wahla, Ahmed, 1081
Wahrhaftig, David I, 1062
Wakeman, Fred, 62
Walden, Michael, 1550
Walden, Michael, 1551
Waldrip, William D., 671
Waldusky, Michelle A, 633
Walecka, John, 1534
Walfish, Marc J, 1209
Walk, Hunter, 941
Walker, Jim, 57
Walker, Clinton W., 494
Walker, James B., 554
Walker, Tom, 1553
Walker, Colin, 2089
Wall, Terrence R, 583
Wall, IV, Thomas R, 1062
Wallace, Brian D, 36
Wallace, Ben, 213
Wallace, Peter, 277
Wallace, Brendan, 727
Wallace, Peggy, 841
Wallace, Jonathan R, 1388
Wallace, Craig, 2131
Wallace III, Ken, 986
Walrath, Michael, 1980
Walsh, Paul, 368
Walsh, Timothy, 433
Walsh, Robert, 699
Walsh, Ryan, 751
Walsh, Kevin T., 946
Walsh, Rob, 1770
Walter, Mark R., 885
Walter Jr., Kenneth G., 902
Walters, Jeffrey M., 1093
Walton, Roger, 422
Walton, Andrew, 2163
Walvoord, John E, 1697
Wan, Mark, 1819
Wanek, David, 1975
Wang, T Chester, 47
Wang, Sona, 452
Wang, Mingyao, 519
Wang, Lucas, 519
Wang, Ted, 552
Wang, Samantha, 563
Wang, Tzyy-Po, 905
Wang, Xiao, 994
Wang, Tiffine, 1269
Wang, Ryan, 1390
Wang, Timothy, 1977
Wang, Tianpeng, 2195
Ward, Carter A., 156
Ward, Sean, 290
Ward, Robert, 1212
Ward, Mike, 1515
Ward, J.R. Kingsley, 2282
Warden, Todd, 907
Warden, Charles M., 1928
Wardlaw, William M., 783
Wardrop, Troy, 9
Ware, Matt, 1160
Ware, Zach, 1912
Warner, Lara J., 554
Warnock, David L., 383
Warnock, Greg, 1204
Warren, Todd, 618
Warren, Jermaine L., 969
Warren, Wilson S, 1112
Warren, Scott, 1234
Warren, Gus, 1611
Washing, Tom, 1653

Washington, Alex, 1990
Washington, Kyle, 2085
Wasserman, Keith, 811
Wassong, David, 1315
Watanabe, Yasuharu, 2007
Watchmaker, Linda, 536
Waters, Steve, 1810
Watkins, John W, 1153
Watkins, Dan, 1206
Watkins, Anita, 1556
Watkins, Timothy, 1902
Watt, Trevor, 924
Watts, William E, 1049
Watts, Michael, 1128
Watts, Katherine, 1712
Waud, Reeve B, 1963
Waugh, Stuart, 2204
Waxberg, Jason, 3270
Waxman, David, 1798
Weaver, Graham, 92
Weaver, Allen A, 1497
Webb, Jeffrey M., 985
Webb, Maynard, 1968
Webb, PhD, Brad, 491
Weber, Kara, 342
Weber, Tony R., 1326
Weber, Ellen, 1577
Weber, Paul, 2210
Weber, MD, Eckard, 621
Wedbush, Eric D, 1969
Weglicki, Tim, 22
Wehrung, Jamie, 176
Wei, Frank Z, 1956
Wei, James, 2007
Weiden, David, 1069
Weil, Burton B, 1919
Weinbar, Sharon, 1626
Weinberg, John, 699
Weiner, Eric, 291
Weiner, Joshua R., 740
Weinfurtner, Ed, 289
Weingarten, Michael, 1676
Weinhoff MD, Gregory M, 474
Weinryb, Merav, 1509
Weinstein, Paul, 215
Weinstein, Joshua S., 403
Weinstein, Brent, 1883
Weintraub, Daniel, 194
Weisenfeld, Andrew J, 1271
Weiser, Marc, 1592
Weisman, Wayne B, 1633
Weiss, Daniel, 126
Weiss, Warren, 770
Weiss, Eli, 819
Weiss, Michael, 862
Weiss, Ira, 962
Weiss, Paul, 1921
Weissenburger, Michael S, 597
Weisskoff PhD, Robert, 710
Weissman, Andy, 1882
Welborn, Miller, 459
Welborn, Kyle, 569
Welborn, Steve M., 2009
Weldon, Thomas D, 40
Weldon, Raymond F, 353
Weldon, Norman, 1418
Weldon, Kent R., 1815
Welling, W Lambert, 1198
Wells, Richard, 1000
Wells, James, 1650
Wells, Richard, 2283
Welsh, Patrick J, 1972
Welsh JD, Jeanette M, 1792
Wendell, Peter, 1670
Wenger, Albert, 1882
Wenzel, Robert J., 74
Werdegar, Maurice, 1975

Wermuth, David J., 1743
Werner, Harold R., 919
Werry, Scott, 2034
Wertheimer, Stephen, 1947
Wertz, Boriz, 2280
Wesson, Bruce, 806
West, Ben, 39
West, Bob, 200
West, Mike, 467
West, Ted, 772
West, Casey, 1732
Westbrook, Thomas H., 746
Westbrook, Kirk, 1011
Wester, Forest, 1857
Westerlind, Victor, 809
Westervelt, Jr., William J., 179
Westley, Peter, 300
Westly, Steve, 1977
Weston, Denny, 753
Weston, Jamie, 1730
Weston CFA, R Patrick, 213
Westphal, Christoph, 1145
Westra, James, 62
Wethington, Jerry D., 1570
Wethington, Bryan M., 1570
Wetzel, Robert B., 196
Whalen, T.J., 786
Whalen Brechtel, Margaret, 1523
Wheaton, Cal, 22
Wheeler, Brian, 257
Wheeler, Kurt C., 495
Wheeler, Andy, 889
Whelan, Edward J., 254
Whelan, J.P., 1066
Whelan, Patrick F, 1424
Whickman, Kirk, 127
Whims, Jim, 93
Whitcomb, Chris, 1369
White, Brandon C., 456
White, Marshall C., 746
White, John D., 774
White, John, 1273
White, Thurman V, 1485
White, Sean C., 1724
White, James N, 1760
White, Gregory A., 1815
White, Aaron, 1939
White, Morty, 2009
White, Jason, 2166
White, Jeff, 2200
White Jr, W Spalding, 1605
Whiteaker, Tom, 912
Whiteaker, Thomas, 967
Whiteley, Phyllis, 1247
Whiteley, Phyllis, 1985
Whitlock, Steve, 1722
Whitney Jr., Ralph R., 900
Whittemore, Alexander D, 1752
Whorf, John, 1294
Whorton, Dave, 1865
Wiacek, Walter, 722
Wiberg, Bill, 59
Wick, Tyler, 21
Wick, Sam, 1883
Wick, William, 1937
Wicker, Damion, 1410
Widder, Ken, 1094
Widmann, Sebastian C., 1130
Widner, Melissa, 1637
Widroe, Gred, 1195
Wiebe, Charles A., 263
Wierck, Ryan, 849
Wiggers, Lane W, 164
Wiggins, Steve, 697
Wigle, Jeff, 2051
Wilcox, Harry, 747
Wild, Jason, 1048

Executive Name Index

Wilde, Peter O., 1496
Wilder, Lawrence, 1936
Wildstein, Evan, 1081
Wilhelm, Klemens, 2126
Wilkerson, L John, 806
Wilkins, Jay, 914
Wilkins, Eric J., 1409
Wilkins, Jr., Herbert P., 1771
Wilkinson, Alan, 64
Wilkosz, Leon R, 583
Willerer, Tom, 1916
Willert, John, 401
Williams, Russ, 16
Williams, Greg, 29
Williams, Brayton, 307
Williams, Ryan, 542
Williams, Greg, 581
Williams, Paul S., 734
Williams, Brent, 894
Williams, Randy, 1061
Williams, Anthony L, 1208
Williams, Terry, 1321
Williams, Ev, 1363
Williams, Jeff, 1728
Williams, Richard J., 1979
Williams, Kristina, 2032
Williams, Peter, 2038
Williams, Tom, 2168
Williams Jr., Robert M., 1037
Williams, III, Edward C., 349
Williamson, Mark N., 368
Williamson, Donna, 452
Williamson, Elizabeth C, 789
Williamson, Glenn, 1290
Williamson PhD, Andrew, 1438
Wilson, Tim, 174
Wilson, Andrew, 200
Wilson, Brent, 462
Wilson, Joshua, 846
Wilson, Peter, 909
Wilson, Karen, 1010
Wilson, Jason, 1491
Wilson, Stoddard M, 1579
Wilson, Tyrone, 1771
Wilson, Adrian N., 1842
Wilson, Adrian, 1842
Wilson, Russ, 1857
Wilson, Fred, 1882
Wilson, Kaley, 2229
Wilson PE, L Edward, 537
Wiltse, Jeannette, 2236
Winblad, Ann, 956
Winblad, Ann, 956
Winder, Caleb, 703
Winefeld, Elena, 41
Winklevoss, Tyler, 1998
Winklevoss, Cameron, 1998
Winn, Christopher, 2194
Winneg, Robert D, 1296
Winship, Chris, 793
Winship, Scott D., 888
Winslow, Frank, 1505
Winterer, Bill, 1417
Winterroth, Seth, 648
Winters, Ana M, 1232
Winters, Kyle, 2201
Wintrob, Jay, 1362
Wirt, Richard, 1393
Wise, Jim P., 893
Witherington, Hunter, 1732
Witherington Jr, James D, 1732

Witte, Curt, 333
Witte, Matthew L, 1168
Witzofsky, Bill, 399
Wizel, Neil A., 740
Wodlinger, David C., 166
Woiwode, Tom, 1928
Wojtowicz, Jean, 382
Wolf, Michael, 280
Wolf, Jen, 991
Wolfe, Josh, 1151
Wolfe, Kirk, 1242
Wolfe, Aaron P, 1753
Wolfe Strouse, Mimi, 39
Wolfe, Ph.D, Daniel B., 6
Wolfond, Henry, 2052
Wolfram, Tyler, 1360
Wolfson, Gene, 427
Wolfson, Rob, 928
Wolin, Harry, 106
Wolkon, Shari H., 1815
Wollaeger, Timothy, 1616
Wolmer, David, 1111
Wolpow, Marc, 194
Womsley, Robert, 1961
Wong, Rich, 28
Wong, Carol, 595
Wong, Henry, 612
Wong, Felix J, 752
Wong, Henry, 807
Wong, Mike, 938
Wong, Raymond L.M., 1730
Wong, Hing, 1951
Wood, Marcus, 744
Wood, Steve, 835
Wood, Jeffrey G, 900
Wood, Steven F., 1014
Wood, Bob, 2001
Woodman, Robbie, 1778
Woodruff, Craig, 48
Woods, Emil, 1115
Woods Jr., Willie E., 969
Woodson, Wade, 1672
Woodward, William, 132
Woodward, Gordon H, 1081
Woodward, Tim, 1355
Woodworth Jr, Alfred S, 647
Woody, Ken, 995
Woody, Jim, 1094
Wooten, Ron, 1349
Worthy, Ford, 1412
Wright, Mark, 287
Wright, Austin, 359
Wright, J.D., 489
Wright, Christopher G., 556
Wright, Tim, 848
Wright, Dalton, 1070
Wu, Jeffrey, 245
Wu, Dennis, 290
Wu, Paul, 870
Wu, Veronica, 942
Wu, Victor L, 1112
Wu, David, 1183
Wu, Tony, 1340
Wurzer, David, 530
Wyant, Jack, 287
Wyatt, Gordon T, 40
Wynperle, William J., 1660

X
Xeuzhao, Dr. Lan, 232
Xie, Chris, 2271

Xu, Peter, 661
Xu, Eric, 823

Y
Yablunsky, Robert G, 1633
Yadav, Ravi, 1315
Yamashita, Kevin, 257
Yang, James, 14
Yang, John, 325
Yang, Hai, 435
Yang, Chris, 879
Yang, Ed, 970
Yang, Geoff, 1534
Yang, Jackie, 1838
Yang, Bruce, 2193
Yang PhD, Lei, 1340
Yanney, Michael, 71
Yarborough, Benjamin W, 1209
Yardley, Daniel, 1422
Yates, Phil, 333
Yau, Philip, 824
Yeager, Caroline, 1019
Yeh, Chris, 1958
Yellurkar, Devdutt, 455
Yen, Tuff, 1655
Yeo, Young, 1864
Yeoham, Paul A, 1484
Yepez, J. Alberto, 1850
Yerushalmi, Oren, 354
Yeshwant, Krishna, 889
Yi, Peter, 968
Yim, Charles, 641
Yoder, Lacey, 1822
Yohe, Matt, 1266
Yoon, Kwan, 296
Yoon, Cene, 333
York, Gwill, 1119
Yosef-Or, Tomer, 21
Yoskovitz, Ben, 2147
Young, John, 154
Young, Eric, 386
Young, David W., 434
Young, William, 495
Young, Tim, 679
Young, Brian D., 686
Young, Matthew, 686
Young, Caroline L., 900
Young, April, 925
Young, Steve, 959
Young, Chris, 1554
Young, Scott F, 1652
Young, Philip M, 1896
Young, Will, 1912
Young, Sarah, 2247
Young PhD, James W, 12
Youngkin, Glenn A, 413
Youngren, Bryce, 1460
Youstra, Bill, 1083
Yovovich, Paul G., 1091
Yu, Simon, 391
Yu, Janie, 796
Yu, Erica, 823
Yu, Ben, 1670
Yu, Dr. Chen, 1941
Yuan, David, 1534
Yuan, David, 1785
Yudkoff, Royce G., 21
Yuen, Homan, 799

Z
Zabbal, Christian, 1729

Zabik, Joseph J., 343
Zachary, George, 455
Zacuto, Adam, 449
Zaczepinski, Guy, 449
Zadourian, Keith, 1022
Zafar, Naeem, 95
Zaki, Kareem, 1821
Zaldivar, Luis, 1403
Zambelli, Anthony W, 1648
Zamsky, Katherine, 408
Zanarini, Jeff, 928
Zang, Lu, 799
Zannino, Richard, 433
Zanone, Joseph, 581
Zaorski, Philip, 782
Zaplatynsky, John, 2218
Zappala, Timothy, 170
Zaslavsky, Dennis, 1964
Zatlukal, David J., 1037
Zaveri, Darshana, 426
Zbar, Brett, 762
Zeisig, Bernie, 2195
Zelaya, Briana J., 1903
Zell, Joseph, 876
Zelnick, Strauss, 2020
Zelter, James, 140
Zemp, Dal, 1542
Zeprun, Howard S., 1850
Zerbib, Nicolas D., 1743
Zhan, Stephanie, 1654
Zhang, Toby, 472
Zhang, Ray, 1467
Zhang, Kevin, 1887
Zhao, Yipeng, 663
Zhou, Lili, 540
Zhou, Sha, 1390
Zhu, Wan Li, 712
Zhuang, Shelley, 4
Zhuo, TX, 728
Zhuo, TX, 1055
Zia, M. Junaid, 2089
Ziebelman, Peter, 1405
Ziegler, Ryan, 655
Zilberman, David, 518
Zilberman, Daniel, 1956
Zilis, Shivon, 284
Zimmerer, Yimin, 1951
Zine, Riadh, 2242
Zine, Imed, 2242
Zink Jr, Darell E, 409
Zinterhofer, Eric, 2252
Ziolkowski, Andy, 570
Zipp, Bob, 114
Zippelius, Pete, 1109
Zisson, Alex, 1817
Zittman, Mark, 1864
Zoellner, Scott, 64
Zohar, Daphne, 1501
Zola, Natty, 1176
Zolfaghari, Paul, 416
Zorich, Robert L., 672
Zou, Kenny, 2083
Zucco, Jim, 505
Zucker, Jeffrey M., 860
Zugaro, Chris, 1856
Zur, Ari M., 348
Zur Muhlen, Adriaan, 1486
Zurek, Andrea, 2010
Zych, Douglas, 1045

Geographic Index

Amsterdam
IDINVEST PARTNERS, 2851

Argentina
ACONCAGUA VENTURES, 2334
ALANTRA, 77
AXVENTURES, 2470
COMPASS GROUP, 522
GE CAPITAL, 808
GRUPO BISA, 2800
LONE STAR FUNDS, 1140

Asia
CISCO INVESTMENTS, 483

Australia
ACCEDE CAPITAL, 2323
ACRUX LIMITED, 2335
ACUMEN VENTURES, 2341
ADVANCE PROPERTY FUND, 2346
AMWIN MANAGEMENT PTY LIMITED, 2398
ANACACIA CAPITAL, 2399
ARCHER CAPITAL, 2420
ARES MANAGEMENT LLC, 159
AUSTRALIAN ETHICAL INVESTMENT LIMITED, 2456
BAIN CAPITAL PRIVATE EQUITY, 220
BLACKBIRD VENTURES, 2520
BLACKSTONE PRIVATE EQUITY GROUP, 277
BLUE COVE VENTURES, 2523
BRANDON CAPITAL PARTNERS, 2536
BROOKFIELD ASSET MANAGEMENT, 2067
CARLYLE GROUP, 413
CATALYST INVESTMENT MANAGERS PTY LIMITED PPM Capital, 2573
CISCO INVESTMENTS, 483
CLEANTECH VENTURES, 2613
CM CAPITAL, 2618
COLONIAL FIRST STATE PRIVATE EQUITY, 2622
CONCEPT FINANCIAL SERVICES, 2627
CONTINENTAL VENTURE CAPITAL LIMITED, 2631
CVC INVESTMENT MANAGERS LIMITED, 2645
DEUTSCHE ASSET MANAGEMENT (AUSTRALIA) LIMITED Deutsche Bank AG, 2659
ENDEAVOUR CAPITAL PTY LIMITED Endeavour Capital, 2699
ENTER VENTURES, 681
EQUITY PARTNERS PTY LIMITED, 2715
FIRST CORPORATE PTY LIMITED, 2743
FIRST INVESTMENT CORPORATION LIMITED, 2744
FORTRESS INVESTMENT GROUP LLC, 767
GE CAPITAL, 808
GREENHILL SAVP, 864
GRESHAM PRIVATE EQUITY LIMITED, 2799
HASTINGS FUNDS MANAGEMENT PTY LIMITED, 2814
HRL MORRISON & COMPANY LIMITED, 2835
INNOVATION CAPITAL LIMITED, 2877
JEGI CAPITAL, 1033
KALORI GROUP INVESTMENTS, 2915
KOHLBERG KRAVIS ROBERTS & COMPANY, 1082
LION SELECTION GROUP LIMITED, 2942
LONE STAR FUNDS, 1140
MACQUARIE DIRECT INVESTMENT LIMITED, 2951
MEDICAL RESEARCH COMMERCIALIZATION FUND, 2959
MOMENTUM FUNDS MANAGEMENT PTY LIMITED, 2975
NANYANG VENTURES PTY LIMITED, 2982
NBC CAPITAL PTY LIMITED, 2988
NEO TECHNOLOGY VENTURES, 2989
NEXTEC DEVELOPMENT CAPITAL LIMITED, 3000
NORTHLEAF CAPITAL PARTNERS, 2204
OneVentures, 3023
PACIFIC EQUITY PARTNERS PTY LIMITED, 3025
PHOSPHAGENICS, 3037
POMONA CAPITAL, 1462
QUINBROOK INFRASTRUCTURE PARTNERS, 1517
RESOURCE CAPITAL FUNDS, 1548
RFC AMBRIAN RFC Group Ltd., 3079
RIVERSIDE COMPANY, 1572
RMB VENTURES LIMITED RMB Australia, 3083
ROTHSCHILD AUSTRALIA - ARROW PRIVATE EQUITY Rothschild Group, 3086
RUSSELL INVESTMENT MANAGEMENT LIMITED, 3089
SCALE INVESTORS, 3102
SENETAS CORPORATION LIMITED Senatas Group, 3110
SOUTHERN CROSS VENTURE PARTNERS, 1711
STARFISH VENTURES, 3138
STARPHARMA POOLED DEVELOPMENT LIMITED, 3139
SYDNEY SEED FUND, 3153
TANK STREAM VENTURES, 3160
TPG CAPITAL, 1835
WILSHIRE PRIVATE MARKETS, 1989
YUUWA CAPITAL, 3248

Austria
3TS CAPITAL PARTNERS, 2309
ALANTRA, 77
ANDLINGER & COMPANY INC, 123
DARBY OVERSEAS INVESTMENTS LTD, 584
ENNOVENT, 2701
G & H KAPITAL PARTNER AG, 2764
GLOBAL EQUITY PARTNERS BETEILIGUNGS-MANAGEMENT, 2783
HORIZONTE VENTURE MANAGEMENT GmbH, 2832
INVEST EQUITY MANAGEMENT CONSULTING GmbH, 2887
ONE EQUITY PARTNERS, 1376
TECNET, 3165
TPA CORPORATE FINANCE CONSULTING GMBH Horwarth International, 3184

Bahrain
ARCAPITA INC, 152
INVESTCORP, 1017

Bavaria
BAYERN KAPITAL, 2495

Belgium
3M UNITEK, 2307
ACKERMANS & VAN HAAREN, 2332
ALLEGRO INVESTMENT FUND, 2366
ANDLINGER & COMPANY INC, 123
AON RISK SOLUTIONS Aon Corporation, 2413
ARKAFUND MEDIA & ICT, 2426
BAEKELAND FUNDS, 2476
CAPRICORN VENTURE PARTNERS NV, 2563
E-CAPITAL MANAGEMENT, 2680
FLANDERS' FOREIGN INVESTMENT OFFICE, 2746
GIMV GIMV, 2780
GIMV NV, 2781
GUIDANT EUROPE SA, 2803
HUMMINGBIRD VENTURES, 2837
INDUFIN, 2862
IPOSCOPE NV/SA, 2895
IT-PARTNERS NV, 2902
LRM - INVESTERINGSMAATSCHAPPIJ VOOR LIMBURG, 2949
MERIFIN CAPITAL, 2963
NAUSICAA VENTURES, 2986
NEW RHEIN HEALTHCARE INVESTORS, 1302
PMV, 3042
PUILAETCO PRIVATE BANKERS KBL Group, 3063
QBIC FUND, 3065
QUEST FOR GROWTH, 3069
RIVERSIDE COMPANY, 1572
SAMBRINVEST SA, 3096
SRIW SA SRIW Group, 3134
TECH TOUR, 3163
VIVES, 3225

Bermuda
ATILA VENTURES, 2442
D.E. SHAW & CO. LP, 579
LONE STAR FUNDS, 1140
WAFRA INC, 1950

1105

Geographic Index

Brazil
ACELERADORA, 2331
ACON INVESTMENTS, 46
ADVENT INTERNATIONAL CORPORATION, 62
AEM CAPITAL, 2349
ASTELLA INVESTMENTS, 2438
ATOMICO, 2446
BR OPPORTUNITIES, 2533
BROOKFIELD ASSET MANAGEMENT, 2067
BRZTECH, 2545
CARLYLE GROUP, 413
COMPANHIA RIOGRANDENSE DE PARTICIPACOES, 2626
DARBY OVERSEAS INVESTMENTS LTD, 584
DUTCHESS CAPITAL, 638
E.BRICKS DIGITAL, 2681
E.VENTURES, 641
EVERCORE CAPITAL PARTNERS, 699
EXPLORADOR CAPITAL MANAGEMENT, 2729
FIR CAPITAL PARTNERS, 2742
GE CAPITAL, 808
GENERAL ATLANTIC PARTNERS, 815
GLOBAL ENVIRONMENT FUND, 834
GREENHILL SAVP, 864
INITIAL CAPITAL, 2872
ITC VENTURES, 2903
LONE STAR FUNDS, 1140
MONASHEES CAPITAL, 2976
NAPKN VENTURES, 2983
PLEXUS VENTURES, 1452
PROJECT A VENTURE GmBH & CO. KG Project A Ventures Latam, 3056
QUALCOMM VENTURES, 1509
REDPOINT VENTURES, 1534
SIGULER GUFF & COMPANY, 1679
TELEFONICA VENTURES, 3169
TMG CAPITAL PARTNERS, 3180
WARBURG PINCUS LLC, 1956

Bulgaria
AXXESS CAPITAL, 2471
ELEVEN, 2696

Canada
LIONHART CAPITAL LTD, 2177
MISTRAL VENTURE PARTNERS, 2195
RELENTLESS PURSUIT PARTNERS, 2237
SANDPIPER VENTURES, 2247

AB
32 DEGREES CAPITAL, 2025
500 STARTUPS CANADA, 2027
ALBERTA ENTERPRISE, 2032
ALBERTA INVESTMENT MANAGEMENT CORP., 2033
ANNAPOLIS CAPITAL, 2038
APECTEC, 2039
ARC FINANCIAL, 2040
AVAC, 2048
AVRIO CAPITAL, 2049
AZIMUTH CAPITAL MANAGEMENT, 2050
AZURE CAPITAL PARTNERS, 215
CBI^2 CAPITAL, 2074
CLARITY CAPITAL, 2611
CROWN CAPITAL PARTNERS, 2091
DISTRICT VENTURES CAPITAL, 2099
ENERTECH CAPITAL, 676
FOUNDATION EQUITY CORPORATION, 2121
INTRINSIC VENTURE CAPITAL, 2160
INVICO CAPITAL CORPORATION, 2162
JOG CAPITAL, 2166
KENSINGTON CAPITAL PARTNERS, 2167
LONGBOW CAPITAL, 2178
MCROCK CAPITAL, 2190
NEXT EQUITIES, 2202
PANACHE VENTURES, 2212
PRIVITI CAPITAL, 2227
REGIMEN PARTNERS, 2235
RENEWABLETECH VENTURES, 1542
SAF GROUP, 2246
THE WESTERN INVESTMENT COMPANY OF CANADA, 2269
TRIWEST, 2275
VENTURE CAPITAL ASSOCIATION OF ALBERTA, 3281
WESTERN AMERICA CAPITAL GROUP, 2286
YALETOWN VENTURE PARTNERS, 2291

BC
7 GATE VENTURES, 2028
AMPLITUDE, 2036
ARDENTON, 2042
BC RENAISSANCE CAPITAL FUND, 2053
BCF VENTURES, 2054
BIOENTERPRISE, 2060
BOND CAPITAL, 2064
CAI CAPITAL PARTNERS, 365
CHRYSALIX, 2078
CM PARTNERS 1021 West Hastings Street, 2083
COPPERLION CAPITAL, 2085
DISCOVERY CAPITAL, 2097
DOVENTI CAPITAL, 2100
EQUUS TOTAL RETURN, 694
EVOK INNOVATIONS, 2111
FOUNDERS GROUP OF FOOD COMPANIES, 2123
FRAMEWORK VENTURE PARTNERS, 2124
FULCRUM CAPITAL PARTNERS, 2126
GOAL HOLDINGS, 2135
GROWTHWORKS, 2143
HARDY CAPITAL PARTNERS, 2144
HEADWATER EQUITY PARTNERS, 2145
HIGHLAND WEST CAPITAL, 2146
HIGHLINE BETA, 2147
KENSINGTON CAPITAL PARTNERS, 2167
LIGHTHEART MANAGEMENT PARTNERS, 2175
LIGHTHOUSE EQUITY PARTNERS, 2176
LUMIRA CAPITAL, 2180
PANGAEA VENTURES LTD, 2213
PARALLEL49 EQUITY, 2214
PENDER WEST CAPITAL PARTNERS, 2218
PIQUE VENTURES, 2223
QUARK VENTURE, 2229
RECAPHEALTH VENTURES, 2233
REGIMEN PARTNERS, 2235
RENEWAL FUNDS, 2238
SAF GROUP, 2246
SCALEUP VENTURES, 2249
SECOND CITY REAL ESTATE, 2253
STERN PARTNERS, 2258
TELUS VENTURES, 2265
TENX VENTURES, 2266
TOP RENERGY INC., 2271
TRICOR PACIFIC CAPITAL, 2274
VANCITY CAPITAL, 2277
VANEDGE CAPITAL PARTNERS, 2278
VERSANT VENTURES, 1928
VERSION ONE VENTURES, 2280
VRG CAPITAL, 2282
YALETOWN VENTURE PARTNERS, 2291
YELLOW POINT EQUITY PARTNERS, 2292

MB
CENTRESTONE VENTURES, 2077
RED LEAF CAPITAL, 2234
RICHARDSON CAPITAL, 2240

NB
ENERGIA VENTURES, 674
NEW BRUNSWICK INNOVATION FOUNDATION, 2200

NL
KILLICK CAPITAL, 2168
PELORUS VENTURE CAPITAL, 2216

NS
BIOENTERPRISE, 2060
BUILD VENTURES, 2068

Geographic Index

GROWTHWORKS, 2143
INNOVACORP, 2155
NOVA SCOTIA BUSINESS INC., 2205
PELORUS VENTURE CAPITAL, 2216
SEAFORT CAPITAL, 2251
TECHNOCAP, 2263

ON

4FRONT CAPITAL PARTNERS, 2026
ACCESS CAPITAL CORPORATION, 2030
AIP PRIVATE CAPITAL, 2031
ALBERTA INVESTMENT MANAGEMENT CORP., 2033
ALTAS PARTNERS, 2034
AMPLITUDE, 2036
ANCIENT STRAINS, 2037
ARCTERN VENTURES, 2041
ARDENTON, 2042
ARGOSY PARTNERS, 2043
ARVA LIMITED, 2044
ASHBRIDGE PARTNERS, 2045
ATLAS PARTNERS, 2046
AUXO MANAGEMENT, 2047
AVRIO CAPITAL, 2049
BANYAN CAPITAL PARTNERS, 2051
BAYSHORE CAPITAL, 2052
BEDFORD CAPITAL, 2056
BERINGER CAPITAL, 2057
BEST FUNDS, 2058
BINGLEY CAPITAL, 2059
BIOENTERPRISE, 2060
BIOINDUSTRIAL INNOVATION CANADA, 2061
BIRCH HILL EQUITY PARTNERS, 2062
BMO CAPITAL MARKETS, 2063
BONNEFIELD FINANCIAL, 2065
BRIGHTSPARK VENTURES, 2066
BROOKFIELD ASSET MANAGEMENT, 2067
CANADIAN BUSINESS GROWTH FUND, 2070
CANADIAN VENTURE CAPITAL ASSOCIATION Canadian Venture Capital & Private Equity Association, 3258
CANOPY RIVERS, 2071
CARPEDIA CAPITAL, 2072
CATALYST CAPITAL GROUP, 2073
CCEI, 2075
CELTIC HOUSE VENTURE PARTNERS, 2076
CIBC CAPITAL MARKETS, 2079
CIBC INNOVATION BANKING, 2080
CLAIRVEST GROUP, 2081
CLEARSPRING CAPITAL PARTNERS, 2082
COBALT CAPITAL, 2084
COVINGTON CAPITAL CORP., 2087
CREDIT MUTUEL EQUITY, 2088
CROSBIE & COMPANY, 2089
CROSSWINDS HOLDINGS INC., 2090
CROWN CAPITAL PARTNERS, 2091
DANCAP PRIVATE EQUITY, 2094
DIFFERENCE CAPITAL, 2096
DISRUPTION VENTURES, 2098
DREAM MAKER VENTURES, 2101
DRI CAPITAL, 2102
DW HEALTHCARE PARTNERS, 639
EDGESTONE CAPITAL PARTNERS, 2103
ELGNER GROUP INVESTMENTS, 2104
ELNOS, 2105
EMERALD TECHNOLOGY VENTURES, 2106
ENERTECH CAPITAL, 676
EPIC CAPITAL MANAGEMENT, 2108
ESPRESSO CAPITAL, 2109
EVENTI CAPITAL PARTNERS, 2110
EVERCORE CAPITAL PARTNERS, 699
EXPORT DEVELOPMENT CANADA, 2112
EXTREME VENTURE PARTNERS, 2113
FASTBREAK VENTURES, 2115
FENGATE, 2116
FIBERNETICS VENTURES, 2117
FIRST ASCENT VENTURES, 2118
FOUNDATION MARKETS, 2122
FRAMEWORK VENTURE PARTNERS, 2124

FREYCINET INVESTMENTS, 2125
FULCRUM CAPITAL PARTNERS, 2126
GARAGECAPITAL, 2127
GCI CAPITAL, 2128
GENESIS CAPITAL CORPORATION, 2129
GENESYS CAPITAL, 2130
GENWEALTH VENTURES, 2131
GEORGIAN PARTNERS, 2132
GIBRALTAR & COMPANY, 2133
GLOBALIVE, 2134
GOLDEN VENTURE PARTNERS, 2137
GOOD NEWS VENTURES, 2138
GRANITE PARTNERS, 2139
GREEN ACRE CAPITAL, 2140
GREENHILL SAVP, 864
GREENSKY CAPITAL INC, 2141
GREENSOIL INVESTMENTS, 2142
HARBOURVEST PARTNERS LLC, 909
HIGHLINE BETA, 2147
HILCO BRANDS, 937
HILL AND GERTNER CAPITAL CORP., 2148
HURON CAPITAL PARTNERS LLC, 960
IANTHUS CAPITAL MANAGEMENT, 966
IGAN PARTNERS, 2149
IMPERIAL CAPITAL, 2150
IMPRESSION VENTURES, 2151
INDURAN VENTURES INC., 2152
INFORMATION VENTURE PARTNERS, 2153
INITIATIVE CAPITAL LIMITED, 2154
INOVIA CAPITAL, 2157
INSTARAGF, 2158
InstarAGF, 2165
INSTITUTIONAL LIMITED PARTNERS ASSOCIATION, 3266
INTEGRATED ASSET MANAGEMENT CORP, 2159
INVESTECO, 2161
IRONBRIDGE EQUITY PARTNERS, 2163
KENSINGTON CAPITAL PARTNERS, 2167
KILMER CAPITAL PARTNERS, 2169
KLASS CAPITAL, 2170
KNIGHT'S BRIDGE CAPITAL PARTNERS, 2171
LAURENCE CAPITAL, 2172
LUGE CAPITAL, 2179
LUMIRA CAPITAL, 2180
MANTELLA VENTURE PARTNERS, 2182
MANULIFE CAPITAL, 2183
MAPLE LEAF ANGELS, 2184
MARIGOLD CAPITAL, 2185
MARKET SQUARE EQUITY PARTNERS, 2186
MARS INVESTMENT ACCELERATOR FUND, 2187
MCCAIN CAPITAL PARTNERS, 2188
MCKENNA GALE CAPITAL, 2189
McLEAN WATSON CAPITAL, 2199
MCROCK CAPITAL, 2190
MERCATOR INVESTMENTS, 2192
MINK CAPITAL, 2193
MMV CAPITAL PARTNERS, 2196
MONTECO STRATEGIC CAPITAL, 2197
MOSAIC CAPITAL PARTNERS, 2198
NEXT CANADA, 2201
NIAGARA BUSINESS & INNOVATION FUND, 2203
NORTHLEAF CAPITAL PARTNERS, 2204
NOVACAP, 2206
OMERS PRIVATE EQUITY, 2207
ONCAP, 2208
ONEX PARTNERS, 2209
ONPOINT VENTURES, 2210
ONTARIO CAPITAL GROWTH CORPORATION, 2211
PANACHE VENTURES, 2212
PARKVIEW CAPITAL PARTNERS, 2215
PELOTON CAPITAL MANAGEMENT, 2217
PENFUND, 2219
PERSISTENCE CAPITAL PARTNERS, 2220
PINNACLE MERCHANT CAPITAL, 2222
PLAZA VENTURES, 2224
PORTAG3 VENTURES, 2225
PRIVEQ CAPITAL FUNDS, 2226
QUANTUM VALLEY INVESTMENTS, 2228

Geographic Index

RADAR CAPITAL, 2230
RBC CAPITAL MARKETS, 2231
REAL VENTURES, 2232
REGIMEN PARTNERS, 2235
RELAY VENTURES, 2236
RESOURCE CAPITAL FUNDS, 1548
RIPPLE VENTURES, 2241
ROADMAP CAPITAL INC., 2242
ROUND 13 CAPITAL, 2243
RUSSELL SQUARE PARTNERS, 2244
RYERSON FUTURES, 2245
SAIL VENTURE PARTNERS, 1603
SARONA ASSET MANAGEMENT, 2248
SCALEUP VENTURES, 2249
SCOTIABANK PRIVATE EQUITY, 2250
SEARCHLIGHT, 2252
SERRUYA PRIVATE EQUITY, 2254
SIGNAL HILL EQUITY PARTNERS, 2255
SKYPOINT CAPITAL, 2256
STANDUP VENTURES, 2257
SUMMERHILL VENTURE PARTNERS, 2259
SWANDER PACE CAPITAL, 1767
TECH CAPITAL PARTNERS, 2262
TERA CAPITAL CORPORATION, 2267
TORQUEST PARTNERS, 2272
TRELLIS CAPITAL CORPORATION, 2273
TRU MANAGEMENT, 1858
VERDEXUS, 2279
VERTU CAPITAL, 2281
VRG CAPITAL, 2282
WATERTON GLOBAL RESOURCE MANAGEMENT, 2283
WELLS FARGO CAPITAL FINANCE, 1970
WESLEY CLOVER, 2284
WESLEY CLOVER, 2284
WHITE SHEEP CORP, 2287
WHITECAP VENTURE PARTNERS, 2288
WHITEHORSE LIQUIDITY PARTNERS, 2289
WYNNCHURCH CAPITAL, 2009
XPV WATER PARTNERS, 2290
YALETOWN VENTURE PARTNERS, 2291

PE
ISLAND CAPITAL PARTNERS, 2164

QC
ACCES CAPITAL QUEBEC, 2029
AMORCHEM, 2035
AMPLITUDE, 2036
ARCTERN VENTURES, 2041
ARGO GLOBAL CAPITAL, 162
AVRIO CAPITAL, 2049
BDC CAPITAL, 2055
BMO CAPITAL MARKETS, 2063
BRIGHTSPARK VENTURES, 2066
CAISSE DE DEPOT ET PLACEMENT DU QUEBEC, 2069
CATO BIOVENTURES, 430
CLEARSPRING CAPITAL PARTNERS, 2082
CORDIANT CAPITAL, 2086
CREDIT MUTUEL EQUITY, 2088
CTI LIFE SCIENCES, 2092
CYCLE CAPITAL MANAGEMENT, 2093
DESJARDINS CAPITAL, 2095
ENERTECH CAPITAL, 676
ENTREPIA VENTURES, 682
ENTREPRENEUR CAPITAL, 2107
ESPRESSO CAPITAL, 2109
FIRST ASCENT VENTURES, 2118
FONDACTION, 2119
FONDS DE SOLIDARITE FTQ, 2120
INNOVOBOT, 2156
INOVIA CAPITAL, 2157
INTEGRATED ASSET MANAGEMENT CORP, 2159
KILMER CAPITAL PARTNERS, 2169
LGC CAPITAL, 2174
LONE STAR FUNDS, 1140
LUGE CAPITAL, 2179
LUMIRA CAPITAL, 2180

MACKINNON, BENNETT & CO., 2181
MEDTEQ+, 2191
MIRALTA, 2194
NORTHLEAF CAPITAL PARTNERS, 2204
NOVACAP, 2206
PANACHE VENTURES, 2212
PERSISTENCE CAPITAL PARTNERS, 2220
PROQUEST INVESTMENTS, 1490
REAL VENTURES, 2232
RHO CANADA VENTURES, 2239
RHO VENTURES, 1558
SANDERLING VENTURES, 1616
SOFINNOVA VENTURES, 1698
SPRING LANE CAPITAL, 1729
TACTICO, 2260
TANDEM EXPANSION FUND, 2261
TELESYSTEM, 2264
TERALYS CAPITAL, 2268
THERILIA, 2270
TVM LIFE SCIENCE MANAGEMENT, 2276
WHITE STAR CAPITAL, 1982
YALETOWN VENTURE PARTNERS, 2291

SK
FARM CREDIT CANADA, 2114
GOLDEN OPPORTUNITIES FUND, 2136
LEX CAPITAL MANAGEMENT, 2173
PFM CAPITAL, 2221
WESTCAP, 2285

Cayman Islands
BBH CAPITAL PARTNERS, 240
CEDRUS INVESTMENTS, 2581
YL VENTURES, 3246

Channel Islands
ACCENT EQUITY PARTNERS, 2325

Chile
AUSTRAL CAPITAL PARTNERS, 2455
AXON PARTNERS GROUP, 2469
COMPASS GROUP, 522
ECUS PRIVATE EQUITY Ecus Private Equity/AXA Capital Chile, 2689
LEXINGTON PARTNERS, 1112
RESOURCE CAPITAL FUNDS, 1548
UDD VENTURES, 3198

China
ADAMS STREET PARTNERS, LLC Adams Street Partners (Beijing) Co., Ltd., 57
ADVENT INTERNATIONAL CORPORATION, 62
ALANTRA, 77
ALOE PRIVATE EQUITY, 2372
ALPINVEST GmbH Alpinvest, 2377
ALPINVEST PARTNERS B.V., 2379
AMALFI CAPITAL MANAGEMENT, 2387
AMERICAN SECURITIES LLC, 110
ANT FINANCIAL, 2404
APAX PARTNERS, 135
ARES MANAGEMENT LLC, 159
ASIAN STRATEGIC INVESTMENTS CORPORATION, 2435
ASIAVEST PARTNERS, 2436
ASTER CAPITAL, 2439
ATOMICO, 2446
AUTHOSIS VENTURES, 2457
BAIDU VENTURES, 219
BAIN CAPITAL PRIVATE EQUITY, 220
BBH CAPITAL PARTNERS, 240
BEIJING HIGH TECHNOLOGY INVESTMENT COMPANY, 2499
BEIJING VENTURE CAPITAL COMPANY LIMITED, 2500
BLACKSTONE PRIVATE EQUITY GROUP, 277
BLUE POINT CAPITAL PARTNERS, 290
BLUERUN VENTURES, 296
BROADLINE PRINCIPAL CAPITAL, 2542
BROOKFIELD ASSET MANAGEMENT, 2067
CANTON VENTURE CAPITAL COMPANY LIMITED, 2557

Geographic Index

CAPITAL TODAY, 2560
CARLYLE GROUP, 413
CATHAYA CAPITAL, 2576
CDH INVESTMENTS, 2579
CEYUAN, 2584
CHENGWEI VENTURES, 2590
CHINA ISRAEL VALUE CAPITAL, 2593
CHINA VEST LIMITED, 2596
CHINA WALDEN MANAGEMENT LIMITED Walden Group, 2597
CHINAVEST, 473
CID GROUP, 2603
CISCO INVESTMENTS, 483
D.E. SHAW & CO. LP, 579
DCM, 596
DEERFIELD MANAGEMENT, 601
DJF DRAGONFUND CHINA, 2667
DUTCHESS CAPITAL, 638
E.VENTURES, 641
EPLANET CAPITAL, 690
FIDELITY GROWTH PARTNERS ASIA, 2733
FORTRESS INVESTMENT GROUP LLC, 767
FUEL CAPITAL, 2761
GCI CAPITAL, 2128
GENERAL ATLANTIC PARTNERS, 815, 2771
GGV CAPITAL, 823
GOBI PARTNERS, 2790
GREENHILL SAVP, 864
GSR VENTURES, 2801
GUANGDONG TECHNOLOGY VENTURE CAPITAL COMPANY, 2802
H&Q ASIA PACIFIC, 892
HARBOURVEST PARTNERS LLC, 909
IDG CAPITAL PARTNERS, 2847
IDG TECHNOLOGY VENTURE INVESTMENT, 2848
IDG-ACCEL, 2850
IDINVEST PARTNERS, 2851
INFOCOMM INVESTMENTS, 2870
JAVELIN INVESTMENTS, 2908
KLEINER PERKINS, 1075
KOHLBERG KRAVIS ROBERTS & COMPANY, 1082
LEGEND CAPITAL, 2936
LIGHTSPEED VENTURE PARTNERS, 1121
MAKERS FUND, 2953
MATRIX PARTNERS, 1181
MITSUI GLOBAL INVESTMENT, 1241
MOUSSE PARTNERS, 1263
NEWMARGIN VENTURE CAPITAL, 2998
NGP CAPITAL, 1327
NORTHERN LIGHT VENTURE CAPITAL, 1340
OAKTREE CAPITAL MANAGEMENT LLC, 1362
ONE EQUITY PARTNERS, 1376
ORBIMED HEALTHCARE FUND MANAGEMENT, 1382
PFINGSTEN PARTNERS LLC, 1435
QIMING VENTURE PARTNERS Qiming Suzhou Office, 3066
QUALCOMM VENTURES, 1509
QUARK VENTURE, 2229
REDPOINT VENTURES, 1534
RICHINA CAPITAL PARTNERS LIMITED, 3082
RIVERSIDE COMPANY, 1572
SAIF PARTNERS, 3093
SAMSUNG VENTURE INVESTMENT CORPORATION, 3098
SB CHINA VENTURE CAPITAL, 3100
SCULPTOR CAPITAL MANAGEMENT Sculptor (Shanghai) Overseas Investment Fund Mgmt Co.,Ltd., 1635
SEQUOIA CAPITAL, 1654
SHANGHAI INFORMATION INVESTMENT INCORPORATED, 3114
SIGULER GUFF & COMPANY, 1679
SINGTEL INNOV8, 3121
STATE STREET GLOBAL ADVISORS, 3140
STEAMBOAT VENTURES, 3142
SUMMIT BRIDGE CAPITAL, 3147
SUN CAPITAL PARTNERS, 1753
SUNEVISION HOLDINGS LIMITED, 3148
TAISHAN CAPITAL CORPORATION, 3156
TALLWOOD VENTURE CAPITAL, 1779
TPG CAPITAL, 1835
TRANSLINK CAPITAL, 1838
TSING CAPITAL, 3194
VANTAGEPOINT CAPITAL PARTNERS, 1906
VENTECH, 3208
VENTURE TECH ALLIANCE, 1922
VINCERA CAPITAL, 3218
VIVO CAPITAL, 1941
WALDEN INTERNATIONAL, 1951
WALL STREET VENTURE CAPITAL, 1953
WARBURG PINCUS LLC, 1956
WESTSUMMIT CAPITAL, 3235
WI HARPER GROUP, 1983
WILSHIRE PRIVATE MARKETS, 1989
ZHENFUND, 3251

Colombia
ACON INVESTMENTS, 46
ACUMEN, 55
ADVENT INTERNATIONAL CORPORATION, 62
COMPASS GROUP, 522
DARBY OVERSEAS INVESTMENTS LTD, 584
HARBOURVEST PARTNERS LLC, 909
SOCIALATOM VENTURES, 3125

Costa Rica
ROOT CAPITAL, 1582

Czech Republic
3TS CAPITAL PARTNERS, 2309
ARX, 2429
CZECH VENTURE PARTNERS SRO K+ Venture Partners B.V., 2648
RIVERSIDE COMPANY, 1572
VENTURE INVESTORS, 3210

Denmark
ATP PRIVATE EQUITY PARTNERS, 2447
BLACKSTONE PRIVATE EQUITY GROUP, 277
DANSK KAPITALANLAEG A/S, 2651
INDUSTRIALIZATION FUND FOR DEVELOPING COUNTRIE, 2865
INVESTMENT FUND FOR CENTRAL & EASTERN EUROPE, 2889
NORTHZONE, 3013
NOVO A/S, 3015
OYSTER INVEST, 3022
SUNSTONE CAPITAL, 3149
VAEKSTFONDEN, 3203

Dubai
ARES MANAGEMENT LLC, 159

England
AEA INVESTORS, 64
AON MERGERS & ACQUISITIONS GROUP, 2412
FORWARD PARTNERS, 2752
LONE STAR FUNDS, 1140
NEW RHEIN HEALTHCARE INVESTORS, 1302
RIVERSTONE, 1573
SAMSUNG VENTURE INVESTMENT CORPORATION, 3098
VALIA, 1900
WAFRA INC, 1950

Estonia
AMBIENT SOUND INVESTMENTS, 2390
BALTCAP MANAGEMENT LTD, 2480

Finland
ABOA VENTURE MANAGEMENT OY, 2318
AURA CAPITAL OY Auratum Group, 2451
BIO FUND MANAGEMENT OY, 2512
BUTZOW NORDIA ADVOCATES LTD, 2552
CAPMAN CAPITAL MANAGEMENT OY, 2562
CLEANTECH INVEST, 2612
CONOR VENTURE PARTNERS OY, 2630
EQVITEC PARTNERS OY, 2716
FENNO MANAGEMENT OY, 2730
FINNISH INDUSTRY INVESTMENT LIMITED, 2740
FINNVERA PLC, 2741
GORILLA VENTURES, 2793
HELMET CAPITAL FUND MANAGEMENT OY, 2820

Geographic Index

INNOFINANCE OY, 2873
LEONIA MB GROUP/MB FUNDS, 2937
MIDINVEST LIMITED, 2966
NEOMARKKA OYJ Neomarkka, 2990
NEXIT VENTURES OY, 2999
NOKIA GROWTH PARTNERS, 1330
NORDIC MEZZANINE LIMITED, 3009
THOMPROPERTIES OY, 3175
VERSOVENTURES, 3213

France

21 PARTNERS, 2293
360 CAPITAL PARTNERS 360 Capital Management SA, 2296
3I GESTION SA 3i Group, 2302
3T CAPITAL, 2308
3i GROUP PLC, 2311
ABM AMRO CAPITAL FRANCE ABN AMRO Group, 2317
ACTIVA CAPITAL, 2338
ACTOMEZZ Groupama Private Equity SA, 2340
ADVENT INTERNATIONAL CORPORATION, 62
AGF PRIVATE EQUITY Allianz Group, 2354
ALANTRA, 77
ALIVE IDEAS, 2365
ALLIANCE ENTREPRENDRE, 2368
ALOE PRIVATE EQUITY, 2372
ALPHA BETEILIGUNGSBERATUNG GmbH, 2375
ALTO INVEST, 2383
ALVEN CAPITAL, 2385
ANVAR, 2408
ARCIS GROUP, 2421
ARES MANAGEMENT LLC, 159
ASTER CAPITAL, 2439
ATRIA CAPITAL PARTENAIRES, 2448
AURIGA PARTNERS, 2453
AVENIR TOURISME, 2459
AXA INVESTMENT MANAGERS PRIVATE EQUITY EUROPE, 2466
BANEXI VENTURES PARTNERS, 2481
BARCLAYS PRIVATE EQUITY FRANCE, 2485
BAYSIDE CAPITAL H.I.G. European Capital Partners SAS, 239
BLACKFIN CAPITAL PARTNERS, 2521
BLACKSTONE PRIVATE EQUITY GROUP, 277
BUTLER CAPITAL PARTNERS FRANCE, 2551
CARLYLE GROUP, 413
CIC FINANCE CIC Group, 2601
CICLAD, 2602
CITA GESTION, 2607
COFINEP, 2620
COMPAGNIE FINANCIERE E DE ROTHSCHILD BANQUE, 2625
CREDIT MUTUEL EQUITY, 2088
DEMETER PARTNERS, 2656
DIRIGEANTS ET INVESTISSEURS, 2665
ELAIA PARTNERS, 2693
EURAZEO, 2719
EUROMEZZANINE CONSEIL, 2721
FINADVANCE, 2735
FINANCIERE DE BRIENNE FCPR, 2738
FONDINVEST CAPITAL, 2747
GALILEO II, 2765
HARBERT MANAGEMENT CORPORATION, 904
IDINVEST PARTNERS, 2851
IFE CONSEIL (INTERMEDIATE FINANCE EUROPE), 2852
ILE-DE-FRANCE, 2855
INNOVACOM SA, 2875
INNOVATION CAPITAL, 2876
INVUS GROUP, 1018
IPBM Group IDI, 2893
IRDI MIDI-PYRENEES, 2896
IRIS CAPITAL, 2897
ISOURCE GESTION, 2899
KOHLBERG KRAVIS ROBERTS & COMPANY, 1082
L CATTERTON PARTNERS, 1088
LBO FRANCE, 2933
LMBO FINANCE, 2945
LONE STAR FUNDS, 1140
MARCEAU INVESTISSEMENTS, 2955
NEXT WORLD CAPITAL, 1319
OAKTREE CAPITAL MANAGEMENT LLC, 1362
OMNES CAPITAL, 3020
PAI MANAGEMENT, 3026
PARTECH INTERNATIONAL, 1416
SAINT-GOBAIN NOVA EXTERNAL VENTURING, 3094
SANOFI-GENZYME BIOVENTURES, 1618
SEVENTURE PARTNERS, 3113
THOMSON-CSF VENTURES, 3176
VENTECH, 3208
WESLEY CLOVER, 2284
WHITE STAR CAPITAL, 1982
XANGE PRIVATE EQUITY, 3239

Georgia

SALFORD CAPITAL PARTNERS, 3095

Germany

3I DEUTSCHLAND GESELLSCHAFT FUR 3i Group, 2299
3I GERMANY GmbH 3i Group, 2301
3I TEUPSCHLAND GmbH 3i Group, 2305
3i GROUP PLC, 2311
ACCERA AG, 2327
ADAMS STREET PARTNERS, LLC Adams Street (Europe) GmbH, 57
ADASTRA, 2343
ADVENT INTERNATIONAL CORPORATION, 62
AEA INVESTORS, 64
ALANTRA, 77
ALLIANZ CAPITAL PARTNERS GmbH, 2370
AMMER PARTNERS, 2393
AON JAUCH & HUBENER GmbH Aon Corporation, 2411
APAX PARTNERS, 135
APOLLO GLOBAL MANAGEMENT, 140
ARES MANAGEMENT LLC, 159
ASTUTIA VENTURES, 2441
AURELIA PRIVATE EQUITY, 2452
B-TO-V PARTNERS, 2475
BAIN CAPITAL PRIVATE EQUITY, 220
BASF VENTURE CAPITAL, 2492
BAY BG BAVARIAN VENTURE CAPITAL CORP, 2494
BAYSIDE CAPITAL H.I.G. European Capital Partners GmbH, 239
BERENBERG PRIVATE CAPITAL, 2502
BERLIN TECHNOLOGIE, 2503
BM-T BETEILIGUNGS MANAGEMENT THURINGEN GmbH, 2527
BMP AKTIENGESELLSCHAFT BMP Venture Capital, 2528
BOEHRINGER INGELHEIM VENTURE FUND, 2530
BONVENTURE, 2531
BRIDGEPOINT CAPITAL GmbH, 2537
CAPITON AG, 2561
CARLYLE GROUP, 413
CATAGONIA CAPITAL, 2569
CINCO CAPITAL, 2604
CIPIO PARTNERS, 2606
CLIFFORD CHANCE PUNDER, 2614
CLOSE BROTHERS EQUITY MARKETS Close Brothers Group, 2616
COMMERZ BETEILIGUNGSGESELLSCHAFT, 2624
CREATHOR VENTURE, 2638
CREDIT MUTUEL EQUITY, 2088
DAIMLERCHRYSLER VENTURE GmbH DaimlerChrysler AG, 2650
DB CAPITAL PARTNERS (ASIA), 2652
DEMETER PARTNERS, 2656
DEUTSCHE ASSET & WEALTH MANAGEMENT, 2658
DEUTSCHE BETEILIGUNGS AG, 2660
DR NEUHAUS TECHNO NORD GmbH, 2673
DVC DEUTSCHE VENTURE CAPITAL, 2679
E.VENTURES, 641
EARLYBIRD, 2682
ECAPITAL ENTREPRENEURIAL PARTNERS AG, 2686
ECONA AG, 2688
EQUINET VENTURE PARTNERS AG, 2713
EVERCORE CAPITAL PARTNERS, 699
FIELDSTONE PRIVATE CAPITAL GROUP, 726
FORBION CAPITAL PARTNERS, 2748
FORTRESS INVESTMENT GROUP LLC, 767
GENERAL ATLANTIC PARTNERS, 815
GENES GMBH VENTURE SERVICES, 2774
GLOBAL LIFE SCIENCE VENTURES GmbH, 2785
GRAZIA EQUITY, 2797
GREENHILL SAVP, 864

HALDER BETEILIGUNGSBERATUNG GmbH, 2805
HALDER HOLDINGS BV, 2806
HANNOVER FINANZ GmbH, 2810
HASSO PLATTNER VENTURES, 2813
HIGH-TECH GRUENDERFONDS, 2824
HOLTZBRINCK VENTURES, 2829
HV HOLTZBRINCK VENTURES, 2838
IBB BETEILIGUNGSGESELLSCHAFT MBH, 2841
KFW-BANKENGRUPPE, 2919
KIZOO TECHNOLOGY CAPITAL, 2921
KPS CAPITAL PARTNERS, 1085
LBBW VENTURE CAPITAL, 2932
LONE STAR FUNDS, 1140
NEUHAUS PARTNERS, 2994
NGN CAPITAL, 1325
OAKTREE CAPITAL MANAGEMENT LLC, 1362
ONE EQUITY PARTNERS, 1376
PARTECH INTERNATIONAL, 1416
PERMIRA, 3033
PERSEUS FUNDS, 1434
PLEXUS VENTURES, 1452
POINT NINE CAPITAL, 3044
POLYTECHNOS VENTURE PARTNERS GmbH, 3046
PROJECT A VENTURE GmBH & CO. KG, 3056
QUADRAN GESTION Deutsche Beteiligungs AG, 3067
RIVERSIDE COMPANY, 1572
S-REFIT GmbH & COMPANY KG, 3090
SAMSUNG NEXT, 1611
SIEMENS VENTURE CAPITAL, 3118
SIGNATURE CAPITAL LLC, 3120
SMAC PARTNERS, 3123
SONY EUROPE, 3129
STAR VENTURES, 3137
STEELHOUSE VENTURES, 3143
T-VENTURE HOLDINGS GmbH Deutsche Telecom, 3155
TARGET PARTNERS, 3161
TENGELMANN VENTURES, 3170
TFG CAPITAL AG, 3172
TRIANGLE VENTURE CAPITAL GROUP, 3188
TRIGENTA CAPITAL GmbH, 3189
TRIGINITA CAPITAL, 3190
TVM CAPITAL, 3196
UCA UNTERNEHMER CONSULT AG, 3197
VENISTA VENTURES, 3207
VERDEXUS, 2279
VON BRAUN & SCHREIBER PRIVATE EQUITY PARTNERS, 3227
WELLINGTON PARTNERS VENTURE CAPITAL GmbH, 3233
WESTTECH VENTURES, 3236
WHEB GROUP, 3237
XANGE PRIVATE EQUITY, 3239

Ghana
MANSA CAPITAL, 1164

Greece
ALANTRA, 77
ALPHA BANK, 2374
GLOBAL FINANCE, 2784

Hong Kong
ANGELO, GORDON & CO., 127
ANGLO CHINESE INVESTMENT COMPANY LIMITED, 2402
APOLLO GLOBAL MANAGEMENT, 140
AQUITAINE INVESTMENT ADVISORS LIMITED, 2418
ARGO GLOBAL CAPITAL, 162
ASIAN INFRASTRUCTURE FUND ADVISERS LIMITED AIF Capital, 2434
BARING PRIVATE EQUITY PARTNERS ASIA, 2488
BASF VENTURE CAPITAL, 2492
BIGFOOT VENTURES, 2511
BLACKSTONE PRIVATE EQUITY GROUP, 277
BOCI DIRECT INVESTMENT MANAGEMENT LIMITED Bank of China, 2529
CARLYLE ASIA INVESTMENT ADVISORS LIMITED Carlyle Group, 2565
CHASE CAPITAL PARTNERS, 2588
CHEUNG KONG INFRASTRUCTURE HOLDINGS LIMITED, 2591
CHINA MERCHANTS CHINA INVESTMENT MANAGEMENT, 2594, 2595
CHINAVEST, 473
CLEARWATER CAPITAL PARTNERS, 504
COATUE MANAGEMENT, 509
CORE PACIFIC - YAMAICHI CAPITAL LIMITED Core Pacific Securities Company Ltd, 2633
CROSBY ASSET MANAGEMENT, 2640
CROSBY CAPITAL LIMITED, 2641
CVC ASIA PACIFIC LIMITED CVC Capital Partners, 2643
D.E. SHAW & CO. LP, 579
DARBY OVERSEAS INVESTMENTS LTD, 584
DIGITAL SKY TECHNOLOGIES, 2663
ELECTRA PARTNERS ASIA LIMITED SFC of Hong Kong, 2694
EVERCORE CAPITAL PARTNERS, 699
EXCELSIOR CAPITAL ASIA, 2727
FUEL CAPITAL, 2761
GE CAPITAL, 808
GENERAL ATLANTIC PARTNERS, 815
GENERAL ENTERPRISE MANAGEMENT SERVICES, 2772
GLOBAL VENTURES MANAGEMENT LIMITED, 2788
GSR VENTURES Golden Sand River (Hong Kong) Limited, 2801
H&Q ASIA PACIFIC, 892
HAMON INVESTMENT GROUP, 2809
HARBOURVEST PARTNERS LLC, 909
HELIANT VENTURES, 2817
HONGKONG LAND INFRASTRUCTURE LIMITED, 2830
HORIZONS VENTURES, 2831
IBRIDGE CAPITAL CORPORATION, 2843
IBUSINESS CORPORATION, 2844
IDG CAPITAL PARTNERS, 2847
INTER-ASIA VENTURE MANAGEMENT LIMITED, 2881
INVUS GROUP, 1018
IT VENTURES LIMITED Digital Heritage Publishing Ltd., 2901
KOHLBERG KRAVIS ROBERTS & COMPANY, 1082
LEXINGTON PARTNERS, 1112
LIGHTHOUSE PARTNERS, 1120
LOMBARD INVESTMENTS, 1139
LOMBARD/APIC (HK) LIMITED, 2946
LONE STAR FUNDS, 1140
MATRIX PARTNERS, 1181
MERRILL LYNCH (ASIA PACIFIC) LIMITED Merrill Lynch Group, 2964
NEW WORLD INFRASTRUCTURE LIMITED, 2996
NORTHERN LIGHT VENTURE CAPITAL, 1340
PAMA GROUP, 3027
PANTHEON VENTURES (US) LP, 1411
POMONA CAPITAL, 1462
PROVIDENCE EQUITY PARTNERS, 1496
PT BNI NOMURA JAFCO MANAJEMEN VENTURA, 3062
QIMING VENTURE PARTNERS Qiming Development HK Limited, 3066
REGENT PACIFIC PRIVATE EQUITY LIMITED Regent Pacific Group Ltd., 3075
ROAD KING INFRASTRUCTURE LIMITED, 3084
ROTH CAPITAL PARTNERS, 1588
SAIF PARTNERS, 3093
SHAW KWEI AND PARTNERS, 3116
SHENZHEN INTERNATIONAL HOLDINGS LIMITED, 3117
SILVER LAKE, 1683
SUNEVISION HOLDINGS LIMITED, 3148
TA ASSOCIATES, 1776
TELECOM VENTURE GROUP LIMITED, 3168
TSING CAPITAL, 3194
VALUE PARTNERS LIMITED, 3204
WARBURG PINCUS LLC, 1956
WHITE STAR CAPITAL, 1982

Hungary
ACME LABS, 2333
CORVINUS NEMZETKOZI BEFEKTETESI RT Corvinus International Investment Ltd., 2634
COVENT INDUSTRIAL CAPITAL INVESTMENT COMPANY, 2635
DARBY OVERSEAS INVESTMENTS LTD, 584
EUROVENTURES CAPITAL, 2725

Iceland
LANDSBANKI VENTURES, 2929
THROUNARFELAG ISLANDS PLC, 3177

Geographic Index

India

3i GROUP PLC, 2311
AAVISHKAAR, 2313
ACCEL, 28
ACUMEN, 55
ADVENT INTERNATIONAL CORPORATION, 62
ALOE PRIVATE EQUITY, 2372
ANZ GRINDLAYS 31 INVESTMENT SERVICES LIMITED, 2409
APAX PARTNERS, 135
APIDC-VENTURE CAPITAL LIMITED, 2416
APOLLO GLOBAL MANAGEMENT, 140
ARTIMAN VENTURES, 174
AVIGO CAPITAL, 2460
BAIN CAPITAL PRIVATE EQUITY, 220
BARING PRIVATE EQUITY PARTNERS INDIA, 2490
BESSEMER VENTURE PARTNERS, 260
BLACKSTONE PRIVATE EQUITY GROUP, 277
BLUESHIFT INTERNET VENTURES Blueshift, 2525
BLUME VENTURES, 2526
BROOKFIELD ASSET MANAGEMENT, 2067
CAPITAL 18, 2558
CARLYLE GROUP, 413
CISCO INVESTMENTS, 483
D.E. SHAW & CO. LP, 579
DARBY OVERSEAS INVESTMENTS LTD, 584
DELTA PARTNERS Delta Partners FZ-LLC, 2654
FIELDSTONE PRIVATE CAPITAL GROUP, 726
FRANKLIN TEMPLETON INVESTMENT, 2756
GE ASIA PACIFIC CAPITAL TECHNOLOGY FUND, 2767
GE CAPITAL, 808
GE CAPITAL SERVICES INDIA LIMITED, 2768
GENERAL ATLANTIC PARTNERS, 815
GLOBAL ENVIRONMENT FUND, 834
GLOBAL TECHNOLOGY VENTURES, 2787
GRAY GHOST VENTURES, 855
GUGGENHEIM PARTNERS, 885
GUJARAT STATE FERTILIZERS COMPANY LIMITED, 2804
HANSUTTAM FINANCE LIMITED, 2811
HELION VENTURE PARTNERS, LLC Helion Advisors Private Limited, 2818
ICF VENTURES PVT LTD, 2846
INDASIA FUND ADVISORS PVT LTD, 2859
INDIAN DIRECT EQUITY ADVISORS PVT LTD, 2861
INDUSTRIAL DEVELOPMENT BANK OF INDIA, 2864
INFOCOMM INVESTMENTS, 2870
INVENTUS, 1013
IXORA VENTURES, 2904
KOHLBERG KRAVIS ROBERTS & COMPANY, 1082
LAUNCHPAD VENTURES, 2931
LEAD ANGELS, 2934
LIGHTSPEED VENTURE PARTNERS, 1121
MATRIX PARTNERS, 1181
NAYA VENTURES, 1285
NEXUS VENTURE PARTNERS, 3001
NORWEST VENTURE PARTNERS, 1346
OJAS VENTURE PARTNERS, 3019
OMIDYAR NETWORK, 1374
ORBIMED HEALTHCARE FUND MANAGEMENT, 1382
PFINGSTEN PARTNERS LLC, 1435
PLUS VENTURES, 3041
PROVIDENCE EQUITY PARTNERS, 1496
QUALCOMM VENTURES, 1509
SAIF PARTNERS, 3093
SAMSUNG VENTURE INVESTMENT CORPORATION, 3098
SEEDFUND, 3109
SEQUOIA CAPITAL Sequoia Capital India Advisors Pvt. Ltd., 1654
SIGULER GUFF & COMPANY, 1679
SRIJAN CAPITAL, 3133
TA ASSOCIATES, 1776
THE MORPHEUS, 3174
TPG CAPITAL, 1835
UNILAZER VENTURES, 3199
USHA MARTIN VENTURES LIMITED, 3202
VENTUREAST, 3211
WALDEN INTERNATIONAL, 1951
WARBURG PINCUS LLC, 1956
ZEPHYR MANAGEMENT LP, 2018

Indonesia

CARLYLE GROUP, 413
PT BHAKTI INVESTAMA TBK, 3061

Ireland

ACT VENTURE CAPITAL LIMITED, 2336
AIB SEED CAPITAL FUND Dublin Business Innovation Centre, 2355
ALANTRA, 77
ATLANTIC BRIDGE, 2443
BBH CAPITAL PARTNERS, 240
BLOOM EQUITY, 2522
CAMPUS COMPANIES VENTURE CAPITAL FUND, 2554
CARLYLE GROUP, 413
CLARENDON FUND MANAGERS, 2610
DRAPER ESPRIT, 2674
EIRCOM ENTERPRISE FUND LIMITED, 2692
ENTERPRISE EQUITY IRELAND LIMITED, 2705
FRONTLINE VENTURES, 2759
GUGGENHEIM PARTNERS, 885
INTELLECTUAL VENTURES, 1005
KERNEL CAPITAL, 2918
LIGHTSTONE VENTURES, 1122
SHANNON COMMERCIAL PROPERTIES, 3115
SIGNATURE CAPITAL LLC, 3120
TRINITY VENTURE CAPITAL TVC Holdings plc, 3191

Israel

ACCELMED, 2324
AFTERDOX, 2352
AGATE MEDICAL INVESTMENTS, 2353
AMANET TECHNOLOGIES LIMITED, 2389
APAX PARTNERS, 135
AQUAGRO FUND, 2417
ASTER CAPITAL, 2439
AURUM VENTURES MKI, 2454
AVIV VENTURE CAPITAL, 2462
BATTERY VENTURES, 235
BLUMBERG CAPITAL, 301
BRIDGE INVESTMENT FUND, 337
BRM SEED, 2541
CARMEL VENTURES, 2566
CATALYST FUND LP, 2571
CEDAR (ISRAEL) FINANCIAL ADVISORS LIMITED Cedar Fund, 2580
CHALLENGE FUNDS - ETGAR LP, 2585
CHINA ISRAEL VALUE CAPITAL, 2593
CISCO INVESTMENTS, 483
CLAL ELECTRONICS INDUSTRIES LIMITED, 2609
CONCORD VENTURES, 2628
CYBERSTARTS, 2647
DELTA VENTURES LIMITED, 2655
DISCOUNT INVESTMENT CORPORATION LIMITED, 2666
EUROFUND LP, 2720
EVERGREEN VENTURE PARTNERS, 2726
FIRST ISRAEL MEZZANINE INVESTORS LIMITED, 2745
FORMULA VENTURES LIMITED Formula Group, 2750
FORUM TECHNOLOGIES VENTURE CAPITAL COMPANY Forum Group, 2751
GAON ASSET MANAGEMENT, 2766
GE CAPITAL, 808
GEMINI ISRAEL VENTURE FUNDS LIMITED, 2770
GENESIS PARTNERS, 2775
GIZA VENTURE CAPITAL, 2782
ICAN ISRAEL-CANNABIS.COM, 2845
INITIAL CAPITAL, 2872
INNOVATION ENDEAVORS, 996
ISRAEL CLEANTECH VENTURES, 2900
JC TECHNOLOGIES LTD, 2909
JERUSALEM VENTURE PARTNERS, 2910
JUMPSEED VENTURES, 2912
KAEDAN INVESTMENTS, 2914
KARDAN LTD, 2916
LIGHTSPEED VENTURE PARTNERS, 1121
LIONBIRD, 2943
LOOL VENTURES, 2947
MAGMA VENTURE PARTNERS, 2952
MARATHON VENTURE CAPITAL FUND LIMITED, 2954

Geographic Index

MATI-HIGH-TECH, 2956
MITSUI GLOBAL INVESTMENT, 1241
MMT MILLENNIUM MATERIALS TECHNOLOGIES FUND LP, 2973
NIELSEN INNOVATE FUND, 3003
NORWEST VENTURE PARTNERS, 1346
ORBIMED HEALTHCARE FUND MANAGEMENT, 1382
PITANGO VENTURE CAPITAL, 3039
POND VENTURES, 3047
PREVIZ VENTURES, 3050
PROSEED, 3059
QUALCOMM VENTURES, 1509
RAFAEL DEVELOPMENT CORPORATION (RDC) LIMITED, 3072
SAMSUNG NEXT, 1611
SAMSUNG VENTURE INVESTMENT CORPORATION, 3098
SBRC INVESTMENT CONSULTATION LIMITED, 3101
SEQUOIA CAPITAL, 1654
SMART BUSINESS CONSULTING, 3124
SONY INNOVATION FUND, 1703
STAGEONE VENTURES, 3136
STAR VENTURES, 3137
TAMAR TECHNOLOGY VENTURES LIMITED, 3158
TAMIR FISHMAN VENTURES, 3159
TELEFONICA VENTURES, 3169
TEUZA MANAGEMENT & DEVELOPMENT LTD, 3171
TRIVENTURES, 3192
VERITAS VENTURE PARTNERS, 3212
VERIZON VENTURES, 1926
VERTEX VENTURE CAPITAL, 3214
VINTAGE INVESTMENT PARTNERS, 3219
VIOLA FINTECH, 3220
VIOLA VENTURES, 3221
WALDEN INTERNATIONAL, 1951
WALDEN ISRAEL VENTURE CAPITAL, 3231
XENIA VENTURE CAPITAL, 3240
XT INVESTMENTS, 3241
YISSUM TECHNOLOGY TRANSFER, 3245
YL VENTURES, 3246
YLR CAPITAL MARKETS LTD, 3247
YVC - YOZMA MANAGEMENT & INVESTMENTS LIMITED, 3249

Isreal
HARBOURVEST PARTNERS LLC, 909
NFX, 1323

Italy
21 PARTNERS, 2293
360 CAPITAL PARTNERS, 2296
ALANTRA, 77
ALICE VENTURES SRL, 2364
AMBIENTA ENVIRONMENTAL ASSETS, 2391
ANGELAB VENTURES, 2401
ANGELO, GORDON & CO., 127
ANNAPURNA VENTURES, 2403
ARGOS SODITIC SPAIN, 2424
BAYSIDE CAPITAL Ih.I.G. European Capital Partners Italy S.r.I., 239
BERRIER CAPITAL, 2504
CARLYLE GROUP, 413
DPIXEL, 2672
FINLOMBARDA SpA, 2739
FRIULIA SpA, 2758
GE CAPITAL, 808
INDUSTRIO VENTURES, 2868
INNOGEST CAPITAL, 2874
PERMIRA, 3033
PLEXUS VENTURES, 1452
PRINCIPIA SGR, 3052
PRIVATE EQUITY PARTNERS SPA, 3053
SYNERGO SGR, 3154

Japan
ADAMS STREET PARTNERS, LLC Adams Street Partners Japan G.K., 57
ADVANTAGE PARTNERS, 2347
ANGELO, GORDON & CO., 127
APAX GLOBIS PARTNERS & COMPANY Globis Capital Partners/Apax, 2414
ASAHI BANK INVESTMENT COMPANY LIMITED, 2430
ASAHI LIFE CAPITAL COMPANY LIMITED, 2431

ATOMICO, 2446
AZCA, 214
B DASH VENTURES, 2474
BAIN CAPITAL PRIVATE EQUITY, 220
BASF VENTURE CAPITAL, 2492
BBH CAPITAL PARTNERS, 240
BLACKSTONE PRIVATE EQUITY GROUP, 277
CARLYLE GROUP, 413
CYBERAGENT VENTURES, 2646
DCM, 596
E.VENTURES, 641
EM WARBURG, PINCUS & COMPANY JAPAN, 2698
ENTREPIA VENTURES, 682
EPIDAREX CAPITAL, 689
FORTRESS INVESTMENT GROUP LLC, 767
FUTURE VENTURE CAPITAL COMPANY LIMITED, 2763
GE CAPITAL, 808
GLOBAL CATALYST PARTNERS, 833
GOGIN CAPITAL COMPANY LIMITED, 2791
GREE VENTURES, 2798
GREENHILL SAVP, 864
GUGGENHEIM PARTNERS, 885
HARBOURVEST PARTNERS LLC, 909
HIKARI TSUSHIN CAPITAL, 2826
IGNITE JAPAN KK Ignite Group, 2854
INFINITY VENTURE PARTNERS, 2869
J-SEED VENTURES INCORPORATED, 2905
JAFCO COMPANY LIMITED JAPAN, 2906
JAPAN ASIA INVESTMENT COMPANY LIMITED, 2907
JTP CORPORATION, 2911
KOHLBERG KRAVIS ROBERTS & COMPANY, 1082
KUBOTA CORPORATION, 2927
LIGHTHOUSE PARTNERS, 1120
LONE STAR FUNDS, 1140
MITSUBISHI UFJ CAPITAL, 2970
MITSUI GLOBAL INVESTMENT, 1241
MITSUI SUMITOMO INSURANCE VENTURE CAPITAL CO, 2971
MOBILE INTERNET CAPITAL, 2974
MVC CORPORATION, 2980
NEOTENY COMPANY LIMITED, 2991
NIF VENTURES COMPANY LIMITED, 3004
NIPPON TECHNOLOGY VENTURE PARTNERS LIMITED, 3005
NISSAY CAPITAL, 3006
OAKTREE CAPITAL MANAGEMENT LLC, 1362
ONO PHARMACEUTICALS COMPANY LIMITED, 3021
PERMIRA, 3033
PINEHURST ADVISORS, 3038
PLEXUS VENTURES, 1452
RIVERSIDE COMPANY, 1572
SAMSUNG VENTURE INVESTMENT CORPORATION, 3098
SONY INNOVATION FUND, 1703
SUNBRIDGE PARTNERS, 1755
TEKINVEST KK, 3166
TEL VENTURE CAPITAL, 1791
TOKIO MARINE CAPITAL COMPANY LIMITED, 3182
TRANS COSMOS INCORPORATED, 3185
TRANSLINK CAPITAL, 1838
UNISON CAPITAL PARTNERS LP, 3201
VCN GROUP INCORPORATED, 3205
WHITE STAR CAPITAL, 1982
YASUDA AND PAMA LIMITED, 3242
YASUDA ENTERPRISE DEVELOPMENT COMPANY, 3243

Kenya
ACUMEN, 55
ROOT CAPITAL, 1582
TLCOM CAPITAL, 3179

Korea
ACE VENTURE CAPITAL LIMITED, 2330
ALTOS VENTURES, 100
ANGELO, GORDON & CO., 127
BLACKSTONE PRIVATE EQUITY GROUP, 277
BLUERUN VENTURES, 296
CARLYLE GROUP, 413
DARBY OVERSEAS INVESTMENTS LTD, 584
H&Q ASIA PACIFIC, 892

1113

Geographic Index

I-PACIFIC PARTNERS, 2840
KOHLBERG KRAVIS ROBERTS & COMPANY, 1082
KOREA FIRST VENTURE CAPITAL CORPORATION, 2924
NHN INVESTMENT, 3002
OAKTREE CAPITAL MANAGEMENT LLC, 1362
QUALCOMM VENTURES, 1509
SAMSUNG NEXT, 1611
SAMSUNG VENTURE INVESTMENT CORPORATION Samsung Electronics, 3098
SOFTBANK VENTURES KOREA, 3127
TONG YANG VENTURE CAPITAL CORPORATION Tong Yang Cement Corporation, 3183
TPG CAPITAL, 1835
TRANSLINK CAPITAL, 1838

Kuwait
WAFRA INC, 1950

Lebanon
BERYTECH FUND, 2506
DAHER CAPITAL, 2649

Lithuania
PRACTICA CAPITAL, 3049

Luxembourg
APOLLO GLOBAL MANAGEMENT, 140
ARCLIGHT CAPITAL PARTNERS, 156
ARES MANAGEMENT LLC, 159
BBH CAPITAL PARTNERS, 240
CARLYLE GROUP, 413
CASTLELAKE, 424
DOTCORP PRIVATE EQUITY FUND, 2669
EUROPEAN INVESTMENT FUND, 2724
KBL FOUNDER SA, 2917
L CATTERTON PARTNERS, 1088
MONITOR CLIPPER PARTNERS, 1248
OAKTREE CAPITAL MANAGEMENT LLC, 1362
RIVERSIDE COMPANY, 1572
STARWOOD CAPITAL GROUP LLC, 1739
SUMMIT PARTNERS, 1752
TPG CAPITAL, 1835
TRILANTIC CAPITAL PARTNERS, 1851

Malaysia
AMANAH VENTURES SDN BHD, 2388
CELADON CAPITAL GROUP, 2582
COMMERCE ASSET VENTURES Sdn Bhd, 2623
DTA CAPITAL PARTNERS S/B, 2675
FIELDSTONE PRIVATE CAPITAL GROUP, 726
GLOBAL MARITIME VENTURES BERHAD, 2786
INTELLIGENT CAPITAL SDN BHD, 2880
MAYBAN VENTURES, 2958
PHILLIP MUTUAL BERHAD, 3035
RHB - H&F MANAGEMENT COMPANY SDN BHD RHB Capital, 3080
TECHNOLOGY PARK MALAYSIA CORPORATION SDN BHD, 3164

Malta
MEDRA CAPITAL, 2960

Mauritius
ADLEVO CAPITAL CIM Fund Services, 2345
AVIGO CAPITAL, 2460
BASIL PARTNERS Kross Border Trust Services Limited, 2493
CHRYSALIS CAPITAL ChrysCapital, 2599
CHRYSCAPITAL MANAGEMENT COMPANIES ChrysCapital, 2600
HELION VENTURE PARTNERS, LLC International Management (Mauritius) Ltd, 2818
HELIX INVESTMENTS, 2819
IDG VENTURES INDIA International Financial Services Limited, 2849

Mexico
ACON INVESTMENTS, 46
ADVENT INTERNATIONAL CORPORATION, 62
ALANTRA, 77
ALTA GROWTH CAPITAL, 2381

ALTA VENTURES MEXICO, 2382
COMPASS GROUP, 522
DARBY OVERSEAS INVESTMENTS LTD, 584
EVERCORE CAPITAL PARTNERS, 699
GE CAPITAL, 808
GENERAL ATLANTIC PARTNERS, 815
NARANYA VENTURES, 2984
NORTHGATE, 1341
ROOT CAPITAL, 1582

Myanmar
SERGE PUN & ASSOCIATES (MYANMAR) LIMITED, 3111

Netherlands
3i GROUP PLC, 2311
AAC CAPITAL PARTNERS, 2312
AESCAP VENTURE, 2350
ALANTRA, 77
ALPINVEST HOLDING NV Alpinvest, 2378
ALPINVEST PARTNERS B.V., 2379
AMPERSAND CAPITAL PARTNERS, 118
ANGELO, GORDON & CO., 127
ANTERRA CAPITAL, 2405
BENCIS CAPITAL PARTNERS, 2501
BIOGENERATION VENTURES, 2514
BRABANTSE ONTWIKKELINGSMIJ NV (BOM), 2534
BROOKLYN VENTURES, 2543
CARLYLE GROUP, 413
COTTONWOOD TECHNOLOGY FUND, 549
DUTCH GROUP, 2678
FORBION CAPITAL PARTNERS, 2748
FRESHWATER VENTURE PARTNERS, 2757
GENERAL ATLANTIC PARTNERS, 815
GILDE INVESTMENT FUNDS, 2779
HENQ, 2822
HOLLAND VENTURE BV, 2828
INDUSTRIEBANK LIOF NV, 2866
LIFE SCIENCES PARTNERS BV, 2939
NESBIC INVESTMENT FUND II, 2992
OAKTREE CAPITAL MANAGEMENT LLC, 1362
ONE EQUITY PARTNERS, 1376
PRIME TECHNOLOGY VENTURES NV, 3051
SABIC VENTURES, 3091
SOLID VENTURES, 3128
TAT CAPITAL PARTNERS LTD., 3162
VENTURE FUND ROTTERDAM BV Indofin Group, 3209
VITULUM VENTURES, 3224
WATERLAND PRIVATE EQUITY INVESTMENT, 3232
WILSHIRE PRIVATE MARKETS, 1989
ZERNIKE SEED FUND BV, 3250

New Zealand
AMP PRIVATE CAPITAL NEW ZEALAND LIMITED AMP Capital, 2395
ANZ PRIVATE EQUITY Private Equity Media, 2410
BIOPACIFIC VENTURES, 2516
BT FUNDS MANAGEMENT LIMITED, 2546
DIRECT CAPITAL PRIVATE EQUITY LIMITED, 2664
IGLOBE PARTNERS, 2853
PWC, 3064
THE CHANNEL GROUP Pacific Channel Ltd., 1808

Northern Ireland
AMICUS CAPITAL PARTNERS, 2392
LOUGH SHORE INVESTMENTS, 2948

Norway
ALLIANCE VENTURE, 2369
BIRK VENTURE, 2519
CONVEXA Tyveholmen AS, 2632
ENERGY VENTURES, 2700
FERD CAPITAL, 2731
FOUR SEASONS VENTURE CAPITAL, 2754
MATURO KAPITAL, 2957
NORTHZONE, 3013
REITEN & CO STRATEGIC INVESTMENTS AS Reiten & Company, 3076

Geographic Index

STATOIL TECHNOLOGY INVEST, 3141
TEKNOINVEST MANAGEMENT, 3167
VIKING VENTURE, 3216

Pakistan
ACUMEN, 55
MINI VENTURES, 2968

Panama
CANALIS CAPITAL, 2555

Peru
CARLYLE GROUP, 413
COMPASS GROUP, 522

Philippines
AB CAPITAL & INVESTMENT CORPORATION The Phinma Group, 2314

Poland
21 PARTNERS, 2293
3TS CAPITAL PARTNERS, 2309
ABRIS CAPITAL, 2319
BARING CORILIUS PRIVATE EQUITY, 2487
BBH CAPITAL PARTNERS, 240
DARBY OVERSEAS INVESTMENTS LTD, 584
ENTERPRISE INVESTORS, 2706
INVEMAX, 2885
PLEXUS VENTURES, 1452
RENAISSANCE PARTNERS, 3077
RIVERSIDE COMPANY, 1572

Portugal
AITEC, 2357
ALANTRA, 77
ESPIRITO SANTO VENTURES, 2717
INTER-RISCO: SOCIEDADE DE CAPITAL DE RISCO, 2882
PATHENA, 3031
PORTUGAL CAPITAL VENTURES Institutional Headquarters, 3048

Qatar
INVESTCORP, 1017

Republic of Korea
ADAMS STREET PARTNERS, LLC Adams Street Partners, LLC (Korea Branch), 57

Romania
3TS CAPITAL PARTNERS, 2309
AXXESS CAPITAL, 2471
SIF TRANSYLVANIA, 3119
TRANSYLVANIA FINANCIAL INVESTMENT COMPANY, 3187

Russia
ABRT VENTURE FUND, 2320
ADD VENTURE, 2344
AIP PRIVATE CAPITAL, 2031
ALFA CAPITAL Alfa Group, 2363
ASTOR CAPITAL GROUP, 2440
AWAY REALTY, 2465
BARING VOSTOK CAPITAL PARTNERS, 2491
BIOPROCESS CAPITAL PARTNERS, 2517
BRIGHT CAPITAL, 2540
BURAN VENTURE CAPITAL, 2549
FINAM GLOBAL, 2736
GENEZIS CAPITAL TECHNOLOGY, 2776
IMI.VC, 2856
INVENTURE PARTNERS, 2886
LETA CAPITAL, 2938
LIFE.SREDA, 2940
PHENOMEN VENTURES, 3034
QUANTUM WAVE FUND, 3068
RABO BLACK EARTH Eagle Venture Partners, 3071
RU-NET VENTURES, 3087
RUNA CAPITAL, 3088

SALFORD CAPITAL PARTNERS, 3095
SIGULER GUFF & COMPANY, 1679
SPINUP VENTURE, 3132
SUPREMUM CAPITAL, 3150
TPG CAPITAL, 1835
TROIKA CAPITAL PARTNERS, 3193
VTB CAPITAL, 3229

Saudi Arabia
INVESTCORP, 1017
SAUDI ARAMCO ENERGY VENTURES, 3099

Scotland
LINK TECHNOLOGIES LIMITED, 2941

Senegal
PARTECH INTERNATIONAL, 1416

Shanghai
AEA INVESTORS, 64

Singapore
3I ASIA PACIFIC 3i Group, 2297
3i GROUP PLC, 2311
ADAMS STREET PARTNERS, LLC Adams Street Partners Singapore Pte. Ltd., 57
AFC MERCHANT BANK, 2351
APOLLO GLOBAL MANAGEMENT, 140
ARCAPITA INC, 152
AZIONE CAPITAL, 2473
B CAPITAL GROUP, 216
BAF SPECTRUM, 2477
BIO*ONE CAPITAL EDMI, 2513
BIOVEDA CAPITAL, 2518
BLACKSTONE PRIVATE EQUITY GROUP, 277
CARLYLE GROUP, 413
EDBI Pte LTD., 2690
ENSPIRE CAPITAL PTE LTD, 2703
EVERCORE CAPITAL PARTNERS, 699
GENERAL ATLANTIC PARTNERS, 815
GET2VOLUME ACCELERATOR, 2778
IGLOBE PARTNERS, 2853
INFOCOMM INVESTMENTS, 2870
JUNGLE VENTURES, 2913
L CATTERTON PARTNERS, 1088
LIGHTSTONE VENTURES, 1122
LONE STAR FUNDS, 1140
OAKTREE CAPITAL MANAGEMENT LLC, 1362
OMERS PRIVATE EQUITY, 2207
PLATINUM EQUITY, 1451
RED DOT VENTURES, 3073
RIVERSIDE COMPANY, 1572
SEQUOIA CAPITAL Sequoia Capital India Advisors, 1654
SINGTEL INNOV8, 3121
SVI VEN CAPITAL, 3151
TPG CAPITAL, 1835
VARDE PARTNERS, 1907
VICKERS FINANCIAL GROUP, 3215
WALDEN INTERNATIONAL, 1951
WARBURG PINCUS LLC, 1956
WILSHIRE PRIVATE MARKETS, 1989

Slovakia
DARBY OVERSEAS INVESTMENTS LTD, 584
EAST FUND MANAGEMENT GmbH GiroCredit, 2683
SLOVAK AMERICAN ENTERPRISE FUND, 3122

South Africa
CLARITY CAPITAL, 2611
ETHOS PRIVATE EQUITY LIMITED: SA, 2718
FIELDSTONE PRIVATE CAPITAL GROUP, 726

South Korea
AIP PRIVATE CAPITAL, 2031
AJU CAPITAL COMPANY, 2358
AMOREPACIFIC VENTURES, 2394

Geographic Index

DRAPER ATHENA, 626
EXCELSIOR CAPITAL ASIA, 2727
GRANITE VENTURE CAPITAL CORPORATION, 2794
HALLIM VENTURE CAPITAL, 2807
HANWHA VC CORPORATION, 2812
HARBOURVEST PARTNERS LLC, 909
HOSEO VENTURE CAPITAL, 2833
HYUNDAI VENTURE INVESTMENT CORPORATION, 2839
IBK CAPITAL CORPORATION Industrial Bank of Korea, 2842
IMM INVESTMENT CORP HCI Private Equity Fund, 2857
KOREA INVESTMENT CORPORATION, 2925
KOREA TECHNOLOGY & BANKING (KTB) NETWORK CORP, 2926
MIRAE ASSET VENTURE ACCELERATOR Mirae Asset Group, 2969
RIVERSIDE COMPANY, 1572
STIC VENTURES CORPORATION LIMITED, 3145

Spain

3I SPAIN 3i Group, 2304
3i GROUP PLC, 2311
ACTIVE VENTURE PARTNERS, 2339
ADARA VENTURE PARTNERS, 2342
ADVENT INTERNATIONAL CORPORATION, 62
ALANTRA, 77
AXIS PARTICIPATIONES EMPRESARIALES, 2467
AXON PARTNERS GROUP, 2469
BARCELONA EMPREN, 2483
BARING PRIVATE EQUITY PARTNERS ESPANA SA, 2489
BAYSIDE CAPITAL H.I.G. European Capital Partners Spain, S.L.U., 239
BIG SUR VENTURES, 2510
BULLNET, 2548
CAIXA CAPITAL RISC, 2553
CARLYLE GROUP, 413
CATALANA D'INICIATIVES CR SA, 2570
CRB INVERBIO, 2636
DEMETER PARTNERS, 2656
DFC LTD, 2661
EVERCORE CAPITAL PARTNERS, 699
GESTION DE CAPITAL RIESGO DEL PAIS VASCO, 2777
HARBERT MANAGEMENT CORPORATION, 904
HIGHGROWTH, 2825
INVEXCEL PATRIMONIO, 2891
KIBO VENTURES, 2920
LANTA DIGITAL VENTURES, 2930
LONE STAR FUNDS, 1140
MERCAPITAL SA, 2962
NAUTA CAPITAL, 2987
PARKWALK ADVISORS, 3028
PERMIRA, 3033
RIVERSIDE COMPANY, 1572
SEAYA VENTURES, 3105
SOCIEDAD REGIONAL DE PROMOCION DEL PRINCIPADO, 3126
TELEFONICA VENTURES, 3169
VITAMINA K VENTURE CAPITAL, 3223

Sri Lanka

ZEPHYR MANAGEMENT LP, 2018

Sweden

3i GROUP PLC, 2311
ALANTRA, 77
ALMI FORETAGSPARTNER AB, 2371
ALTOR EQUITY PARTNERS, 2384
ARES MANAGEMENT LLC, 159
ATOMICO, 2446
AUGMENTA, 2449
COACH & CAPITAL, 2619
CONOR VENTURE PARTNERS OY, 2630
CREANDUM, 2637
EQT PARTNERS AB, 2712
EXPIBEL BV, 2728
FOURIERTRANSFORM, 2755
GREENHILL SAVP, 864
HEALTHCAP Odlander, Fredrikson & Co AB, 2816
INDUSTRI KAPITAL SVENSKA AB, 2863
INDUSTRIFONDEN, 2867
INNOVATIONSKAPITAL, 2878
INVESTMENT AB BURE, 2888
INVESTOR AB, 2890
NORDIC CAPITAL, 3008
NORTHZONE, 3013
NUTEK (NARINGS- OCH TEKNIKUTVECKLINGSVERKET) NUTEK, 3016
PERMIRA, 3033
POD INVESTMENT, 3043
PROCURITAS PARTNERS KB, 3054
RIVERSIDE COMPANY, 1572
SEB VENTURE CAPITAL, 3106
SUNSTONE CAPITAL, 3149
VOLVO GROUP VENTURE CAPITAL, 3226

Switzerland

21 PARTNERS, 2293
3W VENTURES Latour & Zuberbuhler GmbH, 2310
ABB TECHNOLOGY VENTURES, 2315
ACE & COMPANY, 2329
ALANTRA, 77
ALPHA ASSOCIATES, 2373
ALPHAMUNDI GROUP LTD, 2376
ARAVIS VENTURES, 2419
ARGOS SODITIC SA, 2423
ARMADA INVESTMENT GROUP, 2427
ATLANTIC VENTURES, 2444
B-TO-V PARTNERS, 2475
BANK J VONTOBEL COMPANY AG, 2482
BAY CITY CAPITAL LLC, 237
BB BIOTECH VENTURES, 2496
BBH CAPITAL PARTNERS, 240
BIOMED PARTNERS, 2515
CAPVIS EQUITY PARTNERS, 2564
CENTRALWAY, 2583
CREDIT MUTUEL EQUITY, 2088
CREDIT SUISSE PRIVATE EQUITY, 554
DEFI GESTION SA Banque Cantonale Vaudoise, 2653
ECOSYSTEM VENTURES, 650
EMERALD TECHNOLOGY VENTURES, 2106
GLOBAL LIFE SCIENCE VENTURES GmbH, 2785
HBM PARTNERS, 2815
HEALTHCAP, 2816
KK RESEARCH/KK SWISS VALUE INVESTOR, 2922
LAKESTAR, 2928
MONITOR CLIPPER PARTNERS, 1248
MOUNTAIN PARTNERS, 2979
NOKIA GROWTH PARTNERS, 1330
NOVARTIS VENTURE FUNDS, 1350
PARTNERS GROUP, 3029
PLEXUS VENTURES, 1452
POLYTECH VENTURES, 3045
ROCHE VENTURE FUND F. Hoffman-La Roche AG, 3085
SWISSCOM, 3152
TAT CAPITAL PARTNERS LTD., 3162
UNION BANK OF SWITZERLAND, 3200
VERSANT VENTURES, 1928
ZURCHER KANTONALBANK, 3253
ZURMONT MADISON PRIVATE EQUITY, 3254

Taiwan

CHINA DEVELOPMENT INDUSTRIAL BANK CDFH, 2592
H&Q ASIA PACIFIC, 892
HARBINGER VENTURE MANAGEMENT, 905
PAC-LINK MANAGEMENT CORP., 3024
STAGE 1 VENTURES, 1734
TMI, 3181
VIVO CAPITAL, 1941
WALDEN INTERNATIONAL, 1951
WI HARPER GROUP, 1983

Thailand

CSL INVESTMENT & FINANCE, 2642
DOUBLE IMPACT BUSINESS ADVISORY, 2670
LOMBARD INVESTMENTS, 1139
NETROVE ASIA SDN BHD, 2993

Geographic Index

The Netherlands
RIVERSTONE, 1573
SARONA ASSET MANAGEMENT, 2248
STARWOOD CAPITAL GROUP LLC, 1739

Turkey
212 CAPITAL PARTNERS, 2294
3TS CAPITAL PARTNERS, 2309
AKSOY INTERNET VENTURES, 2359
ASLANOBA CAPITAL, 2437
DARBY OVERSEAS INVESTMENTS LTD, 584
HUMMINGBIRD VENTURES, 2837
REVO CAPITAL, 3078

Ukraine
BULL VENTURES, 2547
EASTLABS, 2684
WESTERN NIS ENTERPRISE FUND, 3234

United Arab Emirates
ABU DHABI INVESTMENT AUTHORITY, 2321
AIP PRIVATE CAPITAL, 2031
BLACKSTONE PRIVATE EQUITY GROUP, 277
BROOKFIELD ASSET MANAGEMENT, 2067
CARLYLE GROUP, 413
FULL CIRCLE INVESTMENTS, 2762
GUGGENHEIM PARTNERS, 885
KOHLBERG KRAVIS ROBERTS & COMPANY, 1082
TVM CAPITAL, 3196
WESLEY CLOVER, 2284

United Kingdom
350 INVESTMENT PARTNERS, 2295
3I AUSTRIA BETEILGUNG GmbH 3i Group, 2298
3I EUROPE PLC 3i Group, 2300
3I ITALY 3i Group, 2303
3I UK 3i Group, 2306
3i GROUP PLC, 2311
ABINGWORTH MANAGEMENT LIMITED, 2316
ACACIA CAPITAL PARTNERS, 2322
ACCEL, 28
ACCEL-KKR LLC, 29
ACCENTURE TECHNOLOGY VENTURES, 2326
ACORN GROWTH COMPANIES, 48
ACTIS, 2337
ACUMEN, 55
ADAMS STREET PARTNERS, LLC Adams Street Partners UK LLP, 57
ADVENT INTERNATIONAL CORPORATION, 62
ADVENT VENTURE PARTNERS, 2348
ALANTRA, 77
ALBEMARLE PRIVATE EQUITY LIMITED, 2360
ALBERTA INVESTMENT MANAGEMENT CORP., 2033
ALCHEMY PARTNERS, 2361
ALCUIN CAPITAL PARTNERS LLP, 2362
ALLELE FUNDS, 2367
ALLSTATE INVESTMENTS LLC, 88
ALOE PRIVATE EQUITY, 2372
ALTA BERKELEY ASSOCIATES, 2380
AMADEUS CAPITAL PARTNERS LIMITED, 2386
AMPEZZO PARTNERS, 2396
AMPHION CAPITAL PARTNERS, 2397
ANGEL COFUND, 2400
ANGELO, GORDON & CO., 127
ANTHEMIS GROUP, 2406
ANTRAK CAPITAL, 2407
APAX PARTNERS, 135
APAX PARTNERS ET CIE, 2415
APOLLO GLOBAL MANAGEMENT, 140
APPLE TREE PARTNERS, 143
ARCAPITA INC, 152
ARDENTON, 2042
ARES MANAGEMENT LLC, 159
ARGAN CAPITAL, 2422
ARGUS CAPITAL LTD, 2425
ARTS ALLIANCE, 2428
ASCENSION VENTURES, 2432
ASCLEPIOS BIORESEARCH, 2433
ATLANTIC BRIDGE, 2443
ATOMICO, 2446
AUGMENTUM CAPITAL, 2450
AVANTI CAPITAL, 2458
AVISTA PARTNERS, 2461
AVLAR BIOVENTURES, 2463
AVONMORE DEVELOPMENTS, 2464
AXM VENTURE CAPITAL, 2468
AZINI CAPITAL PARTNERS, 2472
BAIN CAPITAL PRIVATE EQUITY, 220
BAIRD CAPITAL PARTNERS, 222
BALDERTON CAPITAL, 2478
BALLPARK VENTURES, 2479
BARCLAYS LEVERAGED FINANCE, 2484
BARCLAYS VENTURES Barclays, 2486
BARING PRIVATE EQUITY PARTNERS INDIA, 2490
BATTERY VENTURES, 235
BAYSIDE CAPITAL H.I.G. European Capital Partners LLP, 239
BBH CAPITAL PARTNERS, 240
BC PARTNERS LIMITED, 2497
BERINGEA, 251
BERTI INVESTMENTS, 2505
BESTPORT VENTURES, 2507
BIG SOCIETY CAPITAL, 2509
BLACKSTONE PRIVATE EQUITY GROUP, 277
BLUEGEM CAPITAL PARTNERS, 2524
BOTTS & COMPANY LIMITED, 2532
BRAINSPARK PLC, 2535
BRIDGEPOINT CAPITAL LIMITED, 2538
BRIDGES VENTURES, 2539
BROOKFIELD ASSET MANAGEMENT, 2067
BRYAN GARNIER & COMPANY, 2544
BUSINESS GROWTH FUND, 2550
CANDOVER, 2556
CAPITAL INTERNATIONAL Capital Group Companies, 2559
CARLYLE GROUP, 413
CASS ENTREPRENEURSHIP FUND Cass Business School, 2567
CASTLELAKE, 424
CASTROL INNOVENTURES, 2568
CATALYST FUND MANAGEMENT & RESEARCH LIMITED, 2572
CATALYST VENTURE PARTNERS, 2574
CATAPULT VENTURE MANAGERS, 2575
CAZENOVE PRIVATE EQUITY Cazenove Capital, 2577
CCMP CAPITAL, 433
CDC CAPITAL PARTNER CDC Group, 2578
CENTRALWAY, 2583
CHARLOTTE STREET CAPITAL, 2586
CHARTERHOUSE CAPITAL PARTNERS I Charterhouse, 2587
CHELSFIELD PARTNERS, 2589
CHORD CAPITAL, 2598
CINVEN LIMITED, 2605
CISCO INVESTMENTS, 483
CITI VENTURES, 486
CITY OF LONDON INVESTMENT GROUP PLC, 2608
CLARITY CAPITAL, 2611
CLIMATE CHANGE CAPITAL, 2615
CLOSE BROTHERS PRIVATE EQUITY Close Brothers Group, 2617
COLLER CAPITAL LIMITED, 2621
CONNECT VENTURES, 2629
CREDIT SUISSE PRIVATE EQUITY, 554
CVC CAPITAL PARTNERS LTD, 2644
D.E. SHAW & CO. LP, 579
DERBYSHIRE FIRST INVESTMENTS LIMITED, 2657
DFJ ESPRIT, 2662
DN CAPITAL, 2668
DOUGHTY HANSON & CO., 2671
DRAPER ESPRIT, 2674
DUKE STREET CAPITAL Duke Street, 2676
DUNEDIN CAPITAL PARTNERS LIMITED, 2677
DUTCHESS CAPITAL, 638
EC1 CAPITAL LTD, 2685
ECI VENTURES, 2687
EDEN VENTURES, 2691
ELECTRA PARTNERS EUROPE, 2695
EM WARBURG, PINCUS & COMPANY INTERNATIONAL, 2697
ENSO VENTURES, 2702

1117

Geographic Index

ENTERPRISE EQUITY (NI) LTD, 2704
ENTERPRISE VENTURE LIMITED, 2707
ENTERPRISE VENTURES LIMITED, 2708
ENTREE CAPITAL, 2709
ENTREPRENEURS FUND, 2710
EPIDAREX CAPITAL, 689
EPISODE 1 PARTNERS, 2711
EPLANET CAPITAL, 690
EQUISTONE, 2714
ESSEX WOODLANDS HEALTH VENTURES LLC, 697
EUROPEAN ACQUISITION CAPITAL LIMITED, 2722
EVERCORE CAPITAL PARTNERS, 699
F-PRIME CAPITAL PARTNERS, 710
FERRANTI LIMITED, 2732
FIDELITY GROWTH PARTNERS EUROPE, 2734
FIELDSTONE PRIVATE CAPITAL GROUP, 726
FIRST RESERVE, 740
FISHER LYNCH CAPITAL, 744
FORESIGHT VENTURE PARTNERS, 2749
FORTRESS INVESTMENT GROUP LLC, 767
FOUNDATION CAPITAL LIMITED, 2753
FRANCISCO PARTNERS, 779
FRONTLINE VENTURES, 2759
FSE GROUP, 2760
GE CAPITAL, 808
GE EQUITY EUROPE, 2769
GENERAL ATLANTIC PARTNERS, 815
GENERICS GROUP LIMITED Generics Group, 2773
GMT COMMUNICATIONS PARTNERS LLP, 2789
GOLDMAN SACHS INTERNATIONAL UK, 2792
GRANVILLE BAIRD CAPITAL PARTNERS, 2795
GRAPHITE CAPITAL MANAGEMENT LTD, 2796
GREENHILL SAVP, 864
GUGGENHEIM PARTNERS, 885
GV, 889
HAMBRO CAPITAL MANAGEMENT LTD, 2808
HARBERT MANAGEMENT CORPORATION, 904
HARBOURVEST PARTNERS LLC, 909
HELLMAN & FRIEDMAN LLC, 924
HENDERSON PRIVATE CAPITAL, 2821
HG CAPITAL, 2823
HIG CAPITAL HIG European Capital Partners LLP, 928
HILCO BRANDS, 937
HILKO UK LTD/VALCO CAPITAL PARTNERS, 2827
HOXTON VENTURES, 2834
HSBC VENTURES UK LIMITED, 2836
HUMMINGBIRD VENTURES, 2837
IMPERIAL INNOVATIONS, 2858
INDEX VENTURES, 2860
INDUSTRY VENTURES, 986
INGENIOUS VENTURES, 2871
INOVIA CAPITAL, 2157
INTEGRATED TECHNOLOGIES LIMITED, 2879
INTERMEDIATE CAPITAL GROUP PLC, 2883
INTERNATIONAL PRIVATE EQUITY SERVICES LIMITED Guernsey, 2884
INVESTCORP, 1017
INVUS GROUP, 1018
IP GROUP, 2892
IPG GROUP, 2894
ISIS EP LLP F & C, 2898
JEGI CAPITAL, 1033
KLEINWORT CAPITAL LIMITED, 2923
KOHLBERG KRAVIS ROBERTS & COMPANY, 1082
LEGAL AND GENERAL VENTURES LIMITED, 2935
LEXINGTON PARTNERS, 1112
LIGHTHOUSE PARTNERS, 1120
LLOYDS DEVELOPMENT CAPITAL LIMITED, 2944
MACMILLAN DIGITAL EDUCATION, 2950
MEDIMMUNE VENTURES, 1196
MEZZANINE MANAGEMENT LIMITED Mezzanine Management UK Ltd., 2965
MIDVEN, 2967
MMC VENTURES, 2972
MONTAGU PRIVATE EQUITY LIMITED, 2977
MVM LIFE SCIENCE PARTNERS, 2981
NATWEST VENTURES LIMITED, 2985

NAUTA CAPITAL, 2987
NEW MODEL VENTURE CAPITAL, 2995
NEWABLE VENTURES, 2997
NEXT WORLD CAPITAL, 1319
NOMURA PHASE4 VENTURES LTD, 3007
NORTH WEST FUND, 3010
NORTHERN ENTERPRISE LIMITED, 3011
NORTHLEAF CAPITAL PARTNERS, 2204
NORTHSTAR VENTURES, 3012
NOTION CAPITAL, 3014
NVM PRIVATE EQUITY LIMITED, 3017
OAKTREE CAPITAL MANAGEMENT LLC, 1362
OCTOPUS INVESTMENTS, 3018
OMERS PRIVATE EQUITY, 2207
OMIDYAR NETWORK, 1374
ONEX PARTNERS, 2209
PALADIN CAPITAL GROUP, 1400
PANTHEON VENTURES (US) LP, 1411
PARKWALK ADVISORS, 3028
PASSION CAPITAL, 3030
PENTECH VENTURES, 3032
PERMIRA Permira Advisers LLP, 3033
PHOENIX EQUITY PARTNERS LIMITED, 3036
PITON CAPITAL, 3040
PLATINUM EQUITY, 1451
PLEXUS VENTURES, 1452
POMONA CAPITAL, 1462
POND VENTURES, 3047
PRIME TECHNOLOGY VENTURES NV, 3051
PROFOUNDERS CAPITAL, 3055
PROMETHEAN INVESTMENTS LLP, 3057
PROMETHYAN LABS, 3058
PROVIDENCE EQUITY PARTNERS, 1496
QUALCOMM VENTURES, 1509
QUESTER CAPITAL MANAGEMENT LIMITED, 3070
QUINBROOK INFRASTRUCTURE PARTNERS, 1517
REED ELSEVIER VENTURES, 3074
RESOURCE CAPITAL FUNDS, 1548
RIVERSIDE COMPANY, 1572
SAFFRON HILL VENTURES, 3092
SALFORD CAPITAL PARTNERS, 3095
SAMOS INVESTMENTS, 3097
SCHRODER VENTURES HEALTH INVESTORS, 1628
SCOTTISH ENTERPRISE, 3103
SCOTTISH EQUITY PARTNERS, 3104
SCULPTOR CAPITAL MANAGEMENT Sculptor Capital Management Europe Limited, 1635
SEARCHLIGHT, 2252
SEED CAPITAL LIMITED, 3107
SEEDCAMP, 3108
SEVEN SPIRES INVESTMENTS, 3112
SIGNATURE CAPITAL LLC, 3120
SILVER LAKE, 1683
SOVEREIGN CAPITAL, 3130
SPARK VENTURES, 3131
SR ONE LTD, 1731
SSE VENTURES, 3135
STARWOOD CAPITAL GROUP LLC, 1739
STEPSTONE, 3144
STRAND HANSON LIMITED, 3146
SUMMIT PARTNERS, 1752
SUN CAPITAL PARTNERS, 1753
SUPREMUM CAPITAL, 3150
SV HEALTH INVESTORS, 1762
TA ASSOCIATES, 1776
TALIS CAPITAL, 3157
TECHNOLOGY CROSSOVER VENTURES, 1785
TELEFONICA VENTURES, 3169
THE ABRAAJ GROUP, 3173
TIANGUIS LIMITED, 3178
TLCOM CAPITAL, 3179
TPG CAPITAL, 1835
TRANSATLANTIC CAPITAL LTD, 3186
TREVI HEALTH CAPITAL, 1844
TRILANTIC CAPITAL PARTNERS, 1851
TTP VENTURES, 3195
VARDE PARTNERS, 1907

Geographic Index

VENCAP, 3206
VERDEXUS, 2279
VIRGIN GREEN FUND, 3222
VONTOBEL PRIVATE EQUITY MANAGEMENT CAYMAN, 3228
WARBURG PINCUS LLC, 1956
WHEB GROUP, 3237
WHITE STAR CAPITAL, 1982
WILSHIRE PRIVATE MARKETS, 1989
YFM GROUP, 3244
ZOUK VENTURES, 3252

United States

Alabama
ADVANTAGE CAPITAL PARTNERS, 61
C&G CAPITAL PARTNERS, 363
CAMP ONE VENTURES, 384
HARBERT MANAGEMENT CORPORATION, 904
MURPHREE VENTURE PARTNERS, 1273
NEW CAPITAL PARTNERS, 1293
REDMONT VENTURE PARTNERS, 1533
STONEHENGE GROWTH CAPITAL, 1745

Arizona
ACACIA CAPITAL, 25
BILTMORE VENTURES, 264
C3 CAPITAL PARTNERS LP, 364
CANAL PARTNERS, 387
FINAVENTURES, 729
FOGEL INTERNATIONAL, 759
GRAYHAWK CAPITAL, 856
HYPUR VENTURES, 963
LIZADA CAPITAL LLC, 1135
MCKELLAR & COMPANY, 1193
NEST VENTURES, 1290
RESEARCH CORPORATION TECHNOLOGIES, 1543
SOURCE CAPITAL GROUP, 1707
THUNDERBIRD ANGEL NETWORK, 1822
TRU MANAGEMENT, 1858
TRUE NORTH VENTURE PARTNERS, 1859
VALLEY VENTURES LP, 1901
WELLS FARGO CAPITAL FINANCE, 1970

Arkansas
DIAMOND STATE VENTURES LP, 611

California
11.2 CAPITAL, 4
1ST COURSE CAPITAL, 8
500 STARTUPS, 11
5AM VENTURES, 12
7 GATE VENTURES, 2028
A-GRADE INVESTMENTS, 15
ABERDARE VENTURES, 20
ABINGWORTH MANAGEMENT LIMITED, 2316
ABS CAPITAL PARTNERS, 22
ABSTRACT VENTURES, 24
ACACIA CAPITAL, 25
ACARIO INNOVATION, 27
ACCEL, 28
ACCEL-KKR LLC, 29
ACCELEPRISE, 30
ACCELERATOR LIFE SCIENCE PARTNERS, 31
ACCELERATOR VENTURES, 32
ACCENT CAPITAL PARTNERS LLC, 33
ACERO CAPITAL, 41
ACKRELL CAPITAL, 44
ACME CAPITAL, 45
ACON INVESTMENTS, 46
ACORN CAMPUS VENTURES, 47
ACREW CAPITAL, 49
ACT ONE VENTURES, 50
ACUITY VENTURES LLC, 54
ADAMS STREET PARTNERS, LLC Adams Street Partners, Inc., 57
ADOBE VENTURES LP, 58
ADVANCED TECHNOLOGY VENTURES, 59
ADVANTAGE CAPITAL PARTNERS, 61

AGILITY CAPITAL LLC, 69
AHOY CAPITAL, 72
AIRBUS VENTURES, 73
AKERS CAPITAL LLC, 75
ALACRITY VENTURES, 76
ALIGNED PARTNERS, 83
ALLEGIS CYBER CAPITAL, 84
ALLOY VENTURES, 87
ALMAZ CAPITAL, 89
ALPINE INVESTORS, 92
ALSOP LOUIE PARTNERS, 93
ALTA PARTNERS, 94
ALTAIR VENTURES, 95
ALTAMONT CAPITAL PARTNERS, 96
ALTOS VENTURES, 100
ALTURA VENTURES LLC, 103
AMD VENTURES, 106
AME CLOUD VENTURES, 107
AMGEN VENTURES, 112
AMICUS CAPITAL, 114
AMIDZAD PARTNERS, 115
AMKEY VENTURES, 117
AMPLIFY, 120
ANALYTICS VENTURES, 121
ANDREESSEN HOROWITZ, 124
ANGELENO GROUP, 126
ANGELO, GORDON & CO., 127
ANGELS' FORUM LLC, 129
ANNEX VENTURES, 130
ANTHEM VENTURE PARTNERS, 132
ANZU PARTNERS, 133
AOL VENTURES, 134
APHELION CAPITAL, 138
APOLLO GLOBAL MANAGEMENT, 140
APPLIED MATERIALS VENTURES, 144
ARAGON VENTURES, 145
ARCADIAN FUND, 151
ARCH VENTURE PARTNERS, 153
ARCHYTAS VENTURES, 155
ARES CAPITAL CORPORATION, 158
ARES MANAGEMENT LLC, 159
ARGONAUT VENTURES, 163
ARROWHEAD INVESTMENT MANAGEMENT, 168
ARSENAL VENTURE PARTNERS, 171
ARTIMAN VENTURES, 174
ARTIS VENTURES, 175
ASIAVEST PARTNERS, 2436
ASPECT VENTURES, 180
ASSET MANAGEMENT VENTURES, 181
ASTELLAS VENTURE MANAGEMENT, 182
ATA VENTURES, 183
ATEL CAPITAL GROUP, 184
ATHENAEUM FUND, 186
ATRIUM CAPITAL, 192
AUDAX GROUP, 194
AUGUST CAPITAL, 197
AURORA CAPITAL GROUP, 199
AUTO TECH VENTURES, 204
AUTOTECH VENTURES, 205
AVALON VENTURES, 206
AZCA, 214
AZURE CAPITAL PARTNERS, 215
B CAPITAL GROUP, 216
BACKSTAGE CAPITAL, 218
BAIDU VENTURES, 219
BAIN CAPITAL VENTURES, 221
BALMORAL FUNDS, 225
BAND OF ANGELS LLC, 226
BANNEKER PARTNERS, 227
BARODA VENTURES, 228
BASE VENTURES, 229
BASF VENTURE CAPITAL, 2492
BASIS SET VENTURES, 232
BATTERY VENTURES, 235
BAY CITY CAPITAL LLC, 237
BAY PARTNERS, 238
BEE PARTNERS, 243

1119

Geographic Index

BEHRMAN CAPITAL, 245
BENCHMARK, 248
BENHAMOU GLOBAL VENTURES, 249
BERGGRUEN HOLDINGS, 250
BERKELEY VC INTERNATIONAL LLC, 252
BERKELEY VENTURES, 253
BERTRAM CAPITAL, 257
BESSEMER VENTURE PARTNERS, 260
BI WALDEN MANAGEMENT SDN Walden International, 2508
BINARY CAPITAL, 265
BIRCHMERE VENTURES, 272
BISON CAPITAL ASSET MANAGEMENT LLC, 274
BLACK DIAMOND VENTURES, 275
BLACKSTONE PRIVATE EQUITY GROUP, 277
BLADE VENTURES, 278
BLOCKCHAIN CAPITAL, 283
BLOOMBERG BETA, 284
BLUE SKY CAPITAL, 292
BLUEFISH VENTURES, 294
BLUEPOINTE VENTURES, 295
BLUERUN VENTURES, 296
BLUM CAPITAL PARTNERS, 300
BLUMBERG CAPITAL, 301
BMW I VENTURES, 302
BONFIRE VENTURES, 306
BOOST VC, 307
BRAIN TRUST ACCELERATOR FUND, 323
BRAINSTORM VENTURES, 324
BRANDON CAPITAL GROUP, 326
BREAKWATER INVESTMENTS, 330
BREAKWATER MANAGEMENT, 331
BRENTWOOD ASSOCIATES, 334
BREYER CAPITAL, 336
BRIDGESCALE PARTNERS, 339
BRIGHT CAPITAL, 2540
BRIGHTPATH CAPITAL PARTNERS, 340
BRILLIANT VENTURES, 342
BROADHAVEN CAPITAL PARTNERS, 343
BULLPEN CAPITAL, 358
BUNKER HILL CAPITAL, 359
CALCEF CLEAN ENERGY FUND, 367
CALERA CAPITAL, 368
CALIBRATE VENTURES, 370
CALIFORNIA COAST VENTURE FORUM, 3257
CALIFORNIA TECHNOLOGY VENTURES, 371
CALTIUS EQUITY PARTNERS, 373
CALTIUS STRUCTURED CAPITAL, 374
CAMP ONE VENTURES, 384
CAMP VENTURES, 385
CANAAN PARTNERS, 386
CANNA ANGELS LLC, 388
CANNABIS CAPITAL, 389
CANNABIS STRATEGIC VENTURES, 391
CANTOS VENTURES, 395
CANVAS VENTURES, 396
CANYON CREEK CAPITAL, 397
CAPX PARTNERS, 407
CARDINAL VENTURE CAPITAL, 411
CARLYLE GROUP, 413
CARRICK CAPITAL PARTNERS, 416
CASA VERDE CAPITAL, 417
CATAMOUNT VENTURES LP, 428
CATAPULT VENTURES, 429
CATO BIOVENTURES, 430
CELERITY PARTNERS, 439
CENTANA GROWTH PARTNERS, 440
CENTRE PARTNERS MANAGEMENT LLC, 447
CENTURY PARK CAPITAL PARTNERS, 449
CEO VENTURES, 450
CERBERUS CAPITAL MANAGEMENT, 451
CERRACAP VENTURES, 453
CERVIN VENTURES, 454
CHARLES RIVER VENTURES, 455
CHARTER LIFE SCIENCES, 458
CHICAGO PACIFIC FOUNDERS, 469
CHINAROCK CAPITAL MANAGEMENT VENTURES, 472
CHINAVEST, 473

CIPIO PARTNERS, 2606
CIRCLEUP, 482
CISCO INVESTMENTS, 483
CITI VENTURES, 486
CITY HILL VENTURES, 487
CLAREMONT CREEK VENTURES, 491
CLARITY PARTNERS, 494
CLARUS VENTURES, 495
CLEAN PACIFIC VENTURES, 498
CLEANPATH VENTURES, 499
CLEARLAKE CAPITAL, 500
CLEARLIGHT PARTNERS, 501
CLEARSTONE VENTURE PARTNERS, 502
CLEARVIEW CAPITAL, 503
CLYDESDALE VENTURES, 506
COATUE MANAGEMENT, 509
COLUMN GROUP, 517
COMCAST VENTURES, 518
COMET LABS, 519
COMPASS GROUP MANAGEMENT LLC, 523
COMPASS TECHNOLOGY PARTNERS LP, 524
COMSTOCK CAPITAL PARTNERS LLC, 527
CONSOR CAPITAL, 531
CORNERSTONE CAPITAL HOLDINGS, 540
CORNERSTONE HOLDINGS, 542
CORRELATION VENTURES, 544
COSTANOA VENTURE CAPITAL, 547
COSTELLA KIRSCH, 548
COWBOY VENTURES, 552
CREANDUM, 2637
CRESCENDO VENTURE MANAGEMENT LLC, 2639
CRESCENDO VENTURES, 555
CRESCENT CAPITAL GROUP LP, 556
CROSSCUT VENTURES, 561
CROSSLINK CAPITAL, 563
CRUNCHFUND, 564
CUTLASS CAPITAL LLC, 572
CVF CAPITAL PARTNERS, 573
CXO FUND, 574
D.E. SHAW & CO. LP, 579
DAG VENTURES, 581
DATA COLLECTIVE, 585
DBL PARTNERS, 595
DCM, 596
DE NOVO VENTURES, 598
DECIENS CAPITAL, 599
DEEP FORK CAPITAL, 600
DEFTA PARTNERS, 602
DELPHI VENTURES, 604
DFJ VENTURE CAPITAL, 609
DIAMOND TECHVENTURES, 612
DIAMONDHEAD VENTURES, 613
DIGITAL VENTURE CAPITAL ASSOCIATION, 3260
DJF DRAGONFUND CHINA, 2667
DN CAPITAL, 2668
DOCOMO INNOVATIONS, 620
DOMAIN ASSOCIATES LLC, 621
DOT EDU VENTURES, 623
DOUBLE M PARTNERS, 624
DOUBLEROCK VENTURE CAPITAL, 625
DRAPER ATHENA, 626
DRAPER RICHARDS KAPLAN FOUNDATION, 627
DUFF ACKERMAN & GOODRICH, 634
E.VENTURES, 641
ECLIPSE VENTURES, 648
ECOSYSTEM VENTURES, 650
EDBI Pte LTD., 2690
eLAB VENTURES, 2023
ELEVATION PARTNERS, 659
ELYSIUM VENTURE CAPITAL, 661
EMBARK VENTURES, 663
EMERALD OCEAN CAPITAL, 664
EMERGENCE CAPITAL PARTNERS, 665
EMERGENT MEDICAL PARTNERS, 666
ENDEAVOUR CAPITAL, 673
ENERGY CAPITAL PARTNERS, 675
ENERTECH CAPITAL, 676

Geographic Index

ENIAC VENTURES, 679
ENTER VENTURES, 681
EPLANET CAPITAL, 690
ESSEX WOODLANDS HEALTH VENTURES LLC, 697
EVERCORE CAPITAL PARTNERS, 699
EXPERIMENT FUND, 708
EcoR1 CAPITAL, 709
FAIRMONT CAPITAL, 713
FAIRVIEW CAPITAL PARTNERS, 714
FALCON FUND, 715
FELICIS VENTURES, 720
FENOX VENTURE CAPITAL, 721
FIFTH WALL, 727
FIKA VENTURES, 728
FINAVENTURES, 729
FIRELAKE CAPITAL, 730
FIRST ROUND CAPITAL, 741
FISHER LYNCH CAPITAL, 744
FLOODGATE FUND, 751
FOCUS VENTURES, 757
FOG CITY CAPITAL, 758
FORERUNNER VENTURES, 761
FORESITE CAPITAL, 762
FORGEPOINT CAPITAL, 763
FORMATIVE VENTURES, 764
FORREST BINKLEY & BROWN, 765
FORTRESS INVESTMENT GROUP LLC, 767
FORTÉ VENTURES, 768
FORWARD VENTURES, 769
FOUNDATION CAPITAL, 770
FOUNDER PARTNERS, 772
FOUNDERS FUND, 775
FOUR RIVERS GROUP, 777
FOX PAINE & COMPANY LLC, 778
FRANCISCO PARTNERS, 779
FRAZIER HEALTHCARE VENTURES, 782
FREEMAN SPOGLI & CO., 783
FRESH VC, 785
FRIEDMAN, FLEISCHER & LOWE LLC, 787
FRONTIER VENTURE CAPITAL, 791
FRONTIER VENTURES, 792
FTV CAPITAL, 793
FUNDERS CLUB, 795
FUNG CAPITAL USA, 796
FUNK VENTURES, 797
FUSE CAPITAL, 798
FUSION FUND, 799
FUTURE VENTURES, 800
GABRIEL VENTURE PARTNERS, 805
GARAGE TECHNOLOGY VENTURES, 807
GE VENTURES, 809
GENERAL ATLANTIC PARTNERS, 815
GENERAL CATALYST PARTNERS, 816
GENERATION PARTNERS, 818
GENSTAR CAPITAL LP, 819
GEODESIC CAPITAL, 820
GERKEN CAPITAL ASSOCIATES, 822
GGV CAPITAL, 823
GI PARTNERS, 824
GIDEON HIXON FUND, 826
GLADSTONE CAPITAL, 828
GLOBAL CATALYST PARTNERS, 833
GLOBALIVE, 2134
GLOBESPAN CAPITAL PARTNERS, 835
GLYNN CAPITAL MANAGEMENT, 836
GOAHEAD VENTURES, 837
GOLDEN GATE CAPITAL, 839
GOLUB CAPITAL, 844
GRANITE HILL CAPITAL PARTNERS, LLC, 851
GRANITE VENTURES, 852
GRAPHENE VENTURES, 854
GREENHILL SAVP, 864
GREENSPRING ASSOCIATES, 867
GREIF & COMPANY, 869
GREY SKY VENTURE PARTNERS, 870
GREYCROFT PARTNERS, 871
GREYLOCK PARTNERS, 872

GRYPHON INVESTORS, 881
GSR VENTURES, 2801
GSV VENTURES, 883
GUGGENHEIM PARTNERS, 885
GV, 889
GVA CAPITAL, 890
H&Q ASIA PACIFIC, 892
HALLEY VENTURE PARTNERS, 895
HAMILTON BIOVENTURES, 898
HANCOCK PARK ASSOCIATES, 902
HANOVER PARTNERS, 903
HARBERT MANAGEMENT CORPORATION, 904
HARBINGER VENTURE MANAGEMENT, 905
HARRISON METAL, 911
HARVARD CAPITAL GROUP, 913
HEALTHQUEST CAPITAL, 921
HELLMAN & FRIEDMAN LLC, 924
HERCULES TECHNOLOGY GROWTH CAPITAL, INC, 925
HEWLETT PACKARD ENTERPRISE, 927
HIG CAPITAL, 928
HIGHBAR PARTNERS, 933
HIGHLAND CAPITAL PARTNERS, 935
HIGHWAY1, 936
HOMEBREW MANAGEMENT, 941
HONE CAPITAL, 942
HORIZON TECHNOLOGY FINANCE, 946
HORIZON VENTURES LLC, 947
HOULIHAN LOKEY, 948
HOUSATONIC PARTNERS, 949
HUMMER WINBLAD VENTURE PARTNERS, 956
HUNTINGTON CAPITAL, 958
HUNTSMAN GAY GLOBAL CAPITAL, 959
ICON VENTURES, 968
ID VENTURES AMERICA LLC, 970
IDEALAB, 972
IGLOBE PARTNERS, 2853
IGNITION PARTNERS, 974
ILLUMINATE VENTURES, 976
IN-Q-TEL, 979
INCUBE VENTURES, 980
INDEX VENTURES, 2860
INDUSTRIAL GROWTH PARTNERS, 985
INDUSTRY VENTURES, 986
INFOCOMM INVESTMENTS, 2870
INITIALIZED CAPITAL, 991
INITIO GROUP, 992
INNOSPRING, 994
INNOVATION ENDEAVORS, 996
INOVIA CAPITAL, 2157
INSTITUTIONAL VENTURE PARTNERS, 1001
INTEGRAL CAPITAL PARTNERS, 1003
INTEL CAPITAL, 1004
INTELLECTUAL VENTURES, 1005
INTERWEST PARTNERS, 1010
INVENCOR, 1011
INVENT, 1012
INVENTUS, 1013
JACKSON SQUARE VENTURES, 1024
JAVELIN VENTURE PARTNERS, 1028
JAZZ VENTURE PARTNERS, 1029
JC2 VENTURES, 1031
JETBLUE TECHNOLOGY VENTURES, 1035
JF SHEA VENTURES, 1036
JMI EQUITY FUND LP, 1041
K9 VENTURES, 1050
KAIROS VENTURES, 1051
KAISER PERMANENTE VENTURES, 1052
KARLIN VENTURES, 1055
KEARNY VENTURE PARTNERS, 1059
KEIRETSU FORUM, 1061
KERN WHELAN CAPITAL, 1066
KHOSLA VENTURES, 1069
KINSEY HILLS GROUP, 1073
KLEINER PERKINS, 1075
KODIAK CAPITAL, 1079
KOHLBERG KRAVIS ROBERTS & COMPANY, 1082
KOHLBERG VENTURES, 1083

Geographic Index

KPG VENTURES, 1084
KTB VENTURES, 1087
LATTERELL VENTURE PARTNERS, 1094
LAUNCHPAD LA, 1099
LEAPFROG VENTURES, 1102
LEASING TECHNOLOGIES INTERNATIONAL INC., 1103
LEGACY VENTURE, 1106
LEONARD GREEN & PARTNERS LP, 1109
LEVINE LEICHTMAN CAPITAL PARTNERS, 1111
LEXINGTON PARTNERS, 1112
LIGHTHOUSE CAPITAL PARTNERS, 1119
LIGHTSPEED VENTURE PARTNERS, 1121
LIGHTSTONE VENTURES, 1122
LOCUS VENTURES, 1138
LOMBARD INVESTMENTS, 1139
LONGITUDE CAPITAL, 1143
LOS ANGELES VENTURE ASSOCIATION, 3268
LOVELL MINNICK PARTNERS LLC, 1147
LOWERCASE CAPITAL, 1149
LUX CAPITAL, 1151
M12, 1154
MARWIT CAPITAL LLC, 1168
MASCHMEYER GROUP VENTURES, 1170
MATON VENTURE, 1180
MATRIX PARTNERS, 1181
MAVERICK VENTURES, 1182
MAVERON LLC, 1183
MAYFIELD FUND, 1184
MEDIA VENTURE PARTNERS, 1195
MEDIMMUNE VENTURES, 1196
MENLO VENTURES, 1202
MERITECH CAPITAL PARTNERS, 1212
MERITURN PARTNERS, 1213
MERUS CAPITAL, 1218
MESA VERDE PARTNERS, 1221
MHS CAPITAL, 1226
MINDFULL INVESTORS, 1236
MIRAMAR VENTURE PARTNERS, 1237
MISSION BAY CAPITAL, 1238
MISSION VENTURES, 1239
MITSUI GLOBAL INVESTMENT, 1241
MOBILE FOUNDATION VENTURES, 1243
MOHR-DAVIDOW VENTURES, 1247
MONITOR VENTURES, 1249
MONTREUX EQUITY PARTNERS, 1251
MOORE VENTURE PARTNERS, 1253
MORGAN STANLEY EXPANSION CAPITAL, 1255
MORGENTHALER VENTURES, 1257
MOTIV PARTNERS, 1258
MPM CAPITAL, 1268
MS&AD VENTURES, 1269
NATIONAL VENTURE CAPITAL ASSOCIATION, 3272
NAVITAS CAPITAL, 1282
NAXURI CAPITAL, 1284
NEEDHAM CAPITAL PARTNERS, 1288
NEW ENTERPRISE ASSOCIATES, 1297
NEW LEAF VENTURE PARTNERS, 1298
NEWBURY VENTURES, 1311
NEWSCHOOLS VENTURE FUND, 1316
NEXIT VENTURES OY Nexit Ventures Inc., 2999
NEXT WORLD CAPITAL, 1319
NEXUS VENTURE PARTNERS, 3001
NFX, 1323
NGEN PARTNERS, 1324
NGP CAPITAL, 1327
NORTHERN LIGHT VENTURE CAPITAL, 1340
NORTHGATE, 1341
NORTHLEAF CAPITAL PARTNERS, 2204
NORWEST VENTURE PARTNERS, 1346
NOVENTI VENTURES, 1352
NOVO A/S, 3015
NOVUS VENTURES LP, 1354
NTH POWER TECHNOLOGIES, 1355
NVIDIA INCEPTION, 1357
O'REILLY ALPHATECH VENTURES, 1359
OAK HILL CAPITAL PARTNERS, 1360
OAK INVESTMENT PARTNERS, 1361

OAKTREE CAPITAL MANAGEMENT LLC, 1362
OBVIOUS VENTURES, 1363
OCEANSHORE VENTURES, 1365
OCTANe, 1366
ODYSSEY INVESTMENT PARTNERS, 1368
OEM CAPITAL, 1369
OFF THE GRID VENTURES, 1370
OKAPI VENTURE CAPITAL, 1371
OMIDYAR NETWORK, 1374
ONSET VENTURES, 1378
OPUS CAPITAL, 1381
ORBIMED HEALTHCARE FUND MANAGEMENT, 1382
OUTLOOK VENTURES, 1389
OUTPOST CAPITAL, 1390
OWL VENTURES, 1392
OXFORD BIOSCIENCE PARTNERS, 1394
OYSTER VENTURES, 1395
PAC-LINK MANAGEMENT CORP., 3024
PACIFIC COMMUNITY VENTURES, 1396
PACIFIC VENTURES GROUP, 1399
PALADIN CAPITAL GROUP, 1400
PALISADES VENTURES, 1402
PALLADIUM EQUITY PARTNERS, 1403
PALO ALTO VENTURE PARTNERS, 1405
PALO ALTO VENTURE SCIENCE, 1406
PALOMAR VENTURES, 1407
PANORAMA CAPITAL, 1410
PANTHEON VENTURES (US) LP, 1411
PARTECH INTERNATIONAL, 1416
PARTHENON CAPITAL, 1417
PATHBREAKER VENTURES, 1421
PEGASUS CAPITAL GROUP, 1424
PENINSULA VENTURES, 1427
PHILQUO VENTURES, 1437
PHYSIC VENTURES, 1438
PINNACLE VENTURES, 1445
PITANGO VENTURE CAPITAL, 3039
PIVA, 1449
PIVOTNORTH CAPITAL, 1450
PLATINUM EQUITY, 1451
PLEXUS VENTURES, 1452
PLUG AND PLAY VENTURES, 1453
POLARIS VENTURE PARTNERS, 1460
POND VENTURES, 3047
POSEIDON ASSET MANAGEMENT, 1464
PRECURSOR VENTURES, 1471
PRELUDE VENTURES, 1472
PRESIDIO VENTURES, 1474
PRITZKER GROUP PRIVATE CAPITAL, 1479
PRITZKER GROUP VENTURE CAPITAL, 1480
PROGRESS INVESTMENT MANAGEMENT COMPANY, 1485
PROQUEST INVESTMENTS, 1490
PROSPECT VENTURE PARTNERS, 1493
PSILOS GROUP, 1498
QUALCOMM VENTURES, 1509
QUARK VENTURE, 2229
QUEST VENTURE PARTNERS, 1513
QUESTA CAPITAL, 1514
RALLY VENTURES, 1522
REACH CAPITAL, 1527
REDPOINT VENTURES, 1534
REDWOOD CAPITAL CORPORATION, 1535
REEFI CAPITAL, 1537
RELAY VENTURES, 2236
REMBRANDT VENTURE PARTNERS, 1540
RESOLUTE.VC, 1546
RHO VENTURES, 1558
RHYTHM VENTURE CAPITAL, 1559
RIBBIT CAPITAL, 1560
RIDGE VENTURES, 1563
RINCON VENTURE PARTNERS, 1566
RIVERSIDE COMPANY, 1572
RLH EQUITY PARTNERS, 1575
RODA GROUP, 1580
ROSEWOOD CAPITAL, 1587
ROTH CAPITAL PARTNERS, 1588
RUBICON VENTURE CAPITAL, 1595

Geographic Index

SACRAMENTO ANGELS, 1600
SAGEVIEW CAPITAL, 1602
SAIL VENTURE PARTNERS, 1603
SAINTS CAPITAL, 1604
SALESFORCE VENTURES, 1607
SALT CREEK CAPITAL, 1609
SAMSUNG NEXT, 1611
SAMSUNG VENTURE INVESTMENT CORPORATION, 3098
SAN DIEGO VENTURE GROUP, 1612
SAND HILL ANGELS, 1613
SANDBOX INDUSTRIES, 1615
SANDERLING VENTURES, 1616
SAPPHIRE VENTURES, 1620
SCALE VENTURE PARTNERS, 1626
SCIFI VC, 1631
SCRUM VENTURES, 1634
SEACOAST CAPITAL CORPORATION, 1636
SEED MILESTONE FUND, 1644
SEIDLER EQUITY PARTNERS, 1645
SELBY VENTURE PARTNERS, 1646
SEQUOIA CAPITAL, 1654
SHAMROCK CAPITAL ADVISORS, 1660
SHAMROCK HOLDINGS, 1661
SHARESPOST, 1662
SHASTA VENTURES, 1663
SHEPHERD VENTURES, 1664
SHERPALO VENTURES, 1666
SIERRA VENTURES, 1670
SIGMA PARTNERS, 1672
SIGNIA VENTURE PARTNERS, 1678
SILVER LAKE, 1683
SINGTEL INNOV8, 3121
SJF VENTURES, 1689
SK TELECOM VENTURES, 1690
SKYLINE VENTURES, 1691
SKYTREE CAPITAL PARTNERS, 1692
SLOW VENTURES, 1694
SOCIAL CAPITAL, 1696
SOCIAL VENTURE CIRCLE, 3277
SOFINNOVA VENTURES, 1698
SOFTBANK CAPITAL, 1699
SOFTTECH VC, 1700
SONY INNOVATION FUND, 1703
SONY STRATEGIC TECHNOLOGY PARTNERSHIPS, 1704
SORRENTO VENTURES, 1706
SOURCE CAPITAL GROUP, 1707
SOUTHERN CROSS VENTURE PARTNERS, 1711
SPARK CAPITAL, 1715
SPARKLABS GLOBAL VENTURES, 1716
SPECTRUM EQUITY INVESTORS LP, 1717
SPERO VENTURES, 1721
SR ONE LTD, 1731
STAGE 1 VENTURES, 1734
STARTUP CAPITAL VENTURES, 1737
STARWOOD CAPITAL GROUP LLC, 1739
STEAMBOAT VENTURES, 3142
STEELPOINT CAPITAL PARTNERS, 1741
STORM VENTURES, 1747
SUMMIT PARTNERS, 1752
SUN CAPITAL PARTNERS, 1753
SUNBRIDGE PARTNERS, 1755
SUNRISE CAPITAL PARTNERS, 1756
SUNSTONE CAPITAL, 3149
SUSA VENTURES, 1758
SUTTER HILL VENTURES, 1760
SV ANGEL, 1761
SVB CAPITAL, 1764
SWANDER PACE CAPITAL, 1767
SWITCH VENTURES, 1768
SYCAMORE VENTURES, 1769
SYNERGY LIFE SCIENCE PARTNERS, 1772
SYNERGY VENTURES, 1773
TA ASSOCIATES, 1776
TAKEDA VENTURES, 1778
TALLWOOD VENTURE CAPITAL, 1779
TAYRONA VENTURES, 1781
TECH COAST ANGELS, 1784
TECHNOLOGY CROSSOVER VENTURES, 1785
TECHNOLOGY PARTNERS, 1786
TEL VENTURE CAPITAL, 1791
TELEFONICA VENTURES, 3169
TELEGRAPH HILL PARTNERS, 1792
TELESOFT PARTNERS, 1793
TEN ELEVEN VENTURES, 1794
TENAYA CAPITAL, 1796
TENONETEN VENTURES, 1798
THAYER VENTURES, 1806
THE ARCVIEW GROUP, 1807
THE HIVE, 1809
THIRD ROCK VENTURES, 1811
THIRD SECURITY, 1812
THOMA BRAVO LLC, 1814
THOMAS WEISEL VENTURE PARTNERS, 1816
THOMAS, MCNERNEY & PARTNERS, 1817
THOMVEST VENTURES, 1818
THREE ARCH PARTNERS LP, 1819
TOBA CAPITAL, 1829
TONIIC, 1831
TOYOTA AI VENTURES, 1834
TPG CAPITAL, 1835
TRANSLINK CAPITAL, 1838
TRANSMEDIA CAPITAL, 1839
TRIANGLE PEAK PARTNERS, 1846
TRIBE CAPITAL, 1848
TRIDENT CAPITAL, 1850
TRINITY VENTURES, 1853
TRUE VENTURES, 1860
TSG CONSUMER PARTNERS, 1861
TUGBOAT VENTURES, 1865
TVC CAPITAL, 1869
TYLT LAB, 1876
UBIQUITY VENTURES, 1877
UNCORK CAPITAL, 1879
UNITED TALENT AGENCY VENTURES, 1883
UNSHACKLED VENTURES, 1885
UPFRONT VENTURES, 1888
UPWELLING CAPITAL GROUP, 1892
URBAN US, 1894
US RENEWABLES GROUP, 1895
US VENTURE PARTNERS, 1896
VALIA, 1900
VALUEACT CAPITAL, 1903
VANCE STREET CAPITAL, 1904
VANTAGEPOINT CAPITAL PARTNERS, 1906
VCFA GROUP, 1908
VECTOR CAPITAL, 1910
VENBIO, 1914
VENROCK ASSOCIATES, 1916
VENTANA CAPITAL MANAGEMENT LP, 1918
VENTURE TECH ALLIANCE, 1922
VERDEXUS, 2279
VERIZON VENTURES, 1926
VERSANT VENTURES, 1928
VERTICAL GROUP, 1929
VILLAGE GLOBAL, 1933
VISTA EQUITY PARTNERS, 1938
VISTA VENTURE PARTNERS, 1939
VIVO CAPITAL, 1941
VOLVO GROUP VENTURE CAPITAL, 3226
VOYAGER CAPITAL, 1945
WALDEN INTERNATIONAL, 1951
WALDEN VENTURE CAPITAL, 1952
WARBURG PINCUS LLC, 1956
WASABI VENTURES, 1958
WASSERSTEIN & CO., 1960
WAVEMAKER PARTNERS, 1965
WAVEPOINT VENTURES, 1966
WEDBUSH CAPITAL PARTNERS, 1969
WELLS FARGO CAPITAL FINANCE, 1970
WELSH, CARSON, ANDERSON & STOWE, 1972
WEST HEALTH INVESTMENT FUND, 1973
WESTERN ASSOCIATION OF VENTURE CAPITALISTS, 3284
WESTERN STATES INVESTMENT GROUP, 1974
WESTERN TECHNOLOGY INVESTMENT, 1975

1123

Geographic Index

WESTLY GROUP, 1977
WESTON PRESIDIO, 1978
WESTSUMMIT CAPITAL, 3235
WI HARPER GROUP, 1983
WILDCAT VENTURE PARTNERS, 1985
WILSHIRE PRIVATE MARKETS, 1989
WINDWARD VENTURES, 1995
WING VENTURE PARTNERS, 1996
WIREFRAME VENTURES, 2000
WOMEN'S VENTURE CAPITAL FUND, 2003
WOODSIDE FUND, 2005
WORLDVIEW TECHNOLOGY PARTNERS, 2007
WYNNCHURCH CAPITAL, 2009
XSEED CAPITAL MANAGEMENT, 2011
Y COMBINATOR, 2012
YES VC, 2014
YL VENTURES, 3246
YUCAIPA COMPANIES, 2016
ZETTA VENTURE PARTNERS, 2019
ZONE VENTURES, 2021

Colorado

ACCESS VENTURE PARTNERS LLC, 36
ALTA PARTNERS, 94
ALTIRA GROUP LLC, 98
APPIAN VENTURES, 142
ARAVAIPA VENTURES, 146
AWEIDA VENTURE PARTNERS, 210
BBH CAPITAL PARTNERS, 240
BOULDER VENTURES LTD, 315
CANNABIS CAPITAL GROWTH, 390
CANOPY BOULDER, 392
CENTENNIAL VENTURES, 441
CHB CAPITAL PARTNERS, 461
CHEYENNE CAPITAL, 467
CORNERSTONE HOLDINGS, 542
CRAWLEY VENTURES, 553
ENDEAVOUR CAPITAL, 673
FIRST CAPITAL VENTURE, 735
FOUNDRY GROUP, 776
FRASER MCCOMBS CAPITAL, 781
GREEN LION PARTNERS, 860
GROTECH VENTURES, 876
GROWTH FUND PRIVATE EQUITY, 880
HIGH COUNTRY VENTURE, 930
INFIELD CAPITAL, 988
IRON GATE CAPITAL, 1020
KRG CAPITAL PARTNERS, 1086
LACUNA GAP CAPITAL, 1090
LYNWOOD CAPITAL PARTNERS, 1152
MEDIA VENTURE PARTNERS, 1195
MERITAGE FUNDS, 1211
MOBIUS VENTURE CAPITAL, 1245
PARTISAN MANAGEMENT GROUP, 1418
POINT B CAPITAL, 1458
PROGRESS EQUITY PARTNERS, 1484
RESOURCE CAPITAL FUNDS, 1548
ROCKY MOUNTAIN VENTURE CAPITAL ASSOCIATION, 3276
ROSER VENTURES LLC, 1586
SEQUEL VENTURE PARTNERS, 1653
STONEHENGE GROWTH CAPITAL, 1745
TECHSTARS, 1789
TEN ELEVEN VENTURES, 1794
TICONDEROGA PRIVATE EQUITY, 1824
TRANSITION PARTNERS LTD, 1837
VESTAR CAPITAL PARTNERS, 1931
WELLS FARGO CAPITAL FINANCE, 1970
WILSHIRE PRIVATE MARKETS, 1989

Connecticut

1843 CAPITAL, 7
ACCESS MEDICAL VENTURES, 2328
ADVANTAGE CAPITAL PARTNERS, 61
AEA INVESTORS, 64
ALERION PARTNERS, 80
ALTPOINT CAPITAL, 101
ALTUS CAPITAL PARTNERS, 104
ARROWHEAD INVESTMENT MANAGEMENT, 168
AXIOM VENTURE PARTNERS, 212
BLUFF POINT ASSOCIATES, 299
BROOKSIDE EQUITY PARTNERS LLC, 353
BRYNWOOD PARTNERS, 357
CANAAN PARTNERS, 386
CAPITAL PARTNERS, 401
CAVA CAPITAL, 431
CCP EQUITY PARTNERS, 434
CENTRIPETAL CAPITAL PARTNERS, 448
CHL MEDICAL PARTNERS, 474
CLEARVIEW CAPITAL, 503
CLEARWATER CAPITAL PARTNERS, 504
CLOQUET CAPITAL PARTNERS, 505
COHEN PRIVATE VENTURES, 510
COMPASS GROUP MANAGEMENT LLC, 523
CONNECTICUT INNOVATIONS, 530
CORNERSTONE EQUITY INVESTORS LLC, 541
DAVENPORT RESOURCES LLC, 588
DAWNTREADER VENTURES, 592
DUBILIER & COMPANY, 631
EASTVEN VENTURE PARTNERS, 645
ELM STREET VENTURES, 660
EMIL CAPITAL PARTNERS, 668
EQUINOX CAPITAL, 691
EXPANSION CAPITAL PARTNERS, 706
FAIRVIEW CAPITAL PARTNERS, 714
FERRER FREEMAN & COMPANY LLC, 723
FIRST NEW ENGLAND CAPITAL LP, 739
FIRST RESERVE, 740
FORTRESS INVESTMENT GROUP LLC, 767
GALEN PARTNERS, 806
GE CAPITAL, 808
GENERAL ATLANTIC PARTNERS, 815
GENERATION PARTNERS, 818
GILBERT GLOBAL EQUITY PARTNERS, 827
GREAT POINT PARTNERS, 859
GREENHAVEN PARTNERS, 863
GRIDIRON CAPITAL, 873
HAMILTON ROBINSON CAPITAL PARTNERS, 899
HARTFORD VENTURES, 912
HEALTHINVEST EQUITY PARTNERS, 920
HEARTLAND INDUSTRIAL PARTNERS, 923
HERCULES TECHNOLOGY GROWTH CAPITAL, INC, 925
HORIZON TECHNOLOGY FINANCE, 946
IRONWOOD CAPITAL, 1021
JH WHITNEY & COMPANY, 1037
KIDD & COMPANY, 1071
KLINE HILL PARTNERS, 1076
L CATTERTON PARTNERS, 1088
LAUNCHCAPITAL, 1097
LEASING TECHNOLOGIES INTERNATIONAL INC., 1103
LIBERTY CAPITAL PARTNERS, 1114
LITTLEJOHN & COMPANY LLC, 1134
LONGITUDE CAPITAL, 1143
NATURAL GAS PARTNERS, 1278
NGN CAPITAL, 1325
NORTH CASTLE PARTNERS, 1335
OAK HILL CAPITAL PARTNERS, 1360
OAK INVESTMENT PARTNERS, 1361
OAKTREE CAPITAL MANAGEMENT LLC, 1362
OEM CAPITAL, 1369
OLYMPUS PARTNERS, 1372
PERFORMANCE EQUITY MANAGEMENT, LLC, 1431
PLATINUM EQUITY, 1451
RFE INVESTMENT PARTNERS, 1557
ROPART ASSET MANAGEMENT, 1583
SAGEVIEW CAPITAL, 1602
SAUGATUCK CAPITAL COMPANY, 1624
SIGNAL LAKE, 1676
SOURCE CAPITAL GROUP, 1707
SOUTHPORT PARTNERS, 1712
SPENCER TRASK VENTURES, 1720
SPINNAKER CAPITAL PARTNERS, 1723
STARBOARD CAPITAL PARTNERS, 1735
STONE POINT CAPITAL LLC, 1743
SV INVESTMENT PARTNERS, 1763

Geographic Index

THOMAS, MCNERNEY & PARTNERS, 1817
TULLIS HEALTH INVESTORS, 1866
TWJ CAPITAL, 1873
VITAL FINANCIAL LLC, 1940
WARWICK GROUP, 1957
WOMEN'S ASSOCIATION OF VENTURE & EQUITY INC., 3285
WOODBRIDGE GROUP, 2004

Delaware
BBH CAPITAL PARTNERS, 240
DUPONT CAPITAL, 637
INFLECTION POINT VENTURES, 989
SMARTINVEST VENTURES, 1695

District of Columbia
ACCOLADE PARTNERS, 37
ACON INVESTMENTS, 46
ACORN GROWTH COMPANIES, 48
ACTA CAPITAL, 51
ADVANTAGE CAPITAL PARTNERS, 61
AMERICAN INVESTMENT COUNCIL, 3255
ANZU PARTNERS, 133
CALVERT INVESTMENT MANAGEMENT, 376
CAPITAL E, 398
CARLYLE GROUP, 413
CM EQUITY PARTNERS, 507
CORE CAPITAL PARTNERS, 538
DARBY OVERSEAS INVESTMENTS LTD, 584
EMERGING MARKETS PRIVATE EQUITY ASSOCIATION, 3261
EMP GLOBAL, 670
EVERCORE CAPITAL PARTNERS, 699
GRANTHAM CAPITAL, 853
GROSVENOR FUNDS, 875
HALIFAX GROUP LLC, 894
HCI EQUITY PARTNERS, 917
INSTITUTIONAL LIMITED PARTNERS ASSOCIATION, 3266
INTERNATIONAL FINANCE CORPORATION (IFC), 1007
MID-ATLANTIC VENTURE ASSOCIATION, 1227, 3270
NATIONAL VENTURE CAPITAL ASSOCIATION, 3272
OMIDYAR NETWORK, 1374
OXANTIUM VENTURES, 1393
PALADIN CAPITAL GROUP, 1400
QUESTA CAPITAL, 1514
REVOLUTION LLC, 1555
SALEM HALIFAX CAPITAL PARTNERS, 1605
STARWOOD CAPITAL GROUP LLC, 1739
UPDATA VENTURE PARTNERS, 1886
WACHTEL & CO. INC, 1948

Florida
ACCUITIVE MEDICAL VENTURES LLC, 40
ADVANTAGE CAPITAL PARTNERS, 61
AEROEQUITY, 66
ANDLINGER & COMPANY INC, 123
ANTARES CAPITAL CORPORATION, 131
ANZU PARTNERS, 133
ARSENAL VENTURE PARTNERS, 171
ATHENIAN VENTURE PARTNERS, 187
AXON PARTNERS GROUP, 2469
BALLAST POINT VENTURES, 224
BAYSIDE CAPITAL, 239
BIGFOOT VENTURES, 2511
BLAST FUNDING, 279
BROCKWAY MORAN & PARTNERS, 348
CAMBRIDGE CAPITAL, 380
CAPITALA, 405
COMVEST PARTNERS, 528
DARBY OVERSEAS INVESTMENTS LTD, 584
DRESNER COMPANIES, 629
DUBIN CLARK & COMPANY, 632
ENERGY CAPITAL PARTNERS, 675
ENERTECH CAPITAL, 676
EVERCORE CAPITAL PARTNERS, 699
FLORIDA CAPITAL PARTNERS, 752
FLORIDA VENTURE FORUM, 3262
FULCRUM EQUITY PARTNERS, 794
HIG CAPITAL, 928

HORIZON PARTNERS, LTD, 945
INFLEXION PARTNERS, 990
KIRENAGA, 1074
KOHLBERG KRAVIS ROBERTS & COMPANY, 1082
LFE CAPITAL, 1113
LIBERTY CAPITAL PARTNERS, 1114
LIGHTHOUSE PARTNERS, 1120
LM CAPITAL SECURITIES, 1137
LONE STAR FUNDS, 1140
LOVETT MILLER & COMPANY, 1148
NORTH AMERICAN FUND, 1332
PALISADE CAPITAL MANAGEMENT, 1401
PARTISAN MANAGEMENT GROUP, 1418
PENTA MEZZANINE FUND, 1430
PHYTO PARTNERS, 1439
PROQUEST INVESTMENTS, 1490
QUANTUM CAPITAL PARTNERS, 1510
SI VENTURES, 1668
SOURCE CAPITAL GROUP, 1707
SOUTH ATLANTIC VENTURE FUNDS, 1708
STARWOOD CAPITAL GROUP LLC, 1739
STERLING PARTNERS, 1742
STONEHENGE GROWTH CAPITAL, 1745
SUN CAPITAL PARTNERS, 1753
THIRD SECURITY, 1812
TRIVEST PARTNERS, 1857
TULLIS HEALTH INVESTORS, 1866
VINTAGE CAPITAL MANAGEMENT, 1935
VON BRAUN & SCHREIBER PRIVATE EQUITY PARTNERS, 3227
WELLS FARGO CAPITAL FINANCE, 1970
WESTLAKE SECURITIES, 1976

Georgia
ACCEL-KKR LLC, 29
ACCUITIVE MEDICAL VENTURES LLC, 40
ARCAPITA INC, 152
ARES MANAGEMENT LLC, 159
BIP CAPITAL, 271
BLH VENTURE PARTNERS, 282
CAPITALA, 405
CEDAR VENTURES LLC, 437
CEO VENTURES, 450
CORDOVA VENTURES, 537
EGL HOLDINGS, 656
ENGAGE VENTURES, 677
EQUITY SOUTH, 693
FORTRESS INVESTMENT GROUP LLC, 767
FORTÉ VENTURES, 768
FULCRUM EQUITY PARTNERS, 794
GEORGIA OAK PARTNERS, 821
GRAY GHOST VENTURES, 855
GUGGENHEIM PARTNERS, 885
HARBERT MANAGEMENT CORPORATION, 904
HIG CAPITAL, 928
ICV PARTNERS, 969
INVESCO PRIVATE CAPITAL, 1015
KINETIC VENTURES, 1072
MESA CAPITAL PARTNERS, 1219
MSOUTH EQUITY PARTNERS, 1270
NAVIGATION CAPITAL PARTNERS, 1280
NORO-MOSELEY PARTNERS, 1331
PEACHTREE EQUITY PARTNERS, 1423
QUANTUM WAVE FUND, 3068
RED CLAY CAPITAL HOLDINGS, 1529
RELATIVITY CAPITAL, 1539
RIVER CAPITAL, 1570
ROARK CAPITAL GROUP, 1576
SALEM HALIFAX CAPITAL PARTNERS, 1605
STARWOOD CAPITAL GROUP LLC, 1739
TECHOPERATORS, 1788
TTV CAPITAL, 1863
UPS STRATEGIC ENTERPRISE FUND, 1891
WELLS FARGO CAPITAL FINANCE, 1970

Hawaii
HAWAII VENTURE CAPITAL ASSOCIATION, 3263
HMS HAWAII MANAGEMENT, 939

1125

Geographic Index

SOURCE CAPITAL GROUP, 1707
STARTUP CAPITAL VENTURES, 1737

Idaho
RENEWABLETECH VENTURES, 1542

Illinois
ADAMS STREET PARTNERS, LLC, 57
ADVANTAGE CAPITAL PARTNERS, 61
AGMAN PARTNERS, 70
ALLSTATE INVESTMENTS LLC, 88
ALPHA CAPITAL PARTNERS, 90
ALTUS CAPITAL PARTNERS, 104
AMITI VENTURES, 116
ANDERSON PACIFIC CORPORATION, 122
ANGELO, GORDON & CO., 127
APEX VENTURE PARTNERS, 137
ARBOR INVESTMENTS, 147
ARCH VENTURE PARTNERS, 153
ARES MANAGEMENT LLC, 159
BAIRD CAPITAL PARTNERS, 222
BAXTER VENTURES, 236
BBH CAPITAL PARTNERS, 240
BEECKEN PETTY O'KEEFE & COMPANY, 244
BMO CAPITAL MARKETS, 2063
BOUNDS EQUITY PARTNERS, 316
BRIDGE STREET CAPITAL, 338
BROADHAVEN CAPITAL PARTNERS, 343
CAPX PARTNERS, 407
CERBERUS CAPITAL MANAGEMENT, 451
CERES VENTURE FUND, 452
CHICAGO GROWTH PARTNERS, 468
CHICAGO PACIFIC FOUNDERS, 469
CHICAGO VENTURE PARTNERS LP, 470
CHICAGO VENTURES, 471
CIVC PARTNERS, 489
COMVEST PARTNERS, 528
CONCENTRIC EQUITY PARTNERS Financial Investments Corporation, 529
CRESSEY & COMPANY LP, 558
CULTIVIAN SANDBOX VENTURES, 570
CYPRIUM PARTNERS, 577
DN PARTNERS LLC, 619
DRESNER COMPANIES, 629
DUCHOSSOIS CAPITAL MANAGEMENT, 633
DUNRATH CAPITAL, 636
EDGEWATER FUNDS, 654
EVERCORE CAPITAL PARTNERS, 699
FIRST ANALYSIS, 732
FLEXPOINT FORD LLC, 750
FRASER MCCOMBS CAPITAL, 781
FRONTENAC COMPANY, 789
G SQUARED, 802
GLADSTONE CAPITAL, 828
GLENCOE CAPITAL, 830
GOENSE & COMPANY LLC, 838
GOLUB CAPITAL, 844
GREENHILL SAVP, 864
GTCR, 884
GUGGENHEIM PARTNERS, 885
HANCOCK CAPITAL MANAGEMENT, 901
HAWTHORN EQUITY PARTNERS, 916
HCI EQUITY PARTNERS, 917
HERCULES TECHNOLOGY GROWTH CAPITAL, INC, 925
HIG CAPITAL, 928
HIGH STREET CAPITAL, 932
HIGHER GROUND LABS, 934
HILCO BRANDS, 937
HOPEWELL VENTURES, 944
HYDE PARK VENTURE PARTNERS, 962
ILLINOIS VENTURE CAPITAL ASSOCIATION, 3265
ILLINOIS VENTURES, 975
INDEPENDENCE EQUITY, 983
IRISH ANGELS, 1019
JK&B CAPITAL, 1038
JORDAN COMPANY, 1045
JUMP CAPITAL LLC, 1046
KB PARTNERS, 1056
KB PARTNERS LLC, 1057
KNOX CAPITAL, 1078
LAKE CAPITAL, 1091
LASALLE CAPITAL GROUP, 1093
LEO CAPITAL HOLDINGS, LLC, 1108
LIGHTBANK, 1118
LIGHTHOUSE PARTNERS, 1120
LINCOLNSHIRE MANAGEMENT, 1127
LINDEN LLC, 1128
LIONBIRD, 2943
M25 GROUP, 1155
MADISON DEARBORN PARTNERS, 1156
MARANON CAPITAL, 1166
MATH VENTURE PARTNERS, 1178
MERIT CAPITAL PARTNERS, 1209
MIDWEST MEZZANINE FUNDS, 1232
MK CAPITAL, 1242
MODERNE VENTURES, 1246
MOTOROLA SOLUTIONS VENTURE CAPITAL, 1260
MPG EQUITY PARTNERS, 1267
NEEDHAM CAPITAL PARTNERS, 1288
NEWSPRING CAPITAL, 1317
NORTH AMERICAN FUND, 1332
NORTHLEAF CAPITAL PARTNERS, 2204
OCA VENTURES, 1364
ONE EQUITY PARTNERS, 1376
OPEN PRAIRIE VENTURES, 1379
ORIGIN VENTURES, 1384
PARADIGM CAPITAL LTD, 1414
PARALLEL49 EQUITY, 2214
PATRIOT CAPITAL, 1422
PFINGSTEN PARTNERS LLC, 1435
POLESTAR CAPITAL, 1461
PPM AMERICA CAPITAL PARTNERS, 1467
PRAIRIE CAPITAL, 1469
PRISM CAPITAL, 1477
PRITZKER GROUP PRIVATE CAPITAL, 1479
PRITZKER GROUP VENTURE CAPITAL, 1480
PROMUS VENTURES, 1489
PROSPECT PARTNERS LLC, 1492
PRUDENTIAL CAPITAL GROUP, 1497
REDWOOD CAPITAL GROUP, 1536
RLH EQUITY PARTNERS, 1575
ROCK ISLAND CAPITAL, 1578
ROTH CAPITAL PARTNERS, 1588
ROUNDTABLE HEALTHCARE PARTNERS, 1590
SALVEO CAPITAL, 1610
SANDALPHON CAPITAL, 1614
SANDBOX INDUSTRIES, 1615
SECOND CENTURY VENTURES, 1642
SHORE CAPITAL PARTNERS, 1667
SILKROAD EQUITY, 1681
SILVER OAK SERVICES PARTNERS, 1684
STARWOOD CAPITAL GROUP LLC, 1739
STATELINE ANGELS, 1740
STERLING PARTNERS, 1742
SUCSY, FISCHER & COMPANY, 1750
SVOBODA CAPITAL PARTNERS, 1765
THOMA BRAVO LLC, 1814
TRUE NORTH VENTURE PARTNERS, 1859
TWIN BRIDGE CAPITAL PARTNERS, 1871
UBS GLOBAL ASSET MANAGEMENT, 1878
UPHEAVAL INVESTMENTS, 1890
VALOR EQUITY PARTNERS, 1902
VISTA EQUITY PARTNERS, 1938
WALL STREET VENTURE CAPITAL, 1953
WATER STREET HEALTHCARE PARTNERS, 1961
WAUD CAPITAL PARTNERS LLC, 1963
WAVELAND INVESTMENTS LLC, 1964
WELLS FARGO CAPITAL FINANCE, 1970
WILLIS STEIN & PARTNERS LLC, 1986
WILSHIRE PRIVATE MARKETS, 1989
WIND POINT PARTNERS, 1990
WINONA CAPITAL MANAGEMENT, 1999
WYNNCHURCH CAPITAL, 2009

Geographic Index

Indiana
ALLOS VENTURES, 86
CAMBRIDGE VENTURES LP, 382
CARDINAL EQUITY PARTNERS, 409
CARLYLE GROUP, 413
CENTERFIELD CAPITAL PARTNERS, 443
CID CAPITAL, 478
ELEVATE VENTURES, 658
GUGGENHEIM PARTNERS, 885
HAMMOND, KENNEDY, WHITNEY & COMPANY, 900
HIGH ALPHA, 929
HYDE PARK VENTURE PARTNERS, 962
LILLY VENTURES, 1124
MONUMENT ADVISORS, 1252
TRASK INNOVATIONS FUND Purdue Research Foundation, 1840
TRIATHLON MEDICAL VENTURES, 1847
VENTURE CLUB OF INDIANA, 3282

Iowa
AAVIN PRIVATE EQUITY, 17
BROADHORN CAPITAL, 344
INVESTAMERICA VENTURE GROUP, 1016
PALMS & COMPANY, 1404

Kansas
ANGEL CAPITAL ASSOCIATION, 3256
D.E. SHAW & CO. LP, 579
KANSAS VENTURE CAPITAL, 1053

Kentucky
CHRYSALIS VENTURES, 475
HUMANA VENTURES, 955
KENTUCKY HIGHLANDS INVESTMENT CORPORATION, 1064
MERITUS VENTURES, 1214
SOURCE CAPITAL GROUP, 1707
TRIATHLON MEDICAL VENTURES, 1847
VENTURE CONNECTORS, 3283

Louisiana
ADVANTAGE CAPITAL PARTNERS, 61
BVM CAPITAL, 362
CALLAIS CAPITAL MANAGEMENT, 372
ENHANCED CAPITAL, 678
LONGUEVUE CAPITAL LLC, 1144
SAIL VENTURE PARTNERS, 1603
STONEHENGE GROWTH CAPITAL, 1745
VOODOO VENTURES, LLC, 1943
WESTLAKE SECURITIES, 1976

Maine
CEI VENTURES, 438
MAINE VENTURE FUND, 1161
NORTH ATLANTIC CAPITAL CORPORATION, 1333

Maryland
ABELL FOUNDATION VENTURES, 19
ABS CAPITAL PARTNERS, 22
ALLEGIS CYBER CAPITAL, 84
APOLLO GLOBAL MANAGEMENT, 140
ARES MANAGEMENT LLC, 159
ARLINGTON CAPITAL PARTNERS, 166
ASHBY POINT CAPITAL, 179
ATLANTIC CAPITAL GROUP, 190
BOULDER VENTURES LTD, 315
CAMBER CREEK, 377
CAMDEN PARTNERS HOLDINGS LLC, 383
CAPITOL PARTNERS, 406
CATO BIOVENTURES, 430
CNF INVESTMENTS Clark Enterprises, Inc., 508
DFW CAPITAL PARTNERS, 610
ENLIGHTENMENT CAPITAL, 680
EPIDAREX CAPITAL, 689
EVERGREEN ADVISORS, 701
GIC GROUP, 825
GLOBAL ENVIRONMENT FUND, 834
GREENSPRING ASSOCIATES, 867
GROTECH VENTURES, 876
GUGGENHEIM PARTNERS, 885
HERCULES TECHNOLOGY GROWTH CAPITAL, INC, 925
JMI EQUITY FUND LP, 1041
KINETIC VENTURES, 1072
MARYLAND VENTURE FUND, 1169
MEDIMMUNE VENTURES, 1196
MERIDIAN MANAGEMENT GROUP, 1208
NEW ENTERPRISE ASSOCIATES, 1297
NEW MARKETS VENTURE PARTNERS, 1299
NEWSPRING CAPITAL, 1317
NEXTGEN ANGELS, 1320
NORTHPOND VENTURES, 1342
NOVAK BIDDLE VENTURE PARTNERS, 1348
PATRIOT CAPITAL, 1422
QUESTMARK PARTNERS LP, 1515
SAVANO CAPITAL PARTNERS, 1625
SPRING CAPITAL PARTNERS LP, 1727
STERLING PARTNERS, 1742
SYNCOM VENTURE PARTNERS, 1771
TDF, 1782
TEDCO, 1790
TEXADA CAPITAL CORPORATION, 1799
TWJ CAPITAL, 1873
VITAL FINANCIAL LLC, 1940

Massachusetts
(@)VENTURES, 1
.406 VENTURES, 2
5AM VENTURES, 12
ABINGWORTH MANAGEMENT LIMITED, 2316
ABRY PARTNERS, 21
ABS VENTURES, 23
ACCESS BRIDGE-GAP VENTURES, 34
ACCOMPLICE, 38
ADAMS STREET PARTNERS, LLC, 57
ADVANCED TECHNOLOGY VENTURES, 59
ADVANCIT CAPITAL, 60
ADVENT INTERNATIONAL CORPORATION, 62
ALANTRA, 77
AMPERSAND CAPITAL PARTNERS, 118
ANZU PARTNERS, 133
APPLE TREE PARTNERS, 143
ARCLIGHT CAPITAL PARTNERS, 156
ARGO GLOBAL CAPITAL, 162
ASCENT VENTURE PARTNERS, 178
ATLAS VENTURE, 191
ATLAS VENTURE: FRANCE, 2445
AUDAX GROUP, 194
AVALON VENTURES, 206
AXIA CAPITAL, 211
AZCA, 214
BAIN CAPITAL PRIVATE EQUITY, 220
BAIN CAPITAL VENTURES, 221
BATTERY VENTURES, 235
BAYSIDE CAPITAL, 239
BBH CAPITAL PARTNERS, 240
BERKSHIRE PARTNERS LLC, 254
BERWIND PRIVATE EQUITY, 259
BESSEMER VENTURE PARTNERS, 260
BIOVENTURES INVESTORS, 270
BOREALIS VENTURES, 308
BOSTON CAPITAL, 309
BOSTON CAPITAL VENTURES, 310
BOSTON GLOBAL VENTURES, LLC, 311
BOSTON MILLENNIA PARTNERS, 312
BOSTON SEED CAPITAL, 313
BOSTON UNIVERSITY - TECHNOLOGY DEVELOPMENT, 314
BREAKAWAY VENTURES, 329
BROADVIEW VENTURES, 347
BROOK VENTURE FUND, 349
BROOKE PRIVATE EQUITY ASSOCIATES, 350
BUNKER HILL CAPITAL, 359
BV INVESTMENT PARTNERS, 361
CALERA CAPITAL, 368
CAMBRIDGE ASSOCIATES, 379
CAPITAL RESOURCE PARTNERS, 402
CAPX PARTNERS, 407

Geographic Index

CASTANEA PARTNERS, 421
CASTILE VENTURES, 422
CATALYST HEALTH VENTURES, 426
CATO BIOVENTURES, 430
CEDAR FUND, 436
CHARLES RIVER VENTURES, 455
CHARLESBANK CAPITAL PARTNERS, 456
CLARUS VENTURES, 495
CLEAN ENERGY VENTURE GROUP, 497
COLUMBIA CAPITAL, 515
COMMONS CAPITAL, 520
COMMONWEALTH CAPITAL VENTURES LP, 521
CONVERGE VENTURE PARTNERS, 534
CREDIT MUTUEL EQUITY, 2088
CRESCENT CAPITAL GROUP LP, 556
CUE BALL GROUP, 567
CUTLASS CAPITAL LLC, 572
D.E. SHAW & CO. LP, 579
DACE VENTURES, 580
DATA POINT CAPITAL, 586
DDJ CAPITAL MANAGEMENT, 597
DUBIN CLARK & COMPANY, 632
DUTCHESS CAPITAL, 638
EASTWARD CAPITAL PARTNERS, 646
ECHELON VENTURES, 647
EVERCORE CAPITAL PARTNERS, 699
EXCEL VENTURE MANAGEMENT, 703
EXPERIMENT FUND, 708
F-PRIME CAPITAL PARTNERS, 710
FA TECHNOLOGY VENTURES, 711
FAIRHAVEN CAPITAL, 712
FALCON INVESTMENTS, 716
FISHER LYNCH CAPITAL, 744
FLAGSHIP PIONEERING, 747
FLARE CAPITAL PARTNERS, 748
FLETCHER SPAGHT VENTURES, 749
FLYBRIDGE CAPITAL PARTNERS, 754
GE VENTURES, 809
GEMINI INVESTORS, 812
GEN Y CAPITAL PARTNERS Young Entrepreneur Council, 813
GENERAL CATALYST PARTNERS, 816
GLOBESPAN CAPITAL PARTNERS, 835
GRANDBANKS CAPITAL, 848
GREAT HILL PARTNERS LLC, 857
GREYLOCK PARTNERS, 872
GROVE STREET ADVISORS LLC, 879
GRYPHON MANAGEMENT COMPANY, 882
GUGGENHEIM PARTNERS, 885
GUIDE MEDICAL VENTURES, 886
GV, 889
HANCOCK CAPITAL MANAGEMENT, 901
HARBOURVEST PARTNERS LLC, 909
HEALTHCARE VENTURES LLC, 919
HERCULES TECHNOLOGY GROWTH CAPITAL, INC, 925
HERITAGE PARTNERS, 926
HIG CAPITAL, 928
HIGHLAND CAPITAL PARTNERS, 935
HLM VENTURE PARTNERS, 938
HOUSATONIC PARTNERS, 949
IN-Q-TEL, 979
INTERVALE CAPITAL, 1009
INVUS GROUP, 1018
JARVINIAN VENTURES, 1027
JEGI CAPITAL, 1033
JMH CAPITAL, 1040
JW CHILDS ASSOCIATES, 1049
KEPHA PARTNERS, 1065
KERRY CAPITAL ADVISORS, 1067
KNIGHTSBRIDGE ADVISERS, 1077
KODIAK VENTURE PARTNERS, 1080
LAUNCHCAPITAL, 1097
LAUNCHPAD VENTURE GROUP, 1100
LEASING TECHNOLOGIES INTERNATIONAL INC., 1103
LEXINGTON PARTNERS, 1112
LIGHTHOUSE CAPITAL PARTNERS, 1119
LIGHTSTONE VENTURES, 1122
LONG RIVER VENTURES, 1142
LONGWOOD FUND, 1145
LONGWORTH VENTURE PARTNERS, 1146
LUMIRA CAPITAL, 2180
M/C PARTNERS, 1153
MADISON PARKER CAPITAL, 1157
MANSA EQUITY PARTNERS, 1165
MASS VENTURES, 1172
MASSACHUSETTS CAPITAL RESOURCE COMPANY, 1173
MASSACHUSETTS GROWTH CAPITAL CORPORATION, 1174
MASTHEAD VENTURE PARTNERS, 1175
MATERIAL IMPACT, 1177
MATRIX PARTNERS, 1181
MEDIA VENTURE PARTNERS, 1195
MEDIPHASE VENTURE PARTNERS, 1197
MEKETA INVESTMENT GROUP, 1200
MENDOZA VENTURES, 1201
METAPOINT PARTNERS, 1224
MONITOR CLIPPER PARTNERS, 1248
MPE PARTNERS, 1266
MPM CAPITAL, 1268
MVM LIFE SCIENCE PARTNERS, 2981
McCARTHY CAPITAL, 1276
NAUTA CAPITAL, 2987
NEEDHAM CAPITAL PARTNERS, 1288
NEW ATLANTIC VENTURES, 1291
NEW ENGLAND BUSINESS EXCHANGE, 1295
NEW ENGLAND CAPITAL PARTNERS, 1296
NEW ENTERPRISE ASSOCIATES, 1297
NEWBURY, PIRET & COMPANY, 1312
NEXTVIEW VENTURES, 1322
NKM CAPITAL, 1329
NORTH BRIDGE VENTURE PARTNERS, 1334
NORTH HILL VENTURES, 1339
NORTHPOND VENTURES, 1342
NORWICH VENTURES, 1347
NOVARTIS VENTURE FUNDS, 1350
OMEGA FUNDS, 1373
OPENVIEW VENTURE PARTNERS, 1380
OUTCOME CAPITAL, 1388
OXFORD BIOSCIENCE PARTNERS, 1394
PAR CAPITAL MANAGEMENT, 1413
PARTHENON CAPITAL, 1417
PARTNERS HEALTHCARE RESEARCH VENTURES, 1419
PERMAL CAPITAL MANAGEMENT, 1432
PLATINUM EQUITY, 1451
POINT JUDITH CAPITAL, 1459
POLARIS VENTURE PARTNERS, 1460
PROCYON VENTURES, 1483
PROGRESS VENTURES, 1486
PROJECT 11 VENTURES, 1487
PROVIDENCE EQUITY PARTNERS, 1496
PURETECH VENTURES, 1501
QUABBIN CAPITAL, 1503
QUARK VENTURE, 2229
QUARRY CAPITAL MANAGEMENT, 1511
RA CAPITAL MANAGEMENT, 1519
RAPTOR GROUP, 1524
ROCKPORT CAPITAL, 1579
ROMULUS CAPITAL, 1581
ROOT CAPITAL, 1582
ROTH CAPITAL PARTNERS, 1588
ROUGH DRAFT VENTURES, 1589
ROYALTY CAPITAL MANAGEMENT, 1591
SAMSUNG VENTURE INVESTMENT CORPORATION, 3098
SANOFI-GENZYME BIOVENTURES, 1618
SATURN PARTNERS, 1623
SCHOONER CAPITAL LLC, 1627
SCHRODER VENTURES HEALTH INVESTORS, 1628
SEACOAST CAPITAL CORPORATION, 1636
SIGMA PARTNERS, 1672
SIGMA PRIME VENTURES, 1673
SIGNAL LAKE, 1676
SIGULER GUFF & COMPANY, 1679
SOFTBANK CAPITAL, 1699
SOLSTICE CAPITAL LP, 1702
SOURCE CAPITAL GROUP, 1707
SPARK CAPITAL, 1715

1128

Geographic Index

SPECTRUM EQUITY INVESTORS LP, 1717
SPRING LAKE EQUITY PARTNERS, 1728
SPRING LANE CAPITAL, 1729
SR ONE LTD, 1731
STAGE 1 VENTURES, 1734
SUMMIT PARTNERS, 1752
SUPPLY CHAIN VENTURES, 1757
SV HEALTH INVESTORS, 1762
SYMMETRIC CAPITAL, 1770
SYNTHESIS CAPITAL, 1775
TA ASSOCIATES, 1776
TEN ELEVEN VENTURES, 1794
TENAYA CAPITAL, 1796
THIRD ROCK VENTURES, 1811
THOMAS H LEE PARTNERS, 1815
TICONDEROGA PRIVATE EQUITY, 1824
TPG CAPITAL, 1835
TSG EQUITY PARTNERS, 1862
TULLY & HOLLAND, 1867
VELOCITY EQUITY PARTNERS LLC, 1913
VENROCK ASSOCIATES, 1916
VENTURE CAPITAL FUND OF NEW ENGLAND, 1920
VESTAR CAPITAL PARTNERS, 1931
VIDA VENTURES, 1932
VINTAGE CAPITAL MANAGEMENT, 1935
VOLITION CAPITAL, 1942
WALL STREET VENTURE CAPITAL, 1953
WATERMILL GROUP, 1962
WELLS FARGO CAPITAL FINANCE, 1970
WESTON PRESIDIO, 1978
WESTVIEW CAPITAL PARTNERS, 1979
WINDSPEED VENTURES, 1994

Michigan
AMHERST FUND, 113
APJOHN GROUP LLC, 139
ARBORETUM VENTURES, 149
ARSENAL VENTURE PARTNERS, 171
AUGMENT VENTURES, 195
BERINGEA, 251
BIOSTAR VENTURES, 269
BLACKFORD CAPITAL LLC, 276
BRIDGE STREET CAPITAL, 338
DETROIT VENTURE PARTNERS, 607
DRAPER TRIANGLE VENTURES, 628
EDF VENTURES, 652
eLAB VENTURES, 2023
FIRST STEP FUND, 742
FONTINALIS PARTNERS, 760
GELT VC, 811
GENERAL MOTORS VENTURES, 817
GLENCOE CAPITAL, 830
HOPEN LIFE SCIENCE VENTURES, 943
HURON CAPITAL PARTNERS LLC, 960
HURON RIVER VENTURES, 961
INCWELL VENTURE CAPITAL, 981
LIBERTY CAPITAL PARTNERS, 1114
LONG POINT CAPITAL, 1141
LUDLOW VENTURES, 1150
MERCURY FUND, 1206
MICHIGAN VENTURE CAPITAL ASSOCIATION, 3269
MK CAPITAL, 1242
NEMO CAPITAL PARTNERS, 1289
NORTH COAST TECHNOLOGY INVESTORS LP, 1336
PENINSULA CAPITAL PARTNERS LLC, 1426
PLYMOUTH MANAGEMENT COMPANY, 1455
RESONANT VENTURE PARTNERS, 1547
RPM VENTURES, 1592
SENECA PARTNERS, 1649
SOUTHWEST MICHIGAN FIRST LIFE SCIENCE FUND, 1713
TGAP VENTURES, 1802
VENTURE INVESTORS LLC, 1921

Minnesota
AFFINITY CAPITAL MANAGEMENT, 68
ARTHUR VENTURES, 173
BRIGHTSTONE VENTURE CAPITAL, 341

CASTLELAKE, 424
CHERRY TREE COMPANIES, 464
EVERCORE CAPITAL PARTNERS, 699
FIRST GREEN PARTNERS, 738
GOLDNER, HAWN, JOHNSON & MORRISON, 843
GRANITE EQUITY PARTNERS, 850
HCI EQUITY PARTNERS, 917
INVESTAMERICA VENTURE GROUP, 1016
LEMHI VENTURES, 1107
LFE CAPITAL, 1113
MATCHSTICK VENTURES, 1176
MILESTONE GROWTH FUND, 1233
NDI MEDICAL, 1287
NORTHSTAR CAPITAL, 1343
NORWEST EQUITY PARTNERS, 1345
OAK INVESTMENT PARTNERS, 1361
RALLY VENTURES, 1522
SIGHTLINE PARTNERS, 1671
SPELL CAPITAL PARTNERS LLC, 1719
SPLIT ROCK PARTNERS, 1725
THE COLLABORATIVE, 3279
THOMAS, MCNERNEY & PARTNERS, 1817
TRIPLETREE LLC, 1854
VARDE PARTNERS, 1907
VENSANA CAPITAL, 1917
VERSANT VENTURES, 1928
WAYZATA INVESTMENT PARTNERS, 1967
WELLS FARGO CAPITAL FINANCE, 1970

Mississippi
ADVANTAGE CAPITAL PARTNERS, 61
GLASSWING VENTURES, 829
STONEHENGE GROWTH CAPITAL, 1745

Missouri
ADVANTAGE CAPITAL PARTNERS, 61
ASCENSION HEALTH VENTURES LLC, 176
AUGURY CAPITAL PARTNERS, 196
BIOGENERATOR, 267
C3 CAPITAL PARTNERS LP, 364
CAPITAL FOR BUSINESS, INC, 399
CULTIVATION CAPITAL, 569
EVERCORE CAPITAL PARTNERS, 699
FIVE ELMS CAPITAL, 745
GUGGENHEIM PARTNERS, 885
HARBOUR GROUP, 908
INVESTAMERICA VENTURE GROUP, 1016
MEDIA VENTURE PARTNERS, 1195
MISSOURI VENTURE FORUM, 3271
PROLOG VENTURES, 1488
RIVERVEST VENTURE PARTNERS, 1574
SIXTHIRTY, 1688
STONEHENGE GROWTH CAPITAL, 1745

Nebraska
AGMAN PARTNERS, 70
AGRIBUSINESS MANAGEMENT COMPANY, 71
AMERICA FIRST INVESTMENT ADVISORS, 108
DUNDEE VENTURE CAPITAL, 635
EVEREST GROUP, 700
McCARTHY CAPITAL, 1276
TENASKA CAPITAL MANAGEMENT, 1795

Nevada
ADVANTAGE CAPITAL PARTNERS, 61
AUSTRALIS CAPITAL, 203
COLOMA VENTURES, 512
JOHNSTON ASSOCIATES, 1044
REDHILLS VENTURES, 1532
SIERRA ANGELS, 1669
SKYTREE CAPITAL PARTNERS, 1692
VEGAS TECHFUND, 1912

New Hampshire
10X VENTURE PARTNERS, 3
ADVANTAGE CAPITAL PARTNERS, 61
ARETE CORPORATION, 160

1129

Geographic Index

BOREALIS VENTURES, 308
ECOAST ANGEL NETWORK, 649
HARBOR LIGHT CAPITAL PARTNERS, 907

New Jersey
180 DEGREE CAPITAL, 6
BASECAMP VENTURES, 230
BBH CAPITAL PARTNERS, 240
CAMBRIDGE CAPITAL CORPORATION, 381
CARDINAL PARTNERS, 410
CARE CAPITAL, 412
CASABONA VENTURES, 418
CIT GROUP, 484
CRYSTAL RIDGE PARTNERS, 565
D.E. SHAW & CO. LP, 579
DFW CAPITAL PARTNERS, 610
DOMAIN ASSOCIATES LLC, 621
EDELSON TECHNOLOGY PARTNERS, 651
EDISON PARTNERS, 655
ENERGY CAPITAL PARTNERS, 675
ENTREPIA VENTURES, 682
FRIEND SKOLER & COMPANY LLC, 788
JOHNSON & JOHNSON INNOVATION, 1043
JOHNSTON ASSOCIATES, 1044
MERCK GLOBAL HEALTH INNOVATION FUND, 1205
MIDMARK CAPITAL LP, 1230
MUNICH REINSURANCE AMERICA, INC, 1272
NASSAU CAPITAL, 1277
NAVIGATOR PARTNERS LLC, 1281
NEW VENTURE PARTNERS, 1305
NJ TECH COUNCIL, 3274
NJTC VENTURE FUND, 1328
NOVITAS CAPITAL, 1353
OMNICAPITAL GROUP, 1375
ONEX PARTNERS, 2209
OSAGE PARTNERS, 1387
PALISADE CAPITAL MANAGEMENT, 1401
PANGAEA VENTURES LTD, 2213
PLUS VENTURES, 3041
RIDGEWOOD CAPITAL, 1564
SCP PARTNERS, 1633
SELWAY CAPITAL, 1647
SOURCE CAPITAL GROUP, 1707
SWANDER PACE CAPITAL, 1767
SYCAMORE VENTURES, 1769
VERIZON VENTURES, 1926
VERTICAL GROUP, 1929
WILSHIRE PRIVATE MARKETS, 1989
YORK STREET CAPITAL PARTNERS LLC, 2015

New Mexico
COTTONWOOD TECHNOLOGY FUND, 549
FLYWHEEL VENTURES, 756
NATURAL GAS PARTNERS, 1278
NEW MEXICO COMMUNITY CAPITAL, 1300
PSILOS GROUP, 1498
SUN MOUNTAIN CAPITAL, 1754
TECHNOLOGY VENTURES CORPORATION, 1787
VERGE FUND, 1924

New York
3i GROUP PLC, 2311
747 CAPITAL, 14
ABBOTT CAPITAL MANAGEMENT LLC, 18
ACADIA WOODS PARTNERS, 26
ACCELERATOR LIFE SCIENCE PARTNERS, 31
ACCESS CAPITAL, 35
ACCRETIVE LLC, 39
ACI CAPITAL, 42
ACTIVATE VENTURE PARTNERS, 52
ACUMEN, 55
ADAMS STREET PARTNERS, LLC Adams Street Partners, Inc., 57
ADVANCIT CAPITAL, 60
ADVANTAGE CAPITAL PARTNERS, 61
ADVENT INTERNATIONAL CORPORATION, 62
AEA INVESTORS, 64
AEP CAPITAL LLC, 65

AISLING CAPITAL, 74
ALBION INVESTORS LLC, 78
ALEUTIAN CAPITAL PARTNERS, 81
ALPHA VENTURE PARTNERS, 91
ALPINVEST PARTNERS B.V. AlpInvest U.S. Holdings, LLC, 2379
ALTARIS CAPITAL PARTNERS, 97
ALTITUDE INVESTMENT MANAGEMENT, LLC, 99
AMERICAN INDUSTRIAL PARTNERS, 109
AMERICAN SECURITIES LLC, 110
ANDLINGER & COMPANY INC, 123
ANGELO, GORDON & CO., 127
ANGELPAD, 128
AOL VENTURES, 134
APAX PARTNERS, 135
APERTURE VENTURE PARTNERS, 136
APOLLO GLOBAL MANAGEMENT, 140
APPLE TREE PARTNERS, 143
ARBOR INVESTMENTS, 147
ARC ANGEL FUND, 150
ARCHTOP VENTURES, 154
ARCUS VENTURES, 157
ARES MANAGEMENT LLC, 159
ARGENTUM GROUP, 161
ARSENAL CAPITAL PARTNERS, 170
ARTHUR P GOULD & COMPANY, 172
ASCENT BIOMEDICAL VENTURES, 177
ATHYRIUM CAPITAL MANAGEMENT, 188
AUA PRIVATE EQUITY PARTNERS, 193
AUDAX GROUP, 194
AVENUE CAPITAL GROUP, 208
AVISTA CAPITAL PARTNERS, 209
AXXESS CAPITAL, 2471
B CAPITAL GROUP, 216
BABSON CAPITAL MANAGEMENT LLC, 217
BAIN CAPITAL PRIVATE EQUITY, 220
BAIN CAPITAL VENTURES, 221
BAKER CAPITAL, 223
BATTERY VENTURES, 235
BAYSIDE CAPITAL, 239
BBH CAPITAL PARTNERS, 240
BEDFORD FUNDING, 242
BEHRMAN CAPITAL, 245
BERINGER CAPITAL, 2057
BERTELSMANN DIGITAL MEDIA INVESTMENTS, 256
BESSEMER VENTURE PARTNERS, 260
BISON CAPITAL ASSET MANAGEMENT LLC, 274
BLACKSTONE PRIVATE EQUITY GROUP, 277
BLEU CAPITAL, 281
BLOOMBERG BETA, 284
BMO CAPITAL MARKETS, 2063
BNY MELLON CAPITAL MARKETS, 303
BOLDCAP VENTURES LLC, 304
BOLDSTART VENTURES, 305
BOWERY CAPITAL, 317
BOXGROUP, 318
BR VENTURE FUND, 320
BRADFORD EQUITIES MANAGEMENT LLC, 321
BRAEMAR ENERGY VENTURES, 322
BRAND FOUNDRY VENTURES, 325
BRANFORD CASTLE, 327
BREGAL ENERGY, 332
BREGAL SAGEMOUNT, 333
BRERA CAPITAL PARTNERS, 335
BROADHAVEN CAPITAL PARTNERS, 343
BROOKFIELD ASSET MANAGEMENT, 2067
BROOKLYN BRIDGE VENTURES, 351
BROOKS HOUGHTON & COMPANY, 352
BRUCKMANN, ROSSER, SHERRILL & COMPANY, 354
BUSINESS CONSORTIUM FUND, 360
CAI CAPITAL PARTNERS, 365
CALGARY ENTERPRISES, 369
CAMBER CREEK, 377
CANAAN PARTNERS, 386
CANROCK VENTURES, 393
CANTOR VENTURES, 394
CAPITAL Z PARTNERS, 404
CAPX PARTNERS, 407

1130

Geographic Index

CARBON VENTURES, 408
CARLYLE GROUP, 413
CASDIN CAPITAL, 419
CASTLE HARLAN, 423
CASTLELAKE, 424
CATALYST INVESTORS, 427
CAYUGA VENTURE FUND, 432
CCMP CAPITAL, 433
CENTANA GROWTH PARTNERS, 440
CENTERBRIDGE PARTNERS, 442
CENTRE LANE PARTNERS, 446
CENTRE PARTNERS MANAGEMENT LLC, 447
CERBERUS CAPITAL MANAGEMENT, 451
CHARLESBANK CAPITAL PARTNERS, 456
CHART VENTURE PARTNERS, 457
CHAZEN CAPITAL PARTNERS, 460
CHESTNUT HILL PARTNERS, 465
CI CAPITAL PARTNERS, 476
CIRCLE PEAK CAPITAL, 481
CIT GROUP, 484
CITI VENTURES, 486
CITY LIGHT CAPITAL, 488
CLARION CAPITAL PARTNERS LLC, 492
CM EQUITY PARTNERS, 507
COATUE MANAGEMENT, 509
COLUMBUS NOVA, 516
COMCAST VENTURES, 518
COMPASS GROUP, 522
COMPOUND, 525
CONTOUR VENTURE PARTNERS, 533
CONVERSION CAPITAL, 535
CORIOLIS VENTURES, 539
CORNERSTONE VENTURE PARTNERS, 543
CORRELATION VENTURES, 544
CORTEC GROUP, 546
CREDIT MUTUEL EQUITY, 2088
CREDIT SUISSE PRIVATE EQUITY Credit Suisse Group, 554
CRESCENT CAPITAL GROUP LP, 556
CRESTVIEW PARTNERS, 559
CULTIVATE CAPITAL, 568
CYPRESS GROUP, 575
CYPRIUM PARTNERS, 577
D.E. SHAW & CO. LP The D.E. Shaw Group, 579
DAUPHIN CAPITAL PARTNERS, 587
DAVID N DEUTSCH & COMPANY LLC, 589
DEERFIELD MANAGEMENT, 601
DFJ GOTHAM VENTURES, 608
DIFFERENTIAL VENTURES, 614
DRESNER COMPANIES, 629
DUTCHESS CAPITAL, 638
EARTHRISE CAPITAL, 643
EASTON CAPITAL INVESTMENT GROUP, 644
EMIGRANT CAPITAL, 667
EMINENT CAPITAL PARTNERS, 669
ENERGY CAPITAL PARTNERS, 675
ENHANCED CAPITAL, 678
ENSO VENTURES, 2702
ENTREPRENEURS ROUNDTABLE ACCELERATOR, 684
EOS PARTNERS LP, 686
EPIC PARTNERS, 687
ESSEX WOODLANDS HEALTH VENTURES LLC, 697
EVERCORE CAPITAL PARTNERS, 699
EXCELL PARTNERS, INC., 704
EXIUM PARTNERS, 705
EXPANSION VENTURE CAPITAL, 707
FALCONHEAD CAPITAL, 717
FENWAY PARTNERS, 722
FF VENTURE CAPITAL, 724
FGA PARTNERS, 725
FIELDSTONE PRIVATE CAPITAL GROUP, 726
FIRST ATLANTIC CAPITAL LTD., 733
FIRST ROUND CAPITAL, 741
FIRSTMARK CAPITAL, 743
FLEXPOINT FORD LLC, 750
FLYBRIDGE CAPITAL PARTNERS, 754
FORESITE CAPITAL, 762
FORTRESS INVESTMENT GROUP LLC, 767

FOUNDER COLLECTIVE, 771
FOUNDERS EQUITY, 774
FREEMAN SPOGLI & CO., 783
FTV CAPITAL, 793
FdG ASSOCIATES LP, 801
GE CAPITAL, 808
GEFINOR CAPITAL, 810
GENACAST VENTURES, 814
GENERAL ATLANTIC PARTNERS, 815
GENERAL CATALYST PARTNERS, 816
GILBERT GLOBAL EQUITY PARTNERS, 827
GLADSTONE CAPITAL, 828
GLOBALIVE, 2134
GOLDEN SEEDS, 841
GOLDMAN SACHS INVESTMENT PARTNERS, 842
GOLUB CAPITAL, 844
GOTHAM GREEN PARTNERS, 845
GRAND CENTRAL HOLDINGS, 847
GRANITE BRIDGE PARTNERS, 849
GREAT OAKS VENTURE CAPITAL, 858
GREENBRIAR EQUITY GROUP LLC, 862
GREENHILL SAVP, 864
GREENHILLS VENTURES, LLC, 865
GREYCROFT PARTNERS, 871
GRISHIN ROBOTICS, 874
GROVE GROUP MANAGEMENT, 878
GUGGENHEIM PARTNERS, 885
GV, 889
HALYARD CAPITAL, 897
HAMMOND, KENNEDY, WHITNEY & COMPANY, 900
HANCOCK CAPITAL MANAGEMENT, 901
HARBERT MANAGEMENT CORPORATION, 904
HARVEST PARTNERS, 914
HEALTH ENTERPRISE PARTNERS, 918
HEARST VENTURES, 922
HELLMAN & FRIEDMAN LLC, 924
HERCULES TECHNOLOGY GROWTH CAPITAL, INC, 925
HIG CAPITAL, 928
HIGH ROAD CAPITAL PARTNERS, 931
HIGHLAND CAPITAL PARTNERS, 935
HIGHLINE BETA, 2147
HOLDING CAPITAL GROUP, 940
HQ CAPITAL, 952
HT CAPITAL ADVISORS LLC, 953
HUDSON VENTURE PARTNERS, 954
I-HATCH VENTURES LLC, 964
IA VENTURES, 965
IANTHUS CAPITAL MANAGEMENT, 966
IBM VENTURE CAPITAL GROUP, 967
ICV PARTNERS, 969
IDG CAPITAL, 973
IMAGINATION CAPITAL, 977
IMPLEMENT CAPITAL, 978
INNOVATION ENDEAVORS, 996
INSIGHT VENTURE PARTNERS, 1000
INTERLACE VENTURES, 1006
INVESCO PRIVATE CAPITAL, 1015
INVESTCORP, 1017
INVUS GROUP, 1018
IRVING PLACE CAPITAL, 1022
J. BURKE CAPITAL PARTNERS, 1023
JEFFERIES CAPITAL PARTNERS, 1032
JEGI CAPITAL The Jordan Edminston Group, Inc., 1033
JESSELSON CAPITAL CORPORATION, 1034
JLL PARTNERS, 1039
JORDAN COMPANY, 1045
JUMP CAPITAL LLC, 1046
JW ASSET MANAGEMENT, 1048
KBL HEALTHCARE VENTURES, 1058
KELSO & COMPANY, 1062
KESTREL ENERGY PARTNERS, 1068
KIRENAGA, 1074
KOHLBERG & COMPANY LLC, 1081
KOHLBERG KRAVIS ROBERTS & COMPANY, 1082
KPS CAPITAL PARTNERS, 1085
L CATTERTON PARTNERS, 1088
LAUNCHCAPITAL, 1097

1131

Geographic Index

LDV CAPITAL, 1101
LEE EQUITY PARTNERS, 1104
LEEDS EQUITY PARTNERS, 1105
LERER HIPPEAU VENTURES, 1110
LEXINGTON PARTNERS, 1112
LIBERTY CITY VENTURES, 1115
LIBERTY PARTNERS, 1116
LIGHTHOUSE PARTNERS, 1120
LIGHTYEAR CAPITAL, 1123
LINCOLNSHIRE MANAGEMENT, 1127
LINDSAY GOLDBERG, 1129
LINLEY CAPITAL, 1130
LONE STAR FUNDS, 1140
LONG ISLAND CAPITAL ALLIANCE, 3267
LONG POINT CAPITAL, 1141
LONGUEVUE CAPITAL LLC, 1144
LOVELL MINNICK PARTNERS LLC, 1147
LUX CAPITAL, 1151
MANHATTAN INVESTMENT PARTNERS, 1163
MATLINPATTERSON, 1179
MBF CAPITAL CORPORATION, 1188
MCGOVERN CAPITAL, 1191
MERIDA CAPITAL PARTNERS, 1207
MERIWETHER CAPITAL CORPORATION, 1215
MERLIN NEXUS, 1216
MERRILL LYNCH VENTURE CAPITAL, 1217
MESA GLOBAL, 1220
MESA+, 1222
METROPOLITAN PARTNERS GROUP, 1225
MIDOCEAN PARTNERS, 1231
MILLENIUM TECHNOLOGY VALUE PARTNERS, 1235
MORGAN STANLEY EXPANSION CAPITAL, 1255
MOUSSE PARTNERS, 1263
MTS HEALTH INVESTORS, 1271
MURPHY & PARTNERS FUND LP, 1274
NAVY CAPITAL, 1283
NEEDHAM CAPITAL PARTNERS, 1288
NEW ENTERPRISE ASSOCIATES, 1297
NEW LEAF VENTURE PARTNERS, 1298
NEW MOUNTAIN CAPITAL, 1301
NEW SCIENCE VENTURES, 1303
NEW YORK ANGELS, 1306
NEW YORK CITY ENTREPRENEURIAL FUND, 1307
NEW YORK LIFE CAPITAL PARTNERS, 1309
NEW YORK VENTURE PARTNERS, 1310
NEWFIELD CAPITAL, 1313
NEWLIGHT MANAGEMENT, 1314
NEWLIGHT PARTNERS, 1315
NEWSPRING CAPITAL, 1317
NGEN PARTNERS, 1324
NORTH COVE PARTNERS, 1337
NORTHLEAF CAPITAL PARTNERS, 2204
NORTHWOOD VENTURES, 1344
NOVELTEK CAPITAL CORPORATION, 1351
NUVEEN, 1356
NYC SEED, 1358
OAK HILL CAPITAL PARTNERS, 1360
OAKTREE CAPITAL MANAGEMENT LLC, 1362
ODEON CAPITAL PARTNERS, 1367
ODYSSEY INVESTMENT PARTNERS, 1368
OMERS PRIVATE EQUITY, 2207
ONCAP, 2208
ONE EQUITY PARTNERS, 1376
ONEX PARTNERS, 2209
ONONDAGA VENTURE CAPITAL FUND, 1377
ORBIMED HEALTHCARE FUND MANAGEMENT, 1382
PALADIN CAPITAL GROUP, 1400
PALLADIUM EQUITY PARTNERS, 1403
PANTHEON VENTURES (US) LP, 1411
PARTNERSHIP FUND FOR NEW YORK CITY, 1420
PENNELL VENTURE PARTNERS LLC, 1429
PERMAL CAPITAL MANAGEMENT, 1432
PERMIRA, 3033
PERSEUS FUNDS, 1434
PFIZER VENTURE INVESTMENTS, 1436
PINE BROOK ROAD PARTNERS, 1443
PINEBRIDGE INVESTMENTS, 1444

PLATINUM EQUITY, 1451
PLUM ALLEY, 1454
POLARIS VENTURE PARTNERS, 1460
POMONA CAPITAL, 1462
POST CAPITAL PARTNERS, 1465
POUSCHINE COOK CAPITAL MANAGEMENT LLC, 1466
PPM AMERICA CAPITAL PARTNERS, 1467
PRAESIDIAN CAPITAL, 1468
PRIMARY VENTURE PARTNERS, 1475
PROGRESS INVESTMENT MANAGEMENT COMPANY, 1485
PROGRESS VENTURES, 1486
PROSPECT CAPITAL CORPORATION, 1491
PROVIDENCE EQUITY PARTNERS, 1496
PSILOS GROUP, 1498
QUAD PARTNERS, 1504
QUADRANGLE GROUP, 1506
QUILVEST PRIVATE EQUITY, 1516
QUOTIDIAN VENTURES, 1518
RADIUS VENTURES, 1520
RAND CAPITAL CORPORATION, 1523
RAPTOR GROUP, 1524
RECIPROCAL VENTURES, 1528
RED SEA VENTURES, 1530
RELATIVITY CAPITAL, 1539
RESOURCE CAPITAL FUNDS, 1548
RETHINK COMMUNITY, 1550
RETHINK EDUCATION, 1551
RETHINK IMPACT, 1552
REVEL PARTNERS, 1554
RHO VENTURES, 1558
RHODIUM, 3081
RHYTHM VENTURE CAPITAL, 1559
RICHMOND GLOBAL, 1561
RIVERSIDE COMPANY, 1572
RIVERSTONE, 1573
ROSE TECH VENTURES, 1584
ROSECLIFF VENTURES, 1585
ROTH CAPITAL PARTNERS, 1588
RRE VENTURES, 1593
RTP VENTURES, 1594
RU-NET VENTURES RTP Ventures, 3087
RUBICON VENTURE CAPITAL, 1595
RUNTIDE CAPITAL, 1596
SALMON RIVER CAPITAL, 1608
SAMSUNG NEXT, 1611
SANDLER CAPITAL MANAGEMENT, 1617
SARATOGA PARTNERS, 1621
SARONA ASSET MANAGEMENT, 2248
SCHULTZE ASSET MANAGEMENT, 1629
SCOUT VENTURES, 1632
SCULPTOR CAPITAL MANAGEMENT, 1635
SEAPORT CAPITAL, 1638
SEARCHLIGHT, 2252
SEAWAY VALLEY CAPITAL CORPORATION, 1639
SECOND ALPHA, 1640
SENTINEL CAPITAL PARTNERS, 1651
SEYMOUR ASSET MANAGEMENT, 1659
SIGNAL EQUITY PARTNERS, 1674
SIGULER GUFF & COMPANY, 1679
SILICON ALLEY VENTURE PARTNERS, 1680
SILVER LAKE, 1683
SJF VENTURES, 1689
SOFTBANK CAPITAL, 1699
SOGAL VENTURES, 1701
SOURCE CAPITAL GROUP, 1707
SPARK CAPITAL, 1715
SPENCER TRASK VENTURES, 1720
SPIRE CAPITAL PARTNERS, 1724
SPP CAPITAL, 1726
SPRING MOUNTAIN CAPITAL, 1730
STARVEST PARTNERS, 1738
STONE POINT CAPITAL LLC, 1743
STONEBRIDGE PARTNERS, 1744
STONEHENGE GROWTH CAPITAL, 1745
STRIPES GROUP, 1748
SUMMER STREET CAPITAL PARTNERS, 1751
SUN CAPITAL PARTNERS, 1753

Geographic Index

SWAN & LEGEND VENTURES, 1766
SYCAMORE VENTURES, 1769
TAILWIND CAPITAL, 1777
TECHNOLOGY CROSSOVER VENTURES, 1785
TH LEE PUTNAM VENTURES, 1804
THAYER STREET PARTNERS, 1805
THE ABRAAJ GROUP, 3173
THE CHANNEL GROUP, 1808
THREE CITIES RESEARCH, 1820
THRIVE CAPITAL, 1821
TIGER GLOBAL MANAGEMENT, 1826
TIME WARNER INVESTMENT CORPORATION, 1827
TOPSPIN PARTNERS, 1832
TPG CAPITAL, 1835
TRANSCENDENT CAPITAL, 1836
TRESS CAPITAL LLC, 1843
TREVI HEALTH CAPITAL, 1844
TRIBECA VENTURE PARTNERS, 1849
TRILANTIC CAPITAL PARTNERS, 1851
TSG CONSUMER PARTNERS, 1861
TUATARA CAPITAL, 1864
TUSK VENTURES, 1868
TWO SIGMA VENTURES, 1874
UNION CAPITAL CORPORATION, 1881
UNION SQUARE VENTURES, 1882
UNITED TALENT AGENCY VENTURES, 1883
UPSTATE CAPITAL ASSOCIATION OF NEW YORK, 3280
URBAN US, 1894
US RENEWABLES GROUP, 1895
VALAR VENTURES, 1897
VALENCE LIFE SCIENCES, 1898
VALIA, 1900
VARDE PARTNERS, 1907
VCFA GROUP, 1908
VEDANTA CAPITAL LP, 1911
VENBIO, 1914
VENROCK ASSOCIATES, 1916
VERITAS CAPITAL FUND LP, 1925
VERIZON VENTURES, 1926
VERONIS SUHLER STEVENSON, 1927
VERSANT VENTURES, 1928
VESEY STREET CAPITAL PARTNERS LLC, 1930
VESTAR CAPITAL PARTNERS, 1931
VISION CAPITAL, 1937
VISTA EQUITY PARTNERS, 1938
W CAPITAL PARTNERS, 1947
WAFRA CAPITAL PARTNERS INC, 1949
WAFRA INC, 1950
WALL STREET VENTURE CAPITAL, 1953
WAND PARTNERS, 1955
WARBURG PINCUS LLC, 1956
WASSERSTEIN & CO., 1960
WELLS FARGO CAPITAL FINANCE, 1970
WELLSPRING CAPITAL MANAGEMENT LLC, 1971
WELSH, CARSON, ANDERSON & STOWE, 1972
WESLEY CLOVER, 2284
WGI GROUP, 1980
WHEATLEY PARTNERS, 1981
WHITE STAR CAPITAL, 1982
WICKS GROUP OF COMPANIES, LLC, 1984
WILLOWRIDGE PARTNERS, 1987
WINDCREST PARTNERS, 1991
WINDFORCE VENTURES, LLC, 1992
WINDHAM VENTURE PARTNERS, 1993
WL ROSS & CO., 2002
WORK-BENCH, 2006
ZELKOVA VENTURES, 2017
ZEPHYR MANAGEMENT LP, 2018
ZM CAPITAL, 2020
ZS FUND LP, 2022

North Carolina
BBH CAPITAL PARTNERS, 240
BLUE BRIGHT VENTURES, 286
BLUE POINT CAPITAL PARTNERS, 290
CAPITALA, 405
CAROLINA FINANCIAL GROUP, 414
CAROUSEL CAPITAL, 415
CATO BIOVENTURES, 430
CHEROKEE INVESTMENT PARTNERS, 463
COUNCIL FOR ENTREPRENEURIAL DEVELOPMENT, 3259
FIRST FLIGHT VENTURE CENTER, 737
FIVE POINTS CAPITAL, 746
FRANKLIN STREET EQUITY PARTNERS, 780
FRONTIER CAPITAL, 790
GOLDEN PINE VENTURES, 840
GOLUB CAPITAL, 844
GUGGENHEIM PARTNERS, 885
HALIFAX GROUP LLC, 894
HATTERAS VENTURE PARTNERS, 915
IDEA FUND PARTNERS, 971
INTERSOUTH PARTNERS, 1008
MERITURN PARTNERS, 1213
NDI MEDICAL, 1287
NOVAQUEST CAPITAL MANAGEMENT, 1349
PAMLICO CAPITAL, 1409
PAPPAS VENTURES, 1412
PIEDMONT ANGEL NETWORK, 1442
REX HEALTH VENTURES, 1556
RIVER CITIES CAPITAL FUNDS, 1571
SALEM INVESTMENT PARTNERS, 1606
SJF VENTURES, 1689
SOUTHEAST INTERACTIVE TECHNOLOGY FUNDS, 1709
SOUTHERN CAPITOL VENTURES, 1710
SUNBRIDGE PARTNERS, 1755
SYNGENTA VENTURES, 1774
TRELYS FUNDS, 1842
TRIANGLE ANGEL PARTNERS, 1845
WELLS FARGO CAPITAL FINANCE, 1970
WILMINGTON INVESTOR NETWORK, 1988

North Dakota
ARTHUR VENTURES, 173
INVESTAMERICA VENTURE GROUP, 1016
LINN GROVE VENTURES, 1131
NORTH DAKOTA DEVELOPMENT FUND, 1338
NORTHSTAR CAPITAL, 1343

Ohio
ALLOS VENTURES, 86
ARBORETUM VENTURES, 149
ARSENAL VENTURE PARTNERS, 171
ATHENIAN VENTURE PARTNERS, 187
AUSTIN CAPITAL PARTNERS LP, 201
BEVERAGE MARKETING CORPORATION, 261
BLUE CHIP VENTURE COMPANY, 287
BLUE POINT CAPITAL PARTNERS, 290
BRIDGE INVESTMENT FUND, 337
BRUML CAPITAL CORPORATION, 355
CASE TECHNOLOGY VENTURES Case Western Reserve University, 420
CHARTER LIFE SCIENCES, 458
CINCYTECH, 479
CINTRIFUSE, 480
CUSTER CAPITAL, 571
CYPRIUM PARTNERS, 577
DESCO CAPITAL, 606
DRAPER TRIANGLE VENTURES, 628
DRIVE CAPITAL, 630
EARLY STAGE PARTNERS, 642
EDGEWATER CAPITAL PARTNERS, 653
EQUITEK CAPITAL, 692
FORT WASHINGTON CAPITAL PARTNERS GROUP, 766
GLENGARY LLC, 831
HOPEN LIFE SCIENCE VENTURES, 943
JANE VC, 1026
JUMPSTART INC, 1047
LINSALATA CAPITAL PARTNERS, 1132
MPE PARTNERS, 1266
NCT VENTURES, 1286
NDI MEDICAL, 1287
PNC ERIEVIEW CAPITAL, 1456
PRIMUS CAPITAL, 1476
QUEEN CITY ANGELS, 1512
RESERVOIR VENTURE PARTNERS, 1544

1133

Geographic Index

RESILIENCE CAPITAL PARTNERS, 1545
REV1 VENTURES, 1553
RIVER CITIES CAPITAL FUNDS, 1571
RIVERSIDE COMPANY, 1572
RIVERVEST VENTURE PARTNERS, 1574
STONEHENGE GROWTH CAPITAL, 1745
SUNBRIDGE PARTNERS, 1755
TRIATHLON MEDICAL VENTURES, 1847
WALNUT GROUP, 1954

Oklahoma
ACORN GROWTH COMPANIES, 48
DAVIS, TUTTLE VENTURE PARTNERS LP, 591
ENCAP FLATROCK MIDSTREAM, 671
KNIGHTSBRIDGE ADVISERS, 1077
METAFUND, 1223
REGENT PRIVATE CAPITAL, 1538
i2E, 2024

Oregon
ENDEAVOUR CAPITAL, 673
HANOVER PARTNERS, 903
OREGON ANGEL FUND, 1383
OVP VENTURE PARTNERS, 1391
PORTLAND SEED FUND, 1463
SEVEN PEAKS VENTURES, 1656
VEBER PARTNERS LLC, 1909
VENCORE CAPITAL, 1915
VOYAGER CAPITAL, 1945
WELLS FARGO CAPITAL FINANCE, 1970

Pennsylvania
1315 CAPITAL, 5
ACTIVATE VENTURE PARTNERS, 52
ACTUA, 53
ADAMS CAPITAL MANAGEMENT, 56
ARGOSY CAPITAL, 164
AUGUSTUS VENTURES, 198
BBH CAPITAL PARTNERS, 240
BEN FRANKLIN TECHNOLOGY PARTNERS, 246
BERWIND CORPORATION, 258
BIOADVANCE, 266
BIRCHMERE VENTURES, 272
BLUE TREE ALLIED ANGELS, 293
BLUETREE VENTURE FUND, 298
COMCAST VENTURES, 518
CORNERSTONE CAPITAL HOLDINGS, 540
DIMELING SCHREIBER & PARK, 616
DRAPER TRIANGLE VENTURES, 628
ELEMENT PARTNERS, 657
ENERTECH CAPITAL, 676
ENTREPRENEUR PARTNERS, 683
EUREKA GROWTH CAPITAL, 698
FIRST ROUND CAPITAL, 741
GENACAST VENTURES, 814
GLENTHORNE CAPITAL, 832
GRAHAM PARTNERS, 846
GREENHOUSE VENTURES, 866
H KATZ CAPITAL GROUP, 891
HURON CAPITAL PARTNERS LLC, 960
INETWORKS ADVISORS LLC, 987
INNOVATION WORKS, 998
INVERNESS GRAHAM INVESTMENTS, 1014
JAGUAR CAPITAL PARTNERS, 1025
LANCET CAPITAL, 1092
LAUNCHCYTE, 1098
LIFE SCIENCES GREENHOUSE OF CENTRAL PA, 1117
LLR PARTNERS INC, 1136
LOVELL MINNICK PARTNERS LLC, 1147
MAIN STREET CAPITAL HOLDINGS LLC, 1159
MEAKEM/BECKER VENTURE CAPITAL, 1194
MEIDLINGER PARTNERS, 1199
MENTOR CAPITAL PARTNERS LTD, 1203
MID-ATLANTIC VENTURE FUNDS, 1227
MILESTONE PARTNERS, 1234
MISSIONOG, 1240
MVP CAPITAL PARTNERS, 1275

NEW RHEIN HEALTHCARE INVESTORS, 1302
NEWSPRING CAPITAL, 1317
NEXTSTAGE CAPITAL, 1321
NORWICH VENTURES, 1347
ORIGINATE VENTURES, 1385
OSAGE PARTNERS, 1387
PENN VENTURE PARTNERS, 1428
PI CAPITAL GROUP LLC, 1440
PIDC PHILADELPHIA, 1441
PIONEER CAPITAL, 1446
PITTSBURGH EQUITY PARTNERS, 1447
PITTSBURGH LIFE SCIENCES GREENHOUSE, 1448
PITTSBURGH VENTURE CAPITAL ASSOCIATION, 3275
PLEXUS VENTURES, 1452
PNC RIVERARCH CAPITAL, 1457
PROVCO GROUP, 1494
QUAKER BIOVENTURES, 1508
RAF INDUSTRIES, 1521
RITTENHOUSE VENTURES, 1568
ROBIN HOOD VENTURES, 1577
SAFEGUARD SCIENTIFICS, 1601
SCP PARTNERS, 1633
SPIRE CAPITAL PARTNERS, 1724
SPRING CAPITAL PARTNERS LP, 1727
SR ONE LTD, 1731
STONEWOOD CAPITAL MANAGEMENT, 1746
SUSQUEHANNA GROWTH EQUITY, 1759
THINKTIV VENTURES, 1810
TL VENTURES, 1828
WELLS FARGO CAPITAL FINANCE, 1970
WILSHIRE PRIVATE MARKETS, 1989

Rhode Island
ANGEL STREET CAPITAL, 125
MANAGEMENT CAPITAL, 1162
NAUTIC PARTNERS, 1279
PROVIDENCE EQUITY PARTNERS, 1496
SLATER TECHNOLOGY FUND, 1693

South Carolina
AZALEA CAPITAL, 213
BATTELLE VENTURES, 233
VENTURESOUTH, 1923

South Dakota
BIRD DOG EQUITY PARTNERS, 273
BLUESTEM CAPITAL COMPANY, 297
MCGOWAN CAPITAL GROUP, 1192
PRAIRIEGOLD VENTURE PARTNERS, 1470

Tennessee
AM VENTURES, 16
BBH CAPITAL PARTNERS, 240
CHATTANOOGA RENAISSANCE FUND, 459
CLARITAS CAPITAL, 493
CLAYTON ASSOCIATES, 496
COUNCIL CAPITAL, 550
CRESSEY & COMPANY LP, 558
DYNAMO VC, 640
FCA VENTURE PARTNERS, 718
HARBERT MANAGEMENT CORPORATION, 904
INNOVA MEMPHIS, 995
MB VENTURE PARTNERS, 1187
MERITUS VENTURES, 1214
MOUNTAIN GROUP CAPITAL, 1261
PROVENTURE AG, 3060
RED CLAY CAPITAL HOLDINGS, 1529
RIVER ASSOCIATES INVESTMENTS LLC, 1569
SSM PARTNERS, 1732
TENNESSEE COMMUNITY VENTURES, 1797
TVV CAPITAL, 1870
VENTURE ASSOCIATES PARTNERS LLC, 1919

Texas
ADVANTAGE CAPITAL PARTNERS, 61
AM VENTURES, 105
AMERIMARK CAPITAL CORPORATION, 111

Geographic Index

APOLLO GLOBAL MANAGEMENT, 140
ARCH VENTURE PARTNERS, 153
ARDENTON, 2042
ARISTOS VENTURES, 165
ARROWPATH VENTURE PARTNERS, 169
AUSTIN VENTURES, 202
BCM TECHNOLOGIES, 241
BLUE SAGE CAPITAL, 291
BP ALTERNATIVE ENERGY VENTURES, 319
BRAND FOUNDRY VENTURES, 325
BRAZOS PRIVATE EQUITY PARTNERS, 328
CAMBRIA GROUP, 378
CAPITAL SOUTHWEST CORPORATION, 403
CASTLELAKE, 424
CATALYST GROUP, 425
CCMP CAPITAL, 433
CENTERPOINT VENTURE PARTNERS, 444
CENTRAL TEXAS ANGEL NETWORK, 445
CHEVRON TECHNOLOGY VENTURES, 466
CIC PARTNERS, 477
CITARETX INVESTMENT PARTNERS, 485
COLT VENTURES, 514
CORSA VENTURES, 545
CRESCO CAPITAL PARTNERS, 557
CYPRESS GROWTH CAPITAL, 576
DALLAS VENTURE PARTNERS, 582
DAVIS, TUTTLE VENTURE PARTNERS LP, 591
ENCAP FLATROCK MIDSTREAM, 671
ENCAP INVESTMENTS LP, 672
ENERGY CAPITAL PARTNERS, 675
ENERGY VENTURES, 2700
EQUUS TOTAL RETURN, 694
ESCALATE CAPITAL PARTNERS, 695
ESCHELON ENERGY PARTNERS, 696
ESSEX WOODLANDS HEALTH VENTURES LLC, 697
EVERCORE CAPITAL PARTNERS, 699
EVOLVE CAPITAL, 702
FENGATE, 2116
FIRST CAPITAL GROUP, 734
FIRST RESERVE, 740
FORTRESS INVESTMENT GROUP LLC, 767
FRASER MCCOMBS CAPITAL, 781
G-51 CAPITAL LLC, 803
GENERATION PARTNERS, 818
GIDEON HIXON FUND, 826
GREENHILL SAVP, 864
GUGGENHEIM PARTNERS, 885
GULFSTAR GROUP, 888
HADDINGTON VENTURES LLC, 893
HALIFAX GROUP LLC, 894
HANCOCK PARK ASSOCIATES, 902
HARBERT MANAGEMENT CORPORATION, 904
HIG CAPITAL, 928
HOLDING CAPITAL GROUP, 940
HOUSTON ANGEL NETWORK, 950
HOUSTON HEALTH VENTURES, 951
HUNT INVESTMENT GROUP, 957
INCYTE VENTURES, 982
INDEPENDENT BANKERS CAPITAL FUND, 984
INNOVATION PLATFORM CAPITAL, 997
INTERVALE CAPITAL, 1009
JB POINDEXTER & COMPANY, 1030
KENMONT CAPITAL PARTNERS, 1063
KOHLBERG KRAVIS ROBERTS & COMPANY, 1082
LIME ROCK PARTNERS, 1125
LIMESTONE VENTURES, 1126
LONE STAR FUNDS, 1140
MANSA CAPITAL, 1164
MARKPOINT VENTURE PARTNERS, 1167
MERCURY FUND, 1206
MERIT ENERGY COMPANY, 1210
MOBILITY VENTURES, 1244
MURPHREE VENTURE PARTNERS, 1273
NATURAL GAS PARTNERS, 1278
NAYA VENTURES, 1285
NEW CAPITAL PARTNERS, 1293
NGP, 1326

ORIX, 1386
PALOMINO CAPITAL, 1408
PARALLEL INVESTMENT PARTNERS, 1415
PARTHENON CAPITAL, 1417
PEROT JAIN, 1433
PROGRESS EQUITY PARTNERS, 1484
PTV SCIENCES, 1500
QUAKE CAPITAL PARTNERS, 1507
QUINBROOK INFRASTRUCTURE PARTNERS, 1517
RETAIL & RESTAURANT GROWTH CAPITAL LP, 1549
RIDGEWOOD CAPITAL, 1564
RIDGEWOOD ENERGY, 1565
RIVERSIDE COMPANY, 1572
RIVERSTONE, 1573
S3 VENTURES, 1597
SANTE VENTURES, 1619
SATORI CAPITAL, 1622
SAUDI ARAMCO ENERGY VENTURES Aramco Energy Ventures, 3099
SENTIENT VENTURES, 1650
SEVIN ROSEN FUNDS, 1658
SILVER CREEK VENTURES, 1682
SILVERTON PARTNERS, 1685
SOCIAL SECTOR VENTURES, 1697
SPINDLETOP CAPITAL, 1722
STAR VENTURES, 3137
STONEHENGE GROWTH CAPITAL, 1745
TEAKWOOD CAPITAL, 1783
TEXAS EMERGING TECHNOLOGY FUND, 1800
TEXAS VENTURE CAPITAL ASSOCIATION, 3278
TEXO VENTURES, 1801
TGF MANAGEMENT, 1803
THINKTIV VENTURES, 1810
TI VENTURE CAPITAL Texas Instruments Incorporated, 1823
TPG CAPITAL, 1835
TRELLIS PARTNERS, 1841
TRIANGLE PEAK PARTNERS, 1846
TRILANTIC CAPITAL PARTNERS, 1851
TRITON VENTURES, 1855
TRIVE CAPITAL, 1856
TXV PARTNERS, 1875
VISTA EQUITY PARTNERS, 1938
VORTEX PARTNERS, 1944
WAFRA INC, 1950
WARBURG PINCUS LLC, 1956
WELLS FARGO CAPITAL FINANCE, 1970
WESTLAKE SECURITIES, 1976
WINGATE PARTNERS, 1997
YELLOWSTONE CAPITAL, 2013

Utah

42 VENTURES, 9
ALBUM VC, 79
ALTA VENTURES MEXICO, 2382
CHEROKEE & WALKER, 462
CROSS CREEK ADVISORS, 560
DW HEALTHCARE PARTNERS, 639
EPIC VENTURES, 688
INNOVENTURES CAPITAL PARTNERS, 999
KICKSTART SEED FUND, 1070
LONGUEVUE CAPITAL LLC, 1144
MCG CAPITAL MANAGEMENT, 1190
MERCATO PARTNERS, 1204
ORIGIN VENTURES, 1384
PELION VENTURE PARTNERS, 1425
RENEWABLETECH VENTURES, 1542
SENTRY FINANCIAL CORPORATION, 1652
SIGNAL PEAK VENTURES, 1677
SORENSON CAPITAL, 1705
UNIVERSITY VENTURE FUND, 1884

Vermont

FRESHTRACKS CAPITAL, 786
UNDERDOG VENTURES, 1880

Virginia

ALTRIA VENTURES, 102
AMPLIFIER VENTURE PARTNERS, 119

Geographic Index

AVANSIS VENTURES, 207
BIA DIGITAL PARTNERS LP, 263
BLU VENTURE INVESTORS, 285
BLUE HERON CAPITAL, 288
COLUMBIA CAPITAL, 515
COURT SQUARE VENTURES, 551
CROSSHILL FINANCIAL GROUP, 562
DISRUPTOR CAPITAL, 617
EVERGREEN ADVISORS, 701
GLADSTONE CAPITAL, 828
GREEN TOWER CAPITAL, 861
GROTECH VENTURES, 876
HARBERT MANAGEMENT CORPORATION, 904
HARREN EQUITY PARTNERS, 910
HEALTHCARE PRIVATE EQUITY ASSOCIATION, 3264
HORIZON TECHNOLOGY FINANCE, 946
IN-Q-TEL, 979
INDUSTRY VENTURES, 986
LIQUID CAPITAL GROUP, 1133
MCG CAPITAL CORPORATION, 1189
MIDDLEBURG CAPITAL DEVELOPMENT, 1229
MOTLEY FOOL VENTURES, 1259
NEW ATLANTIC VENTURES, 1291
NEW VANTAGE GROUP, 1304
OUTCOME CAPITAL, 1388
PRO-RATA OPPORTUNITY FUND, 1482
QUAD-C MANAGEMENT, 1505
RENAISSANCE VENTURES, 1541
RIDGE CAPITAL PARTNERS LLC, 1562
SAIL VENTURE PARTNERS, 1603
SAVANO CAPITAL PARTNERS, 1625
SINEWAVE VENTURES, 1687
SWAN & LEGEND VENTURES, 1766
THIRD SECURITY, 1812
VALHALLA PARTNERS, 1899
VENSANA CAPITAL, 1917
VENTANA CAPITAL MANAGEMENT LP, 1918
VIRGINIA SMALL BUSINESS FINANCING AUTHORITY, 1936
WASHINGTON CAPITAL VENTURES, 1959
WELLS FARGO CAPITAL FINANCE, 1970
WESLEY CLOVER, 2284

Washington
ACCELERATOR LIFE SCIENCE PARTNERS, 31
ACKERLEY PARTNERS LLC, 43
ALEXANDER HUTTON, 82
ALLIANCE OF ANGELS, 85
ARCH VENTURE PARTNERS, 153
BENAROYA COMPANIES, 247
BIOMATICS CAPITAL, 268
BLUE POINT CAPITAL PARTNERS, 290
BROADMARK CAPITAL, 345
DIVERGENT VENTURES, 618
ENDEAVOUR CAPITAL, 673
FLUKE VENTURE PARTNERS, 753
FLYING FISH, 755
FOUNDER'S CO-OP, 773
FRAZIER HEALTHCARE VENTURES, 782
GREY SKY VENTURE PARTNERS, 870
GUIDE VENTURES, 887
HOLDING CAPITAL GROUP, 940
IGNITION PARTNERS, 974

INTEGRA VENTURES, 1002
INTELLECTUAL VENTURES, 1005
INVESTAMERICA VENTURE GROUP, 1016
LAUNCHBOX DIGITAL, 1096
MADRONA VENTURE GROUP, 1158
MAVERON LLC, 1183
MONTLAKE CAPITAL, 1250
NAYA VENTURES, 1285
OVP VENTURE PARTNERS, 1391
PACIFIC HORIZON VENTURES, 1398
PALMS & COMPANY, 1404
POINT B CAPITAL, 1458
PRIVATEER HOLDINGS, 1481
PSL VENTURES, 1499
SEAPOINT VENTURES, 1637
SECOND AVENUE PARTNERS, 1641
SPEKTRA CAPITAL, 1718
STAENBERG VENTURE PARTNERS, 1733
TIE ANGELS GROUP SEATTLE, 1825
TRILOGY PARTNERSHIP, 1852
VENTURE TECH ALLIANCE, 1922
VOYAGER CAPITAL, 1945
WELLS FARGO CAPITAL FINANCE, 1970
WRF CAPITAL, 2008

West Virginia
MOUNTAINEER CAPITAL, 1262

Wisconsin
4490 VENTURES, 10
BAIRD CAPITAL PARTNERS, 222
CALUMET VENTURE FUND, 375
CAPITAL MIDWEST FUND, 400
CSA PARTNERS, 566
DANEVEST TECH FUND ADVISORS, 583
FCF PARTNERS LP, 719
HORIZON PARTNERS, LTD, 945
KEGONSA CAPITAL PARTNERS, 1060
MASON WELLS, 1171
NEW CAPITAL FUND, 1292
STONEHENGE GROWTH CAPITAL, 1745
VENTURE INVESTORS LLC, 1921
WISCONSIN INVESTMENT PARTNERS, 2001

Wyoming
AEROSTAR CAPITAL LLC, 67

Vietnam
LOMBARD INVESTMENTS, 1139
MEKONG CAPITAL, 2961
VINACAPITAL GROUP, 3217

Wales
FINANCE WALES, 2737

Yugoslavia
SALFORD CAPITAL PARTNERS, 3095

Zimbabwe
CLARITY CAPITAL, 2611

Industry Preference Index / Advertising Technology

AI
ANGELPAD, 128
BOOST VC, 307
DAY ONE VENTURES, 593
ENERTECH CAPITAL, 676
NAYA VENTURES, 1285
YES VC, 2014

API
ANGELPAD, 128

Accessbility
CANTOS VENTURES, 395

Accessories
BREAKAWAY VENTURES, 329

Ad Tech
500 STARTUPS, 11
BERTELSMANN DIGITAL MEDIA INVESTMENTS, 256
QUAKE CAPITAL PARTNERS, 1507

Administration and Accounting
AUSTRALIAN ETHICAL INVESTMENT LIMITED, 2456
VON BRAUN & SCHREIBER PRIVATE EQUITY PARTNERS, 3227

Administrative Automation
HEALTH ENTERPRISE PARTNERS, 918

Advance Polymers
MOUNTAINEER CAPITAL, 1262

Advanced Data Compression Technologies
SONY STRATEGIC TECHNOLOGY PARTNERSHIPS, 1704

Advanced Energy
ARTIS VENTURES, 175

Advanced Manufacturing
ALLOS VENTURES, 86
AMANAH VENTURES SDN BHD, 2388
ELEVATE VENTURES, 658
FIRST STEP FUND, 742
GE VENTURES, 809
IDG CAPITAL PARTNERS, 2847
LEGEND CAPITAL, 2936
SB CHINA VENTURE CAPITAL, 3100

Advanced Manufacturing & Materials
ARCTERN VENTURES, 2041
COUNCIL FOR ENTREPRENEURIAL DEVELOPMENT, 3259

Advanced Marine Applications
CONNECTICUT INNOVATIONS, 530

Advanced Materials
AMHERST FUND, 113
ANGELENO GROUP, 126
ARCH VENTURE PARTNERS, 153
BIRCHMERE VENTURES, 272
BRIGHT CAPITAL, 2540
CHEVRON TECHNOLOGY VENTURES, 466
CHORD CAPITAL, 2598
CLEAN PACIFIC VENTURES, 498
CONNECTICUT INNOVATIONS, 530
DOMAIN ASSOCIATES LLC, 621
ELEMENT PARTNERS, 657
EMERALD TECHNOLOGY VENTURES, 2106
EXPANSION CAPITAL PARTNERS, 706
GENERAL MOTORS VENTURES, 817
GROWTHWORKS, 2143
INNOVATION WORKS, 998
IP GROUP, 2892
MADISON PARKER CAPITAL, 1157
MARS INVESTMENT ACCELERATOR FUND, 2187
NGEN PARTNERS, 1324
OXANTIUM VENTURES, 1393
PANGAEA VENTURES LTD, 2213
PARKWALK ADVISORS, 3028
PI CAPITAL GROUP LLC, 1440
PRESIDIO VENTURES, 1474
REV1 VENTURES, 1553
ROCKPORT CAPITAL, 1579
SABIC VENTURES, 3091
SATURN PARTNERS, 1623
SEVIN ROSEN FUNDS, 1658
SILVERTON PARTNERS, 1685
SOUTHERN CROSS VENTURE PARTNERS, 1711
TANDEM EXPANSION FUND, 2261
TECHNOLOGY PARTNERS, 1786
TENNESSEE COMMUNITY VENTURES, 1797
TRELLIS CAPITAL CORPORATION, 2273
TRIGINITA CAPITAL, 3190
TRITON VENTURES, 1855
WRF CAPITAL, 2008
YISSUM TECHNOLOGY TRANSFER, 3245

Advanced Technologies
B-TO-V PARTNERS, 2475
DISCOVERY CAPITAL, 2097

Advanced Weapons Systems
RAFAEL DEVELOPMENT CORPORATION (RDC) LIMITED, 3072

Advertising
ABU DHABI INVESTMENT AUTHORITY, 2321
AEP CAPITAL LLC, 65
AFTERDOX, 2352
ALLSTATE INVESTMENTS LLC, 88
ANGELPAD, 128
ARCHTOP VENTURES, 154
ARTS ALLIANCE, 2428
ATRIUM CAPITAL, 192
AZURE CAPITAL PARTNERS, 215
BUTLER CAPITAL PARTNERS FRANCE, 2551
CITA GESTION, 2607
COMCAST VENTURES, 518
FAIRHAVEN CAPITAL, 712
FIVE ELMS CAPITAL, 745
GREAT OAKS VENTURE CAPITAL, 858
GREE VENTURES, 2798
GREYCROFT PARTNERS, 871
HARBOURVEST PARTNERS LLC, 909
HUDSON VENTURE PARTNERS, 954
INVENTUS, 1013
KAEDAN INVESTMENTS, 2914
KHOSLA VENTURES, 1069
KOHLBERG VENTURES, 1083
M/C PARTNERS, 1153
MADRONA VENTURE GROUP, 1158
MESA+, 1222
MHS CAPITAL, 1226
NEW ATLANTIC VENTURES, 1291
QUOTIDIAN VENTURES, 1518
RAPTOR GROUP, 1524
SPARK CAPITAL, 1715
STAGE 1 VENTURES, 1734
TELEFONICA VENTURES, 3169
TIME WARNER INVESTMENT CORPORATION, 1827
TRANSMEDIA CAPITAL, 1839
TRIBECA VENTURE PARTNERS, 1849
TUGBOAT VENTURES, 1865
UNION CAPITAL CORPORATION, 1881
VERIZON VENTURES, 1926
WASABI VENTURES, 1958
WICKS GROUP OF COMPANIES, LLC, 1984
ZM CAPITAL, 2020

Advertising Technology
FOUNDER COLLECTIVE, 771
PROJECT A VENTURE GmBH & CO. KG, 3056
RUBICON VENTURE CAPITAL, 1595
SCOUT VENTURES, 1632
VENROCK ASSOCIATES, 1916

Industry Preference Index / Aerospace

Aerospace
BLUE POINT CAPITAL PARTNERS, 290
CATAPULT VENTURES, 429
CM EQUITY PARTNERS, 507
CORNERSTONE CAPITAL HOLDINGS, 540
HAMMOND, KENNEDY, WHITNEY & COMPANY, 900
HANCOCK PARK ASSOCIATES, 902
KILLICK CAPITAL, 2168

Aerospace and Defense
BLAST FUNDING, 279
BRANFORD CASTLE, 327
GREIF & COMPANY, 869
IBM VENTURE CAPITAL GROUP, 967

Aerospace, Defense and Government
ACORN GROWTH COMPANIES, 48
AEROEQUITY, 66
AEROSTAR CAPITAL LLC, 67
ALANTRA, 77
ALEUTIAN CAPITAL PARTNERS, 81
AMERICAN SECURITIES LLC, 110
ANDLINGER & COMPANY INC, 123
ARES MANAGEMENT LLC, 159
ARLINGTON CAPITAL PARTNERS, 166
AURORA CAPITAL GROUP, 199
AZALEA CAPITAL, 213
CAI CAPITAL PARTNERS, 365
CAPITAL FOR BUSINESS, INC, 399
CAPITAL SOUTHWEST CORPORATION, 403
CARLYLE ASIA INVESTMENT ADVISORS LIMITED Carlyle Group, 2565
CARLYLE GROUP, 413
CELERITY PARTNERS, 439
CERBERUS CAPITAL MANAGEMENT, 451
CHART VENTURE PARTNERS, 457
CI CAPITAL PARTNERS, 476
CIT GROUP, 484
CLEARLAKE CAPITAL, 500
COLORADO MILE HIGH FUND, 513
COMSPACE, 526
CONNECTICUT INNOVATIONS, 530
COTTONWOOD TECHNOLOGY FUND, 549
DUBIN CLARK & COMPANY, 632
DUNRATH CAPITAL, 636
ENLIGHTENMENT CAPITAL, 680
FALCON FUND, 715
FINANCIERE DE BRIENNE FCPR, 2738
FIRST ATLANTIC CAPITAL LTD., 733
FIRST NEW ENGLAND CAPITAL LP, 739
FOUNDERS FUND, 775
GOLUB CAPITAL, 844
GREENBRIAR EQUITY GROUP LLC, 862
HARREN EQUITY PARTNERS, 910
HCI EQUITY PARTNERS, 917
HERITAGE PARTNERS, 926
HIG CAPITAL, 928
IRONWOOD CAPITAL, 1021
IXORA VENTURES, 2904
JLL PARTNERS, 1039
JORDAN COMPANY, 1045
KOREA TECHNOLOGY & BANKING (KTB) NETWORK CORP, 2926
LEVINE LEICHTMAN CAPITAL PARTNERS, 1111
LINLEY CAPITAL, 1130
MEZZANINE MANAGEMENT LIMITED Mezzanine Management UK Ltd., 2965
NEW BRUNSWICK INNOVATION FOUNDATION, 2200
NOVA SCOTIA BUSINESS INC., 2205
ODYSSEY INVESTMENT PARTNERS, 1368
ONEX PARTNERS, 2209
OUTCOME CAPITAL, 1388
PARKVIEW CAPITAL PARTNERS, 2215
PIDC PHILADELPHIA, 1441
SCOTTISH ENTERPRISE, 3103
SCP PARTNERS, 1633
SENTINEL CAPITAL PARTNERS, 1651
SPACEVEST, 1714

VANCE STREET CAPITAL, 1904
VENTANA CAPITAL MANAGEMENT LP, 1918
VENTURE ASSOCIATES PARTNERS LLC, 1919
VERITAS CAPITAL FUND LP, 1925
WALNUT GROUP, 1954
WELLSPRING CAPITAL MANAGEMENT LLC, 1971

Aerospace, Defense and Security
RAFAEL DEVELOPMENT CORPORATION (RDC) LIMITED, 3072

Affordable Housing
ENHANCED CAPITAL, 678

Aftermarket Products
CAPITAL PARTNERS, 401

AgTech
QUAKE CAPITAL PARTNERS, 1507

Agribusiness
AMERICA FIRST INVESTMENT ADVISORS, 108
BAY CITY CAPITAL LLC, 237
CATALYST INVESTMENT MANAGERS PTY LIMITED PPM Capital, 2573
GAON ASSET MANAGEMENT, 2766
GIC GROUP, 825
INTERNATIONAL FINANCE CORPORATION (IFC), 1007
NBC CAPITAL PTY LIMITED, 2988
PAI MANAGEMENT, 3026
PENN VENTURE PARTNERS, 1428
RABO BLACK EARTH Eagle Venture Partners, 3071
SIF TRANSYLVANIA, 3119
SRIW SA SRIW Group, 3134
TRANSYLVANIA FINANCIAL INVESTMENT COMPANY, 3187

Agricultural Technologies
AVAC, 2048
BIOENTERPRISE, 2060
FIRST GREEN PARTNERS, 738
GOAL HOLDINGS, 2135

Agriculture
AAVISHKAAR, 2313
ACUMEN, 55
AGRIBUSINESS MANAGEMENT COMPANY, 71
ALBEMARLE PRIVATE EQUITY LIMITED, 2360
ALPHAMUNDI GROUP LTD, 2376
AMERICAN SECURITIES LLC, 110
ANTERRA CAPITAL, 2405
AQUAGRO FUND, 2417
ARTHUR VENTURES, 173
AVRIO CAPITAL, 2049
BASF VENTURE CAPITAL, 2492
BIO FUND MANAGEMENT OY, 2512
BIOGENERATOR, 267
BLUESTEM CAPITAL COMPANY, 297
BOND CAPITAL, 2064
BONNEFIELD FINANCIAL, 2065
CANNA ANGELS LLC, 388
CARBON VENTURES, 408
CHINA MERCHANTS CHINA DIRECT INVESTMENTS LTD., 2594
CHRYSALIX, 2078
CLEAN PACIFIC VENTURES, 498
CULTIVIAN SANDBOX VENTURES, 570
DAHER CAPITAL, 2649
EMP GLOBAL, 670
EXCEL VENTURE MANAGEMENT, 703
FARM CREDIT CANADA, 2114
FOX PAINE & COMPANY LLC, 778
GRANITE EQUITY PARTNERS, 850
GROVE STREET ADVISORS LLC, 879
HALLEY VENTURE PARTNERS, 895
HURON RIVER VENTURES, 961
IANTHUS CAPITAL MANAGEMENT, 966
INNOVA MEMPHIS, 995
ISRAEL CLEANTECH VENTURES, 2900
KHOSLA VENTURES, 1069

Industry Preference Index / Allied Process Industries

KODIAK CAPITAL, 1079
KUBOTA CORPORATION, 2927
LINN GROVE VENTURES, 1131
M25 GROUP, 1155
MERITURN PARTNERS, 1213
NAVY CAPITAL, 1283
NETROVE ASIA SDN BHD, 2993
NEXUS VENTURE PARTNERS Nexus India Capital Advisors Pvt Ltd, 3001
OBVIOUS VENTURES, 1363
PALMS & COMPANY, 1404
PANGAEA VENTURES LTD, 2213
ROOT CAPITAL, 1582
SAIF PARTNERS, 3093
SEAWAY VALLEY CAPITAL CORPORATION, 1639
SKYTREE CAPITAL PARTNERS, 1692
SOCIAL VENTURE CIRCLE, 3277
SOUTHERN CROSS VENTURE PARTNERS, 1711
SUMMIT BRIDGE CAPITAL, 3147
TRUE NORTH VENTURE PARTNERS, 1859
TSING CAPITAL, 3194
UNISON CAPITAL PARTNERS LP, 3201
US VENTURE PARTNERS, 1896
WESTCAP, 2285
WESTERN NIS ENTERPRISE FUND, 3234
YISSUM TECHNOLOGY TRANSFER, 3245
ZERNIKE SEED FUND BV, 3250

Agriculture Technologies
JC2 VENTURES, 1031

Agrochemicals
STARPHARMA POOLED DEVELOPMENT LIMITED, 3139

Air Transportation
CLIFFORD CHANCE PUNDER, 2614

Airlines
THAYER VENTURES, 1806

All Sectors Considered
21 PARTNERS, 2293
3I UK 3i Group, 2306
ABM AMRO CAPITAL FRANCE ABN AMRO Group, 2317
ACKERMANS & VAN HAAREN, 2332
ADVANTAGE PARTNERS, 2347
AGMAN PARTNERS, 70
ALCHEMY PARTNERS, 2361
ALLIANCE ENTREPRENDRE, 2368
ALLIANZ CAPITAL PARTNERS GmbH, 2370
ALMI FORETAGSPARTNER AB, 2371
ALPHA BANK, 2374
ALPHA BETEILIGUNGSBERATUNG GmbH, 2375
ARCIS GROUP, 2421
ARES CAPITAL CORPORATION, 158
ARX, 2429
AVONMORE DEVELOPMENTS, 2464
BACKSTAGE CAPITAL, 218
BARCLAYS LEVERAGED FINANCE, 2484
BERENBERG PRIVATE CAPITAL, 2502
BM-T BETEILIGUNGS MANAGEMENT THURINGEN GmbH, 2527
BRABANTSE ONTWIKKELINGSMIJ NV (BOM), 2534
BROOKS HOUGHTON & COMPANY, 352
CALGARY ENTERPRISES, 369
CATALANA D'INICIATIVES CR SA, 2570
CAYUGA VENTURE FUND, 432
CHARTERHOUSE CAPITAL PARTNERS I Charterhouse, 2587
CICLAD, 2602
CLAIRVEST GROUP, 2081
COFINEP, 2620
COLONIAL FIRST STATE PRIVATE EQUITY, 2622
COMMERZ BETEILIGUNGSGESELLSCHAFT, 2624
CONCEPT FINANCIAL SERVICES, 2627
CORVINUS NEMZETKOZI BEFEKTETESI RT Corvinus International Investment Ltd., 2634
CRESCENT CAPITAL GROUP LP, 556
D.E. SHAW & CO. LP The D.E. Shaw Group, 579

DERBYSHIRE FIRST INVESTMENTS LIMITED, 2657
DEUTSCHE ASSET & WEALTH MANAGEMENT, 2658
DEUTSCHE ASSET MANAGEMENT (AUSTRALIA) LIMITED Deutsche Bank AG, 2659
DISCOUNT INVESTMENT CORPORATION LIMITED, 2666
DOTCORP PRIVATE EQUITY FUND, 2669
E-CAPITAL MANAGEMENT, 2680
ECI VENTURES, 2687
ENTERPRISE VENTURE LIMITED, 2707
ENTERPRISE VENTURES LIMITED, 2708
EUROMEZZANINE CONSEIL, 2721
EUROPEAN ACQUISITION CAPITAL LIMITED, 2722
FAIRVIEW CAPITAL PARTNERS, 714
FINNISH INDUSTRY INVESTMENT LIMITED, 2740
FOGEL INTERNATIONAL, 759
FONDS DE SOLIDARITE FTQ, 2120
FOUR SEASONS VENTURE CAPITAL, 2754
GESTION DE CAPITAL RIESGO DEL PAIS VASCO, 2777
GIMV NV, 2781
GOLDMAN SACHS INTERNATIONAL UK, 2792
H&Q ASIA PACIFIC, 892
HANSUTTAM FINANCE LIMITED, 2811
HG CAPITAL, 2823
HSBC VENTURES UK LIMITED, 2836
IDINVEST PARTNERS, 2851
IFE CONSEIL (INTERMEDIATE FINANCE EUROPE), 2852
INTER-RISCO: SOCIEDADE DE CAPITAL DE RISCO, 2882
IPBM Group IDI, 2893
JANE VC, 1026
KK RESEARCH/KK SWISS VALUE INVESTOR, 2922
LBO FRANCE, 2933
LIGHTHOUSE PARTNERS, 1120
LOMBARD/APIC (HK) LIMITED, 2946
MAINE VENTURE FUND, 1161
MANSA CAPITAL, 1164
MERCAPITAL SA, 2962
MERIFIN CAPITAL, 2963
MILESTONE GROWTH FUND, 1233
NANYANG VENTURES PTY LIMITED, 2982
NATWEST VENTURES LIMITED, 2985
NEW VANTAGE GROUP, 1304
NORDIC CAPITAL, 3008
NORDIC MEZZANINE LIMITED, 3009
OAKTREE CAPITAL MANAGEMENT LLC, 1362
OREGON ANGEL FUND, 1383
PACIFIC EQUITY PARTNERS PTY LIMITED, 3025
PARTNERS GROUP, 3029
PENTA MEZZANINE FUND, 1430
PERFORMANCE EQUITY MANAGEMENT, LLC, 1431
PINEBRIDGE INVESTMENTS, 1444
PROGRESS INVESTMENT MANAGEMENT COMPANY, 1485
PROSPECT CAPITAL CORPORATION, 1491
PROVENTURE AG, 3060
PRUDENTIAL CAPITAL GROUP, 1497
QUEEN CITY ANGELS, 1512
RICHMOND GLOBAL, 1561
RMB VENTURES LIMITED RMB Australia, 3083
RUSSELL INVESTMENT MANAGEMENT LIMITED, 3089
SLOVAK AMERICAN ENTERPRISE FUND, 3122
SOCIEDAD REGIONAL DE PROMOCION DEL PRINCIPADO, 3126
SPRING MOUNTAIN CAPITAL, 1730
TAISHAN CAPITAL CORPORATION, 3156
TRELYS FUNDS, 1842
TRIGENTA CAPITAL GmbH, 3189
TWIN BRIDGE CAPITAL PARTNERS, 1871
UCA UNTERNEHMER CONSULT AG, 3197
UNION BANK OF SWITZERLAND, 3200
UPWELLING CAPITAL GROUP, 1892
VENTURE FUND ROTTERDAM BV Indofin Group, 3209
VIOLA VENTURES, 3221
WILSHIRE PRIVATE MARKETS, 1989
ZURCHER KANTONALBANK, 3253

Allied Process Industries
TIANGUIS LIMITED, 3178

Industry Preference Index / Alternative Energy

Alternative Energy
(@)VENTURES, 1
ACI CAPITAL, 42
ANGELENO GROUP, 126
BERGGRUEN HOLDINGS, 250
BP ALTERNATIVE ENERGY VENTURES, 319
BREAKWATER INVESTMENTS, 330
CHEVRON TECHNOLOGY VENTURES, 466
CNF INVESTMENTS Clark Enterprises, Inc., 508
CROSSLINK CAPITAL, 563
EASTWARD CAPITAL PARTNERS, 646
FIRST RESERVE, 740
FRONTIER VENTURE CAPITAL, 791
INFIELD CAPITAL, 988
INTER-ASIA VENTURE MANAGEMENT LIMITED, 2881
NGEN PARTNERS, 1324
PALADIN CAPITAL GROUP, 1400
SABIC VENTURES, 3091
SOLSTICE CAPITAL LP, 1702
SPINUP VENTURE, 3132
TRELLIS CAPITAL CORPORATION, 2273
TRIANGLE PEAK PARTNERS, 1846
TROIKA CAPITAL PARTNERS, 3193

Alternative Power
ECHELON VENTURES, 647

Analysis
M12, 1154

Analytics
AMD VENTURES, 106
DENALI VENTURE PARTNERS, 605
FIRST ASCENT VENTURES, 2118
LIGHTSPEED VENTURE PARTNERS, 1121

Analytics & Analytical Instruments
AUGMENT VENTURES, 195
CHICAGO VENTURES, 471
GE VENTURES, 809
HENQ, 2822
HORIZONS VENTURES, 2831
JMH CAPITAL, 1040
PROCYON VENTURES, 1483
PROGRESS VENTURES, 1486
YL VENTURES, 3246

Ancillary Services
ELECTRA PARTNERS ASIA LIMITED SFC of Hong Kong, 2694
ENTER VENTURES, 681

Animal Health
BIOGENERATOR, 267
CULTIVIAN SANDBOX VENTURES, 570

Apparel
BREAKAWAY VENTURES, 329
BREAKWATER MANAGEMENT, 331
CERBERUS CAPITAL MANAGEMENT, 451
ENTREPRENEUR CAPITAL, 2107
HOLDING CAPITAL GROUP, 940
KILMER CAPITAL PARTNERS, 2169

Apparel & Footwear
BLUE POINT CAPITAL PARTNERS, 290

Application Software
GRANITE VENTURES, 852
MOTIV PARTNERS, 1258

Applications
ANALYTICS VENTURES, 121
COATUE MANAGEMENT, 509
FIFTH WALL, 727
FOUNDER PARTNERS, 772
FUSION FUND, 799
GEODESIC CAPITAL, 820

GOOD NEWS VENTURES, 2138
INDUSTRY VENTURES, 986
JK&B CAPITAL, 1038
LOCUS VENTURES, 1138
NEW YORK VENTURE PARTNERS, 1310
NKM CAPITAL, 1329
OWL VENTURES, 1392
REACH CAPITAL, 1527
SIGNAL FIRE, 1675
SLOW VENTURES, 1694
SPERO VENTURES, 1721
SWITCH VENTURES, 1768
TEN ELEVEN VENTURES, 1794
UNCORK CAPITAL, 1879
YES VC, 2014

Applications Software & Services
APEX VENTURE PARTNERS, 137
ASSET MANAGEMENT VENTURES, 181
AUSTIN VENTURES, 202
AZURE CAPITAL PARTNERS, 215
BAKER CAPITAL, 223
BOREALIS VENTURES, 308
CHICAGO VENTURE PARTNERS LP, 470
COMCAST VENTURES, 518
COMPAGNIE FINANCIERE E DE ROTHSCHILD BANQUE, 2625
CONCORD VENTURES, 2628
CONNECTICUT INNOVATIONS, 530
FINAVENTURES, 729
FIRSTMARK CAPITAL, 743
GENERAL CATALYST PARTNERS, 816
HUMMER WINBLAD VENTURE PARTNERS, 956
INSIGHT VENTURE PARTNERS, 1000
LONGWORTH VENTURE PARTNERS, 1146
REMBRANDT VENTURE PARTNERS, 1540
SPACEVEST, 1714

Applied Mathematics
JC TECHNOLOGIES LTD, 2909

Applied Science
PATHENA, 3031

Applied Technology
GLENGARY LLC, 831
SYMMETRIC CAPITAL, 1770

Architecture
HILL AND GERTNER CAPITAL CORP., 2148

Aritificial Intelligence
INTEL CAPITAL, 1004

Artificial Intelligence
11.2 CAPITAL, 4
645 VENTURES, 13
ACREW CAPITAL, 49
AMPLIFY, 120
ANALYTICS VENTURES, 121
BAIDU VENTURES, 219
BASIS SET VENTURES, 232
BLUEPOINTE VENTURES, 295
BMW I VENTURES, 302
BOLDSTART VENTURES, 305
BREYER CAPITAL, 336
BRIGHTSPARK VENTURES, 2066
CARBON VENTURES, 408
CATAPULT VENTURES, 429
CHINAROCK CAPITAL MANAGEMENT VENTURES, 472
CHRYSALIX, 2078
COATUE MANAGEMENT, 509
COMET LABS, 519
ECLIPSE VENTURES, 648
ELYSIUM VENTURE CAPITAL, 661
FIFTH WALL, 727
FIKA VENTURES, 728
FIRST ASCENT VENTURES, 2118

1140

Industry Preference Index / Aviation

FLYING FISH, 755
FREYCINET INVESTMENTS, 2125
FUSION FUND, 799
FUTURE VENTURES, 800
GEORGIAN PARTNERS, 2132
GLASSWING VENTURES, 829
GLOBALIVE, 2134
GOLDEN VENTURE PARTNERS, 2137
GOOD NEWS VENTURES, 2138
GROUND UP VENTURES, 877
GV, 889
GVA CAPITAL, 890
HORIZONS VENTURES, 2831
IGAN PARTNERS, 2149
INOVIA CAPITAL, 2157
INTERLACE VENTURES, 1006
LDV CAPITAL, 1101
LOCUS VENTURES, 1138
LUGE CAPITAL, 2179
M12, 1154
MANTELLA VENTURE PARTNERS, 2182
MAPLE LEAF ANGELS, 2184
MARATHON VENTURE CAPITAL FUND LIMITED, 2954
MISTRAL VENTURE PARTNERS, 2195
MOBILE FOUNDATION VENTURES, 1243
MOTLEY FOOL VENTURES, 1259
NEW YORK VENTURE PARTNERS, 1310
NEXT CANADA, 2201
NKM CAPITAL, 1329
OUTPOST CAPITAL, 1390
PATHBREAKER VENTURES, 1421
PLAZA VENTURES, 2224
PORTAG3 VENTURES, 2225
QUAKE CAPITAL PARTNERS, 1507
QUALCOMM VENTURES, 1509
RBC CAPITAL MARKETS, 2231
SAMSUNG NEXT, 1611
SCIENCEVEST, 1630
SMARTINVEST VENTURES, 1695
SONY INNOVATION FUND, 1703
SPERO VENTURES, 1721
SUSA VENTURES, 1758
TEN ELEVEN VENTURES, 1794
THE HIVE, 1809
TOYOTA AI VENTURES, 1834
UBIQUITY VENTURES, 1877
UNCORK CAPITAL, 1879
VANEDGE CAPITAL PARTNERS, 2278
VERIZON VENTURES, 1926
WILDCAT VENTURE PARTNERS, 1985
YALETOWN VENTURE PARTNERS, 2291
ZETTA VENTURE PARTNERS, 2019

Arts
URBAN INNOVATION FUND, 1893

Asset Finance
GRESHAM PRIVATE EQUITY LIMITED, 2799

Asset Management
AMANAH VENTURES SDN BHD, 2388
CHRYSALIX, 2078
CROSSWINDS HOLDINGS INC., 2090
DAVIS, TUTTLE VENTURE PARTNERS LP, 591
HARBOURVEST PARTNERS LLC, 909
JW CHILDS ASSOCIATES, 1049

Assisted Living
CAMBRIDGE CAPITAL CORPORATION, 381

Audio & Video Distribution
SONY STRATEGIC TECHNOLOGY PARTNERSHIPS, 1704

Automation
ACME CAPITAL, 45
AMPLIFY, 120
AXIA CAPITAL, 211

BM-T BETEILIGUNGS MANAGEMENT THURINGEN GmbH, 2527
CATAPULT VENTURES, 429
ENERTECH CAPITAL, 676
FIKA VENTURES, 728
GROUND UP VENTURES, 877
MS&AD VENTURES, 1269
NEWABLE VENTURES, 2997
RTP VENTURES, 1594

Automotive
ALANTRA, 77
ATP PRIVATE EQUITY PARTNERS, 2447
AVIV VENTURE CAPITAL, 2462
BALTCAP MANAGEMENT LTD, 2480
BARING PRIVATE EQUITY PARTNERS ESPANA SA, 2489
BC PARTNERS LIMITED, 2497
BRIDGEPOINT CAPITAL GmbH, 2537
BRIDGEPOINT CAPITAL LIMITED, 2538
CAPVIS EQUITY PARTNERS, 2564
CARLYLE ASIA INVESTMENT ADVISORS LIMITED Carlyle Group, 2565
CARLYLE GROUP, 413
CERBERUS CAPITAL MANAGEMENT, 451
CHINA DEVELOPMENT INDUSTRIAL BANK CDFH, 2592
CLIFFORD CHANCE PUNDER, 2614
CVC ASIA PACIFIC LIMITED CVC Capital Partners, 2643
CVC CAPITAL PARTNERS LTD, 2644
DEFI GESTION SA Banque Cantonale Vaudoise, 2653
DEUTSCHE BETEILIGUNGS AG, 2660
EAST FUND MANAGEMENT GmbH GiroCredit, 2683
ECLIPSE VENTURES, 648
ELGNER GROUP INVESTMENTS, 2104
EQUISTONE, 2714
EUROVENTURES CAPITAL, 2725
FIRST ISRAEL MEZZANINE INVESTORS LIMITED, 2745
FLANDERS' FOREIGN INVESTMENT OFFICE, 2746
FOURIERTRANSFORM, 2755
FRASER MCCOMBS CAPITAL, 781
GENERAL MOTORS VENTURES, 817
HAMMOND, KENNEDY, WHITNEY & COMPANY, 900
HCI EQUITY PARTNERS, 917
IBM VENTURE CAPITAL GROUP, 967
INDUSTRIEBANK LIOF NV, 2866
JAVELIN INVESTMENTS, 2908
JORDAN COMPANY, 1045
LINSALATA CAPITAL PARTNERS, 1132
LITTLEJOHN & COMPANY LLC, 1134
M12, 1154
MOBILE FOUNDATION VENTURES, 1243
NAVIGATION CAPITAL PARTNERS, 1280
PAC-LINK MANAGEMENT CORP., 3024
PRIVATE EQUITY PARTNERS SPA, 3053
PROSPECT PARTNERS LLC, 1492
QUADRAN GESTION Deutsche Beteiligungs AG, 3067
QUALCOMM VENTURES, 1509
RESILIENCE CAPITAL PARTNERS, 1545
SERGE PUN & ASSOCIATES (MYANMAR) LIMITED, 3111
SEVEN SPIRES INVESTMENTS, 3112
STARBOARD CAPITAL PARTNERS, 1735
SUN CAPITAL PARTNERS, 1753
UNISON CAPITAL PARTNERS LP, 3201
VICKERS FINANCIAL GROUP, 3215
VOLVO GROUP VENTURE CAPITAL, 3226

Autonomous Driving
BMW I VENTURES, 302

Autonomous Mobility
TOYOTA AI VENTURES, 1834

Autonomous Vehicles
INTEL CAPITAL, 1004

Aviation
COPPERLION CAPITAL, 2085
GE CAPITAL, 808
HRL MORRISON & COMPANY LIMITED, 2835

1141

Industry Preference Index / Aviation Services

INTERMEDIATE CAPITAL GROUP PLC, 2883
JETBLUE TECHNOLOGY VENTURES, 1035
MVP CAPITAL PARTNERS, 1275
SAMBRINVEST SA, 3096

Aviation Services
ARGOSY CAPITAL, 164

B2B
ENTREPRENEURS ROUNDTABLE ACCELERATOR, 684
GCI CAPITAL, 2128
GENACAST VENTURES, 814
GOOD NEWS VENTURES, 2138
MISTRAL VENTURE PARTNERS, 2195
NAYA VENTURES, 1285
NEWLIGHT PARTNERS, 1315
RED CLAY CAPITAL HOLDINGS, 1529

B2B Services
ARGOSY CAPITAL, 164

B2B Software
FOUNDATION EQUITY CORPORATION, 2121

B2C
ANGELPAD, 128
ENTREPRENEURS ROUNDTABLE ACCELERATOR, 684

Banking
BARING PRIVATE EQUITY PARTNERS INDIA, 2490
CAMBRIDGE CAPITAL CORPORATION, 381
CHINA MERCHANTS CHINA DIRECT INVESTMENTS LTD., 2594
COLLABORATIVE FUND, 511
CROSBY CAPITAL LIMITED, 2641
EPISODE 1 PARTNERS, 2711
IBM VENTURE CAPITAL GROUP, 967
PORTAG3 VENTURES, 2225
RHB - H&F MANAGEMENT COMPANY SDN BHD RHB Capital, 3080
SHANGHAI INFORMATION INVESTMENT INCORPORATED, 3114
SIF TRANSYLVANIA, 3119
TEKINVEST KK, 3166
THOMPROPERTIES OY, 3175
TPA CORPORATE FINANCE CONSULTING GMBH Horwarth International, 3184
VALUE PARTNERS LIMITED, 3204

Beauty & Personal Care
TSG CONSUMER PARTNERS, 1861

Behavioral Health
HEALTH ENTERPRISE PARTNERS, 918

Behavioral Management
FIRST ANALYSIS, 732

Beverages
BEVERAGE MARKETING CORPORATION, 261
BRIDGEPOINT CAPITAL GmbH, 2537
BRIDGEPOINT CAPITAL LIMITED, 2538
CLIFFORD CHANCE PUNDER, 2614
INVESTMENT FUND FOR CENTRAL & EASTERN EUROPE, 2889
RABO BLACK EARTH Eagle Venture Partners, 3071
VINACAPITAL GROUP, 3217

Big Data
42 VENTURES, 9
ARCHTOP VENTURES, 154
AUGMENT VENTURES, 195
BLUEPOINTE VENTURES, 295
CORNERSTONE VENTURE PARTNERS, 543
CORSA VENTURES, 545
DRAPER ATHENA, 626
FIRST ASCENT VENTURES, 2118
G SQUARED, 802
GOOD NEWS VENTURES, 2138
GREEN TOWER CAPITAL, 861
GVA CAPITAL, 890

IMAGINATION CAPITAL, 977
INTEL CAPITAL, 1004
KHOSLA VENTURES, 1069
LIGHTSPEED VENTURE PARTNERS, 1121
M12, 1154
MIDDLEBURG CAPITAL DEVELOPMENT, 1229
MOBILE FOUNDATION VENTURES, 1243
NAYA VENTURES, 1285
NIELSEN INNOVATE FUND, 3003
O'REILLY ALPHATECH VENTURES, 1359
PROCYON VENTURES, 1483
REED ELSEVIER VENTURES, 3074
RTP VENTURES, 1594
RUBICON VENTURE CAPITAL, 1595
SINEWAVE VENTURES, 1687
SUMMIT BRIDGE CAPITAL, 3147
SUSA VENTURES, 1758

Big Data & Analytics
CISCO INVESTMENTS, 483
NFX, 1323
WORK-BENCH, 2006

Bio Materials
CVC INVESTMENT MANAGERS LIMITED, 2645
LATTERELL VENTURE PARTNERS, 1094
LIFE SCIENCES PARTNERS BV, 2939
MMT MILLENNIUM MATERIALS TECHNOLOGIES FUND LP, 2973

Biochemicals & Biomaterials
BIOINDUSTRIAL INNOVATION CANADA, 2061

Bioenergy
BIOINDUSTRIAL INNOVATION CANADA, 2061

Bioengineering
GUANGDONG TECHNOLOGY VENTURE CAPITAL COMPANY, 2802
MIRAE ASSET VENTURE ACCELERATOR Mirae Asset Group, 2969
SAMSUNG VENTURE INVESTMENT CORPORATION Samsung Electronics, 3098

Biofuels
BIOINDUSTRIAL INNOVATION CANADA, 2061
US RENEWABLES GROUP, 1895
VENROCK ASSOCIATES, 1916

Bioinformatics
ALLOY VENTURES, 87
CALUMET VENTURE FUND, 375
LANCET CAPITAL, 1092
NEW VENTURE PARTNERS, 1305
SAND HILL ANGELS, 1613

Biologicals
THE CHANNEL GROUP, 1808

Biomass
FORESIGHT VENTURE PARTNERS, 2749

Biomedical
BAY CITY CAPITAL LLC, 237
ENSO VENTURES, 2702
GOLDEN PINE VENTURES, 840
SPINUP VENTURE, 3132
WRF CAPITAL, 2008

Biometrics
ALTAIR VENTURES, 95
CHORD CAPITAL, 2598

Biopharmaceuticals
5AM VENTURES, 12
ABERDARE VENTURES, 20
ADAMS STREET PARTNERS, LLC, 57
ALTA PARTNERS, 94
APERTURE VENTURE PARTNERS, 136
APJOHN GROUP LLC, 139

Industry Preference Index / Biotechnology

ARCUS VENTURES, 157
ASCENT BIOMEDICAL VENTURES, 177
AUGURY CAPITAL PARTNERS, 196
BAY CITY CAPITAL LLC, 237
CALIFORNIA TECHNOLOGY VENTURES, 371
CARDINAL PARTNERS, 410
CATALYST FUND LP, 2571
CLARUS VENTURES, 495
CTI LIFE SCIENCES, 2092
DOMAIN ASSOCIATES LLC, 621
DRI CAPITAL, 2102
F-PRIME CAPITAL PARTNERS, 710
FLARE CAPITAL PARTNERS, 748
FORWARD VENTURES, 769
FRAZIER HEALTHCARE VENTURES, 782
HAMILTON BIOVENTURES, 898
HATTERAS VENTURE PARTNERS, 915
HEALTHCARE VENTURES LLC, 919
INNOVATION CAPITAL LIMITED, 2877
KBL HEALTHCARE VENTURES, 1058
LANCET CAPITAL, 1092
LIGHTSTONE VENTURES, 1122
LUMIRA CAPITAL, 2180
MBF CAPITAL CORPORATION, 1188
MEDIMMUNE VENTURES, 1196
MEDIPHASE VENTURE PARTNERS, 1197
MONTREUX EQUITY PARTNERS, 1251
MORGAN STANLEY EXPANSION CAPITAL, 1255
MVM LIFE SCIENCE PARTNERS, 2981
NEW ENTERPRISE ASSOCIATES, 1297
NEW LEAF VENTURE PARTNERS, 1298
NOVAQUEST CAPITAL MANAGEMENT, 1349
PAPPAS VENTURES, 1412
PROSPECT VENTURE PARTNERS, 1493
QUAKER BIOVENTURES, 1508
REX HEALTH VENTURES, 1556
RHO VENTURES, 1558
ROBIN HOOD VENTURES, 1577
SPINDLETOP CAPITAL, 1722
SYNTHESIS CAPITAL, 1775
TAKEDA VENTURES, 1778
THREE ARCH PARTNERS LP, 1819
TREVI HEALTH CAPITAL, 1844
TRIATHLON MEDICAL VENTURES, 1847
VENROCK ASSOCIATES, 1916
VENTANA CAPITAL MANAGEMENT LP, 1918

Biopolymers
NOVARTIS VENTURE FUNDS, 1350

Biosciences
CINCYTECH, 479
COTTONWOOD TECHNOLOGY FUND, 549
GIDEON HIXON FUND, 826
HALLEY VENTURE PARTNERS, 895
LIFE SCIENCES GREENHOUSE OF CENTRAL PA, 1117
MOMENTUM FUNDS MANAGEMENT PTY LIMITED, 2975

Biotechnology
5AM VENTURES, 12
ABELL FOUNDATION VENTURES, 19
ABINGWORTH MANAGEMENT LIMITED, 2316
ACADIA WOODS PARTNERS, 26
ACCELERATOR LIFE SCIENCE PARTNERS, 31
ACCES CAPITAL QUEBEC, 2029
ACE VENTURE CAPITAL LIMITED, 2330
ACRUX LIMITED, 2335
ADVENT VENTURE PARTNERS, 2348
AISLING CAPITAL, 74
ALBEMARLE PRIVATE EQUITY LIMITED, 2360
ALFA CAPITAL Alfa Group, 2363
ALTA BERKELEY ASSOCIATES, 2380
ALTA PARTNERS, 94
ALTRIA VENTURES, 102
AMANAH VENTURES SDN BHD, 2388
AMGEN VENTURES, 112
AMKEY VENTURES, 117

AMPERSAND CAPITAL PARTNERS, 118
ANDLINGER & COMPANY INC, 123
ANNEX VENTURES, 130
ANTHEM VENTURE PARTNERS, 132
APAX PARTNERS ET CIE, 2415
APERTURE VENTURE PARTNERS, 136
APPLE TREE PARTNERS, 143
ARBORETUM VENTURES, 149
ASTELLAS VENTURE MANAGEMENT, 182
ATHENAEUM FUND, 186
ATHYRIUM CAPITAL MANAGEMENT, 188
AUSTRALIAN ETHICAL INVESTMENT LIMITED, 2456
AVALON VENTURES, 206
AXIOM VENTURE PARTNERS, 212
AXVENTURES, 2470
AZCA, 214
BAND OF ANGELS LLC, 226
BARCELONA EMPREN, 2483
BASF VENTURE CAPITAL, 2492
BATTERSON VENTURE CAPITAL LLC, 234
BCM TECHNOLOGIES, 241
BEZOS EXPEDITIONS, 262
BIO FUND MANAGEMENT OY, 2512
BIOMED PARTNERS, 2515
BIOPACIFIC VENTURES, 2516
BIOPROCESS CAPITAL PARTNERS, 2517
BLACK DIAMOND VENTURES, 275
BOULDER VENTURES LTD, 315
BRIGHTSTONE VENTURE CAPITAL, 341
BROOK VENTURE FUND, 349
CAMBRIDGE CAPITAL CORPORATION, 381
CAMPUS COMPANIES VENTURE CAPITAL FUND, 2554
CANNA ANGELS LLC, 388
CAPRICORN VENTURE PARTNERS NV, 2563
CARE CAPITAL, 412
CATO BIOVENTURES, 430
CEDRUS INVESTMENTS, 2581
CEI VENTURES, 438
CELADON CAPITAL GROUP, 2582
CHALLENGE FUNDS - ETGAR LP, 2585
CHEVRON TECHNOLOGY VENTURES, 466
CHINA DEVELOPMENT INDUSTRIAL BANK CDFH, 2592
CHL MEDICAL PARTNERS, 474
CITA GESTION, 2607
CLARENDON FUND MANAGERS, 2610
COLT VENTURES, 514
COLUMN GROUP, 517
CONNECTICUT INNOVATIONS, 530
CONTINENTAL VENTURE CAPITAL LIMITED, 2631
CORDOVA VENTURES, 537
CORE PACIFIC - YAMAICHI CAPITAL LIMITED Core Pacific Securities Company Ltd, 2633
CRB INVERBIO, 2636
DELPHI VENTURES, 604
EcoR1 CAPITAL, 709
EDGEWATER FUNDS, 654
ENTERPRISE EQUITY (NI) LTD, 2704
ESSEX WOODLANDS HEALTH VENTURES LLC, 697
EUROPEAN INVESTMENT FUND, 2724
EXPANSION VENTURE CAPITAL, 707
FARM CREDIT CANADA, 2114
FINNVERA PLC, 2741
FIRST CAPITAL VENTURE, 735
FLETCHER SPAGHT VENTURES, 749
FORBION CAPITAL PARTNERS, 2748
FOUNDERS FUND, 775
FRONTIER VENTURE CAPITAL, 791
GENESYS CAPITAL, 2130
GIC GROUP, 825
GIDEON HIXON FUND, 826
GIMV GIMV, 2780
GLOBAL EQUITY PARTNERS BETEILIGUNGS-MANAGEMENT, 2783
GLOBAL LIFE SCIENCE VENTURES GmbH, 2785
GOLDEN PINE VENTURES, 840
GRYPHON MANAGEMENT COMPANY, 882
HALLIM VENTURE CAPITAL, 2807
HANWHA VC CORPORATION, 2812

Industry Preference Index / Biotherapeutics

HARBOURVEST PARTNERS LLC, 909
HBM PARTNERS, 2815
HEALTH ENTERPRISE PARTNERS, 918
HEALTHCAP Odlander, Fredrikson & Co AB, 2816
HELMET CAPITAL FUND MANAGEMENT OY, 2820
HIGH COUNTRY VENTURE, 930
HMS HAWAII MANAGEMENT, 939
HORIZONTE VENTURE MANAGEMENT GmbH, 2832
HYUNDAI VENTURE INVESTMENT CORPORATION, 2839
ICAN ISRAEL-CANNABIS.COM, 2845
ICF VENTURES PVT LTD, 2846
IDG TECHNOLOGY VENTURE INVESTMENT, 2848
INDASIA FUND ADVISORS PVT LTD, 2859
INDURAN VENTURES INC., 2152
INDUSTRIFONDEN, 2867
INITIATIVE CAPITAL LIMITED, 2154
INNOFINANCE OY, 2873
INNOVA MEMPHIS, 995
INNOVATION CAPITAL LIMITED, 2877
INNOVATION CAPITAL, 2876
INNOVATION WORKS, 998
INTERMEDIATE CAPITAL GROUP PLC, 2883
INTERSOUTH PARTNERS, 1008
INVUS GROUP, 1018
IP GROUP, 2892
JAPAN ASIA INVESTMENT COMPANY LIMITED, 2907
JAVELIN INVESTMENTS, 2908
JF SHEA VENTURES, 1036
JOHNSON & JOHNSON INNOVATION, 1043
JOHNSTON ASSOCIATES, 1044
KBL FOUNDER SA, 2917
KEGONSA CAPITAL PARTNERS, 1060
KLEINER PERKINS, 1075
KODIAK CAPITAL, 1079
LATTERELL VENTURE PARTNERS, 1094
LEASING TECHNOLOGIES INTERNATIONAL INC., 1103
LIGHTSTONE VENTURES, 1122
LILLY VENTURES, 1124
LINK TECHNOLOGIES LIMITED, 2941
LONGITUDE CAPITAL, 1143
LRM - INVESTERINGSMAATSCHAPPIJ VOOR LIMBURG, 2949
MAINE ANGELS, 1160
MARATHON VENTURE CAPITAL FUND LIMITED, 2954
MAYFIELD FUND, 1184
MB VENTURE PARTNERS, 1187
MID-ATLANTIC VENTURE FUNDS, 1227
MIDVEN, 2967
MISSION BAY CAPITAL, 1238
MITSUBISHI UFJ CAPITAL, 2970
MITSUI SUMITOMO INSURANCE VENTURE CAPITAL CO, 2971
MMT MILLENNIUM MATERIALS TECHNOLOGIES FUND LP, 2973
MOMENTUM FUNDS MANAGEMENT PTY LIMITED, 2975
MORGENTHALER VENTURES, 1257
MPM CAPITAL, 1268
NEST VENTURES, 1290
NETROVE ASIA SDN BHD, 2993
NEW SCIENCE VENTURES, 1303
NEW YORK CITY ENTREPRENEURIAL FUND New York City Economic Development Corporation, 1307
NEW YORK LIFE CAPITAL PARTNERS, 1309
NEWMARGIN VENTURE CAPITAL, 2998
NGN CAPITAL, 1325
NORTHERN ENTERPRISE LIMITED, 3011
NORTHSTAR VENTURES, 3012
NOVELTEK CAPITAL CORPORATION, 1351
NOVO A/S, 3015
OKAPI VENTURE CAPITAL, 1371
OMEGA FUNDS, 1373
OPEN PRAIRIE VENTURES, 1379
OXFORD BIOSCIENCE PARTNERS, 1394
PAPPAS VENTURES, 1412
PENN VENTURE PARTNERS, 1428
PHOSPHAGENICS, 3037
PIDC PHILADELPHIA, 1441
PITTSBURGH LIFE SCIENCES GREENHOUSE, 1448
PLEXUS VENTURES, 1452
PRAIRIEGOLD VENTURE PARTNERS, 1470

PTV SCIENCES, 1500
QUESTER CAPITAL MANAGEMENT LIMITED, 3070
RESEARCH CORPORATION TECHNOLOGIES, 1543
RHO VENTURES, 1558
SAMSUNG VENTURE INVESTMENT CORPORATION Samsung Electronics, 3098
SANDERLING VENTURES, 1616
SANOFI-GENZYME BIOVENTURES, 1618
SATURN PARTNERS, 1623
SCALE VENTURE PARTNERS, 1626
SCHRODER VENTURES HEALTH INVESTORS, 1628
SCIENCEVEST, 1630
SEED CAPITAL LIMITED, 3107
SHANNON COMMERCIAL PROPERTIES, 3115
SIGNATURE CAPITAL LLC, 3120
SKYLINE VENTURES, 1691
SOCIAL VENTURE CIRCLE, 3277
SORRENTO VENTURES, 1706
SR ONE LTD, 1731
STARBOARD CAPITAL PARTNERS, 1735
STATELINE ANGELS, 1740
STRAND HANSON LIMITED, 3146
SUTTER HILL VENTURES, 1760
SV HEALTH INVESTORS, 1762
SVB CAPITAL, 1764
SYCAMORE VENTURES, 1769
SYNTHESIS CAPITAL, 1775
TAT CAPITAL PARTNERS LTD., 3162
TECH COAST ANGELS, 1784
TECHNOLOGY PARK MALAYSIA CORPORATION SDN BHD, 3164
TERA CAPITAL CORPORATION, 2267
TEUZA MANAGEMENT & DEVELOPMENT LTD, 3171
TFG CAPITAL AG, 3172
THE CHANNEL GROUP, 1808
THOMAS, MCNERNEY & PARTNERS, 1817
TL VENTURES, 1828
TONG YANG VENTURE CAPITAL CORPORATION Tong Yang Cement Corporation, 3183
TPA CORPORATE FINANCE CONSULTING GMBH Horwarth International, 3184
TRANSATLANTIC CAPITAL LTD, 3186
TRANSITION PARTNERS LTD, 1837
TRELYS FUNDS, 1842
TULLIS HEALTH INVESTORS, 1866
TWIN CITIES ANGELS, 1872
UCA UNTERNEHMER CONSULT AG, 3197
USHA MARTIN VENTURES LIMITED, 3202
VAEKSTFONDEN, 3203
VEDANTA CAPITAL LP, 1911
VENTANA CAPITAL MANAGEMENT LP, 1918
VENTURE INVESTORS, 3210
VERSANT VENTURES, 1928
VERTICAL GROUP, 1929
VIDA VENTURES, 1932
VIVO CAPITAL, 1941
WESTERN TECHNOLOGY INVESTMENT, 1975
WI HARPER GROUP, 1983
WILMINGTON INVESTOR NETWORK, 1988
WOODSIDE FUND, 2005
WRF CAPITAL, 2008
YASUDA ENTERPRISE DEVELOPMENT COMPANY, 3243
YISSUM TECHNOLOGY TRANSFER, 3245
YUUWA CAPITAL, 3248
ZERNIKE SEED FUND BV, 3250

Biotherapeutics
SHEPHERD VENTURES, 1664

Bitcoin
500 STARTUPS, 11

Blockchain
AMPLIFY, 120
CHINAROCK CAPITAL MANAGEMENT VENTURES, 472
CHRYSALIX, 2078
ELYSIUM VENTURE CAPITAL, 661
FGA PARTNERS, 725

Industry Preference Index / Business Products & Services

FUTURE VENTURES, 800
LUGE CAPITAL, 2179
MISTRAL VENTURE PARTNERS, 2195
OUTPOST CAPITAL, 1390
OYSTER VENTURES, 1395
QUAKE CAPITAL PARTNERS, 1507
SAMSUNG NEXT, 1611
SCIENCEVEST, 1630
SIGNIA VENTURE PARTNERS, 1678
THE HIVE, 1809

Blockchain/cryptocurrencies
ALTPOINT CAPITAL, 101

Branded Goods
BARING VOSTOK CAPITAL PARTNERS, 2491
BRYAN GARNIER & COMPANY, 2544
CHENGWEI VENTURES, 2590
CLEARVIEW CAPITAL, 503
EMIGRANT CAPITAL, 667
RAPTOR GROUP, 1524

Bridges
ROAD KING INFRASTRUCTURE LIMITED, 3084

Broadband
ALLEGIS CYBER CAPITAL, 84
AZURE CAPITAL PARTNERS, 215
BRAINSTORM VENTURES, 324
CENTENNIAL VENTURES, 441
CLARITY PARTNERS, 494
COLUMBIA CAPITAL, 515
COMCAST VENTURES, 518
FIRST ANALYSIS, 732
I-HATCH VENTURES LLC, 964
KOREA TECHNOLOGY & BANKING (KTB) NETWORK CORP, 2926
NORO-MOSELEY PARTNERS, 1331
PALOMAR VENTURES, 1407
SCALE VENTURE PARTNERS, 1626
SEAPOINT VENTURES, 1637
SIGNAL LAKE, 1676
WI HARPER GROUP, 1983

Broadcasting
ABU DHABI INVESTMENT AUTHORITY, 2321
AEP CAPITAL LLC, 65
ALLSTATE INVESTMENTS LLC, 88
GRUPO BISA, 2800
MACQUARIE DIRECT INVESTMENT LIMITED, 2951
MANHATTAN INVESTMENT PARTNERS, 1163
MCG CAPITAL CORPORATION, 1189
MEDIA VENTURE PARTNERS, 1195
NORTHWOOD VENTURES, 1344
RAPTOR GROUP, 1524
RENAISSANCE PARTNERS, 3077
SOUTH ATLANTIC VENTURE FUNDS, 1708
SYCAMORE VENTURES, 1769
TIME WARNER INVESTMENT CORPORATION, 1827
VENTURE CAPITAL FUND OF NEW ENGLAND, 1920
WICKS GROUP OF COMPANIES, LLC, 1984

Brokering
AMANAH VENTURES SDN BHD, 2388
CHINA MERCHANTS CHINA DIRECT INVESTMENTS LTD., 2594

Building Innovation
GREENSOIL INVESTMENTS, 2142

Building Materials & Resources
SCOTIABANK PRIVATE EQUITY, 2250

Building Materials & Services
ALTUS CAPITAL PARTNERS, 104
AUDAX GROUP, 194
BOUNDS EQUITY PARTNERS, 316
CALERA CAPITAL, 368
CERBERUS CAPITAL MANAGEMENT, 451
DESCO CAPITAL, 606
DUBIN CLARK & COMPANY, 632
DUNEDIN CAPITAL PARTNERS LIMITED, 2677
ENTERPRISE EQUITY (NI) LTD, 2704
GEORGIA OAK PARTNERS, 821
GRAHAM PARTNERS, 846
HIG CAPITAL, 928
INDIAN DIRECT EQUITY ADVISORS PVT LTD, 2861
INDUSTRI KAPITAL SVENSKA AB, 2863
JLL PARTNERS, 1039
JMH CAPITAL, 1040
JORDAN COMPANY, 1045
KOHLBERG & COMPANY LLC, 1081
LINSALATA CAPITAL PARTNERS, 1132
MARCEAU INVESTISSEMENTS, 2955
NAVIGATION CAPITAL PARTNERS, 1280
NAVITAS CAPITAL, 1282
PALOMINO CAPITAL, 1408
SAMBRINVEST SA, 3096
STARBOARD CAPITAL PARTNERS, 1735
STONEBRIDGE PARTNERS, 1744
TRANSYLVANIA FINANCIAL INVESTMENT COMPANY, 3187
WATERMILL GROUP, 1962
XPV WATER PARTNERS, 2290

Building Products
SIGNAL HILL EQUITY PARTNERS, 2255

Building Sciences
FIFTH WALL, 727

Business
GOLDMAN SACHS INVESTMENT PARTNERS, 842

Business & Commercial Services
FIVE POINTS CAPITAL, 746

Business & Consumer Services
IMPERIAL CAPITAL, 2150
SIGNAL HILL EQUITY PARTNERS, 2255

Business & Financial Services
ADVENT INTERNATIONAL CORPORATION, 62
SPRING LAKE EQUITY PARTNERS, 1728

Business Aircraft
CIT GROUP, 484

Business Consulting
CANNA ANGELS LLC, 388

Business Intelligence
YL VENTURES, 3246

Business Model Innovation
ACME CAPITAL, 45

Business Outsourcing
LAKE CAPITAL, 1091
NORO-MOSELEY PARTNERS, 1331
TH LEE PUTNAM VENTURES, 1804

Business Process Outsourcing
CARRICK CAPITAL PARTNERS, 416

Business Products & Services
3I EUROPE PLC 3i Group, 2300
3I GESTION SA 3i Group, 2302
3I ITALY 3i Group, 2303
3TS CAPITAL PARTNERS 3i Group plc, 2309
3i GROUP PLC, 2311
ABRY PARTNERS, 21
ABS CAPITAL PARTNERS, 22
ACI CAPITAL, 42
ACTIVA CAPITAL, 2338
ADAMS STREET PARTNERS, LLC, 57
ADLEVO CAPITAL CIM Fund Services, 2345

Industry Preference Index / Business Products & Services

ADVANTAGE CAPITAL PARTNERS, 61
AEP CAPITAL LLC, 65
AIP PRIVATE CAPITAL, 2031
ALANTRA, 77
ALBION INVESTORS LLC, 78
ALERION PARTNERS, 80
ALEUTIAN CAPITAL PARTNERS, 81
ALTAMONT CAPITAL PARTNERS, 96
ANGELO, GORDON & CO., 127
APAX PARTNERS ET CIE, 2415
APEX VENTURE PARTNERS, 137
APOLLO GLOBAL MANAGEMENT, 140
ARC ANGEL FUND, 150
ARCAPITA INC, 152
ARES MANAGEMENT LLC, 159
ARLINGTON CAPITAL PARTNERS, 166
ARROWHEAD INVESTMENT MANAGEMENT, 168
ASTELLA INVESTMENTS, 2438
AUA PRIVATE EQUITY PARTNERS, 193
AUDAX GROUP, 194
AUGUST CAPITAL, 197
AUSTIN VENTURES, 202
AZALEA CAPITAL, 213
BALMORAL FUNDS, 225
BANNEKER PARTNERS, 227
BBH CAPITAL PARTNERS, 240
BERKSHIRE PARTNERS LLC, 254
BERTRAM CAPITAL, 257
BESTPORT VENTURES, 2507
BEZOS EXPEDITIONS, 262
BIA DIGITAL PARTNERS LP, 263
BIP CAPITAL, 271
BLACKFORD CAPITAL LLC, 276
BLACKSTONE PRIVATE EQUITY GROUP, 277
BLAZER VENTURES, 280
BLUE POINT CAPITAL PARTNERS, 290
BLUEGEM CAPITAL PARTNERS, 2524
BLUESTEM CAPITAL COMPANY, 297
BOUNDS EQUITY PARTNERS, 316
BOWERY CAPITAL, 317
BRAZOS PRIVATE EQUITY PARTNERS, 328
BREAKWATER INVESTMENTS, 330
BREGAL SAGEMOUNT, 333
BRIDGE STREET CAPITAL, 338
BRIDGESCALE PARTNERS, 339
BRIGHTPATH CAPITAL PARTNERS, 340
BRYAN GARNIER & COMPANY, 2544
BRYNWOOD PARTNERS, 357
BUNKER HILL CAPITAL, 359
BUSINESS GROWTH FUND, 2550
CAI CAPITAL PARTNERS, 365
CALERA CAPITAL, 368
CALTIUS EQUITY PARTNERS, 373
CALTIUS STRUCTURED CAPITAL, 374
CALUMET VENTURE FUND, 375
CAMBRIA GROUP, 378
CAMDEN PARTNERS HOLDINGS LLC, 383
CANADIAN VENTURE CAPITAL ASSOCIATION Canadian Venture Capital & Private Equity Association, 3258
CAPITALA, 405
CARLYLE GROUP, 413
CAROUSEL CAPITAL, 415
CARPEDIA CAPITAL, 2072
CATALYST INVESTORS, 427
CENTRE PARTNERS MANAGEMENT LLC, 447
CERES VENTURE FUND, 452
CHEYENNE CAPITAL, 467
CHICAGO GROWTH PARTNERS, 468
CHRYSALIS CAPITAL ChrysCapital, 2599
CI CAPITAL PARTNERS, 476
CIVC PARTNERS, 489
CLARION CAPITAL PARTNERS LLC, 492
CLARITY PARTNERS, 494
CLEARLAKE CAPITAL, 500
CLEARLIGHT PARTNERS, 501
CLEARSPRING CAPITAL PARTNERS, 2082
COLORADO MILE HIGH FUND, 513

CONCENTRIC EQUITY PARTNERS Financial Investments Corporation, 529
CONTOUR VENTURE PARTNERS, 533
CORRELATION VENTURES, 544
CSA PARTNERS, 566
CUE BALL GROUP, 567
CUSTER CAPITAL, 571
CYPRESS GROWTH CAPITAL, 576
DESJARDINS CAPITAL, 2095
DIAMOND STATE VENTURES LP, 611
EDGESTONE CAPITAL PARTNERS, 2103
EMINENT CAPITAL PARTNERS, 669
ENDEAVOUR CAPITAL, 673
ENTREE CAPITAL, 2709
EPIC VENTURES, 688
EUREKA GROWTH CAPITAL, 698
FIRST NEW ENGLAND CAPITAL LP, 739
FIVE ELMS CAPITAL, 745
FOG CITY CAPITAL, 758
FRANCISCO PARTNERS, 779
FRIEND SKOLER & COMPANY LLC, 788
FRONTENAC COMPANY, 789
FRONTIER CAPITAL, 790
FTV CAPITAL, 793
GENERAL ATLANTIC PARTNERS, 815
GENERATION PARTNERS, 818
GEORGIA OAK PARTNERS, 821
GLADSTONE CAPITAL, 828
GLENGARY LLC, 831
GLYNN CAPITAL MANAGEMENT, 836
GOENSE & COMPANY LLC, 838
GOLDNER, HAWN, JOHNSON & MORRISON, 843
GRAHAM PARTNERS, 846
GRANITE PARTNERS, 2139
GRYPHON INVESTORS, 881
GULFSTAR GROUP, 888
HALYARD CAPITAL, 897
HAMILTON ROBINSON CAPITAL PARTNERS, 899
HARBOUR GROUP, 908
HARREN EQUITY PARTNERS, 910
HARVEST PARTNERS, 914
HELLMAN & FRIEDMAN LLC, 924
HERITAGE PARTNERS, 926
HIG CAPITAL, 928
HORIZON VENTURES LLC, 947
HOUSATONIC PARTNERS, 949
HURON CAPITAL PARTNERS LLC, 960
ICV PARTNERS, 969
IMPLEMENT CAPITAL, 978
INDEX VENTURES, 2860
INDEX VENTURES, 2860
INITIAL CAPITAL, 2872
INVERNESS GRAHAM INVESTMENTS, 1014
IRISH ANGELS, 1019
IRONBRIDGE EQUITY PARTNERS, 2163
IRONWOOD CAPITAL, 1021
J. BURKE CAPITAL PARTNERS, 1023
JH WHITNEY & COMPANY, 1037
JLL PARTNERS, 1039
JMH CAPITAL, 1040
JMI EQUITY FUND LP, 1041
KERRY CAPITAL ADVISORS, 1067
KOHLBERG & COMPANY LLC, 1081
KPS CAPITAL PARTNERS, 1085
KRG CAPITAL PARTNERS, 1086
LASALLE CAPITAL GROUP, 1093
LEE EQUITY PARTNERS, 1104
LEEDS EQUITY PARTNERS, 1105
LEONARD GREEN & PARTNERS LP, 1109
LFE CAPITAL, 1113
LIBERTY PARTNERS, 1116
LINLEY CAPITAL, 1130
LLR PARTNERS INC, 1136
LONG POINT CAPITAL, 1141
LONG RIVER VENTURES, 1142
LOVELL MINNICK PARTNERS LLC, 1147
LOVETT MILLER & COMPANY, 1148

Industry Preference Index / Business Software

LYNWOOD CAPITAL PARTNERS, 1152
MADISON PARKER CAPITAL, 1157
MADRONA VENTURE GROUP, 1158
MARANON CAPITAL, 1166
MARWIT CAPITAL LLC, 1168
MASON WELLS, 1171
MCG CAPITAL CORPORATION, 1189
MENTOR CAPITAL PARTNERS LTD, 1203
MIDDLEBURG CAPITAL DEVELOPMENT, 1229
MIDOCEAN PARTNERS, 1231
MIDWEST MEZZANINE FUNDS, 1232
MISSIONOG, 1240
MMC VENTURES, 2972
MONTAGU PRIVATE EQUITY LIMITED, 2977
MONTLAKE CAPITAL, 1250
MOUNTAIN GROUP CAPITAL, 1261
MPG EQUITY PARTNERS, 1267
MSOUTH EQUITY PARTNERS, 1270
MURPHY & PARTNERS FUND LP, 1274
MVP CAPITAL PARTNERS, 1275
NAUTIC PARTNERS, 1279
NAVIGATION CAPITAL PARTNERS, 1280
NEW CAPITAL PARTNERS, 1293
NEW ENGLAND CAPITAL PARTNERS, 1296
NEW MEXICO COMMUNITY CAPITAL, 1300
NEW MOUNTAIN CAPITAL, 1301
NEWSPRING CAPITAL, 1317
NEXUS VENTURE PARTNERS Nexus India Capital Advisors Pvt Ltd, 3001
NORTH AMERICAN FUND, 1332
NORTH ATLANTIC CAPITAL CORPORATION, 1333
NORTHSTAR CAPITAL, 1343
NORWEST VENTURE PARTNERS, 1346
OAK HILL CAPITAL PARTNERS, 1360
ODYSSEY INVESTMENT PARTNERS, 1368
OSAGE PARTNERS, 1387
PALLADIUM EQUITY PARTNERS, 1403
PALOMINO CAPITAL, 1408
PAMLICO CAPITAL, 1409
PARALLEL49 EQUITY, 2214
PARKVIEW CAPITAL PARTNERS, 2215
PARTHENON CAPITAL, 1417
PEACHTREE EQUITY PARTNERS, 1423
PENN VENTURE PARTNERS, 1428
PFINGSTEN PARTNERS LLC, 1435
PIVOTNORTH CAPITAL, 1450
PNC RIVERARCH CAPITAL, 1457
POLARIS VENTURE PARTNERS, 1460
POST CAPITAL PARTNERS, 1465
POUSCHINE COOK CAPITAL MANAGEMENT LLC, 1466
PRAIRIE CAPITAL, 1469
PRIVEQ CAPITAL FUNDS, 2226
QUARRY CAPITAL MANAGEMENT, 1511
RBC CAPITAL MARKETS, 2231
REDMONT VENTURE PARTNERS, 1533
RIDGE CAPITAL PARTNERS LLC, 1562
RIVER ASSOCIATES INVESTMENTS LLC, 1569
RIVER CAPITAL, 1570
RLH EQUITY PARTNERS, 1575
ROARK CAPITAL GROUP, 1576
ROBIN HOOD VENTURES, 1577
ROCK ISLAND CAPITAL, 1578
ROPART ASSET MANAGEMENT, 1583
ROTH CAPITAL PARTNERS, 1588
SALEM INVESTMENT PARTNERS, 1606
SALT CREEK CAPITAL, 1609
SATORI CAPITAL, 1622
SEACOAST CAPITAL CORPORATION, 1636
SEAPORT CAPITAL, 1638
SENTINEL CAPITAL PARTNERS, 1651
SIGMA PARTNERS, 1672
SILVER OAK SERVICES PARTNERS, 1684
SJF VENTURES, 1689
SOUTHEAST INTERACTIVE TECHNOLOGY FUNDS, 1709
SPECTRUM EQUITY INVESTORS LP, 1717
SPIRE CAPITAL PARTNERS, 1724
SPLIT ROCK PARTNERS, 1725

SSM PARTNERS, 1732
STAENBERG VENTURE PARTNERS, 1733
STATELINE ANGELS, 1740
STERLING PARTNERS, 1742
STONEHENGE GROWTH CAPITAL, 1745
STONEWOOD CAPITAL MANAGEMENT, 1746
SUCSY, FISCHER & COMPANY, 1750
SUMMIT PARTNERS, 1752
SUN CAPITAL PARTNERS, 1753
SUNBRIDGE PARTNERS, 1755
SV INVESTMENT PARTNERS, 1763
SVOBODA CAPITAL PARTNERS, 1765
SYMMETRIC CAPITAL, 1770
TA ASSOCIATES, 1776
TAILWIND CAPITAL, 1777
TENNESSEE COMMUNITY VENTURES, 1797
THAYER STREET PARTNERS, 1805
THOMA BRAVO LLC, 1814
THOMAS H LEE PARTNERS, 1815
TL VENTURES, 1828
TOBA CAPITAL, 1829
TORQUEST PARTNERS, 2272
TRIDENT CAPITAL, 1850
TRILANTIC CAPITAL PARTNERS, 1851
TRIVEST PARTNERS, 1857
TRIWEST, 2275
TWJ CAPITAL, 1873
UNION CAPITAL CORPORATION, 1881
UPDATA VENTURE PARTNERS, 1886
VALOR EQUITY PARTNERS, 1902
VEBER PARTNERS LLC, 1909
VENCORE CAPITAL, 1915
VERONIS SUHLER STEVENSON, 1927
VORTEX PARTNERS, 1944
WALNUT GROUP, 1954
WARBURG PINCUS LLC, 1956
WATERMILL GROUP, 1962
WAVELAND INVESTMENTS LLC, 1964
WELSH, CARSON, ANDERSON & STOWE, 1972
WESTERN AMERICA CAPITAL GROUP, 2286
WESTLAKE SECURITIES, 1976
WESTVIEW CAPITAL PARTNERS, 1979
WHEATLEY PARTNERS, 1981
WILLIS STEIN & PARTNERS LLC, 1986
WOODBRIDGE GROUP, 2004
WYNNCHURCH CAPITAL, 2009
XANGE PRIVATE EQUITY, 3239
YELLOW POINT EQUITY PARTNERS, 2292
YFM GROUP, 3244
ZURMONT MADISON PRIVATE EQUITY, 3254

Business Services
ALPINE INVESTORS, 92
BISON CAPITAL ASSET MANAGEMENT LLC, 274
BLUE HERON CAPITAL, 288
BOSTON MILLENNIA PARTNERS, 312
BRANFORD CASTLE, 327
BV INVESTMENT PARTNERS, 361
CAPITAL RESOURCE PARTNERS, 402
CENTURY PARK CAPITAL PARTNERS, 449
CVF CAPITAL PARTNERS, 573
EPIC PARTNERS, 687
GOAL HOLDINGS, 2135
GRANTHAM CAPITAL, 853
HAWTHORN EQUITY PARTNERS, 916
HUNTSMAN GAY GLOBAL CAPITAL, 959
PENDER WEST CAPITAL PARTNERS, 2218
PENFUND, 2219
RIVERSIDE COMPANY, 1572
SAGEVIEW CAPITAL, 1602

Business Software
BENHAMOU GLOBAL VENTURES, 249
ISOURCE GESTION, 2899
SILICON ALLEY VENTURE PARTNERS, 1680

1147

Industry Preference Index / Business Technology

Business Technology
RALLY VENTURES, 1522
WING VENTURE PARTNERS, 1996

Business to Business
ABU DHABI INVESTMENT AUTHORITY, 2321
ACCENTURE TECHNOLOGY VENTURES, 2326
ACTUA, 53
ADAMS STREET PARTNERS, LLC, 57
AEA INVESTORS, 64
ALEXANDER HUTTON, 82
ARGOSY CAPITAL, 164
ARLINGTON CAPITAL PARTNERS, 166
ARSENAL CAPITAL PARTNERS, 170
ARTIMAN VENTURES, 174
BAIRD CAPITAL PARTNERS, 222
BARCLAYS VENTURES Barclays, 2486
BEE PARTNERS, 243
BLU VENTURE INVESTORS, 285
BMP AKTIENGESELLSCHAFT BMP Venture Capital, 2528
BONFIRE VENTURES, 306
BOSTON CAPITAL VENTURES, 310
BOSTON SEED CAPITAL, 313
BRENTWOOD ASSOCIATES, 334
BRUML CAPITAL CORPORATION, 355
C3 CAPITAL PARTNERS LP, 364
CAPITAL MIDWEST FUND, 400
CAPITAL PARTNERS, 401
CARLYLE ASIA INVESTMENT ADVISORS LIMITED Carlyle Group, 2565
CATALYST INVESTMENT MANAGERS PTY LIMITED PPM Capital, 2573
CCP EQUITY PARTNERS, 434
CEI VENTURES, 438
CENTERFIELD CAPITAL PARTNERS, 443
CEO VENTURES, 450
CERVIN VENTURES, 454
CHICAGO VENTURES, 471
CHRYSALIS CAPITAL ChrysCapital, 2599
CHRYSCAPITAL MANAGEMENT COMPANIES ChrysCapital, 2600
CINVEN LIMITED, 2605
CLOSE BROTHERS PRIVATE EQUITY Close Brothers Group, 2617
CORNERSTONE EQUITY INVESTORS LLC, 541
CORTEC GROUP, 546
CRYSTAL RIDGE PARTNERS, 565
DAVID N DEUTSCH & COMPANY LLC, 589
DFW CAPITAL PARTNERS, 610
DIAMONDHEAD VENTURES, 613
DIRECT CAPITAL PRIVATE EQUITY LIMITED, 2664
DUKE STREET CAPITAL Duke Street, 2676
EDGEWATER FUNDS, 654
EM WARBURG, PINCUS & COMPANY INTERNATIONAL, 2697
EM WARBURG, PINCUS & COMPANY JAPAN, 2698
EMIGRANT CAPITAL, 667
ENTER VENTURES, 681
ENTREPRENEUR PARTNERS, 683
ENTREPRENEURS ROUNDTABLE ACCELERATOR, 684
EOS PARTNERS LP, 686
EVERGREEN ADVISORS, 701
FGA PARTNERS, 725
FLOODGATE FUND, 751
FLORIDA CAPITAL PARTNERS, 752
FOUNDER COLLECTIVE, 771
FOUNDERS EQUITY, 774
FRANKLIN STREET EQUITY PARTNERS, 780
FRIEDMAN, FLEISCHER & LOWE LLC, 787
FRONTLINE VENTURES, 2759
FdG ASSOCIATES LP, 801
G-51 CAPITAL LLC, 803
GEMINI INVESTORS, 812
GENACAST VENTURES, 814
GENERATION PARTNERS, 818
GILBERT GLOBAL EQUITY PARTNERS, 827
GLENCOE CAPITAL, 830
GRANVILLE BAIRD CAPITAL PARTNERS, 2795
GRAYHAWK CAPITAL, 856
GREAT HILL PARTNERS LLC, 857
GROTECH VENTURES, 876
GRUPO BISA, 2800
GTCR, 884
HAMILTON ROBINSON CAPITAL PARTNERS, 899
HOLLAND VENTURE BV, 2828
HORIZON PARTNERS, LTD, 945
HUMMER WINBLAD VENTURE PARTNERS, 956
HYDE PARK VENTURE PARTNERS, 962
IRON GATE CAPITAL, 1020
ISIS EP LLP F & C, 2898
LIGHTBANK, 1118
LINSALATA CAPITAL PARTNERS, 1132
LOMBARD INVESTMENTS, 1139
LONGWORTH VENTURE PARTNERS, 1146
MERIT CAPITAL PARTNERS, 1209
MURPHREE VENTURE PARTNERS, 1273
NAYA VENTURES, 1285
NESBIC INVESTMENT FUND II, 2992
NEW MOUNTAIN CAPITAL, 1301
NEWBURY, PIRET & COMPANY, 1312
NEWLIGHT MANAGEMENT, 1314
NORTH DAKOTA DEVELOPMENT FUND, 1338
NORWEST EQUITY PARTNERS, 1345
NTH POWER TECHNOLOGIES, 1355
NUTEK (NARINGS- OCH TEKNIKUTVECKLINGSVERKET) NUTEK, 3016
ODEON CAPITAL PARTNERS, 1367
OLYMPUS PARTNERS, 1372
ORIGIN VENTURES, 1384
OUTLOOK VENTURES, 1389
PALOMAR VENTURES, 1407
PARADIGM CAPITAL LTD, 1414
PARALLEL INVESTMENT PARTNERS, 1415
PENNELL VENTURE PARTNERS LLC, 1429
PERMIRA Permira Advisers LLP, 3033
PRIMUS CAPITAL, 1476
PROGRESS VENTURES, 1486
QUANTUM CAPITAL PARTNERS, 1510
REITEN & CO STRATEGIC INVESTMENTS AS Reiten & Company, 3076
REVO CAPITAL, 3078
SCHOONER CAPITAL LLC, 1627
SEAPORT CAPITAL, 1638
SHASTA VENTURES, 1663
SOFTBANK CAPITAL, 1699
SPRING CAPITAL PARTNERS LP, 1727
STARVEST PARTNERS, 1738
STRIPES GROUP, 1748
TECHOPERATORS, 1788
VOYAGER CAPITAL, 1945
WALL STREET VENTURE CAPITAL, 1953
WEDBUSH CAPITAL PARTNERS, 1969
WESTON PRESIDIO, 1978
WESTTECH VENTURES, 3236
WICKS GROUP OF COMPANIES, LLC, 1984
WIND POINT PARTNERS, 1990
WINGATE PARTNERS, 1997
ZS FUND LP, 2022

Business to Consumer
ENTREPRENEURS ROUNDTABLE ACCELERATOR, 684

Cable
ALLSTATE INVESTMENTS LLC, 88
ANDERSON PACIFIC CORPORATION, 122
ELECTRA PARTNERS ASIA LIMITED SFC of Hong Kong, 2694
FORUM TECHNOLOGIES VENTURE CAPITAL COMPANY Forum Group, 2751
GRUPO BISA, 2800
MACQUARIE DIRECT INVESTMENT LIMITED, 2951
NEOMARKKA OYJ Neomarkka, 2990
SPACEVEST, 1714
TIME WARNER INVESTMENT CORPORATION, 1827
VENTURE CAPITAL FUND OF NEW ENGLAND, 1920
WICKS GROUP OF COMPANIES, LLC, 1984

Industry Preference Index / Chemicals

Cannabis
ACKRELL CAPITAL, 44
ALTITUDE INVESTMENT MANAGEMENT, LLC, 99
ANCIENT STRAINS, 2037
ARCADIAN FUND, 151
ARCHYTAS VENTURES, 155
AUSTRALIS CAPITAL, 203
BASE VENTURES, 229
BLAST FUNDING, 279
BREAKWATER MANAGEMENT, 331
CANALIS CAPITAL, 2555
CANNA ANGELS LLC, 388
CANNABIS CAPITAL, 389
CANNABIS CAPITAL GROWTH, 390
CANNABIS STRATEGIC VENTURES, 391
CANOPY BOULDER, 392
CANOPY RIVERS, 2071
CASA VERDE CAPITAL, 417
CBI^2 CAPITAL, 2074
CJV CAPITAL, 490
CRESCO CAPITAL PARTNERS, 557
CULTIVATE CAPITAL, 568
DOVENTI CAPITAL, 2100
DUTCHESS CAPITAL, 638
EMERALD OCEAN CAPITAL, 664
FIRST CAPITAL VENTURE, 735
FOUNDATION MARKETS, 2122
FRESH VC, 785
GOLDEN OPPORTUNITIES FUND, 2136
GOTHAM GREEN PARTNERS, 845
GREEN ACRE CAPITAL, 2140
GREEN LION PARTNERS, 860
GREEN TOWER CAPITAL, 861
GREENHOUSE VENTURES, 866
GROVE GROUP MANAGEMENT, 878
HALLEY VENTURE PARTNERS, 895
HILL AND GERTNER CAPITAL CORP., 2148
HOUSTON HEALTH VENTURES, 951
HYPUR VENTURES, 963
IANTHUS CAPITAL MANAGEMENT, 966
ICAN ISRAEL-CANNABIS.COM, 2845
INITIATIVE CAPITAL LIMITED, 2154
JW ASSET MANAGEMENT, 1048
KODIAK CAPITAL, 1079
LGC CAPITAL, 2174
LIZADA CAPITAL LLC, 1135
MCGOVERN CAPITAL, 1191
MERIDA CAPITAL PARTNERS, 1207
NAVY CAPITAL, 1283
PHYTO PARTNERS, 1439
POSEIDON ASSET MANAGEMENT, 1464
PRIVATEER HOLDINGS, 1481
REEFI CAPITAL, 1537
SALVEO CAPITAL, 1610
SERRUYA PRIVATE EQUITY, 2254
SKYTREE CAPITAL PARTNERS, 1692
SLOW VENTURES, 1694
TENX VENTURES, 2266
THE ARCVIEW GROUP, 1807
TRESS CAPITAL LLC, 1843
TUATARA CAPITAL, 1864
WHITE SHEEP CORP, 2287

Capital Equipment
ELGNER GROUP INVESTMENTS, 2104
FCF PARTNERS LP, 719

Capital Goods
NEW MOUNTAIN CAPITAL, 1301
RESILIENCE CAPITAL PARTNERS, 1545

Capital Markets
INFORMATION VENTURE PARTNERS, 2153

Carbon Management
BP ALTERNATIVE ENERGY VENTURES, 319

Cargo Handling
NEW WORLD INFRASTRUCTURE LIMITED, 2996

Carpet Yarn
LRM - INVESTERINGSMAATSCHAPPIJ VOOR LIMBURG, 2949

Carriers
ANDERSON PACIFIC CORPORATION, 122
EQT PARTNERS AB, 2712

Cellular Communications
QUAKE CAPITAL PARTNERS, 1507

Cellular Service & Products
ANDERSON PACIFIC CORPORATION, 122
PT BHAKTI INVESTAMA TBK, 3061

Cement Roofing
KUBOTA CORPORATION, 2927
RABO BLACK EARTH Eagle Venture Partners, 3071

Ceramic Tiles
PRIVATE EQUITY PARTNERS SPA, 3053

Chemicals
3I TEUPSCHLAND GmbH 3i Group, 2305
ACTIS, 2337
AEA INVESTORS, 64
AKERS CAPITAL LLC, 75
ALBEMARLE PRIVATE EQUITY LIMITED, 2360
ALLSTATE INVESTMENTS LLC, 88
AMADEUS CAPITAL PARTNERS LIMITED, 2386
AMPERSAND CAPITAL PARTNERS, 118
ANDLINGER & COMPANY INC, 123
APOLLO GLOBAL MANAGEMENT, 140
APPLE TREE PARTNERS, 143
ARROWHEAD INVESTMENT MANAGEMENT, 168
ATHENAEUM FUND, 186
ATRIUM CAPITAL, 192
AUSTIN CAPITAL PARTNERS LP, 201
AVENUE CAPITAL GROUP, 208
AZCA, 214
BASF VENTURE CAPITAL, 2492
BIO FUND MANAGEMENT OY, 2512
BLUE POINT CAPITAL PARTNERS, 290
BRANFORD CASTLE, 327
BRIDGEPOINT CAPITAL GmbH, 2537
BRIDGEPOINT CAPITAL LIMITED, 2538
BROOK VENTURE FUND, 349
BRUML CAPITAL CORPORATION, 355
C3 CAPITAL PARTNERS LP, 364
CANDOVER, 2556
CAPVIS EQUITY PARTNERS, 2564
CENTURY PARK CAPITAL PARTNERS, 449
CLIFFORD CHANCE PUNDER, 2614
CVC ASIA PACIFIC LIMITED CVC Capital Partners, 2643
CVC CAPITAL PARTNERS LTD, 2644
DAVID N DEUTSCH & COMPANY LLC, 589
EAST FUND MANAGEMENT GmbH GiroCredit, 2683
ECI VENTURES, 2687
EDGEWATER CAPITAL PARTNERS, 653
ELECTRA PARTNERS ASIA LIMITED SFC of Hong Kong, 2694
ELEMENT PARTNERS, 657
EMIGRANT CAPITAL, 667
ENTERPRISE EQUITY (NI) LTD, 2704
EQT PARTNERS AB, 2712
EQUISTONE, 2714
EQVITEC PARTNERS OY, 2716
FIRST ANALYSIS, 732
FLANDERS' FOREIGN INVESTMENT OFFICE, 2746
FRIULIA SpA, 2758
GLENCOE CAPITAL, 830
GLENTHORNE CAPITAL, 832
INNOFINANCE OY, 2873
INTERNATIONAL FINANCE CORPORATION (IFC), 1007
INVESTMENT FUND FOR CENTRAL & EASTERN EUROPE, 2889
IP GROUP, 2892

1149

Industry Preference Index / Chemicals & Advanced Materials

JAVELIN INVESTMENTS, 2908
KELSO & COMPANY, 1062
KHOSLA VENTURES, 1069
KOHLBERG KRAVIS ROBERTS & COMPANY, 1082
LITTLEJOHN & COMPANY LLC, 1134
LOMBARD INVESTMENTS, 1139
MERITURN PARTNERS, 1213
MONTAGU PRIVATE EQUITY LIMITED, 2977
NORTHERN ENTERPRISE LIMITED, 3011
ONE EQUITY PARTNERS, 1376
PAI MANAGEMENT, 3026
PARKWALK ADVISORS, 3028
PERMIRA Permira Advisers LLP, 3033
RESILIENCE CAPITAL PARTNERS, 1545
SCOTTISH ENTERPRISE, 3103
SEED CAPITAL LIMITED, 3107
SIF TRANSYLVANIA, 3119
SPELL CAPITAL PARTNERS LLC, 1719
SRIW SA SRIW Group, 3134
TIANGUIS LIMITED, 3178
TORQUEST PARTNERS, 2272
TRANSYLVANIA FINANCIAL INVESTMENT COMPANY, 3187
WATERMILL GROUP, 1962
YISSUM TECHNOLOGY TRANSFER, 3245

Chemicals & Advanced Materials
CHRYSALIX, 2078

Chemistry
TELEGRAPH HILL PARTNERS, 1792

Child Care
OWL VENTURES, 1392

Children
COLLABORATIVE FUND, 511

Civic Technology
DECIENS CAPITAL, 599

Clean Energy
(@)VENTURES, 1
ALTRIA VENTURES, 102
ARCTERN VENTURES, 2041
BERKELEY VENTURES, 253
BMW I VENTURES, 302
BRIGHTPATH CAPITAL PARTNERS, 340
EARTHRISE CAPITAL, 643
ENERTECH CAPITAL, 676
GENERAL CATALYST PARTNERS, 816
MACKINNON, BENNETT & CO., 2181
SIERRA ANGELS, 1669
TERA CAPITAL CORPORATION, 2267
TOP RENERGY INC., 2271

Clean Environment
VENTUREAST, 3211

Clean Technology
(@)VENTURES, 1
350 INVESTMENT PARTNERS, 2295
360 CAPITAL PARTNERS 360 Capital Management SA, 2296
3TS CAPITAL PARTNERS 3i Group plc, 2309
ABB TECHNOLOGY VENTURES, 2315
ACCESS VENTURE PARTNERS LLC, 36
ACERO CAPITAL, 41
ACME LABS, 2333
ACTIVE VENTURE PARTNERS, 2339
ADAMS STREET PARTNERS, LLC, 57
ADARA VENTURE PARTNERS, 2342
ADVANCED TECHNOLOGY VENTURES, 59
ADVANTAGE CAPITAL PARTNERS, 61
AIP PRIVATE CAPITAL, 2031
ALBERTA ENTERPRISE, 2032
ALLIANCE OF ANGELS, 85
ALLOY VENTURES, 87
AMMER PARTNERS, 2393
AMPLIFIER VENTURE PARTNERS, 119
ANDLINGER & COMPANY INC, 123
ANGELS' FORUM LLC, 129
APEX VENTURE PARTNERS, 137
AQUAGRO FUND, 2417
ARAVAIPA VENTURES, 146
ARCH VENTURE PARTNERS, 153
ASTER CAPITAL, 2439
AURUM VENTURES MKI, 2454
AVIV VENTURE CAPITAL, 2462
AXVENTURES, 2470
BATTERY VENTURES, 235
BC RENAISSANCE CAPITAL FUND, 2053
BERINGEA, 251
BERTI INVESTMENTS, 2505
BEST FUNDS, 2058
BEZOS EXPEDITIONS, 262
BIG SUR VENTURES, 2510
BIRCHMERE VENTURES, 272
BLACK DIAMOND VENTURES, 275
BP ALTERNATIVE ENERGY VENTURES, 319
BRIGHTSTONE VENTURE CAPITAL, 341
BUSINESS GROWTH FUND, 2550
CALCEF CLEAN ENERGY FUND, 367
CANADIAN VENTURE CAPITAL ASSOCIATION Canadian Venture Capital & Private Equity Association, 3258
CATHAYA CAPITAL, 2576
CDH INVESTMENTS, 2579
CEDAR FUND, 436
CEDRUS INVESTMENTS, 2581
CELADON CAPITAL GROUP, 2582
CHINA ISRAEL VALUE CAPITAL, 2593
CLEAN ENERGY VENTURE GROUP, 497
CLEAN PACIFIC VENTURES, 498
CLEANTECH INVEST, 2612
CLEANTECH VENTURES, 2613
CLIMATE CHANGE CAPITAL, 2615
COLORADO MILE HIGH FUND, 513
CONNECTICUT INNOVATIONS, 530
CORRELATION VENTURES, 544
COTTONWOOD TECHNOLOGY FUND, 549
COUNCIL FOR ENTREPRENEURIAL DEVELOPMENT, 3259
CREATHOR VENTURE, 2638
CYCLE CAPITAL MANAGEMENT, 2093
DALLAS VENTURE PARTNERS, 582
DAVENPORT RESOURCES LLC, 588
DBL PARTNERS, 595
DOUGHTY HANSON & CO., 2671
DRAPER ATHENA, 626
DYNAMO VC, 640
EARLY STAGE PARTNERS, 642
EARLYBIRD, 2682
EASTWARD CAPITAL PARTNERS, 646
ECOSYSTEM VENTURES, 650
ELEMENT PARTNERS, 657
EMERALD TECHNOLOGY VENTURES, 2106
ENTREPRENEURS FUND, 2710
EPIC VENTURES, 688
ESPIRITO SANTO VENTURES, 2717
EVOK INNOVATIONS, 2111
EXPANSION CAPITAL PARTNERS, 706
FIRST ANALYSIS, 732
FIRST STEP FUND, 742
FLYWHEEL VENTURES, 756
FOUNDATION CAPITAL, 770
FUEL CAPITAL, 2761
FUNK VENTURES, 797
GABRIEL VENTURE PARTNERS, 805
GARAGE TECHNOLOGY VENTURES, 807
GENERAL MOTORS VENTURES, 817
GLOBESPAN CAPITAL PARTNERS, 835
GRAY GHOST VENTURES, 855
GROWTHWORKS, 2143
HARBOR LIGHT CAPITAL PARTNERS, 907
HELION VENTURE PARTNERS, LLC International Management (Mauritius) Ltd, 2818
HERCULES TECHNOLOGY GROWTH CAPITAL, INC, 925

Industry Preference Index / Cloud Computing

HIGH COUNTRY VENTURE, 930
HIGH-TECH GRUENDERFONDS, 2824
HORIZON TECHNOLOGY FINANCE, 946
ICON VENTURES, 968
IDEALAB, 972
IGLOBE PARTNERS, 2853
ILLINOIS VENTURES, 975
INCWELL VENTURE CAPITAL, 981
INDEPENDENCE EQUITY, 983
INETWORKS ADVISORS LLC, 987
INFIELD CAPITAL, 988
INLAND TECHSTART FUND, 993
INNOVATION CAPITAL LIMITED, 2877
ISRAEL CLEANTECH VENTURES, 2900
KEIRETSU FORUM, 1061
KINETIC VENTURES, 1072
KOHLBERG VENTURES, 1083
LEGEND CAPITAL, 2936
LINLEY CAPITAL, 1130
LLOYDS DEVELOPMENT CAPITAL LIMITED, 2944
LONG RIVER VENTURES, 1142
MAINE ANGELS, 1160
MARS INVESTMENT ACCELERATOR FUND, 2187
MASS VENTURES, 1172
MATRIX PARTNERS, 1181
MINDFULL INVESTORS, 1236
MMC VENTURES, 2972
MMV CAPITAL PARTNERS, 2196
MOHR-DAVIDOW VENTURES, 1247
MOTIV PARTNERS, 1258
MOUNTAIN PARTNERS, 2979
NAUSICAA VENTURES, 2986
NAVITAS CAPITAL, 1282
NEEDHAM CAPITAL PARTNERS, 1288
NEO TECHNOLOGY VENTURES, 2989
NEW VENTURE PARTNERS, 1305
NGEN PARTNERS, 1324
NORTHERN LIGHT VENTURE CAPITAL, 1340
NOVA SCOTIA BUSINESS INC., 2205
NOVENTI VENTURES, 1352
ONTARIO CAPITAL GROWTH CORPORATION, 2211
OneVentures, 3023
PANGAEA VENTURES LTD, 2213
PARKWALK ADVISORS, 3028
PARTNERSHIP FUND FOR NEW YORK CITY, 1420
PINNACLE VENTURES, 1445
PITANGO VENTURE CAPITAL, 3039
PMV, 3042
POINT JUDITH CAPITAL, 1459
PRAIRIEGOLD VENTURE PARTNERS, 1470
PRESIDIO VENTURES, 1474
QBIC FUND, 3065
QIMING VENTURE PARTNERS, 3066
RED DOT VENTURES, 3073
RENEWABLETECH VENTURES, 1542
RESERVOIR VENTURE PARTNERS, 1544
ROADMAP CAPITAL INC., 2242
ROCKPORT CAPITAL, 1579
ROTH CAPITAL PARTNERS, 1588
SABIC VENTURES, 3091
SAFFRON HILL VENTURES, 3092
SAIF PARTNERS, 3093
SAIL VENTURE PARTNERS, 1603
SAMOS INVESTMENTS, 3097
SAND HILL ANGELS, 1613
SB CHINA VENTURE CAPITAL, 3100
SCOTTISH EQUITY PARTNERS, 3104
SEQUEL VENTURE PARTNERS, 1653
SIGMA PARTNERS, 1672
SJF VENTURES, 1689
SOLSTICE CAPITAL LP, 1702
SPINUP VENTURE, 3132
SUMMIT BRIDGE CAPITAL, 3147
SUNBRIDGE PARTNERS, 1755
SUPREMUM CAPITAL, 3150
SVB CAPITAL, 1764
TANDEM EXPANSION FUND, 2261

TAO VENTURE CAPITAL PARTNERS, 1780
TECH COAST ANGELS, 1784
TECHNOLOGY PARTNERS, 1786
TENAYA CAPITAL, 1796
TERALYS CAPITAL, 2268
TIE ANGELS GROUP SEATTLE, 1825
TRELLIS CAPITAL CORPORATION, 2273
TRIANGLE VENTURE CAPITAL GROUP, 3188
TROIKA CAPITAL PARTNERS, 3193
TSING CAPITAL, 3194
TYLT LAB, 1876
VANTAGEPOINT CAPITAL PARTNERS, 1906
VENTURE INVESTORS LLC, 1921
VERGE FUND, 1924
VIKING VENTURE, 3216
WALDEN INTERNATIONAL, 1951
WAVEPOINT VENTURES, 1966
WESTLY GROUP, 1977
WESTSUMMIT CAPITAL, 3235
WI HARPER GROUP, 1983
XANGE PRIVATE EQUITY, 3239
XSEED CAPITAL MANAGEMENT, 2011
YALETOWN VENTURE PARTNERS, 2291
YISSUM TECHNOLOGY TRANSFER, 3245
YUUWA CAPITAL, 3248
ZOUK VENTURES, 3252

Clean Transportation
ANGELENO GROUP, 126

Cleantech
ECAPITAL ENTREPRENEURIAL PARTNERS AG, 2686

Clinical Development
BALTCAP MANAGEMENT LTD, 2480

Clinical Research
FIRST ANALYSIS, 732

Cloud
CORNERSTONE VENTURE PARTNERS, 543
SINEWAVE VENTURES, 1687
WILDCAT VENTURE PARTNERS, 1985

Cloud Computing
10X VENTURE PARTNERS, 3
212 CAPITAL PARTNERS, 2294
42 VENTURES, 9
ACCESS VENTURE PARTNERS LLC, 36
ACUMEN VENTURES, 2341
AMITI VENTURES, 116
ARTIS VENTURES, 175
ATLANTIC BRIDGE, 2443
AUGMENT VENTURES, 195
AZURE CAPITAL PARTNERS, 215
BASECAMP VENTURES, 230
BENCHMARK, 248
BESSEMER VENTURE PARTNERS, 260
BEST FUNDS, 2058
BIG SUR VENTURES, 2510
BREGAL SAGEMOUNT, 333
BRIGHTSTONE VENTURE CAPITAL, 341
CAMP ONE VENTURES, 384
CATALYST INVESTORS, 427
CHARLES RIVER VENTURES, 455
CONVERGE VENTURE PARTNERS, 534
CONVEXA Tyveholmen AS, 2632
CORSA VENTURES, 545
DATA COLLECTIVE, 585
DELL VENTURES, 603
DENALI VENTURE PARTNERS, 605
DIVERGENT VENTURES, 618
DOUBLEROCK VENTURE CAPITAL, 625
EDBI Pte LTD., 2690
EMERGENCE CAPITAL PARTNERS, 665
FIDELITY GROWTH PARTNERS EUROPE, 2734
FIRST ASCENT VENTURES, 2118

1151

Industry Preference Index / Cloud Data

FLYING FISH, 755
FOUNDATION CAPITAL, 770
G SQUARED, 802
GEORGIAN PARTNERS, 2132
GGV CAPITAL, 823
GRAYHAWK CAPITAL, 856
GREAT OAKS VENTURE CAPITAL, 858
GROVE STREET ADVISORS LLC, 879
HUMMER WINBLAD VENTURE PARTNERS, 956
ICON VENTURES, 968
ID VENTURES AMERICA LLC, 970
INLAND TECHSTART FUND, 993
IRISH ANGELS, 1019
LIONBIRD, 2943
MERCURY FUND, 1206
NAYA VENTURES, 1285
NEW ENTERPRISE ASSOCIATES, 1297
NORTHZONE, 3013
NOTION CAPITAL, 3014
REVO CAPITAL, 3078
RTP VENTURES, 1594
RUBICON VENTURE CAPITAL, 1595
RUNA CAPITAL, 3088
RUNTIDE CAPITAL, 1596
SALESFORCE VENTURES, 1607
SEVEN PEAKS VENTURES, 1656
SIGMA PRIME VENTURES, 1673
SPARK CAPITAL, 1715
SUMMERHILL VENTURE PARTNERS, 2259
SUMMIT BRIDGE CAPITAL, 3147
SUNBRIDGE PARTNERS, 1755
TECHOPERATORS, 1788
TELEFONICA VENTURES, 3169
UPFRONT VENTURES, 1888
VALAR VENTURES, 1897
VANEDGE CAPITAL PARTNERS, 2278
WESLEY CLOVER, 2284
WING VENTURE PARTNERS, 1996
YL VENTURES, 3246

Cloud Data
BLUEPOINTE VENTURES, 295

Cloud Infrastructure
BENHAMOU GLOBAL VENTURES, 249
CROSSLINK CAPITAL, 563
INTEL CAPITAL, 1004
M12, 1154
RESONANT VENTURE PARTNERS, 1547

Cloud Native Infrastructure
WORK-BENCH, 2006

Cloud Software
GREENHILLS VENTURES, LLC, 865

Cloud Technologies
GVA CAPITAL, 890

Cloud-Based IT Services
COSTANOA VENTURE CAPITAL, 547
EARLYBIRD, 2682
WALDEN VENTURE CAPITAL, 1952

Cloud/SaaS
GOOD NEWS VENTURES, 2138

Coal Processes
MOUNTAINEER CAPITAL, 1262

Commerce
AMPLIFY, 120
BRILLIANT VENTURES, 342
CITI VENTURES, 486
FIRSTMARK CAPITAL, 743
INTERLACE VENTURES, 1006
LIBERTY CITY VENTURES, 1115

RUBICON VENTURE CAPITAL, 1595
VERIZON VENTURES, 1926

Commerce and Trade
DYNAMO VC, 640

Commercial & Industrial
CIT GROUP, 484

Commercial Air
CIT GROUP, 484

Commercial Contracts
BUTZOW NORDIA ADVOCATES LTD, 2552

Commercial Real Estate
SECOND CITY REAL ESTATE, 2253
VIOLA FINTECH, 3220

Commercial Services
BRUCKMANN, ROSSER, SHERRILL & COMPANY, 354
CERBERUS CAPITAL MANAGEMENT, 451
CHEROKEE INVESTMENT PARTNERS, 463
FRONTENAC COMPANY, 789
GROWTHWORKS, 2143
ICV PARTNERS, 969
MPE PARTNERS, 1266
RHB - H&F MANAGEMENT COMPANY SDN BHD RHB Capital, 3080
UNION CAPITAL CORPORATION, 1881

Commercial Software
NFX, 1323

Commercial Transportation
LIONHART CAPITAL LTD, 2177

Commercial and Professional Services
ACCES CAPITAL QUEBEC, 2029

Commodities
APOLLO GLOBAL MANAGEMENT, 140
SAF GROUP, 2246

Communication Technology
AMPLIFIER VENTURE PARTNERS, 119
AUTHOSIS VENTURES, 2457
COLUMBIA CAPITAL, 515
COMMONWEALTH CAPITAL VENTURES LP, 521
EARLYBIRD, 2682
EDBI Pte LTD., 2690
HARBERT MANAGEMENT CORPORATION, 904
IBB BETEILIGUNGSGESELLSCHAFT MBH, 2841
MASTHEAD VENTURE PARTNERS, 1175
MORGAN STANLEY EXPANSION CAPITAL, 1255
MOUNTAINEER CAPITAL, 1262
SARONA ASSET MANAGEMENT, 2248
SUMMIT PARTNERS, 1752
TAMAR TECHNOLOGY VENTURES LIMITED, 3158
TGAP VENTURES, 1802
THIRD SECURITY, 1812
TRELYS FUNDS, 1842

Communications
212 CAPITAL PARTNERS, 2294
3I AUSTRIA BETEILGUNG GmbH 3i Group, 2298
3I DEUTSCHLAND GESELLSCHAFT FUR 3i Group, 2299
3I GERMANY GmbH 3i Group, 2301
3I TEUPSCHLAND GmbH 3i Group, 2305
3T CAPITAL, 2308
ABRY PARTNERS, 21
ABS CAPITAL PARTNERS, 22
ABS VENTURES, 23
ABU DHABI INVESTMENT AUTHORITY, 2321
ACKERLEY PARTNERS LLC, 43
ACONCAGUA VENTURES, 2334
ACT VENTURE CAPITAL LIMITED, 2336
ACTIVE VENTURE PARTNERS, 2339

Industry Preference Index / Communications

ADAMS STREET PARTNERS, LLC, 57
ADOBE VENTURES LP, 58
ADVANTAGE CAPITAL PARTNERS, 61
ADVENT VENTURE PARTNERS, 2348
AEP CAPITAL LLC, 65
AEROSTAR CAPITAL LLC, 67
ALBEMARLE PRIVATE EQUITY LIMITED, 2360
ALICE VENTURES SRL, 2364
ALMAZ CAPITAL, 89
ALPHA CAPITAL PARTNERS, 90
ALTA VENTURES MEXICO, 2382
ALTPOINT CAPITAL, 101
AMADEUS CAPITAL PARTNERS LIMITED, 2386
AMBIENT SOUND INVESTMENTS, 2390
AMERIMARK CAPITAL CORPORATION, 111
AMMER PARTNERS, 2393
ANDERSON PACIFIC CORPORATION, 122
ARGO GLOBAL CAPITAL, 162
ARVA LIMITED, 2044
ASCENT VENTURE PARTNERS, 178
ATHENIAN VENTURE PARTNERS, 187
ATLAS VENTURE, 191
AUGUST CAPITAL, 197
AURELIA PRIVATE EQUITY, 2452
AVISTA CAPITAL PARTNERS, 209
AXIOM VENTURE PARTNERS, 212
BALDERTON CAPITAL, 2478
BALLAST POINT VENTURES, 224
BARING PRIVATE EQUITY PARTNERS INDIA, 2490
BATTERSON VENTURE CAPITAL LLC, 234
BATTERY VENTURES, 235
BBH CAPITAL PARTNERS, 240
BENHAMOU GLOBAL VENTURES, 249
BERKELEY VC INTERNATIONAL LLC, 252
BERKSHIRE PARTNERS LLC, 254
BI WALDEN MANAGEMENT SDN Walden International, 2508
BIGFOOT VENTURES, 2511
BLUE CHIP VENTURE COMPANY, 287
BOTTS & COMPANY LIMITED, 2532
BOULDER VENTURES LTD, 315
BRAINSPARK PLC, 2535
BRIDGESCALE PARTNERS, 339
BRM SEED, 2541
BROADMARK CAPITAL, 345
BURAN VENTURE CAPITAL, 2549
CALIFORNIA TECHNOLOGY VENTURES, 371
CAMP VENTURES, 385
CAMPUS COMPANIES VENTURE CAPITAL FUND, 2554
CANDOVER, 2556
CAPITAL FOR BUSINESS, INC, 399
CAPMAN CAPITAL MANAGEMENT OY, 2562
CARMEL VENTURES, 2566
CASABONA VENTURES, 418
CASTILE VENTURES, 422
CAZENOVE PRIVATE EQUITY Cazenove Capital, 2577
CEDAR (ISRAEL) FINANCIAL ADVISORS LIMITED Cedar Fund, 2580
CEDAR FUND, 436
CELTIC HOUSE VENTURE PARTNERS, 2076
CENTERPOINT VENTURE PARTNERS, 444
CHALLENGE FUNDS - ETGAR LP, 2585
CHARLES RIVER VENTURES, 455
CHARLES RIVER VENTURES, 455
CHARLESBANK CAPITAL PARTNERS, 456
CHENGWEI VENTURES, 2590
CHEVRON TECHNOLOGY VENTURES, 466
CHINA WALDEN MANAGEMENT LIMITED Walden Group, 2597
CIBC CAPITAL MARKETS, 2079
CIC FINANCE CIC Group, 2601
CIT GROUP, 484
CIVC PARTNERS, 489
CLAL ELECTRONICS INDUSTRIES LIMITED, 2609
CLARENDON FUND MANAGERS, 2610
CLARITY PARTNERS, 494
CLEARLAKE CAPITAL, 500
CLOQUET CAPITAL PARTNERS, 505
COLLER CAPITAL LIMITED, 2621
COLORADO MILE HIGH FUND, 513

COLUMBIA CAPITAL, 515
COMCAST VENTURES, 518
COMMERCE ASSET VENTURES Sdn Bhd, 2623
COMMONWEALTH CAPITAL VENTURES LP, 521
COMPASS TECHNOLOGY PARTNERS LP, 524
CONCORD VENTURES, 2628
CONSTELLATION TECHNOLOGY VENTURES, 532
CORAL GROUP, 536
CORDOVA VENTURES, 537
CORE CAPITAL PARTNERS, 538
CORE PACIFIC - YAMAICHI CAPITAL LIMITED Core Pacific Securities Company Ltd, 2633
COURT SQUARE VENTURES, 551
CRESCENDO VENTURE MANAGEMENT LLC, 2639
CRESCENDO VENTURES, 555
DAIMLERCHRYSLER VENTURE GmbH DaimlerChrysler AG, 2650
DAVID N DEUTSCH & COMPANY LLC, 589
DEFTA PARTNERS, 602
DELTA VENTURES LIMITED, 2655
DISCOVERY CAPITAL, 2097
DOCOMO INNOVATIONS, 620
DOUBLE M PARTNERS, 624
DRAPER RICHARDS KAPLAN FOUNDATION, 627
DRESNER COMPANIES, 629
DUCHOSSOIS CAPITAL MANAGEMENT, 633
DUFF ACKERMAN & GOODRICH, 634
E.VENTURES, 641
EASTVEN VENTURE PARTNERS, 645
EASTWARD CAPITAL PARTNERS, 646
ECHELON VENTURES, 647
ECI VENTURES, 2687
ECLIPSE VENTURES, 648
EDISON PARTNERS, 655
EGL HOLDINGS, 656
EIRCOM ENTERPRISE FUND LIMITED, 2692
EM WARBURG, PINCUS & COMPANY INTERNATIONAL, 2697
EM WARBURG, PINCUS & COMPANY JAPAN, 2698
ENTERPRISE EQUITY (NI) LTD, 2704
EPIC VENTURES, 688
EQUINOX CAPITAL, 691
EQVITEC PARTNERS OY, 2716
EURAZEO, 2719
EVERCORE CAPITAL PARTNERS, 699
EVERGREEN VENTURE PARTNERS, 2726
FERRANTI LIMITED, 2732
FINNVERA PLC, 2741
FIRST CAPITAL GROUP, 734
FIRST ISRAEL MEZZANINE INVESTORS LIMITED, 2745
FIRSTMARK CAPITAL, 743
FOCUS VENTURES, 757
FONTINALIS PARTNERS, 760
FORMATIVE VENTURES, 764
FORREST BINKLEY & BROWN, 765
FRANCISCO PARTNERS, 779
FUSE CAPITAL, 798
GABRIEL VENTURE PARTNERS, 805
GALILEO II, 2765
GENERAL ATLANTIC PARTNERS, 2771
GENERATION PARTNERS, 818
GENESIS PARTNERS, 2775
GILDE INVESTMENT FUNDS, 2779
GIMV GIMV, 2780
GIZA VENTURE CAPITAL, 2782
GLADSTONE CAPITAL, 828
GLOBAL EQUITY PARTNERS BETEILIGUNGS-MANAGEMENT, 2783
GLOBESPAN CAPITAL PARTNERS, 835
GMT COMMUNICATIONS PARTNERS LLP, 2789
GRANITE EQUITY PARTNERS, 850
GREAT HILL PARTNERS LLC, 857
GREENSPRING ASSOCIATES, 867
GROTECH VENTURES, 876
GTCR, 884
GUGGENHEIM PARTNERS, 885
HALYARD CAPITAL, 897
HARBINGER VENTURE MANAGEMENT, 905
HELLMAN & FRIEDMAN LLC, 924
HIGHLAND CAPITAL PARTNERS, 935

1153

Industry Preference Index / Communications

HORIZON VENTURES LLC, 947
HOUSATONIC PARTNERS, 949
HUDSON VENTURE PARTNERS, 954
HUMANA VENTURES, 955
I-HATCH VENTURES LLC, 964
ICON VENTURES, 968
ID VENTURES AMERICA LLC, 970
IDEALAB, 972
IGNITE JAPAN KK Ignite Group, 2854
INDASIA FUND ADVISORS PVT LTD, 2859
INDIAN DIRECT EQUITY ADVISORS PVT LTD, 2861
INDUSTRIEBANK LIOF NV, 2866
INDUSTRY VENTURES, 986
INETWORKS ADVISORS LLC, 987
INFLEXION PARTNERS, 990
INSTITUTIONAL VENTURE PARTNERS, 1001
INTERNATIONAL FINANCE CORPORATION (IFC), 1007
INTERSOUTH PARTNERS, 1008
INVENTUS, 1013
INVESCO PRIVATE CAPITAL, 1015
INVESTMENT AB BURE, 2888
INVESTOR AB, 2890
IP GROUP, 2892
IPG GROUP, 2894
IRIS CAPITAL, 2897
ISIS EP LLP F & C, 2898
JEGI CAPITAL The Jordan Edminston Group, Inc., 1033
JERUSALEM VENTURE PARTNERS, 2910
KB PARTNERS LLC, 1057
KBL FOUNDER SA, 2917
KELSO & COMPANY, 1062
KILMER CAPITAL PARTNERS, 2169
KINETIC VENTURES, 1072
KLEINER PERKINS, 1075
KNIGHTSBRIDGE ADVISERS, 1077
KODIAK VENTURE PARTNERS, 1080
KOHLBERG KRAVIS ROBERTS & COMPANY, 1082
LABRADOR VENTURES, 1089
LANDSBANKI VENTURES, 2929
LEAPFROG VENTURES, 1102
LEGAL AND GENERAL VENTURES LIMITED, 2935
LIBERTY PARTNERS, 1116
LIQUID CAPITAL GROUP, 1133
LOVETT MILLER & COMPANY, 1148
M/C PARTNERS, 1153
M12, 1154
MADISON DEARBORN PARTNERS, 1156
MAGMA VENTURE PARTNERS, 2952
MANHATTAN INVESTMENT PARTNERS, 1163
MARATHON VENTURE CAPITAL FUND LIMITED, 2954
MARS INVESTMENT ACCELERATOR FUND, 2187
MARYLAND VENTURE FUND, 1169
MASSACHUSETTS CAPITAL RESOURCE COMPANY, 1173
MASSACHUSETTS GROWTH CAPITAL CORPORATION, 1174
MATRIX PARTNERS, 1181
MAYFIELD FUND, 1184
MCG CAPITAL CORPORATION, 1189
MCGOVERN CAPITAL, 1191
MEDIA VENTURE PARTNERS, 1195
MENLO VENTURES, 1202
MERIDIAN MANAGEMENT GROUP, 1208
MERITECH CAPITAL PARTNERS, 1212
METROPOLITAN PARTNERS GROUP, 1225
MILLENIUM TECHNOLOGY VALUE PARTNERS, 1235
MISSION VENTURES, 1239
MMT MILLENNIUM MATERIALS TECHNOLOGIES FUND LP, 2973
MMV CAPITAL PARTNERS, 2196
MOBIUS VENTURE CAPITAL, 1245
MOHR-DAVIDOW VENTURES, 1247
MOMENTUM FUNDS MANAGEMENT PTY LIMITED, 2975
MONITOR VENTURES, 1249
MOTOROLA SOLUTIONS VENTURE CAPITAL, 1260
McLEAN WATSON CAPITAL, 2199
NAUSICAA VENTURES, 2986
NAUTIC PARTNERS, 1279
NEEDHAM CAPITAL PARTNERS, 1288
NEO TECHNOLOGY VENTURES, 2989

NEOTENY COMPANY LIMITED, 2991
NEST VENTURES, 1290
NEW MOUNTAIN CAPITAL, 1301
NEW VENTURE PARTNERS, 1305
NEW YORK LIFE CAPITAL PARTNERS, 1309
NEWLIGHT MANAGEMENT, 1314
NHN INVESTMENT, 3002
NORTH BRIDGE VENTURE PARTNERS, 1334
NORTH COVE PARTNERS, 1337
NOVAK BIDDLE VENTURE PARTNERS, 1348
OEM CAPITAL, 1369
OEM CAPITAL, 1369
ONTARIO CAPITAL GROWTH CORPORATION, 2211
OPUS CAPITAL, 1381
OUTCOME CAPITAL, 1388
OVP VENTURE PARTNERS, 1391
PAC-LINK MANAGEMENT CORP., 3024
PAI MANAGEMENT, 3026
PALISADES VENTURES, 1402
PAMLICO CAPITAL, 1409
PANTHEON VENTURES (US) LP, 1411
PARKWALK ADVISORS, 3028
PARTECH INTERNATIONAL, 1416
PARTNERSHIP FUND FOR NEW YORK CITY, 1420
PEACHTREE EQUITY PARTNERS, 1423
PELION VENTURE PARTNERS, 1425
PERMAL CAPITAL MANAGEMENT, 1432
PIDC PHILADELPHIA, 1441
PITANGO VENTURE CAPITAL, 3039
POLESTAR CAPITAL, 1461
POLYTECHNOS VENTURE PARTNERS GmbH, 3046
POMONA CAPITAL, 1462
PREVIZ VENTURES, 3050
PRIME TECHNOLOGY VENTURES NV, 3051
PRIMUS CAPITAL, 1476
PRISM VENTUREWORKS, 1478
PROGRESS EQUITY PARTNERS, 1484
PROVCO GROUP, 1494
PROVENANCE VENTURES, 1495
QBIC FUND, 3065
QUADRANGLE GROUP, 1506
QUANTUM VALLEY INVESTMENTS, 2228
QUESTER CAPITAL MANAGEMENT LIMITED, 3070
RAFAEL DEVELOPMENT CORPORATION (RDC) LIMITED, 3072
RAND CAPITAL CORPORATION, 1523
REDPOINT VENTURES, 1534
REMBRANDT VENTURE PARTNERS, 1540
RENAISSANCE PARTNERS, 3077
RHO VENTURES, 1558
RIDGEWOOD CAPITAL, 1564
ROSER VENTURES LLC, 1586
ROYALTY CAPITAL MANAGEMENT, 1591
RRE VENTURES, 1593
RUNTIDE CAPITAL, 1596
SABAN CAPITAL GROUP, 1598
SAINTS CAPITAL, 1604
SALEM INVESTMENT PARTNERS, 1606
SAND HILL ANGELS, 1613
SANDLER CAPITAL MANAGEMENT, 1617
SARATOGA PARTNERS, 1621
SCHOONER CAPITAL LLC, 1627
SCP PARTNERS, 1633
SEACOAST CAPITAL CORPORATION, 1636
SEAPOINT VENTURES, 1637
SEAPORT CAPITAL, 1638
SELBY VENTURE PARTNERS, 1646
SERAPH GROUP, 1655
SEVENTURE PARTNERS, 3113
SEVIN ROSEN FUNDS, 1658
SHAMROCK CAPITAL ADVISORS, 1660
SHANNON COMMERCIAL PROPERTIES, 3115
SI VENTURES, 1668
SIEMENS VENTURE CAPITAL, 3118
SIERRA ANGELS, 1669
SIERRA VENTURES, 1670
SIGMA PARTNERS, 1672
SIGNAL EQUITY PARTNERS, 1674

Industry Preference Index / Computer Hardware & Software

SIGNAL PEAK VENTURES, 1677
SIGNATURE CAPITAL LLC, 3120
SILVER CREEK VENTURES, 1682
SMART BUSINESS CONSULTING, 3124
SONY EUROPE, 3129
SORRENTO VENTURES, 1706
SOURCE CAPITAL GROUP, 1707
SOUTH ATLANTIC VENTURE FUNDS, 1708
SOUTHPORT PARTNERS, 1712
SPECTRUM EQUITY INVESTORS LP, 1717
SPIRE CAPITAL PARTNERS, 1724
SPRING CAPITAL PARTNERS LP, 1727
STAENBERG VENTURE PARTNERS, 1733
STAGEONE VENTURES, 3136
STAR VENTURES, 3137
SUCSY, FISCHER & COMPANY, 1750
SUMMIT PARTNERS, 1752
SUN CAPITAL PARTNERS, 1753
SVB CAPITAL, 1764
SWISSCOM, 3152
T-VENTURE HOLDINGS GmbH Deutsche Telekom, 3155
TAMIR FISHMAN VENTURES, 3159
TAT CAPITAL PARTNERS LTD., 3162
TDF, 1782
TECH CAPITAL PARTNERS, 2262
TECHNOLOGY PARK MALAYSIA CORPORATION SDN BHD, 3164
TEKNOINVEST MANAGEMENT, 3167
TELECOM VENTURE GROUP LIMITED, 3168
TELEFONICA VENTURES, 3169
TELESOFT PARTNERS, 1793
TENAYA CAPITAL, 1796
THOMSON-CSF VENTURES, 3176
THROUNARFELAG ISLANDS PLC, 3177
TL VENTURES, 1828
TRIGINITA CAPITAL, 3190
TRILOGY PARTNERSHIP, 1852
TRINITY VENTURE CAPITAL TVC Holdings plc, 3191
TRINITY VENTURES, 1853
TRITON VENTURES, 1855
TRU MANAGEMENT, 1858
TSG EQUITY PARTNERS, 1862
TVM CAPITAL, 3196
UCA UNTERNEHMER CONSULT AG, 3197
UNITED TALENT AGENCY VENTURES, 1883
US VENTURE PARTNERS, 1896
VAEKSTFONDEN, 3203
VALLEY VENTURES LP, 1901
VELOCITY EQUITY PARTNERS LLC, 1913
VENISTA VENTURES, 3207
VENTECH, 3208
VENTURE CAPITAL FUND OF NEW ENGLAND, 1920
VENTURE INVESTORS, 3210
VERITAS VENTURE PARTNERS, 3212
VERONIS SUHLER STEVENSON, 1927
VESTAR CAPITAL PARTNERS, 1931
VISION CAPITAL, 1937
WALDEN INTERNATIONAL, 1951
WALDEN ISRAEL VENTURE CAPITAL, 3231
WALNUT GROUP, 1954
WARBURG PINCUS LLC, 1956
WASHINGTON CAPITAL VENTURES, 1959
WASSERSTEIN & CO., 1960
WELLS FARGO CAPITAL FINANCE, 1970
WESTERN NIS ENTERPRISE FUND, 3234
WESTERN STATES INVESTMENT GROUP, 1974
WESTERN TECHNOLOGY INVESTMENT, 1975
WESTLAKE SECURITIES, 1976
WHEATLEY PARTNERS, 1981
WHITECAP VENTURE PARTNERS, 2288
WICKS GROUP OF COMPANIES, LLC, 1984
WINDSPEED VENTURES, 1994
WORLDVIEW TECHNOLOGY PARTNERS, 2007
YELLOW POINT EQUITY PARTNERS, 2292
YUUWA CAPITAL, 3248
YVC - YOZMA MANAGEMENT & INVESTMENTS LIMITED, 3249
ZONE VENTURES, 2021

Communications Equipment
ACORN CAMPUS VENTURES, 47
ALEXANDER HUTTON, 82
ALLSTATE INVESTMENTS LLC, 88
AMPERSAND CAPITAL PARTNERS, 118
ANDLINGER & COMPANY INC, 123
ANTHEM VENTURE PARTNERS, 132
APPLIED MATERIALS VENTURES, 144
ARTIMAN VENTURES, 174
ATHENAEUM FUND, 186
AVALON VENTURES, 206
BAKER CAPITAL, 223
HARBERT MANAGEMENT CORPORATION, 904
MACQUARIE DIRECT INVESTMENT LIMITED, 2951

Communications Software
DOT EDU VENTURES, 623
MOBIUS VENTURE CAPITAL, 1245

Community Engagement
THE ABRAAJ GROUP, 3173

Company Law
BUTZOW NORDIA ADVOCATES LTD, 2552

Compliance/Traning/Certification
ENTREPRENEUR PARTNERS, 683

Components & IoT
500 STARTUPS, 11
ADAMS STREET PARTNERS, LLC, 57
ALTA BERKELEY ASSOCIATES, 2380
ATLAS VENTURE: FRANCE, 2445
BARING PRIVATE EQUITY PARTNERS INDIA, 2490
BAY PARTNERS, 238
BLUERUN VENTURES, 296
BRM SEED, 2541
CRESCENDO VENTURES, 555
FINAVENTURES, 729
FRANCISCO PARTNERS, 779
INNOVACOM SA, 2875
INSTITUTIONAL VENTURE PARTNERS, 1001
INVEXCEL PATRIMONIO, 2891
JERUSALEM VENTURE PARTNERS, 2910
LEONIA MB GROUP/MB FUNDS, 2937
MACQUARIE DIRECT INVESTMENT LIMITED, 2951
MARATHON VENTURE CAPITAL FUND LIMITED, 2954
MOBIUS VENTURE CAPITAL, 1245
SEQUOIA CAPITAL, 1654
SPACEVEST, 1714
THOMSON-CSF VENTURES, 3176
VENTURE ASSOCIATES PARTNERS LLC, 1919

Computer Hardware & Software
AB CAPITAL & INVESTMENT CORPORATION The Phinma Group, 2314
ABU DHABI INVESTMENT AUTHORITY, 2321
ACCESS VENTURE PARTNERS LLC, 36
ADAMS STREET PARTNERS, LLC, 57
AKERS CAPITAL LLC, 75
ALEXANDER HUTTON, 82
AMBIENT SOUND INVESTMENTS, 2390
AMPERSAND CAPITAL PARTNERS, 118
ANDLINGER & COMPANY INC, 123
ANTHEM VENTURE PARTNERS, 132
APPIAN VENTURES, 142
APPLIED MATERIALS VENTURES, 144
ARROWPATH VENTURE PARTNERS, 169
ARTIMAN VENTURES, 174
ASSET MANAGEMENT VENTURES, 181
ATHENAEUM FUND, 186
AUSTIN VENTURES, 202
AVALON VENTURES, 206
CAMBRIDGE CAPITAL CORPORATION, 381
ENTERPRISE EQUITY (NI) LTD, 2704
FERRANTI LIMITED, 2732
FIRST ISRAEL MEZZANINE INVESTORS LIMITED, 2745

Industry Preference Index / Computer Related

FRESHWATER VENTURE PARTNERS, 2757
HARBINGER VENTURE MANAGEMENT, 905
ICF VENTURES PVT LTD, 2846
IDG CAPITAL, 973
INDASIA FUND ADVISORS PVT LTD, 2859
INNOVACOM SA, 2875
IPG GROUP, 2894
JAPAN ASIA INVESTMENT COMPANY LIMITED, 2907
KB PARTNERS LLC, 1057
MACQUARIE DIRECT INVESTMENT LIMITED, 2951
MENLO VENTURES, 1202
MVP CAPITAL PARTNERS, 1275
PENN VENTURE PARTNERS, 1428
PROSEED, 3059
RHO VENTURES, 1558
THROUNARFELAG ISLANDS PLC, 3177
TIME WARNER INVESTMENT CORPORATION, 1827

Computer Related
3I AUSTRIA BETEILGUNG GmbH 3i Group, 2298
3I TEUPSCHLAND GmbH 3i Group, 2305
ABU DHABI INVESTMENT AUTHORITY, 2321
AITEC, 2357
ALBEMARLE PRIVATE EQUITY LIMITED, 2360
AMANET TECHNOLOGIES LIMITED, 2389
AUGUST CAPITAL, 197
BARING PRIVATE EQUITY PARTNERS INDIA, 2490
BATTERSON VENTURE CAPITAL LLC, 234
BERKELEY VC INTERNATIONAL LLC, 252
BRIDGEPOINT CAPITAL GmbH, 2537
BRIDGEPOINT CAPITAL LIMITED, 2538
CANDOVER, 2556
CAZENOVE PRIVATE EQUITY Cazenove Capital, 2577
CHICAGO VENTURE PARTNERS LP, 470
CLEARSTONE VENTURE PARTNERS, 502
COMPASS TECHNOLOGY PARTNERS LP, 524
CONCORD VENTURES, 2628
CRESCENDO VENTURE MANAGEMENT LLC, 2639
DAVID N DEUTSCH & COMPANY LLC, 589
DRESNER COMPANIES, 629
ENTERPRISE INVESTORS, 2706
EQVITEC PARTNERS OY, 2716
FINANCIERE DE BRIENNE FCPR, 2738
FORREST BINKLEY & BROWN, 765
GALILEO II, 2765
GE EQUITY EUROPE, 2769
GILDE INVESTMENT FUNDS, 2779
GLOBAL EQUITY PARTNERS BETEILIGUNGS-MANAGEMENT, 2783
GMT COMMUNICATIONS PARTNERS LLP, 2789
HUMANA VENTURES, 955
ID VENTURES AMERICA LLC, 970
IGNITE JAPAN KK Ignite Group, 2854
INDUSTRIFONDEN, 2867
INVESTMENT AB BURE, 2888
JAVELIN INVESTMENTS, 2908
KBL FOUNDER SA, 2917
KLEINER PERKINS, 1075
KNIGHTSBRIDGE ADVISERS, 1077
LANDSBANKI VENTURES, 2929
LANDSBANKI VENTURES, 2929
LEAPFROG VENTURES, 1102
MANHATTAN INVESTMENT PARTNERS, 1163
MASSACHUSETTS CAPITAL RESOURCE COMPANY, 1173
MASSACHUSETTS GROWTH CAPITAL CORPORATION, 1174
MAYFIELD FUND, 1184
MEDIA VENTURE PARTNERS, 1195
MERIDIAN MANAGEMENT GROUP, 1208
NEEDHAM CAPITAL PARTNERS, 1288
NEW YORK LIFE CAPITAL PARTNERS, 1309
NORTH ATLANTIC CAPITAL CORPORATION, 1333
NOVAK BIDDLE VENTURE PARTNERS, 1348
OEM CAPITAL, 1369
OEM CAPITAL, 1369
PALO ALTO VENTURE PARTNERS, 1405
PERMAL CAPITAL MANAGEMENT, 1432
PIDC PHILADELPHIA, 1441
POLESTAR CAPITAL, 1461

POMONA CAPITAL, 1462
PRIME TECHNOLOGY VENTURES NV, 3051
PROVCO GROUP, 1494
RAF INDUSTRIES, 1521
REITEN & CO STRATEGIC INVESTMENTS AS Reiten & Company, 3076
ROYALTY CAPITAL MANAGEMENT, 1591
SEACOAST CAPITAL CORPORATION, 1636
SEAYA VENTURES, 3105
SEQUEL VENTURE PARTNERS, 1653
SHANNON COMMERCIAL PROPERTIES, 3115
SIERRA VENTURES, 1670
SIGMA PARTNERS, 1672
SILVER CREEK VENTURES, 1682
SONY EUROPE, 3129
SOURCE CAPITAL GROUP, 1707
SOUTH ATLANTIC VENTURE FUNDS, 1708
SOUTHPORT PARTNERS, 1712
STARBOARD CAPITAL PARTNERS, 1735
SUTTER HILL VENTURES, 1760
TECHNOCAP, 2263
THOMSON-CSF VENTURES, 3176
THROUNARFELAG ISLANDS PLC, 3177
TRANSITION PARTNERS LTD, 1837
TRINITY VENTURE CAPITAL TVC Holdings plc, 3191
TRINITY VENTURE CAPITAL TVC Holdings plc, 3191
UCA UNTERNEHMER CONSULT AG, 3197
VAEKSTFONDEN, 3203
VENCORE CAPITAL, 1915
VENTURE CAPITAL FUND OF NEW ENGLAND, 1920
VENTURE INVESTORS, 3210
VISION CAPITAL, 1937
WASSERSTEIN & CO., 1960
WESTERN STATES INVESTMENT GROUP, 1974
WESTERN TECHNOLOGY INVESTMENT, 1975
YISSUM TECHNOLOGY TRANSFER, 3245
ZERNIKE SEED FUND BV, 3250

Computer Software
CAMP VENTURES, 385

Computers & Peripherals
BEZOS EXPEDITIONS, 262
STATELINE ANGELS, 1740

Computing
MOBILE FOUNDATION VENTURES, 1243
SIERRA ANGELS, 1669

Concrete
PROCURITAS PARTNERS KB, 3054

Confectionery
LEONIA MB GROUP/MB FUNDS, 2937
RABO BLACK EARTH Eagle Venture Partners, 3071
WESTERN NIS ENTERPRISE FUND, 3234

Connected Mobility
CISCO INVESTMENTS, 483

Conservation
AUSTRALIAN ETHICAL INVESTMENT LIMITED, 2456
BIG SOCIETY CAPITAL, 2509
SENTRY FINANCIAL CORPORATION, 1652
UNDERDOG VENTURES, 1880

Construction
ARVA LIMITED, 2044
ASTOR CAPITAL GROUP, 2440
AVENUE CAPITAL GROUP, 208
BARING PRIVATE EQUITY PARTNERS ESPANA SA, 2489
CATAPULT VENTURES, 429
CHRYSALIX, 2078
CLIFFORD CHANCE PUNDER, 2614
COPPERLION CAPITAL, 2085
CVC ASIA PACIFIC LIMITED CVC Capital Partners, 2643
CVC CAPITAL PARTNERS LTD, 2644

Industry Preference Index / Consumer Internet

DAVID N DEUTSCH & COMPANY LLC, 589
DEUTSCHE BETEILIGUNGS AG, 2660
DUBIN CLARK & COMPANY, 632
DUNEDIN CAPITAL PARTNERS LIMITED, 2677
ELECTRA PARTNERS ASIA LIMITED SFC of Hong Kong, 2694
ENTERPRISE EQUITY (NI) LTD, 2704
EQUISTONE, 2714
FOUNDATION CAPITAL LIMITED, 2753
FdG ASSOCIATES LP, 801
GENESIS CAPITAL CORPORATION, 2129
GOLDEN OPPORTUNITIES FUND, 2136
HANCOCK CAPITAL MANAGEMENT, 901
INVESTMENT FUND FOR CENTRAL & EASTERN EUROPE, 2889
KUBOTA CORPORATION, 2927
LIONHART CAPITAL LTD, 2177
LLOYDS DEVELOPMENT CAPITAL LIMITED, 2944
MARCEAU INVESTISSEMENTS, 2955
MID-ATLANTIC VENTURE FUNDS, 1227
MITSUI SUMITOMO INSURANCE VENTURE CAPITAL CO, 2971
PALMS & COMPANY, 1404
QUADRAN GESTION Deutsche Beteiligungs AG, 3067
RABO BLACK EARTH Eagle Venture Partners, 3071
SAINT-GOBAIN NOVA EXTERNAL VENTURING, 3094
SRIW SA SRIW Group, 3134
STARBOARD CAPITAL PARTNERS, 1735
TGF MANAGEMENT, 1803
WESTERN AMERICA CAPITAL GROUP, 2286
WESTERN NIS ENTERPRISE FUND, 3234

Consumer
1843 CAPITAL, 7
3I EUROPE PLC 3i Group, 2300
3I ITALY 3i Group, 2303
645 VENTURES, 13
ACCEL, 28
ACON INVESTMENTS, 46
ACREW CAPITAL, 49
AMPLIFY, 120
APAX PARTNERS, 135
BESSEMER VENTURE PARTNERS, 260
BRAND FOUNDRY VENTURES, 325
BRANFORD CASTLE, 327
BROOKE PRIVATE EQUITY ASSOCIATES, 350
CANADIAN VENTURE CAPITAL ASSOCIATION Canadian Venture Capital & Private Equity Association, 3258
CEDRUS INVESTMENTS, 2581
EDELSON TECHNOLOGY PARTNERS, 651
FIFTH WALL, 727
FIRST ROUND CAPITAL, 741
FOUNDER COLLECTIVE, 771
GENERAL CATALYST PARTNERS, 816
GOLDMAN SACHS INVESTMENT PARTNERS, 842
GROUND UP VENTURES, 877
HALOGEN VENTURES, 896
INTERLACE VENTURES, 1006
JACKSON SQUARE VENTURES, 1024
KEIRETSU FORUM, 1061
KHOSLA VENTURES, 1069
LDV CAPITAL, 1101
LEE EQUITY PARTNERS, 1104
LIGHTSPEED VENTURE PARTNERS, 1121
LINLEY CAPITAL, 1130
MERCATO PARTNERS, 1204
MIDOCEAN PARTNERS, 1231
NEW ATLANTIC VENTURES, 1291
NKM CAPITAL, 1329
ORIGINATE VENTURES, 1385
PENFUND, 2219
PRITZKER GROUP VENTURE CAPITAL, 1480
QIMING VENTURE PARTNERS, 3066
RECIPROCAL VENTURES, 1528
RIVERSIDE COMPANY, 1572
SAINTS CAPITAL, 1604
SOCIAL CAPITAL, 1696
SPERO VENTURES, 1721
SUSA VENTURES, 1758
TA ASSOCIATES, 1776

THOMAS H LEE PARTNERS, 1815
TIGER GLOBAL MANAGEMENT, 1826
TXV PARTNERS, 1875
VALUEACT CAPITAL, 1903

Consumer Behavior
NIELSEN INNOVATE FUND, 3003

Consumer Brands
SWAN & LEGEND VENTURES, 1766

Consumer Commercial
500 STARTUPS, 11

Consumer Electronics
CATAPULT VENTURES, 429
CHINA ISRAEL VALUE CAPITAL, 2593
INNOVATION WORKS, 998
TYLT LAB, 1876
VOLVO GROUP VENTURE CAPITAL, 3226

Consumer Finance
KAPOR CAPITAL, 1054

Consumer Goods
ACKRELL CAPITAL, 44
BASE VENTURES, 229
BLAST FUNDING, 279
BUSINESS GROWTH FUND, 2550
CIT GROUP, 484
DUTCHESS CAPITAL, 638

Consumer Goods & Services
SARONA ASSET MANAGEMENT, 2248

Consumer Hardware
CREANDUM, 2637

Consumer Internet
A-GRADE INVESTMENTS, 15
AM VENTURES, 16
ACCESS VENTURE PARTNERS LLC, 36
ACTIVE VENTURE PARTNERS, 2339
ADAMS STREET PARTNERS, LLC, 57
AKSOY INTERNET VENTURES, 2359
ANNAPURNA VENTURES, 2403
AOL VENTURES, 134
ASPECT VENTURES, 180
ATA VENTURES, 183
ATLANTIC VENTURES, 2444
ATOMICO, 2446
BAF SPECTRUM, 2477
BALDERTON CAPITAL, 2478
BARODA VENTURES, 228
BASELINE VENTURES, 231
BLACKBIRD VENTURES, 2520
BLH VENTURE PARTNERS, 282
BLUMBERG CAPITAL, 301
BOSTON SEED CAPITAL, 313
BRIDGESCALE PARTNERS, 339
BRIGHTSTONE VENTURE CAPITAL, 341
BULLPEN CAPITAL, 358
CATAMOUNT VENTURES LP, 428
CHARLES RIVER VENTURES, 455
CLYDESDALE VENTURES, 506
CONVEXA Tyveholmen AS, 2632
CROSSLINK CAPITAL, 563
DCM, 596
DEEP FORK CAPITAL, 600
DOUBLEROCK VENTURE CAPITAL, 625
EDBI Pte LTD., 2690
ENTREE CAPITAL, 2709
FELICIS VENTURES, 720
FENOX VENTURE CAPITAL, 721
FLOODGATE FUND, 751
GENACAST VENTURES, 814
GV, 889

Industry Preference Index / Consumer Marketing

ICON VENTURES, 968
INSIGHT VENTURE PARTNERS, 1000
INTEL CAPITAL, 1004
INVENTUS, 1013
KPG VENTURES, 1084
LIGHTBANK, 1118
MADRONA VENTURE GROUP, 1158
MANTELLA VENTURE PARTNERS, 2182
MATRIX PARTNERS, 1181
MERITECH CAPITAL PARTNERS, 1212
MMC VENTURES, 2972
MORADO VENTURE PARTNERS, 1254
NOVAK BIDDLE VENTURE PARTNERS, 1348
OJAS VENTURE PARTNERS, 3019
OMIDYAR NETWORK, 1374
OUTLOOK VENTURES, 1389
PRESIDIO VENTURES, 1474
RUBICON VENTURE CAPITAL, 1595
SCOUT VENTURES, 1632
SEAYA VENTURES, 3105
SERAPH GROUP, 1655
SHERPALO VENTURES, 1666
SILVERTON PARTNERS, 1685
SOFTTECH VC, 1700
SPARKLABS GLOBAL VENTURES, 1716
SRIJAN CAPITAL, 3133
STRIPES GROUP, 1748
SV ANGEL, 1761
TENAYA CAPITAL, 1796
TENAYA CAPITAL, 1796
TUGBOAT VENTURES, 1865
VALAR VENTURES, 1897
VERSION ONE VENTURES, 2280
VILLAGE GLOBAL, 1933
VINE ST VENTURES, 1934
XG VENTURES, 2010

Consumer Marketing
DACE VENTURES, 580

Consumer Marketplace
HYDE PARK VENTURE PARTNERS, 962

Consumer Media
ACTIVE VENTURE PARTNERS, 2339

Consumer Medicine
HEALTHQUEST CAPITAL, 921
TECHNOLOGY PARTNERS, 1786

Consumer Mobile Media
SEAYA VENTURES, 3105

Consumer Networks
DUNDEE VENTURE CAPITAL, 635

Consumer Products
3I GESTION SA 3i Group, 2302
3M UNITEK, 2307
3i GROUP PLC, 2311
ACE & COMPANY, 2329
ACI CAPITAL, 42
ACTIVA CAPITAL, 2338
AEA INVESTORS, 64
ALANTRA, 77
ALBION INVESTORS LLC, 78
ALERION PARTNERS, 80
ALEUTIAN CAPITAL PARTNERS, 81
ALLIANCE OF ANGELS, 85
ALPHA CAPITAL PARTNERS, 90
ALTAIR VENTURES, 95
AMERICAN SECURITIES LLC, 110
ANGELO, GORDON & CO., 127
ANGELS' FORUM LLC, 129
APOLLO GLOBAL MANAGEMENT, 140
ARCAPITA INC, 152
ARES MANAGEMENT LLC, 159

ARROWHEAD INVESTMENT MANAGEMENT, 168
ASIAVEST PARTNERS, 2436
ATRIA CAPITAL PARTENAIRES, 2448
AUA PRIVATE EQUITY PARTNERS, 193
AUDAX GROUP, 194
AVANTI CAPITAL, 2458
AVISTA CAPITAL PARTNERS, 209
AWAY REALTY, 2465
AZALEA CAPITAL, 213
BALMORAL FUNDS, 225
BARING PRIVATE EQUITY PARTNERS INDIA, 2490
BAY BG BAVARIAN VENTURE CAPITAL CORP, 2494
BBH CAPITAL PARTNERS, 240
BERKSHIRE PARTNERS LLC, 254
BERTRAM CAPITAL, 257
BEZOS EXPEDITIONS, 262
BLACKSTONE PRIVATE EQUITY GROUP, 277
BLUEGEM CAPITAL PARTNERS, 2524
BOND CAPITAL, 2064
BRAZOS PRIVATE EQUITY PARTNERS, 328
BREAKAWAY VENTURES, 329
BREAKWATER INVESTMENTS, 330
BREAKWATER MANAGEMENT, 331
BRENTWOOD ASSOCIATES, 334
BRIDGE STREET CAPITAL, 338
BROCKWAY MORAN & PARTNERS, 348
BRUCKMANN, ROSSER, SHERRILL & COMPANY, 354
BRYNWOOD PARTNERS, 357
BUNKER HILL CAPITAL, 359
CAI CAPITAL PARTNERS, 365
CALERA CAPITAL, 368
CALTIUS EQUITY PARTNERS, 373
CALTIUS STRUCTURED CAPITAL, 374
CAMBRIA GROUP, 378
CAPITAL TODAY, 2560
CAPITALA, 405
CAPX PARTNERS, 407
CARDINAL EQUITY PARTNERS, 409
CARLYLE GROUP, 413
CAROUSEL CAPITAL, 415
CASTANEA PARTNERS, 421
CASTLE HARLAN, 423
CATALYST GROUP, 425
CCMP CAPITAL, 433
CEDAR VENTURES LLC, 437
CEI VENTURES, 438
CELERITY PARTNERS, 439
CENTERFIELD CAPITAL PARTNERS, 443
CENTRAL TEXAS ANGEL NETWORK, 445
CENTRE PARTNERS MANAGEMENT LLC, 447
CENTURY PARK CAPITAL PARTNERS, 449
CERBERUS CAPITAL MANAGEMENT, 451
CHARLESBANK CAPITAL PARTNERS, 456
CHAZEN CAPITAL PARTNERS, 460
CHENGWEI VENTURES, 2590
CHEYENNE CAPITAL, 467
CHICAGO VENTURE PARTNERS LP, 470
CHRYSALIS CAPITAL ChrysCapital, 2599
CID CAPITAL, 478
CIRCLE PEAK CAPITAL, 481
CIRCLEUP, 482
CLARION CAPITAL PARTNERS LLC, 492
CLEARLAKE CAPITAL, 500
CLEARLIGHT PARTNERS, 501
CLEARSPRING CAPITAL PARTNERS, 2082
CLYDESDALE VENTURES, 506
COMCAST VENTURES, 518
COMSTOCK CAPITAL PARTNERS LLC, 527
COMVEST PARTNERS, 528
CRYSTAL RIDGE PARTNERS, 565
CYPRESS GROUP, 575
DANCAP PRIVATE EQUITY, 2094
DANEVEST TECH FUND ADVISORS, 583
DARBY OVERSEAS INVESTMENTS LTD, 584
DB CAPITAL PARTNERS (ASIA), 2652
DENALI VENTURE PARTNERS, 605
DESCO CAPITAL, 606

1158

Industry Preference Index / Consumer Products

DIAMOND STATE VENTURES LP, 611
DISTRICT VENTURES CAPITAL, 2099
DRESNER COMPANIES, 629
DRIVE CAPITAL, 630
DUBILIER & COMPANY, 631
DUNEDIN CAPITAL PARTNERS LIMITED, 2677
EMIGRANT CAPITAL, 667
EMIL CAPITAL PARTNERS, 668
EMINENT CAPITAL PARTNERS, 669
ENDEAVOUR CAPITAL, 673
EOS PARTNERS LP, 686
EQT PARTNERS AB, 2712
EQUUS TOTAL RETURN, 694
EUREKA GROWTH CAPITAL, 698
EXCELSIOR CAPITAL ASIA, 2727
FAIRHAVEN CAPITAL, 712
FENWAY PARTNERS, 722
FIDELITY GROWTH PARTNERS ASIA, 2733
FINLOMBARDA SpA, 2739
FIRST ATLANTIC CAPITAL LTD., 733
FIRST STEP FUND, 742
FLORIDA CAPITAL PARTNERS, 752
FLUKE VENTURE PARTNERS, 753
FORREST BINKLEY & BROWN, 765
FOUNDATION CAPITAL, 770
FOUNDATION CAPITAL LIMITED, 2753
FOUNDERS EQUITY, 774
FOX PAINE & COMPANY LLC, 778
FRESH VC, 785
FRIEDMAN, FLEISCHER & LOWE LLC, 787
FRIEND SKOLER & COMPANY LLC, 788
FRONTENAC COMPANY, 789
FULCRUM CAPITAL PARTNERS, 2126
FUNG CAPITAL USA, 796
FdG ASSOCIATES LP, 801
GABRIEL VENTURE PARTNERS, 805
GE ASIA PACIFIC CAPITAL TECHNOLOGY FUND, 2767
GE CAPITAL, 808
GE EQUITY EUROPE, 2769
GEFINOR CAPITAL, 810
GEMINI INVESTORS, 812
GENERAL ATLANTIC PARTNERS, 815
GEORGIA OAK PARTNERS, 821
GIBRALTAR & COMPANY, 2133
GLADSTONE CAPITAL, 828
GLENCOE CAPITAL, 830
GOLDEN GATE CAPITAL, 839
GOLDEN SEEDS, 841
GOLDNER, HAWN, JOHNSON & MORRISON, 843
GOLUB CAPITAL, 844
GRANITE BRIDGE PARTNERS, 849
GRAPHITE CAPITAL MANAGEMENT LTD, 2796
GRAYHAWK CAPITAL, 856
GREAT OAKS VENTURE CAPITAL, 858
GREIF & COMPANY, 869
GROTECH VENTURES, 876
GRYPHON INVESTORS, 881
GULFSTAR GROUP, 888
HALIFAX GROUP LLC, 894
HARBOURVEST PARTNERS LLC, 909
HARREN EQUITY PARTNERS, 910
HARVEST PARTNERS, 914
HERITAGE PARTNERS, 926
HG CAPITAL, 2823
HIG CAPITAL, 928
HIGH-TECH GRUENDERFONDS, 2824
HIGHLAND CAPITAL PARTNERS, 935
HILCO BRANDS, 937
HILL AND GERTNER CAPITAL CORP., 2148
HORIZON PARTNERS, LTD, 945
HUNTSMAN GAY GLOBAL CAPITAL, 959
HURON CAPITAL PARTNERS LLC, 960
ICF VENTURES PVT LTD, 2846
ICV PARTNERS, 969
IDG CAPITAL PARTNERS, 2847
INCWELL VENTURE CAPITAL, 981
INDUSTRIEBANK LIOF NV, 2866

INTERMEDIATE CAPITAL GROUP PLC, 2883
INVESTMENT FUND FOR CENTRAL & EASTERN EUROPE, 2889
INVEXCEL PATRIMONIO, 2891
INVUS GROUP, 1018
IRONBRIDGE EQUITY PARTNERS, 2163
IRONWOOD CAPITAL, 1021
IRVING PLACE CAPITAL, 1022
JAVELIN INVESTMENTS, 2908
JEFFERIES CAPITAL PARTNERS, 1032
JH WHITNEY & COMPANY, 1037
JOHNSON & JOHNSON INNOVATION, 1043
JORDAN COMPANY, 1045
JW CHILDS ASSOCIATES, 1049
KAEDAN INVESTMENTS, 2914
KARLIN VENTURES, 1055
KB PARTNERS, 1056
KENSINGTON CAPITAL PARTNERS, 2167
KERRY CAPITAL ADVISORS, 1067
KIDD & COMPANY, 1071
KILMER CAPITAL PARTNERS, 2169
KNIGHT'S BRIDGE CAPITAL PARTNERS, 2171
KOHLBERG & COMPANY LLC, 1081
KOHLBERG KRAVIS ROBERTS & COMPANY, 1082
KOHLBERG VENTURES, 1083
L CATTERTON PARTNERS, 1088
LAUNCHCAPITAL, 1097
LEGAL AND GENERAL VENTURES LIMITED, 2935
LEGEND CAPITAL, 2936
LEONARD GREEN & PARTNERS LP, 1109
LEVINE LEICHTMAN CAPITAL PARTNERS, 1111
LFE CAPITAL, 1113
LIGHTBANK, 1118
LITTLEJOHN & COMPANY LLC, 1134
LIZADA CAPITAL LLC, 1135
LM CAPITAL SECURITIES, 1137
LUDLOW VENTURES, 1150
MADISON DEARBORN PARTNERS, 1156
MADISON PARKER CAPITAL, 1157
MAINE ANGELS, 1160
MANHATTAN INVESTMENT PARTNERS, 1163
MARANON CAPITAL, 1166
MASSACHUSETTS CAPITAL RESOURCE COMPANY, 1173
MCG CAPITAL CORPORATION, 1189
MEDIA VENTURE PARTNERS, 1195
MEKONG CAPITAL, 2961
MERITURN PARTNERS, 1213
MERRILL LYNCH (ASIA PACIFIC) LIMITED Merrill Lynch Group, 2964
MHS CAPITAL, 1226
MIDWEST MEZZANINE FUNDS, 1232
MINDFULL INVESTORS, 1236
MITSUI SUMITOMO INSURANCE VENTURE CAPITAL CO, 2971
MONITOR VENTURES, 1249
MONTAGU PRIVATE EQUITY LIMITED, 2977
MONTLAKE CAPITAL, 1250
MVP CAPITAL PARTNERS, 1275
NAVY CAPITAL, 1283
NEW ENGLAND CAPITAL PARTNERS, 1296
NEW MEXICO COMMUNITY CAPITAL, 1300
NEW MOUNTAIN CAPITAL, 1301
NEWFIELD CAPITAL, 1313
NEXUS VENTURE PARTNERS Nexus India Capital Advisors Pvt Ltd, 3001
NORTH AMERICAN FUND, 1332
NORTH CASTLE PARTNERS, 1335
NORTHERN LIGHT VENTURE CAPITAL, 1340
NORWEST EQUITY PARTNERS, 1345
NORWEST VENTURE PARTNERS, 1346
OAK INVESTMENT PARTNERS, 1361
PALLADIUM EQUITY PARTNERS, 1403
PAMLICO CAPITAL, 1409
PANTHEON VENTURES (US) LP, 1411
PARALLEL INVESTMENT PARTNERS, 1415
PARALLEL49 EQUITY, 2214
PARTHENON CAPITAL, 1417
PEACHTREE EQUITY PARTNERS, 1423
PENINSULA CAPITAL PARTNERS LLC, 1426
PERMAL CAPITAL MANAGEMENT, 1432

Industry Preference Index / Consumer Products & Services

PERMIRA Permira Advisers LLP, 3033
PHILQUO VENTURES, 1437
PHYSIC VENTURES, 1438
POND VENTURES, 3047
POST CAPITAL PARTNERS, 1465
POUSCHINE COOK CAPITAL MANAGEMENT LLC, 1466
PRAIRIE CAPITAL, 1469
PROSPECT PARTNERS LLC, 1492
PROVCO GROUP, 1494
RAF INDUSTRIES, 1521
RAYMOND JAMES CAPITAL, 1526
RBC CAPITAL MARKETS, 2231
REDWOOD CAPITAL CORPORATION, 1535
RHB - H&F MANAGEMENT COMPANY SDN BHD RHB Capital, 3080
RIDGE CAPITAL PARTNERS LLC, 1562
ROBIN HOOD VENTURES, 1577
ROPART ASSET MANAGEMENT, 1583
ROSEWOOD CAPITAL, 1587
ROTH CAPITAL PARTNERS, 1588
ROYALTY CAPITAL MANAGEMENT, 1591
RRE VENTURES, 1593
SAIF PARTNERS, 3093
SALEM INVESTMENT PARTNERS, 1606
SATORI CAPITAL, 1622
SEACOAST CAPITAL CORPORATION, 1636
SEAWAY VALLEY CAPITAL CORPORATION, 1639
SENTINEL CAPITAL PARTNERS, 1651
SERAPH GROUP, 1655
SOCIAL VENTURE CIRCLE, 3277
SORRENTO VENTURES, 1706
SOURCE CAPITAL GROUP, 1707
SOUTH ATLANTIC VENTURE FUNDS, 1708
STARBOARD CAPITAL PARTNERS, 1735
STATELINE ANGELS, 1740
STEAMBOAT VENTURES, 3142
STRIPES GROUP, 1748
SUCSY, FISCHER & COMPANY, 1750
SUMMIT PARTNERS, 1752
SVOBODA CAPITAL PARTNERS, 1765
SWANDER PACE CAPITAL, 1767
SYMMETRIC CAPITAL, 1770
TECH COAST ANGELS, 1784
TGF MANAGEMENT, 1803
TH LEE PUTNAM VENTURES, 1804
THOMA BRAVO LLC, 1814
THOMSON-CSF VENTURES, 3176
TORQUEST PARTNERS, 2272
TRIVEST PARTNERS, 1857
TSG CONSUMER PARTNERS, 1861
TULLY & HOLLAND, 1867
TYLT LAB, 1876
UNDERDOG VENTURES, 1880
UNIVERSITY VENTURE FUND, 1884
US VENTURE PARTNERS, 1896
VALOR EQUITY PARTNERS, 1902
VENCORE CAPITAL, 1915
VERITAS CAPITAL FUND LP, 1925
VESTAR CAPITAL PARTNERS, 1931
VINCERA CAPITAL, 3218
WALDEN INTERNATIONAL, 1951
WALNUT GROUP, 1954
WASSERSTEIN & CO., 1960
WEDBUSH CAPITAL PARTNERS, 1969
WESTLAKE SECURITIES, 1976
WESTVIEW CAPITAL PARTNERS, 1979
WILLIS STEIN & PARTNERS LLC, 1986
WINONA CAPITAL MANAGEMENT, 1999
WOODBRIDGE GROUP, 2004
YORK STREET CAPITAL PARTNERS LLC, 2015
ZS FUND LP, 2022
ZURMONT MADISON PRIVATE EQUITY, 3254

Consumer Products & Services
ALTAMONT CAPITAL PARTNERS, 96
BALLAST POINT VENTURES, 224
CAPITAL RESOURCE PARTNERS, 402
INNOSPRING, 994

SCOTIABANK PRIVATE EQUITY, 2250

Consumer Retail
MONTAGU PRIVATE EQUITY LIMITED, 2977
SB CHINA VENTURE CAPITAL, 3100
VEBER PARTNERS LLC, 1909

Consumer Services
3i GROUP PLC, 2311
AB CAPITAL & INVESTMENT CORPORATION The Phinma Group, 2314
ABU DHABI INVESTMENT AUTHORITY, 2321
ACCENTURE TECHNOLOGY VENTURES, 2326
ACCESS CAPITAL, 35
ACE & COMPANY, 2329
ADLEVO CAPITAL CIM Fund Services, 2345
AEP CAPITAL LLC, 65
ALBEMARLE PRIVATE EQUITY LIMITED, 2360
ALLIANCE OF ANGELS, 85
ALPHA CAPITAL PARTNERS, 90
ALTA VENTURES MEXICO, 2382
AMBIENT SOUND INVESTMENTS, 2390
AMERIMARK CAPITAL CORPORATION, 111
AMMER PARTNERS, 2393
ANDREESSEN HOROWITZ, 124
APEX VENTURE PARTNERS, 137
ARTHUR P GOULD & COMPANY, 172
AUA PRIVATE EQUITY PARTNERS, 193
AVISTA CAPITAL PARTNERS, 209
BALDERTON CAPITAL, 2478
BARING PRIVATE EQUITY PARTNERS INDIA, 2490
BAY PARTNERS, 238
BBH CAPITAL PARTNERS, 240
BENAROYA COMPANIES, 247
BERKELEY VC INTERNATIONAL LLC, 252
BERTRAM CAPITAL, 257
BLAZER VENTURES, 280
BREGAL SAGEMOUNT, 333
BRENTWOOD ASSOCIATES, 334
BRIDGEPOINT CAPITAL GmbH, 2537
BRIDGEPOINT CAPITAL LIMITED, 2538
BRUCKMANN, ROSSER, SHERRILL & COMPANY, 354
CAI CAPITAL PARTNERS, 365
CALTIUS EQUITY PARTNERS, 373
CALTIUS STRUCTURED CAPITAL, 374
CAMBRIA GROUP, 378
CANYON CREEK CAPITAL, 397
CARLYLE ASIA INVESTMENT ADVISORS LIMITED Carlyle Group, 2565
CAROUSEL CAPITAL, 415
CARPEDIA CAPITAL, 2072
CASTLE HARLAN, 423
CATALYST INVESTORS, 427
CENTRAL TEXAS ANGEL NETWORK, 445
CHASE CAPITAL PARTNERS, 2588
CHAZEN CAPITAL PARTNERS, 460
CHEYENNE CAPITAL, 467
CHICAGO GROWTH PARTNERS, 468
CHINA WALDEN MANAGEMENT LIMITED Walden Group, 2597
CHINAVEST, 473
CI CAPITAL PARTNERS, 476
CINVEN LIMITED, 2605
CIVC PARTNERS, 489
CLEARLAKE CAPITAL, 500
CLEARLIGHT PARTNERS, 501
CLOSE BROTHERS PRIVATE EQUITY Close Brothers Group, 2617
CONCENTRIC EQUITY PARTNERS Financial Investments Corporation, 529
CORRELATION VENTURES, 544
DANCAP PRIVATE EQUITY, 2094
DANEVEST TECH FUND ADVISORS, 583
DAVID N DEUTSCH & COMPANY LLC, 589
DIAMOND STATE VENTURES LP, 611
DOUBLEROCK VENTURE CAPITAL, 625
DRIVE CAPITAL, 630
DUKE STREET CAPITAL Duke Street, 2676
DUNEDIN CAPITAL PARTNERS LIMITED, 2677

Industry Preference Index / Consumer Software

EDGESTONE CAPITAL PARTNERS, 2103
EDGEWATER FUNDS, 654
ELECTRA PARTNERS EUROPE, 2695
EM WARBURG, PINCUS & COMPANY INTERNATIONAL, 2697
EM WARBURG, PINCUS & COMPANY JAPAN, 2698
EMERGENCE CAPITAL PARTNERS, 665
EMIGRANT CAPITAL, 667
EOS PARTNERS LP, 686
EPIC VENTURES, 688
EQT PARTNERS AB, 2712
EQUISTONE, 2714
EURAZEO, 2719
EUREKA GROWTH CAPITAL, 698
EUROVENTURES CAPITAL, 2725
EVERGREEN ADVISORS, 701
FALCONHEAD CAPITAL, 717
FINLOMBARDA SpA, 2739
FIRST ISRAEL MEZZANINE INVESTORS LIMITED, 2745
FIRST NEW ENGLAND CAPITAL LP, 739
FIVE ELMS CAPITAL, 745
FLUKE VENTURE PARTNERS, 753
FOCUS VENTURES, 757
FORREST BINKLEY & BROWN, 765
FOUNDATION CAPITAL, 770
FOUNDATION CAPITAL LIMITED, 2753
FOUNDERS EQUITY, 774
FdG ASSOCIATES LP, 801
GE EQUITY EUROPE, 2769
GEMINI INVESTORS, 812
GENESIS PARTNERS, 2775
GEORGIA OAK PARTNERS, 821
GILBERT GLOBAL EQUITY PARTNERS, 827
GOLDNER, HAWN, JOHNSON & MORRISON, 843
GOLUB CAPITAL, 844
GRAPHITE CAPITAL MANAGEMENT LTD, 2796
GREAT HILL PARTNERS LLC, 857
GRUPO BISA, 2800
GRYPHON INVESTORS, 881
GULFSTAR GROUP, 888
H KATZ CAPITAL GROUP, 891
HALDER HOLDINGS BV, 2806
HALIFAX GROUP LLC, 894
HELION VENTURE PARTNERS, LLC International Management (Mauritius) Ltd, 2818
HG CAPITAL, 2823
HILCO BRANDS, 937
HUMANA VENTURES, 955
HUMMER WINBLAD VENTURE PARTNERS, 956
HURON CAPITAL PARTNERS LLC, 960
IA VENTURES, 965
ICF VENTURES PVT LTD, 2846
ICV PARTNERS, 969
INDUSTRIEBANK LIOF NV, 2866
INNOFINANCE OY, 2873
INVUS GROUP, 1018
IRONBRIDGE EQUITY PARTNERS, 2163
IRVING PLACE CAPITAL, 1022
ISIS EP LLP F & C, 2898
J. BURKE CAPITAL PARTNERS, 1023
KELSO & COMPANY, 1062
L CATTERTON PARTNERS, 1088
LEGAL AND GENERAL VENTURES LIMITED, 2935
LEONARD GREEN & PARTNERS LP, 1109
LFE CAPITAL, 1113
LLR PARTNERS INC, 1136
LOVETT MILLER & COMPANY, 1148
MADISON DEARBORN PARTNERS, 1156
MADRONA VENTURE GROUP, 1158
MARANON CAPITAL, 1166
MAVERON LLC, 1183
MAYFIELD FUND, 1184
MERRILL LYNCH (ASIA PACIFIC) LIMITED Merrill Lynch Group, 2964
MIDDLEBURG CAPITAL DEVELOPMENT, 1229
MIDVEN, 2967
MINDFULL INVESTORS, 1236
MOBIUS VENTURE CAPITAL, 1245
MONTAGU PRIVATE EQUITY LIMITED, 2977

MOUNTAIN GROUP CAPITAL, 1261
MPG EQUITY PARTNERS, 1267
MVC CORPORATION, 2980
NEEDHAM CAPITAL PARTNERS, 1288
NEW MEXICO COMMUNITY CAPITAL, 1300
NEWFIELD CAPITAL, 1313
NEXUS VENTURE PARTNERS Nexus India Capital Advisors Pvt Ltd, 3001
NORTH CASTLE PARTNERS, 1335
NORTH DAKOTA DEVELOPMENT FUND, 1338
NORTHERN ENTERPRISE LIMITED, 3011
NORTHERN LIGHT VENTURE CAPITAL, 1340
NORTHWOOD VENTURES, 1344
NORWEST EQUITY PARTNERS, 1345
NOVELTEK CAPITAL CORPORATION, 1351
NTH POWER TECHNOLOGIES, 1355
PARALLEL49 EQUITY, 2214
PARTHENON CAPITAL, 1417
PEACHTREE EQUITY PARTNERS, 1423
PHILQUO VENTURES, 1437
PHOENIX EQUITY PARTNERS LIMITED, 3036
PIVOTNORTH CAPITAL, 1450
PLUS VENTURES, 3041
POLARIS VENTURE PARTNERS, 1460
POLESTAR CAPITAL, 1461
POMONA CAPITAL, 1462
POND VENTURES, 3047
POUSCHINE COOK CAPITAL MANAGEMENT LLC, 1466
PWC, 3064
QUESTMARK PARTNERS LP, 1515
REITEN & CO STRATEGIC INVESTMENTS AS Reiten & Company, 3076
REVEL PARTNERS, 1554
RHB - H&F MANAGEMENT COMPANY SDN BHD RHB Capital, 3080
ROARK CAPITAL GROUP, 1576
ROSEWOOD CAPITAL, 1587
SAIF PARTNERS, 3093
SAINTS CAPITAL, 1604
SCHOONER CAPITAL LLC, 1627
SENTINEL CAPITAL PARTNERS, 1651
SHASTA VENTURES, 1663
SIERRA VENTURES, 1670
SILVER OAK SERVICES PARTNERS, 1684
SPLIT ROCK PARTNERS, 1725
SSM PARTNERS, 1732
STAENBERG VENTURE PARTNERS, 1733
SWANDER PACE CAPITAL, 1767
TAO VENTURE CAPITAL PARTNERS, 1780
THOMSON-CSF VENTURES, 3176
TRIDENT CAPITAL, 1850
TRILANTIC CAPITAL PARTNERS, 1851
TRINITY VENTURE CAPITAL TVC Holdings plc, 3191
TSG EQUITY PARTNERS, 1862
UNIVERSITY VENTURE FUND, 1884
UPFRONT VENTURES, 1888
VENTURE INVESTORS, 3210
VESTAR CAPITAL PARTNERS, 1931
VISION CAPITAL, 1937
WALDEN INTERNATIONAL, 1951
WALNUT GROUP, 1954
WASSERSTEIN & CO., 1960
WATERLAND PRIVATE EQUITY INVESTMENT, 3232
WAVELAND INVESTMENTS LLC, 1964
WELLSPRING CAPITAL MANAGEMENT LLC, 1971
WESTLAKE SECURITIES, 1976
WESTSUMMIT CAPITAL, 3235
WILLIS STEIN & PARTNERS LLC, 1986
WIND POINT PARTNERS, 1990
WINGATE PARTNERS, 1997
WINONA CAPITAL MANAGEMENT, 1999

Consumer Software

ABRT VENTURE FUND, 2320
CREANDUM, 2637
SEAYA VENTURES, 3105
SEVEN PEAKS VENTURES, 1656

Industry Preference Index / Consumer Technology

Consumer Technology
ELYSIUM VENTURE CAPITAL, 661
FLYBRIDGE CAPITAL PARTNERS, 754
LEAPFROG VENTURES, 1102
LEO CAPITAL HOLDINGS, LLC, 1108
NEW ENTERPRISE ASSOCIATES, 1297
PALO ALTO VENTURE SCIENCE, 1406
SIERRA VENTURES, 1670
VENROCK ASSOCIATES, 1916

Consumer, Retail & Dining
BAIN CAPITAL PRIVATE EQUITY, 220

Consumer/Retail
TPG CAPITAL, 1835

Content
BLOOMBERG BETA, 284
INNOVACOM SA, 2875

Contracting
CATALYST INVESTMENT MANAGERS PTY LIMITED PPM Capital, 2573

Conventional Energy
RIVERSTONE, 1573

Convergent Technologies
LINSALATA CAPITAL PARTNERS, 1132

Copper
SPACEVEST, 1714

Core Financial Applications
INFORMATION VENTURE PARTNERS, 2153

Corporate Advisory
GRESHAM PRIVATE EQUITY LIMITED, 2799

Corporate Insolvency
BUTZOW NORDIA ADVOCATES LTD, 2552

Corporate Services
CORE PACIFIC - YAMAICHI CAPITAL LIMITED Core Pacific Securities Company Ltd, 2633
DAVIS, TUTTLE VENTURE PARTNERS LP, 591
DFC LTD, 2661
ENTER VENTURES, 681
RHB - H&F MANAGEMENT COMPANY SDN BHD RHB Capital, 3080
SOVEREIGN CAPITAL, 3130

Cosmetics
BIOPACIFIC VENTURES, 2516
RABO BLACK EARTH Eagle Venture Partners, 3071
TMG CAPITAL PARTNERS, 3180

Cost-Effective Medicine
TECHNOLOGY PARTNERS, 1786

Cosumer Products
HAMMOND, KENNEDY, WHITNEY & COMPANY, 900

Creative Industries
ASCENSION VENTURES, 2432
CLARITY CAPITAL, 2611
IBB BETEILIGUNGSGESELLSCHAFT MBH, 2841
PORTUGAL CAPITAL VENTURES Institutional Headquarters, 3048

Cryptocurrency
SAMSUNG NEXT, 1611

Culture and Media
CHINA MERCHANTS CHINA DIRECT INVESTMENTS LTD., 2594

Cyber Insurance
GROUND UP VENTURES, 877

Cybersecurity
.406 VENTURES, 2
11.2 CAPITAL, 4
BENHAMOU GLOBAL VENTURES, 249
BESSEMER VENTURE PARTNERS, 260
BOLDSTART VENTURES, 305
COLUMBIA CAPITAL, 515
CYBERSTARTS, 2647
ECAPITAL ENTREPRENEURIAL PARTNERS AG, 2686
ENERTECH CAPITAL, 676
FGA PARTNERS, 725
GENACAST VENTURES, 814
GLASSWING VENTURES, 829
GV, 889
MARYLAND VENTURE FUND, 1169
MS&AD VENTURES, 1269
QUAKE CAPITAL PARTNERS, 1507
SINEWAVE VENTURES, 1687
TEN ELEVEN VENTURES, 1794
VANEDGE CAPITAL PARTNERS, 2278
VERDEXUS, 2279

DNA
IN-Q-TEL, 979

Data
ANGELPAD, 128
BRILLIANT VENTURES, 342
CAMP VENTURES, 385
FIKA VENTURES, 728
INNOVATION ENDEAVORS, 996
PORTAG3 VENTURES, 2225

Data & Cloud
.406 VENTURES, 2

Data Analytics
11.2 CAPITAL, 4
ACCESS VENTURE PARTNERS LLC, 36
AME CLOUD VENTURES, 107
BAIDU VENTURES, 219
BOLDSTART VENTURES, 305
BREYER CAPITAL, 336
CANOPY BOULDER, 392
CHRYSALIX, 2078
CITI VENTURES, 486
CROSSLINK CAPITAL, 563
DELL VENTURES, 603
DOT EDU VENTURES, 623
DYNAMO VC, 640
EXTREME VENTURE PARTNERS, 2113
FIRSTMARK CAPITAL, 743
GERKEN CAPITAL ASSOCIATES, 822
HALYARD CAPITAL, 897
HORIZONS VENTURES, 2831
MISSIONOG, 1240
MOBILE FOUNDATION VENTURES, 1243
MOTIV PARTNERS, 1258
NIELSEN INNOVATE FUND, 3003
PHYTO PARTNERS, 1439
PROGRESS VENTURES, 1486
RUNTIDE CAPITAL, 1596
SAMSUNG NEXT, 1611
SCIFI VC, 1631
SIGNAL FIRE, 1675
TOYOTA AI VENTURES, 1834
UNCORK CAPITAL, 1879
VERIZON VENTURES, 1926
WING VENTURE PARTNERS, 1996

Data Center
CISCO INVESTMENTS, 483
MK CAPITAL, 1242
QUALCOMM VENTURES, 1509
SPRING LAKE EQUITY PARTNERS, 1728

Industry Preference Index / Diagnostics

Data Communications
ALTA BERKELEY ASSOCIATES, 2380
BENAROYA COMPANIES, 247
COMCAST VENTURES, 518
DELTA VENTURES LIMITED, 2655
FORMULA VENTURES LIMITED Formula Group, 2750
FOUNDATION CAPITAL, 770
GE EQUITY EUROPE, 2769
GEMINI ISRAEL VENTURE FUNDS LIMITED, 2770
HARBOURVEST PARTNERS LLC, 909
IN-Q-TEL, 979
INDUSTRIEBANK LIOF NV, 2866
INSTITUTIONAL VENTURE PARTNERS, 1001
NEWBURY VENTURES, 1311
PROCURITAS PARTNERS KB, 3054
WINDWARD VENTURES, 1995

Data Infrastructure
DENALI VENTURE PARTNERS, 605

Data Management
GROUND UP VENTURES, 877
INITIATIVE CAPITAL LIMITED, 2154
MS&AD VENTURES, 1269

Data Mining
GVA CAPITAL, 890
QUANTUM WAVE FUND, 3068

Data Security
ACCESS VENTURE PARTNERS LLC, 36
HEALTH ENTERPRISE PARTNERS, 918
LUGE CAPITAL, 2179
SIGNIA VENTURE PARTNERS, 1678

Data Services
BLOOMBERG BETA, 284
EDGESTONE CAPITAL PARTNERS, 2103
EVERCORE CAPITAL PARTNERS, 699
FIDELITY GROWTH PARTNERS EUROPE, 2734
IN-Q-TEL, 979
MENLO VENTURES, 1202
TELUS VENTURES, 2265

Data Storage
ACCEL-KKR LLC, 29
ALMAZ CAPITAL, 89
AMD VENTURES, 106
ARTIS VENTURES, 175
AWEIDA VENTURE PARTNERS, 210
BOULDER VENTURES LTD, 315
BRIGHTSTONE VENTURE CAPITAL, 341
DATA COLLECTIVE, 585
DELL VENTURES, 603
DIVERGENT VENTURES, 618
FAIRHAVEN CAPITAL, 712
FOUNDATION CAPITAL, 770
MIRAMAR VENTURE PARTNERS, 1237
QUANTUM WAVE FUND, 3068
SIGMA PARTNERS, 1672
US VENTURE PARTNERS, 1896

Data Technology
BASE VENTURES, 229

Data-Defined Security
WORK-BENCH, 2006

Data-driven marketplaces
ALTPOINT CAPITAL, 101

Database Services
ASSET MANAGEMENT VENTURES, 181
CELERITY PARTNERS, 439
DOT EDU VENTURES, 623
EVERGREEN ADVISORS, 701
MVP CAPITAL PARTNERS, 1275

TEXADA CAPITAL CORPORATION, 1799

Debt Management
3I AUSTRIA BETEILGUNG GmbH 3i Group, 2298

Deep Learning
PATHBREAKER VENTURES, 1421

Deep Tech
CXO FUND, 574

Deep Technology
COMET LABS, 519

Defense
CM EQUITY PARTNERS, 507
CORNERSTONE CAPITAL HOLDINGS, 540

Defense & Aerospace
BEHRMAN CAPITAL, 245

Design
500 STARTUPS, 11
645 VENTURES, 13

Developer Platforms
BESSEMER VENTURE PARTNERS, 260

Developer Tools
WESTTECH VENTURES, 3236

Diagnostic & Drug Discovery Platforms
ARCH VENTURE PARTNERS, 153

Diagnostics
ALLOS VENTURES, 86
ASCLEPIOS BIORESEARCH, 2433
ATHYRIUM CAPITAL MANAGEMENT, 188
AVLAR BIOVENTURES, 2463
AZCA, 214
BAY CITY CAPITAL LLC, 237
BIOADVANCE, 266
BIOGENERATION VENTURES, 2514
BIOGENERATOR, 267
BIOMED PARTNERS, 2515
BIOVENTURES INVESTORS, 270
BLADE VENTURES, 278
BROADVIEW VENTURES, 347
CAPITAL FOR BUSINESS, INC, 399
CATALYST HEALTH VENTURES, 426
CENTRESTONE VENTURES, 2077
CHL MEDICAL PARTNERS, 474
DOMAIN ASSOCIATES LLC, 621
EASTON CAPITAL INVESTMENT GROUP, 644
ELM STREET VENTURES, 660
EXCEL VENTURE MANAGEMENT, 703
FIRST ANALYSIS, 732
FLARE CAPITAL PARTNERS, 748
FLETCHER SPAGHT VENTURES, 749
FORESITE CAPITAL, 762
HATTERAS VENTURE PARTNERS, 915
HBM PARTNERS, 2815
HEALTHQUEST CAPITAL, 921
HLM VENTURE PARTNERS, 938
HOPEN LIFE SCIENCE VENTURES, 943
IDEA FUND PARTNERS, 971
INETWORKS ADVISORS LLC, 987
INNOVA MEMPHIS, 995
JOHNSON & JOHNSON INNOVATION, 1043
KAISER PERMANENTE VENTURES, 1052
KB PARTNERS LLC, 1057
LANCET CAPITAL, 1092
LATTERELL VENTURE PARTNERS, 1094
LAUNCHPAD VENTURE GROUP, 1100
LINK TECHNOLOGIES LIMITED, 2941
LONG RIVER VENTURES, 1142
LONGITUDE CAPITAL, 1143

Industry Preference Index / Digital Business Services

MAINE ANGELS, 1160
MARYLAND VENTURE FUND, 1169
MEDIMMUNE VENTURES, 1196
MERCK GLOBAL HEALTH INNOVATION FUND, 1205
MESA VERDE PARTNERS, 1221
MOUNTAIN GROUP CAPITAL, 1261
MVM LIFE SCIENCE PARTNERS, 2981
NEW LEAF VENTURE PARTNERS, 1298
NOVARTIS VENTURE FUNDS, 1350
OKAPI VENTURE CAPITAL, 1371
ONSET VENTURES, 1378
PARTNERS HEALTHCARE RESEARCH VENTURES, 1419
PFIZER VENTURE INVESTMENTS, 1436
PITTSBURGH LIFE SCIENCES GREENHOUSE, 1448
PRISM VENTUREWORKS, 1478
PTV SCIENCES, 1500
PURETECH VENTURES, 1501
RA CAPITAL MANAGEMENT, 1519
ROBIN HOOD VENTURES, 1577
SAND HILL ANGELS, 1613
SCP PARTNERS, 1633
SHEPHERD VENTURES, 1664
SIGNAL PEAK VENTURES, 1677
SPINDLETOP CAPITAL, 1722
TEXO VENTURES, 1801
THE CHANNEL GROUP, 1808
THIRD ROCK VENTURES, 1811
THOMAS, MCNERNEY & PARTNERS, 1817
TWIN CITIES ANGELS, 1872
VALLEY VENTURES LP, 1901
VENROCK ASSOCIATES, 1916
WATER STREET HEALTHCARE PARTNERS, 1961
WELLINGTON PARTNERS VENTURE CAPITAL GmbH, 3233

Digital Business Services
SYNCOM VENTURE PARTNERS, 1771

Digital Cars
BMW I VENTURES, 302

Digital Commerce
SWAN & LEGEND VENTURES, 1766

Digital Content
PIQUE VENTURES, 2223

Digital Convergence
PATHENA, 3031

Digital Health
BREYER CAPITAL, 336
CANVAS VENTURES, 396
CROSSLINK CAPITAL, 563
GCI CAPITAL, 2128
HEALTHQUEST CAPITAL, 921
INNOGEST CAPITAL, 2874
QUALCOMM VENTURES, 1509
SAMSUNG NEXT, 1611
SV HEALTH INVESTORS, 1762
VILLAGE GLOBAL, 1933
WILDCAT VENTURE PARTNERS, 1985
WINDHAM VENTURE PARTNERS, 1993

Digital Health Technology
SEVEN PEAKS VENTURES, 1656

Digital Infrastructure
NEWLIGHT PARTNERS, 1315

Digital Learning
REACH CAPITAL, 1527

Digital Marketing
CROSSLINK CAPITAL, 563
KAEDAN INVESTMENTS, 2914
RUNTIDE CAPITAL, 1596

Digital Media
ACKRELL CAPITAL, 44
CAVA CAPITAL, 431
GOAL HOLDINGS, 2135
IA VENTURES, 965
IMAGINATION CAPITAL, 977
JUMPSTART INC, 1047
PLAZA VENTURES, 2224
RUNTIDE CAPITAL, 1596
SAFEGUARD SCIENTIFICS, 1601
SLOW VENTURES, 1694
VANEDGE CAPITAL PARTNERS, 2278

Digital Media & Marketing
.406 VENTURES, 2
212 CAPITAL PARTNERS, 2294
ABRY PARTNERS, 21
ACCESS VENTURE PARTNERS LLC, 36
ACME LABS, 2333
ADOBE VENTURES LP, 58
ALMAZ CAPITAL, 89
ANGEL STREET CAPITAL, 125
ANNAPURNA VENTURES, 2403
ANTRAK CAPITAL, 2407
APAX GLOBIS PARTNERS & COMPANY Globis Capital Partners/Apax, 2414
ARC ANGEL FUND, 150
ARKAFUND MEDIA & ICT, 2426
ASCENSION VENTURES, 2432
ASTUTIA VENTURES, 2441
AVISTA PARTNERS, 2461
AZIONE CAPITAL, 2473
AZURE CAPITAL PARTNERS, 215
BAF SPECTRUM, 2477
BARODA VENTURES, 228
BASELINE VENTURES, 231
BATTERY VENTURES, 235
BC RENAISSANCE CAPITAL FUND, 2053
BERTELSMANN DIGITAL MEDIA INVESTMENTS, 256
BI WALDEN MANAGEMENT SDN Walden International, 2508
BIG SUR VENTURES, 2510
BLUERUN VENTURES, 296
BLUMBERG CAPITAL, 301
BRIDGESCALE PARTNERS, 339
BRIGHTSTONE VENTURE CAPITAL, 341
BURAN VENTURE CAPITAL, 2549
CAMPUS COMPANIES VENTURE CAPITAL FUND, 2554
CARDINAL VENTURE CAPITAL, 411
CATALYST INVESTORS, 427
CINCYTECH, 479
COLOMA VENTURES, 512
COMMONWEALTH CAPITAL VENTURES LP, 521
COMPOUND, 525
CONNECT VENTURES, 2629
CONSTELLATION TECHNOLOGY VENTURES, 532
CONTOUR VENTURE PARTNERS, 533
CONVERGE VENTURE PARTNERS, 534
CORE CAPITAL PARTNERS, 538
CUE BALL GROUP, 567
DACE VENTURES, 580
DAWNTREADER VENTURES, 592
DEEP FORK CAPITAL, 600
DETROIT VENTURE PARTNERS, 607
DFJ GOTHAM VENTURES, 608
DN CAPITAL, 2668
E.BRICKS DIGITAL, 2681
EASTLABS, 2684
EDEN VENTURES, 2691
ELEVATION PARTNERS, 659
EMERGENCE CAPITAL PARTNERS, 665
ESPRESSO CAPITAL, 2109
EVERGREEN ADVISORS, 701
FAIRHAVEN CAPITAL, 712
FIRESTARTER FUND, 731
FORTÉ VENTURES, 768
FUSE CAPITAL, 798
GENACAST VENTURES, 814

Industry Preference Index / Distributed Electricity

GENESIS PARTNERS, 2775
GENWEALTH VENTURES, 2131
GEORGIAN PARTNERS, 2132
GGV CAPITAL, 823
GLYNN CAPITAL MANAGEMENT, 836
GREYCROFT PARTNERS, 871
GROTECH VENTURES, 876
GUGGENHEIM PARTNERS, 885
HARBOUR GROUP, 908
HELLMAN & FRIEDMAN LLC, 924
HIGHLAND CAPITAL PARTNERS, 935
HORIZONS VENTURES, 2831
HUMMINGBIRD VENTURES, 2837
ICON VENTURES, 968
IDEALAB, 972
IGLOBE PARTNERS, 2853
INSTITUTIONAL VENTURE PARTNERS, 1001
INTEL CAPITAL, 1004
INTERSOUTH PARTNERS, 1008
INVENTUS, 1013
JAVELIN VENTURE PARTNERS, 1028
KAEDAN INVESTMENTS, 2914
KARLIN VENTURES, 1055
KIBO VENTURES, 2920
KODIAK VENTURE PARTNERS, 1080
KOHLBERG VENTURES, 1083
KTB VENTURES, 1087
LABRADOR VENTURES, 1089
LANTA DIGITAL VENTURES, 2930
LONGWORTH VENTURE PARTNERS, 1146
LOOL VENTURES, 2947
MADRONA VENTURE GROUP, 1158
MASS VENTURES, 1172
MERCURY FUND, 1206
MERITECH CAPITAL PARTNERS, 1212
MESA GLOBAL, 1220
MESA+, 1222
MHS CAPITAL, 1226
MIDVEN, 2967
MILLENIUM TECHNOLOGY VALUE PARTNERS, 1235
MK CAPITAL, 1242
MMC VENTURES, 2972
MOTOROLA SOLUTIONS VENTURE CAPITAL, 1260
NEO TECHNOLOGY VENTURES, 2989
NEST VENTURES, 1290
NORO-MOSELEY PARTNERS, 1331
NORTH BRIDGE VENTURE PARTNERS, 1334
NORTHSTAR VENTURES, 3012
NORTHZONE, 3013
ONTARIO CAPITAL GROWTH CORPORATION, 2211
OPENVIEW VENTURE PARTNERS, 1380
PARTECH INTERNATIONAL, 1416
PASSION CAPITAL, 3030
PELION VENTURE PARTNERS, 1425
PENTECH VENTURES, 3032
PINNACLE MERCHANT CAPITAL, 2222
PIQUE VENTURES, 2223
POLARIS VENTURE PARTNERS, 1460
POLYTECH VENTURES, 3045
PRIME TECHNOLOGY VENTURES NV, 3051
PRINCIPIA SGR, 3052
PRISM VENTUREWORKS, 1478
PROFOUNDERS CAPITAL, 3055
PROVENANCE VENTURES, 1495
QUOTIDIAN VENTURES, 1518
RAPTOR GROUP, 1524
REAL VENTURES, 2232
RED DOT VENTURES, 3073
RELAY VENTURES, 2236
REVEL PARTNERS, 1554
SAMOS INVESTMENTS, 3097
SCOTTISH EQUITY PARTNERS, 3104
SELBY VENTURE PARTNERS, 1646
SINGTEL INNOV8, 3121
SK TELECOM VENTURES, 1690
SOCIAL VENTURE CIRCLE, 3277
SOFTBANK CAPITAL, 1699
SOLID VENTURES, 3128
SOUTHERN CAPITOL VENTURES, 1710
SOUTHERN CROSS VENTURE PARTNERS, 1711
SPECTRUM EQUITY INVESTORS LP, 1717
SPRING LAKE EQUITY PARTNERS, 1728
STEAMBOAT VENTURES, 3142
SUMMERHILL VENTURE PARTNERS, 2259
SUNBRIDGE PARTNERS, 1755
SUPREMUM CAPITAL, 3150
TALIS CAPITAL, 3157
TELEFONICA VENTURES, 3169
TELESYSTEM, 2264
TELUS VENTURES, 2265
TENNESSEE COMMUNITY VENTURES, 1797
THINKTIV VENTURES, 1810
TRANSMEDIA CAPITAL, 1839
TRIBECA VENTURE PARTNERS, 1849
TRIDENT CAPITAL, 1850
TRUE VENTURES, 1860
UPFRONT VENTURES, 1888
VALHALLA PARTNERS, 1899
VANTAGEPOINT CAPITAL PARTNERS, 1906
VENTANA CAPITAL MANAGEMENT LP, 1918
VENTECH, 3208
VERTEX VENTURE CAPITAL, 3214
VOYAGER CAPITAL, 1945
VTB CAPITAL, 3229
WALDEN INTERNATIONAL, 1951
WALDEN VENTURE CAPITAL, 1952
WELLINGTON PARTNERS VENTURE CAPITAL GmbH, 3233
WESLEY CLOVER, 2284
WI HARPER GROUP, 1983
WOMEN'S VENTURE CAPITAL FUND, 2003
WORLDVIEW TECHNOLOGY PARTNERS, 2007
XG VENTURES, 2010

Digital Media Delivery
AMITI VENTURES, 116

Digital Networks
ENERTECH CAPITAL, 676

Digital Rights Management
LIQUID CAPITAL GROUP, 1133
SONY STRATEGIC TECHNOLOGY PARTNERSHIPS, 1704

Digital Security
LIQUID CAPITAL GROUP, 1133

Digital Services
FLYWHEEL VENTURES, 756

Digital Technology
DISRUPTION VENTURES, 2098

Digital Transformation
IGNITION PARTNERS, 974

Direct Marketing
AUDAX GROUP, 194
BREGAL SAGEMOUNT, 333
BRENTWOOD ASSOCIATES, 334
ENTREPRENEUR PARTNERS, 683
FREEMAN SPOGLI & CO., 783
LINSALATA CAPITAL PARTNERS, 1132
STERLING PARTNERS, 1742
TEXADA CAPITAL CORPORATION, 1799
UNION CAPITAL CORPORATION, 1881
VENTURE CAPITAL FUND OF NEW ENGLAND, 1920
XANGE PRIVATE EQUITY, 3239
ZM CAPITAL, 2020

Display Technologies
SONY STRATEGIC TECHNOLOGY PARTNERSHIPS, 1704

Distributed Electricity
VENROCK ASSOCIATES, 1916

Industry Preference Index / Distribution

Distribution

3I TEUPSCHLAND GmbH 3i Group, 2305
AAVIN PRIVATE EQUITY, 17
ACCESS CAPITAL, 35
ACTIVA CAPITAL, 2338
AEA INVESTORS, 64
AGRIBUSINESS MANAGEMENT COMPANY, 71
ALEUTIAN CAPITAL PARTNERS, 81
ALLSTATE INVESTMENTS LLC, 88
ALTIRA GROUP LLC, 98
AMERIMARK CAPITAL CORPORATION, 111
APOLLO GLOBAL MANAGEMENT, 140
ARGOSY CAPITAL, 164
ARTHUR P GOULD & COMPANY, 172
ASTOR CAPITAL GROUP, 2440
AUDAX GROUP, 194
AUGUST CAPITAL, 197
AURORA CAPITAL GROUP, 199
AZALEA CAPITAL, 213
BARING PRIVATE EQUITY PARTNERS INDIA, 2490
BBH CAPITAL PARTNERS, 240
BERKELEY VC INTERNATIONAL LLC, 252
BISON CAPITAL ASSET MANAGEMENT LLC, 274
BLACKFORD CAPITAL LLC, 276
BLUE POINT CAPITAL PARTNERS, 290
BLUE SAGE CAPITAL, 291
BLUEGEM CAPITAL PARTNERS, 2524
BOND CAPITAL, 2064
BOUNDS EQUITY PARTNERS, 316
BRADFORD EQUITIES MANAGEMENT LLC, 321
BRANDON CAPITAL GROUP, 326
BRANFORD CASTLE, 327
BRAZOS PRIVATE EQUITY PARTNERS, 328
BRENTWOOD ASSOCIATES, 334
BRIDGE STREET CAPITAL, 338
BROOKSIDE EQUITY PARTNERS LLC, 353
BRUML CAPITAL CORPORATION, 355
BUTLER CAPITAL PARTNERS FRANCE, 2551
C3 CAPITAL PARTNERS LP, 364
CAMBRIDGE CAPITAL, 380
CAMBRIDGE CAPITAL CORPORATION, 381
CAPITAL FOR BUSINESS, INC, 399
CAPITAL PARTNERS, 401
CARDINAL EQUITY PARTNERS, 409
CARPEDIA CAPITAL, 2072
CASTLE HARLAN, 423
CATALYST GROUP, 425
CATALYST INVESTMENT MANAGERS PTY LIMITED PPM Capital, 2573
CENTERFIELD CAPITAL PARTNERS, 443
CERBERUS CAPITAL MANAGEMENT, 451
CHARLESBANK CAPITAL PARTNERS, 456
CHB CAPITAL PARTNERS, 461
CI CAPITAL PARTNERS, 476
CID CAPITAL, 478
CLEARLIGHT PARTNERS, 501
COMPAGNIE FINANCIERE E DE ROTHSCHILD BANQUE, 2625
COMPASS GROUP MANAGEMENT LLC, 523
COMSTOCK CAPITAL PARTNERS LLC, 527
CORTEC GROUP, 546
COVINGTON CAPITAL CORP., 2087
CRYSTAL RIDGE PARTNERS, 565
CUSTER CAPITAL, 571
CYPRIUM PARTNERS, 577
DAHER CAPITAL, 2649
DEFI GESTION SA Banque Cantonale Vaudoise, 2653
DESCO CAPITAL, 606
DN PARTNERS LLC, 619
DRESNER COMPANIES, 629
EAST FUND MANAGEMENT GmbH GiroCredit, 2683
ECI VENTURES, 2687
EDGEWATER CAPITAL PARTNERS, 653
ELGNER GROUP INVESTMENTS, 2104
EMIGRANT CAPITAL, 667
EMIL CAPITAL PARTNERS, 668
EMINENT CAPITAL PARTNERS, 669
EQUITY SOUTH, 693
EQUUS TOTAL RETURN, 694
FAIRMONT CAPITAL, 713
FCF PARTNERS LP, 719
FENWAY PARTNERS, 722
FIRST CAPITAL GROUP, 734
FIRST NEW ENGLAND CAPITAL LP, 739
FLORIDA CAPITAL PARTNERS, 752
FREEMAN SPOGLI & CO., 783
FRIEND SKOLER & COMPANY LLC, 788
FRIULIA SpA, 2758
FdG ASSOCIATES LP, 801
GEMINI INVESTORS, 812
GLADSTONE CAPITAL, 828
GOLDNER, HAWN, JOHNSON & MORRISON, 843
GOLUB CAPITAL, 844
GRANITE EQUITY PARTNERS, 850
GRANTHAM CAPITAL, 853
GRAPHITE CAPITAL MANAGEMENT LTD, 2796
GREENBRIAR EQUITY GROUP LLC, 862
GRUPO BISA, 2800
GTCR, 884
HALIFAX GROUP LLC, 894
HAMILTON ROBINSON CAPITAL PARTNERS, 899
HAMMOND, KENNEDY, WHITNEY & COMPANY, 900
HARBOUR GROUP, 908
HARREN EQUITY PARTNERS, 910
HARVEST PARTNERS, 914
HCI EQUITY PARTNERS, 917
HERITAGE PARTNERS, 926
HIG CAPITAL, 928
HIGH ROAD CAPITAL PARTNERS, 931
HIGH STREET CAPITAL, 932
HOLDING CAPITAL GROUP, 940
HORIZON PARTNERS, LTD, 945
HUMANA VENTURES, 955
INDASIA FUND ADVISORS PVT LTD, 2859
INDEPENDENT BANKERS CAPITAL FUND, 984
INDUSTRI KAPITAL SVENSKA AB, 2863
INTER-ASIA VENTURE MANAGEMENT LIMITED, 2881
INVESTAMERICA VENTURE GROUP, 1016
INVEXCEL PATRIMONIO, 2891
IRONBRIDGE EQUITY PARTNERS, 2163
IRONWOOD CAPITAL, 1021
JAFCO COMPANY LIMITED JAPAN, 2906
JEFFERIES CAPITAL PARTNERS, 1032
KERRY CAPITAL ADVISORS, 1067
KOHLBERG VENTURES, 1083
LEE EQUITY PARTNERS, 1104
LEONARD GREEN & PARTNERS LP, 1109
LINCOLNSHIRE MANAGEMENT, 1127
LINSALATA CAPITAL PARTNERS, 1132
LITTLEJOHN & COMPANY LLC, 1134
LM CAPITAL SECURITIES, 1137
LOMBARD INVESTMENTS, 1139
LONG POINT CAPITAL, 1141
LYNWOOD CAPITAL PARTNERS, 1152
MAIN STREET CAPITAL HOLDINGS LLC, 1159
MARANON CAPITAL, 1166
MARWIT CAPITAL LLC, 1168
MEKONG CAPITAL, 2961
MENTOR CAPITAL PARTNERS LTD, 1203
MERIT CAPITAL PARTNERS, 1209
MERITURN PARTNERS, 1213
MERIWETHER CAPITAL CORPORATION, 1215
MERRILL LYNCH (ASIA PACIFIC) LIMITED Merrill Lynch Group, 2964
MHS CAPITAL, 1226
MIDMARK CAPITAL LP, 1230
MIDWEST MEZZANINE FUNDS, 1232
MILESTONE PARTNERS, 1234
MONUMENT ADVISORS, 1252
MSOUTH EQUITY PARTNERS, 1270
MVP CAPITAL PARTNERS, 1275
NAVIGATION CAPITAL PARTNERS, 1280
NEW ENGLAND CAPITAL PARTNERS, 1296
NORTH AMERICAN FUND, 1332
NORTH BRIDGE VENTURE PARTNERS, 1334
NORTHSTAR CAPITAL, 1343

Industry Preference Index / Drug Development

NORWEST EQUITY PARTNERS, 1345
NTH POWER TECHNOLOGIES, 1355
OAK HILL CAPITAL PARTNERS, 1360
ODEON CAPITAL PARTNERS, 1367
PAI MANAGEMENT, 3026
PALOMINO CAPITAL, 1408
PAMLICO CAPITAL, 1409
PARALLEL49 EQUITY, 2214
PARTHENON CAPITAL, 1417
PEGASUS CAPITAL GROUP, 1424
PENINSULA CAPITAL PARTNERS LLC, 1426
PENN VENTURE PARTNERS, 1428
PERMAL CAPITAL MANAGEMENT, 1432
PFINGSTEN PARTNERS LLC, 1435
PNC ERIEVIEW CAPITAL, 1456
PNC RIVERARCH CAPITAL, 1457
PRIVEQ CAPITAL FUNDS, 2226
PROVCO GROUP, 1494
PT BHAKTI INVESTAMA TBK, 3061
QUAD-C MANAGEMENT, 1505
QUARRY CAPITAL MANAGEMENT, 1511
RESILIENCE CAPITAL PARTNERS, 1545
RFE INVESTMENT PARTNERS, 1557
RIDGE CAPITAL PARTNERS LLC, 1562
RIVER ASSOCIATES INVESTMENTS LLC, 1569
RIVER CAPITAL, 1570
ROCK ISLAND CAPITAL, 1578
SALEM INVESTMENT PARTNERS, 1606
SALT CREEK CAPITAL, 1609
SARATOGA PARTNERS, 1621
SEACOAST CAPITAL CORPORATION, 1636
SEAFORT CAPITAL, 2251
SEIDLER EQUITY PARTNERS, 1645
SENTRY FINANCIAL CORPORATION, 1652
SORRENTO VENTURES, 1706
SOURCE CAPITAL GROUP, 1707
STARBOARD CAPITAL PARTNERS, 1735
STATELINE ANGELS, 1740
STERLING PARTNERS, 1742
STERN PARTNERS, 2258
STONEHENGE GROWTH CAPITAL, 1745
STONEWOOD CAPITAL MANAGEMENT, 1746
SUN CAPITAL PARTNERS, 1753
SVOBODA CAPITAL PARTNERS, 1765
TEKINVEST KK, 3166
TGF MANAGEMENT, 1803
TH LEE PUTNAM VENTURES, 1804
THREE CITIES RESEARCH, 1820
TRIWEST, 2275
TSG CONSUMER PARTNERS, 1861
TULLY & HOLLAND, 1867
TVV CAPITAL, 1870
UNION CAPITAL CORPORATION, 1881
UPFRONT VENTURES, 1888
VEBER PARTNERS LLC, 1909
VISION CAPITAL, 1937
WAND PARTNERS, 1955
WARWICK GROUP, 1957
WATERMILL GROUP, 1962
WAUD CAPITAL PARTNERS LLC, 1963
WAVELAND INVESTMENTS LLC, 1964
WELLS FARGO CAPITAL FINANCE, 1970
WELLSPRING CAPITAL MANAGEMENT LLC, 1971
WESTERN AMERICA CAPITAL GROUP, 2286
WESTLAKE SECURITIES, 1976
WESTVIEW CAPITAL PARTNERS, 1979
WINGATE PARTNERS, 1997
WOODBRIDGE GROUP, 2004
WYNNCHURCH CAPITAL, 2009
ZS FUND LP, 2022

Distribution & Logistics
CVF CAPITAL PARTNERS, 573
FULCRUM CAPITAL PARTNERS, 2126

Distribution Services
RED CLAY CAPITAL HOLDINGS, 1529

Diversified
3I SPAIN 3i Group, 2304
ABU DHABI INVESTMENT AUTHORITY, 2321
ACCENT EQUITY PARTNERS, 2325
ADVENT-MORRO EQUITY PARTNERS, 63
AFC MERCHANT BANK, 2351
ALLSTATE INVESTMENTS LLC, 88
ANDLINGER & COMPANY INC, 123
ANTHEM VENTURE PARTNERS, 132
ARMADA INVESTMENT GROUP, 2427
ATLANTIC CAPITAL GROUP, 190
AVENUE CAPITAL GROUP, 208
BANYAN CAPITAL PARTNERS, 2051
BAYSIDE CAPITAL, 239
BROADLINE PRINCIPAL CAPITAL, 2542
BUSINESS CONSORTIUM FUND, 360
C&G CAPITAL PARTNERS, 363
CAMBRIDGE ASSOCIATES, 379
CAMBRIDGE VENTURES LP, 382
CENTRE LANE PARTNERS, 446
CHATTANOOGA RENAISSANCE FUND, 459
COBALT CAPITAL, 2084
COMPASS GROUP MANAGEMENT LLC, 523
DAVID N DEUTSCH & COMPANY LLC, 589
ENGAGE VENTURES, 677
FORT WASHINGTON CAPITAL PARTNERS GROUP, 766
GELT VC, 811
HONE CAPITAL, 942
INVESTCORP, 1017
KANSAS VENTURE CAPITAL, 1053
KENMONT CAPITAL PARTNERS, 1063
MCGOWAN CAPITAL GROUP, 1192
MCKELLAR & COMPANY, 1193
NAVIGATOR PARTNERS LLC, 1281
PORTLAND SEED FUND, 1463
PPM AMERICA CAPITAL PARTNERS, 1467
RELATIVITY CAPITAL, 1539
RIVER CITIES CAPITAL FUNDS, 1571
SACHS CAPITAL, 1599
SAUGATUCK CAPITAL COMPANY, 1624
SHARESPOST, 1662
SIGULER GUFF & COMPANY, 1679
START GARDEN, 1736
SUN MOUNTAIN CAPITAL, 1754
TRIVE CAPITAL, 1856
UNSHACKLED VENTURES, 1885
WILLOWRIDGE PARTNERS, 1987
ZEPHYR MANAGEMENT LP, 2018

Downstream Technologies
NEWABLE VENTURES, 2997

Drones & 3D
FRONTIER VENTURES, 792

Drug Delivery
ARCUS VENTURES, 157
MVM LIFE SCIENCE PARTNERS, 2981
NOVARTIS VENTURE FUNDS, 1350
ONSET VENTURES, 1378
PARTISAN MANAGEMENT GROUP, 1418
PFIZER VENTURE INVESTMENTS, 1436
SIGNAL PEAK VENTURES, 1677
STARPHARMA POOLED DEVELOPMENT LIMITED, 3139

Drug Delivery Technology
5AM VENTURES, 12

Drug Development
AMHERST FUND, 113
APPLE TREE PARTNERS, 143
ATLAS VENTURE: FRANCE, 2445
BIRCHMERE VENTURES, 272
BRANDON CAPITAL PARTNERS, 2536
CHL MEDICAL PARTNERS, 474
DRI CAPITAL, 2102
EcoR1 CAPITAL, 709

Industry Preference Index / Drug Discovery

HAMILTON BIOVENTURES, 898
INTEGRA VENTURES, 1002
JOHNSTON ASSOCIATES, 1044
KBL HEALTHCARE VENTURES, 1058
MBF CAPITAL CORPORATION, 1188
MESA VERDE PARTNERS, 1221
ORBIMED HEALTHCARE FUND MANAGEMENT, 1382
PAPPAS VENTURES, 1412
RA CAPITAL MANAGEMENT, 1519
STONEWOOD CAPITAL MANAGEMENT, 1746
US VENTURE PARTNERS, 1896

Drug Discovery
ECHELON VENTURES, 647

e-Commerce
ALPHA VENTURE PARTNERS, 91
AMPLIFY, 120
BERTELSMANN DIGITAL MEDIA INVESTMENTS, 256
BLUE POINT CAPITAL PARTNERS, 290
ENTREPRENEURS ROUNDTABLE ACCELERATOR, 684
RUNTIDE CAPITAL, 1596
SIGNIA VENTURE PARTNERS, 1678
ZHENFUND, 3251

E-Commerce & Manufacturing
360 CAPITAL PARTNERS 360 Capital Management SA, 2296
ACCESS VENTURE PARTNERS LLC, 36
ACTUA, 53
ACUMEN VENTURES, 2341
ADASTRA, 2343
ALBUM VC, 79
ALMAZ CAPITAL, 89
AMADEUS CAPITAL PARTNERS LIMITED, 2386
ANGELS' FORUM LLC, 129
ANNAPURNA VENTURES, 2403
ARCHTOP VENTURES, 154
ASLANOBA CAPITAL, 2437
ATILA VENTURES, 2442
AUGMENTUM CAPITAL, 2450
AUTHOSIS VENTURES, 2457
AZURE CAPITAL PARTNERS, 215
BAIRD CAPITAL PARTNERS, 222
BALDERTON CAPITAL, 2478
BARODA VENTURES, 228
BLACKBIRD VENTURES, 2520
BLH VENTURE PARTNERS, 282
BOXGROUP, 318
BRAINSTORM VENTURES, 324
BREAKAWAY VENTURES, 329
BULL VENTURES, 2547
BURAN VENTURE CAPITAL, 2549
CALUMET VENTURE FUND, 375
CATALYST INVESTORS, 427
CAVA CAPITAL, 431
CHARLES RIVER VENTURES, 455
CHARLES RIVER VENTURES, 455
CHICAGO VENTURE PARTNERS LP, 470
CLEARSTONE VENTURE PARTNERS, 502
COMCAST VENTURES, 518
COMPAGNIE FINANCIERE E DE ROTHSCHILD BANQUE, 2625
COMPOUND, 525
DATA POINT CAPITAL, 586
DEEP FORK CAPITAL, 600
DETROIT VENTURE PARTNERS, 607
DFJ GOTHAM VENTURES, 608
DN CAPITAL, 2668
DUBILIER & COMPANY, 631
DUNDEE VENTURE CAPITAL, 635
E.BRICKS DIGITAL, 2681
ECOAST ANGEL NETWORK, 649
EDEN VENTURES, 2691
EDISON PARTNERS, 655
EMIL CAPITAL PARTNERS, 668
EPLANET CAPITAL, 690
EXPANSION VENTURE CAPITAL, 707
FELICIS VENTURES, 720

FIRESTARTER FUND, 731
FIVE ELMS CAPITAL, 745
FORTÉ VENTURES, 768
FOUNDER COLLECTIVE, 771
FRIEND SKOLER & COMPANY LLC, 788
FUNG CAPITAL USA, 796
GENACAST VENTURES, 814
GOLDEN SEEDS, 841
GREAT OAKS VENTURE CAPITAL, 858
GREE VENTURES, 2798
GREYCROFT PARTNERS, 871
HENQ, 2822
IDEALAB, 972
IDG CAPITAL, 973
INFLECTION POINT VENTURES, 989
INLAND TECHSTART FUND, 993
INSIGHT VENTURE PARTNERS, 1000
INVENTURE PARTNERS, 2886
INVENTUS, 1013
INVESCO PRIVATE CAPITAL, 1015
JMI EQUITY FUND LP, 1041
KIBO VENTURES, 2920
LAUNCHPAD VENTURE GROUP, 1100
LEASING TECHNOLOGIES INTERNATIONAL INC., 1103
LIGHTSPEED VENTURE PARTNERS, 1121
LIQUID CAPITAL GROUP, 1133
M25 GROUP, 1155
MAYFIELD FUND, 1184
MESA+, 1222
MHS CAPITAL, 1226
MISSION VENTURES, 1239
MMC VENTURES, 2972
MORADO VENTURE PARTNERS, 1254
MURPHREE VENTURE PARTNERS, 1273
NAUTA CAPITAL, 2987
NEW ATLANTIC VENTURES, 1291
NEWLIGHT MANAGEMENT, 1314
NORTHZONE, 3013
OAK INVESTMENT PARTNERS, 1361
PALO ALTO VENTURE SCIENCE, 1406
PAMLICO CAPITAL, 1409
PARTECH INTERNATIONAL, 1416
PENTECH VENTURES, 3032
PINEHURST ADVISORS, 3038
PITON CAPITAL, 3040
POINT NINE CAPITAL, 3044
PRIMARY VENTURE PARTNERS, 1475
PRIME TECHNOLOGY VENTURES NV, 3051
PRINCIPIA SGR, 3052
QUESTMARK PARTNERS LP, 1515
QUOTIDIAN VENTURES, 1518
RAPTOR GROUP, 1524
REVO CAPITAL, 3078
REVOLUTION LLC, 1555
ROUGH DRAFT VENTURES, 1589
RTP VENTURES, 1594
RU-NET VENTURES, 3087
SAMOS INVESTMENTS, 3097
SATORI CAPITAL, 1622
SATURN PARTNERS, 1623
SHANGHAI INFORMATION INVESTMENT INCORPORATED, 3114
SHASTA VENTURES, 1663
SILICON ALLEY VENTURE PARTNERS, 1680
SOFTBANK CAPITAL, 1699
SORRENTO VENTURES, 1706
SOUTHERN CAPITOL VENTURES, 1710
SRIJAN CAPITAL, 3133
STARBOARD CAPITAL PARTNERS, 1735
STRAND HANSON LIMITED, 3146
SUSQUEHANNA GROWTH EQUITY, 1759
SV ANGEL, 1761
SYCAMORE VENTURES, 1769
TANK STREAM VENTURES, 3160
TARGET PARTNERS, 3161
TENGELMANN VENTURES, 3170
TENNESSEE COMMUNITY VENTURES, 1797
TEXADA CAPITAL CORPORATION, 1799

Industry Preference Index / Education

THINKTIV VENTURES, 1810
TMI, 3181
TRIBECA VENTURE PARTNERS, 1849
TRINITY VENTURES, 1853
TRUE VENTURES, 1860
USHA MARTIN VENTURES LIMITED, 3202
VEDANTA CAPITAL LP, 1911
VENTURE CAPITAL FUND OF NEW ENGLAND, 1920
VERSION ONE VENTURES, 2280
VTB CAPITAL, 3229
WALDEN ISRAEL VENTURE CAPITAL, 3231
WASABI VENTURES, 1958
WESTERN STATES INVESTMENT GROUP, 1974
WHITE STAR CAPITAL, 1982
WI HARPER GROUP, 1983
YL VENTURES, 3246

e-Mobility
BMW I VENTURES, 302

e-Sports
FIRST CAPITAL VENTURE, 735
MCGOVERN CAPITAL, 1191

Earth Sciences
HMS HAWAII MANAGEMENT, 939

Eco-Energies
DEMETER PARTNERS, 2656

Eco-Industries
DEMETER PARTNERS, 2656

Ecommerce
DUTCHESS CAPITAL, 638

Economics
NCT VENTURES, 1286

Education
AAVISHKAAR, 2313
ABRY PARTNERS, 21
ABS CAPITAL PARTNERS, 22
ACCRETIVE LLC, 39
ACUMEN, 55
ALLSTATE INVESTMENTS LLC, 88
ALPHAMUNDI GROUP LTD, 2376
ANTHEM VENTURE PARTNERS, 132
APPIAN EDUCATION VENTURES, 141
ARCHTOP VENTURES, 154
ARLINGTON CAPITAL PARTNERS, 166
ASTELLA INVESTMENTS, 2438
AUDAX GROUP, 194
AUSTRALIAN ETHICAL INVESTMENT LIMITED, 2456
AZURE CAPITAL PARTNERS, 215
BARCLAYS VENTURES Barclays, 2486
BARING PRIVATE EQUITY PARTNERS INDIA, 2490
BEZOS EXPEDITIONS, 262
BIA DIGITAL PARTNERS LP, 263
BIG SOCIETY CAPITAL, 2509
BIGFOOT VENTURES, 2511
BONVENTURE, 2531
BREGAL SAGEMOUNT, 333
BRENTWOOD ASSOCIATES, 334
BRIGHTPATH CAPITAL PARTNERS, 340
CALUMET VENTURE FUND, 375
CALVERT INVESTMENT MANAGEMENT, 376
CAMBRIA GROUP, 378
CAMDEN PARTNERS HOLDINGS LLC, 383
CAMPUS COMPANIES VENTURE CAPITAL FUND, 2554
CAPITAL FOR BUSINESS, INC, 399
CAPITAL PARTNERS, 401
CARBON VENTURES, 408
CASTANEA PARTNERS, 421
CATALYST INVESTMENT MANAGERS PTY LIMITED PPM Capital, 2573
CATALYST INVESTORS, 427

CDH INVESTMENTS, 2579
CENTERFIELD CAPITAL PARTNERS, 443
CHARLESBANK CAPITAL PARTNERS, 456
CHENGWEI VENTURES, 2590
CHICAGO GROWTH PARTNERS, 468
CID CAPITAL, 478
CITY LIGHT CAPITAL, 488
CIVC PARTNERS, 489
CLEARLIGHT PARTNERS, 501
COMMONS CAPITAL, 520
COMVEST PARTNERS, 528
DAY ONE VENTURES, 593
DECIENS CAPITAL, 599
DIRECT CAPITAL PRIVATE EQUITY LIMITED, 2664
EM WARBURG, PINCUS & COMPANY INTERNATIONAL, 2697
EM WARBURG, PINCUS & COMPANY JAPAN, 2698
EMIGRANT CAPITAL, 667
ENDEAVOUR CAPITAL, 673
ENNOVENT, 2701
EPIC PARTNERS, 687
EXPANSION VENTURE CAPITAL, 707
FELICIS VENTURES, 720
FIDELITY GROWTH PARTNERS ASIA, 2733
FIRSTMARK CAPITAL, 743
FRIEDMAN, FLEISCHER & LOWE LLC, 787
GEMINI INVESTORS, 812
GREAT OAKS VENTURE CAPITAL, 858
GRYPHON INVESTORS, 881
GSV VENTURES, 883
HELION VENTURE PARTNERS, LLC International Management (Mauritius) Ltd, 2818
HENDERSON PRIVATE CAPITAL, 2821
HERITAGE PARTNERS, 926
HIG CAPITAL, 928
HOULIHAN LOKEY, 948
IBM VENTURE CAPITAL GROUP, 967
IDG CAPITAL PARTNERS, 2847
INNOVATION PLATFORM CAPITAL, 997
INSIGHT VENTURE PARTNERS, 1000
INTERNATIONAL FINANCE CORPORATION (IFC), 1007
INVENTUS, 1013
IRONWOOD CAPITAL, 1021
ISIS EP LLP F & C, 2898
IXORA VENTURES, 2904
J. BURKE CAPITAL PARTNERS, 1023
JEFFERIES CAPITAL PARTNERS, 1032
JLL PARTNERS, 1039
JORDAN COMPANY, 1045
KAPOR CAPITAL, 1054
KARLIN VENTURES, 1055
KHOSLA VENTURES, 1069
KOHLBERG KRAVIS ROBERTS & COMPANY, 1082
LAUNCHPAD VENTURES, 2931
LEASING TECHNOLOGIES INTERNATIONAL INC., 1103
LEEDS EQUITY PARTNERS, 1105
LIBERTY PARTNERS, 1116
LLR PARTNERS INC, 1136
LOMBARD INVESTMENTS, 1139
M25 GROUP, 1155
MAYFIELD FUND, 1184
MCG CAPITAL CORPORATION, 1189
MHS CAPITAL, 1226
MIDINVEST LIMITED, 2966
MIDWEST MEZZANINE FUNDS, 1232
MURPHY & PARTNERS FUND LP, 1274
NEW MARKETS VENTURE PARTNERS, 1299
NEW MOUNTAIN CAPITAL, 1301
NEWSCHOOLS VENTURE FUND, 1316
NORTH AMERICAN FUND, 1332
NORTHSTAR CAPITAL, 1343
NOVAK BIDDLE VENTURE PARTNERS, 1348
OBVIOUS VENTURES, 1363
OCA VENTURES, 1364
OWL VENTURES, 1392
PARALLEL INVESTMENT PARTNERS, 1415
PARALLEL49 EQUITY, 2214
PARKVIEW CAPITAL PARTNERS, 2215

1169

Industry Preference Index / Education Technology

PEACHTREE EQUITY PARTNERS, 1423
PENN VENTURE PARTNERS, 1428
PHOENIX EQUITY PARTNERS LIMITED, 3036
PLUS VENTURES, 3041
POLESTAR CAPITAL, 1461
POUSCHINE COOK CAPITAL MANAGEMENT LLC, 1466
PRAIRIE CAPITAL, 1469
PREVIZ VENTURES, 3050
PRIMUS CAPITAL, 1476
PROCURITAS PARTNERS KB, 3054
PROSPECT PARTNERS LLC, 1492
QUAD PARTNERS, 1504
QUESTER CAPITAL MANAGEMENT LIMITED, 3070
REACH CAPITAL, 1527
RETHINK COMMUNITY, 1550
RETHINK EDUCATION, 1551
REVOLUTION LLC, 1555
RIVERSIDE COMPANY, 1572
SAIF PARTNERS, 3093
SALMON RIVER CAPITAL, 1608
SARONA ASSET MANAGEMENT, 2248
SCHOONER CAPITAL LLC, 1627
SCOTTISH ENTERPRISE, 3103
SEIDLER EQUITY PARTNERS, 1645
SINEWAVE VENTURES, 1687
SOCIAL CAPITAL, 1696
SOCIAL VENTURE CIRCLE, 3277
SOFTBANK VENTURES KOREA, 3127
SOLSTICE CAPITAL LP, 1702
SOUTHPORT PARTNERS, 1712
SOVEREIGN CAPITAL, 3130
SPIRE CAPITAL PARTNERS, 1724
STERLING PARTNERS, 1742
SUMMER STREET CAPITAL PARTNERS, 1751
SUMMIT PARTNERS, 1752
SUTTER HILL VENTURES, 1760
THE ABRAAJ GROUP, 3173
THOMA BRAVO LLC, 1814
TIE ANGELS GROUP SEATTLE, 1825
TMG CAPITAL PARTNERS, 3180
TONIIC, 1831
TOP RENERGY INC., 2271
URBAN INNOVATION FUND, 1893
VALAR VENTURES, 1897
VALHALLA PARTNERS, 1899
VERONIS SUHLER STEVENSON, 1927
VICKERS FINANCIAL GROUP, 3215
WESTTECH VENTURES, 3236
WHEATLEY PARTNERS, 1981
WICKS GROUP OF COMPANIES, LLC, 1984
WILDCAT VENTURE PARTNERS, 1985
WILLIS STEIN & PARTNERS LLC, 1986
ZHENFUND, 3251

Education Technology
APPIAN EDUCATION VENTURES, 141
MK CAPITAL, 1242
MOUNTAINEER CAPITAL, 1262
PALO ALTO VENTURE SCIENCE, 1406
WILDCAT VENTURE PARTNERS, 1985

Efficient Transport
AUSTRALIAN ETHICAL INVESTMENT LIMITED, 2456

Electric Power
ALTIRA GROUP LLC, 98

Electric Transmission
ENERGY CAPITAL PARTNERS, 675

Electrical Distribution
HT CAPITAL ADVISORS LLC, 953

Electronic Components
3I TEUPSCHLAND GmbH 3i Group, 2305
AKERS CAPITAL LLC, 75
ALEXANDER HUTTON, 82

ALLSTATE INVESTMENTS LLC, 88
AMPERSAND CAPITAL PARTNERS, 118
ANDLINGER & COMPANY INC, 123
ANTHEM VENTURE PARTNERS, 132
ARCH VENTURE PARTNERS, 153
ARTHUR P GOULD & COMPANY, 172
AUGUST CAPITAL, 197
AUSTIN VENTURES, 202
BERKELEY VC INTERNATIONAL LLC, 252
CAPITAL FOR BUSINESS, INC, 399
DEFTA PARTNERS, 602
DRAPER RICHARDS KAPLAN FOUNDATION, 627
DRESNER COMPANIES, 629
KLEINER PERKINS, 1075
MANHATTAN INVESTMENT PARTNERS, 1163
MASSACHUSETTS CAPITAL RESOURCE COMPANY, 1173
MASSACHUSETTS GROWTH CAPITAL CORPORATION, 1174
MAYFIELD FUND, 1184
MOTOROLA SOLUTIONS VENTURE CAPITAL, 1260
NORTH BRIDGE VENTURE PARTNERS, 1334
NOVAK BIDDLE VENTURE PARTNERS, 1348
OEM CAPITAL, 1369
OEM CAPITAL, 1369
PARTECH INTERNATIONAL, 1416
PERMAL CAPITAL MANAGEMENT, 1432
PIDC PHILADELPHIA, 1441
POLESTAR CAPITAL, 1461
PROVCO GROUP, 1494
PT BHAKTI INVESTAMA TBK, 3061
RAF INDUSTRIES, 1521
ROYALTY CAPITAL MANAGEMENT, 1591
SEACOAST CAPITAL CORPORATION, 1636
SEACOAST CAPITAL CORPORATION, 1636
SILVER CREEK VENTURES, 1682
SOURCE CAPITAL GROUP, 1707
SOUTHPORT PARTNERS, 1712
VALLEY VENTURES LP, 1901
VISION CAPITAL, 1937
WESTERN STATES INVESTMENT GROUP, 1974
WESTERN TECHNOLOGY INVESTMENT, 1975
WINGATE PARTNERS, 1997

Electronic Technology
3I AUSTRIA BETEILGUNG GmbH 3i Group, 2298
3I DEUTSCHLAND GESELLSCHAFT FUR 3i Group, 2299
3I GERMANY GmbH 3i Group, 2301
ABOA VENTURE MANAGEMENT OY, 2318
ABU DHABI INVESTMENT AUTHORITY, 2321
ACE VENTURE CAPITAL LIMITED, 2330
ADVENT VENTURE PARTNERS, 2348
AITEC, 2357
AJU CAPITAL COMPANY, 2358
ALTAIR VENTURES, 95
AMADEUS CAPITAL PARTNERS LIMITED, 2386
AMANET TECHNOLOGIES LIMITED, 2389
AMWIN MANAGEMENT PTY LIMITED, 2398
AXA INVESTMENT MANAGERS PRIVATE EQUITY EUROPE, 2466
BALTCAP MANAGEMENT LTD, 2480
BANEXI VENTURES PARTNERS, 2481
BARING PRIVATE EQUITY PARTNERS INDIA, 2490
BI WALDEN MANAGEMENT SDN Walden International, 2508
BROOK VENTURE FUND, 349
CAPRICORN VENTURE PARTNERS NV, 2563
CAPVIS EQUITY PARTNERS, 2564
CAZENOVE PRIVATE EQUITY Cazenove Capital, 2577
CHINA DEVELOPMENT INDUSTRIAL BANK CDFH, 2592
CHINA WALDEN MANAGEMENT LIMITED Walden Group, 2597
CLAL ELECTRONICS INDUSTRIES LIMITED, 2609
COMPAGNIE FINANCIERE E DE ROTHSCHILD BANQUE, 2625
CRESCENDO VENTURE MANAGEMENT LLC, 2639
DAIMLERCHRYSLER VENTURE GmbH DaimlerChrysler AG, 2650
DEFI GESTION SA Banque Cantonale Vaudoise, 2653
EDISON PARTNERS, 655
ENTERPRISE EQUITY (NI) LTD, 2704
EQUISTONE, 2714
EQVITEC PARTNERS OY, 2716
EURAZEO, 2719

Industry Preference Index / Enabling Technology

FERRANTI LIMITED, 2732
FINADVANCE, 2735
FINANCIERE DE BRIENNE FCPR, 2738
FIRST ISRAEL MEZZANINE INVESTORS LIMITED, 2745
FLANDERS' FOREIGN INVESTMENT OFFICE, 2746
FRIULIA SpA, 2758
GENERAL ENTERPRISE MANAGEMENT SERVICES, 2772
GENERICS GROUP LIMITED Generics Group, 2773
GILDE INVESTMENT FUNDS, 2779
GIMV GIMV, 2780
GLYNN CAPITAL MANAGEMENT, 836
GUANGDONG TECHNOLOGY VENTURE CAPITAL COMPANY, 2802
HELMET CAPITAL FUND MANAGEMENT OY, 2820
HT CAPITAL ADVISORS LLC, 953
I-PACIFIC PARTNERS, 2840
ID VENTURES AMERICA LLC, 970
INDUSTRIEBANK LIOF NV, 2866
INDUSTRIFONDEN, 2867
INNOFINANCE OY, 2873
INVEXCEL PATRIMONIO, 2891
JAFCO COMPANY LIMITED JAPAN, 2906
JAVELIN INVESTMENTS, 2908
JC TECHNOLOGIES LTD, 2909
KBL FOUNDER SA, 2917
KOREA FIRST VENTURE CAPITAL CORPORATION, 2924
LEONIA MB GROUP/MB FUNDS, 2937
LMBO FINANCE, 2945
MACQUARIE DIRECT INVESTMENT LIMITED, 2951
MARATHON VENTURE CAPITAL FUND LIMITED, 2954
MARCEAU INVESTISSEMENTS, 2955
MERRILL LYNCH (ASIA PACIFIC) LIMITED Merrill Lynch Group, 2964
MOMENTUM FUNDS MANAGEMENT PTY LIMITED, 2975
NEOTENY COMPANY LIMITED, 2991
NEW YORK LIFE CAPITAL PARTNERS, 1309
NORTHERN ENTERPRISE LIMITED, 3011
PRIME TECHNOLOGY VENTURES NV, 3051
PRIVATE EQUITY PARTNERS SPA, 3053
PROCURITAS PARTNERS KB, 3054
QUESTER CAPITAL MANAGEMENT LIMITED, 3070
RAFAEL DEVELOPMENT CORPORATION (RDC) LIMITED, 3072
RHO VENTURES, 1558
ROSER VENTURES LLC, 1586
SAMBRINVEST SA, 3096
SELBY VENTURE PARTNERS, 1646
SEQUOIA CAPITAL, 1654
SHANNON COMMERCIAL PROPERTIES, 3115
SHAW KWEI AND PARTNERS, 3116
SIERRA VENTURES, 1670
SIGMA PARTNERS, 1672
SIGNATURE CAPITAL LLC, 3120
SONY EUROPE, 3129
SOURCE CAPITAL GROUP, 1707
SOUTH ATLANTIC VENTURE FUNDS, 1708
STARBOARD CAPITAL PARTNERS, 1735
STARVEST PARTNERS, 1738
SVB CAPITAL, 1764
TAT CAPITAL PARTNERS LTD., 3162
TECH CAPITAL PARTNERS, 2262
TECHNOCAP, 2263
TEKNOINVEST MANAGEMENT, 3167
TFG CAPITAL AG, 3172
THOMSON-CSF VENTURES, 3176
THROUNARFELAG ISLANDS PLC, 3177
TRINITY VENTURE CAPITAL TVC Holdings plc, 3191
TRU MANAGEMENT, 1858
TSG EQUITY PARTNERS, 1862
UCA UNTERNEHMER CONSULT AG, 3197
VALLEY VENTURES LP, 1901
VENTURE ASSOCIATES PARTNERS LLC, 1919
VENTURE CAPITAL FUND OF NEW ENGLAND, 1920
VERITAS CAPITAL FUND LP, 1925
WALDEN INTERNATIONAL, 1951
WESTERN STATES INVESTMENT GROUP, 1974
WINDWARD VENTURES, 1995
WINGATE PARTNERS, 1997
WOODSIDE FUND, 2005

Electronics
3M UNITEK, 2307
ALBERTA ENTERPRISE, 2032
ATILA VENTURES, 2442
BEZOS EXPEDITIONS, 262
BM-T BETEILIGUNGS MANAGEMENT THURINGEN GmbH, 2527
BUSINESS GROWTH FUND, 2550
CALIFORNIA TECHNOLOGY VENTURES, 371
CASABONA VENTURES, 418
CONOR VENTURE PARTNERS OY, 2630
CREATHOR VENTURE, 2638
DFJ ESPRIT, 2662
EPLANET CAPITAL, 690
GOLDEN GATE CAPITAL, 839
HORIZON PARTNERS, LTD, 945
HORIZONS VENTURES, 2831
IBM VENTURE CAPITAL GROUP, 967
KILMER CAPITAL PARTNERS, 2169
MITSUBISHI UFJ CAPITAL, 2970
MITSUI SUMITOMO INSURANCE VENTURE CAPITAL CO, 2971
NEW ENTERPRISE ASSOCIATES, 1297
NEWABLE VENTURES, 2997
PAC-LINK MANAGEMENT CORP., 3024
PANGAEA VENTURES LTD, 2213
PARKWALK ADVISORS, 3028
QUEST FOR GROWTH, 3069
SIGMA PARTNERS, 1672
SORRENTO VENTURES, 1706
STATELINE ANGELS, 1740
TEL VENTURE CAPITAL, 1791
TENAYA CAPITAL, 1796
TROIKA CAPITAL PARTNERS, 3193
VERGE FUND, 1924
VIKING VENTURE, 3216
XANGE PRIVATE EQUITY, 3239
YISSUM TECHNOLOGY TRANSFER, 3245

Embedded Software
OJAS VENTURE PARTNERS, 3019

Embedded Systems
CONOR VENTURE PARTNERS OY, 2630
ISOURCE GESTION, 2899

Emerging Markets, Sectors & Technologies
M12, 1154
QUILVEST PRIVATE EQUITY, 1516
TEXAS EMERGING TECHNOLOGY FUND, 1800
TI VENTURE CAPITAL Texas Instruments Incorporated, 1823
VENTURE TECH ALLIANCE, 1922
VENTUREAST, 3211
WALDEN INTERNATIONAL, 1951

Emerging Media
CHINAROCK CAPITAL MANAGEMENT VENTURES, 472

Emerging Technology
NAYA VENTURES, 1285
PRITZKER GROUP VENTURE CAPITAL, 1480

Emissions Control
ANGELENO GROUP, 126

Enabling Software
CONVEXA Tyveholmen AS, 2632

Enabling Technology
(@)VENTURES, 1
ALLEGIS CYBER CAPITAL, 84
BRAINSTORM VENTURES, 324
CORE CAPITAL PARTNERS, 538
EASTVEN VENTURE PARTNERS, 645
FUNG CAPITAL USA, 796
I-HATCH VENTURES LLC, 964
KOHLBERG VENTURES, 1083
MADISON PARKER CAPITAL, 1157
MILLENIUM TECHNOLOGY VALUE PARTNERS, 1235

Industry Preference Index / Energy

NEOTENY COMPANY LIMITED, 2991
NEWSPRING CAPITAL, 1317
OXANTIUM VENTURES, 1393
PHYSIC VENTURES, 1438
SHANGHAI INFORMATION INVESTMENT INCORPORATED, 3114
WESTSUMMIT CAPITAL, 3235

Energy

3M UNITEK, 2307
3TS CAPITAL PARTNERS 3i Group plc, 2309
3i GROUP PLC, 2311
AAVISHKAAR, 2313
ABB TECHNOLOGY VENTURES, 2315
ABELL FOUNDATION VENTURES, 19
ACCERA AG, 2327
ACERO CAPITAL, 41
ACKRELL CAPITAL, 44
ACON INVESTMENTS, 46
ACTIS, 2337
ACUMEN, 55
ADVANTAGE CAPITAL PARTNERS, 61
AEM CAPITAL, 2349
ALBEMARLE PRIVATE EQUITY LIMITED, 2360
ALBERTA ENTERPRISE, 2032
ALLOY VENTURES, 87
ALTIRA GROUP LLC, 98
AMBIENTA ENVIRONMENTAL ASSETS, 2391
ANDLINGER & COMPANY INC, 123
ANGELENO GROUP, 126
ANNAPOLIS CAPITAL, 2038
ARC FINANCIAL, 2040
ARCAPITA INC, 152
ARCLIGHT CAPITAL PARTNERS, 156
ARES MANAGEMENT LLC, 159
ARTHUR P GOULD & COMPANY, 172
ARTHUR VENTURES, 173
ARTIS VENTURES, 175
ASSET MANAGEMENT VENTURES, 181
ASTER CAPITAL, 2439
ATRIUM CAPITAL, 192
AUDAX GROUP, 194
AUGMENT VENTURES, 195
AURORA CAPITAL GROUP, 199
AUSTRALIAN ETHICAL INVESTMENT LIMITED, 2456
AVENUE CAPITAL GROUP, 208
AVISTA CAPITAL PARTNERS, 209
AWAY REALTY, 2465
AZALEA CAPITAL, 213
AZIMUTH CAPITAL MANAGEMENT, 2050
AZIONE CAPITAL, 2473
BAIN CAPITAL PRIVATE EQUITY, 220
BARING PRIVATE EQUITY PARTNERS INDIA, 2490
BARING VOSTOK CAPITAL PARTNERS, 2491
BASF VENTURE CAPITAL, 2492
BATTELLE VENTURES, 233
BEIJING HIGH TECHNOLOGY INVESTMENT COMPANY, 2499
BERKSHIRE PARTNERS LLC, 254
BERTI INVESTMENTS, 2505
BLACKSTONE PRIVATE EQUITY GROUP, 277
BLAST FUNDING, 279
BLUE SAGE CAPITAL, 291
BLUESTEM CAPITAL COMPANY, 297
BOCI DIRECT INVESTMENT MANAGEMENT LIMITED Bank of China, 2529
BP ALTERNATIVE ENERGY VENTURES, 319
BRAEMAR ENERGY VENTURES, 322
BRANFORD CASTLE, 327
BREAKWATER INVESTMENTS, 330
BREGAL ENERGY, 332
BRIGHT CAPITAL, 2540
BRIGHTSTONE VENTURE CAPITAL, 341
C3 CAPITAL PARTNERS LP, 364
CAI CAPITAL PARTNERS, 365
CALCEF CLEAN ENERGY FUND, 367
CALVERT INVESTMENT MANAGEMENT, 376
CANADIAN VENTURE CAPITAL ASSOCIATION Canadian Venture Capital & Private Equity Association, 3258

CAPITAL FOR BUSINESS, INC, 399
CAPITAL SOUTHWEST CORPORATION, 403
CAPITALA, 405
CAPITOL PARTNERS, 406
CAPRICORN VENTURE PARTNERS NV, 2563
CAPX PARTNERS, 407
CARBON VENTURES, 408
CARLYLE GROUP, 413
CASTLE HARLAN, 423
CATALYST GROUP, 425
CEDAR VENTURES LLC, 437
CEDRUS INVESTMENTS, 2581
CEI VENTURES, 438
CHARLESBANK CAPITAL PARTNERS, 456
CHEVRON TECHNOLOGY VENTURES, 466
CHEYENNE CAPITAL, 467
CHICAGO VENTURE PARTNERS LP, 470
CHORD CAPITAL, 2598
CIBC CAPITAL MARKETS, 2079
CIC PARTNERS, 477
CIT GROUP, 484
CITY LIGHT CAPITAL, 488
CLARITY CAPITAL, 2611
CLEAN ENERGY VENTURE GROUP, 497
CLEAN PACIFIC VENTURES, 498
CLEARLAKE CAPITAL, 500
CLIFFORD CHANCE PUNDER, 2614
COACH & CAPITAL, 2619
COLORADO MILE HIGH FUND, 513
COMMONS CAPITAL, 520
CONNECTICUT INNOVATIONS, 530
CRESTVIEW PARTNERS, 559
CVC INVESTMENT MANAGERS LIMITED, 2645
DAG VENTURES, 581
DARBY OVERSEAS INVESTMENTS LTD, 584
DAVENPORT RESOURCES LLC, 588
DISCOVERY CAPITAL, 2097
DUBIN CLARK & COMPANY, 632
DYNAMO VC, 640
EARTHRISE CAPITAL, 643
ECOSYSTEM VENTURES, 650
EDGESTONE CAPITAL PARTNERS, 2103
ELEMENT PARTNERS, 657
EM WARBURG, PINCUS & COMPANY INTERNATIONAL, 2697
EM WARBURG, PINCUS & COMPANY JAPAN, 2698
EMERALD TECHNOLOGY VENTURES, 2106
ENCAP FLATROCK MIDSTREAM, 671
ENERGY VENTURES, 2700
ENNOVENT, 2701
ENTERPRISE EQUITY (NI) LTD, 2704
EOS PARTNERS LP, 686
ESCHELON ENERGY PARTNERS, 696
EXCEL VENTURE MANAGEMENT, 703
EXPANSION CAPITAL PARTNERS, 706
EXPANSION VENTURE CAPITAL, 707
EXPERIMENT FUND, 708
EXPORT DEVELOPMENT CANADA, 2112
FERRANTI LIMITED, 2732
FIELDSTONE PRIVATE CAPITAL GROUP, 726
FINLOMBARDA SpA, 2739
FIRELAKE CAPITAL, 730
FIRST ANALYSIS, 732
FIRST RESERVE, 740
FORESIGHT VENTURE PARTNERS, 2749
FORTRESS INVESTMENT GROUP LLC, 767
FOUNDERS FUND, 775
FOX PAINE & COMPANY LLC, 778
FULL CIRCLE INVESTMENTS, 2762
GE CAPITAL, 808
GE VENTURES, 809
GENERAL ENTERPRISE MANAGEMENT SERVICES, 2772
GENERICS GROUP LIMITED Generics Group, 2773
GIMV GIMV, 2780
GROVE STREET ADVISORS LLC, 879
GRYPHON MANAGEMENT COMPANY, 882
GULFSTAR GROUP, 888
HADDINGTON VENTURES LLC, 893

Industry Preference Index / Energy Efficiency

HAMILTON ROBINSON CAPITAL PARTNERS, 899
HAMMOND, KENNEDY, WHITNEY & COMPANY, 900
HANCOCK CAPITAL MANAGEMENT, 901
HELLMAN & FRIEDMAN LLC, 924
HIG CAPITAL, 928
HOPEWELL VENTURES, 944
HRL MORRISON & COMPANY LIMITED, 2835
HUMANA VENTURES, 955
HURON RIVER VENTURES, 961
IBM VENTURE CAPITAL GROUP, 967
IN-Q-TEL, 979
INETWORKS ADVISORS LLC, 987
INLAND TECHSTART FUND, 993
INNOFINANCE OY, 2873
INNOVATION CAPITAL LIMITED, 2877
INNOVATION PLATFORM CAPITAL, 997
INNOVATION WORKS, 998
INSIGHT VENTURE PARTNERS, 1000
INVICO CAPITAL CORPORATION, 2162
IP GROUP, 2892
IRON GATE CAPITAL, 1020
ISRAEL CLEANTECH VENTURES, 2900
JEFFERIES CAPITAL PARTNERS, 1032
JOG CAPITAL, 2166
JORDAN COMPANY, 1045
KAIROS VENTURES, 1051
KBL FOUNDER SA, 2917
KENSINGTON CAPITAL PARTNERS, 2167
KERRY CAPITAL ADVISORS, 1067
KESTREL ENERGY PARTNERS, 1068
KOHLBERG KRAVIS ROBERTS & COMPANY, 1082
KRG CAPITAL PARTNERS, 1086
LAUNCHPAD VENTURES, 2931
LEX CAPITAL MANAGEMENT, 2173
LIME ROCK PARTNERS, 1125
LINLEY CAPITAL, 1130
LOMBARD INVESTMENTS, 1139
LONGBOW CAPITAL, 2178
LUX CAPITAL, 1151
MACQUARIE DIRECT INVESTMENT LIMITED, 2951
MADISON DEARBORN PARTNERS, 1156
MANHATTAN INVESTMENT PARTNERS, 1163
MASS VENTURES, 1172
MATRIX PARTNERS, 1181
MATURO KAPITAL, 2957
MERIT ENERGY COMPANY, 1210
MERITURN PARTNERS, 1213
MHS CAPITAL, 1226
MITSUI SUMITOMO INSURANCE VENTURE CAPITAL CO, 2971
MMT MILLENNIUM MATERIALS TECHNOLOGIES FUND LP, 2973
MONTAGU PRIVATE EQUITY LIMITED, 2977
MURPHREE VENTURE PARTNERS, 1273
NATURAL GAS PARTNERS, 1278
NEST VENTURES, 1290
NEW BRUNSWICK INNOVATION FOUNDATION, 2200
NEW MEXICO COMMUNITY CAPITAL, 1300
NEW MOUNTAIN CAPITAL, 1301
NEW WORLD INFRASTRUCTURE LIMITED, 2996
NEWLIGHT PARTNERS, 1315
NORTH COVE PARTNERS, 1337
NORTHERN ENTERPRISE LIMITED, 3011
NORTHSTAR VENTURES, 3012
NOVELTEK CAPITAL CORPORATION, 1351
NTH POWER TECHNOLOGIES, 1355
OAK INVESTMENT PARTNERS, 1361
OBVIOUS VENTURES, 1363
ODYSSEY INVESTMENT PARTNERS, 1368
OMERS PRIVATE EQUITY, 2207
OMNES CAPITAL, 3020
ONE EQUITY PARTNERS, 1376
PAI MANAGEMENT, 3026
PAMLICO CAPITAL, 1409
PANGAEA VENTURES LTD, 2213
PANTHEON VENTURES (US) LP, 1411
PARALLEL INVESTMENT PARTNERS, 1415
PARKVIEW CAPITAL PARTNERS, 2215
PARKWALK ADVISORS, 3028
PARTECH INTERNATIONAL, 1416
PENN VENTURE PARTNERS, 1428
PIDC PHILADELPHIA, 1441
PINE BROOK ROAD PARTNERS, 1443
POND VENTURES, 3047
PORTUGAL CAPITAL VENTURES Institutional Headquarters, 3048
PRAIRIEGOLD VENTURE PARTNERS, 1470
PRITZKER GROUP VENTURE CAPITAL, 1480
PRIVITI CAPITAL, 2227
QUAKE CAPITAL PARTNERS, 1507
RAYMOND JAMES CAPITAL, 1526
REITEN & CO STRATEGIC INVESTMENTS AS Reiten & Company, 3076
RENAISSANCE PARTNERS, 3077
RESOURCE CAPITAL FUNDS, 1548
RIDGEWOOD CAPITAL, 1564
RIDGEWOOD ENERGY, 1565
ROBIN HOOD VENTURES, 1577
ROCKPORT CAPITAL, 1579
ROYALTY CAPITAL MANAGEMENT, 1591
RPM VENTURES, 1592
RU-NET VENTURES, 3087
SAF GROUP, 2246
SAIL VENTURE PARTNERS, 1603
SAINT-GOBAIN NOVA EXTERNAL VENTURING, 3094
SAMOS INVESTMENTS, 3097
SARATOGA PARTNERS, 1621
SARONA ASSET MANAGEMENT, 2248
SCOTTISH ENTERPRISE, 3103
SCOTTISH EQUITY PARTNERS, 3104
SEED CAPITAL LIMITED, 3107
SENTRY FINANCIAL CORPORATION, 1652
SEQUOIA CAPITAL, 1654
SEVEN SPIRES INVESTMENTS, 3112
SEVIN ROSEN FUNDS, 1658
SILKROAD EQUITY, 1681
SKYTREE CAPITAL PARTNERS, 1692
SOCIAL VENTURE CIRCLE, 3277
SOURCE CAPITAL GROUP, 1707
SOUTH ATLANTIC VENTURE FUNDS, 1708
SOUTHERN CROSS VENTURE PARTNERS, 1711
SPRING LANE CAPITAL, 1729
SSE VENTURES, 3135
STARBOARD CAPITAL PARTNERS, 1735
STATELINE ANGELS, 1740
STATOIL TECHNOLOGY INVEST, 3141
STEELHOUSE VENTURES, 3143
SUCSY, FISCHER & COMPANY, 1750
SUMMIT PARTNERS, 1752
TECHNOCAP, 2263
TELESOFT PARTNERS, 1793
TENASKA CAPITAL MANAGEMENT, 1795
TPA CORPORATE FINANCE CONSULTING GMBH Horwarth International, 3184
TRIANGLE PEAK PARTNERS, 1846
TRUE NORTH VENTURE PARTNERS, 1859
URBAN INNOVATION FUND, 1893
URBAN US, 1894
US RENEWABLES GROUP, 1895
US VENTURE PARTNERS, 1896
VALUEACT CAPITAL, 1903
VANTAGEPOINT CAPITAL PARTNERS, 1906
VENROCK ASSOCIATES, 1916
VENTANA CAPITAL MANAGEMENT LP, 1918
VICKERS FINANCIAL GROUP, 3215
WAND PARTNERS, 1955
WARBURG PINCUS LLC, 1956
WASABI VENTURES, 1958
WESTERN NIS ENTERPRISE FUND, 3234
WOODSIDE FUND, 2005
WYNNCHURCH CAPITAL, 2009
YELLOW POINT EQUITY PARTNERS, 2292

Energy Efficiency
ANGELENO GROUP, 126
ARAVAIPA VENTURES, 146
BRIGHT CAPITAL, 2540

Industry Preference Index / Energy Equipment & Services

CALCEF CLEAN ENERGY FUND, 367
CHORD CAPITAL, 2598
CLAREMONT CREEK VENTURES, 491
CLEAN PACIFIC VENTURES, 498
CLIMATE CHANGE CAPITAL, 2615
DEMETER PARTNERS, 2656
EARTHRISE CAPITAL, 643
EPLANET CAPITAL, 690
FIDELITY GROWTH PARTNERS EUROPE, 2734
GLOBAL ENVIRONMENT FUND, 834
ID VENTURES AMERICA LLC, 970
ISRAEL CLEANTECH VENTURES, 2900
KOHLBERG VENTURES, 1083
NGEN PARTNERS, 1324
NORTHZONE, 3013
RENEWABLETECH VENTURES, 1542
SAUDI ARAMCO ENERGY VENTURES, 3099
SSE VENTURES, 3135
TSING CAPITAL, 3194
VANTAGEPOINT CAPITAL PARTNERS, 1906
WHEB GROUP, 3237

Energy Equipment & Services
ENERGY CAPITAL PARTNERS, 675

Energy Infrastructure
ENCAP FLATROCK MIDSTREAM, 671

Energy Management
TI VENTURE CAPITAL Texas Instruments Incorporated, 1823

Energy Products
DESCO CAPITAL, 606

Energy Services
BAY PARTNERS, 238
BREGAL ENERGY, 332
FOUNDATION EQUITY CORPORATION, 2121
GENESIS CAPITAL CORPORATION, 2129
GLADSTONE CAPITAL, 828
HARREN EQUITY PARTNERS, 910
SALT CREEK CAPITAL, 1609
TRILANTIC CAPITAL PARTNERS, 1851
VALOR EQUITY PARTNERS, 1902
WESTLAKE SECURITIES, 1976

Energy Storage
ARCTERN VENTURES, 2041
AUTO TECH VENTURES, 204
CLEAN PACIFIC VENTURES, 498
EARTHRISE CAPITAL, 643
NGEN PARTNERS, 1324
OCEANSHORE VENTURES, 1365
TEL VENTURE CAPITAL, 1791
WHEB GROUP, 3237

Energy Technology
.406 VENTURES, 2
FA TECHNOLOGY VENTURES, 711
FLYBRIDGE CAPITAL PARTNERS, 754
FLYWHEEL VENTURES, 756
HOUSTON ANGEL NETWORK, 950
MAYFIELD FUND, 1184
McLEAN WATSON CAPITAL, 2199
NTH POWER TECHNOLOGIES, 1355
RIDGEWOOD CAPITAL, 1564
TANDEM EXPANSION FUND, 2261
TECHNOLOGY PARTNERS, 1786
YELLOWSTONE CAPITAL, 2013

Energy and Resources
CHINA MERCHANTS CHINA DIRECT INVESTMENTS LTD., 2594

Engineered Materials
ARGOSY CAPITAL, 164

Engineered Products
CENTURY PARK CAPITAL PARTNERS, 449

Engineering
360 CAPITAL PARTNERS 360 Capital Management SA, 2296
3I ASIA PACIFIC 3i Group, 2297
ABOA VENTURE MANAGEMENT OY, 2318
ACCESS CAPITAL CORPORATION, 2030
BARING PRIVATE EQUITY PARTNERS ESPANA SA, 2489
BM-T BETEILIGUNGS MANAGEMENT THURINGEN GmbH, 2527
COPPERLION CAPITAL, 2085
EQUISTONE, 2714
EXPIBEL BV, 2728
EXPORT DEVELOPMENT CANADA, 2112
FERRANTI LIMITED, 2732
GENERICS GROUP LIMITED Generics Group, 2773
HANNOVER FINANZ GmbH, 2810
INNOVATION CAPITAL LIMITED, 2877
INNOVATION ENDEAVORS, 996
KAIROS VENTURES, 1051
KB PARTNERS LLC, 1057
LIME ROCK PARTNERS, 1125
MARCEAU INVESTISSEMENTS, 2955
MEZZANINE MANAGEMENT LIMITED Mezzanine Management UK Ltd., 2965
MIDVEN, 2967
PAI MANAGEMENT, 3026
RED DOT VENTURES, 3073
TECHNOLOGY PARK MALAYSIA CORPORATION SDN BHD, 3164
YISSUM TECHNOLOGY TRANSFER, 3245

Enterprise
FIRST ROUND CAPITAL, 741
FRONTLINE VENTURES, 2759
INTEL CAPITAL, 1004
JACKSON SQUARE VENTURES, 1024
KHOSLA VENTURES, 1069
LIGHTSPEED VENTURE PARTNERS, 1121
QUALCOMM VENTURES, 1509
SOCIAL CAPITAL, 1696

Enterprise & Consumer
FRONTIER VENTURES, 792

Enterprise Applications
CASTILE VENTURES, 422
CATAMOUNT VENTURES LP, 428
EDISON PARTNERS, 655
FELICIS VENTURES, 720
GABRIEL VENTURE PARTNERS, 805
MOBIUS VENTURE CAPITAL, 1245
OSAGE PARTNERS, 1387
SALESFORCE VENTURES, 1607
SHEPHERD VENTURES, 1664
STORM VENTURES, 1747
SUMMERHILL VENTURE PARTNERS, 2259

Enterprise Blockchain
RIPPLE VENTURES, 2241

Enterprise IT
CITI VENTURES, 486

Enterprise IT & Infrastructure
VERTEX VENTURE CAPITAL, 3214

Enterprise Mobility
BENHAMOU GLOBAL VENTURES, 249
NEW ENTERPRISE ASSOCIATES, 1297

Enterprise Services
(@)VENTURES, 1
ACCEL-KKR LLC, 29
ADOBE VENTURES LP, 58
ALLEGIS CYBER CAPITAL, 84
ANGELS' FORUM LLC, 129
APEX VENTURE PARTNERS, 137

Industry Preference Index / Entertainment

ASCENT VENTURE PARTNERS, 178
AUSTIN VENTURES, 202
BLUE CHIP VENTURE COMPANY, 287
BLUMBERG CAPITAL, 301
CATALYST FUND LP, 2571
CEDAR (ISRAEL) FINANCIAL ADVISORS LIMITED Cedar Fund, 2580
CEDAR FUND, 436
CHENGWEI VENTURES, 2590
CONSTELLATION TECHNOLOGY VENTURES, 532
DENALI VENTURE PARTNERS, 605
EQUITY PARTNERS PTY LIMITED, 2715
EVERCORE CAPITAL PARTNERS, 699
FORMULA VENTURES LIMITED Formula Group, 2750
GIZA VENTURE CAPITAL, 2782
GROTECH VENTURES, 876
IDG CAPITAL, 973
IDG VENTURES INDIA International Financial Services Limited, 2849
INNOVACOM SA, 2875
JERUSALEM VENTURE PARTNERS, 2910
LONGWORTH VENTURE PARTNERS, 1146
OAK INVESTMENT PARTNERS, 1361
ODEON CAPITAL PARTNERS, 1367
PALO ALTO VENTURE PARTNERS, 1405
REDPOINT VENTURES, 1534
SCALE VENTURE PARTNERS, 1626
SMART BUSINESS CONSULTING, 3124
SPACEVEST, 1714
STAR VENTURES, 3137
STARVEST PARTNERS, 1738
TRITON VENTURES, 1855
UPDATA VENTURE PARTNERS, 1886
VERITAS VENTURE PARTNERS, 3212
VOYAGER CAPITAL, 1945

Enterprise Software
ACTIVE VENTURE PARTNERS, 2339
ACUMEN VENTURES, 2341
ALMAZ CAPITAL, 89
AMBIENT SOUND INVESTMENTS, 2390
AMPLIFIER VENTURE PARTNERS, 119
ANDREESSEN HOROWITZ, 124
ANNAPURNA VENTURES, 2403
ARCHTOP VENTURES, 154
ARTHUR VENTURES, 173
ASPECT VENTURES, 180
ATA VENTURES, 183
AVANSIS VENTURES, 207
AXIA CAPITAL, 211
BAY PARTNERS, 238
BLH VENTURE PARTNERS, 282
BLUEFISH VENTURES, 294
BLUERUN VENTURES, 296
BOSTON CAPITAL VENTURES, 310
BRAINSTORM VENTURES, 324
BREGAL SAGEMOUNT, 333
BRIGHTSTONE VENTURE CAPITAL, 341
BULLPEN CAPITAL, 358
CEDAR FUND, 436
CINCYTECH, 479
COMCAST VENTURES, 518
CORRELATION VENTURES, 544
CRESCENDO VENTURES, 555
DOT EDU VENTURES, 623
EDEN VENTURES, 2691
EGL HOLDINGS, 656
ELAIA PARTNERS, 2693
ENTREE CAPITAL, 2709
EPIC VENTURES, 688
F-PRIME CAPITAL PARTNERS, 710
FA TECHNOLOGY VENTURES, 711
FGA PARTNERS, 725
FLOODGATE FUND, 751
GENESIS PARTNERS, 2775
GEORGIAN PARTNERS, 2132
GV, 889
HELION VENTURE PARTNERS, LLC International Management (Mauritius) Ltd, 2818
HUDSON VENTURE PARTNERS, 954
HUMMER WINBLAD VENTURE PARTNERS, 956
INCWELL VENTURE CAPITAL, 981
INNOVATION WORKS, 998
INSTITUTIONAL VENTURE PARTNERS, 1001
IRISH ANGELS, 1019
KLASS CAPITAL, 2170
MATRIX PARTNERS, 1181
MENLO VENTURES, 1202
MERITECH CAPITAL PARTNERS, 1212
MHS CAPITAL, 1226
MISSION VENTURES, 1239
MISSIONOG, 1240
MORGAN STANLEY EXPANSION CAPITAL, 1255
MORGENTHALER VENTURES, 1257
NAUTA CAPITAL, 2987
NOVUS VENTURES LP, 1354
OJAS VENTURE PARTNERS, 3019
OPUS CAPITAL, 1381
PLAZA VENTURES, 2224
PRITZKER GROUP VENTURE CAPITAL, 1480
RALLY VENTURES, 1522
RELAY VENTURES, 2236
RIPPLE VENTURES, 2241
RRE VENTURES, 1593
SALESFORCE VENTURES, 1607
SERAPH GROUP, 1655
SIGMA PARTNERS, 1672
SIGNAL PEAK VENTURES, 1677
SILVERTON PARTNERS, 1685
SORRENTO VENTURES, 1706
SOUTHEAST INTERACTIVE TECHNOLOGY FUNDS, 1709
SPARKLABS GLOBAL VENTURES, 1716
SPLIT ROCK PARTNERS, 1725
SUNBRIDGE PARTNERS, 1755
SV ANGEL, 1761
TICONDEROGA PRIVATE EQUITY, 1824
TRIDENT CAPITAL, 1850
TRUE VENTURES, 1860
TUGBOAT VENTURES, 1865
TXV PARTNERS, 1875
VALAR VENTURES, 1897
VELOCITY EQUITY PARTNERS LLC, 1913
VENTECH, 3208
WESTTECH VENTURES, 3236
WOODSIDE FUND, 2005
WORLDVIEW TECHNOLOGY PARTNERS, 2007
ZHENFUND, 3251

Enterprise Technology
CLYDESDALE VENTURES, 506
COLUMBIA CAPITAL, 515
JUMP CAPITAL LLC, 1046
OFF THE GRID VENTURES, 1370

Entertainment
360 CAPITAL PARTNERS 360 Capital Management SA, 2296
645 VENTURES, 13
ABRY PARTNERS, 21
ABU DHABI INVESTMENT AUTHORITY, 2321
ACKERLEY PARTNERS LLC, 43
ACKRELL CAPITAL, 44
ADVANCIT CAPITAL, 60
AEP CAPITAL LLC, 65
ARCHTOP VENTURES, 154
BASE VENTURES, 229
BERINGEA, 251
BIA DIGITAL PARTNERS LP, 263
BIGFOOT VENTURES, 2511
BOTTS & COMPANY LIMITED, 2532
BREAKAWAY VENTURES, 329
BREAKWATER MANAGEMENT, 331
BREYER CAPITAL, 336
CANDOVER, 2556
CATALYST INVESTMENT MANAGERS PTY LIMITED PPM Capital, 2573
CEI VENTURES, 438

Industry Preference Index / Environment

CIT GROUP, 484
COMSTOCK CAPITAL PARTNERS LLC, 527
DETROIT VENTURE PARTNERS, 607
DIRECT CAPITAL PRIVATE EQUITY LIMITED, 2664
DYNAMO VC, 640
ELEVATION PARTNERS, 659
FALCONHEAD CAPITAL, 717
FIRSTMARK CAPITAL, 743
GEODESIC CAPITAL, 820
GREIF & COMPANY, 869
GRUPO BISA, 2800
IDEALAB, 972
INDEX VENTURES, 2860
INDEX VENTURES, 2860
INDIAN DIRECT EQUITY ADVISORS PVT LTD, 2861
INGENIOUS VENTURES, 2871
INLAND TECHSTART FUND, 993
INTEL CAPITAL, 1004
IRIS CAPITAL, 2897
KILMER CAPITAL PARTNERS, 2169
LEO CAPITAL HOLDINGS, LLC, 1108
LEVINE LEICHTMAN CAPITAL PARTNERS, 1111
LOMBARD INVESTMENTS, 1139
MAKERS FUND, 2953
MANHATTAN INVESTMENT PARTNERS, 1163
MARS INVESTMENT ACCELERATOR FUND, 2187
MARWIT CAPITAL LLC, 1168
MCG CAPITAL CORPORATION, 1189
MERRILL LYNCH (ASIA PACIFIC) LIMITED Merrill Lynch Group, 2964
MOTOROLA SOLUTIONS VENTURE CAPITAL, 1260
NEW ATLANTIC VENTURES, 1291
NEXTEC DEVELOPMENT CAPITAL LIMITED, 3000
NFX, 1323
ONEX PARTNERS, 2209
PARTNERSHIP FUND FOR NEW YORK CITY, 1420
PRINCIPIA SGR, 3052
PROVIDENCE EQUITY PARTNERS, 1496
QUOTIDIAN VENTURES, 1518
RAPTOR GROUP, 1524
ROBIN HOOD VENTURES, 1577
SABAN CAPITAL GROUP, 1598
SANDLER CAPITAL MANAGEMENT, 1617
SCOUT VENTURES, 1632
SENTRY FINANCIAL CORPORATION, 1652
SHAMROCK CAPITAL ADVISORS, 1660
SIGNAL FIRE, 1675
SOFTBANK VENTURES KOREA, 3127
SONY INNOVATION FUND, 1703
SPECTRUM EQUITY INVESTORS LP, 1717
SUMMIT PARTNERS, 1752
TELESYSTEM, 2264
TORNANTE COMPANY, 1833
TYLT LAB, 1876
UNITED TALENT AGENCY VENTURES, 1883
VENTECH, 3208
VERIZON VENTURES, 1926
WALNUT GROUP, 1954
WESLEY CLOVER, 2284
ZHENFUND, 3251

Environment
3TS CAPITAL PARTNERS 3i Group plc, 2309
AMBIENTA ENVIRONMENTAL ASSETS, 2391
AMERICAN SECURITIES LLC, 110
ASTER CAPITAL, 2439
BATTELLE VENTURES, 233
BIG SOCIETY CAPITAL, 2509
BROOKSIDE EQUITY PARTNERS LLC, 353
CALVERT INVESTMENT MANAGEMENT, 376
CASABONA VENTURES, 418
CATAMOUNT VENTURES LP, 428
CHORD CAPITAL, 2598
CITY LIGHT CAPITAL, 488
COACH & CAPITAL, 2619
COMMONS CAPITAL, 520
CULTIVIAN SANDBOX VENTURES, 570
DISCOVERY CAPITAL, 2097
EARTHRISE CAPITAL, 643
EDELSON TECHNOLOGY PARTNERS, 651
FUEL CAPITAL, 2761
INETWORKS ADVISORS LLC, 987
MATURO KAPITAL, 2957
MIDVEN, 2967
MINDFULL INVESTORS, 1236
MITSUI SUMITOMO INSURANCE VENTURE CAPITAL CO, 2971
MONTAGU PRIVATE EQUITY LIMITED, 2977
NEW MEXICO COMMUNITY CAPITAL, 1300
NGEN PARTNERS, 1324
NORTHSTAR VENTURES, 3012
SAINT-GOBAIN NOVA EXTERNAL VENTURING, 3094
SOUTHERN CROSS VENTURE PARTNERS, 1711
SPRING LANE CAPITAL, 1729
TONIIC, 1831
TSING CAPITAL, 3194
UDD VENTURES, 3198
UNDERDOG VENTURES, 1880
VANCITY CAPITAL, 2277
WOMEN'S VENTURE CAPITAL FUND, 2003
YISSUM TECHNOLOGY TRANSFER, 3245

Environment Products & Services
APEX VENTURE PARTNERS, 137
ASSET MANAGEMENT VENTURES, 181
AUDAX GROUP, 194
CAPRICORN VENTURE PARTNERS NV, 2563
COMPAGNIE FINANCIERE E DE ROTHSCHILD BANQUE, 2625
CONNECTICUT INNOVATIONS, 530
CVC INVESTMENT MANAGERS LIMITED, 2645
FOUNDERS EQUITY, 774
GLOBAL ENVIRONMENT FUND, 834
GRYPHON MANAGEMENT COMPANY, 882
IRONWOOD CAPITAL, 1021
J. BURKE CAPITAL PARTNERS, 1023
MAYFIELD FUND, 1184
NEWMARGIN VENTURE CAPITAL, 2998
NORTHERN ENTERPRISE LIMITED, 3011
PACIFIC COMMUNITY VENTURES, 1396
PARTECH INTERNATIONAL, 1416
PIDC PHILADELPHIA, 1441
POUSCHINE COOK CAPITAL MANAGEMENT LLC, 1466
QUESTER CAPITAL MANAGEMENT LIMITED, 3070
ROARK CAPITAL GROUP, 1576
SAMBRINVEST SA, 3096
SOLSTICE CAPITAL LP, 1702
SOVEREIGN CAPITAL, 3130
SUMMER STREET CAPITAL PARTNERS, 1751
TELESYSTEM, 2264
THOMPROPERTIES OY, 3175
TRIGINITA CAPITAL, 3190

Environmental
COPPERLION CAPITAL, 2085

Environmental & Waste Management
GENESIS CAPITAL CORPORATION, 2129

Environmental Controls
ELEMENT PARTNERS, 657

Environmental Infrastructure
ENERGY CAPITAL PARTNERS, 675
ZOUK VENTURES, 3252

Environmental Protection
ANDLINGER & COMPANY INC, 123
BEIJING HIGH TECHNOLOGY INVESTMENT COMPANY, 2499
BEIJING VENTURE CAPITAL COMPANY LIMITED, 2500
CVC INVESTMENT MANAGERS LIMITED, 2645
GUANGDONG TECHNOLOGY VENTURE CAPITAL COMPANY, 2802
INNOVATION CAPITAL LIMITED, 2877
INTER-ASIA VENTURE MANAGEMENT LIMITED, 2881
KOREA FIRST VENTURE CAPITAL CORPORATION, 2924
TECHNOCAP, 2263
TRANSATLANTIC CAPITAL LTD, 3186

Industry Preference Index / Financial Services

VENTANA CAPITAL MANAGEMENT LP, 1918
WATERMILL GROUP, 1962

Environmental Science
MOUNTAINEER CAPITAL, 1262

Environmental Services
BLUE POINT CAPITAL PARTNERS, 290

Environmental Technology
NEW BRUNSWICK INNOVATION FOUNDATION, 2200
PENN VENTURE PARTNERS, 1428

Equipment
ABU DHABI INVESTMENT AUTHORITY, 2321
AEROSTAR CAPITAL LLC, 67
BAY PARTNERS, 238
CHICAGO VENTURE PARTNERS LP, 470
LEVINE LEICHTMAN CAPITAL PARTNERS, 1111
LIBERTY CAPITAL PARTNERS, 1114
MASSACHUSETTS CAPITAL RESOURCE COMPANY, 1173
MASSACHUSETTS GROWTH CAPITAL CORPORATION, 1174
POMONA CAPITAL, 1462
RAF INDUSTRIES, 1521
SPACEVEST, 1714

Esports
IMAGINATION CAPITAL, 977

Ethnic Products & Services
PACIFIC COMMUNITY VENTURES, 1396

Fabless IC
AUTHOSIS VENTURES, 2457

Family Tech and Education
500 STARTUPS, 11

Family-Owned
AZALEA CAPITAL, 213

Farming
ANTERRA CAPITAL, 2405
BONNEFIELD FINANCIAL, 2065

Fashion
HILL AND GERTNER CAPITAL CORP., 2148
KALORI GROUP INVESTMENTS, 2915
M25 GROUP, 1155
NAXURI CAPITAL, 1284
PIQUE VENTURES, 2223
TYLT LAB, 1876

Fashion/Lifestyle
INNOGEST CAPITAL, 2874

Federal Services
CM EQUITY PARTNERS, 507

Film
ABU DHABI INVESTMENT AUTHORITY, 2321
ARTS ALLIANCE, 2428
NORTHSTAR VENTURES, 3012

FinTech
CORNERSTONE VENTURE PARTNERS, 543
MS&AD VENTURES, 1269
RECIPROCAL VENTURES, 1528
WILDCAT VENTURE PARTNERS, 1985

Finance
ABSTRACT VENTURES, 24
CANTOS VENTURES, 395
CULTIVATE CAPITAL, 568
GOOD NEWS VENTURES, 2138
GROUND UP VENTURES, 877
INNOVATION PLATFORM CAPITAL, 997

M25 GROUP, 1155
MEKETA INVESTMENT GROUP, 1200
MOTIV PARTNERS, 1258
SCOTIABANK PRIVATE EQUITY, 2250
SINEWAVE VENTURES, 1687
THE HIVE, 1809
URBAN US, 1894
VALUEACT CAPITAL, 1903
VIOLA FINTECH, 3220

Financial Data Applications
INFORMATION VENTURE PARTNERS, 2153

Financial Security & Crime Prevention
INFORMATION VENTURE PARTNERS, 2153

Financial Services
360 CAPITAL PARTNERS 360 Capital Management SA, 2296
3I GESTION SA 3i Group, 2302
3i GROUP PLC, 2311
3TS CAPITAL PARTNERS 3i Group plc, 2309
ABU DHABI INVESTMENT AUTHORITY, 2321
ACCESS CAPITAL CORPORATION, 2030
ACE & COMPANY, 2329
ACI CAPITAL, 42
ACME LABS, 2333
ACON INVESTMENTS, 46
ACTIS, 2337
ADVANTAGE CAPITAL PARTNERS, 61
AIG INVESTMENT CORPORATION (ASIA) LIMITED, 2356
AIP PRIVATE CAPITAL, 2031
ALBEMARLE PRIVATE EQUITY LIMITED, 2360
ALLSTATE INVESTMENTS LLC, 88
ALPHA CAPITAL PARTNERS, 90
ALTAMONT CAPITAL PARTNERS, 96
AMANET TECHNOLOGIES LIMITED, 2389
ANGELO, GORDON & CO., 127
ANT FINANCIAL, 2404
ANTHEMIS GROUP, 2406
APAX PARTNERS ET CIE, 2415
APOLLO GLOBAL MANAGEMENT, 140
ARSENAL CAPITAL PARTNERS, 170
ASHBY POINT CAPITAL, 179
ASIAN INFRASTRUCTURE FUND ADVISERS LIMITED AIF Capital, 2434
ASTELLA INVESTMENTS, 2438
ASTOR CAPITAL GROUP, 2440
AUGURY CAPITAL PARTNERS, 196
AUSTIN VENTURES, 202
AUSTRALIAN ETHICAL INVESTMENT LIMITED, 2456
AWAY REALTY, 2465
AZURE CAPITAL PARTNERS, 215
BAIN CAPITAL PRIVATE EQUITY, 220
BALDERTON CAPITAL, 2478
BARCLAYS VENTURES Barclays, 2486
BARING PRIVATE EQUITY PARTNERS INDIA, 2490
BATTERY VENTURES, 235
BAYSHORE CAPITAL, 2052
BERGGRUEN HOLDINGS, 250
BESSEMER VENTURE PARTNERS, 260
BEST FUNDS, 2058
BEZOS EXPEDITIONS, 262
BLACKFIN CAPITAL PARTNERS, 2521
BLACKSTONE PRIVATE EQUITY GROUP, 277
BMP AKTIENGESELLSCHAFT BMP Venture Capital, 2528
BOND CAPITAL, 2064
BOTTS & COMPANY LIMITED, 2532
BRAZOS PRIVATE EQUITY PARTNERS, 328
BREAKWATER INVESTMENTS, 330
BREGAL SAGEMOUNT, 333
BRERA CAPITAL PARTNERS, 335
BRIDGEPOINT CAPITAL GmbH, 2537
BRIDGEPOINT CAPITAL LIMITED, 2538
BROADHAVEN CAPITAL PARTNERS, 343
BROOKSIDE EQUITY PARTNERS LLC, 353
BUTZOW NORDIA ADVOCATES LTD, 2552
CAI CAPITAL PARTNERS, 365

Industry Preference Index / Financial Services

CALERA CAPITAL, 368
CAMBRIDGE CAPITAL CORPORATION, 381
CAMDEN PARTNERS HOLDINGS LLC, 383
CANDOVER, 2556
CAPITAL Z PARTNERS, 404
CARDINAL EQUITY PARTNERS, 409
CARDINAL VENTURE CAPITAL, 411
CARLYLE GROUP, 413
CATALYST FUND MANAGEMENT & RESEARCH LIMITED, 2572
CATALYST INVESTMENT MANAGERS PTY LIMITED PPM Capital, 2573
CCP EQUITY PARTNERS, 434
CEI VENTURES, 438
CENTERFIELD CAPITAL PARTNERS, 443
CENTRE PARTNERS MANAGEMENT LLC, 447
CERBERUS CAPITAL MANAGEMENT, 451
CHARLESBANK CAPITAL PARTNERS, 456
CHASE CAPITAL PARTNERS, 2588
CHEYENNE CAPITAL, 467
CHINA MERCHANTS CHINA DIRECT INVESTMENTS LTD., 2594
CHINA MERCHANTS CHINA INVESTMENT MANAGEMENT, 2595
CHINA VEST LIMITED, 2596
CHRYSALIS CAPITAL ChrysCapital, 2599
CHRYSCAPITAL MANAGEMENT COMPANIES ChrysCapital, 2600
CIBC CAPITAL MARKETS, 2079
CINCO CAPITAL, 2604
CIRCLE PEAK CAPITAL, 481
CITI VENTURES, 486
CIVC PARTNERS, 489
CLEARLIGHT PARTNERS, 501
CLIFFORD CHANCE PUNDER, 2614
CLYDESDALE VENTURES, 506
COLT VENTURES, 514
COMSTOCK CAPITAL PARTNERS LLC, 527
COMVEST PARTNERS, 528
CONCENTRIC EQUITY PARTNERS Financial Investments Corporation, 529
CONTOUR VENTURE PARTNERS, 533
CONVERSION CAPITAL, 535
CORDOVA VENTURES, 537
CRAWLEY VENTURES, 553
CRESTVIEW PARTNERS, 559
DAHER CAPITAL, 2649
DARBY OVERSEAS INVESTMENTS LTD, 584
DAVID N DEUTSCH & COMPANY LLC, 589
DAVIS, TUTTLE VENTURE PARTNERS LP, 591
DECIENS CAPITAL, 599
DFC LTD, 2661
DIRECT CAPITAL PRIVATE EQUITY LIMITED, 2664
DOUBLE IMPACT BUSINESS ADVISORY, 2670
DTA CAPITAL PARTNERS S/B, 2675
DUKE STREET CAPITAL Duke Street, 2676
DUNEDIN CAPITAL PARTNERS LIMITED, 2677
EAST FUND MANAGEMENT GmbH GiroCredit, 2683
ECI VENTURES, 2687
EDISON PARTNERS, 655
ELAIA PARTNERS, 2693
ELECTRA PARTNERS EUROPE, 2695
EM WARBURG, PINCUS & COMPANY INTERNATIONAL, 2697
EM WARBURG, PINCUS & COMPANY JAPAN, 2698
EMIGRANT CAPITAL, 667
ENIAC VENTURES, 679
ENTER VENTURES, 681
ENTERPRISE INVESTORS, 2706
EQUISTONE, 2714
EVERGREEN ADVISORS, 701
EXPIBEL BV, 2728
FAIRHAVEN CAPITAL, 712
FCF PARTNERS LP, 719
FdG ASSOCIATES LP, 801
FELICIS VENTURES, 720
FERRANTI LIMITED, 2732
FIDELITY GROWTH PARTNERS ASIA, 2733
FIELDSTONE PRIVATE CAPITAL GROUP, 726
FIVE ELMS CAPITAL, 745
FLEXPOINT FORD LLC, 750
FORTRESS INVESTMENT GROUP LLC, 767

FOX PAINE & COMPANY LLC, 778
FRIEDMAN, FLEISCHER & LOWE LLC, 787
FTV CAPITAL, 793
FULL CIRCLE INVESTMENTS, 2762
GAON ASSET MANAGEMENT, 2766
GE CAPITAL, 808
GE EQUITY EUROPE, 2769
GEFINOR CAPITAL, 810
GENERAL ATLANTIC PARTNERS, 815
GENERAL ENTERPRISE MANAGEMENT SERVICES, 2772
GENSTAR CAPITAL LP, 819
GERKEN CAPITAL ASSOCIATES, 822
GIC GROUP, 825
GLENCOE CAPITAL, 830
GLENTHORNE CAPITAL, 832
GOLDEN GATE CAPITAL, 839
GOLDEN SEEDS, 841
GRAND CENTRAL HOLDINGS, 847
GRANDBANKS CAPITAL, 848
GRANITE HILL CAPITAL PARTNERS, LLC, 851
GRAPHITE CAPITAL MANAGEMENT LTD, 2796
GRAYHAWK CAPITAL, 856
GREIF & COMPANY, 869
GRUPO BISA, 2800
GTCR, 884
GULFSTAR GROUP, 888
H KATZ CAPITAL GROUP, 891
HALIFAX GROUP LLC, 894
HANNOVER FINANZ GmbH, 2810
HARBOURVEST PARTNERS LLC, 909
HELLMAN & FRIEDMAN LLC, 924
HOLDING CAPITAL GROUP, 940
HORIZON PARTNERS, LTD, 945
HORIZONS VENTURES, 2831
HOULIHAN LOKEY, 948
HUDSON VENTURE PARTNERS, 954
HUNTSMAN GAY GLOBAL CAPITAL, 959
IANTHUS CAPITAL MANAGEMENT, 966
IMPLEMENT CAPITAL, 978
INSIGHT VENTURE PARTNERS, 1000
INTERNATIONAL FINANCE CORPORATION (IFC), 1007
INVENTUS, 1013
ISIS EP LLP F & C, 2898
ITC VENTURES, 2903
J. BURKE CAPITAL PARTNERS, 1023
JAGUAR CAPITAL PARTNERS, 1025
JEFFERIES CAPITAL PARTNERS, 1032
JLL PARTNERS, 1039
JORDAN COMPANY, 1045
JUMP CAPITAL LLC, 1046
KARLIN VENTURES, 1055
KENSINGTON CAPITAL PARTNERS, 2167
KHOSLA VENTURES, 1069
KOHLBERG & COMPANY LLC, 1081
KOHLBERG KRAVIS ROBERTS & COMPANY, 1082
KRG CAPITAL PARTNERS, 1086
LAKE CAPITAL, 1091
LAUNCHPAD VENTURE GROUP, 1100
LEE EQUITY PARTNERS, 1104
LEONARD GREEN & PARTNERS LP, 1109
LEVINE LEICHTMAN CAPITAL PARTNERS, 1111
LIBERTY CAPITAL PARTNERS, 1114
LIGHTYEAR CAPITAL, 1123
LINLEY CAPITAL, 1130
LLOYDS DEVELOPMENT CAPITAL LIMITED, 2944
LLR PARTNERS INC, 1136
LOMBARD INVESTMENTS, 1139
LOVELL MINNICK PARTNERS LLC, 1147
LOVETT MILLER & COMPANY, 1148
MADISON DEARBORN PARTNERS, 1156
MAINE ANGELS, 1160
MANULIFE CAPITAL, 2183
MENTOR CAPITAL PARTNERS LTD, 1203
MERITURN PARTNERS, 1213
MHS CAPITAL, 1226
MISSIONOG, 1240
MITSUI SUMITOMO INSURANCE VENTURE CAPITAL CO, 2971

Industry Preference Index / Fintech

MMC VENTURES, 2972
MONTLAKE CAPITAL, 1250
MOUNTAIN PARTNERS, 2979
NAVIGATION CAPITAL PARTNERS, 1280
NEEDHAM CAPITAL PARTNERS, 1288
NEW CAPITAL PARTNERS, 1293
NEW MOUNTAIN CAPITAL, 1301
NEWFIELD CAPITAL, 1313
NEXTEC DEVELOPMENT CAPITAL LIMITED, 3000
NIPPON TECHNOLOGY VENTURE PARTNERS LIMITED, 3005
NORO-MOSELEY PARTNERS, 1331
NORTH AMERICAN FUND, 1332
NORTH ATLANTIC CAPITAL CORPORATION, 1333
NORTH COVE PARTNERS, 1337
NORTHSTAR CAPITAL, 1343
NORTHWOOD VENTURES, 1344
NORWEST EQUITY PARTNERS, 1345
NORWEST VENTURE PARTNERS, 1346
NOVA SCOTIA BUSINESS INC., 2205
NUTEK (NARINGS- OCH TEKNIKUTVECKLINGSVERKET) NUTEK, 3016
OAK HILL CAPITAL PARTNERS, 1360
OAK INVESTMENT PARTNERS, 1361
OCA VENTURES, 1364
OLYMPUS PARTNERS, 1372
OUTCOME CAPITAL, 1388
PALLADIUM EQUITY PARTNERS, 1403
PAMLICO CAPITAL, 1409
PARALLEL49 EQUITY, 2214
PARKVIEW CAPITAL PARTNERS, 2215
PARTHENON CAPITAL, 1417
PEACHTREE EQUITY PARTNERS, 1423
PINE BROOK ROAD PARTNERS, 1443
POST CAPITAL PARTNERS, 1465
POUSCHINE COOK CAPITAL MANAGEMENT LLC, 1466
PRAIRIE CAPITAL, 1469
PWC, 3064
QUANTUM CAPITAL PARTNERS, 1510
RAYMOND JAMES CAPITAL, 1526
REDMONT VENTURE PARTNERS, 1533
REITEN & CO STRATEGIC INVESTMENTS AS Reiten & Company, 3076
REVOLUTION LLC, 1555
RIBBIT CAPITAL, 1560
RICHINA CAPITAL PARTNERS LIMITED, 3082
RITTENHOUSE VENTURES, 1568
ROBIN HOOD VENTURES, 1577
ROPART ASSET MANAGEMENT, 1583
ROSEWOOD CAPITAL, 1587
ROUGH DRAFT VENTURES, 1589
RRE VENTURES, 1593
SAFEGUARD SCIENTIFICS, 1601
SAGEVIEW CAPITAL, 1602
SAIF PARTNERS, 3093
SAMOS INVESTMENTS, 3097
SARATOGA PARTNERS, 1621
SARONA ASSET MANAGEMENT, 2248
SATORI CAPITAL, 1622
SCP PARTNERS, 1633
SENTRY FINANCIAL CORPORATION, 1652
SEQUOIA CAPITAL, 1654
SERGE PUN & ASSOCIATES (MYANMAR) LIMITED, 3111
SIERRA VENTURES, 1670
SIF TRANSYLVANIA, 3119
SIXTHIRTY, 1688
SOCIAL CAPITAL, 1696
SONY EUROPE, 3129
SOURCE CAPITAL GROUP, 1707
SOUTH ATLANTIC VENTURE FUNDS, 1708
SOUTHPORT PARTNERS, 1712
STATELINE ANGELS, 1740
STONE POINT CAPITAL LLC, 1743
STRAND HANSON LIMITED, 3146
SUCSY, FISCHER & COMPANY, 1750
SUMMIT BRIDGE CAPITAL, 3147
SUMMIT PARTNERS, 1752
SUN CAPITAL PARTNERS, 1753
SUSQUEHANNA GROWTH EQUITY, 1759
SYCAMORE VENTURES, 1769
SYMMETRIC CAPITAL, 1770
TA ASSOCIATES, 1776
TACTICO, 2260
TELEFONICA VENTURES, 3169
TERA CAPITAL CORPORATION, 2267
TH LEE PUTNAM VENTURES, 1804
THAYER STREET PARTNERS, 1805
THOMA BRAVO LLC, 1814
THOMAS H LEE PARTNERS, 1815
THOMPROPERTIES OY, 3175
TORQUEST PARTNERS, 2272
TPA CORPORATE FINANCE CONSULTING GMBH Horwarth International, 3184
TRANSITION PARTNERS LTD, 1837
TRANSYLVANIA FINANCIAL INVESTMENT COMPANY, 3187
TRIBECA VENTURE PARTNERS, 1849
TRILANTIC CAPITAL PARTNERS, 1851
TTV CAPITAL, 1863
UPDATA VENTURE PARTNERS, 1886
UPFRONT VENTURES, 1888
URBAN INNOVATION FUND, 1893
VALLEY VENTURES LP, 1901
VARDE PARTNERS, 1907
VEDANTA CAPITAL LP, 1911
VENTURE INVESTORS, 3210
VESTAR CAPITAL PARTNERS, 1931
VISION CAPITAL, 1937
VITAL FINANCIAL LLC, 1940
VRG CAPITAL, 2282
WAND PARTNERS, 1955
WARBURG PINCUS LLC, 1956
WAVELAND INVESTMENTS LLC, 1964
WELLSPRING CAPITAL MANAGEMENT LLC, 1971
WESTERN NIS ENTERPRISE FUND, 3234
WESTLAKE SECURITIES, 1976
YELLOW POINT EQUITY PARTNERS, 2292

Financial Technology
CHINAROCK CAPITAL MANAGEMENT VENTURES, 472

Finanical Mobile
LIFE.SREDA, 2940

Fintech
.406 VENTURES, 2
ADAMS STREET PARTNERS, LLC, 57
ALTPOINT CAPITAL, 101
BAIN CAPITAL VENTURES, 221
BLUFF POINT ASSOCIATES, 299
BOXGROUP, 318
BREYER CAPITAL, 336
CAMP ONE VENTURES, 384
CANVAS VENTURES, 396
COMVEST PARTNERS, 528
CORRELATION VENTURES, 544
CROSSLINK CAPITAL, 563
CXO FUND, 574
DAY ONE VENTURES, 593
DECIENS CAPITAL, 599
DFJ GOTHAM VENTURES, 608
DIFFERENCE CAPITAL, 2096
DISRUPTION VENTURES, 2098
DRAPER ATHENA, 626
EDISON PARTNERS, 655
ELYSIUM VENTURE CAPITAL, 661
ENTREPRENEURS ROUNDTABLE ACCELERATOR, 684
F-PRIME CAPITAL PARTNERS, 710
FINAVENTURES, 729
FIRST ROUND CAPITAL, 741
FIRSTMARK CAPITAL, 743
FORTÉ VENTURES, 768
GENERAL CATALYST PARTNERS, 816
GOLDEN VENTURE PARTNERS, 2137
GRANDBANKS CAPITAL, 848
GREAT HILL PARTNERS LLC, 857

1179

Industry Preference Index / Fishing

GVA CAPITAL, 890
HARDY CAPITAL PARTNERS, 2144
IMPRESSION VENTURES, 2151
INDEX VENTURES, 2860
INNOGEST CAPITAL, 2874
LIGHTSPEED VENTURE PARTNERS, 1121
LUGE CAPITAL, 2179
MILLENIUM TECHNOLOGY VALUE PARTNERS, 1235
MOTLEY FOOL VENTURES, 1259
NORO-MOSELEY PARTNERS, 1331
NORTH HILL VENTURES, 1339
OBVIOUS VENTURES, 1363
OFF THE GRID VENTURES, 1370
OYSTER VENTURES, 1395
PORTAG3 VENTURES, 2225
RITTENHOUSE VENTURES, 1568
RUBICON VENTURE CAPITAL, 1595
SALMON RIVER CAPITAL, 1608
SATURN PARTNERS, 1623
SIGNIA VENTURE PARTNERS, 1678
SONY INNOVATION FUND, 1703
TACTICO, 2260
TECHNOLOGY CROSSOVER VENTURES, 1785
TENX VENTURES, 2266
URBAN US, 1894
VILLAGE GLOBAL, 1933
WIREFRAME VENTURES, 2000

Fishing
BIO FUND MANAGEMENT OY, 2512
FARM CREDIT CANADA, 2114
WESTERN NIS ENTERPRISE FUND, 3234

Fitness
SIGNIA VENTURE PARTNERS, 1678
STEELPOINT CAPITAL PARTNERS, 1741

Fixed & Mobile Broadband
VERTEX VENTURE CAPITAL, 3214

Flexible Packaging
SUN CAPITAL PARTNERS, 1753

Food
FOUNDERS GROUP OF FOOD COMPANIES, 2123

Food & Agriculture
GLOBAL ENVIRONMENT FUND, 834

Food & Beverage
AGRIBUSINESS MANAGEMENT COMPANY, 71
ALANTRA, 77
AMERICA FIRST INVESTMENT ADVISORS, 108
AMHERST FUND, 113
ARBOR INVESTMENTS, 147
AUDAX GROUP, 194
AUSTRALIAN ETHICAL INVESTMENT LIMITED, 2456
AVRIO CAPITAL, 2049
BALTCAP MANAGEMENT LTD, 2480
BASE VENTURES, 229
BENCIS CAPITAL PARTNERS, 2501
BEZOS EXPEDITIONS, 262
BIO FUND MANAGEMENT OY, 2512
BIOGENERATION VENTURES, 2514
BIOPACIFIC VENTURES, 2516
BOND CAPITAL, 2064
BOULDER VENTURES LTD, 315
BREAKWATER MANAGEMENT, 331
BRIGHTPATH CAPITAL PARTNERS, 340
BROOKSIDE EQUITY PARTNERS LLC, 353
BRYNWOOD PARTNERS, 357
CALIFORNIA COAST VENTURE FORUM, 3257
CANADIAN VENTURE CAPITAL ASSOCIATION Canadian Venture Capital & Private Equity Association, 3258
CAPITAL FOR BUSINESS, INC, 399
CAPITAL PARTNERS, 401
CARPEDIA CAPITAL, 2072
CATALYST INVESTMENT MANAGERS PTY LIMITED PPM Capital, 2573
CEDAR VENTURES LLC, 437
CENTERFIELD CAPITAL PARTNERS, 443
CENTRAL TEXAS ANGEL NETWORK, 445
CENTRE PARTNERS MANAGEMENT LLC, 447
CHARLESBANK CAPITAL PARTNERS, 456
CIC PARTNERS, 477
CID CAPITAL, 478
CLARENDON FUND MANAGERS, 2610
CLYDESDALE VENTURES, 506
COMPAGNIE FINANCIERE E DE ROTHSCHILD BANQUE, 2625
CULTIVIAN SANDBOX VENTURES, 570
CVC ASIA PACIFIC LIMITED CVC Capital Partners, 2643
CVC CAPITAL PARTNERS LTD, 2644
DAVID N DEUTSCH & COMPANY LLC, 589
DIRECT CAPITAL PRIVATE EQUITY LIMITED, 2664
EAST FUND MANAGEMENT GmbH GiroCredit, 2683
ENDEAVOUR CAPITAL, 673
ENNOVENT, 2701
EQUISTONE, 2714
EUROVENTURES CAPITAL, 2725
FALCONHEAD CAPITAL, 717
FARM CREDIT CANADA, 2114
FCF PARTNERS LP, 719
FIRST ATLANTIC CAPITAL LTD., 733
FIRST ISRAEL MEZZANINE INVESTORS LIMITED, 2745
FLANDERS' FOREIGN INVESTMENT OFFICE, 2746
FOUNDATION MARKETS, 2122
FOUNDERS EQUITY, 774
FRONTENAC COMPANY, 789
FULL CIRCLE INVESTMENTS, 2762
GLENCOE CAPITAL, 830
GOLDNER, HAWN, JOHNSON & MORRISON, 843
H KATZ CAPITAL GROUP, 891
HERITAGE PARTNERS, 926
HIG CAPITAL, 928
HILL AND GERTNER CAPITAL CORP., 2148
HORIZON PARTNERS, LTD, 945
HT CAPITAL ADVISORS LLC, 953
ICV PARTNERS, 969
INDUSTRI KAPITAL SVENSKA AB, 2863
INTER-ASIA VENTURE MANAGEMENT LIMITED, 2881
INVUS GROUP, 1018
J. BURKE CAPITAL PARTNERS, 1023
JAVELIN INVESTMENTS, 2908
KILMER CAPITAL PARTNERS, 2169
KOHLBERG VENTURES, 1083
L CATTERTON PARTNERS, 1088
LASALLE CAPITAL GROUP, 1093
LAUNCHPAD VENTURES, 2931
LEGAL AND GENERAL VENTURES LIMITED, 2935
LEVINE LEICHTMAN CAPITAL PARTNERS, 1111
LIBERTY CAPITAL PARTNERS, 1114
LIFE SCIENCES PARTNERS BV, 2939
LITTLEJOHN & COMPANY LLC, 1134
LYNWOOD CAPITAL PARTNERS, 1152
M25 GROUP, 1155
MACQUARIE DIRECT INVESTMENT LIMITED, 2951
MAIN STREET CAPITAL HOLDINGS LLC, 1159
MARCEAU INVESTISSEMENTS, 2955
MCGOVERN CAPITAL, 1191
MIDWEST MEZZANINE FUNDS, 1232
NAVIGATION CAPITAL PARTNERS, 1280
NBC CAPITAL PTY LIMITED, 2988
NESBIC INVESTMENT FUND II, 2992
NEW BRUNSWICK INNOVATION FOUNDATION, 2200
NEW MEXICO COMMUNITY CAPITAL, 1300
NORTH AMERICAN FUND, 1332
ONE EQUITY PARTNERS, 1376
PACIFIC VENTURES GROUP, 1399
PARALLEL49 EQUITY, 2214
PARTHENON CAPITAL, 1417
PENINSULA CAPITAL PARTNERS LLC, 1426
PNC ERIEVIEW CAPITAL, 1456
PROGRESS EQUITY PARTNERS, 1484
PROSPECT PARTNERS LLC, 1492

Industry Preference Index / Gene Therapy

ROOT CAPITAL, 1582
SERRUYA PRIVATE EQUITY, 2254
SHAW KWEI AND PARTNERS, 3116
SHERBROOKE CAPITAL, 1665
SIF TRANSYLVANIA, 3119
SOUTH ATLANTIC VENTURE FUNDS, 1708
SPRING LANE CAPITAL, 1729
SUCSY, FISCHER & COMPANY, 1750
SUMMIT BRIDGE CAPITAL, 3147
SUN CAPITAL PARTNERS, 1753
SWANDER PACE CAPITAL, 1767
TENNESSEE COMMUNITY VENTURES, 1797
TGF MANAGEMENT, 1803
TMG CAPITAL PARTNERS, 3180
TORQUEST PARTNERS, 2272
TRANSYLVANIA FINANCIAL INVESTMENT COMPANY, 3187
TSG CONSUMER PARTNERS, 1861
TULLY & HOLLAND, 1867
TVV CAPITAL, 1870
UNDERDOG VENTURES, 1880
UNION CAPITAL CORPORATION, 1881
WAND PARTNERS, 1955
WELLSPRING CAPITAL MANAGEMENT LLC, 1971
WESTERN NIS ENTERPRISE FUND, 3234
WHITECAP VENTURE PARTNERS, 2288
XPV WATER PARTNERS, 2290
YELLOWSTONE CAPITAL, 2013
YISSUM TECHNOLOGY TRANSFER, 3245
YORK STREET CAPITAL PARTNERS LLC, 2015

Food & Consumer Products
SIGNAL HILL EQUITY PARTNERS, 2255

Food Products & Services
CALERA CAPITAL, 368

Food Safety
CULTIVIAN SANDBOX VENTURES, 570

Food Services
ABU DHABI INVESTMENT AUTHORITY, 2321
AGRIBUSINESS MANAGEMENT COMPANY, 71
ATP PRIVATE EQUITY PARTNERS, 2447
BERINGEA, 251
CLIFFORD CHANCE PUNDER, 2614
ENTREPRENEUR CAPITAL, 2107
FCF PARTNERS LP, 719
FOUNDERS EQUITY, 774
GOLUB CAPITAL, 844
GRUPO BISA, 2800
HOLDING CAPITAL GROUP, 940
JMH CAPITAL, 1040
MOTIV PARTNERS, 1258
PALLADIUM EQUITY PARTNERS, 1403
PRIVATE EQUITY PARTNERS SPA, 3053
SAMBRINVEST SA, 3096
SENTINEL CAPITAL PARTNERS, 1651
SWANDER PACE CAPITAL, 1767

Food Tech & Digital Healthcare
500 STARTUPS, 11

Food Technology
CXO FUND, 574

Food and Beverage
GREIF & COMPANY, 869

Foodtech
ARCTERN VENTURES, 2041
INNOGEST CAPITAL, 2874

Footwear
BREAKAWAY VENTURES, 329

Forensic Science
MOUNTAINEER CAPITAL, 1262

Forestry
BIO FUND MANAGEMENT OY, 2512
FARM CREDIT CANADA, 2114
GLOBAL ENVIRONMENT FUND, 834
LIONHART CAPITAL LTD, 2177
MERITURN PARTNERS, 1213
SOURCE CAPITAL GROUP, 1707
WESTERN NIS ENTERPRISE FUND, 3234
ZERNIKE SEED FUND BV, 3250

Franchising
ARGOSY CAPITAL, 164
BIP CAPITAL, 271
CAPITAL PARTNERS, 401
FOUNDERS EQUITY, 774
H KATZ CAPITAL GROUP, 891
IDG CAPITAL PARTNERS, 2847
LEVINE LEICHTMAN CAPITAL PARTNERS, 1111
SALT CREEK CAPITAL, 1609
SENTINEL CAPITAL PARTNERS, 1651
WOODBRIDGE GROUP, 2004

Frontier
SOCIAL CAPITAL, 1696

Fund Management
CAPMAN CAPITAL MANAGEMENT OY, 2562

Fundraising
CAPMAN CAPITAL MANAGEMENT OY, 2562

Furniture
PRIVATE EQUITY PARTNERS SPA, 3053

Gaming
3W VENTURES Latour & Zuberbuhler GmbH, 2310
ARCHTOP VENTURES, 154
AZURE CAPITAL PARTNERS, 215
BERKELEY VENTURES, 253
BERTELSMANN DIGITAL MEDIA INVESTMENTS, 256
BEZOS EXPEDITIONS, 262
BLAST FUNDING, 279
CLARENDON FUND MANAGERS, 2610
COLOMA VENTURES, 512
DALLAS VENTURE PARTNERS, 582
DATA POINT CAPITAL, 586
EDEN VENTURES, 2691
EPLANET CAPITAL, 690
FELICIS VENTURES, 720
FIRSTMARK CAPITAL, 743
GENACAST VENTURES, 814
GGV CAPITAL, 823
GREAT OAKS VENTURE CAPITAL, 858
GREYCROFT PARTNERS, 871
INGENIOUS VENTURES, 2871
INLAND TECHSTART FUND, 993
INSIGHT VENTURE PARTNERS, 1000
MAKERS FUND, 2953
NHN INVESTMENT, 3002
NORTHSTAR VENTURES, 3012
NOVA SCOTIA BUSINESS INC., 2205
RAPTOR GROUP, 1524
REVO CAPITAL, 3078
ROTH CAPITAL PARTNERS, 1588
SEIDLER EQUITY PARTNERS, 1645
SILKROAD EQUITY, 1681
SONY INNOVATION FUND, 1703
SV ANGEL, 1761
THAYER VENTURES, 1806
TRUE VENTURES, 1860
WASABI VENTURES, 1958
WHITE STAR CAPITAL, 1982
XG VENTURES, 2010

Gene Therapy
MVM LIFE SCIENCE PARTNERS, 2981

1181

Industry Preference Index / General Industrial

General Industrial
3I EUROPE PLC 3i Group, 2300

Genetic Engineering
AMPHION CAPITAL PARTNERS, 2397
ARTHUR P GOULD & COMPANY, 172
MASSACHUSETTS CAPITAL RESOURCE COMPANY, 1173
MASSACHUSETTS GROWTH CAPITAL CORPORATION, 1174
NORTH BRIDGE VENTURE PARTNERS, 1334
PERMAL CAPITAL MANAGEMENT, 1432
PLEXUS VENTURES, 1452
PROVCO GROUP, 1494
ROYALTY CAPITAL MANAGEMENT, 1591
SEED CAPITAL LIMITED, 3107
SEQUEL VENTURE PARTNERS, 1653
SOURCE CAPITAL GROUP, 1707
VERITAS VENTURE PARTNERS, 3212
WASSERSTEIN & CO., 1960
WESTERN TECHNOLOGY INVESTMENT, 1975

Genomics
APPLE TREE PARTNERS, 143
CHL MEDICAL PARTNERS, 474
HEALTH ENTERPRISE PARTNERS, 918
OXFORD BIOSCIENCE PARTNERS, 1394
SPENCER TRASK VENTURES, 1720

Genomics & Bioinformatics
ARCH VENTURE PARTNERS, 153

Glass
SAMBRINVEST SA, 3096
SRIW SA SRIW Group, 3134

Global Equities
DEUTSCHE ASSET MANAGEMENT (AUSTRALIA) LIMITED Deutsche Bank AG, 2659

Global Financial Advisory
ROTHSCHILD AUSTRALIA - ARROW PRIVATE EQUITY Rothschild Group, 3086

Global Industries
CENTENNIAL VENTURES, 441
GREENBRIAR EQUITY GROUP LLC, 862
LINK TECHNOLOGIES LIMITED, 2941
RENAISSANCE PARTNERS, 3077
UBS GLOBAL ASSET MANAGEMENT, 1878

Global Insurance Solutions
DEUTSCHE ASSET MANAGEMENT (AUSTRALIA) LIMITED Deutsche Bank AG, 2659

Global Supply Chains
FIRELAKE CAPITAL, 730

Golf
KB PARTNERS, 1056

GovTech
URBAN US, 1894

Government
CI CAPITAL PARTNERS, 476
ENLIGHTENMENT CAPITAL, 680
INSIGHT VENTURE PARTNERS, 1000
MOTOROLA SOLUTIONS VENTURE CAPITAL, 1260
NAVIGATION CAPITAL PARTNERS, 1280
OMIDYAR NETWORK, 1374
OUTCOME CAPITAL, 1388
PEACHTREE EQUITY PARTNERS, 1423

Government Services
GLADSTONE CAPITAL, 828
RLH EQUITY PARTNERS, 1575

Graphic Arts
CAMBRIDGE CAPITAL CORPORATION, 381
CLAL ELECTRONICS INDUSTRIES LIMITED, 2609
IGNITE JAPAN KK Ignite Group, 2854
MAYFLY CAPITAL, 1185

Graphics
INSIGHT VENTURE PARTNERS, 1000

Green Building
CAPITAL E, 398
ROCKPORT CAPITAL, 1579

Green Energy
EPLANET CAPITAL, 690

Green Technology
10X VENTURE PARTNERS, 3
COUNCIL FOR ENTREPRENEURIAL DEVELOPMENT, 3259
EARTHRISE CAPITAL, 643
GOAL HOLDINGS, 2135
GSR VENTURES, 2801
INFIELD CAPITAL, 988
ISOURCE GESTION, 2899
KLEINER PERKINS, 1075
NGEN PARTNERS, 1324
SCIENCEVEST, 1630
SIERRA ANGELS, 1669
TARGET PARTNERS, 3161
VERTEX VENTURE CAPITAL, 3214
ZELKOVA VENTURES, 2017

Ground Transportation
AUTOTECH VENTURES, 205

Group Finances
CAPMAN CAPITAL MANAGEMENT OY, 2562

HOA Financing
BLAST FUNDING, 279

Handicrafts
AAVISHKAAR, 2313

Hardware
ACCEL-KKR LLC, 29
ACME CAPITAL, 45
ACT VENTURE CAPITAL LIMITED, 2336
AUSTIN VENTURES, 202
BAY PARTNERS, 238
CAZENOVE PRIVATE EQUITY Cazenove Capital, 2577
CIBC CAPITAL MARKETS, 2079
CREANDUM, 2637
ECHELON VENTURES, 647
FIRST ROUND CAPITAL, 741
FIRSTMARK CAPITAL, 743
FLOODGATE FUND, 751
FRANCISCO PARTNERS, 779
G-51 CAPITAL LLC, 803
GENESIS PARTNERS, 2775
HARBOURVEST PARTNERS LLC, 909
HIGHWAY1, 936
HORIZONS VENTURES, 2831
ID VENTURES AMERICA LLC, 970
INNOVATIONSKAPITAL, 2878
LEASING TECHNOLOGIES INTERNATIONAL INC., 1103
MASS VENTURES, 1172
MCROCK CAPITAL, 2190
MERCATOR INVESTMENTS, 2192
MIDVEN, 2967
NEUHAUS PARTNERS, 2994
NEW VENTURE PARTNERS, 1305
OXANTIUM VENTURES, 1393
OYSTER INVEST, 3022
SELBY VENTURE PARTNERS, 1646
STORM VENTURES, 1747
SVB CAPITAL, 1764

Industry Preference Index / Healthcare

SWANDER PACE CAPITAL, 1767

Hardware Technology
McLEAN WATSON CAPITAL, 2199

Hardwood Products
MOUNTAINEER CAPITAL, 1262

Hazardous Waste
VENTANA CAPITAL MANAGEMENT LP, 1918

Health
3M UNITEK, 2307
ACCUITIVE MEDICAL VENTURES LLC, 40
AFFINITY CAPITAL MANAGEMENT, 68
AGATE MEDICAL INVESTMENTS, 2353
ALFA CAPITAL Alfa Group, 2363
ALLOY VENTURES, 87
ALPHA CAPITAL PARTNERS, 90
AMPERSAND CAPITAL PARTNERS, 118
AMWIN MANAGEMENT PTY LIMITED, 2398
ANTHEM VENTURE PARTNERS, 132
APAX PARTNERS ET CIE, 2415
BATTELLE VENTURES, 233
BOULDER VENTURES LTD, 315
BRENTWOOD ASSOCIATES, 334
CALVERT INVESTMENT MANAGEMENT, 376
CHL MEDICAL PARTNERS, 474
FOUNDER COLLECTIVE, 771
GTCR, 884
GULFSTAR GROUP, 888
HALIFAX GROUP LLC, 894
HENDERSON PRIVATE CAPITAL, 2821
HG CAPITAL, 2823
INNOVATIONSKAPITAL, 2878
INTEL CAPITAL, 1004
INTER-ASIA VENTURE MANAGEMENT LIMITED, 2881
KHOSLA VENTURES, 1069
LEASING TECHNOLOGIES INTERNATIONAL INC., 1103
M25 GROUP, 1155
NBC CAPITAL PTY LIMITED, 2988
NORTH ATLANTIC CAPITAL CORPORATION, 1333
NORTHWOOD VENTURES, 1344
PACIFIC COMMUNITY VENTURES, 1396
PACIFIC HORIZON VENTURES, 1398
PANGAEA VENTURES LTD, 2213
PAPPAS VENTURES, 1412
PROSPECT PARTNERS LLC, 1492
REVOLUTION LLC, 1555
SECTION 32, 1643
SENTRY FINANCIAL CORPORATION, 1652
SEQUEL VENTURE PARTNERS, 1653
SIGNIA VENTURE PARTNERS, 1678
SWANDER PACE CAPITAL, 1767
TECHNOCAP, 2263
URBAN INNOVATION FUND, 1893
US VENTURE PARTNERS, 1896
VIVO CAPITAL, 1941

Health & Wellness
645 VENTURES, 13
AMOREPACIFIC VENTURES, 2394
AMPLIFY, 120
ARCHTOP VENTURES, 154
BASE VENTURES, 229
BREAKWATER MANAGEMENT, 331
BRIGHTPATH CAPITAL PARTNERS, 340
CLYDESDALE VENTURES, 506
FUNK VENTURES, 797
GOAL HOLDINGS, 2135
HMS HAWAII MANAGEMENT, 939
KODIAK CAPITAL, 1079
MCGOVERN CAPITAL, 1191
NEW YORK VENTURE PARTNERS, 1310
SOCIAL VENTURE CIRCLE, 3277
SONY INNOVATION FUND, 1703
SPERO VENTURES, 1721

STEELPOINT CAPITAL PARTNERS, 1741
THE HIVE, 1809

Health IT
BIOADVANCE, 266

Health Technology
RELENTLESS PURSUIT PARTNERS, 2237

Healthcare
11.2 CAPITAL, 4
3I ASIA PACIFIC 3i Group, 2297
3I DEUTSCHLAND GESELLSCHAFT FUR 3i Group, 2299
3I EUROPE PLC 3i Group, 2300
3I GERMANY GmbH 3i Group, 2301
3I GESTION SA 3i Group, 2302
3i GROUP PLC, 2311
3I ITALY 3i Group, 2303
3I TEUPSCHLAND GmbH 3i Group, 2305
3W VENTURES Latour & Zuberbuhler GmbH, 2310
5AM VENTURES, 12
AAVIN PRIVATE EQUITY, 17
AAVISHKAAR, 2313
ABELL FOUNDATION VENTURES, 19
ABERDARE VENTURES, 20
ABS CAPITAL PARTNERS, 22
ABS VENTURES, 23
ABSTRACT VENTURES, 24
ACCELERATOR LIFE SCIENCE PARTNERS, 31
ACCOLADE PARTNERS, 37
ACCRETIVE LLC, 39
ACI CAPITAL, 42
ACKRELL CAPITAL, 44
ACREW CAPITAL, 49
ACTIVA CAPITAL, 2338
ACUMEN, 55
ADAMS STREET PARTNERS, LLC, 57
ADVANCED TECHNOLOGY VENTURES, 59
ADVENT INTERNATIONAL CORPORATION, 62
AESCAP VENTURE, 2350
AFFINITY CAPITAL MANAGEMENT, 68
AGATE MEDICAL INVESTMENTS, 2353
AISLING CAPITAL, 74
ALANTRA, 77
ALEXANDER HUTTON, 82
ALLELE FUNDS, 2367
ALTA VENTURES MEXICO, 2382
ALTAMONT CAPITAL PARTNERS, 96
ALTARIS CAPITAL PARTNERS, 97
AMBIENT SOUND INVESTMENTS, 2390
AMICUS CAPITAL PARTNERS, 2392
AMPERSAND CAPITAL PARTNERS, 118
ANGELO, GORDON & CO., 127
ANGELPAD, 128
APAX GLOBIS PARTNERS & COMPANY Globis Capital Partners/Apax, 2414
APAX PARTNERS ET CIE, 2415
APAX PARTNERS, 135
APERTURE VENTURE PARTNERS, 136
APHELION CAPITAL, 138
APJOHN GROUP LLC, 139
APPLE TREE PARTNERS, 143
ARBORETUM VENTURES, 149
ARCAPITA INC, 152
ARCAPITA INC, 152
ARCUS VENTURES, 157
ARES MANAGEMENT LLC, 159
ARGENTUM GROUP, 161
ARLINGTON CAPITAL PARTNERS, 166
ARROWHEAD INVESTMENT MANAGEMENT, 168
ARSENAL CAPITAL PARTNERS, 170
ARTHUR VENTURES, 173
ARTIS VENTURES, 175
ASCENSION HEALTH VENTURES LLC, 176
ASSET MANAGEMENT VENTURES, 181
ASTELLA INVESTMENTS, 2438
ATHYRIUM CAPITAL MANAGEMENT, 188

1183

Industry Preference Index / Healthcare

ATP PRIVATE EQUITY PARTNERS, 2447
ATRIA CAPITAL PARTENAIRES, 2448
AURORA CAPITAL GROUP, 199
AUSTRALIAN ETHICAL INVESTMENT LIMITED, 2456
AVENUE CAPITAL GROUP, 208
AVISTA CAPITAL PARTNERS, 209
AVLAR BIOVENTURES, 2463
AZALEA CAPITAL, 213
AZCA, 214
BAIN CAPITAL PRIVATE EQUITY, 220
BAIN CAPITAL VENTURES, 221
BAIRD CAPITAL PARTNERS, 222
BALLAST POINT VENTURES, 224
BARCLAYS VENTURES Barclays, 2486
BARING PRIVATE EQUITY PARTNERS INDIA, 2490
BAXTER VENTURES, 236
BB BIOTECH VENTURES, 2496
BBH CAPITAL PARTNERS, 240
BC PARTNERS LIMITED, 2497
BEECKEN PETTY O'KEEFE & COMPANY, 244
BERINGEA, 251
BERTRAM CAPITAL, 257
BESSEMER VENTURE PARTNERS, 260
BESTPORT VENTURES, 2507
BIOGENERATION VENTURES, 2514
BIOMED PARTNERS, 2515
BIOVEDA CAPITAL, 2518
BIOVENTURES INVESTORS, 270
BIP CAPITAL, 271
BISON CAPITAL ASSET MANAGEMENT LLC, 274
BLACKSTONE PRIVATE EQUITY GROUP, 277
BLUE CHIP VENTURE COMPANY, 287
BLUE HERON CAPITAL, 288
BLUE POINT CAPITAL PARTNERS, 290
BLUE SAGE CAPITAL, 291
BLUESTEM CAPITAL COMPANY, 297
BOEHRINGER INGELHEIM VENTURE FUND, 2530
BOLDCAP VENTURES LLC, 304
BOND CAPITAL, 2064
BOSTON MILLENNIA PARTNERS, 312
BRAIN TRUST ACCELERATOR FUND, 323
BRAZOS PRIVATE EQUITY PARTNERS, 328
BREAKWATER INVESTMENTS, 330
BREGAL SAGEMOUNT, 333
BRERA CAPITAL PARTNERS, 335
BRIDGE STREET CAPITAL, 338
BRIDGEPOINT CAPITAL GmbH, 2537
BRIDGEPOINT CAPITAL LIMITED, 2538
BROADMARK CAPITAL, 345
BROADVIEW VENTURES, 347
BROOKE PRIVATE EQUITY ASSOCIATES, 350
BRUCKMANN, ROSSER, SHERRILL & COMPANY, 354
BRYAN GARNIER & COMPANY, 2544
BRYANT PARK VENTURES, 356
BULLNET, 2548
BUSINESS GROWTH FUND, 2550
CAI CAPITAL PARTNERS, 365
CALERA CAPITAL, 368
CALTIUS STRUCTURED CAPITAL, 374
CALUMET VENTURE FUND, 375
CAMBRIDGE CAPITAL CORPORATION, 381
CAMDEN PARTNERS HOLDINGS LLC, 383
CANAAN PARTNERS, 386
CANADIAN VENTURE CAPITAL ASSOCIATION Canadian Venture Capital & Private Equity Association, 3258
CANTOS VENTURES, 395
CAPITALA, 405
CAPITOL PARTNERS, 406
CAPRICORN VENTURE PARTNERS NV, 2563
CAPX PARTNERS, 407
CARDINAL EQUITY PARTNERS, 409
CARDINAL PARTNERS, 410
CARLYLE ASIA INVESTMENT ADVISORS LIMITED Carlyle Group, 2565
CARLYLE GROUP, 413
CASDIN CAPITAL, 419
CATALYST HEALTH VENTURES, 426

CATALYST INVESTMENT MANAGERS PTY LIMITED PPM Capital, 2573
CATAPULT VENTURES, 429
CATHAYA CAPITAL, 2576
CCMP CAPITAL, 433
CCP EQUITY PARTNERS, 434
CDH INVESTMENTS, 2579
CEI VENTURES, 438
CELADON CAPITAL GROUP, 2582
CELERITY PARTNERS, 439
CENTERFIELD CAPITAL PARTNERS, 443
CENTRAL TEXAS ANGEL NETWORK, 445
CENTRE PARTNERS MANAGEMENT LLC, 447
CERBERUS CAPITAL MANAGEMENT, 451
CERES VENTURE FUND, 452
CHALLENGE FUNDS - ETGAR LP, 2585
CHARLESBANK CAPITAL PARTNERS, 456
CHASE CAPITAL PARTNERS, 2588
CHENGWEI VENTURES, 2590
CHICAGO GROWTH PARTNERS, 468
CHICAGO PACIFIC FOUNDERS, 469
CHINA ISRAEL VALUE CAPITAL, 2593
CHINA VEST LIMITED, 2596
CHINAVEST, 473
CHL MEDICAL PARTNERS, 474
CHRYSALIS CAPITAL ChrysCapital, 2599
CHRYSALIS VENTURES, 475
CHRYSCAPITAL MANAGEMENT COMPANIES ChrysCapital, 2600
CIBC CAPITAL MARKETS, 2079
CINVEN LIMITED, 2605
CIT GROUP, 484
CITY HILL VENTURES, 487
CLAREMONT CREEK VENTURES, 491
CLARITAS CAPITAL, 493
CLARUS VENTURES, 495
CLAYTON ASSOCIATES, 496
CLEARLAKE CAPITAL, 500
CLEARSPRING CAPITAL PARTNERS, 2082
CLIFFORD CHANCE PUNDER, 2614
COACH & CAPITAL, 2619
COLLABORATIVE FUND, 511
COMMONS CAPITAL, 520
COMVEST PARTNERS, 528
CORAL GROUP, 536
CORDOVA VENTURES, 537
CORNERSTONE EQUITY INVESTORS LLC, 541
CORRELATION VENTURES, 544
COUNCIL CAPITAL, 550
COVINGTON CAPITAL CORP., 2087
CRESSEY & COMPANY LP, 558
CRESTVIEW PARTNERS, 559
CRYSTAL RIDGE PARTNERS, 565
CUSTER CAPITAL, 571
CUTLASS CAPITAL LLC, 572
CVF CAPITAL PARTNERS, 573
CXO FUND, 574
DANCAP PRIVATE EQUITY, 2094
DARBY OVERSEAS INVESTMENTS LTD, 584
DAUPHIN CAPITAL PARTNERS, 587
DAY ONE VENTURES, 593
DE NOVO VENTURES, 598
DIFFERENCE CAPITAL, 2096
DIRECT CAPITAL PRIVATE EQUITY LIMITED, 2664
DRI CAPITAL, 2102
DRIVE CAPITAL, 630
DUKE STREET CAPITAL Duke Street, 2676
DUNEDIN CAPITAL PARTNERS LIMITED, 2677
DW HEALTHCARE PARTNERS, 639
EARLY STAGE PARTNERS, 642
EASTON CAPITAL INVESTMENT GROUP, 644
EASTWARD CAPITAL PARTNERS, 646
ECOAST ANGEL NETWORK, 649
EDF VENTURES, 652
EGL HOLDINGS, 656
ELECTRA PARTNERS EUROPE, 2695
EM WARBURG, PINCUS & COMPANY JAPAN, 2698
EMBARK HEALTHCARE, 662

Industry Preference Index / Healthcare

EMERGENT MEDICAL PARTNERS, 666
EMIGRANT CAPITAL, 667
ENNOVENT, 2701
ENSO VENTURES, 2702
EPLANET CAPITAL, 690
EQUINOX CAPITAL, 691
EQUISTONE, 2714
ESCALATE CAPITAL PARTNERS, 695
ESPIRITO SANTO VENTURES, 2717
ESSEX WOODLANDS HEALTH VENTURES LLC, 697
EVERGREEN VENTURE PARTNERS, 2726
EVOLVE CAPITAL, 702
EXCEL VENTURE MANAGEMENT, 703
EXPERIMENT FUND, 708
EXPIBEL BV, 2728
FCA VENTURE PARTNERS, 718
FELICIS VENTURES, 720
FERRER FREEMAN & COMPANY LLC, 723
FIDELITY GROWTH PARTNERS ASIA, 2733
FIRST ANALYSIS, 732
FIRST CAPITAL VENTURE, 735
FIRST NEW ENGLAND CAPITAL LP, 739
FIRST ROUND CAPITAL, 741
FIRSTMARK CAPITAL, 743
FLAGSHIP PIONEERING, 747
FLETCHER SPAGHT VENTURES, 749
FLEXPOINT FORD LLC, 750
FLUKE VENTURE PARTNERS, 753
FORESITE CAPITAL, 762
FORTRESS INVESTMENT GROUP LLC, 767
FORWARD VENTURES, 769
FOUNDERS EQUITY, 774
FOUNDERS FUND, 775
FRAZIER HEALTHCARE VENTURES, 782
FRESH VC, 785
FRIEDMAN, FLEISCHER & LOWE LLC, 787
FRONTENAC COMPANY, 789
FUEL CAPITAL, 2761
FULCRUM EQUITY PARTNERS, 794
FULL CIRCLE INVESTMENTS, 2762
FUSION FUND, 799
GALEN PARTNERS, 806
GE CAPITAL, 808
GE VENTURES, 809
GEMINI INVESTORS, 812
GENERAL ATLANTIC PARTNERS, 815
GENESYS CAPITAL, 2130
GLENGARY LLC, 831
GLOBALIVE, 2134
GOLDEN OPPORTUNITIES FUND, 2136
GOLUB CAPITAL, 844
GOOD NEWS VENTURES, 2138
GRANVILLE BAIRD CAPITAL PARTNERS, 2795
GRAPHITE CAPITAL MANAGEMENT LTD, 2796
GREAT HILL PARTNERS LLC, 857
GREAT POINT PARTNERS, 859
GREENSPRING ASSOCIATES, 867
GREIF & COMPANY, 869
GREY SKY VENTURE PARTNERS, 870
GROSVENOR FUNDS, 875
GROTECH VENTURES, 876
GROVE STREET ADVISORS LLC, 879
GRYPHON INVESTORS, 881
GV, 889
H KATZ CAPITAL GROUP, 891
HALYARD CAPITAL, 897
HAMILTON BIOVENTURES, 898
HARBERT MANAGEMENT CORPORATION, 904
HARBOR LIGHT CAPITAL PARTNERS, 907
HARBOURVEST PARTNERS LLC, 909
HBM PARTNERS, 2815
HEALTH ENTERPRISE PARTNERS, 918
HEALTHCARE PRIVATE EQUITY ASSOCIATION, 3264
HEALTHCARE VENTURES LLC, 919
HELION VENTURE PARTNERS, LLC International Management (Mauritius) Ltd, 2818
HELLMAN & FRIEDMAN LLC, 924

HERITAGE PARTNERS, 926
HIG CAPITAL, 928
HIGH ROAD CAPITAL PARTNERS, 931
HIGHLAND CAPITAL PARTNERS, 935
HOPEWELL VENTURES, 944
HORIZON TECHNOLOGY FINANCE, 946
HOULIHAN LOKEY, 948
HOUSTON HEALTH VENTURES, 951
HT CAPITAL ADVISORS LLC, 953
HUMANA VENTURES, 955
HUNTSMAN GAY GLOBAL CAPITAL, 959
HURON CAPITAL PARTNERS LLC, 960
IA VENTURES, 965
IANTHUS CAPITAL MANAGEMENT, 966
IBM VENTURE CAPITAL GROUP, 967
ICAN ISRAEL-CANNABIS.COM, 2845
ICV PARTNERS, 969
IDG CAPITAL PARTNERS, 2847
IDG CAPITAL, 973
IDG TECHNOLOGY VENTURE INVESTMENT, 2848
IMPERIAL CAPITAL, 2150
IMPERIAL INNOVATIONS, 2858
INCWELL VENTURE CAPITAL, 981
INDUSTRIFONDEN, 2867
INETWORKS ADVISORS LLC, 987
INLAND TECHSTART FUND, 993
INNOGEST CAPITAL, 2874
INNOVA MEMPHIS, 995
INNOVATION PLATFORM CAPITAL, 997
INSIGHT VENTURE PARTNERS, 1000
INTER-ASIA VENTURE MANAGEMENT LIMITED, 2881
INTERNATIONAL FINANCE CORPORATION (IFC), 1007
INTERWEST PARTNERS, 1010
INVENTUS, 1013
INVESTOR AB, 2890
IRISH ANGELS, 1019
IRON GATE CAPITAL, 1020
IRONWOOD CAPITAL, 1021
ISIS EP LLP F & C, 2898
IXORA VENTURES, 2904
J. BURKE CAPITAL PARTNERS, 1023
JEFFERIES CAPITAL PARTNERS, 1032
JH WHITNEY & COMPANY, 1037
JLL PARTNERS, 1039
JOHNSTON ASSOCIATES, 1044
JORDAN COMPANY, 1045
JUMPSTART INC, 1047
JW ASSET MANAGEMENT, 1048
JW CHILDS ASSOCIATES, 1049
KAISER PERMANENTE VENTURES, 1052
KAPOR CAPITAL, 1054
KARLIN VENTURES, 1055
KEARNY VENTURE PARTNERS, 1059
KEIRETSU FORUM, 1061
KELSO & COMPANY, 1062
KENSINGTON CAPITAL PARTNERS, 2167
KERRY CAPITAL ADVISORS, 1067
KILMER CAPITAL PARTNERS, 2169
KLEINWORT CAPITAL LIMITED, 2923
KOHLBERG KRAVIS ROBERTS & COMPANY, 1082
KRG CAPITAL PARTNERS, 1086
KTB VENTURES, 1087
LAKE CAPITAL, 1091
LATTERELL VENTURE PARTNERS, 1094
LAUNCHCAPITAL, 1097
LAUNCHPAD VENTURE GROUP, 1100
LEGEND CAPITAL, 2936
LEMHI VENTURES, 1107
LEONARD GREEN & PARTNERS LP, 1109
LEONIA MB GROUP/MB FUNDS, 2937
LEVINE LEICHTMAN CAPITAL PARTNERS, 1111
LFE CAPITAL, 1113
LIBERTY PARTNERS, 1116
LINDEN LLC, 1128
LITTLEJOHN & COMPANY LLC, 1134
LLOYDS DEVELOPMENT CAPITAL LIMITED, 2944
LOMBARD INVESTMENTS, 1139

1185

Industry Preference Index / Healthcare

LONGWOOD FUND, 1145
LOVETT MILLER & COMPANY, 1148
LUX CAPITAL, 1151
MADISON DEARBORN PARTNERS, 1156
MANSA EQUITY PARTNERS, 1165
MARS INVESTMENT ACCELERATOR FUND, 2187
MARWIT CAPITAL LLC, 1168
MASSACHUSETTS CAPITAL RESOURCE COMPANY, 1173
MCG CAPITAL CORPORATION, 1189
MEDICAL RESEARCH COMMERCIALIZATION FUND, 2959
MEDIMMUNE VENTURES, 1196
MEDIPHASE VENTURE PARTNERS, 1197
MEKETA INVESTMENT GROUP, 1200
MENTOR CAPITAL PARTNERS LTD, 1203
MERCK GLOBAL HEALTH INNOVATION FUND, 1205
MERIDIAN MANAGEMENT GROUP, 1208
MERLIN NEXUS, 1216
MIDATLANTIC FUND, 1228
MIDINVEST LIMITED, 2966
MISSION BAY CAPITAL, 1238
MITSUBISHI UFJ CAPITAL, 2970
MITSUI SUMITOMO INSURANCE VENTURE CAPITAL CO, 2971
MMC VENTURES, 2972
MONTLAKE CAPITAL, 1250
MONTREUX EQUITY PARTNERS, 1251
MORGAN STANLEY EXPANSION CAPITAL, 1255
MOTIV PARTNERS, 1258
MOTOROLA SOLUTIONS VENTURE CAPITAL, 1260
MPG EQUITY PARTNERS, 1267
MPM CAPITAL, 1268
MS&AD VENTURES, 1269
MURPHY & PARTNERS FUND LP, 1274
MVC CORPORATION, 2980
MVM LIFE SCIENCE PARTNERS, 2981
NAUTIC PARTNERS, 1279
NAVY CAPITAL, 1283
NEMO CAPITAL PARTNERS, 1289
NESBIC INVESTMENT FUND II, 2992
NEW MARKETS VENTURE PARTNERS, 1299
NEW MOUNTAIN CAPITAL, 1301
NEWBURY, PIRET & COMPANY, 1312
NEWLIGHT PARTNERS, 1315
NEWMARGIN VENTURE CAPITAL, 2998
NEWSPRING CAPITAL, 1317
NEXTEC DEVELOPMENT CAPITAL LIMITED, 3000
NFX, 1323
NGN CAPITAL, 1325
NOMURA PHASE4 VENTURES LTD, 3007
NORO-MOSELEY PARTNERS, 1331
NORTH BRIDGE VENTURE PARTNERS, 1334
NORTH COVE PARTNERS, 1337
NORTHERN LIGHT VENTURE CAPITAL, 1340
NORTHSTAR CAPITAL, 1343
NORTHSTAR VENTURES, 3012
NORWEST EQUITY PARTNERS, 1345
NORWEST VENTURE PARTNERS, 1346
NOVARTIS VENTURE FUNDS, 1350
NOVELTEK CAPITAL CORPORATION, 1351
OAK HILL CAPITAL PARTNERS, 1360
OAK INVESTMENT PARTNERS, 1361
OBVIOUS VENTURES, 1363
OLYMPUS PARTNERS, 1372
OMEGA FUNDS, 1373
ONE EQUITY PARTNERS, 1376
OneVentures, 3023
ONEX PARTNERS, 2209
ORIGINATE VENTURES, 1385
OUTCOME CAPITAL, 1388
OWL VENTURES, 1392
PALLADIUM EQUITY PARTNERS, 1403
PAMLICO CAPITAL, 1409
PANTHEON VENTURES (US) LP, 1411
PARALLEL INVESTMENT PARTNERS, 1415
PARALLEL49 EQUITY, 2214
PARTHENON CAPITAL, 1417
PARTNERS HEALTHCARE RESEARCH VENTURES, 1419
PARTNERSHIP FUND FOR NEW YORK CITY, 1420

PEACHTREE EQUITY PARTNERS, 1423
PENFUND, 2219
PERMIRA Permira Advisers LLP, 3033
PERSISTENCE CAPITAL PARTNERS, 2220
PFIZER VENTURE INVESTMENTS, 1436
PHOENIX EQUITY PARTNERS LIMITED, 3036
PINNACLE VENTURES, 1445
PNC ERIEVIEW CAPITAL, 1456
POLARIS VENTURE PARTNERS, 1460
PRIMUS CAPITAL, 1476
PRISM CAPITAL, 1477
PRISM VENTUREWORKS, 1478
PRITZKER GROUP PRIVATE CAPITAL, 1479
PRITZKER GROUP VENTURE CAPITAL, 1480
PROGRESS EQUITY PARTNERS, 1484
PROQUEST INVESTMENTS, 1490
PROSEED, 3059
PSILOS GROUP, 1498
PTV SCIENCES, 1500
QIMING VENTURE PARTNERS, 3066
QUAKER BIOVENTURES, 1508
QUARRY CAPITAL MANAGEMENT, 1511
QUESTER CAPITAL MANAGEMENT LIMITED, 3070
QUESTMARK PARTNERS LP, 1515
RA CAPITAL MANAGEMENT, 1519
RADIUS VENTURES, 1520
RAND CAPITAL CORPORATION, 1523
RAYMOND JAMES CAPITAL, 1526
RECAPHEALTH VENTURES, 2233
REDHILLS VENTURES, 1532
REDMONT VENTURE PARTNERS, 1533
RESERVOIR VENTURE PARTNERS, 1544
RETHINK COMMUNITY, 1550
RHO VENTURES, 1558
RHO VENTURES, 1558
RIVERSIDE COMPANY, 1572
RLH EQUITY PARTNERS, 1575
ROADMAP CAPITAL INC., 2242
ROBIN HOOD VENTURES, 1577
ROTH CAPITAL PARTNERS, 1588
ROUNDTABLE HEALTHCARE PARTNERS, 1590
SAFEGUARD SCIENTIFICS, 1601
SAIF PARTNERS, 3093
SAINTS CAPITAL, 1604
SARONA ASSET MANAGEMENT, 2248
SB CHINA VENTURE CAPITAL, 3100
SCALE VENTURE PARTNERS, 1626
SCOTTISH EQUITY PARTNERS, 3104
SEQUEL VENTURE PARTNERS, 1653
SERGE PUN & ASSOCIATES (MYANMAR) LIMITED, 3111
SEVENTYSIX CAPITAL, 1657
SEVIN ROSEN FUNDS, 1658
SHERBROOKE CAPITAL, 1665
SHORE CAPITAL PARTNERS, 1667
SIERRA ANGELS, 1669
SIGHTLINE PARTNERS, 1671
SIGNATURE CAPITAL LLC, 3120
SILICON ALLEY VENTURE PARTNERS, 1680
SILKROAD EQUITY, 1681
SKYLINE VENTURES, 1691
SKYTREE CAPITAL PARTNERS, 1692
SOCIAL CAPITAL, 1696
SOCIAL VENTURE CIRCLE, 3277
SORRENTO VENTURES, 1706
SOVEREIGN CAPITAL, 3130
SPENCER TRASK VENTURES, 1720
SPLIT ROCK PARTNERS, 1725
STARBOARD CAPITAL PARTNERS, 1735
STERLING PARTNERS, 1742
STONEHENGE GROWTH CAPITAL, 1745
STONEWOOD CAPITAL MANAGEMENT, 1746
SUMMER STREET CAPITAL PARTNERS, 1751
SUMMIT PARTNERS, 1752
SUN CAPITAL PARTNERS, 1753
SV HEALTH INVESTORS, 1762
SYCAMORE VENTURES, 1769
TA ASSOCIATES, 1776

Industry Preference Index / Healthcare Information Technology

TAILWIND CAPITAL, 1777
TAKEDA VENTURES, 1778
TEL VENTURE CAPITAL, 1791
TELEFONICA VENTURES, 3169
TELEGRAPH HILL PARTNERS, 1792
TELESYSTEM, 2264
TEUZA MANAGEMENT & DEVELOPMENT LTD, 3171
TEXO VENTURES, 1801
THE ABRAAJ GROUP, 3173
THOMA BRAVO LLC, 1814
THOMAS H LEE PARTNERS, 1815
THOMAS, MCNERNEY & PARTNERS, 1817
THREE ARCH PARTNERS LP, 1819
TIE ANGELS GROUP SEATTLE, 1825
TMG CAPITAL PARTNERS, 3180
TONIIC, 1831
TOP RENERGY INC., 2271
TPG CAPITAL, 1835
TREVI HEALTH CAPITAL, 1844
TRIATHLON MEDICAL VENTURES, 1847
TRIPLETREE LLC, 1854
TULLIS HEALTH INVESTORS, 1866
TVM CAPITAL, 3196
TXV PARTNERS, 1875
TYLT LAB, 1876
UCA UNTERNEHMER CONSULT AG, 3197
UDD VENTURES, 3198
UNIVERSITY VENTURE FUND, 1884
UPDATA VENTURE PARTNERS, 1886
VALOR EQUITY PARTNERS, 1902
VALUEACT CAPITAL, 1903
VANTAGEPOINT CAPITAL PARTNERS, 1906
VEBER PARTNERS LLC, 1909
VENROCK ASSOCIATES, 1916
VENTURE INVESTORS LLC, 1921
VENTUREAST, 3211
VERSANT VENTURES, 1928
VERTICAL GROUP, 1929
VESTAR CAPITAL PARTNERS, 1931
VICKERS FINANCIAL GROUP, 3215
VIDA VENTURES, 1932
VRG CAPITAL, 2282
WALDEN ISRAEL VENTURE CAPITAL, 3231
WARBURG PINCUS LLC, 1956
WATER STREET HEALTHCARE PARTNERS, 1961
WELLS FARGO CAPITAL FINANCE, 1970
WELSH, CARSON, ANDERSON & STOWE, 1972
WEST HEALTH INVESTMENT FUND, 1973
WESTCAP, 2285
WESTERN TECHNOLOGY INVESTMENT, 1975
WESTLAKE SECURITIES, 1976
WHEATLEY PARTNERS, 1981
WHITECAP VENTURE PARTNERS, 2288
WI HARPER GROUP, 1983
WILLIS STEIN & PARTNERS LLC, 1986
WIND POINT PARTNERS, 1990
WINDHAM VENTURE PARTNERS, 1993
WIREFRAME VENTURES, 2000
WRF CAPITAL, 2008
XT INVESTMENTS, 3241
YELLOW POINT EQUITY PARTNERS, 2292
YELLOWSTONE CAPITAL, 2013
YFM GROUP, 3244
YLR CAPITAL MARKETS LTD, 3247
YORK STREET CAPITAL PARTNERS LLC, 2015

Healthcare Devices
NEW ENTERPRISE ASSOCIATES, 1297

Healthcare Information Technology
.406 VENTURES, 2
ALTARIS CAPITAL PARTNERS, 97
APERTURE VENTURE PARTNERS, 136
ARC ANGEL FUND, 150
ASCENSION HEALTH VENTURES LLC, 176
ASCENT BIOMEDICAL VENTURES, 177
ASPECT VENTURES, 180
AZURE CAPITAL PARTNERS, 215
BEDFORD FUNDING, 242
BIO*ONE CAPITAL EDMI, 2513
BIOGENERATOR, 267
BIOVENTURES INVESTORS, 270
BREGAL SAGEMOUNT, 333
BRIGHTSTONE VENTURE CAPITAL, 341
BROOK VENTURE FUND, 349
CARDINAL PARTNERS, 410
CATALYST INVESTORS, 427
CEDAR VENTURES LLC, 437
CHICAGO VENTURES, 471
CINCYTECH, 479
COUNCIL CAPITAL, 550
DEFTA PARTNERS, 602
DISCOVERY CAPITAL, 2097
DOMAIN ASSOCIATES LLC, 621
EASTON CAPITAL INVESTMENT GROUP, 644
EDBI Pte LTD., 2690
EDISON PARTNERS, 655
ELM STREET VENTURES, 660
F-PRIME CAPITAL PARTNERS, 710
FIDELITY GROWTH PARTNERS EUROPE, 2734
FLETCHER SPAGHT VENTURES, 749
FLYBRIDGE CAPITAL PARTNERS, 754
FRANCISCO PARTNERS, 779
GALEN PARTNERS, 806
GENERATION PARTNERS, 818
GRAND CENTRAL HOLDINGS, 847
GRAYHAWK CAPITAL, 856
GREAT POINT PARTNERS, 859
HATTERAS VENTURE PARTNERS, 915
HLM VENTURE PARTNERS, 938
HOPEN LIFE SCIENCE VENTURES, 943
HORIZON VENTURES LLC, 947
HOUSTON ANGEL NETWORK, 950
HUMANA VENTURES, 955
IGAN PARTNERS, 2149
INETWORKS ADVISORS LLC, 987
JAVELIN VENTURE PARTNERS, 1028
JMI EQUITY FUND LP, 1041
JUMP CAPITAL LLC, 1046
KAISER PERMANENTE VENTURES, 1052
KODIAK VENTURE PARTNERS, 1080
LONG RIVER VENTURES, 1142
MARYLAND VENTURE FUND, 1169
MASS VENTURES, 1172
MEDIMMUNE VENTURES, 1196
MESA VERDE PARTNERS, 1221
MOBIUS VENTURE CAPITAL, 1245
MORGAN STANLEY EXPANSION CAPITAL, 1255
MVM LIFE SCIENCE PARTNERS, 2981
NEMO CAPITAL PARTNERS, 1289
NEW CAPITAL PARTNERS, 1293
OAK INVESTMENT PARTNERS, 1361
OKAPI VENTURE CAPITAL, 1371
ONSET VENTURES, 1378
OSAGE PARTNERS, 1387
PALO ALTO VENTURE SCIENCE, 1406
PFIZER VENTURE INVESTMENTS, 1436
PITTSBURGH LIFE SCIENCES GREENHOUSE, 1448
POINT JUDITH CAPITAL, 1459
POLYTECH VENTURES, 3045
PSILOS GROUP, 1498
REED ELSEVIER VENTURES, 3074
REX HEALTH VENTURES, 1556
RITTENHOUSE VENTURES, 1568
SALMON RIVER CAPITAL, 1608
SANTE VENTURES, 1619
SCHRODER VENTURES HEALTH INVESTORS, 1628
SENECA PARTNERS, 1649
SENTRY FINANCIAL CORPORATION, 1652
SHEPHERD VENTURES, 1664
SOUTHERN CAPITOL VENTURES, 1710
SPINDLETOP CAPITAL, 1722
SPRING LAKE EQUITY PARTNERS, 1728
SYNTHESIS CAPITAL, 1775

1187

Industry Preference Index / Healthcare Innovation

TEXO VENTURES, 1801
VENROCK ASSOCIATES, 1916
VERSANT VENTURES, 1928
WASABI VENTURES, 1958
WEST HEALTH INVESTMENT FUND, 1973
WHEATLEY PARTNERS, 1981

Healthcare Innovation
SANOFI-GENZYME BIOVENTURES, 1618

Healthcare Services
3TS CAPITAL PARTNERS 3i Group plc, 2309
ABRY PARTNERS, 21
ACON INVESTMENTS, 46
ALTARIS CAPITAL PARTNERS, 97
ARBORETUM VENTURES, 149
ARLINGTON CAPITAL PARTNERS, 166
ASCENT BIOMEDICAL VENTURES, 177
ATHYRIUM CAPITAL MANAGEMENT, 188
BEHRMAN CAPITAL, 245
BEZOS EXPEDITIONS, 262
BIOGENERATOR, 267
BLUE CHIP VENTURE COMPANY, 287
BOUNDS EQUITY PARTNERS, 316
BRANFORD CASTLE, 327
CAPITAL RESOURCE PARTNERS, 402
CAROUSEL CAPITAL, 415
CENTERFIELD CAPITAL PARTNERS, 443
CHICAGO GROWTH PARTNERS, 468
CIC PARTNERS, 477
CID CAPITAL, 478
CLARION CAPITAL PARTNERS LLC, 492
CLEARLIGHT PARTNERS, 501
CONCENTRIC EQUITY PARTNERS Financial Investments Corporation, 529
COUNCIL CAPITAL, 550
CRESSEY & COMPANY LP, 558
CUTLASS CAPITAL LLC, 572
DAUPHIN CAPITAL PARTNERS, 587
DBL PARTNERS, 595
DELPHI VENTURES, 604
DFW CAPITAL PARTNERS, 610
DIAMOND STATE VENTURES LP, 611
DUBIN CLARK & COMPANY, 632
EASTON CAPITAL INVESTMENT GROUP, 644
ELM STREET VENTURES, 660
EOS PARTNERS LP, 686
EPIC PARTNERS, 687
ESSEX WOODLANDS HEALTH VENTURES LLC, 697
EUREKA GROWTH CAPITAL, 698
EVERGREEN ADVISORS, 701
FIVE POINTS CAPITAL, 746
FLARE CAPITAL PARTNERS, 748
FORESITE CAPITAL, 762
GENERATION PARTNERS, 818
GENSTAR CAPITAL LP, 819
GLADSTONE CAPITAL, 828
GOLUB CAPITAL, 844
GRANTHAM CAPITAL, 853
GREAT POINT PARTNERS, 859
HARREN EQUITY PARTNERS, 910
HARVEST PARTNERS, 914
HERITAGE PARTNERS, 926
HIGH STREET CAPITAL, 932
HLM VENTURE PARTNERS, 938
HUMANA VENTURES, 955
INETWORKS ADVISORS LLC, 987
INTEGRA VENTURES, 1002
KAISER PERMANENTE VENTURES, 1052
KBL HEALTHCARE VENTURES, 1058
KOHLBERG & COMPANY LLC, 1081
LEE EQUITY PARTNERS, 1104
LLR PARTNERS INC, 1136
LOVETT MILLER & COMPANY, 1148
MARANON CAPITAL, 1166
MBF CAPITAL CORPORATION, 1188
MIDATLANTIC FUND, 1228
MORGAN STANLEY EXPANSION CAPITAL, 1255
MOUNTAIN GROUP CAPITAL, 1261
MTS HEALTH INVESTORS, 1271
MVP CAPITAL PARTNERS, 1275
NAVIGATION CAPITAL PARTNERS, 1280
NEW CAPITAL PARTNERS, 1293
NEW ENTERPRISE ASSOCIATES, 1297
NEWSPRING CAPITAL, 1317
NORO-MOSELEY PARTNERS, 1331
ODEON CAPITAL PARTNERS, 1367
OKAPI VENTURE CAPITAL, 1371
OSAGE PARTNERS, 1387
POST CAPITAL PARTNERS, 1465
POUSCHINE COOK CAPITAL MANAGEMENT LLC, 1466
PSILOS GROUP, 1498
QUAKER BIOVENTURES, 1508
REX HEALTH VENTURES, 1556
ROPART ASSET MANAGEMENT, 1583
SALEM INVESTMENT PARTNERS, 1606
SANTE VENTURES, 1619
SCHRODER VENTURES HEALTH INVESTORS, 1628
SENECA PARTNERS, 1649
SENTINEL CAPITAL PARTNERS, 1651
SEQUOIA CAPITAL, 1654
SILVER OAK SERVICES PARTNERS, 1684
SPINDLETOP CAPITAL, 1722
SSM PARTNERS, 1732
SUCSY, FISCHER & COMPANY, 1750
SYMMETRIC CAPITAL, 1770
SYNTHESIS CAPITAL, 1775
TELEGRAPH HILL PARTNERS, 1792
TICONDEROGA PRIVATE EQUITY, 1824
TREVI HEALTH CAPITAL, 1844
VEDANTA CAPITAL LP, 1911
VERSANT VENTURES, 1928
VESEY STREET CAPITAL PARTNERS LLC, 1930
WATER STREET HEALTHCARE PARTNERS, 1961
WESTVIEW CAPITAL PARTNERS, 1979

Healthcare Technology
BIOMATICS CAPITAL, 268
BLUFF POINT ASSOCIATES, 299
CAPITAL MIDWEST FUND, 400
GREENHILLS VENTURES, LLC, 865
RIPPLE VENTURES, 2241

Healthy Active Lifestyle
CAVA CAPITAL, 431

Heating
ATP PRIVATE EQUITY PARTNERS, 2447
BARING PRIVATE EQUITY PARTNERS ESPANA SA, 2489
BC PARTNERS LIMITED, 2497

High Performance Computing
ARCH VENTURE PARTNERS, 153

High Technology
ACONCAGUA VENTURES, 2334
ALACRITY VENTURES, 76
AMMER PARTNERS, 2393
ANNEX VENTURES, 130
ARAGON VENTURES, 145
AURA CAPITAL OY Auratum Group, 2451
AXIOM VENTURE PARTNERS, 212
AZINI CAPITAL PARTNERS, 2472
BAEKELAND FUNDS, 2476
BATTERSON VENTURE CAPITAL LLC, 234
BAY BG BAVARIAN VENTURE CAPITAL CORP, 2494
BAYERN KAPITAL, 2495
BIOPROCESS CAPITAL PARTNERS, 2517
BUSINESS GROWTH FUND, 2550
CDH INVESTMENTS, 2579
CONNECTICUT INNOVATIONS, 530
CREATHOR VENTURE, 2638
DAIMLERCHRYSLER VENTURE GmbH DaimlerChrysler AG, 2650
ENTREE CAPITAL, 2709

EPIC VENTURES, 688
EQUINET VENTURE PARTNERS AG, 2713
ESPRESSO CAPITAL, 2109
EXCELL PARTNERS, INC., 704
FIRST STEP FUND, 742
FORUM TECHNOLOGIES VENTURE CAPITAL COMPANY Forum Group, 2751
IDG TECHNOLOGY VENTURE INVESTMENT, 2848
INTELLIGENT CAPITAL SDN BHD, 2880
INVESTAMERICA VENTURE GROUP, 1016
KLEINER PERKINS, 1075
LANDSBANKI VENTURES, 2929
LAUNCHPAD VENTURE GROUP, 1100
LIMESTONE VENTURES, 1126
MITSUBISHI UFJ CAPITAL, 2970
MURPHREE VENTURE PARTNERS, 1273
NAUSICAA VENTURES, 2986
NEUHAUS PARTNERS, 2994
NEW YORK LIFE CAPITAL PARTNERS, 1309
PIDC PHILADELPHIA, 1441
RED DOT VENTURES, 3073
RODA GROUP, 1580
SECOND AVENUE PARTNERS, 1641
SEVEN SPIRES INVESTMENTS, 3112
SIERRA VENTURES, 1670
SOCIALATOM VENTURES, 3125
SOUTH ATLANTIC VENTURE FUNDS, 1708
SPINUP VENTURE, 3132
SUTTER HILL VENTURES, 1760
TRIANGLE ANGEL PARTNERS, 1845
TROIKA CAPITAL PARTNERS, 3193
TWO SIGMA VENTURES, 1874
VAEKSTFONDEN, 3203
VENTANA CAPITAL MANAGEMENT LP, 1918
VENTURE CAPITAL FUND OF NEW ENGLAND, 1920
VISION CAPITAL, 1937
VIVES, 3225
WASHINGTON CAPITAL VENTURES, 1959
XENIA VENTURE CAPITAL, 3240
YLR CAPITAL MARKETS LTD, 3247

High Value Added Manufacturing
NEXTEC DEVELOPMENT CAPITAL LIMITED, 3000

Home Improvement
CARDINAL EQUITY PARTNERS, 409

Homeland Security
BRYANT PARK VENTURES, 356
CHART VENTURE PARTNERS, 457
MAIN STREET CAPITAL HOLDINGS LLC, 1159
OUTCOME CAPITAL, 1388
PALADIN CAPITAL GROUP, 1400

Horticulture
CARDINAL EQUITY PARTNERS, 409

Hospitality
CANADIAN VENTURE CAPITAL ASSOCIATION Canadian Venture Capital & Private Equity Association, 3258
FRESH VC, 785
GEODESIC CAPITAL, 820
GOLDEN OPPORTUNITIES FUND, 2136
KALORI GROUP INVESTMENTS, 2915
RAPTOR GROUP, 1524
THAYER VENTURES, 1806
WESTCAP, 2285

Hospitality & Travel
REVOLUTION LLC, 1555

Hospitals
BC PARTNERS LIMITED, 2497
QUANTUM CAPITAL PARTNERS, 1510

Hotel, Tourism & Leisure
TPA CORPORATE FINANCE CONSULTING GMBH Horwarth International, 3184

Hotels
CARPEDIA CAPITAL, 2072
FOUNDATION CAPITAL LIMITED, 2753
STARWOOD CAPITAL GROUP LLC, 1739

Household Goods
CLIFFORD CHANCE PUNDER, 2614
EQUISTONE, 2714
PRIVATE EQUITY PARTNERS SPA, 3053
PROSPECT PARTNERS LLC, 1492
UNION CAPITAL CORPORATION, 1881

Housing
ACUMEN, 55
RETHINK COMMUNITY, 1550
TONIIC, 1831
URBAN INNOVATION FUND, 1893

Human Capital Consulting
AON RISK SOLUTIONS Aon Corporation, 2413

Human Resource Technology
RUBICON VENTURE CAPITAL, 1595

Human Resources
CAPMAN CAPITAL MANAGEMENT OY, 2562
GSV VENTURES, 883

Human Therapeutics
BIOVENTURES INVESTORS, 270

Human Wellness
FREYCINET INVESTMENTS, 2125

Human-Computer Interaction
BLOOMBERG BETA, 284

ICT
CONOR VENTURE PARTNERS OY, 2630

IOT
ZHENFUND, 3251

IP Services
CROSSLINK CAPITAL, 563

IT & Managed Services
CALTIUS EQUITY PARTNERS, 373

IT & Software
TOP RENERGY INC., 2271

IT Consulting
ACCESS CAPITAL, 35

IT Cyber Risk
HALYARD CAPITAL, 897

IT Enabled Services
ACCEL-KKR LLC, 29

IT Infrastructure
AMITI VENTURES, 116
DIAMONDHEAD VENTURES, 613
ENTREPIA VENTURES, 682
NORWEST VENTURE PARTNERS, 1346
PROCYON VENTURES, 1483

IT Security
NEWBURY VENTURES, 1311

IT Services
BEDFORD FUNDING, 242

Industry Preference Index / IT-Intensive Life Science Applications

BEZOS EXPEDITIONS, 262
CROSS CREEK ADVISORS, 560
LIFE SCIENCES PARTNERS BV, 2939
MAINE ANGELS, 1160

IT-Intensive Life Science Applications
MASTHEAD VENTURE PARTNERS, 1175

IT/BIO Convergence
IGLOBE PARTNERS, 2853

Ice Cream
RABO BLACK EARTH Eagle Venture Partners, 3071
WESTERN NIS ENTERPRISE FUND, 3234

Image-Recognition
SONY STRATEGIC TECHNOLOGY PARTNERSHIPS, 1704

Imaging
MEDIMMUNE VENTURES, 1196

Imports/Exports
CROSBY ASSET MANAGEMENT, 2640
EMINENT CAPITAL PARTNERS, 669
FOUNDATION CAPITAL LIMITED, 2753

Industrial
3I ITALY 3i Group, 2303
3M UNITEK, 2307
ACON INVESTMENTS, 46
ADVENT INTERNATIONAL CORPORATION, 62
AMERICAN SECURITIES LLC, 110
APOLLO GLOBAL MANAGEMENT, 140
AURORA CAPITAL GROUP, 199
BAIN CAPITAL PRIVATE EQUITY, 220
BERTRAM CAPITAL, 257
BEZOS EXPEDITIONS, 262
BLACKSTONE PRIVATE EQUITY GROUP, 277
BRANFORD CASTLE, 327
BROOKE PRIVATE EQUITY ASSOCIATES, 350
BROOKSIDE EQUITY PARTNERS LLC, 353
CANADIAN VENTURE CAPITAL ASSOCIATION Canadian Venture Capital & Private Equity Association, 3258
CARLYLE GROUP, 413
CCMP CAPITAL, 433
CENTRAL TEXAS ANGEL NETWORK, 445
CID CAPITAL, 478
CRESTVIEW PARTNERS, 559
DARBY OVERSEAS INVESTMENTS LTD, 584
ECOSYSTEM VENTURES, 650
FOX PAINE & COMPANY LLC, 778
FRANCISCO PARTNERS, 779
HARREN EQUITY PARTNERS, 910
JLL PARTNERS, 1039
KRG CAPITAL PARTNERS, 1086
LAUNCHPAD VENTURE GROUP, 1100
LINLEY CAPITAL, 1130
MASS VENTURES, 1172
MPE PARTNERS, 1266
PORTUGAL CAPITAL VENTURES Institutional Headquarters, 3048
PRAIRIEGOLD VENTURE PARTNERS, 1470
SAINTS CAPITAL, 1604
TECH COAST ANGELS, 1784
TIGER GLOBAL MANAGEMENT, 1826
VINCERA CAPITAL, 3218
WESTVIEW CAPITAL PARTNERS, 1979

Industrial Distribution
ALPHA CAPITAL PARTNERS, 90
HCI EQUITY PARTNERS, 917

Industrial Electronics
ARGOSY CAPITAL, 164

Industrial Equipment
3I TEUPSCHLAND GmbH 3i Group, 2305
ACCESS CAPITAL, 35

ALLSTATE INVESTMENTS LLC, 88
AMERIMARK CAPITAL CORPORATION, 111
AMPERSAND CAPITAL PARTNERS, 118
ANDLINGER & COMPANY INC, 123
ARTHUR P GOULD & COMPANY, 172
AUSTIN CAPITAL PARTNERS LP, 201
AVENUE CAPITAL GROUP, 208
AXIA CAPITAL, 211
BERKELEY VC INTERNATIONAL LLC, 252
BLUE SAGE CAPITAL, 291
BRADFORD EQUITIES MANAGEMENT LLC, 321
BRUCKMANN, ROSSER, SHERRILL & COMPANY, 354
BRUML CAPITAL CORPORATION, 355
CAPITAL FOR BUSINESS, INC, 399
CARDINAL EQUITY PARTNERS, 409
CORDOVA VENTURES, 537
DAVID N DEUTSCH & COMPANY LLC, 589
DRESNER COMPANIES, 629
ENTERPRISE INVESTORS, 2706
EQT PARTNERS AB, 2712
EQUUS TOTAL RETURN, 694
EXPORT DEVELOPMENT CANADA, 2112
FERRANTI LIMITED, 2732
FINANCIERE DE BRIENNE FCPR, 2738
FINLOMBARDA SpA, 2739
FIRST RESERVE, 740
FLORIDA CAPITAL PARTNERS, 752
GE CAPITAL, 808
GENERAL CATALYST PARTNERS, 816
GIMV GIMV, 2780
GLENCOE CAPITAL, 830
GRAHAM PARTNERS, 846
GRANVILLE BAIRD CAPITAL PARTNERS, 2795
HALDER BETEILIGUNGSBERATUNG GmbH, 2805
HALDER HOLDINGS BV, 2806
HAMILTON ROBINSON CAPITAL PARTNERS, 899
HCI EQUITY PARTNERS, 917
HEARTLAND INDUSTRIAL PARTNERS, 923
HT CAPITAL ADVISORS LLC, 953
HUMANA VENTURES, 955
ICV PARTNERS, 969
INDUSTRIEBANK LIOF NV, 2866
INDUSTRIFONDEN, 2867
INNOFINANCE OY, 2873
IRDI MIDI-PYRENEES, 2896
JAVELIN INVESTMENTS, 2908
JB POINDEXTER & COMPANY, 1030
LANDSBANKI VENTURES, 2929
LEGAL AND GENERAL VENTURES LIMITED, 2935
LITTLEJOHN & COMPANY LLC, 1134
LM CAPITAL SECURITIES, 1137
LOMBARD INVESTMENTS, 1139
MANHATTAN INVESTMENT PARTNERS, 1163
MASSACHUSETTS CAPITAL RESOURCE COMPANY, 1173
MASSACHUSETTS GROWTH CAPITAL CORPORATION, 1174
MERIT ENERGY COMPANY, 1210
METAPOINT PARTNERS, 1224
MEZZANINE MANAGEMENT LIMITED Mezzanine Management UK Ltd., 2965
NORTHERN ENTERPRISE LIMITED, 3011
PARTECH INTERNATIONAL, 1416
PERMAL CAPITAL MANAGEMENT, 1432
PERMIRA Permira Advisers LLP, 3033
PLEXUS VENTURES, 1452
RAF INDUSTRIES, 1521
ROYALTY CAPITAL MANAGEMENT, 1591
SARATOGA PARTNERS, 1621
SEACOAST CAPITAL CORPORATION, 1636
SEED CAPITAL LIMITED, 3107
SIEMENS VENTURE CAPITAL, 3118
SKYLINE VENTURES, 1691
SOURCE CAPITAL GROUP, 1707
SOUTH ATLANTIC VENTURE FUNDS, 1708
STARBOARD CAPITAL PARTNERS, 1735
STARWOOD CAPITAL GROUP LLC, 1739
THREE CITIES RESEARCH, 1820
THROUNARFELAG ISLANDS PLC, 3177

Industry Preference Index / Industrial Services

TSG CONSUMER PARTNERS, 1861
VAEKSTFONDEN, 3203
VALLEY VENTURES LP, 1901
VENTURE CAPITAL FUND OF NEW ENGLAND, 1920
VENTURE INVESTORS, 3210
WESTERN NIS ENTERPRISE FUND, 3234
WESTON PRESIDIO, 1978
WINGATE PARTNERS, 1997
ZS FUND LP, 2022

Industrial Goods
SCOTIABANK PRIVATE EQUITY, 2250

Industrial Manufacturing
ARROWHEAD INVESTMENT MANAGEMENT, 168
BRIDGE STREET CAPITAL, 338
CALERA CAPITAL, 368
CATAPULT VENTURES, 429
COMVEST PARTNERS, 528
INCWELL VENTURE CAPITAL, 981
ODYSSEY INVESTMENT PARTNERS, 1368
REDMONT VENTURE PARTNERS, 1533
SENTINEL CAPITAL PARTNERS, 1651
YELLOWSTONE CAPITAL, 2013

Industrial Products
3I GESTION SA 3i Group, 2302
AAVIN PRIVATE EQUITY, 17
ALBEMARLE PRIVATE EQUITY LIMITED, 2360
ANGELS' FORUM LLC, 129
BLUE POINT CAPITAL PARTNERS, 290
BROCKWAY MORAN & PARTNERS, 348
BUNKER HILL CAPITAL, 359
CAMBRIA GROUP, 378
CENTRE PARTNERS MANAGEMENT LLC, 447
DESCO CAPITAL, 606
ECOAST ANGEL NETWORK, 649
EMINENT CAPITAL PARTNERS, 669
EQVITEC PARTNERS OY, 2716
FRIULIA SpA, 2758
GLOBAL EQUITY PARTNERS BETEILIGUNGS-MANAGEMENT, 2783
GOLDNER, HAWN, JOHNSON & MORRISON, 843
HARBOUR GROUP, 908
HELLMAN & FRIEDMAN LLC, 924
HERITAGE PARTNERS, 926
ILE-DE-FRANCE, 2855
INVEST EQUITY MANAGEMENT CONSULTING GmbH, 2887
IRVING PLACE CAPITAL, 1022
JORDAN COMPANY, 1045
MONTAGU PRIVATE EQUITY LIMITED, 2977
NCT VENTURES, 1286
ONEX PARTNERS, 2209
SEED CAPITAL LIMITED, 3107
SERAPH GROUP, 1655
SUMMIT PARTNERS, 1752
SYMMETRIC CAPITAL, 1770
TRELLIS CAPITAL CORPORATION, 2273
TRINITY VENTURE CAPITAL TVC Holdings plc, 3191
VALOR EQUITY PARTNERS, 1902
VELOCITY EQUITY PARTNERS LLC, 1913
WATERLAND PRIVATE EQUITY INVESTMENT, 3232
ZERNIKE SEED FUND BV, 3250
ZURMONT MADISON PRIVATE EQUITY, 3254

Industrial Services
360 CAPITAL PARTNERS 360 Capital Management SA, 2296
3i GROUP PLC, 2311
ALBEMARLE PRIVATE EQUITY LIMITED, 2360
ALTAMONT CAPITAL PARTNERS, 96
AMANAH VENTURES SDN BHD, 2388
AMERICAN INDUSTRIAL PARTNERS, 109
AMICUS CAPITAL PARTNERS, 2392
ARGOSY CAPITAL, 164
ATP PRIVATE EQUITY PARTNERS, 2447
ATRIA CAPITAL PARTENAIRES, 2448
AVISTA CAPITAL PARTNERS, 209
BAIRD CAPITAL PARTNERS, 222
BARING PRIVATE EQUITY PARTNERS INDIA, 2490
BAY BG BAVARIAN VENTURE CAPITAL CORP, 2494
BOTTS & COMPANY LIMITED, 2532
BRUCKMANN, ROSSER, SHERRILL & COMPANY, 354
CALTIUS EQUITY PARTNERS, 373
CARLYLE ASIA INVESTMENT ADVISORS LIMITED Carlyle Group, 2565
CATALYST INVESTMENT MANAGERS PTY LIMITED PPM Capital, 2573
CEI VENTURES, 438
CENTERPOINT VENTURE PARTNERS, 444
CHALLENGE FUNDS - ETGAR LP, 2585
CHEROKEE INVESTMENT PARTNERS, 463
CHICAGO GROWTH PARTNERS, 468
CIC FINANCE CIC Group, 2601
CINVEN LIMITED, 2605
CIVC PARTNERS, 489
CLEARLAKE CAPITAL, 500
CORE PACIFIC - YAMAICHI CAPITAL LIMITED Core Pacific Securities Company Ltd, 2633
CORNERSTONE CAPITAL HOLDINGS, 540
COVENT INDUSTRIAL CAPITAL INVESTMENT COMPANY, 2635
DB CAPITAL PARTNERS (ASIA), 2652
DEUTSCHE BETEILIGUNGS AG, 2660
DFW CAPITAL PARTNERS, 610
DIRECT CAPITAL PRIVATE EQUITY LIMITED, 2664
ELECTRA PARTNERS EUROPE, 2695
ELGNER GROUP INVESTMENTS, 2104
EM WARBURG, PINCUS & COMPANY INTERNATIONAL, 2697
EM WARBURG, PINCUS & COMPANY JAPAN, 2698
ENTERPRISE EQUITY (NI) LTD, 2704
ENTERPRISE INVESTORS, 2706
EQT PARTNERS AB, 2712
EQVITEC PARTNERS OY, 2716
EURAZEO, 2719
EUROVENTURES CAPITAL, 2725
EVOLVE CAPITAL, 702
FERRANTI LIMITED, 2732
FIVE POINTS CAPITAL, 746
FRIEND SKOLER & COMPANY LLC, 788
GENESIS CAPITAL CORPORATION, 2129
GILBERT GLOBAL EQUITY PARTNERS, 827
GLOBAL EQUITY PARTNERS BETEILIGUNGS-MANAGEMENT, 2783
GOLDEN GATE CAPITAL, 839
GRANITE VENTURE CAPITAL CORPORATION, 2794
GRYPHON MANAGEMENT COMPANY, 882
HALDER BETEILIGUNGSBERATUNG GmbH, 2805
HALDER HOLDINGS BV, 2806
HAMMOND, KENNEDY, WHITNEY & COMPANY, 900
HANCOCK CAPITAL MANAGEMENT, 901
HARVEST PARTNERS, 914
HCI EQUITY PARTNERS, 917
HEARTLAND INDUSTRIAL PARTNERS, 923
HG CAPITAL, 2823
HUNTSMAN GAY GLOBAL CAPITAL, 959
INDUSTRIFONDEN, 2867
INNOFINANCE OY, 2873
INVEST EQUITY MANAGEMENT CONSULTING GmbH, 2887
INVESTMENT AB BURE, 2888
INVEXCEL PATRIMONIO, 2891
IRDI MIDI-PYRENEES, 2896
KB PARTNERS LLC, 1057
KENSINGTON CAPITAL PARTNERS, 2167
KIDD & COMPANY, 1071
LANDSBANKI VENTURES, 2929
LIFE SCIENCES PARTNERS BV, 2939
LLOYDS DEVELOPMENT CAPITAL LIMITED, 2944
LMBO FINANCE, 2945
MARATHON VENTURE CAPITAL FUND LIMITED, 2954
MIDMARK CAPITAL LP, 1230
MIDOCEAN PARTNERS, 1231
MIDWEST MEZZANINE FUNDS, 1232
MONTAGU PRIVATE EQUITY LIMITED, 2977
MONUMENT ADVISORS, 1252
NORTH COVE PARTNERS, 1337
NORTHERN ENTERPRISE LIMITED, 3011
NORWEST EQUITY PARTNERS, 1345

1191

Industry Preference Index / Industrial Technology

PAMLICO CAPITAL, 1409
PENINSULA CAPITAL PARTNERS LLC, 1426
PERMIRA Permira Advisers LLP, 3033
PHOENIX EQUITY PARTNERS LIMITED, 3036
POMONA CAPITAL, 1462
PRAIRIE CAPITAL, 1469
RAND CAPITAL CORPORATION, 1523
REITEN & CO STRATEGIC INVESTMENTS AS Reiten & Company, 3076
RIVER ASSOCIATES INVESTMENTS LLC, 1569
SCOTTISH ENTERPRISE, 3103
STONEBRIDGE PARTNERS, 1744
TELESYSTEM, 2264
TGF MANAGEMENT, 1803
TRINITY VENTURE CAPITAL TVC Holdings plc, 3191
TVV CAPITAL, 1870
VISION CAPITAL, 1937
WAND PARTNERS, 1955
WATERLAND PRIVATE EQUITY INVESTMENT, 3232
WELLSPRING CAPITAL MANAGEMENT LLC, 1971
WIND POINT PARTNERS, 1990
WOODSIDE FUND, 2005
WRF CAPITAL, 2008
WYNNCHURCH CAPITAL, 2009
YORK STREET CAPITAL PARTNERS LLC, 2015

Industrial Technology
ARCAPITA INC, 152
BATTERY VENTURES, 235
CAPITAL SOUTHWEST CORPORATION, 403
CHICAGO GROWTH PARTNERS, 468
DVC DEUTSCHE VENTURE CAPITAL, 2679
EARLY STAGE PARTNERS, 642
FORTÉ VENTURES, 768
GENSTAR CAPITAL LP, 819
IBB BETEILIGUNGSGESELLSCHAFT MBH, 2841
INCWELL VENTURE CAPITAL, 981
MENTOR CAPITAL PARTNERS LTD, 1203
RIPPLE VENTURES, 2241

Industrials
NEXT EQUITIES, 2202
TERA CAPITAL CORPORATION, 2267
TPG CAPITAL, 1835

Industry
645 VENTURES, 13
ECAPITAL ENTREPRENEURIAL PARTNERS AG, 2686
FUSION FUND, 799
HIGHLAND WEST CAPITAL, 2146
InstarAGF, 2165
JETBLUE TECHNOLOGY VENTURES, 1035
NOVACAP, 2206
RETHINK COMMUNITY, 1550
SONY INNOVATION FUND, 1703
SUPPLY CHAIN VENTURES, 1757
SUSA VENTURES, 1758
THE HIVE, 1809
URBAN US, 1894
VALUEACT CAPITAL, 1903

Industry Applications
COMET LABS, 519

Industry Software
BESSEMER VENTURE PARTNERS, 260

Info Technology
GREEN TOWER CAPITAL, 861

Information
HUNTSMAN GAY GLOBAL CAPITAL, 959

Information Services
.406 VENTURES, 2
ABRY PARTNERS, 21
BIA DIGITAL PARTNERS LP, 263

BLUESTEM CAPITAL COMPANY, 297
BULLNET, 2548
CAVA CAPITAL, 431
CHARLES RIVER VENTURES, 455
CITY LIGHT CAPITAL, 488
EMERGENCE CAPITAL PARTNERS, 665
FRONTIER VENTURE CAPITAL, 791
IDG TECHNOLOGY VENTURE INVESTMENT, 2848
LEEDS EQUITY PARTNERS, 1105
NORTH ATLANTIC CAPITAL CORPORATION, 1333
POMONA CAPITAL, 1462
PROVIDENCE EQUITY PARTNERS, 1496
QUADRANGLE GROUP, 1506
SALEM INVESTMENT PARTNERS, 1606
SEAPORT CAPITAL, 1638
SILICON ALLEY VENTURE PARTNERS, 1680
SPIRE CAPITAL PARTNERS, 1724
SUMMIT PARTNERS, 1752
TELEGRAPH HILL PARTNERS, 1792
THOMAS H LEE PARTNERS, 1815
TRIDENT CAPITAL, 1850
VOLITION CAPITAL, 1942
WESTLAKE SECURITIES, 1976

Information Technology
(@)VENTURES, 1
360 CAPITAL PARTNERS 360 Capital Management SA, 2296
3I ASIA PACIFIC 3i Group, 2297
3I DEUTSCHLAND GESELLSCHAFT FUR 3i Group, 2299
3I GERMANY GmbH 3i Group, 2301
3I TEUPSCHLAND GmbH 3i Group, 2305
3T CAPITAL, 2308
3TS CAPITAL PARTNERS 3i Group plc, 2309
3W VENTURES Latour & Zuberbuhler GmbH, 2310
AAVIN PRIVATE EQUITY, 17
ABS CAPITAL PARTNERS, 22
ABS VENTURES, 23
ACCEL-KKR LLC, 29
ACCES CAPITAL QUEBEC, 2029
ACCUITIVE MEDICAL VENTURES LLC, 40
ACE VENTURE CAPITAL LIMITED, 2330
ACERO CAPITAL, 41
ACTIS, 2337
ACTIVA CAPITAL, 2338
ADAMS CAPITAL MANAGEMENT, 56
ADASTRA, 2343
ADVANCED TECHNOLOGY VENTURES, 59
ADVANTAGE CAPITAL PARTNERS, 61
AEP CAPITAL LLC, 65
AFTERDOX, 2352
AIP PRIVATE CAPITAL, 2031
AJU CAPITAL COMPANY, 2358
ALEUTIAN CAPITAL PARTNERS, 81
ALICE VENTURES SRL, 2364
ALIGNED PARTNERS, 83
ALLIANCE OF ANGELS, 85
ALLIANCE VENTURE, 2369
ALLOY VENTURES, 87
ALPHA CAPITAL PARTNERS, 90
ALPHA VENTURE PARTNERS, 91
ALSOP LOUIE PARTNERS, 93
ALTA PARTNERS, 94
ALTIRA GROUP LLC, 98
ALVEN CAPITAL, 2385
AMICUS CAPITAL, 114
AMIDZAD PARTNERS, 115
AMITI VENTURES, 116
AMPERSAND CAPITAL PARTNERS, 118
ANDREESSEN HOROWITZ, 124
ANTHEM VENTURE PARTNERS, 132
APAX GLOBIS PARTNERS & COMPANY Globis Capital Partners/Apax, 2414
APAX PARTNERS ET CIE, 2415
APEX VENTURE PARTNERS, 137
APJOHN GROUP LLC, 139
ARBORETUM VENTURES, 149
ARC ANGEL FUND, 150

Industry Preference Index / Information Technology

ARCAPITA INC, 152
ARLINGTON CAPITAL PARTNERS, 166
ARTHUR VENTURES, 173
ASAHI BANK INVESTMENT COMPANY LIMITED, 2430
ASCENSION HEALTH VENTURES LLC, 176
ASCENT VENTURE PARTNERS, 178
ASIAVEST PARTNERS, 2436
ASSET MANAGEMENT VENTURES, 181
ATA VENTURES, 183
ATHENIAN VENTURE PARTNERS, 187
ATILA VENTURES, 2442
ATLANTIC BRIDGE, 2443
ATLAS VENTURE, 191
ATRIA CAPITAL PARTENAIRES, 2448
AUGURY CAPITAL PARTNERS, 196
AUGUST CAPITAL, 197
AURELIA PRIVATE EQUITY, 2452
AURIGA PARTNERS, 2453
AUSTRALIAN ETHICAL INVESTMENT LIMITED, 2456
AUTHOSIS VENTURES, 2457
AVALON VENTURES, 206
AXA INVESTMENT MANAGERS PRIVATE EQUITY EUROPE, 2466
AXIOM VENTURE PARTNERS, 212
AZCA, 214
BAF SPECTRUM, 2477
BALTCAP MANAGEMENT LTD, 2480
BANEXI VENTURES PARTNERS, 2481
BARING PRIVATE EQUITY PARTNERS INDIA, 2490
BASIL PARTNERS Kross Border Trust Services Limited, 2493
BAYSHORE CAPITAL, 2052
BC RENAISSANCE CAPITAL FUND, 2053
BCM TECHNOLOGIES, 241
BEIJING HIGH TECHNOLOGY INVESTMENT COMPANY, 2499
BEIJING VENTURE CAPITAL COMPANY LIMITED, 2500
BERINGEA, 251
BI WALDEN MANAGEMENT SDN Walden International, 2508
BIG SUR VENTURES, 2510
BLUE CHIP VENTURE COMPANY, 287
BLUERUN VENTURES, 296
BLUESHIFT INTERNET VENTURES Blueshift, 2525
BLUETREE VENTURE FUND, 298
BLUMBERG CAPITAL, 301
BM-T BETEILIGUNGS MANAGEMENT THURINGEN GmbH, 2527
BOLDSTART VENTURES, 305
BOSTON MILLENNIA PARTNERS, 312
BOSTON UNIVERSITY - TECHNOLOGY DEVELOPMENT, 314
BOULDER VENTURES LTD, 315
BRAINSPARK PLC, 2535
BREAKWATER INVESTMENTS, 330
BRIDGESCALE PARTNERS, 339
BRIGHTSPARK VENTURES, 2066
BROADMARK CAPITAL, 345
BROOK VENTURE FUND, 349
BUTLER CAPITAL PARTNERS FRANCE, 2551
BV INVESTMENT PARTNERS, 361
CALIFORNIA TECHNOLOGY VENTURES, 371
CANADIAN VENTURE CAPITAL ASSOCIATION Canadian Venture Capital & Private Equity Association, 3258
CANDOVER, 2556
CAPITAL MIDWEST FUND, 400
CAPITOL PARTNERS, 406
CAPMAN CAPITAL MANAGEMENT OY, 2562
CASABONA VENTURES, 418
CASE TECHNOLOGY VENTURES Case Western Reserve University, 420
CATALYST FUND LP, 2571
CATALYST INVESTMENT MANAGERS PTY LIMITED PPM Capital, 2573
CATAMOUNT VENTURES LP, 428
CAZENOVE PRIVATE EQUITY Cazenove Capital, 2577
CDH INVESTMENTS, 2579
CEI VENTURES, 438
CELERITY PARTNERS, 439
CELTIC HOUSE VENTURE PARTNERS, 2076
CENTERFIELD CAPITAL PARTNERS, 443
CERES VENTURE FUND, 452
CEYUAN, 2584
CHARLES RIVER VENTURES, 455

CHEVRON TECHNOLOGY VENTURES, 466
CHICAGO VENTURE PARTNERS LP, 470
CHINA ISRAEL VALUE CAPITAL, 2593
CHINA MERCHANTS CHINA DIRECT INVESTMENTS LTD., 2594
CHINA VEST LIMITED, 2596
CHINA WALDEN MANAGEMENT LIMITED Walden Group, 2597
CHINAVEST, 473
CHRYSALIS CAPITAL ChrysCapital, 2599
CHRYSCAPITAL MANAGEMENT COMPANIES ChrysCapital, 2600
CISCO INVESTMENTS, 483
CLAREMONT CREEK VENTURES, 491
CLARITY PARTNERS, 494
CLIFFORD CHANCE PUNDER, 2614
CM CAPITAL, 2618
COACH & CAPITAL, 2619
COATUE MANAGEMENT, 509
COLLER CAPITAL LIMITED, 2621
COLORADO MILE HIGH FUND, 513
COLUMBIA CAPITAL, 515
COMMERCE ASSET VENTURES Sdn Bhd, 2623
COMPAGNIE FINANCIERE E DE ROTHSCHILD BANQUE, 2625
COMPASS TECHNOLOGY PARTNERS LP, 524
COMSPACE, 526
COMVEST PARTNERS, 528
CONCORD VENTURES, 2628
CONNECTICUT INNOVATIONS, 530
CONSTELLATION TECHNOLOGY VENTURES, 532
CONTINENTAL VENTURE CAPITAL LIMITED, 2631
CONTOUR VENTURE PARTNERS, 533
CONVERGE VENTURE PARTNERS, 534
CORAL GROUP, 536
CORDOVA VENTURES, 537
CORE CAPITAL PARTNERS, 538
CORRELATION VENTURES, 544
CORSA VENTURES, 545
COTTONWOOD TECHNOLOGY FUND, 549
COURT SQUARE VENTURES, 551
COVINGTON CAPITAL CORP., 2087
CREATHOR VENTURE, 2638
CRESSEY & COMPANY LP, 558
DAG VENTURES, 581
DAIMLERCHRYSLER VENTURE GmbH DaimlerChrysler AG, 2650
DANEVEST TECH FUND ADVISORS, 583
DARBY OVERSEAS INVESTMENTS LTD, 584
DBL PARTNERS, 595
DEFTA PARTNERS, 602
DELTA VENTURES LIMITED, 2655
DESJARDINS CAPITAL, 2095
DFC LTD, 2661
DFJ GOTHAM VENTURES, 608
DIRECT CAPITAL PRIVATE EQUITY LIMITED, 2664
DISCOVERY CAPITAL, 2097
DOMAIN ASSOCIATES LLC, 621
DR NEUHAUS TECHNO NORD GmbH, 2673
DRAPER RICHARDS KAPLAN FOUNDATION, 627
DUBILIER & COMPANY, 631
DUCHOSSOIS CAPITAL MANAGEMENT, 633
DVC DEUTSCHE VENTURE CAPITAL, 2679
E.VENTURES, 641
EARLY STAGE PARTNERS, 642
EARLYBIRD, 2682
EAST FUND MANAGEMENT GmbH GiroCredit, 2683
EASTVEN VENTURE PARTNERS, 645
EASTWARD CAPITAL PARTNERS, 646
ECAPITAL ENTREPRENEURIAL PARTNERS AG, 2686
ECI VENTURES, 2687
EDBI Pte LTD., 2690
EDF VENTURES, 652
EDGESTONE CAPITAL PARTNERS, 2103
EDGEWATER FUNDS, 654
EDISON PARTNERS, 655
EGL HOLDINGS, 656
ELAIA PARTNERS, 2693
ELEVATE VENTURES, 658
ELGNER GROUP INVESTMENTS, 2104
EM WARBURG, PINCUS & COMPANY INTERNATIONAL, 2697
EM WARBURG, PINCUS & COMPANY JAPAN, 2698

1193

Industry Preference Index / Information Technology

ENTERPRISE EQUITY (NI) LTD, 2704
ENTREPIA VENTURES, 682
EQUINET VENTURE PARTNERS AG, 2713
ESPIRITO SANTO VENTURES, 2717
ESSEX WOODLANDS HEALTH VENTURES LLC, 697
EURAZEO, 2719
EUROFUND LP, 2720
EUROPEAN INVESTMENT FUND, 2724
EUROVENTURES CAPITAL, 2725
EVERGREEN ADVISORS, 701
EXCEL VENTURE MANAGEMENT, 703
EXPERIMENT FUND, 708
EXPORT DEVELOPMENT CANADA, 2112
FCA VENTURE PARTNERS, 718
FERRANTI LIMITED, 2732
FIFTH WALL, 727
FIRST ANALYSIS, 732
FIRST CAPITAL GROUP, 734
FIRST FLIGHT VENTURE CENTER, 737
FIVE ELMS CAPITAL, 745
FLANDERS' FOREIGN INVESTMENT OFFICE, 2746
FLYBRIDGE CAPITAL PARTNERS, 754
FORTÉ VENTURES, 768
FOUNDATION CAPITAL, 770
FOUNDRY GROUP, 776
FULCRUM EQUITY PARTNERS, 794
FUTURE VENTURES, 800
GCI CAPITAL, 2128
GE CAPITAL, 808
GENERAL ATLANTIC PARTNERS, 815
GENERAL ATLANTIC PARTNERS, 2771
GENERATION PARTNERS, 818
GEORGIAN PARTNERS, 2132
GIZA VENTURE CAPITAL, 2782
GLENGARY LLC, 831
GLOBAL FINANCE, 2784
GLOBESPAN CAPITAL PARTNERS, 835
GOAL HOLDINGS, 2135
GOLDEN GATE CAPITAL, 839
GRAY GHOST VENTURES, 855
GREAT HILL PARTNERS LLC, 857
GREENHILL SAVP, 864
GREENSPRING ASSOCIATES, 867
GROSVENOR FUNDS, 875
GROTECH VENTURES, 876
GROWTHWORKS, 2143
GTCR, 884
GULFSTAR GROUP, 888
HALIFAX GROUP LLC, 894
HALLIM VENTURE CAPITAL, 2807
HALYARD CAPITAL, 897
HARBERT MANAGEMENT CORPORATION, 904
HASSO PLATTNER VENTURES, 2813
HELLMAN & FRIEDMAN LLC, 924
HELMET CAPITAL FUND MANAGEMENT OY, 2820
HIG CAPITAL, 928
HIGH-TECH GRUENDERFONDS, 2824
HIGHLAND CAPITAL PARTNERS, 935
HIKARI TSUSHIN CAPITAL, 2826
HOPEWELL VENTURES, 944
HORIZON TECHNOLOGY FINANCE, 946
HORIZONTE VENTURE MANAGEMENT GmbH, 2832
HOSEO VENTURE CAPITAL, 2833
HOUSTON ANGEL NETWORK, 950
HOUSTON HEALTH VENTURES, 951
HUDSON VENTURE PARTNERS, 954
HYUNDAI VENTURE INVESTMENT CORPORATION, 2839
IBB BETEILIGUNGSGESELLSCHAFT MBH, 2841
ICF VENTURES PVT LTD, 2846
ID VENTURES AMERICA LLC, 970
IDEA FUND PARTNERS, 971
IDG CAPITAL, 973
IGNITION PARTNERS, 974
ILLINOIS VENTURES, 975
ILLUMINATE VENTURES, 976
IN-Q-TEL, 979
INCWELL VENTURE CAPITAL, 981

INDASIA FUND ADVISORS PVT LTD, 2859
INETWORKS ADVISORS LLC, 987
INFLECTION POINT VENTURES, 989
INFOCOMM INVESTMENTS, 2870
INNOVATION CAPITAL, 2876
INNOVATION CAPITAL LIMITED, 2877
INNOVATION WORKS, 998
INNOVATIONSKAPITAL, 2878
INNOVENTURES CAPITAL PARTNERS, 999
INSTITUTIONAL VENTURE PARTNERS, 1001
INTEGRAL CAPITAL PARTNERS, 1003
INTER-ASIA VENTURE MANAGEMENT LIMITED, 2881
INTERMEDIATE CAPITAL GROUP PLC, 2883
INTERNATIONAL FINANCE CORPORATION (IFC), 1007
INTERSOUTH PARTNERS, 1008
INTERWEST PARTNERS, 1010
INVESCO PRIVATE CAPITAL, 1015
INVESTOR AB, 2890
INVEXCEL PATRIMONIO, 2891
IP GROUP, 2892
IPG GROUP, 2894
IPOSCOPE NV/SA, 2895
IRIS CAPITAL, 2897
ISOURCE GESTION, 2899
IT VENTURES LIMITED Digital Heritage Publishing Ltd., 2901
IT-PARTNERS NV, 2902
JAFCO COMPANY LIMITED JAPAN, 2906
JAPAN ASIA INVESTMENT COMPANY LIMITED, 2907
JAVELIN INVESTMENTS, 2908
JEGI CAPITAL The Jordan Edminston Group, Inc., 1033
JK&B CAPITAL, 1038
KAISER PERMANENTE VENTURES, 1052
KALORI GROUP INVESTMENTS, 2915
KAPOR CAPITAL, 1054
KB PARTNERS LLC, 1057
KBL HEALTHCARE VENTURES, 1058
KENSINGTON CAPITAL PARTNERS, 2167
KINETIC VENTURES, 1072
KLEINER PERKINS, 1075
KODIAK VENTURE PARTNERS, 1080
KOREA FIRST VENTURE CAPITAL CORPORATION, 2924
KTB VENTURES, 1087
LABRADOR VENTURES, 1089
LAUDER PARTNERS LLC, 1095
LAUNCHPAD VENTURE GROUP, 1100
LBBW VENTURE CAPITAL, 2932
LEAPFROG VENTURES, 1102
LETA CAPITAL, 2938
LIQUID CAPITAL GROUP, 1133
LIZADA CAPITAL LLC, 1135
LLR PARTNERS INC, 1136
LOCUS VENTURES, 1138
LONG RIVER VENTURES, 1142
LOVETT MILLER & COMPANY, 1148
MANTELLA VENTURE PARTNERS, 2182
MARCEAU INVESTISSEMENTS, 2955
MARS INVESTMENT ACCELERATOR FUND, 2187
MASON WELLS, 1171
MBF CAPITAL CORPORATION, 1188
MCG CAPITAL CORPORATION, 1189
MEAKEM/BECKER VENTURE CAPITAL, 1194
MENLO VENTURES, 1202
MENTOR CAPITAL PARTNERS LTD, 1203
MERITECH CAPITAL PARTNERS, 1212
MERRILL LYNCH (ASIA PACIFIC) LIMITED Merrill Lynch Group, 2964
MIDDLEBURG CAPITAL DEVELOPMENT, 1229
MIRAE ASSET VENTURE ACCELERATOR Mirae Asset Group, 2969
MIRAMAR VENTURE PARTNERS, 1237
MITSUBISHI UFJ CAPITAL, 2970
MOHR-DAVIDOW VENTURES, 1247
MORGAN STANLEY EXPANSION CAPITAL, 1255
MORGENTHALER VENTURES, 1257
MOSAIC CAPITAL PARTNERS, 2198
MOTLEY FOOL VENTURES, 1259
MOTOROLA SOLUTIONS VENTURE CAPITAL, 1260
MOUNTAIN PARTNERS, 2979
MOUNTAINEER CAPITAL, 1262

Industry Preference Index / Information Technology

MPG EQUITY PARTNERS, 1267
MVC CORPORATION, 2980
McLEAN WATSON CAPITAL, 2199
NAUSICAA VENTURES, 2986
NEEDHAM CAPITAL PARTNERS, 1288
NEUHAUS PARTNERS, 2994
NEW BRUNSWICK INNOVATION FOUNDATION, 2200
NEW CAPITAL FUND, 1292
NEW MARKETS VENTURE PARTNERS, 1299
NEW SCIENCE VENTURES, 1303
NEWBURY VENTURES, 1311
NEWMARGIN VENTURE CAPITAL, 2998
NEWSPRING CAPITAL, 1317
NEXTEC DEVELOPMENT CAPITAL LIMITED, 3000
NHN INVESTMENT, 3002
NIPPON TECHNOLOGY VENTURE PARTNERS LIMITED, 3005
NORO-MOSELEY PARTNERS, 1331
NORTH DAKOTA DEVELOPMENT FUND, 1338
NORWEST VENTURE PARTNERS, 1346
NOVAK BIDDLE VENTURE PARTNERS, 1348
NOVELTEK CAPITAL CORPORATION, 1351
NOVUS VENTURES LP, 1354
NTH POWER TECHNOLOGIES, 1355
OAK INVESTMENT PARTNERS, 1361
OEM CAPITAL, 1369
OEM CAPITAL, 1369
OKAPI VENTURE CAPITAL, 1371
ONSET VENTURES, 1378
ONTARIO CAPITAL GROWTH CORPORATION, 2211
ORIGINATE VENTURES, 1385
OSAGE PARTNERS, 1387
OUTLOOK VENTURES, 1389
OXANTIUM VENTURES, 1393
OneVentures, 3023
PAC-LINK MANAGEMENT CORP., 3024
PAI MANAGEMENT, 3026
PALISADES VENTURES, 1402
PALO ALTO VENTURE PARTNERS, 1405
PAMLICO CAPITAL, 1409
PANTHEON VENTURES (US) LP, 1411
PARKWALK ADVISORS, 3028
PARTECH INTERNATIONAL, 1416
PARTNERSHIP FUND FOR NEW YORK CITY, 1420
PATHENA, 3031
PELION VENTURE PARTNERS, 1425
PENNELL VENTURE PARTNERS LLC, 1429
PI CAPITAL GROUP LLC, 1440
PINNACLE MERCHANT CAPITAL, 2222
PINNACLE VENTURES, 1445
PITTSBURGH EQUITY PARTNERS, 1447
PMV, 3042
POLARIS VENTURE PARTNERS, 1460
POLESTAR CAPITAL, 1461
POLYTECH VENTURES, 3045
POLYTECHNOS VENTURE PARTNERS GmbH, 3046
PREVIZ VENTURES, 3050
PRIMARY VENTURE PARTNERS, 1475
PRISM CAPITAL, 1477
PROSPECT PARTNERS LLC, 1492
QBIC FUND, 3065
QED INVESTORS, 1502
QIMING VENTURE PARTNERS, 3066
QUANTUM VALLEY INVESTMENTS, 2228
QUEST FOR GROWTH, 3069
RAFAEL DEVELOPMENT CORPORATION (RDC) LIMITED, 3072
RBC CAPITAL MARKETS, 2231
REDMONT VENTURE PARTNERS, 1533
RENEWABLETECH VENTURES, 1542
RESERVOIR VENTURE PARTNERS, 1544
RESONANT VENTURE PARTNERS, 1547
REV1 VENTURES, 1553
RHO VENTURES, 1558
ROADMAP CAPITAL INC., 2242
ROBIN HOOD VENTURES, 1577
ROSER VENTURES LLC, 1586
RRE VENTURES, 1593
SAIF PARTNERS, 3093

SALMON RIVER CAPITAL, 1608
SAMSUNG VENTURE INVESTMENT CORPORATION Samsung Electronics, 3098
SAND HILL ANGELS, 1613
SAPPHIRE VENTURES, 1620
SATORI CAPITAL, 1622
SATURN PARTNERS, 1623
SCOTTISH EQUITY PARTNERS, 3104
SCP PARTNERS, 1633
SELBY VENTURE PARTNERS, 1646
SELWAY CAPITAL, 1647
SEQUEL VENTURE PARTNERS, 1653
SERAPH GROUP, 1655
SEVENTURE PARTNERS, 3113
SHEPHERD VENTURES, 1664
SI VENTURES, 1668
SIEMENS VENTURE CAPITAL, 3118
SIERRA VENTURES, 1670
SIGNAL PEAK VENTURES, 1677
SIGNATURE CAPITAL LLC, 3120
SILVER CREEK VENTURES, 1682
SLATER TECHNOLOGY FUND, 1693
SOFINNOVA VENTURES, 1698
SOLSTICE CAPITAL LP, 1702
SOUTH ATLANTIC VENTURE FUNDS, 1708
SOUTHEAST INTERACTIVE TECHNOLOGY FUNDS, 1709
SPECTRUM EQUITY INVESTORS LP, 1717
SPENCER TRASK VENTURES, 1720
SPLIT ROCK PARTNERS, 1725
STAR VENTURES, 3137
STARFISH VENTURES, 3138
STATELINE ANGELS, 1740
STIC VENTURES CORPORATION LIMITED, 3145
STORM VENTURES, 1747
SUNBRIDGE PARTNERS, 1755
SV ANGEL, 1761
SVB CAPITAL, 1764
T-VENTURE HOLDINGS GmbH Deutsche Telecom, 3155
TANDEM EXPANSION FUND, 2261
TAO VENTURE CAPITAL PARTNERS, 1780
TECH CAPITAL PARTNERS, 2262
TECH COAST ANGELS, 1784
TECHNOLOGY CROSSOVER VENTURES, 1785
TECHNOLOGY PARK MALAYSIA CORPORATION SDN BHD, 3164
TEKINVEST KK, 3166
TEKNOINVEST MANAGEMENT, 3167
TELESOFT PARTNERS, 1793
TENAYA CAPITAL, 1796
TERALYS CAPITAL, 2268
THOMAS WEISEL VENTURE PARTNERS, 1816
THOMPROPERTIES OY, 3175
THROUNARFELAG ISLANDS PLC, 3177
TL VENTURES, 1828
TMG CAPITAL PARTNERS, 3180
TOBA CAPITAL, 1829
TOKIO MARINE CAPITAL COMPANY LIMITED, 3182
TONG YANG VENTURE CAPITAL CORPORATION Tong Yang Cement Corporation, 3183
TRANS COSMOS INCORPORATED, 3185
TRELYS FUNDS, 1842
TRIANGLE VENTURE CAPITAL GROUP, 3188
TRIDENT CAPITAL, 1850
TRIGINITA CAPITAL, 3190
TRITON VENTURES, 1855
TROIKA CAPITAL PARTNERS, 3193
TRU MANAGEMENT, 1858
TSG EQUITY PARTNERS, 1862
TTV CAPITAL, 1863
TULLIS HEALTH INVESTORS, 1866
TVM CAPITAL, 3196
TWIN CITIES ANGELS, 1872
UNCORK CAPITAL, 1879
UPDATA VENTURE PARTNERS, 1886
USHA MARTIN VENTURES LIMITED, 3202
VALHALLA PARTNERS, 1899
VALLEY VENTURES LP, 1901
VALUEACT CAPITAL, 1903

Industry Preference Index / Information Technology & Media

VANTAGEPOINT CAPITAL PARTNERS, 1906
VEDANTA CAPITAL LP, 1911
VELOCITY EQUITY PARTNERS LLC, 1913
VENTECH, 3208
VENTURE CAPITAL FUND OF NEW ENGLAND, 1920
VENTUREAST, 3211
VERDEXUS, 2279
VERIZON VENTURES, 1926
VRG CAPITAL, 2282
VTB CAPITAL, 3229
WALDEN INTERNATIONAL, 1951
WARBURG PINCUS LLC, 1956
WAVEPOINT VENTURES, 1966
WEBB INVESTMENT NETWORK, 1968
WELSH, CARSON, ANDERSON & STOWE, 1972
WESLEY CLOVER, 2284
WESTVIEW CAPITAL PARTNERS, 1979
WHEATLEY PARTNERS, 1981
WHITECAP VENTURE PARTNERS, 2288
WICKS GROUP OF COMPANIES, LLC, 1984
WING VENTURE PARTNERS, 1996
WRF CAPITAL, 2008
XENIA VENTURE CAPITAL, 3240
XSEED CAPITAL MANAGEMENT, 2011
XT INVESTMENTS, 3241
YALETOWN VENTURE PARTNERS, 2291
YASUDA ENTERPRISE DEVELOPMENT COMPANY, 3243
YVC - YOZMA MANAGEMENT & INVESTMENTS LIMITED, 3249
ZONE VENTURES, 2021

Information Technology & Media
TPA CORPORATE FINANCE CONSULTING GMBH Horwarth International, 3184

Information and Technology
FLYING FISH, 755

Infrastructure
3I AUSTRIA BETEILGUNG GmbH 3i Group, 2298
3i GROUP PLC, 2311
645 VENTURES, 13
ACCEL, 28
ACCEL-KKR LLC, 29
ACCENTURE TECHNOLOGY VENTURES, 2326
ACCESS VENTURE PARTNERS LLC, 36
ACI CAPITAL, 42
ACME CAPITAL, 45
ACUMEN VENTURES, 2341
ADLEVO CAPITAL CIM Fund Services, 2345
ADOBE VENTURES LP, 58
AEM CAPITAL, 2349
AGF PRIVATE EQUITY Allianz Group, 2354
ALBERTA INVESTMENT MANAGEMENT CORP., 2033
ALLEGIS CYBER CAPITAL, 84
ALTAIR VENTURES, 95
ALTUS CAPITAL PARTNERS, 104
AMWIN MANAGEMENT PTY LIMITED, 2398
APEX VENTURE PARTNERS, 137
ARC FINANCIAL, 2040
ATLANTIC BRIDGE, 2443
AXIOM VENTURE PARTNERS, 212
AZIMUTH CAPITAL MANAGEMENT, 2050
BARING PRIVATE EQUITY PARTNERS INDIA, 2490
BATTERY VENTURES, 235
BENAROYA COMPANIES, 247
BESSEMER VENTURE PARTNERS, 260
BLUMBERG CAPITAL, 301
BOCI DIRECT INVESTMENT MANAGEMENT LIMITED Bank of China, 2529
BOSTON CAPITAL VENTURES, 310
BRIDGESCALE PARTNERS, 339
BROOKFIELD ASSET MANAGEMENT, 2067
CAI CAPITAL PARTNERS, 365
CANADIAN VENTURE CAPITAL ASSOCIATION Canadian Venture Capital & Private Equity Association, 3258
CAPITOL PARTNERS, 406
CARLYLE GROUP, 413

CASTILE VENTURES, 422
CEDAR (ISRAEL) FINANCIAL ADVISORS LIMITED Cedar Fund, 2580
CEDAR FUND, 436
CELTIC HOUSE VENTURE PARTNERS, 2076
CENTENNIAL VENTURES, 441
CENTERPOINT VENTURE PARTNERS, 444
CHARLES RIVER VENTURES, 455
CHEUNG KONG INFRASTRUCTURE HOLDINGS LIMITED, 2591
CHINA MERCHANTS CHINA INVESTMENT MANAGEMENT, 2595
CHRYSALIS CAPITAL ChrysCapital, 2599
CISCO INVESTMENTS, 483
CLEARSTONE VENTURE PARTNERS, 502
COLORADO MILE HIGH FUND, 513
COLT VENTURES, 514
COMCAST VENTURES, 518
COMPAGNIE FINANCIERE E DE ROTHSCHILD BANQUE, 2625
CONCORD VENTURES, 2628
CORE CAPITAL PARTNERS, 538
CRESCENDO VENTURES, 555
DAVENPORT RESOURCES LLC, 588
DAWNTREADER VENTURES, 592
DFJ GOTHAM VENTURES, 608
DUBIN CLARK & COMPANY, 632
DUFF ACKERMAN & GOODRICH, 634
DUNRATH CAPITAL, 636
EASTVEN VENTURE PARTNERS, 645
EDBI Pte LTD., 2690
EDGESTONE CAPITAL PARTNERS, 2103
EMP GLOBAL, 670
FIELDSTONE PRIVATE CAPITAL GROUP, 726
FIRST ANALYSIS, 732
FIRSTMARK CAPITAL, 743
FORMATIVE VENTURES, 764
FORMULA VENTURES LIMITED Formula Group, 2750
FORTRESS INVESTMENT GROUP LLC, 767
GABRIEL VENTURE PARTNERS, 805
GE ASIA PACIFIC CAPITAL TECHNOLOGY FUND, 2767
GEMINI ISRAEL VENTURE FUNDS LIMITED, 2770
GENERAL CATALYST PARTNERS, 816
GILBERT GLOBAL EQUITY PARTNERS, 827
GOLDEN OPPORTUNITIES FUND, 2136
GOOD NEWS VENTURES, 2138
GRANDBANKS CAPITAL, 848
GRANTHAM CAPITAL, 853
GREYCROFT PARTNERS, 871
GROTECH VENTURES, 876
GUIDE VENTURES, 887
GULFSTAR GROUP, 888
HAMMOND, KENNEDY, WHITNEY & COMPANY, 900
HARBINGER VENTURE MANAGEMENT, 905
HIG CAPITAL, 928
HRL MORRISON & COMPANY LIMITED, 2835
HUDSON VENTURE PARTNERS, 954
HUMMER WINBLAD VENTURE PARTNERS, 956
IDG CAPITAL, 973
IGNITION PARTNERS, 974
IN-Q-TEL, 979
INDEX VENTURES, 2860
INDEX VENTURES, 2860
INNOVATION PLATFORM CAPITAL, 997
INSIGHT VENTURE PARTNERS, 1000
INTERNATIONAL FINANCE CORPORATION (IFC), 1007
INVESCO PRIVATE CAPITAL, 1015
JEGI CAPITAL The Jordan Edminston Group, Inc., 1033
JK&B CAPITAL, 1038
KALORI GROUP INVESTMENTS, 2915
KB PARTNERS LLC, 1057
KOHLBERG KRAVIS ROBERTS & COMPANY, 1082
KRG CAPITAL PARTNERS, 1086
LIGHTSPEED VENTURE PARTNERS, 1121
LONGBOW CAPITAL, 2178
LONGWORTH VENTURE PARTNERS, 1146
M/C PARTNERS, 1153
MADRONA VENTURE GROUP, 1158
MADRONA VENTURE GROUP, 1158
MARWIT CAPITAL LLC, 1168
MEDIA VENTURE PARTNERS, 1195

Industry Preference Index / Insurance

MENLO VENTURES, 1202
MERCATOR INVESTMENTS, 2192
MERITECH CAPITAL PARTNERS, 1212
METROPOLITAN PARTNERS GROUP, 1225
MILLENIUM TECHNOLOGY VALUE PARTNERS, 1235
MISSION VENTURES, 1239
MOBIUS VENTURE CAPITAL, 1245
MOHR-DAVIDOW VENTURES, 1247
MORGAN STANLEY EXPANSION CAPITAL, 1255
MVP CAPITAL PARTNERS, 1275
NAVIGATION CAPITAL PARTNERS, 1280
NEEDHAM CAPITAL PARTNERS, 1288
NEUHAUS PARTNERS, 2994
NEW MOUNTAIN CAPITAL, 1301
NEW WORLD INFRASTRUCTURE LIMITED, 2996
NEWLIGHT MANAGEMENT, 1314
NORTH BRIDGE VENTURE PARTNERS, 1334
NOVUS VENTURES LP, 1354
OAK INVESTMENT PARTNERS, 1361
OMERS PRIVATE EQUITY, 2207
OPUS CAPITAL, 1381
OUTLOOK VENTURES, 1389
PALOMAR VENTURES, 1407
PELION VENTURE PARTNERS, 1425
PENINSULA VENTURES, 1427
PHYTO PARTNERS, 1439
PITANGO VENTURE CAPITAL, 3039
PMV, 3042
PRISM VENTUREWORKS, 1478
QUAKE CAPITAL PARTNERS, 1507
RECIPROCAL VENTURES, 1528
RED CLAY CAPITAL HOLDINGS, 1529
REDPOINT VENTURES, 1534
REMBRANDT VENTURE PARTNERS, 1540
RPM VENTURES, 1592
S3 VENTURES, 1597
SEAFORT CAPITAL, 2251
SEVIN ROSEN FUNDS, 1658
SHANGHAI INFORMATION INVESTMENT INCORPORATED, 3114
SHASTA VENTURES, 1663
SHEPHERD VENTURES, 1664
SI VENTURES, 1668
SIGNAL LAKE, 1676
SINEWAVE VENTURES, 1687
SMART BUSINESS CONSULTING, 3124
SOFTTECH VC, 1700
SONY STRATEGIC TECHNOLOGY PARTNERSHIPS, 1704
SOUTHEAST INTERACTIVE TECHNOLOGY FUNDS, 1709
SPARK CAPITAL, 1715
STONEBRIDGE PARTNERS, 1744
TECH CAPITAL PARTNERS, 2262
TECHNOLOGY CROSSOVER VENTURES, 1785
TIE ANGELS GROUP SEATTLE, 1825
TOBA CAPITAL, 1829
TRELLIS CAPITAL CORPORATION, 2273
TRUE VENTURES, 1860
UPHEAVAL INVESTMENTS, 1890
URBAN US, 1894
VALHALLA PARTNERS, 1899
VALOR EQUITY PARTNERS, 1902
VARDE PARTNERS, 1907
VELOCITY EQUITY PARTNERS LLC, 1913
VENTECH, 3208
VERIZON VENTURES, 1926
VINACAPITAL GROUP, 3217
VOLITION CAPITAL, 1942
VOYAGER CAPITAL, 1945
WALDEN ISRAEL VENTURE CAPITAL, 3231
WALDEN VENTURE CAPITAL, 1952
WESTCAP, 2285
WINDWARD VENTURES, 1995
WORLDVIEW TECHNOLOGY PARTNERS, 2007
WRF CAPITAL, 2008
YES VC, 2014
YL VENTURES, 3246

Infrastructure Services
HAWTHORN EQUITY PARTNERS, 916
MARKET SQUARE EQUITY PARTNERS, 2186

Infrastructure Software
BAIN CAPITAL VENTURES, 221
BRM SEED, 2541
FLYWHEEL VENTURES, 756
GENESIS PARTNERS, 2775
MOBIUS VENTURE CAPITAL, 1245
ONSET VENTURES, 1378

Infrastructure Technology
CORIOLIS VENTURES, 539

Innovation
CIBC INNOVATION BANKING, 2080
GOLDEN OPPORTUNITIES FUND, 2136
VANCITY CAPITAL, 2277
WESTCAP, 2285

Innovative Products & Services
JERUSALEM VENTURE PARTNERS, 2910
LBBW VENTURE CAPITAL, 2932

Innovative Technology
CELADON CAPITAL GROUP, 2582

Institutional Asset Management
ROTHSCHILD AUSTRALIA - ARROW PRIVATE EQUITY Rothschild Group, 3086

Instrumentation
AXIA CAPITAL, 211
CHL MEDICAL PARTNERS, 474
COMMONWEALTH CAPITAL VENTURES LP, 521
DOMAIN ASSOCIATES LLC, 621
JC TECHNOLOGIES LTD, 2909
LATTERELL VENTURE PARTNERS, 1094
MASSACHUSETTS CAPITAL RESOURCE COMPANY, 1173
MASSACHUSETTS GROWTH CAPITAL CORPORATION, 1174
NOVAK BIDDLE VENTURE PARTNERS, 1348
POLESTAR CAPITAL, 1461
PROVCO GROUP, 1494
RAF INDUSTRIES, 1521
SEED CAPITAL LIMITED, 3107
SILVER CREEK VENTURES, 1682
SOUTHPORT PARTNERS, 1712
TECHNOCAP, 2263
VISION CAPITAL, 1937
WESTERN TECHNOLOGY INVESTMENT, 1975
ZS FUND LP, 2022

Insurance
ABSTRACT VENTURES, 24
AIG INVESTMENT CORPORATION (ASIA) LIMITED, 2356
AMANET TECHNOLOGIES LIMITED, 2389
ARGOS SODITIC SA, 2423
ATRIA CAPITAL PARTENAIRES, 2448
CCP EQUITY PARTNERS, 434
CHINA MERCHANTS CHINA DIRECT INVESTMENTS LTD., 2594
CIVC PARTNERS, 489
CLIFFORD CHANCE PUNDER, 2614
CROSSWINDS HOLDINGS INC., 2090
DFC LTD, 2661
FOX PAINE & COMPANY LLC, 778
GE CAPITAL, 808
HARDY CAPITAL PARTNERS, 2144
HELLMAN & FRIEDMAN LLC, 924
IBM VENTURE CAPITAL GROUP, 967
INTERMEDIATE CAPITAL GROUP PLC, 2883
JORDAN COMPANY, 1045
LUGE CAPITAL, 2179
MS&AD VENTURES, 1269
MUNICH REINSURANCE AMERICA, INC, 1272
NEW CAPITAL PARTNERS, 1293
NEWLIGHT PARTNERS, 1315

1197

Industry Preference Index / Insurance Brokerage

ODYSSEY INVESTMENT PARTNERS, 1368
PORTAG3 VENTURES, 2225
REITEN & CO STRATEGIC INVESTMENTS AS Reiten & Company, 3076
ROBIN HOOD VENTURES, 1577
SONY EUROPE, 3129
SOUTH ATLANTIC VENTURE FUNDS, 1708
SOUTHPORT PARTNERS, 1712
STONE POINT CAPITAL LLC, 1743
THAYER STREET PARTNERS, 1805
THE HIVE, 1809
TPA CORPORATE FINANCE CONSULTING GMBH Horwarth International, 3184
UNISON CAPITAL PARTNERS LP, 3201
VENTURE INVESTORS, 3210
VINACAPITAL GROUP, 3217
VIOLA FINTECH, 3220
VISION CAPITAL, 1937
VRG CAPITAL, 2282
WAND PARTNERS, 1955
WELLSPRING CAPITAL MANAGEMENT LLC, 1971
WESTLAKE SECURITIES, 1976
ZS FUND LP, 2022

Insurance Brokerage
AON RISK SOLUTIONS Aon Corporation, 2413

Integrated Health Solutions
SANOFI-GENZYME BIOVENTURES, 1618

Interactive Media
SPARK CAPITAL, 1715

International/Emerging Markets
500 STARTUPS, 11

Internet
.406 VENTURES, 2
10X VENTURE PARTNERS, 3
212 CAPITAL PARTNERS, 2294
360 CAPITAL PARTNERS 360 Capital Management SA, 2296
ABRT VENTURE FUND, 2320
ACCEL-KKR LLC, 29
ACONCAGUA VENTURES, 2334
ACORN CAMPUS VENTURES, 47
ACTUA, 53
ACUITY VENTURES LLC, 54
ACUMEN VENTURES, 2341
ADASTRA, 2343
ADD VENTURE, 2344
AFTERDOX, 2352
ALACRITY VENTURES, 76
ALBERTA ENTERPRISE, 2032
ALMAZ CAPITAL, 89
ALTA VENTURES MEXICO, 2382
ALTOS VENTURES, 100
ALVEN CAPITAL, 2385
AMBIENT SOUND INVESTMENTS, 2390
AMPEZZO PARTNERS, 2396
ANTHEM VENTURE PARTNERS, 132
ANTRAK CAPITAL, 2407
ARC ANGEL FUND, 150
ARGONAUT VENTURES, 163
ARKAFUND MEDIA & ICT, 2426
ARTIS VENTURES, 175
ASTUTIA VENTURES, 2441
AUSTIN VENTURES, 202
AUTHOSIS VENTURES, 2457
B-TO-V PARTNERS, 2475
BAF SPECTRUM, 2477
BAND OF ANGELS LLC, 226
BANNEKER PARTNERS, 227
BERKELEY VENTURES, 253
BIG SUR VENTURES, 2510
BILTMORE VENTURES, 264
BLACKBIRD VENTURES, 2520
BLUE CHIP VENTURE COMPANY, 287
BLUE COVE VENTURES, 2523
BLUEFISH VENTURES, 294
BLUERUN VENTURES, 296
BOREALIS VENTURES, 308
BOSTON SEED CAPITAL, 313
BREGAL SAGEMOUNT, 333
CALIFORNIA TECHNOLOGY VENTURES, 371
CAPITAL TODAY, 2560
CARMEL VENTURES, 2566
CATAGONIA CAPITAL, 2569
CATALYST INVESTORS, 427
CENTRAL TEXAS ANGEL NETWORK, 445
CENTRALWAY, 2583
CEYUAN, 2584
CLEARSTONE VENTURE PARTNERS, 502
COACH & CAPITAL, 2619
COLOMA VENTURES, 512
COMMONWEALTH CAPITAL VENTURES LP, 521
CONNECT VENTURES, 2629
CONTOUR VENTURE PARTNERS, 533
CONVERGE VENTURE PARTNERS, 534
CREATHOR VENTURE, 2638
CROSS CREEK ADVISORS, 560
CXO FUND, 574
CYBERAGENT VENTURES, 2646
DATA COLLECTIVE, 585
DATA POINT CAPITAL, 586
DAVID SHEN VENTURES, 590
DAWNTREADER VENTURES, 592
DETROIT VENTURE PARTNERS, 607
DFJ ESPRIT, 2662
DIFFERENCE CAPITAL, 2096
DOUBLE M PARTNERS, 624
DPIXEL, 2672
EARLYBIRD, 2682
EASTLABS, 2684
EDELSON TECHNOLOGY PARTNERS, 651
EDEN VENTURES, 2691
ENSPIRE CAPITAL PTE LTD, 2703
EPLANET CAPITAL, 690
EUROPEAN FOUNDERS FUND, 2723
EVERGREEN ADVISORS, 701
EVERGREEN VENTURE PARTNERS, 2726
EXPANSION VENTURE CAPITAL, 707
FF VENTURE CAPITAL, 724
FIVE ELMS CAPITAL, 745
FOCUS VENTURES, 757
FORMATIVE VENTURES, 764
FORTÉ VENTURES, 768
FOUNDER PARTNERS, 772
FOUNDER'S CO-OP, 773
FOUNDERS FUND, 775
FOUNDRY GROUP, 776
FRANCISCO PARTNERS, 779
FREESTYLE, 784
FUNG CAPITAL USA, 796
GENERAL CATALYST PARTNERS, 816
GEORGIAN PARTNERS, 2132
GGV CAPITAL, 823
GLOBESPAN CAPITAL PARTNERS, 835
GLYNN CAPITAL MANAGEMENT, 836
GREE VENTURES, 2798
GRISHIN ROBOTICS, 874
GROTECH VENTURES, 876
GSR VENTURES, 2801
HARBINGER VENTURE MANAGEMENT, 905
HELION VENTURE PARTNERS, LLC International Management (Mauritius) Ltd, 2818
HELLMAN & FRIEDMAN LLC, 924
HIGH COUNTRY VENTURE, 930
HIGHLAND CAPITAL PARTNERS, 935
HOLTZBRINCK VENTURES, 2829
HOXTON VENTURES, 2834
HUDSON VENTURE PARTNERS, 954
HUMMER WINBLAD VENTURE PARTNERS, 956
HV HOLTZBRINCK VENTURES, 2838
IDEALAB, 972

Industry Preference Index / Internet Infrastructure

IDG CAPITAL PARTNERS, 2847
IDG VENTURES INDIA International Financial Services Limited, 2849
IGAN PARTNERS, 2149
ILLUMINATE VENTURES, 976
IMI.VC, 2856
INFINITY VENTURE PARTNERS, 2869
INITIAL CAPITAL, 2872
INLAND TECHSTART FUND, 993
INSTITUTIONAL VENTURE PARTNERS, 1001
INTERSOUTH PARTNERS, 1008
INVENTURE PARTNERS, 2886
IRISH ANGELS, 1019
ISOURCE GESTION, 2899
JAVELIN VENTURE PARTNERS, 1028
JC2 VENTURES, 1031
JMI EQUITY FUND LP, 1041
JUMPSEED VENTURES, 2912
KAEDAN INVESTMENTS, 2914
KEGONSA CAPITAL PARTNERS, 1060
KIBO VENTURES, 2920
KIZOO TECHNOLOGY CAPITAL, 2921
KNIGHT'S BRIDGE CAPITAL PARTNERS, 2171
KODIAK VENTURE PARTNERS, 1080
LANTA DIGITAL VENTURES, 2930
LAUDER PARTNERS LLC, 1095
LAUNCHCAPITAL, 1097
LAUNCHPAD VENTURE GROUP, 1100
LEO CAPITAL HOLDINGS, LLC, 1108
LIONBIRD, 2943
LONG RIVER VENTURES, 1142
LONGWORTH VENTURE PARTNERS, 1146
LOOL VENTURES, 2947
MAGMA VENTURE PARTNERS, 2952
MAINE ANGELS, 1160
MASS VENTURES, 1172
MERCURY FUND, 1206
MILLENIUM TECHNOLOGY VALUE PARTNERS, 1235
MIRAMAR VENTURE PARTNERS, 1237
MOBILITY VENTURES, 1244
MORADO VENTURE PARTNERS, 1254
MORGENTHALER VENTURES, 1257
NAUTA CAPITAL, 2987
NEO TECHNOLOGY VENTURES, 2989
NEXT WORLD CAPITAL, 1319
NEXTVIEW VENTURES, 1322
NEXUS VENTURE PARTNERS Nexus India Capital Advisors Pvt Ltd, 3001
NHN INVESTMENT, 3002
NHN INVESTMENT, 3002
NORWEST VENTURE PARTNERS, 1346
O'REILLY ALPHATECH VENTURES, 1359
OAK INVESTMENT PARTNERS, 1361
OKAPI VENTURE CAPITAL, 1371
OPENVIEW VENTURE PARTNERS, 1380
OPUS CAPITAL, 1381
ORIGINATE VENTURES, 1385
OSAGE PARTNERS, 1387
OUTCOME CAPITAL, 1388
OUTLOOK VENTURES, 1389
PARKWALK ADVISORS, 3028
PARTECH INTERNATIONAL, 1416
PELION VENTURE PARTNERS, 1425
PENTECH VENTURES, 3032
PHENOMEN VENTURES, 3034
PI CAPITAL GROUP LLC, 1440
PINEHURST ADVISORS, 3038
PINNACLE MERCHANT CAPITAL, 2222
PITON CAPITAL, 3040
PLUS VENTURES, 3041
POINT JUDITH CAPITAL, 1459
POINT NINE CAPITAL, 3044
PRINCIPIA SGR, 3052
PROJECT A VENTURE GmbH & CO. KG, 3056
REAL VENTURES, 2232
REED ELSEVIER VENTURES, 3074
REMBRANDT VENTURE PARTNERS, 1540
REVEL PARTNERS, 1554

REVO CAPITAL, 3078
RINCON VENTURE PARTNERS, 1566
RUNA CAPITAL, 3088
SAIF PARTNERS, 3093
SAINTS CAPITAL, 1604
SELBY VENTURE PARTNERS, 1646
SENTRY FINANCIAL CORPORATION, 1652
SEQUOIA CAPITAL, 1654
SEVIN ROSEN FUNDS, 1658
SHASTA VENTURES, 1663
SIGMA PARTNERS, 1672
SIGNAL PEAK VENTURES, 1677
SIGNATURE CAPITAL LLC, 3120
SINGTEL INNOV8, 3121
SK TELECOM VENTURES, 1690
SOFTBANK VENTURES KOREA, 3127
SOLID VENTURES, 3128
SORRENTO VENTURES, 1706
SOUTHERN CROSS VENTURE PARTNERS, 1711
SPECTRUM EQUITY INVESTORS LP, 1717
SPINUP VENTURE, 3132
SPLIT ROCK PARTNERS, 1725
STAGE 1 VENTURES, 1734
STAGEONE VENTURES, 3136
SUMMIT PARTNERS, 1752
SUPREMUM CAPITAL, 3150
SUSQUEHANNA GROWTH EQUITY, 1759
SVB CAPITAL, 1764
TAO VENTURE CAPITAL PARTNERS, 1780
TARGET PARTNERS, 3161
TECH COAST ANGELS, 1784
TECHNOLOGY CROSSOVER VENTURES, 1785
TELESYSTEM, 2264
TENGELMANN VENTURES, 3170
THINKTIV VENTURES, 1810
THRIVE CAPITAL, 1821
TIE ANGELS GROUP SEATTLE, 1825
TIGER GLOBAL MANAGEMENT, 1826
TMI, 3181
TOBA CAPITAL, 1829
TROIKA CAPITAL PARTNERS, 3193
TRUE VENTURES, 1860
TUGBOAT VENTURES, 1865
UNION SQUARE VENTURES, 1882
UNIVERSITY VENTURE FUND, 1884
UPDATA VENTURE PARTNERS, 1886
VALAR VENTURES, 1897
VANTAGEPOINT CAPITAL PARTNERS, 1906
VINE ST VENTURES, 1934
VISION CAPITAL, 1937
VITAMINA K VENTURE CAPITAL, 3223
VITULUM VENTURES, 3224
VOLITION CAPITAL, 1942
VTB CAPITAL, 3229
WALDEN INTERNATIONAL, 1951
WGI GROUP, 1980
WINDSPEED VENTURES, 1994
WORLDVIEW TECHNOLOGY PARTNERS, 2007
WRF CAPITAL, 2008
XANGE PRIVATE EQUITY, 3239
YES VC, 2014
ZELKOVA VENTURES, 2017

Internet Advertising
CORIOLIS VENTURES, 539
TRUE VENTURES, 1860

Internet Applications and Services
GENESIS PARTNERS, 2775
LIFE.SREDA, 2940

Internet Communications
TRUE VENTURES, 1860

Internet Infrastructure
BASECAMP VENTURES, 230
BLUEFISH VENTURES, 294

Industry Preference Index / Internet Infrastructure Services

COLUMBIA CAPITAL, 515
INNOVATION WORKS, 998
MASTHEAD VENTURE PARTNERS, 1175
TGAP VENTURES, 1802

Internet Infrastructure Services
EVENTI CAPITAL PARTNERS, 2110

Internet Technology
(@)VENTURES, 1
ABELL FOUNDATION VENTURES, 19
ACCEL-KKR LLC, 29
ACCESS VENTURE PARTNERS LLC, 36
ACE VENTURE CAPITAL LIMITED, 2330
ACT VENTURE CAPITAL LIMITED, 2336
ADOBE VENTURES LP, 58
AEP CAPITAL LLC, 65
AKERS CAPITAL LLC, 75
ALEXANDER HUTTON, 82
ALICE VENTURES SRL, 2364
ALLEGIS CYBER CAPITAL, 84
ALTAIR VENTURES, 95
AMADEUS CAPITAL PARTNERS LIMITED, 2386
AMWIN MANAGEMENT PTY LIMITED, 2398
ANDERSON PACIFIC CORPORATION, 122
ANGELS' FORUM LLC, 129
ARGO GLOBAL CAPITAL, 162
ARROWPATH VENTURE PARTNERS, 169
ATHENIAN VENTURE PARTNERS, 187
ATRIUM CAPITAL, 192
AURA CAPITAL OY Auratum Group, 2451
AUSTIN VENTURES, 202
AVANSIS VENTURES, 207
AXA INVESTMENT MANAGERS PRIVATE EQUITY EUROPE, 2466
BAIRD CAPITAL PARTNERS, 222
BARCELONA EMPREN, 2483
BASECAMP VENTURES, 230
BOULDER VENTURES LTD, 315
CANAL PARTNERS, 387
CAPITOL PARTNERS, 406
CAPRICORN VENTURE PARTNERS NV, 2563
CASTILE VENTURES, 422
CAZENOVE PRIVATE EQUITY Cazenove Capital, 2577
CEDAR (ISRAEL) FINANCIAL ADVISORS LIMITED Cedar Fund, 2580
CEDAR FUND, 436
CENTENNIAL VENTURES, 441
CHALLENGE FUNDS - ETGAR LP, 2585
CHICAGO VENTURE PARTNERS LP, 470
COLLER CAPITAL LIMITED, 2621
COMMONWEALTH CAPITAL VENTURES LP, 521
CONCORD VENTURES, 2628
CONCORD VENTURES, 2628
CORE CAPITAL PARTNERS, 538
DAIMLERCHRYSLER VENTURE GmbH DaimlerChrysler AG, 2650
DELTA VENTURES LIMITED, 2655
DIAMONDHEAD VENTURES, 613
DOUGHTY HANSON & CO., 2671
DR NEUHAUS TECHNO NORD GmbH, 2673
DRAPER RICHARDS KAPLAN FOUNDATION, 627
ECONA AG, 2688
EDGESTONE CAPITAL PARTNERS, 2103
EDISON PARTNERS, 655
ELECTRA PARTNERS ASIA LIMITED SFC of Hong Kong, 2694
ENTERPRISE EQUITY (NI) LTD, 2704
EPIC VENTURES, 688
EPISODE 1 PARTNERS, 2711
EURAZEO, 2719
EUROFUND LP, 2720
EVERCORE CAPITAL PARTNERS, 699
FERRANTI LIMITED, 2732
FORMULA VENTURES LIMITED Formula Group, 2750
FOUNDATION CAPITAL, 770
FRESHWATER VENTURE PARTNERS, 2757
GALILEO II, 2765
GEMINI ISRAEL VENTURE FUNDS LIMITED, 2770
GENESIS PARTNERS, 2775
GILBERT GLOBAL EQUITY PARTNERS, 827

GMT COMMUNICATIONS PARTNERS LLP, 2789
GRANDBANKS CAPITAL, 848
GRAYHAWK CAPITAL, 856
GREENHILL SAVP, 864
HALLIM VENTURE CAPITAL, 2807
HIKARI TSUSHIN CAPITAL, 2826
HYUNDAI VENTURE INVESTMENT CORPORATION, 2839
ID VENTURES AMERICA LLC, 970
IDG CAPITAL, 973
IDG TECHNOLOGY VENTURE INVESTMENT, 2848
IDINVEST PARTNERS, 2851
IGNITE JAPAN KK Ignite Group, 2854
IN-Q-TEL, 979
IPG GROUP, 2894
ITC VENTURES, 2903
JAPAN ASIA INVESTMENT COMPANY LIMITED, 2907
JK&B CAPITAL, 1038
KALORI GROUP INVESTMENTS, 2915
KB PARTNERS LLC, 1057
KINETIC VENTURES, 1072
KNIGHTSBRIDGE ADVISERS, 1077
KOREA FIRST VENTURE CAPITAL CORPORATION, 2924
LEASING TECHNOLOGIES INTERNATIONAL INC., 1103
MACQUARIE DIRECT INVESTMENT LIMITED, 2951
MADRONA VENTURE GROUP, 1158
MANHATTAN INVESTMENT PARTNERS, 1163
MASSACHUSETTS CAPITAL RESOURCE COMPANY, 1173
MASSACHUSETTS GROWTH CAPITAL CORPORATION, 1174
MASTHEAD VENTURE PARTNERS, 1175
MATRIX PARTNERS, 1181
MAYFIELD FUND, 1184
MENLO VENTURES, 1202
MERITECH CAPITAL PARTNERS, 1212
METROPOLITAN PARTNERS GROUP, 1225
MIRAE ASSET VENTURE ACCELERATOR Mirae Asset Group, 2969
MISSION VENTURES, 1239
MOBILE INTERNET CAPITAL, 2974
MOSAIC CAPITAL PARTNERS, 2198
NEW YORK CITY ENTREPRENEURIAL FUND New York City Economic Development Corporation, 1307
NEWBURY VENTURES, 1311
NEWLIGHT MANAGEMENT, 1314
NORTH ATLANTIC CAPITAL CORPORATION, 1333
NORTHWOOD VENTURES, 1344
NOVAK BIDDLE VENTURE PARTNERS, 1348
PITANGO VENTURE CAPITAL, 3039
PRIME TECHNOLOGY VENTURES NV, 3051
REDPOINT VENTURES, 1534
RHO VENTURES, 1558
RRE VENTURES, 1593
SAMSUNG VENTURE INVESTMENT CORPORATION Samsung Electronics, 3098
SEAYA VENTURES, 3105
SEQUEL VENTURE PARTNERS, 1653
SHANGHAI INFORMATION INVESTMENT INCORPORATED, 3114
SIERRA VENTURES, 1670
SMART BUSINESS CONSULTING, 3124
SONY EUROPE, 3129
SONY STRATEGIC TECHNOLOGY PARTNERSHIPS, 1704
SORRENTO VENTURES, 1706
SOUTHPORT PARTNERS, 1712
STAGE 1 VENTURES, 1734
SUNEVISION HOLDINGS LIMITED, 3148
SYCAMORE VENTURES, 1769
TAMIR FISHMAN VENTURES, 3159
TELUS VENTURES, 2265
TEUZA MANAGEMENT & DEVELOPMENT LTD, 3171
TIME WARNER INVESTMENT CORPORATION, 1827
TWJ CAPITAL, 1873
UNION SQUARE VENTURES, 1882
US VENTURE PARTNERS, 1896
VOYAGER CAPITAL, 1945
WALDEN ISRAEL VENTURE CAPITAL, 3231
WASSERSTEIN & CO., 1960
WELLINGTON PARTNERS VENTURE CAPITAL GmbH, 3233
WESTERN STATES INVESTMENT GROUP, 1974
WESTERN TECHNOLOGY INVESTMENT, 1975

1200

Industry Preference Index / Life Sciences

WINDWARD VENTURES, 1995
YLR CAPITAL MARKETS LTD, 3247

Internet of Things
CHRYSALIX, 2078
EXTREME VENTURE PARTNERS, 2113
GOOD NEWS VENTURES, 2138

Internet-Enabled Hardware
CATALYST INVESTORS, 427

Internet/Mobile/Media
GIZA VENTURE CAPITAL, 2782

Internet/Web Services
BEZOS EXPEDITIONS, 262

Invention
INTELLECTUAL VENTURES, 1005

Investment Analysis and Research
AUSTRALIAN ETHICAL INVESTMENT LIMITED, 2456

Investor Relations
CAPMAN CAPITAL MANAGEMENT OY, 2562

IoT
CISCO INVESTMENTS, 483
CORNERSTONE VENTURE PARTNERS, 543
FOUNDER PARTNERS, 772
INTEL CAPITAL, 1004
MS&AD VENTURES, 1269
QUALCOMM VENTURES, 1509
SAMSUNG NEXT, 1611
SONY INNOVATION FUND, 1703
SWITCH VENTURES, 1768
WILDCAT VENTURE PARTNERS, 1985

Labour Law
BUTZOW NORDIA ADVOCATES LTD, 2552

Language Processing
CARBON VENTURES, 408
PATHBREAKER VENTURES, 1421

Laser
NEUHAUS PARTNERS, 2994

Law Enforcement
BRYANT PARK VENTURES, 356

Legal
COVENT INDUSTRIAL CAPITAL INVESTMENT COMPANY, 2635
M25 GROUP, 1155

Legal and Compliance
CAPMAN CAPITAL MANAGEMENT OY, 2562
VON BRAUN & SCHREIBER PRIVATE EQUITY PARTNERS, 3227

Leisure
3I ASIA PACIFIC 3i Group, 2297
ACTIS, 2337
APOLLO GLOBAL MANAGEMENT, 140
AVANTI CAPITAL, 2458
BARCLAYS VENTURES Barclays, 2486
BENCIS CAPITAL PARTNERS, 2501
BOTTS & COMPANY LIMITED, 2532
CANDOVER, 2556
CINVEN LIMITED, 2605
CLOSE BROTHERS PRIVATE EQUITY Close Brothers Group, 2617
CLYDESDALE VENTURES, 506
DUKE STREET CAPITAL Duke Street, 2676
DUNEDIN CAPITAL PARTNERS LIMITED, 2677
FALCONHEAD CAPITAL, 717
GRAPHITE CAPITAL MANAGEMENT LTD, 2796
HAMBRO CAPITAL MANAGEMENT LTD, 2808
HENDERSON PRIVATE CAPITAL, 2821
HG CAPITAL, 2823
MERRILL LYNCH (ASIA PACIFIC) LIMITED Merrill Lynch Group, 2964
NORTHERN ENTERPRISE LIMITED, 3011
PHOENIX EQUITY PARTNERS LIMITED, 3036
PROSPECT PARTNERS LLC, 1492
QUESTER CAPITAL MANAGEMENT LIMITED, 3070
SCHOONER CAPITAL LLC, 1627
SOVEREIGN CAPITAL, 3130
SWANDER PACE CAPITAL, 1767
WESLEY CLOVER, 2284

Leisure & Hospitality
BUSINESS GROWTH FUND, 2550

License Communications
SYNCOM VENTURE PARTNERS, 1771

Life Sciences
3I TEUPSCHLAND GmbH 3i Group, 2305
5AM VENTURES, 12
ABINGWORTH MANAGEMENT LIMITED, 2316
ABOA VENTURE MANAGEMENT OY, 2318
ACCELERATOR LIFE SCIENCE PARTNERS, 31
ACCELMED, 2324
ACME LABS, 2333
ACORN CAMPUS VENTURES, 47
ACT VENTURE CAPITAL LIMITED, 2336
ADAMS STREET PARTNERS, LLC, 57
ADVANTAGE CAPITAL PARTNERS, 61
AGF PRIVATE EQUITY Allianz Group, 2354
AISLING CAPITAL, 74
ALBERTA ENTERPRISE, 2032
ALICE VENTURES SRL, 2364
ALLIANCE OF ANGELS, 85
ALLOY VENTURES, 87
ALPINVEST GmbH Alpinvest, 2377
ALPINVEST HOLDING NV Alpinvest, 2378
ALTA PARTNERS, 94
AMANET TECHNOLOGIES LIMITED, 2389
AMBIENT SOUND INVESTMENTS, 2390
AMGEN VENTURES, 112
AMIDZAD PARTNERS, 115
AMPHION CAPITAL PARTNERS, 2397
ANGELAB VENTURES, 2401
APPLE TREE PARTNERS, 143
ARAVIS VENTURES, 2419
ARBORETUM VENTURES, 149
ASCLEPIOS BIORESEARCH, 2433
ATHENIAN VENTURE PARTNERS, 187
ATLAS VENTURE, 191
ATLAS VENTURE: FRANCE, 2445
AUGURY CAPITAL PARTNERS, 196
AURELIA PRIVATE EQUITY, 2452
AURIGA PARTNERS, 2453
AURUM VENTURES MKI, 2454
AUSTRAL CAPITAL PARTNERS, 2455
AVALON VENTURES, 206
AWEIDA VENTURE PARTNERS, 210
AZCA, 214
BAIRD CAPITAL PARTNERS, 222
BAND OF ANGELS LLC, 226
BANEXI VENTURES PARTNERS, 2481
BATTELLE VENTURES, 233
BAY BG BAVARIAN VENTURE CAPITAL CORP, 2494
BAY CITY CAPITAL LLC, 237
BC RENAISSANCE CAPITAL FUND, 2053
BCM TECHNOLOGIES, 241
BEIJING HIGH TECHNOLOGY INVESTMENT COMPANY, 2499
BIOMED PARTNERS, 2515
BIOPACIFIC VENTURES, 2516
BIOVEDA CAPITAL, 2518
BIOVENTURES INVESTORS, 270
BIRK VENTURE, 2519
BLADE VENTURES, 278
BM-T BETEILIGUNGS MANAGEMENT THURINGEN GmbH, 2527
BMP AKTIENGESELLSCHAFT BMP Venture Capital, 2528
BOEHRINGER INGELHEIM VENTURE FUND, 2530

Industry Preference Index / Life Sciences

BOSTON UNIVERSITY - TECHNOLOGY DEVELOPMENT, 314
BOULDER VENTURES LTD, 315
BRAIN TRUST ACCELERATOR FUND, 323
BRANDON CAPITAL PARTNERS, 2536
BRIGHTSTONE VENTURE CAPITAL, 341
BROADMARK CAPITAL, 345
BROADVIEW VENTURES, 347
BRYAN GARNIER & COMPANY, 2544
BUSINESS GROWTH FUND, 2550
CALIFORNIA TECHNOLOGY VENTURES, 371
CANADIAN VENTURE CAPITAL ASSOCIATION Canadian Venture Capital & Private Equity Association, 3258
CAPITAL MIDWEST FUND, 400
CAPMAN CAPITAL MANAGEMENT OY, 2562
CARDINAL PARTNERS, 410
CARE CAPITAL, 412
CASDIN CAPITAL, 419
CASE TECHNOLOGY VENTURES Case Western Reserve University, 420
CATALYST HEALTH VENTURES, 426
CATALYST INVESTMENT MANAGERS PTY LIMITED PPM Capital, 2573
CATO BIOVENTURES, 430
CEDAR VENTURES LLC, 437
CELERITY PARTNERS, 439
CENTRESTONE VENTURES, 2077
CHARTER LIFE SCIENCES, 458
CHASE CAPITAL PARTNERS, 2588
CLARITY CAPITAL, 2611
CLARUS VENTURES, 495
CM CAPITAL, 2618
CNF INVESTMENTS Clark Enterprises, Inc., 508
COLUMN GROUP, 517
COMMERCE ASSET VENTURES Sdn Bhd, 2623
COMPAGNIE FINANCIERE E DE ROTHSCHILD BANQUE, 2625
CONCORD VENTURES, 2628
CORAL GROUP, 536
CORDOVA VENTURES, 537
CORRELATION VENTURES, 544
COUNCIL FOR ENTREPRENEURIAL DEVELOPMENT, 3259
CRB INVERBIO, 2636
CREATHOR VENTURE, 2638
CROSS CREEK ADVISORS, 560
CTI LIFE SCIENCES, 2092
CULTIVATION CAPITAL, 569
DAG VENTURES, 581
DANEVEST TECH FUND ADVISORS, 583
DE NOVO VENTURES, 598
DIRECT CAPITAL PRIVATE EQUITY LIMITED, 2664
DISCOVERY CAPITAL, 2097
DOMAIN ASSOCIATES LLC, 621
DVC DEUTSCHE VENTURE CAPITAL, 2679
EASTON CAPITAL INVESTMENT GROUP, 644
EDELSON TECHNOLOGY PARTNERS, 651
ELEVATE VENTURES, 658
ELM STREET VENTURES, 660
EM WARBURG, PINCUS & COMPANY JAPAN, 2698
EMBARK VENTURES, 663
EMERALD OCEAN CAPITAL, 664
EMERGENT MEDICAL PARTNERS, 666
ENSO VENTURES, 2702
ENTREPRENEURS FUND, 2710
EPIC VENTURES, 688
EPIDAREX CAPITAL, 689
EQUINET VENTURE PARTNERS AG, 2713
ESSEX WOODLANDS HEALTH VENTURES LLC, 697
EVOLVE CAPITAL, 702
EXCEL VENTURE MANAGEMENT, 703
FARM CREDIT CANADA, 2114
FIRST CAPITAL GROUP, 734
FIRST FLIGHT VENTURE CENTER, 737
FIRST STEP FUND, 742
FLAGSHIP PIONEERING, 747
FLANDERS' FOREIGN INVESTMENT OFFICE, 2746
FLETCHER SPAGHT VENTURES, 749
FORBION CAPITAL PARTNERS, 2748
FORWARD VENTURES, 769
FRAZIER HEALTHCARE VENTURES, 782

GE ASIA PACIFIC CAPITAL TECHNOLOGY FUND, 2767
GENERICS GROUP LIMITED Generics Group, 2773
GENESYS CAPITAL, 2130
GENSTAR CAPITAL LP, 819
GIZA VENTURE CAPITAL, 2782
GLENTHORNE CAPITAL, 832
GLOBAL LIFE SCIENCE VENTURES GmbH, 2785
GOLDEN PINE VENTURES, 840
GOLDEN SEEDS, 841
GRANITE HILL CAPITAL PARTNERS, LLC, 851
GREAT POINT PARTNERS, 859
GREENSPRING ASSOCIATES, 867
GROVE STREET ADVISORS LLC, 879
GROWTHWORKS, 2143
GUIDE VENTURES, 887
GV, 889
HAMILTON BIOVENTURES, 898
HATTERAS VENTURE PARTNERS, 915
HEALTHCAP Odlander, Fredrikson & Co AB, 2816
HEALTHCARE VENTURES LLC, 919
HERCULES TECHNOLOGY GROWTH CAPITAL, INC, 925
HIGH COUNTRY VENTURE, 930
HIGH-TECH GRUENDERFONDS, 2824
HOPEN LIFE SCIENCE VENTURES, 943
HOPEWELL VENTURES, 944
HORIZON TECHNOLOGY FINANCE, 946
HOUSTON ANGEL NETWORK, 950
IBB BETEILIGUNGSGESELLSCHAFT MBH, 2841
IDG TECHNOLOGY VENTURE INVESTMENT, 2848
ILLINOIS VENTURES, 975
INCUBE VENTURES, 980
INDASIA FUND ADVISORS PVT LTD, 2859
INDUSTRIEBANK LIOF NV, 2866
INFLEXION PARTNERS, 990
INNOVATION CAPITAL, 2876
INNOVATION WORKS, 998
INOVIA CAPITAL, 2157
INTEGRA VENTURES, 1002
INTEGRAL CAPITAL PARTNERS, 1003
INTERSOUTH PARTNERS, 1008
INVESCO PRIVATE CAPITAL, 1015
IPOSCOPE NV/SA, 2895
JUMPSTART INC, 1047
KERNEL CAPITAL, 2918
KLEINER PERKINS, 1075
KRG CAPITAL PARTNERS, 1086
LAUNCHCYTE, 1098
LAUNCHPAD VENTURE GROUP, 1100
LBBW VENTURE CAPITAL, 2932
LEASING TECHNOLOGIES INTERNATIONAL INC., 1103
LIFE SCIENCES GREENHOUSE OF CENTRAL PA, 1117
LIFE SCIENCES PARTNERS BV, 2939
LIGHTHOUSE CAPITAL PARTNERS, 1119
LIGHTSTONE VENTURES, 1122
LINDEN LLC, 1128
LINK TECHNOLOGIES LIMITED, 2941
LINN GROVE VENTURES, 1131
LONGITUDE CAPITAL, 1143
LUMIRA CAPITAL, 2180
LUX CAPITAL, 1151
MANULIFE CAPITAL, 2183
MARS INVESTMENT ACCELERATOR FUND, 2187
MARYLAND VENTURE FUND, 1169
MAYFIELD FUND, 1184
MB VENTURE PARTNERS, 1187
MEAKEM/BECKER VENTURE CAPITAL, 1194
MEDIPHASE VENTURE PARTNERS, 1197
MERCURY FUND, 1206
MERITURN PARTNERS, 1213
MERLIN NEXUS, 1216
MESA VERDE PARTNERS, 1221
MMV CAPITAL PARTNERS, 2196
MOHR-DAVIDOW VENTURES, 1247
MONTREUX EQUITY PARTNERS, 1251
MORGENTHALER VENTURES, 1257
MOUNTAIN GROUP CAPITAL, 1261
MURPHREE VENTURE PARTNERS, 1273

Industry Preference Index / Logistics

MVM LIFE SCIENCE PARTNERS, 2981
MVP CAPITAL PARTNERS, 1275
NEW BRUNSWICK INNOVATION FOUNDATION, 2200
NEW CAPITAL FUND, 1292
NEW SCIENCE VENTURES, 1303
NEWABLE VENTURES, 2997
NOVA SCOTIA BUSINESS INC., 2205
NOVARTIS VENTURE FUNDS, 1350
NOVO A/S, 3015
OKAPI VENTURE CAPITAL, 1371
OMNES CAPITAL, 3020
ONTARIO CAPITAL GROWTH CORPORATION, 2211
ORBIMED HEALTHCARE FUND MANAGEMENT, 1382
OUTCOME CAPITAL, 1388
OVP VENTURE PARTNERS, 1391
OXFORD BIOSCIENCE PARTNERS, 1394
OneVentures, 3023
PAC-LINK MANAGEMENT CORP., 3024
PACIFIC HORIZON VENTURES, 1398
PANORAMA CAPITAL, 1410
PAPPAS VENTURES, 1412
PARKWALK ADVISORS, 3028
PARTNERS HEALTHCARE RESEARCH VENTURES, 1419
PENN VENTURE PARTNERS, 1428
PFIZER VENTURE INVESTMENTS, 1436
PI CAPITAL GROUP LLC, 1440
PIEDMONT ANGEL NETWORK, 1442
PITTSBURGH EQUITY PARTNERS, 1447
PITTSBURGH LIFE SCIENCES GREENHOUSE, 1448
PMV, 3042
POLARIS VENTURE PARTNERS, 1460
POLYTECHNOS VENTURE PARTNERS GmbH, 3046
PORTUGAL CAPITAL VENTURES Institutional Headquarters, 3048
PRAIRIEGOLD VENTURE PARTNERS, 1470
PRISM VENTUREWORKS, 1478
PROLOG VENTURES, 1488
PTV SCIENCES, 1500
QBIC FUND, 3065
QUAKER BIOVENTURES, 1508
QUEST FOR GROWTH, 3069
QUESTER CAPITAL MANAGEMENT LIMITED, 3070
RA CAPITAL MANAGEMENT, 1519
RBC CAPITAL MARKETS, 2231
RENEWABLETECH VENTURES, 1542
RESEARCH CORPORATION TECHNOLOGIES, 1543
RIVERVEST VENTURE PARTNERS, 1574
ROADMAP CAPITAL INC., 2242
ROCHE VENTURE FUND F. Hoffman-La Roche AG, 3085
SAND HILL ANGELS, 1613
SANOFI-GENZYME BIOVENTURES, 1618
SANTE VENTURES, 1619
SCHRODER VENTURES HEALTH INVESTORS, 1628
SCOTTISH EQUITY PARTNERS, 3104
SCP PARTNERS, 1633
SEB VENTURE CAPITAL, 3106
SERAPH GROUP, 1655
SEVENTURE PARTNERS, 3113
SEVIN ROSEN FUNDS, 1658
SHEPHERD VENTURES, 1664
SIGNAL PEAK VENTURES, 1677
SLATER TECHNOLOGY FUND, 1693
SOFINNOVA VENTURES, 1698
SOLSTICE CAPITAL LP, 1702
SOUTHWEST MICHIGAN FIRST LIFE SCIENCE FUND Southwest Michigan First, 1713
SPENCER TRASK VENTURES, 1720
SPINDLETOP CAPITAL, 1722
SPLIT ROCK PARTNERS, 1725
STAR VENTURES, 3137
STAR VENTURES, 3137
STARFISH VENTURES, 3138
STONEHENGE GROWTH CAPITAL, 1745
SUMMIT PARTNERS, 1752
SUNSTONE CAPITAL, 3149
SVB CAPITAL, 1764
SYNERGY LIFE SCIENCE PARTNERS, 1772
TAMIR FISHMAN VENTURES, 3159

TANDEM EXPANSION FUND, 2261
TECH COAST ANGELS, 1784
TECHNOLOGY PARTNERS, 1786
TEKNOINVEST MANAGEMENT, 3167
TEL VENTURE CAPITAL, 1791
TELEGRAPH HILL PARTNERS, 1792
TERALYS CAPITAL, 2268
TGAP VENTURES, 1802
THE CHANNEL GROUP, 1808
THIRD ROCK VENTURES, 1811
THIRD SECURITY, 1812
THOMAS, MCNERNEY & PARTNERS, 1817
THREE ARCH PARTNERS LP, 1819
TRASK INNOVATIONS FUND Purdue Research Foundation, 1840
TRELYS FUNDS, 1842
TRIANGLE ANGEL PARTNERS, 1845
TRIATHLON MEDICAL VENTURES, 1847
TRIGINITA CAPITAL, 3190
TULLIS HEALTH INVESTORS, 1866
TVM CAPITAL, 3196
US VENTURE PARTNERS, 1896
VALENCE LIFE SCIENCES, 1898
VALLEY VENTURES LP, 1901
VEDANTA CAPITAL LP, 1911
VENBIO, 1914
VENCORE CAPITAL, 1915
VENTUREAST, 3211
WATER STREET HEALTHCARE PARTNERS, 1961
WESTERN TECHNOLOGY INVESTMENT, 1975
WHEATLEY PARTNERS, 1981
WISCONSIN INVESTMENT PARTNERS, 2001
XENIA VENTURE CAPITAL, 3240
XSEED CAPITAL MANAGEMENT, 2011
YELLOWSTONE CAPITAL, 2013
YISSUM TECHNOLOGY TRANSFER, 3245
YUUWA CAPITAL, 3248
YVC - YOZMA MANAGEMENT & INVESTMENTS LIMITED, 3249

Lifestyle & Recreation
BEZOS EXPEDITIONS, 262
FUNK VENTURES, 797

Light Manufacturing
CARDINAL EQUITY PARTNERS, 409
CI CAPITAL PARTNERS, 476
EMINENT CAPITAL PARTNERS, 669
GRANTHAM CAPITAL, 853
SARONA ASSET MANAGEMENT, 2248

Lighting
CROSSLINK CAPITAL, 563

Litigation
BUTZOW NORDIA ADVOCATES LTD, 2552

Lodging
THAYER VENTURES, 1806

Logistics
ACI CAPITAL, 42
ACTIS, 2337
ALANTRA, 77
ALEUTIAN CAPITAL PARTNERS, 81
ANGELENO GROUP, 126
AURORA CAPITAL GROUP, 199
BARCLAYS VENTURES Barclays, 2486
BISON CAPITAL ASSET MANAGEMENT LLC, 274
BRIDGE STREET CAPITAL, 338
BULL VENTURES, 2547
BUTLER CAPITAL PARTNERS FRANCE, 2551
CAMBRIDGE CAPITAL, 380
CANTOS VENTURES, 395
CHINA VEST LIMITED, 2596
CHINAVEST, 473
CHRYSALIX, 2078
CLOSE BROTHERS PRIVATE EQUITY Close Brothers Group, 2617
DEFI GESTION SA Banque Cantonale Vaudoise, 2653

1203

Industry Preference Index / Low Capex Semiconductor

DEUTSCHE BETEILIGUNGS AG, 2660
EAST FUND MANAGEMENT GmbH GiroCredit, 2683
ENDEAVOUR CAPITAL, 673
ENTREPRENEUR CAPITAL, 2107
ENTREPRENEURS ROUNDTABLE ACCELERATOR, 684
EOS PARTNERS LP, 686
EQUISTONE, 2714
EUROVENTURES CAPITAL, 2725
FENWAY PARTNERS, 722
FIDELITY GROWTH PARTNERS ASIA, 2733
FLANDERS' FOREIGN INVESTMENT OFFICE, 2746
FOUNDERS EQUITY, 774
FdG ASSOCIATES LP, 801
GE CAPITAL, 808
GEORGIA OAK PARTNERS, 821
GRANTHAM CAPITAL, 853
GREENBRIAR EQUITY GROUP LLC, 862
GULFSTAR GROUP, 888
HALIFAX GROUP LLC, 894
HARBOUR GROUP, 908
HCI EQUITY PARTNERS, 917
HIGH STREET CAPITAL, 932
INDASIA FUND ADVISORS PVT LTD, 2859
INTER-ASIA VENTURE MANAGEMENT LIMITED, 2881
JEFFERIES CAPITAL PARTNERS, 1032
KERRY CAPITAL ADVISORS, 1067
LEE EQUITY PARTNERS, 1104
M25 GROUP, 1155
MERIT CAPITAL PARTNERS, 1209
NAVIGATION CAPITAL PARTNERS, 1280
NCT VENTURES, 1286
NESBIC INVESTMENT FUND II, 2992
NEW MOUNTAIN CAPITAL, 1301
NORO-MOSELEY PARTNERS, 1331
PARADIGM CAPITAL LTD, 1414
PARALLEL49 EQUITY, 2214
PARTHENON CAPITAL, 1417
PENDER WEST CAPITAL PARTNERS, 2218
PHOENIX EQUITY PARTNERS LIMITED, 3036
POST CAPITAL PARTNERS, 1465
PRIVATE EQUITY PARTNERS SPA, 3053
PROCURITAS PARTNERS KB, 3054
PT BHAKTI INVESTAMA TBK, 3061
QUAKE CAPITAL PARTNERS, 1507
SALT CREEK CAPITAL, 1609
SARONA ASSET MANAGEMENT, 2248
SONY INNOVATION FUND, 1703
TH LEE PUTNAM VENTURES, 1804
VRG CAPITAL, 2282
WESTLAKE SECURITIES, 1976
WESTVIEW CAPITAL PARTNERS, 1979
WOODBRIDGE GROUP, 2004
WYNNCHURCH CAPITAL, 2009
XANGE PRIVATE EQUITY, 3239
ZURMONT MADISON PRIVATE EQUITY, 3254

Low Capex Semiconductor
OJAS VENTURE PARTNERS, 3019

Low Carbon and Renewable Energy Infrastructure
QUINBROOK INFRASTRUCTURE PARTNERS, 1517

Low Technology
PEGASUS CAPITAL GROUP, 1424
ROSER VENTURES LLC, 1586

Low-Capital Intensity Manufacturing
PACIFIC COMMUNITY VENTURES, 1396

Low-Tech Manufacturing
BLACKFORD CAPITAL LLC, 276

Loyalty
CHICAGO VENTURES, 471

Luxury Goods
EMINENT CAPITAL PARTNERS, 669

Luxury/Lifestyle
AVISTA PARTNERS, 2461

Machine Intelligence
FRONTIER VENTURES, 792

Machine Learning
AMD VENTURES, 106
ANALYTICS VENTURES, 121
CARBON VENTURES, 408
CHINAROCK CAPITAL MANAGEMENT VENTURES, 472
CITI VENTURES, 486
COMET LABS, 519
DELL VENTURES, 603
DRAPER ATHENA, 626
FIRST ASCENT VENTURES, 2118
FLYING FISH, 755
FRONTLINE VENTURES, 2759
GREEN TOWER CAPITAL, 861
IGNITION PARTNERS, 974
IMAGINATION CAPITAL, 977
LDV CAPITAL, 1101
M12, 1154
PATHBREAKER VENTURES, 1421
QUAKE CAPITAL PARTNERS, 1507
UBIQUITY VENTURES, 1877
WILDCAT VENTURE PARTNERS, 1985

Machinery
BALTCAP MANAGEMENT LTD, 2480
CHINA VEST LIMITED, 2596
CORNERSTONE CAPITAL HOLDINGS, 540
DEUTSCHE BETEILIGUNGS AG, 2660
HALLIM VENTURE CAPITAL, 2807
JB POINDEXTER & COMPANY, 1030
LEONIA MB GROUP/MB FUNDS, 2937
PALMS & COMPANY, 1404
PWC, 3064
QUADRAN GESTION Deutsche Beteiligungs AG, 3067
SIF TRANSYLVANIA, 3119
TRANS COSMOS INCORPORATED, 3185
TRANSYLVANIA FINANCIAL INVESTMENT COMPANY, 3187
ZURMONT MADISON PRIVATE EQUITY, 3254

Managed Services
ISOURCE GESTION, 2899

Management
ACCENTURE TECHNOLOGY VENTURES, 2326
CHINA MERCHANTS CHINA DIRECT INVESTMENTS LTD., 2594
DIRIGEANTS ET INVESTISSEURS, 2665
ENTER VENTURES, 681
EQUITY PARTNERS PTY LIMITED, 2715
GENERICS GROUP LIMITED Generics Group, 2773
INNOVATION CAPITAL LIMITED, 2877
J-SEED VENTURES INCORPORATED, 2905
NIPPON TECHNOLOGY VENTURE PARTNERS LIMITED, 3005
WESTERN NIS ENTERPRISE FUND, 3234

Management Buyouts
WESTCAP, 2285

Manufacturing
3I ASIA PACIFIC 3i Group, 2297
AAVIN PRIVATE EQUITY, 17
ACI CAPITAL, 42
ACTIS, 2337
ADVANTAGE CAPITAL PARTNERS, 61
AEA INVESTORS, 64
ALBERTA ENTERPRISE, 2032
ALEUTIAN CAPITAL PARTNERS, 81
ALEXANDER HUTTON, 82
ALLSTATE INVESTMENTS LLC, 88
ALPHA CAPITAL PARTNERS, 90
AMERICAN INDUSTRIAL PARTNERS, 109
AMERIMARK CAPITAL CORPORATION, 111
AMHERST FUND, 113

Industry Preference Index / Manufacturing

AMPERSAND CAPITAL PARTNERS, 118
AMWIN MANAGEMENT PTY LIMITED, 2398
ANDLINGER & COMPANY INC, 123
APOLLO GLOBAL MANAGEMENT, 140
ARES MANAGEMENT LLC, 159
ARGENTUM GROUP, 161
ARGOSY CAPITAL, 164
ARLINGTON CAPITAL PARTNERS, 166
ARSENAL CAPITAL PARTNERS, 170
ARVA LIMITED, 2044
ASHBRIDGE PARTNERS, 2045
ASIAN INFRASTRUCTURE FUND ADVISERS LIMITED AIF Capital, 2434
ASIAVEST PARTNERS, 2436
ASTOR CAPITAL GROUP, 2440
AURORA CAPITAL GROUP, 199
AUSTIN CAPITAL PARTNERS LP, 201
AVENUE CAPITAL GROUP, 208
AZALEA CAPITAL, 213
BALMORAL FUNDS, 225
BARCLAYS VENTURES Barclays, 2486
BENAROYA COMPANIES, 247
BENCIS CAPITAL PARTNERS, 2501
BERINGEA, 251
BERKSHIRE PARTNERS LLC, 254
BLUE POINT CAPITAL PARTNERS, 290
BLUE SAGE CAPITAL, 291
BLUESTEM CAPITAL COMPANY, 297
BOCI DIRECT INVESTMENT MANAGEMENT LIMITED Bank of China, 2529
BOND CAPITAL, 2064
BOUNDS EQUITY PARTNERS, 316
BRADFORD EQUITIES MANAGEMENT LLC, 321
BRANDON CAPITAL GROUP, 326
BRAZOS PRIVATE EQUITY PARTNERS, 328
BREAKWATER INVESTMENTS, 330
BRIDGEPOINT CAPITAL GmbH, 2537
BRIDGEPOINT CAPITAL LIMITED, 2538
BRIGHTPATH CAPITAL PARTNERS, 340
BROOKSIDE EQUITY PARTNERS LLC, 353
BRUML CAPITAL CORPORATION, 355
BRYNWOOD PARTNERS, 357
C3 CAPITAL PARTNERS LP, 364
CAI CAPITAL PARTNERS, 365
CAMBRIA GROUP, 378
CAMBRIDGE CAPITAL, 380
CAMBRIDGE CAPITAL CORPORATION, 381
CANADIAN VENTURE CAPITAL ASSOCIATION Canadian Venture Capital & Private Equity Association, 3258
CANDOVER, 2556
CAPITAL FOR BUSINESS, INC, 399
CAPITAL MIDWEST FUND, 400
CAPITAL PARTNERS, 401
CAPX PARTNERS, 407
CARBON VENTURES, 408
CARPEDIA CAPITAL, 2072
CASTLE HARLAN, 423
CATALYST GROUP, 425
CATALYST INVESTMENT MANAGERS PTY LIMITED PPM Capital, 2573
CELADON CAPITAL GROUP, 2582
CELERITY PARTNERS, 439
CENTERFIELD CAPITAL PARTNERS, 443
CERBERUS CAPITAL MANAGEMENT, 451
CHARLESBANK CAPITAL PARTNERS, 456
CHENGWEI VENTURES, 2590
CHEROKEE INVESTMENT PARTNERS, 463
CHEYENNE CAPITAL, 467
CHINA MERCHANTS CHINA DIRECT INVESTMENTS LTD., 2594
CHINA MERCHANTS CHINA INVESTMENT MANAGEMENT, 2595
CHINAVEST, 473
CHRYSALIS CAPITAL ChrysCapital, 2599
CHRYSALIX, 2078
CIBC CAPITAL MARKETS, 2079
CID CAPITAL, 478
CLEARLIGHT PARTNERS, 501
CLEARSPRING CAPITAL PARTNERS, 2082
CLEARVIEW CAPITAL, 503
CLOSE BROTHERS PRIVATE EQUITY Close Brothers Group, 2617
COACH & CAPITAL, 2619
COLORADO MILE HIGH FUND, 513
COMPAGNIE FINANCIERE E DE ROTHSCHILD BANQUE, 2625
COMPASS GROUP MANAGEMENT LLC, 523
CORNERSTONE CAPITAL HOLDINGS, 540
CORNERSTONE EQUITY INVESTORS LLC, 541
CORTEC GROUP, 546
COVINGTON CAPITAL CORP., 2087
CRAWLEY VENTURES, 553
CRYSTAL RIDGE PARTNERS, 565
CUSTER CAPITAL, 571
CVC ASIA PACIFIC LIMITED CVC Capital Partners, 2643
CVC CAPITAL PARTNERS LTD, 2644
CVF CAPITAL PARTNERS, 573
CYPRESS GROUP, 575
CYPRIUM PARTNERS, 577
CZECH VENTURE PARTNERS SRO K+ Venture Partners B.V., 2648
DAHER CAPITAL, 2649
DANCAP PRIVATE EQUITY, 2094
DAVID N DEUTSCH & COMPANY LLC, 589
DESCO CAPITAL, 606
DESJARDINS CAPITAL, 2095
DIAMOND STATE VENTURES LP, 611
DIMELING SCHREIBER & PARK, 616
DIRECT CAPITAL PRIVATE EQUITY LIMITED, 2664
DN PARTNERS LLC, 619
DOUBLE IMPACT BUSINESS ADVISORY, 2670
DUBIN CLARK & COMPANY, 632
DUFF ACKERMAN & GOODRICH, 634
DUNEDIN CAPITAL PARTNERS LIMITED, 2677
EARLY STAGE PARTNERS, 642
ECI VENTURES, 2687
ECLIPSE VENTURES, 648
EDGESTONE CAPITAL PARTNERS, 2103
EDGEWATER CAPITAL PARTNERS, 653
ELECTRA PARTNERS ASIA LIMITED SFC of Hong Kong, 2694
ELEMENT PARTNERS, 657
ELGNER GROUP INVESTMENTS, 2104
EMBARK VENTURES, 663
EMIGRANT CAPITAL, 667
ENDEAVOUR CAPITAL, 673
ENTERPRISE EQUITY (NI) LTD, 2704
ENTERPRISE INVESTORS, 2706
EQUITY SOUTH, 693
EUREKA GROWTH CAPITAL, 698
EXCELSIOR CAPITAL ASIA, 2727
EXPANSION CAPITAL PARTNERS, 706
EXPORT DEVELOPMENT CANADA, 2112
FAIRMONT CAPITAL, 713
FCF PARTNERS LP, 719
FINLOMBARDA SpA, 2739
FIRST CAPITAL GROUP, 734
FIRST NEW ENGLAND CAPITAL LP, 739
FLORIDA CAPITAL PARTNERS, 752
FOUNDATION EQUITY CORPORATION, 2121
FOUNDERS EQUITY, 774
FRIEND SKOLER & COMPANY LLC, 788
FULCRUM CAPITAL PARTNERS, 2126
FdG ASSOCIATES LP, 801
GEFINOR CAPITAL, 810
GEMINI INVESTORS, 812
GENESIS CAPITAL CORPORATION, 2129
GEORGIA OAK PARTNERS, 821
GLADSTONE CAPITAL, 828
GLENTHORNE CAPITAL, 832
GLOBAL EQUITY PARTNERS BETEILIGUNGS-MANAGEMENT, 2783
GLOBAL FINANCE, 2784
GOLDNER, HAWN, JOHNSON & MORRISON, 843
GOLUB CAPITAL, 844
GRAHAM PARTNERS, 846
GRANITE BRIDGE PARTNERS, 849
GRANITE EQUITY PARTNERS, 850
GRANITE PARTNERS, 2139
GRAPHITE CAPITAL MANAGEMENT LTD, 2796
GREIF & COMPANY, 869

Industry Preference Index / Manufacturing

GRIDIRON CAPITAL, 873
GRUPO BISA, 2800
GRYPHON INVESTORS, 881
GULFSTAR GROUP, 888
HALDER BETEILIGUNGSBERATUNG GmbH, 2805
HALIFAX GROUP LLC, 894
HAMILTON ROBINSON CAPITAL PARTNERS, 899
HAMMOND, KENNEDY, WHITNEY & COMPANY, 900
HANCOCK PARK ASSOCIATES, 902
HANNOVER FINANZ GmbH, 2810
HANOVER PARTNERS, 903
HARBOUR GROUP, 908
HARREN EQUITY PARTNERS, 910
HARVEST PARTNERS, 914
HEADWATER EQUITY PARTNERS, 2145
HERITAGE PARTNERS, 926
HIG CAPITAL, 928
HIGH ROAD CAPITAL PARTNERS, 931
HIGHLAND WEST CAPITAL, 2146
HOLDING CAPITAL GROUP, 940
HOPEWELL VENTURES, 944
HORIZON PARTNERS, LTD, 945
HOULIHAN LOKEY, 948
HT CAPITAL ADVISORS LLC, 953
HURON CAPITAL PARTNERS LLC, 960
HURON RIVER VENTURES, 961
IBM VENTURE CAPITAL GROUP, 967
ICV PARTNERS, 969
INDEPENDENT BANKERS CAPITAL FUND, 984
INDUSTRI KAPITAL SVENSKA AB, 2863
INDUSTRIAL GROWTH PARTNERS, 985
INNOVENTURES CAPITAL PARTNERS, 999
INTERMEDIATE CAPITAL GROUP PLC, 2883
INTERVALE CAPITAL, 1009
INVERNESS GRAHAM INVESTMENTS, 1014
INVEST EQUITY MANAGEMENT CONSULTING GmbH, 2887
INVESTAMERICA VENTURE GROUP, 1016
INVESTOR AB, 2890
IRISH ANGELS, 1019
IRONBRIDGE EQUITY PARTNERS, 2163
IRONWOOD CAPITAL, 1021
InstarAGF, 2165
J. BURKE CAPITAL PARTNERS, 1023
JAFCO COMPANY LIMITED JAPAN, 2906
JEFFERIES CAPITAL PARTNERS, 1032
KEGONSA CAPITAL PARTNERS, 1060
KELSO & COMPANY, 1062
KENSINGTON CAPITAL PARTNERS, 2167
KENTUCKY HIGHLANDS INVESTMENT CORPORATION, 1064
KERRY CAPITAL ADVISORS, 1067
KLEINWORT CAPITAL LIMITED, 2923
KOHLBERG & COMPANY LLC, 1081
KOREA FIRST VENTURE CAPITAL CORPORATION, 2924
KPS CAPITAL PARTNERS, 1085
LINLEY CAPITAL, 1130
LLR PARTNERS INC, 1136
LOMBARD INVESTMENTS, 1139
LONG POINT CAPITAL, 1141
LYNWOOD CAPITAL PARTNERS, 1152
M25 GROUP, 1155
MACQUARIE DIRECT INVESTMENT LIMITED, 2951
MADISON DEARBORN PARTNERS, 1156
MADISON PARKER CAPITAL, 1157
MAIN STREET CAPITAL HOLDINGS LLC, 1159
MANULIFE CAPITAL, 2183
MARANON CAPITAL, 1166
MARWIT CAPITAL LLC, 1168
MASSACHUSETTS CAPITAL RESOURCE COMPANY, 1173
MCROCK CAPITAL, 2190
MEDRA CAPITAL, 2960
MERIT CAPITAL PARTNERS, 1209
MERITURN PARTNERS, 1213
MERITUS VENTURES, 1214
MERIWETHER CAPITAL CORPORATION, 1215
MESA CAPITAL PARTNERS, 1219
METAPOINT PARTNERS, 1224
MIDDLEBURG CAPITAL DEVELOPMENT, 1229

MIDINVEST LIMITED, 2966
MIDMARK CAPITAL LP, 1230
MIDVEN, 2967
MIDWEST MEZZANINE FUNDS, 1232
MILESTONE PARTNERS, 1234
MOMENTUM FUNDS MANAGEMENT PTY LIMITED, 2975
MPE PARTNERS, 1266
MSOUTH EQUITY PARTNERS, 1270
NAUTIC PARTNERS, 1279
NAVIGATION CAPITAL PARTNERS, 1280
NBC CAPITAL PTY LIMITED, 2988
NEW BRUNSWICK INNOVATION FOUNDATION, 2200
NEW ENGLAND CAPITAL PARTNERS, 1296
NEW MEXICO COMMUNITY CAPITAL, 1300
NEWBURY, PIRET & COMPANY, 1312
NORTH AMERICAN FUND, 1332
NORTH DAKOTA DEVELOPMENT FUND, 1338
NORTHERN ENTERPRISE LIMITED, 3011
NORTHERN LIGHT VENTURE CAPITAL, 1340
NORTHSTAR CAPITAL, 1343
NORTHWOOD VENTURES, 1344
NORWEST EQUITY PARTNERS, 1345
NOVA SCOTIA BUSINESS INC., 2205
NUTEK (NARINGS- OCH TEKNIKUTVECKLINGSVERKET) NUTEK, 3016
ODEON CAPITAL PARTNERS, 1367
ONE EQUITY PARTNERS, 1376
PALLADIUM EQUITY PARTNERS, 1403
PAMLICO CAPITAL, 1409
PANTHEON VENTURES (US) LP, 1411
PARALLEL49 EQUITY, 2214
PARKVIEW CAPITAL PARTNERS, 2215
PARTHENON CAPITAL, 1417
PEACHTREE EQUITY PARTNERS, 1423
PEGASUS CAPITAL GROUP, 1424
PENN VENTURE PARTNERS, 1428
PFINGSTEN PARTNERS LLC, 1435
PNC ERIEVIEW CAPITAL, 1456
PNC RIVERARCH CAPITAL, 1457
POST CAPITAL PARTNERS, 1465
POUSCHINE COOK CAPITAL MANAGEMENT LLC, 1466
PRISM CAPITAL, 1477
PRITZKER GROUP PRIVATE CAPITAL, 1479
PROCURITAS PARTNERS KB, 3054
QUAD-C MANAGEMENT, 1505
QUAKE CAPITAL PARTNERS, 1507
QUANTUM CAPITAL PARTNERS, 1510
QUARRY CAPITAL MANAGEMENT, 1511
RAF INDUSTRIES, 1521
RAYMOND JAMES CAPITAL, 1526
RBC CAPITAL MARKETS, 2231
RED CLAY CAPITAL HOLDINGS, 1529
RESILIENCE CAPITAL PARTNERS, 1545
RFE INVESTMENT PARTNERS, 1557
RICHINA CAPITAL PARTNERS LIMITED, 3082
RIVER ASSOCIATES INVESTMENTS LLC, 1569
RIVER CAPITAL, 1570
RIVERSIDE COMPANY, 1572
ROBIN HOOD VENTURES, 1577
ROCK ISLAND CAPITAL, 1578
ROSER VENTURES LLC, 1586
ROTHSCHILD AUSTRALIA - ARROW PRIVATE EQUITY Rothschild Group, 3086
RPM VENTURES, 1592
SAIF PARTNERS, 3093
SALEM INVESTMENT PARTNERS, 1606
SAMBRINVEST SA, 3096
SATORI CAPITAL, 1622
SCOTIABANK PRIVATE EQUITY, 2250
SEACOAST CAPITAL CORPORATION, 1636
SEAFORT CAPITAL, 2251
SEAWAY VALLEY CAPITAL CORPORATION, 1639
SELBY VENTURE PARTNERS, 1646
SHAW KWEI AND PARTNERS, 3116
SONY INNOVATION FUND, 1703
SOUTH ATLANTIC VENTURE FUNDS, 1708
SPELL CAPITAL PARTNERS LLC, 1719

Industry Preference Index / Marketplaces

SPLIT ROCK PARTNERS, 1725
STARBOARD CAPITAL PARTNERS, 1735
STERLING PARTNERS, 1742
STERN PARTNERS, 2258
STONEHENGE GROWTH CAPITAL, 1745
STONEWOOD CAPITAL MANAGEMENT, 1746
SUCSY, FISCHER & COMPANY, 1750
SUN CAPITAL PARTNERS, 1753
SUPPLY CHAIN VENTURES, 1757
TAT CAPITAL PARTNERS LTD., 3162
TENNESSEE COMMUNITY VENTURES, 1797
TGF MANAGEMENT, 1803
THREE CITIES RESEARCH, 1820
TOP RENERGY INC., 2271
TORQUEST PARTNERS, 2272
TPA CORPORATE FINANCE CONSULTING GMBH Horwarth International, 3184
TRANS COSMOS INCORPORATED, 3185
TRELLIS CAPITAL CORPORATION, 2273
TRIWEST, 2275
TSG EQUITY PARTNERS, 1862
UNION CAPITAL CORPORATION, 1881
UNISON CAPITAL PARTNERS LP, 3201
VALOR EQUITY PARTNERS, 1902
VANCE STREET CAPITAL, 1904
VEBER PARTNERS LLC, 1909
VELOCITY EQUITY PARTNERS LLC, 1913
VERITAS CAPITAL FUND LP, 1925
WALNUT GROUP, 1954
WARWICK GROUP, 1957
WATERMILL GROUP, 1962
WAUD CAPITAL PARTNERS LLC, 1963
WAVELAND INVESTMENTS LLC, 1964
WEDBUSH CAPITAL PARTNERS, 1969
WELLS FARGO CAPITAL FINANCE, 1970
WESTERN AMERICA CAPITAL GROUP, 2286
WESTLAKE SECURITIES, 1976
WESTON PRESIDIO, 1978
WESTVIEW CAPITAL PARTNERS, 1979
WILLIS STEIN & PARTNERS LLC, 1986
WINGATE PARTNERS, 1997
WOODBRIDGE GROUP, 2004
YELLOW POINT EQUITY PARTNERS, 2292
YORK STREET CAPITAL PARTNERS LLC, 2015
ZONE VENTURES, 2021

Manufacturing & Distribution
INNOVATION PLATFORM CAPITAL, 997
PENDER WEST CAPITAL PARTNERS, 2218

MarTech
TACTICO, 2260

Marine
BRANFORD CASTLE, 327

Marine Services
GLOBAL MARITIME VENTURES BERHAD, 2786
PROSPECT PARTNERS LLC, 1492

Marine Transportation
COPPERLION CAPITAL, 2085

Maritime
CIT GROUP, 484

Maritime Industry
AZIONE CAPITAL, 2473

Market Research
NIELSEN INNOVATE FUND, 3003

Marketing
3TS CAPITAL PARTNERS 3i Group plc, 2309
ACCENTURE TECHNOLOGY VENTURES, 2326
ACTUA, 53
ALERION PARTNERS, 80
AMANET TECHNOLOGIES LIMITED, 2389
ANGELPAD, 128
BLUE CHIP VENTURE COMPANY, 287
BMP AKTIENGESELLSCHAFT BMP Venture Capital, 2528
BOSTON CAPITAL VENTURES, 310
BRENTWOOD ASSOCIATES, 334
BRILLIANT VENTURES, 342
BULL VENTURES, 2547
BUTLER CAPITAL PARTNERS FRANCE, 2551
CASTANEA PARTNERS, 421
CAVA CAPITAL, 431
CELERITY PARTNERS, 439
CINCO CAPITAL, 2604
CINCYTECH, 479
CITI VENTURES, 486
COVENT INDUSTRIAL CAPITAL INVESTMENT COMPANY, 2635
DACE VENTURES, 580
DUBILIER & COMPANY, 631
EDISON PARTNERS, 655
ENTREPRENEURS ROUNDTABLE ACCELERATOR, 684
EVERGREEN ADVISORS, 701
FOG CITY CAPITAL, 758
FOUNDERS EQUITY, 774
FRIEDMAN, FLEISCHER & LOWE LLC, 787
GGV CAPITAL, 823
GREYCROFT PARTNERS, 871
HALYARD CAPITAL, 897
HELLMAN & FRIEDMAN LLC, 924
HUDSON VENTURE PARTNERS, 954
INGENIOUS VENTURES, 2871
INSIGHT VENTURE PARTNERS, 1000
JEGI CAPITAL The Jordan Edminston Group, Inc., 1033
JUMP CAPITAL LLC, 1046
L CATTERTON PARTNERS, 1088
LAKE CAPITAL, 1091
LAUNCHPAD VENTURES, 2931
M25 GROUP, 1155
MHS CAPITAL, 1226
NCT VENTURES, 1286
NIELSEN INNOVATE FUND, 3003
NIPPON TECHNOLOGY VENTURE PARTNERS LIMITED, 3005
NORTH HILL VENTURES, 1339
PARKVIEW CAPITAL PARTNERS, 2215
PENN VENTURE PARTNERS, 1428
PROGRESS EQUITY PARTNERS, 1484
SAF GROUP, 2246
SCALE VENTURE PARTNERS, 1626
SHASTA VENTURES, 1663
STAGE 1 VENTURES, 1734
SUPPLY CHAIN VENTURES, 1757
TECHNOLOGY PARK MALAYSIA CORPORATION SDN BHD, 3164
TRANSMEDIA CAPITAL, 1839
UNION CAPITAL CORPORATION, 1881
UPFRONT VENTURES, 1888
VENISTA VENTURES, 3207
VERONIS SUHLER STEVENSON, 1927
YLR CAPITAL MARKETS LTD, 3247
ZM CAPITAL, 2020

Marketing Technology
BAIN CAPITAL VENTURES, 221
DETROIT VENTURE PARTNERS, 607
PROGRESS VENTURES, 1486

Marketing/Sales Services
VRG CAPITAL, 2282

Marketplace
MISTRAL VENTURE PARTNERS, 2195
OYSTER VENTURES, 1395

Marketplace/On-Demand Services
CHICAGO VENTURES, 471

Marketplaces
BESSEMER VENTURE PARTNERS, 260
BOXGROUP, 318

1207

Industry Preference Index / Material Handling

CANVAS VENTURES, 396
DECIENS CAPITAL, 599
GOOD NEWS VENTURES, 2138
JACKSON SQUARE VENTURES, 1024
ORIGIN VENTURES, 1384
REVOLUTION LLC, 1555
RUBICON VENTURE CAPITAL, 1595

Material Handling
ALANTRA, 77

Material Science
EMBARK VENTURES, 663
INDEPENDENCE EQUITY, 983

Materials
M25 GROUP, 1155

Materials Technology
ALBEMARLE PRIVATE EQUITY LIMITED, 2360
AMPLIFIER VENTURE PARTNERS, 119
ATHENAEUM FUND, 186
ATRIUM CAPITAL, 192
AUSTIN CAPITAL PARTNERS LP, 201
AVENUE CAPITAL GROUP, 208
AZINI CAPITAL PARTNERS, 2472
BATTERSON VENTURE CAPITAL LLC, 234
BEIJING VENTURE CAPITAL COMPANY LIMITED, 2500
BRIDGEPOINT CAPITAL GmbH, 2537
BRIDGEPOINT CAPITAL LIMITED, 2538
CANDOVER, 2556
CONVEXA Tyveholmen AS, 2632
ENTERPRISE EQUITY (NI) LTD, 2704
EQT PARTNERS AB, 2712
EQVITEC PARTNERS OY, 2716
FAIRHAVEN CAPITAL, 712
FIRELAKE CAPITAL, 730
GARAGE TECHNOLOGY VENTURES, 807
GENERICS GROUP LIMITED Generics Group, 2773
GUANGDONG TECHNOLOGY VENTURE CAPITAL COMPANY, 2802
HIGH-TECH GRUENDERFONDS, 2824
IDEA FUND PARTNERS, 971
INNOVACOM SA, 2875
LOMBARD INVESTMENTS, 1139
MASON WELLS, 1171
NEWMARGIN VENTURE CAPITAL, 2998
NORTH ATLANTIC CAPITAL CORPORATION, 1333
NORTHERN ENTERPRISE LIMITED, 3011
OKAPI VENTURE CAPITAL, 1371
RPM VENTURES, 1592
SEED CAPITAL LIMITED, 3107
SHAW KWEI AND PARTNERS, 3116
VIKING VENTURE, 3216
VINACAPITAL GROUP, 3217

Mechanical Products
CALIFORNIA COAST VENTURE FORUM, 3257

Media
360 CAPITAL PARTNERS 360 Capital Management SA, 2296
3TS CAPITAL PARTNERS 3i Group plc, 2309
3i GROUP PLC, 2311
ABRY PARTNERS, 21
ABS CAPITAL PARTNERS, 22
ACCEL, 28
ACI CAPITAL, 42
ACKERLEY PARTNERS LLC, 43
ACON INVESTMENTS, 46
ACTIVA CAPITAL, 2338
ADOBE VENTURES LP, 58
ADVANCIT CAPITAL, 60
AEP CAPITAL LLC, 65
ALBERTA ENTERPRISE, 2032
ALERION PARTNERS, 80
ALLIANCE VENTURE, 2369
ALVEN CAPITAL, 2385
AMERICAN SECURITIES LLC, 110
AMICUS CAPITAL PARTNERS, 2392
ANDERSON PACIFIC CORPORATION, 122
APAX PARTNERS ET CIE, 2415
APOLLO GLOBAL MANAGEMENT, 140
ARCHTOP VENTURES, 154
ARKAFUND MEDIA & ICT, 2426
ARLINGTON CAPITAL PARTNERS, 166
AUA PRIVATE EQUITY PARTNERS, 193
AUDAX GROUP, 194
AURA CAPITAL OY Auratum Group, 2451
AVISTA CAPITAL PARTNERS, 209
AWAY REALTY, 2465
BALDERTON CAPITAL, 2478
BALLPARK VENTURES, 2479
BARCELONA EMPREN, 2483
BARCLAYS VENTURES Barclays, 2486
BARING PRIVATE EQUITY PARTNERS ESPANA SA, 2489
BARING PRIVATE EQUITY PARTNERS INDIA, 2490
BARING VOSTOK CAPITAL PARTNERS, 2491
BATTERY VENTURES, 235
BENCIS CAPITAL PARTNERS, 2501
BERINGEA, 251
BIA DIGITAL PARTNERS LP, 263
BLACKSTONE PRIVATE EQUITY GROUP, 277
BLADE VENTURES, 278
BLUE CHIP VENTURE COMPANY, 287
BLUE SAGE CAPITAL, 291
BLUERUN VENTURES, 296
BM-T BETEILIGUNGS MANAGEMENT THURINGEN GmbH, 2527
BOTTS & COMPANY LIMITED, 2532
BRAZOS PRIVATE EQUITY PARTNERS, 328
BREAKWATER MANAGEMENT, 331
BRIDGEPOINT CAPITAL GmbH, 2537
BRIDGEPOINT CAPITAL LIMITED, 2538
BRILLIANT VENTURES, 342
BRYAN GARNIER & COMPANY, 2544
BULL VENTURES, 2547
BULLNET, 2548
CANADIAN VENTURE CAPITAL ASSOCIATION Canadian Venture Capital & Private Equity Association, 3258
CANDOVER, 2556
CANYON CREEK CAPITAL, 397
CARLYLE ASIA INVESTMENT ADVISORS LIMITED Carlyle Group, 2565
CARMEL VENTURES, 2566
CATALYST GROUP, 425
CAZENOVE PRIVATE EQUITY Cazenove Capital, 2577
CEDRUS INVESTMENTS, 2581
CEI VENTURES, 438
CENTENNIAL VENTURES, 441
CENTRE PARTNERS MANAGEMENT LLC, 447
CHALLENGE FUNDS - ETGAR LP, 2585
CHARLESBANK CAPITAL PARTNERS, 456
CHASE CAPITAL PARTNERS, 2588
CHENGWEI VENTURES, 2590
CHEYENNE CAPITAL, 467
CHICAGO VENTURE PARTNERS LP, 470
CHINA VEST LIMITED, 2596
CHINAVEST, 473
CIC FINANCE CIC Group, 2601
CINCO CAPITAL, 2604
CITA GESTION, 2607
CIVC PARTNERS, 489
CLARITY PARTNERS, 494
CLEARLAKE CAPITAL, 500
CLIFFORD CHANCE PUNDER, 2614
COACH & CAPITAL, 2619
COLUMBIA CAPITAL, 515
COMCAST VENTURES, 518
COMPAGNIE FINANCIERE E DE ROTHSCHILD BANQUE, 2625
COMSTOCK CAPITAL PARTNERS LLC, 527
CONSTELLATION TECHNOLOGY VENTURES, 532
CORAL GROUP, 536
CORE PACIFIC - YAMAICHI CAPITAL LIMITED Core Pacific Securities Company Ltd, 2633
COURT SQUARE VENTURES, 551
CREATHOR VENTURE, 2638

Industry Preference Index / Media

CRESTVIEW PARTNERS, 559
CYPRESS GROUP, 575
DELTA PARTNERS Delta Partners FZ-LLC, 2654
DEUTSCHE BETEILIGUNGS AG, 2660
DOUBLE IMPACT BUSINESS ADVISORY, 2670
DOUBLE M PARTNERS, 624
DUBILIER & COMPANY, 631
DUFF ACKERMAN & GOODRICH, 634
DUNEDIN CAPITAL PARTNERS LIMITED, 2677
E.VENTURES, 641
EAST FUND MANAGEMENT GmbH GiroCredit, 2683
ECONA AG, 2688
ELECTRA PARTNERS ASIA LIMITED SFC of Hong Kong, 2694
ELEVATION PARTNERS, 659
EM WARBURG, PINCUS & COMPANY JAPAN, 2698
ENSPIRE CAPITAL PTE LTD, 2703
ENTREPRENEURS ROUNDTABLE ACCELERATOR, 684
EOS PARTNERS LP, 686
EUROVENTURES CAPITAL, 2725
EVERGREEN VENTURE PARTNERS, 2726
EXCELSIOR CAPITAL ASIA, 2727
FALCONHEAD CAPITAL, 717
FELICIS VENTURES, 720
FIDELITY GROWTH PARTNERS ASIA, 2733
FOG CITY CAPITAL, 758
FORMULA VENTURES LIMITED Formula Group, 2750
FRIEDMAN, FLEISCHER & LOWE LLC, 787
GE CAPITAL, 808
GENERAL ENTERPRISE MANAGEMENT SERVICES, 2772
GENERATION PARTNERS, 818
GEODESIC CAPITAL, 820
GLADSTONE CAPITAL, 828
GLENCOE CAPITAL, 830
GLOBAL FINANCE, 2784
GLOBALIVE, 2134
GMT COMMUNICATIONS PARTNERS LLP, 2789
GOLDEN GATE CAPITAL, 839
GOLUB CAPITAL, 844
GRANDBANKS CAPITAL, 848
GRANITE EQUITY PARTNERS, 850
GREAT HILL PARTNERS LLC, 857
GREENHAVEN PARTNERS, 863
GREIF & COMPANY, 869
GTCR, 884
H KATZ CAPITAL GROUP, 891
HAMBRO CAPITAL MANAGEMENT LTD, 2808
HANNOVER FINANZ GmbH, 2810
HARBOURVEST PARTNERS LLC, 909
HAWTHORN EQUITY PARTNERS, 916
HEARST VENTURES, 922
HELION VENTURE PARTNERS, LLC International Management (Mauritius) Ltd, 2818
HELLMAN & FRIEDMAN LLC, 924
HG CAPITAL, 2823
HIG CAPITAL, 928
HIGH ROAD CAPITAL PARTNERS, 931
HOPEWELL VENTURES, 944
HOUSATONIC PARTNERS, 949
HUDSON VENTURE PARTNERS, 954
I-PACIFIC PARTNERS, 2840
ICF VENTURES PVT LTD, 2846
INDASIA FUND ADVISORS PVT LTD, 2859
INDIAN DIRECT EQUITY ADVISORS PVT LTD, 2861
INDUSTRI KAPITAL SVENSKA AB, 2863
INGENIOUS VENTURES, 2871
INLAND TECHSTART FUND, 993
INNOVATION CAPITAL LIMITED, 2877
INSIGHT VENTURE PARTNERS, 1000
INVENTUS, 1013
IRIS CAPITAL, 2897
ISIS EP LLP F & C, 2898
ITC VENTURES, 2903
JAGUAR CAPITAL PARTNERS, 1025
JEFFERIES CAPITAL PARTNERS, 1032
JEGI CAPITAL The Jordan Edminston Group, Inc., 1033
JERUSALEM VENTURE PARTNERS, 2910
KELSO & COMPANY, 1062
KENSINGTON CAPITAL PARTNERS, 2167
KERRY CAPITAL ADVISORS, 1067
KILMER CAPITAL PARTNERS, 2169
KLEINWORT CAPITAL LIMITED, 2923
KOHLBERG KRAVIS ROBERTS & COMPANY, 1082
L CATTERTON PARTNERS, 1088
LAUNCHPAD VENTURE GROUP, 1100
LEE EQUITY PARTNERS, 1104
LEONARD GREEN & PARTNERS LP, 1109
LIBERTY CITY VENTURES, 1115
LIGHTSPEED VENTURE PARTNERS, 1121
LOMBARD INVESTMENTS, 1139
LONG RIVER VENTURES, 1142
M/C PARTNERS, 1153
M25 GROUP, 1155
MADISON DEARBORN PARTNERS, 1156
MAGMA VENTURE PARTNERS, 2952
MAINE ANGELS, 1160
MAYFIELD FUND, 1184
MCG CAPITAL CORPORATION, 1189
MCGOVERN CAPITAL, 1191
MERRILL LYNCH (ASIA PACIFIC) LIMITED Merrill Lynch Group, 2964
MEZZANINE MANAGEMENT LIMITED Mezzanine Management UK Ltd., 2965
MURPHY & PARTNERS FUND LP, 1274
MVP CAPITAL PARTNERS, 1275
NAVIGATION CAPITAL PARTNERS, 1280
NESBIC INVESTMENT FUND II, 2992
NEW MOUNTAIN CAPITAL, 1301
NEW YORK ANGELS, 1306
NEWFIELD CAPITAL, 1313
NEXTEC DEVELOPMENT CAPITAL LIMITED, 3000
NEXUS VENTURE PARTNERS Nexus India Capital Advisors Pvt Ltd, 3001
NORTH COVE PARTNERS, 1337
NORTHERN LIGHT VENTURE CAPITAL, 1340
NORTHZONE, 3013
OAK HILL CAPITAL PARTNERS, 1360
ONE EQUITY PARTNERS, 1376
ONTARIO CAPITAL GROWTH CORPORATION, 2211
PAI MANAGEMENT, 3026
PALISADES VENTURES, 1402
PALLADIUM EQUITY PARTNERS, 1403
PAMLICO CAPITAL, 1409
PARTNERSHIP FUND FOR NEW YORK CITY, 1420
PEACHTREE EQUITY PARTNERS, 1423
PENN VENTURE PARTNERS, 1428
PHOENIX EQUITY PARTNERS LIMITED, 3036
PINEHURST ADVISORS, 3038
POMONA CAPITAL, 1462
POST CAPITAL PARTNERS, 1465
POUSCHINE COOK CAPITAL MANAGEMENT LLC, 1466
PRESIDIO VENTURES, 1474
PROVENANCE VENTURES, 1495
PROVIDENCE EQUITY PARTNERS, 1496
QUADRANGLE GROUP, 1506
QUESTER CAPITAL MANAGEMENT LIMITED, 3070
RAPTOR GROUP, 1524
REED ELSEVIER VENTURES, 3074
ROTH CAPITAL PARTNERS, 1588
RRE VENTURES, 1593
SABAN CAPITAL GROUP, 1598
SAFFRON HILL VENTURES, 3092
SALEM INVESTMENT PARTNERS, 1606
SANDLER CAPITAL MANAGEMENT, 1617
SCALE VENTURE PARTNERS, 1626
SCOUT VENTURES, 1632
SCP PARTNERS, 1633
SEAPORT CAPITAL, 1638
SECOND ALPHA, 1640
SEVIN ROSEN FUNDS, 1658
SHAMROCK CAPITAL ADVISORS, 1660
SIGNAL EQUITY PARTNERS, 1674
SOFTBANK CAPITAL, 1699
SOUTHEAST INTERACTIVE TECHNOLOGY FUNDS, 1709
SPECTRUM EQUITY INVESTORS LP, 1717
SPENCER TRASK VENTURES, 1720

Industry Preference Index / Media & Entertainment

SPIRE CAPITAL PARTNERS, 1724
STAGEONE VENTURES, 3136
STONEWOOD CAPITAL MANAGEMENT, 1746
SUMMIT PARTNERS, 1752
SUN CAPITAL PARTNERS, 1753
SUPPLY CHAIN VENTURES, 1757
SYCAMORE VENTURES, 1769
TAO VENTURE CAPITAL PARTNERS, 1780
TDF, 1782
TECH COAST ANGELS, 1784
TELECOM VENTURE GROUP LIMITED, 3168
TELESYSTEM, 2264
THAYER STREET PARTNERS, 1805
THIRD WAVE DIGITAL, 1813
THOMAS H LEE PARTNERS, 1815
THRIVE CAPITAL, 1821
TIGER GLOBAL MANAGEMENT, 1826
TLCOM CAPITAL, 3179
TMG CAPITAL PARTNERS, 3180
TORNANTE COMPANY, 1833
TRUE VENTURES, 1860
UNISON CAPITAL PARTNERS LP, 3201
UNITED TALENT AGENCY VENTURES, 1883
USHA MARTIN VENTURES LIMITED, 3202
VENCORE CAPITAL, 1915
VENROCK ASSOCIATES, 1916
VERIZON VENTURES, 1926
VERONIS SUHLER STEVENSON, 1927
VESTAR CAPITAL PARTNERS, 1931
VICKERS FINANCIAL GROUP, 3215
VINACAPITAL GROUP, 3217
WALNUT GROUP, 1954
WARBURG PINCUS LLC, 1956
WASABI VENTURES, 1958
WASSERSTEIN & CO., 1960
WESTON PRESIDIO, 1978
WESTVIEW CAPITAL PARTNERS, 1979
WICKS GROUP OF COMPANIES, LLC, 1984
WILLIS STEIN & PARTNERS LLC, 1986
WINDSPEED VENTURES, 1994
ZELKOVA VENTURES, 2017
ZM CAPITAL, 2020
ZONE VENTURES, 2021

Media & Entertainment
CLARION CAPITAL PARTNERS LLC, 492
KRG CAPITAL PARTNERS, 1086
SILKROAD EQUITY, 1681

Media & Telecommunications
ACCESS BRIDGE-GAP VENTURES, 34
BRANFORD CASTLE, 327
MIDOCEAN PARTNERS, 1231
TPG CAPITAL, 1835

Media Distribution
BLOOMBERG BETA, 284

Media Technology
DIFFERENCE CAPITAL, 2096
PROGRESS VENTURES, 1486
RIPPLE VENTURES, 2241
RUBICON VENTURE CAPITAL, 1595
WESTTECH VENTURES, 3236

Medical
ABINGWORTH MANAGEMENT LIMITED, 2316
ALICE VENTURES SRL, 2364
ALTA PARTNERS, 94
AMPERSAND CAPITAL PARTNERS, 118
AMWIN MANAGEMENT PTY LIMITED, 2398
ANTHEM VENTURE PARTNERS, 132
APJOHN GROUP LLC, 139
CAPRICORN VENTURE PARTNERS NV, 2563
COMPAGNIE FINANCIERE E DE ROTHSCHILD BANQUE, 2625
CONCORD VENTURES, 2628
CORAL GROUP, 536

DEFTA PARTNERS, 602
ENTREPRENEUR CAPITAL, 2107
GEMINI ISRAEL VENTURE FUNDS LIMITED, 2770
GENERICS GROUP LIMITED Generics Group, 2773
GLENTHORNE CAPITAL, 832
GOAL HOLDINGS, 2135
GUANGDONG TECHNOLOGY VENTURE CAPITAL COMPANY, 2802
HOLLAND VENTURE BV, 2828
INDUSTRIFONDEN, 2867
INNOFINANCE OY, 2873
JAFCO COMPANY LIMITED JAPAN, 2906
JAPAN ASIA INVESTMENT COMPANY LIMITED, 2907
JC TECHNOLOGIES LTD, 2909
MACQUARIE DIRECT INVESTMENT LIMITED, 2951
MANHATTAN INVESTMENT PARTNERS, 1163
MERRILL LYNCH (ASIA PACIFIC) LIMITED Merrill Lynch Group, 2964
PLEXUS VENTURES, 1452
PRIVATE EQUITY PARTNERS SPA, 3053
SAMSUNG VENTURE INVESTMENT CORPORATION Samsung Electronics, 3098
SKYLINE VENTURES, 1691
SVB CAPITAL, 1764
TAT CAPITAL PARTNERS LTD., 3162
TRANSATLANTIC CAPITAL LTD, 3186
WAVEPOINT VENTURES, 1966

Medical & Health Related
ACCESS CAPITAL, 35
ALBEMARLE PRIVATE EQUITY LIMITED, 2360
AMADEUS CAPITAL PARTNERS LIMITED, 2386
ARBORETUM VENTURES, 149
ARTHUR P GOULD & COMPANY, 172
ASCENSION HEALTH VENTURES LLC, 176
AURIGA PARTNERS, 2453
BARING PRIVATE EQUITY PARTNERS ESPANA SA, 2489
BARING PRIVATE EQUITY PARTNERS INDIA, 2490
BATTERSON VENTURE CAPITAL LLC, 234
BEECKEN PETTY O'KEEFE & COMPANY, 244
BERKELEY VC INTERNATIONAL LLC, 252
BIO FUND MANAGEMENT OY, 2512
CIC FINANCE CIC Group, 2601
CID CAPITAL, 478
CONCORD VENTURES, 2628
CONTINENTAL VENTURE CAPITAL LIMITED, 2631
DE NOVO VENTURES, 598
DELPHI VENTURES, 604
DRESNER COMPANIES, 629
ENTERPRISE EQUITY (NI) LTD, 2704
EQUUS TOTAL RETURN, 694
FERRER FREEMAN & COMPANY LLC, 723
GEFINOR CAPITAL, 810
GIMV GIMV, 2780
GLYNN CAPITAL MANAGEMENT, 836
GUIDANT EUROPE SA, 2803
HUMANA VENTURES, 955
INDUSTRIEBANK LIOF NV, 2866
INNOVATION CAPITAL LIMITED, 2877
INVESTMENT AB BURE, 2888
IPG GROUP, 2894
KBL FOUNDER SA, 2917
KLEINER PERKINS, 1075
KNIGHTSBRIDGE ADVISERS, 1077
LEGAL AND GENERAL VENTURES LIMITED, 2935
LIFE SCIENCES PARTNERS BV, 2939
LM CAPITAL SECURITIES, 1137
MASSACHUSETTS CAPITAL RESOURCE COMPANY, 1173
MASSACHUSETTS GROWTH CAPITAL CORPORATION, 1174
MAYFIELD FUND, 1184
NEW YORK LIFE CAPITAL PARTNERS, 1309
NORTHERN ENTERPRISE LIMITED, 3011
ONO PHARMACEUTICALS COMPANY LIMITED, 3021
PAMLICO CAPITAL, 1409
PARTECH INTERNATIONAL, 1416
PERMAL CAPITAL MANAGEMENT, 1432
PIDC PHILADELPHIA, 1441
PITANGO VENTURE CAPITAL, 3039
POMONA CAPITAL, 1462

Industry Preference Index / Medical Devices

PROVCO GROUP, 1494
RAF INDUSTRIES, 1521
REITEN & CO STRATEGIC INVESTMENTS AS Reiten & Company, 3076
ROYALTY CAPITAL MANAGEMENT, 1591
SANDERLING VENTURES, 1616
SEACOAST CAPITAL CORPORATION, 1636
SEED CAPITAL LIMITED, 3107
SHANNON COMMERCIAL PROPERTIES, 3115
SHAW KWEI AND PARTNERS, 3116
SIEMENS VENTURE CAPITAL, 3118
SKYLINE VENTURES, 1691
SOURCE CAPITAL GROUP, 1707
SOUTH ATLANTIC VENTURE FUNDS, 1708
SOUTHPORT PARTNERS, 1712
SR ONE LTD, 1731
SUTTER HILL VENTURES, 1760
TEKNOINVEST MANAGEMENT, 3167
THROUNARFELAG ISLANDS PLC, 3177
TRANSITION PARTNERS LTD, 1837
TULLY & HOLLAND, 1867
VAEKSTFONDEN, 3203
VALLEY VENTURES LP, 1901
VENTANA CAPITAL MANAGEMENT LP, 1918
VENTURE INVESTORS, 3210
VERITAS VENTURE PARTNERS, 3212
WASSERSTEIN & CO., 1960
WATERLAND PRIVATE EQUITY INVESTMENT, 3232
WESTERN STATES INVESTMENT GROUP, 1974
WESTERN TECHNOLOGY INVESTMENT, 1975
WOODSIDE FUND, 2005
ZERNIKE SEED FUND BV, 3250
ZS FUND LP, 2022

Medical Devices
AAVIN PRIVATE EQUITY, 17
ABELL FOUNDATION VENTURES, 19
ABERDARE VENTURES, 20
ACCELMED, 2324
ACCESS MEDICAL VENTURES, 2328
ACCUITIVE MEDICAL VENTURES LLC, 40
ACONCAGUA VENTURES, 2334
ADAMS STREET PARTNERS, LLC, 57
ADVENT VENTURE PARTNERS, 2348
AESCAP VENTURE, 2350
AFFINITY CAPITAL MANAGEMENT, 68
AGATE MEDICAL INVESTMENTS, 2353
ALBERTA ENTERPRISE, 2032
ALEUTIAN CAPITAL PARTNERS, 81
ALFA CAPITAL Alfa Group, 2363
ALLOS VENTURES, 86
ALTARIS CAPITAL PARTNERS, 97
AMHERST FUND, 113
AMKEY VENTURES, 117
AMPERSAND CAPITAL PARTNERS, 118
ANDLINGER & COMPANY INC, 123
ANGELS' FORUM LLC, 129
ANNEX VENTURES, 130
APERTURE VENTURE PARTNERS, 136
APJOHN GROUP LLC, 139
ARBORETUM VENTURES, 149
ARCH VENTURE PARTNERS, 153
ASCENSION HEALTH VENTURES LLC, 176
ASCENT BIOMEDICAL VENTURES, 177
ATHYRIUM CAPITAL MANAGEMENT, 188
ATLAS VENTURE: FRANCE, 2445
AUGURY CAPITAL PARTNERS, 196
AUSTIN CAPITAL PARTNERS LP, 201
AVIV VENTURE CAPITAL, 2462
AVLAR BIOVENTURES, 2463
AZCA, 214
BAY CITY CAPITAL LLC, 237
BB BIOTECH VENTURES, 2496
BCM TECHNOLOGIES, 241
BEECKEN PETTY O'KEEFE & COMPANY, 244
BIOADVANCE, 266
BIOGENERATION VENTURES, 2514

BIOGENERATOR, 267
BIOSTAR VENTURES, 269
BIOVENTURES INVESTORS, 270
BIRCHMERE VENTURES, 272
BLACK DIAMOND VENTURES, 275
BLADE VENTURES, 278
BRANDON CAPITAL PARTNERS, 2536
BREAKWATER INVESTMENTS, 330
BRIDGE INVESTMENT FUND, 337
BRIGHTSTONE VENTURE CAPITAL, 341
BROADVIEW VENTURES, 347
BROOK VENTURE FUND, 349
CALIFORNIA TECHNOLOGY VENTURES, 371
CAPITAL FOR BUSINESS, INC, 399
CARDINAL PARTNERS, 410
CATALYST FUND LP, 2571
CATALYST HEALTH VENTURES, 426
CEDAR VENTURES LLC, 437
CENTRESTONE VENTURES, 2077
CHALLENGE FUNDS - ETGAR LP, 2585
CHINA DEVELOPMENT INDUSTRIAL BANK CDFH, 2592
CHL MEDICAL PARTNERS, 474
CIBC CAPITAL MARKETS, 2079
CID CAPITAL, 478
CITARETX INVESTMENT PARTNERS, 485
CLARENDON FUND MANAGERS, 2610
COMPASS TECHNOLOGY PARTNERS LP, 524
CONNECTICUT INNOVATIONS, 530
CUTLASS CAPITAL LLC, 572
DE NOVO VENTURES, 598
DEFTA PARTNERS, 602
DELPHI VENTURES, 604
DELTA VENTURES LIMITED, 2655
DOMAIN ASSOCIATES LLC, 621
EASTON CAPITAL INVESTMENT GROUP, 644
ECHELON VENTURES, 647
EDBI Pte LTD., 2690
EGL HOLDINGS, 656
ELM STREET VENTURES, 660
EMERGENT MEDICAL PARTNERS, 666
ENTREE CAPITAL, 2709
ESCALATE CAPITAL PARTNERS, 695
ESSEX WOODLANDS HEALTH VENTURES LLC, 697
EVENTI CAPITAL PARTNERS, 2110
EVERGREEN ADVISORS, 701
EXCEL VENTURE MANAGEMENT, 703
F-PRIME CAPITAL PARTNERS, 710
FCF PARTNERS LP, 719
FIRST ANALYSIS, 732
FLARE CAPITAL PARTNERS, 748
FLETCHER SPAGHT VENTURES, 749
FORBION CAPITAL PARTNERS, 2748
FORESITE CAPITAL, 762
FORWARD VENTURES, 769
FRAZIER HEALTHCARE VENTURES, 782
FUNK VENTURES, 797
GALEN PARTNERS, 806
GRANTHAM CAPITAL, 853
GREAT POINT PARTNERS, 859
GREENHILLS VENTURES, LLC, 865
GUIDE MEDICAL VENTURES, 886
HAMILTON BIOVENTURES, 898
HAMMOND, KENNEDY, WHITNEY & COMPANY, 900
HATTERAS VENTURE PARTNERS, 915
HBM PARTNERS, 2815
HEALTHQUEST CAPITAL, 921
HIGH COUNTRY VENTURE, 930
HLM VENTURE PARTNERS, 938
HOPEN LIFE SCIENCE VENTURES, 943
HOPEWELL VENTURES, 944
ID VENTURES AMERICA LLC, 970
IDEA FUND PARTNERS, 971
IDG VENTURES INDIA International Financial Services Limited, 2849
INCUBE VENTURES, 980
INDUSTRIO VENTURES, 2868
INETWORKS ADVISORS LLC, 987
INLAND TECHSTART FUND, 993

Industry Preference Index / Medical Devices & Implants

INNOVA MEMPHIS, 995
INNOVATION WORKS, 998
INTEGRA VENTURES, 1002
INVUS GROUP, 1018
IP GROUP, 2892
JAPAN ASIA INVESTMENT COMPANY LIMITED, 2907
JF SHEA VENTURES, 1036
JMH CAPITAL, 1040
JOHNSON & JOHNSON INNOVATION, 1043
KAISER PERMANENTE VENTURES, 1052
KALORI GROUP INVESTMENTS, 2915
KB PARTNERS LLC, 1057
KBL HEALTHCARE VENTURES, 1058
KEARNY VENTURE PARTNERS, 1059
KEGONSA CAPITAL PARTNERS, 1060
LANCET CAPITAL, 1092
LATTERELL VENTURE PARTNERS, 1094
LAUNCHPAD VENTURE GROUP, 1100
LFE CAPITAL, 1113
LIGHTSTONE VENTURES, 1122
LONG RIVER VENTURES, 1142
LONGITUDE CAPITAL, 1143
LOVETT MILLER & COMPANY, 1148
MARATHON VENTURE CAPITAL FUND LIMITED, 2954
MARYLAND VENTURE FUND, 1169
MASS VENTURES, 1172
MB VENTURE PARTNERS, 1187
MBF CAPITAL CORPORATION, 1188
MEDIMMUNE VENTURES, 1196
MERITECH CAPITAL PARTNERS, 1212
MESA VERDE PARTNERS, 1221
MONTREUX EQUITY PARTNERS, 1251
MORGENTHALER VENTURES, 1257
MOUNTAIN GROUP CAPITAL, 1261
MOUNTAINEER CAPITAL, 1262
MPM CAPITAL, 1268
MTS HEALTH INVESTORS, 1271
MURPHREE VENTURE PARTNERS, 1273
MVM LIFE SCIENCE PARTNERS, 2981
NDI MEDICAL, 1287
NEEDHAM CAPITAL PARTNERS, 1288
NEW LEAF VENTURE PARTNERS, 1298
NEW SCIENCE VENTURES, 1303
NEWSPRING CAPITAL, 1317
NGN CAPITAL, 1325
NHN INVESTMENT, 3002
NOMURA PHASE4 VENTURES LTD, 3007
NORWICH VENTURES, 1347
NOVO A/S, 3015
OKAPI VENTURE CAPITAL, 1371
OMEGA FUNDS, 1373
ONSET VENTURES, 1378
ORBIMED HEALTHCARE FUND MANAGEMENT, 1382
ORIGINATE VENTURES, 1385
OXFORD BIOSCIENCE PARTNERS, 1394
PAPPAS VENTURES, 1412
PARTISAN MANAGEMENT GROUP, 1418
PARTNERS HEALTHCARE RESEARCH VENTURES, 1419
PELION VENTURE PARTNERS, 1425
PITTSBURGH LIFE SCIENCES GREENHOUSE, 1448
PREVIZ VENTURES, 3050
PRISM VENTUREWORKS, 1478
PROSPECT VENTURE PARTNERS, 1493
PTV SCIENCES, 1500
PURETECH VENTURES, 1501
QUAKER BIOVENTURES, 1508
QUESTMARK PARTNERS LP, 1515
RA CAPITAL MANAGEMENT, 1519
RAFAEL DEVELOPMENT CORPORATION (RDC) LIMITED, 3072
RESEARCH CORPORATION TECHNOLOGIES, 1543
REX HEALTH VENTURES, 1556
RHO VENTURES, 1558
ROBIN HOOD VENTURES, 1577
ROUNDTABLE HEALTHCARE PARTNERS, 1590
SAND HILL ANGELS, 1613
SBRC INVESTMENT CONSULTATION LIMITED, 3101
SCALE VENTURE PARTNERS, 1626

SCHRODER VENTURES HEALTH INVESTORS, 1628
SCP PARTNERS, 1633
SENECA PARTNERS, 1649
SHEPHERD VENTURES, 1664
SHERBROOKE CAPITAL, 1665
SIGHTLINE PARTNERS, 1671
SIGNAL PEAK VENTURES, 1677
SKYLINE VENTURES, 1691
SORRENTO VENTURES, 1706
SPINDLETOP CAPITAL, 1722
SPLIT ROCK PARTNERS, 1725
STATELINE ANGELS, 1740
SUCSY, FISCHER & COMPANY, 1750
SV HEALTH INVESTORS, 1762
SYNERGY LIFE SCIENCE PARTNERS, 1772
SYNERGY VENTURES, 1773
SYNTHESIS CAPITAL, 1775
TELEGRAPH HILL PARTNERS, 1792
TEXO VENTURES, 1801
THE CHANNEL GROUP, 1808
THIRD ROCK VENTURES, 1811
THOMAS, MCNERNEY & PARTNERS, 1817
THREE ARCH PARTNERS LP, 1819
TI VENTURE CAPITAL Texas Instruments Incorporated, 1823
TIE ANGELS GROUP SEATTLE, 1825
TREVI HEALTH CAPITAL, 1844
TRIANGLE VENTURE CAPITAL GROUP, 3188
TRIATHLON MEDICAL VENTURES, 1847
TULLIS HEALTH INVESTORS, 1866
TWIN CITIES ANGELS, 1872
US VENTURE PARTNERS, 1896
VEDANTA CAPITAL LP, 1911
VENROCK ASSOCIATES, 1916
VERSANT VENTURES, 1928
VERTICAL GROUP, 1929
WESTERN TECHNOLOGY INVESTMENT, 1975
WHEATLEY PARTNERS, 1981
WILMINGTON INVESTOR NETWORK, 1988
WINDWARD VENTURES, 1995
XENIA VENTURE CAPITAL, 3240
YASUDA ENTERPRISE DEVELOPMENT COMPANY, 3243
ZURMONT MADISON PRIVATE EQUITY, 3254

Medical Devices & Implants
NOVARTIS VENTURE FUNDS, 1350

Medical Devices and Equipment
PRAIRIEGOLD VENTURE PARTNERS, 1470

Medical Equipment
SECTION 32, 1643

Medical Equipment and Instruments
ACCES CAPITAL QUEBEC, 2029

Medical Imaging
LDV CAPITAL, 1101

Medical Products
FIRST CAPITAL GROUP, 734
ROUNDTABLE HEALTHCARE PARTNERS, 1590
SEIDLER EQUITY PARTNERS, 1645
VANCE STREET CAPITAL, 1904

Medical Products & Services
CENTURY PARK CAPITAL PARTNERS, 449
NORTH AMERICAN FUND, 1332
WATER STREET HEALTHCARE PARTNERS, 1961

Medical Research
SECTION 32, 1643

Medical Supply
HOUSTON HEALTH VENTURES, 951

Medical Technology
360 CAPITAL PARTNERS 360 Capital Management SA, 2296

Industry Preference Index / Mobile

ABS VENTURES, 23
ACCUITIVE MEDICAL VENTURES LLC, 40
AGATE MEDICAL INVESTMENTS, 2353
BANEXI VENTURES PARTNERS, 2481
BIOMED PARTNERS, 2515
BIOSTAR VENTURES, 269
BLUETREE VENTURE FUND, 298
CASABONA VENTURES, 418
CHORD CAPITAL, 2598
CLARUS VENTURES, 495
DFJ ESPRIT, 2662
DVC DEUTSCHE VENTURE CAPITAL, 2679
EARLYBIRD, 2682
EPLANET CAPITAL, 690
ESSEX WOODLANDS HEALTH VENTURES LLC, 697
F-PRIME CAPITAL PARTNERS, 710
GLOBAL LIFE SCIENCE VENTURES GmbH, 2785
GREY SKY VENTURE PARTNERS, 870
HEALTHCAP, 2816
HEALTHCAP Odlander, Fredrikson & Co AB, 2816
HLM VENTURE PARTNERS, 938
INTERSOUTH PARTNERS, 1008
KALORI GROUP INVESTMENTS, 2915
MEDICAL RESEARCH COMMERCIALIZATION FUND, 2959
MEDIMMUNE VENTURES, 1196
MPM CAPITAL, 1268
NAUSICAA VENTURES, 2986
NEMO CAPITAL PARTNERS, 1289
NEWABLE VENTURES, 2997
ONSET VENTURES, 1378
PARKWALK ADVISORS, 3028
PSILOS GROUP, 1498
RED DOT VENTURES, 3073
REV1 VENTURES, 1553
SAMOS INVESTMENTS, 3097
SANTE VENTURES, 1619
SIGHTLINE PARTNERS, 1671
STAENBERG VENTURE PARTNERS, 1733
SUMMIT BRIDGE CAPITAL, 3147
SYNTHESIS CAPITAL, 1775
TRIVENTURES, 3192
TWIN CITIES ANGELS, 1872
VENBIO, 1914
WELLINGTON PARTNERS VENTURE CAPITAL GmbH, 3233
WHITECAP VENTURE PARTNERS, 2288
WINDHAM VENTURE PARTNERS, 1993

Medicine
ANALYTICS VENTURES, 121
EMERGENT MEDICAL PARTNERS, 666

Merchant Banking
ROTHSCHILD AUSTRALIA - ARROW PRIVATE EQUITY Rothschild Group, 3086

Metals
ABOA VENTURE MANAGEMENT OY, 2318
BRUML CAPITAL CORPORATION, 355
FIRST ISRAEL MEZZANINE INVESTORS LIMITED, 2745
HELMET CAPITAL FUND MANAGEMENT OY, 2820
IBM VENTURE CAPITAL GROUP, 967
JB POINDEXTER & COMPANY, 1030
JORDAN COMPANY, 1045
KUBOTA CORPORATION, 2927
MERITURN PARTNERS, 1213
RESILIENCE CAPITAL PARTNERS, 1545
RESOURCE CAPITAL FUNDS, 1548
SAMBRINVEST SA, 3096
SPELL CAPITAL PARTNERS LLC, 1719
SRIW SA SRIW Group, 3134
WATERMILL GROUP, 1962
WATERTON GLOBAL RESOURCE MANAGEMENT, 2283

Metals & Mining
CHRYSALIX, 2078
SAF GROUP, 2246

Microcontrollers
QUANTUM WAVE FUND, 3068

Microelectronics
180 DEGREE CAPITAL, 6
CORE CAPITAL PARTNERS, 538
EUROFUND LP, 2720
JC TECHNOLOGIES LTD, 2909
MMT MILLENNIUM MATERIALS TECHNOLOGIES FUND LP, 2973
POLYTECHNOS VENTURE PARTNERS GmbH, 3046
TRIGINITA CAPITAL, 3190
VALLEY VENTURES LP, 1901

Microfinance
ALPHAMUNDI GROUP LTD, 2376
GRAY GHOST VENTURES, 855

Microprocessors
QUANTUM WAVE FUND, 3068

Microsystems
NEUHAUS PARTNERS, 2994

Midstream
BREGAL ENERGY, 332

Midstream Growth
HADDINGTON VENTURES LLC, 893

Midstream Oil & Gas
ENERGY CAPITAL PARTNERS, 675

Military
ALTUS CAPITAL PARTNERS, 104
CELERITY PARTNERS, 439
QUANTUM WAVE FUND, 3068

Minerals
CLARITY CAPITAL, 2611
RESOURCE CAPITAL FUNDS, 1548

Mining
CIBC CAPITAL MARKETS, 2079
COPPERLION CAPITAL, 2085
GE CAPITAL, 808
INTERNATIONAL FINANCE CORPORATION (IFC), 1007
LIME ROCK PARTNERS, 1125
LION SELECTION GROUP LIMITED, 2942
LIONHART CAPITAL LTD, 2177
MERITURN PARTNERS, 1213
PALMS & COMPANY, 1404
RESOURCE CAPITAL FUNDS, 1548
RFC AMBRIAN RFC Group Ltd., 3079
SOUTHERN CROSS VENTURE PARTNERS, 1711
WATERTON GLOBAL RESOURCE MANAGEMENT, 2283

Mobile
10X VENTURE PARTNERS, 3
42 VENTURES, 9
ACCEL, 28
ACUMEN VENTURES, 2341
ALBUM VC, 79
ALLIANCE VENTURE, 2369
ALPHA VENTURE PARTNERS, 91
ALTOS VENTURES, 100
AMHERST FUND, 113
ANGELPAD, 128
ANNAPURNA VENTURES, 2403
ANTRAK CAPITAL, 2407
ARC ANGEL FUND, 150
ARCHTOP VENTURES, 154
ASLANOBA CAPITAL, 2437
ASPECT VENTURES, 180
AZURE CAPITAL PARTNERS, 215
B-TO-V PARTNERS, 2475
BAF SPECTRUM, 2477
BALLPARK VENTURES, 2479

1213

Industry Preference Index / Mobile & Internet

BARODA VENTURES, 228
BENCHMARK, 248
BERKELEY VENTURES, 253
BESSEMER VENTURE PARTNERS, 260
BIRCHMERE VENTURES, 272
BLACKBIRD VENTURES, 2520
BLUMBERG CAPITAL, 301
BRIGHTSPARK VENTURES, 2066
BRIGHTSTONE VENTURE CAPITAL, 341
CARMEL VENTURES, 2566
CATAGONIA CAPITAL, 2569
CATALYST INVESTORS, 427
CAVA CAPITAL, 431
CENTRAL TEXAS ANGEL NETWORK, 445
CLEARSTONE VENTURE PARTNERS, 502
COLOMA VENTURES, 512
CONNECT VENTURES, 2629
CONVERGE VENTURE PARTNERS, 534
CORSA VENTURES, 545
DATA POINT CAPITAL, 586
DCM, 596
DFJ ESPRIT, 2662
DFJ GOTHAM VENTURES, 608
DN CAPITAL, 2668
DOUBLEROCK VENTURE CAPITAL, 625
E.BRICKS DIGITAL, 2681
EASTLABS, 2684
EC1 CAPITAL LTD, 2685
EDEN VENTURES, 2691
ENIAC VENTURES, 679
ESCALATE CAPITAL PARTNERS, 695
EXTREME VENTURE PARTNERS, 2113
FAIRHAVEN CAPITAL, 712
FELICIS VENTURES, 720
FINAVENTURES, 729
FIRST ASCENT VENTURES, 2118
FIRSTMARK CAPITAL, 743
FOUNDER COLLECTIVE, 771
FOUNDER PARTNERS, 772
FOUNDER'S CO-OP, 773
GABRIEL VENTURE PARTNERS, 805
GENACAST VENTURES, 814
GENWEALTH VENTURES, 2131
GGV CAPITAL, 823
GOLDEN VENTURE PARTNERS, 2137
GOOD NEWS VENTURES, 2138
GRAYHAWK CAPITAL, 856
GREAT OAKS VENTURE CAPITAL, 858
GREE VENTURES, 2798
HELION VENTURE PARTNERS, LLC International Management (Mauritius) Ltd, 2818
HENQ, 2822
HORIZONS VENTURES, 2831
HOXTON VENTURES, 2834
ICON VENTURES, 968
IDG VENTURES INDIA International Financial Services Limited, 2849
IMI.VC, 2856
INFINITY VENTURE PARTNERS, 2869
INLAND TECHSTART FUND, 993
INNOVATION WORKS, 998
INSTITUTIONAL VENTURE PARTNERS, 1001
INVENTURE PARTNERS, 2886
INVENTUS, 1013
IRISH ANGELS, 1019
KIZOO TECHNOLOGY CAPITAL, 2921
LANTA DIGITAL VENTURES, 2930
LAUNCHCAPITAL, 1097
LAUNCHPAD VENTURE GROUP, 1100
LIONBIRD, 2943
MASS VENTURES, 1172
MERCURY FUND, 1206
MHS CAPITAL, 1226
MOBILITY VENTURES, 1244
MORADO VENTURE PARTNERS, 1254
NARANYA VENTURES, 2984
NAUTA CAPITAL, 2987
NAYA VENTURES, 1285

NEW ATLANTIC VENTURES, 1291
NEXIT VENTURES OY, 2999
NEXIT VENTURES OY Nexit Ventures Inc., 2999
NEXT WORLD CAPITAL, 1319
NEXTGEN ANGELS, 1320
NHN INVESTMENT, 3002
NIELSEN INNOVATE FUND, 3003
O'REILLY ALPHATECH VENTURES, 1359
OMIDYAR NETWORK, 1374
OYSTER INVEST, 3022
PALO ALTO VENTURE SCIENCE, 1406
PENTECH VENTURES, 3032
PINEHURST ADVISORS, 3038
PLUS VENTURES, 3041
POINT NINE CAPITAL, 3044
PREVIZ VENTURES, 3050
PRIME TECHNOLOGY VENTURES NV, 3051
PRINCIPIA SGR, 3052
PROGRESS VENTURES, 1486
PROJECT A VENTURE GmBH & CO. KG, 3056
QUALCOMM VENTURES, 1509
QUOTIDIAN VENTURES, 1518
REAL VENTURES, 2232
REED ELSEVIER VENTURES, 3074
RELAY VENTURES, 2236
RRE VENTURES, 1593
RUNA CAPITAL, 3088
SAIF PARTNERS, 3093
SCOUT VENTURES, 1632
SCRUM VENTURES, 1634
SEQUOIA CAPITAL, 1654
SERAPH GROUP, 1655
SIERRA ANGELS, 1669
SIGMA PRIME VENTURES, 1673
SILICON ALLEY VENTURE PARTNERS, 1680
SILVERTON PARTNERS, 1685
SK TELECOM VENTURES, 1690
SOFTBANK VENTURES KOREA, 3127
SOFTTECH VC, 1700
SOUTHERN CAPITOL VENTURES, 1710
SPARK CAPITAL, 1715
SPINUP VENTURE, 3132
SPRING LAKE EQUITY PARTNERS, 1728
SRIJAN CAPITAL, 3133
STAGE 1 VENTURES, 1734
TANK STREAM VENTURES, 3160
TARGET PARTNERS, 3161
THIRD WAVE DIGITAL, 1813
TIE ANGELS GROUP SEATTLE, 1825
TMI, 3181
TRIBECA VENTURE PARTNERS, 1849
VERDEXUS, 2279
VERSION ONE VENTURES, 2280
VINE ST VENTURES, 1934
VITULUM VENTURES, 3224
WASABI VENTURES, 1958
WESLEY CLOVER, 2284
WESTSUMMIT CAPITAL, 3235
WHITE STAR CAPITAL, 1982
WOMEN'S VENTURE CAPITAL FUND, 2003
XANGE PRIVATE EQUITY, 3239
XG VENTURES, 2010

Mobile & Internet
BURAN VENTURE CAPITAL, 2549
MENLO VENTURES, 1202

Mobile & Tablet
500 STARTUPS, 11

Mobile Apps
BLACK DIAMOND VENTURES, 275
CAMP VENTURES, 385
DALLAS VENTURE PARTNERS, 582
EONCAPITAL, 685
IGLOBE PARTNERS, 2853
INVENTUS, 1013

Industry Preference Index / Nanotechnology

KAEDAN INVESTMENTS, 2914
OJAS VENTURE PARTNERS, 3019
RHO CANADA VENTURES, 2239
SALESFORCE VENTURES, 1607
SERAPH GROUP, 1655
SPEKTRA CAPITAL, 1718
UPFRONT VENTURES, 1888

Mobile Broadband
MOTOROLA SOLUTIONS VENTURE CAPITAL, 1260

Mobile Commerce
OCA VENTURES, 1364

Mobile Communications Devices
AURA CAPITAL OY Auratum Group, 2451
AZIONE CAPITAL, 2473
BLUERUN VENTURES, 296
DOUGHTY HANSON & CO., 2671
GILDE INVESTMENT FUNDS, 2779
IDG CAPITAL, 973
INDUSTRIEBANK LIOF NV, 2866
JAVELIN VENTURE PARTNERS, 1028
PITANGO VENTURE CAPITAL, 3039
REDPOINT VENTURES, 1534
SALESFORCE VENTURES, 1607
SPENCER TRASK VENTURES, 1720

Mobile Computing
ALTA VENTURES MEXICO, 2382
LIQUID CAPITAL GROUP, 1133
SHEPHERD VENTURES, 1664
SIGMA PARTNERS, 1672
SIGNAL PEAK VENTURES, 1677
WING VENTURE PARTNERS, 1996

Mobile Data Services
I-HATCH VENTURES LLC, 964

Mobile Energy Transmission
INFIELD CAPITAL, 988

Mobile Enterprise
IGNITION PARTNERS, 974

Mobile Entertainment
TRUE VENTURES, 1860

Mobile Infrastructure
UPFRONT VENTURES, 1888

Mobile Internet
ZHENFUND, 3251

Mobile Media
BOREALIS VENTURES, 308
GRANDBANKS CAPITAL, 848

Mobile Services
ADARA VENTURE PARTNERS, 2342
DACE VENTURES, 580
GENESIS PARTNERS, 2775
RUNTIDE CAPITAL, 1596
TRUE VENTURES, 1860

Mobile Software
GREENHILLS VENTURES, LLC, 865

Mobile Technology
AMITI VENTURES, 116
AUTHOSIS VENTURES, 2457
BRIDGESCALE PARTNERS, 339
CALUMET VENTURE FUND, 375
GLOBESPAN CAPITAL PARTNERS, 835
GV, 889
MIDATLANTIC FUND, 1228
NGP CAPITAL, 1327

PLAZA VENTURES, 2224
POINT JUDITH CAPITAL, 1459
RELAY VENTURES, 2236
TRUE VENTURES, 1860
WINDFORCE VENTURES, LLC, 1992
YL VENTURES, 3246

Mobility
ABRT VENTURE FUND, 2320
ARCTERN VENTURES, 2041
ASTER CAPITAL, 2439
BOLDSTART VENTURES, 305
CAMP ONE VENTURES, 384
CARDINAL VENTURE CAPITAL, 411
CASTROL INNOVENTURES, 2568
CLAREMONT CREEK VENTURES, 491
DELL VENTURES, 603
ENTREPIA VENTURES, 682
FORTÉ VENTURES, 768
G SQUARED, 802
GREYCROFT PARTNERS, 871
HURON RIVER VENTURES, 961
INTEL CAPITAL, 1004
MOBILE FOUNDATION VENTURES, 1243
MS&AD VENTURES, 1269
OBVIOUS VENTURES, 1363
ONSET VENTURES, 1378
RUBICON VENTURE CAPITAL, 1595
SAMSUNG NEXT, 1611
SEIDLER EQUITY PARTNERS, 1645
SONY INNOVATION FUND, 1703
SUMMERHILL VENTURE PARTNERS, 2259
URBAN US, 1894
WILDCAT VENTURE PARTNERS, 1985

Mortgages
VARDE PARTNERS, 1907

Multimedia
AMD VENTURES, 106
APAX PARTNERS ET CIE, 2415
CALIFORNIA TECHNOLOGY VENTURES, 371
COMPAGNIE FINANCIERE E DE ROTHSCHILD BANQUE, 2625
ENTREPIA VENTURES, 682
EURAZEO, 2719
MIRAE ASSET VENTURE ACCELERATOR Mirae Asset Group, 2969
NEUHAUS PARTNERS, 2994
SBRC INVESTMENT CONSULTATION LIMITED, 3101
SCOTTISH ENTERPRISE, 3103
SYNCOM VENTURE PARTNERS, 1771

Music
INGENIOUS VENTURES, 2871
NORTHSTAR VENTURES, 3012
RAPTOR GROUP, 1524
SECTION 32, 1643
ZM CAPITAL, 2020

Nano- and Microtechnologies
ARCH VENTURE PARTNERS, 153

Nanotechnology
180 DEGREE CAPITAL, 6
ASSET MANAGEMENT VENTURES, 181
BASF VENTURE CAPITAL, 2492
CEDRUS INVESTMENTS, 2581
CORE CAPITAL PARTNERS, 538
COTTONWOOD TECHNOLOGY FUND, 549
CREATHOR VENTURE, 2638
FRONTIER VENTURE CAPITAL, 791
HIGH-TECH GRUENDERFONDS, 2824
LUX CAPITAL, 1151
MAINE ANGELS, 1160
MMT MILLENNIUM MATERIALS TECHNOLOGIES FUND LP, 2973
NEW VENTURE PARTNERS, 1305
OXANTIUM VENTURES, 1393
PELION VENTURE PARTNERS, 1425

Industry Preference Index / Natural Gas

QUESTER CAPITAL MANAGEMENT LIMITED, 3070
RED DOT VENTURES, 3073
SOUTHERN CROSS VENTURE PARTNERS, 1711
SPINUP VENTURE, 3132
YISSUM TECHNOLOGY TRANSFER, 3245

Natural Gas
APECTEC, 2039
ENCAP FLATROCK MIDSTREAM, 671
HADDINGTON VENTURES LLC, 893
MOUNTAINEER CAPITAL, 1262
NATURAL GAS PARTNERS, 1278
PRIVITI CAPITAL, 2227

Natural Resources
ARTHUR P GOULD & COMPANY, 172
ATRIUM CAPITAL, 192
AVENUE CAPITAL GROUP, 208
BARING PRIVATE EQUITY PARTNERS INDIA, 2490
CEDRUS INVESTMENTS, 2581
CROSBY ASSET MANAGEMENT, 2640
EM WARBURG, PINCUS & COMPANY INTERNATIONAL, 2697
EM WARBURG, PINCUS & COMPANY JAPAN, 2698
EMP GLOBAL, 670
FIELDSTONE PRIVATE CAPITAL GROUP, 726
FOUNDATION MARKETS, 2122
GENERAL ENTERPRISE MANAGEMENT SERVICES, 2772
HUMANA VENTURES, 955
LYNWOOD CAPITAL PARTNERS, 1152
MID-ATLANTIC VENTURE FUNDS, 1227
MIDDLEBURG CAPITAL DEVELOPMENT, 1229
NEW BRUNSWICK INNOVATION FOUNDATION, 2200
PIDC PHILADELPHIA, 1441
ROYALTY CAPITAL MANAGEMENT, 1591
SAMOS INVESTMENTS, 3097
SARATOGA PARTNERS, 1621
SEED CAPITAL LIMITED, 3107
SOURCE CAPITAL GROUP, 1707
SOUTH ATLANTIC VENTURE FUNDS, 1708
STARBOARD CAPITAL PARTNERS, 1735
SUN CAPITAL PARTNERS, 1753
TERA CAPITAL CORPORATION, 2267
WAND PARTNERS, 1955
WOODSIDE FUND, 2005

Natural Resources & Chemicals
ACCESS BRIDGE-GAP VENTURES, 34

Network Infrastructure
FAIRHAVEN CAPITAL, 712
INNOVATION WORKS, 998
SEAPOINT VENTURES, 1637

Network Infrastructure & Security
ADAMS CAPITAL MANAGEMENT, 56
ARCH VENTURE PARTNERS, 153
DYNAMO VC, 640
FIRST ANALYSIS, 732
STAENBERG VENTURE PARTNERS, 1733

Network Technology
FUSION FUND, 799

Networking
ACORN CAMPUS VENTURES, 47
ADOBE VENTURES LP, 58
AKERS CAPITAL LLC, 75
ALEXANDER HUTTON, 82
ALTAIR VENTURES, 95
AMADEUS CAPITAL PARTNERS LIMITED, 2386
AMBIENT SOUND INVESTMENTS, 2390
ANGELS' FORUM LLC, 129
ANTHEM VENTURE PARTNERS, 132
ARROWPATH VENTURE PARTNERS, 169
ARTIS VENTURES, 175
ASCENT VENTURE PARTNERS, 178
ASSET MANAGEMENT VENTURES, 181
ATHENAEUM FUND, 186
AVALON VENTURES, 206
AZURE CAPITAL PARTNERS, 215
BAND OF ANGELS LLC, 226
BATTERY VENTURES, 235
BENHAMOU GLOBAL VENTURES, 249
BLUMBERG CAPITAL, 301
CEDAR (ISRAEL) FINANCIAL ADVISORS LIMITED Cedar Fund, 2580
CEDAR FUND, 436
CEI VENTURES, 438
CELTIC HOUSE VENTURE PARTNERS, 2076
CHEVRON TECHNOLOGY VENTURES, 466
CHICAGO VENTURE PARTNERS LP, 470
COMCAST VENTURES, 518
CORE CAPITAL PARTNERS, 538
DALLAS VENTURE PARTNERS, 582
DELL VENTURES, 603
DUCHOSSOIS CAPITAL MANAGEMENT, 633
EASTVEN VENTURE PARTNERS, 645
ECLIPSE VENTURES, 648
FOUNDATION CAPITAL, 770
GILBERT GLOBAL EQUITY PARTNERS, 827
GOOD NEWS VENTURES, 2138
HARBINGER VENTURE MANAGEMENT, 905
IDG TECHNOLOGY VENTURE INVESTMENT, 2848
JERUSALEM VENTURE PARTNERS, 2910
LIQUID CAPITAL GROUP, 1133
MADRONA VENTURE GROUP, 1158
MATRIX PARTNERS, 1181
MBF CAPITAL CORPORATION, 1188
MENLO VENTURES, 1202
MERCATOR INVESTMENTS, 2192
MILLENIUM TECHNOLOGY VALUE PARTNERS, 1235
MIRAMAR VENTURE PARTNERS, 1237
MONITOR VENTURES, 1249
MOTOROLA SOLUTIONS VENTURE CAPITAL, 1260
NEOTENY COMPANY LIMITED, 2991
NEW VENTURE PARTNERS, 1305
O'REILLY ALPHATECH VENTURES, 1359
PELION VENTURE PARTNERS, 1425
PENN VENTURE PARTNERS, 1428
PITANGO VENTURE CAPITAL, 3039
PROCYON VENTURES, 1483
SAND HILL ANGELS, 1613
SCALE VENTURE PARTNERS, 1626
SHEPHERD VENTURES, 1664
SIGNAL LAKE, 1676
SIGNAL PEAK VENTURES, 1677
SILICON ALLEY VENTURE PARTNERS, 1680
SINEWAVE VENTURES, 1687
SOFTBANK CAPITAL, 1699
SPACEVEST, 1714
STATELINE ANGELS, 1740
STORM VENTURES, 1747
SYCAMORE VENTURES, 1769
TELUS VENTURES, 2265
TI VENTURE CAPITAL Texas Instruments Incorporated, 1823
TIME WARNER INVESTMENT CORPORATION, 1827
TL VENTURES, 1828
VERITAS VENTURE PARTNERS, 3212
VERIZON VENTURES, 1926
WASHINGTON CAPITAL VENTURES, 1959
WESLEY CLOVER, 2284
WHEATLEY PARTNERS, 1981
WOODSIDE FUND, 2005
ZONE VENTURES, 2021

Networking & Equipment
ZM CAPITAL, 2020

Networks
CALUMET VENTURE FUND, 375
TAMAR TECHNOLOGY VENTURES LIMITED, 3158

Networks and Communities
BLOOMBERG BETA, 284

Industry Preference Index / Oil & Gas

Neural Networks
GVA CAPITAL, 890

Neurotechnology
TECHNOLOGY PARTNERS, 1786

New Age Media
G SQUARED, 802

New Energy
COTTONWOOD TECHNOLOGY FUND, 549
IDG CAPITAL PARTNERS, 2847
IDG TECHNOLOGY VENTURE INVESTMENT, 2848
RHO VENTURES, 1558

New Enterprise
CANVAS VENTURES, 396

New Materials
360 CAPITAL PARTNERS 360 Capital Management SA, 2296
CONOR VENTURE PARTNERS OY, 2630
CREATHOR VENTURE, 2638
ECAPITAL ENTREPRENEURIAL PARTNERS AG, 2686
QBIC FUND, 3065
QUANTUM WAVE FUND, 3068
QUEST FOR GROWTH, 3069
SB CHINA VENTURE CAPITAL, 3100
SPINUP VENTURE, 3132
TROIKA CAPITAL PARTNERS, 3193

New Media
3W VENTURES Latour & Zuberbuhler GmbH, 2310
ABRT VENTURE FUND, 2320
ACCESS VENTURE PARTNERS LLC, 36
ACKERLEY PARTNERS LLC, 43
AMPLIFIER VENTURE PARTNERS, 119
ANGELAB VENTURES, 2401
ANTHEM VENTURE PARTNERS, 132
ARTIS VENTURES, 175
AUSTIN VENTURES, 202
AVANSIS VENTURES, 207
BIG SUR VENTURES, 2510
BIGFOOT VENTURES, 2511
CORIOLIS VENTURES, 539
GENERAL CATALYST PARTNERS, 816
IDG CAPITAL, 973
IDG CAPITAL PARTNERS, 2847
KNIGHT'S BRIDGE CAPITAL PARTNERS, 2171
LAUNCHBOX DIGITAL, 1096
NEW ATLANTIC VENTURES, 1291
NIELSEN INNOVATE FUND, 3003
ONSET VENTURES, 1378
OUTCOME CAPITAL, 1388
OneVentures, 3023
POND VENTURES, 3047
REED ELSEVIER VENTURES, 3074
REMBRANDT VENTURE PARTNERS, 1540
RHO CANADA VENTURES, 2239
RHO VENTURES, 1558
VERDEXUS, 2279
WESTSUMMIT CAPITAL, 3235

New Organizational Models
BLOOMBERG BETA, 284

New Service Models
RUBICON VENTURE CAPITAL, 1595

New Technology
ARCHTOP VENTURES, 154

New Therapeutics & Platforms
NOVARTIS VENTURE FUNDS, 1350

Next Generation Computing
ENTREPIA VENTURES, 682

Next Generation Materials
IGLOBE PARTNERS, 2853

Next Generation Software
.406 VENTURES, 2

Niche Manufacturing
AUDAX GROUP, 194
BBH CAPITAL PARTNERS, 240
CELERITY PARTNERS, 439
CHB CAPITAL PARTNERS, 461
FCF PARTNERS LP, 719
FIVE POINTS CAPITAL, 746
GEORGIA OAK PARTNERS, 821
GOLDNER, HAWN, JOHNSON & MORRISON, 843
HIGH STREET CAPITAL, 932
JH WHITNEY & COMPANY, 1037
JMH CAPITAL, 1040
LIBERTY PARTNERS, 1116
LINCOLNSHIRE MANAGEMENT, 1127
MAIN STREET CAPITAL HOLDINGS LLC, 1159
MIDOCEAN PARTNERS, 1231
MONUMENT ADVISORS, 1252
MPG EQUITY PARTNERS, 1267
MVP CAPITAL PARTNERS, 1275
NEW CAPITAL FUND, 1292
PALOMINO CAPITAL, 1408
PRAIRIE CAPITAL, 1469
PRIVEQ CAPITAL FUNDS, 2226
RIDGE CAPITAL PARTNERS LLC, 1562
STONEBRIDGE PARTNERS, 1744
SUMMER STREET CAPITAL PARTNERS, 1751
TRIVEST PARTNERS, 1857
TVV CAPITAL, 1870
WYNNCHURCH CAPITAL, 2009

Non-profit & Public Authorities
TPA CORPORATE FINANCE CONSULTING GMBH Horwarth International, 3184

Nontechnology
INFIELD CAPITAL, 988

Nutraceuticals
FARM CREDIT CANADA, 2114
MOUNTAIN GROUP CAPITAL, 1261

Nutrition
BAY CITY CAPITAL LLC, 237
BIOGENERATOR, 267
BIOPACIFIC VENTURES, 2516
BOULDER VENTURES LTD, 315
NORTH CASTLE PARTNERS, 1335

O2O
ZHENFUND, 3251

Office Imaging & Technology
CIT GROUP, 484

Oil & Gas
32 DEGREES CAPITAL, 2025
3I ASIA PACIFIC 3i Group, 2297
AEM CAPITAL, 2349
AIP PRIVATE CAPITAL, 2031
ALFA CAPITAL Alfa Group, 2363
ALTIRA GROUP LLC, 98
AMANET TECHNOLOGIES LIMITED, 2389
ANNAPOLIS CAPITAL, 2038
APECTEC, 2039
ARC FINANCIAL, 2040
ARCLIGHT CAPITAL PARTNERS, 156
ASTOR CAPITAL GROUP, 2440
AZIMUTH CAPITAL MANAGEMENT, 2050
BARING VOSTOK CAPITAL PARTNERS, 2491
BASF VENTURE CAPITAL, 2492
BLAST FUNDING, 279

Industry Preference Index / Oilfield Services

BOND CAPITAL, 2064
BRANFORD CASTLE, 327
CHENGWEI VENTURES, 2590
CHEVRON TECHNOLOGY VENTURES, 466
CHRYSALIX, 2078
CIBC CAPITAL MARKETS, 2079
CNF INVESTMENTS Clark Enterprises, Inc., 508
COLT VENTURES, 514
CONVEXA Tyveholmen AS, 2632
CROSBY ASSET MANAGEMENT, 2640
ENCAP FLATROCK MIDSTREAM, 671
ENCAP INVESTMENTS LP, 672
ENERGY VENTURES, 2700
EQUISTONE, 2714
ESCHELON ENERGY PARTNERS, 696
FIRST RESERVE, 740
FOX PAINE & COMPANY LLC, 778
HUNT INVESTMENT GROUP, 957
IBM VENTURE CAPITAL GROUP, 967
INDASIA FUND ADVISORS PVT LTD, 2859
INTERNATIONAL FINANCE CORPORATION (IFC), 1007
INTERVALE CAPITAL, 1009
JOG CAPITAL, 2166
KALORI GROUP INVESTMENTS, 2915
KESTREL ENERGY PARTNERS, 1068
LEX CAPITAL MANAGEMENT, 2173
LIME ROCK PARTNERS, 1125
LIONHART CAPITAL LTD, 2177
LONGBOW CAPITAL, 2178
MANULIFE CAPITAL, 2183
MCROCK CAPITAL, 2190
MERIT ENERGY COMPANY, 1210
NATURAL GAS PARTNERS, 1278
NGP, 1326
PALMS & COMPANY, 1404
PRIVITI CAPITAL, 2227
RBC CAPITAL MARKETS, 2231
RFC AMBRIAN RFC Group Ltd., 3079
RIDGEWOOD CAPITAL, 1564
SAUDI ARAMCO ENERGY VENTURES, 3099
SOURCE CAPITAL GROUP, 1707
STATOIL TECHNOLOGY INVEST, 3141
VIKING VENTURE, 3216
WESTERN AMERICA CAPITAL GROUP, 2286
WESTLAKE SECURITIES, 1976
XPV WATER PARTNERS, 2290

Oilfield Services
ARC FINANCIAL, 2040
LONGBOW CAPITAL, 2178

Oncology
SANOFI-GENZYME BIOVENTURES, 1618

Online Advertising
GENACAST VENTURES, 814
PROGRESS VENTURES, 1486
SPECTRUM EQUITY INVESTORS LP, 1717

Online Applications
SPARK CAPITAL, 1715

Online Consumer Services
EARLYBIRD, 2682

Online Content
ALEXANDER HUTTON, 82
ANTHEM VENTURE PARTNERS, 132
BATTERY VENTURES, 235
ID VENTURES AMERICA LLC, 970
PALO ALTO VENTURE PARTNERS, 1405

Online Education
MACMILLAN DIGITAL EDUCATION, 2950

Online Marketing
ARTS ALLIANCE, 2428

Online Marketplaces
MISTRAL VENTURE PARTNERS, 2195

Online Media
SALMON RIVER CAPITAL, 1608

Online Publishing
TRUE VENTURES, 1860

Online Services
NEW ATLANTIC VENTURES, 1291

Online To Offline Offerings
DECIENS CAPITAL, 599

Online Video
500 STARTUPS, 11

Open Source
.406 VENTURES, 2
AZURE CAPITAL PARTNERS, 215
SUNBRIDGE PARTNERS, 1755

Optical
HARDY CAPITAL PARTNERS, 2144
PAC-LINK MANAGEMENT CORP., 3024

Optical Networks and Components
TAMAR TECHNOLOGY VENTURES LIMITED, 3158

Optical Technology
BANEXI VENTURES PARTNERS, 2481
BROOK VENTURE FUND, 349
CORE CAPITAL PARTNERS, 538
DEFTA PARTNERS, 602
ELECTRA PARTNERS ASIA LIMITED SFC of Hong Kong, 2694
GILBERT GLOBAL EQUITY PARTNERS, 827
GUANGDONG TECHNOLOGY VENTURE CAPITAL COMPANY, 2802
JC TECHNOLOGIES LTD, 2909
NOVAK BIDDLE VENTURE PARTNERS, 1348
SCALE VENTURE PARTNERS, 1626
SCOTTISH ENTERPRISE, 3103
SI VENTURES, 1668
SPACEVEST, 1714
SPENCER TRASK VENTURES, 1720
WI HARPER GROUP, 1983

Optics
CONOR VENTURE PARTNERS OY, 2630
CRAWLEY VENTURES, 553

Optics & Photonics
ARCH VENTURE PARTNERS, 153

Other Energy Related Assets
ENERGY CAPITAL PARTNERS, 675

Outsourced Solutions
HALYARD CAPITAL, 897

Outsourcing & Efficiency
ARGENTUM GROUP, 161
ARLINGTON CAPITAL PARTNERS, 166
BRERA CAPITAL PARTNERS, 335
BRYAN GARNIER & COMPANY, 2544
BUSINESS GROWTH FUND, 2550
CELERITY PARTNERS, 439
CHRYSALIS CAPITAL ChrysCapital, 2599
CHRYSCAPITAL MANAGEMENT COMPANIES ChrysCapital, 2600
COMSTOCK CAPITAL PARTNERS LLC, 527
DUKE STREET CAPITAL Duke Street, 2676
ECI VENTURES, 2687
ELECTRA PARTNERS ASIA LIMITED SFC of Hong Kong, 2694
FCF PARTNERS LP, 719
FIRST ANALYSIS, 732
FIVE ELMS CAPITAL, 745
FOUNDERS EQUITY, 774

Industry Preference Index / Pharmaceuticals

GENERAL ATLANTIC PARTNERS, 2771
GENERATION PARTNERS, 818
HAMILTON ROBINSON CAPITAL PARTNERS, 899
HELION VENTURE PARTNERS, LLC International Management (Mauritius) Ltd, 2818
HIGH STREET CAPITAL, 932
MTS HEALTH INVESTORS, 1271
NTH POWER TECHNOLOGIES, 1355
OAK INVESTMENT PARTNERS, 1361
ODEON CAPITAL PARTNERS, 1367
RITTENHOUSE VENTURES, 1568
ROSEWOOD CAPITAL, 1587
RU-NET VENTURES, 3087
SENTRY FINANCIAL CORPORATION, 1652
SEQUOIA CAPITAL, 1654
TEXADA CAPITAL CORPORATION, 1799
TGF MANAGEMENT, 1803
UPDATA VENTURE PARTNERS, 1886
WATERLAND PRIVATE EQUITY INVESTMENT, 3232

Packaging
ALTRIA VENTURES, 102
AMERICA FIRST INVESTMENT ADVISORS, 108
AMERICAN SECURITIES LLC, 110
APOLLO GLOBAL MANAGEMENT, 140
ARROWHEAD INVESTMENT MANAGEMENT, 168
ASHBRIDGE PARTNERS, 2045
CAMBRIDGE CAPITAL, 380
CVC INVESTMENT MANAGERS LIMITED, 2645
DEUTSCHE BETEILIGUNGS AG, 2660
ELECTRA PARTNERS ASIA LIMITED SFC of Hong Kong, 2694
FCF PARTNERS LP, 719
GEORGIA OAK PARTNERS, 821
GLENTHORNE CAPITAL, 832
GRAHAM PARTNERS, 846
HORIZON PARTNERS, LTD, 945
IRVING PLACE CAPITAL, 1022
JAVELIN INVESTMENTS, 2908
JORDAN COMPANY, 1045
MASON WELLS, 1171
MERITURN PARTNERS, 1213
PENDER WEST CAPITAL PARTNERS, 2218
PROSPECT PARTNERS LLC, 1492
RESILIENCE CAPITAL PARTNERS, 1545

Paper
AMERICAN SECURITIES LLC, 110
CERBERUS CAPITAL MANAGEMENT, 451
FCF PARTNERS LP, 719
MERITURN PARTNERS, 1213
SRIW SA SRIW Group, 3134

Parenting
CANTOS VENTURES, 395

Patient Safety
HEALTH ENTERPRISE PARTNERS, 918

Payment Services
ASHBY POINT CAPITAL, 179

Payments & Financial Services
500 STARTUPS, 11
CHICAGO VENTURES, 471
INFORMATION VENTURE PARTNERS, 2153
MISSIONOG, 1240

Pensions
ARGOS SODITIC SA, 2423
DFC LTD, 2661

Peripherals
STATELINE ANGELS, 1740

Personal Care
ASHBRIDGE PARTNERS, 2045

Personal Finance
PORTAG3 VENTURES, 2225

Pet Products
HERITAGE PARTNERS, 926

Petrochemicals
GRYPHON MANAGEMENT COMPANY, 882
JAVELIN INVESTMENTS, 2908
MEZZANINE MANAGEMENT LIMITED Mezzanine Management UK Ltd., 2965

Pharma Data
HEALTH ENTERPRISE PARTNERS, 918

Pharmaceutical Services
PFIZER VENTURE INVESTMENTS, 1436

Pharmaceuticals
3TS CAPITAL PARTNERS 3i Group plc, 2309
ACRUX LIMITED, 2335
ACTIVA CAPITAL, 2338
ALBERTA ENTERPRISE, 2032
ALFA CAPITAL Alfa Group, 2363
ALTARIS CAPITAL PARTNERS, 97
AMANAH VENTURES SDN BHD, 2388
AMANET TECHNOLOGIES LIMITED, 2389
AMGEN VENTURES, 112
AMKEY VENTURES, 117
AMPERSAND CAPITAL PARTNERS, 118
AMPHION CAPITAL PARTNERS, 2397
ANDLINGER & COMPANY INC, 123
ANTHEM VENTURE PARTNERS, 132
APJOHN GROUP LLC, 139
APPLE TREE PARTNERS, 143
ARBORETUM VENTURES, 149
ARCH VENTURE PARTNERS, 153
ASCLEPIOS BIORESEARCH, 2433
ASTELLAS VENTURE MANAGEMENT, 182
ATHENAEUM FUND, 186
ATHYRIUM CAPITAL MANAGEMENT, 188
AVALON VENTURES, 206
AZCA, 214
BAXTER VENTURES, 236
BAY CITY CAPITAL LLC, 237
BIOMED PARTNERS, 2515
BIOPACIFIC VENTURES, 2516
BIOPROCESS CAPITAL PARTNERS, 2517
BIOVEDA CAPITAL, 2518
BLACKSTONE PRIVATE EQUITY GROUP, 277
BOEHRINGER INGELHEIM VENTURE FUND, 2530
CARDINAL EQUITY PARTNERS, 409
CARE CAPITAL, 412
CATO BIOVENTURES, 430
CHL MEDICAL PARTNERS, 474
CIBC CAPITAL MARKETS, 2079
CITA GESTION, 2607
CLIFFORD CHANCE PUNDER, 2614
COLLABORATIVE FUND, 511
COLUMN GROUP, 517
DOMAIN ASSOCIATES LLC, 621
EDGEWATER CAPITAL PARTNERS, 653
EDISON PARTNERS, 655
EMBARK HEALTHCARE, 662
ESSEX WOODLANDS HEALTH VENTURES LLC, 697
FERRANTI LIMITED, 2732
FIRST ANALYSIS, 732
FLAGSHIP PIONEERING, 747
FORWARD VENTURES, 769
GALEN PARTNERS, 806
GLOBAL LIFE SCIENCE VENTURES GmbH, 2785
GREAT POINT PARTNERS, 859
HBM PARTNERS, 2815
HEALTHCAP, 2816
HEALTHCAP Odlander, Fredrikson & Co AB, 2816
INCUBE VENTURES, 980
INDASIA FUND ADVISORS PVT LTD, 2859

Industry Preference Index / Photonics

INDUSTRY VENTURES, 986
INETWORKS ADVISORS LLC, 987
INTERSOUTH PARTNERS, 1008
INVESTMENT FUND FOR CENTRAL & EASTERN EUROPE, 2889
IP GROUP, 2892
JK&B CAPITAL, 1038
JOHNSON & JOHNSON INNOVATION, 1043
JOHNSTON ASSOCIATES, 1044
JW ASSET MANAGEMENT, 1048
KEARNY VENTURE PARTNERS, 1059
KEGONSA CAPITAL PARTNERS, 1060
KODIAK CAPITAL, 1079
LATTERELL VENTURE PARTNERS, 1094
LILLY VENTURES, 1124
LINK TECHNOLOGIES LIMITED, 2941
LONGITUDE CAPITAL, 1143
LONGWOOD FUND, 1145
LRM - INVESTERINGSMAATSCHAPPIJ VOOR LIMBURG, 2949
LUMIRA CAPITAL, 2180
MANHATTAN INVESTMENT PARTNERS, 1163
MMT MILLENNIUM MATERIALS TECHNOLOGIES FUND LP, 2973
MPM CAPITAL, 1268
NEW SCIENCE VENTURES, 1303
NEWSPRING CAPITAL, 1317
NOMURA PHASE4 VENTURES LTD, 3007
PAI MANAGEMENT, 3026
PALMS & COMPANY, 1404
PARTNERS HEALTHCARE RESEARCH VENTURES, 1419
PRIVATE EQUITY PARTNERS SPA, 3053
PROGRESS EQUITY PARTNERS, 1484
PTV SCIENCES, 1500
RITTENHOUSE VENTURES, 1568
ROUNDTABLE HEALTHCARE PARTNERS, 1590
SAMBRINVEST SA, 3096
SAND HILL ANGELS, 1613
SANDERLING VENTURES, 1616
SCHRODER VENTURES HEALTH INVESTORS, 1628
SCP PARTNERS, 1633
SOFINNOVA VENTURES, 1698
SPINDLETOP CAPITAL, 1722
TAKEDA VENTURES, 1778
THE CHANNEL GROUP, 1808
THOMAS, MCNERNEY & PARTNERS, 1817
TPA CORPORATE FINANCE CONSULTING GMBH Horwarth International, 3184
TRANSITION PARTNERS LTD, 1837
TULLIS HEALTH INVESTORS, 1866
TWIN CITIES ANGELS, 1872
VALLEY VENTURES LP, 1901
VERSANT VENTURES, 1928
WATER STREET HEALTHCARE PARTNERS, 1961
WESTERN NIS ENTERPRISE FUND, 3234

Photonics
CONNECTICUT INNOVATIONS, 530
LDV CAPITAL, 1101
MURPHREE VENTURE PARTNERS, 1273
NEUHAUS PARTNERS, 2994
TECH CAPITAL PARTNERS, 2262

Physical Sciences
CASE TECHNOLOGY VENTURES Case Western Reserve University, 420
GENERICS GROUP LIMITED Generics Group, 2773
GUANGDONG TECHNOLOGY VENTURE CAPITAL COMPANY, 2802
ILLINOIS VENTURES, 975
QUANTUM WAVE FUND, 3068

Plastics
BASF VENTURE CAPITAL, 2492
BROOKSIDE EQUITY PARTNERS LLC, 353
C3 CAPITAL PARTNERS LP, 364
CAPITAL FOR BUSINESS, INC, 399
DESCO CAPITAL, 606
EMIGRANT CAPITAL, 667
FIRST ATLANTIC CAPITAL LTD., 733
FIRST ISRAEL MEZZANINE INVESTORS LIMITED, 2745
GRAHAM PARTNERS, 846

HORIZON PARTNERS, LTD, 945
LEONIA MB GROUP/MB FUNDS, 2937
LINSALATA CAPITAL PARTNERS, 1132
LITTLEJOHN & COMPANY LLC, 1134
MCG CAPITAL CORPORATION, 1189
PHOSPHAGENICS, 3037
RESILIENCE CAPITAL PARTNERS, 1545
SPELL CAPITAL PARTNERS LLC, 1719
TGAP VENTURES, 1802
VENTURE ASSOCIATES PARTNERS LLC, 1919

Platform As A Service
SPEKTRA CAPITAL, 1718

Pollution
HT CAPITAL ADVISORS LLC, 953
INDUSTRIEBANK LIOF NV, 2866
NGEN PARTNERS, 1324
VAEKSTFONDEN, 3203
VENTANA CAPITAL MANAGEMENT LP, 1918

Power
AMERICAN SECURITIES LLC, 110
CANADIAN VENTURE CAPITAL ASSOCIATION Canadian Venture Capital & Private Equity Association, 3258
CARLYLE GROUP, 413
CIBC CAPITAL MARKETS, 2079
CLIMATE CHANGE CAPITAL, 2615
ISRAEL CLEANTECH VENTURES, 2900
KOHLBERG VENTURES, 1083
MCROCK CAPITAL, 2190
NORTH COVE PARTNERS, 1337
OXANTIUM VENTURES, 1393

Power Generation
ARC FINANCIAL, 2040
ENERGY CAPITAL PARTNERS, 675
HCI EQUITY PARTNERS, 917
US RENEWABLES GROUP, 1895

Power Infrastructure
ANGELENO GROUP, 126

Power Management
TI VENTURE CAPITAL Texas Instruments Incorporated, 1823

Power Storage
HADDINGTON VENTURES LLC, 893

Power Technologies
ACCESS CAPITAL CORPORATION, 2030
ALTIRA GROUP LLC, 98
ARCLIGHT CAPITAL PARTNERS, 156
BLUEFISH VENTURES, 294
CHEUNG KONG INFRASTRUCTURE HOLDINGS LIMITED, 2591
CHEVRON TECHNOLOGY VENTURES, 466
EMP GLOBAL, 670
NEW MOUNTAIN CAPITAL, 1301
NTH POWER TECHNOLOGIES, 1355
WYNNCHURCH CAPITAL, 2009

Predictive Medicine Technology
FLARE CAPITAL PARTNERS, 748

Premium Consumer Products
SJF VENTURES, 1689

Preventative Health and Services
SINEWAVE VENTURES, 1687

Prevention
JOHNSON & JOHNSON INNOVATION, 1043

Printing
ACCESS CAPITAL, 35
AVIV VENTURE CAPITAL, 2462
DEUTSCHE BETEILIGUNGS AG, 2660

IGNITE JAPAN KK Ignite Group, 2854
MASON WELLS, 1171
MAYFLY CAPITAL, 1185
QUADRAN GESTION Deutsche Beteiligungs AG, 3067
SAMBRINVEST SA, 3096
SRIW SA SRIW Group, 3134
UNION CAPITAL CORPORATION, 1881
XANGE PRIVATE EQUITY, 3239

Private Education
BOND CAPITAL, 2064

Private Equity
3I AUSTRIA BETEILGUNG GmbH 3i Group, 2298
747 CAPITAL, 14
BROOKFIELD ASSET MANAGEMENT, 2067
BUTZOW NORDIA ADVOCATES LTD, 2552
CHINA VEST LIMITED, 2596
COHEN PRIVATE VENTURES, 510
GRESHAM PRIVATE EQUITY LIMITED, 2799

Process Controls
DESCO CAPITAL, 606

Processing
DFC LTD, 2661
DIRECT CAPITAL PRIVATE EQUITY LIMITED, 2664
ELECTRA PARTNERS ASIA LIMITED SFC of Hong Kong, 2694
EUROVENTURES CAPITAL, 2725
ICV PARTNERS, 969
INDUSTRI KAPITAL SVENSKA AB, 2863
INTER-ASIA VENTURE MANAGEMENT LIMITED, 2881
LEVINE LEICHTMAN CAPITAL PARTNERS, 1111
LITTLEJOHN & COMPANY LLC, 1134
LLR PARTNERS INC, 1136
MERITURN PARTNERS, 1213
NORTH DAKOTA DEVELOPMENT FUND, 1338

Productivity
M12, 1154

Products & Technology
CAPITAL RESOURCE PARTNERS, 402

Professional Services
MOBIUS VENTURE CAPITAL, 1245

Property Development
BOSTON CAPITAL, 309
GRESHAM PRIVATE EQUITY LIMITED, 2799

Property Management
AMANAH VENTURES SDN BHD, 2388
CHEROKEE INVESTMENT PARTNERS, 463
CONTINENTAL VENTURE CAPITAL LIMITED, 2631
COVENT INDUSTRIAL CAPITAL INVESTMENT COMPANY, 2635
ENTREPRENEUR CAPITAL, 2107
GRAPHITE CAPITAL MANAGEMENT LTD, 2796
PWC, 3064
REDWOOD CAPITAL GROUP, 1536
STARWOOD CAPITAL GROUP LLC, 1739
TECHNOLOGY PARK MALAYSIA CORPORATION SDN BHD, 3164

Property Transactions
BUTZOW NORDIA ADVOCATES LTD, 2552

Proprietary Industrial Products & Services
CAPITAL RESOURCE PARTNERS, 402

Proprietary Products
WARWICK GROUP, 1957

Pub Tech
BERTELSMANN DIGITAL MEDIA INVESTMENTS, 256

Public Health & Safety
URBAN US, 1894

Publishers
ENTREPRENEUR PARTNERS, 683

Publishing
ADOBE VENTURES LP, 58
AEP CAPITAL LLC, 65
ALLSTATE INVESTMENTS LLC, 88
APPIAN EDUCATION VENTURES, 141
ARCHTOP VENTURES, 154
ATRIUM CAPITAL, 192
BC PARTNERS LIMITED, 2497
BMP AKTIENGESELLSCHAFT BMP Venture Capital, 2528
BROOK VENTURE FUND, 349
BRUML CAPITAL CORPORATION, 355
BUTLER CAPITAL PARTNERS FRANCE, 2551
CARDINAL EQUITY PARTNERS, 409
CASTANEA PARTNERS, 421
DAVID N DEUTSCH & COMPANY LLC, 589
DOUBLE IMPACT BUSINESS ADVISORY, 2670
DUBILIER & COMPANY, 631
ECI VENTURES, 2687
GREENHAVEN PARTNERS, 863
HENDERSON PRIVATE CAPITAL, 2821
JEGI CAPITAL The Jordan Edminston Group, Inc., 1033
KERRY CAPITAL ADVISORS, 1067
MACQUARIE DIRECT INVESTMENT LIMITED, 2951
MEDIA VENTURE PARTNERS, 1195
MERITURN PARTNERS, 1213
MVP CAPITAL PARTNERS, 1275
NESBIC INVESTMENT FUND II, 2992
POST CAPITAL PARTNERS, 1465
QUOTIDIAN VENTURES, 1518
SARATOGA PARTNERS, 1621
SOUTHPORT PARTNERS, 1712
SRIW SA SRIW Group, 3134
TECHNOLOGY PARK MALAYSIA CORPORATION SDN BHD, 3164
THREE CITIES RESEARCH, 1820
TIME WARNER INVESTMENT CORPORATION, 1827
WESTON PRESIDIO, 1978
WESTVIEW CAPITAL PARTNERS, 1979
WICKS GROUP OF COMPANIES, LLC, 1984
ZM CAPITAL, 2020

Publishing & Printing
STERN PARTNERS, 2258

Quantum
DAY ONE VENTURES, 593

Quantum Computing
FUTURE VENTURES, 800

Radio
ALLSTATE INVESTMENTS LLC, 88
BREAKWATER MANAGEMENT, 331
GRUPO BISA, 2800
LEVINE LEICHTMAN CAPITAL PARTNERS, 1111
MEDIA VENTURE PARTNERS, 1195
TIME WARNER INVESTMENT CORPORATION, 1827
VENTURE CAPITAL FUND OF NEW ENGLAND, 1920
WICKS GROUP OF COMPANIES, LLC, 1984

Rail
CIT GROUP, 484

Rail Transportation
COPPERLION CAPITAL, 2085

Railroad Services
SEIDLER EQUITY PARTNERS, 1645

Reagent Suppliers
TELEGRAPH HILL PARTNERS, 1792
THE CHANNEL GROUP, 1808

Real Estate
ACACIA CAPITAL, 25

Industry Preference Index / Real Estate Rehabilitation

ACCESS BRIDGE-GAP VENTURES, 34
ACKRELL CAPITAL, 44
ALBERTA INVESTMENT MANAGEMENT CORP., 2033
ASTOR CAPITAL GROUP, 2440
ATLANTIC CAPITAL GROUP, 190
AVENUE CAPITAL GROUP, 208
BARING PRIVATE EQUITY PARTNERS INDIA, 2490
BAYSHORE CAPITAL, 2052
BERGGRUEN HOLDINGS, 250
BLUE SKY CAPITAL, 292
BLUESTEM CAPITAL COMPANY, 297
BOCI DIRECT INVESTMENT MANAGEMENT LIMITED Bank of China, 2529
BOSTON CAPITAL, 309
BROOKFIELD ASSET MANAGEMENT, 2067
CAMBER CREEK, 377
CANTOS VENTURES, 395
CAPMAN CAPITAL MANAGEMENT OY, 2562
CARLYLE ASIA INVESTMENT ADVISORS LIMITED Carlyle Group, 2565
CATALYST FUND LP, 2571
CERBERUS CAPITAL MANAGEMENT, 451
CHALLENGE FUNDS - ETGAR LP, 2585
CHELSFIELD PARTNERS, 2589
CHEROKEE INVESTMENT PARTNERS, 463
CHINA MERCHANTS CHINA INVESTMENT MANAGEMENT, 2595
CIBC CAPITAL MARKETS, 2079
CLARITAS CAPITAL, 493
COHEN PRIVATE VENTURES, 510
CORDOVA VENTURES, 537
COVENT INDUSTRIAL CAPITAL INVESTMENT COMPANY, 2635
CREDIT SUISSE PRIVATE EQUITY Credit Suisse Group, 554
DAVID N DEUTSCH & COMPANY LLC, 589
ELGNER GROUP INVESTMENTS, 2104
EM WARBURG, PINCUS & COMPANY INTERNATIONAL, 2697
EM WARBURG, PINCUS & COMPANY JAPAN, 2698
ENTREE CAPITAL, 2709
ENTREPRENEURS ROUNDTABLE ACCELERATOR, 684
FGA PARTNERS, 725
FIFTH WALL, 727
FULL CIRCLE INVESTMENTS, 2762
GE CAPITAL, 808
GENERAL ENTERPRISE MANAGEMENT SERVICES, 2772
GLOBALIVE, 2134
GOAL HOLDINGS, 2135
GREIF & COMPANY, 869
H KATZ CAPITAL GROUP, 891
HARDY CAPITAL PARTNERS, 2144
HQ CAPITAL, 952
HUNT INVESTMENT GROUP, 957
INITIO GROUP, 992
INVICO CAPITAL CORPORATION, 2162
IRON GATE CAPITAL, 1020
KB PARTNERS, 1056
KEIRETSU FORUM, 1061
LEVINE LEICHTMAN CAPITAL PARTNERS, 1111
LRM - INVESTERINGSMAATSCHAPPIJ VOOR LIMBURG, 2949
MANHATTAN INVESTMENT PARTNERS, 1163
MANULIFE CAPITAL, 2183
MID-ATLANTIC VENTURE FUNDS, 1227
MITSUI SUMITOMO INSURANCE VENTURE CAPITAL CO, 2971
NEWFIELD CAPITAL, 1313
PLAZA VENTURES, 2224
PMV, 3042
QUILVEST PRIVATE EQUITY, 1516
REDWOOD CAPITAL GROUP, 1536
REEFI CAPITAL, 1537
REITEN & CO STRATEGIC INVESTMENTS AS Reiten & Company, 3076
RICHINA CAPITAL PARTNERS LIMITED, 3082
ROBIN HOOD VENTURES, 1577
SCULPTOR CAPITAL MANAGEMENT, 1635
SEAWAY VALLEY CAPITAL CORPORATION, 1639
SECOND CENTURY VENTURES, 1642
SERGE PUN & ASSOCIATES (MYANMAR) LIMITED, 3111
SILKROAD EQUITY, 1681
SONY EUROPE, 3129
STARBOARD CAPITAL PARTNERS, 1735
STARWOOD CAPITAL GROUP LLC, 1739
THOMPROPERTIES OY, 3175
TPA CORPORATE FINANCE CONSULTING GMBH Horwarth International, 3184
UNISON CAPITAL PARTNERS LP, 3201
URBAN US, 1894
VARDE PARTNERS, 1907
VENTURE INVESTORS, 3210
VICKERS FINANCIAL GROUP, 3215
VINACAPITAL GROUP, 3217
WALNUT GROUP, 1954
WELLS FARGO CAPITAL FINANCE, 1970
WESLEY CLOVER, 2284

Real Estate Rehabilitation
ENHANCED CAPITAL, 678

Real Estate Technology
ALBUM VC, 79
TACTICO, 2260

Real-Time Data
.406 VENTURES, 2

Reconfigurable Processors
SONY STRATEGIC TECHNOLOGY PARTNERSHIPS, 1704

Recreation
URBAN INNOVATION FUND, 1893

Recreational Vehicles
CARDINAL EQUITY PARTNERS, 409

Recycling
ALTRIA VENTURES, 102
AUSTRALIAN ETHICAL INVESTMENT LIMITED, 2456
AUTO TECH VENTURES, 204
CAMBRIDGE CAPITAL, 380
PENDER WEST CAPITAL PARTNERS, 2218
WHEB GROUP, 3237

Recycling Systems
AZCA, 214

Renewable Energy
ACCERA AG, 2327
ALPHAMUNDI GROUP LTD, 2376
ALTIRA GROUP LLC, 98
AMBIENTA ENVIRONMENTAL ASSETS, 2391
ANGELENO GROUP, 126
ARAVAIPA VENTURES, 146
ARAVIS VENTURES, 2419
BERTI INVESTMENTS, 2505
BP ALTERNATIVE ENERGY VENTURES, 319
BREGAL ENERGY, 332
BRIGHT CAPITAL, 2540
BUSINESS GROWTH FUND, 2550
CALCEF CLEAN ENERGY FUND, 367
CAPITAL E, 398
CASABONA VENTURES, 418
CHORD CAPITAL, 2598
CLARENDON FUND MANAGERS, 2610
CLEAN PACIFIC VENTURES, 498
CLEANPATH VENTURES, 499
CM CAPITAL, 2618
CONNECTICUT INNOVATIONS, 530
CONTINENTAL VENTURE CAPITAL LIMITED, 2631
CYCLE CAPITAL MANAGEMENT, 2093
DAVENPORT RESOURCES LLC, 588
DEMETER PARTNERS, 2656
EARTHRISE CAPITAL, 643
ENHANCED CAPITAL, 678
FIRST RESERVE, 740
FSE GROUP, 2760
GLOBAL ENVIRONMENT FUND, 834
HERCULES TECHNOLOGY GROWTH CAPITAL, INC, 925

Industry Preference Index / Retail, Consumer & Leisure

HG CAPITAL, 2823
INVESTECO, 2161
IP GROUP, 2892
LLOYDS DEVELOPMENT CAPITAL LIMITED, 2944
MEDRA CAPITAL, 2960
MINDFULL INVESTORS, 1236
OMNES CAPITAL, 3020
PMV, 3042
PROSEED, 3059
RENEWABLETECH VENTURES, 1542
RIDGEWOOD CAPITAL, 1564
RIVERSTONE, 1573
SABIC VENTURES, 3091
SAUDI ARAMCO ENERGY VENTURES, 3099
SPRING LANE CAPITAL, 1729
TEL VENTURE CAPITAL, 1791
TSING CAPITAL, 3194
URBAN INNOVATION FUND, 1893
US RENEWABLES GROUP, 1895
WHEB GROUP, 3237
ZOUK VENTURES, 3252

Renewable Energy & Environment
BRYAN GARNIER & COMPANY, 2544

Renewable Infrastructure
ZOUK VENTURES, 3252

Renewable Power
BROOKFIELD ASSET MANAGEMENT, 2067
PARKWALK ADVISORS, 3028

Renewable Resources
AGRIBUSINESS MANAGEMENT COMPANY, 71
COLORADO MILE HIGH FUND, 513
MARWIT CAPITAL LLC, 1168

Research
CANNA ANGELS LLC, 388
NCT VENTURES, 1286

Research & Development
AWAY REALTY, 2465
CHEROKEE INVESTMENT PARTNERS, 463
INVESTMENT FUND FOR CENTRAL & EASTERN EUROPE, 2889
LATTERELL VENTURE PARTNERS, 1094
OXFORD BIOSCIENCE PARTNERS, 1394
VENTANA CAPITAL MANAGEMENT LP, 1918

Research Provider
CHINA VEST LIMITED, 2596

Research Services
BIOGENERATOR, 267

Research Tools
BIOADVANCE, 266
BIOGENERATOR, 267

Resource Efficiency
ROCKPORT CAPITAL, 1579
WELLINGTON PARTNERS VENTURE CAPITAL GmbH, 3233
ZOUK VENTURES, 3252

Resource Productivity Technologies
INVESTECO, 2161

Resource Services
SIGNAL HILL EQUITY PARTNERS, 2255

Resource Use & Efficiency
ARCTERN VENTURES, 2041

Resources
WESTCAP, 2285

Restaurants
AMERICAN SECURITIES LLC, 110
AMHERST FUND, 113
BRANFORD CASTLE, 327
BRUCKMANN, ROSSER, SHERRILL & COMPANY, 354
CARPEDIA CAPITAL, 2072
CIC PARTNERS, 477
CIT GROUP, 484
CLIFFORD CHANCE PUNDER, 2614
CLYDESDALE VENTURES, 506
FAIRMONT CAPITAL, 713
FREEMAN SPOGLI & CO., 783
GEORGIA OAK PARTNERS, 821
GOLDEN GATE CAPITAL, 839
GOLUB CAPITAL, 844
HARREN EQUITY PARTNERS, 910
JAFCO COMPANY LIMITED JAPAN, 2906
JEFFERIES CAPITAL PARTNERS, 1032
L CATTERTON PARTNERS, 1088
MADISON PARKER CAPITAL, 1157
POUSCHINE COOK CAPITAL MANAGEMENT LLC, 1466
RBC CAPITAL MARKETS, 2231
RETAIL & RESTAURANT GROWTH CAPITAL LP, 1549
ROBIN HOOD VENTURES, 1577
ROSEWOOD CAPITAL, 1587
SEAWAY VALLEY CAPITAL CORPORATION, 1639
SUN CAPITAL PARTNERS, 1753
SWAN & LEGEND VENTURES, 1766
THAYER VENTURES, 1806
TSG CONSUMER PARTNERS, 1861
WALNUT GROUP, 1954
WELLS FARGO CAPITAL FINANCE, 1970

Restructuring
BUTZOW NORDIA ADVOCATES LTD, 2552

Retail
645 VENTURES, 13
ACREW CAPITAL, 49
BRAND FOUNDRY VENTURES, 325
BROOKE PRIVATE EQUITY ASSOCIATES, 350
FIFTH WALL, 727
GROUND UP VENTURES, 877
IBM VENTURE CAPITAL GROUP, 967
INTERLACE VENTURES, 1006
LDV CAPITAL, 1101
NFX, 1323
RIVERSIDE COMPANY, 1572
SERRUYA PRIVATE EQUITY, 2254
STERN PARTNERS, 2258

Retail Services
SWAN & LEGEND VENTURES, 1766

Retail, Consumer & Leisure
3TS CAPITAL PARTNERS 3i Group plc, 2309
AAVIN PRIVATE EQUITY, 17
ACON INVESTMENTS, 46
ADVENT INTERNATIONAL CORPORATION, 62
ALANTRA, 77
ALBUM VC, 79
ALPINE INVESTORS, 92
AMICUS CAPITAL PARTNERS, 2392
AMMER PARTNERS, 2393
APAX PARTNERS ET CIE, 2415
APOLLO GLOBAL MANAGEMENT, 140
ASTOR CAPITAL GROUP, 2440
AVANTI CAPITAL, 2458
BALLPARK VENTURES, 2479
BALMORAL FUNDS, 225
BENCIS CAPITAL PARTNERS, 2501
BLACKSTONE PRIVATE EQUITY GROUP, 277
BLUEGEM CAPITAL PARTNERS, 2524
BLUESTEM CAPITAL COMPANY, 297
BREAKAWAY VENTURES, 329
BUSINESS GROWTH FUND, 2550
CAMBRIA GROUP, 378

1223

Industry Preference Index / Retail, Restaurants & Distribution

CAPITAL TODAY, 2560
CARLYLE GROUP, 413
CIC PARTNERS, 477
CIT GROUP, 484
DENALI VENTURE PARTNERS, 605
GRANITE HILL CAPITAL PARTNERS, LLC, 851
HOLDING CAPITAL GROUP, 940
INDEX VENTURES, 2860
IRON GATE CAPITAL, 1020
IRVING PLACE CAPITAL, 1022
J. BURKE CAPITAL PARTNERS, 1023
KALORI GROUP INVESTMENTS, 2915
KOHLBERG KRAVIS ROBERTS & COMPANY, 1082
KRG CAPITAL PARTNERS, 1086
LEE EQUITY PARTNERS, 1104
LEONARD GREEN & PARTNERS LP, 1109
LINLEY CAPITAL, 1130
MAINE ANGELS, 1160
MARWIT CAPITAL LLC, 1168
NAXURI CAPITAL, 1284
NEXTEC DEVELOPMENT CAPITAL LIMITED, 3000
PALLADIUM EQUITY PARTNERS, 1403
POUSCHINE COOK CAPITAL MANAGEMENT LLC, 1466
QIMING VENTURE PARTNERS, 3066
RBC CAPITAL MARKETS, 2231
ROSEWOOD CAPITAL, 1587
SAINTS CAPITAL, 1604
SIGNAL FIRE, 1675
TECH COAST ANGELS, 1784
TH LEE PUTNAM VENTURES, 1804
TULLY & HOLLAND, 1867
VEDANTA CAPITAL LP, 1911
WALNUT GROUP, 1954
WESTVIEW CAPITAL PARTNERS, 1979
YFM GROUP, 3244

Retail, Restaurants & Distribution
CALIFORNIA COAST VENTURE FORUM, 3257

Retail, Restaurants & Franchising
ALTAMONT CAPITAL PARTNERS, 96

Retailing
ACCES CAPITAL QUEBEC, 2029
ALANTRA, 77
AMANAH VENTURES SDN BHD, 2388
ANGELO, GORDON & CO., 127
APAX GLOBIS PARTNERS & COMPANY Globis Capital Partners/Apax, 2414
APAX PARTNERS ET CIE, 2415
APEX VENTURE PARTNERS, 137
ARSENAL CAPITAL PARTNERS, 170
ATRIA CAPITAL PARTENAIRES, 2448
AVENUE CAPITAL GROUP, 208
BARCLAYS VENTURES Barclays, 2486
BAY BG BAVARIAN VENTURE CAPITAL CORP, 2494
BERINGEA, 251
BERKSHIRE PARTNERS LLC, 254
BOSTON CAPITAL VENTURES, 310
BOULDER VENTURES LTD, 315
BRADFORD EQUITIES MANAGEMENT LLC, 321
BREAKWATER INVESTMENTS, 330
BRUCKMANN, ROSSER, SHERRILL & COMPANY, 354
BRUML CAPITAL CORPORATION, 355
BRYAN GARNIER & COMPANY, 2544
CARLYLE ASIA INVESTMENT ADVISORS LIMITED Carlyle Group, 2565
CARPEDIA CAPITAL, 2072
CATALYST INVESTMENT MANAGERS PTY LIMITED PPM Capital, 2573
CENTRE PARTNERS MANAGEMENT LLC, 447
CIC FINANCE CIC Group, 2601
CINVEN LIMITED, 2605
COMPASS GROUP MANAGEMENT LLC, 523
DAVID N DEUTSCH & COMPANY LLC, 589
DIRECT CAPITAL PRIVATE EQUITY LIMITED, 2664
DOUBLE IMPACT BUSINESS ADVISORY, 2670
DUKE STREET CAPITAL Duke Street, 2676
EMP GLOBAL, 670
ENTREPRENEUR PARTNERS, 683
EQT PARTNERS AB, 2712
EQUISTONE, 2714
FAIRMONT CAPITAL, 713
FENOX VENTURE CAPITAL, 721
FOUNDATION CAPITAL LIMITED, 2753
FREEMAN SPOGLI & CO., 783
FRIEND SKOLER & COMPANY LLC, 788
FRIULIA SpA, 2758
FUNG CAPITAL USA, 796
FdG ASSOCIATES LP, 801
GAON ASSET MANAGEMENT, 2766
GE CAPITAL, 808
GENERAL ENTERPRISE MANAGEMENT SERVICES, 2772
GLOBAL FINANCE, 2784
GOLDEN GATE CAPITAL, 839
GOLUB CAPITAL, 844
GRAPHITE CAPITAL MANAGEMENT LTD, 2796
GREIF & COMPANY, 869
GRUPO BISA, 2800
HANCOCK PARK ASSOCIATES, 902
HELMET CAPITAL FUND MANAGEMENT OY, 2820
HILCO BRANDS, 937
HILKO UK LTD/VALCO CAPITAL PARTNERS, 2827
HORIZON PARTNERS, LTD, 945
HOULIHAN LOKEY, 948
HUMMER WINBLAD VENTURE PARTNERS, 956
INDUSTRI KAPITAL SVENSKA AB, 2863
IRISH ANGELS, 1019
JAFCO COMPANY LIMITED JAPAN, 2906
JH WHITNEY & COMPANY, 1037
JW CHILDS ASSOCIATES, 1049
KELSO & COMPANY, 1062
KENSINGTON CAPITAL PARTNERS, 2167
KNIGHT'S BRIDGE CAPITAL PARTNERS, 2171
L CATTERTON PARTNERS, 1088
LLOYDS DEVELOPMENT CAPITAL LIMITED, 2944
LLR PARTNERS INC, 1136
LMBO FINANCE, 2945
LOMBARD INVESTMENTS, 1139
LOVETT MILLER & COMPANY, 1148
MACQUARIE DIRECT INVESTMENT LIMITED, 2951
MADISON PARKER CAPITAL, 1157
MANULIFE CAPITAL, 2183
MEKONG CAPITAL, 2961
MERRILL LYNCH (ASIA PACIFIC) LIMITED Merrill Lynch Group, 2964
MID-ATLANTIC VENTURE FUNDS, 1227
MIDMARK CAPITAL LP, 1230
MONTLAKE CAPITAL, 1250
MVP CAPITAL PARTNERS, 1275
NEEDHAM CAPITAL PARTNERS, 1288
NORTH ATLANTIC CAPITAL CORPORATION, 1333
NORTHWOOD VENTURES, 1344
OAK INVESTMENT PARTNERS, 1361
PARTNERSHIP FUND FOR NEW YORK CITY, 1420
PENINSULA CAPITAL PARTNERS LLC, 1426
PHOENIX EQUITY PARTNERS LIMITED, 3036
QUANTUM CAPITAL PARTNERS, 1510
QUARRY CAPITAL MANAGEMENT, 1511
RESILIENCE CAPITAL PARTNERS, 1545
RETAIL & RESTAURANT GROWTH CAPITAL LP, 1549
SAMOS INVESTMENTS, 3097
SORRENTO VENTURES, 1706
SPLIT ROCK PARTNERS, 1725
STATELINE ANGELS, 1740
SUN CAPITAL PARTNERS, 1753
SWANDER PACE CAPITAL, 1767
TENNESSEE COMMUNITY VENTURES, 1797
THREE CITIES RESEARCH, 1820
UNISON CAPITAL PARTNERS LP, 3201
UPFRONT VENTURES, 1888
WELLS FARGO CAPITAL FINANCE, 1970
WESTON PRESIDIO, 1978
YLR CAPITAL MARKETS LTD, 3247
ZS FUND LP, 2022

Industry Preference Index / SaaS

Risk Management
AON RISK SOLUTIONS Aon Corporation, 2413

Robotics
11.2 CAPITAL, 4
360 CAPITAL PARTNERS 360 Capital Management SA, 2296
ABSTRACT VENTURES, 24
AXIA CAPITAL, 211
BOOST VC, 307
CARBON VENTURES, 408
CATAPULT VENTURES, 429
CHRYSALIX, 2078
COMET LABS, 519
DRAPER ATHENA, 626
DYNAMO VC, 640
EMBARK VENTURES, 663
FA TECHNOLOGY VENTURES, 711
FRONTIER VENTURES, 792
FUTURE VENTURES, 800
GOLDEN VENTURE PARTNERS, 2137
GRISHIN ROBOTICS, 874
GV, 889
INNOVATION WORKS, 998
KHOSLA VENTURES, 1069
LDV CAPITAL, 1101
MASS VENTURES, 1172
MEDRA CAPITAL, 2960
OUTPOST CAPITAL, 1390
PATHBREAKER VENTURES, 1421
QUAKE CAPITAL PARTNERS, 1507
SAMSUNG NEXT, 1611
SCIENCEVEST, 1630
SECTION 32, 1643
SONY INNOVATION FUND, 1703
SPINUP VENTURE, 3132
SUPPLY CHAIN VENTURES, 1757
TENX VENTURES, 2266
TOYOTA AI VENTURES, 1834
TRELLIS CAPITAL CORPORATION, 2273
UNCORK CAPITAL, 1879

Rubber
DESCO CAPITAL, 606

Rural Innovations
AAVISHKAAR, 2313

SMB Productivity & Cloud Services
500 STARTUPS, 11

SaaS
10X VENTURE PARTNERS, 3
42 VENTURES, 9
ABRT VENTURE FUND, 2320
ACCEL, 28
ACCELEPRISE, 30
ACCESS VENTURE PARTNERS LLC, 36
ACTUA, 53
ADAMS STREET PARTNERS, LLC, 57
ADD VENTURE, 2344
ALBUM VC, 79
ALPHA VENTURE PARTNERS, 91
ALTA VENTURES MEXICO, 2382
AMPLIFY, 120
ANTRAK CAPITAL, 2407
ASCENT VENTURE PARTNERS, 178
ASLANOBA CAPITAL, 2437
ASPECT VENTURES, 180
AUGMENT VENTURES, 195
AZURE CAPITAL PARTNERS, 215
BANNEKER PARTNERS, 227
BARODA VENTURES, 228
BAY PARTNERS, 238
BENHAMOU GLOBAL VENTURES, 249
BEST FUNDS, 2058
BIP CAPITAL, 271
BIRCHMERE VENTURES, 272
BLACKBIRD VENTURES, 2520
BLUMBERG CAPITAL, 301
BOLDSTART VENTURES, 305
BOSTON SEED CAPITAL, 313
BOXGROUP, 318
BREGAL SAGEMOUNT, 333
BURAN VENTURE CAPITAL, 2549
CALUMET VENTURE FUND, 375
CAMP ONE VENTURES, 384
CANAL PARTNERS, 387
CARDINAL VENTURE CAPITAL, 411
CARMEL VENTURES, 2566
CARRICK CAPITAL PARTNERS, 416
CATALYST INVESTORS, 427
CEDAR FUND, 436
CELTIC HOUSE VENTURE PARTNERS, 2076
CEO VENTURES, 450
CHARLES RIVER VENTURES, 455
CISCO INVESTMENTS, 483
CLYDESDALE VENTURES, 506
CONVERGE VENTURE PARTNERS, 534
CYPRESS GROWTH CAPITAL, 576
DUNDEE VENTURE CAPITAL, 635
EDBI Pte LTD., 2690
EDEN VENTURES, 2691
EMERGENCE CAPITAL PARTNERS, 665
EONCAPITAL, 685
EVENTI CAPITAL PARTNERS, 2110
FAIRHAVEN CAPITAL, 712
FELICIS VENTURES, 720
FIRESTARTER FUND, 731
FIVE ELMS CAPITAL, 745
GCI CAPITAL, 2128
GENACAST VENTURES, 814
GENWEALTH VENTURES, 2131
GLASSWING VENTURES, 829
GOLDEN VENTURE PARTNERS, 2137
GREAT OAKS VENTURE CAPITAL, 858
GREYCROFT PARTNERS, 871
HUMMER WINBLAD VENTURE PARTNERS, 956
IDG VENTURES INDIA International Financial Services Limited, 2849
ILLUMINATE VENTURES, 976
INFORMATION VENTURE PARTNERS, 2153
INVENTUS, 1013
JACKSON SQUARE VENTURES, 1024
KAEDAN INVESTMENTS, 2914
KIZOO TECHNOLOGY CAPITAL, 2921
KLASS CAPITAL, 2170
LIGHTHOUSE EQUITY PARTNERS, 2176
LIGHTSPEED VENTURE PARTNERS, 1121
LOVETT MILLER & COMPANY, 1148
M12, 1154
MERCURY FUND, 1206
MERITECH CAPITAL PARTNERS, 1212
MHS CAPITAL, 1226
MIRAMAR VENTURE PARTNERS, 1237
MORADO VENTURE PARTNERS, 1254
NAYA VENTURES, 1285
NEW ATLANTIC VENTURES, 1291
NEW ENTERPRISE ASSOCIATES, 1297
NEXTGEN ANGELS, 1320
NOTION CAPITAL, 3014
ORIGIN VENTURES, 1384
OSAGE PARTNERS, 1387
OYSTER VENTURES, 1395
OneVentures, 3023
PENTECH VENTURES, 3032
POINT NINE CAPITAL, 3044
PRIMARY VENTURE PARTNERS, 1475
PROCYON VENTURES, 1483
QUAKE CAPITAL PARTNERS, 1507
REAL VENTURES, 2232
RELAY VENTURES, 2236
RIDGE VENTURES, 1563
RTP VENTURES, 1594
RUBICON VENTURE CAPITAL, 1595
SIGMA PARTNERS, 1672

1225

Industry Preference Index / SaaS & Data Services

SIGMA PRIME VENTURES, 1673
SIGNIA VENTURE PARTNERS, 1678
SINEWAVE VENTURES, 1687
SPEKTRA CAPITAL, 1718
SRIJAN CAPITAL, 3133
STAGE 1 VENTURES, 1734
STRIPES GROUP, 1748
SUNBRIDGE PARTNERS, 1755
SUSQUEHANNA GROWTH EQUITY, 1759
TAO VENTURE CAPITAL PARTNERS, 1780
TARGET PARTNERS, 3161
THINKTIV VENTURES, 1810
TICONDEROGA PRIVATE EQUITY, 1824
TRIDENT CAPITAL, 1850
TRUE VENTURES, 1860
TUGBOAT VENTURES, 1865
UPFRONT VENTURES, 1888
VALHALLA PARTNERS, 1899
VANEDGE CAPITAL PARTNERS, 2278
VERGE FUND, 1924
VERSION ONE VENTURES, 2280
VILLAGE GLOBAL, 1933
VOLITION CAPITAL, 1942
WESLEY CLOVER, 2284
WILDCAT VENTURE PARTNERS, 1985
ZELKOVA VENTURES, 2017

SaaS & Data Services
BAIN CAPITAL VENTURES, 221

SaaS Businesses
TACTICO, 2260

Safety
ALTRIA VENTURES, 102

Safety and Graphics
3M UNITEK, 2307

Safety, Testing & Inspection
BLUE POINT CAPITAL PARTNERS, 290

Sales & Marketing SaaS
CHICAGO VENTURES, 471

Sales and Marketing
AUSTRALIAN ETHICAL INVESTMENT LIMITED, 2456

Sanitation
AAVISHKAAR, 2313

Satellite Communications
ANDERSON PACIFIC CORPORATION, 122
APOLLO GLOBAL MANAGEMENT, 140
SPACEVEST, 1714

Satellite Imaging
LDV CAPITAL, 1101

Seafood
ARTHUR P GOULD & COMPANY, 172

Security
(@)VENTURES, 1
10X VENTURE PARTNERS, 3
645 VENTURES, 13
ACCEL, 28
ACTIVE VENTURE PARTNERS, 2339
ALEUTIAN CAPITAL PARTNERS, 81
ALTA VENTURES MEXICO, 2382
ALTAIR VENTURES, 95
AMD VENTURES, 106
AMMER PARTNERS, 2393
AMPLIFIER VENTURE PARTNERS, 119
AUXO MANAGEMENT, 2047
AVIV VENTURE CAPITAL, 2462
AZURE CAPITAL PARTNERS, 215

BALDERTON CAPITAL, 2478
BATTELLE VENTURES, 233
BLAST FUNDING, 279
BLUMBERG CAPITAL, 301
CELERITY PARTNERS, 439
CHART VENTURE PARTNERS, 457
CID CAPITAL, 478
CISCO INVESTMENTS, 483
CITI VENTURES, 486
CITY LIGHT CAPITAL, 488
CLAREMONT CREEK VENTURES, 491
DELL VENTURES, 603
DRAPER ATHENA, 626
DUNRATH CAPITAL, 636
EMBARK VENTURES, 663
ENLIGHTENMENT CAPITAL, 680
EUROFUND LP, 2720
FAIRHAVEN CAPITAL, 712
FOUNDERS EQUITY, 774
FRANCISCO PARTNERS, 779
GOOD NEWS VENTURES, 2138
GRANDBANKS CAPITAL, 848
GRAYHAWK CAPITAL, 856
GULFSTAR GROUP, 888
HOLLAND VENTURE BV, 2828
HORIZONS VENTURES, 2831
ICON VENTURES, 968
IDEALAB, 972
IGNITION PARTNERS, 974
IN-Q-TEL, 979
INNOFINANCE OY, 2873
INTEL CAPITAL, 1004
IT-PARTNERS NV, 2902
JACKSON SQUARE VENTURES, 1024
JC2 VENTURES, 1031
LDV CAPITAL, 1101
LEVINE LEICHTMAN CAPITAL PARTNERS, 1111
LIGHTSPEED VENTURE PARTNERS, 1121
LRM - INVESTERINGSMAATSCHAPPIJ VOOR LIMBURG, 2949
M12, 1154
MENLO VENTURES, 1202
MIRAE ASSET VENTURE ACCELERATOR Mirae Asset Group, 2969
MOTOROLA SOLUTIONS VENTURE CAPITAL, 1260
MS&AD VENTURES, 1269
NAUTA CAPITAL, 2987
NORO-MOSELEY PARTNERS, 1331
NOVA SCOTIA BUSINESS INC., 2205
NOVAK BIDDLE VENTURE PARTNERS, 1348
PALADIN CAPITAL GROUP, 1400
PREVIZ VENTURES, 3050
QUANTUM WAVE FUND, 3068
QUESTER CAPITAL MANAGEMENT LIMITED, 3070
SAMSUNG NEXT, 1611
SCP PARTNERS, 1633
SIGNAL PEAK VENTURES, 1677
SONY INNOVATION FUND, 1703
SOUTHERN CROSS VENTURE PARTNERS, 1711
STAGE 1 VENTURES, 1734
STORM VENTURES, 1747
TAO VENTURE CAPITAL PARTNERS, 1780
TELEFONICA VENTURES, 3169
VERIZON VENTURES, 1926
WALNUT GROUP, 1954
WESTERN TECHNOLOGY INVESTMENT, 1975
WINDSPEED VENTURES, 1994
YES VC, 2014

Seed
WAVEMAKER PARTNERS, 1965

Select Retail
RIVER ASSOCIATES INVESTMENTS LLC, 1569

Self-Driving Cars
DAY ONE VENTURES, 593

Industry Preference Index / Sensors

Semiconductors
3I DEUTSCHLAND GESELLSCHAFT FUR 3i Group, 2299
3I GERMANY GmbH 3i Group, 2301
ACCESS VENTURE PARTNERS LLC, 36
ACE VENTURE CAPITAL LIMITED, 2330
ACKRELL CAPITAL, 44
ACORN CAMPUS VENTURES, 47
ADAMS CAPITAL MANAGEMENT, 56
ADARA VENTURE PARTNERS, 2342
ALICE VENTURES SRL, 2364
ALLIANCE VENTURE, 2369
ALTA BERKELEY ASSOCIATES, 2380
ALTAIR VENTURES, 95
AMBIENT SOUND INVESTMENTS, 2390
AMWIN MANAGEMENT PTY LIMITED, 2398
APPLIED MATERIALS VENTURES, 144
ARCH VENTURE PARTNERS, 153
ARTIS VENTURES, 175
ASIAVEST PARTNERS, 2436
ASSET MANAGEMENT VENTURES, 181
ATLANTIC BRIDGE, 2443
AUSTIN VENTURES, 202
AUTO TECH VENTURES, 204
BALDERTON CAPITAL, 2478
BAND OF ANGELS LLC, 226
BANEXI VENTURES PARTNERS, 2481
BATTERY VENTURES, 235
BAY PARTNERS, 238
BI WALDEN MANAGEMENT SDN Walden International, 2508
BIRCHMERE VENTURES, 272
BLACK DIAMOND VENTURES, 275
BLUERUN VENTURES, 296
CALIFORNIA TECHNOLOGY VENTURES, 371
CAMP VENTURES, 385
CARMEL VENTURES, 2566
CENTERPOINT VENTURE PARTNERS, 444
CHALLENGE FUNDS - ETGAR LP, 2585
CHINA DEVELOPMENT INDUSTRIAL BANK CDFH, 2592
CHINA WALDEN MANAGEMENT LIMITED Walden Group, 2597
CID GROUP, 2603
CISCO INVESTMENTS, 483
CLAL ELECTRONICS INDUSTRIES LIMITED, 2609
CONCORD VENTURES, 2628
CORE CAPITAL PARTNERS, 538
DRAPER ATHENA, 626
DUCHOSSOIS CAPITAL MANAGEMENT, 633
DVC DEUTSCHE VENTURE CAPITAL, 2679
EASTVEN VENTURE PARTNERS, 645
ECAPITAL ENTREPRENEURIAL PARTNERS AG, 2686
ECHELON VENTURES, 647
ECLIPSE VENTURES, 648
EMBARK VENTURES, 663
EPLANET CAPITAL, 690
FAIRHAVEN CAPITAL, 712
FINAVENTURES, 729
FOCUS VENTURES, 757
FORMATIVE VENTURES, 764
FORMULA VENTURES LIMITED Formula Group, 2750
FOUNDATION CAPITAL, 770
FRANCISCO PARTNERS, 779
GEFINOR CAPITAL, 810
GEMINI ISRAEL VENTURE FUNDS LIMITED, 2770
GIZA VENTURE CAPITAL, 2782
GOLDEN GATE CAPITAL, 839
GRAYHAWK CAPITAL, 856
GSR VENTURES, 2801
GUGGENHEIM PARTNERS, 885
HARBERT MANAGEMENT CORPORATION, 904
HARBINGER VENTURE MANAGEMENT, 905
ID VENTURES AMERICA LLC, 970
IGLOBE PARTNERS, 2853
INDUSTRIFONDEN, 2867
INTEL CAPITAL, 1004
INTERSOUTH PARTNERS, 1008
JERUSALEM VENTURE PARTNERS, 2910
JF SHEA VENTURES, 1036
JK&B CAPITAL, 1038
KB PARTNERS LLC, 1057
KHOSLA VENTURES, 1069
KODIAK VENTURE PARTNERS, 1080
KOREA FIRST VENTURE CAPITAL CORPORATION, 2924
LABRADOR VENTURES, 1089
MAGMA VENTURE PARTNERS, 2952
MATRIX PARTNERS, 1181
MBF CAPITAL CORPORATION, 1188
MENLO VENTURES, 1202
MERITECH CAPITAL PARTNERS, 1212
MIRAMAR VENTURE PARTNERS, 1237
MITSUI SUMITOMO INSURANCE VENTURE CAPITAL CO, 2971
MOHR-DAVIDOW VENTURES, 1247
MORGAN STANLEY EXPANSION CAPITAL, 1255
MURPHREE VENTURE PARTNERS, 1273
NEEDHAM CAPITAL PARTNERS, 1288
NETROVE ASIA SDN BHD, 2993
NEW VENTURE PARTNERS, 1305
NEWLIGHT MANAGEMENT, 1314
NHN INVESTMENT, 3002
NOVUS VENTURES LP, 1354
OKAPI VENTURE CAPITAL, 1371
OPUS CAPITAL, 1381
PAC-LINK MANAGEMENT CORP., 3024
PARKWALK ADVISORS, 3028
PI CAPITAL GROUP LLC, 1440
PITANGO VENTURE CAPITAL, 3039
PRESIDIO VENTURES, 1474
PRIME TECHNOLOGY VENTURES NV, 3051
QUEST FOR GROWTH, 3069
RIDGEWOOD CAPITAL, 1564
RPM VENTURES, 1592
SAINTS CAPITAL, 1604
SAMSUNG VENTURE INVESTMENT CORPORATION Samsung Electronics, 3098
SAND HILL ANGELS, 1613
SCALE VENTURE PARTNERS, 1626
SELBY VENTURE PARTNERS, 1646
SHASTA VENTURES, 1663
SIERRA VENTURES, 1670
SIGMA PARTNERS, 1672
SIGNATURE CAPITAL LLC, 3120
SILVERTON PARTNERS, 1685
SOUTHERN CROSS VENTURE PARTNERS, 1711
STATELINE ANGELS, 1740
STORM VENTURES, 1747
SUMMIT BRIDGE CAPITAL, 3147
SUMMIT PARTNERS, 1752
SUNBRIDGE PARTNERS, 1755
SYCAMORE VENTURES, 1769
TALLWOOD VENTURE CAPITAL, 1779
TECH CAPITAL PARTNERS, 2262
TEL VENTURE CAPITAL, 1791
TENAYA CAPITAL, 1796
TEUZA MANAGEMENT & DEVELOPMENT LTD, 3171
TI VENTURE CAPITAL Texas Instruments Incorporated, 1823
TRELLIS CAPITAL CORPORATION, 2273
US VENTURE PARTNERS, 1896
VENCORE CAPITAL, 1915
VENTECH, 3208
VENTURE TECH ALLIANCE, 1922
WALDEN INTERNATIONAL, 1951
WESTERN TECHNOLOGY INVESTMENT, 1975
WESTLAKE SECURITIES, 1976
WINDWARD VENTURES, 1995
WOODSIDE FUND, 2005
WORLDVIEW TECHNOLOGY PARTNERS, 2007
XPV WATER PARTNERS, 2290

Semiconductors & Materials
RHO CANADA VENTURES, 2239

Semis/Coretech
CROSSLINK CAPITAL, 563

Sensors
AXIA CAPITAL, 211

1227

Industry Preference Index / Service Industries

Service Industries
ALLEGIS CYBER CAPITAL, 84
AMERIMARK CAPITAL CORPORATION, 111
BLUE SAGE CAPITAL, 291
CARDINAL EQUITY PARTNERS, 409
CARDINAL PARTNERS, 410
EDGEWATER FUNDS, 654
GLADSTONE CAPITAL, 828
GRANITE EQUITY PARTNERS, 850
HANNOVER FINANZ GmbH, 2810
HANOVER PARTNERS, 903
INVESTAMERICA VENTURE GROUP, 1016
KOHLBERG & COMPANY LLC, 1081
MIDMARK CAPITAL LP, 1230
NORTHERN ENTERPRISE LIMITED, 3011
NORTHWOOD VENTURES, 1344
QUANTUM CAPITAL PARTNERS, 1510
SIERRA VENTURES, 1670
SPLIT ROCK PARTNERS, 1725
THREE CITIES RESEARCH, 1820

Services
AAVIN PRIVATE EQUITY, 17
ACE VENTURE CAPITAL LIMITED, 2330
APAX PARTNERS, 135
BAKER CAPITAL, 223
BARING VOSTOK CAPITAL PARTNERS, 2491
BRANDON CAPITAL GROUP, 326
BRAZOS PRIVATE EQUITY PARTNERS, 328
BRIDGEPOINT CAPITAL GmbH, 2537
BRIDGEPOINT CAPITAL LIMITED, 2538
BROCKWAY MORAN & PARTNERS, 348
CATALYST GROUP, 425
CELADON CAPITAL GROUP, 2582
COMPASS GROUP MANAGEMENT LLC, 523
CZECH VENTURE PARTNERS SRO K+ Venture Partners B.V., 2648
DEFI GESTION SA Banque Cantonale Vaudoise, 2653
DIMELING SCHREIBER & PARK, 616
DN PARTNERS LLC, 619
DUNEDIN CAPITAL PARTNERS LIMITED, 2677
EDGEWATER FUNDS, 654
ELECTRA PARTNERS EUROPE, 2695
EQUITY SOUTH, 693
FAIRMONT CAPITAL, 713
FLORIDA CAPITAL PARTNERS, 752
FRIEND SKOLER & COMPANY LLC, 788
FULCRUM CAPITAL PARTNERS, 2126
GEFINOR CAPITAL, 810
GLOBAL FINANCE, 2784
GRANITE BRIDGE PARTNERS, 849
GRAPHITE CAPITAL MANAGEMENT LTD, 2796
GRIDIRON CAPITAL, 873
HARBERT MANAGEMENT CORPORATION, 904
HIGH ROAD CAPITAL PARTNERS, 931
ILE-DE-FRANCE, 2855
INDIAN DIRECT EQUITY ADVISORS PVT LTD, 2861
INDUSTRI KAPITAL SVENSKA AB, 2863
IRON GATE CAPITAL, 1020
LIBERTY PARTNERS, 1116
MARWIT CAPITAL LLC, 1168
MESA CAPITAL PARTNERS, 1219
MILESTONE PARTNERS, 1234
NEWLIGHT MANAGEMENT, 1314
NORWEST VENTURE PARTNERS, 1346
PANTHEON VENTURES (US) LP, 1411
PNC ERIEVIEW CAPITAL, 1456
PRISM CAPITAL, 1477
PRITZKER GROUP PRIVATE CAPITAL, 1479
PT BHAKTI INVESTAMA TBK, 3061
QUAD-C MANAGEMENT, 1505
RESONANT VENTURE PARTNERS, 1547
RETAIL & RESTAURANT GROWTH CAPITAL LP, 1549
RFE INVESTMENT PARTNERS, 1557
SAMBRINVEST SA, 3096
SHANGHAI INFORMATION INVESTMENT INCORPORATED, 3114
SOUTHEAST INTERACTIVE TECHNOLOGY FUNDS, 1709
SRIW SA SRIW Group, 3134

STERN PARTNERS, 2258
TECH COAST ANGELS, 1784
WARWICK GROUP, 1957
WAUD CAPITAL PARTNERS LLC, 1963

Silicon-Related Technologies
COMPASS TECHNOLOGY PARTNERS LP, 524

Site Remediation
DEMETER PARTNERS, 2656

Skincare
MCGOVERN CAPITAL, 1191

Smart Buildings
CATAPULT VENTURES, 429

Smart Cities
CHINAROCK CAPITAL MANAGEMENT VENTURES, 472
MACKINNON, BENNETT & CO., 2181

Social
LIGHTSPEED VENTURE PARTNERS, 1121

Social Applications
KIZOO TECHNOLOGY CAPITAL, 2921

Social Determinants
HEALTH ENTERPRISE PARTNERS, 918

Social Enterprises
BIG SOCIETY CAPITAL, 2509
FSE GROUP, 2760
IRISH ANGELS, 1019

Social Impact
VANCITY CAPITAL, 2277

Social Media
10X VENTURE PARTNERS, 3
ARCHTOP VENTURES, 154
BENCHMARK, 248
BIRCHMERE VENTURES, 272
BLACKBIRD VENTURES, 2520
BLUERUN VENTURES, 296
BLUMBERG CAPITAL, 301
BREYER CAPITAL, 336
BULLPEN CAPITAL, 358
CAMP ONE VENTURES, 384
CAVA CAPITAL, 431
CLEARSTONE VENTURE PARTNERS, 502
COLOMA VENTURES, 512
CORSA VENTURES, 545
DATA POINT CAPITAL, 586
DETROIT VENTURE PARTNERS, 607
EDEN VENTURES, 2691
EMERGENCE CAPITAL PARTNERS, 665
G SQUARED, 802
GENWEALTH VENTURES, 2131
GOLDEN SEEDS, 841
GREAT OAKS VENTURE CAPITAL, 858
GREE VENTURES, 2798
HORIZONS VENTURES, 2831
INLAND TECHSTART FUND, 993
JC2 VENTURES, 1031
LAUNCHPAD VENTURE GROUP, 1100
LIGHTBANK, 1118
LOOL VENTURES, 2947
M25 GROUP, 1155
MHS CAPITAL, 1226
MOTOROLA SOLUTIONS VENTURE CAPITAL, 1260
NFX, 1323
PENTECH VENTURES, 3032
QUAKE CAPITAL PARTNERS, 1507
RAPTOR GROUP, 1524
REVEL PARTNERS, 1554
SOFTTECH VC, 1700

Industry Preference Index / Software

SPARK CAPITAL, 1715
SRIJAN CAPITAL, 3133
SUMMERHILL VENTURE PARTNERS, 2259
SV ANGEL, 1761
TECHOPERATORS, 1788
TENGELMANN VENTURES, 3170
THINKTIV VENTURES, 1810
TOP RENERGY INC., 2271
TRIDENT CAPITAL, 1850
VENROCK ASSOCIATES, 1916
WASABI VENTURES, 1958
WHITE STAR CAPITAL, 1982
WINDFORCE VENTURES, LLC, 1992
WOMEN'S VENTURE CAPITAL FUND, 2003
XG VENTURES, 2010

Social Services
BONVENTURE, 2531
NIELSEN INNOVATE FUND, 3003
RUBICON VENTURE CAPITAL, 1595

Software
(@)VENTURES, 1
212 CAPITAL PARTNERS, 2294
3I AUSTRIA BETEILGUNG GmbH 3i Group, 2298
3I DEUTSCHLAND GESELLSCHAFT FUR 3i Group, 2299
3I GERMANY GmbH 3i Group, 2301
3TS CAPITAL PARTNERS 3i Group plc, 2309
42 VENTURES, 9
AM VENTURES, 16
AAVIN PRIVATE EQUITY, 17
ABELL FOUNDATION VENTURES, 19
ABRT VENTURE FUND, 2320
ABS VENTURES, 23
ABSTRACT VENTURES, 24
ACCEL-KKR LLC, 29
ACCELEPRISE, 30
ACCESS CAPITAL, 35
ACKRELL CAPITAL, 44
ACONCAGUA VENTURES, 2334
ACT ONE VENTURES, 50
ACT VENTURE CAPITAL LIMITED, 2336
ACUITY VENTURES LLC, 54
ACUMEN VENTURES, 2341
ADVENT VENTURE PARTNERS, 2348
AFTERDOX, 2352
AGF PRIVATE EQUITY Allianz Group, 2354
AITEC, 2357
ALBERTA ENTERPRISE, 2032
ALLEGIS CYBER CAPITAL, 84
ALLIANCE VENTURE, 2369
ALLOS VENTURES, 86
ALPHA VENTURE PARTNERS, 91
ALPINE INVESTORS, 92
ALTOS VENTURES, 100
AMD VENTURES, 106
AMPLIFIER VENTURE PARTNERS, 119
AMPLIFY, 120
ANALYTICS VENTURES, 121
ANGELS' FORUM LLC, 129
APAX GLOBIS PARTNERS & COMPANY Globis Capital Partners/Apax, 2414
APEX VENTURE PARTNERS, 137
ARC ANGEL FUND, 150
ASCENT VENTURE PARTNERS, 178
ATLAS VENTURE: FRANCE, 2445
ATRIUM CAPITAL, 192
AUGMENT VENTURES, 195
AURA CAPITAL OY Auratum Group, 2451
AURORA CAPITAL GROUP, 199
AUTHOSIS VENTURES, 2457
AVANSIS VENTURES, 207
AWEIDA VENTURE PARTNERS, 210
AXA INVESTMENT MANAGERS PRIVATE EQUITY EUROPE, 2466
AXIOM VENTURE PARTNERS, 212
AXVENTURES, 2470
AZINI CAPITAL PARTNERS, 2472

BALDERTON CAPITAL, 2478
BALLAST POINT VENTURES, 224
BAND OF ANGELS LLC, 226
BANNEKER PARTNERS, 227
BARCELONA EMPREN, 2483
BATTERY VENTURES, 235
BERKELEY VENTURES, 253
BEST FUNDS, 2058
BI WALDEN MANAGEMENT SDN Walden International, 2508
BLACKBIRD VENTURES, 2520
BLAST FUNDING, 279
BLU VENTURE INVESTORS, 285
BLUESHIFT INTERNET VENTURES Blueshift, 2525
BLUETREE VENTURE FUND, 298
BLUMBERG CAPITAL, 301
BMP AKTIENGESELLSCHAFT BMP Venture Capital, 2528
BOLDSTART VENTURES, 305
BONFIRE VENTURES, 306
BOSTON CAPITAL VENTURES, 310
BREGAL SAGEMOUNT, 333
BRIDGEPOINT CAPITAL GmbH, 2537
BRIDGEPOINT CAPITAL LIMITED, 2538
BRIGHTSPARK VENTURES, 2066
BUSINESS GROWTH FUND, 2550
CALUMET VENTURE FUND, 375
CAMBER CREEK, 377
CAMPUS COMPANIES VENTURE CAPITAL FUND, 2554
CANAL PARTNERS, 387
CANDOVER, 2556
CANROCK VENTURES, 393
CARDINAL VENTURE CAPITAL, 411
CARMEL VENTURES, 2566
CASTILE VENTURES, 422
CATALYST FUND LP, 2571
CAZENOVE PRIVATE EQUITY Cazenove Capital, 2577
CEDAR (ISRAEL) FINANCIAL ADVISORS LIMITED Cedar Fund, 2580
CEI VENTURES, 438
CENTENNIAL VENTURES, 441
CENTRAL TEXAS ANGEL NETWORK, 445
CERVIN VENTURES, 454
CHALLENGE FUNDS - ETGAR LP, 2585
CHARLES RIVER VENTURES, 455
CHARLES RIVER VENTURES, 455
CHAZEN CAPITAL PARTNERS, 460
CHENGWEI VENTURES, 2590
CHICAGO VENTURE PARTNERS LP, 470
CHINA WALDEN MANAGEMENT LIMITED Walden Group, 2597
CIBC CAPITAL MARKETS, 2079
CIBC INNOVATION BANKING, 2080
CLOQUET CAPITAL PARTNERS, 505
COATUE MANAGEMENT, 509
COLOMA VENTURES, 512
COLUMBIA CAPITAL, 515
COMVEST PARTNERS, 528
CONCORD VENTURES, 2628
CONTOUR VENTURE PARTNERS, 533
CONVERGE VENTURE PARTNERS, 534
CORAL GROUP, 536
CRAWLEY VENTURES, 553
CREANDUM, 2637
CRESCENDO VENTURE MANAGEMENT LLC, 2639
CRESCENDO VENTURES, 555
CROSSLINK CAPITAL, 563
CSA PARTNERS, 566
CXO FUND, 574
CYPRESS GROWTH CAPITAL, 576
DAG VENTURES, 581
DALLAS VENTURE PARTNERS, 582
DATA COLLECTIVE, 585
DAWNTREADER VENTURES, 592
DEFTA PARTNERS, 602
DELL VENTURES, 603
DELTA VENTURES LIMITED, 2655
DETROIT VENTURE PARTNERS, 607
DFJ ESPRIT, 2662
DFJ VENTURE CAPITAL, 609
DN CAPITAL, 2668

Industry Preference Index / Software

DOUBLEROCK VENTURE CAPITAL, 625
DR NEUHAUS TECHNO NORD GmbH, 2673
DRAPER ATHENA, 626
DRAPER RICHARDS KAPLAN FOUNDATION, 627
DUCHOSSOIS CAPITAL MANAGEMENT, 633
DYNAMO VC, 640
EARLYBIRD, 2682
EASTVEN VENTURE PARTNERS, 645
ECAPITAL ENTREPRENEURIAL PARTNERS AG, 2686
ECHELON VENTURES, 647
EDELSON TECHNOLOGY PARTNERS, 651
EDEN VENTURES, 2691
EDGESTONE CAPITAL PARTNERS, 2103
EDGEWATER FUNDS, 654
EDISON PARTNERS, 655
ELEVATION PARTNERS, 659
EQUITY SOUTH, 693
ESCALATE CAPITAL PARTNERS, 695
EUROPEAN FOUNDERS FUND, 2723
EVERCORE CAPITAL PARTNERS, 699
EVERGREEN VENTURE PARTNERS, 2726
FALCON FUND, 715
FENOX VENTURE CAPITAL, 721
FF VENTURE CAPITAL, 724
FIDELITY GROWTH PARTNERS EUROPE, 2734
FIFTH WALL, 727
FINADVANCE, 2735
FINANCIERE DE BRIENNE FCPR, 2738
FINAVENTURES, 729
FLOODGATE FUND, 751
FLYWHEEL VENTURES, 756
FOCUS VENTURES, 757
FOG CITY CAPITAL, 758
FORMULA VENTURES LIMITED Formula Group, 2750
FOUNDATION CAPITAL, 770
FOUNDER PARTNERS, 772
FOUNDERS FUND, 775
FOUNDRY GROUP, 776
FRANCISCO PARTNERS, 779
FRONTIER VENTURE CAPITAL, 791
FTV CAPITAL, 793
FUSION FUND, 799
G-51 CAPITAL LLC, 803
GABRIEL VENTURE PARTNERS, 805
GARAGE TECHNOLOGY VENTURES, 807
GE VENTURES, 809
GEFINOR CAPITAL, 810
GENACAST VENTURES, 814
GENERAL CATALYST PARTNERS, 816
GENERAL ENTERPRISE MANAGEMENT SERVICES, 2772
GENSTAR CAPITAL LP, 819
GGV CAPITAL, 823
GILDE INVESTMENT FUNDS, 2779
GIZA VENTURE CAPITAL, 2782
GLOBESPAN CAPITAL PARTNERS, 835
GLYNN CAPITAL MANAGEMENT, 836
GOLDEN GATE CAPITAL, 839
GRANDBANKS CAPITAL, 848
GRANITE VENTURE CAPITAL CORPORATION, 2794
GRAYHAWK CAPITAL, 856
GREAT HILL PARTNERS LLC, 857
GREENHAVEN PARTNERS, 863
GREENHILL SAVP, 864
GREYLOCK PARTNERS, 872
GROTECH VENTURES, 876
GROUND UP VENTURES, 877
GUGGENHEIM PARTNERS, 885
GULFSTAR GROUP, 888
GV, 889
HARBERT MANAGEMENT CORPORATION, 904
HARBINGER VENTURE MANAGEMENT, 905
HARBOURVEST PARTNERS LLC, 909
HASSO PLATTNER VENTURES, 2813
HELLMAN & FRIEDMAN LLC, 924
HIGH COUNTRY VENTURE, 930
HORIZON VENTURES LLC, 947
HOXTON VENTURES, 2834

HUDSON VENTURE PARTNERS, 954
HUMMER WINBLAD VENTURE PARTNERS, 956
HUMMINGBIRD VENTURES, 2837
HUNTSMAN GAY GLOBAL CAPITAL, 959
HYUNDAI VENTURE INVESTMENT CORPORATION, 2839
I-PACIFIC PARTNERS, 2840
IA VENTURES, 965
ICON VENTURES, 968
ID VENTURES AMERICA LLC, 970
IDEA FUND PARTNERS, 971
IDEALAB, 972
IDG TECHNOLOGY VENTURE INVESTMENT, 2848
IDG VENTURES INDIA International Financial Services Limited, 2849
IGAN PARTNERS, 2149
IGNITE JAPAN KK Ignite Group, 2854
IGNITION PARTNERS, 974
INCWELL VENTURE CAPITAL, 981
INDIAN DIRECT EQUITY ADVISORS PVT LTD, 2861
INETWORKS ADVISORS LLC, 987
INFLEXION PARTNERS, 990
INITIALIZED CAPITAL, 991
INLAND TECHSTART FUND, 993
INNOSPRING, 994
INNOVACOM SA, 2875
INNOVATION WORKS, 998
INNOVATIONSKAPITAL, 2878
INSTITUTIONAL VENTURE PARTNERS, 1001
INTEL CAPITAL, 1004
INTER-ASIA VENTURE MANAGEMENT LIMITED, 2881
INTERSOUTH PARTNERS, 1008
INVENTURE PARTNERS, 2886
INVENTUS, 1013
INVEXCEL PATRIMONIO, 2891
INVUS GROUP, 1018
IPOSCOPE NV/SA, 2895
IRISH ANGELS, 1019
ISOURCE GESTION, 2899
JAFCO COMPANY LIMITED JAPAN, 2906
JC TECHNOLOGIES LTD, 2909
JERUSALEM VENTURE PARTNERS, 2910
JF SHEA VENTURES, 1036
JK&B CAPITAL, 1038
JMI EQUITY FUND LP, 1041
JUMPSTART INC, 1047
KAEDAN INVESTMENTS, 2914
KALORI GROUP INVESTMENTS, 2915
KBL FOUNDER SA, 2917
KERRY CAPITAL ADVISORS, 1067
KLASS CAPITAL, 2170
KODIAK VENTURE PARTNERS, 1080
LABRADOR VENTURES, 1089
LANDSBANKI VENTURES, 2929
LAUNCHCAPITAL, 1097
LAUNCHPAD VENTURE GROUP, 1100
LBBW VENTURE CAPITAL, 2932
LEAPFROG VENTURES, 1102
LEASING TECHNOLOGIES INTERNATIONAL INC., 1103
LEVINE LEICHTMAN CAPITAL PARTNERS, 1111
LIBERTY CAPITAL PARTNERS, 1114
LIBERTY PARTNERS, 1116
LLR PARTNERS INC, 1136
LOCUS VENTURES, 1138
LONG RIVER VENTURES, 1142
LOVETT MILLER & COMPANY, 1148
LRM - INVESTERINGSMAATSCHAPPIJ VOOR LIMBURG, 2949
M/C PARTNERS, 1153
M25 GROUP, 1155
MAINE ANGELS, 1160
MANTELLA VENTURE PARTNERS, 2182
MARATHON VENTURE CAPITAL FUND LIMITED, 2954
MARYLAND VENTURE FUND, 1169
MASON WELLS, 1171
MASSACHUSETTS CAPITAL RESOURCE COMPANY, 1173
MASTHEAD VENTURE PARTNERS, 1175
MAYFIELD FUND, 1184
MBF CAPITAL CORPORATION, 1188
MCROCK CAPITAL, 2190

Industry Preference Index / Software

MEDRA CAPITAL, 2960
MERCATOR INVESTMENTS, 2192
MERCURY FUND, 1206
MERITUS VENTURES, 1214
MERUS CAPITAL, 1218
METROPOLITAN PARTNERS GROUP, 1225
MIDINVEST LIMITED, 2966
MIDVEN, 2967
MILLENIUM TECHNOLOGY VALUE PARTNERS, 1235
MISSION VENTURES, 1239
MISSIONOG, 1240
MISTRAL VENTURE PARTNERS, 2195
MK CAPITAL, 1242
MMV CAPITAL PARTNERS, 2196
MOHR-DAVIDOW VENTURES, 1247
MOMENTUM FUNDS MANAGEMENT PTY LIMITED, 2975
MONITOR VENTURES, 1249
MOUNTAINEER CAPITAL, 1262
NAVITAS CAPITAL, 1282
NEEDHAM CAPITAL PARTNERS, 1288
NEST VENTURES, 1290
NEUHAUS PARTNERS, 2994
NEW ATLANTIC VENTURES, 1291
NEW MOUNTAIN CAPITAL, 1301
NEW VENTURE PARTNERS, 1305
NEW YORK CITY ENTREPRENEURIAL FUND New York City Economic Development Corporation, 1307
NEW YORK LIFE CAPITAL PARTNERS, 1309
NEW YORK VENTURE PARTNERS, 1310
NEWLIGHT MANAGEMENT, 1314
NEXT WORLD CAPITAL, 1319
NFX, 1323
NKM CAPITAL, 1329
NORTH ATLANTIC CAPITAL CORPORATION, 1333
NORTH BRIDGE VENTURE PARTNERS, 1334
NORWEST VENTURE PARTNERS, 1346
NOVAK BIDDLE VENTURE PARTNERS, 1348
NYC SEED, 1358
OAK INVESTMENT PARTNERS, 1361
OKAPI VENTURE CAPITAL, 1371
OLYMPUS PARTNERS, 1372
OPENVIEW VENTURE PARTNERS, 1380
OPUS CAPITAL, 1381
OSAGE PARTNERS, 1387
OVP VENTURE PARTNERS, 1391
OWL VENTURES, 1392
OXANTIUM VENTURES, 1393
OYSTER INVEST, 3022
PAC-LINK MANAGEMENT CORP., 3024
PALISADES VENTURES, 1402
PALO ALTO VENTURE PARTNERS, 1405
PALOMAR VENTURES, 1407
PARTECH INTERNATIONAL, 1416
PELION VENTURE PARTNERS, 1425
PENINSULA VENTURES, 1427
PENN VENTURE PARTNERS, 1428
PENNELL VENTURE PARTNERS LLC, 1429
PI CAPITAL GROUP LLC, 1440
PIEDMONT ANGEL NETWORK, 1442
PINNACLE MERCHANT CAPITAL, 2222
PITANGO VENTURE CAPITAL, 3039
POND VENTURES, 3047
PRESIDIO VENTURES, 1474
PRIME TECHNOLOGY VENTURES NV, 3051
PRISM VENTUREWORKS, 1478
PRIVATE EQUITY PARTNERS SPA, 3053
PROJECT 11 VENTURES, 1487
PROMUS VENTURES, 1489
QUEST FOR GROWTH, 3069
QUESTER CAPITAL MANAGEMENT LIMITED, 3070
QUESTMARK PARTNERS LP, 1515
RAFAEL DEVELOPMENT CORPORATION (RDC) LIMITED, 3072
REACH CAPITAL, 1527
RECIPROCAL VENTURES, 1528
REDPOINT VENTURES, 1534
REED ELSEVIER VENTURES, 3074
RESONANT VENTURE PARTNERS, 1547

REVEL PARTNERS, 1554
RIDGE VENTURES, 1563
RIDGEWOOD CAPITAL, 1564
ROPART ASSET MANAGEMENT, 1583
ROSER VENTURES LLC, 1586
ROUGH DRAFT VENTURES, 1589
RPM VENTURES, 1592
RRE VENTURES, 1593
RUNA CAPITAL, 3088
S3 VENTURES, 1597
SAINTS CAPITAL, 1604
SAMSUNG VENTURE INVESTMENT CORPORATION Samsung Electronics, 3098
SAND HILL ANGELS, 1613
SANDBOX INDUSTRIES, 1615
SATORI CAPITAL, 1622
SBRC INVESTMENT CONSULTATION LIMITED, 3101
SCALE VENTURE PARTNERS, 1626
SELBY VENTURE PARTNERS, 1646
SEQUOIA CAPITAL, 1654
SEVIN ROSEN FUNDS, 1658
SHANNON COMMERCIAL PROPERTIES, 3115
SHASTA VENTURES, 1663
SHEPHERD VENTURES, 1664
SIERRA ANGELS, 1669
SIERRA VENTURES, 1670
SIGMA PARTNERS, 1672
SIGNATURE CAPITAL LLC, 3120
SMART BUSINESS CONSULTING, 3124
SMARTINVEST VENTURES, 1695
SOCIAL VENTURE CIRCLE, 3277
SOLID VENTURES, 3128
SOUTHEAST INTERACTIVE TECHNOLOGY FUNDS, 1709
SOUTHERN CAPITOL VENTURES, 1710
SPACEVEST, 1714
SPECTRUM EQUITY INVESTORS LP, 1717
SPENCER TRASK VENTURES, 1720
SPERO VENTURES, 1721
SPLIT ROCK PARTNERS, 1725
SPRING LAKE EQUITY PARTNERS, 1728
STAENBERG VENTURE PARTNERS, 1733
STAGEONE VENTURES, 3136
STARTUP CAPITAL VENTURES, 1737
STARVEST PARTNERS, 1738
STATELINE ANGELS, 1740
STORM VENTURES, 1747
SUCSY, FISCHER & COMPANY, 1750
SUMMIT BRIDGE CAPITAL, 3147
SVB CAPITAL, 1764
SWITCH VENTURES, 1768
SYCAMORE VENTURES, 1769
SYMMETRIC CAPITAL, 1770
TAMAR TECHNOLOGY VENTURES LIMITED, 3158
TAMIR FISHMAN VENTURES, 3159
TANK STREAM VENTURES, 3160
TARGET PARTNERS, 3161
TEAKWOOD CAPITAL, 1783
TECH COAST ANGELS, 1784
TECHNOCAP, 2263
TECHNOLOGY CROSSOVER VENTURES, 1785
TELESOFT PARTNERS, 1793
TELESYSTEM, 2264
TEN ELEVEN VENTURES, 1794
TENAYA CAPITAL, 1796
TENX VENTURES, 2266
TEUZA MANAGEMENT & DEVELOPMENT LTD, 3171
TFG CAPITAL AG, 3172
TGAP VENTURES, 1802
THOMA BRAVO LLC, 1814
THOMSON-CSF VENTURES, 3176
TIE ANGELS GROUP SEATTLE, 1825
TL VENTURES, 1828
TRANS COSMOS INCORPORATED, 3185
TRANSITION PARTNERS LTD, 1837
TRIBECA VENTURE PARTNERS, 1849
TRINITY VENTURE CAPITAL TVC Holdings plc, 3191
TRINITY VENTURES, 1853

Industry Preference Index / Software & IT

TRITON VENTURES, 1855
TRU MANAGEMENT, 1858
TRUE VENTURES, 1860
TSG EQUITY PARTNERS, 1862
TVC CAPITAL, 1869
UNCORK CAPITAL, 1879
UPDATA VENTURE PARTNERS, 1886
US VENTURE PARTNERS, 1896
VALAR VENTURES, 1897
VALLEY VENTURES LP, 1901
VELOCITY EQUITY PARTNERS LLC, 1913
VENCORE CAPITAL, 1915
VENTURE CAPITAL FUND OF NEW ENGLAND, 1920
VERDEXUS, 2279
VERITAS VENTURE PARTNERS, 3212
VERIZON VENTURES, 1926
VIKING VENTURE, 3216
VISION CAPITAL, 1937
VITAL FINANCIAL LLC, 1940
VORTEX PARTNERS, 1944
VOYAGER CAPITAL, 1945
WALDEN INTERNATIONAL, 1951
WALDEN ISRAEL VENTURE CAPITAL, 3231
WALDEN VENTURE CAPITAL, 1952
WESTERN AMERICA CAPITAL GROUP, 2286
WESTLAKE SECURITIES, 1976
WESTSUMMIT CAPITAL, 3235
WESTVIEW CAPITAL PARTNERS, 1979
WHEATLEY PARTNERS, 1981
WILDCAT VENTURE PARTNERS, 1985
WINDWARD VENTURES, 1995
WOODBRIDGE GROUP, 2004
WOODSIDE FUND, 2005
WORLDVIEW TECHNOLOGY PARTNERS, 2007
WRF CAPITAL, 2008
XANGE PRIVATE EQUITY, 3239
YFM GROUP, 3244
YL VENTURES, 3246
YUUWA CAPITAL, 3248
ZM CAPITAL, 2020
ZONE VENTURES, 2021

Software & IT
RIVERSIDE COMPANY, 1572

Software & Information Services
CAPITAL RESOURCE PARTNERS, 402

Software & Internet
CALIFORNIA COAST VENTURE FORUM, 3257
TRIBE CAPITAL, 1848

Software & Services
DCM, 596
REVOLUTION LLC, 1555

Software (incl. SaaS)
RHO CANADA VENTURES, 2239

Software Development
HENQ, 2822

Software Services
3I ASIA PACIFIC 3i Group, 2297
ADARA VENTURE PARTNERS, 2342
ALTA BERKELEY ASSOCIATES, 2380
ARGENTUM GROUP, 161
CENTERPOINT VENTURE PARTNERS, 444
CHRYSALIS CAPITAL ChrysCapital, 2599
CHRYSCAPITAL MANAGEMENT COMPANIES ChrysCapital, 2600
CITA GESTION, 2607
COMMONWEALTH CAPITAL VENTURES LP, 521
ELECTRA PARTNERS ASIA LIMITED SFC of Hong Kong, 2694
GMT COMMUNICATIONS PARTNERS LLP, 2789
GRANDBANKS CAPITAL, 848
INSIGHT VENTURE PARTNERS, 1000
LIBERTY PARTNERS, 1116
MADRONA VENTURE GROUP, 1158
McLEAN WATSON CAPITAL, 2199
SOUTHERN CROSS VENTURE PARTNERS, 1711

Software Systems
CALIFORNIA TECHNOLOGY VENTURES, 371

Solar Energy
ANGELENO GROUP, 126
AZCA, 214
ENERTECH CAPITAL, 676

Solar Infrastructure
FORESIGHT VENTURE PARTNERS, 2749

Space
11.2 CAPITAL, 4
CORNERSTONE CAPITAL HOLDINGS, 540
KHOSLA VENTURES, 1069

Space Technology
BESSEMER VENTURE PARTNERS, 260
BOOST VC, 307
FRONTIER VENTURES, 792
GOOD NEWS VENTURES, 2138
NEWABLE VENTURES, 2997

Specialist Financial Businesses
ROTHSCHILD AUSTRALIA - ARROW PRIVATE EQUITY Rothschild Group, 3086

Specialized Services
CLEARVIEW CAPITAL, 503

Specialty Chemicals
AMERICAN SECURITIES LLC, 110
BROOKSIDE EQUITY PARTNERS LLC, 353
CAPITAL FOR BUSINESS, INC, 399
CAPITAL SOUTHWEST CORPORATION, 403
CENTERFIELD CAPITAL PARTNERS, 443
FCF PARTNERS LP, 719
GLADSTONE CAPITAL, 828
GRYPHON MANAGEMENT COMPANY, 882
HERITAGE PARTNERS, 926
HIG CAPITAL, 928
HORIZON PARTNERS, LTD, 945
JMH CAPITAL, 1040
MOUNTAINEER CAPITAL, 1262
POUSCHINE COOK CAPITAL MANAGEMENT LLC, 1466

Specialty Consumer
HAWTHORN EQUITY PARTNERS, 916

Specialty Consumer Brands
CUE BALL GROUP, 567

Specialty Consumer Products
GRIDIRON CAPITAL, 873
PARALLEL INVESTMENT PARTNERS, 1415

Specialty Distribution
VALOR EQUITY PARTNERS, 1902
WATER STREET HEALTHCARE PARTNERS, 1961

Specialty Finance
BIP CAPITAL, 271
CLARION CAPITAL PARTNERS LLC, 492
SALT CREEK CAPITAL, 1609
WELLS FARGO CAPITAL FINANCE, 1970

Specialty Food Products
PACIFIC COMMUNITY VENTURES, 1396

Specialty Healthcare
ALLOS VENTURES, 86

Industry Preference Index / Tech-Enabled Business Services

Specialty Lending
NEWLIGHT PARTNERS, 1315

Specialty Manufacturing
ALBION INVESTORS LLC, 78
CALTIUS STRUCTURED CAPITAL, 374
GLADSTONE CAPITAL, 828
NEWSPRING CAPITAL, 1317
SIGNAL HILL EQUITY PARTNERS, 2255
STONEBRIDGE PARTNERS, 1744
TGAP VENTURES, 1802

Specialty Manufacturing & Distribution
BEHRMAN CAPITAL, 245

Specialty Packaging
STONEBRIDGE PARTNERS, 1744

Specialty Retail
BUNKER HILL CAPITAL, 359
CASTANEA PARTNERS, 421
CLARION CAPITAL PARTNERS LLC, 492
GRYPHON INVESTORS, 881
HARVEST PARTNERS, 914
INVUS GROUP, 1018
SEIDLER EQUITY PARTNERS, 1645
TWJ CAPITAL, 1873

Specialty Services
LAKE CAPITAL, 1091
PEGASUS CAPITAL GROUP, 1424

Specialty Staffing
CALTIUS STRUCTURED CAPITAL, 374

Speech and Natural Language
FLYING FISH, 755

Sports
ACKRELL CAPITAL, 44
BREAKAWAY VENTURES, 329
DETROIT VENTURE PARTNERS, 607
FALCONHEAD CAPITAL, 717
INTEL CAPITAL, 1004
KB PARTNERS, 1056
PROSPECT PARTNERS LLC, 1492
RAPTOR GROUP, 1524
SWANDER PACE CAPITAL, 1767
UNITED TALENT AGENCY VENTURES, 1883

Sports, Media & Entertainment
REVOLUTION LLC, 1555

Staffing
ACCESS CAPITAL, 35

Stem Cell Therapy
SPENCER TRASK VENTURES, 1720

Storage
ELECTRA PARTNERS ASIA LIMITED SFC of Hong Kong, 2694
EVERCORE CAPITAL PARTNERS, 699
FORMULA VENTURES LIMITED Formula Group, 2750
GENESIS PARTNERS, 2775
GOOD NEWS VENTURES, 2138
GRANDBANKS CAPITAL, 848
JACKSON SQUARE VENTURES, 1024
KHOSLA VENTURES, 1069
NEW VENTURE PARTNERS, 1305
NTH POWER TECHNOLOGIES, 1355
OAK INVESTMENT PARTNERS, 1361
PITANGO VENTURE CAPITAL, 3039
REDPOINT VENTURES, 1534

Storage & Computing
MENLO VENTURES, 1202

Storage Networking
ACCEL-KKR LLC, 29

Stored Energy
INFIELD CAPITAL, 988

Superannuation
AUSTRALIAN ETHICAL INVESTMENT LIMITED, 2456

Supply Chain Management
ODYSSEY INVESTMENT PARTNERS, 1368
TOP RENERGY INC., 2271

Supply Chain Technology
CAMBRIDGE CAPITAL, 380

Sustainability
ALTRIA VENTURES, 102
CULTIVIAN SANDBOX VENTURES, 570
DBL PARTNERS, 595
FLAGSHIP PIONEERING, 747
GRANITE HILL CAPITAL PARTNERS, LLC, 851
MINDFULL INVESTORS, 1236
MITSUI SUMITOMO INSURANCE VENTURE CAPITAL CO, 2971
PANGAEA VENTURES LTD, 2213
SJF VENTURES, 1689
SPRING LANE CAPITAL, 1729
URBAN INNOVATION FUND, 1893

Sustainable Energy
ATLANTA VENTURES, 189
CASTROL INNOVENTURES, 2568
KHOSLA VENTURES, 1069

Sustainable Food and Agriculture
INVESTECO, 2161

Sustainable Living
PHYSIC VENTURES, 1438

Sustainable Materials
WHEB GROUP, 3237

Sustainable Products
COLLABORATIVE FUND, 511

Sustainable Technologies
SELBY VENTURE PARTNERS, 1646

Sustainable Transportation
FUTURE VENTURES, 800

Systems & Hardware
GABRIEL VENTURE PARTNERS, 805
NORWEST VENTURE PARTNERS, 1346

Systems & Peripherals
GLOBESPAN CAPITAL PARTNERS, 835

Systems & Software
MASS VENTURES, 1172

TMT
3I GESTION SA 3i Group, 2302
SB CHINA VENTURE CAPITAL, 3100
ZHENFUND, 3251

Tech Enabled Services
ACTIVE VENTURE PARTNERS, 2339

Tech Services
CALTIUS STRUCTURED CAPITAL, 374

Tech-Enabled Business Services
BLUE HERON CAPITAL, 288

1233

Industry Preference Index / Technology

Technology
(@)VENTURES, 1
.406 VENTURES, 2
1843 CAPITAL, 7
212 CAPITAL PARTNERS, 2294
3TS CAPITAL PARTNERS 3i Group plc, 2309
3i GROUP PLC, 2311
645 VENTURES, 13
A-GRADE INVESTMENTS, 15
AAVISHKAAR, 2313
ACACIA CAPITAL PARTNERS, 2322
ACADIA WOODS PARTNERS, 26
ACCEDE CAPITAL, 2323
ACCEL-KKR LLC, 29
ACCELEPRISE, 30
ACCELERATOR VENTURES, 32
ACCENTURE TECHNOLOGY VENTURES, 2326
ACCESS VENTURE PARTNERS LLC, 36
ACCOLADE PARTNERS, 37
ACCOMPLICE, 38
ACE & COMPANY, 2329
ACKRELL CAPITAL, 44
ACREW CAPITAL, 49
ACT ONE VENTURES, 50
ACTIVE VENTURE PARTNERS, 2339
ADAMS CAPITAL MANAGEMENT, 56
ADAMS STREET PARTNERS, LLC, 57
ADVANCIT CAPITAL, 60
ALBUM VC, 79
ALLEGRO INVESTMENT FUND, 2366
ALLELE FUNDS, 2367
ALLIANCE VENTURE, 2369
ALMAZ CAPITAL, 89
ALPINVEST GmbH Alpinvest, 2377
ALPINVEST HOLDING NV Alpinvest, 2378
ALTA BERKELEY ASSOCIATES, 2380
ALTA PARTNERS, 94
ALTOS VENTURES, 100
AMANET TECHNOLOGIES LIMITED, 2389
AME CLOUD VENTURES, 107
AMICUS CAPITAL PARTNERS, 2392
AMPHION CAPITAL PARTNERS, 2397
ANALYTICS VENTURES, 121
ANT FINANCIAL, 2404
APAX GLOBIS PARTNERS & COMPANY Globis Capital Partners/Apax, 2414
ARAVAIPA VENTURES, 146
ARBOR VENTURES, 148
ARGENTUM GROUP, 161
ARMADA INVESTMENT GROUP, 2427
ARTHUR P GOULD & COMPANY, 172
ASCENT VENTURE PARTNERS, 178
ASTELLA INVESTMENTS, 2438
ATLANTA VENTURES, 189
ATLANTIC VENTURES, 2444
ATLAS VENTURE: FRANCE, 2445
ATOMICO, 2446
AUDAX GROUP, 194
AUGMENTUM CAPITAL, 2450
AUSTRAL CAPITAL PARTNERS, 2455
AUTO TECH VENTURES, 204
AVAC, 2048
AWAY REALTY, 2465
AXVENTURES, 2470
AZINI CAPITAL PARTNERS, 2472
BALLPARK VENTURES, 2479
BARCLAYS VENTURES Barclays, 2486
BARING VOSTOK CAPITAL PARTNERS, 2491
BASE VENTURES, 229
BASECAMP VENTURES, 230
BATTELLE VENTURES, 233
BATTERY VENTURES, 235
BC PARTNERS LIMITED, 2497
BEN FRANKLIN TECHNOLOGY PARTNERS, 246
BERINGER CAPITAL, 2057
BERLIN TECHNOLOGIE, 2503
BERTRAM CAPITAL, 257
BESTPORT VENTURES, 2507
BIGFOOT VENTURES, 2511
BIP CAPITAL, 271
BIRCHMERE VENTURES, 272
BISON CAPITAL ASSET MANAGEMENT LLC, 274
BLACK DIAMOND VENTURES, 275
BLACKSTONE PRIVATE EQUITY GROUP, 277
BLAST FUNDING, 279
BLOOM EQUITY, 2522
BLU VENTURE INVESTORS, 285
BLUE BRIGHT VENTURES, 286
BLUE HERON CAPITAL, 288
BLUEFISH VENTURES, 294
BLUETREE VENTURE FUND, 298
BLUMBERG CAPITAL, 301
BLUME VENTURES, 2526
BMP AKTIENGESELLSCHAFT BMP Venture Capital, 2528
BOLDCAP VENTURES LLC, 304
BOOST VC, 307
BOREALIS VENTURES, 308
BOSTON CAPITAL VENTURES, 310
BOSTON GLOBAL VENTURES, LLC, 311
BRADFORD EQUITIES MANAGEMENT LLC, 321
BRIGHTSTONE VENTURE CAPITAL, 341
BRILLIANT VENTURES, 342
BROADHAVEN CAPITAL PARTNERS, 343
BROADHORN CAPITAL, 344
BROOKLYN BRIDGE VENTURES, 351
BRUML CAPITAL CORPORATION, 355
BRYANT PARK VENTURES, 356
BUILD VENTURES, 2068
CALIFORNIA COAST VENTURE FORUM, 3257
CAMP ONE VENTURES, 384
CAMP VENTURES, 385
CANAAN PARTNERS, 386
CANOPY BOULDER, 392
CANROCK VENTURES, 393
CANYON CREEK CAPITAL, 397
CAPMAN CAPITAL MANAGEMENT OY, 2562
CAPX PARTNERS, 407
CARBON VENTURES, 408
CARDINAL VENTURE CAPITAL, 411
CARLYLE ASIA INVESTMENT ADVISORS LIMITED Carlyle Group, 2565
CARLYLE GROUP, 413
CASABONA VENTURES, 418
CASTROL INNOVENTURES, 2568
CAVA CAPITAL, 431
CEDAR VENTURES LLC, 437
CEO VENTURES, 450
CERBERUS CAPITAL MANAGEMENT, 451
CHARLOTTE STREET CAPITAL, 2586
CHASE CAPITAL PARTNERS, 2588
CHAZEN CAPITAL PARTNERS, 460
CHEVRON TECHNOLOGY VENTURES, 466
CHRYSALIS VENTURES, 475
CIBC CAPITAL MARKETS, 2079
CIBC INNOVATION BANKING, 2080
CINCO CAPITAL, 2604
CINTRIFUSE, 480
CLARITAS CAPITAL, 493
CLAYTON ASSOCIATES, 496
CLEARLAKE CAPITAL, 500
CLEARSPRING CAPITAL PARTNERS, 2082
CNF INVESTMENTS Clark Enterprises, Inc., 508
COATUE MANAGEMENT, 509
COLLABORATIVE FUND, 511
COLLER CAPITAL LIMITED, 2621
COLT VENTURES, 514
COMPANHIA RIOGRANDENSE DE PARTICIPACOES, 2626
COMPOUND, 525
CONTINENTAL VENTURE CAPITAL LIMITED, 2631
CONTOUR VENTURE PARTNERS, 533
CONVERSION CAPITAL, 535
CONVEXA Tyveholmen AS, 2632
CORE PACIFIC - YAMAICHI CAPITAL LIMITED Core Pacific Securities Company Ltd, 2633

Industry Preference Index / Technology

COSTELLA KIRSCH, 548
COTTONWOOD TECHNOLOGY FUND, 549
COWBOY VENTURES, 552
CRUNCHFUND, 564
CULTIVATION CAPITAL, 569
CULTIVIAN SANDBOX VENTURES, 570
CUSTER CAPITAL, 571
CXO FUND, 574
CapitalG, 578
DANCAP PRIVATE EQUITY, 2094
DANEVEST TECH FUND ADVISORS, 583
DAVENPORT RESOURCES LLC, 588
DAVID N DEUTSCH & COMPANY LLC, 589
DAYLIGHT PARTNERS, 594
DB CAPITAL PARTNERS (ASIA), 2652
DE NOVO VENTURES, 598
DEFTA PARTNERS, 602
DEUTSCHE BETEILIGUNGS AG, 2660
DFJ VENTURE CAPITAL, 609
DIAMOND TECHVENTURES, 612
DISCOVERY CAPITAL, 2097
DISRUPTOR CAPITAL, 617
DJF DRAGONFUND CHINA, 2667
DRAPER ESPRIT, 2674
DRAPER TRIANGLE VENTURES, 628
DRESNER COMPANIES, 629
DRIVE CAPITAL, 630
DUCHOSSOIS CAPITAL MANAGEMENT, 633
DUNDEE VENTURE CAPITAL, 635
DUTCHESS CAPITAL, 638
E.BRICKS DIGITAL, 2681
EASTVEN VENTURE PARTNERS, 645
ECOAST ANGEL NETWORK, 649
ECOSYSTEM VENTURES, 650
EDELSON TECHNOLOGY PARTNERS, 651
EDGEWATER CAPITAL PARTNERS, 653
EGL HOLDINGS, 656
EM WARBURG, PINCUS & COMPANY INTERNATIONAL, 2697
EM WARBURG, PINCUS & COMPANY JAPAN, 2698
EMERALD OCEAN CAPITAL, 664
EMIGRANT CAPITAL, 667
ENERTECH CAPITAL, 676
ENSPIRE CAPITAL PTE LTD, 2703
ENTREPIA VENTURES, 682
EQUITEK CAPITAL, 692
EQUITY PARTNERS PTY LIMITED, 2715
EUROPEAN FOUNDERS FUND, 2723
EUROPEAN INVESTMENT FUND, 2724
EVERCORE CAPITAL PARTNERS, 699
EXPERIMENT FUND, 708
EXPIBEL BV, 2728
FA TECHNOLOGY VENTURES, 711
FAIRHAVEN CAPITAL, 712
FCA VENTURE PARTNERS, 718
FGA PARTNERS, 725
FIDELITY GROWTH PARTNERS ASIA, 2733
FIDELITY GROWTH PARTNERS EUROPE, 2734
FIKA VENTURES, 728
FINAM GLOBAL, 2736
FINANCE WALES, 2737
FIRST CAPITAL VENTURE, 735
FIRST FLIGHT VENTURE CENTER, 737
FIRST NEW ENGLAND CAPITAL LP, 739
FLAGSHIP PIONEERING, 747
FLUKE VENTURE PARTNERS, 753
FOCUS VENTURES, 757
FOG CITY CAPITAL, 758
FORREST BINKLEY & BROWN, 765
FOUNDATION MARKETS, 2122
FOUNDER PARTNERS, 772
FRANKLIN STREET EQUITY PARTNERS, 780
FRESH VC, 785
FRESHTRACKS CAPITAL, 786
FREYCINET INVESTMENTS, 2125
FRONTENAC COMPANY, 789
FTV CAPITAL, 793
FULCRUM EQUITY PARTNERS, 794

FULL CIRCLE INVESTMENTS, 2762
GABRIEL VENTURE PARTNERS, 805
GARAGE TECHNOLOGY VENTURES, 807
GE ASIA PACIFIC CAPITAL TECHNOLOGY FUND, 2767
GEMINI INVESTORS, 812
GEMINI ISRAEL VENTURE FUNDS LIMITED, 2770
GENACAST VENTURES, 814
GENES GMBH VENTURE SERVICES, 2774
GEODESIC CAPITAL, 820
GET2VOLUME ACCELERATOR, 2778
GLASSWING VENTURES, 829
GLOBAL CATALYST PARTNERS, 833
GOLDEN OPPORTUNITIES FUND, 2136
GOLDEN SEEDS, 841
GOLDEN VENTURE PARTNERS, 2137
GOLDMAN SACHS INVESTMENT PARTNERS, 842
GRANITE HILL CAPITAL PARTNERS, LLC, 851
GRANITE VENTURES, 852
GREENSPRING ASSOCIATES, 867
GREIF & COMPANY, 869
GROTECH VENTURES, 876
GROVE STREET ADVISORS LLC, 879
GSV VENTURES, 883
GUGGENHEIM PARTNERS, 885
GULFSTAR GROUP, 888
HALLEY VENTURE PARTNERS, 895
HALOGEN VENTURES, 896
HANCOCK CAPITAL MANAGEMENT, 901
HARBERT MANAGEMENT CORPORATION, 904
HARBOR LIGHT CAPITAL PARTNERS, 907
HARBOURVEST PARTNERS LLC, 909
HARRISON METAL, 911
HAWTHORN EQUITY PARTNERS, 916
HEARST VENTURES, 922
HELIANT VENTURES, 2817
HELLMAN & FRIEDMAN LLC, 924
HERCULES TECHNOLOGY GROWTH CAPITAL, INC, 925
HG CAPITAL, 2823
HIGH COUNTRY VENTURE, 930
HIGHER GROUND LABS, 934
HOPEWELL VENTURES, 944
HORIZON TECHNOLOGY FINANCE, 946
HORIZON VENTURES LLC, 947
HOUSTON HEALTH VENTURES, 951
HOXTON VENTURES, 2834
HUDSON VENTURE PARTNERS, 954
HYPUR VENTURES, 963
I-HATCH VENTURES LLC, 964
IBM VENTURE CAPITAL GROUP, 967
IDEALAB, 972
ILE-DE-FRANCE, 2855
IMPERIAL INNOVATIONS, 2858
INDUSTRIO VENTURES, 2868
INDUSTRY VENTURES, 986
INITIATIVE CAPITAL LIMITED, 2154
INNOSPRING, 994
INNOVA MEMPHIS, 995
INNOVACORP, 2155
INNOVATION ENDEAVORS, 996
INNOVATION PLATFORM CAPITAL, 997
INNOVATION WORKS, 998
INOVIA CAPITAL, 2157
INSTITUTIONAL VENTURE PARTNERS, 1001
INTERLACE VENTURES, 1006
INVENT, 1012
ISIS EP LLP F & C, 2898
ISOURCE GESTION, 2899
ITC VENTURES, 2903
IXORA VENTURES, 2904
J-SEED VENTURES INCORPORATED, 2905
JAGUAR CAPITAL PARTNERS, 1025
JAVELIN VENTURE PARTNERS, 1028
JC2 VENTURES, 1031
JETBLUE TECHNOLOGY VENTURES, 1035
K9 VENTURES, 1050
KALORI GROUP INVESTMENTS, 2915
KEIRETSU FORUM, 1061

1235

Industry Preference Index / Technology

KENSINGTON CAPITAL PARTNERS, 2167
KEPHA PARTNERS, 1065
KERNEL CAPITAL, 2918
KERRY CAPITAL ADVISORS, 1067
KILLICK CAPITAL, 2168
KILMER CAPITAL PARTNERS, 2169
KLEINWORT CAPITAL LIMITED, 2923
KOHLBERG KRAVIS ROBERTS & COMPANY, 1082
KPG VENTURES, 1084
LAKE CAPITAL, 1091
LASALLE CAPITAL GROUP, 1093
LAUDER PARTNERS LLC, 1095
LAUNCHBOX DIGITAL, 1096
LAUNCHCAPITAL, 1097
LAUNCHPAD LA, 1099
LAUNCHPAD VENTURES, 2931
LDV CAPITAL, 1101
LEO CAPITAL HOLDINGS, LLC, 1108
LEONIA MB GROUP/MB FUNDS, 2937
LIBERTY CITY VENTURES, 1115
LIGHTHOUSE CAPITAL PARTNERS, 1119
LIGHTHOUSE EQUITY PARTNERS, 2176
LINLEY CAPITAL, 1130
LOVETT MILLER & COMPANY, 1148
LUDLOW VENTURES, 1150
LUX CAPITAL, 1151
M/C PARTNERS, 1153
MADRONA VENTURE GROUP, 1158
MAPLE LEAF ANGELS, 2184
MARYLAND VENTURE FUND, 1169
MASSACHUSETTS CAPITAL RESOURCE COMPANY, 1173
MATCHSTICK VENTURES, 1176
MATH VENTURE PARTNERS, 1178
MATON VENTURE, 1180
MCG CAPITAL CORPORATION, 1189
MCGOVERN CAPITAL, 1191
MEDIA VENTURE PARTNERS, 1195
MEDRA CAPITAL, 2960
MERCATO PARTNERS, 1204
MERITUS VENTURES, 1214
METROPOLITAN PARTNERS GROUP, 1225
MIRALTA, 2194
MISSION VENTURES, 1239
MISSIONOG, 1240
MMT MILLENNIUM MATERIALS TECHNOLOGIES FUND LP, 2973
MMV CAPITAL PARTNERS, 2196
MONTLAKE CAPITAL, 1250
MOTIV PARTNERS, 1258
MOUNTAIN GROUP CAPITAL, 1261
MOUNTAINEER CAPITAL, 1262
MOZART VENTURE PARTNERS, 1264
MS&AD VENTURES, 1269
NAVY CAPITAL, 1283
NBC CAPITAL PTY LIMITED, 2988
NEEDHAM CAPITAL PARTNERS, 1288
NEOTENY COMPANY LIMITED, 2991
NEW ATLANTIC VENTURES, 1291
NEW YORK ANGELS, 1306
NEW YORK VENTURE PARTNERS, 1310
NEWBURY VENTURES, 1311
NEWBURY, PIRET & COMPANY, 1312
NEXTSTAGE CAPITAL, 1321
NEXUS VENTURE PARTNERS Nexus India Capital Advisors Pvt Ltd, 3001
NFX, 1323
NKM CAPITAL, 1329
NORO-MOSELEY PARTNERS, 1331
NORTH WEST FUND, 3010
NORTHERN LIGHT VENTURE CAPITAL, 1340
NORTHGATE, 1341
NORTHSTAR VENTURES, 3012
NORWEST EQUITY PARTNERS, 1345
NOVENTI VENTURES, 1352
NYC SEED, 1358
OAK HILL CAPITAL PARTNERS, 1360
OCA VENTURES, 1364
OCEANSHORE VENTURES, 1365

ONE EQUITY PARTNERS, 1376
OPEN PRAIRIE VENTURES, 1379
OPENVIEW VENTURE PARTNERS, 1380
OPUS CAPITAL, 1381
ORIGIN VENTURES, 1384
OUTCOME CAPITAL, 1388
OUTPOST CAPITAL, 1390
OWL VENTURES, 1392
OYSTER INVEST, 3022
PALADIN CAPITAL GROUP, 1400
PALOMAR VENTURES, 1407
PANORAMA CAPITAL, 1410
PAPPAS VENTURES, 1412
PARKWALK ADVISORS, 3028
PASSION CAPITAL, 3030
PENINSULA VENTURES, 1427
PERMIRA Permira Advisers LLP, 3033
PHENOMEN VENTURES, 3034
PHYTO PARTNERS, 1439
PI CAPITAL GROUP LLC, 1440
PIEDMONT ANGEL NETWORK, 1442
POLARIS VENTURE PARTNERS, 1460
PORTUGAL CAPITAL VENTURES Institutional Headquarters, 3048
PRAIRIEGOLD VENTURE PARTNERS, 1470
PRITZKER GROUP VENTURE CAPITAL, 1480
PROFOUNDERS CAPITAL, 3055
PROJECT 11 VENTURES, 1487
PSL VENTURES, 1499
QUANTUM CAPITAL PARTNERS, 1510
RAND CAPITAL CORPORATION, 1523
RAPTOR GROUP, 1524
RBC CAPITAL MARKETS, 2231
REACH CAPITAL, 1527
RECIPROCAL VENTURES, 1528
RED SEA VENTURES, 1530
REED ELSEVIER VENTURES, 3074
REMBRANDT VENTURE PARTNERS, 1540
RETHINK IMPACT, 1552
REVO CAPITAL, 3078
RIDGE VENTURES, 1563
RITTENHOUSE VENTURES, 1568
RIVERSIDE COMPANY, 1572
ROADMAP CAPITAL INC., 2242
ROPART ASSET MANAGEMENT, 1583
ROTH CAPITAL PARTNERS, 1588
RPM VENTURES, 1592
S3 VENTURES, 1597
SAFEGUARD SCIENTIFICS, 1601
SAFFRON HILL VENTURES, 3092
SAGEVIEW CAPITAL, 1602
SAINTS CAPITAL, 1604
SCALE VENTURE PARTNERS, 1626
SCALEUP VENTURES, 2249
SCIFI VC, 1631
SCOTIABANK PRIVATE EQUITY, 2250
SEAPORT CAPITAL, 1638
SEAWAY VALLEY CAPITAL CORPORATION, 1639
SEB VENTURE CAPITAL, 3106
SECOND ALPHA, 1640
SECTION 32, 1643
SEQUEL VENTURE PARTNERS, 1653
SEVEN PEAKS VENTURES, 1656
SEVENTYSIX CAPITAL, 1657
SEVIN ROSEN FUNDS, 1658
SHAW KWEI AND PARTNERS, 3116
SI VENTURES, 1668
SIERRA ANGELS, 1669
SIGNAL EQUITY PARTNERS, 1674
SIGNAL FIRE, 1675
SILKROAD EQUITY, 1681
SILVER LAKE, 1683
SINEWAVE VENTURES, 1687
SKYTREE CAPITAL PARTNERS, 1692
SLOW VENTURES, 1694
SMAC PARTNERS, 3123
SMARTINVEST VENTURES, 1695
SONY INNOVATION FUND, 1703

Industry Preference Index / Technology-Enabled Services

SORRENTO VENTURES, 1706
SOUTHEAST INTERACTIVE TECHNOLOGY FUNDS, 1709
SPARK VENTURES, 3131
SPERO VENTURES, 1721
SPRING CAPITAL PARTNERS LP, 1727
STEAMBOAT VENTURES, 3142
STEELHOUSE VENTURES, 3143
STERLING PARTNERS, 1742
STONEHENGE GROWTH CAPITAL, 1745
STONEWOOD CAPITAL MANAGEMENT, 1746
STRAND HANSON LIMITED, 3146
SUMMIT BRIDGE CAPITAL, 3147
SUN CAPITAL PARTNERS, 1753
SUNEVISION HOLDINGS LIMITED, 3148
SUNSTONE CAPITAL, 3149
SUPREMUM CAPITAL, 3150
SUSA VENTURES, 1758
SWITCH VENTURES, 1768
SYDNEY SEED FUND, 3153
TA ASSOCIATES, 1776
TACTICO, 2260
TAMAR TECHNOLOGY VENTURES LIMITED, 3158
TANK STREAM VENTURES, 3160
TAYRONA VENTURES, 1781
TDF, 1782
TECH CAPITAL PARTNERS, 2262
TECH COAST ANGELS, 1784
TECHNOCAP, 2263
TECHNOLOGY VENTURES CORPORATION, 1787
TECHOPERATORS, 1788
TECNET, 3165
TELECOM VENTURE GROUP LIMITED, 3168
TELEFONICA VENTURES, 3169
TELESOFT PARTNERS, 1793
TEN ELEVEN VENTURES, 1794
TENONETEN VENTURES, 1798
TFG CAPITAL AG, 3172
TH LEE PUTNAM VENTURES, 1804
THAYER STREET PARTNERS, 1805
THE ABRAAJ GROUP, 3173
THOMA BRAVO LLC, 1814
TIGER GLOBAL MANAGEMENT, 1826
TLCOM CAPITAL, 3179
TOMORROW VENTURES, 1830
TOP RENERGY INC., 2271
TPG CAPITAL, 1835
TRANSCENDENT CAPITAL, 1836
TRANSLINK CAPITAL, 1838
TRASK INNOVATIONS FUND Purdue Research Foundation, 1840
TRELLIS CAPITAL CORPORATION, 2273
TRIANGLE PEAK PARTNERS, 1846
TRIANGLE VENTURE CAPITAL GROUP, 3188
TRILOGY PARTNERSHIP, 1852
TRIPLETREE LLC, 1854
TTP VENTURES, 3195
TWO SIGMA VENTURES, 1874
TYLT LAB, 1876
UNITED TALENT AGENCY VENTURES, 1883
UNIVERSITY VENTURE FUND, 1884
UPHEAVAL INVESTMENTS, 1890
VANTAGEPOINT CAPITAL PARTNERS, 1906
VEBER PARTNERS LLC, 1909
VECTOR CAPITAL, 1910
VENROCK ASSOCIATES, 1916
VENTANA CAPITAL MANAGEMENT LP, 1918
VENTURE INVESTORS LLC, 1921
VERGE FUND, 1924
VERIZON VENTURES, 1926
VERTICAL GROUP, 1929
VICKERS FINANCIAL GROUP, 3215
VINCERA CAPITAL, 3218
VIOLA FINTECH, 3220
VITAL FINANCIAL LLC, 1940
VITAMINA K VENTURE CAPITAL, 3223
WACHTEL & CO. INC, 1948
WASABI VENTURES, 1958
WASHINGTON CAPITAL VENTURES, 1959
WAVEMAKER PARTNERS, 1965
WELLS FARGO CAPITAL FINANCE, 1970
WESTON PRESIDIO, 1978
WESTSUMMIT CAPITAL, 3235
WI HARPER GROUP, 1983
WILDCAT VENTURE PARTNERS, 1985
WILMINGTON INVESTOR NETWORK, 1988
WIREFRAME VENTURES, 2000
WISCONSIN INVESTMENT PARTNERS, 2001
YELLOW POINT EQUITY PARTNERS, 2292
YES VC, 2014
YVC - YOZMA MANAGEMENT & INVESTMENTS LIMITED, 3249
ZETTA VENTURE PARTNERS, 2019
ZONE VENTURES, 2021

Technology & Telecommunications
APAX PARTNERS, 135
APAX PARTNERS ET CIE, 2415

Technology Platforms
BLOOMBERG BETA, 284

Technology, Media & Telecommunications
ADVENT INTERNATIONAL CORPORATION, 62
BAIN CAPITAL PRIVATE EQUITY, 220
BRYAN GARNIER & COMPANY, 2544
NOVACAP, 2206

Technology-Enabled Business
ACTIVATE VENTURE PARTNERS, 52
ALLOS VENTURES, 86
NORWEST VENTURE PARTNERS, 1346
OJAS VENTURE PARTNERS, 3019
SILVER LAKE, 1683
SSM PARTNERS, 1732
VOLITION CAPITAL, 1942

Technology-Enabled Products
HELION VENTURE PARTNERS, LLC International Management (Mauritius) Ltd, 2818
TENNESSEE COMMUNITY VENTURES, 1797

Technology-Enabled Services
.406 VENTURES, 2
1843 CAPITAL, 7
ABS VENTURES, 23
ACERO CAPITAL, 41
ACUMEN VENTURES, 2341
ALTIRA GROUP LLC, 98
ARC ANGEL FUND, 150
ARTS ALLIANCE, 2428
AURORA CAPITAL GROUP, 199
BALLAST POINT VENTURES, 224
BERLIN TECHNOLOGIE, 2503
BIG SUR VENTURES, 2510
BLH VENTURE PARTNERS, 282
BLUME VENTURES, 2526
CHICAGO GROWTH PARTNERS, 468
CINCYTECH, 479
CONCENTRIC EQUITY PARTNERS Financial Investments Corporation, 529
CORE CAPITAL PARTNERS, 538
CYPRESS GROWTH CAPITAL, 576
DAWNTREADER VENTURES, 592
DRIVE CAPITAL, 630
EMERGENCE CAPITAL PARTNERS, 665
ESCALATE CAPITAL PARTNERS, 695
GREENSPRING ASSOCIATES, 867
HEALTHQUEST CAPITAL, 921
INVENTUS, 1013
MADISON DEARBORN PARTNERS, 1156
MERITAGE FUNDS, 1211
NEW ENTERPRISE ASSOCIATES, 1297
NORO-MOSELEY PARTNERS, 1331
NORTH ATLANTIC CAPITAL CORPORATION, 1333
OPENVIEW VENTURE PARTNERS, 1380
PARTHENON CAPITAL, 1417

Industry Preference Index / Technology-Enabled Software

PLUS VENTURES, 3041
RITTENHOUSE VENTURES, 1568
SANDBOX INDUSTRIES, 1615
SIGMA PRIME VENTURES, 1673
SILVERTON PARTNERS, 1685
TEAKWOOD CAPITAL, 1783
TEXO VENTURES, 1801
THAYER STREET PARTNERS, 1805

Technology-Enabled Software
BREGAL SAGEMOUNT, 333
TECHOPERATORS, 1788

Telecommunications
360 CAPITAL PARTNERS 360 Capital Management SA, 2296
3I ASIA PACIFIC 3i Group, 2297
3TS CAPITAL PARTNERS 3i Group plc, 2309
3W VENTURES Latour & Zuberbuhler GmbH, 2310
3i GROUP PLC, 2311
AB CAPITAL & INVESTMENT CORPORATION The Phinma Group, 2314
ABELL FOUNDATION VENTURES, 19
ACCESS VENTURE PARTNERS LLC, 36
ACE VENTURE CAPITAL LIMITED, 2330
ACON INVESTMENTS, 46
ACORN CAMPUS VENTURES, 47
ACTIS, 2337
ADAMS CAPITAL MANAGEMENT, 56
ADARA VENTURE PARTNERS, 2342
ADASTRA, 2343
AEP CAPITAL LLC, 65
AEROSTAR CAPITAL LLC, 67
AFTERDOX, 2352
AGF PRIVATE EQUITY Allianz Group, 2354
AKERS CAPITAL LLC, 75
ALEXANDER HUTTON, 82
ALFA CAPITAL Alfa Group, 2363
AMANET TECHNOLOGIES LIMITED, 2389
ANDERSON PACIFIC CORPORATION, 122
ANDLINGER & COMPANY INC, 123
ANTHEM VENTURE PARTNERS, 132
APAX PARTNERS ET CIE, 2415
APEX VENTURE PARTNERS, 137
ARROWPATH VENTURE PARTNERS, 169
ARTIS VENTURES, 175
ARVA LIMITED, 2044
ASSET MANAGEMENT VENTURES, 181
ATHENAEUM FUND, 186
ATILA VENTURES, 2442
AURA CAPITAL OY Auratum Group, 2451
AUSTRALIAN ETHICAL INVESTMENT LIMITED, 2456
AVALON VENTURES, 206
AVANSIS VENTURES, 207
AVENUE CAPITAL GROUP, 208
AWAY REALTY, 2465
AXA INVESTMENT MANAGERS PRIVATE EQUITY EUROPE, 2466
AZCA, 214
BAIRD CAPITAL PARTNERS, 222
BALTCAP MANAGEMENT LTD, 2480
BAND OF ANGELS LLC, 226
BARCELONA EMPREN, 2483
BARCLAYS VENTURES Barclays, 2486
BARING PRIVATE EQUITY PARTNERS INDIA, 2490
BARING VOSTOK CAPITAL PARTNERS, 2491
BATTERY VENTURES, 235
BENAROYA COMPANIES, 247
BIA DIGITAL PARTNERS LP, 263
BLACK DIAMOND VENTURES, 275
BLACKSTONE PRIVATE EQUITY GROUP, 277
BMP AKTIENGESELLSCHAFT BMP Venture Capital, 2528
BOSTON CAPITAL VENTURES, 310
BRAZOS PRIVATE EQUITY PARTNERS, 328
BREAKWATER INVESTMENTS, 330
BRERA CAPITAL PARTNERS, 335
BULLNET, 2548
CALIFORNIA TECHNOLOGY VENTURES, 371
CAPITOL PARTNERS, 406

CARLYLE ASIA INVESTMENT ADVISORS LIMITED Carlyle Group, 2565
CARLYLE GROUP, 413
CATALYST FUND LP, 2571
CATALYST GROUP, 425
CEDAR (ISRAEL) FINANCIAL ADVISORS LIMITED Cedar Fund, 2580
CEDAR FUND, 436
CENTERFIELD CAPITAL PARTNERS, 443
CENTRAL TEXAS ANGEL NETWORK, 445
CHASE CAPITAL PARTNERS, 2588
CHICAGO VENTURE PARTNERS LP, 470
CHINA DEVELOPMENT INDUSTRIAL BANK CDFH, 2592
CHINAVEST, 473
CIBC CAPITAL MARKETS, 2079
CID GROUP, 2603
CINCO CAPITAL, 2604
CIVC PARTNERS, 489
CM CAPITAL, 2618
CNF INVESTMENTS Clark Enterprises, Inc., 508
COACH & CAPITAL, 2619
COLLER CAPITAL LIMITED, 2621
COMPAGNIE FINANCIERE E DE ROTHSCHILD BANQUE, 2625
COMSPACE, 526
CONCORD VENTURES, 2628
CONVEXA Tyveholmen AS, 2632
CORDOVA VENTURES, 537
CREATHOR VENTURE, 2638
CROSBY ASSET MANAGEMENT, 2640
CVF CAPITAL PARTNERS, 573
DARBY OVERSEAS INVESTMENTS LTD, 584
DB CAPITAL PARTNERS (ASIA), 2652
DELTA PARTNERS Delta Partners FZ-LLC, 2654
DESJARDINS CAPITAL, 2095
DOCOMO INNOVATIONS, 620
DR NEUHAUS TECHNO NORD GmbH, 2673
DRAPER RICHARDS KAPLAN FOUNDATION, 627
DVC DEUTSCHE VENTURE CAPITAL, 2679
EDBI Pte LTD., 2690
EDELSON TECHNOLOGY PARTNERS, 651
EDEN VENTURES, 2691
EDGESTONE CAPITAL PARTNERS, 2103
EMP GLOBAL, 670
ENSPIRE CAPITAL PTE LTD, 2703
ENTERPRISE INVESTORS, 2706
EPLANET CAPITAL, 690
EQT PARTNERS AB, 2712
EUROFUND LP, 2720
EXPORT DEVELOPMENT CANADA, 2112
FALCON FUND, 715
FIBERNETICS VENTURES, 2117
FIDELITY GROWTH PARTNERS ASIA, 2733
FIELDSTONE PRIVATE CAPITAL GROUP, 726
FINADVANCE, 2735
FLANDERS' FOREIGN INVESTMENT OFFICE, 2746
FORMULA VENTURES LIMITED Formula Group, 2750
FOUNDATION CAPITAL, 770
GALILEO II, 2765
GE CAPITAL, 808
GEFINOR CAPITAL, 810
GEMINI ISRAEL VENTURE FUNDS LIMITED, 2770
GENERAL ENTERPRISE MANAGEMENT SERVICES, 2772
GENERICS GROUP LIMITED Generics Group, 2773
GILBERT GLOBAL EQUITY PARTNERS, 827
GLOBAL FINANCE, 2784
GLOBALIVE, 2134
GMT COMMUNICATIONS PARTNERS LLP, 2789
GOAL HOLDINGS, 2135
GRAYHAWK CAPITAL, 856
GREENHILL SAVP, 864
GRUPO BISA, 2800
GTCR, 884
HALIFAX GROUP LLC, 894
HANNOVER FINANZ GmbH, 2810
HARBOURVEST PARTNERS LLC, 909
HIKARI TSUSHIN CAPITAL, 2826
HMS HAWAII MANAGEMENT, 939
HOSEO VENTURE CAPITAL, 2833

Industry Preference Index / Therapeutics

I-PACIFIC PARTNERS, 2840
IDG TECHNOLOGY VENTURE INVESTMENT, 2848
INCYTE VENTURES, 982
INFLECTION POINT VENTURES, 989
INLAND TECHSTART FUND, 993
INNOVACOM SA, 2875
INNOVATION CAPITAL, 2876
INNOVATION CAPITAL LIMITED, 2877
INNOVATIONSKAPITAL, 2878
INSIGHT VENTURE PARTNERS, 1000
INVEXCEL PATRIMONIO, 2891
ISOURCE GESTION, 2899
IT-PARTNERS NV, 2902
JAGUAR CAPITAL PARTNERS, 1025
JAVELIN INVESTMENTS, 2908
JEFFERIES CAPITAL PARTNERS, 1032
JK&B CAPITAL, 1038
JORDAN COMPANY, 1045
KALORI GROUP INVESTMENTS, 2915
KB PARTNERS LLC, 1057
KENSINGTON CAPITAL PARTNERS, 2167
LBBW VENTURE CAPITAL, 2932
LEASING TECHNOLOGIES INTERNATIONAL INC., 1103
LEVINE LEICHTMAN CAPITAL PARTNERS, 1111
LMBO FINANCE, 2945
LONG RIVER VENTURES, 1142
LOVETT MILLER & COMPANY, 1148
MACQUARIE DIRECT INVESTMENT LIMITED, 2951
MADISON DEARBORN PARTNERS, 1156
MARCEAU INVESTISSEMENTS, 2955
MAYFIELD FUND, 1184
MBF CAPITAL CORPORATION, 1188
MERRILL LYNCH (ASIA PACIFIC) LIMITED Merrill Lynch Group, 2964
MITSUI SUMITOMO INSURANCE VENTURE CAPITAL CO, 2971
MOTOROLA SOLUTIONS VENTURE CAPITAL, 1260
MURPHREE VENTURE PARTNERS, 1273
NEEDHAM CAPITAL PARTNERS, 1288
NEUHAUS PARTNERS, 2994
NEW YORK CITY ENTREPRENEURIAL FUND New York City Economic Development Corporation, 1307
NEWBURY VENTURES, 1311
NEWFIELD CAPITAL, 1313
NORTH ATLANTIC CAPITAL CORPORATION, 1333
NORTHERN LIGHT VENTURE CAPITAL, 1340
NORTHWOOD VENTURES, 1344
NOVELTEK CAPITAL CORPORATION, 1351
OAK HILL CAPITAL PARTNERS, 1360
OAK INVESTMENT PARTNERS, 1361
OJAS VENTURE PARTNERS, 3019
OneVentures, 3023
PAI MANAGEMENT, 3026
PALOMAR VENTURES, 1407
PENN VENTURE PARTNERS, 1428
PENTECH VENTURES, 3032
PI CAPITAL GROUP LLC, 1440
PNC RIVERARCH CAPITAL, 1457
PRIME TECHNOLOGY VENTURES NV, 3051
PRITZKER GROUP VENTURE CAPITAL, 1480
PROCURITAS PARTNERS KB, 3054
PROVIDENCE EQUITY PARTNERS, 1496
QUANTUM WAVE FUND, 3068
QUEST FOR GROWTH, 3069
RABO BLACK EARTH Eagle Venture Partners, 3071
RBC CAPITAL MARKETS, 2231
RHO VENTURES, 1558
SAMSUNG VENTURE INVESTMENT CORPORATION Samsung Electronics, 3098
SATORI CAPITAL, 1622
SBRC INVESTMENT CONSULTATION LIMITED, 3101
SCOTTISH ENTERPRISE, 3103
SCP PARTNERS, 1633
SECOND ALPHA, 1640
SELWAY CAPITAL, 1647
SEQUEL VENTURE PARTNERS, 1653
SHANGHAI INFORMATION INVESTMENT INCORPORATED, 3114
SIGNAL LAKE, 1676
SIGNATURE CAPITAL LLC, 3120

SKYPOINT CAPITAL, 2256
SMAC PARTNERS, 3123
SOLID VENTURES, 3128
SOUTHEAST INTERACTIVE TECHNOLOGY FUNDS, 1709
SOUTHERN CROSS VENTURE PARTNERS, 1711
SPENCER TRASK VENTURES, 1720
STAR VENTURES, 3137
STRAND HANSON LIMITED, 3146
SWISSCOM, 3152
SYCAMORE VENTURES, 1769
T-VENTURE HOLDINGS GmbH Deutsche Telecom, 3155
TAILWIND CAPITAL, 1777
TECH CAPITAL PARTNERS, 2262
TECHNOCAP, 2263
TELUS VENTURES, 2265
TEUZA MANAGEMENT & DEVELOPMENT LTD, 3171
TIGER GLOBAL MANAGEMENT, 1826
TIME WARNER INVESTMENT CORPORATION, 1827
TLCOM CAPITAL, 3179
TMG CAPITAL PARTNERS, 3180
TRIGINITA CAPITAL, 3190
TVV CAPITAL, 1870
TWJ CAPITAL, 1873
TYLT LAB, 1876
USHA MARTIN VENTURES LIMITED, 3202
VENCORE CAPITAL, 1915
VENTANA CAPITAL MANAGEMENT LP, 1918
VERITAS CAPITAL FUND LP, 1925
VINACAPITAL GROUP, 3217
VOLVO GROUP VENTURE CAPITAL, 3226
WESLEY CLOVER, 2284
WILLIS STEIN & PARTNERS LLC, 1986
WINDWARD VENTURES, 1995
WOODSIDE FUND, 2005
WORLDVIEW TECHNOLOGY PARTNERS, 2007
XANGE PRIVATE EQUITY, 3239
YFM GROUP, 3244
YLR CAPITAL MARKETS LTD, 3247

Telecommunications & Media
IBM VENTURE CAPITAL GROUP, 967

Television
INGENIOUS VENTURES, 2871
MEDIA VENTURE PARTNERS, 1195
NORTHSTAR VENTURES, 3012

Test & Measurement
HCI EQUITY PARTNERS, 917
HERITAGE PARTNERS, 926

Textiles
CAPVIS EQUITY PARTNERS, 2564
CHINA VEST LIMITED, 2596
CITA GESTION, 2607
FIRST ISRAEL MEZZANINE INVESTORS LIMITED, 2745
INDIAN DIRECT EQUITY ADVISORS PVT LTD, 2861
INTERMEDIATE CAPITAL GROUP PLC, 2883
LITTLEJOHN & COMPANY LLC, 1134

Therapeutics
ABERDARE VENTURES, 20
AISLING CAPITAL, 74
AMGEN VENTURES, 112
ASTELLAS VENTURE MANAGEMENT, 182
BIOADVANCE, 266
BIOGENERATION VENTURES, 2514
BIOGENERATOR, 267
BRAIN TRUST ACCELERATOR FUND, 323
BROADVIEW VENTURES, 347
CENTRESTONE VENTURES, 2077
EASTON CAPITAL INVESTMENT GROUP, 644
EDBI Pte LTD., 2690
ELM STREET VENTURES, 660
EcoR1 CAPITAL, 709
F-PRIME CAPITAL PARTNERS, 710
FLAGSHIP PIONEERING, 747

1239

Industry Preference Index / Tools

FORESITE CAPITAL, 762
HAMILTON BIOVENTURES, 898
HOPEN LIFE SCIENCE VENTURES, 943
JOHNSTON ASSOCIATES, 1044
KAISER PERMANENTE VENTURES, 1052
LANCET CAPITAL, 1092
LIGHTSTONE VENTURES, 1122
LONGWOOD FUND, 1145
LUMIRA CAPITAL, 2180
MAINE ANGELS, 1160
NEW SCIENCE VENTURES, 1303
OMEGA FUNDS, 1373
OXFORD BIOSCIENCE PARTNERS, 1394
PFIZER VENTURE INVESTMENTS, 1436
PITTSBURGH LIFE SCIENCES GREENHOUSE, 1448
PRISM VENTUREWORKS, 1478
PURETECH VENTURES, 1501
RESEARCH CORPORATION TECHNOLOGIES, 1543
SANDERLING VENTURES, 1616
SOFINNOVA VENTURES, 1698
SYNERGY LIFE SCIENCE PARTNERS, 1772
THIRD ROCK VENTURES, 1811
VENBIO, 1914
VENTANA CAPITAL MANAGEMENT LP, 1918
WELLINGTON PARTNERS VENTURE CAPITAL GmbH, 3233

Tools
ASSET MANAGEMENT VENTURES, 181
ATLAS VENTURE: FRANCE, 2445

Tourism
ACTIS, 2337
AMANET TECHNOLOGIES LIMITED, 2389
AVENIR TOURISME, 2459
BUSINESS GROWTH FUND, 2550
CLOSE BROTHERS PRIVATE EQUITY Close Brothers Group, 2617
COMPAGNIE FINANCIERE E DE ROTHSCHILD BANQUE, 2625
ELECTRA PARTNERS ASIA LIMITED SFC of Hong Kong, 2694
ENTREPRENEUR CAPITAL, 2107
EQUISTONE, 2714
NEW MEXICO COMMUNITY CAPITAL, 1300
PARTNERSHIP FUND FOR NEW YORK CITY, 1420
PORTUGAL CAPITAL VENTURES Institutional Headquarters, 3048
SIF TRANSYLVANIA, 3119
SRIW SA SRIW Group, 3134
UCA UNTERNEHMER CONSULT AG, 3197
UNION CAPITAL CORPORATION, 1881

Toxic Materials Handling
MOUNTAINEER CAPITAL, 1262

Toys
BALTCAP MANAGEMENT LTD, 2480

Trade
TPA CORPORATE FINANCE CONSULTING GMBH Horwarth International, 3184

Training
CASTANEA PARTNERS, 421
EPIC PARTNERS, 687
LEEDS EQUITY PARTNERS, 1105
SCHOONER CAPITAL LLC, 1627

Transaction Processing
CARRICK CAPITAL PARTNERS, 416
VEDANTA CAPITAL LP, 1911

Transformational Businesses
RUBICON VENTURE CAPITAL, 1595

Transmission
BREGAL ENERGY, 332

Transportation
3I ASIA PACIFIC 3i Group, 2297
ACCESS CAPITAL, 35

ACI CAPITAL, 42
ACTIS, 2337
AIP PRIVATE CAPITAL, 2031
ALEUTIAN CAPITAL PARTNERS, 81
ALEXANDER HUTTON, 82
APOLLO GLOBAL MANAGEMENT, 140
ASTER CAPITAL, 2439
ASTOR CAPITAL GROUP, 2440
ATP PRIVATE EQUITY PARTNERS, 2447
AURORA CAPITAL GROUP, 199
AUTO TECH VENTURES, 204
AUTOTECH VENTURES, 205
AVENUE CAPITAL GROUP, 208
BERKSHIRE PARTNERS LLC, 254
BLAST FUNDING, 279
BLUE POINT CAPITAL PARTNERS, 290
BOCI DIRECT INVESTMENT MANAGEMENT LIMITED Bank of China, 2529
BOND CAPITAL, 2064
BOSTON CAPITAL VENTURES, 310
CAMBRIA GROUP, 378
CAMBRIDGE CAPITAL, 380
CANADIAN VENTURE CAPITAL ASSOCIATION Canadian Venture Capital & Private Equity Association, 3258
CARBON VENTURES, 408
CARLYLE ASIA INVESTMENT ADVISORS LIMITED Carlyle Group, 2565
CARLYLE GROUP, 413
CARPEDIA CAPITAL, 2072
CATALYST INVESTMENT MANAGERS PTY LIMITED PPM Capital, 2573
CERBERUS CAPITAL MANAGEMENT, 451
CHRYSALIX, 2078
CLIMATE CHANGE CAPITAL, 2615
CLOSE BROTHERS PRIVATE EQUITY Close Brothers Group, 2617
COLLABORATIVE FUND, 511
COMVEST PARTNERS, 528
CVC INVESTMENT MANAGERS LIMITED, 2645
DAIMLERCHRYSLER VENTURE GmbH DaimlerChrysler AG, 2650
DEFI GESTION SA Banque Cantonale Vaudoise, 2653
DUBIN CLARK & COMPANY, 632
ECI VENTURES, 2687
ELGNER GROUP INVESTMENTS, 2104
EMP GLOBAL, 670
ENDEAVOUR CAPITAL, 673
ENERTECH CAPITAL, 676
ENTERPRISE EQUITY (NI) LTD, 2704
EOS PARTNERS LP, 686
EQUISTONE, 2714
EUROVENTURES CAPITAL, 2725
EXPANSION CAPITAL PARTNERS, 706
EXPORT DEVELOPMENT CANADA, 2112
FENWAY PARTNERS, 722
FIELDSTONE PRIVATE CAPITAL GROUP, 726
FLANDERS' FOREIGN INVESTMENT OFFICE, 2746
FONTINALIS PARTNERS, 760
FORTRESS INVESTMENT GROUP LLC, 767
FOURIERTRANSFORM, 2755
FRASER MCCOMBS CAPITAL, 781
FdG ASSOCIATES LP, 801
GE CAPITAL, 808
GENERAL ENTERPRISE MANAGEMENT SERVICES, 2772
GENERAL MOTORS VENTURES, 817
GEORGIA OAK PARTNERS, 821
GLADSTONE CAPITAL, 828
GLENTHORNE CAPITAL, 832
GOLDNER, HAWN, JOHNSON & MORRISON, 843
GRAHAM PARTNERS, 846
GRAND CENTRAL HOLDINGS, 847
GRANTHAM CAPITAL, 853
GREENBRIAR EQUITY GROUP LLC, 862
GULFSTAR GROUP, 888
GV, 889
HALDER HOLDINGS BV, 2806
HALIFAX GROUP LLC, 894
HARREN EQUITY PARTNERS, 910
HCI EQUITY PARTNERS, 917

Industry Preference Index / Waste & Recycling

HIG CAPITAL, 928
IBM VENTURE CAPITAL GROUP, 967
INFIELD CAPITAL, 988
INVESTMENT FUND FOR CENTRAL & EASTERN EUROPE, 2889
JB POINDEXTER & COMPANY, 1030
JEFFERIES CAPITAL PARTNERS, 1032
JORDAN COMPANY, 1045
KELSO & COMPANY, 1062
KHOSLA VENTURES, 1069
KPS CAPITAL PARTNERS, 1085
MACKINNON, BENNETT & CO., 2181
MCROCK CAPITAL, 2190
MERRILL LYNCH (ASIA PACIFIC) LIMITED Merrill Lynch Group, 2964
NAVIGATION CAPITAL PARTNERS, 1280
NORTHERN ENTERPRISE LIMITED, 3011
NOVELTEK CAPITAL CORPORATION, 1351
OMERS PRIVATE EQUITY, 2207
PARKVIEW CAPITAL PARTNERS, 2215
PENDER WEST CAPITAL PARTNERS, 2218
PHOENIX EQUITY PARTNERS LIMITED, 3036
PORTUGAL CAPITAL VENTURES Institutional Headquarters, 3048
POST CAPITAL PARTNERS, 1465
RED CLAY CAPITAL HOLDINGS, 1529
RESILIENCE CAPITAL PARTNERS, 1545
REVOLUTION LLC, 1555
ROAD KING INFRASTRUCTURE LIMITED, 3084
ROCKPORT CAPITAL, 1579
SAMOS INVESTMENTS, 3097
SARONA ASSET MANAGEMENT, 2248
SHAW KWEI AND PARTNERS, 3116
SIF TRANSYLVANIA, 3119
SIGNIA VENTURE PARTNERS, 1678
SOUTHPORT PARTNERS, 1712
SUN CAPITAL PARTNERS, 1753
THROUNARFELAG ISLANDS PLC, 3177
TPA CORPORATE FINANCE CONSULTING GMBH Horwarth International, 3184
TRANS COSMOS INCORPORATED, 3185
TRANSYLVANIA FINANCIAL INVESTMENT COMPANY, 3187
TSING CAPITAL, 3194
URBAN INNOVATION FUND, 1893
URBAN US, 1894
WATERMILL GROUP, 1962
WELLS FARGO CAPITAL FINANCE, 1970
WYNNCHURCH CAPITAL, 2009

Transportation Solutions
INVESTECO, 2161

Transportation and Infrastructure
BRANFORD CASTLE, 327

Travel
DYNAMO VC, 640
NFX, 1323

Travel & Leisure
ARCHTOP VENTURES, 154
BLACKSTONE PRIVATE EQUITY GROUP, 277
LLOYDS DEVELOPMENT CAPITAL LIMITED, 2944
ONE EQUITY PARTNERS, 1376
RAPTOR GROUP, 1524
TPG CAPITAL, 1835

Underground Hydrocarbon Storage
HADDINGTON VENTURES LLC, 893

Utilities
AWAY REALTY, 2465
CHEUNG KONG INFRASTRUCTURE HOLDINGS LIMITED, 2591
NTH POWER TECHNOLOGIES, 1355

Utilities & Electric Power
CHRYSALIX, 2078

Utilities & Farming
CALIFORNIA COAST VENTURE FORUM, 3257

Vaccines
SANOFI-GENZYME BIOVENTURES, 1618

Value-Added Distribution
ALBION INVESTORS LLC, 78
ARROWHEAD INVESTMENT MANAGEMENT, 168
ARROWHEAD INVESTMENT MANAGEMENT, 168
BALMORAL FUNDS, 225
CID CAPITAL, 478
FIVE POINTS CAPITAL, 746
JMH CAPITAL, 1040
MPG EQUITY PARTNERS, 1267

Vehicle Technology
VENROCK ASSOCIATES, 1916

Venture Capital
INDUSTRY VENTURES, 986

Vertical
OYSTER VENTURES, 1395

Veterinary Medicine
TWIN CITIES ANGELS, 1872

Video Gaming
ALBUM VC, 79
SONY STRATEGIC TECHNOLOGY PARTNERSHIPS, 1704

Video Industry
TECH CAPITAL PARTNERS, 2262

Video Surveillance
AUXO MANAGEMENT, 2047

Virtual Reality
AMPLIFY, 120
BLUEPOINTE VENTURES, 295
BOLDSTART VENTURES, 305
BRIGHTSTONE VENTURE CAPITAL, 341
LDV CAPITAL, 1101
OUTPOST CAPITAL, 1390
PATHBREAKER VENTURES, 1421
QUAKE CAPITAL PARTNERS, 1507
SAMSUNG NEXT, 1611
SIGNIA VENTURE PARTNERS, 1678
SONY INNOVATION FUND, 1703
SUSA VENTURES, 1758
VERIZON VENTURES, 1926

Virtual Reality & Augmented Reality
AMD VENTURES, 106
BERTELSMANN DIGITAL MEDIA INVESTMENTS, 256
BOOST VC, 307
DAY ONE VENTURES, 593
FINAVENTURES, 729
FRONTIER VENTURES, 792
PRESENCE CAPITAL, 1473

Virtualization
ATLANTIC BRIDGE, 2443
NEW ENTERPRISE ASSOCIATES, 1297
STORM VENTURES, 1747

Vocational Training
APPIAN EDUCATION VENTURES, 141

Waste & Recycling
AMBIENTA ENVIRONMENTAL ASSETS, 2391
ANGELENO GROUP, 126
AUDAX GROUP, 194
CLARENDON FUND MANAGERS, 2610
CLIMATE CHANGE CAPITAL, 2615
DEMETER PARTNERS, 2656
GEMINI INVESTORS, 812
HENDERSON PRIVATE CAPITAL, 2821
NORTH ATLANTIC CAPITAL CORPORATION, 1333

Industry Preference Index / Waste & Resources

PARALLEL49 EQUITY, 2214
PROCURITAS PARTNERS KB, 3054
SOVEREIGN CAPITAL, 3130
SPRING LANE CAPITAL, 1729
STRUCTURE CAPITAL, 1749
TPA CORPORATE FINANCE CONSULTING GMBH Horwarth International, 3184
TRUE NORTH VENTURE PARTNERS, 1859
WHEB GROUP, 3237
WOODBRIDGE GROUP, 2004

Waste & Resources
ENERTECH CAPITAL, 676

Waste Management
CARBON VENTURES, 408

Waste Water Treatment
AZCA, 214

Water
AAVISHKAAR, 2313
ACUMEN, 55
ALTRIA VENTURES, 102
AQUAGRO FUND, 2417
AUDAX GROUP, 194
CLEAN PACIFIC VENTURES, 498
CLIMATE CHANGE CAPITAL, 2615
CULTIVIAN SANDBOX VENTURES, 570
DEMETER PARTNERS, 2656
EARTHRISE CAPITAL, 643
ELEMENT PARTNERS, 657
EMERALD TECHNOLOGY VENTURES, 2106
EMP GLOBAL, 670
ENNOVENT, 2701
EXPANSION CAPITAL PARTNERS, 706
FIRELAKE CAPITAL, 730
FIRST ISRAEL MEZZANINE INVESTORS LIMITED, 2745
FLYWHEEL VENTURES, 756
FREYCINET INVESTMENTS, 2125
ISRAEL CLEANTECH VENTURES, 2900
MCROCK CAPITAL, 2190
MEIDLINGER PARTNERS, 1199
NEW WORLD INFRASTRUCTURE LIMITED, 2996
POND VENTURES, 3047
PROCURITAS PARTNERS KB, 3054
SAIL VENTURE PARTNERS, 1603
SAUDI ARAMCO ENERGY VENTURES, 3099
SOUTHERN CROSS VENTURE PARTNERS, 1711
SPRING LANE CAPITAL, 1729
TEL VENTURE CAPITAL, 1791
TRUE NORTH VENTURE PARTNERS, 1859
WASSERSTEIN & CO., 1960
WHEB GROUP, 3237
XPV WATER PARTNERS, 2290

Water Purification
ALTUS CAPITAL PARTNERS, 104

Water Technologies
INVESTECO, 2161
TECHNOLOGY PARTNERS, 1786

Water Treatment
CARDINAL EQUITY PARTNERS, 409

Wealth
PORTAG3 VENTURES, 2225

Wealth & Asset Management
LUGE CAPITAL, 2179
VIOLA FINTECH, 3220

Wealth Management & Trust
ROTHSCHILD AUSTRALIA - ARROW PRIVATE EQUITY Rothschild Group, 3086

Web Applications & Services
ARTHUR VENTURES, 173
BAND OF ANGELS LLC, 226
DALLAS VENTURE PARTNERS, 582
EC1 CAPITAL LTD, 2685
ENTREPIA VENTURES, 682
KLASS CAPITAL, 2170
MITSUI SUMITOMO INSURANCE VENTURE CAPITAL CO, 2971
NETROVE ASIA SDN BHD, 2993
OJAS VENTURE PARTNERS, 3019

Web Infrastructure
.406 VENTURES, 2

Web Platforms
SPARK CAPITAL, 1715

Web Related
NEXTGEN ANGELS, 1320

Web Services
SERAPH GROUP, 1655

Web-Enabled Services
SJF VENTURES, 1689
US VENTURE PARTNERS, 1896

Web/Mobile Applications
Y COMBINATOR, 2012

Wellness
APHELION CAPITAL, 138
BIG SOCIETY CAPITAL, 2509
FALCONHEAD CAPITAL, 717
JOHNSON & JOHNSON INNOVATION, 1043
OBVIOUS VENTURES, 1363
SWAN & LEGEND VENTURES, 1766
WIREFRAME VENTURES, 2000

Wholesale
ALLSTATE INVESTMENTS LLC, 88
BAY BG BAVARIAN VENTURE CAPITAL CORP, 2494
BENCIS CAPITAL PARTNERS, 2501
BOND CAPITAL, 2064
BRUML CAPITAL CORPORATION, 355
CINCO CAPITAL, 2604
FOUNDATION CAPITAL LIMITED, 2753
GAON ASSET MANAGEMENT, 2766
GRUPO BISA, 2800
GULFSTAR GROUP, 888
INDUSTRI KAPITAL SVENSKA AB, 2863
LOMBARD INVESTMENTS, 1139
MACQUARIE DIRECT INVESTMENT LIMITED, 2951
MERRILL LYNCH (ASIA PACIFIC) LIMITED Merrill Lynch Group, 2964
NORTH ATLANTIC CAPITAL CORPORATION, 1333
QUANTUM CAPITAL PARTNERS, 1510
SAMBRINVEST SA, 3096
WELLS FARGO CAPITAL FINANCE, 1970

Wholesale Distribution
AUSTIN CAPITAL PARTNERS LP, 201

Wind Power
ABB TECHNOLOGY VENTURES, 2315
BP ALTERNATIVE ENERGY VENTURES, 319

Winegrowing & Agriculture
TPA CORPORATE FINANCE CONSULTING GMBH Horwarth International, 3184

Wireless
10X VENTURE PARTNERS, 3
ACTIVE VENTURE PARTNERS, 2339
APOLLO GLOBAL MANAGEMENT, 140
ARCH VENTURE PARTNERS, 153
CALUMET VENTURE FUND, 375
CARMEL VENTURES, 2566

Industry Preference Index / Workforce Development

CATALYST INVESTORS, 427
CEYUAN, 2584
CID GROUP, 2603
COLUMBIA CAPITAL, 515
COMMONWEALTH CAPITAL VENTURES LP, 521
CONVEXA Tyveholmen AS, 2632
DIAMOND TECHVENTURES, 612
DOUBLEROCK VENTURE CAPITAL, 625
EPLANET CAPITAL, 690
ESCALATE CAPITAL PARTNERS, 695
EUROPEAN FOUNDERS FUND, 2723
FIRST ANALYSIS, 732
FORMATIVE VENTURES, 764
GSR VENTURES, 2801
GUGGENHEIM PARTNERS, 885
IDG CAPITAL PARTNERS, 2847
JARVINIAN VENTURES, 1027
KODIAK VENTURE PARTNERS, 1080
LAUNCHPAD VENTURE GROUP, 1100
LEAPFROG VENTURES, 1102
LEO CAPITAL HOLDINGS, LLC, 1108
MOBILITY VENTURES, 1244
NEXIT VENTURES OY, 2999
NEXIT VENTURES OY Nexit Ventures Inc., 2999
NORTHWOOD VENTURES, 1344
OKAPI VENTURE CAPITAL, 1371
OPUS CAPITAL, 1381
OXANTIUM VENTURES, 1393
PELION VENTURE PARTNERS, 1425
REMBRANDT VENTURE PARTNERS, 1540
SEAPOINT VENTURES, 1637
SHEPHERD VENTURES, 1664
STORM VENTURES, 1747
SUNBRIDGE PARTNERS, 1755
TELESOFT PARTNERS, 1793

Wireless Applications
BLUEFISH VENTURES, 294

Wireless Architectures
TI VENTURE CAPITAL Texas Instruments Incorporated, 1823

Wireless Communications
DOT EDU VENTURES, 623

Wireless Infrastructure
RHO CANADA VENTURES, 2239

Wireless Services
GRANDBANKS CAPITAL, 848

Wireless Software
GREENHILLS VENTURES, LLC, 865

Wireless Systems
CROSSLINK CAPITAL, 563

Wireless Technologies
ACCENTURE TECHNOLOGY VENTURES, 2326
ACORN CAMPUS VENTURES, 47
ACTA CAPITAL, 51
AKERS CAPITAL LLC, 75
ALLEGIS CYBER CAPITAL, 84
ARGO GLOBAL CAPITAL, 162
ASIAVEST PARTNERS, 2436
ATA VENTURES, 183
ATLANTIC BRIDGE, 2443
ATRIUM CAPITAL, 192
AUTHOSIS VENTURES, 2457
AVALON VENTURES, 206
AVANSIS VENTURES, 207
AZIONE CAPITAL, 2473
BAY PARTNERS, 238
BLUMBERG CAPITAL, 301

BRIGHTSPARK VENTURES, 2066
CASTILE VENTURES, 422
CEDAR (ISRAEL) FINANCIAL ADVISORS LIMITED Cedar Fund, 2580
CEDAR FUND, 436
CHINA DEVELOPMENT INDUSTRIAL BANK CDFH, 2592
CLARITY PARTNERS, 494
COMSPACE, 526
CRAWLEY VENTURES, 553
DELTA VENTURES LIMITED, 2655
DOCOMO INNOVATIONS, 620
FCA VENTURE PARTNERS, 718
GABRIEL VENTURE PARTNERS, 805
GENESIS PARTNERS, 2775
GRANDBANKS CAPITAL, 848
GROSVENOR FUNDS, 875
GUIDE VENTURES, 887
HARBINGER VENTURE MANAGEMENT, 905
HORIZON VENTURES LLC, 947
I-PACIFIC PARTNERS, 2840
IDG CAPITAL, 973
IGLOBE PARTNERS, 2853
INNOVATION CAPITAL LIMITED, 2877
JAVELIN INVESTMENTS, 2908
KOREA TECHNOLOGY & BANKING (KTB) NETWORK CORP, 2926
M/C PARTNERS, 1153
MADRONA VENTURE GROUP, 1158
MANTELLA VENTURE PARTNERS, 2182
MATRIX PARTNERS, 1181
MEDIA VENTURE PARTNERS, 1195
MERITECH CAPITAL PARTNERS, 1212
MOBILE INTERNET CAPITAL, 2974
MOTOROLA SOLUTIONS VENTURE CAPITAL, 1260
NAUTA CAPITAL, 2987
NEST VENTURES, 1290
NEWBURY VENTURES, 1311
NORTHERN LIGHT VENTURE CAPITAL, 1340
PITANGO VENTURE CAPITAL, 3039
REAL VENTURES, 2232
REDPOINT VENTURES, 1534
RIDGEWOOD CAPITAL, 1564
RPM VENTURES, 1592
SELBY VENTURE PARTNERS, 1646
SHASTA VENTURES, 1663
SI VENTURES, 1668
SIGMA PARTNERS, 1672
SKYPOINT CAPITAL, 2256
SMART BUSINESS CONSULTING, 3124
SONY STRATEGIC TECHNOLOGY PARTNERSHIPS, 1704
STAR VENTURES, 3137
T-VENTURE HOLDINGS GmbH Deutsche Telecom, 3155
TAMAR TECHNOLOGY VENTURES LIMITED, 3158
TECH CAPITAL PARTNERS, 2262
TELUS VENTURES, 2265
TI VENTURE CAPITAL Texas Instruments Incorporated, 1823
TRILOGY PARTNERSHIP, 1852
US VENTURE PARTNERS, 1896
VELOCITY EQUITY PARTNERS LLC, 1913
VENCORE CAPITAL, 1915
VENTANA CAPITAL MANAGEMENT LP, 1918
VOYAGER CAPITAL, 1945
WESTERN TECHNOLOGY INVESTMENT, 1975
WI HARPER GROUP, 1983
WORLDVIEW TECHNOLOGY PARTNERS, 2007
ZONE VENTURES, 2021

Wood Industries
INVESTMENT FUND FOR CENTRAL & EASTERN EUROPE, 2889
SAMBRINVEST SA, 3096
SRIW SA SRIW Group, 3134
WATERMILL GROUP, 1962

Workforce Development
URBAN US, 1894

Portfolio Companies Index

A

A & A Manufacturing Company, 194
A Head For Profits, 493
A la Carte Delivery, 1507
A Little Market, 3239
A Place for Mom, 1956
A Stucki Company, 1505
A Touch of Country Magic, 1606
A&A Trading, 2114
A&B American Style, 622
A&B Electronics, 438
A&D Environmental Services, 443, 1343
A&G Pharmaceutical, 1169
A&R Logistics, 1171
A&W, 2272
A+ Network, 1752
A-D Technologies, 194
A-Gas, 1082, 2944
A-Lab Oy, 2966
A-Life Medical, 1706
A-Max, 2771
A-ROSA, 3232
A-SaaS, 1607
A-Saas, 148
A-Solutions, 3022
A-Star, 2646
A-TEK, 507
A., 2444
A. & D. Prevost, 2095
A. & L. Pinard, 2120
A. Silva & Silva, 3048
A.A. Kachtan, 2389
A.R.E. Accessories, 565
A.S. Group, 2354
A.S. Nettoyage, 2120
A.S.T. Soldering Technologies, 2389
A.T.L.A.S. Aeronautique, 2095
A.V. Gauge & Fixture, 2163
A/B Tasty, 3239
A10 Capital, 928
A10 Networks, 905, 1752, 2703
A123 Systems, 171, 1157, 1334, 2717
A2M, 2213
A2SEA, 2651
A4 Health Systems, 1409
A5, 364
A8 Music Group, 2850
AA Asphalting, 1250
AA Consulting & Associates, 3261
AAA Slaes & Engineering, 1422
AAB Smart Tools LLC, 908
AAC Acoustic, 1760, 2590
AAC Holdings Inc., 403
AAC Technologies, 823
Aaccredited Home Lenders, 404
AAD, 1350
AaDya, 13
AAG Energy Limited, 1956
AAMP of America, 194, 969
Aaptiv, 1000, 1768
Aardvark, 197, 231
AardvarQ, 998
Aarki, 384, 1634, 1655, 1952
Aarohi Communications, 1793
Aaron Industries, 746
Aarowhead, 1041
Aarrowcast, 1037
Aarusha Homes, 55
Aasaan Jobs, 1013
AAT, 2422
Aavangs Fiskehus, 3203
AAVID, 1986
Aavishkaar, 483
Aavya Health, 1615
AB SA, 2706
Abacas Insights, 2
Abaco PR, 63

Abaco Systems, 1925
Abacus, 13, 260, 889
Abacus Group LLC, 1979
Abacus.AI, 1666
Abakus Solar, 3020
Abasco Energy Technologies, 1573
ABATEC Electronics AG, 2783
Abaton.com, 955
Abaxia, 2855
abaxx, 2771
ABB Optical Group, 1301
Abbey Healthcare Staffing, 1067
Abbey Post, 1097
Abbey Road Consulting, 3259
ABC Cosmétique, 3239
Abc Environnement, 2120
abc Financial, 1344
ABC Home Medical Supply, 639
ABC Industries, 327, 439, 478
ABC Laboratories, 439
ABC Learning Centres Ltd, 2456
ABC Supply, 62
ABC TEST, 3261
Abcd, 2448
AbCelex Technologies, 570
AbCellera, 1666
Abcia, 3020
Abe's Market, 2566
Abec Group, 2985
Abeja, 1607
AbelConn, 164
AbelConn Holdings, 1557
Abengoa, 740
Abeo, 1417, 2754, 3203
Aberdeen Group, 521, 897
Abertis, 385, 2379
Abgentis, 2967, 3107
ABI, 2935
ABI (UK) Ltd., 2677
Abide Therapeutics, 410
Abierto Networks, 1160, 1161
Ability, 909, 1360
ABILITY Network, 1752, 3279
Ability Network, 221
Ability One, 1128
AbilTo, 938
Abingdon Health, 2858
AbioGenix, 1615
Abiomed, 2748
Abionic, 3045
Abipa Canada, 2120
Abiquo, 2987
Abirnet, 3231
ABK Biomedical, 1988, 2155
Abl, 741, 1392, 1527, 1551
ABL Technic, 1937
Ablathion Frontiers, 1975
Ablative Solutions, 269
Able, 707
Able Health, 858
Able Home Health, 406
Able Lending, 544
Able Planet, 61
AbleTo, 2
Ablexis, 371, 1436, 1811
Ablynx, 94, 2316, 2780, 2781
ABM Industris Inc., 869
AbMart, 1340
Abmit Biosciences, 1196
Abode Healthcare, 782
ABODO, 635
AboGen, 1160
Abom, 1061
Abotic, 2531
About.com, 596, 1103
About.me, 358, 776, 784, 889, 1700, 1860
AboutOne, 841

ABPathFinder, 635
ABR Innova Oy, 2873
Abra, 148, 307, 741, 924, 1110, 1222, 1465
ABRA Auto Body, 3279
ABRA Auto Body & Glass, 1403
Abrado Welbore Services, 2700
Abrams Fensterman, 3267
Abravax, 1507
Abre. Action Streamer, 479
ABRH, 1970
Abridean, 2196
Abridge, 1882
Abrigo, 29
Abrisa Industrial Glass, 1456
Abrisa Technologies, 846
Abrisud, 2338, 2340, 2448
Abrium, 2551
Abrizio, 1975
Abry, 2897
Abryx, 386
ABS Capital Partners, 3270
ABS Materials, 6
ABS Materials Inc., 1047
AbSci, 1383, 2008
Absolute Commerce, 1693
Absolute Dental, 244
Absolute Dental Management, 158
Absolute Engery, 2873
Absolutely Custom Group, 1492
Absorbent Technologies, 1915
Abstract, 552, 741, 2280
Absynthe Minded, 3042
ABT Molecular Imaging, 1008
ABT Molecular Imaging Evermind, 1261
ABTL, 1496
Abu Dhabi Investment Authority, 3261
Abundant Robotics, 519, 889
Abusix, 3161
Abuzz Technologies, 1702
AbVitro, 1619
Abyssal, 3048
Abzena, 1972
AC Busines Media, 1719
AC Label, 667
AC Lordi, 468
AC&A, 66
ACA Compliance Group, 1301
Acacia, 521, 1181
Acacia Communications, 1752
ACACIA Venture Partners, 1760
Acacia Venture Partners, 3284
AcaciaPharma, 710
AcadeMedia, 1496
Academia, 3070, 3131
Academia.edu, 1715, 1860
Academic Management Services, 1752, 1770
Academic Management Systems, 1333
Academic Merit, 1160
Academic Partnerships, 1000
Academy for Urban School Leadership, 1316
Academy Sports + Outdoors, 1082
Acadia Healthcare, 1963
ACADIA Pharmaceuticals, 1394, 1452, 2651, 2748, 3007
Acal Energy, 192, 2295, 3028
Acalvia, 889
Acalvio, 28, 974, 2239
Acapela Group, 2897
Acapella, 514
Acarix, 3113, 3149
ACAS Equity Holdings Corporation, 158
ACAS Real Estate Holdings Corporation, 158
Acasa, 3108
ACB (India), 1956
ACC Systems, 1663
Acca Networks, 2854
Accantia, 2676

1245

Portfolio Companies Index

Accedian Networks, 1752
Accel, 37
Accel Entertainment, 2081
Accel Graphics, 36
Accel Growth Fund, 623
Accel IX Strategic Partners, 623
Accel KKR, 37
Accel Partners, 3284
Accel Semiconductor Corporation, 2597
Accela, 21, 254, 333, 1475
Accela Media, 3041
Accela Technology, 1755
Accelecare Holdings, 1628
Accelecare Wound Centers, 221
Accelera, 1715
Accelerant Holdings, 96
Accelerate Fund, 2032
Accelerate Learning, 1392
Accelerated Companies, 1415
Accelerated Networks, 1378
Accelerated Oil Technologies, 1082
Accelerated Orthopedic Technologies, 660, 678
Accelerated Rehabilitation Centers, 881
Accelerated Technologies, 2748
Acceleration Systems, 1061
AcceleratorIQ, 6
Accelerator Corp., 2008
Accelerator Corporation, 1043
Accelergy, 1355, 1786
Accelero Pharma, 59
Acceleron, 1122
Acceleron Pharma, 206, 260, 747, 762, 925, 1460, 1760, 1916
Accella, 170
Accellent, 209, 220, 1086
Accello, 1273
Accellos, 441
AccelOps, 1237
Accelops, 183, 1896
Accent, 1779, 3235
Accent Energy, 42
Accent Equity 2003 Ltd, 2651
Accent Ood Services, 1684
Accent Therapeutics, 709
AccentCare, 62, 1360
AccentHealth, 1153
Acceo Solutions, 2095, 2120
Accept Software, 1738
Acceptd, 1553
Acces, 2851
Acces 360, 1747
ACCESS, 1704
Access, 254, 824, 892, 949
Access Cash, 1256
Access Closer, 986
Access Closure, 1378, 1445
Access Health, 52, 1227
Access Information Management, 21, 1752
Access Insurance, 96
Access Intelligence, 1927
Access Medical, 2936
Access MediQuip, 1961
Access Physicians, 918
Access Point Financial, 1743
Access Spectrum LLC, 1506
Access Sports Media, 515, 1239
Access Technology Ventures, 34
Access Venture Partners, 3276
Access360, 1975
AccessBio, 3145
AccessData, 1640, 1705
AccessESP, 1125
AccessLine, 805
AccessOne, 790
Accessories Marketing, 1456
Accessories Marketing Inc., 788
Accio Energy, 742, 1547

Accion, 107, 3261
Accion Systems, 1694
Acciona Energia Internacional, 1082
Accipiter, 1008, 1709, 2226
Accipiter Systems, 998
Accium Biosciences, 85, 2008
Acclara, 97
Acclarent, 1212
Acclaris, 1850, 1886, 2196
ACCO, 3020, 3047
Acco, 770, 1416
ACCO Material Handling Solutions, 1082
Accolade, 39, 124, 416, 518, 560, 695, 1158
Accolo, 548
Accomodations Plus Technologies, 158
Accompany, 552
Accompany Beta, 974
Accomplice, 70
Accord, 3137
Accord Networks, 59
Accordant Health Systems, 1008
Account Now, 856
Accountabil IT, 1979
Accounting SaaS Japan Co., 2974
AccountNow, 1850
AccountsIQ, 2355
Accoustical Material Services, 1505
Accovion, 2638
Accredible, 1054
Accredo Health, 1972
Accreon, 1165
Accretive Commerce, 39
Accretive Health, 39, 176
Accriva Diagnostics, 237, 1956
Accruent, 819, 1776, 1975
ACCT Holdings, 1726
Accu Metrics, 946
Accubuilt, 1400
Accucam Machining, 2126
Accudyne Industries, 413
Acculis, 622
Acculynk, 1361
Accume Partners, 222
Accumen, 39
Accumeter Labs, 1295
Accumetrics, 1057, 1574, 1792
Accupac, 928, 1037
Accuracy Microsensors, 1377
Accurate, 949
Accurate Component Sales, 931, 1343
Accurate Group, 1240
Accurate Group Holdings, 22, 1189
Accurate Metal Fabrications, 716
Accuratus Lab Services, 118
AccuRev, 1913
Accurev, 521
Accuri, 747
Accuri Cytometers, 1975
AccurIC, 2967
Accuride, 1134
Accuride Corporation, 559
Accuris, 2443, 3147
Accuro, 1619, 1972
Accuronix, 267
Accuscore, 1784
AccuSource Solutions, 984
AccuSpec Electronics, 1159
Accutest Laboratories, 654
Accutrainee, 2567
Accuvally Inc., 1509
AccuVein, 260, 946, 2981
AccuWater, 445
ACE Cash Express, 1039
ACE Cogeneration, 156
Ace Gathering Holdings LLC, 403
Ace Learning, 1551
Ace Metrix, 1102, 1407

ACE*COMM, 865
ace2three.com, 2081
Aceable, 751, 1602, 1985
Acelero Learning, 1021
AcelRx Pharmaceuticals, 925, 1445, 1691, 1819
Acema Importations, 2095
AceMetrix, 956
Acention Digital, 622
Acer, 892, 2436
Acer Group, 1769
Acerta, 1154
Acerta Pharma, 782
Acertus, 1777
Aces, 101
ACES Quality Management, 1293
Acesion, 347
Acessa Health Inc., 158
Acessozero, 2331
Acetelion, 191
Aceva, 1975
ACG, 909, 3233
ACG Materials, 928
ACH BRITO & CIA, 3048
Achaogen, 12, 153, 621, 762, 1916
Achates Power, 1579, 1846
Acheogen, 782
Achica, 2662
Achieve 3000, 1000
Achieve3000, 1328
AchieveIt, 271
Achievement Preparatory Academy, 1316
Achievers, 848
Achillion, 530, 1412, 1508, 2445
Achillion Pharmaceuticals, 495, 621, 1058, 1490, 1775
Achronix, 1303
Achronix Semiconductor, 682, 925
Achronix Semicondutor Corp., 682
ACI, 1041, 2089
ACI Brands, 2126
Acier Fastech, 2120
Acier Majeau, 2095, 2120
Aciex Therapeutics, 237
Acino, 209
ACIS, 373
Acision, 2443
ACIST Medical Systems, 1409
Acko, 28
ACL, 1346
ACL Airshop, 213
ACL Wireless, 2881
Aclara, 118, 1753
Aclara Biosciences, 1412
Aclaris Therapeutics, 74, 136, 710, 762, 1519, 1698, 1941
Aclima, 1696
Aclime, 1552
ACM Research Corporation, 1769
ACME Cryogenics, 828
Acme Cryogenics, 846
Acme Fine Furniture Natra Group, 2814
Acme Finishing Company, 1606
Acme Packet, 59
Acme Technologies, 547
ACMI, 778
Acodec, 71
Acologix, 2970
Acompli, 1534
Aconex, 605, 779
Aconite, 751, 1390
Acopia, 28
Acopia Networks, 455, 3137
Acorda, 954
Acorda Therapeutics, 769, 1002, 1271, 2748
Acordis, 2644
Acorn, 101
Acorn Applications, 3259

Portfolio Companies Index

Acorn International, 3093
Acorn Systems, 202
Acorns, 641, 858, 1178, 1741
Acosta, 413
Acoustic Sensing Technology, 2295
Acoustic Technologies, 1873
Acoustic Zoom, 2700
AcousticEye, 2900
Acova, 2883
ACPI, 109
ACQI, 3257
Acquia, 37, 1297, 1334, 1672, 1673, 1725, 1796
Acquired.io, 661, 890
Acquisio, 2120
ACR Capital Holdings, 2300, 2311
ACR Electronics, 1332
ACR Group, 1045
ACRA Control, 2336
Acre Trader, 1554
Acreage Holdings, 390
Acres Cultivation & Cannabis, 557
Acrisure, 21, 819, 909, 1927
Acro Vape, 392
Acrobatiq, 628, 922
Acrodea, 58
Acrodyne Communications, 1314
Acrohone Ltd., 2707
Acromedia Inc., 623
AcroMetrix, 1792
Acronis, 89, 1235, 2320
Acrotec, 1516
Acrow Bridge, 631
AcryMed, 753
ACS, 2392
Acsis, 1604
ACT Biotech, 1325
ACT Lighting Inc., 577
Act On, 1896
Act!, 655
Act-On, 1785
Act-On Software, 1853, 1945
Acta, 1017
Acta Groupe, 2851
Acta Technology, 757
Acta Vascular Systems, 865
ActaCell, 144
Actano Ltd, 3162
Actar International SA, 2653
Actel, 59, 214
Actelioln, 2607
Actelion, 2607, 2625
Actelis, 183, 1975, 2875, 3123, 3231
Actelis Argus Cyber Security, 3214
Actelis Networks, 57, 833, 1604, 2508, 2565
Acteon, 1082, 2317
Actex, 1345
ACTi, 905
Actiance, 1038, 1626, 1760
Actifio, 59, 124, 1334, 1625, 1785
Actility, 483, 2851
Actimis, 1241
Actimize, 793
Actinobac Biomed, 1051
Action, 1751, 2311
Action Carting, 1021
Action For Children, 2539
Action Labs Inc., 465
Action Mecanique, 2095
Action Target, 632, 812
Action X, 1699, 2137
Actional Corporation, 197
Actionality, 2671
ActionBar, 3108
ActionCOACH, 3267
Actiondesk, 795
ActionIQ, 317, 743, 1654
ActionSprout, 1383

ActionX, 1926
Actis, 3261
ACTIV Financial Systems, 260
Activ Surgical, 1703
Activ8, 2967
Activa Resources, 477
Activaero, 2515
Activamt, 924
Activant, 1041
Activate Capital Ltd., 1082
Activate Healthcare, 1271
Activate Networks, 703
Active 24 ASA, 2754
Active Aero Group Holdings Inc., 862
Active Circle, 2875
Active Control eXperts, 1702
Active Endpoints, 1334, 2445
Active Industrial Solutions, 2215
Active Interest Media, 1990
Active Live Scientific, 1784
Active Mind Technology, 51, 1254
Active Minerals International, 1209
Active Network, 23, 202, 1480, 1780, 1994
Active Networks, 455
Active Optical MEMS, 1352
Active Power, 202, 444, 1558
Active Reactor Company, 2613
Active Semiconductors, 1646
Active Software, 757, 1975
Active Sportswear International, 2651
Active Voice, 1752
Active-Semi, 1646, 1796
Active.com, 1057, 1334, 1780
Active8, 2953
ActiveCard., 2544
Actived, 1923
Activehours, 1560
ActiVein, 3240
Actively Learn, 189
ActiveProspect, 745
ActiveSky, 2877
ActiveStyle, 1572
Activiews, 2726
Activiomics, 2892
Activity Hero, 1013
Actix, 1752
ACTO, 2113, 2138, 2187, 2212
Acto, 2184
ActoGeniX, 2350, 2476, 2939
ActOn, 1346
Acton Pharmaceuticals, 1228
Actona, 2462
Actown-Electrocoil, 1332
ACTR (GeoStrut), 1542
Actual Experience, 2892
ActualMeds, 1757
Actuate, 28, 1247
Actuera, 3232
Acturis, 1752
Actus Corporation, 2347
ACTV8me, 297
Acucela, 2970
AcuFocus, 40, 413, 1082, 1628, 1762, 1975, 2565
Acuity, 2058
Acuity Ventures, 3284
Acumatica, 89, 3088
Acumen, 282
Acumen Brands, 815
Acumentrics, 466, 497
Acumentrics Holding Corporation, 407
Acunote, 2329
Acunu, 2691, 2858, 3032
Acura Pharmaceuticals Inc., 806
Acurex, 1770
Acusphere, 1975
Acusto Oy, 2873

AcuStream, 1020
Acutas Medical, 2737
AcuteLogic Corporation, 2414
Acutus, 1382
Acutus Medical, 809
Acylin Therapeutics, 153, 2008
Ad Hawk Microsystems, 1004
Ad Lightning, 755
Ad Mass, 545
AD PathLabs, 765
AD Technology, 2857
Ad Valem Technologies, 3208
Ad Venture Interactive, 166
AD-Tech Plastic Systems, 465
Ad.ly, 871
Ad2pro, 3211
ADA Carbon Solutions, 675
Ada Support, 2280
AdAdapted, 113
Adagene, 710
Adalta, 3248
Adam Software, 2426
Adama Materials, 1737
Adamas, 634, 1247
Adamas Nanotechnologies, 3259
Adamas Pharmaceuticals, 581, 2513, 2690
Adamation, 1461
Adamence, 3020
Adams Brush Manufacturing, 1295
Adams Capital Management, 3275
Adams Childrenswear, 2537, 2538
Adams Harris, 57
Adams Pharma, 1341
Adams Publishing Group, 403
Adams Respiratory Therapeutics, 74
Adams Street Partners, 3255, 3261
Adams Street Partners LLC, 3265
Adande Refrigeration, 2306
Adansonia Management Services Limited, 3261
Adao Global, 984
Adap.TV, 1715
Adap.Tv, 260
Adap.tv, 1534
Adapsyn Bioscience, 2130
Adapt Media, 1306
Adapt-N, 432
AdaptaMat, 2451
Adaptify, 1008
Adaptimmune, 710, 762, 1297, 1382
Adaptive, 418
Adaptive Biotechnologies, 762
Adaptive Blue, 264
Adaptive Computing, 688, 1728
Adaptive Insights, 411, 1041, 1378, 2153
Adaptive Mobile, 1004, 2671
Adaptive Ozone Solutions, 1837
Adaptive Planning, 1249, 1975
AdaptivEnergy, 979
Adaptix, 223, 1596
Adaptly, 695, 1110, 1827, 1899
ADAPX, 85
Adapx, 979, 1391, 1400, 1425
ADAR IT, 1242
Adara, 231, 1378, 1515, 1806
Adara Media, 197, 1257
Adare Pharmaceuticals, 1835
Adarza, 267, 704
Adarza BioSystems, 569
Adavium Medical, 149, 1916
Adaytum, 1725, 2079
Adazza, 2834
ADB Airfield Solutions, 3026
AdBm Technologies, 445
AdBrain, 3018
AdBrite, 548, 1241
Adcade, 858, 1518, 1632
Adchemy, 197, 623

Portfolio Companies Index

ADCO Global, 199
ADCO Group, 135
Adco Products Inc, 832
Adco Technologies, 832
Adconion, 2797
Adconion Media Group, 2604
ADD, 2342
Add, 641
Addenda Capital, 2120
Addepar, 301, 724, 1902
AddEvent, 772
Addex Pharmaceuticals, 2513, 2690
Addex Therapeutics, 1271, 1297
ADDI, 1933
Addiction Campuses of America, 794
Addiko Bank, 62
Addison Group, 1368
Addison Lee Group, 413
Addison McKee, 78
Addison Software, 2823
Additech, 946
Addoz, 2873
Addressable, 1421
Addressograph-Bartizan, 1746
AddSecure, 21
Addstructure, 1176
AddThis, 1001, 1348, 1502, 1558
Addum, 2863
AdDuplex, 3049
Addus Healthcare, 686
Addvocate, 625
Addy, 1998
ADECN, 1354
Adelard Soucy, 2120
AdelaVoice, 1734
Adeliade Bank Ltd, 2456
Adelior, 2607
Adello Biologics, 400
Adelphic, 287, 1181
Aden & Anais, 1645, 1767
Adenia Partners, 3261
Adenios, 320
Adenium Biotech, 3149, 3203
Adenosine Therapeutics LLC, 184
Adenovir Pharma, 2449
Adeo Health Science, 1519
Adept, 563
Adept Plastic Finishing, 917
Adeptra, 23, 2348
Adeptus Health, 1742
Aderant, 779
Aderant Holdings, 1156
Adernant, 1491
AdEspresso, 1912
Adesso, 2293
Adesso Systems, 2565
Adesto, 57
Adesto Technologies, 6, 144, 153, 183, 184
ADF Restaurant Group, 158
AdFin, 394
Adfinitum, 2143
Adforce, 192, 1405, 1975
ADG, 222
AdGent, 2618
adglow, 1982
Adgrok, 2329
AdHawk, 1176, 1703
AdHawk Microsystems, 2066
Adheron Therapeutics, 112, 1196
Adhersis, 2601
Adhezion Biomedical, 1385
Adiana, 769, 925
Adicet Bio, 1350
Adictiz, 3020
Adience, 2914
Adient Medical, 347, 950, 951
ADiFY, 1916

Adify, 1896
Adikteev, 3208
Adimab, 308, 1382, 1460, 1628, 1762
Adina, 1396
Adistry, 392
Aditazz, 174
Adjara Hotel, 3095
adjust, 3161
Adkeeper, 1715
Adknowledge, 1041, 1327, 1474, 1785
Adku, 1860
ADL Technology, 2962
Adler and Allen, 2944
Adler Hot Oil Service, 1719
Adlucent, 1810
Adludio, 2478
Adly, 1888, 1965
ADM Capital, 3261
Adma Biologics Inc., 74
AdMarvel, 1244
Admbit, 74
Admedo, 2967
Admeld, 1715
Admiral, 272
AdmitHub, 1527, 1551, 2236
Admittance Technologies, 445
Admitted.ly, 1518
Admittedly, 544
AdMob, 1341, 1654
Admob, 28, 581, 634
AdMobius, 1747
Admovate, 772
AdNear, 386
Adnexus, 747, 1916
Adnexus Therapeutics, 191
Adobe Healthcare, 1777
Adobe Systems Inc., 1903
Adocia, 2851
Adolor, 153
Adolor Corporation, 94
Adometry, 202, 1663
Adomic, 624, 1099, 1965
Adomo, 1975
AdOn Network, 1011
Adop, 100
Adore, 1764
Adore Me, 1532, 1888, 3208
Adored, 3
AdoRx Therapeutics, 689
ADP Dental Company Ltd, 2722
ADP Primary Care, 2379
AdPay, 142
Adperfect, 2176
Adra Match, 3043
Adracare, 2149
Adreima, 333, 1963
AdRelevance, 887
Adrenaline, 374
Adria, 2392
Adrian, 59
Adrich, 1703
AdRise, 295
Adroit Digital, 286
AdRoll, 28, 770, 1218, 1975
Adroll, 751, 1001
Ads Native, 1378
ADS Technologies Inc., 465
Adscale, 2829
AdsNative, 622
Adspace Networks, 324, 596, 1954
Adspert, 256
adsquare, 3161
AdStage, 624, 1311, 1926, 2010
Adstage, 306, 768, 784
Adstrix, 3003
ADstruc, 608, 1700
AdSwerve, 21

ADT CAPS Co., 413
ADT Security, 744
adtarget.me, 3049
AdTheorent, 1926
AdTheos, 121
ADTI, 1753
Adult & Pediatric Dermatology, 1963
Adura Technologies, 1324, 1906
Aduro, 21, 2978
Adva-Net, 550
AdvaCare, 1752
Adval Tech, 77
Advalight, 3203
Advancce Health, 1752
Advance Auto Parts, 783
Advance Energy Partners, 672
Advance Engineered Products, 2163
Advance Group, 1970
Advance Health, 909
Advance ICU Care, 149
Advance Medical, 1752
Advance Technology Services, 465
AdvanceCOR, 2824
Advanced, 2021
Advanced Accelerator Applications, 3113
Advanced Accessory Systems, 439
Advanced Adnimal Diagnostics, 570
Advanced Analog Technology, 892
Advanced Analogic Technologies, 1180, 1769, 2603
Advanced Animal Diagnostics, 1008
Advanced AV, 812
Advanced Bio Development, 1088
Advanced BioCatalytics, 319
Advanced Biomarker, 1571
Advanced Biomarker Technologies, 1008
Advanced BioNutrition, 1169, 1665, 2106, 2492
Advanced Career Technologies, 787
Advanced Cath, 1014
Advanced Catheter Therapies, 459, 995
Advanced Cell Diagnostics, 1298, 2978
Advanced Cell Diagnostics, 1752
Advanced Ceramic X Corp, 3218
Advanced Circuits, 523
Advanced Circulatory Systems, 3279
Advanced Composite Group, 2657
Advanced Computer Systems, 2535
Advanced Cyclone Systems, 2717
Advanced Dermatology & Cosmetic Surgery, 194, 914
Advanced Diamond Technologies, 975, 983, 1740
Advanced Digital Broadcast, 2922
Advanced Digital Internet Corp., 187
Advanced Discovery, 1857
Advanced Disposal Services, 746
Advanced Drainage Systems, 254
Advanced Duplication Services, 1343, 1503
Advanced Electron Beams, 747
Advanced Equities Financial Corp., 137
Advanced Farm Technologies, 429
Advanced Fibre, 536
Advanced Fibre Communication, 1728
Advanced Finance & Investment Group LLC, 3261
Advanced H2O, 1209
Advanced ICU Care, 1850, 1975
Advanced Image Enhancement, 1693
Advanced Industrial Devices, 1578
Advanced Inquiry Systems, 144
Advanced Instruments Inc., 909
Advanced Interactive Systems, 2079
Advanced LEDs, 2400
Advanced Lighting Technologies Inc., 1621
Advanced M, 779
Advanced Material Process Corporation, 1336
Advanced Medical Personnel Services, 503

Portfolio Companies Index

Advanced Metering Data Systems, 1144
Advanced Micro-Fabrication Equipment, 833
Advanced Microgrid Solutions, 595, 809
Advanced Network Solutions, 378, 678
Advanced Pain Management, 468
Advanced Payment Solutions, 1850
Advanced Photonix, 979, 1918
Advanced Physical Therapy, 443
Advanced Power Electronics Corporation, 2603
Advanced Practice Strategies, 176, 1173
Advanced Processing and Imaging, 224
Advanced Recycling Systems, 1021
Advanced Scientifics, 1452
Advanced Sleep Medicine Services, 931
Advanced Software Applications, 1227
Advanced Solar Power, 1340
Advanced Solutions, 333
Advanced Structural Alloys, 958
Advanced Systems Automation, 892
Advanced Technology Healthcare Solutions, 1448
Advanced Technology Services, 1557
Advanced Technology Services UK Limited, 1979
Advanced Vision Technology, 3137
Advancell, 2483
AdvancePath, 548
Advancis Pharmaceutical Corp., 212
Advancis/Middle Brook, 1558
AdvanDx, 1205
Advano, 395, 1630
Advanova, 2824
Advanstar, 1927
Advanstar Communications, 924
Advanta, 778
Advantage, 2073
Advantage Home Health, 406
Advantage Home Telehealth, 704
Advantage Medical Electronics, 405
Advantage Payroll Service, 1986
Advantage Sales & Marketing, 135, 1109
Advantaged Sintered Metals & Contact, 1209
Advantedge Healthcare Solutions, 774
Advantice Health, 1590
Advantmed, 274
Advantor Systems Corporation, 1276
Advarra, 1128
Advasense, 2782
Advekit, 120
Advent, 1965
Advent Aerospace Inc., 902
Advent International, 869, 3264
Advent Software, 1835
Adventa, 114
Adventr, 1507
Adventrx Pharmaceuticals, 1784
Adventuer Ventures, 2855
Adventure Gold, 2120
Adventure Sports Products, 1837
AdventureLink, 1915
Adventures, 3108
AdverCar, 386
Advertising.com, 876, 2754
Advertory, 2921
Adverum, 1928
Advidxchange, 909
Advion, 74, 1460
Advion BioSciences, 432, 1691
Advion Inc., 810
Advision Media Holdings, 3093
Advisor Group, 1123
Advisors Excel, 1978
Advocus, 1099
AdvoServ, 824
Adway, 1507
Adways, 596
Adwerx, 876

Adwo, 1838
Adyen, 815
Adynxx, 621, 1271
Adzerk, 1845
Adzuna, 3030
AEB, 2445
AED-SICAD, 235
Aegea Medical, 87, 604
Aegerion Pharmaceuticals, 925, 1775
Aegis, 181, 949
Aegis AI, 622
Aegis Business Credit, 3262
Aegis Chemical Solutions, 1009
Aegis Legal Consulting, 3276
Aegis Sciences Corporation, 21
Aegle Gear, 459
Aeglea Biotherapeutics, 1124, 1519
Aehr Text Systems, 1752
Aelin Therapeutics, 1350
Aeluros, 1241, 1975
Aemass, 307
AEMI, 3020
AEMT, 131
Aeolus Re, 1956
AEP Networks, 1175, 1227
AePONA, 2386, 3191
Aepona, 1460
Aera, 1297, 2132
Aera 1, 968
Aeration Industries, 850
Aereo, 743
Aereon, 1846
AerGen Leasing, 862
Aerial, 1004
Aerial Access Equipment, 405
Aerial Biopharma, 1556
Aerie, 495
Aerie Pharmaceuticals, 94, 762, 1698
Aerin Medical, 590, 1097
Aeris, 505
Aeris Communications, 548
AerisTech, 2967
Aernnova, 744
Aero, 823, 1968
Aero Communications, 1545
Aero Corporation, 1262
Aero Interiors Company, 225
Aero Mechanical Industries, 1300
Aero Products, 1017
Aero Systems Engineering, 443
Aero Thermal, 2295
Aero-Mark MRO, 1533
AeroCare, 1628, 1762
AeroCare Holdings, 723, 1271
Aerocrine, 2562, 2728, 2890
Aerocrine AB, 1382, 2816
Aerodesigns, 1460
Aeroflex, 839, 1925, 2460
AeroFS, 206
Aerofs, 2329
Aerogen, 1896, 1975
AeroGen-TEK, 540
Aeroglide Corporation, 523
Aerohive, 777, 1121, 1340
Aerohive Networks, 581, 634, 1001, 1297
Aeromics, 347
Aeronics, 293
Aeroport International De Mont-Tremblant, 2120
Aeropost, 1334
AeroPrecision, 1368
AeroPRISE, 2382
AeroScout, 536, 1202, 1975, 3137
Aerosol Services Company Inc., 869
Aerosol Servives Holdings Corp., 869
Aerospace Products International, 1545
Aerospares 2000, 48
Aerospike, 93, 1297

Aerostar Global Logistics, 443
Aerostructures Corporation, 2565
Aerothermal Group, 2539
Aerovance, 1325, 2496
Aerovox, 1295
Aerpio, 1382
Aerpio Therapeutics, 187, 479, 1059, 1847, 1921
AerSale Holdings, 1109
AERT, 928
Aeryon Labs, 1752
AES, 2918
AescAp Venture, 3042
Aesgen, 1975
AESSEAL, 2311
Aesynt, 779
AET, 1295
Aether Bio, 318
Aether Partners, 1167
AetherPal, 1305, 1459
Aethon, 176, 628, 998, 1440, 1520, 1850
Action, 1297
Aeva, 4, 1151
Aevere Systems, 1202
Aevitae, 3232
AEye, 1004
Aeye, 1075
AF Global Corporation, 740
Afaqs!, 3109
Afara Websystems, 1975
Afb, 2406
AFC, 2007
AFC Enterprises, 783
Afero, 721
Affare Del Giorno, 2672
Affdex, 2831
Affectis Pharmaceuticals AG, 2350
Affectiv, 3018
Affectiva, 721, 1075, 1259
AffectoGenimap, 2562
AffectoGenimap Group Oyj, 2716
Affera, 1347
Afferent Pharmaceuticals, 621, 1298, 1412, 1811, 3085
Affibody, 2728, 2890
Affibody AB, 2816
Affiliated Power Services, 908
AffiliateShop, 1681
Affinaquest, 1697
Affinergy, 1810, 1988, 3259
Affinia Group Inc., 575
Affinimark Technologies, 1097
Affinio, 2068, 2243
Affinion Group, 815
AffiniPay, 857
Affinitiv, 1166
Affinity, 858
Affinity Capital Management, 3279
Affinity Dental Management, 1231
Affinity Engiens, 2457
Affinity Express, 925
Affinity Healthcare, 2676
Affinity Jobs, 1853
Affinity Lab, 678
Affinity Labs, 1323
Affinity Networks, 132
Affinity Neworks, 1965
Affinity Specialty Apparel, 1545
Affinity VideoNet, 925
Affinium Pharmaceuticals, 769
Affinnova, 747, 1665
Affinor Growers, 1079
Affirm, 124, 235, 823, 1069, 1121
Affirma Capital, 3261
Affirmed, 455, 1181, 1382
Affirmed N.V., 1297
Affirmed Networks, 1121
Affirmify, 863

1249

Portfolio Companies Index

Affitech, 2754, 3167
Affomix Corp., 530
Affomix Corporation, 660
Affordable Care, 254
Affordable Interior Systems, 194, 349, 1970
Affordable Luxury Network, 3215
Affy Tapple, 338
Affymax, 260, 2970
Afina, 322
Afiniti Ventures, 1915
Afinity, 397
Afinity Life Sciences, 2048
Afmedica, 139
Afram Plantation Limited, 834
AFrame, 2691
Aframe, 3012, 3018
Afraxis, 206
Afresh, 231, 996
Africa Check, 1374
Africa50, 3261
African Capital Alliance, 3261
African Infrastructure Investment Managers Pty (Lt, 3261
African Lakes Ethiopia, 2889
African Leadership Academy, 1374
African Media Initiative, 1374
AfricInvest, 3261
Afs Technologies, 161
AFS Technologies Inc., 21
After School, 552, 1611
AfterBOT, 475
AfterCollege, 756
Aftermarket Technology, 199
Aftermath, 21
AfterSteps, 1655
AG Associates, 2775
AG Data, 415
AG Global, 1573
AG Kings Holdings Inc., 403
AG Kühnle Kopp & Kausch, 2712
AG Semi, 127
Ag Trucking, 828
Ag2, 2626, 2626
Aga Khan Rural Support Program, 55
AGA Medical, 1972
Agada Bioscience, 2155
Against Gravity, 741, 1183, 1654
AgaMatrix, 723
Agami Systems, 925
Agape Package Manufacturing, 2590, 3062
Agari, 87, 235, 603, 741, 1346, 1626
Agarrius, 2604
Agate Logic, 47
AgBiome, 6, 153
AGC AeroComposites, 48
Ageia Technologies, 925
Agena Bioscience, 1792
Agena Technologies, 1919
Agence De Securite Mirado, 2095
Agencyport Software, 1815
AgencyQ, 61
Agendia B/V, 2785
AgenDx, 1019
AgenDx Biosciences, 658
Agent, 889, 1260
Agent Ace, 1846
Agent IQ, 1670
Agent Media Corporation, 1465
Agent Provocateur Limited, 2311
Agentase, 998
AgentDesks, 128
Agentdesks, 994
Agentero, 707
Agentics Inc., 2775
AgentIQ, 1595
Agentiq, 472
Agentology, 784

Agents Inspired, 2483
Agentscape, 2673
Agentum Technologies, 2451
Ageras, 1017
Agere, 202
AGF Group, 2120
Aggamin, 347
Aggregage, 1784
Aggregate Knowledge, 581, 634, 770, 1406
Aggregated Knowledge, 358
AGI, 473, 2918
AGI Dermatics, 1844
Agilance, 422
Agile, 1247
Agile Financial Technologies, 2849
Agile Materials & Technologies Inc., 371
Agile Media Network, 2974
Agile Networks, 28
Agile Planet, 445
Agile Sciences, 3259
Agile Software, 28, 757, 1288, 1654
Agile Systems, 706, 2058
Agile Therapeutics, 74, 412, 1490, 1941
Agile Upstream, 98
AGILEci, 2406
AgileNano, 1784
Agilence, 852, 1321, 2196
Agilence Inc., 29
Agilex Fragrances, 1231
Agilic, 3203
Agilis, 1812
Agility, 904, 1045, 1235
Agility Communications Inc., 252
Agility Fuel Systems, 657
Agility Recovery, 1136
Agility Robotics, 1703
Agilix, 1677
Agilix Corporation, 2518
Agilliance Group, 3118
AgilOne, 1184, 1319, 1654, 1796
Agilone, 777
Agilux Labs, 118
Agilyx, 3092
Agios, 747
Agios Pharmaceuticals, 153, 1811
AGIS, 61, 1405, 1737
Agistics, 1975
Agito Networks, 422
AGL, 1350
Aglity Communications, 3118
AgLocal, 635
AGM Automotive, 1856
Agman Capital, 70
AgnioChem, 2196
Agnitio, 2987
Agnito, 2693
Agolo, 1154
Agora, 318, 3125
Agora Communication, 2120
Agora Fund, 3277
Agora.io, 823
Agoura Technologies, 1915
Agouron Pharmaceuticals, 1918
AGR Enhanced Drilling Systems, 3141
AGR Group, 2384
Agralogics, 1061
Agramkow Fluid Systems, 2651
AgraQuest, 304
Agreement Express, 790
Agreemint, 30
AgriBiotics, 2049
Agribiotics Inc., 2114
Agrileum, 1820
Agrilink Holdings, 2622
Agrilink Holdings Pty Limited, 2715
Agrilyst, 7, 351, 525
Agrimetis, 1519

Agrinos, 1774
Agripharm, 2071
Agrisoma Biosciences, 2093
AgriSync, 995
Agritibi R.H., 2120
Agrivert, 2362
Agrivida, 570, 581, 634, 802, 1470, 1474, 1774
Agro Arms, 3262
Agro-100 Ltee, 2120
Agro-Bio Controle, 2120
Agrocentre Belcan, 2120
AgroGeneration, 2372
Agroils, 2874
Agromillora, 1017
Agronomic Technology, 173
Agros Nova Sp. z o.o., 2706
AgroSavfe, 3065
Agrosavfe, 3042
Agrostar, 28
AGS, 869
AGS Health, 97
AgSmarts, 995
AgSolver, 582
AGTC, 1008, 1010, 1731
Aguamarina, 1069
Aguamur, 2489
AGV Logistica, 834
Agworld, 3248
AGY Holding Corporation, 1081
AGY Therapeutics, 2780, 2781
AH Harris, 789
AH Parallel Fund III-Q, 623
Aha, 1916
Aha!ogy, 479
AHAlife, 596
Ahalogy, 962, 1384
AHF Products, 109
Ahhaaa!, 2754
Ahlijasa, 721
Ahlsell, 2379
AHM, 166
AHP Billing, 349
Ahura Scientific, 153, 422, 798, 880
ai, 807
Ai Build, 3108
AI Exchange, 1097
AI Fund, 872
aI METRIX, 2771
Aiara, 3127
Aibang.com, 1181
Aibel, 2731
Aicent, 1776, 1983, 2697, 2853
AiCO Technologies Co. Ltd, 2347
Aiconn Technology, 1922
AiCure, 222, 268, 1480
AidIn, 1531
Aidin, 1581
Aidox Oy, 2716
Aiera, 754
Aif Capital Ltd, 3261
Aifi, 942
Aigle, 2415
Aigotec, 3137
AiHit, 3229
Aiko Biotechnology, 1161
Aikosolar, 973
Aileron, 1731
Aileron Solutions, 1824
Aileron Therapeutics, 703, 1124, 3085
Aim Above, 3262
AIM Aviation, 2944
AIM Health Group, 2058, 2150
AIM Software, 1972
Aim Technology, 2472
Aimbridge, 815
Aimbridge Hospitality, 62, 1104
AIMCo, 3258

Portfolio Companies Index

Aimia Inc., 300
Aimmune Therapeutics, 762, 1143, 1519
AIMotive, 483
AIMS, 1382
Aims, 286
AimSteady, 1507
Aimune Therapeutics, 74
Aimware Limited, 2705
Aingel, 1370
Ainsworth Lumber, 2067
Ainsworth Pet Nutrition, 1088
Aiotv, 2155
AIP Aerospace, 109
AIP Private Capital, 3258
aiPod, 972
Aiptek International, 2603
AIQ, 124
Air Castle, 767
Air Chef, 1275
Air Energi, 2935
Air Italy, 3154
Air Lease Corp., 869
Air Lease Corporation, 159
Air Map, 1480
Air Media, 130
Air Medical Group Holdings, 220, 1275
Air Methods, 110
Air Monitor Corporation, 908
Air Movement Systems, 742
Air Serv, 1770
Air Tailor, 1176
Air Waves, 364
Air Waves Inc., 1344
Air Works, 1297
Air-Inc, 1920
Air-sea Survival Equipment, 2361
Air2Web, 2875
Air2Web Asera, 3118
Aira, 149
Aira.io, 1151
aira.io, 720
Airband, 21, 2196
airBand Communications, 2639
Airband Communications Holdings, 555
Airbanq, 243
Airbase, 1933
Airbiquity, 85, 974, 1733
Airbnb, 45, 124, 262, 578, 679, 743, 775, 815, 816, 820, 823, 872, 1075, 1524, 1654, 1761, 1766
AirBoard, 307
Airborne 1, 1915
Airborne Entertainment, 1926
Airborne Intl., 2213
Airborne1, 1784
Airbud, 622
Airbug, 1121
Aircall, 2478
AirCell, 1769
Aircell, 1480
AirClic, 765
Airclic, 1041, 1305
Aircraft Fasteners, 949, 1491
Aircraft Technical Publishers, 1166
AircraftLogs, 1553
Aircuity, 1920
aire, 1982
Airespace, 1087, 1255, 1747, 2926
Airex Energy, 2093
Airfordable, 218
Airgo Networks, 28, 1975
AirHelp, 721, 1749, 2010
Airis Wellsite Services, 1125
Airlease, 2329
Airline Services, 2944
Airln Space, 2491
AirLogix, 955

Airmada, 622, 1487
AIRMAP, 1696
AirMap, 816, 1509, 1703
Airmap, 219, 358, 519, 1151, 1154
Airnet Communications, 56
Airobotics, 296, 1154
Aironet, 212
AirPair, 852
Airpax, 468
AirPlug, 1747, 1838
Airport Technology Center, 2565
Airpower Insurance, 264
AirPR, 544, 1247, 1607
AirSense, 2987
AirSense Wireless, 2668
Airship, 1926
Airside, 876
Airsis, 1784
Airspace, 851, 1663
Airspace Link, 607
Airspace Technologies, 1509
Airspan, 1509, 1637, 3137
Airspan Networks, 1361, 1558, 1769
Airsphere, 2775
Airstone Labs, 1860
Airstream, 2113
AirStrip, 1654
Airstrip, 1509
Airswift, 1971
Airtable, 15, 318, 784, 942, 1694
Airtag, 3113
AirTight Networks, 1850, 2508
Airtime, 889, 1075, 1110, 1833
Airtreks, 506, 1535
Airvana, 1235, 2020
AirVine Scientific, 1095
AirVM, 2068
Airware, 124, 730, 1489
Airwatch, 28
Airwave, 889
Airwavz Solutions, 1409, 3259
Airway Services, 529
Airway Therapeutics, 479
Airweb, 2662
Airwide Solutions, 212, 1080, 1167
Airwork, 2664
Airworx Construction Equipment & Supply, 1053
Airxcel Holdings Inc., 354
AirXpanders, 544, 1488, 1941
Airy3D, 1004
Airy:3D, 472, 1983
Aisera, 1202, 1666
Aisle411, 569
Aisle50, 1384
Aislelabs, 1607, 2239, 2243
Aisys Ltd., 2954
AIT, 2209
AIT Bioscience, 658
AIT Worldwide Logistics, 1505
Aito Technologies, 2630, 2637
Aitua, 2967
Aiva Health, 50
AIXTRON Semiconductor Technologie, 2810
Aizon, 395
Ajax Health, 74, 1082
Ajax Health. Alcresta Therapeutics, 921
Ajax Intel, 995
Ajker Deal, 721
AJP Motos, 3048
AK Valley, 1701
Akadémos, 1083
Akamai, 223
Akamai Technology, 1103
Akamedia, 2383
Akari Therapeutics, 762, 1297, 1941
AkaRx, 1760

Akash Systems, 1069
Akebia Therapeutics, 187, 479, 1059, 1143, 1512, 1847, 1921
Akerman LLP, 3262
Akero, 1928
Akero Therapeutics, 143
Akeros Silicon, 1786
Akers Group, 2384
Akiban Technologies, 1334
Akibia, 521
Akido, 858
Akido Labs, 994
Akili Software, 3259
Akimbi, 1416
Akimbo Systems, 1975, 2021
Akin, 519, 1026
Akin Gump Strauss Hauer & Feld LLP, 3261
Akindo Sushiro, 3033
Akindo Sushiro Co., 2379
Akinova, 1269
Akiva, 1784
Akiva Inc., 371
Aknol, 2776
Akonix Systems, 1407
Akonni Biosystems, 1169
Akorda, 1554
Akorri, 1334
Akouos, 12, 1297, 1350, 1519
Akoya, 1740
AKQA, 2079
Akqa, 779
Akros, 595
Akros Silicon, 1896
Aksh Optifibre Ltd. (India), 2694
Akshara Foundation, 1374
Aksys, 1760
Akta US LLC, 77
Aktana, 1601
Aktano, 3138
Aktino, 1237, 1682, 1918
AktiVax, 930
Aktive, 1890
Aktrion, 2796
Aktua, 442
Akubio, 2316
Akulaku, 148
Akumina, 3
Akustikken, 3203
AKVASmart, 3167
Akwan, 2742
Al Film, 34
AL Gulf Coast Terminals, 156
Al Nabil Food Industries, 413
Al Rajhi Capital, 152
AL Shore, 156
Al-F-Hitech, 2969
Alabama Theater, 1681
Alacritech Inc., 252, 1288
Aladdin, 1910
AlaFair, 1801
Alain Afflelou, 2721
Alamar Foods, 413
Alamito Minerals, 514
Alamo Drafthouse Cinema, 96
Alamosa Solar Generating Project, 413
Alan, 2225
Alando, 3233
Alantium, 2454
Alantos Pharmaceuticals, 2682, 2748
Alapage.com, 2765, 3208
Alarm.cOm, 1785
Alarm.com, 22
Alarmguard Holdings, 1067
Alarts.com, 724
Alary, 2120
Alaska Airlines, 1970
Alaska Communications Systems, 778

1251

Portfolio Companies Index

Alasko, 1088
Alate Partners, 2236
Alatest, 2475
Alation, 547, 968, 1798
Alauda.cn, 1004
Alauda.io, 2439
Alawar Entertainment, 89
AlayaCare, 2157, 2170, 2184, 2233
ALBA 1, 2857
ALBA Therapeutics, 184
Alba Therapeutics, 1628, 2816
Albany Molecular Research, 1452
Albarelle, 2338
Albeo, 322
Albert, 942, 2225
Albert Perron, 2095
Alberta Enterprise Corporation, 3258
Alberta Newsprint Company, 2258
Alberta Teachers' Retirement Fund, 3258
Albertville Quality Foods, 928
Albion Medical Holdings, 1526
Albireo, 3196
Albireo Energy, 960
Albridge Solutions, 212, 361, 954
Albrieo, 3007
Albright Capital Management LLC, 3261
AlbéA, 1753
ALC Concierge Service, 1583
Alcala Farma, 1775
Alcami, 1156
Alcentra, 2361
Alces, 219
Alces Technology, 36, 519
Alchemia, 2618
Alchemist Accelerator, 483, 809
Alchemista, 1487
Alchemy, 1370, 1572
Alchemy 43, 707, 761
Alchemy Semiconductor, 202
AlchemyAPI, 36
Alchimer, 2354
Alchip, 3123
Alchip Technologies, 3093
Alcholo Monitoring Systems, 1572
Alci, 2296
Alcide, 1004
ALCOM, 214
Alcon Computing, 1004
Alcontrol, 2556
Alcor Micro, 3218
Alcresta, 1811
Alcresta Therapeutic, 782
Alcumus Group, 3130
Alcyone Lifesciences, 907
Aldagen, 1008, 1442, 1842
Aldaph, 2889
Aldea Pharmaceuticals, 386
Aldeia da Pedralva - Empreend. Turisticos, 3048
Alder Biopharmaceuticals, 604, 762, 1658, 2008
Aldera, 22
Aldeyra Therapeutics, 621
Aldila Therapeutics, 709
Aldis, 233, 1273
Aldus, 753
Aleafia, 2254
Alector, 762, 889, 1238, 1382
Aledade, 268, 889, 1169
Aledadem Amino, 1916
Aledia, 322, 1004
Alegra AG, 2427
Alegus Technologies, 1123
Alektrona, 1693
Alelion Batteries, 2755
Alemite LLC, 908
Alentic Miscroscience, 2155
Alephd, 1416
AleraGroup, 819

Alere Medical, 1975
Alere Medical Inc., 572
Alereon, 441, 678, 1244
Alerion Biomedical, 1543
Aleris AB, 2712
Alert 360, 1752
Alert Life Sciences Computing, 3048
Alert Logic, 36, 986, 1364, 1886, 1972
Alert1, 1852
Alertek, 998
AlertEnterprise, 1381
AlertMe, 1906
AlertTech, 1810
Aleva, 2515
Aleva Neurotherpeutics, 2496
AlexandAlexa, 2972
Alexander Mann Solutions, 1301, 2207
Alexander Tank, 1430
Alexar Therapeutics, 1303
Alexion, 530
Alexis Biochemicals, 118
Alexis Bittar, 1861
Alexo Therapeutics, 1122
Alexza, 12
Alexza Molecular Delivery Corporation, 2316
Alexza Pharmaceuticals, 925
Alfa, 2725
Alfabet, 2377
Alfacam, 2780
AlfaLight, 652, 1921
Alfalight, 59, 153, 979
Alfresco, 28, 1184, 1235
Alfresco Software Alteryx, 1620
Alfy, 536
ALG USA Holdings, 1491
Algal Scientific, 742, 983
Algas Industries, 111
Algebra Ventures, 483
Algentis, 2976
Algeta, 2519
Algeta AS, 2816
Algety Telecom, 555
Algiax, 2824
Algo Access, 3073
Algolia, 28, 1747, 3044
Algolux, 817, 2109
AlgometR, 418
Algomi, 2834
Algomi Ltd., 2928
Algopix, 1006
Algorand, 1882
Algorithmia, 600, 1158, 2006
Algorithmics, 2079
ALI Solutions, 1863
Ali Solutions, 137
ALI Technologies, 2097
Alianza, 856, 1070, 1427, 1677, 1884
Aliaxis, 3069
Alibaba, 823, 986, 2733, 3100
Alibaba Group, 802, 1235, 1683
Alibaba.com, 1678
Alibre, 197, 1558
Alibris, 1083
Alice, 13, 395, 1218
Alice.com, 583
Alien Technology, 57, 692, 947, 1558, 1755
Alien Technology Corp., 1297
Alien Vault, 1001, 1024
AlientVault, 823
AlienVault, 544, 1850, 2342
Aligence, 2439
Align, 333
Align Aerospace Holdings Inc., 862
Align Global Consulting, 3259
Align Technology, 1360
Alignable, 313, 1184, 1322, 1623
AlignAlytics, 1568

Aligned Carbon, 1613
Aligned Energy/Inertech, 1376
Aligned Telehealth, 1628
Aligned Teleheath, 1762
Alignment Healthcare, 815
Alignment Software, 947
Alignvest Management Corporation, 2134
Aligos, 1928
Alimentary Health, 2918
Alimentation Coop Port-Cartier, 2120
Alimentation Francis Gravel, 2095
Alimentation L'epicier, 2120
Aliments Urbains, 2120
Alimera Sciences, 621, 1008, 1297, 1460, 1626, 1698, 1916
Alinea, 747
Alinea Pharma, 1628
Alinean, 1745
Alinta Energy, 1835
Alinta Ltd, 2456
Alion, 1925
Alios BioPharma, 3015, 3085
Alipay, 2404
ALIS, 1080
Alis, 153
Alitacare, 1081
Alithya, 2265
AliveCor, 1069, 1509
Alix Partners, 924
AlixPartners, 1017
Alizyme, 2823
Alkami, 1240, 1597
Alkar-RapidPak, 719
Alkira, 1075
Alku, 1979
All Aboard America, 812
All Aboard America!, 439
All American Group, 928
All Around Roustabout, 407
All Def Digital, 60, 1813
All Elements, 3259
All Flex, 850
All Funds Bank, 924
All Gold Imports, 2235
All Island Media, 849
All Metro Health Care Services, 1279
All of It IT, 2449
All Safe, 1719
All Seasons Services, 1114
All Star Directories, 202
All States Ag Parts, 1166
All Tech/IESCO, 1343
All Traffic Data, 1638
All Traffic Solutions, 655
All Turtles, 816, 1607
All-Clad Holdings Inc., 492
All-State, 291
All-Tag Security, 2862
All3Media, 2537, 2538
All4, 1040
All4Staff, 1178
AllAboardToys, 685
AllAbout, 596
Allakos, 94, 1297, 1574, 3085
Allami Nyomda, 2487
Allant, 1231
Allay, 128, 1768
Allbirds, 325, 707, 858, 1110, 1183, 1530, 1585
allbirds, 1694
Allbound, 387
AllBusiness, 1760
Allbusiness.com, 1906
Allcargo, 277
AllCloud, 1034
AllConnect, 1355, 3133
Allconnect, 695, 1709
AllDefDigital, 60

1252

Portfolio Companies Index

Allecra Therapeutics, 2748
Allegiance, 1540
Allegiance Hospice Group, 1628
Allegience Software, 349
Allego, 816
Allegra Direct Communications, 830
Allegro, 744, 909, 1334, 1910, 2823
Allegro Development Corp, 1728
Allegro Diagnostics, 426, 1080
Allegro Venture Partners, 1766
Allen Afflelou, 2852
Allen Edmonds, 334, 378
Allen Edmonds Shoe Corp., 843
Allen Foods Inc., 869
Allena Pharmaceutials, 1811
Allena Pharmaceutials, 260, 782
Allergan, 1349
Allevi, 266
AlleWin Technologies, 1558
AllFacilities Energy Group, 998
AllHeart, 788
AllHere, 1551
Alliance, 1209
Alliance Boots, 2379
Alliance Boots plc, 413
Alliance Business Lending, 1512, 1970
Alliance Care, 406
Alliance Corp., 2163
Alliance Data Systems, 1972, 2379
Alliance Data Systems Corp., 1903
Alliance for Affordable Internet, 1374
Alliance for College-Ready Public Schools, 1316
Alliance Health, 688, 1204, 1438
Alliance Health Networks, 1945
Alliance Healthcare Services, 1271
Alliance Hotelerie, 2792
Alliance Laundry Systems LLC, 354
Alliance Medical, 2537, 2538, 2796
Alliance Medical Ltd, 3186
Alliance Pharma, 2981
Alliance Pharmaceutical, 1918
Alliance Sports Group, 403
Alliance Steel Service, 1719
Alliance Tire Company, 1970
AllianceCare, 402, 1628
Alliant, 909
Alliant Group, 1516
Alliant Insurance Services, 1129
Alliantgroup, 21
Allied 100 All Island Media, 1232
Allied Aerofoam Products, 1111
Allied Alloys, 1970
Allied Defense Group, 1491
Allied Glass Containers, 2617
Allied Reliability Group, 1435
Allied Resource Corporation, 1397
Allied S/A, 1376
Allied Technologies, 2372
Allied Vision Group Inc., 900
Allied Waste, 869
Alliedbarton Security, 881
AlliedPRA, 476
Alligator Bioscience, 3149
Allinea, 2967
Allinea Software, 3107
Allion Healthcare, 716
Allison Marine, 1127
Allison Publications, 828
Allison Transmission Holdings Inc., 1903
Allituition, 1615
Allm, 2857
Allmyapps, 2693
Allocade, 602
Allocadia, 100, 976, 2157, 2266
Allocation Specialists, 425
Allocine, 2607
AlloCure, 3015

Allopartis, 2011
Alloptic, 187
Allos Therapeutics, 74
Allos Ventures, 3269
Allosteros, 347
Allot, 2775
Allot Comm, 3159
Allot Communication Ltd., 3158
Allot Communications, 3231
Allovue, 1054, 1551
Alloy, 37, 544, 679, 1202, 2020
Alloy Die Casting, 828
Alloy Merchant Finance LP, 3261
Alloy Ventures, 3284
AlloyCorp Mining, 1548
Allozyne, 153
Allpets.com, 2021
AllPoints, 1435
Allrecipes.com, 378
Allscripts, 260, 1255
Allsec Technologies, 413, 805
Allset, 124, 525
Allston Trading, 779
Allstream, 2073
allSystem, 3154
Alltec Global, 123
Alltech, 2579
ALLTELL, 1835
AllTheRooms, 1306, 1310, 3125
Alltop Tech, 3218
AllTrails, 385, 1717
Alltrails, 128
Alltricks.com, 1416
Alltrope Medical, 951
Alltrust Networks, 1388
Allume, 823
Allure Security, 2019
Allure Security Technology, 829
Allure Systems, 1138
Allurion Technologies, 1581
Alluvium, 1151, 2006
Alluxio, 124
Allvoices, 1906
AllWest Insurance Services, 2146, 2165
Allworx, 432, 1475
AllyAlign Health, 918
Allyes Information Technology, 2847
Allylix, 570, 1615, 1784, 2492
Allylix Canada, 2049
ALM Media, 1960
ALM Positioners, 1053
Alma, 720, 741
Alma Campus, 1346
AlmaBox, 2984
AlmaConnect, 2904
Almadtrac, 1448
Almalence, 1004
Almaz Capital, 483
Almaz Capital Partners, 3284
Alminder, 1865
Almond Systems, 1181
Almonde, 2079
Almotech, 2355
Alnara Pharmaceuticals, 260, 782, 1145, 1268, 1811
Alnylam, 2445
Alnylam Pharmaceuticals, 153, 191, 410
Alo, 2384
Alo7, 1509, 3215
AloDokter, 721
Alogent, 235
ALOHA, 1998
Aloha, 668, 720, 741, 858, 935, 1663
Alok Textile Industries Limited, 2861
ALON and XL Associates, 1422
Alongside, 2128, 2200
Alooma, 1121

Alopa Networks, 1975
Alopexx Pharmaceuticals, 1419
AloStar Bank of Commerce, 1443, 1743
Alothon Group, 3261
Alpaca, 661
Alperton Ford & Truck, 2985
Alpex Pharma, 2496
Alpha, 563
Alpha & Omega Semiconductor, 905
Alpha Associates, 3261
Alpha Bay, 1677
Alpha Comm Enterprises, 1276
Alpha Draft, 120, 784, 1888
Alpha Foods, 811
Alpha Guardian, 1231
Alpha II, 1979
Alpha Imaging, 443
Alpha Innotech, 69
Alpha Media, 330, 331, 673
Alpha Networks, 2329, 2603
Alpha Outpost, 1150
Alpha Packaging, 1022
Alpha Ring, 1983
Alpha Sheets, 1487
Alpha Smart, 1752
Alpha Source Inc., 222
Alpha Therm, 2978
Alpha Vertex, 724
Alpha vision tech, 2969
Alphabet Energy Inc., 491
Alphabet Inc., 1666
Alphabeta Therapeutics, 943
Alphablock, 2266
AlphaBlox, 1003
Alphablox, 23, 986
Alphabox, 28
Alphabroder, 1134
AlphaDraft, 1563
Alphaeon, 1143
AlphaICs, 2106
Alphamed, 1148
Alphamin, 2862
Alphamosaic, 2662, 2671, 3195
Alphanim, 2897
AlphaPoint, 1577
Alpharank, 956
AlphaSense, 996
AlphaStaff, 39
Alphatec, 1730
Alphatronix, 131, 1708
Alphion, 212
Alphion Corp., 1779
Alpine Data Labs, 1239
Alpine Immune Sciences, 782
Alpine Oral Tech, 1069
Alpine Risk Services, 2362
Alps, 1147
Alreverie, 525
ALRISE, 2841
Alrise Biosystems, 2638
Alro, 2949
ALS Resolvion, 794
Alsalar, 1655
Alsay Inc., 984
Alsbridge, 1136
Alsentis, 1736
Alsid, 2296
Also, 2922
Also Energy, 2081
Alstom Power Conversion, 2714
Alston & Bird, 3259
Alsyon Technologies, 3113
Alt School, 124, 231
Alt United Garment Service, 2810
Alt12Apps, 1010
Alta, 634
Alta Analog Inc., 130

1253

Portfolio Companies Index

Alta Devices, 197, 560, 581, 1474
Alta Growth Capital, 3261
Alta Rock Energy, 59
Alta Semper Capital, 3261
Altair engineering, 2771
Altair Global, 1276
Altair Semiconductor, 260, 2782
Altair Therapeutics, 1817
Altaire, 2100
Altamira, 515
Altamont Capital Partners, 3255
Altan China Co Ltd, 2499
Altaravision, 3259
AltaRock Energy, 1069
Altasciences, 2169
Altaven, 3239
Altead, 2448
Altec, 937
Altec Lansing, 1096
Altech Inspections, 1456
Altegra Health, 1417
Altegris, 819
Altegrity, 1496
Altela, 1924
Alteon Health, 782
Alteon Health LLC, 158
Alteon WebSystems, 757, 1087, 1378, 1682, 1760
Alter Eco America, 3277
Alter G, 491, 797, 1600, 1928
Altera, 385
Alterest, 3108
Alterface, 3225
AlterGeo, 89, 1004, 2344
Alteria Automation, 1507
Alterna, 1861
Alterna LLC, 97
Alternative, 1587
Alternative Biomedical Solutions, 446
Alternative Fuels Group, 989
Alternative Hose LLC, 1040
Alternative Solutions, 557
Alternative Technology Inc., 461
AlterPoint, 202, 1038, 1407
Alterra Power Corp., 1324
Alteryx, 1000, 1212, 1829
Altex Energy, 2050
Althea, 1784
Althea Technologies, 925, 1792
AltheaDx, 1792
Atheos, 3015
Altia Systems, 1004, 1285
Altice S.A., 413
Altieri Bakery, 1639
Altierre, 183, 184, 1975
Altierre Corporation, 1089
Altiga, 260
Altiga Networks, 521
Altilia, 3052
Altimate Medical, 850
Altiostar Networks, 483
Altiris, 1677, 2382
Altiris Therapeutics, 2618
Altiscale, 313, 1654
Altitude, 1634, 2010, 2897, 2897
Altitude Digital, 1204
Altitude Telecom, 3208
Altitun, 2878
AltiusEd, 1715
Alto, 120
Alto Pharmacy, 942, 1024
Alto Plastics, 2410
AltoBeam, 1896, 2667
AltoCom, 1752
Altopa Inc., 2287
Altor, 634
Altor BioScience, 1616, 3196

Altor Networks, 581
Altos Ventures, 3284
Altostra, 1768
Altra, 402
Altraverda, 2598, 2717
Altrec, 958
Altria, 2614
Altrium CNI, 2857
Altruik, 608, 1306, 2017
Altruist, 3001
Altruja, 2824
AltSchool, 741, 775, 1531
AltspaceVR, 792, 1151
Altura Communication Solutions, 1684
Altura Medical, 59, 1298
Altus Pharamceuticals, 3007
Altwork, 275
Alucid Technologies, 1218
Alukon, 2795
Alum.ni, 1463
Alumni Educational Solutions, 2163
Alumnify, 459
Alung, 86
ALung Technologies, 293, 298, 998, 1448
Alural Group, 2332
Alure, 652
Alutrans Canada, 2095
Alva, 2567
Alvarez & Marsal Capital, 3255
Alvarion, 2585, 3118, 3137
Alvarri, 1872
AlveolUs, 184
Alverix, 1305
AlVest, 2851
Alvey, 3042
Alvine, 1698
Alvine Pharmaceuticals, 747, 1010, 1410, 1493
Alvogen, 1134
Alwarebytes, 935
Always Hired, 1054
Always In Touch, 400
Always Market, 1244
Always Prepped, 1860
AlwaysOn, 1061
Alwaysprepped, 1530
AlwazPro, 995
Alyce, 2137
Alyotech Canada, 2095
Alzeca Biosciences, 445
Alzheimers Research & Treatment Center, 746
AM Conservation Group, 1857
AM Pharma, 2496
AM-BEO, 2348
Am-Pharma, 2748
AmacaThera, 2180
Amadesa, 2566
Amadeus, 2497, 2605
Amadeus Capital Partners, 3261
Amaethon, 2892
Amakem, 2748, 2949, 3020
Amakem Therapeutics, 3042
Amalfi Semiconductor, 596
Amalgamated Bean Coffee Trading Company, 584
Amalyst, 2967
Amann, 2795
Amann Girrbach AG, 1776
Amaranth Medical, 458
Amarillo Biosciences, 1837
Amarin, 1382, 1698, 1817
Amart All Sports, 2420
Amas, 2863
Amasten, 1097
Amatek, 2644
Amati, 1257
Amatis, 2142
Amaya Gaming Group, 2095

Amazon, 1865
Amazys, 2922
Amba, 2818
Amba Defence, 2967
Ambarella, 581, 634, 1181, 1341
Ambassador, 173, 1150, 1176, 1736, 2017
Ambassador Theatre Group, 1496
Ambea AB, 1082
Amber Networks, 1747, 1975
Amber Road, 1886
Amber Taverns, 2935
Amber Technology, 2622
Amberdata, 956
AmberPoint, 563, 1760
Amberst Holdings, 1743
AmberWave, 1793
Ambient, 1306
Ambient Air, 1726
Ambient Clinical Analytics, 297
Ambient Devices, 1584
Ambienta Biomasse, 2391
Ambion, 1792
Ambiq Micro, 202, 483, 961, 1206, 2690
Ambiqmicro, 1075
Ambit, 762, 2780, 2781
Ambit Biosciences, 206, 769, 1382, 1520, 3085
Ambition, 889, 1489
Ambition Solutions, 459
Ambow Education, 2603
Ambow Education Holding, 3062
Ambra Health, 474
Ambric, 798
Ambrose, 3267
Ambrx, 12, 2419, 3085
Ambuja Cement, 2697
Ambulance Medilac, 2095
Ambulatory Services of America, 1129
Ambyint, 809, 1206
Ambys Medicines, 1778
AMC Entertainment, 220
Amc10, 322
Amcare, 2936
AMCC, 1654, 1922
AmCom, 1725
Amcor, 2389
AMCS, 1000
AMD Holdings, 750
Amdocs Ltd., 1972
AMEC, 238, 1010
Amec, 1121, 1509, 1534
Amecci, 2120
Ameda, 1166
Amedeo Capital Limited, 1443
Amedia, 34
Amedisys Resource Management Division, 406
Amedo, 2824
Amedrix, 2824
Amee, 1359
Amen, 15, 3149
Amenity Analytics, 1004
Ameos, 3020
Amercable Inc., 985
AmerCareRoyal, 917
America Golf, 1753
America Isreal Cannabis Association, 860
America Latina Logistica, 834
America Rotor Company, 1533
America's PowerSports, 90, 1990
America's Thrift Stores, 92
Americam Physician Partners, 240
American & Efird LLC, 1085
American Academic Suppliers, 1435
American Achievement, 722
American Achievement Corporation, 1884
American Advisors Group, 787
American Alliance Dialysis Holdings, 969
American Apparel, 869

1254

Portfolio Companies Index

American Asphalt & Grading, 765
American Auto Auction Group, 222
American Axle & Manufacturing, 110
American Bath Group, 1275
American Beacon, 1062, 1835
American BioCare, 1423
American Broadband, 1491
American Candy, 1295
American Cannabis Company, 638
American Capital, 380
American Card Services, 1719
American Cellular Corporation, 818
American Clay, 1300
American Clinical Solutions, 405
American Community Newspapers, 1409, 1724
American Consolidated Media, 374
American Construction Source, 500
American CyberSystems, 21
American Dental Partners, 1039
American Disposal Services, 1465
American Dryer Corporation, 1744
American Efficient, 498
American Endovascular, 1346
American Energy Partners, 1846
American Energy Permian Basin, 740
American Engineered Components, 843
American Exteriors, 405, 1484
American Federal Bank, 260
American Felt & Filter, 1295
American Freight, 1045
American Fuel Cell, 704
American Furniture Manufacturing, 465, 523
American Giant, 668
American Gilsonite, 1403, 1491
American Greetings Interactive, 2897
American Higher Educaion Development, 849
American Home/American Furniture Company, 902
American Honors, 508, 1299, 1782
American Hospice, 1572
American Huts, 164
American Independent Companies, 1955
American Industrial Machine, 17
American Industrial Partners, 1871
American Institute of Technology, 716
American Internet Corp, 521
American Israeli Paper Mills2, 2609
American Leather, 164, 401
American Legal Fund, 264
American LegalNet, 1600
American Lighting Supply, 765
American Lock, 843
American Log Handlers, 678
American Made, 1623
American Marketing Industries Holdings Inc., 575
American Medical Systems, 3279
American Messaging Services, 982
American Millwork Corporation, 1521
American Mirrex, 832
American Nuts, 403
American Patholoy Partners, 1297
American Pipe & Plastics, 1624
American Piping Products, 654, 1424
American Prison Data Systems, 1551
American Products Co., 465
American Rec, 1753
American Renal, 442
American Renal Associates, 1136, 1409
American Reprographics Inc., 300
American Residential, 1372, 1972
American Residential Services, 456
American Resource Development, 672
American Roadprinting, 998
American Roland Foods, 1931
American Scholar, 1745
American Screen Art, 693

American Seafoods LP, 447
American Signcrafters, 812
American Skiing Company, 1360
American Stencil, 465
American Stock Transfer & Trust Company, 1572, 3025
American Superconductor, 260
American Surgical Professionals, 859
American Threshold Industries, 1570
American Tire, 1017
American Tire Distributors, 456
American Tire Distributors Inc., 862
American Wholesale, 57
AmeriCann, 1135
AmericasOne, 344
AmeriCast Technologies, 1085
Americo Manufacturing, 291
AmeriFile, 683
Amerifit Nutrition, 237
Amerigroup Real Solutions, 1760
Amerijet International, 928
AmeriMark, 405
Amerimed, 2381, 2382
AmeriPath, 1972
Ameriqual, 1134
AmeriQual Group LLC, 159
AmerisourceBergen Corporation, 354
AmeriSphere, 1276
Ameristop, 1954
Ameritox, 221, 1271, 1654, 1742, 1760
AMES, 1967
Ames, 1753
Ames Taping Tools, 199, 378
Ameta s.r.o., 3122
Amethis Finance, 3261
Ametros Financial Corp., 492
AMF, 654, 869
Amfora Packaging, 46
AMG, 1633
Amgen, 181
Amh Canada Ltee, 2120
AMHC Healthcare, 1061
Amherst Fund, 3269
Amherst Pierpont Securities, 815
AMI, 1758
AMI Holdings Inc., 1590
AMI Semiconductor, 779
Amiato, 585
Amicus, 782, 1358, 1374, 1475, 1518
Amicus Therapeutics, 1297, 1493, 1508, 1520
Amigo Insurance Holding Corporation, 1465
Amigo Technology, 3218
Amimon, 116, 436, 2726, 3231
Amino, 28, 49, 180, 318, 741, 889, 1323, 1882
Amino Technologies, 2472
Aminoagro, 1516
Aminolabs, 3042
Amionx, 1509
Amira, 1760
Amira Learning, 883, 1392
Amira Pharma, 1928
Amira Pharmaceuticals, 1493, 3015
Amitree, 28, 107, 942, 1254
Amkor Technology, 827, 1633, 2728, 2890
AML RightSource, 492
Amlogic, 973, 2850
Ammeraal Beltech, 2851
AMN Healthcare, 1372
Amnis, 85, 1002
Amobee, 3169
Amobee Media Systems, 28
Amonix, 57
Amor GmbH, 2311
Amorfix Life Sciences, 1837
Amorphology, 1051
Amour Vert, 668
Amourvert, 428

Amp Electrical Distribution Services, 657
AMP Robotics, 219, 519
AMP Therapeutics, 2530
Amp'd Mobile, 1558
AMPAC, 928
AMPAC Packaging, 716
Ampad, 152
Ampaire, 1613
Ampathy, 1507
Amper, 60, 776
Amper Music, 351
Amperex Technology, 892
Amperion Cayman, 162
Amperity, 773, 1158
Ampersand, 124
Amphivena Therapeutics, 1268
Amphora, 466
Amphora Medical, 222, 710, 1143, 1872
Ampire Co, 3218
Ampla Pharmaceuticals, 1002, 1775
Ample, 525, 942
Ample Communications, 1558, 1975
Ample Hills, 1110
Ample Hills Creamery, 351, 1530
Ample Medical, 1975
Ample Organics, 2140, 2287
Ampler, 70
Amplero, 974, 1607, 1985
Amplexor, 2563
Amplidata, 2837, 3152
Amplience, 3018
Amplified Technology Holdings, 631
Amplified Wind Solutions, 1047
Amplifinity, 628, 642
Amplifire, 1105
Amplify, 228, 397, 600, 641, 1965
Amplify Partners, 37
Amplify.ai, 547
Amplimed Corporation, 1901
Amplio Filtration Group, 2391
Amplion, 1656
AmpliPhi, 1812
Amplitude, 235, 248, 318, 1001, 1212, 1218, 1654, 1694, 1761, 2851
Amplitude Ventures, 3258
Amplity Health, 96
Amplus Communication Pte Ltd, 2703
Amply, 1363
Amplyx Pharmaceuticals, 841
AmpMe, 2027
Ampool, 454
Amprius, 1075, 1850, 1906
AmPro Mortgage Corporation, 591
Ampulse, 1975
AmQuip, 500
Amr Systems, 2483
AmRest, 1956
Amri, 909
AMRM, 19
Amromco Energy, 740
AmSafe Partners Inc., 862
Amsky Technology, 3062
AmSpec, 1372
amSTATZ, 1097, 2943
Amt, 2748
AMT3D Limited., 2705
AMTD, 2844
Amtec Precision Products, 1332
Amtech Corporation, 81
Amtek Auto, 1956
Amtex, 917
AMTEX Radiátory, 2648
Amtran, 2436
AMTrust, 2851
AMU Holdings, 1491
Amura, 2463
Amvonet, 1047

Portfolio Companies Index

Amware Fulfillment LLC, 403
AmWINS Group, 1301
Amylin, 1654, 1760
Amynta Group, 1156
Amyris, 184, 634
Amyris Biotechnologies, 581
Amzur Technologies, 3262
An Giang Plant Protection, 2961
AnaBios Corporation, 1061, 1784
AnaCatum, 2630
Anacle, 2477, 2853
Anaconda, 816, 2874
Anacor, 762, 946
Anacor Pharma, 1916
Anacor Pharmaceuticals, 1558
Anadigm, 2445
Anadys, 2445
Anadys Pharmaceuticals, 1775
Anaergia, 2261
AnAerobics, 1377
Anaeropharma Science, 1241
Anafocus, 2548
Anafore, 2477
Anagin, 709
Anagnostics Bioanalysis, 3165
Anagram, 395
Anaheim, 846
AnaJet, 468
Analect Instruments, 187
AnalizaDX LLC, 1047
Analog Inference, 1243
Analogic, 97
Analogic Tech, 1180
Analogix, 596, 835
Analogix Semiconductor, 1975, 2005
Analyte Health, 1247, 1480
Analyte Media, 137
Analytical Space, 622, 754, 1329
Analyticon Discovery GmbH, 3190
Ananas, 392
Anandia Labs, 2140
Anant Raj, 260
Anantara, 2818
Anaplan, 509, 560, 852, 1212, 1663
Anaptys Bio, 782
Anaptys Biosciences, 206
AnaptysBio, 87, 3015
Anaqua, 1000
Anaren, 1925
Anark Corporation, 1273
Anasazi, 1255
Anaxsys, 2967
Ancera Corporation, 660
Ancestry, 1212, 1717
Ancestry.com, 57, 227, 563, 925, 986, 1677, 2379, 2382, 3033
Anchange Productions, 1437
Anchor, 28, 679, 889, 1045, 1721
Anchor BanCorp Wisconsin Inc., 404
Anchor Glass, 1967
Anchor Glass Container, 1085
Anchor Intelligence, 1038, 1975
Anchor Media Investors, 1360
Anchor Therapeutics, 919, 3196
Anchorage, 661
Ancient Mosaic Studios, 378
Ancile Solutions, 1166
Ancillary Advantage, 723
Ancora, 1884
AnD APT Inc., 1004
AND Automotive Navigation Data, 3209
Anda Tool and Fasterner Ltd., 908
Andale, 1975
ANDalyze, 975, 1199
AnDAPT, 483
Andela, 79, 883, 889, 1607, 1716, 1758, 2147
Andera, 655, 1693

Anderson & Stowe, 3255
Anderson Aerospace, 1047
Anderson Group, 2095
Anderson Pacific Corporation, 3265
Andes Biotechnologies, 2455
Andia, 392
Andigilog, 1664, 1975
Andium, 408
Andjaro, 2478
Ando, 544
Andpad, 1607
Andre Potvin Cuisine/Salle De Bain, 2095
Andreessen Horowitz, 37
Andreessen Horowitz Fund II-A, 623
Andrena, 13
Andrew, 1305
Andrew Davidson & Company, 2196
Andrew Page, 3036
Andrew Technologies, 1328
Andrews International Holdings, 1275
Andrews International Inc., 465
Andritz, 3069
Androit, 132
Andromedia, 1038, 1563
Anduril, 816
Andy Transport, 2120
Anello Photonics, 429
Anergis, 2515, 3149
Anesco, 3104, 3252
Anesiva, 212, 1775
Anessa, 2200
AneuRx, 1378
Anevia, 2876, 3113
AnexBusiness, 1376
Anfacto, 620
Angagio, 1346
Angaza, 1552, 1607
Angaza Design, 756
Angel food Systems, 3182
Angel Springs, 2944
Angela Bruderer, 2475
Angelini Group, 1452
Angelle, 1726
AngelList, 38, 70, 609, 650, 707, 792, 889, 1054, 1075, 1150, 1323, 1839, 1998, 2236, 2280
Angellist, 229, 751, 1694
AngelPad, 295
Anges Quebec Capital, 3258
AnGesMG, 2970
Angie's, 1665
Angie's List, 560, 641, 1119, 1477, 2928
Angiob, 3245
Angiodroid, 2874
AngioDynamics, 209
Angiogenix, 3167
AngioScore, 371, 986, 1425, 1498, 1792
Angioslide, 269, 2353, 3192, 3241
Angiosyn, 94
Angiotech, 1134
Angle, 816
Angle Technologies, 872
Angler Labs, 293
Anglian Group, 2361
Anglian Group Plc., 575
Anglian PLC, 2361
Anglo Suisse Offshore Partners, 156
Anglr, 1155
Angstrom, 1784
Angstrom Pharmaceuticals, 1702
Angstrom Power, 898, 1906, 2053
Angstrom Publishing, 1191
Angury, 648
Angus Fire, 2944
ANI Pharmaceuticals, 732, 1275
ANI Printing Inks, 3009
Ani-Mat, 2120
AniBoom, 2726

Anika Therapeutics, 212
Anilinker Oy, 2716
Animal Adventure, 1719
Animal Health International, 456, 1109
Animal Supply Company, 894
AnimaPlus, 2220
Animart LLC, 843
Animated Dynamics Inc., 658
Animated Speech Corporation, 1669
Animex, 2562
Animon, 2580
Animoto, 1158, 1700, 1717
Anite Travel, 2944
Anitox, 1572
Aniways, 2831
Anji, 1340
Anji-Micro, 3235
Anju Software, 21
Anjuke.com, 1181
Ankasa, 544
Ankeena, 1853
Anker, 973
Anki, 124, 1874
Ankura, 1156
Anmestix, 323
Ann Arbor Angels, 3269
Ann Williams Group, 742
Ann's House of Nuts, 1372
Anna's Linens, 1587
AnneLutfen.com, 3208
Annexon, 1297
Annexon Bioscience, 1350
Annexon Biosciences, 495, 544
Annie's, 925
Annonay Productions France, 3020
Annovation Biopharma, 191, 1419
Annularspace, 2310
Anodyne, 349
Anokion, 1350, 1928
Anokiwave Inc., 810
Anomali, 816, 889, 1001
Anonymous Content, 1766
Anord Mardix, 257
Anova Data, 935
Anova Fertility & Reproductive Health, 2220
Anover.net, 1459
Anpute, 3194
Anquanbao, 1340
Ansa, 1558
Ansa Software, 206
Ansaar Management Company, 55
Ansamed Ltd, 2705
Ansaris, 1452
Ansaro, 883
Ansell Ltd, 2456
ANSIRA, 1086
Ansley at Roberts Lake, 1219
Ansley Commons, 1219
ANSR, 28
Answer IQ, 1158
AnswerDash, 1945, 2008
AnswerLogic, 1348
Answers, 1752, 1776
Answers Corporation, 135
Answers.com, 592, 1534
AnswerSoft, 202, 1558
Answersoft, 3137
Ansyr, 85
ANT, 2894
Ant Financial Cloud, 2404
Ant Fortune, 2404
Antares Holdings Limited, 1123
Antares Pharma, 1452, 2196
Antavo, 3108
AnTech, 3099
Anteis, 2496
Antengo, 1306

Portfolio Companies Index

Antenna, 971, 1459, 1596
Antenna International, 1984
Antenna Software, 521, 1297, 1334, 1460
Antenna79, 1088
Antenova, 2472, 3070
Anteo Diagnostics, 2618
Anterios, 514
Antero Resources, 1956
Anteryon, 1509, 3069
Antheia, 1666
Anthemis Gropu, 2940
Anthera Pharmaceuticals, 925, 1268, 1412, 1698, 1898, 1906
Anthony, 199
Anthony Machine, 984
Anthony's Coal Fired Pizza, 1088
Anthony's Pizza, 1516
Anthos, 37
Antibe Therapeutics, 2048
Antibiotice, 3187
Antig Technology Co, 2590
Antio Therapeutics, 2180
Antispameurope, 2824, 2994
Antiva Biosciences, 2180
Antler, 2944
Anton Capital Entertainment SCA, 716
Antriabio, 237
AntVoice Group, 2385
Anudip Foundation, 1374
Anuluex Technologies, 1725
Anuncie La, 2331
Anusbisnetworks, 3048
Anutra Medical, 904
Anvato, 1306, 1393
Anvendeo Designwelt, 2824
Anvil, 747
Anvil Holdings, 354
Anvil International, 1777
Anvil Semiconductors, 2967
Any Media, 3042
Any Vision, 1509
Any.do, 301, 720
AnyBody Technology, 3203
Anyka, 2436
AnyMeeting, 1784
Anymeeting, 397
Anyplace, 795
AnyPresence, 1072
Anypresence, 876
AnyRiver, 131
Anyscale, 4
Anysource Media, 1321
AnyTime Access, 52
Anytime Access, 1227
Anytime Fitness, 1576
Anyware, 3113
ANZ, 2978
ANZ Banking Corp, 2659
Anzamune, 2516
AOD Software, 1476
AOMS, 2066
AON, 3262
AON3D, 1370
aon3D, 2212
AOptix, 502, 1860
Aoptix, 1341
Aoptix Technologies, 581
Aorato, 28
AorTx Inc., 269
AOSP, 2579
aovo Touristik AG, 3197
AP Aqua, 2725
AP Benson Ltd, 2894
AP Technical Textiles, 2392
Ap+m, 1435
Apach Network, 2897
Apache, 1922, 2965

Apacheta Corporation, 1402
Apalya Technologies, 2849
Apama, 347
Apama Medical, 176
APANA, 1893
Aparium Hotel Group, 70
Apartment Data Services, 378, 1719
Apartment List, 942
ApartmentJet, 293, 298
ApartmentList, 1181
ApaTech, 2662
Apatech, 2674
Apax CAES, 893
Apax Partners, 3264
APC Automotive Technologies, 914
Apcela, 493
Apcera, 585, 1860
APCOA, 1017
APCT, 1624
APDS, 3277
Apeel Science, 124
Apeel Sciences, 1784, 1888, 3257
Apeks, 2058
Apellis, 919, 2978
Apellis Pharma, 1941
Apellis Pharmaceuticals, 689
Apere, 1975
Aperia, 1600
Aperia Technologies, 195, 1669
Aperio, 586
Aperto Networks, 1038, 2875
Aperture, 529, 1720
Aperture Credentialing, 955
Apervita, 222, 809, 1178, 1480
Apesoft, 2553
Apex, 819
Apex Analytix, 415
Apex Companies, 1777
Apex Construction Systems, 1915
Apex Fund Services, 793
Apex Learning, 520, 1242
Apex Microtecnology, 1232
Apex Parks Group, 413, 654
Apex Revenue Technologies, 1979
Apex Service Partners, 92
Apex Towers, 542
Apex.AI, 1834
Apexian Pharmaceuticals, 658
APF - WFCF, 1970
APH Property Holdings, 1491
Apherma Corporation, 1180
Aphria, 390, 1135, 2254
API Healthcare, 779, 1970
API Heat Transfer, 194, 985
API Heat Transfer Inc., 1971
API Maintenance Systems, 3203
API Outsourcinv, 1113
Apiary, 231
Apiary.io, 2010
Apica, 3192
Apidos CLO, 1491
Apigee, 238, 757, 1620
APIM Therapeutics, 2519
Apique, 1023
Apire Health, 1261
Apitope, 2949, 3042
APJeT, 448
Apjohn Ventures, 3269
Apkudo, 1169
Apl Next Ed, 658
Aplix, 892
APMG, 2576
Apnapaisa Private, 3062
Apneon Inc., 572
ApoCell, 1752
Apogee, 839
Apogee IT Services, 288, 349

Apogee Translite, 1606
Apogen, 2008
ApoGen Biotechnologies, 31
Apogen Technologies, 166
Apolife, 742
Apollo Computers, 1760
Apollo Endosurgery, 1500
Apollo Enterprise Solutions, 278
Apollo Fusion, 872
Apollo Global Management, 1271, 3255
Apollo International, 2728, 2890
Apollo MedFlight, 403
Apollo Medical Devices, 1047
Apollo Solar, 973
Aporeto, 1346
Aporta Digital, 3203
Apos, 2462
Apotek Hjartat, 2384
Apothecare, 503
Apothecare LLC, 1735
Apothecarry, 392
Apothecary Products, 1345
Apoxis SA, 2816
App Annie, 641, 973, 1001, 1654, 2850, 2869
App Central, 296
App in the Air, 2856
App Press, 658
App.ic, 1513
App.io, 1634
App47, 1899
Appalachian Lighting Systems, 998
AppAnnie, 871
Apparel Media Group, 1097, 1364
Appart City, 2851
AppAttach, 85, 2008
appAttach, 1458
Appature, 773
Appbistro, 1655
Appboy, 32, 301, 486, 1522
AppBus, 52, 768
Appcast, 222, 1019
Appcelerator, 1184, 1474, 1540, 1747, 1838
AppCityLife, 756
Appconomy, 1860
Appcore, 344
Appcues, 1670
AppDetex, 1384
AppDirect, 776, 1738, 2157
AppDome, 1202
Appdome, 603
AppDynamics, 560, 815, 986, 1001, 1121
Appear Here, 727, 2972
Appear Networks, 3013
Appear TV, 2637
Appear [here], 2478
Appear[Here], 2752
Appelberg, 2888
Appen Butler Hill, 2399
Apperian, 260, 534, 1097, 1334
Apperio, 3108
Appetas, 1406
AppFirst, 743
Appfluent, 1886
Appfluent Technology, 1348
AppFog, 773
Appfog, 974
Appfolio, 641
Appfuel, 307
Appgate, 2878
Appglu, 1958
AppHero, 2137
Appia, 596, 1331, 1333, 1830, 1850, 1916
Appian, 1297, 1348
Appian Communications, 1668
Appied Adhesives, 1232
Appier, 2690
Appili Therapeutics, 2155

1257

Portfolio Companies Index

Appilog, 436, 2655
Appilog Inc., 2580, 2775
Appinions, 320
Appionics Holdings, 1004
Appiphony, 1607
AppIQ, 59, 1334
Appirio, 815, 823, 1516, 1654
Appium, 2875
Applaud Medical, 1051, 1238
Applause, 1146, 1172, 1515, 1626, 3236
Applauze, 1054, 1860
Apple, 1654
Apple Computers, 1257
Apple Leisure Group, 1082
Apple Pie Capital, 384
Apple Toon, 1534
Apple Valley Waste, 1751
AppleBoard, 174
Applegate, 1767
ApplePie Capital, 1502
Appleseed's, 839
Appletoon, 3215
Appletree Institute for Education Innovation, 1316
Appletree.com, 791
Appleyards Plastics Ltd., 3011
Applicam, 2521
Application Networks, 59, 2779
Application Security, 1080, 1400
Applie Pie Capital, 784
Applied, 578, 924, 1041
Applied Adhesives, 843, 1765
Applied Aerospace Structures, 1919
Applied Automation, 1708
Applied Biocode, 970
Applied BioMath, 3
Applied Biosystems, 181, 1896
Applied CleanTech, 1623
Applied Composites, 1919
Applied Consultants, 1279
Applied Energy, 2796
Applied Genetic Technologies, 1008, 1196
Applied Genetics, 1730
Applied Graphene Materials, 3012
Applied Intuition, 124, 751, 1151, 1848
Applied Isotope Technologies, 1448
Applied Micro, 181, 1896
Applied MicroStructures, 524, 947
Applied Molded Products, 1919
Applied Molecular Evolution, 769
Applied Nano Surfaces Sweden, 2755
Applied Optoelectronics, 905, 1769
Applied Process, 932
Applied Proteomics, 621, 1946
Applied Science Fiction, 444, 1558, 1855, 3137
Applied Sensor, 2728, 2890
Applied Sensor AB, 3162
Applied Silver, 1865
Applied Solar Technologies, 260
Applied Spectral Imaging, 3162, 3241
Applied Systems, 220
Applied Visions, 3267
Applied Wave Research, 95, 880
Applieddata.net, 161
Applifier, 1226
AppLift, 3051
Applimation, 1407
Applitools, 1670, 2952
Applix, 2401, 3052
AppLovin, 1082, 1968
Apply, 318
Apply Board, 1047
Apply Financial, 1860
Apply Kit, 1958
ApplyBoard, 2027, 2128, 2137
AppMesh, 1010, 1782
AppNeta, 221, 1041

AppNexus, 539, 741, 1080, 1849, 1916
Appnexus, 1785
Appnique, 1285
Appnomic, 1346
Appolicious, 137
Apponboard, 1613
AppOrbit, 547
Apporbit, 1075
Apportable, 1254, 2329
Appotronics, 3093
Appplied Precision, 1792
Appreciate, 2952
Apprenda, 974, 1475
Apprente, 1421
Apprentice, 1480
Apprion, 466
Appriss, 221, 500, 909, 1000, 1041, 1346, 1991
Appro Healthcare, 1377
Appro Systems, 1770
Approach Software, 1336
Approva, 1348
Approvia, 2605
Approvisionnement Populaire, 2095
Apprupt, 2994
Apps Associates, 361
Apps.com, 1994
Appsbuilder, 2403
APPScomm, 1004
AppScotch, 89
Appsfire, 2851
AppsFlyer, 710, 2952
AppsFreedom, 856
Appshed, 2586
AppSheet, 1297
APPsolute Mobility, 2527
appssavvy, 1860
Appstores Inc., 650
AppStream, 1038
AppTap, 1291, 1771
Apptec Laboratory Services, 1817
Apptegy, 745
Apptentive, 85, 773, 856, 889, 1384, 2137
Apptera, 87
Appthority, 544, 1896, 1916
Appthwack, 1463
Apptient, 580
Apptimize, 547, 889, 1218, 2010
Apptio, 124, 483, 872, 1663
Apptis Holdings, 1301
Apptitude, 3118
Apptive, 445
Apptix, 2632
Apptonomy Mobile Technologies, 2155
Apptopia, 707
Appuri, 231
Appurify, 585
Appvance, 1028, 2960
Appy Couple, 724
AppZen, 1534
APR Energy, 46, 1315
Aprea, 12, 1928
Aprecia Pharmaceuticals, 287
Aprecia Pharma, 1271
Apria Healthcare Group, 2379
Apricot Forest, 296
April, 100
Aprimo, 86, 1672, 1733
aPriori, 1672, 1673
Apropos Technology, 153
Apropose, 1297
APS Investments, 3261
Apsalar, 544, 596, 773, 1254, 1818
APSE, 48
Apsmart, 2668
APT, 57, 3191
APT Pharmaceuticals, 1445, 1543
Aptalis Pharma, 1835

Aptanomics, 2354
AptDeco, 13, 858
Apteligent, 1626, 1663
Aptible, 785, 1151
Aptim, 1925
Aptinyx, 782, 1094, 1143, 2130
Aptis, 260, 1257
Aptitude Investment Management, 1129
Aptiv Solutions, 894, 1628
AptivIO, 1507
Apto, 1206
Aptoide, 641, 3048
Aptology, 538, 2019
Aptomar AS, 3141
Apton Biosystems Inc., 1069
Aptuit, 1972
Apture, 502
Aptus, 851
Aptus Endosystems, 1772, 1896
Apus, 1534
APW Yarn Technologies, 2392
APX, 1072, 1378, 2005
APX Labs, 1320, 1483, 1687
Apyon, 2626
Apyon, 2626
AQDOT, 3028
Aqua, 49, 180, 1154
Aqua Capital, 3261
Aqua Mobile, 2469
Aqua Pharmaceuticals, 1590
Aqua Security, 1121
Aqua Systems, 409
Aqua-Flo LLC, 449
Aquaai, 218
AquaBlok, 1553
AquaBounty Technologies, 237
Aquabyte, 547, 1297
AquaChem, 1166
Aquacue, 498
AquaGen, 2754
AquAgro Lab, 2417
Aqualisa, 2617
Aqualitas, 1807, 2140, 2155
Aquamar Holdings, 960, 1609
Aquamarine Power, 2315, 3135
AquaMelon Water, 3262
Aquamiel Tequilla, 2122
AquaMost, 2001
Aquamundi, 2626
Aquantia, 115, 1121, 1297, 1922
Aquantia Corporation, 1445
Aquantina Corp., 1951
aQuantive, 1637, 1945
Aquapharm BioDiscovery, 2350
Aquarelle.com, 2385
Aquaria Inc., 869
Aquarius Technologies, 2726
Aquasana, 678
AquaSprouts, 1507
AquaSpy, 570, 658, 2717
Aquaspy, 1615
Aquatic Informatics, 2290
AquaVenture Holdings, 657
AquaVentures Holdings LLC, 63
Aquea Scientific, 304
Aqueduct, 2008
Aqueduct Critical Care, 1061
Aquent, 1173, 1970
Aqueos, 984
Aquera, 1202, 1663, 1758
AqueSys, 40, 1558
Aquicore, 727, 1282
Aquilex, 1134
Aquilex Corporation, 914
Aquinox, 1436
Aquion, 1171
Aquion Energy, 59, 407, 770, 946, 1075

1258

Portfolio Companies Index

Aquion Water Treatment, 1963
Aquire, 242
Aquis, 1157
Aquto, 1181, 1334
Aqwise, 2900
AR Carton, 2325
Arabela Holding, 413
Arable, 395
Araccel, 2380
Arago, 1082
Aragon, 307
Aragon Pharmaceuticals, 74
Aragon Surgical, 237, 1003
Arakis, 3007
Arakis Aridhia, 3104
Aralez Pharmaceuticals, 1048
AraLight, 1305
Aramark, 433, 1815, 1956
Aramsco, 1368
Aramsco Holdings Inc., 64
Arandell, 1719
Arandell Corporation, 407
ArangoDB, 3161
Arann Healthcare, 2355
Aras, 649
Aras Corp., 809
Arasys Technologies, 1672
Aratana, 1615
Aratana Therapeutics, 206, 570, 1268
Aravo, 483
Aravo Solutions, 129, 324, 756
Arbe Robotics, 2296
Arbell Electronics, 2095
Arbinet, 184
ArBlast, 1452
ARBOC Specialty Vehicles, 928
Arbonne, 686
Arbor, 858
Arbor Health Care, 1708
Arbor Investments, 3265
Arbor Networks, 652, 1121, 1474
Arbor Partners, 3269
Arbor Pharmaceuticals, 1082
Arbor/Hyperion, 1654
Arboretum Ventures, 3269
ArborMetrix, 149, 961, 1592
Arbortext, 1336
Arbovax, 1442, 1988
Arbutus Biopharma, 762, 1271
Arby's, 1576
Arby's Restaurant Group, 1970
ARC Center, 344
ARC Machines, 1168
Arc Terminals, 1846
ARC UAE Logistics II, 152
ARCA Biopharma, 315, 1271
ArcadeMonk, 2294
Arcadia, 318, 695, 809, 1613
Arcadia Biosciences, 2492
Arcadia Communications, 1066
Arcadia Data, 1004, 1184
Arcadia Healthcare Solutions, 723
Arcadia Power, 488
Arcadian Management, 1255
Arcadian Networks, 1025
Arcadis, 3069
Arcanvs, 1011
Arcapita International Luxury Residential Develope, 152
Arcapita Qatar Real Estate Investment I, 152
Arcapita US Residential Development II, 152
Arcapita US Residential Developmental III, 152
Arcapita Ventures I Limited, 152
Arcarios, 2476, 2514, 2949, 3020, 3042
Arcato Laboratories, 840
ArcCore, 2755
Arcellx, 1731

Arceo Analytics, 851
Arch, 519, 1045, 1218
Arch Aluminum and Glass, 1141
Arch Capital Group Ltd., 924
Arch Innotek, 267
ARCH Venture Partners, 2492, 3265
Arch Venture Partners, 986
ArcheMedX, 119
Archemix, 1558, 2445
Archemix Corp., 187
Archer, 1125
Archer Aviation, 1613
Archer Education, 1384
Archer Rppse, 1701
ArcherDX, 1145
Archermind, 973
Archermind Technology, 2850
Archetype Ventures Fund, 483
Archimede Technology Group, 1558
Archimedes Health Investors, 3264
Archimica, 74
Archipelago, 2771
Architizer, 1894
Archivas, 1334, 1702
Archive Systems, 655, 1328
ArchivesOne, 21, 949
Archon Woodworks, 1503
Archrock, 1663
Archstone Smith, 152
Archway Digital Solutions Inc, 2508
Archway Marketing Services, 1017, 1777
Arcion Therapeutics, 1010
ArcLight Capital Partners, 3255
ARCMail Technology, 61
Arcmail Technology, 362
Arco, 2426
Arco Bodegas, 2537, 2538
Arcomet, 2780
Arcor Group, 1007
ARCOS, 1572
Arcos, 3240
Arcosa Inc., 1903
Arcot, 28, 58, 1378, 1911
Arcot Systems, 852
ArcSight, 1003, 1235, 1474
Arcsight, 1001
Arcsoft, 1728
Arctic, 171
Arctic Chiller Group, 2126
Arctic Glacier, 1491
Arctic Glacier Holdings, 928
Arctic Oilfield Equipment, 1491
Arctic Wolf, 1121
ArcticDX, 2058
Arcus Biosciences, 74, 709, 762
Arcxis, 979
Ardais, 1092
Ardana, 2748
Ardelyx, 112, 762, 1297
Ardence, 402
Ardenham Energy, 2539
Ardent Health Services, 723, 1972
Ardent Hire Solutions, 2252
Ardent Services, 1144
ArdentCause, 742
Ardentia, 2967
Ardenton Capital Corporation, 3258
Ardeo Imaging, 2077
Arder Holdings, 1360
Ardian, 1725
Ardica Technologies, 1746
Ardmore Shipholding Ltd., 862
Ardonagh Group, 1156
Ardyne, 1125
Are You A Human, 607, 742
Area 1, 84, 552, 741
Area Wide Protective, 290

Area1, 1075
Arecor, 3107
Arel Communication and Software Ltd., 2954
Arena, 1041, 1412, 1626
Arena Group, 2965
Arena Gulf, 1125
Arena Solutions, 1975
Arendsoog, 3042
Ares Management LLC, 3264
Areso, 2674
Arevo, 1069
ARG, 2381
Argen-X, 2748
arGEN-X, 1382, 2514, 3113
Argent, 567
Argent (Ford Alloy Wheel Plant), 2410
Argenta Discovery, 3195
arGentis, 995
Argenx, 762
ArgNor Wireless Ventures BV, 162
Argo, 2978
Argo Group, 404
Argo Medical Technologies, 3059
Argo Tea, 330, 1954
Argo Tea Inc., 331
Argo-Tech Corporation, 862
ArgoMed, 1412
Argon Medical Devices, 1590
Argon Networks, 1334
Argos, 946
Argos Therapeutics, 1008, 1398, 2748, 3196
Argotec, 1990
Argus, 2952
ARGUS Software, 1123
Argyle Data, 41, 183, 1690
Argyle Security, 2965
Arhaus, 783
Aria, 603, 1010, 1460, 2285
Aria CV, 347, 426
Aria CV Inc., 269
Aria Insights, 1151
Aria Systems, 221, 956, 1916
Ariad, 206, 769
Ariane Systems, 3020
Ariat, 334
Aricam, 2489
Aricent, 2654
Ariel Networks, 2854
Ariel Re, 1372
Arieso, 2295, 2662
Arieso Ltd, 2894
Arigo G360, 349
Arima Communications, 473
Arima Computer Corp., 3218
Ario Pharma, 1303, 2748
Ariosa Diagnostics, 1212, 1916
Aris Teleradiology, 859
Arisdyne, 466, 642
Arise, 39
Arisem, 2354
Arista, 28, 206, 1534
Arista MD, 544
Arista Networks, 986, 3121
Aristacom, 1558
Ariston Global, 263, 1724
Aristos Logic, 1975, 2005
Aristotle Circle, 1306, 1558
Aristotle Corporation, 1166
Arit Optronics, 2389
Aritech, 1725
Ariterm, 3054
Arivale, 1183
Arizona Center for Cancer Care, 1271
Arizona Nutritional Supplements, 673
Arizona Technology Enterprises, 3268
Ark, 455, 707, 1118, 1839
Ark Holding Company, 245

Portfolio Companies Index

Ark Naturals, 213
Ark Therapeutics, 3007
Ark-Angels Fund, 3042
Ark-La-Tex Wireline Services, 1491
Arkadium, 655
Arkados Group, 2031
Arkal Medical, 1817
Arkansas Automatic Sprinklers, 1214
Arkavund Media, 3042
ARKeX, 2700
Arkex, 2731, 3104
ARKimedes, 3042
Arkin, 295
Arkis Biosciences, 995
Arkivum, 2892, 3028
ARKLATEX Energy Services, 910
Arkmicro Technologies, 3062
Arkoma Pipeline Partners, 156
Arkoon, 3208
Arkopharma, 2977
Arlant, 3048
Arlettie, 3113
ARM-Harith Infrastructure Investments Ltd, 3261
Arma Beheer BV, 2806
Armacell, 1017
Armada.ai, 640
Armadio Verde, 2874
ArmaGen, 1241
ArmaGen Technologies, 2530
Armand Agra, 2123
Armaron Bio, 3138
Armatis, 3020
Armatis-Laser Contact, 2338
Armax Gaz SA, 3187
Armeco, 2120
Armed Response Team, 1300
ArmedAngels, 2475
Armel Corporation, 2052
Armenia Tomato, 1007
Armenian Datacom Company, 2654
Armgo Pharma Inc., 74
ARMO Biosciences, 1382
Armoire, 896
Armon, 3137
Armonix, 1397
Armor Group, 2795
Armor Holding II, 1491
Armor Security, 1233
Armor5, 3001
Armored Things, 829, 1172, 2157
Armorize, 2390
ArmorText, 454
Armory, 229, 563, 1028, 1613
Armstrong, 1835
Armstrong Energy, 1795
Armstrong Flooring Inc., 1903
Armstrong Franklin, 1114
Armstrong World Industries Inc., 1903
Armtec Limited, 2067
Armune BioScience, 139
Arneg SPA, 77
Arnold Logistics, 1144
Arnold Magnetic Technologies, 194, 523
Arnott, 368
Aromyx, 625, 1218
Arosa+LivHome, 958
Arotech, 862
Arovia, 226
ARPAC, 606
Arpatia India Growth Capital I, 152
Arpeggio Biosciences, 795
Arpida, 2607, 2922
Arpida AG, 2651
Arquati, 3154
Arque, 2342
ArQule, 191, 1898

Arqule, 2445
Arradial, 314
Arradiance, 1237
Arraiy, 472, 1151
ArraVasc, 1241
Array, 334
Array BioPharma, 153, 315, 782, 1103, 1775
Array Health, 85, 773, 1331
Array Networks, 892
Array Power, 730
ArrayComm, 541, 1704
Arrayent, 596
Arresto Biosciences, 634, 1341
Arris, 1334
Arris Pharmaceutical, 260
Arriva Pharmaceuticals, 2079
Arrive, 251
Arrive BioVentures, 1556
Arrivo, 24
ARRM Holdings, 1491
Arro Corporation, 407
ArroHealth, 938
Arrow Material Handling Products, 399, 1053
Arrow Storage Products, 1967
Arrow Therapeutics, 191, 2780, 2781
Arrow Tru-Line, 1141, 1456
Arrow Tru-Line. Bar Louie, 1753
Arroweye, 222
ArrowEye Solutions, 57
Arrowhead, 1017
Arrowhead Brass Products, 373
Arrowhead Electrical Products, 1435
ArrowPath Venture Partners, 986
Arrowpoint, 28
ArrowPoint Communications, 1334
ArrowSpan, 2703
Arroyo, 596
Arroyo Video Solutions, 1975
Arsais, 1628
Arsanis, 1460, 1643, 1762
Arsanis Biosciences, 1382
Arsenal, 184
Arsenal Capital Partners, 1271, 3264
Arsenal Digital Studios, 1709
Arsenal Medical, 1008, 1334, 1460
Arsenal Venture Partners, 3262, 3269
Arsenic, 561
ARSS Infrastructure Ltd, 2859
Arstasis, 177
ART, 260
ART Advanced Recognition Technologies, 2720
Art For Everyday, 2043
ART Group, 584
Art of Click, 1965
Art Technology Group, 1728, 2610
Art.com, 1235, 1460, 1604, 1710, 1748
Art19, 256, 1883
Art2Wave, 1945
Artcraft, 2985
Arteaus Therapeutics, 191
Artel Video, 314
Artel Video Systems, 455
Artemis, 1070
Artemis Pharmaceuticals, 1775
Artemis Pharmaceuticals GmbH, 2785
Artemys, 318
Arteriocyte, 695
Arteriocyte Inc., 420
Arteriocyte Medical Systems, 639
Arteriors, 1345
Arteris, 555, 620, 2639, 3208
Arterys, 107, 181, 809, 1254, 1347
Artesian, 3018
Artfinder, 3013
Artful Home, 1640
ArtGo Holdings, 413
Artha Partners, 3261

Arthena, 770
Arthrosurface, 312
Arthus-Bertrand, 2602
Artic Wolf, 1534
Article, 2243
Articulinx, 1896
ArtiCure, 1008
Artielle, 1616
Artifact Entertainment, 765
Artifact Software, 1227
Artificial Muscle, 153, 1324
Artima SA, 2706
ArtimiCambridge Broadband, 2386
Artios, 1350, 1628, 1762
Artis Exploration, 2025
Artisan Components, 1896
Artisan Entertainment, 194
Artisan Partners, 924, 1760
Artisan Pharma, 1325, 2513, 2690
Artistic Holdings, 1141
Artisto Music, 2476
ArtistOnGo, 684
Artists Wanted, 1359
Artivest, 600, 1531, 1631
ArtLab, 2857
ARTMS, 2229
ARTONE Manufacturing, 78
Artrendex, 1069
Arts Alliance Media, 2428
Artsicl, 1518
Artspace, 386
ArtSquare, 995
Artsy, 318, 973, 1088, 1524
Artus Labs, 915
ArtusLabs, 1710
Aruba, 1654
Aruba Networks, 175, 757, 1853
ARUHI Corporation, 413
Arula Systems, 805
Arvegenix, 267, 569
Arvento, 1017
Arvia Technology, 3028
Arvinas, 12, 386, 1519
Arvinas Corporation, 660
Arvirago, 2548
Arweave, 1882
Arxan, 652, 1400
Arxan Technologies, 1776, 1782
Arxas Technologies, 1850
Arxis Capital Group, 559
ARXX, 1355
Arxx Building Products, 2196
ARXX ICF, 2058
Arxxus, 1607
Ary Therapeutics, 177
Aryaka, 1010, 1247, 1247, 1474, 1853, 3001
ARYX Therapeutics, 184
ARYx Therapeutics, 1119, 3007
Arzan, 1702
Arzeda Corp., 2008
ArzonSolar, 126
AS Groupe, 2354
AS International Group, 2851
AS Roma, 1524
ASA Events, 869
ASA Foodnesia, 1241
Asahi Tec Corporation, 3201
Asahi Tec/Trimas, 846
ASAlliances Biofuels, 1895
Asalus, 2737, 2892
Asana, 124, 248, 775, 1054
Asana Rebel, 641
Asankya, 979, 1655, 3212
Asante, 3149
Asante Capital Group, 3261
Asante Solutions, 598, 1817, 3015
Asap54, 641

1260

Portfolio Companies Index

Asarina, 2851
ASAY, 1701
Asbury Automotive Group, 783
ASC Signal, 1545
ASC Specialty Vehicle, 902
Ascade Telecom Software, 2562
Ascend Learning, 1496
Ascend Media, 1927
Ascend Wellness, 1464, 1610
Ascend.io, 28, 720
Ascendancy Healthcare, 237
Ascendant Advisors Group, 1503
Ascendant Spirits, 1784
Ascendas India Trust, 152
Ascendent Telecommunications, 765
Ascendify, 483, 809
Ascendis Pharma, 74, 762, 1519, 1698, 1941
Asceneuron, 1043, 1731
Ascension Insurance, 439, 1417
Ascension Orthopedics, 782
Ascensus, 819
Ascent 360, 36
Ascent Aviation Services Corporation, 1144
Ascent Bio-Nano Technologies, 737
Ascent Capital Partners, 3261
Ascent Healthcare Solutions, 1590, 1901
Ascent Pediatrics, 1067
Ascent Resources, 740
Ascent Venture Partners, 3273
Ascenta Health, 2049
Ascenta Therapeutics, 621, 1626, 1698, 1896
Ascenz, 3073
Ascom, 2922
Ascot Resources, 1548
Asempra, 184, 1896
Asentium Capital, 1946
Aseptia, 1689
Asera, 1003, 1975
Asetek, 3013, 3149, 3203
ASG, 92
ASG Security, 1417, 1963
ASG Technologies, 1134
AsGoodAsNew, 3208
Ash & Erie, 1019
Ash Access, 1418
ASH Technologies, 2336
Ashburton Investments, 3261
Ashby Industries, 908
Ashcroft Inc., 1085
Asher House Wellness, 391
Ashley Stewart, 500
Ashot Ashkelon (metal), 2389
Ashtead Technology, 3036
Ashtech, 1542
Ashvattha, 1169, 1613
Ashworth, 1742
ASI, 2585, 3249
Asia Alternatives Management, 3261
Asia Books, 1139
Asia Books Company, 2946
Asia Broadcast Satellite, 3033
Asia Chemical Corporation, 2961
Asia Ec, 2697
Asia Foods, 2881
Asia Grown Capital Advisors (S) Pte Ltd, 3261
Asia Info, 2590
Asia Opportunity Fund LP, 1007
Asia Pacific Carbon Fund, 3042
Asia Partners, 3261
Asia Renal Care, 2297, 2733, 2881
Asia Renal Care Ltd, 2728, 2890
Asia Satellite Telecom Holdings, 413
Asia Travelmart Ltd. (Malaysia), 2694
Asia Vital Components, 2603
AsiaEC.com, 2698
AsiaInfo, 473
Asiainfo, 2998

AsiaInfo & Aicent, 2698
Asiakastieto, 1017
Asian Development Bank, 3261
Asian Food Channel, 3215
Asian Genco, 815
Asian Health Alliance, 55
Asian Infrasturcture Investments Bank, 3261
Asian Mineral Resources, 2942
Asianinfo, 2733
Asiaray Media Group, 1088
Asiasoft, 1139
Asiasoft Corporation, 2946
AsiaTelco Technologies, 973
ASIMCO, 220
Asimov, 124
Asius Technologies, 1061
ASK, 2544, 2853
Ask, 1896, 2343, 2348, 2876
Askey, 2436
AskMe, 986
Askola USA Corporation, 1975
AskWonder, 305
Ask|Net, 2343
ASLAN Pharmaceuticals, 2518
Asmacure, 2120
ASML, 1004
Asocs, 3214
Asoka, 1747, 3152
ASP, 1114, 2936
aSpecial, 3073
Aspect, 1910, 3137
Aspect Biosystems, 2213
Aspect Development, 1654
Aspect Medical Systems, 1760
Aspect Ratio, 1728
Aspect Software, 839, 1361
Aspect Ventures, 483
Aspective, 1017
Aspectrics, 1405
ASPEED Software, 422
Aspen, 2697
Aspen Aerogels, 184, 768, 1579, 2492
Aspen Avionics, 852, 1300, 1677
Aspen Dental, 110
Aspen Dental Management, 159, 402, 1109
Aspen Education Group, 374
Aspen Energy Partners, 1278, 1326
Aspen Heigths, 1622
Aspen Insurance, 2556
Aspen Laser & Technologies, 1837
Aspen Marketing Group, 334
Aspen Marketing Services, 1086
Aspen Medical Products, 546
Aspen Midstream, 671
Aspen Pumps, 2311
Aspen Re, 1372
Aspen Surgical, 1590
Aspen Tech, 1173
Aspex Semiconductor, 3070, 3131
Aspinity, 293
Aspire Financial Services, 793
Aspire Food Group, 1031
Aspire Health, 94, 889
Aspire Home Care, 702
Aspire Medical, 1975
Aspire Public Schools, 1316
AspireIQ, 942, 956
Aspireo Pharmaceuticals, 3196
AspireU, 1316
Aspiring Minds, 1374
Aspirion, 271
Asplundh Tree Expert Co., 832
Aspocomp Group Oyj, 2990
Asprevea Pharmaceuticals, 212, 2097
Assay Designs, 118
AssayMetrics, 2737
ASSE, 2361

Assembly, 569, 799, 1882
Assent, 2118
Asset Acceptance Capital Corp., 1505
Asset Allocation & Management Company, 1743
Asset Control, 2734
Asset Enhancement Solutions LLC, 3267
Asset International, 202
Asset Living, 1851
Asset Management Company, 3284
Asset Management Outsourcing, 187
Asset Matrix, 2058
AssetMark, 1147
AssetNation, 1724
ASSIA, 3152
Assia, 3169
Assicom, 2293
Assima, 2875, 3239
Assis Medical, 3192
Assistant Coach, 950
AssistGuide, 1011, 2457
Assistive Technologies, 1728
Associa, 1752
Associated Chemist Inc., 985
Associated Chemists, 1909
Associated Container Terminals Ltd, 2859
Associated Content, 1699
Associated Foods, 193
Associated Freezers Corporation, 2150
Associated Materials, 924, 1017, 1456
Associated Materials Inc., 914
Associated Partners, 1082
Association Financial Services, 1430
Association for Democratic Reforms, 1374
Association Member Benefits Advisors, 819
Association of Asiona American Investment Managers, 3285
Association of Certified Anti-Money Laundering Spe, 1956
Assure X Health, 86
Assured Risk Cover, 1013
AssuredPartners, 135
Assurely, 1632
AssureRx, 479, 1512
AssureRx Health, 1553
Assurerx Health, 491
Assurex Health, 560, 1654, 2000
AssurOne, 3113
Assystem, 2851
AST, 1777
Astadia, 1080, 1607, 1728
Astaro, 3233
Astech, 1770
Astellia, 2875
Aster Data, 623, 968, 1654
Aster Data Systems, 741, 1001
Asterand Bioscience, 919
Asteres, 1616
Astex Pharmaceuticals, 94, 986
Astex Therapeutics, 1775, 2780
Asthmatx, 1241, 1251
Astor Corporation, 199
Astound, 1809
Astound Inc., 2267
Astra Augmedix, 1613
Astral AR, 218
Astral Point Communications, 1975
Astranis, 107, 124, 318, 395, 720, 1151, 1329
AstraZeneca, 1452
Astro, 180, 707, 1534, 1998
Astro Electroplating, 1745
Astro Gaming, 1975
Astroboundary, 1846
AstroDigital, 890
Astrodyne Corporation, 194
Astronomer, 128, 479, 1670, 2000
AstroWatt, 1297
Astute Medical, 598, 621, 1268

1261

Portfolio Companies Index

Astute Networks, 1896
AsuraGen, 1205, 1500
Asuragen, 1792
Asure Software, 1114
Asurion, 254, 949, 1496, 1852, 1972
Asurion Corporation, 1156
ASUSTek Computer, 1769
Async, 1708
Asyntis Gmbh, 2682
AT Internet, 3020
At Last Software, 308
AT&T, 1096
At-Bay, 1069
ATA, 3093
ATA Groiup, 2965
Atai Life Sciences, 800
Atakama Labs, 2455
Atani, 3007
Atara Bio, 112, 634, 709
Atara Biotherapeutics, 581, 621
Atari, 1654
Atavium, 341, 876, 1384
Atbusiness, 2562
ATC Drivetrain, 559
AtCor Medical, 2622
Atea, 2978
Atelier D'Usinage Quenneville, 2120
Atelier Progun, 2120
Atelier Tangente, 2120
Ateliers Cfi Metal, 2095
Ateliers Jean Del'Cour, 3134
Atelka, 2169
Ateme, 3208, 3239
Atempo Group, 2531
Aten International, 3218
Aternity, 3214
ATG Access, 2944
ATG Rehab, 194
Atheer Labs, 1236
Athelas, 622, 1654, 1663, 2419
Athena, 1925
Athena Club, 567
athena Controls, 834
Athena Design, 2005
Athena Design Systems, 1975
Athena Diagnostics, 245
Athena Feminine Technologies, 1677
Athena Health, 180, 609
Athena Semiconductors, 1288
athenahealth, 823
Athenix, 312, 1008
AtheroGenics, 1398
Atherogenics, 1616
AtheroMed, 1896
Atheromed, 1929
Atheros Communications, 197, 1474
Atherotech, 524, 986, 1288, 1533
Atherotech Diagnostics, 245
Athersys, 548, 1412, 1520, 1975
Athieva, 3062
Athilon Group Holdings Corp., 1123
Athleon, 85
Athletes' Performance, 402
Athletes' Performance, 1460
Athletica Sport Systems, 2126
Athletico, 914
Athlon Holdings, 300
AtHoc, 57, 964
Athos, 1121, 1696
Athos Services Commemoratifs, 2120
ATI, 1456
ATI Physical Therapy, 1086
Atico Mining, 1548
Atieva, 3194
Atifon (Packaging prod.), 2389
Atipica, 1054
Atiti, 2271

Ativa Medical, 1872
Atlanta Cable Systems, 575
Atlanta Tech Village, 189
Atlantech, 3104
Atlantic Asset Management, 1147
Atlantic Beverage Company, 960, 1166
Atlantic Broadband, 21
Atlantic Broadband Group, 1360
Atlantic Capital Bancshares, 1743
Atlantic Cedar Products, 2049
Atlantic Cellular Company LP, 1621
Atlantic Diagnostic Laboratories, 164
Atlantic Horticulture, 2114
Atlantic Motor Labs, 2155
Atlantic Plywood, 1141
Atlantic Power Holdings, 156
Atlantic Wind Connection, 332
Atlantis Computing, 57, 1416, 1522, 1975
Atlantis Healthcare Group, 1491
Atlantium, 2439
Atlas, 307, 1099, 1527
Atlas 3D, 658
Atlas Aerospace, 1705
Atlas Aerospace LLC, 413
Atlas Apps, 1784
Atlas Connectivity, 1578
Atlas Genetics, 2496, 2939
Atlas Material Testing Solutions, 985
Atlas Obscura, 751
Atlas Organics, 1923
Atlas Partners LP, 3258
Atlas Venture, 70, 3273
Atlas Water, 349
Atlas-SSI, 2290
Atlassian Software, 28
Atlast Homewares Inc., 908
AtlasWatersystems, 649
AtlEn Opportunity, 1764
Atlice, 744
ATMA Software, 114
atmarkIT, 2854
ATMI, 530
Atmosera, 1638
Atmosphere Networks, 757
Atmospheric Plasma Solutions, 3259
ATMU, 413
Ato Bio, 1731
ATO Solution Co., 3002
AtoBe, 2779
Atom, 395
Atom Computing, 318, 1916
Atomation, 267
Atomic, 858
Atomic Reach, 2131
Atomicorp, 285
Atomos Nuclear and Space, 1890
Atomwise, 107
Aton Pharma, 74, 1730
Atonometrics, 445
Atonomics, 3149
Atop Holdings, 892
Atoptech, 47
Atos, 3026
Atosho, 3150
Atox Bio, 3245
ATP-PEP, 3261
Atrato, 210
Atreaon, 2978
Atreca, 709, 1238
Atrenta, 925, 1017
Atria, 1257
Atria Yhtymä Oyj, 2990
Atrica, 1038, 1975, 2585, 2770, 2875, 2890, 2897
Atrica Axcan Pharma, 2728
Atricath, 2874
Atricia, 249

AtriCure, 1896
ATRIN Pharmaceuticals, 1577
Atrinet Ltd., 3213
Atritech, 1478, 1817
Atritech Inc., 269
Atrium, 124, 741, 816, 839, 942, 1024, 1663
Atrium Companies, 1456
Atrium Innovations, 2120, 3033
Atrium Underwriting Group, 1743
Atronix, 1343
ATRP Solutions, 998, 1448
Atrributor, 1672
Atrua, 645
ATS Advanced Telematic Systems, 970
ATS Medical, 94
AtScale, 107, 1747
Atscale, 518
Atsu, 1158
ATT, 2436
AttachedApps, 1061, 1924
Attachmate, 779, 1041, 1814
Attachmate Group, 839
AttackIQ, 1509, 1607
Attainia, 1737
Attano, 2818
AtTask, 1380, 1604, 1705
Attena Neurosciences, 206
Attenda, 1153
Attendease, 2027
Attendo, 2537, 2538
Attends, 1085
Attenex, 1945
Attensa, 1945
Attensite Corporation, 1407
Attenti, 135, 779
Attero, 3232
Attero Recycling, 851
Atticus, 728
Attivio, 1361, 1810
ATTO-TEC GmbH, 3190
Attol, 2544
Attolight AG, 650
Attom Data Solutions, 1147
Attraction Media, 2095
Attributor, 114, 968, 1646
Attune, 1346, 1416, 1488
Attune Pharmaceuticals, 1519
Attune Technologies, 1509
Attunity, 3059
ATW, 1923
ATX Networks, 928, 1409
Atyati, 3211
Atyr Pharma, 1460
aTyr Pharma, 410, 621, 709
Atys, 2551
Atzuche, 922
Au Bon Pain Inc., 354
Au Financiers, 1956
Au Forum du Batiment, 3239
Auberge Et Spa Le Nordik, 2120
Auberge Relais Lac Cache, 2120
Auberge Resorts Collection, 425
Auburn Armature, 1422
Aucfan, 2798
Aucionata, 2838
AucSale, 1755
Auction Holdings, 521
Auction.com, 1743
Auctionata, 2829
Auctionpay, 142
Audacious, 3012
Audacy, 994
Audax Private Equity, 3264
Auden McKenzie, 1452
Audentes, 12, 74, 181, 762, 1519, 1928
Audentes Therapeutics, 1382, 1698
Audible, 256

Portfolio Companies Index

Audible Reality, 2212
Audience, 1779, 1922, 1946
Audience Partners, 1502
Audience Science, 184, 1247
AudienceFUEL, 1710
AudiencePoint, 459
AudienceScience, 1184, 1641
Audiencescience Inc., 623
Audiense, 3108
Audinate, 3138
Audio Network, 1748
Audio Precision, 235, 903
Audio Visual Services Corporation, 1062
Audiocodes Ltd., 2775
Audiocure, 2824
Audiodraft, 1489
AudioGo, 2362
AudioMicro, 1099
Audiomojo, 1915
Audiosocket, 247
AudioTalk Networks, 947
AudioVroom, 1306
Audisoft, 2029, 2851
AuditBoard, 50, 235
AuditFile.com, 307
Auditude, 852, 1534
Audius, 816, 1075, 1121
Audm, 1768
Audyssey, 132
Audyssey Laboratories, 2974
Augement Therapy, 293
Augeo, 2779
Augeo FI, 1123
Augmate, 384, 704
AugMedix, 858
Augmedix, 94, 665
Augmenix, 176, 426
Augment, 1607
Augment Ventures, 3269
Augmented Pixels, 1809
Augmented Radar Imaging, 1554
Augmentix, 202
Augtera Networks, 49
Augur, 2149
Augure, 3208
Augury, 741, 1110, 1480
August, 552, 1183, 1518, 1558, 1700, 1998
August Capital, 37, 3284
August Capital Management V, 623
August Lock, 1254
Augusta Sportswear, 1062
Augusta Sportswear Group, 1505
Augusta Systems, 1470
Augustus Energy Partners II, 1125
Aujas Netowks, 2849
Auld Phillips, 2258
Aulera Autentication, 429
Aunt Bertha, 3277
Auntie Anne's, 1576
Auntie Dolores, 1135
AUPU Group Holding Company, 584
Aura, 552, 1527, 1555
Aura Health Corp., 2122
Aura Life, 3259
Aura Light International AB, 2537, 2538
Auramicro, 1922
Auransa, 4, 1151
Aureon Labrotories, 2445
Auricup Resources, 2942
Aurigen, 1315, 2103
Aurigen Capital Limited, 1443
Aurinia, 1941
Aurinia Pharmaceuticals, 1297, 2180
Aurion Pro Solutions, 646
Aurionpro, 69
Auris, 1151, 1643
Auris Medica, 1698

Aurizon Mines Ltd, 2120
Aurizon Ultrasonics, 1292
Auro Robotics, 792
Aurochs Brewing, 293
AuroMira Energy, 2490
Auror Algae, 1352
Aurora, 872
Aurora Algae, 805, 1361
Aurora Biosciences Corp., 206
Aurora Cannabis, 203, 390
Aurora Cannabis Inc., 2136
Aurora Diagnostics, 1086, 1752
Aurora Discovery, 1792
Aurora Flight Sciences, 680, 834
Aurora Flower Co., 557
Aurora Foods, 722
Aurora Labs, 707
Aurora Networks, 422, 1474
Aurora Organic Dairy, 456
Aurora Products Group, 1081
Aurora SFC Systems, 138, 371
Aurora Solar, 727
Aurora Systems, 1017
AuroraNetics, 1080
Aurum, 1626
Aurum Software, 1255
Aurum Technologies, 1986
Aurvista Gold Corporation, 2120
Ausenco, 1548
Aushon Biosystems, 1334
Auspex, 541, 762, 1410
Auspex Pharmaceuticals, 1817
Auspherix, 2959
Auspion, 1051
Austal Ships, 2398
Austin Coctails, 293
Austin Entrepreneurs Foundation, 1650
Austin Fitness Group, 501
Austin Technology Incubator, 1650
Austral Capital Partners, 3261
Australian Central Credit Union, 2456
Australian Education, 2456
Australian Geographics, 2420
Australian Kitchen Industries, 2622
Australian Pipeline Trust, 2456
Australian Venue Co., 1082
Austri, 1340
Austriamicrosystems, 2922
Autekbio, 47
Auterion, 547
Auterra, 711, 786, 1475
Auth0, 773, 1050, 1212
AuthenTec, 1314, 1745
Authentic Brands Group, 1109, 2171
Authentic8, 776, 1218
Authentica, 1334
Authentiq, 3108
Authentix, 413
Authentor Systems, 1668
Authntk, 1299
AuthO, 1463
Author Solutions, 257
Authorea, 724, 1151, 1306, 1310
Authoria, 242
Authority Brands, 135
AuthorityLabs, 92
Authy, 585, 1998, 3125
Auticon, 2260
Autifony, 1436, 1762
Autifony Therapeutics, 1628, 2858
Autinform GmbH, 2537, 2538
Autism Learning Partners, 859
AutismSees, 622
Autit, 640, 829
Auto Data Network, 1558
Auto Meter Products Inc., 908
Auto Radio, 596, 2936

Auto Trader Group, 135
Auto22, 2539
Autoaid, 2824
AutoAlert, 959
Autobar, 2379, 2587
Autobooks, 222, 607
Autobus Dionne, 2095
Autobus Dufresne, 2095
Autobus Lion, 2120
Autobutler, 2637
Autocam, 199
Autoda, 2569, 2829
Autodis, 2721
AutoDistribution, 2551
Autodistribution, 1017
Autoequip, 2489
AutoESL Design Technologies, 56
AutoFi, 679, 1110
Autofi, 563
autoGraph, 1285, 1945
autograph, 2249
AutoGrid, 770, 1945
Autoland Inc., 447
Autoloader, 2824
Autolog Systems, 3203
Autology World, 2468
Automak Automotive Company, 1017
Automat, 518, 2236
Automatan LLC, 899
Automated Fuel Systems Group, 2709
Automated Insights, 551, 1364, 1387, 1899
Automated Systems Design, 443
Automatic, 114, 1860
Automatic Betterment, 2406
Automatics, 1592
Automation Anywhere, 1297
AutomationHero, 219
AutomationQA, 2320
Automattic, 1000, 1149, 1460
Automic, 2851
Automile, 1000, 1607
Automobile Protection Coporation, 1743
Automotive Mastermind, 1041
Automsoft, 2322
AutoNavi, 2936
Autonet Mobile, 650, 1734
Autoniq, 781
Autonomic, 518, 1696
Autonomic Materials, 975, 983
Autonomic Technologies, 1010
Autonomix Medical Inc., 269
Autonomous Marine Systems Inc., 497
Autonomous Partners, 510, 1882
Autopay, 781
Autopilot, 1540, 1607, 1711
AutoServe1, 2197
AutoSource, 2209
AutoSource Motors, 2208
Autosplice, 1037, 1456
Autotalks, 116, 781, 1241, 2952
Autotask, 933, 1041
Autotask Corporation, 1333
Autotether, 678
Autotube, 2325
AutoVirt, 1672
Autowraptec, 445
Autumn Years at Newport Mesa, 958
Autumn Years at Ojai, 958
Auust Technology Corporation, 1288
Auvents W. Lecours, 2120
Auvik, 2076, 2239
Aux Money, 770
Auxadyne, 3262
Auxilium, 1725
Auxilum, 74
Auxmoney, 1416, 1882
Auxon, 305

Portfolio Companies Index

AV Lab, 121
Av Smoot, 61
AVA, 2278
Ava, 622, 1110, 1323
Avaak, 1102
Avaamo, 4, 295, 1004, 1540, 1983
AVAC Ltd., 3258
Avacta, 2892
Avad Energy, 1278, 1326
Avadim Technologies Inc., 1923
Avago, 1683
Avail Media, 1676
Avail-TVN, 247
Availant, 310
Availink, 296, 777, 1297
Availity, 779
Avalanche Biotech, 1916
Avalanche Insights, 934
Avalanche Technology, 260, 946, 1818, 1946, 3229
Avalara, 173, 247, 1152, 1602
Avalent Technologies, 1769
Avalign Technologies, 166, 1128, 1590
Avalon, 779, 2136
Avalon Advisors, 413
Avalon Cable, 21
Avalon Pharmaceuticals, 2780
Avamar, 1121, 1255, 1975
AVANAN, 3136
Avancen, 3277
Avanex, 1654
Avangate, 2309
Avani Bio Energy, 55
Avanir, 495, 762
AvanStrate, 413
Avant, 815, 1384
Avant Credit, 37, 1502
Avant Healthcare Professionals, 1113
AVANT Immunotherapeutics, 212
Avant Immunotherapeutics, 3007
Avant!, 1760
AvantCredit, 1593
Avante Health Solutions, 654
Avantec Vascular, 1018
Avantech Testing Services, 1093
AvantGo, 58, 852, 1405
Avanti Marble & Granite, 1745
Avanticare, 2708
Avantis Medical Systems, 269, 1251
Avantium, 2378, 2662
Avantium BV, 2350
Avantium International B.V., 2577
Avantor Performance Materials Holdings, 1301
Avanz Capital, 3261
Avanza, 2572
Avanza Laboratories, 74
Avanzar Medical, 1722
AVAST Software BV, 1752
Avatar Alliance, 35
Avatar International, 1572, 1927
Avaxia Biologics, 841, 1160, 1784
Avaya, 1683, 2379
Avaz, 1013
AvData Systems, 1708
Aveanna Healthcare, 1037, 2219
Avec Lab, 1755
Avecia, 1017
Avecto, 1041
Avedro, 136, 308, 598, 647, 747, 921, 1478
Avega Systems, 3062
Avegant, 1004
Aveillant, 2662, 2674
Aveksa, 455, 743, 793
Avelas Biosciences, 206
Avella Specialty Pharmacy, 1575
Avelo, 2944
Avena Foods, 2163

Avendus Capital, 1082
Aveni, 2851
Avenir Finance, 2625
Avent, 2587
Aventail, 757, 1235, 1853
Avention, 884
Aventium, 2439
Aventura, 703, 938
Aventure, 2602
Avenue A Razorfish, 1896
Avenue Ltd, 2705
Avenues: The World School, 1116, 1136
Aveo, 747, 2970
AVEO Oncology, 1297
AVEO Pharmaceuticals, 260, 925, 1394, 1493
AvePoint, 1752
Aver, 809, 1286
Aver Inc., 630
Aver Informatics, 2001
Averail, 1747
Avere, 2079
Avere Systems, 1121, 1796
Averify, 582
Averna, 2261
Averon, 1269
Avertec, 2481
Avery Haelth, 2796
Averys, 2851
Aveta, 127
Avetta, 1346, 1972
Avexegen, 1238
Avexis, 762, 1519, 1812
AVG Technologies, 57, 1776
Avgol (Plastics), 2389
AvhanaHealth, 1731
AVI Networks, 1202
Avi Networks, 483, 634, 872
Avi Networksm Barefoot Networks, 1121
AVI-SPL, 1683
AVIA, 1046
Avia, 1480
Avia Boisystems, 438
Aviacode, 790
Aviaion Inflatables, 1430
Aviary, 262, 1715
Aviate, 784
Aviation Partners, 2085
Aviation Technologies, 1368
Aviator, 2325
Aviatrix, 974
Avici Systems, 28, 1728
Avicin Therapeutics Ltd., 430
Avid, 94, 1760
Avid Radiopharmaceuticals, 1124
Avid Ratings, 251
Avidal, 2824
AvidBots, 720, 823
Avidbots, 2027, 2137
Avidia, 112, 1691
Avidimer Therapeutics, 747, 1336
Avidity NanoMedicines, 709
Avidity Nanomedicines, 710
AvidXchange, 1442
Avidxchange, 776
Avidyne, 935
Avila Therapeutics, 191
Avilinks, 2875
Avillion, 495
Avinity, 2837
Avinity Systems B.V., 3128
Aviom, 1227
Avior Integrated Products, 2120
Aviron, 153
Avisare, 218
Avisena, 2196
Aviso, 552, 741, 1626, 1663
Avist, 974

Avista, 1295
Avista Oil, 1230
Avista Pharma, 118
Avita Biomedical, 371
Avitas Systems, 809
Avitec, 2562
Avitide, 308, 1382, 1628, 1762
Avito, 28, 3013
Aviv REIT, 1129
Aviva Communications, 47
Avizent, 1086
Avizia, 285, 288, 921, 1320
Avjet Holding, 2095
AVK, 3234
AVM, 2362
AVMedical Dialysis Access Management, 2328
Avnera, 260, 581, 634, 968
Avnera Corporation, 1445
AVO Carbon Holdings, 1230
Avocado, 231
Avocado Systems, 574
Avolent, 1558
Avolon Aerospace Limited, 1360
Avomeen, 932
Avonmore Pásztó, 2725
Avoxi, 224
Avrij, 2200
Avrio Capital, 2032
Avro Life Science, 1630, 1758
Avro Life Sciences, 663
AvroBio, 1628
Avrobio, 191, 495, 1762
Avset, 2451
Avst, 1640
AVTEC, 1956
Avure Food Processing, 1234
Avvasi, 2262
Avvir, 1894
Avvo, 581, 634, 974
AW Leil, 2251
Awake Security, 872
AWAKENS, 1703
Awarables, 19
Aware Point, 206
Awareness, 1334
Awareness Technologies, 739
Awarepoint, 968, 1298, 1556
AWAS, 57
Away, 28, 518, 525, 761, 858
Away.com, 1480
Awcloud, 1004
Awe.sm, 1888
AWECO, 2810
Awesomeness TV, 1480, 1883
AwesomenessTV, 1242
aWhere, 146, 3277
AWL, 819
AwoX, 2662
AWS Convergence Technologies, 1422
AWT Labels & Packaging, 1171
AXA Stenman, 2501
Axalta Coating Systems, 413
Axcan Pharma, 74, 2033, 2890
Axcel Photonics, 1915
Axcella, 747
Axcess, 3022
AXCESS International Inc., 2397
Axcient, 1427, 1818
AXDRAFT, 795
Axeda, 1041, 2196
Axeda Systems, 1227, 3231
Axel, 2447
Axel Springer, 924
Axel Springer Digital Classifieds, 815
Axela, 2196
AxelaCare Holdings Inc., 914
Axelliance, 2851

Portfolio Companies Index

Axent, 655
Axentra Corporation, 2058
Axerra, 3179
Axesnetwork Solutions, 2095
Axia Energy, 1278, 1326
Axial, 518, 655, 741, 1110, 1534, 1991
Axial BioTech, 184
Axial Biotech, 1915
Axial Biotherapeutics, 1051, 1145
Axial Exchange, 386, 904, 1988, 3259
Axial Healthcare, 2
Axialog, 2466
AxiaMed, 918
Axicon Technologies, 1227
AxieTech International Holdings, 413
Axikin Pharma, 1241
Axikin Pharmaceuticals, 1616
Axine, 1580
Axine Water Technologies, 2078
Axio, 425
Axio Biosolutions, 28
Axiom, 634, 1410, 1828, 1896, 1922, 2386, 2577, 2823, 2854
Axiom CME, 1228
Axiom Global, 581
Axiom Law, 416
Axiom Legal, 627
Axiom Microdevices, 132, 1779
Axiom Space, 1613
Axioma, 1608, 1623
Axiomatics, 2619
AxioMed, 2728
AxioMed Spine, 642, 1187, 1544, 1817
AxioMx, 660, 1940
Axiomx, 530
Axion, 2348
Axion Power International, 643
Axios, 641, 1110
Axip Energy Services, 1835
Axipointe Inc., 300
Axis, 2138
Axis Capital Funding II, 1970
Axis Energy Services, 1125
Axis Group Integrated Services, 3130
AXIS Industrial Services, 1745
Axis Network Technology, 260
AxisPoint Health, 528
AxisRooms, 3109
AxisThree, 2610
Axitron, 1784
Axium Healthcare Pharmacy, 415
Axius, 1183
Axle.AI, 1507
AxleHire, 243, 648
Axlon International, 2754
AxoGen, 40, 184, 697
Axogen, 598
Axolotl, 1103
Axon AI, 285
Axoni, 124
Axonia Medical, 1379, 1713
Axonics Modulation Technologies, 1143
Axonify, 339, 1041
Axonize, 543
Axsol, 2527
Axsun Technologies, 1235, 1906
Axter Agroscience, 2049
Axxana, 1474, 2566
Axxessit, 2632
Axxima, 2377
Ayalogic, 642, 1047
Ayannah, 1965
Ayar Labs, 1004
Ayasdi, 358, 486, 751, 809, 1001, 1075
Aydanaya, 2284
Aye, 578
Ayehu, 249

Ayla, 563
Ayla Networks, 483, 1689, 1945
Aylus Networks, 1181, 1334
Ayogo, 703
AyoxxA, 2824
AYTB, 1017
AYZH, 3277
Azahar Coffee, 55
Azaire Networks, 2005
Azalea, 1008
Azaleos, 1641
AZB & Partners, 3261
Azellon, 2892
Azelon Pharmaceuticals, 1119
Azentic, 2095
Azerx, 1901
Azevan Pharmaceuticals, 177, 1117
Azimo, 641
Azimut Exploration, 2120
Azimuth, 1334
Azimuth Capital Management, 3258
Azimuth Systems, 1080
Azimuth Technology, 984, 1144
Azonic, 2058
Azorus, 2143, 2205
Azoti, 1286
Aztech Systems, 892
Aztek Networks, 876, 1782
Azuik, 1672
Azuki, 1065
Azul Brazilian Airlines, 1978
Azul Systems, 1474
Azumio, 720
Azuqua, 609, 974, 1000
Azure Capital Partners, 986, 2032, 3258
Azure Films, 2574
Azure Power, 770, 2818
Azure Solutions, 1305
Azurity, 1349
Azuro, 1237, 1975, 3195
AZVIcode, 1710
AZZLY, 3262

B

B DNA, 1311
B Media, 542
B Media Group, 1638
B&B Hotels, 413
B&B Merger Corp., 1927
B&B Roadway Security Solutions, 960
B&C Foods Inc., 354
B&E Group, 1266
B&H Education, 21, 1504
B&W Quality Growers, 405
B+B SmartWorx, 846, 1014
B+H International LP, 2056
B+T Group, 828
B-152, 2776
B-Band, 2873
B-Dry, 828
B-Hive, 1916
B-Line, 839
B-Process, 3208
B-Sm@rk, 2522
B-Stock, 1717
B-Stock Solutions, 1759, 1860
B-Way Holding, 1156
B.B. Hobbs, 1689
B.E.T. - er Mix, 1209
B.M.B., 2120
B.R. Lee Industries Inc., 152
B12, 816
B12 Transportation Group, 1053
B2B Center, 3088
B2eMarkets, 2079
B2R Technologies, 2313
B2X, 1244

B2X Care Solutions, 2797
B8ta, 518, 679, 1006
b8ta, 727
BA Insight, 52, 1385
Ba&sh, 1088
BA-Insight, 1387
Baarb, 1507
Bab.La, 2979
BabaBoo, 3058
Babajob, 855
Babba Co., 1118
Babbaco, 1087, 1615
Babbel, 1327, 2921
Babeeta, 3215
Babies, 1923
Babington, 2539
Babla, 2824
Babson CLO, 1491
Baby Belle, 3042
Baby Gourmet, 2048, 2049
Baby Plus, 658
Baby Quip, 1507
Baby Scripts, 1019
Baby-Mart.de, 3170
Baby.com.br, 1821, 2976
BabyCare, 2590
BabyCenter, 1853
Babycenter, 260, 1563
BabyEarth, 349
BabyList, 1371
Babylon, 2834
Babyscript, 811
BabyTree, 1181
BabyUniverse, 925
Bac2 Ltd, 2464
Baccarat, 1088
Bacharach, 787
Bachman Information Systems, 1255
Back At You Media, 1642
Back in Motion, 2163
Back To Nature, 357
Back To The Roots, 1530
Back to the Roots, 2238
Back Werk, 2851
Back-und Kondit, 2810
Back9 Network, 869
Backlot Cars, 1384
BackOps, 585, 641, 1489
Backplane, 231, 1524
Backtrace, 1522
Backtrace I/O, 1849
Backtype, 784
BackupAgent B.V., 3128
Backupify, 206
BackWeb, 1853
Backyard Products, 443
Backyard Products LLC, 577
BACOM, 291
Bacrac Supply Company, 378
Bacterin, 1382
BacterioScan, 267
Bactusense, 3245
Badenia Bettcomfort GmbH & Company KG, 2806
Badgeville, 1010, 1522, 1853, 1968
Badoo, 2736
Baebies, 293, 1556
Baekeland Fonds, 3042
Baert, 2501
Bag Balm, 812
Bag Borrow or Steal, 1741
BAG Med, 2810
Bagcheck, 1254
Bagchi Law, 3259
BagDoom.com, 721
Bagel Nash, 3244
Bagnali Court, 2539

1265

Portfolio Companies Index

Bagrationi, 71
Bagwell Supply, 2045
Bahcesehir Schools, 413
Bahrain Bay, 152
Bai Du, 1084
BAI Global, 1295
Baichuan, 3194
Baidu, 609, 690, 2850
Baierl & Demmelhuber Innenausbau GmbH, 2494
Baihe, 1340, 1796
Baihe Holding Corp., 1297
Baihe.com, 1184
Baike.com, 596
Bailey 44, 1346
Bailey International, 1435
Bailiwick, 1345
Bailtrand, 3020
Baimos Technologies, 2824
Bain Capital, 3264
Bainbridge, 152, 1173
Bainbridge Health, 266
BAInsight, 1400
Baird Capital, 3265, 3269
Bairo, 3262
Baixing, 1796
Baja Broadband, 1153
Bakcell, 1244
Baker & Taylor, 423, 1986
Baker Communications, 986
Baker Hughes Inc., 1903
Baker Manufacturing, 1578
Baker McKenzie, 3261
Baker Technologies, 151, 229, 1439, 1464, 1610, 1843
Baker Tilly, 3275, 3279
BakerCorp, 1123, 3033
Bakewise Brands, 1209
Bako, 118
Bakpax, 1363, 1392
Baku Coca-Cola Bottlers II, 1007
BAL, 2455
BalaDyne, 1336
Balance, 85, 384
Balance Bar, 357
Balance Therapeutics, 1247, 1412
Balance Water, 668
Balanced, 229
Balances M. Dodier, 2095
Balbix, 1031, 1184
Balboa Water Group, 1505
Balcas Ltd, 2704
BalconyTV, 871
Balconytv, 1460
Baldor Electric Co, 2456
Balena, 609, 809
Balenda, 180
Baligam, 2914
Balihoo, 1090, 1380
Balkrishna Industries, 2599, 2600
Ballard, 214
Ballard Leasing, 1494
Ballard Medical Products, 1708
Ballast Point Ventures, 3262
BallerTV, 79
Ballet Jewels, 788
Ballot Ready, 1155
BallotReady, 934
Ballston Plaza II, 2565
Bally Engineering, 354
Ballygowan, 2823
Balnea Erlebnisbäder GmbH & Co. Chieming/Obb, 2494
Balsa, 318
Baltic Rim Fund Ltd., 2651
Baltoro Capital, 3261
Balyo, 2296, 3113

Balzac Coffee, 2795
Balzac's Coffee, 2099
Bambecco, 1169, 1291
Bambeco, 22
Bambi/Banat, 3095
Bamboo HR, 1705
Bamboo Rose, 1276
Banana Boat, 1096
Banca FarmaFactoring, 442
Banca Romenesca, 2471
BancBoston Capital, 1295
Banco Best, 2717
Banco Indusval & Partners, 1956
BancWest Bancorp, 131, 1708
Band of Angels, 3118
Bandals, 742
Bandcamp, 1860
Bandit Vehicle Security, 2709
BandPage, 1247, 1563
Bandsintown, 51, 286
Bandura Systems, 285
Bandwagon, 218, 1310
BandWD, 3240
Bandwidth 10, 970
Banebys, 2339
Bang Er Medical, 710
Bangbite, 3052
Bangcle, 1534
Banjo, 296, 1297, 1912, 2478
Bank Invest, 2447
Bank of America Merrill Lynch, 3262
Bank of Innovation, 2646
Bank Of N.T. Butterfield & Son, 413
Bank of Qeensland, 2456
Bank of Western Australia, 2456
Bank United, 442
Bankers Systems, 843
BankFacil, 641
Bankier, 2528
Bankity, 3125
Bankrate, 131
Bankruptcy Management Solutions, 456
BankThai, 300
BankUnited, 1403
Banner Bank, 787
Banner Service Corp., 443
Banner Services, 1477
Banner Services Corporation, 932
Banner Solutions, 1777
Bannerman, 785
Bannerman Resources, 1548
Banqsoft, 2754
Banshee Bungee, 85, 1784
Banshee Wines, 1734
Banter, 2195
Banyan, 1070
Banyan Energy, 41
Banyan Technology, 1047
Banyan Water, 428, 567
Banza, 788, 1585, 3052
Banzai, 1613
Baobab, 60, 318, 518
Baobab Resources, 638
Baobab Studies, 1473
Baobab Studios, 472, 1611
Baobao, 823
Baofeng.com, 2850
Baoya Estates, 2487
Baozen, 842
Bar Harbor Biotechnology, 1161
Bar-Plate Manufacturing, 1521
Bara Energia do Brasil Petróleo e Gás, 1573
BARBRI, 1105
Barcalounger, 902
Barco New, 2780
Barcodes, 1368
Barcodes Inc., 546

Barcoo, 2444
Bard's Tale Beer, 1872
Bardy Diagnostics, 918, 2180
BardyDX, 1556
BardyDx, 176, 1628, 1762
Bare Escentuals, 168, 2015
Bare Snacks, 668, 1324
Barefoot Landing, 1681
Barefoot Networks, 124, 603, 1654
BareFruit, 2049
Barilla Draw, 514
Baring Hellenic Ventures SA (BHV), 2784
Baring Private Equity Asia Ltd, 3261
Baring Vostok Capital Partners, 3261
Barjan, 1435
Bark, 1055
Bark & Co., 1593
Bark Box, 1110
BarkBox, 1546
Barkbox, 1460
Barkly, 1297
Barn & Willow, 896
Barnacle Seafood, 1213
Barnellan Equity Advice Ltd, 3261
Barnes & Thornburg, 3279
BarNotes, 1943
Barnraiser, 325
Barofold, 315, 2815
BAROnova, 935, 1619, 2180
Baronova, 1143, 1378
Barosense, 1412, 1884
Barra Energia, 740
Barracuda, 2587, 2823
Barracuda Networks, 57, 757, 779, 1654
Barrel Park Investments, 1370
Barried Therapeutics Inc., 74
BarrierSafe Solutions International, 1128, 1368
BarrirerSafe Solutions International, 654
BARRx, 925
Barrx Medical, 782, 1760
Barry Callebaut, 2922
Bartab, 650
Barteca, 815
Bartech, 2862
Bartech System Corp, 2653
Bartek, 2272
Barthel Pauls, 3134
Bartlett Holdings Inc., 914
Barton Nelson, 61
BarTrendr, 1061
Barvista Homes, 1745
BAS Broadcasting, 828
Base, 1364, 1593, 1696, 1721
Base 10 Group, 2218
Base Case Management, 2824
Base Culture, 668
BASE Engineering Inc., 908
BASE Entertainment, 494
Base Operations, 829
Base Pair Biotechnologies, 2110
Base Venture, 1370
Base-2 Capital, 1364
Base79, 60, 2972
Baseball Express, 734
Basecamp, 262
Basecamp Fitness, 1576
Baseclick, 2492
Basefarm, 21
BaseKit, 2691, 2987
Baselayer, 1480
Basepaws, 226
Basho, 1988
Basic 3C, 988
Basic-Fit, 2311
Basin Properties, 1125
Basis, 124, 596, 889, 1427
Basis Technology, 979

1266

Portfolio Companies Index

Basis.io, 1121
BASIX Group, 2313
Basix Krishi, 55
Bask, 22
Basket Savings, 679
Basler, 2375
Basno, 1222
Basso, 2436
Batanga, 1442, 1710, 1728
Batanga Inc., 158
Bateel, 1088
Bathrooms.com, 2450
Batigroup, 2922
Batitech, 2095
Baton, 1528
Baton System, 93
Bats, 1717
BATS Global Markets, 1776
Batteries Plus Bulbs, 783, 1576
Batterii, 479
Battery Solutions, 443
Battery Streak, 50
Battery Ventures, 986, 3273, 3284
BattleBin, 459
Battlefly, 85
Battlefy, 120, 600
Bauble Bar, 871
BaubleBar, 28, 1110
Baublebar, 180, 518
BaubleBar Inc., 49
Baud Data Communications, 2850
Bauer AG, 2660
Bauer Marketplace, 2172
Bauer Performance Sports Ltd., 1081
Baurer, 2343
Bausch & Lomb, 1817, 1972
BAWAG, 1730
Baxano, 187, 1445, 1819
Baxano Surgical, 1059, 1493
Baxi Group, 2497
Baxter Group Ltd, 2456
Baxter International, 1271
Baxter Manufacturing, 1557
Bay Club, 1082
Bay Dynamics, 416, 518
Bay Labs Inc., 1069
Bay MicroSystems, 1288
Bay Microsystems, 979, 1604, 1646
Bay Partners, 3284
Bay State Physical Therapy, 368
Bay Tech, 1315
BayanT, 3168
Bayantel, 2434
Baydin, 1050
Baydon Solutions Ltd, 2554
Baydrive Limited, 2821
Bayhill Therapeutics, 1412, 1896
Baylor Home Care, 406
Baylor Home Infusion Therapy, 406
Baynes Electric Supply, 1173
Baynote, 623, 1038, 3121
Bayonne Energy Center, 156
BayPackets, 1793
Bayshore, 249
Bayshore Networks, 1611
Baystone Software, 536
Bayview Financial, 277, 838
Bayview Hospitality Group, 2043
Bayview Systems, 1461
Bazaar, 351
Bazaarvoice, 202, 741, 751, 815, 1810
BB Hotels, 2852
BBAM, 2209
BBE, 798
BBJ Rentals, 1166
BBN Technologies, 28, 521
BBox, 1657

BBOXX, 2181
BBS, 3194
BBVA Compass, 3259
BBy Inc., 1507
BC Decker Inc., 2094
BC Naturals, 2100
BC Partners VIII, 2447
BC Tech Fund, 3258
BC Technical, 1270
BC2Environmental Corp., 274
BC3 Technologies, 1507
BCD, 1916
BCD Semiconductor, 1534, 3062
BCF Ventures, 3258
BCG, 1317
BCI Broadband, 1516
BCI Burke, 894
BCode, 2618
BCombs, 3259
bContext, 1632
BCR Solid Solutions, 2290
BD Accuri, 113
BDC Capital, 3258
BDNA, 555, 1052, 1677
bDNA, 2639
BDO, 3259
BDO USA, 3267
BDP International, 862
BDS, 1135, 1227
BDS Analytics, 99, 151, 392
BDTNDR, 392
Be, 197, 3137
Be Green Packaging, 1572
Be Jane, 1915
Be Power Tech, 747
Beach, 1082
BeachMint, 1118, 1235, 1853
Beacon, 2265
Beacon Analytical Systems, 438
Beacon Communications, 443
Beacon Fire & Safety, 949, 1396
Beacon Healthcare, 1784
Beacon Promotions, 316
Beaconhome, 858
Beagle, 3108
Beam, 148, 630, 855, 1075, 1363
Beam Dental, 2132
Beam Express, 3045
Beam Impact, 342
Beam Messenger, 2113
Beamery, 128, 1154
BeamExpress, 2899
Beamr, 996, 1926
BeamReach Networks, 252, 2508, 3118
Beanitos, 1088
Beanworks, 2223
Bear, 1551
Bear Down Brands, 330, 331
Bear Flag Robotics, 707
Bear Naked, 243
Bear Paw Energy, 893
Bearcom, 257
Bearence Management Group, 1276
BearingPoint, 787
Beast, 307
Beast Brands, 1613
Beat, 100
BeatBox, 1194
BeatCraft, 2991
BeatTheBushes, 2856
Beauceron Security, 2200
Beaudry & Theroux, 2095
Beautiful AI, 741, 1663
Beauty Bakerie, 13
Beauty Booke, 1306
Beauty Box 5, 445
Beauty Counter, 7

Beauty First, 1549
Beauty in Fashion, 2936
BeautyCon, 896, 1813
Beautycounter, 1263, 1830
Beautylish, 1118
BeautyStat.com, 418
BeautyTouch, 981
Beaver Visitec, 1590
Beaver-Visitec International, 1835
BeavEx, 686
Bebe, 869
Bebestore, 2446
Bebop, 124
bebop, 1654
Beceem, 620, 1087, 1922
Beceem Communications, 833
Beceem Firetide, 1241
Becker Underwood Inc., 449
BeckerBs Healthcare, 1409
Beckett Corp., 465
Beckfield College, 1504
Beckon, 386, 1522, 1916
Becton, 1452
BedaBox, 3262
Bedford Capital Limited, 3258
Bedrijvencentrum Waasland, 3042
Bedrock, 976, 1766
Bedrock Analytics, 454
Bedrock Capital, 879
BedRocket Media, 1297
Bee Free Honee, 1149
Bee-keeping Dedinsk[2]., 3122
Beecher Carlson, 202
Beecken Petty O'Keefe & Company, 3264, 3265
Beef 'O' Brady's, 1111
Beefeaters, 2150
Beefsteak, 1766
Beekeeper, 1611
BeeKeeper Labs, 2001
Beeline, 3108
Beelogics, 3245
Beeminder, 1463
Beenz, 810
Beepi, 1589
Beeswax, 776, 935
Befar Group, 2542
BeFree, 1103, 2005
Begin, 883
BeGo, 2967
Behalf, 1240
BehaveCare, 1993
Behavioral Health Group, 378, 789
Behavioral Interventions, 1505
Behavioral Signals, 1051
BehavioSec, 483, 2630, 3018
Behaviour Interactive, 2095
Behavioural Centers of America, 1128
Behavox, 2834
Behrens Manufacturing, 828
Bei Jing Lepro Seva, 2436
Beijing Amcare Women's & Children's Hospital, 1956
Beijing Capital Juda, 1082
Beijing Hua Yu Network Technology Development, 3093
Beijing Ibase Software Co Ltd, 2499
Beijing International Power Development & Investme, 2500
Beijing International Trust and Investment Co, 2500
Beijing Jingeng Clean Energy, 3093
Beijing King's Orient Hi-Tech Group Co Ltd, 2499
Beijing Lepro Seva Da Technologiy Development, 3093
Beijing Med-Pharm Co. Ltd., 2397, 2397
Beijing MMIM Technologies, 2850

1267

Portfolio Companies Index

Beijing Odyssey Chemicals, 2542
Beijing Phylion Battery Co Ltd, 2499
Beijing Rising Technology Co., 3093
Beijing Ryzur Exiom Medical Investment Co., 3093
Beijing Tianyu Communications Equipment, 1956
Beijing UniSoc Technology Ltd., 1004
Beijing Yangpuweiye Technology Development, 2850
Beijing Yize Jianyuan Technology Co., 3093
BeInSync, 2462, 2720
Beintoo, 2874, 3179
BEL USA, 528
BelAir Networks, 2196, 3155
Belair Networks, 1410
Belazee, 721
Belcan, 66
Belden & Blake Corporation, 1573, 2565
Belenus, 3233
Belfast International Airport, 2823
Belga-Films, 3134
BeliefNet, 2196
Believe, 3208, 3239
Belkin, 1770
Belkin International, 1752
Bell ActiMedia, 2079
Bell and Howell, 1979
Bell Automotive Products, 443, 1477
Bell Biosystems, 129, 1238
Bell Nursery Holdings, 1129
Bell Robotics, 1509
Bell Sports, 334
Bell'O International, 752
Bell-Park Co., 2907
Bella Pictures, 1915
BellaBeat, 721
Bellabeat, 1489
BellBrook Labs, 2001
BELLE Michigan, 3269
Bellerophon, 12
Bellerophone Therapeutics, 1301
Bellhops, 858, 1149
Bellicum, 762
Bellicum Pharmaceuticals, 1519
Bellisio Food LLC, 447
Bellisio Foods, 716
Bellsystem24, 220
Bellwave, 2833, 2857
Bellwether Bio, 2008
Belly, 483, 1118, 1297
Belmont Meat Products, 1751, 2089
Belmont Technology, 1334
BeLocal, 2569
Beloola, 307
Belstar Investment, 2313
Belwater Capital Fund, 623
Belwind, 3042
Beme, 1121
BeMyEye, 2296
Benaissance, 1276
Benbria, 1926
Benbria Loop, 2284
Bench, 100, 533, 1110, 1475, 1518, 2157
Benchling, 124, 1202
Benchmark, 1067, 3215
Benchmark Capital, 3284
Benchmark Revenue Management, 1784
Benchmark Storage Innovations, 210
Benchmarq, 202
Benchmarq Microelectronics, 3137
BenchPrep, 1118, 1555
Benchprep, 1297, 1392
BenchSci, 2027, 2137, 2157
Bend, 2
Bendigo Bank Ltd, 2456
Bendon, 1022, 1984

BeneChill, 1325
Benechill Inc., 2816
Benefit, 1736
Benefit Express, 1136
Benefit Informatics, 550
Benefit Mall, 1255
Benefitfocus, 1361
BenefitMall, 202, 909
BenefitMall.com, 955
Benefitter, 181
Benefix, 52
Benefood NV, 2806
Benefuel, 2061
Benestra, 909, 1153
BeneStream, 150, 1054
BeneSys, 932, 1572
Benetech, 468
Benetel, 2355
Benevis, 787, 1777
Benevis Practice Services, 1134
Benevity, 1041
Benex, 3182
Benihana, 127
Benivo, 2997
Benjamin River Productions, 3049
Benlowe Group Ltd, 2486
Bennedikthegaard, 3203
Bennedsgaard, 3203
Bennett Tool & Die Company, 399, 1053
Bennington Marine, 225
Benson Group, 2944
Benson Hill Biosystems, 267, 569, 889, 1206
Bensussen Deutsch & Associates, 577
Bentek, 595
Bentek Corporation, 1396
Benten Bio Services, 1428
Benthic Geotech, 2975
Bentley Pharmaceuticals, 1452
Bentley Place, 1219
Bento, 518, 2943
Bento for Business, 1240
Bento Nouveau, 2049
Bento Sushi, 2049
Bentobox, 358
Benu, 1715, 1760
Benu Networks, 518, 1728
Benvenue, 598
Benvenue Medical, 621, 1786
Benzinga, 607, 1118
Bequam, 2851
Bercomac Limitee, 2120
BERD, 3048
beRecruited, 1157
Berg Earth, 3006
Bergamotte, 2296
Bergen Medical Products, 293, 841
BerGenBio, 2519
Berger Singerman LLP, 3262
Berggi, 2342
Berggruen Car Rentals, 250
Bergteamet, 2325
Bering Media, 2262
Beringea, 3269
Beringer, 1835
Beringer Energy, 2040
Berkana, 2936
Berkana Wireless, 1237, 1747, 2926
Berkanna Wireless, 1087
Berkeley Capital Management, 1147
Berkeley Contract Packaging, 940
Berkeley Design Automation, 260, 1975, 2005
Berkeley Lights, 107, 275, 1654
Berkeley Lights Inc., 1951
Berkenhoff, 2795
Berkshire, 168
Berkshire Grey, 1069
Berlin Packaging, 1017, 1360

Berliner Verlag, 1927
Berna Biotech, 2922
BERNAMA Systems And Solutions Advisor Sdn Bhd, 3164
Bernard Robinson & Company, 3259
Berry, 846
Berry Aviation, 48
Berry Aviation Inc., 984
Berry Family Nurseries, 465
Berry Plastics, 140
BerryAvenue, 2829, 2838
Berrygenomics, 2936
Bertram, 2823
Bertrand Ducks, 2120
Bertrandt, 3069
Bertucci's Corporation, 1111
Beru AG, 2565
Beryllium, 812
Bespoke Furniture Ltd., 2657
Bespoke Global, 841
Bespoke Post, 13, 1632
Bessemer Venture Partners, 3273
Best Doctors, 240, 646, 1460, 1627
Best Elite International, 3093
Best Health, 1251
Best Kids (YeeHoo Baby World), 2944
Best Lawyers, 1111
Best Lighting Products, 849
Best Maid Cookie Co., 147
Best Teacher, 2646
Best Version Media, 257
Best!, 655
Bestar, 2120, 2206
BeStylish, 2797
BET and WIN.com, 2783
Beta O2, 1604
Betable, 358, 1254, 1860
Betabrand, 776, 1254, 1359
BetaCat Pharmaceuticals, 1619
BetaGlue Technologies, 2874
BetaWorks, 641
Betaworks, 590, 1004, 1110, 1593, 1699
Betfair, 3097
Betfair.com, 2711
BeTheBeast.com, 1965
BeTrend, 1755
Bettcher Industries, 1266
Better, 1075
Better Bean, 1463
Better Finance, 1700
Better Life Medical, 710
Better Life Partners, 2
Better Life Technology LLC, 449
Better Mobile Security, 1306
Better Online Solutions, 3101
Better Place, 2900
Better Software Company, 2195
Better Than Cash Alliance, 1374
Better Things, 1964
Better Voicemail, 445
Better Walk, 1187
Better Workplace, 398
Better World, 2576
BetterBody Foods, 999
BetterCloud, 282, 641, 754, 871, 1235, 1849
Bettercloud, 28
BetterCompany, 296, 454, 1992
BetterDoctor, 1222, 1297, 1700
Betterez, 1035
Betterfly, 471, 1118
BetterLesson, 935, 1299, 1316, 1392
Betterlesson, 1527
Bettermarks, 2531
Betterment, 260, 486, 779, 1202, 1531
BetterUp, 563, 609, 784
Betterup, 1121
BetterView, 525, 942

Portfolio Companies Index

Betterview, 13
BetterWalk, 995
Betterware, 2537, 2538
BetterWare de Mexico, 46
BetterWorks, 1075
Betterworks, 544
BetweenMarkets, 202
Beverage House, 654
Beverage Innovations, 1191
Bevesys Oy, 2873
Bevi, 497, 622
BeVisible, 218
Bevo Agro, 2051
Bevocal, 1896, 1975
BevSpot, 622
Beynd, 79
Beyond, 1749
Beyond 12, 1316
Beyond Games, 45, 707, 1118
Beyond Limits, 319
Beyond Meat, 511, 1075, 1095, 1363
Beyond Pricing, 358
Beyond The Rack, 2196
Beyond the Rack, 1410
Beyond View, 1421
BeyondCore, 1202
BeyondNow Technologies, 1837
BeyondTrust, 1925
BeyondTrust Software, 1970
BeyondView, 1473
BEZ Systems, 1913
Bezar, 351, 1222
BEZRK, 3071
BF Acquisitions Company LLC, 869
BFF GEMZ, 1615
BFG Supply, 2214
Bfinance, 222, 2565
BFL Capital, 3279
BFM, 2375
BFS Capital, 655
BGB, 3194
BGE, 2936
BGI, 1340, 3100
BGIS, 433
BGMedicine, 747
bGroupe Berkem, 2851
BH Cosmetics, 1231
Bharat Box Factory, 2460
Bharat Light and Power (BLP), 3211
Bharat Matrimony, 386
Bharat Serums and Vaccines, 1382
Bharti Enterprise, 2697
Bharti Infratel, 1082
Bharti Tele-Ventures, 2434
BHI Energy, 66
Bhoruka Power, 584
BHP Billiton, 2659
BHS Getriebe GmbH, 2712
BHS Specialty Chemical Products, 1730
BHS Specialty Chemicals, 1465
Bi Coastal Media, 669
Biametrics, 2824, 2932
BiancaMed, 3113
BianoGMP, 2527
Bias Power, 1740
Biba, 1010, 1853
Biba Apparels, 1956
BiblioMondo, 2263
Bibutek, 3052
Bicske-M1 Industrial Park And Logistic Centre, 2635
Bicycle Therapeutics, 182, 191, 1145, 1350, 1628, 1731, 1762
BID Group, 2146, 2165
Bid4assets, 324
Bidadoo Auctions, 85
BidClerk, 58

Bidclerk, 852
Bidgely, 532, 1069, 2132
BidPal, 86, 1242
Bidtellect, 287
Bidu.com.br, 2976
Bielsko Business Center, 3077
Bien Cuit, 1420
Biex, 1255
BiFab, 3135
Bifold Group, 2944
BIG, 2810
Big, 124
Big 3 Precision Products, 1870
Big Bang Ventures, 3042
Big Box, 1183, 1390, 1663
Big Button, 2967
Big Cafe, 1087
Big City Farms, 3277
Big Fish Games, 1608
Big Frame, 132, 1480
Big Frame. Bonds.com, 2649
Big Heart Pet Brands, 1931
Big Issue Invest, 2509
Big Matrix Research Institute, 2970
Big Night Entertainment Group, 638
Big River, 1047
Big Rock Sports LLC, 274
Big Sandy Equipment Company, 156
Big Sandy Peaker, 1795
Big Sky Farms, 2049
Big Squid, 1070
Big Switch Networks, 603, 1004, 1257, 1534
Big Teams, 1766
BigBand Networks, 436, 455, 2580, 3137
BigBasket, 260
Bigbelly Solar, 1173
BigCommerce, 816, 823
Bigcommerce, 751, 1235, 1699, 1725, 1796
BigDoor, 773
Biger Boat, 2021
Bigfinite, 563
BigFix, 214, 967, 1212, 1646, 1975
Bigfix, 1725
Bigfoot Captial, 3276
Bigfoot Interactive, 954
Bigfoot Networks, 1334
BigFrame, 791, 1099
Bigger Pockets, 1276
Bigham Brothers, 1870
BigHand, 2944
BigHealth, 1052
BigID, 305, 518, 814, 2153
BigLeaf, 1383
BigMachines, 1041
BigMouth, 405, 478
BigPanda, 235, 1184
Bigpanda, 836
Bigpoint GmbH, 1752, 1776
Bigscreen, 1473
BigStage, 1646
Bigstream, 1004
BigSwitch, 1069
Bijoux Terner, 152
BikeStation, 1784
Bil-Jax, 443
Bilguiden, 3013
Bilibili, 973
Bill & Melinda Gates Foundation, 3261
Bill Trust, 655
Bill.Com, 197
Bill.com, 596, 665, 968, 1626, 1863
Bill4Time, 92
Billabong, 96
BillDesk, 502
Billeo, 183, 491
Billetto, 3203
BillGuard, 260

Billian, 3013
Billing Services Group, 21
BillingPlatform, 515
Billions Chemicals, 2542
BillMeLater, 215, 1888
BillPay, 2829, 2838
BilltoMobile, 1257
Billtrust, 221
Bimedia, 2851
BINA, 1236
Binaris, 603, 1121
Binary Event Network, 343
Binary Fountain, 938
BinaryVR, 307
Bind, 1107
BIND Biosciences, 925, 1419
Bind Biosciences, 153, 747
Bind Therapeutics, 1460
Bindview, 1041
Bing Outdoor Media, 445
Bingdian, 1534
BingoBox, 823
BinOptics, 61, 432, 810, 1523
Binpress, 1489, 1634
Binswanger Glass, 403
Binti, 318, 741, 1054, 1149
biNu, 1830
Binwise, 1596
BIO - Belgian Investment Company for Developing Co, 3261
Bio Agri Mix, 2062
Bio Futures PLC, 2708
Bio Gas Bree, 2949
Bio Gate, 2979
Bio Imagene, 176
Bio Protect, 3240
Bio Systems, 1060
Bio Theranostics, 921
Bio Trove, 426
Bio-Nobile Oy, 2318
Bio.Logis, 2569
Bioabsorable Therapeutics Inc., 269
BioAbsorbable Therapeutics, 1975
BIOAGE, 942
Bioage, 124
Bioage Labs, 720
BioAlliance Pharma, 2563, 3113
BioAmber, 1241, 2049
BioAnaLab, 3107
BioArray Solutions, 212, 1325
BioAstra Technologies, 2273
BioAtlantis, 2918
BioBeats, 679, 1611
Biobeats, 1524
BioBehavioral Diagnostics, 1419, 1658
Biobot Analytics, 1421
Biobras, 2742
Biocancell Therapeutics, 3245
Biocartis, 3042
Biocartis SA, 2350
Biocell, 2979
Biocept, 1288
Bioceptive, 3277
BioCeros, 2514
Bioceros, 2748
BioCision, 1543
Biocius Life Sciences, 426, 703
BioClinica, 118, 1039, 1961
Biocode-Hycel, 2680
BioCollection, 622
BioConnect Systems, 710
BioConsortia, 1069
BioControl Limited, 1452
BioCore Holdings, 1628
BioCote, 3107
Biocroi, 2918
BioCryst Pharmaceuticals, 1918

Portfolio Companies Index

Biodelivery Sciences, 762
Biodesy, 12, 1436, 3085
BioDetego, 266
Biodiesel Producers., 2645
BioDigital, 351, 743
BioDuro, 62
Bioelectron, 1241
Bioenergy Development Company, 1315
Bioenvision, 74
Bioerix SRL, 584
Biofer, 3042
Bioferma, 2489
BioFire Diagnostics, 188
BioForm, 3167
Bioform Medical, 1500
Bioformix, 1512
BioGanix, 2031
Biogazelle, 3065
Biogen Idec, 181
Biogenic Reagents, 694
Biognosys, 1774
Biogroup LCD, 2851
Biohaven, 530
Biohaven Pharma, 1941
BioHaven Pharmaceuticals, 74, 136
Biohaven Pharmaceuticals, 762, 1519
BioHitech America, 1428
BioImagene, 2457
Bioindustrial Innovation Canada, 3258
Bioinvent, 2878
BioIQ, 921
BIOIVT, 170
Biokey, 117
BioKier, 347, 3259
BioLeap, 1774
Bioleap, 1508
Biolex, 1508
Biolex Therapeutics, 1008, 1842
Bioline Rx, 3137
BioLineRx, 1382
Biolinq, 870
Biolite, 55
Biologics, 1577
BiologicsMD, 950
Biologische Analysensystem, 2810
Biologos, 702
Biolonix, 2001
BioLumic, 2071
BiOM, 1673
Biomarin, 1268
BioMarker Strategies, 19
BioMASON, 3259
Biomass CHP, 2610, 3012
Biomatlante, 3113
Biomatrica, 979, 1221
BioMCN, 3232
Biomedical Development Corporation, 734
Biomedical Structures, 1770
Biomedican, 2287
Biomeme, 1577
BioMendics, 1047
Biomerix, 177
Biomet, 2379
Biometric Access Co., 190
Biometrix, 1975
Biometron, 2619
Biomimedica, 666
BioMimetic, 212
Biomimetic, 1187, 1500
BioMimetic Therapeutics, 3015
Biomode, 3048
Biomonitor, 3149
BioMoti, 3107
BioNano Genomics, 233, 621
BioNanovations, 995, 1187
Bionic Sight, 1420
Bioniche Life Sciences, 2049, 2120

Bioniche Pharma, 1590
Bionova, 995
Bionumerik, 36
BioNumerik Pharmaceuticals, 734
BioParadox, 598
Biopharmacopae, 2029
Biopharmacopae Design International, 2049
BioPharmX, 1941
BioPhytis, 3113
Bioplexus, 530
Bioprocess H2O, 1693
Bioptigen, 293, 1442
BiOptix, 315
Bioreason, 1011
Bioreclamation, 1343
BioRegen, 710
BioReliance, 209
BioRelix, 660
Biorem, 706
BioRen, 237
Biorender, 795
Bioresearch, 222
BioResource International, 3259
BioRexis, 1508, 1866
BioRob, 2824
BioRx, 1770
BIOSAFE, 293, 998
BioSafe, 1448
BioScale, 946, 1303, 1306, 2978
Bioscale, 1584
Bioscience, 2470
BioScrip, 1081
BioSeek, 237
Biosense, 3249
BioSensia, 2443
Biosensia, 2918
Biosensor, 2754
Biosensor Application AB, 3245
Biosensors International, 892
Biosensors International Group, 3093
BioSensory, 1162
Bioserve, 3211
BioSet, 652, 1187, 1299
BioStable Science & Engineering, 1619
Biostar, 1837
BioStorage Technologies, 1520
BioStratum, 2816
Biosurface Technologies, 1929
Biosurfit, 3048
BioSurplus, 1689
Biosyntech, 1412
BioSyntha, 2967
Biosynthetic Technologies, 319
Biota Technology, 2011
Biotage, 2728, 2890
Biotage AB, 2816
Biotec Pharmacon, 2754
Biotech Fonds Vlaanderren, 3042
Biotie, 1928
Biotie Therapies, 762, 2419, 2662, 2851
BioTie Therapies Oyj, 2318
Biotix, 723
Biotoscana, 697, 744
BioTrace Medical, 1371
BioTransplant, 1558
Biotrend - Inovacao e Engenharia Em Biotecnologia, 3048
Biotronic NeuroNetwork, 859
BioTrove, 647, 703
Biovalve, 2682
BioVascular, 2496
Biovation, 3104
Biovend, 2975
BioVentrix, 1792
Bioventus, 94, 118, 697, 1722, 3259
Biovertis, 3196
Biovest International, 1760

BioVex, 3104
Biovex, 1847, 2748
Bioview Ltd, 2954
BioVigilant, 233
Bioville, 2949
BioWare/Pandemic Studios, 659
BioWish Technologies, 1623
Bioworks, 1377
Biox, 2049
BIOX Corporation, 2114
BiOxyDyn, 3010
BiPar Sciences, 181, 1119, 1946
Birch Box, 28
Birch Hill Equity Partners Management, 3258
Birch Permian LLC, 158
Birch Telecom, 1927
BirchBox, 2385
Birchbox, 325, 518, 741, 761, 836, 1531
Birchmere Ventures, 3275
Bird, 28, 641, 1480, 1654, 2236
Bird Rock Bio, 12, 1731
Birdback, 3030
BirdBox, 685, 930
BirdDog Solutions, 949
BirdEye, 107
Birdi, 1054
birdi, 1701
Birdies, 761, 1346
Birdly, 2296
Birdstep, 3043
Birdstep Technology ASA, 162
Birmingham BioPower, 2749
Birst, 581, 634
Birthday Express, 1672
BIS, 3124
Bis-Technics 2000, 2949
Biscayne Neurotherapeutics, 2229
BISCO Environmental, 1636
Biscotti, 1407
Bishop Auckland Hospital, 2749
Bishop Rock Software, 506
BiSN, 319, 809
Bison, 2651
Bisuness Search Technologies, 682
BISYS Group, 1972
Bit Bliz, 1180
Bit Cauldron, 3262
Bit Computer, 2924
Bit Pagos, 2984
Bit.ly, 590, 1700
Bit9, 2445
Bitaksi, 2437
BitArmor Systems, 998
BitAuto, 596, 2457, 2936
Bitband, 2462
BitBand Ltd, 2585
Bitbar, 1509, 2662, 2674
Bitbond, 3044
Bitboys Oy, 2318
Bitcasa, 1425
Bitcase, 2831
BitCentral, 986
Bitcoin, 124, 1998
BitDefender, 2471
BitDeli, 585
Bite, 341
Bite Squad, 333
Bitec Southeast, 1708
Bitesize, 1370
Bitesnap, 724
BitFone, 2926
Bitfone, 1087, 1352, 1994, 2999
Bitfusion, 1547, 2278
Bitglass, 1297, 1346, 3121
BitGo, 339, 1115, 1534
BitHeads, 2058
Bitium, 120, 306, 624, 1055, 1546

Portfolio Companies Index

Bitly, 1054, 1359, 1593, 1717
Bitmain, 1121, 2690
Bitmaker, 2244
BitMinutes, 505
Bitmovin, 2446
Bitnet, 1968
Bitoya, 1696
BitPay, 1202
Bitpay, 107, 1593, 1863, 2831
bitpay, 720
Bitpipe, 1175
Bitproof.io, 307
Bitquick, 307
BitRefill, 307
Bitsbox, 756
BitSight, 518, 521, 754, 835
BitSight Technologies, 823, 1202
Bitsqr, 1830
Bitstrips, 2831
BitTorrent, 581, 596, 1474
Bittware, 2610
BitVault, 1222
Bitvore Corporation, 1784
BitWall, 307
Bitwave Semiconductor, 1975
Bitwise, 1259
Bitwise Industries, 1527
BitYota, 1254, 1968
Bityota, 563
Bitzer Mobile, 41
BiVACOR, 3023
Bivio, 1682
Bivio Networks, 1975
BIW, 2662
Bix, 115, 1760, 1853
Bix Produce, 1166, 1345
Bix Produce Company, 1343
Biz360, 1975
Bizbuyer, 1784
BizBuyer.Com, 1255
Bizer, 1607
Bizible, 1226
BizLink Holdings, 1769
Bizly, 351, 707, 1035
Biznet Solutions, 2610
Bizo, 260, 563, 1916, 1946
Bizongo, 28
BizReach, 1607
BizTel One, 1599
Bizzabo, 1323, 2352, 2914
Bizzuka, 61
BJ's Wholesale Club, 1109, 1970
BJB Education/Jade, 1516
Bjond, 628
BjondHealth, 943
bk Medical, 97
BKA Restoration, 838
bKash, 855
BKS Cable, 2309
Bkstg, 600, 1110
BL Healthcare, 1926
Bla-Bla.com, 954
Blaast, 2390
BlaBlaCar, 28, 1000, 2860, 2860
Black Bear Power, 156
Black Book Magazine, 460
Black Diamond, 1928
Black Diamond IT Services, 235
Black Diamond Therapeutics, 1519
Black Dog Investment, 3279
Black Duck, 1620, 1725
Black Duck Software, 757
Black Knight Financial Services, 1815
Black Letter Discovery, 1234
Black Mountain Sand, 1278, 1326
Black Point Petroleum, 156
Black Rock Systems, 1915

Black Sage, 48
Black Sand Technologies, 202, 1334
Black Sea Oil & Gas SRL, 413
Black Spider Technologies, 2674
Black Swan Energy, 1956
Blackarrow, 1184, 1460
Blackbaud, 924, 1041
Blackbeard Operating LLC, 1278, 1326
Blackbird Ventures, 483
Blackboard, 1348, 1360, 1496, 2565
BlackBook, 1632
Blackbuck, 28
BlackDuck, 695, 747
Blackeagle Energy Services, 606
Blacket, 819
BlackFog, 69
Blackfoot, 1975
BlackHawk Industrial, 328
BlackHorse Solutions, 1794
BlackJet, 229
Blackjewel, 1125
BlackLake Technology, 823
Blacklane Limiusines, 2475
BlackLine, 1683
BlackLogus, 1810
Blackmore, 1834
Blackmores Ltd, 2456
Blackpeak Group, 3261
Blacksmith Brands, 456
BlackSpider Technologies, 2577, 2662
Blackstone Group, 3264
BlackStratus, 1747
BlackThorn Therapeutics, 268, 889, 1206
Blacktrace, 2006
Blackwave, 1672
Blackwood Seven, 3203
Blade, 3, 85, 228, 816, 1110, 1268
Blade Games World Inc., 371
Blade Therapeutics, 3023
Bladelogic, 260, 1242
Blagden, 2361
Blair, 839
Blake & Pendleton, 1765
Blameless, 28
Blanc Labs, 2113
Blanclink, 2113
Blank Label, 1757
Blankpage AG, 2310
Blaschak Coal Corp., 403
Blaschak Coal Corporation, 1234
Blast, 107
Blast Motion, 107
Blast Movement Technologies, 1548
BlastPoint, 293
Blau Mobilfunk GmbH, 2673
Blausen Medical Communications, 950
Blavity, 889
BLAZE, 50
Blaze Entertainment, 1975
Blaze Mobile, 253
Blaze Pizza, 334
Blaze Software, 305, 1255
Blaze.io, 313
BlazeMeter, 3246
Blazent, 933, 1952
BlazingDB, 1611
Bleach Group, 330
Bleach Group Inc., 331
Bleacher Report, 563
Blekko, 231, 1700, 1896, 1975
Blend, 535, 727, 872, 1121, 1297, 1716, 2010
Blend Labs, 1631
Blenderhouse, 1448
Blendid, 942
Blendoor, 218
Blendspace, 1316
Bleximo, 679

bLife, 1860
BlikBook, 2752
Blink, 518, 2479, 2920, 3208
Blink Biomedical, 2851
Blink Health, 318
Blink Twice, 1915
Blinker, 2962
Blinkfire, 3223
Blinkist, 641, 1000
Blinks Labs, 2841
BlinkTrade, 307
Blinkx, 44
BLiNQ, 2259
BLiNQ Networks, 1305
Blip.TV, 221
Blip.tv, 2390
Blippy, 197, 1546
Blis, 251
Blismedia, 2479
Blispay, 743, 1297
Blisplay, 383
Bliss, 1088
Blissfully, 956
Blitsy, 471, 508, 586, 731
Blitz, 561
BlitzESports, 60
Blivio, 2543
Bloc, 231, 1663
Block, 1110
Block 45, 2202
Block Cypher, 721, 770, 896
Block Renovation, 1363
Block Six Analytics, 60, 317, 1155
Blockable, 308, 1259, 1894
BlockApps, 148
Blockboard, 1054
Blockchain, 889, 1121
Blockchain Innovations Inc., 2122
BlockCypher, 107, 1297
Blockcypher, 307, 852
BlockDaemon, 305
Blockdaemon, 518, 814
Blockline, 2991
BlockScore, 1291
Blockscore, 307
Blockspring, 124
Blockstack, 525, 622, 942, 1151, 1395, 1882, 2280
BlockStream, 1069
Blockstream, 107, 721, 1809
Blocktower Capital, 1882
BlocPower, 1054, 1894, 3277
BlocWatch, 2195
blogfoster, 2841
BlogHer, 1916
Bloglovin', 1110, 1982
Blokable, 1054
Blood Monitoring Solutions, 995
Blood Montoring Solutions, 1187
Bloodbuy, 1810
Bloom, 1359
Bloom Automation, 392
Bloom Energy, 137, 184, 398, 581, 802, 1245, 1297, 1341, 1755
Bloom Farms, 1694
Bloom Health, 1271, 1615
Bloom Technologies, 1054
BloomAPI, 773, 1643
BloomBoard, 272
Bloomenergy, 634, 1031
Bloomfire, 202, 1682
Bloomin' Brands, 220
Bloomlife, 50
BloomNation, 471, 1715
BloomReach, 235, 1297
Bloomreach, 221, 1121, 1607
Bloomscape, 607, 1555

1271

Portfolio Companies Index

Bloomthat, 761
Bloomz, 544, 724
Blossom, 307, 1983, 3108
Bloud Tecnology Partners, 1592
Blount International, 110
Bloxr, 1425
Bloxroute Labs, 754
BLS Revecore, 2204
Blu Dot, 461
Blu Homes, 340
Blu Jay, 779
Blue 7 Communications, 130
blue acorn iCi, 2057
Blue Agave Software, 1672
Blue Ant Media, 2133, 2236
Blue Apron, 741, 1748
Blue Ash Therapeutics, 479
Blue Belt Technologies, 998
Blue Bird, 110
Blue Bottel Coffee, 1860
Blue Bottle, 1524
Blue Bottle Coffee, 511, 1138, 1694
Blue Bottle Coffee Co., 397
Blue Bottle Coffee Company, 1083
Blue Box Group, 1945
Blue Buffalo, 1018
Blue Calypso, 1244
Blue Capital, 722
Blue Cedar, 249
Blue Chip Partners Surgery Centers, 493
Blue Chip Surgery Centers Partners, 287
Blue Cliff College, 1504
Blue Coat, 779, 1871, 1896
Blue Coat Systems, 1491, 1814
Blue Cod Technologies, 646, 655
Blue Danube Systems, 1654
Blue Dog Bakery, 378, 1250
Blue Dot Energy Services, 1144
Blue Fever, 896
Blue Gas Marine, 3259
Blue Heron, 1002
Blue Heron Paper Company, 1085
Blue Heron Technologies, 1915
Blue J Legal, 2195, 2236
Blue Jeans Network, 28, 235, 1297
Blue Jeans Networks, 1996
Blue Lava Group, 1915
Blue Light, 459
Blue Line Logistics, 2949
Blue Line Protection Group, 963
Blue Lithium, 1952
Blue Lobster Software, 954
Blue Matador, 1070
Blue Medical, 224
Blue Medora, 1736
Blue Microphones, 1572
Blue Mountain Village, 2254
Blue Nile, 260, 1003, 1853
Blue Nile Bluevine, 1121
Blue Ocean Network, 2579
Blue Origin, 262
Blue Pillar, 86, 171, 491, 658, 676
Blue Pixels Media, 3267
Blue Point Capital Partners III(A) LP, 2094
Blue Pumpkin Software, 1646, 3118
Blue Pumpkin Software/Witness Systems, 1288
Blue Ribbon Baking Inc., 869
Blue Ribbon Dispatch, 1609
Blue Ridge Asphalt, 156
Blue Ridge ESOP Associates, 834
Blue Ridge Numerics, 834
Blue Ridge Paper Products Inc., 1085
Blue Ridge Pharmaceuticals, 1760
Blue River Technology, 996
Blue Rock, 1928
Blue Rubicon, 2944
Blue Sky Research, 69

Blue Spark Technologies, 642, 1755
Blue Sprig Pediatrics, 1082
Blue Star (Acquired By Us Office Products), 2664
Blue Star Solutions, 1255
Blue Star Sports, 819
Blue Talon, 171
Blue Triangle, 1019
Blue Triangle Technologies, 285
Blue Vector Systems, 627
Blue Vision, 1473
Blue Wave, 1570
Blue Wolf Capital Fund II, 158
BlueAc, 1257
BlueArc, 466, 563
Bluearc, 2472
BlueArc Corporation, 560
BluEarth Renewables, 2040
Bluebank, 1004
Bluebeam Software, 1784
Blueberry, 1323
Blueberry Broadcasting, 1726
Bluebird, 892
Bluebird Bio, 153, 644, 1811, 2748, 3196
BlueBirdBio, 1519
BlueBox, 1563
Bluebox Security, 1796
BlueCamroo, 1061
BlueCart, 296
BlueCasa, 306
BlueCat Networks, 339, 1156, 1850
Bluecava, 1597
BlueCedar, 856
Bluechip Technologies, 2610
Bluechip Technologies Holdings Ltd, 2704
BlueConic, 1673
Bluecore, 720, 743, 773, 942, 2132
Bluecrew, 858
BlueCross BlueShield Venture Partners, 3265
Bluedata, 603, 974
Bluefield, 1885
Bluefields, 1912, 2479
Bluefin, 383
BlueFin Labs, 1534
Bluefin Labs, 1524, 1699
Bluefire Security Technologies, 1038
Bluefish Holdings LLC, 1820
Bluefly, 500, 1558
BlueFox, 231
Bluefox, 799
BlueFox.io, 1006
Bluegiga Technologies, 2451
BlueGill Technologies, 793, 1257
Bluegrass Dairy and Food, 1209
Bluegrass Dairy And Food Inc., 631
Bluegrass Materials Company, 1129
Bluehole Studio, 100
BlueJeans, 1346
BlueKai, 823, 1534, 1725, 1926
Bluekai, 641
BlueKat, 1445
Blueknight Energy Partners, 456
BlueLane, 634, 1474
BlueLeaf, 1592
Blueleaf, 2406
Bluelight, 1615
BlueLine Grid, 1260
Bluemercury, 1018, 1599
BlueMountain Capital, 3264
Bluenog, 1571
Bluenose Analytics, 1696
BlueOrchard Finance, 3261
BluePay Processing, 1776
BluePay Processing Inc., 158
BluePeak Private Capital, 3261
Bluepoint Solutions, 1863
Blueprint, 2196

Blueprint Health, 1993
Blueprint Income, 622
Blueprint Medicines, 762, 1519, 1811
Blueprint Power, 727, 1894
Blueprint Registry, 1176
Blueprint Software Systems, 2261
Blueprint Ventures, 986
Blueprinter, 3203
BlueRoads, 1975
BlueRun Ventures, 3284
Bluerush, 2243
BlueShift, 1297, 1334, 2445
Blueshift, 858
BlueSky Equities, 3258
Bluesmart, 721, 1329
BlueSnap, 857, 1417
BlueSocket, 1975
Bluesocket, 315
Bluespace, 799
BlueSpace Software, 1126
BlueSpace Software Corp., 810
Bluespec, 1334, 2445
BlueSpire, 931
BlueStacks, 106, 974, 1004, 1474
Bluestacks, 1509
Bluestar Solutions, 1975
Bluestar.com, 79
BlueStem Brands, 405
Bluestem Brands, 221
Bluestone, 28, 2944
BlueStone Natural Resources, 1326
Bluestone Software, 56
BlueStrata EHR, 569
Bluestreak, 1738
Bluestreak Media, 734
Bluestreak Technology, 682
Bluestreak Technology Inc., 682
BlueStripe, 1853, 1899
BlueTalon, 268
BlueTarp Financial, 438, 754, 1161, 1853
BlueTown, 3022
Bluetrain Mobile, 1097
BlueTrap Financial, 935
BlueTree Allied Angels, 3275
BlueVine, 486, 1154, 1202
BlueVine Capital, 544
Bluewater Bio International, 3107
BlueWhale, 1906
Bluewolf, 1575
BlueYield, 1502
Blujays Brand, 392
Blumberg Capital, 986
Blume Ventures Fund, 3199
Blurb, 132, 386, 925, 1604
Blutag, 50
Bluum, 418
BluVector, 1136
BluWireless Technology, 2997
BluWrap, 730, 2405
Blycos Biotechnologies, 826
Blyncsy, 1070
Blyth, 413
BMB Corp, 2347
BMC, 1082
Bmd, 2354
bMenu, 2369
BMI Asia, 2590
BMI Asia Inc, 2728
Bmi Canada, 2120
BML Pharmaceuticals, 131
BMM Compliance, 330, 331
BMO Capital Partners, 3258
BMR Financial Group, 1708
BMS Reimbursement, 1239
BNI, 1409
BNI Video, 422, 483
BNN Holdings, 1491

1272

Portfolio Companies Index

Bnocular, 341
BNX Systems, 2565
BNY Mellon Wealth Management, 3275
BOA Group, 64
Board Vantage, 770
Board Vitals, 792
BoardBookit, 293
BoardOnTrack, 1172
BoardVantage, 238
BoarwalkTech, 1254
Boat International Publications, 2821
Boatbound, 707, 1749, 2960
Boathouse Sports, 1665
Boats Group, 135
Boatsetter, 858
Boaz Energy LLC, 1278
Bob, 148
Bobcat Gas Storage, 893
Bobo, 3251
BOC Edwards, 2379
BOC International Limited, 2936
Boca, 202
Boca Executive Beauty, 378
BOCADA, 887
Bocada, 1975
Bocasa, 2949
Bock & Clark, 932
Bodegas Campo Burgo, 2985
Bodegas Lan, 2962
Bodo, 799
Body & Labs, 743
Body and Mind, 203
Body Central, 1979
Body Evolution, 362
Body Media, 176
Body Phyx, 1047
BodyFX, 796
Bodymat, 3134
BodyMedia, 980
Bodymedia, 1623
Bodytech, 1088
Boekhandels Groep Nederland Holding BV, 2992
Boemer BV, 2992
Boftel Oy, 3213
Bogart Associates, 507
Bohemia Interactive Simulations, 1572
Bohemia Prints, 2683
Bohemian Guitars, 1749
Bohner-EH, 2824
Boingo Wireless, 184, 1241, 1741
Boisaco, 2095
Boise Cascade Company, 1156
Bojangles', 1045
Boka Sciences, 826
Bokecc, 3142
Boku, 124, 581, 634, 1069, 1297, 3169
Bol.com, 3155
Bolb Inc., 1951
Bold, 2243
Bold Commerce, 2288
Bold Energy III, 672
BOLD Guidance, 1047
Bold Metrics, 545
Bold Threads, 770
Bolder Healthcare Solutions, 654
Bolder Industries, 146
BOLDstart Ventures, 986
Bolero, 2472
Boloco, 1157, 1999
Boloni, 2936
Bols Royal Distilleries, 2644
Bolstr, 1054
Bolstra, 86, 658
Bolt, 37, 483, 858, 874, 942, 946, 1416
Bolt Financial, 751
Bolt Insurance, 1640
Bolt Threads, 775, 996, 1238

Bolthouse Farms, 1156
Boly Media Communications, 47
Boma International, 3042
Bombardier, 2120
Bombardier Recreational Products, 220
Bombas, 857
BombBomb, 1642
BombFell, 590
Bombfell, 1581
Bomedus, 2824
Bomfell, 858
Bomgar, 779
BoMill, 1774
Bon Voyaging, 1310
Bon'App, 1615
Bona Film Group, 3093
Bonanza, 773, 1945
Bonck Education, 2936
Bond Capital, 3258
Bond Street, 276
BondDesk, 2379
Bonded Filter, 812
Bonded Holdings LLC, 65
Bonded Kayit Sistemleri AS, 250
Bonded Services Group, 1984
BondMart, 791
Bonesupport AB, 2816
Bonfaire, 1118, 1853
Bonfire, 124, 563
Bonfire Wings, 950
Bongarde Holdings, 863
Bonitasoft, 3208
Bonmarché, 1753
Bonna Sabla, 2317, 2863
Bonne O, 2230
Bonneterie Richelieu, 2095
Bonobos, 28, 325, 761, 836, 858, 1121, 1531
Bonotel, 413
Bonovo, 2936
Bonovo Orthopedics, 1382
Bonsai, 1154
Bonson Inormation Technology, 2850
Bonti, 514
Bonti Inc., 487
Bonusbox, 2444
Bonusly, 743
Boo-Box, 2976
Boohee, 1509
Book A Tiger, 3236
Book Jam, 100
Book-It Oy, 2873
BookBub, 206, 1322
Booker, 876, 1046, 1782
Booker Software, 221, 646, 1940
BookFresh, 231
Bookham Technology, 2662
Booking Pal, 384
Bookly.co, 1070
BookMyShow, 28
BookNook, 1527, 1893
Bookyap, 1615
Boom, 307, 561, 942, 977, 1118, 1329, 1593
boom, 792
Boom Entertainment, 826
Boom Fantasy, 622, 1595
Boom Studios, 791
Boom! Studios, 1592
Boom.tV, 741
BoomBotix, 1952
Boombotix, 231, 548
Boomerage Commerce, 1663
Boomerang Commerce, 1158
Boomerang's, 445, 950
Boomi, 246, 743
BoomTime, 1924
BoomTown, 1759
Boomtown, 384, 784

Boomtown!, 707
Boomtrain, 295
Boomz, 773
Boon & Gable, 561
Boon + Gable, 942, 1183
Boon Supply, 1363
Boone, 869
Boosey & Hawkes, 2823
booshaka, 792
Boost, 1115
Boost Biomes, 525
Boost CTR, 1968
Boost Insurance, 1346
Boost Juice Bars, 2550
Boost Media, 235, 1028
Boostable, 1254, 1634
Boosted, 792, 1694, 2157
Boosted Boards, 1069
Booster, 535, 707, 1158, 1183, 1923
Booster Fuels, 2280
Boostermedia, 3128
Boostr, 256
BoostUp, 981
Bootlegger Clothing, 2258
Bootup Labs, 2143
Booya Fitness, 622
Booz Allen Hamilton, 413
Booztgroup, 3149
Bop.fm, 721
Bopack NV, 2806
Boqii, 842, 3062
Borchers, 1045
Borchers Americas Inc., 158
Border Construction Specialties, 1765
Border X Lab, 1075
Borderware, 2005
Boreal - Informations Strategiques, 2120
Boreal Drilling, 2120
Boreal Genomics, 979, 1059, 2053, 2143
Borean Pharma, 2419, 2748
Borer City Media, 1632
Borg & Bigum, 3203
Borjomi, 3095
Bormioli Rocco, 1937
Borqs, 1004, 1509
Borro, 386, 1502, 1560, 2450, 2691
Borrow, 1894
Borrowell, 1982, 2125, 2225
BorrowMyDoggy, 3108
Bortech, 649
Bos, 2571
Bosideng, 2850
Bosley's, 1576
Bosmans Graphics, 2949
BOSS, 842
BOSS (Business Operations & Software Solutions), 2715
Bossa Nova, 869
Bossa Nova Beverages Group, 1915
Bossa Nova Concepts, 998
Bossa Studios, 2446
Bossa Studios UK, 2953
Bossanova, 1004
Bossard Metrics Inc., 908
Bosslady, 3038
Bostlnno, 313
Boston Biomedical, 1241
Boston Celtics, 1524
Boston Children's Hospital, 1271
Boston Color Graphics, 259
Boston Duck Tours, 1623
Boston Heart Diagnostics, 221
Boston Market, 1753
Boston Medical Technologies, 314
Boston Power, 1916
Boston Proper, 334
Boston Seed Capital, 3273

Portfolio Companies Index

Boston Ship Repair, 616
Boston-Power, 805, 1361
Bot MD, 751
Botaneco, 2048, 2049
Botanical Labs, 1460
BotChain, 829
Botlex, 3171
Boto International, 2565
Bottica.com, 2972
Bottle Rock Power, 413, 1573
Bottle Rocket Power, 1895
Bottlenose, 1384, 1798, 1839
BottleRocket, 622
Bottomline Technologies, 2662
Boudless, 776
Bouffard Sanitaire Et Acier Bouffard, 2095
Boulder, 741
Boulder Ionics, 1711
Boulder Scientific Company, 1505
Boulder Ventures, 986, 3270, 3276
Bouldin Creek Distillery, 445
Boulevard, 306
Bounce, 28
Bounce Exchange, 560, 1358, 1475
BounceExchage, 533
BounceX, 235, 2239
Bouncy, 307
Bound, 1384
Boundary, 1626
Boundless, 773, 1065, 1260, 1322, 1916, 2278
Boundless Mind, 1310
Boundless Network, 202, 1685, 1810
BountyJobs, 872, 1592
Bourgeois Guitars, 1161
Bourn Hall International, 3196
Bourne Leisure, 2556, 2935
Bout'chou, 3042
Boutique La Vie En Rose, 2120
Boutique Le Pentagone, 2095
Bouxtie, 129
Bow & Drape, 150, 1757, 1912
Bow River Capital, 3276
Bow Valley BBQ, 2099
Bowater Building Products Limited, 2306
Bowater Home Improvements Limited, 2306
Bowers & Wilkins, 107
Bowery, 377, 600, 707, 728, 741, 754, 816, 889, 1110, 1282, 1589
Bowery Farming, 823
Bowlin Group, 1605
Bowman Power Group, 2760
Bowstreet, 1255
Bowtech, 1345
Bowtie, 724
Box, 124, 260, 509, 609, 665, 788, 815, 1212, 1620, 1626, 1696
Box-It, 3018
Box.Net, 925
Boxbee, 1150
Boxbot, 174, 1834
BoxC, 171, 1297, 1998
BoxCast, 1047
Boxed, 107, 318, 679, 741, 823, 871
Boxed Wholesale, 600, 1678
Boxee, 1699, 1715
Boxer, 445, 1760
Boxer Cross, 524, 1288
Boxercraft, 1569
Boxever, 2522
Boxfish, 1285
BoxFox, 1155
Boxtal, 2851
BOXX Technologies, 734
Boyd Corp., 819
Boyd Industries, 1609
Bozoka.com Sweden, 2754
Bozzetto Group, 3154

BP Express, 364
BP3, 1810
BParts, 3048
BPL Communications, 3168
BPL Global, 998, 1355
BPL Mobile Comunications, 1793
BPSC, 235
Bqteicg, 2658
Braavo, 318, 641
BRAC, 1374
Brace Industrial Gorup, 1742
BraceAbility, 1860
Bracket, 762, 1417
Bracket Computing, 84
BracNet, 602
Brad's Raw Foods, 246, 1585
Bradford Health Services, 447
Bradford Networks, 1886, 1994
Bradshaw Home, 2208
Bradshaw International, 2183
BradshawHome, 2209
Brady Enterprises, 812
Braeburn, 143, 209, 1519
Brahms, 2377
Braigo Labs, 623, 1004
Brain Corporation, 1509
Brain Sentry, 1306
Brain X, 1784
Brain.fm, 1694
Brainbees Technologies, 2849
BrainBits, 1267
BrainCells, 1412, 1786, 2970
BRAINcoBiopharma, 1452
BrainFx, 2149
BrainGEM L.L.C, 2861
Brainiac, 2296
Brainient, 2428
Brainly, 816, 3044
Brainomix, 3028
Brainpower, 2625
BrainRush, 301
Brainscape, 1632
BrainScope, 2096
BrainScope Company, 323, 1169
BrainSellers.com, 2991
BrainsGate, 2353
Brainshark, 1668, 1915
BrainSpec, 622
Brainstorm, 1070
Braintree, 28
BrainyWorks, 2347
Braitrim, 2823
Brakes Group, 220
Brami, 1110
Brammer Bio, 118
Branch, 50, 124, 306, 552, 607, 942, 972, 1138, 1158, 1176, 1611
branch, 1155
Branch Brook Holdings, 1767
Branch Messenger, 561
Branch Metrics, 1297
Branch Technology, 459
BranchOut, 44
Branchout, 1323
BranchTrack, 3108
Brand Affinity Technologies, 1237
Brand AI, 773
Brand Calculus, 2818
Brand Connections, 1927
Brand Connections LLC, 575
Brand Events Holdings, 2871
Brand Group Holdings, 413
Brand Networks, 64
Brand Thunder, 1553
Brand Yourself, 1291
Brand.net, 757
Brandable, 1121

BrandAmerica, 1784
Brandbase Holdings Inc., 461
Brandcast, 544, 1663
Branded Online, 1020
BrandFX, 746, 1744
Branding Brand, 1000
Brandless, 45, 552, 889, 1534, 1694
Brandlive, 1383, 1463
BrandMaker GmbH, 2686
Brandmuscle, 1572
BrandRapport Group, 2871
Brands4Friends, 3170
Brandscreen, 1711
BrandsforFriends.com, 1416
Brandtex Group A/S, 2712
Brandtone, 1774
Brandwatch, 1602, 2987
Brandweek Adweek, 2057
BrandYourself, 1310, 2017
Branless, 1297
Brant Instore Corp., 900
Brash Entertainment, 21
Brasilmobile, 2626
Brass Monkey, 1518
Brass Smith Innovations, 1111
Brasseler USA, 415
Brat, 1110
Brat TV, 318
Brava, 552
Bravanta, 69
Brave, 942
Brave Commerce, 2182
Brave Software, 24
Bravely, 351, 544
BraveNew Talent, 3013
Bravida, 220
Bravo Brio Restaurant Group Inc., 354
Bravo Health, 560, 782
Bravo Natural Resources LLC, 1326
Bravo Sierra, 318
Bravo Sports, 447, 1767
Bravo Target Safety, 2292
Bravo Wellness, 22
Brawler, 1846
Brawler Industries, 1777
Braxton Technologies, 925
Brayton Point Power, 675
Braze, 235, 358, 525, 560, 1212, 1563
Brazen, 1060
BRCK, 1894
BRD, 1115
BrdgAI, 800
Brdr. Sommer, 3203
Bread, 567, 1183, 1202, 1222
Breadless, 607
Break Trail Ventures, 3276
Break-Up Alert, 512
Breaker, 1965
Breaking Free, 2967
BreakingPoint Systems, 202
Breakthrough, 858, 1054, 1254, 1696
Breakthrough Energy Ventures, 3273
Breakup Goods, 1736
Breathe, 1075
Breathe for Change, 1527
Breathe Technologies, 1773
BreatheAmerica Inc., 697
Breather, 889, 1202, 1593, 1694, 2147
Breathing Buildings, 2972
Breathometer, 1749
BRECIS Communications Corporation, 252
Breedit, 3245
Breen & Carolina Color, 170
Breethe, 19
Breeze Industrial Products Corp., 985
Breeze Tecnhologies, 3229
Breezeworks, 2011

1274

Portfolio Companies Index

BreezoMeter, 2851
Breezy, 243, 679, 720, 1700
Breg, 697, 1961
Breguet, 1017
Breinify, 574
Breitenfeld, 1256
Brendmoe & Kirkestuen, 2754
Brenntaq, 220
Brentax Inc., 465
Brentwood Associates Private Equity IV LP, 2094
Brentwood Associates Private Equity V LP, 2094
Breslow & Walker LLP, 3267
Bresnan Broadband, 1506
Breveon, 1180
Brew Dr. Kombucha, 421
Brewpublik, 1585
Brewster, 858
BRG Sports, 722
BRG Sports Inc., 158
Bri-Chem Supply, 2286
Bri-Mar Manufacturing LLC, 903
Bricata, 655
Brick, 946
Brickell Biotech, 1401
Brickman Group, 2015
Brickstream, 646, 1247
Brickwood NYC, 1764
Brickwork, 60, 552, 761
Bride Story, 721
Bridea, 100
Brideside, 251
Bridg, 228, 397, 1965
Bridg. Brightfunnel, 1055
Bridge, 1226, 1240
Bridge Bank, 3259, 3262, 3276
BRIDGE Energy Group, 1886
Bridge International Academies, 1069, 1297, 1374, 1551
Bridge International Academy, 1551
Bridge Semiconductor, 998
Bridge2Solutions, 946
Bridgebio, 74
BridgeBio Pharma, 1082
Bridgefy, 981
BridgeLux, 548
Bridgelux, 596, 1906, 1922
Bridgepoint Education, 1956
Bridgepoint Medical, 1460
Bridgeport Tank Trucks, 194
Bridger, 1573
Bridger Energy Funding, 156
Bridges Ventures, 2509
Bridgespan, 1975
BridgeStream, 1461
BridgeU, 3108
BridgeWave Communications, 538, 1637
Bridgit, 2278
Bridj, 786, 1322
Brief, 101
BriefCam, 2462
Briefcam, 3245
Briefcase, 635
Brierley + Partners, 1760
Brigadier Oil & Gas, 672
Brigham Resources, 1443, 1956
Bright, 720, 741, 1758
bright box, 2938
Bright Cellars, 566, 1555
Bright Computing, 2674, 3051
Bright Edge, 1004
Bright Farms, 668
Bright Frams, 398
Bright Greens, 285
Bright Health, 560, 641, 1297, 1534
Bright Horizons, 220, 260, 1853
Bright Hub, 1008

Bright Light Systems, 794
Bright Machines, 648, 1151, 2690
Bright Now! Dental, 881
Bright Pattern, 454
Bright Peak, 1928
Bright Source, 319
Bright Tiger Technologies, 1334
Bright View Technologies, 3259
Bright.md, 1383, 1463, 1480, 1656
BrightBox, 2011
BrightBytes, 1000, 1316, 1551
BrightCloud, 1780
BrightContext, 1710
Brightcord Investment, 1769
Brightcove, 28, 922
Brightcrowd, 1323
Brightdoor, 971, 1388
BrightEdge, 235, 1000
Brightedge, 100, 976
Brighten, 120
Brighter, 634, 1184, 1796
Brighter Dental, 1832
Brightex Industries, 584
BrightFarms, 427
Brightfarms, 1324
Brightfield, 1923
BrightFlag, 2759
BrightFunnel, 114
Brightfunnel, 563
Brighthaul (Israel) Ltd., 3249
BrightHeart, 374, 1136
BrightHouse, 1937
BrightInsights, 648
Brightleaf, 776
Brightmail, 28, 933
Brightmont Academy, 1242
BrightNest, 1364
Brighton Best International, 2603
Brightpearl, 2691, 2972, 3014
BrightPet Nutrition Group, 846
BrightReasons, 2823
BrightRoll, 57, 1084, 1319, 1626, 1850, 1860
Brightside, 518, 2709
Brightside Academy, 1136, 1227, 1689
BrightSource, 609
BrightSource Energy, 466, 595, 925, 1906
Brightspace, 777
Brightspark Ventures, 3258
BrightSpring, 2209
BrightStar, 716
Brightstar Corp., 1129
Brightstorm, 1087
BrightTalk, 1334
BrightView, 1082
BrightVolt, 322
Brightware, 36
Brightwell Payments, 1280
Brightwheel, 563, 679, 823, 1149, 2137
Brightwork, 2918
Brill Street, 1364
Brill Street + Company, 452
Brille24, 2604
Brilliance Financial Technology, 654
Brilliant, 1054, 1138, 1696
Brilliant Bicycles, 325
Brilliant Telecommunications, 627
Brim, 97
brim, 2151
Bringg, 1607
Bringhub, 397
BringIt, 1655
BringMeThat, 1518
BringShare, 1553
Brinkhof Group International NV, 2828
Brinks Home Security, 473
Brintons Carpets, 413
Brio Technology, 1728

Brion, 968
Brion Technologies, 1257, 1975
Briq, 679
Briqueteries de Ploegsteert, 3134
Brisbane Materials, 1711
brisbane Materials, 1305
Brisk.io, 2637
Bristol Compressors International Inc., 1085
Bristol Farms, 673, 869
Bristol Technology, 530
Brit + Co, 1004
Brit + Co., 1926
Brit Media, 1361
Brit+Co, 1110
Brit+Co., 552
Britannia Pharmaceuticals Limited, 1452
Brite, 1346
Brite Health, 1885
Brite Semiconductor, 1010
Briter Electronics, 2975
British Columbia Investment Management Corporation, 3258
British Marine Holdings Ltd., 404
British Salt, 2944
British Telecom, 2621
BritishEco, 2760
Britt Allcroft Group, 2823
Brix Networks, 422, 455, 3137
Brixton, 96
BrizzTV, 3019
Broad Daylight, 1975
Broad Hollow Bioscience Park, 3267
Broad Oak Energy II, 672
Broad River Power, 675
Broadband Access Systems, 1334
Broadband Communications, 1180
Broadband Services, 2079
Broadbase Software, 757, 1247
Broadbus, 3137
Broadbus Technologies, 455, 1445
Broadcast Electronics, 21
Broadcast Media Group, 2951
Broadcast Pix, 1160
Broadcast.com, 922
BroadcastAmerica.com, 438
Broadcasting Partners, 1141, 1927
Broadcom, 385
BroadHop, 315, 856, 1427
Broadhorn Farm, 344
BroadJump, 202
Broadlane, 1628
BroadLight, 2655
Broadlight, 215, 3137
BroadLogic, 197, 1558, 1827
Broadly, 776, 1297
Broadnet, 2962
Broadreach, 55
BroadRiver Communications, 536
Broadsoft, 260, 455, 555, 612, 876, 986, 1212, 2639
BroadSound, 905
BroadStar Energy, 678
Broadview Network Holdings, 1297
Broadview Networks, 223
Broadview Networks Holdings, 1189
Broadview Ventures, 3273
BroadVision, 1760
Broadware Technologies, 1672
Broadway Networks, 3047
Broadway Roulette, 896
Broadxent Pte Ltd, 2508
Brocade, 933, 1121
Brocade Communications, 238, 1975
Brocase, 1247
Brock, 109
Broda Group, 2275
Broder Bros., 1491

1275

Portfolio Companies Index

Broder Brothers Co., 220
Broderbound, 563
Brodmann17, 1611, 2947
Broetje-Automation GmbH Wiefelstede, 3067
Brogea, 2632
Brom compositions, 2389
Brome Financial Corporation, 2120
Bromium, 124, 974, 1004, 1121, 1212
Bromlum, 935
Bronco Manufacturing, 565
Bronco Midstream Holdings, 156
Broncus Technologies, 269, 1241, 1975
Brook Furniture Rental, 70
Brookdale Senior Living, 767
Brookdale Senior Living Inc., 404
Brookfield Asset Management, 3255, 3258, 3261, 3264
Brookfield Real Estate & Relocation Services, 2067
Brookhaven Instruments, 235
Brooklin Concrete, 2163
Brooklinen, 622, 743
Brooks & Whittle Limited, 1557
Brooks Equipment Company, 245
Brooks Fiber Properties Inc., 1211
Brooks Instrument, 109
Brooks Service Group, 2361
Brooks24x7, 521
Brookside, 2049
Brookside Mill CLO, 1491
Brookson, 1572
Brookstone, 214, 1970
Brookstreet, 2284
Brooktree Corporation, 1918
Bros Catering, 3093
Brouwerij Bosteels, 3232
Brouwerij Martens, 2949
Brown & Joseph, 1093
Brown Advisory, 508
Brown Industries, 17
Brown Integrated Logistics, 1280
Brown Jordan International, 1134
Browntape, 3109
Browserstack, 28
Browz, 2649
BRPH Architects-Engineers, 131
Brubakken, 3076
Bruce Foods Corporation, 77
Brud, 1654
Bruha, 2138
Bruin II, 1045
Brunner Mond, 3178
Bruno Invest, 2949
Bruno Saint Hilarie, 2338
Brunswick Bowling Products, 828
Brunton, 1096
Brushstrokes, 2073
Bruxie, 1088
Bruzd Foods, 622
Bryant & Stratton College, 1417
Bryant Stibel, 3268
Bryte, 1613
BryterCX, 178
BSB, 3001
BSF/HOME, 2107
BSI2000, 1837
BSL Wood Products, 2120
BSM, 46
BSM Wireless, 2058
BSN Glasspack, 2644
BSN Medical, 2977
BSO, 21
BT Imaging, 144
BT Wood, 2612
BTC Jam, 1560
BTCC, 1121
bTendo, 2566

BTG, 21, 52
BTI Photonic Systems, 1080
BTI Studios, 413
BTI Systems, 221, 2196
BTM Company, 405
BTX Group, 1753
Bubble, 1070
Bubble Gum, 3138
Bubble Motion, 2870, 3062, 3121
Bubbles & Beyond, 2824, 2932
Bubbli, 197
Bubbly, 1407
Bubl, 981
Buchanan Ingersol & Rooney, 3275
Buckeye Cellulose Corporation, 1156
Buckeye Nutrition, 402
Buckeye Partners, 1573
Buckner Equipment Rental, 465
Buckzy, 2195
Bucyrus, 109
Budco, 830
Budding Enterprise Fund, 1135
Buddy, 85, 1839, 3051
Buddy Media, 238, 823, 1001, 1699
BuddyTV, 85
Budget Propane, 2095
BudgIT, 1374
Budhire, 391
Budnitz Bicycles, 786
BudTender, 392
Bueda, 998
Buenavision Cable TV, 869
Buffalo Coal, 1548
Buffalo Games, 1171
Buffalo Wild Wings, 1576
Buffer, 128, 229, 1640
Bug Labs, 551, 1715, 1926
Bugbuster, 3045
BugCrowd, 1400, 1416
Bugcrowd, 547, 1522, 1607
Bugsee, 1050
Bugsnag, 889
Bugukgangbyung Co., 584
build Ops, 877
Build Stream, 1894
Build-a-Bear Workshop, 1954
BuildaBrand, 2567
BuildCraft Homes, 1709
BuildDirect, 1247
BuildDirect Technologies, 2143
Builders FirstSource, 1039, 1956
Builders VC, 2032
BuildForge, 202
Building Connected, 563, 941, 1121
Building Energy, 1061, 3154
Building Engines, 1100
Building For Good, 2978
Building Material Distributors, 1970
Building Materials Holding Corporation, 1970
Building Products & Services Company, 1270
Building Robotics, 1531, 1977
Building Systems Design, 374
BuildingConnected, 243, 784, 942
BuildingDNA, 735
BuildingEngines, 377
BuildingIQ, 398, 1400, 2439
BuildLinks, 1709, 3133
BuillionVault.com, 2450
Built In, 1480
Built In Chicago, 635
BUILT Robotics, 727
Built Robotics, 858, 1297
Built Technologies, 727
Builtr Labs, 308
Bujagali Hydropower Project, 277
BuldumBuldum.com, 2437
Bulitt, 2550

Bulk Handling Systems, 374
Bulk MRO, 1768
Bull Capital Partners Pte Ltd, 3261
Bull City Forward, 3259
Bull City Venture Partners, 483
Bull Moose Capital, 2275
Bulldog, 1810
Bulldog Group, 2058
Bulldog Solutions, 1732, 1745
Bulletin, 707, 721, 754, 896, 1075
Bulletin Intelligence, 631
Bullhorn, 819, 925, 1000, 1970
BullionVault, 3040
Bullish, 3276
Bullpen Capital, 295
BuluBox, 635
Bumba, 3042
Bumble Bee Foods LP, 447
Bumble Bee Seafoods, 869, 1871
Bumblebee, 1894
Bumblebee Spaces, 1834, 1893, 1933
Bump, 1075, 1905
Bunchball, 852, 1846
BundleTech, 3040
Bundy Refrigeration, 1753
Bungalow, 622, 1069
Bunker, 518, 1721
Bunker Ex, 3108
Bunker's, 2382
Bunker's Group, 2381
Bunndle, 1254
Bureau van Dijk, 2556
Burgaflex, 276
Burgaflex Holdings, 405
Burger King, 1835
Burke America Parts Group, 405
Burke Williams, 958
Burl Software, 1008
Burlington Coat Factory, 220
Burlywood, 26
Burn Manufacturing, 55
Burner, 1798, 1916
Burning Glass, 1551
Burns e-Commerce Solutions, 2823
Burns Scalo Real Estate, 3275
Burren Energy, 2491
Burrow, 325, 1297, 1577
Burrow Global, 984
Burst, 1810
Burstly, 306, 1699, 1888, 2649
BurstPoint Networks, 1994
Burtek Enterprises, 2009
Burton Flower & Garden, 1456
Burton Saw & Supply, 1435
Bus Online, 2847
Bus.com, 302, 1024, 2184
Busaba Eathai, 3036
Busbud, 1555, 2157, 2224
Buse Industries, 399
Bush Equities dba Cuddledown, 438
Bushnell, 2379
Business & Decision, 3208
Business Advirory Service, 2796
Business Backers, 1512, 1784
Business Computer News, 214
Business Connect China, 751
Business Engine, 1255, 1975
Business Exchange, 635
Business Infusions, 2048
Business Insider, 262, 1001, 1083, 1593
Business Intelligence Advisors, 2
Business Layers, 807
Business Materis, 2375
Business Monitor International, 1717
Business Networking International, 378
Business of Fashion, 3097
Business Ready Solutions, 3259

Portfolio Companies Index

Business Search Technologies Corp., 682
Business Service Corporatiom, 3182
Business Signatures, 114, 1865
Business.com, 1001, 1733
Businessland, 260
Businessolver, 1041
Business_Doc, 2765
Buster, 1530
Bustle, 816, 1696, 1827
Bustle Digital Group, 823
busuu, 3055
Butler, 1423
Butler Schein Animal Health, 1360
Butler's Pantry, 61
Buttercoin, 2583
Butterfield Fulcrum Group, 361
Butterfly, 386, 2782
Butterfly Fields, 2313
Butterfly VLSI, 2775
Button, 38, 1222, 1346
Button Down Solutions LLC, 3267
Button Inc., 1534
Buuldcon, 3108
Buy Back Booth, 2066
Buy Properly, 2245
Buy.at, 2662
Buy.com, 500
Buyat, 2674
BuyerQuest, 732
Buyerquest, 161
Buyers Edge Platform, 333
BuyersEdge, 114
BuyerZone, 260, 521
BuyFi, 1632
BuyHappy, 493
BuySafe, 876
Buysafe, 912
buySAFE, 538
Buysight, 1378
BuySquare, 253
Buytime Media, 494
Buzz Media, 925
Buzz Points, 525, 871
Buzz Referrals, 1615
Buzz Solutions, 1286
Buzzbil, 3127
Buzzerd.com, 2976
BuzzFeed, 124, 771, 815, 922, 1110, 1593, 1699
Buzzfeed, 1297
BuzzLogic, 1975
BuzzMedia, 757
BuzzParadise, 1516
Buzzsaw.com, 1255
Buzzstarter, 625, 1965
BVG India, 2311
BVRP, 2354
BW Landco LLC, 158
BW Manufacturing, 1606
BWGS, 1753
Bwise BV, 2828
BXM Holding Company, 1491
By Humankind, 318
ByAllAccounts, 422, 521
Bybe, 1176
ByBox, 779, 2464
bydsign, 1755
Byecity.com, 3208
Byerly's, 843
Byggmax, 2384
BYJC, 2936
BYJU's, 1121
Byju's, 1392
Byliner, 206, 784
Bynder, 1000
BYNDL, 1061
Byndl, 1825
ByPay Information, 3062

Byram Healthcare, 778
Byram Holdings Inc., 572
Byrider, 96
Byrider Systems, 1491
Byte, 1473, 3154
Byte Cubed, 680
Byte Dance, 2690
Byte Foods, 171
Bytedance, 1297
ByteGain, 4
Bytegain, 1149
ByteGrid, 101
Bytelight, 756
ByteMobile, 623, 645
Bytemobile, 1850
Bytemobile Inc., 162
BytePlay, 3097
byTourexcel, 2851

C

C And Co., 351
C MAC Microtechnology, 779
C&C Energia, 2040
C&D Technologies, 1085
C&J Energy Services, 815
C&K, 1159, 1753
C&M Corporation, 1962
C&V Portable, 2255
C&W Manufacturing and Sales, 1053
C-4 Analytics, 77, 361
C-Dilla, 2380
C-guys Inc, 2414
C-K Composites Co., 1746
C-Lecta, 2824
c-LEcta, 2527
C-Mine Crib, 2949
C-P Flexible Packaging, 733
C-Platform, 1340
C-Port, 260, 3137
C-Port Corporation, 314
C-Pro, 1769
C-sATS, 773
C-Side, 3048
C-Takt AB, 2718
C. Light Technologies, 622
C.B. Fleet Laboratories, 881
C.H.I. Overhead Doors, 168, 413
C.R.O.I., 2095
C.R.S/Vamic, 2095
C/R Energy Jade, 1573
C10 Connect, 3259
C1X, 148
C2 Micro, 2593
C2 Microsystems, 2566
C2 SmartLight Oy, 2966
C2 Therapeutics, 598, 1773
C2Call, 2824
C2cube, 2974
C2F, 730
C2FO, 486, 2259
C2RO, 2128
C3 Energy, 532, 1010, 1760
C3 IoT, 336
C3 Metrics, 1306
C3.ai, 1985
C3/CustomerContactChannels, 1743
C360, 293, 298
C360 Live, 1657
C4 Distro, 99
C7, 1677
C7 Data Centers, 1070, 1189
C8 Sciences, 1097
C9, 1010, 1184
CA Customer Alliance, 2824
Caarbon, 707, 1050, 1416
CaaScade, 1885
CaaStle, 1666

Caavo, 872, 922
Caavo Inc, 1095
Cabaletta Bio, 12
CABB, 3033
Cabela's, 433
Cabi, 1037
Cabify, 1531, 1998, 3105
Cabinet M, 841
CabinetM, 1100, 1757
Cable Management Ireland, 1927
Cable Sense, 2295
CableMatrix, 3231
CableOrganizer, 405
Cables Ben-Mor, 2095
Cabo Telecom, 46
Cabochon Aesthetics, 1493
Cabovisao, 2073
Cabrellis Pharmaceuticals, 769, 1574
Cacafly, 3038
Cacao De Colombia, 55
Cache IQ, 445
Cactus Commerce, 2095, 2120
Cadant, 1057
Cade (Dental Care), 3180
Cadena Bio, 747
Cadence, 1081, 1554, 1928
Cadence Aerospace, 166
Cadence Aerospace LLC, 158
Cadence Biomedical, 85
Cadence Capital Management, 1275
Cadence Pharmaceuticals, 237, 782, 1786, 2496
Cadent, 3137
Cadent Technologies, 1628
Cadent Therapeutics, 191
Cadforce, 306, 362, 1915
Cadia Networks, 1334
Cadient Group, 655
Cadiogen Sciences, 181
Cadmus, 680
Cadre, 124, 142, 816, 842, 1069, 1694
Cadre Technologies, 315
CadrioDx, 1412
Caelux Corporation, 1069
Caerphilly, 1340
CAES Development Company, 893
Caesars Entertainment, 140, 869, 2379
Cafe Communications, 1004
Cafe Costume, 3042
Cafe Enterprises, 1234
Cafe Express, 1549
Cafe Faro, 2120
Cafe Media, 935
Cafe Nero, 2362
Cafe Press, 2829
Cafe Rio, 783
Cafe X, 994
CafeMedia, 21
Cafepress, 1654
CafeX Communications, 483, 976
Caffe Bene, 3002
Caffeine, 124, 872
Cagenix, 995
CAI, 3259
CAI Capital Partners, 3258
CAIA Association, 3285
Caiman Energy II, 671
Cairn Ventures, 3279
Caisse de Depot et Placement du Quebec, 3261
Caisse de depot et placement du Quebec, 3258
Caithness Energy, 156
Cake, 79, 1070
Cake Financial, 231
Cake Marketing, 69
CakeStyle, 1615
Cal Pacific, 1997
Cala Health, 107, 1151
Calabrio, 1082, 1725, 3279

1277

Portfolio Companies Index

Caladrius Biosciences, 1271
CalAmp, 1239
Calan, 1227
Calastone, 28, 3018
Calchan Holdings, 1298, 1628
CalciMedica, 1616, 1731
Caldan Therapeutics, 689
Caldwell & Gregory, 415
Calectro, 2602
Calednra, 3113
Caledonia Spirits, 786
Caledonian Building Systems Ltd., 2677
Caleel and Hayden, 1491
Calendly, 189, 981
Calendra, 3208
Calera, 925, 1069, 1558
Calero, 500
Calgary Scientific, 2048
Cali Bamboo, 931
Caliber Collision, 1109, 2207, 2219
Caliber Infosolutions, 998, 1448
Calibra Medical, 782, 1008
Calibrium, 12, 782
Calico Commerce, 1975
Calico Energy Services, 247, 1458
Calidora, 753
Calient Networks, 1793, 1975
Calient Technologies, 432, 1474
Calient Technologies Inc., 810
California Bank of Commerce, 506
California Check Cashing Stores, 839
California Comfort Corp., 908
California Cryobank, 1143
california Cryobank, 1349
California Cryobank Life Sciences, 824
California Gold Inc., 2122
California Linear Devices, 1918
California Manufacturing Enterprises, 869
California Medical Evaluators, 443
California Pizza Kitchen, 405, 839
California Pizza Kitchen Inc., 354, 403
California Power, 1967
California Safe Soil, 3277
California Trusframe, 2275
Caliopa, 2476, 3042
Caliper Life Sciences, 153, 153
Calista Technologies, 1121, 1975
Calistoga, 112, 782, 1094
Calistoga Pharma, 94
Calistoga Pharmaceuticals, 1445
Calithera, 1122, 1238
Calithera Biosciences, 59, 604, 1145, 1298, 1896
Calix, 215, 536, 770, 1003, 1072, 1725, 1793
Calix Networks, 1975
Calixa Therapeutics, 782
Call Connect, 536
Call My Name, 386
Call Rail, 282
Call-Net Enterprises Inc., 2073
Call2Action, 1697
Call9, 858, 1054
CallApp, 1759
Callaway Golf, 1896
Callbritannia, 2539
CallConnect Communications, 765
Callcredit Information Group, 884, 2379
Callery, 653
CallFire, 1255
CallGate, 626
Callidus, 1911
Callidus Capital Corporation, 2073
Callidus Software, 1378
Calligo, 1017
Calliper, 206
CallMiner, 979, 990, 1008, 1672, 1673
Callpod, 338, 338
CallRail, 387, 1602

CallRecall, 2526
Callserve, 2577
Callsign, 84
Callsign Inc, 28
Callstream, 3244
CallTime, 934
CallTower, 333
Calm, 1000
CalmImmune, 1519
CalmSea, 976
CalNet Technology Group, 378
Calo, 949
Calon Cardio, 2737
Calorics, 1460
Calosyn Pharma, 362, 1187
CalPeak Power, 413
CalPERS, 3261
Calpine Co., 2073
Calpine Corporation, 675
Calpulli Inc, 3178
Calsonic Kansei, 1082
Calstar, 1355
Calstar Products, 398, 1977
CalSTRS, 3261
Calsys, 2936
Caltex Resources, 1278, 1326
Calumet Energy, 1795
CalUniversity, 3215
Calupso Medical, 237
Calvert Education Serices, 508
Calvert Education Services, 1299
Calvert Healthcare Partners, 406
Calvet, 2883
Calvin Capital, 1082
Caly Networks, 3118
Calypso Medical Technologies, 1002, 1241, 1574, 2496
Calypso Technology, 1970
Calypte, 1915
Calypte Biomedical, 1786
Calypto, 968
Calypto Design Systems Inc., 1779
Calysta, 2213
Calysta Energy Inc., 1951
Calyx, 963, 1135, 1630
Calyx Therapeutics, 1412
Calyx Transportation Group, 2009
Cam-Trac Sag-Lac, 2095
Camber, 1301
Camber Creek, 3270
Cambium Learning Group, 1925, 1927
Cambium Networks, 1910
Cambly, 889, 1749, 3125
Cambria Security, 1038
Cambrian BioPharma, 800
Cambrian Genomics, 1531, 1798, 1998
Cambrian Intelligence, 724
Cambridge, 3215
Cambridge Associates LLC, 3261
Cambridge Biotechnology, 2463
Cambridge Blockchain, 567, 1100
Cambridge Broadband, 2779
Cambridge Broadband Networks, 2342
Cambridge CMOS Sensors, 3028
Cambridge Cognition, 3244
Cambridge Display, 986
Cambridge Epigenetix, 889
Cambridge Heart, 1255
Cambridge International Inc., 985
Cambridge Major Laboratories, 166
Cambridge Medical & Rehabilitation Center, 3196
Cambridge Positioning Systems, 162, 2380, 2662
Cambridge Positioning Systems Limited, 3118
Cambridge Semiconductor, 3195
Cambridge Silicon Radio, 2386, 2662, 3118
Cambridge Solutions, 3262

Cambridge Sound Management, 828
Cambridge Wowo, 1509
CambridgeSoft, 655
Cambrios, 87, 184, 206, 1474
Cambrios Technology, 153, 979
Cambrooke Therapeutics, 806
Cambus Medical, 2355
Came Automatismes, 2653
CAMECA, 2565
Camelback Ventures Fellowship Program, 1316
Camelbak, 523
Camelot Education, 1572
Cameo, 679, 858, 1384, 1480
Cameo Communications, 2508
Camera IQ, 50, 1473, 1663
CameraIQ, 342
Camero, 3231
Cameron Health, 136, 1445, 1500, 1574, 1706, 1975, 2496, 2728, 2890
Cameron's Coffee & Distribution Co., 843
Camiant, 1334
Camile Products, 1336
Camillion Solutions, 2196
Camino Modular Systems, 1557
Camino Natural Resources, 1278
Camio, 751, 1101
Camiocam, 784
Camoplast Solideal, 2095, 2120
Camp, 1110
CAMP Systems, 884, 2698
CAMP Systems International, 361
Camp4, 124
Campaign, 1150
Campaign Monitor, 1000, 2266
Campaignmonitor, 28
Campalyst, 2822
Campanda, 2475, 2851
Campania International, 1521
Campbell Grinder Company, 830
Campfire, 392
CampGroup, 373, 374
Camping World Holdings, 559
Campolo Middleton & McCormick LLP, 3267
Campsystems, 2697
Campus Book Rentals, 462
Campus Energy, 2062
Campus Explorer, 306, 1364, 1566
Campus Founders Fund, 1070
Campus Management, 1105
Campuslogic, 883
CampusTap, 638
Camras Vision, 737
Camsavon, 2889
CamSemi, 2295, 2662, 2674, 3104
CAMSIE Leasing, 1764
Camstar, 856
Camtainer, 2889
Camus Hydronics Ltd., 908
CaméRus, 3020
Can Art Aluminum Extrusion, 2204, 2272
Can Capial, 1502
CAN Capital, 1212, 1560
Can Capital, 28
Can-Do National Tape, 932, 1570
Can-Fite BioPharma, 1452, 3249
Canaan Partners, 3284
Canada Film Capital, 2218
Canada Metal (Pacific), 2163
Canada Metal Pacific, 327
Canada Moteurs Importations, 2120
Canada Pension Plan Investment Board, 3258
Canada Pooch Ltd., 354
Canadia Solar, 3062
Canadian Appliance Source, 2292
Canadian Bureau of Investigations & Adjustments, 2196
Canadian Business Growth Fund, 3258

Portfolio Companies Index

Canadian Forestry Equipment, 2286
Canadian Helicopters, 2120
Canadian National Stock Exchange, 2058
Canadian Northern Outfitters, 2168
Canal Guyane, 2897
Canal Partners, 3276
Canal Web, 2765
Canal+, 223, 1596
Canalyst, 2278
Canam, 109
Canamax Energy, 2025
Canapar, 2071
Canara, 515
Canary, 351, 1306, 1874
Canary Connect Inc., 1069
Canary Medical, 2229, 2237
CanAscen Group, 1864
CANBank, 2266
CanBas, 2970
CanBiocin, 2048
Canbriam Energy, 1956, 2040
Cancer Advances Inc., 430
Cancer Targeting Systems, 2978
CancerVax, 1975
Candela, 135, 1058
Candera, 187
Candex, 1226
Candid Co., 641
Candidate Labs, 318
Candis, 1121
Candlescience, 3259
Cando Rail Services, 2272
Candor Midstream, 671
Candy Club, 972
CandyClub, 561
Candyking, 2325
CanEra Resources, 1573
Canes., 2565
CanGen, 461
CanGen Holdings, 1343
Canimix, 3170
CanImGuide, 2449
Canmec Group, 2095
Cann Trust Direct, 2094
Canna Zoning, 392
Cannabinit, 2845
Cannabis Big Data, 392, 2287
Cannabis Mercantile Trading Exchange, 2845
Cannabis Now, 1843
Cannabix Technologies, 2031
Cannactrl, 392
Cannalysis, 417
CannaPharmaRx, 1079
CannaRoyalty Corp., 1135
Cannasure, 963
CannaSys Inc., 1079
Canndescent, 99, 1207
Cannect Communications, 1837
Cannell Communications LP, 1621
Cannella Media, 1403
Cannella Response Television, 1927, 2020
Cannera Consulting, 2100
CannLabs, 1135
CannRx Technology Inc., 2845
CannTrust Holdings, 390
Canon Communications, 1927
Canopy, 600, 688, 858, 971, 1181, 1297, 3259
Canopy at Belford Park, 1219
Canopy Biosciences, 267
Canopy Boulder, 1135
Canopy Labs, 1897, 2125
Canopy Servicing, 318
Canotic, 1499
CanPro Ingredients, 2285
Canstar Restorations, 2126
Cantaloip, 770
Cantaloupe Systems, 834

Cantex Pharmaceuticals, 621
Canto, 192
Canva, 720, 1181, 1663, 2520
Canvas, 377, 1380, 1387, 1571, 1813
Canvas Technology, 107
Canvaspop, 2076
Canvass, 2232
Canvia, 62
Canvs, 52, 1150, 1595
Canvs+, 1958
Canwest, 2073
Canyon Services Group, 2040
CAP (Children at Play) Toys, 1954
Cap Energie II, 3134
Cap Vert Finance, 2448
Cap Vert Finance SA, 413
cap-XX, 2877
Capa Finance, 2471
Capchase, 318
Cape, 1158, 1297
Cape Analytics, 1151
Cape By The Sea, 2120
Cape byron Power, 1517
Cape Clear, 2336
Cape Electrical Supply, 1765
Cape Energy, 2772
Cape Pine Investment Holdings, 834
Cape Productions, 2011
Capell Barnett Matalon & Schoenfeld, 3267
Capella, 275, 622, 764, 826
Capella Education, 1183
Capella Education Company, 1608
Capella Photonics, 1604
Capella Space, 107
Capella Space Inc., 174
Caper, 795
Caperfly, 2967
Capevo, 3203
Capewell Aerial Systems, 164
Capewell Holdings, 1021
Capical, 2824
Capillary, 1346
Capillary Technologies, 1509
Capio, 243, 2379
Capio Exploration, 2040
Capitain D's, 716
Capital, 800
Capital Bank Financial, 559
Capital Biochip Corporation, 2499
Capital Community Angels Investors, 3269
Capital Consulting, 2795
Capital Contractors Inc., 1403
Capital Drywall, 838
Capital Dynamics, 3261
Capital Economics, 2944
Capital Education Group, 1348
Capital Farm Credit, 16
Capital First Limited, 1956
Capital Nature, 3059
Capital Pawn, 403
Capital SLI Group, 1288
Capital Sports Holdings, 716
Capital Sports Ventures, 1766
Capital Stream, 247, 1945
Capital Teaching Residency, 1316
Capital Tool & Design, 1505
Capital Vision Services, 2034, 2046
Capital-E, 3042
CapitalLand, 152
CapitalSource, 787, 1156, 1587
CapitalSouth Partners, 3262
Capitol Broadcasting Company, 3259
Caplinked, 1958, 1965
Caplugs, 258
CapMAC, 1621
CapMAC Holdings, 1769
Capnamic Ventures, 483

Capnia, 1941, 2369
Cappella, 1241, 3046
Capria Ventures LLC, 3261
Capricoast, 28
Capricor, 347
Capricorn, 2949
Capricorn Cleantech Co-Investments, 3069
Caprion Proteomics, 468, 859
Capriza, 124, 455
CapRock Holdings, 21
Caprotec, 2638
Caps Visual Communications, 1881
Capsa Healthcare, 1111
Capsa Solutions, 1232
Capsalus, 707
Capsant, 2892
Capshare, 1070
Capsilon, 779
Capson, 1615
Capston Logistics, 1491
Capstone, 1045, 3137
Capstone Logistics, 853, 1270
Capstone Natural Resources II, 1125
Capstone Turbine, 1355
Capstone Turbine Corporation, 1558
Capsugel, 909
Capsule, 1041
Capsulution NanoScience AG, 3190
Captain Dash, 2899
Captain Ed's Lobster Trap, 1213
Captain Tortue Group, 1088
Captain Up, 3081
Captain401, 858
Captalis, 2752
Captek Softgel, 1469
Captini, 3108
Caption Data, 2967
Caption Health, 4
Captiv8, 1883
Captivate Network, 818
Captive Resources, 1104
Captor N.V., 2902
Captora, 221
Captricity, 38, 1054, 1696
Captronic Systems, 2469
Captura Software, 1728, 1945
Capture Education, 1553
Capture.io, 661
Capula, 2537, 2538
CapWay, 218
CapX Partners, 3265
Car 2 U, 3012
Car Dekho, 578
Car IQ, 226
Car King, 222, 2936
Car Quids, 3108
Car Wash Partners, 260
Cara Health, 1615
Cara Therapeutics, 177, 530, 1558, 2981
Cara Vita, 1002
Caralo Global, 1047
Caraustar, 1967
Caraustar Industries, 928
Caravan Health, 1927
Carbon, 302, 358, 809, 889, 1654
Carbon 38, 508, 1613
Carbon Black, 38, 70, 935, 942, 1181, 1654
Carbon Cure, 2142
Carbon Design, 1181
Carbon Design Systems, 521
Carbon Health, 1028, 1613
Carbon Media Group, 1242
Carbon Robotics, 1101, 1509
Carbon38, 896, 1998
Carbon60, 1153
Carbonated, 2137
CarbonCure, 2213

1279

Portfolio Companies Index

Carboncure, 2155
Carbonfire, 319
Carbonite, 563, 777, 1734, 1838
Carbonite Inc., 1202
Carbylan Biosurgery, 1010
Carbylan Therapeutics, 1941
Carchex, 190
Card, 120
Card Compliant, 1764
Card Establishment Services, 541, 1972
Card Personalization Solutions, 669
Card.com, 132, 179, 1502, 1546, 1965
CarDash, 720
Cardax, 1002
Cardax Pharmaceuticals, 61, 1011, 1786
Cardconnect, 793
Cardeas Pharma, 206, 604, 2008
Cardenas, 1082
Cardero, 347
Cardeus Pharmaceuticals, 1241
CardFlight, 724, 858, 1178
Cardia Access, 1872
Cardiac Dimensions, 136, 1010, 1460, 2180, 2970
Cardiac Insight, 2008
Cardiac Pathways, 1255
CardiaLen, 347
Cardialen, 267, 569, 1872
Cardiapex, 2324
CardiAQ, 1382
CardiAQ Valve, 347
CardiAQ Valve Technologies, 1928
Cardica, 560, 1760, 1975
Cardiff Software, 852
Cardikine, 2079
Cardinal Business Media Inc., 334
Cardinal Commerce, 831, 1476
Cardinal Gas Storage Partners, 675
Cardinal Medical Ltd, 3186
Cardinal Midstream III, 671
Cardinal Power Funding, 156
Cardinal Resources, 3277
Cardio 3 Biosciences, 3134
Cardio Dimensions, 149
Cardio Focus, 1975
Cardiocomm Solutions Inc, 2097
Cardiocore, 136
CardioCreate, 1784
CardioDX, 181, 634, 1143, 1247
CardioDx, 581
Cardiodx, 2540
CardioFocus, 40, 314, 749, 1058, 1604, 1628, 1762
Cardiogram, 124
CardioInsight, 1047
CardioInsight Technologies Inc., 420
Cardiokine Biopharma, 74
CardioKinetix, 1112, 1410, 1896, 1915
Cardiokinetix, 1298
CardioKinetix Inc., 572
Cardiologs, 2851
Cardiome Pharma, 1394
CardioMEMS, 312, 748
Cardiomems, 136, 644
Cardiometrics, 85
CardioNet, 748, 1616
Cardionomic, 1297
CardioNOW, 1975
CardioPhotonics, 1097
Cardiosolutions, 270
CardioSolv Ablation Technologies, 886
CardioSpectra, 514
Cardiovascular Systems, 1241
CardiOx, 1553
Cardiox, 642
Cardioxyl, 1382
Cardioxyl Pharmaceuticals, 1297

Cardium, 530
Cardiva, 806
Cardiva Medical, 117, 905, 1500, 1769, 1975, 3192
Cardlife, 3108
Cardlytics, 386, 1072, 1460, 1863
Cardmobil, 3031
CardonetCommtouch, 3249
Cardoz, 2748
Cardoz AB, 2816
Cardpool, 784, 858
CardScan, 521
CardSpring, 585
Cardspring, 28, 1254
CardStar, 51, 119, 1097, 1926
Carduus, 2539
Cardvalue, 3215
CardZee, 1681
Care, 1832
Care Concepts, 1837
Care Hospice, 1166
Care Hospice Inc., 158
Care Kinesis, 1385
Care Management Technologies, 474, 691
Care Services LLC, 1293
Care Thread, 1693
Care Wave, 870
Care Well Urgent Care, 544
Care.com, 560, 578, 1001, 1181, 1853, 2829, 2838
Care/of, 842
Care2, 1733
Care2.com, 378
Care4Data NV, 2806
CareAcademy, 218, 1551
CareAngel, 3262
Careanyware, 1148
CareCap, 1061
CareCentrix, 909, 1615, 1752, 1961
CareCloud, 57, 1004, 1346, 1796
CareCru, 2266
CareCycle Solutions, 984
Caredent, 1088
Caredox, 741
CareDx, 1003
Caredx, 1298
Careem, 91, 509
Career Choices, 1139, 2946
Career Education, 300
Career JSM, 2284
Career Now, 981
Career Point Infosystems, 584
Career Rewards, 1227
CareerBuilder, 1405
CareerFoundry, 2841
Careerminds, 150
CareerStep, 746
CareerTu, 1138
Carefree, 442
CareFusion, 300
CareFx, 856
Carefx, 142, 1702
CareGain, 52, 989, 1227, 1314
Caregiver Inc., 550
Caregiver Services, 405, 1498
Carego, 2043
CareGuide, 2157, 2224
CareHubs, 1615
CareIT, 995
Carekinesis, 1520
Careland International, 3093
Careline, 202
Caremerge, 171, 809, 1000
CareMore Health, 433
Carena, 753
CareNet, 892
CarePartners Plus, 266

CarePoint Health, 405
CarePoint Partners, 1963
CarePort, 231, 792
Careport Health, 313
CarePredict, 3262
Careray, 2936
CareSimply, 1615
CareSouth Health System, 406
CareSpot Express Healthcare, 1972
Carestack, 28
Carestream, 2209
Caresync, 904
Caretaker Medical, 1019
Careteam, 2223
CareWell Urgent Care, 474, 1844
CareWire, 1615
CareWise, 1398
CareWorx, 2224
CareX, 2781
Carex Health Brands, 1209
CareZone, 1297, 1363
Carezone, 428
Carfit, 249
Cargal, 2609
Cargo, 472, 607, 1006, 1547, 1585
Cargo Airport Services, 443, 1491
Cargo Airport Services USA, 969
Cargo Chief, 129
CargoGuard, 2824, 2932
Cargomatic, 1254, 1749, 1876, 1998
CargoSense, 1019, 1229
CargoTech, 898, 1784
CargoX, 1509
CarHop, 92
Caribbean Restaurants, 423, 1360
Caribe, 1244
Caribeean Restaurants, 1505
Caribore Coffee, 152
Caribou Biosciences, 710, 1238
CariHeal, 2324
Carillion, 949
Caring Brands International, 894, 1111
Caring People, 465
Caring.com, 596, 1663, 1725
Caringo, 202, 1303
Caris Life Sciences, 1037
Carl Bro, 2888
Carl Data Solutions, 2031
Carl Zeiss Vision GmbH, 2712
Carlease, 1118
Carlile Bancshares, 1104, 1743
Carlipa Systems, 2855
carlisle Wide Plank Floors, 1040
Carloan 4U, 3104
Carlson Products, 1053
Carlton Corporate Finance, 2732
Carlyle Asia Partners III LP, 2094
Carmel Pharma, 2728
Carmel Ventures, 3118
Carmell Therapeutics, 293, 907, 998, 1448
Carmen Systems, 2779, 2878
Carmera, 889, 1222
Carmichael Training Systems, 810
Carmody MacDonald, 3271
Carmot Therapeutics, 517
Carna Biosciences, 2970
Carnegie, 2384
Carnegie Fabrics, 368
Carnegie Mellon University, 3275
Carnegie Speech, 979, 1306
Carnegie Speech Company, 998
Carnival Mobile, 317
Carnot, 1519
Carolina Beverage Group LLP, 357
Carolina Skiff, 1523
Carolus Therapeutics, 206
Caroobi, 302

1280

Portfolio Companies Index

Carousel Capital, 1871
Carousell, 2690
CarPark, 2537, 2538
Carparts/ADN, 1558
Carpathia Hosting, 1724
CarPay, 120
Carpe, 1595
CarPrice, 89, 641
CarProof, 924
Carr Separations/Kendro Lab Products, 1103
Carre Blanc, 2965
Carrefour, 2614
Carrere Group, 2544
Carrick Therapeutics, 889
Carrier Access Corporation, 212
Carrier Energy Partners, 1573
Carrier IQ, 1247, 1474
CarrierChoice.com, 1227
Carriere Neigette, 2120
CarrierIQ, 455, 2987
Carroll Cuisine, 413
Carrosserie Pro 2010, 2120
Carrot, 218
Carrot Fertility, 707
Carrot Inc., 1069
Carrum Health, 1458, 1985
CARS, 1988
Carsabi, 585
Carsablanca, 2475
Carsala, 1097
Carsala Inc., 1089
CarServ, 1507
CARsgen Therapeutics, 1087
Carson, 3255
Carson Life, 566, 2001
CARSTAR, 1576
Carstar, 693
Carta, 1202, 1329, 1613, 1696, 1848, 3276
Carta Finana, 3203
Carta Worldwide, 2168
Cartagenia, 3042
Cartasite, 274
Cartavi, 471, 731, 1364, 1458, 1480
CartCrunch, 2943
Cartegraph, 1409
Carter Haston JV, 1082
Carter's, 1017
Carter-Waters, 1209
Cartera Commerce, 528, 580, 1920
Cartes Networks, 288
Cartesis, 1416, 2348
Carthage Agricultural Company, 2329
Carthage Specialty Paperboard, 1422
CarThrottle, 3030
Cartica AI, 1834
Cartica Management LLC, 3261
Carticept Medical, 621, 1297
Cartier Resouces, 2120
Cartiere del Garda, 2644, 2883
CartiHeal, 2328
Cartiva, 94, 621, 1993
Carto, 28, 1607
Cartodb, 3223
Cartogram, 226, 1507
Cartonplast Group, 3154
CarTrade, 386
Cartrawler, 1000
Carvel, 1576
Carvoyant, 1734
CarWale, 3109
Carwoo, 301
Carwoo!, 2329
Carwow, 28, 2478, 3097
Cary Street Partners, 3259
Caryl Baker Visage, 2045
CAS Medical Systems, 1817
Casa, 525, 1110, 2539

Casa Madera, 331
Casa Systems, 1752
Casabella Holdings, 2022
Casabu, 2871
Casamba, 21
Casavant Brothers, 2120
Casavo, 2296
Cascade, 1604
Cascade Bancorp, 1109, 1123
Cascade Drilling LP, 667
Cascade Entertainment Group, 492
Cascade Pacific Pulp, 1967
Cascade Prodrug, 1383
Cascade Sensior Living, 1082
Cascade Windows, 96
Cascadia Windows & Doors, 2238
Cascadian Therapeutics, 1297
Casda Biomaterials, 220
Case Continuum, 1097
Case Logic, 1086
Case Text, 563
CaseCentral, 949, 1733
Casella, 2348
Casemaker, 1720
CaseNET, 1672
Casentric, 1047
Casero, 162
CaseStack, 301, 494, 1784
Casetext, 318, 1530, 1758
Cash Cycle Solutions, 263
Cash Management Solutions, 1343
Cash River, 3062
CashEdge, 2079
Cashie Commerce, 1784
CashShield, 823
CashStar, 793, 1339
Casi, 984
Casimir Partners, 557
Casino Royal, 3232
Casino VR Poker, 307
Cask, 974
Casnov@, 2439
Casper, 544, 563, 1001, 1110, 1297, 1346, 1480, 1694
Caspida, 741, 1534
CAST, 2544
Cast, 2662, 2851
Cast & Crew, 21, 1683, 1927, 2020
Cast Futura, 3154
Cast Iron, 1911
CAST Software, 2043
Cast Steel Products, 2292
Cast21, 995
Castel Portfolio, 1082
Castell Oil Company, 1326
Castex Energy, 477
CastGrabber, 998, 1440
Castify Networks, 2380
Castion Corp., 588
CastIron, 1796
Castle, 741
Castle Biosciences, 921, 1261, 1722
Castle Connolly, 847
Castle Networks, 260
Castle Pines Capital, 793
Castlebeck, 2823
Castlecare, 2795
Castlefield, 190
Castlerock, 1326
Castlerock Exploration, 1278
Castlewood Surgical, 3277
Castlight, 20
Castlight Health, 1896, 1916
Castro Cheese, 1403
CastStack, 807
Casual Living and Trigon Plastics, 164
Casugel, 2379

CAT Forsknings-og Teknologipark, 2651
Catabasis, 1122, 1196, 1628, 1762
Catabsis, 59, 495
Catacel, 1047
Catalant, 809, 816
Catalent, 74
Catalia Health, 24, 799, 942
Catalina, 909, 924
Catalist, 1584
Catalliances, 2466
Catalog, 107, 395, 1297
Catalog DNA, 219
Catalog Technologies, 1421
Catalyst, 525, 793
Catalyst Biosciences, 919, 1122, 1543, 1698
Catalyst Clinical Research, 1349
Catalyst Law Group, 3276
Catalyst Oncology, 1915
Catalyst Orthosience, 1019
Catalyte, 1606
Catalytic, 305, 770, 1118, 1297, 1480
Catalytic Solutions, 1324, 1474
Catalyze.io, 471
Catamaran, 1747, 1793
Catamaran Communications, 1975
Catapult, 1326
Catapult Growth, 3276
Catapult Health, 918
Catapult Learning, 413, 1041
Catapult Services, 1278
CatapultX, 1507
Catari, 3048
Catastrophe Solutions International, 529
Catavolt, 496, 718, 1829
Catawiki, 28, 3056
Catch, 703, 877, 1655, 1893
Catchafire, 1054, 1552
CatchApp, 2921
Catchpoint Systems, 235
Catellus, 1835
Catena Networks, 252, 1257
Caterna, 2824
Caterplus, 3244
Cath Kidston, 1776
Cathay Capital NA LLC, 3258
Cathay Industrial Biotech, 2815
Cathay Industrial Biotech Ltd., 1297
Cathbuddy, 622
Catherines, 1017
Catheter Connections, 138, 1070, 1884
Catheter Innovations, 1706
Catheter Robotics, 1375
CathRx, 2618
CathWorks, 2229
CathWorks Ltd., 269
Catlant, 935
Catlight Health, 1361
Catlin, 456, 575
Catlin Group Limited, 404
Catlin Westgen Group, 447
Cato Networks, 49, 180, 872
Cattle Care, 1138
Cattlog, 995
Cattron Group, 1557
Causes, 115, 1975
Cava, 1766
Cavale Steel Company, 2949
Cavalia, 2095
Cavalier Fire Protection LLC, 1562
Cavalier Telephone, 746, 1153
Cavalry Investments, 1970
Cavario, 631
Cavendish Kinetics, 1509, 1779
Caveon, 1915
Cavidi Tech AB, 2728, 2890
Cavion, 1124, 1350
Cavium Networks, 613, 1540

1281

Portfolio Companies Index

Cawnetworks, 933
CAXA Technology, 2850
Cayenna Medical, 1725
Cayenne Medical, 749, 1187
Caymas Systems, 798
Caymas Systemts, 1975
Cazena, 124
CB News, 2607
CB Richard Ellis Services, 783
Cbana Labs, 975
cbanc Network, 57
Cbazaar, 1013, 3019
CBD Tech Ltd, 2585
Cbeyond, 57, 1156
Cbeyond Communications, 1906
Cbeyond Inc., 224
CBI (ARTE), 2609
CBI Health Group, 2082, 2207, 2219, 2292
CBIT, 3203
CBIZ, 3262
CBR, 2605
CBRE Group, 300
CBRE Group Inc., 1903
CBS Payroll Services, 1770
CBT Technologies, 164
CBT Technology, 1557
CBx, 2149
Cc:Betty, 1655
CCA Floors & Interiors, 698
CCAM Biotherapeutics, 1382
CCapture, 2892
CCBN, 36
CCC, 1017
CCC Information Services, 1109, 1835
CCC Information Services Inc., 62
CCD Holdings, 1279
CCELP Holding, 553
CCI Telecom, 734
CCID, 2936
CCIG, 3276
cClearly, 1563
CCM Benchmark, 2851
CCM Hockey, 2062
CCM Pharma Sdn Bhd, 3164
CCMP Capital Advisors, 3255
CCMX, 2415
Ccmx, 2721
Ccobox, 24
CCPI Holdings, 1491
CCS, 1964, 2033, 2079
CCS Medical, 1086
CCTM, 3194
CD Diagnostics Inc., 269
CD Dignostics, 1940
CD Networks, 2857
CD Park, 2857
CDC, 2375
CDG, 823, 2579
CDI Computer Dealers, 2089
CDIM, 2936
CDIm FMI, 66
CDM MAX LLC, 413
CDM Resource Management, 1573
CDNow, 876
CDP, 2733
CDS, 933
CDS Outsourcing, 3259
CDW, 1156, 1496
CDX, 1135
CE LA VI, 1088
CE Rental, 443
CE2 Carbon Capital, 675
Ceapro, 2048
Cebix, 1010, 1698, 1817, 2816
Cecilware, 739
CEDA, 2207
Cedar Capital, 793, 1136

Cedar Creek, 456
Cedar Electronics, 405
Cedar Gate Technologies, 884
Cedar Point Communications, 455, 757, 3137
CedarCrestone, 2361
Cedarcrestone, 839
CedarPoint Communications, 184
Cedarpoint Investments, 3258
CeDe Group, 2755
Cedexis, 59
Cedip Infared Systems, 2383
Cedrepa, 2620
CEEK VR, 218
CeeQTM, 3153
CEFIC, 3178
Cegeka, 2949
Cegelec Holdings, 2587
CEGX, 1303, 1654
CEI Coastal Ventures III, 1160
Ceipal, 2195
CEL LEP, 928
CEL Polska, 526
CEL Procurement, 2944
Cel.ly, 1463
CelAccess, 445
Celarix, 202, 1003
Celaton, 2550
Celator Pharma, 1271
Celator Pharmaceuticals, 621, 1508, 1817, 1828, 1898
Celco, 3203
Celco Controls, 931
Celcore, 260
Celcuity, 341
CelebrateExpress.com, 153
Celebration Restaurant Group, 1344
Celebrity Inc., 1086
Celect, 796
Celectis, 2354
Celemi, 2888
Celeno, 483
Celentail.ai, 994
Celequest, 1121
Celera, 747
Celerica, 3137
Celerion, 221, 1628
Celerion Holdings, 1271
Celeris AG, 2427
Celeritek, 1760
Celerity Pharmaceuticals, 1961
Celero Accelerated Commerce, 1136
Celery, 307
Celestial Semiconductor, 2508, 2597
Celestial Tiger Entertainment, 1598
Celestica, 2209
Celestite, 96
Celestry, 2853
Celetronix, 839
Celevity, 318
Celexion, 747
Celgen Biopharmaceutical Co., 2593
Celi APS, 3049
Celiant, 1305
Celight & Blade fusion, 3159
Celilo Group Media, 85
Celions, 28
Cell Based Delivery, 2748
Cell Biologics, 1087
Cell Biosciences, 3015
Cell Co., 58
Cell Design Labs, 1238
Cell Medica, 2858
Cell Microsystems, 737
Cell Networks, 2769
Cell Pathways, 1786
Cell Ventures, 2769
CellAccess, 260

Celladon, 1268, 1436, 1916
CellAegis, 347
Cellaegis Devices, 2092
Cellatope, 1508
CellBazaar, 855
CellCentric, 2978
Cellcentric, 2967
Cellcon, 2666
Cellectar, 2001
Cellectar Biosciences, 1921
Cellective Therapeutics, 1008, 1094
Cellectricom AB, 2718
Cellectricon, 2728
CellEra, 2475
Cellera, 2900
CellerateRX, 425
Celleration, 1303, 1477, 1847, 1921
Celletra, 2770, 3137
Cellfacts, 2967
CellFE, 663
Cellfire, 1202, 1682, 1747, 1926, 1975
Cellfor, 362
CellGate, 1975
Cellicon, 314
Cellink, 1769
Cellit, 131
Cellity, 2475
CellMax Life, 174
Cellnovo, 2748, 3020
Cello Lighting, 226
Cellomics, 212
Cellotape, 953
CellPathways, 1398
CellRox, 3050
Cellrox, 3088
Cellscape, 1975
CellScope, 491
CellSeed, 2970
Celltick, 1352
Celltick Software Technologies, 2910
CellTrak, 1242
Celltrion Healthcare, 1376
Celltrix, 3015
Cellufuel, 2155
Cellular Line, 1088
Cellular Research, 12
CellularOne, 1153
Cellulosic Sugar Producers Co-Operative, 2061
Celluman, 998
Cellwand Communications, 2172
Cellwize, 3221
Cellworks, 174
Celly, 1383
CellzDirect, 856, 986, 1702
Cellzdirect, 1901
Cellzone, 1775
Celo, 124, 2280
Celon Pharma, 1452
Celoxia, 2348
Celoxica, 2577
Celoxica Holdings, 3070
Celsense, 1098, 1448
Celsia Technologies, 990
Celsion Corp., 946
Celsius, 1191
Celsius Therapeutics, 889
Celsus Therapeutics, 1271
Celsys, 596
Celtaxsys, 621, 2180
Celtel, 260
Celtic House Venture Partners, 3258
Celtic Inns, 2677
Celtic Manor, 2284
Celtra, 712, 1699
Celtra Technologies, 848
Celtrade, 2043
Celtrak Ltd, 2705

Portfolio Companies Index

Celtro, 1558, 2580
Celtro Inc., 2775
Celtronix, 3171
Celtx, 2068, 2168
Celularity, 1643
Celunol, 1558
Celxpert Energy Corp., 3218
CEMA, 52
CEMA Technologies, 1227
CEME, 1017
CEME Group, 2714
Cemengal, 3154
Cementos Balboa, 1082
Cempra, 74, 1508
Cempra Pharmaceuticals, 1008
Cems, 2436
Cencom Cable, 1211
Cendura, 563
Cendyn, 29
Cenega N.V., 2429
CeNeRx, 1412
CeNeS, 2463
Cengage, 2033
Cengage Learning, 135, 2252
Censia, 574
Censis, 1572
Censys, 872, 889
Cent 17 CLO, 1491
Centage, 1869
Centagenetix, 314
Centah, 2109
Centara Hotels and Resorts, 1139, 2946
Centaur Communications, 1927
Centauri Health Solutions, 1628, 1762
Centennial Communications, 63, 1682
Centennial HealthCare, 1708
Centennial Healthcare Corporation, 1148
Centennial Resource Development LLC, 1278
Centennial Towers, 1156
Center For Discover & Adolescent Change, 869
Center for Financial Services Innovation, 1374
Center for Global Development, 1374
Center for Research and Teaching in Economics, 1374
Center for Vein Restoration, 546
Center on Democracy, 1374
Center Parcs, 277, 2852
Center Rock, 812
Center Square Investment Management, 1147
Center to Support Excellence in Teaching, 1316
CenterBeam, 757, 1297
Centerbeam, 548, 2472
Centerline Communications, 1344
Centerplate Inc., 1372
Centerpoint, 37
CenterPoint Ventures, 986
CenterPointe Behavioral Health, 918
CenterPost, 212
Centerre Healthcare, 1574, 1819
CenterRun, 1288
Centerrun, 563
CenterRun Software, 1654
CenterStone Technologies, 315, 553
Centiba, 995
Centice, 1348, 3068
Centillium, 1087
Centillium Communications, 1896, 2508
Centor Software, 954
Centra, 1227, 1334
Centra Industries, 926
Centra Software, 521
Central Can Company, 619
Central Desktop, 925
Central Logic, 1204
Central Pacific Bank, 1737
Central Parking Services, 3211
Central Pattana, 1139, 2946

Central Power, 1578
Central Security Group, 1752
Central States Bus Sales, 399, 1053
Central Technology Services, 2235
Centrale Partners, 2544
Centrality Communications, 757, 905
CentralReach, 1000
Centrax, 77
Centre De Peinture L.B.G., 2120
Centre De Tri, 2095
Centre Des Congres De Sept-Œles, 2095
Centre Jardin Lac Pelletier, 2120
Centre Medical Le Mesnil, 2095
Centre Pacific Holdings LLC, 447
Centrexion Therapeutics, 1297
Centri, 1097
Centri Technology, 85
Centric, 2361
Centric Software, 310, 796, 1175, 1361
Centrify, 28, 620, 1024, 1184, 1672
CentriLogic, 1141
Centripetal, 1420
Centrix, 2974
Centrl, 567
Centro, 793
Centro Médico Teknon, 2497
Centron, 400
Centrotec, 3069
Centrue Financial Corporation, 404
Centrul Medical Unirea, 2309
Centrum Communic, 2508
Centurion Capital Group, 1147
Centurion Wireless Technologies, 541
Century 21. CRL, 869
Century Equity Partners, 3264
Century Fire Protection, 849
Century Graphics Corporation, 1505
Century Maintenance Supply, 783
Century Midstream, 740
Century Payments, 202
Century Resources, 1606
Century Wheel @ Rim, 1919
CENX, 560, 1926, 2195
Cenx, 596, 935
Cenzic, 59, 1038, 1247
Ceon Corporation, 252
Ceon Corporation/Convergys Corporation, 1288
Cephalon, 1452
Cepheid, 59, 385
Cepstral, 998
Ceptaris, 1387
Ceptaris Therapeutics, 136
Ception Therapeutics, 136
Cequel Communications, 1506
Cequence Energy, 2040
Cequence Security, 1663
Cequent Pharmaceuticals, 1412
Cequint, 43, 553
CERAC, 719
Ceradis, 2405
Ceradyne, 1288
Ceragon Networks, 2770, 3137
Cerahelix, 1160, 1161
Ceramem, 1157
Ceramic/Apolo Group, 2423
Cerapedics, 1196, 1325, 1382
Ceraver Osteal, 2625
Cerba European Lab, 3026
Cerberian, 1677
Cerebra, 1407
Cerebral Assessment Systems, 704
Cerebras Systems, 648
Cerebri, 1154
Cerebro Tech Medical Systems, 950
Cerebrotech, 1261
Cerecor, 1268
Cerecor Inc., 1297

Ceregene, 898
Ceregene Inc., 371
Cerego, 324
Cerelia, 2851
Cerenicimo, 2311
Cerenis Therapeutics, 94, 1382, 2816, 3196
Cerensis Therapeutics, 652
Cerent, 1793, 1975
CEREP II Mezzanine Loan Partners LP, 2094
Ceres, 1394, 1956, 1975
Ceres Power, 2892
CereScan, 735
CeresImaging, 1000
Cereve, 1786
Cerexa, 782, 1251, 1412
Cergaon Networks Ltd, 3158
Ceridian, 1815, 1972, 2033
Ceridian Corp, 300
CeriFi, 1105
Cerillion, 2795
Cerillion Technologies, 2662
Cerimon Pharmaceuticals, 3007
Cerion, 322
Cerion Energy, 704
Cerity Partners, 1123
Cernostics, 1448
Ceroc, 876
Ceros, 508, 871, 1673, 1738
Certain Lending, 1933
Certara, 170, 1910
Certeon, 1672
Certes Networks, 1321
Certica, 349
Certicom, 1940
Certifacame.com, 2382
Certified Recycling, 2214
Certified Safety, 917
Certified Security Solutions, 1455
CertifiedMail, 954
CertifiGroup, 3259
Certify, 1161
Certify Inc., 438
CertiPath, 553
Certiport, 1724
Certisign, 1004
CertiVox, 3018, 3032
Certn, 2284
certn, 2212
Certona, 695
Certona Corp., 23
Certpoint, 954
Certus Energy Solutions, 1009
Cerulean, 1151
Cerulean Pharma, 260, 1124, 1460
Cerulean Technology, 521
Cerus, 536
Cerus Endovascular, 1044
Cerved, 220
Cervelo Pharmaceuticals, 2496
CervilLenz, 1047
Cervo-Polygaz, 2095
Cerylid, 2975
CESA, 2537, 2538
Cesa, 2962
Cesar, 2551
Cesura, 1558
CET, 2677
Cetaccean Networks, 314
Cetacean Networks, 455
Cetera Financial Group, 1123
Ceterix, 12
Ceterix Orthopaedics, 1928
Cetero Research, 1086
Ceterus, 876
Cethar Vessels, 2490
Cetrea, 3203
Cetrifuge Systems, 1348

1283

Portfolio Companies Index

CEVA Logistics, 140, 2379
CEVA Santé Animale, 2863
Cevec, 2638
CEYX Technologies, 1664
CF Stinson, 361
CFares, 807
CFEngine, 2731
CFGI, 750
CFM Religion Publishing Group, 1984
CFMG, 928
CFN, 2089
CFP Flexible Packaging, 2537, 2538, 2852
CFRC Water and Energy Solutions Inc., 1047
CFS Brands, 1045
CGCG, 905
Cgen, 1534
Cgen Diital Media Company Limited, 3062
CGI, 530, 747
CGI Pharmaceuticals, 1124, 1574, 1906
CGL Manufacturing Inc., 2167
Cgtrader, 1004
CGTrader.Om, 3049
Ch Group Limited Partnership, 2120
CH4 Energy, 1278, 1326
Ch4e, 2892
Ch5 Finland Oy, 2873
Cha Cha, 925
CHA Consulting, 1141, 1166
Chabert-Duval, 2423
ChaCha, 1558, 1906
Chacha, 262
Chai Labs, 1218
Chain, 486, 1069, 1593
Chain Bureau, 2266
CHAINalytics, 834
Chainsaw, 2139
Chair-man Mills, 2139
Chairish, 772, 1359
Chairman Mom, 751
Chakshu Research, 1975
Chalk, 2184
Chalkable, 707
Chalkfly, 1736
Challenge Post, 1584
Chamate, 1361, 2850
Chamberlain Gard, 465
Chamberlin Edmonds & Associates, 1850
Chameleon, 395
Chameleon Systems, 1975
Chamelic, 2892
Chamilia, 334
Champagne Gardet, 2620
Champion, 984
Champion Manufacturing, 1111
Champion Medical Technologies, 1046
Champion Petfoods LP, 2056
Champion Technologies Inc., 461
Champion Windows, 1752
Champions Oncolody, 1271
Champions Oncology, 235, 1297
Champlin Wind, 332
Champtek, 2436
Chancenwerk, 2531
Chancery Software, 2196
Chandler Industries, 1422
Chandler Signs, 403
Chandler/May, 166
Chang Hwa Bank, 2633
Changba, 296
Change Collective, 1322
Change Dynamix, 86
Change Healthcare, 924, 1241, 1331, 1615
Change Heroes, 2233
Change Research, 934
Change.org, 1363, 1374, 1552
ChangePoint, 2058
Changetip, 1998

Changing Paradigms, 1954
ChangingWorlds, 3191
Chango, 525, 2182
Channel Advisor, 59
Channel Breeze, 296
Channel Control Marchants, 1082
Channel Insight, 1558
Channel Intelligence, 210
Channel IQ, 630
Channel Medsystems, 136, 1145
Channel Technologies Group, 828
Channel Technology, 36
Channel Wind, 3257
ChannelAdvisor, 1710, 3259
ChannelAdvisor Corporation, 1080
ChannelEyes, 317
Channeleyes, 976
ChanneLogics, 1709
ChannelSoft Holdings, 2597, 3093
Chantemor, 2601
ChanTest, 118, 1770
Chaoli, 823
Chaologix, 1988
Chaordix, 2291
CHAOSSEARCH, 2
ChaosSearch, 829
Chaoticom, 1080
Chaparral Energy, 433
Chaparral Network Storage, 187, 210
ChapDrive, 3013
Character Lab, 1316
Charcoal Group, 2172
Charcuterie L. Fortin Ltee, 2095
Chargbee, 1000
Charge Master, 302
Charge Point, 302, 1344
Chargeback, 1070
Chargebee, 28
ChargeItSpot, 1577
ChargePoint, 532, 1157, 1558, 1945
Chargepoint, 322
ChargePoint Inc., 158
Charger Oil & Gas, 156
Chargifi, 1004
Chariot, 472
Chariot Acquisition LLC, 158
Chariots Elevateurs Du Quebec, 2095
Charismathics, 2994
Charitweet, 1589
Charitygift, 1855
CharityStars, 2296
Charles Chocolates, 1655
Charles River, 209
Charles Voegele, 2922
Charleston Newspaper, 21
CharlestonPharma, 1923
Charli, 2291
CharlieHR, 3108
Charlotte Research Institute, 3259
Charlotte Russe Holdings Inc., 63
Charlotte Tilbury, 3097
Charlotte Tilbury, 1654
Charlotte's Web Holdings, 390
Charm Engineering, 2807
Charming Charlie, 902
Charrington Fuels, 2985
Chart Industries, 194
Chart.io, 206, 563
ChartBeat, 1149
Chartbeat, 609, 784, 1110, 1359, 1700
ChartBoost, 1690
Chartboost, 729, 1654, 1838, 2010
Chartcube, 1663
Charter Board Partners, 1316
Charter Brokerage, 170
Charter Communications, 559, 1946
Charter Life Sciences, 3284

Charter NEX Films, 1171
Charter Nex Films, 1109
Chartio, 358, 858
Chartone, 1915
Chartwell Healthcare, 111
ChartWise Medical Systems, 496, 718
Chase Medical, 734
Chase Pharmaceuticals, 323
Chasella Capital Partners, 3267
Chassis Breaks International, 1085
Chat Sports, 799
Chatalytic, 1323
ChatBlazer, 1681
ChatBook, 1607
Chatbooks, 1070
Chatdesk, 728, 1758
Chateau Bonne Entente, 2120
Chateau M.T., 2120
Chatfish, 1709
ChatGrid, 567
Chatgrid, 679
Chatham Technologies, 753, 1071
Chatitive, 1158
Chatkit, 2027, 2182
Chatous, 2011
ChatQuery, 1507
Chatter, 2187, 2245
Chatter Research, 2027, 2113
Chatters, 2208, 2209
Chaumet, 1017
Chauvet, 546
CHC, 3194
CHC Helicopter Corporation, 740
Che Behavioral Health Services, 96
Che101, 1121
Cheap Data Communications, 3049
Check, 777, 1257
Check Point, 1896
Check Point HR, 655
Check Point Software Technologies LTD., 772
Check24, 28
Checkbook, 307, 650
Checkers Drive-In Restaurants, 1651
Checkers Drive-In Restaurants Inc., 1971
CheckiO, 1912
Checkmark, 1000
Checkmarx, 3241
CheckMobile, 2932
Checkpoint, 2823
CheckPoint HR, 2196
CheckPoint Pumps & Systems, 61
Checkpoint Surgical, 732, 1047, 1287
CheckR, 28
Checkr, 889, 1001, 2012
Checks and Balances Bookkeeping, 3267
Cheddar, 518, 569, 1121
Cheddar Up, 1070
Cheddar's Restaurants, 328
Cheddars, 1361
Cheese, 120
Cheetah, 648
Cheetah Digital, 1910
Cheetah Medical, 176
Cheetah Medical Holdings, 2981
Cheetah Technology, 751
Cheezburger, 206, 1699
Chef, 235, 486, 974, 1235
Chef Code Can, 609, 1626
Chef'n, 478
Chef's Cut Real Jerky, 500
Chef's Plate, 668
ChefHero, 2137
Chefit, 2280
Chefsfeed, 175
Chegg, 581, 634, 751, 770, 805, 986, 1235, 1445
Chelford Group PLC, 2732
Chelsea, 846

Portfolio Companies Index

Chelsey Henry, 85
Chelsio Communications, 184, 947, 1297, 2974
Chemaid Laboratories, 1971
Chemco, 2120
ChemConnect, 986, 1255
ChemDAQ, 1448
Chemdex, 237
ChemDry, 222
Chemical Computing Group, 97
Chemical Express, 2985
Chemical Manufacturing and Refining, 2985
Chemical Week, 1927
Chemist Direct, 2446
ChemoCentryx, 2816
Chemogen, 438, 1161
ChemQuest chemicals, 653
Chemrec AB, 1906
Chemseco, 465
Chemson, 2887
Chemtura, 1134
Chengwei Capital, 1760
Cheniere, 277
Chenming Mold Industrial Corporation, 2603
Cheq, 235
Cheq Fm, 2095
Chequed.com, 1523
Chereau, 2851
Cheribundi, 432, 668
Cherin Law Offices, 3275
Chernin Group, 1496
Cherokee Partners, 156
Cherre, 1282
Cherry Bekaert LLP, 3262
Cherry Labs, 890
Cherry Road Technologies, 223
Cherrypick, 342
Cherwell, 1000
Cherwell Software, 1082
Chesapeake Energy, 1846
Chestnut Medical, 1773
Chevron Phillips, 2690
Chewse, 776
Chewy.com, 867, 1942
CHF Solutions, 176, 2728, 2890
CHG Healthcare, 1493
CHG Healthcare Services, 159, 782, 1109
CHI, 787
CHI Overhead Doors, 1082, 1141
Chia, 124
Chiarezza, 2521
Chiaro Networks, 1558, 2655, 3118
Chiasma, 153, 1268, 3245
Chic by Choice, 3048
Chicago Deferred Exchange, 1469
Chicago Deferred Exchange Company, 529
Chicago Miniature Lighting, 1856
Chicago Pacific Founders, 3264
Chicago Ventures, 3265
ChicagoLand Commissary, 940
Chicagoland Smile Group, 1667
Chicisimo, 3223
Chickapea Pasta, 2099
Chicken Kingdom, 71
Chicken Salad Chick, 334
Chicory, 1749
Chief, 754
Chief Executive Group, 863
Chieftain Sand and Proppant, 675, 1152
Child Development Schools, 830
Children & Teen Dental Group, 1270
Children's Cable Network, 1837
Children's Dental Health Associates, 610
Children's Discovery Center, 1255
Chill Factor, 2539
Chimani, 1161
Chime, 180, 552, 563, 761, 941, 1019
Chime Bank, 1202

Chime Banking, 49
Chime Entertainment LLC, 506
Chimei Innolux, 892
Chimera Bioengineering, 129, 1051
Chimerix, 74, 94, 386, 1298, 1412, 1616, 2978, 3259
Chimerix Inc., 782
Chimeros, 791
China Agritech, 413
China Auto Rental, 1956
China Biologic Products, 1956
China Biologic Products Inc., 973
China Broad Media Corp, 3093
China Cablecom, 1025
China CYTS Tours Holding Co Ltd., 2500
China Digital TV Holding Co., 3093
China Dredging, 2593
China Finance Online, 2850
China Fire & Security Group, 220
China Fishery Group, 413
China Genetics Holdings, 371
China GrenTech Holdings Limited, 3062
China Gtel Limited, 1297
China Homerun, 2978
China Int'l Capital Corp. Ltd., 1082
China Kidswant, 1956
China Materialia, 809
China Medicine, 1376
China Merchants Bank, 2594
China Merchants Bank Co. Ltd, 2595
China Merchants Plaza (Shanghai) Property C, 2595
China Merchants Securities Co. Ltd., 2594
China Motion Telecom International ltd, 2597
China Netcom, 2614
China Outfitters Holdings, 1082
China Rapid Finance, 1502
China Recycling Energy Group, 413
China Resources Cement Holdings Limited, 2402
China Search, 2936
China Senior Care, 1766
China SpeedNet, 2936
China Stem Cell, 1087
China Sunergy, 3194
China Synthetic Mica Technology, 3062
China Talent Group, 823
China Veg, 2881
China Wireless, 3062
Chinada, 3127
ChinaEdu, 260, 2850
ChinaInvent, 2936
Chinalliances, 2998
Chinatron Group Holdings, 162
Chinaway, 3215
Chinook Book, 1383
Chinook Energy, 2040
Chinook Therapeutics, 143
Chiome Bioscience, 3006
Chip and Pepper, 2254
Chip Express Corporation, 1255
Chip Hope Co., 3218
Chip X Corp (Chip Express), 1288
Chip-Man Technologies, 2451
Chipbond, 2436
ChipCare, 2184
Chipcon, 411, 2754
Chipidea, 2717
Chipita, 2784
Chipmore, 2436
Chips & Media, 1087, 2833
Chipsbank, 1004, 2936
ChipSensors, 2918
ChipX, 1906
Chiracon GmbH, 3190
Chirotouch, 1963
Chirpify, 1623, 1945
Chirpme, 301

Chisel, 1916
Chloe & Isabel, 720
Chloe + Isabel, 1531, 1699
Chlorogen, 1533
Chlorophylle, 2029, 2095
CHMack, 1512
Chmerix Inc., 181
Chobani, 1835
Chobo Labs, 2010
Chockstone, 1915
Chocolat Jean-Talon, 2095
Choice, 1717
Choice Brands Adhesives, 1209
Choice Pet, 448
Cholestech, 1786
Cholestech Corp., 947
Chomp, 438
Chongqing Broadband, 2936
Chongqing New Standard, 2936
Chooch AI, 1613
Choose Energy, 1324
Choosy, 761, 1297
Chooze, 1807
Choozle, 858
Chopt, 1088
Chordiant Software, 1728
Choreo, 2058
Choridiant Software, 757
Chorum Technologies, 692, 1558
Chorus, 1534, 1883
Chorus Fitness, 776
Chorus.ai, 2132
Chosen, 3081
ChosenSecurity, 422
Choupettes, 3042
Chow Town, 362
Chowbotics, 776
Chowly, 1890
Chowly Inc., 1155
ChowNow, 306, 397, 427, 624, 1055, 1099, 1888
Chownow, 2649
Christ, 2311
Christiansopigens Sild, 3203
Christmas Tradition, 2094
Chroma Therapeutics, 925, 3007
ChromaCode, 1297
Chromaflo Technologies, 110, 170
Chromalox, 433
ChromaTan, 293, 298
Chromatan, 1117
Chromatic Research, 1255, 1336
Chromatik, 228, 1099, 1489
Chromatin, 319, 975, 1438, 1921
Chromatis Networks, 2910
Chrome River, 732
Chromeriver, 161
Chromis Fiberoptics, 841, 1306, 1584
Chromium Graphics Inc., 869
ChromoTek, 2824
Chronic Health Metrics, 1448
Chronix Biomedical, 1470
Chrono, 12, 809
Chrono Therapeutics, 1238
Chrono.gg, 282
Chrono24, 1000
Chronocam, 2296
Chronogen, 2196
Chronometriq, 339
Chronos Life Group, 1081
Chronos/Checkforte, 2626
Chrysalis, 260, 1257, 2058, 2079
Chrysalis Ventures, 3265, 3269
Chrysalix, 2032, 2492
Chrysalix Venture Capital, 986
Chrysler Holdings, 1730
CHS Capital LLC, 3265
CHT Group, 77

1285

Portfolio Companies Index

Chubb, 473
Chubb Insurance Group, 3259
Chubbies, 1110, 1563
Chukong Technologies, 823, 1340, 1509
Chumby, 1175, 1359
Chumby Industries, 1038
Chung's, 969
Chunyu, 296
Church Street Health Management, 152
Church's Chicken, 152, 787
Churchill Financial Group, 1372
Churchill Pharma, 1271
Churnzero, 876
Chushou TV, 823
Chute, 776, 784, 1896
ChyronHego, 1910
CI Medical Technologies, 97
Cianna Medical, 666
Ciao, 3233
Ciao Bella, 1665
Ciband, 3044
CIBC, 3276
CIBC Innovation Banking, 3258
Cibiem, 1628, 1762, 1811
Cibiem Inc., 269
CiBo, 747
CIBT, 21, 1081
CIBT Global, 194
CIC Capital Canada, 3258
CIC Capital Ventures, 3258
CIC Minerals, 477
CicekSepeti, 2837
Ciceroos, 2672, 3052
Ciclon Semiconductor, 1916
Cidade, 953
Cidara, 12
Cidara Therapeutics, 74, 782, 1519
CiDi, 219
Cido, 1770
CiDRA, 212, 1913
Cidra, 1604
Cielo, 29
Cielo24, 724
Ciena, 260, 1121, 1558, 1720, 2007, 3137
Ciespace, 153, 192
Ciespace Corporation, 998
Cif Metal Ltd, 2095
CIFC, 456
CIG Logistics, 675
Cigital, 1136, 1227
Cignex, 2493
Cignifi, 1374
CigniTens, 3137
Cii Technology, 3259
Ciitizen, 124
Cima Nanotech, 2973
CIMB Group Holding, 300
CIMCON, 1100
CIMCON Lighting, 497
Ciment Blanc d'Algerie, 1007
CIMON Medical, 2867
CIMS, 2292
Cinario Ltd, 2554
Cinarra, 483
Cinarra Systems, 89
Cinchapi, 1421
Cincinnati Bell, 1360
Cinco Oil & Gas, 672
Cincon Electronics, 3218
CinCor, 12
Cindu International, 2332
Cine+, 2984
Cine-tal Systems, 1544
Cinedigm DC, 1491
Cinedigm Digital Cinema, 1230
Cinegif, 950
Cinelease, 194

Cinemacraft, 2913
Cinemagram, 1202
Cinemaki, 2446
Cinemark, 1156, 1506
Cinemark USA Inc., 575
Cinetopia, 1636
Cinnabon, 1576
Cinnafilm, 756
Cinnos, 2184
Cinova, 183
Cint, 2637, 3051
Cintel, 1087
Cinven, 3264
CIP Technologies, 2598
Cipher Surgical, 2967
Cipher Trace, 180
Cipher Trust, 1896
CipherCloud, 124
Ciphergen Biosystems, 1255, 1975
Cipherium Systems Co, 2703
CipherOptics, 212, 1080, 1975
CipherTrace, 49
Ciqual Limited, 1830
CiraNova, 1975
CiRBA, 1672, 2196
Cirba, 1673
Circ Medtech, 55
CIRCA, 1999
Circa, 625, 685, 721, 1150, 1518, 1632
Circa Corporation of America, 910
Circadian, 260
Circadiance, 998, 1448
Circassia, 2858
Circet Groupe, 62
Circle, 336, 816, 973, 1181, 2236
Circle Back, 508
Circle Cardiovascular Imaging, 2121, 2291
Circle Ci, 1626
Circle Internet Financial, 1662
Circle Internet Financial Limited, 1361
Circle K, 1017
Circle Medical, 196
Circle of Moms, 1975
Circle Pharma, 1238
Circle Up, 1323
CircleBack, 876
CircleCI, 231, 585, 609
Circles, 922
CircleSt, 1099
CircleUp, 889, 1183, 1584
Circon Systems Corp, 2097
Circuit, 1894
Circuit World, 2089
CircuitHub, 889
CircuitMeter, 2041
Circuitronics, 828
Circularis, 395
Circulate, 358, 858
Circulite, 2748
CircusTrix, 1403
Ciris Energy, 1558
CirisEnergy, 322
Cirius Therapeutics, 782
Cirpack, 2897
Cirque Dreams, 193
Cirque Du Soleil, 1835
Cirquest, 995
Cirro, 1237, 1829
Cirro Secure, 1055, 2011
Cirrus, 152
Cirrus Logic, 563
Cirrusdata, 150
CirrusWorks, 1632
Cirtec Medical LLC, 449
Cirtemo, 1923
CIS, 48
CIS Secure Computing, 405

Cisco, 1096, 1654
Cisco Systems, 3212, 3259
Cision, 884
Cisse Cocoa, 841
Cissoid, 3225
Cista, 1297
CIT GAP Funds, 3270
Cita Neuro Pharmaceutical, 2196
Citadel, 959, 1121
Citadel Architectural Products, 1252
Citadel Communications, 21
Citadel Outsource Group, 1343
Citadel Plastics, 456
Citat, 2888
CITB, 2889
Citco, 815
Citco III, 1743
Citel Tech, 2348
Citelighter, 1306
Citiesocial, 3181
Citigroup Inc., 1903
Citilog, 2876
CitiPower I Pty Ltd, 2591
CitiusTech, 815
Citiva, 966
CitiXsys, 21
Citizant, 507
Citizen, 1054, 1151, 1654
Citizen Hex, 2280
Citra Health Solutions, 859
Citrine, 2011
Citrine Informatics, 107, 996, 1254
Citrix Systems, 3262
Citron Hygiene, 2062
Citrus Lane, 231, 823, 1054, 1865
Cittio, 925
Citus Data, 358, 1069
CitusData, 585
City Barbeque, 783
City Bebe, 445
City Carting & Recycling, 61
City Carting Holding, 1021
City Center, 869
City Cloud International, 483
City Gear, 405
City Media, 1340
City Mortgage Corporation, 111
City on a Hill, 1316
City Pantry, 2997
City Place, 70
City Sports, 1970
City Ventures LLC, 159
City Wide Towing, 2255
Citybox, 823
CityFlyer Express, 2823
Cityfront Partners LLC, 122
CityGrowsm Contentplace, 1507
CityIndex, 779
Citymapper, 2478, 2629
CityMart, 1894
Citymesh, 3042
Cityneo, 2897
Citynews, 3052
CityNorth, 1967
Cityscan, 1384
CityShop, 823
CitySmart, 1507
CitySocializer, 2685, 3055
CitySoft, 438, 1689
Cityspace, 2577
CitySquares, 649
Cityvoter, 580
Cityzen, 3259
CivaTech Oncology, 3259
CIVCO, 1086
Civcom Inc., 2750
Civic Eagle, 218, 934

1286

Portfolio Companies Index

Civic Partners, 1871
Civic Science, 998
CivicConnect, 2133
CivicPlus, 361
CivicScience, 1291
Civil Maps, 107, 472
Civilized, 2071
Civis Analytics, 630, 1926
Civitas Learning, 202, 665, 720, 741, 751, 1299, 1551
Civitas Solutions, 1931
Civitas Therapeutics, 237, 386, 1519, 1698
Civitech, 934
Civolution, 3051
CJ Entertainemnt, 2857
CJ Entertainment, 2833
CJ Fallon, 1111
CJ Foods Inc., 1037
CJ HelloVision Co., 2727
CK Mechanical Plumbing & Heating, 678
CKE Restaurants, 1576
CKH Food & Health Limited, 2727
CKL Design Automation, 69
CL Educate, 851
Clad-Rex, 316
Cladwell, 1155
Claim Compass, 2138
Claim-Maps, 85
ClaimForce, 1384
Claire By 30 Seconds To Fly, 1035
Claire's, 140
Claire-Sprayway, 843
ClairMail, 968, 986, 1389
Clairsonic, 85
Clairvest Group, 3258
Clairvoyant Networks, 737
Clairvoyante, 1646, 1646
Clal Industries Ltd., 34
Clara, 24, 395, 622, 942, 1534
Clara Labs, 232
ClaraBridge, 315
Clarabridge, 816, 876, 904, 1008, 1625, 1752
Claranet, 21, 967
Clare, 741
ClareMedica Health Partners, 244
Claremont, 1558
Claremont Creek Ventures, 3284
Claresys, 2967
Claret Medical, 644, 1122, 1619
Clari, 1654
Claria, 807
Clariant, 2922
Claricom Solutions, 1067
Clarifai, 889, 1101, 1151, 1202
Clarifi, 1509
Clarify, 1378
Clarify Health Solutions, 1082
Clarify Medical, 297
Clarigent Health, 479
Clario Medical, 1600
Clarion Brands, 1767
Clarion Events, 1927, 2379, 2823
Clarion Industries, 1403
Clarion Partners, 1123
Clariondoor, 173
ClariPhy, 986, 1378
Clariteam, 2322
Claritics, 454
Clariton, 3249
Claritum, 2574
Clarity, 784
Clarity Health, 1334
Clarity Money, 24, 724, 1183
Clarity Payment Solutions, 2717
Clarity Solution Group, 1575
Clarity Visual Systems/Planar Systems, 1288
ClarityHealth, 85

Claritymoney, 486
Clarivate Analytics, 2209
ClariVest Asset Management, 1147
Clarivoy, 1553
Clarizen, 581, 634, 2566, 3221
Clark, 1067, 1121, 1551, 2225
Clark Brands, 1964
Clark Nexsen, 3259
Clarkston Consulting, 3259
Claros Diagnostics, 520
Claroty, 996
Clarus, 1760
Clarus Glassboards, 257
Clarus Therapeutics, 1490, 1817
Clarus Ventures, 37
ClarVista Medical, 1993
ClasDojo, 1054
Class Box, 641
Class Dojo, 720, 1110, 1254
Class Technology, 1755
Classcraft, 2066
ClassDojo, 816, 883, 1316, 1527, 1663, 1675, 1700
ClassDoko, 1879
Classic Accessories, 478
Classic Chevy International, 908
Classic Events, 1745
Classic Hospitals, 2935
Classic Party Rentals, 949
Classic Specs, 813
Classic Sports Network, 1728
Classified Verticals, 1192
Classkick, 858, 1054, 1118
Classmarkets, 2829, 2838
Classmates, 928
Classmates Online, 153
ClassOne Group, 1606
ClassOwl, 192
ClassPass, 280, 295, 727, 816, 889, 1184, 1694
Classpass, 318, 1581
Classroom Connect, 334, 378
Classting, 3127
ClassTracks, 1701
ClassWallet, 334, 1316
Classwatch, 2574
Classy, 358, 1041, 1552, 1607
Clause, 3108
Clavert Education Services LLC, 383
Clavis Insight, 2674, 3104
Clay, 305, 318
Claymore Capital Management, 2058
Clayton Dubilier & Rice, 3264
Cleaire Advanced Emissions Control, 1730
Clean Air Partners, 2079
Clean Air Power, 3028
Clean Coal Technologies Inc., 1191
Clean Diesel Technologies, 1579, 2492
Clean Earth, 523, 1134
Clean Emission Fluids, 742
Clean Energy Fuels, 1109
Clean Fiber, 1100
Clean Power Finance, 498
Clean Power Finance Inc., 491
Clean Technology Solutions, 1603
Clean Water Works, 2186
Clean Well, 1977
Clean World Partners, 1600
Cleancut, 318
CleanFish, 1236
Cleanify, 11, 229, 358, 650, 858, 1054
Cleanly, 1150
CleanRisk, 2143
CleanScapes, 1689
CleanSlate, 921
Cleantech America, 506
Cleantech Group, 1603
CleanVolt Energy, 737

Clear Access, 278
Clear Align, 1306
Clear Blade, 545
Clear Catheter Systems, 1543
Clear Channel Communications, 220
Clear Choice, 1753
Clear Comfort, 146
Clear Contract, 1267
Clear Creek Midstream, 671
Clear Data, 748
Clear Flight Solutions, 549
Clear Flow Inc., 371
Clear Genetics, 525
Clear Labs, 720, 889, 1202
Clear NDA, 1267
Clear Object, 658
Clear Path Robotics, 809
Clear Scholar, 658
Clear Shape Technologies, 1896
Clear Slide, 1829
Clear Spring, 115
Clear Standards, 1072, 1348
Clear Story Data, 124
Clear Swift, 2674
Clear Technology, 1769
Clear Urban Energy, 1558
Clear Vascular Inc., 157
Clear Water, 222
Clear-Cut Medical, 3050
Clear-to-Send Electronics, 131
Clear2Pay, 2837, 3042
ClearAccess, 1383
ClearAccess IP, 612
ClearAccessIP, 807
Clearant, 1166
ClearBalance, 127
ClearBanc, 2225
Clearbanc, 2137
Clearbit, 741, 2019
ClearBlade, 445
Clearblanc, 2157
Clearbridge BioMedics, 2518
ClearCare, 235, 1945
ClearChoice Holdings LLC, 1088
ClearCommerce, 202, 1945
ClearCount, 1448
ClearCount Medical Solutions, 998
Clearcover, 1118
ClearCube, 202, 757
Clearcube, 1400
ClearDATA, 703, 938, 1346
ClearDATA Networks, 1205
ClearEdge, 377
ClearEdge 3D, 1442
ClearEdge Partners, 1458
ClearEdge Power, 144, 1083
ClearedIn, 1269
Clearent, 196, 646, 793
Clearent/FieldEdge, 62
Cleareon Fiber Networks, 631
CLEAResult, 815
Clearfit, 848
ClearFlame Engines, 1613
ClearFlow, 138, 1383
Clearfly Communications, 502
ClearForest, 3231
Clearforest, 23
ClearFuels Technology, 807, 807
ClearGov, 1172
ClearGraph, 858
ClearGuage, 192
ClearLab, 138
Clearlake Capital Group, 3255
ClearLaw AI, 1613
ClearLeap, 1331
Clearleap, 1759, 1853
Clearlink, 1409

1287

Portfolio Companies Index

Clearly.ca, 2144
ClearlySo, 2509
ClearMedical, 1002
ClearMedicare, 995
ClearMetal, 648, 1297
Clearmetal, 996
Clearminster, 2796
ClearMotion, 1154, 1297, 1509
Clearn Membranes, 2978
ClearOrbit, 1855
Clearpath, 2157
ClearPath Diagnostics, 1667
Clearpath Robotics, 648, 1061, 2172
ClearPoint, 655
ClearPoint Metrics, 1038
Clearpool, 655
ClearRoad, 1894
ClearSaleing, 1553
Clearscope, 967
ClearServe, 1632
ClearSide, 1696
Clearside Biomedical, 915, 1261
ClearSky, 816, 935
Clearslide, 260
ClearSource, 1708
Clearspring Capital Partners, 3258
ClearStory, 634, 1075
ClearStory Data, 581, 889
ClearStream, 975
Clearswift, 2386, 2662
Clearswift Corporation, 2577
Cleartrip, 581
Clearview, 2967
Clearview Capital Fund II LP, 2094
ClearVoice, 79
Clearwater, 97, 473, 1972
Clearwater Analytics, 1752
Clearwell, 634, 1341, 1534
Clearwell Systems, 1654
Clearwire, 306, 596
Cleatrip, 634
Cleave, 12
Cleave Bioscience, 1297
Cleave Biosciences, 157, 182, 495, 1382, 1896
Cleaver Brooks Inc., 1971
Cleaver-Brooks Inc., 908
Clef, 1254
Clek Inc., 2087
Clementia, 709, 1297, 1382, 1519
Clementon Park Splash Worlld, 1991
Clenarm, 3097
Cleo, 92, 720, 761, 872, 2478
cleo fashions, 2258
Cleor, 2293
Cless Cosméticos, 1376
Clesse, 123
Clevamama, 2355
Cleveland HeartLab, 703, 831, 919, 1205
Cleveland Medical Polymers, 642
Clever, 751, 883, 889, 1054, 1121, 1654, 1700, 2012
CleverCoin, 307
Cleversafe, 234, 979, 1364, 1474, 1480
Cleversense, 1118
Cleverset, 85
Clevertap, 28
CLI Studios, 883
Clic, 2095
Click, 779
Click Commerce, 1668
Click Diagnostics, 174
Click Energy, 126
Clickability, 2196
ClickAd, 2309
Clickatell, 581, 634, 1654
Clickbooth, 403, 446
ClickDimensions, 29

Clicker, 968, 1534
ClickFox, 436, 925, 2580, 2655, 3212
ClickingHouse Pte Ltd, 2473
ClickMechanic, 11
ClickPay, 52
Clickpay Services, 1385
Clickshare Service, 438
Clicksign, 641
Clicksoftwar, 2775
ClickSquared, 2196
Clicksquared Inc., 23
Clicktale, 1082
Clicktivated Video, 981
Clidec, 3180
Client Distribution Services, 1372
Client Outlook, 2187
ClientSoft, 954
ClientSuccess, 79, 1656
Clifford Thames, 2944
Clifton, 2390, 3068
CliftonLarsonAllen, 3262, 3275
Climacell, 1035
ClimaCheck, 2619
Climastar, 2489
Climate Energy, 2615
Climatewell, 3013
Climatisation Mixair, 2095
Climax Portable Machine Tools, 985
Climos, 322
Climpact, 2693
Clinc, 630
Cline Driving Solutions, 746
Clinical Assessment Services, 2537, 2538
Clinical Genomics, 3023
Clinical Ink, 496, 718, 1349
Clinical Innovations, 1479, 1590
Clinical Logistics, 2155
Clinical Products, 1261
Clinical Research Investments, 1764
Clinical Research Laboratories LLC, 274
Clinical Sensors, 737
Clinical Supplies Management, 859
Clinicient, 427
Cliniconex, 2284
Clinipace Worldwide, 904, 915, 1255, 1406, 3259
Clinique D'Optometrie Vu, 2095
Clinique Développement, 3239
CliniSys, 2977
Clinitron, 1509
Clinkle, 688
Clinovia, 2796
Clinovo, 1061, 1600
Clinverse, 655, 915, 1940
CLIO, 1088
Clio, 2280, 3044
Clip, 968, 1240, 1518
Clip Industie, 235
Clipboard, 773
ClipCall, 1926, 2947
Clipcomm, 3127
Clipper Marine, 937
Cliptone, 1437
Cliq Designs Ltd, 2708
Cliqloc, 2824
CliQr, 770
CliqStudios, 857
Clique, 306
Clique Media, 624
Clique Media Group, 60, 641, 1110, 1222
Cliqz.com, 2604
Clir, 2041
Clix, 909
Clixtr, 115
CLK Design Automation, 1257
Cloakware, 712
Clobotics, 823, 1087

Clockwork Fox, 2168, 2216
Clockwork Solutions, 1783
Clondalkin, 1956
Close.io, 1715
Closedloop Solutions, 1760
Closely, 114, 125, 685, 876
CloserStill, 3036
Closet Works, 1435
Closet world, 374
Clothes Horse, 533, 1358, 1475
Clothia, 280, 1334, 1518
Cloud Access, 1965
Cloud Agronomics, 195
Cloud Apps, 2674
Cloud Bees, 178
Cloud Business, 2567
Cloud Control, 2638
Cloud Cruiser, 1378, 1600, 1669, 1966
Cloud Elements, 876, 904, 1522
Cloud Elemts, 36
Cloud Genix, 1004
Cloud Health Technologies, 1626
Cloud Lending, 688
Cloud Made, 3149
Cloud MedX, 1151
Cloud Moment, 1121
Cloud Passage, 518, 544
Cloud Pharmaceuticals, 3259
Cloud Physics, 968
Cloud Simple, 1154
Cloud Technology Partners, 91, 1361, 1480
Cloud Temple, 967
Cloud.com, 1534, 3001
Cloud4Wi, 1381
Cloud66, 603
Cloud9, 1883
Cloud9 Analytics, 1102
Cloudability, 585, 776, 1463, 1789, 1853
Cloudamize, 1240
Cloudant, 206
CloudApps, 2662
CloudArena, 2437
CloudBeds, 569
CloudBees, 1181, 1926
Cloudbees, 1121
CloudBolt Software, 1000
CloudByte, 3001
CloudCheckr, 2195
CloudCherry, 483
CloudEndure, 603, 2952
CloudEngine, 3174
Cloudera, 28, 581, 634, 836, 979, 1212
CloudFare, 1297, 1509
Cloudfiling, 602
CloudFlare, 867, 1425
Cloudflare, 578, 1882, 1916
CloudFX, 483
CloudGenix, 1184
cloudGuide SA, 650
CloudHealth Technologies, 1212, 1673
CloudHelix, 1968
Cloudian, 1004
Cloudify, 1004
CloudIQ, 2539
Cloudkick, 206
CloudLanes, 1154
CloudLock, 436
Cloudmark, 32, 793, 974, 1327, 1474, 1752, 1975
Cloudmeter, 1194
Cloudnexa, 52
CloudOn, 770, 1540, 1696, 1838
CloudOne, 1455
CloudPassage, 777, 1212, 1663, 1796
CloudPay, 1558
CloudPhysics, 1075, 1184
Cloudreach, 1235

1288

Portfolio Companies Index

Cloudscaling, 1853
CloudSense, 1607, 1910
Cloudshare, 455
CloudShield, 1975
Cloudshield, 1400
CloudShield Technologies, 798
Cloudstitch, 1589
CloudStreet Oy, 3213
CloudSwitch, 521
CloudTags, 971
CloudVelocity, 1425
CloudVelox, 1184
CloudWave, 1979
Cloudwords, 1747
CloudX, 678
Cloudyn Code Fresh, 3221
Clourdera, 1311
Clove, 325
Clover, 85, 839, 942, 1254, 1760, 1985
Clover Health, 107, 741, 751, 889, 1654
Clover Imaging Group, 1345
Clover Letter, 896
Clover Tx, 395
Cloverhill Bakery, 1505
Cloverleaf, 2775
Clovis, 2711
Clovis Oncology, 20, 74, 94, 621, 782, 1297, 1436, 1928
Clowe & Cowan of El Paso, 1343
Cloyes, 1085
Cloze, 1322
CLP Resources, 468
CLS Holdings USA, 1283
Cls Info, 2095
CLT Research, 1295
Club Champion, 1056
Club Company, 2935
Club Staffing, 1372
Club W, 1965
ClubCorp Inc., 575
Clubessential, 235
Clubhosue, 1110
Clubhouse, 235, 351
ClubReady, 235
Clue, 2674
Clupedia, 1915
Cluster, 231
Cluster Seven, 3070
Clustree, 2851
Clustrix, 183, 933, 1896
Clutch, 1317, 1601, 1758
Clutter, 120, 727, 777, 889, 1028, 1654, 2446
Clyde Bergemann, 2965
Clyde Bergemann Group, 2660
Clyde Biosciences, 689
Clyde-Bergemann-Gruppe Wesel/Glasgow/Delaware, 3067
Clypd, 38, 313, 586, 784, 1839
clypd, 1849
CM Energy, 675
CMC, 383, 1387
CMC Biologics, 1248
CMD Bioscience, 678, 1097
Cmed, 3104
CMG, 567
CMG Health, 955
CMG Holdings, 1957
CMG Silhouette Sports Club, 2293
CMI, 2436
CMI Limited, 401
CMI-Dutchview, 2501
CML Group, 1295
CML HealthCare, 2233
CMOSIS, 1776
Cmosis, 3042
CMP Pharma, 97
CMP.LY, 1385

CMR Group, 3020
CMRA, 679
CMS, 168
CMS Management Solutions, 1569
Cmune, 596, 2446
CMW, 2436
CMWare, 1886
CNC, 2590, 2998
CNC Global, 788
CNCdata, 958
CNDAA, 1573
CNEI, 2944
CNEX Labs, 483, 1154, 1670
CNEX LABS Inc., 1951
CNEXLabs, 603
CNK Telecom, 2434
CNM Technologies, 2686
Cnn, 2721
CNNH NeuroHealth, 550
CNOOC, 2772
CNote, 226
CNS Response, 1603
CNS Therapeutics, 1817
CNSX Markets, 2058
CO Everywhere, 2978
Co Star, 977
Co-Tech Copper Foil, 1769
co.don, 2377
CO2 GRO, 2061
Co3Systems, 912
Coach America, 722
Coach Up, 3
CoachUp, 329, 816
Coachup, 1459, 1789
CoActive Technologies, 1134
CoAdna Photonics, 970
Coagulex Inc., 485
Coal, 3018
Coal Fire, 222
Coal Products, 2883
Coalescent Surgical, 1251, 1975
Coalfields Enterprise Fund, 2708
Coalfire Systems, 413
CoAlign Innovations, 87
Coalision, 2169
CoalTek, 322
Coapt Systems, 312
Coast Access, 623
Coast Appliances, 2275
Coast Composites, 443
Coast Crane, 194
Coast Gas Industries, 199
Coast of Maine, 1161
Coast of Maine Organic Products, 438
Coastal Carolina Clean Power, 1573
Coastal Carolina Clean Power LLC, 413
Coastal Community Bank, 1250
Coastal Companies, 1166, 1270
Coastal Credit, 1417
Coastal Drilling, 1409
Coastal Drilling Company, 1745
Coastal Sunbelt, 1270
Coastal Ventures, 1548
Coastal Waste & Recycling, 529
Coastal.com, 2144
Coates Hire, 413
Coating Excellence International, 1171
Cobalt, 307, 519, 772, 2697, 2698, 2939
Cobalt Biofuels, 1
Cobalt Boats, 1587
Cobalt International Energy, 413, 740, 1573
Cobalt Light Systems, 2967
Cobalt Networks, 197
Cobalt Office Park, 1967
Cobalt Robotics, 727, 1654, 1834
Cobalt Technologies, 1445, 1906
Cobb Slater Ltd., 2657

Cobblestone Fayette, 1219
Cobblestone Golf Group, 378
Cobelguard CIT, 2949
Cobion, 3233
Cobli, 727
Cobotics, 1057
Cobra, 3154
Cobra Waire & Cable, 1209
Cobre Capital, 3276
Coca-Cola, 473, 2389
COCAT, 1484, 1745
Cockroach Labs, 743, 889, 1534, 2006
Cocoa China, 3142
Cocona, 712
Cocone, 3127
Coconut Calendar, 2249
Coconut Software, 2153
CoCubes.Com, 3019
Cod Farmers, 2475
Coda, 107, 872, 1268
CODA Holdings, 1573
Coda Project Inc., 1069
Coda Signature, 735
CoDa Therapeutics, 621, 2516
Codacy, 3108
Coddle, 574
Code 42 Software, 3279
Code A Site, 3259
Code Climate, 1110, 1322, 1882
Code Combat, 721
Code Fights, 641
Code for America, 1374
Code Fresh, 1154
Code Green Networks, 238
Code42, 1041, 1297, 1640, 1725
Code42 Software, 28
Codeacademy, 317, 1359
Codecademy, 754, 1075, 1694, 1882
CodeCombat, 124
Codecov, 318
CodeEval, 253
Codefights, 544, 1222
Codeherent, 2284
CodeHS, 1054, 1316, 1656
Codekingdoms, 1716
Codel Holding Company, 1492
Codementor, 3181
Codenomicon, 3051
Codenomicon Oy, 2716
CodeNow, 1316
Codenvy, 1829
CodeRed, 61
CodeRise, 3125
CodeRyte, 520, 1702, 1916
CodeSealer, 3203
Codeship, 313, 710, 1673, 3108
Codesignal, 720
CodeSpark, 799, 972
Codespark, 1054
codeSpark, 1893
Codetoys, 3233
Codetoys Oy, 2716, 2873
Codeverse, 567
Codexis, 466, 2690
CODi, 1234
Codiak, 709, 747
Codice Software, 2548
Codigo Entertainment LLC, 63
Coding, 1121
Coding Technologies, 2754
Codiscope, 1136
Codon Devices, 747
Cody, 773, 1632
CoEdition, 325, 1297
coeo, 293
Cofactor Genomics, 107, 176, 267, 1202
COFCO Meat, 1082

1289

Portfolio Companies Index

Coferon, 915, 1196
Coffee Circle, 3170
Coffee Day Resorts, 1082
Coffee Meets Bagel, 596, 1118, 1983
Coffin Turbo Pump, 1275
Coficern/Sagem, 2601
CoFoundersLab, 1169
CoFoundit, 2856
Cogent Communications, 315, 2007, 2910
Cogent Healthcare, 1239, 1963
Cogent Midstream, 671
Cogentrix Power Management, 413
Cogiscan, 2095
Cogit.com, 1119
Cogito, 1607
Cognate Bioservices, 697
Cognet, 132, 1668
Cognetix, 1412
Cogni, 574
Cogniac, 204, 205
Cognical, 1849
Cognima, 2639, 3179
Cognio, 23, 1334
Cognita Schools, 1082
CogniTens, 3231
Cognition Therapeutics, 293, 841, 998, 1448, 1784
Cognition Therapeutics Inc., 987
CognitionIP, 795
Cognitiv, 342
Cognitive Concepts, 1057
Cognitive Match, 2407
Cognitive Networks, 596
Cognitive Scale, 1004, 1154
Cognitive Toy Box, 1551
Cognitive Toybox, 622
CognitiveScale, 1346
Cognivue Corporation, 2058, 2058
Cognoa, 2978
Cognoptix, 1100, 1160
Cogoport, 28
CogRx, 1306
CogX, 574
Cohda Wireless, 483
Cohealo, 1581, 1757
Cohen & Company, 3275
Cohen & Grigsby, 3275
Cohera Medical, 998, 1066, 1082, 1448
Cohere Technologies, 107, 1121, 1297
Coherent, 181
Coherent Path, 305, 534, 848, 1673, 1734
Coherex Medical, 1677, 1884
Cohero Health, 266, 1611
Coherus BioSciences, 1082
Coherus Biosciences, 1124, 1519, 1698
Cohesity, 28, 175, 235, 483, 770, 889, 1255, 1509, 1654
Cohesive Network Systems, 1972
CohesiveFT, 1364
Cohn & Gregory, 984
Coi Pharmaceuticals, 206
COIFF'Idis, 3020
Coimbra Genomics, 3048
COIN, 1708
Coin, 1700
Coin Jar, 307
Coinage, 307
Coinapoly, 684
Coinbase, 49, 124, 235, 307, 620, 872, 1001, 1531, 1560, 1643, 1761, 2012, 2280, 2885
Coinbunble, 1768
CoinFlip, 1035
Coinfloor, 3030
Coinhako, 307
Coining of America, 1159
Coinjar, 2520
Coinplug, 626

Coinprism, 307
Coinsetter, 1849
CoInspec, 1894
Coinstar, 247, 753, 753, 856
Cointerra, 3097
Coinut, 307
Cojoin, 1099
Coker Tire, 1022
Col-Met Spray Booths, 1745
CoLab, 795
CoLab Software, 2168
Colab Software, 2212
Colabot, 1809
CoLabs, 226
Colbar, 2775
Colby Pharmaceuticals, 1328
Cold Chain Technologies, 199
Cold Genesys, 1983
Cold PackSystem, 1891
Cold Spring Harbor Laboratory, 1271
ColdSpark, 1038
Coldwater Creek, 839
ColdWatt, 202
Coldwell Banker, 368
Cole Haan, 135
Cole Information, 349
Cole Real Estate Investments, 869
Cole Taylor Bank, 529
Cole-Parmer Instrument Company, 884
Coleman Swenson Booth, 986
Colerain RV, 1071
Coles Myer, 2659
Coletica, 2466
Coley, 2377
Coley Pharmaceutical Group, 1817, 2785
Colford Capital, 1248
Colgate Energy, 1278, 1326
Coliant Corporation, 742
Colibra, 235
Colibri, 622, 1505
Colibria, 2754, 3013
Colibrys Ltd, 3162
Colingo, 1254, 2920
Colisee, 909, 2851
CollabNet, 1136
CollabNet VersionOne, 1910
Collaborate.com, 1097
Collaborative Medical, 3267
Collaborative Practice Solutions, 1289
Collaborative Solutions, 1979
Collabornet, 1512
Collabrify, 1592
Collage, 2225
CollaGenex Pharmaceuticals, 74
Collanos AG, 650
Collarity, 1975
CollateBox, 3133
Collax, 2813, 3233
Collect, 307
Collect America, 1203
Collect Rx, 1293
Collectif, 392
Collection Papillon Gemme, 2095
Collections Marketing Center, 1385
Collective, 871
Collective Bias, 1886
Collective Health, 775, 858, 889, 1297, 1534
Collective Intellect, 142, 553, 876
Collective IP, 930
Collective Retreats, 318, 741, 1694
Collective Therapeutics, 769
CollectiveHealth, 1696
CollectiveIP, 685
Collectively, 1310
CollectiveMedical, 1075
CollectiveMedical Technologies, 1052
Collectors Universe, 1288

College Ave Student Loans, 518
College Enterprises/Blackboard, 1288
College Factual, 119
College of Natural Sciences Advisory Council, 1650
College Pharmaceuticals, 136
College Portfolio, 1810
Collegebacker, 1527
CollegeProwler.com, 1194
Collegiate Funding Services, 1123
Collegium, 312
Collegium Pharmaceutical, 709, 782, 1519, 1691
Coller Capital, 3258
Collgard, 3249
Collider, 459, 1126
Collider Media, 1810
Colligo, 2109
Collingwood Ethanol, 413
Collinor Software, 2824
Colloquis, 592
Collplant, 3245
COLO, 1627
Cologix, 515, 867
ColoHub LLC, 122
Colomer Group, 2644
Colonial Claims, 529
Colonial Pipeline Co., 1082
Colony Hardware, 64, 1777
Colony Sardegna, 3154
Color, 518, 762, 816, 996, 1663
Color Genomics, 107, 721, 1069, 1675
Color Kinetics, 1288
Color Labs Enterprises, 958
Colorado Boxed Beef Company, 96
Colorado Technology Association, 3276
Colorbok, 1336
ColorChip, 2720, 3046, 3214
Colorchip, 3231
Colorcon, 258
Colorcraft Packaging, 832
Colore Science, 919, 1251
Coloredge, 1604
Colorescience, 74, 621, 1145, 1725
Colormatrix, 194
Colorme Info, 2850
Coloscuem, 2558
Colourlovers, 1254
Coloursmith, 2168
Colson Group, 1651
Colt CTX Resources, 514
Colt Mineral Interests, 514
Colt Unconventional Resources, 514
Colt WTX Resources, 514
Colter Energy, 2275
Colu Technologies, 318
Colubris Networks, 1227, 1782
CoLucid, 1412
CoLucid Pharma, 1271
CoLucid Pharmaceuticals, 621, 1847
Columbia Capital, 986, 3270
Columbia Green, 243
Columbia Green Technologies, 2291
Columbia Northwest, 293
Columbia Power Technologies, 1383
Columbus Manufacturing, 147
Columbus Recycling, 1857
Colusa Power Development, 156
com, 3251
Com 21, 757
Com Tech Communications, 2951
COM21, 1558
Com21, 1087
Com2Us, 1087
Com2uS, 1747
Com6, 3208
Comact Equipment, 2095
CoManage, 56

Portfolio Companies Index

Comar, 846
Comark Building Systems, 328
Comark Services, 2258
Comat, 2460
ComAv, 573
Combat Gent, 1912
Combat Medical, 3107
Combat Networks, 2058
Combatant Gentleman, 1099
Combatant Gentlemen, 280, 871, 1226
Combatant Gentlement, 3044
CombiChem, 1706
Combichem, 769
Combinati, 226
CombinatoRx, 312
Combined Public Communications, 164
Combined Solar, 2978
Combined Systems, 413
Combinenet, 137
Combinent BioMedical Systems, 520
ComBrio, 989, 1920
comCables, 1837
Comcen Computer Supplies Ltd, 2836
Comcore Semiconductor, 765
Comdata, 541
Comedy.com, 1952
CoMentis, 458, 1616
Comentis, 495
Comergent, 1255
Comerica, 3284
Comerica Bank, 3258, 3279
Comes Bois, 3134
Comet Bio, 2061
Comet Ridge Resources, 1443
Comet Solutions, 187, 756
Comet Systems, 502, 954
Comfy, 491, 1154, 1282
Comgates, 2585
COMgroup International, 1837
Comic Rocket, 1463
Comilion, 1896
ComiXology, 1310
Comixology, 1584
Comlase, 2878
Comlinkdata, 92
Comm-Art International, 2949
Comm-Works Holdings, 1343
Comma, 124
Command Alkon, 1516
Command Audio, 1244, 1733
Command Health, 1023
Command Information, 1348, 1400
Command Security Corporation, 1837
CommandDot, 318
Commerce 5, 1896
Commerce Connect Media, 21
Commerce Decisions, 2711, 3107
Commerce Decisions Ltd, 2894
Commerce Guys, 2385
Commerce One, 757, 1038, 1255, 1558, 1975, 1983
CommerceSync, 384
Commercetools, 2441, 2824
Commercial Bank of Ceylon, 3151
Commercial Bearing Service, 2286
Commercial Credit, 1147
Commercial Defeasance, 1752
Commercial Financial Services, 111
Commercial Solutions, 2049
Commercial Steel Trating Corporation, 917
Commercial Tribe, 36
Commercialware, 402
Commericial Advance, 869
Commericial Tribe, 876
Commerz, 2810
Commil ltd, 2770
Commil Ltd., 2750

Commit, 2451
CommitChange, 307
Committee to Protect Journalists, 1374
Commodites Corp., 541
Commodity Blenders, 932
Common, 1149, 1183, 1346, 1694
Common Assets, 1810
Common Curriculum, 19
Common Networks, 648, 816, 1151
Common Resources III, 672, 1443
Common Sensing, 1509, 1618
CommonBond, 1696, 1849
CommonCents, 622
Commonfloor.com, 578
CommonTime, 2407
Commonwealth Bank, 2659
Commonwealth Business Media, 21, 1557
Commonwealth Chesapeake, 1795
Commonwealth Fusion Systems, 800
Commonwealth Network Technologies, 314
Commonwealth Sprague, 1295
Commonwealth Sprague Capacitor, 1751
Commpario, 2899
Commprize, 2775
CommProve, 3179
CommQuest, 247
Commrail, 1915
CommScope, 413
Commsoft, 1621
Communauto, 2181
Communicado (Now Screentime Communicado), 2664
Communication Science, 1532
Communications & Power Industries Inc., 575
Communications Products and Services, 1152
Communications Supply Corporation, 914
Communispace, 856
Community & Southern Bank, 1270
Community & Southern Bank Holdings, 1123
Community Broadcasters LLC, 1344
Community Cars, 678
Community Energy, 1689
Community First, 260
Community Health TV, 995
Community Home Health, 406
Community Investment Management, 1258
Community Investors, 1189
Community Links, 2539
Community Medicla Services, 503
Community of Science, 1599
Community Sift, 2157
Community Sourced Capital, 3277
Community Trust Financial Corp., 1443
Community Veterinary Partners, 546
CommunityBrands, 1000
CommunityOne Bancorp, 413
Communo, 2212
CommutAir, 1422
Commuter Advertising, 628
CommVerge Solutions, 1361, 1474, 2597
ComNet, 1136
Comoto Holdings, 1049
Compaas, 1054
Compact Particle Acceleration, 1379
Compact Particle Acceleration Corporation, 583
Compact Power, 2169
Compagnie Européenne de Prestations Logistique, 152
Compal Communications, 3218
Companeo, 413
Companion, 1121
Company.com, 793
Compaq, 1558
Compaq Computer, 197
Comparably, 306, 518, 561, 563, 1149, 1888
Comparaonline.com, 1560
compare, 2361

CompareAsia, 842
Compas, 2446
CompAS Controls, 1440
Compass, 2, 842, 1001, 2772, 3055, 3081
Compass EOS, 1334
Compass Therapeutics, 268, 308, 889
Compass Water Solutions, 1275, 1281
Compassion-First Pet Hospitals, 1505
Compatible Systems, 315
Compel, 869
Compellent Technologies, 555, 2639
Compellon, 1051
Compendium, 658
Compete, 468, 521, 925, 1725
Competentia, 3076
Competitive Power Ventures Holdings, 1956
Competitive Technology, 352
Competitor Group, 683
Competitor Sports Technology, 2850
Compex, 1963
Compin Group, 3020
Complete Genomics, 184, 1493
Complete Holdings Group, 1732
Complete Innovations, 1770
Completel, 1211
CompleteXrm, 1884
Complex Media, 28, 202
Complex Media Network, 1597
Complexa, 293, 1448
ComplexCare Solutions, 1956
Complexe Funeraire Ste-Bernadette, 2095
Complexe Sportif Interplus, 2095
Complia Health, 416
Compliance Assurance Corporation, 998
Compliance Control, 3010
Complion, 251, 1047
Complix, 2949, 3020, 3042
Complix Alphabody Therapeutics, 2476
Comply 365, 630
Comply Advantage, 2478
ComplySci, 655
Complyserv, 2967
Compology, 1054, 1097
Component Sourcing International, 164
ComponentArt, 2058, 2058
CompoSecure, 1136
Composit Ltd., 2750
Composite Software, 623, 1407, 1796
Composite Systems, 502
Composite Technologies, 1275
Compositence, 2824
Compound, 124, 295, 525, 1933
ComPower Systems, 2058
Compower Systems, 2058
Comprehend, 563, 644, 1121, 1518, 1654
Comprehensive Addiction Programs, 1275
Comprehensive Clinical Development, 474
Comprehensive NeuroScience, 691
Comprehensive Pharmacyservices, 176
Comprehensive Prosthetics & Orthotics, 3211
Compression Kinetics, 995, 1187
Compression Polymers Group, 465
Compressor Controls Corp., 465
Compro Pago, 2984
CompStak, 386
Compstak, 377, 707
Compucare, 1255
CompuCom Systems, 1815
CompuDyne Corporation, 500
Compugen, 1896
Compugroup, 2771
CompuLink, 2465
Compumotor, 260
Compund Therapeutics, 2445
CompuPlay, 1986
CompUSA, 202
Compusearch, 166, 1041

Portfolio Companies Index

Computable, 525, 1151, 1363
Computacenter, 2796
Computer Aided Services, 536
Computer Aided Technology, 489
Computer Generation Inc., 152
Computer Motion, 69
Computer Science Innovations, 1708
Computerized Electricity Systems, 2417
computershare, 2771
Computex Technology Solutions, 1280
Computility, 344
Computime, 61
CompuTrain Europe B.V, 2537, 2538
Compuware, 37, 901
Compuware Corporation, 1814
ComRent, 834
ComRent InternationaldCLI, 2379
COMS Interactive, 1752
ComScore, 1677
Comscore, 28
Comscore Networks, 1001
ComSong Interactive Technologies, 2910
ComSpace, 1558
Comstellar, 494
Comstock Resources, 1082
Comstock Systems Corporation, 1008
Comsys, 1409, 2775
Comtempo Ceramic Tile, 468
Comverge, 928, 1355, 1579
Comvest Partners, 3264
Comview, 2775
Comware, 2807
Con-Fom, 3076
Conamix, 704
Conatus Pharmaceuticals, 237, 1268, 3085
Concent, 2537, 2538
Concentra, 558, 1255, 1972, 3014
Concentric, 1100
Concentric Educational Solutions, 1316
Concentric Equity Partners, 3262
Concentrx Pharmaceuticals, 3259
Concept 10 Inc., 623
Concept Mat, 2095
Concept Shopping, 1003
Concept Therapeutics, 1261
concept3D, 1090
Conceptboard, 2824, 2932
ConceptDrop, 1155
Conception Gsr, 2095
Conception Technology, 1837
Concepts Direct, 1837
Conceptua Math, 1061
Conceptus, 1378, 1906
Concerro, 136, 1052
Concert Industries, 2067
Concert Pharmaceuticals, 747, 1197, 1298, 1691, 1819, 3196
Concert Window, 1306
ConcertoHealth, 943
Concha, 395
Concierge Choice, 1584
Concierge Stat, 622
Concillium, 2709
Concord Communications, 314, 805
Concord Enviro, 834
Concord Foods, 147
Concord Health Partners, 3264
Concord Medical Service Co., 413
Concorde Career Colleges, 1116
Concordia Coffee Company, 753
Concordia Fibers, 1693
Concours Mania Groupe, 2851
Concours Mold, 559
Concrete Technologies Worldwide, 1081
Concung, 1139
Concur, 1534
Concur Japan, 1755

Concur Technologies, 1001
Concurrent, 1540, 1860
Concurrent Electronic Design Automation, 998
Concurrent Manufacturing, 225
Concurrent Real-Time, 235
Concurrent Thinking, 2967, 3107
Conditioned Air, 812
conditorei Coppenrath & Wiese GmbH & Co., 77
Condo Control Central, 2170
Condor Systems, 245
Conductor, 427, 646, 743, 1181
Conductor (Credit Card Processing), 3180
Conduit, 858
Conectt, 2626
Conelec, 1159
Conenza, 85
Conerstone, 724
ConertoHealth, 149
Conexance, 3239
Conexant, 839
Conexant Systems, 2005
ConexED, 1070
Conexia Energy, 3020
CoNextions, 270, 1070
Conexus Energy, 1278, 1326
Confer, 770, 1181
Confer Health, 1696
Confetti, 814
Confide, 741, 889, 1110, 2928
Confident Cannabis, 358
Confident Financial Solutions, 781
Confie Seguros, 21
ConfigureSoft, 1041
Confirm.io, 431, 2239
Confirma, 753, 1792, 1915, 1975
Confirma Software, 21
Conflucence Solar, 2632
Confluence Outdoor, 1037
Confluence Resources, 1278, 1326
Confluence Solar, 1365
Confluence Technologies, 1460
Confluences Life Sciences, 689
Confluent, 118, 248, 1654
Confluent Health, 654
Confluent Surgical, 176, 1445
Conforma Therapeutics, 769, 1574
Conformative, 202
Conformative Systems, 1445
ConforMIS, 1975
Confortvisuel.com, 3020
Confovis, 2824
Confuence Pharmaceuticals, 658
Conga, 1000, 1607
Congebec, 2095
Conger & Elsea, 1423
Congress Inns, 1404
Congressional Bank, 1599
Congruency, 2585
Congruex Holdings, 559
Coniq, 3097
Conject, 3113
ConjuGon, 2001
Conjur, 206
Connance, 1334
Connaught Group Ltd, 2836
Connect, 1626
Connect America Holdings, 716
Connect Group, 2949
Connect Managed Servies, 2944
Connect Part, 2446
Connect Resource Services, 740
Connect South, 1255
Connect Towers, 1734
Connect-Air International, 556
Connect.me, 3152
ConnectBlue, 2439
Connected, 223, 852, 1702, 1738, 1853

Connected Backup, 2709
Connected Living Inc., 831
Connected Signals, 249, 1613, 1834
Connected2fiber, 178
ConnectedHealth, 2778
ConnectEDU, 1114
ConnectHQ, 1798
Connecticut Color, 321
Connecticut Innovations, 3273
Connectifier, 1099
Connectify, 979
Connection Brands, 1615
Connection Engine, 1760
ConnectiveRx, 762, 819
Connectivity, 1566, 1798, 2662
Connectivity Wireless, 1606
ConnectM, 2849
Connectria, 333
Connecture, 475, 779, 859, 1732, 1863
ConnectYourCare, 22
Connelly-Boland and Associates, 3275
Conner, 541, 1853
Conner Perphirals, 1211
Connetbeam, 805
Connetics Corporation, 94
Connexina, 2967
Connexion Point, 1927
Connexions Asia, 2690
Connexity, 306
Connextions, 1301
Connor Bros, 1456
Connotate, 422, 1478
ConnXus, 479
Conoisseur Communications, 21
Conoptica, 2754
Conor Medsystems, 136, 644
Conpoto, 1736
Conquer Mobile, 2155
Consecutive Capital, 751
Consejosano, 55
Consel On Call, 873
Conselytics, 858
Consensus, 79
Consensus Orthopedics, 330, 331
Consensus Point, 841
Consensys Imaging Services, 806
Consentry, 1911
Consero Consulting, 2967
Consero Global, 361
Consert, 1926
Conserv, 1954
Conservis, 570
Consilient Health, 1452
Consilio & Advanced Discovery, 824
Consilium Software, 3062
Consistel, 3062
Consodata, 2765
Consol, 909
Consolidated Container Company, 220
Consolidated Energy Systems, 1542
Consolidated Equipment Group, 903
Consolidated Fire Protection, 373, 881
Consolidated Precision Products, 290, 1956
Consolidated Precision Products Corp., 166, 254
Consolidayed Precision Products Corp., 985
ConsoliDent, 1557
Consolitated Theatres, 21
Consoltex, 109
Consorte, 2632
Consorte Media, 1760
ConsortNT, 2466
Constant Contact, 521, 954, 1146, 1255, 1623
Constant Therapy, 1054
Constanta, 3187
Constantia Flexibles, 1376
Constella, 1409
Constellar, 1558

1292

Portfolio Companies Index

Constellation Pharma, 1916
Constellation Pharmaceuticals, 517, 1731, 1811
Constellation Services International, 715
Construct, 307
Construction Control, 2089
Construction L.F.G., 2095
Construction Labor Contractors, 465, 1684
Construction Leclerc Et Pelletier, 2095
Construction Software Technologies, 1824
Constructive Media, 928
Constructor, 2019, 2384
Constructor.io, 799
Consultative Group to Assist the Poor, 1374
Consulting Solutions, 529
Consumer Brands, 275
Consumer Media Network, 21
Consumer Physics, 668, 1069
ConsumerReview, 1646
Consumerunited, 1715
Consumr, 1222
Consure Medical, 28
Conta Azul, 2983
ContaAzul, 11, 1560
Contac Services, 2091
Contact, 2717
Contact East, 1295
Contact Engine, 2997
Contact Solutions, 1334
Contactually, 313, 544, 876, 3044
Container Consultants & Systems, 2334
ContainerShip, 272
Contastic, 1483
Contec, 220
Contec Medical, 3007
Contech, 2881
Contech Engineered Solutions, 1134
Contego Fraud, 2967
Contego Fraud Solutions, 2567
Contego Medical, 915
Contego Services Group, 61
Contendo, 1796
Content Analytics, 89
Content Fleet, 2994
Content Flow, 2841
Content Raven, 649, 1100
Contentful, 816, 2478, 3044
Contently, 533, 724, 1024, 1118, 1358, 1673, 1789
Contents Japan, 2991
ContentWise, 2751
Contessa Premium Foods Inc., 465
Contex A/S, 2712
Contexo Media, 1927
Context Integration, 402
Context Logic, 1254
Context Media, 56
Contextin, 1715
ConteXtream, 1926
Contextream, 249
Continental, 926
Continental Airlines, 1835
Continental Business Credit, 1970
Continental Cablevision, 314
Continental Coal Ltd., 638
Continental Energy Systems LLC, 1129
Continental Fire & Safety, 949
Continental Medical, 541
Continental North Penn Technology, 869
Continental Services, 1578
Continental Structural Plastics, 477, 1343
Continental Warehousing, 1956
Continental Windpower, 1784
Contino, 515
Contintental Electronics Corp., 1925
Continuity, 29, 585, 1097
Continuity Control, 741, 1571
Continuous Computing, 1407

Continuous Computing Corp, 905
Continuum, 493, 551, 1752
Continuum Energy, 914
Continuum Photonics, 1038
ContinuumRx, 918, 1241, 1533
Contorion, 3056
Contour Aerospace, 869
Contour Energy Systems, 979, 1896
Contour Industries, 409
Contour Semiconductor, 712
Contract Land Staff, 1343
Contract Security, 1154
Contract Services Limited, 465
Contraline, 24
Contrast, 3149
Contrast Security, 41, 235, 816
Control Circle, 3104
Control Delivery Systems, 1255
Control Device, 1343
Control Devices LLC, 843
Control Systems BV, 2806
Control Works, 1915
Control4, 770, 1204, 1677, 1884
ControlCase, 1293
Controlex, 2795
Controlled Contamination Services, 702, 1422
Controlled Products, 503
Controls Southeast Inc., 985
ControlScan, 695, 904, 946, 1863
Controltec, 1784
Contros, 2824
Convansys Inc (Us/India), 2694
ConvaTec, 209, 413
Convene, 727
Convenience Food Systems, 2883
Convenient Power HK Limited, 1241
ConvenientMD, 378
Conventor, 1288
Conventus Orthopaedics, 297
Conventus Orthopaedics Inc., 269
Convera, 979
Convercent, 1558, 1620
Converd, 2978
Converge, 1611
Converge Medical, 898
Converge Venture Partners, 3273
Convergence Pharmaceuticals, 1298
ConvergeNet, 1793
Convergent, 1423
Convergent Dental, 329, 1142
Convergent Group, 1668
ConvergeOne, 500
Convergex, 884
Convergint Technologies, 1086
Convergys Corp., 300
Converity, 770
Converium, 2922
Conversant, 1742
Converser, 2948
Conversion Logic, 1110
ConversionLogic, 306, 561
Conversocial, 2662, 2674, 3018
Convert.com, 2382
Convertergy, 3194
Converting, 1171
Convertro, 260, 634, 1226
Converus, 79, 1070
Convery Computer, 1010
Convex, 1558
Convey, 36, 322, 545
Convey Computer, 1558
Convey Health Solutions, 528
Convictional, 795, 1138
Convio, 57, 58, 184, 202, 852, 1540
CONVIVA, 1425
Conviva, 770, 823, 1297, 1604, 1827
Convo, 1257

Convoy, 262, 578, 872, 1530
ConWeaver, 2824
Cooee, 2452
Cook & Boardman Group, 1134
Cook It, 2099
Cook Taste Eat, 301
Cookies, 3236
Cookin, 622
Cooking.com, 263, 502, 765
Cookitfor.us, 1615
Cookstr, 1306
Cookwizme, 2856
Cool Dry, 3098
Cool Energy, 972
Cool Gear International, 46, 1521
Cool Planet Energy Systems, 532, 889
Cool Sculpting, 59
Cooladata, 1607, 3221
Coolan, 1696
CoolBrands International, 2254
CoolChip Technolgies, 1912
CoolChip Technologies, 643, 981
Cooledge, 809, 2291
CoolEdge Lighting, 153, 2053
Cooledge Lighting, 2143
Coolerado, 259
Coolerado Corporation, 1730
Cooley, 3259, 3276
Coolfire Solutions, 1019
Coolibar, 1113
Cooliris, 620, 1977
CoolIT, 457
CoolIT Systems, 2048, 2157
Coolman Entertainment, 1087
CoolPlanet, 1334
Coolr, 1945
CoolSpotter, 1641
CoolTech, 19
Cooltech Applications, 3020
Cooper Equipment Rentals, 2251
Cooper-Standard Automotive Inc., 575
Cooperative De Travailleurs Actionnaire De Negotiu, 2095
Cooperative De Travailleurs Actionnaire De Tec, 2095
Cooperative Forestiere De Girardville, 2095
Cooperative Forestiere De L'Outaouais, 2095
Cooperative Funeraire De, 2095
CooperSmith, 1708
Cooptalis, 2851
Coord, 1894
Coordinated Care Solutions, 1103
Copa90, 641
Copac, 415
Copado, 1000
Copan Systems, 202
Copano Energy, 1835, 1846
Copart Inc., 300
CoPatient, 2233
Copia, 1329
Copient Health, 189
Copilot, 1888
Copiun, 1097, 1348
Coplex, 3276
Copper, 231, 889, 1082, 1346
Copper Key, 2021
Copper Mountain, 757, 1087, 1558, 1760
Copper Mountain Beverages, 1512
CopperEgg, 1810
CopperEye, 979
Copperfield Chimney Supply, 908
Coppergate, 3221
Copperleaf Technologies, 2143
Coprosain, 3134
COR, 1760
Cor4 Oil, 1125
Cora Health Services, 881

1293

Portfolio Companies Index

Coradiant, 596, 1237
Coraid, 1072
Coral Eurobet, 2587
Coral Network, 1558
Coral Systems, 1398
Coral Therapeutics, 1628
Coralog, 2855
CorAssist, 2726, 3241, 3249
Corassist, 2454
CorasWorks, 1348
Coravin, 1993
Corbus Pharmaceuticals, 1160
Corcept Therapeutics, 1760, 1786
Corda Campus, 2949
Cordance, 85
Cordant, 1963
Cordata, 86, 479
Cordial, 1888
Cordium, 3130
Corduro, 889
Core, 1721
Core BTS, 1777
Core Business Technology Solutions, 774
Core Capital Partners, 3270
Core Commnications, 1599
CORE Diagnostics, 174
Core Innovation Capital, 1374
CORE Interactive, 3267
Core Line Pipe, 2025
Core OS, 2006
CORE Outdoor Power, 1623
Core Pacific Group, 2633
Core Pharma, 1590
Core Photonics, 2831, 2952
Core Security Technologies, 1255, 2334
Core Solutions, 1568, 1577
Core Tigo, 1670
CoreCare Systems, 1203
Coredial, 230, 1136
CoreHr, 1041
Corel, 1910
CoreLab, 118
CoreLab Partners, 57, 1628
Corelight, 28, 816
CoreLink Data Centers, 1153
CoreLogic, 300
CoreMedia, 3155
Coremetrics, 793, 1646
Corengi, 1615
Corensic, 2008
CoreObjects, 1407
CoreOptics, 555, 986, 2639
CoreOS, 2012
CorePharma Holdings, 1456
Corephotonics, 116
CorePower Yoga, 1088
CorePROFIT Solutions, 1227
CoreSpring, 1316
CoreStreet, 1886
CoreTek, 56, 1038
Coretelligent, 1927
Coreteq Systems, 3141
CoreTrace, 1916
Coretronic, 2436
CoreValue Software, 223
Corevia Medical, 816
CoreView, 1000
Coreworks, 2717
Coreworx, 2109
Corex, 2571
Corfin Industries LLC, 245
Corgenix, 1837
Corgreen Technologies, 1079
Corhythm, 980
Corindus Vascular Robotics Inc., 269
Corio, 757
Coriolis Networks, 314

Cority, 1346, 2132
Cority Software Inc., 158
Corium, 138
Corix Group, 2051
Corixa, 769, 782, 1760
Cormetech, 675
Cormetrics, 28
Cormier Textile Products, 438
Corn. Van Loocke, 2332
Corneliani, 1017
Corner Bakery Cafe, 1576
Cornerjob, 641, 2874
Cornershop, 28, 1024
Cornerstone, 238
Cornerstone Automation Systems, 477
Cornerstone Brands, 1156
Cornerstone Chemical, 928
Cornerstone Chemical Company, 1134
Cornerstone Concrete, 462
Cornerstone Fund Services, 3276
Cornerstone Medical & Technology Financial, 3259
Cornerstone Natural Resources, 672
Cornerstone On Demand, 32
Cornerstone OnDemand, 260, 1212
Cornhusker Energy, 42
Cornice, 925
Cornice Corporation, 2079
Corona Labs, 1218
Corona Optical Systems, 1057
Coronado Curragh Pty., 967
Coronis, 2481
Coronis Health, 349
Coronis Systems, 2466
Corpak Medsystems, 1128
Corpmart.com, 2993
Corporate Trael International, 2944
Corporate Visions, 405
CorporateRewards, 1572
Corporation Dermoaesthetica (Spain), 2784
Corpus Medical, 118
Correct Care Solutions, 194, 884
CorrectNet, 2196
Corredge Networks, 1676
Correlated Magnetics Research, 1028
Correlia Biosystems, 2213
Correlix, 3240
CorrelSense, 3059
Correlsense, 3214
Corridor Pharmaceuticals, 1196
CorridorPharma, 1508
Corrigo, 114, 777, 1733, 1769
Corrmoran, 2824
Corrona, 859
Corsa, 2076
Corsa Technology, 2242
Corsair, 779
Corsair Communications, 1682
Corsica Innovations Inc., 490
Corsicana Mattress Company, 1141
Corso UK, 2967
CorSolutions Medical Corporation, 955
Cort, 354
CorTec, 2824, 2932
Cortefiel, 909, 3033
Cortene, 1095
Cortera, 235, 1830
Cortex, 641, 1758
Cortex Pharmaceuticals, 975
Cortexica Vision Systems, 2858
Cortexyme, 1654, 1778
Corthera, 1898
Corti, 2851
Cortica, 2831
Cortigroupe, 3134
Cortilla, 2672
Cortina, 87, 386, 596, 968

Cortina Systems, 1080, 1257, 1911
Corton Precision Optical Company, 1558
Corus Health Realty, 1599
Corus Pharma, 132, 1002
Corval Energy, 2025
Corvara, 2325
Corvas International, 1706, 1918
Corventis, 1247, 1500
Corvia Medical, 2180
Corvida Medical, 1061
Corvidia Therapeutics, 143
Corvil, 483, 1522, 2472
Corvis, 2007
Corvita Corporation, 1378
Corvium, 570
Corvus, 2
Corvus Insurance, 1363
Corwave, 3113
CoScale, 3065
Cosemi Technologies, 1784
Cosential, 52
Cosentry, 1776
CoSine Communications, 757, 1793
Coskata, 59, 835, 1474
Cosm Care, 2149
Cosmetic Essence Innovations, 1134
Cosmic Cart, 635
Cosmosbay, 2354
Cosmosbay Vectis, 2354
Cosmotech, 2439
Cost:bart, 3203
Costanoa Venture Capital, 1760
Costco, 1096
Costco Wholesale, 869
Costella Kirsch, 3284
Costello, 658
CoStim, 1419
CoStim Pharmaceuticals, 191, 1268
Cota, 697
Cota Capital, 295
CoTap, 455
Cotap, 665
Cote Sud Invetissement, 2601
CoTEch Ventures, 3262
Cotendo, 1474
Cotera, 621
Cotherics, 782
Cotherix, 94
Cotiviti, 1925
Cotopaxi, 325, 544, 727, 761, 1070, 1110, 2144
Cottan Cosmetic GmbH, 2494
Cotterlaz, 2317
Cotton Patch Cafe, 96
Cotton Tracks, 2984
Cottonwood Capital, 462
CoTweet, 231
Coty Inc., 744
COUB, 890
Couchbase, 28, 57, 620, 836, 974, 1184, 1334, 3235
CouchDB Relax, 1534
CouchSurfing, 816, 1202, 3044
Couchsurfing, 248, 1374
CouchUp, 586
Coulomb Technologies, 912
Council Oak Resources, 672
Counsel On Call, 493, 1166
Counsel Press, 828, 1191
Counselytics, 525
Counsyl, 775, 858
Countable, 934
Counterpane Internet Security, 260
CounterPath, 2284
CounterPoint Health Solutions, 970
CounterStorm, 1038, 1348
CounterTack, 171, 712, 1241, 2690
Countertop Foods, 120

1294

Portfolio Companies Index

Countly, 3108
Country Club Enterprises, 828
Country Fresh, 686
Country Pure Foods, 290, 619
Country Road Communications, 21
CountryBanc, 1372
Countryside Hospice, 932
Countryside Power Income Fund, 2073
Countrywide plc, 140
Coupa, 235, 296, 563, 1212, 1247, 1522
Coupang, 91, 100, 560, 771, 976, 1475, 2709
Coupling Wave Solutions, 2385
CouponRani, 3133
Coupons.com, 1846
CoupSmart, 1512
CoUrbanize, 308
Courion, 1041, 1400, 1515
Course Hero, 115, 858, 883, 1183
Course Report, 1551
CourseHorse, 1306, 1310, 1358
Coursera, 802, 883, 1075, 1297, 1640, 2690
CourseStorm, 1161
Coursicle, 995
Court Buddy, 741
Court Square Capital Partners, 3264
Court Square Capital Partners III LP, 2094
Courtagen, 732
Courtagen Life Sciences, 907
CourtLink, 85
CourtTrax, 1226
Cova, 2136
Covacsis, 483
Covalent Health, 926
Covariant, 219
Covariant AI, 4, 1611
Covario, 793, 1945
Covaro Networks, 444
Covast, 2779, 3233
Cove.tool, 1894
Covelight Systems, 1008
Covenant Care, 447
Covenant Healthcare, 2695
Covenant Review, 1105
Covenant Surgical Partners, 1082
Coventor, 812
CoVenture, 858
Coventya, 2965
Coveo, 2264
Coveo Solutions, 2029, 2261
Cover, 858, 1183, 1359, 1531, 1663, 1696, 1848
Cover FX, 1088
Cover My Test, 1169
Coverall, 969, 1491
Covercraft Industries LLC, 449
Coverfox, 28
CoverHound, 301, 358, 1593
Coverhound, 128
Coveright Surfaces GmbH, 2660
Coveright Surfaces Holding GmbH, 914
Coveris, 1753
Coverity, 452
CoverMyMeds, 779, 1047
Coveroo, 531, 1540
Covertix, 2669
CoverWallet, 770, 1882
Covestor, 238, 1715
Covics, 2936
covina Biomedical, 2155
CoWare, 1288
Coware Inc., 2902
Cox Insurance, 2676
Coxon, 2436
Coya, 641
Coyne Textile Services, 402
Coyote Logistics, 1956
Coyuchi, 548, 3092
Cozart, 2463

Cozi Group, 925
Cozy, 816, 889, 1656, 1696
Cozzini Bros, 194, 2062
Cozzini Bros., 158
CP Energy, 559
CP Media LLC, 669
CP Secure, 905
CP Well Testing, 1491
CPA, 2967
CPA Global, 744, 1109
CPC, 192, 3020
CPCEP, 3194
CPF Living Communities; Florida Elite Medical Grou, 469
CPG International, 64, 901, 1037
CPG International Inc., 159
CPI, 168, 787, 2695
CPI Card Group, 2214
CPI International, 1925
CPI Luxury Group, 17
CPI. Crown Van Gelder, 123
CPL Industries, 1937
CPM Holdings, 827
CPO Commerce, 1841
CPower, 260, 706, 928
Cpower, 2439
CPS, 786, 2674
CPS Houston, 984
CPS Products Inc., 908
CPT, 2710
CPUsage, 1254
CPV Maryland Holding Company II, 158
CPV Wind Ventures, 156
CPX Lone Tree Hotel, 1020
CPX Security, 2, 178
CQMS Razer, 109
CQS, 2709
Cquia, 1359
CQuotient, 221
CR Brands, 1545
CR Media Group, 2487
CR-X, 2975
CR2, 2336, 3191
CRA Continental Realty Advisors, 297
Crackle, 1323
Cradle Technologies, 925
Cradle Techologies, 1676
CradlePoint, 1204
Cradlepoint Technology, 1391
Craegmoor, 2935
Craft Dragon, 2967
Craft International, 514
Craft Media Network, 375
CraftArtEdu, 375
CraftMark Bakery, 477
Craftrad, 3236
Craftsmen Industries, 1477
Craftsvilla, 1121
Craftsvilla.com, 3001
Craftsy, 36, 1748
Craftyful, 1965
Craigcare Group, 2814
Crain Hot Old Services, 1053
Cramster.com, 1099
Crane & Co., 77, 1129
Crane 1, 1435
Crane Company, 832
Craneware, 3104
Cranial Technologies, 244
Cranite Systems, 1038
Cranium, 1183, 1865
Cranswick Pet and Aquatics (Tropical Marine Center, 2944
Crash, 1527
Crashlytics, 231
CrashMob, 1291
Crate, 2674

Crate.io, 2019
Crater, 226, 1323
Crave Labs, 1486
Crawfish Cogen, 156
Crawley Ventures LLC, 3276
Craxel, 851
Crayon, 231
CRB Innovations, 1558
CRC Health, 373, 374
CRC Health Group, 220
CRC Industries Inc., 258
CRCM Ventures, 483
Cre Apps, 2984
Creaform, 2029
Creal, 2338
Crealta Pharmaceuticals, 884
Crealytics, 2824, 2932, 2979
Creas Carolinas, 3259
Creatcomm, 1509
Create Electronic Optical Co, 2703
Create&Learn, 883
Create1, 1585
Creation Holdings Inc., 158
Creation Technologies, 2079, 2082
Creative Artists Agency, 1835
Creative Circle, 1256
Creative Deign Systems, 626
Creative Forming, 1171
Creative Labs, 3108
Creative Live, 518, 720
Creative Market, 1146, 1655, 2027
Creative Mines, 846
Creative Multimedia, 753, 1398
Creative Peptides Sweden AB, 2816
Creative Solutions Group, 1295
CreativeDrive, 257
CreativeGig, 1958
CreativeLIVE, 1696, 2428
CreativeLive, 872
Creativelive, 883
creativeLIVE, 889
CreativeWorx, 1306
Creativity Software, 2972
Creator, 519, 889
CreatorDen, 2284
CREDANT Technologies, 555
Credant Technologies, 202, 986
Credence, 59
Credence Resources, 2136
Credence Systems, 202, 1682
Credential, 2539
Credential Solutions, 334
Crederity, 3211
Credibly, 750
CrediFi, 235, 3221
Credit Benchmark, 2478
Credit Central, 1491
Credit Infonet Group, 1651
Credit Karma, 578, 720, 1502, 1759
Credit Key, 306
Credit Sesame, 384, 835, 1013, 1202
CreditCall Limited, 2507
CreditCards.com, 202
CreditEase, 973
CreditKarma, 1560
CreditSights, 711
CreditStacks, 1370
Credivalores, 46
Credo West, 514
CredoRax, 2974
Credorax, 301, 793
CredSimple, 317, 1475, 1993
CreekPath Systems, 1793
Creekstone Farms, 1753
Creganna, 97
Creganna-Tactx Medical, 3033
Crehana, 1551

1295

Portfolio Companies Index

Crelate Talent, 745
Cremascoli Ortho, 2676
Creme de la Creme, 65
Creme Mel, 928
Creo Products, 3137
CREPAPER GmbH, 2686
Cresa, 3279
Crescendo, 2772
Crescendo Biologics, 182, 1778, 2463, 2967
Crescendo Biosciences, 1247
Crescendo Bioscience, 1691
Crescendo Communications, 1853, 1896
Crescendo Networks, 2472
Crescendo Ventures, 986
Crescent, 415
Crescent City Schools, 1316
Crescent Diagnostics, 2918
Crescent Entertainment, 494
Crescent Sleep Products, 843
CrescentDx, 2355
Crescerance, 271
CRESecure, 1863
Cresilon, 622
Cressey & Company, 3264, 3265
Crestcom, 1281
Crestcom International, 1484
CrestMarc, 2978
Crestmark, 1219
Crestview Partners, 3255
Crestwood, 1846
Crestwood Midstream Partners, 277
Crete Energy, 1795
Crevet Limited, 2951
Crew, 49, 180, 872, 1097, 1654, 1721
Crexendo, 1583
CREXi, 784, 1055
Crexi, 228, 1024, 1110
CRFS Services, 932
CRG, 2113
CRH Healthcare, 783
CRI Worldwide, 118, 1628
Cribspot, 961
Cricket Health, 318, 741, 1323, 1656
Cril Telecom Software, 2354, 2781
CrimeReports, 202
Crimson Hexagon, 841, 858, 1437, 1584, 1757, 2017
Crimson Pipeline LP, 1278, 1326
Crimson Well Services Inc., 902
Crinetics, 12, 1519, 1928
Crioestaminal, 1572
Crisi Medical Systems, 1784
Crisp Media, 539, 1211
Crisplant Industries, 2863
Crispr, 1928
Crispr Therapeutics, 1731
Cristal Delivery, 2514
Criteo, 57, 260, 1699, 2693, 2851, 2860, 2860
Criteria Investment Partners LLC, 623
Criteria Labs, 1915
Criterion Brock, 1969
Critical Alert Systems, 1969
Critical Blue, 3032
Critical Links, 3048
Critical Media, 494
Critical Mention, 1306, 1584, 1680, 1745
Critical Path, 1247
Critical Perfusion, 1600
Critical Signal Technologies, 633, 636
Critical Solutions International, 1651, 1870
Critical Start, 333
CriticalFit, 450
Criticalpath, 2771
Critigen, 126, 839
Crius Energy, 126, 707
CRMnext, 1346
Crocodoc, 1581

Crocs, 277
Crocus, 2876
Crocus Technology, 3208
CrodFlower, 1513
Crom, 1270
Crompco Corp., 465
Crono, 998
Cronofy, 942, 3108
Cronos, 1062
Crop Design, 2781
Croptimize Inc., 392
Cropx, 996
Crosman Acquisition Corporation, 765
Crosman Corporation, 1971
Cross, 492
Cross Fader, 1749
Cross Fernandez & Riley, 3262
Cross Mediaworks, 492, 518, 1104
Cross River, 124
Cross River Bank, 235
Cross Trees Medical, 177
Cross-Country Infrastructure Services Inc., 1368
Crossbar, 174, 544, 1075, 1340
Crossbeam, 741
Crossbeam Systems, 314, 455, 455, 521, 757, 1181, 1728
Crossboard Mobiel, 1593
Crossboard Mobil, 1291
Crossbow, 1400
Crossbow Technology, 378, 1257
CrossCHX, 630
CrossCom, 316
Crosscom National, 838
CrossComm, 3259
CrossEngage, 2841
CrossEyes, 3203
Crossfader, 721
CrossFiber, 171, 1305, 1711
Crossing Automation Inc., 1779
Crossing Rocks Energy, 1326
CrossLand Mortgage Corp., 541
Crosslayer Networks, 1180
CrossLoop, 103
Crossman Corporation, 1491
Crossmark, 1956
Crossmatch, 779
CrossMedia Services, 161, 805
Crossover, 607
Crossplane Capital, 14
Crossrider, 1323
CrossRoads, 1187
Crossroads Systems, 202
Crosstown Traders, 839
Crosstown Traders Inc., 433
Crosstrees Medical, 1558
Crossvertise, 2824
Crossway Media Solutions, 2333
Crosswire, 2831
Crothall Healthcare, 1136
Crowd AI, 318
Crowd Architects, 2527
Crowd Compass, 85
Crowd Cow, 1158, 1183
Crowd Factory, 1747
Crowd Guru, 2841
Crowd Strike, 578
Crowd Supply, 1656
Crowd Technologies, 2967
CrowdAI, 107, 525, 1758
Crowdamp, 1121
Crowdanalytix, 28
Crowdbooster, 1513
Crowdcare, 2113
Crowdcast, 1323
CrowdCompass, 1383
CrowdComputing Systems, 871
Crowdcube, 2478

Crowdcube.com, 2674
Crowded, 150
CrowdEngineering, 2672, 3052
CrowdFlower, 260, 396, 784, 1050, 1853
CrowdHall, 1912
CrowdJustice, 741
Crowdly, 1100, 1306, 2017
CrowdMed, 1297
Crowdpac, 544
CrowdProcess, 3108
CrowdRiff, 2133
CrowdRise, 1882, 1883
Crowdrise, 1118
CrowdStar, 946, 1827
Crowdster, 393
CrowdStreet, 1656
CrowdStrike, 28, 1371, 1956
CrowdTangle, 60, 1306
Crowdtap, 776, 1849
Crowdtest, 2331
Crowdtilt, 596
CrowdTwist, 685, 712, 1699, 1738
Crowdtwist, 1789
CrowdVision, 2400
CrowdWorks, 2646
Crowdz, 195
Crowe Horwath, 3262
Crowe Paradis Servicing Corp., 492
Crowe UK LLP, 3276
Crown Affair, 325
Crown Bioscience, 47, 1382
Crown Brands, 446
Crown Castle International, 1211
Crown Column, 415
Crown Fiberglass, 1919
Crown Group, 606
Crown Laboratories, 1251
Crown Pacific, 368
Crown Plastics, 61
Crown Products & Services, 1209
Crownit, 28
Crownpeak, 1024
CrownPeak Technology, 1672
CrownRock, 1125
CrownRock Minerals, 1125
CrownWheel Partners, 1143
CRS CraneSystems, 2235
CRS Proppants, 686
CRS Reprocessing Services, 164
CRS Temporary Housing, 1166
CRT Midco, 1491
CRU Kafe, 3108
CRU-DataPort, 1909
Crucell, 191, 1775, 2378, 2748
CrucialTec, 1087
Cruise, 771, 942, 1329, 1678
Cruise Automation, 4
Crunch, 127
CrunchBase, 720
Crunchbase, 665, 1184, 1607
Crunchbutton, 785
Cruncher, 24
CrunchFund, 202
CrunchTime!, 235
Crunchvase, 552
Crunchyroll, 1916
Crushpath, 455
Crux Biomedical, 666, 925
Cruzar Medical, 426
CRV, 3273
Cryo-Cell, 1681
CryoCor, 184, 468, 1786
Cryocor, 560
Cryogen, 1786
Cryogenic Services, 1708
Cryothermic Systems, 293, 1047, 1553
Cryotherpeutics, 2824

Portfolio Companies Index

CryoVascular Systems, 1896
Crypt, 1110
Crypt TV, 60
CryptoKitties, 124, 525
CryptoMove, 1421
Cryptomove, 1696
CryptoNumerics, 4
Crysalin, 2892
CrystAI-N, 2824
Crystal, 272, 1607
Crystal & Company, 3267
Crystal CG, 2733, 2936
Crystal Decisions, 197
Crystal Dynamics, 131
Crystal Financial, 1315
Crystal IS, 1151
Crystal Jade, 1088
Crystal Optech, 2542
Crystal Orange Hotel Holdings, 413
Crystal Packaging, 1837
Crystal Semi, 1558
Crystal Semiconductor, 202
Crystal Semiconductor, 1682
Crystal Solar, 1365, 1791
Crystal-IS, 153
Crystalplex, 1098, 1448
Crystalsol, 2630
Crystaplex Corporation, 998
Crystax, 2483
Crystechcoating, 2667
Crysteel Manufacturing, 619
CS Identity, 594, 950
CS Indemnity, 406
CSA Medical, 176, 288, 732, 886, 1008, 1299, 1628, 1762
CSA Service Solutions, 667
CSafe Global, 97
CSALC, 1340
CSAT Solutions, 365
CSC Media Group, 1927
CSDVRS, 1153, 1496
CSG Systems International, 1850
CSI Leasing, 456
CSID, 445
CSIdentity, 1017
CSK Auto, 1017
CSL, 3145
CSL DualCom, 3018
CSM Bakery Solutions, 405
CSP Business Media, 1422
CSP Holdings, 553
CSP II Destressed Opportunities Trust, 623
CSR, 2386, 3104
CSRHub, 3277
CST Images, 1837
CSTV, 43
CT Acquisition Corp., 1252
CT Therapeutics, 181
CTACCEL, 1004
CTEK Creator Group, 2384
CTERA, 483
Ctera, 1916
CTi Biopharma, 1297
CTI Foods, 1134, 1815
CTI Life Sciences Fund, 3258
CTI Semiconductor, 2924
CTI Towers, 518
CTM Group Inc., 843
CTO.ai, 2212, 2291
CTP Hydrogen, 520
CTP Offshore-C Feeder Fund Ltd., 2094
Ctrip, 973, 2850
CTRL, 3150
CTRL-Labs, 889, 1151
Ctrlio, 3108
CTS, 1126
Cuadrilla Resources Holdings, 1573

Cub Digital, 2936
Cube, 585
Cube Biotech, 2638
Cube Optics, 1658
Cube Optics AG, 3137
Cube26, 1958
CubeTree, 1853
CubeWorks, 1004
Cubex, 958
Cubical, 2824
Cubie, 3038
Cubie Messenger, 2474
Cubility, 466, 2700
Cubist Pharmaceuticals, 410, 1452, 1775
Cuboh, 2138
Cubyn, 2296
Cuculus, 2824
Cudahy Tanning Co., 1213
Cue, 45, 1821
Cue & Co., 1082
Cuebiq, 150, 2874
Cuemath, 578
Cuff-Gard, 995
Cuff-Mate, 1187
CugarCRM Inc., 1951
Culcherd, 2099
Culinary Agents, 1222
Culinary Standards, 1332
Cullinan Oncology, 1268
Cultivian Sandbox, 3269
Culture Amp, 720
CultureIQ, 229, 1110, 1912
CultureiQ, 1480
CultureLabel, 2685
Culturelabel.com, 2586
CultureMob, 85
CulturVate, 2284
Culver's, 1576
Cumbak, 3109
Cumberland Consulting Group, 1777
Cumberland Therapy Services, 1667
Cumming Acquisition, 1456
Cumming Group, 1141, 1777
Cumulocity, 2824
Cumulocity GmbH, 3213
Cumulus, 124
Cumulus Media, 220, 559, 1815
Cumulus Networks, 235, 1654, 1996
Cunningham Lindsey, 1134
Cunningham Lindsey Group Limited, 1743
Cupo Nation, 2838
Cupoint, 2470
Cuponation, 1297
Cura Software, 2709
Curacity, 1554
Curacyte, 2377
Curagen, 530
Curai, 816
Curalate, 741, 1297
Curam Software, 2734
CuraSeal, 1993
Curaseal, 177
Curasen Therapeutics, 1143
Curaspan Health Group, 1173
Curative Orthopaedics, 622
Curb, 445
curbFlow, 1893
Curbide, 1798
Curbio, 1169
Cure Match, 121
CureAtr, 1993
Cureatr, 52, 1420
Curebase, 708
Cureeo, 1615
CureFab, 2824
Curefab, 2475
Curefit, 28

Curejoy, 28
CureLauncher, 981
Cureo, 1047
Cureon, 2878
Curetis, 2515, 2748, 2939, 3085
Cureus, 491
Curie Co., 395
Curiosity, 1384
Curiosity.com, 1480
Curious AI Company, 2478
Curious.com, 1534
Curisium, 1297
CurlMix, 218
Curo, 787
Curology, 45, 761
Curon Medical, 1378
Curoverse, 534, 915, 1459
Currency, 1147
Currency Capital, 405
Currency Cloud, 38
Currencycloud, 889
Currencyfair, 2759
Currensee, 1334
Current Analysis, 137
Current Media, 300
Current Motor Company, 742
Current TV, 1083
CurrentAnalysis, 989
Curriculet, 1316
Curriculum Associations, 254
Currie Medical, 1232
Currie Medical Specialties Inc., 1040
Curse, 823, 1700, 2851, 3208
Cursogram, 3055
CURT Manufacturing, 1435
Curtis Bay Energy, 1021
Curtis Bay Medical Waste Services, 1751
Curtis Industries Holdings, 1279
Curtis Papers Inc., 1085
Curtis Screw Company, 1970
Curvature, 1505
Curve, 3108
Curve Dental, 235
Curves, 1335
Curvo, 658
Cuseum, 799
Cushcraft Corporation, 691
Cushman & Wakefield, 1835, 2204, 3259
Custom Composites, 1223
Custom Control Concepts, 1422
Custom Engineered Wheels Inc., 899
Custom Ink, 857, 1766
Custom Made, 1627
Custom Marketing, 399
Custom Molded Products, 752, 1457
Custom Profile, 276
Custom Sensors & Technologies, 413, 3026
Custom Steel Processing, 364
Custom Welding Services, 2286
Custom Wholesale Floors, 1215
Custom Window Systems, 1279
Custom Wood Products, 849
CustomAir, 365
CustomControl Concepts, 1705
Customer Alliance, 2979
Customer Matrix, 2439
Customer XPs Software Private Limited, 3062
Customer.io, 318, 1383, 1656, 2017
CustomerLink Systems Inc., 75
CustomMade, 1097, 1322
CustomVine, 1320
Custora, 770, 816, 1899
Cut, 518
Cute Metrix, 121
Cute Town, 2856
Cutera, 94
Cutex, 1422

1297

Portfolio Companies Index

CutisCare, 274
CutisPharma, 118
Cutler Repaving Inc., 1053
Cutters, 1127
Cutters Wireline Services, 1067
Cutting Edge Gamer, 445
Cuvva, 3108
Cuyana, 386
CV Finer Foods, 438
CV Holdings, 1423
CV Ingenuity, 1773
CV Ingenuity Corp., 269
CV Lab, 2874
CV Properties LLC, 1735
CV Therapeutics, 1775
CVA, 36
cValue, 3003
CVC Brasil Operadora e Agencia de Viagens S.A., 413
CVC Capital Partners, 3255, 3264
CVC Private Equity, 2631
CVC Sustainable, 2631
CVCI Growth Partnership II, 2094
CVE Technology Group Inc., 274
Cvent, 272, 1599
CVI, 2978
cVidya, 3137
cVidya Networks, 2566, 3136
CVRx, 23, 1059, 1297, 1993
CVT, 2584
CVT Corp., 2093
CVT Therapeutics, 782
CVTCORP, 2264
CVWarehouse, 2837
CW Environmental, 2362
CW Financial Services, 767
CWC Well Services, 2067
CWK Network, 1954
CWP Coloured Wood Products Oy, 2873
CWR Mobility, 2822
Cx, 1830
CXO Systems, 1080
CxS Corporation, 413
Cy World, 2857
Cyalume, 170
Cyalume Technologies, 1422
Cyan, 215, 1072, 1782, 1796
Cyan Optics, 757
Cyanide, 2899
Cyanogen, 1509, 1534
Cyara, 867
Cybeats, 2184, 2241
Cyber Physical Systems, 1261
Cyber Rain, 69, 797, 1784
Cyber-Ark, 3214
Cyber-Care, 212
Cyber-Patrol, 1428
Cyber-Rain, 187
Cybera, 57, 493, 1727
CyberAlert, 123
CyberCore Technologies, 680, 1400
CyberGrants, 1963
CyberGRX, 84, 889, 1794
Cyberhawk, 3104
CyberHeart, 666
Cyberian Outpost, 530
Cyberinc, 249
Cyberis Group, 865
Cyberkinetics, 1693
Cyberkinetics Inc., 2785
Cybernetiq, 2184
Cyberpoint, 1727
Cyberrinc, 1028
CyberShift, 1136
CyberSmart, 3108
CyberSource, 1888
CyberSpa, 19

CyberSponse, 285
Cybersports, 2837
CyberX, 724, 1346
Cybex Computer Products, 1708
Cybex Computer Products Corporation, 1148
Cybiocare, 2029
Cybrant, 555
Cybrary, 173, 285
Cybrid, 2936
CYC Fitness, 1585
Cyclacel, 3104
Cyclacel Pharmaceuticals, 2690
Cycle Capital Management, 3258
Cycle Gear Inc., 914
Cycle Taiwan, 3038
Cycleenergy, 2309
Cycleon, 2475
Cyclonaire Holding Corporation, 1492
Cyclone Commerce, 161
Cyclo‹des, 2271
Cyco Software, 2779
Cycognito, 116
Cydan, 237, 1143, 1297, 1436
Cydas, 1607
Cydcor, 839
CyDex Pharmaceuticals, 1574
Cyence, 1001
Cyfe, 92
CyFir, 967
Cygate, 2888
CyGene Inc., 588
Cygent, 555
Cygilant, 1916
Cygnal, 202
Cygnal Technologies, 2058
Cygnus Hospitals, 710
Cygnus Solutions, 197
Cyient, 413
Cylacel Pharmaceuticals, 2513
Cylance, 486, 603, 712, 1000, 1069, 1082, 1794
Cylene Pharmaceuticals, 1241, 1543, 1616
Cylera, 1611
Cylex, 304, 376
CymaBay, 1928
CymaBay Therapeutics, 237, 762, 1906
Cymabay Therapeutics, 1916
Cymat, 2058, 2058
Cymax, 2144
Cymbet Corp, 2973
Cymbet Corporation, 184
Cymedica Orthopedics, 138
Cymer, 1918
Cymmetria, 45, 720, 3108
Cymphonix, 1204
Cymtec, 2737
Cynapsus, 74
Cynet, 1346
CYNGN, 124
Cynosure, 314
Cynvenio Biosystems, 132
CyOptics, 2720, 2875, 2910
Cyota, 260
Cyperus, 2415
CypherWorX, 704
Cyphort, 620, 770, 1181
CyPhy, 816
Cyphy, 1260
Cyphy Works, 720
Cypress, 1654
Cypress Cellular LP, 122
Cypress Communications, 152
Cypress Semiconductor, 563, 1558
Cypress.io, 282
Cyrano, 3208
Cyras, 2007
Cyras Systems, 1202, 1779
Cyren, 3101

CYRK, 796
CyrusOne, 21
Cysal, 2686, 2824
Cyteir Therapeutics, 1271, 1916
Cytheris, 2466, 2748, 3020
Cytimune Sciences, 1169
CytoAgents, 293
Cytochroma, 3015
Cytogel, 448
Cytogen Corp., 1044
Cytokinetics, 94
CytoLogix Corporation, 314
CytoMed, 1558
Cytomedix, 1169
CytomX Therapeutics, 386, 1811, 3085
Cytoo, 2710
CytoPherx, 138, 400, 642, 666, 1336, 1378
Cytos, 74
Cytos Biotechnology AG, 2785
Cytosolv, 1693
CytoSorbents, 1328
Cytosport, 1861
Cytovale, 219
Cytovance Biologics, 859
Cytovas, 266
Cytovia, 765
Cytoville, 710
Cytox, 2967
Cytrellis, 268
CYTYC, 59
Cytyc, 56
Cyvek, 530
CyVera, 1913
Cyvera, 301, 530
CYVision, 1004
Czech On Line, 2429
Cür, 1079

D

D Square, 2949
D&D London, 2944
D&F Solution, 2857
D&M Holdings, 220
D&S Community Services, 528
D&S Residential Services, 1422, 1484
D'Lisi Food Systems, 1745
D-Eye, 2874
D-gate Semiconductor, 2833
D-Labs, 2813
D-Link, 892
D-Pharm, 2585, 2770, 3231
D-Share, 3052
D-Wave, 262
D-Wave Systems, 6, 2143
D.Light, 55, 2439, 3001
d.light, 855
D.Light Design, 791
D.light Design, 807
D.M. Robichaud, 2186
D.S. Brown, 443
D.Western Therapeutics, 2970
D1G1T, 2113
D1g1t, 2225
D2 Audio, 202
D2 Hawkeye, 349
D2Audio, 444
D2E Capital, 2949
D2Hawkeye, 1067
D2S, 581, 634
D3O, 251
D3O, 2710
D4C Dental Brands, 244
Dabbl, 89
dabble, 1155
Dabee, 2976, 2983
DAC, 2847
Dac, 2436

Portfolio Companies Index

Dacentec, 3042
Dacentec/Awingu, 2837
Dachis Group, 202
Dacor, 869
Dadam Game, 3127
Daddies Board Shop, 1964
DadLabs, 594
Dae-in-lnfo sys, 2969
Daechun Greenwater, 584
Daekyung Machinery & Engineering, 2857
Daesan Energy, 584
Daesung Eltec, 3145
Daewon Special Wire Co, 2807
DAFCA, 1080, 1305
Dafiti, 2829, 2838, 3170
Dagne Dover, 622
Daguu, 2869
Daher Lhotellier, 2721
Dahlam Rose & Co., 1147
Dailey Grommet, 1097
DaileyCred, 889
Daily Harvest, 1121, 1595
Daily Juice, 445
Daily Secret, 641, 871
DailyBreak, 455
DailyBurn, 685
DailyCall, 3113
DailyLook, 1888
DailyMe, 1403
Dailyme, 3236
dailyme TV, 2841
Dailymotion, 1416, 2851
DailyObjects, 3109
DailyPay, 1640, 2118
DailyPerfect, 2390
DailyWOrth, 1830
DailyWorth, 608
DailyWorth.com, 3277
Dainese, 1017
DairyMart, 1067
Daisy Manufacturing Co., 354
Daisytek International, 468
Dakim, 806
Dakine, 96
Dakota, 2946
Dakota Arms, 378, 1915
Dakota Bodies, 2978
Dakota Minnesota & Eastern Railroad, 1139
Dakotaland Autoglass, 1192
Dakotaland Manufacturing, 297
Daktari, 1205
Daktari Diagnostics, 1347, 1419
Dal Bolognese Ristorante, 2401
Dalbo, 1067
Dalbo Holdings, 1127
Dalcor Pharmaceuticals, 2092
Dale Gas Partners, 477
Dale Power Solutions, 2944
Daleen Technologies, 1038
Dalet, 1991, 2354
Dali Wireless, 1303, 2457
Dali Wireless Systems, 1737
Dalia, 3236
Dalia Research, 2478, 2841
Dalie, 2602
Dalipal Pipe Company, 892
DalRybProm, 2491
Daltys, 2293, 3020
Dalus, 2382
Damac, 1824
Damac Products, 1469
Damar Aerosystems, 82
Damark International, 536
Damballa, 57, 301, 1010, 1400, 1407, 1672, 1673
Damon X Labs, 2113
Dan Howard Industries, 447
Dan-Loc, 164

Dan-Loc Bolt & Gasket, 1503
dan.com, 967
Dana, 442
Dana Hospitality, 2126
Dana-Farber Cancer Institute, 1271
Dancap Family Investment Office, 3258
DanceOn, 1099, 1813
DanChem, 653
Dancing Deer Baking, 841, 1021
Danco Machine, 828
Dandelion, 877, 1297
Dandelion Energy, 308, 511
Danforth Advisors LLC, 403
Dangdang, 2850
Dangdang.com, 596
Danger, 115, 613, 1001, 1212, 2875, 3155
Danger Inc, 184
Daniel's Jewelers, 1403
Danilait, 2889
Dank Business Systems Plc., 575
Danna McKitrick PC, 3271
Danone, 473
Dansk Erhvervsinvestering, 2447
Danskin, 796
Dantec Dynamics, 235
Dantom Systems Inc., 654
Dantz, 933, 1637
Dantz Development Corporation, 753
Danville, 1014
Danziger Innovations, 3245
Dao Aviation, 3203
Daojia, 1340
Dapper, 1916, 2280
Dapper Labs, 1611, 1882
Daptiv, 85
DARAG Group, 559
DarbeeVision, 2778
Darby Smart, 761, 1183
Darfon Electronics, 892
Dark, 305
Dark Cubed, 285
Dark Owl, 745
Dark Water Studios, 2610
Darks Club, 2924
Darkstore, 1933
DarkTrace, 1000, 2834
Darktrace, 1082, 1794
DarkVision Technologies, 2111
Darmiyan, 721
DarQroom, 2899
Darrow Associates, 3267
DART Aerospace, 862
Darwin AI, 2138, 2157
DarwinAI, 1363
Darwinbox, 1121
Dash, 600, 622, 1306, 1894
Dash Hudson, 2068, 2155
Dash Navigation, 555
Dashbell, 1734
Dashbid, 448
DashBin, 1581
Dashboard Director, 863
Dashbot, 724, 1611
Dashdash, 28
Dasher, 1254
Dashlane, 260, 743, 1558
DashWire, 85
Dasient, 249
Data Allegro, 968
Data Analytics Media, 617
Data Council, 668
Data Direct, 839
Data Display Systems, 1606
Data Domain, 1760
Data Driven Delivery Systems, 1271
Data Fusion Technologies, 378
Data Gram, 1507

Data Hug, 2674
Data Iku, 743
Data Inventions, 479, 1286
Data Nerds, 776
Data Net Corporation National Health Care Systems, 1708
Data Physics, 235
Data Plus Math, 518
Data Pop, 32
Data Race, 734
Data Respons, 3076
Data Return LLC, 1621
Data Robot, 1004
Data Role, 479
Data Science International, 560
Data Sciences, 1460
Data Sciences International, 68, 386
Data Security Systems Solutions, 2870, 3062
Data Smoothie, 3108
Data Synapse, 1680
Data TV Networks, 1057
Data Vision Resources, 582
Data.World, 751, 1611, 1663
DataBank, 654, 1765
DataBanq, 990
Databetes, 622
Databricks, 124, 235, 820, 1297, 1761
DataCamp, 173, 1717
DataCandy, 2132
Datacare Software Group, 2705
Datacastle, 2618
DataCenter Technologies, 2837
Datacitics, 2610
Datacom Systems, 812
Datacoral, 1158, 1696
DataCore, 1000
DataCore Software, 1886
Datacraft Solutions, 1860
Datacratic, 2109
DataCycles, 524
DataDirect Networks, 2897
DataDog, 1212, 1380
Datadog, 533, 814, 1358, 1594
Datadog Inc., 965
DataEssence, 3059
Dataflow, 3107
DataFlyte, 459
Dataform, 1848
DataFox, 889
DataGravity, 455
Datagres, 3001
Dataguise, 1611, 1829
Datahug, 2662
Dataiku, 235
Dataium, 781
DataKraft, 2355
DataLase, 3244
Datalase, 2492
Datalink, 822
DATAllegro, 56, 757, 1407, 1916
Datalogix, 547, 1001
Datalogue, 754
Datalot, 231, 1123
Datameer, 486, 1075, 1319, 1534
DataMentors, 21
Dataminr, 318, 535, 560, 600, 707, 836, 1001, 1916
DataMotion, 954
Datamyx, 897
DataNet Communications, 1506
Datanyze, 889, 1563
DataOnline, 787
Datapath.io, 3161
Datapine, 2979
datapine, 3207
Datapipe, 21, 29, 1235
Datapoint, 584, 2361

1299

Portfolio Companies Index

DataPop, 306
Datapop, 1099, 1242, 1524, 1566
dataQorp, 1837
Dataquest, 1487
DataRobot, 38, 483, 942, 965, 1297
DataRPM, 1055
DataSage, 59
Datascan Berhad, 3164
DataScience, 561
Dataside, 1167
DataSift, 2649
Datasift, 2760
Datasnap.Io, 964
DataSource, 932, 1014
DataSphere, 974
DataSphere Technologies, 732
Datastax, 518, 560, 563, 1075, 1121, 1212, 1319, 1626
DataSynapse, 1745
Datatel, 1850
DataTorrent, 1254
DataTrak International, 212
Datavail, 257, 315, 427, 1211
Datavantage Corporation, 1621
Dataview Solutions, 1837
Datavisor, 1297
Dataware Technologies, 192
Datawire Communication Networks, 2079, 2196
DataXu, 38, 70, 754, 1202, 1818
Datec Coating Corporation, 2273
Datek Online, 63
Datera, 1069
DATEV eG, 967
Dathena Science, 1269
Datica, 173, 222
Datical, 202, 1206
Datiphy, 935
DATIS HR Cloud, 3262
Datometry, 603
Datorama, 436, 996, 1121
Datos IO, 1121
Datou, 2733
Datran Media, 1906
Datrium, 1121, 1297
Datsphere Technologies, 1391
DATTUS, 1155
Dattus, 86, 566
Datuit, 3279
Daum Communications corp, 2839
Davalor, 276
Davco Restaurants LLC, 354
Dave, 1643
Dave & Buster's, 1360
Dave & Buster's Inc., 1971
Davenport Newberry Holdings, 1573
Daverci, 1383
DavexLabs, 373
David Energy, 318
David's Bridal, 1109
Davies Group, 959, 2944
Davis Standard, 2209
Davis-Standard, 2208
Davo Technologies, 1688
Davra Networks, 2355
DaWanda, 2829, 2838, 3040, 3044
DAX Solutions, 69
Dax Solutions, 1784
Daxko, 824, 1409
Daxsonics Ultrasound, 2155
Daxton, 2285
Day One Response, 841
Day4 Energy, 2097
Daya CNS, 267
Dayak, 1321
Dayforce, 339
Daylight Forensic & Advisory, 793
Daylight Studios, 3073

DayNine, 1409
Days, 1531
Daysoft.com, 3104
Dayton Parts LLC, 64
Dayton Superior Corporation, 1368
Daz 3D, 515
Daz3D, 620
Daz3d, 1884
Dazel, 202
DB and SOFT, 2839
DB Networks, 486, 876, 1069
DBD Deutsche Breitband Dienste GmbH, 3046
Dbix Systems, 2623
DBmaestro, 2947
DBS Communications Inc., 654
DBS Nationwide, 2985
DBSH, 543
Dbvu, 2479
DC Devices, 1811
Dc Preparatory Academy, 1316
DC Public Charter School Board, 1316
DC Safety, 631
DC School Reform Now, 1316
DCG Systems, 3002
DCI Holdings, 722
DCL Medical Laboratories, 443
DCN Media Inc., 392
DCS Sanitation Management, 465
DCX, 1837
DDF, 1689
De Boelekes, 3042
De Kleine Kikker, 3042
De Kleine Wereld, 3042
De Novo Pharmaceuticals, 2463
De Toverboom, 3042
De Vecchi Group, 2423
De Zebra, 3042
De-Ice, 941
Dead Sea Industries (Chemicals), 2389
Deal United, 2824, 3170
Deal$ Nothing Over a Dollar, 1954
DealCloud, 569
DealCurrent, 1784
Dealer HQ, 781
Dealer Tire, 1129, 1776
Dealer-FX, 959
DealerHQ, 445
DealerSocket, 1212
Dealertrack Technologies, 1888
Dealflicks, 1595, 1965, 2010
Dealgenius.com, 937
Dealhub, 543
Dealised, 3248
Dealix, 772
Dealogic, 413
Dealsandyou.com, 1327
Dealsquare, 301
Dear Health, 1051
Dearborn Mid-West Conveyor Company, 77, 716
Deb Shops, 1104
DebiTech, 2754
Debix, 1841
Deborah Centrum, 3042
Debut Bio, 395
Deca, 2446
Decalog, 2383
Decalog B.V., 3137
deCarta, 385, 411, 1245, 1690, 1838
Decartes Labs, 707
DecaWave, 2918
Decell, 2828
DeCell Technologies, 2155
Decibel Therapeutics, 889, 1731
Decide.com, 1183
DecImmune Therapeutics, 182
Deciphera, 1628, 1762
Deciphera Pharmaceuticals, 1837

Decision Dynamics, 2196
Decision Engines, 1809
Decision One, 1972
Decision Resources Inc., 361
DecisionNext, 129, 1522
DecisionPoint, 3259
DecisionView, 58
Decisive Farming, 2048, 2190
Decisyon, 946
Deck, 934
Declicmedia, 2365
DecImmune, 347
DecImmune Therapeutics, 919
DeCODE Genetics, 94
deCODE Genetics, 153, 191, 925, 1460, 1775
Decolar, 1654
Decolar.com, 815
Decru, 979, 3137
Dedenbear Products, 908
Dedendo, 2638
Dedicate Transport, 1422
Dedicated Computing, 1171
Dedicated Network Partners Oy, 3213
Dedicated Transport, 443
Dedigate, 2837
Dedrone, 720, 1031, 3161
Deduct, 1642
Dee Development Engineers, 413
Deem, 724, 1361, 1604
Deep, 1734, 3221
Deep Blue Medical Advances, 226
Deep Brain Innovations, 1287
Deep Breeze, 1633
Deep Casing Tools, 2700
Deep Casting Tools, 3104
Deep Domain, 85
Deep Eddy, 445
Deep Forest Media, 1809
Deep Genomics, 4, 800
Deep Genomics Inc., 1069
Deep Gulf Energy, 740
Deep Imaging, 1206
Deep Imaging Technologies, 950
Deep Lens, 1670
Deep Motion, 472
Deep Secure, 3244
Deep Sentinal, 1663
Deep Sentinel, 1151
Deep Vein Medical Inc., 270
Deep Vision, 519
DeepBreeze, 2462
DeepCrawl, 745
Deepfield, 1547, 1592
DeepFlex, 466, 2700
DeepGram, 307
Deepgram, 525, 721, 1329
Deepgreen, 392
Deeplocal, 998
DEEPMAP, 124
Deepmind, 2831
DeepNines Technologies, 592
Deepscale, 107, 204, 205
Deer Ridge Centre, 2172
Deerac Fluidics, 2918
Deerfield Management, 3264
Deerland, 1590
Deerpath Energy, 1579
Deeya Energy Inc, 184
Deezer, 2669
Defacto, 2875
Defense Mobile, 848
DefenseStorm, 2132
Défiance Stamping Company, 828
Define My Style, 1512
DefinedCrowd, 1703
Definiens AG, 2079
DefiniGEN, 3028

1300

Portfolio Companies Index

Definition 6, 1280
Definition6, 438
Definitive Healthcare, 62, 1717
Definity Health, 1906
Deflecto, 654
Defy, 1615
Defy Media, 22
DEG, 1607
DegreeChamp, 622
Degreed, 79, 883, 1392, 1551
DEI Holdings, 456
Dejero, 2224
Dejero Labs, 2058
Dejima Inc., 986
DEKA Medical, 1708
Deka-Brushes, 2805
Dekko, 301, 590, 650
Dekko.co, 1097
Deko, 1240
Del Amo Diagnostic Center, 869
Del Monte, 2379
Del Monte Foods, 354, 1516
Del Real Foods, 1403
Del Taco, 456
Del Taco Holdings, 1109
Del.Icio.Us, 641
DelaGet, 3279
Delair, 1004
Delaware North, 16
Delco Corp., 1053
Delectable, 600
Delego, 2058
Delek Refining, 1970
Delenex, 2815
Delenex Therapeutics, 495
Delete, 3020
Delfigo Security, 1734
DELFMEM, 3225
Delfoi, 2451
Deli'en, 3203
Delia Systems, 2855
Delighted, 889
Delimex, 722
Delinea, 1901
Delinia, 191
Deliv, 961, 1592, 1853, 1888
DeliverCareRx, 80
Delivering Happiness Group/Daredu, 3215
Deliveroo, 816, 2834
Delivery Agent, 536, 757, 2797
Delivery Hero, 1000, 2829, 2838, 3044, 3170, 3236
Delivery-club.ru, 2344
Delivery.com, 394
DeliveryAgent, 184, 411, 1311
Dell, 56, 385, 541, 1683
Dell Technologies, 3273
Dellwood, 1017
Deloitte, 967
Deloitte & Touche, 3276
Deloitte LLP, 3259
Delonex Energy, 1956
Delorio Foods, 1093
Delpharm, 2851
Delphi Behavioral Health Group, 403, 894
Delphia, 2137
Delphin Shipping, 1062
Delphinus, 251, 742
Delphinus Medical Technologies, 149, 943
Delphix, 235, 872, 968, 1121, 1752
Delpor, 1051
Delsey, 2422
Delsitech, 2873
DelStar Technologies, 1557
Delsys Pharmaceutical, 1558
Delta Career Education Corp., 881
Delta Data Software, 29

Delta ID, 3098
Delta Innovative Enterprises Limited, 2861
Delta Method, 641
Delta Rigging & Tools, 202
Delta Systems, 1689
Delta-Q Technologies Corp., 2053
Delta-V Partners, 3276
DeltaBank, 2465
DeltaCredit, 2465
Deltak, 843
Deltaknot, 2993
DeltaLease-Far East, 2465
Deltamed, 2855
Deltanoid Pharmaceuticals, 1921, 2001
DeltaRail, 1937
Deltek, 1301, 1491, 1516, 1814
Deltona Corporation, 1404
Delve Networks, 85, 1089
DEM Solutions, 3070, 3131
Demand Base, 1626
Demand Media, 818, 1361
DemandBase, 1607, 1725, 1760
Demandbase, 58, 100, 547, 867, 1024, 1602, 1672
DemanderJustice.com, 1416
Demandforce, 751
DemandMedia, 132
DemandPoint, 1014, 1891
DemandQ, 532
DemandSage, 679
Demandtec, 626
Demandware, 1334
Demantra Ltd., 2585, 2750
DeMaT TransAsia, 2434
Dematic, 64
Demdex, 814, 1663
Deme Blue Energy, 3042
Demegen, 1746
Demegen Inc, 588
Demers Ambulances, 2082
DeMet's Candy Company, 357
Demilec, 1753
Demisto, 872
Democracy.com, 1810
Democrcy Prep Public School, 1316
Demodesk, 795
Demyst Data, 148
DemystData, 1240, 3121
DEN, 2558
Den Berenboot, 3042
DeNA China, 2869
Denali Therapeutics, 262, 268, 709, 710, 747
Denby, 937
Dendreon, 85, 1558, 1616
Dendrite, 655
Denion Pharmaceuticals, 1232
Denison, 2796
Dennis Conncer Sports, 1837
Denodo, 959
Denon & Marantz, 220
DeNovaMed, 2155
DENOVO, 2936
Denovo, 1004, 1153, 1340
Denovo Sciences, 742
DeNovo Ventures, 3284
Denplan, 2796
Densify, 2261
Densitas, 2155
Density, 1150, 1888
Dent Wizard, 873
Dental Care Alliance, 914, 1505
Dental Services Group, 558, 654
Dental Technologies, 2051
Dentek, 1861
Dentem, 2113
Dentidesk, 1507
Dentigenix, 85

Dentistanbul, 834
Dentolo, 2841
Dentons, 3272
Denver Biomedical, 194
Deny all, 3020
Deolan, 2365
DEOS, 530
Depict, 1524
Depop, 2478, 2838
Deposco, 1891
Deposit Solutions, 641
DepoTech, 1706
Dequingyuan, 834
Derby Jackpot, 358
DerbyJackpot, 1475
DerbySoft, 1340
Dering Hall, 607, 1110, 1699
Derive Systems, 834
Derksen Printers, 2258
Derma Sciences, 806, 1452
Dermaflage, 995
DermaRite, 1777
Dermatology Associates of Tyler, 1727
Dermatology Group, 1166
Dermira, 74, 237, 386, 762, 1297
Dermlink, 1615
DermTech International, 1784, 1974
Des-Case Corp., 985
Des-Case Corporation, 1435
Desalitech, 2417
Desantis, 2401
Descartes Labs, 544, 563, 570
Descartes Systems Group, 1757
Desch Plantpak, 1127
Descomplica, 1696
Descript, 124
Desenvolvimento de Colucoes Digitais, 3048
Desert Artisans, 2313
Deserve, 180
Deserve Cards, 49
Desi, 193
Desicrew, 3211
Design Art Networks, 3221
Design EXchange Co., 2907
Design Flux Technologies, 1047
Design Genie, 512
Design Ideas, 1970
Design Molded Plastics, 1870
Design Space, 1209
Design/Craft Fabric Holdings, 1279
DesignArt Networks, 2566, 2952
DesignBuddy, 1306
DesignCrowd, 3138
Designer Carbon Materials, 3107
Designer Protein, 1344
Designers House, 132
DesignMedix, 1383
Desire2Learn, 1297
+Desk.com, 358
DeskConnect, 1589
Deskera, 483
DeskForce, 543
Desktime, 1642
Desktone, 1699
Desktop Geneti, 1615
Desktop Metal, 302, 809, 889, 1151, 1297
Deskwolf, 3203
Desmos, 660, 889, 1054, 1527
Despegar, 28
Despegar.com, 1000
Despoke Post, 858
Desser Tire, 846
Desso, 2501
Desti, 2831
Destination Cinema, 1477
Destination Maternity, 1275, 1970
Destineer, 979

1301

Portfolio Companies Index

Destiny Pharma, 1452
DeTeBe AG, 3197
Detechtion Technologies, 657
Detectify, 1000
Detector Technology, 118
DeTelefoongids BV, 1927
Deter Magnetic Technologies, 1111
Determina, 1896
Detroit Innovate, 3269
detroit Labs, 607
Detroit Venture Partners, 3269
Deutsch-Dagan (Elect.), 2389
Deutsche Glasfaser, 1082
Deutsche Messe Interactive, 2569
Deutsche Rohstoff AG, 2492
Deutsche Startups, 2829, 2838
Dev/Con Detect, 995
Devas Multimedia, 515
Devax, 1896
Devax Inc., 269
Devcon, 839
DevCon Detect, 1370
Devcon Detect, 829
Deveinfo Oy, 2873
DeveloGen, 3007
DeveloGen AG, 2785
DevelopIP, 2760
Development and the Rule of Law, 1374
Devenson, 1607
Devergy, 55
Device Anywhere, 2196
Device Authority, 93
Device Fidelity, 582
Device Innovation Group, 915
Device Scape, 968
DeviceFidelity, 1261
Devicescape, 144
Devicescape Software, 197
DeviceVM, 1737
Devie Medical, 2527
DeVilbiss Healthcare, 1931
Devmynd, 1260
Devo, 1000
Devonway, 563
Devoted Health, 1363, 1916
Devotion New Energy, 3194
Devpost, 539, 1381
Devver, 1359
DeWayne's Quality Metal, 1606
Dewey's Bakery, 1606
Dewhurst/Angloarch, 2796
Dewpointx, 996
Dex Media, 1972
Dex One, 1134
DexCom, 1725
Dexela, 3107
Dexerials, 3201
DexKo Global, 1085
Dexter + Chaney, 1409
Dexterra, 1672
Dextrys, 779
Deyu Agri, 3100
Dezima Pharma, 1303, 2514, 2748
Dezurik, 850
DF King World Wide, 21
DFA Capital Management, 1146
DFine, 1382, 1493, 1725
DFINITY, 124
Dfinity, 180
DFJ Venture Capital, 986
DFR, 1965
DFT Microsystems, 692, 2196
DG Industries, 2855
DG Power, 156
DG3, 170
DGAM, 2033
DGF, 2293

DGI Clinical, 2155
DgR, 1708
DGS Retail, 1578
DGS SA, 2706
DGSI, 235
DHA, 3107, 3107
Dharmacon, 315, 1792
Dhebhuk, 3088
DHI Group Inc., 1506
Dhingana, 1013
DHISCO, 928
DHL, 380
Dhrama, 395
Di'an, 3100
Dia & Co., 771, 942, 1110, 1183
Dia&Co, 1654
Diabetes Care Group, 1261, 1331
Diabetica, 2918
Diabetomics, 1383
Diablo Technologies, 1896, 2196, 2813
DiaDexus, 1626
diaDexus, 1558
Diagnosis One, 655
Diagnosoft, 3259
Diagnostek, 35
Diagnostic Imaging, 1971
Diagnostic Photonics, 975
Diagnostic Technology, 3171
Diagnotes, 658
Diagnovus, 1261
Dialogic, 1017
DialogMuseum, 2531
DialogTech, 1384
Dialogue, 2118, 2225
Dialogue Marketing, 830
DialOnce, 249
Dialpad, 124, 720, 889, 1643, 2006
Diam, 3020
Diamanti, 609
Diamedica, 2077
Diamedica Ltd, 3162
Diameter Health, 52
Diametrics Medical, 1398
Diamond Assets LLC, 1435
Diamond Bank, 413
Diamond Cable, 2792
Diamond Contract Services, 958
Diamond Factory, 890
Diamond Foundry, 1363
Diamond Hard Surfaces, 3107
Diamond Innovations, 1134
Diamond Kinetics, 1657
Diamond Lane, 1682
Diamond Packaging, 1021
Diamond Rental, 949
Diamond S, 740
Diamond Software, 2967
Diamondback, 1491
Diamondback Drugs, 1777
DiaMonTech, 2841
Diamyd, 998
Diandian Yangche, 823
Dianji, 2733, 2936
Dianon Systems Inc., 300
Dianping, 1121
Dianrong, 1340
Diapers.com, 260
Diasome, 1452, 1508
DiAthegen, 187
Diatomix, 1613
Diatos, 2354
Diatron Group, 1572
DiBcom, 2662, 2674
Dibs, 218
diCarta/Emptoris, 1288
Dice, 1982
DiceInc, 2771

Dicerna, 1519
Dicerna Pharmaceuticals, 621, 925, 1394, 1691
Dicerna Pharmaceuticals, 1731
Dick's Sporting Goods, 260, 1970
Dickinson, 276
Dickinson and Company, 1452
Dickinson Frozen Foods, 374, 1152
Dickinson Frozen Foods Inc., 449
Dickson Construction, 1705
DICOM Grid, 474
Dicom Grid, 386
Dicom Transportation Group, 1990
DicoverRx, 1255
Didatuan, 2850
Didera, 954
DiDi, 107
Didi, 45
Didi Chuxing, 823, 1095, 1181, 1297
Didix, 3232
Die Cuts With a View, 928
DIEL, 2616
Diesel Marine International Ltd, 2486
Diet to go, 2874
Diffbot, 720, 1968
Different Hotels Group, 2949
Differential Diagnostics, 1558
Diffinity Genomics, 704, 1097
Diffusion Pharma, 1271
Difinity Health, 94
Difter Entertainment, 1421
DiFusion Technologies, 445
Digabit, 756, 930
Digby, 594
Digex, 876
digg, 1982
Digi-Prex, 1138
Digibonus, 2385
DigiCert, 1776
Digicert, 1460
Digicon Technologies, 721
Digidesign, 1760
DigiFlex, 3059, 3214
Digify, 3073
Digilab, 2626
Digilens, 93, 1703
Digimarc, 58, 852
DigiPath Inc., 1135
Digirad, 1616, 1706
Digit, 231, 816, 889
DIGIT Wireless, 1306
Digital Air Strike, 665, 1663, 1888, 2649
Digital Alloys, 1069
Digital Angel, 865
Digital Artists, 600
Digital Arts, 2826
Digital Assent, 282
Digital Bridges, 162
Digital Campaigns, 2021
Digital Capital Partners LLC, 122
Digital China, 2771
Digital China Jinxin, 2936
Digital Chocolate, 1389, 1760, 2590, 2668
Digital Claim, 1507
Digital Cognition Technologies, 563
Digital Compliance, 221
Digital Currency Group, 743, 1696
Digital Domain, 716, 2266
Digital Envoy, 807
Digital Fortress, 897, 1211
Digital Founatin, 1704
Digital Fountain, 58, 807, 1181
Digital Fuel, 757, 2472
Digital Fuel Technologies, 1672
Digital Generation Systems, 536
Digital Genius, 525, 1110, 1607
Digital Golf Technologies, 1178
Digital Graphics, 530

Portfolio Companies Index

Digital Guardian, 712, 1136
Digital H2O, 738
Digital Health Department, 1655
Digital Healthcare, 2693
Digital Island, 238, 1239, 1728
Digital Legends, 2548
Digital Life Technologies, 1160
Digital Lumens, 1327, 2439
Digital Magics, 2874
Digital Map Products, 1869
Digital Market, 1853
Digital Marketing Institute, 1717
Digital Media Agency, 403
Digital Media Professionals, 596
Digital Media Professionals Inc., 2414
Digital Media Solutions, 2081, 2899
Digital Medica Services, 443
Digital Motorworks, 734
Digital Music Network, 1672
Digital Objects, 1149
Digital Ocean, 407, 646, 1789
Digital Onboarding, 607
Digital Optics, 1008
Digital Orchid, 1664
Digital Payment Technologies, 2090, 2196
Digital Performance, 1566
Digital Pharmacist, 52
Digital Pickle, 1097
Digital Reality, 824
Digital Reasoning, 979, 1107, 1420
Digital Research, 1853
Digital River, 403
Digital Room, 1166
Digital Route, 162, 2662
Digital Royalty, 1912
Digital Shadows, 1794, 3030
Digital Signal, 946, 1348
Digital Signal Corporation, 1400
Digital Solid State Propulsion, 979
Digital Theatre, 2871
Digital Traffic Systems, 1583
Digital Transmission Systems, 1708
Digital Virgo, 2293
DigitalBridge Communications, 263, 1348, 1400
DigitaleSeiten, 3044
DigitalFuel, 976, 1024
DigitalGenius, 593, 1149
DigitalOcean, 124, 965
Digitalpath.net, 100
DigitalPersona, 192
DigitalScirocco, 85
DigitalThink, 58, 852, 2007
Digitalwork, 137
Digitas, 924
Digitech, 1409
Digitouch, 2837
DigiTour, 1813
Digitrace/Sleepmed Inc., 1103
Digiturk, 1496
DigiTx Partners, 1268
Digium, 1181, 1796
Digium|Asterik, 61
Digmine, 623
Digney York Associates, 1209
Dignify Therapeutics, 737, 3259
DigyScores, 735
Dil Mil, 942
Dilaz, 2889
Diligence Labs, 704
Diligent, 500, 1000
Diligent Power Private, 1956
Diligent Robotics, 1421, 1877
Diligent TechnologiesAllot, 2770
Dilithium Networks, 2323, 3062
Dilitronics, 2824
DilMil, 623
Dilthium Networks, 2618

Dimdim, 3001
DIME, 251
Dimension IO, 307
Dimension Therapeutics, 710, 1271, 1382, 1519
Dimensional Dental, 1963
Dimensional Tools Inc., 908
DIMO Corp., 48
Dimora, 1045
Dinalit System, 2969
Dinamundo, 1860
Dinda, 1897
dinda, 720
Dine Market, 994
Dinghartinger Apfelstrudel Productions-UND Vertrie, 2494
Dinghy, 2478
Dink, 3042
Dino Lift Oy, 2318
DinoDirect, 1340
Dinoflex, 2218
Dinova, 790
Dinsmore, 3275
Diomed Holdings, 925
Diomet, 1835
Dionex, 1760
Dip Devices, 860
DipJar, 1487
Dipole Materials, 19
Diposta, 3259
Direct 2 Internet, 2754
Direct Buy, 1183
Direct Capital, 1970
Direct Chassis Link Inc., 1134
Direct Connect Lofistix, 960
Direct Flow, 1298
Direct Flow Medical, 748, 946, 1906
Direct General, 368, 1331
Direct Group, 2944
Direct Health Delivery, 3268
Direct Hit Technologies, 521
Direct Lending Investments, 1061
Direct Marketing Company, 2094
Direct Marketing Solutions, 443
Direct Medical Knowledge, 852
Direct Scale, 876
Direct Tavel, 1684
Direct Travel, 21
Direct Vet Marketing, 907
DirectBuy, 2079
DirectedAI, 2113
DirectedSensing, 1303
DirectEHR, 1289
DirectFlow Medical, 652
Directly, 547, 1154, 1611, 1829, 1860
DirectPath, 1166
Directr, 60, 313, 858
DirectScale, 1070, 1384
DirectVetMarketing, 1261
Directworks, 628
Directworks Inc., 158
Diresco, 2949
DIREVO Industrial Biotechnology, 3196
Dirtt, 706
DIRTT Environmental Solutions, 1324
Dirtt Environmental Solutions, 137
Dirty Lemon, 229
Disa Holding, 3054
Disarm Therapeutics, 191
Disaster Kleenup International, 812
Discera, 548, 947
DisclosureNet, 2058
DISCO, 2132
Disco, 1013, 1070
Disconnect, 743, 935
Discord, 872, 1563
Discote, 3249
Discourse, 741

Discover Books, 1515
Discover Exploration, 413
Discover Video, 530
Discover.ly, 858
DiscoverMusic, 818
DiscoverOrg, 333
DiscoveRx, 1197, 1691
Discovery Data, 333
Discovery Education, 779
Discovery Foods, 787
Discovery Group, 2923
DiscoveryLabs, 1508
Disease Diagnostic Group, 1047
Disetronic, 2564
Dish.fm, 2856
Dishcarft, 1352
Dishcraft Robotics, 231, 741
Dishero, 1050
Disksites, 3159
Diskyver, 2284
Dispatch, 124, 848, 1607, 1821
Dispatch Health, 94
Dispatch Management Services, 131
Dispatch Tracking Solutions, 1784
Dispatch Transportation, 225
Dispatch.io, 2017
Dispatcher, 2011
Dispatchr, 751
Dispensarly, 392
DispenseSource, 765
DisperSol, 457
Dispersol Technologies, 26
Displair, 2938, 3132
Displanplan, 3244
Display Data, 2674
Display Design & Instore Marketing, 2810
Display Link, 2478
Playdata, 2662
DisplayLink, 581, 634, 2662, 2674
DisplayPoints, 445
Displaytech, 1288, 2652
Disqo, 306
Disqus, 1334
Disrupt Beam, 1581
Disruption, 1518
Disruption Corporation, 1320
Disruptor Beam, 534, 889
Disston Precision, 1521
Distacom, 2719
Distant Lands Trading Co., 447
Distech Systems, 61
Distil Networks, 544, 724, 776, 971, 1789
Distocraft, 2562
Distractify, 60
Distribion, 9
Distribution Alimentaire, 2029
Distribution International, 194
District of Columbia International School, 1316
DITA Exchange, 3203
Dittmers Korrosionsschutz, 2810
DITTO, 197
Ditto, 567, 1734
Diveo, 1211
Divergence, 570, 1488, 1615
Diversa Corp., 212
Diverse World, 2967
Diversi Foods, 3232
Diversified, 1270, 1777
Diversified Composites, 1919
Diversified Foodservice Supply, 1086
Diversified Graphics, 443
Diversified Human Resources, 373, 374
Diversified Machine Systems, 1484
Diversified Maintenance Systems, 789
Diversified Metal Engineering, 2082
Diversigen, 241
DiversiTech, 932

Portfolio Companies Index

Diverza, 2382
Divide, 305, 814, 1475
Divido, 3108
Divio, 3218
Divisions Maintenance Group, 374
DiVitas, 502
DiVitas Networks, 1119
Divolution, 2824
DivorseSecure, 995
Divshot, 306, 1099, 1566, 1798, 2649
Divvy, 49, 79, 1000
Divvy Investments, 3259
DivvyCloud, 538, 1240
DivvyHQ, 635
DIVX, 411
DivX, 2021
Divx, 1983
Dixie Chemical Company, 830
Dixie Electric, 740
Dixie Elixirs, 638
Dixie Southern, 1745
DIY, 1075, 1715
DIYSEO, 594
Dizzion, 36, 544, 876
DJ Pharma, 468
DJI, 1075
DJO, 277, 2325
Djr Energy LLC, 1851
DJTunes.com, 2824
DJZ, 1222, 1546, 1749, 1860
DKT, 3100
DL Industries, 734
DLA Piper, 3272
dlhBowles, 1266
DMA, 1572
Dmailer, 2383
DMC Stratex Networks, 2005
DMF Medical, 2155
DMN Installations, 3017
DMO Systems, 1896
DMS, 2876
DMT, 1602
DMTG, 3100
DMTI Spatial, 2196
DNA Diagnostics Center, 1271
DNA Group, 3259
DNA Research, 2662
DNA Response, 247, 553
DNANexus, 1700
DNAnexus, 491, 720, 741, 762, 889, 1050, 2000
DNAtrix Therapeutics, 1206
DNCA Finance SA, 1776
Dnium Pte Ltd, 2703
DNS Services, 1906
DNS:NET Internet Service GmbH, 3067
Doane Pet Care Enterprises Inc., 354
DOAR Communications, 1927
Dobie Media, 493
Dobler Metallbau GmbH, 2494
Doc AI, 519
Doc Authority, 724
Doc Doc, 2913
Docalytics, 566
Doccom, 2691
Docebo, 2170, 3052
Docent Health, 1297
Docker, 107, 248, 560, 872, 974, 1000, 1121, 1149, 1654, 1853, 2012
DocOnYou, 2469
Docphin, 1581
DocPlanner, 3040
Docplanner.com, 3044
Docracy, 1518
DocRun, 1546
DocSend, 552, 1110
Docsend, 1700
DocSynk, 1285

Doctor Evidence, 548
Doctor On Demand, 45, 889, 1509
Doctor on Demand, 91, 842, 1046, 1110, 1830, 1916
Doctor's Best, 1335
Doctor's Choice Home Care, 702
Doctors, 1507
DocTracker, 534
Doctrackr, 2365
Doctrakr, 1460
Docu Sign, 518
Docufide, 1784
Docufree, 1891
Docufree Corporation, 1148
DocuLynx, 1021
Document Depository Corp., 1577
Document Technologies, 413, 1505
DocuSign, 28, 85, 260, 486, 560, 603, 729, 836, 974, 1000, 1024, 1626, 1642, 1672, 2690
DocuWare, 1255
DocVerse, 231
Dodla Dairy, 3211
Dodoni, 2784
DOF Subsea, 740
Dog Parker, 896
Doggyloot, 1384, 1615
Dogswell, 869, 1861
DogVacay, 228
DogVacey, 770
Doit International, 456
Dojo Madness, 1809
Dolan Media Company, 21
Dolce Hotels & Resorts, 378
Dolead Dynadmic, 3239
Dolex, 57
DolEx Dollar Express Inc., 1403
Doll Capital Management, 3284
Dollar Express, 63
Dollar General Corporation, 2379
Dollar Shave Club, 124, 552, 761, 1480, 1663, 1785, 1916
Dollarama, 220
Dolls Kill, 544, 1183
Dolly, 1183, 2280
Dolphine Marine International, 1745
Dolphinsearch Inc., 371
Domaille Engineering, 399
Domain Elite Holdings, 621
Domain Surgical, 548, 1382
Domain Therapeutics, 2851, 3113
DomainHoldings, 1899
Domainiac, 2851
Domaininvest, 2426
Doman Surgical Inc., 269
Domdex, 1584
Dome Coffees, 2420
Dome9, 1381
DOmedia, 1286
DOmedic, 2265
Domenia Credit, 2471
Dometic, 2497, 3009
Domfinans, 3150
Domicile, 1158
Domidep, 2340
Dominion Diagnostics, 1693
Domino, 1097
Domino Data Lab, 1654, 1694, 2019
Domino's Pizza, 473
Domino's Pizza Japan, 220
Domio, 1595
DOMO, 823, 1839
Domo, 262, 836, 872, 1001, 1204, 2019
Domo Retail, 2471
Domo Safety, 2310
Domo Technologies, 1425
Domus, 2362
Domuso, 593

Domuso Inc., 811
DomusVi, 3026
Donato, 2638
Donaza, 2352
Donde, 471
dondeEsta, 1734
Done By None, 3109
Done Right!, 197
Dong Jiang, 3194
Dongwoon Anatech, 3002
Donlar Corp., 1986
Donnadolce Service SRL, 2419
Donnelley Financial Solutions, 3275
DonorPath, 635
Donortap, 3125
Donseed, 2355
Donson, 2667
Donup, 1088
Donuts, 21, 202, 665, 695, 818, 1828
Doo, 3161
Doobic, 3002, 3127
Doodad, 1964
Dooland, 2936
Dooly, 318
dooly, 2212, 2249
DoorDash, 1069, 1075, 1654, 1662, 1761, 2012
Doordash, 1323
Doorr, 2138
Doorstat, 2202
Doorstead, 1138
Dopbox, 1654
DOPE Magazine, 963
Doppelganger, 184
Dopplr.com, 2604
Dor, 2019
Dorado, 184, 1407, 1728
Dorado E&P, 672
Doray Minerals, 2942
DORC, 2977
Dori Media, 3101
Doright Fashion, 2850
Dorland Health, 1275
Dormeo, 646
Dorna Promocion del Deporte, 2644
Dorner Holding Corp., 158
dorsaVi, 3138
Dorsey & Whitney, 3279
Dorsey Schools, 812, 1504
DoSomething.org, 1374
Dot & Bo, 1254, 1361, 1853
dot Blockchain Music, 2027
Dot Health, 2113
Dot Hill, 3101
Dot Loop, 1853
Dot Medical, 3010
Dot Product, 1004
Dot Wireless, 132
DOTC United, 1121
DotCloud, 2329
Dotcom Therapy, 1293
DotDashPay, 519
Dote, 1121
dotFX, 1966
Dotgo, 688
DotNetNuke, 1425
Dotnetnuke, 197
Dotomi, 1896
Dotomi Direct Messaging, 1913
Dots, 720, 1993
DOTS Technology Corp, 1297
Dotster, 223
Dottikon, 2922
Dou-Dou, 3042
Douban, 2584
Double Bridge Technology, 2850
Double Click, 924, 1041, 1121
Double Dutch, 32, 1097

Portfolio Companies Index

Double E Company, 556
Double Fusion, 1827
Double Robotics, 874
DOUBLE Trade, 2544
Double-Scope, 3006
DoubleBeam, 384
DoubleDutch, 1082
Doubledutch, 358, 751, 1118
DoublePositive, 1388, 1710
DoubleTrade.com, 1668
Doubletwist, 3013
DoubleVerify, 301, 741, 814, 1001, 1041
Dough, 1118
Dough.com, 1785
Douglas Dynamics, 199
Douglas Products, 96
Douglas Steel Supply, 1970
Douguo, 823
Doum & Nanum, 2857
DoveConviene, 3052
Doveconviene/Shopfully, 2296
Dover Microsystems, 1509
Dovetail, 743
Dow Kokam, 1603
Dow Pharmaceutical Sciences, 1691
Dow Venture Capital, 3269
Dowley Security, 1273
Dowley Security Systems, 1745
Down, 307, 858
Downeast LNG, 1068
Downtyme, 1589
Doxel, 124
Doxim, 824
Doxim Inc., 158
Doximity, 609, 665, 1010, 1257
Doxis Lighting Factory, 2949
Doxo, 262, 1024, 1247
DOZ, 1749
DPA Microphones, 1572
dPharm, 3241
DPI Specialty Foods, 147
DPM, 655
DPS Inc., 69
DPW Van Stolk Holding, 3209
DPx, 1039
Dr Lal PathLabs, 1776
Dr. Comfort, 1209
Dr. Dental, 21
Dr. Martens, 3033
Dr. On Demand, 1663
Dr. Wu, 1088
Dr.2, 1121
DR2, 3277
Draft, 60, 329, 650, 1888
Draft Day, 1118
Draft Kings, 313, 743
DraftKings, 38, 70, 823, 1534
draganfly, 2134
Dragdis, 3049
Dragnet Solutions, 524, 791
Dragon Army, 189
Dragon Innovation, 1110
Dragonfly, 970
DragonPlay, 2709
DragonsMeet, 2869
DragonWave, 2058
Dragos Inc., 84
Drais, 1010, 1760
Drake Automotive, 960
Drake Equipment, 1609
Draker, 202, 786, 1097
DramaFever, 1242
Dramafever, 858, 3127
Draper Espirit, 986
Draper Fisher Jurvetson, 3284
Draper James, 761
Draper Richards, 3284

Draper Triangle, 3275
Draper Triangle Ventures, 3269
Draper's & Damon's, 839
DraTek Technologies, 2667
Drawbridge, 1075, 1082, 1654
Drawbridge Health, 809
Drawbridge Networks, 317, 1475
Dray Alliance, 50
Dray Now, 518
Drayer Physical Therapy Institute, 1128
DrayNow, 814
DRB Systems, 1469
DRDx, 2824
Dream Dinners, 506
Dream Execution, 2857
Dream Giveaway, 17
Dream Link Entertainment, 721
Dream Maker Ventures, 3258
Dream Square, 1340
Dreambox, 1392
DreameGGs, 799
DreamLine, 1266
Dreamlines, 101, 2441
Dreamlines.de, 2813
DreamLocal, 1161
DreamPayments, 2128
Dreams, 1753
Dreamscape, 1883
DreamWater, 2263
DreamWorks Animation SKG, 1946
Dremio, 483, 1121, 1346, 1534
Dresser, 1368, 1573
Dresser-Rand Group; Exterran Energy Corp., 1903
Drever Capital Management, 1061
Drew Foam Companies, 828
Drew Foam Companies Inc., 327
Drex-Chem Malaysia, 1572
Drexcode, 2874
Dreyfus-Corney, 678
DrFirst, 1625
DRG Limited, 2871
DRI Holdings Limited, 621
DribbleUp, 622
Drie Pees, 3042
Driessen Aerospace, 2378
Drift, 741, 816, 965, 1110, 1654
Drifter Entertainment, 1473
Driftrock, 2752
Driftwood Dairy Holding, 1168
DrillingInfo, 1000
Drillinginfo, 560, 1166
drillMap, 1579
Drimki, 2390
Drimmi, 2320
DRINKmaple, 786
Drip, 24, 351
Dripkit, 1507
Drish Shoes Limited, 2861
Drishtee, 55
Drishti, 124, 249
Drishyam AI, 30
Drive Factor, 1502
Drive For Me, 2851
Drive Motors, 358
Drive.ai, 823, 994
DriveAble Assessment Centres, 2121
Driveline Retail, 1091
Driven Brands, 168, 415, 1576
Driven Brands Inc., 914
Driven Inc., 403
Driven Performance Brands, 1232
DrivenBrands, 1871
Driver Hire, 2944
DriverSide, 912
Drivetime, 720
Drivetribe, 2446

Drivewyze, 665, 2157
Drivezy.com, 1758
Drivin, 1118
Driving Curve, 3181
Drivr, 3203
Drizly, 329, 431, 712
Drizzle, 2099
DRL, 1110
Drobo, 757, 1341, 1593, 1760
Drofika, 1507
Droice Labs, 622
Drone Base, 792, 1888
Drone Deploy, 128, 1626
Drone Racing League, 472, 922, 1151, 1813
DroneBase, 1480
Dronebase, 1882
DroneDeploy, 665, 1700, 1879
Dronen Consulting, 1252
DroneSeed, 1696, 1721
Drop, 218, 724, 1670, 1983, 2147, 2224, 2225
drop, 93, 1982
Drop.io, 608
Dropbox, 28, 115, 248, 455, 802, 836, 1001, 1761, 2012, 2860, 2860
DropCam, 238
Dropcam, 28, 1001, 1054
DropCountr, 1893
DropFire, 1734
DropGifts, 2829
Droplet, 1238
Droplr, 1463, 1656
Dropoff, 544
Dropout Labs, 305
DropThought, 2011
Drover, 319, 2280
Drug Emporium, 753
DrugAbuse Sciences, 3007
Drugstore.com, 922, 1003, 1183, 1865
Drum, 1985
Drumglass High School, 2749
Drummond Gold Limited, 1548
Drunc, 858
Druva, 603, 1654, 1796, 2690, 3001
Dry Soda, 841
Dry Soda Co., 85
Drybar, 421, 1576
Dryden Human Capital, 3244
DS Medical, 1963
DS Services, 559
DS-IQ, 1247
DSA/Phototech, 378
DSC, 1004
DSCI, 1276
dscout, 251
DSG, 1344
DSI Holding Company, 1456
DSI Renal, 782
DSL.Net, 757
DSM Green Power, 2761
DSM-AGI Corporation, 3062
DSO Interactive, 3113
DSP Concepts, 302
DSP Concepts Inc., 1951
DSP Group, 260
DSP Group Inc, 2585
DSP Holdings, 2975
DSpace, 2618
Dsquare, 3042
DSST Public Schools, 1316
Dstillery, 431, 533, 539, 695, 1317, 1486, 1896, 1916
DSTLD, 120, 1965
DSTLD Premium Denim Co., 228
DSW Homes, 984
DTC Logistics, 673
Dtex Systems, 777, 1346
DTI, 901

1305

Portfolio Companies Index

DTI Inc., 914
DTIQ, 361
DTl Transportation, 1423
DTLR Inc., 354
DTMS, 2299, 2301, 2305
DTN, 869, 1927
DTT Surveillance, 812, 1465
DTx, 131
DTX Studios, 2931
Du Pareil Au Meme, 2423
Dual Therapeutics, 1420
Dualtec, 2438
Duane Reade, 1360
Dub, 1771
Dubai Investment Park, 152
DuBois Chemicals, 199, 378, 2046
Dubset, 567
Dubsmash, 679, 1149, 2478
Ducati, 3154
Ducati Motor Holding Spa, 1835
Ducatt, 2949, 3042
Duchossois Capital Management, 3265
Duck Creek Technologies, 135
DuckDuckGo, 1882
Duckhorn, 824
Ducksboard, 2920
Duco, 1000
Dude Solutions, 500, 3259
DueDil, 3030
Duedil, 1361
DueGo, 3030
Duett AS, 29
Duetto, 235, 968, 1806
Duff & Phelps, 413, 1147, 1743, 3272
Dufry, 2922
Dugun.com, 2437
Duimelotje, 3042
Duke Realty, 1954
Dulce Vida, 445
Dumur Industries, 2163
Dunamu, 1509
Duncan Media Group, 506
Dundee Venture Capital, 3265
Dune, 2454
Dune Networks, 1896, 2380
Dunkin Brands, 220
Dunlop, 2851
Dunn Paper, 1166, 1213, 1997
Dunn Paper Inc., 403
Dunrath Capital, 3265
Dunwello, 1322
Duo, 820, 889, 1212
Duo Security, 1534, 1547, 1860
Duolingo, 578, 630, 1075, 1882
Duolog Ltd, 2705, 2705
Duoyuan, 834
Dupont, 2851
Durata, 74
Durata Therapeutics, 386, 1508, 1698, 1941
Duratap, 1766
DuraTherm, 3222
Duravant, 1368
Durcon, 1505
Durham Graphene, 2892
Durham Scientific Crystals Limited (DSC), 2397
DuritCast, 3048
Duropak, 1376
Dusan Co. LTD, 2839
Dust Identity, 1075
Dust Networks, 555, 979, 2639
Dustin, 2384
Dusty, 395
Dusty Robotics, 231
Dutch, 1776
Dutchie, 417
Dutton-Forshaw, 2644
Duvas Technologies, 2760

DVDO, 1747
DVN Holdings, 1769
DVS Sciences, 12, 1247, 1436
DVT Corp., 152
DVTEL, 1647
DVTel, 1633
DW Healthcare Partners, 3264
DWave, 609
Dwell, 1694
Dwellable, 1183
Dwll.in, 3174
DWOLLA, 124
Dwolla, 607, 776
DWT-Engineering Oy, 2318
Dx Biosciences, 791
DxUpClose, 841
DXY.com, 596
Dyadic, 486
Dyax, 762, 1092, 1558
Dydacomp, 1234
dYdX, 124
DyeCat, 2892
DYM, 1334
Dym Co., 3002
Dymant, 1416
DYN, 1334
Dyn, 308
Dyna Crane Services, 2136, 2285
Dynacare Kasper, 2082
Dynacure, 2851
Dynadec, 1114, 1693
DynaGen, 2205
DynaGrid Construction Group, 477
DynaIndustrial, 2136, 2285
Dynamatic, 364
Dynament, 235
Dynamic Change, 2967
Dynamic Communicaties, 403
Dynamic Details, 439
Dynamic Extractions Historic Futures, 3107
Dynamic Industries, 413, 1573
Dynamic Medical Systems Inc., 869
Dynamic Mobile Data Systmes, 954
Dynamic Offshore Resources, 1573
Dynamic Organic Light, 1915
Dynamic Precision Group, 413
Dynamic Quest, 1724
Dynamic Signal, 483, 1154, 1540, 1916
Dynamic Sinal, 1827
Dynamic Systems, 917
Dynamic Yield, 996
DynamicImaging, 402
DynamicOps, 1319
Dynamics, 56, 221
DynamicSignal, 1853
Dynamo, 779
DynaOptics, 1669
Dynaoptics, 1600
Dynapac, 3009
Dynapel Systems, 2754
Dynapower, 1435
DynaPump, 466
DynaRoad Oy, 2716
DynaScan Technology Corp, 2703
Dynasty, 741
Dynatect Manufacturing, 2311
Dynatherm Medical, 1616
Dynatrace, 238, 901, 1814
Dynatrace Inc., 158
Dynavax, 769
Dynavax Corp., 212
Dynavax Technologies, 1616, 2518
Dynavec, 2970
DynCorp International, 1925
Dynea Oy, 2379
Dynegy, 675
Dynex Technologies, 118

Dynisco, 194
Dyno Holdings, 359
Dyno Nobel A, 3009
Dynogen, 1412, 2445
Dynogen Pharmaceuticals, 2316
Dynojet, 846, 1022
DynoSense, 1983
DYSIS, 1978
Dysonics, 1004
DéCor Gravure, 1570
Défoncé, 44

E

E 1023, 1524
E Band Communications, 206
E Ink, 922, 1702
E&B Technology Co., 2924
e+ Cancer Care, 1081
e+ CancerCare, 789
E-Band Communications, 925
E-Blink, 2899
E-Capital, 2724
E-Chromic Technologies, 119
E-Conolight, 1209
e-Courier Software, 92
E-Data Sift, 1626
e-Dialog, 521
E-Future, 2998
e-Glue, 436, 2580
e-Government Solutions, 1957
e-infoda.com, 1837
e-Medical System, 1755
E-mice, 2772
E-Motion, 3154
E-Motion Medical Ltd., 2328
E-Motion Ventures, 2967
E-Net, 2897
E-One Moli, 1906
E-One Moli Energy, 2053
E-printing Company, 2855
e-Rewards, 1760, 1776
E-Scape Bio, 1350
E-Security, 59
e-Security, 1886
E-Senza Technologies, 2824
e-Sharing, 1956
E-SIM, 3249
E-Supportlink ltd, 2854
e-Therapeutics, 3018
E-Tran, 954
e-trees Japan Inc., 2414
E-Z Shipper Racks, 752
E.A.R.T.H., 1393
E.B. Bradey Co., 869
E.D. Smith & Sons, 2150
E.E. Stringer Funeral Homes, 111
E.L. Haynes Public Charter School, 1316
e.l.f. Cosmetics, 1861
E.Piphany, 1865
E/O Networks, 536
E14, 2386
e27, 3038
e2E Materials, 432
e2e Materials, 320
E2E Networks, 2526
E2E Rail, 3211
E2open, 1000, 1038, 1911
e2Open, 560
E3Bank, 3277
E4 Health, 1165
E4X, 2655
E5 Systems Inc., 803
E8 Security, 84
e994, 2473
EA, 1382
EA Pharma, 3020
EAA Inspection Services, 3267

Portfolio Companies Index

eAccess, 1769
Eachnet, 2850
EachScape, 533, 848
Eachscape, 1358
Eachwin Capital, 841
EACOM Timber, 1062
EAG Laboratories, 1368
Eagaveev, 307
Eager, 754
EagerPanda, 622
Eagle, 260
Eagle Battery, 409
Eagle Business Solutions, 3267
Eagle Crest Energy, 1888
Eagle Crest Energy Company, 2649
Eagle Energy Company of Oklahoma, 1573
Eagle Energy Exploration, 1573
Eagle Eye Analytics, 743
Eagle Filter, 2873
Eagle Foods, 1062
Eagle Genomics, 2967
Eagle Hardware & Garden, 753
Eagle Oil & Gas Co., 508
Eagle Pharmaceutical, 1490
Eagle Point Credit Management, 1743
Eagle Precision, 1053
Eagle Quest International, 1270
Eagle River Homes, 1455
Eagle Vision Pharmaceuticals, 266
EagleBurgmann, 2155
Eagleview, 500
EagleView Technologies, 1717
EAI-Vista, 1558
eAngler.com, 1668
Earbits, 243
Eargo, 272, 563, 1183, 1530
EarLens, 1122
Earlens, 74, 1993
Earlydoc, 3224
EarlySense, 337, 3059
Earn, 1509
Earn Up, 384, 1054
Earn.com, 124
Earnest, 38, 306, 544, 560, 724, 1183, 1566
Earnest Research Company, 1387
Earnin, 124, 384, 720, 1181
Earnix, 2750
EarnUp, 599
Earnup, 55, 544
Earny, 518, 1184
Earshot, 272, 1458
Earth AI, 395
Earth Animal, 448
Earth Class Mail, 85
Earth Fare, 1360
Earth Networks, 1388, 1460
Earth Tech, 1521
EarthClean, 3279
EarthCube, 2296
Earthlink Network Inc., 1103
EarthLite, 327
EarthSense, 995
Ease, 307, 566
Ease Central, 600
Ease Entertainment Services, 274
Easecentral, 525, 784
eAsic, 946, 2726
EasilyDo, 1184, 1896
Easou, 3100, 3208
eAssist Global Solutions, 2079
East Balt Bakeries, 1376
East Club, 1965
East District, 3038
East Hampton Sandwich Co., 477
East Shore Aircraft, 1967
East West Manufacturing, 667
Eastern Broadcasting Company, 413

Eastern Elevator, 1404
EastMachinery, 1121
Easton Capital, 986
Easton-Bell Sports, 2015
EastPoint Sports, 316, 1171
Eastport Holdings, 405
Eastvillage, 3042
Easy Bike, 2439
Easy Buy, 1139, 2946
Easy Market, 1352
Easy Metrics, 1689
Easy Post, 889
Easyart.com, 2535
EasyAsk, 1672
Easyaula, 2950
easyCar, 3055
EasyCopay, 1306
Easyfinance.ru, 2344
EasyLap, 1844
EASYLINK, 1769
Easynet & MDNX, 2944
Easynvest, 62
EasyPak, 846
EasyPost, 1222, 1666
Easyship, 1595
Easyvoyage, 3113
EAT Club, 741
Eat Club, 858, 1097
Eat Makhana, 622
Eat Street, 858
Eatalynet, 2296
Eatem Foods, 1456
Eatem Foods Co., 1132
Eatime Inc., 623
Eating Recovery Center, 433, 1104
Eaton Veterinary Pharmaceutical, 958
EatonTowers, 909
Eatsa, 1643
EatStreet, 566, 983
Eau Ecarlate, 2423, 2852
Eave, 567
Eaze, 417, 785, 858, 1694, 1807
Eazytec, 1004
EB Brands, 1234
eBags, 986, 1785
eBANK, 2772
eBaoTech, 793
Ebara, 214
Ebates, 197, 386, 770
eBay, 248, 1183
Ebb, 1928
Ebb Tehrapeutics, 149
Ebb Therapeutics, 1082
Ebbu, 557, 1135, 1807
Ebel, 1017
eBenx, 1041
Eberle, 846
Eberly Design Inc., 328
eBest, 1180
EBI Life Sciences, 1921
Ebiquity, 1927
ebix.com, 536
Eblana Photonics, 3179
EbLens, 1049
EBlink, 2385, 3113
EBM Solutions, 1412
EBOOST, 1681
EBR Systems, 176, 1628, 1725, 1762
EBR Systems Inc., 604
eBrevia, 792
EBS Technologies, 2824
EBT, 2781
eBureau, 946, 1445, 1534, 1725, 1796
Ebury Partners, 2400
eBus.TV, 2913
EC Waste, 1465
ECA Medical Instruments, 1144

Ecamion, 2187
eCareOne.com, 406
Ecast, 757
Eccentex, 3229
Ecco Safety Group, 258
Eccrine Systems, 479
eCentria, 1255
ECG Management Consultants, 881
eChalk, 646, 2196
eChalk.com, 460
Echelon, 260, 1247
Echelon Aviation, 1491
Echelon Insights, 617
Echo, 548, 1982
Echo 360, 508, 551, 1633
Echo Active Learning, 633
Echo Health Ventures, 3273
Echo Nest, 521
Echo Pixel, 1004
Echo11, 656
Echo360, 1699, 1766
Echodyne, 1151, 1158, 2278
Echodyne Corp., 1005
Echogen Power Systems, 1047
Echolab, 669
EchoNous, 1082
Echopass, 386, 1389
EchoPixel, 6
EchoSign, 665, 1747
Echostar Corp., 300
Echoworx Corporation, 2058
Echtman Engineering Co., 2389
ECI, 1017, 2609
ECI Engineering & Construction, 3173
ECi Software Solutions, 135, 413
ECI Technology, 3274
ECI The Elastic Network, 3221
eCift, 2475
Eckler Industries, 908
Eckler's, 222
Eckler's Enterprises Inc., 449
Eclat, 1558
Eclectic Bars Limited, 2458
Eclerot and Ziegler AG, 3172
Eclipse, 1082
Eclipse Advantage, 1093
Eclipse Aviation, 692
Eclipse Resources, 672, 1846
Eclipse Therapeutics Inc., 487
Eclypsium, 1004, 1158, 1877
ECNlive, 3018
Eco Consumer Services, 2778
Eco Digitec, 2271
Eco Logic, 2058
Eco Online, 3216
ECO Products, 3257
Eco Projects, 3042
ECO Technologies, 2128
Eco-Dan, 2562
Eco-Site, 1270, 3259
Eco4Cloud, 2672, 3052
eCoast Marketing, 1299
eCoast Sales Solutions, 1605
EcoATM, 491, 716, 1780
ecoATM, 184
Ecobee, 2204, 2262
ecobee, 2236
Ecoboard Holdings, 1745
Ecoboard Industries Limited, 2861
EcoEnvelopes, 1872
EcoFactor, 491, 1579, 2439
Ecohaus, 1646
Ecoin Co Ltd, 2839
EcoIntense, 1255, 2824
EcoInteractive, 92
Ecolibrium Solar, 1553, 1988
Ecollege, 402

Portfolio Companies Index

eCollege, 1480
EcoLogic, 184
Ecologic Brands, 340, 595
EcoLogicLiving, 2295
Ecom Food Industries, 2139
EcoMade, 3194
Ecometrica, 2505
eCommHub, 1673
eCommission, 1123
eCommission Financial Services, 1234
Ecomo, 1894
EcoMotors, 925
EconCore, 2366
Econex, 2839
Econic Technologies, 2858
Ecopackers, 2137
EcoPhos, 2563
EcoPlant, 249
Ecoprod, 3234
eCopy, 438
Ecore, 657
Ecoscape Solutions, 465
EcoScraps, 595, 1070
Ecosec, 2284
Ecosense, 747
Ecosense Lighting, 646
EcoSmart, 642
Ecosmart, 768
EcoSMART Technologies, 537, 1579
ECOSO, 3100
EcoSurg, 995, 1187
EcoSynthetic, 2061
ECOtality, 2315
EcoTensil, 3277
Ecotensil, 1600
Ecotone AS, 3141
Ecoult, 2613
Ecount, 1175
Ecova, 1096
Ecovacs Robotics, 973
Ecovation, 432
Ecovision Renewables, 2505
ECP/CH Industries, 746
Ecrebo, 3018
ECRM Holdings, 361
Ecron Acunova, 1382
ECS Environmental Solutions, 164
ECS Federal, 1129
ECS Learning Systems, 17
ECS Refining, 2022
ECS Tuning, 257
ECTel, 2609
ECtelecom, 2807
eCullet, 126
Ecutronic, 2342
eccVision, 796
Ecwid, 3088
Ed Laboratory, 2924
ED MAP, 1689
Ed Map, 1364
Ed., 1123
EDAC Technologies, 862
Edagora, 3020
Edai.com, 3100
Edaijia, 1121
EDAN, 3100
Edaris Health, 387, 1172
eDarling, 2829, 2838
eData Sift, 1888
eData Source, 1873
Edcamp Foundation, 1316
EdCast, 454, 1054, 1699
Edcentric, 1105
EDCO, 297, 361
Edcon, 220
EDDA Technology, 2667
Eddie Bauer, 839

Eddingpharm, 1382
Eddingpharm International Holdings Limited, 621
Eddy Packing, 1171
eDealya, 3003
Edelman Financial Services, 924
Edelweiss Financial Services, 413
Eden, 396, 518, 679, 727
Eden Health, 13, 49, 325
Eden Park Illmination, 1592
Edenbridge, 1777
EdeniQ, 126, 184
Edeniq, 609, 1977
EdenPark Illumination, 975
Edenspace, 1774
Edesa Biotech, 2180
eDev, 495
EDF Ventures, 3269
Edge, 2826
Edge Adhesives Holdings, 828
Edge Case Research, 293
Edge Compute, 799
Edge Connex, 518
Edge Fitness Clubs, 1345
Edge Intelligence, 107
Edge Makers, 206
Edge Medical Devices Ltd, 3158
Edge Systems, 1978
Edge Technologies, 1606
Edge Trade, 655
Edgecase, 202, 533
EdgeCast, 306
EdgeConneX, 240, 1782
EdgeConnex, 1860
Edgeconnex, 1211
Edgefolio, 3108
Edgemont, 1219
Edgen Corporation, 1745
Edgenet, 1116
Edgespring, 1121
Edgeware, 2637
Edgewater Markets, 793
Edgewater Networks, 646, 1407, 1522
EdgeWave, 183, 1869
EdgeWave Software, 69
Edgewise Networks, 2
Edgewood Partners Holdings, 413, 1743
Edgeworx, 1611
Edgile, 21
Edgwater Midstream, 671
Edgy Bees, 180
Edgybees, 1926
EDH Groupe des Ecoles, 2851
EDHC, 445
EDI, 853
Edible Arrangements, 1088
Edico Genome, 603
Edif Group, 3036
Edify, 1421
EDIGMA.com, 3048
Edimer, 1618, 1811
Edinburgh Molecular Imaging, 689
Edioma, 445, 594
Edison, 1184, 2978
Edison Agrosciences, 267
Edison Learning, 1116
Edison Partners, 3274
Edisun Microgrids, 101, 972
Editas, 1811
Editas Medicine, 709, 747, 762, 1419
Edition F, 3236
Editions Montparnasse, 2897
Editions Oberthur, 2340
Editorially, 351
Edj Analytics, 475
Edlio, 1136
edly, 2195

Edmark Corporation, 1398
EDMC, 1496
Edmentum, 1491, 1814
Edmit, 1551
Edmodo, 1796
Edmund & Associates, 1136
EDN, 1784
edo Interactive, 1906
Edo Japan, 2292
eDoc Architects, 1668
edocs, 757, 2427
Edovo, 1054
EDR, 235, 530
eDreams, 596
eDreams Edusoft, 1013
edriving, 1166
EDS Docdata B.V., 2902
EdSurge, 428, 1316, 2003
EDT Learning, 2890
Edtech Holdings, 361
Edthena, 3277
Edubridge, 55
Educate, 1742
Educate Online, 1742
Education Affiliates, 1039
Education Corporation of America, 1937, 1986
Education Dynamics, 897
Education Elements, 946, 1316, 1551, 1865
Education Futures Group, 1492
Education Management Corporation, 1105, 2379
Education Networks of America, 1270
Education One D/B/A Penn Foster, 716
Education Overseas Ltd, 3146
Education Partners, 1986
Education.com, 371, 1793
Educational Holdings LLC, 77
Educational Initiatives, 1348
Educents, 563, 600, 883, 1054
Educreations, 28, 1316
Edudo, 2967
Edududes Ltd., 2967
Edufii, 826, 1585, 1784
EduK, 720
EduK Group, 21, 1105
Edunav, 1381
EduSports, 3109
EDUSS, 687
Edvantage Group, 3013
Edvantage Group AS, 2369
Edward Don & Company, 744
Edward W. Brooke Charter School, 1316
Edwards Group, 433
Edwin, 658
Edwin Watts Golf, 168
Edwin Watts Golf Shops, 1971
EdXact, 2899
EDY International, 2471
Edyn, 721
ee4, 386
EEC Incorporated, 1208
Eedoo, 2936
Eefoof, 1784
EELCEE, 2755
EELF, 2471
Eemax, 1572
EEMCO, 3194
Eero, 107, 741, 858, 874, 1534, 1663, 1694
eEye Digital Security, 260
EFC International, 1505
Effective Measure, 1558, 1711
eFFECTOR, 1350, 1731
eFFECTOR Therapeutics, 182, 517, 1238, 1896
Efferent Labs, 704
Efficere, 1915
Efficient Finance, 386
Efficient Forms, 949
Efficient Networks, 856, 1407

1308

Portfolio Companies Index

EfficientFrontier, 1534
Efficity, 3113
EffiMat, 3203
Efflux Systems, 851
EFI, 58
EFI Electronics for Imaging, 3137
Eficia, 2439
EFileCabinet, 1677
eFileCabinet, 84
EFJohnson, 779
eflow, 2974
eFolder, 695
EFP Corp., 1030
Efreightsolutions, 29
EFront, 779
Eftia OSS Solutions, 162
Eftpos New Zealand, 2664
eFuneral, 1047
EG Gilero, 3259
eGain, 1599
eGain Communications, 1360
eGalax, 2603
Egalet, 2702, 3149
Egalet Corp., 191
EGAR Technology, 2465
EGB Investments, 2293
Egea Biosciences, 898
EGeen, 2390
Egenera, 202, 1080
eGenesis, 1069
eGenesis Bio, 268
Eggdetect, 3245
EggDrop, 1853
Eggrock, 1142
EGHC, 383
Egis Technology, 2703
Egis Tecnology, 3062
Egistec, 2436
eGistics, 1850
eGix, 443
Egnyte, 751, 889, 1075, 1460, 1682
eGO, 1693
egreetings.com, 1480
eGroups, 1626
Eguana Technologies, 2671
eGuardian, 1784
eGym, 2824
EHANG, 823
Ehang, 3251
eHarmony, 1235, 1785
Ehealth, 1121
eHealth Global Technologies, 1745
eHealth Technologies, 52, 1205
eHedge AG, 2528
eHi Car Services, 3062
EI Technologies, 2876
EIC, 2965
Eichrom Technologies, 153
Eider, 2423
Eideticom, 2157
Eidex Education Analytics, 1736
Eidogen, 186
Eidos, 762, 1519
EidoSearch, 1546
Eigen Innovations, 2128, 2200
Eiger, 1010, 1941
Eiger Biopharmaceuticals, 1519
Eight, 1069
8 Enterprises, 378
Eight O'Clock Coffee, 881
8 Rivers Capital, 3259
8 Security, 1809
Eight Sleep, 785, 1329
8 Solutions, 3130
Eight Spokes, 1097
860 South, 1219
886 Food, 3181

88Rising, 1813
89, 256, 307
89 Energy, 1278, 1326
89bio, 1143, 1519
8D World, 1715
8digits, 3078
8Fit, 3223
8I, 60
8i, 219, 792, 922, 1611, 1926, 3023
8th Wall, 1663
8thBridge, 1850
8tracks, 1700
eInstruction, 468
eIQ Energy, 1324
Eisai, 1349, 1452
Eisenworld, 2795
Eisfeld Datentechnik, 2713
Eisner Amper, 3274
EisnerAmper LLP, 3267
eJamming, 1584
eJammingAudiiO, 1306
Ejasent, 555
Eka, 3001
Eka Systems, 126, 1579
Ekahau, 946
Ekinops, 3208
Ekkia, 2448
eKnitting, 1535
Eko, 175, 996, 1965
Eko Studio, 1611
EKomi, 3170
Ekona Power, 2111
EKOS, 260, 925, 1325
Ekos, 153, 176, 1786
Ekos Corporation, 1241
EkoStinger, 432, 704
EKR Therapeutics, 1136, 1268, 1508
Ekstop.com, 2913
Ekstrem Lavpris, 2863
Ektron Inc., 438
ekWateur, 2439
El Dorado Ventures, 3284
El Ganso, 1088
El Pharma, 1051
El Pollo Loco, 783
El Rancho, 2985
El Rayan Danfarm, 2889
El Super, 1720
El-Forest, 2755
EL-OP (Optics), 2389
ElaCarte, 590, 1118, 1581
Elan, 1452
Elan Languages, 2949
Elance, 757
Elance ODek, 1748
Elantec Semiconductors, 2380
Elara Caring, 1062
Elastagen, 2536
elastic, 248
Elastic Path, 1602, 2291
ElasticRun, 1346
Elasticsearch, 585
Elastifile, 235, 483, 1121
Elastix, 2342
Elastomeric Technologies, 52, 1227
Elatica, 1184
Elatifile, 603
Elation Health, 609, 1054
ElationEMR, 20
ELAXY, 2616
Elbi, 2389
Elbion, 2354
Elbit, 3211
Elcely Therapeutics, 1786
Elcelyx, 1122
Elco-Brandt Group, 2745
Elcom, 2775

Elcom Technologies, 2454
Eldat, 2720
Eldon Holding AB, 2712
Eldorado Bancshares. Ennis-Flint, 1372
Eldorado Stone, 846
Ele.me, 1181
Election, 37
Electra Bicycle Company, 373
Electra Vehicles, 1100
Electrawinds, 3042
Electric, 823
Electric AI, 317
Electric Cloud, 1184, 1540, 1593, 1896
Electric Imp, 1149, 1534
Electrical Components International, 1085
Electrical Source Holdings, 862
electrIQ Power, 2142
Electro Energy, 979
Electro-Motion Inc., 1609
Electro-Motive Diesel Inc., 862
Electro-Radiation Inc., 418
Electrochaea, 267
ElectroChemical Systems Inc., 737
ElectroCore, 644, 1205
ElectroCraft, 1636
Electrokoppar, 2883
Electromed, 3279
Electron Beam Technologies, 321
Electron Database Company, 1047
Electronic, 2556
Electronic Arts, 836, 1654, 1785
Electronic Data Resources, 1745
Electronic Packaging Products Inc., 985
Electronic Systems Protection, 873
Electronics, 111
Electronics for Imaging, 300
Electrophotonics, 2267
Electrosteel Steels, 584
Electrovaya, 2058
Electrum Partners, 1135
Elegant Desserts, 193
Elegant Hotels Group, 1937
Elektron AB, 2718
Elektronabava, 967
Elektronik+Kabeltechnik Gmbh & Co., 2616
Eleme Medical, 652
Eleme Petrochemical, 2086
Elemedia, 1305
Element, 1004, 1154, 1269
Element 14, 3195
Element 5, 2299, 2301, 2305
Element AI, 2027
Element Analytics, 809, 2439
Element Data, 755
Element Energy, 491
Element Fleet Management Corp., 1903
Element Materials Technology, 2311
Element Petroleum, 156
Element Science, 1811
Element14, 260
Elemental, 85
Elemental Technologies, 979, 1383, 1945
Elementary Robotics, 1834, 1877
ElementLabs, 706
Elements Behavioral Health, 782
Elements Casino, 2081
Elementum, 107, 809, 1121
Elemis, 1088
Elemtnal, 620
Elentec Semiconductor, 1896
Elephant Drive, 306, 1099
Elephant Oil & Gas, 1851
ElephantDrive, 1566, 1784
Eletrobras, 1730
Eletromidia, 928
Elettrostudio Energia, 3020
Elettrostudio Energia Infrastructure, 3020

Portfolio Companies Index

Eleutian, 2390
Elevar Equity, 1374
Elevate, 679, 720, 1054, 1255, 1522, 1654
Elevate Accessories, 392
Elevate Credit, 1654, 1785
Elevate Digital, 61
Elevate K-12, 1019
Elevate Security, 547
Elevation Labs, 503
Elevation Partners, 43
Elevation Pharma, 1221
Elevation Resource Holdings, 1443
Elevator, 301
Eleven Biotherapeutics, 747, 1811
eleven-x, 2138
Elevian, 1095
Elevoc, 1509
Eley Group, 2944
Elgin Equipment Group, 194
Elgin Fastener Group, 194
Eli Research, 263
Eliason Corporation, 1234
Elicit, 724, 871
Eligo Bioscience, 1069
ElimiDateapp.com, 2885
eLink Communications, 526
Eliokem Materials & Concepts, 1134
Elira Therapeutics, 267
Elis II, 2497
Elit Teknoloji, 2309
Elite, 2489
Elite Advanced Laser Corporation, 2603
Elite Comfort Solutions, 170
Elite Daily, 1530, 1583
Elite Education Media Group, 2850
Elite One Source, 118
Elitel, 2897
Elitra, 1412
Elity Systems, 536, 954
ELIX Polymers, 1753
ELIXIA, 2384
Elixir, 1438
Elixir Pharmaceuticals, 925
Elixirs, 1135
Eliza Corporation, 1417
Elizabeth Arden, 1549
Ella Health, 474, 1460
Ellacoya, 2445
Ellen Tracy, 2171
Eller Media, 924
Ellery Homestyles, 1857
Ellevation, 1316, 1527, 1551
Ellevest, 533, 1607, 1631
Ellibs Oy, 2873
Ellie, 301, 1965
Ellie Mae, 115, 986
Elliegrid, 1507
Elliot, 317, 1758
Ellipse, 3203
Ellipse Technologies Inc., 269
Ellipsis Health, 1069
Elliptic, 3018, 3108
Ellis Communication Group, 1062
Ellison Bakery, 276, 529
Ello, 776, 786
Ellucian, 924, 1041, 1109, 1835
Ellumniate, 2196
Elm City Food Cooperative, 678
Elmira Pet Products, 2056
Elmo-Calf, 3008
Elmville, 2883
Elo Touch Solutions, 559
Elo7, 28, 1000, 2976
Eloan, 793
eLoan, 595
eLocal, 1136
Elogex, 722

Elona Bio Technologies, 1452
Elopak, 2731
Eloqua, 238, 260, 514, 1041
Eloqua Corp., 986
Eloquent, 1378
Eloquii, 896
eLoupes, 1004
Eloxx Pharmaceuticals, 2229
Elprint, 2754
Elron, 2666
Elroy Air, 429, 942, 1663
Elstar Therapeutics, 143
Elsy, 829
Eltek Group, 2384
Eltel Networks Oy, 2311
Elto.com, 2520
Elucent Medical, 222
Elusys Therapeutics, 1196, 1452
Ely Medical Group, 2918
Elysium, 816, 1183
Elytra, 2366
EM Kinetics, 644
Em Teck, 2839
EM4, 223, 2196, 2562
Emachines, 2826
eMachines, 1558
Emageon, 176, 1533, 1619
Emagia, 1672
Emagine IT, 680
Emagix, 2155
Email Data Source, 1306, 1584
Emailage, 306, 720
Emailvision, 3113
Emano, 2867
EMarketer, 1748
Emarsys, 1910
Emay, 2850
Embarcadero Maritime, 1082
Embarcadero Technologies, 1814
Embark, 107, 302, 596, 784, 942, 1643
Embark General, 96
Embark Trucks, 1654
Embarke, 1489
Embedded Linux Technology Inc., 2414
Embedded Planet, 692
Ember Corporation, 979
Ember Resources, 466, 2067
Ember Technologies, 2613
Embera Neurotherapeutics, 362, 1061
EMBL Technology Fund, 2452
Emblem Corp., 390
Embodi, 1615
Embodied, 874, 1004, 1703, 1834
Embodied Intelligence, 1151
Embollic Protection, 1378
embotics, 2267
Embrace, 679, 795
EMBrace Design, 995
Embrace Pet Insurance, 1047
Embrace.io, 228, 306, 318
Embrane, 1334, 1474
Embrella, 915
Embrella Cardiovascular Inc., 269
Embroker, 243
EMC (Emmy), 2841
EmCasa, 622
Emcore, 1970
Emdeon, 277, 2379
Emdot, 2892
Emeco, 2420
EMED, 1770
eMed Technologies, 312
Emediamarketing, 3052
Emefcy, 2900, 3047
Emerald, 1412
Emerald BioAgricultre Corp., 90
Emerald Clean Power, 1573

Emerald Expositions, 2209
Emerald Media, 1082
Emerald Performance Materials, 110
Emerald Solutions, 1112, 1558
Emerald Textiles, 2204
Emerald Therapeutics, 775, 1627
Emeraude Chimie International, 2340
Emeraude International, 2340
Emerge, 3277
Emergence BioEnergy, 855
Emergency Communications Network, 1572
Emergency Essentials, 1645
Emergent, 792, 889
Emergent Discovery, 1161
Emergent One, 707
Emergent Payments, 743
Emergent Respiratory Products, 1664
Emergent Trading, 470
Emerging Markets Communications, 21
Emerging Threats, 658
EmergingMed, 61
Emergo Therapeutics, 1556
Emeritus Corporation, 1621
Emerus, 1972
Emerus Hospital Partners LLC, 202
eMeter, 595, 1341
EMeter. Enernoc, 770
EMG, 3026
Emic, 2451
Emida, 1888
Emids, 222
Emids Experience Partnership, 550
Emillion Oy, 2873
eMindful, 1113
Emine Software, 2703
Emissary, 305, 889, 1222, 1322
EMIT Corporation, 485
Emjag Digital, 2401
EMLSI, 2857
Emmaus Life Science Inc., 69
Emme, 2380
Emme E2MS, 678
Emmerge, 1254
Emmes Corporation, 245
EMMI Solutions, 1476
Emnotion, 967
EMO Labs, 1920
emocha, 1701
emocha Mobile Health, 1054
EMoov, 3108
eMotion, 1188
Emotive Communications, 1348
Empathica, 1041, 1705
Empathy, 1004
Empatica, 2874
Empaua, 1607
Emperative, 314
EMPG, 1166
Emphirix, 1181
Empire Brushes, 1954
Empire CLS, 869
Empire Generating, 675
Empire Global, 1079
Empire Petroleum Holdings, 1599
Empire Today, 1491
EmpirecLS Worldwide Chauffeured Services, 274
Empiricom, 2892
Empirix, 1796, 1814
Emplify, 86, 569
Employ Bridge, 1270
EmployBridge, 1256
Employease, 1148
Employee Channel, 544, 1247
Employer's Direct Insurance Company, 839
EmployerDirect, 1801
Employment Hero, 3023

1310

Portfolio Companies Index

Employment Staffinf, 493
EmployUs, 3259
EMPO Corporation, 1233
Empolyease, 1405
Empow Networks, 178
Empower, 2322, 2577
Empower Energies, 817
Empower Interactive Group, 162
Empower RF Systems, 1752
Empowered, 1010
Empowered Careers, 852
empowertel, 1793
Empresa Generadora de Electricidad Haina, 584
Empresas Verdes Argentina, 834
Empyr, 544, 1024
Empyrean, 493, 793
Emrgy, 1923
EMS, 1041
Ems Chemie, 2922
EMS Management & Consultants, 1343
Emsemble Therapeutics, 747
EMSI, 244
Emstone Engineering, 2449
Emtec, 1423
Emu Solutions, 285
Emu Technology, 1019, 1229
Emulate, 942
EN Engineering, 815, 1871
En Gibton, 3245
ENA, 1733
Enable Injections, 479, 1418
Enable M, 2859
Enable Semiconductor, 3218
Enanta, 1092, 2815
Enanta Pharmaceuticals, 986, 1775, 2379, 3196
EnAqua Solutions, 1484
Enara Networks, 1715
Enata Pharmaceuticals, 1394
Enbala, 676, 809, 1363
enbala, 2078
Enbrel, 2102
Encanto, 1037
Encanto Restaurants Inc., 914
Encap, 2369
EnCap Investments, 3255
Encelle, 1008
Encentiv Energy, 298, 1447
Encentivenergy, 272
Encentuate, 197, 805
Encepta, 2284
Encino Energy, 1020
Encirq, 1354
Encoda Systems, 1724
Encoded Genomics, 94, 1916
Encoded Therapeutics, 1202
Encodia, 268
Encoding.com, 1841, 2017
Encore Capital Group Inc., 492
Encore Dermatology, 697, 1143
Encore Fitness, 797
Encore Interactive, 2200
Encore Media Systems B.V., 2902
Encore Networks, 2284
Encore Paper, 468
EncoreAlert, 1320
EnCorps, 1316
Encos, 2892
Encover, 1672
enCross Partners, 2857
Encycle, 676, 2184, 2187
Encycle Therapeutics, 2187
End The Lix, 950
End2End, 23, 690, 2386
Endaga, 1054
Endame, 1075
Endeavor, 744, 1857
Endeavor Robots, 166

Endeavor Schools, 1105
Endeavour, 1846, 2493
Endeavour Healthcare, 2622
Endeca, 260, 823
Endeca Technologies, 1796
Endeco, 2355
Ender's Fund, 3127
Endforce, 986
Endgame, 515, 1400, 1625, 1788
EndHub, 1642
Endicott Biofuels, 893
Endo Stim, 1619
Endo Vasix, 2728
Endo Via, 426
EndoArt Ltd, 3162
Endocardial Solutions, 1378
Endocare, 97
EndoChoice, 550, 1571, 1654
Endocontrol, 3113
EndoCross, 3241
Endocyte, 287, 1616, 1847
EndoGastric Solutions, 59, 386, 468, 1122, 1520
EndoInsight, 995
Endoinsight, 1187
Endologix, 697, 1268
EndoMedix, 1558
Endonetics, 1706
Endorsify, 1507
Endosense SA, 1325
Endoshape, 930
EndoSpan, 2324
EndoSphere, 1512, 1553
EndoStim, 1488
Endotex, 1378
Endotronix, 136, 270, 1047, 1628, 1762, 2180
EndPlay, 1906
Endres Processing, 1040
Endurance Energy, 1956
Endurance International, 1915
Endurance International Group, 194
Endurance Lift Holdings, 559
Endurance Specialty Holdings Ltd., 404
Endurance Specialty Insurance, 839
Endurance Wind Power, 2053
Enduro Resource Partners, 1573
Enduro Resource Partners II, 1573
EndWave, 1672
Endwave, 1257
Enecsys, 2615
Enefco, 1727
Enefco International, 164
Eneida, 3048
Ener-core, 1603
EnerAge, 1244
Enerbee, 2296
Enercast, 2824
Enercomp, 2612
EnerCorp, 1009
EnerG2, 730, 1391, 2008
Energate, 2093
Energetic Insurance, 497
Energetic Solutions, 594
Energetics, 2715
Energex, 657
Energia Zachod, 3209
Energreen, 2700
Energy Cache, 491
Energy Capital Partners, 3255
Energy Cool, 3203
Energy Credit Partners, 740
Energy Developments, 3025
Energy Distribution Partners, 529
Energy Drilling, 2700
Energy Financial and Physical, 553
Energy Fishing & Rental Services, 910
Energy Future Holdings, 2379
Energy Life One SRL, 2419

Energy Manufacturing, 1456
Energy Micro, 3013
Energy Network, 584
Energy Services Group, 29
Energy Solutions International, 1014
Energy Solutons, 1491
Energy Source, 853
Energy Source Partners, 678
Energy Storage Systmes, 1463
Energy Trade, 1517
EnergyCo. Holdings, 1270
EnergyHub, 44, 1438
Energyn Corporation, 2382
EnergySage, 497, 1100
EnergySolutions, 675, 1129
Energytics, 1810
Enerkem, 322, 1558, 1977, 2093
Enerkem Technologies, 184
Enermont, 3127
EnerNOC, 322
Enernoc, 609
Enerpulse, 1603
Enerqos, 2615
Enersciences, 61
Enersize, 2612
Enertech, 2208
EnerTech Capital, 3258
EnerTech Environmental, 1393
Enertia Software, 553
Enertiv, 727
EnerVault, 1241, 1365
Enervee, 1363
Enesco LLC, 225
eNeura, 383
eNeura Therapeutics, 19
Enevate, 184, 1239, 1474, 3194
EnEvolv, 570
Enexion, 2824
Enfield Logistics, 402
Enfora, 57, 1080
Enforcer eCoaching, 1047
Enfore, 107
Enforta, 260
Enfusen, 1047
Enfusion, 793
Engage, 1147
Engage Therapeutics, 2180
Engage2Excel, 873
Engage2Excell, 1166
Engage3, 275
Engagio, 741, 743
Engauge, 897
Engeltjes & Bengeltjes, 3042
Engendren Corporation, 1209
enGene, 2180
EnGene IC, 2975
Engility, 1082
Engine, 1091
Engine Bio, 219
Engine Efficiency, 322
Engine ML, 429
Engine Yard, 238, 581, 634, 1474, 1915
Engineered Propulsion Systems, 1872
Engineering Ingegneria Informatica, 1376
Enginge Biosciences, 2690
Enginsight, 2527
English Bay Batter, 2183
English Boiler Tube, 1053
English Central, 889, 1690
English Color, 1979
English Ninjas, 2284
EnglishHelper, 1374
EnglishUp, 2950
Englobe, 2208, 2209
Engrade, 707, 1028, 1054, 1316, 1551
Enhanced Capital Partners, 1946
Enhanced Capital/Tree Line, 1743

1311

Portfolio Companies Index

Enhanced Drilling, 3216
Enhanced Energy Group, 1693
Enhatch, 751
enherent, 1558
Enigma, 518, 563, 707, 754, 1358, 2469
Enigma Information Systems, 3231
Enigma Software, 2725
Enigmatec, 2386
Eniram, 2630, 2731
Enium, 2857
Eniware, 3277
Enjay Converters, 2107
Enjovia, 2284
Enjoy, 802, 935, 1075
Enjoy Beer, 787
Enjoy Technology, 1361
Enkata, 548
Enkata Technologies, 137, 1600, 1672
Enki Technology, 144, 1579
Enlibrium, 544
Enlighten, 99, 1864
Enlightened, 1579
Enliken, 243
EnLink Geoenergy Services, 591
Enlink Midstream, 1278, 1835
Enlitic, 1656
Enlivant, 1835
Enlyton, 445
Enmass, 1558
Ennis-Flint, 328
eNNOV, 1991
Enocean, 2106, 3233
EnosiX, 1047
Enosix, 86
ENOTECA, 3201
Enotria, 2524
Enovix, 596, 1004, 1509, 1579, 1853
eNow, 3262
Enphase Energy, 144, 184, 238, 925, 946, 1579
Enpiorion, 925
Enplug, 972
Enpocket, 296
Enprecis, 333
Enprego Ligado, 2872
EnRoute, 85
EnrTech Capital, 2032
Ensamblage, 3042
Ensatus, 28
Ensemble Communications, 555
Ensemble Therapeutics, 153
Ensenda, 87
Ensenta, 2457
Enservio, 221, 1181
Ensighten, 129, 1000, 1942
Ensilo, 1121, 3221
Ensim, 757, 1378
Ensiz Technology, 2857
Enso Relief, 107
EnSolve Biosystems, 3277
Ensono, 456, 1153
Enspire DBS Therapy, 886
Enstar Group, 1743
Enstigo, 1784
EnStorage, 386
Enstream, 2265
Ensure Medical, 1094, 1896
Ensus, 413
Ensus Ethanol, 1573
Enswers, 3127
Ensyn, 2049, 2161
Ensyn Technologies, 2114
Entac Medical, 995
ENTACT, 1479, 1803
Entact, 202
Entangled Ventures, 1551
Entasis Therapeutics, 495, 782
Entegra, 1009

EntegraBlu, 1244
EnteGreat, 678
Entegreat, 1533
Entellios, 2824
Entellus Medical, 867, 1082, 1725
Entelo, 235, 544, 1663
Entelos, 315
Enter Crews, 2474
Entera, 555
Enteraction TV, 2662
Entercept Security Technologies, 613, 1038
Entergy Industrial, 3218
Enteric Medical Technologies, 1251
Enterix, 2877
EnterMedicare, 318
Enterome, 3020, 3113
EnteroMedics, 237, 458, 1378
Enterprise DB, 1838
Enterprise Electronics Corporation, 1925
Enterprise Florida, 3262
Enterprise Link, 36
Enterprise Macay, 2048
Enterprise Therapeutics, 689, 1350, 1928
EnterpriseDB, 455, 1234, 1899, 2196
Enterprises DB, 1317
Enterproid, 1358
Enterra Feed, 2049
Entertainment Cruises, 969, 1479
EnterVault, 1791
Entevo, 1348
Entevo Corp., 315
Enthrill Distribution, 2048
Enthuse, 243
Entigral Systems, 1442, 1845
Entire Technology, 2603
Ento Bio, 1047
Entomo, 85, 1637
Entone, 536, 1626
Entone Technologies, 1407
Entorian Technologies, 202
Entouch, 2439
EnTouch Controls, 1689
Entrack, 980
Entrada, 12, 493, 695, 1268
Entrada Health, 718
Entrade, 986
Entrans International, 109
EntreMed, 2419
Entrepreneur First, 872
Entrigue Surgical, 136, 1478
ENTrique Surgical, 925
Entrisphere, 1906, 3137
Entropic, 757, 1926
Entropic Communications, 132, 729, 852, 898, 1239
Entropix, 770
EntropySoft, 2385
Entryless, 3125
Entrypoint VR, 1611
Entuity, 3092
ENTvantage Diagnostics, 445
Enuma, 1050, 1054
Enuvis, 197
Enval, 2400
Envara, 2782
Enven Energy Corporation, 508
Envenio, 2076, 2128
Envera, 904
Enverus, 29
Envestnet, 137, 770, 1888
Envestra Limited, 2591
Envia Systems, 238
Enviance, 235
Enview, 563
Envirelation, 678
Enviro Vac, 1166
Envirocon, 2085

Envirogen, 1044
Environcom, 2372
Environment Furniture, 958
Environmental Express, 1457
Environmental Lighting Concepts, 1745
Environmental Lights, 1435
Environmental Operating Solutions, 1199
Environmental Pest Service, 403
Environmental Pest Services, 529
Environmental Planning Group, 1276
Environmental Recovery Corporation, 1578
Environmental Services Provider, 1605
Environmental Support Solutions, 856
Environments@Work LLC, 649
EnvironWorks, 1067
EnviroScent, 80
EnviroSolutions, 1837
Envirosystems, 2183
Envis Corp, 1672
Envisagenics, 1154, 1158
Envisia, 386, 1412, 2978
Envisia Therapeutics, 1271
Envisics, 817
Envision, 881
Envision Healthcare, 1082
ENVision Mobile, 30
Envision Pharma Group, 894
EnvisionNet Computer Services, 438
EnvisionRX, 1835
Envista, 308, 1459
Enviva Holdings, 1573
Envivio, 555, 986, 1180, 2443, 2875
Envivo, 905
Envizi, 29
Envkey, 795
Envocore, 403, 610
Envoi, 2138
Envox, 3013
Envox Group AB (publ.), 2716
Envoy, 12, 124, 427, 488, 816, 1149, 1202
Envoy Networks, 521
Envy Modular Systems, 742
Enwoven, 101
ENXSuite, 1324
Enyvision, 1417
Enzen Global Solutions, 584
Enzerna Biosciences, 3259
Enzium, 266
Enzymedica, 1324
Enzymotec, 2973, 3241
Enzytech, 260
Eoconix, 1922
Eocycle, 2093
Eodom, 3113
Eoidio, 2562
Eolite, 2851
EOLO, 2252
Eolring Dynamic Cell Network, 2354
eOne Globe, 2771
Eonian Technology, 3262
eonMedia, 685
Eontec Limited, 2079
EoPlex Technologies, 627
EoPlex Technologies Inc., 1089
eOriginal, 1136
EOS, 319
Eos, 237
EOS Climate, 730
EOS Fitness Holdings LLC, 354
EOS SpA, 2350, 3052
Eosense, 2155
Eosex, 3008
EOSi, 2290
Eosi, 1615
EoStar, 1638
EP Canada Film Services, 2218
EP Energy, 34, 1573

1312

Portfolio Companies Index

Ep Minerals, 839
EP Sciences, 347
ePact, 2291
ePACT Network, 2223
ePanstwo Foundation, 1374
ePartners, 402, 1288
ePawn, 2693
EPD-visionk, 2514
Epedal, 3048
ePet World, 301
ePetWorld GmbH, 2979, 3044
EPharmix, 267
Ephesoft, 1204
EPI, 3211
Epi-V, 2944
Epic, 1527, 1968
Epic at Cub Run, 190
Epic Burger, 567
Epic Games, 1075, 1121
EPIC Insurance Brokers & Conultants, 3274
Epic Sciences, 157, 621, 1436, 3085
Epic Therapeutics, 260
Epic Ventures, 3276
Epic!, 1983
EpiCare, 400
EpiCept, 925
Epicor, 1082
Epicor Software, 1850
Epics, 977
Epiderma, 2029
EpiEP, 841, 1097
Epigan, 2949
Epigenesis, 2728
EpiGenesis Pharmaceuticals, 312
Epigenomics, 2299, 2301, 2305
Epigram, 59, 1247
Epiodyne, 1202, 1238
Epion, 989
Epiphany Dermatology, 476
Epiphany Solar Water Systems, 998
Epiq, 914, 2207
Epirus, 12
Epirus Biopharmaceuticals, 1251
Episencial, 3277
Episensor, 2355
EPiServer, 3013
Episerver, 1000
Episode 1, 2674
Episodic, 852
EpiStar, 905
EpistoGraph, 2549
Epithany, 2008
Epitome Biosystems, 747
Epitomics, 117, 1769
EpiTop, 1340
Epivalley, 2857
EpiVax, 1693
EpiWorks, 1108
Epix, 260
EPIX Pharmaceuticals, 312
Epizyme, 112, 237, 762, 1268
EPL, 2889
EPO.com, 2572
Epocal, 2196
Epoch, 220
Epoch Biosciences, 237
Epoch Systems, 1087
Epocrates, 237, 609, 986, 1235
EPOS, 3231
Epox Computer, 3218
Epoxy, 60, 871, 1827, 1888
Epredix Campus Tele Video, 402
ePrint Factory GmbH, 2673
Eprise Corporation, 212
eprofessional GmbH, 2528
EPropertyData, 1642
EProspects, 3013

Epsagon, 1121
Epsilon, 742
Epsilon Power Holdings, 156
Epsitech Group, 2855
Eptam Plastics, 926
Eptica, 3020
Epuramat, 2540
EPV Solar, 2327
EqcoLogic, 2366
Eqise, 2478
EQOS, 2348
EQT, 3264
Equal Media, 2446
Equal Opportunity Schools, 1316
Equality Specialities Inc., 1621
EqualLogic, 712, 757, 1024, 1672
Equallogic, 455
Equalum, 809
Equanet, 2796
Equastream, 3262
Equator, 115, 964
Equator Technologies, 1704, 2079
Eques, 1509
Equian, 859
Equibrand Holding Corporation, 1562
Equicare Health, 2291
Equidate, 1749
Equifax, 1903
eQuilibrium, 497
Equilis, 3134
Equinix, 563
Equinox, 297, 1088
Equinox Fitness, 1109
Equiom, 2944
Equipboard, 1685
EquipmentShare, 858, 1613
Equipmentshare, 1395
EquipmentShare.co.nz, 1000
EquiPower Resources Corp., 675
Equipwell, 250
Equita GmbH & Co. Holdings, 77
Equitalk, 3107
Equitant, 39
Equitas, 386, 2313
Equitrac, 541
Equity Broadcasting, 1769
Equity Trust, 2556
EquityLock Solutions, 1863
EquitySim, 79
Equityzen, 1097
Equivalent Data, 364
Equivest, 2616
Equus Energy, 694
Equus Media Development Company, 694
ER, 2851
ER Energy Group, 672
ER Experts, 838
Era, 315
ERA Biotech, 3020
Era-plantech, 2483
Eracom, 1558
EraGen, 1488
EraPlay, 2271
Eratech, 2043
Eratome, 3020
ERC midwest, 1578
ERC Wiping Products Inc., 465
Ercio, 1352
Ercom, 2385
eRecyclingCorps, 1324
eResearch Technology, 1136, 2379
Erewards, 1460
ERG, 1128
ERG Services, 584
Ergalis-Selpro-Plus RH, 2338
Ergis, 2429
Ergo Genesis, 984

Ergobaby, 523
ErgoGenesis, 1422
ergoTrade AG, 2528
ERI Solutions, 1724
Erickson, 1134
Eridan, 395
Eris Exchange, 710
Erlang Technology, 2457
ERM, 2207
ERMS Corporation, 2058
Erno Laszlo, 778
Ernst & Young, 3274
eRoom Technology, 1334
ERPLY, 720
Erply, 1534
ERT Systems, 742
Eruditor Group, 1004
ErVaxx Limited, 1628
Erydel, 2874
Erytech, 2851
ES Robbins, 1970
(es) Corporation, 2474
ES-Plastic GmbH, 2494
Esanex, 1008, 1124
esanex, 1124
Esately, 85
Esaturnus, 3042
ESBATech, 495
Escalade Energy, 156
Escalate, 839
Escape Rescue Systems, 3212
Escapia.com, 85
Escher Reality, 1473
Escient Pharmaceuticals, 12
ESCO Corporation, 673
Escorts Construction Equipment, 584
eSecLending, 1417
eSellerProf, 3014
Esentire, 655, 2153
eSentire, 2132
EServices, 1726
eServices, 1422, 1727
eSfot, 1837
ESG, 2311, 3194
eShakti.com, 2849
eShares, 707, 1050, 2010
eShip-4U, 3249
Esi Group SA, 2601
ESI Lighting, 1492
ESI Software, 1706
eSight, 2149, 2187
eSilicon, 428, 483
eSilicon Corporation, 2639, 2890
Esim Chemicals, 1753
Esionic, 1520
eSionic, 36, 688
Eska, 123, 1255
Esmalglass, 1017
Esmark, 1578
Esmertec, 2922
ESO, 29
ESO Solutions, 202, 445
Eso-Technologies, 583
Esoko, 55
eSolar, 972, 1361
eSolutions, 779, 1979
Esoterix Inc., 245
Esox s.r.o., 3122
ESP Pharma, 94
ESP Technologies, 2196
eSpark, 1242, 1316, 1480
eSpark Learning, 1527
Espaçolaser, 1088
Esper, 1421, 1877
Esperance, 1618
Esperance Pharmaceuticals, 61, 362, 1543
Esperanto Technologies, 519

1313

Portfolio Companies Index

Esperion Therapeutics, 74, 94, 181, 621
Espial Group, 2196
Esports, 1191
Esports Entertainment Group, 735
Esports One, 679
Esports Tickets, 2245
EsportsOne, 1507
Espresa, 563, 1563
Espressif, 1004
Espressive, 816
Espresso Capital, 3258
Espresso Logic, 1013
EspriGas, 550
Esprit Holidays Ltd, 2486
Esprit Pharma, 94
Esquire, 892
Esquire Bank, 707
ESS Inc., 2093, 2213
Ess Kay Finance, 1346
ESSA, 495
Essanelle Hair Group AG, 2806
Essence Group, 1615
EssenceHealthcare, 1075
Essent Group, 1315, 1443
Essentia, 421
Essential Cabinetry Group, 873
Essential Products, 1534
Essentialis, 1786, 1941
Essentialis Therapeutics, 769
Essention, 1641
Essess, 1483
Essex, 834
Essex WoodlandsFund, 955
Essner Manufacturing, 540
Est, 413
Establishment Labs, 890, 1048
EStarCom, 210
Estate Assist, 295
Estately, 1700
Estech, 1792
Estify, 120, 724, 1070, 1581
Estimize, 533, 1146
Estimote, 272, 1028
Estore, 2826
Estorian, 85, 315
Estrakon, 742
Estrohaze, 392
estudy Site, 439
eStyle, 2021
eSUB Construction Software, 1555
ESupply Systems, 781
Esurance, 1405
Esurg Corporation, 2079
ESV Digital, 3056
ET Solar, 3194
ETA Compute Inc., 1951
Etacts, 2329
EtaGen, 1069
Etam, 2607
Etanco, 2311
eTang, 1558
ETC, 35, 2795
Etcetera Edutainment, 998
ETE Medical, 118
eTeamz, 1784
Eternygen, 689, 2841
ETF Securities, 793, 1235, 1759
ETG, 2949
Ethelo, 2233
Ether Optronics, 2579, 3062
Ether Optronics Inc, 2703
Ethereum, 124
Etherscan, 307
Etherstack, 979
Ethertronics, 1255, 1658
Ethex, 1286
Ethic, 395, 1054, 1893

Ethical Coffee Company, 2293
Ethical Pharmaceuticals Ltd, 3186
Ethical Property, 2509
Ethiochicken, 55
EthnicGrocer.Com, 1057
Ethoca, 1717
eThor, 2048
Ethos, 607, 889, 1654
Ethos Lending, 1069
ETI, 36, 123, 142
eTime Capital, 2652
Etive Technologies, 2967
ETix, 1710
Etohum, 2437
Etonenet, 1241
Etoos, 2857
EToro, 2406
Etoro, 1715
Etouch, 596
ETouches, 871
Etouches, 431
etouches, 161, 959
eToys.com, 260
Etrans, 3100
etrials, 1314
Etronic, 3218
Etronica, 1784
ETSA Utilities, 2591
ETSolar, 2584
Etsy, 28, 336, 836, 1882, 2860, 2860
ETT, 374
ETX, 654
EU Networks, 508
Eucalyptus, 641
Euclid, 2010
Euclises, 267
Euclises Pharmaceuticals Inc., 569
Eumakh, 3181
euNetworks, 515
Euphonix, 1378
EUR Systems Inc., 1621
Eureka II LP, 2094
Eureka Resources, 893
Eureka Therapeutics, 47
Eurekite, 549
Euretco NV, 2806
Euro Carter, 2384
Euro Part, 2851
Euro Services Laboratory, 2855
Euro-atomizado., 2489
EURO-DIESEL, 2311
EuroChlor, 3178
EuroDesign Cabinets, 1141
Euroelektro International Oy, 2873
EuroFem, 1774
Euroflow, 2574
Eurofresh Inc., 354
Euroimmun, 2713
Euromate, 2378
Euromedic, 834
Euromedic International, 2977
Euromerchant Balkan Fund (EBF), 2784
Euronet, 2725
Europe Apotheek, 2503
Europe Snacks, 2851
Europe Technologies, 2466
European Colour plc, 3178
European Directory Assistance, 2426
European Games Group, 3020
European Homes, 2448, 2851, 3239
European Investor Services, 3146
European Locomotive Leasing, 1082
European Secondary Development Fund IV LP, 2094
European Telecommunication Holding E.T.H. AG, 2528

European Telecommunications & Technology, 2577, 2662
European Wax Center, 328
Europroteome AG, 2682
Euroscreen, 3134
Euroseas, 514
Eurospect Manufacturing Inc., 2103
Euroventures III, 2724
EUSA Pharma, 697, 1452
Eutech, 2772
Eutech Medical, 2562
Eutech Medical AB, 2718
Eutechnyx, 3051
Eutelsat, 2605, 2719
EUTEX European Telco Exchange, 2673
Euthymics Bioscience, 1921
EV Connect, 624, 1061, 3277
EV Energy Partners, 672
Eva, 307
Eva Airways, 2436
Evalve, 1725
Evalve Inc., 23, 572
Evander Group, 2944
evandtec, 1324
Evaneos, 3239
Evans, 368
Evans & Dixon, 3271
Evans & Sutherland, 2005
Evans and Sutherland, 1257
Evanston Capital Management, 1776
Evanta, 1105
Evariant, 918, 1121, 1607
Evatic, 3216
EVault, 550
Evault, 2058
EVCI Career Colleges, 528
Evco Research, 1689
EvConnect, 306
EVE, 2662
Eve, 2674, 2944
Eve Medical, 981
EVE NY, 2850
Eve Tab, 2113
Eve.com, 1121
Eved, 452, 1242, 1480
Evelo Bioscience, 889
Evelo Biosciences, 747
Even, 384, 1069, 1509
EVEN Financial, 710
Even Financial, 351, 1110
Evenflo Company, 1978
Evenflo Company Inc., 914
Event Hi, 392
Event Photography Group, 1526
Event Rental Group, 2139
Event Zero, 1003
Eventbase, 1158
Eventbrite, 581, 634, 1654, 1796
Eventful, 238, 3169
Eventovate, 2355
EventReviews.com, 1905
Events Core, 2473
Events.com, 1830, 1905
Eventup, 566, 1118
Eventyard, 2696
eVenues, 1254
EVEO, 1239
Ever, 968, 2354, 2466
Ever Compliant, 148, 3221
Ever EdTech, 3259
Everalbum, 720
Everbank Financial Coporation, 1148
EverBank Financial Corporation, 1301
Everbee, 2354, 2897
Everbridge, 23, 646, 1640, 2671
Evercare, 2936
Everclaw, 1202

Portfolio Companies Index

Evercontact, 3108
Everdream, 1480, 1558
Everest Software, 315, 1886
Everex Systems, 1336
EverFi, 1551, 1830
Everfi, 262, 1552
Evergage, 59, 1459
Evergig, 1416
Evergreen, 869, 1134
Evergreen Group, 2936
Evergreen Holdings, 611
Evergreen Lodge, 1396
Evergreen Media Corporation, 575
Evergreen Services Group, 92
Evergreen Solar, 214, 1355, 1579, 1702
Evergreen Tank Solutions, 1368
Evergreen Transport, 1766
Everite Machine Products, 698
Everlance, 107
Everlane, 1069, 1110, 1183, 1694
Everlasting Wardrobe, 1507
Everlaw, 124, 1050, 1401
Everly, 459
Everly Well, 1701
Evernote, 107, 620, 836, 1212, 1254, 1257, 1607, 1654, 1694
Everplans, 1263, 1632
Everquote, 1625, 1640
Eversholt Leasing, 2556
Eversight, 665
Eversound, 3
Everspin, 688
Everspin Technologies, 1151, 1305, 1672
Everspring, 39, 416
Everstream, 1153
Everstring, 1121, 3251
EverTeam, 1416
EverTrue, 1480
Evertrue, 221, 313, 1531
EverWatch, 680
Everwise, 396, 777, 1654, 1968
Everwrite, 2983
Every Move, 85
Every Screen Media, 539
Everyaction, 1000
EverybodyFights, 329
Everyclick, 2967
EveryDay Health, 3137
Everyday Health, 770, 925, 1558, 1626
Everyday Learning, 153
Everyday Solutions, 747
Everykey, 981
EveryMove, 1615
Everymove, 1789
Everyone Counts, 69
Everypath, 2079
EveryScape, 580, 1100, 1291
EveryScreen Media, 533
Everytable, 55, 1110
Everything, 2446
Everything Benefits, 173
Everything But The House, 867
Everything but the House, 641
Everything.me, 2831, 3121
eVestment, 1608
Evi, 3018
evian, 473
Evichat, 2245
EviCore Healthcare, 815
Evidation, 181, 809, 1552, 1628, 1762
Evident, 49, 282
Evident Software, 1321
Evident.io, 1860, 1916
Evidon, 1956
Evie, 741
Eviivo, 1017
Evikon, 2390

Evino, 3056
eVisit, 856, 1070
Evite, 197
EVO, 655
Evo Electric, 2858
EVO Payments International, 1156
Evocalize, 1158
Evocatal, 2824
Evocutis, 2892
Evodos, 2686
Evogene, 2417
Evok Innovations, 3258
Evoke, 1094
Evoke Pharma, 621
Evoke Software Corp., 212
Evol Foods, 243, 1446
Evolable Asia, 721
Evolita, 3003
Evolution Equity, 483
Evolution Markets, 434
Evolution Midstream, 671
eVolution Networks, 809
Evolv, 823, 1121, 1906
Evolv Sports & Designs, 354
Evolv Technologies, 1005
Evolv Technology, 816, 1151
Evolva, 2419, 2515, 2710, 3149, 3211
Evolve, 1745
Evolve Energy, 1894
Evolve IP, 857
Evolved Intelligence, 2691
Evolving Systems, 2754
Evotec, 2816, 3196
Evotec NeuroSciences GmbH, 3137
Evox Therapeutics, 889
Evoz, 590, 2872
EVP EyeCare, 546
Evree, 2113
evree, 2212
Evrest Broadband Networks, 314
Evriholder Products, 443
EVRS, 2574
Evrythng, 483
EVS Broadcast Equipment, 3069
eVu, 1668
Evvnt, 2960
EW Healthcare Partners, 3264
EwayTech, 2128
EWC, 550
eWise, 1863
EWT, 2106
Ex Libris, 839, 3231, 3245
Ex Libris Global Holdings, 1970
Ex Libris Ltd., 3158
EXA, 651
Exa Corporation, 310
Exabeam, 49, 180, 483, 968, 1121, 1346
Exablox, 596, 1896
Exacom, 1638
Exacq Technologies, 1057
Exact Imaging, 2149, 2180
Exact Media, 2239
Exact Target, 1626
Exactbid, 1717
Exactech, 1835
Exacter, 1286, 1553
Exactis.com, 315
Exactium, 2720
ExactTarget, 231, 560
EXACTUALS, 1863
Exadigm, 636
Exagen Diagnostics, 549, 688, 1221
Exago, 3031
Exagrid, 935
ExaGrid Systems, 1672, 1673, 1796
Exal, 901
Exal Group, 1744

Exalt, 1010, 1853
Examination Management Services, 1271
Examity, 857
ExamSoft, 1717
ExamWorks, 1109
Exanet, 536
ExaProtect, 3020
Exaro Energy III, 1602
Exasol, 2979
Excaliard Pharmaceuticals, 1574
Excalibur Resources, 672
Excara, 1558
Exceed Midlands Advantage Fund, 2944
Excel Academy Charter Schools, 1316
Excel Engineering, 1578
Excel Fitness, 96
Excel Manufacturing, 1705
Excel Polymers, 42
Excel Technology, 2844
Excelan, 238
Excelcom, 2434
Excelerate Health Ventures, 737
Excelerate Labs, 1364
Excelero, 235, 1509
Excelitas Technologies, 1925
Excellere Capital Partners LP, 2094
excelleRx, 1136
Excelligence, 378, 1334
Excelligence Learning Corp., 334
excellRx, 1409
Excelsior Medical, 1456, 1590
ExCentos, 2824
Exception Wild Bunch, 2897
Excera, 2978
Excera Materials Group, 1336
Exchange Resources, 214
Exchange Solutions, 178, 1339, 1899, 2196
Exchangery, 1615
Excico, 2366, 2949
Excico Group, 3042
Excision Biotherapeutics, 175
Exclaim, 1769, 2196
Exclara, 1579, 1922
Exclusive Networks, 3020
Exco inTouch, 3104
EXCO Resources, 159
Exco Resources, 1082
Excosoft, 2890
ExecOnline, 1291, 1387
ExecThread, 1028
Executive Greetings Inc., 245
Executive Health Resources, 21, 1927, 1979
Executive Strategies Group LLC, 3267
Exegy, 1317
Exelate, 1317, 3221
eXelate, 1850, 2566
Exelis, 191
Exelixis, 1394, 1775
Exelixis Pharmaceuticals, 212
Exelixis Pharmaceuticals Inc., 2785
Exemplify, 1924
Exent, 483, 1827
Exentive F.B. Technology, 2855
Exergen, 1173
Exergyn, 1061
Exeter Finance Corporation, 1280
Exfm, 1715
Exhale, 334
Exie, 2312
Exie AS, 2754
Exigen, 757
Eximia, 3052
Eximias, 1508
Eximo Medical, 2324
Exinda, 867, 1380
Exini Diagnostics, 2449
Exist, 1965

1315

Portfolio Companies Index

eXist db, 1798
Exit Games, 2994, 3123
Exit Games GmbH, 2673
Exithera Pharmaceuticals, 1627
EXL Service, 793
Exl Services, 1360
ExLibris, 779
Exlinea, 2551
eXML, 2708
Exmplar, 1913
EXO, 1736
Exo Imaging, 1703
Exocor, 1624
Exodus, 805, 922
Exodus Communications, 238, 1038
ExoGenesis, 989, 1920
Exonhit, 2354
ExonHit Therapeutics, 1394
Exoplatform, 3239
Exoprise Systems, 712
EXOS, 22, 374
Exosect, 2710
Exosome Diagnostics, 157, 1325, 1419, 2748
Exosun, 3020
Exotec, 2296
Exotrail, 2296
Exp, 815
Expa, 1110
Expan, 3054
Expand Network, 3159
Expander, 2309
Expanding Orthopedics, 644, 1187, 1847
Expanse, 1758
Expansion Therapeutics, 12, 1075, 1350, 1519
Expect Labs, 1513, 1798
Expedi, 317
Expel, 235, 1118
Expensable, 493
ExpenseBot, 1047
Expensify, 231, 1459, 1534, 2080
Expera Specialty Solutions, 1085
Experient, 1456
Experiment, 1874
Experiment 7, 1473
Expert Global Solutions, 1376
Expert Janitorial Services, 1422
Expert NJS, 1423
Expert Plan, 52, 161, 1275
Experteer, 2829, 2838
Experteer.dE, 641
ExpertFile, 2184
Experticity, 221, 1677
Experts Exchange, 1810
Expeto, 2111, 2195
Expii, 858
Expion, 3259
Explara, 3133
Explay-Japan, 2974
Explocity, 2846
Explora Petroleum, 1956
Explore Schools, 1316
EXPLORER, 1155
ExplORer Surgical, 1630
Explorer Surgical, 138
Explorys, 748
Explorys Inc., 202
Explorys Medical, 1619
Expo, 1478
Expocolour, 2985
Exponential Entertainment, 1061, 1825
Exponor Digital, 3048
Exporo, 641
Export Development Canada, 3258
Exposoft Solutions, 2196
ExpoTV, 1175
ExpreS2ion Biotechnologies, 3203
Express, 839

Express Energy Services, 869, 1134
Express Engineering, 2944
Express Food Group, 1139
Express KCS, 1623
Express Oil Change & Service Center, 415
Express Oil Change and Service Center, 168
Express Packaging, 917
Express Window Films, 812
ExpressCells, 1577
ExpressCoin, 1681
Expressions Furniture, 713
expresso, 1354
Expresso Education Limited, 2458
Expressor Software, 521
Expressor Software Corp, 1672
Expro, 2379
ExproSoft, 3216
Expway, 2876, 2899
Expé, 3239
ExSar Corporation, 1188
Exsequor, 2881
Extant Components, 1956
Extend, 1528
Extend Media, 1916
ExtendCredit, 1784
Extended Care Information Network, 654
Extended Stay America, 442
Extended Systems, 986
ExtendMedia, 1474
Extenet, 441
ExteNet Systems, 654, 1407
Extenet Systems, 1315
Extennet, 1658
Extensibility, 1008
Extensity, 1121, 1474
Exteria, 846
Enterprise, 202, 1855
Exterro, 1105
Extole, 1346, 1534, 1626, 1663, 1850
Extra Space Storage, 865
ExtraHop, 1158, 1212
ExtraHop Networks, 1785
Extranomical Tours, 1609
ExtraOrtho, 995
Extraprise, 521
Extreme Communications, 734
Extreme DA, 115
Extreme Innovations, 2113
Extreme Networks, 1474, 1853
Extreme Packet Devices, 1080
Extreme Reach, 560, 1142, 1717
Extreme Venture Partners, 3258
ExtremeReach, 871
Extricity, 1910
Extricity Software, 757
Extrumed, 1014
Extrusion Dies Industries, 257
Exult, 39, 2652
Exuvis, 3042
Exvivo, 721
Exxcelia, 909
Exxelia Magnetics, 2851
Exym, 92
EY, 3272, 3275, 3279
Eyang Holdings, 2936
eYantra, 3211
Eye Care Centers Of America, 839
Eye Health America, 1136
Eye Q, 545
Eye Smart Technology, 1004
Eye-Fi, 1838
Eye-q, 2818
Eyebobs, 1345
eyeBrain Medical, 297
Eyebright Medical, 710
eyecandylab, 226
Eyecare Partners, 787

EyeCare Services Partners, 914
EyeEm, 2444
Eyefactive, 2824
Eyeka, 3208
eYeka, 2899
Eyelation, 582
EyelCo, 1097
EyeM, 3030
Eyemart Expreess, 787
Eyeonics, 23
Eyeota, 3056
EyePoint Pharmaceuticals Inc., 697
EyeQ, 3001
EyeQuant, 2995
Eyequant, 2479
EYES, 3100
EyeSense, 2939
EyeSight Mobile Technologies, 1241
Eyesight&Vision, 2824
EyeSouth, 1166
Eyesquad, 2342
EyeTechCare, 3020
Eyevensys, 2229
Eyeview, 1121, 2987
Eyewitness News, 1927
Eyewitness Surveillance, 378, 1136
EyeWonder, 263
Eykona Technolgies, 3028
EYP Architecture & Design, 1141
Eyrus, 1259
EZ Apps, 1784
EZ Chip Technologies, 1038
EZ Lube, 869
EZ-DSP Ltd, 2704
Ez-Ways.Com, 847
EZ-WHEEL, 2296
ezboard, 1733
EzCater, 1000
ezCater, 1100, 1160
EZCertify.com, 1208
EZchip, 3137
Eze Software Group, 1835
EZE Trucking, 1477
Ezeep, 2824
Ezetap, 1696
Eziba, 1558
Ezibuy, 2664
Ezoic, 2478
Ezono, 2527
eZono AG, 2981
Ezra, 1101
EzRez Software, 2457
EZShield, 2103
eZuce, 1375

F

F&B Asias, 1627
F+W Media, 21
F-Prime Capital, 3273
F-Star, 1731, 3196
F-Star Alpha Limited, 191
f-star GmbH, 2350
f-star GmbH, 3015
F.B. Leopold Company, 693
F.T. Silfies, 190
F/ELD, 2254
F2G, 74, 3149
F5, 1563
Faab-Fabicauto, 2340
FAAH Pharma, 3196
Fab, 620, 1184, 1437, 1594, 1700, 1821, 2446, 2475, 3121
Fab Furnish, 3170
FAB Pharma, 2876
Fab.com, 2017, 2604, 3229
Fabco Automotive, 2009
FabEnCo/BlueWater, 812

1316

Portfolio Companies Index

FabFitFun, 1821, 1888
FabHotels, 842, 1509
Fabl, 286
Fable, 1390
Fable Studio, 1663
Fabric, 996, 1183, 1530
Fabric Genomics, 237
Fabrinet, 892
FabSource, 3259
Face U, 1121
Face.com, 3081
Facebook, 124, 336, 650, 659, 775, 836, 842, 986, 1212, 1235, 1785, 2663, 2723, 2831, 2928
Facebook Investment Fund LLC, 2604
Facecake, 2010
Faces Human Capital Management, 557
Facet, 2953
Facet Pricing, 865
FaceTime Communications, 1038
Faceware, 3092
FacilitySource, 1956
FACIT, 3258
Fact Based Communication Ltd, 2754
FactGem, 1286
Faction, 1211
Facton, 2813
Factor Trust, 1240
FactorTrust, 22
Factory Connection, 90
Factory Four, 19
Factory Logic, 56
FactSquared, 934
Factual, 101, 124, 972, 1237, 1604, 1888
Factual Beta, 720
Factury, 307
Faena Group, 34
FAF Inc., 1162
Fair, 45, 300, 302, 802, 1028, 1363
Fair Information Services BV, 2992
Fairchild Industrial Products Company, 556
FairClaims, 728
Fairclaims, 563
Faire, 761, 1069, 1121, 1654, 2137
Fairfield Collectibles, 1422
Fairfield Energy, 1573, 1956
Fairhaven Pharmaceuticals, 2130
Fairline Boats Holdings Ltd, 2306
FairLoan, 32
Fairly, 1323
Fairmarkit, 1172
Fairmont Hotels, 300
Fairmount Santrol, 110
FairPay Solutions, 734
Fairr.De, 2841
FairShake, 318
Fairway, 1231
Fairway America, 1061
Fairway Architectural Railing Solutions, 164
Fairway Biomed, 995
Fairway Energy, 893
Fairway Medical Technologies, 950
Fairway Outdoor, 884
Fairways Group (UK), 2306
Fairweather, 2254
Fairygodboss, 883
Faith Street, 1115
FaithStreet, 1518
Falanx AS, 2369
Falby Design, 3203
Falcon, 1017
Falcon Computing, 219, 1670
Falcon First Communications LP, 1986
Falcon Gas Storage, 152
Falcon Genomics, 1448
Falcon Social, 3203
Falcon-Vision, 2487

Falconstor, 2436
Falkonry, 232, 2019
Fallbrook Technologies, 1324
Fallon Visual Products, 1127
Falls Fabricating, 1719
Falmac, 892
Falrion Technologies, 455
Fama, 120, 306
Fame and Partners, 743, 1888
FameBit, 1813, 2147
Famigo, 1685
Familia, 1584
Familia Dental, 894
Families for Excellent Schools, 1316
Familonet, 3207, 3236
Family Arc, 344
Family Care, 406
Family Home Health Services, 654, 1902
Family Plan, 1507
Family Tech, 479
FamilyID.com, 313
Familylink, 2382
FamilyMint, 742
FamilyTime, 1668
Famo.us, 1028
Famoco, 2851
Famosa, 1753
Famoso, 2254
Famous, 1000, 1611
FamPlus, 2824
Fan AI, 472
Fan Duel, 518
Fan.tv, 1534
FanAI, 707, 1585
Fanaticall, 1830
Fanatics, 124, 1000, 1683
FanBank, 561
Fanbank, 384, 1528
FanBread, 120
Fanbread, 1965
FanBridge, 1700
Fanbridge, 1149
Fancred, 1912
Fancy, 816, 1524, 1530
Fancy Hands, 1110, 1460, 1546
Fandango, 39
Fandango Inc., 2402
Fandeavor, 1912
FanDuel, 867, 1082, 1660, 3032, 3040
Fanduel, 295, 358, 578
Fanfare, 757
FanFare Media Works, 21
FangDD, 1121
Fango, 1615
Fanhattan, 871
FanIQ, 1906
FanNation, 1641
Fannin Partners, 950
FanoFineFood, 2378
FanPlayr, 605
Fantasmo, 1101
Fantastic, 869
Fantasy Entertainment, 402
Fantasy Moguls, 1641
Fantasy Shopper, 2475
FantasySalesTeam, 445
Fantom, 2355, 2522
Fantrail, 594
Fantuan Delivery, 2128
FanTV, 641
FanXChange, 371
FanXchange, 2224
fanxchange, 2133
Fanzila, 301
FAOPEN, 1755
FAPS, 1636
Far Chemical Inc., 653

Far Niente, 824
Far Sounder, 1693
Faraday, 786, 1097, 2008
Farecast, 1445, 1760
FareChase, 310
Farechase, 23
Farfaria, 1013
FarFetch, 641
Farfetch, 973
Farm Burger, 821
Farm Dog, 2947
Farm Fresh, 354
Farm Fresh Pet Foods, 2099
Farm Hill, 1115
Farm Market iD, 349
Farma Holding, 3054
Farman, 2672
Farmdrop, 2446
Farmeasy, 1509
FarmerBs Fridge, 996
Farmeron, 1101, 1322, 1700, 3108
Farmers Business Network, 595, 889, 1075
Farmers Hope, 55
FarmersEdge, 2049
FarmHopping, 3108
Farmhouse Culture, 1383, 2238
Farmhouse Fare Ltd, 2708
Farmigo, 1665
Farminers Startup Academy, 2856
Farmland Keeper, 823
Farmland LP, 3277
FarmLogix, 505
FarmLogs, 607, 630, 742, 961, 962
FarmQA, 1131
Farmshots, 1923
Farmstr, 1852
FarmWise, 232
Farnese Vini, 2293
Farralon Medical, 1915
Farran Technology, 2918
Farrell Fritz PC, 3267
Farther Farms, 622
Fashion and You, 1327
Fashion Cents, 788
Fashion for Home, 2829, 2838
Fashion One, 2511
Fashion Playres, 1097
Fashion Project, 1475, 1627
Fashionara, 1121
Fashionette, 2441
Fast, 9
Fast BioMedical, 658
Fast Booking, 2897
Fast Goods Groups UAB, 3049
Fast Lane Ventures, 3229
Fast Pace Urgent Care, 1667
Fast Pay Partners, 1970
Fast Sandwich LLC, 403
Fast Track Systems, 153
FastAsset, 649
Fastback Networks, 770, 852
FastCAP Systems, 1686
Fastcase, 1720
FastChannel, 43
Fastchip Inc., 252
FASTech Integration, 206, 314
Fasten, 89
Fasteners for Retail, 1456
Faster, 2422
Fastfox, 1121
Fastfrate, 722
Fastly, 235, 1563
FastMed Urgent Care, 21
FastPay, 486
Fastrax Oy, 2716
FastScale, 183
FASTSIGNS, 783

1317

Portfolio Companies Index

FASTSIGNS International, 1111
FastSoft, 69, 1237
Fastsoft, 192
FastSpring, 29, 378, 1824
FASTTAC, 998, 1584
FastTrac, 1306
FastWeb, 2667
Fastyl, 1359
Fat Llama, 13
Fat Pipe, 1677
Fat Spaniel Technologies, 144, 1397
Fatbrain.com/Barnesandnoble.com, 1288
Fate Therapeutics, 153, 1391, 1419, 1460, 1618, 1916
Fatherly, 256, 563, 858, 1110, 1883
FATHOM, 2290
Fathom, 858, 1721, 2265
Fathom Computing, 1421
FatWire, 1314
Fauna, 535, 547, 889
Faust Pharma, 2354
Favor, 307, 545, 1685
Favrille, 1288
Faxitron, 1014
FaxSav, 536
Fazoli's, 1753
FB Brands, 1232
FBC Device, 3149, 3203
FBGS, 2527
FBL Group LLC, 122
FBR & Co., 559
FC Holdings, 1039
FCA, 1477
FCA Packaging, 1469
FCF Fox Corporate Finance, 2979
FCI, 220, 1516, 2857
FCL Graphics, 619
FCS, 2806
FCV, 2474
FCX Performance, 1456
FCX Performance Inc., 914
FDG-Gruppe, 3067
FDH, 949
FDH Velocitel, 1986
FDN Communications, 441
FE3 Medical, 129
Fe3 Medical, 980
Fearless, 307
FeastFox, 622
Feastly, 307, 593, 1749, 1977
Feather, 995, 1075
Feature Labs, 754
FeatureSpace, 2858
febit, 979
Federal, 1086
Federated Foods, 3146
Federated Media Publishing, 315, 1410
Federated Sample, 1943
FedEx Ground, 17
Fedora, 1998
FedTax, 345
FeedBurner, 609, 1760
Feedhenry, 2918
Feedly, 1323
Feedvisor, 816
Feedzai, 486, 585
FeeFighters, 1364
Feefighters, 1615
Feeney Brothers Utility Services, 365
Feetz, 1069
FEEX, 301
Felins USA, 1252
Felix & Paul, 472
Felix & Paul Studios, 518
Felix Energy, 672
Fellow, 2157

Fellowship for Race and Equity in Education, 1316
Felt, 459
FEM, 1222
FEM Inc., 1028
Femco Machine, 1021
FEMCO Machine Co., 1624
Femeda Ltd, 2708
FemSelect, 1577
Femtosense, 2278
Fenavic, 2352
Feneral Paramterics, 1558
Fenergo, 1000
Fengguang Bio-Fan, 3194
Fengkai Machinery, 2936
Fenix Opportunity, 2052
Fennebresque, 3259
Fenno Rahasto Ky, 2740
FenSense, 1507
Fenwal, 1835
Fenway Summer, 384
Fenwick, 2601
Ferche Millwork, 1521
Ferfics, 2355
Fero Labs, 317
Ferrara Candy Company, 1088
Ferrara Fire Apparatus, 1209
Ferrell Companies, 1837
Ferrera DeStefano & Caporusso, 3267
Ferric Semiconductor, 1303
Ferring Pharmaceuticals, 1452
Ferris, 1888
Ferroelectric Memory GmbH, 2686
FerroKin Biosciences, 495, 2816
Ferrosan Medical Devices, 2384
Fertility Focus, 2967
Fertiseeds, 2454
Festicket, 3055
Fetch, 858
Fetch Back, 525
Fetch Robotics, 1663
Fetch Technologies, 979
Fetcher, 1554
FetchNotes, 1736
Fetco Home Decor, 1230
Fetise, 3109
Fever Tree, 2944
FeVo, 1530
Fevo, 2239
Fewmo Tech Limited, 1241
FF Pharmaceuticals, 2949
FFC, 37
FFI Contracting Services, 3262
FFI Holdings Inc., 63
FFL Partners, 3264
FFO Home, 1753
Ffpharma, 3042
FG Microtek, 3188
FGA Media, 594
FGL, 1965
Fh, 2696
FI Info Net, 253
Fi Smart Dog Collar, 1310
Fi-on, 2969
fi360, 299
Fiagon, 2824
Fianciere Felix, 2721
Fiber By-Products, 251
Fiber Composites, 1232
Fiber Optic Network Systems, 1257
Fiber-Line, 1021
Fiberex, 2202
FiberForge, 1837
Fiberight, 526
FibeRio, 1685
FibeRio Technology Corporation, 549
Fiberline, 3203

Fiberlink, 655
Fibernet, 2697
Fiberoptic Components, 211
Fibers, 2317
Fibersense Technology, 194
Fiberxon, 3062
FiberZone Networks, 1348
FiBest, 1755
Fibest., 2854
Fibocom Wireless, 1004
Fibroblast, 1615
Fibrocell Science, 1812
FibroGen, 762, 2970
Fibrotech, 2536
Fibrotech Therapeutics, 2959
Fictiv, 1004
Fiddlehead, 2068
Fiddlehead Technology, 2200
Fidelia Technology, 1994
Fidelica Microsystems, 1918
Fidelis, 989, 1054, 1359, 1459
Fidelis Education, 1348
Fidelis Insurance Holdings Limited, 559
Fidelis Security Systems, 1169, 1728
Fidelis SeniorCare, 935
Fidelis Seniorcare, 474
Fidelity Investments, 3259
Fidelity National Financial Inc., 1903
Fidelity National Financial Services, 1835
Fidelity Payment Services, 1166
Fidlock, 2824
Fido Labs, 1437
Fidor, 2406, 3239
Fidor Russia, 2940
Field Agent, 745
Field Day, 934
Field Lens, 1306, 1380
Field Solutions, 3279
FieldAware, 1380
Fieldaware, 3147
Fieldbrook Foods Corporation, 147
FieldCentrix, 192, 765, 1672, 1706
FieldCLIX, 684
FieldDay, 561
Fieldglass, 876, 1156, 1738
Fieldiens, 1358
FieldLens, 533, 1475, 1518, 1699
Fieldlens, 308
FieldTest, 306
FieldView, 1689
FieldView Solutions, 1387
Fieldwire, 128
Fieldwood Energy, 1573
Fien En Mile, 3042
Fiesta Mart, 46
Fifth Creek Energy, 1278, 1326
FiftyOne, 57
Fight My Monster, 871
FightCamp, 2212
Figma, 872, 1075
FIGS, 1524
Figs, 397, 1055, 1247
Figtagram, 1883
Figure, 231, 535
Figure 1, 1611, 2239, 2280
figure 1, 2187
Figure 8, 666
Figure 8 Wireless, 206
Figure Eight, 720, 1154, 1607
Figure8 Surgical, 293
Fiix, 2132, 2172
Fiksu, 455
Filament, 218, 358, 563, 1547, 1611, 1926
Filament Brands Inc., 447
Filament Labs, 1592
Filco Carting, 1745
Filecoin, 124, 307, 1630, 1666

1318

Portfolio Companies Index

FileFacets, 2076, 2128
Filefacets, 2284
Fileforce, 1004
Filement, 2696
Filesx, 2775
FileTrek, 132, 2058
Filevine, 79
Filip, 2831
Fill Factory, 2674
Fillattice, 2423
Filld, 1028
FillFactory, 2662
Fillfactory N.V., 2902
Fillmore Advisory, 2646
Film Monkey, 2184
Film Track, 1000
FilmLoop, 807
Filmwerks LLC, 1638
Filoukes, 3042
Filson, 334, 378
Filter Easy, 171
Filter Minder, 1719
Filter Squad, 3248
FilterEasy, 971
FIMC, 949
FIN Engineering Group Ltd, 2704
Fin Robotics, 623
Fin Tyre, 3154
Finaeo, 2027, 2149
Final, 397, 1150
Finalcad, 2439
Finale, 1114
Finali Corporation, 315
FinalPrice, 89
Finalsite, 1717
Finance New Europe, 2648
FinanceAcar, 2406
FinanceIt, 1863
Financial Directions Group, 3259
Financial Engines, 757, 770, 836, 1360
Financial Guaranty Insurance Company, 575
Financial Guard, 462
Financial Health Services, 1466
Financial Investments Corporation, 3265
Financial Technology Ventures, 3284
FinancialContent, 238
FinancialForce, 1607
Financiere Orefi, 2985
Financière C.T. (Captain Tortue)., 2653
Financière Fouquet II, 2653
Finanical Engines, 793
Finanzcheck.De, 909
Finanzchef24, 3161
Finanzchek, 2475
Finastra, 744
FiNC, 721
Find-Me Technologies, 3023
Finderly, 1860
Findify, 3108
Findis, 1516, 2338
FindIt, 471, 962
Findit, 1589
FindMatic, 450
Findspace, 2224
Fine Line Services LLC, 3268
Fine Sounds Group, 3020
Fine Tubes, 1962
FineHeart, 347
FineLine Technologies, 468, 1846
Finery, 896
Finest City Broadcasting LLC, 21
Finetune, 1161
Finfox, 622
Fingi, 1061
Finicity, 607
Finisar, 2323
Finite Carbon, 1828

Finite State, 2019
Finix, 49
Finix Payments, 50, 941
Finjan, 249
Finjan Vital Security, 909
FinLeap, 1269
FinLocker, 569
Finn AI, 7, 2291
Finn Corp, 1820
Finn Lamex Safety Glass Oy, 2318
Finn.ai, 755
Finnair Oyj, 2990
Finnish Chemicals, 3178
Finnlines Oyj, 2990
Fino, 1004
Finova Financial, 525
Finrise, 1323
Finsecur, 2466
FINsix, 1686, 1916
FINsix Corp., 497
Finsphere Corporation, 1247
Fintech, 2492
FinTech Innovation Lab, 533
Fintech Lab, 1558
Fintyre, 2524
Finxera, 231, 751, 770
Fios, 753, 2051
Fire & Life Safety America, 290, 746, 1086
Fire Apps, 974
Fire Door Solutions, 667
Fire Grill, 1168
Fire Rock, 678
FIRE Solutions, 1828
FIRE1, 1122
FireApps, 695, 1852
Firearms Training Systems Inc., 447
Firebase, 585, 707
Firebirds Restaurants, 127
Firebox.com, 3070, 3131
Firebrand Media, 2574
Firecomms, 3152
Firecraft Products, 2168
Firedoor, 2878
FireEye, 581, 634, 777, 968, 979, 1654
Firefly, 622
Firefly Energy, 1057
Firefly LED Lighting, 445
Firefly Solar Generators, 2505
Fireglass, 1121
Firehole Composites, 36
FireHUD, 622
FireKing Security Group, 1435
FireLayers, 3246
Fireman's Brew, 1061
Firemon, 1000
Firepoint, 387
Firepond, 2005
FirePower Debt GP, 3258
FireRein, 2061
FireRock, 61
Firesale, 392
Fireside Glamping, 678
Firestar Software Inc., 2397
Firestone Diamonds, 1548
Firetide, 536, 939
Fireweed Fund, 623
FireWheel Energy, 672
Firich Enterprises, 3218
Firm 58, 1334
Firm AS, 2079
Firm58, 1480
First, 971
First Access, 55, 2910
First Access Entertainment, 34
First Active Media, 2468
First Aid Shot Therapy, 1698
First Allied, 1147

First American Financial, 300
First American Payment Systems, 1129
First American Records Management, 949
First American Title Company of Marin, 869
First Analysis, 3265
First Ascent Ventures, 3258
First Asset Management, 2079
First Bancorp, 1815
First Bauxite, 1548
First Crush, 704
First Data, 2379
First Data Corp., 1082
First Data Holdings, 1743
First Eagle Investment Management, 1776
First Equity, 1920
First Green Partners, 1956
First Health Group Corp., 300
First Hill Partners, 3276
First Insight, 56
First Insight Inc., 158
First Light Fusion, 3028
First Light Hospitality, 3277
First Marketing, 1770
First National Digital Currency, 2266
First Nickel, 1548
First Opinion, 720, 1489, 1634
First Orange Contact, 2451
First Point Holdings, 3062
First Quality, 473
First Republic Bank, 368, 824, 1654, 3272
First Source, 443
First Sun Capital, 1123
First Tower, 1491
First Watch, 62
First Wave Products Group, 1523
First West Capital, 3258
First Western Financial, 553
First Wind Holdings, 1156
FirstBest, 1317
FirstBest Systems, 646
FirstFuel, 235
FirstFuel Software, 1355, 1579
FirstLight HomeCare, 1281
FirstLight Power Enterprises, 675
Firstquote Masson Financial Services, 2572
FirstRain, 1361
FirstSense Software, 1334
Firth Rixon, 67
Firth Rixson, 1360
Fisbones AS, 3141
Fiscal Note, 890
Fiscalia Privada, 2455
FiscalNote, 13, 107, 535, 622, 785, 1613, 1998
Fischbein, 1491
Fischben, 1270
Fischer Block, 285
FISERV, 1972
Fiserv., 2674
Fish2BE, 2949
Fishbowl, 655, 695, 1899
Fishbrain, 3108
Fisher Scientific, 209
Fisher Unitech, 1166
Fisher/Unitech, 1572
FishNet Security, 654
Fishtree, 1299
Fision, 768
Fisk, 853
FISOC, 594
Fispan, 2212
Fit & Fresh, 478
FIT Biotech Oyj, 2318
Fit Solutions, 3078
Fit XR, 1183
Fitamins, 391
Fitbit, 1620, 1699, 1700, 1860
Fitc&Color, 2437

1319

Portfolio Companies Index

FitLinxx, 1021, 2196
Fitmob, 707, 1323
fitmob, 1184
Fitn, 1784
Fitness Connection, 1576, 1979
Fitness First, 2605
Fitness Interactive Experience, 362
Fitness on Request, 1113
Fitnesskeeper, 1359
Fitnet, 1812
FitNexx, 995
Fitocracy, 679, 707, 1364, 1581
Fitorbit, 1715
Fitplan, 1110
Fits.me, 2630, 2710
FitStar, 60, 1222
Fitstar, 1853
Fitting Valve and Control Corporation, 111
Fitzroy, 1099
Five, 622
Five Across, 852
Five Apes, 1865
Five Below, 1136
Five Prime, 59, 2816
Five Prime Therapeutics, 595, 621, 2513, 2690
Five Star Finance, 1346
Five Star Food Service, 783, 909
Five Star Foods, 746
Five Star Franchising, 999
Five Star Technologies, 466, 2196
Five Start Manufacturing, 1570
Five to Nine, 622, 1507
5 à Sec BV, 2722
5.11, 1776
500 Startups, 1965
500friends, 563, 796, 858, 1513, 1958
500px, 724
500V, 721
51 Deco, 3062
5173.com, 2850
51edu, 2850
51edu.com, 2850
51Fanli.com, 3142
51job, 596
51offer, 1297
51Talk, 596
51talk, 3251
51VR, 1121
51wan.com, 3208
55.1 Tactical, 523
555 Mansell, 1219
56.com, 58, 3142
57 Stars, 3261
58 Daojia, 1082
58.com, 596, 1956
Five9, 184
FiveAcross, 58
5AM Ventures, 3269
5aSec, 1516
5i Medical, 1061
5iSciences, 278
5Medical Marketing, 1228
5miles, 973
5mina, 590
5minMedia, 1715, 2914
5Nine, 1000
FivePrime, 1928
FivePrime Therapeutics, 2970
Fiverr, 28, 260, 1118
FiveRun, 243
FiveRuns, 202
5Square Systems, 1975
FiveStar, 1257
FiveStars, 2012
Fivestars, 596, 1121
5th Element Tracking, 694
5to1, 798

5V Technologies, 1922
Fixed, 1218, 1749
Fixes 4 Kids, 1070
Fixmo, 1400, 1410, 2831
Fixya, 1184
Fizzback, 2987
Fjord Marin, 2754
Fk-Biotecnologia, 2626
Fketchfab, 1416
Flaaming Oy, 2966
Flabeg, 1753
Flachsland Zukunftsshulen, 2531
Flaconi, 2441, 2475
FLAG Therapeutics, 3259
Flagship Pioneering, 879
Flagship Ventures, 3269
Flagstone Foods, 881
Flagstone Reinsurance Holdings Limited, 1123
Flair, 1894
Flamel Technologies FoldRx, 94
Flamingo Horticulture, 1753
Flanco International, 2429
Flanders' Drive, 3042
Flare Capital Partners, 3273
Flare Technologies, 622
Flaregames, 28
Flarion, 260, 1305
Flarion Technologies, 692, 3155
Flash Delivery, 922
Flash Networks, 116, 909, 1926, 2726, 2782, 3123, 3124, 3155
Flash Valet, 202
FlashBase, 592
FlashFoto, 54
Flashline, 56
FlashNetworks Ltd, 2585
Flashnotes, 1699, 1734
Flashpoint, 483, 2132
FlashSoft, 32, 358
Flashtalking, 1601, 1776
Flat Iron Energy Partners, 542
Flat Out of Heels, 218
Flat World, 1899
Flat World Knowledge, 1849
FlatFrog, 3149
Flatiron, 858
Flatiron Health, 741
Flatiron School, 1821
Flatlay, 1507
Flatout Flatbread, 1335
Flatstack, 1943
Flattr, 3030
FlatWorld Knowledge, 1475
Flavor Infusion LLC, 77
Flavor1, 1753
Flavors Holdings, 405
Flayvr, 2914
Flect, 1607
Fleecs, 2776
Fleet Complete, 1156
Fleet One, 793, 1136
Fleet Worth Solutions, 161
FleetCor, 61, 220
FleetCor Technologies, 1752
Fleetgistics Enterprises Inc., 908
FleetMatics, 1480
Fleetmatics, 1001, 1017
FleetMatics USA, 1970
Fleetops, 2138, 2212
FleetPride, 199, 378, 1017
FleetPride Inc., 334
Fleetpride Inc., 1835
FleetPro, 3232
Fleetsmith, 1202
Fleetwash, 1491
Fleetwood, 77
Fleksy, 679, 1075

FLENS, 2974
Fletcher Spaght Ventures, 3269
Fleux Pine, 1378
Flex, 1654
Flex Logix, 1151
Flex Logix Technologies, 648
Flex Pharma, 260, 1122, 1145
Flex Pharma Inc., 487
Flex-P Industries, 2623
Flexa, 972
Flexan, 1128
Flexday, 2144
FLEXE, 1641
Flexe, 1534
FlexEnergy, 1009
Flexential, 744, 824
Flexera Software, 1814
FlexGen, 2514, 3020
FlexGen Power Systems, 98, 809
Flexicath, 1448
Flexion, 12, 1928
Flexion Therapeutics, 1436
Flexitech, 1753
Flexiti Financial, 2134
Flexitive, 2144, 2249
Flexium Interconnect, 2603
FlexLight Networks, 536
FlexLogics, 623
FlexMinder, 2008
FlexNetworks, 2062
flexperto, 2841
FlexPharma, 544, 709
FlexPlay, 43
Flexpoint Ford, 3264
Flexport, 318, 720, 741, 775, 889, 942, 991, 1370, 1666, 1758, 1876
FlexRay, 1111
FlexReceipts, 125
FlexSpark, 995
Flexstar Technology, 194, 378
FlexTrip, 685
Flexuspine, 1929
Fliaz, 1846
Flickr, 1323
Fliggo, 1655
Flight Deck, 1047
Flight Office, 1061
Flight Options, 1545
Flight Training Acquisitions, 1127
Flight Trampoline Parks, 828
FlightCar, 823, 858, 1699
FlightCaster, 2329
Flightdocs, 161
Flightman, 3032
FlightWave Aero, 429, 811
Fliit, 2841, 3236
Flingo, 197
Flinks, 2179
flinks, 2212
Flinn Scientific Inc., 909
Flint, 1427, 1860
Flint Mobile, 1747
Flint Trading Inc., 746
Flip, 1121
Flipboard, 518, 823, 1000, 1075, 2860, 2860
Flipd, 2245
FlipGive, 2149
Flipgloss, 1099
Flipgrid, 173, 341
Flipkart, 28
Flipkart.com, 1946
Flipp, 1000
Flipside, 307
Flipter, 2984
FlipTop, 585
Fliptop, 1146, 1524
Fliptu, 1632

Portfolio Companies Index

Flirtey, 1149, 1329, 1509
Flirtic, 89
Flixbus, 815, 2838
Flixel, 2113, 2182
Flixel Cinemagraph, 2200
FlixMaster, 685
Flixster, 1121, 1445
FlixWagon, 2352
Flo, 661, 2551
Float, 384
Floating Point Group, 622
Flocabulary, 1551
Flocations, 3121
FloDesign, 2492
Flogit4u, 3092
Flojos, 364
FloNetwork, 1769
Flood Data Services, 131
Floodgate, 202
Floop, 678
Floor & Decor, 783
Floor & Decor Outlets of America, 159, 1873
Floor & Décor, 1970
Floor & DéCor Outlets of America, 1624
Floored, 351, 871, 1531, 1593, 1874
FloQast, 120, 1000, 1829, 1965
Floravere, 325, 1768
Florence Healthcare, 243
Floreo, 1473
Florida Autism Center, 1667
Florida Bank, 224
Florida Bank Group, 1148
Florida Blue, 3262
Florida East Coast Industries, 767
Florida East Coast Railway, 767
Florida Food Products, 1231
Florida Funders, 3262
Florida Gulfshore Capital, 3262
Florida Marine Group, 1745
Florida Pallative Homecare, 406
Florimex Group, 2501
Flosonics Medical, 2130, 2149, 2187
FloSports, 256
FloType, 585
Flourish, 622
Flow, 761, 796, 813, 1632
Flow ++, 219
Flow Control Group, 257
Flow Control Solutions Inc., 158
Flow Dry Technology, 164
Flow Hub, 151, 1439
Flow Kana, 845, 1464, 1610
Flow Solutions, 1557
Flow State Media, 1716
Flow Traders BV, 1752
Flow-Dry, 1021
FlowBelow, 445
FlowCadia Inc., 782
FlowCardia, 1412
Flowchem, 170
Flowdock, 1563
FlowForward Medical, 1379
Flowhub, 99, 1807
Flowmedica, 2748
Flowonix, 495
Flowonix Medical, 1375
Flowplay, 69, 1004, 2390
FlowTech Feuling, 678
Flowtown, 231, 1054
Flowtune, 622
Floyd, 251, 325
floyd, 607
FloydHub, 1611
FLRish, 557, 1135
FLS Transportation, 21
Flud, 1150
Fludicon, 2932

Fludrive, 402
Fluencr, 1912
Fluency Voice Technology, 2577
Fluensee, 975
Fluent Home, 333
Fluent.AI, 2184
Fluent.ai, 2027
Fluid, 544, 842, 876
Fluid Clarification, 2136, 2285
Fluid Delivery Solutions LLC, 1851
Fluid Screen, 195
Fluidic Analytics, 2674, 3028
Fluidigm, 560, 979, 1010
Fluidmesh Networks, 1964
Fluids Inc., 2291
Flume, 195
Flunt Industries, 1209
Fluoptics, 2899
Fluorous Technologies, 998
Flurry, 180, 308, 563, 609, 627, 741, 1010
Flutter, 1983
Flux, 308, 641, 889
FluxDrive, 85
Fluxion, 1238
Fluxion Biosciences, 491, 1080
Fluxome Sciences, 3113
Fluxus, 1416, 2354
Fluxx, 720
FLX Bio, 517, 889, 1075
Fly, 1530
Fly The Wave, 1161
Flybits, 2153, 2225, 2273
Flybridge Capital Partners, 3273
Flyby Media, 457
FlyCast, 293
Flycast, 260, 1725
FlyCleaners, 2017
Flyhomes, 1663
Flying Colours Corp., 926
Flynn Pharma, 1844
Flynn Restaurant Group, 1978, 2183
Flyp Technologies Inc., 2094
Flyr, 1035
Flyshot, 2245
FlyteComm, 1354
Flytrex, 249
Flywheel, 322, 1150
Flywheel Software, 1579
FlyWire, 313
Flywire, 710, 1183
FM Sylvan, 290
FM:Systems, 29, 3259
FMA France, 2805
FMC, 3069
FMH Aerospace, 985
FMI, 653
FMI International, 1086
FMP, 1097
FMS Advanced Systems Group, 979
FNB United, 1360
FNEX, 658
FNF Construction Inc., 1037
FNZ, 815
Foam Fabrications, 523
Foam Rubber Products, 1252
Foamix, 1941
Focal, 1398
Focal Point Data Risk, 897, 1345
Focal Point Pharmaceuticals, 1187
Focal Systems, 547, 2019
Focal Therapeutics, 666, 1371
FocalTech Sytems, 2703
Focus, 2676
FOCUS Brands, 1576
Focus Brands, 1491
Focus Diagnostics, 209
Focus Financial, 1460

Focus Financial Partners, 1082, 1752
Focus Genetics, 2516
Focus Media, 690, 1087, 2297, 3100
Focus Motion, 1634
Focus Solutions, 2472
Focus Solutions Group, 2894
Focus Technology Consulting, 1605
Focus Ventures, 986, 3284
Focus:Trainr, 1099
Focused Health Solutions, 1128
FocusEdu.cn, 596
Fogbreak Software, 1672
Fogg, 2886
FogHorn, 603, 809, 1809
Foghorn Therapeutics, 747
FogLogic, 1663
Fogo De Chao, 1815
FogPharma, 889
Foko, 2195
Foldax, 1051
Foldax Inc., 269
Foley & Lardner LLP, 3262
Foley's, 2292
Folica, 1748
Folicum, 3149
FolioDynamix, 655
Foliot Furniture, 2206
Follica, 1460
Follow The Coin, 307
FollowAnalytics, 180, 1607, 2019
Followap Telecommunications, 3221
Folloze, 396, 454, 856
FON, 2446
Fon, 536
Fonality, 1226, 1235
Fondaction, 3258
Fondis Electronic, 3020
Fonds de soliderite FTQ, 3258
Fondu, 280, 679
Fonecta Oy, 1927
Foneric, 1509
Fongo, 2262
Fontainebleau, 869
Fontinalis Partners, 3269
Fontself.com, 2310
Food 52, 1110
Food Distributor, 1422
Food For All, 1894
Food Freshness Technology, 2405
Food Genius, 114, 471, 731, 1615, 1992
Food Matters Market, 3277
Food On The Table, 202
Food Should Taste Good, 1665
Food.ee, 85, 2291
Fooda, 1118, 1902
Foodbuzz, 308
Foodee, 2144
FoodGenius, 962
Foodient T/A Whisk, 2967
Foodini, 1615
FoodLogiQ, 2238
FoodMaster, 71
FoodMesh, 2223
foodpanda, 842
Foodspotting, 296
Foodware Group, 1372
Football For Good, 2125
Foothills Creamery, 2269
Foothold Technology, 92
Footnote, 1677
Footprint Retail Services, 468
Footways, 3113
For Days, 1006
For Us All, 770
Fora Financial, 1403
ForAtable.com, 2310
Foray, 561

1321

Portfolio Companies Index

Forbes, 659
Forbes Travel Guide, 282, 493, 1830
Forbius, 2180, 2187
Force, 1000
Force 10, 1896
Force 10 Networks, 1257
Force10, 563, 596, 1212, 1676
Force10 Networks, 196, 536, 1728
Forcepoint, 1112
Ford Models, 101
Ford Wholesale Co. Inc., 869
Forecast Health, 3259
ForeFlight, 1683
Forefront Dermatology, 2207, 2219
ForeFront Education, 374
Forelinx, 811
Forendo Pharma, 1350
Forensic Logic, 2978
Forenvia Venture I Ky, 2740
ForeScout, 28, 49, 180, 560, 1212
ForeScout Technologies, 925
ForeSee, 1886
Foresee Results, 2196
Foreside, 1147
Foreside Company, 438
Foresight, 538
Foresight AI, 232
Foresight Reserves, 1573, 1730
Forest Device, 622
Forest Holidays, 2944
Forest2Market, 643
Forethought, 1933
Forever, 1849
Forgame Holdings Limited, 1776
Forge, 622, 977, 1696
Forge Communications, 3259
Forge Energy, 672, 1443
Forge Global, 1395
Forged Metals, 67
ForgeRock, 28, 770, 1082
Forgerock, 1212
Foria, 638
Forkly, 685
Form Labs, 996
Form Technologies, 109
FORMA Therapeutics, 2513, 2690
Forma Therapeutics, 184, 1124, 1350
Forma-Dis, 2293, 2340
Formac Pharmaceuticals, 2366, 3042
Formation Capital, 3264
Formation Data Systems, 1425
Formation Energy, 1129
Formation Systems, 23
Formative, 1551
Formel D GmbH, 3067
Formex, 2878
FormFactor, 1247
Formica Corporation, 1621
Formisimo, 3108
FormLabs, 776, 1097
Formlabs, 1054
Formolgy, 2967
Formosa Epitaxy, 2603, 3218
Formosa International, 2436
Formscape Group, 2662
Formspring, 231
Formspring.Me, 1460
Formula 1, 924
Formula E, 1509
Formula Systems, 2745
Forno d'Asolo, 2293
Foro Energy, 466, 809, 1334
Forsake, 1686
ForSight Newco II, 1725
ForSight Vision 4, 1928
ForSight Vision 5, 1928
ForSight VISION4, 1122

ForSight VISIONS, 1122, 1786
Forst Point Power, 156
Fort Awesome, 708
Fort Dearborn Company, 1086
Fort Garry Brewing Co., 2136
Fort James, 260
Fort Scale, 1004
FORTE, 1657
FORTE Industrial Equipment Systems, 77
Forte Media, 1004
Forte Research Systems, 1292
Forte Tools, 1760
ForteBio, 1094
Fortegra Financial, 1752
Fortemedia, 2853
Forter, 4, 148, 1607, 1626
Forterro, 235
Forth Dimension Displays, 2671
Forthfield, 1469
Forticom, 2663
Fortify, 408, 1024
Fortify Software, 581, 634, 1672
Fortinet, 596, 602, 986, 1212, 1474
Fortis Energy Services, 830
Fortius Financial, 462
Fortius Sport & Health, 2265
Fortress, 77, 518
Fortress Technologies, 418, 1087, 1116
FortressIQ, 305, 679
Fortum Oyj, 2990
Fortumo, 871, 1004
Fortune Cookie, 2535
Fortune Greek Gas Gathering and Processing, 332
Fortus Medical Inc., 341
Forty Cloud, 2952
Forty Seven, 495, 1121
Forté, 1853
Forté Media, 620
FortéBio, 1268
Forum Pharmaceuticals, 710
Forus Health, 28, 2849
Forward, 741, 1069
Forward Health Group, 2001
Forward Networks, 124, 609
Forward Water Technologies, 2061
Fos4x, 2824
Foseco, 2605, 2605
Fosen IKT, 967
Foss Manufacturing Company, 2009
Fossil Creek Resources, 672
Foster + Partners, 2300
Foster Findlay Associates, 2700
Fosun, 473
Fotango Ltd, 3013
Fotech, 319
Fotech Solutions, 2700, 3104
Fotokyte, 2296
Fotolia Holdings, 1776
Fotolog, 641
Fotoshkola, 2540
Fougera Pharmaceuticals, 986
Found Ocean, 2391
Foundation Capital, 986, 3284
Foundation Consumer Healthcare, 1062
Foundation DB, 1760
Foundation Medicine, 1811, 3085
Foundation Partners Group, 1742
Foundation Radiology Group, 475
Foundation Risk Partners Corp., 158
Foundation9, 779
Foundationworks, 1915
Founder Collective, 3273
Founder Sport Group, 433
Founder Suite, 724
FounderDating, 1054, 1700
FounderFuel, 51

Founders Advantage Capital, 2134
Foundry Group, 986, 3276
Foundry Networks, 596
Foundstone, 2051
Fount Therapeutics, 762
Fountain, 563, 1384, 1879
Fountain Medical Development, 2667
4 Energy, 2295
Four Eyes, 1965
Four Mine, 724
Four Seasons Health Care, 2361
Four Soft, 3211
Four Star Lighting Co., 465
Four Wheel Campers, 1609
4-Antibody, 2797
40 South Energy, 2874
410 Labs, 1860
410Labs, 1169
411.ca, 2224
41st Parameter, 968
42, 1716
42 Floors, 260, 377, 1531
42 North Dental LLC, 158
420 Klean, 392
42Floors, 1297
42matters, 3056
45M, 1334
480 Biomedical, 347, 1008, 1334, 1460
4AZA Bioscience, 2563
4C, 1046
4Charity.com, 1011
4doctor, 721
4Free WiFi, 3181
4Front, 1807
4Gas Holding B.V., 1573
4Gas Holding BV, 413
4GI, 2697
4HAMCOGEN, 2949
4Home, 1926, 3047
4INFO, 1646
4info, 1241, 1946
4IQ, 249
4JET Technologies, 2686
4moms, 293, 421
FourPhase Systems, 260
Fourpost, 1758
FourQ, 631
4R Systems, 1804, 1862
4Refuel, 1062
FourSquare, 1341
Foursquare, 124, 1359, 1715, 1882
4subsea, 3216
4Tell, 1463
Fourth, 1000
4th Pass, 1017
FourthWall Media, 1633
4w MarketPlace, 3052
4Wall Entertainment Inc., 1368
4Wheel Drive Hardware, 1435
Fove, 792
Fovea, 2316, 2748
Foviance, 2674
Foviance Group, 2662
Fox Head, 96
Fox Photo, 354, 1017
Fox Racing Shox, 523
Fox River Fiber, 928
Fox Rothschild, 3268, 3275
Fox Technologies, 2716, 3013
Fox Thermal Instruments Inc., 908
Foxborn NMR, 3171
Foxcom, 2720
Foxcom Wireless, 2775
Foxfire, 1689
FoxHollow Technology, 23
Foxlink, 892
Foxquilt Insurance, 2113

1322

Portfolio Companies Index

FoxTrot, 1110
Foxtrot, 727, 1757
Foxtrot Code, 86
Foxy's Pash, 3257
FP Newspapers, 2258
FPEE, 2448
FPG, 1491
FPMI Solutions, 1400
FPS Group, 299
FPT Corporation, 2961
FPX, 959
FR Midstream Holdings, 740
Fr8, 1370
FRA/Business Interactif, 2466
Fractal, 2858
Fractal Analytics, 135
Fractal Analytics Private Limited, 1776
Fractal Design, 852
Fractal Systems, 322, 1558
Fractus, 2483, 2987
Fractyl, 260, 816
Fractyl Laboratories, 621
Fragmob, 69, 1583
Fraikin, 2719, 2852
Frame, 1154
Frame Technology, 197
Frame.ai, 535, 743
Frame.io, 743, 1663, 1675
Framebridge, 1766
Framehawk, 544, 1846
FrameMax, 560
Framer, 1138
Framespot AB, 2718
Framework Venture Partners, 3258
France Champignon, 2551
France Géothermie, 3020
France Hélices SA, 2653
France Portes, 2985
Francesca's Collection, 433
Franchise, 1753
FranchiseKnowHow LLC, 3267
Francis Drilling Fluids, 828
Francising Works, 2509
Franco Signor, 361
Frank, 1527
Frank & Oak, 256, 1118, 2239, 2280
Frank Entertainment Group, 1636
Frank., 877
Franklin Energy, 21, 1081
Franklin Energy Services, 1456
Franlin Templeton Investments, 924
Frans Bonhomme, 2601
Franshion Properties, 1956
Frantic Films, 2196, 2226
Fraser River Pile & Dredge, 2275
FraudMetrix, 2439
FraudSciences, 1534
Fraudwall/Anchor Intelligence, 623
Fraugster, 3108
Frauscher Sensor Technology, 862
Frazier Healthcare Partners, 3264
Freak'n Genius, 1912, 1992
Freck, 231
Fred Sands, 869
Free, 1607
Free Awesome, 1632
Free Decision, 847
Free Flow Power, 259, 1895
Free Monee, 1760
Free Wheel, 770
FreeAgent, 1118
FreeBalance, 2263
Freebird, 816
FreeBorders, 438
Freeborders, 536
FreeBrie, 2856
Freedom Communication Technologies, 903

Freedom Group, 1970
Freedom Innovations, 1777, 1792
Freedom Medical, 1521
Freedom Meditech Inc., 1047
Freedom Mobile, 2254
Freedom Robotics, 1834
Freedom Scientific, 849
FreedomPay, 296, 538
FreedomPop, 596
Freee, 596, 641
FreeForm, 1563
Freeform, 32
FreeHand Surgical, 2598
Freelancers Union, 1420
Freeletics, 431
FreeLinc, 682, 682
FreeMarkets, 272, 1623
Freenome, 124, 181, 889, 996, 1643
Freeosk, 251, 732
Freepath, 1600
Freepoint Commodities, 1743
FreeRange Games, 544, 1563
Freesbee, 2607
Freescale, 3033
Freespree, 3149
Freestyle Solutions, 1234
FreeTextbooks.Com, 1533
FreeWave Technologies, 1776
Freewebs, 115
FreeWill, 622
Freight Farms, 1097
Freight Tiger, 1121
Freightliner, 152
Freightos, 809
FreightWaves, 1480
Fremach Groep, 2949
Fremont Ventures, 3284
French Founders, 1006
French Girls, 60, 784
FRENDS Technology Oy, 2716
Frenzoo, 1965, 2390
Fresca Mexican Foods, 1250
Fresenius, 3069
Fresh Choice, 1896
Fresh Dining, 1396
Fresh Dining Concepts, 405
Fresh Express, 869
Fresh Food Concepts, 443
Fresh Hemp Foods, 2049
Fresh Nation, 1110
Fresh Origins, 1093
Fresh Squeeze, 1615
FreshBooks, 70, 1361, 2132, 2204
FreshDirect, 2079
FreshGrade, 1316, 2236
Freshgrade, 1527
Freshly, 935, 1000, 1982
FreshMenu, 1121
Freshpak, 1753
Freshpet, 1231
FreshPlanet, 1563, 1700
FreshPlum, 585
Freshstone Brands, 2123
FreshTemp, 1632
Freshworks, 578
Fresno, 1696
Fresvii, 2474
Freudenberg, 77
Freycinet Investments, 3258
FRH Consumer Services, 1841
Frichti, 2851
FriCSo, 2462
Frictionless Commerce, 466
Friday, 3048
Friend.ly, 1323
Friend2friend, 324
FriendBuy, 871

Friendi, 690
Friendly's Garden Fresh Restaurant Corp., 1753
Friends & Allies Brewing, 445
Friends of Choice in Urban Schools, 1316
FriendsAbroad.com, 2711
Friendship Public Charter Schools, 1316
Friendsly, 1110
Friendsurance, 641, 2831
Frigoscandia, 3009
Frigotechnica, 2471
Fring, 1334
fring, 3212
Fringe81, 2646
Fringilunch, 3042
Frintit, 1615
Frissul, 3048
Fritz AI, 679
FrogApps, 2646
From the Ground Up, 500
FromAtoB.com, 3113
Front, 305, 609, 1654, 1694, 1696, 1700, 1848, 1879
Front Bridge, 1626
Front Desk, 1641
Front Porch Digital, 916
Front Range Biosciences, 99, 392, 895, 1439, 1610, 1613
Front Row, 1054
FrontBridge, 757
FrontCall, 2875
Frontdesk Connect, 995
Frontenac Company, 3265
Frontera Energy, 2073
Frontier Bank of Texas, 445
Frontier Capital, 3262
Frontier Car Group, 204, 205, 781
Frontier Drilling, 1573
Frontier Firewood, 1262
Frontier Markets, 55, 3109
Frontier Packaging, 828
Frontier Silicon, 2380, 2472
Frontier Spinning Mills, 110
Frontier Strategy Group, 1715
Frontier Ventures, 986
Frontier Waste Solutions, 291
FrontierIP, 2892
FrontierMedEx, 2965
FrontierVision Partners LP, 1372
Frontline Performance Group, 21
Frontline Selling, 1240
Frontrange, 779
FrontStream Payments, 1331, 1732
Frost Fighter, 2145
Frozen Specialties, 1767
FRS, 1361
Fruition Partners, 1850
Fruux, 2824
FRVR, 2953
FRX Polymers, 2900
Fry's Electronics, 214
FSA Store, 52, 1385, 1459
FSB Global Holdings, 1129
FSI, 678
FSL 3D, 1751
Fsona Communications, 692
FSV Payment Systems, 224
FT Partner, 986
FTAPI SecuTransfer, 2824
FTE, 2616
FTL, 2574
FTRANS, 1849
Ftrans, 1863
Ftuan, 2936
FTV Capital, 986
Fu Sheng Industrial, 1139, 2946
Fubar Radio, 2967
Fubon Financial, 2436

1323

Portfolio Companies Index

Fuego, 1853
Fuego Tech, 3137
Fuel 3D, 3028
Fuel 50, 306
Fuel Powered, 1311
Fuel Systems, 328
Fuel Systems Solutions Inc., 274
FuelQuest, 2079, 3157
Fuentek, 3259
Fugoo, 69
Fugue, 538, 1169
Fuhu, 1255
Fuisz Media, 1222
Fuji Food Products, 797
Fuji Machinery Mfg. & Electronics Co. Ltd., 2347
Fulano, 2626
Fulcrum, 319, 1407
Fulcrum Bioenergy, 1604, 1895
Fulcrum Capital Partners, 3258
Fulcrum Composites, 1336
Fulcrum Equity Partners, 3262, 3270
Fulcrum Microsystems, 852
Fulcrum Technologies, 214
Fulcrum Therapeutics, 762
Fulham, 322
Full Circle, 85
Full Circle Feed, 704
Full Circle Insights, 1607
Full Circle Technologies, 1047
Full Contact, 930
Full Harvest, 570, 2000
Full Sail University, 1776
Full Scale Solutions, 3259
Full Spectrum, 1435
Full Vision, 111, 1053
FULLBEAUTY Brands, 135
Fullbeauty Brands, 456
Fullbridge, 1830
Fullcast.io, 552, 728
FullContact, 222, 685, 776, 1789, 2017
Fullerton, 374
Fullhan, 2936
FullSeven Technologies, 1710
FullStory, 889
Fullstory, 1075, 1607
Fullterton Technology, 2603
FullTilt Solutions, 2196
Fultec Semiconductor, 555, 798
Fulwisdom Capital, 3267
Fun+, 1678
Fun-Life, 1755
Funambol, 422
Funanga, 2838
Funcom, 3013
Function of Beauty, 823, 1701
functionability, 2220
Functional Neuromodulation, 748, 2130
Fundacion Ciudadano Inteligente, 1374
Fundbox, 148, 262, 816, 1069, 2943
Fundera, 741, 1069, 1110, 1502
Funders Club, 1004
FundersClub, 720, 741, 1715
Funding Circle, 1560, 2860, 2860
Funding Gates, 567
Funding University, 599
Fundly, 1054, 1150, 1257, 1655
Fundrise, 377
Funds India, 770, 1013
Fundtech, 2775, 2910, 3137
FundThrough, 2249
FundWell, 1642
Fungible, 235, 1184
Funizen, 100
Funko, 46, 378
Funkyfunky, 2857
FunMobility, 1108

Funnel, 2478
Funnel Cake, 2273
Funny or Die, 581, 634
Funny or Die (Sabse Technologies Inc.), 623
FunPlus, 3142
Funsherpa, 1958
Funxional Therapeutics, 3015
Funzio, 1563
Funzio G-Bits, 973
Furhat Robotics, 2478
Furie Operating Alaska, 675
Furnishare, 1110
Fusar Technologies, 418
Fuse, 515
Fuse Capital, 986
Fuse Energy, 672
Fuse.it, 1323
fusebill, 2249
Fusepoint, 1153
Fushe Kruje Cement, 1007
Fushion-IO, 1121
Fushun Cogen Power Plants, 2591
Fusient Media Ventures, 876
Fusio-Io, 1204
Fusion, 1105, 1477
Fusion Ads, 2473
Fusion Antibodies, 2610
Fusion Coolant, 742
Fusion Coolant Systems, 113
Fusion Education Group, 1999
Fusion Pharmaceuticals, 2130
Fusion Risk Management, 427
Fusion-io, 1212, 1474, 1846
Fusion.io, 124
Futalis, 2824
Futrli, 641
Futuragene, 3245
Future Ad Labs, 2479, 3030
Future Advisor, 858
Future Drinks, 2400
Future Family, 49, 180
Future Finance, 1502
Future Fuel, 1527
Future Is Now Schools, 1316
Future Point Systems, 1994
Future Publishing, 683
Future Publishing/Edicorp, 2415
Future Tech Holdings, 1605
Future.Fit, 1875
FutureAdvisor, 396, 1054, 1654
Futuredontics, 567
FutureE, 2710
FutureFamily, 2157
Futuremark, 2999
FutureMark Group Manistique, 1962
FutureNet Group, 1455
Futureo, 3208
FuturePlay, 483
Futures, 3020
Futurestate IT, 2184
FutureStay, 1310
FutureTech Holdings, 1423
FutureTrade, 807
FutureVault, 306
Futurice Oy, 2873
Futuris, 500
Fuze Network, 599, 1070, 1181
Fuzhou Skyunion Digital, 2850
Fuzic, 86
Fuzz Pet Health, 679
Fuzzbuzz, 1758
FVF, 3262
FX Bridge, 1863
FXCM, 2649
FXGear, 3127
FXI Technologies, 2369
Fyber, 1327

Fyfe Group LLC, 274
Fynaz, 2017
Fyrfly, 1766
Fysical, 942
fyto, 2991

G

G Connect, 2775
G&H Orthodontics, 97, 654, 1572
G-Log, 757
G-Mode, 1755
G-TEC Natural Gas Systems, 1523
G.I. Group, 2126
G.I. View, 2655
G/O Media, 857
G1 Dynamics, 426
G1 Therapeutics, 915, 1196, 1261, 1519, 2180
G10 Entertainment Korea, 2850
G2 Crowd, 1480
G2 Microsystems, 2323
G2 Web Services, 1476
G20 Ventures, 3273
G2One, 238
G2X Energy, 1151, 1786
G3 Global Energy, 156
G3P, 3048
G5, 867, 1234, 1942
GA Communications, 405
GA Pack, 220
GAB Robins, 335
Gabbro, 222
Gabriel Logan, 1526
Gabriel Performance Products, 443, 653
Gabriel Venture Partners, 3284
GadgetSpace, 1709
Gadzoox Networks, 1378
GaeaSoft. ICO Inc. & Imas Co Ltd., 2839
Gaffey Healthcare, 97
GAGA, 1056
Gai Energy, 3104
Gaia Interative, 1001
Gaia Online, 1534, 1827
Gaiam, 869
GaiaTech, 1270
GaiaWorks, 1826
GaiaX, 1755
Gailileo Processing, 1204
Gain Capital, 655
GAIN Capital Group, 1906
Gain Capital Group, 1728
Gain Credit, 1247
GainFitness, 1010
Gainful, 622
GainSight, 221
Gainsight, 235, 483, 569, 1000, 1121, 1607, 1752
GainSpan, 385, 1305, 2974
Gainspan, 979
GainSpan Corp, 1672
Gala, 2605
Gala Biotech, 1921
Gala Group, 2556
Gala Therapeutics, 143
GalaGen, 1918
Galantos Pharma, 2824
Galapagos, 2378, 2748
Galatea, 307
Galaxy Desserts, 1396
Galaxy Far East, 3218
Galaxy II, 1491
Galaxy Tool Corporation, 828
Galbani, 2497
Gale Technologies, 1378
Galecto Biotech, 3149
Galera Therapeutics, 267, 544, 569, 1519
Galera Therapeutics Inc., 1350
Galey & Lord, 354
Galil Medical, 1817, 1929, 3072, 3279

Portfolio Companies Index

Galileo, 1070
Galileo Global Education, 1496
Galileo Processing, 1915
Galileo Technology, 1121
Galleher, 1505
Galleon, 1122
Galleon Oil & Gas, 156
Gallery Watch, 1855
Galley, 2019
Gallo Holdings, 1927
Gallop, 2137, 2182
Galls, 456, 476
Galoob, 796
Galt Associates, 312
Galva Union, 2302
Galyan's Trading, 783
GamaLife, 135
Gamalon, 2, 720, 1004
Gambling Compliance, 3070, 3131
Gambol Pet Group, 1082
Game, 2796
Game Closure, 107
Game Duell, 2829, 2838
Game Equipment, 61
Game Insight, 2856
Game Mix, 1055
Game Plan, 1262
Game Plan Technologies, 1470
Game Ready, 797, 1580
Game Salad, 791, 871
Game Trust, 1873
Game Ventures, 2477, 2870
GameChanger, 547, 685, 1852, 2017
GameCo, 1028, 1310
GameFlip, 358, 1118
GameFly, 777, 1242, 1654, 1796
GameForge, 28
GameGenetics, 2824
Gamelayers, 1359
Gamelet, 3038
GameLogic, 925
Gamemage Interactive, 3062
GameMo, 2473
Gamer Sensei, 472, 1384
Gamersensei, 313
GamersFirst, 641
GamersFirt, 871
Games Are Social, 3052
Games Warehouse Ltd., 908
Games2Win.com, 502
GameSalad, 724, 1206
Gamet Sp. z o.o., 2706
Gametime, 889
GameTrust, 1680
Gamevice, 371
GameWisp, 1178
GAMFG Precision, 1171
Gamigo, 3155
Gamigo AG, 2528
Gamma Medica-Ideas, 402, 1498
Gamma Optical, 2603
Gamma spol. s r.o., 3122
Gammon, 2599, 2600
Gamo, 1516
Gamo Outdoor SL, 354
GAN Integrity, 655, 1240
GaN Systems, 1579, 2078, 2093
Gan Systems, 302
Ganache Brands, 2123
Gander Mountain, 1970
Ganeden Biotech, 402
Ganesh Housing, 260
GangaGen, 184
Gangagen, 2846
Gangavaram Port, 1956
Gangwon Wind Power, 584
Ganjaboxes, 392

Ganji, 296, 1327
Ganni, 1088
Ganymede Software, 1708
Ganzhou Dingsheng Water Technological Co., 2727
GAPbuster Worldwide, 732
Garage Technology Ventures, 986
Garantia Data, 221
Garapon, 1241
Garard Pasquier, 2602
Garbanzo Mediterranean Grill, 812
Gardein, 1861
Garden Fresh Holdings, 447
Garden Fresh Restaurant, 713, 1706
Garden Organics, 1784
Garden Ridge, 64
Gardena, 2863
Gardeners, 3233
Gardio, 2619
Gardner Aerospace, 2677
Gardner Denver, 1082
Gardner Denver Inc., 1903
Garena, 815
Garlik, 2662, 2671, 2674
Garneau Welding and Fabricating, 2286
Garner, 2058
Garretson Resolution Group, 914, 1435
Garrison Manufacturing, 1609
Gartmore, 924
Gartner, 260, 1209
Gartner Inc., 1903
Gary Platt Manufacturing, 1343
Gary's Tux Shops, 869
Gas Control Equipment, 2422
Gas Gas, 2891
Gas Secure, 3216
Gas Station TV, 251, 716
GasBuddy, 1810
Gate Rocket, 1142
Gate5, 2444
GateGuru, 1632
Gatekeeper Innovation, 1807
Gatekeeper Innovation Inc., 1439
Gatekeeper Systems Inc., 900
Gatekeepr Innovation, 1669
Gateway Casinos & Entertainment, 2073
Gateway EDI, 21
Gateway Healthcare, 1332
Gateway Rail Freight, 277
Gather, 1150
GatherUp, 92
Gatik, 996
GATR Technologies, 979
GATX Logistics, 1360
GAUDRE, 3049
Gauge Insights, 622
Gauntlet, 741
Gauss Surgical, 1489, 1556
Gautier, 2852
Gavel & Gown, 2094
GawkBox, 1158
Gaze, 2014
Gazelle, 1438, 1579, 1916
GazelleLab, 1784
Gazillion, 781
gazillion, 1425
Gazillion Entertainment, 1361, 2329
Gazzang, 202, 1682
GB Auto Service Inc., 862
GB Foods, 909
Gbits Network Technology, 2850
GBT, 1519
GC Aesthetics, 1251, 1382
GC Partners Interational Ltd., 2094
GC-Rise Pharmaceutical, 1382
GCA Service Solutions, 1275
GCA Services Group, 1114

GCAN Insurance Company, 2079
GCL, 2579
GCLOUD, 2646
GCM, 2987
GCM Grosvenor, 924
GCM Grosvenor LS Power Equity Partners II, 2094
GCMW, 2491
GCommerce, 54, 69
GCoreLab, 3073
GCR Holdings Ltd, 2792
GCR Inc., 900
Gcrypt, 2400
GCS, 909
GCT, 620, 1983
GD Interactive, 2667
GDG Environnement Groupe, 2029
GDGT, 1715
GDI, 2062
GDM Electronics, 3042
GDS, 3100
GE Current, 109
Gealean Holding GmbH, 2806
Gearworks, 536
Geary LSF, 958
GebIBET, 3048
Gecko, 2029
Gecko Biomedical, 3020
GeckoCap, 1615
GED Integrated Solutions, 104
Gee Holdings, 959
Geeklist, 2938
Gehl, 214
Geisinger Health System, 967
GEKA GmbH, 2311
Geka-brush GmbH, 2806
Gekko Systems Pty Limited, 2398
Gelato Fiasco, 1160, 1161
Gelson's Market, 1835
Geltor, 570
Gem, 120, 228, 272, 525, 741, 972, 1222, 1604, 1965
Gem Mobile Treatment Services, 1742
Gem Shopping Network, 1753
Gema Diagnostics, 1336
Gemandforce, 1405
Gemba, 2200
Gemba Solutions, 2967
Gemcap Lending I, 1970
Gemcom, 1041
Gemcor II, 1523
Gemfire, 1922
Geminare, 2058
Gemini Equipment & Rents, 250
Gemini Solar and Battery Storage Project, 1517
Gemini Therapeutics, 191
Geminus, 1809
Geminx, 1898
Gemmus Pharma, 298, 1784, 1988
Gemphire Therapeutics, 400, 703
Gemstone Biotherapeutics, 19
GemTek, 905
Gemvara, 386
gen-E, 958
Gen.Video, 608
Gen3 Marketing, 1093
Genagro, 2329
Genaissance Pharmaceuticals, 530, 3218
Genalta Power, 2091
Genalyte, 491, 1069, 1791
Genasys, 2342
Genbad, 826
GENBAND, 1361, 1658, 3137
Genband, 538, 1072, 1376, 1604, 1841, 1911
Genbook, 2989
GENCO Distribution System Inc., 862
Gencove, 1721, 2280

Portfolio Companies Index

Gendai Games, 1099
Gendel Ltd, 2704
Gene Grafts, 3059
Gene Logic, 1394
Geneart, 2713
Geneba Properties N.V., 2073
GeneCentric, 915
Genecis, 2128
Genedata, 1350
GenEdit, 1654
Geneoscopy, 622
Genepeeks, 946
GenePharm, 117
GenePreDiT, 3048
GeneQuine, 2824
Gener8tor, 566
Generac, 2033
Generac Power Systems, 433
General American, 1171
General Assembly, 262, 1001, 1183, 1524, 1551, 1912
General Atlantic, 3264
General Bandwidth, 1103
General Blood, 3279
General Catalyst, 37
General Catalyst Partners, 3273
General Compression, 1470, 1895
General Donlee, 2794
General Electric, 1295
General Finance Corp., 274
General Fusion, 262, 322, 2078, 2143, 2710
General Healthcare, 2605
General Healthcare Group, 2497
General Healthcare Group Limited, 135
General Moile, 3121
General Photonics, 729
General Products, 1230
General Sentiment, 393
General Tools & Instruments, 931
General Trailers, 1134
General Wireless, 162
GeneralRadar, 1075
Generate, 798
Generation Bio, 762
Generation Brands, 1505
Generation Capital Partners, 986
Generation Create, 2991
Generation Health, 1067
Generation5, 2196
GeneriCo, 267
Genesant Technologies Inc., 810
GeneSciences, 1051
Genesis, 1244
Genesis (Gen), 2664
Genesis Energy, 1082
Genesis Financial Solutions, 654, 673, 1388
Genesis Luxury, 1088
Genesis Media, 287
Genesis Networks, 1146, 1175
Genesis Offshore, 1745
Genesis Private Equity Fund, 2724
Genesis Worldwide Inc., 1085
GeneSpectrum, 1693
Genesys, 227, 924, 1785, 2379, 3033, 3208
Genesys Capital Management, 3258
Genetesis, 479
Genetic Finance, 2831
Genetic Therapy, 1394, 1558
Geneticure, 2000
GeneWeave, 2011
GeneWEAVE Inc., 491
Genewiz, 118
Genex, 1044
Genextropy, 1161
Gengo, 1004, 1054, 2446, 3044
Geni, 455
Geni Tech, 2969

Genia Photonics, 979
Geniachip, 1101
Genic, 3145
Genicon Inc., 438
Genie, 623
Genie Network Resource Management Inc, 2703
Geniee, 721, 2798
Genieo, 3059
Genies, 229, 525, 770, 858, 1110, 1183, 1530
Genius, 124, 600, 607, 721, 1110, 1699, 1839, 2012
Genius Genomatics, 1247
Genius Plaza, 1054
Genius Sports, 135
Genkey, 3051
Genmedica Therapeutics, 2433, 2553
Genoa, 197
Genoa Healthcare, 753, 2051
Genocea, 1731, 2978
Genocea Biosciences, 1460, 1691
GenoLogics, 1391
Genomar, 2754
Genomatica, 87, 609, 1906
Genome Compiler, 1323, 2943
Genome DX Biosciences, 222
Genome Medical, 809
Genome Profiling LLC, 6
GenomeDx, 1205
Genomenon, 1019
Genomera, 1097
Genomic Expression, 3277
Genomica, 153, 315
Genomics Collaborative, 747
Genomics Medicine Ireland, 889
Genomics PLC, 762
Genomind, 493
GenomOncology, 1047
Genopaver, 1812
GenoProt Ltd, 2924
Genoptix, 118, 468
Genova Diagnostics, 1111
Genovique Specialties, 170
Genoway, 2876
Genpact, 2771
Genpact Limited, 1360
GenPat77 Pharmacogenetics AG, 3190
GenPharm, 206
GenPrime, 85
GenPro, 1577
GenPro Profiling, 266
Gens, 2626
GenServe, 164
Genset S.A., 1394
Gensia Pharmaceuticals, 1706
GenSight, 1928
Genstar Capital, 3255
Gensyn Technologies, 642
Genta, 157, 1896
Gental Monster, 1088
Genticel, 2851
Gentis, 1412
Gentium, 1898
Gentle Monster, 973
Gentleware, 2673
Gentra Systems, 1113
Gentronix, 3244
GenturaDx, 237
Genturi, 4
Genuisly, 3125
Genus, 1896
Genvault, 560
GenVec, 652, 1558
Genvec, 153
Genvid, 2953
Genwi, 1013, 1513, 3001
GenXcomm, 1004
Genzion BioSciences, 2816

Geo Mcquesten, 1295
Geo-Solutions, 1521
Geocea Biosciences, 1151
GeoCom TMS, 2196
GeoComm, 850
Geodelic Systems, 502
Geodex Communications, 834
GeoDigital, 676, 2106, 2161
Geodigital, 817
Geoforce, 2080
GeoIQ, 979
GeoiQ, 457
Geologic Systems LTD., 361
Geologistics, 380
Geoloqi, 1463, 1945
Geomagic, 1899
Geomagical, 1084
Geomind, 2857
Geong, 2998
GeoOrbital, 1100
Geopacific Resources, 1548
GeoPage, 85
Geophysical, 2910
Geophysical Research Company, 1223
Geopii, 2948
Georg Jensen, 1017
Georgian Partners, 483, 3258
GeoScience International, 2967
Geosemble, 979
Geosim Systems, 2535
Geosite, 1269
Geositian AB, 2718
Geospago, 1885
Geospiza, 85
Geostellar, 1169
Geotek, 850, 3137
GeoTix, 195
GeoTrace, 541
Geotrace Technologies, 1361
GeoTrust, 422
GeoVector, 385
GeoVera, 750
GeoVera Holdings Inc., 787
GeoVera Insurance, 924, 1293
GeoVideo Networks, 1305
GeoVS, 2737
GeoVue, 1227
Geoworks, 238
GEPPERT, 2979
Gerard Darel, 3020
Gerber Scientific, 1910
Gerber Technology, 109
German Auto Labs, 2841, 3161
Germanos, 2784
Germguardian, 831
Geroline, 2045
Geron Corporation, 1394
Geronimo Alloys, 812
Gerresheimer, 1017, 3069
Gerson Lehrman Group, 260
Gesco Group of Companies, 290
Gespac, 2625
Gesplan, 2626
Gestalt, 1136
Gestigon, 2824
GestureTek, 620
Gesundheit Foods, 557
Get AS, 1506
Get Back, 909
Get Fresh Kit, 1615
Get Point, 1530
GET Power, 2460
Get Real Health, 2265
Get Satisfaction, 1010, 1054, 1359, 1700
Getable, 1489
Getafive, 1615
GetAgent, 3108

Portfolio Companies Index

Getaround, 15, 91, 322, 544, 1202, 1254, 1592, 1662, 1846
Getaway, 1088
GetBulb, 2674
Getech, 2892
Getemed AG Medizin- und Informationstechnik, 3190
GetFeedback, 1607
GetGlue, 1558
GetGOing, 585
GetGoing, 1118, 2886
Gethuman, 544
GetInsured.com, 260
Getinsured.com, 1416, 1853
GETiT, 2818
GetLenses.co.uk, 3018
Getmapping, 3107
Getmobile, 2604
Getninjas, 2976
GETPAID, 1886
GetRelevant, 1535
GetSocial, 3048
Getsurance, 2841
GetTaxi, 2886
GetThis, 1784
Getty Images, 924
Getwell Network, 1899
GetWellNetwork, 176, 633, 986, 1142, 1459, 1972
GetYourGuide, 235, 1082, 3055
Getyourguide, 1715
Gevaert Bandweverij, 2680
Gevity HR Inc., 1903
Gevo, 3222
GFarmalabs, 1135
GfK SE, 1082
Gfnmediber, 2824
GForce Group, 344
GFRC Cladding Systems, 828
Gfycat, 93
GGVS, 2493
GHD, 2851
GHN Online, 224
Gho Holding, 2748
GHO Ventures, 3274
Ghost, 1069
GHP Group, 2206
GHS Interactive, 1832
GI Dynamics, 621
Gi Dynamics, 59
GI Dynamics Inc., 572
GI Partners, 3264
GI Plastek, 828, 1727
GI Windows, 347
GI-Therapies, 2959
Giant, 1660
Giant Hemu, 3194
Giant Realm, 655
Giant Swarm, 318
Giant.AI, 1069
Gibbon, 3224
Gibbons Refractories, 2985
Gibraltar, 2134
Gibraltar Capital Holdings, 1622
Gibson Energy, 1573
Gicare Pharma, 2748
Gicram Groupe, 152
Gidsy, 2444, 3149
GIF, 2311
Gifi, 2415
Gifnote, 1344
Gift Boogle, 737
Gift Certificate Center, 536
Gift Talk, 1509
Giftango, 1383
Giftbit, 784
Giftcard Zen, 1150

GiftCertificates.com, 1226, 1633
Giftly, 231, 751, 1592
Giftspot, 85
Gifty, 3049
GIGA, 651
Giga Information Group, 1348
Giga Spaces, 793, 1004
Giga-Tronics, 1730
GigaComm, 1604
GigaDevice, 1340, 3235
GigaGen, 491
Gigamon, 935
GigaNet, 852
Gigante Central Wet-Mill, 55
GigaOM, 1860
Gigarant, 3042
Gigared, 1633
GigaSpaces, 2541
GigaTrust, 190, 1604
Gigi Hill, 1853
Gigit, 1749
Gigle Networks, 3047, 3104
GigOptix, 1314
Gigoptix, 69
Gigster, 124, 720, 1534
Gigwalk, 32, 197, 1327, 1700
Gigya, 58, 508, 560, 581, 623, 634, 741, 867, 1184
Gila, 1456
Gila Therapeutic, 347
Gilat Satellite Networks, 3212
Gilbarco Veeder-Root, 354
Gilchrist & Soames, 1767, 1871
Gild, 231, 835
Gilead Sciences Inc., 1202
Gill, 3244
Gill Mix Green, 1088
Gilt, 646
Gilt Groupe, 815, 1181, 1445, 1699, 1946
GILUPI, 2452
Gilupi, 2824
Gimahot, 2824
Gimbal, 51
Gimlet Media, 1149
Gimme, 189
Gimmie, 1965
Ginegar Plastic Products Ltd, 2745
Giner.io, 1581
Ginger, 679, 2831
Ginger.io, 1052, 1054, 1069, 1097, 1860
Ginkgo Bioworks, 4, 720, 970, 1172
GinkgoTree, 1736
Ginni Designs, 1784
Ginsenga, 3042
Ginsey Holdings, 828
Giosis, 1361
Giphy, 816, 823, 836, 889, 1001, 1110, 1121, 1694
Gipis, 2856
Giraffic, 3050
Giraud International, 2551
Girissima, 3048
Girlboss, 1121
Girls Labs, 1701
GirlSense, 1108
GIS, 959
Giska, 823
Gislaved Folic, 3008
Gist, 1946
GitHub, 124, 1654
Github, 1001
GitLab, 889, 1069
Giuseppe Zanotti, 1088
Give & Go, 2219
Give More Media, 526
GiveCampus, 1701
GiveForward, 731, 1615

GiveGab, 432, 704
GiveLegacy, 1848
Given Imaging, 3072
Givit, 183
Gixo, 552, 872
Gizmo, 1958
Gizmo Beverages, 378
Gizmo5, 592
Gizwits, 1509
GKC Projects, 584
GL Education, 1111
GL Education Group, 1017
Glacier Bay Technology, 488
Gladiator Entertainment, 650
Gladius Pharmaceuticals, 1731, 2180
Gladly, 872, 1035
Gladly Software, 823
Glam Media, 57, 581, 871, 925, 1235
Glam.com, 1952
Glambot, 229
Glambox, 2872
GlamLoop, 2838
Glamour Sales Holding, 1241
GLAMSQUAD, 1699
Glamsquad, 1110
Gland Pharma, 3211
Glanola, 1734
Glass America, 774
Glass Container Company (GCC), 3234
Glass2Energy, 3152
Glassbreakers, 7, 1054
Glassdoor, 248, 578, 581
Glassdoor.com, 634, 1760
Glasshouse, 392
GlassHouse Technologies, 1080, 1672
GlassMasters Autoglass, 2269
Glassnetic Inc., 1641
Glassock Company, 746
GlassPoint, 1579, 1604, 2078
Glasspoint Solar, 1355
Glassybaby, 262
Glauconix, 704
Glaukos, 782, 1010, 1212, 1251, 1382, 1928
Glaukos Corporation, 621
GlaxoSmithKline, 1452, 3259
Glazer-Kennedy Insider's Circle, 1684
Gleam, 3048
Glean.in, 2685
Gleason, 1931
Gleason Research Associates, 680
Glenaden Shirts Limited, 2392
Glenmark Pharmaceuticals, 2337
Glenrose Instruments, 300
Glenveigh Medical, 459
Glide, 1202
Glide Pharma, 3107
Glidepath Power Solutions, 1517
Glider, 1463
Glidian, 1701
Glidr, 1766
Gliknik, 19
Glimmerglass, 144, 1378
Glimpse, 883
Glint, 260, 1212, 1663
Gliph, 307
Glitzi, 50
GLM, 374
GLM Industries, 2033
GLMX, 1760
glo AB, 1906
Global Active, 2717
Global Advanced Metals, 1548
Global Analytics, 563, 1102, 1502
Global Armour, 2392
Global Asset Alternatives, 1114
Global Atlantic Financial Group, 1443
Global Benefits Group Inc., 274

1327

Portfolio Companies Index

Global Bioenergies, 3113
Global Blood Therapeutics, 762, 1811
Global Blue, 1683, 2329
Global Brass and Copper Inc., 1085
Global Cash Access, 1728
Global Closure Systems, 3026
Global Collect, 3051
Global Communication Semiconductors, 2703
Global Communications, 729
Global Connection, 1234
Global Consumer Products, 1241
Global Custom Commerce, 1255
Global Eagle, 2252
Global Easy Water Products, 55
Global Education Learning Holdings, 1828
Global Employment Solutions, 1086, 1491
Global european Pharma, 1349
Global Exchange Services, 1558
Global Financial, 1147
Global Financial Technology, 1906
Global Forest Products, 834
Global Franchise Group, 1111, 2254
Global Garden Products, 2852, 3009
Global Geophysical Services, 1062
Global Graphics, 123
Global Group, 2979
Global Healthcare Exchange, 1814
Global ID Group, 1014, 1113
Global Indemnity Limited, 778
Global Integrity, 1374
Global Jet Capital, 66
Global Kinetics, 2536, 2959
Global Knowledge, 1166, 1231
Global Knowledge Network, 1972
Global Link Logistics, 1372
Global MailExpress, 57
Global Market Group, 3062
Global Market Insie, 1945
Global Material Exchange, 445
Global Media Online, 2826
Global Mediacom, 3061
Global Medical Isotope Systems, 1532
Global Medical Response, 1082
Global Mixed-Mode Technology, 2603, 3218
Global Name Registry, 2754, 3013
Global Navigation Solutions, 3036
Global Orthopaedic Technologies, 1572
Global Peersafe, 1121
Global Power Systems, 985
Global Radio, 526
Global Restoration Holdings, 330, 331
Global Savings Group, 641
Global Scanner, 823
Global Scanning, 3054
Global Signal, 767
Global Solutions, 2695
Global Sugar Art, 81
Global Sun Technology, 1769
Global Supply Chain Finance, 250
Global Talent Track, 483
Global Tel Link, 1925
Global Tel*Link, 110
Global Telecom & Technology, 263
Global Traffic Network, 884
Global Transport Services, 3061
Global Tranz, 1759
Global Tubing, 2040
Global Value Commerce, 1606, 1710
Global Vantedge, 2599, 2600
Global Voices, 1374
Global Wireless Unified Messaging, 865
Global Woods, 834
Global-e, 135
Global360, 1041
Globalblood Therapeutics, 74
GlobalCast, 1305
GlobalCollect, 1972

GlobaliD, 148
Globalive, 3258
GlobaliveXMG, 2134
GlobalMedic, 2263
GlobalOptions, 225
GlobalOutlook, 1285
GlobalServe, 954
Globalserve, 2196
GlobalSight, 2652
GlobalSIM, 2382
GlobalSim, 1677
GlobalSoft, 1676
GlobalSpec, 2698
Globalspec, 2697
GlobalTranz, 1496, 1942
GlobalView, 434
GlobalWide Media, 673
Globant, 793
Globe, 2680
Globe Sherpa, 1463
Globe Wirelss, 1752
Globecomm Systems, 1960
GlobeImmune, 57, 1122, 1124, 2008
Globeleq, 2337
GlobeOp, 2965
GlobeSherpa, 1383
Globesherpa, 85
Globespan Capital Partners, 3284
Globetouch, 1926
Globevestor, 307
Globoforce, 2478
Globus Medical, 495
Globys, 378, 1852
Glooko, 1611, 1696, 2132
gloProfessional, 1767
Glori Energy, 61, 1394
Glory, 3100
Glosil, 3002
Glossi, 132
Glossier, 761, 1001, 1110
GlossyBox, 2829, 2838
Gloucester Pharmaceuticals, 1493, 1558
Glow, 124, 3056
Glow and Affirm, 1631
Glow Concept, 823
Glow Digital Media, 2464
GlowForge, 776
Glowing.io, 1138
Glowpoint, 695
GLS Companies, 1970
Glu, 1626
Glu Mobile, 823, 1445
GlucosAlarm, 995
GlucoVista, 724, 1730
Glue Networks, 129, 1600, 1669
Gluecode Software, 1407
Gluetech, 1507
Glunt Industries, 1209
Gluster, 3001
Glutinatus, 3154
GLWL Research, 3196
Glycart, 2748
Glycart AG, 2785
GlyciFi, 308
GlycoFi, 312
Glycomed, 1896
GlycoMimetics, 1500, 1618
Glycominds Ltd, 2973
GlycoProx, 307
Glyde, 455, 1592
Glympse, 974, 1285, 1474, 1926, 2010
Glynlyon, 1132
Glynn Capital Management, 3284
GlySens, 1993
Glysure, 2978
Glythera, 2892
GM Ventures, 3269

GMC Television Broadcasting, 1189
GME, 2824
GMedia, 1121
GMI, 793
GMIS, 260
GMZ Energy, 1241
GNAP, 789
+ GNEO, 307
GNI, 2970
Gninx, 3088
Gnip, 741
Gnosis Analytics, 3073
GNS Healthcare, 320
Go, 1069
GO Albert Group, 2855
Go Daddy, 1082, 1785
Go Electric, 658
Go Fish, 304
Go Global Travel, 135
GO Outdoors, 2311, 3244
Go Plant, 2796
Go React, 745
Go Software, 1148
Go To Logistics, 917
Go Toast, 685
GO-JEK, 2278
Go-Jek, 1082
Go-Now, 418
Go2mo, 2308
GoAhead Software, 1945
Goal Zero, 1204, 1705
Goal.com, 260, 3097
Goalbook, 1316, 3277
GOAT, 1181
Goat, 741, 1888
GoBalto, 2690
goBalto, 1241, 1509, 2513
Gobble, 124, 720, 721, 1254
Gobbler, 1592
Gobee.Bike, 874
Gobi Partners, 483
Gobiquity Mobile Health, 1010
GoButler, 15
Goby, 325, 544, 1065, 1110, 1530, 1585, 2142
GoCardless, 28, 2329, 2478, 3030
GoCatch, 3160
GoChime, 685
GoCo, 1607
GoCoin, 1681
GoDaddy, 1683
Goddess Garden, 2238
GoDigital Networks, 536
GoDundMe, 1212
Goednavond, 3042
GoEuro, 235, 842, 1075, 2446, 2813, 2928
GoFar, 3153
Goffin NV, 2806
Goformz, 751
GoForward Inc., 1666
GoFundMe, 872
Gogo, 1340
Gogo Bot, 1323
GoGoGab, 1749
Gogotech, 378
GoGrab, 218
GoHealth, 1345
Going Green, 1061
GoingOn Networks Inc., 371, 2427
GoInstant, 231, 305
Gojee, 1010, 1054
Gokaldas Exports Limited, 277
Golazo, 2401
Gold Bank Communications, 2924
Gold Health Cre, 2136
Gold Lasso, 1169
Gold Medal Services, 1021
Gold Road Resources, 1548

Portfolio Companies Index

Gold Standard Baking, 1166, 2214
Gold Star Foods, 423, 869
Gold's Gym, 462
Goldbach Media, 2783
Goldbely, 1004
Goldbook, 2924
Goldco, 1457
Golden Corral, 354
Golden Data, 1082
Golden Eye, 2936
Golden Gate, 37
Golden Gate Capital, 1760
Golden Harvest, 584
Golden Health Care, 2269, 2285
Golden Key, 1323
Golden Seeds, 3267
Golden State Overnight, 894
Golden State Towers, 1927
Golden State Vintners, 765
Golden Telecom, 2491
Golden Tulip, 2796
Golden Ventures, 3258
Golder Investment Management LLC, 3265
Goldhat Advisors, 3259
Golding Farms Foods Inc., 447
Goldleaf Financial Solutions, 1123
Goldman Sachs, 3255
Goldner Hawn, 1295
GoldStar, 1244
Goldwind, 1906
Golf In Corporation, 1404
GolferPass, 3062
GolfNet, 650
GolfNow, 264
Golfnow, 856
Golfzon, 3145
Goli, 3211
Goliath Solutions, 1954
Golinks, 795
Golnstant, 784
Golsun, 3194
GOME Electrical Appliances, 220
Gomez, 925, 2343, 2671
Gomez Inc., 23
Gone App, 3125
Gonet, 2775
GoNet Systems, 2974
GoNetworks, 249
Gong, 483
Gong.io, 1346
GoNoodle, 475
GoNoodle Inc., 810
Gonzo, 892
Good, 184, 206, 563, 1183, 1235, 1626, 1865
Good Boy Studies, 1507
Good Buy Gear, 1555, 2236
Good Company, 1507
Good Data, 710, 1004, 1359
Good Deal, 2553
Good Dog, 318
Good Eggs, 231, 248, 544, 1054, 1258, 1363, 1654, 1977
Good Harbour Laboratories, 2197
Good Health Advertising, 1306
Good Health Natural Foods, 1605
Good Health Natural Products, 1234
Good Morning Securities, 892
Good Morning Shinhan Securities, 1139, 2946
Good Natured, 2291
Good News Ventures, 3258
Good Readers, 1323
Good Shepherd Entertainment, 545
Good Start Genetics, 1382
Good Stock, 325
Good Technology, 278, 502, 609, 1255, 1361, 1540, 1623
Good Uncle, 741, 1110, 1480

Good Way Rubber Industries, 2623
Good Way Technologies, 1004
Good.co, 1716
Goodbaby, 3100
Goodbeans, 2829, 2838
Goodbelly, 668
Goodcover, 318
GoodData, 89, 124, 816, 1319, 1796, 1991
Goodeed, 1006
Goodfair, 120
GoodGuide, 1438
Goodlife, 3038
GoodLife Fitness, 2183, 2219
Goodlux Technology, 1160
Goodman, 924
Goodmans, 1970
Goodpack, 1082
Goodpatch, 1607
Goodpath, 1768
Goodr, 896
Goodreads, 1798
GoodRx, 779, 1717, 1888
Goodship, 1481
Goodsie, 1322
Goodtime, 883
Goodview International, 2850
GoodWest Industries Inc., 1403
Goodwill Group, 2826
Goodworld, 384
Goodybag, 445
Goody's, 2784
Google, 1654, 1865
Goom Radio, 1416, 2693
Goop, 1121
Gooten, 724
Gopago, 1655
Gopher Resource, 675
GoPresent, 450
GoPro, 1896, 3142
GoPuff, 91, 641
GordianTec, 3248
Gordmans, 1753
Gordon Murray Design, 1247
Gortz & Schiele, 2375
GoSecure, 1794
Goshi, 1615
Gospel, 1607
GoSpotCheck, 685, 1000
GoSquared, 2586, 3030
GossamerBio, 709
GoTenna, 351, 1882
goTenna, 1306, 1310
GotGame, 2184
Gotha Cosmetics, 909
Gotham Therapeutics, 1731, 1928
Gotive, 3122
Goto Software, 2302
GoToCall.com, 536
GoToMeeting, 305, 641
GoToMyPC, 592
GoTRIBE, 1507
Gotuit Media, 2445
GouKW, 1509
Gould & Lamb, 21
Gourmet Culinary Partners, 193
Gourmet Foods, 193
Gourmet Kitchen, 193
Gourmet Settings, 2043
Gousto, 2972
Govini, 1607
GoWorkaBit, 3108
GoWrench, 2138
Goyoo, 641
Goyoo Networks, 2869
GPA, 1765
GPA Acquisition Company, 1343
GPC Biotech, 1775

GPE II LP., 2926
Gpredictive, 3161
GPRS, 1166
GPS Insight, 333
GPS Trackit, 1014
GPSI Holdings, 717
GQ Life Sciences, 52
GR Energy Services Holdings, 1443
Gr8 People, 178
Grab, 11, 823, 1121, 1662
Grab Media, 1146, 1699
Grab Networks, 1633
Grabango, 24, 519, 1563
Grabb-It, 1138
GrabCAD, 1789
GrabCad, 455, 1181
GrabGreen, 69
Grabr, 1323, 1675
Grace, 2772
Grace Hill, 1572
Grace THW Holdings, 892
Gracel, 2839
Gracenote, 260, 1994
Gracious Eloise, 841
Graco Supply & Integrated Services, 984
Gracon, 542
GracoRoberts, 507
Gradall, 1141
Grade Us, 92
GradeCheck, 742
Gradescope, 784, 883, 1050, 1527
GradeSlam, 272, 1527
Gradient, 87, 306, 624, 755
Gradient X, 228
GradLeaders, 364
GradSave, 971
Graduation Alliance, 202, 1299, 1677
Graduway, 1323
Graematter, 267
Graffiti Labs, 2010
Graham Waste, 17
GRAIL, 268, 1145
Grail, 262, 762, 889, 1481
Grain Bulk Handlers, 2337
Grain Communications Group, 1760
Grakon, 985
Grakon International Inc., 862
Gram, 392
Gram Equipment, 3054
Grameen America, 1420
Grameen Intel Social Business, 1004
Grameen Koota, 2313
Grameenphone, 2337
Gramercy Beverage, 3257
Gramex 2000, 584
Grammarly, 816, 1001, 1675
GrammaTech, 746
GrammaTech Inc., 403
Granada Learning Group, 1927
Grand Angels, 3269
Grand Cathay Securities, 2436
Grand Chip Microelectronics, 1004
Grand Circus, 607
Grand Cru, 1327, 2851
Grand Equipment, 276
Grand Frais, 2851
Grand Junction, 238, 1760
Grand Junction Networks, 197
Grand Peaks, 34
Grand Power Systems, 276
Grand Prairie Foods, 1192
Grand River Aseptic Manufacturing, 166
Grand Rounds, 872, 1916
Grand st., 1222
Grand-Hotel du Cap-Ferrat, 34
GrandCentrix, 2824
Grande, 441

Portfolio Companies Index

Grande Cashe Coal, 2067
Grande Communications, 21, 202
Grandes Distilleries de Charleroi, 3134
Grandis, 144
Grandoil, 1340
Grandpoint, 368, 1231
Grandpoint Capital, 1743
Grands Vins De Girande, 2302
Grandsys Technologies & Service, 3062
Grandview Gallery, 478
Granicor, 2029
Granicus, 1041
Granify, 1897, 2113, 2170
Granite & Marble Holdings Inc., 984
Granite City Food & Brewery, 477, 1192
Granite City Tool Company Inc., 908
Granite Growth Health Partners, 3264
Granite Seed Company, 1168
Granny's Kitchen Ltd., 465
GranQuartz, 984
GranQuartz Holdings LLC, 908
Grant Peaking Power, 156
Grant Thornton, 3274, 3279
Grant Thornton LLP, 3259, 3262
Grant Victor, 673
Grantium, 2058
Granula, 2873
Granular, 124, 720
GrapeviceLogic.com, 313
Grapevine, 1172
Graph Effect, 791
GraphAlchemist, 1463
Graphcore, 603, 770, 1654, 2446, 2674
Graphene Technologies, 1061
Graphenix Development, 704
Graphic Controls, 1751, 1979
Graphic.ly, 650
GraphicIQ, 1480
Graphics Arts Equipment, 2985
GraphIQ, 1075
Graphite Software, 2076, 2128
GraphPad Software, 1000
GraphScience, 1524
GraphSQL, 1254
Graphus, 285
Graphwear, 1238
Grass Valley, 779
Grass-Pass, 392
Grassi & Co., 3267
Grassroots, 99
Grassroots Greenhouse, 99
Grassroots Herbology, 99
Grassroots Unwired, 358, 1577
Grassroots Vermont, 966
GrassWire, 79
Gravie, 20, 341, 743, 809, 1725
Gravitant, 545, 1597
Graviton, 1668, 2682
Gravitude AS, 3141
Gravity, 197, 307, 1087, 1534, 1888, 2833
Gravity Oilfield Services Inc., 500
Gravy Analytics, 1728
Gravyty, 226, 1100
Gray Bug, 1169
Gray Energy Services, 447
Gray Line of Tennessee, 1529
Gray Peak Technologies, 1728
Gray Wolf Industrial, 456
GrayBug, 19
Graybug, 915
Grayhawk Capital LLC, 3276
Graylog, 641, 1206
GrayMatter LLC, 899
Graze, 2662, 2674
Graze.com, 3018
Great Ajax, 750
Great Call, 551

Great Clips, 1557
Great Expressions Dental Centers, 194, 1576
Great Gate Network, 1361
Great HealthWorks, 1430
Great Jones, 563
Great Lakes Angels, 3269
Great Lakes Carbon, 109
Great Lakes Caring Home Health & Hospice, 1971
Great Lakes Dredge & Dock Corporation, 1156
Great Lakes Health Plan, 1251
Great Lakes Pharmaceuticals, 420, 458, 642, 943, 1047, 1553, 1921
Great Northwest Insurance Co., 492
Great Oakland Public Schools Leadership Center, 1316
Great Point Energy, 59
Great Point Power, 156
Great Point Ventures, 59
Great Wall, 2850
Great Western Holdings, 2883
Great Western Leasing & Sale, 164
Great Wolf Lodge, 442
GreatAmerica, 1409
GreatCall, 1741
Greatcall, 455
GreatHorn, 2, 724
Greatist, 751
GreatPoint Energy, 925, 1474
Greats, 1475
GreatSchools, 1316
Greatville Limited, 3062
Greatwide Logistics, 722
Grede Casting, 1967
Greek and Roman mythology, 2857
Greeley Company, 897
Green & Tonic, 668
Green Bancorp, 1443
Green Bancorp Inc., 914
Green Bank, 787
Green Bio, 1340
Green Biologics, 2295, 2978
Green Bits, 417
Green Box, 596
Green Bureau, 2308
Green Chemicals, 2892
Green Compass, 364
Green Creative, 1209
Green Creative LLC, 908
Green Cross Biotech, 2857
Green Diamond Sand Products, 17
Green Distribution, 1430
Green Dot, 986, 1235, 1654, 1796, 1863, 1864
Green Earth Fuels, 1573
Green Energy Biofuels, 55
Green Fig, 1985
Green Flower, 99, 1439, 1807
Green Flower Media, 1135
Green For Life, 916
Green Highland, 3104
Green Light Auto Solutions, 462
Green Matters, 1110
Green Motion, 2574
Green Mountain Technology, 29
Green Organic Dutchman, 390
Green Pacific Biologicals, 2455
Green Patch, 1853
Green Peak, 2674
Green Power Labs, 2155
Green SQL, 3081
Green Tank Technologies, 417, 2140
Green Thumb Industries, 390, 557, 1135
Green Tree, 442
Green Wave Systems, 2690
Green Wizard, 398
Green Zebra Grocery, 1383
Green-eye Technology, 2212

Greenberg Traurig, 3262
GreenBone Ortho, 2874
Greenbureau, 3020
GreenCore, 2061
Greencore Group Plc, 77
Greenergetic, 2686
Greenergy, 834
Greenfiber Tech, 3048
GreenField Ethanol, 2094
Greenfield Global, 2062
Greenfield Midstream, 671
Greenfield Networks, 833
Greenfly, 1813
Greengate, 1324
GreenGoose, 1254, 2017
Greenhouse, 1306, 1546, 1696
Greenhouse Juice, 2071
Greenhouse.io, 720
Greenko, 834
Greenko Group Plc, 2372
GreenLancer, 1736
Greenleaf Biofuels, 61, 678
Greenleaf Book Group, 17
Greenlight, 2236
GreenLight Biosciences, 1080
Greenlight Guideline, 1613
Greenlight Technologies, 1747
Greenling, 114, 445, 950
Greenlots, 3151
Greenman Gaming, 2691
GreenMan Technologies, 1730
GreenMantra, 2041, 2187
GreenMantra Technologies, 2061
Greenmantra Technologies, 2093
Greenmountain, 1855
GreenPeak, 2366
GreenPeak Technologies, 2662
GreenPeptide, 2970
Greenphire, 743
Greenplum, 305, 592, 652, 954, 1212, 1239
GreenPrint, 189, 459
GreenQ, 1894
GreenRoad, 912, 3222
GreenScreens, 392
Greensfelder, 3271
Greensight Agronomics, 1630
GreenSky, 1502
Greenslate, 1927
GreenSoil Building Innovation Fund, 3258
GreenSQL, 2952
Greenstar Plant Products, 2258
GreenTec Bio-Pharmaceuticals, 2100
Greentech Innovation, 2504
GreenThrottle, 1853
Greenvironment Oy, 2873
GreenVolts, 2315
GreenWatt, 3225
GreenWave Systems, 1977
Greenway, 1409
Greenway Grameen, 55
GreenWorld Restoration, 445
Greenzie, 189
Greetz, 3051
Greg C. Rigamer & Associates, 465
Gregg Drilling & Testing, 2059
Gregor Diagnostics, 741
Gremlin, 1688
Gremlin Social, 569
Gremln, 1784
Grenadier Energy Partners II, 672
Grenslandhallen, 3042
Greo, 622, 751
GReply, 623
Gretech, 3127
Gretel, 3262
Greybug Vision, 495
Greycells18, 2558

Portfolio Companies Index

Greyline Instruments Inc., 908
Greylock Partners, 3276
Greylock XII Limted, 623
Greystripe, 1249
Greyter Water Systems, 2061
GreyWall Software, 678
GreyWater, 3001
Grid, 1254
Grid Dynamics, 249, 3229
Grid Expert, 2354
Grid Net, 483, 809
Gridants Inc., 623
GridApp Systems Inc., 810
GRIDbot, 445
Gridco Systems, 1334, 1579
gridComm, 2778
GridGain, 89, 1594
GridIron, 1853
Gridium, 1282
GridNet, 428
Gridnet, 322
GridNt, 2667
GridPlex, 1584
GridPlex Networks, 1306
GridPoint, 61
Gridpoint, 3097
Gridraster, 1885
Gridsmart Technologies, 1214
Gridspace, 792
Gridstone Research, 3041
Gridstore, 1378
Gridsum, 1327, 3142
Gridtential, 1580
Gridtest, 3277
Gries Deco, 2299, 2301, 2305
Grilstad, 3076
Grin, 795, 1663
Grin Scooters, 1138
Grind Networks, 1699
Griplock Systems, 374, 1609
Gristone, 495
Griswold, 1466
Griswold Home Care, 378
Griti, 1004
Gritston Oncology, 1928
Gritstone Oncology, 20, 237, 517, 782, 889
Gro, 282
GRO Biosciences, 996
Gro-Well Brands, 407, 834
Grocer, 3108
Grocery Outlet, 1491
Grocery Outlet Bargain Market, 924
Grocery Shopping Network, 1906
Grockit, 1003, 1316
Grohe, 1835
Grohmann GmbH Prum, 3067
Grokker, 180, 518, 544, 741, 1069
Grokr, 1896
GroLens, 30
Groome, 164
Groome Transportation, 546
Groove Biopharma, 153, 2008
Groove Mobile, 649, 1080, 3137
Groq, 1696
GroSocial, 1070
groSolar, 1689
Grosvenor Capital Management, 3269
Grouby, 2109
Ground Truth, 1001, 1154
GroundBase, 934
Groundhog Technologies, 892
GroundLink, 528
GroundMetrics, 1784
GroundWork, 1184, 1620
Groundwork, 386
Group Commerce, 2566
Group Dekko, 1456

Group Dekko Holdings Inc., 447
Group Intelligentia Oy, 2873
Group K Diagnostics, 266
Group Nine, 1110
Group Trade, 2769
Group Transportation Services, 917
Group Uriach, 77
Group14, 2008
Group360 Inc., 985
Group360 Worldwide, 61
GroupAero, 1422
Groupalia, 2553, 2987
Grouparoo, 679
Groupe Bertrand, 2851
Groupe Bio7, 2851
Groupe BPS, 3020
Groupe Caillé, 2945
Groupe Conseil, 2029
Groupe Cyrus, 2521
Groupe d'Emballages Souples, 2722
Groupe De Presse Michel Hommell, 2601
Groupe Doucet, 2317
Groupe Emera SA, 2653
Groupe Eurilogic, 2625
Groupe Eyssautier, 3020
Groupe Hermés-Métal Yudigar, 3020
Groupe IP, 3239
Groupe J.L. Leclerc, 2029
Groupe Lucien Barriere, 2079
Groupe Moreau, 2009
Groupe Proclif, 2676
Groupe Rougnon, 2340
Groupe Segex, 2851
Groupe Soloc, 2985
Groupe SQLI, 2875
Groupe Unafinance, 3020
Groupement JV, 2365
Grouper, 634
Groupie, 2113
Groupize, 841, 1806
Grouply, 32, 1359
Groupmatics, 1047
GroupMe, 741, 1821
Groupon, 124, 641, 1183, 2663
Groupon Japan, 2869
GroupRaise, 1054
GroupSense, 285
Groupsense.io, 1019
Groupsite, 1965
Groupsite.com, 1169
Groupsize, 1100
Groupspaces, 2464
Grove, 720, 741, 1149, 1184, 1888
Grove Collaborative, 358, 942, 1346
Grove Labs, 622, 1589
Grover, 1611
Grovo, 52, 547, 1110, 1531, 1700
Grow, 1070
Grow Generation, 845, 1207
Grow Healthy, 557
Grow Journey, 1923
Grow Now, 155
Grow Progress, 934
GrowBLOX Science, 1135
Growcentia, 1135, 1807
Grower's Secret, 3277
Growers Holdings, 995
GrowGeneration, 1283
GrowHealthy, 966
GrowLab Ventures, 2053
Grownetics, 392, 1439, 1843
GrowSumo, 2125
Growth Networks, 1121
Growth Ventures Group, 344
GrowX, 229
GrubHub, 114, 581, 1108, 1121, 1384, 1748
Grubhub, 248, 1717

GrubHub Seamless, 1956
GrubHub.com, 634
GrubMarket, 799, 823, 858, 2128
Grubwithus, 1968, 2649
Grun Style, 364
Grunspar, 2979
Grupo Abaco Menorquin Yachts, 2962
Grupo ARG, 2382
Grupo Corporativo Ono, 1506
Grupo Cortefiel, 3026
Grupo Phoenix, 1376
Grupo Sala, 46
Grupo Salvador Caetano, 3048
Grupo Terratest, 2851
Grupo TorreSur, 1496
Grupo Visabeira, 3048
Grupos, 2626
Gryphon Networks, 1770
GRYT, 704
GSE Environmental, 1134
GSEI, 2379
GSI, 398, 442
GSI Group Inc., 77
GSI Health, 1568
GSM, 3127
GSMA Mobile for Development Intelligence, 1374
GSMA Mobile Money for the Unbanked, 1374
GSO, 1991
GST Holdings Ltd, 2297
GT Advanced Technologies, 126
GT Nexus, 796, 1956, 2079, 2698
Gt Nexus, 2697
GTar, 721
GTCR, 3255
GTCR LLC, 3265
Gten, 3233
GTESS Corporation, 1080
GTI, 2206
GTI Capital, 1241
GTI Capital Group, 1830
GTI Medivenures, 1830
GTK UK, 3244
GTP Operations, 1491
GTS, 260, 1153
GTS CE Holdings, 1361
GTT, 924, 2674, 2818
GTx, 74, 1187
GTX Messaging, 3207
GTxcel, 1303
Gu Sheng Tang, 710
Guadalupe Power, 1967
Guangdong Fendhua High-Tech, 2850
Guangdong Hongtu Technology, 2802
Guangdong Ronsen Super Micro-wire, 2802
Guangdong Yashii Group, 2542
Guardant Health, 942, 1069, 1121, 1654
Guardent, 954
Guardhat, 607
Guardian, 55, 787
Guardian Analitics, 770
Guardian Analytics, 547, 1725, 1760, 1846
Guardian Capital Partners, 14
Guardian Compliance, 353
Guardian Pharmacy, 409
Guardian Technologies, 831
GuardianEdge, 411
GuardiCore, 235, 483, 603
Guardium, 436, 3212
Guardium Inc., 2580
Guardly, 2113
GuardTime, 2870
Guardtime, 2390, 2831
Guava Technologies, 925, 1002
GuavaPass, 1701
Guavus, 1515, 1838
Gucci, 1017

1331

Portfolio Companies Index

GUD, 1888
Guerilla RF, 1442
Guesser, 2280
Guestcentric Systems, 3048
Guesty, 2952
Guide, 1099
Guidebook, 1226
Guided Delivery Systems, 177
Guided Interventions, 1047
Guidehouse, 1925
Guideline, 708, 720, 1110
Guideline Research, 1295
Guidelines, 1826
Guidemark Health, 931
Guidepath Medical, 445
GuideSpark, 1212, 1563, 1747
Guidespromos.Com, 2669
Guidewire, 1896
Guidewire Software, 238
Guild, 552, 720, 1534, 1551, 1607, 1921
Guild Mortage Company, 1276
Guilded, 1758
Guildery, 552
Guillaume-Teco, 2680
Guitar Center, 220
Guldfynd Holding, 2863
Gulf American Land Corporation, 1404
Gulf Coast Coca-Cola Bottling Company, 1621
Gulf Coast Energy Resources, 1956
Gulf Coast LNG, 893
Gulf Coast Machine and Supply, 1491
Gulf Coast Shipyard Group, 1134
Gulf Cryo, 1017
Gulfstream, 1045
Gulfstream Services, 1745
Gulu Agricultural Development Company, 55
GumGum, 561, 741, 1255
Gumgum, 1099, 1888
Gummicube, 841
Gump's, 1952
Gumroad, 741
Gun, 307
Gunderson Dettmer, 3272
Guns & Oil Brewing, 445
Gunslinger Studios, 1813
Gunther International, 1188
GupShup, 1796, 2818
Gupshup, 455
Gupta Daniel, 392
Guru, 197, 743, 1607
GuruNet Corp., 807
Gushan Environmental, 1087
Gushcloud, 1965
Gusion, 2892
Gust, 1310, 1584
Gusto, 49, 107, 180, 560, 578, 665, 792, 816, 889, 942, 1075, 1607, 1631, 1666, 1694, 1761, 2012
GutCheck, 876, 1522
Gute TV Laune, 2829, 2838
Guvenrehberi, 2437
Guy & O'Neill Inc., 447
GV Meditech, 2313
GVA, 2944
GVK Power, 2434
GVO, 2979
GW Anglin Manufacturing, 2051
GW Pharmaceuticals, 390, 1135
gWallet, 57
GWC, 1509
Gweepi Medical, 1615
Gwynnie Bee, 378, 623, 946, 1766
Gwynnie Bee., 431
GxG Management LLC, 3267
GXS, 779
Gxs, 839
Gyant, 3108

Gyeonggi Expressway, 584
Gyft, 1055, 1581
Gymboree, 2252
Gymboree China, 220
Gymboree Corporation, 220
Gympact, 1546
Gympass, 641
Gymtrack, 1982
Gynesonics, 59, 544, 925, 1010, 2316
GynoPharma, 1558
Gyrodata, 732
Gyros, 2890
Gyros Protein, 118
Gyroscope, 785

H
H&E Equipment Services Inc., 354
H&S, 653
H-D Manufacturing, 1572
H-E Parts International, 789
H-Log, 3239
H.C. Berger Brewing Company, 1837
H.C. Carbon, 2824
H.J. Meyers & Co., 1837
H.M. Dunn AeroSystems Inc., 873
H2Gen Innovations, 376, 520
H2HCare, 2918
H2O Audio, 1784
H2Oil Energy, 559
H2Scan, 1784
H2X, 1745
H3 Sportgear, 1234
H4-Global, 2967
H5, 1001, 1952
H5 Technologies, 2457
Haansoft, 3168
Haarslev Industries, 2384
HAAS Alert, 1286
Haas Alert, 1894
Haas School of Business, 214
Haawk, 306
Habana, 1004
Habana Labs, 235, 260
Haband, 839
Habit Analytics, 795
Habitation Mgr Deschenes, 2029
HabitAware, 218
Habiteo, 2439
Habito, 2446
Habx, 2851
Hachi, 1912
Hacker Automation, 2527
HackerOne, 248
HackHands, 994
Hackworks, 2113
Hadapt, 530, 678, 1097
Haemair, 2737
Haematologic Technologies, 653
Haemonetics Corp., 300
Haemostatix, 3070
Haggen, 528
Hahl, 2795
HAHT Commerce, 1709, 2079
Haht Commerce, 69
Haihong Hydraulic Science, 2542
Haikou Qili Pharmaceutical, 2802
Haiku Deck, 1852
Hail, 2446
Hailify, 684
Hailo, 28, 1531, 2752, 2978
Hainan Airline, 892
Hainan Hailing Chemipharma Corporation, 1241
Hairun, 3100
Haitai Confectionery and Foods, 2643
Haitou, 994
Haitunjia, 823
Haiyuan Group, 3194

HAL Trust, 1494
Halathion, 1340
Halation Photonics, 144, 1241
HalCash North America, 179
Halcon Resouces, 672
Halcyon Loan Advisors, 1491
Hale and Hearty Soups, 405
Hale Hamilton, 2923
HALE.Life, 6
Halex, 2851
Halfpenny Technologies, 52, 1387, 1568, 1940
Halfpops, 1665
HalfWave, 2700
Halifax Biomedical, 2205
Halin, 2378
Halite Energy Group, 588
Hall Research, 276
Hallcon, 2206
Hallcrest, 1435
Halliburton Co., 1903
Halo, 2539
Halo Branded Solutions, 523
Halo Business Intelligence, 1869
Halo Filters, 391
Halo Innovations, 1113
Halo Labs, 155, 266
Halo Neuro, 708
Halo Neuroscience, 567, 1151, 1700
Halogen Software, 1041
Halozyme, 1812
Halozyme Therapeutics, 514
Halp, 2245
HalSource, 1438
Halston, 937
Halter, 1877
Hamer LLC, 903
Hamilton Captive Management, 330, 331
Hamilton Insurance Group Ltd., 404
Hamilton Lane, 3258
Hamilton Robinson Captial Partners, 14
Hamilton State Bancshares, 1777
Hamilton State Bank, 127
Hammer & Chisel, 1827
Hammerhead Navigation, 1056
Hammerstone Corp., 2067
Hampton Creek, 2831
Hamster, 1755
Hamstersoft, 2938
Han net, 2969
HANA Micron, 892
Hanaro Telecom, 3168
Hancock's Wholesale Supply, 908
Hancor Inc., 354
Hand & Stone, 1111
Hand In Gag, 2531
Hand-In-Hand Home Health Care, 406
Handel Information Technologies Inc., 36
Handel's Ice Cream, 501
Handi Quilter, 903, 1884
Handle, 1183
Handle Financial, 751, 1054
Handmade, 2671, 2987
Handmark, 162, 308
Handminder, 995, 1187
HANDS HQ, 2685
HandShake, 1226
Handshake, 305, 665, 883, 1075, 1121, 1149, 1475, 1527, 1700, 3044
Handshake VR, 2273
Handsman Co., 2907
HandStands, 1857
Handwriting.io, 896
Handy Expert Home Services, 935
HandyLab, 652
Hanegal, 3203
Hangar Technology, 1151
Hangry, 2184

Portfolio Companies Index

Hangtime, 1010, 1968
Hank's Maintenance, 2163
Hanley Wood, 21
Hanley Wood/Meyers Research, 1231
Hanley-Wood, 897, 1927
Hanleywood, 1134
Hanna Anderson, 1753
Hanna Andersson, 1088
Hannetware, 2857
Hannon Hill, 189
Hans Anders, 2379
Hans bio med., 2969
Hanseatische Verlags-Beteiligung, 2810
Hansen, 839
Hansen Engine, 826
Hansen Medical, 426, 598, 1493, 1691
Hanshow, 1121
Hansol Gyoyook Company, 1139, 2946
Hansons, 960
Hanting Inns & Hotels, 2850
Hantro, 2999
Hanweck, 161
Haocen, 3194
HaoDF, 2584
HaoDF.com, 596
HaoHaoZhu, 823
Hapara, 1316, 1551, 1865
Hapila, 2527, 2824
Happich Fahzeug-und Industrieteile GmbH, 2806
Happier, 1546, 1916
Happiest Babby, 889
Happiest Baby, 720, 1151, 1363
Happiest Minds, 386
Happify, 2475
Happist Minds, 1004
Happlink, 2886
Happy Cloud, 1034
Happy Elements, 596, 2936
Happy Floors, 1132
Happy Hour Creative, 352
Happy Joe's, 17
Happy Returns, 342, 1149, 1183, 1888
Happy Toy Machine, 1306
HappyCo, 1282
Happyview.fr, 2385
Hapten Sciences, 1187
HaptX, 1890
HapYak, 534
Hara, 1355
Hara Software, 757
Harbar, 1173
Harbert Growth Partners, 3270
Harbert Management, 3262
Harbert Venture Partners, 3262
Harbinger, 69
Harbo Technologies, 2111
Harbor, 124, 727
Harbor Community Bank, 909, 1062
Harbor Freight, 1970
Harbor View Advisors, 3262
Harborside Health Center, 1135, 1610
Harborside Healthcare, 1017
Harborside Inc., 2122
HarborTechnologies, 1161
Harbortouch Holdings of Delaware, 1491
Harbour, 1282
Harbour Antibodies, 191
Harbour Landing Village, 2221
Harbour Networks, 3168
Harbourgate Resort & Marina, 1681
HarbourVest Partners, 2375, 3255, 3258
Harbr, 2168
harbr, 2212
Harden Manufacturing, 1132, 1456
HardMetrics, 1387
Hardmetrics, 1321
Hardware Resources, 908, 1456

Hardwear, 2613
Hargray Holdings, 1506
Haripur Power Project, 1007
Hark, 1534
Harley Marine Services, 1491
Harman International, 260
Harmar, 546
Harmless Harvest, 1263
Harmon.ie, 3101
Harmonic, 1896
Harmonic Inc., 947
Harmonix, 776, 1473
Harmonix Music Systems, 1173
Harmony Biosciences, 1941
Harmony Information Systems, 1886
Harmony Information Systems Inc., 1041
Harmony Toy, 1295
Harmonycom, 2775
Harness, 1202
Harper Wilde, 342, 622
Harpoon, 1268
Harpoon Medical, 19, 689, 1169
HarQen, 400, 841, 2001
Harren Equity Partners, 3264
Harri, 397
Harrington Holdings Inc., 654
Harris Connect, 1984
Harris Hill, 3244
Harris Research, 374
Harrison Metal, 37
Harrison Street Capital, 3265
Harron Communications LP, 361
Harry Winston, 722
Harry's, 318, 325, 935, 1018, 1531, 2928
Harry's Fresh Foods, 1159
Hart InterCivic, 928, 1855
Hart Systems, 1832
Hartmann, 492
Hartzell Manufacturing, 843
Harver, 1000
Harvery Automation, 1615
Harvest, 634, 3239, 3257
Harvest Automation, 570, 1172, 2709, 2939
Harvest Cannabis Co., 557
Harvest Hill Beverage Company, 357
Harvest Labs, 622
Harvest Partners, 3264
Harvest Partners III L.P., 2660
Harvest Partners IV L.P., 2660
Harvest Power, 581
HarvestMark, 183
HarvestPort, 570
Harvey, 1696
Harvey Gulf, 1045
Harvey Jones, 3244
Harvey Tool, 1572
Hasec, 2527
Hashgo, 641, 871
HashiCorp, 823, 1184, 1534
Hashrabbit, 307
Hashtag Paid, 2125, 2138
Haskell Jewels, 940
Haskins Electric, 940
Hassle.com, 3208
Haste, 282
Hastings Holdings Corporation, 1557
Hat Tricks Group, 2923
Hatch Apps, 1026
Hatch Baby, 1149
Hatch Loyalty, 124
Hatchbuck, 569
Hatchtech, 3023
Hatfield & McCoy Whiskey, 1019
Hathway, 1496
Hatsize, 841, 2058
Hatteras Networks, 798
Haus, 325

Hausway, 2271
Haute Hijab, 218, 342, 567
Haute Hippie, 937
Hautelook, 1235
Hava Health, 1507
Havco Wood Products, 843
Haven, 563, 741, 942
Haven Behavioral, 496
Haven Behavioral Healthcare, 176, 240, 558
Havenly, 776, 1070
Haverfield, 834
Havok, 3191
Hawaii Biotech, 61, 939, 1002, 1011
Hawaiian Wireless Inc., 1621
Hawk Medical, 1972
Hawkeye Renewables, 1815, 1967
Hawkpoint, 2965
Hawkwood Energy, 1956
Hawthorne Effect, 1675
HaxAsia, 3132
Haxiot, 1244
Haydon Enterprises Inc., 908
Hayes Medical, 1769
Hayneedle, 1654
Haynes International, 1141
Haystack, 1166
Haystagg, 1958
Hayward, 433
Hayward Gordon, 657
Hazel, 684
Hazel Health, 1392
Hazelcast, 221
Hazinem, 2294
Hazinem Pirlanta, 2437
Hazy, 1154
HB Performance Systems Holdings, 1279
HB&G Building Products, 164
HB&G Building Products Inc., 846
HC Semitek, 973
Hc1.com, 658
HC360, 406
HCA, 220
HCBF Holding Company, 1743
HCCA International, 493
HCG Energy, 940
HCI Systems, 438
HCJ, 2949
HCOA Fitness, 1832
HCT Group, 2539
HCTec Partners, 493
HD Biosciences, 1436, 2978
HD Supply, 220
HD Vest, 1417
HD Vest Financial Services, 744, 1147
HDH Advisors, 3279
HDmessaging, 1119, 2999
HDR, 2936
HDT Global, 456, 1134
HDT Inc, 2590
HDVI, 204, 1118
Head Country, 828
Head Light, 1481
Headliner, 1680
Headnote, 1323
HeadOut, 1150
Headout, 2280
Headsense, 809
Headset, 963, 1610, 1843, 2071
HeadSpace, 60
Headspace, 1717, 1761
HeadSpin, 889
Headspin, 1670
Headstrong, 892, 1972
Headwater Equity, 3258
Headway Technologies, 892, 1896
Heal, 1095
Heal.com, 163

1333

Portfolio Companies Index

Healcerion, 3127
Healhcare Financial Resources Inc., 949
Healint, 1965
Healinx, 1668, 2775
Healionics, 85
Healogics, 1626
Healogram, 1589
Health, 181
Health & Bliss, 995, 1187
Health & Safety Institute, 1166
Health Allies, 1558
Health and Fitness Central Europe (HFCE), 2648
Health AP, 858
Health at Home, 406
Health Cap, 2447
Health Carechain, 1915
Health Catalust, 1052
Health Catalyst, 688, 1346, 1654
Health Communications Network Limited, 2915
Health Credit Services, 793
Health Data Insights, 1532, 1888
Health Data Vision Inc., 1532, 1888
Health Diagnostic Laboratory, 1271
Health Dialog, 1720
Health eFilings, 2001
Health Enterprise Partners, 3264
Health Essentials, 260
Health Extras Inc., 404
Health Fidelity, 458
Health Guru, 1142
Health Hero, 1507
Health Hero Network, 371, 1003
Health Information Designs, 475
Health Innovations Group, 2233
Health Integrated, 171, 1571, 1745, 2196
Health iPASS, 1267
Health iPass, 718
Health IQ, 124, 741, 770
Health Language, 1796
Health Management Associates, 541
Health Market Science, 246, 655
Health Monitor Network, 1979
Health Monitoring Systems, 998, 1448
Health Outcomes Sciences, 856
Health Outcomes Worldwide, 2155, 2205
Health Payment Systems, 373
Health QR, 2155
Health Reveal, 809
Health Sherpa, 1054
Health Systems Technologies, 1398
Health Watch Holdings, 1557
Health-E Commerce, 244
Health2works, 2967
HealthAllies, 502
Healthcall Optical Services, 2507
Healthcare Anywhere, 658
Healthcare Asset Network, 86
Healthcare Brands International, 2662, 2674
Healthcare Finance Group, 1136
Healthcare First, 1409
Healthcare Funding Corp., 1837
Healthcare Highways, 1619
Healthcare Interactive, 876
Healthcare Interative, 904
Healthcare Management Systems, 1456
Healthcare Recoveries, 955
Healthcare Solutions, 328, 1148
Healthcare Waste Solutions, 97
Healthcare.Com, 1640
HealthCareSolutions, 652
HealthcareSource, 779
HealthCatalyst, 1705
HealthChannels, 921
HealthClinicPlus, 1615
HealthComp Holdings, 92
HealthDelivery, 1615
HealthEdge, 1498

Healthedge, 946
HealthEdge Investment Partners, 3264
HealthEJourney, 2233
Healtheon-WebMD, 1103
HealthExpense, 1046
HealthFinch, 471
Healthfinch, 1364
Healthfuse, 1293
HealthFusion, 506
Healthgrades, 697, 909, 1931
HealthGuru, 422
Healthguru, 580
HealthHelp, 1002, 1271
HealthHiway, 872
Healthie, 272, 622
Healthify, 52, 55, 1054
Healthify Me, 1013
HealthifyMe, 1611
HealthiNation, 1242
HealthInvest Equity Partners, 3264
Healthium MedTech, 135
Healthizen, 3109
HealthKart, 1374
Healthland, 779
Healthline, 1052
Healthline Networks, 1906
HealthLoop, 396, 1054, 1830
HealthLoop. Impinj, 1438
HealthMEDX, 1850
HealthMedX, 1717
HealthPlan, 374
HealthPlan Holdings, 1961
HealthPlanOne, 743, 871
Healthplus Corporation, 354
HealthPort, 21
HealthPrize Technologies, 1165
HealthQuest Capital, 3264
HealthQx, 918
Healthrageous, 1142, 1334
HealthSavings Administrators, 299
Healthscope, 1835
HealthSCOPE Benefits, 21
HealthScribe, 876
HealthSense, 1165
Healthsense, 1205, 1520
Healthshare Technology, 59
HealthSlate, 1641
HealthSpot, 642
Healthspring, 1615, 1619
HealthSTAR, 928
HealthSun, 1403
HealthSynq, 1558
HealthTap, 1184
Healthtap, 1247
healthTap, 1865
HealthTeacher, 1732
HealthTech Holdings, 1456
HealthTell, 298, 1400, 1940
HealthTrans, 21
Healthtrax, 1021, 1751
Healthtrends Medical Investments, 2477
HealthTronics, 97
HealthTronics IT Solutions, 97
Healthvana, 228
Healthvison, 2771
HealthWarehouse.com, 1291
HealthWiz, 622
HealthWyse, 949
HealthX, 695, 1041
Healthy Directions, 42
Healthy Headie Lifestyle, 392, 1135
Healthy Pet, 374
Healthy Pets, 2099
Healthy Roots, 218
Healthy Roster, 1286
Healthy.io, 1611
HealthyOut, 1632

Healx, 2478
Hearland, 442
Hearsay, 1625
Hearsay Sustems, 1654
Hearsay Systems, 720
Heart & Paw, 1963
Heart Center, 2881
Heart Graffiti, 742
Heart This, 784
Heart to Heart Hospice, 1752
HeartBar, 1665
Heartbeat, 1110
HeartFlow, 666, 1615, 1896
Hearthside Food Solutions, 456, 1931
Heartlab, 1114
Heartland, 1753
Heartland Automotive Services, 1505
Heartland Communications Group, 828
Heartland Dental Care, 1082
Heartland Payment Systems, 1136
Heartland Resources, 1784
Heartland Steel Products, 443
Heartsine Technologies, 2610
HeartStent, 1786
HeartThis, 1416
HeartVista, 1069
HeartWork, 552
Heartwork, 231
HeatGenie, 445, 1061
Heatwave Interactive, 1771
Heavybit, 1149
HeavyBit Industries, 585
Heckyl, 3109
Hedgeable, 1688
HedgeStreet, 925
Hedvig, 1363, 1860, 2690
Heemang Dream Haksa Co., 584
Heeros Systems Oy, 2873
Heffron Consulting, 605
Heguang International, 3062
Heidrich, 3020
Heineken, 473
Heinz, 473
Heleo, 518
Heliatek, 2492, 2686, 2824
Helicon Re, 654
Helicos, 2445
Helicos BioSciences Corp., 747
Helie Power, 319
Helinet Aviation Services LLC, 274
HelioCampus, 1409
Heliocentris Energiesysteme GmbH, 2528
Helion, 1760
Helios Coatings, 944
HelioVOlt, 1400
Heliovolt, 678
Helium, 395, 743, 889, 1097, 1701
Helium Systems, 1069
Helius, 1677
Helix, 609, 1075
Helix Sleep, 858
Helixis, 59, 1371
Hellas Direct, 2225
HellaWaller, 876
Hellman & Friedman, 3255, 3264
Hello ChuXing, 823
Hello Fresh, 1000, 2829, 2838
Hello Giggles, 792, 1813, 1883
Hello Machines, 2855
Hello People Ops, 392
Hello Tech, 544
Hello Vera, 724
HelloAva, 1701
HelloGiggles, 1480
HelloHome, 995
HelloNature, 3127
HelloSign, 889

Portfolio Companies Index

Hellosign, 776, 1968
HelloSoft, 712, 1241
HelloTech, 120, 228, 561, 707, 972, 1055, 1158, 1888
HelloTechm Gyft, 397
HelloWallet, 1782
HelloWorld, 1088
Helly Hansen, 2384
Helly Hensen, 1017
Helmedix, 2959
Help, 1531
Help Around, 1993
Help At Home Inc., 1971
Help Scout, 776
Help Shift, 1004, 1154
Help Social, 545
Help Systems, 1725
Help/Systems, 194, 1752
Helpful, 2137
Helpr, 567
HelpSaude, 2438
HelpScout, 2017
HelpShift, 1607
Helpshift, 483, 1860, 3001
HelpSystems, 928
Helpsystems, 456
Helveta, 2295
Helvetic.com AG, 2427
Hem, 2446
Hema Source, 949
HemaSource, 846
Hematris Wound Care, 2452, 2824
Hemen Kiralik, 2294
Hemen Kiralikm, 2437
Hemisphere Media Group, 2252
Hemodynamic Therapeutics Inc., 430
Hemophelia Resources of America, 1770
Hemosphere, 666
Hemosphere Inc., 572
Hemoteq Gmbh, 2682
Hemp Business Journal, 392
Henan, 2591
HengFu Logistics, 1906
Hengxin Electric, 1340
HengZhi, 2475
Heniff Transportation Systems, 240
Heniff Transportation Systems LLC, 1372
Henley-Putnam University, 1116
Hennessy Capital Solutions, 352
Henniges Automotice Holdings, 2009
Hennings Automotive, 1134
Henry, 846
Henry Company, 110
Henry Silverman Jewelers, 1708
Henry The Dentist, 325, 2202
Hensoldt, 1082, 2851
HEP Tech, 905
Hepaco, 415, 881
Hepregen, 233
Heptagon, 1327, 2875, 2878, 3214
Heptagon/AMS, 823
Heptares Therapeutics, 495, 2981
Heptio, 1121
Hera Health Solutions, 995
Herald Media Holdings, 194
Herantis, 347
Herb, 358, 858, 1110
Herbal Magic, 2079
Herbalgem, 2862
Herbalife, 839
Herban Planet, 1135
Herbert, 2071
HerbPharm, 1250
Hercules, 801
Hercules Technology Growth Capital, 3262
HerdDogg, 995
Here, 1004

Heresy, 3108
Heritage Foodservice Group, 909
Heritage Group, 3264
Heritage Home Group, 1085
Heritage Inks International, 832
Heritage-Crystal Clean Inc., 354
Herld Media, 897
Hermes Precisa Australia, 2951
Hermois, 1676
Hermés Métal, 3020
Hero Digital, 476
Hero Investments, 220
Heroku, 231, 1534, 2012
HeroX, 488
HEROZ, 2974
Hertel Holding, 2332
HES Beheer, 3209
HeSaLight, 3203
Hess Print Solutions Inc., 1971
Het Engeltje, 3042
Hetan Technologies, 2979
HeTexted, 1306, 1310
HeTian Hospital Management, 1082
Hetras, 3104
HETSCO, 1252
Hetworth Corp., 2094
Heureka Software, 1286
Heuresis, 2978
Hewitt, 2771
Hewlett-Packard, 1096
Hex Performance, 788
Hexadite, 1794, 3246
Hexagon Bio, 1666
HexaTech, 1008, 1658
Hexcel Corporation, 862
Hexion Specialty Chemicals, 140
Hey, 1715
Hey Group, 2841
Hey Orca!, 2216
HeyCater, 2296
Heyday, 727, 1110, 1585
Heyfair, 2527
Heymama, 1310
HeyMarket, 1563
Heyo, 1812
HeyOrca, 2168
Heysan, 2446
Heysta Energy, 1573
Heytex Bramsche GmbH Bramsche, 3067
HF2 SRL, 2419
HFFC, 260
HFSC Holdings, 765
HG Data, 306, 688
HGB, 1705
HGData, 1566
HGHI, 241
HGI Holdings, 1456
HH Ventures, 17
HHA eXchange, 1276
HHI Holdings LLC, 1085
Hi Bruno, 2296
Hi Corp., 596
Hi Fidelity Genetics, 737
Hi Media, 3113
Hi Technologies, 1509
Hi-G-Tek, 233
Hi-Grade Welding & Manufacturing, 399
Hi-Lo Automotive Inc., 1621
Hi-mart, 892
Hi-Media, 641
Hi-Rel Group, 1159
Hi-Tec Profiles, 2221
Hi-Tech, 3100
Hi-Tech Manufacturing, 1477
Hi-Tech Rubber Inc., 449
Hi-Tech Wealth, 2772
hi5 Networks, 925

Hiberna Corporation, 315
Hibernator, 2473
Hibernia Atlantic, 263
Hibernia Energy, 1278, 1326
Hichain, 2936
HiChina, 2850
Hickery Farms, 465
Hickory, 1551
Hickory Farms, 1753
Hicks Broadcasting Partners, 734
Hickson & Welch, 2677
Hiconics, 2936
Hidden City, 43
Hidden Level, 1095
Hidrate Spark, 1701
Hidrotenecias, 46
HIG Capital, 3264, 3265
Higginbotham Insurance Agency, 1743
High Alpha, 665
High Beauty, 2071
High Branch Software, 655
High Brow Cat, 514
High Desert Power, 1795
High End Systems, 818
High Fidelity, 889, 1054, 1860
High Gear Media, 28, 581
High Ground Energy, 1443
High Ground Solutions, 1533
High Park, 1481
High Performance Building Systems, 998
High Power Lithium, 690
High Pressure Equipment Company, 1960
High Q, 1255
High QA, 52
High Ridge Brands, 357
High Roads, 1080
High Sierra Energy Partners, 1053
High Street Capital, 3265
High Street Capital Partners, 557
High Street Insurance Partners, 960
High Times, 151, 1135
High Tower Software, 1116
High Wind, 3042
High-Mobility, 2841
High-Tech Grunderfonds, 3155, 3170
Highdeal, 2875
Highdef, 2475
Higher Education Partners, 1248
Higher Gear Group, 928
Higher Logic, 1041
Higher Power Nutrition, 1234
HigherNext, 1321
HigherOne, 1991
Highest Reward, 392
HighFive, 1121
Highfive, 816, 889
Highgate Hotels, 1851
Highgate Labs, 2685
HighGear Media, 634
HighGround, 1118
HighJump, 925, 1725
Highland Capital Partners, 3273, 3284
Highlands Bank, 514
Highlight, 609, 871
HighlightCam, 1050, 1513, 2329
Highlighter, 685
Highline, 2239, 2291
HIGHLINE Canada Accelerator, 2143
Highline Financial, 1724
Highline Media, 1724
Highline Wealth Management, 1599
Highmark Energy, 1326
HighPoint Solutions, 1136
HighRoads, 925, 2196
Highroads, 23
HighSpot, 1607
Highspot, 1158, 1663

1335

Portfolio Companies Index

Hightail, 37, 87, 665, 1024, 1658
Hightower, 1531, 1821
HighWave, 2875
Highwinds, 171
HighWire, 29
HIIG, 2379
Hijauan Bengkoka, 834
Hijoki, 2921
Hijro, 307, 561, 724
HijUp, 721
Hiku, 1254
HIL Applied Medical, 3245
Hilb Group, 21
Hilco Technologies, 812
Hilding Anders, 1017, 1082, 3008
Hile Bio-pharma, 2733
Hilite Industries, 1456
Hill & Valley, 481, 1477
Hill and Valley, 1516
Hill Country Holdings, 374
Hill Leigh Group, 2985
Hill Ward Henderson, 3262
Hillary's Group, 2617
Hillcrest, 646
Hillcrest Labs, 876
Hillier's, 937
Hillman Group, 1360
Hillsdale Furniture, 353
Hillsidecandy, 953
Hillstone, 1340, 3215
Hilton Worldwide, 869
Himadri, 220
himagine Solutions, 244
Himalayan Handmade Candles, 1606
HiMama, 2243
Himark Bogas, 2048
Himax Technologies, 3218
Himex Limited, 3199
HIMS, 334, 3098
Hims, 761
Hinge, 679, 858, 1531, 1663
Hinge Health, 4, 1000, 2446
Hingeto, 1054
HIP Digital, 871
Hip Digital, 1850
Hip Shot Dot, 1736
Hipbone, 947
Hipcamp, 1694
Hipclub, 3044
Hipdot, 1323
Hiperos, 1752
HiperScan, 2824
HipGeo, 1254
Hipmunk, 1001, 1327, 1361, 1806, 1968
Hipoges, 1082
Hippo, 24, 518, 720, 727, 1323
Hippo Insurance, 1095
Hippocrates Associates, 1837
HipSnip, 2400
Hipster, 1118
HipSwap, 871
HipVan, 1965
HiQ, 306, 624
Hiramatsu Inc., 2347
Hire An Esquire, 13
Hire Counsel & Mestel, 1141
Hire Dynamics, 1270
Hire IQ, 1788
Hire Vue, 1070
Hire.com, 202
HireArt, 720, 1010
Hired, 45, 518, 563, 858, 1670, 1700
HiRel Systems LLC, 461
HireMojo, 100
HireNetworks, 3259
Hireology, 222, 731, 1118
Hirequip Projex, 2420

HireRight, 596, 1725
HireVue, 852, 1654
HIRO, 436
Hirslanden Holdings, 2497
HIS, 2545
Hisarlar, 584
Hiscox, 2796
Hisoar Pharma, 2542
HiSoft Technology International, 690, 3062
Hispanic Yellow Pages, 21
Histogenics, 989, 1725
Histogenics Corporation, 312
Histogenics Hyperion Therapeutics, 1698
Histoire d'Or, 2375
Historic Futures, 2539
HistoRX, 349
HistoRx, 520
HistoSonics, 642, 749, 1802, 1921, 2180
Histosonics, 915
Hitachi Kokusai Electric, 1082
Hitch, 3108
HitCheck, 226
Hitech, 2969
HitecVision AS, 77
HitFix, 841, 1784
HitFox, 3170
HitFox Group, 2829, 2838
Hitmeister, 2475
HitRecord, 1613
HITS, 1109
hiu! Media, 3062
Hive, 128, 816
Hive II, 623
HiveIO, 1522
HiveLive, 876
Hivemapper, 32
HiveUAV, 792
hiwire, 2021
Hixme, 1075
Hiya, 2478
Hjem Is Europa, 2863
Hjem-IS, 3203
HJMT Communications LLC, 3267
HJR Asphalt, 2285
HK Ruokatalo Oyj, 2990
HL Leasing, 2810
HLine Digital Media, 1228
HLM, 37
HMC+, 2824
HMicro, 2011
HMP, 1759
HMR Foods, 2089
HMS Healthcare, 1086
HMT, 1777
HNA Group, 473
HNB, 3151
HNI Healthcare, 1619
HNW, 534, 592, 2196
Hoak Media Corporation, 441
Hobbico Inc., 577
Hobbs, 2306, 2311
Hobbs Bonded Fibers, 1021
Hobbs Rental Corporation, 364
Hobnob, 1346
Hobo Labs, 852, 1663
Hochtemperatur Engineering GmbH, 2660
Hockeystick, 2138
Hodges Ward Elliott, 1622
Hodges-Mace, 1743
Hodinkee, 751, 1149, 1758
Hodo, 473
Hodo Soy Beanery, 1097
Hoffiges, 2721
Hoffman & Baron LLP, 3267
Hoffman Media, 263, 1533
Hoffmaster Group, 168, 1456
Hoffmaster Group Inc., 1971

Hojoki, 2638
HOKO, 3108
Hoku Scientific, 807, 939
Hola, 1852
HOLA Home Furnishing, 1769
Hola!, 2831, 2952
Holaira, 59, 1122, 1725
Holberton, 1527
Holberton School, 107
Hold Jinn Electronics, 3218
Hole 19, 1982
Hole19, 3108
Holganix, 293, 1385
Holiday Enterainment, 2436
Holiday Inn Express, 2539
Holiday Retirement, 767
HolidayIQ, 28
Holland & Hart, 3276
Holland & Knight LLP, 3262
Holland Energy, 1795
Holland Services, 928
Hollander, 959
Hollander Sleep Products, 1651
Hollar, 518, 761, 1075, 1121, 1480
Holley, 1127
Hollinee, 316
Hollinger, 2073
Hollywood Tans, 42
Holman Boiler Works, 908
Holmes Place, 2962
Holmris, 3203
Holoclara, 1051
Hologram, 630
Holographix, 314
Holor, 1983
HolyTax, 2936
Homag Group AG, 2660
Homann Chilled Foods, 2821
Homax, 1372
Home & Legacy, 2677
Home 24, 2829
Home Appliances, 2399
Home Bistro, 1689
Home Care of St. Francis, 406
Home Chef, 69, 1088
Home Decor Holdings, 1456
Home Dialysis, 1956
Home Dialysis Plus, 1929
Home Director, 954
Home Health Holdings, 1422
Home Helpers, 1132
Home Inns, 2850
Home Inns & Hotel Management, 1769
Home Products International, 1954
Home Skinovations, 1844
Home Solutions, 1086
Home Technology Healthcare, 1986
Home Town Cable, 21
Home.is, 1611
Home24, 2838
Home61, 593
HomeAway, 202, 1001, 1534, 1850, 2723
Homebase, 231, 552, 761, 1069
HomeBay, 770
HomeBistro Foods, 438
HomeCare, 1970
HomeCare.com, 1169, 1259
HomeCentric Healthcare, 1727
HomeCourt.ai, 1138
HomeEquity Bank, 2062
HomeGrocer.com, 85
Homegrown Natural Foods, 374
Homejoy, 1546
HomeLight, 358, 486, 889, 1202
Homelight, 563
HomeMe.ru, 2320
Homeperf, 2851

Portfolio Companies Index

HOMEQ Corp., 2183
Homer, 351, 858, 1110, 1585
Homeroom, 1183
Homeschool, 1463
Homeshift, 3108
Homesnap, 1555
Homesoft Oy, 2873
HomeSphere, 1849
HomeSpotter, 341
HomeStars, 2109
Homesuite, 622
HomeSun, 2505
Hometap, 816
Hometeam, 1151
HomeToGo, 1000
HomeTouch, 1615
Hometown Communications, 1570
Hometown Food Company, 357
HomeVestors, 1111
Homewood Health, 2082
Homey, 995
Homie, 79, 607, 1070
Homigo, 2027
Homology Medicines, 12, 1932
Hone, 1527
Hone Comb, 1463
Honest Buildings, 308, 1247, 1282, 1579, 1977, 2142
Honest Networks, 727
Honest Tea, 190
Honey, 1150
Honey Smoked Fish, 1276
HoneyApps, 1865
Honeybee, 1758
Honeybee Health, 120
HoneyBook, 397, 1346
Honeybook, 1323
HoneyComb, 1061
Honeycomb.io, 641
Honeycommb, 1595
HoneyTree Films, 1160
Honeywell, 473
Hong Bang, 3194
Hong Kong Broadband Network, 2379
Hongchizhineng, 1121
HongHua Co., 1573
Honghua Group Limited, 3218
Hongkong Electric, 2591
Honk, 101, 306, 707, 1055, 1749, 1798
HONKON, 509
Honor, 124, 941, 1054, 1323, 1694
Honor Medical Staffing, 1606
Honors Holdings, 1049
Hoodinn Interactive Limited, 2703
Hoodong, 1340
Hooja, 506
Hook Logic, 221, 796
Hook Mobile, 51, 119, 2850
Hooked, 552, 1150
Hooked Media Group, 1896
Hookipa Biotech, 2748
Hookipa Biotech AG, 1778
Hookit, 1741
Hooks, 2325
Hoopla, 976, 1601, 1607, 1853
Hooters Restaurants, 1494
HootSuite, 28, 301, 922, 1235
Hootsuite, 1000, 2080
Hooven Heat Treating, 465
Hoover Group, 740
Hopdpddy, 1088
Hope, 934
Hope20, 3257
Hopen Life Sciences Venture, 3269
Hopkins, 2209, 2219
Hopkins Capital Group, 3262
Hopkins Manufacturing, 788, 1456, 2208

Hopper, 38, 2066
Hopscotch, 751, 1054, 1222, 1546
HopSkipDrive, 743, 896, 1183, 1480, 1888
Hopster, 1292, 2997
HopStop, 3081
Horizon, 2206, 2674, 3085
Horizon Cellular Group, 260
Horizon Development, 1954
Horizon Digital Enterprise, 1755
Horizon Discovery, 2662, 3028
Horizon Discovery Limited, 2981
Horizon Food Equipment Inc., 899
Horizon Mud Comapny, 1422
Horizon Organic, 542
Horizon Organic Dairy, 856
Horizon Packaging, 1229
Horizon Partners, 3284
Horizon Pharma, 188, 191, 1271, 1325, 1508, 1626, 1760, 2785, 3196
Horizon Robotics, 1004
Horizon Science, 2516
Horizon Semiconductors, 2782
Horizon Services, 1753
Horizon Systems, 1229
Horizon Therapeutics, 925
Horizon Ventures, 986
Hormos Medical Ltd Oy, 2318
Hornblower Holdings, 559
Hornet Group, 1745
Horse Network, 313, 786
Horseburgh & Scott Co., 654
Horsehead, 1134
HorsePower, 1172
Hortau, 2049
Hortex, 2422
Hortonworks, 248, 1796, 2860, 2860
Hospice Advantage Holdings, 1651
Hospice Link, 1331
Hospira, 1349
Hospital Corporation of America, 493
Hospital IQ, 1146
Hospital Therapy Services, 1837
Hospitalists Management Group LLC, 64
Hospitalists Now, 1722
Hospitality Associates, 1633
Hospitality Mints, 1132, 1456
Host Analytics, 59, 569, 646, 1319, 1738, 1850, 1910
Hosted Solutions, 21
Hostfully, 218
Hosting, 1409
Hostspot, 2984
Hostway, 1134, 1927
Hot Bread Kitchen, 1420
Hot Potato, 1821
Hot Rail/Conexant/Skyworks, 1288
Hot Topic, 1706
Hotbar.com, 23, 2720, 3158
HotChalk, 695, 883
Hotchalk, 1247
Hotel Booking Solutions, 563
Hotel El Convento, 63
Hotel Tonight, 49, 180, 761, 771, 1896
Hotel Urbano, 1000
Hotelbar.Com, 2626
Hotelogix, 28
HotelRunner, 2294
Hotelscene Limited, 2507
HotelTonight, 28, 235, 741, 823
HotJobs.com, 260
Hotjobs.com, 818
HotLink, 1102
Hotmail, 609
HotPads, 1194
HotRail, 1646
Hotrail, 36
HotSchedules, 224, 1072

Hotsip AB, 162
Hotspir Technologies Inc., 269
HotSpot Merchants, 2200
Hotspur Technologies, 1378
Hotswap, 1073
HotU, 1011
Hotwire.com, 1835
Houghton International Inc, 832
Houghton Mifflin Harcourt, 21
Houghton NYC, 218
Houlihan's Restaurants Inc., 843
House of Anita Dongre, 815
House of Blues, 1681
House of HR, 2851
House of Matriach, 1061
HouseBites, 2685
HouseCall, 641
Housecall Pro, 222
Housejoy, 1509
Houseparty, 518, 872, 1323, 1654, 1694, 1883
HouseTrip, 28
HouseValues, 468
Housing Development Finance Corporation, 2337
Houston Health Ventures, 950
Houston Medical Robotics Inc., 485
Houwelings Nurseries, 2049
Houzz, 518, 823, 858, 1075, 1654
HOVER, 889
Hover, 89, 93
How About We, 1358
How.do, 2831
HowAboutWe.com, 724, 1226
Howcast, 43, 580, 1798
HowGood, 743, 858
HowStuffWorks, 1709
Hozelock, 2644
HPC Energy Services, 2025
HPR, 314
HPS Holding Company, 1279
HQ Medical Technology, 710
HQ Raleigh, 3259
HqO, 1282, 1480
HR New Media, 2824, 2994
HRA Pharma, 1452, 1572
HRI, 61, 795
HROI, 492
HRP Refrigerants, 2985
HSBC, 3276
HSE24, 1496
Hsin Yung Chien Co., 3218
HSIO Technologies, 3279
Hsiri Therapeutics, 266
HSS, 97, 374
HTBASE, 2138
HTG, 1731
HTG Molecular Diagnostics, 1702, 1901
HTI, 3020
HTI Technologies Holding Corporation, 1557
HTP, 1553
Hua Medicine, 153, 710, 1916
Huaqin, 1004
Huaxun Technology, 2733
Huaya Technology, 2590
Huayue Education, 135
HUB, 924
Hub International, 909, 2034, 2046, 3262
Hubb, 745, 1383
Hubba, 842, 2066, 2125, 2224
Hubbardton Forge, 359
Hubble, 743, 3108
Hubble Telemedical, 1187
Hubbub, 2752
HubCast, 521
Hubdoc, 2243
HubHaus, 816, 1696
HubPages, 1747

Portfolio Companies Index

Hubspan, 1626, 1637, 2079, 2196
HubSpot, 455, 1181, 1654, 1796
Hubspot, 560, 1626
Hubster, 1894
Hubub, 508
HubX, 310
Huckleberry, 563, 641, 858, 1721
Huddle, 271, 634, 968, 1181, 2691
Huddle House, 1505, 1651
Hudong, 2667
Hudson Baking Company, 147
Hudson Bay Company, 2067
Hudson Lock LLC, 1964
Hudson Medical Communications, 1228
Hudson Products, 2015
Hudson Products Corporation, 1573
Hudson Respiratory Care, 783
Huga Optotech, 1906
Hughes, 1232
Hughes Broadcasting Partners, 1927
Hughes Pittman & Gupton LLP, 3259
Hugin, 3013
Hugo Boss, 3033
Huhtamäki Oyj, 2990
Huicheng Pectechnology, 2936
Huiseoul, 181
Huiying Medical Technology, 1004
Huji, 2593
Hulafrog, 1524
Hullabalu, 858, 1115, 1632, 1716
Hullmark Stafford, 2148
Huma.ai, 799
Human Agency, 934
Human API, 124
Human Code, 202
Human Demand, 150
Human DX, 741
Human Dx, 1054
Human Eyes, 2541
Human Genome Science, 1558
Human Genome Sciences, 1394
Human Inference, 3051
Human Interest, 1758
Human Longevity Inc., 609
Human.co, 3224
Humana, 2422
HumanAPI, 128, 296
Humane, 395
HumanEyes Technologies, 3245
HumanFirst, 2212
Humanforce, 29
Humangride, 2824
Humanize, 313
Humanoid, 1958
HumanZyme, 2978
Humax, 2924
Humble & Fume, 2140
Humble Bundle, 1654
Humble Dot, 1758
Humedica, 1205, 1334
Humedics, 2824, 2841, 3113
Humense, 1390
Humi HR, 2027
Humin, 1830
Humirel, 2481
Hummer Winblad Venture Partners, 3284
Hummingbird, 941, 2818
Hummingbird Technologies, 2997
Humon, 622
Hunch, 231, 260
Hungama.com, 1004
Hungarocamion Rt., 2429
Hunger Computer, 2924
Hungry, 1613
HUNGRY Marketplace, 1259
Hungry Root, 351, 563, 858, 1110, 1222
HungryRoot, 1121

Hunkemoller, 3026
Hunt Marcellus, 1062
Hunt Valve, 1166
Hunter Boot, 2252
Hunter Business Law, 3262
Hunter Defence Technologies, 245
Hunter Fan, 1231
Hunter Fan Holdings, 2379
Hunter's Specialties, 443
HuntForce, 635
Huntress, 2796
Huntress Labs, 285
Huntswood CTC Ltd, 2306
Huodongxing, 596
Hupnos, 226
Hurix Systems, 2818
Huron, 1856
Huron Energy Corporation, 2040
Huron River Ventures, 3269
Hurray, 2733
Hurrier, 2147
Hurrikan Power, 156
Husk Power Systems, 55
Huskie Tools, 1343
Hustle, 770, 883, 889, 934, 1000, 1054, 1607, 1696, 1721
Hut Six Security, 2284
Huterra, 1292
HUVRData, 445
HVault Storage, 1676
HVH Transportation, 917
HVMN, 124
HVT Group, 1526
Hweden, 1753
HX Technologies, 1321
Hy Cite Enterprises LLC, 1403
HY Trust, 1004
Hy-Bon Engineering Company, 1435
Hy-Lok, 3145
Hyalto, 2239, 2284
HYAS, 1154, 1758
Hyas, 2284
Hybolic, 3194
Hybond AS, 3141
Hybrid Apparel, 96
Hybrid Cluster, 2685
Hybrid Energy, 2918
Hybrid Graphics, 2999
HybridCluster, 2586
Hybrigenics, 2415, 2625
Hybris, 959
Hybritech, 1760
Hyco International Inc., 447
Hycor, 1128
Hycrete, 1324, 1579
Hyde Park Capital Partners, 3262
Hyde Park Venture Partners, 3265, 3269
Hydra Biosciences, 59, 1122, 1124, 1196, 1460
Hydra Studios, 727
Hydrade, 591
HydraDx, 791
Hydrant, 622
Hydrasun, 1017
Hydraulex Global, 1744
Hydrexia, 1711
HydroChem, 442
HydroChemPSC, 1134
HydroCision, 270
Hydrocision, 1847
Hydrocore, 3262
HydroDive, 1164
Hydrofarm, 2254
Hydrogenics Corporation, 2079
Hydroid, 211
HydroMassage, 80
HydroNovation, 498
HydroPoint, 2106

HydroPoint Data Systems, 730, 1249, 1579
Hydrostor, 2041
Hydrovoima, 2318
Hydrox Pipeline Oy, 2873
Hygenic, 1456
Hygenica, 251
Hykso, 811
HYLA, 1593
HYLA Mobile, 1689
Hyland Software, 1814
Hylete, 1741
Hynes Industries, 1545
Hyosung Wind Power Holdings, 584
Hype!, 3108
Hyper, 60
Hyper Giant, 2057
Hyper Strong, 973
Hyper9, 1181, 1916
HyperActive Technologies, 998
Hyperchip, 2263
Hypercom, 779
Hyperconnect, 100
HyperEdge, 1171
HyperGrid, 41
Hyperink, 1097
Hyperion, 1082
Hyperion Insurance Group, 815
Hyperion Therapeutics, 237, 1410
Hyperion Therpeutics, 2008
HyperKey, 226
Hyperlite Mountain Gear, 438, 1161
Hyperloop One, 809, 1329
Hyperloop Transportation Technologies, 1095
Hyperoptic, 1315
Hyperplane, 879
Hyperpublic, 1821
Hyperpulic, 1699
HyperQuality, 1237
HyperQuest, 1480
HyperScience, 107, 720, 743, 1613
Hypersonix, 1666
Hypertrust N.V., 2902
HyperVerge, 1285
HyperVR, 120
Hyperwallet Systems, 1476
Hyperwave, 2298
Hyperwear, 445
Hyperweek.net, 2310
Hyphen, 1006
Hypnion, 59, 747, 769
HypothenkenZentrum AG, 77
HYPR, 2, 305, 1611
HYPRES, 2369
Hypur, 963
Hyr, 754
Hysko, 2027
Hysolate, 996
Hythro Power Corporation, 2460
HyTrust, 483, 688, 852, 1850
Hytrust, 2278
Hyundai Oil Terminal, 3145
Hyunjin Materials and Yonghyun Base Materials, 892
Hyva, 2375
Hywire Ltd., 3249
HZO, 6, 1020, 1838
HzO, 2831

I

I and C-Cruise.Co, 721
I G Doors, 3017
I Need MD, 650
I'm Sick Mobile, 951
I-Concerts, 3152
I-Deal Optics, 1159
I-Film, 212
I-Food Chains, 2931

1338

Portfolio Companies Index

I-Logix, 23, 1334, 2779
i-Logix, 521
I-Mab Biopharma, 2690
i-merge, 2563
I-Neumaticos, 2553
i-Nexus, 2407
i-Optics BV, 2350
I-Payment, 493
I-Solutions Global, 2967
I-STAT, 1044
i-Team, 1097
I-Um, 100
i-Wireless, 1715
I.AM+, 890
I/OMagic Corporation, 865
I/Pro, 922
I/SCRIBES Corp., 588
i2, 2015
I20 Pharma, 2454
i2s, 3031
i2X, 1269
i3 Broadband, 1638
i3 Equity Partners, 809, 1154
i3 Mobile, 1704
I3 Precision, 3073
I4CP, 754
i4cp, 1250
i4i, 2199
IA Ventures, 37
Iaam, 2509
IAC, 2965
IACX Energy, 893
iAdvise, 2385
IAG Research, 260
Iagnosis, 1448
IAM Registry, 649
IAM Robotics, 519
Iamba, 436, 2782
iAmplify, 1080
IAMRobotics, 799
Ian's Natural Foods, 2238
Ianacare, 567
ianet, 2466
iAngel, 1323
ianTECH, 297
Ianthus, 390
iAnthus, 845
iAppPay, 1340
IASI, 3187
IASIS Healthcare, 894, 1039
Iasis Healthcare, 1835
IASIS Healthcare Corporation, 1271, 2379
IAT Automobile Technology, 1241
Iatroquest, 979
iAutomation, 1572
iBAHN, 1906
iBahn, 69
iBalance Medical, 1691
iBase, 3208
iBBS, 1409
iBeat, 488, 544, 1183
Ibeatyou.com, 1099
Iberchem, 2489, 2851
Ibex, 1335
Ibexis Technologies, 3107
Ibfx.com, 1717
IBI Biosensors, 2939
iBinom, 2938
iBiquity, 876
iBiquity Digital, 1305
IBIS Networks, 1061
Ibistic, 3013
IBK Bioanalytik, 2824
IBM, 473, 3212
Ibotta, 823, 858
iBoxPay, 2446
Ibpil, 260

iBreva, 310
IBS Software Services, 815
IC Axon, 723
IC Data Com, 742
IC Media, 3218
IC Potash, 1548
IC Works, 1087, 1896
iCAD, 1303
ICAP Media, 2355
iCardiac Technologies, 61, 1745
iCare.com, 3262
iCarsclub, 3073
Icarus, 3134
Icatus RT, 392
ICC Nexergy, 1014
ICC Wales, 2284
ICE, 1751
Ice Energy, 1603
Ice Group, 34
Ice Mobility, 916
Ice Protection, 222
Ice Tech, 1004
Ice.Com, 1460
Icebreaker, 934
IceCure Medical, 337
icejam, 2068
Iceline/Darko, 2471
iCentera, 1470
iCentris, 1583
Iceotope, 2439
Icera, 712, 2196, 2662, 2674
Icertis, 560, 641, 974
Icertis Applied, 1212
iCetana, 3248
ICG Commerce, 846
Ichor Systems, 109, 779
Ici, 3259
ICI Holding Company, 1492
iCims, 1759
IClean, 834
iClick, 954
iclick, 85
Icm, 2765
ICM Partners, 559
ICM Products Inc., 449
ICMS, 2366
Icom Cmt, 1728
Icon, 181, 858
ICON Health & Fitness, 1491
Icon Identity Solutions, 1209
Icon Vapor, 1079
Icon Ventures, 3284
Icon.me, 1810
Icona, 2892
iConclude, 1663
Iconectiv, 779
Iconery, 120, 397, 561
Iconfinder, 3203
Iconic Group, 788
Iconic Labs, 1850
Iconic Therapeutics, 660, 1268
Iconix, 791
Iconixx, 224, 904
Iconoculture, 536, 1952
iContact, 1333, 1886
Icontainers, 3223
IContracts, 655
iControl Networks, 455
Icopal, 1017
Icot, 260
Icovia, 308
ICPR Junior College, 63
Icq Holding, 2391
iCracked, 124
iCreate Software, 2849
ICREO Co. Ltd., 2347
iCrossing, 818, 1738

iCRTec, 1305
ICS, 2361
ICsense, 2366
ICurrent, 563
ICX Media, 876
Icynene, 787
iCYT, 975
iCyt, 1379
ID, 1334
ID Analytics, 1235, 1239, 1853
ID By DNA, 24
ID by DNA, 175
ID Entropy, 52
ID INCU, 3127
ID Quantique, 3068
ID Watchdog, 548
ID.me, 285, 793, 1531, 1632
ID5, 2296
ID90, 1806
ID90 Travel, 228
Idaciti, 1070
Idaho Pacific, 1166
Idanit, 2720
Idapted, 1600
IDbyDNA, 1613
IDC, 1705
Iddiction, 935
Idea, 626
IDEA AG, 2816
Idea AG, 3069
Idea Cellular, 1496
Idea Point, 329
Idea.me, 1518
ideaForge, 1509
IdeaFoundry, 3275
Ideal Binary, 2355
Ideal Crane, 1223
Ideal Image, 1088
Ideal Protein, 135
Ideal Response, 9
Ideal Spot, 545
Ideal Standard, 220
Ideal-Tridon, 985
Idealab, 502
Idealista, 135
Idealists, 624
Ideas, 1725
Ideas Revenue Organization, 1760
Ideaya Bioscience, 889
Ideaya Biosciences, 12
IDEC Pharmaceuticals, 1706
Ideeli, 567, 590, 1080, 1738, 1766
iDeeli, 1319
Idelic, 272, 408, 1384
Idelix Software, 979, 2097
Idemama, 2437
Idenix, 1268, 2513, 2690, 3007
IdentalSoft, 718
Identec Group, 1004
Identec Solutions, 2106
Identified, 378, 724, 1906
Identified Technologies, 272
Identifix/SRS, 1972
Identify, 2750
Identify Sotware, 2682
Identify3D, 243
Identilock, 488
Identity Engines, 947
Identity Group Holdings Corporation, 1209
Identity Mind, 249
Identity Software, 3137
Identive Group, 2979
Identropy, 1387
IdenTrust, 1558
IDERA, 959
Idera, 202
Idesta, 2863, 2863

1339

Portfolio Companies Index

Idetic, 1706
IDEV, 1500
Idev, 237
IDev Techologies, 1574
Idevices, 530
Idevio, 2619
Idex, 2863
Idexx, 1760
Idexx Laboratories, 747
IDG Capital Partners, 336
IDG Energy, 973
IDG Ventures India, 483
IDG Ventures SF, 3284
IDH, 2935
IDI, 1870
Idibon, 2978
Idinvest Partners, 483
Idiom, 1334
Idiom Technologies, 1672
IDIS, 1087, 2617
Idle Free, 1060
IDOC, 1189, 1572, 2332
iDoneThis, 1010, 1912
IDQ, 170
IDQ Holdings, 1491
IDreamSky, 1534
iDro, 392
IDS, 2899, 3239
IDS/Morshinkaya, 3095
Idun, 206
iDun, 1760
Idun Pharmaceuticals, 153, 1493, 1706, 1918, 2518
IDV Solutions, 1455
IDX, 46
IE CHP, 3135
IE-Engine, 1080
IEI Technologies., 2590
IEnergizer Limited, 403
iEntertainment Network, 1709
IEP Technologies, 1651
IEver, 1121
IEX, 260
IEX Group, 1782, 2132
If You Can, 89, 595
IF&P Foods, 443
if(we), 1119, 1184
Ifbyphone, 137, 1317, 1571, 1642, 1732
IfChange, 1121
Ifeelgoods, 1513, 1865
Ifesca, 2527
IFILM, 1704
iFire, 214
Iflix, 2690
iFLYTEK, 2936
IFM Therapeutics, 191
IfOnly, 15, 1524
Iforce, 2472
iForem, 805
IFOTEC, 2875
IFrameApps, 2669
iFreecomm, 1340
IFTTT, 124, 751, 1110, 1346, 1607
IGEM Therapeutics, 689
Igeneon, 2299, 2301, 2305
Igenica, 1382
Igenica Biotherapeutics, 517
Igenu, 809
IGG, 922, 973
iglo Group, 3033
Igloo, 790, 1037, 2153
Igloo Education, 2967
Igloo Products, 46
Igloo Vision, 2967
IGM Specialties, 170
Igneous, 1158, 1534
Ignis Careers, 55

Ignis Innovation, 2194
Ignite Technologies, 202
Ignition, 37
Ignition Group, 716
Ignition One, 1625
IgnitionOne, 22, 946, 1699
Ignyta, 514, 782
Ignyta Inc., 487
IGPS, 1516
IGPS Logistics LLC, 225
Igrok, 826
IguanaFix, 1509
Iguazio, 603, 1926, 2224
IGuiders, 1047
iGuitar, 1584
IHaveU, 1121
iHaveU, 2850
IHAVEU.com, 3062
IHC, 834
IHC Merwede Group, 3209
iHealtHome, 1061
iHear, 138
iHear Medical, 1119
iHeartMedia, 1815
iHello, 954
IHQ, 2857
Ihr Partner Software, 2713
IHS Markit, 3272
IHSInc, 2771
iimak, 104
iItoo, 1191
iiWisdom, 1627
IJenko, 2899
iJento, 2972, 2987
iJet, 1146
iJET Intelligent Risk Systems, 2196
IJReview, 617
IkamvaYouth, 1374
iKang, 690
Ikano Communications, 925
Ikano Therapeutics, 710
Ikanos, 1922
Ikanos Communications, 1474, 1793
Ikaria, 12, 153, 188, 1156, 1301, 1491, 1916, 2008, 2419
Ikaros Solar, 3020
Ikaros Solar Fund, 3042
ikaSystems, 1496
IKEA, 1096, 2881
Iken, 2574
iKingdom, 2048
Ikivo, 2754
Iknaos, 1779
iKobo, 2196
Ikon Science, 857
Ikon Semiconductor, 2918
IKOS, 1853
Ikos, 272
IL & FS Investment Limited, 805
IL MAKIAGE, 1088
Il Mare, 1087
IL&FS, 260
IL&FS Transportation, 867
ILAC, 2208
ILC Dover, 245
iLearning Engines, 1169
Ilerasoft, 218
Ilesfay, 479
ILEX, 312
ILEX Oncology, 1775
ILFS Technologies, 483
ILIAS-Medical, 2824
iLight, 1764
iLight Technologies, 378
Ilink, 2850
iLink Global, 1057
iLinkMD, 1915

Ilkos Therapeutics, 2092
Illinois Central Corporation, 575
Illinois Neurospine Institute, 61
IllinoisVENTURES LLC, 3265
IlloSpear, 2332
illuma Drive, 2142
Illumenix, 650
Illumeo, 358, 751
Illumigen Biosciences, 1398
Illumina, 153, 1394, 1604
Illuminate, 2342
Illuminate Education, 1000, 1136
Illumine Radiopharmaceuticals, 1577
Illumingen, 85
IlluminOss, 703, 1145, 1412
Illuminoss, 1693, 1731, 2939
Illuminoss Medical, 1298
Illumio, 107, 124, 816
Illumitex, 137, 144, 210, 826, 981, 1774
Illumix, 1121, 1183
Illumobile, 243
Illusense, 2278
Illusive, 996, 1154
Illusive Networks, 486
illusive networks, 483
Illustra, 1257, 1853
ILMO Products, 61
Ilos, 1176
iloxx GmbH, 3137
ILP, 168
ILSC Education Group, 1504
Ilum-A-Lite, 2613
Ilumin, 23
iLumin Corporation, 2652
iLumin Software, 315
Ilumno, 1000
ILX Holdings, 1573
ILX Holdings II, 1573
Ilypsa, 12, 1896
Im In, 130
im3D Clinic South, 3052
iM3dical, 3048
iM3MDICAL, 3031
IMA, 2446
Ima Engineering, 2873
ImaCor, 666
Image API, 1234
Image Cafe, 161
Image Centre, 2664
Image Metrics, 1239, 3092
Image Searcher, 1784
Image Skincare, 1231
Image Vision Labs, 1952
Image Ware Systems, 853
Image-Guided Neurologics, 1745
ImageBrief, 858
ImageFIRST, 368
Imagenet, 374
ImageQuix, 92
Imagetalk Oy, 2873
ImageVision, 1028
ImageX, 85
Imagimed, 1423
ImaginAb, 1350
Imaginatik Limited, 2760
Imagine, 679, 2577
Imagine Air, 1310
Imagine Communications, 2566, 2662
Imagine Health, 938
Imagine K12, 51
Imagine Learning, 1705
Imagine Nation, 2944
Imagine Technology Group, 838
ImagineAir, 1306
Imagineer Systems, 3107
Imaginetics, 443, 1071

Portfolio Companies Index

Imagitas (TMSI-Targeted Marketing Solutions), 1954
Imago BioSciences, 112, 782
Imago Biosciences, 495
Imalux, 642, 1544
Imanis Data Inc., 1004
Imara, 237
iMark, 202
iMarketing Solutions Group, 2043
Imax, 2073
IMAX Corp., 492
Imbellus, 1392, 1888
Imbera, 3013
Imbera Electronics, 2630
Imbria Pharmaceuticals, 1519
Imbruvica, 74, 495
IMC Limited, 1956
IMCD, 220, 2378
IMCO, 1374
IMCO Technologies, 1740
IMCS Group, 448
IMDS, 170
Imedex, 1930
Imedia, 3137
iMediation, 2415
iMedX, 3211
iMedX Holdings, 1557
ImeeGolf, 2355
Imeem, 1257
imeem, 58
Imergy, 595
IMERGY Power Systems, 1786
IMG, 21
IMG Midstream, 332
Imge, 617
Imgnation, 307
Imgur, 124, 1604
IMI AG, 2785
IMI Exchange, 1361
IMI Express, 832
IMI Intelligent Medical Implants AG, 3046
IMImobile, 743, 3070, 3131
IMinent, 2899
Imiplex, 266
Imix, 3149
imIX, 1593
IML, 1632
iML, 1747
Imlek Group, 3095
IMlogic, 563, 1080
Imm, 2715
Immaculate Baking Co., 1113, 1665
Immatics, 2475, 2797
Immedia, 2972
Immedia Semiconductor, 223
Immediately, 1885
Immediatelyapp.com, 1958
Immersed, 1004
Immersive Media, 2266
Immersive Media Tactical Solutions, 405
Immersv, 770, 792
Immgenics, 3007
Immidio, 3128
Immobilienscout24, 3233
Immortals, 561, 1813
Immotor, 823
Immucor, 1835
Immucor Inc., 1903
Immudicon, 622
Immulogic, 260
Immune Cellular, 181
Immune Design, 94, 517, 1490, 1618
Immune Targeting Systems, 2816
Immune Works, 658
Immunet, 1788
Immunetrics, 998, 1098, 1448
Immunix, 807

Immuno Gum, 1784
Immuno Photonics, 267, 569
ImmunoBiology, 2463, 2598, 3107, 3244
Immunogen, 1271
Immunome, 266, 1577
Immunomedics, 762
Immunomic Therapeutics, 1061, 1117
Immunovaccine, 2155
Immunovaccine Inc., 2092
Immunovalent Therapeutics, 870
Immunservice, 2824
ImmusanT, 1271
Immuta, 285, 535, 630
IMN, 349, 1334
IMO, 176
iMobileMagic, 3031
Imobox, 2438
iModules, 1105
IMoney, 721
Imonomi, 2646
iMove, 979, 1393
Impact, 37, 1114
Impact Applications, 3107
Impact Confections, 328
Impact Economics, 1286
Impact Fire Services, 373
Impact Group, 476
Impact HQ, 260
Impact Radius, 1534
Impact Technologies, 1377
ImpactGames, 998
Impacto, 2626
ImpactXoft, 310
Imparto Software, 626
Impath, 206
Impath Networks, 2058, 2143, 2205
Impaxx, 199
ImpediMed, 3138
Impel Microchip, 2417
Impel NeuroPharma, 1346, 1941
Impel Neuropharma, 12, 85
Impella Cardiosystems, 2748
Imperative Energy, 2295
Imperfect, 754
Imperfect Produce, 544, 1183, 1663
Imperial Machining, 1021
Imperial Plastics Inc., 843
Imperium Renewables, 1786
Impermium, 784, 1254
Impero, 1017
Imperva, 180
iMPERVA, 1212, 1896
Imperva Bot Management, 1286
Impeto Medical, 3113
Impinj, 153, 880, 1245, 1460, 1891
Impinq, 1922
Implandata Opthalmic Products, 2824
Implanet, 3113
Implantable Provider Group, 383
Implex Corporation, 1275
Impli, 626
Implus, 16, 168, 254
Imply, 124, 1069
Impopharma, 1916, 2130
Import.io, 107
Impossible, 511
Impossible Aerospace, 648
Impossible Foods, 107, 889, 1069
Impossible Software, 2604
ImpreMedia, 494
impreMedia, 897
Impress, 2377
Impression-Show, 2847
ImpressPages, 3049
Imprint Energy, 1613
Imprivata, 1460
Improbable, 124, 535

Improveline, 2380
Impulse Monitoring, 1866
Impulse Monitoring Inc., 176
IMRSV, 679, 1518
IMS, 541, 596, 2058
IMS Health, 1109, 2379
Ims Health, 1835
IMScouting, 2352
IMSRV, 1736
Imstem Biotechnology, 530
IMSWorkX, 704
Imt, 1626
Imtex, 2197
Imubit, 851
imusic-school, 3113
IMV, 2602
Imvelo Forests, 834
IMVision, 2419
IMVU, 339
IMX, 3127
In Addition, 649
In Crowd, 2987
In Go, 1070
In Go Money, 508
In The Swim, 194
In The Swim Inc., 774
In-Q-Tel, 3270, 3273
In.vision Research, 1745
In2itive Bsuiness Solutions LLC, 1053
Inadco, 1896
Inapac, 2436
Inapac Technologies, 1354
Inaplex, 3107
Inari, 747, 1928
Inasoft, 455
Inboard, 1888
InboundWriter, 764
Inbox, 418, 544
INC 500 Companies, 35
INC Research, 57, 209
INCA, 2348
InCarda Therapeutics Inc., 181
InClassToday, 1527
inCode Telecom, 757
inCode Telecom Group, 162
InComm, 224, 1956
InContext Solutions, 106, 251, 962, 1004, 1455
InCrowd, 1100
InCube Ventures, 1124
Indalo Therapeutics, 267
Indco, 1870
INDEECO, 61
Indeed, 1882
Indegy, 49, 180
InDemand Interpreting, 918
Independa, 1221, 1237
Independa Inc., 487
Independence, 2857
Independence Care System, 1420
Independent Bank, 638
Independent Commercial, 2709
Independent Imaging, 1606
Independent Living Solutions, 1361
Independent Living Systems, 1165
Independent Network Television Holdings, 2465
InDex, 2562
Index IQ, 793
Index Stock Imagery, 1275
Indextank, 32, 231, 784
Indexus Biomedical, 737
Indi, 222, 1010, 2144
Indi Molecular, 181
Indi Semiconductor, 274
India Resources Limited, 1548
Indiagames, 58
IndiaHomes, 2818
Indialdeas.com, 1776

1341

Portfolio Companies Index

Indiamart.com, 1004
Indian Dreams, 2783
Indian Energy Exchange, 1121
indian Energy Exchange, 834
Indiana Business Bank, 1964
Indiana Limestone Company, 2009
IndiaProperty.com, 386, 1184
Indicee, 2053
INDICO, 1589
Indico, 2
Indico.co, 313
Indie Semiconductor, 204
IndieGoGo, 1226, 1563
Indiegogo, 243, 525, 724, 1000, 1001, 1075, 1968, 2280
Indigenous Media, 60
Indigo, 747, 2058
Indigo Agriculture, 20
Indigo Biosciences, 1117
Indigo Biosystems, 702
Indigo Natural Resources LLC, 1851
Indigo Pipelines, 3104
Indigo Vision, 3104
InDinero, 384
inDinero, 229, 1054
Indio, 525, 1202, 1218
Individual.com, 260
Indix, 206, 2406
IndMusic, 1813
Indo-European Foods, 443, 1343
Indochino, 1158, 2280
Indoo.rs, 3165
Indoor Atlas, 1244
Indoor Direct, 1771
IndoStar Capital Finance, 1627
IndoTraq, 1244
Indow Windows, 1463, 3277
Indulge Desserts, 193
Indus, 1721
Indusind Bank, 815
Industrial Access, 2471
Industrial Accoustics Company, 64
Industrial Air Tool, 2022
Industrial Bank Co. Ltd, 2594, 2595
Industrial Ceramic Solutions, 1261
Industrial Container Services, 901
Industrial Defender, 2315
Industrial Lighting Products, 1435
Industrial Magnetics, 1343, 1569
Industrial Media, 559
Industrial Piping, 276, 1726
Industrial Safety Technologies, 1189
Industrial Securities Co. Ltd, 2594
Industrial Securities Co. LtdChina Merchants Secur, 2595
Industrial Service Solutions, 654
Industrial Services Group, 1605
Industrial Toys, 1480
Industrial Valley Title, 832
Industrial Water Treatment Solutions, 1469
Industrias Y Fundiciones Iglesias, 2985
Industrical Container Services, 199
Industrios Software, 2058
Industrious, 727
Industry Partners: Deloitte, 3272
Industry Weapon, 998, 1447
INEA, 1956
Ineda Systems, 483, 1509
Inest, 1384
iNest, 807, 1379
iNet Interactive, 378
INETCO Systems, 2143
INetU Holdings, 361
inexio Informationstechnologie und Telekommunikati, 3067
INF Tech Enterprises, 1837
Infacare, 191

InfaCare Pharmaceutical, 919
inFakt, 3044
Infantium, 1061
Infarm, 2478
Inficomm, 466
Infilaw, 1742
InfiLaw System, 21
Infiltrator Systems, 846, 1456
Infiltrator Systems Inc., 1014
Infinate Z, 979
Infinera, 144, 278, 536, 968, 1760, 1884
Infineta, 1334
Infinia ML, 416
Infinian Corp, 1460
Infinicon, 563
Infinio, 935
InfiniRoute Networks, 184, 947
Infinit, 2365
Infinite, 445
Infinite Analytics, 1483
Infinite Electronics Inc., 819
Infinite English, 822
Infinite Graphics, 3279
Infinite Power Solutions, 144, 538, 979, 1460
Infinite Road, 3273
Infinite Uptime, 622
Infinity, 74
Infinity Broadcasting Corporation, 575
Infinity CCS, 2967
Infinity Finance Ltd., 2788
Infinity Laser Centers, 63
Infinity Natural Resources, 1278, 1326
Infinity Pharmaceuticals, 1493
Infinity Quick, 2137
Infitel, 2377
Infitel International N.V., 2673
Inflammatix Inc., 1069
InflaRX, 2527
InflaRx, 1519
Inflazome, 1143, 1350
Inflection, 547, 1181, 1760
Inflection Energy, 332
Inflow, 541, 2856
inflow Control, 3099
Inflow Group, 897
Inflow Inc., 1724
Influe, 2765
Influence Health, 1683
Influitive, 32, 534, 741, 976, 1121, 1546, 2113, 2132, 2137, 2236
Influxdata, 235
InfluxDB, 1184
Info Pro Solutions, 3041
Info Talk, 2890
Info Trust, 210
Infoaxe, 115, 1089
Infobase, 446, 1927
InfoBionic, 347, 703, 1601, 1784
Infobionic, 1100
Infobjects, 2735
Infoblox, 633, 757, 1348, 1379, 1654, 1796, 1853
Infobright, 2153
InfoChimp, 724
Infocrossing, 865
InfoDif, 2437
Infodustry, 2607
Infoether, 989
InfoGear Technology, 852
InfoGenesis, 2698
InfoGin, 536
Infogix, 928
Infoglide Software, 1008
Infogr.am, 3044
Infogroup, 433, 1166
InfoHighway, 1136
Infokom Elektrindo, 3061

InfoLibria, 314
InfoLogix, 925
Infomark, 3127
Infomart International, 1241
Infomedics, 1334
Infomove, 85
Infonaut, 2058
Infoniqa, 2887
Infopaginas Inc., 63
Infopress, 2487
Infor, 839
Infor Global Solutions, 1752
InfoReady Corporation, 742
Inform Diagnostics, 209
Informatica, 238, 1121, 1607
Information Builders, 333
Informative, 1003, 3231
Informed DNA, 1349
InformedDNA, 3262
Informu, 1507
InfoScout, 221
InfoSec, 2590
Infosec, 2998
Infosum, 1888
InfoTalk Corporation, 2079
Infotrieve, 402, 1850
Infoucs Health Ltd, 2894
InfoUSA, 192
InfoVista S.A., 1814
Infra, 1604
Infra Group/Verbraeken, 3232
Infracommerce, 754
Infrafone, 2619
Inframetrics, 521
Infrant, 2436
InfraReDx, 1616
InfraScale, 548
Infrascale, 416
InfraScan, 266
Infrasoft, 1295
Infrasoft Technologies, 2490
Infrasonics, 1706
Infrastructure and Industrial Constructors USA, 801
Infrastructure Networks, 98
InfraTrac, 3092
Infusio, 2481
Infusion Biosciences, 1843
Infusion Soft, 173, 1070
Infusionsoft, 1247, 1677
Infusystem, 1970
Infutor, 1346
ING Vysya Bank, 2599, 2600
InGameAd, 3121
Ingemas, 2489
Ingenero, 2618
Ingenica, 1811
Ingenio, 92, 608, 1003
Ingenious Med, 176, 271, 550, 1052
Ingenuity, 1558
Ingenuity Systems, 237, 986
Ingenuityprep, 1316
InGo, 383
Ingo Money, 1240
Ingrain, 2700
Ingresse, 1509
Ingrian, 933
INgrooves, 69
Ingulex, 1382
Inhalon Biopharma, 1613
Inhance Media Audiolife, 1784
Inhance Technologies, 170, 199
InheritedHealth, 1099
InHerSight, 1259
Inhibitex, 1398
Inhibox, 2892
InhibRx, 1519

Portfolio Companies Index

Inhibrx LLC, 487
INI Farms, 2313, 3199
ini3, 3127
Ininal, 2437
Inion, 2562
Inion Ltd., 2816
InishTech, 2522, 2918
Init Innovation, 3069
Init Live, 2284
Init.ai, 305
Initech, 3168
Initiate, 1400, 1615
Initiate Systems, 1672
Injae Tongil Village Co., 584
Injured Workers Pharmacy, 46, 194, 1491
Injury Sciences, 734
Ink, 229, 585
Inka Oy, 2966
Inkbox, 1183, 2137
Inkd, 1641
Inked, 256, 271
Inked Brands, 896
Inkine Pharmaceutical Company, 1394
Inkling, 968, 1054, 1654, 1796
InkSpin1, 2390
Inland, 901
Inland American Real Estate Trust Inc., 869
Inland Container Express, 1605
Inlet Medical, 1113
Inlet Technologies, 538, 1782
InLight Communications, 2910
Inlustra, 1784
Inlustra Technologies, 1915
InMage, 115
Inman Investment Management, 3284
Inmar, 1301, 2207
Inmark, 1505
Inmark Services, 35
Inmarsat, 135
INMATEC Technologies GmbH, 2686
inMediata, 921
InMobi, 1460, 1666
inmobly, 1553
Inmotion Entertainment Group, 354
Inn Road, 1584
InnaMed, 622
InnaPhase, 1136
Innara Health, 1379
Innate Pharma, 1516, 2466
Inncercool Therapies, 1786
Inner City Broadcasting, 1409
Inner City Media Corporation, 897
Inner Loop Capital, 3270
Inner Wireless, 1244
Inneractive, 2726
InnerChange, 558
iNNERHOST, 1724
Innerpac, 1456
Innerpass, 1734
InnerProduct Partners, 1157
InnerPulse, 177
Innerspace, 2027
Innerstave, 940
Innervate, 773
InnerVision Medical Technologies, 2048
InnerWireless, 441, 1017, 1558
Innes, 2308
InNetwork, 2155
Innis & Gunn, 1088
Inno Light, 578
InnoCentive, 1124
Innocentive, 979, 1720
Innochip Technology, 2857
Innocoli, 1698
InnoCOMM Wireless, 764
Innocor, 1753
Innocrin, 1008, 1124

Innocrin Pharmaceuticals, 182
Innocutis, 224
InnoCyte, 2824
Innofact, 2829
Innofact AG, 2838
Innofidei, 1534
Innofidei Corporation, 2974
InnoGraft, 1604
Innography, 202
innogreen, 2936
Innolight, 1121
Innolume, 144
Innolume GmbH, 3046
InnoMake, 1509
Innometrix, 995, 1187
InnoMotix, 2824
InnoPad, 712, 1913
InnoPath, 1244, 1604, 3214
InnoPath Software, 1241, 1906
InnoPharma, 188, 1817
Innorex Technologies, 3145
Innospark Ventures, 3273
Innostream, 2833
InnoTech, 765
Innotech Solar, 3013
Innotrac, 1742
Innouvo, 3273
Innov-X Systems, 438
Innova, 36, 753, 1607
Innova B2B Logistics, 2859
Innova Card, 2875
Innova Corporation, 1398
Innova Dynamics, 1558
Innova Light, 2632
Innovaccer, 1121
InnovAge, 1972
Innovalight, 153, 184, 1855
Innovari, 1906
Innovasic, 856
Innovasic Semiconductor, 1901
Innovatel, 493
Innovatia Medical Systems, 3262
Innovatient, 1097
Innovatient Solutions, 678
Innovation, 753
Innovation Capital, 986
Innovation Works, 3275
Innovative, 959, 969, 1041
Innovative Aftermarket Systems, 819
Innovative Biosensors, 1299
Innovative Building Systems, 928
Innovative Chemical Products, 1166
Innovative Food Processors, 118
Innovative Health Products, 528
Innovative Healthcare Systems, 1708
Innovative Micro Technologies, 69
Innovative Micro Technology, 1237
Innovative Pressure Technologies, 211
Innovative Robotics, 807, 1180
Innovative Silicon, 202
Innovative Solutions & Support, 52, 56, 1227
Innovative Supply Solutions, 266
Innovative Technology, 1604
Innovectra, 1146
Innovectra Corporation, 2196
Innoveer Solutions, 521
Innovent Biologics, 710
Innovent Systems, 1918
Innovest, 299
Innovex Downhole Solutions, 1009
Innovia, 1604
Innovid, 483
Innovion, 1288
Innovis, 1327
InnoVision Imagine Laboratory, 737
Innovium, 872, 1509
Innovium Inc., 1951

Innoviz, 116, 2296
Innoz, 3109
Innozen, 1784
innRoad, 288, 1306
Inocucor Technologies, 2093
Inogen, 40, 206, 3015
Inopen, 3211
Inotec AMD, 3028
Inotek, 946, 1558, 2970
Inotek Pharmaceuticals, 925, 1196
Inova Labs, 1094, 1819
Inova Payroll, 459
Inovateus Solar, 1229
iNovia Capital, 2032
Inovis, 1672
Inovise Medical Inc, 3162
Inovision, 1128
Inovus Solar, 1458
Inovys Corporation, 1407
Inozyme Pharma, 1143
Inpact, 2481
Inpaq Technology, 2603
Inpensa, 1577
InPhase, 1676
InPhenix, 1929
Inpher, 317, 563
Inphi Corp., 1087, 1779, 2457
Inphi Corporation, 1951, 2926
InPhonic, 538, 1227
Inplat, 3150
inPlug, 1509
inPowered, 1558, 2236
Inpria, 1004, 1383
Inpulse, 2329
InQ, 954
InQuira, 1760, 2079
INRange Management Systems, 293
INRange Systems, 452, 944, 1117
InReach, 1783
InRentive, 1178
INRFOOD, 951
INRIX, 126, 221, 1916
Inrix, 197, 1004
INS, 1654
INS SA, 2828
Insales, 2344
Inscentinel, 2967
Insception Biosciences, 2196
Insception Lifebank, 2043
Inscope, 658
Inscopix, 107, 751
Inscripta, 762, 1916
Inseal Medical, 1460
Inseec, 2851
Insense, 3107
InSense Inc., 1951
Inserm Transfert Initiative, 2530
Insert Therapeutics, 371
Inside Contactless, 2380
Inside Higher Ed, 61, 1504
Inside Real Estate, 9
Inside Secure, 1327
Inside Tracker, 1172
Inside-Secure, 3235
Inside.Com, 1654
Insidehack, 1530
InsidePacket, 648
Insider Technologies, 3244
InsideSales.com, 1607, 2019
Insidesales.com, 688, 1896
InsideSherpa, 795
InsideTrack, 1522
InsideView, 665, 770, 1540, 1725, 1728
Insieve, 3019
Insight, 206
Insight 2 Design, 1606
Insight Communications, 559

1343

Portfolio Companies Index

Insight Engines, 563
InSight Eye Care, 378
Insight Global, 159, 374
Insight Global Inc., 914
InSight Health Services Corp. Inc., 894
Insight Health Solutions, 1693
InSight Management, 505
InSight Mobile Data, 29
Insight Plus, 2646
Insight Squared, 260, 609, 1322
Insight Technologies Network Academy, 2709
Insight2Profit, 610
Insightera, 1121
insightexpress, 2771
InsightGlobal, 1109
Insightly, 665
Insightpool, 1782
Insightra Medical, 3097
InsightRX, 519
InsightSquared, 38, 534, 1607
Insignia Energy, 2067
Insignia Systems, 3279
Insikt, 32, 743
Insilico Medicine, 1701
Insilixa, 2978
InSite Medical Technologies, 666
InSite One, 184
Insite Wireless Group, 427
Insited, 2638
Insitro, 124, 762
insitro, 889
Insitu, 85
Insitu Group, 1641
InSleep Technologies, 1993
Insmed, 762, 1508, 2748
Insmed Inc., 1008
InSoft, 56
Insolu, 3262
InSound Medical, 371
Insound Medical, 138
Insource Contract Services, 556, 1469
InSpa, 85, 595
inSparq, 1632
Inspection Oilfield Services, 1422
Inspectorio, 1176
Insperity, 1770, 3267
Inspherion, 1047
InspiraFarms, 2439
Inspirato, 36, 581, 634, 741, 1001, 1075, 1235
Inspire, 136, 306, 561, 1363
Inspire Brands, 1576
Inspire Living, 995
Inspire Medical Systems, 1382, 1772, 1802, 1896
Inspire Pharmaceuticals, 1008
Inspired Group Ltd, 2361
Inspired Teaching Demonstration School, 1316
Inspiron Logistics, 1047
Inspo Network, 1499
Inspur-Cisco Networking Technology, 483
Insta Health Solutions, 1013
Instabank, 2940
Instabase, 124, 872
Instabridge, 2478
Instacart, 124, 386, 518, 802, 1069, 1075, 1654, 1761, 2012
instacart, 1662
InStadium, 80, 944, 1802
Instadium, 1606
InstaEDU, 544, 1696
Instagift, 773
Instagram, 124, 231, 248, 265, 1654, 1821
Installation Made Easy, 1576
Installed Building Products, 1134
Installs Inc., 405
InstaMed, 179, 416, 1328, 1387
Instamotor, 707, 994
Instana, 3161

Instant, 1072, 2965
Instant Web, 1491
Instantis, 1038, 1896
Instantly, 791
Instapage, 1255
Instaread, 1768
Instart, 124
Instart Logic, 777, 1760, 1796
Instartlogic, 820, 1075
Instavest, 1329
Instawares, 224
Instawork, 625
Instill, 986, 1672
Instill Corporation, 455
Instinctiv, 432, 1584
Instinctive, 679
Institute For Integrative Nutrition, 1345
Institute of Finance & Management, 863
Institutional Shareholder Services, 819, 1931, 2698
Institutional Venture Partners, 3284
Instituto Cidade Democratica, 1374
Instnt, 1554
Instore, 607, 1150
InStore Finance, 1047
InStream, 534
InStream Media, 1734
Instructables, 231, 1359
Instructure, 688, 826, 1830, 1884
Instrument Development Corporation, 1252
Instrument Sales and Service, 1422
Instrumental, 648, 741
Instylla, 176
Insulcheck, 2355
Insulet Corp., 138
Insurance Auto Auctions, 713, 1252
Insurance Auto Auctions Inc., 1903
Insurance Claims Management, 1572
Insurance Technologies, 9
Insurance Technologies Corporation, 29
Insurance.com, 912, 1738
Insuranceforchildren.ca, 2128
InsureCert Systems, 2266
Insureon, 39
Insurity, 819, 1970
Insurrection Media, 1813
Insymphony, 264
Insyncro, 2623
Intacct, 260, 547, 665, 1024, 1725, 1760
Intacct Corporation, 1038, 1672
Intact Medical Corps., 23
Intact Vascular, 1508
Intalio, 1416, 2005
Intamac, 2295, 3244
Intana Bioscience, 2824
InTANK, 1573
Intapp, 857
Intarcia, 762, 1516, 1519
Intarcia Therapeutics, 94, 237, 867, 986, 1298
Intec, 2771
Intec Pharma, 3245
Intec Telecom Systems, 2709
InTech Aerospace, 213
Intechra, 667, 1689
INTEG Process Group, 998
Integen, 115
IntegenX, 560, 621, 946, 979, 1094, 1515
Intego, 260
Integra, 21
Integra Life Sciences, 1494, 1918
Integra Securities, 2490
Integracare, 2226
Integragen, 2354, 2851, 2876
Integral, 954, 1255, 1425
Integral Access, 536
Integral Ad Science, 38, 539, 560, 1486
Integral Development, 57

Integral Development Corporation, 2196
Integral Energy Management, 1895
Integral Wave, 1558
Integrant Technologies, 1087, 2807
Integrate, 518, 768, 776
Integrate.ai, 2132, 2225
Integrated Advantage Group, 984
Integrated Aerospace Manufacturing, 611
Integrated Biosystems, 1251
Integrated Cable Assembly Holdings, 849
Integrated Chipware, 1227
Integrated Defense Technologies, 1925
Integrated Dental Holdings, 2944
Integrated Diagnostic Centers, 806
Integrated Energy Services, 187
Integrated Global Services, 985
Integrated Healthcare Strategies, 374
Integrated Materials Incorporated, 1089
Integrated Packaging Group, 2814
Integrated Photovoltaics, 1089
Integrated Polymer Solutions, 985
Integrated Portfolio Management Services, 1745
Integrated Power Services, 1368
Integrated Silicon Systems, 1008
Integrated Spatial Information Solutions, 1837
Integrated Turf Solutions, 1343
Integrated Vascular Systems, 1896
Integration Management, 2622
Integration Technologies, 63
Integrex, 753
Integri Chain, 52
IntegriChain, 29, 1328
IntegriCo Composites, 457
Integrien, 502
Integriertes Resource Management, 2783
Integris Software, 49, 180, 1158
Integrity, 959
Integrity Marketing Group, 914
Integrity Services, 406
Integro, 1368, 1978
Intel, 836
Intela Global Limited, 2507
Intelenet, 277
IntelePeer, 184, 652, 925, 1906
Intelerad, 2206
Intelesens, 2610
Intelex, 909, 1041
Intelipost, 3056
InteliSecure, 790
Intelisum, 1884
Intelius, 928
Intelivote Systems, 2184
Intelizon Energy, 3211
Intellasset, 3182
Intelle Innovations, 2966
Intellectual Technology, 374
Intellectual Ventures, 455, 1676
Intellefex, 2005
Intelleflex, 912, 1257, 1305, 1646
IntelleGrow, 1374
Intellia Therapeutics, 191, 709
Intellibridge, 954
Intellicare, 1532
Intellicare America, 438
IntelliCare america Inc., 572
IntelliCyt, 1300, 1488, 1924
Intelliden, 925
Intelliflux, 297
Intelligence Controls, 1336
Intelligent Beauty, 925
Intelligent Bio-Systems, 1347
Intelligent Clearing Network, 642, 1097
Intelligent Energy, 3135
Intelligent Epitaxy Technology, 1180
Intelligent Flying Machines, 622
Intelligent InSites, 173
Intelligent ION, 85

1344

Portfolio Companies Index

Intelligent Markets, 2005
Intelligent Medical Devices, 1915
Intelligent Mobile Support, 1047, 1447, 1553
Intelligent Office, 3244
Intelligent Reasoning Systems, 153
Intelligent Retinal Imaging Systems, 224
Intelligent Soil Recycling, 2186
IntelligentReach, 3104
Intelligrated, 881, 1728, 3033
Intellihot, 400
Intellihot Green Technologies, 983
Intellijoint, 2187
Intellikine, 1896
Intelliment Security, 3108
Intellimize, 941, 942
Intellinet, 656
Intellinote, 876
Intellio Therapeutics, 762
IntelliPack, 734
Intelliquest, 202
Intellirod Spine, 1047
Intelliseek, 979
Intellispace, 187
Intellispark, 883
Intellisports, 2245
Intelliteach, 361, 1343
IntelliView Technologies, 2048
IntelliVision, 249, 1013
Intellivote Systems, 2205
Intelliworks, 1348, 2196
Intellus Learning, 1551
Intelocate, 2138
Intelomed, 1448
IntelRa, 3127
Intelsat, 683, 1156, 1683
Intelsat Holdings, 3201
Intelsoft Technologies, 85
Intelyt, 93
Intematix, 563, 609, 791
INTENIUM, 2994
Intenium GmbH, 2673
Intense, 2662, 2674
Intense Photonics, 2336
Intent, 1596
Intent Media, 1000, 1181, 1534
Intent Technologies, 3239
Inter Ana, 1154
Inter Co., 2907
Inter V Medical, 2107
inter-touch, 3168
Interact Public Safety Systems, 238
Interact.io, 3108
InterAct911, 1681
Interaction Laboratories, 1599
Interactions, 518, 1339, 1672, 1673, 1699, 1886
Interactive Advisory Software, 1788, 1863
Interactive Data, 1956
Interactive Health, 787
Interactive Investor, 2972
Interactive Investor International, 1494
Interactive Media Holdings, 1604
Interactive Supercomputing, 747
Interactive Television, 1734
Interagon, 2369
Interana, 107, 235
Interational Equipment Solutions, 1085
Interative Retail Management Inc., 588
Interative.ai, 1138
Interaxon, 2068, 2831
InterBay Technologies, 1171
Interbest, 3232
Interbest Holding B.V., 2379
InterCall, 1708
Intercasting Corporation, 1175
Intercell, 3007
Intercell AG, 2785, 3137
Intercept, 74, 1382

Intercept Pharmaceuticals, 495
Intercept Technology, 2527
InterChina Network Software, 3062
interCloud, 3208
Intercom, 889, 1075, 1696
Interconnect Devices, 1234
Intercos, 1088
Intercus, 2527
InterDent, 928
Interdent, 1491
Interface, 1792
Interface Biologics, 2087
Interface Security Systems, 333
Interface Solutions, 1990
Interfolio, 285, 1000
Intergraph, 924, 1041, 1835
Intergraph Corp., 1903
Intergrasco, 2369
Interim, 541
Interior Define, 727, 858, 1480
Interior Heavy Equipment Operator School, 2145
Interior Logic Group, 1134, 1270
Interior Specialists, 1086
Interior Specilists Inc., 869
Interlace Medical, 136
Interlacken Capital, 1295
Interland, 315
Interleukin Genetics, 237, 946
Interlink Communications, 1986
Interlinq Software, 753
Interlogix, 1141
Interlude, 1004
Interluxe Holdings, 1104
Intermad, 2923
Intermarine, 1301
Intermatix, 1474
Intermed, 2824
Intermedia, 1156, 1327
Intermedia.net, 1360
Intermedix, 1815
Intermex Holdings, 1129
InterModal Data, 1072
InterMolecular, 1896
Intermolecular, 1534
InterMune, 94
InterMune Pharmaceuticals, 1616
Intern, 1830
Internap, 596, 852, 1255, 1637
International, 1295, 2556
International Aerospace Coatings, 1904
International Asset Systems, 1956
International Budget Partnership, 1374
International Car Wash Group, 1576
International Components, 1728
International Decision Systems, 1763
International Development, 1422
International Education Corporation, 250
International Fitness Holdings, 2275
International Logging, 1573
International Market Centers, 220
International Meal Company Holdings SA, 63
International Media Group, 1769
International Media Partners, 1927
International Medical Group, 1837
International Mortgage Bank, 3234
International Quantum Epitaxy, 1227
International Silver, 494
International Telecommunication Data Systems, 530
International Test Technologies, 2705
International Textile Group, 500
Internationella Engelska Skolan, 1776
InterNations, 2441, 2829, 2838
Internet Auction, 1087
Internet B, 1082
Internet Brands, 924, 1041, 1534
Internet Broadcasting, 1725

Internet Is Fun, 2352
Internet Number Corporation, 1704
Internet Photonics, 1305, 1793
Internet Profiles, 1850
Internet Secure, 2058
Internet Sports Marketing, 2709
InternetCorp, 2309
Internetwork AG/Q Inc, 2682
Internext, 3208
Interntional Coffee Group, 459
InterOptic, 1480
Interoute Communications, 559
Interperse, 1407
Interplay, 2669
Interplay Learning, 1670
Interrad Medical, 1802
InterResolve, 2478
Interroll, 2922
InterSAN, 1133
Intersan, 592
Intersec, 483
Intersect, 1500
Intersect ENT, 1445
Intersect Enterprises, 1896
Intersect Labs, 795
Intersent Ent., 74
InterServ Services Corporation, 1708
Interset, 132
Intership, 1164
Intersil, 260
InterSpec, 1161
Intersperse, 502
Interstate, 839
Interstate Hotels & Resorts, 1081
Interstate Soutwest, 225
InterSwitch Limited, 2345
InterTrust, 2005
Intertug, 584
Intervalv, 1986
InterVene, 1097
Intervene, 544
Intervention Insights, 251, 475, 943
Interventional Imaging Inc., 420
Interventional Spine, 176
Interventional Spine Inc., 269
Interventional Technologies, 1760
InterVideo Corp., 947
Interviewed, 858, 1329
Interviewing.io, 1054, 1758
InterVisions Systems, 960
InterWave, 939
Interwell, 2731
InterWest Partners, 3284
Interwise, 925, 2079, 2781, 3124
Interwoven, 349, 757, 1038
InterWrap, 1505
InterXion, 986
Interxion, 223, 1596
Intesource, 856
Intezer, 1004, 1611
Intezyne, 266
inthinc, 462
Intigua, 436
Intility, 3013
Intimate Bridge 2 Conception, 998
Intime Software, 2682
Intineris, 3042
Intio, 747
Intiva, 1191
Intiva Biopharma, 1191
Into Networks, 1604
INTO University Partnerships, 1105
IntoNow, 1534
IntoPIX, 3225
inTouch, 1286
InTouch Health, 251, 806
Intown Golf Club, 189

Portfolio Companies Index

Intoxalock, 1972
Intra Links, 853
Intra-Cellular Therapies, 1328, 1420
Intradiem, 1041, 1571
Intradigm Corporation, 1124
Intrado, 1038
Intrafusion Holding Corporation, 1189
IntraLase, 652, 1921
Intralign, 97
Intralink Concept Sdn Bhd, 3164
IntraLinks, 1409, 1558, 1776
Intralinks, 23
Intransa, 1558, 1896
IntraOp Medical Corporation, 1090
IntraPac, 2208, 2209
IntraPace, 980
Intrapace, 129
IntraPoint, 989
Intraprise Health, 918
Intratech Medical, 3241
Intravascular Imaging Inc., 347
Intrepid, 3262
Intrepid Learning, 793
Intrepid Learning Solutions, 1250
Intresco, 2961
Intrexon, 514, 1812
Intricately, 1758
Intrinergy, 1273
Intrinsa, 1474
Intrinsic, 741, 1516, 2769
Intrinsic Graphics, 1704
Intrinsic ID, 3051
Intrinsic Therapeutics, 867, 1298
Intrinsiq Materials, 432
Intrinsity, 56
IntroFly, 1615
IntroHive, 2143
Introhive, 1607, 2068, 2200
Intrommune, 1577
Intronis, 1380
Introspective Systems, 1160
IntruGuard, 2853
IntruVert Networks, 1853
INTTRA, 22
Intucell, 260
Intuit, 197
Intuition Robotics, 1611, 1834
Intuitive Creations, 3073
Intuitive Health, 96
Intuitive Surgical, 1691
Intuity Medical, 40, 666, 1817, 1896, 1928
Intuityy Medical, 1916
Intune Networks, 1715, 2918
Inturn, 761, 1110
IntuView, 3240
Intuwave, 2781
Intvnet, 2857
Intwine Connect, 420
Inui Health, 107
Invaluable, 178, 646, 1000
Invaragen, 2513
Invarium, 1378, 1791
Invatron Systems, 1777
Invendo Medical, 3196
Invenia, 1613, 2019
Invenias, 2972
Invenio Imaging, 1238
InvenLux, 3194
Invenra, 1292, 2001
InvenSense, 620
Invensys Plc., 1903
Invensys Sealing Systems, 2644
Inventables, 567, 635, 1860
inVentiv Health, 1815
Inventory Connections, 622
InVenture, 707, 1222
Inventus, 500, 1503

Inventus Capital Management, 623
Inventus Power, 1086
Inventys, 1580, 2078
Inventys Thermal, 1241
Inveresk, 2556
Inverness Medical Innovations, 1394
Inversa Systems, 2200
Inversago Pharma, 2130
Inverse, 563
Inverstiere.ch, 2310
Inveshare, 1025
Invest Cloud, 793
Invest Detroit, 3269
Invest Michigan, 3269
Invest Southwest, 3276
Investa Företagskapital, 2867
Investar, 264
InvestCloud, 1066
Investcorp International, 3255
InvestEdge, 998
Investedin, 1055, 1965
Investiere.ch, 650
Investis, 2472
InvestLab, 1906
Investor Members: 3TS Capital Partners, 3270
InvestX, 2266
Invi, 2831
InVia Robotics, 306, 663
Invibed, 1551
Invicta Medical, 648
Invidi, 1010, 1926
INVIDI Technologies, 1202
InView Technology Corporation, 979
Invincea, 876, 904, 1291
Invinia, 678
inVino, 1097, 1958
Invinsec, 173
Inviragen, 458, 1921, 2690
Invirsa, 479
Invisable Hand Networks, 314
InVisage, 171, 455, 1010, 1327, 1579
InvisibleCRM, 2320
InVision, 235
Invision, 22, 743, 820, 1314
InvisionHeart, 1261
Invitae, 1382, 1817
Invitae Corp., 2130
Invitalia Ventures, 483
Invite Media, 858
Invited Media, 814
Invitrogen, 118
InVivo AI, 2066, 2212
Invivo Data, 1354
Invivodata, 548, 947, 2196
Invivolink, 1615
Invixium, 2190
Invo Healthcare, 1465
Invoca, 28, 306, 1566, 1607, 1888
InvoCare, 2951
Invodo, 1597, 1658
Invoice2go, 1560
InvoiceLink, 1008
Invoke Solutions, 925
Involta, 1153
Involver, 260, 454
InvolveSoft, 306
Involvio, 483
Invro, 3107
Invuity, 1010, 1898, 1993
Inxent, 1818
Inxight, 979
Inxight Software, 23, 1906
Inxite Software, 925
InXpo, 925
Inxpo, 935
Inzign Private, 3062
IO, 1480, 1742

IO Education, 1136
IO Pipe, 1158
IO Turbine, 1121
Iobit, 973
Iobox, 3179
ioBox, 2380
IOCORE, 2709
IOD, 1136
Iodine, 1222, 1716
iOffice, 1963
Iogen Corporation, 2058
Ioline Corporation, 753
Iolon Inc., 1003
Iomai, 1786
Iomando, 1061
Iome, 2229
Iomega, 1896
IOMX, 1268
ION Investment Group, 1776
Ion Torrent, 237
IonField Systems, 230
Ionic, 173, 724, 816, 1075, 1118, 1212
Ionic Liquid Solutions, 1229
Ionic Materials, 712
Ionic Polymer Solutions, 2967
Ionic Security, 282, 889, 968, 1788, 1794, 1968
Ionisos, 2340, 2448
IonQ, 889
Iontas Ltd, 2705
iOpener Media, 3188
IOpipe, 305, 544
Ioppolo Law Group, 3262
iOR Partners, 364
Iora, 1460
iOra, 2577
Iora Health, 2, 710, 748, 809
iORGA Group, 2383
IOSIL Energy, 2717
IOTA Engineering, 985
IOTAS, 1383
Iotas, 7, 1004
Iotera, 1595
IoTium, 809, 1031
IOTurbine, 1218
IOU Financial Inc., 2094
Iovance Biotherapeutics, 782
Iovation, 679, 688
iovation, 1620
Iovox, 3018
Iowa Approach, 1619
Ioxus, 184, 322, 432, 544, 1977, 2439
IP Access, 3104
IP Commerce, 142, 1863
IP Flex, 2772
IP Infusion, 75, 764
IP Infusion Inc., 2991
IP Mobile, 1334
IP MobileNet, 1706
IP Unity, 1704
IP Wireless, 494, 1715
IP2IPO Group, 2894
IP3 Networks, 807
IPA, 925
iPacesetters, 1021, 1071, 1727
Ipanema, 2662, 2674
iParadigms, 1956
Iparc, 3042
iPass, 69, 1235
IPATH, 1157
iPay Technologies, 1717
IPC, 260, 442, 3154
IPCentury, 3188
Ipcom, 3232
IPCore Tecnologies, 1769
IPD Global, 2056
Ipdia, 3113
iPeer Multimedia International, 3062

Portfolio Companies Index

iPerceptions, 2264
IPeria, 162
Iperian, 184
iPerian, 1268, 2970
IPFS, 307
IPG, 1654
IPH, 3026
IPH Group, 1017
iPharro Media, 3188
iPhrase, 712
IPI Scrittura, 954
Ipida, 3051
ipinfusion, 411
iPipeline, 1317, 1785, 1942
IPivot, 596
Iplas, 1121
IPlight, 436
IPNet Solutions, 765
IPourIt, 1784
IPQ2, 2856
Ipreco, 1927
Ipreo, 271
iPrint.com, 592
Iprobelabs Inc., 737
iProf Learning Solutions, 2849
iProgress, 2354
IPS Corporation, 368
Ipsen, 1271
Ipsilon, 1247
Ipsogen, 3113
Ipsogen Cancer Profiler, 530
Ipsum Networks, 1558
Ipsy, 45, 358
IPT, 192
Ipt, 3149
IPtronics, 2637
IPValue, 2771
IPVALUE Management, 1910
ipvision, 3203
IPWireless, 805, 1360
IQ Brands, 960
IQ Evolution, 2824
IQ Financial Systems, 23
IQ Labs, 2682
iQ License, 1475
IQ Media, 655
IQ Systems, 1188
IQE, 52
IQinvision, 715
IQMS, 227, 1785
IQNavigator, 223, 884
iQor, 959
IQS Inc., 137
iQu, 2837
iQuartic, 1097
iquartic, 1615
IQur, 2892
IQVIA, 744
IQVia, 1109
Iracore International Inc., 787
iRestify, 2138, 2184
iRex Technologies, 2312
iRhythm, 762, 1247
Irhythm Technnologies, 1298
iRhythm Technologies, 1772
IRI, 1301
Iridex, 1786
Iridian Technologies, 853
Iridigm, 805
Iridigm Display Corp, 197
Iris, 260, 924, 1480
Iris Automation, 243
Iris Mobile, 962, 1364
Iris Nova, 823
Iris Plans, 52
Iris PR Software, 387
IRIS.TV, 1813

Iris.TV, 1486
Irisa, 1481
IrisCube, 1352
iRise, 1255
IrisVision, 226
IrisVR, 786
IRL, 751
IRLan Ltd, 2954
IRM Systems, 2543
Iroc, 2481
iRoc, 2466
Iroko Pharmaceuticals, 1382
Iron Age, 722
Iron Gaming, 459
Iron Gate Capital, 3276
Iron Horse Midstream, 1278, 1326
Iron Horse Tools, 1745
Iron Ox, 519, 679, 1421
Iron Pearl, 1323
Iron Planet, 28, 1235
IRON Solutions, 1730
Iron Solutions, 1738
Iron Source, 3221
Iron.io, 231
Iron.MQ, 618
Ironform Holdings, 2009
IronKey, 1102
Ironman, 1496
IronNet Cybersecurity, 1075
IronPlanet, 560
IronPort, 114, 1540
Ironport, 84
Ironport Systems, 466
Ironshore, 368
IronSource, 2439
ironSource, 1598, 2566
Ironstone Resources, 3097
Ironwood, 2513, 2690
Ironwood Midstream Energy Partners II, 671
Ironwood Pharmaceuticals, 188, 1261, 1460
Irri-Al-Tal Ltd., 2122
IrriGreen, 226
IRT, 995
Irth Solutions, 333
IRule, 607
Irvin Automotive Products Inc., 577
Irving Tanning, 1213
iRxReminder, 1047
IRYStec, 2260
IS enterprise, 2822
IS/Pins, 2837
iS5 Communications, 2273
Isaac & Company, 300
Isabl, 1613
Isara, 1663
iSatori, 1837
Isatori Inc, 331
ISB Accelerator, 153
ISC Water Solutions, 378
Iscare AS, 2353
Ischemia Care, 347, 1512
Ischemia Technologies, 1057
iScience Interventional, 1398
Isco International, 153
IsCool, 3113
iScreen, 995
iScreen Vision, 1187
isee, 679
iSeek, 130
iSelect.com.au, 1717
iSend, 855
iSense, 1915
ISFC, 3001
iSheriff, 1886
iShipdit, 995
ISI Detention Contracting Group, 1209
Isidore Electronics Recycling, 3277

Isilon, 823, 2445
Isilon Systems, 757, 1654, 1796
iSine, 3267
ISIS, 786, 1760, 3134
Island Chemical, 832
Island Oasis, 1726
Island Water Technologies, 2155
Islanet Communications, 63
Isle Utilities, 2290
ISN, 783
iSnap, 1600
ISO Group, 22, 131
Isocket, 301, 547
iSocket, 32, 1513, 1546
Isoco, 2483
Isodiol International, 2254
iSoft, 2771
Isoftstone, 2436
iSoftstone, 2733
Isolation Network, 1660
ISolved HCM, 29
iSonar, 436
Isonics, 1915
IsoRay Medical, 1915
IsoStem, 1801
IsoTis, 2378
ISPC, 3042
iSpeak, 2584
ISpeech, 1784
iSpeech, 1306
iSpot, 1828
iSpot.tv, 1000, 1158
ISPsoft, 1305
iSqFt, 1544
ISR, 2051
Isreal Plant Sciences, 1191
Iss, 2697
Issuu, 3149
Ista, 909
Ista International GmbH, 744
ISTA Pharmaceuticals, 1616
Istar Medical, 3134
ISTO, 2939
ISTO Technologies, 176
Istra Research, 235
iStreamPlanet, 1515
istyle, 1755
iSuppli Corporation, 2079
Isys Interactive, 2967
iSystems, 1684
IT Assist Inc., 1609
IT Convergence, 2493
IT Cosmetics, 1861
IT Provider, 2447
It's Just Lunch, 1572
IT-Ernity, 1927
IT-Pac Romania SA, 3187
Ita Software, 1717
iTAC, 2713
iTAC Software AG, 1620
Italian Rose Gourmet Products, 290
Italic, 518
Italmatch Chemicals, 2851
Italtel, 335
Itamar Medical, 237
Itax Group, 856
ItBit, 386
itBit, 1115
ITC, 1954
ITC Capital Partners, 1072
ITC Cellular Holdings, 1708
ITC Compounding Pharmacy, 475
ITC DeltaCom, 1708
ITC Holding Company, 1708
ITE Group, 1927
iTeam, 1100
Iteksa Venture., 2867

Portfolio Companies Index

iTellio, 432
ITEMBASE, 2979
Itembase, 3236
Itemmaster, 655
Iteos, 3225
iTeos, 1268
Iterable, 13, 128, 1218
Itero, 1410
Itero Biopharmaceuticals, 3211
Iteros, 195, 293
Iterum Therapeutics, 237, 782
Itho, 2378
Itho Daalderop, 2501
ITinvolve, 202
ITL Canis, 3239
ITM, 2602
ITM Power, 3018
ITMedia, 1755
ITN Nanovation, 2638
ITN Networks, 1927, 2020
iTOKiNET, 1677
itrac LLC, 349
iTRACS Corporation, 944
iTradeNetwork Inc., 21
iTraffic, 954
itriage, 94
Itron, 696
Itronix, 839
ITS, 2936
ITS Compliance, 732
Itsbyu, 1176
Itslearning, 2637
ItsMyNews, 1532
ITSolutions, 654
ItsOn, 483, 1796
ITSworld Sicilia, 3052
ITT Educational Services, 300, 1496
Iturmo, 2489
ITW, 473
ItzBig, 1558
Itzcash Card, 1121
Iubenda, 2672
Iuka, 2892
iUNU, 1286
IVAC, 209
Ivanti, 500
Ivantis, 604, 1519, 2690
Ivantis. MedWentive, 176
iVelocity LLC, 122
Iven, 2284
Ivenix, 710
IvenSense, 1922
Iventis, 762
Ividence, 3020
iView Therapeutics, 266
iVillage, 1558, 2079
iVita Financial, 1910
iVivity, 1038
iViZ Techno Solutions, 2849
Ivize, 378
iVMD, 2001
Ivrea Pharmaceuticals, 2445
Ivxinevotech, 596
Ivy, 1323
Ivy Rehab, 1963
Ivycorp, 2003
IW Financial, 1160
IWATech, 2604
IWAtech, 2475
IWatt, 612
iWatt, 925, 947, 1672, 1906
IWC, 2700
iWin.com, 130
iWitness/Zantaz, 1793
IWJW, 823
Iwoca, 3157
iWorlds Simulations, 1915

IWS, 1751
IX Europe PLC, 2722
Ix Innovations, 742
Ixaris, 3107
IXI, 538
IXI Mobile, 3179
IXI Mobile Inc, 2770
Ixia, 869
Ixico, 2858
IXIGO, 2477
Ixigo, 2475
Ixoraa Media Inc., 623
IXS, 1372
Ixsight, 3109
Iyia Technologies, 1784
iYogi, 386, 609, 1620
IyziCo, 2294
IZEA, 990
iZENEtech, 1361
IZettle, 3013
iZettle, 2637, 3252
Izorok, 3071
iZotope, 22
Izypeo, 2308
IZZE, 1665

J

J Brand, 916
J&J Produce, 405
J&L Specialty Steel, 354
J&S, 2851
J&W Scientific Inc., 1621
J-B Weld, 374
J-Tell, 2969
J. Crew, 1835
J. Hilburn, 231, 235, 339
J. Jill, 152, 839
J.America, 828
J.B. Williams Company, 357
J.Hilburn, 695
J.Mclaughlin, 334
J.S. Held, 1166
JAB Broadband, 21
Jab Broadband, 925
JabberSmack, 1108
Jabbit, 3058
Jabong, 2838
JAC Holding Corporation, 1491
JAC Products, 2009
Jacada, 3137
Jack and Jake's, 3277
Jack Be, 904
Jack Erwin, 563, 1663
Jack Rabbit, 1070
Jack Rogers, 1344
Jack Threds, 1585
Jack Wolfskin, 277, 2714
Jack's, 2209
JackBe, 538
Jackbox Games, 1024
JackCards, 1097
Jacked, 805
Jackpocket, 358, 1613
JackRabbit, 828
Jackrabbit, 1424
Jackson Hewitt Tax Service, 1041
Jackson Offshore Holdings, 1144
Jackson Vending Ltd., 2707
Jackson's Honest, 1113
Jacob Ash, 338
Jacobi, 976
Jacobson Companies, 1360
Jacobson Machine Works, 843
JacquelineBs Gourmet Cookies, 77
Jacques Vert, 2361
Jacques Vert Group, 1753
Jacuzzi, 500

Jacuzzi Brands, 140
Jacuzzi Brands Corp., 159
Jada Beauty, 658
JADE Equipment Corporation, 1203
Jade Solutions, 1837
JadeTrack, 1286
Jafora, 2609
JAG-ONE, 1409
Jagex Games Studio, 1717
Jaggaer, 29
Jahabow, 61, 611
Jail Education Solutions, 3277
Jajah Jasper Technologies, 986
Jam Hub, 1160
Jama, 1158, 1853
Jama Software, 1000, 1383
Jamba Juice, 1576, 1587, 1853, 2254
James, 2759
James Communications, 1621
James E. Wagner Cultivation Corporation, 2071
James Heal, 235
JamesEdition, 3040
Jameslist.com, 2604
Jameson, 415
JAMF Software, 802, 1752, 3279
JamHub, 445
Jamieson Wellness, 433
Jamii, 2569
Jamo, 3009
Jan Pro, 812
JANA, 1715
Jana, 756, 1509, 1926
Janaagraha, 1374
Jancee Screw Products, 2094
Jandi, 3127
Jane Norman, 2796
Jane Software, 2080
Jane West, 1135
Janeeva, 1455
Janiis, 1070
JanRain, 791
Janrain, 665, 688, 933, 1235, 1592, 1607, 1725
Janrain User Management Platform, 132
Jansy Packaging, 698
Janton, 2422
Janus, 500
Janus Capital Group, 300
JANUS Research Group Inc., 507
JanusRV, 1530
JanusVR, 60, 307, 1110
Japan Carlife Assist, 2974
Japan Communications, 596
Japan Internet Ventures, 847
Japan Medical Data Centre, 3182
Japan Telecom, 3168
Japan Tissue Engineering, 2970
Jarden, 2697
Jardine Transport, 2251
Jardine's, 984
Jareva Technologies, 1038
Jargon, 1877
Jari Pharmaceuticals, 2748
Jarllytec Co., 3218
Jarvis Hotels, 2556
JASK, 1794
Jask, 235, 603, 1075
Jason Incorporated, 716
Jaspan Schlesinger LLP, 3267
Jasper, 1003, 1654, 3013
Jasper @ Cisco, 555
Jasper Infotech Pvt Ltd., 1004
Jasper Soft, 1626
Jasper Wireless, 339, 581, 634, 1445, 1996, 3121
JasperSoft, 57
Jaspersoft, 596, 1257
Jaulna, 2445
Jauni, 1534

Portfolio Companies Index

Jaunt, 792, 889, 935
Jaunt VR, 994
Java Detour, 506
Javelin, 365
Javelin Pharmaceuticals, 1325
Javelin Venture Partners, 3284
Javlin Capital, 1364
Javo Beverage Company, 717
Jawabu Microhealth, 55
Jawbone, 596, 625, 729, 1184, 1654, 1727, 2446
Jaxtr, 115, 197, 623
Jays, 2637
Jaza, 2184
JAZD Markets, 521
Jazinga, 2066
Jazz, 272, 724, 1607
Jazz Pharma, 1271
Jazz Pharmaceuticals, 57, 839, 1493, 1963
JazzHR, 306
JB Hi Fi, 2951
JBLCo, 1262
JBoss, 1445
jCatalog Software, 2452
JCC, 2944
JCK KG, 3067
Jcrew Group, 1109
JD Holding, 3062
JDA Software, 300
JDA Software Group, 1301
JDR, 1937
JDR Recovery Corporation, 402
JDS Pharmaceuticals, 97
JDS Therapeutics, 1044
Jebbit, 313, 586, 1172, 1757
JEC, 2317
Jecure, 1928
Jeda Networks, 1237, 1896
Jeda Technologies, 130
Jedox, 2686
Jeepers! Inc., 447
Jeepglint, 3251
Jeevanti, 3109
Jeeves, 235, 3109
Jefferson Capital International, 750
Jefferson Dental Care, 334
JEL Hydraulics, 3145
Jelastic, 89, 3088
Jeld-Wen, 2209
Jelf Group Plc., 404
Jelfa SA, 1452
Jellagen, 2997
Jelly Button, 2914
Jelly in the News, 1715
Jellyfish, 1060
Jellyvision, 1024, 1672
Jen Sen Hughes, 881
JeNaCell, 2527, 2824
JenAffin, 2824
Jenali, 762
JenaValve, 191
Jenavalve, 3149
Jenetric, 2527
Jeni's, 421
jenID Solutions, 2527
Jenny Craig, 1335
Jenoptik, 2527
Jenrin Discovery, 266, 362, 1543
Jens Jorgensen, 3203
Jensen Hughes, 1166
JeNu, 1641
Jenzabar, 1067
Jericho Capital Corp., 3267
Jericho Sciences, 737
Jerini AG, 1325, 2528
Jerr-Dan, 1134
Jersey Precast, 812
Jersey Watch, 479

Jessops Ltd., 2677
Jet, 486, 509, 761, 1475, 1821
Jet Finance, 2471
Jet Health, 918, 1628, 1762
Jet Insight, 1323
Jet Metal, 2439
Jetasonic, 2155
JetCell, 1747
Jetchange.fr, 2899
JetClosing, 1183, 1499
JetLenses, 795
JetLore, 2838
Jetlore, 93, 721
Jetpac, 1254
Jetpack Workflow, 1155
JetPay, 750
Jetro Cash & Carry, 433, 1109
Jetset Sports, 1705
Jetsetter, 1181
JetSmarter, 500
Jetta Corp, 553
Jettable, 2462
Jetul, 2325
Jewelbots, 218, 981
Jewlr, 2066
Jexys Pharmaceuticals, 3245
Jeyes, 2935
JFDI.Asia, 3132
JFIN Business Credit Fund, 1970
JFrog, 235, 603, 1000, 1626
JG Wentworth, 1039
JGB Enterprises, 97
JGWPT Holdings, 1136
JHP Pharmaceuticals, 1956
JHT Holdings, 109
Jiahua, 3100
Jiangli, 3100
Jiangxi Guohong Group, 2542
Jiayuan, 2584
Jiayuan.com, 3251
JIBE, 608, 2017
Jibe, 1110, 1146, 1460, 1620
Jibjab, 1460
Jibo, 712, 721, 754
Jida Pharmaceuticals, 1956
Jido, 1390
Jiff, 1323, 1916
Jiffy, 2137
Jifiti, 1034
Jig Space, 307
Jigsaw Data Corp., 202
Jiguang, 973
Jihua.fm, 2869
Jiko, 663, 1888
Jilcraft, 1295
Jill-e Designs LLC, 669
Jim 'N Nick's Bar-B-Q, 1576
Jimdo, 1717
Jimmy Buffet's Margaritaville, 1681
Jimmy John's, 1576, 1978
Jimu Box, 3208
Jin-Magic, 2974
Jinfengyuan, 3194
Jing Jin Electric, 2667
Jing-Jin Electric, 3215
JingDong 360 Buy Online, 2560
Jingtum, 1390
Jinhe Industrial, 2542
JinkoSolar Holdings, 2593
JinSheng International, 220
JinTronix, 1158
Jinu, 2857
Jinx, 325
Jirafe, 743, 1359
Jist.tv, 994
Jitterbit, 1607
Jitterbug, 2987

JITx, 795
JiuDing China, 2850
Jive, 1334, 1654
Jive Software, 756, 1341, 2144
Jivox, 1381, 2818
JiWire, 1850
JK Group, 1759
JK&B Capital, 986
JL Darling, 1343
JMH International, 1343
JMI Equity, 37, 986, 3270
JMJ Associates, 2311
JML Optical Industries, 746
JMTY, 641, 2869
Jnana, 1928
JNM Group, 2126
JNTC, 3145
Jo-Ann Stores, 1109
Joany, 272, 776
Job Cannon, 445
Job Direct, 530
Job partners, 2544
Jobalign, 773, 1158
Jobaline, 1852
Jobandtalent, 2446, 2920
Jobber, 2280, 3044
JobCase, 1625
JobCoin, 103
JobDig, 1113
Jobdisabili, 2296
JOBDOH, 3108
Jobe's, 446
Jobintree, 2385
JobLeads, 2824
JobPartners, 2779
JobPlanet, 1509
Jobplanet, 100
Jobr, 679, 1809
Jobro Platkomponenter, 2755
Jobs For Vets, 811
jobs2web, 1886
Jobson Healthcare Information, 716, 1984
JobSync, 1099, 1784
JobUFO, 2841
Jobvite, 183, 427, 1850
Joby, 107
Joby Aviation, 1004, 1035, 1834, 2690
Jodel, 751
Joe, 755
Joe Hudson's Collision Center, 415
Joerns, 199
Joerns Healthcare, 1134, 1505
Joey's Fine Foods, 193
Jofel, 2962
John Barker Group, 2985
John Deere, 473
John H. Harland Company, 300
John Hardy, 1088
John Laing Partnership, 3017
John West Foods, 2420
Johnny on the Spot, 632
Johnny Rockets, 1753
Johnny Was, 673
Johnny's Fine Foods, 1999
Johnson & Johnson, 1096
Johnson & Johnson Innovation, 3273
Johnson and johnson, 2803
Johnson Biomedical Capital, 3262
Johnston Fabrics & Finishing, 1213
Joicaster, 971
JointlyHealth, 1784
Joist, 38, 486, 2137, 2182
Joiz, 2638
Jojonomic, 721
Jolata, 183
Joliet Equipment, 1021
Joliet Holdings, 164

1349

Portfolio Companies Index

Jolife, 2562
Jolimark Holdings, 2936
Jolimont Global Mining Systems, 1548
Jolt, 79
Jolyn, 1346
Jon M Hall Company, 1281
Jonah Energy LLC, 1835
Jonathan Engineered Services, 468
Jonathan Engineered Solutions, 985, 1111
Jones, 877
Jones & Frank, 746, 1231
Jones Lang LaSalle, 3276, 3279
Jones Naturals, 213
Jones Rail Industries, 2266
Jones The Grocer Group, 1088
JonesTrading, 787
Jonway Automobile, 2576
Joonko, 1054
JOOR, 235
Joor, 386, 858, 1110, 1530
Jopa, 3088
Jopari Solutions, 1669, 1979
Jopwell, 567, 1054, 1721
Jordan Health Services, 1403
Jordens DC, 2949
Joriki, 2272
Jorn Ditlevsen, 3203
Jornaya, 518, 655, 814
Joseph Ribkoff, 2206
Joseph's Frozen Foods, 357
Josephine, 1054
Jostens, 1017
José Andrés ThinkFoodGroup, 1766
Jott, 43, 1110, 1183
Joule, 747
Joules, 2944
Joulex, 1788
Jounce, 762
Jounce Therapeutics, 1811
Journera, 124, 1480
Journey Meditation, 1310
Journey Sales, 1240
Jove Equity Partners, 3267
Jow, 641
Joy, 1363
Joya, 100
Joya Communications Inc., 1879
Joyent, 688, 871, 1522, 3169
Joyfride, 784
Joyful Frog Digital Incubator, 721
JoyLux, 293
Joymode, 941, 1149
Joyoung, 2579
Joyride, 552
JoyRun, 1346
Joyrun, 751
JoyStream, 307
JoyTunes, 1000, 2914
Joyus, 28, 1010, 1827
JP Mobil, 2890
JP Morgan Private Bank, 3267
JPC Holdings LLC, 1735
JR Automation, 559
JRD Communication, 3062
JRG Securities, 2490
JRL Systems, 131, 1708
JS Digitech, 2807
JS Held, 1147
JSA Healthcare Corporation, 955
JSC Krasalkor Aluminiystroi Krasnoyarsk, 1404
JScrambler, 3048
JSI NV, 2992
JSI Store Fixtures, 1557
JSK Therapeutics, 1070, 2382
JTF, 2796
Judas Theatreproducteies, 3042
Judicata, 1069

Judson Technologies, 1295
Judy, 325
Judy's Book, 43
Juhudi Kilimo, 55
Juice Plus, 16
Juice Press, 1585
Juice Tyme Acquisition Corp, 1456
Juix, 2128
Jukedeck, 3028
Jukin Media, 256, 397, 1055, 1099, 1813
Julep, 85, 124, 1226, 1524
Juli, 2593
Julia Computing, 816
Juliet Marine Systems Inc., 206
July Systems, 1886
Jumbo, 2784
Jumei.com, 3208, 3251
Jumia, 3170
Jumio, 729, 1235
JUMP, 1202
Jump, 307, 2881
Jump Cloud, 776
Jump Ramp, 358, 946
Jump Ramp Games, 679, 1699
Jump.ca, 2285
JumpCam, 889
JumpCloud, 1563
Jumpcut, 858, 1183
Jumpstart Foundy, 1187
Jumptap, 1534, 1899
Jun Group, 897
Junar, 2455
Junction Solutions, 1242
June, 741, 776, 942, 1110
June Life, 648
Junggwan Library Operation Co., 584
Jungla, 124
Junglee Games, 238
Jungo, 1793
Juniper Financial, 2079
Juniper Networks, 1001
Juniper Resources, 1326
Juniper Square, 720, 942
Junkless, 1507
Juno, 762
Juno Energy, 156
Juno Lighting, 368
Juno Online Services, 1769
Juno Rising, 438
Juno Therapeutics, 262, 1519, 1916, 2008
Junyo, 1054, 1316
Jupiter, 1768
Jupiter Fund Management, 1776
Jupiter Intelligence, 1269
Jupiter Shop Channel, 220
Jurag Separation, 3149
Jurnal, 721
Juro, 3108
JUSP, 3052
Just, 101
Just A Pinch Recipe Club, 1261
Just Book, 2668
Just Brakes, 812
Just Childcare, 3036
Just Eat, 1534
Just Fabulous, 1785
Just in Time Tourist, 3048
Just Inc., 107, 1069
Just Learning, 2361
Just Marketing International, 1724
Just Park, 302
Just Retirement, 3033
Just the Right Book, 1097
JustBook, 2637
JustCommodity, 2870
JustEnough Software, 2709
JustEva.ru, 2549

JustFabulous, 1181
JustFav, 1558
JustFoodForDogs, 1088
Justice Design Group, 1964
Justin's, 953
JustOne, 1254
Justworks, 1534
Juswin Technologies, 2975
Jut, 28
Jutian Fund Management Co, 2594
Jutian Fund Management Co. Ltd, 2595
Jutian Securities Co. LtdHoulder China Insurance B, 2595
Jutron Oy, 2740
Juvantia Pharma Ltd Oy, 2318
Juvaris BioTherapeutics, 1628
Juvena Therapeutics, 1758
Juvenescence, 762
Juventas Therapeutics, 642, 831, 1047, 1303, 1544, 1847, 1921
Juvo, 784, 1611, 1675
Juxta Labs, 1070, 2382
JVC, 1344
JVH Gaming, 3232
Jvion, 918
JW Aluminum Company, 1971
JW Player, 567, 641, 867
JWD, 1139
JWD Machine, 1705
JWPlayer, 871
Jydsk Aluminum Industrial, 3203
Jydsk Planteservice, 3203
Jyothy Laboratories, 2337
Jyve, 305, 561, 1563, 1675

K

K Health, 518
K Mobile, 3208
K&A Water, 1191
K&F Industries, 199
K&F Industries Inc., 575
K&G Men's Center, 1708
K&G Men's Centers, 1148
K&N Engineering Inc., 881
K-MAC, 1372
K-Tek, 1770
K-Vault Software Ltd (KVS), 2577
K.G. Box Inc., 465
K.Wah International Holdings Limited, 2402
K12, 1785
K2, 260, 779
K2 Cyber Security, 663
K2 Global, 1593
K2 Industrial Services, 402, 894, 1605
K2 Insurance Services, 673
K2 Intelligence, 1299
K2 Internet S.A., 2528
K2 Optronic, 2348
K2 Pure Solutions LP, 447
K2-MDV Holdings, 1081
K2M, 723, 1972
K3, 3244
K4Connect, 1670
K9 Resorts, 1281
KA International Group, 2962
Kaai, 1445
Kaarta, 2142
KabaFusion Holdings, 240
Kabam, 184, 386, 729, 1534, 1690
Kabbage, 296, 1247, 1699, 1818, 1891
Kabbee, 3018, 3097
Kabira, 2875, 3137
Kabira Technologies, 162
Kaboa, 2994
Kabobs, 193
Kaboodle, 807
Kabron, 3042

Portfolio Companies Index

Kabu.com, 596
Kabul Serena Hotel, 1007
Kace, 757, 1024
KaDang, 1534
Kadel's Auto Body, 1232
Kadena, 525
Kadent/Landau, 1516
Kadient, 1080
Kadiri, 1945
Kaditt, 2646
Kadmon, 1941
Kaggle, 585, 1798, 2019
Kagoor Networks, 1906
Kahala Brands, 2254
Kahala Code Factory, 2457
KAHLA Porzellan, 2527
Kahoot!, 1154
Kahr Medical, 1618
Kahuna, 547, 720, 777, 1489, 1654, 1700
KAI Pharmaceuticals, 1008, 1691
Kai Square, 3121
Kai Yuan, 3208
Kaiam, 595
KAIAM Corporation, 1786
Kaiam Corporation, 1896
Kaibae, 3257
Kaidara., 2625
Kaiima, 609, 2831
Kaiima Bio Agritech, 1241
KaiLight Photonics, 3249
Kairos, 218, 1054, 1701
Kaiser Permanente, 214
Kaitone, 2936
Kaixin001, 1340
Kajeet, 805
Kakao, 596
Kakehashi, 1607
Kala Pharmaceuticals, 1811
Kala Pharmaceuticals, 1119, 1143, 1151, 1460, 1519, 1941
KalaBios, 12
Kaleidacare, 92
Kaleido, 747
Kaleido Biosciences, 20
Kaleidoscope Medical, 426
Kaleo, 306, 871, 904, 972, 1055, 1509, 1604, 1798
Kaleo Software, 624
KalGene Pharmaceuticals, 2180
Kalibrr, 1374, 1965
Kalid, 2445
Kalido, 1181
Kalion, 841, 1100
Kalisaya, 460
Kalkitech, 834
Kalkomey, 1014
Kallik, 2967
KallOut, 103
Kallyope, 517, 1151
Kalo, 836
KaloBios, 87, 1618, 1698, 2970
KaloBios Pharmaceuticals, 2513, 2690
Kalpan Hydro, 1459
Kalpana, 1202
Kalpsys, 2690
Kaltura, 2, 206, 1004, 1241, 1327, 1620, 1625, 3001
KalVista, 1519
KalVista Pharma, 1941
Kalvista Pharma, 1628
KalVista Pharmaceuticals, 1145
Kalypsys, 2419, 2513
Kalypto Medical, 1760
Kalyra, 1784
Kamada, 925
Kambr, 1875
Kamcord, 1218, 1838, 2010

Kaminario, 184, 835, 1241, 1796
Kampyle, 2566, 3221
Kana, 69
Kana Software, 1558, 1672
Kanaly Trust, 1147
Kanam Lifescript, 69
Kanbox, 596
Kanchli, 2579
Kandy Pens, 638
KaNDy Therapeutics, 1143
Kaneq Bioscience, 3196
Kanetix, 1248
KangaDo, 1749
Kango, 226
Kangol, 2923
Kanisa/Knova, 1288
Kanler, 751
Kantana Group, 1139, 2946
Kantox, 2851
Kanvas, 150, 1632
Kanvas Labs, 679
Kanyos Bio, 1350, 1928
Kaon, 1146
Kaonetics Technologies, 735
Kaperio, 1574
Kapitol, 2680
Kapost, 36, 567, 751, 781, 930, 1020, 1607, 1789, 2017
Kapow, 630
Kapow Events, 471, 731
Kappa Packaging, 2644
Kappoki Games LTD, 2554
Kapta, 1176, 1522
Kaptivo, 249
Kapwing, 1075, 1663, 1933
Kar's Nuts, 1403
Karachi Electric Supply Company, 3173
Karadi Tales Company, 2313
Karat, 1346
Kardia Therapeutics, 241
KareInn, 3108
Kareo, 508, 695, 867, 1251, 1380, 1748
KargoCard, 833
Karhu Sporting Goods, 2873
Karius, 996, 1121
Karius Inc., 1069
Karl Lagerfeld, 135
Karma, 641, 3224
Karma Communications Group, 3036
Karma Gaming, 2239
Karma Sphere, 1896
Karmaback.com, 445
Karmaloop, 407
Karmasphere, 1474
Karmic, 148, 544, 2493
Karmic Labs, 93, 384, 1097, 1592
Karobi, 307
Karos Pharmaceuticals, 1298, 1420
Karoui&Karoui World, 2654
Karsen, 2697
Karuna Health, 318, 741
Karus Therapeutics, 1298, 1628, 2892
Karve Energy, 2025
Karyopharm Therapeutics, 604
Kasbah Resources, 2942
Kascend, 935
Kasenna, 1352
Kaseya, 1000
Kashf School Sarmaya, 55
Kasisto, 1306, 1420
Kasko, 3108
Kason, 222
Kastle Therapeutics, 750
Kaszek Ventures, 483
Katabat, 52
Katahdin Inc., 1862
Katahdin Industries, 1021

Katalyst Surgical, 267
Katch, 1626
Kateeva, 595, 1303, 1672, 1715, 3098
Katerra, 107, 1282
Katerra Inc., 1069
Katy Industries, 1081
Katz Sapper & Miller, 3267
Katzkin Leather Interiors Inc., 501
Kauf.da, 641
Kaufman & Broad, 3026
Kaufman Hall & Associates, 1156
Kaval Wireless, 2058
Kaval Wireless Technologies, 2079
Kavin Engineering, 1164
Kawi Safi Ventures, 623
Kawin Technology, 2936
KAYAC, 2646
KAYAK, 1654
Kayak, 1001, 1850
Kayak.com, 1796
Kayden Industries, 2275
Kaydon Corp., 77
Kayentis, 3113, 3239
Kaymbu, 1527
Kayo Conference Series, 3285
Kaz Inc., 447
Kazan Networks, 1004
Kazeon, 502, 757
Kazeon Systems, 1038, 1445
Kazuhm, 121
KBC Arkiv, 3042
KBI, 2978
KBI Biopharma, 224, 1915
KBOS, 2826
KBP Foods, 1430
KCAEP, 374
KCAS, 1053
KCG, 815
KCI, 209
KCom, 2674
KCS, 29, 2564
KD 1, 1558
KD1, 202
kDa Group, 2220
KdocTV Los Angeles, 1062
Kds, 655
KDS China, 1004
KDS International, 28
Keane, 1147, 1166
Keas, 38
Keatext, 2027
Keaton Row, 1202, 1306
Kebony, 2428, 3113
Kebotix, 663, 754
Keclon, 2470
Kedu Healthcare, 222
Keduo, 1340
KEE Action Sports, 127
Kee Safety, 2944
Keebitz, 2921
Keebler, 1018
Keeley Asset Management, 1776
Keemotion, 3225
Keen Home, 325
Keen IO, 306, 585, 1425, 1566, 2010
KeenHigh Technologies, 2593
KeenSkim, 2696
Keep, 124, 823
Keep Holdings, 596, 1860
Keep Holdings/AdKeeper, 1361
Keep Truckin, 1626
Keepcon, 2334, 2976
Keeps, 741, 781, 1183
KeepSafe, 181
Keepsafe, 751
KeepTrax, 1285
KeepTruckin, 889

1351

Portfolio Companies Index

Keepy, 1998
Keesing, 2851
Keezy. K Health, 1110
Kefta, 114
Keg Logistics, 333, 1638
Keiretsu, 3262
Keisense, 530
Keit, 2967
Keith Prowse, 3017
Kekemeke, 3044
Kel-Tech, 170
Keldelice, 3020
Kelkoo, 2481
Kelle's Transport Service, 405
Kellermeyer Bergensons Services, 824, 1081
Kellogg Company, 473
Kellstrom Aerospace, 66
Kellwood Company, 1753
Kelsius Limited, 2610
Kelso & Company, 3255, 3264
Kelst, 3042
Kelvin Inc., 2111
Kemartek, 2355
Kemberton, 1136
Kemco Systems, 1578
Kemia, 898
Kemira GrowHow Oyj, 2990
Kemira Oyj, 2990
Kemistry, 512
Kemp Technologies, 655
Kemper Corporation, 404
Ken Taub, 3267
Kenan Advantage, 2207
Kenan Advantage Group, 1134, 1557
Kenan Advantage Group Inc., 442
Kenandy, 1121
Kendall Vegetation Services, 290
Kendra Scott, 254, 1346
Kendrick Electric, 716
Kendrion, 3069
Kendro Laboratory, 1128
Kenesto, 436, 2813
kenexa, 1040
KENGURU, 445
Kenlin Pet Supply, 788
Kenna Security, 547
Kennedy Information, 863
Kenra, 1861, 2150
KenSci, 974
Kensho, 336, 708, 1489
Kensho Technologies, 710
Kenshoo, 1323, 1654, 2428
Kenshoo Kodiak Networks, 1796
Kensington & Sons, 2401
Kensington Flats, 2285
Kentik, 741
Kentrox, 1017
Kenzie Academy, 1551
Kenzington Brewing Company, 2184
Keoghs, 2944
Keonn, 1061
Keopsys, 3208
KEP Technologies, 2851
Kepler, 547
Kepler Academy, 2202
Kepler Capital Markets, 2521
Kepler Equities, 1123
Kepro, 135, 1166
KeraFAST, 496, 718
Kerb, 2535
Kerberos Proximal Solutions, 1445, 1543
Kerenix, 2910
Kereos, 458, 1187, 1574, 1847
Keri Systems, 636
Kericure, 1507
Keriton, 266, 622
Kerk Motion Products Inc., 908

Kerogen Energy Holdings, 1573
Keronite, 2472
Keros Therapeutics, 2229
Kerr Group, 368
Kerrera Company, 584
Keryx, 1059
Keryx Biopharma, 1271
Kesios Therapeutics, 1628
Kesko Oyj, 2990
Kespry, 483, 792, 1121
Kestrel Heat, 1068
Ketai, 2850
KeTech, 3018
Ketera, 1003
Kether, 2851
Ketos, 1552
Kettle & Fire, 482
Kewl, 950
Key, 1985
Key Associates, 3262
Key Brandon Entertainment Inc., 2094
Key Concierge, 545
Key Energy, 156
Key Health, 276, 333
Key Investment, 3279
Key Living, 2224
Key Plastics, 1967
Key Retirement, 3036
Key Safety Systems, 559
Key-Trak, 1148
KEY/VISYS, 2949
Key2Act, 1136
Keybase, 124
KeyBay Pharmaceutical, 998
Keycast, 1572
Keychain Logistics, 280, 599, 1222, 1475, 1518, 1531, 1699
Keyes Packaging Group, 147
KeyImpact Sales & Systems, 686
KeyImpact Sales and Systems, 1049
Keylime Software, 1706
KeyMe, 235, 518, 1982
Keymile, 1572
Keynote, 260
Keynote Systems, 1814
Keyo, 1363
KeyPoint Government Solutions, 901, 1925
Keyport Solutions, 2347
Keyrocket, 2824
Keyssa, 93, 1004, 1427
Keystone, 541
Keystone Automotive Operations, 220, 1134
Keystone Communications, 2079
Keystone Dental, 1817, 1956
Keystone Foods Holdings, 1129
Keystone Heart, 1382
Keystone Ranger Holdings, 1275
Keystone Retaining Wall Systems, 1343
KeyTech Limited, 274
KeyTone Cloud, 483
Keytouch Corporation, 2754
Keytruda, 2102
KEYW, 834
Keywee, 996
Kezar Life Sciences, 20, 237, 709
KFC, 334
KFX Medical, 1251
KFx Medical, 87, 149, 458, 1187
KG Telecom, 3218
Kgb, 1017
kgb, 1785
KGen Power, 156
KGH Customs Services, 3054
KH Connect, 1004
Khan Academy, 1316
Khancera, 626
Kheiron Medical Technologies, 1095

Khimetrics, 310
Khosla Ventures LLC, 3284
Kiadis, 2662
Kiadis Pharma, 94, 2518, 2674, 2939, 3069
Kiala, 2354, 2662, 2851
Kiana, 890
Kiana Analytics, 129
KickApps, 1699, 1715
KickApps (KIT Digital), 1333
Kickback, 858, 1150
Kickboard, 1299, 1874, 3277
Kicking Horse Coffee, 1767
Kicksend, 1860
Kickstart Seed Fund, 2382, 3276
Kickstarter, 511, 1149, 1882
Kickup, 1527
Kid Interiør, 2863
KidAdmit, 1050
Kidaptive, 1202, 1316, 1634
Kidaro, 1747
Kidblog, 3279
Kiddom, 1069, 1392
Kidfresh, 668
Kidizen, 1019, 1176, 1384
KidKraft, 1231
KIDOZ, 2947
Kidpass, 1028
Kidrobot, 1741
Kids Care Dental, 374
Kids Care Dental Group, 1742
Kids Garden, 3042
Kids Kitchen, 3042
Kids On 45th, 325
Kids on 45th, 1183, 1701
Kids123.com, 1461
Kidsline, 869
Kidsline Inc., 449
KidsLink, 282
Kidsmart, 869
Kidspotter, 2355
KidsToPros, 1613
kidsunlimited, 2944
Kidz Bop, 21
Kidzui, 1584
Kieffer & Co., 399, 1343
Kigo, 2638
Kii, 181, 483, 721
Kiian Group, 3154
Kiio, 2001
Kiip, 956, 1839, 1860, 1926
Kiite, 708
Kik, 770, 802, 1235, 1593, 1604, 1715
KIK Custom Products, 442
KIKA Medical, 1325
Kildare Capital, 3267
Kilimanjaro Energy, 153
Kilimo, 995
Kilkenny, 260
Kill Cliff, 1665
Killick Aerospace, 2168
KiloLambda, 3249
Kilombero Valley, 834
Kilopass, 2853
Kilopass Klocwork, 1896
Kilosoft Oy, 2966
Kiloutou, 3026
Kim Susan, 1745
Kimaya Fashions, 584
Kimberly Access Limited, 2944
KIMBIA, 445
Kimbia, 950, 1597
Kimble, 29
KimKim, 1323
Kimomex Markets, 1915
Kimono, 1055, 1998
Kimotion., 2875
KIMS GCC, 1382

Portfolio Companies Index

KIMS India, 1382
KIN, 1496
Kin, 2225
Kin Community, 668, 816
Kinamu Business Solutions, 3165
Kinaxis, 2263
Kinburn Corp, 447
Kincora Group, 3097
Kind, 1766
Kindara, 313, 1656
Kinder Morgan, 1573
Kindly, 852
Kindly Care, 751, 1024
Kindred, 4, 648, 741, 889
Kindred at Home, 1972
Kindred Bio, 709
Kindred Healthcare, 1835, 1972
Kindred.ai, 107
Kindstar, 2978
Kindstar Global, 222
Kinduct, 1004
Kinectrics, 1937
Kinema Systems, 648
Kinematics, 126
Kinematix, 3048
Kinestral, 12, 129
Kineta, 1061
Kinetic, 488, 563
Kinetic Books Company, 1148
Kinetic Commerce, 2110
Kinetic Computer Corporation, 1461
Kinetic Concepts, 368
Kinetic Concepts Inc., 300
Kinetic Social, 287, 1361, 1748, 1776
Kinetic Ventures, 3270
Kinetica, 486, 1212
Kinetika, 3154
Kinetikos Medical, 1792
Kinetix Living, 1183
Kineto, 1637, 1747
Kineto Wireless, 1241, 1760, 3155
Kinetrex Energy, 2214
Kinex Medical Company, 1209
Kinex R&M Rehabilitation, 1209
King, 2860, 2860
King Juice Company, 1171
King Tester Corporation, 1609
KING&I, 2857
King-Reed & Associates, 2794
Kingdee, 973
Kingfield Health, 2935
Kings County Distillery, 1420
Kings Foodmart, 127
Kingsclear, 2796
Kingsdown, 2206
Kingsgate Consolidated, 1548
Kingsoft WPS, 823
KingStar, 750
KingYee, 3100
Kinloch Holdings, 434
Kinnek, 128, 563, 858, 1670
Kinney Group, 658
Kinnikinnick Foods, 2049
Kinsa, 743, 965, 1075
Kinside, 1026
Kinsus Interconnect Technology Corporation, 2603
Kintana, 823
Kinvey, 38, 206, 313, 1789, 1926
Kinvolved, 704
Kio Networks, 324
Kiodex Inc., 986
Kiomix, 1377
Kionix, 432, 1126
Kionix Inc., 810
Kip, 858
KIPP DC, 1316

KIPP MA, 1316
Kipsu, 1176
Kira, 1000
Kira Talent, 2236
KiraKira3D, 1004, 1551
Kiran Energy, 260
Kirby Lester Group, 838
Kirin Pharmaceutical, 1452
Kirkland's, 402
Kirona, 2944
Kirtas Technologies, 1057
Kirusa, 28, 645, 2818, 3001, 3274
KISCO Solutions, 2347
Kishlay Snacks, 1346
KISI, 1222
KisoJi Biotechnology, 2180
Kiss No Frog, 2838
KissKissBankBank, 3239
KISSmetrics, 720, 1860
KissMetrics, 1700
Kissmetrics, 1460, 1546
KissMyAds, 3207
Kissnofrog, 2829
Kit Check, 1298, 1556
Kit Digital, 3169
Kitalive, 1607
Kitan Consolidated, 2609
KitCheck, 2943
Kitcheck, 644, 1052
Kitched United, 889
Kitchen Collection, 1970
Kitchen Surfing, 1715
KitchenMate, 679, 2137, 2138
Kite, 325, 784
Kite & Lightingm, 307
Kite & Lightning, 1390
Kite Phrama, 94
Kith Kitchen, 1435
Kitman Labs, 296
KitSplit, 622
Kitsy Lane, 1146, 1459
KITT.ai, 773
Kitt.ai, 1701
Kittery, 1507
Kittyhawk, 306
Kity, 852
Kiva, 1374
Kiva Software, 1121, 1853
Kiva Systems, 1194
Kiveda, 2829, 2838
Kiverdi, 1054
Kivuto, 2155
Kiwa, 3257
KIWI, 1894
Kiwi, 1654
Kiwi Co., 325
Kiwi Crate, 1061
Kiwi Wearables, 981
KiwiCo, 518, 720, 741, 761
Kiwigrid, 2824
Kixer, 1798
KIXEYE, 1853
Kixeye, 946, 968, 1121, 1563
Kiyatec, 1923
KJK, 1121
KJUS, 1999
Kkeye, 2850
KKR, 3264
Klala, 3104
Klang, 2953
Klar, 49
Klara, 1110
Klarna, 668, 815, 1001, 1502, 1654, 2446, 2446, 2663, 2928
Klash, 3207
Klashwerks, 2187
Klaxoon, 1982

KLD Energy, 594
KLDiscovery, 1979
Kleiner Perkins Caufield Byers, 3284
KlikDaily, 721
Kline Hill Partners, 3255
Klip, 1181
Klipfolio, 305, 2195
Klipsch Audio, 1906
Klir Technologies, 753
Klmeta, 2824
Klockner Pentaplast, 2616
Klone Lab, 1157
Klook, 2690
Kloudless, 1983, 1992, 2010
Kloudpics, 2856
Klout, 724, 871, 1001, 1916
KLP, 71
KLUE, 2233
Klune Industries, 1904
Klustera, 724
Kluttr, 623
KlÖckner & Co. AG, 1129
Klöckner Pentaplast, 2605
KM Labs, 1004, 1051
KMC Mining, 2033
KMCO, 164
Kmofin Arkiv, 3042
KMX, 2061
Knack, 590, 661, 1075
Knape & Vogt, 1990
Kneebone, 2058
Kneron, 1509
Knewsapp, 1825
Knewton, 28, 741, 743, 775, 2446, 2690
KNF Corporation, 1203
Kngine, 3098
Knight & Carver Wind Group, 834
Knight Oil Tools, 500
Knight Packaging Group, 1492
Knight-Hub Computing, 526
Knights Apparel, 1209, 1234, 1970
Knightscope, 807
KnipBio, 981, 1100, 3277
Knjaz Milos, 3095
Knoa, 178, 2978
Knoa Corporation, 954
Knoa Software, 678, 678, 711, 1523
Knoa Software Inc., 810
Knobbe Martens, 3268
Knobbe Martens Olson & Bear, 3268
Knock, 544, 858
Knod, 688
Knodes, 1518
Knoll, 2697
Knology, 224, 1708
KNOLOGY Holdings, 1708
Knolskape, 1013
Knopp Biosciences, 1448, 1623
Knopp Biosciences LLC, 1098
Knopp Neurosciences, 998
Knotable, 3236
Knotch, 858, 1010, 1749
Knotel, 1346, 3236
Knotet, 2027
Knotice, 1047
Knovel, 52, 567, 1680, 1745
Know Better Foods, 1251
KnowBe4, 1794
Knowde, 395
Knowhere, 564
Knowledge Adventure, 1793
Knowledge Architechts, 1529
Knowledge Factor Nobel Learning Communities, 1105
Knowledge Power, 2572
Knowledge Revolution Inc., 947
Knowledge to Practice, 1551

1353

Portfolio Companies Index

Knowledge Transmission, 2960
Knowledge Tree, 1571
Knowledge Vision, 848
KnowledgeHound, 1155
Knowledgemill, 2972
KnowledgeNet, 1257
KnowledgeNet Inc., 252
KnowledgeStorm, 1863
KnowledgeTree, 538, 1406
Knowlix, 2382
Knowlton Development Corporation, 2183
KnowMe, 260
Knowre, 1087, 1716, 3127
Knowsy, 858
Knowtions Research, 2153
Knozen, 871
KNS, 3127
KNTV, 596
Knutson Mortgage, 843
KNXit, 392
Koala.ch, 2385
Koan, 563
Koan Agroscience, 557
Kobalt, 889, 1643, 2280, 2478
Kobalt Music, 3070, 3131
Kobus Services, 2967
Koch & Associates Inc., 908
Kochek, 1224
Koda Distribution Group, 194
KodaCloud, 518, 2076
Kodak Dental Systems, 1096
Kodiak Networks, 1515
Kodiak Robotics, 235, 1121
Koding, 871, 1069, 1181, 1594
Kodotel, 3071
Koemei, 1634
Kogent Surgical, 267
Kognitiv, 2230
Kognitiv Corporation, 2172
Kognitiv Spark, 2200
Koh Founders, 228
Kohlberg Kravis Roberts & Co., 3255
Koho, 2225
Kohort, 786, 1475, 2017
Koinify, 729
Koio, 325
Kokam, 1603
Kokko, 1176
Koko, 1721
Kokowa, 307
Kokunai Shi, 2347
Kolbe-Coloco, 2887
Kold-Draft, 293
Kollective, 560, 1242, 1480
Kolltan Pharmaceuticals, 660
Kolpin Outdoors, 719
Kolpin Powersports, 719
Koltan Pharmaceuticals, 2815
Komax, 2564
Komex, 2309
Komiko, 773
Komli, 3001
Komli Media, 2818
Komodo, 3012
Komodohealth, 720
Komptech Farwicks, 2683
Kona Bay Marine Resources, 939, 1011
Kona International, 3145
Kona Medical, 621, 1122, 1604
Kona Medical Inc., 269
Konarka Technologies, 126, 466
Konecta, 2851
Kong, 124
Kong.net, 2850
Kongregate, 1121
Koning, 704
Koninklijke Swets and Zeitlinger BV, 2992

KonMari, 1183
KonTEM, 2824
Kontera, 548, 1796, 3221
Kontera Technologies, 2566
Kontiki, 58, 852, 1242, 1445
KontrollFreek, 282
Kontron, 1956
Kontron Embedded AG, 2299, 2301, 2305
Kony, 1000, 1699
Kooba, 1767
Koolbit, 386
KoolSpan, 1169, 1584, 1873
Koolspan, 1306
Kooltra, 1607, 2243
Koomi, 2184
Koontz-Wagner Electronic, 932
Koowo, 1340
Kopari, 1088
Kopari Beauty, 15
KopoKopo, 1028
Koppers Inc., 1621
Korbit, 3127
Kore Wireless Group, 21
Kore.ai, 1285
Korea First Bank, 300
Korea OTC, 2857
Korea Petrochemical, 892
Korem, 2029
Korn Ferry, 787
Koronis Pharma, 1398
Korra, 623
Korrelated, 206
Korrio, 974
Koru, 488, 741, 1183
Korvis, 1645
KOS Corp, 2051
Kosan Biosciences, 94
Kosmix, 180, 1121
Kosmos Energy, 1956
Kostek Systems, 3002
Kotak, 144
Kotidata, 2966
KOTURA, 798
Kotura, 153, 880
Kouchzauber, 3056
Koudai, 1181
Koudai Shopping, 1956
Koupon, 1206
Kovars, 1600
Kovax, 3245
Kovio, 581, 634, 925, 1241
Koyj, 1087
Koza Gida, 584
KP Aviation, 225
KP Corporation, 812
KP Holdings, 1343
KP1, 2375
KPA, 489
KPG Ventures, 57
KPI Consulting, 378
KPMG, 214, 3272, 3274, 3275, 3276
KPop Stage, 3181
KPS Capital Partners, 3255
Kraco, 1753
Krak, 3108
Kramerk Junction, 1573
Kratos Defense & Security Solutions, 1361
Kraus Global, 2226
Krause's Sofa Factory, 713
Krauss Craft, 465
Krauthammer, 2378
Krayden, 1505
Kreatel, 2888
Kreditech, 301, 3044
Kreeda Games, 2849
Kreker, 3071
Kretschmer, 357

KRG Capital Partners, 77
KrisEnergy Holdings, 740
Krisp, 1670
Krispy Kreme UK, 2362
Kristalpark III, 2949
Kriya, 307
Krohnert Infotecs, 2824
Kroll BondRatings, 1299, 1593
KromaTiD, 735
Kronos, 924, 1041, 1166
Kronos Foods, 1492
KRP Properties, 2284
Krueger-Gilbert Health Physics, 378
Kruk SA, 2706
Krungthep Land, 1139, 2946
Krush, 324, 1524
Krux, 28, 1563, 1620, 1827
Kryptiq, 1945
Kryptiq Corporation, 241
Krypton, 547
KSARIA, 245
kSaria, 1334
kSaria Corporation, 315
KSep Systems, 224
KSM Castings, 2695
KSNET, 1139, 2946
KSNet, 892
Kspine, 1725
KSQ, 747
KTH Seed Capital, 2867
Ku6, 823
Kuaidian, 823
Kuaipay, 1361
Kuali, 1392
Kuato, 2831
Kubos, 307
Kudu, 1835
Kuehne Nagel, 380
Kujiale, 823, 922
Kula, 2856
Kula Bio, 318, 663
Kuli Kuli, 2161
Kumu Networks, 483, 1069, 1926
Kun Wha Pharmaceutical, 1452
Kung Fu Fast Food Chain, 2560
Kunterbunt, 2531
Kuona, 2984
KupiVIP, 28, 2320, 2928
KupiVip.ru, 1004
Kupivip.ru, 2478
Kura Oncology, 709
Kurbo Health, 1489, 1678
Kurgyvenu.It, 3049
Kurion, 730, 1151
Kuros Biosurgery, 2876
Kurt Geiger, 2714
Kurt Versen, 168, 194
Kurtosys, 1846, 1860
Kuschco Holdings, 390
Kush Bottles, 151, 1207
Kustomer, 305, 483
Kuusama Design Oy, 2873
Kuvare, 96
Kuvee, 771, 816
Kuwait Energy, 3173
Kuzneski Financial Group, 3275
KV Custom Window and Doors, 2215
KV Games, 3251
KVS, 793, 2662, 2674
Kwater, 1072
Kwicr, 1673, 1916
Kwik, 544, 1323, 1346
Kwipped, 1923
KX Industries, 1191
KXEN, 925
Kxen, 3239
Kyjen, 1572

Portfolio Companies Index

Kylie.ai, 1701
Kyligence, 483
Kylin Therapeutics, 840
Kyma, 3072
Kyma Technologies, 1915
Kymata, 1793, 2336
Kymera International, 1403
Kymera Therapeutics, 191, 1124
Kymeta, 1005, 1151
Kyn Therapeutics, 191
KynderMed, 3262
Kynectiv, 1568
Kyotec Group, 2862
Kyowa Hakko Kirin, 1452
Kypha, 267
Kyriba, 1888
Kyruus, 710, 935, 1151, 1607, 1916
Kyte, 620, 627, 795, 2446, 3152
Kythera Biopharmaceuticals, 153, 1493
Kyto, 3056
Kytogenics, 2205
KZO, 1899
KZO Innovations, 242, 979

L

L&C Trucking, 2163
L&L Foods, 477
L&S Industries, 940
L&S Mechanical, 316
L'Anza, 1979
L'ArcoBaleno, 2838
L'Artisan Parfumeur, 778
L'Azurde, 1017
L'Occitane, 402
L., 896
L.B. Maple Treat Corporation, 2056
L.B. White Company, 1171
L.I.T. Surgical, 1167
L.P., 2022
L2C, 1502
l2C Technologies, 1553
L3 Technology, 2967
L4 Epsilon, 3113
L7 Logistics, 995
L99, 2850
LA 411, 863
La Cuisine du Web, 2365
LA Digital Post, 1605
La Dove, 373
LA Fitness, 2379
LA Fitness International, 1156, 1343, 1645
La Jolla Pharmaceutical, 514
La Jolla Pharmaceutical Company, 1706, 1918
La Lumière, 1766
La Luna, 3042
la Madeline, 1751
La Petite Bretonne, 2049
La Place, 1753
La Ruche qui dit Oui!, 3239
La Tavola Fine Linen Rental, 789
LAB InterLink, 1837
Lab42, 1615
LAB4U, 1527
Labaster, 2478
Labco, 3020
Labcyte, 595, 809, 925, 1298
Labcyte Inc., 87, 604
LabDoor, 981
Labdoor, 544, 751, 994
Label Insight, 569, 1206
Label-Aire, 869
Labelbox, 942, 1075
Labelink, 2215
Labeyrie Fine Foods, 3026
labfolder, 2841
Labgas Instrument Company, 2873
LabGenius, 1363

Labmeeting, 1073
LabOne, 1972
LaboPharm, 925
Laboratoire M2, 2093
Laboratorios Sanifit, 2553
Laboratory Corp. of America, 300
LaborChart, 745
Laborie Medical Technologies, 194
Labormed, 1452
Labournet, 55
Labrador Mobile, 43
Labrador Ventures, 3284
Labrys Biologics, 386, 1010
Labsco, 782
Labstep, 3108
Labster, 1392
LabVantage, 333
Laces, 1166, 2209
Laces Group, 2208
LaCima, 2053
Ladder, 1121
Ladder Capital, 824
Lady In Leisure Ltd, 2836
LaFarge Surma Cement, 1007
Lagan, 2662, 2674
Lagan Technologies, 2610
Lagarrique, 2340
Lagoa, 38
Lagotek, 85, 650
Lagrange Systems, 1247
Laho Equipement, 2714
Laho Equipment, 2721
Laird Limited, 62
LAIX, 823
Laiye, 1121
Lakala, 2936
Lake City Acquisition, 1252
Lake County Press, 407
Lake Shore Group, 1578
LakePharma, 118
Lakeview Health, 1166
Lakoteka, 2696
LAM Research Company, 1706
Lamar, 1188
Lambada School, 889
Lambda, 811
Lambda School, 823
Lambda Technologies, 1008
Lambert Somec, 2029
Lamina Technologies, 3101
Lamination Services, 1606
Lamoda, 2829, 2838, 3170
Lamont Digital System, 402
Lampiris, 3134
Lanair Holdings, 399
Lancashire Holdings, 559
Lancashire Holdings Limited, 404
Lancashire Rosebud Fund, 2708
Lancaster Laboratories, 843
Lancaster Pollard Holdings, 1743
Lancope, 386, 550
Land Insight, 3108
Landdrill International, 2091
LANDesk, 1910
LANDESK Software, 1814
LANDesk Software, 1677, 1871
Landis, 942
Landit, 547, 708
Landmark, 192, 779
Landmark Equity Partners XIV LP, 2094
Landmark Equity Partners XV LP, 2094
Landmark Graphics, 1558
Landmark Irrigation Holding Services, 1492
LANDR, 2224
Landroller, 1784
Landry's, 869
Landsham, 2494

Landshire Inc., 77
Landslide Technologies, 56, 998
Landt, 567
Landune International, 1769
Landways, 515
Lane, 2212
Lane Supply Inc., 984
Lanetix, 1024
Laney Drilling, 1516
Lang Technologies, 2613
Langhaus Financial, 2172
Language Labs, 2931
Language Management, 1295
Language Weaver, 1402, 1784
Languagelabs.com, 2464
Lanjing Technology, 2998
Lannett Company, 188
Lansmont, 235
LANtech, 1837
Lantern, 120, 1184, 1700
Lantern Communications, 1003
Lantheus Medical Imaging, 209
Lanthio Pharma, 2514
Lantiq, 839
Lantos Technologies, 426, 703, 946, 1519
Lanx, 468
Lanzatech NZ, 1445
Lapmaster International, 716
Lapolla Industries, 678, 678
Lara Networks, 1288, 1793
Larada Sciences, 1784
Laramie Energy, 672
Laredo Hospitality, 2254
Laredo Petroleum Holdings, 1956
Largan Precision, 3218
Larian Publishing, 3042
Larian Studios, 2426
Lario Oil & Gas Company, 529
Lark, 181, 721, 841
Larky, 742
LARQ, 195
Las Vegas Cannaplex, 1135
Las Vegas Color Graphics, 1719
Las Vegas Film Festival, 512
LaSalle Capital, 3265
Lasem, 2962
Laser Diagnostic Technologies, 1706
Laser Diagnostic Technology, 1672
Laser Diagnostics, 947
Laser Light Engines, 322
Laser Projection Technologies, 349
LaserCure Sciences, 278
Laserhip, 1491
LaserShip, 862, 1248
Lashou, 2979
LASO, 596
Lasso, 1615, 1896
Last Second Tickets, 2586
Last.flicloud, 2446
Last.Fm, 2446
LastLine, 641
Lastline, 603, 1474, 1534
Lastminute, 2386, 3013
Lastminute.com, 1323, 1888
Laszlo Systems, 1241, 2196
LAT Apparel, 1562
Latapack, 2086
Latch, 377, 707, 1151
Late Great Chevy, 908
Latent AI, 800
Lateral, 3108
Latex International, 1466
Latham & Watkins, 3272
Latham International, 1134
LaTherm, 2824
Latin Healthcare Fund, 955
Latino Communications Network, 1233

1355

Portfolio Companies Index

Latista, 285, 377
Latite Holdings, 1127
Latite Roofing & Sheetmetal Company, 838
Latitude Geographics, 235
Latrima Medical, 2328
Lattice Power, 2436
LatticePower, 1184
Lattive Engines, 1654
Lauder Partners, 3284
Laudio, 2
Laughing Glass Cocktails, 129
Laughlin & Associates, 3262
Laughly, 218
Launch Darkly, 609
Launch Learning, 742
LaunchBit, 1912
Launchbox Digital, 51
LaunchCapital, 3273
Launchcyte, 1448
LaunchDarkly, 1534, 1879
Launcher, 307
LaunchKey, 679, 1912
Launchkey, 1150
LaunchKit, 231, 784
LaunchPad, 1097
Launchpad, 1943
Launchpad Global Consulting, 2931
Launchpad LA, 228, 306
Launchpad.la, 1566
LaunchPoint, 416
Launchrock, 1518
Laundry Mart Inc., 447
Laureate Education, 1946
Laureate International Universities, 1742
Laurel & Wolf, 1055, 1749, 1965
Laurel & Wolf Interior Design, 896
Laurel Health Care Co., 1271
Lauren Loft Social, 1047
Laurus Labs, 710
Lava, 1928
Lavalife, 2079
Lavante, 183, 1620, 1916
Lavino Shipping Company, 832
Lavo, 1767
Lavu, 688
Law Business Research, 1111
LawGeex, 2947
LawLogix, 1457
Lawmatics, 679, 1554
Lawn Doctor, 1111
Lawn Guru, 397
Lawnmower, 307
LawnTap, 995
LawPal, 1716
LawPivot, 1958
Lawrence Group, 61
Lawrenceville Plasma Physics, 19
Laws of Motion, 622
Lawson, 839, 1725
Lawyaw, 1554
Layar, 3051, 3149
Layer, 107, 132, 641, 871, 941, 1154, 1254, 1489, 1607
Layer Vault, 1524
Layered Technologies, 1915
LayerVault, 1531
Layerwise, 3042
Layetana Real Estate, 152
Lazada, 2829, 2838, 3170
Lazart Production, 1521
Lazer Spot, 556
Lazer Spot Inc., 862, 914
Lazook, 3030
Lazy Acres Merket, 869
Lazydays, 1967
LBL Lighting Inc., 908
LBP Manufacturing, 1166, 1479

LCM XIV CLO, 1491
LD COM, 2497
LD Vision Group, 2144
LDC, 3097
LDetek, 235
LDiscovery, 1456
LDK, 2579, 3194
LDK Solar, 3062
LDL Technology, 2481
LDR, 1500, 1792
LDR Medical, 202
LDR Spine, 1619
Le Bronze Industriel, 2423
Le Figano, 2601
Le Figaro, 2625
Le Gourmet Chef, 1549
Le Kan, 3121
Le Monde Holdings Ltd, 2486
Le Souk, 858
Le Tigre, 937
LE TOTE, 11
Le Tote, 171, 688, 889, 946, 1110, 1634
Lea, 2851
Lea com, 2354
Leacom, 2354
LEAD, 1412
Lead Group, 1717
Lead Pages, 173
Lead Point, 1534
Leadcorp, 584
Leader Gasket of Slovakia s.r.o., 3122
Leader Technologies, 378
Leaderflush, 2796
Leaders, 567, 1323
Leadership Public Schools, 1316
LeadFlip, 307
LeadGenius, 243, 1054, 1670
LeadiD, 1849
Leading Edge Geomatics, 2206
Leading Edge Innovations, 1023
Leading Edge Labels, 2796
Leading Educators, 1316
LeadingResponse, 969, 1232
LeadPages, 630
Leadpages, 776
LeadQual, 949
LeadSift, 1607, 2155
Leadspace, 235, 3214
Leadtone Limited, 3062
Leadtrend, 1922
Leaf, 392, 1439, 1807
Leaf Cart, 392
Leaf Forward, 2140
Leaf Link, 1110, 1439
LeafLink International, 2071
LeafList, 860
Leafly, 1481
Leaftail Labs, 1183, 1663
League, 770, 2225, 2265
League Apps, 13
LeagueApps, 533, 1530, 1632
LeagueLink, 1057
Leagues, 1965
Lean Plastics, 2527
LeanData, 544, 720, 1663
LeanEco, 3203
LeanIX, 1000
LeanNova Engineering, 2755
Leanplum, 1075, 1346, 1663
LeanTaaS, 1000
Leanworks, 2400
Leap, 325, 547, 1323
LEAP Auto Loans, 202
Leap Motion, 935, 3055
Leap Therapeutics, 919
Leap.It, 635
Leapfin, 317

Leapfrog, 1334
LeapFrog Investments, 1374
Leaplife, 1563
Leapmind, 994, 1004
Leapset, 1097
LeapYear Technologies, 622
Lear Corporation, 575
Leara, 1416
Learfield Sports, 1496
Learmont Pharmaceuticals, 662
Learn Behavioural, 1136
Learn It Systems, 1234, 1719
Learn To Live, 1176
Learn Vest, 180
Learn Zillion, 596
LearnBoost, 455
learndirect, 2944
Learners Guild, 55, 1054
Learnfield (Skoove), 2841
Learning, 1491
Learning Care Group, 110, 1256
Learning Games Network, 1316
Learning Labs, 2967
Learning Machines, 737
Learning Seat, 1572
Learning.com, 732
Learnium, 2284
LearnLaunch, 1097
LearnLux, 622
Learnmetrics, 981, 1004
Learnosity, 235
Learnpedia, 2904
LearnUp, 1663
LearnVest, 28, 493, 535, 581, 634, 1584
LearnWell, 349
LearnZillion, 1316, 1392, 3277
Learnzillon, 1359
Lease Accelerator, 1000
Lease Term Solutions, 1072
LeaseExchange, 1535
LeaseLock, 1613, 1985
Leaselock, 1784
LeaseQ, 1160
LeaseQuery, 189
Leather Resources of America Inc., 201
LeatherXchange, 2386
LecTec, 214
Lectrus Corporation, 1557
Lecturi, 2838
Lecturio, 2829
LED Engin, 1416
LED Medical Diagnostics, 2077
LED Roadway Lighting, 2093, 2205
Ledbury, 617, 904
LeddarTech, 2029, 2899
Ledge, 120
Ledger, 561
Ledger Investing, 942, 1675
LedgerX, 889
Ledgerx, 1121
Lediberg, 3154
Ledlight Group, 2428
Ledlite, 2949
Lee Equity Partners, 3264
Leeflink, 417
Leejam, 1017
Leena AI, 795
Leengate Valves, 3244
Leepet, 2936
Leerink, 1147
Leerink Transformation Partners, 37
Leet, 307
Leeward Renewable Energy, 156
LefEngin, 947
Lefora, 491, 1097
Left at Albuquerque, 1549
Left Hand Robotics, 429

Portfolio Companies Index

LeftHand Networks, 315, 807, 1480, 1899
Lefthand Networks, 142
LeftRight Studios, 998
Legacy at Sandhill, 1219
Legacy Cabinets Holdings II, 1189
Legacy Connect, 1632
Legacy Investments, 2131
Legacy Ridge, 1219
Legacy Technologies, 399
Legacy Technologies Inc., 1053
Legacy Venture, 3284
Legal Communications, 1275
Legal Sifter, 272
Legal Zoom, 1001
LegalMation, 1259
LegalShield, 1231
LegalSifter, 293
LegalZoom, 779, 1075, 3033
Legalzoom, 560, 1460
LegalZoom.com, 1235
Legato, 1760
Legend Communications of Wyoming, 828
Legend Films, 198
Legend Natural Gas, 1573
Legend Pictures, 1830
Legend Production Holdings, 1573
Legend3D, 198
Legendary, 28, 336, 973, 1153
Legendary Pictures, 21
Legends of Learning, 488
Legerity, 779
Leggett & Platt Incorporated, 77
Legion, 741, 1346
Legit, 395, 679
Legit Patents, 3108
LegitParents, 707
Legra Systems, 1080
LeGuide.com, 3113
LegUp, 1004
Legworks, 951
Lehigh Technologies, 946
Leica, 277, 1017
Leisure Concepts, 869
Leisure link, 2676
Leisure Link Holdings Limited, 2821
Leisure-Hunt, 2386
LeisureLink, 1239, 1784, 1915
Leisurelink, 502
LeisureQ, 3127
Leiter's, 782
Leiters, 1628, 1762
Lekolar, 2311, 3054
Lele Global, 1121
Lele Ketang, 1392
LEM Holding, 3069
Lema21, 1696
LeMaitre, 949
Lemhi Ventures, 3279
Lemon Tree, 1956
Lemonade, 295, 707, 816, 889
LemonAid Health, 1350
Lemonaid Health, 544
LemonBox, 1138
Lemongrass, 515
Lemontech, 29
Lenco, 2337
Lenda, 1595, 1998
Lendamend, 1784
LendCare, 489
Lenddo, 301, 525, 1374
Lending Club, 238, 509, 578, 1258, 1346
Lending Front, 1554
Lending Standard, 1688
LendingClub, 115, 386, 770, 1257, 1818, 2583
LendingFront, 2153
LendingHome, 552, 741, 770
LendingPoint, 63

LendInvest, 2446
Lendio, 79, 518, 1849
LendIt, 100
LendKey, 1886
Lendkey, 608, 609, 1863
LendMed, 995
LendStreet, 1054
LendUp, 773, 889, 1054, 1502, 1758, 1818, 2012
Lenel Systems International, 2902
Lengow, 2385
Lenimed, 2824
Lenley Holdings, 3262
Lenovo, 2771
Lenox, 492
Lensabl, 120
Lensar, 74
Lenscare AG, 3190
Lenskart, 2204
Lenslet, 1038
Lenslet Ltd., 3158
LensVector, 979, 1241, 1915
Lensway.com, 2144
Lensway.se, 2144
LenSx, 1921
Lenta, 1835
LENTECHS, 297
Lentil, 2137
Leo, 784
Leo Health, 1585
Leocorpio, 378
Leon Hansen Maskinfabrik, 3203
Leonard Green & Partners, 3264
Leosphere, 2851
Leostream, 1194
Leptos Biomedical, 1786
Leqee, 2690
Lerer Ventures, 1699
Les Fréres Blanc, 3020
Leslie's, 1088
LeSlipFrançais, 2296
LESS, 650
Lesser Evil, 2161
Lesson Nine (Babbel), 2841
Lessonly, 86, 1551
Let's Do This, 1663
Letao, 2584
Lethbridge Biogas, 2048
Lets, 2857
LetsBab, 937
LetsLunch, 3125
LetsVenture, 28
Lettuce, 228, 306, 624, 1099, 2017
LeukoSite, 1558
Leuven Air, 2366
Lev, 364
LevaData, 1757
LevdUp, 585
Level, 1095
Level 10 Energy, 2000
Level 5 Networks, 2386
Level 7 Systems, 805
Level Access, 1041
Level Equity, 37
Level Ex, 1480
Level Four Orthotics and Prosthetics, 1430
Level Platforms, 2043
Level Ten Energy, 773
Level10 Comics, 3109
LevelEleven, 607, 962, 1286, 1607
LevelOps, 679
Levels Beyond, 1869
LevelTen Energy, 532
LevelUp, 889, 935, 1839
Levensohn Venture Partners, 3284
Lever, 544, 942, 991, 1181, 1626
Levin HomeCare, 752
Levlad Inc., 869

Levo League, 813, 858, 896
Levy Acq., 1681
Lewis Electric Supply, 111
Lewis-Goetz and Company, 194
LEX Energy Partners, 2136
Lex Machina, 547, 567, 2011
Lex Markets, 1613
Lexaria Energy, 1135
Lexibridge, 530
Lexicon, 237, 839
Lexicon Marketing, 1505
Lexington Home Brands, 1753, 2015
Lexington Medical, 1347
Lexington Partners, 3284
Lexipol, 1572
Lexitas, 135
Lexity, 1715
Lexmark, 928
Lexop, 2212
Leyden Energy, 1672
Leyhs Pharma, 2527
Leyline, 1315
Leyou, 1241, 2436
LFE Capital, 3262, 3279
LG Lugar de Gente, 928
LGC, 2935
LGC Wireless, 162, 612, 2462
LgDb, 685
LGM Pharma, 403
LGS Innovations, 1156
LGT, 2509
LHC Holdings, 1491
LHP Hospital Group, 433
LHS, 2771
Li-Cycle, 2061
LIA Diagnostics, 1577
Lia Diagnostics, 293
Liaison, 768, 1205, 1331, 1626
Liaison International, 1460, 1956
Liaison Technologies, 1891
Lian Luo, 1121
LianLian, 1340
Lianlian Pay, 1361
Liason Acquisition LLC, 158
LiaZon, 221
Liberate, 2585
Liberation Entertainment, 494
Libero, 2329
LiberoVision, 3152
Libersy, 2822
Libertas, 557
Liberty, 2524
Liberty Bell Power, 156
Liberty Cannabis, 99
Liberty Dialysis, 1086
Liberty Global Ventures, 3276
Liberty Hydro, 1199
Liberty Latin America, 2252
Liberty Oilfield Services, 529, 1573
Liberty Plaza, 1681
Liberty Pressure Pumping, 1315
Liberty Resources, 1573
Liberty Resources II, 1573
Liberty Safe, 523
Liberty Safe & Security Products, 1456
Liberty Tax Service, 655
Liberty Tire Recycling, 1114
LibertyX, 1487
Libit, 2782
Library Solutions, 1376
Library Systems & Services, 164, 1503
LibraTax, 1115
Librato, 231, 552
LibreDigital, 56, 1846
Librestream, 2106
Librestream Technologies Inc., 2136
Librify, 1306

Portfolio Companies Index

Libryo, 3108
LicenseStream, 43
Lida Holdings Limited, 2727
Lidyana, 1594
Lieberman Research Worldwide, 1777
Lieferheld, 3044, 3170
Liekki Oy, 2873
Lien Nation, 1923
Lier Chemical Co., 2542
Life 360, 760, 1323
Life Care Services, 1276
Life Detection Systems, 995
Life Express, 2936
Life Guard Games, 1589
Life House, 518
Life Image, 1172, 1419
Life Imaging Systems, 2058
Life Line Screening, 1460
Life Links, 995
Life Media, 1241
Life Share Technologies, 86
Life Sprout, 19
Life Style, 2336
Life Technologies Corp., 1903
Life Time, 1835
Life.io, 1568
Life36, 1097
Life360, 302, 358, 596, 707, 1054, 1119, 1611, 1655
Lifeblob, 3109
LifeBond, 2454
Lifebond, 2604
Lifecake, 2685
LifeCell, 2818
Lifecode, 1654
Lifecodes, 530
Lifecore Biomedical, 3279
LifeCrowd, 1478
Lifecrowd, 1118
LifeCycle Pharma, 3015
LifeHive Systems, 2184
LifeIMAGE, 806, 1142
Lifeline Scientific, 2710
Lifeline Systems Inc., 1903
Lifelines Technology, 651
LifeLinkMD, 1599
LifeLock, 385, 986, 1235
Lifelock, 264, 560, 1001
LifeMinders, 1348
LifeMine, 762
LifeMine Therapeutics, 889
LifeNet Systems, 3262
LifePAD, 2940
LifePay, 2940
LifePort, 1705
Lifesafer, 1343
Lifescan, 1760
Lifescript, 646
LifeShield Security, 1226, 1348
LifeSize, 1760
Lifesize, 1212, 1534
LifeSize Communications, 202, 1445, 1796
Lifespring, 55
LifeSprout, 1169
LifeStream, 1128
Lifestream Diagnostics, 1837
Lifestyle Family Fitness, 224
Lifestyle Media, 734
Lifesum, 1716, 2674
LifeSync Corporation, 68, 362
LifetecNe, 1558
LifeTime, 1109
Lifetime Fitness, 744
LifeWave, 1600
Lifeways, 2207
Lift, 1715
Lift Auto Group, 2070

Lift for Life Academy, 61
Liftbump, 617
LiftIgniter, 306
Liftoff, 231
Liftoff Mobile, 378, 1583
Liftopia, 741, 1149, 1594, 1806
LiftSeat Corporation, 1740
LIG, 3145
Ligado Networks, 442
Ligand Pharma, 1271
Ligature, 3249
Ligchine International, 291
Light, 648, 889
Light Based Technologies, 2053
Light Blue Optics, 2662, 2674
Light Chaser, 823
Light Field Lab, 45, 1926
Light In The Box, 2584
Light Integra Technology, 2266
Light Sail Energy, 2155
Light Sciences Oncology, 57, 925, 3015
Light Step, 1534
Light Wave Dental Management, 92
Lightbend, 872, 1663
LightChip Inc., 252
Lightelligence, 219
Lighter Capital, 773, 1945
Lightera, 1747
Lightfoot, 998
LightForm, 1151
Lightform, 519, 1473
LightHaus Logic, 2143
Lighthouse, 107, 720, 1675, 1724
Lighthouse Autism Center, 21
Lighthouse Capital Partners, 3284
Lighthouse Community Charter School, 1316
Lighthouse Resources, 1548
Lighting Technologies International, 1664
LightingScience, 3252
LightInTheBox.com, 3251
Lightlife Foods, 357
Lightneer, 883, 1527
Lightning Hybrids, 319
Lightning Network, 1809
Lightning Systems, 146
Lightningcast, 1133
Lightower, 1153, 1409
Lightpoint, 1061
Lightpoint Medical, 3107
LightPost Digital, 387
Lightricks, 1000, 3221
LightRiver Technologies, 573
Lightship Telecom, 184
Lightspan, 1704
LightSpeed, 28, 2157
Lightspeed, 2080
Lightspeed Financial, 1728
Lightspeed Venture Partners, 986, 3284
LightStep, 552, 1654
Lightstream, 1480
LightSurf, 212
Lightswitch, 1118
Lightt, 324
LighTuning, 905
LightUp, 622
LightUp Technologies AB, 2718
Lightyear Holdings, 156
Ligier-Microcar, 2293
Ligistics Exchange, 751
Lignetics, 828
LigoCyte Pharmaceuticals, 187, 769
Lihua Group, 2936
Liingo Eyewear, 79
Lijit Networks, 315
Like.com, 238, 563
LikeList, 1771
Likely, 2586

Likewise, 1853
Lilakutu, 2437
Lilium, 1363
Lilium Aviation, 2446
Lilliput Kidswear, 220
Lilliputian Systems, 925
Lilly, 1096, 1349
LiLoE, 995
Lilt, 1654, 2019
Lilu, 1507
Lily, 1885
Lily's Kitchen, 1088
Lilypad Scales, 1589
Lima, 1416
Lima Corporate, 2851
Limata, 2824
Limbach Facility Services, 801
Limbix, 1473, 1654
Limbix Health, 1421
Limburg Gas, 2949
Limburg Win (D) T, 2949
Limburgs Klimaatfonds, 2949
Lime, 91, 124, 232, 727, 889
Lime Energy Co., 274
Lime Microsystems, 2662, 2674, 3028
Limeade, 85, 1869
LimeBike, 1643
Limeelife, 1249
Limejump, 3030
Limelight, 2149, 2243
Limelight Bio, 143
Limelight Networks, 1361
LimelightHealth, 2225
Limerick Investments, 3265
Limestone II Holding Company, 672
Limestone Pharma, 2077
Linas Matkasse, 2637
Linc Software, 2846
Lincare Holdings Inc., 1903
Lincoln Clean Energy, 202
Lincoln Educational Services, 300
Lincoln Generating, 1795
Lincoln Helios Ltd., 908
Lincoln International Corporation, 908
Lincoln Investment, 1147
Lincoln Peak Partners, 786
Lincoln Peaking Power, 156
Lincoln Snacks, 357
Lincor, 655
Linden Capital Partners, 3264, 3265
Linden Lab, 184, 262, 428, 835, 1054, 1374, 1604
Lindoc, 2474
Lindora, 869
Lindorff Group, 2384
Lindsstrom LLC, 908
Line 6, 1760
Line-Up, 3108
Line-X, 846
Lineage Grow Co., 2122
LineaGen, 1616
Lineagen, 921, 1070, 1221, 1406, 1470, 1884
Linear Technology, 541, 1654, 1760
Linedata Services, 2876
LineKong, 1340
Linekong, 2850
Linen King, 1638
LineStream, 642
LineStream Technologies, 1896
Lineus Medical, 995
Lingia, 1965
Linglong Tire, 2936
Lingo Live, 1392
LingoChamp, 922
Lingokids, 1527
Lingoland, 307
Lingotek, 756, 979, 1677

1358

Portfolio Companies Index

LinguaLeo, 3088
Linguee, 2475
Linio, 2829, 2838, 3170
Link Care Services, 2899
Link Evolution, 2414
Link Labs, 285
Link Market Services, 3025
Link Medicine, 495
Link Mobility, 21
Linkable, 287
Linkable Networks, 221, 486, 534, 1065
Linkage, 164, 3100
LinkDoc, 2439
LinkedIn, 1654, 1839
Linkedin, 836, 2723
Linkett, 2113
LinkSmart, 1760
Linksoft, 530
LinkStorm, 1584
Linkstorm, 1061, 1160, 1306
Linktone, 2733
LinkWell Health, 1715
Linkwell Health, 646, 938
Linqia, 1028
LinQuest Corporation, 1156
Lintes, 1004
Linus Academy, 173
Linuxx Global Solutions, 1606
Linx Technologies, 164
Liola, 1791
Lion Semiconductor Inc., 1951
Lion Street, 202
Lionbridge, 402, 541, 1166
Lionbridge Capital, 909
Lionhead Studios, 2322
Lipella Pharmaceuticals, 1448
Lipetski Khladokombinat, 3071
Lipman, 2745
Lipocalyx, 2824
Lipocine, 762
Lipomics, 1915
LipoScience, 1412, 1819
LipoSonix, 40, 1445
Lipton Corporate Child Care Centers, 1702
Liquavista, 144, 1305, 3051
Liquent, 852
Liqui-Box, 1372
Liquid Audio, 1474
Liquid Data Intelligence, 3048
Liquid Environmental Solutions, 22
Liquid Grids Swarmology, 1784
Liquid Light, 1906
Liquid M, 181
Liquid Machines, 1175
Liquid Robotics, 1906
Liquid Web, 1156
Liquida Technologies, 1412
LiquidCool Solutions, 400
Liquidia, 2978
Liquidia Technologies, 386, 730
Liquidity Ventures, 3265
Liquidity Wines, 2144
LiquidLEDs, 1922
Liquidmetal Technologies, 1244
LiquidPlanner, 85, 1869
LiquidSky, 1611
LiquidSpace, 275, 1061, 1323
Liquidspace, 751, 1663
Liquidware Labs, 3, 1038, 1829
LiQuifix, 1097
LiquiGlide, 2242
Liquor.Com, 590
Liquor.com, 1097
Liqvid, 3151
Lise Watier, 2150
Lisi group, 2616
LISNR, 1046, 1047, 1595

Lisnr, 479, 1004, 1206, 1486
Listen, 197
Listen Current, 1316, 3277
Listen First, 790
Listen MD, 36
Listen.com, 202
Listenloop, 307
ListenWise, 1100
Listn, 1099
Listo, 55
Listo!, 130
LitBit, 1254
Litbit, 107, 544, 976
Litecontrol, 1173
LitePoint, 1654
LiteScape, 115, 301, 1699, 1793
Litescape, 1911
Lithells, 2863
Lithion Power Group, 2275
Lithium, 634, 665, 724, 1028, 1522, 1604, 1663
Lithium Technologies, 248, 581, 867, 1620, 1796
Lithium Technology, 651
Litmus, 1717
Little Bird, 1383
Little Bits, 1110
Little Borrowed Dress, 1358
Little Ducks Organics, 1905
Little Eye Labs, 3211
Little Green Pharma, 2174
Little Labs, 120, 1149
Little Passports, 841, 1757
Little Pim, 841
Little Spoon, 1701
Little Star Media, 1703
Little Tucker, 2099
littleBits Electronics, 776, 874, 1359, 1860, 1874
LittleBorrowedDress, 1097
LittleLabs, 561
Liv Riverale, 1219
LivBlends, 1634, 2010
Live Better With, 2995
Live By Touch, 2936
Live Gamer, 455, 1080, 1849
Live Look, 1306
Live Objects, 1809
Live Person, 1680
Live Well Financial, 1339
Live.Me, 973
LiveAction, 483, 1000
LiveBarn, 2239
Livebid.com, 85
LiveCapital, 411, 1646
Livedome, 2824
Livefyre, 567, 724, 871, 1896, 2017
Livehive, 41
LiveIntent, 91, 235, 358, 695, 741, 793, 1110, 1663
LiveLOOK, 1584
LiveLoop, 1968
Lively, 32, 324, 395, 547, 823
LiveMetric, 1890
Livemocha, 197
LiveNinja, 486
Livenlenz, 2155
LiveOps, 197, 581, 634, 1001, 1202, 1235
Livepeer, 525
LivePerson, 305, 460
LiveRail, 3047
LiveRamp, 1323, 1334, 1540
Liverperson, 592
LiveSafe, 488, 922
LiveScribe, 1474
Livescribe, 563, 595, 1626, 1838, 1906
Livestar, 1054, 1254
Livestock Water Recycling, 2048
LiveStories, 773, 974, 1894
LiveTune, 3240

LiveU, 386, 2566, 3221
LiveVox, 294
LivHome, 1626
Living Earth Technology, 1689
Living Gluten Free, 103
Living Proof, 1460
Living Social, 1896
Livingly Media, 1202
Livingsocial, 876
Livingston International, 1742
Livity Africa, 1374
Livly, 1282
Livongo, 609, 816, 1075, 1154, 2690
Livongo Health, 1694
LivWell International Corp., 2074
LJL BioSystems, 237
LJL Biosystems, 94
LK Bennett, 3036
LK DEsign Automation, 2445
LKC Technologies, 285
LL Games, 3215
LLamasoft, 1242
Llamasoft, 195, 742, 1757, 1835
LLC, 506
LLOG, 277
Lloyd's Barbeque Company, 1159
LLP Holding Corporation, 908
LLR Partners, 3264
LLS Internet (loopline), 2841
LM, 809
LM Foods, 378
LMC Diabetes & Endocrinology, 2220
Lmeca, 1087
LMF, 2887
LN Holdings, 1804
LNC, 3113
Load Dynamix, 249, 538, 933, 1237
Loadmaster Derrick & Equipment, 2009
Loadstar Sensors, 130, 1288
Loanbase, 307
loanDepot, 1417
LoanLogics, 1577, 1942
LoanSnap, 231
Loar Group, 1039
LOB, 751
Lob, 741, 1138, 1150, 1634
Lobby7, 2611
LOC-AID, 1008
Locafox, 2838
Local, 721
Local Bushel, 235, 1893
Local Crate, 1176
Local ID, 228
Local Libations, 545
Local Lift, 1589
Local Logic, 2027, 2093
Local Market Launch, 306, 1566
Local Media, 515
Local Media of America, 1814
Local Motion, 1254, 1912
Local Motors, 1632, 1912
Local Offer Network, 975
Local Orbit, 742, 1736
Local Response, 608, 871, 1249, 1968
Local TV, 1360
Local Voice, 288
Local Yokel Media, 678
Local.com, 922
Localdirt, 1359
Locale, 1758
Localeur, 218, 445
Locali, 3257
Locality, 1118, 1181
Localize, 1176
LocalMind, 2147
LocalWise, 243

1359

Portfolio Companies Index

Localytics, 91, 679, 770, 1097, 1100, 1306, 1460, 1486, 1789
Locamex, 2607
Locamoda, 1474
Locanis, 3161
LocAsian Networks, 2473
Locatible, 640
Location, 1693
Location Labs, 296, 609, 1241
Location Smart, 1008
Locationlabs, 1641
LocationSmart, 1869
Locaweb, 1683
Locbox, 1010
Locemia, 270
Locemia Solutions, 1993
Lochgilphead Hospital, 2749
LOCJ, 1097
Lock8, 2831
Lockdown Networks, 1003
Locke Lord LLP, 3262
Lockerdome, 569
Locket, 858
Locketgo, 2184
LockPath, 1522
Lockpath, 1968
Lockr, 635
Lockyer, 1517
LocoJoy, 2936
Locomation, 799
LocoMobi, 981
Locomobi, 32
Locomotiv, 1316
Locox, 1533
LOCR, 2979
Locr, 2824
Locu, 1118, 1798
Locus, 184, 1452, 1626
Locus Biosciences, 175
Locus Corporation (Korea), 2694
Locus Energy, 2017, 3277
Locus Insights, 1507
LocusPlay, 1734
Lodestone Data Technologies, 392
Lodgify, 3108
LODH Private Equity Euro Choice III LP, 2094
LODH Private Euro Choice III, 2094
Lodi Gas Storage, 893
Lodo Therapeutics, 6, 31
Loehmann's Medifax EDI, 152
Loenbro, 1777
Loft, 727
Loft Orbital, 1877
Loftium, 609, 773
LoftSmart, 707
Loftsmart, 128
Lofty, 858, 2604
Logan Energy, 3135
Logan's Roadhouse, 354, 1062
LogCheck, 351, 1894
LogDNA, 1395
Logentrics, 2759
Logentries, 1460
Logfire, 655, 794
Loggi, 727, 1509
Loggly, 1860
Loggly LoopNet, 1853
Logi Analytics, 1136, 1752, 1886
Logibec, 824
Logic Blox Predictix, 1072
Logic PD, 461
Logic Vision, 1288
Logic.ink, 1238
Logical Therapeutics, 3015
LogicLibrary, 1348
LogicTree, 2196
LogicVision, 1769

Logim, 2887
Login Analytics, 876
Login Radius, 1154
LoginRadius, 2291
Logistics Marketplace, 1757
Logistik, 2082
Logistik Unicorp, 2043
Logistyx Technologies, 1071
LogiSynn, 1047
Logitech, 214
Logitrade, 2338
LogLigic, 757
LogLogic, 1793
LogMatrix, 954
LogMeIn, 1460, 2309
LogMeIn, 1003
Logo Athletics, 1954
LogoGarden, 496, 718
Logojoy, 2027
LogoSportswear, 828
Logoworks, 1663
LogPoint, 3203
LogRhythm, 36, 876, 930, 2690
LogRocket, 622
LogZilla, 3262
Lohika, 100, 627
Lois Law Library, 402
Lokafy, 2113
Loki Studios, 596
Loku, 445
Lola, 325, 707, 816, 889, 1110
Lolli, 761, 2280
Lollicam, 770
Lolly Wolly Doodle, 743
Lomb Scientific, 2399
Lombard Medical, 74
Lombard Medical Technologies, 2981
Lombardi Software, 202, 1407
Lomo Market, 3277
Lomond, 2965
Lomonosov Porcelain Plant, 2465
Loncin, 3100
London & Henley, 2796
Lone Peak, 1777
Lone Star, 64
Lone Star Land & Energy II, 672
Lone Star Overnight, 328
Lonestar Heart, 1847
Long Game, 1363
Long John Silver's, 405
Long Range Systems, 1783
Long-Term Stock Exchange, 1363
LongBoard Inc., 252
Longcheer Holdings Limited, 2850
Longeviti, 19
Longevity, 3048
Longhorn Health Solutions, 1622
Longhurst Group, 3017
Longitude Capital, 3284
Longitude Licensing, 1742
Longmaster Information & Technology, 2850
Longmen, 3194
Longmen Group, 2372
Longs Pharmacy Solutions, 1777
LongShine, 973
Longshine Information Technology, 2850
Longtail Video, 32
Longview Fibre Paper & Packaging, 2067
LongWatch, 989
Lontra, 2967
Lonza Biologics, 2513, 2690
Loock, 219
Look's Gourmet Food, 438
Look.io, 120
Lookback, 2928
LookBookHQ, 655
Looker, 560, 578, 741, 820, 1075, 1212, 1534

Looking Glass, 93, 776, 1151
Lookingglass Cyber Solutions, 1940
Lookk, 2691
Lookmark, 1101
LookNook, 1810
Lookout, 28, 124, 1069, 1149, 1235, 1509, 1852, 2860, 2860
Looks Gourmet Food Company, 1161
Looksharp, 1054
Looksmar, 2398
Loom, 816, 858
Loom Vision, 1151
Loom.AI, 1473
Loomia, 623
Loop & Tie, 1607
Loop Genomics, 4, 799
Loop It, 206
Loop Me, 2479
Loopcam, 2444, 3030
Loopline Systems, 3056
LoopNet, 368, 869, 1534
Loopt, 581, 634
Looptify, 799
Loot, 2225
Loot Crate, 330
Loot Crate Inc., 331
Lophius Biosciences, 2824
Loral Aerospace Holdings Inc., 575
Lorem, 754
Lorica Solutions, 1745
Loris.AI, 751
Loris.ai, 488
Lorus Therapeutics, 1452
Losant, 479
Lose It!, 816
Lost Crates, 1615
LostMyName, 889
Losán, 2489
Lot18, 28, 743
Lot18mimesis Republic, 2669
Lota.cloud, 2284
Lotame, 235, 665, 946, 1625
Lotame Solutions, 1445
Lotaris, 3045, 3215
Lotek, 2238
LotLinx, 1540
Lottay, 791
Lottery Now, 1613
Lotus Clinical Research, 610
Lotus Flare, 318, 525
Lotus Leaf Coatings, 756
Lotus Midstream, 671
Lotus Tissue Repair, 1811
LotusFlare, 1696
LOUD Technologies, 1753
Loudr, 1437
Louis Plung & Company, 3275
Louisiana Crane Company, 1745
Louisiana Tuggs, 1745
Loup, 1563
Love & Quiches, 193
Love Goodly, 1507
Love With Food, 858, 1054
Love'em Ingham, 909
Lovecrafts, 2478
LOVEFiLM, 2662
LoveFilm.com, 2674
Lovefilm.com, 3018
Loveholidays.com, 2586
LoveHomeSwap, 2972
Lovell Minnick Partners, 1871
Lovely, 280, 1749
Lovepop, 622, 935
Lover.ly, 1839
Loverly, 858, 1518
Loverly/Dubblee Media, 1699
LoveSac, 1954

Portfolio Companies Index

Lovesac, 841
Lovevery, 1183, 1527, 1701
Lovin' Scoopful, 2401
Loving Care Agency, 1271
Low Carbon Lighting, 3012
LowerMyBills, 1725
Loxam, 2311, 2375
Loxi, 2475
Loxo Oncology, 74, 762, 1382
Loyalty Bay, 2752
Loyalty Builders, 173
Loyalty Lab, 1389
Loyalty Rewardz, 386, 3211
Loyaltyworks, 402, 693
LoóNa, 661
LP Innovations, 1913, 1920
LP33, 1097
Lpath, 1974
LPInnovations, 989
LPL Financial, 924, 1835
LPR, 2448
LRM, 3042
Lrn, 1105
LRV Health, 3273
LS, 1705
LS Polaris Innocation Fund, 3273
LS9, 184, 747
LSAT, 1958
LSI, 1001
LSI Logic, 1654, 1760
LSQ Funding, 1147
LSR Group, 2851
Lssi, 2697
LSSi Data, 852
LT Solutions, 1755
LTB4 Sweden AB, 2816
LTC, 3002
LTCG, 1743
LTI, 1618
LTO, 3085
LTS Scale Company, 1159
LTSE, 124, 511, 1149
LTX Corporation, 1103
Lua, 60
Luca Technologies, 2492
Lucane Pharma, 3113
LucasFilm Animation, 2690
Lucent Digital Video, 1305
Lucent Polymers, 1343
Lucent Sky, 2125, 2125
Lucent Technologies, 2621
Luceo Technologies, 2824
Luceor Wimesh Systems, 2308
LuciaWind AG, 2419
Lucibel, 1311, 2439
Lucid, 69, 130, 231, 909, 1212, 1427, 1717, 1916, 2782
Lucid Dimensions, 1837
Lucid Green, 1439
Lucid Imagination, 979
Lucid Software, 856, 1070
Lucidchart, 1050
Lucideus, 1031, 1269
Lucideworks, 852
Lucidity Lights, 2329
LucidMedia, 2196
Lucidmedia, 1599
LucidPort Technologies, 627
Lucidux, 1693
Lucidworks, 84, 1663
LucidWorks Inc., 1951
Lucina Health, 149, 475
Lucintech, 2106
Lucira Health, 4, 648
Lucite International, 2587
Lucix, 1402
Lucix Corporation, 1664

Luciz, 869
Lucky, 1760
Lucky Brand, 869, 1109
Lucky Fish, 3221
Lucky Pai, 1796
Lucky Strike, 374
Lucky Strikes Entertainment, 1971
Lucky Voice Private Karaoke, 2428
Lucy, 1183
Ludei, 2920, 3223
Ludic Labs, 1084
Ludlow Ventures, 3269
Ludus, 3187
Lufa Farms, 2093
Lufax/Lu.com, 148
LuHua Chemical Co., 2593
Luka, 1150
LulaWed, 1161
Lulu, 3030, 3055
Luma, 229
Luma Sleep, 3262
Lumapps, 2851
LumaSense Technologies, 657, 1361
Lumata, 779
LumaTax, 552
Lumatax, 1158
Lumavate, 86, 658
Lumavita, 2496
Lumavita AG, 2816
Lumec, 2001
Lumec Control Products, 1740
LumeJet, 2400, 2967
Lumen Learning, 1383
Lumena, 1412
Lumena Pharmaceuticals, 1519, 1574
Lumenaré Networks., 2639
Lumenaza, 2841
Lumencor, 85, 1383
Lumend, 23
LumEnergi, 322
Lumenetix, 195, 1427
Lumenier, 1435
Lumenis, 2353, 3212, 3241
Lumens, 1087
Lumension, 1626
Lumentus, 1642
Lumere, 718
LumeRx, 647
Lumesis, 1321, 1601
Lumeta, 1305
Lumetrics, 1745
Lumexis, 2021
Lumi, 596, 761, 941, 1149, 1150
Lumi Holdings, 3062
Lumiata, 1004, 1069
Lumicell, 1080
Lumidigm, 1011, 1702
Lumiere Hotel, 190
Lumiette, 1365
Lumigent, 1334
LumiGrow, 498
Lumigrow, 1207
Lumilog, 2481
Lumin, 972
Lumin-oZ Co. Ltd., 2414
Lumina Looue, 3215
Lumina Networks, 1926
Luminae, 834
Luminaire, 3215
Luminal, 1169
Luminar, 890
Luminate, 197, 215, 1654
Luminescent, 1658
Luminescent Technologies, 56
Luminex Home Decor & Fragrance, 446
Luminist, 107
Luminoso, 9, 26

Luminostics, 951
Luminous Medical, 57, 1574
LuminUltra, 2290
Luminus, 322, 1400
Lumiode, 144
Lumitec, 2867
LumiThera, 1061
Lumity, 609, 1696
Lummi Indian Nation, 1404
Lumo, 1035, 1254
Lumoid, 358
Lumos Networks, 1506
Lumos Pharma, 495, 1619
Lumosity, 743, 1202, 1346
Lumotune, 2027
Luna Lights, 1155
Luna Technologies, 1348
Lunada Bay Corp., 1624
Lunar, 24, 707
Lunata Hair, 2133
Lunchgate.ch, 2310
Lunchio, 2841
Lund Van Dyke, 378
Lune, 525
Luneau Technology, 3239
Lunera, 69, 1977, 2142
Lunera Lighting, 1083, 3068
Lunewave, 1894
LunGuard, 3050
Luno, 2478
Lunova, 2867
Luphos, 2824
Lutebox, 1958
Luther Pendragon, 3018
Lutheran Family Services, 1837
Lutonix, 1445, 1574, 1896
Lux Assure, 3141
Lux Biosciences, 2815, 3015
Lux Research, 333, 1151
Luxar, 753
Luxe, 679, 770, 792, 1888, 1916
Luxe Energy, 1278, 1326
LuxeValet, 1534
Luxfer, 1134
Luxim, 1579, 1784
Luxin Evotech, 2936
Luxine, 1915
Luxodo, 2475
Luxola, 1965, 2798
Luxology, 1584
LuxResearch, 428
Luxtech, 1577
Luxtera, 197, 946, 1151, 1406, 1658, 1791
Luxuery Presence, 1768
Luxul, 1677, 2667
Luxul Technology, 1838
Luxury Garage Sale, 586
Luxury Optical Holdings, 481
Luze Minerals, 1278
Luzitin, 3048
LVI Services, 716, 818
LVL Technologies, 1095
lvl5, 593
LVL7, 1896
LVL7 Systems, 1119
Lxchelsis, 3196
LXR and Co., 2133
Lycera, 153, 495, 652, 1010
Lyceum Capital Fund II, 2094
Lycored, 77
Lycus Ltd., 653
Lydall Inc., 77
Lydian Trust, 1733
LYFE Kitchen, 1830
LyfeStart International, 3257

1361

Portfolio Companies Index

Lyft, 107, 124, 204, 205, 509, 511, 518, 578, 751, 775, 799, 1050, 1184, 1258, 1323, 1329, 1372
lyft, 101
Lygos, 741
Lymphact, 3048
Lynatox, 2527
Lyncean, 1004
Lynda.com, 28, 1212, 1717, 1835
Lyndra, 2229
Lyndy Biosciences, 293
Lyngsaa, 3203
Lynk, 1760
LYNK Capital, 1061
Lynq, 150
Lynx Grills Inc., 449
Lynx Medical Systems, 779
Lynx Network Group, 1455
Lynx Photonic Networks, 1793
Lyon and Post, 1585
LyondellBasell Industries, 140
LyondellBesell, 34
Lyonnaise de Garantie, 3020
Lypanosys Limited, 2853
Lyra, 1916
Lyra Health, 872
Lyra Therapeutics, 1519
Lyrebird, 124
Lyric, 727, 1363
Lyric Pharmaceuticals, 136, 1619
Lysomal Therapeutics, 1124
Lysosomal Therapeutics, 915
Lysosomal Therapeutics Inc., 191
Lyst, 28, 1758, 2478, 2662, 2674
Lytics, 518, 1540, 1945
Lytro, 124, 544, 1050, 1334
Lytron, 1173
Lytx, 500, 1041, 1846, 1972
Lytx Inc., 1003
Lyxr, 391
Lódz, 2706

M

M and M Direct, 1776
M Cubed, 667
M Cubed Technologies, 1954
M Level, 271
M&M Food Market, 2252
M&M Manufacturing, 1803
M&M Pump & Supply, 619
M&M Resources, 2163
M&Q Packaging Corp., 401
M&W, 2998
M*Modal, 1376
M-Biz Global, 3002
M-D Building Products, 577
M-DAQ, 486
M-Daq, 3215
M-Factor, 1445, 1896
M-Files, 2674
M-Flow, 2050
M-Kopa, 855
M-Real Oyj, 2990
M-Service, 842
M-Spatial, 2380
M.A. Gedney, 1113
M.G.V.S, 2462
M.Gemi, 329, 761, 816
M.I.T.R.A, 3199
M.K Electron Co. Ltd, 2924
M.S Solutions, 3183
M.T.R.E, 2585
M/A-COM Technology Solutions Holdings, 1752
M15, 1340
M2, 722
M2 Holdings Limited, 3062
M2 Renewables, 1603
M2i, 2851
m2M Strategies, 794
M2p-Labs, 2824
M2S, 97, 308, 1142, 1436
M33 Grwoth, 879
M5, 52, 655
M5 Midstream LLC, 1851
M7, 1352
M7 Group, 1496
M86 Security, 1886
M87, 1158, 1509
M:Metrics, 964
Ma Maison Fleur, 3042
Ma-Papaterie, 2383
MAA Laboratories Inc., 737
Maaco, 1576
Maana, 809, 1004
Maapilim, 3221
MaaS360, 946
MaaT Pharma, 3113
MAAX, 2067
Mabaya, 2947
Mabion, 1452
Mac IT Solutions, 3170
Macada, 2910
Macaroni Grill, 839
Maccine, 2513, 2690
MacDermid Holdings, 2379
MacDougalls' Cape Code Marine Service, 259
Macgregor, 194
MacGregor Group, 521
MACH, 2698
Mach, 2697
Machang Bridge, 584
Macheen, 1334
Machiels Building Solutions, 2949
Machine Laboratory, 1234
Machine Metrics, 1172
Machine Zone, 2012
MachineryLink, 57
MachineZone, 231
Machinify, 235
Machinima, 1242, 1534, 1846
machtfit, 2841
MacKay CEO Forums, 2292
Mackenzie-Childs, 421
Mackinac Commercial Credit, 1970
Mackle Brothers, 1404
Maclogix, 3085
MacNeill Pride Group, 447
Macro Art, 3244
Macro Meta, 1663
MacroGenics, 1010, 1574, 1941, 2970
MacroGenics Inc., 94
Macrolide Pharmaceuticals, 1350, 1731
Macromedia, 238, 536
Macrometa, 249, 799
MacroMill, 1755
Macronix International, 892
Macrosan, 1340
MACTEC, 461
Mactec, 1409
MacTrac, 2950
MacuCLEAR, 445
MacuLogix, 259, 1117
Mad Catz Interactive, 352
Madaket, 1151, 1607
Madaket Health, 710
MadaLuxe Group, 937
Madan Plastics Inc., 788
Madcap Learning Adventure, 2184
Made, 641
Made.com, 3055
Madefire, 132, 544, 563, 1860
Madeira Madeira, 754, 2976
Madfiber, 85
Madhouse, 3062
Madison Dearborn Capital Partners VI LP, 2094
Madison Dearborn Capital Partners VII LP, 2094
Madison Dearborn Partners, 3255, 3264, 3265
Madison Logic, 492
Madison Park Funding IX, 1491
Madison Reed, 518, 727, 1183, 1346, 1860
madison Reed, 1613
Madison Vaccines, 2001
Madison Vaccines Inc., 1921
MadKast, 685
Madoc, 3042
Madorra, 3023
Madrigal Pharma, 1271
Madrigal Pharmaceuticals, 237
Madrona Solutions Group, 82
Mads, 2822
Madvapes, 1213
mAdvertise, 301
Maeglin, 2876
MAEH, 834
Maestro, 1595, 1657
Maestro Commerce, 2709
Maestro Health, 94
Maestrodev, 1965
MaestroIQ, 600
MaestroIQ, 770
MaestroQA, 622, 679
MAG Interactive, 1327
MAG Technology, 892
Magadi Soda, 3178
MagCam, 2366
Magella, 1972
Magellan, 118
Magellan Health, 1058
Magellan Health Services Inc., 300
Magellan Midstream Partners, 1156
Magellan Midstream Services II, 1573
Magellan Power Holdings, 156
Magellan Sp. z o.o., 2706
Magen Biosciences, 1151
Magenta Therapeutics, 191, 709
Magento, 227
Mageon, 1052
Magic AI, 1509
Magic Leap, 124, 1075, 1363, 1509, 1946, 2690
Magicalia, 2711
MagicBus, 607
Magiceyes, 2857
MagicTab, 3108
MagicWheels, 85
Maginaatics, 2443
Maginatics, 3235
Magink, 2750
Magisto, 1509, 2831, 2952
Magma, 563, 2050
Magma Flooring, 1292
Magma Global, 2550
Magna Energy Services, 542
Magna Legal Services, 489
Magnablend, 202
Magnamosis, 1238
Magnap, 1238
Magnate Worldwide, 489, 1166
Magnatech, 2978
Magnemotion, 1173
Magnet, 124
Magnet Banking, 1863
Magnet Communications, 536
Magnetic, 455, 539, 655, 1358
Magnetic Insight, 12, 219
Magnify Networks, 1584
Magnify.net, 1306, 1734
Magnify360, 1226
Magnitude Internet, 2527
Magnitude Software, 1524
Magnolia Bluffs Casino, 1111
Magnolia Broadband, 608, 1244, 1633

1362

Portfolio Companies Index

Magnolia Medical Technologies, 921
Magnolia NeuroSciences, 31
Magnolia Petroleum Co., 477
Magnomics, 3048
Magnum, 1087
Magnum Energy, 893
Magnum Materials, 123
Magnum NGLS, 893
Magnum Semiconductor, 197, 1017
Magnum System, 291
Magnus, 2985
Magonlia Broadband, 1647
Magoosh, 243, 1054
MagPower, 2717
MagSil, 682
MagSil Corp., 682
Magwel, 3069
Mahana, 445
Mahana Therapeutics, 1151
Mahi Networks Inc., 252
Mahmee, 218
Mahoot, 1865
Maidbot, 519
maidbot, 792
Maiden Lane Ventures, 38
Mailchannels, 85
Mailcloud, 3018
MailFrontier, 1202
Mailjet, 2385
MailMag, 2437
MailSouth, 1301
Mailtime, 721
Mailtrack, 3223
Maily, 3108
Maimonidex RA, 3245
Main Bank Corporation, 1148
Main Street Dairy, 1017
Main Street One, 934
Main Venture Capital Funds, 2609
MainBancorp, 1708
Maincontrol, 2750, 3249
maincontrol, 3137
Maine Beverage Company, 1129
Maine Craft Distilling, 438, 1161
Maine Trailer, 438
Maine Wealth Partners, 1160
Mainframe, 724, 1070, 2834
MainStay Medical, 1872
Mainstay Medical, 3113
Mainstem, 1207
Mainstreet Networks, 197
MAINtag, 2851
MainTech, 1837
Maison Le Grand, 2161
Maisonette, 1480
Maisons Babeau-Seguin, 2851
Maisons du Monde, 2714
Maiyet, 595
MAJEC Ventures, 3262
Majestic Oaks, 1219
Majestic Star, 1967
Major League Gaming, 1361
Major League Hacking, 816
Major Leasing, 1708
Makara, 1663
Make a Mind Co., 1393
Make It Work, 1784
Make Music, 2625
Make School, 1054
Make.tv, 1154
Makemereach, 2385
MakeMyTrip.com, 805
Makena Capital, 1760
Makena Capital Management, 1946
Makeover Solutions, 308
Maker, 124, 871, 1888, 2649
Maker Labs, 3257

Maker Media, 751
Maker Meia, 1359
Maker Studios, 60, 641, 1830, 2928, 3121
Maker's Row, 707, 1054
Makerbot, 262
Makers Academy, 2752
MakersKit, 1222, 1849
MakeSpace, 1149, 1475, 1749, 1888
Makespace, 1359
MakeTime, 89
Maketime, 776
Maketion, 1509
MakieLab, 3149
MAKO Surgical, 1691, 1769
Mako Surgical Corp., 94, 136, 1251
Makr, 351
Makua Foods Oy, 2937
Makucell, 1784
Malabar Investments, 940
Malaria.com, 163
Malaysia Steel Works, 2623
Malcovery Security, 293
Malhot Industries, 2206
Malibu Grand Prix, 869
Mallard Exploration, 1278, 1326
Mallet, 969
Mallet & Company, 556
Malliouhana Resort, 70
Malmöhus Invest, 2867
Malo Clinic, 2717
Malone Mortgage Co., 869
Malteurop International SA, 2620
Malthus, 3076
Maluuba, 3098
MAMA & Company, 2944
Mama Earth Organics, 2238
MaMa Rosa's, 959
MamaEarth Organics, 2161
MamaMancini's, 650
Mamapedia, 1865
Mamava, 786
Mambu, 2921, 3044
Mamma Chia, 3277
Mammoth Biosciences, 107, 1184, 1238, 2000
Mammoth Diagnostics, 1323
Mammoth Media, 872
Mamoca, 1784
Mamsy, 3208
Mamut, 3013
Man Crates, 1344
Man Infraconstruction, 3173
Man Outfitters, 1507
Manac, 109
ManageCO2, 2522
Managed By Q, 1054
Managed by Q, 1694
Managed Health Care Associates, 2015
Management Consulting Group, 2524
Management Health Solutions, 646, 1520
ManagerComplete, 445
ManageSoft, 2323
Managing Editor, 852
Manappura, 851
Manappuram Finance Limited, 135
Manas Resources, 2942
Mandalay Sports Media, 515
Manda^, 1509
Mander Portman Woodward Limite, 1111
Mando, 892
Mandrel Oy, 2873
Mangahigh, 3055
Mangar International, 3244
Mangatar, 2672
MangirKart, 2444
Mango Games, 1696
Mango Health, 231, 358, 741, 751, 1075
Mango Plate, 1716

Mango Technologies, 3019
Mango Telecom, 1004
MangoPlate, 1509
Mangoplate, 3127
Mangrove, 3137
Mangstor, 1303
Manhattan Beachwear, 1456
Manhattan Beachwear LLC, 1132
Manhattan Physicians Laboratories, 1844
Mania Technologies, 1017
Manifest, 552
Manifest Digital, 263
Manifold, 305, 2068, 2280
Manistique Papers, 1209
Manitoba Harvest, 523
Manitowoc Tool & Machining, 1209
Manna Molecular Science LLC, 1207
MannaPro, 61
Mannatech, 638
Mannesmann Plastics Machinery, 3209
Manny's Tortas, 1233
Mano daktaras, 3049
Manor House Retirement Centers Inc., 447
Manov, 2751
Manroland Goss, 109
Mansion Hotel, 2850
Mansour Mining Technologies, 2059
Manta Media, 187, 1544
Mantara, 343, 548, 1711, 2618
Manthan Software Services, 2849
Manthan Systems, 1346
Manti Exploration, 672
Manticore Games, 544, 564
Mantis Vision, 1509
Mantle, 4
Mantra Bio, 318
Mantra Dairy, 2313
Manuel, 2489
ManufactOn, 1100
Manufactured, 120
Manugistics, 2698
Manx, 1491
Manzama, 1656
Manzil Health Care Services, 3196
Map My Beauty, 981
Map My Fitness, 202
Map My India, 3001
MAP Pharmaceuticals, 1691
Map Pharmaceuticals, 74
MAP Pharmaceuticals Inc., 237
Mapado, 2365
MapAnything, 904, 1607
Mapbar, 2850
Mapbox, 595, 776, 1480
MAPI, 2544
Mapillary, 1101, 1323, 1654, 2446
Maple, 514, 1475, 1821, 2187
Maple Assist, 2245
Maple Farm Media, 1734
Maple Hill Creamery, 2161
Maple Tree Networks, 314
Maples, 2490
Mapletree, 152
Maplin, 2796
Maplin Electronics, 2977
Mapmy Fitness, 52
MapMyIndia, 1509
MappedIn, 2128
Mapper, 180, 272
Mapper Lithography, 3069
Mapquest.com, 192, 1850
MapR, 1509
Mapr, 483, 578, 1534
MapR Technologies, 867, 1184
Maps on Us, 1305
Mapsense, 120, 1798
Maptuit, 2196

1363

Portfolio Companies Index

MAR Systems, 642, 1047
Marasesti, 3187
Marathon, 1146, 1623
Marathon Data Systems, 468, 529
Marathon Group, 1008
Marathon Pharmaceuticals, 1902
Marathon Products, 214
Maravai LifeSciences, 884
Marble, 564, 1247, 1655
Marble Robot, 811
Marble Security, 563
Marbles, 1615
Marcadia Biotech, 12, 782
Marcanet, 2489
Marcegaglia, 1970
Marcel & Fils, 3239
March Capital Partners, 3268
Marchim SA, 3187
Marco, 1345
Marco Aldany, 1516
Marco Genics, 157
Marcolin, 3026
MarcoPolo Learning, 3108
Marcum LLP, 3267
Mardil Medical, 3211
Marfeel, 256, 2987
Margan Business Development Ltd., 2954
Margaritaville, 1430
Margaritaville Holdings, 353
Margin Edge, 1019
Margin Point, 161
MarginPoint, 1014, 1239
MariaDB, 371
Marian Heath Greeting Cards, 1954
Marianna Industries, 910, 1605
Marie Brizard, 2676
Marie-Laure PLV, 2340
Marietta Corporation, 159
Marijuana Doctor, 1439
MariMed, 1283
Marin Software, 114, 563, 581, 634, 757
Marina, 1412
Marinello, 812
Mariner Finance, 1234
Mariner Village, 190
Marino Med, 2419
Marinus Pharmaceuticals, 386, 621, 1698
Maris Group, 2949
Maritech International, 2754
MariTEL, 849
Maritime Biologgers, 2155
Mark Andy, 109
Mark IV Industries, 2497
Mark Logic, 1796
Mark VII Equipment, 843
Mark43, 262, 816, 1099, 1149, 1589, 1715, 1894
Markafoni, 2928
Markant Sdwest Handel, 2810
MarkaVIP, 2837, 3051
Marken, 2379
Markers Workstation, 1047
Market Dial, 1070
Market Express, 529
Market Force Information, 315, 925, 1248
Market Fresh Produce, 364
Market Leader, 1641
Market Strategies International, 1927
Market Street Advisors, 1317
Market Tech Media Corporation, 263
Market Track, 199
Market Wagon, 658
Market6, 1658
MarketBrief, 286
MarketCast, 1081
Marketdial, 563
Marketech International, 1769
MarketFactory, 743

Marketfish, 85
MarketForce, 695
MarketForce Information, 441
Marketing Evolution, 1000, 2019
Marketing Technology Solution: (MTS), 954
Marketing Technology Solutions, 1420
Marketingfx, 9
MarketingIsland.com, 2196
MarketLab, 1961
MarketLive, 835, 1672
Marketlive, 192, 968, 1024
MarketMan, 1323, 2947
Marketmax, 1862
MarketMuse, 1554, 2212
Marketo, 358, 1001, 1010, 1427, 1747
Marketocracy, 764
MarketPage, 2359
Markets and Markets, 793
MarketShare, 659, 793
MarketSoft, 954
Marketsync, 85
Markett, 120
MarketTools, 856
MarketTrack, 378
MarketWare, 79
Marketwired, 1236, 2183
Marketworks, 563
MarketXS, 3051
MarkForged, 1181
Markforged, 1154
Markit, 815, 2390
Markit Medical, 622
Markkit, 1055, 1118, 1965
Markland Technologies, 2754
MarkLogic, 1235, 1654
MarkMonitor, 757, 770
Markmonitor, 1001
Markov, 1721
Marks Bros. Jewelers, 1986
Marlen International, 1435
Marley Natural, 1481
Marley Spoon, 1882, 3236
Marlin, 2732
Marlin Business Services Corp., 1423
Marlin Mobile, 1097
Marlin Resources, 672
Marlin Software, 1846
Marmalade Café, 1415
Marmot, 1853
Marner, 1872
Maroon Group, 476
Marope Algarve, 3048
Marotech, 2029
Marqeta, 852
MarqueMedicos, 61
Marqueta, 2943
Marquette Business Credit SPE I, 1970
Marquette Transportation, 1086
Marquette Transportation Company, 2379
Marquette Transportation Finance, 1970
Marquii, 1507
Marriott Praia D'El Rey, 3048
Marrone Bio Innovations, 498, 1089, 1241, 1774, 1966
Marrone Organic Innovators, 1669
Mars Reel, 218
Marsala Biotech, 2077
Marsh, 1753
Marsh Bellofram Corporation, 606
Marshall & Swift, 869
Marshall & Swift Holdings, 361
Marshall & Williams Co., 908
Marshall Excelsior Company, 908
Marshall Retail Group, 334, 354, 378, 969
Marshall Tube, 1173
Marstone, 7
Marsulex Environmental Technologies, 2062

Martello, 2284
Martex Fiber, 1234
Martha Stewart Living Omnimedia Inc., 1903
Martialone Ltd., 2554
Martin Color-Fi, 616
Martin Currie, 559
Martin Pharmaceuticals, 662
Martinez Geospatial, 1233
Martis Capital, 3264
Martmania, 2776
Martsoft, 1180
Marubi, 1088
Marussia F1 Team, 2944
Marval Bioscience, 791
Marvaomedical, 2355
Marvel, 336
Marvell Technology Group, 1779
Marvin Manufacturing, 96
Marvin's, 1970
Marxent, 607, 1734
Masa, 2481
Masa Maso, 1340
Masabi, 760, 2972
Masada Security, 131
Masada Security Holdings, 1708
Mascara Sales & Marketing, 1578
Mascoma, 747, 1906
Mascoma Corporation, 1445
Masergy, 21, 254, 441, 1211
Masergy Holdings Inc., 158
Mashable, 1299, 1886
Mashav, 2609
Mashburn, 282
Masher Media, 1784
Mashery, 623, 741, 764, 1584
Mashgin, 1758
MashNetworks, 171
Mashwork, 1992
Maskd, 1830
Mason, 4
Mason Finance, 1075
Mason Manufacturing, 61
Mason Steel, 1606
Mass Relevance, 202, 525
Mass Roots, 638, 1135
Massage Envy, 1576
Massage Heights, 16
Massana, 2336
MassCEC, 3273
MassDevelopment, 3273
Massdrop, 552, 741, 1184
Masse, 1183
Massey Fair, 932
Massif, 839
Massif Oil & Gas, 1278
Massif Oil & Gas II, 1326
MassInvestor, 3262
Massiv Konzept, 2475
Massive, 608, 1247, 1314
Massive Impact, 3121
Massman Automation, 850
Massmarket, 3013
MassVentures, 3273
Mast Kalandar, 2818
Mast Therapeutics, 1490
Master, 2206, 2649
Master Capital Group, 2649
Master Financial Management, 2382
Master PIM, 2527
MasterClass, 60, 1028, 1395, 1883
Masterclass, 883, 1001, 1138, 1613
MasterCraft, 1967
MasterImage 3D, 3098
Mastermind Toys, 2062
Masternaut, 779
MasterpieceVR, 2212
Masterskill, 1516

Portfolio Companies Index

Mastery Connect, 883
MasteryConnect, 428
Mastro's Restaurants, 1970
Matagorda Island Gas Ops, 156
Matatu, 2978
Matchbook, 1518
Matches, 3104
Matchmove, 3215
MATE Ltd, 2585
Materialist, 1323
MaterialNet, 1133
Materials Marketing, 1521
MatexNet, 2846
MATH Venture Partners, 3265
Mathcore, 2878
Mathey Dearman, 828
MathHarbor, 3174
Mathpix, 1527
Maths Doctor, 2950
Mathsoft, 655
Mathzee, 1615
Mati, 622, 1613
Matic, 132, 397
Matilda Jane, 478
Matilda Jane Clothing, 443
Matisse Networks, 2005
Matlet Group, 1636
MatlinPatterson Global Opportunities Partners III, 2094
Mato-Erno.com, 1158
Matox, 2612
Matriavax, 2978
Matrics, 1133, 1348, 1599
Matrimony.com, 1184
MatriSys Bioscience, 870
Matritech, 1896
Matrix, 2944
Matrix Industries, 1613
Matrix Medical Network, 224, 782, 1972
Matrix Memory, 634
Matrix Partners, 3273, 3284
Matrix Semiconductor, 1003, 1793
Matrix Sensors, 1237
Matrixx, 928, 1728, 1865, 3152
Matrixx Initiatives, 1491
Matrixx Software, 872
Mattco Forge, 290
Matter, 1524
Matter Port, 1282
Mattereum, 525
MatterMark, 585
Mattermark, 776, 1749
Mattermost, 942
Matternet, 519, 1138, 1703, 1998
Matterport, 106, 107, 720, 1151, 1509, 1531, 2012, 2853
matterport, 792
Mattersight, 1760
Matthews, 1516, 1871
Matthews Asia, 1147
Matuse, 1741
Mauna Kea Technologies, 1498, 3113
Mauritsklinieken, 3232
Mavatar, 1749
Maven, 858, 1654
Maven Link, 1829
Mavencare, 2113
mavencare, 2249
Mavenir, 560
Mavenir Systems, 87, 197, 202, 1334
MavenLink, 416
Maverick, 1268
Maverick Air Center, 1192
Maverick Healthcare, 894, 1491
Maverick Healthcare Equity, 1189
Maverick Media LLC, 447
Maverix Biomics, 181

Maveron Equity Partners, 986
Mavin, 1263
Maviro, 2272
Mavrck, 1065
Mavrx, 563
Mavu Pharma, 782
MAX, 2168
Max, 135
Max Environmental, 104
Max Matthiessen, 2384
Max Media, 839
Max Truck, 2755
Maxager, 214
Maxcess, 258
Maxcress, 257
MaxCyte, 904, 1008
Maxeda, 2379
Maxeda DIY Group, 3033
MaxFunds.com, 1336
Maxi Canada, 96
Maxia Pharmaceuticals Inc., 237
Maxim, 1922
Maxim Pharmaceuticals, 1918
Maxima Corporation, 765
Maximiles, 3113
Maximum Throughput, 2196
MaxLinear, 1239, 1896
Maxment, 2824
Maxor, 244
MaxPoint, 1853
MaxStream, 1677
Maxsys Ltd, 2372
Maxta, 124, 1796
Maxteck Technology, 3218
Maxtena, 1169
Maxthon, 455
Maxtor, 238
MaxVision, 925
Maxwell, 395
Maxwell Health, 426, 548, 1110, 1849
Maxwell Systems, 1136
Maxxam Analytics, 2082
Maxxim Medical, 778
Maxymiser, 3032
May Mobility, 607, 707, 811, 1834
Maya Cinemas, 21
Maya Entertainment Group, 1771
Maya's Mom, 1323
Mayborn Group, 2300, 2311
Mayfield Associates Fund, 623
Mayfield Fund, 3284
Mayflower Medicinals, 966
Mayi, 1906
Maystreams, 1167
Mayvenn, 11, 124, 229, 1097
Mayvien, 1632
Maz, 707
MAZ Germany, 2994
Mazu Networks, 1738
MB Aerospace, 166
MB Aerospace Holdings II Corp., 158
MB Equity Fund II Ky, 2740
MB Equity Fund Ky, 2740
MB Financial Bank, 529
MB Industries, 1745
MB Innovations, 1187
MB2 Dental Solutions LLC, 158
MBA & Company, 2972, 3040
MBA Polymers, 2372, 2391, 2703
Mbaobao.com, 596
MBAPolymers, 2671
MBF Healthcare Partners, 3264
MBH Enterprises, 1020
MBH Settlement Group, 1343
Mbi, 2697
MBI Energy Services, 1129
MBIA, 1956

MBlox, 1626
Mblox, 946
mBlox, 1354, 1850, 2458
Mbm Systems, 2824
MBooster, 2874
MBRP, 2163
MBS Media Campus, 34
MBT Ag, 2785
MC Assembly, 577
MC Group, 1139
MC Group PLC, 2946
MC Laboratory, 2970
MC MC, 1727
MC Pelican Fund LP, 623
MC Sign, 373
MC Sign Company, 373
MC Technology, 2833
MC10, 20, 1241
Mc10, 1334
mc10, 1993
MC2, 686
Mc2i, 2448
MCA Dental Group, 2220
MCA Solutions, 1146
McAfee, 744
McAffee, 1835
McAlister's Deli, 1576
McAobao, 2936
mCarbon, 386
McBride Plc., 575
MCC Control Systems, 373
McCaw Cellular, 1211
McClarin Plastics, 276
McCormick & Schmick's Seafood Restaurants Inc., 354
McCoy Global, 2121
McCoy Sales, 1477
McCubbin Hosiery, 1422
McData, 202
McDonald's, 473, 2881
McGraw-Hill, 1551
McGraw-Hill Education, 140
MCGZ, 2949
MChek, 3001
MCI, 1085
McIntosh Perry, 2255
MCK Group, 2420
McKechnie Aerospace, 1256
McKeil Marine, 2272
McKenzie Creative Brands, 158
McKenzie Sports Products, 873, 1557
Mckenzie Sports Products, 1111
McLarens, 96
MCMC, 1275
Mcmurry/TMG, 1984
McMynn Leasing, 2258
MCN, 1965
MCN Bio-Products, 2049
MCN Bioproducts, 2114
McNally Industries, 399
McNeil Technologies, 1925
MCNex, 1087
MCP, 3013
MCRA, 374
McRae's Environmental Services, 2258
McRock Capital, 2032
McRock Capital iNFund, 483
MCS, 2462
MCS Property Group., 2814
MCS/Medical Compression Systems, 2324
MCT, 3049
MCube, 634
Mcube, 581
mCube, 970, 1075, 1474
Mcube Works, 1747
MCubeWorks, 1087
MD, 206

1365

Portfolio Companies Index

MD Beauty, 2015
MD Now, 334, 348
MD VIP, 1109
MDalgorithms Inc., 1069
Mdaq, 2690
mdBriefCase, 2220
MDC Vacuum Products, 446
MDDF, 710
mDhil, 855
MDLive, 242
MDM, 1452
MdotLabs, 471
MDS, 2265
MDS Gateways, 2336
MDS Inc., 1903
MDS Technology, 3145
MDT, 631
MDT Software, 606
MDX Health, 2851, 3113
MDY, 655
ME 3I, 3048
Me.com, 324
Meadow, 151, 397, 994, 1694, 1807
Mealey's Furniture, 1415
MealPal, 518, 1202
Meals & Media, 2967
Meals to Live, 445
MeaningMine, 2355
Mearthane Products, 1636
Measurabl, 308, 532, 561, 1607
Measured, 1384
Measureful, 1463
Mebelorama, 3170
Mebias Discovery, 266
MEC Dynamics, 1915
Mec.com, 2683
MEC3, 1572
Meca-Teno, 2415
Mecatronix, 3098
Meccatronicore, 2868
Mecfor, 2251
Mech Mocha, 3133
Mechanical Dynamics, 1336
Mechanical Rubber Products, 1404
Mechanical Zoo, 623
Mechanische Componenten, 2810
Mechanodontics, 226
Meciria, 3107
Mecmesin, 235
Mecoswiss, 2810
Mecs, 109
Med America Recycling, 654
Med Data, 415
Med Solutions, 1776
Med-Legal, 910
Med-Pharmex, 639
Med3000 Group, 1148
Meda Pharmaceuticals, 1452
MedAdherence, 678
MedAffinity, 3262
Medafor, 3279
Medagate, 183
Medal Playlabs, 2953
Medallia, 679, 1604, 1654
Medallion Analytics, 1385, 1387
Medallion Anayltics, 998
MedAptus, 312, 312
Medarex, 237, 865
MedAssets, 876, 1040
MedAssets America, 1972
MedAssist, 1590
MedAux, 1551
MedAvante, 1730, 1844
MedAware, 809
Medaware Solutions, 267
MedBox, 1135
Medbridge, 1136

MedCap, 1409
MedCath, 1972
Medcenter, 2458
MedCenterDisplay, 1261
MedChart, 2149, 2187
Medchart, 2137
MedChronic, 3031
MedCity Media, 1047
Medcorder, 800
MedCPU, 1205
MedCrypt, 679
Medcrypt, 1601
Meddle, 1306
MedE America, 1972
MedeAnalytics, 221, 986
Medeanalytics, 665
Medecision, 876
MedECUBE Healthcare, 174
Medeikonos, 2878
Medeikonos AB, 2718
Medenovo LLC, 487
Medeo, 2233
Medeor Therapeutics, 1519, 1941
Mederi, 946
MedEViewing, 847
MedExpress, 1654
Medexus Pharmaceuticals, 2180
Medfinders, 881
Medforth Global Healthcare Education, 2034, 2046
Medfusion, 915
Medgenics, 3245
MedHaul, 995
MedHok, 1717
Medhost, 1476
Medi Tate, 3240
Media Armor, 871, 1310
Media China Corp, 2847
Media Development Investment Fund, 1374
Media Group of America, 617
Media Lano, 3179
Media Lario Technologies, 3046
Media Matchmaker, 1784
Media Math, 508
Media Nusantara Citra, 1598, 3061
Media Platform, 1249
Media Radar, 221
Media Recovery, 734
Media Rights Capital, 21
Media Spike, 1524
Media Surface, 2769
Media-Streams.Com, 3162
Media4Care, 2841
Mediaboost, 3214
Mediachain Labs, 1101
Mediacontech, 3154
Mediacore, 2278
MediaDev, 2466
Mediaflex, 2857
MEDIAI Co, 2807
Medial Cancer Screening, 2831
Medialets, 608
MediaMath, 427, 1486, 1502, 1601, 1689
Mediamath, 1728
Mediamo, 2504
Median, 2851
MediaNation Inc., 2402
Medianet, 223
Mediant, 732
Mediant Communications, 161
MediaOmics, 3048
Mediapacs, 1221
MediaPass, 624
Mediaplatform, 1728
MediaPlex, 2907
Mediapps, 2354
MediaPro, 790

Mediaprobe Inc., 2991
Mediaquest, 3173
MediaRadar, 790
MediaResponseGroup, 1927
MediaShare, 596
Mediasilo, 1627
Mediasmart, 2920
MediaSolv, 1299
Mediaspan, 3133
MediaSpan Group, 1709
Mediaspectrum, 1000
Mediasurface, 2386
Mediatech Inc., 859
MediaTek, 1922
Mediatel, 192, 1927
MediaTile, 1306, 1584
MediaV, 823
MediBeacon, 267, 1046
MediBic, 2970
Medic Vision, 337, 3059
Medicago, 2029
Medical Arts Press, 683
Medical Card System, 1039
Medical Card Systems, 63
Medical Care Corporation, 320
Medical Depot, 723
Medical Device Innovation, 2463
Medical Imaging Australasia Group Limited, 2398
Medical Indicators, 606
Medical Management of New England, 312
Medical Metrix Solutions, 520, 1459
Medical Payment Exchange, 1572
Medical Pharmacies, 2082
Medical Port, 3048
Medical Present Value, 3137
Medical Science & Computing, 1136
Medical Solutions, 1276
Medical Specialties Distributors, 1301
Medical Tracking Solutions, 3262
Medical University of the Americas, 691
Medicalis, 938
Medication Delivery Devices, 1706
Medicinal Genomics, 359
Medicine Man, 1807
Medicine Man Technologies, 1135
Medicinia, 641, 2976
MediciNova, 2970
Medico, 743
Medico (Hong Kong) Limited, 621
Medicode, 1850
Medicom Medical, 2918
MediConnect Global, 1204, 1677
Medicure, 2077
Medicus, 2381
Medicus Healthcare Solutions, 244
Medicus IT, 349
Medicus Technologies, 1494
MedidaMetrics, 747
Medidata, 52, 1680
Medidata Solutions, 1745
Medify, 1945
MediGene, 3196
MediGene AG, 3137
Medigus, 1382, 2655
Medikidz, 915
Medikly, 644, 721
MediMedia, 2605
MediMedia USA, 1931
MEDINET, 2970
Medingo, 3072
Medio, 1247, 1926
Medio Systems, 28, 623
Mediornet, 2781
MediQuest, 1002
MediQuest Therapeutics, 3015
MediQuire, 496, 718

1366

Portfolio Companies Index

MediSafe, 2947
Medisafe, 1509
Medisas, 124, 942, 1069
Medisse, 2514, 3020
MEDITECH, 1752
Meditory, 981
Medium, 124, 872, 1149, 1363
Medivance, 1691
Medivo, 1205
Mediware Information Systems, 1814
Medizinaltechnik Ltd, 3162
MedLEARNING AG, 3197
Medley Global Advisors, 361
MedLumics, 2874
Medlumics, 2553
MedManage, 560
MedManage Systems, 753, 1664
MedMark, 1508
Medmark, 1136
MedMark Services, 402, 474
MedMen, 1135
MedNews, 163
Medolac, 3277
Medopad, 1615
MedOptions, 909, 949, 1459
Medovent, 2824
Medpace, 433
MedPage Today, 1689
Medpage Today, 52
MedPlast, 1571
MedPointe, 782
MedPointe Inc., 575
MedPricer, 1792
MedPro Safety Products, 188
MedQuist Inc., 1903
MedRepublic, 120
MedRespond, 1448
MedRhythms, 1161
Medrium, 1325
Medrobotics, 293, 1448, 1693
medSage, 293
MedSage Technologies, 1448
medSage Technologies, 998, 1440
MedSave, 1850
Medscape, 922
Medseek, 550
MedServe, 209
MedService Repair, 1267
MedShape Solutions, 979
Medsite, 1954
MedSocket, 267
Medsouth Health Care, 1708
Medspa Partners, 2220
MedSpan, 312
Medsphere, 688, 946
MedSphere International, 905
Medsphere International Holding, 3062
Medstack, 2212
MEDSTIM, 1287
Medsurant Health, 1293
MedSynergies, 793
Medtechnica, 2745
MedTorque, 2214
Medtouch, 1173
Medtrex, 52, 1227
Medudem.com, 2310
Medumo, 1100
Medusa Medical Technologies Inc., 2155
MedVance Institute, 818
Medvantix, 153
MedVantx, 1021, 1802
Medvantx, 1460
MedVentive, 538, 703, 1142
MedVenture, 118, 1379
MedVenture Associates, 3284
MedWaves Incorporated, 117
Medwell, 710

Medycyna Rodzinna SA, 2706
Medytox, 3145
Meebo, 968, 1087
Meedor, 3022
Meelo, 448
Meer Corp., 465
Meero, 1982
Meesho, 1138
MeetElise, 877
Meetic, 2354, 2851
MeetingSense Software, 1869
Meetrics, 2841
Meetup, 1374
MeeVee Inc., 1089
Meez, 132
MEG Energy, 1956
MEGA Brands, 1970
Mega Lifesciences, 1139, 2946
Mega Zebra, 2671
MegaBots, 1183
Megabots, 107
Megadyne, 2851
Megahoot LLC, 725
Megamedia, 2717
MegaPath, 1896
MegaPath Networks, 1402, 1850
Megaphone TV, 3127
Megastudy, 892
MegaZebra, 2921
Meghmani Organics Ltd. (India), 2694
Meglan, 2047
Mego, 307
Mei Ah Entertainment, 2847
MEI Group, 220
MEI Labels Holdings, 1765
MEI Pharma, 74, 458, 1298, 1819, 1941
Meiban, 2690
Meicai, 823
Meicai.cn, 3251
Meican, 842, 1327
Meico Crown Entertainment, 869
Meihua, 823
Meili/Mogu, 823
Meilishuo, 296
Meilleire Gestion, 2851
Meilleurmobile.com, 2851
MeilleursAgents.com, 2385
Meilleurtaux.com, 3208
Mein Auto, 3239
MeinAuto, 2838
MeinAuto.de, 2829
Meineke, 168, 1576
Meineke Car Care Center, 415
Meineke Car Care Centers, 894
MeinProspekt, 2824
Meiosys, 3233
Meister Plus, 2696
Meituan, 815, 1340
Meituan-Dianping, 509
Meiya Power Company, 2434
Meize Energy Industries Holding Limited, 3062
Mejuri, 2027, 2232
Mekanist, 3047
Mekics Co., 3002
Melco Electric, 838
Melco International Development Limited, 2402
Meldium, 773
Melele, 3251
Melexis, 3069
Melinta Therapeutics, 1956
Melior Discovery, 266, 1915, 3211
Melita, 1153
Melixa, 2868
Mellanox, 1654, 2770
Mellanox Technologies, 1896, 3231
Mellitus, 347
MELODEA, 3245

Melodeo, 1945
Melon, 1099
Meltwater, 772, 1910
Member Suite, 1555
MemberClicks, 745
MemberHealth, 1972
Members: 104 West, 3276
Members: 17 Asset Management, 3261
Members: A&M Capital Partners, 3264
Members: Abingworth, 3273, 3284
Members: ACON Investments, 3255
Members: Applied Facts, 3268
Members: DLA Piper, 3274
Memblaze, 1509
MembranePRO, 297
Memc Electronic Materials, 1835
Memebox, 100, 552, 721, 1716, 1998, 2012
Memebox Corporation, 1263
MeMed, 1696, 2831
Memed, 641, 1509
MemfoACT, 2369, 3216
Memiray, 1051
Memo Right, 1838
Memobox, 2383
Memoir, 784, 1518, 1534, 1821
Memolane, 197
Memora, 2851
Memora Inversiones Funerarias, 2311
Memora Services Funerarias, 2300
Memorial MRI & Diagnostic, 1824
Memory Inc., 2785
Memory Medallion, 998
Memory Pharmaceuticals, 925, 2518
Memphis Meats, 609, 800, 2446
memphis Meats, 318
MeMPile Ltd, 2973
Memrise, 206, 2478
Memry, 530
MEMS Drive Inc., 1951
Memscap, 3124
Memsic, 2850
MemSQL, 28, 741, 858, 965, 1069, 2663
Memsql, 585
MemVerge, 1051
Menara, 646
Menara Networks, 144, 1672
Mendeley, 2390
Mendix, 2822, 3051
Mendocino Farms, 1088
Mendor, 2939
Mengniu Dairy, 2337
Meninvest Kantox, 1416
Menlo Entrepreneurs Fund X, 623
Menlo Security, 816
Menlo Therapeutics, 237, 1941
Menlo Therpeutics, 74
Menlo Ventures, 3284
Menlomicro, 809
Mensch & Natur AG, 588
Mentad, 301
Mental Canvas, 1154
Mention, 3044
Mentor, 2795
Mentor Corp., 1903
Mentor Graphics, 1760
Mentored, 1286
Mentum, 2851
Menu Next Door, 1000
Meow Mix Company, 575
MeQuilibrium, 475
Mequilibrium, 1601
Mer Group, 2745
Mera Career Guide, 3199
MeraDoctor, 2313
Meraki, 634, 1341, 1654
Meraki Networks Inc., 623
Merant, 2005

1367

Portfolio Companies Index

Mercado, 3137
Mercado Software, 3231
Mercados SUVIANDA, 1396
Mercantile Adjustment Bureau, 1523
Mercaris, 1054
Mercateo, 3161
Mercato Partners, 3276
Mercator MedSystems, 138
Mercatus, 195
Mercaux, 1589
Merced Systems, 1760
Mercent, 85, 1869
Mercer Advisors, 374, 819, 1147, 1166, 2204
Mercer County Community College, 3274
Mercer Foods, 789, 846
Merchant Atlas, 301, 1839
Merchant Capital Solutions, 1743
Merchant eSolutions, 1850
Merchant Warehouse, 1417
MerchantAtlas, 1097
Merchantry, 641, 871
Merchbar, 1749
Mercuri International, 2888
Mercury Fund, 950, 3265, 3269
Mercury Media, 686
Mercury Security, 1136
Mercury Taverns, 2985
Merenda Limited, 2705
Merex Group, 632
Merfish Pipe and Supply and Pipe Exchange, 1376
Mergent, 415
Mergers & Acquisitions, 3285
Merical, 1128
Meridian, 1383
Meridian Rack & Pinion, 828
Meridian Rail Services, 1372
Meridian Surgical Partners, 152, 374
Meridien Research, 439
Merill Industries, 61
Meriplex Communications, 2081
Merisant, 1967
MeriStar Investment Partners Lesee, 1360
Meristem Therapeutics, 2302, 2354
Merit, 1758
Merit Health Systems Corporation, 1986
Merit Industries Inc., 908
Merit Service Solutions, 1232
Meritage, 1094
Meritage Energy, 1020
Meritage Pharma, 1929
Meritas, 1742
Meritex, 380
Meritize, 488
Meritron Networks, 1906
Merkle Group, 1785
Merlin, 816
Merlin 200, 465
Merlin Enterainments Plc., 1903
Merlin Entertainments, 277
Merlin Metalworks, 1295
Merlin Securities, 1654
Merlin Technologies, 1886, 2196
MerLion, 2513
MerLion Pharma, 2690
Merlion Pharma, 2419
MerLion Pharmaceuticals, 2452, 2518
Merlion Pharmaceuticals, 3062
Merlon Intelligence, 2006
Mermaid Maritime, 1139, 2946
Merrco Payments, 2144
Merrick Pet Care, 1248, 1767
Merrill Lynch, 2614
Merrimack, 1438
Merrimack Pharmaceuticals, 925, 1884
Merrion, 2918
Merrion Pharmaceuticals, 925

Merry Jane, 417, 1813
Mersana, 6
Mersana Therapeutics, 710, 1436, 1490
Mersive Technologies, 944
Mertz Manufacturing, 1423
Meru, 1249
Meru Networks, 502, 623, 1796, 2603
Merus, 237, 1043, 1436, 1519, 2939
Merus Audio, 3203
MESA and Asteral, 3033
Mesaplexx, 1711, 2618
Mesatronic, 2481
Meshify, 445
Mesirow Financial Private Equity, 3265
Mesker, 1014
MesoCoat, 1047
Mesosphere, 124, 770, 1069
Mesquite Power, 156
Message Bus, 1460, 1860
Message Missile, 3107
Message Pad, 2662
Message Systems, 1317
Message Yes, 755
MessageBird, 2446
MessageBus, 1334
MessageLabs, 306
MessageMe, 1546
MessageOne, 1738
MessageVine, 3155
MessageVine Montilio, 2580
Messenger, 1469
Mestergruppen, 2731
Mesura, 2737
MET, 3107, 3107
MET Innovations, 1047
MET-TEST, 656
Meta, 518, 721, 792, 994, 2149, 2700, 3216
Meta Financial Group, 96, 353
Meta Group, 1041
Meta Resolver, 679
Meta Server, 530
Metabase Inc., 1666
Metablo, 2899
Metabogal Ltd., 2954
Metabolex, 3015
Metaboli, 2385
Metabolic Explorer, 3113
METabolic EXporer, 3020
Metabolic Solutions Development Company, 943, 1379, 1713
Metabolik Technologies, 2111
Metabolon, 184, 383, 697, 749, 1658, 1774, 1842
MetaBrite, 384
MetaCarta, 466, 1702
Metacarta, 979
MetaCDN, 3138
MetaCloud, 1425, 1747
Metacloud, 386
Metacrine, 709
Metactive, 1379
MetaFlo, 2187
Metafor, 2278
Metaforic, 3104
Metagenics Inc., 274
Metaio, 2443
Metal Nanopowders, 3107
Metal Networks, 1597
Metal Powders & Process, 3107
Metaldyne, 923
Metalicity, 1548
Metalico, 1557
MetaLINCS, 1540
Metall Technologie Holding GmbH, 2712
Metallkraft, 2615
Metallwarenfabrik Gemmingen, 1937
Metalogix, 3033
Metals Technology Corp., 321

Metaltec Steel Abrasive, 1422
MetalWood Bats, 1262
Metalysis, 2598, 2662, 2674
Metamachinix, 623
Metamarkets, 1524, 1860, 2406
Metamaterial Technologies, 2230
Metamaterial Technologies Inc., 2155
MetaMatrix, 1003
Metamerge, 2632
MetaMetrics, 135, 1409
MetaMind, 1069
Metanautix, 1654
Metapa, 954
MetaPack, 2535
Metapack, 2577
Metapack Ltd, 2894
Metaphor, 1306
Metaphor Solutions, 1584
Metaphysics VR, 307
Metaplace, 555
Metaps, 721
Metara, 524
Metaresolver, 231
Metasolv, 202
MetaSource, 1093
Metasphere Ltd., 2290
MetaStabble Capital, 1882
MetaStable, 1654
MetaStable Capital, 2280
MetaStorm, 212
Metastorm, 986
Metaswitch, 779
Metaswitch Networks, 1654
Metatomix, 1913
MetaTV, 192
Metavante, 1103
Metavention, 1928
Metawave, 204, 205, 1834
Metaweb, 634
Metcase Consulting Oy, 2966
Meteo Protect, 2181
Meteo-Logic, 2831
MeteoGroup, 815
Meteor, 85, 124, 585, 1968
Meteor Learning, 1728
Meteor Solutions, 1089
Metfilmschool, 2428
MetGen, 2612
Metgen, 2106
Method CRM, 2170
Method Holdings, 1430
MethodCare, 818
Methodology, 743
Methylation Sciences, 2143
Metis Secure Solutions, 998
Metonic Real Estate Solutions, 70
Metra Biosystems, 206
Metrasens, 3018
MetraTech, 28
Metrc, 417
Metrekare, 2437
Metreos Corporation, 1126
Metric Insights, 741, 1110, 2006
Metric Medical Devices, 950
Metric Stream, 278
Metricly, 317
MetricStream, 500, 1052, 1602, 2079, 2690
Metricstream, 979
Metrigo, 3056
Metrika, 1360
Metriv, 126
Metrix Systems, 2735
Metro Franchising, 1516
Metro Group, 2614
Metrobility Optical Systems, 438
Metrofi, 197
MetroGistics, 1422

1368

Portfolio Companies Index

Metrolight, 2900, 3222
Metrologic, 779
Metromile, 720, 741
Metron Aviation, 315
Metron Systems, 85
Metronet, 2944
Metronome, 177
Metronome Therapeutics, 1760
Metronor, 2754
MetroPCS, 494, 1153, 1156, 1409, 1682
Metropolis Healthcare Limited, 1956
Metropolitan Market, 673
Metropolitan National Bank, 1991
Metros Corp., 810
MetSchools, 1927
Mettermark, 858
Mettl, 2526
Mettle Midstream Partners, 1278, 1326
Meu Rio, 1374
MeUndies, 1998
Meus Pedidos, 1509
Mevotech, 2219
Mewave, 1786
Mey Alcoholic Beverages, 1835
Meya.ai, 2027
Meyer Industries, 734
Meyer Materials, 1114
Meyer Unkovic & Scott, 3275
MeYou Health, 224
Mezmeriz, 61, 432, 704, 1523
Mezz Cap, 434
Mezzia, 1057
MF Fire, 19
MFG.com, 262, 2733
MFM, 164
Mforma, 2451
MFormation, 1334
Mformation, 500
mFormation, 560
Mfuse Limited, 2507
MFX Solutions, 1374
MGC Diagnostics, 104
MGid, 2736
MGM Resorts, 869
MGS Manufacuring, 1171
MGS Mfg. Group Inc., 577
MGVS, 3241
MHR Institutional Partners III, 2094
MHR Institutional Partners IV LP, 2094
Mi Bioresearch, 157
MI International, 2795
Mi-Factory, 2527
Mi-Pay, 3018
Mi5 Networks, 1089
Miami Green, 190
Miaozhen Systems, 1534
Miartech, 2667, 3194
Miasole, 184, 807, 1445
MiaSolé, 69, 1906
Miba Plast, 3101
Mic, 1110
MIC Group, 1030
Mic Network, 60
Mica Sense, 3257
MiCardia Corp., 269
Micarga.com, 3125
Micel, 1747
Micello, 590
Michael Foods, 843
Michael Huber Gmbh, 832
Michael Verheyden, 3042
Michael's Bakery Products LLC, 958
Michaels, 220
Michaels Stores, 277
Michell Instruments, 235
Michelson Diagnostics, 3018
Michigan Accelerator Fund, 3269

Michigan Angel Fund, 3269
Michigan eLab, 3269
Michigan Induction Inc., 465
Michigan Ladder, 113
michigan Landscape Professionals, 1609
Michigan Power, 156
Micira, 124
Mickey Forest, 1507
MicksGarage, 2355
Micoy, 344
Micrima, 2400
Micro DataStat, 1047
Micro Drip, 55
Micro Focus, 161, 839
Micro Inks, 2599, 2600
Micro Interventional Devices, 52, 233, 1385
Micro Inverventional Devices, 1117
Micro Linear, 1896
Micro Networks/Andersen Laboratories, 131
Micro Office, 1991
Micro Power, 1402
Micro Precision, 405
Micro Prose, 876
Micro Technology, 2673
Micro Vision, 214
Micro Warehouse, 783
Micro-LAM, 1019
Micro-Poise Measurement Systems, 109
Microban International, 240
Microbial Solutions, 2967
MicroBilt, 1863
Microbiologics, 850
Microbion Corporation, 2229
Microchip, 1257, 1604
Microchip Technology, 1654
MicroCHIPS, 314
Microchips, 1460
Microchips Biotech, 1008
Microcision, 1523
Microcosm Commnications, 3047
Microcosm Communications, 2662
Microdisplay Corporation, 197
Microduino, 1509
Microdynamics Group, 849, 1232
MicroE Systems, 52, 314, 1227
MicroEdge, 333
Microelectronics, 1922
MicroEnergy Credits, 3277
Microenergy Credits, 841
MicroEnsure, 1374
MicroEra Power, 1507
Microfabrica, 184, 466, 1010, 2021
Microgame, 1248
MicroGreen, 61
MicroGREEN Polymers, 2008
MicroGreen Polymers, 85
Microgrid Labs, 737
MicroGroup, 1456
MicroHeart, 1896
Microland, 1850
Microland Limited, 3062
Microlytic, 3203
MicroMass, 443
Micromatic, 505
Micromax Informatics Limited, 1776
MicroMed Technology, 2079
Micromed Technology, 3186
Micromet, 187, 191, 769, 1325
Micromet., 2877
Micron Technologies, 166
MicroNet, 3279
MicroNet Automation, 2824
Micronics Filtration Holdings, 1904
Micronotes, 907
Microoptical Devices, 153
MicroPact, 680
Micropact, 166

Microphage, 1915
Micropoint, 1340
Micropole Univers, 2876
Microporous Products, 985
Micropower, 1784
MicroProbe, 756
Microquai Techno, 3062
MicrOrganic Tech., 704
Microsaic Systems, 3028
MicroSave, 1374
Microscreen, 2978
MicroSeismic, 466, 1579, 1776
Microshade, 3203
Microshare, 1259
Microsoft, 197, 1096
Microsoftware, 3127
Micross Components, 1904
MicroStar, 783
Microstar Logistics, 158
Microstim, 2824
Microsystems, 529
Microtask, 3149
MicroTech Systems Inc., 69
MicroTransponder, 445
Microtrip, 307
Microvention, 59, 1896
Microventures LLC, 650
Microvisk, 2967
Microwave Networks, 734
Microwave Photonics, 1305
Microwave Vision, 3113
MicuRx, 2978
MicVac AB, 2718
Mid America Brick, 61
Mid Atlantic Capital, 1166
MID Labs, 1382
Mid Oaks Investments LLC, 3265
Mid Valley Industries LLC, 843
Mid-America Entertainment, 843
MidAmerica Administrative & Retirement Solutions L, 92
Midas Vision, 1227
MIDAS Vision Systems, 954
MidAtlantic Broadband, 1208
Midcap Financial, 1104
MidCap Funding IV, 1970
Middle Peak Medical, 3113
Middle Tennessee Home Health Services, 406
Mideast Youth, 1374
Midgard, 1967
Midi, 1057
Midi Compliance & Ethics Solutions, 1364
Midigator, 1136
midland appliances, 2163
Midland Cogeneration Venture, 156
Midland Container, 443
Midland Industrial Glass, 2967
Midnight Pharma LLC, 1556
MidNox, 2329
Midori Capital, 2148
Midori Health, 747
Midstates Petroleum, 740
MidStream Technologies, 753
Midverse Studios, 1655
Midway Pharmaceuticals, 266
Midwest Automotive Designs, 1424
Midwest Dental, 787
Midwest Iron & Metals, 1209
Midwest MicroDevices, 1553
Midwest Plastic Products, 1719
Midwest Supplies, 378
Midwest Technical Institute, 1751
Midwest Vision Partners, 92
Midwestern BioAg, 274
Midwestern Manufacturing Company, 1209
Miele Events, 392
Mifratel, 2426

Portfolio Companies Index

MIG, 2850
MIGfast, 2613
Mighty, 79, 883, 1384
Mighty AI, 1158
Mighty Ai, 776
Mighty Cast, 1108
Mighty Meeting, 679, 2010
Mighty Nest, 731
Mighty Networks, 552, 741, 751
MightyBell, 858, 871
Mightybell, 641
MightyHive, 720
MightyNest, 1178
Mightytext, 972
Migo, 972
MiiCard, 1688
Miikana, 12
Miikana Therpeutics, 2419
Mikawaya, 828
Mike & Mike's Organics, 2139
MikMak, 1883
Mikotor, 1706
Milacron, 433, 1970
Milagro Exploration, 46
Milan Supply Chain Solutions, 917
Milcom Technologies, 2717
Miles, 1035, 1703, 1894
Milestone AV Technologies, 633, 1479
Milestone Aviation Group, 1279
Milestone Environmental Services, 1009
Milestone Pharmaceuticals, 621, 1412
Milestone Technologies, 928
Milestones, 2254
Military Advantage, 1896
Milk & Honey, 668, 1099
Milk Specialties Co., 354
Milk Specialties Global, 110
Milk Stork, 1893
Milk the Sun, 2686
Milkman, 2296
Mill River Labs, 1073
Millendo, 12
Millendo Therapeutics, 782, 1145
Millenial Media, 51
Millenium Laboratories, 1776
Millenium Pharmacy Systems, 474
Millennial Media, 358, 455
Millennial Net, 1080
Millennium Care Inc., 2094
Millennium Custom Foods, 443
Millennium Outdoors, 1745
Millennium Pharmacy System Inc., 176
Millennium Pharmacy Systems, 184, 315
Millennium Trust, 21, 1166
Miller Fabrication, 470
Miller Heiman, 881, 1166, 1496, 2015
Miller's Ale House, 1576
Millers Fashion Group, 2951
Millers Self Storage, 2951
Millibatt, 721
Millicore, 2562
Milling Hotels, 3203
Millipede, 1619
Millstone, 1627
Millworks, 796
MilMar Food Group, 1745
Milo, 115
Milo Biotechnology, 1047
MILSPRAY Military Technologies, 1521
Milstone AV Technologies Inc., 787
Milton Industries, 1166
Milyoni, 183, 1361, 1818
MIM-Hayen, 1446
Mimecast, 1000
MiMedx, 1842
Mimeo.com, 608, 909, 1422
Mimetica, 3138

Mimetogen, 1627
Miminally Invasive Devices, 1512
Mimio, 1733
Mimir Networks, 2155
Mimix Broadband, 734, 1126
Mimix Broadband Inc., 810
Mimoatec Co. Ltd, 2924
Mimoni, 238, 1374
MimoOn, 2824
Mimosa, 757
Mimosa Networks, 1361
Mimosa Systems, 197, 502, 623, 968, 1119
Mimub, 2920
Minar, 2742
MinBox, 1150
Minbox, 2113
MinCell, 2824
Mincom, 779
Mincom Limited, 2622
Mind Candy, 28, 3070, 3131
Mind Lab, 28, 1226, 2976
Mind Palette Co., 2646
Mind.com, 634
Mindbites, 1860
MindBody, 1251
Mindbody, 1001
Mindbody Software, 1784
MindBridge, 2232
Mindbridge, 1528
Mindcet, 2366
MindClick, 624
MindFlow Technologies, 1855
MindFrame Inc., 176
MindGuard, 3159
Mindmatics, 2829, 2838
MindMatics & Mobile Commerce, 3155
MindMatrics, 2662
Mindmatters, 1227
MindMeld, 721, 1084, 1563
Mindmeld, 3098
MindMixer, 635
Mindray Medical, 1087
Mindreef, 1080
Minds'Eye, 1306
Mindshare Medical, 1701
Mindshare Technologies, 1705
Mindshift Technologies, 1782
Mindshow, 307, 609, 1480
Mindstrong, 762, 816
MindSumo, 585, 1945
MindTickle, 28, 1509
Mindworks, 2818
Mineloader, 2733
Mineral Fusion, 1335
Mineral Tree, 857
MineralTree, 2
Minerva, 1604, 2949
Minerva Networks, 1352, 1896
Minerva Surgical, 1928, 1941
MineSense, 2093
minesense, 2078
Minetta Brook, 1061
Minettabrook, 1463, 1825
mInfo, 1733
Ming Yi Zhu Dao, 472
Mingle Analytics, 438
Mingle Healthcare Solutions, 1161
Mingleverse Laboratories, 2053
Mingoa, 2355
MingPlan.com, 371
Minh Hoang Garment, 2961
Mini Storage Self Storage Center, 2918
Mini-Skool, 2082
Minibanda, 2344
Minibar, 858, 1998
Minicom Digital, 2462
Minigate, 626

Miniluxe, 567
Minim, 754
Minimally Invasive Devices, 386, 458, 1520, 1544, 1553
Minimarketsimasys, 2619
Minimax, 1017
Minimax Viking Group, 3020
MinInvasive Orthopedic Solutions, 2328
Minio, 107, 603
Ministore, 1306
Ministry Brands, 29, 819, 909, 1000
Ministry of Cake, 2944
Ministry of Supply, 1912
MinistryHub.com, 344
Minit Asia Pacific, 3201
Minivator, 2967
MINKABU, 2974
Minnesota & Eastern Railroad, 2946
Minnesota Educational Computing, 1332
Minnetonka Tankers, 1967
Minnetronix, 97
Mino Games, 858
Mino Monsters, 707
MiNodes, 3056
Minomonsters, 2329
Minoryx, 2851
Minova Insurance Holdings Ltd., 404
Minova International, 2617
Minox Technology, 2754
Minsheng Energy, 2936
Mint, 741, 1663
Mint Farm Energy, 1967
Mint House, 1555
Mint Solutions, 2939, 3113
Minted, 248, 1202, 1346, 1563, 1785
Mintera, 3137
Mintigo, 57
Mintra Trainingportal, 1572
Mintz Group, 1979
Minubo, 3108
Minute Media, 235
Minute Menu Systems, 92
MinuteBuzz, 3113
MinuteKey, 646
minuteKEY, 1181
Minuto Seguros, 641
Minutrade, 641
Mio, 679
Mios e-Solutions Oy, 2318
Miovision, 2181, 2190, 2224, 2238
miovision technologies, 2161
MIOX, 1791
Miox, 596
MIOX Corporation, 756, 1300
MIP, 2051
Mips, 1760
MIPS AB, 2816
MIQ Logistics, 202
Mira Rehab, 1615
Mirabilis Medica, 458, 1677
Miracle Linux, 1755
Miradia, 757
Mirador Biomedical, 85, 2008
Mirador Financial, 563
Mirage Network, 56
MiRagen, 112, 347
MiRagen Therapeutics, 191, 315
Mirageworks, 3127
Mirakl, 2693
Miramar Labs, 560, 621, 1122
Miramarlabs, 74
Miramix, 622
Mirantis, 603, 1000, 1620, 3235
Mirapoint, 933
Mirati, 1412
Mirati Therapeutics, 1382
MIRE, 2366

Portfolio Companies Index

miReven, 2959
Miria Systems, 1568
Mirics Semiconductor, 2322
MIRNA Therapeutics, 1436
Mirna Therapeutics, 544, 1500, 1619, 1698
Miromatrix, 341
Mironid, 689
Mirow, 1507
MirriAd, 3107
Mirror, 307, 544, 741, 1110, 1150
Mirror 42, 3128
Mirror.me, 975
MirrorMe, 679
Mirth, 1807
Mirth Provisions, 1135
MIS Implants Technologies, 1776
Misco, 937
Misco Robotics Kitchen Assistant, 397
MiserWare, 979, 1899
MisFit, 226
Misfit, 775, 823, 2831
Misfit Wearables, 1359, 1798
Mishor, 301, 2831
Mision Critical Software, 1041
Mismi, 1623
Miso, 1138
Miso Music, 590
Mission, 329
Mission Barns, 395
Mission Bio, 129, 1184, 1613
Mission Community Bank, 1403
Mission Critical, 202
Mission Mark, 1323
Mission Motors, 988, 1700
MISSION Therapeutics, 1436
Mission Therapeutics, 1731, 2858, 3085
Mission U, 743
Mission Ventures, 3284
MissionBio, 799
MissionMode, 1681
Missions Controls Automation, 1915
MissionU, 1551
Missouri Metals, 1295
Mist, 1075, 1346
Mist Systems, 483
Mister, 2219
Mister Bell, 3020
Mister Car Wash Holdings, 1109
Mister Cookie Face, 147
Mister Spex, 2441, 2668, 2797, 2824, 3044, 3104, 3239
MisterAssur, 2521
Mistral, 3001
Mistral Energy, 1573
Mistral Pharma, 2196
Mistral Solutions, 3062
Misty Robotics, 776, 1916, 2000
Mitchell, 199, 378, 924, 1041
Mitchell Gold + Bob Williams, 849
Mitchell Rubber Products, 828
MITEC Automotive, 2527
Mitel, 779, 2252
Mithmitree, 1139
Mitobridge, 1145
Mitokinin, 1238
Mitokyne, 1268
Mitotix, 1334
Mitra, 2878
Mitra Biotech, 28, 1519
Mitra Medical, 2888
Mitralighn, 1847
Mitralign, 946, 1604, 2748
Mitrionics, 2637
Mitro, 1181
Mits, 1852
Mitsubishi, 214
Mitten, 846

Mitu, 1813, 1888
MITY Enterprises, 1705
MITY Holdings of Delaware, 1491
MiTú, 60
Miva, 274
Mivenion, 2824
Mix, 1666
Mix.com, 2851
Mixamo, 852
Mixaroo(Boxfish), 3098
Mixbook, 445, 772, 1089
Mixcomm, 1051
Mixed Dimensions, 93
Mixed Signals, 1407
Mixel, 1460
Mixer Labs Inc., 623
MixerLabs, 231
MixLab, 325
Mixlr, 3030
Mixmax, 751
Mixonic, 506
Mixpanel, 124, 2012
Mixpo, 2291
Mixpo Portfolio Broadcasting, 2143
MixRank, 585
Mixrank, 1655
MixRank Inc., 650
Mixt, 1363
Mixx Entertainment Inc, 3166
Mixxt, 2979
Miyabaobei, 3251
Miyoko's Kitchen, 1363
Mizzen & Main, 1912
Mizzen+Main, 1088
MJ Freeway, 1807
MJ Hybrid Solutions, 392
MJ's Fine Foods, 2049
MJardin, 1807
MJIC, 1135
mjoy, 3207
MK Capital, 3265, 3269
MKM Building Supplies, 2311
MKS, 2058, 2267
MKTG, 1881
ML-C, 2824
ML-CSP II Trust, 623
Mlab, 776, 2869
mLab, 231
MLL Telecom, 2044
Mlog, 2974
MLS Media, 1496
MLstate, 3113
MLT, 2857
Mlvch, 890
MM Guardian, 418
MM Pipeline Services, 1705
MMB Networks, 2041, 2224, 2242
MMC, 2007
MMC Networks, 197, 1534, 1896
MMI Holdings, 405
MMIST, 2087
MMIT, 1759, 1972
MMS, 2796
MMS - A Medical Supply Company, 1970
MMV Financial, 434
MNC Asset Management, 3061
MNC Asuransi Indonesia, 3061
MNC Bank, 3061
MNC Energy, 3061
MNC Finance, 3061
MNC Kapital Indonesia, 3061
MNC Land, 3061
MNC Life Assurance, 3061
MNC Securities, 3061
MNC Sky Vision, 1598, 3061
MnEBay, 2993
MNectar, 544, 721, 2010

Mnemosyne, 1693
mnubb, 1982
Mnubo, 2190
MNX, 1572
Mo'Minis, 1241
MOAC, 1390
Moasis, 1334
mOasis, 1580
MOAT, 1226
Moat, 60, 317, 741, 1184, 1699
Moatech, 2924
Mob Scene, 611
Mobalytics, 89
Mobango, 2671
MoBank, 2400
Mobassurance, 3049
Mobbit Systems, 2545
Mobbles, 1896
Mobcent, 2869
MobCrete, 2936
MobCrush, 60, 561
Mobcrush, 306, 741, 1075, 1149
MoBeam, 1241
Mobeam, 626
Mobee, 1010, 1097, 1734, 1988
Mobestream Media, 202
Mobi PCS, 1153
MOBI Wireless, 333
MOBI.Money, 3229
Mobicart, 2778
MobiCash, 1061
MobiCom Corporation, 939
Mobideo, 377
Mobidoo, 1611
Mobien Technologies, 3211
Mobify, 1206, 2224
Mobikon, 2913
Mobilaris, 2754
MobilCom Holding, 2810
Mobile 1, 2914
Mobile 365, 609, 1001, 1906, 2999
Mobile Access, 3124
Mobile Action, 720
Mobile Arq, 418
Mobile Aspects, 998
Mobile Cause, 1784
Mobile City, 2475
Mobile Commerce, 2662, 2674
Mobile Commons, 1437
Mobile Embrace, 1596
Mobile Fusion, 1693
Mobile Health Engagement Strategies, 794
Mobile Mantra Inc., 650
Mobile Medical International Corporation, 349
Mobile Messenger, 1853
Mobile Parts, 2126
Mobile Posse, 515, 551, 904, 1502, 1699
Mobile Price Card, 1161
Mobile Roadie, 1099, 1992, 2668
Mobile Storage Systems, 2206
Mobile System7, 538
Mobile Teacher, 2950
Mobile Travel Technologies, 2662
Mobile World, 2961
Mobile Xoom, 418
Mobile.com, 1760
Mobile.de, 2795
Mobile2Win, 2662
MobileAccess Networks, 2720
Mobileaware, 2987
MobileDay, 1699, 1700
MobileDevHQ, 773
MobileFusion, 998
MobileIron, 770, 1346, 1747, 3121
Mobileiron, 1001
MobileLogix, 387
Mobilemode, 2451

1371

Portfolio Companies Index

MobilePeak Systems, 596, 2850
MobileRQ, 1383, 1926
Mobiles Republic, 2638
Mobiles Republick, 3239
MobileSmith, 344
MobileSpan, 1860
MobileStorm, 69, 685
Mobiletag, 2385
Mobileum, 596
MobileWalla, 1158
Mobilewalla, 2870, 3062
Mobileway, 1017
Mobileworks, 1634
MobileXL, 1784
MobilEye, 3101, 3245
Mobileye.com, 2604
Mobilibuy, 3003
Mobilicity, 1506, 2073
Mobilife, 2438
Mobilike, 3044
Mobilite, 1660
Mobilitus, 1463
Mobilize, 751, 934
Mobilize.me, 1991
Mobilizer, 995, 1187
Mobiltel ., 2784
Mobiltel EAD, 2309
Mobiltex, 2290
Mobilygen, 1796
Mobim Technologies, 2667
Mobimo, 2922
Mobinex, 3215
Mobiquity, 1146, 1317, 1673
MobiSante, 85
Mobisante, 2008
Mobiserve, 1244, 2654
MobiTV, 922, 1126, 1361
Mobitv Inc., 1534
Mobius, 384, 408
Mobius Imaging, 1100
Mobius Technologies, 1600
Mobius Therapeutics, 267, 569
Mobius Venture Capital, 986
Mobix, 596
Mobixell, 1244
Mobixell Networks, 2472, 2662
Mobliss, 43, 85, 964
Moblize, 466
Mobotix, 2713
Mobovivo, 2048
MobPartner, 2385
MobSquad, 2212, 2236
MobStac, 28, 483
Mobvoi, 3251
Moby Mart, 1701
Mocana, 809, 1663, 1711, 1850
Mocapay, 685, 1090
Mocavo, 685, 1789
Mochi, 1663
MOCON, 3279
MocoSpace, 1699
Mocuis, 1452
Mod Operandi, 1593
Moda Midstream, 671
Moda Operandi, 135, 1291
MODA Technology Partners, 1321
Moda Technology Partners, 1387
Modal, 1390
Modanisa, 2437
ModbiTV Inc., 810
ModBot, 107, 1254
Modbot, 936
ModCloth, 858, 998
Mode, 525, 770
Mode Diagnositics, 2892
Mode DX, 3028
Mode.ai, 1183

Model Metrics, 1596
Model N, 28, 1212
Model N Inc., 986
Modemore, 2857
Modern Animal, 318
Modern Fertility, 318, 741, 1183, 1882
Modern Luxury, 494
Modern Machinery, 2085
Modern Meadow, 175, 1531
Modern Resources, 672
Modern Water, 2892
Moderna, 747, 1519, 2690
ModernHealth, 96
Modernizing Medicine, 1752
Modest, 229
Modewalk, 1218
Modify Watches, 243
Modius, 1400
Modiv Media, 1637
Modjoul, 574
Modjoy, 3062
Modnique, 869
Modo Labs, 1747
Modria, 59, 1054
Modsy, 272, 518, 525, 1346, 1758
Modtech, 1086
Modular Energy Devices, 1693
Modular Robotics, 776
Modular Space Corporation, 22
Modulated Imaging, 870
Modulus Video, 1853
ModuMetal, 428, 841
Modumetal, 7, 85, 319, 1641, 2008
Modus, 213
ModViz, 192, 1646
Moe's Southwest Grill, 1576
Moeke, 3042
Moeller Aerospace, 66, 909
Mogarde, 2602
Mogi, 206
MOGL, 1061
Mogl, 1784
Mogo, 2144
MOGO BankConnect, 2995
Mogreet, 791, 1099
Mogul, 1329, 1701
Mohomine, 898
Mohr Davidow Ventures, 3284
Mojilala, 858
Mojio, 2236, 2265
Mojiva, 1425
Mojix, 1361, 1637
Mojo, 1255
Mojo Motors, 38, 1322, 1592
Mojo Networks, 852, 1951
Mojo Vision, 799, 1069, 1613
MojoPages, 202, 1784 '
Mojoworks, 2478
Moka, 721, 823, 2260, 2690
MokaFive, 1324
Moki, 84, 688
Moki Mobility, 1425
Moksha8, 1251
Mold-Rite Plastics, 1022
Moldflow Corporation, 1608
Molecuar Glasses, 704
Molecular, 166
Molecular Assemblies, 4
Molecular Connections, 2490, 2490
Molecular Detection, 1784
Molecular Devices, 1760
Molecular Imaging Research, 742
Molecular Imaging Technology, 1281
Molecular Imprints, 87, 1151, 1791
Molecular Logix, 241
Molecular Match, 950
Molecular Partners, 2496

Molecular Sensing, 569
Molecular Staging, 2079
Molecular Templates, 703, 1143
Molecular Templates Inc., 1619
MolecularMD, 224
Moleculera Labs, 1488
MolecuLight, 2149
Moleculo, 585
Molekule, 563, 942, 1879
Molio, 60, 79
Mollie Stone's Markets, 869
Molly, 896
Moloco, 1087
Molotov.tv, 2851
Molplex, 3010
Molycop, 109
Mom Trusted, 272, 301
MoMelan Technologies, 1419
MoMeland Technologies, 1097
Moment, 773, 1151, 1183
Moment Snap, 317
Moment.Me, 301
Moment.me, 3121
Momenta, 762
Momenta Pharmaceuticals, 191, 410
MomentFeed, 306, 624, 791, 1798
Momentfeed, 2649
Momentive Performance Materials, 140
Momentous, 512
Momentum, 384, 1166, 2058
Momentum Healthware, 2196
Momentum Machines, 858, 1069, 1983
Momentum Technologies Sdn Bhd, 3164
MommyMixer, 445
Momo, 1181
Mona, 272
MonaLiza, 2655
Monarch Industries Limited, 1209
Monarch Machine Tool, 61
Monarch Marking Systems, 1368
Monarch Teching Technologies Inc., 831
Monark, 1991
Monarx, 1070
Monashees, 483
MONCLER, 3020
Moncler, 973
Monday.com, 1000
Mondee, 884, 1255
Mondi Foods, 2781
Mondial Risk Management, 2709
Mondo, 1575
Mondo Media, 1813
Mondo Minerals, 2851
Mondosoft, 2779
Mondrian Investment Partners Ltd., 924
Moneris, 3048
Monese, 3108
Monet Software, 69
Monetate, 246, 741, 751, 1380, 1584
Money Design, 721
Money Forward, 721
moneydesktop, 1863
MoneyExpery, 2972
MoneyFarm, 2403, 3052
MoneyGram International, 300, 1815
MoneyLion, 655
Moneymail, 2736
Moneysights, 2526
Moneytree, 1607
MongoDB, 754
MongoHQ, 585
MongoLab, 1888
Mongolab, 784
Monitor Group, 374
Monitronics, 402
Monitronics International, 202
Moniture, 1001

Portfolio Companies Index

Monolith, 2050, 2822
Monolith Materials, 738
Monopoly Media, 2683
Monoqi, 2444, 2813
Monosnap, 2856
MonoSol RX PharmFilm Technology, 508
Monospace, 1099
MonoSphere, 798
Monpelier RE, 787
Monroe Capital, 3265
Monroe Engineering, 1765
Monroe Truck Equipment, 1166
Monscierge, 593
Monsoon Commerce, 1360
Monstar Lab, 721, 2974
Monster Media, 1727
Monster Mosquito Systems, 950
Monster XP, 364
Monstrous, 1958
Mont Blanc, 2325
Montage, 222, 2436
Montage Embry Hills, 1219
Montage Talent, 375
Montage Technology, 1838
Montana Rail & Southern Railway of British Columbi, 2085
Montana Resources, 2085
Montana Silversmiths, 17
Montavista, 1704, 1896
Monte Alto Forestall, 834
Monte Nido, 1111
Monte Nido Holdings LLC, 447
Monte Rosa, 1928
Monterey, 2436
Monteris, 1379
Monteris Medical, 1713, 1928
Montigo, 365
Montpelier RE, 456
Montpelier Re Holdings, 300, 827, 1368
Montpelier Re Holdings Ltd., 575
Montreaux Equity Partners, 3284
Monzo, 816
Moo, 38
Moodbyme, 1416
Moodify, 1834
Moodlerooms, 1146, 1169
Moody International, 1017
Moody's Corp., 1903
Moogsoft, 483, 603, 1534
MooMee, 1681
Moonfrye, 871, 1222
Moonlighting, 51
Moonshine Farms, 1627
Moonshoot, 2870
Moore, 2664
Moore Gallagher, 2664
Moore Landscapes, 501
MooreCo, 556
Moosejaw Mountaineering, 1415
Mootwin, 3113
Moovit, 302
Moovweb, 968
Mooyah, 225
Mopec, 276
MoPowered, 2406
Moprise, 85
MoPro, 695
Mopub, 968
Moran Printing, 1745
Moravia, 492
Morbax, 1507
MORE Health, 219
More.com, 1405
MoreCom, 3214
Moreens, 690
Moregidge, 2184
Moreover, 592

Moreover Technologies, 2711
Moreton and Company, 3276
Morflora, 3245
Morgan Auto Group, 862
Morgan Contracting, 1021
Morgan Corp., 1030
Morgan International, 2415
Morgan Lewis, 3272, 3274, 3275
Morgan Olson, 1030
Morgan Solar, 2041
Morgan Stanley, 1903
Morgan Stanley Capital Partners, 3264
Morgan Street, 1615
Morgenthaler Ventures, 3284
Morhterhood Maternity, 869
Mormak, 2145
Mornin' Glory, 2441
Morningside Venture Group, 1040
MorningStar, 152
Morph Labs, 1965
Morpheus Technologies, 1160
Morphic Therapeutic, 709, 1731
Morphics Technology, 555
Morphie, 786
Morphisec, 809
Morpho, 3006
Morphochem, 3007
MorphoSys, 191
Morphotek, 246, 769
Morphotek Inc., 747
Morria Biopharmaceuticals, 3245
Morris Homes, 2985
Morrison & Foerster, 3272
Morrone Organic Innovations, 1915
Morse Shoe Inc., 354
Morta Security, 585
Mortar, 858
Mortar Data, 814
Mortgage Contracting Services, 110, 529
Mortgage Hippo, 3125
Mortgagebot, 1717
MortgageIT, 592
MortgageIT.com, 1133
Morthier Catering, 3042
Morton Grove Pharmaceuticals, 468
Morton Industrial Group, 328
Morton's The Steakhouse, 327
MOS, 3127
Mosaic, 325, 1363, 1666, 1958
Mosaic Biosciences, 919, 930, 1122
Mosaic Manufacturing, 2125
Mosaic Material, 2111
Mosaica Education Inc., 1274
Moschip, 3211
Moseo, 114
Moser Baer, 2599, 2600
Moser Baer India Ltd. (India), 2694
Mosh, 2936
Moshimo, 721
Mosquito Control Services, 1343
Moss Adams, 3268
Moss Holding Company, 1456
Moss Inc., 449
Moss Software, 371
Mosss, 272
Most Oil, 2202
Mosyle, 79
Mothers Work, 1275
MothersClick, 650
Motia, 212, 1080
Motif Biosciences Inc., 2397
Motif Investing, 770, 1346
MotifInvesting, 974
Motifworks, 1958
Motimatic, 883
Motion, 596
Motion Computing, 678, 803

Motion Industries (Saeco and Precision Bearings), 2410
Motion Math, 1054, 1958
Motion Recruitment, 1134
Motion Recruitment Partners, 873
Motion Specialties, 2062
MotionDSP, 979
Motionet AG, 2979
Motionpoint, 1255
Motionsoft, 655, 695
MotionTech Automation, 409
Motista, 377, 1599
Motiv, 852, 1075
Motiva, 1701
Motivate, 1323
Motive, 202, 514
Motive Medical Intelligence, 93, 1255
Motivity Labs, 1285
Motivo, 1013
Motoczysz, 1915
Motoractive, 2471
MotoRefi, 1259
Motorleaf, 2027
Motorola, 214, 1096
Motorola Solutions, 1683
Motorola Solutions Venture Capital, 3265
Motorsport Aftermarket Group, 1109, 2015
MotoSport, 184
Motovario, 3154
Motricity, 278, 1710
MotrPart, 3174
Mount Cleverest, 724
Mount Wilson Ventures, 972
Mountain Alarm, 1636
Mountain Hub, 1070
Mountain Muffler, 1252
Mountain View CLO, 1491
Mountain Warehouse, 2944
Mountain Waste & Recycling, 529
Mountaineer Gas Holdings, 156
Mountaineer Keystone, 740
MountainView Capital, 404
Mousam Valley, 1161
MouseHouse, 1267
MouseStats, 2155
Mout de POM, 2049
Mouth, 1306, 1912
Mouth Off Health, 684
Mov.ai, 3221
Movable, 1047
Movable Ink, 525, 533, 724
Movandi, 1670
Movati Athletic, 1345
Movato, 1798
Movaya, 85
Move, 659, 1642
Move Loot, 858
Movea, 2899
MoveButter, 622
MoveInSync, 1013, 1509
Moveline, 1518, 1789, 1876, 1912
Moven, 1306, 1524, 2406, 2940
Mover, 624, 2291, 2960
Mover.io, 120
MoveWith, 761, 1487
Movidius, 2355, 2674
Movie Pass, 150
Movie Pong, 1825
MoviePass, 1749, 1860
Moviepilot, 2674, 2797
Movik, 1334
Movik Networks, 1112, 1361
Moving Image 24, 2531
Moving iMage Technologies, 69
Moving Solutions, 1396
MovingIMAGE24, 2452
MovingImage24, 2979

1373

Portfolio Companies Index

MovingWorlds, 3277
Movio Network, 1306
Movirtu, 855, 3179
Movity, 2329
Movius, 536, 1445
Movius Interactive, 1474
MoVoxx, 1099
Moxe, 1601
Moxie, 770
Moxie Patriot LLC, 158
Moxie Software, 1361
MoxieJean, 1615
Moximed, 1122
MoxiWorks, 1910
Moxtra, 483
Moyo Game, 2869
MoyoGame, 641
Moz, 776, 974, 1158
mozaiq operations, 483
Mozak, 995
Mozat, 2477, 3062
Mozes, 1334
Mozido, 1503
Mozio, 181, 1035
Mozwood, 834
MP Hygiene, 2851
MP3.com, 502
mParticle, 317, 679, 1696, 2137
mPay Gateway, 142
MPE, 244, 1435
Mpex, 57
Mpex Pharmaceuticals, 1574
MPHARMA, 1696
Mphasis, 2490
MPI, 206
MPI Products, 1997
MPM Capital, 3273
MPoint, 1306
Mporai, 85
MPOWERD, 3277
mPrest, 809
mPrest New Forests, 126
MPStor, 2918
mPulse, 306
mPulse Mobile, 938
Mr Taddy, 2474
Mr Wolf, 2428
Mr. Cat, 928
Mr.Ted Ltd. Macaw BV, 2828
MRA Medical Reimbursements of America, 718
MReadBooks, 3113
mReferral, 2844
MRGK, 3150
MRI Flexible Packaging, 1230
MRI Robotics, 3279
MRI Software, 824
Mrs Wordsmith, 1527
Mrs. Gooch's, 869
MS2 Array, 1448
MSA, 869
MSC Software Corp., 1903
MSC Wellness Experts, 2962
MSD Ignition, 881
Msg.ai, 60, 1607
msg.ai, 317
MSI Acquisition, 111
mSpoke, 998, 1440
mSpot, 1853
MST, 3192
Mstar Semiconductor, 2603
MState, 305
MSU Business Incubator, 2938
MSX International, 716
MT MembraTec, 3203
mTAB, 1234
MTAR, 277
MTEM, 3104

MTI, 2826
MTI Film, 1693
MTI International, 1209
MTI Wireless Edge, 2571
MTL, 1708, 2883
MTPV, 497
MTPV Power Corp., 144
MTT, 2674
MTV Japan, 892
MTW Corp., 894
Mu Dynamics, 634
Mu Sigma, 793, 815
Mubadala Investment Company, 3264
Mubert, 890
MUBI, 2972
Mucci Farms, 2206
MuciMed, 139
Mucker Capital, 37
Mucosis, 2514
Mudlick Mail, 503
MuDynamics, 757
Mueller Electric Company, 606
Mueller Prost, 3271
Muffin Mam, 213
Muir Engineering Group, 2399
Muk Air, 2889
MuleSoft, 238, 1212, 1257, 1620
Mulesoft, 1001
Mullinix Packages, 1171
Multex.com, 192
Multi Packaging Solutions, 168, 1156
Multi-Channel Communications, 2079
Multi-Flow Industries, 717
Multi-Media Digilab, 2855
Multi-Portions, 2049
Multiacao (Call Center), 3180
MultiAd, 1881
Multicaja, 2455
Multicast Media, 1242
Multicoin Capital, 1882
Multifonds (IGEFI Group Sarl), 1752
MultiGEN Diagnostics, 1915
Multilayer Coating Technologies, 1962
Multimac, 3203
MultiPhy, 3214, 3221
Multiphy, 2566
MultiPlan, 578, 744, 909, 924, 1109, 1325, 1972
Multiplan, 1516
Multiple, 2225
Multiplex, 3233
Multiplicom, 3042, 3065
Multiply, 1459, 1906
Multiply Labs, 721
MultiSensor Sci., 1100
Multisensor Scientific, 497
Multisorb Technologies, 1751
Multispan, 117
Multitec, 3020
MultiView, 1956
Multiwave, 2548, 2717
Mumo, 275
Munchery, 641
Munder Capital Management, 559
Mundus Energia SRL, 2419
Municipal Communications II, 1638
Murally, 2382
Murermester Jon Rasmussen, 3203
Murfie, 2001
MuriGen Therapeutics, 3138
Murj, 1143
Murray Supply Company, 1605
Muse, 720, 724
Muse & Co., 641, 2869
MuseAmi, 2011
MuseFind, 2223
Musement, 2296
Music Audience Exchange, 1178

Music Dealers, 566
Music DNA, 2527
Music Of Your Life, 1079
Music Reports Inc., 21
Music Securities, 2974
Music Semiconductors, 892
Musical Overture, 189
Musical.ly, 472, 823
MusiCapital, 1766
musicMagpie.co.uk, 2944
MusicPlayr, 2829, 2838
MusicShake, 1838
Musiwave, 3208
Muskegon Angels, 3269
Mustang Ventures, 1850
Mustek, 892
Musto, 3036
Mutabilis, 2466
MuteeGaming.com, 2308
Muth Mirror Systems, 862
Muthoot Finance, 2490
Mutiny, 552
Mutual Mobile, 646
Mutual-Pak, 1922
MUUT, 1463
Muut, 1383
Muve, 630
Mux, 60, 60, 1149, 1758
Muyingzhijia.com, 222
Muzak, 21, 818
Muzak Limited Partnership, 447
Muze, 318
Muzik, 1764
Muzit, 226
Muzy, 1054
Muzzley, 3048
mValent, 455
MVC Capital, 694, 3265
MVConnect, 274
MVD House, 1327
MVI Technology, 2967
MVMNT, 431
MVP, 3152
MVP Group International, 1873
MW Group Ltd, 2722
MW Industries, 110, 168, 1505
MW Manufacturers, 1017
MW Windows, 722
MWI Veterinary Supply Inc., 354
MX, 79, 1339
MX Logic, 856
MXD3D, 626
MXD3D Inc., 650
MXData, 2662
mxHero, 226
MXLogic, 212
My Alarm Center, 1021
My Alerts, 876
My Blog Media GmbH, 3197
My Coupon Doc, 1615
My Damn Channel, 1437, 2017
My Dentist, 3109
My Docket, 1899
My Event Insurance, 1905
My Fit Foods, 1861
My GO Games, 1716
My Health Terms, 1977
My Heritage, 2390, 2813
My Job Chart, 264
My New Financial Advisor, 1965
My Payment Network, 998
My Perfect Gig, 1334
My Real Trip, 100
My Senior Portal, 3262
My Social Book, 2669
My Therapy Company, 1667
My-Apps, 2940

Portfolio Companies Index

My-apps, 2856
Mya, 770
myAgway, 405
MyAlerts, 1384
Myanmar Innovation Greenhouse, 1374
MYbank, 2404
myBestHelper, 2223
Mybet.com, 2475
myBlee, 3208
MyBurger, 1229
MyBuys, 1407
Myca, 1615, 2029
MyChild, 3048
Mycocann, 392
MyCodeSchool, 3174
MycoDev Group, 2200
Mycogen, 2927
Mycogen Corporation, 1706
MyCoi, 658
myCOI, 1019
MYCOM OSI, 500
Mycotech Corp., 588
MycoTechnology, 1613
MycoWorks, 1758
MyDeco, 3070, 3131
Mydeco, 2446
Mydeco.com, 2428
Mydish, 2468
MyDocket, 202
Mydoma Studio, 2284
MyDx, 1079
MyEdu, 221
Myelin Health, 222
Myelo, 2841
MyEnergy, 398, 1459
MyEnergyn, 497
Myers Motors, 1047
MyETone, 2457
MyEyeDr., 1248
Myeyedr., 456
Myfab, 2385
MyFitnessPal, 28
MyFP, 1906
MyGall, 2841
MyGeek.com, 1011
Mygola, 301
MyHealthDIRECT, 475
MyHealthDirect, 149
MyHeritage, 560, 1323, 2994
Myia, 2019
Myine Elecronics, 742
MyKardia, 1811
myLAB Box, 951
Mylearnadfriend, 3012
Mylestoned, 313
MyLife.com, 1361
MyLikes, 1839
Mylikes, 2010
Mymedcoupons.com, 1448
MyMoneyButler, 1688
MYMORIA, 2841
Mynd, 1024
MyNewPlace, 1725, 1760, 1853
myNEXUS, 1271
Myngle, 2822
Myntra, 28
Myntra.com, 2849
MYOB, 220
Myobis, 3113
Myocor, 536
MyOffers, 192
Myogen, 74
MyoKardia, 762
MyOmics, 1693
Myomo, 1261
MyOn, 779
Myonexus, 479

MyOpenJobs, 1783
Myopowers, 1350
MyoScience, 40, 598
Myosotis, 1044
MyOwnMed, 1766
Myozyme, 2102
MyPermissions, 2947
MyPlay, 1003
Myra Labs, 751
MyRecovery, 3108
Myresjöhus, 2863
Myriad, 1516, 1720
Myriad Development, 810
Myriad Genetics, 856
Myriax, 3138
Myro, 1363
myRoundUp, 951
Mysa, 2168
MyShape, 1784
Mysitcom Ltd, 2782
MySmartPrice, 28, 2818
mySociety, 1374
MySpace, 1445
Myspace, 1534
Myspace/Intermix Media, 1906
Mysportbrands & Mysportworld, 2441
Mysportgroup, 2797, 2987, 3239
MYSQL, 1001
MySQL, 1474
MySteel.com, 2542
Mystery Science, 1527
MysticCom, 2910
MyStrain, 392
MyStrom, 3152
MyStudyWeb Sdn Bhd, 3164
MyTango, 192
Mythic, 609, 800, 1151
MyThings, 1323, 2566
Mythings, 2669
myThings, 646
Mytime, 32, 1888
MyTomorrows, 2478
Mytonomy, 1054, 3277
MyTopia, 249
Mytrade, 264
Myungsung Environment, 584
MyUS.com, 171
MyVBO, 3
Myvyllage, 55
MyWallSt, 1259
Mywaves, 115
MyWebGrocer, 959, 1748
MyWishBoard, 2940
myWobile Pte Ltd, 2473
Myxer, 1734, 1734
MyYearbook, 1896
MZI Resources, 1548
Mölnlycke Health Care, 3008
MäsospiÜ, 3122
Médi-Partenaires, 2714
München, 2494, 2494

N

N B Education, 1274
N&W, 1017
N-Dimension, 676
N-Dimension Solutions, 2058
N-of-One, 534, 703
N-Tec, 2710
N-Trig, 2726
N-trig, 386
N-Triq, 2454
N.E.W. Customer Service, 1348
N2 Broadband, 1728
N2 Imaging Systems, 540
N26, 235, 1000
N2K, 1728

N30 Pharma, 946
N3N, 483
N3twork, 679, 751, 1075
N5 Sensors, 285
Naadam, 707
Naaptol, 386
NABCO Inc., 1159
Naborly, 1758, 2144
naborly, 2249
Nabriva, 1143, 2815
Nabriva Therapeutics, 709, 1941, 3007
Nabriva Therapeutics AG, 2785
Nabsys, 1459, 1693
NACOLAH Holding Corporation, 404
Nactis, 2965
Nada Moo!, 2099, 2161
Nadella, 2293
Naf Naf, 1576
NAFA, 851
NAFACO, 3218
NailSnaps, 218, 1701
NAJA, 325
Naja, 229, 896, 1183
Naked, 460
Naked Biome, 50, 1268
Naked Objects, 3107
NakedPoppy, 1069
Nakina Systems, 2196
Naldo, 3127
Nallatech, 3104
Nalu Medical, 1143
NAM, 1602
Nam Long Investment Corporation, 2961
NameCoach, 1875
Namely, 358, 777, 823, 867, 1110, 1181, 1626, 1860
Namet, 1017
Namo Media, 1758
Namotech, 2857
Namshi, 2829, 2838
Nan Ya PCB, 892
Nanda Tech, 2475
Nandi Proteins, 3028
Nanigans, 638
Nanit, 1888
Nanjing Kingfriend Biochemical Pharmaceutical Co., 1452
Nanjing Sample Technology Co. Ltd., 2633
Nanny Caddy, 1097
Nano Detection Technology, 479
Nano Endoluminal, 2626
Nano Magnetics, 2066
Nano MR, 1677
Nano Opto, 608
Nano Photonics, 47
Nano String Technologies, 180
Nano-C, 760
Nano-Meta Technologies, 3068
Nano-Tex, 730
NanoBio, 1921
Nanobiomatters, 2469
Nanobiotix, 3113
Nanobox, 1070
NanoCarrier, 2970
Nanochip, 1038
NanoClear Technologies, 1051
Nanoco, 3244
Nanocomp, 946, 1160
Nanocomp Technologies Inc., 3
Nanoconduction, 2005
Nanocopoeia, 3279
Nanofactory Instruments AB, 2718
NanoFilm, 2690
Nanogate Technologies, 2713
Nanogen, 214
NanoGram, 1241, 1791
NanoGram Corporation, 184

1375

Portfolio Companies Index

NanoGram Devices, 1579
Nanogram Devices, 1355
NanoH2O, 1119
NanoHorizons, 1117, 1428
NanoLambda, 1448
nanoLambda, 998
Nanolayers, 2973
Nanoleaf, 2831
Nanomagnetics, 2386
Nanomagnetics Ltd., 2750
NanoMas Technologies, 643, 2492
NANOMED, 3100
NanoMedex, 1060
NanoMedical Diagnostics, 422
Nanomedical Diagnostics, 1613
NanoMedical Systems, 445
Nanomix, 144, 1604
Nanomotion Ltd., 2954
NanoMR, 703
Nanonet, 623
NanoNexus, 524
Nanonics Imaging, 3245
Nanoom Tech, 3002
NanoPack Inc., 1577
NanoPass, 3241
Nanophase Technologies, 153
Nanophthalmics, 995
Nanopore, 2892
Nanopore Diagnostics, 267
Nanopthalmics, 1187
NanoRacks, 445, 715
NanoRep, 1323
Nanoscale Powders, 1627
Nanosolar, 925, 2717
Nanospectra Biosciences, 950
Nanosphere, 1324
NanoSpun, 2831
NanoStatics, 400, 983, 1553
NanoSteel, 676, 712, 2078
Nanosteel, 817, 946
Nanostim, 666, 1896
Nanostream, 747
NanoString, 762
NanoString Technologics, 495
NanoString Technologies, 1255, 1391
NanoSys, 153
Nanosys, 6, 620, 979, 1151, 1460, 1493
Nanosys Inc., 144
Nanotech Semiconductor, 3047
Nanotecture, 2892
Nanotecture Ltd, 2894
NaNotics, 1095
Nanotion, 2310
Nanotion AG, 650
Nanotron Technologies, 3252
Nanotron Technologies GmbH, 3046
Nanotronics Imaging, 775
Nanovi, 3203
Nantero, 455, 455, 483, 603, 835, 1291
Nanum Technologies, 2857
Nanya Technology, 3218
NapaJen Pharma, 1241
NapaStyle, 1733
Napatech, 2731
NAPO Pharmaceuticals, 1011
Napo Pharmaceuticals, 715, 1002
Naprotek, 653
Naptech, 3013
NAR REach, 1642
Nara-Sarang Co., 584
Naritiv, 1813, 1965
NARR8, 2856
Narragansett Bay, 1315
Narragansett Beer, 1191, 1524
Narrativ, 50
Narrative, 1101, 1860, 3030
Narrative Science, 235, 1620

NarrativeDx, 569
NarrativeScience, 1046
Narrator AI, 754
Narus, 986, 3231
Narvar, 235, 561, 796, 1607
NAS, 152
Nascar Members Club, 43
Nascentric, 1288
NASCOM, 2949
Nasdaq, 924
Naseeb Networks, 690
Nash Finch, 1970
Nash_Elmo, 194
Nasioncom, 2623
Naskeo, 3239
Nasra Public School, 55
Nassau Broadcasting Partners LP, 1724
Nassko, 2878
Nasty Gal, 2860, 2860
Nasuni, 603, 754, 1334, 1673
Nasuni Corporation, 1672
NasVax, 3245
Nasville Shores Water Park, 1991
Nasza-Klasa, 2723
NAT Inc., 1621
Natera, 491, 762, 1382, 1519
Natero, 1218
Natia, 2924
Natilus, 1390
Natilus Inc., 811
National Australia Bank, 2659
National Auto Care, 1147, 1857
National Bedding Company LLC, 159
National Billing Partners, 1364
National Cable Networks, 2465
National Car Parks, 2306
National Cardiovascular Partners, 221
National CC, 557
National Data Corp., 300
National Deli, 1569
National Dentex, 1972
National Dentex Corporation, 68
National Display Systems LLC, 556
National Distribution & Contracting, 1684
National Energy Equipment, 2258
National Entertainment Network, 1248
National Funding, 1970
National Gift Card, 1093
National Healing, 1002
National HME, 1777
National Home Healthcare Corp., 127
National Laboratory Center, 1708
National Logistics Services, 2126
National Medical Health Card Systems, 1301
National Mentor Holdings, 1156
National P.E.T., 1423
National Packaging Systems, 52, 1227
National Pasteurized Eggs, 944
National Pen, 1127
National Penn Bancshares, 1956
National Power, 364
National Print Group, 1141
National Product Services, 131
National Prostaff, 2113
National Re Corporation, 404
National Research Institute, 439, 1824
National Rural Support Program, 55
National Seating & Molbility, 1971
National Security Partners, 1963
National Semiconductor, 1103
National Spine & Pain Centers, 209, 1166, 1651
National Spinning Company, 1970
National Stock Exchange, 815
National Stock Exchange of India, 1346
National Surgical Care, 328
National Surgical Hospitals, 456
National Technical Systems, 199, 378

National Tele-Communications (NTC), 35
National Veterinary Associates, 1752, 2207
National Video Monitoring Corporation, 378
National Warranty Corporation, 839
National Westminster Bank, 2621
NationBuilder, 124, 1374
Nations Energy, 893
Nations Hearing, 16
NationStar, 767
Nationwide Acceptance Holdings, 1491
Nationwide Credit Inc., 447
Nationwide Distribution, 1252
Nationwide Graphics, 591
NationWide Healthcare, 1346
Nationwide Industries, 164
Nationwide Marketing Group LLC, 158
Native, 215
Native Energy, 438, 786
Native Foods Cafe, 1324
Native Foods Café, 958
Native Minds, 1535
Native Networks, 2380, 2910, 3159
Native Tap, 397
Native Voice, 1554
NativeMinds, 947
Nativo, 256, 641, 871, 1222, 1965
Natron Energy, 1069
NatSteel, 2772
Nattagansett Beer, 1114
Natue, 3056
Natunola Health Biosciences, 2049
Natural Balance Pet Foods Inc., 465
Natural Communications, 2854
Natural Convergence, 2196
Natural Cycles, 641
Natural Dental Implants, 2496, 2841
Natural Food Holdings, 916
Natural Insight, 52
Natural Markets Food Group, 2073
Natural Motion, 2711
Natural Order Supply, 860
Natural Products Group Inc., 914
Natural Systems Utilities, 2290, 3277
NaturalInsight, 1385
Nature et D'couvertes, 2601
NatureBox, 1699
Naturebox, 816
Naturol, 3211
NAU Country Insurance Company, 1123
Naumann/Hobbs Material Handling, 917
Naurex, 709, 1094
Nautic Partners, 3264
Nauticus Networks, 455
Nautilus Neurosciences, 1777
Nautilus Plus, 2206
Nauto, 302, 817, 872, 1834
Nav, 79, 563, 942, 1070, 1075
Navabi, 3113
Navacord, 1156
Navantis, 916
Navayuga Engineering Company, 2311
Navdy, 936, 1150, 1222, 1489, 1592, 1595, 1888, 1992
Navegg, 2438
Navera, 665
Naviant, 202
Navico, 2384
Navicore Ltd, 2716
Navicure, 1041
Navidea Biopharmaceuticals, 925
Navigating Cancer, 1722
Navigator Publishing, 438
NaviHealth, 176, 1615, 1972
Navimo, 2676
NaviNet, 1334
Navini Networks, 202, 852, 1244, 1796
Naviscan, 1616

1376

Portfolio Companies Index

Naviscan PET Systems, 1169
Navistone, 358, 479, 1072
Navitas Lease, 1331
Navitor Pharmaceuticals, 191, 1043, 1731
Navix Holdings Corporation, 1492
Naviya Entertainment, 2857
Navmii Holdings, 3157
Navotek, 337
Navotek Medical, 2353
NavStar, 1837
Navtech, 1927
Navtrck, 1680
NavVis, 3161
Navy Power, 156
Nawboi Technologies, 3262
NAWEC, 19
Nawotec, 3233
Naya, 896, 1088
Naylor, 494
Nayya, 684
NB Golf Cars, 1192
NB Therapeutics, 1508
NBA.com China, 2831
NBD, 1757
NBD Nano, 3, 313
NBIC Holdings, 1443
NBIZ, 3127
NBP Capital LLC, 250
NBS Design, 1915
NBT Solutions, 438, 1161
NBX Corp., 521
NBX Corporation, 1257
nChannel, 1553
Ncino, 1607
nCino, 1000
nCipher, 2894
nCircle, 641, 887
NCircle Entertainment, 1202
nCircle Network Security, 1038
NCM Services, 238
NComputing, 1515
nContact, 904, 1008
NCP, 2605
NCP Finance, 1491
NCR Corp., 300
NCrease, 995
nCrowd, 282, 1331
nCrypted Cloud, 851
NCS Energy Services, 1705
NCSG Crane & Heavy Haul, 675
NCTI, 1086
NDLI Logistics, 828
NDS, 846, 853
NDT CCS, 1017
NDT Systems, 235
NE Photonics, 183
Nea, 1460
Neah, 85
Neah Power Systems, 422
Near Me, 1749
Near Pte Ltd, 483
Near Space Labs, 2000
Nearbuy, 525
NearGroup, 307
Nearify, 3109
Nearly Natural Inc., 447
Nearpod, 883, 1000, 1527
Nearstream, 1860
Nearwoo, 1798
NEAS, 3076
Neat, 246, 646, 655, 2225
Neat Receipts, 2196
Neat Stitch, 3240
Neat Work, 1384
Neato Robotics, 1352, 1915
NEBC, 1021
NEBCO Insurance Services, 1743

Nebraska Book Company, 1372
Nebula, 1968
Nebula Genomics, 708, 1993
Nebulab, 1701
NECCO Realty Investments, 158
Necessity LLC, 3257
Necho Systems, 2058
Nectar, 525
Nectar Power, 1579
nedl, 218
Nedstat, 3051
Nedway Air Ambulance, 1209
neea, 1096
Need, 3207
Needle, 695, 1070, 1118, 1540, 1663
Needls, 2001
Needs & Senses, 2543
Needs Entertainment, 2857
Neff Corp., 1368
Negotiatus, 13, 795, 1701
NEHP, 786
NEI Treatment Systems, 275
Neighbor, 79
Neighbor.ly, 1749
Neighborhood Cable, 3168
Neighborhood Fuel, 1110
Neighborhood Goods, 761, 877, 1183
Neighborland, 1110, 1860, 1943
Neighborly, 24, 243, 914
Neilsoft, 278, 1850
Neiman Marcus, 1835
Neiman Marcus Group LTD Inc., 159
Nekoosa, 1997
Nekso, 2113
Nektar, 214, 1378
Nektar Therapeutics, 1452
Nelipak, 1171
Nellix Endovascular Inc., 269
Nellson, 1134
Nellson Nutraceutical, 1081
Nellson Nutraceutical LLC, 901
Nellymoser, 1699
Nelson Cash, 70
Nelson Communications, 1954
Nelson Global Products, 1990
Nelson Mullins, 3272
Nelson Pipeline, 1281
Nemaha Environmental, 364
Nematron Corporation, 1336
Nemera, 2977
Nemetschek, 3069
Nemgenix, 1774
neMob, 1607
Neo Tech, 456
Neo Technology, 2630
Neo-Neon, 3194
Neo4j, 710
NeoBear, 1509
Neocera, 1728
NeoChord, 943, 1802
Neochord, 222
Neocis, 1643
NeoClone, 2001
Neoconix, 1410, 1896
Neodata Group, 3052
Neodrill AS, 3141
NeoEdge Networks, 2196
Neoen Netzoptiker, 3020
Neogas, 834
Neohapsis, 1305, 1400, 1850
Neolane, 3239
Neolinear, 272, 1008
Neologin, 455
NeoMend, 3015
Neomend, 495, 1493
Neomobile, 2524
NEON, 1837

Neon, 1041, 1247, 1860, 2011
Neonga, 2841, 3170
Neonode, 1244
NeoNova, 215, 925
Neonova, 339
NeoPath, 1398
NeoPath Networks, 805
Neopath Networks, 197, 596, 933
NeoPhotonics, 1579, 2662
Neophotonics, 1288, 1918
NeoPhotonics Corporation, 1361
NeoRx, 206
Neorx, 237
NEOS, 581
Neos Geosolutions, 634
NEOSE Technologies, 2496
Neosensory, 703
Neosil, 925
Neoss, 2972
NeoStem, 514
Neostrata, 1191
NeoSurgical, 2918
NeoSystems Corp., 1605
Neotechnology, 3149
Neoteny Labs, 1374
Neoteny Venture Development, 2991
Neothetics, 495, 621
Neotonus, 131
NeoTract, 867
Neotract, 508, 1516, 1993
Neotropix, 1508
Neovest, 1863
Neoware Systems, 1203
Neoworld, 444
NEP Broadcasting, 683
NEP Group, 559
Nepes Display, 3002
Nephera, 2454, 2726
NephRx, 1713
Neptco, 541
Neptune, 1017, 1915
Neptune Technology Group, 2015
Neptune-Benson, 194
Nerd Street Gamers, 1657
Nerdio, 1242
NerdWallet, 1001
Nereus, 769, 1412, 2815
Nereus Pharmaceuticals, 1775
Nerites, 1921
Nero, 909, 2443
Neroc, 2501
NERv, 622
Nervana, 609
Nervana Systems, 1151
Nerve, 460
NESCO, 675
Nesher1, 2609
NESS, 3171
Ness, 2748
Ness Computing, 1830
Ness Display, 2857
Nest, 1459, 1530, 1663, 1694, 1916
Nesta Impact Investments, 2509
Nester Hosiery, 1209
Nestio, 784, 1150, 1518, 1632
Nestor Sales, 415
NestReady, 2027
Net Asia, 1755
Net Biscuits, 2638
Net Display Systems, 3209
Net Effect Systems, 1853
Net Health, 1717
NET Midstream, 156
Net Movie, 2850
Net Perceptions, 1725
Net Power, 3194
Net Power & Light, 3121

Portfolio Companies Index

Net Power & Lighting, 1427
Net Systems Informatics, 2313
NET Technologies, 1676
Net Trans, 928
Net Translations, 2483
Net TV, 2857
Net Vision, 2666
Net-Hopper, 1364
Net-Marketing Corporation, 2974
Net2000 Communications, 1227
Net263 Holdings, 1769
Net2Net Corp., 521
Net4, 1516
Net4Call AS, 2369
Net6, 1626
Netafim, 3033
NetAmbit, 2818
Netaphor Software, 1677
Netas, 1376
NETASQ, 2851
NetasQ, 2439
Netasq, 3113
NetBase, 100, 979, 1818, 3235
NetBase Solutions, 2196
Netbase Solutions, 1728
NetBio, 646
Netbiscuits, 1748
Netboa, 161
NetBoost, 852
NetBoss Technologies, 698
Netbot, 153
NetBotz, 202, 444
Netbreeze, 2393
NetByTel, 2079
Netcell, 197
Netcentrex, 555
NetCentrics, 654
Netcitadel, 851
NetClarity, 1160
NetClerk, 1003
Netcontinuum, 1407
NetConversions, 807
NetCore, 1334
netCostumer, 455
Netcycler, 2612
NetDevices, 422, 798
NetDocuments, 500, 688
Netdragon, 2850
Netease.com, 865
Neteconomy, 2662
NetEffect, 202
Netentsec, 935
Netezza, 455, 1212
Netflective Technology, 2383
NetFlip, 1853
Netflix, 770, 1001, 1785
NetForensics, 592
netForensics, 1133
Netformx, 1759
NetFortris, 1724
NetG Networks, 805
NETGEAR, 897
NetGear, 1096
Netgem, 2765
NetGenesis, 1626
NetGraph Information Technology SA, 2354
Netguardians, 3045
Nethra, 130
Netian, 2924
Netik, 2348
Netilla Networks, 1227
Netinbiz, 2857
Netino, 3113
NetKey, 954, 1886, 2196
Netkey, 530
Netki, 229
Netli, 823, 1257

Netlify, 124, 1075
NetLogic, 1922
Netmagic, 3001
Netmania, 2967
NetMed, 2784
Netmining, 2426
Netmobile, 3233
Netmoshere, 757
NetMotion, 1637
NetMotion Wireless, 753, 1241
Netmotion Wireless, 1640
Netmovie, 3142
NetNearU, 1108
NetNoir, 1461
NetNumber, 1873
Netonomy, 2662
Netopia, 197
NetOps, 1314
Netork Physics, 1407
Netotiate, 436
NetPlenih, 1632
NetPlenish, 1150
NetPodium, 1945
Netpower, 3215
Netpro, 1041
Netprospex, 655, 1728
Netpulse, 197, 620, 791, 1028
Netqin, 2733
NetQuote, 1717, 1748
Netra, 1100
Netradyne, 1154
NetRegulus, 1057
Netretail Holding, 2309
Netro Corporation, 1087, 2910
Netronome, 483, 2662, 2674
Netronome Systems Ltd, 2894
NetScaler, 757, 805, 1747
Netscaler, 823
Netscalibur Limited, 3179
Netscape, 58, 922
NetScreen, 1474, 1717
Netscribes, 2493
NetSeer, 1239, 1378
Netsertive, 871, 904, 1593
NetSkope, 1696
Netskope, 603, 820
Netsmart, 824
Netsmart Technologies, 1608
NetSocket, 1658, 1682, 1921
Netsol, 2613
NetSolve, 56
NetSpend, 1126, 1235
NetSpend Corp., 810
NetSpira, 2548
NetStream, 202
NetSuite, 1212, 1738
Netsurion, 445
Netuitive, 560, 946, 1242, 1540
NetVision, 1677
NetWin, 2584
Network Alchemy, 1853
Network Allies, 1173
Network Appliance, 1760
Network Chemistry, 979
Network Commerce, 1461
Network Communications, 2379
Network Development Group, 737
Network Distributors, 1609
Network Electronics ASA, 2369
Network For Good, 383
Network for Good, 19
Network Global Logistics, 1505
Network Instruments, 1970
Network Intelligence, 422
Network Intelligence Corp., 1041
Network International, 466, 815, 3173
Network Merchants, 333

Network Specialists, 1188
Network Switching Systems, 206
Network Vision, 211
Network-1 Software & Technology, 1188
Networked Insights, 1060
NetworkPlay, 2558
Networks, 1383
Networks in Motion, 1239, 1760, 1926
Networks Insights, 842
Networth Services, 1837
NetZero Inc., 1103
NEU, 622
Neucel Specialty Cellulose LTD., 1971
NeueHouse, 431, 539
Neuf Telecom, 2375
Neul, 1241, 2662, 2674
Neumayer Tekfor, 2714
NeuMitra, 1254
Neumitra, 970
Neumob, 679, 1118, 1663
NeuMoDx, 1921
NeuMoDx Molecular, 149, 222
NeuProtect, 1196
Neura, 1786, 2615
Neural Analytics, 1784
Neural Technologies Ltd., 162
Neurala, 1260, 2296, 2851
Neuralink, 800
Neuralitic, 3214
Neuraltus Pharmaceuticals, 57, 1906
Neurana Pharmaceuticals, 1143
Neuraxpharm, 135
Neurex, 1760
Neurex Corp., 947
Neuro 3D, 2466
Neuro-Bio, 1051
NeuroAccess Technologies, 886
NeuroChaos Solutions, 445
Neurocrine, 206
NeuroDerm, 762
NeuroFlow, 418
NeuroFluidics, 323
Neurogastrx, 12
Neurogenetics, 1706
NeurogesX, 925
Neurogesx, 153, 560
Neurogesx Inc., 2785
NeuroInterventions, 998
Neurolink, 980
Neurologix, 1401
NeuroLutions, 176, 267
Neurolutions, 1488
NeuroMesh, 622
NeuroMetrix, 521
Neuromonics, 1455, 2877
Neurona Therapeutics, 517
Neuronetics, 40, 1010, 1058, 1298, 1378, 1418, 1436, 1460, 1508, 1819
NeuroNova AB, 2816
Neuronyx, 1452
NeuroPace, 621, 1010, 1786
Neuroptics, 138
Neuroptix, 1915
Neuros Medical, 136, 293, 1047, 1553, 1574
Neuros Medical Inc., 420, 831
NeuroStar, 176
Neurosynaptics, 3211
Neurotech, 1087, 1693, 2354
NeuroTherapeutics Pharma, 3015
Neurotherapeutics Pharma, 1817
NeuroTherm, 1132, 1456
Neurotic Media, 1655
Neurotrack, 107, 1069, 1552, 1696
NeuroTronik, 915
NeuroTronik Limited, 1261
Neurovance, 1921
Neurovigil, 791

1378

Portfolio Companies Index

NeuroVision, 2518
Neuspera, 1993
Neustar, 2697
Neutec Pharma, 2748
Neutekbio Ltd, 2705
Neutral Connect Networks, 1153
Neutral Path Communications LLC, 122
Neutral Tandem, 560, 596
Neutrino, 2296
Neutronics, 1234
Neutun, 1585
NeuVector, 799, 956
Neuvis, 530
NeuWave, 1921
NeuWave Medical, 1928
Nevales, 3109
Neven Vision, 2021
Nevenvision, 132
Never.no, 2369
Nevercode, 3108
Neverfail, 2734
Neverfail Water, 2951
Neverware, 1551
Nevion, 3013
Nevro, 40, 237, 1268, 1819
New Age Exploration, 1548
New Age Meats, 1613
New Archery Products Corp., 354
New Brand Analytics, 1806
New Breed Logistics, 380, 1956
New Carbon, 1262
New Career Skills, 2539
New Century Financial Corporation, 856
New Century Health, 1961
New Century Hospice, 1626
New Century Transportation, 1491
New Channel, 2850
New China Life, 2936
New Citizen (Centre UA), 1374
New Co., 784
New Coffee Co. II, 3048
New Constructs, 1688
New Covert Generating, 1795
New Eagle, 742
New Earth Solutions, 2295
New Energy, 353
New England 800 dba Taction, 438
New England Audio Resource, 438
New England Envelope, 1295
New England Growth Fund, 1295
New England Linen, 1021
New England Linen Supply, 61
New England Orthotic & Prosthetic Systems, 1751
New Enterprise Associates, 986, 3265, 3270, 3273, 3284
New Era of Networks, 153, 2005
New Era Portfolio, 1732
New Era Technology, 1166
New Evolution Ventures, 1937
New Flyer, 1085
New Flyer Industries Ltd., 914
New Focus Auto, 3145
New Fortress Energy, 767
New Foxus, 1257
New French Bakery, 147
New Frontier, 1135
New Frontier Data, 1207, 1439
NEW Global Talent, 64
New Haven Pharmaceuticals, 678
New Hope Bariatric, 202
New Horizons, 383, 2677, 2881
New Horizons Program, 2539
New Image Group, 1570
New IT Venture, 1755
New Knowledge, 823, 1151
New Leaf Paper, 1396

New Look, 3033
New Matter, 93, 972
New Media Gateway, 9
New Momentum LLC, 506
New Mountain Capital, 3255
New Mountain Learning, 1984
New Oak, 1334
New Ocean Capital Management, 1743
New Ocean Health Solutions, 173
New Path, 2599, 2600
New Point IV/V/VI, 1743
New Polar, 1252
New Relic, 248, 581, 634, 1796, 1853
New Relic. AssureRx Health, 777
New River Innovation, 1008
New Seasons Market, 673
New Vine Logistics, 1733
New Vision, 2936
New Vision TV LP, 1986
New Vitality, 222
New Voice Media, 1785, 2691, 3014
New Wave Broadcasting, 818
New Wave Foods, 1613
New Whey Nutrition, 1832
New World Angels, 3262
New World Application, 2861
New World Natural Brands, 364
New World Trading, 2944
New York & Company, 1022
New York Butcher Shoppe, 1923
New York Digital Health Accelerator, 1508
New York Genome Center, 1420
New York Sports Clubs, 1587
New Zealand King Salmon, 2516
New Zealand Pharmaceuticals, 2516
NewACT, 436
Newark Energy, 433
NeWAY, 1135
Neways, 839
Newbay, 2734
NewBay Media, 1984
Newberry Geothermal, 1895
NewBold, 1746
Newbook, 101
Newbury Equity Partners LP, 2094
Newbury Second Fund LP, 2094
Newburyport Brewing Company, 1734
NewCare Solutions, 1440, 1448
NewCity Communications, 536
Newco, 1101
NewCold, 1134
NewComLink, 1738
NewConnect, 285
Newcrete, 2051
NewCross Technologies, 531
NewEdge, 538
Newfield Design, 1160, 1161
Newforma, 235, 308, 1080, 1334
Newfront, 1758
Newgen, 690
Newgen Knowledge Works, 584
Newgen Software, 1620
Newgistics, 1134, 1738
NewHound, 132, 707, 1489
Newhound, 1830
Newk's Eatery, 1651
NewKota Energy Group, 611
Newlanis, 1400
NewLeaf Symbiotics, 1379, 1579, 2213
Newlife, 2772
Newlight Management, 986
Newline Products Inc., 461
Newlisi, 2296
NewPace Ltd., 269
Newpath Network, 1211
NewPath Ventures, 57
Newpoint Technologies, 1314

NewPort Communications, 1003, 1779
Newport Group, 1062
Newport Media, 199, 581, 634, 833, 1445, 1916
Newpro, 812
Newron Pharmaceuticals, 3196
Newronika, 2874
News Distribution Network, 768, 1830
Newscale, 563
newScale, 560
NewSchools Venture Fund, 1865
NewsCrafted, 345
NewsCred, 60, 743, 793, 871, 965, 1010, 1110, 1184
Newscred, 751
NewsEdge, 192
Newsela, 1054, 1075, 1392, 1527
Newser, 1477
NewsGator Technologies, 1175
NewSignature, 515
Newsle, 609, 1183
Newsletter Publishing, 3146
Newsquest, 2605
NewStar Financial, 1770
Newstep Networks, 2058
Newstore, 816
Newsvine, 1641
Newtec, 3042
Newtention Extended Networks GmbH, 2673
Newterra, 2290
newterra, 126
NewtonX, 708, 1768
Newtron, 2713, 2829, 2838
Newtron AG, 2528
NewVoiceMedia, 2972
NewWave Communications, 1409
NewWoods Petroleum, 740
New'Mode, 934
Nexabit Networks, 852
Nexage, 922, 3121
Nexamp, 1459
Nexant, 1355, 1361, 1793
Nexar, 707, 809, 1611, 1694
Nexaweb, 1913
Nexaweb Technologies, 1175
Nexcon, 3201
Nexcore Technology, 1071
Nexcura, 153
Nexenta, 603, 777, 1028, 1474, 1838, 3235
Nexeo Solutions, 1835
Nexeon, 2858
Nexercise, 1734
Nexersys iPower Trainer, 445
Nexess, 3113
NexGen, 2354
NexGen Medical Systems, 1600
Nexgen Storage, 36, 876, 1319
Nexgenia, 2008
Nexia Device, 626
Nexidia, 537, 1400, 1615
Nexient, 454
NexImmune, 112
Nexinto, 2944
Nexis Vision, 1122
Nexkey, 1888
Nexlas, 544
Nexleaf Analytics, 1226
NexlWeb, 1052
Nexmo, 1705
Nexom, 2290
Nexosis, 1176, 1554
Nexpa, 483
NexPlanar, 184, 946
NexPlanner, 1010
Nexsan Technologies, 1906
Nexsteppe, 322
Nexstim Ov, 2816
Next, 1013, 3257

1379

Portfolio Companies Index

Next Big Sound, 965, 1700, 1789
Next Door Lending, 2031
Next Force Technology, 295
Next Games, 1563
Next Healthcre, 1131
Next Instrument, 2857
Next Jump, 1666
Next Kraftwerke, 2994
Next Level Apparel, 290
Next Level Learning Inc., 63
Next Model Management, 839
Next New Networks, 798
Next Step Living, 322, 646, 1906
Next Step Robotics, 19
Next Thing Co., 1236
Next Wave, 74
Next Wave Energy, 675
Next Wave Pharmaceuticals, 237
NexTag, 1785
Nextance, 1405
Nextbio, 115
Nextbit, 28
NextCaller, 721
NextCard, 765, 1725, 1853
NextCat, 742
Nextdocs, 1380
Nextdoor, 262, 518, 581, 634, 872, 1000, 1075, 1212, 1534, 1662, 1663
Nextec Applications, 212
Nextech, 779
Nextek Inc, 3162
NEXTEL, 1257
Nextel Partners, 1156
Nextera, 2519
Nexterra Systems, 2040, 2053
Nextest System Corporation, 132
Nextest/Teradyne, 1288
Nextfoods, 1183
NextForce, 623
NextG Networks, 1156, 1305, 1534
NextGen Solar LLC, 234
NextGenTel, 3013
NextGreatPlace, 1853
NextHealth Technologies, 1346
NexTier Networks, 650
NextInput, 1670
NextIO, 1038, 1922
Nextivity, 810
Nextlabs, 1352
NextLight Renewable Power, 675
Nextly, 685
NextMark, 438, 1920
NextNav, 842, 1361
Nextnav, 515
NextNet Wireless, 536, 3137
Nextnew Networks, 1715
NextNine, 3241, 3249
NexTone Communications, 1227
Nextpage, 2079
Nextpeer, 679
NextPharma, 1753
Nextplus, 1888
NEXTracker, 595
NexTraq, 779
NextRay, 971
Nextreme Thermal Solutions, 457, 979, 1915
NextRequest, 1768
nextResort, 1535
NextShift Robotics, 1757
Nextsilicon, 116
NextSource, 928
Nextumi, 1544
NextView Ventures, 3273
NextVR, 518
Nextware Ltd., 2907
NextWave, 1067
NextWave Hire, 622

NextWave Pharmaceuticals, 1410
Nexus, 2826, 3069
NEXUS Biosystems, 1792
Nexus Gas Parttners, 447
Nexus Mutual, 2280
Nexusedge Technologies, 2623
Nexvet, 762
Nexwave, 3233
NexWave Solutions, 2312
Nexway, 2851, 3239
NEXX Systems, 925
Nexx Systems, 1672
Nexxo, 1760
NF Holding Company, 1708
Nfluence, 85
Nfocus, 980
Nfocus Neuromedical, 865, 1786
NFP Automotive, 1753
NFP Corporation, 1156
NFR Security, 655
NFWare, 89
NG Advantage LLC, 497
NG Data, 2851
NGageContent, 1047
NGD Systems, 249
NGen Enabling Technologies Funds, 2492
NGI Holdings, 1171
Ngine, 3127
Nginx, 641
NGM Biopharmaceuticals, 517, 1493
NGMOCO, 751, 1001
Ngpay, 2818
NGRAIN, 2053
NGrain, 916
nGUVU, 2066
NGX Bio, 6
NHW Holding, 553
Niacet, 1166
Niagara Generation, 1895
Niagara Thermal Products, 1745
Niantic, 93, 306, 1212
Niantic Inc., 235
Niantic Labs, 1028
Niara, 1916
Nibe, 3069
NibMor, 668
Nibo, 641
Nic and Zoe, 1524
Nic+Zoe, 329
Nice, 3251
Nice Actimize, 3221
Nice People At Work, 2469
Niceberg Studios, 2949, 3042
Nicecom, 3137
Niche, 60, 1700
Niche.com, 298
Nichols Portland, 104
Nickle Bus, 418
Nickson Industries, 1224
NICO, 1571
Nicoat, 373
Nicolette, 218
Nicoya, 2288
Nicoya Lifesciences, 2184, 2187
Nido Surgical, 347
Nielsen, 924
Nielsen & Bainbridge, 1081, 1456
Nielsen Company, 2379
Nielsen-Kellerman, 503, 654
Nieuws.Be, 2426
Nifty Thrifty, 871
Nigel Wright, 222
Nightingale, 1589
Nihon Eslead Corp, 2907
Nihon Trim Co., 2907
Nijgh Periodieken, 2378
Nikas, 2784

Nikkiso, 214
Niko Niko, 1943
Niko Resources Ltd., 834
Nikola Labs, 1286
Nikoma, 2604
Niku, 757, 1910, 1952
Nile Guide, 1084
NileGuide, 2196
Nilex, 2126
Nima, 776, 1888
Niman Ranch, 520, 1396
Nimaya, 1886
Nimbic, 2008, 2455
Nimbit, 1584, 1734
Nimbix, 1682
Nimble, 622, 685
Nimble Commerce, 69, 1715
Nimble Pharmacy, 741, 1069
Nimble Storage, 28, 175, 823, 836, 1996
Nimblefish Technologies, 1672
NimbleGen, 1691
NimbleGen Systems, 1921
NimbleRX, 634
NimbleTV, 871
Nimbus, 466, 483
Nimbus CD International Inc., 245
Nimbus Discovery, 1124
Nimbus Partners, 2662
Nimbus Therapeutics, 191, 1122, 1731
Nimia, 1286
Nimsoft, 1041, 1760, 3013
NIN Ventures, 3265
Nina McLemore, 460
Nine Four Ventures, 529
Nine Plus, 1865
Nine Point Medical, 946
Nine Star, 1784
9 Story Limited, 2020
9.9 Media, 2818
900 Dwell, 1219
908 Devices, 153
90East, 3168
911 Industrial Response, 2145
99 Cents Only Stores, 159
99 Designs, 28
99.co, 721
99Bill, 1121
99Bill.com, 596
99Cloud, 1004
9fin, 3108
9flats, 3055
9flats.com, 641, 871
9GAG, 741, 1860
9gag, 784, 871, 1149
9Lenses, 1072, 1522
NinePoint Medical, 1419, 1493, 1811
9Ren Group, 740
Nines, 1613
NineSigma, 642, 1571, 2196
Nineteenth Amendment, 325
9Tong, 1534
Nineyu, 3208
Ning, 1235
Ningans, 206
Ningo, 2331
Ninian Solutions, 581
Ninja Blocks, 2520, 3121
Ninja Metrics, 1061, 1784
Ninjacart, 1509
Ninox, 3240
Nintex, 1625, 1886
Nintex Group, 1776
Ninth Decimal, 518, 1346
Ninth Street Advisors, 3265
NinthDecimal, 791, 1410
Ninza Turtle, 2857
Nioptics, 153

1380

Nipendo, 2831, 2952
Nippon Dry-Chemical, 3006
Nippon Steel, 214
Niron Magnetics, 174
Nirvana, 751
Nirvana Science, 1923
NIRvana Sciences Inc., 737
Nirvanix, 1899
Nisamest Oy, 2318
Niska Gas Storage, 1573
Nistica, 2196
Nitero, 106, 1711
Nitgen Technologies, 892
NiTi Surgical Solutions, 2726
Nitiloop, 2328
Nito, 1306
Nitramonia SA, 3187
Nitrex, 2206
Nitrex Chemicals, 2337
Nitrio, 976
Nitro med, 314
Nitro Software, 235, 3138
Nitrogenics, 267
Nitronex, 153, 314, 1008, 1709
NIU, 823
Nival, 89, 2663
Nivalis, 1519
Nivel, 1062
Nivel Holdings, 194
Niveus Medical, 138, 666, 1097
Nix Hydra, 776
Nixon, 1491
NiYO, 1696
Nizam Energy, 55
Njorsk Gjenvinning, 2384
Nkarta Therapeutics, 1731
NKT Therapeutics, 1196, 1419, 1628
nLayers, 3231
NLIGHT, 2008
nLight, 1247, 3098, 3123
nLight Photonics, 1361
nLine Systems Corp, 3162
NLS Holdings, 1279
NLT Spine, 2324
NLX, 166
NLynx Systems, 1708
Nlyte Software, 2478
nlyte Software, 1324
NM Group Global LLC, 90
NMC, 2332
NMDG Engineering, 3042
NMI, 779, 857, 946
NMusic, 3031
NNG, 1000
Noah's Bagels, 1587
Nobao, 3194
Nobel Learning Communities, 1017
Nobia, 2863
Nobil, 2664
Nobis, 2795
Noble BioMaterials, 1828
Noble Biomaterials, 1568
Noble Blends, 1135
Noble Foods, 2206
Noble Logistic Services, 190
Noble Transmission, 1749
Nobles Worldwide, 1014, 1111
Noblivity, 1615
NOBRA, 2889
NoBroker, 1087
Nocibe, 1516
Nocopo, 3203
NOCpulse, 1334
NOD Inc., 1951
NOD Pharmaceuticals, 2518
Nodality, 1436
Nodality Inc., 158

Node, 206, 661, 1035, 1269
Node Capital, 1507
Node.io, 243
Node4, 2944
NodeFly, 1663
NodePrime, 1595
Nodesource, 563
Nodexus, 870
NodThera, 12, 689
Noel Leeming, 2664
Noel-Levitz, 1504
Noetix, 1460, 1672
Noga Dairy, 193
Nohla, 2008
Nohla Therapeutics, 12
NoiseToys, 650
Nok Airlines, 1139, 2946
Nok Nok Lab, 1260
Nok Nok Labs, 596, 1378
Nokeena, 502
Nokeena Networks, 623
Noken, 622
Nolio, 436
Nom, 296
Nomacorc, 1622, 1752
Nomad Health, 2, 741
Nomadic, 1183, 1473
Nomi, 871, 1531
Nomiku, 218
Nominum, 59, 835, 1257, 1474
Nomios, 3020
Nomis Solutions, 197, 221, 646
Nomnomnom, 641
Nomorerack.com, 1361
Non Linear Dynamics Ltd, 3011
Non-Linear Dynamics, 2400
Nonabox, 2920
None Networks, 2302
Nongshim, 2857
Nonni's, 1990
Nonstop Games, 2637
Nonstopyacht, 2483
Noodle, 1766
Noodle Partners, 1392
NoodleMarkets, 1551
Noodles & Co., 1088
Noom, 1509, 1593, 1634, 1838
Noon, 1151, 1663
Noos, 3179
Nopassword, 890
Nor-Cal Products, 673
Nor1, 1806
Nora Therapeutics, 1493, 1941
Noranco, 1231, 2056
Noranda, 1134
Norbain, 2379
Norbord, 2067
Norcos, 2799
Norcraft Companies, 316, 1435
Norcross Safety Products, 1368
Nord Sense, 306
Nordax Finans, 1937
Nordco Holdings LLC, 862
Nordco Inc., 158
Nordic, 1762
Nordic Capital IV, 2447
Nordic Consulting, 918, 938
Nordic Consulting Partners, 1628
Nordic Energy Services, 2632
Nordic Mezzanine, 2447
Nordic Nanovector AS, 2519
Nordic Packaging and Container International, 1156
Nordic Telephone Company, 2379
Nordic Venture Partners, 2447
Nordisk Terapi, 2754
Nordnav Technologies, 2662

Nordofin Resources, 3209
Nordstrom, 869
NoRedInk, 883, 962, 1054, 1178, 1551, 2010
Norel Systems, 2936
Norian Corporation, 1398
Noriel, 2471
Norland Technology, 3014
Norm Thompson, 839
Norma Group, 2300
Normal, 1524
Normal Ears, 1876
Normerica Building Systems, 2044
NormOxys, 412
Noro-Moseley Partners, 3262
Noront Resources, 1548
Norquin, 1643
Norse, 1361
Norshield Security Products, 1719
Norsk Titanium, 144
Norstel, 2637, 2755, 3013
Norstrem Associates, 3262
Norsun Foods, 1295
Nortech Sytems, 1970
Nortek, 159
Nortev, 2355
North, 741, 2157
North America Cable Equipment, 1203
North America Central School Bus LLC, 843
North American Archery, 722
North American Baking, 1954
North American Breweries, 1085
North American Dental Group, 21
North American Partners in Anesthesia, 110, 1109
North American Rescue, 680, 1651
North American Substation Services, 985
North American Video, 894
North Bridge Growth Equity, 37
North Coast Composites, 48
North Coast Minerals, 1545
North Coast Technology Investors, 3269
North Dakota Holdings, 897
North of England Gas Distribution Network, 2591
North Sea Infrastructure Holdings, 156
North Sea Midstream Partners, 156
North Star Seafood, 1857
North Trade, 3054
Northburd, 1843
Northcentral University, 716
Northeast Dental Management, 1651
Northeastern Nonwovens, 1224
Northeastern Ohio Energy Hotel Fund, 1020
Northern Biologics, 1928
Northern Blizzard Resources, 1573
Northern Brewer, 683
Northern Contours, 1275
Northern Digital, 194
Northern Equity Investments, 1160
Northern Mat & Bridge, 2275
Northern Michigan Angels, 3269
Northern Power Systems, 1355, 1579
Northern Tier Energy, 1835
Northern Trust Private Equity, 3265
Northfield, 782
Northfield Industries, 1857
Northgate Capital LLC, 623
Northland Material Handling, 2286
NorthPage, 1065
Northpole, 2697
Northshore Bio, 1383
NorthStar, 2384
Northstar Aerospace, 2009
Northstar Travel, 1166
Northstar Travel Media, 1984
Northwave Technology, 1915
Northwest Cascade, 1636

1381

Portfolio Companies Index

Northwest Coatings, 373
Northwest Hardwoods, 109, 1134
Northwest Plan Services, 1979
Northwestern Management Services, 1128
Northwood Ventures, 3267
Norwegian Cruise Line, 1835
Norwesco, 1372
Norwest Equity Partners, 3279
Norwest Pallet Supply, 960
Norwest Productions, 2399
Norwest Venture Partners, 3284
Nosan, 1452
Noscira, 1452, 1452
Nosto, 2851
Not Your Average Joe's Inc., 354
Notable Health, 872
Notable Labs, 4, 741, 858, 1138
Notable Solutions, 655
Notal Vision, 2726
Notarize, 727, 1150
Notation Caption, 37
Notch Therapeutics, 2180
NoteSwift, 297
Noteworth, 525
Nothing Bundt Cakes, 1111
NotifyMD, 550
Notifymd, 1334
Notion, 377, 741, 942, 1383, 1666
Notion Capital, 483
Notis Global, 1135
Notiva, 197
Notonthehighstreet.com, 3131
Nototehighstreet.com, 3070
Noun Project, 1055, 1149
Nouncy, 3224
Nouriz, 2936
NousCom, 1928
Nouscom, 12
Nova, 721, 816, 2609, 3159, 3171
Nova Analytics Corp., 521
Nova Cardia, 1251
Nova Cimangola, 1007
Nova Corp., 300
Nova Credit, 741
Nova Instruments, 235
Nova Metrix, 235
Nova Ratio AG, 2713
Nova Science, 2918, 3191
Nova Scientific, 178
Nova Zyme Pharmaceuticals, 426
Novabase, 2717
Novacap, 220, 2167
NovaCardia, 94, 769, 1691
NovaCentrix, 807
Novacept, 1493
NovaCopper, 1548
Novacta, 2967
Novacta Biosystems, 3107
NovaDel Pharma, 1452, 1452, 1490
Novadigm Therapeutics, 621
Novadip, 3225
NovaDx, 1837
Novaerus, 710
Novagali Pharma SA, 3245
Novagraaf, 2378
Novak Biddle, 986
Novalar, 312
Novalux, 1915
NovaMed, 2733
NovaMin, 904
NovaMin Technology, 1008
Novapost, 2385
NovaPump, 2527
Novare, 666, 1459
Novariant, 502
Novarra, 1038
Novartis, 1452

Novartis Venture Fund, 3273
Novasentis, 1117, 3098
Novasic, 2481
Novasite Pharmaceuticals, 1002
NovaSom, 666, 1508, 1601
NovaSparks, 1416
NovaSterilis, 320
Novasys Medical, 87, 176, 925, 1378
Novate, 2918
Novate Medical, 3020
Novatel Wireless, 541
Novatex, 2489
NovaTorque, 730
NovaTract, 61, 1097
NovaTract Surgical, 678, 841, 1940
Novavax, 1493
Novawatt, 3239
Novazyme Pharmaceuticals, 74
Novel Effect, 408, 1151
Novel Therapeutic Technologies, 3245
Novelda, 2369
Novelics, 2778
Novell, 2005
Novell Inc., 300
NovellusDx, 1993
Novelos, 61
Novelos Therapeutics, 2702
Novera Optics, 1087, 2926
Novetta, 166
Novexel, 191, 2316
Novi, 2447
Novian Health, 987
Novidea, 1607
Novihum Technologies, 570
Novik, 503, 2029
NovImmune, 2419
Novinda, 1305
Novinium, 85
Novint Technologies, 506
NovioGendix, 2514
Novira, 12, 1928
Novira Therapeutics, 386
Novitex Enterprise Solutions, 140
NOVO 1, 830
NOVO Energy, 1895
NovoCure, 1043, 1436
Novocure, 1993
NovoDynamics, 979
NovoED, 547, 1183
NovoEd, 1054
Novogi, 2748
Novogy, 570, 1097
Novolex, 1990
Novologix, 1725
Novolyte Technologies, 170
Novomanip, 3122
Novome, 12
Novomer, 747, 1391, 1438, 3099
Novonix, 2155
Novoron Bioscience, 218
NovoStent, 1616
Novostent, 1251, 1600
NovoStent Corporation, 1241
Novotyr Therapeutics, 3245
Novovil, 3042
Novozymes, 1271
Novozymes AS, 77
Novozymes Malaysia Sdn Bhd, 3164
Novus, 221
Novus Health, 2058
Novus Leisure, 2935
NOVX Systems, 2196
Now Public, 1244
Nowait, 272, 630
NowMedia, 506
NowSecire, 222
NowSecure, 1046, 1178

NowThis News, 1699
NowThisMedia, 1361
Noxilizer, 19
Noxxon, 3113
NOXXON Pharma, 3196
NOXXON Pharma AG, 1325, 3190
Noyo, 728
Nozomi, 823
Nozomi Networks, 1151
Nozomi Photonics Co. Ltd., 2414
NP Photonics, 1664
Np Text, 779
NPC International, 1372
Nperspective, 3262
NPH Property Holdings, 1491
NPI Medical, 1719
NPIC, 2978
nPlatform, 3127
nPoint, 2001
NPS Pharmaceuticals, 1452
NPSG, 894
NPX Technologies Ltd., 2541
nQuire Software, 596
NRS Healthcare, 2944
NS1, 754, 823, 1607
NS8, 148, 285
NSA International, 1360
NSC Minerals, 2034, 2046, 2183
NSC Technologies, 529
Nscaled, 2671
nScaled, 89
Nsgene, 3149
NSi, 353
Nsight, 493, 1777
nSite Software, 1389
Nsknox, 3221
NSM Music Group, 908
NSS, 2325
nStack, 107
NStreams Technologies, 47
NTE Aviation LLC, 1964
NTELOS Holdings, 1506
NTent, 223
Nth Degree, 405, 828
NthOrbit, 623
nThrive Inc., 158
nTopology, 564
nTouch Research, 1008
NTRON, 235
NTRU Cryptosystems, 1704
NU Bank, 1502
Nu Energy, 2613
Nu Sirt Sciences, 915
Nu Skin Enterprises, 300
Nu Visions Manufacturing, 374
Nu3, 2928
nu3, 3056
Nualight, 2615
Nuance, 181, 3212
Nuance Communications, 1257
Nubank, 1534
Nubera, 2987
Nubisio, 221
Nubo, 1260
Nubundle, 1118
NuCana, 1698
Nucana, 2978
Nuclear Engineering Services, 2944
Nucleonics Inc., 2816
Nucleus, 1530
NuCO2, 199, 378
Nucore, 563
NuCORE Technology, 947
Nucore Technology, 1672
NuCurrent, 400
Nucurrent, 983
Nucypher, 525, 799

Portfolio Companies Index

Nudge Rewards, 2066
Nudo Products, 1557
Nueclear, 1346
Nuelle, 1993
Nuera, 23
Nuera Communications, 162
Nueva Cocina Foods, 131
Nuevo Midstream Dos, 671
Nuevolution, 3015, 3149
Nufern, 212, 530
NuGen, 1760
NuGEN Technologies, 87, 925
Nugen Technologies, 1520
NuHabitat, 445
Nuji, 3097
Nujira, 2386, 2615
Nulabel, 150
NuLink, 897
Nulogy, 2170
Numadic, 640
Numara Software, 1886
Numarine, 3173
Numascale AS, 3141
NumberFire, 544, 1524
Numberfour AG, 2604
Numbrs, 2583
Numedii Inc., 491
Numerai, 51, 741, 1329
Numerate, 191, 1124
Numerated, 1916
Numeric Investors, 1776
Numericable, 3020
Numerical Technologies, 1247
Numerify, 777
Numet, 1071
Numet Machining, 1021
Numet Machining Techniques, 1727
Numetric, 1000
Numi Organic Tea, 428
Numina, 1663
Numira, 1677
Numira Biosciences, 1784
Numonyx, 779
Numotion, 1136
Nuna, 1075
NUO Therapeutics, 508
NuoDB, 956, 1146, 1257
NuOrder, 161, 552, 871, 1888
Nuovo Film, 1340
NuPathe, 1508
NuPathes, 237
NuPotential, 362
NuPulse, 347
Nur, 3137
Nura, 153, 2419
Nurego, 1809
NuRelm, 998
Nuritas, 570, 1061
Nurix, 517, 1811
Nuro, 872
Nursefinders, 2079
NurseGrid, 1463
Nursery Supplies Inc., 1127
NursIT, 2841
Nurtur Me, 950
Nurture Life, 1019
NurturMe, 445
Nurx, 942, 1075, 1149
NuScriptRX, 678
NuscriptRx, 995
NuSil Technology, 1301, 1505
NuSirt, 1261
Nuskool, 418
NuSpace, 540
Nuspire, 21
Nusym Technologies, 627
Nusym Technology, 1945

Nut Pods, 482
Nutanix, 32, 235, 301, 867, 1255, 1620
NuTek Salt, 1069
Nutfield Technology, 1920
Nutmeg, 2478, 3032
Nutonian, 38
nuTonomy, 3098
Nutrabolt, 1231
Nutraceutical, 959
NutraClick, 646
Nutragenesis, 77
Nutri Ventures, 3048
Nutrigreen, 2717
Nutrinsic, 930
Nutrionix, 3113
NutriSystem Inc., 300
Nutrition Physiology Company LLC, 894
Nutrition Physiology Corporation, 1605
Nutritional High, 1079, 1135, 2122
Nutrivise, 590, 1097
NutshellMail, 950
Nuun, 85
nuuvera, 2134
Nuvaira, 1725, 1928, 1993
NuVasive, 468, 1412
Nuve, 445, 1685
Nuveen Investments, 1156, 2379
Nuvei, 1166, 2206
Nuvelo, 2079
Nuvelution, 495
Nuventix, 322, 1010
Nuvi, 688, 1070
Nuvisio, 2910
NuVision Engineering, 1937
Nuvita, 1924
Nuvita Professional, 1924
Nuvo TV, 1827
Nuvolo, 809
Nuvoloso, 1218
NuvoMed, 1061
Nuvon, 1028
NuvoSun, 69
NuVox, 1409
Nuvox, 1153, 1211
NuVox Communications, 1506
Nuvyyo, 2076
Nuwest Communities, 2202
Nuzzel, 1254, 1563, 1585, 1700
NVIDIA, 2007
Nvidia, 1922
nVidia, 1760
NView, 799
nVision, 149, 426, 1655
nVision Medical, 841
Nvite, 1320
NVMdurance, 1305
NVoicePay, 2003
NVP Brightstar, 2621
NVT Group, 235
Nwave Technologies, 226
NWay, 3251
nWay, 231, 552, 1563, 1838, 2010
nway, 1983
Nwestco, 1979
NWP Services, 563, 1769
NWPolymers, 1909
NxEdge, 596
NxGen Electronics, 1915
NXP, 220, 2379
NXP Semiconductor, 57
NXP Semiconductors, 744
NxStage Medical, 560
NXT Capital, 1743, 1743
NXT Capital Funding IV, 1970
NXT-ID, 530
NxtControl, 3165
NxtGen Emission Controls, 192

NxThera, 149, 1241, 1488
NxtMile Sports Insoles, 1736
NY Accelarator Corp., 1420
Ny Department Stores, 1017
Nycomed, 209, 2379
Nycomed Pharma, 3008, 3009
NYDJ Apparel, 559
NYF, 3100
Nyge Aero, 2863, 2863
NYIT, 3267
Nylas, 564, 858, 1595
Nyle Systems, 1161
NYLIM Jacob Ballas India Fund III LLC, 2094
Nylon Corporation of America, 1224
Nymbus, 1000
Nymi, 974, 1607, 2236
Nymirum, 943
Nyota Minerals, 1548
NYSE Blue, 1786
Nyshex, 809
NYX Security, 3013
Nécessaire, 761, 1183

O

O Luxe Holdings Limited, 1088
O Premium Waters, 439
O&S Doors, 1753
O'Brien Corp., 985
O'Brien Veterinary Management, 378
O-In Design Automation, 1672
O.K. 4U KIDDO, 1708
O.school, 218
O2 Canada, 2128
O2 Cool, 1964
O2B Kids, 1724
O2Micro, 892
O3b Networks, 1334
Oak Financial, 658
Oak HC/FT, 3264, 3273
Oak Hill Advisors, 815
Oak Investment Partners, 3279
Oak Pacific Interactive, 2936
Oak Street Funding, 127
Oak Street Health, 1315
Oak Valley Resources, 672
Oakcreek Golf, 2051
Oakley Networks, 634
OakNorth, 2690
Oakstone Holdings, 3262
Oanda Coorperation, 2427
Oar AG, 3172
Oasis, 949
Oasis Atlantico - Hotelaria e Turismo, 3048
Oasis Children's Services, 687
Oasis Labs, 232, 1151
Oasis Marinas, 19, 493
Oasis Media Corporation, 650
Oasis Outsourcing, 97, 1062, 1279
Oasys, 747
Oasys Water, 59
Oath, 329
OATSystems, 925
OB Hospitalist Group, 159, 176, 881
Ob10, 2472
Obalon, 275, 1010
Obalon Therapeutics, 621, 1371
Obaz, 1118
Oberon Media, 2472
Oberthur, 2293
Oberthur Card Systems, 2852
Oberthur Smart Cards, 2721
Obie, 795
Obie.ai, 2027
OBike, 874
Obillex, 2972
Obizible, 1626
Object Reservoir, 1273

1383

Portfolio Companies Index

Object Video, 1, 1133
Objective Logistics, 1322
Objectivity, 58
ObjectStar, 1017
ObjectVideo, 627, 1348, 1886
Oblend, 2287
Oblix, 757
Oblong, 809
Oblong Industries Inc, 776
OBMedical, 1923
Obo, 1985
Obopay, 1378
ObsEba, 1698
Observe Medical, 3203
ObserveIt, 221
Observeit, 1728
ObservePoint, 79, 1204
Obseva, 74
Obsidian, 1778
Obsidian Security, 872
Obsidian Therapeutics, 191
Obsidian/Applied Materials, 1288
OC Robotics, 3107
OC Robotics Ltd, 2464
OCA Venture Partners, 3265
Ocado, 3097
Ocarina Network, 1474
Ocarina Networks, 968
Ocata Therapeutics, 132
Occam Networks, 925
Occam Sciences, 660
Occam Systems, 2967
Occasion Brands, 1234
Occidental Hotels Allegro Resorts, 2962
Occipital, 776, 874, 1050, 1789
OccuRx, 2959
Ocean Approved, 1161
Ocean Breeze Water Park, 1991
Ocean Butterflies, 2847
Ocean Current Energy, 3262
Ocean Executive, 2155
Ocean Installer, 1164
Ocean Outdoor, 2944
Ocean Renewable Power Co., 1160
Ocean Sales, 2269
Ocean Sparkle, 3211
Ocean Watch, 286
Ocean's Halo, 431
Oceana Therapeutics, 94, 782
Oceanlinx, 2613, 2717
Oceans Healthcare, 816
OCENSA, 584
OCENSA Transportation Rights, 584
Ocera, 1010, 1698
Ocera Therapeutics, 560, 621, 867, 1271, 1533, 1817, 1941
Oceus Networks, 1777
OCI Solar, 584
OCJ, 3100
Ockam, 800
OCM Print Management Solutions, 2574
Octagon, 52
Octagon Investment Partners, 1491
Octagon Research Soltuions Inc., 655
Octalica, 436
Octane AI, 307
Octane Fitness, 1335
Octane Lending, 533
Octane Software, 1003
Octane5 International LLC, 693
Octasic, 2206
Octasoft, 1180
Octave, 720, 1363
Octave Group, 2252
Octi, 1663
Octio AS, 3141
Octiv, 86

October, 2851
Octopus.com, 114
Octoshape, 2999
Ocuity, 3195
Ocular Dynamics, 1238
Ocular Technologies, 1271
Ocular Therapeutix, 176, 1445, 1460, 1628, 1762
Ocularis Pharma, 400
Oculeve, 1928
OcuLex, 237
Oculex Pharmaceuticals, 74, 524
Oculii, 519, 1483
OCULIR, 1664
Oculis, 1350
Oculis Labs, 979, 1988
Oculus Health, 703
Oculus VR, 124, 1181, 1715
ODC Nimbus, 631
ODENBERG, 2336
Odeo, 114
Odeon/UCI Cinemas, 2379
Odersun, 1397, 3222
oDesk Corporation, 1672
Odessa Power Holdings, 675
OdigeO, 3033
Odim, 2754
Odimo, 3124
Odin, 89, 3137
Odin Technologies, 3231
OdontoPrev, 1018
Odontoprev, 3180
Odoo, 3239
Odyssey, 1045, 1593
Odyssey Health Care, 402
Odyssey Investment Partners, 1871
Odyssey Logistics & Technology, 380, 1850
Odyssey Technologies, 1208
Odyssey Thera, 2815
Odyssey Thera Inc., 2816
Oenalliance, 2625
Oerthalign Inc., 371
OEwaves, 729, 1828
Oferteo.pl, 3044
Off Grid Electric, 595
Off.Grid:Electric, 1374
Offbeatguides, 2604
Offensive Security, 1717, 1794
Offerdat, 3262
OfferIQ, 724
OfferLogic, 313
Offermatica, 223
Offermobi, 150
Offerpop, 534, 1991
Offers.com, 1759
Offerton Liveshopping, 2339
OfferUp, 124, 518, 823, 1024
Office Baroque Gallery, 3042
Office Media Network, 818
Office Practicum, 1409
Office Total, 928
OfficeMax, 1096
OfficeSource, 765
OfficeTiger, 779
Offset Gerhard Kaiser, 2375
Offshore Inland Marine & Oilfield Services, 1415
Ofo, 2446
OG Planet, 626
Ogee, 786
Ogee Inc., 438
Oggifinogi, 533
Ogin, 1786, 1906
Ogin Energy, 595
Ogmento, 457
Ogury, 3208
OGX Holding II, 672
OH Aircraft Acquisition, 1360

Ohai, 197
Ohi, 782
OHM Connect, 180
OHMConnect, 751
OhmConnect, 488
Oil Purification Systems, 190
Oilfield Water Logistics, 1326
Oilgear Company, 1171
OilSERV, 1125
Oilstudios.com, 2574
Oinky, 3108
Oja.la, 2984, 3125
Ojai Energy Systems, 3257
Ojo, 1593
OK Indutries, 1557
Okairos, 1928, 2530
Okanjoya, 231
Okapi Sciences, 3042
Okcupid, 858
Okena, 1702
Okera, 720
Oki, 214
Okko Hotels, 2851
Okmetic Oyj, 2990
OKpanda, 1054, 1546
OKTA, 751
Okta, 124, 836, 1069, 1968
OKTOGO, 2320
Oktogo, 3208
Oktogo.ru, 3229
OKWave, 1755
Ola, 1181, 1826
Olam International, 2434
Olam-Africa, 1007
Olapic, 858, 1146, 1406, 1632
Old Dominion Freight Line, 380
Old Hickory Smokehouse, 1345
Old london, 631
Old Time Pottery, 528
Old World Christmas, 828
Old World Industries, 901
Ole & Steen, 1088
Oleon Holding, 2332
Olfactor Laboratories, 1784
Oliberte, 3277
Olicar, 2524
OliLux Biosciences, 622
Olista Software Corporation, 2770
Olive, 1286
Olive Devices, 266
Olive Medical, 1784
Olive Software, 3123
Olivenoel, 3170
Oliver, 1006
Oliver Printing & Packaging Co., 1435
Oliver Products, 258, 1171
Oliver Solution, 2952
Ollie, 150, 544, 668, 1110, 1585
Ollie's Bargain Outlet, 433
Olly, 229, 1363
OLO, 538
Olo, 1826
Olon Industries, 1456
Olono, 1985
Olook, 2976
OLSet, 2010
OLSON, 1086
Olvi Oyj, 2990
OLX, 3001
Olympia Chimney Supply, 164
Olympic Physical Therapy, 82
Olympix, 2696
Olympus Re Holdings, 827
OM Signal, 2109
OM1, 816
Omada, 124, 809, 1052, 1929
Omada Health, 1054, 1346

Portfolio Companies Index

Omadi, 79
Omadi Mobile Management, 1070
Omaha National, 70
Omaze, 256, 561, 724, 743, 1623, 1833
Ombitron, 1784
Omedix, 1142
Omega Diagnostics, 3028
Omega Energia Renovael S.A., 1956
Omega Environmental Technologies, 1343, 1569
Omega Funds One Way Ventures, 3273
Omega Health Systems, 1275
Omega Ingredients, 2760
Omega Pharma, 3232
Omega Red, 2944
Omega Wirless, 1153
OmegaTech, 237
Omegawave, 2630
Omeicos, 2841
Omek, 724
omelas, 2241
Omeros, 153, 1844, 1946, 2419
OMERS Private Equity, 3264
OMERS Ventures Fund II, 483
Ometric, 1842
OMGPOP, 1699, 1715
OMGPop, 231
OMNE Partners, 70
Omneon, 1402, 1911
Omneon Video Networks, 59
Omni, 754, 935, 1837
OMNI Design, 1837
Omni Energy Services Corp., 1971
Omni Labs, 318
OMNI Retail Group, 2003
Omni-ID, 809
Omnia, 2754
Omnia Communications, 3137
Omniata, 1024
Omnicell, 176, 1760
Omnichain, 1554
Omnico Plastics, 3017
Omnidian, 488
OmniEarth, 308
Omniex, 1670
Omniflow, 3048
OmniGuide, 1498
OmniGuide Inc., 269
OmniGuide Surgical, 1382
Omnilink, 876
Omniome, 268
OmniOx, 709
Omniplex, 96
Omnipoint, 1793
OmniSci, 1926
Omnisci, 2278
Omniscience, 890
OmniSonics Medical Technologies, 3007
Omnispace, 515
OmniSpeech, 218
OmniSYS, 477
OMNITICKET network, 2544
Omniture, 563, 1626, 1705, 1884
Omnity, 1149, 1218
OmniVision, 1180
OmniVision Entertainment, 1371
Omny, 1218
Omrix, 2571, 3101
Omrix Biopharmaceuticals, 2563
OMsignal, 2195
Omtrix Biopharmaceuticals, 925
OMX, 2184
On Campus Marketing, 1724
On Deck Capital, 741
On Device Research, 2479, 3030
On Display, 563
On Farm Systems, 1600
On It, 950

On Second Thought, 218
On Shift, 831
ON Technology, 56
On The Border, 839
On-Chip Biotechnologies, 1241
On-Motion Oy, 2873
On-set, 2571
On-Site Fuel Service, 405
On-X Life Technologies, 1500
ON24, 184, 1604
On24, 386, 1640
OnApp, 2944
Onapsis, 2, 171, 1136
Onaro, 436, 2580
Onavo, 2831, 2952
OnBoard Security, 349
ONCampus Media, 958
Oncap, 2167
Once Innovations, 1872
Once24 Inc., 986
oncgnostics, 2527
Onco Health, 1988
Onco Med Pharmaceuticals, 604
Onco Vision, 2548
Onco-Screen, 2172
OncoFactor, 1391
Oncofactor, 153, 2008
OncoGenex Pharma, 1271, 1941
OncoGenex Technologies, 1543
OncoHealth, 666
Oncology Molecular Imaging, 1484
OncoMed, 238, 1094, 1122
Oncomed, 1929
OncoMed Pharmaceuticals, 57, 598, 3007
Onconova Therapeutics, 3211
Oncontract.com, 3199
Oncora Medical, 266, 622
OnCore Manufacturing Services, 439
Oncore Manufacturing Services, 839
Oncorus, 1268
Oncorus Inc., 182
Oncos Therapeutics Ltd., 2816
Oncoscope, 144, 157
OncoStem Diagnostics, 174
Oncue, 317
Ondango, 2629
Ondax, 1915
OnDeck, 533, 770, 1593, 1620
Ondeck Capital, 1001
OnDemand Therapeutics, 1010
Ondeso, 2475
Ondevice Research, 2586
Ondotek, 1440
ONE, 2379, 2384, 2914
One, 892
One & Only Ocean Club, 34
One Access, 2876
ONE Access Networks, 2354
One Agency, 2426
One Animation, 2913
One Asia Resources, 2942
One Call Medical, 1368
ONE Campaign, 1374
One Caring Team, 307
One Cavo, 1837
One Chronos, 318
One clickHR, 2894
One Concern, 564, 1894
One Distribution, 257
1 Doc Way, 181, 858
One Door, 1728
One Floral Group, 916
ONE Group, 1681
One Inc., 384
One Kings Lane, 1001
One Kloud, 272
One Logos Education Solutions, 987

One Medical, 248, 1138, 1604
One Medical Group, 581, 634, 1361
One Medical Passport, 496, 718
One Mobikwik Systems Private Ltd., 483
One Month, 1998
One On One, 716
One On One Ads, 1375
One Page, 1595
One Path, 1270
One Potato, 896
One Radio, 2008
One Smart, 2978
One Spa World, 1088
One Spot, 1247
One Stop Systems, 1784
One Tap Away, 318
One Two Four, 2944
One Up, 100
One Up Sports, 1883
One Wave, 2998
One World Fitness PFF, 447
One World Foods, 2099
1-2-3.TV, 2897, 3233
1-800 Contacts, 722
1-800 Radiator, 1576
1-800-CONTACTS, 1815
1-800-Dentist, 221
1-Page, 792
10 for Humanity, 3259
10% Happier, 544
100 Thieves, 607, 1654
1000 Museums, 85, 1306, 1310, 1632
1000mercis, 2851
1001 Listes, 2551
100Kin10, 1316
100KM Foods Inc., 2161
101, 293, 622
101 Mobility, 546
10C Technologies, 1244
10sheet, 1358
10th Magnitude, 1409
10th Street LLC, 158
10X, 1740
10X Engineered Materials, 1286
10X Genomics, 1212, 1916
10x Genomics, 762
10X Technologies, 1940
10x Technologies, 1400
10x Technology, 983
11 Honore, 1888
11 Honoré, 761
1105 Media Holdings, 1279
117go.com, 1534
1200 Pharma, 1051
121cast, 3121
121nexus, 1185
12snap AG, 162
12Soft, 2857
1322 North, 1219
1366 Technologies, 809, 1334, 1460, 1906
13th Lab, 2637
140 Proof, 296
15Five, 1384, 1749, 3044
16fun, 2936
17 Media, 1087
17TeraWatts, 1507
1901 Group, 680
One97, 1620
1A Smart Start LLC, 158
OneAccess, 2662, 2851
OneBreath, 3211
OneCause, 1242
OneChip Photonics, 596, 1257
OneClick HR, 2972
OneCommand, 695, 1000
Onedio, 3078
OneDome, 226

1385

Portfolio Companies Index

OneFineStay, 386
onefinestay, 3055
Onefootball, 1882
Oneforty, 114
Onehub, 85, 974
Oneida Molded Plastics, 164
OneKloud, 1370
Onel, 2612
1Life Healthcare, 1445
Oneline Radiology, 949
OneLink Communications, 559
OneLogin, 1696
Onelogin, 1626
1Mage Software, 1837
OneMain, 767
1Mainsteam, 596
OneMed Group, 2311
OneMob, 129, 249
1More Design, 823
OneNeck IT Services, 1979
ONEofTHEM, 2646
OnePath, 1166
OnePath Networks, 2079, 2454, 2926
OnePath Systems, 1857
OnePIN, 711, 1734
OneRiot, 142, 521, 1715
Oneshape Inc., 521
OneSignal, 1675
OneSource Distributors, 926
OneSource Virtual, 897
OneSpace, 935
Onespin, 2472
OneSpot, 445, 1682
1st Credit, 2537, 2538
1st Virtual Communications, 1235
1stdibs, 248, 1000, 1715
Onestop, 796
OneTouchPoint, 969, 1232
OneTwoSee, 1240
Onetwotrip, 2446
1upHealth, 679
OneWave Inc, 2590
OneWeb, 1509
Onewed, 773
OneWest Bank, 1315
OneWest Bank Group, 1743
Onewheel, 1894
1World Online, 602
Onex Communications, 3137
OnExchange, 1672
OnFarm, 1097
OnFiber, 1793
OnFiber Communications, 1994
Onfido, 1154, 1607
Onfleet, 622
OnFocus, 1261
OnForce, 1333
Onformonics, 2355
Ongig, 1749
ONI Systems, 1247, 1474, 1682
ONICON Incorporated, 908
Onics, 1061
Online Benefits, 847
Online Partners, 2711
Online Tech, 530
Online Tech Stores, 276, 529
Online Tours, 641
OnlineMarket, 2437
Onlineprinters GmbH, 1776
OnlineTours, 2886
OnlineTradesmen.ie, 2355
Onmia Molecular, 2553
OnMobile, 2264
OnMobile Systems, 162
Ono, 525
Ono Food Co., 1421
ONO Labs, 2841

Ono-Auna, 2379
OnPharma, 548
OnPoint Group, 914
OnPrem Networks Corporation, 765
OnPulse, 1810
Onramp, 949
Onramp Branding, 1681
OnScale, 226, 1613
OnSeen, 1286
Onset Medical Corp., 269
Onset Ventures, 3284
Onshape, 124
OnShift, 500, 628, 642, 938, 1047
Onsite Dental, 1346
Onsite Health, 949
Onsite Systems, 2005
Onsolve, 1925
Onstation Corporation, 947
ONStor, 798
OnStream Networks, 1760
OnSwipe, 1502, 1789, 1821
Onswipe, 679, 1118, 1254, 1715
OnTarget, 1885
onTargetjobs, 1956
Ontario Excavac, 2186
Ontario Systems, 166
Ontario Teachers' Pension Plan, 3264
OnTech, 791
Ontela, 1637
Ontex International, 1835
Ontic, 1933
OnTime Networks, 2632
Ontoforce, 2949
Ontology, 2691
ONTOPx, 2475
OnTrak Software, 1512
OnTruck, 2446
Onventis, 1620
Onward Healthcare, 1972
OnX, 1235
OnX Enterprise Solutions, 2058
ONXEO, 2851
Onymos, 249
Onyx, 206
Onyx Payments, 928, 1491
Onyx Pharmaceuticals, 769
ONZO, 3135
OnúCall, 2241
Oo, 3262
Ooda Health, 609
Oodle, 600, 968
OOHA Wilkins, 378
Ooma, 627, 1406, 1782, 1983, 2196
Ooma Pharmacyclics, 181
Oomba, 69
Oomnitza, 317, 625
Ooska News, 631
Oosterhof Dairy, 3203
Ooyala, 378, 1540
Op Source, 563
op5, 3043
Opal, 1158, 1383, 1463, 1656
OPAQ Networks, 515
Opcity, 968
OPDA, 2936
Open, 972
Open Data Institute, 1374
Open Data Nation, 1894
Open DNS, 634
Open Energi, 2295
Open Energy Efficiency, 488
Open English, 754, 1534, 1785
Open Garden, 1926
Open Government Partnership, 1374
Open Health Network, 1507
Open Interface, 247
Open Kernel Labs, 2989

Open Knowledge, 1374
Open Lending, 333
Open Media, 515
Open Mineral, 2106
Open Networks, 2664
Open Networks Engineering, 1336
Open Peak, 1593
Open Road, 1317
Open Road Entertainment, 330, 331
Open Road Integrated Media, 1083
Open Road Media, 841
Open Sensors, 3108
Open Sky, 935, 1524
Open Solutions, 212, 530, 1202, 1910
Open Span, 793
Open Sponsorhip, 1585
Open Wide, 2439
Open-E, 1380
Open-Xchange, 2686
OpenAir, 964
Openbay, 313, 1524, 1734
OpenBazaar, 124
Openbc, 3233
OpenBet Technologies, 2379
Openbit Oy, 2873
OpenBravo, 2342
OpenBucks, 871
Openbucks, 107, 1254
OpenCare, 724, 2187
OpenConnect Systems, 1682
OpenDataSoft, 2439
OpenDNS, 581, 836, 1760
OpenDoor, 823, 1631
Opendoor, 720, 727, 1069, 1346, 1761
OpenDrives, 306
OpenEnglish, 1000
Openet, 2478
OpenField, 934
OpenGamma, 743
OpenGov, 1095
Opengov, 45, 124, 1031
Opengov.com, 378
Openharbor.com, 2711
Openhomes, 566
OpenInvest, 124, 2000
Openlane, 197
OpenLink, 924
OpenLogic, 142
OpenMarkets, 1364, 1801
Openmind, 751, 2443
OpenNetwork Technologies, 1668
OpenPages, 184, 1672
OpenPath, 306, 1480
Openpath, 728
OpenPeak, 650
Openplain, 2355
OpenQ, 876
OpenReach, 494
OpenServices, 954, 1227
OpenSesame, 1416
OpenSignal, 1509, 3030
Opensignal, 1359
OpenSite Technologies, 1008, 1709
OpenSky, 386, 1496
OpenSpace, 219, 318, 1151, 1282
Openspace, 770
OpenSpan, 835, 979, 1181, 1672, 1673
OpenSponsorship, 811
Opensynergy, 2813
OpenTable, 248, 324, 1003
Opentext Corporation, 2267
Opentrons, 1069, 1110
Openwater, 703, 1095
Openwave Systems, 1038
OpenX, 634, 741, 1474, 1620, 1640, 1965, 3070, 3131
Openx, 1359

Portfolio Companies Index

OpenX Software, 581, 1241
OpenZeppelin, 318
Opera Solutions, 680, 1683
Operational Results, 1070
Operative, 655, 779
Operator, 872
Operator of Full Service Restaurants, 353
Operator Systems, 3203
Opexa Therapeutics, 241
OpGen, 560, 979
Ophidion, 1577
Ophthonix, 560
Ophthotech, 495
Ophthotech Corporation, 1698, 3015
OPi, 3113
Opinion Research Corporation, 1136
OpinionLab, 1732
OPKO Health, 2970
Oplayp, 2451
Oplink, 1180
Oplus, 602
Oplus Technologies, 2541, 2782
Opnext, 494
Opocrin, 1452
Oportun, 581, 634, 858, 872, 1001
OPOWER, 1226
Opower, 1996
Oppa, 2976
Opportunity Bancshares Inc., 404
Opposing Views, 1784
Oppten, 3125
OPS Solutions, 400
Opsani, 2019
Opsclarity, 1254
Opscode, 1968
OpSec, 1017
Opsens, 2029, 2180
Opsidio, 266
Opsmatic, 607, 784, 976, 1254
OpsMx, 603
Opsona Therapeutics, 2918, 3020, 3085
OpSource, 184, 925
OpsTechnology, 514, 1944
Opsware, 757, 986, 1003
Optanix, 779
Optaros, 455, 946
Optasia Medical, 3092
Optasite, 1142, 1459, 1862
OptConnect, 846
Optellios, 56
OPTEM, 642
Opternative, 1046, 1480, 1849
Optessa, 2058
Opthalmopharma, 2717
Optherion, 1412, 1508
Opththotech, 2815
Opti, 2238
Optiant, 422
Optibase Ltd., 2954
Optibus, 1000, 1926
Optical Data Systems, 1682
Optical Experts Manufacturing, 224, 1477
Optical Solutions, 536
Optichron, 1922
OptiComp Corporation, 1669
Opticon, 1295
Opticon M, 1784
OpTier, 2566
Optify, 1846
Optigenex, 1191
Optii Solutions, 377
Optilly, 721
Optilly/Install Monitizer, 1839
Optim.al, 625
Optima Global Solutions, 3274
Optimal, 3221
Optimal IMX, 678, 1533

Optimal Solutions Integration, 1777
Optimal Test, 2462, 2566, 2726
OptimalQ, 543
Optimas, 109
Optimax Systems, 1702
OptiMedica, 634
Optimedica, 87
Optimer, 1742
Optimer Pharmaceuticals, 2496
OptiMine, 375, 956, 2001, 2019
Optimine, 1292
Optimizely, 124, 221, 235, 248, 486, 544, 545, 720, 1010, 1054, 1149, 1607, 2012
Optimo Route, 2834
OptimoRoute, 1421
Optimum Outcomes, 1963
Optimus EMR Inc., 331
Optimus Ride, 743, 781, 1254
Optinel Systems, 1348, 2754
Optinex Inc, 2954
OptiNose, 2710
Optinose, 209, 762
Optinuity, 1916
Option 3, 1543
Option Care, 1156
OptionEase, 1237
Optionis Group, 2965
Options City, 655
Options Technology, 333
OptionsHouse, 815
OptionWay, 1370
Optireno, 2439
OptiScan, 176
Optiscan, 1122
OptiScan Biomedical, 1241, 1325
Optissimo, 3154
Optiv, 1017, 1794
Optivia Medical, 1442
Optiwind, 678
Opto Atmosphere, 961
Opto Tech, 892
Optomec, 809
Optoro, 876, 1169, 1502, 1689, 1766
Optos, 2386
Optos PLC, 2386
Optosecurity, 2029
Optosense, 2369
OptoTrace Technologies, 3062
Optovia, 925
Optovue, 892, 970, 1844
Optovue Corporation, 47
OpTrip, 115
Optum, 541
Optum Ventures, 3273
OpTun's, 2655
Optuvt AB, 2816
Optware Corporation, 2414
Opulan, 2436
Opus 12, 395, 2111
Opus Global Holdings, 884
Opus Medical, 1493
Opus One Solutions, 2238
Opus12, 890
OPX Biotechnologies, 595, 1895
OpxBio, 2011
Opxbio, 322, 1247
Ora VéHicules Electriques, 2945
Orabrush, 1860
Orachiotek, 270
Oracle, 1334
Oracle Care Limited, 2507
Oracle Packaging, 446
Oracle Responsys, 770
Oracle/Skywire, 1676
Oradian, 3108
Oragenics, 1812
OraHealth, 85

Oral Care, 3054
OraMetrix, 946, 3137
Oramir, 3171
Orange Groves/OCP Holding Company, 1764
Orange Plastics, 869
Orange Retail Finance India, 851
Orange Slovensko, 2309
Orange Theory Fitness, 334
Orangebus, 3012
Orangetheory Fitness, 1576
OraPharma Inc., 782
Orascom Telecom Algeria, 2337
Orasi Medical, 2077
Oratio, 3108
Orative, 613, 1853
Oraya Therapeutics, 621, 1626, 1772
Orb, 307, 3252
Orb Energy, 55
Orb Networks, 1257
ORB Packing, 932
Orbeus, 472, 1615
Orbility, 2851
OrbiMed Healthcare Fund Management, 37
Orbis Biosciences, 1764
Orbis Education, 1136
Orbis Technologies Inc., 349
Orbit Commerce, 1057
Orbit Fab, 1613
Orbit Garant, 2255
Orbital, 3104
Orbital Insight, 820, 1151
Orbital Optics, 2967
Orbital Sidekick, 4
Orbital Tool Technologies, 1422
Orbitera, 306
Orbius, 1321
Orbona, 1452
Orbotix, 1789
Orbus Therapeutics, 1143
Orca Systems, 3211
Orcamp, 2475
Orch1d, 525
Orchard, 351, 386, 535, 1282, 1502, 1715, 2184
orchard, 2212
Orchard Brands, 839
Orchard Information Systems Ltd, 3011
Orchard Therapeutics, 1519
Orchestra, 1054, 3208
Orchestra Networks, 2693
Orchestrate, 1547
Orchestrate.io, 1860
Orchestream, 2386
Orchestria, 757, 1400, 2671
Orchestro, 1299, 1348
Orchid, 124, 2014
Orchid BioSciences, 1394
Orchid Labs, 1138
Orchid Orthopedic Solutions, 2384
Orchid Underwriters, 881
Orchids Paper Products Company, 616
Orckit Communications Ltd, 2585
Order Corner, 445
Order Groove, 796
Order With Me, 641, 2869
OrderAhead, 858, 1531
OrderDynamics, 690
Orderful, 1421
OrderGroove, 243, 1110
OrderGrove, 1766
Ordermark, 50
OrderMotion, 1886, 2196
OrderUp, 707
OrderWithMe, 1912
Ordinal, 2439
Ordoro, 445
Ordr, 1794
Ordr.In, 1150

1387

Portfolio Companies Index

Ordway, 1110
Orege, 2615
oregon Chai, 1665
Oregon Ice Cream, 1767
Oreko Metal Mining, 250
Oren Semiconductor, 602, 1704
Orex Technologies, 3101
OrexiGen, 762
Orexigen, 1251, 1626
OREXIGEN Therapeutics, 560
Orexigen Therapeutics, 621
Orexo, 3020
Orexo AB, 2816
Organic Holdings, 1430
Organic Meadow, 2049
Organic Style, 506
Organic To Go, 797
Organica, 2290, 2851
Organika Health Products, 354
Organix, 966
Organosys, 2771
Orgentec, 1961
Orggit, 1615
Ori, 1069
Oric Pharmaceuticals, 517, 709, 762
Orica, 2659
Oridion, 2922
Oriel Therapeutics, 1817
OrienGene, 2978
Orient Speech Therapy, 710
Oriental Standard, 596
Oriental Trading, 334
Oriental Trading Company, 378
ORIG3N, 6, 1087
Orig3n, 602, 915
Origami Logic, 581, 634, 968, 3221
Origami Risk, 1717
OriGene, 973
Origene, 2978
Origin, 751
Origin BioMed, 2205
Origin Biomed, 2049
Origin Fertility Care, 2392
Origin Games, 100
Origin Holdings, 1785
Origin House, 390
Origin Materials, 2061
Origin Ventures, 3265
Original, 1912
Original Additions, 2944
Orion, 206, 706, 1260
Orion Equity Partners, 3273
Orion Healthcorp, 1970
Orion Holding, 584
Orion ICG, 447
Orion Labs, 161, 1563
Orion Media, 2944
Orion Technologies, 1430
Orion Technology, 3145
Orion Telescopes & Bionoculars, 1741
Orionis Biosciences, 703
Oris4, 2205
Orius Corporation, 1986
Orizon, 654
Orka Group, 1017
Orliman, 1572
Orlucent, 666
Ormigga, 1507
ORMvision, 2781
Ornet, 3231
Ornet Data Communication, 2770
Ornikar, 2851
Ornim, 809
Ornim Medical, 1382
Oro Negro, 159
Orolia, 3239
Orono Spectral Solutions, 1161

OROS, 1286
OrphaZyme, 3149
Orphazyme ApS, 2350
Orpheris, 383
Orpheus Interactive, 1061
Orphgen Pharmaceuticals, 1915
Orpiva, 1244
ORQIS Medical, 560
Orquest, 1398
ORS Nasco, 328
OrSense, 1604, 3137
Orsus, 436
Orsus Solutions, 2580
Ortec International, 2563
Ortega InfoSystems, 1769
Ortega Innfosystems, 1180
OrthAlign, 1371, 1543
Orthalign, 1571
Ortho Accel, 950
Ortho Kinematics, 445, 1187, 1500, 1801
Ortho Organizers, 118, 439
Ortho Space, 3240
Ortho-Space Ltd., 269
OrthoAccel Technologies, 1597
OrthoBethesda, 403
Orthocare Innovations, 1627
OrthoClassic, 373
Orthocon, 2496
OrthoFi, 29
Orthogem, 2967, 3107
Ortholite Holdings LLC, 1851
Orthopaedic Synergy, 2876
Orthos, 2737
OrthoScan, 138
Orthoscan Inc., 371
Orthovita, 2563
Orthovita., 2563
Orthspace, 3192
Ortiva Wireless, 206, 1239
Ortodisc Technology, 1769
OSA Technologies, 1747, 1769
Osage Venture Partners, 3270
Osaro, 24, 107, 518, 525, 721, 1254
Osby Glas, 3054
Oscar, 578, 775, 816, 836, 1110, 1531
Oscar Mike Games, 514
OsComp Systems, 466, 2700
OSF Commerce, 1607
OSHAP, 3137
Oshkosh Floor Designs, 719
OSI, 1516
OSIsoft, 1785
Oskando, 2390
Oski Energy, 1895
OSM Environmental, 704
Osmo, 1050, 1888
Osmose, 1081
Osmosis, 1701
Osmotica Pharmaceutical, 209
OsoBio, 97
Osper, 535
Osprey, 783, 2196
Osprey Informatics, 2111
Osprey Medical, 2536, 2618, 2959, 3279
Osprey Publishing, 2362
Osprey Ventures, 3284
OSRAM, 973
Ossia, 721
Ossianix, 266
Ossium Health, 741
Osso VR, 1473, 1675
Ostara, 1906
Ostara Nutrient Recovery Techologies, 2053
Osteobiologics, 36, 1500, 1817
OsteoQC, 2180
Osteotech, 1769
Ostergard, 3203

Ostrovok, 2446
Osum Oil Sands, 1956
Osuuspankkien Keskuspankki Oyj, 2990
OTEC International, 19
Otelic, 384
OTG, 909
OTG Software, 1886
Other Inbox, 1841
OtherInbox, 1810
Others Online, 85
Otherwise, 2296
Othot, 52
Otic Pharma, 1382
Otifex, 2959
Otis Spunkmeyer, 168, 2079
OTO Systems Inc., 1006
OTO.ai, 799
Otogami, 3223
OtoNexus, 841
OtoNexus Medical Technologies, 1061
Otonomo, 603, 922
Otonomy, 206, 621, 1382, 1574, 3015
OtoSense, 519, 1061, 3277
Otsuka Pharma, 1271
Ott-Lite, 1477
Ottakar's, 2796
Otter Valley Foods, 2049
Otto Gourmet, 3170
Otto Sauer Achsenfabrik GmbH, 2660
Ouicar, 2851
Ounce Labs, 521
Our Family Clinic, 55
Ouroboros Medical, 177
Ourofino Saude Animal, 815
OurStage.com, 1097
Ouster, 532, 942
Out of Milk, 1226
Outback Steakhouse, 131, 1708
Outbound Engine, 100, 1331
OutboundDengine, 751
OutboundEngine, 1685
Outbox, 707
Outbrain, 909, 2566, 3081
Outcome Health, 842, 1480
Outdoor Exchange, 418
Outdoor Project, 1383
Outdoor Seasons, 1141
Outdoor Voices, 511, 761, 816, 1530
Outdoorsy, 204, 205, 1323
Outer Bay, 757
OuterBay, 1626
Outfit, 745
Outfittery, 2829, 2838, 2841
Outfox AI, 934
Outlast, 591
Outlast Technologies, 1769
Outlaw, 317
Outlier, 4, 741, 941, 1563, 1758
Outlook Group, 1234
Outlyer, 235
Outmatch, 432
OutMathc, 383
Outokumpu Oyj, 2990
Outplay Entertainment, 3032
Outpost Games, 60
Outpost Medicine, 782, 1778, 1941
Outreach, 751, 773, 777, 1154, 1184, 2280
OutreachCircle, 934
Outrigger, 1738
Outrigger Energy, 1278, 1326
Outrigger Media, 1730
Outright, 1663
Outschool, 1527
Outside Intelligence, 2131
Outside The Classroom, 1665
Outsmart Ltd, 2770
Outsolve, 746

1388

Portfolio Companies Index

Outsourcing Services Group, 869
Outspark, 590, 1771
OutStart, 314, 520, 1672, 1702
OutSystems, 2717
Outsystems, 3048
OUTtv Network, 2258
Outvote, 934
Outward, 1218
Outward Hound, 1049
OUYA, 1184
Ova Science, 1519
Oval Technologies, 2590
OvaScience, 1145, 1812
Ovation Logistics, 2107
Ovelin, 1860
Overcast Media, 85
Overclock Labs, 564
Overdog, 282
Overlake Capital, 1061
Overland, 274
Overland Container Transportation Services, 2218
Overland Solutions, 1301
Overlap, 814
Overlay Media, 2892
Overlay.tv, 2262
Overnight, 228, 561
Overseas Dragon China, 1139, 2946
Oversee.net, 1360
Oversi, 3221
OverSi Networks, 2662
Oversi Networks, 2566
Oversight Systems, 58, 852, 1672, 1673
Overstat, 1028
Overtime, 124, 544, 977, 1613
Overton's, 194
Overtone, 23
Overture, 876, 946, 1389, 1888
Overture Networks, 835, 1008, 1257, 1515, 1796, 2427
Overture Services, 502
Overture Technologies, 1133, 1299
Ovetime, 13
OVGuide, 228
Ovia Health, 1118
Oviinbyrd Forest, 2172
Oviinbyrd Golf Club, 2172
OVO Mobile, 3023
Ovuline, 1097, 1118, 2943
Ovum Hospitals, 1346
OWCP Pharmaceutical Research, 1079
Owen Equipment Holdings, 1492
Owensboro Grain, 61
Owera, 2369
OWIT Global, 1577
Owl, 45
Owl AI, 1613
Owl Analytics, 532
Owl Cameras Inc., 1069
Owl Cybersecurity, 1152
Owl Manor Veterinary, 658
Owler, 1346, 1853
Owlet, 79, 679, 724
Owlet Baby Care, 648
Owliance, 2521
Owlized, 1061
Own, 797
OWN POS, 742
Own Products, 1305
OwnBackup, 1000, 1607
OwnCloud, 710
ownCloud, 534
OwnEnergy, 533, 1420
Owner Listens, 1489
OwnerIQ, 38, 534, 695, 1065, 1146, 1172, 1734
Ownershipp, 307
OwnLocal, 231, 1110

OwnThePlay, 981
Ownza, 1226
OWYN, 500
Oxagen, 1268
Oxagen Limited, 1628
Oxane, 466
Oxane Materials, 2700
Oxatis, 3020
Oxbow Carbon, 559
Oxford Advanced Surfaces, 2892
Oxford BioMedica, 2662
Oxford Cannabinoid Technologies, 417
Oxford Catalysts, 2892
Oxford Collection Agenecy, 1745
Oxford Diffraction, 3195
Oxford Finance, 1972
Oxford Health Plans, 209, 1835
Oxford Immunotec, 495, 2662, 2674, 2858, 3070
Oxford Immunotec Ltd, 2894
Oxford Performance Materials, 678
Oxford RF Sensors, 2892
OxfordPV, 3028
Oxid Esales, 2932
Oxide, 648
Oximeter Plus, 3267
Oxis Energy, 3107
Oxlo, 142
Oxlo Systems, 1592
OxOnc Development, 1382
Oxonica, 2492
Oxord Immunotec, 1298
Oxsensis, 2295, 2967
Oxtex, 2997, 3028
OxThera, 2851
OxThera AB, 2816
OxTox, 3107
Oxtox, 2892
OXX, 981
Oxygen, 1138
Oxygen Media, 494
Oxynade, 2426
Oxyntix, 2892
Oxyrane, 1303, 2748, 2978
Oxysure Systems, 1915
Oy 4Pharma Ltd, 2716
Oy Plusdial Ab, 2873
Oy Stinghorn, 2873
Oy Wireless Media Finland, 2873
Oyo, 2936
OYO Sportstoys, 38
Oyster Point Pharma, 1928
Oyster.com, 32, 221
OZ Communications, 51, 1906
OZ Holding, 2922
Ozd Industrial Park, 2635
Ozmo, 852
Ozmo Devices, 1779, 2443
Ozon, 483
Ozon.ru, 641, 1459, 2829, 2838
Ozonator, 1532
Ozone Media Solutions, 2849
OzSonotek, 3248
Ozvision, 2462
Ozz Electric, 3252
Ozzy, 1323

P

P&A, 1599
P&H Solutions, 1770
P&R Dental Strategies, 1293
P-Com, 856
P-Cube, 823, 833
P.A. Semi, 1916
P.F. Chang's, 1516, 1853
P.M. Power Group Inc., 2136
P1.CN, 3013
P2 Science, 660

P2Binvestor, 1211
P2i, 2967
P3 Logistic Parks, 1835
P4RC, 1965
P97, 2106
PA Semi, 757
PacBio, 762
Pace, 493
Pace Analytical, 199
Pacer Electronics, 1770
Pacfic World, 1491
Pachyderm, 770, 1758
Pacific & Cutler, 274
Pacific Architects and Engineers, 1129
Pacific Biosciences, 87, 634, 1247, 1760
Pacific Biosciences of California, 581
Pacific Brands, 2643
Pacific Catch, 334
Pacific Coast Publishing, 2150
Pacific Coffee (Holdings) Limited, 2402
Pacific College of Oriental Medicine, 1504
Pacific Communications Sciences, 1706
Pacific Construction, 973
Pacific Crest, 374
Pacific Design, 2854
Pacific DirectConnect, 939
Pacific Edge Software, 753
Pacific GMP, 1915
Pacific Handy Cutter, 1111
Pacific Interpreters, 1909
Pacific Island Resources, 939
Pacific Island Restaurants Inc., 334
Pacific Light Technologies, 1383
Pacific Mandarin Assets Ltd., 2788
Pacific Paper, 1609
Pacific Pharmacy Group, 1396
Pacific Pools, 1751
Pacific Print Group, 2410
Pacific Rim Palm Oil, 2337
Pacific Shoring, 960, 1609
Pacific Star Communications, 753
Pacific Sunwear, 839
Pacific Wave Systems, 1111
Pacific West Land, 1061
Pacific Western Bank, 3272
Pacific World Corporation, 1111
Pacificflight Catering, 2664
Paciolan, 161
Pacira Pharmaceuticals, 1268, 1616
Packagd, 761, 1075
Packaging Concepts & Design, 1232
Packaging Coordinators, 867, 1817
Packaging Corporation of America, 1156
Packaging Dynamics, 1081
Packaging Plus LLC, 449
Packers Holdings LLC, 914
Packers Provision, 63
Packet, 603, 1611
Packet Design, 1175, 1597
Packet Island, 306, 612, 807
Packeteer, 1378
PacketExchange, 2662
Packetexchange, 2674
Packetfront, 3179
PacketFrpont, 2386
PacketHop, 798
PacketMotion, 187, 2196
PacketSled, 285
Packettrap, 197
PacketVideo, 1704
PacketZoom, 231
PackExpo.com, 1227
PackLate, 814
PackLink, 2339
Pacon Corp., 1171
PacStar, 457
Pact, 2972

1389

Portfolio Companies Index

Pact Apparel, 3277
Pact Pharma, 762
Pactas, 2441, 3239
Pactera, 823
Pactolus Communications, 521
Pactolus Communications Software, 1227
PactSafe, 658, 1155, 1206
Padcom, 1116
Paddle8, 1263, 1998
Paddock Pools Patios & Spas, 1067
Padhaaro, 3174
PADI, 1127, 2034, 2046
Padlet, 1527
Padlock Therapeutics, 191, 1043
Paetec International, 514
Paga, 1374, 2345
Pagatech, 55
Pagaya, 3221
PagePlanner, 2369
Pager. Pinscreen, 1151
PagerDuty, 2012
Pagerduty, 124, 231, 1761, 1968
PageScience, 431
PageUp, 235
PageVamp, 622
PAGEVAULT, 1155
PageVault, 1019
Pagineer, 3181
Paging Network of Canada, 982
Pague Menos, 815
Pahteon Inc., 63
PAI Erope V LP, 2094
Pai+, 973
PAICE, 19
Paid Piper, 301
Paidos Health Management Services, 955
Paidy, 148
Paige, 1861
Pain Doctor, 1088
Pain Therapeutics, 187
Painless, 984
PainReform, 3241
Painting by Nakasone, 1233
PaintZen, 1518
Paintzen, 128, 295, 358, 586, 707, 1110, 1322, 1530
PAION, 2463
Pair, 15
PairGain Technology, 1918
Pairingo, 3051
Pajarito Powder, 1924
Paju Yangju Tongil Village Co., 584
Paketin, 2527
Pako Bay, 2889
PakSense, 85
PAL, 1850
Paladin Capital Group, 3270
Paladin Cyber, 877, 1118
Paladin Ethanal Acquistion, 1400
Paladina Health, 94
Palamida, 1241, 1952
Palantir, 775, 802, 836, 851, 2000
Palantir Technologies, 979, 1593
Palatin, 1941
Palatin Technologies Inc., 946
Palette, 2113
Palisade, 344
Palladian, 1751
Palladio, 1335
Palladium Group, 1248
Palleon Pharmaceuticals, 1731, 1778
PalletOne Inc., 694
Palletways, 3036
Palliser Estate, 2664
Palm, 249, 659, 1760
Palm Beach Tan, 16
Palm Commerce, 1087

Palm Commerce Holdings, 3062
Palm Inc., 947
Palmax, 3218
Palmers, 2293
Palmetto, 1110
Palmetto Exchange, 1219
Palms Casino Resort, 1109
Palo Alto, 1341
Palo Alto Health Sciences, 138
Palo Alto Networks, 1796
Paloalto, 968
Paloma Partners IV, 672
Palomar Specialty, 819
Palringo, 690
Palvella Therapeutics, 266
Palyon, 2496
Palyon Medical, 157
Pameco Corp., 1134
Pamira, 1493
Pamyra, 2527
Panache Ventures, 2032
Panacos, 118, 1241, 1412
Panalpina, 2922
Panasas, 441, 757, 1247, 1348
Panaseer, 483
Panasonic, 214
Panaya, 2813
Pancetera, 1378
Pancon, 1234
Panda Security, 2443
Panda Whale, 721
PandaDoc, 100, 1154
PandaPay, 622
Pandion, 1928
Pandion Therapeutics, 1731
Pando, 1110
Pando Daily, 229
Pando Logic, 3221
Pando Networks, 2541
Pandoodle, 1923
Pandora, 563, 595, 807, 823, 922, 1952
Pandora Media, 1445, 1646
Pandora Media Inc., 1089
Pandora.TV, 100, 596
Pangaea Ventures, 2492
Pangea, 471, 731, 1046, 1364
Pangea World Corporation, 506
PanGenetics, 3020
Pangenetics, 2748
PanGeo Subsea, 466, 2700
Panhandle Oilfield, 164
Panhandle Oilfield Service Companies, 1605
Panjiva, 1584
Panjo, 1222, 1715
Pankaku, 2646
Panlabs International, 753
Panmira, 206
Panna, 60, 132, 1099, 1110, 1183, 1634
Panomics, 12, 237, 2419
Panopta, 745
Panoptic Security, 1070, 2382
PanOptica, 1628, 1811
Panopticon, 1646
Panopto, 1261, 1623
Panorama, 1968
Panorama Education, 1392, 1700, 1879
Panoramic Power, 2900
Panoratio Database Images, 3046
PANOS Brands, 931
PANOS Brands LLC, 900
Pantech & Curitel, 1087
Pantero, 608
PanTerra Networks, 129
Pantex International, 1937
Pantheon, 231, 741, 751, 776, 1380
Pantheon Ventures, 3255
Panther, 13, 3100

Panther Capital, 1135
Panther Expedited, 722
Panther Expedited Services, 2015
Panther Labs, 1138
Pantry, 552, 1634
Panvideo, 608
Panviva, 2975, 3151
Panzura, 466, 1181, 1212, 1381
Pap, 2306
Papa Johns, 894
Papa Murphy's, 456
Papa Murphy's International, 1104
Papaya, 596, 728, 972
Paper and Tea, 2841
Paper Battery Company, 1876
Paper G, 1097
Paper House Productions, 1157
Paper Machinery Corp., 577
Paper Source, 334, 1017
Paper.li, 3045
Paper.li/Smallrivers, 1699
Paperchase, 2796
Paperless, 1593, 2455
Paperless Post, 1666
Paperlit, 2403
Papernest, 2851
PaperSpace, 318
Paperspace, 799, 994, 1150
PaperWorks, 1753
Papillon D'Or, 2426
Paprika, 721
Papyrus, 2384
PAR, 2965
Par Accel, 1780
Par Pharmaceutical, 1452, 1835
Par Pharmaceutical Companies, 2379
PAR3, 1733
Parable Health, 622
Parabola, 1218
Parachute, 342, 754, 1099, 1222, 1758, 1888
Parachute Health, 1000
Paracosm, 600
Parade, 229, 2436, 2936
Paradigm, 1041, 2207, 3137
Paradigm B.V., 778
Paradigm Capital, 3265
Paradigm Genetics, 1008
Paradigm Group, 1343
Paradigm Healthcare Corporation, 955
Paradigm Management Services, 1123
Paradigm Packaging, 1132, 1456
Paradigm Spine, 1844
Paradigm Tax Group, 1572
Paradigm Therapeutics, 2463
Paradigm4, 841, 1065, 1673, 1757, 2652
Paradise Electronics, 197
Paradise Rentals, 1764
Paradromics, 799
Paragen Bio, 3023
Parago, 1314, 1804
Paragon, 392, 530, 1603, 2676, 3249
Paragon Bioservices, 383
Paragon Development Systems, 1171
Paragon Energy Solution, 164
Paragon Films, 1971
Paragon Medical, 97
Paragon Networks International, 1038
Paragon Products, 378
Paragon Robotics, 1047
Paragon Technology, 958
Parakey, 231, 1359
ParaLife, 855
Paraline Group, 1955
Parallaz Capital Partners LLC, 161
Parallel, 3221
Parallel Domain, 547, 1834, 1877
Parallel Geometry, 1437

Portfolio Companies Index

Parallel Products, 1820
Parallel Universe, 2872
Parallel Wireless, 751
Parallel49 Equity, 2167
ParAllele, 115, 1247
Parallels, 89, 1000, 1625
Paramit, 97
Paramount Healthcare, 406
Paramount Hotels, 2361
Paramount Services, 468
Paranet, 196
Parasut, 1560, 3078
Paratek, 23, 74, 1169, 1348, 2815
Paratek Microwave, 979, 1257
Paratek Pharmaceuticals, 2518, 3007
Paratinova.com, 1099
Parature, 1133, 1899
PARC, 214
Parca Deposu, 2294
Parcel, 858, 1115
ParcelGenie, 2760
Parchment, 1348, 1608, 2080
Parcours, 2448
Parcxmart, 649
ParElastic, 534
Parelastic, 1097, 1734
Parella, 2851
Parental Health, 995
Parenthoods, 1115
ParentMedia, 871
Parento, 684
Parents.com, 724
Pareto Health, 857
Parexel, 312
Parian Capital Corporation, 2258
Parian Logistics, 2258
Paribus, 535, 770
ParinGenix, 1543
Paris Presents, 1171, 1960
Paris RE, 924
Paris Re Holdings, 1301
Paris Saclay Fund, 483
Paris Town, 1752
Parisa Group, 2644
Parish Publishing Solutions, 1963
Parisian Inc., 575
Parity, 2041
Park & Diamond, 1894
Park Cake, 1937
Park Foods, 1435
Park Place, 456
Park Place Technologies, 1824, 1979
Park Resorts, 2617
Park Scientific, 1087
Parkalgar, 3048
Parkdean Resorts, 2209
Parker, 1753
ParkiFi, 876
Parkifi, 377
Parking Company America, 374
Parklet, 1747
Parkloco, 1100
ParkMe, 126, 760, 1563
Parkmobile, 760
Parko, 1716
Parkway Products, 401
Parkway Properties, 1835
ParkWhiz, 222, 962, 1046
Parlano, 1146
ParLevel, 445
Parliament Pointe, 2285
Parmaco Oy, 2937
Paro, 1555
Parrable, 582
Parrot, 3113
Parsable, 741
Parse, 585

Parse.ly, 301, 724
Parsec, 243, 1110, 1829
Parsegon, 622
Parsely, 876
Parsley Health, 1613
ParStream, 223, 585
PART Point, 678
Partake Foods, 218
Partech, 483
Partech International, 3284
Partenaires Livres, 2607
Partender, 1595, 1998
Parterre Flooring Systems, 1040
Particle, 306, 1509
Particle Dynamics, 653
Partify, 1507
Partner Communications, 1598
Partnered, 1749
Partnerpedia Solutions, 2053
PartnerRe, 559
Partners in Leadership Inc., 900
Partpic, 150
Parts Authority, 1045
Parts Market, 708
Parts Town, 254
Partsearch Technologies, 1745
PartsSource, 857, 1476
Partssource, 1460
PartStore, 1680
PartTec, 658
Party City, 1815
Party Packagers, 2051
PartySlate, 896
PAS International Holdings, 77
PAS Technologies, 873, 1086
Pascal Metrics, 617
Pascal's Pocket Corporation; Social Fabric Corpora, 715
Pashas, 1516
Passage AI, 4
Passage Bio, 1928
Passageways, 745
Passave, 2541
Passave Technologies, 2720, 3231
Passbase, 679, 1890
PasseiDireto, 641
Passmark Security, 613
Passport, 876, 1138, 1242
Passport Corporation, 455
Passport Food Group, 1969
Passport Health Communications, 1717
Passport Systems, 520
Passport Systems Inc., 144
PassRight, 30
Passworks, 3048
Pasta Chips, 668
Pastair, 2449
Pastceram, 3048
Pasteuria Bioscience, 61
Patagonia BioEnergia, 1573
Patara Pharma LLC, 487
Patch, 795
Patch Products, 1832
Path, 231, 609, 1323, 1663
Path Ex, 995
Path Intelligence, 1359
Path Scale, 95
Path-Tec, 794
Pathable, 85
PathAI, 816
Pathbrite, 1551
PathFactory, 2168
Pathfinder Health Innovations, 496, 718
Pathfinder Technologies, 915
Pathfinder Therepeutics, 1261
Pathfire, 69
Pathgather, 533

PathGroup, 1166, 1271, 1476
Pathlight, 432
Pathlight Technologies, 1918
Pathlight Technology, 954
Pathmatics, 228, 256, 306, 1055, 1888
PathogenDx, 99, 1610
PathoGenetix, 176
Pathology, 22
PathoQuest, 2851
PathScale, 455, 466
Pathsenors, 1169
Pathsensors, 285
PathSource, 1958
PathSpot, 728
PathStream, 1551
Pathway, 1094
Pathway Diagnostics, 237
Pathway Medical Technologies, 2748
Pathwork Diagnostics, 1354, 1915
Patient Connect Service Limited, 2981
Patient Education Media Inc., 447
Patient Engagement Systems, 786
Patient Innovations, 3267
Patient Safe Solutions, 383
PatientCo, 1615
Patientco, 29
PatientKeeper, 94, 1197
PatientPing, 710, 741
Patientping, 124
PatientPoint, 1088, 2252
Patients Know Best, 2478
PatientSafe, 2265
Patientsafe, 2690
PatientSafe Solutions, 1205, 1498, 1600
Patientsafe Solutions, 933
Patreon, 38, 1323, 1883
patreon, 991
Patrick Hackett Hardware Company, 1639
Patriot Capital, 3265
Patriot Environmental Services, 126, 1636
Patriot Media, 1724
Patriot National Bancorp, 1730
Patriot Storage, 1573
PatriotOne Technologies, 2200
Pattern Energy Group, 1573
Pattern Insight, 1921
Pattern89, 1019
PatternEx, 1069
Patton Surgical Corp., 810
Paul Fabs, 48
Paul Fredrick, 501
PaulaBs Choice, 257
Paulee Cleantec, 3245
Pavilion Data, 174
Pavilion Medical Innovations, 426
Pavilion Technologies, 734
Paviliondata, 1075
Pavlok, 981
Pavlov, 622
PAVmed, 1983
Pavève, 1623
Pawngo, 36, 594, 1118
Paxar Corp., 300
Paxata, 483, 1154, 1829, 2690
Paxata Inc., 1951
Paxos, 1115
PaxVax, 974
Pay Off, 858
Pay With My Bank, 2478
Pay-O-Matic, 1516
Pay-O-Matic Corporation, 774
Payable, 784
PayasUgym, 2972
paybright, 2070
PayByGroup, 1716
Paycom, 1972
Paycor Inc., 135

1391

Portfolio Companies Index

PayCycle, 596, 1863
Paycycle, 197
PayDay One, 2457
Paydiant, 1334, 1734
Paydici, 1383
PayEase, 506
Payer Compass, 918, 1717
PayFone, 1593
Payfone, 1381, 1926, 2236
Payformance, 1745
PayGo, 1810
Paygo Energy, 2439
PayJoy, 942
Payjoy, 525, 1882
PayK12, 658
PayKey, 641
PayKii, 179
PayLease, 779
Payless, 839
Payless ShoeSource, 300
Payleven, 2829, 2838
PayLink Payment Plans, 1234
Paylocity, 57
Paymap, 1251
Payment America Systems, 678
Paymentus, 29
Paymetric, 779
Paymetrics, 1407
Paymill, 301, 2829, 2838, 3149
PayNearMe, 358, 547, 1069, 1860
Paynearme, 197
Payoff, 743, 1716, 2406
Payoneer, 1306, 1759, 2566, 3221
PayPal, 296, 502, 1156
Paypal, 115
PayPerks, 596, 2406
Payperks, 1306
PayPlug, 2329
PayRock Energy, 672
Paysafe, 779
PaysafeCard.com, 2783
PayScale, 1853
Payscale, 753
PaySimple, 548, 695, 1759
PaySpan, 22
Payspan, 938
Paystack, 2329
PayStand, 454
Paystream, 22
Paysys, 402
PaySys International Inc., 693
Paytrail Oyj, 2966
Paytronix Systems Inc., 857
Paywhere, 3073
Payzer, 51, 876
Pazoo, 1079
PB Works, 1247
PBA, 2936
PBF Pita Bread Factory, 147
PBV Partners, 277
PBWorks, 1655, 1958
PC Depot Corp, 2907
Pc Dir, 2664
PC Helps, 439
PC On Call, 2652
PC-Soft, 2452
PCC Technology, 530
PCH International, 560, 757, 1346, 1846
PChem, 653
PCI Biotech, 2519
PCI Holding Corporation, 1493
PCI Pharma Services, 782
PCIX, 287
PCl Group, 2616
PCN Network, 1422
PCX Aerostructures, 1557
PD Services Ltd, 2306

PDC Brands, 1109
PDHI, 1285
PDI, 819
PDJ Group, 2944
PDQ South Texas, 224
PDR Network, 1104
PDS Biotechnology, 658
PDSHeart, 224
pdv Wireless, 1344
PDV-Systeme, 2527
Peach, 668, 1100, 1158, 1183
Peach Works, 86, 171
Peachtree Business Products, 683
PeachWorks, 961
Peachy, 325
Peacock Engineering Company, 245
Peacock Foods, 456
PEAK Broadcasting, 378
Peak Builders, 678
Peak Games, 2837
Peak Power, 2187
PEAK Sports, 2936
PEAK Surgical, 1916
Peak Timbers, 834
Peak Ventures, 3276
Peak Well Systems, 1752
Peak10, 1972
Peakon, 2478
Peanut Labs, 641
PeanutPress, 954
Peanutpress.Com, 847
Peapod, 247
Pear, 493, 724
Pear Therapeutics, 12, 149, 2690
Pearfection, 2979
Pearl, 12, 495, 959
Pearl Capital, 404
Pearl Hydrogen, 1340
Pearl Izumi, 765
Pearl Meyer & Partners, 374
Pearlchain.net, 2949
Pearlman Industries Inc., 908
Pears Portfolio, 2792
Pearson's, 357
Peate Institute for Entrepreneurs, 3268
Pebble, 455
Pebble Post, 1070
PebblePost, 946, 2182
Pebblepost, 724
Pebby, 1507
PECA Labs, 293
PECH, 584
PECO Pallet, 1242, 1479, 1745, 1954
Pecora Corporation, 832
Pedalite, 2574
Pedestal Networks, 596
Pediatria, 1230
Pediatric Health Choice, 503
Pediatrix Medical Group Inc., 300
Pedidos Ya, 2446
Peek, 707, 858, 896
Peekk Travel, 1323
Peel, 231, 1054, 1534, 1838
Peel Away Labs, 1310
Peel-Works, 1013
Peeled Snacks, 1905
Peepoople, 3277
Peer, 625
Peer 1, 439
Peer IQ, 1258
Peer Medical, 2726
Peer39, 592
Peeractive, 1577
PeerApp, 436, 1752, 2580, 2726
PeerIndex, 2406, 2407
Peerj, 1359
Peerless Industrial Group, 1979

Peerless Network, 695
Peerless Networks, 57
Peerlyst, 976
PeerMedical, 2324
PeerNova, 623
PeerNova Inc., 810
Peerspace, 1749
PeerStreet, 124, 720, 1282
peerTransfer, 1502, 1715
PeerView, 1203
Peespace, 770
PEG, 2439
Peg, 55
Pegasense, 1589
Pegasus, 29, 3249
Pegasus Solar, 1371
Pegasus Solutions, 300
Pegasus Technologies Ltd., 2954
Pegasus TransTech, 415
PegEx, 400
Peixeurbano, 2976
PEKU Publications, 1958
Pelagicore, 2755
Pelamis, 2295
Pelamis Wave Power, 520
Pelham Homes, 2985
Pelican, 2348
Pelican AutoFinance, 750
Pelican Imaging, 835, 979, 1010
Pelican Products, 245, 1491
Pelican Water Systems, 1857
Pelion Venture Partners, 3276
Pellepharm, 709
Pellet Systems International, 2049
Pellion, 1069, 1260
Peloton, 272, 319, 325, 762, 823, 909, 1075, 1088, 1865
Peloton Computer Enterprises, 2275
Peloton Technology, 1613
Peloton Therapeutics, 517
Pelss, 1990
Pelvalon, 1347
Pemba Sun and Mozwood, 834
PEMCO, 1753
Peminic, 954
Pen.io, 1254
PenAndFree, 3127
PenBay Solutions, 438, 1161
Penblade, 1070
Pencil, 243
Penda Corporation, 1134
PendaForm, 1545
PenDataSoft, 1607
Pendo, 235, 533, 971, 1212, 1607
Pendo.io, 538, 560
Pendulab, 1681
Pendum, 928
Penederm, 1378
Penguin Computing, 1677
Penhaigon's, 778
Penhall International Inc., 354
Peninsula, 1251
Peninsula Energy, 1548
Peninsula Packaging Company, 1368
Peninsula Pharmaceuticals, 595, 1412
Peninsula Ventures, 3284
Penlon, 97
Penn Warranty Corporation, 378
PennAlt Organics Inc., 987
Pennant Foods Corp., 348, 1372
Pennant Sp, 1533
PennEnergy Resources, 672
PennTech Machinery Corporation, 908
Penny, 1696
Penrice, 2622
Penrice Soda Products, 3178
Penrose Landfill Gas Conversion LLC, 1895

1392

Portfolio Companies Index

PenSimple, 392
Penta Securities Systems, 892
Pentaho, 581, 634, 1235
Pentalum, 436, 2315, 2726
Pentec Health, 782, 1345
Pentech, 1633
Pentheon, 1626
Penthera Partners, 998
Penton Media, 1231, 1960
Pentzer Corporation, 1295
People, 807
People Data Labs, 1758
People Matter, 1626
People Pattern, 1247
People Power, 1655
People Support, 180
People's Motor International, 1769
People.ai, 890
People.co, 1546, 1998
PeopleAdmin, 1752
Peopleclick, 242, 1148
PeopleCube, 2837
PeopleGrove, 883, 1527
PeopleLinx, 871, 1387
PeopleMater, 1257
PeopleMatter, 85, 1008, 1331, 1738
PeopleSupport, 502
PeopleTec, 1533
PEP Industries, 1279
Pepcom GmbH, 1927
Pepe Jeans, 1088
Peplin, 1268
Pepo, 544
Pepper Dining, 1372
Pepper Hamilton, 3275
PepperBall Technologies, 69
PepperData, 107, 547, 1678
Pepperdata, 1254, 1968
Pepperdata Networks, 486
Pepperfry, 1346
Pepperjam, 227
Pepperlane, 1100
Peppermint Technology, 29
Peppers & Rogers, 1003
Peptech, 1543
Pepticom, 3245
Peptilogics, 293
Peptor, 3231
Peptron, 2857
Peracon, 526
Peraso, 2128, 2157
Peraso Technologies, 2076, 2242
Peraton, 1925
PerBlue, 1118
Perceive 3D, 3048
Percello, 852
PerceptiMed, 644, 1094, 1303
Perception Software, 445
Perceptive Automata, 741, 1834
Perceptive Navigation, 19
Perceptive Pixel, 979
Perceptive Software, 1255
Perch, 307
Percipient.ai, 1916
Percolata, 519, 1055, 1595, 1758, 1809, 1983
percolata, 612
Percolate, 60, 741, 823, 1110, 1694, 1839
Percona, 826
Percsys, 1251
PercuSurge, 1786
Percutaneous Systems, 524
Peregrine Semiconductor, 1257, 1288, 1402
Peregrine Semiconductor, 1314
Perennial Energy, 399
Perennial Energy LLC, 1053
Perennials and Sutherland LLC, 257
PerfAction, 3059

Perfect Commerce, 592
Perfect Company, 1383
Perfect Fit, 1134
Perfect Point, 1061
Perfect Sense, 416
Perfect Timing, 1753
PerfectMarket, 1853
Perfecto, 793, 3221
Perfecto Mobile, 835, 2566, 3214
PerfectServce, 1571
Perfectus Biomed, 2967
Perferred Pet Care, 1730
Perfint, 1346
Perfint Healthcare, 2849
Perforce Software, 500
Perform, 34
Performance, 2015
Performance Assessment Network Inc., 1724
Performance Bicycles, 1335
Performance Fabrics, 338
Performance Fibers, 1753
Performance Food, 277
Performance Food Group, 744, 1516, 1971
Performance Health, 873, 1156
Performance Health & Wellness, 353
Performance IQ, 235
Performance Logic, 847
Performance Plants, 2136
Performance Team Freight Systems Inc., 274
PerformanceRetail, 2079
Performant Financial Corporation, 1417
Performax Physical Therapy, 1228
Performics, 1057
PerformLine, 741
Performline, 1584
Peribit, 770
Pericom Technology, 2457
PeriGen, 806, 1608, 1850
Perimeter eSecurity, 1863
Perimeter Internetworking, 1191
Perimeter Labs, 1011
Perimeter Medical Imaging, 2242
Perimter Protection Group, 3054
Periodical, 1099
PeriOptimum, 998
PeriRx, 266
Periscope, 707, 771, 1183, 1218, 1758
Periscope Data, 128, 295, 609
Periscope Equity, 14
Periscope Holdings, 1417
Peritus AI, 1809
Perk Health, 1872
Perkbox, 2674
Perkin Elmer, 1295
Perkins & Marie Callender's, 1970
Perkins Coie, 3272
Perkins Restaurant & Bakery, 1967
Perl Street, 1894
Perlan Therapeutics, 1706
Perlara, 1238
Perlara PBC, 1694
Perlegen, 2513, 2690
Perlego, 85, 553
Permacharge Corp, 210
Permanent General Company Inc., 404
Permasense, 2858
Permatec, 1452
Permeon Biologics, 153
Permeon Biologics, 747
Permian Tank & Manufacturing, 1573
Permlight, 69
Permutation, 858
Pernix Therapeutics, 74, 1134
Pernix Therapeutics Holdings, 188
Peronetics, 3221
Perora GmbH, 2686
Perosphere Inc., 530

Perpetua, 535
Perpetual Ventures, 3276
Perpetuum, 2892, 3028, 3070
Perquest, 1730, 1738
Perricone MD, 1861
Persado, 221, 486, 646
Persante, 1343
Persante Health Care, 910
PerSe, 541
Persea Bio, 1812
Persephone Biome, 870, 1758
Perseus Proteomics, 2970
Persian Acceptance Corp., 2254
Persianas, 2337
Persio, 1384
Persist Technologies, 626
Persistence Data Mining, 995
Persistence Software, 1288
Persistent Sentinel, 2450
Persistent Systems, 805
Persivia, 938
Persona, 668, 2079
Personal Capital, 544, 563, 1001, 1046, 1916
Personal Genome Diagnostics, 19, 1169, 1993
Personal Medsystems, 3113
Personal Wine, 950
Personali, 436, 1346
Personalis, 1247
Personalized Media, 1375
PersonalPath Systems, 1986
Personetics, 2566
Personify, 106, 975, 1409
PerspecSys, 1400
Perspecta, 1925
Perspica, 1809
Perstorp, 3026
Persystent Enterprise, 990
Pertemps Network Group, 2944
Pervacio, 1142, 1940
Pervasis, 747
Pesanlab, 721
Pestana Berlin, 3048
Pet 360, 1136
Pet Center Comercio and Participacoes S.A., 1956
Pet IQ, 79
Pet Loss Center, 378
Pet Love, 2976
Pet Smart, 1970
Pet Supermarket, 1576, 2219
Pet Valu, 1576
Pet's Choice, 753
Pet360, 1886
Petal, 24, 351, 858, 1585, 1613
PetaSense, 720
Petcircle.com.au, 779
Petco Animal Supplies, 1109, 1835
PetCoach, 1183
Petcube, 89
PetDesk, 387
Pete Health, 120
Peter Butz, 2810
Peter Geeson Ltd., 2657
Peter Tosh, 1135
Peterhouse Group, 2985
Petermann Bus Co., 843
Petersen Companies, 1986
Petersen Pet Provisions, 1745
Peterson Party Center, 632
PetHub, 1061
Petkit, 823
Petmate, 1372, 1990
Petmatrics LLC, 788
PetMedicus Laboratories, 1777
Petnet, 69, 874, 1097, 1716
Petra Pharma, 6, 31
Petra Solar, 2717

1393

Portfolio Companies Index

Petra Systems, 171, 657
Petrecycle, 2975
Petro Harvester, 1835
Petro Shopping Centers, 368
PetroChoice, 1086
PetroChoice Holdings Inc., 862
PetroCloud, 542
Petroleum Service Corporation, 199
PetroLiance, 1270
PetroLogistics, 1129
Petroplus Holdings, 1573
PetroSkills, 361
PetroStreamz, 3216
Petrotank, 156
Petrowest Energy Services Trust, 2091
Petrus Resources, 1278, 1326
PetsDx Imaging, 998
Petsense, 1999
PETsys Electronics, 3048
PetVet Care Centers, 1088
Pevion Biotech, 2496
Pevonia, 1861
Pex, 567, 976, 1758
PEX Card, 196, 299, 1306, 2157
Pexco, 901, 1368
PF Baseline Fitness, 783
PF Group, 3203
Pfingsten Publishing, 897, 1435
Pfizer, 1096
Pfizer Inc., 1349
Pflegeplatz-manager, 2527
PFP Cybersecurities, 285
PGI International, 654
PGOA Media, 221, 1660
PGP, 596
phanfare, 215
Phantom Fireworks, 577
PhantomAlert, 1734
PhantomCyber, 770
Pharm Akea Therapeutics, 237
Pharm-Olam, 1505
Pharma 73, 3048
Pharma Diagnostics, 2366
Pharma Engineering, 3107
Pharma Logic, 853
Pharma Marketing Ltd., 1372
Pharmaca, 1438
Pharmaca Integrate Pharmacy, 935
PharmAcbine, 1382
Pharmaceutic Litho & Label Company, 1021, 1624
Pharmaceutical SymBio, 3006
Pharmacie Lafayette, 2851
Pharmacopeia, 206
Pharmacy Partners, 1963
PharmAdva, 704
Pharmadyne, 314
PharmaEste, 3052
PharmaFluidics, 3065
Pharmagen Healthcare Ltd., 55
Pharmagest Interactive, 3069
PharmaNetics, 1008
Pharmanex, 237, 2733
Pharmaq, 3033
PharmArc Analytics, 2490
PharmaResearch, 468
Pharmaron, 74, 596, 2936
PharmaSecure, 855
Pharmasset, 1268
PharmaStem, 1044
Pharmatrin Ltd, 2554
Pharmawizard, 2403
Pharmaxis, 1349, 2618
Pharmetics, 1248
PHARMetrics, 1334
PharmHouse, 2071
Pharminax, 2892

Pharming, 1775
Pharmion, 237, 3007
Pharmitas, 85
PharmMD, 1261, 1572
Pharmos, 1044
Pharmright, 1923
PharmRight Corporation, 981
Pharsight, 1288, 1702
Phase Four, 93, 811
Phase Genomics, 2008
Phase One Consulting Group, 680
Phase Vision, 2400
PhaseBio, 915
PhaseBio Pharmaceuticals Inc., 182
Phasebridge, 502
Phaserx, 153
Phasor Solutions, 2967, 3018
PhatNoise, 807
PHC, 746, 1067, 2978
Phelps Industries, 849
Phemi, 2092, 2229
Phemi Health Systems, 2291
Phenex, 2638
Phenex Pharmaceuticals, 2932
Phenex Pharmaceuticals AG, 2713
Phenom TRM Cloud Platform, 1670
Phenome Networks, 3245
Phenometrix, 1244
Phenomic, 395
Phenomix, 2618, 3007
Phg, 871
Phi, 734
Phiar, 1346
Phil, 563, 761
Philadelphia Energy Solutions, 2329
Philadelphia Financial Group, 832
Phillips & Temro, 1166
Phillips & Temro Industries, 194
Phillips & Temro Industries Inc., 908
Phillips Energy Partners III, 672
Phillips Pet Food & Supplies, 64, 1815
Phillips Screw Company, 812, 1173
Phillips-Medisize Corporation, 1081
Philm, 823
Philo, 608, 708, 720, 754, 1334, 1613
Philoptics, 3098
Philz Coffee, 552, 650, 1752
Phish Labs, 1136
PhishLabs, 794
PhishMe, 1400
PhiSkin, 892
Phizzle, 69, 93
PHNS, 881
Phobos Corporation, 187
Phoenix, 631
Phoenix American Financial, 3272
Phoenix Aromas and Essential Oils, 812
Phoenix Brands, 1127
Phoenix Children's Academy, 194
Phoenix Energy Technologies, 69
Phoenix Exploration Company, 1573
Phoenix Health & Safety, 2967
Phoenix Innovations Corp., 2084
Phoenix Labs, 823, 1563
Phoenix Microsystems, 1708
Phoenix New Media, 2978
Phoenix Nuclear Labs, 1292, 2001
Phoenix S&T, 266
Phoenix Services LLC, 1372
Phonak, 2564
Phone.com, 724, 3274
Phone2Action, 635
Phonedeck, 2444
PhoneSpots, 1637
Phonespots, 563
Phonetic Systems, 2952
Phonetic Systems Ltd., 2750

Phonezoo Communications Inc., 1089
Phonio, 243
Phonofile, 2369
Phononic, 823, 1556, 1916
Phorest, 2355, 2522
Phoseon Technology, 753
Phosphonics, 3113
Phosphorus, 743
Photo Dynamic, 2155
PhotoBox, 867
Photobox, 1516
Photoboxm QD Vision, 935
Photochannel Networks, 2097
PhotoCreate, 2646
Photodigm, 524
PhotoKharma, 1306
Photolynx, 92
PhotoMania, 2952
Photon Dynamics Inc., 947
Photonic Bridges, 2936
Photonic Bridges Holdings, 3062
Photonic Devices, 1361
Photonic Technologies SAS, 1491
Photonics Applications, 530
PhotoniXnet Corporation, 2414
Photonyx, 3013
Photopharmica, 2892
PhotoPharmics, 1070
Photoshelter, 816
Photoswitch Biosciences, 1238
PhotoThera, 898
Photothera Inc., 371
Photronics, 865
Phrase Technologies, 455
Phreesia, 176, 695, 938, 1136, 1142, 1460, 1615, 1906
PHRQL, 1448
PHT, 312
Phthisis Diagnostics, 1442
Phu Nhuan Jewelry, 2961
Phunware, 445, 483, 781, 1597, 1965
PHX, 655
Phycal, 1047
Phychips, 3127
PhyFlex Networks, 162
Phylagen, 6, 570
Phylion Battery, 2936
Phyllom Bioproducts, 1600
Phylos, 1694
PHYND, 582
Phynd Technologies, 1556
Physcient, 293, 298, 971, 1097, 1845, 1923, 1988
Physical Property Testing, 235
Physical Rehabilitation Network, 1684
Physician IMS Control, 969
Physician Sales & Service, 1866
Physician Software Systems, 400
Physicians Dialysis, 1271
Physicians Endoscopy, 1062, 1409
Physicians Immediate Care, 1136
Physicians Pharmacy Alliance, 1572
PhysiciansNet.com, 163
Physics Ventures, 955
PhysiHome, 2943
Physio Control, 220
PhysIQ, 2229
physIQ, 2943
Phytel, 1460
Phytelligence, 2008
Phythea, 2448
Phyworks, 2348, 2662, 2674
Pi Charging, 776
Pi Therapeutics, 2229
Pi Variables, 1894
PI Worldwide, 812

1394

Portfolio Companies Index

Pi-Cardia, 2874
Pi-R Squared, 2324
Piab, 2384
PIADA Italian Street Food, 1088
Piaggio/Derbi Record, 2962
Piazza, 720, 1054
Pica, 563
Pica 8, 1241
Pica8, 1906
Picaboo, 385
Picanova, 3208
Picard, 744, 2379, 2497
Picarda Holdings Sdn. Bhd, 2958
Picarro, 581, 634, 757
Picasso Labs, 858
PicCollage, 784, 1513, 2010
Piccollage, 751
Pickie, 608, 1115, 1222
Pickit, 1154
Pickle Robot, 2280
Pickle Robot Co., 318
PICKUP, 293
Pickwick & Weller, 231
Picmonic, 387
PicMonkey, 1717
PicnicHealth, 858
Picoboo, 115
PicoCandy, 1965
PicoChip, 3047
Picochip, 2472, 3104
PicoLight, 455
Picolight, 536
PicoNetics, 1180
PicsArt, 1000
Pictarine, 1615
Pictela, 206
Pictoris, 2765
Picturelife, 471, 1715
PictureTel, 541
PictureTree, 2841
Pie, 1965
Pie Insurance, 49
Pieberry, 1607
Piece of Cake, 2646
Piedmont Aviation Services, 1570
Piedmont Candy Company, 1578
Piedmont Pharmaceuticals, 1442, 1915, 2618
Piedra Resources III, 672
Pienso, 679
Pier Systems, 85
Pierce, 3054
Piercom, 2336
PierianDx, 79
Pieris, 2748
Pieris AG, 1382, 2785
PIERIS Proteolab, 2312
Pierpoint Securities, 1743
Pierre Fabre, 1452
Pietro Rosa TBM, 77
PIFC, 2796
Pigeonly, 229, 1054
PiinPoint, 1282
Piio, 30
Pijon, 785
Pika Energy, 497, 1160, 1161
Pika Energy Inc., 438
Pike Electric Corporation, 1129
Pilgrim Software, 1745
Pillar Processing, 1777
Pillo, 266
Pillow, 79, 307, 707
PillPack, 38, 45, 771, 1202, 1694
Pillpack, 1789
Pilot, 776
Pilot Multimedia (M) Sdn Bhd, 3164
Pilot Software Inc., 803
Pilot Thomas Logistics, 1963

Pilotly, 218
Pin Drop Security, 1480
PIN Pharma, 1325, 1420
Pinarello, 1088
PINC Solutions, 947, 1760
Pindrop, 124, 560, 720, 820, 1001, 1031, 2690
Pindrop Security, 486, 1534, 1968
Pine Environmental Services, 1521
Piney Woods Resources, 1548
Ping, 741
Ping Communications, 2369
Ping Identity, 142, 609, 710, 1620, 1846
Ping Indentity, 1794
Ping++, 2439
Pingboard, 1685
Pinger, 581, 634, 1075
Pingg, 306
Pingora Asset Management, 1742
PingPad, 130
Pingpad, 751, 1390
PingStamp, 2984
PingThings, 306, 809
Pingup, 206
Pink.oi, 641
Pinkberry, 1183, 2254
Pinkgirls, 678
Pinkoi, 772
Pinnacle, 909, 2209
Pinnacle Automotive Hospitally, 383
Pinnacle Direct Marketing, 1954
Pinnacle Electronics, 1159
Pinnacle Energies, 1241
Pinnacle Engines, 988
Pinnacle Foods, 277
Pinnacle Medical Solutions, 1214
Pinnacle Renewable Energy, 2208
Pinnacle Security, 839
Pinnacle Treatment, 1491
Pinnacle Treatment Centers, 439, 812, 1128
Pinnacle Ventures, 3284
Pinova, 2204
Pinpoint, 305
Pinpoint Care, 1364
Pinpoint Software, 2001
Pinteon, 2978
Pinterest, 124, 623, 743, 802, 842, 1075, 1235, 1306, 1310, 1694, 1761
Pioneer Bank, 445
Pioneer Metal Finishing, 1469
Pioneer Recycling, 573
Pioneer Sand Company, 1039
Pioneer Square Labs, 262, 776, 1183
Pioneer Surgical Technology, 944
Pionyr Immunotherapeutics, 1238, 1628, 1932
Pipax Environment, 2857
Pipdrive, 2446
Pipe, 2479
PipeDrive, 295
Pipedrive, 128, 1000, 1540, 1747
Pipeline, 1928
Pipeline DB, 1798
Pipeline Integrity, 2556
Piper, 1392, 1527
Piper Aircraft, 616
Piper Bioscience, 20
Piper Inc., 593
Pipestem Energy Group, 1895
Pipilu, 1340
Pipp Mobile Storage Solutions, 443
Pippa Jean, 2829, 2838
PIQ, 89, 2296
Piqora, 100, 231, 2010
Pique Tea, 741
Pique Therapeutics, 840, 1442, 1988
Piqur, 1928
Pirate3D, 3073
PIRCH, 1088

Pirios, 3077
Pirtek, 894
Pirtek Europe, 1937
Pirus Networks, 455
Pisano, 2284
Pishoniac, 3127
Pisla Oy, 2966
Pison Technology, 622
Piston Cloud, 1860
Piston Cloud Computing, 585, 3152
Piston Enterprise OpenStack, 618
Pitango Venture Capital, 3284
Pitch Deck, 1509
PitchBook, 3272
PitchPoint Solutions, 2058
Pitchpoint Solutions, 2134
Pitstop, 2113, 2241
PittaRosso, 2293
PittMoss, 293
Pittsburgh Equity Partners, 3275
Pittsburgh Glass Works, 1081
Pittsburgh Iron Oxides, 998
Pittsburgh Life Sciences Greenhouse, 3275
Pittsburgh Technology Council, 3275
Pitzi, 754, 2872
Pivitol Health Solutions, 297
Pivot, 608, 626, 1010, 1699, 2196
Pivot Medical, 1251
Pivot North Capital, 37
Pivot Physical Therapy, 476
Pivot Solutions, 304, 954
Pivot3, 757, 1597, 1682
Pivotal Commware, 1151
Pivotal Laboratories, 3017
Pivotal Systems, 1828
Pivotdesk, 1789
PivotLink, 1738, 1850
Pixability, 655, 1046, 1100, 1160, 1459, 1486
Pixable, 1202
Pixalate, 397, 1028, 1055
Pixel Magic Imaging, 1709
Pixel Ripped, 307
Pixel Underground, 2139
Pixel Velocity, 628
Pixelexx Systems, 153
Pixelink, 2058
Pixelligent, 19
Pixelmetrix Corporation, 2703
Pixelux Entertainment, 1437
Pixelworks, 652, 757
PixFusion, 1745
PIXIA, 680
Pixie, 436
Pixim, 192, 979, 1922
Pixim Inc., 1779
Pixium, 3020
Pixium Vision, 3113
Pixlee, 890, 2011
piXlogic, 979
Pixonic, 2344
Pixorize, 622
Pixspan, 285
Pixsta, 2604
Pixtronix, 634, 880
Pixvana, 483, 1154, 1158
Pixways, 3239
PJS Publications, 1927
PKL Group, 2985
PKWare, 1166
Pkware, 2206
PL Midstream, 1129
Pl-x, 3124
Place IQ, 1899
Placecast, 508, 1378, 1945
Placed, 1874
Placefirst, 2295
Placeholder, 1882

1395

Portfolio Companies Index

PlaceIQ, 965, 1524
Placemark Investments, 2153
Placemeter, 1634
Placenote, 4, 2280
Placester, 1581, 1757, 1789
PlaceWare, 805
Placeware, 1911
PlaCor, 1872
Plae, 1416
Plaid, 486, 720, 842, 1075, 1346, 1715
Plain Vanilla, 641, 871, 1563
PlainID, 3221
Plains GP Holdings, 1846
Plan, 622, 1758
Plan Me Up, 2308
Plan Member Services, 1147
Plan Vanilla, 1222
Plan4Demand, 1746
Planalytics, 1275
Planck Re, 148
Planday, 2851
Planet, 996, 1363, 1662, 2439
Planet A.T.E., 132
Planet ATE, 1664
Planet Biopharmaceuticals Inc., 74
Planet Blue, 330, 331
Planet DDS, 378
Planet Fitness, 1861, 2379
Planet Labs, 107, 585, 595, 609, 741, 792, 1359
Planet Las, 1151
Planet Payment, 383
Planet Risk, 790
Planet Services, 2399
Planet Soho, 1257
Planet., 720
Planetary Resources, 535, 874
PlanetHS, 594
PlanetScale, 318
PlanetTran, 567
Planetveo, 2385
PlanGlid, 229
PlanGrid, 280, 2012, 2329
Planitax, 791
PlanMember Financial, 374
Planner5D, 2856
PlanSource, 1107
Plant Prefab, 1363
Plant Systems & Services PSS GmbH, 3067
Plantation Petroleum Holdings V, 672
Plantation Products, 783
Plantcml, 839
Planted Supply Co., 557
PlantEXT, 1191
Plantic Technologies, 2645
Plantiga, 2278
Planto, 2225
Plantronics, 1096
PlantSense, 805
Planview, 909, 1000
Planwise, 1642
Plarium, 1323
Plasc Card, 981
Plasco Energy Group, 159
Plaskolite, 456
Plasma Antennas, 3107
Plasmanet, 2732
Plasmonix, 1169
Plassein Packaging, 374
Plast Team, 3203
Plastc, 856
Plastc Card, 1427
Plastic Components, 1266
Plastic Engineered Components, 1986
Plastic Logic, 1361, 2386, 2492
Plasticity, 622, 1061
Plasticos, 2625
Plastics Industries Inc., 245

Plastifab Industries, 2235
Plastiq, 38, 754, 858, 1069, 1075
Plastomics, 267
Plate Joy, 770
Plateau, 1255
Plated, 641, 646, 724, 858, 1728, 1789
Platfora, 84, 486, 585, 979, 1226, 1760, 1796
Platform Solutions, 1017
Platform.sh, 249, 2851
Platform9, 1202, 1534
Platinex Inc., 2122
Platinum Energy Solutions, 500
Platiq, 1322
Platmin, 2337
Plattform Advertising, 1742
Plaxica, 2858
Plaxo, 634, 905
Play By Play Sports Broadcasting Camps, 1657
Play the Future, 2027, 2113
Play Vox, 3125
Play Vs., 1097
Playa Viva, 398
Playbuzz, 3221
Playcast, 1242, 3240
PlayCore, 1651
Playdeck, 600
Playdek, 724, 871
Playdo, 3013
Playdom, 1480, 1678
Player Tokens, 1158
Players' Lounge, 622
Playfire, 2446
PlayFirst, 596, 1853
PlayFull, 226
Playground Energy, 2696
PlayHaven, 641
PlayJam, 58, 2400
Playlore, 2976
Playmob, 2967
Playnery, 3127
Playnomics, 32, 743, 2011, 2278
PlayOn, 1331
PlayOn! Sports, 271
Playpeli, 3215
PlayPhone, 411
PlayPhone Inc., 1089
PlayPower, 1134
PlayRaven, 2637
Playrific, 841, 1160
Plays TV, 634
Plays.tv, 1663
PlaySay, 1348
PlaySight, 1926
Playsino, 1830, 1965
Playspan, 1235
PlaySpanTM, 650
Playstudios, 596, 968
Playswell, 1983
Playtex, 1096
Playtex Products Inc., 300
Playtika, 1323, 2914
PlayToTV, 2822
PlayVox, 745
PlayVS, 1611
Plazes, 2444, 2475, 2671
Plazz Entertainment, 2527
Pleasants Energy, 1795
Please Assist Me, 218, 995
Pledgeling, 306
Plenty, 262, 996, 1323
Plenum Media, 3105
Pleo, 3108
Plesk, 89
Plethora, 1151, 1262
Plews & Edelmann, 2219
Plex, 779, 2170
Plexigen, 1412

Plexo Capital, 483
Plexpress, 2630
Plextronics, 144, 730, 998
Plexus, 2878, 2892
Plexus Entertainment, 1632
Plexuss, 799
Plexx, 1181
Plexxi, 1334
Plexxikon, 59, 94, 1412
Pley, 544, 751
PLH Group, 675
Plianced, 1551
Pliant, 1967
Pliant Therapeutics, 1202
Pligus, 2331
Plinga, 3113
Plista, 2444
Plixer, 235
Plixi, 132
Plooto, 2137
plooto, 2249
Plotech, 3218
Plotly, 2239, 2278
PlotWatt, 107
plotwatt, 720
Pluck Corporation, 1445
Pluck Tea, 2244
Plug.dj, 1028
Plugar, 2626
Plugg, 2403
Plum, 43, 824, 1061, 1069, 3018
Plum Baby, 2760
Plum Choice, 655, 1153
Plum Organics, 339, 428, 1488
Plum Perfect, 841, 1054
Plum Print, 351, 1923
Plumble, 2851
PlumChoice, 646
Plume, 1024
PLUMgrid, 1146
PlumSilce, 1072
Plumtree, 852
Plunify, 2778
Pluot, 525
PluralSight, 1000
Pluralsight, 560, 883, 994, 1551, 1705
Pluribus Networks, 1202, 1247
PLUS, 1283, 2254
Plus One Robotics, 1110, 1480
PlushCare, 823, 994
Plusmo, 623
PlusPlus, 1613
PlusTV, 223, 1596
Pluto, 858, 1158, 1183, 1883, 1885
Pluto Mail, 1589
Pluto.TV, 1480, 1813
Plutoshift, 519
PLx Pharmaceutical, 1002
Ply Gem Industries, 476
Plyfe, 1632
PLYmedia, 1798
Plymouth Opportunity REIT, 1067
Plymouth Ventures, 3269
PLZ Aeroscience, 1479
PLZ Aeroscience Corporation, 1372
PLZ Holding Corporation, 64
PM Diagnostics, 267
PMA PhotoMetals of Arizona Inc., 984
PMC, 181, 1506, 1983
PMC-Sierra, 1760
PMW Pharma, 1010
PNC, 3274
PNE/Ecogas, 2881
PneumRx, 57, 94, 1058, 1792
Pneumrx, 2748
Pneuron, 1387
Poached Jobs, 1383

Portfolio Companies Index

POC Medical Systems Inc., 270
Pocket, 231, 770
Pocket Science, 3174
Pocket Watch, 1883
Pocketbook, 3160
PocketFM, 2960
PocketGems, 858, 1534
PocketThis, 1637
Poco, 2850
Pod Foods, 1885
Pod Inn, 2936
Pod Pack International, 1144
Pod Point, 2674
Podaddies Inc., 1089
Podimetrics, 1347
Podio, 3149
Podium, 79, 622, 1070
Podo Labs, 3108
Pods, 152
POET, 297
POET Software, 1672
POF, 2548
Pogo Resources, 477
Pogoplug/Cloud Engines, 1699
PogoSeat, 1749, 1876
Pogoseat, 295, 2010
Pohjola-Yhtymä Oyj, 2990
Poindexter Systems, 954
Point, 124, 1150
Point B Capital LLC, 3276
Point Biomedical, 468
Point Blank Enterprises, 1039, 1753
Point Judith Capital, 3273
Point One Navigation, 519
Point Park Properties, 152
PointCare, 349
PointClickCarem PowerPlan, 1041
Pointcloud, 219
PointRight, 29
Points International, 2079
Pointus Partners, 2260
Pointy, 3108
Poka, 2157
Pokelabo, 596
Poken, 3152
PokitDok, 1107, 1291
Pokkt, 3121
Polaar, 3113
Polar, 552, 1254, 2132
Polar Beverages, 402, 1173
Polar Molecular Corporation, 1837
Polar Oled, 2892
Polar Plastics Ltd., 465
Polar Sapphire, 2041, 2061, 2187
Polar Windows, 1572
Polaris, 168, 2447, 3113
Polaris Alpha, 166
Polaris Networks, 2926
Polaris Partners, 3273
Polaris Pool Holdings, 1505
Polaris Wireless, 609, 627, 1402
Polarmatic Oy, 2966
Polaroid, 378, 2171
Polatis, 2380, 2662, 2674
Polatix, 1038
Polestar, 1753
Polfa Kutno SA, 1452
Policolor, 2471
Policy Bazaar, 1013
Policy Bazaar.com, 1560
Policy Genius, 228, 728, 1055, 1555
PolicyGenius, 1758, 1768
Policygenius, 1346
PolicyMic, 1531
PolicyStat, 658
poLight, 2369, 3216
Poligof, 2293

Poligrafia SA, 2487
Polimedia, 2857
Poliogg, 1749
Poliris, 2466
Poll Everywhere, 1149
Pollen, 3108
Pollenizer, 1965
Pollex Mobile, 3062
Polly Portfolio, 1983
PollyEx, 727
Poly Remedy, 59
Poly-Wood, 409
PolyActiva, 2536, 2959
PolyAd Services, 653
Polyair Inter Pack, 830
Polycera, 50
PolyCera Membranes, 297
Polychain Capital, 24, 124, 307, 1882, 2280
Polycom, 1001, 3212
Polyconcept, 456, 909, 1017, 2311
Polycor, 2204, 2272
Polyfibron Technologies Inc., 354
Polyform Products Company, 1111
PolyFuel, 1786
Polyfuel, 1087
Polygene Ltd, 2954
Polygenta, 2372, 3211
Polygon Pictures Inc., 2347
Polygrafoformlenie, 2465
Polygraph, 71
Polymer Additives, 1045
Polymer Corporation, 1332
Polymer Holding, 1492
Polymer Solutions Group, 170
Polymer Technology, 399
Polymita Technologies, 2342
Polymorph, 622
Polynt, 909, 2379
PolyOne, 1970
Polypack, 3071
Polyphalt, 2058
PolyPid, 3240
PolyPipe, 894
Polypore, 2697
polySpectra, 2213
Polystream, 1095
Polystyvert, 2093
Polytec Holding AG, 2564
Polytex Environmental Inks, 373
PolyTherics, 2858
Polytronics, 3218
PolyUp, 890
Polyvera, 3194
PolyVision, 530
PolyVision Inc., 693
Polyvore, 634, 1181
Pom-Co, 432
Pomelo, 721, 1139
Pomeroy, 500
Pomifer Power Funding, 156
Pomme de Pain, 3020
Pomocni.pl, 3044
Ponce de Leon Pharmaceuticals, 1418
Poncho, 24, 1110
Pond Biofuels, 2187
Pond Ventures, 2472
Pond5, 1306, 1584, 1748
Pondurance, 1315
Ponfac, 2626
Pongolo, 397
Pontis, 2726
Pony Lumber, 1909
Pony.ai, 518
Pooch, 650
Poof-Slinky, 1516
Poorman-Douglas, 1770
Pop, 60

Pop Art, 1070
Pop Cap, 1212
Pop Chest, 307
Pop Displays, 1753
Pop Dust, 1110
Pop Medical, 3192
Pop-Up Pantry, 1099
PopCom, 218, 1286
Popcorn Metrics, 3108
Popdog, 2953
Popdust, 1699
Popego, 2334
PopExpert, 707
Popexpert, 1749
PopLegal, 721
Poppin, 741
Poppin., 1663
Poppins, 2649
PopSQL, 795
PopStarClub, 1108
Popsugar, 1001
Poptent, 1242
Poptip, 1699
Popular Pays, 251, 858
PopularPays, 799
Population Genetics, 1774
Populus, 1554, 2236
Populus Global, 2200
PopUp, 51
Poq, 3108
Por ti, 1584
Porch, 1604
Porcher, 2607
Porcher Industries, 3020
Porex Corporation, 199
Pork Farms, 1937
Porpoise, 2200
Port Arthur Steam Energy, 109
Port Hawkesbury Paper, 2258
Port Logistics Group, 673
Portable Energy Products, 651
Portable Medic, 1615
Portadam, 1727
Portal, 12
Portal de Documentos, 1376
Portal Educacao, 2438
Portal Entertainment, 2967
Portalarium, 1632
PortalPlayer, 1017, 2079
Portapure, 3277
Portea, 1509
Porter & Chester Institute, 1814
Porter Aviation Holdings, 2094, 2103
Porter Group, 1503
Porter Lancastrian, 2985
Porter Road, 858
Porterbrook, 2944
Portero, 1113
Portfolio Group, 404, 789
Portfolio Litigation Fund, 2094
Portfolio Solutions, 1114
Porthaven Care Homes, 3036
Portico, 655, 937
Portico Systems, 2196
Portillo's, 254
PortIT, 3013
Portland Orthopaedics Pty Limited, 2715
Portman Travel, 1937
Portola, 59, 1760, 1967
Portola Pharmaceuticals, 782, 1493, 2316
Portrait Innovations, 405
Portrait Software, 2472
Portside, 1138
PortWise, 2662, 2754
Portworx, 809, 1184
Posco Energy, 3145
POSE, 1860, 2872

1397

Portfolio Companies Index

Pose, 596, 1099
Poseida Therapeutics, 1143
Poseidon, 2266
Poshly, 841, 1983
Poshmark, 560, 823, 1013, 1184, 1323, 1700, 1879
PosiGen, 532
Posiq, 1806
Positionly, 3044
Poss, 2114
Poss Design, 2049
Possmedia, 2857
Post Factory NY, 2139
Post Impressions, 2732
Post University, 818
Post-N-Track, 530
Post.Bid.Ship., 1458
PostBeyond, 2153, 2224
Postcard on the Run, 624
Poste Imo, 3020
Posterous, 968, 1054, 1853
Posterous Spaces, 1534
Postie, 306, 342
Postini, 197
Postling, 1584, 1958
Postmaster, 2017
Postmastes, 1826
PostMates, 1700
Postmates, 128, 295, 563, 707, 802, 961, 1395, 1662, 1694, 1879
PostPath, 968, 2007
PostProcess, 1259
Postrocket, 1460
PostX, 1405
Pot Pots, 557
Pot Scientist, 392
Potbelly, 248, 1183
Potel & Chabot, 2293
Potentia Renewables, 2181
Potentia Semiconductor, 1080
Potenza Therapeutics, 1268
PotGuide.com, 392
Potloc, 2066
Potomac Research Group, 617
Potter Electric, 1232
Poundland, 1956
Poundworld Retail LTD, 1835
Povo, 2428
POW, 85
Pow Bio, 395
Powder OLEDs, 3107
PowderMed, 2316
Powell Johnson, 1147
Power & Composite Technologies, 917
Power 2 Switch, 1364
Power Analog, 1922
Power Assure, 979, 2315
Power Automation AG, 3172
Power By Proxy, 3098
Power Design Services, 702
Power Distribution, 257
Power Genius, 2936
Power Holdings, 959
Power Hour Fitness, 1267
Power I.T. LLC, 1053
Power Inbox, 1146
Power Innovations, 1677
Power Medical Interventions, 1325
Power Paper, 2386, 3046
Power Paper Ltd, 2973
Power Plus Communications, 2615
Power Practical, 1070
Power Precise Solutions Inc., 171
Power Products, 1651
Power Products LLC, 819
Power Protection Products Inc., 985
Power Reviews, 22, 2446

Power Services Group, 213
Power Survey, 676, 1328, 2093
Power To Fly, 563
Power to Fly, 1110
Power2sme, 1013
Power2Switch, 253, 471, 1615
PowerBand Global, 2087
Powerband Global, 2058
Powerbilt, 937
Powercast Corporation, 998
Powercell, 294
Powercell Sweden, 2755
PowerChord, 224
PowerCloud Systems, 1028, 1952
Powercom, 2337
Powercor Australia Ltd, 2591
PowerD, 3101
PowerDMS, 224, 790
PowerDsine, 2571, 2585
Powerdsine, 23
Powerfile, 1682
PowerGen Renewable Energy, 1830
PowerGenix, 171, 322, 595, 2761
PowerGenix Systems, 126, 1786
Powerhouse Dy Dynamics, 418
Powerhouse Dynamics, 497, 534, 643, 946, 1100, 1459, 2106
PowerInbox, 235, 650
Powerit Holdings, 1
Powerit Solutions, 706
Powerlase, 2662
Powerleader Science & Technology Ltd., 2633
PowerLight Corporation, 595
Powermat, 817, 1282, 1730, 2015
Powermet, 995
PowerOasis, 3244
PowerOne Media, 954
POWERPRECISE, 1922
PowerQuest, 654, 856
PowerReviews, 777, 1796, 2005
Powers Equipment Company, 540
PowerSchool, 2209
Powerset, 115
Powershares by Invesco, 793
Powerspan, 1324
PowerSteering Software, 954, 2196
PowerStop, 1166
PowerTeam Services, 1062
PowerTech, 85
PowerTech Group, 1637
PowerTel, 3168, 3168
Powertel, 1148, 1708
PowerToFly, 922
PowerU, 3194
Powervar, 1435
Powervation, 322, 1922
PowerVision, 1112, 1916
Powervision, 59, 74, 544, 782, 1122, 1410
PowerWay, 443
Powhow, 1358
Powwr, 745
Poxel, 1271, 3020
Poynt, 1181
PPA, 2936
pParoc, 3009
PPC Industries Inc., 64
PPC Partners, 3264
PPD, 924
PPI-Time Zero, 1422
PPI/Time Zero Inc., 1624
PPM America Capital Partners, 3265
PPS, 1572, 2584
PPTV, 296, 3100
PPU Maconomy, 3137
PQ Corp., 168
PQ Corporation, 433
PR Wireless, 1153

Pr0Net, 734
Practically Green, 534
Practice, 488
Practice Fusion, 1257, 1382
Practice Insight, 897
Practice Plan Group Ltd., 2677
Practicefusion, 720
PracticePanther, 92
Practo, 578
Praditus, 3113
Praekelt Foundation, 1374
Praemo, 2190
Pragmatech Software, 1080
Prairie Capital, 3265
Prairie Fava, 2099
Prairie Meats, 2285
Prairie Soil Services, 2221
Prairie Storm Energy Corp, 1326
Prairie Storm Energy Corp., 1278
Praized, 1965
Pramata, 1427
Prana, 2238, 3001
PrarieGold Solar, 1470
Prattle, 544
Praxis, 751, 1751
PRCL Research, 3196
PRE Resources, 259
Preact, 243, 305, 1055
Preact.io, 1099
Precede, 2726
PrecedentHealth, 1801
Preceptis Medical, 1418
Precidian Investments, 235
Precious, 795, 1138
Precipio Diagnostics, 678
Precise, 3100
Precise Light Surgical, 644, 1711
Precise Packaging, 1856
Precise Software Solutions, 3137
Precisi Therapeutics, 946
Precision, 828, 1293, 2209, 2965
Precision Aviation Group, 752, 1457
Precision Biosciences, 710, 1519
Precision Components, 1067
Precision Dermatology, 74
Precision Dermatology, 782, 1508
Precision for Medicine, 1037
Precision fOr Medicine Holdings, 1361
Precision Global, 2208
Precision Hawk, 1235
Precision Image Analysis, 1061
Precision Manufacturing Group LLC, 556
Precision Medicine Group, 254
Precision Mounting, 2145
Precision NanoSystems, 12
Precision Nutrition, 361
Precision Partners Holding Company, 1234
Precision Products Group, 1141
Precision Southeast, 828
Precision Spine Care, 403
Precision Therapeutics, 221, 304, 1508, 1746, 3196
Precision Ventures, 1100
PrecisionDemand, 871, 1738
PrecisionHawk, 518, 532, 1926
PrecisionLender, 1000
Precithera, 2092
Preclick, 1689
Precog, 1547
Precognitive, 754
Precom, 2936
PreCon, 2587
Precursor Energetics, 1355
Precyse, 97
Predata, 535, 655
Predfast, 793
Predict Spring, 720

Portfolio Companies Index

PredictHQ, 180
Prediction IO, 2010
Predictive Networks, 314
Predictive Service, 831
PredictWise, 934
Predikto, 1788
Predix Pharmaceuticals, 769
Predixion, 69, 1829
Predixion Software, 791, 1237, 1407
Preemadonna, 896, 2280
Preempt, 816
PreEmptive Meds, 400
PreEmptive Solutions, 1047, 1553
Preen.me, 2831
Preferred Compounding, 1997
Preferred Concepts, 1743
Preferred Freezer Services, 722
Preferred Rubber, 653
Preferred System Solutions, 507
Preferred Systems, 530
Preferred Systems Solutions, 1388
Prefix, 325
Preflexibel, 2862
Pregis, 1372
Pregis Corporation, 64
Preh GmbH, 2660
Prelert, 712, 3058
Prellis, 395
PremFina, 1595, 2674
Premia, 1062
Premier Global Services Inc., 403
Premier Kids Care, 1957
Premier Needle Arts, 290
Premier Pacific Pharmaceutical Industries, 1769
Premier Performance Products, 401, 1605
Premier Precision Group, 1719
Premier Store Fixtures, 1144
Premiere Cinemas Corporation, 1708
Premiere Global Sports, 1435
Premiere Page, 1986
PremierXD, 1777
Premise, 52, 317, 530, 989, 1696, 2406
Premise Health, 1961, 2207
Premise One, 940
Premium Brands, 2051, 2218
Premium Franchise Brands, 1232
Premium Power, 1906, 3135
Premix, 1171
Premiys, 1257
PRENAV, 519
Prenav, 563
Prenax Global, 2754
Prenda, 79
Preo, 981
Prepac, 2272
Prepaid Capital, 2717
Prepaid Direct, 2079
Prepaid Media, 2717
Prepaid Technologies, 224
Prepared Response, 85, 247
PreparedHealth, 1480
PrePlay, 1852
Presage Biosciences, 1778
PreScience Labs, 383
Prescient Healthcare Group, 222
Prescient Systems, 954
Prescott Group, 152
Presence AI, 1006
Presence From Innovation, 399, 1053
Presence Learning, 272, 288, 428
Presence.ai, 1370
PresenceLearning, 427, 1299
President Engineering, 3244
Presidential, 1252
Presidential Holdings, 1252
Presidio, 793, 1212
Presidio Pharmaceuticals, 1410

Presidio Pharmaceuticals Inc., 237
Presidio Systems, 1378
Presidion Inc., 897
Presidium, 655
Press A Point, 969
Press Ganey, 909
Press Ganey Associates, 1931
Press Index, 2551
Pressly, 2109
PressPass, 2978
Pressure Technologies, 3244
PrestaShop, 3113, 3239
Presteve Foods, 2123
Prestiamoci, 2874
Prestige Brands International, 2015
Prestige Insurance Holdings Limited, 404
Presto, 502
Presto Engineering, 3113
PrestoBox, 1463
Preston Hollow Capital, 909
Preston-Eastin, 399
PrestoSports, 235
Pret a changer, 3239
Preteckt, 995
Pretio Interactive, 2284, 2291
Pretium Packaging, 819
Pretty Simple, 2851
Prettylitter, 566
PrevaCept Infection Control, 400
Prevail Therapeutics, 709, 1519
Prevailion, 84
Prevalent, 794, 1000
Prevedere, 770, 1154, 1346
Preventice, 1205, 3279
Preventice Solutions, 173
Preventicus, 2527
Preview Networks, 3149
Preview System, 115
Previser, 974
PreVisor, 402
Previstar, 1348, 1400
Prevoty, 306, 624, 1055, 1099
Prevtec, 2029
Prevtec microbia, 2264
Prewise Group Oy, 2873
Prexa Pharmaceuticals, 1775
Prezi, 1717, 3149
Prezi.inc, 2604
Prezzo, 1835
PRGX Global, 300
PRI Group, 1422
PriCare, 1708
Price Spider, 790
Price.com, 807
Pricelock, 132
PriceMatch, 1416
Priceonomics, 280, 585, 1715, 2329
PriceRunner, 3013
PriceWaiter, 459
Pricing Engine, 707
PricingAssistant, 1416
Pridenta, 3196
Priject Time & Cost, 902
Prima Capital Advisors, 1743
Primanex Corporation, 1180
Primanti Bros., 1088
Primary Access, 1760
Primary Access Corporation, 1706
Primary Data, 436, 603, 688, 1204, 1425
Primary Packaging, 619
Primary.com, 941
PrimaTable, 585
Primavera, 779
Primavista, 2669
Primax Electronics, 892
Primaxx, 69
Prime Advantage, 1372, 1733

Prime Bank, 1494
Prime Discovery, 318
Prime Distribution, 1171
Prime Equipment, 1017
Prime Health Services, 1144
Prime Leather, 1213
Prime Network Inc., 2907
Prime Risk Partners, 1815
Prime Rock Resources, 1125
Prime Sense, 386
Prime Student Loan, 534
Prime System, 2826
PrimeCo, 494
PrimeCo Wireless Communications, 619
PrimeCredit Limited, 473
PrimeLine Utility Services, 740
Primeloop, 1655, 1912
Primer, 107, 563, 1151
Primera Biosystens, 212
PrimeraDx, 1010
PrimeRevenue, 240, 1593, 2196
Primerevenue, 235
PrimeSport, 500, 1491
Primestream, 812
Primet, 184, 432
Primet Oy, 2873
PriMetrica, 958
Primex Technologies, 2176
Primis, 1708
PRIMIS Marketing Group, 468
Primitive, 307
Primo Water, 1681
Primrose Schools, 1576
Primus, 1837
Primus International, 1360
Primus Pacfic Partners I LP, 2094
Primus Pharmaceuticals, 1452
Primus Power, 595, 2078
Prince, 1134
Prince International Corporation, 1403
Prince Mineral Holding Corporation, 1491
Princepa Biopharma, 1731
Princeps Therapeutics, 1731
Princess Yachtz International, 1088
Princeton Financial Systems, 655
Princeton Optronics, 1348
Princeton Softech, 1136
Principia, 1122, 1238
Principia Biopharma, 1298, 1382, 1698
Princo, 2436
Print Direction, 405
Print Polska, 2429
Print Syndicate, 508, 586
Printo, 3109
PrintOne, 2891
Printpaks, 197
PrintWithMe, 1155
Prior Data Sciences, 2079
PriorAuthNow, 607, 1286
Priori Data, 3108
Priori Legal, 858
Priority Express, 654
Priority Holdings, 528
Priority Solutions, 170, 782
Prism, 1563
Prism Education Group, 434, 938
Prism Medical UK, 2944
Prism Network, 2967
PRISM Plastics, 443
Prism Skylabs, 132, 585, 1474, 1489, 1830, 1846
Prism Vision Group, 1505
Prisma, 661, 1075
Prisma Medios de Pagos S.A., 62
Prismatic, 1028, 1798
PrismHR, 29
Pristine, 1597
Pritikin, 374

Portfolio Companies Index

Pritzker Group, 3265
Privacy Analytics, 2278
Privalia, 815, 2987
Privalla, 2553
Privamista Group, 2338
Private Bancorp Inc., 654
Private Company, 1477
Private Core, 770
Private Label Cosmetics, 1605
Privateer Holdings, 99
Privategriffe, 2401
PrivateLot, 3239
Privilege Unerwriters, 1743
Privitar, 1607
Privlo, 1502
Privoro, 1031
Privus, 1595
Privé Revaux, 2144
Priyo.com, 721
PrizeLogic, 1409
Prizeo, 1489, 1634
Pro Active Therapy, 1557
Pro Group, 402
Pro Hydration Therapy, 995
Pro Mach, 1368
Pro Oilfield Services, 1009
Pro Player Connect, 1797
Pro PT, 859
Pro Service Hawaii, 949
PRO Unlimited, 914, 1017
Pro-Fab Group, 2009
PRO-PAC Packaging, 2645
Pro-Pet, 928
Pro.com, 609, 1158, 1183
ProAct Services Corp., 900
Proacta, 3085
ProactiveNet, 592
Proampac, 1971
Proaxion, 1923
Probiodrug, 2815, 3196
Probity Medical Transcription, 1428
Procaps, 2150
Procaptura, 2754
Procarta, 2978
Procarta Biosystems, 2967
ProcedureFlow, 2068
Procelerate Technologies, 1305
Procertus, 1921
Process Fab, 1904
Process Map, 171
Process Sensing Technologies, 235
Process Systems Enterprise, 2858
Process'ware, 3048
ProcessClaims, 1910
Processing.com, 1093
Prochips Inc., 2924
Procite, 1336
ProClarity Corporation, 1535
Proclivity, 796
Proclivity Systems, 1771
Procognia, 3137
Procomp Informatics, 2907
Procompra, 3056
ProCore, 1798
Procore, 1282, 1826
ProCredit Bank, 3234
ProCredit Group, 2086
ProCredit Moldova, 3234
ProctorFree, 1072, 1923
Procured Health, 710, 1046
Procurement Advisors, 333
Procuri, 831
Procurifiy, 2153
Prodagio Software, 1783
Prodea, 536
Prodealcenter, 3020
Prodigy, 24, 564, 1613

Prodigy Finance, 2478
Prodomax Automation Ltd., 2167
ProdPerfect, 679
ProdThink, 871
Produced Water Absorbents, 2700
ProducePay, 622
Product Health, 1251
Product Hunt, 124, 552, 1150
Product Software Development, 834
ProductBIO, 1749
Productboard, 1075
Production Resource Group, 1045
Production Resource Group LLC, 158
Production Science, 466
Producto Protegido, 2455
ProEnergy Holdings, 46
ProEnergy Services, 686
Profeshion, 2948
Profesia, 3122
Professional Bull Riders, 1724
Professional Capital Services, 1136
Professional Environmental Engineers, 364
Professional Press, 1275
Professional Rental Tools, 1021, 1144
Professional Service Industries, 1372
Professional Systems, 1605
Professional Warranty Service, 1776
Profex, 1850
Profi, 909
Profi.ru, 3088
Proficiency, 455
Proficient Auto, 1745
Proficio Bank, 801
Profile Systems, 1142
Profility, 3050
ProFind, 1913
Profine, 152
Profit Systems, 828
Profita Fund I Ky, 2740
Profitect, 249, 856
Profitlogic, 626
Proformex, 1026
Profound Medical, 2130, 2187
Profound Medical Corp., 2092
Profounder, 1097
ProfoundNano, 3279
PROFUSA, 1613
Profusa, 181
ProgenIQ, 2477
Progeniq, 2390
Progenity, 188
Progenteq, 2892
Progentix Orthobiology, 2514
Progexia, 3020
Progility, 3018
Progistics Distribution, 958
Prognolic, 2856
Prognos, 150, 1601
Progression Therapeutics, 241
Progressive Acute Care, 1192
Progressive Concepts, 1549
Progressive Finance, 1752
Progressive Group, 2079
Progressive Moulded Products, 1360
Progressive REI, 512
Progressive-PMSI, 1062
Progressly, 1701
Progresso Financiero, 455
Progressus Therapy, 1742
Progrexion, 928
Progrexion Holdings, 1491
ProGuides, 120
Progyny, 1075, 1731
PROHBTD, 44, 1135
PROHBTED, 2254
Proj, 1374
Project Applecart, 622

Project Arriendo, 909
Project Cohort, 544
Project Decor, 1097
Project Frog, 491, 1579
Project Leadership Associates, 439, 698
Project Management Academy, 1105
Project44, 1000
project44, 1480
Projector, 231
Projectpartner, 2853
Projitech, 1047
ProKarma, 673
ProKyma, 2967
Prolacta Bioscience, 74, 94, 627, 697, 791, 797, 826, 1600, 1915
Prolamina Corporation, 1971
Proletariat, 743
Prolexic, 1850
Prolific Earth Sciences, 995
Prolific Technology, 2603
Prolific Works, 1100
ProLogis, 152
Prolojik, 2967
Prolong Pharmaceuticals, 1058
Prolupin GmbH, 2686
Promach, 1109
Promatory, 1793
Promatory Communications, 818
Promax Nutrition, 1168
ProMed, 598
Promedior, 644, 919, 1122, 1460, 2748
Promega, 1921
Promenade, 2254
Promentis Pharmaceuticals Inc., 74
Promethean Surgical Devices, 1773
Promethera, 2530, 2949, 3225
Promethera Biosciences, 1241
Prometheus, 1409
Prometheus Group, 779, 1776
Prometheus Laboratories, 402, 1725
Prometheus Therapeutics & Diagnostics, 209
Promethium, 2019
Prominence Networks, 3124
Promic, 3107
Promise, 741
Promise Healthcare, 1271
Promise Pictures, 512
PromisePay, 1688
Promo Boxx, 178
Promoboxx, 313, 534, 876, 1097, 1734
Promociones Farma, 3223
PromocionesFarma.com, 2920
Promopost Holding, 2491
Prompt.ly, 306, 1655
Promt.ly, 1566
ProNAi, 1382
ProNAi Therapeutics, 943, 1941
ProNatura, 2338
ProNerve, 1963
ProNet, 1682
Proniras, 31
Pronota, 2476, 2939
Pronoun, 206, 231
Pronova BioPharma, 2519
Pronto, 79, 795
Pronto Insurance, 1403
ProntoForms, 2284
ProofPilot, 351, 567
Proofpoint, 248, 339, 581, 634, 968, 1212, 1247, 1341
Propane Taxi, 1502
ProParts, 908
Propel, 124, 1346, 1607
Propel Baltimore Fund, 19
Propel Biofuels, 1, 1355
Propel IT, 987
Propel Orthodontics, 1228

1400

Portfolio Companies Index

Propeller, 547, 792, 858, 1054, 1731
Propeller Health, 1696
Propeller Industries, 1315
PropelPLM, 1675
Proper, 1138
Properly, 181, 1110, 2137
Propero, 2572
Properties, 1505
Property Detective, 2995
Property Network, 2871
Property Partner, 3108
Property Partners, 3018
Property Solutions, 999
Propertybase, 2994
PropertyBrands, 1000
PropertyBridge, 491
PropertyView Solutions, 1354
ProPetro Services, 675
Propex, 1967
ProPharma Group, 1046, 1128
ProPhase Labs, 638
Prophecy, 1205
Prophet 21, 1136
Propoly, 3108
Proposal Software.com, 383
Proposify, 2155
Proprietary Fund, 2958
Proprius Pharmaceuticals, 769
Proptec Renewables, 2526
PropTiger, 1509
Proragonist Therapeutics, 74
PROS, 1970
Pros, 1041
Prosci, 1105
Proscia, 754, 799, 1577, 1701
Prose, 544, 761, 1000, 1110, 1183, 1530
ProSeeder, 841
Prosensa, 2851
ProSep, 6
ProService Hawaii, 787
ProSiebenSat1 Media SE, 924
ProSight, 2541
Prosight Specialty Insurance, 1835
ProSites, 1572
Proskauer, 3272
Prosky, 1054
Prosolia, 658
Prosonix, 2710, 3069
ProSource, 478
Prospect Brands, 1276
Prospect Medical, 1965
Prospect Medical Holdings, 1109
Prospect Mortgage, 1742
Prospect Partners LLC, 3265
Prospect Pools Group, 1492
Prospect Water, 1492
ProspectWise, 561
Prospectwise, 1099
Prosper, 563, 710, 779, 1001, 1212, 1374, 1502, 1830
Prospera, 483, 1509
Prostalund, 2562
Prostar Energy, 2275
ProStor Systems, 315
ProStrakan, 1349
Prota Therapeutics, 3023
ProtAffin, 2710
ProtAffin Biotechnologic AG, 2350
Protag, 3073
Protagonist, 762, 3138
Protagonist Therapeutics, 1043, 1124, 1519
Protalix Biotherapeutics, 1271
Protean, 962
Protean Electric, 1361
ProteanTecs, 3221
ProTec, 77
Protect America, 716

Protect My Car, 559
Protect Plus Air Holdings, 900, 958
Protect Wise, 563
Protection One, 1506
Protective Packaging Corporation, 734
Protectwise, 171
Protedyne, 1142
Protege Energy III, 672
Protego Medical, 2959
Protego Networks, 1237
Protegrity Advisors, 3267
Protegys Group, 2375
Protein Bar and Kitchen, 1088
Protein Discovery, 1187
Protein Laboratories Rehovot, 3245
Protein Sciences, 1583
Protein Simple, 1241
ProteinQure, 2137
ProteinSimple, 1094, 1929
Protel, 111
Protellindo, 254
Protelus, 85
Protemo, 2008
Protenergy, 2167
Protenus, 173, 1052
Proteocyte AI, 2125
Proteogenix, 1915
Proteolix, 59, 1094, 3007
Proteologics, 2454
Proteom, 2463
Proteome, 312
Proteon Therapeutics, 1268, 1478, 1691, 3196
Proteon Therpeutics, 1008
Proteostasis, 710, 1618
Proterra, 302, 532, 817, 1241, 1363, 1923
Proterro, 233, 322, 570
Proteus, 2466
Proteus Biomedical, 57
Proteus Digital Health, 68, 181, 749, 1052
Protez Pharmaceuticals, 237, 1508
Prothena Corporation, 1698
ProThera Biologics, 1693
ProTip, 3113
Proto Labs, 1334, 3279
Proto Software, 304
Protochips, 1442, 1606, 1988
Protocol Driven Healthcare Inc., 54
Protocol Global Systems, 928
Protocol Labs, 942, 1666, 1882
Protocol Systems, 238
Protocom Development Systems Pty Limited, 2715
Proton, 530
Proton Energy Systems, 893, 1355, 1702, 2079
Proton Media, 1385
Protonex, 520, 1702, 1920
ProtonMedia, 1387
Protraining, 2765
Protus IP Solutions, 2058
Provade VMS, 181
ProVale, 1548
Provalliance-Franck Provost, 1018
Provant, 687
Provasculon, 347, 1419
Provation, 500
ProVation Medical Inc., 158
Prove Inc., 1640
Proven, 590, 1054
Proven., 124
Proven.com, 1254, 1958
Provendi, 3239
ProVest, 1469
Provide Commerce, 1793
Providea Conferencing, 1979
Providence Equity Partners, 3255
Providence Equityt, 2167
Providence Medical Technology, 138

Provident Companies Inc., 404
ProviderTrust, 718
Providien Medical, 673
Provigent, 2655, 2952
ProVita International Medical Center, 3196
Provivi, 1051
Provocraft, 1705
Provogue, 805
Provox Technologies, 1227
ProxBox, 995
Proxim, 1398
Proxim Wireless, 3137
Proxima, 1918
Proxima Therapeutics, 94
Proxima Therapeutics RXStrategies, 1148
Proximagen, 2892
Proximal Data, 206, 618
Proximetry, 1540, 1995
Proximiant, 2978
Proximic, 2829, 2838
Proximities, 212, 990
Proxio, 2003
Proxiserve, 2851
Proxpur Labs, 253
Proxy, 1075
ProxyClick, 745
PRT Growing Services, 2275
Prudent Energy, 1241, 1340
Prudential Capital Group, 77
Pruska Real Estate, 1139, 2946
PRV Metals, 1166
Pryor Cashman LLP, 3267
Prysm, 174, 1416, 1810
PRZM, 50
PS Dept, 1475
PS Production Services, 2139
PS Soft, 2354
PSA Worldwide, 1606
PSafe, 641, 1534
Psagot, 135
PSAV, 1372
PSC, 1134
PSC Holdings I, 1129
PSD Group, 2796
PSI, 1963
PSIA, 2807
Psionic, 807
PSIOxus, 1731
PsiOxus Therapeutics, 2858
pSivida, 1271
PSM Investments, 584
PSS, 1727
PSS Systems, 58, 215, 852
Psyadon Pharma, 1271
PsyTechnics, 1305
Psytechnics, 2662, 2674
PT Berrybenka, 2798
PT Bukalapak.com, 2798
PT Marga Mandalasaki, 2434
PT Pricearea Andalan Prestasi, 2798
PTC, 2815
PTC Therapeutics, 237, 1145, 1946, 2816, 3015
PTRx, 1915
Public, 395
Public Engines, 2382
Public Financial Management, 832
Public Funds Investment Tracking and Reporting, 1688
Public Mobile, 455, 1153
Public Recruitment Group, 2795
Public Relay, 1988
Public Stuff, 743
PublicEngines, 1677
PublicStaff, 1310
PublicStuff, 1306, 2604
Publishing, 2556
Publishing Group of America, 1506

1401

Portfolio Companies Index

PubMatic, 1327
Pubmatic, 197, 3001
PubNub, 483, 1626, 2236
Puddle, 1254
Pudget, 243
Pueblo Mechanical & Controls, 960
Puerto Rico ASC Holdings Co. Inc., 63
Puerto Rico Waste Investment LLC, 158
Pull Request, 728
PullString, 741, 872
Pulmagen, 2662
Pulmagen Therapeutics, 2748, 2981, 3195
Pulmatrix, 12, 153, 1460
Pulmocide, 710, 1145, 1628, 1731
Pulmokine, 347
Pulmonary Apps, 1047
PulmonX, 1251
Pulmonx, 598, 1094
PulmonX Corp., 2816
Pulpo Media, 1226
Puls, 1611, 3221
Pulsant Limited, 1360
Pulsar Vascular, 1616
Pulse, 641, 1534
Pulse 8, 1169
Pulse Data, 941
Pulse Point, 608
Pulse Systems, 470
Pulse Therapeutics, 267, 569
Pulse Ventures, 3273
Pulse Veterinary Technologies, 1832
Pulse.io, 384, 1416
Pulsecore Semiconductor, 197
Pulselabs, 1158
PulsePoint, 1291, 1886, 1906
Pulsetech Products Corporation, 734
PulseVet, 327
PulseWave, 1244
Pulsic, 3051
PulsoSocial, 3125
Pulsus, 3127
Pulumi, 1158
Puman, 3181
Pump Audio, 1475
Pumps & Pressure, 2145
Pumps and Controls, 1562, 1578
PumpUp, 2125
Pumpup, 816
Punch Bowl Social, 1088
Punch Powertrain, 2949
Punchbowl, 649, 1100
Punchbowl Software, 533
Punchh, 454, 1782
PunchTab, 1247
Pundar, 1374
Pundit, 622
Puppet, 483, 1075, 2690
Puppet Labs, 1846, 1860
Purch, 22, 44
Purchasing Power, 333, 716
Pure Barre, 1088
Pure Canadian Gaming, 2208, 2209
Pure Dental Brands, 960
Pure Digital, 757, 986
Pure Digital Technologies, 555, 1906
Pure Energies Group, 1324
Pure Fishing, 1037
Pure Growth Organics, 1585
Pure Gym, 433
Pure Incubation, 1173
Pure Leapfrog, 2509
Pure Life Renal, 1251, 1331
Pure Organix, 391
Pure People, 2851
Pure Storage, 836, 1001, 1534, 2860
Pure Swiss Water AG, 650
Pure Wafer, 653

Pure Wow, 858
PureCars, 1734
PureEnergy Solutions, 457
Puregym, 1109
Purely Proteins, 2463
PureRED, 1735
PureRed Integrated Marketing, 1557
PureSight Inc., 807
PureStorage, 1760
PureTech Systems, 1837
PureWave, 1102
PureWave Networks, 183
PureWow, 1480
PureWRX, 1331, 1685
Purigen, 12
PuriLens, 212
Purisma, 852
Purissima, 226, 1610
Purity Life Health Produts, 2051
PurMeo, 3044
Purmeo, 2638
Purple Communications, 500
Purple Cows, 656
Purple Land Management, 1622
Purple Squirrel, 561
Purpose, 1552
PurposeEnergy, 497
PursueCare LLC, 1735
PUSH, 2125
Push Doctor, 2674
Push Wellness, 1615
Push.io, 60
Pusher, 2478, 3030
Pushlife, 2182
Puttman Infrastructure, 529
PVI Industries, 1209
PVPower, 1615
PVR Partners, 1573
PVRI, 55
Pwnie Express, 712
PWRF, 1244
PXP, 1846
PXP Group, 2309
Py, 622
Pyatt, 345
Pyatt/Broadmark Management, 1061
Pygg, 1711
Pymetrics, 1069, 1607
Pyramid Healthcare, 503, 1343
Pyramid Investors LLC, 158
Pyramid Management Advisors, 158
Pyramid Research, 863
Pyramid Technologies Inc., 903
Pyrotek Special Effects, 2084
Pythagoras, 2726, 2900
Pytheas, 3073
Python, 980
Pyxis, 1760
Pyxis - Helpmate Robotics, 1103
Pyxis Technology, 764

Q

Q, 941
Q Bio, 124, 1069
Q Chip, 2737
Q Group, 1633
Q Holding, 2311
Q Holding Company, 985
Q Link Technologies, 608
Q Networks, 1496
Q Therapeutics, 688, 1677
Q'Max Solutions, 2051
Q-Centrix, 1742
Q-CTRL, 1670
Q-GO, 3051
Q-go.com B.V., 162
Q-layer, 2837

Q-Sense AB, 2718
Q-Sensei, 1926, 2527
Q-Sera, 2959
Q1 Labs, 1702
Q2 Publishing Inc., 447
Q2ebanking, 57
Q3DM, 898
Q4, 909, 2109, 2118, 2153, 2224
Q9 Networks, 1156
Qadium, 107, 1001
Qapa, 2296
Qapa.fr, 1416
Qarnot Computing, 3208
QASymphony, 271, 1000
Qazzow, 2008
QBotix, 730
QC Supply, 456
QC Supply LLC, 158
QCI Marine Offshore, 374
QCL Holdings, 1583
QD Laser, 1241
QD Vision, 979, 1334
QDrinks, 1097
QED, 1228
Qeep, 3239
Qeexo, 1670
QF Holdings, 158
QGenda, 779
QHR Technologies, 2233
Qiandai.com, 3208
Qiave Technologies, 521
Qihoo, 1181
Qihoo 360, 1534
Qik, 89
Qinous, 2841
Qinyang Power Plants, 2591
Qinyuan, 3194
QK Holdings, 1636
QLess, 50
Qliance, 262, 1291, 1641
Qlight Nanotech, 3245
QLL, 3038
Qmatic, 2384
QMax, 1403
Qmax Solutions, 2051
QMC Media, 63
Qminder, 3108
Qnary, 1905
Qnovo, 532, 1579
Qognify, 235
QOL Medical, 224
QoL Meds, 1279
QOOP, 506
Qopius, 2296
Qordoba, 180, 306
QOSMOS, 2674
Qosmos, 2385, 2662
Qpass, 823, 1003, 1637, 2079
QPID, 1419
QPID Health, 1181, 1298
QPS Pharmaceutical Services LLC, 732
QQ, 2850
QR Pharma, 266
Qr8 Health, 886
QRA, 2155
Qriously, 934, 1715, 2387
Qronus Interactive Ltd., 2954
Qrunch, 2646
QRxPharma, 2877
QSC AG, 223
Qsent, 1945
QSI Restaurant Partners, 220
QSIL, 2527
Qspeed Semiconductor, 56, 1779
QSpex Technologies, 1722
QSr, 184
QStar, 672

1402

Portfolio Companies Index

QStream, 1100
Qstream, 703, 2759
Qstrios, 2100
QTC Medical Services, 1717
Qteros, 1142
QTS, 815
QTVascular, 2690
Quad Learning, 1291, 1766
Quad/Graphics, 2073
Quadel Consulting Corporation, 917
QuaDPharma, 1523
QuadraMed, 779, 1394, 1866
Quadranet, 1927
Quadrangle Architects Limited, 2148
Quadrant, 2922
Quadrant Software, 1173
QuadraSpec, 652
Quadratic 3D, 1670
Quadriga Capital III, 2094
Quadrimex, 2851
Quadstone, 2386
Quaker Capital Investments, 3275
Quaker Fabric, 1141
Quala, 62
Qualaroo, 1371, 1460, 1860
Qualas Power Services, 1171
QUALCOM, 1922
Qualcomm, 385
QualDerm Partners, 558
Quali, 603
Qualia, 60, 679, 724, 1202, 1486, 1524, 2113
QualiSystems, 2726
Qualitor, 1971
Quality Aluminium Products, 276
Quality Alumnum Products, 1606
Quality Care Solutions, 856
Quality Coach Inc., 832
Quality Distribution, 135
Quality Farm & Country, 722
Quality Green, 203
Quality HVAC, 2271
Quality Metric, 955
Quality Powder Coating, 812
Quality Senior Living Partners, 1144
Quality Uptime Services, 1638
Quality Valve, 1435
Quality Wood Products, 61
QualityHealth, 954
Quallaby, 1334
Qualson, 3127
Qualtera, 3020
Qualtre, 646
Qualtrics, 1000
Qualtré, 1181
QualVu, 930
Qualys, 23, 1850, 1888
Quancheng, 148
Quandl, 2149
Quandoo, 3040
Quanergy, 1311
Quanhtum Bridge Communications, 314
Quanta, 151, 2475, 3113
Quanta Display, 2603
Quanta Fluid Solutions, 2918
Quanta Storage, 2603
QuantaLife, 1940
Quantalife, 1400
Quantance, 385, 620, 852, 1010, 1782
Quantapore, 799
Quantcast, 483, 775, 1460
Quantec, 2199
Quantem, 1727
Quantenna, 115, 646, 1916, 2797, 3152, 3169
Quantenna Communcations, 1406
Quantenna Communications, 581, 634, 1672, 1711, 2540
Quanterix, 153, 221, 747, 979

Quantic Industries, 374
Quantic Mind, 1601
Quanticel, 1928
QuanticMind, 454, 770
QuantiFind, 107, 1534
Quantifind, 518
Quantion, 1061
Quantiva, 422, 608
Quantopian, 1069, 1715
QuantPower, 41
Quantros, 176, 779
Quantum, 197, 214
Quantum Benchmark, 2278
Quantum Compliance, 2967
Quantum Diamon Technologies, 870
Quantum Energy Partners, 879
Quantum Health, 39, 97, 857
Quantum Machines, 235
Quantum Medical Imaging, 853
Quantum Metric, 1000
Quantum Ops, 1448
Quantum Pharmaceuticals, 2944
Quantum Secure, 636
Quantum Spatial, 166
Quantum Workplace, 1276
Quantum14, 1791
Quantum4D, 979
QuantumBio, 1117
QuantumClean, 1727
QuantumScape, 1069, 1075
Quantumsphere, 1915
Quanzhou Jinhua Edible Oil Co., 2727
Quark Games, 1242, 1540
Quark VR, 307
Quarri, 445
Quarrio, 218
Quarry Technologies, 314
Quarterly, 1716, 1860, 1912
Quartet Health, 710
Quartus Capital Partners, 2660
Quartzy, 1069, 1110
Quasar, 1901
Quasar Ventures, 665
Quatermove, 2466
Quatris Healthco, 1638
QuatRx, 1010, 1916
Quatrx, 782
QuatRx Pharmaceuticals, 1059, 1828
Qubell, 249, 1522
Qubera Solutions, 69
Qubit, 1607, 2478
Qubole, 455, 1001, 1346
Qucit, 1894
Quellan, 968, 1922
Quelleenergie.fr, 2385
Quellos, 1183
Quench, 2184
Quench USA, 657, 828, 3222
Quench USA Inc., 63
Quentis, 1928
Queralt, 678
Queremos/WeDemand, 3157
Querium, 445, 3277
Queromedia, 2426
QueryObject Systems, 954
Quest, 168, 744, 779
Quest Events LLC, 843
QuEST Global Services, 62
Quest Specialty Chemicals, 194
Quest.ii, 2441
Questar Assesment, 1299
QuestBack, 3076
Questco, 2214
Questcor Pharma, 1251
Questex, 1231, 1660
Questrade, 2058
Queueco, 3108

Quiave, 1041
Quic, 1041
Quick Attach Attachments, 1343
Quick Base, 1972
Quick Med Claims, 746
Quick Sensor, 2426
Quick Study Radiology, 1915
QuickAirLink, 1958
Quickarrow, 36
QuickBRCare, 1507
Quickcue, 459
QuickGifts, 1810
Quickhit, 2196
Quickie Manufacturing Corp, 447
QuickLogic, 1257
Quickly, 607
Quickoffice, 1664
QuickPay, 59, 760
QuickPlay Media, 1156
Quickplay Media, 2096
QuickSilver Technology, 1672
Quicksilver Technology, 692
Quickturn Design, 1087
Quid, 175, 2236, 2446, 2870
Quidbit, 2195
Quidnet Energy, 497, 2111
Quidsi, 1445
Quiet.ly, 624
Quietly, 306
Quigley's, 1135
Quigo, 724
Quigo Technologies, 1001
Quikly, 1150
Quikr, 1327, 1346, 1374
Quilt, 679, 770
Quin Street, 1725
Quincy, 590, 1097
Quinnova Pharmaceuticals, 1817
Quinsis, 2949
QuinStreet, 757, 823, 1760
Quint, 2089
Quinta da Marinha Leisure, 3048
Quintana Shipping, 1573
Quintessence Biosciences, 2001
Quintic, 1779
Quintiles, 74, 220, 1835
Quintiles Transnational, 2311
Quintiq, 1136
QuintoAndar, 1509
Quintus Technologies, 1234
Quinyx, 235
Quip, 45, 1613, 1916
Quipper, 2446
Quippi International Gift Card Center, 206
Quirch, 1403
Quire, 995
Quirky, 38, 786, 1524, 1593
Quiron Hospital Group, 2962
Quithelp, 622
QuitNet, 314
Quitt.ch, 2310
Quixey, 823, 1838, 1968, 2443
Quizlet, 100, 547, 1392, 1882
Quizno's, 1549
QuizUp, 1222
Qulture.Rocks, 795
QUMAS, 2079, 2336, 2734
Qumas, 2918
Qumranet, 1445
Qumu, 59, 807, 1747, 2196, 3279
Qumulo, 585, 935, 1075, 1158, 1899
Qunar, 823, 1683, 1796
Qunar.com, 1184
Qunomedical, 1269
Quntiles, 2300
Quobyte, 3161
Quora, 511, 1181, 1334

1403

Portfolio Companies Index

Quorum, 1829
Quorum Business Solutions, 1573, 1683
Quorum Health Group, 1972
Quorum Systems, 555, 1445
Quotatis, 2481
Quote.com, 1770
Quotient Biodiagnostics Holdings, 806
Quotient Diagnostics, 2760
Quottly, 148
Quovo, 1607, 2225
Qurasense, 2280
Qurasense Relativity Space, 1613
Quri, 428, 1066, 1181
QuVis, 1636
Qv21 Technologies, 505
Qvella, 915
QVentus, 721
Qventus, 1184, 1346
Qvidian, 521, 1080, 1334
Qvivo, 3121
Qwick, 79
QwikCart, 1458
Qwikcilver, 2818
Qwiki, 533, 1118, 1655
Qwil, 395, 890, 1528
Qwilr, 3153
Qwilt, 483, 1534
QWS Holdings LLC, 63
QxMD, 2266
Qynergy, 979
Qype, 2475, 2604
Qyuki, 483
QZZR, 1592
qZZR, 1070

R

R & V, 3062
R Studio, 816
R Taco, 1576
R&B Technology Holding Corporation, 3062
R&D Circuits, 1422
R&H Supply, 1422
R&R Ice Cream, 3020, 3026
R-2solid to Warburg Pincus, 1918
R-Square, 3127
R-Tech Ueno, 2970
R.E.D.D., 1161
R.G.E. Group Ltd., 34
R.H. Electronics, 2745
R.M. Williams, 1088
R.Rouvari Oy, 2873
R/c Sugarkane, 1573
R2 Acquisition Corp., 158
R2 Semiconductor, 1257, 1672
R2 Technology, 153
R24 Lumber, 1689
R2G, 2584
R2I, 222
R2Net, 779, 1323
R2P, 2851
R3 Communications, 2841
R3 Education, 1469
RA Capital, 70, 3273
RA EL, 2006
Ra Pharma, 1122
Ra pharma, 112
Rabbit, 124
Rabbit Farm, 3122
Rabbit Tractors, 995
RABBL, 1061
Raben Tire, 1403
RAC, 3020
Raccortubi Group, 3154
Racemi, 52, 1400
Racemi Inc., 904
Rachio, 377, 1237, 1894
Racing Champions Corporation, 1986

Racing-Live, 3208
Rack Attack, 2051
RackSpace, 2252
Racktop, 1169
RackWare, 1387
Rackware, 1070
Racotek, 536
RacoWireless, 1014
Ractiv, 3073
Ractivity, 2837
Rad Locks, 1295
RAD Technologies, 1401
Radar Networks, 798
Radar Relay, 1528
Radara, 2995
RADCOM, 3137
Radcom, 3231
Raden, 1585
Radiac Abrasives, 1456, 1979
Radial, 218
Radial Engineering, 2235
Radial3D, 1507
RadialPoint, 1540
Radialpoint, 1776
Radian Capital, 37
Radiance Technologies, 466
Radians Innova, 2878
Radianse, 176
Radiant Logistics, 374
Radiant Medical, 237
Radiant Range, 2623
Radiant Research, 374
Radiant RFID, 218
Radiant Systems, 3274
Radiate Media, 871, 1070, 1677
Radiation Therapy Services, 1931
Radiator Labs, 622, 1894
Radiaus Innova AB, 2718
Radicle, 2071
Radient 360, 2068
Radient Technologies, 2048
radient360, 2168
Radio Therapeutics Corporation, 524
Radio Time, 2457
RadioFrame Networks, 645
RadioPharmacy Investors, 1189
RadioPulse, 3127
RadioRx, 1010
Radiotel, 3249
Radiotel Ltd., 2750
Radiowalla, 3019
Radisens Diagnostics, 2918
Radish, 1149, 1883
Radisphere, 946
Radisphere National Radiology Group, 1361
Radisys, 1604
Radium One, 2662
RadiumOne, 1853
Radiumone, 563
Radius, 107, 296, 351, 775, 836, 919, 1268, 1670
Radius Aerospace Inc., 158
Radius Global Growth Experts, 222
Radius Health, 2496
Radius Intelligence, 1427
Radius Networks, 538
Radius8, 150
Radlan Computer Communications, 197
Radlan Ltd., 2750
Radley, 3036
Radnet Ltd, 2770
RadPad, 1965
Radpad, 600
Radview, 1334
Radview Software Ltd., 2750
RADVision, 3158
Radware, 2585
Radwin, 2720

RAE Systems, 1910
Raet, 2378
Rafay Systems, 751
Rafferty's Garden, 2399
Rafter, 757, 1119, 1747
Raftr, 1095, 1392
Rag & Bone, 1022
RagingMobile, 1334
Rags, 1070
RAIDCore, 1146
Raidtec Corporation, 2336
Railcomm, 1627
Railroad Controls Limited, 916
RailWorks, 1990
Rain Neuromorphics, 795
Rain Systems, 1507
Rainbow Child Care Centre, 1724
Rainbow Early Education, 1505
RainDance, 1247, 1247
Raindance, 2611
RainDance Technologies, 87, 1508
Rainforest, 306, 650, 1254
Rainforst QA, 563
RainKing, 1717
Rainmaker, 1346
Rainmaker Systems, 1354
RainStar, 2671
RainStor, 1747
Rainvow, 307
Raisbeck, 48
Raisbeck Engineering, 984
RaiseMe, 741, 883, 1392, 1534, 1607
Raisio Yhtymä Oyj, 2990
Raj Manufacturing, 1767
Rajant, 233
Raken, 306, 679
Raketu, 1314
Raleigh, 853
Raley's, 1970
Ralfi/Estima Finance, 2471
Ralink Technology, 892, 1769
Rally, 1247, 1839, 2138, 2168
Rally Point, 181
Rally Rd., 2236
Rally Software, 315, 538, 1212, 1245
Rallybio, 12
RallyOn, 1655
RallyPoint, 595
Ralph, 307
RAM Medical Innovations, 226
Ramaco Resources, 675
Ramada Plaza, 2285
Ramanas Farms, 834
Rambus, 1247
Ramco Oil Services, 2944
Rameder, 1572
Ramet Trom, 135
Ramky Infrastructure, 3173
RAMMP Hospitality, 2292
RAMP, 521, 922, 1738
Ramp, 518, 712, 2690
Ramp Networks, 757
Ramsey Industries, 873, 1345
Ramsway (JSC), 626
RaNA, 1419
Rancard Solutions, 2345
Rancher, 1184
Rand Logistics, 109
Randall & Reilly, 2204
Randall-Reilly, 199, 1017, 1409
Randian, 1507
Randori, 2
Randy's Worldwide Automotive, 1132
RANDYS Worldwide Automotive, 1777
Range Fuels, 1397
Range Me, 784
Range Networks, 855, 1374

Portfolio Companies Index

Range Resources Ltd., 638
Rangeland Energy III, 671
Ranger Aerospace, 164
Ranger AirShop, 164
Ranger International Services Group, 739
Ranger Marketing, 3232
Ranger Wirless Solutions, 1622
Rangespan, 3018
Rangusutra, 2313
Rani Therapeutics, 980
Ranir, 383, 1128
Rank, 2273
Ranked Media & Technologies, 1507
Ranker, 306, 358, 585, 1099, 1149, 1566, 1798, 1965
RankMyApp, 1370
RankScience, 318
Ranpak, 1368
Ranpak Corp., 168
Rantizo, 995
Rapchat, 229
RaPharma, 1519
Rapid Diagnostek, 400, 1292
Rapid Financial Services, 1970
Rapid Micro Biosystems, 1143, 2690, 3196
Rapid Miner, 1146
Rapid Ratings, 1136
Rapid RMS, 459
Rapid7, 221, 1785
RapidAir, 1435
RapidAPI, 124
RapidBuyr, 1194
RapidCare Clinic, 1667
RapidDeploy, 1611
RapidMicro Biosystems, 1508
Rapidminer, 178
RapidScan, 2978
Rapidscan, 181
RapidSOS, 488, 622, 768, 1260
Rapidsos, 935, 1154
Rapidstream, 3218
RapidStream Inc., 947
Rappi, 124, 751, 770, 942
Rapportive, 305
Rapsodia, 1088
Rapt, 7
Rapt Media, 841, 2010
Raptor Pharmaceuticals, 1775
Raptor Sports Properties, 1524
Raptor Supplies, 2834
Raptor Technologies LLC, 158
Raptr, 106, 581, 1796
Rare, 2076
Rare Bits, 741
Rare.io, 2195
RareCyte, 12, 1792
Raritan, 1317
Ras Therapeautics, 1117
Rasa, 232
RAScom, 3137
Rasilient Systems, 47
Rasiris, 1398
Rasko, 71
Rate Us, 3153
RathGibson, 1967
Ratio, 1740
Rautaruukki Oyj, 2990
Rav Galai, 3245
RAVE, 1673
Rave Mobile Safety, 221, 1593
Rave Wireless, 1672
Ravel, 708, 1334
Ravelli, 2391
Raven, 2076, 2184
Raven Biotechnologies, 1002
Raven Pack, 2674
Raven Power Holdings, 1573

Raven Window, 146
Raven360, 1172
Ravenflow, 1407
Ravisent Technologies, 52
Ravti, 941, 1282
Raw Essentials, 1442
Rawstream, 3108
Rax Restaurants Inc., 354
Ray Sat, 418
Ray Sono AG, 2783
Raybern's, 1861
Raydiance, 184, 609
Raydiant Oximetry, 226
Rayfay, 547
Raymond Express International, 928
Raymundos, 193
Rayne, 1324, 1438
Rayne Water, 1579
Rayner Foods, 2923
Raysat, 2472
Raytel Medical, 955
RayV, 3241
Rayv, 525
RayVio, 195, 596
Raza MicroElectronics, 1080
Raze, 1883
Raze Therapeutics, 1268
Raze Therapeutics Inc., 182
RazorGator, 1361
Razorpay, 1138
RazorSight, 946
Razorsight, 2196
Razz, 807
RBC Bearings, 199, 1037
RBC Signals, 24, 219, 243, 519
RBN, 2543
RCG Global Services, 686
RCN, 909, 1717
RCN Grande, 1835
RCP Advisors, 3265
Rd Rabbit, 1054
Rd.Md, 1663
RDA, 973
RDA Microelectronics, 2850
RDD Pharma, 1382
Rdio, 2446
RDM Corporation, 2144
RDMD, 1151
RDR, 2892
RDX, 333, 1156
Re Commmunity Recycling, 909
Re-Leash, 3257
Re.mu, 3181
RE2, 628
Rea Metrix, 2490
Reaads, 1837
Reach, 1985
Reach Air Medical, 926
REACH Health, 550
Reach Influence, 607
Reach Labs, 622
Reach Robotics, 1509
Reach Surgical, 2936
Reach150, 1642, 1829
Reachable, 2382
Reachdesk, 745
ReachForce, 1242
ReachHealth, 271
Reachli, 2017
ReachLocal, 1906
ReachOut Healthcare America, 1256
ReactEvent, 2284
Reaction, 1070
Reaction Biology, 1098
Reaction Commerce, 306, 561
Reactivity, 613, 1038
Reactor Labs, 1992

READ, 3216
Read ASA, 2754
READ Cased Hole, 2700
Readeo, 1615
Reading Bridges, 2355
Reading Room, 3018
Reading Truck Body, 1030, 1136
ReadMe, 710, 858
Readmill, 2444
Ready Mixed Concrete, 194
Ready Pac Produce, 928
Ready Responders, 488
Ready Robotics, 679
Ready Set Food, 120
Ready Set Surgical, 479
ReadyCart, 459
Readyforzero, 1460
ReadyPulse, 1522
Real Eyes, 2710
Real Foundations, 1944
Real Gravity, 1083
Real Image, 483
Real Imaging, 3050
Real Mex Restaurants Inc., 354
Real Musical, 2891
Real People Investment Holdings, 2086
REAL SAMURAI, 2974
Real Savvy, 545
Real Time Content, 1305
Real Ventures, 51
Real Vision, 341
Real-Time Collaboration Solutions By PlaceWare, 1626
Real-Time Radiography, 3245
Real-time Radiography Ltd, 2973
Real5D, 625
Realbest, 2841
Realcom, 2854
REALD, 553
RealDirect, 1475, 1849
Realflair, 2574
Realine, 205
Realities.io, 307
Reality Female Condom, 1837
Reality Mobile, 466, 2700
Realm, 1069, 1110, 1626
Realm Therapeutics, 1271
RealManage, 310, 1944
RealMatch, 2566
Realmatch, 655
RealNetworks, 1910
Realogy, 140
RealOps, 1407, 1899
RealPractice, 1237
RealScout, 596
RealSelf, 1641
Realstar Management, 2079
Realtime, 2545
Realtime Robotics, 1834
Realton Corporation, 1382
RealtyShares, 11, 560, 1882
RealVue, 1668
RealWinWin, 1227, 1689
Realworld.co, 2646
realync, 1155
Realytics, 2503
ReaMetrix, 1245
REAN Cloud, 361
Reapit, 29
Reapplix, 3203
Rearden Commerce, 1235
Reata Pharmaceuticals, 3015
Rebag, 525, 563, 816
Rebar, 1288
Rebecca Taylor, 1753
Rebel Coast Winery, 307
Rebel Mail, 305

1405

Portfolio Companies Index

Rebel Mouse, 1110, 1361
Rebellion, 996
Rebelmail, 600
RebelMouse, 741, 1699
Rebit, 36, 876
Rebllion Energy, 1278, 1326
Reborn Beauty, 1954
Rebtel, 2478
Rebus, 1507
Rebuy, 2979
ReBuy.de, 2813
ReceiptBank, 1000
Receivable Solutions, 1979
Receivables Exchange, 710, 1478, 1738
Receivables Management Partners, 1343
ReCept Pharmacy, 818
Receptiv, 655, 946
Receptos, 153, 747, 1124, 1460, 1916
Recharge, 679, 707, 751
Recisio, 2365
Reckitt Benckiser, 1452
Recko, 1138
ReckOne Inc., 623
Recochem, 1767, 2183
Recogni, 1834
Recognia, 1306
Recoletos, 2962
Recombine, 743
Recommerce Solutions, 2308, 3113
Recommind, 1620
RECON Holdings III, 1129
Recon Instruments, 2278
Reconda International, 1142
Recondo, 946
Recondo Technology, 333, 1107
Reconnex, 197
ReconRobotics, 1872
Record 360, 92
Recordati S.p.A., 1452
Recorded Books, 1960
Recorded Future, 38, 965, 979, 1000, 2478
RecordSetter, 1149, 1912
Recount Media, 1882
Recoup Fitness, 1507
Recourse Technologies, 596
Recover Energy Services, 2050
RecoverX, 858, 1585
Recovery Technology Solutions, 1895
RecoveryDirect Acquisition, 158
Recros Medica, 1145
RecruiterNet, 438
RecruitingTrends, 863
RecruitTalk, 459
Recupyl, 2372
Recurly, 641, 710, 784, 1460
Recurrent Energy, 1247
Recursion, 445
Recursion Pharma, 107
Recursion Pharmaceuticals, 1151, 1202, 1363
Recursion Pharmeceuticals, 720
Recurve, 1579
RecycleBank, 1672
Recyclebank, 184, 1438, 1593, 1673, 1977
Red 7 Media, 1927
Red Ambiental, 834
Red Aril, 976, 1853
Red Bag Solutions, 794
Red Balloon Security, 1480
Red Bend Software, 536, 2566
Red Brick Systems, 238
Red Bridge Capital, 462
Red Bubble, 1323
Red Built, 1344
Red Canary, 36
Red Door Spa, 1335
Red Foundry, 1364
Red Hawk Fire & Security, 528

Red Herring, 1865
Red IQ, 377
Red Kite, 2674
Red Mango, 477
Red Oak Power, 675
Red Paper Group, 2420
Red Rabbit, 1420
Red River Waste, 1422
Red River Waste Solutions, 1021
Red Robin Gourmet Burgers, 1505
Red Rock Biofuels, 747
Red Sift, 1982
Red Storm Entertainment, 1709
Red Swoosh, 563
Red Technology Alliance, 1573
Red Tricycle, 707, 1183, 1852
Red Vector, 1745
Red Ventures, 815, 1502, 1683
Red Vision, 655
Red Wolf Security, 2184
Red-C, 436, 2580
Red-M, 2386
Redback Networks, 1996
Redbeacon, 1916
Redbend, 3221
RedBird Capital Partners, 70
Redbooth, 101, 206
RedBrick Health, 938
Redbrick Health, 935
Redbubble, 605
RedBus, 3109
Redbus.in, 1013
RedCap, 1700
Redcap, 707
Redd, 786
Redd & Whyte, 2760
Reddit, 511, 1821, 2012
reddit, 991
Reddo Mobility, 38
RedDot, 2616
ReddPath Integrated Pathology, 1448
Reddy Ice Inc., 158
Redeam, 1035
Redecam Group, 3154
Redecam Group SpA, 2821
RedEenvelope, 192
REDEF, 60
ReDeTec, 2184
Redfern Integrated Optics, 1779
Redfield Proctor, 392
Redfin, 609, 835, 836, 1946
Redfish Rentals, 928
Redgate Communications, 1708
Redgate Media, 1769
RedHelper, 2938
Redhill Biopharma, 1382
RedHook Ale Brewery, 753
Redington Gulf, 1017
Redis Labs, 3221
Redislabs, 603
Redkite Financial Markets, 2662
Redknee, 2196
Redlen Technologies, 2143, 2213, 2291
Redline Communications, 880
Redline Networks, 59, 455
Redline Trading Solutions, 567
Redmart, 3127
reDock, 2027, 2212
Redowl, 535
RedOwl Analytics, 84, 1632
Redox, 2, 754
RedPack Logistics, 998
RedPath, 990
RedPath Integrated Pathology, 293, 998
RedPoint, 876
Redpoint Bio, 1328
Redpoint eventures, 483

Redpoint Ventures, 986, 3284
RedPost, 658
RedPrairie, 779
RedRover, 2017
RedSeal, 968, 1102, 1178, 1391, 1916
RedSeal Systems, 979
RedSky Technologies, 636
Redstone, 2007
Redstone Communications, 1334
Redtail Solutions, 1920
Redtree People, 3010
Reduxio, 3221
RedVision Systems, 1886
Redwave Medical, 2527
Redwood Systems, 1241
Redwood Trust Inc., 1903
RedZone, 1161
RedZone Robotics, 1199, 1234
Redzone Robotics, 22
RedZone Roboticss, 998
RedZone Wireless, 438
Reebok Spartan Race, 1524
Reebonz, 823
Reed City Tool, 164
Reed Group, 194
Reed Smith, 3275
Reedsy, 3108
Reef, 168, 2544, 2544
ReefEdge, 645
Reel Genie, 1169
Reel Power International, 632
Reelcraft Industries, 908
Reelgood, 544
Reelio, 641
Reelwell, 1125
Reemo, 995
ReEnergy Holdings, 1573
Reeves Extruded Products, 1606
Reevoo, 2691, 2972
Refac Optical Group, 46
Refer.com, 972
Referral Saasquatch, 2284
Refinery 29, 1110
Refinery29, 741, 751, 1748
Reflect, 773
Reflectent, 1913
Reflectent Software, 1672
Reflectivity, 1704, 1922
Reflektion, 235
Reflektive, 124
Reflex Photonics, 2196
Reflexion, 1916
Reflexion Network Solutions, 310
Reflexis, 857, 1602
Reformation, 761
Reframe It, 1600, 1669
Refresco, 2204
Refresco Gerber, 2311
Refresh, 455, 1534
Refresh Body, 1701
Refresj, 770
Refrigerated Holdings, 722
REG, 171
Regado, 1508
Regado Biosciences, 1898
Regal, 3203
Regal Cinemas, 1708
Regalii, 721, 1054, 1998
Regard, 2965
ReGear, 1746
ReGear Life Sciences, 998, 1448
ReGelTec, 19
ReGen Biologics, 1616
REGEN Energy, 1324
Regency, 1846
Regency Beauty Institute, 1469
Regency Energy Partners LP, 914

1406

Portfolio Companies Index

Regency Entertainment, 3020
Regency Gas Services, 456
Regency Hospital Company, 1963
Regency Midwest, 297
Regenemed, 1600
Regeneron Pharmaceuticals, 1616
Regenesis Biomedical, 794, 1702, 1901
Regent, 1299, 1991
Regent Cabinetry, 917
Regent Communications, 1708
Regent Education, 405, 475, 508
Regent Education Inc., 158
Regent Holding, 783
Regentis Biomaterials, 3059
ReGenX Biosciences, 710
REGENXBIO, 1941
RegenXBio, 1916
RegenxBio, 762
Regesis Biomedical, 1802
Regimend MD, 1191
Regional Growth Capital, 3271
Regional Management Corp., 1403
Regional Rail, 1111
Register.com, 1899, 1910
Registrar Corp., 257
Regroup, 1160
regroup, 1155
Regulatory and Quality Solutions, 610
Regulatory Datacorp, 221
Regulus, 1670
Rehive, 307
REI, 680
Reichert, 1751
Reify, 181
ReigoHelden, 2979
Reille24, 2475
Reilly's Hempvet, 786
Reima, 1572
Reimagine Holdings Group, 361
Reinnervate, 3028
Reischling Press, 958
Reisefeber, 3013
Rekoo, 641, 2869, 3002
Rekoo Japan, 2869
Reladyne Inc., 64
RelateIQ, 1534
Relationship Science, 922, 1607
Relativity, 397, 1696
Relativity Space, 1329
Relay, 1317, 1446
Relay Foods, 1830, 3277
Relay Network, 741
Relay Therapeutics, 709
Relay Ventures, 2032, 2172
Relay2, 626
RelayFoods.com, 235
RelayHealth, 1668
RelayRides, 707, 760, 1531, 1968
Relayrides, 197
Relegence, 954
Relevad, 772
Relevant Rental Solutions, 403
Relevant Solutions, 781
Relevate, 349
Relevium Technologies, 2031
Relevvant, 1839
Reliable Biopharmaceutical Corporation, 828
Reliable Parts, 1765
Reliable Robotics, 648, 1421
Reliance Electric, 354
Reliant Healthcare Professionals, 492
Reliant Home Health, 1209
Reliant Hospital Partners, 1279
Reliant Medical Products, 1533
Reliant Pharmaceuticals Inc., 237
Reliant Rehabilitation, 639
Reliant Renal Care, 639, 723

Reliant Technologies, 1445
Reliaquest, 793
Relias Learning, 1136
Relievant, 386, 1378
Relievant MedSystems, 241
Relievant Medsystems, 666, 1122
ReliOn, 1397
Reliving, 2284
Relmada RiboNova, 266
Relogix, 2195
Relovv, 342
Reltio, 2, 563
Relume, 742
Relypsa, 12, 1197, 1298, 1382
Relypsa Inc., 604
ReMark, 2378
Remarkable, 1985
Rembrandt Photo Services, 447
Rembrandt Venture Partners, 986, 3284
Remcan, 2292
Remco Maintenance Corp., 465
Remedi S, 1970
Remedi Seniorcare, 1742
Remedly, 718
Remedy, 93, 347
Remedy Health, 1460
Remedy Health Media, 1927
Remedy Informatics, 768, 1205
Remedy Interactive, 548
Remedy Partners, 1728
Remedy Pharmaceuticals, 662
Remedy Systems, 1830
Remerge, 2841, 3236
Remesh, 816
Remi, 1276
Remicade, 2102
Remind, 741, 883, 1075, 1392, 1696
Remita Health, 1628, 1762
RemitDATA, 1331, 1732
RemitDATA Inc., 810
Remitly, 262, 685, 773, 1502, 1789, 1830, 1852
Remity, 609
Remma Consulting, 2526
Remon Medical Technologies, 1847
Remora Petroleum, 1326
Remote Analysis, 2873
Remote Co., 2974
Remote Year, 754, 935
Remote.it, 306, 525
Remotely, 1114
RemoteMDx, 506
RemoteReality, 233, 457
Remotive, 1789
RemoTV, 1676
REMP AG, 2564
Rempex Pharmaceuticals, 782
Remtec Inc., 1053
Renaissance, 578, 779, 924
Renaissance BV, 2722
Renaissance Lighting, 1324, 1579
Renaissance Mark, 170, 1954
Renaissance Pharma, 1590
Renaissance Venture Capital Fund, 3269
Renal Advantage, 1972
Renal Care Group, 300
Renal Care Partners, 1251
Renal Solutions, 117, 1448, 1847
RenalSolutions, 184
RenaMed Biologics, 1336
Rend, 2155
Renegade Brands, 96
Reneo, 1519
ReNet Japan Group, 2974
Renew, 1158, 1916
Renew Financial, 126, 322, 2000
Renew Inserts, 1143
Renew Power, 834

Renewable Energy Group, 1895
Renewable Energy Products, 1400
Renewable Funding, 491, 1324
RenewLife, 1871
Renex Holdings, 2613
Renfro, 1062
Reniac, 358, 1483, 1890
Renix, 2061
Renkoo, 623
Renle, 3194
Renmatix, 946
Rennhack Marketing Services, 328, 928
RenoNorden, 2325
RenoRun, 1363, 2157
Renovar, 1292
Renovate America, 1579, 1902
Renovia, 1145
Renovis, 747, 2513, 2518, 2690
Renovis Inc., 2816
Renoviso, 942
Renovo, 1926, 2518
RenovoRx, 129, 841
Renren, 596, 1244, 2936
RenRench.com, 1534
RenRui, 2936
Rensa Filtration, 654
Rent The Runway, 221, 935, 1075
Rent the Runway, 45, 1785
Rentabilities, 1150
Rentalutions, 569
Rentbits, 1114
RentBureau, 855
Rented, 1024
Renthop, 1874
Rentify, 2478
RentJuice, 1097
Rentlytics, 306, 563, 567, 942, 1566
Rentmatix, 1075
Rentokil Initial Plc., 1903
RentPath, 1496
Rentpath Inc., 1835
RentPayment, 756
RentStuff, 459
ReNu Power, 156
Reonomy, 1475, 1546, 1699, 2132
ReovoRX, 1600
REP, 2551, 2607
Rep, 761
Rep The Squad, 858
Repable, 2128, 2200
Repair Pal, 319
Repairogen, 1051, 1420
RepairPal, 1865, 1958
Repare, 1268, 1928
Repco, 2951
Repco Group, 2420
RepconStrickland, 156
Repeater Technology, 757
RepEquity, 61, 678
Repetto International, 2302
Replaid, 3038
Replay Solutions, 1672
Replenish, 858
Replica, 996
Replica Labs, 3125
Replicated, 305
Replicon, 665, 1696
Replika, 45, 1069
Replimune, 191, 762
Replit, 1527
Reply, 1389
Reply.com, 184, 1235
ReportGrid, 1097
Reportive, 3233
Reposit, 3108
Repositive, 3108
Reposito, 2921

Portfolio Companies Index

Repost, 120
ReproCELL, 2970
Reprogenesis, 1412
Repros Therapeutics, 1059
Repsly, 1100
Republic Doors & Frames, 606
Republic Midstream, 156
Republic National Cabinet Corporation, 575
Republic Project, 1222
Republic.co, 1395
Repulic Insurance, 328
Reputation Institute, 427
Reputation.Com, 197, 751
Reputation.com, 176, 757, 968, 1075, 1700
ReputationLoop, 92
Reputology, 92
ReqMed Company, 2970
ReQuest, 1475
Request Broadband, 3168
Request Now, 1589
Requisite Technology, 1235
Reroyal Holdings LP, 354
RES Software, 1886
RESC, 306
Rescale, 262, 585, 724, 1154, 2329
Rescare, 1557
ReSci, 761, 1247
ReScie, 1888
Resco Products Inc., 832, 1971
Rescue Forensics, 995
RescueTime, 1149
RescueTimy, 1860
Research Enhanced Design + Development Inc., 438
Research Horizons, 2022
Research Now Group Inc., 403
ResearchGate, 15, 248, 775, 777, 842, 1796
Reserve, 60
Reset Therapeutics, 237
ReShape, 1628, 1762
ReShape Medical, 1921
Reshape Medical, 1298
Residence Inn by Marriott, 190
Resident, 13
Residential Design Services, 958
Residential Mortgage Services, 686
Residential Services Group Inc., 1971
Resilient, 712
Resilient Systems, 646
Resilinc, 1013, 1607, 1663, 1757
Resiver, 2029
ResLab Holding, 2754
Reslink, 2754
Resman AS, 3141
Resolute, 2655
Resolute AI, 1555
Resolute Games, 995
Resolute Networks, 2782
Resolution Health, 1850
ReSolutionTx, 2229
Resolve Systems, 1000
Resolve Therapeutics, 644, 1303, 2008
Resolver, 2170, 2674
Resolvyx, 747, 1419
Resolvyx Pharmaceuticals, 412
Resonado, 226, 429, 622
Resonance, 2509
Resonant, 1206
Resonant Medical, 2196
Resonant Venture Partners, 3269
Resonate, 161, 871
Resonate Networks, 2157
Resource Ammirati, 1979
Resource Label Group, 733
ReSource Pro, 610
Resourcekraft, 2918
Respect Network, 1061

Respectance B.V., 3128
Respicardia, 40, 68, 1460, 1819, 3279
Respicardia Inc., 158
Respira Therapeutics, 549
Respiratory Motion, 1061, 1160, 1988
RespirTech, 3279
Respond2 Communications Holdings, 1279
Respondly, 306, 1968
Response Analytics, 1427
Response Analytics Inc., 856
Response BioMedical, 1382
Response Linl, 949
Response Networks, 1227
Response Tap, 2691
Response Team 1, 838
ResponseTek Networks, 2196
Responsetek Networks, 2143
Responsfabrikken, 3022
Responsys, 560, 836, 1024, 1119, 1672
ResQ, 2137, 2149
Resson Aerospace, 2068, 2200, 2239
Rest Devices, 708
Restalo, 2339, 3105
Restaurant Associates Corporation, 354
Restaurant Kritic, 2838
Restaurant Technologies, 199, 3279
Restaurant Technology, 378
Restaurant-Kritik.de, 2829
Restaurants Unlimited, 1753
Restopolitan, 2669
Restorando, 665, 754, 1747, 2446
Restoration + Recovery, 610
Restoration Parts Unlimited, 632
Restoration Robotics, 87, 495, 1010
Restore, 2949
Restore Medical, 995
Restore Medical Solutions, 1187
Restorix Health, 1109
RestorixHealth, 558
Resultados Digitais, 641
Results Physiotherapy, 1742
REsurety, 497, 1097
Resverlogix, 1325
Resy, 1110
Resy Network, 1694
Retail Associated Mgt., 1295
Retail Decisions, 2379
Retail Me Not, 57, 1001
Retail Next, 2690
Retail Optimization, 660, 1142
Retail Shopping Systems, 418
Retail Solutions, 1620, 1913, 1916
RetailExchange's, 422
Retailigence, 1236, 1513
RetailNet, 1738
RetailNext, 1327, 1509
Retailnext, 197
Retailo, 3113
Retea, 2888
ReTel Technologies, 685
Retention Science, 228, 624, 1055, 1247, 1480
Rethink, 149, 1551
Rethink Autism, 1551
ReThink Medical, 1347
Rethink Robotics, 262, 455, 935, 1673, 1874
RethinkDB, 114, 206, 935, 1968, 2329
Retica Systems, 1672
Retif, 2317, 2375
Retina AI, 518
RetiSpec, 2149
ReTrans, 1777
Retrica, 100
Retriever Communications, 2975
Retroficiency, 1459
Retrofit, 471, 609, 731, 1480
Retronaut, 2586, 2685
Retrophin, 188

Retroscreen Virology, 2892
Retrosense, 1221
Retrotope, 1044
RetroVascular, 1773
Retty, 2646
Retty.com, 2798
Return on Intelligence, 1025
Return Path, 460, 547, 776, 777, 1245, 1620
ReturnCentral, 56, 989
ReturnLogic, 1577
Reunion, 1604
ReUrban, 3279
REV, 109
Rev, 835, 1374
Rev H20, 81
Rev Worldwide, 751
Reva, 834
REVA Medical, 621
Reva Systems, 1334
Reval, 521, 1334
Revance, 2513
Revance Therapeutics, 1664, 1786, 1941, 2690
Revascular Therapeutics, 57, 458, 1094
ReVascular Therapeutics Inc., 269
RevCascade, 342
Revcascade, 1563
Reveal, 349
Reveal Design Automation, 742
Reveal Energy Services, 1125
Reveal Media, 622
Reveal Mobile, 971
Reveal Technology Inc., 1089
Reveel, 454
Revel, 1834
Revel Body, 85
Revel Systems, 596, 792, 1972
Revelstoke Capital Partners, 3264
Revenew International, 1111
Revenue Cycle Solutions, 402
Revenue Science, 623, 1733
Revenue Technologies, 56
Revenue.Com, 1012
RevenueCat, 795
Rever, 302, 2019
Revera, 183, 563
Reverb, 231, 1118, 1247
ReverbNation, 1348, 1710
Revere, 231, 1110, 1281
Revere Packaging, 1484
Reverie Labs, 318, 2000
Reverie Language Technologies, 1509
Reverse Logistics GmBH, 1248
Reverse Medical, 666
Reverse Medical Corp., 269, 642
ReverseVision, 1869
ReversingLabs, 979
Revfluence, 129
Review Centre Limited, 2871
Review Pro, 2339
Review Trackers, 566
Reviews 42, 3211
Revionics, 301, 695, 1600
Revip, 229
Revise, 3028
Revision, 1490
Revision App, 3108
ReVision Optics, 621
Revision Optics, 386, 1010
Revision Skincare, 1590
ReVision Therapeutics, 1775
Revisios, 2514
Revit Technology, 1334
Revitas, 1136
Revival, 545
Revive Personal Products, 164
Revivio, 455, 1119
Revivn, 1054, 1894

Portfolio Companies Index

Revlo, 1329, 2113, 2249
Revmetrix, 377, 814, 1320
RevoLights, 1669
Revolights, 195, 1600
ReVolt Technology, 3013
Revolut, 2478, 3108
Revolution Analytics, 1334, 1474
Revolution Credit, 228, 1110, 1240
Revolution Foods, 428, 595, 1977
Revolution Growth, 3270
Revolutions Foods, 1438
REVOLV, 1861
Revolv, 1789
Revolver, 2646
Revolymer, 2892, 3028
Revotar Biopharmaceuticals AG, 2528
Revry, 218
Revsite, 1766
Revstone, 1067
Revulytics, 178, 538
RevUp, 1721
Revup, 1607
Revuze, 3003
RevX, 1346
ReWalk, 3050
Reward Gateway, 857
Reward Group Ltd, 2836
Rewards Now, 655
REWARDS21, 1155
RewardsPay, 1254
RewewData, 184
Rewind.me, 1680
Reworld Media, 2851
Rex, 1883
Rexel, 2719
Rexnord, 140
Rexter, 1965
Reynold Greenleaf & Associates, 966
Reynolds & Reynolds Co., 1903
Reynolds American, 16
Reynolds Plymer, 364
Reynolds Polymer Technologies, 1053
Rezatec, 2997
RezSolutions, 1850
Rezzcard, 3277
Rf Magic, 2436
RF Micro Devices, 3137
RF Surgical, 1725
rFactr, 1632
RFArrays, 1303
RFE Investment Partners, 77
RFG Enterprises, 908
RFHIC, 3145
RFIB, 368
RFID Global Solutions, 1388
RFJ Auto, 1045
RFmagic, 132
RFMD, 59, 1676
RFnano, 1393
RFP360, 745
RFS Goldings, 716
RGB Networks, 757, 1241, 1445
RGL Reservoir Management, 456
RGM Advisors, 1776
RGM Group, 1575
Rhapso, 2899
Rhebo GmbH, 2686
Rhein Biotech, 2748
Rheo, 1421
Rheonix, 432, 1126, 1523
Rheonix Inc., 810
Rhetorical, 3104
Rhiag Group, 2379
Rhino, 724
RhinoCyte, 1512
Rhinotek Heavy Duty Computer Products, 276
Rhiza, 173, 384, 628

RHK. Salient Surgical Technologies, 555
RHM Klinik und Pflegeheime, 3232
Rhomobile, 2382
Rhone, 1088
Rhumbix, 836, 872
Rhysto, 3052
Rhythm, 762, 1268, 1811
Rhythm NewMedia, 1257, 1540
Rhythm Pharmaceuticals, 1436
Rhythm Superfoods, 445, 482, 950
Rhythm Xience, 2149
Rhythmia Medical, 1347
Rhythmlink, 926
Rialto, 704, 3108
Rib-X Pharmaceuticals, 23, 212, 410
Ribbit, 856, 1084, 1427, 1437, 2017
Ribbon, 872, 1965
Ribometrix, 1628
Ribon Therapeutics, 1778
RibX, 1604
Rice Garden, 147
Rice's Honey, 443
Rich Relevance, 603, 609, 720
Richard Brady & Associates, 1040
Richardeyres, 953
Richardson Foods, 774
Richcore, 3211
Richelieu Foods Inc., 357
RichFX, 536
Richrelence, 563
RichRelevance, 1594, 1865
richrelevance, 872
Richtek Technology, 2603
RichWave, 1922
Ricki's Fashions, 2258
RickIQ, 235
Ricmedia, 2974
Ricoh, 214
Ride Health, 266
Ride Report, 941, 1893
RideCell, 302
Ridecell, 1703
RideKleen, 1507
RidePal, 491
Ridgebury Tankers, 1573
Ridgeline Midstream Holdings, 156
Ridgeway, 2386
Ridgewood Energy Fund, 1764
Ridgeworth Investments, 1123
Ridgmont, 2796
Ridley - Race Productions, 2949
Ridlr, 1509
Rienfer, 3108
Riffa Views, 152
Riffsy, 784
RiffTrax, 198
Rifiniti, 13
Rifkin Acquisition Partners, 1927
Rig Up, 809
Rigado, 1158, 2278
Rigel, 782
Rigetti, 124, 720, 721, 1254, 1758
Rigetti Computing, 107, 1151
Righscale, 1796
Right Brain, 2949
Right Brain + Left Brain, 3275
Right Health, 2149, 2265
Right Media, 1445, 1534
Right Networks, 361
Right Pointe, 489
Right Scale, 634
Right Time Heating and Air Conditioning, 2081
Right Vision, 2601
Right90, 947
RightAnswers, 1328
RightCare Solutions, 621
RightHand Robotics, 1202

Righthook, 741
Rights Flow, 52
RightScale, 581, 1474
RightsFlow, 1385
Rightside, 818, 1717
Rightware, 2999
RigNet, 1235
Rigor, 189
RigUp, 858
Riide, 1585
Riipen, 1527
RillaVoice, 684
RIM China Company, 1769
RIMCO Royalty Partners, 1503
Rimini Street, 57
Rimor, 2944
Rimrock, 78
Rimrock Construction, 462
Rimrock Midstream, 675
Rinac India, 2460
Rinant Neuroscience, 1493
Rinat Neuroscience, 1786
Rincon Industries, 439
Ring, 741, 842, 874, 874, 1888
Ring Central, 581, 634, 1626
Ring2Conferencing, 2342
RingCentral, 1341
Ringly, 351, 936, 1222
Ringo, 3267
RingYa, 2352
Rinovum, 293, 1448
Rinovum Women's Health, 298
Rinse, 32, 229, 707, 724, 858, 1028, 1222
RIO, 1711
RIO Brands, 443
Rio Nogales Power, 1795
Rio Ranch Markets, 611
Rio SEO, 631, 1945
Rio Seo, 793
Rio Tinto, 2659
Riot Games, 743
Ripcord, 219, 519, 968, 1075, 1151
Ripe Metrics, 392
Ripfire, 524
Ripio, 307
Riplay, 1416
Ripple, 24, 384, 472, 1329, 1662
Ripple Labs, 107
Ripples, 249
Rippling, 942
RIPS Technologies, 2686
Riptide, 1323
Riptide Tek, 2197
Riri, 3154
Riscica Associates, 3267
Rise, 552, 858, 2200
Rise Art, 858
Rise Baking Company, 1372
Rise Brewing Co., 1191
Rise Health, 748, 1619
RiseSmart, 548, 1747
Rishabh Instruments, 834
Rising Star Resources, 2025
RisingStars Growth Fund, 2708
Risk Alyze, 793
Risk I/O, 1865
Risk International, 361
Risk Lens, 603
Risk Methods, 3044
Risk Recon, 603
Risk Strategies, 1062
Risk Strategies Company, 909, 1081
Riskclick, 2386
riskdata, 2491
RiskIQ, 1752, 2132
Riskmatch, 1118
RiskMetrics, 23

1409

Portfolio Companies Index

RiskMetrics Group, 1717
Riskrecon, 816
RistCall, 995
RiT, 3137
Rita's, 164
Rita's Water Ice Franchise Company, 717
Ritani, 394
RITC, 1315
Rite In The Rain, 82
RITEK, 892
Ritter Pharmaceuticals, 1028
Ritual, 761, 872, 1000, 1346, 1888, 1985, 2132, 2137, 2182, 2195
Riva Boats, 1404
Rival Health, 794, 1923
Rive Technology, 59, 455, 1241, 1355, 3099
River Cities Capital Funds, 3269, 3270
River Medical, 206
River Point Farms, 378, 477
River Ranch Fresh Foods, 2015
River Studios, 792
Riverbed, 385, 909, 1212
Riverchase Dermatology, 1469
Riverhead Networks Inc, 2770
RiverMeadow, 483
RiverMend Health, 1346
Rivermine, 1146, 1699, 1899
RiverMuse, 1853
Rivermuse, 3058
RiverPay, 2113
Rivers Agile, 3275
Riversdale Resources, 1548
Riverside Engineering, 719
Riverside Insights, 92
Riverside Products, 719
RiverSilica, 3019
Riverstone, 1219
Rivertop Renewables, 570, 738, 3277
Riverview Power LLC, 158
Rivet & Sway, 231
Rivet Smart Audio, 1019
Riviera Broadcast Group, 1927
Riviera Travel, 3036
Rivkin Radler LLP, 3267
Rivs Digital Interviews, 1019
Rixty, 784, 1028
Rize, 1146
Rizing, 1136
RJ Metrics, 1700, 2017
RJE International, 958
RJMetrics, 1531, 1853
RJO Holdings Corp., 403
RKD Group, 361
RLabs, 1374
RM Techtronics, 1021
RMB SA, 2564
RMC, 2375
RMDY, 325
Rmi, 2697
RMI Corp. Seeking Alpha, 634
RMI Corporation, 1080
Rmoni, 2366
Rmoni Wireless, 2949
RMP Group Inc., 158
RMS Group, 3244
RMSS, 1711
RMX Resources, 477
Rna Diagnostics, 2149
RNA Networks, 1383
RNAgri, 267
Rndex, 1459
Ro, 816, 1694
Ro-Flow Compressors, 1292
Road Angel, 2662
Road Trippers, 479
RoadBotics, 1894
RoadLink, 722

RoadMap, 3028
RoadMunk, 2137
Roadmunk, 720
Roadrunner Pharmacy, 118
RoadRunner Recycling Inc., 56
Roadrunner Transportation Systems, 917
Roads, 1305
RoadSafe Traffic Systems, 716
Roadster, 547
Roadtrippers, 630, 1150
Roam, 307, 472, 977, 1758
Roam & Wander, 3181
Roam Robotics, 1721
Roanwell Corporation, 17
Robbins Brothers, 528
Robbins-Gioia, 48
Robbinskertsten Direct, 349
Robert Allen Duralee Group, 96
Robert Graham, 2171
Robert Lee Morris, 940
Roberts Company, 1021
Roberts Radio, 1728
Roberts Tool Company, 1705
Robertshaw, 1753
Robin, 305, 600, 743
Robin Care, 1758
Robin Systems, 751
Robin Therapeutics, 191
Robinhood, 45, 578, 792, 1075, 1329, 1560, 1662, 1694, 1758
Robinson Department Store, 1139, 2946
Robison and Davidson, 2985
Roblox, 100, 741, 772, 872, 1212
RoboCV, 890, 2938
Robotic Drilling Systems AS, 3141
Robotic Skies, 1070
Robotiq, 235
Robots Lab, 874
Robust Intelligence, 1666
Rochal Industries, 425
Rock Health, 858, 1052
Rock Mobile, 2936, 3123
Rock Mobile Corp, 2662
Rock My Run, 950
Rock Ridge Stone, 378
Rock Your Life, 2531
Rock-It Cargo, 368
Rock-Ola, 908
Rockbot, 32, 306, 607, 1758, 2010
Rockerbox, 1306
Rocket Dog, 481, 839
Rocket Fuel, 560, 1752
Rocket Jump, 1813
Rocket Lawyer, 197, 946, 1255
Rocket Pharma, 514
Rocket Racing League, 1584
Rocket Seals, 1152
Rocket Softwa, 1491
RockeTalk, 1239
RocketBolt, 622
RocketFuel, 623
Rocketfuel, 287, 1247, 1327, 1341
Rocketfuel Inc., 1089
Rocketmiles, 471
Rocketrip, 814
RocketRoute, 319
Rockets Of Awesome, 318
Rockets of Awesome, 325, 761, 816, 1110
Rockies Venture Fund, 3276
Rocklands, 834
Rockport, 456
RockPort Capital Partners, 3284
Rockport Georgetown Partners, 156
Rocksbox, 646, 1181, 1675
Rocksbox Jewelry, 942
Rockset, 872
Rockwekll Automation, 473

Rockwell Collins Inc., 1903
Rockworth Companies, 462
Rocky Mountain Financial Corporation, 447
Rocky Mountain Helicopters, 616
Rocky Mountain Portable Storage, 1745
RockYou, 515, 729, 1690
Rockyou, 596, 1416
Rococo Software, 3191
Roctest, 235
Roctool, 2876
Rod and Tubing Services, 378
Rodeo Therapeutics, 31, 2008
Rodgers Plant Hire, 2985
Rodvig Kro & Badehotel, 3203
Roehm, 62
Roehm Marine, 443
Roenest Group, 3154
Roger Garments, 1248
Rogers Corporation, 77
RogersCasey, 402
Rogue, 1310
Rogue Valley Microdevices, 1915
ROI DNA, 231
Roka BioScience, 1382
Roka Bioscience, 74
Rokid, 973
Roku, 835, 922, 1202
Roland, 909
RolePoint, 585, 1839
Rolepoint, 128
ROLI, 2478
Roli, 743, 776
Rolith, 3229
Roll Rite, 164, 401
Rolland, 928
rollApp, 2938
Rollbar, 1546
RollEase, 1343
Rollick, 204, 205
Rolling Hills Generating, 1795
Rolls-Royce Holdings Plc., 1903
RollStream, 876
Rollstream, 538
Rolltech, 229, 1912
Roly International Holdings, 892
ROM Corp., 449
Roman Decorating Products, 378
Roman Products LLC, 1609
Romania, 2706
Romanoco-Gruppe Karlsruhe, 3067
Romar Partners, 3265
Rombah Wallace, 2392
Romet, 2255
Romotive, 1254, 1912
RomoWind, 2475
Rompetrol Rafinare SA, 3187
Romprest Service SA, 2309
Romulus Capital, 3273
Rondele Specialty Foods, 719
Rongshu.com, 2998
Ronnoco Beverage Solutions, 960
Ronveaux, 3134
Roofsafe, 2399
Roofstock, 942, 1069
Rooftop Media, 215
Rook Media, 716
Rookwood Pavillion, 1954
Room Beats, 2638
Room Choice, 1070
Room Sketcher, 3216
Room Temperature Superconductors Inc. (ROOTS), 588
Room77, 1524
Roomi, 858, 1585, 1958
Roomorama, 3044, 3215
Roompot, 909
Roonets, 1755

Portfolio Companies Index

Roosland, 3209
Roost, 519, 1178, 2280
Rooster, 1323
RoosterBio, 2278
Roostock, 858
Root, 630
Root Metrics, 378
Root Music, 1341
Root Wireless, 1583
Root3, 171, 491
Roots, 2252
RootsRated, 459
Rootstock Software, 1607
Rope, 3211
Roposo, 1826
Rorus, 622
Roscoe Manufacturing, 465
Rose America Corp., 443
Rose City Printing and Packaging, 1569
Rose Hills, 869
Rose Paving, 1209
Rosemont Holdings, 2379
Rosemont Solebury Co-Investment Fund LP, 2094
roserocket, 2249
Rosetta LLC, 1129
Rosie, 13, 1663
Ross, 2157
Ross Aviation, 447
Ross Education, 1039
ROSS Intelligence, 2232
Ross PPD Corporation, 1185
Ross Stores, 300
Ross Systems, 2881
Ross-Simons, 783
Rostik Restaurants Ltd, 2491
Rostra Tool Company, 1021
Rosum, 455
Rotam Global AgroSciences, 2603
Rotating Machinery Services Inc., 546
Rotation Medical, 1412, 2939
Roti, 567
Rotimatic, 2690
Rotographik, 2891
Rotoliptic, 2111
RotoMetrics, 1651
Rotorcraft Leasing Company, 928, 1745
Rotronic, 235
Rough Country, 873
Rough Country Suspension Systems, 168
Roundabout Markets, 995
Roundbox, 538, 1460, 1593
RoundCorner, 1607
RoundPegg, 36, 635, 1458
Rounds, 3081
RoundTable Healthcare Partners, 3265
RoundTrip, 1259
Roundy's, 2379
RoundyBs Supermarkets, 1986
Roupe Pommier, 3020
Route, 79
Route 66 Ventures, 3270
Routehappy, 533, 1475
RouteLambda, 1755
RouteThis, 2243
Rover, 91, 560, 741
Rover.com, 776, 1158, 1202
Rovi Inc., 300
Roving, 954
Roving Planet, 142
Rovio, 2446
Rovsing Dynamics, 3149
Row Sham Bow, 1008
Rowan University, 3274
Rowe, 1753
Rowe Farms, 2161
Rowe International Inc., 908

Rowies, 2862
Rowland Coffee Roasters, 402
Rowmark, 257
Rox, 1350
ROX Medical, 621
Roxar, 152
Roxgold, 2942
Roximity, 685, 721, 781, 1150
ROXRO Pharma, 1493
Roxus, 2998
Royal Adhesives, 1456
Royal Adhesives & Sealands, 653
Royal Adhesives & Sealants, 170, 1505
Royal Baths Manufacturing, 1456
Royal Cactus, 3259
Royal Camp Services, 900
Royal Die and Stamping Co., 985
Royal Group Technologies Limited, 2073
Royal Mat, 2206
Royal Mosa BV & Freecom Technologies BV, 2828
Royal Pet Supplies, 1511
Royal Robbins Inc., 354
Royal Sanders, 2501
Royal Sign Supply, 1837
Royal Wolf Australia, 274
Royalimages.in, 3211
Royall & Company, 468
Royalty Exchange, 876
Royalty Pharma, 1400, 1516
RoyaltyShare, 1850
Royole, 973, 2850
RP Scherer Corporation, 575
Rpath, 1334
RPI, 958
RPM Technologies, 2052
RPM Ventures, 3269
RPO, 2989, 3062
RPX, 455
RQI, 222
RQX Pharmaceuticals, 206, 544
RRT Global, 2540
RS LiveMedia, 238
RSA Engineered Products, 540, 1209
RSam, 1041
RSC Holdings, 1360
RSG, 2209
RSI, 1355, 1751, 2876, 2892
RSM US, 3276
RSportz, 1061
RT Sourcing Asia Limited, 2402
RT-SET Ltd, 2585
RTG Asia, 3215
RTHM, 2099
RTI Surgical, 1961
RTIME, 1398
RTL-Westcan, 2033
RTS, 1516, 1585
RTS Holdings Inc., 77
RtTech Software, 2190
ru-Net Holdings, 2491
Rubica, 1110, 1888
Rubicon, 493
Rubicon Pharmacies, 2272
Rubicon Project, 502, 685, 1184
Rubicon Technology, 184, 1057, 1915
Rubikloud, 2157, 2831
rubikloud, 2118
Rubio Therapeutics, 747
Rubitection Separation Design Group, 1448
Rubius Therapeutics, 709
Rubrick, 1269
Rubrik, 872, 1001, 1031, 1069
Ruby Groupe, 2974
Ruby Ribbon, 595, 1247, 1853
Rucker's, 61
Ruckus Wireless, 730, 757, 1212, 1241, 3121

Rudjer Boskovic Institute, 2832
Rudy's Barbershop, 1344
Rue du Commerce, 2375
Rue Lala, 329
Ruesch Systems, 1972
RuffaloCODY, 1334, 1504, 1752, 1979
Rugby Manufacturing Company, 903
Rugs Direct, 1606
RuiYi, 2419
Rule, 1067
Rules Based Medicine, 560
RulesPower, 538, 1080
RuleStream Corporation, 1175
Rum Jungle Resources, 2942
Ruma, 1374
Rumble, 858
Rumble Automation, 2089
Rumble Media, 2829, 2838
Rumcom, 3212
RuMe, 841
Run 3D, 3107
Run Service, 3062
Runa, 1218, 1607, 3277
Runa HR, 795
RunaHR, 1758
Runcom, 3179
Rune Labs, 226
RunKeeper, 313, 1097, 1715
Runnable, 1546
Runpath, 1259
Runrun, 634
Runscope, 1860
Runyon Equipment Rental, 1578
Rupari Food Services, 407
Rupari Foods, 1990
Rupeetalk, 3109
Rupture, 231, 623
Rural Broadband Investments, 884
RushFiles, 3203
Ruskin Moscou Faltischek, 3267
Russell Hendrix, 290
Russian Navigation Technologies, 3229
Rustic Crust, 438, 1689, 2238
Rusts of Cromer, 2985
Rutgers University, 3274
Ruth's Hospitality Group, 354, 1156
Rutherford Polk McDowell Home Health, 406
Ruthinium Group, 2622
Rutland Plastics, 1572
RV Technology, 162
rVita, 650
RWI Construction, 1705
Rx Drug Mart, 2220
Rx Label Technology, 916, 1435
Rx Safes, 1079
Rx Savings Solutions, 1276
Rx30, 884
RxBenefits, 857
RxHope, 1769
RxKinetix, 210
RxSight, 762, 1143, 1519
RxVantage, 1028, 1693, 1965
Ryan, 2209
Ryan Herco Flow Solutions, 862
Ryan Murphy Inc., 1837
Ryan's Express Transportation Services Inc., 449
Ryder TRS, 1156
Rye Studio, 2936
Ryko, 1857
Ryla, 1689
Rylo, 232
RYNO Motors, 1383
Rypos, 946, 1173
Rypple, 339
Rysta LifeScience, 3033
Ryver, 856
Ryvers, 1070

1411

Portfolio Companies Index

S

S Gympass, 2446
S&N Communications, 1753
S&P Syndicate, 1139, 2946
S&R Cabinets, 1605
S&S Industries, 1134
S&S Tech, 1087
S*Bio, 2419, 2513, 2690
S*BIO Pte., 1241
S-cubism Holdings, 2974
S. Pack & Print, 1139, 2946
S.I. Jacobson, 78
S.R. Accord, 135
S2 Interactive, 995, 1187
S3C, 1915
S4, 569
S4 Agtech, 267
Saadiyat, 152
Saama, 416
SAAS, 3051
SaaS Capital, 529
Saasuma, 1507
Saatchi Art, 641, 3056
SABA, 563
Saba, 909, 1910
Saba Medical Group LP, 1986
Saba University, 691
Sabal Medical, 1923
Sabalo Energy, 672
Saban Brands LLC, 1598
Saban Films, 1598
SABE Online, 3048
SABEResPODER, 1396
Saberr, 3108
Sabex, 1590
Sabimedical, 2553
Sabine Oil & Gas, 740
Sabio Labs, 115
Sabre, 816, 1045, 1683, 1835
Sabre Communications, 212
Sabre Holdings, 57, 1850
Sabre Industries, 1081
Sabrix, 777, 1247, 1853
SabrTech Inc., 2155
Sabse Technologies, 2066
Sackets Harbor Brewing Company, 1639
Sadbhav, 1346
Sadler's Smokehouse, 328
Sadra Medical, 40, 1378
Saegis Pharmaceuticals, 1786
Saehan Enertech, 3168
SaehWa, 3145
Saehwa IMC, 3002
Saelvigbugtens Camping, 3203
SAF, 3233
Safe, 909
SAFE Boats International, 1276
Safe In Sound Hearing, 1609
Safe Life, 1906
Safe Security, 969
Safe Shepherd, 1364
Safe-Guard, 1406
Safe-H2O, 1061
Safe-id, 3233
SafeAI, 663
SAFEbuilt, 1572
SafeDK, 1611
SafeGraph, 1563, 1675
SafeGuard, 2972
Safeguard America, 1295
SafeGuard Cyber, 84
Safeguard Global, 29
Safehub, 799
Safello, 1982
Safely You, 1421
Safemark Systems, 1234
Safend, 3231

SafeNet, 1899, 1910
Safeonline, 2572
SafePeak, 3240
SafePorche, 1097
SafeRent, 315
SafeRide, 120
Saferide, 306
Safetel, 3216
SafeTraces, 488, 1721
SafeTrek, 569, 1183
Safety Culture, 2520
Safety Infrastructure Solutions, 746, 1744
Safety Quick Light, 638
Safety Seven, 2136
Safetykleen, 135
SafetyPay, 2717
SafeView, 233, 1348, 1400
Safeway plc, 2614
Safeway Safety Step, 1512
Safic Alcan, 2375
Saft Groupe, 3069
Safway Group Holding, 1368
SAGA, 2379
Saga, 2587
Saga (Acromas), 3033
Saga Resource Partners, 46
Sagantea, 3171
SAGE, 1792
Sage, 398, 469, 762
Sage Automotive, 1970
Sage Automotive Interiors, 500
Sage Bin, 1070
Sage Electrochromics Inc., 144
Sage Hospice, 1166
Sage Midstream, 1573
Sage Products, 1156
Sage Therapeutics, 709, 1382
Sage Therepeutics, 1811
Sagent Pharmaceuticals, 1941
SageQuest, 944, 1553
Sagetis Biotech, 2553
Sageview-Wolff Real Estate, 1602
Sagitta, 3159
Sago Energy, 893
Sagres Discovery, 212
Sagrotel - Sociedade Imobiliaria, 3048
Saguaro Resources, 1443
Saguna, 3240
Sahale Snacks, 1403
Saham Finances, 3173
Sai, 1268
Sai Sudhir, 3211
Saia Burgess, 2922
Saia-Burgess, 2564
Saifun, 2609
Sail, 1439
Sail Internet, 1315
SAILDRONE, 1696
Saildrone, 1151
Sailfish Boats, 821
Sailogy, 2960
Sailpoint, 1685
SailPoint Technologies, 1814
Sailthru, 248, 317, 608, 1110, 1593
SailTthru, 1626
Saint Springs, 71, 2465
Saisha Tehnology, 465
Saisudhir, 834
Sajan, 1192
Sajar Plastics, 1159
Sakhinterlesprom, 2491
Saks Inc., 1017
Sakti, 557
Sakura Enterprises, 1769
Salad Signature, 909
Saladax, 703, 841
Saladax Biomedical, 1117

Saladworks, 446
Salbro Bottle Group, 2090
Salem International University, 1828
Sales Beach, 1364
Sales Force Pardot, 189
Sales Gossip, 2479
Sales Performance International, 1209
Sales Portal, 1458
Sales Rabbit, 1070
SalesconX, 1306
Salesfloor, 1982
Salesforce, 1212
Salesforce Japan, 1755
Salesforce.com, 665, 1755
SalesforceIQ, 836
SalesFusion, 1331
Salesfusion, 282
SalesGoose, 1958
SalesHero, 519
SalesLoft, 189, 665, 1000
SalesLogix, 947
SalesPortal, 183
SalesRabbit, 79
Salesvue, 569, 658
SalesWarp, 377
SALIDO, 32
Salido, 1310
Salient CRGT, 789, 1925
Salient Partners, 1752
Salient Pharmaceuticals, 445, 950
Salient Surgical, 1187
Salient Surgical Technologies, 1574, 1844
Saline Lectronics Inc., 113
Salins, 2317
Salins du Midi, 2375
Salix Pharmaceuticals, 1394, 1452
SalmData, 756
SALO, 3279
Salon Share, 512
Salon.com, 852
Salorix, 3001
Salsa, 655, 964
Salsa Labs, 29
Salsify, 1181, 1334, 1916
SALT, 2967
Salt Lake Brewing Company, 1605
Salt of Life AG, 2528
Salt Union, 2796
Salter Labs, 654, 1590
Salton Inc., 447
Saltside, 1323
SaltStack, 79, 1204
Saltworks, 319
Salu, 1733
Salunda, 3028
Salusion, 684
Salvage Direct, 1689
Salveo, 1698
Salveo Specialty, 1819
SAM, 2889
Sam Seltzer's Steakhouse, 402
SAMAG Group, 2527
SAManage, 2566
Samanage, 1607, 3221, 3240
Samara, 940
Samara Innovations, 660
Samba Ads, 2872
Samba Safety, 909, 1824
Samba Sensors, 2878
Samba TV, 1613
SambaAds, 3081
SambaCloud, 1334
SAMBASafety, 1503
Samedi.de, 2604
SameSide, 934
Sammumed, 3215
Samo, 307

1412

Portfolio Companies Index

Sample6, 386, 946
Sample6 Technologies, 466
Sampler, 2125, 2138
Samplify, 455
Samplify Systems, 764
Samsara, 124, 816
Samson Neuro Sciences, 2328
Samson Resources, 559
Samstock Oy, 2716
Samsung, 1096
Samuel Lawrence Furniture Co., 843
Samurai International, 2646
SAN Home Entertainment, 2974
San Jacinto Minerals, 1125
San Shing Fastech Corporation, 1139, 2946
San Vicente Group, 2535
Sana, 1183
Sana Packaging, 392
SanaBit, 704
SanaExpert, 2339
Sanako Corporation, 2318, 2716
Sanctum, 3231
Sand 9, 521
Sand Hill Exchange, 1589
Sand Tech, 2058
Sand9, 1946
Sandata, 1748
Sandata Technologies, 29
Sandbox, 959, 2583
Sandbox Industries, 3265
Sandbox Learning, 1442
Sandbox VR, 1473
Sandbridge Technologies, 422
Sandbridge Technologies Inc., 1779
Sandburst Corporation, 314
Sandcraft, 1704
SandForce, 596, 1747, 1838
Sandinvest, 2719
Sandisc, 3212
Sandler O'Neill & Partners, 1062
Sandlot Solutions, 1107
Sandow Media, 1927
Sandpiper Networks Inc, 947
Sandpiper Software, 1011
SandRidge, 1846
Sandridge Energy, 159
Sands Capital Ventures, 3270
SandVideo, 223
Sandvine, 779, 3212
Sandwell Schools, 2749
Sandymount Technologies, 1757
Sanepar, 834
Sanera Systems, 1747
Sanergy, 55
Sanfer, 815
Sangamo, 762
Sangamo Biosciences, 2463
Sanguine Biosciences, 1012
Sani-Matic, 719
Sani-Service, 2254
Sanitors, 1770
Sanlight, 933
Sano, 721, 741, 751, 1254
Sano Corporation, 131
Sano Intelligence, 720
sanofi, 1349
Sanommune, 2077
Sanona, 2400
Sanova Dermatology, 118
Sanovia Corporation, 938
SANSAN, 2646
Santa Cruz Nutritionals, 1590
Santa Fe Relocation, 473
Santa Rosa Consulting, 383
Santander Asset Management, 815
Santander Consumer USA, 442
Santaris A/S, 2785

Santaris Pharma, 2748, 3015, 3113, 3149
Santarus, 898, 1725
Santerra, 1244
Santessima, 3113
Santhera Pharmaceuticals, 1394
Santhera Pharmaceuticals AG, 1325
SANTIER, 1424
Santur, 1906
Santur Corporation, 1119
Sanyang Electronics, 2857
Saol Therapeutics, 610
SAP, 3069
Sapala, 3211
Sapato, 641
saperatec, 2686
Saphena Medical, 426
Sapho, 93, 107, 720, 858, 1254, 1563, 1700
Sapias, 807
Sapiens Data Science, 822
Sapient Health Networks, 1398
Sapient Industries, 1894
Sapphire Digital, 918
Sapphire Energy, 153, 262, 1916
Sapphire Power Holdings, 1573
Sapphire Technology, 3145
Sapphire Therapeutics, 312, 1493
Saprogal, 2962
Sara Lee Corp., 1903
Sara Lee Frozen Bakery, 1081
Saraplast, 2313
Saraware Oy, 2716
Sarcode Bioscience, 94, 495
Sarcos, 809
Sarda Technologies, 971
Sardex, 2874
Sardex.net, 2672
Sarens, 3232
Sarnova, 1961
Sarolina Staff, 1751
Sartorius, 3069
Sarvega, 1057
SAS Sistema de Ensino, 815
SASE Company, 290
Sasets, 3107
Sash, 85
Sasken, 2846
Sasseur, 1088
Sasun, 1745
Satago, 3108
Satcom, 651
Sate, 2850
Sate Auto, 2936
Sateco, 3020
Satelec, 2602
Satiety, 666
Satiogen, 1221
Satmetrix, 777
Satmex, 442
Satoris, 323
Satrec Initiative, 1087
Satsuma, 1519
Satsuma Pharmaceuticals, 2180
Saturday Shoes, 2936
Sauce Labs, 1001, 1829
Saucelabs, 1607
Saucey, 11, 101, 358
Sauiba Sensors AB, 2718
Saul Ewing Arnstein & Lehr, 3275
Saunders & Associates, 828
Saunders Inc., 693
Saurer, 2922
Sav-On, 734
Savaari Car Rentals, 1013
Savage Sports, 1141, 1456
SavaJe Technologies, 1305
Savana, 1321
Savantis Systems, 1672

Savara, 445
Savara Pharmaceuticals, 1061
Savari, 817
SavATree, 476
Save a Lot Food Stores, 2209
Saveology, 716
Savers, 1109
SaveUp, 282, 1860
Savi Technology, 1910
Savigent, 1192
Saving Star, 754
SavingStar, 596, 741, 946
Savio, 2379
Savioke, 4, 107, 720, 994, 1254, 2690
Savitude, 1176, 1370
SAVO, 1620
Savo, 1742
Savo-Solar, 2612
Savonix, 799, 1070
Savoteur, 641
Savoy Entertainment Group, 651
Savvion, 214, 1906
SAVVIS, 1972
Savvymoney, 1865
Sawtek, 1708
Saxbys Coffee, 1275
Saxo Bank, 815, 1835
Saxx, 334
SAY Media, 197, 757
Say Media, 1584
Sayduck, 3108
Saygent, 1055
Saykara, 1158
Saylent, 745, 1339
Saylent Technologies, 1388, 1920
SayNow, 1663, 1865
Sayspring, 408, 525
SBA Materials, 1711
SBG Capital, 2148
SBI Fine Chemicals, 2048
SBJ, 2796
SBJ Group Limited, 404
SBM Co., 2727
SBP Holdings LP, 64
SBR Health, 751
SBS Broadcasting, 2380
SBS Industries, 828
SBV Venture Partners, 3284
SC Labs, 1843
Scala Energy, 672
Scale, 2011
Scale Arc, 544
Scale Computing, 22, 86, 287, 732, 1544, 1626
Scale Factor, 1176
Scale Venture, 3284
ScaleARc, 3001
ScaleArc, 1853
ScaleBase, 221
Scaled Inference, 720, 1069, 1151
Scaled Networks, 2960
Scalefast, 249
ScaleMP, 646, 2462
Scalent Systems, 1038
Scaleo Chip, 3113
ScaleOut, 2474
ScaleOut Software, 85
Scali, 2754
Scality, 1202, 3020
Scalpr, 307
Scalyr, 1663, 1758
Scalyr Inc., 1666
Scan Therapeutics, 1145, 1350
Scana Noliko, 2949
Scanadu, 721, 1236
Scanalytics, 566
Scanalytics Inc., 1155
Scanbio, 2754

1413

Portfolio Companies Index

Scanbot (by Doo), 3161
ScanBuy, 954
Scanbuy, 1146, 1175
ScanCafe, 1024, 1672
Scancell, 3107
ScandBook, 2325
Scandic Hotels, 2325
Scandit, 2446
Scandlines, 2311
Scandura Holdings, 1557
Scandza AS, 1129
Scanntech, 2455
Scanrope, 2754
ScanSafe, 1626
ScanScout, 115, 231
Scanse, 792
Scansite 3D, 799
Scanvacc, 2754
Scanwell, 2280
Scarpblog, 1146
Scatter, 1151
Scayl, 85
Scene Sharp, 2200
SceneDoc, 1260, 2149
Scense, 3128
Scent Air Technologies, 1605
Scentbird, 1150
Scenti Bio, 1202
Scentys, 3113
Schaltbau Holding, 3069
Scharffen Berger Chocolate Maker, 1083
Schema, 2541, 2720, 3231
Schema Ltd, 2585, 2770
SchemaLogic, 466
Schematic Labs, 721, 1699, 1860
Schenck Process, 909
Schiller Bikes, 1061
Schiller International University, 1828
Schlotzsky's, 1576
Schmersahl Treloar & Co., 3271
Schnader Attorneys at Law, 3275
Schneidersohne, 2616
Schneller, 846
Schoeller Arca Systems, 1376
Schofield Media Group, 1927
Scholar Locker, 1581
Scholar Rock, 709
ScholarCentric, 400
ScholarMe, 883
ScholarPro, 1615
Scholly, 622
School Imrpovement Network, 1770
School Loop, 1306, 1584
School Loop Inc., 1310
School of Management and Business Advisory Council, 1650
School of Rock, 1742
School Stickers, 2539
SchooLa Inc., 650
SchoolChapters, 1940
SchoolMessenger, 468
SchoolMint, 1054, 1527
Schoolmint, 563, 942
Schoology, 743, 858, 1041, 1194
Schoolzilla, 1054, 1527
Schooner Capital, 3273
Schoox, 1072
Schrader International, 1156
Schuepbach Energy, 477
Schulerhilfe Gelsenkirchen, 3067
Schulman Associates, 2150
Schulz Catering, 135
Schumacher, 2209
Schur Flexible, 1516
Schutt Sports, 873
SCHUTZKLICK, 2979

Schweiger Dermatology Group, 1136, 1628, 1762
Schylling, 828
SCI Solutions, 1984
SciApps, 678
SciAps Inc., 438, 810
Science, 228, 561, 922, 1965
Science 37, 1151
Science Exchange, 1110
Science Exchange, 563, 1254, 1346, 1359, 1882, 1968, 1993, 2010
Science Inc., 286
Science37, 836
Science4You, 3048
ScienceBased Health, 145
SCIenergy, 1846, 1977
Scienova, 2527
Sciens Building Solutions, 960
Scientech, 373, 374, 2436
Scientific Games, 818
Scientific Games Holdings Corp, 447
Scientific Magnetics, 3098
Scientific Media, 1830
Scientific Protein Laboratories, 170
Scientific Publishers, 2429
Scientist.com, 12
Sciessent, 2492
Scietific Systems, 2336
Scifiniti, 87, 730
Scigineer, 596
SciKon Innovation, 737
Scinfiniti, 1427
Scint-X, 2630
Scintera, 197, 1658
Scintera Networks, 623
Scioderm, 1122, 1786
Scion, 314
Scion Pharmaceuticals, 1092
Scipher Medicine, 1069
SciQuest, 1008, 1853
Scitex, 2666
Scitex3, 2609
Scitor Corporation, 1109
Scivantage, 655
Scivex, 1086
Sckipio, 116
SCM Insurance Services, 2272
Scodix, 126, 235, 2900
Sconce, 2870
Sconce Solutions, 2913
Scondoo, 3044
Scoo, 2380
Scoop, 302
Scoop.it, 1416, 2693
Scoopshot, 2630
Scoot, 1183, 1632
Scoot Science, 318
Scooter's Coffee, 1276
Scope AR, 1473, 1758
ScopeAI, 1607
ScopeAR, 1675
Scopely, 132, 306, 560, 624, 641, 720, 871, 935, 1237, 1480, 1531
Scopix, 2455
Scopus, 2571
Score Data, 623
Score Stream, 206
Scorebig, 221
Scoreboard, 1227
Scorista, 2940
SCORT, 2544, 2544
Scotch & Soda, 1753
Scotia Technology, 812
Scott Technologies Inc., 300
Scottish Equity Partners, 2944
Scottish Re Group Limited, 575
Scottish-American Insurance, 378

Scout, 781
Scout 24, 924
Scout Clean Energy, 1517
Scout Mob, 1110
Scoutables, 972
Scoutible, 858
ScoutLabs, 1028
Scoutmob, 1291
Scovill Fasteners Inc., 1621
SCP Ltd., 1229
scPharmaceuticals, 12
Scrap Partners, 364
Scratch Kitchen, 325
Scratch Music Group, 533, 1420
Scratch Wireless, 534
Scratch-It, 1061
Scratch-it, 1656
Scrazzl, 2522
Scream Point, 398
Screenlife, 43
Screenreach, 3012
Screenvision, 1660
Scribble, 2132
Scribble Live, 544
ScribbleLive, 2118, 2259
Scribd, 455, 1069, 1073, 1906
Scribd., 1534
Scribe America, 468
Scribe Software, 308
ScribeAmerica, 1930
Scrible, 3277
Scrip Companies, 403
Scripted, 1534
ScriptRock, 1897
Scriptswitch, 2967
Scrittura, 954
ScrollMotion, 567, 660
Scrubgrass, 156
Scrybe, 58
SCS Financial Serices, 1743
SCT, 443
SCT Stem Cell Technology, 3245
SCT Telecom, 3020
Scuf Gaming LLC, 810
Sculpteo, 3239
SculptiVR, 307
ScyllaDB, 1509
Scynexis, 762, 1731, 2876
Scytl, 1620, 1946, 2478, 2987
SDC Materials, 2492
SDG, 2493
SDI, 1466
SDI Gas, 1125
SDI Health, 1136, 1777
SDI Inc., 1136
SDI Special Devices, 1967
SDK Biotechnologies, 650
SDLtridion, 2671
SEA, 2735
Sea Bags, 1161
Sea Island Lake Cottages, 1219
Sea Machines, 679, 1101
Sea Machines Robotics, 1834
Sea Transportation-Dry Bulk, 1967
Seabed Geophysical, 2754
Seaboard International Inc., 985
Seabrook International, 77, 801
Seabulk International, 1573
Seafolly, 1088
Seaformatics, 2168
Seagate, 385, 1096, 1733
Seagate Technologies, 1001
Seagate Technology, 197, 1835
Seagate Technology Plc., 1903
SeAH Besteel, 2434
Seahawk Biosystems Corporation, 979
Seahorse App, 3125

Portfolio Companies Index

Seahorse Bioscience, 521, 1303, 2939
Seahorse Biosciences, 747
Seakeeper, 551
SEAL, 1845
Seal, 1829
Seal Innovation, 3277
Sealand Natural Resources, 1741
SeaLife Pharma, 3165
Sealine, 2796
SealSkinz, 2539
Seaman Paper, 1173
Seamicro, 563, 609
Seamless Docs, 1260, 1306
Seamless Receipts, 608
Seamless Toy Company, 1489
SeamlessDocs, 1894
SeaProducts, 1507
Search Lateral, 1547
Searchandise Commerce, 608, 989
Searchmetrics, 2994
Searchspace, 3104
Sears Canada, 1970
Seaside National Bank & Trust, 1147, 1417
Seasoned Staq, 1072
Seaspan Marine corporation, 2085
SeaStar Solutions, 110
SeaSuite By Goby, 1642
SeaSwift, 909
SEAT, 2497
SeatAdvisor, 1706
Seaters, 3257
SeatGeek, 771, 836, 1110, 1263, 1358, 1531
Seatme, 1183
Seattle Metrics Inc., 908
Seattle Sensor Systems, 85
Seattle Shellfish, 1446
Seattle Systems, 719
Seattle's Best International, 1576
Seatwave, 2734, 2829, 2838
Seaurat Technologies, 817
Seaview Petroleum Co. LP, 447
Seaway Networks, 1038
Seaway Restaurant Group, 1639
Seaworld Parks and Entertainment, 277
Sebacia, 40, 621, 1419, 1928
Sebela Pharmaceuticals, 610
Sebia, 909, 2601
Secfi, 1310
Seche/Tredi, 2625
Sechrist Industries Inc., 654
Seclore, 2818, 3211
Second Accent, 1551
Second Closet, 2288
Second Cup Coffee Co., 2254
Second Genome, 59, 1122, 1655, 1731, 1966
Second Home, 3097
Second Life, 1323
Second Measure, 1346, 1663
Second Porch, 1383
Second Spectrum, 1798
SecondKeys, 995
Secondmarket, 743, 2831
SecondMind, 724
SecondSol, 2527
Secoo, 2850, 3208
Secor, 166
Secova Services, 2490
Secret Cinema, 1696
Secret Double Octopus, 249
Secret Escapes, 3018, 3207
Secret Sales, 2629
SecretBuilders, 1097
SecretSales, 3032
Secretsales, 2671
SecretSales.com, 1416
Sectigo, 779
Seculert, 3246

Securadyne Systems, 1409
SecurAmerica, 1970
Secure, 876
Secure Data in Motion, 1116
Secure Directory, 2333
Secure Food Solutions, 995
Secure Key, 2052
Secure Meters Limited, 2861
Secure Soft, 2857
Secure Software, 1886
Secure-24, 909, 1409
Secureauth, 1829
SecureKey Technologies, 2265
SecureLink, 1017, 2862
SecureLogix, 734
SecureMedia, 1704
Securent, 1378
Securesafe, 2583
Securicy, 2212
Securiguard, 2292
Securimax, 2410
Securistyle, 2923
Securitas Direct, 220
Security, 1832
Security 7, 3249
Security American Financial Enterprises, 1343
Security Innovation, 349
Security Networks, 1360
Security Scorecard, 305
Security Solutions of America, 405
Securitypoint Media, 1524
Securly, 994, 1392
Securus Medical Group, 1047, 1574
Securus Technologies, 744, 909
SecurView, 483
Secusmart, 2393, 2979
Sedal, 2489
Sedan, 2889
Sedemac, 3001
Sedgwick, 924, 1743
SEE Forge, 544
See Forge, 950
See Me, 707, 1489
See.me, 1358
Seebo, 1480, 3221
SeeChange Health, 1498
Seeclickfix, 1359
SeeCommerce, 1945
SeeControl, 1427
Seed, 351, 2225
Seed Education Corp., 55
Seed Holdings, 1557
Seed Infotech, 851
Seed Invest, 858
Seed Media Group, 1954
Seed&Spark, 218
Seedcamp, 2296, 2406, 2586, 2674, 2822, 3018, 3097
SeedInvest, 1632
SeedLegals, 3108
Seedling, 7, 896, 1222, 1888
Seeds, 218, 307
SEEFT Ventures, 2724
SEEGRID Corporation, 998
Seek Communications Limited, 2398
Seeking Alpha, 581
SeeMore Interactive, 1553
Seen Digital Media, 1553
SEEO, 1474
Seeq, 98, 1158, 1641
Seequent, 29
SeeRoseGo, 1507
Seesaw, 231
Seesmic, 2446
Seevibes, 3045
Sefaira, 322
Sefas, 2354

Segall Bryant & Hamill, 1814
Segetis, 3279
Segment, 641, 1075, 2012
Segmentify, 2284
Segmint, 1047
Segra, 99
Segrest, 1215
Segue Manufacturing Services, 211
Seibold, 2683
Seikagaku, 1452
Seisint, 1717, 2079
Seismic, 1024, 1041
Seismic Games, 624, 791
Seismos, 1028
Seitel Inc., 1903
Seitz, 123
Sekal, 3099
Sekal AS, 3141
SEKO Logistics, 862
SELA, 3072
Selah Genomics, 1923
Selavo Machinery, 2936
Seldin Company, 70
Select Energy Services, 559
Select Medical, 1972
Select Product Group, 477
Select Rehabilitation, 374
Select Technology, 3107, 3107, 3107
Selecta Biosciences, 747, 1382, 1419, 1460, 1941
Selectable Media, 206
Selectbidder, 2200
SelecTec, 1689
Selectica, 1038
SelectQuote, 353, 1764
SelectX Pharmaceuticals, 3196
Selektessen, 3170
Selenis, 2489
Selenity Therapeutics, 1350
Selexys Pharmaceuticals, 1268
Self Esteem Brands, 1576
Self Lender, 1070
Selfapy, 2841
Selfie Networks, 317
SelfMade, 1006, 1585
Selfmade, 743
Selfnet, 3014
SelfScore, 1716
Selig Sealing Products, 245
Seligman Spectrum Focus Fund, 623
Selima, 3244
Sellars, 1719
Sellbrite, 972
Seller Crowd, 1110
SellerCrowd, 1699
Sellercrowd, 813
Selligent, 959
Selligy, 609
SellPoints, 852
Sellpoints, 1202
Selltag, 3223
Selltis, 61
Selmic Oy, 2716
Seloger, 2375
SeluxDx, 1519
Selva Medical, 1693
Selventa, 747, 1412
Selway Partners, 1633
Selènia, 3154
Semafone, 3018
Semagtx, 1405
Semantifi, 1097
Semasio, 256, 2829, 2838, 3056
Semba Biosciences, 1060
Sembiosys, 237
Sembiosys Genetics, 2049
Sembiosys genetics Inc., 2114

1415

Portfolio Companies Index

Semetric/Musicmetric, 3032
Semicoa, 1904
Semiconductor Manufacturing International, 892
Semiconductor Manufacturing International Corporat, 1769, 2603
Semiconductors, 729
SemiNex, 649
Seminis, 778
SemiProbe, 1097
Semitech Semiconductor, 2613, 2778
Semknox, 3236
Semma, 1268
Semma Therapeutics, 710
Semnur, 386
Semnur Pharma, 1941
Semnur Pharmaceuticals, 782
SemperCare, 402, 2079
Semprae, 1508
Sempre Health, 1552
Semprius, 144, 153, 946, 975, 979, 1008
Semprus, 12
SEMRE, 1696
Semrush, 641
Semtek, 1916
Senator Investment Group, 70
Sence360, 743
Sencha, 968
Senco Brands, 2009
Sencorp, 1162
Send Me Mobile, 1846
Send Word Now, 1401
SendBird, 1663
SendbyBag, 2948
Sendero Midstream Partners, 675
Senders, 1006
SendGrid, 1700
Sendgrid, 1789
SendHub, 1054, 1655
Sendio, 187, 1664
Sendmail, 58, 1255
Sendme, 1715
Sendori, 115, 231
Sendwithus, 231
Seneca Systems, 552
Senet, 907
Senet. ShotSpotter, 488
Senforce, 1677, 2382
Senhouse Capital, 3097
Senic, 272, 3161
SENIOcare, 3232
Senior Helpers, 97, 1111
Senior Whole Health, 550, 1776
SeniorBridge, 373
SeniorLink, 521
Seniorlink, 1334
Seniovo, 2841
Sennder, 640
Senneca Holdings, 1081
Senodia Technologies, 2667
Senomyx, 1493
Senomyx. Sunesis, 237
Senr.net, 1715
Senreve, 896
Senrio, 1383
SensAble, 1334, 1915
SenSage, 1241
Sensas, 2625
Sensata Technologies, 220
Sensay, 120
Senscient, 445, 950, 1306, 1584
Sense, 852, 976, 1563
Sense Networks, 1028
Sense.ly, 721
Sense360, 306, 525, 624, 1509
Sensee, 1416
Senseg, 2390
SenseiHub, 307

Senselogix, 2295
SenseLogix Limited, 3010
SenseOmics, 181
Senseonics, 604, 3085
SenseStream Ltd., 162
SenseTime, 1509
SenseWare, 285
Sensiba San Filippo, 3272
Sensibill, 2118, 2151, 2153, 2195
Sensible Organics, 2238, 2329
Sensible Problems, 500
Sensibo, 2947
Sensicast, 834
Sensicore, 1324, 1786
Sensics, 285, 1169
SensiHub, 1885
Sensika, 2696
Sensimed, 2353
Sensinode, 2630
Sensipar, 2102
Sensis, 1288
Sensity, 89, 1247, 1682
Sensity Systems, 483
Sensl, 2355
Sensopia, 1416
Sensor Films, 704
Sensor Solutions Holdings, 654
Sensor Tower, 128
Sensorberg, 2503, 3236
Sensorly, 2693
SensorNet, 235
Sensoro, 219
SensorSuite, 2142
Sensorsuite, 2113
Sensortec, 2598
SensorTower, 1218, 1540
SensorTran, 1745
Sensortran, 706
SensorUp, 2278
Sensory Analytics, 1442, 1923, 1988
Sensory Networks, 2323
Sensory Technologies, 2058
Sensotrade, 3245
Sensu, 235, 776
Sensy, 1013
Sensys, 1412
Sensys Networks, 947, 1945
Sentelic, 1922
Sentenai, 754, 1487
Senti Biosciences, 1613
Sentiar, 267
SentiBiosciences, 1151
Sentient, 809
Sentient Biosciences, 1693
Sentient Energy, 770
Sentient Medical Systems, 632, 1232
SentientScience, 2132
Sentieon, 973
Sentilla, 491, 1378, 1966
Sentillion, 1008, 1725
Sentiment Alpha, 393
Sentinal Alert, 2216
Sentinel, 585, 1977
Sentinel Capital Partners, 1871
Sentinel Data Centers, 1062
Sentinel Healthcare, 1613
Sentinel Offender Services LLC, 274
Sentinel One, 1534
Sentinel Vision, 524
Sentinella Pharmaceuticals, 412
SentinelOne, 851, 1687
Sentinl, 981
Sentito Networks, 1080, 1227
Sentons, 1340
Sentori, 655, 1227
SentreHEART, 1445, 1493, 1941
SentriLock, 1642

Sentrix, 2952
Sentry Energy, 1009
Senvion, 442
Senyi, 472
Senzari, 2813
SEO Pledge, 393
SEOshop, 2822
Seoul Beltway Corporation, 584
Separators, 1252
Sepaton, 757, 1899
SEPIAtec GmbH, 3190
Sepracor, 1044
SEPS Pharma, 2949
Septentrio N.V., 2902
SeqOnce, 663
Sequa, 1134
SeQual, 176
Sequana, 206, 769
Sequana Medical, 2515, 2710, 2939
Sequans, 3152
Sequans Communicatinos, 2899
Sequation, 1038
Sequel Youth & Family Services, 96
Sequella, 1169
Sequence Bio, 2168, 2216
Sequence Design, 197, 757, 1672
Sequence Health, 1293
Sequenom, 3007, 3137
Sequenom Inc., 2785
Sequent Medical, 604, 621
Sequent Software, 1381
Sequenta, 1247
Sequitur Energy Resources, 46
Sequoia, 52, 2285
Sequoia Communications, 1918
Sequoia Software, 223
Sequoia Tech Partners, 623
Sequoia Vaccines, 569
SequoiaSoft, 3239
Sequr, 189
Sera Prognostics, 426, 621
Sera Prognostics, 1010
SeraCare Life Sciences, 1128
Serafim Silva - Atividades Hoteleiras, 3048
Serafina Energy, 1443
Seragen, 314
Seragon Pharmaceuticals, 74
Serap, 2423
SeraStar, 1676
Serco, 2674
Seren, 2892
Serena, 959
Serena & Lily, 235, 761
Serene Green, 392
Serenex, 1008
Seres Health, 2702
Seres Therapeutics, 747, 1519
Sericol Inc., 1621
Seriforge, 941, 1363
Serious Energy, 1906
Serious Integrated, 2190
Seriously, 1888
Sermatech International, 170
Sermo, 1146, 1699
SERPs.com, 1463
Sertoli Technologies, 1543
Serus, 613
Servals Automation, 2313
Servi Group, 2731
Service, 708, 1183
Service Champ, 894, 1605
Service Design Associates, 1252
Service Express, 914, 1409
Service Finance Company, 750
Service Frame, 2918
Service Metrics, 1563
Service Partners, 1505

1416

Portfolio Companies Index

Service Radio Rentals, 1040
Service Source, 949
Service Strategies Interntional, 111
Service2Media, 3051
ServiceBench, 1041, 1133
ServiceBot Software, 995
ServiceChannel, 1689
ServiceLink, 1815
ServiceMax, 57, 560, 665, 1184, 1515, 1853
Servicemax, 563, 1212
ServiceNow, 1041
ServiceNow Inc., 514
Servicesoft Technologies, 2079
Servicys, 176
Servion, 483
Servion Global Solutions, 187
ServOne, 909
Servosity, 1923
Sesil, 1087
Session M, 935
Session Title Services, 678
SessionM, 455, 1075, 1607
Sessions, 2520
Sessions.edu, 1720
Set Media, 563
Set Scouter, 2125
Set.fm, 2137
Setagon Inc., 269
SetJam, 1584
SetPoint Medical, 748, 1122
SetSight, 3279
Settle, 2940
Sev1Tech, 610
SEVE, 3020
SEVEN, 2716
Seven Bridges Genomics, 1483
Seven Continents, 2148
7 Cups of Tea, 599
7 Days Group Holdings, 413
7 Gate Ventures, 3258
Seven Generations, 1846
Seven Generations Energy, 2040
Seven Lakes Technologies, 416
Seven Media, 1087
Seven Oaks Biosystems, 426
Seven Rosen, 2658
Seven Seas, 3222
Seven Seas Water, 657
7 Shifts, 307
Seven Technologies, 3244
7-Technologies, 2651
70 Millions Staffing, 1507
Seven10, 1276
71LBS, 1615
71lbs, 971, 1364
7234, 2936
724 Solutions, 202
727 Solutions, 1704
72Lux.com, 1306
798 Entertainment, 2850
7AC Technologies, 497
7AC Technology, 1100
7d Software GmbH & Co., 2673
SevenFifty, 1480
7Gege, 2936
SevenInvensun, 1509
7k7k, 823
Sevenly, 1966
SevenR Rooms, 518
7shifts, 2236
7signal, 86, 1047
7signal Solutions, 1553
SevenSpace, 1853
7Summits, 1607
Seventh Generation, 428, 1627, 2329
Seventh Sense Biosystems, 979, 1460
7thOnline, 460, 1745

SeventhSense Biosystems, 747, 1811
7TM Pharma, 3015
Sevenval, 2503
Sevin Rosen, 37
Sevin Rosen Funds, 986
SevOne, 221, 1387
Sewa Grih Rin, 55
Sewon Telecom, 2924
SEWORKS, 1509
Seworks, 3127
Sextant Education Corporation, 64
Sexy Hair, 1861
Seymour Investment Management, 2292
Sfara, 569, 1110, 1926
SFERRA, 1111
SFI, 495
SFO Technologies, 584
SFOX, 1696
Sfox, 307, 1848
SG Fleet Services, 2622
SG360, 364, 969
SGA, 812
SGA Production Services, 632
SGB, 1817
SGE, 1340
SGGHM - Soc. Geral Gestao Hoteis de Mocambique, 3048
SGN, 115
SGS Co., 2209
SGX Pharmaceuticals, 1493
SGX Sensortech, 222
Shaanxi Northwest New Technology Industry Co. Ltd., 2633
Shacham, 2751
Shade Up, 567
Shadow Government, 2310
Shadow Networks, 1400
Shadowfax, 1509
Shaerworks, 3272
Shake, 307, 1222, 1593, 1699
Shake Shack, 1109
Shakr Media Company, 1951
Shakti, 834
Shakti Battery, 1083
Shanahan's, 2051
Shandong Winery, 892
Shanghai Chunge Glass Co., 2542
Shanghai Framedia Advertisement, 2847
Shanghai Global Baby Products, 1241
Shanghai Harvest Network Technology, 179
Shanghai Hintsoft Software, 2850
Shanghai Huahong, 2936
Shanghai iRay, 1340
Shanghai Mining Software Company, 2998
Shanghai Shen-Li High Tech, 2542
Shanghai Superrfid Electronics Technology, 2850
Shanghai Yi Shang Network Information Company, 1241
Shanghai-Haier-IC, 3235
Shangpin, 3142
Shangri-La, 2285
Shanon, 2974
Shansong (FlashEX), 1119
Shape, 231, 1035, 1149, 1916, 2690
Shape Security, 84, 1075, 1346, 1670, 1830
Shape Technologies, 109
Shape.AG, 2736
Shaper, 519, 679
ShapeShift, 36
Shapeshift, 877
ShapeUp, 703
Shapeways, 124, 1151
SHARE, 1286
Share Microfin, 2313
Share This, 1839
Shareable Ink, 1107
Shareablee, 7, 841, 1699, 1899

Shareaholic, 313, 1065, 1322
Sharebuilder, 887
ShareCare, 493
Sharecare, 171, 251, 806, 922, 1830
Shared Spectrum Company, 508
ShareGrove, 660
Shareholder InSite, 678
ShareLaTeX, 3108
Sharelink, 2796
SharePost, 1810
SharePractice, 1634
shareThat, 1734
ShareThis, 287, 609, 721, 975, 1046, 1206, 1592
Sharethrough, 751, 1334
Sharewise, 2475
Shari's Management Corporation, 481, 713
Shari's Restaurants, 716
Shark, 2448
Sharklet Technologies, 1126
Sharp Analytics, 9
Sharpen, 658
Sharps, 1753
Shasun, 1382
Shayne International Holdings, 584
Shayog, 55
Shazam, 1001, 2322, 2428, 2472, 2668, 2711
Shearer's Foods, 1990
ShearShare, 218
Sheer Networks, 1038, 3137
Sheerly Genius, 2133
Sheertex, 2041
SheFly, 622
SheKnows, 518
Shelby.tv, 206
Shelf Drilling, 423, 1125
Shelf Engine, 773
Shelfari, 85
Shelfmint, 1721
Shell, 214
Shell Oil, 2621
ShellHound, 1613
SheIn, 973
Shelter Distribution, 328
Shelter Luv, 1218
ShelterLogic Investment, 1557
ShelterPoint Life, 686
Shemin, 1372
Shenandoah Growers, 2290
Shengtang Entertainment, 2590
Shenogen Pharma Group, 973
Shenwu, 3100
Shenzhen Green Materials Hi-tech, 2802
Shenzhen Guanri Telecom, 2850
Shenzhen Kingdee Software, 2850
Shenzhen Kingsky, 2850
Shenzhen Sunlord Electronics, 2802
Shenzhen Tsinghua Tongfang Co Ltd, 2499
Shenzhen WuZhouLong Motors, 2802
Shenzhen Yinboda Telecommunication Technology, 2802
Shenzhen Yuton, 2936
Shenzhoufu, 3208
Shenzhoufu.com, 2850
Sheplers, 881
Sheridan, 924
Sheridan Group Inc., 354
Sherman & Reilly Inc., 693
Shermans Travel, 57
Sherpa, 745, 2236
Sherpaa, 1359, 1699
Shertrack, 1336
Shevirah, 285
Shezhen Shenzinlong Industry, 3062
Shicoh Engineering, 1755
Shida Shenghua Chemical, 2542
Shield AI, 124, 941
ShieldAI, 622

1417

Portfolio Companies Index

ShieldX, 180
Shielf Tech, 418
Shift, 124, 228, 302, 306, 609, 624, 842, 858, 935, 942, 1566, 1965, 2010
Shift Payments, 1054
Shift Technology, 816
Shift4 Payments, 2252
Shiftboard, 85
ShiftForward, 3048
ShiftGig, 731
Shiftgig, 471, 823, 1480
Shiftgig Silver Spring Networks, 560
ShiftLeft, 1184
ShiftMessenger, 1054
SHIFTMobility, 1829
ShiftPlanning, 1226, 3044
Shilpa Medicare, 2490
Shimmur, 1703
Shimojani, 644
Shimon Systems, 130
Shin Kong International, 2850
Shin Kong Mitsukoshi Department Store, 1769
Shin Nippon Biomedical Laboratories, 2970
Shine, 518, 679, 754, 2831, 2872
SHINE Medical Technologies, 2001
ShineOn, 1184
Shineon, 1340
Shinesty, 282
Shiningstar Energy, 2040
Shinrai, 2333
Shinsung Solar Energy, 3145
Shionogi & Co., 1271
Shionogi Inc., 1349
Ship Mate, 120
Ship Supply, 928
Shipamax, 395, 640
ShipBob, 1202
ShipHawk, 204, 397, 1055, 1965
Shipmonk, 1757
Shippable, 618, 1158, 2008
Shippable Simply Measured, 773
Shippabo, 306
Shippert Medical, 1667
Shippo, 1700, 1879, 1882, 2280
Shiprocket, 1613
Shipsi, 896
Shipt, 641, 904
Shipwell, 727, 741, 1933, 2132
Shipwire, 1194
Shire, 1271
Shirtinator, 2979
Shiva, 238
Shixianghui, 1119
SHL, 1927
Shnier, 2255
Sho My Homework, 3030
ShoCard, 107, 544, 1254
Shocking Technologies, 183
Shockwatch, 734
Shockwave Medical, 1519, 1916
Shoe Corp. of America, 461
Shoe Sensation, 1049
Shoeboxed, 1348
Shoeboxed.com, 286
Shoebuy, 1728
Shoeby - Lakeside, 2501
Shoedazzle, 1410
Shoedazzle.Com, 1460
Shoefitr, 293, 1940
Shoelace, 2027
Shoes For Crews, 64
Shoes for Crews, 433
Shoes of Prey, 1711, 2520
Shogun, 795
Shomiti Systems, 1682
Shoof Technologies, 1075
Shop Genius, 1965

Shop Hers, 1546
Shop It To Me, 1865
Shop Your World, 2853
Shopa, 3018
Shopatron, 1810
Shopcaster, 2182
ShopClues, 2818, 2943
ShopClues.com, 3001
ShopEx, 2936
Shopgate, 2638
Shopify, 743
ShopIgniter, 1853
Shopitur, 3048
ShopKeep, 533, 1863
Shopkeep, 946, 1849
ShopKeepPOS, 386
Shopkick, 486
Shopko, 1753
ShopLogic, 585
Shopmium, 3208, 3239
Shopnation, 1099
shopobot Inc., 650
ShopPad, 1101
Shoppers Drug Mart, 209, 456
Shopping.Com, 197
Shopping.com, 212, 641
Shoppo, 823
Shoprocket, 3108
ShopSavvy, 397
ShopShops, 761, 1882
ShopSocial.ly, 1899
ShopSpot, 3121
Shopturn, 1176
Shopular, 770
ShopWell, 712, 1305, 1488
ShopWiki, 818
ShopYourWorld.com, 1965
Shore Capital Partners, 37, 3265
ShoreGroup, 779
Shoreline Solutions, 378
ShoreMaster, 932
ShoreTel, 757, 770, 1796
Shortlist, 1615, 1885
Shoshin, 214
Shot Tracker, 1019
Shotgun Picture, 2528
Shots, 1150, 1888, 2010
Shots Studio, 1983
ShotSpotter, 491
Shotspotter, 826
Shotspotter Inc., 1089
ShotTracker, 1657
Shotzr, 36
Shoutlet, 1108, 1384
Show Battery, 2155
Show Kicker, 1463
Show Long Fashion Gourmet Co, 2542
Showa Yakuhin Kako, 3201
Showbie, 2291
Showbizdata, 2021
Showcard Print, 2944
Showcase-TV, 2974
ShowClix, 998, 1447
ShowEvidence, 192, 756
Showfields, 1766
ShowGrow, 203
ShowingTime, 29
ShowMe, 679
Showpad, 1000
Showroom Logic, 781
ShowUHow, 1771
ShowWorld Holding, 3062
Showyou, 1860
ShoZu, 555
Shred All, 443
Shred-It, 2183
Shred-it, 57

Shree Kamdhenu Electronics, 2313
Shriram City Union Finance, 135
Shuangcheng Pharma, 973
Shubham, 2818
Shuddle, 707
Shukinko, 1499
Shun On Electronic, 2603
Shunra Software, 2566
ShurCo Acquisition, 1343
Shurgard Self-Storage, 152
Shurpa, 995
Shutl, 641, 1891, 2837, 3014
Shutterfly, 58, 339, 1183, 1247
Shutterly, 852
Shvydko, 3234
Shyft, 226, 1158
Shyft Analytics, 52
Shyp, 785, 1749, 1998, 2010
SI Auto, 2481
SI Corp., 1017
Si Time, 968
SI-BONE, 149, 1691
Si-Bone, 1382
Si-Bone, 1251
Si-Cat, 2187
Si2, 3211
Si2 Microsystems, 3062
SIA Abrasives, 2564
Siamab, 1100
Siamab Therapeutics, 1160
Siamons International, 2049
Siano, 1604, 3137, 3231
Siara Systems, 1474
Siaras, 183
Siargo, 47
SiBeam, 1151
Sibley & Associates, 2794
SiC Processing, 3252
Sichuan Tomorrow Fine Chemical Co., 2434
Sicom, 1136, 2754
Sicomed, 2784
SiCortex, 1038
Sicoya, 3161
Side by Side, 505
SideCar, 742
Sidecar, 178, 206, 721, 904, 1321, 1387, 1577, 1699
Sidecare, 150
Sidedolla, 1585
Sidel, 2607
Sidense, 2262, 3214
Sideqik, 243, 306, 1566
Sideris Pharmaceuticals, 915, 1268
SideStep, 1796
Sidestep, 1850
SideTrade, 3239
Sidetrade, 3113
Sidley Austin, 3272
Siebel System, 58
Siebel Systems, 852
Siebel Systems Inc., 1903
Siembraviva, 55
Siemens AG, 3212
Siemplify, 2132
Siempo, 218
Siena Funding, 1970
Sienna Biopharmaceuticals, 94
Sientra, 495, 1382
Sienza, 1051
Sierra Atlantic, 1013
Sierra Design, 1793
Sierra Hamilton, 405
Sierra Industries, 678
Sierra Labs, 728
Sierra Lifestyle, 3257
Sierra Monolithics, 1747
Sierra Nevada Solar, 1669

1418

Portfolio Companies Index

Sierra Oil & Gas, 672
Sierra Oncology, 139, 400, 782, 1519, 1941
Sierra Systems, 839
Sierra Ventures, 214
Sierra Wireless, 385, 852, 2097, 2267
Siesta Medical, 138
Siffron, 1372
SIFI, 2293
SiFotonics Technologies, 970
Sift, 607
Sift Science, 1000
Sifteo, 1860
Siftery, 32, 107
Siftit, 1788
SIG, 2209
SIG Holding, 2616
Sigasi, 2476
SiGe Semiconductor, 712, 2079
SiGen, 892
SigFig, 596
Sigfox, 1416, 1607, 2693
SIGG, 1572
Sigh Machine, 961
Sight Machine, 809, 1206, 1359, 1703
sight4all, 297
Sighten, 1363
Sightline Technologies, 1325
Sightly, 1830, 1992
SightMD, 469
Sightpath Medical, 456
Sightward, 753
Sigilon Therapeutics, 747
SIGMA, 789
Sigma Estimates, 3203
Sigma International General Medical Apparatus, 1148
Sigma Offshore, 2700
Sigma-Tau Pharmaceutical, 1452
SigmaFlow, 1783
SigmaTel, 1793
Sigmatel, 596
SigmaX Limited, 2705
Sign-Zone, 1435
Sign-Zone Inc., 909
SignaCert, 807
Signal, 222, 688, 922, 1480, 1830
Signal 88 Security, 1276
Signal AI, 2759
Signal Bay Inc., 1079
Signal Innovations Group, 979
Signal Outdoor Advertising, 1270
Signal Peak Ventures, 3276
Signal Sciences, 1359
Signal Storage Innovations, 1837
Signal Tree Solutions, 166
SignalFX, 816
SignalSense, 1852
SignalSoft, 964
SignalWire, 1611
Signase, 1412
Signature Bank, 3272
Signature Bank NY, 3276
Signature Coast, 573
Signature Control Systems Inc., 834
Signature Destinations, 85
Signature Genomic, 118
Signature Hospice and Home Health, 1271
Signature Security Group, 2420
Signature Systems Group, 1132
SigNav, 2989
SignaVine, 181
Signavio, 135
Signet Accel, 655
Signet Jewelers, 1109
Signiant, 310, 695, 1334, 2199
Signicast, 1479
Signicat, 3216

SigniFAI, 544
Signifai, 935
Signifi, 2058
Signifyd, 84, 585, 1202, 1502, 1546
Signio, 1850
Signix, 946
Signma, 1983
SignmaQuest, 115
SignNow, 1371
Signostics, 2536
SignPost, 2132
Signpost, 1380, 1632
SignStorey, 1306
Signstorey, 839
Signum Technology, 3036
SignUp.com, 724
Sigouria Groupe, 865
Sigstr, 658
Sigtec Pty, 2622
Sigus Slovakia, 2683
SigValue Technologies Inc., 2828
Sihayo Gold, 2942
Sihe Wood, 596, 2936
Siigo, 29
Siimpel, 2021
Siine, 2446
Sikka, 183
Sikka Software Corporation, 1670
Siklu, 116, 1509, 2726
Sila, 1181
Silatronix, 1292, 1921, 2001
Silbond Corp., 443
Silecs, 2662
Silego, 1747
Silego Technology, 1978
Silent, 3104
Silent Preferred Partners, 194
Silex Microsystems, 3013
Silex., 2562
Silexica, 1218
Silicium Energy, 1069
Silicon Architects, 197
Silicon Bandwidth, 2079
Silicon Blue, 563, 2853
Silicon Clocks, 764, 1151, 1779
Silicon Cloud, 2778
Silicon Dimensions, 1080
Silicon Energy, 893, 1003, 1355
Silicon Energy Corp, 2079
Silicon Frontline Technology, 970
Silicon Hive, 1305, 3051
Silicon Image, 197
Silicon Laboratories, 1685
Silicon Labs, 444
Silicon Media, 2386
Silicon Metrics, 1288
Silicon Mitus, 690
Silicon Motion Inc., 947
Silicon Navigator Corp., 810
Silicon Optix, 757
Silicon Packets, 1646
Silicon Space Technology, 1303
Silicon Spice, 2007
Silicon Systems, 1237
Silicon Touch Technology, 3218
Silicon Valley Bank, 3276
Silicon Value, 2720
Silicon Value Ltd, 3158
Silicon Video Inc., 432
SiliconSystems, 1664
Siliconware Precision Industries, 892
Silicor Materials, 59, 835
Silicycle, 2029
Silikids, 1736
Siliquent, 2380
Siliquent Technologies, 1445
Silitech, 2436

Silixa, 466, 1125
Silixa Ltd., 3141
Silk, 2446
Silk Greenhouse, 1708
Silk Labs, 625
Silk Road, 563
Silk Road Medical, 1346, 1929
Silkan, 3113
SilkRoad, 770, 946, 3235
SilkRoad Japan, 1755
SilkRoad Realty Capital, 1681
SilkRoad Technology, 1681, 1796
Silkspan, 1139
Silniva Inc., 174
Silot, 148
SILQ, 995
Siluria, 1474, 3099
Siluria Technologies, 87, 153, 1151
Silver, 60
Silver Aero, 225
Silver Bullet, 146
Silver Creek, 1057
Silver Creek Oil & Gas, 559
Silver Creek Permian, 559
Silver Creek Systems, 1407
Silver Jeans Co., 2258
Silver Kite, 2580
Silver Lake, 3255
Silver Lining, 1358
Silver Lining Solutions, 2967
Silver Oak Energy, 672
Silver Peak, 248, 634, 1341, 1625
Silver Peak Systems, 581, 872, 1445
Silver Regulatory Associates, 3268
Silver Spring Networks, 634, 770
Silver State Materials, 194
Silver Storm Technologies, 538
Silver Stream Software, 1038
Silver Tail Systems, 548, 979
Silverado Senior Living, 1575
Silverback Exploration, 672
SilverBack Technologies, 314
Silverback Technologies, 1334
Silvercare Solutions, 718
SilverCarrot, 1314
Silvercrest, 1946
Silvergate Pharmaceuticals Inc., 782
Silverline, 1409, 1607
Silverlink, 1052, 1673
Silverlink Communications, 1672
Silvernest, 7, 896
SilverPOP, 184
Silverpop, 1863
SilverRail, 349, 386
SilverRail Technologies, 848
SilverSheet, 50
Silversheet, 306, 1888
SilverSky, 1748
Silversky, 530
SilverSpring Networks, 581
Silverspring Networks, 1341
SilverStorm Technologies, 212, 422
SilverStream, 1334
SilverTil, 1102, 1655
Silvertip Completion Services, 1125
SilverTrail Systems, 486
SilverVue, 1480
Silvue, 523
Silvus, 1045
SIM Digital, 2139
SIM Partners, 1046, 1571
Simbe, 519, 1473
Simbe Robotics, 1421
Simbi, 24, 972, 1183
Simbionix, 642
Simbol Materials, 730, 988, 1247
SIMCO Ltd., 908

1419

Portfolio Companies Index

SimCraft, 656
Simcro, 1572
Sime Diagnostics, 3107
Simeio Solutions, 1972
Simibio, 2514
Simlife, 2850
Simmerson Holdings, 2523
Simmons, 722, 1017
Simmons Bedding Company, 159
Simms Fishing Products, 421
Simon Data, 2
SimonDelivers, 1113, 1954
Simonds Industries, 1279
SIMP, 3020
Simperium, 679
Simpirica, 598
Simplaex, 3161
Simple, 965, 1663, 1821, 2406, 2940
Simple Citizen, 1070
Simple Disability Insurance, 384
Simple Emotion, 1463
Simple Energy, 1789, 1977
Simple Feast, 2478
Simple Habit, 1138
Simple Health, 24
Simple Legal, 599
Simple Reach, 1965
Simple Star, 1916
Simple Tuition, 1339
Simplee, 1696
SimpleGeo, 784
SimpleIT, 2385
SimpleLegal, 306, 1758
SimpleNexus, 1000
Simpler, 585
SimpleReach, 38, 1242, 1475
SimpleRelevance, 471, 962
SimpleTax, 2685, 3108
Simpletax, 2586
Simpletuition, 946
Simpleview, 9, 1045
Simplex Solutions, 2007
Simplexity, 1348
Simpli.fi, 533, 1486
Simplibuy, 650
Simplicissius Book Farm, 3052
Simplifeye, 128, 720
Simplified Logistics, 476
SimpliField, 745
Simplify Compliance, 1105, 1166
Simplifya, 963, 1207
SimplifyMD, 1008
Simplivity, 455, 646, 1212
Simplus, 560, 1607
Simply Good Jars, 1577
Simply Hired, 807, 1563
Simply Incredible Foods, 1292
Simply Measured, 777, 1226
Simply Smart Group, 2677
Simply Vital Health, 307
SimplyCast, 2155
SimplyHired, 770
Simplyhired Inc., 623
SimplyShe, 69, 910
SimplyTapp, 1926
SimplyWell, 1837
Simponi, 2102
Simpplr, 1346, 1607
Simpson Performance Products, 354, 415
SimpTek Technologies, 2200
Simscale, 1882
SimSuite, 1532
SIMtone, 1080
Simtra Aerotech Spotfire, 2878
Simulmedia, 206, 1827
Simworx, 2967
Sin Delantal, 3105

SINA Corporation, 1474
Sincerely, 455, 1715
SinDelantal.com, 2920
Sinequa, 3239
Singapore Advanced Biologics, 2518
Singapore Suzhou Township Development, 2690
Singer Equities, 1136
Single Digits, 333, 1728
Single Platform, 608
SingleOps, 189, 745
SinglePipe Communications, 1214
SinglePlatform, 1480
SinglePoint, 48, 1637
SingleToken Security, 649
Singly, 784, 1358, 1860
Singpost, 1715
Singular, 816, 1346
Singular BIO, 1929
Singulex, 1488
Sinitic, 2128
Sinldo, 1340
Sino Forest, 1087
Sino-Forest, 2772
SinoBnet, 2850
Sinocampus, 3208
Sinocom, 2936
Sinofusion, 2998
SinoGen International, 892
SinoLending, 585
Sinomedia Holding Limited, 220
Sinopsys, 930
Sinopsys Surgical, 1206
Sinosol AG, 2979
SinoSun Technology, 823
Sinovia Technologies, 721
Sinoway Herbal Skin Care, 2560
Sinphoniq, 2868
SintecMedia, 3231
SinterFire, 164
SiOnyx, 1946
Sionyx, 563, 1460
siOPTICA, 2527
SioTex, 950
Sipera, 3137
Siperian, 132
Siping Cogen Power Plants, 2591
SiPort, 1305, 1445
Sipp, 668
Sipwise, 3165
Sipx, 1247, 2011
Siraga, 2602
SIRAKOSS, 689
Sirchie Fingerprint Laboratories, 1526
Sircon, 652
Siren Care, 1701
Siren Care Inc., 1069
Sirenum, 640
SiRF Technology, 1922
SiRF Technology Holdings Inc., 1779
Sirga Advanced BioPharma, 737
Siri, 1257, 2831
Sirific, 1244
Sirigen, 1915
Sirion Biotech, 2638
SIrion Therapeutics, 74
Sirion Therapeutics, 1775
Sirius, 1062
Sirius Computer Solutions, 909, 1814
Sirius Decisions, 1041
Sirocco, 1928
Siromed, 1049
Sirona Dental Systems, 1156
SironRX, 642
SironRX Therapeutics, 1047
SironRx Therapeutics, 1553, 1847
Sirrus, 171, 322, 479, 1241
SirsiDynix, 164, 969

Sirti, 2293
Sirtris Pharmaceuticals, 410, 1691
SIRVA, 1156
Sisal, 3033
SiSense, 1594, 1670
Sisense, 1381
Sisterson, 3275
Sistina Software, 555
Sisu Global Health, 19, 383
Sitara Networks, 455, 1668
Site Hands, 793
Site Jabber, 1655
SiteAware, 2947
Sitecare, 2854
Sitecore Corporation, 1785
Sitel, 1134
Sitematic, 1239
SiteMinder, 1785
SiteOne Therapeutics, 1238
Siterra, 441
SiteScape, 647
Sitetracker, 1607
Sitewit, 1734
Siteworx, 1575
SiTime, 385, 2797
Sitka Biopharma, 2229
Sitka Exploration, 2025, 2040
Sitoa, 2457
Sitrion, 1245
Sitryx Therapeutics, 1145, 1628
SitScape, 979
Sittercity, 137, 1459, 1480
Sittercity.com, 222
Siva, 2011
Siva Power, 595, 730, 1850
Sivdon Diagnostics, 2638
Siverge, 2726
SiVerio Inc., 810
SiVerion, 1126
Siverion, 856, 1901
Sivyer Steel Corporation, 719
Six Apart, 197, 757, 2991
Six Degrees, 456
Six Degrees Games, 502
6 River Systems, 648, 1202, 1346
Six Rooms Holdings, 1241
6 Sence, 229
Six Waves, 1460
6 Wind, 2876
60 Erie St. Jersey City NJ, 190
64-x, 741
64x Bio, 318
Sixa, 811
6connect, 956
6d, 249
6D.AI, 751, 816
6D.ai, 1663
Sixdof Space, 543
Sixense, 807, 1611
SixFix, 995
6fusion, 1008
Sixpack Mobile Applications, 3128
6Scan, 3246
6Sense, 1607
6sense, 235, 547, 1916
6SensorLabs, 1700
6sicuro, 3052
Sixth Sense Media, 1640
6th Treet Inc., 1169
Sixtron Advanced Materials, 184
SixUp, 32
Sixup, 1551
6Waves, 1000
6WIND, 483
6wunderkinder, 2446
Size Technologies, 1646
Sizzling Platter, 1902

1420

Portfolio Companies Index

SJ Irvine Fine Foods, 2049
SJ Semi, 1509
SJI Holdings, 361
Sjtu Sunway Software Industry Ltd., 2633
SK FireSafety Group, 2501
SK Sinsegi Telecom, 2857
SK Spruce, 1670
Skale Labs, 751
Skansogaard, 3203
Skaphandrus, 3048
SKC Communication Products, 1276
Skechers, 869
Skedulo, 547
Skeed, 2974
Skerou, 2308
SketchDeck, 942, 1768
SketchFab, 308
Sketchfab, 743, 2478
Skift, 60, 1110, 1222
Skill Survey, 52
Skillist, 754
Skilljar, 1184, 1663
Skillo, 607
Skillshare, 318, 1715, 1721, 1912
SkillSoft, 220, 1672
Skillsoft, 1668
Skillsoft PLC, 300
SkillSurvey, 989, 1476
Skillz, 38, 70, 1322, 1613
Skimlinks, 256, 871
Skin Analytics, 2001
Skin Medica, 1251
Skinkers, 2322
SkinMedica, 74, 1725
Skinphonic, 1191
Skip, 724, 1006, 1834
Skip the Dishes, 2137
Skipta, 1165
SKLZ, 1741
SkopeNow, 1269
Skopos Financial, 1104
Skorpios Technologies, 549
SKOut, 1965
Skout, 1323
Skrill, 1017
SKS, 1516
Skuid, 1607
Skullcandy, 1204
Skully Helmets, 1311
Skupos, 640
Skura, 2058
Skurt, 302, 707, 1888
SkuVault, 224
Sky Europe, 2683
SKY Harbor Capital Management, 1743
Sky Squirrel Technologies, 2155
Sky Vision, 892
SkyAtlas, 3078
SkyBitz, 1014
Skybox Imaging, 181, 386
Skybox Security, 1540, 1759, 2566, 3221
Skybuilt Power, 979
Skycast, 85
Skycatch, 206, 243, 724, 1269, 1509, 1894
Skycision, 995
Skycredit, 2978
SkyCross, 620, 805, 1828
Skycure, 770, 1663
SkyDeck Accelerator, 1670
Skydex, 36
Skydex Technologies, 553
SkyDrop, 1670
Skydrop, 640
Skye Chesapeake Bay Roating Company, 1599
Skye Mineral Partners, 494
SkyePharma, 1616
Skyera, 1690

SkyeTek, 142
Skyfire, 1410, 1853
SkyFuel, 756
SkyGrid, 791
Skyhook Wireless, 221, 534
Skyhour, 1035
Skyland Exchange, 1219
Skylar Body, 120, 342
Skylark, 220, 2379
Skylight Healthcare Systems, 1425, 1664
Skylight.net, 1954
SkyLights, 1473
Skylights, 1370
Skyline, 37, 148, 2155
Skyline Home Loans, 1888
Skyline Innovations, 61, 398
Skyline Solar, 1365
Skyline Windows, 1209
SkyMall, 1724
Skymedi Corporation, 2603
Skynamo, 745
Skyonic, 322
Skype, 385, 609, 690, 800, 2446, 2831, 2928
SkyPilot, 2999
Skypilot, 197
SkyPilot Networks, 1646
SkyPipeline, 378
Skyroam, 3215
SkyRyse, 488
Skyryse, 395, 648, 1916
SkySafe, 1530
Skyscanner, 3104
Skysheet, 2329
Skysoft, 58
SkySpecs, 113, 961, 981
SKYstream, 1097
SkyStream Networks, 823
Skysun LLC, 1047
Skytap, 974, 1158, 1380, 2008
Skytide, 852
SkyTran, 996
Skytream Networks, 1001
Skytree, 1028, 1891
SkyVu, 858, 1118, 1322
SkyWard, 773
Skyward, 1945
Skyware Global, 654
SkyWatch, 2137
Skyway, 2427
Skyword, 946, 1486
Skyworks Interactive, 418
Slack, 45, 107, 518, 823, 1001, 1075, 1149, 1694, 1696, 1761
Slacker, 1239
Slacker Radio, 515
Slackers, 441
SLAMcore, 1834
SlamData, 1656, 1663
Slamdata, 36
Slang, 1696
SlashNext, 1346
Slater Technology Fund, 1693
SLED Mobile, 298
Sleek Medspa, 1954
Sleep Country, 722
Sleep Country Canada, 2183
Sleeperbot, 272
SleepMed, 224, 1398
Sleepy's, 368
SLG Recycling, 3020
Slice, 560, 596, 823, 996, 1035
Slide, 707
Slide Rocket, 215
SlideShare, 1916
Slightly Nutty, 3257
Slim Ops Studios, 998
Sling, 305

Sling Media, 184, 596, 922, 2936
Slive, 195
SLIVER.tv, 994
Sliver.tv, 1611, 1670
sliver.tv, 1703
SLM Corporation, 1903
SloanLED, 222, 908
Slocum Adhesives, 1209
Slon Lofts Group, 788
Slope, 640, 1641
Slovlepex, 3122
Slovpack Bratislava, 3077
SLR Consulting Limited, 2311
SLT Logic, 1676
Slyce, 1306
Slyde, 3045
SM Logistics, 2769
SM&A, 373, 374
SM&A Holdings, 1368
Smackhigh, 313
Small Bone Innovations, 212, 1325, 1844
Small Box Energy, 856
Small Demons, 2010
Small Door, 325
Small Giant Games, 3055
Small World, 2972, 3097
Smallable, 2385
Smallstep, 305
Smalltown, 764
Smarfin, 2886
Smarkets, 3030
Smarking, 1329, 1483, 1589
Smarsh, 1829
Smart & Final Stores LLC, 159
Smart Ace, 3002
Smart Autonomous Solutions, 2031
Smart Communications, 29
Smart Destinations, 1317, 1339
Smart Document Solutions, 152
Smart Education, 2869
Smart Energy Instruments, 2041
Smart Eye, 2755
Smart Focus, 779
Smart Furniture, 1273
Smart Host, 2841
Smart Hydro Power, 2686
Smart Link Ltd, 2782
Smart Loyalty, 2979
Smart Lunches, 586, 1100, 1581
Smart Medical Systems, 621
Smart Mocha, 1463
SMART Modular, 1683
Smart Modular Technologies, 779
Smart Pants Vitamins, 1255
Smart Picture, 781
Smart Picture Solution, 445
Smart Planet Technologies, 1061
Smart Recruiter, 1607
Smart Recruiters, 1540
Smart Reno, 2027
Smart Sand, 500
Smart Scheduling, 1615
Smart Skin, 2200, 2239
Smart Skin Technologies, 2068, 2143
Smart Sparrow, 3023
Smart Storage, 2539
Smart Telecom, 2918
Smart Vision Labs, 1530
Smart Warehousing, 745
Smart Wave, 3072
Smartanalyst, 52, 655
SmartAngels, 3239
Smartassel, 1334
SmartAsset, 1518
Smartasset, 1028
SmartBear, 779
Smartbear, 1829

1421

Portfolio Companies Index

Smartbin, 2355
SmartBix, 1916
Smartbiz, 231
SmartCover Systems, 2290
SmartDrive Systems, 1361
SmartDyeLivery, 2527
Smarter Alloys, 2041
Smarter Grid Solutions, 3104
Smarter HQ, 658
Smarter Sorting, 408
Smarterer, 1551, 1860
SmarterHQ, 1728
SmarteSoft, 445, 594
Smartesting, 2899
Smartfile, 658
SmartFlow Technologies, 1014
Smartfrog, 641
Smarthouse, 2686
SmartKem, 3018
SmartKids, 2438
SmartLane, 120
Smartlaw, 2838
Smartlight Ltd, 2585
Smartling, 32, 720, 1563, 1796, 1916
Smartlink, 1719
SmartMI, 823
Smartner, 2386
SmartNews, 2446
SmartOps, 56
Smartots, 3127
SmartPackets, 649
SmartPak Equine, 438, 1360
SmartPark Equine, 1334
SmartPath, 1008
Smartpods, 2200
Smartrac Technology, 1376
SmartRecruiters, 1184, 1991
SmartRG, 791, 1250, 1383
SmartRM, 2672
SmartRx, 3211
Smarts Japan, 1755
SmartShare, 3203
Smartsheet, 1158
SmartSheet10 Technology, 1289
SmartShoot, 1700
Smartsky, 1211
SmartSource Holdings, 1456
SmartSpot, 1675
SmartSynch, 233, 1355
SmartTrade, 2685
SmartVid.io, 1100
Smartvid.io, 308, 1480
SmartWool, 1748
Smarty Content, 2920
Smarty Pants, 482
Smarty Pants Vitamins, 330
SmartyPants Inc., 331
SmartyPig, 582
SmartZip, 1642
Smartzip, 1028
SmartZip Analytics, 491
SmartZip Analytics Inc., 567
SMASH, 998
Smash.gg, 1149
Smashburger, 1020
Smashfly, 1380
Smava, 2994
SMB Machinery Systems, 931
sMedio, 2974
Smeet, 2813
SMG, 319, 2209
SMI, 1516
SMIC, 596
Smic, 2436
SmilarWeb, 1323
Smile Brands, 881, 1972
Smile Brands Inc., 1134

Smile Direct Club, 1075
Smile Doctors, 1166
Smile Doctors Braces, 16, 1128
Smile Identity, 1758
Smile Maker, 2646
Smile Reminder, 1677
SmileBack, 1518
Smiles Services, 849
Smilo, 325, 1346
SMiT, 1184
Smith Broadcasting Group, 897
Smith Co., 77
Smith Pipe, 514
Smith System Driver Improvement Institute, 1111
Smith-Cooper International, 746
SmithRx, 858
Smokey Bones, 1753
Smoothstone, 1242
Smore, 773, 2280
Smove, 1965
SMS Assist, 842, 1480
SMS GupShup, 835
SmS Tnzotherm, 3229
SMT Dynamics, 1915
SMT Kingdom, 1041
SMTC Corporation, 439
SMTP, 638
Smulders Group, 2501
Smule, 751, 852, 1663
Smule UParts, 781
Smurfit Kappa, 1156
Smurfit-Stone, 1967
Smyte, 206
Smyte., 231
Smyth, 2206
Småföretagsinvest, 2867
SN Tech, 1603
Snadec, 3239
Snag A Slip, 493
SnagaJob, 646
Snagajob, 197, 222, 904, 1008, 1725
SnagAJob.com, 57
SnagFilms, 518
Snakblox, 1306
Snap, 578
Snap Av, 924
Snap Financial Group, 787
Snap Kitchen, 1088
Snap Sheet, 1480
Snap Strat, 1663
Snap-On Inc., 1903
SnapAV, 815
SnapChat, 509
Snapchat, 248, 265, 802, 820, 1001, 1212, 1839
Snapdeal.com, 3001
Snapdocs, 32, 784
Snapflow, 1463
SnapGear, 1459
Snapin, 85
SNAPin Software, 1637
SnapLogic, 454, 548, 974
Snaplogic, 751
snapLogic, 1846
Snaplytics, 51
SnapNames, 85
Snapp Digital, 392
Snappcloud, 1299, 1460
SnappyTV, 784
SnapRetail, 56
SnapRoute, 1346
Snaproute, 1154
Snaps, 3127
SnapScreen, 2245
Snapsheet, 1118, 1364
Snapt, 3221
SnapTell, 1038
Snaptell, 623

SnapTrack, 852
SnapTravel, 243, 1118, 2157
Snapwire, 226
Snark.ai, 1848
SNC Former, 1139, 2946
SNDR, 1228
Snell, 2944
Snell and Wilcox, 2348
Snips, 679, 1809
SNL Financial, 1301
SNL Securities, 1927
SnoBar Cocktails, 1061
Snocap, 114
Snooze, 1978
Snow Companies, 1979
Snow Lakes Resources Ltd., 2122
Snow+Rock, 2935
Snowball, 2137
Snowball Group Limited, 2715
Snowbear, 2073
Snowflake, 1158
Snowflake Computing, 1534
Snowhite, 276
Snowshoe, 1149, 1150, 1222
Snowshoe Stamps, 2001
SnowShore, 455
SNU Precision, 1087
SnugMug, 1604
SNUPI Technologies, 2008
Snyder Industries Inc., 1372
Snyk, 305
So1, 3161
SOA Software, 1400, 1402, 1965
Soane Energy, 466, 1009
SoapBox, 2137
Soapbox, 1766
SOASTA, 764
Soasta, 386, 1425
Sobe, 1191
SOCAR, 511
SoccerScout.com, 2696
SOCi, 856
Sociable Labs, 2239
Sociable Labs Stipple, 1513
Sociagram, 1047
Social Annex, 397, 1055
Social Chorus, 1083, 1992
Social Construct, 1894
Social Finance, 1592
Social Gaming Network, 1348
Social Imprints, 3277
Social Insight, 2856
Social Intelligence, 946
Social Matterz, 545
Social Native, 50
Social Radar, 876, 1766
Social SafeGuard, 904
Social Sentinal, 786
Social Sentinel, 378, 1110
Social Service Coordinators, 1417
Social Solutions, 1388
Social Stock Exchange, 2509
Social Toaster, 1169
Social Touch, 823
SocialAnnex, 1965
SocialBicycles, 1306
SocialBomb, 1584
SocialBro, 3104
Socialbro, 2464
SocialFlow, 432, 712, 1523, 1699
Socialflow, 1593
SocialFlow Inc., 810
Socialize, 721, 1054
Socialkaty, 1118
Socialmedian, 1083
SocialPandas, 1860
Socialpoint, 2987

Portfolio Companies Index

Socialradar, 1320
SocialRank, 60, 305
Socialrel8, 3012
SocialSafeGuard, 1607
Socialsci, 1097
SocialShield, 1916
SocialSign.in, 351, 1306
SocialSignIn, 1178
SocialTables, 1806
Socialtext, 242, 1884
Socialthing, 685
SocialToaster, 285, 1958
Socialwalk, 3073
Socialware, 803, 1255, 1685, 1810
SocialWeekend, 1632
SocialWire, 32, 1700
Socinser, 2489
Sociocast, 1306
Socionado, 1507
SoCloz, 2385
SoCore Energy, 1118
Socotra, 1269
Socrata, 1257, 1380, 1620
Socrates AI, 1346
Socrates.ai, 1916
Socratic, 1663, 1715
Socratic Labs, 707
Socrative, 1860
Socrex, 3125
Socure, 91, 724, 2006
Sodacard, 3121
SodaHead, 1239, 1247, 1798
Sodastream, 2796
Sodium Solutions, 2286
Sofa Carpet Specialist, 1753
SoFactory, 3113
Sofar Sounds, 1882, 3018
Sofatronic, 2994
Sofatutor, 2841
Sofdesk, 676
Soff-Cut, 374
Soffio Medical, 1347, 1628
SOFI, 1001
SoFI, 996
SoFi, 231, 596, 1502, 1818
Sofialys, 2638
Sofitech AS, 3141
Soft Module, 538
Soft Surroundings, 334, 378
Soft Switching Technologies, 61
Soft-Switch, 1275
Softbank Broadband Fund, 3152
Softbank Capital, 986
SoftBank Group, 3255
SoftBook Press, 524
Softbox Systems, 859
Softbrands, 402
Softchoice, 2062, 2183
Softcom, 3137
Softek, 1017, 1886
SOFTEK Storage Solutions, 1288
Softgames, 2841, 3236
Softgate Systems, 655
Softlayer, 824
Softmax, 2969
Softrax, 1227
Softricity, 712, 1146, 1167
Softscope, 40
Softscope Medical Technologies, 1817
SoftTech VC, 986
Software, 454
Software Architects, 368
Software Integrity, 248
Software Technology, 1633
Software Transformation Inc., 206
Software Unlimited, 349
Software.com, 724

Softway, 3180
SoftWriters, 1776
SOG Specialty Knives & Tools, 828, 1250
SOGEM, 2419
Soha Systems, 454
Sohan Lal Commodity, 3001
Sohu, 2850
Soikea Solutions Oy, 2966
Soil Nerd, 995
Soil Safe Conduit, 2379
SoilSafe, 894
Soilwise, 2645
SoJeans, 3208
Sojern, 757, 1346, 1846, 1850
Sojournix, 782, 1519
Sokanu, 2291
Sokrati, 1013
Sol, 1736
Sol Cuisine, 2161
SOL Republic, 1236
Sol-Gel, 2585
Sol-Gel Ltd, 2973
Sol-Gen, 3245
Solace, 2261, 2284
Solace Systems, 909, 916
Soladigm, 1672
SolAero Technologies, 680, 901, 1925
Solaicx, 144, 1089
Solairdirect, 2439
Solais, 786
Solais Lighting, 1142
Solantro, 1474
Solantro Semiconductor Corp., 497
Solapoint, 2703
Solar Array Ventures, 1393
Solar Century, 3104
Solar Change, 678
Solar Edge, 3214
Solar Energies, 3020
Solar Implant Techn9logies, 2632
Solar Participations, 3020
Solar Plastics, 1970
Solar Silicon Technology, 835
Solar Universe, 1579
SolarBridge Technologies, 975
Solarcentury, 1906, 3252
SolarCity, 595, 609
SolarEdge, 1381
Solarex Photovaltaic, 2881
Solarflame Communications, 2322
Solarflare, 132
Solarflare Communications, 646, 1237, 1361
SolarFun, 2936
Solargigia, 2436
Solaria, 57, 184, 548, 1324, 1672
Solaria Corporation, 1241
Solariat, 1084
Solaris Midstream Holdings LLC, 1851
Solarnow, 55
SolarOne, 786
SolarOne Solutions, 1862
SolarReserve, 332, 1397, 1895
Solarsilicon Recycling Services LLC, 274
Solarvista, 1340
SolarVista Media, 1327
Solarwinds, 751, 909, 1244
Solasia, 1268
Solazyme, 322, 1906
SolBright Renewable Energy, 2031
Sold., 313
SoldPrint Europe, 3128
Soldsie, 641, 1700
Soleno Therapeutics, 1941
Soleo Communications, 749
Soleo Health, 928
SolePower, 1507
Solera Holdings Inc., 744

Solera Networks, 84, 560, 1677, 1850
Soleras, 438
Soleras Advanced Coatings, 657
Soleras Advances Coatings, 2379
Solexa, 2386
Solexel, 581, 595, 1786, 1977
Solfo, 624
SolFocus, 184, 1324
Solfocus, 137
Solgaz, 3077
Soliant, 1372, 1579
SoliCore, 1303
Solicore, 730
Solid Biosciences, 762, 1519
Solid Carbon Products, 285, 1542
Solid Energy, 817
Solid Partners, 1115
Solid State Equipment, 1752
Solid State Pharma Inc., 2155
Solid X Partners Inc., 1530
Solidcore, 968
SolidEnergy, 144
SolidFire, 867, 1348
Solidfire, 1899
Solidia Technologies, 319, 2492
Solidica, 1336
Solidscape, 556, 903
SolidSpace, 1681
SolidStage, 585
SOLIDUS Investment Fund, 1374
Solidware Technologies, 975
SolidWorks, 1334
Soligenix, 1079, 1812
SoLink, 2249
Solink, 2144, 2284
Solis Mammography, 782, 1156
Solis Women's Health, 402, 1168
Solisite, 622
Solita, 135
Soliton, 2058
Solius, 1095
Solix BioSystems, 988
SolmeteX, 812
Solo Growth Corp., 2140
Solo Stove, 257
Sologear, 583
SOLOMO, 2001
Solomon Systech, 2436, 2603
SoLoMoTo, 890
Solovis, 655, 1240
Solrec, 2985
Sols, 707, 792
SOLS Systems, 1151
Solsoft, 2607
Solstas Lab Partners, 176, 1972
Solstice, 622
Solstice Capital, 520
Solstice Energy Solutions, 218
Solstice Medical, 658
Solstice Neurosciences, 1817
Solstice Software, 538
Solsys Medical, 1628, 1762
Solta Medical, 1786
Solta Medical Tocagen, 762
Solterra Recycling Solutions, 1576
Soltrus, 2079
Solucient, 1927
Solueta Co., 3002
Solugen, 395
Solulink, 1455
Solus Biosystems, 2457
Solution Builders Limited, 2760
Solutionary, 500
SolutionReach, 688
Solutionreach, 1677, 1752
Solutions Vending International, 392
Soluto, 2872

1423

Portfolio Companies Index

Solv, 49, 180, 872, 1323
Solvaira Specialties, 170
Solve Media, 1291, 1489
SolveBio, 625
SolveDirect Service Management, 2309
Solvis, 123
Solvoyo, 2294
Solvvy, 1626
SOLX, 644
Solx, 2981
Solyndra, 1445, 3222
Soma, 231, 552, 1110, 1222, 1236
Soma Analytics, 1615
Soma Networks, 1918
Somaca, 908
SomaDetect, 2149, 2200
SomaLogic, 1490
Somatix, 769
SOMAVAC, 995
Somaxon Pharma, 1251
Somaxon Pharmaceuticals, 1493
Somboom Advance Technology, 1139
Somboon Advance Technology, 2946
Somelos Tecidos, 3048
Somero Enterprises, 1770
Somerset Gas Transmission Company, 1523
Something Navy, 318
Sometrics, 1099
Somo, 2752
Somo Global, 2972
SoMoLend, 1358, 1512
Somoto, 2914
SOMS Technologies, 1523
Sona, 415
Sona Group, 2923
SonaCare Medical, 806
Sonar, 301
Sonar Entertainment Inc., 2073
SonarMed, 445, 658, 1512
Sonas, 3054
Sonatype, 238, 508, 956, 1257
Sonavex, 19, 472, 799, 870
Sonavex Surgical, 1701
Sonavi Labs, 1613
Sonder, 262, 872, 2144, 2157, 2249
Sonedo, 1212
Sonetik, 2496
Sonexa, 1626
Sonexis, 1103, 1913
Songbird, 115
Songkick, 1700
Songwhale, 998
Songwoo, 3145
Songza, 525, 600
Sonia, 563
Sonian, 1380, 1478, 2259
Sonic, 1576
Sonic Notify, 15, 1524
Sonic Sleep, 1507
Sonicbids, 655
SonicCloud, 1157
Sonicliving, 1359
Sonics, 835, 1314
SonicWALL, 238
SonicWall, 744, 779
Sonify Biosciences, 19
Sonim, 2472
Sonim Technologies, 641
Sonion, 2384
Sonitrol Corporation, 1409
Sonitrol Inc., 1724
Sonitus Medical, 115, 979
Sonneborn Refined Products, 1376
Sonnen, 809
Sonnen GmbH, 2686
Sonnendo, 1382
Sonobi, 1601

Sonoma, 176
Sonoma Creamery, 378
Sonoma Orthopedic, 732
Sonoma Orthopedic Products, 652, 666
Sonoma Orthopedics, 980
Sonoma Orthpedic, 1725
Sonoma Pharma, 1251
Sonos, 129, 641, 751, 867, 1534
SonoVol, 737
Sonrai, 2200
Sonrai Security, 1794
Sonru, 2918
Sonus, 422
Sonus Networks, 1087, 1334
Sony, 214
Sookasa, 1547
SoonR, 1474, 1818
Soonr, 502, 933
Soothe, 1563
Sopherion Therapeutics, 1298, 1490, 1828
Sopherion Therapeutics Inc., 2816
Sophia Genetics, 2296, 2478
Sophos, 135, 1017
Sopris Health, 567
Sopsy, 2437
Soraa, 126, 946, 1069, 1324
Sorbent Therapeutics, 153
Sorbisense, 3203
Sorenson Communications, 1156
Sorenson Media, 1611
Soricimed, 2200
Sorra, 184
Sorrento, 74
Sorrento Networks, 461
SortSpoke, 2249
SOS Security, 2022
Sosei, 1394
Sosh, 1460
Soshi Games, 2967
SoSocio, 2543
Sote Logistics, 1885
SOTEC, 2826
Sotera Defense Solutions, 159, 1134
Sotera Wireless, 1616, 2513, 2690
Sotralu, 2340
Soudsonic, 2564
SouFun, 2850
Soulbrain, 3145
Soulco, 2949
SoulCycle, 1109
Sound Agriculture, 570, 1238
Sound Building Supply, 1609
Sound Fuhua, 3194
Sound Lounge, 164
Sound Seal Inc., 899
Sounday, 2672, 3052
SoundBite, 1334
SoundBite Communications, 521
SoundCloud, 432, 679, 823, 1075, 1882, 2860, 2860
Soundcloud, 1001, 2444, 2671
Soundflavor, 114
Soundhawk, 1860
SoundHound, 115, 833, 1838
SoundHound Inc., 720, 1952
SoundHouse LLC, 515
Soundpays, 2195
Soundrop, 3013
Soundskrit, 2260
Soundstim Therapeutics, 870
Soundsupply, 1118
Soundtrack Your Brand, 2478
Soundtracker, 1581
SoundVamp, 2696
Soundview Advice, 3267
Soundview Maritime LLC, 1134
Soundview Technology, 1389

SoundWall, 296
Soundwave, 1716
Source 4 Teachers, 1599
Source Code, 793
Source Defence, 84
Source Energy Partners, 1443
Source Energy Services, 2275
Source Fire, 538
Source Medical, 1533
Source Photonics, 779
Source3, 13, 533, 544
Source4Style, 841
Sourcebits Technologies, 2849
SOURCEBYNET, 1769
Sourced, 2243
SourceDogg, 2522
Sourceeasy, 358
SourceFire, 989
Sourcefire, 560, 1212
Sourcegraph, 1534
SourceHOV, 1910
SourceIQ, 649
SourceMedia, 1017
SourceMedical, 1927
Sourcepoint, 776
Sourcery, 1254, 1595
Sources Refrigeration & HVAC Inc., 170
SourceTrace Systems, 855
Sourcify, 1554
Souris Mini, 2029
Sousacamp, 2717
South Bay Mental Health Center, 1189
South Beach Diet, 1231
South Dakota Innovation Partners, 1192
South Lakeland Parks, 2935
South Memory Restaurant Co., 2542
South Side, 782
South Staffordshire Place, 152
South-Tek Systems, 1435
Southampton Photonics, 2386
Southcoast-Boca Associates, 1148
Southcross, 675
Southcross Energy, 456
Southeast, 158
Southeast Directional Drilling, 1422, 1705
Southeast Guardrail, 1606
Southeast Health Plan, 1708
Southeast Healthplan, 1148
Southeast PowerGen, 156
Southeast TechInventures, 1442, 1923
Southeast Venture Capital Limited II, 1708
Southeastern Automotive Aftermarket Service Holdin, 415
Souther Lithoplate, 1526
Southerland, 164
Southern Ag Carriers, 917
Southern Air Holdings, 1360
Southern Assisted Living, 1526
Southern Care Hospice Services, 1255
Southern Carlson, 1062
Southern HVAC, 1270
Southern Management Corporation, 1234
Southern Petroleum Laboratories, 828
Southern Petroleum Laboratories Inc., 654
Southern Pines, 156
Southern Quality Meats, 928
Southern Spine Institute, 364
Southern States, 940
Southern Systems, 1708
Southern Technical College, 1984
Southern Theaters, 678, 1927
Southern Tide, 328
Southern Towing Company, 1856
Southern Veterinary Partners, 1667
SouthernCare, 1081
Southland Log Homes, 152, 2978
Southland Royalty Company, 672

Portfolio Companies Index

Southpaw Live, 529
Southwall Technologies, 1288
Southwaste Serivces, 1503
Southwest Nanotechnologies, 259
Southwest Value Partners, 1276
Southwest Windpower, 466, 1579
Sova Pharmaceuticals, 206
Sovereign Brands, 1954
Sovereign Woodmet, 2486
Sovrn, 776, 1112
sovrn, 1374
sovrn Holdings, 1361
Sown To Grow, 1026
Soylent, 1110
soylent, 991
SoYoung, 135
SP Industries, 846, 1343
SP Industries Inc., 908
SP Surgical, 666
SPA, 2556
Spaas Kaarsen, 2949
Space Adventures/Zero-G, 1584
Space Ape Games, 2629
Space Exploration Technologies, 1902
Space Monkey, 585, 1254, 1460, 2017
Space Tango, 395
Space-Ime Insight, 3252
Space-Time Research, 2622
Spaceape Games, 3013
Spacebel, 3134
SpaceClaim, 1288
Spaceclaim, 308, 1334
SpaceClaim Corporation, 1080
SpaceCurve, 618
Spaces, 307, 518
Spacesys, 307
Spacetec IMC Corp., 465
SpaceWatts, 2263
SpaceX, 595, 609, 650, 775, 792, 799, 800, 1890, 2278
Spacex, 802
Spacious, 1110
Spada Media, 1114
Spadac, 743
Spanfeller Media, 1849
Spanfeller Media Group, 1699, 1906
Spanlink, 1725
Spansive, 679
SPAR Middle Volga, 2465
SPAR Moscow Holdings, 2465
SPARC, 1807
Sparcana, 2967
Sparcyz, 2646
Spare, 392
SpareFoot, 1685
Sparefoot, 751
Spark, 1359
Spark Networks, 2841
Spark Post, 1136
Spark Therapeutics, 1698
SparkBase, 1553
Sparkbuy, 247
Sparkcentral, 1024, 1725, 2949
SparkCognition, 1926
Sparkcognition, 1031
Sparked, 1054, 1860
Sparkfund, 532
Sparkir, 30
Sparkow, 3239
Sparkpr, 3272
Sparkt, 987
Sparky Animation, 2853
SPARQ, 2187
Sparq, 2041
Sparqd, 1940
Sparrowhawk Media, 2306
Sparrows Group, 64

Sparsha Learning, 2526
Sparta Science, 1509
Sparta Systems, 97, 1752, 1814
Spartan College of Aeronautics and Technology, 1742
Spartan Energy Services, 910
Spartan Foods of America, 1132, 1456
Spartan MTech, 725
Spartan Race, 329, 922
Spartanova, 2476
Spartatn, 2184
Spartech, 170
Spartoo, 935
SPATIAL, 1155
Spatial, 2157
Spatial Stae, 1611
Spatial Wireless, 1167, 1906
Spaulding Composites, 1224
SPC TelEquip, 1503
Speakaboos, 60
Speakeasy, 852
Speakeasy Political, 934
SpeakerText, 1958
Speakr, 1632, 1829
Spear Therapeutics, 1775
SpearFysh, 1047
Specialdocs Consultants, 1667
Specialist Heating Components Ltd, 2708
Specialized Desanders, 900
Specialized Education Services, 468, 1469
Specialized Elevator Services, 489
Specialized Medical Services, 1572
Specialty Applicances, 746
Specialty Bakers, 1744
Specialty Brands, 368
Specialty Care, 1081
Specialty Commerce Corp., 2103
Specialty Commodities Inc., 843
Specialty Filaments, 402
Specialty Finance Company, 1086
Specialty Healthcare Services, 541
Specialty Manufacturing Inc., 449
Specialty Sales, 1166
Specialty Vehicles Group, 1030
SpecialtyCare, 97
Specific Media, 779
SpecificMEDIA, 1664
Specified Fittings, 1250, 1343
Specle, 2464
Specright, 728
Spectel, 1017
Spector & Co., 290
Spectra, 192
Spectra Biomedical Inc., 206
Spectra Securities Software, 2058
SpectraFluidics, 979
SpectraGenetics, 1448
Spectral Dimensions, 349, 1689
Spectral Edge, 2967
SpectraLinear, 798, 947
Spectralink, 1753
SpectraLink Corp., 947
Spectralus Corporation, 650
SpectraSensors, 466, 548, 765, 1355
Spectrawatt, 1397
Spectrio, 257, 1572
Spectrum, 1110, 1762
Spectrum Athletic Clubs, 334
Spectrum Bridge, 1782, 1860, 2717
Spectrum Five, 1344
Spectrum Health Care, 2082, 2206
Spectrum Healthcare Services, 541
Spectrum K12, 1886
Spectrum K12 School Solutions, 1348
Spectrum Lubricants, 1343
Spectrum Motors, 1764
Spectrum Network Systems, 3168

Spectrum Professional Services, 244, 1628
Spectrum Resources Towers, 1927
Spectrum Staffing, 821
Speech Recognition, 2662
Speech4Good, 1589
SpeechCycle, 1153
SpeechTrans, 418
Speechworks, 1626
SpeeCo, 1435
Speed Plastics, 2967
SpeedBit, 3124
SpeedCast, 1776, 3168
Speedel, 2922
Speedera Networks, 1853
SpeedInfo, 548
Speedline Technologies, 1085
Speedscan, 2622
SpeedTracs, 656
Speedy Packets, 1483
Speek, 1320, 1899
Spell, 648, 2014
Spellacy Universal Ltd., 2788
Spencer Supports Canada, 2107
Spensa, 658
Spently, 2113
Spepharm Holding, 3196
Sperical Defence, 535
SpermCheck, 1442
Spero Therapeutics, 191, 1419, 1519, 1731
Sperry & Rice, 1609
SPG International, 1424
SPG Solar, 834
SPGPrints Group B.V., 1017
Sphaera Pharma, 2490
Sphera, 819, 3179
Sphere, 922, 1084, 1806, 1963
Sphere Drake Holdings Limited, 447
Sphere Energy, 2025
Sphere Fluidics, 2997, 3028
SPHERE Technology Solutions, 3274
Spherics, 1412
Spheris, 1040
Sphero, 776, 874, 1204
Spheros GmbH, 3067
Sphinx Pharmaceuticals, 1008
SPI Polyols, 168
Spi Technologies Inc, 2694
Spice Chain Corporation, 789
Spice World, 1403
Spiceworks, 751, 1001, 1663, 1796
Spicus, 100
Spicy Horse, 3215
SpiderCloud Wireless, 455, 1181
Spidr Tech, 272
Spiff, 79
Spig, 2391
Spikes Security, 249, 1940
Spiketrap, 1421
Spill Magic Inc., 465
Spin, 874
Spinal Concepts, 1378
Spinal Dynamics, 1786
Spinal Elements, 1081
Spinal Kinetics, 598, 938, 1255, 1626, 1628
Spinal MetRX, 1448
Spinal Modulation, 598, 980
SpinalKinetics, 177
SpinalMotion, 1059, 1691, 1819
Spindle Labs, 1460
Spindletop Capital, 3264
Spindrift, 1488
Spine Form, 1512
Spine Wave, 386, 558, 1122, 1187, 1298
Spine Wave Inc., 371
Spine-Tech, 1725
SpineAlign, 915
SpineGuard, 3020

1425

Portfolio Companies Index

Spinelab, 2475
Spineology, 68
SpineView, 177, 1325
SpineVision, 2354
SpineVision SA, 2816
SpinGo, 688, 1070
Spinifex, 2536
SpinLaunch, 429, 1075, 1095
SpinMedia, 132, 1782
Spinnaker Networks, 1202
Spinnaker Support, 374
Spinnakr, 1320, 3044
Spinner, 1563
Spinrite, 1166, 1651
Spinzo, 2143
Spiracur, 598, 1298, 1445, 1773
Spiral Genetics, 609
Spiras Health, 718
Spire, 874, 1046, 1489, 1509, 1593, 1634, 1663
Spire Global, 1241
Spireon, 257
Spireon Inc., 862
SpireSano, 1047
Spirion, 1014
Spirit Brands, 402
Spiritshop, 566
Spiritsoft, 2572
Spiro, 3
Spiro Technologies, 1172
Spirogen, 1543
Spirox, 74, 136, 544, 921, 1916
Spirus Medical, 1459
SPL, 985
SPlacer, 3221
Splacer, 1323, 1509
Splash, 60, 178, 1110, 1183, 1530, 1883, 2249, 3055, 3108
Splashtop, 1218, 1474, 1620, 1747, 2667
Splen, 2680
Splendia, 2385, 3020
Splice, 754, 1110, 1607, 1860
Splice Machine, 544, 1010, 1247
Split Rail Fence & Supply Co., 330
Splitwise, 3, 358, 1563
Splonum, 2832
Splunk Technology, 197
Splyce, 704
SPM, 3002
Spock, 502
spocket, 2212
Spoke, 720, 872, 3108
SPOKE Custom Products, 364
Spoken, 974
SpokenLayer, 1150
Spongecell, 1524
Sponsia, 2696
SponsorHub, 1518
Sponsorhub, 599
SponsorPay, 2813, 3044
Sponsors: ACG New York, 3285
Sponsors: Activate Venture Partners, 3275
Sponsors: BDO, 3271
Spontaneous Order, 2841
Spoolex, 123
Spoon University, 1178
Sporple, 1885
Sport 2000, 2338
Sport Hero, 204
Sport Ngin, 1522, 3279
Sport Pursuit, 2674
Sport Testing, 2131
Sport Universal Process, 3239
Sport1, 2723
Sportcraft, 316
Sportgenic, 1084
SportHero, 91
Sportica, 2936

SportlogiQ, 2118, 2184, 2239
Sportlogiq, 2260
Sportnex GmbH, 3197
SportPursuit, 2662
Sports & Recreation, 1017
Sports & Recreation Inc., 693
Sports Tradex, 445
Sportskeeda, 3109
SportsLine.com, 131
Sportsman Tracker, 961, 1155
Sportsman's Warehouse, 1645
SportsNest, 2526
Sportsplex Japan, 3182
Sportsrocket, 1110
Sportsvite, 1306
SportVision, 695
Sportvision, 1480, 1640
Sportxast, 1924
Spot, 1269
Spot Crowd, 1176
Spot Hero, 205, 358
SpotAHome, 1075
Spotfire, 466
Spotflux, 1291
SpotHero, 641, 1118, 1364, 1480
Spothero, 1615
Spotify, 775, 802, 842, 1235, 1346, 1524, 1785, 2637, 2663, 2831, 2928
Spotless, 3025
Spotless Group Limited, 2379
Spotlife, 114
SpotOn, 280
Spotright, 36, 876
Spotsetter, 1028
SpotTaxi.com, 43
Spotter, 684
SpotterRF, 979
Spotzot, 454, 770
Spotzot Mobile Shopping, 1013
SPPTH, 3048
SPR Therapeutics, 1047, 1287
Sprayglo, 465
SpreadTrum, 385
Spreadtrum, 1087, 1340, 2936
Spredfast, 1010, 1380, 1810
Spredfest, 867
Spree Commerce, 1531, 1821, 1860, 1912
Spreecast, 1194
Sprig, 1150
Spring, 471, 720, 1046, 1110, 1552
Spring Air Sommex Corporation, 2056
Spring by Pivetal, 1212
Spring CM, 770
Spring Consulting, 2754
Spring Discovery, 816, 1758
Spring Flower, 2378
Spring Labs, 1480
Spring Lake, 1219
Spring Loaded, 2068, 2155
Spring Metrics, 286, 2017
Spring Mobile, 1620
Spring Path, 1534
Spring Source, 634
Spring Tide Networks, 1474
Spring Venture Group, 745
Spring.me, 3160
SpringBig, 895
Springbig, 99
Springboard, 547, 2479
Springbok Energy, 1278, 1326
Springbot, 904, 1788, 1863
SpringBot Commerce, 768
Springbuk, 658, 921
SpringCharts, 950
SpringCM, 297
Springcm, 946
Springcoin, 817

Springer, 2605
Springlane, 2838
Springs, 923
SpringSource, 238
Springstone, 1972
Sprinklr, 1031, 2690
Sprint Industrial Holdings, 733
Sprooki, 2778
Sprout, 1255, 1293, 2265
Sprout Health Group, 949
Sprout Social, 1118
SproutBox, 658
Sproutling, 32, 743, 761
Sproxil, 55
Spruce, 231, 552, 1075
Spruce Media, 1502
Spruce Up, 1158
Sprucebot, 1176
Spryker, 3056
SPS, 1340
SPS Commerce, 57, 212, 1725
SPSS Inc., 1103
SPUD, 2238
Spyce, 1183, 1509
Spyce Inc., 1069
Spyder Active Sports, 461, 2379
Spykar, 2460
Spyke Media, 3207
Spyor Safe Mobile Security, 119
Spyryx Biosciences, 915
SQAD, 492
SQLstream, 760
Sqrl, 962
Sqrrl, 38, 1522, 1728
Squabbler, 1965
Squadra VC, 3270
Squadrun, 24
Square, 486, 823, 1069, 1620, 1766
Square 1 Bank, 1273
Square Gourmet, 2855
Square Roots, 488
Square Space, 1761, 2860
Square Trade, 220, 221
SquareClock, 3113
Squarespace, 815, 2860
SquareTrade, 1733, 1978
SquareTwo Financial, 732
Squawka, 2752
Squee, 2696
Squelch, 1663
Squire, 13
Squirro, 1607
Squirro AG, 650
Squla, 1111
Sqwiggle, 1150, 1489
SQZ Biotech, 2229
SR One, 3273
SR Technics, 2299, 2301, 2305
SR Telecom & Co., 2073
SRA International, 1496
Sram, 168
SRCH2, 1798
Srch2, 585
Srckode, 2271
SRDS Media Information LP, 1986
SRE Solutions, 55
SREI Infrastructure Finance Ltd, 2086
Sresta, 3211
SRET, 3100
SRK, 2867
SRL Global, 2450
SRP Companies, 199
SRS, 1857
SRS Acquiom, 1147, 3272, 3276
SRS Distribution, 254, 1109
SRS Medical, 1627
SRS Software, 1814

Portfolio Companies Index

SS8, 1348, 1378
SS8 Networks, 2005
SSB, 2795
SSE Rogerstone, 3135
SSI, 959, 1213, 2732
SSI Holdings, 361
SSP, 924
SST, 1260
St George Bank, 2659
St Residental, 1835
St-Hubert, 2977
St-Pierre Et Durocher Arpenteurs Geometres, 2120
St. Croix Hospice, 1343
St. George Logistics, 1141, 1144
St. George Warehouse, 1021
St. John Knits, 1931
St. John's Hop On Hop Off, 2168
St. Louis Arch Angels, 3271
St. Marche Group, 1088
St. Matthew's University, 687, 691
Staccot Communications, 455
Stack, 479
Stack Commerce, 1965
Stack Driver, 221
STACK Ltd., 908
STACK Media, 1047
Stack Overflow, 262
StackAdapt, 2224
StackCommerce, 120
StackEngine, 1685
Stackery, 773, 956
StackExchange, 1715
Stackhut, 1254
StackIQ, 132, 206, 856
StackMob, 231, 1853
Stackpole International, 559
Stackshare, 641
StackStorm, 2011
StadiaNet Sports, 131
Stadion Money Management, 1776
Stadium Goods, 761
Stae, 724
Staff Leasing, 1505
Staffbase, 641
Staffmark, 523
Staffordshire Schools, 2749
StaffRanker, 1965
Stafix Oy, 2966
Stag-Parkway, 1132
Stag-Parkway Inc., 862
Stage1 Beteiligungs Invest, 2783
StageMark, 293
Staghorn Petroleum, 672
Staging Concepts, 276, 405
Staging Connections, 2951
Stagnito Business Information, 1832
Stahl, 1017
Stainton Metals, 3017
Stake Center, 1753
Stakeholder Midstream, 671
Stallion, 1134, 1967
Stalwart, 2796
Stamford Bridge Power, 156
Stamped, 525, 1830
Stampede Meat, 713
Stampery, 307
Stamplay, 3108
Stamps.com, 765
Stanadyne, 109
Stanadyne Corporation, 1081
STANCE, 1202
Stance, 45, 1070, 1075, 1204, 1663
Standadyne Corporation, 1456
Standard Aero, 1925
Standard Bank, 3095
Standard Bariatrics, 479

Standard Bots, 318
Standard Cognition, 1138
Standard Cyborg, 395, 811
Standard Diagnostics, 1087
Standard Locknut, 443
Standard Networks, 3127
Standard Parking Corporation, 1081
Standard Precast, 17
Standard Treasury, 1489, 2583
Standcard Bancshares, 1743
Standex International, 1295
Standing Stone, 530
Standingcloud, 206
StandoutJobs, 1306
Stanford Microdevices/Sirenza, 1288
Stanmore Implants, 2858
Stant Corporation, 928, 1343
Stantec, 2150
Stanton Carpet, 1505
Stanton Carpet Corp, 1456
Stantum, 2876
Stanza, 525
Staples, 909, 937, 1096
STAQ, 1554
Staq, 538, 814, 1809
Star, 3014
Star Career Academy, 812
Star CJ, 1496
STAR EnviroTech Inc., 908
Star Festival, 2798
Star Market, 1017
Star Seed, 828
Star Tribune Media Holdings, 1967
Star-Glo Industries, 940
Star2Star Communications, 1317
Starboard, 2797
Starbucks, 247, 753
Starbucks Beijing, 892
Starbucks Coffee, 1853
STARC Systems, 288
Starcard, 2886
StarCite, 184
Starcity, 1894
Stardog, 538
Stardog Union, 876
Starent Networks, 757
Starface, 325
Starfish Oil & Gas, 2349
Starfish Retention Solutions, 1299, 1348
Starflyer, 596
Stargaze, 2558
StarGen, 314
Stargus, 422
Starhome, 2472, 2770
Starksky Robotics, 640
Starkware, 751
Starline, 2423
Starling, 3072
Starmaker, 2010
StarMaker Interactive, 2853
StarMobile, 1968
Starmount, 1271
Starnet Interactive, 1108
Starpoint Health, 373
STARR Life Sciences, 998
Starr Life Sciences, 1448
Starrino, 1340
Starry, 743
Starship, 874, 1663
Starsky Robotics, 24, 429, 811, 942, 1663
Starskyrobotics, 1885
StarStreet Inc., 650
Start Garden, 3269
StartApp, 436
Startapp, 178
STARTech, 1197
Startflyer, 3006

Startingdot, 2385
Startip + Health, 1052
Startmate, 2520
Startronics, 220
Startup Bootcamp, 3236
Startup Weekend Trójmiasto, 2885
Startup.Lt, 3049
Startupbootcamp, 3207
Startupi.com.br, 2872
Startwire, 222
StarWind Software, 89, 2320
Staselog Oy, 2873
Stash Energy, 2200
Stashbox, 392
State National Companies, 654
StatEasy, 1447
StatementOne, 1465
States Title, 727
Statfl, 2109
Statflo, 2113, 2243
STATinMed, 403
Statisfy, 712, 1958
Statista, 2797
Statlab Medical Products, 1469
StatMuse, 243
Statmuse, 1883
STATs ChipPac Taiwan Semiconductor Corporation, 2603
Statsbot, 679
StatSocial, 649
Statsocial, 150
Status, 101
StatX, 1013
Stauber, 1505
Stauber Performance Ingredients Inc., 969
Stax, 231
Stay Alfred, 529
Stay Tuned, 325
Stay22, 2138
Stayful, 386
StayNTouch, 1169
StayOnline, 960
STC Wireless Resources Inc., 1621
Stdlib, 2184
SteadyServ Technologies, 658
Steak & Ale Restaurant, 354
Steak 44, 364
Steak-ummm, 1159
Stealth, 1060, 1150
Stealth Monitoring, 2047
Stealth Peptides, 2978
Stealth Space Company, 45
Stealthbits, 1829
Stealz, 1845
Steam Logistics, 640
Steambolico, 3048
Steamist, 1521
StearClear, 418
Stedi, 1758
Steel & OBbrien Manufacturing, 654
Steel Brick, 1663
Steel Reef Infrastructure Corp., 2221
SteelBrick, 665
Steelbrick, 1001
STEELE Compliance Solutions, 333
Steele Solutions, 1209
Steelhead Composite, 146
Steelhead LNG, 2050
SteelHouse, 306, 871, 1204, 2649
Steelhouse, 228, 1566
Steelhouse Stellapps Technologies, 1509
SteelPoint, 787
SteelSeries, 1088
Steelwedge, 1672
Steep Hill, 1135, 1207, 1439, 1807
Steereo, 1507
Steifel Laboratories, 277

1427

Portfolio Companies Index

Steiger, 2683
Stein Rose Investment Counsel, 1147
Stein World, 1997
Steiner Education Group, 1088
Stelara, 2102
Stelco, 2067
Stelco Inc., 2073
Stella, 1323, 2544
Stella & Chewy's, 1748
Stella & Dot, 1865
Stella D'Oro, 357
Stella May Contracting, 1208
Stella Service, 518, 608, 768
Stellar, 384
Stellar Loyalty, 1782
Stellar Materials LLC, 843
Stellar Outdoor Media, 828
StellaService, 1346
Stellic, 1527
Stem, 49, 126, 180, 532, 809, 1150, 1813, 1883, 1888
Stem Cell Theranostics, 1655
Stem Village, 2113
Stemcentrx, 175, 775
StemCyte, 69, 1769
Stemgent, 1122
Stemia Biomarker Discovery, 583
Stemina Biomarker Discovery, 2001
Stemless, 1507
Stemmatters, 3031
Stemnion, 1092
Stemonix, 341
Stensul, 1149
Stentntor, 1092
Stentys, 3020, 3104
STEP Energy Services, 2040
STEP Labs, 805, 807
Step Labs, 184
Step-In, 2669
Step2, 1116
Stephan Machinery GmbH, 3067
Stephen's Rental Servies Inc., 2103
STEPLabs, 612
StepLeader, 1571
Stepmind, 2354
StepOne, 1685
Steppe Resources Inc., 1326
StepStone, 2329
Stepstone, 3013
StepStoneMed, 241
StepUp Commerce, 852
Stereocake, 2333
Stereotaxis, 118, 176, 1616, 1619
Stericycle, 1156
SteriFx, 362
Sterigenics, 884
Steril Med, 176
SterilMed, 3279
Sterix Limited, 2463
Sterling, 901
Sterling Energy, 1256
Sterling Foods, 969, 1803
Sterling InfoSystems, 818
Sterling Partners, 3255, 3265
Sterling Pork Farms, 2049
Sterling Technology, 2985
Sterling Trading Tech, 1136
SterlingBackcheck, 368
Sternhill, 37
Sterno Group, 523
Steudle, 2887
Steve Nash Fitness Clubs, 127
Stevens, 1037
Stevens Institute of Technology, 3274
Stevie, 2831
Steward Advanced Materials, 123
STI, 1647

Stic, 2436
Stick Tech, 2451
Sticks'n'Sushi, 3203
Sticky, 2630, 3013
StickyADS.tv, 3208
Stiffel, 1159
Stik.com, 742
Stillwater Scientific Instruments, 438
Stim Wave, 1628, 1762
Stimsonite Corporation, 1505
Stimwave, 1988
Stimwave Technologies, 666
STING Capital, 3043
Stingray, 2264
Stingray Digital, 466
Stion, 322
Stirling Cooke Browne, 2792
Stirling Schools, 2749
Stitch, 784, 1110, 1700, 1716, 1749
Stitch Fix, 231
Stitch Labs, 547, 1860
Stixi Ag, 832
STK, 2254, 2309
Stkr.it, 981
Stobhill Hosptial, 2749
Stockbyte, 2336
Stockpile, 768, 1184, 2195
StockTwits, 776, 1860
Stockwell, 761, 941
StockX, 607
Stohlquist Waterware, 111
Stoke, 634, 757, 1003, 1087, 1341, 1474
Stoke Therapeutics, 143, 143, 1519
Stokes Bio, 2918
Stokes Sauces, 2760
Stokomani, 2375
Stolle Machinery, 1134
Stolle Machinery Company, 109
Stoller, 16
Stone Canyon Entertainment Corporation, 575
Stone Goff Partners, 1344
Stone Panels, 1224
Stone Point Materials, 1753
Stone Source, 774
Stone Tool Supply Inc., 908
StoneCastle, 456
StoneFly Inc., 555
Stonegate Mortgage, 2649
Stonegate Production Company, 1443
Stonegate Production Company II, 1443
StoneLock, 2260
StoneRidge Insurance Brokers, 489
StoneRiver Holdings, 1743
Stonewall Kitchen LLC, 447
Stony Brook University, 3267
Stop Breathe & Think, 120, 1893
Stop&Walk, 2920
StopDDoS, 1499
Stora Enso Oyj, 2990
Storactive, 69, 1180
Storage Genetics, 210
StorageApps, 187
Stord, 640, 1758
Store Fixtures Group, 1295
Store-Locator.com, 2310
Store2be, 2841
StoreFinancial, 1764
Storefront Inc., 650
StoreLynkm StreamSpot, 479
STOREMAVEN, 11
Storent Holding, 584
StoreNVY, 1715
Storeroom Solutions, 1227
Storiant, 322, 1181
Storify, 1489
Storigen, 455
StoriiCare, 30

Storj.iO, 890
Stork Prints, 2501
StormBlok, 1686
Stormpath, 1425, 1626
StoroMedia, 541
Storsimple, 1534
Storwize, 1796
Story Magic, 1254
Story Xpress, 1176
Storyblaster, 50
StoryFirst, 2491
StoryFirst Co, 2465
Storyhunter, 1323
StoryVine, 1306
Stouse, 364
Stouse LLC, 843
Stout Industries, 61
Stout Street Capital, 3276
StowAway, 525
Stowga, 3108
STP, 1516
STR, 1097
Straatum, 2918
Stradeblu Srl, 2653
Strahman Valves, 478
StraighterLine, 475, 1146, 1299, 1551
Straighterline, 488, 743
Strala, 79
Stram Global Services, 159
Strand Energy, 696
Strasbaugh, 69
Strata, 846
Strata Decision, 1927
Strata Dx, 1128
Strata Oncology, 149, 222
Strata Worldwide, 1997
StrataCloud, 282
StrataCom Inc., 1202
StrataDx, 1271
Stratalight, 563
Stratatech Corporation, 2001
StrataTech Education Group, 828
Stratavia, 181
Strategia, 242
Strategic Equipment and Supply, 328
Strategic Funding Source, 1443
Strategic Investment Group, 787
Strategic Legal Solutions, 1230
Strategic Marketing, 1765
Strategic Materials, 1134, 1937, 1986
Strategic Outsourcing Inc., 492
Strategic Partners, 209
Strategikon Pharma, 226
Stratetic Insight, 819
StratEx, 897
Stratford School, 1504
Stratifyd, 799, 2132
Stratim, 302
Stratix, 1777
Stratophase, 2892
Stratos, 1547, 1829, 3085
Stratoscale, 1509
Stratus Computer, 197
Stratus Technologies, 1017
Strava, 1024
Stravina, 1234
Stray Light, 658
Strayer Education, 1301
Streak, 1149
Stream, 173, 707
Stream Global Services, 1970
Stream Machine, 1779
Stream Processors, 2005
Streambase, 946
StreamBase Systems, 979
StreamCore, 2354
StreamElements, 1611

Portfolio Companies Index

StreamLabs, 561
Streamlabs, 641
Streamline, 2796
Streamline Circuits, 439
Streamline Health, 1331
Streamlined Ventures, 295
StreamLink Software, 285, 1047
Streamloan, 811
StreamOcean, 2667
Streamserve, 2472
StreamSets, 974
StreamVine, 445
Streamweaver, 1261
Streem, 755, 3125
Street Contxt, 2157, 2225
Street Light Data, 44
StreetAcademy, 2974
StreetCred, 317
StreetHub, 3018
Streetline, 760, 1579, 1860
StreetTrend, 937
Strengthportal, 307
StressWave, 85
Stride, 883, 1035, 1916
Stride Health, 710, 2225
Stride Tool, 405
StrideBio, 1778
Striim, 603
Striiv, 970
Strike Brewing Company, 950
Strike Group, 2275
StrikeAd, 397, 1055, 1700, 1798, 1965, 2662
Strikingly, 641
String, 2984
String AI, 120
StrionAir, 1702
Strip, 816, 1075
Stripe, 578, 775, 1069, 1149, 1534, 1607, 1666, 1826, 2012, 2446
Stripes Holdings LLC, 1971
Striva, 59
StriVectin, 1088
STRIVR, 60
Strivr, 302
Strix Systems, 1407
Strobe, 1359
Strohal, 2887
Stroidetal, 3071
Stroili Oro Group, 2293
Stroma, 2944
Stromedix, 70, 191, 782
Strong Hold, 3127
Strong Ventures, 1965
StrongArm Tech., 704
StrongArm Technologies, 1703
Strongbridge Biopharma, 946, 1271, 1941
StrongLoop, 1663
Strongpoint, 2109
Strongsalt, 799
StrongView, 634
StrongView Systems, 581
Stroz Friedberg, 1301
Structo, 823, 1965
Structural, 1176
Structural and Steel Products, 1209
Structural Concepts, 1171
Structure Vision, 2892
Structured Polymers, 445
Structured Web, 161
Struq, 3032
Stryde, 799
STS Aviation Group, 862
Stubbs Alderton & Markiles LLP, 3268
StubHub, 1733
Student Loan Genius, 445, 1054, 1595
Student Loan Hero, 707
Student Opportunity Center, 1551

Studer Group, 1041
Studio, 79
Studio Design, 1070
Studio Direct, 796
Studio Moderna, 815
StudioNow, 493, 496, 718
Studitemps, 2475, 2829, 2838, 3113, 3239
StudiVZ, 2444
Study Edge, 1183
Study Group, 1496
Study Soup, 397
StudyEdge, 2329
Studypool, 1110
StudySoup, 32
Studytube, 2822
StumbleUpon, 231, 1445
Stumbleupon, 197
Stumbleupon Inc., 623
Stupeflix, 3108
Sturm Foods, 1171
STx Healthcare Services, 1422
Styla, 3236
Style for Hire, 1306
Style Seat, 229
Style Seek, 1054
Style-Passport.com, 2400
Stylecaster, 607
StyleCraft Home Collection, 1469
Stylecraze, 3211
StyleFeeder, 1627
Stylefruits.de, 2638
Stylefy, 1810
Stylekick, 981
Stylemarks, 3207
StyleSaint, 561, 641
StyleSeat, 552, 1149, 1700, 3044
StyleSight, 567
StyleTread, 2797
Stylight, 2829, 2838, 3170
Stylus, 922
Styron, 220
Styrotherm, 2832
Sub-One Technology, 466
SubCenter.io, 272
Sube, 2671
Subex, 1305
Subitec, 2686
Subledger, 599
Sublimity Therapeutics, 1143
Submittable, 756
Subotica, 3095
Subscription Services, 1837
Subspace, 1151, 1613
Substack, 795
Subtle Medical, 219, 799
Suburban Team, 932
Sucampo Pharmaceuticals, 2970
SuccessEd, 364
SuccessFactors, 411, 665, 823, 1865
Sucreries de Berneuil, 2620
Sucriere De Bernevil, 2601
SucSeed, 2168
Suddenlink Communications, 2379
Suddenly Social, 1655
Suez Portfolio, 2792
Sugar23. SV Angel, 1766
SugarCRM, 29, 609, 679, 1235
Sugarfina, 896
SugarSync, 609, 1646, 1672
Sugru, 2960
Suhyang Networks, 64
SuitedMedia, 2184
Suiteness, 358
SuitePad, 2841
Suitpad, 3161
Suki, 1916
Sulekha, 1346

Sulia, 871
SULO, 2420
Sulvaris, 2049
Sum Up, 2475, 3170
Sumazi, 1749
Sumerian, 3104
Suminter India Organics, 3001
Sumisura, 3203
Summary Analytics, 1243
Summer, 1058
Summerland Energy, 2025
Summit, 3137
Summit Behavioral Healthcare, 750
Summit BHC, 787
Summit Broadband, 61
Summit Business Media, 686
Summit Companies, 476
Summit Estates, 958
Summit Financial Services Group, 131
Summit Fire Protetcion, 1492
Summit Global Partners, 402
Summit Interconnect, 917
Summit Materials, 277
Summit Medical, 1667
Summit Medical Group, 1572
Summit Microelectronics, 197
Summit Midstream Partners, 675
Summit Partners, 3264
Summit Sync, 408
SummitIG, 515
Summly, 1821, 2831
Sumo Logic, 560, 1001
Sumologic, 872
SumoShift, 2284
Sumridge Partners, 1364
SumUp, 2940
Sumzero, 1998
Sun & Earth, 438, 520, 1689
Sun & Sea, 2850
Sun Art Retail Group, 815
Sun Basket, 37, 231, 544
Sun Behavioural Health, 1136, 1628, 1762
Sun Catalytix, 1460
Sun Culture, 2439
Sun Earth Ceramics Limited, 2861
Sun Graphics, 399
Sun Healthcare, 1557
Sun Microsystems, 197, 836
Sun Mountain Capital, 3276
Sun Orchard Inc., 447
Sun Products, 1931
Sun Select, 2049
Sun Source, 1134
Sun-Jin Boramae Co., 584
Sunac, 220
SuNAM Co., 144
Sunbelt Medical, 1606
Sunbelt Modular, 321
Sunbelt National Mortgage Corporation, 1986
Sunbelt Steel, 1745
Sunbelt Supply, 500
Sunbelt-Solomon Solutions, 1851
Sunbio, 2978
Sunburst Farms, 61
Sunburst Media-Louisiana, 828
Sunbury Textile Mills, 1141
Suncayr, 2184
Sunchron, 1672
SunCommon, 786
Suncrest Solar, 1705
Sunda, 1681
Sundae, 1758
Sundance, 42, 378
Sundance Energy Inc., 158
Sundar, 544
Sunday Sky, 3221
Sunday's Nederland BV, 2828

1429

Portfolio Companies Index

SundaySky, 518, 835, 1346, 2566
Sunderstorm, 99
Sundevil Power, 1967
Sundia, 2436
Sundolier, 146, 3277
SunEdison, 144
Sunesis, 74, 946, 1898
Suneva Medical, 697
Sunflower New Co., 623
Sunfun (iPart), 3215
SunFunder, 3277
Sung Industrial, 2807
SunGard, 220, 1496
Sungard, 1835
SunGard Data Systems, 2379
Sungevity, 340, 675, 730
Sunglass, 1531
Sungy Mobile, 3062
Sunhouse, 218
Suninfo, 3100
Suning.com, 473
Suniva, 137
Sunless, 1572
Sunlight, 1527, 3108
Sunlight Ltd, 3162
SunLink, 498
Sunlink Corporation, 126
Sunlit, 1340
Sunlux Energy, 3062
Sunniva, 1135
Sunnova, 675, 1846
Sunnovations, 398
Sunny Sky Products, 1645
SunPharm Corporation, 1008
SunPower, 214
Sunpreme, 3194
Sunquest, 959
Sunrain Energy, 2542
Sunrise, 19, 152, 1322, 1546
Sunrise Oilfield Supply, 1997
Sunrise Strategic Partners LLC, 1851
Sunrise Windows, 1572
Sunrop Fuels, 1361
SunRun, 581, 770
Sunset Tower Hotel, 34
Sunshine, 1254, 1998
Sunshine Heart, 2618
Sunshine Media Holdings, 828
Sunshine Paper, 2936
Sunshine Restaurant Partners, 2015
Sunstream Boat Lifts, 85
SunSun Lighting, 1361
Sunteck, 528
SunTek, 722
Suntel, 3168
SunTelephone, 220
SunTouch, 519
SunTree Snack Foods, 1622
Suntron Corp., 300
Sunverge, 1711
Sunworks Farm, 2049
SunZia Southwest Transmission Project, 675
Suomen Kuitulava Suvisoft Oy, 2873
Suomen Teollisuusosa Oy, 2873
Suomen Transval Oy, 2937
Suometry, 2184
SUPA, 218
Super, 707
Super Awesome, 2834
Super Bac, 2717
Super Bit Machines, 1563
Super Dragon Technology, 2603
Super Evil Megacorp, 561, 816, 1678, 3251
Super Heat Games, 791
Super Max, 909
Super Truper, 2920
Super-Medium, 395

Superalloy, 2436
Supercell, 1001, 2446, 2860, 2860
Superconductor Technologies, 69
Superconductor Technologies Inc., 1103
Superdata, 2953
Superdata Technology, 2850
Superfish, 3240
Superhard Materials, 3107
Superhuman, 351, 1421, 1595
Superhuman Labs, 305
Superior Automotive, 353
Superior Automotive Group, 1415, 1415
Superior Boiler Works Inc., 1053
Superior Chaircraft Corporation, 111
Superior Contract Cleaners, 465
Superior Controls, 77
Superior Fabrication, 1214
Superior Fibers, 338, 932
Superior Group of Companies, 2136, 2285
Superior Plant Rentals, 425
Superior Recreational Products, 853, 1435
Superior Tool Holding Company, 1492
Superior Tube, 1962
Superior Vision, 442
Superior Vision Holding Company, 1279
Supermedium, 1390
Supermercato 24, 2296
Supermercato24, 2874
Supernus, 946
SuperPedestrian, 1715
Superpedestrian, 816
Superpeer, 679
SuperPhone, 811
Superplastic, 1933
SuperService, 1967
SuperSonic Imagine, 3020
Superstar Games, 1019
Supertron Technologies, 2397
Supervalu, 380
Suplari, 1158, 1663
Supplemental Health Care, 1197
Supplemental Health Care Services, 587
SupplierInsight, 831
Supply Edge, 69
Supply Hog, 1097
Supply Shift, 1757
SupplyAI, 1554, 1757
SupplyEdge Inc., 371
SupplyFrame, 502
SupplyHog, 459, 1518
Supplyhog, 590, 1364
SupplyOne Holding, 1275
SupplyShift, 317
SupplySolution, 1672
Supponor, 3013
Supponor Systems, 2630
Support Logic, 1670
Supportkids.com, 402
SupportPay, 1592
Supreme, 3170
Supreme Corq, 846
Supreme Imports, 2677
Supreme NewMedia, 2604
Supresoft, 2850
Suprmasv, 2406
Supyo, 623
Sur La Table, 405, 753, 783, 783, 1017
Sura Asset Management, 815
Suralink, 1070
Sure, 724
Sure Fit Home Decor, 446
Sure Shot Drilling, 611
Sure Storage, 2860
SureAuto, 3194
Surebits, 307
SureDone, 1306
Surefield, 1463

Surefire Local, 52
Surefire Medical, 930, 1189, 1418
Surekam, 2936
SureLogic, 1623
SurePoint Holdings, 1492
Surepoint Technologies Group, 2009
SurePrep, 333
SureSource, 1927
Surf Air, 228
Surf Communication Solutions, 2571, 2782
Surf Watch, 508
Surface Logix, 1438
Surface Oncology, 112, 191, 710, 1124
Surface Pharmaceuticals, 297
SurfAir, 1749, 1798, 1912, 1965
Surfair, 132, 724
SurfEasy, 2182
SurfKitchen, 162
Surge, 950
Surgent Professional Education, 1724
Surgery Partners, 928
Surgical Care Affiliates, 1835
Surgical Information Systems, 1345
Surgical Solutions, 1742
Surgical Specialties, 1941
Surgicount Medical, 138
Surgient, 563
Surgiquest, 138, 1571
SurgiQuest Inc., 371
Surgis, 1301
SurgRx, 1493
Surgrx Inc., 371
Surkus, 2144
Surple, 2284
Surreal, 307
Surrey Nanosystems, 2892, 3018, 3028
Sursen, 2850
Surun, 1235
Survata, 1563, 1700
Survery Monkey, 578
Survey 160, 934
Survey Monkey, 1717
Survey Sampling International, 1496
SurveyMonkey, 1696
Survios, 720, 852, 1151, 1611, 1663
Survitec, 2209
Survly, 1099
Surya, 1382
Suryoday Micro Finance, 2313
Suse, 2343
Susiecakes, 1742
Suspa, 123
Sustainability Roundtable, 398
Sustainable Minds, 3277
Sustainable Produce Urban Delivery, 2048
Sustainable Real Estate, 678
Sustainable Real Estate Manager, 1097
Sustainable Resource Solutions, 2892
SustainX, 1579
Sustainx, 1460
Susty Party, 3277
Sutro, 981
Sutro Biopharma, 94, 112, 800, 1124, 1628, 1691
Sutrovax, 782, 1143, 2092
SutureExpress, 1128
Suturtek, 1847
Suumologic, 836
SUVACO, 2974
Suvidhaa, 1346
Suvola, 445
SuVolta, 197
Suvolta, 2540
Suzhou Anjie Technology, 2936
Suzhou HiPro Polymers, 220
Suzlon, 2599, 2600
Suzo-Happ, 1435
Suzo-Happ Group, 46

1430

Portfolio Companies Index

SV Academy, 1392, 1551
SV Angel III, 623
SV Health Investors, 3264, 3273
SVAcademy, 488
Svaya Nanotechnologies, 1672
Svelte, 1303
Svelte Medical Systems, 508, 1347
Sverica, 37
Sverica Capital Management, 3264
Sverve, 1632
SVI Public, 892
SVM Cards, 179
SVNetwork, 1445
Svoboda Capital Partners, 3265
SVOX, 2662
SVOX AG, 650
SVP, 3020
SVP Worldwide, 1081
Svpply, 1715
Svrf, 1183
SVTC, 1922
SVTC Technologies, 1360
SWAAY, 1701
Swagbucks, 1785
Swallow Solutions, 1292, 2001
Swan Global Investments, 793
Swander Pace Capital, 1871
SwanLabs, 249, 596
Swanson Industries, 901
Swanson Industries Inc., 64
SwapBox, 229
Swapbox, 983
Swapcom, 3113
SwapDrive, 533, 538
Swapit, 3047
Swarm, 1696
Swarm 64, 3161
Swarm Vision, 1370
Swas Healthcare, 2313
Swayable, 934
SWC Technology Partners, 1765
Sweaty Betty, 1088
Swedish Institute, 1504
Sweep, 1054
Sweet, 607
Sweet Additions, 364
Sweet Garden, 3182
Sweet Green, 508, 1530
Sweet Leaf Iced Teas, 950
Sweet Relish, 51, 286
SweetBio, 995
Sweetbio, 1187
Sweetch, 2943
Sweeten, 1282
Sweetgreen, 329
sweetgreen, 511
SweetIM, 1323
SweetIQ, 2224
Sweetlabs, 1359
Sweetriot, 841
SweetSpring Salmon, 3257
Swell, 609, 1010, 1323
Swell Advantage, 2155
Swell Energy, 1894
Swell Rewards, 307
Swensen's, 2254
Swept, 2027, 2155, 2157
Swiff-Train Co., 443
Swift Biosciences, 149, 749, 1206
Swift Fine Foods Limited, 2705
Swift Medical, 2180, 2187, 2232, 2236
Swift Navigation, 648, 720, 1509
Swift Shift, 563, 784
Swiftera, 1894
Swiftly, 307, 1611, 2238
Swiftmile, 1926
Swiftpage, 1046

SwiftPay MD, 1615
SwiftShift, 317, 3108
SwiftStack, 1184, 1380, 1747
Swiftype, 585
SwifyKey, 3018
Swiggy, 1346
SwineTech, 995
Swing by Swing, 1099
Swing Education, 1054, 1392, 1696
SwingPal, 1261
Swink.tv, 791
SwipBox, 3203
Swipe, 3030
Swipeclock Workforce Management, 9, 1014
Swipely, 1322
SwipeSense, 648, 1364, 1480, 1615, 1801
Swirl, 816, 922, 1146
Swirl Networks, 1699
Swish Analytics, 1657
Swiss Farm Stores, 1275
Swiss Farms, 1727
Swiss Smile, 2496
Swiss VC/PE Investment, 3152
Swiss-American Products, 1469
Swisshaus, 1937
Swissport, 3026
Switch, 525, 1906, 3081
Switch & Data Facilities, 1728
Switch Materials, 2143, 2213
Switch.co, 625
Switchback Energy Acquisition, 1278
Switchfly, 386, 1737, 1738, 1806
SwitchGear, 1792
SwitchNote, 1958
Swivel, 751
Swivel Beauty, 218
Swivi, 874, 3181
Swix Sport, 2731
Swoon Editions, 3018
Swoop, 1899
Swoopo, 197
Sword Diagnostics, 658, 1328, 1915
Swrve, 41, 2355, 2443
SWS Group, 1360
Swyft, 1061
Swype, 247
Swyper, 620
SWYX, 3233
Swyx, 1693
Syabas, 95
Syapse, 176, 809, 1601, 1696
Sybase, 197, 214
Sycara, 685
SyChip, 1167, 1305
Sygate, 1352, 1853
Sygate Technologies, 1850
Syktyvkar, 2491
Sylantro, 1626
Sylantro Systems Corporation, 162
Sylvatex, 841
Symantec, 197
SYMBII, 462
Symbio, 395, 793
Symbio Robotics, 648
Symbiomix, 710
Symbiomix Therapeutics, 1382
Symbion, 559, 1708, 1743, 2447
Symbios Holdings, 944
Symbiot Business Group, 1677
Symbiotec Pharmalab, 584
Symbiotix Biotherapies, 1051
Symbium, 956
Symcat.com, 1874
Symend, 2195
Symetis, 2419
Symetrica, 3028
Symform, 1146

Symic, 1241
Symic Biomedical, 1124
Symicbio, 1238
Symmetry Medical, 1372
Symmetry Surgical, 1590
Symon, 839
Symphogen, 1303, 3015, 3085, 3149, 3203
Symphonic Distribution, 224
Symphony, 1218
Symphony Commerce, 221, 525, 743
Symphony Evolution, 2815
Symphony Services, 1804
Sympli, 365
Symplified, 84, 852
Symplr, 500, 1409
Symwave, 1080
Symyx, 237
Syn Mun Kong Insurance, 1139
Synacast, 2667
Synack, 84, 823, 968, 1075, 1154
Synacor, 6, 61, 807, 1333, 1523
Synacor Inc., 1951
Synad, 2380
Synairgen, 2892
Synamedia, 1910
Synap, 222
SynapDx, 748
Synapdx, 221
Synapse, 708
Synapse BioMedical, 1941
Synapse Biomedical Inc., 420, 1047
Synapse Design, 69
SynapseMX, 640
SynapSense, 791, 1355
Synapsense, 563
Synaptic Digital, 1475, 1699
Synaptics, 206
Synarc-Biocore Holdings, 188
Sync-Rx, 3072
Syncapay, 1240
Syncapse, 1410
SynCardia Systems, 188, 452
Syncardia Systems, 1020
Synced Care, 241
SyncHR, 26, 856
Synchris, 989, 1348
Synchrologic, 314, 876, 1038
Synchroneuron, 2978
Synchronoss, 23, 1001
Synchronoss Technologies, 3274
Synchronous Aerospace Group, 902, 1134
Syncro, 2553
Syncro Medical Innovations, 1347
Syncronex, 1733
Syncsort, 500, 1991
Syndax, 206, 709, 769, 1268, 1412
Syndax Pharmaceuticals, 621
Syndicate, 1315
Syndigo, 1045
Synecor, 177, 1772
Synerchip, 3062
SynergEyes, 87, 604, 1995
Synergeyes, 598
SynergEyes Inc., 269
Synergx, 2206
Synergy, 74
Synergy Beverages, 1306
Synergy HomeCare Franchising LLC, 158
Synerlab, 2293
Synermore, 2978
Synervoz, 1149, 2027
Synerway, 2607
Synethic Biologics, 1812
SynGen, 237
Synico, 1233
Synlogic, 191
Synopsys, 1257, 1922

1431

Portfolio Companies Index

Synopsys Inc., 300
Synoptek, 746, 1829
Synosia, 12
Synosia Therapeutics, 3015
Synosia Therpeutics, 2419
Synovex, 1419
Synovia Solutions, 178, 760
SYNQ3, 297
SYNQY, 1061
Synstar International, 2644
Synta Pharma, 1271
Syntax, 2206
Syntaxin, 2316, 3113
Syntem, 2415
Synteract, 1343
SynteractHCR, 439
Synteratchr, 881
Synthace, 4
Synthego, 1202, 1983
Synthematix, 1710
SynTherix, 452
Synthesia, 1101
Synthetic Games, 791
Synthetic Genomics, 319, 609, 703, 800
SynthOrx, 1519
SynthoRX, 544
Synthorx, 206
Syntiant, 663, 1154
Syntimmune, 143
Syntonix, 237, 1412
Syntonix Pharmaceuticals, 1188
Syntricity, 1995
Synventive, 1134
Synvest., 2332
Synyron Maerial Handling, 1111
Syon, 1295
Syquest, 2380
Syrgis Performance Initiators, 653
Syros, 74, 153, 747
Syrrx, 237, 2079
Sys Cloud, 1013
Syscan, 1180
Syscon Justice Systems, 2051
Sysdaq, 2857
Sysgo, 2713
Systeam, 2888
Systec Corp., 899
Systech, 946
Systech International, 631
System, 2962
System C Healthcare Ltd, 2486
System Heat, 2776
System One, 1231, 1927
Systems & Networks, 536
Systems Maintenance Services, 1752, 1815
Systems Planning and Analysis, 507
Systinet Corporation, 2309
Systran, 3127
Sysview Technology, 865
Syzygy Plasmonics, 2111

T

T&K Machine, 61, 1745
T-Base Communications, 2058
T-Bird Restaurant Group, 928
T-Pro Solutions, 1553
T-Rex, 1601
T2 Biosystems, 136, 747, 979, 1419, 1438, 1460
T2 Systems, 1409
T2Biosystems, 74, 157
T2Cure, 2710
T3, 307
T3Media, 57, 1660
T3S Technologies, 1070
T4 Media Group, 3018
T4 Spatial, 3257
TA, 7

TA Associates, 3255, 3264
TA Associates Battery, 2658
Taamkru, 3073
Taavura1, 2609
Taaz, 553
Tab, 596, 3236
TAB Products, 1066
Tabacarcen, 584
TabbedOut, 1841
Tabcon, 2271
Tableau Software, 1212
Tablewerks Inc., 953
Tablus, 1850
Taboola, 518, 2726
Tabsquare, 2778
TabTale, 1509, 2952
Tabula Rasa, 646
Tabula Rasa Healthcare, 52, 1568
Tabur/Bricogite, 2601
Tacala, 96
Tacati, 3052
TacBright, 3145
Tachyon, 1270
Tachyus, 961
Tacit, 69
Tacit Innovations, 2128
Tacit Software, 2005
Tacit Technologies, 466
Tackk, 724, 961, 1595
Tackpoint, 2285
Taco Bueno, 1403
Taco Mac, 477
Tact.aI, 1607
Tact.ai, 1154, 1534, 1888
Tactic, 2029
Tactile Systems Technology, 806, 1520
Tactix, 1909
TactoTek, 2630
Tactus, 1818
Tacurion Pharma Inc., 182
TaDa Innovations, 768
Tadaa, 2479
Tadelon Holding Group, 2542
Tadem Capital, 295
Tadir-Gan, 2745
Tadiran Com Ltd., 2745
tado§, 3161
Tae Life Sciences, 175
Tae-san Techno, 2807
Taejin, 2772
Taeyang 3C, 2857
Taft, 727
Tag Commander, 3239
Tag Pop, 972
TagArray, 1737
Tagga, 2266
Tagged, 1839
Tagkast, 1118
TagMan, 871
Tagman, 2464
Tagnetics, 983
Tagnos, 249
Tagstand, 1518
Tagsys, 2466
Tagsys RFID, 2662
Tagsys Rfid, 3092
Tahoma Ventures, 3276
Taifas, 3048
Taiflex Scientific, 2603
Taiger, 1269
Tails.com, 2674, 3018
Taimei Medical Technology, 1826
Tainet Communcation Systems, 2603
Taipale Telematics, 2873
Taisho Pharmaceutical Co., 1452
Taiwan Cellular Corp, 2907
Taiwan IC Packaging, 1769

Taiwan Semiconductor Manufacturing Company, 892
Taiwan Sumida Electronics, 892
Taizhou Reflecting Materials, 2542
TaKaDu, 2106, 2315
Takara Bio, 2970
Take 5, 1857
Take 5 Oil Change, 1576
Take Lessons, 563, 1118
Take the Interview, 1568, 1738
Take-Two Interactive, 2020
Takeaway.com, 3051
Takeda, 1349
TakeLessons, 1700, 1846
Takelessons, 1965, 1968
Takeoff, 1958
TAKF, 3071
Takko, 135
Takumi Technology, 144
Takwak, 3188
Takyca, 2921
TAL International, 654
Tala, 511, 1001, 1149
Talari Networks, 777, 1202, 1682
Talarian, 206
Talbot Underwriting, 1372
Talech, 107, 1254
Talecom, 2967
Talecris, 118
Talena, 386
TalenBin, 455
Talend, 1683
Talent Academy, 222
Talent Bin, 1118
Talent Reef, 790
Talent Sky, 129
Talent Sonar, 544, 974, 1054
Talent Sprint, 3001
Talent Systems, 373
Talent Wunder, 3236
Talenta, 721
TalentBin, 1655
TalentGuard, 445
Talenthouse, 69
TalentShare, 679
TalentSoft, 2383, 3113
TalentSpring, 85
TalentWorks, 773, 1149
Talenya, 2947
Talenz, 2473
Tales2Go, 1169, 1993
TalexMedical, 266
Taligen Therapeutics, 495
Talisma, 1637
Talix, 518, 1052
Talk Desk, 609
Talk Route, 173
talk2me, 2754
Talkable, 32
Talkative, 2284
TalkDesk, 1747
Talkdesk, 11, 1607
Talking Blocks, 1024
TalkingData, 1340
TalkingNets, 455
TalkIQ, 180, 1626
Talko, 1054
Talkpush, 3108
TalkShoe, 293, 1306, 1584
Talkspace, 525, 1346, 1699
Tall Oak Learning, 673
Tall Oak Midstream, 671
Tall Tree Foods, 96
Talla, 206, 351
Tallarium, 1528
Tallgrass Energy, 1062, 1846
Tally, 552, 1075, 1663

Portfolio Companies Index

Tally Systems, 521
TallyGenicom, 170
TallyGo!, 306
Talmetrix, 479
Talon Oil & Gas II, 672
Talyst, 1391
Tama Broadcasting, 897
Tamak, 3071
Tamara Mellon, 342
Taminco, 2379
Tammac, 1633
Tamr, 809, 851, 1687, 2006
Tanaza, 3108
Tandem, 641
Tandem Computers, 181
Tandem Diabetes Care, 604, 621, 938, 1059
Tandem Health Care, 245
Tandem Medical, 1398
Tandus Flooring, 1505
Tandvitaal, 2501
Tanenbaum-Harber Insurance Group, 1372
Tangdou, 823
Tangent Energy Solutions, 676
Tangentix, 3028
Tangerine Technologies, 294
Tangible Play, 2010
Tangible Science, 1238
Tangle Creek Energy, 2040
Tango, 106, 609, 790, 1509, 1597, 1838
Tango Card, 751, 1766
Tango Networks, 1873
Tango/High Country Venture, 3276
Tangoe, 212, 655, 2144
Tanium, 358, 486, 820, 1001
Tank & Rast, 2379
Tank Holdings Corp., 1109
Tank Services, 1746
Tantaline, 259, 3203
Tantalus, 1534
Tantalus Systems Corp, 2097
Tantivy Communications, 1348
Tanyuan Tech, 2936
Tao, 1704
Taobao, 3100
Taomee, 1598
Taos, 359
Tap 'n Tap, 1291
Tap Commerce, 525
Tap Influence, 36
Tap Rock Resources, 1278
Tap to Learn, 679
Tap.tv, 908
Tapad, 206, 525, 743, 1518
Tapatalk, 751
Tapcanvas, 1050
Tapcart, 50, 120
Tapco International, 368
TapCommerce, 679
Tapdaq, 2478
Tapfwd, 1416
TapInfluence, 876
Tapingo, 1069, 2566, 3221
Tapio, 1024
TapJoy, 1010
Tapjoy, 1865
Tapp Label Technologies, 2218
Tapper Candies, 1954
TapRoot Systems, 1008
Tapsense, 1968, 2010
Taptalk, 1998
Taptap, 2987
Taptolearn, 2329
Taptu, 2662, 2674
Tapulous, 32, 933
Tapulous/GoGoApps, 623
Taqua, 1017, 1459
Taqua Systems, 455

TARA, 6
Tara, 883
Tara AI, 49
tara Technologies, 225
Taral Networks, 1080
Taranis, 3221
Tarari, 1237
Taraspan, 2284
Taratec, 1136
Tarena, 842, 3062
Tarena International, 2850
Targa Resources, 675
Targacept, 1394, 3007
Targamite, 658
TargAnox, 177, 1419
TargeGen, 468, 769, 1412, 1906, 2496
Targent, 1044
Target Compiler Technologies N.V., 2902
Target Data, 137
Target Pharma Solutions, 1923
Target PharmaSolutions, 1346
Target Pharmasolutions, 1556
Targeted Genetics Corp., 1916
Targeted Growth, 1002, 2008
TargetRx, 1508
Targetspot, 221
TargetX, 1504
Targovax, 2519
Targus, 722
Targus Group International, 2015
Tari, 180
Taris, 747, 1519
Taris Biomedical, 1460, 1811
Tarpon Towers, 1724
Tarquin Plc., 404
Tarsa Therapeutics, 1508, 2981, 3015
Tarsus Medical, 1725
Tartan Canada Corporation, 2051
Tartec, 655
Tartine et Chocolat, 2302
Tarveda, 747, 1928
Tarveda Therapeutics, 1271
TAS Energy, 657
TAS Environmental Services, 290
TAS Environmental Services LP, 61
Tasi Group, 258
Tasit.Com, 2437
Task Easy, 377
Task Force X Capital Management, 51
Taskeasy, 36, 876, 1070
Tasker Ventures, 2362
TaskRabbit, 231, 1322, 1531, 1663, 1833
Taskrabbit, 751
Tasktop, 2291
Tasman Building Products, 2420
Tasnet, 1708
TASQ Technology, 881
TASSL, 1577
TasteMade, 1813
Tastemade, 518, 1534
TastemakerX, 231, 1860
Tasti D-Lite, 1741
Tasting Room, 545, 1655
Tasty Banking Company, 832
TastyTrade, 1118
Tastytrade, 1785
TastyWorks, 1118
TAT Technologies Ltd., 2745
Tatango, 85
Tate's Bake Shop, 1572
Tatron, 3183
Tattersall Sound and Picture, 2139
Tattile, 2391
Tattva, 2974
Tau-Metrix, 115
Taulia, 129, 581, 634, 1181, 1515, 1853, 2265, 2690, 2928

Taunt, 776, 1499
Taurex Drill Bits, 1009
Taurus, 678
Tausendkind, 2841
Tavour, 773
Tavve Software, 57
Tax Advisors Group Inc., 403
Tax Credit, 1927
Tax Guard, 1166
TaxBit, 79
TaxiForSure, 2818
TaxJar, 306
Tay Two Co., 2907
Taykey, 1699, 1796
Taylor Logistics LLC, 894
Taylor Morrison Home Corporation, 1835
Taylor Precision Products, 405
Taylor-Wharton International, 1990
TaylorMade, 1085
Taymax Group Holdings LLC, 1851
Tazznet, 933
TB Biosciences, 1385
TB12, 567
TBA Global, 1465
TBD Fusion, 2760
TBH, 544
tbh, 243
TC3, 1041
TCDS.com, 2043
tCell, 1202
TCF Financial Corp., 300
TCG RX, 782
TCHO, 668
TCI, 161, 443, 1477
TCP Communications, 897
TCP Venture Capital, 3270
TCR, 1230
TCR2, 1268
TCSC, 1726
TCT, 2733
TCV, 37
TDF, 2587
TDF Ventures, 3270
TDS, 917
TDS Logistics, 1505
Tdsoft, 2770
TDX, 1017
Tea Drops, 567, 896
Tea Leaf, 770
Teach for India, 1374
Teach.com, 153
TeachBoost, 567
Teacher Gaming, 2953
TeacherMatch, 1469
Teachers Pay Tachers, 1717
TeachFX, 1527
Teaching Company, 378
Teaching Strategies, 468
Teachscape, 22
Teachtown, 85
Teads, 1700
Teads.tv, 1416
Teaforia, 994
Teal, 1070
Teal Natural Resources, 1278
Tealeaf, 238
Tealet, 1912
Tealium, 486, 1474, 1796, 2132
Team 8, 1509
Team BS, 2795
Team Drive-Away, 478
Team Health Holdings, 1156
Team Liquid, 1118
Team Olivia, 3054
Team Snap, 776, 1829
TEAM Software, 29
Team Technologies, 1572

1433

Portfolio Companies Index

Team Technologies Inc., 500
Team Viewer, 909
Team8, 996, 1154
Teambox, 585
Teambuy.ca, 2058
Teamer, 2918
TeamEx, 450
TeamHealth, 541, 1271
teamly, 1912
TeamMates, 1837
Teamo.ru, 641
TeamOne Logistics, 821
TeamSnap, 685
TeamSystem, 220, 924
TeamViewer, 867, 3033
Teamwork.ai, 307
Teamworks, 189, 816
Teapot Inc., 623
Tear Film Innovations, 297
TearClear, 297
TearScience, 598, 1508
Teasdale Foods Inc., 1403
Tecan, 1775
Tech, 1922
Tech Air, 476
Tech Cast Holdings, 1719
Tech Holdings, 1135
Tech Launch, 418
Tech Lighting LLC, 908
Tech Pak, 1295
Tech Pharmacy Services, 806
Tech Rentals, 1423
Tech Stars, 776
TechDerm, 1228
Techdirt, 115
TeChen, 2936
Techfaith Wireless, 2850
TechForward, 1099
TechInvent AS, 3141
Techlink Entertainment, 2205
Technibus, 1435
Technical Compression Services, 1745
Technical Gas Products, 1521
Technical Innovation, 1270, 1423
Technical Machine, 1589, 1860
Technical Solutions Holdings Inc., 654
Technicolor, 1910
Technikom Polska, 526
Technimark, 1479, 1505
TechninAsia, 721
Technische Handelsmaatschappij Marchand-Andriessen, 3209
Technisource, 456
Technisyst, 2622
Technium Labs, 3109
Techno-Aide, 1343
Technocer, 2945
Technoflex, 3239
Technolas, 2710, 2932
Technolas Perfect Vision GmbH, 2816
Technologies, 285
Technologies Co. Ltd., 2633
Technology IQ US LLC, 623
Technology Tarena, 973
Technology Village, 3279
Technomatix, 3137
Technorati, 184, 197, 1965, 2446
Techorati, 1245
Techpoint, 2974
TechProcess, 1327
TechProcess Solutions, 872
TechPubs, 1837
TechRx, 954
TechSee, 1607
TechSkills, 1364
Techstar, 608
TechStars, 206, 685, 1699

Techstars, 1019, 1020, 1097, 1594
Techstars Ventures, 635, 3276
TechStyle, 561, 1181
TechTarget, 1785
TechTemple, 641
TechTrader, 1227
Techverse Inc., 737
Techwell, 2603
Teckal, 3154
Teckro, 1643
Tecnomen Oyj, 2990
Tecnowind Group, 3154
Tecomet, 188, 456
Tecon Rio Grande SA, 2086
Tecpro Systems, 2460
Tecta America, 2034, 2046, 2209
Tectonic, 1607
Tectonic Audio Labs, 1061
Tectonic Ventures, 3273
Tecumseh Products, 2067
Tecverde, 834
Teddy Bear Portraits, 654
Tedea, 2745
Tediber, 2296
Tee Life, 3006
Teecinno, 3257
Teekay, 1846
Teem, 79, 1070, 1384
TEEM PH, 2481
Teem Photonics, 223, 2439, 2876
Teens and Toddlers, 2539
Teeology, 1460
Teespring, 2012
TeesuVac, 3203
Teewinot Life Sciences, 1864
Teforia, 1263
TEG, 2539
Tega Industries, 1776
Tegic, 247, 1637
Tegic Communications, 753, 1945
Tegile, 560
Tegile Systems, 197
Tego, 1160
Tegra Medical, 853
Tehuti Networks, 3059
Teidem - Jomo, 2501
Teikon, 2626
Tejas Networks, 805, 1184
TEK Supply, 1295
Tek-Air Systems, 606
Tekelec, 1910
Tekion, 107
Tekion Cloud, 295
Teklatech, 3203
TekLinks, 1409, 1770
Tekni-Plex, 765
Tekniplex, 819
Teknovus, 757, 880, 1922
Tektagen, 312
Tektronix Inc., 1903
TEKVOX, 445
Tel-loin, 2969
TELA Bio, 1382
Tela Innovations, 275
Teladoc, 520, 867, 938, 968, 1228, 1515, 1850
Telaria, 1235
Telarix, 655
Telcom Semicon, 1087
TELCOR, 29
Teldio, 2284
Tele Atlas, 1212, 1244, 1793
Telecity Group, 1360
Telecolumbus, 2497
Telecom Design, 2401
Telecom Transport Management, 1637
Telecom USA, 1708
Telecomia Venture I Ky, 2740

TeleComputing, 2632
Telecomputing, 2731
telecon, 2082
TeleCTG, 721
Teleflex Inc., 832
Telegate, 2782, 3249
Telegent Systems, 1340, 2457
Telegesis, 3107
Telegram, 661
Telegraph Hill, 37
Telehealth Solutions, 1293
Telekenex, 1952
Telemetric Corporation, 75
TeleNav, 1769, 1796
Telenav, 1202, 2853
Telenet, 2781, 3095
TelePacific, 1017
TelePacific Communications, 184
Telepizza, 3033
Teleport, 3108
Teleportd, 2629
TeleportMe, 2885
Telera, 757, 1747
Telera Inc., 252
Telerik, 1752
Telerivet, 1028
TelerX, 1205
TeleSign Holdings, 1752
Telesofia, 2943
Telesoft, 37
Telestream, 819, 1814
Teletrac, 1910
Televero, 445
Televero Health, 1801
Telibrahma, 3019
Teligent Inc., 158
Telik, 1775
Teliport Me, 972
Telisma, 2354, 2544
Telitas US, 2754
Telkore, 1689
Tellagence, 1463
TellApart, 231
Tellapart, 221
Tellermate Holdings, 353
Telleroo, 3108
Tellium, 2007
Tellja, 2638, 2994
TellMe, 1235
Telltale, 1563
Telltale Games, 852
Tellwise, 1852
Telly, 1965, 2010
Telnyx, 1178, 1458
Telocity, 197
Telogis, 126, 560, 1970
Telogy, 23
Telogy Networks, 1348
TeLoRmedix, 1490
Telormedix, 2419
Telos Corporation, 680
Telos Entertainment, 2058
Telovations, 1148
Telrad Connegy, 2782
TelRock, 1244
Teltech Resource Network, 536
Teltron Telecommunications & Electronics, 2807
telweb, 2263
Telx, 824
Tembec, 1967
Temenos, 2784, 2881
Temescal Wellness, 1135
temicon GmbH, 2686
Temis, 3020
Temp Automation, 1061
Tempered Networks, 974, 1563
Tempest, 1694, 1928

Portfolio Companies Index

Tempest Re, 1372
Templar Energy, 740
Tempo, 585, 2137, 2831
Tempo AI, 679, 1237
Tempo Auto, 107
Tempo Automation, 841, 1151, 1879
Tempo Payments, 1646
Tempo.AI, 3121
TempoDB, 471, 618, 756, 962
Temporal, 2187
Tempow, 2478
Tempronics, 1355
Temptime, 1961
Tempur World, 168
Tempur-Pedic, 787
Tempus, 1118
Ten Marks, 272, 428
Ten-X, 578
Ten10, 135
Tenaska Poer Fund II LP, 2094
TenCar, 704
Tencent, 973
Tender Greens, 1166
Tender Products, 1492
Tender Tree, 707
TenderTree, 599
Tendril, 36, 142, 809, 979, 1593, 1906
TenEighty, 3276
Tenere, 1962
Tenet Home Care, 406
Tenex Greenhouse, 1616
Tenfen, 3215
Tenfu, 815
Tengchuang, 2936
Tengion, 1508
Tengion Inc., 2816
Tengwu, 2850
Tenjin, 942
tenKsolar, 1470
Tennis Channel, 221
Tennis Point, 3020
Tenor, 552, 972, 1534
Tenovos, 1554
Tensar, 152
Tensar Corporation, 423
Tensator, 1572
Tenscorcomm, 36
Tensilica, 620, 1212, 2007
Tensor Surgical, 459, 995
TensorFlight, 307
Tenstorrent, 648
Tenstreet, 1717
Tentrr, 896, 1363
TenXc, 1038
Tenxer, 1968
tenXer, 1860
Tenzing, 2110
TEOCO, 1776
Tepha, 1002, 1929
tEQuitable, 1259
Ter Hulst, 2949
Tera Semiconductor, 1087
Tera-Barrier Films, 144
Terabit Radios, 384
Teracent, 1084
Teracent Corp., 623
Teraco, 849
Teraco Data Environments, 254
TeraConnect, 1080
Teradata, 59
Teradian, 2857
Teradiant Networks, 765
Teradici, 87, 979, 2143, 2380
TeraDiode, 77
Teradyne, 1295
Terago, 1640
TeraLogic, 1704

TeraLogic Pharmaceuticals, 112
Teralytics, 2446, 2928
Teranetics, 833
Terapede, 1611
Terapia, 2683
Terapio, 1619
TeraPore, 174
Terapore, 1519
Teraspan Networks, 2273
TeraSquare, 3127
TeraView, 2386, 3098, 3195
TeraView Limited, 2760
Terawave, 1087
Terawave Communications, 2926
TeraXion, 2029
Terayon, 1087, 1952, 3231
Terbium Labs, 2, 829
Tercica, 1493
Tergal, 2317
Teridian Semiconductor, 839
Teridion, 2952
Terminal, 1075
Terminal49, 318
TerminalFour, 2355
Terminus, 173, 189, 655
Teros, 466, 1626
Terra Firma, 2329
Terra Firma Capital Partners III, 2094
Terra Grain Fuels, 2049
Terra Grain Fuels Inc., 2136
Terra Motors, 721
Terra-Gen, 675
Terra-Gen Power, 156
Terracare Associates, 1422, 1484
Terraclear, 1158
Terracotta, 634, 1474
TerraEchos, 1860
TerraGo, 508
TerraGo Technologies, 979
TerraLink Horticulture, 2258
TerraLUX, 553
Terramar, 1219
TerraMarc Industries, 1086
Terramera, 2041, 2238
TerraPact, 515
Terrapass, 1355
TerraPower, 455, 1005, 1069
Terrapure Environmental, 2062
TerrAscend, 1048, 2071
TerraServer, 1709
TerrAvion, 1218
TerraXML, 210
Terreal, 2719
Terres, 2602
Territory, 1888
Territory Foods, 1259
Terszol, 834
Tertio Service Management Systems, 2754
Tervela, 1339, 1672, 1673
Tervita, 1062, 1931
TES, 2876
TES Global, 1835
TESARO, 1412, 1698
Tesaro, 1010
Tesla, 595, 800, 2155, 2796
Tesla Exploration Ltd., 2040
Tesla Motors, 524, 609, 1786, 1906
Tesora, 1459
Tesorio, 751, 1329
TesoRx Pharma, 1061
Tespo, 505
Tessa Therapeutics, 2690
Tessian, 2478
Tessolve, 144
Tessolve Solutions, 3062
Test Object, 3236
Test.ai, 641, 2019

TestAmerica, 928
Testbirds, 3113
Testek Inc., 1368
TestEquity, 733
TestFire, 743
Testfreaks, 3013
Testhub, 3236
Testing Services Holdings, 654
Testive, 1100
Testmunk, 1513
TestQuest, 1288
TestRigor AI, 30
Testroom, 2994
TestSoup, 1958
Tether Technologies, 1061
Tetherex, 1268
Tethis, 286
Tethr, 876, 1240
Tethys Bioscience, 560, 791, 1341
Teton Gravity Research, 678
Tetra Discovery Partners, 139
TetraData, 655
Tetragenetics, 704, 1100
TetraLogic, 915, 1094, 1436, 1508
TetraLogic Pharmaceuticals, 495, 1929
Tetraphase, 237, 747
Tetraphase Pharmaceuticals, 703, 1197, 1691
TetraScience, 751, 1055
Tetrate, 1611
Tetravitae Bioscience, 975
Teva, 1452
TEVET Process Control Technologies, 2720
Texada Software Inc, 2097
Texas Advanced Optoelectronic, 1915
Texas B&B, 111
Texas Genco, 924, 1835
Texas Land & Cattle, 1549
Texas Ventures, 950
Texcel Medical, 196
Texchange (Austin), 1650
Texel, 543
Texerity, 349
Text IQ, 1421, 1670
Text Now, 784
Text+, 2649
Texta America, 1086
Textech Industries, 166
TextEngine, 218
Texterity, 1920
Textile Based Delivery, 1061
Textilia, 2888
Textio, 552, 665, 1626
TextIQ, 751
TextMaster, 2385
textPlus, 1181
TextRecruit, 1675
Textronics, 1324, 1438
TextureMedia, 445
TFF, 3279
TGap Ventures, 3269
TGaS Advisors, 812
TGBS, 3194
TGI Fridays, 473, 1651
TGI Systems Corporation, 407
TGR Financial, 945
TGR Industrial Services, 1209
TGT Oilfield Services, 1125
Thaddeus Medical Systems, 995
Thai Cane Paper Public, 892
Thalchemy, 1921
Thalento, 2949
Thales, 1922
Thalmic Labs, 1473, 1715
Thankful AI, 120
Thankx, 751
Thanx, 968, 1028, 1531, 1700, 2010
THaT, 1079

1435

Portfolio Companies Index

Thatcher Tubes, 832
thatgamecompany, 1509
Thayer Ventures, 228
The Access Group, 1248
The Ace, 1219
The Active Network, 1389
The Aladdin Group, 673
The Alaska Club, 1127
The Alberleen Group, 841
The American Academy, 2382
The Americas Card, 1502
The Arbor Company, 152
The ARC Group, 1743
The Arcview Group, 1135
The Art of Shaving, 402
The Art Store, 1549
The Athletic, 60, 256, 518, 1768
The Atlas Group, 846
The Backplane, 1830
The Bayou Companies, 96
The Beak Beyond, 392
The Bee Corp, 658
The Beer Café, 851
The Berkman Law Firm, 3267
The Better Software Company, 724
The Big Know, 1113
The Bisys Group, 300
The Black Tux, 561, 1110, 1202
The Blackstone Group, 3255
The Block, 1595
The BondFactor Company, 1830
The Boring Company, 800
The Bouqs Company, 120
The Bowery Saving Bank, 1621
The Brixton, 2285
The Brock Group, 1129
The Browser Company of New york, 318
The Bruery, 421
The Business of Fashion, 60
The Business Software Center, 2574
The Canadian National Institute of Health Inc., 2254
The Carlson Company Inc., 1053
The Carlstar Group, 109
The Carlyle Group, 3255
The Cayman, 2285
The Center for Vein Restoration, 1963
The Center for Wound Healing, 274
The Chartis Group, 1575
The Chia Co., 1516
The Chicago Athletic Association, 70
The Cipher Brief, 93
The Cleaning Authority, 1457, 1599
The Climate Corp., 2446
The Climate Corporation, 836, 1798, 2406
The Cloud, 2662, 2674
The Clymb, 688, 1383, 1952
The Community Company, 297
The ComplEAT Food Group, 2944
The Concery Network, 506
The Container Store, 1109, 1360
The Convenience Network, 459
The Copernicus Group IRB, 556
The Core Institute, 782
The Corner Vet, 445
The Corporate University Xchange, 1428
The Cranemere Group, 3264
The Cranemere Group Ltd., 1258
The Crosby Group, 1082
The Crown Group, 931
The Currency Cloud, 2406, 3014, 3239
The Dating Ring, 1749
The Delaney Hardware Company, 917
The Detection Group, 129
The Difference, 218
The Diplomat Group, 680
The Dirty Bird, 2254

The Dodo, 871, 1699
The Door, 218
The Dwyer Group, 1572
The Eastman Egg Company, 1155
The Echo Nest, 1181
The Echonest, 1524
The Edelman Financial Group, 1104
The Edgewater Funds, 3255, 3265
The Efficiency Network Inc., 56
The Employment Group, 2501
The Engine, 3273
The Engineering Company, 3108
The Eton Group Ltd, 2722
The Evans Network of Companies, 64
The Executive Centre, 2772
The Execu|Search Group, 926
The Expectations Project, 1316
The Expert Institute, 1717
The Fabric, 1926
The Faction Collective, 3018
The Fairways Group, 1275
The Family, 641
The Fanfare Group, 1445
The Farmer's Dog, 511, 761, 1663
The Feedroom, 1913
The Felters Group, 985
The Filter, 2691
The Finial Company, 984
The Flatiron School, 1181
The Flavor of california LLC, 1609
The Flex Company, 120, 896
The Focus Corporation, 1086
The Fragrance Outlet, 1415
The Friendly Stranger, 2140
The Gallery, 1219
The Galtney Group, 1770
The Gelato Fiasco, 438
The GI Alliance, 1963
The GigaOM Network, 87
The Goal Group, 2136
The Golden Financial Group Inc., 447
The Good Promise, 445
The Goodship, 1807
The Graph, 1528
The Great Gourmet, 1208
The Green Organic Dutchman, 99
The Green Solutions, 966
The Grid, 107, 1055
The Grow Network, 1018
The Guild, 1183, 1613
The Gym, 2539, 3036
The Harris Agency, 3274
The Harrisburg Senators, 1428
The Herbalista Set, 392
The High Note, 845
The Hillman Group, 433
The Hilsinger Company, 969
The Hippo Kitchen, 951
The History Press, 3018
The Hive, 295, 809, 1926
The Home Decor Companies, 1132
The Honest Company, 816, 1001, 1480
The Hotels Network, 1323
The Huffington Post, 1699
The Hunt, 1028
The Hut Group, 2478
The Hydrafacial Company, 1128
The Iconic, 3170
The Independent Group, 2944
The Inside, 761, 1110
The Intersect Group, 1270
The Investment Fund For Central and Eastern Europe, 2865
The Investment Fund for Emerging Markets, 2865
The Iron Horse Hotel, 70
The Iron Yard, 1923

The Jay Group, 1636
The Johnny Rockets Group, 447
The Jordan Company, 3255
The Juice Plus Company, 96
The Kela Group, 1910
The Kendal Group, 3018
The Kernel Group, 1886
The King Edward, 2254
The Kive Company, 120
The Langley Corporation, 1295
The LeadCorp, 892
The League, 1563, 2011
The Learning Company Inc., 447
The Learning Egg LLC, 1047
The Learning Experience, 1021, 1504
The Leather Shop, 1295
The Level Playing Field Corporation, 507
The Liberation Group, 2935
The Limited, 1753
The Linc Group, 824
The Lion Brewery, 746
The Listening Co., 2662
The Lodge, 796
The Logic Group, 1759
The Los Angeles Film Schook, 1776
The Lovesac Company, 1622
The Lucky Group, 132
The Lynch Law Group, 3275
The Mad Video, 3223
The Madera Group, 330
The Marktets LLC, 902
The Masonry Group, 846
The Medical Cit, 2946
The Medical City, 1139
The Mentor Method, 218
The Merit Group, 446
The Metropolitan Switch Board Company, 1745
The Mighty, 823, 1888
The Mill at New Holland, 1219
The Mobility House, 3252
The Mochi Ice Cream Company, 449
The Mom Project, 1019
The Money Finder, 2068, 2155
The Motley Food, 263
The Motley Fool, 807, 1422
The Muse, 49, 180, 595, 968
The NanoSteal Company, 171
The Neck and Back Clinics, 1824
The Neiman Marcus Group, 2697
The New Motion, 2710
The New Orleans Exchange, 646
The NewsMarket, 304
The Nielsen Company, 1815
The Noun Project, 60, 1222
The Nuance Group, 3026
The Oceanaire Inc., 492
The Official Information Company, 1927
The ONE, 3251
The One Health Company, 266, 1601
The One Of Them, 2869
The One Page Company, 301
The Online Backup Company, 3013
The Orange Chef Co., 1716
The Original Cakerie, 881
The Outline, 60, 1530
The Outsource Group, 556
The Overlook, 1219
The Pairie Club, 297
The Pallet Network, 2944
The Pantry, 783
The Paper Store, 1979
The Paramont, 1219
The Pedowitz Group, 656
The PFM Group, 969
The Phia Group, 1979
The Phoenix at James Creek, 1219
The Pill Club, 1663

1436

Portfolio Companies Index

The Planet Group, 1231
The Plastics Group, 1962
The Player's Tribune, 1001
The Players Tribune, 1883
The Plunge, 1437
The Podcast App, 795, 1527
The Poma Companies, 1111
The Portables Exhibit Systems, 2258
The Poseidon Companies, 1062
The Practice, 2972
The Prairie Club, 1192
The Praxis Companies, 1275
The Press Gallery, 2202
The Princeton Review, 456, 1372
The Private Clinic Group, 2524
The PromptCare Companies, 894, 1230
The Property Software, 2944
The Pros Closet, 776
The Pub, 1430
The RapcoHorizon Company, 1232
The Real Real, 641
The RealReal, 49, 386, 595, 707, 857, 871
The Realtime Group, 514
The Receivables Exchange, 221
The Reject Shop, 2951
The Relish, 896
The Remi Group, 1276
The Renewal Workshop, 1019
THE RESET, 69
The Resolute Fund II, 2094
The Resumator, 1566, 1942
The Retreat at Grand Lake, 1219
The Richardson Group, 402
The Ride, 1623
The Right People Construction Group, 1270
The Right.Fit, 1701
The Ritedose Corporation, 1372
The Riverside Company, 3255, 3264
The Riveter, 342, 773, 1158
The Rocky Mountain School of Design, 1776
The Rogue Initiative, 1390, 1473
The Roof, 1423
The Rounds, 2155
The RunThrough, 1306
The Sails Company, 785
The Sandbox Group, 1422
The Saxton Group, 1141
The Sceptre Group, 2574
The Search Agency, 1041
The Service Companies, 1937
The ServiceMaster Company, 1456
The Shade Store, 1109
The Shelby Group, 1979
The Sheridan Group, 168
The Shoe Box, 937
The Shore, 2948
The Shriram Group, 2599, 2600
The SIA Group, 2863
The Signature Group, 1040
The Sill, 896
The Skimm, 896
The Socialite Family, 2296
The SPIRIT Project, 1912
The Sports Authority, 1109
The SR Group, 222
The Stakeholder Company, 3073
The Stanley Works, 1295
The State Group, 2292
The Still, 325
The Succession Fund LP, 2094
The Sun Exchange, 307
The Sun Valley Group, 1086
The T System, 779
The Tab, 2478
The TASI Group, 985
The TEAM Companies, 2272
The Templar Hotel, 2254

The Tensar Corporation, 1086
The TharpeRobbins Company, 1624
The Tie Bar, 468
The Tile Shop, 2978
The Tire Rack, 1109
The Topps Company, 1156
The Town Kitchen, 1893
The Town of Wasaga Beach, 2254
The Townsend Group, 884
The Trade Desk, 624
The Trade Desk Inc., 965
The Training Room, 2944
The Tranzonic Co, 1456
The Traxys Companies, 1062
The tuesday Company, 934
The Veggie Grill Inc., 331
The Village Green Bookstore, 1837
The Visual Revenue Platform, 1406
The VOID, 1926
The Void, 1509
The Waddington Group, 1372
The Warranty Group, 1835
The Water Initiative, 1191
The Wave VR, 1888
The Weather Channel, 220, 2379
The Wellness Group, 3215
The Winebow Group, 348
The Wing, 325, 351, 1075
The Wireless Stores, 1764
The Wonder, 325
The Wood Heating Company, 3012
The Works, 2171
The Wrap, 1183
The Wrench Group, 1017
The Young Turks, 641
The Zebra, 224, 272, 751, 1685
Theatermania, 724
Theatro, 1069, 1682
Thebizmo, 649
TheBlogTgv, 3179
TheBouqs.com, 1965
theBouqs.com, 1513
TheBrain Technologies Corporation, 2079
Theeb, 1017
Thefind, 221
TheFutureFM, 707
TheGreenBridge.com, 1097
TheGuarantors, 1982
TheHappyCloud, 206
Theia Interactive, 981
Thelial Technologies, 3048
Themis, 3020
TheNeura, 3121
Theorem Clinical Research Holdings, 1279
thePlatform, 818, 1715
Therabis, 1135
Therachon, 1928
Theraclone Sciences, 153, 386, 919
Theragen, 224
Theranos, 183, 275
Theranostics Health, 1169
Therapeutic Human Polyclonals, 1543
Therapeutic Monitoring Systems, 2130
Therapeutic Research Center, 779, 1111
TheraPlay, 1735
Theraplay, 610
Therapure Biopharma Inc., 2073
Therapy Brands, 1123
Therasolve, 2949
Therasos Therapeutics, 59
TheraTogs, 930
Theratome Bio, 658
Theravance, 23, 1691
TheraVasc, 1047
TheraVase, 1553
TheraVida, 1616
TheraVir, 3245

TheRealReal, 180, 1010
Theregen Corporation, 1616
TheRetailPlanet.com, 756
Theriana Pharmaceuticals, 1519
Therion Biologicals Corporation, 1398
Therma-Tru Doors, 1141
Therma-Wave, 214
Thermacore, 1428
Thermafiber, 443
Thermal Product Solutions, 1545
Thermal Sensing Products Inc., 985
Thermal Solutions Manufacturing, 1545
Thermalin, 1577
Thermalin Diabetes, 1229
Thermalin Diabetes LLC, 1047
ThermaSource, 1895
ThermaSys, 1516
ThermImage, 259
Thermo Ceramix, 807
Thermo Fisher Scientific, 1452
Thermo-Tech Windows, 316
ThermoChem Recovery International, 19
Thermoforming Technology Group, 1719
Thermogenics, 2163
Thermon Industries, 194
Thermondo, 2841
Therodiag, 2876
Theron Pharmaceuticals, 129
TherOptix, 297
TherOx, 560, 1003
Therox, 136, 1303
Thesan Pharma, 1628
theScore, 2236
Thesis Couture, 218
TheSkimm, 941
TheSquare, 954
TheSquareFoot, 1475
TheStreet Inc., 6
TheStreet.com, 1103, 1785
Theta Microelectronics, 947
TheTapLab, 1581
Thetaray, 809
theTradeDesk, 306, 771
Thetus, 1355
Theva, 3161
THEVA DüNnschichttechnik GmbH, 2686
TheWaveVR, 307, 1390, 3108
TheySay, 3028
Thiel Cheese & Ingredients, 719
ThinAir, 1254
Thinair, 229
ThinCI, 823
Thinglefin, 371
Things Engraved, 2254
Things Remembered, 225, 1156
Things Remembered Inc., 354
ThingThing, 3108
Think Data Works, 2273
Think Finance, 1737, 1785
Think Research, 2149, 2180
Think Through Learning, 1299, 1689
Think Through Math, 883, 1623
Think Vine, 479
ThinkCERCA, 192, 1178
ThinkData Works, 2113, 2118
Thinkful, 751, 1392, 1518
Thinkfuse, 773
Thinking Phone Networks, 59
Thinking Screen Media, 1146
Thinkingbox, 2258
ThinkingPhones, 1785
ThinkIQ, 306
ThinkLabs, 3109
THINKmd, 786
ThinkNear, 305, 724
Thinknear, 525
Thinknum, 13

1437

Portfolio Companies Index

ThinkRF, 2284
ThinkSpider, 1061
thinkThin, 1861
Thinkup, 1518
ThinkVine, 628
Thinkware, 2857
Thinkwell, 1604
ThinOptX, 1262
THINQ Learning Solutions, 1994, 2079
Thinsters, 500
Third Bridge, 909
Third Channel, 796
Third Love, 721
Third Point Re, 1062
Third Point Reinsurance, 1443
Third Rock Ventures, 3273
Third Screen Media, 712
Third Wave Automation, 648, 1834
Third Wave Technologies, 1921
ThirdEye, 3108
Thirdlove, 720, 1563, 2010
ThirdStream BioScience, 234
Thirstystone Resources, 1521
Thirty madison, 1613
This Is l, 799
ThisClicks, 641, 871
Thislife, 1254
Thismoment, 1850
ThisNext, 502
Thoma Bravo, 37, 1871, 3255, 3265
Thomas H. Lee Partners, 3264
Thomas Steelwork, 2985
Thompson Industrial Services, 746, 1270
Thomson, 300
Thomson Directories, 2883
Thomson Plastics, 104
Thomsons Online Benefits, 1927
THOR Technologies, 1850
Thor Technologies, 310, 1146, 2153
Thorco, 1578
Thorley Industries, 1915
Thorn Lighting, 1017
Thornbury Nursing Services, 2676
Thorne Research, 1728, 1979
Thorne Research Inc. & Diversified Natural Product, 556
Thought Division, 512
Thought Equity, 36
Thought Equity Motion, 142, 1771
ThoughtExchange, 2291
Thoughtexchange, 2153
ThoughtSpot, 816, 909
Thoughtspot, 820
ThoughtWire, 2233, 2243, 2291
ThoughtWorks, 135
Thousand Eyes, 1607
ThousandEyes, 777
Thrasos, 1412
Thrasos Therapeutics, 1122
Thread, 298, 628, 2478, 3030, 3277
Threadbox, 1916
Threadflip, 231
Threads, 623
Threat Metrix, 2618
Threat Stack, 2, 38, 1626
ThreatConnect, 876
ThreatMATRIX, 1796
Threatmetrix, 197
ThreatQuotient, 285
ThreatStream, 1400
Thred Up, 935, 1322, 1888
ThredUp, 1534, 1853
thredUp, 842
3 Day Blinds, 1587, 1752
Three Eagles Communications Company, 1409
Three Leaf Ventures, 3269
Three Ring, 1299

Three Rings, 114
Three Sixty Sourcing, 334
3-D Machining, 1477
3-V Biosciences, 1075, 1297
32 Degrees Capital, 2032
33 Across, 858
33Across, 754, 2157
33across, 741, 871, 1425, 1502, 1584
360, 2579
360 Fly, 1088
360 Insights, 2170
360 PT Management, 439, 812
360 Safe, 2584
360Commerce, 1148
360insights, 1602
360ip, 214
360ip Pte. Ltd., 233
360pi, 1685
360T Group, 1752
361 Capital, 1147
365 Data Centers, 563
365 Retail Markets, 1276, 1455
365Media, 2709
365Scores, 2938
365Scores.com, 436
36Kr, 641
37 Signals, 262
37.5, 171, 928
39.net, 2850
3alioty Technica, 500
3AM Innovations, 1894
3B Scientific, 1037
3BG Supply Co., 658
3Birds, 282
3C Logic, 285, 377, 1169
3ci, 2095
3Com, 1654
3com, 249
3D Corporation Solutions, 1372
3D Hubs, 2478
3D Perception, 2369
3D Robotics, 776, 1359, 1860
3D-SensIR, 307
3DBio, 1051
3DD Pharma, 2949
3Derm, 1988
3DFortify, 622
3DFS Power Solutions, 3259
3Di, 2626, 2626
3DP, 1558
3DR, 1323
3DR Laboratories, 61
3DRobotics, 1184, 1874
3DSoc, 2849
3Dsolve, 2991
3DV, 3072
3E Company, 1239
3E Nano, 2061
3form, 1194, 1623
3G, 2850
3GA, 2021
3GPP, 2584
3Guu.com, 3208
3HACK.PL, 2885
3legs, 3097
3LM, 28
3mensio, 2780
3mensio Medical Imaging, 3051
3PAR, 2007, 2853
3PARdata, 1975
3Pillar Global, 1317
3Play Media, 1100
3QMatrix, 1837
3Scale, 3040
3scale, 547, 1028
3scan, 519, 1151
3seventy, 818

3SI Security Systems, 1136
3Sourcing, 721
3T Biosciences, 181, 1202
3Tier, 1459
3TS Capital Partners, 483, 3261
3V, 1863
3VR, 581, 634, 757, 979
3VR Security, 1906
3ware, 1646
Threewide, 1262
Threshold Pharmaceuticals, 782
Threshold Power, 1324
Thrifty Lavanderia, 402
Thrilling, 1894
Thrillist Media Group, 1361
Thriva, 3108
Thrive, 1054
Thrive Global, 60, 1001, 1110
Thrive Market, 171, 525, 641, 1883
Thrive Networks, 1153
ThriveMetrics, 393
Thron, 2874
ThroughPut, 995
ThruPoint, 1255
Thrupore, 1577
Thumb, 1699
Thumbplay, 560, 964
Thumbplay Music, 1926
Thumbtack, 578, 1028, 1226
Thunder, 181, 1983
ThunderSoft, 1340
Thurst, 218
Thymes, 421
Thyrocare, 1346
TI Health, 897
Tia, 525, 941
Tiama, 3020
Tiandi Energy, 1850
Tiange Technology, 2850
Tianji New Materials, 2936
Tiannong, 2850
Tianpin, 3100
Tiantian Online, 2850
Tianya, 2936
Tiaris, 1080
Tiatros, 129, 756
TIB, 3145
TIBC, 2674
Tibco, 380
Tibersoft, 1920
Tibion, 1819
Tic, 2984
Ticket Evolution, 580, 1524
Ticket Mob, 1099
Ticket Monster, 867
Ticketbase, 1912
TicketBiscuit, 224
Ticketea.com, 3105
Ticketfly, 533, 560, 1247, 1358, 1475, 1620
Ticketleap, 1321
TicketManager.com, 1459
TicketsNow, 1480
Ticketstream, 3077
Tickle, 197, 1323
Tickr, 1108
TICON Industrial, 1139, 2946
TICON Industrial Connection Public, 892
Tictail, 2478, 3056
TIDAL Software, 1906
Tidal Software, 1354
Tidal Systems, 1340
Tidal Wave Technology, 1187
TidalScale, 768, 956
TidalTV, 315
TIDBT, 1632
Tide, 1269
Tidel, 846, 1134, 1910

1438

Portfolio Companies Index

Tidelift, 776, 816
Tidemark, 1796
TidePool, 1546
Tidewater Equipment Company, 1021
Tidewater Midstream and Infrastructure, 2062
Tideway, 3104
TIDI, 1590
TIDI Products, 1037
Tidi Products, 168
TiE LaunchPad, 623
Tie Society, 590
Tiendas 3B, 1516
Tier 1 Energy Solutions, 1009
Tier One Relocations, 1753
Tier1Asset, 3203
TierlCRM, 1607
Tierpoint, 3274
Tiff's Treats, 477
Tiff's Treats Cookie Delivery, 1255
Tiffany & Co., 300
TiFiC AB, 2369
TiGenix, 2563, 3085
Tigenix, 2949
Tiger Calcium, 2214
Tiger Connect, 1251, 1663
Tiger Iron Capital, 3273
Tiger Text, 37
Tigera, 1158
TigerConnect, 1346
TigerGraph, 4, 107, 1758
Tigerlily, 3113
TigerOptics, 706
TigerText, 644, 1382
Tigertext, 1298, 1303
Tigo Energy, 946, 1391, 2900
Tigris Pharmaceuticals, 1325
Tijuana Flats, 193
Tikl, 1110
Tikona Digital Networks, 1361
Tile, 107, 823, 1069, 1183, 1694
Tilera, 249, 1922, 3235
Tilia, 14
Tiller, 2296
Tilley, 2133
Tilney Bestinvest, 3033
Tilray, 1481
Tilson Technology Management, 438
Tilt, 2012
Tiltan Pharma, 3245
Tilting Motor Works, 1061
TIM Group, 521, 848
Timber Automation, 291
Timberland Corp., 300
Timbuk2, 1396
Timbuktu, 1306
Time Domain, 1704, 1733
Time Packaging Limited, 2861
time play, 2134
Timebyping, 318
Timecast, 1716
TimeClock Plus Inc., 158
TimeHero, 2137
Timehop, 1359, 1663, 1715
Timelines, 137
TimeSight Systems, 650
TimesLED, 1340
TimesTen, 1257
TimeSys, 1746
Timetovisit.ru, 2344
TimeTrade, 534, 1100
Timetrade, 178
Tin Drum Asian Kitchen, 271
Tinde, 3013
Tinder, 248
Tindie, 773
Tinea Pharmaceuticals, 1493
Tinfoil Security, 1254, 1563, 1594

Tinker Garten, 351
Tinkercad, 308
Tinkergarden, 1392
Tinkergarten, 488, 1527
Tinnerman Palnut Engineered Products Inc., 862
Tinoro, 121
Tinsel, 218
Tint, 972
Tinted, 896
Tintri, 777
Tiny Build, 2953
Tiny Pulse, 173
Tinybop, 351, 1054, 1593, 1874
Tinychat, 15
Tinypay.me, 2359
TINYpulse, 231
TIO, 1923
TIO Networks Corporation, 1406
Tioga Energy, 791, 1324, 1355
Tioga Pharmaceuticals, 769, 1298, 1817, 2130, 2496
Tioma Therapeutics, 267, 569
Tip Hive, 1923
Tipa, 2462
Tipico, 2423
TiqIQ, 533
TIR Systems, 2097
Tirendo, 3056
Tiryaki Agro, 1017
TIS, 3161
Tissue Analytics, 792
Tissue Regeneration Systems, 1921
Tissue Regenix, 2892
Tissue Repair Company, 1398
Tissuemed, 1604
TissueTech, 224, 697
Tissuetech, 1571
Tital Fitness LLC, 556
Titan, 327
Titan Fastener Products Inc., 908
Titan Fitness, 1456
Titan Health Corporation, 572
Titan Pharmaceuticals, 946
TitanFil, 2155
Titanium Energy Services, 2251
Titanobel, 3020
TitanX, 2755
TITUS AG, 3190
Titus Oil & Gas LLC, 1278, 1326
Tiversa, 1194
TIVIT, 135
Tivity Health, 94, 97
TIVO, 563
TiVo, 1704
Tivo, 1001
Tivoli, 2007
Tivoli Audio, 1752, 2254
Tivra Corp., 2213
Tiway Oil, 1516
Tixr, 1876
Tizona, 1268
Tizona Therapeutics, 182
Tizor, 623
Tizra, 1693
TJ Brent, 3017
TJ Hale, 812
TJS Insurance Group, 3275
Tk20, 1685
TKH Group, 3069
TLC Companies, 932
TLC Health Network, 152
TLC Vision, 928
TLContact, 944
TLK Group, 1599
TLL, 101
TMAC Resources, 1548
Tmax soft, 2969

TMCI Padovan, 3154
TMI International, 1343
TMP Worldwide Advertising & Communications, 1927
TMRC, 2970
TMRW, 12
TMS Brokers, 2309
Tmsuk, 602
TMT Coaxial Network, 2782
Tmunity, 1075
TMX, 3276
TN Stillhouse, 459
TNT, 2965
TNT Crane & Rigging, 740, 1368
TNW Systems, 1409
to-BBB BV, 2350
TOA Technologies, 642
Tobii, 3013
Tobira Therapeutics, 386, 782, 1251, 3015
Tobles AG, 2564
Toca Madera, 331
Tocaya Organica, 331
Tock, 1384, 1480
TodaCell, 2352
Today Tix, 1595
TodayTix, 857, 1876
Todd Combustion, 402
Todou, 1087
Tods Aerospace, 48
Toera Therapeutics, 1713
Together, 795
Together Work, 824
Togg, 1885
Toggle, 1894
Toguh, 1876
Tok & Stok, 2329
Tok.tv, 2010
Tokalas, 1221
Tokamak Energy, 2967
TokBok Inc., 623
TokBox, 115
Tokbox, 634
Toke With, 1807
Tokeheim Corp., 300
Token, 1888
Tokia.It, 3049
Tokitaki, 3133
Toko, 1848
Tokopedia, 3127
Toktumi, 548
Tokyo Joe's, 873
Tokyo Smoke, 1610, 1807, 2140
Tolemi, 728, 1768
Tolera, 1379
Tolera Therapeutics, 1847
Tolingo, 2994
Tollgrade, 839
Tom Tailor, 2375
TOMA Biosciences, 1400, 1488, 1940
Tomaisins, 2417
ToMarket, 1507
Tomfoolery, 1254
Tommie Cooper, 2401
Tommy Hilfiger, 135
Tommy John, 743, 1306, 1310
Tomophase, 1616
Tomorrow, 755, 1269
TomorrowInnovations, 1830
TomoTherapy, 176, 1379, 1619, 1921
Tomra Systems, 3069
Tonal, 1184, 1663
Tonbo Imaging, 174, 1509
Tongbanjie, 2936
TongCard Holdings, 2667
Tongdun, 973
Tongtech, 2850
Tonian, 455

1439

Portfolio Companies Index

Tonic.ai, 708
TONIX Pharmaceuticals, 1786
Tonka Equipment Company, 1215
Tonoga, 1645
Tonomy, 136
Tonx, 397, 1055
Tonys Farm, 3194
Too Faced Cosmetics, 815
Too Faced Holdings, 1978
Too.Step, 2444
TooJay's Restaurant & Deli, 327
ToolingU, 831
ToolsGroup, 29
. Toolwire, 947
Toolwire, 524, 1354, 1389, 1604, 1672
Toopher, 545
Toot, 1551
Toothpick, 2685, 3030
Top Canventure, 2271
Top Corp, 684
Top Driver, 1999
Top Flight Technologies, 724
Top Gain, 3194
Top Hat, 665, 720, 1700, 1879, 1882, 2132, 2137, 2157, 2184, 2280
Top Image, 584
Top in Nature, 2271
Top Knobs USA Inc., 908
Top Rx, 750, 1166
Top Tier Software, 215
Top10, 2752
Topack Fittings, 1967
Topanga, 1355
Topanga Technologies, 1445
Topas Therapeutics, 689
Topaz, 74
Topcoder, 488
TopFan, 36
TopHatter, 455
Topica, 197, 3179
Topica Pharmaceuticals, 1493, 1811
Topio, 1672, 3137
TopiVert, 1628, 2858
Topline Game Labs, 394
Toplogis, 47
TopNoggin, 462
Topo Athletic, 1346
Topokine, 1627
TopOPPS, 569
TopoTarget A/S, 2816
Topps, 1833
Topray Technologies, 2603
Tops Foods, 2781
Tops Markets, 1256
Topshop/Topman Holdings, 1109
Topspin Communications, 1474
TopSportLab, 2949
Topsy, 296
Topway Industries, 2487
Torax, 1616
Torax Medical, 40, 1817
Torbit, 1853
TORC Oil & Gas, 2136
Torch, 934
Torchlite, 1607
Tordivel, 2754
Torigen, 1701
Torill's Table, 2099
Torino Power Solutions, 2031
Tornate Animation, 1833
Tornier, 1725, 1929, 3279
Toro Gold, 2942
Toro Gold Limited, 1548
Toronto Fashion Week, 2148
Toronto Stock Exchange, 3268
Torqeedo, 2979
Torque, 747

Torque Tension Systems Ltd, 3011
Torrent Oil, 1278, 1326
Torrent Resources, 1141
Torrent Systems, 1348
Torrex Equipment Corporation, 524
Tortilla, 1516
Tortoise, 1147
Tortuga AgTech, 1721, 1758
Tortuga Logic, 648
Torun, 2706
Torus Insurance Holdings, 1743
Tory Burch, 815
Tosca Services, 135
Toss, 1075
Toss Lab, 1509
Total Attorneys, 263
Total Care RX, 439
Total Expert, 173
Total Fitness, 2677
Total Home Health Care, 406
Total Immersion, 1416, 2693, 2899
Total Management & Earlybird Courier, 1954
Total Pave, 2200
Total Safety, 1134
Total Woman, 1575
TotalExpert, 2132
Totality, 223, 2079
TotallyMoney.com, 3104
TotalMobile, 2972
Totango, 249, 396, 856
Totemic Labs, 4
Totems, 3108
Totes ISOTONER, 1017
Totes Isotoner Corporation, 354
Totspot, 1099, 1749
Totsy, 608
Toucan, 883, 2137
Touch Commerce, 1416, 1640
Touch Micro-System, 1922
Touch Of Modern, 751
Touch Surgery, 2478
TouchBistro, 2134, 2236, 2243
TouchCommerce, 665, 954
Touchdown Technologies, 56, 715, 1911, 1915
Touching Lives Adult Day Services, 1233
TouchOfModern, 1416
TouchPath, 9
TouchPay Holdings, 1745
Touchstone Exploration, 2091
Touchtown.ch, 2310
TouchTunes Interactive Networks, 1906
Toudou.com, 2850
Toughglass Holdings Ltd, 2704
Tourneau, 1109
Tournus, 2965
Tourradar, 2834
Tout, 1585
ToutApp, 11, 1024, 1358
Tovala, 1384, 1480
Tovarnity, 2683
Tower Cloud, 224, 1072, 1331
Tower Co., 1946
Tower Light, 2391
TOWER Software Engineering, 2715
Tower Technology, 2951
Tower Ventures, 1459, 1862
Tower Vision, 1506
TowerCare Technologies, 841
TowerCo, 1315, 1777
Towercom Development, 1148
TowerCom Development L.P., 1708
Towercom Enterprises, 1148
TowerCom Limited, 1708
Towercom Limited, 1148
TowerView Health, 266
Town Place, 1219
town shoes, 2082

Town Sports International Inc., 354
Towne Park, 909, 1776
Townsend, 678
Townsquared, 751
Towry, 1516
Toxicology Holdings, 698
ToxiMet, 2760
Toymail, 1149
Toys 'R Us, 220
ToyTalk, 455, 1860
Toytalk, 1069
TP Therapeutics, 1731
TPC Group, 740
TPC Wire & Cable, 1435
TPF, 3134
TPG, 3255, 3264
TPI Composites, 126, 657
Tpo, 2436
TPx, 494
Tr, 1110
TR Fleet, 2967
TR-Tech. Int Oy, 2318
TRA, 1080
Tra-con, 1295
Traackr, 1097
Trace, 120, 325, 561, 1004
Trace One, 2662
TraceAssured, 2610
TraceLink, 710, 743, 2132
TraceME, 1585
TraceMe, 1158
Tracer Net, 526
Trachte, 1266
TracID AS, 3141
Track.com, 724
Track4C, 3065
TrackBill, 569
TrackDuck, 3049
Tracker Resources Development III, 672
TrackIF, 2001
TrackMaven, 317
TrackR, 776, 981, 1958
Tracks N Teeth, 1507
Tracksmith, 1110, 1530
TrackTik, 2132, 2157, 2170
TrackVia, 36, 712, 756, 1146
Trackvia, 720
TrackX, 1206
Tracon Pharma, 157
Tracsis, 2892, 3028
Tractable, 974, 2019
Tractech Inc., 653
Traction, 1839
Traction Guest, 1607
Traction Software, 979, 1693
TractManager, 170, 1728
Tractor Zoom, 995
Tracx, 383, 646, 655, 754
Tracy Biomass, 1895
TradAir, 2566
Tradair, 3221
Trade & Invest British Columbia, 3268
Trade Desk, 646
Trade Gecko, 1965
Trade Harbor, 179
Trade It, 486
Trade Me, 135
Trade Sparq, 1965
TradeBeam, 1780
Tradebeam, 1672
TradeBlock, 710
TradeCapture, 466
TradeDoubler, 2754
TradeGlobal, 333
TradeIt, 1528
Tradeka Ltd., 2863
TradeKing, 1364

Portfolio Companies Index

TradeLanes, 995
Trademark Global, 257
Trademark Now, 2478
Trademob, 3170
Tradeo, 1323, 2328
Tradepoint Atlantic, 937
TRADER, 135
Traderion, 3108
TraderServe, 2535
TraderTools, 646, 655
Tradeshift, 3014
Tradesmen, 1971
Tradesmen Enterprises, 2126
TradeSource, 1624
Tradesy, 243, 306, 624, 1075, 1099, 1566, 2649
Tradewinds Forest Products, 1909
Tradex Technologies, 800
Tradier, 710
Trading View, 1019
Tradingcom Europe, 2625
TradingScreen, 1785
Tradiv, 392
Tradoria, 3113
Trados, 2343
Traefik, 2296
Traeger Pellet Grills LLC, 1851
Traffic Roots, 392
Traffic Station, 2021
Traffic Technologies, 2645
TrafficCast China, 583
TrafficCast International, 452, 583, 1292
Trafficware, 1086
Trafi, 3049
Tragara, 1122
Tragara Pharmaceuticals, 621, 1490
Tragus, 2935
Trail, 3108
Trainers Vault, 1507
Training Partners USA Limited, 331
Trait Biosciences, 2140
Traitwise, 445
Traity, 2831, 3108
Trajectory IQ, 2121
Trak Communications, 1925
TRAKAmerica, 928
TrakLok, 995
TRAKnet, 1289
Trala, 1384
Tran Switch, 59
Trancept Systems, 1008
Tranquis Therapeutics Inc., 1731
Trans American Rubber, 1745
Trans-o-Flex, 2375
Trans-Trade, 1234
Trans1, 59
TranS1 Inc., 572
TransACT, 3168
Transaction Services, 368
Transaction Wireless, 1239, 1371
Transactis, 525, 724, 1306, 1601, 1738
TransAlta Corp., 2033
Transatel, 3113
Transave, 1493, 2748
Transaxle, 846
Transbiodiesel, 2417
Transcast Media, 2703
Transcend, 1094
Transcend Medical, 386, 938, 1122, 1725, 1786
Transcend Robotics, 519
Transcend Therapeutics, 62
Transcendent, 92
Transcept, 1010, 1251
Transcept Pharmaceuticals, 898
TransChip, 1239
TransCom, 734
TransCore, 1086
TransCorp, 652

TransCorp Spine, 666
Transcorp Spine, 943
TranscribeMe, 129, 1061, 1600, 1669, 1988
Transcriptic, 107, 965
TransDigm, 254, 1368
Transdigm, 2697
TransEngen, 1107
TransEnterix, 74, 1008, 1508, 1628
Transera, 1747
Transera Communications, 1119
Transervice Logistics, 2022
Transfer Tool Products, 17, 611, 1053
TransferGo, 3049, 3049
TransferSoft, 1965
TransferWise, 1761
Transferwise, 1001, 1897, 2674, 3108
TransFirst, 1972
Transfix, 317, 396, 600, 707, 1110
TransForce Inc., 1403
Transform Materials, 1009
TransformativeMed, 2008
Transgaming, 2058
Transgene, 2544
TransGenic, 2970
TransGo, 746
Transifex, 1829
Transit Labs, 2184
Transit Screen, 408
Transit Wireless, 1777
Transitive, 555, 2472, 3047
Translarity, 1828
Translate Bio, 191
TranslateBio, 1731
TransLattice, 596
Translent Plasma Systems, 1051
Translink, 380
TransMedic, 269
TransMedics, 1665, 1906
Transmedics, 747
TransMeta, 1103
Transmeta, 1704
Transmeta Corporation, 1728
Transmode, 3043
Transmolecular, 136, 1398
Transnational Corporation, 2300
Transnational Foods, 364
Transolutions, 443
Transom Capital Group, 14
Transonic Combustion, 1916
Transpac, 1132
Transpac Imports, 1456
Transparent Healthcare, 1097, 3277
Transperra, 1089
Transphorm, 1151
Transplace, 1835
Transplace Holdings, 862
Transpond, 1884
Transporeon, 1572, 1757, 1835
Transport Corp. of America Inc., 843
Transport Holdings Inc., 404
Transport Industries, 722
Transport Labor Contract, 1505
Transport Labor Holding Company, 250
Transport Models, 2708
Transport Technology Systems, 1906
Transportation Safety Technologies Inc., 152
Transtar, 787
Transtar Industries, 1456
Transtech control, 2750
TransUnion, 62, 1156
Transwestern Publishing Company LP, 1986
TranSwitch, 3137
Transwitch, 1728
TRANZACT, 897, 1927
Tranzonic, 1684
Tranzyme Pharma, 1508, 1817
Trap!T, 2831

Trapeze Networks, 422, 1445
Trapezoid, 2006
Traphaco, 2961
Trapp Technology, 333
Traptic, 941, 1933
TrapX Security, 1381
Trash Warrior, 1613
Trask Contracting, 2047
Traslational Cancer Drugs Pharma, 1452
Traumatec, 445
Trausch Industries, 654
Travador, 3239
Travel Joy, 229, 1323
Travel Nurse Across America, 873
Travel Store, 3048
TravelCenters of America, 1360, 1372
Travelcircus, 2841
TravelClick, 1814
Travelclick, 221
Travelmob, 2913
Travelmuse Inc., 371
Travelnuts, 1912
Travelport, 1785
TravelPotst.com, 114
TravelPrice, 2769
Travelprice.com, 2354
Travelpro Group, 1231
TravelTab, 171
Traverse Biosciences, 704
Traverse Networks Incorporated, 1089
Travis Peak Resources, 672
Travo, 228
Travora, 646
Travora Media, 1738
Trax, 1571
Trax Group, 1724
Traxo, 1682, 1806
Tray, 306
Tray.io, 128, 3030
Traycer Systems, 1553, 1740
Trazzler, 231, 1584
TRDATA, 3108
Trea Asset Management, 1147
Tread, 2241
Tread Corporation, 828
Trean Corporation, 97
Treasure Data, 1626
Treasure Valley Business Group, 1605
Treasury Prime, 1758
Treat U, 3048
TreaTec21, 3245
Treater, 1642
Treatful, 324, 851
Treatibles, 1135
Treatment X, 392
Treato, 1298, 1382
Treatspace, 272
Treau, 1894
Trebeca, 228
Treble.ai, 795
Tred, 773, 1149
Tredi, 2415
Tree House, 1374
Tree Island Industries, 1970
Treehouse, 1696
TreeRing, 1641
Treez, 151, 1610
Trefoil Therapeutics, 544
Trei, 3154
TREK Diagnostic, 118
Trek10, 658
Trellis, 417, 779
Trellis Bioscience, 644, 1303
Trellis Research Group, 392
Trelys, 738
Trema, 23, 1017
Tremor Media, 1175

1441

Portfolio Companies Index

Tremor Video, 386, 609, 1846
Trending, 307
TrendKite, 1685
Trendkite, 1206
TrendMD, 1758, 2125, 2273
Trends for Friends Brands, 3208
Trendy Foods Finances, 3134
Trendy International Group, 1088
Trendyol.com, 1075
Trendzone Construction, 2542
Trescal, 77, 2207
TresseNoire, 218
Tresu, 3203
Tresys Technology, 245
Trevena, 919, 1460, 1941
Treventis Corp., 266
Trevi Holdings, 2985
Trevi Therapeutics, 136
Trexel, 63
Trey Whitfield School, 1420
TRG Screen, 1409
Tri Alpha Energy, 1916
Tri-Link Technologies Inc, 2097
tri-Star Aerospace, 1368
Tri-Star Electronics, 374
Tri-Star Protector, 1040
Tri-Wire, 1173
Tria, 74, 237
TRIA Beauty, 598, 1941
Tria Beauty, 138, 188, 1786
Triad 700, 1153
Triad Behavioral Health, 550
Triad Isotopes, 1417
Triad Life Sciences, 425
Triad Retail Media, 716
Triad Semiconductor, 646
Triage, 1222, 2149, 2539
Triage Management Services, 131
Triage Staffing, 1276
TrialCard, 1368
TrialPay, 231, 581, 1515, 1839
Trialpay TRUSTe, 634
TrialReach, 3018
Trials AI, 120
TrialScope, 655
Triana Energy, 1256
Triangle Ice, 746
Triangle Pharmaceuticals, 769
Triax Midwest Associates, 1927
Triax Southeast Assocites, 1927
Tribar Manufacturing, 917
Tribe, 1150
Tribe Mobile, 690
Tribeca Flashpoint Media Arts Academy, 1742
TribeHR, 1181
Triblio, 1065, 1146
Tribogenics, 756
Tribold, 2662, 2691
Tribridge, 1136
Tribune Company, 3265
Tribute Direct, 1090
Tricast, 288
Trice Medical, 921, 1601
Trice Medical Inc., 269
Tricho-Med Corp.; Global Canna Labs; Etea Sicurezz, 2174
Tricida, 762, 1143, 1941
Trico Products, 1081
Tricoci University, 529
Tricog, 1013
Tricord Systems, 536
TriCore Solutions, 361
Tricoya, 319
Tridelta plc, 2554
Tridemensional Engenharia, 2349
Trident, 37
Trident Group, 3267

Trident Pharmaceuticals, 1775
Trident University International, 1752
Trident USA Health Services, 782
Trident V Credit Holdings, 1743
Tridien Medical, 523
Tridion, 2779, 3051
Trieza, 1268
Trifacta, 585, 872, 974, 1563, 2011
Triformix, 1646
Trig, 1633
Trigen Ltd., 2816
Triggit, 1333, 1715, 1798
TriggrHealth, 630
Trigo, 32, 2448
Trikon Technologies, 765
Trilibis Mobile, 183
TrilibisMobile, 100
Trilio, 2
Triller, 1149, 1563
Trillian Surgical, 425
Trilliant, 809, 1906, 2315, 3252
Trillium College, 1504
Trilogy, 1378
Trilogy Education Services, 488, 935, 1551
Trilogy International Partners, 1496, 2134
Trilogy Midstream, 1278, 1326
Trilumina, 1070
Trim, 2280
Trim Parts, 1343
Trimac Industries, 1837
Trimark Usa, 194
TriMas, 1970
Trimas, 923
Trimb Healthcare, 209
TriMech, 1276
TriMedx, 176
Trimeris, 1398
Trimlite Manufacturing, 2275
Trinean, 2476
TriNet, 815, 3267
TriNetX, 1268
Trinity, 928
Trinity Capital Investment, 3276
Trinity CO2, 1256
Trinity Consultants, 881, 1111
Trinity Convergence, 1008, 1227, 1288
Trinity Hospice, 1086
Trinity Industries Inc., 1903
Trinity Mobile Networks, 306, 972
Trinity Watthana, 1139, 2946
Trinity3 Technology, 403
TriNorthern Security Distribution, 328
Trintech, 1717
Trintel, 402
Trio Labs Inc., 737
Trio Video, 263
Trion, 518, 596, 1604, 1827, 1853
Trion Coating, 1229
Trip Tribe, 285
Trip Trotting, 1655
Trip.com, 1534
TriPath Imaging, 118
TripBam, 1806
Tripbirds, 2637
TripConnect, 1175
Tripex Pharma, 1271
Triphase, 2366
Tripifoods, 1295
Tripit, 215, 1359
Triple, 770
Triple Canopy, 7
Triple G Systems, 2058
Triple M Housing, 2275
Triple Point Technology, 1041, 1972
Triple Ring Technologies, 69
TripleByte, 720
Triplebyte, 991

TripleLift, 655, 1115, 1222, 1322, 1860, 2157
TripleSeat, 635
TripleShot, 534
TripLingo, 282
Triposo, 1010
TRIPP, 1473
Tripp, 1184
Tripping, 590, 1097, 1513
Trippy, 641, 1798
Tripshare, 1306
Triptrotting, 1099
Tripwire, 59, 807, 1001, 1626, 1814
TriReme Medical, 57, 1819
Trisara, 2772
Triscend Corporation, 252
Trispan, 542
TriStar, 441
Tristar, 3018
Tristar 600, 493
Tristar License Group, 493
TriState Capital, 1147
Tristream Energy, 893
Tritec Performance Solutions, 653
Tritech, 787
TriTech Software Systems, 1979
Tritech Software Systems, 909
Triton, 909, 1793
Triton BioSystems., 2973
Triton Container, 1931
Triton Digital, 1910
Triton Network Systems, 1103
Triton Power Partners, 675
Triton Water, 1199
Triton Web Properties, 539
TritonWear, 2128, 2184
Triumfant, 538, 989, 1348
Triumph Group Inc., 354
Triumpth Higher Education Group, 383
Trius Therapeutics, 1478, 1915
TriVascular, 867, 1059, 1445
Trivascular, 23, 604, 1268
Trive Capital, 879
TriVentures II Fund; V-Wave Ltd., 269
Triversity, 2079
Trividia, 36
TriVirix, 1842, 2704
Trivitron Healthcare, 710
Trivnet, 2952, 3137, 3212
Triwater Holdings, 654
TriWest Capital Partners, 2167
TriZetto Group, 955
TriZetto Group Inc., 1903
Trizic, 784
Trnql, 1254
Troax, 2325
Troika Networks, 132, 898
Trois Petits Cochons, 812
Trojan Battery, 456
Trojan Lithograph Corporation, 147
Troll Communications LLC, 1986
Trolltech, 3013
Trolly, 2526
Tronair, 1086, 1111, 1570
Tronair Holdings, 1456
Tronic's Micro Systems, 2876, 3020
Tronics, 2439
Tronox, 1134
Troodon, 3142
Troon, 1109
Troops, 49, 180, 720, 942, 1758
Troopwork, 1888
TrophpSYS, 2527
Tropic Biosciences, 2106
Tropic Networks, 555, 1080
Tropical Smoothie Cafe, 271
Tropikal Pet, 1572
Tropitone, 1435

Portfolio Companies Index

Tropos Networks, 1003, 1945
Troux Technologies, 1445, 2754
Trov, 508, 2406
Trove, 630, 872, 1958
Trover Solutions, 1927
Troverie, 2202
Trovix, 32, 852
Troxell Communication Inc., 64
Troy, 1262
Troy Energy, 1795
Troyanda, 3234
TRP Energy LLC, 1851
Trrivest, 2167
Tru, 2691
Tru Fit Athletic Clubs, 439
Tru Hearing, 1705
Tru Optik, 1486
Tru Star Technology, 180
Truaxis, 1853
Trubion Pharma, 153, 1916
Trubion Pharmaceuticals, 782, 1493
TruBrain, 341
Truck Accessories Group, 1030
Truck Bodies & Equipment International, 1456
Truck Driver Power, 995
Truck Hero, 433
Truck-Lite, 1062, 1456
Truck24, 3233
Truckish, 995
TruckPro LLC, 914
Truckstop.com, 333
TruckTrack, 3108
Trucktrack, 3030
True, 552, 1753, 2006
True & Co., 280, 563, 1699
True Accord, 1069, 1631
True Anthem, 1595, 1883
True Body, 1097
True Botanicals, 567
True Citrus, 80
True Facet, 942, 1183
True Fit, 329, 560, 1046, 1677, 2132
True Gault, 432
True Home Value, 374
True Link, 1054, 1055
True Link Financial, 599
True North Therapeutics, 1268
True Office, 533, 1420
True Oil Company LLC, 159
True Partners, 1963
True Potentional LLP, 793
True Science, 686
True Share Vault, 865
True Temper, 827
True Temper Sports, 1127
True Ultimate Standards Everywhere, 581
True Vault, 721
True X Media, 968, 1534
True&Co., 1700, 1912
TrueAccord, 148, 318, 720, 1968
Truearc, 2267
Truebil, 1013
Truebill, 593, 1329
TrueCaller, 1075
Truecaller, 2446
TrueCar, 132, 1810, 1888, 1946, 2649
TrueChoice, 397
TrueCommerce, 29
Truecommerce, 655
TrueData, 226
trueEx, 1420
TrueFacet, 773, 784, 1825
TrueLeaf, 2155
TrueLemon, 989
TrueLens, 534
TrueLook, 1681
TrueMotion, 816

TrueNet Communications, 1569
TrueNorth Therapeutics, 1238
TrueSAN Networks, 1535
TrueSpan, 1747, 1779
TrueTemper Sports, 541
TrueVault, 1099
TrueVision Systems Inc., 69
Truework, 564, 1069
Trufa, 770
Trufood, 193
Truist, 1689
Trulia, 180, 600, 1323, 1460
Trulioo, 301
Trulite, 1753
Trulogica, 514
TRULY, 2685
Truly, 305
Truly Wireless, 128
Trumaker, 1028, 1531
Trumaker & Co., 544, 1593, 1595
Trumba, 197, 1637
Trumid, 148
Trumo, 1254
Trunk Archive, 3149
Trunk Club, 137, 871
Trupanion, 1183
TruSecure Corporation, 1668
TruSignal, 1534, 1725
Trusona, 1075, 1154
Truspan, 563
Trusper, 596
Truss, 1282
Trussle, 3108
Trussway Holdings Inc., 461
Trust & Will, 896
Trust Arc, 968
Trust Digital, 171, 538, 712
Trust Metrics, 1486
Trust Pilot, 2674
Trust You, 2838
TruStar Technology, 49
TrustArc, 333
TRUSTe, 231
Trusted, 525
Trusted Computer Solutions, 1348
Trusted Edge, 1348
Trusted Insight, 1254, 1809
Trusted Metrics, 1988
Trusted Network Technologies, 1038
Trusted Shops, 3020
TrustedID, 1884
TrustedInsight, 585, 625
TrustEgg, 1958
Trustev, 871
TrustGo, 1340
Trusthouse Services Group, 881
TrustID, 1853
Trustifi, 1532
Trustify, 1585, 1701
Truston, 2779
Trustpilot, 3013, 3203
TrustRadius, 1184
Trustribe, 3049
Trustwave, 161, 793, 1041, 1477, 1672, 1886
TrustWeaver, 2637
TrustYou, 2829, 3020
TruTouch, 1100
Trutouch, 1924
TruTouch Technologies, 756, 1300
TruU, 574, 1809
Truven Health Analytics, 1925
Truveris, 1291, 1298, 1849
Truvian Health, 663
Truviso, 613, 1378
TRX Systems, 1169, 1260
Try, 1150
Try.Com, 751

Try.com, 3108
Trylon-TSF, 2044
Tryoop, 2438
Tryton Medical, 946, 1500, 1574
Tryzens Group, 3104
TS3 Technology, 1232
TSA Consulting Group, 299
Tsang Yow, 905
Tse Sui Luen Jewellery Limited, 2402
TSI, 166
Tsinghua Tongfang Artificial Environment Co Ltd, 2499
TSL, 2795
TSM, 2953
TSM Corporation, 917
Tsmc, 2436
TSO Logic Inc., 643
TSS Solutions, 48
TST Media, 1872
Tstar 600, 1344
Tsumobi, 627, 1690, 2010
Tsunami Visual Technologies, 1180
TT dotCom Sdn Bhd, 3164
TTA, 2362
TTH Holdings, 111
TTPOD, 2978
TTR - Transactional Track Record, 3048
TTTech, 809
TTYL, 751
Tuache.com, 935
Tube City IMS Corporation, 1971
Tubel Technologies, 466
TubeMogul, 243, 358, 560, 770, 1853, 2171, 3121
Tubi, 770
Tubular, 743
Tubular Labs, 1813
Tubular Textile, 405, 908
Tucana Technologies, 526
Tucker Arsenberg Attorneys, 3275
Tucows, 1882
Tudou, 1916, 3062
Tueo Health, 1701
Tuesday Morning, 1156
Tufin, 3101
Tuilux, 2438
Tuition.io, 306, 1099, 1247, 1985
Tuizzi, 3048
Tujia, 823
Tula, 817, 1088
Tularik, 782
Tule, 1069
Tulip, 1075, 1607
Tulip Corporation, 1624
Tulip Medical, 2353
Tulip Molded Plastics, 1021
Tulip Retail, 796, 1046, 1489, 1700, 2157
Tulsa Inspection Resources, 1605, 1726
Tulsa Welding School, 1751
Tumbleweed Communications, 58, 192, 197, 852
Tumblr, 1235
tumblr, 1715
Tumri, 1663
Tunable Photonics Corporations, 765
Tune, 773, 968
Tune Wiki, 620
TuneIn, 518, 1737
Tunein, 816, 968
Tunespeak, 569
Tuniein, 1001
Tuniu.com, 596, 935
Tunnel, 2646
Turbine, 823, 1728
Turbine Engine Specialists, 2168
Turbine Inc., 371
Turbo Appeal, 377
Turbo International, 958

1443

Portfolio Companies Index

Turbonetics, 653
Turbonomic, 935
TurboSquid, 61
Turing Video, 232
Turn, 757, 867, 1663, 1850
Turner, 959
Turning Art, 1322
Turning Technologies, 348
Turnitin, 883, 1346
TurnKey, 1685
Turnleaf, 210
Turnstone, 1928
Turntable.Fm, 1460
Turo, 707, 1075, 1663
Turtle Beach, 52, 1748
Turtle Beach Systems, 1227
Turtle Entertainment GmbH, 3020
Turtle Island Recycling, 2167
Tuscany Apartments, 70
Tusker Therapeutics, 143
Tut Systems, 161
Tutela, 2291
Tution.io, 1222
Tutor.com, 592
tutoria, 2950
Tutorspree, 1821
Tutum, 1594
TuVox, 58
.tv, 724
TV Three, 2336
TV Time, 525
TVA Medical, 1597, 1619
TVB, 1496
TVC, 3049
TVH, 3239
Tvinci, 2914
TVision, 2137
TVision Insights, 799, 1101, 1487
TVR Communications, 402
Tvrecheck, 2355
TVSmiles, 641, 2475, 3208
TVtrip, 1416
TVTY, 1416, 2296
TVU, 3127
TVU Networks, 100, 1291, 1604
TVU Pack, 3127
Tweed Tree Lot, 2071
Twelve, 1122, 1725, 1928
Twelvefold, 43
Twelvefold Media, 548
TwelveStone Health Partners, 493
Twentify, 2284
Twenty-First Century Fox Inc., 1903
Twenty20, 358
TwentyBN, 1243
Twentybn, 1154
Twentyeight Seven, 1350
Twentyeight-Seven, 182, 1145
TWG Plus, 1783
Twilio, 11, 609, 1050, 1054, 1534, 1761
Twilo, 2870
Twin Cities Business, 3279
Twin Med, 1776
Twin Med LLC, 274
Twin Rivers Technologies, 1623
Twin Vee, 1745
Twin-Star International, 1857
Twindom, 307
Twine, 3108
Twine Health, 1524
Twinlab Consolidated Holdings, 1430
Twinstrata, 206
Twist, 1585
Twist Bioscience, 107, 144, 153, 181, 237, 268, 1400, 1940
Twisted Pair, 538
Twisted Pair Solutions, 457

Twistle, 918
Twistlock, 603, 1794
Twitch, 751, 1761, 1821, 2012, 3235
Twitmusic, 1965
Twitt2go, 2984
Twitter, 231, 248, 262, 265, 455, 650, 751, 802, 1001, 1235, 1524, 1882
Twitter Urban Airship, 1839
Two Bit Circus, 776
Two Bridges Design, 860
Two Moms in the RAW, 1324
Two Pore Guys Inc., 1069
Two Roads Brewing Company, 678
Two Tap, 1839
2-10 Home Buyers Warranty, 335
2-20 Records Management, 1832
20 East End, 34
20-20 Technologies, 2095
20/20 GeneSystems, 1061, 1169
200-208 Sixth St. Jersey City NJ, 190
2020, 1910
2020 Marketing, 3279
21 Buttons, 2296
21 Centrale Partners, 2544
212 Resources, 1, 657
21Buttons, 2851
21cake, 2936
21Diamonds, 2829, 2838, 3208
21Net, 2967, 3018
21sportsgroup, 2841
21st Century Creations, 737
21st Century Telecom Group, 1038
21ViaNet, 2850
21Vianet, 823
21vianet.com, 1853
23 and Me, 623
2359 Media, 3121
23andMe, 708, 802, 889, 1268, 1297, 1654, 1662, 3085
23andme, 1640
24 Hour Fitness, 1622
24-7 Intouch, 2219
24-7 Intouch Inc., 1851
24/7 Real Media, 1853
24access Solutions B.V., 3128
24M, 455
24symbols, 3108
24x7 Learning, 2558
250OK, 173
265.com, 2850
28-7, 1268
2bSURE.com Pte Ltd, 2508
2C2P, 148
2can, 89
2CheckOut, 1850
2Checkout, 468, 779
TwoCubes Inc., 392
2degrees, 1852
2DIALOG, 1697
Twofish, 1916
Twofour Group, 2944
2Mundos, 2983
2nd Address, 235, 770, 889
2nd Ave LLC, 354
2nd Watch, 515, 1158
2Rivers/Yesplan, 3042
2sens, 1611
TwoSix Labs, 876
2TD, 2700
2U, 260, 488, 1348, 1502, 1534, 1551
TwoWay Media, 2754
2Wire, 28, 596, 1212
2XU, 1088
2|Beans, 668
Twyla, 1001
TX, 2584
Txcell, 2876, 3113

TXCOM, 2383
TXEntre, 1650
TxPort, 1708
Txtr, 2444
TxVia, 2717
Tyan, 905
TydenBrooks, 257
Tyfone, 3019
Tylted, 1146
Tynec, 2569
Tynker, 454, 720, 883, 1527, 2010
Tynt, 1410
Tynt Multimedia, 2048
Tyntec, 909
Typeform, 3044
Typekit, 784
Typenex Medical, 470
Typesafe, 3045
Typhoon Studios, 2953
Tyres on the Drive, 2972
Tyrrells, 1017
TYRX, 495, 1412
Tysabri, 2102
Tyto, 2943
tyze, 2233
Tzero Technologies, 197
Tzetzo Bros., 1727
Töging am Inn, 2494

U

U Grok It, 1061
U Pol, 2796
U-Center, 3232
U-Line, 1132
U-Line Corporation, 1456
U-Nav Microelectronics, 807
U-Nest, 226
U-Systems, 117, 548, 1769
U.S. Anesthesia Partners, 254
U.S. Auto Parts Network, 1361
U.S. Education Corporation, 468
U.S. Environmental Services, 894
U.S. Fence Solutions, 331
U.S. Intergrity, 1657
U.S. LBM, 1062
U.S. Lumber, 1156
U.S. Minerals, 1209
U.S. Pole Company, 374
U.S. Power Generating Company, 1156
U.S. Retirement & Benefits Partners, 1081
U.S. Risk, 1081
U.S. Silica, 839
U.S. Tape, 1521
U3 Pharama, 94
U3 Pharma, 191
u51.com, 823
UAS Laboratories, 3279
UAV Navigation, 2548
UAVenture Capital, 3276
Ubby, 307
uBeam, 1150, 1888
Ubeeko, 3236
Uber, 45, 248, 262, 509, 668, 770, 771, 802, 815, 820, 842, 1054, 1075, 1095, 1138, 1149, 1202
uberall, 3056
UberMedia, 287, 518, 972
UberSense, 313
Ubertweek, 2569
UberVU, 2691
UBF Mittelstandfinanzierungs AG, 2724
Ubicast, 2308
Ubicom, 197
Ubidyne, 2671
UBiome, 1054
uBiome, 107, 1694
Ubique, 1516, 2113, 3249
Ubique Networks, 2155

1444

Portfolio Companies Index

Ubiquiti Networks, 1752
Ubiquity Software Corporation, 1038
Ubiquity Solar, 2061
Ubisoft, 2184
Ubitricity, 2841
UBIX, 1945
UBK, 2924
uBlox, 2853
UBmatrix LLC, 506
Ubona, 2558
Ubooly, 1838
UBuildNet, 418
UC, 2584
UC RUSAL, 34
Ucandoo, 2527
UCann, 1079
UCIC, 2184
UCIT, 2047
UCloud, 596
UCode, 972
Uconnect, 3, 1958
Ucopia, 3239
UCT Coatings, 1655
UCWeb, 823
Udacity, 455, 630
udelv, 1893
Udemy, 358, 1118, 1226, 1346
UDH Healthcare, 3069
UEI Global, 250
UEPAA!!, 2310
UFO, 2781
UFO Movies India, 1496
UFO Movietz Pvt, 2311
Ufora, 533, 1358, 1874
UGint, 3002
Ugo, 1680
UGO Networks, 954
Ugs, 2697
Uhuroo, 3109
UHY Advisors, 374
UICO, 251, 1455
Uinta Brewing Company, 1572
UiPath, 578, 1075, 1158, 1212, 3108
UiTV, 2733
Uizard, 1101, 1310
Ujam, 2813
Ujet, 1075, 2236
Uju Electronics, 2833
UK Support Services, 2695
UK2, 2944
Uken, 2113
Ukko, 996
Ukko Inc., 1069
uKnow, 1306, 1320
ULi, 2436
uLocate, 1080
Ulta Beauty, 1888
Ulterra Drilling Technologies, 110
Ultimus Fund Solutions, 1136
UltiSat, 1136
UltiZen Games, 3062
Ultra Angkle, 658
Ultra Clean Technology, 779
Ultra SoC Technologies, 3018
Ultra-Fit Manufacturing, 2044
UltraCell, 171, 2717
Ultracell, 497
UltraCision, 1227
Ultracision, 52
UltraCom, 3137
Ultracor, 812
UltraDNS, 2709
Ultrageny Pharmaceutical, 1618
Ultragenyx, 1412
Ultralase, 2795
UltraLink, 765
Ultranat, 2612

UltraSoc Technologies, 2760
UltraSPECT, 3212
Ultrazonix DNT AB, 2816
Ultriva, 627
Ultriva Inc., 1089
Ultromex, 2295
Uluru, 1079
UMA Enterprises, 1141, 1456
uMake, 296, 942
Umano, 272
Umanto.com, 3208
Umba, 1912
Umbono, 2921
Umicore, 3069
Uminova Invest, 2867
UMN Pharma, 2970
Umpqua Holdings Corporation, 1815
Umuse, 1663
Un Jour Aileurs, 2448
Unaptent, 307
Unata, 2182
Unbabel, 1154, 1607, 1611
Unblockable, 1663
Unbounce, 773, 2109, 2280, 3044
Unbound, 996, 1701, 1768, 2674, 2752
Unbound Concepts, 707
UnboundID, 1380, 1685
Unbxd, 1013
Uncharted Power, 218, 1054
Uncle Julio's, 1037, 1088, 1549
Uncle Milton, 1232
Uncommon Cacao, 55
Unconventional Gas Resources, 2040
Unconventional Resources, 672
Uncovet, 1965
Under Armour, 1587
Under the Canopy, 937
Under The Mango Tree, 55
Under the Roof Decorating, 2048
Underground Solutions, 1599
Underscore, 3273
Understory, 566, 1912
Undertone, 1041
Undock, 684
Unearth, 1158
Unequal Technologies LLC, 987
Unglue, 228
Uni Group Inc., 869
Uni Key, 181
Uni2 Hold Tight, 2967
Uni5.Com, 2626
Unibioscreen & Zetes, 2680
Unica, 1041
Unicell, 2936
Unico, 1753
Unicoaero, 1035
Unicoba, 1376
Unicon, 3001
Unident, 3180
UniDesk, 1181
Unidym, 1791
Unifeye Vision Partners, 1963
Unifi, 1626
Unified Patents, 1979
Unified Physician Management LLC, 159
Unified Power, 1435
Unifiller Systems Inc., 899
Unifrax, 110, 500
Unify2, 1825
Unifyo, 2685
UniKey, 724, 1095
Unikey, 1611
Unikrn, 60, 1595
Unilabs, 135
Unilend, 2296
Unilife, 1382
Unimersiv, 307

Union Agriculture Group, 2329
Union Bank of California, 214
Union Biometrica, 349
Union Crate, 1758
Union Digital, 2057
Union Metal, 843
Union Mobile Pay, 2831
Union Square Hospitality Group, 1109
Union Tractor, 1343
Union-Optech, 3235
Unionamerica Insurance Company Limited, 404
Unioncy, 2696
Unipart Rail Holdings, 2883
Uniphore, 574, 1031
UniPlaces, 2446, 3018
Uniq Investigation & Security Services, 2931
Unique Ltd., 2205
Unique Pub Company, 2935
Unique Pubs, 2605
Uniquify, 69
UniQure, 762
Unique, 2748
Unirac, 834
UNIRISX, 1025
Uniscape, 324, 3218
Uniscon, 1244
Unishippers Global Logistics, 746
UNIsite, 1038, 1038
Unisound, 1509
Unisource, 220
Unisource Network Services, 1461
Unitah Engineering & Land Serveying, 1345
Unitas Global, 1242
UniTask, 642, 742
Unite House, 2944
Unite US, 1632
Unitech Aerospace, 374, 654
Unitech Composites and Structures, 48
United American Energy Corp., 778
United BioSource, 209, 1037
United Brass Works, 321
United By Blue, 3277
United by Blue, 668
United Capital, 1602
United Catalyst, 841
United Claim Solutions, 859
United Confectioneries, 2491
United Copper Industries, 1085
United Country Real Estate, 402
United Dental Care, 1148, 1708
United Dental Partners, 368
United Dermpartners, 782
United Distribution Group, 110
United Flexible, 166, 828
United House Developments, 2944
United Imaging Healthcare, 2761
United Initiators, 1937
United Legal Services, 2944
United Living Group, 2944
United Logistics, 42
United Metro Media, 263
United Milk Company, 2784
United New Mexico Financial Corporation, 447
United Online, 502
United PanAm Financial Corporation, 1443
United Pet Group Inc., 168, 788
United Piece Dye Works, 1505
United Pipe & Steel Corp., 1266
United Plastics Group, 199
United Platform Technologies, 1769, 2457
United Preference, 1615
United Real Estate Group, 1276
United Recovery Systems, 194
United Retail Grop Inc., 447
United Road, 1085
United Road Services, 456, 1465
United Road Towing, 1234

1445

Portfolio Companies Index

United Roadbuilders, 2286
United Rotary Brush Corporation, 1343
United Site Services, 368, 1368
United States Embassy Residential Community, 3095
United States Environmental Services, 752
United States Infrastructure Corporation, 1109
United States Pipe and Foundry Company, 2009
United Studios Ltd, 2861
United Surgical Partners International, 909, 1972
United Tactical Systems, 501
United Telephone Company, 1270
United Therapies Holding LLC, 274
United Villages, 855, 1891
UnitedHealth Group, 869
UnitedLex, 386, 2818
Unitek, 1134
Unitek Information Systems, 558
Uniti, 2252
Unitive, 751, 3162
Unito, 2027, 2195
UniTrends, 904, 1400, 1842
Unitronics, 2891
Unity, 3235
Unity Biotechnology, 709, 1916
Unity Influence, 593
Unity Semiconductor, 197, 1257
Unity Technologies, 2853
UnityWorks Media, 1872
Univa, 142, 538, 1364, 1571
Univa UD, 153
Univacco Technology, 2603
Universal Ad, 3231
Universal American, 762, 1104, 1271, 1972
Universal American Financial Corporation, 404
Universal Avenue, 1607
Universal Biosensors, 188, 2618
Universal Education, 2936
Universal Fiber Systems, 928, 1505
Universal Hospital Services, 894
Universal Lighting Technologies, 1134
Universal Media Group, 1769
Universal Pure, 846
Universal Rail Systems, 2272
Universal Services, 70
Universal Services Of America, 374
Universal Software, 349
Universal Solutions International, 746
Universal Standard, 1530
Universal Technical Institute, 456
Universal Turbine Parts LLC, 843
UniversalPegasus International, 1086
Universe Media, 2936
University Beyond, 1507
University Netcasting, 1706
University of Denver, 3276
University of Law, 2977
University of Massachusetts Medical School, 1271
University of Pittsburgh Innovation Institute, 3275
University of Sint Eustatius School of Medicine, 687
University of South Australia - The Mawson Institu, 2959
University of St. Augustine for Health Sciences, 2046
University Park Energy, 1795
UniversityNow, 732, 1348
Univfy, 1552
Uniview, 220
Univision, 57
Univision Communications, 1156, 1496, 1598, 1815, 1835, 2379
Univision Technology, 1769
Uniwave, 2457
Unleash Immuno Oncolytics, 267

Unlimited Sports Group, 2501
Unmetric, 3001, 3062
Unmute, 561
UNO Danmark, 3203
Uno Restaurant Holdings Corp, 447
Uno Restaurant Holdings Corp., 465
Unocoin, 307
Unopiu, 3154
Unravel, 1154
Unravel Data, 823, 1202
Unreal Candy, 1524
Unser Heimatbacker Holding GmbH, 3067
Unsplash, 1101
Untangle, 1204
Untethered Labs, 418
UNTICKit, 727
UntuckIt, 1075
Unum Therapeutics, 191, 710, 1618
Unveillance, 285
Unwind Me, 785
Unwired Group Limited, 354
Unwired Nation, 810
UNX, 343, 1147
UOL Publishing, 1008
Up My Game, 2155
Up Out, 1669
Up Skill, 508, 809, 1607
UP&UP Inc., 404
Upad, 2400
UPC Renewable, 834
UpChain, 2118
UpCity, 471, 731, 1019
Upcomer, 977
UpCounsel, 295
Upcounsel, 128, 525, 547, 941
Updata Partners, 3270
Update Legal, 881
Update Logic, 538
Update Software, 2732
Updater, 1642, 1699
UPEK, 613
UPF Services, 1152
Upfront Digital Media, 301, 1899
Upgrade, 743
UpLevel, 2006
UpLift, 1563
Uplifting Entertainment, 65
Upload, 1473
UploadVR, 1390
Uplogix, 56, 594
UPM-Kymmene Oyj, 2990
UPMC Enterprises, 3275
Upnext, 150
UpOut, 1563
Upper, 1079
Upper Crust, 1503
Upper Hand Managed Sports, 658
Uprise Medical, 1615
Uprising, 1258
Uproxx, 1001, 1883
Upruc Ctr SA, 3187
Upruc Tap-Sdv SA, 3187
Upserve, 872, 1663
Upserver, 1480
Upshift, 1894
Upshot.com, 59
Upside, 569, 1688
Upside Health, 1507
Upsie, 1176
Upsight, 100, 641, 2113
UPSKILL, 1101
UpSkill, 2006
Upskill, 1259
Upslope Capital Management, 3276
Upspring Baby, 445
UpStart, 1075
Upstart, 511, 544

Upstart Network, 1069
Upstream, 3179
Upstream Commerce, 1968, 3246
Upstream Health, 1656
Upswing, 1551
Uptake, 1118, 1853
Uptake Medical, 68, 1378, 1600, 1773, 2008
UPTI, 3137
Uptivity, 655
UpTo, 1150, 1921
Uptown Network, 150
Uptycs, 518, 814
Upverter, 2137
upwell, 1204
UpWork, 1625
Upwork, 248, 581, 634, 743, 835, 1024, 1666
Upworthy, 428, 1715
Urachip, 2936
Uraniom, 307
Uranium Resources, 1548
Urban Airship, 358, 773, 776, 1149, 1860
Urban Barn, 2258
Urban Engines, 623
Urban Labs, 392
Urban Remedy, 1363
Urban Rivals, 2385
URBANARA, 2979
Urbanara, 301, 2475, 2797
UrbanBound, 876, 1738
UrbanFootprint, 1696
Urbanlogiq, 2027
UrbanSitter, 180, 386, 595, 1202
Urbansitter, 44
UrbanStems, 1259
Urbanstems, 876, 1766
Urbantag, 1655
Urbasolar, 3020
Urbint, 727, 1894
Urbium, 2695
uReach Technologies, 162
Urgant, 285
Urgent Team, 1571, 1762
Urgent.ly, 768, 1926
UrgentTeam, 1628
Urjanet, 544, 876
Urli.st, 2629
Urnex, 546
UroGene, 2563
Urology Management Associates, 1049
Urova, 995
Urova Medical, 1187
UROValve, 1306
Ursa, 792
Ursa Major Tech, 93
US Acute Care Solutions, 94, 1972
US Anesthesia Partners, 1972
US Auto Sales, 1234
US Behavioral Health, 955
US Bioservices, 1037
US Builder Services, 838
US CareNet, 406
US Century Bank, 353
US Corrugated, 1967
US Development Group, 675
US eDirect, 29
US Eye, 1409
US Foodservice, 1456
US Health Works, 97
US HealthVest, 710, 1844
US HealthWorks, 2079
US Investigation Services, 1972
US Labs, 378
US LEC, 1506
US Lec Corp., 221
US Manufacturing Corporation, 2009
US MED, 928
US Medical, 1837

1446

Portfolio Companies Index

US Oncology, 1972
US One Communications Corporation, 1986
US Pharmcia, 1452
US Pipe, 528
US Power Generating, 1795
US Radiology Specialist, 1972
US Radiosurgery, 1409
US Renal Care, 558, 782, 1109, 1628, 1762
US Salt, 1166
US Search, 935
US Silica Company, 914
US Tarp, 1606
US Unwired, 1017
US Well Services, 405, 559
USA Bouquet, 801
USA Capital Holdings Inc., 461
USA Compression Partners, 1409
USA Datanet, 1751
USA Discounters, 1415
USA Environment, 1997
USA Television Holdings, 1270
USADATA.com, 1668
UsAmeriBank, 529
uSamp, 871, 1380
USC Stevens Center for Innovation, 3268
USCO Logistics, 380
USDS, 1010
UsedCardboardBoxes.com, 797
User 1st, 543
User Friendly Media, 1927
User Replay, 2685
User Voices, 590
UserBliss, 103
Userfarm, 3179
Userfox, 3044
Userful, 2048
UserIQ, 282
Userlane, 745
Usermind, 455, 1202
UserTesting, 502, 1066, 1640, 1958
Uservoice, 231
USGI Medical, 57
Usha Martin, 3168
Ushi.cn, 2979
Uship, 1075
uShip, 581, 634, 1685
Ushr, 768, 2106
USI, 876
USI Holdings Corporation, 404
USI Insurance Services Corp., 1621
UsingMiles Inc., 553
USNR, 673
USP Hospitales, 2962
USPT, 2658
USSC, 632
UST-Aldetec Group, 540
UStar, 2936
UStec, 1377, 1751
Ustraap, 3125
UStream, 596, 646, 1089, 1958
Ustream, 1700
USU Software, 3069
uSwitch, 2944
UTAC, 2436
uTales, 2619
Utbrain, 3221
UTC Retail, 698
uTest, 1991
Utex Industries, 194
Utildata, 3099
Utilidata, 322
Utility, 322
Utility Pipeline, 240
Utility Telecom, 573
Utimaco, 1017
Utique, 1407
Utkarsh Microfinance, 2313

UTP, 969
Utrecht Art Supplies, 556, 1157
Utrecht Manufacturing, 1832
UTV LLC, 623
UUCun, 3215
UUSee, 3142
Uview Ultraviolet Systems Inc., 908
Uvision360, 1923
Uwanna?, 206
Uway, 3127
UX, 563
UX Specialized Logistics, 1636
UXPin, 784, 1563
Uzerzoom, 2339

V

V Resorts, 3109
V Ships, 2617
V&D, 1753
V-Bank, 2441
V-Enable, 1706
V-Grid Energy Systems, 532
V-Kernel, 649
V-ME Media, 1771
V-Wave, 2229
V.Group, 2207
V.I.O., 338
V12 Data, 349
V12 Group, 1328
V2, 3154
V2 Technology, 2993
V2W Fun4kids, 3042
V3 Systems, 1886
VA Linux, 1563
VA Linux Systems, 1474, 1862
Va-Q-Tec, 3252
Vaatsalya, 2313, 3109
Vaca Energy, 494
Vacant Property Security Limited, 2821
Vacatia, 243, 324, 1028, 1183
Vaccine Tech, 2978
Vaco, 1505
Vacuum Technologies Corporation, 678
Vadio, 1463
Vagabond, 1019, 1229
Vagabond Vending, 285
Vahan, 1138
Vailmail, 1663
Vaimi, 3127
Vaioptic, 3046
Valant, 69
Valcare Medical, 2324
Valen Analytics, 538, 1502
Valen Technologies, 142
Valence Health, 748
Valence Surface Technologies, 812, 1856
Valencell, 1782, 1860
Valens Semiconductor, 116, 1241, 2462, 2952
Valent, 16, 1305
Valent Aerostructures, 461
Valenti Capital, 3269
Valentine Paper, 1213
Valentis, 3245
Valentus Specialty Chemicals, 960
ValenTx, 68, 652, 1628, 1802
Valeo, 473
Valere Power, 1796
Valerion Therapeutics, 1618
Valeritas, 59, 938, 1268, 1378, 1972, 2353
Valet Living, 914
Valet Park, 1173
Valet Waste, 1301
Valet.io, 1589
Valfix, 226
Valgen, 2526
ValiCert, 2079
Valicert, 197, 1087

Valid Information Systems, 3107
Validic, 1052, 1689, 1988, 3277
Validity, 563, 1410, 1922
Validity Sensors, 1793
Validus DC Systems, 2315
Validus Holdings, 1301
Validus IVC, 2944
Valign, 1358
Valimail, 754
Valiosys, 2354
Valista, 2386, 3191
Valitas Health Services, 1156
Vallent, 645
Vallent Corporation, 162
Valley Agriceuticals, 1207
Valley Fastener Group, 1578
Valley Meats, 1332
Valley National Bank, 3274
Valley Vessel Fabricators, 1719
Valley-Dynamo, 722
Valor Water Analytics, 1893
Valore, 38
Valorem, 3020
Valquip Corporation, 832
Valtech Cardio, 1325
Valterra Products, 353
Valtris Specialty Chemicals, 928
Valttori Oy, 2966
Value Creators & Company, 3127
Value Partners, 940
Value Payment Systems, 1261
Value Retail, 2949
Valued Investing, 1589
Valuedesign, 2646
ValueOptions, 559
Valuewait, 2543
Valvitalia, 3154
Valyoo Technologies, 2849, 3199
Van Dyke Energy Company, 1164
Van Houtte Cafe, 1134
Van-Lang Foods, 193
Vana Vidyut Private Ltd, 2313
Vanbridge, 1743
VanceInfo, 596, 2936
Vancl, 2584, 2850
Vanco, 857
Vanda, 2690
Vanda Pharmaceuticals, 1493, 2513
Vandalia Research, 1262
Vanderbilt, 1136
Vanderveer Plastics, 812
Vandolay, 1966
Vandor, 1477
VanDyne SuperTurbo, 988
Vangent, 1925
VanGogh Imaging, 285
Vangst, 1439
Vangst Talent Network, 417
Vanguard A.G., 2653
Vanguard Graphics International, 399, 1053
Vanguard Healthcare, 2965
Vanguard Modular, 164
Vanguard Scientific, 557
Vanguard Space Technologies, 680
Vanilla, 685
Vanksen, 1516
Vanner Inc., 201
Vantage, 1045
Vantage Data Centers, 1683
Vantage Media, 263, 1422, 1728
Vantage Mobility International, 374
Vantage Oncology, 434, 938, 1360
Vantage Power, 2960
Vantage Robotics, 792, 942
Vantia Limited, 2981
Vantia Pharma, 1628
Vantia Therapeutics, 3015

Portfolio Companies Index

Vantium Management, 140
Vantos, 69, 753, 1389
Vantrix, 682, 682, 1038, 2259
Vantrix Corporation, 1728
Vanu, 455, 646
Vapogenix, 1019
Vapor IO, 254
Vapor Power, 1232
Vapor Slide, 392, 1135
Vapotherm, 560, 1122, 1515
Vapps, 215
Varana Health, 809
VArchive, 307
Vardon, 2796
Varel International, 152, 1086
Varentec, 1069
Vari-Form, 1753
Variable, 459
Variable Message Signs, 2306
Variable Wind Solutions, 2417
Variagenics, 1412, 1775
VariBlend Dual Dispensing Systems, 668, 1023
Varicent, 793, 2153
Variowell Development, 2686
Varix Medical Corp., 1543
vArmour, 84, 935, 2006, 2278
Varolii, 296, 1146
Varonis, 2726
Varro Technologies, 294
Varsity Brands, 456
Varsity Healthcare Partners, 3264
Varsity News Network, 171, 1736
Varuna, 1894
VarVee, 553
VASA Fitness, 1684
Vasco.de, 2813
Vascular Graft Solutions, 347
Vascular Pathways, 157, 176, 2981
Vascular Pharmaceuticals, 1008, 1268
Vascular Therapies, 508
Vaska Tech, 1589
Vasona Networks, 1305
Vasonova, 138, 1543
Vasonova Inc., 371
VasoPharm, 2710
Vasoptic Medical, 19
VasoStar, 3192
Vast, 502, 548, 1102, 1346, 1810
Vast Broadland, 1409
Vathys, 795
Vatica Health, 857
Vativ Technologies, 765
Vator.tv, 1965
Vatterott College, 1971
Vatterott Educational Centers, 1776
Vault, 678
Vault.com, 1927
Vaultive, 1303
VaultLogix, 739, 1979
Vaurum, 1489
Vauto, 221
Vaward Communications, 649
Vaxart, 238, 412
Vaxent, 995
Vaxess Technologies, 1347
Vaxiion Therapeutics, 1974
Vaximm, 2496, 2515, 3149
Vaxin, 1533
VaxInnate, 386, 1196, 1298
Vaxxas, 919, 2536, 2959, 3023
Vaya Vision, 3221
Vayable, 1546, 2329
Vayusa, 1637
Vayyar, 116
Vazata, 224
VB&P, 722
VBI, 495

VBI Vaccines, 12, 153
VBL Therapeutics, 2454
VBrick Systems, 56, 1255
VC-Net, 2972
VC3, 1979
VCC Optoelectronics, 1969
VCG Inc., 693
VChain, 3108
VCharge, 497
vCharge, 1693
VCON., 2571
Vcopious, 1568
VCortex, 3240
VCST, 778, 2949
Vdoo, 1269
Vdopia, 623, 3001
Ve24, 1459
Veber Solar I, 1909
Vecta, 2454
Vector, 850, 1663
Vector Capital, 3255
Vector Disease Control, 378
Vector Holding, 2623
Vector International, 2754
Vector Media, 1724
Vector Solutions, 1136
Vectorious, 347
VectorLearning, 1496
Vectorply, 1270, 1343
Vectra, 107, 634
Vectra AI, 965
Vectra Networks, 581
Veda, 3025
Vedero Software, 377
Veduca, 2950
Vee24, 178, 586
Veeam Software, 2320
Veebeam, 764
Veelo, 1383
Veem, 307
VEENOME Inc., 650
VeeR, 1611, 1670
Veev, 648
Veeva Systems, 665
Vega-Chi, 3018
Veggie Grill, 330, 334, 1149
Vehicle Trasportation Service, 3182
Vehicular Technologies, 651
Vela, 342
Vela Pharmaceuticals, 1188
Vela Systems, 521
Velano Vascular, 1054, 1601
Veldeman Group, 2949
Velicept Therapeutics, 1143, 1271
Velio, 833
Vella, 1519
Velo, 1340
Velo3D, 1069
VeloBit, 712, 1146
Velocidata, 1317
Velocify, 1942
Velocimed, 1574
Velocitel, 1937
Velocity, 1724
Velocity Aerospace Holding Group, 1492
Velocity Outdoor Corporation, 523
Velocity Technology Solutions, 1189, 1683, 1728
VelocityShares, 793
VeloCloud, 1916
Velomat Assembly Automation, 1352
Velomedix, 1966
Velos, 607, 1524, 1532
Velox Power, 1517
Veloxum, 1734
Veltek Associates, 1203
Velum Global Credit Mgmt., 405
VeluwseBron, 3232

Velvac Holdings, 1492
Velvet Energy LTD, 1851
Velvet Taco, 1088
Vemba, 1888
Vena Solutions, 2170
Venado Oil & Gas, 672
Venafi, 770, 1204, 1425
Venanpri Group, 2208, 2209
Venari, 1045
Venari Resources, 1062
VenatoRx, 266, 762, 1928
Vence, 395, 679, 1070
Vencore, 1925
Vend, 1897, 3044
Venda, 880
Vendasta, 2278
Vendavo, 596, 765, 779, 1010, 1672, 1725
Vendetta Mining, 1548
Vending System, 3154
Vendor Registry, 86, 459, 1923
Vendormate, 1456
VendorSafe Technologies, 1496
Vendstar, 92
Venerable Holdings, 559
Venga, 320
Vengo, 1632
Veniam, 1882, 1926
Veniti, 222, 569, 1488
Venminder, 1240
Vennli, 658, 1019
VennWorks LLC, 2783
Venous Health Systems, 666
Venrock, 3273
Vensafe, 2731
Vensun Pharmaceuticals, 1048
Ventaleon, 2515, 2939
Vente-Privee, 1752
Ventealapropriete.com, 1416
Vention, 1982
Vention Medical, 1086
VentiRx, 153, 621, 782
VentiRx Pharmaceuticals, 1196
Ventiv Technology, 1777
VentriNova, 347
Ventritex, 1786
Ventura Associates, 1881
Venture Bank, 3279
Venture Fellows, 1650
Venture Investors, 3269
Venture Sales Group, 1578
Venture Steel, 63
Venture Technology Groups, 443
Venture/Life Sciences Agendia, 2466
VentureBeat, 115, 1226, 1522
VentureScanner, 243
Venturesity, 3133
Venturi Wireless, 947, 1354, 1747
Venturion Limited Partnership, 2079
VenueBook, 432
Venuemob, 3121
Venus Concept, 697, 921, 1143
VenusConcept, 136
Venustech, 2584
VenX, 1261
Venyu, 1157
Veo Robotics, 1151
Veolia, 152
VER, 1088
Ver Se Innovation, 584
Veracicom, 536
Veracity Medical Solutions, 1187
Veracode, 38, 70, 560, 979, 1212, 1738
Veracross LLC, 361
Veracyte, 621
Verafin, 1717, 2153, 2168
Veran, 809, 1488, 1928
Veran Medical Technologies, 61, 1556

Portfolio Companies Index

Verana Health, 268
Verance, 287, 386, 551, 1604
Verano Holdings, 2254
Verari Systems, 439
Verastem, 59, 410, 1145, 1268
Verato, 515
Verax BioMedical, 270, 1142
Verax Biomedical, 508, 1057
Verb, 445
VerbalizeIt, 685
Verbling, 358, 397, 2329
Verdande Technology AS, 3141
Verdant, 2126
Verdeeco, 1923
VerdEng Connectors, 2760
Verdezyne, 319, 1249, 1391
Verdiem Corporation, 126
Verdigris, 1926
Verelst, 2501
Verengo Solar, 126
Verenium, 188, 322, 455
Verge Genomics, 232, 609, 1055, 1694
Verge Health, 349
Verge Solutions, 954
Vergesense, 1421
Veri, 378
Veriato, 909, 1979
Verical, 1899
Vericare, 938
Vericept, 1672
Vericlaim, 750
Verico Technology, 109
Vericred, 718
Veridiem, 310
Verient, 620, 833
Verificient, 1054
Verificient Technologies, 707
Verified Person, 1658
Veriflow, 1202
VeriFone, 1257
Verifone, 779
VerifyValid, 1736
Verilogue, 655
Verilume, 1235
Verimatrix, 548, 1038, 1239
Verinata Health, 1247, 1341
Verinetics, 737
Verio, 1211
Verious, 2010
Verisight, 1743
VeriSign, 1244
VeriSilicon, 905, 1087, 1796, 1906, 2850, 2853, 2936, 3235
VeriSilicon Holdings Company Ltd., 1951
VeriSIM Life, 1758
Verisity, 757, 2720
Verisma, 288
Verismic, 1677
Verista Imaging, 2077
Veristat, 967
Veristone Capital, 1061
Verisure Smart Alarms, 924
Verisys, 1717
Veritas, 1172
Veritas Finance, 1346
Veritext, 1017, 1109
Veritext Holding Company, 1456
Veritone, 1237
Veritonic, 977, 1766
Veritract, 1070, 1884
Verity, 876
Verity Solutions, 974
Verity Wine Partners, 1023
Verivo, 521
VeriVue, 1181, 1715
Veriware, 2005
Verizon, 3274

Vermed, 2602
Vermont Smoke & Cure, 1213
Vermont Teddy Bear, 786, 1862
Verna Group, 2935
VerneGlobal, 816
Vero, 1998
Verodin, 563, 1794
Verold, 2143
Verona Pharma, 74, 762, 1271, 1941
Verplex Systems, 3218
Verrex, 17
Versa, 351, 1518
Versa Networks, 175, 1184, 1926
VersaMed, 2751
VersaPharm, 1777
Versartis, 74, 1298, 1519, 1698
Versata, 1672
Versatile, 1793
Versatile Natures, 1894
Versatile Processing Group, 1209
Verse, 641
Verse Music Group, 1984
Versify, 1689
VersionONe, 1380
Versium, 1825
Versive, 2006
Versly, 231
Verso Paper, 140
Versusgame, 1507
Versé, 1374
Vert, 1069
Vert Mirabel, 2071
Vertafore, 924, 1041, 1835
Vertaris, 2372
Vertascale Software, 1966
Vertellus Specialties, 170, 1990
Verterra, 460, 608
Vertex, 206
Vertex Aerospace, 109, 1925
Vertex Business Services, 403
Vertex Data Science, 1360
Vertex Downhole, 676, 2261
Vertex Management Israel, 1633
Vertex Networks, 947
Vertex Resource Group, 2025
VertexOne, 610
Vertical Acuity, 1072
Vertical Bridge, 654, 1045
Vertical Communications, 536
Vertical Management Systems, 958
Vertical Mass, 397
Vertical Networks, 1003
Vertical Performance Partners, 1699
Vertical Power, 1924
Vertical Techmedia, 3236
Vertical Wind Energy, 2610
Verticalnerve, 9
VertiCann, 392
Vertiflex, 1817
Vertis Neuroscience Inc, 3162
Verto Education, 318, 883
Vertos Medical, 210, 1228, 1378
Vertrue, 563
Verus, 793
Verus Pharmaceuticals, 187
Verusen, 2019
Verva, 2536
Verva Pharmaceuticals, 2959
Verve, 296, 781, 1327, 1509, 2674, 2759
Verve Health, 658
Verve Mobile, 561
Very Good Security, 1138
Veryan, 2858
Veryfi, 50
Vesey Street Capital Partners, 3264
Vesiflo, 345
Vesper, 942

Vesper Technologies, 219
Vessel, 785, 1001, 1749, 1813
Vessel Co., 3002
Vessix, 1099
Vesta, 100, 1361, 1590, 1910
Vesta GMS, 23
VESTA Modular, 225
Vesta Retail Network, 1080
Vesta Therapeutics, 1915
Vestagen, 921
Vestar Capital Partnrs, 3255
Vestaron, 570, 1379, 1379, 1713, 2213
Vestcom, 456, 541, 909
Vested Health, 1262
Vestiaire Collective, 2478, 3208
Vestmark, 287, 1625
Veston Nautical, 1409
Vestorly, 1306
VetCentric, 1665, 1733
VetCloud, 2696
Vetco International, 2556
VetCor, 558, 914
VetDC, 1061
Veterinary Practice Partners, 1409
Vetevo, 2841
Vetra Energia, 46
Vets First Choice, 308, 938, 1460
Vetta, 290
Vette, 1080
Vetted Petcare, 120
Vetter, 101
Vettery, 1118, 1480
Vettro, 1672
Vetty, 1507
Vetus den Ouden, 2378
VeVeo, 1181
Veveo, 1375
Vexata, 1184
Vexos, 446
VFA, 655
VFG Plc, 2836
vFunction, 1663
VGo Communications, 422
Vhoto, 1183
VHSquared, 1628
VHsquared, 1731
VHT, 944
Vi-Jon, 254
VIA, 1477
Via, 707, 922, 1054
Via Separations, 663
Via Transportation, 1095
Viabizzuno, 2293
Viacell, 3007
ViaCyte, 1398, 1519, 1616, 1929
Viadeo, 3208
Viagene, 1706
Viagogo, 1965, 2401, 2446, 2503
ViaHero, 1507
Viajala, 3125
ViajaNet, 641
Viajanet, 816
Viajanet.com.br, 1534
Viakoo, 1061
Viamedia, 1091
Viamet, 915
Viamet Pharmaceuticals, 182, 1008, 1124
ViaNovus, 1461
Viasto, 2841
Viathan, 753
Viatime, 1340
Viatris, 1775
ViaWest, 1360
Viawest, 824, 1677
VIBE, 892
Vibe HCM, 790
Vibe/Spin Ventures, 783

1449

Portfolio Companies Index

Wavelet, 1070
Wavelink Corporation, 1728, 1979
Wavemark Technologies, 1991
WaveMetrix, 51
Wavesmith Networks, 521
WaveStream, 132
WaveTec Vision, 40, 598, 762, 1928
WAVi, 1837
Wavii, 1798
Wavin, 2644
Wavion, 2541
Waxing the City, 1576
Way Up, 1183, 1530
Wayfair, 909, 1715
Wayfarer, 1087
Wayfinder Resources, 1125
Waylo, 307
Waymark WSC Sports, 607
WAYN, 2662
Wayn, 3104
Wayne Trademark Printing & Packaging, 399
WayPay, 2027
Waypoint Homes, 824
Waypoint Leasing, 1315
Wayport, 1235, 1626, 1911, 3137
Wayside Technology Group, 3274
WayUp, 318, 816, 1694
Wayve, 525, 648
Waywire (Magnify Networks), 1321
Waze, 296, 2831, 2952
Wazee Digital, 1017
Wazoku, 2995
Wazoo Sports, 1214
WC Leasing, 678
WCCT, 949
WCG, 170
WCS Europe, 2284
WD Diamonds, 960
WDP Holdings Corporation, 1492
WDT, 1771
We Are Colony, 3108
We Are Pop Up, 2428
We Hostels, 3208
WE Magazine, 2584
We Pay, 1968
We7, 2691
Weaber Inc., 577
Wealth Access, 1688
Wealth Engine, 646
Wealth Enhancement Group, 1123
WealthAccess, 569
WealthEngine, 1348, 1502
WealthForge, 1259
Wealthfront, 581, 634, 872, 1560, 1694, 1696
WealthKernel, 3108
Wealthminder, 625
WealthNavi, 641
Wealthpoint Health Services, 2172
Wealthsimple, 2151, 2184, 2225
Wealthtracking, 1191
WealthTrust, 716
Wearable Intelligence, 3099
Wearwell, 556
WearWorks, 1507
Weasler Engineering Inc., 985
Weather Analytics, 1072, 1169
Weather Trends International, 1080
Weatherhaven, 2126
Weathernews Inc, 3182
WeatherPredict, 1693
Weathershield, 1455
Weave, 79, 427, 563, 941, 942
Web Geo Services, 3113
Web Methods, 32
Web Reservations International, 924
Web Tpa, 591
Webabcus Ltd, 2894

WebAction, 1752
Webbankir, 3150
Webchutney, 2558
WebCollage, 436
WebCollage and HSCG, 2779
WebCollage Inc., 2580
WebCriteria, 1668
WebDialogs, 1913
Webdyn, 2481
Webedia, 3208, 3239
WebEquity, 92
Webify Solutions, 2662
WebInterpret, 3113
WebLayers, 3212
WebLinc, 946, 1544, 1601
Webline, 59
WebLink International, 86
WebLogic, 238
WebMethods, 954
Webmoco, 2967
WebOrder, 807
Webputty, 221
WebRadar, 1509
Webraska Mobile Technologies SA, 162
Webroot, 1184, 1604
Webroot Software, 1785
Webs, 1348
WebScal, 876
WebScale, 1247
Webscale, 249
Websense, 300, 1112
Webshots, 784, 1149, 1546, 1860
Websitebutler, 2841
Webspective, 1257
Webstep, 3076
Webtide, 1965
Webtrends, 779
WebVisible, 757
Webware, 2113
Wecash, 973
WeChi, 206
weComm, 2407
Weconnect, 417
WeddingChannel.com, 1853
Weddington Way, 1028, 1531, 1853
WeddingWire, 427, 1710
Weddingwire, 1717
Wedeco Seed Fund I Ky Kb, 2740
Wedge Networks, 2048
Wedgewood Hospitality Group, 1492
Wedgewood Pharmacy, 1166
Wedgies, 60, 397, 1222
wedgies, 1912
Wedia, 3239
Wedit, 742
WeDo, 561, 2972, 3030
WedPics, 358, 971, 1364, 1845
Wedspire, 218
Weebly, 231, 751, 2012
Weeby.co, 935
WeeCare, 120, 728, 1696
WeedMD, 1191
Weekend Company, 3052
Weeks Service Company, 17
Weem, 1075
Weener Plastic GmbH, 1129
Weener Plastic Packaging Group, 2311
Weengs, 3108
Wefox, 1607, 3108
Weft, 1483
WeGather, 1615
WeGrow, 392
WeHeartIt, 1226, 1563, 1827
WeHeartPics, 2856
Wei Chai Shi, 1327
WEIC, 2974
Weight Watchers, 1018, 1134

Weilos, 1099
Weiman, 546
Weiyun, 2936
Weizuche, 817
weka.io, 1509
WekaIO, 1346
Welbe Health, 1143
WelbeHealth, 2
Welch ATM, 1578
Welcome, 743
Welcome Break, 1017
Welcome Dairy, 926
Welcu, 1830
Weldobot, 418
Welkin Health, 181
Well Bridge Health, 1448
Well Street Urgent Care, 787
Well-Foam, 439, 812
WellAWARE Systems, 1899
Wellbeats, 1113
Wellbore Solutions, 2632
Wellborn Forest, 917
Wellborn Forest Products, 1132, 1456
Wellcentive, 904, 1331
Wellco, 839
WellDoc, 181, 703, 1205, 1993
WellDog, 212, 1600
Weller, 325
Wellesley Pharmaceuticals, 1061
Wellfount, 149, 658
Wellframe, 609
WellGen Inc., 2397
Wellgood, 1584
Wellist, 2
Wellkeeper, 1300, 1924
Wellman, 1970
Wellman Plastics, 1037
Wellness Centers, 1191
WellnessFX, 1028, 1945
Wello, 1254, 1437
Wellogix, 734
WellPartner, 1002
Wellpartner, 1197, 1250
Wellpass, 55
Wells-CTI, 1017
WellSheet, 266
WellSky, 1835
WellSpring Pharmaceutical Corporation, 1651
Wellspring Worldwide, 1242
Welltec International, 1752
WellTok, 1371
Welltok, 665, 748, 754, 938, 1010, 1237, 1509, 2132, 2690
WellTrack, 2200
Welltrack, 2027
WellTrackOne, 266, 644
Welly, 1363
Welocalize, 1136, 1345
Welsh, 3255
Weltrend Semiconductor, 892
Welzorg, 2863
Wencor, 1368
Wendy's, 473
Wengo, 3208
Wenner Bread Products, 789
Wentorth Technology, 1161
Wentworth Senior Living Services, 462
Wentworth Technology Inc., 438
Wenzel, 445
Wenzel Spine, 987, 1801
Weole Ene, 3020
Weotta, 585, 1798
Wep, 2936
WePay, 197, 793, 974, 2012
WePow, 596, 1518
Wercker, 3224
WeRecover, 318

Portfolio Companies Index

Werecover, 563
Werewolf, 1268
Werk, 896, 1701
Wermland Paper AB, 3054
Werner Holdings, 1111
Wertkarten AG, 2783
Wesabe, 1359
WESCO Aircraft, 67
WESCO International Inc., 575
Weskey Graphics, 2258
Wesley Clover Solutions, 2284
WeSpire, 497, 1100
Wespro, 2558
West Academic, 1111
West Academic Publishing, 698
West Allen Capital, 3275
West American Rubber Company, 985
West Coast Fitness, 421
West Corporation, 1506, 1815
West Dermatology LLC, 158
West Glen Town Center, 70
West Pharmaceuticals, 1452
West Point Resources, 2031
West Star Aviation, 1345
Westar Aerospace & Defense Group, 654
Westbrook, 1607
Westcoast Entertainment, 1295
Westec Interactive, 494
Westerlund Group, 2781
Western Building Centres Limited, 2136
Western Dentral, 1301
Western Emulsions, 1168
Western Forest Products, 2067, 2079
Western Glove Works, 2258
Western Industries, 335, 846
Western Jet Aviation, 439
Western Marketing, 1997
Western Nonwovens, 199
Western Oilfield Equipment Ltd., 676
Western Oilfield Equipment Rentals, 2025
Western Peterbilt Inc., 862
Western Reserve Products, 843
Western Seed, 55
Western Windows Systems, 405
Western Wireless Corp., 300
Westeryly Wind, 1895
WestFace Medical, 870
Westfalia, 2795
Westlake Hardware Inc., 843
Westland Technologies, 828
Westminster Foods, 1093
Westminster Healthcare, 1972
Westmoreland Advanced Materials, 293
Westmount Storefront Systems, 2043
Westny Building Products Company, 201
Weston Medical, 3007
Westpac Banking, 2659
Westridge Cabinets, 2255
Westwave Communications Inc., 252
Westwing, 2829, 2838, 3044
WestwoodOne, 869
Wet Point, 634
Wethos, 351, 754, 934
Wetpaint, 581
Wetzel's Pretzels, 1111
Wevat, 3108
WeVideo, 1642
Wevorce, 599, 721, 770
WEVR, 305
WeVR, 1611, 1813
Wevr, 107, 600, 792
WeWork, 248, 581, 634
WexEnergy, 704
WFI, 2007
WGT, 968
Wha Tap, 1509
Whale Communications, 2541

Whale Imaging, 1382
Whaleback Managed Services, 422
Wharfedale Hospital, 2749
Wharton Economics, 221
What 3 Words, 1985
What's In My Handbag, 2691
What's On India, 3001
WhatCounts, 1572
Wheel Pros, 500
Wheelabrator Technologies, 675
Wheelhouse, 351, 772, 1323
Wheels Up, 1585
Wheelwell, 1323
Wheelys, 1701
Whelan Refining Ltd, 2539
When I Work, 173, 630, 641
When.com, 1405
WHERE, 1080
Where, 1916
WhereNet, 555
Whereonearch, 2386
WhimseyBox, 1615
Whip Networks, 1001
Whip Tail Technologies, 1730
Whipclip, 751
Whisbi, 256, 2339
Whisk, 724, 1965
Whisper, 1663, 1758
Whistle, 596, 1531
Whistle Sports, 668
Whistler, 1295
Whitcraft Group, 862, 1132, 1456
White Cap Industries, 1086
White Oak Resources, 46
White Ops, 4
White Ops., 1400
White Pine Company, 713
White Source, 1154
White Swan Environmental Ltd., 2167
White Systems, 1162
Whitebridge Pet Brands, 789
WhiteCoat, 972
WhiteDove Herbals, 1837
WhiteFence, 57
WhiteGlove Health, 678
Whitehall Specialties, 1171
Whitechat Jr., 1392
WhiteHat Security, 100, 807, 947, 1041, 1737, 2457
WhiteOps, 876
WhiteSky, 1478
WhiteSmoke, 2914
WhiteSource, 1306
WhiteSwell, 980, 1519
Whitetruffle, 1254
Whitney International University System, 22
Whittl, 1364, 1384
Whitworth Tool, 399, 611
Whizz Kid Entertainment, 2871
Whizztek, 3048
Who Is Happy, 392
Who What Wear, 871, 1222, 1833
Who Works Around You Pte Ltd, 2473
WhoBet, 1860
Whodini, 1513
Whoknows, 799
Whole Biome, 107
Wholesale Floors, 1726
Wholeshare, 595, 1254
Wholesome Goodness, 1046
Wholesome Pet Care, 1767
Wholesome Sweetners, 1516
WHOOP, 1263
Whoop, 1489
Whos Here, 1118
WhoSay, 1475
Whoseyourlandlord, 1507

Wibbitz, 256, 2831, 2872, 2947
Wibidata, 386
Wibotic, 2008
WiBotics, 519
WiChorus, 1445, 1534
Wicked Quick, 1383
Wicket Labs, 1158
Wickr, 93
Wicks Educational Publishing, 1984
Wide Corporat, 2414
Wide Open Spaces, 635
WiDeFi, 212, 990
WideOpenWest, 1360
WideOrbit, 871, 922, 1184
WiderThan, 1133
Widerthan, 964
Widespace, 3013
Widetronix, 608, 1475
Widevine Technologies, 1906
Widyard, 1879
Wifi Slam, 1655
Wifidabba, 623
Wigwag, 942
Wikia, 1001, 1374, 1865
Wikicell, 1460
Wikitude, 3165
WIL Research Laboratories, 245
Wiland, 334
Wilbanks Trucking and Wilbanks Leasing, 1376
Wilcon, 1409
Wild Earth, 720
Wild Pocketsm Xactly, 976
Wild Sports, 409, 443
Wild Tangent, 59, 2079
Wild Things, 287, 1954
Wild Type, 1238
Wild VR, 1383
Wildcard, 1699
Wildcat Discovery Technologies, 988, 3222
Wildcat Discovery Technology, 12
Wildcomm, 1239
Wildfang, 218, 1383, 1912
Wildfire, 1838
Wildflower, 644
Wildflower Health, 915, 918
WildTangent, 872, 1158, 1235, 1704
Wildworks, 1677
Wilex AG, 3196
Wiliot, 1346, 1509
Wilke-Rodriguez, 796
Wilks Broadcast Group, 1984
Will Ventures, 3273
Willa Skincare, 1905
Willamette Broadband, 263
Willcall, 1749
WillCare, 1751
Willert Home Products, 61, 61
Willful, 2260
William Blair, 3272
William Hill, 2605, 2644
Williams Controls, 109
Williams Healthcare, 1295
Williams Scotsman, 1368
Williams Scotsman Inc., 575
Williams Scotsman International Inc., 1903
Williams Sonoma, 300
Willie's Grill & Icehouse, 477
Willie's Reserve, 963, 1864
Willing, 15
Willis Towers Watson Plc., 1903
Willo, 1075
Willow, 1993
Willtek, 1017
WilmerHale, 3272
Wilmington Pharmaceuticals, 1988
Wilocity, 1779
Wilson, 503

1455

Portfolio Companies Index

Zellwerk GmbH, 3190
Zeltic, 782
ZELTIQ, 1419
Zeltiq, 74, 1916
Zemanta, 2691
Zemax, 166
Zembula, 1656
Zen Holdings, 2857
Zenalytic Laboratories, 2100
Zenasis, 95
Zenbox, 1546
Zencity, 1154
Zend, 215, 1620
Zend Technologies, 3231
Zendesk, 248, 455, 1001, 1181, 1534
ZenDrive, 302, 707
Zendrive, 45, 107
Zenefits, 518, 1001
Zenflow, 841
Zenfolio Inc., 403, 446
ZeniMax Media, 1496
Zenith, 1256
Zenith Adminstators, 374
Zenith American Solutions, 244
Zenith Energy, 1062
Zenith Products Corp., 456
Zenith Vehicle Contracts Ltd., 2677
Zenith-Leaerive, 2944
Zenium, 1315
ZenMate, 3056
Zenomics, 737
Zenoss, 119, 315, 876, 1008, 1169, 1752
Zenoti, 1346
ZenPayroll, 585
Zenph Sound Innovations, 1008
Zenplaya, 1306
ZenPrint, 1070
Zenprise, 238, 1540, 1663
Zenprop, 2709
Zenput, 1024, 2280
Zenrex, 175
Zensar Technologies, 135
Zensar Technologies Ltd, 2694
Zenso, 2366
Zention Limited, 2981
Zentiva, 62
Zentri, 249
Zenverge, 596, 1926, 2005
Zenysis, 1329
ZeOmega, 333
Zeomega, 1615
Zep Solar, 548
Zepheira, 2195
Zephyr, 115, 454
Zephyr Health, 968
Zephyr Investments Limited, 152
Zephyr Technology, 2853
Zephyrus, 1238
Zeplin, 751
Zerbee's, 1705
ZergNet, 256
Zerista, 1070
Zero, 679, 1118
01 Communique, 2058
Zero G, 1306
000 Mile, 465
Zero Stack, 770
0-In Design, 1975
Zero2IPO, 1737, 2457
02 RegenTech, 1047
ZeroChroma, 1169
ZeroFOX, 538, 935
ZeroFox, 814
zeroheight, 795
ZeroLight, 3051
ZeroTurnaround, 221
ZeroVM, 1547

Zerply, 1370, 1518
Zerto, 1001, 1594
Zerve, 1291
Zest, 1560
Zest Dental, 209
Zest Finance, 646, 754, 1798, 1888
Zest Health, 582, 1118
Zesta, 2010
ZestFinance, 1119, 1181
Zestful, 318
Zesty, 761, 3030
Zeta Global, 1670
Zeta Interactive, 1017
ZetrOZ, 1745
Zetta, 1024
Zetta.net, 115, 770
ZettaCom, 1017
Zettaset, 933
Zettics, 1046, 1945
Zeus, 243, 317, 751, 1323, 2674, 3104
Zeus Technology, 2662
Zeuss, 768, 1169
Zevia, 1324, 1344
Zhaogang.com, 3251
Zhena's, 1524
Zhilabs, 2548
Zhima Credit, 2404
Zhizhen Node, 2850
Zhone, 69
Zhongdian Biotech, 2584
Zhongsheng Group, 815
Zhongsou, 2850
Zhuhai Power Plant, 2591
Zhuhai Yueke Tsinghua Electronic Ceramics, 2802
Zi-Lift, 466
Ziani's, 2732
Ziarco, 112
Zibby, 1240
ZicroData, 949
Ziebel, 2700, 3216
Zift Solutions, 1072, 1710
Ziften, 1841
Zigfu, 1581
Ziggo, 57, 744
Ziggs.com, 190
Zigzag, 100
Ziibra, 307
Ziiproom, 1100
Zikon, 650
Zilift, 2700, 3099, 3216
Zilker Brewing, 445
Zillabyte, 609, 1222
Zilliant, 411, 1841
Zim's Crack Creme, 631
Zimbio, 32
Zimbra, 634, 1474, 1534
Zimmer Spine, 3279
Zimory, 2638
Zimperium, 1611, 1670
ZIN s.r.o., 3122
Zinc, 809, 922
ZincFive, 126
Zinch, 1323, 1480
Zing, 448
ZING Systems, 1445
ZingBox, 603, 2439
ZingFront, 219
Zingle, 306, 561
Zinio Systems, 521, 1402
Zinion, 946
Zinkia, 2469
ZinniaTek, 2978
Zinwave, 3104
Zio, 658
Zip The Strip, 512
Zip2, 922, 1247

Zipbooks, 79
ZipCar, 248, 1445
Zipcar, 1212
Zipdrug, 525, 1151, 1530
Zipfit Denim, 1019
Zipit, 1214, 1923
Zipit Wireless, 1755, 1994
Zipline, 318, 720
ZipLine Medical, 491, 2011
ZipList, 1699
Ziplogix, 1642
Zipmark, 533, 1358, 1406, 1475, 1632
Zipments, 471, 743
Zipnosis, 173, 176, 1601
Zipongo, 243, 703, 1184, 1522
Zippity, 1100
Zipprecruiter, 1001
Zippy App, 1669
ZipRealty, 649
ZipScene, 479, 1046
Ziptronix, 1008
Zipwhip, 1154
ZipZap, 301
Ziqitza Health Care Ltd., 55
Zira.ai, 318
Zirmed, 818
Zirtual, 1798, 1912
Zitra, 3170
Ziva Software, 3019
Zivame.com, 2849
Zive, 293
Zivix, 3279
Zixi, 1627
Zkey.com, 2021
Zlango, 581, 634
Zmags, 1333
Zmanda, 2818
ZMP Inc., 2414
Znode, 1553
ZocDoc, 262, 775, 2446
Zodiac, 525
Zodius, 295
Zoetis, 16
Zogenix, 468, 495, 1626, 1817
Zola, 396, 518, 761, 842
Zola Electric, 809
Zolk, 2918
Zollo, 3003
Zolo Technologies, 548
Zomay Marine and Logistics, 1164
Zonare, 176
Zone Holding, 3054
Zone Labs, 1038, 1626
Zone Reactor, 2021
Zone2, 293
Zone3, 2264
Zonnecentrale Limburg, 2949
Zonoff, 1899
Zonton, 1340
zoocasa, 2134, 2151
Zoom, 107, 665, 2831
Zoom Information, 521
Zoom Media Group, 22
Zoom+, 673
Zoom.ai, 2113, 2138
ZoomCar India, 1329
ZoomData, 518
ZoomInfo, 1916
ZoomThru, 995
Zoona, 1374
Zoopla Property Group, 3018
ZoOpt, 2417
Zoorate, 3052
Zoosk, 115, 183, 386, 548
ZooskottaMark, 183
Zootrock, 1749
Zoove, 1410

Portfolio Companies Index

Zoox, 609, 800, 1151
Zooz, 384, 2011, 2947, 3081
Zopa, 2450, 2478, 2752, 3233
Zoran, 536
Zorch, 338
Zorch International, 452, 1622
Zorg Domein, 1111
Zosano Pharma, 1490, 3007
Zowdow, 101, 972
Zozi, 1097, 1311
Zrinse, 942
ZS Pharma, 1519, 1574, 1698
Zscaler, 578, 603
ZSi-Foster, 1435
zSpace Inc., 174
ZT3 Technologies, 730
Ztar Mobile, 1348
ZTEC Instruments, 1924
Zubie, 319, 1327
Zubio, 650
Zuga Medical, 1047
Zui.com, 1239
Zula, 1323
Zuli, 1998, 2010

Zulily, 197, 1183, 1212
Zum, 128
Zumata, 1965
Zumbro Discover, 347
Zume Pizza, 107, 1183, 1675
Zumiez, 334
Zumobi, 1361, 1637
Zumper, 708, 1075
Zunlei, 2584
Zuora, 248, 581, 634, 1319, 1534, 1663, 1796, 1946, 1968
Zurex Pharma Inc., 222, 2001
Zuu, 721
Zvents, 1906
Zwift, 1663
Zycada Delivery Network, 1670
Zycada Networks, 454
Zyfin, 2406
Zyga, 1187
Zyga Technology, 621, 1725
Zylo, 1202, 1607
Zylo Media, 1160
Zylo Tech, 1554
Zylotech, 829, 1595

Zyme, 1759
Zymenex, 3149
Zymergen, 107, 609, 996, 1238, 1363
ZymeTx, 1837
Zymeworks, 1271, 2092, 2180
Zymo Genetics, 782
Zympay, 822
Zyncro, 2339
Zynga, 32, 206, 358, 581, 634, 1001, 1699, 1882, 2475, 2604, 2663
Zynstra, 3018
ZYNX Networks, 1180
Zype, 1554
Zyper, 761
Zyray Wireless, 652, 764, 1239
Zyrobotics, 218
ZyStor Therapeutics, 1921
Zytech Building Systems, 2275
Zytiga, 2102
Zywave, 199, 901
Zywie LLC, 1044
ZZ Biotech, 347

SALEM PRESS

2021 Title List

SALEM PRESS

Visit www.SalemPress.com for Product Information, Table of Contents, and Sample Pages.

Flash Fiction
Gender, Sex and Sexuality
Good & Evil
The Graphic Novel
Greed
Harlem Renaissance
The Hero's Quest
Historical Fiction
Holocaust Literature
The Immigrant Experience
Inequality
LGBTQ Literature
Literature in Times of Crisis
Literature of Protest
Magical Realism
Midwestern Literature
Modern Japanese Literature
Nature & the Environment
Paranoia, Fear & Alienation
Patriotism
Political Fiction
Postcolonial Literature
Pulp Fiction of the '20s and '30s
Rebellion
Russia's Golden Age
Satire
The Slave Narrative
Social Justice and American Literature
Southern Gothic Literature
Southwestern Literature
Survival
Technology & Humanity
Violence in Literature
Virginia Woolf & 20th Century Women Writers
War

Critical Insights: Film
Bonnie & Clyde
Casablanca
Alfred Hitchcock
Stanley Kubrick

Critical Approaches to Literature
Critical Approaches to Literature: Feminist
Critical Approaches to Literature: Moral
Critical Approaches to Literature: Multicultural
Critical Approaches to Literature: Psychological

Critical Surveys of Literature
Critical Survey of American Literature
Critical Survey of Drama
Critical Survey of Graphic Novels: Heroes & Superheroes
Critical Survey of Graphic Novels: History, Theme, and Technique
Critical Survey of Graphic Novels: Independents and Underground Classics
Critical Survey of Graphic Novels: Manga
Critical Survey of Long Fiction
Critical Survey of Mystery and Detective Fiction
Critical Survey of Mythology & Folklore: Gods & Goddesses
Critical Survey of Mythology & Folklore: Heroes and Heroines
Critical Survey of Mythology & Folklore: Love, Sexuality, and Desire
Critical Survey of Mythology & Folklore: World Mythology
Critical Survey of Poetry
Critical Survey of Poetry: Contemporary Poets
Critical Survey of Science Fiction & Fantasy Literature
Critical Survey of Shakespeare's Plays
Critical Survey of Shakespeare's Sonnets
Critical Survey of Short Fiction
Critical Survey of World Literature
Critical Survey of Young Adult Literature

Cyclopedia of Literary Characters & Places
Cyclopedia of Literary Characters
Cyclopedia of Literary Places

Introduction to Literary Context
American Poetry of the 20th Century
American Post-Modernist Novels
American Short Fiction
English Literature
Plays
World Literature

Magill's Literary Annual
Magill's Literary Annual, 2021
Magill's Literary Annual, 2020
Magill's Literary Annual, 2019

Masterplots
Masterplots, Fourth Edition
Masterplots, 2010-2018 Supplement

Notable Writers
Notable African American Writers
Notable American Women Writers
Notable Mystery & Detective Fiction Writers
Notable Native American Writers & Writers of the American West
Novels into Film: Adaptations & Interpretation
Recommended Reading: 600 Classics Reviewed

Grey House Publishing | Salem Press | H.W. Wilson | 4919 Route, 22 PO Box 56, Amenia NY 12501-0056

SALEM PRESS

2021 Title List

Visit www.SalemPress.com for Product Information, Table of Contents, and Sample Pages.

HISTORY

The Decades
- The 1910s in America
- The Twenties in America
- The Thirties in America
- The Forties in America
- The Fifties in America
- The Sixties in America
- The Seventies in America
- The Eighties in America
- The Nineties in America
- The 2000s in America
- The 2010s in America

Defining Documents in American History
- Defining Documents: The 1900s
- Defining Documents: The 1910s
- Defining Documents: The 1920s
- Defining Documents: The 1930s
- Defining Documents: The 1950s
- Defining Documents: The 1960s
- Defining Documents: The 1970s
- Defining Documents: American Citizenship
- Defining Documents: The American Economy
- Defining Documents: The American Revolution
- Defining Documents: The American West
- Defining Documents: Business Ethics
- Defining Documents: Capital Punishment
- Defining Documents: Civil Rights
- Defining Documents: Civil War
- Defining Documents: The Cold War
- Defining Documents: Dissent & Protest
- Defining Documents: Drug Policy
- Defining Documents: The Emergence of Modern America
- Defining Documents: Environment & Conservation
- Defining Documents: Espionage & Intrigue
- Defining Documents: Exploration and Colonial America
- Defining Documents: The Formation of the States
- Defining Documents: The Free Press
- Defining Documents: The Gun Debate
- Defining Documents: Immigration & Immigrant Communities
- Defining Documents: The Legacy of 9/11
- Defining Documents: LGBTQ+
- Defining Documents: Manifest Destiny and the New Nation
- Defining Documents: Native Americans
- Defining Documents: Political Campaigns, Candidates & Discourse
- Defining Documents: Postwar 1940s
- Defining Documents: Prison Reform
- Defining Documents: Secrets, Leaks & Scandals
- Defining Documents: Slavery
- Defining Documents: Supreme Court Decisions
- Defining Documents: Reconstruction Era
- Defining Documents: The Vietnam War
- Defining Documents: U.S. Involvement in the Middle East
- Defining Documents: World War I
- Defining Documents: World War II

Defining Documents in World History
- Defining Documents: The 17th Century
- Defining Documents: The 18th Century
- Defining Documents: The 19th Century
- Defining Documents: The 20th Century (1900-1950)
- Defining Documents: The Ancient World
- Defining Documents: Asia
- Defining Documents: Genocide & the Holocaust
- Defining Documents: Nationalism & Populism
- Defining Documents: Pandemics, Plagues & Public Health
- Defining Documents: Renaissance & Early Modern Era
- Defining Documents: The Middle Ages
- Defining Documents: The Middle East
- Defining Documents: Women's Rights

Great Events from History
- Great Events from History: The Ancient World
- Great Events from History: The Middle Ages
- Great Events from History: The Renaissance & Early Modern Era
- Great Events from History: The 17th Century
- Great Events from History: The 18th Century
- Great Events from History: The 19th Century
- Great Events from History: The 20th Century, 1901-1940
- Great Events from History: The 20th Century, 1941-1970
- Great Events from History: The 20th Century, 1971-2000
- Great Events from History: Modern Scandals
- Great Events from History: African American History
- Great Events from History: The 21st Century, 2000-2016
- Great Events from History: LGBTQ Events
- Great Events from History: Human Rights

Great Lives from History
- Computer Technology Innovators
- Fashion Innovators
- Great Athletes
- Great Athletes of the Twenty-First Century
- Great Lives from History: African Americans
- Great Lives from History: American Heroes
- Great Lives from History: American Women
- Great Lives from History: Asian and Pacific Islander Americans
- Great Lives from History: Inventors & Inventions
- Great Lives from History: Jewish Americans
- Great Lives from History: Latinos
- Great Lives from History: Scientists and Science
- Great Lives from History: The 17th Century
- Great Lives from History: The 18th Century
- Great Lives from History: The 19th Century
- Great Lives from History: The 20th Century
- Great Lives from History: The 21st Century, 2000-2017
- Great Lives from History: The Ancient World
- Great Lives from History: The Incredibly Wealthy
- Great Lives from History: The Middle Ages
- Great Lives from History: The Renaissance & Early Modern Era
- Human Rights Innovators
- Internet Innovators
- Music Innovators
- Musicians and Composers of the 20th Century
- World Political Innovators

Grey House Publishing | Salem Press | H.W. Wilson | 4919 Route, 22 PO Box 56, Amenia NY 12501-0056

2021 Title List

Visit www.HWWilsonInPrint.com for Product Information, Table of Contents, and Sample Pages.

The Reference Shelf
Affordable Housing
Aging in America
Alternative Facts, Post-Truth and the Information War
The American Dream
American Military Presence Overseas
Arab Spring
Artificial Intelligence
The Business of Food
Campaign Trends & Election Law
College Sports
Conspiracy Theories
Democracy Evolving
The Digital Age
Dinosaurs
Embracing New Paradigms in Education
Faith & Science
Families - Traditional & New Structures
Food Insecurity & Hunger in the United States
Future of U.S. Economic Relations: Mexico, Cuba, & Venezuela
Global Climate Change
Graphic Novels and Comic Books
Guns in America
Hate Crimes
Immigration
Internet Abuses & Privacy Rights
Internet Law
LGBTQ in the 21st Century
Marijuana Reform
National Debate Topic 2014/2015: The Ocean
National Debate Topic 2015/2016: Surveillance
National Debate Topic 2016/2017: US/China Relations
National Debate Topic 2017/2018: Education Reform
National Debate Topic 2018/2019: Immigration
National Debate Topic 2019/2021: Arms Sales
National Debate Topic 2020/2021: Criminal Justice Reform
National Debate Topic 2021/2022
New Frontiers in Space
The News and its Future
Policing in 2020
Politics of the Oceans
Pollution
Prescription Drug Abuse
Propaganda and Misinformation
Racial Tension in a Postracial Age
Reality Television
Representative American Speeches, Annual Edition
Rethinking Work
Revisiting Gender
Robotics
Russia
Social Networking
The South China Sea Conflict
Space Exploration and Development
Sports in America
The Supreme Court
The Transformation of American Cities
The Two Koreas
U.S. Infrastructure
Vaccinations
Whistleblowers

Core Collections
Children's Core Collection
Fiction Core Collection
Graphic Novels Core Collection
Middle & Junior High School Core
Public Library Core Collection: Nonfiction
Senior High Core Collection
Young Adult Fiction Core Collection

Current Biography
Current Biography Cumulative Index 1946-2021
Current Biography Monthly Magazine
Current Biography Yearbook

Readers' Guide to Periodical Literature
Abridged Readers' Guide to Periodical Literature
Readers' Guide to Periodical Literature

Indexes
Index to Legal Periodicals & Books
Short Story Index
Book Review Digest

Sears List
Sears List of Subject Headings
Sears: Lista de Encabezamientos de Materia

History
American Game Changers: Invention, Innovation & Transformation
American Reformers
Speeches of the American Presidents

Facts About Series
Facts About the 20th Century
Facts About American Immigration
Facts About China
Facts About the Presidents
Facts About the World's Languages

Nobel Prize Winners
Nobel Prize Winners: 1901-1986
Nobel Prize Winners: 1987-1991
Nobel Prize Winners: 1992-1996
Nobel Prize Winners: 1997-2001
Nobel Prize Winners: 2002-2018

Famous First Facts
Famous First Facts
Famous First Facts About American Politics
Famous First Facts About Sports
Famous First Facts About the Environment
Famous First Facts: International Edition

American Book of Days
The American Book of Days
The International Book of Days

Grey House Publishing | Salem Press | H.W. Wilson | 4919 Route, 22 PO Box 56, Amenia NY 12501-0056